THE EUROPA WORLD YEAR BOOK 2008

VOLUME I

PART ONE: INTERNATIONAL ORGANIZATIONS
PART TWO: AFGHANISTAN–JORDAN

LONDON AND NEW YORK

First published 1926

© Routledge 2008
Albert House, 1–4 Singer Street, London, EC2A 4BQ, United Kingdom
(Routledge is an imprint of the Taylor & Francis Group, an Informa business)

All rights reserved. No part of this
publication may be photocopied, recorded,
or otherwise reproduced, stored in a retrieval
system or transmitted in any form or by any
electronic or mechanical means without the
prior permission of the copyright owner.

ISBN13: 978-1-85743-451-4 (The Set)
978-1-85743-452-1 (Vol. I)
ISBN10: 1-85743-451-X (The Set)
1-85743-452-8 (Vol. I)
ISSN: 0071-2302
Library of Congress Catalog Card Number 59-2942

Senior Editor: Joanne Maher

Statistics Editor: Philip McIntyre

Regional Editors: Lynn Daniel, Katie Dawson, Lucy Dean, Iain Frame,
Imogen Gladman, Dominic Heaney, Juliet Love, Jillian O'Brien, Jacqueline West

International Organizations Editors: Catriona Appeatu Holman, Helen Canton

Associate Regional Editors: Meena Khan, Kirstie Macdonald,
Christopher Matthews, Anna Thomas

Assistant Editors: Kim Chamberlain, Laura Davis, David Gruar,
Catriona Marcham, Simon Molony, Adrian Reynolds,
Janine Tenzer, Gareth Vaughan, Elli Woollard

Associate Editor, Directory Research: James Middleton

Editorial Director: Paul Kelly

Typeset in New Century Schoolbook

Typeset by Data Standards Limited, Frome, Somerset

Printed and bound in Great Britain by Polestar Wheatons, Exeter

FOREWORD

THE EUROPA WORLD YEAR BOOK was first published in 1926. Since 1960 it has appeared in annual two-volume editions, and has become established as an authoritative reference work, providing a wealth of detailed information on the political, economic and commercial institutions of the world.

Volume I contains a comprehensive listing of some 1,900 international organizations and the first part of the alphabetical survey of countries of the world, from Afghanistan to Jordan. Volume II contains countries from Kazakhstan to Zimbabwe. An Index of Territories covered in both volumes is to be found at the end of Volume II.

The International Organizations section gives extensive coverage to the United Nations and its related agencies and bodies. There are also detailed articles concerning other major international and regional organizations; entries for many affiliated organizations appear within these articles. In addition, the section includes briefer details of some 1,500 other international organizations. A comprehensive Index of International Organizations is included at the end of Volume I.

Each country is covered by an individual chapter, containing: an introductory survey including recent history, economic affairs, government, defence, education, and public holidays; an economic and demographic survey using the latest available statistics on area and population, health and welfare, agriculture, forestry, fishing, industry, finance, trade, transport, tourism, the media, and education; and a directory section listing names, addresses and other useful facts about organizations in the fields of government, election commissions, political parties, diplomatic representation, judiciary, religions, the media, telecommunications, banking, insurance, trade and industry, development organizations, chambers of commerce, industrial and trade associations, utilities, trade unions, transport, and tourism.

The entire content of the print edition of THE EUROPA WORLD YEAR BOOK is available online at www.europaworld.com. This prestigious resource incorporates sophisticated search and browse functions as well as specially commissioned visual and statistical content. An ongoing programme of updates of key areas of information ensures currency of content, and enhances the richness of the coverage for which THE EUROPA WORLD YEAR BOOK is renowned.

Readers are referred to the nine titles in the Europa Regional Surveys of the World series: AFRICA SOUTH OF THE SAHARA, CENTRAL AND SOUTH-EASTERN EUROPE, EASTERN EUROPE, RUSSIA AND CENTRAL ASIA, THE FAR EAST AND AUSTRALASIA, THE MIDDLE EAST AND NORTH AFRICA, SOUTH AMERICA, CENTRAL AMERICA AND THE CARIBBEAN, SOUTH ASIA, THE USA AND CANADA, and WESTERN EUROPE, available both in print and online, offer comprehensive analysis at regional, sub-regional and country level. More detailed coverage of international organizations is to be found in THE EUROPA DIRECTORY OF INTERNATIONAL ORGANIZATIONS.

The content of THE EUROPA WORLD YEAR BOOK is extensively revised and updated by a variety of methods, including direct mailing to all the institutions listed. Many other sources are used, such as national statistical offices, government departments and diplomatic missions. The editors thank the innumerable individuals and organizations world-wide whose generous co-operation in providing current information for this edition is invaluable in presenting the most accurate and up-to-date material available.

May 2008

ACKNOWLEDGEMENTS

The editors gratefully acknowledge particular indebtedness for permission to reproduce material from the following sources: the United Nations' statistical databases and *Demographic Yearbook*, *Statistical Yearbook*, *Monthly Bulletin of Statistics*, *Industrial Commodity Statistics Yearbook* and *International Trade Statistics Yearbook*; the United Nations Educational, Scientific and Cultural Organization's *Statistical Yearbook* and Institute for Statistics database; the *Human Development Report* of the United Nations Development Programme; the Food and Agriculture Organization of the United Nations' statistical database; the statistical databases of the World Health Organization; the International Labour Office's statistical database and *Yearbook of Labour Statistics*; the World Bank's *World Bank Atlas*, *Global Development Finance*, *World Development Report* and *World Development Indicators*; the International Monetary Fund's statistical database, *International Financial Statistics* and *Government Finance Statistics Yearbook*; the US Geological Survey; the International Telecommunication Union; the World Tourism Organization's *Compendium* and *Yearbook of Tourism Statistics*; and *The Military Balance 2008*, a publication of the International Institute for Strategic Studies, Arundel House, 13–15 Arundel Street, London WC2R 3DX. Statistics Canada information is used with the permission of Statistics Canada. Users are forbidden to copy this material and/or redisseminate the data, in an original or modified form, for commercial purposes, without the expressed permission of Statistics Canada. Information on the availability of the wide range of data from Statistics Canada can be obtained from Statistics Canada's Regional Offices, its website at www.statcan.ca, and its toll-free access number 1-800-263-1136.

HEALTH AND WELFARE STATISTICS: SOURCES AND DEFINITIONS

Total fertility rate Source: WHO Statistical Information System. The number of children that would be born per woman, assuming no female mortality at child-bearing ages and the age-specific fertility rates of a specified country and reference period.

Under-5 mortality rate Source: WHO Statistical Information System. Defined by WHO as the probability of a child born in a specific year or period dying before the age of five, if subject to the age-specific mortality rates of that year or period.

HIV/AIDS Source: UNAIDS. Estimated percentage of adults aged 15 to 49 years living with HIV/AIDS. < indicates 'fewer than'.

Health expenditure Source: WHO Statistical Information System.
US $ per head (PPP)
International dollar estimates, derived by dividing local currency units by an estimate of their purchasing-power parity (PPP) compared with the US dollar. PPPs are the rates of currency conversion that equalize the purchasing power of different currencies by eliminating the differences in price levels between countries.
% of GDP
GDP levels for OECD countries follow the most recent UN System of National Accounts. For non-OECD countries a value was estimated by utilizing existing UN, IMF and World Bank data.
Public expenditure
Government health-related outlays plus expenditure by social schemes compulsorily affiliated with a sizeable share of the population, and extrabudgetary funds allocated to health services. Figures include grants or loans provided by international agencies, other national authorities, and sometimes commercial banks.

Access to water and sanitation Source: WHO/UNICEF Joint Monitoring Programme on Water Supply and Sanitation (JMP) (Mid-Term Assessment, 2004). Defined in terms of the percentage of the population using improved facilities in terms of the type of technology and levels of service afforded. For water, this includes house connections, public standpipes, boreholes with handpumps, protected dug wells, protected spring and rainwater collection; allowance is also made for other locally defined technologies. Sanitation is defined to include connection to a sewer or septic tank system, pour-flush latrine, simple pit or ventilated improved pit latrine, again with allowance for acceptable local technologies. Access to water and sanitation does not imply that the level of service or quality of water is 'adequate' or 'safe'.

Human Development Index (HDI) Source: UNDP, *Human Development Report* (2007/08). A summary of human development measured by three basic dimensions: prospects for a long and healthy life, measured by life expectancy at birth; knowledge, measured by adult literacy rate (two-thirds' weight) and the combined gross enrolment ratio in primary, secondary and tertiary education (one-third weight); and standard of living, measured by GDP per head (PPP US $). The index value obtained lies between zero and one. A value above 0.8 indicates high human development, between 0.5 and 0.8 medium human development, and below 0.5 low human development. A centralized data source for all three dimensions was not available for all countries. In some such cases other data sources were used to calculate a substitute value; however, this was excluded from the ranking. Other countries, including non-UNDP members, were excluded from the HDI altogether. In total, 177 countries were ranked for 2005.

CONTENTS

Abbreviations — Page ix
International Telephone Codes — xiii

PART ONE
International Organizations*

The United Nations	3
Members	3
Permanent Missions	4
Observers	8
Information Centres/Services	9
Conferences	10
Co-ordinating Bodies	10
Finance	11
Secretariat	11
General Assembly	12
Security Council	14
Trusteeship Council	19
Economic and Social Council—ECOSOC	19
International Court of Justice	20

United Nations Fundamental Treaties
Charter of the United Nations	23
Universal Declaration of Human Rights	31

United Nations Regional Commissions — 33
Economic Commission for Europe—ECE	33
Economic and Social Commission for Asia and the Pacific—ESCAP	35
Economic Commission for Latin America and the Caribbean—ECLAC	38
Economic Commission for Africa—ECA	40
Economic and Social Commission for Western Asia—ESCWA	43

Other United Nations Bodies — 46
Office for the Co-ordination of Humanitarian Affairs—OCHA	46
United Nations Office on Drugs and Crime—UNODC	47
Office of the United Nations High Commissioner for Human Rights—OHCHR	49
United Nations Human Settlements Programme—UN-Habitat	50
United Nations Children's Fund—UNICEF	52
United Nations Conference on Trade and Development—UNCTAD	55
United Nations Development Programme—UNDP	58
United Nations Environment Programme—UNEP	62
United Nations High Commissioner for Refugees—UNHCR	66
United Nations Peace-keeping	77
United Nations Peace-building	89
United Nations Population Fund—UNFPA	92
United Nations Relief and Works Agency for Palestine Refugees in the Near East—UNRWA	94
United Nations Training and Research Institutes	96
World Food Programme—WFP	98

Specialized Agencies within the UN System — 102
Food and Agriculture Organization—FAO	102
International Atomic Energy Agency—IAEA	107
International Bank for Reconstruction and Development—IBRD (World Bank)	112
International Development Association—IDA	118
International Finance Corporation—IFC	118
Multilateral Investment Guarantee Agency—MIGA	Page 120
International Civil Aviation Organization—ICAO	121
International Fund for Agricultural Development—IFAD	123
International Labour Organization—ILO	124
International Maritime Organization—IMO	127
International Monetary Fund—IMF	129
International Telecommunication Union—ITU	135
United Nations Educational, Scientific and Cultural Organization—UNESCO	137
United Nations Industrial Development Organization—UNIDO	142
Universal Postal Union—UPU	144
World Health Organization—WHO	145
World Intellectual Property Organization—WIPO	152
World Meteorological Organization—WMO	155
World Tourism Organization—UNWTO	159

African Development Bank—ADB	162
African Union—AU	164
Andean Community of Nations	170
Arab Fund for Economic and Social Development—AFESD	174
Arab Monetary Fund	175
Asia-Pacific Economic Co-operation—APEC	176
Asian Development Bank—ADB	182
Association of South East Asian Nations—ASEAN	185
Bank for International Settlements—BIS	194
Caribbean Community and Common Market—CARICOM	196
Central American Integration System	201
Common Market for Eastern and Southern Africa—COMESA	205
The Commonwealth	206
The Commonwealth of Independent States—CIS	215
Co-operation Council for the Arab States of the Gulf (Gulf Co-operation Council—GCC)	219
Council of Arab Economic Unity	222
Council of the Baltic Sea States—CBSS	224
The Council of Europe	225
Economic Community of West African States—ECOWAS	232
Economic Co-operation Organization—ECO	238
European Bank for Reconstruction and Development—EBRD	239
European Space Agency—ESA	241
European Union—EU	244
The Franc Zone	306
Inter-American Development Bank—IDB	308
Intergovernmental Authority on Development—IGAD	311
International Chamber of Commerce—ICC	312
International Criminal Court	314
International Olympic Committee	315
International Organization for Migration—IOM	317
International Red Cross and Red Crescent Movement	319
International Committee of the Red Cross—ICRC	320
International Federation of Red Cross and Red Crescent Societies—IFRCS	322
International Seabed Authority	323
International Trade Union Confederation—ITUC	324
Inter-Parliamentary Union—IPU	326
Islamic Development Bank	329
Latin American Integration Association—LAIA	331
League of Arab States	332
Mercosur/Mercosul—see Southern Common Market	
North American Free Trade Agreement—NAFTA	338
North Atlantic Treaty Organization—NATO	340
Organisation for Economic Co-operation and Development—OECD	347
International Energy Agency—IEA	351
OECD Nuclear Energy Agency—NEA	352

---
* A complete Index of International Organizations is to be found on p. 2545.

CONTENTS

Organization for Security and Co-operation in Europe—OSCE	Page 354
Organization of American States—OAS	360
Organization of Arab Petroleum Exporting Countries—OAPEC	366
Organization of the Black Sea Economic Co-operation—BSEC	367
Organization of the Islamic Conference—OIC	369
Organization of the Petroleum Exporting Countries—OPEC	373
OPEC Fund for International Development	376
Pacific Community	377
Pacific Islands Forum	380
South Asian Association for Regional Co-operation—SAARC	384
Southern African Development Community—SADC	386
Southern Common Market (Mercosur/Mercosul)	391
World Council of Churches—WCC	393
World Federation of Trade Unions—WFTU	395
World Trade Organization—WTO	396
Other International Organizations	401

PART TWO
Afghanistan–Jordan

Afghanistan	475
Albania	502
Algeria	522
Andorra	549
Angola	556
Antarctica	575
Antigua and Barbuda	577
Argentina	587
Armenia	616
Australia	634
Australian External Territories:	
Christmas Island	670
Cocos (Keeling) Islands	672
Norfolk Island	674
Other Australian Territories	678
Austria	680
Azerbaijan	708
The Bahamas	727
Bahrain	738
Bangladesh	755
Barbados	780
Belarus	790
Belgium	810
Belize	840
Benin	851
Bhutan	869
Bolivia	885
Bosnia and Herzegovina	906
Botswana	931
Brazil	946
Brunei	980
Bulgaria	992
Burkina Faso	1012
Burma—see Myanmar, Vol. II	
Burundi	1029
Cambodia	1048
Cameroon	1070
Canada	1088
Cape Verde	1128
The Central African Republic	1137
Chad	1153
Chile	1171
The People's Republic of China	1197
Chinese Special Administrative Regions:	
Hong Kong	1248
Macao	1270
China (Taiwan)	1284
Colombia	1317
The Comoros	1342
The Democratic Republic of the Congo	Page 1354
The Republic of the Congo	1375
Costa Rica	1391
Côte d'Ivoire	1407
Croatia	1431
Cuba	1451
Cyprus	1475
The Czech Republic	1501
Denmark	1521
Danish External Territories:	
Faroe Islands	1546
Greenland	1552
Djibouti	1558
Dominica	1567
The Dominican Republic	1576
East Timor—see Timor-Leste, Vol. II	
Ecuador	1594
Egypt	1618
El Salvador	1649
Equatorial Guinea	1666
Eritrea	1676
Estonia	1689
Ethiopia	1708
Fiji	1729
Finland	1745
Finnish External Territory:	
Åland Islands	1768
France	1772
French Overseas Possessions:	
French Overseas Regions and Departments:	
French Guiana	1825
Guadeloupe	1832
Martinique	1840
Réunion	1846
French Overseas Collectivities:	
French Polynesia	1854
Mayotte	1866
Saint-Barthélemy	1871
Saint-Martin	1871
Saint Pierre and Miquelon	1872
The Wallis and Futuna Islands	1875
Other French Overseas Territories:	
The French Southern and Antarctic Territories	1882
New Caledonia	1883
Gabon	1896
The Gambia	1912
Georgia	1926
Germany	1949
Ghana	1999
Greece	2019
Grenada	2040
Guatemala	2050
Guinea	2070
Guinea-Bissau	2086
Guyana	2100
Haiti	2113
Honduras	2134
Hungary	2149
Iceland	2170
India	2183
Indonesia	2242
Iran	2282
Iraq	2315
Ireland	2348
Israel	2374
Italy	2415
The Ivory Coast—see Côte d'Ivoire	
Jamaica	2455
Japan	2471
Jordan	2521

Index of International Organizations 2545

An Index of Territories is to be found at the end of Volume II.

ABBREVIATIONS

AB	Aktiebolag (Joint-Stock Company); Alberta	bte	boîte (box)	CTCA	Confederación de Trabajadores Centro-americanos
Abog.	Abogado (Lawyer)	Bul.	Bulvar (boulevard)	Cttee	Committee
Acad.	Academician; Academy	bulv.	bulvarīs (boulevard)	cu	cubic
ACP	African, Caribbean and Pacific (countries)			cwt	hundredweight
ACT	Australian Capital Territory	C	Centigrade		
AD	anno Domini	c.	circa; cuadra(s) (block(s))	DC	District of Columbia; Distrito Capital; Distrito Central
ADB	African Development Bank; Asian Development Bank	CA	California		
		CACM	Central American Common Market	d.d.	delniška družba, dioničko društvo (joint stock company)
ADC	aide-de-camp	Cad.	Caddesi (Street)		
Adm.	Admiral	CAP	Common Agricultural Policy	DE	Delaware; Departamento Estatal
admin.	administration	cap.	capital		
AfDB	African Development Bank	Capt.	Captain	Dec.	December
AG	Aktiengesellschaft (Joint-Stock Company)	CAR	Central African Republic	Del.	Delegación
		CARICOM	Caribbean Community and Common Market	Dem.	Democrat; Democratic
AH	anno Hegirae			Dep.	Deputy
a.i.	ad interim	CBSS	Council of Baltic Sea States	dep.	deposits
AID	(US) Agency for International Development	CCL	Caribbean Congress of Labour	Dept	Department
		Cdre	Commodore	devt	development
AIDS	acquired immunodeficiency syndrome	CEMAC	Communauté économique et monétaire de l'Afrique centrale	DF	Distrito Federal
				Dgo	Durango
AK	Alaska	Cen.	Central	Diag.	Diagonal
Al.	Aleja (Alley, Avenue)	CEO	Chief Executive Officer	Dir	Director
AL	Alabama	CET	common external tariff	Div.	Division(al)
ALADI	Asociación Latinoamericana de Integración	CFA	Communauté Financière Africaine; Coopération Financière en Afrique centrale	DM	Deutsche Mark
				DMZ	demilitarized zone
Alt.	Alternate			DNA	deoxyribonucleic acid
AM	Amplitude Modulation	CFE	Treaty on Conventional Armed Forces in Europe	DN	Distrito Nacional
a.m.	ante meridiem (before noon)			Doc.	Docent
amalg.	amalgamated	CFP	Common Fisheries Policy; Communauté française du Pacifique; Comptoirs français du Pacifique	Dott.	Dottore/essa
Apdo	Apartado (Post Box)			DPRK	Democratic People's Republic of Korea
APEC	Asia-Pacific Economic Co-operation				
				Dr	Doctor
approx.	approximately	Chair.	Chairman/person/woman	Dr.	Drive
Apt	Apartment	Chih.	Chihuahua	Dra	Doctora
AR	Arkansas	CI	Channel Islands	Dr Hab.	Doktor Habilitowany (Assistant Professor)
ARV	advanced retroviral	Cia	Companhia		
AŞ	Anonim Şirketi (Joint-Stock Company)	Cía	Compañía	dr.(e)	drachma(e)
		Cie	Compagnie	DR-CAFTA	Dominican Republic-Central American Free Trade Agreement
A/S	Aktieselskab (Joint-Stock Company)	c.i.f.	cost, insurance and freight		
		C-in-C	Commander-in-Chief		
ASEAN	Association of South East Asian Nations	circ.	circulation	Drs	Doctorandus
		CIS	Commonwealth of Independent States	DU	depleted uranium
asscn	association			dwt	dead weight tons
assoc.	associate	CJD	Creutzfeldt-Jakob disease		
ASSR	Autonomous Soviet Socialist Republic	cm	centimetre(s)		
		cnr	corner	E	East; Eastern
asst	assistant	CO	Colorado	EBRD	European Bank for Reconstruction and Development
AU	African Union	Co	Company; County		
Aug.	August	c/o	care of		
auth.	authorized	Coah.	Coahuila	EC	European Community
av., Ave	Avenija, Avenue	Col	Colonel	ECA	(United Nations) Economic Commission for Africa
Av., Avda	Avenida (Avenue)	Col.	Colima; Colonia		
Avv.	Avvocato (Lawyer)	COMESA	Common Market for Eastern and Southern Africa	ECE	(United Nations) Economic Commission for Europe
AZ	Arizona				
		Comm.	Commission; Commendatore	ECLAC	(United Nations) Economic Commission for Latin America and the Caribbean
		Commdr	Commander		
b.b.	bez broja (without number)	Commdt	Commandant		
BC	British Columbia	Commr	Commissioner	ECO	Economic Co-operation Organization
BC	before Christ	Cond.	Condiminio		
Bd	Board	Confed.	Confederation	Econ.	Economics; Economist
Bd, Bld, Blv., Blvd	Boulevard	Cont.	Contador (Accountant)	ECOSOC	(United Nations) Economic and Social Council
		COO	Chief Operating Officer		
b/d	barrels per day	Corp.	Corporate	ECOWAS	Economic Community of West African States
BFPO	British Forces' Post Office	Corpn	Corporation		
Bhd	Berhad (Public Limited Company)	CP	Case Postale, Caixa Postal, Casella Postale (Post Box); Communist Party	ECU	European Currency Unit
				Edif.	Edificio (Building)
Bldg	Building			edn	edition
blk	block	CPSU	Communist Party of the Soviet Union	EEA	European Economic Area
Blvr	Bulevar			EFTA	European Free Trade Association
BP	Boîte postale (Post Box)	Cres.	Crescent		
br.(s)	branch(es)	CSCE	Conference on Security and Cooperation in Europe	e.g.	exempli gratia (for example)
Brig.	Brigadier			EIB	European Investment Bank
BSE	bovine spongiform encephalopathy	CSTAL	Confederación Sindical de los Trabajadores de América Latina	EMS	European Monetary System
				EMU	Economic and Monetary Union
BSEC	(Organization of the) Black Sea Economic Co-operation			eMv	electron megavolt
		CT	Connecticut	Eng.	Engineer; Engineering

ABBREVIATIONS

EP	Empresa Pública	HSC	Harmonized System Classification	küç	küçasi (street)
ERM	Exchange Rate Mechanism			kv.	kvartal (apartment block); kvartira (apartment)
ESACA	Emisora de Capital Abierto Sociedad Anónima	HSH	His/Her Serene Highness	kW	kilowatt(s)
Esc.	Escuela; Escudos; Escritorio	Hwy	Highway	kWh	kilowatt hours
ESCAP	(United Nations) Economic and Social Commission for Asia and the Pacific	IA	Iowa	KY	Kentucky
		IBRD	International Bank for Reconstruction and Development		
ESCWA	(United Nations) Economic and Social Commission for Western Asia			LA	Louisiana
		ICC	International Chamber of Commerce; International Criminal Court	lauk	laukums (square)
esq.	esquina (corner)			lb	pound(s)
est.	established; estimate; estimated			LDCs	Least Developed Countries
etc.	et cetera	ICFTU	International Confederation of Free Trade Unions	Lic.	Licenciado
EU	European Union			Licda	Licenciada
eV	eingetragener Verein	ICRC	International Committee of the Red Cross	LNG	liquefied natural gas
excl.	excluding			LPG	liquefied petroleum gas
exec.	executive	ICT	information and communication technology	Lt, Lieut	Lieutenant
Ext.	Extension			Ltd	Limited
		ICTR	International Criminal Tribunal for Rwanda		
F	Fahrenheit	ICTY	International Criminal Tribunal for the former Yugoslavia	m	metre(s)
f.	founded			m.	million
FAO	Food and Agriculture Organization	ID	Idaho	MA	Massachusetts
		IDA	International Development Association	Maj.	Major
f.a.s.	free alongside ship			Man.	Manager; managing
Feb.	February	IDB	Inter-American Development Bank	MB	Manitoba
Fed.	Federal; Federation			mbH	mit beschränkter Haftung (with limited liability)
feds	federations	IDPs	internally displaced persons		
FL	Florida	i.e.	id est (that is to say)	MD	Maryland
FM	frequency modulation	IFC	International Finance Corporation	MDG	Millennium Development Goal
fmr(ly)	former(ly)			MDRI	multilateral debt relief initiative
f.o.b.	free on board	IGAD	Intergovernmental Authority on Development	ME	Maine
Fr	Father			Me	Maître
Fr.	Franc	IHL	International Humanitarian Law	mem.(s)	member(s)
Fri.	Friday	IL	Illinois	MEP	Member of the European Parliament
FRY	Federal Republic of Yugoslavia	ILO	International Labour Organization/Office		
ft	foot (feet)			Mercosul	Mercado Comum do Sul (Southern Common Market)
FTA	free trade agreement/area	IMF	International Monetary Fund		
FYRM	former Yugoslav republic of Macedonia	IML	International Migration Law	Mercosur	Mercado Común del Sur (Southern Common Market)
		in (ins)	inch (inches)		
		IN	Indiana	Méx.	México
		Inc, Incorp.			
g	gram(s)	Incd	Incorporated	MFN	most favoured nation
g.	gatve (street)	incl.	including	mfrs	manufacturers
GA	Georgia	Ind.	Independent	Mgr	Monseigneur; Monsignor
GATT	General Agreement on Tariffs and Trade	INF	Intermediate-Range Nuclear Forces	MHz	megahertz
				MI	Michigan
GCC	Gulf Co-operation Council	Ing.	Engineer	MIA	missing in action
Gdns	Gardens	Insp.	Inspector	Mich.	Michoacán
GDP	gross domestic product	Int.	International	MIGA	Multilateral Investment Guarantee Agency
Gen.	General	Inzå.	Engineer		
GeV	giga electron volts	IP	intellectual property	Mil.	Military
GM	genetically modified	IPU	Inter-Parliamentary Union	Mlle	Mademoiselle
GmbH	Gesellschaft mit beschränkter Haftung (Limited Liability Company)	Ir	Engineer	mm	millimetre(s)
		IRF	International Road Federation	Mme	Madame
		irreg.	irregular	MN	Minnesota
GMO(s)	genetically modified organism(s)	Is	Islands	mnt.	mante (road)
GMT	Greenwich Mean Time	ISIC	International Standard Industrial Classification	MO	Missouri
GNI	gross national income			Mon.	Monday
GNP	gross national product	IT	information technology	Mor.	Morelos
Gov.	Governor	ITU	International Telecommunication Union	MOU	memorandum of understanding
Govt	Government			MP	Member of Parliament
Gro	Guerrero	ITUC	International Trade Union Confederation	MS	Mississippi
grt	gross registered tons			MSS	Manuscripts
GSM	Global System for Mobile Communications	Iur.	Lawyer	MT	Montana
				MW	megawatt(s); medium wave
Gto	Guanajuato	Jal.	Jalisco	MWh	megawatt hour(s)
GWh	gigawatt hours	Jan.	January		
		Jnr	Junior		
		Jr	Jonkheer (Esquire); Junior	N	North; Northern
ha	hectares	Jt	Joint	n.a.	not available
HE	His/Her Eminence; His/Her Excellency			nab.	naberezhnaya (embankment, quai)
hf	hlutafelag (Limited Company)	Kav.	Kaveling (Plot)	NAFTA	North American Free Trade Agreement
HI	Hawaii	kg	kilogram(s)		
HIPC	heavily indebted poor country	KG	Kommandit Gesellschaft (Limited Partnership)	nám.	náměstí (square)
HIV	human immunodeficiency virus			Nat.	National
hl	hectolitre(s)	kHz	kilohertz	NATO	North Atlantic Treaty Organization
HM	His/Her Majesty	KK	Kaien Kaisha (Limited Company)		
Hon.	Honorary, Honourable	km	kilometre(s)	Nay.	Nayarit
hp	horsepower	kom.	komnata (room)	NB	New Brunswick
HPAI	highly pathogenic avian influenza	kor.	korpus (block)	NC	North Carolina
		k'och.	k'ochasi (street)	NCD	National Capital District
HQ	Headquarters	KS	Kansas	NCO	non-commissioned officer
HRH	His/Her Royal Highness				

ABBREVIATIONS

ND	North Dakota	Prof.	Professor	SITC	Standard International Trade Classification
NE	Nebraska; North-East	Propr	Proprietor	SJ	Society of Jesus
NEPAD	New Partnership for Africa's Development	Prov.	Province; Provincial; Provinciale (Dutch)	SK	Saskatchewan
NGO	non-governmental organization	prov.	provulok (lane)	Skt	Sankt (Saint)
NH	New Hampshire	pst.	puistotie (avenue)	SLP	San Luis Potosí
NJ	New Jersey	PT	Perseroan Terbatas (Limited Company)	SMEs	small and medium-sized enterprises
NL	Newfoundland and Labrador, Nuevo León	Pte	Private; Puente (Bridge)	s/n	sin número (without number)
NM	New Mexico	Pty	Proprietary	Soc.	Society
NMP	net material product	p.u.	paid up	Sok.	Sokak (Street)
no	numéro, número (number)	publ.	publication; published	Son.	Sonora
no.	number	Publr	Publisher	Şos.	Şosea (Road)
Nov.	November	Pue.	Puebla	SP	São Paulo
nr	near	Pvt.	Private	SpA	Società per Azioni (Joint-Stock Company)
nrt	net registered tons			Sq.	Square
NS	Nova Scotia			sq	square (in measurements)
NSW	New South Wales	QC	Québec	Sr	Senior; Señor
NT	Northwest Territories	QIP	Quick Impact Project	Sra	Señora
NU	Nunavut Territory	Qld	Queensland	Srl	Società a Responsabilità Limitata (Limited Company)
NV	Naamloze Vennootschap (Limited Company); Nevada	Qro	Querétaro		
		Q. Roo	Quintana Roo	SSR	Soviet Socialist Republic
NW	North-West	q.v.	quod vide (to which refer)	St	Saint, Sint; Street
NY	New York			Sta	Santa
NZ	New Zealand			Ste	Sainte
		Rag.	Ragioniere (Accountant)	STI(s)	sexually transmitted infection(s)
		Rd	Road	str.	strada, stradă (street)
OAPEC	Organization of Arab Petroleum Exporting Countries	R(s)	rand; rupee(s)	str-la	stradelă (street)
		reg., regd	register; registered	subs.	subscribed; subscriptions
OAS	Organization of American States	reorg.	reorganized	Sun.	Sunday
OAU	Organization of African Unity	Rep.	Republic; Republican; Representative	Supt	Superintendent
Oax.	Oaxaca			SUV	sports utility vehicle
Oct.	October	Repub.	Republic	sv.	Saint
OECD	Organisation for Economic Cooperation and Development	res	reserve(s)	SW	South-West
		retd	retired		
OECS	Organisation of Eastern Caribbean States	Rev.	Reverend		
		RI	Rhode Island	Tab.	Tabasco
Of.	Oficina (Office)	RJ	Rio de Janeiro	Tamps	Tamaulipas
OH	Ohio	Rm	Room	TAŞ	Turkiye Anonim Şirketi (Turkish Joint-Stock Company)
OIC	Organization of the Islamic Conference	RN	Royal Navy		
		ro-ro	roll-on roll-off	Tas	Tasmania
OK	Oklahoma	RP	Recette principale	TD	Teachta Dàla (Member of Parliament)
ON	Ontario	Rp.(s)	rupiah(s)		
OPEC	Organization of the Petroleum Exporting Countries	Rpto	Reparto (Estate)	tech., techn.	technical
		RSFSR	Russian Soviet Federative Socialist Republic	tel.	telephone
opp.	opposite			TEU	20-ft equivalent unit
OR	Oregon	Rt	Right	Thur.	Thursday
Org.	Organization			TN	Tennessee
ORIT	Organización Regional Interamericana de Trabajadores			tř	třída (avenue)
	S	South; Southern; San	Treas.	Treasurer
		SA	Société Anonyme, Sociedad Anónima (Limited Company); South Australia	Tue.	Tuesday
OSCE	Organization for Security and Cooperation in Europe			TV	television
				TX	Texas
		SAARC	South Asian Association for Regional Co-operation		
p.	page	SACN	South American Community of Nations		
p.a.	per annum			u.	utca (street)
PA	Palestinian Authority; Pennsylvania	SAECA	Sociedad Anónima Emisora de Capital Abierto	u/a	unit of account
				UAE	United Arab Emirates
Parl.	Parliament(ary)	SADC	Southern African Development Community	UEE	Unidade Económica Estatal
per.	pereulok (lane, alley)			UEMOA	Union économique et monetaire ouest-africaine
PE	Prince Edward Island	SAR	Special Administrative Region		
Perm. Rep.	Permanent Representative	SARL	Sociedade Anônima de Responsabilidade Limitada (Joint-Stock Company of Limited Liability)	UK	United Kingdom
PF	Postfach (Post Box)			ul.	ulica, ulitsa (street)
PICTs	Pacific Island countries and territories			UM	ouguiya
				UN	United Nations
PK	Posta Kutusu (Post Box)	SARS	Severe Acute Respiratory Syndrome	UNAIDS	United Nations Joint Programme on HIV/AIDS
Pl.	Plac, Plads (square)				
pl.	platz; place; ploshchad (square)	Sat.	Saturday	UNCTAD	United Nations Conference on Trade and Development
PLC	Public Limited Company	SC	South Carolina		
PLO	Palestine Liberation Organization	SD	South Dakota	UNDP	United Nations Development Programme
		Sdn Bhd	Sendirian Berhad (Private Limited Company)		
p.m.	post meridiem (after noon)			UNEP	United Nations Environment Programme
PMB	Private Mail Bag	SDR(s)	Special Drawing Right(s)		
PNA	Palestinian National Authority	SE	South-East	UNESCO	United Nations Educational, Scientific and Cultural Organization
POB	Post Office Box	Sec.	Secretary		
pp.	pages	Secr.	Secretariat		
PPP	purchasing-power parity	Sen.	Senior; Senator	UNHCHR	UN High Commissioner for Human Rights
PQ	Québec	Sept.	September		
PR	Puerto Rico	SER	Sua Eccellenza Reverendissima (His Eminence)	UNHCR	United Nations High Commissioner for Refugees
pr.	prospekt, prospekti (avenue)				
Pres.	President	SFRY	Socialist Federal Republic of Yugoslavia	UNICEF	United Nations Children's Fund
PRGF	Poverty Reduction and Growth Facility			Univ.	University
		SGP	Stability and Growth Pact	UNODC	United Nations Office on Drugs and Crime
Prin.	Principal	Sin.	Sinaloa		

ABBREVIATIONS

UNRWA	United Nations Relief and Works Agency for Palestine Refugees in the Near East	v-CJD	new variant Creutzfeldt-Jakob disease	WEU	Western European Union
				WFP	World Food Programme
		Ven.	Venerable	WFTU	World Federation of Trade Unions
UNWTO	World Tourism Organization	Ver.	Veracruz		
Urb.	Urbanización (District)	VHF	Very High Frequency	WHO	World Health Organization
US	United States	VI	(US) Virgin Islands	WI	Wisconsin
USA	United States of America	Vic	Victoria	WSSD	World Summit on Sustainable Development
USAID	United States Agency for International Development	Vn	Veien (Street)		
		vol.(s)	volume(s)	WTO	World Trade Organization
USSR	Union of Soviet Socialist Republics	VT	Vermont	WV	West Virginia
		vul.	vulitsa, vulytsa (street)	WY	Wyoming
UT	Utah				
		W	West; Western		
VA	Virginia	WA	Washington (State); Western Australia		
VAT	value-added tax			yr	year
VEB	Volkseigener Betrieb (Public Company)	WCL	World Confederation of Labour	YT	Yukon Territory
		Wed.	Wednesday	Yuc.	Yucatán

xii

INTERNATIONAL TELEPHONE CODES

To make international calls to telephone and fax numbers listed in *The Europa World Year Book*, dial the international code of the country from which you are calling, followed by the appropriate country code for the organization you wish to call (listed below), followed by the area code (if applicable) and telephone or fax number listed in the entry.

	Country code	+ or − GMT*
Afghanistan	93	+4½
Albania	355	+1
Algeria	213	+1
Andorra	376	+1
Angola	244	+1
Antigua and Barbuda	1 268	−4
Argentina	54	−3
Armenia	374	+4
Australia	61	+8 to +10
Australian External Territories:		
Australian Antarctic Territory	672	+3 to +10
Christmas Island	61	+7
Cocos (Keeling) Islands	61	+6½
Norfolk Island	672	+11½
Austria	43	+1
Azerbaijan	994	+5
Bahamas	1 242	−5
Bahrain	973	+3
Bangladesh	880	+6
Barbados	1 246	−4
Belarus	375	+2
Belgium	32	+1
Belize	501	−6
Benin	229	+1
Bhutan	975	+6
Bolivia	591	−4
Bosnia and Herzegovina	387	+1
Botswana	267	+2
Brazil	55	−3 to −4
Brunei	673	+8
Bulgaria	359	+2
Burkina Faso	226	0
Burundi	257	+2
Cambodia	855	+7
Cameroon	237	+1
Canada	1	−3 to −8
Cape Verde	238	−1
Central African Republic	236	+1
Chad	235	+1
Chile	56	−4
China, People's Republic	86	+8
Special Administrative Regions:		
Hong Kong	852	+8
Macao	853	+8
China (Taiwan)	886	+8
Colombia	57	−5
Comoros	269	+3
Congo, Democratic Republic	243	+1
Congo, Republic	242	+1
Costa Rica	506	−6
Côte d'Ivoire	225	0
Croatia	385	+1
Cuba	53	−5
Cyprus	357	+2
'Turkish Republic of Northern Cyprus'	90 392	+2
Czech Republic	420	+1
Denmark	45	+1
Danish External Territories:		
Faroe Islands	298	0
Greenland	299	−1 to −4
Djibouti	253	+3
Dominica	1 767	−4
Dominican Republic	1 809	−4

	Country code	+ or − GMT*
Ecuador	593	−5
Egypt	20	+2
El Salvador	503	−6
Equatorial Guinea	240	+1
Eritrea	291	+3
Estonia	372	+2
Ethiopia	251	+3
Fiji	679	+12
Finland	358	+2
Finnish External Territory:		
Åland Islands	358	+2
France	33	+1
French Overseas Regions and Departments:		
French Guiana	594	−3
Guadeloupe	590	−4
Martinique	596	−4
Réunion	262	+4
French Overseas Collectivities:		
French Polynesia	689	−9 to −10
Mayotte	262	+3
Saint-Barthélemy	590	−4
Saint-Martin	590	−4
Saint Pierre and Miquelon	508	−3
Wallis and Futuna Islands	681	+12
Other French Overseas Territory:		
New Caledonia	687	+11
Gabon	241	+1
Gambia	220	0
Georgia	995	+4
Germany	49	+1
Ghana	233	0
Greece	30	+2
Grenada	1 473	−4
Guatemala	502	−6
Guinea	224	0
Guinea-Bissau	245	0
Guyana	592	−4
Haiti	509	−5
Honduras	504	−6
Hungary	36	+1
Iceland	354	0
India	91	+5½
Indonesia	62	+7 to +9
Iran	98	+3½
Iraq	964	+3
Ireland	353	0
Israel	972	+2
Italy	39	+1
Jamaica	1 876	−5
Japan	81	+9
Jordan	962	+2
Kazakhstan	7	+6
Kenya	254	+3
Kiribati	686	+12 to +13
Korea, Democratic People's Republic (North Korea)	850	+9
Korea, Republic (South Korea)	82	+9
Kosovo	381†	+3
Kuwait	965	+3
Kyrgyzstan	996	+5
Laos	856	+7
Latvia	371	+2

INTERNATIONAL TELEPHONE CODES

	Country code	+ or − GMT*
Lebanon	961	+2
Lesotho	266	+2
Liberia	231	0
Libya	218	+1
Liechtenstein	423	+1
Lithuania	370	+2
Luxembourg	352	+1
Macedonia, former Yugoslav republic	389	+1
Madagascar	261	+3
Malawi	265	+2
Malaysia	60	+8
Maldives	960	+5
Mali	223	0
Malta	356	+1
Marshall Islands	692	+12
Mauritania	222	0
Mauritius	230	+4
Mexico	52	−6 to −7
Micronesia, Federated States	691	+10 to +11
Moldova	373	+2
Monaco	377	+1
Mongolia	976	+7 to +9
Montenegro	382	+1
Morocco	212	0
Mozambique	258	+2
Myanmar	95	+6½
Namibia	264	+2
Nauru	674	+12
Nepal	977	+5¾
Netherlands	31	+1
Netherlands Dependencies:		
Aruba	297	−4
Netherlands Antilles	599	−4
New Zealand	64	+12
New Zealand's Dependent and Associated Territories:		
Tokelau	690	−10
Cook Islands	682	−10
Niue	683	−11
Nicaragua	505	−6
Niger	227	+1
Nigeria	234	+1
Norway	47	+1
Norwegian External Territory:		
Svalbard	47	+1
Oman	968	+4
Pakistan	92	+5
Palau	680	+9
Palestinian Autonomous Areas	970 or 972	+2
Panama	507	−5
Papua New Guinea	675	+10
Paraguay	595	−4
Peru	51	−5
Philippines	63	+8
Poland	48	+1
Portugal	351	0
Qatar	974	+3
Romania	40	+2
Russian Federation	7	+2 to +12
Rwanda	250	+2
Saint Christopher and Nevis	1 869	−4
Saint Lucia	1 758	−4
Saint Vincent and the Grenadines	1 784	−4
Samoa	685	−11
San Marino	378	+1
São Tomé and Príncipe	239	0
Saudi Arabia	966	+3
Senegal	221	0
Serbia	381	+1
Seychelles	248	+4
Sierra Leone	232	0

	Country code	+ or − GMT*
Singapore	65	+8
Slovakia	421	+1
Slovenia	386	+1
Solomon Islands	677	+11
Somalia	252	+3
South Africa	27	+2
Spain	34	+1
Sri Lanka	94	+5½
Sudan	249	+2
Suriname	597	−3
Swaziland	268	+2
Sweden	46	+1
Switzerland	41	+1
Syria	963	+2
Tajikistan	992	+5
Tanzania	255	+3
Thailand	66	+7
Timor-Leste	670	+9
Togo	228	0
Tonga	676	+13
Trinidad and Tobago	1 868	−4
Tunisia	216	+1
Turkey	90	+2
Turkmenistan	993	+5
Tuvalu	688	+12
Uganda	256	+3
Ukraine	380	+2
United Arab Emirates	971	+4
United Kingdom	44	0
United Kingdom Crown Dependencies	44	0
United Kingdom Overseas Territories:		
Anguilla	1 264	−4
Ascension Island	247	0
Bermuda	1 441	−4
British Virgin Islands	1 284	−4
Cayman Islands	1 345	−5
Diego Garcia (British Indian Ocean Territory)	246	+5
Falkland Islands	500	−4
Gibraltar	350	+1
Montserrat	1 664	−4
Pitcairn Islands	872	−8
Saint Helena	290	0
Tristan da Cunha	290	0
Turks and Caicos Islands	1 649	−5
United States of America	1	−5 to −10
United States Commonwealth Territories:		
Northern Mariana Islands	1 670	+10
Puerto Rico	1 787	−4
United States External Territories:		
American Samoa	1 684	−11
Guam	1 671	+10
United States Virgin Islands	1 340	−4
Uruguay	598	−3
Uzbekistan	998	+5
Vanuatu	678	+11
Vatican City	39	+1
Venezuela	58	−4½
Viet Nam	84	+7
Yemen	967	+3
Zambia	260	+2
Zimbabwe	263	+2

* The times listed compare the standard (winter) times in the various countries. Some countries adopt Summer (Daylight Saving) Time—i.e. +1 hour—for part of the year.

† Mobile telephone numbers for Kosovo use the country code for Monaco (377).

Free trial available!

Europa World *Plus*
Europa World and the Europa Regional Surveys of the World online
www.europaworld.com

Europa World *Plus* enables you to subscribe to Europa World together with as many of the nine Regional Surveys of the World online as you choose, in one simple annual subscription.

The Europa Regional Surveys of the World complement and expand upon the information in Europa World with in-depth, expert analysis at regional, sub-regional and country level.

Providing:

* An interactive online library for all the countries and territories of each of the world regions
* Impartial coverage of issues of regional importance from acknowledged experts
* A vast range of up-to-date economic, political and statistical data
* Book and periodical bibliographies - direct you to further research

* Extensive directory of research institutes specializing in the region
* Ability to search by content type across regions
* Thousands of click-through web links to external sites

The nine titles that make up the series are as follows: *Africa South of the Sahara; Central and South-Eastern Europe; Eastern Europe, Russia and Central Asia; The Far East and Australasia; The Middle East and North Africa; South America, Central America and the Caribbean; South Asia; The USA and Canada; Western Europe.*

For further information and to register for a free trial please contact us at:
Tel: + 44 (0) 20 7017 6062
Fax: + 44 (0) 20 7017 6720
E-mail: reference.online@tandf.co.uk

free trial available!

Europa World Plus
Europa World and the Europa Regional Surveys of the World online
www.europaworld.com

Europa World Plus enables you to subscribe to Europa World together with as many of the nine Regional Surveys of the World online as you choose, in one simple annual subscription.

The Europa Regional Surveys of the World complement and expand upon the information in Europa World with in-depth, expert analysis at regional, sub-regional and country level.

Providing:

* An interactive online store for all the entities and territories of each of the world's bodies
* In-depth coverage of issues of regional importance from a knowledgeable expert
* A vast range of up-to-date economic, political and statistical data
* Book and periodical bibliographies - direct route to further research

Plus:

* Extensive directory of research institutes specialising in the region
* Ability to search by content type across apportions
* Hyperlinked click-through web links to external sites

The nine titles that make up the series are as follows: Africa South of the Sahara, Central and South-Eastern Europe, Eastern Europe, Russia and Central Asia, The Far East and Australasia, The Middle East and North Africa, South America, Central America and the Caribbean, South Asia, The USA and Canada, Western Europe.

For further information and to register for a free trial please contact us at:
Tel: +44 (0) 20 7017 6027
Fax: +44 (0) 20 7017 6720
E-mail: reference.online@tandf.co.uk

Routledge
Taylor & Francis Group

PART ONE
International Organizations

PART ONE

International Organization

THE UNITED NATIONS

Address: United Nations, New York, NY 10017, USA.
Telephone: (212) 963-1234; **fax:** (212) 963-4879; **internet:** www.un.org.

The United Nations was founded in 1945 to maintain international peace and security and to develop international co-operation in addressing economic, social, cultural and humanitarian problems.

The United Nations was a name devised by President Franklin D. Roosevelt of the USA. It was first used in the Declaration by United Nations of 1 January 1942, when representatives of 26 nations pledged their governments to continue fighting together against the Axis powers.

The United Nations Charter was drawn up by the representatives of 50 countries at the United Nations Conference on International Organization, which met at San Francisco from 25 April to 26 June 1945. The representatives deliberated on the basis of proposals put forward by representatives of China, the USSR, the United Kingdom and the USA at Dumbarton Oaks in August–October 1944. The Charter was signed on 26 June 1945. Poland, not represented at the Conference, signed it later but nevertheless became one of the original 51 members.

The United Nations officially came into existence on 24 October 1945, when the Charter had been ratified by China, France, the USSR, the United Kingdom and the USA, and by a majority of other signatories. United Nations Day is celebrated annually on 24 October.

The UN's chief administrative officer is the Secretary-General, elected for a five-year term by the General Assembly on the recommendation of the Security Council. He acts in that capacity at all meetings of the General Assembly, the Security Council, the Economic and Social Council, and the Trusteeship Council, and performs such other functions as are entrusted to him by those organs. He is required to submit an annual report to the General Assembly and may bring to the attention of the Security Council any matter which, in his opinion, may threaten international peace.

Secretary-General: BAN KI-MOON (Republic of Korea) (2007–11).

Membership

MEMBERS OF THE UNITED NATIONS
(with assessments for percentage contributions to the UN budget for 2007–09, and year of admission)

Country	Assessment	Year
Afghanistan	0.001	1946
Albania	0.006	1955
Algeria	0.085	1962
Andorra	0.008	1993
Angola	0.003	1976
Antigua and Barbuda	0.002	1981
Argentina	0.325	1945
Armenia	0.002	1992
Australia	1.787	1945
Austria	0.887	1955
Azerbaijan	0.005	1992
Bahamas	0.016	1973
Bahrain	0.033	1971
Bangladesh	0.010	1974
Barbados	0.009	1966
Belarus[1]	0.020	1945
Belgium	1.102	1945
Belize	0.001	1981
Benin	0.001	1960
Bhutan	0.001	1971
Bolivia	0.006	1945
Bosnia and Herzegovina	0.006	1992
Botswana	0.014	1966
Brazil	0.876	1945
Brunei	0.026	1984
Bulgaria	0.020	1955
Burkina Faso	0.002	1960
Burundi	0.001	1962
Cambodia	0.001	1955
Cameroon	0.009	1960
Canada	2.977	1945
Cape Verde	0.001	1975
Central African Republic	0.001	1960
Chad	0.001	1960
Chile	0.161	1945
China, People's Republic	2.053	1945
Colombia	0.105	1945
Comoros	0.001	1975
Congo, Democratic Republic	0.003	1960
Congo, Republic	0.001	1960
Costa Rica	0.030	1945
Côte d'Ivoire	0.009	1960
Croatia	0.050	1992
Cuba	0.054	1945
Cyprus	0.044	1960
Czech Republic[2]	0.281	1993
Denmark	0.739	1945
Djibouti	0.001	1977
Dominica	0.001	1978
Dominican Republic	0.024	1945
Ecuador	0.021	1945
Egypt	0.088	1945
El Salvador	0.020	1945
Equatorial Guinea	0.002	1968
Eritrea	0.001	1993
Estonia	0.016	1991
Ethiopia	0.003	1945
Fiji	0.003	1970
Finland	0.564	1955
France	6.301	1945
Gabon	0.008	1960
The Gambia	0.001	1965
Georgia	0.003	1992
Germany	8.577	1973
Ghana	0.004	1957
Greece	0.596	1945
Grenada	0.001	1974
Guatemala	0.032	1945
Guinea	0.001	1958
Guinea-Bissau	0.001	1974
Guyana	0.001	1966
Haiti	0.002	1945
Honduras	0.005	1945
Hungary	0.244	1955
Iceland	0.037	1946
India	0.450	1945
Indonesia	0.161	1950
Iran	0.180	1945
Iraq	0.015	1945
Ireland	0.445	1955
Israel	0.419	1949
Italy	5.079	1955
Jamaica	0.010	1962
Japan	16.624	1956
Jordan	0.012	1955
Kazakhstan	0.029	1992
Kenya	0.010	1963
Kiribati	0.001	1999
Korea, Democratic People's Republic	0.007	1991
Korea, Republic	2.173	1991
Kuwait	0.182	1963
Kyrgyzstan	0.001	1992
Laos	0.001	1955
Latvia	0.018	1991
Lebanon	0.034	1945
Lesotho	0.001	1966
Liberia	0.001	1945
Libya	0.162	1955
Liechtenstein	0.010	1990
Lithuania	0.031	1991
Luxembourg	0.085	1945
Macedonia, former Yugoslav republic	0.005	1993
Madagascar	0.002	1960
Malawi	0.001	1964
Malaysia	0.190	1957
Maldives	0.001	1965
Mali	0.001	1960
Malta	0.017	1964
Marshall Islands	0.001	1991
Mauritania	0.001	1961
Mauritius	0.011	1968
Mexico	2.257	1945
Micronesia, Federated States	0.001	1991
Moldova	0.001	1992
Monaco	0.003	1993
Mongolia	0.001	1961

INTERNATIONAL ORGANIZATIONS — United Nations

Country	Contribution	Year
Montenegro[3]	0.001	2006
Morocco	0.042	1956
Mozambique	0.001	1975
Myanmar	0.005	1948
Namibia	0.006	1990
Nauru	0.001	1999
Nepal	0.003	1955
Netherlands	1.873	1945
New Zealand	0.256	1945
Nicaragua	0.002	1945
Niger	0.001	1960
Nigeria	0.048	1960
Norway	0.782	1945
Oman	0.073	1971
Pakistan	0.059	1947
Palau	0.001	1994
Panama	0.023	1945
Papua New Guinea	0.002	1975
Paraguay	0.005	1945
Peru	0.078	1945
Philippines	0.078	1945
Poland	0.501	1945
Portugal	0.527	1955
Qatar	0.085	1971
Romania	0.070	1955
Russia[4]	1.200	1945
Rwanda	0.001	1962
Saint Christopher and Nevis	0.001	1983
Saint Lucia	0.001	1979
Saint Vincent and the Grenadines	0.001	1980
Samoa	0.001	1976
San Marino	0.003	1992
São Tomé and Príncipe	0.001	1975
Saudi Arabia	0.748	1945
Senegal	0.004	1960
Serbia[3]	0.021	2000
Seychelles	0.002	1976
Sierra Leone	0.001	1961
Singapore	0.347	1965
Slovakia[2]	0.063	1993
Slovenia	0.096	1992
Solomon Islands	0.001	1978
Somalia	0.001	1960
South Africa	0.290	1945
Spain	2.968	1955
Sri Lanka	0.016	1955
Sudan	0.010	1956
Suriname	0.001	1975
Swaziland	1.071	1968
Sweden	0.998	1946
Switzerland	1.216	2002
Syria	0.016	1945
Tajikistan	0.001	1992
Tanzania	0.006	1961
Thailand	0.186	1946
Timor-Leste	0.001	2002
Togo	0.001	1960
Tonga	0.001	1999
Trinidad and Tobago	0.027	1962
Tunisia	0.031	1956
Turkey	0.381	1945
Turkmenistan	0.006	1992
Tuvalu	0.001	2000
Uganda	0.003	1962
Ukraine[1]	0.045	1945
United Arab Emirates	0.302	1971
United Kingdom	6.642	1945
USA	22.000	1945
Uruguay	0.027	1945
Uzbekistan	0.008	1992
Vanuatu	0.001	1981
Venezuela	0.200	1945
Viet Nam	0.024	1977
Yemen[5]	0.007	1947/67
Zambia	0.001	1964
Zimbabwe	0.008	1980

Total Membership: 192 (April 2008)

[1] Until December 1991 both Belarus and Ukraine were integral parts of the USSR and not independent countries, but had separate UN membership.

[2] Czechoslovakia, which had been a member of the UN since 1945, ceased to exist as a single state on 31 December 1992. In January 1993, as Czechoslovakia's legal successors, the Czech Republic and Slovakia were granted UN membership, and seats on subsidiary bodies that had previously been held by Czechoslovakia were divided between the two successor states.

[3] Montenegro was admitted as a member of the UN on 28 June 2006, following its declaration of independence on 3 June; Serbia retained the seat formerly held by Serbia and Montenegro.

[4] Russia assumed the USSR's seat in the General Assembly and its permanent seat on the Security Council in December 1991, following the USSR's dissolution.

[5] The Yemen Arab Republic (admitted to the UN as Yemen in 1947) and the People's Democratic Republic of Yemen (admitted as Southern Yemen in 1967) merged to form the Republic of Yemen in May 1990.

SOVEREIGN STATES NOT IN THE UNITED NATIONS
(April 2008)

China (Taiwan)   Vatican City (Holy See)

Diplomatic Representation

PERMANENT MISSIONS TO THE UNITED NATIONS
(April 2008)

Afghanistan: 360 Lexington Ave, 11th Floor, New York, NY 10017; tel. (212) 972-1212; fax (212) 972-1216; e-mail afgwatan@aol.com; Permanent Representative Dr ZAHIR TANIN.

Albania: 320 East 79th St, New York, NY 10075; tel. (212) 249-2059; fax (212) 535-2917; e-mail albania@un.int; Permanent Representative ADRIAN NERITANI.

Algeria: 326 East 48th St, New York, NY 10017; tel. (212) 750-1960; fax (212) 759-5274; e-mail mission@algeria-un.org; internet www.algeria-un.org; Permanent Representative YOUCEF YOUSFI.

Andorra: 2 United Nations Plaza, 25th Floor, New York, NY 10017; tel. (212) 750-8064; fax (212) 750-6630; e-mail andorra@un.int; Permanent Representative CARLES FONT-ROSSELL.

Angola: 125 East 73rd St, New York, NY 10021; tel. (212) 861-5656; fax (212) 861-9295; e-mail ang-un@angolamissionun.org; internet www.angolamissionun.org; Permanent Representative ISMAEL ABRAÃO GASPAR MARTINS.

Antigua and Barbuda: 610 Fifth Ave, Suite 311, New York, NY 10020; tel. (212) 541-4117; fax (212) 757-1607; e-mail antigua@un.int; internet www.un.int/antigua; Permanent Representative JOHN W. ASHE.

Argentina: 1 United Nations Plaza, 25th Floor, New York, NY 10017; tel. (212) 688-6300; fax (212) 980-8395; e-mail argentina@un.int; internet www.un.int/argentina; Permanent Representative JORGE ARGÜELLO.

Armenia: 119 East 36th St, New York, NY 10016; tel. (212) 686-9079; fax (212) 686-3934; e-mail armenia@un.int; internet www.un.int/armenia; Permanent Representative ARMEN MARTIROSIAN.

Australia: 150 East 42nd St, 33rd Floor, New York, NY 10017; tel. (212) 351-6600; fax (212) 351-6610; e-mail australia@un.int; internet www.unny.mission.gov.au; Permanent Representative ROBERT HILL.

Austria: 823 United Nations Plaza, 8th Floor, New York, NY 10017; tel. (212) 949-1840; fax (212) 953-1302; e-mail austria@un.int; internet www.un.int/austria; Permanent Representative GERHARD PFANZELTER.

Azerbaijan: 866 United Nations Plaza, Suite 560, New York, NY 10017; tel. (212) 371-2559; fax (212) 371-2784; e-mail azerbaijan@un.int; Permanent Representative AGSHIN MEHDIYEV.

Bahamas: 231 East 46th St, New York, NY 10017; tel. (212) 421-6925; fax (212) 759-2135; e-mail bahamas@un.int; Permanent Representative PAULETTE A. BETHEL.

Bahrain: 866 Second Ave, 14th/15th Floor, New York, NY 10017; tel. (212) 223-6200; fax (212) 319-0687; e-mail bahrain@un.int; internet www.un.int/bahrain; Permanent Representative TAWFEEQ AHMED KHALIL ALMANSOOR.

Bangladesh: 227 East, 45th Street, 14th Floor, New York, NY 10017; tel. (212) 867-3434; fax (212) 972-4038; e-mail bangladesh@un.int; internet www.un.int/bangladesh; Permanent Representative ISMAT JAHAN.

Barbados: 800 Second Ave, 2nd Floor, New York, NY 10017; tel. (212) 867-8431; fax (212) 986-1030; e-mail barbados@un.int; Permanent Representative CHRISTOPHER F. HACKETT.

Belarus: 136 East 67th St, 4th Floor, New York, NY 10021; tel. (212) 535-3420; fax (212) 734-4810; e-mail belarus@un.int; internet missions.un.int/belarus; Permanent Representative ANDREI DAPKIUNAS.

Belgium: 823 United Nations Plaza, 4th Floor, New York, NY 10017; tel. (212) 378-6300; fax (212) 681-7618; e-mail belgium@un.int;

internet www.un.int/belgium; Permanent Representative JOHAN C. VERBEKE.

Belize: 800 Second Ave, Suite 400G, New York, NY 10017; tel. (212) 593-0999; fax (212) 593-0932; e-mail blzun@undp.org; Permanent Representative STUART LESLIE.

Benin: 4 East 73rd St, New York, NY 10021; tel. (212) 249-6014; fax (212) 988-3714; e-mail benin@un.int; internet www.un.int/benin; Permanent Representative JEAN-MARIE EHOUZOU.

Bhutan: 2 United Nations Plaza, 27th Floor, New York, NY 10017; tel. (212) 826-1919; fax (212) 826-2998; e-mail pmbnewyork@aol.com; Permanent Representative DAW PENJO.

Bolivia: 211 East 43rd St, 8th Floor, Rm 802, New York, NY 10017; tel. (212) 682-8132; fax (212) 682-8133; e-mail bolivia@un.int; Permanent Representative E. HUGO SILES-ALVARADO.

Bosnia and Herzegovina: 866 United Nations Plaza, Suite 580, New York, NY 10017; tel. (212) 751-9015; fax (212) 751-9019; e-mail bosnia@un.int; internet www.un.int/bosnia; Permanent Representative MILOS PRICA.

Botswana: 103 East 37th St, New York, NY 10016; tel. (212) 889-2277; fax (212) 725-5061; e-mail botswana@un.int; Permanent Representative SAMUEL OTSILE OUTLULE.

Brazil: 747 Third Ave, 9th Floor, New York, NY 10017; tel. (212) 372-2600; fax (212) 371-5716; e-mail braun@delbrasonu.org; internet www.un.int/brazil; Permanent Representative MARIA LUIZA RIBEIRO VIOTTI.

Brunei: 771 First Ave, New York, NY 10017; tel. (212) 697-3465; fax (212) 697-9889; e-mail info@bruneimission-ny.org; Permanent Representative EMRAN BAHAR.

Bulgaria: 11 East 84th St, New York, NY 10028; tel. (212) 737-4790; fax (212) 472-9865; e-mail bulgaria@un.int; internet www.un.int/bulgaria; Permanent Representative RAYKO STRAHILOV RAYTCHEV.

Burkina Faso: 115 East 73rd St, New York, NY 10021; tel. (212) 288-7515; fax (212) 772-3562; e-mail burkinafaso@un.int; Permanent Representative MICHEL KAFANDO.

Burundi: 336 East 45th St, 12th Floor, New York, NY 10017; tel. (212) 499-0001; fax (212) 499-0006; e-mail burundi@un.int; Permanent Representative JOSEPH NTAKIRUTIMANA.

Cambodia: 866 United Nations Plaza, Suite 420, New York, NY 10017; tel. (212) 223-0676; fax (212) 223-0425; e-mail cambodia@un.int; internet www.un.int/cambodia; Permanent Representative SEA KOSAL.

Cameroon: 22 East 73rd St, New York, NY 10021; tel. (212) 794-2296; fax (212) 249-0533; e-mail info@cameroonmission.org; internet www.cameroonmission.org; Permanent Representative MARTIN BELINGA EBOUTOU.

Canada: 1 Dag Hammarskjöld Plaza, 885 Second Ave, 14th Floor, New York, NY 10017; tel. (212) 848-1100; fax (212) 848-1195; e-mail canada@un.int; internet www.un.int/canada; Permanent Representative JOHN MCNEE.

Cape Verde: 27 East 69th St, New York, NY 10021; tel. (212) 472-0333; fax (212) 794-1398; e-mail capeverde@un.int; Permanent Representative ANTONIO PEDRO MONTEIRO LIMA.

Central African Republic: 386 Park Ave South, Rm 1114, New York, NY 10016; tel. (212) 679-8089; fax (212) 545-8326; e-mail caf@un.int; Permanent Representative FERNAND POUKRE-KONO.

Chad: 211 East 43rd St, Suite 1703, New York, NY 10017; tel. (212) 986-0980; fax (212) 986-0152; e-mail chad@un.int; Permanent Representative MAHAMAT ALI ADOUM.

Chile: 3 Dag Hammarskjöld Plaza, 305 East 47th St, 10th/11th Floor, New York, NY 10017; tel. (212) 832-3323; fax (212) 832-0236; e-mail chile@un.int; internet www.un.int/chile; Permanent Representative JUAN GABRIEL VALDES.

China, People's Republic: 350 East 35th St, New York, NY 10016; tel. (212) 655-6100; fax (212) 634-7626; e-mail chinamission_un@fmprc.gov.cn; internet www.china-un.org; Permanent Representative WANG GUANGYA.

Colombia: 140 East 57th St, 5th Floor, New York, NY 10022; tel. (212) 355-7776; fax (212) 371-2813; e-mail colombia@colombiaun.org; internet www.colombiaun.org; Permanent Representative CLAUDIA BLUM.

Comoros: 420 East 50th St, New York, NY 10022; tel. (212) 972-8010; fax (212) 983-4712; e-mail comoros@un.int; internet www.un.int/comoros; Permanent Representative MOHAMED TOIHIRI.

Congo, Democratic Republic: 866 United Nations Plaza, Suite 511, New York, NY 10017; tel. (212) 319-8061; fax (212) 319-8232; e-mail drcongo@un.int; internet www.un.int/drcongo; Permanent Representative CHRISTIAN ILEKA ATOKI.

Congo, Republic: 14 East 65th St, New York, NY 10021; tel. (212) 744-7840; fax (212) 744-7975; e-mail congo@un.int; Permanent Representative BASILE IKOUEBE.

Costa Rica: 211 East 43rd St, Rm 903, New York, NY 10017; tel. (212) 986-6373; fax (212) 986-6842; e-mail pmnu@rree.go.cr; internet www.un.int/costarica; Permanent Representative JORGE URBINA.

Côte d'Ivoire: 46 East 74th St, New York, NY 10021; tel. (212) 717-5555; fax (212) 717-4492; e-mail ivorycoast@un.int; internet www.un.int/cotedivoire; Chargé d'affaires ILAHIRI ALCIDE DJEDJE.

Croatia: 820 Second Ave, 19th Floor, New York, NY 10017; tel. (212) 986-1585; fax (212) 986-2011; e-mail croatia@un.int; internet www.un.int/croatia; Permanent Representative NEVEN JURICA.

Cuba: 315 Lexington Ave and 38th St, New York, NY 10016; tel. (212) 689-7215; fax (212) 779-1697; e-mail cuba@un.int; internet www.un.int/cuba; Permanent Representative ORLANDO REQUEIJO GUAL.

Cyprus: 13 East 40th St, New York, NY 10016; tel. (212) 481-6023; fax (212) 685-7316; e-mail cyprus@un.int; internet www.un.int/cyprus; Permanent Representative ANDREAS D. MAVROYIANNIS.

Czech Republic: 1109–1111 Madison Ave, New York, NY 10028; tel. (646) 981-4000; fax (646) 981-4099; e-mail un.newyork@embassy.mzv.cz; internet www.mfa.cz/un.newyork; Permanent Representative MARTIN PALOUS.

Denmark: 1 Dag Hammarskjöld Plaza, 885 Second Ave, 18th Floor, New York, NY 10017; tel. (212) 308-7009; fax (212) 308-3384; e-mail nycmis@um.dk; internet www.missionfnnewyork.um.dk/en/; Permanent Representative CARSTEN STAUR.

Djibouti: 866 United Nations Plaza, Suite 4011, New York, NY 10017; tel. (212) 753-3163; fax (212) 223-1276; e-mail djibouti@nyct.net; Permanent Representative ROBLE OLHAYE.

Dominica: 800 Second Ave, Suite 400H, New York, NY 10017; tel. (212) 949-0853; fax (212) 808-4975; e-mail dominica@un.int; Permanent Representative SIMON PAUL RICHARDS.

Dominican Republic: 144 East 44th St, 4th Floor, New York, NY 10017; tel. (212) 867-0833; fax (212) 986-4694; e-mail drun@un.int; internet www.un.int/dr; Permanent Representative ERASMO LARA-PEÑA.

Ecuador: 866 United Nations Plaza, Rm 516, New York, NY 10017; tel. (212) 935-1680; fax (212) 935-1835; e-mail ecuador@un.int; internet www.un.int/ecuador; Permanent Representative MARIA FERNANDA ESPINOSA GARCES.

Egypt: 304 East 44th St, New York, NY 10017; tel. (212) 503-0300; fax (212) 949-5999; e-mail egypt@un.int; Permanent Representative MAGED ABDELFATTAH ABDELAZIZ.

El Salvador: 46 Park Ave, New York, NY 10016; tel. (212) 679-1616; fax (212) 725-7831; e-mail elsalvador@un.int; Permanent Representative CARMEN MARÍA GALLARDO HERNÁNDEZ.

Equatorial Guinea: 57 Magnolia Ave, Mount Vernon, NY 10553; tel. (914) 667-8999; fax (914) 667-8778; e-mail eqguinea@un.int; Permanent Representative LINO SIMA EKUA AVOMO.

Eritrea: 800 Second Ave, 18th Floor, New York, NY 10017; tel. (212) 687-3390; fax (212) 687-3138; e-mail eritrea@un.int; internet www.un.int/eritrea; Permanent Representative ARAYA DESTA.

Estonia: 600 Third Ave, 26th Floor, New York, NY 10016; tel. (212) 883-0640; fax (212) 883-0648; e-mail mission.newyork@mfa.ee; Permanent Representative TINA INTELMANN.

Ethiopia: 866 Second Ave, 3rd Floor, New York, NY 10017; tel. (212) 421-1830; fax (212) 754-0360; e-mail ethiopia@un.int; internet www.un.int/ethiopia; Permanent Representative DAWIT YOHANNES.

Fiji: 630 Third Ave, 7th Floor, New York, NY 10017; tel. (212) 687-4130; fax (212) 687-3963; e-mail fiji@un.int; internet www.fijiprun.org; Permanent Representative Dr TUPENI BABA.

Finland: 866 United Nations Plaza, Suite 222, New York, NY 10017; tel. (212) 355-2100; fax (212) 759-6156; e-mail sanomat.yke@formin.fi; internet www.un.int/finland; Permanent Representative KIRSTI LINTONEN.

France: 1 Dag Hammarskjöld Plaza, 245 East 47th St, 44th Floor, New York, NY 10017; tel. (212) 308-5700; fax (212) 421-6889; e-mail france@un.int; internet www.un.int/france; Permanent Representative JEAN-MAURICE RIPERT.

Gabon: 18 East 41st St, 9th Floor, New York, NY 10017; tel. (212) 686-9720; fax (212) 689-5769; e-mail gabon@un.int; Permanent Representative DENIS DANGUE RÉWAKA.

The Gambia: 800 Second Ave, Suite 400F, New York, NY 10017; tel. (212) 949-6640; fax (212) 808-4975; e-mail gambia@un.int; Permanent Representative TAMSIR JALLOW.

Georgia: 1 United Nations Plaza, 26th Floor, New York, NY 10021; tel. (212) 759-1949; fax (212) 759-1832; e-mail georgia@un.int; internet www.un.int/georgia; Permanent Representative IRAKLI ALASANIA.

Germany: 871 United Nations Plaza, New York, NY 10017; tel. (212) 940-0400; fax (212) 940-0402; e-mail germany@un.int; internet www.germany-info.org/un; Permanent Representative Dr THOMAS MATUSSEK.

INTERNATIONAL ORGANIZATIONS — United Nations

Ghana: 19 East 47th St, New York, NY 10017; tel. (212) 832-1300; fax (212) 751-6743; e-mail ghanaperm@aol.com; Permanent Representative Leslie Kojo Christian.

Greece: 866 Second Ave, 13th Floor, New York, NY 10017; tel. (212) 888-6900; fax (212) 888-4440; e-mail mission@greeceun.org; internet www.greeceun.org; Permanent Representative John Mourikis.

Grenada: 800 Second Ave, Suite 400K, New York, NY 10017; tel. (212) 599-0301; fax (212) 599-1540; e-mail grenada@un.int; Permanent Representative Dr Angus Friday.

Guatemala: 57 Park Ave, New York, NY 10016; tel. (212) 679-4760; fax (212) 685-8741; e-mail guatemala@un.int; internet www.un.int/guatemala; Permanent Representative Jorge Skinner-Klée Arenales.

Guinea: 140 East 39th St, New York, NY 10016; tel. (212) 687-8115; fax (212) 687-8248; e-mail guinea@un.int; Permanent Representative Mamady Traoré.

Guinea-Bissau: 211 East 43rd St, Rm 704, New York, NY 10017; tel. (212) 338-9394; fax (212) 293-0264; e-mail guinea-bissau@un.int; Chargé d'affaires a.i. Alfredo Lopes Cabral.

Guyana: 866 United Nations Plaza, Suite 555, New York, NY 10017; tel. (212) 527-3232; fax (212) 935-7548; e-mail guyana@un.int; Permanent Representative Samuel R. Insanally.

Haiti: 801 Second Ave, Rm 600, New York, NY 10017; tel. (212) 370-4840; fax (212) 661-8698; e-mail haiti@un.int; Permanent Representative Léo Mérorès.

Honduras: 866 United Nations Plaza, Suite 417, New York, NY 10017; tel. (212) 752-3370; fax (212) 223-0498; e-mail m.suazo@worldnet.att.net; internet www.un.int/honduras; Permanent Representative Jorge Arturo Reina Idiaquez.

Hungary: 227 East 52nd St, New York, NY 10022; tel. (212) 752-0209; fax (212) 755-5395; e-mail hungary@un.int; internet www.un.int/hungary; Permanent Representative Gábor Bródi.

Iceland: 800 Third Ave, 36th Floor, New York, NY 10022; tel. (212) 593-2700; fax (212) 593-6269; e-mail icecon.ny@utn.stjr.is; internet brunnur.stjr.is/embassy/newyork.nsf/pages/index.html; Permanent Representative Hjalmar W. Hannesson.

India: 235 East 43rd St, New York, NY 10017; tel. (212) 490-9660; fax (212) 490-9656; e-mail india@un.int; internet www.un.int/india; Permanent Representative Nirupam Sen.

Indonesia: 325 East 38th St, New York, NY 10016; tel. (212) 972-8333; fax (212) 972-9780; e-mail ptri@indonesiamission-ny.org; internet www.indonesiamission-ny.org; Permanent Representative Raden Mohammad Marty Muliana Natalegawa.

Iran: 622 Third Ave, 34th Floor, New York, NY 10017; tel. (212) 687-2020; fax (212) 867-7086; e-mail iran@un.int; internet www.un.int/iran; Permanent Representative Mohammad Khazaee.

Iraq: 14 East 79th St, New York, NY 10021; tel. (212) 737-4433; fax (212) 772-1794; e-mail missionofiraq@nyc.rr.com; internet www.iraqi-mission.org; Permanent Representative Hamid al-Bayati.

Ireland: 1 Dag Hammarskjöld Plaza, 885 Second Ave, 19th Floor, New York, NY 10017; tel. (212) 421-6934; fax (212) 752-4726; e-mail ireland@un.int; internet www.un.int/ireland; Permanent Representative Paul Kavanagh.

Israel: 800 Second Ave, New York, NY 10017; tel. (212) 499-5510; fax (212) 499-5516; e-mail israel@un.int; internet www.israel-un.org; Permanent Representative Dan Gillerman.

Italy: 2 United Nations Plaza, 24th Floor, New York, NY 10017; tel. (212) 486-9191; fax (212) 486-1036; e-mail italy@un.int; internet www.italyun.org; Permanent Representative Marcello Spatafora.

Jamaica: 767 Third Ave, 9th Floor, New York, NY 10017; tel. (212) 935-7509; fax (212) 935-7607; e-mail jamaica@un.int; internet www.un.int/jamaica; Permanent Representative Raymond Osbourne Wolfe.

Japan: 866 United Nations Plaza, 2nd Floor, New York, NY 10017; tel. (212) 223-4300; fax (212) 751-1966; e-mail mission@un-japan.org; internet www.un.int/japan; Permanent Representative Yukio Takasu.

Jordan: 866 United Nations Plaza, Suite 552, New York, NY 10017; tel. (212) 832-9553; fax (212) 832-5346; e-mail jordan@un.int; Permanent Representative Mohammed F. al-Allaf.

Kazakhstan: 866 United Nations Plaza, Suite 586, New York, NY 10017; tel. (212) 230-1900; fax (212) 230-1172; e-mail kazakhstan@un.int; internet www.un.int/kazakhstan; Permanent Representative Byrganym Aitimova.

Kenya: 866 United Nations Plaza, Rm 486, New York, NY 10017; tel. (212) 421-4740; fax (212) 486-1985; e-mail kenya@un.int; internet www.un.int/kenya/; Permanent Representative Zachary Dominic Muburi-Muita.

Korea, Democratic People's Republic: 820 Second Ave, 13th Floor, New York, NY 10017; tel. (212) 972-3105; fax (212) 972-3154; e-mail dprk@un.int; Permanent Representative (vacant).

Korea, Republic: 335 East 45th St, New York, NY 10017; tel. (212) 439-4000; fax (212) 986-1083; e-mail korea@un.int; internet www.un.int/korea; Permanent Representative Hyun Chong Kim.

Kuwait: 321 East 44th St, New York, NY 10017; tel. (212) 973-4300; fax (212) 370-1733; e-mail kuwait@kuwaitmission.com; internet www.kuwaitmission.com; Permanent Representative Abdullah Ahmed Mohamed al-Murad.

Kyrgyzstan: 866 United Nations Plaza, Suite 477, New York, NY 10017; tel. (212) 486-4214; fax (212) 486-5259; e-mail kyrgyzstan@un.int; Permanent Representative Nurbek Jeenbaev.

Laos: 317 East 51st St, New York, NY 10022; tel. (212) 832-2734; fax (212) 750-0039; e-mail lao@un.int; internet www.un.int/lao; Permanent Representative Phommachanh Kanika.

Latvia: 333 East 50th St, New York, NY 10022; tel. (212) 838-8877; fax (212) 838-8920; e-mail irppanony@aol.com; Permanent Representative Solveiga Silkalna.

Lebanon: 866 United Nations Plaza, Rm 531–533, New York, NY 10017; tel. (212) 355-5460; fax (212) 838-2819; e-mail lebanon@un.int; Permanent Representative Nawaf A. Salam.

Lesotho: 204 East 39th St, New York, NY 10016; tel. (212) 661-1690; fax (212) 682-4388; e-mail lesotho@un.int; internet www.un.int/lesotho; Permanent Representative Lebohang Fine Maema.

Liberia: 820 Second Ave, 13th Floor, New York, NY 10017; tel. (212) 687-1033; fax (212) 687-1035; e-mail liberia@un.int; Permanent Representative Nathaniel Barnes.

Libya: 309–315 East 48th St, New York, NY 10017; tel. (212) 752-5775; fax (212) 593-4787; e-mail libya@un.int; internet www.libya-un.org; Permanent Representative Giadalla Azzuz Belgassem Ettalhi.

Liechtenstein: 633 Third Ave, 27th Floor, New York, NY 10017; tel. (212) 599-0220; fax (212) 599-0064; e-mail liechtenstein@un.int; internet www.un.int/liechtenstein; Permanent Representative Christian Wenaweser.

Lithuania: 420 Fifth Ave, 3rd Floor, New York, NY 10018; tel. (212) 354-7820; fax (212) 354-7833; e-mail lithuania@un.int; internet www.un.int/lithuania; Permanent Representative Dalius Cekuolis.

Luxembourg: 17 Beekman Pl., New York, NY 10022; tel. (212) 935-3589; fax (212) 935-5896; e-mail luxun@undp.org; internet www.un.int/luxembourg; Permanent Representative Jean-Marc Hoscheit.

Macedonia, former Yugoslav republic: 866 United Nations Plaza, Suite 517, New York, NY 10017; tel. (212) 308-8504; fax (212) 308-8724; e-mail macedonia@un.int; internet www.un.int/macedonia; Permanent Representative Slobodan Tasovski.

Madagascar: 820 Second Ave, Suite 800, New York, NY 10017; tel. (212) 986-9491; fax (212) 986-6271; e-mail repermad@ren.com; internet www.un.int/madagascar; Permanent Representative Zina Andrianarivelo-Razafy.

Malawi: 600 Third Ave, 21st Floor, New York, NY 10016; tel. (212) 949-0180; fax (212) 599-5021; e-mail malawiun@aol.com; Permanent Representative Steve Dick Tennyson Matenje.

Malaysia: 313 East 43rd St, New York, NY 10017; tel. (212) 986-6310; fax (212) 490-8576; e-mail malaysia@un.int; internet www.un.int/malaysia; Permanent Representative Hamidon bin Ali.

Maldives: 820 Second Ave, Suite 800C, New York, NY 10017; tel. (212) 599-6195; fax (212) 661-6405; e-mail mdv@undp.org; internet www.un.int/maldives; Permanent Representative Ahmed Khaleel.

Mali: 111 East 69th St, New York, NY 10021; tel. (212) 737-4150; fax (212) 472-3778; e-mail malionu@aol.com; Permanent Representative Cheick Sidi Diarra.

Malta: 249 East 35th St, New York, NY 10016; tel. (212) 725-2345; fax (212) 779-7097; e-mail mltun@un.int; Permanent Representative Saviour F. Borg.

Marshall Islands: 800 Second Ave, 18th Floor, New York, NY 10017; tel. (212) 983-3040; fax (212) 983-3202; e-mail marshallislands@un.int; Permanent Representative Alfred Capelle.

Mauritania: 116 East 38th St, New York, NY 10017; tel. (212) 986-7963; fax (212) 986-8419; e-mail mauritania@un.int; internet www2.un.int/public/mauritania; Permanent Representative Abderrahim Ould Hadrami.

Mauritius: 211 East 43rd St, 15th Floor, New York, NY 10017; tel. (212) 949-0190; fax (212) 697-3829; e-mail mauritius@un.int; internet www.un.int/mauritius; Permanent Representative Somduth Soborun.

Mexico: 2 United Nations Plaza, 28th Floor, New York, NY 10017; tel. (212) 752-0220; fax (212) 688-8862; e-mail mexico@un.int; internet www.un.int/mexico; Permanent Representative Claude Heller.

Micronesia, Federated States: 820 Second Ave, Suite 17A, New York, NY 10017; tel. (212) 697-8370; fax (212) 697-8295; e-mail

INTERNATIONAL ORGANIZATIONS — United Nations

fsmun@fsmgov.org; internet www.fsmgov.org/fsmun; Permanent Representative Masao Nakayama.

Moldova: 35 East 29th St, New York, NY 10016; tel. (212) 447-1867; fax (212) 447-4067; e-mail unmoldova@aol.com; internet www.un.int/moldova; Permanent Representative Alexei Tulbure.

Monaco: 866 United Nations Plaza, Suite 520, New York, NY 10017; tel. (212) 832-0721; fax (212) 832-5358; e-mail monaco@un.int; internet www.un.int/monaco; Permanent Representative Gille Noghes.

Mongolia: 6 East 77th St, New York, NY 10021; tel. (212) 737-3874; fax (212) 861-9460; e-mail mongolia@un.int; internet www.un.int/mongolia; Permanent Representative Ochir Enkhtsetseg.

Montenegro: 420 East 54th St, Apt. 18H, New York, NY 10022; tel. (212) 753-9255; Permanent Representative Neboyša Kaludjerović.

Morocco: 866 Second Ave, 6th and 7th Floors, New York, NY 10017; tel. (212) 421-1580; fax (212) 980-1512; e-mail morocco@un.int; internet www.un.int/morocco; Permanent Representative Al Mustapha Sahel.

Mozambique: 420 East 50th St, New York, NY 10022; tel. (212) 644-5965; fax (212) 644-5972; e-mail mozambique@un.int; internet www.un.int/mozambique; Permanent Representative Filipe Chidumo.

Myanmar: 10 East 77th St, New York, NY 10021; tel. (212) 535-1310; fax (212) 737-2421; e-mail myanmar@un.int; Permanent Representative Kyaw Tint Swe.

Namibia: 135 East 36th St, New York, NY 10016; tel. (212) 685-2003; fax (212) 685-1561; e-mail namibia@un.int; internet www.un.int/namibia; Permanent Representative Dr Kaire Munionganda Mbuende.

Nauru: 800 Second Ave, Suite 400D, New York, NY 10017; tel. (212) 937-0074; fax (212) 937-0079; Permanent Representative Marlene Inemwin Moses.

Nepal: 820 Second Ave, Suite 17B, New York, NY 10017; tel. (212) 370-3988; fax (212) 953-2038; e-mail nepal@un.int; internet www.un.int/nepal; Permanent Representative Madhu Raman Acharya.

Netherlands: 235 East 45th St, 16th Floor, New York, NY 10017; tel. (212) 697-5547; fax (212) 370-1954; e-mail netherlands@un.int; internet www.pvnewyork.org; Permanent Representative Franciscus Antonius Maria Majoor.

New Zealand: 1 United Nations Plaza, 25th Floor, New York, NY 10017; tel. (212) 826-1960; fax (212) 758-0827; e-mail nz@un.int; internet www.nzmissionny.org; Permanent Representative Rosemary Banks.

Nicaragua: 820 Second Ave, Suite 801, New York, NY 10017; tel. (212) 490-7997; fax (212) 286-0815; e-mail nicaragua@un.int; internet www.un.int/nicaragua; Permanent Representative Maria Rubiales de Chamorro.

Niger: 417 East 50th St, New York, NY 10022; tel. (212) 421-3260; fax (212) 753-6931; e-mail nigerun@aol.com; internet www.un.int/niger; Permanent Representative Aboubacar Ibrahim Abani.

Nigeria: 828 Second Ave, New York, NY 10017; tel. (212) 953-9130; fax (212) 697-1970; e-mail nigeria@un.int; Permanent Representative Aminu Bashir Wali.

Norway: 825 Third Ave, 39th Floor, New York, NY 10022; tel. (212) 421-0280; fax (212) 688-0554; e-mail delun@mfa.no; internet www.un.norway-un.org; Permanent Representative Johan Ludvik Lovald.

Oman: 866 United Nations Plaza, Suite 540, New York, NY 10017; tel. (212) 355-3505; fax (212) 644-0070; e-mail oman@un.int; Permanent Representative Fuad Mubarak al-Hinai.

Pakistan: 8 East 65th St, New York, NY 10021; tel. (212) 879-8600; fax (212) 744-7348; e-mail pakistan@un.int; internet www.un.int/pakistan; Permanent Representative Munir Akram.

Palau: 866 UN Plaza, Suite 575, New York, NY 10017; tel. (212) 813-0310; fax (212) 813-0317; e-mail mission@palauun.org; internet www.palauun.org; Permanent Representative Stuart Beck.

Panama: 866 United Nations Plaza, Suite 4030, New York, NY 10017; tel. (212) 421-5420; fax (212) 421-2694; e-mail emb@panama_msun.org; Permanent Representative Ricardo Alberto Arias.

Papua New Guinea: 201 East 42nd St, Suite 405, New York, NY 10017; tel. (212) 557-5001; fax (212) 557-5009; e-mail pngmission@pngun.org; Permanent Representative Robert Guba Aisi.

Paraguay: 211 East 43rd St, Suite 400, New York, NY 10017; tel. (212) 687-3490; fax (212) 818-1282; e-mail paraguay@un.int; Permanent Representative Eladio Loizaga.

Peru: 820 Second Ave, Suite 1600, New York, NY 10017; tel. (212) 687-3336; fax (212) 972-6975; e-mail peru@un.int; Permanent Representative Jorge Voto-Bernales.

Philippines: 556 Fifth Ave, 5th Floor, New York, NY 10036; tel. (212) 764-1300; fax (212) 840-8602; e-mail misunphil@aol.com; internet www.un.int/phillipines; Permanent Representative Hilario G. Davide.

Poland: 9 East 66th St, New York, NY 10021; tel. (212) 744-2506; fax (212) 517-6771; e-mail poland@un.int; internet www.un.int/poland; Permanent Representative Andrzej Towpik.

Portugal: 866 Second Ave, 9th Floor, New York, NY 10017; tel. (212) 759-9444; fax (212) 355-1124; e-mail portugal@un.int; internet www.un.int/portugal; Permanent Representative João Manuel Guerra Salgueiro.

Qatar: 809 United Nations Plaza, 4th Floor, New York, NY 10017; tel. (212) 486-9335; fax (212) 758-4952; e-mail newyork@mofa.gov.qa; Permanent Representative Nassir Bin Abdulaziz Al-Nasser.

Romania: 573–577 Third Ave, New York, NY 10016; tel. (212) 682-3273; fax (212) 682-9746; e-mail romania@un.int; internet www.un.int/romania; Permanent Representative Mihnea Ioan Motoc.

Russia: 136 East 67th St, New York, NY 10021; tel. (212) 861-4900; fax (212) 628-0252; e-mail rusun@un.int; internet www.un.int/russia; Permanent Representative Vitaly Churkin.

Rwanda: 124 East 39th St, New York, NY 10016; tel. (212) 679-9010; fax (212) 679-9133; e-mail rwanda@un.int; Permanent Representative Joseph Nsengimana.

Saint Christopher and Nevis: 414 East 75th St, 5th Floor, New York, NY 10021; tel. (212) 535-1234; fax (212) 535-6854; e-mail sknmission@aol.com; internet www.stkittsnevis.org; Permanent Representative Delano Frank Bart.

Saint Lucia: 800 Second Ave, 9th Floor, New York, NY 10017; tel. (212) 697-9360; fax (212) 697-4993; e-mail slumission@aol.com; internet www.un.int/stlucia; Permanent Representative Anthony Bryan Severin.

Saint Vincent and the Grenadines: 801 Second Ave, 21st Floor, New York, NY 10017; tel. (212) 687-4490; fax (212) 949-5946; e-mail stvg@un.int; Permanent Representative Camillo M. Gonsalves.

Samoa: 800 Second Ave, Suite 400J, New York, NY 10017; tel. (212) 599-6196; fax (212) 599-0797; e-mail samoa@un.int; Permanent Representative Ali'ioaiga Feturi Elisaia.

San Marino: 327 East 50th St, New York, NY 10022; tel. (212) 751-1234; fax (212) 751-1436; e-mail sanmarinoun@hotmail.com; Permanent Representative Daniele Bodini.

São Tomé and Príncipe: 400 Park Ave, 7th Floor, New York, NY 10022; tel. (212) 317-0533; fax (212) 317-0580; e-mail stp@un.int; Chargé d'affaires a.i. Ovidio Manuel Barbosa Pequeno.

Saudi Arabia: 405 Lexington Ave, 56th Floor, New York, NY 10017; tel. (212) 697-4830; fax (212) 983-4895; e-mail saudi-mission@un.int; internet www.saudi-un-ny.org; Permanent Representative Fawzi bin Abd al-Majeed Shobokshi.

Senegal: 238 East 68th St, New York, NY 10021; tel. (212) 517-9030; fax (212) 517-3032; e-mail senegal.mission@yahoo.fr; internet www.un.int/senegal; Permanent Representative Paul Badji.

Serbia: 854 Fifth Ave, New York, NY 10021; tel. (212) 879-8700; fax (212) 879-8705; e-mail yugoslavia@un.int; internet www.un.int/serbia; Chargé d'Affaires Pavle Jevremović.

Seychelles: 800 Second Ave, Rm 400C, New York, NY 10017; tel. (212) 972-1785; fax (212) 972-1786; e-mail seychelles@un.int; Permanent Representative Ronald Jean Jumeau.

Sierra Leone: 245 East 49th St, New York, NY 10017; tel. (212) 688-1656; fax (212) 688-4924; e-mail sierraleone@un.int; Permanent Representative Joe Robert Pemagbi.

Singapore: 231 East 51st St, New York, NY 10022; tel. (212) 826-0840; fax (212) 826-2964; e-mail singapore@un.int; internet www.mfa.gov.sg/newyork; Permanent Representative Vanu Gopala Menon.

Slovakia: 801 Second Ave, 12th Floor, New York, NY 10017; tel. (212) 286-8418; fax (212) 286-8419; e-mail slovakia@un.int; internet www.un.int/slovakia; Permanent Representative Peter Burian.

Slovenia: 600 Third Ave, 24th Floor, New York, NY 10016; tel. (212) 370-3007; fax (212) 370-1824; e-mail mny@mzz-dkp.gov.si; internet www.un.int/slovenia; Permanent Representative Sanja Stiglic.

Solomon Islands: 800 Second Ave, Suite 400L, New York, NY 10017; tel. (212) 599-6193; fax (212) 661-8925; e-mail solomonislands@un.int; Permanent Representative Colin D. Beck.

Somalia: 425 East 61st St, Suite 702, New York, NY 10021; tel. (212) 688-9410; fax (212) 759-0651; e-mail somalianet@hotmail.com; internet www.iaed.org/somalia; Permanent Representative Elmi Ahmed Duale.

South Africa: 333 East 38th St, 9th Floor, New York, NY 10016; tel. (212) 213-5583; fax (212) 692-2498; e-mail soafun@worldnet.att.net; internet www.southafrica-newyork.net/pmun; Permanent Representative Dumisani Shadrack Kumalo.

Spain: 823 United Nations Plaza, 9th Floor, New York, NY 10017; tel. (212) 661-1050; fax (212) 949-7247; e-mail spain@spainum.org;

internet www.spainun.org; Permanent Representative Juan Antonio Yáñez-Barnuevo.

Sri Lanka: 630 Third Ave, 20th Floor, New York, NY 10017; tel. (212) 986-7040; fax (212) 986-1838; e-mail srilanka@un.int; Permanent Representative Prasad Kariyawasam.

Sudan: 655 Third Ave, Suite 500–510, New York, NY 10017; tel. (212) 573-6033; fax (212) 573-6160; e-mail sudan@un.int; Permanent Representative Abdalmahmood Abdalhaleem Mohamad.

Suriname: 866 United Nations Plaza, Suite 320, New York, NY 10017; tel. (212) 826-0660; fax (212) 980-7029; e-mail suriname@un.int; internet www.un.int/suriname; Permanent Representative Henry Leonard MacDonald.

Swaziland: 408 East 50th St, New York, NY 10022; tel. (212) 371-8910; fax (212) 754-2755; e-mail swaziland@un.int; Permanent Representative Phesheya Mbongeni Dlamini.

Sweden: 1 Dag Hammarskjöld Plaza, 885 Second Ave, 46th Floor, New York, NY 10017; tel. (212) 583-2500; fax (212) 832-0389; e-mail sweden@un.int; internet www.un.int/sweden; Permanent Representative Anders Lidén.

Switzerland: 633 Third Ave, 29th Floor, New York, NY 10017; tel. (212) 286-1540; fax (212) 286-1555; e-mail vertretung-un@nyc.rep.admin.ch; internet www.uno.admin.ch/sub_uno/e/uno.html; Permanent Representative Peter Maurer.

Syria: 820 Second Ave, 15th Floor, New York, NY 10017; tel. (212) 661-1313; fax (212) 867-3985; e-mail syria@un.int; internet www.syria-un.org; Permanent Representative Bashar Ja'Afari.

Tajikistan: 136 East 67th St, New York, NY 10021; tel. (212) 744-2196; fax (212) 472-7645; e-mail tajikistan@un.int; Permanent Representative Sirodjidin Mukhridinovich Aslov.

Tanzania: 201 East 42nd St, 17th Floor, New York, NY 10017; tel. (212) 972-9160; fax (212) 682-5232; e-mail tzrepny@aol.com; Permanent Representative Augustine Philip Mahiga.

Thailand: 351 East 52nd St, New York, NY 10022; tel. (212) 754-2230; fax (212) 754-2535; e-mail thailand@un.int; Permanent Representative Don Pramudwinai.

Timor-Leste: 866 Second Ave, 9th Floor, New York, NY 10017; tel. (212) 759-3675; fax (212) 759-4196; e-mail timor-leste@un.int; internet www.un.int/timor-leste; Permanent Representative Nelson Santos.

Togo: 112 East 40th St, New York, NY 10016; tel. (212) 490-3455; fax (212) 983-6684; e-mail togo@un.int; e-mail onu@republicoftogo.com; Permanent Representative Roland Yao Kpotsra.

Tonga: 250 East 51st St, New York, NY 10022; tel. (917) 369-1025; fax (917) 369-1024; e-mail tongaunmission@aol.com; Permanent Representative Fekitamoeloa 'Utoikamanu.

Trinidad and Tobago: 820 Second Ave, 5th Floor, New York, NY 10017; tel. (212) 697-7620; fax (212) 682-3580; e-mail tto@un.int; Permanent Representative Philip R. A. Sealy.

Tunisia: 31 Beekman Pl., New York, NY 10022; tel. (212) 751-7503; fax (212) 751-0569; e-mail tunisia@un.int; internet www.tunisiaonline.com/tunisia-un/index.html; Permanent Representative Habib Mansour.

Turkey: 821 United Nations Plaza, 10th Floor, New York, NY 10017; tel. (212) 949-0150; fax (212) 949-0086; e-mail turkey@un.int; internet www.un.int/turkey; Permanent Representative Baki Ilkin.

Turkmenistan: 866 United Nations Plaza, Suite 424, New York, NY 10021; tel. (212) 486-8908; fax (212) 486-2521; e-mail turkmenistan@un.int; Permanent Representative Aksoltan T. Ataeva.

Tuvalu: 800 Second Ave, Suite 400B, New York, N.Y. 10017; tel. (212) 490-0534; fax (212) 808-4975; Permanent Representative Enele Sosene Sopoaga.

Uganda: 336 East 45th St, New York, NY 10017; tel. (212) 949-0110; fax (212) 687-4517; e-mail ugandaamb@aol.com; internet www.un.int/uganda; Permanent Representative Francis Butagira.

Ukraine: 220 East 51st St, New York, NY 10022; tel. (212) 759-7003; fax (212) 355-9455; e-mail mail@uamission.org; internet www.uamission.org; Permanent Representative Yuriy A. Sergeev.

United Arab Emirates: 747 Third Ave, 36th Floor, New York, NY 10017; tel. (212) 371-0480; fax (212) 371-4923; e-mail uae@un.int; Permanent Representative Ahmed Abdulrahman al-Jerman.

United Kingdom: 1 Dag Hammarskjöld Plaza, 885 Second Ave, New York, NY 10017; tel. (212) 745-9200; fax (212) 745-9316; e-mail uk@un.int; internet www.ukun.org; Permanent Representative Sir John Sawers, John Sawers.

USA: 799 United Nations Plaza, New York, NY 10017; tel. (212) 415-4000; fax (212) 415-4443; e-mail usa@un.int; internet www.un.int/usa; Permanent Representative Zalmay Khalilzad.

Uruguay: 866 United Nations Plaza, Suite 322, New York, NY 10017; tel. (212) 752-8240; fax (212) 593-0935; e-mail uruguay@un.int; internet www.un.int/uruguay; Permanent Representative Elbio O. Rosselli.

Uzbekistan: 866 United Nations Plaza, Suite 326, New York, NY 10017; tel. (212) 486-4242; fax (212) 486-7998; e-mail uzbekistan@un.int; Permanent Representative Alisher Vohidov.

Vanuatu: 866 United Nations Plaza, 3rd Floor, New York, NY 10017; tel. (212) 425-9600; fax (212) 425-9653; e-mail vanuatu@un.int; Permanent Representative Donald Kalpokas.

Venezuela: 335 East 46th St, New York, NY 10017; tel. (212) 557-2055; fax (212) 557-3528; e-mail venezuela@un.int; internet www.un.int/venezuela; Permanent Representative Javier Arias Arias Cárdenas.

Viet Nam: 866 United Nations Plaza, Suite 435, New York, NY 10017; tel. (212) 644-0594; fax (212) 644-5732; e-mail vietnamun@aol.com; internet www.un.int/vietnam; Permanent Representative Le Luong Minh.

Yemen: 413 East 51st St, New York, NY 10022; tel. (212) 355-1730; fax (212) 750-9613; e-mail yemen@un.int; internet www.un.int/yemen; Permanent Representative Abdullah M. as-Saidi.

Zambia: 237 East 52nd St, New York, NY 10022; tel. (212) 888-5770; fax (212) 888-5213; e-mail zambia@un.int; internet www.un.int/zambia; Permanent Representative Lazarous Kapambwe.

Zimbabwe: 128 East 56th St, New York, NY 10022; tel. (212) 980-9511; fax (212) 308-6705; e-mail zimbabwe@un.int; Permanent Representative T. J. B. Boniface Guwa Chidyausiku.

OBSERVERS

Inter-governmental organizations, etc., which have received an invitation to participate in the sessions and the work of the General Assembly as Observers, maintaining permanent offices at the UN:

African Union: 346 East 50th St, New York, NY 10022; tel. (212) 319-5490; fax (212) 319-7135; Permanent Representative Amadou Kébé.

Asian-African Legal Consultative Organization: 404 East 66th St, Apt 12C, New York, NY 10021; tel. (212) 734-7608; e-mail aalco@un.int; Permanent Representative K. Bhagwat-Singh (India).

Caribbean Community: 97/40 62nd Drive, 15K, Rego Park, NY 11374-1336; tel. and fax (718) 896-1179; Permanent Representative Miles Stoby.

Commonwealth Secretariat: 800 Second Ave, 4th Floor, New York, NY 10017; tel. (212) 599-6190; fax (212) 808-4975; e-mail comsec@thecommonwealth.org.

European Community (European Commission Delegation in New York): 305 East 47th St, New York, NY 10017; tel. (212) 371-3804; fax (212) 758-2718; e-mail euinfo@delusny.cec.eu.int; internet www.europa-eu-un.org.

European Community (Liaison Office of the General Secretariat of the Council of Ministers of the European Union): 345 East 46th St, 6th Floor, New York, NY 10017; tel. (212) 292-8600; fax (212) 681-6266; the Observer is the Permanent Representative to the UN of the country currently exercising the Presidency of the Council of Ministers of the European Union.

La Francophonie: 801 Second Ave, Suite 605, New York, NY 10017; tel. (212) 867-6771; fax (212) 867-3840; e-mail francophonie@un.int; Permanent Representative Moussa Makan Camara.

Holy See: 25 East 39th St, New York, NY 10016; tel. (212) 370-7885; fax (212) 370-9622; e-mail office@holyseemission.org; internet www.holyseemission.org; Permanent Representative Most Rev. Celestino Migliore (Titular Archbishop of Canosa).

International Committee of the Red Cross: 801 Second Ave, 18th Floor, New York, NY 10017; tel. (212) 599-6021; fax (212) 599-6009; e-mail log.nyc@icrc.org; Head of Delegation Dominique Buff.

International Federation of Red Cross and Red Crescent Societies: 630 Third Ave, Suite 2104, New York, NY 10017; tel. (212) 338-0161; fax (212) 338-9832; e-mail redcross@un.int; Permanent Representative Encho Gospodinov.

International Organization for Migration: 122 East 42nd St, Suite 1610, New York, NY 10168; tel. (212) 681-7000; fax (212) 867-5887; e-mail unobserver@iom.int; Permanent Representative Luca Dall'Oglio.

International Seabed Authority: 1 United Nations Plaza, Rm 1140, New York, NY 10017; tel. (212) 963-6470; fax (212) 963-0908; e-mail seaun@un.org.

International Tribunal for the Law of the Sea: 1 United Nations Plaza, Rm 1142, New York, NY 10017; tel. (212) 963-6480; fax (212) 963-0908.

Inter-Parliamentary Union: 200 East 42nd St, Suite 3102, New York, NY 10017; tel. (212) 557-5880; fax (212) 557-3954.

IUCN—The World Conservation Union: 406 West 66th St, New York, NY 10023; tel. and fax (212) 734-7608.

INTERNATIONAL ORGANIZATIONS   *United Nations*

League of Arab States: 747 Third Ave, 35th Floor, New York, NY 10017; tel. (212) 838-8700; fax (212) 355-3909; e-mail las@un.int; Permanent Representative YAHIA AL-MAHMASSANI.

Palestine: 115 East 65th St, New York, NY 10021; tel. (212) 288-8500; fax (212) 517-2377; e-mail palestine-observer-mission@un.int; internet www.un.int/palestine; Permanent Representative RIYAD H. MANSOUR.

Organization of the Islamic Conference: 130 East 40th St, 5th Floor, New York, NY 10016; tel. (212) 883-0140; fax (212) 883-0143; e-mail oic@un.int; internet www.oicun.org; Permanent Representative MOKHTAR LAMANI.

Sovereign Military Order of Malta: 216 East 47th St, 8th Floor, New York, NY 10017; tel. (212) 355-6213; fax (212) 355-4014; e-mail sm-malta@un.int; Permanent Representative JOSÉ ANTONIO LINATI-BOSCH.

The following inter-governmental organizations have a standing invitation to participate as Observers, but do not maintain permanent offices at the United Nations: African, Caribbean and Pacific Group of States; African Development Bank; Agency for the Prohibition of Nuclear Weapons in Latin America and the Caribbean; Andean Community; Asian Development Bank; Association of Caribbean States; Association of Southeast Asian Nations; Central American Integration System; Collective Security Treaty Organization; Common Fund for Commodities; Commonwealth of Independent States; Communauté économique des états de l'Afrique centrale; Community of Sahel-Saharan States; Comunidade dos Países de Língua Portuguesa; Council of Europe; East African Community; Economic Community of West African States; Economic Co-operation Organization; Eurasian Economic Community; GUAM: Organization for Democracy and Economic Development; Hague Conference on Private International Law; Ibero-American General Secretariat; Indian Ocean Commission; Inter-American Development Bank; International Centre for Migration Policy Development; International Criminal Court; International Criminal Police Organization (Interpol); International Development Law Organization; International Hydrographic Organization; International Institute for Democracy and Electoral Assistance; Islamic Development Bank; Latin American Economic System; Latin American Integration Association; Latin American Parliament; OPEC Fund for International Development; Organisation for Economic Co-operation and Development; Organisation of Eastern Caribbean States; Organization for Security and Co-operation in Europe; Organization of American States; Organization of the Black Sea Economic Co-operation; Pacific Islands Forum; Partners in Population and Development; Permanent Court of Arbitration; Shanghai Co-operation Organization; South Asian Association for Regional Co-operation; Southern African Development Community; World Customs Organization.

United Nations Information Centres/Services

Algeria: 9A rue Emile Payen, Hydra, Algiers; tel. (21) 48-08-71; fax (21) 69-23-15; e-mail unic.dz@undp.org; internet algiers.unic.org/.

Argentina: Junín 1940, 1°, 1113 Buenos Aires; tel. (11) 4803-7671; fax (11) 4804-7545; e-mail buenosaires@unic.org.ar; internet www.unic.org.ar; also covers Uruguay.

Armenia: 375001 Yerevan, 2 Petros Adamyan St, 1st Floor; tel. (10) 560-212; fax (10) 561-406; e-mail dpi@undpi.am; internet www.undpi.am.

Australia: POB 4045, 46–48 York St, 5th Floor, Sydney, NSW 2000; tel. (2) 9262-5111; fax (2) 9262-5886; e-mail unic@un.org.au; internet www.un.org.au; also covers Fiji, Kiribati, Nauru, New Zealand, Samoa, Tonga, Tuvalu and Vanuatu.

Austria: POB 500, Vienna International Centre, 1400 Vienna; tel. (1) 26060-4666; fax (1) 26060-5899; e-mail unis@unvienna.org; internet www.unis.unvienna.org; also covers Hungary, Slovakia and Slovenia.

Azerbaijan: 1001 Baku, UN 50th Anniversary St 3; tel. (12) 498-98-88; fax (12) 498-32-35; e-mail dpi@un-az.org; internet www.un-az.org.

Bahrain: POB 26004, Bldg 69, Rd 1901, Manama 319; tel. 17311676; fax 17311692; e-mail unic.bahrain@undp.org; internet www.undp.org.bh/unic; also covers Qatar and the United Arab Emirates.

Bangladesh: POB 3658, Dhaka 1000; tel. (2) 8117868; fax (2) 8112343; e-mail unic.dhaka@undp.org; internet www.unicdhaka.org.

Belarus: 220050 Minsk, 17 Kirov St, 6th Floor; tel. (17) 227-48-76; fax (17) 226-03-40; e-mail dpi_unit.by@undp.org; internet www.un.by.

Belgium: Residence Palace, rue de la Loi, Quartier Rubens, Block C2, 1040, Brussels; tel. (2) 788-84-84; fax 788-84-85; e-mail info@unric.org; internet www.unric.org.

Bolivia: Calle 14 esq. S. Bustamante, Ed. Metrobol II, Calacoto, La Paz; tel. (2) 2624512; fax (2) 2795820; e-mail unicbol@nu.org.bo; internet www.nu.org.bo/cinu.

Brazil: Palacio Itamaraty, Avda Marechal Floriano 196, 20080-002 Rio de Janeiro; tel. (21) 2253-2211; fax (21) 2233-5753; e-mail infounic@unicrio.org.br; internet www.unicrio.org.br.

Burkina Faso: BP 135, 14 ave de la Grande Chancellerie, Secteur no 4, Ouagadougou; tel. 50-30-60-76; fax 50-31-13-22; e-mail cinu.oui@fasonet.bf; internet www.ouagadougou.unic.org; also covers Chad, Mali and Niger.

Burundi: BP 2160, ave de la Révolution 117, Bujumbura; tel. (2) 225018; fax (2) 241798; e-mail unicbuj@undp.org; internet bujumbura.unic.org.

Cameroon: PB 836, Immeuble Tchinda, rue 2044, Yaoundé; tel. 221-23-67; fax 221-23-68; e-mail unic.cm@undp.org; internet yaounde.unic.org; also covers the Central African Republic and Gabon.

Chile: Edif. Naciones Unidas, Avda Dag Hammarskjöld, Casilla 179-D, Santiago; tel. (2) 210-2000; fax (2) 228-1947; e-mail dpisantiago@eclac.cl.

Colombia: Calle 100, No. 8A-55, 10°, Edificio World Trade Center, Torre C, Bogotá 2; tel. (1) 257-6044; fax (1) 257-7936; e-mail unicbogota@cinucol-un.org; internet www.onucolombia.org; also covers Ecuador and Venezuela.

Congo, Democratic Republic: PB 7248, blvd du 30 juin, Kinshasa; tel. 884-5537; fax 884-3675; e-mail unic.kinshasa@undp.org.

Congo, Republic: POB 13210, ave Foch, Case ORTF 15, Brazzaville; tel. 661-20-68; fax 81-27-44; e-mail prosper.mihindou@undp.org; internet brazzavile.unic.org.

Czech Republic: nam. Kinských 6, 150 00 Prague 5; tel. 257199831; fax 257316761; e-mail unicprg@osn.cz; internet www.unicprague.cz.

Egypt: 1 Osiris St, Garden City, Cairo; tel. (2) 7900022; fax (2) 7953705; e-mail info@unic-eg.org; also covers Saudi Arabia.

Eritrea: Andinet St, Zone 4 Admin. 07, Airport Rd, Asmara; tel. (1) 151166; fax (1) 151081; e-mail mohammed.salih@undp.org; internet asmara.unic.org.

Ethiopia: POB 3001, Africa Hall, Addis Ababa; tel. (11) 5515826; fax (11) 5510365; e-mail ecainfo@un.org.

Ghana: POB GP 2339, Gamel Abdul Nassar/Liberia Rds, Accra; tel. (21) 665511; fax (21) 665578; e-mail info@unic-ghana.org; internet www.accra.unic.org; also covers Sierra Leone.

Georgia: 380079 Tbilisi, Eristavi St 9; tel. (32) 998558; fax (32) 250271; e-mail registry.ge@undp.org; internet www.undp.org.ge.

India: 55 Lodi Estate, New Delhi 110 003; tel. (11) 24628877; fax (11) 24620293; e-mail unicindia@unicindia.org; internet www.unic.org.in; also covers Bhutan.

Indonesia: Gedung Surya, 14th Floor, 9 Jalan M. H. Thamrin Kavling, Jakarta 10350; tel. (21) 3983-1011; fax (21) 3983-1014; e-mail unic-jakarta@unic-jakarta.org; internet www.un.or.id.

Iran: POB 15875-4557; 39 Shahrzad Blvd, Darrous, Tehran; tel. (21) 228-72837; fax (21) 228-73395; e-mail unic@unic.un.or.ir; internet www.unic-ir.org.

Japan: UNU Bldg, 8th Floor, 53–70 Jingumae 5-chome, Shibuya-ku, Tokyo 150 0001; tel. (3) 5467-4451; fax (3) 5467-4455; e-mail unic@untokyo.jp; internet www.unic.or.jp.

Kazakhstan: 480100 Almaty, Tole bi 67; tel. (727) 269-53-27; fax (727) 258-26-45; e-mail registry.kz@undp.org; internet kazakhstan.unic.org.

Kenya: POB 30552, United Nations Office, Gigiri, Nairobi; tel. (20) 7623292; fax (20) 7624349; e-mail nairobi.unic@unon.org; internet www.unicnairobi.org; also covers Seychelles and Uganda.

Lebanon: Riad es-Solh Sq., POB 11-8575-4956, Chouran, Beirut; tel. (1) 981301; fax (1) 981516; e-mail unic-beirut@un.org; also covers Jordan, Kuwait and Syria.

Lesotho: POB 301, Maseru 100; tel. (22) 312496; fax (22) 310042; e-mail unic.maseru@undp.org; internet maseru.unic.org.

Liberia: Dubar Bldg, Virginia, Monrovia; tel. 2260195; fax 205407; e-mail registry.1r@undp.org.

Libya: POB 286, Khair Aldeen Baybers St, Hay al-Andalous, Tripoli; tel. (21) 4770521; fax (21) 4777343; e-mail tripoli@un.org.

Madagascar: PB 1348, 22 rue Rainitovo, Antasahavola, Antananarivo; tel. (20) 2224115; fax (20) 2233315; e-mail unic.ant@dts.mg; internet www.antananarivo.unic.org.

INTERNATIONAL ORGANIZATIONS *United Nations*

Mexico: Presidente Masaryk 29, 6°, México 11 570, DF; tel. (55) 5263-9718; fax (55) 5203-8638; e-mail unicmex@un.org.mx; internet www.cinu.org.mx; also covers Cuba and the Dominican Republic.

Morocco: BP 601; rue Tarik ibn Zyad 6, Rabat; tel. (7) 76-86-33; fax (7) 76-83-77; e-mail unicmor@unicmor.ma; internet www.unicmor.ma.

Myanmar: 6 Natmauk Rd, Tamwe P.O., Yangon; tel. (1) 542910; fax (1) 542634; e-mail unic.myanmar@undp.org.

Namibia: Private Bag 13351, Paratus Bldg, 372 Independence Ave, Windhoek; tel. (61) 233034; fax (61) 233036; e-mail unic@un.na; internet windhoek.unic.org.

Nepal: POB 107, UN House, Kathmandu; tel. (1) 524200; fax (1) 523991; e-mail registry.np@undp.org.

Nigeria: POB 1068, Alfred Rewane Rd, Ikoyi, Lagos; tel. (1) 269-4886; fax (1) 269-1934; e-mail uniclag@unicnig.org; internet lagos.unic.org.

Pakistan: POB 1107, House No. 26, 88th St, G-6/3, Islamabad; tel. (51) 2270610; fax (51) 2271856; e-mail unic@dsl.net.pk; internet www.un.org.pk/unic.

Panama: POB 6-9083, El Dorado; UN House Bldg 154/155, Ciudad del Saber, Clayton, Panama City; tel. (7) 302-4522; fax (7) 305-4521; e-mail cinup@un.org.pa; internet www.cinup.org.

Paraguay: Casilla de Correo 1107; Edif. Naciones Unidas, Avda Mariscal López, Asunción; tel. (21) 614443; fax (21) 611988; e-mail unic.py@undp.org.

Peru: POB 14-0199, Lord Cochrane 130, San Isidro, Lima 27; tel. (1) 441-8745; fax (1) 441-8735; e-mail informes@uniclima.org.pe; internet www.uniclima.org.pe.

Philippines: POB 7285 ADC (DAPO), Pasay City, Metro Manila; tel. (2) 338-5520; fax (2) 338-0177; e-mail infocentre@unicmanila.org; internet www.unicmanila.org; also covers Papua New Guinea and Solomon Islands.

Poland: 00-608 Warsaw, Al. Niepodległości 186; 02-514 Warsaw, POB 1; tel. (22) 8255784; fax (22) 8257706; e-mail unic.pl@undp.org; internet www.unic.un.org.pl.

Romania: 011975 Bucharest, Bd. Primaverii 48A; tel. (21) 201-78-77; fax (21) 201-78-80; e-mail unic@undp.ro.

Russia: 4/16 Glazovsky per., 119002 Moscow; tel. (495) 241-2894; fax (495) 230-2138; e-mail dpi-moscow@unic.ru; internet www.unic.ru.

Senegal: BP 154, rues de Thann et Dajorne, Dakar; tel. 889-11-89; fax 822-14-06; e-mail unicdakar@cinu-dakar.org; internet dakar.unic.org; also covers Cape Verde, Côte d'Ivoire, The Gambia, Guinea, Guinea-Bissau and Mauritania.

South Africa: Metro Park Bldg, 351 Schoemann St, POB 12677, Pretoria 0126; tel. (12) 354-8506; fax (12) 354-8501; e-mail unic@un.org.za; internet pretoria.unic.org.

Sri Lanka: POB 1505, 202/204 Bauddhaloka Mawatha, Colombo 7; tel. (1) 580691; fax (1) 501396; e-mail mohan.samaranayake@undp.org.

Sudan: POB 1992, UN Compound, Gamma'a Ave, Khartoum; tel. (11) 773121; fax (11) 773772; e-mail registry.sd@undp.org; also covers Somalia.

Switzerland: Palais des Nations, 1211 Geneva 10; tel. 229172300; fax 229170030; e-mail press_geneva@unog.ch; internet www.unog.ch; also covers Bulgaria.

Tanzania: Msimbazi Creek Housing Estate Ltd, King's Way, Mafinga St, Plot 134/140, Kinondoni, Dar es Salaam; tel. (22) 2199297; fax (22) 2668749; e-mail maravanyika@un.org; internet daressalaam.unic.org.

Thailand: ESCAP, United Nations Bldg, Rajadamnern Nok Ave, Bangkok 10200; tel. (2) 288-1866; fax (2) 288-1052; e-mail unisbkk.unescap@un.org; internet www.unescap.org/unic; also covers Cambodia, Hong Kong, Laos, Malaysia, Singapore and Viet Nam.

Togo: BP 911, 107 blvd du 13 janvier, Lomé; tel. and fax 221-23-06; e-mail cinutogo@cafe.tg; also covers Benin.

Trinidad and Tobago: 16 Victoria Ave, Port of Spain; tel. 623-4813; fax 623-4332; e-mail unicpos@unicpos.org.tt; internet www.unicpos.org.tt; also covers Antigua and Barbuda, the Bahamas, Barbados, Belize, Dominica, Grenada, Guyana, Jamaica, the Netherlands Antilles, Saint Christopher and Nevis, Saint Lucia, Saint Vincent and the Grenadines, and Suriname.

Tunisia: BP 863, 61 blvd Bab-Benat, Tunis; tel. (71) 560-203; fax (71) 568-811; e-mail onu.tunis@planet.tn; internet www.unictunis.org.tn.

Turkey: PK 407, Birlik Mahallesi, 2 Cad. No. 11, 06610 Cankaya, Ankara; tel. (312) 4541051; fax (312) 4961499; e-mail unic@un.org.tr; internet 195.142.135.65/unic/unic_eng.asp.

Ukraine: 01021 Kyiv-21, Klovsky Uzviz, 1; tel. (44) 253-93-63; fax (44) 253-26-07; e-mail registry@un.org.ua; internet www.un.org.ua.

USA: 1775 K St, NW, Suite 400, Washington, DC 20006; tel. (202) 331-8670; fax (202) 331-9191; e-mail unicdc@unicwash.org; internet www.unicwash.org.

Uzbekistan: 700029 Tashkent, 4 Taras Shevchenko St; tel. (71) 133-09-77; fax (71) 120-34-50; e-mail registry.uz@undp.org; internet www.undp.uz.

Western Europe: United Nations Regional Information Centre, Residence Palace, Bloc C, Level 7, 155 rue de la Loi/Wetstraat, 1040 Brussels, Belgium; tel. (2) 788-84-84; fax (2) 788-84-85; e-mail info@unric.org; internet www.unric.org; serves Belgium, Cyprus, Denmark, Finland, France, Germany, Greece, The Holy See, Iceland, Ireland, Italy, Luxembourg, Malta, Monaco, the Netherlands, Norway, Portugal, San Marino, Spain, Sweden, United Kingdom; also provides liaison with the institutions of the European Union.

Yemen: POB 237; St 5, off Al-Boniya St, Handhal Zone, San'a; tel. (1) 274000; fax (1) 274043; e-mail unicyem@y.net.ye; internet www.unicyem.org.

Zambia: POB 32905, Lusaka 10101; tel. (1) 228478; fax (1) 222958; e-mail unic@zamtel.zm; internet lusaka.unic.org; also covers Botswana, Malawi and Swaziland.

Zimbabwe: POB 4408, Sanders House, 2nd Floor, First St/Jason Moyo Ave, Harare; tel. (4) 777060; fax (4) 750476; e-mail unic@mweb.co.zw.

Conferences

Global conferences are convened regularly by the United Nations. Special sessions of the General Assembly assess progress achieved in the implementation of conference action plans. The following global conferences and special sessions were scheduled for 2008–09:

Conference on Disarmament, 2008 session (Jan.–March, May–June, July–Sept.: Geneva, Switzerland);

High-level Meeting of the General Assembly to review comprehensively the progress achieved in realizing the Declaration of Commitment on HIV/AIDS and the Political Declaration on HIV/AIDS (June 2008: New York);

High-level Meeting of the General Assembly for a Mid-term Review of the Almaty Programme of Action, on the theme 'Addressing the Special Needs of Landlocked Developing Countries' (Oct. 2008, New York);

Follow-up International Conference on Financing for Development to Review the Implementation of the Monterrey Consensus (Nov.–Dec. 2008: Doha, Qatar);

Plenary meeting of the General Assembly to commemorate the sixtieth anniversary of the Universal Declaration of Human Rights (Dec. 2008: New York);

Conference on Disarmament, 2009 session (Jan.–March, May–June, July–Sept.: Geneva, Switzerland);

High-level UN Conference on South-South Co-operation (early 2009: Argentina);

Special meeting of the General Assembly to review activities undertaken during the International Year of Human Rights Learning (Dec. 2009: New York).

Co-ordinating Bodies

The Senior Management Group, a committee of senior UN personnel established in 1997, acts as the Secretary-General's cabinet and as the central policy-planning body of the United Nations. The 28-member United Nations System Chief Executives Board for Co-ordination—CEB, founded in 1946 as the Administrative Committee on Co-ordination and renamed in 2001, convenes at least twice a year under the chairmanship of the Secretary General to co-ordinate UN system-wide policies, activities and management issues. The United Nations Development Group (UNDG), established in 1997, unites, under the chairmanship of the Administrator of UNDP, the heads of some 28 UN funds, programmes and departments concerned with sustainable development, in order to promote coherent policy at country level. Project management services are provided throughout the UN system of entities and organizations, as well as to certain bilateral donors, international financial institutions and governments, by the United Nations Office for Project Services—UNOPS. UNOPS, founded in 1995 and a member of the UNDG, is self-financing, funded by fees earned from the services that it provides. The Inter-Agency Standing Committee—IASC, founded in 1992, comprises the executive heads of 17 leading UN and other agencies and NGO consortia, who convene at least twice a year under the leadership of the Emergency Relief Co-ordinator (see OCHA). It co-

Finance

The majority of the UN's peace-keeping operations are financed separately from the UN's regular budget by assessed contributions from member states.

In recent years the UN has suffered financial difficulties, owing to an expansion of the organization's political and humanitarian activities and delay on the part of member states in paying their contributions. In 1993 the UN Secretary-General formulated a series of economy measures to be applied throughout the organization, in order to avert a financial crisis. However, the fragility of the UN's financial situation has persisted, partly owing to delays in the process between approval of a peace-keeping operation and receipt of contributions for that budget. In December 1997 a UN Development Account was established to channel administrative savings achieved as a result of reforms to the UN's administrative structure towards financing development projects. In December 2000 the General Assembly approved a restructuring of scale of assessment calculations, the methodology and accuracy of which had been contested in recent years, particularly by the USA. From 2001 the level of US contributions to the regular annual budget was reduced from 25% to 22%, while annual contributions were raised for several nations with rapidly developing economies. At 31 October 2007 126 member states had paid their regular budget assessments in full, while the remaining members owed some US $836m. Of the total amount of unpaid assessments the USA owed $786m. In addition, many member states owed outstanding assessment contributions to the peace-keeping and international tribunal budgets at that time. The scale of assessment calculations were reviewed most recently in 2006.

In 1997 a US business executive, Ted Turner, announced a donation of US $1,000m. to finance UN humanitarian and environmental causes. The donation has been paid in instalments and administered through his 'UN Foundation', and a UN Fund for International Partnerships (UNFIP) was established by the UN Secretary-General in 1998 to facilitate relations between the UN system and the UN Foundation. The Foundation, which is also sustained by resources from other partners and by grassroots donors, supports the UN through advocacy, grant-making, and the implementation of public-private partnerships.

The proposed UN budget for 2008–09 amounted to US $4,195.2m.

PROPOSED TWO-YEAR BUDGET OF THE UNITED NATIONS
(US $'000)

	2008–09
Overall policy-making, direction and co-ordination	662,675.9
Political affairs	815,291.6
International justice and law	80,872.8
International co-operation for development	379,189.2
Regional co-operation for development	442,842.2
Human rights and humanitarian affairs	242,367.7
Public information	179,349.0
Common support services	537,273.3
Internal oversight	38,768.9
Jointly-financed activities and special expenses	105,318.0
Capital expenditures	55,157.5
Safety and security	196,870.2
Development Account	16,480.9
Staff Assessment	442,785.8
Total	**4,195,243.0**

United Nations Publications

Basic Facts About the United Nations.
Demographic Yearbook.
Index to Proceedings (of the General Assembly; the Security Council; the Economic and Social Council; the Trusteeship Council).
International Law Catalogue.
Monthly Bulletin of Statistics.
Population and Vital Statistics Report (quarterly).
Statement of Treaties and International Agreements (monthly).
Statistical Yearbook.
UN Chronicle (quarterly).
United Nations Disarmament Yearbook.
United Nations Juridical Yearbook.
World Economic and Social Survey.
World Situation and Prospects.
World Statistics Pocketbook.
Yearbook of the United Nations.
Other UN publications are listed in the chapters dealing with the agencies concerned.

Secretariat

According to the UN Charter the Secretary-General is the chief administrative officer of the organization, and he may appoint further Secretariat staff as required. The principal departments and officers of the Secretariat are listed below. The chief administrative staff of the UN Regional Commissions and of all the subsidiary organs of the UN are also members of the Secretariat staff and are listed in the appropriate chapters. The Secretariat staff also includes a number of special missions and special appointments, including some of senior rank.

The Secretary-General chairs the Senior Management Group (SMG), a committee of senior UN personnel that acts as his cabinet and as the central policy-planning body of the United Nations. Two subsidiary committees of the SMG, the Policy Committee and the Management Committee, were inaugurated in 2005 to enhance the efficiency of high-level decision-making.

The Secretariat comprises about 15,000 staff holding appointments continuing for a year or more, but excluding staff working for the UN specialized agencies and subsidiary organs.

In July 1997 the Secretary-General initiated a comprehensive reform of the administration of the UN and abolished some 1,000 Secretariat posts. The reforms aimed to restructure the Secretariat's substantive work programme around the UN's five core missions, i.e. peace and security, economic and social affairs, development co-operation, humanitarian affairs and human rights. During 1997 the Centre for Human Rights and the Office of the High Commissioner for Human Rights were consolidated into a single office under the reform process, while a new Office for Drug Control and Crime Prevention was established, within the framework of the UN Office in Vienna, to integrate efforts to combat crime, drug abuse and terrorism; this was subsequently renamed the UN Office on Drugs and Crime. In December a new post of Deputy Secretary-General was created to assist in the management of Secretariat operations, in particular the ongoing reform process, and represent the Secretary-General as required.

In December 2001, on the recommendation of the Secretary-General, the General Assembly established the Office of the High Representative for the Least Developed Countries, Landlocked Developing Countries and Small Island Developing States. In May 2002 the Secretary-General appointed the first United Nations Security Co-ordinator. A new Department for Safety and Security, headed by an Under-Secretary-General for Safety and Security and replacing the Office of the United Nations Security Co-ordinator, was established in February 2005, taking over responsibility for the safety of UN personnel.

In June 2004 a Panel of Eminent Persons on Civil Society and UN Relationships—appointed by the Secretary-General in February 2003, as part of the ongoing UN reform process, with a mandate to explore and make recommendations on the interaction between civil society, private-sector enterprise, parliaments and the UN—issued its final report. A High-Level Panel on Threats, Challenges and Change, appointed by the Secretary-General in November 2003 (in the aftermath of the deaths in August of 21 UN staff members, including Sergio Vieira de Mello, UN High Commissioner for Human Rights, in a terrorist attack in Baghdad, Iraq) to evaluate the ability of the UN to address threats to the peace and security of the international community and to recommend relevant policy and institutional changes, including reforms to the Security Council, published its findings in December 2004. The report of the Secretary-

INTERNATIONAL ORGANIZATIONS

United Nations

General entitled 'In Larger Freedom: Towards Development, Security and Human Rights for All', issued in March 2005 after consideration of the High-Level Panel's report, proposed a realignment of the Secretariat's structure, entailing the establishment of a peace-building support office and strengthening support within the body for mediation by the Secretary-General (his 'good offices'), democracy, and the rule of law. He also determined to establish a cabinet-style decision-making executive within the Secretariat, supported by a small subsidiary cabinet secretariat, and proposed a higher level of managerial authority for the role of Secretary-General. Further proposals included the appointment of a Scientific Adviser to the Secretary-General, mandated to supply strategic scientific advice on policy matters, and a comprehensive review of the functioning of the Office of Internal Oversight Services. The Secretary-General's reform proposals were reviewed by the World Summit of UN heads of state held in September (see General Assembly). In December an Ethics Office responsible for applying a uniform set of ethical standards was established within the Secretariat. From January 2008 the UN ethical code was extended to cover employees of all UN funds and programmes. In March 2006 the Secretary-General issued a report entitled 'Investing in the United Nations' in which he outlined proposals to strengthen the role of the Secretariat through a realignment of staff skills, involving relocating personnel and core practices away from headquarters; increasing management accountability and introducing a single comprehensive annual report of its activities; upgrading information technology capabilities; and streamlining the budget. In July 2007 a new Department of Field Support was established within the Secretariat to provide expert administrative and logistical support for UN peace operations in the field.

The UN Secretariat and Iraqi Government jointly chair the International Compact for Iraq, a five-year framework for co-operation between Iraq and the international community that was launched in May 2007.

Secretary-General: BAN KI-MOON (Republic of Korea).
Deputy Secretary-General: Dr ASHA-ROSE MIGIRO (Tanzania).

Executive Office of the Secretary-General
Under-Secretary-General, Chief of Staff: VIJAY K. NAMBIAR (India).
Deputy Chef de Cabinet, Assistant Secretary-General: WOO-SON KIM (Republic of Korea).

Department for Disarmament Affairs
Under-Secretary-General: SERGIO DE QUEIROZ DUARTE (Brazil).

Department for Safety and Security
Under-Secretary-General: Sir DAVID VENESS (United Kingdom).

Department of Economic and Social Affairs
Under-Secretary-General: SHA ZUKANG (People's Republic of China).
Assistant Secretary-General, Economic Development: KWAME SUNDARAM JOMO.
Assistant Secretary-General, Special Adviser on Gender Issues and the Advancement of Women: RACHEL MAYANJA.
Assistant Secretary-General, Policy Planning: ROBERT ORR.
Assistant Secretary-General, Policy Co-ordination and Inter-Agency Affairs: THOMAS STELZER (Austria).

Department of Field Support
Under-Secretary-General: SUSANNA MALCORRA (Argentina).
Assistant Secretary-General: JANE LUTE (USA).

Department of General Assembly and Conference Management
Under-Secretary-General: MUHAMMAD SHAABAN (Egypt).
Assistant Secretary-General: YOHANNES MENGESHA.

Department of Management
Under-Secretary-General: ALICIA BÁRCENA IBARRA (Mexico).

Department of Peace-keeping Operations
Under-Secretary-General: JEAN-MARIE GUÉHENNO (France).
Assistant Secretary-General: EDMOND MULET.
Assistant Secretary-General, Rule of Law and Security: DMITRY TITOV.

Department of Political Affairs
Under-Secretary-General: B. LYNN PASCOE (USA).

Department of Public Information
Under-Secretary-General: KIYOTAKA AKASAKA (Japan).

Office for the Co-ordination of Humanitarian Affairs
Under-Secretary-General for Humanitarian Affairs and Emergency Relief Co-ordinator: JOHN HOLMES (United Kingdom).

Office on Drugs and Crime
Under-Secretary-General: ANTONIO MARIA COSTA (Italy).

Office of Oversight Services
Under-Secretary-General: INGA-BRITT AHLENIUS (Sweden).

Office of the High Representative for the Least Developed Countries, Landlocked Developing Countries and Small Island Developing States
Under-Secretary-General and High Representative: CHEICK SIDI DIARRA (Mali).

Office of Legal Affairs
Under-Secretary-General, The Legal Counsel: NICOLAS MICHEL (Switzerland).
Assistant Secretary-General, Legal Affairs: LARRY D. JOHNSON.

Office of the Special Representative of the Secretary-General for Children and Armed Conflict
Under-Secretary-General: RADHIKA COOMARASWAMY (Sri Lanka).

Office of the United Nations High Commissioner for Human Rights
Palais des Nations, 1211 Geneva 10, Switzerland; tel. 229179000; fax 229179010; internet www.unhchr.ch.
High Commissioner: LOUISE ARBOUR (Canada) (until 30 June 2008).
Deputy High Commissioner: KYUNG-WHA KANG (Republic of Korea).

Peace-building Support Office
Assistant Secretary-General: CAROLYN MCASKIE (Canada).

Geneva Office
Palais des Nations, 1211 Geneva 10, Switzerland; tel. 2291071234; fax 229170123; internet www.unog.ch.
Director-General: SERGEI ORDZHONIKIDZE (Russia).

Nairobi Office
POB 30552, Nairobi, Kenya; tel. (20) 7621234.
Director-General: ANNA TIBAIJUKA (Tanzania).

Vienna Office
Vienna International Centre, POB 500, 1400 Vienna, Austria; tel. (1) 26060; fax (1) 263-3389; internet www.un.or.at.
Director-General: ANTONIO MARIA COSTA (Italy).

General Assembly

The General Assembly was established as a principal organ of the United Nations under the UN Charter. It first met on 10 January 1946. It is the main deliberative organ of the United Nations, and the only one composed of representatives of all the UN member states. Each delegation consists of not more than five representatives and five alternates, with as many advisers as may be required. The Assembly meets regularly for three months each year, and special sessions may also be held. It has specific responsibility for electing the Secretary-General and members of other UN councils and organs, and for approving the UN budget and the assessments for financial contributions by member states. It is also empowered to make recommendations (but not binding decisions) on questions of international security and co-operation.

The regular session of the General Assembly commences in mid-September. After the election of its President and other officers, the Assembly opens its general debate, a two-week period during which the head of each delegation makes a formal statement of his or her government's views on major world issues. Since 1997 the Secretary-General has presented his report on the work of the UN at the start of the general debate. The Assembly then begins examination of the principal items on its agenda: it acts directly on some agenda items, but most business is handled by the six Main Committees (listed below), which study and debate each item and present draft resolutions to the Assembly. After a review of the report of each Main Committee, the Assembly formally approves or rejects the Committee's recommendations. On designated 'important questions', such as recommendations on international peace and security, the admission of new members to the United Nations, or budgetary questions, a two-thirds majority is needed for adoption of a resolution. Other questions may be decided by a simple majority. In the Assembly, each member has one vote. Voting in the Assembly is sometimes replaced by an effort to find consensus among member states, in order to strengthen support for the Assembly's decisions: the President consults delegations in private to find out whether they are willing to agree to adoption of a resolution without a vote; if they are, the President can declare that a resolution has been so adopted.

Special sessions of the Assembly may be held to discuss issues which require particular attention (e.g. illicit drugs) and 'emergency special sessions' may also be convened to discuss situations on which the UN Security Council has been unable to reach a decision. The Assembly's 10th emergency special session, concerning Illegal Israeli Actions in Occupied East Jerusalem and the rest of the Occupied Palestinian Territory, commenced in April 1997 and has been subsequently reconvened intermittently. The 23rd meeting of the session, called in December 2003 by Arab and non-aligned countries, requested that the International Court of Justice (ICJ) render an advisory opinion on the legal consequences arising from the construction of a wall by Israel in the Occupied Palestinian Territory including in and around East Jerusalem; this action was taken by the General Assembly following two failures by the Security Council to adopt resolutions on the matter. The 24th meeting of the session was convened in July 2004 to discuss the ICJ's ruling on this matter, which had been delivered earlier in that month. A special session on children, reviewing progress made since the World Summit for Children, held in 1990, and the adoption in 1989 of the Convention on the Rights of the Child, was convened in May 2002. In January 2005 a special session took place to commemorate the 60th anniversary of the liberation of the Nazi concentration camps.

The Assembly's 55th session (from September 2000) was designated as the Millennium Assembly. In early September a Millennium Summit of UN heads of state or government was convened to debate 'The Role of the United Nations in the 21st Century'. The Millennium Summit issued the UN Millennium Declaration, identifying the values and principles that should guide the organization in key areas including peace, development, environment, human rights, protection of the vulnerable, and the special needs of the African continent; and specified six fundamental values underlying international relations: freedom; equality; solidarity; tolerance; respect for nature; and a sense of shared responsibility for the global economy and social development. The summit adopted the following so-called Millennium Development Goals (MDGs), each incorporating specific targets to be attained by 2015: the eradication of extreme poverty and hunger; attainment of universal primary education; promotion of gender equality and empowerment of women; reduction of child mortality rates; improvement in maternal health rates; combating HIV/AIDS, malaria and other diseases; ensuring environmental sustainability; and the development of a global partnership for development. Reform of the Security Council and the need for increased UN co-operation with the private sector, non-governmental organizations and civil society in pursuing its goals were also addressed by the summit. Progress in attaining the MDGs was to be reviewed on a regular basis. A five-year review conference of the Millennium Declaration was convened in September 2005 at the level of heads of state and of government.

In October 2003 the President of the Assembly appointed six facilitators to oversee discussions on means of revitalizing the Assembly, and in mid-December the Assembly adopted a landmark resolution that, while reaffirming relevant provisions of the UN Charter and the UN Millennium Declaration, outlined a number of reforms to the Assembly's operations. The changes, aimed at enhancing the Assembly's authority, role, efficiency and impact, were to take effect following broad consultations over the next two years. The resolution provided for a regular meeting of the Presidents of the Assembly, Security Council and ECOSOC, with a view to strengthening co-operation and complementarity in the respective work programmes of the three bodies. In July 2004 the Assembly adopted a resolution on further revitalization of its work, with provisions for streamlining its agenda, sharpening the focus of the six Main Committees, and reducing paperwork.

In March 2005 the Secretary-General presented to the General Assembly a report entitled 'In Larger Freedom: Towards Development, Security and Human Rights for All'. Building on the September 2000 Millennium Declaration, the report focused on three main pillars, defined as: 'Freedom from Want', urging developing countries to improve governance and combat corruption, and industrialized nations to increase funds for development assistance and debt relief and to provide immediate free market access to all exports from least developed countries; 'Freedom from Fear', urging states to agree a new consensus on security matters and adopting a definition of an act of terrorism as one 'intended to cause death or serious bodily harm to civilians or non-combatants with the purpose of intimidating a population or compelling a government or an international organization to do or abstain from doing any act'; and 'Freedom to Live in Dignity', urging the international community to support the principle of 'responsibility to protect'. The report also detailed a number of recommendations for strengthening the UN, which were subsequently considered by the September 2005 World Summit of UN heads of state. These included: rationalizing the work of the Assembly (see above) and focusing its agenda on substantive topical issues, such as international migration and the conclusion of a new comprehensive international strategy against terrorism; restructuring the Secretariat; expanding the membership of the Security Council; and establishing a new UN Human Rights Council to replace the Commission on Human Rights. In December the General Assembly, acting concurrently with the Security Council, authorized the establishment of an intergovernmental advisory Peace-building Commission, which had been recommended in September by the World Summit. In March 2006 the Assembly authorized the establishment of the new Human Rights Council. Both the Peace-building Commission and Human Rights Council were inaugurated in June. In February 2007 the Assembly appointed five ambassadors to host negotiations aimed at advancing the process of Security Council reform.

President of 62nd Session: SRGJAN KERIM (FYR Macedonia).

MAIN COMMITTEES

There are six Main Committees, on which all members have a right to be represented. Each Committee includes an elected Chairperson and two Vice-Chairs.

First Committee: Disarmament and International Security.
Second Committee: Economic and Financial.
Third Committee: Social, Humanitarian and Cultural.
Fourth Committee: Special Political and Decolonization.
Fifth Committee: Administrative and Budgetary.
Sixth Committee: Legal.

OTHER SESSIONAL COMMITTEES

General Committee: f. 1946; composed of 28 members, including the Assembly President, the 21 Vice-Presidents of the Assembly and the Chairs of the six Main Committees.

Credentials Committee: f. 1946; composed of nine members appointed at each Assembly session.

POLITICAL AND SECURITY MATTERS

Special Committee on Peace-keeping Operations: f. 1965; 34 appointed members.

Disarmament Commission: f. 1978 (replacing body f. 1952); 61 members.

UN Scientific Committee on the Effects of Atomic Radiation: f. 1955; 21 members.

Committee on the Peaceful Uses of Outer Space: f. 1959; 61 members; has a Legal Sub-Committee and a Scientific and Technical Sub-Committee.

Ad Hoc Committee on the Indian Ocean: f. 1972; 44 members.

Committee on the Exercise of the Inalienable Rights of the Palestinian People: f. 1975; 25 members.

Special Committee on the Implementation of the Declaration on Decolonization: f. 1961; 24 members.

Ad Hoc Committee on Terrorism: f. 1996.

DEVELOPMENT

Commission on Science and Technology for Development: f. 1992; 33 members.

Committee on Energy and Natural Resources Development: f. 1998; 24 members.

United Nations Environment Programme (UNEP) Governing Council: f. 1972; 58 members.

LEGAL QUESTIONS

International Law Commission: f. 1947; 34 members elected for a five-year term; originally established in 1946 as the Committee on the Progressive Development of International Law and its Codification.

INTERNATIONAL ORGANIZATIONS

Advisory Committee on the UN Programme of Assistance in Teaching, Study, Dissemination and Wider Appreciation of International Law: f. 1965; 25 members.

UN Commission on International Trade Law: f. 1966; 36 members.

Special Committee on the Charter of the United Nations and on the Strengthening of the Role of the Organization: f. 1975; composed of all UN members.

There is also a UN Administrative Tribunal and a Committee on Applications for Review of Administrative Tribunal Judgments.

ADMINISTRATIVE AND FINANCIAL QUESTIONS

Advisory Committee on Administrative and Budgetary Questions: f. 1946; 16 members appointed for three-year terms.

Committee on Contributions: f. 1946; 18 members appointed for three-year terms.

International Civil Service Commission: f. 1972; 15 members appointed for four-year terms.

Committee on Information: f. 1978, formerly the Committee to review UN Policies and Activities; 95 members.

There is also a Board of Auditors, Investments Committee, UN Joint Staff Pension Board, Joint Inspection Unit, UN Staff Pension Committee, Committee on Conferences, and Committee for Programme and Co-ordination.

SUBSIDIARY BODIES

Human Rights Council: f. 2006, replacing the fmr Commission on Human Rights (f. 1946); inaugural meeting held 19 June 2006; mandated to promote universal respect for the protection of all human rights and fundamental freedoms for all; addresses and makes recommendations on situations of violations of human rights; promotes the effective co-ordination and mainstreaming of human rights within the UN system; supports human rights education and learning and provides advisory services, technical assistance and capacity-building support; serves as a forum for dialogue on thematic issues connected with human rights; makes recommendations to the General Assembly for the advancement of international human rights law; promotes the full implementation of human rights obligations undertaken by states; aims to contribute, through dialogue and co-operation, towards the prevention of human rights violations, and to ensure prompt responses to human rights emergencies; 47 mems; Pres. DORU COSTEA (Romania).

Peace-building Commission: f. 2006; inaugural meeting held 23 June 2006; an intergovernmental advisory body, subsidiary simultaneously to both the General Assembly and the Security Council; mandated to focus international attention on reconstruction, institution-building and sustainable development in countries emerging from conflict and to advise on and propose integrated strategies for post-conflict recovery; 31 mem. states; Chair. YUKIO TAKASU (Japan).

Security Council

The Security Council was established as a principal organ under the United Nations Charter; its first meeting was held on 17 January 1946. Its task is to promote international peace and security in all parts of the world.

MEMBERS

Permanent members: People's Republic of China, France, Russia, United Kingdom, USA. The remaining 10 members are normally elected (five each year) by the General Assembly for two-year periods (five countries from Africa and Asia, two from Latin America, one from eastern Europe, and two from western Europe and others).

Non-permanent members in 2008: Belgium, Indonesia, Italy, Panama, South Africa (term expires 31 December 2008); and Burkina Faso, Costa Rica, Croatia, Libya, Viet Nam (term expires 31 December 2009).

Rotation of the Presidency in 2008: Libya (January); Panama (February); Russia (March); South Africa (April); United Kingdom (May); USA (June); Viet Nam (July); Belgium (August); Burkina Faso (September); People's Republic of China (October); Costa Rica (November); Croatia (December).

Organization

The Security Council has the right to investigate any dispute or situation which might lead to friction between two or more countries, and such disputes or situations may be brought to the Council's attention either by one of its members, by any member state, by the General Assembly, by the Secretary-General or even, under certain conditions, by a state which is not a member of the United Nations.

The Council has the right to recommend ways and means of peaceful settlement and, in certain circumstances, the actual terms of settlement. In the event of a threat to or breach of international peace or an act of aggression, the Council has powers to take 'enforcement' measures in order to restore international peace and security. These include severance of communications and of economic and diplomatic relations and, if required, action by air, land and sea forces.

All members of the United Nations are pledged by the Charter to make available to the Security Council, on its call and in accordance with special agreements, the armed forces, assistance and facilities necessary to maintain international peace and security. These agreements, however, have not yet been concluded.

The Council is organized to be able to function continuously. The Presidency of the Council is held monthly in turn by the member states in English alphabetical order. Each member of the Council has one vote. On procedural matters decisions are made by the affirmative vote of any nine members. For decisions on other matters the required nine affirmative votes must include the votes of the five permanent members. This is the rule of 'great power unanimity' popularly known as the 'veto' privilege. In practice, an abstention by one of the permanent members is not regarded as a veto. Any member, whether permanent or non-permanent, must abstain from voting in any decision concerning the pacific settlement of a dispute to which it is a party. Any member of the UN that is party to a dispute under consideration by the Council may participate in the Council's discussions without a vote.

The allocation of the Security Council's permanent seats reflects the post-Second World War international situation. It is envisaged that reforms to the Council should be implemented aimed at establishing a more equitable regional representation and recognizing the current global balance of power. Consideration of such reform commenced in 1993 at the 48th Session of the General Assembly, which established a Working Group to assess the issue. Agreement on the size and composition of an expanded Security Council has been hindered by conflicting national and regional demands. Brazil, India, Japan and Germany (the 'Group of Four') have requested the status of permanent members without veto rights; while Italy, Pakistan and other middle-ranking countries (known as 'Uniting for Consensus') have requested a 25-member Council with 10 new non-permanent seats; and the African Union has contended that African states should receive two permanent seats with veto power, and that there should be four further new permanent seats and five non-permanent seats. In September 2000 the UN Millennium Summit declared support for continued discussions on reform of the Council. The report of the High-Level Panel on Threats, Challenges and Change (see Secretariat), issued in December 2004, stated that the role of the developed countries that contribute most to the UN financially (in terms of contributions to assessed budgets), militarily (through participation in peace-keeping operations), and diplomatically should be reflected in the Council's decision-making processes, as well as the interests of the broader membership (particularly those of developing countries). The report proposed two models for the expansion of the Council. The first entailed the provision of six new permanent seats (broadening the current regional representation on the Council), with no veto, and of three non-permanent seats with a two-year term; while the second entailed the establishment of a new category of eight 'semi-permanent' seats to be occupied for periods of four years. In his report entitled 'In Larger Freedom: Towards Development, Security and Human Rights for All', issued in March 2005 (see General Assembly), the Secretary-General supported the High-Level Panel's proposals on Security Council reform. The proposals were reviewed by the World Summit of UN heads of state convened by the General Assembly in September. In February 2007 the General Assembly appointed five ambassadors to advance the process of Security Council reform by hosting negotiations on the following five key issues: composition of the Council; veto power; regional representation; the size of an enlarged Council; and the working methods of the Council and its relationship with the General Assembly. In March 2008 an interim proposal was made to expand the Security Council from 15 to 22 members, with the 192 UN member states to determine which countries should occupy the remaining seats and future negotiations to address the issue of veto power.

Activities

As the UN organ primarily responsible for maintaining peace and security, the Security Council is empowered to deploy UN forces in the event that a dispute leads to fighting. It may also authorize the use of military force by a coalition of member states or a regional organization. A summit meeting of the Council convened during the Millennium Summit in September 2000 issued a declaration on ensuring an effective role for the Council in maintaining international peace and security, with particular reference to Africa. In June 2006 an intergovernmental advisory UN Peace-building Commission (see below) was inaugurated as a subsidiary advisory body of both the Security Council and the General Assembly, its establishment having been authorized by the Security Council and General Assembly, acting concurrently, in December 2005. The annual reports of the Commission were to be submitted to the Security Council for debate. During 2007 the Security Council continued to monitor closely all existing peace-keeping and political missions and the situations in countries where missions were being undertaken, and to authorize extensions of their mandates accordingly. The Council authorized the establishment of the UN Integrated Office in Burundi (BINUB) and UN Mission in Nepal (UNMIN) in January 2007, the AU/UN Hybrid Operation in Darfur (UNAMID) in July 2007, and the UN Mission in the Central African Republic and Chad (MINURCAT) in September of that year.

On 12 September 2001 the Security Council expressed its unequivocal condemnation of the terrorist attacks against targets in the USA, which had occurred on the previous day. It expressed its readiness to combat terrorism and reiterated the right to individual or collective self-defence in accordance with the UN Charter. At the end of September the Council adopted Resolution 1373 establishing a Counter-Terrorism Committee (CTC) to monitor a range of measures to combat international terrorism, including greater international co-operation and information exchange and suppressing the financing of terrorist groups. A special session of the Council at ministerial level was convened on the issue of terrorism in November. The Council continued to review the work of the CTC and to urge all states to submit reports on efforts to implement Resolution 1373, as well as to ratify relevant international conventions and protocols. In January 2003 the Council met at ministerial level to discuss international terrorism, including the issue of particular states maintaining stocks of weapons of mass destruction. The meeting adopted a resolution urging intensified efforts to combat terrorism and full co-operation with the CTC. The CTC has made efforts to strengthen contacts with international, regional and sub-regional organizations, and in March 2003 it convened a meeting of 57 such groupings and agreed on a co-ordinated approach to the suppression of terrorism. A follow-up meeting was convened in March 2004. In that month the Council adopted a resolution to strengthen the CTC by classifying it as a special subsidiary body of the Council, headed by a Bureau and assisted by an Executive Directorate (the Counter-Terrorism Committee Executive Directorate—CTED). In March 2008 the Council extended the mandate of the CTED until 31 December 2010. In April 2004 the Council adopted Resolution 1540—which considered the threat posed by the possible acquisition and use by non-state actors, particularly terrorists, of weapons of mass destruction, and urged all states to establish controls to prevent the proliferation of such weapons—and established the '1540 Committee' to monitor its implementation. The December 2004 report of the High-Level Panel on Threats, Challenges and Change stated that, confronted by a terrorism 'nightmare scenario', the Council would need to take earlier, more pro-active and more decisive action than hitherto.

The imposition of sanctions by the Security Council as a means of targeting regimes and groupings that are deemed to threaten international peace and security has increased significantly in recent years and has been subjected to widespread scrutiny regarding enforceability and the potential adverse humanitarian consequences for general populations. In the latter respect the Council has, since 1999, incorporated clauses on humanitarian assessment in its resolutions; the sanctions that took effect against the Taliban regime in Afghanistan and al-Qa'ida in January 2001 were the first to entail mandatory monitoring of the humanitarian impact. In 2000 a proposal was submitted to the Council regarding the establishment of a permanent body to monitor sanctions violations. The UN Secretary-General established a working group in April 2000 to evaluate sanctions policy. Draft versions of the group's final report have recommended that future Security Council resolutions enforcing sanctions should clearly specify intended goals and targets, include incentives to reward partial compliance, and focus in particular on the finances and movements of leaders (so-called 'smart sanctions'). The group's work was ongoing in 2008. In April 2000 the Council authorized the establishment of a temporary monitoring mechanism to investigate alleged violations of the sanctions imposed against the UNITA rebels in Angola, owing to their failure to implement earlier Council resolutions demanding compliance with the obligations of the peace process in that country. In July 2000 the Council voted to prohibit the exportation of all rough diamonds from Sierra Leone that had not been officially certified by that country's Government. (It had become evident that the ongoing conflicts in Sierra Leone and Angola were fuelled by rebel groups' illegal exploitation of diamond resources and use of the proceeds derived there from to purchase armaments.) In December a panel of experts appointed by the Council issued a report on the connections between the illicit exportation of diamonds from Sierra Leone and the international trade in armaments. In March 2001 the Council banned the purchase of diamonds exported from Liberia, and demanded that the Liberian authorities refrain from purchasing so-called 'conflict diamonds' from illegal sources and cease providing support to rebel organizations, with particular reference to the main rebel grouping active in Sierra Leone. The Council also re-imposed an embargo on the sale or supply of armaments to Liberia and imposed diplomatic restrictions on high-level Liberian government officials, with effect from May. In January 2003 the Council endorsed a new diamond certification scheme, known as the Kimberley Process, which had entered into effect on 1 January following an agreement reached by some 30 governments to regulate the trade in rough diamonds and eliminate the illegal sale of diamonds to fund conflicts. In May the Council imposed, additionally, a ban on the sale of timber products originating in Liberia. In December the Council endorsed the imposition against Liberia of a revised sanctions regime, to complement developments in the peace process there. The sale or supply of arms and related materiels to Liberia (except for use by the UN Mission in Liberia—UNMIL) and the purchase of rough diamonds and timber products from that country remained prohibited, and restrictions remained in force on travel by designated Liberian individuals. In June 2006 the Council terminated the sanctions on the purchase of timber products from Liberia, and in April 2007 the sanctions on the purchase of rough diamonds from that country were withdrawn. In May 2002 the Council suspended the travel restrictions on senior officials of the UNITA movement in Angola, following the signing of a cease-fire agreement ending hostilities in that country. All sanctions against UNITA were removed in December and the relevant Sanctions Committee, established pursuant to a resolution adopted in 1993, was dissolved. In September 2003 the Council voted to end punitive measures imposed against Libya in 1992 and 1993 relating to the destruction of a commercial airline flight over Lockerbie, United Kingdom, in December 1988. In July 2003 the Council banned the sale or supply of armaments and other military assistance to militias in the Democratic Republic of the Congo (DRC), and in November an arms embargo, travel restrictions and an assets freeze were imposed on designated individuals and entities in Côte d'Ivoire.

In March 2005, following the signing of a Comprehensive Peace Agreement between the Government of Sudan and the Sudan People's Liberation Movement/Army in January, the Council authorized the establishment of the UN Mission in Sudan (UNMIS) to support and monitor implementation of the accord. In July 2004 the Security Council imposed an arms embargo against non-governmental entities and individuals—including the Janjaweed militias—in Darfur, Sudan, and demanded that the Sudanese Government disarm the militias. During 2007 the Security Council consulted closely on the Darfur situation with the UN Secretariat, the AU and the Sudanese Government, authorizing in July the deployment of UNAMID.

In April 2005 the Security Council authorized the establishment of an independent commission to assist the Lebanese authorities with their investigation into a terrorist attack perpetrated in February that had killed 15 people, including the former Prime Minister of that country, Rafik Hariri. In October the investigating commission reported that it suspected officials and other individuals from both Lebanon and Syria of involvement in the fatal attack. Consequently, in that month, the Security Council adopted a resolution imposing travel and economic sanctions against such suspected individuals, and requiring the Syrian authorities to detain named Syrian suspects and to co-operate fully and unconditionally with the commission. In March 2006 the Council adopted a resolution requesting the UN Secretary-General to negotiate an agreement with the Lebanese Government on the establishment of an international tribunal to try those suspected of involvement in the February 2005 terrorist attack. The resulting agreement on the Special Tribunal for Lebanon was endorsed by the Security Council in May 2007. The Tribunal, based in The Hague, Netherlands, was to comprise both international and Lebanese judges and was to apply Lebanese (not international) law. The UN Secretary-General appointed a Registrar to the Tribunal in March 2008. In August 2006, following eruption in the previous month of full-scale conflict in southern Lebanon between the Israeli armed forces and the militant Shi'a organization Hezbollah, the

Council adopted a resolution calling for a full cessation of hostilities and the immediate withdrawal of all Israeli forces.

In October 2006 the Security Council demanded that the Democratic Republic of Korea abandon all programmes related to nuclear weapons, ballistic missiles and other weapons of mass destruction in a complete, verifiable and irreversible manner; an embargo was imposed by the Council on the supply of arms, military technology and luxury goods to that country, and the foreign assets of personnel connected to its weapons programme were frozen.

In December 2006 the Security Council imposed sanctions against Iran, including an embargo related to that country's nuclear and ballistic missile programmes and punitive measures targeted at individuals and entities connected to the programmes. In March 2007 the Council adopted a further resolution imposing a ban on the export of arms from Iran, and, in March 2008, an additional resolution was adopted authorizing inspections of any cargo to and from Iran suspected of concealing prohibited equipment; strengthening the monitoring of Iranian financial institutions; and adding names to the existing list of individuals and companies subject to asset and travel restrictions.

In December 1996 the Security Council approved the implementation of Resolution 986, which was adopted in April 1995, to provide for the limited export of Iraqi petroleum to enable the purchase of humanitarian supplies and the provision of contributions to the UN Compensation Committee (which had been established to settle claims against Iraq resulting from the 1990 Gulf War). The Council was responsible for renewing the mandate of the agreement and for approving contracts for the sale of petroleum and the purchase of food and medical goods. In October 1999 the Council adopted Resolution 1284, establishing a new policy towards Iraq. The resolution provided for an unlimited ceiling on petroleum exports under the agreed humanitarian programme, and for a suspension of sanctions dependent upon Iraq's co-operation with a new arms inspection body, the UN Monitoring, Verification and Inspection Commission (UNMOVIC) that was to replace the UN Special Commission (UNSCOM, established in 1991 to monitor the disposal of weapons), whose inspectors had withdrawn from Iraq in December 1998. At the end of March 2000 the Council doubled the maximum permitted revenue that Iraq might use to purchase petroleum industry spare parts and other equipment under the ongoing programme. A new sanctions regime was discussed during 2001. This envisaged facilitating the transfer of civilian and humanitarian goods to Iraq, while tightening border checks for military or other illegal trading. Disagreements among Council members concerned the extra responsibility placed on Iraq's neighbouring countries and the compilation of a list of 'controlled' items requiring special approval to be imported into Iraq. The existing oil-for-food scheme was extended in July, after Russia confirmed that it would veto the new proposals, and again in November. At that time, however, the Council approved a draft Goods for Review List (GRL), which it intended to enter into effect in the following year, subject to further negotiations. In May 2002 the Council adopted Resolution 1409 to implement the new sanctions regime. The programme was extended for a further 180 days in December, although negotiations continued regarding adjustments to the GRL, advocated by the USA to tighten the restrictions on military-related items. Further goods to be subject to approval were agreed by the Council at the end of that month.

In September 2002 the US President, George W. Bush, expressed concern that Iraq was challenging international security owing to its non-compliance with previous UN resolutions relating to the elimination of weapons of mass destruction. Subsequently, diplomatic discussions intensified regarding the need for a new UN resolution on Iraq, amidst increasing pressure from the US administration to initiate military action. An open debate was held in the Security Council in October, at the request of the Non-aligned Movement. On 8 November the Council adopted Resolution 1441 providing for an enhanced inspection mission and a detailed timetable according to which Iraq would have a final opportunity to comply with its disarmament obligations. Following Iraq's acceptance of the resolution, inspectors from UNMOVIC and the IAEA arrived in Iraq in late November, with Council authorization to have unrestricted access to all areas and the right to interview Iraqi scientists and weapons experts. In early December Iraq submitted a declaration of all aspects of its weapons programmes, as required under Resolution 1441. In early January 2003 UNMOVIC's then Executive Chairman, Dr Hans Blix, briefed the Council on Iraq's declaration and the inspection activities. A full update was presented to the Council on 27 January, as required by Resolution 1441 60 days after the resumption of inspections. The Director-General of the IAEA, Dr Mohammad el-Baradei, called for an ongoing mandate for his inspectors to clarify the situation regarding nuclear weapons. However, Blix declared that Iraq had potentially misled the UN on aspects of its chemical and biological weapons programmes and urged more active and substantive co-operation on the part of the Iraqi authorities to determine the existence or otherwise of proscribed items and activities. On 14 February Blix reported to the Council that the Iraqi authorities had recently become more active in proposing and undertaking measures to co-operate with UNMOVIC, and on 7 March he noted that Iraq had started to destroy, under UNMOVIC supervision, its Al Samoud 2 missiles and associated items, having accepted the conclusion of an international panel that these exceeded the permissable range decreed by the Council. Blix declared that the destruction to date of 34 Al Samoud 2 missiles and other items represented a 'substantial measure of disarmament', and that a significant Iraqi effort was under way to clarify a major source of uncertainty regarding quantities of biological and chemical weapons that had been unilaterally destroyed in 1991. Blix stated that UNMOVIC inspectors would require a number of further months in which to verify sites and items, analyse documents, interview relevant persons and draw conclusions, with a view to verifying Iraq's compliance with Resolution 1441. Meanwhile, extensive debate was conducted in the Council regarding Iraq's acceptance of its disarmament obligations and appropriate consequent measures, including the need for a new Council resolution to enforce Resolution 1441. On 24 February the USA, United Kingdom and Spain submitted a draft resolution to the Council stating that Iraq had failed to co-operate 'immediately, unconditionally and actively' with UNMOVIC, as required by Resolution 1441, and insisting upon immediate full co-operation, failing which military force should be used to remove the incumbent regime; France, Germany and Russia, however, demanded that UNMOVIC should be given more time to fulfil its mandate. On 18 March UNMOVIC personnel were withdrawn from Iraq in view of the abandonment by the USA, United Kingdom and Spain of efforts to win the Council's support for their draft resolution and consequent ultimatum by the USA that the Iraqi leadership should leave the country immediately or face a military invasion. Unilateral military action by US, British and allied forces commenced on 19 March. On that day, presenting to the Council UNMOVIC's draft work programme (required under Resolution 1284 to be formulated within a fixed period after the commencement of inspection activities), Blix stated that the Commission's experts had found that the Iraqi authorities had hitherto supplied only limited new information that would be of substantial assistance in resolving outstanding issues of concern. Upon the initiation of military action Iraq's petroleum exports under the oil-for-food programme were suspended immediately. On 28 March the Security Council adopted a resolution enabling technical adjustments to the oil-for-food programme and authorizing the UN Secretary-General to facilitate the delivery and receipt of goods contracted by the Iraqi Government for the humanitarian needs of its people.

On 22 May 2003, following the overthrow of Saddam Hussain in April, the Security Council adopted Resolution 1483, withdrawing economic sanctions against Iraq, and providing for the resumption of petroleum exports and the phasing-out, by November, of the oil-for-food programme. The resolution also supported the formation by the Iraqi people, assisted by the 'Coalition Provisional Authority' (the occupying powers under unified command) and a new Special Representative of the Secretary-General, of an Iraqi-run interim administration, pending the establishment by the Iraqi people of an internationally recognized, representative government that would assume the responsibilities of the Authority. On the same day an open meeting of the Council was briefed on the post-conflict situation in Iraq by several UN agencies conducting humanitarian operations there and also by the International Committee of the Red Cross. The Council reaffirmed in Resolution 1483 that Iraq must meet its disarmament obligations and declared that the Council would revisit the mandates of UNMOVIC and the IAEA in this regard. Reporting on UNMOVIC's activities in June, shortly before retiring as the Commission's Executive Chairman, Blix stated that, although responsibility for weapons inspections in Iraq had been taken over by a US-led Iraq Survey Group, UNMOVIC remained available to continue its work in the field. Blix declared that while significant quantities of proscribed items remained unaccounted for in Iraq and might exist, it was not justifiable to assume that they must exist. In mid-August the Council authorized the establishment of the UN Assistance Mission for Iraq (UNAMI), which was mandated to support the Secretary-General in fulfiling his responsibilities under Resolution 1483. Shortly afterwards the newly-appointed Special Representative of the Secretary-General for Iraq (and UN High Commissioner for Human Rights), Sergio Vieira de Mello, and 21 other UN staff were killed in a terrorist attack on the UNAMI headquarters in Baghdad. In response the Council adopted a resolution strongly condemning all forms of violence against participants in humanitarian operations and urging that perpetrators thereof should be brought to justice. Subsequently, until the formation of the Iraqi Interim Government at the end of June 2004 (see below), UNAMI operated primarily from outside Iraq. In mid-October 2003 the Council authorized a multinational peace-keeping force, under unified command, to help maintain security in Iraq and to support UNAMI and the institutions of the Iraqi interim administration. (The mandate of the multinational force was most recently extended to August 2008.) In November 2003 the Council adopted a resolution that stressed the importance of continuing to enforce the ban on trade in armaments with Iraq and authorized the establishment of a sanctions committee to identify those individuals and entities holding the outstanding financial assets of the former Saddam Hussain regime. In April 2004 the Council adopted a resolution welcoming the decision of the Secretary-General in the previous month to appoint a high-level panel to investigate allegations of fraud and corruption in the administration of the oil-for-food programme. The panel's final report, released in October 2005, found that there had been serious manipulation of the humanitarian aims of the programme: the Saddam Hussain regime was accused of having diverted US $1,800m. in illicit surcharges and bribes from the scheme, and more than 2,000 companies were reported to have received illicit payments. Resolution 1546, adopted by the Council in June 2004, endorsed the newly-formed Iraq Interim Government and outlined a timetable for Iraq's transition to democratic government. The resolution was approved after several weeks of discussions mainly concerned with the extent of Iraqi sovereignty and the continued presence of multinational forces in that country. In August the Council renewed UNAMI's mandate for one year. The Council welcomed the elections held in January 2005 to the new Iraq Transitional National Assembly, while reaffirming the role of the Special Representative of the Secretary-General and UNAMI in support of Iraqi efforts to promote national dialogue, and urging the international community to continue to provide advisers and technical support towards UN activities in Iraq. The Council has reiterated demands for the repatriation of all Kuwaiti and third-country nationals who had been missing since the 1990 Gulf War and for the return of their property. In June 2007 the Security Council voted to terminate UNMOVIC's mandate, noting testimonials that all of Iraq's known weapons of mass destruction had been deactivated and that the Iraqi Government had declared its support for international non-proliferation regimes. The Council also terminated the mandate of the IAEA weapons inspectors in Iraq.

During 2007 the Council continued to provide a forum for discussion of the situation in the Middle East and violence in the West Bank and Gaza and in Israel and to support a comprehensive and just settlement to the situation based on relevant Council resolutions, the outcome (including the principle of 'land for peace') of the Madrid Conference held in October–November 1991, agreements previously reached by the parties, and the peace initiative of Saudi Crown Prince Abdullah that was endorsed by the Arab League summit in March 2002. In the latter month the Council adopted Resolution 1397 which envisaged two separate states of Israel and Palestine existing within secure and recognized borders. In November 2003 the Council endorsed the adoption in April by the so-called 'Quartet' comprising envoys from the UN, European Union, Russia and USA of a 'performance-based roadmap to a permanent two-state solution to the Israeli-Palestinian conflict'. The Council welcomed the summit meeting held in February 2005, in Sharm el-Sheikh, Egypt, between the Palestinian and Israeli leaders, at which they reaffirmed commitment to the stalled roadmap initiative, and the Council also welcomed conciliatory actions subsequently taken by both sides. In July the Council convened an open debate on the situation in the Middle East, at the request of Arab member states of the UN. In December 2006 the Council endorsed a presidential statement expressing deep concern over the continuing insecurity in the Middle East and restating the key role of the Quartet. Addressing an open debate on the Middle East situation in March 2008, the UN Secretary-General reaffirmed commitment to the ongoing framework for resolving the conflict and, noting that the Israeli and Palestinian leaders had in the previous month made a commitment to reaching a settlement by the end of 2008, urged that momentum towards a resolution of the conflict be maintained.

In 2007 consideration of African issues, crises and post-conflict situations was a major priority of the Security Council's agenda. Numerous meetings were held to consider African matters, with a focus on the humanitarian situation, development strategies, conflict prevention, crisis management and peace-building. In June of that year the Council conducted a mission to the Democratic Republic of the Congo, Côte d'Ivoire, Ethiopia, Ghana and Sudan.

Discussions on the future status of Kosovo remained a high priority for the Security Council in 2007–08. In February 2008 the Council met in emergency session in reaction to Kosovo's unilateral declaration of independence from Serbia. Pending new guidance from the Council, Resolution 1244 governing the UN Interim Administration in Kosovo and Metohija (UNMIK) was to remain in force.

The Security Council monitored and considered the situation in Haiti during 2007, and stressed the importance of the activities of the UN Stabilization Mission in Haiti (MINUSTAH) in supporting the ongoing constitutional and political process, all-inclusive dialogue and police activities against armed gangs.

In February 2006 the Security Council endorsed the Afghanistan Compact, which had been adopted in the previous month as a Framework for the partnership between Afghanistan and the international community. The Security Council addressed the situation in Afghanistan at regular intervals during 2007. In March 2008 the Council extended the mandate of the UN Assistance Mission in Afghanistan (UNAMA, established in March 2002) until March 2009. It has also successively extended the mandate of the International Security Assistance Force in Afghanistan.

In November 2001 the Council adopted as a resolution specific commitments and measures to protect children from the effects of armed conflict and to meet their humanitarian needs. The abuse of children in armed conflicts was the subject of a further presidential statements issued in May 2002 and an open debate in January 2004. A new resolution on children and armed conflict was adopted in April of that year. In February 2005 the Council convened a further open debate on the issue and in July it adopted a resolution urging the prompt establishment of a mechanism to monitor and report on matters connected with children and armed conflict. In July 2006 the Council issued a statement welcoming the progress made since the July 2005 resolution. Children and armed conflict were the subject of a further open debate and presidential statement in November 2006. A presidential statement issued in October 2002 proposed that countries formulate national registers of arms brokers to counter illicit brokering of small arms and impose stricter penalties for illicit trading activities. In March 2003 the Council adopted a declaration on the threat to peace and security in West Africa caused by the proliferation of small arms and light weapons and by mercenary activities; open debates on small arms were held in January 2004, February 2005 and February 2006. In June 2007 a presidential statement was adopted that requested the UN Secretary-General to submit a biennial report on the small arms situation, starting in 2008. A Council presidential statement issued in March 2002 identified core objectives for the protection of civilians in conflict situations. Open debates on the subject were held in December 2002, December 2004, June and December 2005, December 2006, and June 2007; in April 2006 the Council adopted a resolution in which it demanded actions concerning the protection of civilians in armed conflict. Other ongoing themes considered by the Council in recent years have included women, the role of the UN in supporting justice and the rule of law, security sector reform, the relationship between the Council and regional organizations, the role of the Council in addressing humanitarian crises, and the role of the UN in post-conflict national reconciliation.

SPECIAL SUBSIDIARY BODIES

Counter-Terrorism Committee (CTC): f. 2001, pursuant to Security Council Resolution 1373 (2001) and, in March 2004, in accordance with Resolution 1535 (2004), elevated to a special subsidiary body; comprises a Plenary (composed of the Council member states) and a Bureau; assisted by an Executive Directorate (the Counter-Terrorism Committee Executive Directorate—CTED, which became operational in December 2005); since Sept. 2005 the CTC has also been mandated to monitor member states' implementation of Resolution 1624 (2005), concerning incitement to commit acts of terrorism.

The UN Peace-building Commission, which was inaugurated in June 2006, its establishment having been authorized by the Security Council and General Assembly in December 2005, is a subsidiary advisory body of both the Council and Assembly.

COMMITTEES

In March 2008 there were three **Standing Committees**, each composed of representatives of all Council member states:

Committee of Experts on Rules of Procedure (studies and advises on rules of procedure and other technical matters);

Committee on the Admission of New Members;

Committee on Council Meetings away from Headquarters.

Ad hoc Committees, which are established as needed, comprise all Council members and meet in closed session:

Governing Council of the UN Compensation Commission established by Security Council Resolution 692 (1991);

1540 Committee established pursuant to Security Council Resolution 1540 (2004).

Within this category are the Sanctions Committees, which may be established to oversee economic or political enforcement measures, imposed by the Security Council to maintain or restore international peace and security. At March 2008 the following committees were operational:

Security Council Committee established pursuant to Resolution 1737 (2006) concerning Iran;

Security Council Committee established pursuant to Resolution 1718 (2006) concerning the Democratic People's Republic of Korea;

Security Council Committee established pursuant to Resolution 1636 (2005) concerning Syria;

Security Council Committee established pursuant to Resolution 1591 (2005) concerning Sudan;

Security Council Committee established pursuant to Resolution 1572 (2004) concerning Côte d'Ivoire;

Security Council Committee established pursuant to Resolution 1533 (2004) concerning the Democratic Republic of the Congo;

Security Council Committee established pursuant to Resolution 1521 (2003) concerning Liberia;

Security Council Committee established pursuant to Resolution 1518 (2003) concerning the financial assets of the former Iraqi regime;

Security Council Committee established pursuant to Resolution 1267 (1999) concerning al-Qa'ida and the Taliban and associated individuals and entities;

Security Council Committee established pursuant to Resolution 1132 (1997) concerning Sierra Leone;

Security Council Committee established pursuant to Resolution 918 (1994) concerning Rwanda;

Security Council Committee established pursuant to Resolution 751 (1992) concerning Somalia.

A Working Group on General Issues on Sanctions was established in 2000, on a temporary basis, to consider ways of improving the effectiveness of UN sanctions. A Working Group established pursuant to Resolution 1566 (2004) is mandated to consider practical measures to be imposed upon individuals, groups or entities involved in or associated with terrorist activities, other than those designated by the Committee on al-Qa'ida and the Taliban; and the possibility of establishing an international fund to compensate victims of terrorist acts and their families.

AD HOC INTERNATIONAL TRIBUNALS AND SPECIAL COURT

INTERNATIONAL CRIMINAL TRIBUNAL FOR THE FORMER YUGOSLAVIA—ICTY

Address: Registry: Public Information Unit, POB 13888, 2501 EW The Hague, Netherlands.

Telephone: (70) 512-5343; **fax:** (70) 512-5355; **internet:** www.un.org/icty.

In May 1993 the Security Council, acting under Article VII of the UN Charter, adopted Resolution 827, which established an ad hoc 'war crimes' tribunal. The so-called International Tribunal for the Prosecution of Persons Responsible for Serious Violations of International Humanitarian Law Committed in the Territory of the Former Yugoslavia (also referred to as the International Criminal Tribunal for the former Yugoslavia—ICTY) was inaugurated in The Hague, Netherlands, in November. The ICTY consists of a Chief Prosecutor's office, and 16 permanent judges, of whom 11 sit in three trial chambers and five sit in a seven-member appeals chamber (with the remaining two appeals chamber members representing the ICTR, see below). In addition, a maximum at any one time of nine *ad litem* judges, drawn from a pool of 27, serve as required. Public hearings were initiated in November 1994. The first trial proceedings commenced in May 1996, and the first sentence was imposed by the Tribunal in November. In July and November 1995 the Tribunal formally charged the Bosnian Serb political and military leaders Radovan Karadžić and Gen. Ratko Mladić, on two separate indictments, with genocide, crimes against humanity, violation of the laws and customs of war and serious breaches of the Geneva Conventions. In July 1996 the Tribunal issued international warrants for their arrest. Amended indictments, confirmed in May 2000, and announced in October and November, respectively, included the withdrawal of the fourth charge against Mladić. Karadžić and Mladić remained at large in March 2008. In April 2000 Momčilo Krajišnik, a senior associate of Karadžić, was detained by the ICTY, charged with genocide, war crimes and crimes against humanity. Biljana Plavšić, a further former Bosnian Serb political leader, surrendered to the Tribunal in January 2001, also indicted on charges of genocide, war crimes and crimes against humanity. In the following month three Bosnian Serb former soldiers were convicted by the ICTY of utilizing mass rape and the sexual enslavement of women as instruments of terror in wartime. In February 2003 Plavšić was sentenced to eleven years' imprisonment, having pleaded guilty in October 2002 to one of the charges against her (persecutions: a crime against humanity). (Under a plea agreement reached with the Tribunal the remaining charges had been withdrawn.) In mid-1998 the ICTY began investigating reported acts of violence against civilians committed by both sides in the conflict in the southern Serbian province of Kosovo and Metohija. In early 1999 there were reports of large-scale organized killings, rape and expulsion of the local Albanian population by Serbian forces. In April ICTY personnel visited refugee camps in neighbouring countries in order to compile evidence of the atrocities, and obtained intelligence information from NATO members regarding those responsible for the incidents. In May the then President of the then Federal Republic of Yugoslavia (FRY, which was renamed Serbia and Montenegro in February 2003, and divided into separate states of Montenegro and Serbia in 2006), Slobodan Milošević, was indicted, along with three senior government ministers and the chief-of-staff of the army, charged with crimes against humanity and violations of the customs of war committed in Kosovo since 1 January 1999; international warrants were issued for their arrests. In June, following the establishment of an international force to secure peace in Kosovo, the ICTY established teams of experts to investigate alleged atrocities at 529 identified grave sites. The new FRY administration, which had assumed power following legislative and presidential elections in late 2000, contested the impartiality of the ICTY, proposing that Milošević and other members of the former regime should be tried before a national court. In April 2001 Milošević was arrested by the local authorities in Belgrade. Under increasing international pressure, the Federal Government approved his extradition in June, and he was immediately transferred to the ICTY, where he was formally charged with crimes against humanity committed in Kosovo in 1999. A further indictment of crimes against humanity committed in Croatia during 1991–92 was confirmed in October 2001, and a third indictment, which included charges of genocide committed in Bosnia and Herzegovina in 1991–95, was confirmed in November 2001. In February 2002 the Appeals Chamber ordered that the three indictments be considered in a single trial. The trial commenced later in that month. Milošević, however, continued to protest at the alleged illegality of his arrest and refused to recognize the jurisdiction of the Court. The case was delayed repeatedly owing to the ill health of the defendent, and in March 2006 he died in captivity. In August 2001 the ICTY passed its first sentence of genocide, convicting a former Bosnian Serb military commander, Gen. Radislav Kristić, for his role in the deaths of up to 8,000 Bosnian Muslim men and boys in Srebrenica in July 1995. In January 2003 Fatmir Limaj, an ethnic Albanian deputy in the Kosovo parliament and former commander of the Kosovo Liberation Army (KLA), was indicted by the ICTY on several counts of crimes against humanity and war crimes that were allegedly committed in mid-1998 against Serb and Albanian detainees at the KLA's Lapusnik prison camp. Limaj was arrested in Slovenia in February 2003 and transferred to ICTY custody in early March. At March 2008 49 people remained accused by the Tribunal, of whom 45 were in custody and four were at large. Of those who had appeared in proceedings before the Tribunal, nine had been acquitted, 53 had received a final guilty sentence, and 29 had been referred to national jurisdications. Five indictments had been withdrawn following the transfer of the accused to the Tribunal. Some 17 people had completed their sentences. It was envisaged that the Tribunal's trial activities would be terminated by 2010. The Tribunal assisted with the establishment of the War Crimes Chamber within the Bosnia and Herzegovina state court, which became operational in March 2005, and also helped Croatia to strengthen its national judicial capacity to enable war crimes to be prosecuted within that country.

President of the ICTY: FAUSTO POCAR (Italy).

ICTY Prosecutor: SERGE BRAMMERTZ (Belgium).

ICTY Registrar: HANS HOLTHUIS (Netherlands).

INTERNATIONAL CRIMINAL TRIBUNAL FOR RWANDA—ICTR

Address: Registry: Arusha International Conference Centre, POB 6016, Arusha, Tanzania.

Telephone: (212) 963-2850; **fax:** (212) 963-2848; **e-mail:** ictr-press@un.org; **internet:** www.ictr.org.

In November 1994 the Security Council adopted Resolution 955, establishing an International Criminal Tribunal for Rwanda (ICTR) to prosecute persons responsible for genocide and other serious violations of humanitarian law that had been committed in Rwanda and by Rwandans in neighbouring states. Its temporal jurisdiction was limited to the period 1 January to 31 December 1994. The Tribunal consists of 11 permanent judges, of whom nine sit in four trial chambers (based in Arusha, Tanzania) and two sit in the seven-member appeals chamber that is shared with the ICTY and based at The Hague. In August 2002 the UN Security Council endorsed a proposal by the ICTR President to elect a pool of 18 *ad litem* judges to the Tribunal with a view to accelerating its activities and bringing them to a conclusion by 2008–10. In October 2003 the Security Council increased the number of *ad litem* judges who may serve on the Tribunal at any one time from four to nine. A high security detention facility had been built within the compound of the prison in Arusha. The first plenary session of the Tribunal was held in The Hague in June 1995; formal proceedings at its permanent headquarters in Arusha were initiated in November. The first trial of persons charged by the Tribunal commenced in January 1997, and sentences were imposed in July. In September 1998 the former Rwandan Prime Minister, Jean Kambanda, and a former mayor of Taba, Jean-Paul Akayesu, both Hutu extremists, were found guilty of genocide and crimes against humanity; Kambanda subsequently became the first person ever to be sentenced under the 1948 Convention on the Prevention and Punishment of the Crime of Genocide. In October 2000 the Tribunal rejected an appeal by Kambanda. In November 1999 the Rwandan Government temporarily suspended co-operation with the Tribunal in protest at a decision of the appeals chamber to release an indicted former government official owing to procedural delays. (The appeals chamber subsequently reversed this decision.) In 2001 two ICTR investigators employed on defence teams were arrested and charged with genocide, having been found to be working at the Tribunal under assumed identities. Relations between the Rwandan Government and the ICTR deteriorated again in 2002, with the then Chief Prosecutor accusing the Rwandan authorities of failing to facilitate the travel of witnesses to the Tribunal and withholding access to documentary materials, and counter accusations by the Rwandan Government that the Tribunal's progress was too slow, that further suspected perpetrators of genocide had been inadvertently employed by the Tribunal and that Rwandan witnesses attending the Tribunal had not received sufficient protection. Reporting to the UN Security Council in July, the then Chief Prosecutor alleged that the Rwandan non-co-operation ensued from her recent decision to indict former members of the Tutsi-dominated Rwanda Patriotic Army for human rights violations committed against Hutus in 1994. In September 2003 the trial of Théoneste Bagosora, a former military commander accused of masterminding the genocide, commenced, after considerable procedural delays. In January 2004 a former minister of culture and education, Jean de Dieu Kamuhanda, was found guilty on two counts of genocide and extermination as a crime against humanity. In the following month Samuel Imanishimwe, a former military commander, was convicted on seven counts of genocide, crimes against humanity and serious violations of the Geneva Conventions. Two others were acquitted of similar charges. In early May 2004 Yussufu Munyakazi, accused of directing mass killings by the Interahamwe militia in Cyangugu and Kibuye Provinces, was arrested in the Democratic Republic of the Congo. By March 2008 the Tribunal had delivered judgments against 35 accused, of whom five were acquitted. A further 27 people were on trial at that time, while nine indictees were awaiting trial. Some 13 of those accused remained at large.

Both the ICTY and ICTR are supported by teams of investigators and human rights experts working in the field to collect forensic and other evidence in order to uphold indictments. Evidence of mass graves resulting from large-scale unlawful killings has been uncovered in both regions.

President of the ICTR: DENNIS BYRON (Saint Christopher and Nevis).
ICTR Prosecutor: HASSAN BUBACAR JALLOW (The Gambia).
ICTR Registrar: ADAMA DIENG (Senegal).

SPECIAL COURT FOR SIERRA LEONE

Address: Jomo Kenyatta Rd, New England, Freetown, Sierra Leone.
Telephone: (22) 297000; **fax:** (22) 297001; **e-mail:** scsl-mail@un.org; **internet:** www.sc-sl.org.

The Court was established in January 2002 by agreement of the United Nations and the government of Sierra Leone, pursuant to a Security Council resolution of August 2000 to establish an independent Special Court to prosecute those 'bearing the greatest responsibility for committing violations against humanitarian law' since 20 November 1996. Trial proceedings commenced in June 2004. By March 2008 a total of 13 people had been indicted by the Special Court, although two indictments were withdrawn in December 2003 following the deaths of two of the accused, and following the death of another of the accused a further indictment was terminated in May 2007. In April 2006 the Special Court for Sierra Leone and the International Criminal Court concluded a memorandum of understanding in accordance with which the Special Court was to use the courtroom and detention facilities of the International Criminal Court for the planned trial of Charles Taylor, the former president of Liberia, on charges of crimes against humanity. Taylor, who had been arrested in Nigeria and transferred to the Special Court in March, was transferred to the Criminal Court's detention centre in The Hague in June. Taylor's trial commenced in June 2007. It was adjourned shortly afterwards and reconvened in January 2008.

President of the Court: GEORGE GELAGA KING (Sierra Leone).
Chief Prosecutor: STEPHEN RAPP (USA).
Registrar: HERMAN VON HEBEL.

Trusteeship Council

The Trusteeship Council (comprising the People's Republic of China—a non-active member until May 1989, France, Russia, the United Kingdom and the USA) was established to supervise United Nations Trust Territories through their administering authorities and to promote the political, economic, social and educational advancement of their inhabitants towards self-government or independence (see Charter). On 1 October 1994 the last territory remaining under UN trusteeship, the Republic of Palau (part of the archipelago of the Caroline Islands), declared its independence under a compact of free association with the USA, its administering authority. The Security Council terminated the Trusteeship Agreement on 10 November, having determined that the objectives of the agreement had been fully attained. On 1 November the Trusteeship Council formally suspended its operations; thereafter it was to be convened on an extraordinary basis as required. The report of the UN Secretary-General entitled 'In Larger Freedom: Towards Development, Security and Human Rights for All', issued in March 2005, proposed that the Trusteeship Council should be terminated.

Economic and Social Council—ECOSOC

ECOSOC promotes world co-operation on economic, social, cultural and humanitarian problems. (See Charter of the United Nations.)

MEMBERS

Fifty-four members are elected by the General Assembly for three-year terms: 18 are elected each year. Membership is allotted by regions as follows: Africa 14 members, western Europe and others 13, Asia 11, Latin America 10, eastern Europe 6.
President: LÉO MÉRORÈS (Haiti) (2008).

ORGANIZATION

The Council, which meets annually for four weeks in July, alternately in New York and Geneva, is mainly a central policy-making and co-ordinating organ. It has a co-ordinating function between the UN and the specialized agencies, and also makes consultative arrangements with approved voluntary or non-governmental organizations which work within the sphere of its activities. The Council has functional and regional commissions to carry out much of its detailed work. ECOSOC's purview extends to more than 70% of the human and financial resources of the UN system. The Council was given a leading role in following up the implementation of the Monterrey Consensus, adopted by the March 2002 International Conference on Financing for Development.

The report of the UN Secretary-General entitled 'In Larger Freedom: Towards Development, Security and Human Rights for All', issued in March 2005, outlined a number of proposed changes to ECOSOC aimed at improving its effectiveness. These included: the organization by the Council of annual ministerial-level progress reviews (AMRs) of agreed development goals, in particular the Millennium Development Goals pledged by UN heads of state and government in September 2000 (the theme of the 2008 AMR was 'implementing the internationally agreed goals and commitments in regard to sustainable development'; the inauguration of a regular high-level development co-operation forum (see below); the organization by the Council, whenever required, of meetings to assess and promote co-ordinated responses to threats to development, such as famines, epidemics and major natural disasters; and the develop-

INTERNATIONAL ORGANIZATIONS

ment of a permanent structure within the Council for monitoring the economic and social dimensions of conflicts, with the aim of improving prospects for long-term recovery, reconstruction and reconciliation, and working in co-operation with a proposed new Peace-building Commission.

Every April ECOSOC holds high-level consultations with the IMF, World Bank, WTO and UNCTAD. The theme of the April 2008 meeting was 'coherence, co-ordination and co-operation in the context both of the implementation of the Monterrey Consensus and of the outcome of the World Summit convened by the UN General Assembly in September 2005'.

DEVELOPMENT CO-OPERATION FORUM—DCF

The biennial high-level Development Co-operation Forum (DCF) was inaugurated in July 2007. The Forum is mandated to advance the implementation of all internationally agreed development goals, including the Millennium Development Goals, and to promote dialogue to find effective ways of supporting international development. The first Forum was scheduled to be convened in July 2008, in New York, with participation by UN bodies, bilateral development agencies, regional development banks, civil society and private sector representatives.

SESSIONAL COMMITTEES

Each sessional committee comprises the 54 members of the Council: there is a First (Economic) Committee, a Second (Social) Committee and a Third (Programme and Co-ordination) Committee.

FUNCTIONAL COMMISSIONS

Commission on Crime Prevention and Criminal Justice: f. 1992; aims to formulate an international convention on crime prevention and criminal justice; 40 members.

Commission on Narcotic Drugs: f. 1946; mainly concerned in combating illicit traffic; 53 members; there is a Sub-Commission on Illicit Drug Traffic and Related Matters in the Near and Middle East.

Commission on Population and Development: f. 1946; advises the Council on population matters and their relation to socio-economic conditions; 47 members.

Commission on Science and Technology for Development: f. 1992; works on the restructuring of the UN in the economic, social and related fields; 33 members.

Commission for Social Development: f. 1946 as the Social Commission; advises ECOSOC on issues of social and community development; 46 members.

Commission on the Status of Women: f. 1946; aims at equality of political, economic and social rights for women, and supports the right of women to live free of violence; 45 members.

Commission on Sustainable Development: f. 1993 to oversee integration into the UN's work of the objectives set out in 'Agenda 21', the programme of action agreed by the UN Conference on Environment and Development in June 1992; 53 members.

Statistical Commission: Standardizes terminology and procedure in statistics and promotes the development of national statistics; 24 members.

United Nations Forum on Forests: f. 2000; all states members of the United Nations and its specialized agencies.

STANDING COMMITTEES

Commission on Human Settlements: f. 1977.

Committee on Negotiations with Intergovernmental Agencies: f. 1946.

Committee on Non-Governmental Organizations: f. 1946.

Committee for Programme and Co-ordination: f. 1962.

In addition there are expert bodies on: the transport of dangerous goods and the globally harmonized system of classification and labelling of chemicals; geographical names; development policy; public administration; international co-operation in tax matters; economic, social and cultural rights; and indigenous issues; there is an ad hoc open-ended working group on informatics; an ad hoc intergovernmental group experts on energy and sustainable development; and there are also the following other ad hoc mechanisms: advisory groups on African countries emerging from conflict and on Haiti, the UN ICT Task Force, the Public-Private Alliance for Rural Development, and Committee on Negotiations with Intergovernmental Agencies.

REGIONAL COMMISSIONS
(see United Nations Regional Commissions)

Economic Commission for Africa (ECA).

Economic Commission for Europe (ECE).

Economic Commission for Latin America and the Caribbean (ECLAC).

Economic and Social Commission for Asia and the Pacific (ESCAP).

Economic and Social Commission for Western Asia (ESCWA).

RELATED BODIES

Board of Trustees of the International Research and Training Institute for the Advancement of Women (INSTRAW): 11 members.

International Narcotics Control Board: f. 1964; 13 members.

Programme Co-ordination Board for the Joint UN Programme on HIV/AIDS (UNAIDS): f. 1995; 22 members.

UNDP/UNFPA Executive Board: 36 members, elected by ECOSOC.

UNHCR Executive Committee: 53 members, elected by ECOSOC.

UNICEF Executive Board: 36 members, elected by ECOSOC.

WFP Executive Board: one-half of the 36 members are elected by ECOSOC, one-half by FAO; governing body of the World Food Programme.

International Court of Justice

Address: Peace Palace, Carnegieplein 2, 2517 KJ The Hague, Netherlands.
Telephone: (70) 302-23-23; **fax:** (70) 364-99-28; **e-mail:** information@icj-cij.org; **internet:** www.icj-cij.org.

Established in 1945, the Court is the principal judicial organ of the UN. All members of the UN are parties to the Statute of the Court. (See Charter.)

THE JUDGES
(March 2008; in order of precedence)

	Term Ends*
President: ROSALYN HIGGINS (United Kingdom)	2012
Vice-President: AWN SHAWKAT AL-KHASAWNEH (Jordan)	2009
Judges:	
RAYMOND RANJEVA (Madagascar)	2009
SHI JIUYONG (People's Republic of China)	2012
ABDUL G. KOROMA (Sierra Leone)	2012
GONZALO PARRA-ARANGUREN (Venezuela)	2009
THOMAS BUERGENTHAL (USA)	2009

—continued	Term Ends*
HISASHI OWADA (Japan)	2012
BRUNO SIMMA (Germany)	2012
PETER TOMKA (Slovakia)	2012
RONNY ABRAHAM (France)	2014
KENNETH KEITH (New Zealand)	2015
BERNARDO SEPÚLVEDA AMOR (Mexico)	2015
MOHAMMED BENNOUNA (Morocco)	2015
LEONID SKOTNIKOV (Russia)	2015

* Each term ends on 5 February of the year indicated.

Registrar: PHILIPPE COUVREUR (Belgium).

The Court is composed of 15 judges, each of a different nationality, elected with an absolute majority by both the General Assembly and the Security Council. Representation of the main forms of civilization and the different legal systems of the world are borne in mind in their election. Candidates are nominated by national panels of jurists.

The judges are elected for nine years and may be re-elected; elections for five seats are held every three years. The Court elects its President and Vice-President for each three-year period. Members may not have any political, administrative, or other professional occupation, and may not sit in any case with which they have been otherwise connected than as a judge of the Court. For the purposes of

INTERNATIONAL ORGANIZATIONS

United Nations

a case, each side—consisting of one or more states—may, unless the Bench already includes a judge with a corresponding nationality, choose a person from outside the Court to sit as a judge on terms of equality with the Members. Judicial decisions are taken by a majority of the judges present, subject to a quorum of nine Members. The President has a casting vote.

FUNCTIONS

The International Court of Justice operates in accordance with a Statute which is an integral part of the UN Charter. Only states may be parties in cases before the Court; those not parties to the Statute may have access in certain circumstances and under conditions laid down by the Security Council.

The Jurisdiction of the Court comprises:

1. All cases which the parties refer to it jointly by special agreement (indicated in the list below by a stroke between the names of the parties);

2. All matters concerning which a treaty or convention in force provides for reference to the Court. About 700 bilateral or multilateral agreements make such provision. Among the more noteworthy: Treaty of Peace with Japan (1951), European Convention for Peaceful Settlement of Disputes (1957), Single Convention on Narcotic Drugs (1961), Protocol relating to the Status of Refugees (1967), Hague Convention on the Suppression of the Unlawful Seizure of Aircraft (1970);

3. Legal disputes between states which have recognized the jurisdiction of the Court as compulsory for specified classes of dispute. Declarations by the following 65 states accepting the compulsory jurisdiction of the Court are in force (although many with reservations): Australia, Austria, Barbados, Belgium, Botswana, Bulgaria, Cambodia, Cameroon, Canada, the Democratic Republic of the Congo, Costa Rica, Côte d'Ivoire, Cyprus, Denmark, Dominica, the Dominican Republic, Egypt, Estonia, Finland, The Gambia, Georgia, Greece, Guinea, Guinea-Bissau, Haiti, Honduras, Hungary, India, Japan, Kenya, Lesotho, Liberia, Liechtenstein, Luxembourg, Madagascar, Malawi, Malta, Mauritius, Mexico, Nauru, the Netherlands, New Zealand, Nicaragua, Nigeria, Norway, Pakistan, Panama, Paraguay, Peru, the Philippines, Poland, Portugal, Senegal, Serbia, Somalia, Spain, Sudan, Suriname, Swaziland, Sweden, Switzerland, Togo, Uganda, the United Kingdom and Uruguay.

Disputes as to whether the Court has jurisdiction are settled by the Court.

Judgments are without appeal, but are binding only for the particular case and between the parties. States appearing before the Court undertake to comply with its Judgment. If a party to a case fails to do so, the other party may apply to the Security Council, which may make recommendations or decide upon measures to give effect to the Judgment.

Advisory opinions on legal questions may be requested by the General Assembly, the Security Council or, if so authorized by the Assembly, other United Nations organs or specialized agencies.

Rules of Court governing procedure are made by the Court under a power conferred by the Statute.

In July 1993 the Court established a seven-member Chamber for Environmental Matters, in view of the world-wide expansion of environmental law and protection.

CONSIDERED CASES

Judgments

Since 1946 more than 130 cases have been referred to the Court relating to legal disputes or legal questions. Some were removed from the list as a result of settlement or discontinuance, or on the grounds of a lack of basis for jurisdiction. Cases which have been the subject of a Judgment by the Court include: Monetary Gold Removed from Rome in 1943 (Italy v. France, United Kingdom and USA); Sovereignty over Certain Frontier Land (Belgium/Netherlands); Arbitral Award made by the King of Spain on 23 December 1906 (Honduras v. Nicaragua); Temple of Preah Vihear (Cambodia v. Thailand); South West Africa (Ethiopia and Liberia v. South Africa); Northern Cameroons (Cameroon v. United Kingdom); North Sea Continental Shelf (Federal Republic of Germany/Denmark and Netherlands); Appeal relating to the Jurisdiction of the ICAO Council (India v. Pakistan); Fisheries Jurisdiction (United Kingdom v. Iceland; Federal Republic of Germany v. Iceland); Nuclear Tests (Australia v. France; New Zealand v. France); Aegean Sea Continental Shelf (Greece v. Turkey); United States of America Diplomatic and Consular Staff in Tehran (USA v. Iran); Continental Shelf (Tunisia/Libya); Delimitation of the Maritime Boundary in the Gulf of Maine Area (Canada/USA); Continental Shelf (Libya/Malta); Application for revision and interpretation of the Judgment of 24 February 1982 in the case concerning the Continental Shelf (Tunisia v. Libya); Military and Paramilitary Activities in and against Nicaragua (Nicaragua v. USA); Frontier Dispute (Burkina Faso/Mali); Delimitation of Maritime Boundary (Denmark v. Norway); Maritime Boundaries (Guinea-Bissau v. Senegal); Elettronica Sicula SpA (USA v. Italy); Land, Island and Maritime Frontier Dispute (El Salvador/Honduras, in one aspect of which Nicaragua was permitted to intervene) (also, in 2003, Application for Revision of the 1992 Judgment in the Case concerning the Land, Island and Maritime Frontier Dispute, requested by El Salvador); Delimitation of Maritime Boundary in the area between Greenland and Jan Mayen island (Denmark v. Norway); Maritime Delimitation and Territorial Questions between Qatar and Bahrain (Qatar v. Bahrain); Territorial Dispute (Libya/Chad); East Timor (Portugal v. Australia); the Gabčíkovo–Nagymaros Hydroelectric Project (Hungary v. Slovakia, aspects of which were still under consideration in 2008); Fisheries Jurisdiction (Spain v. Canada); Delimitation of the Boundary around Kasikili Sedudu Island (Botswana v. Namibia); La Grand case (Germany v. USA); Arrest Warrant of 11 April 2000 (Democratic Republic of the Congo—DRC v. Belgium); Land and Maritime Boundary between Cameroon and Nigeria (Cameroon v. Nigeria, with Equatorial Guinea intervening); Sovereignty over Pulau Ligatan and Pulau Sipadan (Indonesia/Malaysia); Destruction of Oil Platforms (Iran v. USA); Avena and other Mexican Nationals (Mexico v. USA); Legality of Use of Force (Serbia and Montenegro v. Belgium; Canada; France; Germany; Italy; the Netherlands; Portugal; and the United Kingdom); Certain Property (Liechtenstein v. Germany); Armed Activities on the Territory of the Congo (DRC v. Burundi; Rwanda; and Uganda, aspects of which were still under consideration in 2008); Frontier Dispute (Benin/Niger); Application of the Convention on the Prevention and Punishment of the Crime of Genocide (Bosnia and Herzegovina v. Serbia and Montenegro); and Territorial and Maritime Dispute in the Caribbean Sea (Nicaragua v. Honduras).

Other cases under consideration, or pending before the Court, in 2008 were: a case brought by Croatia against the Federal Republic of Yugoslavia (FRY, renamed Serbia and Montenegro in 2003 and divided into separate states of Montenegro and Serbia in 2006) concerning the application of the 1948 Convention on the Prevention and Punishment of the Crime of Genocide; a case brought by Guinea against the Democratic Republic of the Congo (DRC) concerning the treatment of a Guinean business executive, Ahmadou Sadio Diallo; cases concerning the legality of the use of force brought by the FRY against Spain and the USA; a case brought by Nicaragua against Colombia concerning territory and maritime delimitation in the western Caribbean; a case brought by the Republic of the Congo against France seeking an annulment of investigations and criminal proceedings under way in France concerning the alleged involvement of several high-ranking Congolese officials in crimes against humanity reportedly perpetrated in the Republic of the Congo; a case brought by Malaysia and Singapore concerning the sovereignty of Pedra Branca/Pulau Batu Puteh, Middle Rocks and South Ledge; a case brought by Romania against Ukraine concerning Maritime Delimitation in the Black Sea; a case brought by Costa Rica against Nicaragua concerning Navigational and Related Rights; a case brought by Argentina against Uruguay concerning the construction of pulp mills on the River Uruguay; a case brought by Djibouti against France concerning certain questions of mutual assistance in criminal matters; and a case brought by Peru against Chile on maritime delimitation in the Pacific ocean. In September 2003 two cases brought by Libya against the United Kingdom and the USA (Questions of Interpretation and Application of the 1971 Montreal Convention arising from the Aerial Incident at Lockerbie) were withdrawn at the request of the three parties.

Advisory Opinions

Matters on which the Court has delivered an Advisory Opinion at the request of the United Nations General Assembly include the following: Condition of Admission of a State to Membership in the United Nations; Competence of the General Assembly for the Admission of a State to the United Nations; Interpretation of the Peace Treaties with Bulgaria, Hungary and Romania; International Status of South West Africa; Reservations to the Convention on the Prevention and Punishment of the Crime of Genocide; Effect of Awards of Compensation Made by the United Nations Administrative Tribunal (UNAT); Western Sahara; Application for Review of UNAT Judgment No. 333; Applicability of the Obligation to Arbitrate under Section 21 of the United Nations Headquarters Agreement of 26 June 1947 (relating to the closure of the Observer Mission to the United Nations maintained by the Palestine Liberation Organization); Legality of the Use or Threat of Nuclear Weapons; and Legal Consequences of the Construction of a Wall by Israel in the Occupied Palestinian Territory.

An Advisory Opinion has been given at the request of the Security Council: Legal Consequences for States of the continued presence of South Africa in Namibia (South West Africa) notwithstanding Security Council resolution 276 (1970).

In 1989 (at the request of the UN Economic and Social Council—ECOSOC) the Court gave an Advisory Opinion on the Applicability of

INTERNATIONAL ORGANIZATIONS

Article 6, Section 22, of the Convention on the Privileges and Immunities of the United Nations. The Court has also, at the request of UNESCO, given an Advisory Opinion on Judgments of the Administrative Tribunal of the ILO upon Complaints made against UNESCO, and on the Constitution of the Maritime Safety Committee of the Inter-Governmental Maritime Consultative Organization, at the request of IMCO. In July 1996 the Court delivered an Advisory Opinion on the Legality of the Use by a State of Nuclear Weapons in Armed Conflict, requested by WHO. In April 1999 the Court delivered an Advisory Opinion, requested by ECOSOC, on the Difference Relating to Immunity from Legal Process of a Special Rapporteur of the Commission on Human Rights.

Finance

The UN budget appropriation for the Court for the two year period 2008–09 amounted to US $41.2m.

Publications

Acts and Documents, No. 5 (contains Statute and Rules of the Court, the Resolution concerning its internal judicial practice and other documents).
Bibliography (annually).
Pleadings ((Written Pleadings and Statements, Oral Proceedings, Correspondence): series).
Reports ((Judgments, Opinions and Orders): series).
Yearbook.

UNITED NATIONS FUNDAMENTAL TREATIES

Charter of the United Nations

(Signed 26 June 1945)

(Note: The report of the UN Secretary-General entitled 'In Larger Freedom: Towards Development, Security and Human Rights for All', issued in March 2005, proposed the following amendments to the Charter: the elimination of the 'enemy' clauses in Articles 53 and 107; the deletion from the Charter of Chapter XIII, 'The Trusteeship Council'; and the deletion of Article 47 on The Military Staff Committee and related references.)

WE THE PEOPLES OF THE UNITED NATIONS DETERMINED

to save succeeding generations from the scourge of war, which twice in our lifetime has brought untold sorrow to mankind, and to reaffirm faith in fundamental human rights, in the dignity and worth of the human person, in the equal rights of men and women and of nations large and small, and

to establish conditions under which justice and respect for the obligations arising from treaties and other sources of international law can be maintained, and

to promote social progress and better standards of life in larger freedom,

AND FOR THESE ENDS

to practise tolerance and live together in peace with one another as good neighbours, and

to unite our strength to maintain international peace and security, and

to ensure, by the acceptance of principles and the institution of methods, that armed force shall not be used, save in the common interest, and

to employ international machinery for the promotion of the economic and social advancement of all peoples,

HAVE RESOLVED TO COMBINE OUR EFFORTS TO ACCOMPLISH THESE AIMS.

Accordingly, our respective Governments, through representatives assembled in the city of San Francisco, who have exhibited their full powers found to be in good and due form, have agreed to the present Charter of the United Nations and do hereby establish an international organization to be known as the United Nations.

I. PURPOSES AND PRINCIPLES

Article 1

The Purposes of the United Nations are:
1. To maintain international peace and security, and to that end: to take effective collective measures for the prevention and removal of threats to the peace, and for the suppression of acts of aggression or other breaches of the peace, and to bring about by peaceful means, and in conformity with the principles of justice and international law, adjustment or settlement of international disputes or situations which might lead to a breach of the peace;
2. To develop friendly relations among nations based on respect for the principle of equal rights and self-determination of peoples, and to take other appropriate measures to strengthen universal peace;
3. To achieve international co-operation in solving international problems of an economic, social, cultural, or humanitarian character, and in promoting and encouraging respect for human rights and for fundamental freedoms for all without distinction as to race, sex, language, or religion; and
4. To be a centre for harmonizing the accusations of nations in the attainment of these common ends.

Article 2

The Organization and its Members, in pursuit of the Purposes stated in Article 1, shall act in accordance with the following Principles.
1. The Organization is based on the principle of the sovereign equality of all its Members;
2. All Members, in order to ensure to all of them the rights and benefits resulting from membership, shall fulfil in good faith the obligations assumed by them in accordance with the present Charter;
3. All Members shall settle their international disputes by peaceful means in such a manner that international peace and security, and justice, are not endangered;
4. All Members shall refrain in their international relations from the threat or use of force against the territorial integrity or political independence of any state, or in any manner inconsistent with the Purposes of the United Nations;
5. All Members shall give the United Nations every assistance in any action it takes in accordance with the present Charter, and shall refrain from giving assistance to any state against which the United Nations is taking preventive or enforcement action;
6. The Organization shall ensure that states which are not Members of the United Nations act in accordance with these Principles so far as may be necessary for the maintenance of international peace and security;
7. Nothing contained in the present Charter shall authorize the United Nations to intervene in matters which are essentially within the domestic jurisdiction of any state or shall require the Members to submit such matters to settlement under the present Charter; but this principle shall not prejudice the application of enforcement measures under Chapter VII.

II. MEMBERSHIP

Article 3

The original Members of the United Nations shall be the states which, having participated in the United Nations Conference on International Organization at San Francisco, or having previously signed the Declaration by United Nations of January 1, 1942, sign the present Charter and ratify it in accordance with Article 110.

Article 4

1. Membership in the United Nations is open to all other peace-loving states which accept the obligations contained in the present Charter and, in the judgement of the Organization, are able and willing to carry out these obligations.
2. The admission of any such state to membership in the United Nations will be effected by a decision of the General Assembly upon the recommendation of the Security Council.

Article 5

A member of the United Nations against which preventive or enforcement action has been taken by the Security Council may be suspended from the exercise of the rights and privileges of membership by the General Assembly upon the recommendation of the Security Council. The exercise of these rights and privileges may be restored by the Security Council.

Article 6

A Member of the United Nations which has persistently violated the Principles contained in the present Charter may be expelled from the Organization by the General Assembly upon the recommendation of the Security Council.

III. ORGANS

Article 7

1. There are established as the principal organs of the United Nations: a General Assembly, a Security Council, an Economic and Social Council, a Trusteeship Council, an International Court of Justice, and a Secretariat.
2. Such subsidiary organs as may be found necessary may be established in accordance with the present Charter.

Article 8

The United Nations shall place no restrictions on the eligibility of men and women to participate in any capacity and under conditions of equality in its principal and subsidiary organs.

IV. THE GENERAL ASSEMBLY

Composition

Article 9

1. The General Assembly shall consist of all the Members of the United Nations.

2. Each Member shall have not more than five representatives in the General Assembly.

Functions and Powers
Article 10
The General Assembly may discuss any questions or any matters within the scope of the present Charter or relating to the powers and functions of any organs provided for in the present Charter, and, except as provided in Article 12, may make recommendations to the Members of the United Nations or to the Security Council or to both on any such questions or matters.

Article 11
1. The General Assembly may consider the general principles of co-operation in the maintenance of international peace and security, including the principles governing disarmament and the regulation of armaments, and may make recommendations with regard to such principles to the Members or to the Security Council or to both.
2. The General Assembly may discuss any questions relating to the maintenance of international peace and security brought before it by any Member of the United Nations, or by the Security Council, or by a state which is not a Member of the United Nations in accordance with Article 35, paragraph 2, and, except as provided in Article 12, may make recommendations with regard to any such question to the state or states concerned or to the Security Council or both. Any such question on which action is necessary shall be referred to the Security Council by the General Assembly either before or after discussion.
3. The General Assembly may call the attention of the Security Council to situations which are likely to endanger international peace and security.
4. The powers of the General Assembly set forth in this Article shall not limit the general scope of Article 10.

Article 12
1. While the Security Council is exercising in respect of any dispute or situation the functions assigned to it in the present Charter, the General Assembly shall not make any recommendations with regard to that dispute or situation unless the Security Council so requests. 2.
2. The Secretary-General, with the consent of the Security Council, shall notify the General Assembly at each session of any matters relative to the maintenance of international peace and security which are being dealt with by the Security Council and shall similarly notify the General Assembly, or the Members of the United Nations if the General Assembly is not in session, immediately the Security Council ceases to deal with such matters.

Article 13
1. The General Assembly shall initiate studies and make recommendations for the purpose of:
(a) promoting international co-operation in the political field and encouraging the progressive development of international law and its codification;
(b) promoting international co-operation in the economic, social, cultural, educational, and health fields, and assisting in the realization of human rights and fundamental freedoms for all without distinction as to race, sex, language, or religion.
2. The further responsibilities, functions and powers of the General Assembly with respect to matters mentioned in paragraph 1(b) above are set forth in Chapters IX and X.

Article 14
Subject to the provision of Article 12, the General Assembly may recommend measures for the peaceful adjustment of any situation, regardless of origin, which it deems likely to impair the general welfare or friendly relations among nations, including situations resulting from a violation of the provisions of the present Charter setting forth the Purposes and Principles of the United Nations.

Article 15
1. The General Assembly shall receive and consider annual and special reports from the Security Council; these reports shall include an account of the measures that the Security Council has decided upon or taken to maintain international peace and security.
2. The General Assembly shall receive and consider reports from the other organs of the United Nations.

Article 16
The General Assembly shall perform such functions with respect to the international trusteeship system as are assigned to it under Chapters XII and XIII, including the approval of the trusteeship agreements for areas not designated as strategic.

Article 17
1. The General Assembly shall consider and approve the budget of the Organization.
2. The expenses of the Organization shall be borne by the Members as apportioned by the General Assembly
3. The General Assembly shall consider and approve any financial and budgetary arrangements with specialized agencies referred to in Article 57 and shall examine the administrative budgets of such specialized agencies with a view to making recommendations to the agencies concerned.

Voting
Article 18
1. Each Member of the General Assembly shall have one vote.
2. Decisions of the General Assembly on important questions shall be made by a two-thirds majority of the members present and voting. These questions shall include: recommendations with respect to the maintenance of international peace and security, the election of the non-permanent Members of the Security Council, the election of the Members of the Economic and Social Council, the election of Members of the Trusteeship Council in accordance with paragraph 1(c) of Article 86, the admission of new Members to the United Nations, the suspension of the rights and privileges of membership, the expulsion of Members, questions relating to the operation of the trusteeship system, and budgetary questions.
3. Decisions on other questions, including the determination of additional categories of questions to be decided by a two-thirds majority, shall be made by a majority of the members present and voting.

Article 19
A Member of the United Nations which is in arrears in the payment of its financial contributions to the Organization shall have no vote in the General Assembly if the amount of its arrears equals or exceeds the amount of the contributions due from it for the preceding two full years. The General Assembly may, nevertheless, permit such a Member to vote if it is satisfied that the failure to pay is due to conditions beyond the control of the Member.

Procedure
Article 20
The General Assembly shall meet in regular annual sessions and in such special sessions as occasion may require. Special sessions shall be convoked by the Secretary-General at the request of the Security Council or of a majority of the members of the United Nations.

Article 21
The General Assembly shall adopt its own rules of procedure. It shall elect its President for each session.

Article 22
The General Assembly may establish such subsidiary organs as it deems necessary for the performance of its functions.

V. THE SECURITY COUNCIL
Composition
Article 23
1. The Security Council shall consist of 11 Members of the United Nations. The Republic of China, France, the Union of Soviet Socialist Republics, the United Kingdom of Great Britain and Northern Ireland, and the United States of America shall be permanent members of the Security Council. The General Assembly shall elect six other Members of the United Nations to be non-permanent members of the Security Council, due regard being specially paid, in the first instance to the contribution of Members of the United Nations to the maintenance of international peace and security and to the other purposes of the Organization, and also to equitable geographical distribution.
2. The non-permanent members of the Security Council shall be elected for a term of two years. In the first election of the non-permanent members, however, three shall be chosen for a term of one year. A retiring member shall not be eligible for immediate re-election.
3. Each member of the Security Council shall have one representative.

Note: From 1971 the Chinese seat in the UN General Assembly and its permanent seat in the Security Council were occupied by the People's Republic of China. In December 1991 Russia assumed the former USSR's seat in the UN General Assembly and its permanent seat in the Security Council.

Functions and Powers

Article 24

1. In order to ensure prompt and effective action by the United Nations, its Members confer on the Security Council primary responsibility for the maintenance of international peace and security, and agree that in carrying out its duties under this responsibility the Security Council acts on their behalf.
2. In discharging these duties the Security Council shall act in accordance with the Purposes and Principles of the United Nations. The specific powers granted to the Security Council for the discharge of these duties are laid down in Chapters VI, VII, VIII and XII.
3. The Security Council shall submit annual and, when necessary, special reports to the General Assembly for its consideration.

Article 25

The Members of the United Nations agree to accept and carry out the decisions of the Security Council in accordance with the present Charter.

Article 26

In order to promote the establishment and maintenance of international peace and security with the least diversion for armaments of the world's human and economic resources, the Security Council shall be responsible for formulating, with the assistance of the Military Staff Committee referred to in Article 47, plans to be submitted to the Members of the United Nations for the establishment of a system for the regulation of armaments.

Voting

Article 27

1. Each member of the Security Council shall have one vote.
2. Decisions of the Security Council on procedural matters shall be made by an affirmative vote of seven members.
3. Decisions of the Security Council on all other matters shall be made by an affirmative vote of seven members including the concurring votes of the permanent members; provided that, in decisions under Chapter VI, and under paragraph 3 of Article 52, a party to a dispute shall abstain from voting.

Procedure

Article 28

1. The Security Council shall be so organized as to be able to function continuously. Each member of the Security Council shall for this purpose be represented at all times at the seat of the Organization.
2. The Security Council shall hold periodic meetings at which each of its members may, if it so desires, be represented by a member of the government or by some other specially designated representative.
3. The Security Council may hold meetings at such places other than the seat of the Organization as in its judgment will best facilitate its work.

Article 29

The Security Council may establish such subsidiary organs as it deems necessary for the performance of its functions.

Article 30

The Security Council shall adopt its own rules of procedure, including the method of selecting its President.

Article 31

Any Member of the United Nations which is not a member of the Security Council may participate, without vote, in the discussion of any question brought before the Security Council whenever the latter considers that the interests of that Member are specially affected.

Article 32

Any Member of the United Nations which is not a member of the Security Council or any state which is not a Member of the United Nations, if it is a party to a dispute under consideration by the Security Council, shall be invited to participate, without vote, in the discussion relating to the dispute. The Security Council shall lay down such conditions as it deems just for the participation of a state which is not a Member of the United Nations.

VI. PACIFIC SETTLEMENT OF DISPUTES

Article 33

1. The parties to any dispute, the continuance of which is likely to endanger the maintenance of international peace and security, shall, first of all, seek a solution by negotiation, enquiry, mediation, conciliation, arbitration, judicial settlement, resort to regional agencies or arrangements, or other peaceful means of their own choice.
2. The Security Council shall, when it deems necessary, call upon the parties to settle their disputes by such means.

Article 34

The Security Council may investigate any dispute, or any situation which might lead to international friction or give rise to a dispute, in order to determine whether the continuance of the dispute or situation is likely to endanger the maintenance of international peace and security.

Article 35

1. Any Member of the United Nations may bring any dispute, or any situation of the nature referred to in Article 34, to the attention of the Security Council or of the General Assembly.
2. A state which is not a Member of the United Nations may bring to the attention of the Security Council or of the General Assembly any dispute to which it is a party if it accepts in advance, for the purposes of the dispute, the obligations of pacific settlement provided in the present Charter.
3. The proceedings of the General Assembly in respect of matters brought to its attention under this Article will be subject to the provisions of Articles 11 and 12.

Article 36

1. The Security Council may, at any stage of a dispute of the nature referred to in Article 33 or of a situation of like nature, recommend appropriate procedures or methods of adjustment.
2. The Security Council should take into consideration any procedures for the settlement of the dispute which have already been adopted by the parties.
3. In making recommendations under this Article the Security Council should also take into consideration that legal disputes should as a general rule be referred by the parties to the International Court of Justice in accordance with the provisions of the statute of the Court.

Article 37

1. Should the parties to a dispute of the nature referred to in Article 33, fail to settle it by the means indicated in that Article, they shall refer it to the Security Council.
2. If the Security Council deems that the continuance of the dispute is in fact likely to endanger the maintenance of international peace and security, it shall decide whether to take action under Article 36 or to recommend such terms of settlement as it may consider appropriate.

Article 38

Without prejudice to the provisions of Articles 33 to 37, the Security Council may, if all the parties to any dispute so request, make recommendations to the parties with a view to a pacific settlement of the dispute.

VII. ACTION WITH RESPECT TO THREATS TO THE PEACE, BREACHES OF THE PEACE, AND ACTS OF AGGRESSION

Article 39

The Security Council shall determine the existence of any threat to the peace, breach of the peace, or act of aggression and shall make recommendations, or decide what measures shall be taken in accordance with Articles 41 and 42, to maintain or restore international peace and security.

Article 40

In order to prevent an aggravation of the situation, the Security Council may, before making the recommendations or deciding upon the measures provided for in Article 39, call upon the parties concerned to comply with such provisional measures as it deems necessary or desirable. Such provisional measures shall be without prejudice to the rights, claims, or position of the parties concerned.

The Security Council shall duly take account of failure to comply with such provisional measures.

Article 41
The Security Council may decide what measures not involving the use of armed force are to be employed to give effect to its decisions, and it may call upon the Members of the United Nations to apply such measures. These may include complete or partial interruption of economic relations and of rail, sea, air, postal, telegraphic, radio, and other means of communication, and the severance of diplomatic relations.

Article 42
Should the Security Council consider that measures provided for in Article 41 would be inadequate or have proved to be inadequate, it may take such action by air, sea, or land forces as may be necessary to maintain or restore international peace and security. Such action may include demonstrations, blockade, and other operations by air, sea, or land forces of Members of the United Nations.

Article 43
1. All Members of the United Nations, in order to contribute to the maintenance of international peace and security, undertake to make available to the Security Council, on its call and in accordance with a special agreement or agreements, armed forces, assistance, and facilities, including rights of passage, necessary for the purpose of maintaining international peace and security.
2. Such agreement or agreements shall govern the numbers and types of forces, their degree of readiness and general location, and the nature of the facilities and assistance to be provided.
3. The agreement or agreements shall be negotiated as soon as possible on the initiative of the Security Council. They shall be concluded between the Security Council and Members or between the Security Council and groups of Members and shall be subject to ratification by the signatory states in accordance with their respective constitutional processes.

Article 44
When the Security Council has decided to use force it shall, before calling upon a Member not represented on it to provide armed forces in fulfilment of the obligations assumed under Article 43, invite that Member, if the Member so desires, to participate in the decisions of the Security Council concerning the employment of contingents of that Member's armed forces.

Article 45
In order to enable the United Nations to take urgent military measures, Members shall hold immediately available national airforce contingents for combined international enforcement action. The strength and degree of readiness of these contingents and plans for their combined action shall be determined, within the limits laid down in the special agreement and agreements referred to in Article 43, by the Security Council with the assistance of the Military Staff Committee.

Article 46
Plans for the application of armed force shall be made by the Security Council with the assistance of the Military Staff Committee.

Article 47
1. There shall be established a Military Staff Committee to advise and assist the Security Council on all questions relating to the Security Council's military requirements for the maintenance of international peace and security, the employment and command of forces placed at its disposal, the regulation of armaments, and possible disarmament.
2. The Military Staff Committee shall consist of the Chiefs of Staff of the permanent members of the Security Council or their representatives. Any Member of the United Nations not permanently represented on the Committee shall be invited by the Committee to be associated with it when the efficient discharge of the Committee's responsibilities requires the participation of that Member in its work.
3. The Military Staff Committee shall be responsible under the Security Council for the strategic direction of any armed forces placed at the disposal of the Security Council. Questions relating to the command of such forces shall be worked out subsequently.
4. The Military Staff Committee, with the authorization of the Security Council and after consultation with appropriate regional agencies, may establish regional sub-committees.

Article 48
1. The action required to carry out the decisions of the Security Council for the maintenance of international peace and security shall be taken by all the Members of the United Nations or by some of them, as the Security Council may determine.
2. Such decisions shall be carried out by the Members of the United Nations directly and through their action in the appropriate international agencies of which they are members.

Article 49
The Members of the United Nations shall join in affording mutual assistance in carrying out the measures decided upon by the Security Council.

Article 50
If preventive or enforcement measures against any state are taken by the Security Council, any other state, whether a Member of the United Nations or not, which finds itself confronted with special economic problems arising from the carrying out of those measures shall have the right to consult the Security Council with regard to a solution of those problems.

Article 51
Nothing in the present Charter shall impair the inherent right of individual or collective self-defence if an armed attack occurs against a Member of the United Nations, until the Security Council has taken measures necessary to maintain international peace and security. Measures taken by Members in the exercise of this right of self-defence shall be immediately reported to the Security Council and shall not in any way affect the authority and responsibility of the Security Council under the present Charter to take at any time such action as it deems necessary in order to maintain or restore international peace and security.

VIII. REGIONAL ARRANGEMENTS

Article 52
1. Nothing in the present Charter precludes the existence of regional arrangements or agencies for dealing with such matters relating to the maintenance of international peace and security as are appropriate for regional action, provided that such arrangements or agencies and their activities are consistent with the Purposes and Principles of the United Nations.
2. The Members of the United Nations entering into such arrangements or constituting such agencies shall make every effort to achieve pacific settlement of local disputes through such regional agencies before referring them to the Security Council.
3. The Security Council shall encourage the development of pacific settlement of local disputes through such regional arrangements or by such regional agencies either on the initiative of the states concerned or by reference from the Security Council.
4. This Article in no way impairs the application of Articles 34 and 35.

Article 53
1. The Security Council shall, where appropriate, utilize such regional arrangements or agencies for enforcement action under its authority. But no enforcement action shall be taken under regional arrangements or by regional agencies without the authorization of the Security Council, with the exception of measures against any enemy state, as defined in paragraph 2 of this Article, provided for pursuant to Article 107 or in regional arrangements directed against renewal of aggressive policy on the part of any such state, until such time as the Organization may, on request of the Governments concerned, be charged with the responsibility for preventing further aggression by such a state.
2. The term enemy state as used in paragraph I of this Article applies to any state which during the Second World War has been an enemy of any signatory of the present Charter.

Article 54
The Security Council shall at all times be kept fully informed of activities undertaken or in contemplation under regional arrangements or by regional agencies for the maintenance of international peace and security.

IX. INTERNATIONAL ECONOMIC AND SOCIAL CO-OPERATION

Article 55
With a view to the creation of conditions of stability and well-being which are necessary for peaceful and friendly relations among

nations based on respect for the principle of equal rights and self-determination of peoples, the United Nations shall promote:
(a) higher standards of living, full employment, and conditions of economic and social progress and development;
(b) solutions of international economic, social, health, and related problems; and international cultural and educational co-operation; and
(c) universal respect for, and observance of, human rights and fundamental freedoms for all without distinction as to race, sex, language, or religion.

Article 56

All Members pledge themselves to take joint and separate action in co-operation with the Organization for the achievement of the purposes set forth in Article 55.

Article 57

1. The various specialized agencies, established by intergovernmental agreement and having wide international responsibilities, as defined in their basic instruments, in economic, social, cultural, educational, health, and related fields, shall be brought into relationship with the United Nations in accordance with the provisions of Article 63.
2. Such agencies thus brought into relationship with the United Nations are hereinafter referred to as specialized agencies.

Article 58

The Organization shall make recommendations for the co-ordination of the policies and activities of the specialized agencies.

Article 59

The Organization shall, where appropriate, initiate negotiations among the states concerned for the creation of any new specialized agencies required for the accomplishment of the purposes set forth in Article 55.

Article 60

Responsibility for the discharge of the functions of the Organization set forth in this Chapter shall be vested in the General Assembly and, under the authority of the General Assembly, in the Economic and Social Council, which shall have for this purpose the powers set forth in Chapter X.

X. THE ECONOMIC AND SOCIAL COUNCIL

Composition

Article 61

1. The Economic and Social Council shall consist of 18 Members of the United Nations elected by the General Assembly.
2. Subject to the provisions of paragraph 3, six members of the Economic and Social Council shall be elected each year for a term of three years. A retiring member shall be eligible for immediate re-election.
3. At the first election, 18 members of the Economic and Social Council shall be chosen. The term of office of six members so chosen shall expire at the end of one year, and of six other members at the end of two years, in accordance with arrangements made by the General Assembly.
4. Each member of the Economic and Social Council shall have one representative.

Functions and Powers

Article 62

1. The Economic and Social Council may make or initiate studies and reports with respect to international economic, social, cultural, educational, health, and related matters and may make recommendations with respect to any such matters to the General Assembly, to the Members of the United Nations, and to the specialized agencies concerned.
2. It may make recommendations for the purpose of promoting respect for, and observance of, human rights and fundamental freedoms for all.
3. It may prepare draft conventions for submission to the General Assembly, with respect to matters falling within its competence.
4. It may call, in accordance with the rules prescribed by the United Nations, international conferences on matters falling within its competence.

Article 63

1. The Economic and Social Council may enter into agreements with any of the agencies referred to in Article 57, defining the terms on which the agency concerned shall be brought into relationship with the United Nations. Such agreements shall be subject to approval by the General Assembly.
2. It may co-ordinate the activities of the specialized agencies through consultation with and recommendations to such agencies and through recommendations to the General Assembly and to the Members of the United Nations.

Article 64

1. The Economic and Social Council may take appropriate steps to obtain regular reports from the specialized agencies. It may make arrangements with the Members of the United Nations and with specialized agencies to obtain reports on the steps taken to give effect to its own recommendations and to recommendations on matters falling within its competence made by the General Assembly.
2. It may communicate its observations on these reports to the General Assembly.

Article 65

The Economic and Social Council may furnish information to the Security Council and shall assist the Security Council upon its request.

Article 66

1. The Economic and Social Council shall perform such functions as fall within its competence in connection with the carrying out of the recommendations of the General Assembly.
2. It may, with the approval of the General Assembly, perform services at the request of Members of the United Nations and at the request of specialized agencies.
3. It shall perform such other functions as are specified elsewhere in the present Charter or as may be assigned to it by the General Assembly.

Voting

Article 67

1. Each member of the Economic and Social Council shall have one vote.
2. Decisions of the Economic and Social Council shall be made by a majority of the members present and voting.

Procedure

Article 68

The Economic and Social Council shall set up commissions in economic and social fields and for the promotion of human rights, and such other commissions as may be required for the performance of its functions.

Article 69

The Economic and Social Council shall invite any Member of the United Nations to participate, without vote, in its deliberations on any matter of particular concern to that Member.

Article 70

The Economic and Social Council may make arrangements for representatives of the specialized agencies to participate, without vote, in its deliberations and in those of the commissions established by it, and for its representatives to participate in the deliberations of the specialized agencies.

Article 71

The Economic and Social Council may make suitable arrangements for consultation with non-governmental organizations which are concerned with matters within its competence. Such arrangements may be made with international organizations and, where appropriate, with national organizations after consultation with the Member of the United Nations concerned.

Article 72

1. The Economic and Social Council shall adopt its own rules of procedure, including the method of selecting its President.
2. The Economic and Social Council shall meet as required in accordance with its rules, which shall include provision for the convening of meetings on the request of a majority of its members.

XI. NON-SELF-GOVERNING TERRITORIES

Article 73

Members of the United Nations which have or assume responsibilities for the administration of territories whose peoples have not yet attained a full measure of self-government recognize the principle that the interests of the inhabitants of these territories are paramount, and accept as a sacred trust the obligation to promote to the utmost, within the system of international peace and security established by the present Charter, the well-being of the inhabitants of these territories, and, to this end:

(a) to ensure, with due respect for the culture of the peoples concerned, their political, economic, social, and educational advancement, their just treatment, and their protection against abuses;
(b) to develop self-government, to take due account of the political aspirations of the peoples, and to assist them in the progressive development of their free political institutions, according to the particular circumstances of each territory and its peoples and their varying stages of advancement;
(c) to further international peace and security;
(d) to promote constructive measures of development, to encourage research, and to co-operate with one another and, when and where appropriate, with specialized international bodies with a view to the practical achievement of the social, economic, and scientific purposes set forth in this Article; and
(e) to transmit regularly to the Secretary-General for information purposes, subject to such limitations as security and constitutional considerations may require, statistical and other information, of a technical nature relating to economic, social, and educational conditions in the territories for which they are respectively responsible other than those territories to which Chapters XII and XIII apply.

Article 74

Members of the United Nations also agree that their policy in respect of the territories to which this Chapter applies, no less than in respect of their metropolitan areas, must be based on the general principles of good-neighbourliness, due account being taken of the interests and well-being of the rest of the world, in social, economic, and commercial matters.

XII. INTERNATIONAL TRUSTEESHIP SYSTEM

Article 75

The United Nations shall establish under its authority an international trusteeship system for the administration and supervision of such territories as may be placed thereunder by subsequent individual agreements. These territories are hereinafter referred to as trust territories.

Article 76

The basic objectives of the trusteeship system, in accordance with the Purposes of the United Nations laid down in Article 1 of the present Charter, shall be:

(a) to further international peace and security;
(b) to promote the political, economic, social, and educational advancement of the inhabitants of the trust territories, and their progressive development towards self-government or independence as may be appropriate to the particular circumstances of each territory and its peoples and the freely expressed wishes of the peoples concerned, and as may be provided by the terms of each trusteeship agreement;
(c) to encourage respect for human rights and for fundamental freedoms for all without distinction as to race, sex, language, or religion, and to encourage recognition of the interdependence of the peoples of the world; and
(d) to ensure equal treatment in social, economic, and commercial matters for all Members of the United Nations and their nationals, and also equal treatment for the latter in the administration of justice, without prejudice to the attainment of the foregoing objectives and subject to the provisions of Article 80.

Article 77

1. The trusteeship system shall apply to such territories in the following categories as may be placed thereunder by means of trusteeship agreements.
(a) territories now held under mandate;
(b) territories which may be detached from enemy states as a result of the Second World War; and
(c) territories voluntarily placed under the system by states responsible for their administration.

2. It will be a matter for subsequent agreement as to which territories in the foregoing categories will be brought under the trusteeship system and upon what terms.

Article 78

The trusteeship system shall not apply to territories which have become Members of the United Nations, relationship among which shall be based on respect for the principle of sovereign equality.

Article 79

The terms of trusteeship for each territory to be placed under the trusteeship system, including any alteration or amendment, shall be agreed upon by the states directly concerned, including the mandatory power in the case of territories held under mandate by a Member of the United Nations, and shall be approved as provided for in Articles 83 and 85.

Article 80

1. Except as may be agreed upon in individual trusteeship agreements, made under Articles 77, 79, and 81, placing each territory under the trusteeship system, and until such agreements have been concluded, nothing in this Chapter shall be construed in or of itself to alter in any manner the rights whatsoever of any states or any peoples or the terms of existing international instruments to which Members of the United Nations may respectively be parties.
2. Paragraph 1 of this Article shall not be interpreted as giving grounds for delay or postponement of the negotiation and conclusion of agreements for placing mandated and other territories under the trusteeship system as provided for in Article 77.

Article 81

The trusteeship agreement shall in each case include the terms under which the trust territory will be administered and designate the authority which will exercise the administration of the trust territory. Such authority, hereinafter called the administering authority, may be one or more states or the Organization itself.

Article 82

There may be designated, in any trusteeship agreement, a strategic area or areas which may include part or all of the trust territory to which the agreement applies, without prejudice to any special agreement or agreements made under Article 43.

Article 83

1. All functions of the United Nations relating to strategic areas, including the approval of the terms of the trusteeship agreements and of their alteration or amendment, shall be exercised by the Security Council.
2. The basic objectives set forth in Article 76 shall be applicable to the people of each strategic area.
3. The Security Council shall, subject to the provisions of the trusteeship agreements and without prejudice to security considerations, avail itself of the assistance of the Trusteeship Council to perform those functions of the United Nations under the trusteeship system relating to political, economic, social, and educational matters in the strategic areas.

Article 84

It shall be the duty of the administering authority to ensure that the trust territory shall play its part in the maintenance of international peace and security. To this end the administering authority may make use of volunteer forces, facilities, and assistance from the trust territory in carrying out the obligations towards the Security Council undertaken in this regard by the administering authority, as well as for local defence and the maintenance of law and order within the trust territory.

Article 85

1. The functions of the United Nations with regard to trusteeship agreements for all areas not designated as strategic, including the approval of the terms of the trusteeship agreements and of their alteration or amendment, shall be exercised by the General Assembly.
2. The Trusteeship Council, operating under the authority of the General Assembly, shall assist the General Assembly in carrying out these functions.

XIII. THE TRUSTEESHIP COUNCIL

Composition

Article 86

1. The Trusteeship Council shall consist of the following Members of the United Nations:
(a) those Members administering trust territories;

(b) such of those Members mentioned by name in Article 23 as are not administering trust territories; and
(c) as many other Members elected for three-year terms by the General Assembly as may be necessary to ensure that the total number of members of the Trusteeship Council is equally divided between those Members of the United Nations which administer trust territories and those which do not.

2. Each member of the Trusteeship Council shall designate one specially qualified person to represent it therein.

Note: On 1 October 1994 the Republic of Palau, the last remaining territory under UN trusteeship, became independent. The Trusteeship Council formally suspended operations on 1 November; subsequently it was to be convened, as required, on an extraordinary basis.

Functions and Powers
Article 87
The General Assembly and, under its authority, the Trusteeship Council, in carrying out their functions, may:
(a) consider reports submitted by the administering authority
(b) accept petitions and examine them in consultation with the administering authority
(c) provide for periodic visits to the respective trust territories at times agreed upon with the administering authority; and
(d) take these and other actions in conformity with the terms of the trusteeship agreements.

Article 88
The Trusteeship Council shall formulate a questionnaire on the political, economic, social, and educational advancement of the inhabitants of each trust territory, and the administering authority for each trust territory within the competence of the General Assembly shall make an annual report to the General Assembly upon the basis of such questionnaire.

Voting
Article 89
1. Each member of the Trusteeship Council shall have one vote.
2. Decisions of the Trusteeship Council shall be made by a majority of the members present and voting.

Procedure
Article 90
1. The Trusteeship Council shall adopt its own rules of procedure, including the method of selecting its President.
2. The Trusteeship Council shall meet as required in accordance with its rules, which shall include provision for the convening of meetings on the request of a majority of its members.

Article 91
The Trusteeship Council shall, when appropriate, avail itself of the assistance of the Economic and Social Council and of the specialized agencies in regard to matters with which they are respectively concerned.

XIV. THE INTERNATIONAL COURT OF JUSTICE
Article 92
The International Court of Justice shall be the principal judicial organ of the United Nations. It shall function in accordance with the annexed Statute, which is based upon the Statute of the Permanent Court of International Justice and forms an integral part of the present Charter.

Article 93
1. All Members of the United Nations are *ipso facto* parties to the Statute of the International Court of Justice.
2. A state which is not a Member of the United Nations may become a party to the Statute of the International Court of Justice on condition to be determined in each case by the General Assembly upon the recommendation of the Security Council.

Article 94
1. Each Member of the United Nations undertakes to comply with the decision of the International Court of Justice in any case to which it is a party.
2. If any party to a case fails to perform the obligations incumbent upon it under a judgment rendered by the Court, the other party may have recourse to the Security Council, which may, if it deems necessary, make recommendations or decide upon measures to be taken to give effect to the judgment.

Article 95
Nothing in the present Charter shall prevent Members of the United Nations from entrusting the solution of their differences to other tribunals by virtue of agreements already in existence or which may be concluded in the future.

Article 96
1. The General Assembly or the Security Council may request the International Court of Justice to give an advisory opinion on any legal question.
2. Other organs of the United Nations and specialized agencies, which may at any time be so authorized by the General Assembly, may also request advisory opinions of the Court on legal questions arising within the scope of their activities.

XV. THE SECRETARIAT
Article 97
The Secretariat shall comprise a Secretary-General and such staff as the Organization may require. The Secretary-General shall be appointed by the General Assembly upon the recommendation of the Security Council. He shall be the chief administrative officer of the Organization.

Article 98
The Secretary-General shall act in that capacity in all meetings of the General Assembly, of the Security Council, of the Economic and Social Council, and of the Trusteeship Council, and shall perform such other functions as are entrusted to him by these organs. The Secretary-General shall make an annual report to the General Assembly on the work of the Organization.

Article 99
The Secretary-General may bring to the attention of the Security Council any matter which in his opinion may threaten the maintenance of international peace and security.

Article 100
1. In the performance of their duties the Secretary-General and the staff shall not seek or receive instructions from any government or from any other authority external to the Organization. They shall refrain from any action which might reflect on their position as international officials responsible only to the Organization.
2. Each Member of the United Nations undertakes to respect the exclusively international character of the responsibilities of the Secretary-General and the staff and not to seek to influence them in the discharge of their responsibilities.

Article 101
1. The staff shall be appointed by the Secretary-General under regulations established by the General Assembly.
2. Appropriate staffs shall be permanently assigned to the Economic and Social Council, the Trusteeship Council, and, as required, to other organs of the United Nations. These staffs shall form a part of the Secretariat.
3. The paramount consideration in the employment of the staff and in the determination of the conditions of service shall be the necessity of securing the highest standards of efficiency, competence, and integrity. Due regard shall be paid to the importance of recruiting the staff on as wide a geographical basis as possible.

XVI. MISCELLANEOUS PROVISIONS
Article 102
1. Every treaty and every international agreement entered into by any Member of the United Nations after the present Charter comes into force shall as soon as possible be registered with the Secretariat and published by it.
2. No party to any such treaty or international agreement which has not been registered in accordance with the provisions of paragraph 1 of this Article may invoke that treaty or agreement before any organ of the United Nations.

Article 103
In the event of a conflict between the obligations of the Members of the United Nations under the present Charter and their obligations under any other international agreement, their obligations under the present Charter shall prevail.

Article 104

The Organization shall enjoy in the territory of each of its Members such legal capacity as may be necessary for the exercise of its functions and the fulfilment of its purposes.

Article 105

1. The Organization shall enjoy in the territory of each of its Members such privileges and immunities as are necessary for the fulfilment of its purposes.
2. Representatives of the Members of the United Nations and officials of the Organization shall similarly enjoy such privileges and immunities as are necessary for the independent exercise of their functions in connection with the Organization.
3. The General Assembly may make recommendations with a view to determining the details of the application of paragraphs 1 and 2 of this Article or may propose conventions to the Members of the United Nations for this purpose.

XVII. TRANSITIONAL SECURITY ARRANGEMENTS

Article 106

Pending the coming into force of such special agreements referred to in Article 43 as in the opinion of the Security Council enable it to begin the exercise of its responsibilities under Article 42, the parties to the Four-Nation Declaration signed at Moscow, October 30, 1943, and France, shall, in accordance with the provisions of paragraph 5 of that Declaration, consult with one another and as occasion requires with other Members of the United Nations with a view to such joint action on behalf of the Organization as may be necessary for the purpose of maintaining international peace and security.

Article 107

Nothing in the present Charter shall invalidate or preclude action, in relation to any state which during the Second World War has been an enemy of any signatory to the present Charter, taken or authorized as a result of that war by the Governments having responsibility for such action.

XVIII. AMENDMENTS

Article 108

Amendments to the present Charter shall come into force for all Members of the United Nations when they have been adopted by a vote of two-thirds of the members of the General Assembly and ratified in accordance with their respective constitutional processes by two-thirds of the Members of the United Nations, including all the permanent members of the Security Council.

Article 109

1. A General Conference of the Members of the United Nations for the purpose of reviewing the present Charter may be held at a date and place to be fixed by a two-thirds vote of the members of the General Assembly and by a vote of any seven members of the Security Council. Each Member of the United Nations shall have one vote in the conference.
2. Any alteration of the present Charter recommended by a two-thirds vote of the conference shall take effect when ratified in accordance with their respective constitutional processes by two-thirds of the Members of the United Nations including all the permanent members of the Security Council.
3. If such a conference has not been held before the tenth annual session of the General Assembly following the coming into force of the present Charter, the proposal to call such a conference shall be placed on the agenda of that session of the General Assembly, and the conference shall be held if so decided by a majority vote of the members of the General Assembly and by a vote of any seven members of the Security Council.

XIX. RATIFICATION AND SIGNATURE

Article 110

1. The present Charter shall be ratified by the signatory states in accordance with their respective constitutional processes.
2. The ratifications shall be deposited with the Government of the United States of America, which shall notify all the signatory states of each deposit as well as the Secretary-General of the Organization when he has been appointed.
3. The present Charter shall come into force upon the deposit of ratifications by the Republic of China, France, the Union of Soviet Socialist Republics, the United Kingdom of Great Britain and Northern Ireland, and the United States of America, and by a majority of the other signatory states. A protocol of the ratifications deposited shall thereupon be drawn up by the Government of the United States of America which shall communicate copies thereof to all the signatory states.
4. The states signatory to the present Charter which ratify it after it has come into force will become original Members of the United Nations on the date of the deposit of their respective ratifications.

Article 111

The present Charter, of which the Chinese, French, Russian, English, and Spanish texts are equally authentic, shall remain deposited in the archives of the Government of the United States of America. Duly certified copies thereof shall be transmitted by that Government to the Governments of the other signatory states.

IN FAITH WHEREOF the representatives of the Governments of the United Nations have signed the present Charter.

DONE at the city of San Francisco the twenty-sixth day of June, one thousand nine hundred and forty-five.

AMENDMENTS

The following amendments to Articles 23 and 27 of the Charter came into force in August 1965.

Article 23

1. The Security Council shall consist of 15 Members of the United Nations. The Republic of China, France, the Union of Soviet Socialist Republics, the United Kingdom of Great Britain and Northern Ireland, and the United States of America shall be permanent members of the Security Council. The General Assembly shall elect 10 other Members of the United Nations to be non-permanent members of the Security Council, due regard being specially paid, in the first instance to the contribution of Members of the United Nations to the maintenance of international peace and security and to the other purposes of the Organization, and also to equitable geographical distribution.
2. The non-permanent members of the Security Council shall be elected for a term of two years. In the first election of the non-permanent members after the increase of the membership of the Security Council from 11 to 15, two of the four additional members shall be chosen for a term of one year. A retiring member shall not be eligible for immediate re-election.
3. Each member of the Security Council shall have one representative.

Article 27

1. Each member of the Security Council shall have one vote.
2. Decisions of the Security Council on procedural matters shall be made by an affirmative vote of nine members.
3. Decisions of the Security Council on all other matters shall be made by an affirmative vote of nine members including the concurring votes of the permanent members; provided that, in decisions under Chapter VI and under paragraph 3 of Article 52, a party to a dispute shall abstain from voting.

The following amendments to Article 61 of the Charter came into force in September 1973.

Article 61

1. The Economic and Social Council shall consist of 54 Members of the United Nations elected by the General Assembly.
2. Subject to the provisions of paragraph 3, 18 members of the Economic and Social Council shall be elected each year for a term of three years. A retiring member shall be eligible for immediate re-election.
3. At the first election after the increase in the membership of the Economic and Social Council from 27 to 54 members, in addition to the members elected in place of the nine members whose term of office expires at the end of that year, 27 additional members shall be elected. Of these 27 additional members, the term of office of nine members so elected shall expire at the end of one year, and of nine other members at the end of two years, in accordance with arrangements made by the General Assembly.
4. Each member of the Economic and Social Council shall have one representative.

The following amendment to Paragraph 1 of Article 109 of the Charter came into force in June 1968.

Article 109

1. A General Conference of the Members of the United Nations for the purpose of reviewing the present Charter may be held at a date and place to be fixed by a two-thirds vote of the members of the General Assembly and by a vote of any nine members of the Security Council. Each Member of the United Nations shall have one vote in the conference.

Universal Declaration of Human Rights

(Adopted 10 December 1948)

Whereas recognition of the inherent dignity and of the equal and inalienable rights of all members of the human family is the foundation of freedom, justice and peace in the world,

Whereas disregard and contempt for human rights have resulted in barbarous acts which have outraged the conscience of mankind, and the advent of a world in which human beings shall enjoy freedom of speech and belief and freedom from fear and want has been proclaimed as the highest aspiration of the common people,

Whereas it is essential, if man is not to be compelled to have recourse, as a last resort, to rebellion against tyranny and oppression, that human rights should be protected by the rule of law,

Whereas it is essential to promote the development of friendly relations between nations,

Whereas the peoples of the United Nations have in the Charter reaffirmed their faith in fundamental human rights, in the dignity and worth of the human person and in the equal rights of men and women and have determined to promote social progress and better standards of life in larger freedom,

Whereas Member States have pledged themselves to achieve, in cooperation with the United Nations, the promotion of universal respect for and observance of human rights and fundamental freedoms,

Whereas a common understanding of these rights and freedoms is of the greatest importance for the full realization of this pledge, Now, therefore,

The General Assembly

Proclaims this Universal Declaration of Human Rights as a common standard of achievement for all peoples and all nations, to the end that every individual and every organ of society, keeping this Declaration constantly in mind, shall strive by teaching and education to promote respect for these rights and freedoms and by progressive measures, national and international, to secure their universal and effective recognition and observance, both among the peoples of Member States themselves and among the peoples of territories under their jurisdiction.

Article 1

All human beings are born free and equal in dignity and rights. They are endowed with reason and conscience and should act towards one another in a spirit of brotherhood.

Article 2

Everyone is entitled to all the rights and freedoms set forth in this Declaration, without distinction of any kind, such as race, colour, sex, language, religion, political or other opinion, national or social origin, property, birth or other status.

Furthermore, no distinction shall be made on the basis of the political, jurisdictional or international status of the country or territory to which a person belongs, whether it be independent, trust, non-self-governing or under any other limitation of sovereignty.

Article 3

Everyone has the right to life, liberty and security of person.

Article 4

No one shall be held in slavery or servitude; slavery and the slave trade shall be prohibited in all their forms.

Article 5

No one shall be subjected to torture or to cruel, inhuman or degrading treatment or punishment.

Article 6

Everyone has the right to recognition everywhere as a person before the law.

Article 7

All are equal before the law and are entitled without any discrimination to equal protection of the law. All are entitled to equal protection against any discrimination in violation of this Declaration and against any incitement to such discrimination.

Article 8

Everyone has the right to an effective remedy by the competent national tribunals for acts violating the fundamental rights granted him by the constitution or by law.

Article 9

No one shall be subjected to arbitrary arrest, detention or exile.

Article 10

Everyone is entitled in full equality to a fair and public hearing by an independent and impartial tribunal, in a determination of his rights and obligations and of any criminal charge against him.

Article 11

1. Everyone charged with a penal offence has the right to be presumed innocent until proved guilty according to law in a public trial at which he has had all the guarantees necessary for his defence.
2. No one shall be held guilty of any penal offence on account of any act or omission which did not constitute a penal offence, under national or international law, at the time when it was committed. Nor shall a heavier penalty be imposed than the one that was applicable at the time the penal offence was committed.

Article 12

No one shall be subjected to arbitrary interference with his privacy, family, home or correspondence, nor to attacks upon his honour and reputation. Everyone has the right to the protection of the law against such interference or attacks.

Article 13

1. Everyone has the right to freedom of movement and residence within the borders of each state.
2. Everyone has the right to leave any country, including his own, and to return to his country.

Article 14

1. Everyone has the right to seek and to enjoy in other countries asylum from persecution.
2. This right may not be invoked in the case of prosecutions genuinely arising from non-political crimes or from acts contrary to the purposes and principles of the United Nations.

Article 15

1. Everyone has the right to a nationality.
2. No one shall be arbitrarily deprived of his nationality nor denied the right to change his nationality.

Article 16

1. Men and women of full age, without any limitation due to race, nationality or religion, have the right to marry and to found a family. They are entitled to equal rights as to marriage, during marriage and at its dissolution.
2. Marriage shall be entered into only with the free and full consent of the intending spouses.
3. The family is the natural and fundamental group unit of society and is entitled to protection by society and the State.

Article 17

1. Everyone has the right to own property alone as well as in association with others.
2. No one shall be arbitrarily deprived of his property.

Article 18

Everyone has the right to freedom of thought, conscience and religion; this right includes freedom to change his religion or belief, and freedom, either alone or in community with others and in public or private, to manifest his religion or belief in teaching, practice, worship and observance.

Article 19

Everyone has the right to freedom of opinion and expression; this right includes freedom to hold opinions without interference and to seek, receive and impart information and ideas through any media and regardless of frontiers.

Article 20
1. Everyone has the right to freedom of peaceful assembly and association.
2. No one may be compelled to belong to an association.

Article 21
1. Everyone has the right to take part in the government of his country, directly or through freely chosen representatives.
2. Everyone has the right of equal access to public service in his country.
3. The will of the people shall be the basis of the authority of government; this will shall be expressed in periodic and genuine elections which shall be by universal and equal suffrage and shall be held by secret vote or by equivalent free voting procedures.

Article 22
Everyone, as a member of society, has the right to social security and is entitled to realization, through national effort and international co-operation and in accordance with the organization and resources of each State, of the economic, social and cultural rights indispensable for his dignity and the free development of his personality.

Article 23
1. Everyone has the right to work, to free choice of employment, to just and favourable conditions of work and to protection against unemployment.
2. Everyone, without any discrimination, has the right to equal pay for equal work.
3. Everyone who works has the right to just and favourable remuneration ensuring for himself and his family an existence worthy of human dignity, and supplemented, if necessary, by other means of social protection.
4. Everyone has the right to form and to join trade unions for the protection of his interests.

Article 24
Everyone has the right to rest and leisure, including reasonable limitation of working hours and periodic holidays with pay.

Article 25
1. Everyone has the right to a standard of living adequate for the health and well-being of himself and of his family, including food, clothing, housing and medical care and necessary social services, and the right to security in the event of unemployment, sickness, disability, widowhood, old age or other lack of livelihood in circumstances beyond his control.
2. Motherhood and childhood are entitled to special care and assistance. All children, whether born in or out of wedlock, shall enjoy the same social protection.

Article 26
1. Everyone has the right to education. Education shall be free, at least in the elementary and fundamental stages. Elementary education shall be compulsory. Technical and professional education shall be made generally available and higher education shall be equally accessible to all on the basis of merit.
2. Education shall be directed to the full development of the human personality and to the strengthening of respect for human rights and fundamental freedoms. It shall promote understanding, tolerance and friendship among all nations, racial or religious groups, and shall further the activities of the United Nations for the maintenance of peace.
3. Parents have a prior right to choose the kind of education that shall be given to their children.

Article 27
1. Everyone has the right freely to participate in the cultural life of the community, to enjoy the arts and to share in scientific advancement and its benefits.
2. Everyone has the right to the protection of the moral and material interests resulting from any scientific, literary or artistic production of which he is the author.

Article 28
Everyone is entitled to a social and international order in which the rights and freedoms set forth in this Declaration can be fully realized.

Article 29
1. Everyone has duties to the community in which alone the free and full development of his personality is possible.
2. In the exercise of his rights and freedoms, everyone shall be subject only to such limitations as are determined by law solely for the purpose of securing due recognition and respect for the rights and freedoms of others and of meeting the just requirements of morality, public order and the general welfare in a democratic society.
3. These rights and freedoms may in no case be exercised contrary to the purposes and principles of the United Nations.

Article 30
Nothing in this Declaration may be interpreted as implying for any State, group or person any right to engage in any activity or to perform any act aimed at the destruction of any of the rights and freedoms set forth herein.

UNITED NATIONS REGIONAL COMMISSIONS

Economic Commission for Europe—ECE

Address: Palais des Nations, 1211 Geneva 10, Switzerland.
Telephone: 229171234; **fax:** 229170505; **e-mail:** info.ece@unece.org; **internet:** www.unece.org.

The UN Economic Commission for Europe (ECE) was established in 1947 and was, with ECAFE (now ESCAP), the earliest of the five regional economic commissions set up by the UN Economic and Social Council (ECOSOC). The Commission promotes pan-European economic integration. It provides a regional forum for dialogue and co-operation on economic and sectoral issues for governments from European countries, as well as central Asian republics, the USA, Canada and Israel. It provides analysis, policy advice and assistance to governments, gives focus to UN global mandates on economic issues, and establishes norms, standards and conventions to facilitate international co-operation within and outside the region.

MEMBERS

Albania
Andorra
Armenia
Austria
Azerbaijan
Belarus
Belgium
Bosnia and Herzegovina
Bulgaria
Canada
Croatia
Cyprus
Czech Republic
Denmark
Estonia
Finland
France
Georgia
Germany
Greece
Hungary
Iceland
Ireland
Israel
Italy
Kazakhstan
Kyrgyzstan
Latvia
Liechtenstein
Lithuania
Luxembourg
Macedonia, former Yugoslav republic
Malta
Moldova
Monaco
Montenegro
Netherlands
Norway
Poland
Portugal
Romania
Russia
San Marino
Serbia
Slovakia
Slovenia
Spain
Sweden
Switzerland
Tajikistan
Turkey
Turkmenistan
Ukraine
United Kingdom
USA
Uzbekistan

Organization
(March 2008)

COMMISSION

The Commission, the highest decision-making body of the organization, holds annual formal sessions in Geneva to review the economic situation and decide on activities for the coming year. The 63rd session was to take place in April 2009. As well as taking strategic decisions the Commission provides a forum for senior-level dialogue on regional economic development policy.

EXECUTIVE COMMITTEE

The Executive Committee prepares the formal sessions of the Commission, implements the decisions of the Commission, and acts on behalf of the Commission between the sessions of that body. The Executive Committee also reviews and approves the programmes of work of the sectoral committees, which report at least once a year to the Executive Committee.

SECRETARIAT

The Secretariat services the meetings of the Commission and its sectoral committees and publishes periodic surveys and reviews, including a number of specialized statistical bulletins (see list of publications below). The Executive Secretary carries out secretarial functions for the executive bodies of several regional conventions and their protocols (see below).
Executive Secretary: MAREK BELKA (Poland).

SECTORAL COMMITTEES

Committee on Economic Co-operation and Integration;
Committee on Environmental Policy;
Committee on Housing and Land Management;
Committee on Inland Transport;
Committee on Sustainable Energy;
Committee on Timber;
Committee on Trade;
Conference of European Statisticians.

Activities

ECE's original purpose, when it was established by ECOSOC in 1947, was to give effective aid to the countries devastated by the Second World War. It was granted permanent status in 1951. During the 'cold war' period it served as the only major instrument of economic dialogue and co-operation linking the communist countries of central and eastern Europe with the countries of western Europe, and achieved the harmonization of a number of aspects of transport and trade, such as road signs, safety and anti-pollution standards for motor vehicles, standards for the transport of perishable or dangerous goods, and agreements on customs procedures. During the 1990s, when political changes in central and eastern Europe had allowed countries there to undergo transition from a centrally planned economy to a market economy, ECE adopted the role of assisting these countries, including the newly independent countries that had formerly been part of the USSR and Yugoslavia, and it extended its activities to the central Asian countries, which became members of both ECE and ESCAP.

The guiding principle of ECE activities is the promotion of sustainable economic growth among its 56 member countries. To this end it provides a forum for communication among states; negotiates international legal instruments concerning trade, transport and the environment; and supplies statistics and economic and environmental analysis. The implications for ECE of the enlargement of the European Union (EU) implemented in May 2004 and January 2007, and ongoing developments in member states with economies in transition, generated significant debate during the mid-2000s on the future direction of the Commission's work. The 59th session of ECE, convened in February 2004, commissioned a comprehensive, external evaluation on the state of ECE. The report, which was published in June 2005, included the following recommendations: more effective governance and management of the Commission, including restructuring work divisions and sub-programmes and identifying specialized areas of competence; raising the political profile of the Commission; co-ordinating the regional implementation of the UN Millennium Development Goals (MDGs); improving co-operation with other organizations, in particular a partnership with UNDP and with other regional commissions; and strengthening the participation of the private sector and non-governmental organizations in the Commission. Greater priority was to be given to the environment and transport, and to the specific problems affecting countries with economies in transition. The 61st session of ECE, convened in December 2005, adopted the resulting Work Plan on ECE Reform. The reform process, implemented in 2006, was to be reviewed by the Commission in 2009.

Economic Co-operation and Integration: The programme on Economic Co-operation and Integration, which is implemented by the Committee on Economic Co-operation and Integration and was established under the reform process approved in December 2005, has the following thematic focuses: strengthening the competitiveness of member states' economies by promoting the knowledge-based economy and innovation; facilitating the development of entrepreneurship and the emergence of new enterprises; facilitating effective regulatory policies and corporate governance, including those in the financial sector; promoting public-private partnerships for domestic and foreign investment; maintaining intellectual property rights; and other relevant aspects of international economic co-operation and integration. The Committee has created two teams of experts, on innovation and competitiveness policies, and on intellectual property, who meet annually in support of work in these areas. During 2007 it focused on establishing networks of experts in other relevant fields, to allow dialogue and the exchange of information, with the particular aim of providing support for low-income countries undergoing economic transition.

Environment: ECE aims to facilitate and promote co-operation among member governments in developing and implementing policies for environmental protection, the rational use of natural resources, and sustainable development. It supports the integration of environmental policy into sectoral policies, seeks solutions to environmental problems, particularly those of a transboundary nature, and assists in strengthening environmental management capabilities, particularly in countries in transition. A programme of Environmental Performance Reviews helps to improve the effectiveness of environmental management and policies in individual countries. The Committee on Environmental Policy brings governments together to formulate policy and provides a forum for the exchange of experience and good practices. It prepares the Environment for Europe ministerial-level conferences (normally held every four years: the 2007 conference took place in Belgrade, Serbia) and supports a Pan-European Programme on transport, health and the environment. ECE promotes the implementation of international agreements on the environment and assesses national policies and legislation. In addition, it has negotiated five conventions relating to the environment and serves as their secretariat: the Convention on Long-range Transboundary Air Pollution (which entered into force in 1983 and has been extended by eight protocols); the Convention on the Protection and Use of Transboundary Watercourses and International Lakes (Water Convention, entered into force in 1996, two protocols); the Convention on Environmental Impact Assessment in a Transboundary Context (Espoo Convention, entered into force in 1997, one protocol); the Convention on the Transboundary Effects of Industrial Accidents (entered into force in 2000, one protocol); and the Convention on Access to Information, Public Participation in Decision-making and Access to Justice in Environmental Matters (Aarhus Convention, entered into force in 2001, one protocol).

Forestry and Timber: ECE's Timber Committee works closely, through an integrated programme, with the European Forestry Commission of the FAO to promote sustainable forest management. It compiles data and analyses long-term trends and prospects for forestry and timber; keeps under review developments in the forest industries, including environmental and energy-related aspects; and publishes an annual market review of forest products. The Committee meets annually to review the programme, as well as to discuss policy and market trends and outlook. Assistance in the form of workshops and expert advice is provided to help countries that are undergoing economic transition to develop their forestry sectors. During 2007 a workshop was conducted on the subject of the increasing competition between timber processing and the generation of energy from wood, and a ministerial conference on the protection of forests in Europe took place.

Housing, Land Management and Population: ECE's Committee on Housing and Land Management aims to improve housing conditions, spatial planning and land administration policies. In particular, it promotes the provision of adequate housing, both in the countries of eastern Europe that are undergoing socio-economic transition, and also in deprived neighbourhoods in western Europe. The Committee and its Working Party on Land Administration have prepared guidance on urban renewal, condominium management, housing finance, land administration and social housing. The Committee organizes sub-regional workshops and seminars, and provides policy advice in the form of country profiles on the housing sector and land administration reviews, undertaken by experts. ECE's Generations and Gender Programme, begun in 2000, conducts research on population and demographic change. In November 2007 ECE organized a Conference on Ageing to discuss the implications of fertility rates that have fallen below replacement level, and a further conference of experts and policy-makers, on the causes and consequences of demographic change, was to take place in 2008.

Statistics: The Conference of European Statisticians (CES) and ECE's Statistical Division have the task of co-ordinating international statistical activities in the region, by reviewing the most topical statistical areas, identifying gaps and duplication, and looking for issues not yet addressed. The CES plenary sessions and seminars offer a forum for senior statisticians, often leading to work in new areas and the preparation of new standards and recommendations. The CES and the Statistical Division work to develop methodology in compiling and disseminating economic, social and demographic statistics, for example in harmonizing methods of compiling the gross domestic product, national accounts and other economic indicators; measuring the distorting effect of globalization on national statistical systems; and finding sound methods of measuring sustainable development. The Division helps countries, especially those undergoing economic transition, to improve their statistical systems in accordance with the UN Fundamental Principles of Official Statistics, by advising on legislation and institutions and on how to ensure the independence and impartiality of official statistics. It maintains an on-line statistical database, allowing comparison of major economic and social indicators, and publishes guide-lines on the editing of statistical data.

Sustainable Energy: ECE's Committee on Sustainable Energy provides a forum for intergovernmental dialogue, supports research by groups of experts, and provides technical assistance. Its chief concern is maintaining energy security, which is threatened by volatile petroleum prices and by disruptions in supply. It undertakes research on the classification and evaluation of energy reserves; improving energy efficiency so as to reduce dependence on imports and reduce greenhouse gas emissions; cleaner electricity production from coal and other fossil fuels; exploiting methane gas from coalmines; and the use of natural gas.

Trade: ECE's Committee on Trade received a new mandate following the reforms undertaken in 2006: it was to focus on the facilitation of international trade by means of simpler and better-integrated trade procedures, electronic business methods, common agricultural quality standards and the harmonization of technical regulations. The Committee was to continue working closely with other UN and non-UN organizations, and to provide a forum for dialogue between public and private sectors. The UN Centre for Trade Facilitation and Electronic Business (UN/CEFACT, established in 2002 as part of ECE) works to reduce delays and costs in international transactions by simplifying the necessary procedures. ECE's Working Party on Agricultural Quality Standards develops and updates commercial quality standards for fruit, vegetables and other agricultural products, in cooperation with OECD, and promotes the application of these standards through regional seminars and workshops. The Working Party on Regulatory Co-operation and Standardization Policies aims to harmonize diverse product regulations and standards, which can seriously impede trade, especially among the countries undergoing economic transition, for example when certificates accompanying goods are not recognized by the importing country. It has developed an international model for technical harmonization to assist countries wishing to standardize their rules on specific products or sectors. ECE's Advisory Group on Market Surveillance aims to combat the proliferation of counterfeit and pirated goods.

Transport: ECE aims to promote a coherent, efficient, safe and sustainable transport system through the development of international agreements, conventions, norms and standards relating to road, rail, inland water and combined transport. These international legal instruments, which are developed by intergovernmental specialized working parties with participation from transport equipment manufacturers and consumers and road users, include measures for improving vehicle safety and limiting vehicle emissions, simplifying border crossing procedures, improving road traffic safety, setting the conditions for developing coherent infrastructure networks, and providing for the safe transport of dangerous goods. One of the working groups, the World Forum for Harmonization of Vehicle Regulations, has global participation. In addition to these regulatory activities, ECE addresses transport trends and economics and compiles transport statistics; and it provides a forum for the exchange of technical and legal expertise. The Commission also assists eastern and southeastern European countries and ECE member states from central Asia with the development of their transport systems and infrastructures. In 2005 a plan was elaborated, with ECE support, for investment in the Trans-European Motorway (TEM) and the Trans-European Railway (TER) projects, which were to develop the road and rail networks in 21 central, eastern and southeastern European countries. Another project, undertaken jointly with ESCAP, aims to develop Euro-Asian transport links. With the Europe Office of WHO, ECE administers a Transport, Health and Environment Pan-European Programme, in order to promote sustainable transport policies and systems.

SUB-REGIONAL PROGRAMME

Special Programme for the Economies of Central Asia (SPECA): initiated in 1998 as a joint programme of ECE and ESCAP, SPECA aims to strengthen sub-regional co-operation, by enabling the discussion of regional issues and offering technical assistance. Six Project Working Groups cover: transport and border crossing; water and energy; trade; information and communications technology for development; statistics; and gender and economy. The SPECA Economic Forum meets annually: in 2007 it discussed trade and investment links between Central Asia and trading partners in Asia and Europe. In 2002 the SPECA Business Advisory Council was inaugurated to bring together business representatives from participating countries and from their major trading and economic partners. Participating countries: Afghanistan, Azerbaijan, Kazakhstan, Kyrgyzstan, Tajikistan, Turkmenistan and Uzbekistan.

ECE also provides technical assistance to the Southeast European Co-operative Initiative.

Finance

The allocation for ECE's regular budget in 2008 was US $28.3m.

Publications

UNECE Report (annually).
UNECE Weekly.
UNECE Compendium of Legal Instruments, Norms and Standards.
UNECE Countries in Figures.
Report of the Conference of European Statisticians (annually).
Trade Promotion Directory (annually).

For its different areas of activity (see above) ECE produces statistical bulletins, reports, performance reviews, country profiles, standards, agreements, recommendations, discussion papers, guidelines and manuals.

Economic and Social Commission for Asia and the Pacific—ESCAP

Address: United Nations Bldg, Rajadamnern Nok Ave, Bangkok 10200, Thailand.
Telephone: (2) 288-1234; **fax:** (2) 288-1052; **e-mail:** unisbkk.unescap@un.org; **internet:** www.unescap.org.

The Commission was founded in 1947, at first to assist in post-war reconstruction, and subsequently to encourage the economic and social development of Asia and the Far East; it was originally known as the Economic Commission for Asia and the Far East (ECAFE). The title ESCAP, which replaced ECAFE, was adopted after a reorganization in 1974. From 2002 ESCAP's administrative structures and programme activities underwent a process of intensive restructuring.

MEMBERS

Afghanistan
Armenia
Australia
Azerbaijan
Bangladesh
Bhutan
Brunei
Cambodia
China, People's Republic
Fiji
France
Georgia
India
Indonesia
Iran
Japan
Kazakhstan
Kiribati
Korea, Democratic People's Republic
Korea, Republic
Kyrgyzstan
Laos
Malaysia
The Maldives
Marshall Islands
Micronesia, Federated States
Mongolia
Myanmar
Nauru
Nepal
Netherlands
New Zealand
Pakistan
Palau
Papua New Guinea
Philippines
Russia
Samoa
Singapore
Solomon Islands
Sri Lanka
Tajikistan
Thailand
Timor-Leste
Tonga
Turkey
Turkmenistan
Tuvalu
United Kingdom
USA
Uzbekistan
Vanuatu
Viet Nam

ASSOCIATE MEMBERS

American Samoa
Cook Islands
French Polynesia
Guam
Hong Kong
Macao
New Caledonia
Niue
Northern Mariana Islands

Organization
(March 2008)

COMMISSION

The main legislative organ of ESCAP is the Commission, which meets annually at ministerial level to examine the region's problems, to review progress, to establish priorities and to decide upon the recommendations of the Executive Secretary or the subsidiary bodies of the Commission. It reports to the UN Economic and Social Council (ECOSOC). Ministerial and intergovernmental conferences on specific issues may be held on an ad hoc basis with the approval of the Commission, although no more than one ministerial conference and five intergovernmental conferences may be held during one year.

COMMITTEES AND SPECIAL BODIES

The following Committees advise the Commission and help to oversee the work of the Secretariat. The Committees meet every two years, and their sub-committees meet in the intervening years.

Committee on Poverty Reduction: has sub-committees on Poverty Reduction Practices and Statistics.
Committee on Managing Globalization: has sub-committees on International Trade and Investment, Transport Infrastructure and Facilitation and Tourism, Environment and Sustainable Development, and Information, Communications and Space Technology.
Committee on Emerging Social Issues: has sub-committees on Socially Vulnerable Groups and Health and Development.
Special Body on Least Developed and Landlocked Developing Countries: meets every two years.
Special Body on Pacific Island Developing Countries: meets every two years.

In addition, an Advisory Committee of permanent representatives and other representatives designated by members of the Commission functions as an advisory body; it generally meets every month.

SECRETARIAT

The Secretariat operates under the guidance of the Commission and its subsidiary bodies. It consists of the Office of the Executive Secretary and two servicing divisions, covering administration and programme management, in addition to the following substantive divisions: Development of Pacific Island Countries and Territories; Environment and Sustainable Development; Information, Communication and Space Technology; Poverty and Development; Social Development (including Emerging Social Issues); Statistics; Trade and Investment; and Transport and Tourism. The Secretariat also includes a Least Developed Countries Co-ordination Unit, and the UN Information Service/Bangkok.

Executive Secretary: NOELEEN HEYZER (Singapore).

SUB-REGIONAL OFFICE

ESCAP Pacific Operations Centre (EPOC): Private Mail Bag, Suva, Fiji; tel. 3319669; fax 3319671; e-mail epoc@un.org; internet www.unescap.org/epoc; f. 1984, relocated to Fiji 2005; responsible for ESCAP's sub-programme on Development of Pacific Island Countries and Territories; assists Pacific island governments in forming and implementing national sustainable development strategies, particularly poverty reduction programmes that create access to services by socially vulnerable groups; conducts research, promotes regional co-operation and knowledge-sharing, and provides advisory services, training and pilot projects.

Activities

ESCAP acts as a UN regional centre, providing the only intergovernmental forum that includes the whole of Asia and the Pacific, and executing a wide range of development programmes through technical assistance, advisory services to governments, research, training and information. In 1992 ESCAP began to reorganize its programme activities and conference structures in order to reflect and serve the region's evolving development needs. The approach that was adopted focused on regional economic co-operation, poverty alleviation through economic growth and social development, and environmental and sustainable development. In May 2002, having considered the recommendations of an intergovernmental review meeting held in March, ESCAP determined to implement a further restructuring of its conference structures and thematic priorities. Three main thematic programmes were identified: poverty reduction (comprising sub-programmes on poverty and development, and on statistics), managing globalization (with sub-programmes on trade and investment, environment, and space technology); and emerging social issues (with sub-programmes on health and development, gender and development, and population and social integration). In May 2007 the Commission, convened in Almaty, Kazakhstan, commemorated the 60th anniversary of ESCAP and reaffirmed its central role in fostering regional and sub-regional co-operation.

Emerging Social Issues: ESCAP's Emerging Social Issues Division comprises three sections: Health and Development, Gender and Development, and Population and Social Integration. The Division's main objective is to assess and respond to regional trends and challenges in social policy and human resources development, with particular emphasis on the planning and delivery of social services and training programmes for disadvantaged groups, including the poor, youths, women, the disabled, and the elderly. It aims to strengthen the capacity of public and non-government institutions to address the problems of marginalized social groups and to foster partnerships between governments, the private sector, community organizations and all other involved bodies. The Health and Development section promotes health for all as a critical condition for economic growth and social stability: it supports the strengthening of human resources, adequate health financing, improved delivery of health services, access to affordable medicines, and health promotion. In 2008 ongoing projects included promotion of sustainable strategies for universal access to health care, particularly in the Greater Mekong sub-region; and strengthening life skills to reduce young people's vulnerability to HIV and AIDS and to substance abuse. The Gender and Development section promotes the advancement of women by helping to improve their access to education, economic resources, information and communication technologies and decision-making; it is also committed to combating violence against women, including trafficking. The Population and Social Integration section provides technical assistance to national population programmes, conducts research and assists the exchange of information; promotes the rights of people with disabilities; supports improvement of access to social services by poor people; and helps governments to form policies that take into account the increasing proportion of older people in the population. The Division implements global and regional mandates, such as the Programme of Action of the World Summit for Social Development and the Jakarta Plan of Action on Human Resources Development. The Biwako Millennium Framework for Action towards an Inclusive, Barrier-free and Rights-based Society for Persons with Disabilities in Asia and the Pacific was adopted by ESCAP as a regional guide-line underpinning the Asian and Pacific Decade of Disabled Persons (2003–12). In 1998 ESCAP initiated a programme of assistance in establishing a regional network of Social Development Management Information Systems (SOMIS). ESCAP collaborated with other agencies towards the adoption, in November 2001, of a Regional Platform on Sustainable Development for Asia and the Pacific. The Commission undertook regional preparations for the World Summit on Sustainable Development, which was held in Johannesburg, South Africa, in August–September 2002. In following-up the summit ESCAP undertook to develop a bio-diversity park, which was officially inaugurated in Rawalpindi, Pakistan, in January 2005. The Commission also prepares specific publications relating to population and implements the Programme of Action of the International Conference on Population and Development. The Secretariat co-ordinates the Asia-Pacific Population Information Network (POPIN). The fifth Asia and Pacific Population Conference, sponsored by ESCAP, was held in Bangkok, Thailand, in December 2002. In September 2004 ESCAP convened a senior-level intergovernmental meeting on the regional review and implementation of the Beijing Platform for Action (Beijing + 10), relating to gender equality.

Environment and Sustainable Development: ESCAP is concerned to strengthen national capabilities to achieve environmentally sound and sustainable development by integrating economic concerns, such as the sustainable management of natural resources, into economic planning and policies. The Environment and Sustainable Development Division comprises sections on Energy Resources, Environment, and Sustainable Development and Water Resources. The Division was responsible for implementation of the Regional Action Programme for Environmentally Sound and Sustainable Development for the period 2001–05. Other activities have included the promotion of integrated water resources development and management, including water quality and conservation and a reduction in water-related natural disasters; strengthening the formulation of policies in the sustainable development of land and mineral resources; and the consideration of energy resource options, such as rural energy supply, energy conservation and the planning of power networks. Through the Division ESCAP prepares a report entitled State of the Environment in Asia and the Pacific which is published at five-yearly intervals, most recently in 2005. Following the massive earthquake and consequent devastating sea movements, or tsunamis, that occurred in late December 2004 in the Indian Ocean, ESCAP assisted other UN and international agencies with an initial emergency response and undertook early reviews of the impact of the event. In January 2005 the Executive Secretary appointed a Task Force on Tsunami Disaster Management to assist countries to address issues relating to natural disaster management, and to raise those issues at a regional level. The chairman of the Task Force was also appointed co-chair of an Inter-Agency Regional Task Force on Tsunami Relief and Rehabilitation that was established at a heads of agency meeting, convened by ESCAP later in that month, with particular responsibility to exchange information relating to rehabilitation and reconstruction in the aftermath of the tsunami disaster and to more general capacity-building on disaster preparedness. At the end of January a ministerial meeting, in Phuket, Thailand, approved the establishment of a regional tsunami early-warning system. ESCAP administers the voluntary, multi-donor Tsunami Regional Trust Fund which was inaugurated in late 2005 to support reconstruction and national and regional efforts to establish the early-warning system. ESCAP helped to organize a ministerial conference on environment and development, which was convened in Seoul, Republic of Korea, in March 2005. Representatives of the 52 countries attending the meeting adopted a Regional Implementation Plan for Sustainable Development in Asia and the Pacific (2006–10) and a Seoul Initiative on Environmentally Sustainable Economic Growth. The Division supports efforts to co-ordinate and monitor implementation of these initiatives. In particular, it received a mandate to work on issues related to climate change caused by global warming: it collates information, conducts regional seminars on adapting to climate change, and provides training in clean technology and guidance on reduction of harmful gas emissions. The inaugural meeting of the Asia-Pacific Regional Platform on Climate Change and Development was organized by ESCAP in March 2008.

Information, Communication and Space Technology: ESCAP's Information, Communication and Space Technology Division comprises the following sections: Information and Communication Technology (ICT) Policy, ICT Applications, and Space Technology Applications. The Division aims to strengthen capacity for access to and the application of ICT and space technology, in order to maximize the benefits of globalization. It supports the development of cross-sectoral policies and strategies, and also supports regional cooperation aimed at sharing knowledge between advanced and developing economies and in areas such as cyber-crime and information security. In May 2005 the Commission approved the establishment, in the Republic of Korea, of the Asian and Pacific Training Centre for ICT for Development (APCICT); APCICT was inaugurated in June 2006 (see below). In June 2005 the Division convened a senior-level meeting of experts to consider technical issues relating to disaster management and mitigation in Asia and the Pacific. The Division organized several conferences in preparation for the second phase of the World Summit on the Information Society (WSIS), which took place in November 2005, and co-ordinates regional activities aimed at achieving WSIS targets for the widespread use of ICT by 2015. During 2007 the Division organized projects and workshops in various countries of the region on the provision of ICT for rural communities, in particular for women entrepreneurs. It helps members to include space technology in their development planning, for example the use of satellites in meteorology, disaster prevention, remote sensing and distance learning. In August 2007 the Division hosted an international meeting on the use of space technology to combat avian influenza and other infectious diseases. A meeting of national policy-makers on disaster management was convened in March 2008 to discuss access to satellite information as a means of predicting and managing natural disasters.

Poverty and Development: The work of the Poverty and Development Division is undertaken by the following sections: Development Policy, Socio-economic Analysis and Poverty Reduction. The Division aims to increase the understanding of the economic and social development situation in the region, with particular attention given to the attainment of the UN Millennium Development Goals (MDGs), sustainable economic growth, poverty alleviation, the integration of environmental concerns into macroeconomic decisions and policy-making processes, and enhancing the position of the region's disadvantaged economies, including those Central Asian countries undergoing transition from a centrally-planned economy to a market economy. The Division is responsible for the provision of technical assistance, and the production of relevant documents and publications. The 63rd Commission, meeting in Almaty, Kazakhstan, in May 2007, endorsed a regional plan, developed by ESCAP, UNDP and the Asian Development Bank, to support poorer member countries to achieve the MDGs. Assistance was to be provided in the following areas: knowledge and capacity-building; expertise; resources; advocacy; and regional co-operation in delivering public goods (including infrastructure and energy security). The Commission also approved a resolution urging greater investment in health care in all member countries.

Statistics: ESCAP's Statistics Division provides training and advice in priority areas, including national accounts statistics, poverty indicators, gender statistics, population censuses and surveys, and the strengthening and management of statistical systems. It supports co-ordination throughout the region of the development, implementation and revision of selected international statistical standards, and, in particular, co-ordinates the International Comparison Programme (ICP) for Asia and the Pacific (part of a global ICP initiative). The Division disseminates comparable socio-economic statistics, with increased use of the electronic media, promotes the use of modern technology in the public sector and trains senior-level officials in the effective management of ICT. Training is provided by the Statistical Institute of Asia and the Pacific (see below).

Trade and Investment: ESCAP aims to help members to benefit from globalization by increasing global and regional flows of trade and investment. Its Trade and Investment Division provides technical assistance and advisory services. It aims to enhance institutional capacity-building; gives special emphasis to the needs of least-developed, land-locked and island developing countries, and to Central Asian countries that are in transition to a market economy, in accelerating their industrial and technological advancement, promoting their exports, and furthering their integration into the region's economy; supports the development of electronic commerce and other information technologies in the region; and promotes the intra-regional and inter-subregional exchange of trade, investment and technology through the strengthening of institutional support services such as regional information networks. The Division functions as the secretariat of the Asia-Pacific Trade Agreement (APTA), concluded in 1975 to promote regional trade through mutually agreed concessions by the participating states (in 2008 they comprised Bangladesh, the People's Republic of China, India, Laos and Sri Lanka). Since 2004 the Division has organized an annual Asia-Pacific Business Forum, involving representatives of governments, the private sector and civil society. It operates the Asia-Pacific Trade and Investment Agreements Database, the Trade and Transport Facilitation Online Database and an on-line Directory of Trade and Investment-Related Organizations, and publishes the Asia-Pacific Trade and Investment Review twice a year. The Division acts as the Secretariat of the Asia-Pacific Research and Training Network on Trade (ARTNeT), established in 2004, which aims to enhance the region's research capacity. ESCAP, with the World Trade Organization (WTO), implements a technical assistance programme, helping member states to implement WTO agreements and to participate in ongoing multilateral trade negotiations.

Transport and Tourism: ESCAP's Transport and Tourism Division aims to improve the regional movement of goods and people, and to strengthen the role of tourism in economic and social development. The Division has three sections: Transport Infrastructure, Transport Facilitation, and Transport Policy and Tourism. Its principal task is the implementation of the Asian Land Transport Infrastructure Development (ALTID) programme, initiated in 1992. ALTID projects include the development of the Trans-Asian Railway and of the Asian Highway road network. Other activities are aimed at improving the planning process in developing infrastructure facilities and services, in accordance with the Regional Action Programme (Phase II, 2002–06) of the New Delhi Action Plan on Infrastructure Development in Asia and the Pacific, which was adopted at a ministerial conference held in October 1996, and at enhancing private sector involvement in national infrastructure development through financing, management, operations and risk-sharing. The Division aims to reduce the adverse environmental impact of the provision of infrastructure facilities and to promote more equitable and easier access to social amenities. A Ministerial Conference on Infrastructure Development was organized by ESCAP in November 2001. An Intergovernmental Agreement on the Asian Highway Network (adopted in 2003, identifying some 141,000 km of roads in 32 countries) came into effect in July 2005. The first meeting of a working group on the highway, which was to convene twice a year, was held in December. By November 2007 about 10,000 km of the highway network had been upgraded to meet the minimum standards set by the Agreement, and in that month an Asian Highway Investment Forum was convened by ESCAP to finance the improvements still required on a further 12,000 km of the network. In November ESCAP organized an intergovernmental meeting to conclude a draft agreement on the establishment of a Trans-Asian Railway Network, comprising some 80,900 km of rail routes. The intergovernmental accord was adopted in April 2006. In 2004 ESCAP and the UN Economic Commission for Europe (ECE) initiated a project for developing Euro-Asian transport linkages, aiming to identify and overcome the principal obstacles (physical and otherwise) along the main transport routes linking Asia and Europe. In November 2003 ESCAP approved a new initiative, the Asia-Pacific Network for Transport and Logistics Education and Research (ANTLER), to comprise education, training and research centres throughout the region. In November 2006 a Ministerial Conference on Transport was held in Busan, Republic of Korea. The Busan Declaration, adopted by the meeting, outlined a long-term development strategy for regional transport and identified investment priorities. The meeting also adopted a Ministerial Declaration on Road Safety which pledged to implement safety measures to save some 600,000 lives in the region in the period 2007–15. Tourism concerns include the development of human resources, improved policy planning for tourism development, greater investment in the industry, and minimizing the environmental impact of tourism. A Plan of Action for Sustainable Tourism in the Asia and Pacific Region (1999–2005) was adopted in April 1999, and a second phase of the Plan was to cover the period 2006–12. A Network of Asia-Pacific Education and Training Institutes in Tourism, established in 1997, comprised 211 institutes and organizations in 2008. Throughout all its activities the Division devotes particular attention to the needs and concerns of least-developed, land-locked and island developing nations, and economies in transition in the region.

CO-OPERATION WITH OTHER ORGANIZATIONS

ESCAP works with other UN agencies and non-UN international organizations, non-governmental organizations, academic institutions and the private sector; such co-operation includes joint planning of programmes, preparation of studies and reports, participating in meetings, and sharing information and technical expertise. In July 1993 a memorandum of understanding (MOU) was signed by ESCAP and the Asian Development Bank, outlining priority areas of co-operation between the two organizations. These were: regional and sub-regional co-operation; issues concerning the least-developed, land-locked and island developing member countries; poverty alleviation; women in development; population; human resource development; the environment and natural resource management; statistics and data bases; economic analysis; transport and communications; and industrial restructuring and privatization. The two organizations were to co-operate in organizing workshops, seminars and conferences, in implementing joint projects, and in exchanging information and data on a regular basis. A new MOU between the two organizations was signed in May 2004 with an emphasis on achieving poverty reduction throughout the region. In 2001 ESCAP, with the Bank and UNDP, established a regional partnership to promote the MDGs (see above); a joint regional report on implementation of the goals was prepared by the partnership and published in June 2005 prior to a global review, conducted at the UN General Assembly in September, and a further regional review was published in 2007. In May 2007 ESCAP endorsed a regional plan developed by the partnership with the aim of addressing regional challenges (in particular those faced by poorer countries) to the achievement of the MDGs. The UN Special Programme for the Economies of Central Asia (SPECA), begun in 1998, is implemented jointly by ESCAP and ECE: SPECA helps the participating countries to strengthen regional co-operation, particularly in the areas of water resources, energy and transport, and creates incentives for economic development and integration into the economies of Asia and Europe. In May 2007 ESCAP signed an MOU with ECE and the Eurasian Economic Community to strengthen co-operation in sustainable development, in support of the MDGs. In the following month ESCAP signed an MOU with the International Organization for Migration to provide for greater co-operation and co-ordination on international migration issues.

REGIONAL INSTITUTIONS

Asian and Pacific Centre for Agricultural Engineering and Machinery (APCAEM): A-7/F, China International Science and Technology Convention Centre, 12 Yumin Rd, Chaoyang District, Beijing 100029, People's Republic of China; tel. (10) 8225-3581; fax (10) 8225-3584; e-mail info@unapcaem.org; internet www.unapcaem.org; f. 1977 as Regional Network for Agricultural Engineering and Machinery, elevated to regional centre in 2002; aims to reduce poverty by enhancing environmentally sustainable agriculture and food production, applying 'green' and modern agro-technology for the well-being of producers, and consumers; work programmes comprise agricultural engineering, food chain management, and agro-enterprise development and trade; undertakes research, training, technical assistance and the exchange of information. Active mems: Bangladesh, People's Republic of China, Democratic People's Republic of Korea, Fiji, India, Indonesia, Iran, Mongolia, Nepal, Pakistan, Philippines, Republic of Korea, Sri Lanka, Thailand, Viet Nam; Dir Dr JOONG-WAN CHO; *APCAEM Policy Brief* (quarterly).

Asian and Pacific Centre for Transfer of Technology: APCTT Bldg, POB 4575, C-2 Qutab Institutional Area, New Delhi 110 016, India; tel. (11) 26966509; fax (11) 26856274; e-mail postmaster@apctt.org; internet www.apctt.org; f. 1977 to assist countries of the ESCAP region by strengthening their capacity to develop, transfer and adopt technologies relevant to the region, and to identify and promote regional technology development and transfer; operates Business Asia Network (www.business-asia.net) to promote technology-based co-operation, particularly between small and medium-sized enterprises; Dir Dr KRISHNAMURTHY RAMANATHAN; publs *Asia Pacific Tech Monitor*, *VATIS Updates on Biotechnology*, *Food Processing*, *Ozone Layer Protection*, *Non-Conventional Energy*, and *Waste Management* (each every 2 months).

Asian and Pacific Training Centre for ICT for Development (APCICT): Bonbudong, 3rd Floor Songdo Techno Park, 7-50 Songdo-dong, Yeonsu-gu, Incheon City, Republic of Korea; tel. 245-1700; fax 245-7712; e-mail staff@unapcict.org; internet www.unescap.org/icstd/applications/apcict.asp; f. 2006 to provide training to ICT policy-makers and professionals, advisory services and analytical studies, to promote best practices in the field of ICT, and to contribute to narrowing the digital divide in the region; Dir HYUEN-SUK RHEE.

INTERNATIONAL ORGANIZATIONS

Centre for Alleviation of Poverty through Secondary Crops' Development in Asia and the Pacific (CAPSA): Jalan Merdeka 145, Bogor 16111, Indonesia; tel. (251) 343277; fax (251) 336290; e-mail capsa@uncapsa.org; internet www.uncapsa.org; f. 1981 as CGPRT Centre, current name adopted April 2004; initiates and promotes socio-economic and policy research, training, dissemination of information and advisory services to enhance the living conditions of rural poor populations reliant on secondary crop agriculture; Dir Dr TACO BOTTEMA (Netherlands); publs *CAPSA Flash* (monthly), *Palawija News* (3 a year), working paper series, monograph series and statistical profiles.

Statistical Institute for Asia and the Pacific (SIAP): JETRO-IDE Building, 2–2 Wakaba 3-chome, Mihama-ku, Chiba-shi, Chiba 2618787, Japan; tel. (43) 2999782; fax (43) 2999780; e-mail staff@unsiap.or.jp; internet www.unsiap.or.jp; f. 1970 as Asian Statistical Institute, present name 1977; became a subsidiary body of ESCAP in 1995; trains government statisticians at the Institute and in various co-operating countries in Asia and the Pacific; prepares teaching materials, assists in the development of training on official statistics in national and sub-regional centres; Dir DAVAASUREN CHULTEM-JAMTS (Mongolia); publ. *SIAP Newsletter* (annually).

ASSOCIATED BODIES

ESCAP/WMO Typhoon Committee: PAGASA, 4th Floor, Science Garden, Agham Rd, Diliman, Quezon City, Philippines; tel. and fax (632) 4349026; e-mail tcs@philonline.com; internet www.tcsphilippines.org; f. 1968; an intergovernmental body sponsored by ESCAP and the World Meteorological Organization for mitigation of typhoon damage; aims to establish efficient typhoon and flood warning systems through improved meteorological and telecommunication facilities; promotes disaster preparedness, trains personnel and co-ordinates research. The committee's programme is supported from national resources and also by UNDP and other international and bilateral assistance. Mems: Cambodia, People's Republic of China, Hong Kong, Japan, Democratic People's Republic of Korea, Republic of Korea, Laos, Macao, Malaysia, Philippines, Singapore, Thailand, USA, Viet Nam; Co-ordinator Dr ROMAN L. KINTANAR.

WMO/ESCAP Panel on Tropical Cyclones: Technical Support Unit (TSU), c/o Pakistan Meteorological Dept, POB 1214, H-8/2, Islamabad, Pakistan; tel. (51) 9257314; fax (51) 4432588; e-mail tsupmd@hotmail.com; internet www.tsuptc-wmo.org; f. 1972 to mitigate damage caused by tropical cyclones in the Bay of Bengal and the Arabian Sea. Mems: Bangladesh, India, the Maldives, Myanmar, Oman, Pakistan, Sri Lanka, Thailand; TSU Co-ordinator Dr QAMAR-UZ-ZAMAN CHAUDHRY.

United Nations (Regional Commissions)

Finance

For the two-year period 2006–07 ESCAP's programme budget, an appropriation from the UN budget, was US $71.9m. The regular budget is supplemented annually by funds from various sources for technical assistance.

Publications

Annual Report.
Asia-Pacific Development Journal (2 a year).
Asia-Pacific in Figures (annually).
Asia-Pacific Population Journal (3 a year).
Asia-Pacific Trade and Investment Review (2 a year).
Bulletin on Asia-Pacific Perspectives (annually).
Economic and Social Survey of Asia and the Pacific (annually).
Environment and Sustainable Development News (quarterly).
ESCAP Energy News (2 a year).
ESCAP Human Resources Development Newsletter (2 a year).
ESCAP Population Data Sheet (annually).
ESCAP Tourism Review (annually).
Foreign Trade Statistics of Asia and the Pacific (every 2 years).
Key Economic Developments and Prospects in the Asia-Pacific Region (annually).
Population Headliners (several a year).
Poverty Alleviation Initiatives (quarterly).
Socio-Economic Policy Brief (several a year).
State of the Environment in Asia and the Pacific (every 5 years).
Statistical Indicators for Asia and the Pacific (quarterly).
Statistical Newsletter (quarterly).
Statistical Yearbook for Asia and the Pacific.
Technical Co-operation Yearbook.
Trade and Investment Information Bulletin (monthly).
Transport and Communications Bulletin for Asia and the Pacific (annually).
Water Resources Journal (annually).
Manuals; country and trade profiles; commodity prices; statistics; Atlas of Mineral Resources of the ESCAP Region (country by country)

Economic Commission for Latin America and the Caribbean—ECLAC

Address: Edif. Naciones Unidas, Avda Dag Hammarskjöld 3477, Vitacura, Casilla 179D, Santiago, Chile.
Telephone: (2) 2102000; **fax:** (2) 2080252; **e-mail:** secepal@eclac.cl; **internet:** www.eclac.org.

The UN Economic Commission for Latin America was founded by the UN Economic and Social Council (ECOSOC) in 1948 to co-ordinate policies for the promotion of economic development in the Latin American region. The current name of the Commission was adopted in 1984.

MEMBERS

Antigua and Barbuda	El Salvador	Peru
Argentina	France	Portugal
Bahamas	Germany	Saint Christopher and Nevis
Barbados	Grenada	Saint Lucia
Belize	Guatemala	Saint Vincent and the Grenadines
Bolivia	Guyana	Spain
Brazil	Haiti	Suriname
Canada	Honduras	Trinidad and Tobago
Chile	Italy	United Kingdom
Colombia	Jamaica	USA
Costa Rica	Japan	Uruguay
Cuba	Korea, Republic	Venezuela
Dominica	Mexico	
Dominican Republic	Netherlands	
Ecuador	Nicaragua	
	Panama	
	Paraguay	

ASSOCIATE MEMBERS

Anguilla	Montserrat	Turks and Caicos
Aruba	Netherlands Antilles	United States
British Virgin Islands	Puerto Rico	Virgin Islands

Organization

(March 2008)

COMMISSION

The Commission normally meets every two years at ministerial level in one of the regional capitals. The 31st session was held in Montevideo, Uruguay, in March 2006 and the 32nd session was scheduled to be held in Santo Domingo, Dominican Republic, in 2008. The Commission has established the following permanent bodies:

Caribbean Development and Co-operation Committee;
Committee on South-South Co-operation;
Regional Conference on Women;
Regional Council for Planning of ILPES (see below);
Statistical Conference of the Americas.

SECRETARIAT

The Secretariat employs more than 500 staff and is headed by the Offices of the Executive Secretary and of the Secretary of the Commission. ECLAC's work programme is carried out by the following divisions: Economic Development (including a Development Studies Unit); Economic and Social Planning (ILPES, see below); International Trade and Integration; Natural Resources and Infrastructure (including a Transport Unit); Population (CELADE, see below); Production, Productivity and Management (including an Agricultural Development Unit, a joint ECLA/UNIDO Industrial and Technological Development Unit and a Unit on Investment and Corporate Strategies); Social Development; Statistics and Economic Projections; Sustainable Development and Human Settlements; and Women and Development. There are also units for information and conference services, and special studies, an electronic information section, and support divisions of administration, of documents and publications, and of programme planning and management.

Executive Secretary: JOSÉ LUIS MACHINEA.

SUB-REGIONAL OFFICES

Caribbean: 1 Chancery Lane, POB 1113, Port of Spain, Trinidad and Tobago; tel. 623-5595; fax 623-8485; e-mail neil.pierre@cepal.org; internet www.eclacpos.org; f. 1956; covers non-Spanish-speaking Caribbean countries; functions as the secretariat for the Caribbean Development and Co-operation Committee; Dir NEIL PIERRE.

Central America and Spanish-speaking Caribbean: Avda Presidente Masaryk 29, Apdo Postal 6-718, 11570 México, DF; tel. (55) 5250-1555; fax (55) 5531-1151; e-mail jorge.matter@cepal.org; internet www.eclac.org.mx; f. 1951; covers Central America and Spanish-speaking Caribbean countries; Officer-in-Charge JORGE MÁTTAR.

There are also national offices, in Buenos Aires, Argentina; Brasilia, Brazil; Bogota, Colombia; and Montevideo, Uruguay, and a liaison office in Washington, DC.

Activities

ECLAC collaborates with regional governments in the investigation and analysis of regional and national economic problems, and provides guidance in the formulation of development plans. The activities of its different divisions include research, monitoring of trends and policies, and comparative studies; analysis; publication of information; provision of technical assistance; organizing and participating in workshops, seminars and conferences; training courses; and co-operation with national, regional and international organizations, including non-governmental organizations and the private sector. In April 1996 the Commission, meeting in San Jose, Costa Rica, considered means of strengthening the economic and social development of the region, within the framework of a document prepared by ECLAC's Secretariat, and adopted a resolution which defined ECLAC as a centre of excellence, charged with undertaking an analysis of specific aspects of the development process, in collaboration with member governments. The 27th session of the Commission, held in Oranjestad, Aruba, in May 1998, approved the ongoing reform programme, and in particular efforts to enhance the effectiveness and transparency of ECLAC's activities. ECLAC's 28th session, convened in Mexico City in April 2000, debated a document prepared by the Secretariat which proposed that the pursuit of social equity, sustainable development and 'active citizenship' (with emphasis on the roles of education and employment) should form the basis of future policy-making in the region. ECLAC's 29th session, which was held in Brasilia, Brazil, in May 2002, focused on the process of globalization. The meeting adopted the Brasilia Resolution, which outlined a strategic agenda to meet the challenges of globalization. Proposed action included the consolidation of democracy, strengthening social protection, the formulation of policies to reduce macroeconomic and financial vulnerability, and the development of sustainable and systemic competitiveness. The objectives of the agenda were to achieve a guaranteed supply of general public goods, to overcome, steadily, the imbalances in the world order, and to build, gradually, an international social agenda based on rights. The Resolution requested that ECLAC strengthen its work in the relevant areas. The 30th session was held in June–July 2004 in San Juan, Puerto Rico. Among the issues discussed were proposals in a new ECLAC study entitled Productive Development in Open Economies, and activities to be undertaken, with UNESCO, to promote education in the region. The Commission's 31st session, convened in March 2006, in Montevideo, Uruguay, approved the proposals outlined in a document entitled 'Shaping the Future of Social Protection', which addressed social conditions in member countries. A new work programme for ECLAC, covering the period 2008–09, was adopted by the 31st session; it focused on a number of regional priorities, including: consolidating macroeconomic stability, improving integration into the global economy, increasing social cohesion, and developing sustainable development policies. The session also adopted a resolution supporting the UN Stabilization Mission in Haiti and recognizing efforts undertaken by the Commission on behalf of the Mission.

ECLAC works closely with other agencies within the UN system and with other regional and multinational organizations. ECLAC co-operated with the Organization of American States (OAS) and the Inter-American Development Bank in the servicing of intergovernmental groups undertaking preparatory work for the establishment of a Free Trade Area of the Americas (FTAA). ECLAC also supports member countries in negotiations of bilateral or sub-regional free-trade agreements, in particular with the USA. In January 2002 ECLAC hosted an Interregional Conference on Financing for Development, held in Mexico City, which it had organized as part of the negotiating process prior to the World Summit on Financing for Development, held in March. In June senior representatives of ECLAC, UNDP, the World Bank and the Inter-American Development Bank agreed to co-ordinate activities in pursuit of the development goals proclaimed by the so-called Millennium Summit meeting of the UN General Assembly in September 2000. ECLAC was to adapt the objectives of the goals to the reality of countries in the region. In July 2004 the 30th session of the Commission approved the establishment of an intergovernmental forum to monitor the implementation of decisions emerging from the World Summit on Sustainable Development, held in Johannesburg, South Africa, in September 2002. In January 2006 ECLAC organized the first Regional Implementation Forum on Sustainable Development, as mandated by the UN Commission on Sustainable Development. ECLAC provides regional support to the UN Information and Communication Technologies Task Force, which was established in November 2001. A working meeting on the establishment of a regional network under the Task Force, in order to plan and monitor the development of digital technology in the region, was held in June 2002. In January 2003 a regional conference was convened, in the Dominican Republic, in preparation for the World Summit on the Information Society (WSIS), the first phase of which was held in December, in Geneva, Switzerland. In July 2004 delegates to the 30th session of the Commission requested that ECLAC co-ordinate a regional preparatory meeting to define objectives and proposals for the second phase of the Summit in 2005. The regional ministerial meeting was convened in Rio de Janeiro, Brazil, in June 2005, and a Regional Action Plan, eLAC 2007, was approved, for which ECLAC was to be the Technical Secretariat; eLAC supports national and regional projects that incorporate information and communications technology for use in economic and social development in the region. A second plan, eLAC 2010, was adopted by ministers in February 2008. In November 2003 ECLAC launched REDESA, a web-based network of institutions and experts in social and environmental statistics. The first phase of a Macroeconomic Dialogue Network (REDIMA I) was established in 2003, to assist communication on macroeconomic issues between economists from the region's central banks and ministries of finance: a second phase, REDIMA II, was initiated in 2005. In July 2007 ECLAC organized the fourth Statistical Conference of the Americas, which is convened every two years to promote the development and improvement of national statistics (in particular their comparability), and to encourage co-operation between national statistical offices and regional and international organizations: the fourth Conference discussed the monitoring of progress towards the UN's Millennium Development Goals in the region, and preparations for the 2010 round of national population censuses. ECLAC organizes an annual competition to encourage small-scale innovative social projects in local communities.

In July 2006 Japan became the first Asian nation to be granted full membership of ECLAC. The membership of the Republic of Korea was formally approved in July 2007.

Latin American and Caribbean Institute for Economic and Social Planning (Instituto Latinoamericano y del Caribe de Planificacion Economica y Social—ILPES): Edif. Naciones Unidas, Avda Dag Hammarskjöld 3477, Vitacura, Casilla 179d, Santiago, Chile; tel. (2) 2102000; fax (2) 2060252; e-mail secretaria.se@cepal.org; internet www.eclac.org/ilpes/; f. 1962; supports regional governments through the provision of training, advisory services and research in the field of public planning policy and co-ordination; Dir JUAN CARLOS RAMIREZ.

Latin American Demographic Centre (Centro Latinoamericano y Caribeno de Demografia—CELADE): Edif. Naciones Unidas, Avda Dag Hammarskjöld 3477, Casilla 179D, Santiago, Chile; tel. (2) 2102000; fax (2) 2080252; e-mail celade@eclac.cl; internet www.eclac.org/celade; f. 1957, became an autonomous entity within ECLAC in 1971 and was fully incorporated into ECLAC as its Population Division in 1997; provides technical assistance to governments, universities and research centres in demographic analysis, population policies, integration of population factors in development planning, and data processing; conducts courses on demographic analysis for development and various national and

INTERNATIONAL ORGANIZATIONS

regional seminars; provides demographic estimates and projections, documentation, data processing, computer packages and training; Dir DIRK JASPERS-FAIJER.

Finance

For the two-year period 2006–07 ECLAC's proposed regular budget, an appropriation from the UN, amounted to US $97.2m. In addition, extra-budgetary activities are financed by governments, other organizations, and UN agencies, including UNDP, UNFPA and UNICEF.

Publications

(in English and Spanish)

CEPAL Review (3 a year).
Demographic Observatory (2 a year).
ECLAC Notes (every 2 months).
Economic Survey of Latin America and the Caribbean (annually).
FAL Bulletin (Trade Facilitation and Transport in Latin America (monthly).
Foreign Investment in Latin America and the Caribbean (annually).
Latin America and the Caribbean in the World Economy (annually).
Notas de Población (2 a year).
Preliminary Overview of the Economies of Latin America and the Caribbean (annually).
Social Panorama of Latin America (annually).
Statistical Yearbook for Latin America and the Caribbean.
Water Resources Newsletter (2 a year).
Studies, reports, bibliographical bulletins.

Economic Commission for Africa—ECA

Address: Menelik II Ave, POB 3001, Addis Ababa, Ethiopia.
Telephone: (11) 5517200; **fax:** (11) 5514416; **e-mail:** ecainfo@uneca.org; **internet:** www.uneca.org.

The UN Economic Commission for Africa (ECA) was founded in 1958 by a resolution of the UN Economic and Social Council (ECOSOC) to initiate and take part in measures for facilitating Africa's economic development.

MEMBERS

Algeria	Eritrea	Niger
Angola	Ethiopia	Nigeria
Benin	Gabon	Rwanda
Botswana	The Gambia	São Tomé and
Burkina Faso	Ghana	Príncipe
Burundi	Guinea	Senegal
Cameroon	Guinea-Bissau	Seychelles
Cape Verde	Kenya	Sierra Leone
Central African	Lesotho	Somalia
Republic	Liberia	South Africa
Chad	Libya	Sudan
Comoros	Madagascar	Swaziland
Congo, Democratic	Malawi	Tanzania
Republic	Mali	Togo
Congo, Republic	Mauritania	Tunisia
Côte d'Ivoire	Mauritius	Uganda
Djibouti	Morocco	Zambia
Egypt	Mozambique	Zimbabwe
Equatorial Guinea	Namibia	

Organization

(March 2008)

COMMISSION

The Commission may only act with the agreement of the government of the country concerned. It is also empowered to make recommendations on any matter within its competence directly to the government of the member or associate member concerned, to governments admitted in a consultative capacity, and to the UN Specialized Agencies. The Commission is required to submit for prior consideration by ECOSOC any of its proposals for actions that would be likely to have important effects on the international economy.

CONFERENCE OF AFRICAN MINISTERS

The Conference, which meets every year, is attended by ministers responsible for finance, planning and economic development, representing the governments of member states, and is the main deliberative body of the Commission. The Commission's responsibility to promote concerted action for the economic and social development of Africa is vested primarily in the Conference, which considers matters of general policy and the priorities to be assigned to the Commission's programmes, considers inter-African and international economic policy, and makes recommendations to member states in connection with such matters.

OTHER POLICY-MAKING BODIES

Five intergovernmental committees of experts attached to the Sub-regional Offices (see below) meet annually and report to the Commission through a Technical Preparatory Committee of the Whole, which was established in 1979 to deal with matters submitted for the consideration of the Conference.

Seven other committees meet regularly to consider issues relating to the following policy areas: women and development; development information; sustainable development; human development and civil society; industry and private sector development; natural resources and science and technology; and regional co-operation and integration.

SECRETARIAT

The Secretariat provides the services necessary for the meeting of the Conference of Ministers and the meetings of the Commission's subsidiary bodies, carries out the resolutions and implements the programmes adopted there. It comprises the Office of the Executive Secretary and the following divisions: Food Security and Sustainable Development; Governance and Public Administration; ICT, Science and Technology; NEPAD and Regional Integration; Trade, Finance and Economic Development; the African Centre for Gender and Social Development; and the African Centre for Statistics.

Executive Secretary: ABDOULIE JANNEH (The Gambia).

SUB-REGIONAL OFFICES

The Sub-regional Offices (SROs) aim to enable member states to play a more effective role in the process of African integration and to facilitate the integration efforts of the other UN agencies active in the sub-regions. In addition, the SROs act as the operational arms of ECA at national and sub-regional levels with a view to: ensuring harmony between the objectives of sub-regional and regional programmes and those defined by the Commission; providing advisory services; facilitating sub-regional economic co-operation, integration and development; collecting and disseminating information; stimulating policy dialogue; and promoting gender issues. Under the radical restructuring of the ECA, completed in 2006, the SROs were given an enhanced role in shaping the Commission's agenda and programme implementation, and were also designated as privileged partners of the regional economic communities. (The following five of Africa's regional economic communities are regarded as the pillars of the envisaged African Economic Community: the Common Market for Eastern and Southern Africa—COMESA, the Communauté économique des états de l'Afrique centrale—CEEAC, the Economic Community of West African States—ECOWAS, the Southern African Development Community—SADC, and the Union of the Arab Maghreb.)

Central Africa: POB 14935, Yaoundé, Cameroon; tel. 23-14-61; fax 23-31-85; e-mail srdc@camnet.org; Officer-in-Charge HACHIM KOUMARÉ.

East Africa: POB 4654, Kigali, Rwanda; tel. 586549; fax 586546; e-mail mdiouf@uneca.org; Dir MBAYE DIOUF.

North Africa: 22 rue Jabal Al Ayachi, POB 827, Méchouar-Rabat, Morocco; tel. (3) 767-45-95; fax (3) 767-52-82; e-mail srdc-na@uneca.org; internet www.uneca-na.org; Dir KARIMA BOUNEMRA BEN SOLTANE.

Southern Africa: POB 30647, Lusaka, Zambia; tel. (1) 231062; fax (1) 236949; e-mail uneca@zamnet.zm; internet www.uneca.org/eca-sa; Officer-in-Charge JENNIFER KARGBO.

West Africa: POB 744, Niamey, Niger; tel. 72-29-61; fax 72-28-94; e-mail srdcwest@eca.ne; Dir HALIDOU OUEDRAOGO.

Activities

The Commission's activities are designed to encourage sustainable socio-economic development in Africa and to increase economic co-operation among African countries and between Africa and other parts of the world. The Secretariat has been guided in its efforts by major regional strategies, including the Abuja Treaty on the establishment of an African Economic Community, signed under the aegis of the Organization of African Unity (OAU, now African Union—AU) in 1991, the UN System-wide Special Initiative on Africa (launched in 1996, see below), and the UN New Agenda for the Development of Africa, which covered the period 1991–2000. In 2006 the Executive Secretary of ECA appointed a Task Force to assist with reorganizing the Commission, with a view to better supporting efforts to advance development in Africa, and also to address means of strengthening ECA's presence at sub-regional level and to examine the Commission's partnership with other regional stakeholders. A radical restructuring of ECA's divisions was implemented in that year, with more emphasis to be placed on knowledge generation and networking; advocacy; and advisory services and technical co-operation. The two main aims of ECA's work programme for 2007–09 were: promoting regional integration in support of the AU's vision and priorities; and meeting Africa's special needs and the emerging global challenges. Within these two areas, the Commission was to focus on the following: regional integration, infrastructure and trade; meeting the UN's Millennium Development Goals (MDGs), with a special emphasis on poverty reduction and growth, sustainable development and gender; promoting good governance and popular participation; information and communications technology (ICT) and science and technology for development; and statistics and statistical development. A particular priority over the three-year period was to support and build the capacity of the regional economic communities to implement programmes under the New Partnership for Africa's Development (NEPAD), which was established by the AU in 2001. ECA planned to strengthen its collaboration with the NEPAD secretariat, with the AU and with the African Development Bank during 2007–09.

ICT, SCIENCE AND TECHNOLOGY

The ICT (Information and Communications Technology), Science and Technology Division has responsibility for co-ordinating the implementation of the Harnessing Information Technology for Africa project (in the context of the UN System-wide Special Initiative on Africa) and for implementing the African Information Society Initiative (AISI), which was started in 1996 to support the creation of an African information and communications infrastructure. ECA is responsible for overseeing quality enhancement and dissemination of statistical databases; for improving access to information by means of enhanced library and documentation services and output; and for strengthening geo-information systems for sustainable development. In addition, ECA encourages member governments to liberalize the telecommunications sector and stimulate imports of computers in order to enable the expansion of information technology throughout Africa. ECA manages the Information Technology Centre for Africa (see below). The Commission administers the Partnership for Information and Communication Technologies in Africa (PICTA), which was established in 1999 as an informal grouping of donors and agencies concerned with developing an information society in Africa. ECA provided institutional and logistical support to an African Ministerial Committee which was established in April 2004 to consider proposals of the first phase of the World Summit on Information Society (WSIS), convened in December 2003. ECA co-ordinated preparations for the African Regional Preparatory Conference in February 2005 for the second phase of the WSIS, which was convened in Tunis, Tunisia, in November of the same year. In 1999 ECA's Committee on Development Information established the African Virtual Library and Information Network (AVLIN) as a hub for the exchange of data among African researchers and policy-makers. In August 2000 ECA launched the Africa Knowledge Networks Forum (AKNF). The Forum, to be convened on an annual basis under ECA auspices, was to facilitate co-operation in information-sharing and research between professional research and development networks, and also between these and policy-makers, educators, civil society organizations and the private sector. It was to provide technical support to the African Development Forum (see below). In May 2003 the Committee on Development Information, convened to address the theme 'Information for Governance', urged governments to make consistent use of information systems in decision-making and in the decentralization of services and resources. During that month ECA launched the e-Policy Resource Network for Africa, under the Global e-Policy Resource Network initiative aimed at expanding the use and benefits of information and communication technologies. In August 2007 ECA and the World Health Organization (WHO) commissioned, within the framework of the AISI, a joint regional needs assessment and study in respect of WHO's Africa Health Infoway (AHI) programme, which supports the collection of sub-national health data and statistics for analysis, dissemination and use to support decision-making in the health sector, and aims to strengthen the capacity of African countries in using information in decision-making. An ICT Forum was organized by ECA in February 2008 to encourage investment in the ICT sector in Africa. The ECA Science and Technology Network (ESTNET) provides an information service on science and technology for African policy-makers and others. In March 2008 ECA organized a conference entitled Science with Africa to link African science-based organizations and businesses with their global counterparts.

GOVERNANCE AND PUBLIC ADMINISTRATION

The role of ECA's Governance and Public Administration Division is to improve member states' capacity for good governance and development management. The Division provides support for the African Peer Review Mechanism, a NEPAD initiative whereby participating member governments mutually assess compliance with a number of codes, standards and commitments that uphold good governance and sustainable development. The Division also helps civil society organizations to participate in governance; supports the development of private-sector enterprises; and helps to improve public administration in member states. To achieve these aims the Division provides technical assistance and advisory services, conducts studies, and organizes training workshops, seminars and conferences at national, sub-regional and regional levels for ministers, public administrators and senior policy-makers, as well as for private and non-governmental organizations. In October 1999 the first African Development Forum (ADF) was held in Addis Ababa, Ethiopia. The ADF process was initiated by ECA to formulate an agenda for effective, sustainable development in African countries through dialogue and partnership between governments, academics, the private sector, donor agencies, etc. It was intended that regular ADF meetings would consider a specific development issue. The first Forum was convened on the theme 'The Challenge to Africa of Globalization and the Information Age'. It reviewed the AISI (see above) and formulated country action plans and work programmes. The second ADF, convened in October 2000 on the theme 'AIDS: the Greatest Leadership Challenge', addressed the impact on Africa of the HIV/AIDS epidemic and issued a Consensus and Plan of Action. The third ADF, held in March 2002, addressed the theme 'Defining Priorities for Regional Integration'. ADF IV took place in October 2004 with the theme of 'Governance for a Progressing Africa'. ADF V, convened in November 2006, adopted a Consensus Document, which included proposals for launching an African Youth Volunteer Corps to encourage skills development and to address manpower shortages, and an African Youth Exchange Programme to promote the idea of citizenship and a common identity. In 1997 ECA, jointly with UNDP, hosted the first of a series of meetings on good governance, in the context of the UN System-wide Special Initiative on Africa. The second African Governance Forum (AGF II) was held in Accra, Ghana, in June 1998. The Forum focused on accountability and transparency, which participants agreed were essential elements in promoting development in Africa and should involve commitment from both governments and civil organizations. AGF III was convened in June 1999 in Bamako, Mali, to consider issues relating to conflict prevention, management and governance. The fourth AGF, which took place in Kampala, Uganda, in September 2000, focused on parliamentary processes and their role in consolidating good governance on the continent. AGF V, addressing the role of local government in reducing poverty in Africa, was held in Maputo, Mozambique, in May 2002. The sixth AGF was held in Kigali, Rwanda, in April 2006, and focused on NEPAD's implementation of the African Peer Review Mechanism. AGF VII was convened in Ouagadougou, Burkina Faso, in October 2007, on the theme 'Building the Capable State in Africa'. In 2005 the first African Governance Report was published by ECA, monitoring progress towards good governance in 27 countries; a second report, covering 40 countries, was due to be published in 2008.

AFRICAN CENTRE FOR GENDER AND SOCIAL DEVELOPMENT

ECA aims to improve the socio-economic prospects of women through the promotion of equal access to resources and opportunities, and equal participation in decision-making. An African Centre for Gender and Development (renamed as above in 2006) was established in 1975 to service all national, sub-regional and regional bodies involved in development issues relating to gender and the advancement of women. The Centre manages the African Women's Development Fund, which was established in June 2000. The preliminary results of a new African Gender and Development Index were presented in January 2005, measuring how far member states had met their commitments towards international agreements on gender equality and women's advancement. A Commission on HIV/AIDS and Governance in Africa, with its secretariat based at ECA headquarters, was launched in September 2003. The Commission, an initiative of the UN Secretary-General, was mandated to assess the impact of the HIV/AIDS pandemic on national structures and African economic development and to incorporate its findings in a Final Report; this was issued in October 2005.

FOOD SECURITY AND SUSTAINABLE DEVELOPMENT

ECA's Food Security and Sustainable Development Division aims to strengthen the capacity of member countries to design institutional structures and implement policies and programmes, in areas such as food production, population, environment and human settlements, to achieve sustainable development. It also promotes the use of science and technology in achieving sustainable development. In 1995 ECA published its first comprehensive report and statistical survey of human development issues in African countries. The Human Development in Africa Report, which was to be published every two years, aimed to demonstrate levels of development attained, particularly in the education and child health sectors, to identify areas of concern and to encourage further action by policy-makers and development experts. Other reports and surveys monitor, review and disseminate information regarding development research and activities. ECA promotes food security in African countries through raising awareness of the relationship between population, food security, the environment and sustainable development; encouraging the advancement of science and technology in member states; and providing policy analysis support and technical advisory services. The strengthening of national population policies forms an important element of ECA's objective of ensuring food security in African countries. Population Information Africa (POPIA) was established in 1999 as an on-line resource to provide information for policy-makers, planners and researchers on matters related to population. From 2005 ECA increased its work devoted to the changes in climate caused by global warming, and the resulting threat posed by drought, floods and other extreme events. In 2006, with the AU and the African Development Bank, it established a 10-year Climate for Development in Africa Programme (Clim-Dev Africa) to improve the collection of climate-related data and assist in forecasting and risk management. ECA provides the technical secretariat for Clim-Dev Africa. In December 2007 ECA announced the establishment of an African Centre for Climate Policy Studies, to help member states to incorporate climate-related concerns in their development policies so as to counter the impact of climate change.

STATISTICS

The African Centre for Statistics was established in 2006 as a new division of ECA, to encourage the use of statistics in national planning, to provide training and technical assistance for the compilation, analysis and dissemination of statistics, and to prepare members for the 2010 round of population censuses. The Advisory Board on Statistics in Africa, which was inaugurated in 2004 and comprises 15 experts from national statistical offices, sub-regional bodies and training institutes, meets annually to advise ECA on statistical developments in Africa and guide its activities. The Statistical Commission for Africa (StatCom-Africa), comprising representatives of national statistical offices, regional and international institutions and development partners, met for the first time in January 2008: it was to meet every two years as the principal body overseeing statistical development in Africa, with annual working groups monitoring progress and deciding on activities. ECA assists its member states in population data collection and data processing; analysis of demographic data obtained from censuses or surveys; training demographers at the Regional Institute for Population Studies (RIPS) in Accra, Ghana, and at the Institut de formation et de recherche demographiques (IFORD) in Yaounde, Cameroon; formulation of population policies and integrating population variables in development planning, through advisory missions and through the organization of national seminars on population and development; and dissemination of demographic information.

TRADE, FINANCE AND ECONOMIC DEVELOPMENT DIVISION

ECA's Trade, Finance and Economic Development Division, established in 2006, is concerned with issues relating to macroeconomic analysis, and also deals with international trade, international trade negotiations, finance and financial sector policies, debt, aid, investment, and industrial policies. The Division comprises: the Financing Development Section, the Industry and Sectoral Policies Section, the Macroeconomic Analysis Section, the Trade and International Negotiations Section, and the African Trade Policy Centre (ATPC). The Financing Development Section is responsible for researching and analysing challenges in the area of development finance relating to the attainment of sustained growth and poverty reduction. The Section provides support to member states, regional and national institutions, academics, and private-sector and civil society interests, and also engages in policy advocacy work. Principal focus areas are: foreign aid, debt, private capital flows, and savings and remittances. The Section produces publications and provides training, seminars and workshops. The Industry and Sectoral Policies Section assists African countries to formulate and implement effective industrial policies, strategies and programmes aimed at enhancing their competitiveness in the global production system. The Section undertakes policy research and outreach activities and aims to improve the access of local policy researchers to analytical tools and information. The Macroeconomic Analysis Section assists member states to improve their capacity to formulate, implement and monitor sound macroeconomic policies and better institutional frameworks, with a view to achieving sustainable development. The Section also focuses on policy advocacy and collaboration with development organizations and institutions, produces publications and provides training, conferences and workshops. It undertakes macroeconomic research and policy analysis in the following areas: macroeconomic modelling and planning, growth strategies, fiscal and monetary policies and debt management. The Section also prepares background documents for the annual Conference of African Ministers of Finance, Planning, and Economic Development. The Trade and International Negotiations Section conducts research and outreach activities aimed at ensuring best practice in trade policy development and undertakes research and dissemination activities on bilateral and international trade negotiations (such as the ongoing multilateral trade negotiations under the World Trade Organization) with a view to helping African countries to benefit from globalization through trade. The African Trade Policy Centre (ATPC), established in May 2003, aims to strengthen the human, institutional and policy capacities of African governments to formulate and implement sound trade policies and participate more effectively in international trade negotiations. The Centre takes both a national and regional perspective, and provides a rapid response to technical needs arising from on-going trade negotiations. ECA provides guidance to the policy-making organs of the UN and the AU on the formulation of policies supporting the achievement of Africa's development objectives. It contributes to the work of the General Assembly and of specialized agencies by providing an African perspective in the preparation of development strategies. In March 1996 the UN announced its System-wide Special Initiative on Africa to mobilize resources and to implement a series of political and economic development objectives over a 10-year period. ECA's Executive Secretary was appointed the Co-Chairperson, with the Administrator of UNDP, of the Steering Committee for the Initiative. In November 2000 an informal 'Big Table' meeting, convened between ministers of finance from African countries and OECD ministers of development co-operation, focused on transforming Africa's relationship with its development partners; in October 2001 the Big Table addressed means of establishing a new African co-operation framework and in January 2003 it considered the role played by the IMF in low-income countries. In February 2007 a Big Table meeting was held to discuss the management of Africa's natural resources. In February 2008 it was announced that the Big Table was to be replaced by the Coalition for Dialogue on Africa (CoDA). In April 2003 ECA and the African Development Bank synchronized their annual meetings in an effort to find a common position on addressing the principal challenges confronting the continent. They concluded that development was constrained by national debt, a persistent decline in exports, and weak economic growth rates. They also urged a thorough review of development strategies to determine whether poor outcomes were the result of bad policy, poor implementation or external factors. In 2006 ECA and the Bank organized the first African Economic Conference, to allow an annual exchange of ideas among economists and policy-makers. ECA publishes an annual Economic Report on Africa.

NEPAD AND REGIONAL INTEGRATION DIVISION

The New Partnership for Africa's Development (NEPAD) was established by the AU in 2001, and ECA was assigned the task of co-ordinating UN support for NEPAD at the regional level. ECA's NEPAD and Regional Integration Division, formed in 2006, comprises the NEPAD Support Unit and two other sections, one covering regional integration and the other supporting infrastructure and natural resources development. ECA supports the implementation of the AU's regional integration agenda, through research; policy analysis; strengthening capacity and the provision of technical assistance to the regional economic communities; and working on transboundary initiatives and activities across a variety of sectors. In June 2002 ECA issued its first Annual Report on Regional Integration. ECA was appointed lead agency for the second United Nations Transport and Communications Decade in Africa (UNTACDA II), covering the period 1991–2000. The principal aim of UNTACDA II was the establishment of an efficient, integrated transport and communications system in Africa. ECA and the World Bank jointly co-ordinate the sub-Saharan Africa Transport Programme (SSATP), established in 1987, which aims to facilitate policy development and related capacity-building in the continent's transport sector. A meeting of all participants in the programme is held annually. In September 2004 the SSATP conference, hosted by ECA, recognized the importance of the transport sector in achieving the MDGs and proposed a ministerial review to ensure the integration of transport issues in MDG strategies. The regional Road Management Initiative (RMI) under the SSATP seeks to encourage a partnership between the public and private sectors to manage and maintain road infrastructure more efficiently and thus to improve country-wide communications and transportation activities. An Urban Mobility component of the SSATP aims to improve sub-Saharan African urban transport services, while a Trade and Transport component aims to enhance the international competitiveness of regional economies through the establishment of more cost-effective services for shippers. The Railway Restructuring element focuses on the provision of financially sustainable railway enterprises. In December 2003 the first Central African Forum on Transport Infrastructure and Regional Integration was convened by ECA. In November 2005 a meeting of sub-Saharan African ministers of transport, convened in Bamako, Mali, on the fringes of the SSATP Annual General Meeting, adopted a resolution aimed at developing Africa's transport infrastructure, focusing on the importance of incorporating transport issues into poverty reduction strategies, ensuring sustainable financing for Africa's road programmes, and prioritizing road safety issues. The African Road Safety Conference, convened in Accra, Ghana, in February 2007 by African ministers responsible for transport and health, reaffirmed road safety as a key development priority and pledged to set and achieve measurable national targets for road safety and the prevention of traffic injuries in all member states. The Fourth Regional Conference on the Development and Utilization of Mineral Resources in Africa, held in March 1991, adopted an action plan that included the formulation of national mineral exploitation policies; and the promotion of the gemstone industry, small-scale mining and the iron and steel industry. The Southern and Eastern African Mineral Centre, established by ECA in Dar-es-Salaam, Tanzania, in 1977, opened its membership to all African states in 2007. The Centre provides data-processing, training, analytical services and research on mineral applications. An international study group to review African mining was convened by ECA for the first time in October 2007. ECA's Energy Programme provides assistance to member states in the development of indigenous energy resources and the formulation of energy policies to extricate member states from continued energy crises. In May 2004 ECA was appointed as the secretariat of a new UN-Energy/Africa initiative which aimed to facilitate the exchange of information, good practices and knowledge-sharing among UN organizations and with private sector companies, non-governmental organizations, power utilities and other research and academic institutions. ECA assists member states in the assessment and use of water resources and the development of river and lake basins common to more than one country. ECA encourages co-operation between countries with regard to water issues and collaborates with other UN agencies and regional organizations to promote technical and economic co-operation in this area. In 1992, on the initiative of ECA, the Interagency Group for Water in Africa (now UN-Water/Africa) was established to co-ordinate and harmonize the water-related activities of the UN and other organizations on the continent. ECA has been particularly active in efforts to promote the integrated development of the water resources of the Zambezi river basin and of Lake Victoria. In December 2003 ECA hosted the Pan-African Implementation and Partnership Conference on Water (PANAFCON).

ASSOCIATED BODY

Information Technology Centre for Africa (ITCA): POB 3001, Addis Ababa, Ethiopia; tel. (11) 5514534; fax (11) 5510512; e-mail itca@uneca.org; internet www.uneca.org/itca; f. 1999 to strengthen the continent's communications infrastructure and promote the use of information and communications technologies in planning and policy-making; stages exhibitions and provides training facilities.

Finance

For the two-year period 2008–09 ECA's proposed regular budget, an appropriation from the UN budget, was estimated at US $117.8m., while extra-budgetary resources from grants provided by donors were expected to amount to $100.5m., bringing ECA's total funding requirement for the period to $278.3m.

Publications

African Governance Report.
African Statistical Yearbook.
African Women's Report.
Africa's Sustainable Development Bulletin.
ATPC News.
The ECA Echo.
ESTNET Newsletter (annually).
GenderNet (two a year).
Insight (quarterly Southern Africa Office newsletter).
One Africa.
PICTA Bulletin (monthly).
Sustainable Development Report on Africa (every two years).
Assessing Regional Integration in Africa (ARIA) report series, country reports, policy and discussion papers, reports of conferences and meetings, training series, working paper series.

Economic and Social Commission for Western Asia—ESCWA

Address: Riad es-Solh Sq., POB 11-8575, Beirut, Lebanon.
Telephone: (1) 981301; **fax:** (1) 981510; **e-mail:** webmaster-escwa@un.org; **internet:** www.escwa.org.lb.

The UN Economic Commission for Western Asia was established in 1974 by a resolution of the UN Economic and Social Council (ECOSOC), to provide facilities of a wider scope for those countries previously served by the UN Economic and Social Office in Beirut (UNESOB). The name 'Economic and Social Commission for Western Asia' (ESCWA) was adopted in 1985.

MEMBERS

Bahrain	Palestine
Egypt	Qatar
Iraq	Saudi Arabia
Jordan	Syria
Kuwait	United Arab Emirates
Lebanon	Yemen
Oman	

Organization

(March 2008)

COMMISSION

The Commission meets every two years in ministerial session to determine policy and establish work directives. Representatives of UN bodies and specialized agencies, regional organizations, other UN member states, and non-governmental organizations having consultative status with ECOSOC may attend as observers. The 25th ministerial session of the Commission was to be convened in May 2008.

PREPARATORY COMMITTEE

The Committee has the task of reviewing programming issues and presenting recommendations in that regard to the sessions of the Commission. It is the principal subsidiary body of the Commission and functions as its policy-making structure. Seven specialized inter-governmental committees have been established to consider specific areas of activity, to report on these to the Preparatory Committee and to assist the Committee in formulating ESCWA's medium-term work programmes: they meet every two years, except for the Committee on Transport, which meets annually.

SECTORAL COMMITTEES

Statistical Committee: established in 1992;

Committee on Social Development: established in 1994;

Committee on Energy: established in 1995;

Committee on Water Resources: established in 1995;

Committee on Transport: established in 1997;

Committee on Liberalization of Foreign Trade and Economic Globalization: established in 1997;

Committee on Women: established in 2003.

In addition, an Advisory Committee meets every four months at ESCWA headquarters: it comprises the heads of diplomatic missions in the host country, and a senior representative of the host country, and fulfils a consultative role, while providing a means of communication between member governments and the ESCWA Secretariat. The Consultative Committee on Scientific Technological Development and Technological Innovation was established in 2001 and meets every two years. It comprises experts from public institutions, the private sector, civil society and research centres.

SECRETARIAT

The Secretariat comprises an Executive Secretary, a Deputy Executive Secretary, a Secretary of the Commission, a Statistics Co-ordination Unit, a UN Information Centre, an Administrative Services Division and a Programme Planning and Technical Co-operation Division. The following divisions supervise ESCWA's work programmes: the Economic Analysis Division, the Globalization and Regional Integration Division, the Information and Communication Technology Division, the Social Development Division and the Sustainable Development and Productivity Division. Each Division is headed by a Chief, who is accountable to the Executive Secretary. In addition, there is an ESCWA Centre for Women (established in 2003, formerly part of the Social Development Division), and a Unit for Emerging and Conflict Related Issues, established in 2006.

Executive Secretary: BADER OMAR AL-DAFA (Qatar).

Activities

ESCWA is responsible for proposing policies and actions to support development and to further economic co-operation and integration in western Asia. ESCWA undertakes or sponsors studies of economic, social and development issues of the region, collects and disseminates information, and provides advisory services to member states in various fields of economic and social development. It also organizes conferences and intergovernmental and expert group meetings and sponsors training workshops and seminars.

Much of ESCWA's work is carried out in co-operation with other UN bodies, as well as with other international and regional organizations, for example the League of Arab States, the Co-operation Council for the Arab States of the Gulf (GCC) and the Organization of the Islamic Conference (OIC). ESCWA's 24th ministerial session, convened in May 2006, considered the topic 'New Challenges in the Region and their Impact on the Work of ESCWA'; progress towards the achievement of the UN Millennium Goals in the region; and youth unemployment (see below). ESCWA adopts biennial strategic frameworks as the basis for its programme planning.

ECONOMIC ANALYSIS

The Economic Analysis Division aims to increase the capacity of member countries to co-ordinate economic policies and achieve sustainable economic development. The overall objective is to improve economic management by enhancing the coverage, availability and use of indicators, statistics, and other financial data and trends. The Division makes continuous assessments of the region's macroeconomic performances; conducts economic research, modelling and forecasting; monitors the region's progress towards the UN's Millennium Development Goals; and disseminates its findings to support dialogue at various regional meetings.

EMERGING AND CONFLICT-RELATED ISSUES

In January 2006 a Unit for Emerging and Conflict-related Issues (ECRI) was established to consolidate and develop ESCWA's activities in conflict and post-conflict countries and areas, including Iraq, the Palestinian territories and, initially, southern Lebanon. In view of the extensive damage resulting from the Israeli military strikes that targeted the Lebanese bases of the militant Shi'a organization Hezbollah in July–August of that year, the mandate of ECRI was expanded to cover all of Lebanon. ECRI's priority areas include analysis and policy formulation for reducing the causes of conflict; capacity-building to improve the effectiveness of public administration and the rule of law forging partnerships among civic entities at local and regional level; and working with other ESCWA divisions to meet the special needs of countries affected by conflicts. ESCWA administers an E-Caravan mobile computer school programme, to provide ICT training to communities in southern Lebanon. Other projects include: provision of regional and local 'networking academies' in Iraq, to give training in information technology; the Smart Communities Project, providing modern technology for villages in Iraq; improvement of statistics related to gender in Iraq; and support of the Coalition of Arab-Palestinian Civil Society Organizations.

ESCWA CENTRE FOR WOMEN

The ESCWA Centre for Women was established in October 2003. Its main focus of activities is the empowerment and advancement of women. It also aims to incorporate issues relating to gender in regional projects and programmes. The Centre monitors developments, compiles country profiles on the status of women, provides support for formulating relevant legislation, raises awareness by publishing reports and studies, and organizes conferences. In December 2003 ESCWA issued its first Status of Arab Women Report; this was to assess the situation of Arab women at two-yearly intervals.

GLOBALIZATION AND REGIONAL INTEGRATION

ESCWA aims to assist member states to achieve sustainable economic development in the region and to integrate more fully into the world economy. The Globalization and Regional Integration Division aims to facilitate trans-boundary flows of goods, services, people and capital, by integrating regional markets, responding to global trade liberalization (such as the challenges and opportunities created by the World Trade Organization and the Greater Arab Free Trade Area), and helping member countries to increase their exports and to encourage domestic and foreign investment. The work of the Division's Transport Team includes the development of an integrated transport system in the Arab Mashreq region; development of a regional transport information system; formation of national and regional transport and trade committees, representing both the private and public sectors; simplification of cross-border trading procedures; and the use of electronic data exchange for more efficient transport and trade. The Regional Integration and Financing for Development Team works to encourage domestic, intra-regional and foreign investment, and to help member countries improve their debt management. The Maritime Transport Team helps member states to develop their merchant fleets and sea-ports, and to harmonize maritime policies.

INFORMATION AND COMMUNICATION TECHNOLOGY

The Information and Communication Technology Division works to increase the capabilities of ESCWA member countries in harnessing information and communication technology (ICT) in support of sustainable development and regional integration. It aims to narrow the so-called digital gap between Arab countries and other regions, and, consequently, to improve the competitiveness of local industries and the effectiveness of local services. It supports the formation of ICT policies and infrastructure, by providing technical assistance, pilot projects, studies and meetings of experts. ESCWA was responsible for advising member countries on the implementation of recommendations issued by the World Summit on the Information Society, held in December 2003, and on preparations for the second phase of the Summit, which was convened in Tunis, Tunisia, in November 2005.

SOCIAL DEVELOPMENT

ESCWA's Social Development Division encourages regional co-operation in promoting comprehensive and integrated social policies, so as to achieve greater social equality and well-being, and to alleviate poverty, social exclusion, gender imbalances and social tension. It advises governments on the importance of integrating social analysis into policy-making, identifies methods for the effective formulation, implementation and monitoring of social policy, and assists national and regional research on social development. ESCWA's objectives with regard to population are to increase awareness and understanding of links between population factors and poverty, human rights and the environment, and to strengthen the capacities of member states to analyse and assess demographic trends and migration. In the area of participatory development ESCWA aims to further the alleviation of poverty and to generate a sustainable approach to development through greater involvement of community groups, institutions and users of public services in decision-making. The Division's work on social policy in the city analyses urban problems, such as poverty, unemployment, violence, and failure to integrate vulnerable and marginal groups, and aims to assist policy-makers in ensuring that all city-dwellers have equal access to public services. ESCWA provides a forum for preparatory and follow-up meetings to global conferences. In February 2002 ESCWA organized a ministerial preparatory meeting for the World Assembly on Ageing, which was convened, in Madrid, Spain, in April. The meeting adopted an Arab Plan on the Elderly up to the Year 2012. In May 2006 ESCWA's 24th ministerial session urged member states to make available current and accurate national statistics on youth employment and unemployment and to collate data on other youth-related issues, such as education and health, with a view to establishing national databases on the youth labour situation.

STATISTICS

ESCWA helps to develop the statistical systems of member states in accordance with the UN Fundamental Principles of Official Statistics, in order to improve the accuracy and comparability of economic and social data, and to make the information more accessible to planners and researchers. It aims to improve human and institutional capacities, in particular in the use of statistical tools for data analysis, to expand the adoption and implementation of international statistical methods, and to promote co-operation to further the regional harmonization of statistics. ESCWA assists members in preparing for the 2010 round of population and housing censuses.

SUSTAINABLE DEVELOPMENT AND PRODUCTIVITY

The work of ESCWA's Sustainable Development and Productivity Division is undertaken by five Teams, covering: energy for sustainable development; water management; sustainable management of the environment; technology and enterprise development; and sustainable agriculture and rural development. ESCWA aims to counter the problem of an increasing shortage of freshwater resources and deterioration in water quality resulting from population growth, agricultural land use and socio-economic development, by supporting measures for more rational use and conservation of water resources, and by promoting public awareness of and community participation in water and environmental protection projects. The Division assists governments in the formulation and implementation of capacity-building programmes and the development of surface and groundwater resources. ESCWA promotes greater co-operation among member and non-member countries in the management and use of shared water resources. ESCWA supports co-operation in the establishment of electricity distribution and supply networks throughout the region and promotes the use of alternative sources of energy and the development of new and renewable energy technologies. It places a special emphasis on increasing the access of poor people to cheap energy and water, and on the creation of new jobs.

The Division promotes the application of environmentally sound technologies in order to achieve sustainable development, as well as measures to recycle resources, minimize waste and reduce the environmental impact of transport operations and energy use. ESCWA collaborates with national, regional and international organizations in monitoring and reporting on emerging environmental issues and to pursue implementation of Agenda 21, which was adopted at the June 1992 UN Conference on Environment and Development, with particular regard to land and water resource management and conservation.

Finance

ESCWA's projected share of the UN budget for the two years 2006–07 was US $56.3m.

Publications

ESCWA Annual Report.
UN-ESCWA Weekly News.
Analysis of Performance and Assessment of Growth and Productivity in the ESCWA Region.
Annual Review of Developments in Globalization and Regional Integration.
Compendium of Environment Statistics.
Compendium of Social Statistics and Indicators.
Country and Regional Profiles for Sustainable Development Indicators.
ESCWA Centre for Women Newsletter (monthly).
Estimates and Forecasts for GDP Growth in the ESCWA Region.
External Trade Bulletin of the ESCWA Region (annually).
Review of Industry in ESCWA Member Countries.
Review of Information and Communication Technology and Development.
Status of Arab Women Report (every 2 years).
Survey of Economic and Social Developments in the ESCWA Region.
Transport Bulletin.
Weekly News.

ESCWA publishes reports, case studies, assessments, guides and manuals on the subjects covered by its various Divisions.

OTHER UNITED NATIONS BODIES

Office for the Co-ordination of Humanitarian Affairs—OCHA

Address: United Nations Plaza, New York, NY 10017, USA.
Telephone: (212) 963-1234; **fax:** (212) 963-1312; **e-mail:** ochany@un.org; **internet:** ochaonline.un.org.

OCHA was established in January 1998 as part of the UN Secretariat, with a mandate to co-ordinate international humanitarian assistance and to provide policy and other advice on humanitarian issues. It replaced the Department of Humanitarian Affairs, established in 1992.

Organization
(March 2008)

OCHA has headquarters in New York, and in Geneva, Switzerland. It maintains regional support offices in Dakar, Senegal (for west Africa), Johannesburg, South Africa (southern Africa) and Nairobi, Kenya (central and east Africa); and deploys regional disaster response advisers in Panama (for Latin America and the Caribbean), Kobe, Japan (Asia), and Suva, Fiji (the Pacific). OCHA also maintains field presences in Africa, Europe, Asia and Latin America. In 2008 there were 1,585 staff posts, of which one-third were based at the headquarters.

Under-Secretary-General for Humanitarian Affairs and Emergency Relief Co-ordinator: JOHN HOLMES (United Kingdom).

Activities

OCHA's mandate is to work with UN agencies, governments, inter-governmental humanitarian organizations and non-governmental organizations to ensure that a prompt, co-ordinated and effective response is provided to complex emergencies and natural disasters. OCHA monitors developments throughout the world and undertakes contingency planning. It liaises with UN Resident Co-ordinators, Humanitarian Co-ordinators and country teams, and reaches agreement with other UN bodies regarding the division of responsibilities, which may include field missions to assess requirements, organizing Consolidated Inter-agency Appeals for financial assistance (see below), and mobilizing other resources. The Emergency Relief Co-ordinator is the principal adviser to the UN Secretary-General on humanitarian issues. He chairs the Inter-Agency Standing Committee (IASC), which co-ordinates and administers the international response to humanitarian disasters and the development of relevant policies. The Co-ordinator also acts as Convener of the Executive Committee for Humanitarian Affairs, which provides a forum for humanitarian agencies, as well as the political and peace-keeping departments of the UN Secretariat, to exchange information on emergency situations and humanitarian issues. From 2001 OCHA implemented the recommendations of an internal review process aimed at strengthening its three core functions of co-ordination, advocacy and policy development. In 2001 a new strategic planning process was also initiated. From 2006 a new biennial planning and budgeting strategic framework was introduced. OCHA's strategic framework for 2007–09 incorporated the following three goals: consolidated humanitarian reform to ensure an adequate and relevant humanitarian response; maintaining a recognized leadership role in humanitarian advocacy policy; and developing a more effective and efficient organization.

OCHA's Early Warning Unit identifies and monitors potentially emerging humanitarian crises, as well as humanitarian emergencies at risk of deterioration and potentially resurgent humanitarian emergencies. Analysis by the Unit determines the at-risk areas to which inter-agency contingency planning missions should be directed.

OCHA maintains internet-based Integrated Regional Information Networks (IRINs). The first IRIN was created in 1995 in Nairobi, Kenya, to disseminate information on the humanitarian situation in central and east Africa. Additional IRINs have since been established in Abidjan, Côte d'Ivoire (covering west Africa), Johannesburg, South Africa (for southern Africa) and Islamabad, Pakistan (for central Asia). The IRINs provide new coverage of a total of 46 countries in sub-Saharan Africa and eight countries in central Asia. A complementary service, ReliefWeb, launched in 1996, monitors crises and publishes information on the internet.

OCHA's Humanitarian Emergency and Response Co-ordination branches (based, respectively, at the New York and Geneva headquarters) co-operate in mobilizing and co-ordinating international emergency assistance. The Response Co-ordination branch facilitates and participates in situation assessment missions; prepares briefings and issues Situation Reports to inform the international community on ongoing humanitarian crises, the type and level of assistance required and action being undertaken; and provides administrative support to OCHA field offices. The Emergency Services branch, based at the Geneva headquarters, undertakes disaster-preparedness activities and manages international rapid response missions in the field. UN Disaster Assessment and Co-ordination (UNDAC) teams, established by OCHA with the aid of donor governments, are available for immediate deployment to help to determine requirements and to co-ordinate assistance in those countries affected by disasters, for example by establishing reliable telecommunications and securing other logistical support. OCHA maintains a Central Register of Disaster Management Capacities, which may be available for international assistance. In addition, a stockpile of emergency equipment and supplies is maintained at the UN Humanitarian Response Depot in Brindisi, Italy, ready for immediate dispatch. The Field Co-ordination Support Section of the Emergency Services Branch acts as the secretariat of INSARAG, an inter-governmental network dealing with urban search and rescue (USAR) issues. INSARAG facilitates information exchange, defines standards for international USAR assistance, and develops methodology for international co-ordination in earthquake response. A joint OCHA/UNEP Environment Unit mobilizes and co-ordinates international assistance in environmental emergency situations. In 2007 a new UN inter-agency Displacement and Protection Support Section (DPSS), reporting to the Emergency Relief Co-ordinator, was established, with the aim of strengthening and co-ordinating the inter-agency collaborative response to the plight of people displaced from their homes by civil conflict and natural disasters.

The focal point within the UN system for co-ordinating disaster reduction activities in the socio-economic, humanitarian and development fields is the International Strategy for Disaster Reduction (ISDR), which has an Inter-Agency Secretariat (UN/ISDR) based in Geneva. The UN Emergency Relief Co-ordinator presides over the ISDR's Inter-Agency Task Force on Disaster Reduction (IATF/DR), which comprises 25 UN, international, regional and civil society organizations and is the principal body within the UN system responsible for developing disaster reduction policy. In January 2005 the UN/ISDR organized a World Conference on Disaster Reduction, held in Kobe, Japan, which launched the International Early Warning Programme (IEWP), comprising UN bodies and agencies including the ISDR, UNEP, WFP and the WMO. The IEWP was to improve global resilience to natural disasters (such as droughts, wildland fires, volcanic eruptions, earthquakes, tsunamis—tidal waves, floods and hurricanes) by improving the exchange of observational data, promoting education on disaster preparedness, and ensuring an effective response mechanism to be activated on the issue of warnings. The Kobe Conference also adopted the Hyogo Declaration and the Hyogo Framework of Action covering the period 2005–15, which had the following strategic goals: integrating disaster risk reduction into sustainable development policies and planning; development and strengthening of institutions, mechanisms and capacities to build resilience to hazards; and the systematic incorporation of risk reduction approaches into the implementation of emergency preparedness, response and recovery programmes.

OCHA facilitates the Consolidated Inter-agency Appeal Process (CAP), which aims to organize a co-ordinated response to resource mobilization following humanitarian crises. Participants in the process include UN bodies and agencies and other international governmental and non-governmental organizations (including the International Red Cross and Red Crescent Movement). Under guide-lines adopted by the IASC in 1994, the CAP was clearly defined as a programming mechanism rather than simply an appeal process. Technical guide-lines adopted in 1999 established a framework for developing a Common Humanitarian Action Plan (CHAP) to address a crisis, co-ordinating the relevant inter-agency appeal (on the basis of the CHAP), and preparing strategic monitoring reports. CAP appeals for 2008, seeking an estimated US $3,800m., were issued in December 2007; they concerned complex humanitarian crises affecting some 25m. people in 24 countries and regions.

In December 2005 the UN General Assembly adopted a resolution establishing a new Central Emergency Response Fund (CERF), expanding the former Central Emergency Revolving Fund (founded in 1991) to comprise a US $450m. grant facility, in addition to the existing $50m. revolving element, with a view to ensuring a more predictable and timely response to humanitarian crises. Both the grant and revolving facilities were to be financed by voluntary contributions from member states. Up to two-thirds of the grant facility was to be devoted to life-saving rapid response initiatives. The upgraded Fund, administered on behalf of the UN Secretary-General by the Emergency Relief Co-ordinator in consultation with humanitarian agencies and relevant humanitarian co-ordinators, had three principle objectives: promotion of early action and response to save lives in the case of newly emerging crises or deterioration of existing complex crises, through an initial injection of funds before further donor contributions become available; enhanced response to time-crucial requirements based on demonstrable needs; and strengthening core elements of humanitarian response in underfunded crises. UN agencies and their implementing partners were to be able to access the Fund within 72 hours of the onset of a crisis. The new CERF became operational in March 2006, and by February 2008 had committed $634.8m. for the implementation of 804 projects in 60 countries.

In November 2007 the CERF authorized US $14.7m. in urgent humanitarian support for the 8.7m. people affected by damage inflicted by Cyclone Sidr, which had struck coastal areas of south and southwestern Bangladesh. In January 2008 OCHA appealed for $41.9m. to fund projects aimed at providing humanitarian assistance to victims of violent civil unrest in Kenya that had erupted in the aftermath of a disputed presidential election at the end of the previous month, and had resulted in more than 800 fatalities, had left many thousand people injured, and had rendered some 500,000 civilians in need of emergency aid, including 250,000 people who were displaced from their homes.

GLOBAL CLUSTER LEADS

During 2005 the IASC developed a concept of co-ordinating agency assistance to IDPs through the institutionalization of a 'Cluster Approach', currently comprising 11 core areas of humanitarian activity, with designated global cluster lead agencies:

Agriculture: FAO.
Camp Co-ordination/Management: UNHCR (conflict situations), IOM (natural disasters).
Early Recovery: UNDP.
Education: UNICEF, Save The Children.
Emergency Shelter: UNHCR (conflict situations), International Federation of Red Cross and Red Crescent Societies (natural disasters).
Emergency Telecommunications: OCHA, UNICEF, WFP.
Health: WHO.
Logistics: WFP.
Nutrition: UNICEF.
Protection: UNHCR (IDPs in conflict situations and natural disasters/non-IDP civilians in conflict situations), OHCHR, UNICEF (IDPs in natural disasters/non-IDP civilians in conflict situations).
Water, Sanitation and Hygiene: UNICEF.

Finance

OCHA's budgetary requirements for 2008 were an estimated US $213m.

Publications

Annual Report.
OCHA in 2008.
OCHA News (weekly).

United Nations Office on Drugs and Crime—UNODC

Address: Vienna International Centre, POB 500, 1400 Vienna, Austria.
Telephone: (1) 26060-0; **fax:** (1) 26060-5866; **e-mail:** unodc@unodc.org; **internet:** www.unodc.org.

The UN Office on Drugs and Crime (UNODC) was established in November 1997 (as the Office for Drug Control and Crime Prevention—ODCCP) to strengthen the UN's integrated approach to issues relating to drug control, crime prevention and international terrorism. A reform programme was launched in 2002 aimed at integrating further the Office's areas of activity. The Office was renamed in October of that year. It comprises two principal components: the United Nations Drug Programme and the United Nations Crime Programme.

Organization
(March 2008)

UNODC comprises the following four divisions: Operations; Treaty Affairs; Research and Public Affairs; and Management. There is a UNODC liaison office in New York and there are 21 field offices world-wide.
Executive Director: Antonio Maria Costa (Italy).

Activities

UNITED NATIONS DRUG PROGRAMME

The UN Drug Programme was established in 1991 as the UN International Drug Control Programme (UNDCP) and was renamed in 2002. It is responsible for co-ordinating the activities of all UN specialized agencies and programmes in matters of international drug control. The structures of the former Division of Narcotic Drugs, the UN Fund for Drug Abuse Control and the secretariat of the International Narcotics Control Board (see below) were integrated into the Programme. Accordingly, it became the focal point for promoting the UN Decade Against Drug Abuse (1991–2000) and for assisting member states to implement the Global Programme of Action that was adopted by the UN General Assembly in 1990 with the objective of achieving an international society free of illicit drugs and drug abuse. At a special summit meeting of the General Assembly, held in June 1998, heads of state and representatives of some 150 countries adopted a global strategy, formulated on the basis of UNDCP proposals, to reduce significantly the production of and demand for illicit substances over the next decade. UNDCP subsequently launched the Global Assessment Programme on Drug Abuse (GAP), which aimed to establish one global and nine regional drug abuse data systems to collect and evaluate data on the extent of and patterns of illegal substance abuse. In the context of drug supply reduction the Illicit Crop Monitoring Programme (ICMP) supports the development of comprehensive monitoring systems in the six countries believed to account for some 90% of illicit opium and coca production (Afghanistan, Bolivia, Colombia, Laos, Myanmar and Peru); a global monitoring component of the ICMP provides technical assistance to the national monitoring systems. The ICMP is facilitated by a combination of satellite sensing (with the assistance of the European Space Agency), aerial surveillance and ground-level surveys, which provide a reliable collection and analysis mechanism for data on the production of illicit substances. The Alternative Development Programme supports projects to create alternative sources of income for farmers economically dependent on the production of illicit narcotic crops. The UN Drug Programme aims to suppress trafficking in these substances and supports efforts to enhance regional and cross-border co-operation in implementing law enforcement initiatives. It serves as an international centre of expertise and information on drug abuse control, with the capacity to provide legal and technical assistance in relevant areas of concern. It supports governments in efforts to strengthen their institutional capacities for drug control (for example, drug identification and drug law enforcement training) and to prepare and implement national drug control 'action plans'.

The Programme's approach to reducing demand for illicit drugs combines strategies in the areas of prevention, treatment and rehabilitation. It sponsors activities to generate public awareness of the harmful effects of drug abuse, for example through its Global Youth Network project, which aims to involve young people in prevention activities, and through the system of goodwill ambassadors associated with its 'Sports Against Drugs' campaign. The Programme works with governments, as well as non-governmental and private organizations and local community partners, in the detection, treatment, rehabilitation and social reintegration of drug addicts. It also undertakes research to monitor the drugs problem: for example, assessing the characteristics of drug-takers and the substances being used in order to help identify people at risk of becoming drug-takers and to enhance the effectiveness of national programmes to address the issue (see also GAP, above).

The Programme promotes implementation of the following major treaties which govern the international drug control system: the Single Convention on Narcotic Drugs (1961) and a Protocol amending the Convention (1972); the Convention on Psychotropic Substances (1971); and the UN Convention against Illicit Traffic in Narcotic Drugs and Psychotropic Substances (1988). Among other important provisions, these treaties aim to restrict severely the production of narcotic drugs, while ensuring an adequate supply for medical and scientific purposes, to prevent profits obtained from the illegal sale of drugs being diverted into legal usage and to secure the extradition of drug-traffickers and the transfer of proceeds for criminal prosecution. The Programme assists countries to adapt their national legislation and drug policies to facilitate their compliance with these conventions and to enhance co-ordinated inter-governmental efforts to control the movement of narcotic drugs. It services meetings of the International Narcotics Control Board (INCB), an independent body responsible for promoting and monitoring government compliance with the provisions of the drug control treaties, and of the Commission on Narcotic Drugs, which, as a functional committee of ECOSOC, is the main policy-making organ within the UN system on issues relating to international drug abuse control. The INCB is promoting co-ordinated global action to prevent illicit internet sales of internationally-controlled prescription drugs by so-called 'online pharmacies'.

UNODC co-operates closely with other international, regional and non-governmental organizations and maintains dialogue with agencies advocating drug abuse control. It is a co-sponsor, with ILO, UNDP, UNESCO, UNFPA, UNICEF, WHO, the World Bank and UNHCR of the Joint Programme on HIV/AIDS (UNAIDS), which was established on 1 January 1996. UNODC's participation is in recognition of the importance of international drug control efforts in preventing the spread of HIV/AIDS. In October 2004 UNODC and the World Customs Organization launched a joint Container Control Programme aimed at improving port control measures in developing countries.

UNODC supports the Central Asia Regional Information and Co-ordination Centre (CARICC), which was established in Almaty, Kazakhstan in February 2006 to combat illicit drugs-trafficking in that region. In April UNODC and the Collective Security Treaty Organization (comprising Armenia, Belarus, Kazakhstan, Kyrgyzstan, Russia and Tajikistan) signed a protocol on developing joint projects and sharing information with the aim of addressing drugs-trafficking, terrorism and transborder crime in Central Asia.

UNITED NATIONS CRIME PROGRAMME

Through the United Nations Crime Programme, which is implemented by the Centre for International Crime Prevention (CICP), established in 1997, UNODC is responsible for crime prevention, criminal justice and criminal law reform. The Programme oversees the application of international standards and norms relating to these areas, for example the Minimum Rules for the Treatment of Prisoners, Conventions against Torture, and Other Cruel, Inhuman or Degrading Treatment or Punishment, and Safeguards Guaranteeing the Protection of the Rights of Those Facing the Death Penalty. The Programme provides member states with technical assistance to strengthen national capacities to establish appropriate legal and criminal justice systems and to combat transnational organized crime (see below). It supports the Commission on Crime Prevention and Criminal Justice, a functional committee of ECOSOC, which provides guidance in developing global anti-crime policies. The Programme manages the Global Programme against Corruption, a Global Programme on Organized Crime, which aims to analyse emerging transnational criminal organizations and assist countries to formulate strategies to combat the problem, and a Global Programme against Trafficking in Human Beings (trafficking in human beings for sexual exploitation or forced labour is regarded as the fastest-growing area of international organized crime). In March 2007 UNODC and partners initiated the Global Initiative to Fight Human Trafficking (UN-GIFT), with the aim of raising awareness world-wide of the phenomenon, promoting effective preventative measures, and improving law enforcement methods. In February 2008 UN-GIFT organized the Vienna Forum to Fight Human Trafficking, with participation by UN member states and agencies, other international organizations, academics, and representatives of the private sector and civil society. The CICP supported member states in the preparation of the UN Convention against Transnational Organized Crime; the so-called Palermo Convention, with three additional Protocols on trafficking in human beings, the smuggling of migrants, and controlling the proliferation of firearms, was opened for signature in December 2000 at a UN conference on combating organized crime held in Sicily, Italy, and entered into force in September 2003. The Programme assisted with the formulation of the UN Convention against Corruption, which was opened for signature in December 2003 in Merida, Mexico, and entered into force in December 2005.

The UN Crime Programme promotes research and undertakes studies of new forms of crime prevention, in collaboration with the UN Interregional Crime and Justice Research Institute (UNICRI). It also maintains a UN Crime and Justice Information Network database (UNCJIN), which provides information on national crime statistics, publications and links to other relevant intergovernmental agencies and research and academic institutes.

The UNODC's Terrorism Prevention Branch, established in 1999, researches trends in terrorist activity and assists countries to improve their capabilities to investigate and prevent acts of terrorism. The Branch promotes international co-operation in combating the problem, is compiling a database on global terrorism, and has initiated a study into the connections between terrorist activity and other forms of crime.

The UN Global Programme against Money Laundering (GPML), established in March 1999, assists governments with formulating legislation against money laundering and establishing and maintaining appropriate frameworks to counter the problem. GPML activities include the provision of technical assistance, training, and the collection, research and analysis of crime data. The Programme, in collaboration with other governmental organizations, law enforcement agencies and academic institutions, co-ordinates the International Money Laundering Information Network (IMoLIN), an internet-based information resource (accessible at www.i-molin.org). IMoLIN incorporates the Anti-Money Laundering International Database (a comprehensive database on money-laundering legislation throughout the world that constituted a key element in the Office's activities in support of the elaboration of the International Convention against Transnational Organized Crime—see above). At the first GPML Forum, held in the Cayman Islands in March 2000, the governments of 31 participating 'offshore' financial centres agreed in principle to adopt internationally-accepted standards of financial regulation and measures against money laundering.

UNODC organized several regional preparatory meetings prior to the 11th UN Congress on Crime Prevention and Criminal Justice, which was held in Bangkok, Thailand, in April 2005.

Finance

UNODC receives an allocation from the regular budget of the UN, although voluntary contributions from member states and private organizations represent the majority (about 90%) of its resources. The proposed consolidated budget for the two-year period 2008–09 amounted to some US $212.3m., including programme expenditure of $173.2m., of which $152.1m. was to be allocated to technical assistance and advice activities, $5.8m. to services relating to policy-making and treaty adherence, and $14.3m. to research, analysis and advocacy activities.

Publications

Bulletin on Narcotics.
Forum on Crime and Society.
Global Report on Crime and Justice.
Multilingual Dictionary of Narcotic Drugs and Psychotropic Substances Under International Control.
Technical Series.
The United Nations and Juvenile Justice: A Guide to International Standards and Best Practices.
UNODC Update (quarterly).
World Drug Report.

INTERNATIONAL ORGANIZATIONS

United Nations (Other Bodies)

Office of the United Nations High Commissioner for Human Rights—OHCHR

Address: Palais des Nations, 1211 Geneva 10, Switzerland.
Telephone: 229179000; **fax:** 229179022; **e-mail:** infodesk@ohchr.org; **internet:** www.ohchr.org.

The Office is a body of the UN Secretariat and is the focal point for UN human rights activities. Since 1997 it has incorporated the Centre for Human Rights. OHCHR is guided by relevant resolutions of the General Assembly, the Charter of the United Nations, the Universal Declaration of Human Rights and subsequent human rights instruments, the Vienna Declaration and programme of action adopted by the 1993 World Conference on Human Rights (see below), and the outcome document of the 2005 World Summit of the General Assembly.

Organization
(March 2008)

HIGH COMMISSIONER

In December 1993 the UN General Assembly decided to establish the position of a United Nations High Commissioner for Human Rights (UNHCHR) following a recommendation of the World Conference on Human Rights, held in Vienna, Austria, in June of that year. The High Commissioner, who is the UN official with principal responsibility for UN human rights activities, is appointed by the UN Secretary-General, with the approval of the General Assembly, for a four-year term in office, renewable for one term. The High Commissioner is assisted by a Deputy High Commissioner for Human Rights.

High Commissioner: LOUISE ARBOUR (Canada) (until 30 June 2008).
Deputy High Commissioner: KYUNG-WHA KHANG (Republic of Korea).

ADMINISTRATION

OHCHR's Executive Direction and Management comprises the following units: the Executive Office of the High Commissioner; the Policy, Planning, Monitoring, and Evaluation Section; the Communications Section; the Civil Society Unit; the Field Safety and Security Section; and the Donor and External Relations Section. OHCHR's headquarters contains the following four substantive Divisions: Field Operations and Technical Co-operation; Research and Right to Development; Special Procedures; and the Human Rights Council and Treaties Division. There is also a Programme Support and Management Services unit, and a branch office in New York, USA, that aims to ensure that human rights issues are fully integrated into the broader UN development and security agenda.

FIELD PRESENCES

As the Office's involvement in field work has expanded, in support of UN peace-making, peace-keeping and peace-building activities, a substantial structure of field presences has developed. In early 2008 there were OHCHR regional offices in Addis Ababa, Ethiopia (covering East Africa); Bangkok, Thailand (Southeast Asia); Beirut, Lebanon (the Middle East); Bishkek, Kyrgyzstan (Central Asia); Panama City, Panama (Central and South America, assisted by a small liaison office in Santiago, Chile); Pretoria, South Africa (Southern Africa); and Suva, Fiji (the Pacific); as well as an OHCHR Regional Centre for Human Rights and Democracy for Central Africa, based in Yaoundé, Cameroon. OHCHR country offices with human rights promotion and protection mandates were being maintained in Angola, Bolivia, Cambodia, Colombia, Guatemala, Mexico, Nepal, the Palestinian territories, Serbia (including Kosovo), Togo and Uganda. The Office was also supplying human rights advisers to several UN country teams; was responsible for the human rights components of 17 UN peace missions; and was undertaking a number of technical co-operation projects.

Activities

The mandate of OHCHR incorporates the following functions and responsibilities: the promotion and protection of human rights throughout the world; the reinforcement of international co-operation in the field of human rights; the promotion of universal ratification and implementation of international standards; the establishment of a dialogue with governments to ensure respect for human rights; and co-ordination of efforts by other UN programmes and organs to promote respect for human rights. Upon request OHCHR undertakes assessments of national human rights needs, in consultation with governments. Through the provision of guidance and training it supports the establishment of independent national human rights institutions. The Office may also study and react to cases of serious violations of human rights, and may undertake diplomatic efforts to prevent violations. It also produces educational and other information material to enhance understanding of human rights. OHCHR co-operates with academic bodies and non-governmental organizations working the area of human rights.

OHCHR was the lead agency in undertaking preparations for the World Conference against Racism, Racial Discrimination, Xenophobia and Related Intolerance, convened in Durban, South Africa, in August–September 2001 and attended by representatives of 168 governments. The following five core themes were addressed at Durban: sources, causes, forms and contemporary manifestations of racism; victims; prevention, education and protection measures; provision of remedies and redress (i.e. compensation); and future strategies to achieve full and effective equality. The Conference adopted the 'Durban Declaration' and a Programme of Action, in accordance with which national plans of action were to be implemented by participating states: universal ratification of the International Convention on the Elimination of all Forms of Racism (ICERD) was to be prioritized, with the broadest possible ratification of other human rights instruments, and national legislation was to be improved in line with the ICERD. OHCHR was to play a leading role in following up the implementation of the Programme of Action; on the recommendation of the Conference an interim Anti-discrimination Unit was established within the Office for this purpose.

In 2005 the High Commissioner published a Plan of Action for the future development of the Office and the development of the UN's human rights agenda. The Plan proposed greater involvement of the Office in both setting and ensuring—through improved monitoring and public reporting of violations and the provision of sustained technical assistance and advice at country level—the implementation of human rights norms. The World Summit of heads of state and government convened by the General Assembly in December 2005 noted the Plan of Action and made a commitment to the expansion of the UN human rights programme and to increasing the Office's funding. The High Commissioner subsequently issued strategic management plans for the Office covering the periods 2006–07 and 2008–09; over the period of the second plan efforts were to be made to widen the Office's funding base.

OHCHR assisted with the preparation of the International Convention for the Protection of All Persons from Enforced Disappearance, which was opened for signature in February 2007 and was to enter into force after ratification by 20 signatory states. By February 2008 the Convention had been signed by 72 countries and ratified by one (Albania).

During 2005 the UN's Inter-Agency Standing Committee (IASC), concerned with co-ordinating the international response to humanitarian disasters, developed a concept of organizing agency assistance to IDPs through the institutionalization of a 'Cluster Approach', currently comprising 11 core areas of activity. OHCHR, with UNHCR and UNICEF, was designated joint lead agency for the cluster on Protection.

The Office acts as the secretariat for three grant-making humanitarian funds: the UN Voluntary Fund for Victims of Torture, which was established in 1981; the Voluntary Fund for Indigenous Populations (established in 1985); and the Voluntary Fund on Contemporary Forms of Slavery (established in 1991).

OHCHR field offices and operations ('field presences'—see above) undertake a variety of activities, such as training and other technical assistance, support for Special Rapporteurs (usually appointed by the Commission on Human Rights to investigate human rights emergencies), monitoring and fact-finding. Increasingly they provide support to conflict prevention, peace-making, peace-keeping and peace-building activities. OHCHR co-operates with the UN Department of Peace-keeping Operations and Department of Political Affairs in developing the human rights component of peace-keeping and peace-building missions. In early 2008 OHCHR was servicing 28 thematic mandates and 10 geographic mandates (the most recent of which included investigations into the human rights situations in Sudan and Uzbekistan, both launched in 2005, and mandates extended in that year for ongoing investigations into the human rights situations in Belarus, Burundi, Cambodia, the Democratic

Republic of the Congo, the Democratic People's Republic of Korea, Myanmar and the Palestinian territories).

The OHCHR quick response desk co-ordinates urgent appeals for assistance in addressing human rights emergencies. The High Commissioner issues reports on human rights emergencies to the Commission on Human Rights.

TECHNICAL CO-OPERATION PROGRAMME

The UN Technical Co-operation Programme in the Field of Human Rights was established in 1955 to assist states, at their request, to strengthen their capacities in the observance of democracy, human rights, and the rule of law. Examples of work undertaken within the framework of the programme include training courses and workshops on good governance and the observance of human rights, expert advisory services on the incorporation of international human rights standards into national legislation and policies and on the formulation of national plans of action for the promotion and protection of human rights, fellowships, the provision of information and documentation, and consideration of promoting a human rights culture. In recent years the Programme, one of the key components of OHCHR's activities, has expanded to undertake UN system-wide human rights support activities, for example in the area of peacekeeping (see above).

Finance

OHCHR's activities are financed from the regular budget of the UN, as well as by voluntary contributions (which are channelled through the Trust Fund for the Support of the Activities of the UNHCHR and the Voluntary Fund for Technical Co-operation in the Field of Human Rights), and the three humanitarian trust funds administered by the Office. For the two years 2008–09 the approved regular budget appropriation for OHCHR amounted to US $115.3m. In addition, to cover expenditure over that period, the Office was to appeal to the international community for voluntary contributions of $173.3m., and the humanitarian trust funds were forecast to provide $24.1m.

Publications

Annual Report.
Fact sheet series.
Human Rights Quarterly.
Human rights study series.
Professional training series.
Other reference material, reports, proceedings of conferences, workshops, etc.

United Nations Human Settlements Programme— UN-Habitat

Address: POB 30030, 00100 Nairobi, Kenya.
Telephone: (20) 7623120; **fax:** (20) 7623477; **e-mail:** infohabitat@unhabitat.org; **internet:** www.unhabitat.org.

UN-Habitat (formerly the United Nations Centre for Human Settlements, UNCHS-Habitat, established in October 1978 to service the intergovernmental Commission on Human Settlements) became a full UN programme in January 2002. UN-Habitat serves as a focus for human settlements and sustainable urban development activities in the UN system. UN-Habitat was mandated by the Second UN Conference on Human Settlements, Habitat II, which was held in Istanbul, Turkey, in June 1996, to pursue the Habitat Agenda, focusing on the objectives of adequate shelter for all and sustainable human settlements in an urbanizing world; further mandates are derived from the September 2000 UN Millennium Forum Declaration and Agenda for Action, and from the June 2001 Habitat II review conference's Declaration on Cities and other Human Settlements in the New Millennium.

Organization
(March 2008)

GOVERNING COUNCIL

The Governing Council (formerly the Commission on Human Settlements) meets once every two years and has 58 members, serving for four years. Sixteen members are from Africa, 13 from Asia, 10 from Latin America and the Caribbean, six from eastern European countries, and 13 from western European and other countries. The Committee of Permanent Representatives to UN-Habitat, which meets at least four times a year, functions as an inter-sessional subsidiary body of the Governing Council. The Governing Council reports to the UN General Assembly through ECOSOC.

SECRETARIAT

The Secretariat services the Governing Council, implements its resolutions and ensures the integration and co-ordination of technical co-operation, research and policy advice. It comprises the Office of the Executive Director; the Regional and Technical Co-operation Division; the Monitoring and Research Division; the Shelter and Sustainable Human Settlements Development Division; and the Financing Human Settlements Division.

Executive Director: Anna Kajumulo Tibaijuka (Tanzania).

Activities

In February 2008 the UN Secretariat forecast that by the end of that year at least one-half of the world's population would be resident in towns and cities (compared with about one-third in 1950). Of the world's urban population, about one-third (nearly 1,000m. people) lives in slums without access to basic sanitation. UN-Habitat supports and conducts capacity-building and operational research, provides technical co-operation and policy advice, and disseminates information with the aim of strengthening the development and management of human settlements. It is mandated to support the UN Millennium Development Goals (MDGs) of halving, by 2015, the proportion of people without sustainable access to safe drinking water and improving significantly the lives of at least 100m. slum dwellers by 2020. In October 2003 the Programme predicted that, owing to unprecedented urban growth accompanied by poverty and social inequalities, the number of slum dwellers world-wide would double to about 2,000m. by 2030, rendering the above MDG a minimum objective. The September 2005 World Summit of UN heads of state approved the development of a Slum Upgrading Facility (SUF). In that year more advanced monitoring systems were introduced to track the progress made in improving living condition in slums.

In June 1996 representatives of 171 national governments and of more than 500 municipal authorities attending Habitat II adopted a Global Plan of Action (the 'Habitat Agenda'), which incorporated detailed programmes of action to realize economic and social development and environmental sustainability, and endorsed the conference's objectives of ensuring 'adequate shelter for all' and 'sustainable human settlements development in an urbanizing world'. UN-Habitat provides the leadership and serves as a focal point for the implementation of the Agenda. In 1999 UNCHS (Habitat) approved a set of 23 resolutions to reduce poverty, improve shelter and environmental conditions, promote good governance, and improve the status of women. In 1999 UNCHS (Habitat) and the World Bank jointly launched the Cities Alliance, which also comprises G-7 and other governments, UNEP, the Asian Development Bank, the European Union, and local authorities, and aims, through its Cities without Slums Action Plan (endorsed by the September 2000 UN Millennium Summit), to increase resources reaching the urban poor by improving ongoing urban programmes, and by strengthening links between grant-funded urban development co-operation and investment follow-up. A special session of the UN General Assembly, entitled Istanbul + 5, was held in June 2001 to report on the implementation of the recommendations of the Habitat II conference. The special session adopted a Declaration on Cities and Other Human Settlements in the New Millennium that reaffirmed commitment to the objectives of the Habitat Agenda and urged an intensification of efforts towards eradicating widespread poverty, which was identified as the main impediment to achieving these, and towards promoting good governance. The special session also resolved to increase international co-operation in several other areas, including addressing HIV/AIDS, urban crime and violence, environmental issues, and the problems posed by conflicts and refugees; and recommended the enhancement of the status and role of UNCHS (Habitat). Consequently, in December 2001 the General Assembly authorized the elevation of the body to a full UN programme with a strengthened mandate to address and implement the Habitat Agenda and, in January 2002, UN-Habitat was inaugurated.

UN-Habitat's activities over the six-year period 2008–13 are governed by a medium-term strategic and institutional plan, adopted in April 2007, that aims by 2013 to help establish the necessary conditions for arresting the growth of slums and to set the stage for the subsequent reduction in and reversal of the number of slum dwellers world-wide. The plan focuses on: advocacy and monitoring; affordable land and housing; environmentally-sound basic infrastructure and services; participatory urban planning, management and governance; and innovative human settlements finance, with each focus area accompanied by a set of strategic objectives and achievement indicators. In addition, a peer-review mechanism comprising several Habitat Agenda partners was to be established during the period of the plan as a means of monitoring progress and achievement.

UN-Habitat's work programme for 2008–09 incorporates the following priority areas, as defined by the Governing Council: adequate shelter for all and sustainable human settlements development; monitoring the Habitat Agenda; regional and technical co-operation; and human settlements financing.

UN-Habitat maintains a Global Urban Observatory (GUO) to monitor implementation of the Habitat Agenda and to report on and support local and national plans of action and ongoing research and development. The Observatory operates through GUONet, a global network of regional, national and local urban observatories, and through partner institutions that provide training and other capacity-building expertise. The Observatory also maintains the GUO databases of urban indicators, statistics and city profiles. The Observatory works closely with the Best Practices and Local Leadership Programme, which was established in 1997 to support the implementation of the Habitat Agenda through the use of information and networking. The UN Housing Rights Programme (UNHRP), launched jointly by UN-Habitat and OHCHR in April 2002, supports states and other stakeholders with the implementation of their Habitat Agenda commitments to realizing the universal right to adequate housing. In 2004 UN-Habitat established an Advisory Group on Forced Evictions, with a mandate to monitor forced evictions of people with no or inadequate legal security of tenure, and to identify and promote alternatives including in situ upgrading of accommodation and negotiated resettlement. UN-Habitat's programme on Rapid Urban Sector Profiling for Sustainability (RUSPS) involves an accelerated action-oriented assessment of urban conditions in particular cities in seven thematic areas (governance; slums; gender and HIV/AIDS; urban environment; local economic development; basic urban services; and cultural heritage), with a view to developing and implementing tailor-made urban poverty reduction policies. Through its Strengthening Training Institutions programme UN-Habitat supports regional and national training institutions by organizing regional workshops to develop capacity-building strategies and to analyse training need assessments; by designing new training manuals and other tools; by developing, jointly with partners, generic training manuals and handbooks; by training trainers; and by supporting institutions with the design and implementation of national training programmes.

UN-Habitat participates in implementing the human settlements component of Agenda 21, which was adopted at the UN Conference on Environment and Development in June 1992, and is also responsible for the chapter of Agenda 21 that refers to solid waste management and sewage-related issues. The Programme implements a programme entitled 'Localizing Agenda 21', to assist local authorities in developing countries to address local environmental and infrastructure-related problems, with a particular focus on secondary cities. It also collaborates with national governments, private-sector and non-governmental institutions and UN bodies to achieve the objectives of Agenda 21. The Settlement Infrastructure and Environment Programme was initiated in 1992 to support developing countries in improving the environment of human settlements through policy advice and planning, infrastructure management and enhancing awareness of environmental and health concerns in areas such as water, sanitation, waste management and transport. In October 2002 UN-Habitat launched a Water and Sanitation Trust Fund to support a new Water and Sanitation Programme, with the aim of supporting the goal of halving the proportion of the world's population lacking access to basic sanitation or clean water by 2015, that was set by the World Summit on Sustainable Development (WSSD), held in Johannesburg, South Africa, during August–September 2002 to assess strategies for strengthening the implementation of Agenda 21. The Water and Sanitation Programme promotes policy dialogue, information exchange, water education and awareness-raising; monitors progress towards achieving the MDG targets on improving access to safe water and sanitation; and designs replicable model-setting initiatives, i.e. the Lake Victoria Region Water and Sanitation initiative and the Mekong Regional Water and Sanitation initiative. The Water and Sanitation Programme incorporates two regional sub-programmes. The Managing Water for African Cities programme, jointly co-ordinated by UN-Habitat and UNEP, promotes efficient water demand management, capacity-building to alleviate the environmental impact of urbanization on freshwater resources, information exchange on water management and conservation issues, and the exchange of best practices in urban water management. In March 2003 UN-Habitat and the Asian Development Bank (ADB) signed an agreement on the establishment of the parallel Water for Asian Cities programme. The ADB was to provide US $10m. in grants and $500m. in loans in support of the programme over a five-year period. A global Urban Management Programme aims to strengthen the contribution of cities and towns in developing countries towards human development, including economic growth, social advancements, the reduction of poverty and the improvement of the environment. The Programme (active in 140 cities in 58 countries) is an international technical co-operation project, of which UN-Habitat is the executing agency, the World Bank is an associated agency, while UNDP provides core funding and monitoring. The Programme is operated through regional offices, in collaboration with bilateral and multilateral support agencies, and brings together national and local authorities, community leaders and representatives of the private sector to consider specific issues and solutions to urban problems. The related Safer Cities Programme was initiated in 1996. By 2008 23 Safer Cities Programme initiatives had been launched in cities, countries and regions, including a regional initiative launched in 2006 to improve urban safety through local government capacity-building in Asia and the Pacific. A Sustainable Cities Programme, operated jointly with UNEP, is concerned with incorporating environmental issues into urban planning and management, in order to ensure sustainable and equitable development. The Programme is active in some 30 cities world-wide, although a prepared series of policy guide-lines is used in many others. Some 95% of the Programme's resources are spent at city level to strengthen the capacities of municipal authorities and their public-, private- and community-sector partners in the field of environmental planning and management, with the objective that the concepts and approaches of the Programme are replicated throughout the region. UN-Habitat provided the secretariat of the inaugural World Urban Forum, held in April–May 2002 with participation by national governments and Habitat Agenda partners. The Forum, which represents a merger of the former Urban Environment Forum and International Forum on Urban Poverty, aims to promote international co-operation in shelter and urban development issues. The second World Urban Forum was held in Barcelona, Spain, in September 2004; the third in Vancouver, Canada, in June 2006; and the fourth was to be convened in Nanjing, People's Republic of China, in 2008. In addition, UN-Habitat supports training and other activities designed to strengthen management development (in particular in the provision and maintenance of services and facilities) at local and community level. UN-Habitat's Global Campaign for Secure Tenure and Global Campaign on Urban Governance both emphasize urban poverty reduction. UN-Habitat focused on the theme of 'Sustainable Urbanization' as its main contribution to the WSSD held in August–September 2002 (see above).

In November 2004 UN-Habitat hosted the first meeting of the Global Research Network on Human Settlements (HS-Net). HS-Net was to act as a forum for human settlements researchers, research institutions and networks, and was to advised the UN-Habitat Secretariat on the preparation of its two 'flagship reports', the *Global Report on Human Settlements* and *State of the World's Cities*.

Increasingly UN-Habitat is being called upon to contribute to the relief, rehabilitation and development activities undertaken by the UN in areas affected by regional and civil conflict. UN-Habitat also provides assessment and technical support in the aftermath of natural disasters. Reconstruction and recovery activities are co-ordinated by the Risk and Disaster Management Unit. In December 2003 UN-Habitat signed a Memorandum of Understanding with UNHCR that covered several areas of co-operation including sheltering refugees and returnees, settlement and infrastructure planning, and property rights.

Finance

UN-Habitat's work programme is financed from the UN regular budget, and from voluntary contributions to the UN Habitat and Human Settlements Foundation and to the Programme's technical co-operation activities. The approved budget for the two-year period 2008–09 amounted to US $246m., comprising a regular budget allocation of $18.9m., contributions to the Habitat and Human

Settlements Foundation forecast at $105.7m., and expected contributions totalling $121.4m. for technical co-operation activities.

Publications

Global Report on Human Settlements (annually).
State of the World's Cities (every 2 years).
Habitat Debate (quarterly).
Water for Cities (quarterly).
UMP e-Newsletter (quarterly).
Technical reports and studies, occasional papers, bibliographies, directories.

United Nations Children's Fund—UNICEF

Address: 3 United Nations Plaza, New York, NY 10017, USA.
Telephone: (212) 326-7000; **fax:** (212) 887-7465; **e-mail:** info@unicef.org; **internet:** www.unicef.org.

UNICEF was established in 1946 by the UN General Assembly as the UN International Children's Emergency Fund, to meet the emergency needs of children in post-war Europe. In 1950 its mandate was expanded to respond to the needs of children in developing countries. In 1953 the General Assembly decided that UNICEF should become a permanent branch of the UN system, with an emphasis on programmes giving long-term benefits to children everywhere, particularly those in developing countries. In 1965 UNICEF was awarded the Nobel Peace Prize.

Organization
(March 2008)

EXECUTIVE BOARD

The Executive Board, as the governing body of UNICEF, comprises 36 member governments from all regions, elected in rotation for a three-year term by ECOSOC. The Board establishes policy, reviews programmes and approves expenditure. It reports to the General Assembly through ECOSOC.

SECRETARIAT

The Executive Director of UNICEF is appointed by the UN Secretary-General in consultation with the Executive Board. The administration of UNICEF and the appointment and direction of staff are the responsibility of the Executive Director, under policy directives laid down by the Executive Board, and under a broad authority delegated to the Executive Director by the Secretary-General. In January 2007 there were more than 8,000 UNICEF staff positions, of which about 85% were in field offices.

Executive Director: ANN M. VENEMAN (USA).

UNICEF OFFICES

UNICEF has a network of eight regional and 126 field offices serving 156 countries and territories. Its offices in Tokyo, Japan, and Brussels, Belgium, support fund-raising activities; UNICEF's supply division is administered from the office in Copenhagen, Denmark. A research centre concerned with advocacy for child rights and development is based in Florence, Italy.

Belgium: rue Montoyer 14, 1000 Brussels; tel. (2) 513-22-51; fax (2) 513-22-90; e-mail brussels@unicef.be; internet unicef.be.

Japan: UNU Headquarters Bldg, 8th Floor, 53–70, Jingumae 5-chome, Shibuya-ku, Tokyo 150-0001, Japan; tel. (3) 5467-4431; fax (3) 5467-4437; e-mail tokyo@unicef.org; internet www.unicef.or.jp.

Regional Office for the Americas and the Caribbean: Apdo 0843-03045, Panamá, Panama; tel. (507) 301-7400; fax (507) 317-0258; e-mail afranco@unicef.org; internet www.uniceflac.org.

Regional Office for Central and Eastern Europe and the Commonwealth of Independent States: Palais des Nations, 1211 Geneva 10, Switzerland; tel. 229095111; fax 229095909; e-mail info@unicef.ch; internet www.unicef.org/ceecis.

Regional Office for East Asia and the Pacific: POB 2-154, Bangkok 10200, Thailand; tel. (2) 2805931; fax (2) 2803563; e-mail eapro@unicef.org.

Regional Office for Eastern and Southern Africa: POB 44145, Nairobi, Kenya 00100; tel. (20) 621234; fax (20) 622678; e-mail unicefesaro@unicef.org.

Regional Office for the Middle East and North Africa: POB 1551, UNICEF House, Tla'a al-Ali al Dahak Bin Soufian St, 11821 Amman, Jordan; tel. (6) 5539977; fax (6) 5538880; e-mail menaro@unicef.org.jo.

Regional Office for South Asia: POB 5815, Leknath Marg, Kathmandu, Nepal; tel. 4419082; fax 4419479; e-mail rosa@unicef.org.

Regional Office for West and Central Africa: POB 29720, Dakar-Yoff, Senegal; tel. 869-58-58; fax 820-89-65; e-mail wcaro@unicef.org.

UNICEF Innocenti Research Centre: Piazza SS. Annunziata 12, 50122 Florence, Italy; tel. (055) 20330; fax (055) 2033220; e-mail florence@unicef.org; internet www.unicef-irc.org; f. 1988.

UNICEF Supply Division: UNICEF Plads, Freeport 2100, Copenhagen, Denmark; tel. 35-27-35-27; fax 35-26-94-21; e-mail supply@unicef.org; internet www.unicef.org/supply.

NATIONAL COMMITTEES

UNICEF is supported by 37 National Committees, mostly in industrialized countries, whose volunteer members, numbering more than 100,000, raise money through various activities, including the sale of greetings cards. The Committees also undertake advocacy and awareness campaigns on a number of issues and provide an important link with the general public.

Activities

UNICEF is dedicated to the well-being of children, adolescents and women and works for the realization and protection of their rights within the frameworks of the Convention on the Rights of the Child, which was adopted by the UN General Assembly in 1989 and by 2007 was almost universally ratified, and of the Convention on the Elimination of All Forms of Discrimination Against Women, adopted by the UN General Assembly in 1979. Promoting the full implementation of the Conventions, UNICEF aims to ensure that children world-wide are given the best possible start in life and attain a good level of basic education, and that adolescents are given every opportunity to develop their capabilities and participate successfully in society. The Fund also continues to provide relief and rehabilitation assistance in emergencies. Through its extensive field network in some 156 developing countries and territories, UNICEF undertakes, in co-ordination with governments, local communities and other aid organizations, programmes in health, nutrition, education, water and sanitation, the environment, gender issues and development, and other fields of importance to children. Emphasis is placed on low-cost, community-based programmes. UNICEF programmes are increasingly focused on supporting children and women during critical periods of their life, when intervention can make a lasting difference. UNICEF is actively involved in global-level partnerships for child protection, including the Inter-Agency Co-ordination Panel on Juvenile Justice; the Inter-Agency Working Group on Unaccompanied and Separated Children; the Donors' Working Group on Female Genital Mutilation/Cutting; the Better Care Network; the Study on Violence Against Children; the Inter-Agency Standing Committee (IASC) Task Force on Protection from Sexual Exploitation and Abuse in Humanitarian Crises; and the IASC Task Force on Mental Health and Psychological Support in Emergency Settings. In 2006 UNICEF allocated 11% of its total programme assistance towards policy advocacy and partnerships for children's rights.

In July 2005 some 64 young people from G8 member states (Canada, France, Germany, Italy, Japan, Russia, the United Kingdom and the USA) participated in the first Junior 8 (J8) summit, organized, with support from UNICEF, on the fringe of the annual G8 summit, convened in that year in Gleneagles, Scotland. The J8 summit addressed issues including education, energy, HIV/AIDS, and tolerance. Young people participating in the second J8 summit, organized to coincide with the 2006 G8 summit, held in St Petersburg, Russia, directly addressed a meeting of G8 leaders. The third J8 summit was convened in Wismar, Germany, in June 2007, and included a meeting with leaders attending the parallel G8 summit convened in nearby Heiligendamm; and the fourth J8 summit meeting was scheduled to take place in Tokyo, Japan, in July 2008.

The five principal themes of UNICEF's medium-term strategic plan for the period 2006–09 are: young child survival and development; basic education and gender equality, including the Fund's continued leadership of the UN Girls' Education Initiative (UNGEI); HIV/AIDS and children, including participation in the Joint UN Programme on HIV/AIDS (UNAIDS—see below); child protection from violence, exploitation and abuse; and policy advocacy and partnerships for children's rights. These priorities are guided by the relevant UN Millennium Development Goals (MDGs) adopted by world leaders in 2000, and by the 'A World Fit for Children' declaration and plan of action endorsed by the UN General Assembly Special Session on Children in 2002 (see below).

UNICEF served as the substantive secretariat for, and played a leading role in helping governments and other partners prepare for, the UN General Assembly Special Session on Children, which was held in May 2002 to assess the outcome of the World Summit for Children convened in 1990 (which had made commitments to reducing mortality rates for infants and children; reducing the maternal mortality rate; reducing severe malnutrition amongst children under five; ensuring universal access to safe drinking water and to sanitary means of excreta disposal; and ensuring universal access to basic education) and to determine a set of actions and objectives for the next 10 years. At the Session the General Assembly adopted a declaration entitled 'A World Fit for Children', reaffirming its commitment to the agenda of the 1990 summit, and outlining a plan of action that resolved to achieve as yet unmet World Summit goals by 2010 and to work towards the attainment by 2015 of 21 new goals and targets supporting the MDGs in the areas of education, health and the protection of children. The latter included: a reduction of mortality rates for infants and children under five by two-thirds; a reduction of maternal mortality rates by three-quarters; a reduction by one-third in the rate for severe malnutrition among children under the age of five; and enrolment in primary education by 90% of children. In December 2007 a special session of the UN General Assembly reviewed progress attained so far towards 'A World Fit for Children'. UNICEF's annual publication *The State of the World's Children* includes social and economic data relevant to the well-being of children. In 1995 UNICEF developed its Multiple Indicator Cluster Survey (MICS) method of data collection, which was in the 2000s being used as a main tool in measuring progress towards the achievement of the UN MDGs.

In 2000 UNICEF launched a new initiative, the Global Movement for Children—comprising governments, private- and public-sector bodies, and individuals—which aimed to rally world-wide support to improve the lives of all children and adolescents. In April 2001 a 'Say Yes for Children' campaign was adopted by the Global Movement, identifying 10 critical actions required to further its objectives. These were: eliminating all forms of discrimination and exclusion; putting children first; ensuring a caring environment for every child; fighting HIV/AIDS; eradicating violence against and abuse and exploitation of children; listening to children's views; universal education; protecting children from war; safeguarding the earth for children; and combating poverty. In 2003 UNICEF, WHO, the World Bank and other partners established a new Child Survival Partnership, which was to act as a forum for the promotion of co-ordinated action in support of efforts to reduce the level of child mortality in 42 targeted developing countries.

UNICEF, in co-operation with other UN agencies, promotes universal access to and completion of basic and good quality education. The Fund, with UNESCO, UNDP, UNFPA and the World Bank, co-sponsored the World Conference on Education for All, held in Thailand in March 1990, and undertook efforts to achieve the objectives formulated by the conference, which included the elimination of disparities in education between boys and girls. UNICEF participated in and fully supports the objectives and framework for action adopted by the World Education Forum in Dakar, Senegal, in April 2000. The Fund supports education projects in sub-Saharan Africa, South Asia and countries in the Middle East, North Africa, and Latin America and the Caribbean, and leads and acts as the secretariat of the United Nations Girls' Education Initiative (UNGEI), which aims to increase the enrolment of girls in primary schools in more than 100 countries. In 2006 about 115m. school-age children world-wide, of whom more than one-half were girls, remained deprived of basic education. Some 21.3% of the Fund's programme assistance was allocated to basic education and gender equality in 2006. Major 'back-to-school' campaigns and enrolment drives were launched in countries struck by the December 2004 Indian Ocean tsunamis; within three months of the disaster 90% of affected children had returned to school. In 2005 approximately 500,000 girls in Afghanistan were enrolled in schools for the first time, and in March 2007 an UNGEI project (the Afghanistan Girls' Education Initiative—AGEI) was launched in that country. UNICEF's annual publication *The State of the World's Children* includes social and economic data relevant to the well-being of children. It was reported in this publication in 2007 that one of the most powerful constraints to realizing children's rights and achieving the MDGs was discrimination against women.

UNICEF works to improve safe water supply, sanitation and hygiene, and thereby reduce the risk of diarrhoea and other water-borne diseases. In partnership with other organizations the Fund supports initiatives to make schools in more than 90 developing countries safer through school-based water, sanitation and hygiene programmes. UNICEF places great emphasis on increasing the testing and protection of drinking water at its source as well as in the home. In 2006 UNICEF and partners established the Global Task Force on Water and Sanitation with the aim of providing all children with access to safe water, and accelerating progress towards MDG targets on safe drinking water and basic sanitation.

UNICEF aims to break the cycle of poverty by advocating for the provision of increased development aid to developing countries, and aims to help poor countries obtain debt relief and to ensure access to basic social services. UNICEF is the leading agency in promoting the 20/20 initiative, which was endorsed at the World Summit for Social Development, held in Copenhagen, Denmark, in March 1995. The initiative encourages the governments of developing and donor countries to allocate at least 20% of their domestic budgets and official development aid respectively, to healthcare, primary education and low-cost safe water and sanitation.

UNICEF estimates that the births of some 50m. children annually are not officially registered, and promotes universal registration in order to prevent the abuse of children without proof of age and nationality, for example through trafficking, forced labour, early marriage and military recruitment. It estimates that some 218m. children were involved in exploitative labour (excluding domestic work) in 2004, and approximately 126m. children aged five–17 were believed to be engaged in hazardous work. It is estimated that, annually, around 1.2m. children world-wide are trafficked. The Fund, which vigorously opposes the exploitation of children as a violation of their basic human rights, works with ILO and other partners to promote an end to exploitative and hazardous child labour, and supports special projects to provide education, counselling and care in developing countries. UNICEF co-sponsored and actively participated in the Second Congress Against Commercial Sexual Exploitation of Children held in Yokohama, Japan, in December 2001. Some 10.2% of the Fund's direct programme assistance was allocated to the improved protection of children in 2006.

In 2006 UNICEF allocated 51% of its programme assistance to young child survival and development. The Fund estimated that around 9.7m. children under five years of age died in 2006 (compared with some 20m. and 13m. child mortalities in, respectively, 1960 and 1990), mainly in developing countries, and the majority from largely preventable causes. UNICEF has worked with WHO and other partners to increase global immunization coverage against the following six diseases: measles, poliomyelitis, tuberculosis, diphtheria, whooping cough and tetanus. In 2003 UNICEF, WHO, the World Bank and other partners established a new Child Survival Partnership, which acts as a forum for the promotion of co-ordinated action in support of efforts to save the children's lives in 42 targeted developing countries. In September 2005 UNICEF, WHO and other partners launched the Partnership for Maternal, Newborn and Child Health, formed to accelerate progress towards MDGs four and five, which aim to reduce child and maternal mortality respectively. In 2000 UNICEF, WHO, the World Bank and a number of public- and private-sector partners launched the Global Alliance for Vaccines and Immunization (GAVI, subsequently renamed the Gavi Alliance), which aims to protect children of all nationalities and socio-economic groups against vaccine-preventable diseases. GAVI's strategy includes improving access to sustainable immunization services, expanding the use of existing vaccines, accelerating the development and introduction of new vaccines and technologies and promoting immunization coverage as a focus of international development efforts.

The results of integrated approaches to child health, such as the Accelerated Child Survival and Development (ACSD) strategy and community-based Integrated Management of Childhood Illnesses (IMCI) programme, have demonstrated new potential to reduce child mortality. The ACSD strategy, implemented by UNICEF since 2002, is an intensive combination of life-saving interventions including the promotion of antenatal care, vaccination and breast-feeding, volunteer health-worker follow-up of newborns and the distribution of insecticide-treated mosquito nets. Focused in 97 high-mortality districts in 11 mainly West African countries, ACSD has reached around 16m. people, including 2.8m. children under the age of five.

In 2006 UNICEF issued a report entitled *Pneumonia: The Forgotten Killer of Children*, which identified pneumonia as the primary medical cause of all deaths of children under five years of age.

At the UN General Assembly Special Session on Children, in 2002, goals were set to reduce measles deaths by 50%. Expanded efforts by UNICEF, WHO and other partners led to a reduction in world-wide measles deaths by around 60% between 1999 and 2005.

UNICEF-assisted programmes for the control of diarrhoeal diseases promote the low-cost manufacture and distribution of prepackaged salts or home-made solutions. The use of 'oral rehydration therapy' has risen significantly in recent years, and is believed to prevent more than 1m. child deaths annually. During 1990–2000 diarrhoea-related deaths were reduced by one-half. UNICEF also promotes the need to improve sanitation and access to safe water supplies in developing nations in order to reduce the risk of diarrhoea and other water-borne diseases (see 20/20 initiative, above). To control acute respiratory infections, another leading cause of death in children under five in developing countries, UNICEF works with WHO in training health workers to diagnose and treat the associated diseases. Around 1m. children die from malaria every year, mainly in sub-Saharan Africa. In October 1998 UNICEF, together with WHO, UNDP and the World Bank, inaugurated a new global campaign, Roll Back Malaria, to fight the disease. UNICEF is actively engaged in developing innovative and effective ways to distribute highly-subsidized insecticide-treated mosquito nets at local level, thereby increasing the proportion of children and pregnant women who use them.

According to UNICEF estimates, around 25% of children under five years of age are underweight, while each year malnutrition contributes to about one-half of the child deaths in that age group and leaves millions of others with physical and mental disabilities. More than 2,000m. people world-wide (mainly women and children in developing countries) are estimated to be deficient in one or more essential vitamins and minerals, such as vitamin A, iodine and iron. UNICEF supports national efforts to reduce malnutrition, for example, fortifying staple foods with micronutrients, widening women's access to education, improving the nutritional status of pregnant women, improving household food security and basic health services, providing food supplies in emergencies, and promoting sound childcare and feeding practices. Since 1991 more than 19,000 hospitals in about 130 countries have been designated 'baby-friendly', having implemented a set of UNICEF and WHO recommendations entitled '10 steps to successful breast-feeding'. In 1996 UNICEF expressed its concern at the impact of international economic embargoes on child health, citing as an example the extensive levels of child malnutrition recorded in Iraq. UNICEF remains actively concerned at the levels of child malnutrition and accompanying diseases in Iraq and in the Democratic People's Republic of Korea, which has also suffered severe food shortages.

UNICEF estimates that more than 500,000 women die every year during pregnancy or childbirth, largely because of inadequate maternal healthcare. For every maternal death, approximately 30 further women suffer permanent injuries or chronic disabilities as a result of complications during pregnancy or childbirth. With its partners in the Safe Motherhood Initiative—UNFPA, WHO, the World Bank, the International Planned Parenthood Federation, the Population Council, and Family Care International—UNICEF promotes measures to reduce maternal mortality and morbidity, including improving access to quality reproductive health services, educating communities about safe motherhood and the rights of women, training midwives, and expanding access to family planning services. Under the Global Partnership for Maternal, Newborn and Child Health, UNICEF works with WHO, UNFPA and other partners in countries with high maternal mortality to improve maternal health and prevent maternal deaths. UNICEF and partners work with governments and policy-makers to ensure that emergency obstetric care is a priority in national health plans. In 200 UNICEF activities in this area included support for obstetric facilities and training in, and advocacy of, women's health issues such as avoiding child marriage, eliminating female genital mutilation/cutting (FGM/C), and preventing malaria and promoting the uptake of tetanus toxoid vaccinations and iron and folic acid supplements among pregnant women.

UNICEF is concerned at the danger posed by HIV/AIDS to the realization of children's rights and in 2006 allocated 5.5% of its programme expenditure to this area. At the end of 2007 it was estimated that 2.1m. children under the age of 15 were living with HIV/AIDS world-wide. During that year some 420,000 children under the age of 15 were estimated to have been newly infected with the HIV virus, while 290,000 died as a result of AIDS and AIDS-related illnesses. It is believed that more than 15m. children worldwide have lost one or both parents to AIDS since the start of the pandemic. UNICEF's priorities in this area include prevention of infection among young people (through, for example, support for education programmes and dissemination of information through the media), reduction in mother-to-child transmission, care and protection of orphans and other vulnerable children, and care and support for children, young people and parents living with HIV/AIDS. UNICEF works closely in this field with governments and co-operates with other UN agencies in the Joint UN Programme on HIV/AIDS (UNAIDS), which became operational on 1 January 1996. In July 2002 UNICEF, UNAIDS and WHO jointly produced a study entitled *Young People and HIV/AIDS: Opportunity in Crisis*, examining young people's sexual behaviour patterns and knowledge of HIV/AIDS. UNICEF advocates Life Skills-Based Education as a means of empowering young people to cope with challenging situations and encouraging them to adopt healthy patterns of behaviour. In July 2004 UNICEF and other partners produced a *Framework for the Protection, Care and Support of Orphans and Vulnerable Children Living in a World with HIV and AIDS*. In October 2005 UNICEF launched Unite for Children, Unite Against AIDS, a campaign that was to provide a platform for child-focused advocacy aimed at reversing the spread of HIV/AIDS amongst children, adolescents and young people; and to provide a child-focused framework for national programmes based on the following four pillars: the prevention of mother-to-child HIV transmission, improved provision of paediatric treatment, prevention of infection among adolescents and young people, and protection and support of children affected by HIV/AIDS. In January 2007 UNICEF issued *Children and AIDS: A stocktaking report* detailing the progress and challenges of the previous year.

UNICEF provides emergency relief assistance to children and young people affected by conflict, natural disasters and food crises. In situations of violence and social disintegration the Fund provides support in the areas of education, health, mine-awareness and psychosocial assistance, and helps to demobilize and rehabilitate child soldiers. In recent years several such operations have been undertaken, including in Afghanistan, Burundi, Democratic Republic of the Congo, Iraq, Liberia, the Palestinian territories, Sierra Leone, Somalia and Sudan. In December 2007 UNICEF appealed for some US $237.4m. through the UN Consolidated Inter-Agency Appeal Process to fund emergency assistance to children and women in emergencies in 2008. In 1999 UNICEF adopted a Peace and Security Agenda to help guide international efforts in this field. Emergency education assistance includes the provision of 'Edukits' in refugee camps and the reconstruction of school buildings. In the area of health the Fund co-operates with WHO to arrange 'days of tranquility' in order to facilitate the immunization of children in conflict zones. Psychosocial assistance activities include special programmes to support traumatized children and help unaccompanied children to be reunited with parents or extended families.

In 2006 UNICEF provided primary health care to some 2.1m. people in Darfur, Sudan, and worked with partners to supply camps with safe water and basic sanitation to the region. During that year UNICEF also conducted a 'Go to School' campaign in Darfur, and 1.2m. children were also immunized against polio and given vitamin A supplements.

In the mid-2000s UNICEF country offices prepared contingency plans for a possible future avian influenza pandemic among humans, with a particular focus on children, as part of the inter-agency response to the threat.

An estimated 250,000 children are involved in armed conflicts as soldiers, porters and forced labourers. UNICEF encourages ratification of the Optional Protocol to the Convention on the Rights of the Child on the involvement of children in armed conflict, which was adopted by the General Assembly in May 2000 and entered into force in February 2002, and bans the compulsory recruitment of combatants below the age of 18. The Fund also urges states to make unequivocal statements endorsing 18 as the minimum age of voluntary recruitment to the armed forces. It is estimated that land-mines kill and maim between 8,000 and 10,000 children every year. The Convention on the Prohibition of the Use, Stockpiling, Production and Transfer of Anti-Personnel Mines and on their Destruction was adopted in December 1997 and entered into force in March 1999. By March 2008 the Convention had been ratified by 155 countries. UNICEF is committed to campaigning for its universal ratification and full implementation, and also supports mine-awareness campaigns.

During 2005 the UN's Inter-Agency Standing Committee (IASC), concerned with co-ordinating the international response to humanitarian disasters, developed a concept of organizing agency assistance to IDPs through the institutionalization of a 'Cluster Approach', currently comprising 11 core areas of activity. UNICEF was designated the lead agency for the clusters on Education (jointly with Save The Children); Emergency Telecommunications (jointly with OCHA and WFP); Nutrition; Protection of IDPs in natural disaster situations and of non-IDP civilians in conflict situations (with UNHCR and OHCHR); and Water, Sanitation and Hygiene.

Finance

UNICEF is funded by voluntary contributions from governments and non-governmental and private-sector sources. UNICEF's income is divided into contributions for 'regular resources' (used for country programmes of co-operation approved by the Executive Board, programme support, and management and administration costs) and contributions for 'other resources' (for special purposes, including expanding the outreach of country programmes of co-operation and ensuring capacity to deliver critical assistance to women and children, for example during humanitarian crises). Total income in 2006 amounted to US $2,781m., of which 64% was from

governments and intergovernmental organizations, and 29% from private-sector sources.
UNICEF's total expenditure in 2006 was estimated at US $2,343m.

Publications

Progress for Children (in English, French and Spanish).

The State of the World's Children (annually, in Arabic, English, French, Russian and Spanish and about 30 other national languages).
UNICEF Annual Report (in English, French and Spanish).
UNICEF at a Glance (in English, French and Spanish).
Young People in Changing Societies (annually).

Reports and studies; series on children and women; nutrition; education; children's rights; children in wars and disasters; working children; water, sanitation and the environment; analyses of the situation of children and women in individual developing countries.

United Nations Conference on Trade and Development—UNCTAD

Address: Palais des Nations, 1211 Geneva 10, Switzerland.
Telephone: 229175809; **fax:** 229170051; **e-mail:** info@unctad.org; **internet:** www.unctad.org.

UNCTAD was established in December 1964. It is the principal instrument of the UN General Assembly concerned with trade and development, and is the focal point within the UN system for integrated activities relating to trade, finance, technology, investment and sustainable development. It aims to maximize the trade and development opportunities of developing countries, in particular least-developed countries, and to assist them to adapt to the increasing globalization and liberalization of the world economy.

Organization
(March 2008)

CONFERENCE

The Conference is the organization's highest policy-making body and normally meets every four years at ministerial level in order to formulate major policy guide-lines and to decide on UNCTAD's forthcoming programme of work. The 11th session was held in São Paulo, Brazil, in June 2004 and the 12th session was scheduled to be held in Accra, Ghana, in April 2008. As well as its 192 members, many intergovernmental and non-governmental organizations (NGOs) participate in UNCTAD's work as observers.

TRADE AND DEVELOPMENT BOARD

The Trade and Development Board is the executive body of UNCTAD. It comprises elected representatives from 146 UNCTAD member states and is responsible for ensuring the overall consistency of UNCTAD's activities, as well as those of its subsidiary bodies. The Board meets for a regular annual session lasting about 10 days, at which it examines global economic issues. It may also meet a further three times a year in order to address management or institutional matters.

COMMISSIONS

The Trade and Development Board has three Commissions: the Commission on Trade in Goods and Services and Commodities; the Commission on Investment, Technology and Related Financial Issues; and the Commission on Enterprise, Business Facilitation and Development. The Commissions meet once a year in regular session and may convene up to 10 Expert Meetings a year on specific issues.

SECRETARIAT

The secretariat comprises the following Divisions: Globalization and Development Strategies; Investment, Technology and Enterprise Development; International Trade in Goods and Services, and Commodities; Services Infrastructure for Development and Trade Efficiency; Africa, Least Developed Countries and Special Programmes; and Management.

The UNCTAD secretariat, comprising some 402 staff, undertakes policy analysis; monitoring, implementation and follow-up of decisions of intergovernmental bodies; technical co-operation in support of UNCTAD's policy objectives; and information exchanges and consultations of various types.

Secretary-General: Dr Supachai Panitchpakdi (Thailand).

Activities

UNCTAD activities are underpinned by the three major pillars of consensus-building; research and policy analysis; and technical assistance. The Conference has five main programmes of work: Globalization and development strategies; Investment, technology and enterprise development; International trade in goods and services, and commodities; Services infrastructure and trade efficiency; and Africa, least developed countries and special programmes.

In February 2000 the 10th session of the Conference, held in Bangkok, Thailand, adopted the Bangkok Declaration, which stated the importance of promoting equitable and sustainable development in view of increasing global interdependence, trade liberalization and advances in technology. The Declaration emphasized UNCTAD's commitment to a fair, non-discriminatory and fully-integrated multilateral trading system that would not tolerate the marginalization of the world's least developed economies, and urged that the next round of multilateral trade negotiations address development issues. The Declaration noted the need for increased policy coherence at national and international level, and for more effective co-operation and co-ordination among multilateral institutions. It recommended open debate on global development issues by all development partners, including the private sector, NGOs, academics and politicians. The Conference also adopted the Bangkok Plan of Action which assessed the consequences of globalization for development, recommended measures to be implemented by the international community, and provided a strategic framework for UNCTAD's future work programme. The 11th session of the Conference was convened in São Paulo, Brazil, in June 2004, on the theme of 'Enhancing coherence between national development strategies and global economic processes towards economic growth and development'. The 11th session issued the São Paulo Consensus, which determined that the Bangkok Plan of Action should continue to serve as a strategic framework for the work of the organization and established specific policy direction for the next four years; and emphasized that development strategies should be formulated with a view to minimizing the negative social impact of globalization, urging that efforts should converge at the international level on working towards the attainment of the UN Millennium Goals. In October 2005 the UNCTAD Secretary-General established a Panel of Eminent Persons, which was to consider strategies for enhancing UNCTAD's development role and impact and for fulfilling the Conference's development mission and the mandates contained in the Bangkok Plan of Action and the São Paulo Consensus; in June 2006 the Panel issued a report detailing its findings.

GLOBALIZATION AND DEVELOPMENT STATEGIES

UNCTAD works to promote policies and strategies at national and international level in support of development, and analyses issues, such as financial crises, to support sustainable economic management. It contributed to the implementation and review of the UN New Agenda for the Development of Africa in the 1990s (UNNADF). UNCTAD provides assistance to developing countries in the area of debt-management, and in seeking debt relief from their creditors. UNCTAD is responsible for the software component of a joint programme with the World Bank to extend technical co-operation to developing countries in the field of debt management. The assistance is based on the development and distribution of software (the Debt Management and Financial Analysis System—DMFAS) designed to enable debtor countries to analyse data, make projections, and to plan strategies for debt repayment and reorganization. By March 2008 the programme had supported 66 countries, involving 99 institutions. UNCTAD provides training for operators in the use of the software, and for senior officials, to increase their awareness of institutional reforms which might be necessary for effective debt management. In November 2007 the Sixth UNCTAD Debt Management Conference was held in Geneva with participation by debt managers and policy makers including representatives of governments, international organizations, the private financial and legal sector, academia and civil society from more than 70 countries.

In 1995 UNCTAD initiated a programme of technical assistance to support the Palestinian people, within the context of involvement with Palestinian economy which had begun in 1979 with a study of the economic situation in the occupied territories.

The 2006 edition of UNCTAD's annual *Trade and Development Report*, published in August of that year, urged that international measures be taken to lessen global trade imbalances in order to avoid potential future financial crises in developing countries. The *Report* emphasized the need to alter the orientation of aid to enable it better to contribute to the establishment of enterprises and production systems that could generate employment for people moving from rural to urban areas. It was noted that insufficient urban employment prospects in developing countries were resulting in a high level of emigration to industrialized countries. The *Report* also proposed that developing countries should be allowed greater 'policy space' and recommended that their governments foster industrial policies aimed at promoting economic growth and structural change in order to generate employment and raise living standards over the long term. This was considered to be a departure from the climate of the 1980s and 1990s, in which international organizations had urged developing nations to give precedence to market forces.

The 2007 edition of the *Trade and Development Report*, published in September 2007 with the subtitle *Regional Co-operation for Development*, urged the strengthening of regional co-operation between developing countries, but also recommended a cautious approach towards the adoption of North-South bilateral or regional preferential trade agreements, on the grounds that, alongside expanding market access and foreign direct investment (FDI), these could also restrict national 'policy space'.

INTERNATIONAL TRADE IN GOODS AND SERVICES, AND COMMODITIES

The International Trade Centre in Geneva is operated jointly by the World Trade Organization—WTO and UNCTAD. UNCTAD has supported 27 countries through the process of accession to the WTO. The UNCTAD Secretariat provided technical assistance to developing countries in connection with the Uruguay Round of multilateral trade negotiations, and in February 2002 UNCTAD initiated a new capacity-building and technical assistance programme to help developing countries in the Doha Development Round of trade negotiations.

UNCTAD has provided a forum for the negotiation of, and monitors and facilitates, international agreements on commodities, including cocoa, jute, rubber and tropical timber. (Such agreements are designed to ensure the stabilization of conditions in the trade of the commodities concerned.) The establishment of the Common Fund for Commodities was agreed by UNCTAD in 1980, and the Fund came into operation in 1989. More recently UNCTAD has been concerned to assist countries to adopt risk management and financial strategies against commodity dependence and price fluctuation, and to encourage diversification to reduce dependence on single commodities. Under the Bangkok agreements, UNCTAD was committed to improve market transparency and the availability of information, in particular through the improved use of technology.

Since the 1970s UNCTAD has been actively involved in work relating to restrictive business practices. In 1980 the UN General Assembly adopted a set of mutually agreed equitable principles and rules for the control of restrictive business practices, which had been negotiated under UNCTAD auspices. An Intergovernmental Group of Experts monitors and reviews its implementation. UNCTAD provides technical assistance to developing countries in the formulation and enforcement of competition legislation and consumer protection law and policies. It is also responsible for reviewing the developmental impact of international agreements on competition law. Through its Programme on Dispute Settlements UNCTAD provides training on aspects of settlement in international trade, investment and intellectual property disputes. UNCTAD has established a Commercial Diplomacy Programme to provide training and capacity-building to strengthen the participation and effectiveness of developing member countries in international and regional trade negotiations.

During the 1990s UNCTAD undertook research into the design and implementation of a multilateral system to trade emissions of so-called greenhouse gases. UNCTAD's Carbon Market Programme analyses the impact of measures to address climate change through the reduction of greenhouse gas emissions and works to promote a fair and effective global carbon market. In June 1997, in co-operation with the Earth Council, UNCTAD established a Greenhouse Gas Emissions Trading Policy Forum to support the development of a plurilateral emissions market. In June 1999 the International Emissions Trading Association (IETA) was established, sponsored by UNCTAD and the Earth Council. The IETA, which was envisaged as a successor to the Forum, comprised commercial companies, business organizations and regional and national trading associations, as well as invited international organizations, research institutes and NGOs. It was to serve as a forum for the exchange of information and ideas relating to international emissions trading and as a means of developing the market in emission permit trading, which was scheduled to be launched in 2008. During the initial phase of the IETA's operations UNCTAD provided temporary secretariat support. In September 2007 UNCTAD became one of the first UN agencies to adopt a Carbon Neutral Initiative.

UNCTAD is responsible for the Generalized System of Preferences (GSP), initiated in 1971, whereby a proportion of both agricultural and manufactured goods that are exported by developing countries receive preferential tariff treatment by certain developed countries, Russia and several central European countries. UNCTAD monitors changes in and amendments to national GSP schemes and reviews the use of these schemes by beneficiary developing countries. In addition, the Commission on Trade in Goods and Services and Commodities (see above) is responsible for providing a forum to examine the operation of schemes, the benefits they offer and the future role of the GSP. In March 2001 the European Union introduced a new initiative, the so-called Everything but Arms scheme, to amend the GSP regime in member countries to provide free market access to all products from LDCs (see below), except arms and munitions, and with special provisions for rice, sugar and bananas. UNCTAD's database of trade control measures has been made available through a Trade Analysis and Information System (TRAINS). A Trade Analysis Branch aims to improve the understanding of current and emerging issues in international trade of concern to developing countries. UNCTAD and the World Bank jointly developed the World Integrated Trade Solution (WITS), providing access to trade data through the internet.

In January 2008 UNCTAD issued a report entitled *Erosion of trade preferences in the post-Hong Kong framework: From 'trade is better than aid' to 'aid for trade'*, addressing the trade preference situation since the WTO's Sixth Ministerial Conference held in Hong Kong in December 2005.

In 1996 UNCTAD launched a BioTrade Initiative to stimulate trade and investment in biological resources, as a basis for equitable, sustainable development. Under the Initiative UNCTAD has established partnerships with national and regional organizations, using their local knowledge and expertise to develop and implement biodiversity programmes. The Initiative also supports the development of appropriate policies and legislation to support the sustainable trade and investment in biodiversity, i.e. to address issues such as benefit sharing, intellectual property rights and poverty alleviation. In 2002 UNCTAD and the International Trade Centre jointly launched a BioTrade Facilitation Programme, which aimed to promote the trade in biodiversity products and services through arrangements that would enhance sustainable bio-resources management, product development, value-adding processing and marketing.

INVESTMENT, TECHNOLOGY AND ENTERPRISE DEVELOPMENT

UNCTAD has been mandated as the organ within the UN system responsible for negotiating a multilateral framework governing FDI that would protect the interests of the poorest countries, taking account of the work already undertaken by OECD in this area. In UNCTAD's revised approach, encouragement of FDI and of domestic private enterprise in developing countries and countries in transition have become central to the agency's work. UNCTAD is increasingly seeking the input and participation of non-governmental groups, such as academics, NGOs and business representatives, in its intergovernmental machinery, where appropriate. UNCTAD's Division of Investment, Technology and Enterprise Development organizes regional meetings, technical symposia and training courses in aspects of international investment agreements. It also conducts Investment Policy Reviews to assess and promote a country's investment potential. Within the Division the Advisory Service on Investment and Training (ASIT) executes the technical assistance programme for investment promotion strategies. UNCTAD'S Commission on Investment, Technology and Related Financial Issues undertakes the functions of the former ECOSOC Commission on International Investment and Transnational Corporations, which aimed to provide an understanding of the nature of FDI and transnational corporations, to secure effective international agreements and to strengthen the capacity of developing countries in their dealings with transnational corporations through an integrated approach, including research, information and technical assistance. A subsidiary body—the Intergovernmental Group of Experts on International Standards of Accounting and Reporting—aimed to improve the availability of information disclosed by transnational corporations. In November 1997 the UN General Assembly endorsed a proposal of the UN Secretary-General that the Group report directly through the UNCTAD Commission on Investment, Technology and Related Financial Issues.

The Commission on Enterprise, Business Facilitation and Development advises countries on policy-related issues and training activities concerning the development of entrepreneurship. It facilitates the exchange of experiences on the formulation and implementation of enterprise development strategies, including privatization, public-sector co-operation and the special problems relating to enterprise development in countries in economic transition. Since 1996 UNCTAD has administered EMPRETEC, initially started as a pilot programme in 1988, which undertakes capacity-building activities to develop institutional structures supportive of enterprise and small business ventures. The programme also aims to foster business links with other transnational corporations (TNCs). The 2006 *Report on Trade and Development* noted the increasing influence of TNCs based in developing countries, particularly in Asia, and the focus of such corporations on channelling FDI in the sphere of South-South investment.

UNCTAD services the ECOSOC Commission on Science and Technology for Development, which provides a forum for discussion of the following issues relating to science and technology for development: technology for small-scale economic activities to address the basic needs of low-income countries; gender implications of science and technology for developing countries; science and technology and the environment; the contribution of technologies to industrialization in developing countries; and the role of information technologies, in particular in relation to developing countries.

SERVICES INFRASTRUCTURE AND TRADE EFFICIENCY

Activities to enhance transport and trade logistics constitute an important component of UNCTAD's efforts to improve the participation of developing countries in international trade. It convenes expert meetings, extends technical support and organizes specialized training activities. In March 1999, at a diplomatic conference held under the auspices of UNCTAD and the International Maritime Organization (IMO), an International Convention on the Arrest of Ships was adopted. Other initiatives have resulted in the adoption of the UN Convention on the Carriage of Goods by Sea (Hamburg Rules—1978), the UN Convention on International Multimodal Transport (1980), the UN Convention on a Code of Conduct for Liner Conferences (effective from 1983), the UN Convention on Conditions for Registration of Ships (1986), and the International Convention on Maritime Liens and Mortgages. UNCTAD administers a Port Training Programme, as part of its TrainforTrade initiative, which emphasizes the need for human resources and capacity-building activities to support trading efforts by developing countries. UNCTAD promotes the use of e-commerce as a means of development. It publishes an annual *E-Commerce and Development Report* which analyses issues that influence the expansion of e-commerce in developing countries and identifies means of promoting its use in order to support economic and social development. UNCTAD organized a meeting on e-finance at the UN International Conference on Financing for Development, which was held in Monterrey, Mexico, in March 2002. During the 1980s UNCTAD developed an Automated System for Customs Data (ASYCUDA), which by March 2008 was operational in more than 80 countries and regions. It serves as a customs management system, using international standards, covering essential trade procedures, such as customs declarations, accounting procedures and transit documentation. In March 2002 UNCTAD inaugurated a fully electronic version of ASYCUDA to enable transactions to be undertaken using the internet. A software package, Advance Cargo Information System (ACIS), enables shipping lines and railway companies to track the movement of cargo. Through the use of ACIS and ASYCUDA UNCTAD aims to enhance the effective exchange of information in order to counter customs fraud.

In November 2002 the Global Trade Point Network (GTPNet), which was launched by UNCTAD in 1994 as an electronic source of trade-related information for use by small and medium-sized enterprises, was transferred to the World Trade Point Federation, an organization established by UNCTAD in 2000 to represent the programme's beneficiaries and to maintain the network of trade points.

The 2006 *Report on Trade and Development*, reviewing trends in information and communication technology, noted that in the business world broadband internet access was acquiring the status of an essential utility, and that it was essential to expand access to this in developing countries.

AFRICA, LEAST DEVELOPED COUNTRIES AND SPECIAL PROGRAMMES

UNCTAD aims to give particular attention to the needs of the world's 50 (at March 2008) least developed countries (LDCs—as defined by the UN). At March 2008 some 34 of the LDCs were in Africa. The Conference also places particular focus on the special problems and challenges faced by small island states, landlocked developing countries, economies in transition, and so-called structurally weak, vulnerable and small economies. The eighth session of the Conference requested that detailed analyses of the socio-economic situations and domestic policies of the LDCs, their resource needs, and external factors affecting their economies be undertaken as part of UNCTAD's work programme. The ninth session determined that particular attention be given to the problems of the LDCs in all areas of UNCTAD's work. The 10th session focused on the impact of globalization on developing economies and on means of improving trade opportunities for the LDCs. The 11th session noted the increasing marginalization of the LDCs in the global economy and urged UNCTAD to consider solutions to this. UNCTAD serves as the secretariat for the UN Conference on the Least Developed Countries, which are convened every 10 years. The (most recent) Third UN Conference on the Least Developed Countries, which took place in Brussels, Belgium, in May 2001, was attended by more than 6,500 participants from governments, NGOs and other elements of civil society, and considered issues including governance, peace and social stability, enhancing productive capacities, intellectual property and development, infrastructure development, and financing growth and development. A Brussels Programme of Action for 2001–10, which had been elaborated by LDCs and their development partners, was adopted by the Third Conference. UNCTAD was mandated to assist with its implementation, with particular emphasis on the needs of land-locked and small island developing states. UNCTAD issues an annual report on the Brussels Programme of Action presenting relevant policy research, and offers targeted technical assistance and co-operation in support of the Programme.

UNCTAD co-operates closely with the New Partnership on Africa's Development (NEPAD). In July 2005, meeting in Gleneagles, Scotland, the annual summit of G8 leaders determined to double assistance to Africa by 2010, as first recommended by UNCTAD in 2000. In September 2006 UNCTAD issued a report entitled *Economic Development in Africa—Doubling Aid: Making the 'Big Push' Work*, in which the Conference welcomed the pledges of the G8 leaders, while also noting serious shortcomings in the existing aid delivery system. The report proposed the establishment of a new architecture for the application of official development assistance, recommending that the multilateral nature of such support should be strengthened and that it should be channelled through a UN funding window. In September 2007 UNCTAD published *Economic Development in Africa—Reclaiming Policy Space: Domestic Resource Mobilization and Development States*, in which it recommended the promotion of a 'diversity of policies' tailored to specific national situations, rather than the application of a one-size-fits-all approach to policy-making on economic development in Africa.

Finance

The operational expenses of UNCTAD are borne by the regular budget of the UN, and amount to approximately US $50m. annually. Technical co-operation activities, financed from extra-budgetary resources, amount to some $25m. annually.

Publications

Development and Globalization: Facts and Figures.
E-commerce and Development Report (annually).
Economic Development in Africa Report.
Information Economy Report.
Least Developed Countries Report (annually).
Trade and Development Report (annually).
Trade and Environment Review.
UNCTAD Handbook of Statistics (annually, also available on DVD-Rom and online).
UNCTAD News (3 a year).
World Commodity Survey.
World Investment Report (annually).

United Nations Development Programme—UNDP

Address: One United Nations Plaza, New York, NY 10017, USA.
Telephone: (212) 906-5295; **fax:** (212) 906-5364; **e-mail:** hq@undp.org; **internet:** www.undp.org.

The Programme was established in 1965 by the UN General Assembly. Its central mission is to help countries to eradicate poverty and achieve a sustainable level of human development, an approach to economic growth that encompasses individual well-being and choice, equitable distribution of the benefits of development, and conservation of the environment. UNDP advocates for a more inclusive global economy. UNDP is the focus of UN efforts to achieve the Millennium Development Goals.

Organization
(March 2008)

UNDP is responsible to the UN General Assembly, to which it reports through ECOSOC.

EXECUTIVE BOARD

The Executive Board is responsible for providing intergovernmental support to, and supervision of, the activities of UNDP and the UN Population Fund (UNFPA). It comprises 36 members: eight from Africa, seven from Asia and the Pacific, four from eastern Europe, five from Latin America and the Caribbean and 12 from western Europe and other countries. Members serve a three-year term.

SECRETARIAT

Offices and divisions at the Secretariat include: an Operations Support Group; Offices of the United Nations Development Group, the Human Development Report, Development Studies, Audit and Performance Review, Evaluation, and Communications; and Bureaux for Crisis Prevention and Recovery, Resources and Strategic Partnerships, Development Policy, and Management. Five regional bureaux, all headed by an assistant administrator, cover: Africa; Asia and the Pacific; the Arab states; Latin America and the Caribbean; and Europe and the Commonwealth of Independent States.

Administrator: KEMAL DERVİŞ (Turkey).
Associate Administrator: AD MELKERT (Netherlands).

COUNTRY OFFICES

In almost every country receiving UNDP assistance there is an office, headed by the UNDP Resident Representative, who usually also serves as UN Resident Co-ordinator, responsible for the co-ordination of all UN technical assistance and operational development activities, advising the Government on formulating the country programme, ensuring that field activities are undertaken, and acting as the leader of the UN team of experts working in the country. The offices function as the primary presence of the UN in most developing countries.

Activities

UNDP provides advisory and support services to governments and UN teams with the aim of advancing sustainable human development and building national development capabilities. Assistance is mostly non-monetary, comprising the provision of experts' services, consultancies, equipment and training for local workers. Developing countries themselves contribute significantly to the total project costs in terms of personnel, facilities, equipment and supplies. UNDP also supports programme countries in attracting aid and utilizing it efficiently. A network of nine Sub-regional Resource Facilities (SURFs) has been established to strengthen and co-ordinate UNDP's role as a global knowledge provider and channel for sharing knowledge and experience.

During the late 1990s UNDP undertook an extensive internal process of reform, 'UNDP 2001', which placed increased emphasis on its activities in the field and on performance and accountability. In 2001 UNDP established a series of Thematic Trust Funds to enable increased support of priority programme activities. In accordance with the more results-oriented approach developed under the 'UNDP 2001' process UNDP introduced a new Multi-Year Funding Framework (MYFF), which outlined the country-driven goals around which funding was to be mobilized, integrating programme objectives, resources, budget and outcomes. The MYFF was to provide the basis for the Administrator's Business Plans for the same duration and enables policy coherence in the implementation of programmes at country, regional and global levels. A Results-Oriented Annual Report (ROAR) was produced for the first time in 2000 from data compiled by country offices and regional programmes. In September 2000 the first ever Ministerial Meeting of ministers of development co-operation and foreign affairs and other senior officials from donor and programme countries, convened in New York, USA, endorsed UNDP's shift to a results-based orientation.

In accordance with the second phase of the MYFF, covering 2004–07, UNDP focused on the following five practice areas: democratic governance; poverty reduction; energy and the environment; crisis prevention and recovery; and combating HIV/AIDS. Other important 'cross-cutting' themes, to be incorporated throughout the programme areas, included gender equality and the empowerment of women, information and communication technologies, and human rights. UNDP's Strategic Plan for the period 2008–11 emphasized UNDP's 'overarching' contribution to achieving sustainable human development through capacity development strategies, to be integrated into all areas of activity. Other objectives identified by the Plan included strengthening national ownership of development projects and promoting and facilitating South-South co-operation.

From the mid-1990s UNDP assumed a more active and integrative role within the UN system-wide development framework. UNDP Resident Representatives—usually also serving as UN Resident Co-ordinators, with responsibility for managing inter-agency co-operation on sustainable human development initiatives at country level—were to play a focal role in implementing this approach. In order to promote its co-ordinating function UNDP allocated increased resources to training and skill-sharing programmes. In 1997 the UNDP Administrator was appointed to chair the UN Development Group (UNDG), which was established as part of a series of structural reform measures initiated by the UN Secretary-General, with the aim of strengthening collaboration between all UN funds, programmes and bodies concerned with development. The UNDG promotes coherent policy at country level through the system of UN Resident Co-ordinators (see above), the Common Country Assessment mechanism (CCA, a country-based process for evaluating national development situations), and the UN Development Assistance Framework (UNDAF, the foundation for planning and co-ordinating development operations at country level, based on the CCA). Within the framework of the Administrator's Business Plans for 2000–03 a new Bureau for Resources and Strategic Partnerships was established to build and strengthen working partnerships with other UN bodies, donor and programme countries, international financial institutions and development banks, civil society organizations and the private sector. The Bureau was also to serve UNDP's regional bureaux and country offices through the exchange of information and promotion of partnership strategies.

MILLENNIUM DEVELOPMENT GOALS

UNDP, through its leadership of the UNDG and management of the Resident Co-ordinator system, has a co-ordinating function as the focus of UN system-wide efforts to achieve the so-called Millennium Development Goals (MDGs), pledged by 189 governments attending a summit meeting of the UN General Assembly in September 2000. The objectives were to establish a defined agenda to reduce poverty and improve the quality of lives of millions of people and to serve as a framework for measuring development. There are eight MDGs, as follows, for which one or more specific targets have been identified:

i) to eradicate extreme poverty and hunger, with the aim of reducing by 50% the number of people with an income of less than US $1 a day and those suffering from hunger by 2015, and to achieve full and productive employment and decent work for all, including women and young people;

ii) to achieve universal primary education by 2015;

iii) to promote gender equality and empower women, in particular to eliminate gender disparities in primary and secondary education by 2005 and at all levels by 2015;

iv) to reduce child mortality, with a target reduction of two-thirds in the mortality rate among children under five by 2015;

v) to improve maternal health, specifically to reduce by 75% the numbers of women dying in childbirth and to achieve universal access to reproductive health by 2015;

vi) to combat HIV/AIDS, malaria and other diseases, with targets to have halted and begun to reverse the incidence of HIV/AIDS, malaria and other major diseases by 2015 and to achieve universal access to treatment for HIV/AIDS for all those who need it by 2010;

vii) to ensure environmental sustainability, including targets to integrate the principles of sustainable development into country policies and programmes, to reduce by 50% the number of people without access to safe drinking water by 2015, to achieve significant improvement in the lives of at least 100m. slum dwellers by 2020;

viii) to develop a global partnership for development, including efforts to deal with international debt, to address the needs of least developed countries and landlocked and small island developing states, to develop decent and productive youth employment, to provide access to affordable, essential drugs in developing countries, and to make available the benefits of new technologies.

UNDP plays a leading role in efforts to integrate the MDGs into all aspects of UN activities at country level and to ensure the MDGs are incorporated into national development strategies. The Programme supports efforts by countries, as well as regions and sub-regions, to report on progress towards achievement of the goals, and on specific social, economic and environmental indicators, through the formulation of MDG reports. These form the basis of a global report, issued annually by the UN Secretary-General since mid-2002. UNDP also works to raise awareness of the MDGs and to support advocacy efforts at all levels, for example through regional publicity campaigns, target-specific publications and support for the Millennium Campaign to generate support for the goals in developing and developed countries. UNDP provides administrative and technical support to the Millennium Project, an independent advisory body established by the UN Secretary-General in 2002 to develop a practical action plan to achieve the MDGs. Financial support of the Project is channelled through a Millennium Trust Fund, administered by UNDP. In January 2005 the Millennium Project presented its report, based on extensive research conducted by teams of experts, which included recommendations for the international system to support country level development efforts and identified a series of Quick Wins to bring conclusive benefit to millions of people in the short-term. International commitment to achieve the MDGs by 2015 was reiterated at a World Summit, convened in September. In November 2007 the UN, in partnership with two major US companies, launched an online MDG Monitor to track progress and to support organizations working to achieve the goals.

DEMOCRATIC GOVERNANCE

UNDP supports national efforts to ensure efficient and accountable governance, to improve the quality of democratic processes, and to build effective relations between the state, the private sector and civil society, which are essential to achieving sustainable development. As in other practice areas, UNDP assistance includes policy advice and technical support, capacity-building of institutions and individuals, advocacy and public information and communication, the promotion and brokering of dialogue, and knowledge networking and sharing of good practices.

UNDP works to strengthen parliaments and other legislative bodies as institutions of democratic participation. It assists with constitutional reviews and reform, training of parliamentary staff, and capacity-building of political parties and civil organizations as part of this objective. UNDP undertakes missions to help prepare for and ensure the conduct of free and fair elections. Increasingly, UNDP is also focused on building the long-term capacity of electoral institutions and practices within a country, for example voter registration, election observation, the establishment of electoral commissions, and voter and civic education projects.

Within its justice sector programme UNDP undertakes a variety of projects to improve access to justice, in particular for the poor and disadvantaged, and to promote judicial independence, legal reform and understanding of the legal system. UNDP also works to promote access to information, the integration of human rights issues into activities concerned with sustainable human development, as well as support for the international human rights system.

Since 1997 UNDP has been mandated to assist developing countries to fight corruption and improve accountability, transparency and integrity (ATI). It has worked to establish national and international partnerships in support of its anti-corruption efforts and used its role as a broker of knowledge and experience to uphold ATI principles at all levels of public financial management and governance. UNDP publishes case studies of its anti-corruption efforts and assists governments to conduct self-assessments of their public financial management systems.

In March 2002 a UNDP Governance Centre was inaugurated in Oslo, Norway, to enhance the role of UNDP in support of democratic governance and to assist countries to implement democratic reforms in order to achieve the MDGs. The mandate for the work of the Centre during the period 2005-2009 incorporated activities in the following areas: governance and poverty eradication; governance and conflict prevention; civil society, empowerment and governance; and learning and capacity development.

Within the democratic governance practice area UNDP supports more than 300 projects at international, country and city levels designed to improve conditions for the urban poor, in particular through improvement in urban governance. The Local Initiative Facility for Urban Environment (LIFE) undertakes small-scale projects in low-income communities, in collaboration with local authorities, the private sector and community-based groups, and promotes a participatory approach to local governance. UNDP also works closely with the UN Capital Development Fund to implement projects in support of decentralized governance, which it has recognized as a key element to achieving sustainable development goals.

UNDP aims to ensure that, rather than creating an ever-widening 'digital divide', ongoing rapid advancements in information technology are harnessed by poorer countries to accelerate progress in achieving sustainable human development. UNDP advises governments on technology policy, promotes digital entrepreneurship in programme countries and works with private-sector partners to provide reliable and affordable communications networks. The Bureau for Development Policy operates the Information and Communication Technologies for Development Programme, which aims to promote sustainable human development through increased utilization of information and communications technologies globally. The Programme aims to establish technology access centres in developing countries. A Sustainable Development Networking Programme focuses on expanding internet connectivity in poorer countries through building national capacities and supporting local internet sites. UNDP has used mobile internet units to train people even in isolated rural areas. In 1999 UNDP, in collaboration with an international communications company, Cisco Systems, and other partners, launched NetAid, an internet-based forum (accessible at www.netaid.org) for mobilizing and co-ordinating fundraising and other activities aimed at alleviating poverty and promoting sustainable human development in the developing world. With Cisco Systems and other partners, UNDP has worked to establish academies of information technology to support training and capacity-building in developing countries. UNDP and the World Bank jointly host the secretariat of the Digital Opportunity Task Force, a partnership between industrialized and developing countries, business and non-governmental organizations that was established in 2000. UNDP is a partner in the Global Digital Technology Initiative, launched in 2002 to strengthen the role of information and communications technologies in achieving the development goals of developing countries. In January 2004 UNDP and Microsoft Corporation announced an agreement to develop jointly information and communication technology (ICT) projects aimed at assisting developing countries to achieve the MDGs.

POVERTY REDUCTION

UNDP's activities to facilitate poverty eradication include support for capacity-building programmes and initiatives to generate sustainable livelihoods, for example by improving access to credit, land and technologies, and the promotion of strategies to improve education and health provision for the poorest elements of populations (with a focus on women and girls). UNDP aims to help governments to reassess their development priorities and to design initiatives for sustainable human development. In 1996, following the World Summit for Social Development, which was held in Copenhagen, Denmark, in March 1995, UNDP launched the Poverty Strategies Initiative (PSI) to strengthen national capacities to assess and monitor the extent of poverty and to combat the problem. All PSI projects were to involve representatives of governments, the private sector, social organizations and research institutions in policy debate and formulation. Following the introduction, in 1999, by the World Bank and IMF of Poverty Reduction Strategy Papers (PRSPs), UNDP has tended to direct its efforts to helping governments draft these documents, and, since 2001, has focused on linking the papers to efforts to achieve and monitor progress towards the MDGs. In early 2004 UNDP inaugurated the International Poverty Centre, in Brasília, Brazil, which aimed to foster the capacity of countries to formulate and implement poverty reduction strategies and to encourage South-South co-operation in all relevant areas of research and decision-making. In particular, the Centre aimed to assist countries to meet Millennium goals and targets through the research and implementation of pro-poor growth policies and social protection and human development strategies, and the monitoring of poverty and inequality.

UNDP country offices support the formulation of national human development reports (NHDRs), which aim to facilitate activities such as policy-making, the allocation of resources and monitoring progress towards poverty eradication and sustainable development. In addition, the preparation of Advisory Notes and Country Co-operation Frameworks by UNDP officials helps to highlight country-specific aspects of poverty eradication and national strategic priorities. In January 1998 the Executive Board adopted eight guiding principles relating to sustainable human development that were to be implemented by all country offices, in order to ensure a focus to UNDP activities. Since 1990 UNDP has published an annual *Human Development Report*, incorporating a Human Development Index, which ranks countries in terms of human development, using three key indicators: life expectancy, adult literacy and basic income required for a decent standard of living. In 1997 a Human Poverty Index and a Gender-related Development Index, which assesses gender equality on the basis of life expectancy, education and income, were introduced into the Report for the first time. Also in 1997 a UNDP scheme to support private-sector and community-based initiatives to generate employment opportunities, MicroStart, became operational.

UNDP is committed to ensuring that the process of economic and financial globalization, including national and global trade, debt and capital flow policies, incorporates human development concerns. It was actively concerned to ensure that the Doha Development Round of World Trade Organization (WTO) negotiations achieve an expansion of trade opportunities and economic growth to less developed countries. With the UN Conference on Trade and Development (UNCTAD), UNDP manages a Global Programme on Globalization, Liberalization and Sustainable Human Development, which aims to support greater integration of developing countries into the global economy. UNDP manages a Trust Fund for the Integrated Framework for trade-related technical assistance to least-developed countries, which was inaugurated in 1997 by UNDP, the IMF, the International Trade Centre, UNCTAD, the World Bank and the WTO, and is the lead agency for its capacity development component.

In 1996 UNDP initiated a process of collaboration between city authorities world-wide to promote implementation of the commitments made at the 1995 Copenhagen summit for social development and to help to combat aspects of poverty and other urban problems, such as poor housing, transport, the management of waste disposal, water supply and sanitation. The so-called World Alliance of Cities Against Poverty was formally launched in October 1997, in the context of the International Decade for the Eradication of Poverty. The first Forum of the Alliance was convened in October 1998, in Lyon, France; it has subsequently been held every two years.

UNDP sponsors the International Day for the Eradication of Poverty, held annually on 17 October.

ENVIRONMENT AND ENERGY

UNDP plays a role in developing the agenda for international co-operation on environmental and energy issues, focusing on the relationship between energy policies, environmental protection, poverty and development. UNDP promotes the development of national capacities and other strategies that support sustainable development practices, for example through the formulation and implementation of Poverty Reduction Strategies and National Strategies for Sustainable Development.

UNDP recognizes that desertification and land degradation is a major cause of rural poverty and promotes sustainable land management, drought preparedness and reform of land tenure as means of addressing the problem. It also aims to reduce poverty caused by land degradation through implementation of environmental conventions at a national and international level. In 2002 UNDP inaugurated an Integrated Drylands Development Programme which aimed to ensure that the needs of people living in drylands are met and considered at a local and national level. The Drylands Development Centre implements the programme in 19 African, Arab and West Asian countries. UNDP is also concerned with sustainable management of forestries, fisheries and agriculture. Its Biodiversity Global Programme assists developing countries and communities to integrate issues relating to sustainable practices and biodiversity into national and global practices. Since 1992 UNDP has administered a Small Grants Programme, funded by the Global Environment Facility (GEF), to support community-based initiatives concerned with biodiversity conservation, prevention of land degradation and the elimination of persistent organic pollutants. The Equator Initiative was inaugurated in 2002 as a partnership between UNDP, representatives of governments, civil society and businesses, with the aim of reducing poverty in communities along the equatorial belt by fostering local partnerships, harnessing local knowledge and promoting conservation and sustainable practices.

UNDP promotes clean energy technologies (through the Clean Development Mechanism) and aims to extend access to sustainable energy services, including the introduction of renewable alternatives to conventional fuels, as well as access to investment financing for sustainable energy. In December 2005 UNDP launched an MDG Carbon Facility, which aimed to channel increased carbon financing to projects that contribute directly to achieving MDGs in developing countries. The first projects under the MDG Carbon Facility were inaugurated in February 2008, in Uzbekistan, the former Yugoslav republic of Macedonia, Yemen and Rwanda. UNDP supports other efforts to promote international co-operation in the management of chemicals. It was actively involved in the development of a Strategic Approach to International Chemicals Management which was adopted by representatives of 100 governments at an international conference convened in Dubai, UAE, in February 2006.

UNDP works to ensure the effective governance of freshwater and aquatic resources, and promotes co-operation in transboundary water management. It works closely with other agencies to promote safe sanitation, ocean and coastal management, and community water supplies. In 1996 UNDP, with the World Bank and the Swedish International Development Agency, established a Global Water Partnership to promote and implement water resources management. UNDP, with the GEF, supports an extensive range of projects which incorporate development and ecological requirements in the sustainable management of international waters. These include the Global Mercury Project, The Yellow Sea Large Marine Ecosystem project, the Dnipro Basin Environment Programme, and projects in the Gulf of Guinea, Lake Tanganyika, and the Red Sea and Gulf of Aden.

CRISIS PREVENTION AND RECOVERY

UNDP collaborates with other UN agencies in countries in crisis and with special circumstances to promote relief and development efforts, in order to secure the foundations for sustainable human development and thereby increase national capabilities to prevent or mitigate future crises. In particular, UNDP is concerned to achieve reconciliation, reintegration and reconstruction in affected countries, as well as to support emergency interventions and management and delivery of programme aid. It aims to facilitate the transition from relief to longer-term recovery and rehabilitation. Special development initiatives in post-conflict countries include the demobilization of former combatants and destruction of illicit small armaments, rehabilitation of communities for the sustainable reintegration of returning populations and the restoration and strengthening of democratic institutions. UNDP is seeking to incorporate conflict prevention into its development strategies. UNDP has established a mine action unit within its Bureau for Crisis Prevention and Recovery in order to strengthen national and local demining capabilities including surveying, mapping and clearance of anti-personnel landmines. UNDP also works closely with UNICEF to raise mine awareness and implement risk reduction education programmes, and manages global partnership projects concerned with training, legislation and the socio-economic impact of anti-personnel devices.

UNDP is the focal point within the UN system for strengthening national capacities for natural disaster reduction (prevention, preparedness and mitigation relating to natural, environmental and technological hazards). UNDP's Bureau of Crisis Prevention and Recovery, in conjunction with the Office for the Co-ordination of Humanitarian Affairs and the secretariat of the International Strategy for Disaster Reduction, oversees the system-wide Capacity for Disaster Reduction Initiative (CADRI), which was inaugurated in 2007, superseding the former United Nations Disaster Management Training Programme. In February 2004 UNDP introduced a Disaster Risk Index that enabled vulnerability and risk to be measured and compared between countries and demonstrated the correspondence between human development and death rates following natural disasters. UNDP was actively involved in preparations for the second World Conference on Disaster Reduction, which was held in Kobe, Japan, in January 2005. Following the Kobe Conference UNDP initiated a new Global Risk Identification Programme. During 2005 the Inter-Agency Standing Committee, concerned with co-ordinating the international response to humanitarian disasters, developed a concept of providing assistance through a 'cluster' approach, comprising core areas of activity. UNDP was designated the lead agency for the Early Reconstruction and Recovery cluster, linking the immediate needs following a disaster with medium- and long-term recovery efforts.

HIV/AIDS

UNDP regards the HIV/AIDS pandemic as a major challenge to development, and advocates for making HIV/AIDS a focus of national planning and national poverty reduction strategies; supports decentralized action against HIV/AIDS at community level; helps to strengthen national capacities at all levels to combat the disease; and aims to link support for prevention activities, education and treatment with broader development planning and responses. UNDP places a particular focus on combating the spread of HIV/AIDS through the promotion of women's rights. UNDP is a co-sponsor, jointly with WHO, the World Bank, UNICEF, UNESCO, UNODC, ILO, UNFPA, WFP and UNHCR, of the Joint UN Programme on HIV/AIDS (UNAIDS), which became operational on 1 January 1996. UNAIDS co-ordinates UNDP's HIV and Development Programme. Since 2003 UNDP has worked in partnership with the Global Fund to Fight HIV/AIDS, TB and Malaria, in particular to support the local principal recipient of grant financing and to help to manage fund projects.

UNDP administers a global programme concerned with intellectual property and access to HIV/AIDS drugs, to promote wider and cheaper access to antiretroviral drugs. In December 2005 the World Trade Organization agreed to amend the agreement on Trade-Related Aspects of Intellectual Property Rights (TRIPS) to allow countries without a pharmaceutical manufacturing capability to import generic copies of patented medicines.

Finance

UNDP and its various funds and programmes are financed by the voluntary contributions of members of the United Nations and the Programme's participating agencies, as well as through cost-sharing by recipient governments and third-party donors. In 2008–11 total voluntary contributions were projected at US $20,600m., of which $5,300m. constituted regular (core) resources, $5,000m. bilateral donor contributions, $5,500m. contributions from multilateral partners and $4,800m. cost-sharing by programme country governments.

Publications

Annual Report of the Administrator.
Choices (quarterly).
Human Development Report (annually).
Poverty Report (annually).
Results-Oriented Annual Report.

Associated Funds and Programmes

UNDP is the central funding, planning and co-ordinating body for technical co-operation within the UN system. A number of associated funds and programmes, financed separately by means of voluntary contributions, provide specific services through the UNDP network. UNDP manages a trust fund to promote economic and technical co-operation among developing countries.

CAPACITY 2015

UNDP initiated Capacity 2015, as a successor to its Capacity 21 scheme, at the World Summit for Sustainable Development, which was held in August–September 2002. Capacity 2015 aims to support developing countries in expanding their capabilities to meet the Millennium Development Goals. An information and learning network was to be established to promote and facilitate the participation of civil society and local communities in the sustainable development process.

GLOBAL ENVIRONMENT FACILITY (GEF)

The GEF, which is managed jointly by UNDP, the World Bank (which hosts its secretariat) and UNEP, began operations in 1991 and was restructured in 1994. Its aim is to support projects concerning climate change, the conservation of biological diversity, the protection of international waters, reducing the depletion of the ozone layer in the atmosphere, and (since October 2002) arresting land degradation and addressing the issue of persistent organic pollutants. The GEF acts as the financial mechanism for the Convention on Biological Diversity and the UN Framework Convention on Climate Change. UNDP is responsible for capacity-building, targeted research, pre-investment activities and technical assistance. UNDP also administers the Small Grants Programme of the GEF, which supports community-based activities by local non-governmental organizations, and the Country Dialogue Workshop Programme, which promotes dialogue on national priorities with regard to the GEF. In August 2006 some 32 donor countries pledged US $3,130m. for the fourth periodic replenishment of GEF funds (GEF-4), covering the period 2007–10. At February 2008 UNDP GEF-funded projects amounted to $7,470m. for 560 initiatives. An additional $479.7m. had been committed under the Small Grants Programme.

Chair. and CEO: MONIQUE BARBUT (France).
Executive Co-ordinator UNDP-GEF Unit: YANNICK GLEMAREC; 304 East 45th St, 9th Floor, New York, NY 10017, USA; fax (212) 906-6998; e-mail gefinfo@undp.org.

MONTREAL PROTOCOL

Through its Montreal Protocol Unit UNDP collaborates with public and private partners in developing countries to assist them in eliminating the use of ozone-depleting substances (ODS), in accordance with the Montreal Protocol to the Vienna Convention for the Protection of the Ozone Layer, through the design, monitoring and evaluation of ODS phase-out projects and programmes. In particular, UNDP provides technical assistance and training, national capacity-building and demonstration projects and technology transfer investment projects. By December 2005 the Executive Committee of the Montreal Protocol had approved grants for projects and activities that had resulted in the elimination of an estimated 190,661 metric tons of ODS production.

UNDP DRYLANDS DEVELOPMENT CENTRE (DDC)

The Centre, based in Nairobi, Kenya, was established in February 2002, superseding the former UN Office to Combat Desertification and Drought (UNSO). (UNSO had been established following the conclusion, in October 1994, of the UN Convention to Combat Desertification in Those Countries Experiencing Serious Drought and/or Desertification, Particularly in Africa; in turn, UNSO had replaced the former UN Sudano-Sahelian Office.) The DDC was to focus on the following areas: ensuring that national development planning takes account of the needs of dryland communities, particularly in poverty reduction strategies; helping countries to cope with the effects of climate variability, especially drought, and to prepare for future climate change; and addressing local issues affecting the utilization of resources.

Director: PHILIP DOBIE (United Kingdom); POB 30552, 00100 Nairobi, Kenya; tel. (20) 7624640; fax (20) 7624648; e-mail ddc@undp.org; internet www.undp.org/drylands.

PROGRAMME OF ASSISTANCE TO THE PALESTINIAN PEOPLE (PAPP)

PAPP, established in 1978, is committed to strengthening newly-created institutions in the Israeli-occupied Territories and emerging Palestinian autonomous areas, to creating employment opportunities and to stimulating private and public investment in the area to enhance trade and export potential. Examples of PAPP activities include the following: construction of sewage collection networks and systems in the northern Gaza Strip; provision of water to 500,000 people in rural and urban areas of the West Bank and Gaza; construction of schools, youth and health centres; support to vegetable and fish traders through the construction of cold storage and packing facilities; and provision of loans to strengthen industry and commerce. In 2007 programme expenditure amounted to US $57.5m., of which more than half was for infrastructure, employment generation and poverty reduction projects.

UNDP Special Representative in the Occupied Palestinian Territories: JENS ANDERS TOYBERG-FRANDZEN (Denmark); POB 51359, Jerusalem; tel. (2) 6268200; fax (2) 6268222; e-mail registry.papp@undp.org; internet www.undp.ps.

UNITED NATIONS CAPITAL DEVELOPMENT FUND (UNCDF)

The Fund was established in 1966 and became fully operational in 1974. It invests in poor communities in least-developed countries through local governance projects and microfinance operations, with the aim of increasing such communities' access to essential local infrastructure and services and thereby improving their productive capacities and self-reliance. UNDCF encourages participation by local people and local governments in the planning, implementation and monitoring of projects. The Fund aims to promote the interests of women in community projects and to enhance their earning capacities. A Special Unit for Microfinance (SUM), established in 1997 as a joint UNDP/UNCDF operation, was fully integrated into UNCDF in 1999. UNDCF/SUM helps to develop financial services for poor communities and supports UNDP's MicroStart initiative. UNCDF was a co-sponsor of the International Year of Microcredit in 2005 and hosts the UN high-level Advisors Group on Inclusive Financial Sectors. In 2006 UNCDF supported local development programmes and funds in 23 countries. Programme expenditure in that year amounted to US $25.2m.

Executive Secretary a.i.: HENRIETTE KEIJZERS (Netherlands); Two United Nations Plaza, 26th Floor, New York, NY 10017, USA; fax (212) 906-6479; e-mail info@uncdf.org; internet www.uncdf.org.

UNITED NATIONS DEVELOPMENT FUND FOR WOMEN (UNIFEM)

UNIFEM is the UN's lead agency in addressing the issues relating to women in development and promoting the rights of women worldwide. The Fund provides direct financial and technical support to enable low-income women in developing countries to increase earnings, gain access to labour-saving technologies and otherwise improve the quality of their lives. It also funds activities that include women in decision-making related to mainstream development projects. UNIFEM has supported the preparation of national reports in 30 countries and used the priorities identified in these reports and in other regional initiatives to formulate a Women's Development Agenda for the 21st century. Through these efforts, UNIFEM played an active role in the preparation for the UN Fourth World Conference on Women, which was held in Beijing, People's Republic of China, in September 1995. UNIFEM participated at a special session of the General Assembly convened in June 2000 to review the conference, entitled Women 2000: Gender Equality, Development and Peace for the 21st Century (Beijing + 5). In March 2001 UNIFEM, in collaboration with International Alert, launched a Millennium Peace Prize for Women. UNIFEM maintains that the empowerment of women is a key to combating the HIV/AIDS pandemic, in view of the fact that women and adolescent girls are often culturally, biologically and economically more vulnerable to infection and more likely to bear responsibility for caring for the sick. In March 2002 UNIFEM launched a three-year programme aimed at making the gender and human rights dimensions of the pandemic central to policy-making in 10 countries. A new online resource (www.genderandaids.org) on the gender dimensions of HIV/AIDS was launched in February 2003. Following the massive earthquake and tsunami that struck parts of the Indian Ocean in late December 2004, UNIFEM undertook to promote the needs and rights of women and girls in all emergency relief and reconstruction efforts, in particular in Indonesia, Sri Lanka and Somalia, and supported capacity-building of grass-roots organizations. UNIFEM was a co-founder of WomenWatch (accessible online at www.un.org/womenwatch), a UN system-wide resource for the advancement of gender equality. UNIFEM manages the UN's Trust Fund in Support of Actions to Eliminate Violence Against Women (established in 1996), which by early 2008 had awarded grants in excess of US $19.0m. in support of more than 263 initiatives in around 115 countries. In November 2007 UNIFEM launched a year-long campaign, 'Say NO to Violence against Women', to raise awareness of the issue and generate world-wide support for efforts to end violence against women. Programme expenditure in 2005 totalled $55.8m.

Director a.i.: JOANNE SANDLER; 304 East 45th St, 15th Floor, New York, NY 10017, USA; tel. (212) 906-6400; fax (212) 906-6705; e-mail unifem@undp.org; internet www.unifem.org.

UNITED NATIONS VOLUNTEERS (UNV)

The United Nations Volunteers is an important source of middle-level skills for the UN development system supplied at modest cost, particularly in the least-developed countries. Volunteers expand the scope of UNDP project activities by supplementing the work of international and host-country experts and by extending the influence of projects to local community levels. UNV also supports technical co-operation within and among the developing countries by encouraging volunteers from the countries themselves and by forming regional exchange teams comprising such volunteers. UNV is involved in areas such as peace-building, elections, human rights, humanitarian relief and community-based environmental programmes, in addition to development activities.

The UN International Short-term Advisory (UNISTAR) Programme, which is the private-sector development arm of UNV, has increasingly focused its attention on countries in the process of economic transition. Since 1994 UNV has administered UNDP's Transfer of Knowledge Through Expatriate Nationals (TOKTEN) programme, which was initiated in 1977 to enable specialists and professionals from developing countries to contribute to development efforts in their countries of origin through short-term technical assignments. In March 2000 UNV established an Online Volunteering Service to connect development organizations and volunteers using the internet. As at November 2006 some 9,000 volunteers from 169 countries had been engaged in online collaborations.

At the end of October 2007 5,391 UNVs were serving in 128 countries. At that time the total number of people who had served under the initiative amounted to more than 30,000 in over 140 countries.

Executive Co-ordinator: AD DE RAAD (Netherlands); POB 260111, 53153 Bonn, Germany; tel. (228) 8152000; fax (228) 8152001; e-mail information@unvolunteers.org; internet www.unv.org.

United Nations Environment Programme—UNEP

Address: POB 30552, Nairobi, Kenya.
Telephone: (20) 621234; **fax:** (20) 624489; **e-mail:** cpiinfo@unep.org; **internet:** www.unep.org.

The United Nations Environment Programme was established in 1972 by the UN General Assembly, following recommendations of the 1972 UN Conference on the Human Environment, in Stockholm, Sweden, to encourage international co-operation in matters relating to the human environment.

Organization
(March 2008)

GOVERNING COUNCIL

The main functions of the Governing Council, which meets every two years, are to promote international co-operation in the field of the environment and to provide general policy guidance for the direction and co-ordination of environmental programmes within the UN system. It comprises representatives of 58 states, elected by the UN General Assembly, for four-year terms, on a regional basis. The Council is assisted in its work by a Committee of Permanent Representatives.

HIGH-LEVEL COMMITTEE OF MINISTERS AND OFFICIALS IN CHARGE OF THE ENVIRONMENT

The Committee was established by the Governing Council in 1997, with a mandate to consider the international environmental agenda and to make recommendations to the Council on reform and policy issues. In addition, the Committee, comprising 36 elected members, was to provide guidance and advice to the Executive Director, to enhance UNEP's collaboration and co-operation with other multilateral bodies and to help to mobilize financial resources for UNEP.

SECRETARIAT

Offices and divisions at UNEP headquarters include the Office of the Executive Director; the Secretariat for Governing Bodies: Offices for Evaluation and Oversight, Programme Co-ordination and Management, and Resource Mobilization; and divisions of communications and public information, early warning and assessment, policy development and law, policy implementation, technology and industry and economics, regional co-operation and representation, environmental conventions, and Global Environment Facility co-ordination.

Executive Director: ACHIM STEINER (Germany).

REGIONAL OFFICES

Africa: POB 30552, Nairobi, Kenya; tel. (20) 624292; fax (20) 623928; e-mail roainfo@unep.org; internet www.unep.org/roa.

UNEP Arab League Liaison Office: POB 212, Cairo, Egypt; tel. (2) 3934046; fax (2) 3950119; e-mail unep-allo@link.net.

Asia and the Pacific: United Nations Bldg, 2nd Floor, Rajadamnern Nok Ave, Bangkok 10200, Thailand; tel. (2) 288-1234; fax (2) 280-3829; e-mail uneproap@un.org; internet www.roap.unep.org.

Europe: 11–13 chemin des Anémones, 1219 Châtelaine, Geneva, Switzerland; tel. 229178279; fax 229178024; e-mail roe@unep.ch; internet www.unep.ch/roe.

Latin America and the Caribbean: blvd de los Virreyes 155, Lomas Virreyes, 11000 México, DF, Mexico; tel. (55) 5202-6394; fax (55) 5202-0950; e-mail enlace@pnuma.org; internet www.pnuma.org.

North America: 1707 H St NW, Washington, DC 20006, USA; tel. (202) 785-0465; fax (202) 785-2096; e-mail uneprona@un.org; internet www.rona.unep.org.

UNEP New York Office: DC-2 Bldg, Room 0803, 2 United Nations Plaza, New York, NY 10017, USA; tel. (212) 963-8210; fax (212) 963-7341; e-mail info@nyo.unep.org; internet www.nyo.unep.org; Dir JUANITA CASTRANO.

West Asia: POB 10880, Manama, Bahrain; tel. 17812777; fax 17825110; e-mail uneprowa@unep.org.bh; internet www.unep.org.bh.

OTHER OFFICES

Convention on International Trade in Endangered Species of Wild Fauna and Flora (CITES): 15 chemin des Anémones, 1219 Châtelaine, Geneva, Switzerland; tel. 229178139; fax 227973417; e-mail info@cites.org; internet www.cites.org; Sec.-Gen. WILLEM WOUTER WIJNSTEKERS (Netherlands).

Global Programme of Action for the Protection of the Marine Environment from Land-based Activities: POB 16227, 2500 BE The Hague, Netherlands; tel. (70) 3114460; fax (70) 3456648; e-mail gpa@unep.nl; internet www.gpa.unep.org; Officer-in-Charge ANJAN DATTA (Bangladesh).

Regional Co-ordinating Unit for East Asian Seas: UN Bldg, 2nd Floor, Rajadamnern Nok Ave, Bangkok 10200, Thailand; tel. (2) 288-1860; fax (2) 281-2428; e-mail kleesuwan.unescap@un.org; internet www.cobsea.org; Co-ordinator Dr SRISUDA JARAYABHAND.

Regional Co-ordinating Unit for the Caribbean Environment Programme: 14–20 Port Royal St, Kingston, Jamaica; tel. 922-9267;

fax 922-9292; e-mail uneprcuja@cwjamaica.com; internet www.cep.unep.org; Co-ordinator NELSON ANDRADE COLMENARES.

Secretariat of the Basel Convention: CP 356, 13–15 chemin des Anémones, 1219 Châtelaine, Geneva, Switzerland; tel. 229178218; fax 227973454; e-mail sbc@unep.ch; internet www.basel.int; Exec. Sec. KATHERINA KUMMER PEIRY.

Secretariat of the Mediterranean Action Plan on the Implementation of the Barcelona Convention: Leoforos Vassileos Konstantinou 48, POB 18019, 11610 Athens, Greece; tel. (210) 7273100; fax (210) 7253196; e-mail unepmedu@unepmap.gr; internet www.unepmap.gr; Co-ordinator PAUL MIFSUD.

Secretariat of the Multilateral Fund for the Implementation of the Montreal Protocol: 1800 McGill College Ave, 27th Floor, Montréal, QC, Canada H3A 3J6; tel. (514) 282-1122; fax (514) 282-0068; e-mail secretariat@unmfs.org; internet www.multilateralfund.org; Chief Officer MARIA NOLAN.

UNEP/CMS (Convention on the Conservation of Migratory Species of Wild Animals) Secretariat: Hermann-Ehlers-Str. 10, 53113 Bonn, Germany; tel. (228) 8152402; fax (228) 8152449; e-mail secretariat@cms.int; internet www.cms.int; Exec. Sec. ROBERT HEPWORTH.

UNEP Chemicals: International Environment House, 11–13 chemin des Anémones, 1219 Châtelaine, Geneva, Switzerland; tel. 229178192; fax 227973460; e-mail chemicals@unep.ch; internet www.chem.unep.ch; Dir Dr MAGED YOUNES.

UNEP Division of Technology, Industry and Economics: Tour Mirabeau, 39–43, Quai André Citroën, 75739 Paris Cédex 15, France; tel. 1-44-37-14-41; fax 1-44-37-14-74; e-mail unep.tie@unep.fr; internet www.unep.fr; Dir SILVIE LEMMET (France).

UNEP International Environmental Technology Centre (IETC): 2–110 Ryokuchi koen, Tsurumi-ku, Osaka 538-0036, Japan; tel. (6) 6915-4581; fax (6) 6915-0304; e-mail ietc@unep.or.jp; internet www.unep.or.jp; Exec. Dir PER MENZONY BAKKEN (Norway).

UNEP Ozone Secretariat: POB 30552, Nairobi, Kenya; tel. (20) 762-3850; fax (20) 762-4691; e-mail ozoneinfo@unep.org; internet ozone.unep.org; Exec. Sec. MARCO GONZÁLEZ (Costa Rica).

UNEP-SCBD (Convention on Biological Diversity—Secretariat): 413 St Jacques St, Office 800, Montréal, QC, Canada H2Y 1N9; tel. (514) 288-2220; fax (514) 288-6588; e-mail secretariat@cbd.int; internet www.cbd.int; Exec. Sec. AHMED DJOGHLAF (Algeria).

UNEP Secretariat for the UN Scientific Committee on the Effects of Atomic Radiation: Vienna International Centre, Wagramerstrasse 5, POB 500, 1400 Vienna, Austria; tel. (1) 26060-4330; fax (1) 26060-5902; e-mail malcolm.crick@unscear.org; internet www.unscear.org; Sec. Dr MALCOLM CRICK.

Activities

UNEP serves as a focal point for environmental action within the UN system. It aims to maintain a constant watch on the changing state of the environment; to analyse the trends; to assess the problems using a wide range of data and techniques; and to promote projects leading to environmentally sound development. It plays a catalytic and co-ordinating role within and beyond the UN system. Many UNEP projects are implemented in co-operation with other UN agencies, particularly UNDP, the World Bank group, FAO, UNESCO and WHO. About 45 intergovernmental organizations outside the UN system and 60 international non-governmental organizations have official observer status on UNEP's Governing Council, and, through the Environment Liaison Centre in Nairobi, UNEP is linked to more than 6,000 non-governmental bodies concerned with the environment. UNEP also sponsors international conferences, programmes, plans and agreements regarding all aspects of the environment.

In February 1997 the Governing Council, at its 19th session, adopted a ministerial declaration (the Nairobi Declaration) on UNEP's future role and mandate, which recognized the organization as the principal UN body working in the field of the environment and as the leading global environmental authority, setting and overseeing the international environmental agenda. In June a special session of the UN General Assembly, referred to as 'Rio + 5', was convened to review the state of the environment and progress achieved in implementing the objectives of the UN Conference on Environment and Development (UNCED), held in Rio de Janeiro, Brazil, in June 1992. The meeting adopted a Programme for Further Implementation of Agenda 21 (a programme of activities to promote sustainable development, adopted by UNCED) in order to intensify efforts in areas such as energy, freshwater resources and technology transfer. The meeting confirmed UNEP's essential role in advancing the Programme and as a global authority promoting a coherent legal and political approach to the environmental challenges of sustainable development. An extensive process of restructuring and realignment of functions was subsequently initiated by UNEP, and a new orga-

nizational structure reflecting the decisions of the Nairobi Declaration was implemented during 1999. UNEP played a leading role in preparing for the World Summit on Sustainable Development (WSSD), held in August–September 2002 in Johannesburg, South Africa, to assess strategies for strengthening the implementation of Agenda 21. Governments participating in the conference adopted the Johannesburg Declaration and WSSD Plan of Implementation, in which they strongly reaffirmed commitment to the principles underlying Agenda 21 and also pledged support to all internationally-agreed development goals, including the UN Millennium Development Goals adopted by governments attending a summit meeting of the UN General Assembly in September 2000. Participating governments made concrete commitments to attaining several specific objectives in the areas of water, energy, health, agriculture and fisheries, and biodiversity. These included a reduction by one-half in the proportion of people world-wide lacking access to clean water or good sanitation by 2015, the restocking of depleted fisheries by 2015, a reduction in the ongoing loss in biodiversity by 2010, and the production and utilization of chemicals without causing harm to human beings and the environment by 2020. Participants determined to increase usage of renewable energy sources and to develop integrated water resources management and water efficiency plans. A large number of partnerships between governments, private-sector interests and civil society groups were announced at the conference.

In May 2000 UNEP sponsored the first annual Global Ministerial Environment Forum (GMEF), held in Malmö, Sweden, and attended by environment ministers and other government delegates from more than 130 countries. Participants reviewed policy issues in the field of the environment and addressed issues such as the impact on the environment of population growth, the depletion of earth's natural resources, climate change and the need for fresh water supplies. The Forum issued the Malmö Declaration, which identified the effective implementation of international agreements on environmental matters at national level as the most pressing challenge for policy-makers. The Declaration emphasized the importance of mobilizing domestic and international resources and urged increased co-operation from civil society and the private sector in achieving sustainable development. The second GMEF, held in Nairobi in February 2001, addressed means of strengthening international environmental governance, establishing an Open-Ended Intergovernmental Group of Ministers or Their Representatives (IGM) to prepare a report on possible reforms. GMEF-6, held in February 2006 in Dubai, United Arab Emirates, considered energy and the environment and chemicals management.

ENVIRONMENTAL ASSESSMENT AND EARLY WARNING
The Nairobi Declaration resolved that the strengthening of UNEP's information, monitoring and assessment capabilities was a crucial element of the organization's restructuring, in order to help establish priorities for international, national and regional action, and to ensure the efficient and accurate dissemination of emerging environmental trends and emergencies.

In 1995 UNEP launched the Global Environment Outlook (GEO) process of environmental assessment. UNEP is assisted in its analysis of the state of the global environment by an extensive network of collaborating centres. The fourth umbrella report on the GEO assessment process (GEO-4) was issued in October 2007. The following regional and national *GEO* reports have been produced in recent years: *Africa Environment Outlook* (2002), *Brazil Environment Outlook* (2002), *Caucasus Environment Outlook* (2002), *North America's Environment* (2002), *Latin America and the Caribbean Environment Outlook* (2003), *Andean Environment Outlook* (2003), *Pacific Environment Outlook* (2005), *Caribbean Environment Outlook* (2005), *Atlantic and Indian Oceans Environment Outlook* (2005), and *Africa Environment Outlook -2* (2006). UNEP is leading a major Global International Waters Assessment (GIWA) to consider all aspects of the world's water-related issues, in particular problems of shared transboundary waters, and of future sustainable management of water resources. UNEP is also a sponsoring agency of the Joint Group of Experts on the Scientific Aspects of Marine Environmental Pollution and contributes to the preparation of reports on the state of the marine environment and on the impact of land-based activities on that environment. In November 1995 UNEP published a Global Biodiversity Assessment, which was the first comprehensive study of biological resources throughout the world. The UNEP—World Conservation Monitoring Centre (UNEP—WCMC), established in June 2000, provides biodiversity-related assessment. UNEP is a partner in the International Coral Reef Action Network—ICRAN, which was established in 2000 to manage and protect coral reefs world-wide. In June 2001 UNEP launched the Millennium Ecosystems Assessment, which was completed in March 2005. Other major assessments undertaken included GIWA (see above); the Assessment of Impact and Adaptation to Climate Change; the Solar and Wind Energy Resource Assessment; the Regionally-Based Assessment of Persistent Toxic Substances; the Land Degradation Assessment in Drylands; and the Global Methodology for Mapping Human Impacts on the Biosphere (GLOBIO) project. In July 2007 UNEP launched the 2010 Biodiversity Indicator Partnership (2010BIP), which aimed to monitor conservation efforts to protect global biological diversity.

UNEP's environmental information network includes the Global Resource Information Database (GRID), which converts collected data into information usable by decision-makers. The UNEP-INFOTERRA programme facilitates the exchange of environmental information through an extensive network of national 'focal points'. By March 2008 177 countries were participating in the network. Through UNEP-INFOTERRA UNEP promotes public access to environmental information, as well as participation in environmental concerns. UNEP aims to establish in every developing region an Environment and Natural Resource Information Network (ENRIN) in order to make available technical advice and manage environmental information and data for improved decision-making and action-planning in countries most in need of assistance. UNEP aims to integrate its information resources in order to improve access to information and to promote its international exchange. This has been pursued through UNEPnet, an internet-based interactive environmental information- and data-sharing facility.

UNEP's information, monitoring and assessment structures also serve to enhance early-warning capabilities and to provide accurate information during an environmental emergency.

POLICY DEVELOPMENT AND LAW

UNEP aims to promote the development of policy tools and guide-lines in order to achieve the sustainable management of the world environment. At a national level it assists governments to develop and implement appropriate environmental instruments and aims to co-ordinate policy initiatives. Training workshops in various aspects of environmental law and its applications are conducted. UNEP supports the development of new legal, economic and other policy instruments to improve the effectiveness of existing environmental agreements.

UNEP was instrumental in the drafting of a Convention on Biological Diversity (CBD) to preserve the immense variety of plant and animal species, in particular those threatened with extinction. The Convention entered into force at the end of 1993; by March 2008 189 states parties and the European Community were parties to the CBD. The CBD's Cartagena Protocol on Biosafety (so called as it had been addressed at an extraordinary session of parties to the CBD convened in Cartagena, Colombia, in February 1999) was adopted at a meeting of parties to the CBD held in Montréal, Canada, in January 2000, and entered into force in September 2003; by March 2008 the Protocol had been ratified by 142 states parties and the European Community. The Protocol regulates the transboundary movement and use of living modified organisms resulting from biotechnology in order to reduce any potential adverse effects on biodiversity and human health. It establishes an Advanced Informed Agreement procedure to govern the import of such organisms. In January 2002 UNEP launched a major project aimed at supporting developing countries with assessing the potential health and environmental risks and benefits of genetically modified (GM) crops, in preparation for the Protocol's entry into force. In February the parties to the CBD and other partners convened a conference, in Montréal, to address ways in which the traditional knowledge and practices of local communities could be preserved and used to conserve highly threatened species and ecosystems. The sixth conference of parties to the CBD, held in April 2002, adopted detailed voluntary guide-lines concerning access to genetic resources and sharing the benefits attained from such resources with the countries and local communities where they originate; a global work programme on forests; and a set of guiding principles for combating alien invasive species. UNEP supports co-operation for biodiversity assessment and management in selected developing regions and for the development of strategies for the conservation and sustainable exploitation of individual threatened species (e.g. the Global Tiger Action Plan). It also provides assistance for the preparation of individual country studies and strategies to strengthen national biodiversity management and research. UNEP administers the Convention on International Trade in Endangered Species of Wild Flora and Fauna (CITES), which entered into force in 1975 and comprised 172 states party at January 2008.

In May 2001 UNEP launched the Great Apes Survival Project (GRASP), which supports, in 23 countries in Africa and South-East Asia, the conservation of gorillas, chimpanzees, orang-utans and bonobos. GRASP's first intergovernmental meeting, held in Kinshasa, Democratic Republic of the Congo in September 2005, was attended by representatives of governments of great ape habitat states, donor and other interested states, international organizations, NGOs, and private-sector and academic interests. The meeting adopted a Global Strategy for the Survival of Great Apes, and the Kinshasa Declaration pledged commitment and action towards achieving this goal.

In October 1994 87 countries, meeting under UN auspices, signed a Convention to Combat Desertification (see UNDP Drylands Development Centre), which aimed to provide a legal framework to counter the degradation of drylands. An estimated 75% of all drylands have suffered some land degradation, affecting approximately 1,000m. people in 110 countries. UNEP continues to support the implementation of the Convention, as part of its efforts to protect land resources. UNEP also aims to improve the assessment of dryland degradation and desertification in co-operation with governments and other international bodies, as well as identifying the causes of degradation and measures to overcome these.

UNEP is the lead UN agency for promoting environmentally sustainable water management. It regards the unsustainable use of water as the most urgent environmental and sustainable development issue, and estimates that two-thirds of the world's population will suffer chronic water shortages by 2025, owing to rising demand for drinking water as a result of growing populations, decreasing quality of water because of pollution, and increasing requirements of industries and agriculture. In 2000 UNEP adopted a new water policy and strategy, comprising assessment, management and co-ordination components. The Global International Waters Assessment (see above) is the primary framework for the assessment component. The management component includes the Global Programme of Action (GPA) for the Protection of the Marine Environment from Land-based Activities (adopted in November 1995), and UNEP's freshwater programme and regional seas programme. The GPA for the Protection of the Marine Environment for Land-based Activities focuses on the effects of activities such as pollution on freshwater resources, marine biodiversity and the coastal ecosystems of small-island developing states. UNEP aims to develop a similar global instrument to ensure the integrated management of freshwater resources. It promotes international co-operation in the management of river basins and coastal areas and for the development of tools and guide-lines to achieve the sustainable management of freshwater and coastal resources. UNEP provides scientific, technical and administrative support to facilitate the implementation and co-ordination of 14 regional seas conventions and 13 regional plans of action, and is developing a strategy to strengthen collaboration in their implementation. The new water policy and strategy emphasizes the need for improved co-ordination of existing activities. UNEP aims to play an enhanced role within relevant co-ordination mechanisms, such as the UN open-ended informal consultation process on oceans and the law of the sea.

In 1996 UNEP, in collaboration with FAO, began to work towards promoting and formulating a legally binding international convention on prior informed consent (PIC) for hazardous chemicals and pesticides in international trade, extending a voluntary PIC procedure of information exchange undertaken by more than 100 governments since 1991. The Convention was adopted at a conference held in Rotterdam, Netherlands, in September 1998, and entered into force in February 2004. It aims to reduce risks to human health and the environment by restricting the production, export and use of hazardous substances and enhancing information exchange procedures.

In conjunction with UN-Habitat, UNDP, the World Bank and other organizations and institutions, UNEP promotes environmental concerns in urban planning and management through the Sustainable Cities Programme, as well as regional workshops concerned with urban pollution and the impact of transportation systems. In 1994 UNEP inaugurated an International Environmental Technology Centre (IETC), with offices in Osaka and Shiga, Japan, in order to strengthen the capabilities of developing countries and countries with economies in transition to promote environmentally sound management of cities and freshwater reservoirs through technology co-operation and partnerships.

UNEP has played a key role in global efforts to combat risks to the ozone layer, resultant climatic changes and atmospheric pollution. UNEP worked in collaboration with the World Meteorological Organization to formulate the UN Framework Convention on Climate Change (UNFCCC), with the aim of reducing the emission of gases that have a warming effect on the atmosphere, and has remained an active participant in the ongoing process to review and enforce the implementation of the Convention and of its Kyoto Protocol. UNEP was the lead agency in formulating the 1987 Montreal Protocol to the Vienna Convention for the Protection of the Ozone Layer (1985), which provided for a 50% reduction in the production of chlorofluorocarbons (CFCs) by 2000. An amendment to the Protocol was adopted in 1990, which required complete cessation of the production of CFCs by 2000 in industrialized countries and by 2010 in developing countries. The Copenhagen Amendment, adopted in 1992, stipulated the phasing out of production of hydrochlorofluorocarbons (HCFCs) by 2030 in developed countries and by 2040 in developing nations. In 1997 the ninth Conference of the Parties (COP) to the Vienna Convention adopted a further amendment which aimed to introduce a licensing system for all controlled substances. The 11th COP, meeting in Beijing, People's Republic of China, in November–December 1999, adopted the Beijing Amendment, which imposed tighter controls on the import and export of HCFCs, and on the production and consumption of bromochloromethane (Halon-1011, an industrial solvent and fire extinguisher). The Beijing Amendment entered into force in December 2001. At the 19th COP (also the 20th anniversary meeting of the adoption of the Montreal Protocol), held in September 2007, states parties to the Vienna Convention agreed to advance the deadline for the elimination of HCFCs: production and consumption were to be frozen by 2013, and were to be phased out in developed countries by 2020 and in developing countries by 2030. A Multilateral Fund for the Implementation of the Montreal Protocol was established in June 1990 to promote the use of suitable technologies and the transfer of technologies to developing countries. UNEP, UNDP, the World Bank and UNIDO are the sponsors of the Fund, which by March 2007 had approved financing for about 5,500 projects and activities in 144 developing countries at a cost of around US $2,000m. Commitments of $400.4m. were made to the sixth replenishment of the Fund, covering the three-year period 2006–08. (The total budget for 2006–08 was $470.0m., the remainder deriving from the following sources: $59.6m. to be carried over from the 2003–05 triennium and $10m. to be provided from interest accruing.)

POLICY IMPLEMENTATION

UNEP's Division of Environmental Policy Implementation incorporates two main functions: technical co-operation and response to environmental emergencies.

With the UN Office for the Co-ordination of Humanitarian Assistance (OCHA), UNEP has established a joint Environment Unit to mobilize and co-ordinate international assistance and expertise for countries facing environmental emergencies and natural disasters. In mid-1999 UNEP and UN-Habitat jointly established a Balkan Task Force (subsequently renamed UNEP Balkans Unit) to assess the environmental impact of NATO's aerial offensive against the then Federal Republic of Yugoslavia. In November 2000 the Unit led a field assessment to evaluate reports of environmental contamination by debris from NATO ammunition containing depleted uranium. A final report, issued by UNEP in March 2001, concluded that there was no evidence of widespread contamination of the ground surface by depleted uranium and that the radiological and toxicological risk to the local population was negligible. It stated, however, that considerable scientific uncertainties remained, for example as to the safety of groundwater and the longer-term behaviour of depleted uranium in the environment, and recommended precautionary action. In December 2001 UNEP established a Post-conflict Assessment Unit, which replaced, and extended the scope of, the Balkans Unit. In 2008 the Post-conflict Assessment Unit was engaged in Afghanistan, Indonesia, Lebanon, Liberia, Maldives, Nigeria, the Palestinian territories, Somalia, Sri Lanka and Sudan. It had completed a programme in Iraq, producing a *Desk Study on the Environment in Iraq* in 2003 and an *Assessment of Environmental 'Hot Spots' in Iraq* in 2005.

UNEP, together with UNDP and the World Bank, is an implementing agency of the Global Environment Facility (GEF), which was established in 1991 as a mechanism for international co-operation in projects concerned with biological diversity, climate change, international waters and depletion of the ozone layer. UNEP services the Scientific and Technical Advisory Panel, which provides expert advice on GEF programmes and operational strategies.

TECHNOLOGY, INDUSTRY AND ECONOMICS

The use of inappropriate industrial technologies and the widespread adoption of unsustainable production and consumption patterns have been identified as being inefficient in the use of renewable resources and wasteful, in particular in the use of energy and water. UNEP aims to encourage governments and the private sector to develop and adopt policies and practices that are cleaner and safer, make efficient use of natural resources, incorporate environmental costs, ensure the environmentally sound management of chemicals, and reduce pollution and risks to human health and the environment. In collaboration with other organizations and agencies UNEP works to define and formulate international guide-lines and agreements to address these issues. UNEP also promotes the transfer of appropriate technologies and organizes conferences and training workshops to provide sustainable production practices. Relevant information is disseminated through the International Cleaner Production Information Clearing House. UNEP, together with UNIDO, has established 34 National Cleaner Production Centres to promote a preventive approach to industrial pollution control. In October 1998 UNEP adopted an International Declaration on Cleaner Production, with a commitment to implement cleaner and more sustainable production methods and to monitor results. In 1997 UNEP and the Coalition for Environmentally Responsible Economies initiated the Global Reporting Initiative, which, with participation by corporations, business associations and other organizations and stakeholders, develops guide-lines for voluntary reporting by companies on their economic, environmental and social performance. In April 2002 UNEP launched the 'Life-Cycle Initiative', which aims to assist governments, businesses and other consumers with adopting environmentally sound policies and practice, in view of the upward trend in global consumption patterns.

UNEP provides institutional servicing to the Basel Convention on the Control of Transboundary Movements of Hazardous Wastes and their Disposal, which was adopted in 1989 with the aim of preventing the disposal of wastes from industrialized countries in countries that have no processing facilities. In March 1994 the second meeting of parties to the Convention determined to ban the exportation of hazardous wastes between industrialized and developing countries. The third meeting of parties to the Convention, held in 1995, proposed that the ban should be incorporated into the Convention as an amendment. The resulting so-called Ban Amendment (prohibiting exports of hazardous wastes for final disposal and recycling from states and/or parties also belonging to OECD and, or, the European Union, and from Liechtenstein, to any other state party to the Convention) required ratification by three-quarters of the 62 signatory states present at the time of adoption before it could enter into effect; by March 2008 the Ban Amendment had been ratified by 63 parties. In 1998 the technical working group of the Convention agreed a new procedure for clarifying the classification and characterization of specific hazardous wastes. The fifth full meeting of parties to the Convention, held in December 1999, adopted the Basel Declaration outlining an agenda for the period 2000–10, with a particular focus on minimizing the production of hazardous wastes. At March 2008 the number of parties to the Convention totalled 170. In December 1999 132 states adopted a Protocol to the Convention to address issues relating to liability and compensation for damages from waste exports. The governments also agreed to establish a multilateral fund to finance immediate clean-up operations following any environmental accident.

The UNEP Chemicals office was established to promote the sound management of hazardous substances, central to which has been the International Register of Potentially Toxic Chemicals (IRPTC). UNEP aims to facilitate access to data on chemicals and hazardous wastes, in order to assess and control health and environmental risks, by using the IRPTC as a clearing house facility of relevant information and by publishing information and technical reports on the impact of the use of chemicals.

UNEP's OzonAction Programme works to promote information exchange, training and technological awareness. Its objective is to strengthen the capacity of governments and industry in developing countries to undertake measures towards the cost-effective phasing-out of ozone-depleting substances. UNEP also encourages the development of alternative and renewable sources of energy. To achieve this, UNEP is supporting the establishment of a network of centres to research and exchange information of environmentally sound energy technology resources.

REGIONAL CO-OPERATION AND REPRESENTATION

UNEP maintains six regional offices. These work to initiate and promote UNEP objectives and to ensure that all programme formulation and delivery meets the specific needs of countries and regions. They also provide a focal point for building national, sub-regional and regional partnership and enhancing local participation in UNEP initiatives. Following UNEP's reorganization a co-ordination office was established at headquarters to promote regional policy integration, to co-ordinate programme planning, and to provide necessary services to the regional offices.

UNEP provides administrative support to several regional conventions, for example the Lusaka Agreement on Co-operative Enforcement Operations Directed at Illegal Trade in Wild Flora and Fauna, which entered into force in December 1996 having been concluded under UNEP auspices in order to strengthen the implementation of the CBD and CITES in Eastern and Central Africa. UNEP also organizes conferences, workshops and seminars at national and regional levels, and may extend advisory services or technical assistance to individual governments.

CONVENTIONS

UNEP aims to develop and promote international environmental legislation in order to pursue an integrated response to global environmental issues, to enhance collaboration among existing convention secetariats, and to co-ordinate support to implement the work programmes of international instruments.

UNEP has been an active participant in the formulation of several major conventions (see above). The Division of Environmental Conventions is mandated to assist the Division of Policy Development and Law in the formulation of new agreements or protocols to existing conventions. Following the successful adoption of the Rotterdam Convention in September 1998, UNEP played a leading role in formulating a multilateral agreement to reduce and ultimately eliminate the manufacture and use of Persistent Organic Pollutants (POPs), which are considered to be a major global environmental hazard. The agreement on POPs, concluded in December 2000 at a conference sponsored by UNEP in Johannesburg, South Africa, was adopted by 127 countries in May 2001 and entered into force in May 2004.

UNEP has been designated to provide secretariat functions to a number of global and regional environmental conventions (see above for list of offices).

COMMUNICATIONS AND PUBLIC INFORMATION

UNEP's public education campaigns and outreach programmes promote community involvement in environmental issues. Further communication of environmental concerns is undertaken through the media, an information centre service and special promotional events, including World Environment Day, photography competitions, and the awarding of the Sasakawa Prize (to recognize distinguished service to the environment by individuals and groups) and of the Global 500 Award for Environmental Achievement. In 1996 UNEP initiated a Global Environment Citizenship Programme to promote acknowledgment of the environmental responsibilities of all sectors of society.

Finance

UNEP derives its finances from the regular budget of the United Nations and from voluntary contributions to the Environment Fund. A budget of US $144m. was proposed for the two-year period 2006–07, of which $122m. was for programme activities, $5.8m. for programme support, $10.2m. for management and administration, and $6m. for fund programme reserves.

Publications

Annual Report.
APELL Newsletter (2 a year).
Cleaner Production Newsletter (2 a year).
Climate Change Bulletin (quarterly).
Connect (UNESCO-UNEP newsletter on environmental degradation, quarterly).
Earth Views (quarterly).
Environment Forum (quarterly).
Environmental Law Bulletin (2 a year).
Financial Services Initiative (2 a year).
GEF News (quarterly).
Global Water Review.
GPA Newsletter.
IETC Insight (3 a year).
Industry and Environment Review (quarterly).
Leave it to Us (children's magazine, 2 a year).
Managing Hazardous Waste (2 a year).
Our Planet (quarterly).
OzonAction Newsletter (quarterly).
Tierramerica (weekly).
Tourism Focus (2 a year).
UNEP Chemicals Newsletter (2 a year).
UNEP Update (monthly).
UNEP Year Book (annually).
World Atlas of Biodiversity.
World Atlas of Coral Reefs.
World Atlas of Desertification.
Studies, reports, legal texts, technical guide-lines, etc.

United Nations High Commissioner for Refugees—UNHCR

Address: CP 2500, 1211 Geneva 2 dépôt, Switzerland.
Telephone: 227398111; **fax:** 227397312; **e-mail:** unhcr@unhcr.org; **internet:** www.unhcr.org.

The Office of the High Commissioner was established in 1951 to provide international protection for refugees and to seek durable solutions to their problems. In 1981 UNHCR was awarded the Nobel Peace Prize.

Organization
(March 2008)

HIGH COMMISSIONER

The High Commissioner is elected by the United Nations General Assembly on the nomination of the Secretary-General, and is responsible to the General Assembly and to the UN Economic and Social Council (ECOSOC).
High Commissioner: ANTÓNIO MANUEL DE OLIVEIRA GUTERRES (Portugal).
Deputy High Commissioner: L. CRAIG JOHNSTONE (USA).

EXECUTIVE COMMITTEE

The Executive Committee of the High Commissioner's Programme (ExCom), established by ECOSOC, gives the High Commissioner policy directives in respect of material assistance programmes and advice in the field of international protection. In addition, it oversees UNHCR's general policies and use of funds. ExCom, which comprises representatives of 66 states, both members and non-members of the UN, meets once a year.

ADMINISTRATION

Headquarters include the Executive Office, comprising the offices of the High Commissioner, the Deputy High Commissioner and the Assistant High Commissioner. The Inspector General, the Director of the UNHCR liaison office in New York, and the Director of the Department of International Protection report directly to the High Commissioner. The other principal administrative units are the Division of Financial and Supply Management, the Division of Human Resources Management, the Division of External Relations, the Division of Information Systems and Telecommunications, the Division of International Protection Services, and the Department of Operations, which is responsible for the five regional bureaux covering Africa; Asia and the Pacific; Europe; the Americas and the Caribbean; and Central Asia, South-West Asia, North Africa and the Middle East; and also includes the Division of Operational Services and the Emergency and Security Service. At July 2006 there were 263 UNHCR offices in 116 countries world-wide. At that time UNHCR employed 6,540 people (including short-term staff), of whom more than 80% were working in the field. In that year a Structural and Management Change Process was initiated, with the aim of reviewing and improving UNHCR's processes and structures.

Activities

The competence of the High Commissioner extends to any person who, owing to well-founded fear of being persecuted for reasons of race, religion, nationality or political opinion, is outside the country of his or her nationality and is unable or, owing to such fear or for reasons other than personal convenience, remains unwilling to accept the protection of that country; or who, not having a nationality and being outside the country of his or her former habitual residence, is unable or, owing to such fear or for reasons other than personal convenience, is unwilling to return to it. This competence may be extended, by resolutions of the UN General Assembly and decisions of ExCom, to cover certain other 'persons of concern', in addition to refugees meeting these criteria. Refugees who are assisted by other UN agencies, or who have the same rights or obligations as nationals of their country of residence, are outside the mandate of UNHCR.

In recent years there has been a significant shift in UNHCR's focus of activities. Increasingly UNHCR has been called upon to support people who have been displaced within their own country (i.e. with similar needs to those of refugees but who have not crossed an international border) or those threatened with displacement as a result of armed conflict. In addition, greater support has been given to refugees who have returned to their country of origin, to assist their reintegration, and UNHCR is working to enable local communities to support the returnees, frequently through the implementation of Quick Impact Projects (QIPs). In 2004 UNHCR led the formulation of a UN system-wide Strategic Plan for internally displaced persons (IDPs). During 2005 the UN's Inter-Agency Standing Committee (IASC), concerned with co-ordinating the international response to humanitarian disasters, developed a concept of organizing agency assistance to IDPs through the institutionalization of a 'Cluster Approach', currently comprising 11 core areas of activity. UNHCR is the lead agency for the clusters on Camp Co-ordination and Management (in conflict situations; IOM leads that cluster in natural disaster situations), Emergency Shelter, and (jointly with OHCHR and UNICEF) Protection.

In the mid-2000s UNHCR widened its scope from its mandate to protect and assist people fleeing persecution and violence in response to the enormous impact of two devastating natural disasters. Following the series of tidal waves (tsunamis), emanating from an earthquake in the Indian Ocean, that devastated coastal regions in 14 countries in South and South-East Asia and East Africa in December 2004, UNHCR requested emergency funding totalling US $77m. in support of a 12-month relief operation to provide shelter, non-food relief supplies and logistical support for survivors in Aceh, Indonesia (close to the epicentre of the earthquake), Sri Lanka and Somalia. This was part of a pan-UN inter-agency appeal for $1,100m. In October 2005 UNHCR provided an immediate response to support survivors of the South Asian earthquake that struck northern Pakistan and bordering areas of India and Afghanistan.

UNHCR has been increasingly concerned with the problem of statelessness, where people have no legal nationality, and promotes new accessions to the 1954 Convention Relating to the Status of Stateless Persons and the 1964 Convention on the Reduction of Statelessness. UNHCR maintains that a significant proportion of the global stateless population has not hitherto been systematically identified. In October 2006 ExCom urged member states to share with UNHCR data on stateless persons and on persons with undetermined nationality.

Addressing the annual meeting of ExCom in October 2007 the High Commissioner, while emphasizing that UNHCR was not mandated to manage migration, urged a concerted international effort to raise awareness and comprehension of the broad patterns (including the scale, complexity, and causes—such as poverty and the pursuit of improved living standards) of global displacement and migration. In order to fulfil UNHCR's mandate to support refugees and others in need of protection within ongoing mass movements of people, he urged better recognition of the mixed nature of many 21st century population flows, often comprising both economic migrants and refugees, asylum-seekers and victims of trafficking who required detection and support. It was also acknowledged that conflict and persecution—the traditional reasons for flight—were being increasingly compounded by factors such as environmental degradation and detrimental effects of climate change.

At December 2006 the total population of concern to UNHCR, based on provisional figures, amounted to 32.9m., significantly higher than the 20.8m. recorded in the previous year (attributable in part to the enhancement of UNHCR's engagement with IDPs, following the development in 2005 of the IASC's Cluster Approach, see above, although the Office continued to count only conflict-generated IDPs in its statistical data). At the end of 2006 the refugee population world-wide totalled 9.9m. UNHCR was also concerned with some 733,622 recently returned refugees, 12.8m. IDPs, 5.8m. stateless persons, 740,165 asylum-seekers, 1.9m. returned IDPs, and 1.0m. others. UNHCR maintains an online statistical population database, accessible at www.unhcr.org/statistics/populationdatabase.

World Refugee Day, sponsored by UNHCR, is held annually on 20 June.

INTERNATIONAL PROTECTION

As laid down in the Statute of the Office, UNHCR's primary function is to extend international protection to refugees and its second function is to seek durable solutions to their problems. In the exercise of its mandate UNHCR seeks to ensure that refugees and asylum-seekers are protected against *refoulement* (forcible return), that they receive asylum, and that they are treated according to internationally recognized standards. UNHCR pursues these objectives by a variety of means that include promoting the conclusion and ratification by states of international conventions for the protection of refugees. UNHCR promotes the adoption of liberal practices of asylum by states, so that refugees and asylum-seekers are granted admission, at least on a temporary basis.

The most comprehensive instrument concerning refugees that has been elaborated at the international level is the 1951 United Nations Convention relating to the Status of Refugees. This Convention, the scope of which was extended by a Protocol adopted in 1967, defines the rights and duties of refugees and contains provisions dealing with a variety of matters which affect the day-to-day lives of refugees. The application of the Convention and its Protocol is supervised by UNHCR. Important provisions for the treatment of refugees are also contained in a number of instruments adopted at the regional level. These include the 1969 Convention Governing the Specific Aspects of Refugee Problems adopted by the Organization of African Unity (now the African Union—AU) member states in 1969, the European Agreement on the Abolition of Visas for Refugees, and the 1969 American Convention on Human Rights.

UNHCR has actively encouraged states to accede to the 1951 United Nations Refugee Convention and the 1967 Protocol: 147 states had acceded to either or both of these basic refugee instruments by March 2008. An increasing number of states have also adopted domestic legislation and/or administrative measures to implement the international instruments, particularly in the field of procedures for the determination of refugee status. UNHCR has sought to address the specific needs of refugee women and children, and has also attempted to deal with the problem of military attacks on refugee camps, by adopting and encouraging the acceptance of a set of principles to ensure the safety of refugees. In recent years it has formulated a strategy designed to address the fundamental causes of refugee flows. In 2001, in response to widespread concern about perceived high numbers of asylum-seekers and large-scale international economic migration and human trafficking, UNHCR initiated a series of Global Consultations on International Protection with the signatories to the 1951 Convention and 1967 Protocol, and other interested parties, with a view to strengthening both the application and scope of international refugee legislation. A consultation of 156 Governments, convened in Geneva, in December 2001, reaffirmed commitment to the central role played by the Convention and Protocol. The final consultation, held in May 2002, focused on durable solutions and the protection of refugee women and children. Subsequently, based on the findings of the Global Consultations process, UNHCR developed an Agenda on Protection with six main objectives: strengthening the implementation of the 1951 Convention and 1967 Protocol; the protection of refugees within broader migration movements; more equitable sharing of burdens and responsibilities and building of capacities to receive and protect refugees; addressing more effectively security-related concerns; increasing efforts to find durable solutions; and meeting the protection needs of refugee women and children. The Agenda was endorsed by ExCom in October 2002. In September of that year the High Commissioner for Refugees launched the *Convention Plus* initiative, which aimed to address contemporary global asylum issues by developing, on the basis of the Agenda on Protection, international agreements and measures to supplement the 1951 Convention and 1967 Protocol.

UNHCR is one of the 10 co-sponsors of UNAIDS.

ASSISTANCE ACTIVITIES

The first phase of an assistance operation uses UNHCR's capacity of emergency response. This enables UNHCR to address the immediate needs of refugees at short notice, for example, by employing specially trained emergency teams and maintaining stockpiles of basic equipment, medical aid and materials. A significant proportion of UNHCR expenditure is allocated to the next phase of an operation, providing 'care and maintenance' in stable refugee circumstances. This assistance can take various forms, including the provision of food, shelter, medical care and essential supplies. Also covered in many instances are basic services, including education and counselling.

As far as possible, assistance is geared towards the identification and implementation of durable solutions to refugee problems—this being the second statutory responsibility of UNHCR. Such solutions generally take one of three forms: voluntary repatriation, local integration or resettlement in another country. Where voluntary repatriation, increasingly the preferred solution, is feasible, the Office assists refugees to overcome obstacles preventing their return to their country of origin. This may be done through negotiations with governments involved, or by providing funds either for the physical movement of refugees or for the rehabilitation of returnees once back in their own country. UNHCR supports the implementation of the Guidance Note on Durable Solutions for Displaced Persons, adopted in 2004 by the UN Development Group.

When voluntary repatriation is not an option, efforts are made to assist refugees to integrate locally and to become self-supporting in their countries of asylum. This may be done either by granting loans to refugees, or by assisting them, through vocational training or in other ways, to learn a skill and to establish themselves in gainful occupations. One major form of assistance to help refugees re-establish themselves outside camps is the provision of housing. In cases where resettlement through emigration is the only viable solution to a refugee problem, UNHCR negotiates with governments in an endeavour to obtain suitable resettlement opportunities, to encourage liberalization of admission criteria and to draw up special immigration schemes. During 2006 an estimated 27,700 refugees (as well as 1,860 family reunification cases) were resettled under UNHCR auspices.

In the 1990s UNHCR consolidated efforts to integrate certain priorities into its programme planning and implementation, as a standard discipline in all phases of assistance. The considerations include awareness of specific problems confronting refugee women, the needs of refugee children, the environmental impact of refugee programmes and long-term development objectives. In an effort to improve the effectiveness of its programmes, UNHCR has initiated a process of delegating authority, as well as responsibility for operational budgets, to its regional and field representatives, increasing flexibility and accountability. A Policy Devolopment and Evaluation Service reviews systematically UNHCR's operational effectiveness.

All UNHCR personnel are required to sign, and all interns, contracted staff and staff from partner organizations are required to acknowledge, a Code of Conduct, to which is appended the UN Secretary-General's bulletin on special measures for protection from sexual exploitation and sexual abuse. The post of Senior Adviser to the High Commissioner on Gender Issues, within the Executive Office, was established in 2004.

EAST ASIA AND THE PACIFIC

In early 1998 the Hong Kong authorities formally terminated the policy of granting a port of first asylum to Vietnamese 'boat people'. In February 2000 UNHCR welcomed a decision by the Hong Kong authorities to offer permanent residency status to the occupants of the last remaining Vietnamese detention camp (totalling 973 refugees and 435 'non-refugees'). By the end of May, when the camp was closed, more than 200 Vietnamese had failed to apply for residency. At 31 December 2006 UNHCR was providing assistance to some 8,045 of an estimated further 300,897 Vietnamese refugees in mainland People's Republic of China (PRC). In 1995, in accordance with an agreement concluded with the PRC Government, UNHCR initiated a programme to redirect its local assistance to promote long-term self-sufficiency in the poorest settlements, including support for revolving-fund rural credit schemes. UNHCR favours the local integration of the majority of the Vietnamese refugee population in the PRC as a durable solution to the situation.

In 2007 UNHCR reported that there were as yet no effective domestic mechanisms in place in the Hong Kong Special Administrative Region to apply the 1951 United Nations Convention relating to the Status of Refugees (of which the PRC is a signatory), despite the area attracting mixed inflows of refugees, asylum-seekers and economic migrants.

From April 1991 increasing numbers of Rohingya Muslims in Myanmar fled into Bangladesh to escape brutality and killings perpetrated by the Myanma armed forces. UNHCR launched an international appeal for financial aid for the refugees, at the request of Bangladesh, and collaborated with other UN agencies in providing humanitarian assistance. UNHCR refused to participate in a programme of repatriation of the Myanma refugees agreed by Myanmar and Bangladesh, on the grounds that no safe environment existed for them to return to. In May 1993 a memorandum of understanding between UNHCR and Bangladesh was signed, whereby UNHCR would be able to monitor the repatriation process and ensure that people were returning of their own free will. In November a memorandum of understanding, signed with the Myanma Government, secured UNHCR access to the returnees. The first refugees returned to Myanmar with UNHCR assistance at the end of April 1994. They and all subsequent returnees were provided with a small amount of cash, housing grants and two months' food rations, and were supported by several small-scale reintegration projects. Attempts by UNHCR to find a local solution for those unwilling to return to Myanmar have been met with resistance by the Bangladeshi Government. By the end of December 2006 an estimated 26,268 Myanma refugees remained in camps in Bangladesh, of whom 21,716 were receiving basic care from UNHCR. There were also some 21,544 Myanma refugees in Malaysia (all UNHCR-assisted) at that time, compared with 14,208 at the start of the year.

In the early 1990s members of ethnic minorities in Myanmar attempted to flee attacks by government troops into Thailand; however, the Thai Government refused to recognize them as refugees or to offer them humanitarian assistance. In December 1997 Thailand and Myanmar agreed to commence 'screening' the refugees to determine those who had fled persecution and those who were economic migrants. Screening activities were suspended during 2001–04. In February 2004 the Myanma Government granted UNHCR access to areas along the Myanmar-Thailand border, thereby potentially enabling the large-scale voluntary repatriation of the Myanma (mainly Karen/Kayin) refugee population remaining in camps there. The Myanma Government requested that UNHCR should plan for the return and reintegration of IDPs as well as refugees. UNHCR, however, decided to postpone repatriation and reintegration operations pending the conclusion of an internationally acceptable peace agreement between the Myanma authorities and militants that would secure the safety of returnees. At 31 December 2006 some 132,241 Myanmar refugees remained encamped in Thailand, including 15,779 spontaneous arrivals during the year; all were receiving assistance from UNHCR. In 2006 more than 4,700 Myanma Thailand refugees were resettled in third countries.

In April 1999, following the announcement by the Indonesian Government, in January, that it would consider a form of autonomy or independence for East Timor, some 26,000 Indonesian settlers left their homes as a result of clashes between opposing groups and uncertainty regarding the future of the territory. The popular referendum on the issue, conducted at the end of August, and the resulting victory for the independence movement, provoked a violent reaction by pro-integration militia. UNHCR, along with other international personnel, was forced to evacuate the territory in early September. At that time there were reports of forced mass deportations of East Timorese to West Timor, while a large number of others fled their homes into remote mountainous areas of East Timor. In mid-September UNHCR staff visited West Timor to review the state of refugee camps, allegedly under the control of militia, and to persuade the authorities to permit access for humanitarian personnel. It was estimated that 250,000–260,000 East Timorese had fled to West Timor, of whom some 230,000 were registered in 28 camps at the end of September. At that time there were also an estimated 190,000–300,000 people displaced within East Timor, although the International Committee of the Red Cross estimated that a total of 800,000 people, or some 94% of the population, had been displaced, or deported, during the crisis. The arrival of multinational troops, from 20 September, helped to stabilize the region and enable the safe receipt and distribution of food supplies, prompting several thousands to return from hiding. Most homes, however, along with almost all other buildings in the capital, Dili, had been destroyed. In early October UNHCR, together with the International Organization for Migration, initiated a repatriation programme for the refugees in West Timor. However, despite an undertaking by the Indonesian Government in mid-October that it would ensure the safety of all refugees and international personnel, persistent intimidation by anti-independence militia impeded the registration and repatriation processes. UNHCR initially aimed to complete the repatriation programme by mid-2001, prior to the staging of elections to a Constituent Assembly by the UN Transitional Administration in East Timor (UNTAET), which assumed full authority over the territory in February 2000). However, in September 2000 UNHCR suspended its activities in West Timor, following the murder by militiamen there of three of its personnel. A UN Security Council resolution, adopted soon afterwards, deplored this incident and strongly urged the Indonesian authorities to disable the militia and to guarantee the future security of all refugees and humanitarian personnel. In mid-September UNTAET and the Indonesian Government signed a Memorandum of Understanding on co-operation in resolving the refugee crisis. However, despite a subsequent operation by the Indonesian security forces to disarm the militia, intimidation of East Timorese refugees reportedly persisted, and UNHCR did not redeploy personnel to West Timor. The Office did, however, liaise with other humanitarian organizations to facilitate continuing voluntary repatriations, which have been encouraged by the Indonesian authorities. UNHCR's operation in East Timor aimed to promote the safe voluntary repatriation of refugees, monitor returnees, support their reintegration through the implementation of QIPs, pursue efforts towards sustainable development and the rehabilitation of communities, and promote reconciliation and respect for human rights. In mid-May East Timor (now Timor-Leste) achieved independence. At that time almost 205,000 East Timorese refugees were reported to have returned since October 1999. UNHCR and the newly elected administration were co-operating to encourage further repatriation, as well as to assist with Timor-Leste's accession to the international instruments of protection and with the development of new national refugee protection legislation. On 31 December 2002 UNHCR terminated the refugee status of people who fled East Timor in 1999. Some 11,000 unsettled former East Timorese refugees reportedly remained in West Timor in 2007; UNHCR has assisted them in areas including food security and health and education provision while working to ensure durable solutions to their situation.

Renewed violent unrest in Timor-Leste that erupted in April 2006 resulted in significant new population displacement within the country, and, at 31 December 2006, some 155,231 Timorese IDPs were of concern to UNHCR. During May–August 2006 the Office provided immediate relief to the newly uprooted IDPs, in the form of non-food items such as tents, and from September 2006 onwards UNHCR remained involved in IDP protection and reconciliation activities. It was estimated at March 2008 that an estimated 100,000 people remained displaced within Timor-Leste, of whom around 30,000 were encamped near Dili and approximately 70,000 were being accommodated by host families and communities.

UNHCR endeavours to facilitate safe passage to the Republic of Korea for people who have fled from the Democratic People's Republic of Korea to the PRC and other countries in the region.

SOUTH ASIA

From 1979, as a result of civil strife in Afghanistan, there was a massive movement of refugees from that country into Pakistan and

Iran creating the world's largest refugee population, which reached a peak of almost 6.3m. people in 1990. In 1988 UNHCR agreed to provide assistance for the voluntary repatriation of refugees, both in ensuring the rights of the returning population and in providing material assistance such as transport, immunization, and supplies of food and other essentials. In April 1992, following the establishment of a new Government in Afghanistan, refugees began to repatriate in substantial numbers, although, meanwhile, large numbers of people continued to flee into Pakistan as a result of persisting insecurity. From October 1996 an escalation of hostilities in northern and western regions of Afghanistan resulted in further massive population displacement. The total number of returnees from Iran and Pakistan during the decade 1988–98 amounted to more than 4.2m. UNHCR, with other UN agencies, attempted to meet the immediate needs of IDPs and recent returnees in Afghanistan through systematic monitoring and, for example, by initiating small-scale multi-sectoral QIPs to improve shelter, rural water supply and local infrastructure; organizing income-generating and capacity-building activities; and providing food and tools. However, the ongoing civil conflict, as well as successive severe droughts and harsh winter conditions, caused renewed population displacement, precluding a settlement of the refugee situation and entailing immense difficulties in undertaking comprehensive relief efforts. Activities were disrupted by periodic withdrawals of UN international personnel owing to security concerns.

The humanitarian crisis in Afghanistan worsened considerably during 2000. In mid-2001 UNHCR warned that the food insecurity in the country was continuing to deteriorate and that population movements were ongoing. In September, prompted by the threat of impending military action directed by a US-led global coalition against targets in the Taliban-administered areas of Afghanistan, UNHCR launched a US $252m. appeal to finance an emergency relief operation to cope with the potentially large further movement of Afghan refugees and IDPs. Although all surrounding countries imposed 'closed border' policies (with Pakistan reportedly permitting limited entry to Afghans in possession of correct travel documentation), it was envisaged that, were the security situation to deteriorate significantly, large numbers of Afghans might attempt to cross into the surrounding countries (mainly Iran and Pakistan) at unsecured points of entry. UNHCR urged the adoption of more liberal border policies and began substantially to reinforce its presence in Iran and Pakistan. Activities undertaken included the supply of basic relief items, such as tents and health and hygiene kits, and assistance with the provision of community services, such as education for school-age children. The construction and maintenance of new camps near the Pakistan-Afghanistan border was initiated in co-operation with the Pakistan Government and other agencies, and new refugee shelters were to be constructed in Iran. Emergency contingency plans were also formulated for a relief initiative to assist a projected further 500,000 IDPs (in addition to the large numbers of people already displaced) inside Afghanistan. Large population movements out of cities were reported from the start of the international political crisis. An estimated 6m. Afghans (about one-quarter of the total population) were believed to be extremely vulnerable, requiring urgent food aid and other relief supplies. In mid-September all foreign UN field staff were withdrawn from Afghanistan for security reasons; meanwhile, in order to address the humanitarian situation, a Crisis Group was established by several UN agencies, including UNHCR, and a crisis management structure came into operation at UNHCR headquarters. In October (when air-strikes were initiated against Afghanistan) UNHCR opened a staging camp at a major crossing point on the Afghanistan-Pakistan border, and put in place a system for monitoring new refugee arrivals (implemented by local people rather than by UNHCR personnel). It was estimated that from October 2001–January 2002 about 50,000 Afghan refugees entered Pakistan officially, while about 150,000 crossed into the country at unofficial border points; many reportedly sought refuge with friends and relatives. Much smaller movements into Iran were reported. Spontaneous repatriations also occurred during that period (reportedly partly owing to the poor conditions at many camps in Pakistan), and UNHCR-assisted IDP returns were also undertaken. UNHCR resumed operations within Afghanistan in mid-November 2001, distributing supplies and implementing QIPs, for example the provision of warm winter clothing. From that month some 130,000 Afghan refugees in Pakistan were relocated from inadequate accommodation to new camps. On 1 March 2002, following the adoption in December 2001 by the international community of the Bonn Agreement on provisional arrangements for stabilizing Afghanistan, UNHCR initiated, jointly with the new interim Afghan administration, an assisted repatriation programme. UNHCR also concluded tripartite accords on repatriation with the Afghan authorities and with Iran and Pakistan. In March 2002 UNHCR signed a new agreement with the Iranian Government to grant access to Afghans in detention centres throughout that country and to undertake a screening programme for asylum-seekers, in order to deal with the problem of undocumented refugees. At 31 December 2006 some 1.0m. UNHCR-assisted Afghan refugees remained in Pakistan (in addition to an estimated 2.1m. Afghans believed to be refugees residing outside camps), 914,260 UNHCR-assisted refugees remained in Iran (in addition to about 1m. unregistered refugees, some of whom were to be deported during 2008), and 9,472 remained in India (all UNHCR-assisted). By early 2008 around 4.7m. refugees had returned from Pakistan and Iran since early 2002; of these, 386,667 returned during 2006 (138,618 with UNHCR assistance). UNHCR provides returning refugees with transport and an initial reintegration package, including a cash grant and food and basic household items, and monitors their situation. Particular focus is placed upon the situation of returnee women and prevention of gender-based violence, and on encouraging the return of professional workers, especially doctors and teachers. The Office also works to improve local infrastructure and water supply facilities, and by the end of 2007 had completed the construction of more than 200,000 shelter units. UNHCR aims to strengthen the capacity of the Afghan Government to manage the return and sustainable reintegration of refugees and IDPs. In early 2006, following the termination in September 2005 of the process determined by the 2001 Bonn Agreement and the adoption by the UN-sponsored London Conference on Afghanistan, convened on 31 January–1 February 2006, of the Afghanistan Compact as a framework for international assistance until end-2010, UNHCR developed an outline strategy for its Afghan operations over 2007–09, during which period it envisaged the voluntary return of a further 1.6m. Afghans.

In September 2005 Afghanistan acceded to the 1951 Convention relating to the Status of Refugees and its 1967 Protocol.

In October 2005 parts of northern Pakistan and bordering areas of India and Afghanistan were struck by a devastating earthquake, killing more than 80,000 people, injuring an estimated 74,000, rendering more than 3m. homeless, destroying local infrastructure and, owing to mountainous terrain and the isolation of many affected communities, causing unprecedented logistical challenges to aid agencies. UNHCR, with capabilities already on the ground as a result of its operations in support of Afghan refugees (see above), provided an immediate response, distributing to survivors tents and blankets from stores within the country. Further shelter materials were then brought in from global stockpiles, and UNHCR also provided stoves and kerosene for heating to help survivors to cope with severe winter conditions at 144 camps in the earthquake zone. In August 2006 UNHCR transferred responsibility for managing the camps to the Pakistan authorities; nevertheless, the Office was to continue to participate in planning and capacity-building activities.

In 1991–92 thousands of people of Nepalese ethnic origin living in Bhutan sought refuge from alleged persecution by fleeing to eastern Nepal. In December 2000 Bhutan and Nepal reached agreement on a joint verification mechanism for the repatriation of the refugees, which had been hitherto the principal issue precluding a resolution of the situation. The first verification of Bhutanese refugees was undertaken in March 2001. By March 2008 there remained around 107,000 Bhutanese refugees residing in seven camps in Nepal, all of whom were receiving UNHCR assistance in the form of food, shelter, medical care and water, and 25,000 of whom were registered for resettlement. At the end of that month UNHCR launched an operation to resettle more than 10,000 of the Nepalese refugees, mainly to the USA. During 2007 the Nepalese Government extended citizenship to some 2.6m. of the 3.5m. stateless people hitherto resident in Nepal.

During 1983–2001 hostilities between the Sri Lankan Government and Tamil separatists resulted in the displacement of more than 1m. Sri Lankan Tamil refugees (who sought shelter in India) and IDPs. Ongoing efforts by UNHCR to repatriate the Sri Lankan refugees were disrupted in late 1995 by an offensive by Sri Lankan government troops against the northern Jaffna peninsula, which caused a massive displacement of the local Tamil population. Increasing insecurity from late 1999 prompted further population movements.However, following the conclusion of a cease-fire agreement between the Sri Lankan Government and Tamil separatists in February 2002, the number of spontaneous returns accelerated. From April 2006 conflict between Tamil separatists and the Sri Lankan Government escalated once again, prompting a new wave of internal displacement and refugee movements to India during 2006–07. In 2006–07 UNHCR provided emergency relief items to most of the estimated 190,000 new Sri Lankan IDPs; monitored the human rights situation and advised the Sri Lankan authorities about the treatment of the displaced population; and established about 60 sites to accommodate the new IDPs. During 2006 UNHCR also supported the relocation of some 900 long-standing Sri Lankan IDP families. At 31 December 2006 there were 469,165 Sri Lankan IDPs of concern to UNHCR and 89,405 recently returned IDPs, as well as an estimated 69,609 Sri Lankan refugees remaining in camps in southern India. At end-December 2006 India's total refugee population of some 158,366 also included 77,200 refugees from the People's Republic of China (mainly Tibetans).

CENTRAL ASIA

In late 1992 people began to flee civil conflict in Tajikistan and to seek refuge in Afghanistan. During 1993 an emergency UNHCR operation established a reception camp to provide the 60,000 Tajik refugees with basic assistance, and began to move them away from the border area to safety. In December a tripartite agreement was concluded by UNHCR and the Tajik and Afghan Governments regarding the security of refugees returning to Tajikistan. UNHCR monitored the repatriation process and provided materials for the construction of almost 20,000 homes. The operation was concluded by the end of 1997. Nevertheless, at the end of 2000, there were still nearly 60,000 Tajik refugees remaining in other countries of the former USSR. In the early 2000s an initiative was implemented to integrate locally up to 10,000 Tajik refugees of Kyrgyz ethnic origin in Kyrgyzstan and 12,500 Tajik refugees of Turkmen origin in Turkmenistan; this process was facilitated by the conclusion in mid-2003 of a Kyrgyz-Tajik agreement on a simplified procedure for citizenship acquisition. From 1 July 2006 UNHCR terminated refugee status for exiled Tajiks, although the Office continued to support their voluntary repatriation. By the end of that year most of the former Tajik refugees in Kygyzstan and Turkmenistan had become naturalized citizens of those countries, as planned. From late 2001 about 9,000 Afghan refugees repatriated from Tajikistan under the auspices of UNHCR and the International Organization for Migration. During 2006 nearly 1,500 Afghan refugees were resettled from Tajikistan to third countries, leaving a remaining Afghan refugee poplation in that country of about 1,000 at 31 December. UNHCR expressed concern following the adoption by the Tajikistan authorities in May 2002 of refugee legislation that reportedly contravened the 1951 Convention relating to the Status of Refugees and its 1967 Protocol. In 2003 UNHCR agreed to participate in an EU/UNDP Border Management Programme in Central Asia (BOMCA); BOMCA was ongoing in 2008. At the request of the Uzbekistan Government UNHCR closed its Uzbekistan office in April 2006.

UNHCR planned to open a regional office in Almaty, Kazakhstan, during 2008.

NORTH AFRICA AND THE MIDDLE EAST

UNHCR co-ordinates humanitarian assistance for the estimated 165,000 Sahrawis registered as refugees in four camps in the Tindouf area of Algeria. In September 1997 an agreement was reached on implementing the 1991 Settlement Plan for the Western Sahara. Accordingly, UNHCR was to help organize the registration and safe return of some 120,000 Sahrawi refugees provisionally identified as eligible to vote in the planned referendum on the future of the territory. In addition, UNHCR was to facilitate the reintegration of the returnees and monitor their rehabilitation. By 2008, however, little progress had been achieved towards the implementation of the Settlement Plan and subsequent alternative settlement proposals. UNHCR was continuing to provide basic relief items and to facilitate family visits and telephone communications for the residents of the Tindouf camps.

In June 1992 people fleeing the civil war and famine in Somalia began arriving in Yemen in large numbers. UNHCR set up camps to accommodate some 50,000 refugees, providing them with shelter, food, water and sanitation. As a result of civil conflict in Yemen in mid-1994, a large camp in the south of the country was demolished and other refugees had to be relocated, while the Yemen authorities initiated a campaign of forcible repatriation. During 1998–mid-2000 the refugee population in Yemen expanded, owing to an influx of Somalis fleeing civil conflict and, to a lesser extent, people displaced by the 1998–2000 Eritrea–Ethiopia border conflict. The relocation of refugees to a newly constructed camp at al-Kharaz, central Yemen, was undertaken during 2000–01. Yemen has continued to receive a steady flow of mixed groups of migrants from the Horn of Africa. At December 2006 Yemen was hosting an estimated 96,655, mostly Somali, refugees; the majority of these were residing in urban areas, while some 9,000 were accommodated in the al-Kharaz camp. Ongoing violent conflict in northern Yemen was also generated internal displacement at that time.

In April 1994 UNHCR initiated a programme to provide food and relief assistance to Turkish Kurds who had fled into northern Iraq. In September 1996 fighting escalated among the Kurdish factions in northern Iraq. By the time a cease-fire agreement was concluded in November some 65,000 Iraqi Kurds had fled across the border into Iran. UNHCR, together with the Iranian Government, provided these new refugees with basic humanitarian supplies. By the end of the year, however, the majority of refugees had returned to Iraq, owing to poor conditions in the temporary settlements, security concerns at being located in the border region and pressure from the Iranian authorities. In December UNHCR announced its intention to withdraw from the Atroush camp in northern Iraq, which housed an estimated 15,000 Turkish Kurds, following several breaches of security in the camp. UNHCR proceeded to transfer 3,500 people to other local settlements, and continued to provide humanitarian assistance to those refugees who had settled closer to Iraqi-controlled territory but who had been refused asylum. During 1997–2000 some 2,200 Turkish Kurds repatriated from Iraq with assistance from UNHCR. In January 2004 UNHCR reached a preliminary agreement with Turkey and the USA on the voluntary repatriation of 13,000 Turkish Kurds remaining as refugees in Iraq; there were still around 10,000 Turkish Kurd refugees in Iraq at January 2007.

In March–May 1991, following the 1990 war against Iraq by a multinational force, and the subsequent Iraqi suppression of resistance in Kurdish areas in the north of the country, there was massive movement of some 1.5m., mainly Kurdish, Iraqi refugees into Iran and Turkey. UNHCR was designated the principal UN agency to attempt to alleviate the crisis. In May the refugees began to return to Iraq in huge numbers and UNHCR assisted in their repatriation, establishing relief stations along their routes from Iran and Turkey. Following the war to liberate Kuwait UNHCR gave protection and assistance to Iraqis, *bidoun* (stateless people) and Palestinians who were forced to leave that country. In May 2000 the Kuwaiti authorities determined that all *bidoun* still resident in the country should register officially with the national authorities by 27 June; while it was agreed that citizenship requirement restrictions would be eased for some 36,000 *bidoun* who had been enumerated at a population census in 1965, the remaining stateless residents (numbering an estimated 75,000) were to be required to apply for short-term residency permits. At 31 December 2006 there remained 109,661 people in Kuwait of concern to UNHCR, mainly *bidoun* (totalling 88,086), Iraqis and Palestinians.

In March 2003, in view of the initiation of US-led military action against the Saddam Hussain regime in Iraq, UNHCR and the International Federation of Red Cross and Red Crescent Societies signed an agreement on co-operation in providing humanitarian relief in Iraq and neighbouring countries. From mid-2003, following the overthrow of the Saddam Hussain Government, UNHCR developed plans for the eventual phased repatriation of more than 500,000 of the large population of Iraqis exiled world-wide, and for the return to their homes of some 800,000 IDPs, contingent, however, upon the stabilization of the political and security situation in the country. The Office assumed responsibility for assisting about 50,000 refugees from other countries (some 34,000 Palestinians, as well as Iranians and Syrians) who had been supported by the previous Iraqi administration but were now suffering harassment; many had abandoned their homes in Iraq owing to insufficient security and inadequate supplies. Negotiations with Iran were initiated in mid-2003 to enable Iranian refugees to repatriate across the Iraq–Iran border. From March–May 2003, and following the bomb attack in August on the UN headquarters in Baghdad, all international UN humanitarian personnel were withdrawn from Iraq, leaving national staff to conduct operations on the ground. During 2003–05 some 315,000 spontaneous returns by Iraqi refugees and asylum-seekers and 496,000 returns by IDPs were reported. However, owing to the ongoing unstable security situation, UNHCR and the Iraqi Interim Government (inaugurated in June 2004) discouraged Iraqi refugees from returning home, and UNHCR warned governments hosting Iraqi refugees against repatriation, as well as advising continued protection of Iraqi asylum-seekers. During early 2006–end-2007, owing to escalating violent sectarian unrest, it was reported that more than 1.5m. Iraqis had become newly displaced and that many people—including skilled and professional workers—had left Iraq, further inhibiting the national recovery process. In mid-April 2007 an International Conference on Addressing the Humanitarian Needs of Refugees and Internally Displaced Persons inside Iraq and in Neighbouring Countries was convened in Geneva by the UN High Commissioner for Refugees. During 2007 UNHCR expanded its operations in Iraq and refocused its assistance activities to target support particularly at the most vulnerable IDPs, including female-headed households, the elderly, children, and families without resources. UNHCR remained highly concerned for foreign refugees remaining in Iraq (totalling 44,406 at end-2006). At March 2008 UNHCR estimated that some 2.8m. Iraqis were displaced internally. In addition, it was estimated that up to 2m. Iraqis were sheltering in neighbouring countries, mainly Syria (around 1.2m.) and Jordan (around 700,000), placing considerable strain on local infrastructure and services. In 2006 more Iraqis sought asylum in Europe than any other nationality.

As a consequence of the full-scale conflict that erupted in southern Lebanon in mid-July 2006 between the Israeli armed forces and the militant Shi'a organization Hezbollah, it was estimated that, in total, around 900,000 Lebanese civilians were displaced from their homes, of whom about 180,000 sought shelter in Syria. During that month UNHCR reinforced its field staff in the region, monitored the situation on the Lebanon-Syria border, and appealed for US $18.9m. in donations from the international community to provide basic relief items, such as tents, mattresses, blankets and plastic sheeting, for 100,000 of the most vulnerable IDPs in Lebanon and 50,000 of those sheltering in Syria. Following the conclusion of a cease-fire in mid-August most IDPs returned to their homes;

UNHCR continued to distribute emergency items to people dispossessed by the conflict, and to provide psycho-social support to traumatized adults and children, and provided warehouse facilities and transport support to the UN Mine Action Service. Jointly with other humanitarian organizations the Office embarked upon a second phase of assistance aimed at supporting the rebuilding of houses and rehabilitation of devastated communities.

SUB-SAHARAN AFRICA

UNHCR has provided assistance to refugee and internally displaced populations in many parts of the continent where civil conflict, violations of human rights, drought, famine or environmental degradation have forced people to flee their home regions. The majority of African refugees and returnees are located in countries that are themselves suffering major economic problems and are thus unable to provide the basic requirements of the uprooted people. Furthermore, UNHCR has often failed to receive adequate international financial support to implement effective relief programmes. In March 2004 a UNHCR-sponsored Dialogue on Voluntary Repatriation and Sustainable Reintegration in Africa endorsed the creation of an international working group—comprising African governments, UN agencies, the AU and other partners—to support the return and sustainable reintegration of refugees in several African countries, including Angola, Burundi, the Democratic Republic of the Congo (DRC), Eritrea, Liberia, Rwanda, Sierra Leone, Somalia and Sudan. At 31 December 2006 there were an estimated 4.9m. people of concern to UNHCR in sub-Saharan Africa.

The Horn of Africa, afflicted by famine, separatist violence and ethnic conflict, has experienced large-scale population movements in recent years. Following the overthrow of the regime of former Somali president Siad Barre in January 1991 hundreds of thousands of Somalis fled to neighbouring countries. In 1992 UNHCR initiated a repatriation programme for the massive Somali and Ethiopian refugee populations in Kenya, which included assistance with reconstruction projects and the provision of food to returnees and displaced persons. However, continuing instability in many areas of Somalia impeded the completion of the repatriation process to that country and resulted in further population displacement. Repatriations accelerated in the early 2000s owing to advances in the peace process. During 1992–mid-2006 more than 1m. Somali refugees returned to their country, of whom about 485,000 received UNHCR assistance. However, many areas of the country have remained unstable, drought-affected and lacking in basic services. The Office, with other partners, has implemented community-based QIPs, aimed at facilitating long-term self-reliance by improving local education and health provision, water supply and productive capacity. It was hoped that the inauguration of a new transitional Somali parliament in August 2004 might lead to improved stability and an eventual increase in voluntary returns. Nevertheless, the humanitarian situation in Somalia remained poor from 2005 onwards, owing to severe drought in the region, and deteriorated further in early 2007 as a result of increased insecurity. Intense fighting between government forces and local militia in Mogadishu during February–mid-April 2007 prevented UNHCR personnel from accessing basic supplies warehoused there for distribution to the displaced civilian population. The Somalian IDP population totalled an estimated 750,000 at end-2007. At the end of 2006 there remained an estimated total Somali refugee population of 464,038, of whom 173,702 were in Kenya and 91,587 in Yemen. During 2008 UNHCR aimed to help new Somali IDPs through the provision of basic shelter materials and relief items; and to strengthen the protection of/promote durable solutions for IDPs, returnees and others of concern.

By late 1997 UNHCR estimated that some 600,000 Ethiopians had repatriated from neighbouring countries, either by spontaneous or organized movements. The voluntary repatriation operation of Ethiopian refugees from Sudan (which commenced in 1993) was concluded in mid-1998. With effect from 1 March 2000 UNHCR withdrew the automatic refugee status of Ethiopians who left their country before 1991. Transportation and rehabilitation assistance were provided for 9,321 of these, who wished to repatriate. At 31 December 2006 there remained an estimated total Ethiopian refugee population of 74,026; some 16,428 Ethiopians remained in Kenya and 11,009 were in Sudan. At that time Ethiopia itself was hosting a total of 96,980 refugees (of whom the majority were Sudanese), while Kenya was sheltering 272,531 (mainly Somalis). During 2007 Kenya enacted a Refugee Act, in accordance with which it was to assume a more active role in managing the registration and status determination of refugees. Consequently UNHCR was to shift the focus of its operations towards a more advisory function.

From 1992 some 500,000 Eritreans took refuge in Sudan as a result of separatist conflicts; however, by 1995 an estimated 125,000 had returned spontaneously, in particular following Eritrea's accession to independence in May 1993. A UNHCR repatriation programme to assist the remaining refugees, which had been delayed for various political, security and funding considerations, was initiated in November 1994. Its implementation, however, was hindered by a shortfall in donor funding and by differences between the Eritrean and Sudanese Governments, and Sudan continued to host substantial numbers of Eritrean refugees. Renewed conflict between Eritrea and Ethiopia, which commenced in 1998, had, by mid-1999, resulted in the displacement of some 350,000 Eritreans and 300,000 Ethiopians. In mid-2000, following an escalation of the conflict in May, UNHCR reported that some 95,000 Eritreans had sought refuge in Sudan, while smaller numbers had fled to Djibouti and Yemen. Following the conclusion of a cease-fire agreement between Eritrea and Ethiopia in June, UNHCR initiated an operation to repatriate the most recent wave of Eritrean refugees from Sudan, and also inaugurated a scheme to repatriate 147,000 long-term refugees. UNHCR and other agencies collaborated to rehabilitate areas of Eritrea that were receiving returnees. During 2001 UNHCR withdrew assistance to Eritrean IDPs, whose numbers had declined from a peak of 300,000 to about 45,000 by May. At the end of 2002 UNHCR terminated the refugee status of Eritreans who fled their country since 1993. During mid-2000–end-2003 UNHCR assisted 54,000 voluntary repatriations of Eritrean refugees from Sudan. Thereafter UNHCR aimed to support the repatriation of a further 35,000 Eritrean refugees and to close 16 of the 18 camps for Eritreans in Sudan, maintaining the two remaining camps to shelter Eritreans with continuing eligibility for international protection. The initial deadline of end-2004 for achieving this was not met owing to inadequate funding. At 31 December 2006 the total number of Eritreans still sheltering in Sudan was estimated at 157,220, of whom 108,120 were receiving UNHCR assistance.

At 31 December 2006 an estimated 686,311 Sudanese were exiled as refugees, mainly in Chad, Uganda, Ethiopia, Kenya, the DRC and the Central African Republic (CAR), owing to a history of civil unrest in southern Sudan and the emergence in early 2003 of a new conflict zone in the western Sudanese province of Darfur (see below). At end-2006 some 550,337 Sudanese refugees were receiving assistance from UNHCR. The Ugandan Government, hosting an estimated 215,675 Sudanese refugees at that time (171,565 UNHCR-assisted), has provided new resettlement sites and, jointly with UNHCR and other partners, has developed a Self-Reliance Strategy, which envisages achieving self-sufficiency for the long-term refugee population through integrating services for refugees into existing local structures. In 2006 the Ugandan Government adopted a new Refugee Act that included gender-based persecution as a grounds for granting refugee status. In view of the conclusion of a comprehensive peace agreement between the Sudanese Government and rebels in January 2005 UNHCR, in collaboration with other humanitarian agencies, planned to support the future voluntary repatriation and reintegration of some 380,000 refugees to southern Sudan from neighbouring countries. It was envisaged that UNHCR would assist the voluntary repatriation of 50,000 refugees from Uganda to Sudan in 2008. During that year UNHCR also aimed, in view of an improvement in the security situation in northern Uganda, to support the return to their places of origin of 500,000 Ugandan IDPs. In February 2006 UNHCR and Sudan signed tripartite agreements with Ethiopia, the DRC and the Central African Republic to provide a legal framework for the repatriation of Sudanese refugees remaining in those countries.

From April 2003 more than 200,000 refugees from Sudan's western Darfur region sought shelter across the Sudan-Chad border, having fled an alleged campaign of killing, rapes and destruction of property conducted by pro-government militias against the indigenous population. In addition, an estimated 2m. people became displaced within Darfur. The Office has organized airlifts of basic household items to the camps, has aimed to improve and expand refugees' access to sanitation, healthcare and education, to manage supplementary and therapeutic feeding facilities in order to combat widespread malnutrition, to provide psychosocial support to traumatized refugees, and to promote training and livelihood programmes. The operation has been hampered by severe water shortages resulting from the arid environment of the encampment areas, necessitating costly UNHCR deliveries of stored water, and by intense insecurity. A significant deterioration during 2006 in the security situation in the eastern areas of Chad bordering Darfur (where resources were already stretched to the limit), as well as in Darfur itself, led to further population displacement in the region, including the displacement of significant numbers of Chadians. By early 2008 some 27,000 Chadians had fled into Darfur, and there were also some 180,000 Chadian IDPs who had fled inwards from the Chad-Sudan border region. At that time Chad was still hosting 240,000 refugees from Darfur, accommodated in 12 UNHCR camps. UNHCR established a presence within western Darfur in June 2004, and was operating from six offices there in early 2008, at which time it was providing protection activities to around 500,000 of the 800,000 local IDPs, as well as the Chadian refugees, in the region. Following the establishment of the AU/UN Hybrid Operation in Darfur (UNAMID) in December 2007, UNHCR planned to open a liaison office near the UNAMID base in northern Darfur. UNHCR teams have undertaken efforts to train Sudanese managers of camps in Darfur in the areas of protection and human rights. The Office has also established in the area a number of women's centres providing support to survivors of sexual violence, and several centres for IDP youths, as well as rehabilitating conflict-damaged schools.

Following an outbreak of civil conflict in the CAR in early 2003, resulting in a *coup d'état* in March, some 41,000 CAR refugees fled to southern Chad. Continuing insecurity in northern CAR resulted in further population displacement and influxes of refugees into Chad during 2005–early 2008. In 2006 UNHCR initiated a protection strategy in the CAR, which it aimed to strengthen in 2008. At December 2007 45,000 CAR refugees were accommodated by UNHCR in four camps in Chad, and there were an estimated 197,000 IDPs inside the CAR.

Significant population displacements have occurred in West Africa in recent years, particularly since the outbreak in 1989 of enduring violent conflict in Liberia. Rebel insurgencies, fuelled by the illegal trade in 'conflict diamonds' and a proliferation of small arms, subsequently spread to Sierra Leone, Guinea and, latterly, Côte d'Ivoire (see below). During 1992 and the first half of 1993 refugees fleeing unrest in Senegal and Togo, as well as Liberia, increased the regional refugee population substantially. In accordance with a Liberian peace agreement, signed in July 1993, UNHCR was responsible for the repatriation of Liberian refugees who had fled to Guinea, Côte d'Ivoire and Sierra Leone. UNHCR also began to provide emergency relief to the displaced population within the country. Persisting political insecurity prevented any solution to the refugee problem, and in mid-1996 UNHCR suspended its preparatory activities for a large-scale repatriation and reintegration operation of Liberian refugees, owing to an escalation in hostilities. In early 1997 the prospect of a peaceful settlement in Liberia prompted a spontaneous movement of refugees returning home, and in April UNHCR initiated an organized repatriation of Liberian refugees from Ghana. The establishment of a democratically elected Liberian government in August and the consolidation of the peace settlement were expected to accelerate the return of refugees and other displaced persons. However, the process was hindered by logistical difficulties, the persisting volatility particularly of some border regions, and alleged atrocities perpetrated by Liberian troops. During 1998 and 1999 an estimated 15,000 Liberians fled to Guinea from insecurity in the Lofa area of northern Liberia; meanwhile, UNHCR was forced to suspend its operations in Lofa. By the end of 2000 nearly 400,000 Liberians were reported to have repatriated, more than one-third with UNHCR assistance. UNHCR organized QIPs to facilitate the reintegration of the returnees. Mounting insecurity in southern Guinea from September 2000 (see below) accelerated the return of Liberian refugees from camps there. However, during 2001 some 80,000 Liberians were displaced from their homes, and refugee camps for Sierra Leoneans were disrupted, owing to an escalation of violence particularly in the Lofa and Gbarpolu areas. In mid-2003 a further 147,000 Liberian refugees fled to neighbouring countries following an escalation in hostilities. However, owing to progress subsequently achieved in the Liberian peace process (including, in August 2003, the deployment of an ECOWAS peace-keeping force—ECOMIL—to the country, the exile of President Charles Taylor, and the conclusion of a peace agreement by the parties to the conflict; the deployment in October of a UN peace-keeping force, replacing ECOMIL; the peaceful staging of legislative and presidential elections in, respectively, October and November 2005; and the arrest and detention of Taylor in March 2006), mass voluntary spontaneous returns by Liberian refugees were reported in 2004–06. In February 2006 UNHCR altered its policy from 'facilitating' voluntary returns by Liberian refugees to 'actively promoting' large-scale returns. At 31 December 2006 there remained an estimated 160,548 Liberian refugees (118,146 UNHCR-assisted), of whom 21,816 were in Guinea (all UNHCR-assisted). At that time there were 237,822 returned Liberian IDPs of concern to UNHCR. The large-scale repatriation of refugees to Liberia was officially completed in June 2007. By the end of that year most Liberian IDPs were reported to have returned to their origins, and UNHCR planned to consolidate and phase out its reintegration activities by the end of 2008.

Further large-scale population displacement in West Africa followed an escalation of violence in Sierra Leone in early 1995. By December 1996 there were nearly 370,000 Sierra Leonean refugees in Liberia and Guinea, while a further 654,600 internally displaced Sierra Leoneans were of concern to UNHCR. The repatriation of Sierra Leonean refugees from Liberia was initiated in February 1997. However, the programme was suspended in May, owing to renewed political violence, which forced UNHCR staff to evacuate the country, and the seizure of power by military forces. Thousands of people fled to other parts of the country, as well as to neighbouring countries to escape the hostilities. Following the intervention of the ECOMOG multinational force (authorized by ECOWAS) and the conclusion of a peace agreement in October, residents of the Sierra Leone capital, Freetown, who had been displaced by the conflict, began to return. In February 1998 ECOMOG troops took control of Freetown from the rebel military forces, and in the following month the elected President, Ahmed Tejan Kabbah, was reinstated as Head of State. None the less, large numbers of Sierra Leoneans continued to cross the borders into neighbouring countries, owing to ongoing violence in the northern and eastern regions of the country and severe food shortages. In early 1999 anti-government forces again advanced on Freetown, prompting heavy fighting with ECOMOG troops and the displacement of thousands more civilians. In February a reported 200,000 people fled the town of Kenema in south-eastern Sierra Leone following attacks by rebel militia. In May a cease-fire agreement was concluded between the Government and opposition forces, and a formal peace accord was signed in early July, under which the rebels were to be disarmed and demobilized; however, the agreement broke down in May 2000. The resumption of hostilities delayed a planned repatriation operation and displaced an estimated 50,000 people from their homes. A new cease-fire agreement was signed by the Sierra Leone Government and the principal rebel group in early November. Meanwhile, persistent insecurity in northeastern and some border areas of Sierra Leone prompted further movements of Sierra Leonean refugees to Guinea during 2000. From September, however, unrest in southern Guinea (see below) caused some Sierra Leonean refugees who had been sheltering in camps there to repatriate. In 2001 UNHCR, while assisting, with the International Organization for Migration, returns by sea from the Guinean capital Conakry to Freetown, organized radio broadcasts to southern Guinea warning Sierra Leoneans against attempting to escape the unrest there by returning over the land border into volatile northeastern and other border areas of Sierra Leone. The successful staging of legislative and presidential elections in May 2003 and the consolidation of the peace process accelerated refugee returns. UNHCR terminated voluntary repatriation operations for Sierra Leonean refugees at 31 July 2004, by which time the Office had assisted about 180,000 of a total 280,000 returns since 2000. Thereafter, refugee status was to be determined on an individual basis for those who had not yet returned. At the end of 2005 UNHCR and partners terminated a four-year programme of reintegration assistance, mainly in the form of community development projects, aimed at providing a stable and self-supporting environment for returnees to Sierra Leone.

In August 2000 the security situation in southern border areas of Guinea deteriorated owing to increasing insurgencies by rebels from Liberia and Sierra Leone, which displaced a large number of Guineans from their homes and also endangered an estimated 460,000 mainly Liberian and Sierra Leonean refugees (see above) accommodated in Guinean camps. In mid-September UNHCR and other aid organizations withdrew their international personnel and suspended food distribution in these areas following the murder by armed rebels of a member of UNHCR staff. Insecurity, hunger and mounting hostility from elements of the local population subsequently led significant numbers of refugees to flee the unprotected camps. Many sought to reach northern Guinea, while some returned spontaneously to their countries of origin. Following an escalation in fighting between Guinean government forces and insurgent rebels in early December refugee movements intensified; however, it was reported that an estimated 180,000 refugees and 70,000 IDPs remained stranded without humanitarian assistance in the south-western Bec de Perroquet area. Later in December UNHCR dispatched emergency teams to assist with the relocation of refugees who had escaped the conflict zone. In February 2001 the High Commissioner negotiated with the parties to the conflict for the establishment of a humanitarian 'lifeline' to enable the delivery of assistance to and possible evacuation of the refugees and IDPs trapped at Bec de Perroquet: conveys of food aid began to reach the area at the end of that month. Meanwhile, UNHCR opened five new refugee settlements in central Guinea and, supported by the Guinean authorities, dispatched search teams into Bec de Perroquet in an attempt to find and evacuate refugees still stranded there. UNHCR withdrew from Bec de Perroquet at the end of May.

UNHCR provided assistance to 120,000 people displaced by the extreme insecurity that developed in Côte d'Ivoire from September 2002. About 25,000 Côte d'Ivoire refugees fled to southern Liberia, and others sought shelter in Ghana, Guinea and Mali. In addition, during November–January 2003 an estimated 40,000 Liberian refugees in Côte d'Ivoire repatriated, in both spontaneous and partly UNHCR-assisted movements, having suffered harassment since the onset of the conflict. UNHCR initiated a number of QIPs aimed at rehabilitating the infrastructure of communities that were to receive returned Côte d'Ivoire refugees. At 31 December 2006 there remained 709,228 IDPs in Côte d'Ivoire. It was envisaged that the signing of the Ouagadougou peace agreement in March 2007 by the Côte d'Ivoire President and the main rebel grouping would lead to an increase in refugee returns during 2008; UNHCR was to monitor the conditions of return and the reintegration of the former refugees.

UNHCR's activities in assisting refugees in West Africa have included a focus on the prevention of sexual and gender-based violence in refugee camps—a regional action plan to combat such violence was initiated in 2002—and collaboration with other agencies to ensure continuity between initial humanitarian assistance and long-term development support.

Since 1993 the Great Lakes region of central Africa has experienced massive population displacement, causing immense operational challenges and demands on the resources of international humanitarian and relief agencies. In October of that year a military coup in Burundi prompted some 580,000 people to flee into Rwanda and Tanzania, although many had returned by early 1994. By May 1994, however, an estimated 860,000 people from Burundi and Rwanda had fled to neighbouring states (following a resurgence of ethnic violence in both countries), including 250,000 mainly Rwandan Tutsi refugees who entered Tanzania over a 24-hour period in late April in the most rapid mass exodus ever witnessed by UNHCR. In May UNHCR began an immediate operation to airlift emergency supplies to the refugees. For the first time in an emergency operation UNHCR organized support to be rendered in the form of eight defined 'service packages', for example, to provide domestic fuel, road servicing and security or sanitation facilities. Despite overcrowding in camps and a high incidence of cholera and dysentery (particularly in camps in eastern Zaire, where many thousands of Rwandan Hutus had sought refuge following the establishment of a new Government in July) large numbers of refugees refused to accept UNHCR-assisted repatriation, owing to fears of reprisal ethnic killings. In September reports of mass ethnic violence in Rwanda, which were disputed by some UN agencies, continued to disrupt UNHCR's policy of repatriation and to prompt returnees to cross the border back into Zaire. Security in the refugee camps, which was undermined by the presence of military and political elements of the former Rwandan regime, remained an outstanding concern for UNHCR. A resurgence of violence in Burundi, in February 1995, provoked further mass population movements. However, in March the Tanzanian authorities, reportedly frustrated at the lack of international assistance for the refugees and the environmental degradation resulting from the camps, closed Tanzania's border with Burundi, thus preventing the admission into the country of some 100,000 Rwandan Hutu refugees who were fleeing camps in Burundi. While persisting disturbances in Rwanda disrupted UNHCR's repatriation programme, in April Rwandan government troops employed intimidation tactics to force some 90,000 internally displaced Hutus to leave a heavily populated camp in the south-west of the country; other small camps were closed. In August the Zairean Government initiated a short-lived programme of forcible repatriation of the estimated 1m. Rwandan and 70,000 Burundian Hutu refugees remaining in the country, which prompted as many as 100,000 refugees to flee the camps into the surrounding countryside. In September Rwanda agreed to strengthen its reception facilities and to provide greater security and protection for returnees, in collaboration with UNHCR, in order to prepare for any large-scale repatriation. UNHCR, meanwhile, expanded its information campaign, to promote the return of refugees, and enhanced its facilities at official border entry points. In December UNHCR negotiated an agreement between the Rwandan and Tanzanian authorities concerning the repatriation of the estimated 500,000 Rwandans remaining in camps in Tanzania. UNHCR agreed to establish a separate camp in north-west Tanzania in order to accommodate elements of the refugee population that might disrupt the repatriation programme. The repatriation of Rwandan refugees from all host countries was affected by reports of reprisals against Hutu returnees by the Tutsi-dominated Government in Rwanda. In February 1996 the Zairean Government renewed its efforts to accelerate the repatriation process, owing to concerns that the camps were becoming permanent settlements and that they were being used to train and rearm a Hutu militia. In July the Burundian Government forcibly repatriated 15,000 Rwandan refugees, having announced the closure of all remaining refugee camps. The repatriation programme was condemned by UNHCR and was suspended by the country's new military authorities, but only after many more thousands of refugees had been obliged to return to Rwanda and up to 30,000 had fled to Tanzania.

In October 1996 an escalation of hostilities between Zairean government forces, accused by Rwanda of arming the Hutu *Interahamwe* militia, and Zairean (Banyamulenge) Tutsis, who had been the focus of increasingly violent assaults, resulted in an extreme humanitarian crisis. Some 250,000 refugees fled 12 camps in the east of the country, including 90,000 Burundians who returned home. An estimated 500,000 refugees regrouped in Muganga camp, west of Goma, with insufficient relief assistance, following the temporary evacuation of international aid workers. UNHCR appealed to all Rwandan Hutu refugees to return home, and issued assurances of the presence of human rights observers in Rwanda to enhance their security. In November, with the apparent withdrawal of *Interahamwe* forces and the advance of the Tutsi-dominated Alliance des forces démocratiques pour la libération du Congo-Zaïre (AFDL), an estimated 600,000 refugees unexpectedly returned to Rwanda; however, concern remained on the part of the international community for the substantial number of Rwandan Hutu refugees at large in eastern Zaire. Further mass movement of Rwandan refugee populations occurred in December, owing to the threat of forcible repatriation by the Tanzanian Government, which had announced its intention of closing all camps by the end of the year. UNHCR initiated a repatriation programme; however, 200,000 refugees, unwilling to return to Rwanda, fled their camps. The majority of the refugees were later identified by the Tanzanian national army and escorted to the Rwandan border. By the end of December some 483,000 refugees had returned to Rwanda from Tanzania.

In February 1997 violence in Zaire intensified, which prompted some 56,000 Zaireans to flee into Tanzania and disrupted the distribution of essential humanitarian supplies to refugees remaining in Zaire. An estimated 170,000 refugees abandoned their temporary encampment at Tingi-Tingi, fearing attacks by the advancing AFDL forces. About 75,000 reassembled at Ubundu, south of Kisangani, while the fate of the other refugees remained uncertain. In March and April continued reports of attacks on refugee camps by AFDL forces and local Zaireans, resulted in large numbers of people fleeing into the surrounding countryside, with the consequent deaths of many of the most vulnerable members of the refugee population from disease and starvation. At the end of April the leader of the AFDL, Laurent-Désiré Kabila, ordered the repatriation of all Rwandan Hutu refugees by the UN within 60 days. Emergency air and land operations to evacuate some 185,000 refugees who had regrouped into temporary settlements were initiated a few days later. The repatriation process, however, was hindered by administrative and logistical difficulties and lack of co-operation on the part of the AFDL forces. By June an estimated 215,000 Rwandans were still missing or dispersed throughout the former Zaire (renamed the Democratic Republic of the Congo—DRC—by the AFDL in May). In the following months relations between the Kabila Government and UNHCR deteriorated as a result of several incidences of forcible repatriations of refugees to Rwanda and reports that the authorities were hindering a UN investigation into alleged abuses of human rights, committed against the Rwandan Hutu refugees by AFDL forces. In August an agreement was concluded to provide for the voluntary repatriation of some 75,000 refugees from the DRC remaining in Tanzania, under UNHCR supervision. However, the conflict that erupted in the DRC in August 1998 (see below) led to further large population movements. The repatriation of the estimated 260,000 Burundians remaining in Tanzania was also impeded, from early 1998, by an escalation of violence, which destabilized areas of return for both refugees and IDPs. In December 1997 a tripartite agreement was signed to provide for the organized repatriation of the remaining former Zairean refugees in Rwanda, with both Governments agreeing to observe strict conditions of security for the refugees on both sides of the border.

During the late 1990s UNHCR resolved to work, in co-operation with UNDP and WFP, to rehabilitate areas previously inhabited by refugees in central African countries of asylum and undertook to repair roads, bridges and other essential transport infrastructure, improve water and sanitation facilities, and strengthen the education sector. However, the political stability of the region remained extremely uncertain, and, from August 1998, DRC government forces and rebels became involved in a civil war in which the militaries of several regional governments were also implicated. From late 1998 substantial numbers of DRC nationals fled to neighbouring countries (mainly Tanzania and Zambia) or were displaced within the DRC. Meanwhile, the DRC, in turn, was hosting a significant refugee population. Although a cease-fire agreement was signed by all parties to the conflict in July 1999, this did not begin to be implemented until early 2001, when Kabila was assassinated and succeeded as President by his son, Maj.-Gen. Joseph Kabila. Following the DRC Government's adoption of peace agreements, in July and August 2002, with, respectively, the Rwandan and Ugandan Governments, nearly all Rwandan and Ugandan forces were withdrawn before the end of that year. Meanwhile, troop withdrawals were also initiated by Angola, Burundi, Namibia and Zimbabwe. In view of the conclusion, in December, of a peace agreement providing for the staging of elections in the DRC after a transition period of 24 months, UNHCR planned for eventual mass refugee returns. The Office, in co-operation with UNDP, the UN Mission in the DRC (MONUC) and the World Bank, was to assist efforts to demobilize, disarm and repatriate former combatants. Insecurity continued to prevail, however, during 2003–07, in north-eastern areas of the DRC, resulting in continuing population displacements. In September 2005 UNHCR and the DRC and Tanzanian Governments signed a tripartite agreement on facilitating returns of DRC refugees from Tanzania. It was envisaged that further returns would be prompted by the holding of legislative and a first stage of presidential elections in the DRC in July 2006, although the security situation subsequently remained unstable and reintegration efforts were also restricted by insufficient funding. A tripartite agreement on assistance was concluded by the Burundian and Tanzanian Governments and UNHCR in August 2003. UNHCR concluded similar accords during that year with the Rwandan Government and other states hosting Rwandan refugees, paving the way for significant voluntary refugee returns to Rwanda during 2004–06. In 2006 UNHCR assisted a total of 44,652 refugee returns to Burundi and 29,070 to the DRC. A further 84,000 refugees returned to the DRC during January–September 2007. During

January–June 2007 some 675,000 IDPs returned to their origins in the DRC (mainly in Ituri, South Kivu and Katanga), although a further 300,000 were displaced, owing to incessant rebel activity in North Kivu. The major populations of concern to UNHCR in the Great Lakes region at 31 December 2006 were, provisionally, as follows: 1.1m. IDPs, 208,371 refugees and 490,000 returned refugees in the DRC; 48,144 returned refugees in Burundi; 49,192 refugees in Rwanda; and a refugee population of 485,295 (287,061 UNHCR-assisted) in Tanzania, the largest concentration of refugees on the continent, though reduced from 602,088 at end-2004. UNHCR has provided education, environmental protection and healthcare programmes at camps in Tanzania, with a focus on the empowerment of women, eliminating gender-based violence and controlling the spread of HIV/AIDS. UNHCR also provides support to those refugees permitted by the Tanzanian Government to resettle permanently in that country. The security of international aid personnel in the Great Lakes region has been of concern and UNHCR assists the Tanzanian authorities with ensuring that camps retain a humanitarian, civilian ethos and exclude infiltrators without entitlement to humanitarian protection.

UNHCR is a leading participant in two main HIV/AIDS initiatives in the Great Lakes region, both of which should benefit refugees, returnees, IDPs and host communities: the Great Lakes Initiative on HIV/AIDS and the Congo-Oubangui-Chari Initiative.

In mid-1997 an estimated 40,000 refugees from the Republic of the Congo fled to the DRC, following a short-lived outbreak of civil conflict. In December a memorandum of understanding was signed by representatives of the two Governments and of UNHCR, providing for their immediate repatriation. From late 1998 the resumption of conflict in the Republic of the Congo disrupted UNHCR humanitarian efforts in that country and caused significant numbers of Congolese to seek refuge in the DRC and Gabon, and the internal displacement of as many as 500,000 people. Following the agreement of a cease-fire in December the majority of IDPs returned home. More than 60,000 Congolese refugees had repatriated by the end of 2000. A tripartite accord on the voluntary repatriation of Congolese refugees from Gabon was concluded by UNHCR and the Congolese and Gabon Governments during 2001. The Office continued to assist with their repatriation and reintegration in 2004–06, following the conclusion of a peace accord between the Congolese Government and rebels in March 2003. At December 2006 Congolese refugees remaining in Gabon numbered 7,178 (all of whom were being assisted by UNHCR). During 2000 more than 80,000 refugees from the DRC sought protection in the Republic of the Congo. At the end of 2006 that country was still hosting some 46,341 refugees from the DRC. In 2008 most refugees in the Republic of the Congo were largely self-sufficient and working as farmers and fishermen. During that year UNHCR was to offer assistance packages to families to encourage voluntary repatriation to the DRC; the Office also aimed to promote the local integration of those unwilling to return.

In 1994 continuing civil conflict in Angola caused some 370,000 people to leave their home areas. Prior to the signing of a peace settlement in November, UNHCR provided assistance to 112,000 internally displaced Angolans and returnees, although military activities, which hindered accessibility, undermined the effectiveness of the assistance programme. In mid-1995, following a consolidation of the peace process in Angola, UNHCR appealed for US $44m. to support the voluntary repatriation of some 300,000 Angolan refugees through a two-and-a-half-year operation. By June 1996 implementation of the repatriation programme was delayed, reportedly owing to poor accommodation and other facilities for returnees, limited progress in confining and disarming opposition troops and the continued hazard of land-mines throughout the country. During 1997 an estimated 53,000 Angolans voluntarily returned from the DRC and Zambia, bringing the total returnees to some 130,000 since mid-1995. In November 1997 UNHCR resolved to implement an operation to provide for the repatriation and reintegration of the remaining Angolan refugees by June 1999. UNHCR allocated $15.7m. to support the repatriation process and other activities in Angola, including strengthening the country's road infrastructure, monitoring areas of return, the implementation of reintegration projects and promoting links with other development programmes. In May 1998, however, the security situation in Angola deteriorated, and at the end of June UNHCR declared a temporary suspension of the repatriation operation. The renewed violence also resulted in further population displacement, with refugee movements into the DRC continuing during 1998–2001. In July 2000 UNHCR expanded its operations in Angola to support IDPs by providing emergency humanitarian assistance and helping IDP communities and local administrations with the provision of basic services, demining and the rehabilitation of local infrastructures. Following the signing of the Luanda Peace Agreement in April 2002 between the Angolan Government and rebels of the União Nacional para a Independência Total de Angola, UNHCR made preparations for the voluntary repatriation of a projected 400,000 Angolan refugees sheltering elsewhere in southern Africa. It was estimated that in all more than 4.3m. Angolans were displaced from their homes during the 1980s and 1990s, and by the end of 2005 a total of nearly 4.4m. IDPs, refugees and demobilized fighters had reportedly returned home. By the end of 2004 the Office had rehabilitated the nine main repatriation corridors into Angola. UNHCR has assisted the Angolan Government with the development of a Sustainable Reintegration Initiative for returned refugees. At 31 December 2006 UNHCR was providing assistance to some 47,017 Angolan returned refugees. Meanwhile, an estimated 206,501 Angolans were still sheltering in neighbouring countries at that time, including 132,295 in the DRC and 42,675 in Zambia. HIV/AIDS- and mine-awareness training have been made available by UNHCR at refugee reception centres.

THE AMERICAS AND THE CARIBBEAN

In May 1989, when an International Conference on Central American Refugees (CIREFCA) was held in Guatemala, there were some 146,400 refugees receiving UNHCR assistance (both for emergency relief and for longer-term self-sufficiency programmes) in the region, as well as an estimated 1.8m. other refugees and displaced persons. UNHCR and UNDP were designated as the principal UN organizations to implement the CIREFCA plan of action for the repatriation or resettlement of refugees, alongside national co-ordinating committees. UNHCR QIPs were implemented in the transport, health, agricultural production and other sectors to support returnee reintegration (of both refugees and IDPs) into local communities, and to promote the self-sufficiency of the returning populations. Implementation of UNHCR's programme for the repatriation of some 45,000 Guatemalan refugees in Mexico began in January 1993. UNHCR initiated projects to support the reintegration of Guatemalan returnees, and in 1994–95 undertook a campaign to clear undetonated explosives in forest areas where they had resettled. The CIREFCA process was formally concluded in June 1994, by which time some 118,000 refugees had voluntarily returned to their countries of origin under the auspices of the programme, while thousands of others had integrated into their host countries. In December a meeting was held, in San José, Costa Rica, to commemorate the 10th anniversary of the Cartagena Declaration, which had provided a comprehensive framework for refugee protection in the region. The meeting adopted the San José Declaration on Refugees and Displaced Persons, which aimed to harmonize legal criteria and procedures to consolidate actions for durable solutions of voluntary repatriation and local integration in the region. UNHCR's efforts in the region subsequently emphasized legal issues and refugee protection, while assisting governments to formulate national legislation on asylum and refugees. From 1996 several thousand Guatemalan refugees have received Mexican citizenship under a fast-track naturalization scheme; the programme to naturalize long-standing Guatemalan refugees was terminated in 2005.

In November 2004 regional leaders met in Mexico City to commemorate the 20th anniversary of the Cartagena Declaration, and launched a new initiative, the Mexico Plan of Action, which aimed to address current population displacement problems in Latin America, with a particular focus on the humanitarian crisis in Colombia and the border areas of its neighbouring countries (see below), and the increasing numbers of refugees concentrated in urban centres in the region. The Cities of Solidarity pillar of the Mexico Plan of Action assists UNHCR with facilitating the local integration and self-sufficiency of people in urban areas who require international protection; the Borders of Solidarity pillar addresses protection at international borders; and the Resettlement in Solidarity pillar promotes co-operation in resettling refugees. At December 2006 3,319 refugees remained in Mexico.

In 1999 the Colombian Government approved an operational plan proposed by UNHCR to address a massive population displacement that has arisen in that country in recent years (escalating from 1997), as a consequence of ongoing internal conflict and alleged human rights abuses committed by armed groups. Significant cross-border movements of Colombian refugees into neighbouring countries prompted UNHCR to intensify its border-monitoring activities during the early 2000s to enhance its capacity to forecast and react to new population movements. UNHCR has assisted with the implementation of an IDP registration plan, provided training in emergency response to displacements, and supported ongoing changes in Colombia's legislative framework for IDPs. UNHCR has also co-operated with UNICEF to improve the provision of education to displaced children. During 2008 UNHCR aimed to provide legal and humanitarian support to more than 400,000 IDPs within Colombia. The Office also planned to provide legal protection and educational and medical support to around 500,000 Colombians who had fled to but not sought asylum in neighbouring countries. The Office's strategy for supporting countries receiving displaced Colombians (of whom the majority were not registered as refugees) have included border-monitoring activities, entailing the early warning of potential refugee movements, and provision of detailed country-of-origin data. Within Colombia UNHCR's protection activities have included ensuring an adequate, functioning legal framework for the protection of IDPs and enabling domestic institutions to supervise compliance with national legislation regarding the rights of IDPs; strengthening representation for IDPs and other vulnerable people; and developing local protection networks. UNHCR also aimed to advise on public policy formulation in the areas of emergency response, IDP registration, health, education, housing, income-generation and protection of policy rights; and to promote durable solutions for IDPs, in particular local integration. Conditions in most areas are regarded as unsafe for voluntary returns. The Office has built up stockpiles of relief items in neighbouring countries and has developed contingency plans with other partners to enable the rapid deployment of personnel to border areas should the exodus of refugees from Colombia intensify further. At the end of 2006 an estimated 3m. IDPs within Colombia (some 200,000 newly displaced during that year) remained of concern to UNHCR. By January 2008 an estimated 250,000 Colombians had fled to Ecuador, while 200,000 were sheltering in Venezuela; the majority of these had not sought official protection.

Canada and the USA are major countries of resettlement for refugees. UNHCR provides counselling and legal services for asylum-seekers in these countries. At 31 December 2006 the estimated refugee populations totalled 151,827 in Canada and 843,498 in the USA, while asylum-seekers numbered 23,593 and 124,223 respectively.

CENTRAL AND SOUTH-EASTERN EUROPE

The political changes in Central and Eastern Europe during the early 1990s resulted in a dramatic increase in the number of asylum-seekers and displaced people in the region. UNHCR was the agency designated by the UN Secretary-General to lead the UN relief operation to assist those affected by the conflict in the former Yugoslavia. It was responsible for the supply of food and other humanitarian aid to the besieged capital of Bosnia and Herzegovina, Sarajevo, and to Muslim and Croatian enclaves in the country, under the armed escort of the UN Protection Force. Assistance was provided not only to Bosnian refugees in Croatia and displaced people within Bosnia and Herzegovina's borders, but also, in order to forestall further movements of people, to civilians whose survival was threatened. The operation was often seriously hampered by armed attacks (resulting, in some cases, in fatalities), distribution difficulties and underfunding from international donors. The Dayton peace agreement, which was signed in December 1995 bringing an end to the conflict, secured the right for all refugees and displaced persons freely to choose their place of residence within the new territorial arrangements of Bosnia and Herzegovina. Thus, the immediate effect of the peace accord was further population displacement, including a mass exodus of almost the entire Serb population of Sarajevo. Under the peace accord, UNHCR was responsible for planning and implementing the repatriation of all Bosnian refugees and displaced persons, then estimated at 2m.; however, there were still immense obstacles to freedom of movement, in particular for minorities wishing to return to an area dominated by a different politico-ethnic faction. Returns by refugees and IDPs (including significant numbers of refugees returning to areas where they represented minority ethnic communities) accelerated from 2000, owing to an improvement in security conditions. In July 2002 the heads of state of Bosnia and Herzogovina, Croatia and the Federal Republic of Yugoslavia (FRY, which was renamed 'Serbia and Montenegro' in 2003, and was divided into separate sovereign states of Montenegro and Serbia in June 2006) met in Sarajevo with a view to resolving a number of outstanding issues including the return of remaining refugees. In January 2005 the concerned parties adopted the Sarajevo Declaration, committing to resolve remaining population displacement issues promptly through the 'Sarajevo Process' (also known as the '3X3 Initiative'). The repossession by their rightful owners and reconstruction of illegally appropriated properties have been key issues for returned refugees to the region. By December 2006 there was still an estimated total Bosnian refugee population of 199,946, of whom some 34,608 were receiving assistance from UNHCR. The majority of the Bosnian refugee population were in the USA, Germany and Serbia. At the end of 2006 there were 4,184 returned IDPs of concern to UNHCR in Bosnia and Herzegovina and 135,500 IDPs who had yet to return home. In 2008 UNHCR was working to find durable solutions for extremely vulnerable returned refugees and IDPs in that country.

From March 1998 attacks by Serbian forces against members of a separatist movement in the southern Serbian province of Kosovo and Metohija resulted in large-scale population displacement. Of particular concern were some 50,000 people who had fled to the surrounding mountains, close to the Albanian border, without shelter or adequate provisions. In October the withdrawal of Serbian troops and the involvement of the international community in the provision of aid and monitoring of the situation in Kosovo was thought to have prompted substantial numbers to have returned home. However, in December there were reports of renewed attacks by Serbian forces on the local Albanian population, which persisted into 1999. The failure of peace negotiations prompted further displacement, and in late March an estimated 95,000 people fled their homes following the withdrawal of international observers of the OSCE and the commencement of a NATO operation, which aimed to halt the Serbian attacks and compel the FRY to agree to a peace settlement. By mid-April UNHCR estimated that up to 1.3m. Kosovar Albanians had been displaced since the fighting began in 1998, with reports that thousands had been forcibly expelled by Serbian troops in recent weeks. UNHCR attempted to provide emergency relief to the thousands of refugees who fled to neighbouring countries, and expressed concern for those remaining in the province, of whom up to 400,000 were thought to be living without shelter. In early April 1999 UNHCR condemned the decision of the authorities in the former Yugoslav republic of Macedonia (FYRM) forcibly to evacuate some 30,000 refugees from camps in Blace, near the FRY border, and subsequently to close the border to further refugees. At that time UNHCR helped to co-ordinate an international effort to evacuate substantial numbers of the refugees to third countries, and issued essential identity and travel documents. In Albania UNHCR funded transport to relocate an estimated 250,000 people from the border town of Kukës, where resources and the local infrastructure were strained by the massive population influx, to other sites throughout the country. At the start of June the Kosovar refugee population totalled some 443,300 people in Albania, 247,800 in the FYRM, 69,300 in Montenegro, and 21,700 in Bosnia and Herzegovina, while under a joint Humanitarian Evacuation Programme with the International Organization for Migration, more than 90,000 refugees had been evacuated to 29 countries. UNHCR organized host families to receive a large proportion of the refugees, while additional shelter was provided in the form of tented camps and collective centres. In mid-June, following a cease-fire accord and an agreement by the FRY to withdraw all forces and paramilitary units, UNHCR initiated a large-scale registration operation of Kosovar refugees and began to deliver emergency provisions to assist the displaced population within Kosovo. Despite warnings of anti-personnel devices and lack of shelter, UNHCR estimated that some 477,000 refugees had returned in a spontaneous repatriation movement by the end of June. Meanwhile, it was reported that a total of 170,000 Serbs left Kosovo, fearing reprisal attacks by returning ethnic Albanians; in addition, some 50,000 members of the Roma minority moved out of the province. In September UNHCR estimated that one-third of all homes in Kosovo had been destroyed or seriously damaged during the conflict, prompting concerns regarding the welfare of returning refugees and IDPs in the coming winter months. UNHCR distributed 'shelter kits' to assist the process of reconstruction of homes, and proceeded to accelerate the distribution of blankets and winter clothing, as well as of fuel, food, water, and the provision of medical care throughout Montenegro and Serbia. In mid-2000 UNHCR scaled down its emergency humanitarian activities in Kosovo and provided a UN Humanitarian Co-ordinator to oversee the transition to long-term reconstruction and development, in co-operation with the UN Interim Administration Mission in Kosovo (UNMIK). UNHCR and OSCE have periodically jointly assessed the situation of minority communities in Kosovo; minority returns (numbering nearly 18,000 during 2000–end-2007) and integration have reportedly been impeded by discrimination against and intimidation of minorities in the province. At the end of 2006 there were still 227,590 IDPs in Serbia. In addition, Serbia was hosting 174,027 refugees, of whom 27,414 were from Bosnia and Herzegovina and 71,111 from Croatia. In 2006 UNHCR initiated a civil registration programme for undocumented IDPs in Kosovo and Serbia.

In response to the mounting insecurity in the FYRM from early 2001, as conflict escalated between ethnic Albanian rebels and government troops, 81,000 Macedonian refugees fled to Kosovo (of whom several thousand repatriated promptly) and 12,000 to southern Serbia during February–August, while over that period more than 50,000 people became displaced within the FYRM. In June UNHCR appealed for funds to finance the provision of emergency humanitarian assistance to the Macedonian refugees, and opened a registration centre in Kosovo. Repatriations accelerated following the conclusion in August of a framework peace agreement between the opposing parties, however many people remained displaced owing to fears they would return to communities in which they would belong to an ethnic minority.

EASTERN EUROPE

In December 1992 UNHCR dispatched teams to establish offices in both Armenia and Azerbaijan to support more than 1m. people displaced from 1988 as a result of the war between the two countries, including some 360,000 ethnic Armenians who fled Azerbaijan for Armenia. A cease-fire agreement was signed between the two sides in May 1994, although violations of the accord were subsequently reported and relations between the two countries remained tense. The preliminary findings of a census of the ethnic Armenian Azerbaijani refugee population in Armenia conducted by the Armenian Government in 2006, with the support of UNHCR, indicated that by that time many of the ethnic Armenian Azerbaijani refugees had either become naturalized Armenian citizens (this process having been facilitated by UNHCR-supported legislation introduced by the Armenian Government in 1995) or had resettled in third countries. At the end of 2006 113,324 ethnic Armenian Azerbaijani refugees remained in Armenia. Azerbaijan was still supporting a massive population of 686,586 IDPs. UNHCR's humanitarian activities have focused on improving shelter, in particular for the most vulnerable among the refugee population, and promoting economic self-sufficiency and stability. During 2006 UNHCR provided protection to some 1,900 Chechen refugees in Azerbaijan.

In Georgia, where almost 300,000 people left their homes as a result of civil conflict from 1991, UNHCR has attempted to encourage income-generating activities among the displaced population, to increase the Georgian Government's capacity to support those people and to assist the rehabilitation of people returning to their areas of origin. At 31 December 2006 there were 245,980 Georgian IDPs, affected by the ongoing conflicts in Abkhazia and South Ossetia. During 2006 UNHCR supported the Georgian Government in the preparation of a national IDP strategy, focusing on the right of IDPs to integrate locally without prejudicing their right eventually to return to their home communities. In late 1999 an estimated 7,000 refugees fleeing insecurity in Chechnya entered Georgia. UNHCR has delivered food to the Chechen refugees and the host families with whom the majority are staying, and has also assisted the refugees through shelter renovation, psychosocial support and the provision of child-care facilities and health and community development support, as well as monitoring refugee-host family relations. UNHCR planned to terminate during 2008 its food support programme to the Chechen refugees remaining in Georgia (numbering about 1,500 in 2007).

From 1994 UNHCR pursued a process to establish a comprehensive approach to the problems of refugees, returnees, IDPs and migrants in the Commonwealth of Independent States (CIS). A regional conference convened in Geneva, Switzerland, in May 1996, endorsed a framework of activities aimed at managing migratory flows and at developing institutional capacities to prevent mass population displacements. At that time it was estimated that more than 9m. former citizens of the USSR had relocated since its disintegration as a result of conflict, economic pressures and ecological disasters. The structures put in place by the 1996 CIS regional conference were terminated in October 2005. By 2008 all CIS member states excepting Uzbekistan had acceded to the 1951 Convention.

In March 1995 UNHCR initiated an assistance programme for people displaced as a result of conflict in the separatist republic of Chechnya (the Chechen Republic of Ichkeriya), the Russian Federation, as part of a UN inter-agency relief effort, in collaboration with the International Committee of the Red Cross (ICRC). UNHCR continued its activities in 1996, at the request of the Russian Government, at which time the displaced population within Chechnya and in the surrounding republics totalled 490,000. During 1997 UNHCR provided reintegration assistance to 25,000 people who returned to Chechnya, despite reports of sporadic violence. The security situation in the region deteriorated sharply in mid-1999, following a series of border clashes and incursions by Chechen separatist forces into the neighbouring republic of Dagestan. In September Russian military aircraft began an aerial offensive against suspected rebel targets in Chechnya, and at the end of the month ground troops moved into the republic. By November an estimated 225,000 Chechens had fled to neighbouring Ingushetiya. UNHCR dispatched food supplies to assist the IDPs and, from February 2000, periodically sent relief convoys into Chechnya, where there was still a substantial displaced population; the poor security situation, however, prevented other UNHCR deployment within Chechnya. During the first half of 2004 the Russian authorities closed the three tented refugee camps that had been operational in Ingushetiya at December 2003. Temporary lodging (consisting of rooms in accommodation centres or in private homes) was to be provided for those refugees who did not wish to return home. The Russian authorities implemented an information campaign to encourage Chechen refugees to return from Ingushetiya. At 31 December 2006 UNHCR estimated that 18,468 Chechen refugees remained in Ingushetiya. During 2006 some 3,362 Chechen returns from Ingushetia were reported, while a further 760 such returns were reported during the period January–August 2007. UNHCR has conducted interviews of returnees in order to ensure that returns were voluntary rather than enforced. At 31 December 2006 there remained an estimated 57,349 IDPs within Chechnya.

CO-OPERATION WITH OTHER ORGANIZATIONS

UNHCR works closely with other UN agencies, intergovernmental organizations and non-governmental organizations (NGOs) to increase the scope and effectiveness of its operations. Within the UN system UNHCR co-operates, principally, with the World Food Programme in the distribution of food aid, UNICEF and the World Health Organization in the provision of family welfare and child immunization programmes, OCHA in the delivery of emergency humanitarian relief, UNDP in development-related activities and the preparation of guide-lines for the continuum of emergency assistance to development programmes, and the Office of the UN High Commissioner for Human Rights. UNHCR also has close working relationships with the International Committee of the Red Cross and the International Organization for Migration. In 2005 UNHCR worked with 578 NGOs as 'implementing partners', enabling UNHCR to broaden the use of its resources while maintaining a co-ordinating role in the provision of assistance.

TRAINING

UNHCR organizes training programmes and workshops to enhance the capabilities of field workers and non-UNHCR staff, in the following areas: the identification and registration of refugees; people-orientated planning; resettlement procedures and policies; emergency response and management; security awareness; stress management; and the dissemination of information through the electronic media.

Finance

The United Nations' regular budget finances a proportion of UNHCR's administrative expenditure. The majority of UNHCR's programme expenditure (about 98%) is funded by voluntary contributions, mainly from governments. The Private Sector and Public Affairs Service aims to increase funding from non-governmental donor sources, for example by developing partnerships with foundations and corporations. Following approval of the Unified Annual Programme Budget any subsequently identified requirements are managed in the form of Supplementary Programmes, financed by separate appeals. The total Unified Annual Programme Budget for 2007 was projected at US $1,043m.

Publications

Global Trends (annually).
Refugees (quarterly, in English, French, German, Italian, Japanese and Spanish).
Refugee Resettlement: An International Handbook to Guide Reception and Integration.
Refugee Survey Quarterly.
Refworld (annually).
Sexual and Gender-based Violence Against Refugees, Returnees and Displaced Persons: Guide-lines for Prevention and Response.
The State of the World's Refugees (every 2 years).
Statistical Yearbook (annually).
UNHCR Handbook for Emergencies.
Press releases, reports.

Statistics

POPULATIONS OF CONCERN TO UNHCR BY REGION
('000 persons, at 31 December 2006, provisional figures)

	Refugees*	Asylum-seekers	Returned refugees†	Others of concern‡
Africa	2,608	244	312	6,588
Asia	4,538	90	409	9,874
Europe	1,747	252	13	1,693
Latin America/Caribbean	41	16	1	3,486
North America	995	148	—	—
Oceania	84	2	—	—
Total	**9,878**	**744**	**734**	**21,510**

* Includes persons recognized as refugees under international law, and also people receiving temporary protection and assistance outside their country but who have not been formally recognized as refugees.
† Refugees who returned to their place of origin during 2006.
‡ Mainly internally displaced persons (IDPs), former IDPs who returned to their place of origin during 2006, and stateless persons.

POPULATIONS OF CONCERN TO UNHCR BY COUNTRY*
('000 persons, at 31 December 2006, provisional figures)

	Refugees†	Asylum-seekers	Returned refugees†	Others of concern†
Africa				
CAR	12.4	1.9	0.1	147.0
Chad	286.7	0.0	0.0	112.7
Côte d'Ivoire	27.3	2.3	0.0	709.4
DRC	208.4	0.1	41.2	1,565.3
Egypt	88.0	16.4	0.0	0.1
Kenya	272.5	18.5	—	100.0
Liberia	16.2	0.1	108.0	237.8
Somalia	0.7	1.2	1.8	400.0
South Africa	35.1	131.1	0.0	—
Sudan	196.2	4.5	42.3	1,379.3
Tanzania	485.3	0.4	0.0	—
Uganda	272.0	5.8	5.0	1,886.2
Zambia	120.3	0.2	—	—
Asia				
Afghanistan	0.0	0.0	387.9	139.8
Bangladesh	26.3	0.8	—	300.0
China, People's Republic‡	301.0	0.1	0.0	0.0
India	158.4	0.7	0.0	—
Iran	968.4	1.0	0.1	—
Iraq	44.4	2.1	20.2	2,114.4
Jordan	500.2	19.2	—	0.0
Kuwait	0.1	0.5	—	109.1
Lebanon	20.2	2.6	—	750.1
Malaysia	37.2	9.2	—	61.3
Myanmar	—	—	—	728.0
Nepal	128.2	1.5	—	3,510.4
Pakistan§	1,044.4	2.7	0.0	—
Sri Lanka	0.1	0.1	0.4	558.6
Saudi Arabia	240.8	0.3	—	70.0
Syria	702.2	5.2	0.0	300.0
Thailand	133.1	18.4	—	0.3
Timor-Leste	0.0	0.0	—	167.0
Europe				
Armenia	113.4	0.1	—	—
Azerbaijan	2.6	0.1	0.0	689.3
Bosnia and Herzegovina	10.3	0.1	1.4	139.7
Estonia	0.0	0.0	—	119.2
France	146.0	39.6	—	0.9
Georgia	1.4	0.0	0.0	308.3
—continued	Refugees†	Asylum-seekers	Returned refugees†	Others of concern†
Germany	605.4	52.8	—	10.0
Latvia	0.0	0.0	—	393.0
Netherlands	100.6	13.1	—	4.5
Russian Federation	1.4	0.3	0.1	450.7
Serbia	99.0	0.0	6.1	314.0
Sweden	79.9	12.4	—	5.6
United Kingdom	301.6	—	12.4	0.2
Latin America/Caribbean				
Colombia	0.1	0.1	0.0	3,000.0
Ecuador	11.8	5.5	—	250.0
Venezuela	0.7	7.8	—	200.0
North America				
Canada	151.8	23.6	—	—
USA	843.5	124.2	—	—

* The list includes only those countries having 100,000 or more persons of concern to UNHCR.
† See table above for definitions.
‡ Excluding Hong Kong Special Administrative Region.
§ Excluding Afghans sheltering outside camps.

ORIGIN OF MAJOR POPULATIONS OF CONCERN TO UNHCR*
('000 persons, 31 December 2006, provisional figures)

Origin	Population of concern to UNHCR
Colombia	3,561.8
Iraq	3,518.9
Afghanistan	2,750.5
Sudan	2,124.5
DRC	2,040.2
Uganda	1,914.3
Somalia	889.9
Lebanon	765.5

* Data exclude some 4.3m. Palestinian refugees who come under the mandate of UNRWA, although some (at 31 December 2006) 341,533 Palestinians who are outside the UNRWA area of operation, for example those in Iraq and Libya, are considered to be of concern to UNHCR.

United Nations Peace-keeping

Address: Department of Peace-keeping Operations, Room S-3727-B, United Nations, New York, NY 10017, USA.
Telephone: (212) 963-8077; **fax:** (212) 963-9222; **internet:** www.un.org/Depts/dpko/.

United Nations peace-keeping operations have been conceived as instruments of conflict control. The UN has used these operations in various conflicts, with the consent of the parties involved, to maintain international peace and security, without prejudice to the positions or claims of parties, in order to facilitate the search for political settlements through peaceful means such as mediation and the good offices of the UN Secretary-General. Each operation is established with a specific mandate, which requires periodic review by the UN Security Council. United Nations peace-keeping operations fall into two categories: peace-keeping forces and observer missions.

Peace-keeping forces are composed of contingents of military and civilian personnel, made available by member states. These forces assist in preventing the recurrence of fighting, restoring and maintaining peace, and promoting a return to normal conditions. To this end, peace-keeping forces are authorized as necessary to undertake negotiations, persuasion, observation and fact-finding. They conduct patrols and interpose physically between the opposing parties. Peace-keeping forces are permitted to use their weapons only in self-defence.

Military observer missions are composed of officers (usually unarmed), who are made available, on the Secretary-General's request, by member states. A mission's function is to observe and report to the Secretary-General (who, in turn, informs the Security Council) on the maintenance of a cease-fire, to investigate violations and to do what it can to improve the situation. Peace-keeping forces and observer missions must at all times maintain complete impartiality and avoid any action that might affect the claims or positions of the parties.

A UN Stand-by Arrangements System (UNSAS) became operational in 1994; at April 2005 some 83 countries were participating in the system by making available specialized civilian and military personnel, as well as other services and equipment. In January 1995 the UN Secretary-General presented a report to the Security Council, reassessing the UN's role in peace-keeping. The document stipulated that UN forces in conflict areas should not be responsible for peace-enforcement duties, and included a proposal for the establishment of a 'rapid reaction' force which would be ready for deployment within a month of being authorized by the Security Council. In September 1997 the UN Secretary-General established a staff to plan and organize the formation of the so-called UN Stand-by Forces High Readiness Brigade (SHIRBRIG), based in Denmark, was declared available to the UN in January 2000 and became fully operational later in that year with the deployment of troops to the newly authorized UN Mission in Ethiopia and Eritrea (UNMEE) for a duration of six months. In March 2003 a SHIRBRIG team supported ECOWAS in planning the deployment of the ECOMICI peace-keeping mission to Côte d'Ivoire. In September of that year SHIRBRIG deployed some 20 personnel to the newly established UN Mission in Liberia (UNMIL). During 2005–06 SHIRBRIG assisted with preparations for the deployment of the UN Mission in Sudan (UNMIS). By mid-2007 Argentina, Austria, Canada, Denmark, Finland, Ireland, Italy, Lithuania, the Netherlands, Norway,

INTERNATIONAL ORGANIZATIONS

Poland, Portugal, Romania, Slovenia, Spain, and Sweden had formally committed troops to the force, while Chile, Croatia, Czech Republic, Egypt, Hungary, Jordan, Latvia and Senegal were participating as observers.

In August 2000 a report on UN peace-keeping activities prepared by a team of experts appointed by the Secretary-General assessed the aims and requirements of peace-keeping operations and recommended several measures to improve the performance of the Department of Peace-keeping Operations (DPKO), focusing on its planning and management capacity from the inception of an operation through to post-conflict peace-building activities, and on its rapid response capability. Proposed reforms included the establishment of a body to improve co-ordination of information and strategic analysis requirements; the promotion of partnership arrangements between member states (within the context of UNSAS) enabling the formation of several coherent multinational brigades, and improved monitoring of the preparedness of potential troop contributor nations, with a view to facilitating the effective deployment of most operations within 30 days of their authorization in a Security Council resolution; the adoption of 'on-call' reserve lists to ensure the prompt deployment of civilian police and specialists; the preparation of a global logistics support strategy; and a restructuring of the DPKO to improve administrative efficiency. The study also urged an increase in resources for funding peace-keeping operations and the adoption of a more flexible financing mechanism, and emphasized the importance of the UN's conflict prevention activities. In November the Security Council, having welcomed the report, adopted guide-lines aimed at improving its management of peace-keeping operations, including providing missions with clear and achievable mandates. In June 2001 the Council adopted a resolution incorporating a Statement of principles on co-operation with troop-contributing countries, which aimed to strengthen the relationship between those countries and the UN and to enhance the effectiveness of peace-keeping operations. A new Rapid Deployment Level within UNSAS was inaugurated in July 2002. In 2004 the Department established a Special Investigation Team, at the request of the UN Secretary-General, which, in November, visited the Democratic Republic of the Congo to examine allegations of sexual exploitation and abuse committed by peace-keeping personnel. In July 2007 a new Department of Field Operations was established within the UN Secretariat to provide expert support and resources to enhance personnel, budget, information and communication technology and other logistical aspects of UN peace operations in the field. At the same time the Department of Peace-keeping Operations was restructured.

The UN's peace-keeping forces and observer missions are financed in most cases by assessed contributions from member states of the organization. In recent years a significant expansion in the UN's peace-keeping activities has been accompanied by a perpetual financial crisis within the organization, as a result of the increased financial burden and some member states' delaying payment. At 30 November 2007 outstanding assessed contributions to the peace-keeping budget amounted to some US $3,150m.

By 31 January 2008 the UN had deployed a total of 63 peace-keeping operations, of which 13 were authorized in the period 1948–88 and 50 since 1988. At 31 January 2008 119 countries were contributing some 90,429 uniformed personnel to the ongoing operations, of whom 76,529 were peace-keeping troops, 11,218 civilian police and 2,682 military observers.

In 2008 the Department of Peace-keeping Operations was directly supporting three political and peace-building missions (in addition to those maintained by the Department of Political Affairs): the UN Assistance Mission in Afghanistan (established in March 2002), the UN Integrated Office in Sierra Leone (established in January 2006 as a successor to the UN peace-keeping operation in that country), and the UN Integrated Office in Burundi (established in January 2007, again succeeding a UN peace-keeping operation).

In 1988 the United Nations Peace-keeping Forces were awarded the Nobel Peace Prize.

Hybrid African Union (AU)/UN Operation in Darfur—UNAMID

Address: El Fasher, Sudan.

Joint AU-UN Special Representative: RODOLPHE ADADA (Republic of the Congo).

Force Commander: Gen. MARTIN LUTHER AGWAI (Nigeria).

UNAMID was established by a resolution of the UN Security Council in July 2007, authorized to take necessary action to support the implementation and verification of the Darfur Peace Agreement signed in May 2006 by the Sudanese Government and a rebel faction in Darfur, southern Sudan. UNAMID was also mandated to protect civilians, to provide security for humanitarian assistance, to support an inclusive political process, to contribute to the promotion of human rights and rule of law, and to monitor and report on the situation along the borders with Chad and the CAR. UNAMID was scheduled to have its management, command and control structures in place by October and to assume command of the AU Mission in Sudan (AMIS) at the end of the year. A Joint Support Co-ordination Mechanism (JSCM) in Addis Ababa, comprising liaison officers and communications equipment, was to ensure effective consultation between the UN and AU headquarters. By February 2008 UNAMID had absorbed 1,380 police officers from AMIS. The UN Secretary-General reported in that month that the UN and AU were finalizing an exchange of letters defining their partnership with regard to UNAMID.

In December 2007 UNAMID, the UN Mission in Sudan (UNMIS) and the AU-UN Joint Mediation Support Team for Darfur (JMST) formed a joint task force to recommend policies and mechanisms for enhancing co-operation. UNMIS was to provide logistical support to UNAMID.

UNAMID had an authorized strength of up to 19,555 military personnel and 6,432 police. The mission's operational strength at 31 January 2008 comprised 7,156 troops, 220 military observers and 1,704 police officers, supported by 66 UN Volunteers. The budget for UNAMID amounted to US $128m. for the period 1 July 2007–30 June 2008, funded from a Special Account comprising assessed contributions from UN member states.

United Nations Disengagement Observer Force—UNDOF

Address: Camp Faouar, Syria.

Force Commander: Maj.-Gen. WOLFGANG JILKE (Austria).

UNDOF was established for an initial period of six months by a UN Security Council resolution in May 1974, following the signature in Geneva of a disengagement agreement between Syrian and Israeli forces. The mandate has since been extended by successive resolutions. The initial task of the Force was to take over territory evacuated in stages by the Israeli troops, in accordance with the disengagement agreement, to hand over territory to Syrian troops, and to establish an area of separation on the Golan Heights.

UNDOF continues to monitor the area of separation; it carries out inspections of the areas of limited armaments and forces; uses its best efforts to maintain the cease-fire; and undertakes activities of a humanitarian nature, such as arranging the transfer of prisoners and war-dead between Syria and Israel. The Force operates exclusively on Syrian territory.

At 31 January 2008 the Force comprised 1,045 troops; it is assisted by approximately 57 military observers of UNTSO's Observer Group Golan, and supported by 145 international and local civilian personnel. Further UNTSO military observers help UNDOF in the performance of its tasks, as required. The General Assembly appropriated US $39.7m. to cover the cost of the operation for the period 1 July 2007–30 June 2008.

United Nations Integrated Mission in Timor-Leste—UNMIT

Address: Dili, Timor-Leste.

Telephone: 3312210; **fax:** 3322007; **internet:** www.unmit.org.

Special Representative of the UN Secretary-General and Head of Office: ATUL KHARE (India).

Police Commissioner: RODOLFO ASER TOR (Philippines).

In succession to the UN Mission in Support of East Timor (UNMISET), the UN Transitional Administration in East Timor (UNTAET) and the UN Office in Timor-Leste (UNOTIL), the UN Integrated Mission in Timor-Leste (UNMIT) was established by UN Security Council Resolution 1704 in August 2006 to support the Timor-Leste authorities with consolidating stability, promoting democratic governance and facilitating the process of national reconciliation. The mission was to co-operate with the Australian-led International Stabilization Force (ISF, also comprising troops from Malaysia, New Zealand and Portugal), which had been deployed to Timor-Leste in late May 2006 to secure key installations following an eruption of violent unrest in the previous month. The mission was authorized to assist with all aspects of the staging of the 2007 presidential and legislative elections, with restoring and maintaining public security, and with the promotion of human rights and justice. In January 2007 UNMIT signed a trilateral agreement with the Timorese authorities and Australian Government to enhance co-ordination of all security-related activities. During the first half of 2007 the UNMIT police presence was expanded to provide full support to the Timorese national police and ISF in facilitating public security during the electoral process. In May UNMIT reported that the presidential elections, conducted in April and May, had been 'free and fair'. Parliamentary elections were conducted in late June, and in early August the Special Representative of the UN Secretary-General welcomed the establishment of a new coalition government.

The inauguration of the new government, however, prompted renewed violent unrest in several districts of the country. Consequently, during August, UNMIT convened a meeting of representatives of national political groupings to address means of calming the unrest, and also offered practical assistance to the Timorese authorities towards restoring security and delivering humanitarian aid to those affected by the violence. In November a delegation of the UN Security Council visited the country. In February 2008 the UN condemned violent attacks against the Prime Minister and President in Timor-Leste. In that month, in extending UNMIT's mandate by one year, the Security Council requested that UNMIT continue to assist the government in enhancing the effectiveness of the judiciary, to review and reform the security sector, to co-ordinate donor co-operation for institutional capacity-building and to assist in the formulation of poverty reduction and economic growth strategies.

At 31 January 2008 UNMIT comprised 1,444 police officers and 32 military liaison officers; at 31 December 2007 it was assisted by a team of 336 international staff, 791 local civilian staff and 117 UN Volunteers. The General Assembly apportioned US $153.16m. to finance the operation during the period 1 July 2007–30 June 2008.

United Nations Interim Administration Mission in Kosovo—UNMIK

Address: Priština, Kosovo.

Special Representative of the UN Secretary-General and Head of Mission: JOACHIM RÜCKER (Germany).

Principal Deputy Special Representative of the UN Secretary-General: LARRY ROSSIN (USA).

Police Commissioner: RICHARD MONK (United Kingdom).

In June 1999 NATO suspended a 10-week aerial offensive against the then Federal Republic of Yugoslavia (which was renamed 'Serbia and Montenegro' in 2003 and divided into separate sovereign states of Montenegro and Serbia in June 2006), following an agreement by the Serbian authorities to withdraw all security and paramilitary forces from the southern province of Kosovo and Metohija, where Serbian repression of a separatist movement had prompted a humanitarian crisis and co-ordinated international action to resolve the conflict. On 10 June the UN Security Council adopted Resolution 1244, which outlined the terms of a political settlement for Kosovo and provided for the deployment of international civilian and security personnel. The security presence, termed the Kosovo Peace Implementation Force (KFOR), was to be led by NATO, while the UN was to oversee all civilian operations. UNMIK was established under the terms of Resolution 1244 as the supreme legal and executive authority in Kosovo, with responsibility for all civil administration and for facilitating the reconstruction and rehabilitation of the province as an autonomous region. For the first time in a UN operation other organizations were mandated to co-ordinate aspects of the mission in Kosovo, under the UN's overall jurisdiction. The four key elements, or Pillars, of UNMIK were (I) humanitarian affairs (led by UNHCR); (II) civil administration; (III) democratization and institution-building (OSCE); and (IV) economic reconstruction (EU). At the end of the first year of UNMIK's presence the element of humanitarian assistance was phased out. A new Pillar (I), concerned with police and justice, was established in May 2001, under the direct leadership of the UN. On arriving in the province at the end of June 1999 UNMIK and KFOR established a Joint Implementation Commission to co-ordinate and supervise the demilitarization of the Kosovo Liberation Army. UNMIK initiated a mass information campaign (and later administered new radio stations in Kosovo) to urge co-operation with the international personnel in the province and tolerance for all ethnic communities. A Mine Co-ordinating Centre supervised efforts to deactivate anti-personnel devices and to ensure the safety of the returning ethnic Albanian population. In July the UN Secretary-General's Special Representative took office, and chaired the first meeting of the Kosovo Transitional Council (KTC), which had been established by the UN as a multi-ethnic consultative organ, the highest political body under UNMIK, to help to restore law and order in the province and to reintegrate the local administrative infrastructure. In August a Joint Advisory Council on Legislative Matters was constituted, with representatives of UNMIK and the local judiciary, in order to consider measures to eliminate discrimination from the province's legal framework. At the end of July UNMIK personnel began to supervise customs controls at Kosovo's international borders. Other developments in the first few months of UNMIK's deployment included the establishment of joint commissions on energy and public utilities, education, and health, a Technical Advisory Commission on establishing a judiciary and prosecution service, and, in October, the establishment of a Fuel Supervisory Board to administer the import, sale and distribution of petroleum. Central financial institutions for the province were inaugurated in November. In the same month UNMIK established a Housing and Property Directorate and a Claims Commission in order to resolve residential property disputes. In September the KTC agreed to establish a Joint Security Committee, in response to concerns at the escalation of violence in the province, in particular attacks on remaining Serbian civilians. In mid-December the leaders of the three main political groupings in Kosovo agreed on provisional power-sharing arrangements with UNMIK. The so-called Kosovo-UNMIK Joint Interim Administrative Structure established an eight-member executive Interim Administrative Council and a framework of administrative departments. The KTC was to maintain its consultative role. In January 2000 UNMIK oversaw the inauguration of the Kosovo Protection Corps, a civilian agency comprising mainly former members of the newly demilitarized Kosovo Liberation Army, which was to provide an emergency response service and a humanitarian assistance capacity, to assist in de-mining operations and contribute to rebuilding local infrastructure. In August UNMIK, in view of its mandate to assist with the regeneration of the local economy, concluded an agreement with a multinational consortium to rehabilitate the Trepca nonferrous mining complex. During mid-2000 UNMIK organized the voter registration process for municipal elections, which were held in late October. In mid-December the Supreme Court of Kosovo was inaugurated, comprising 16 judges appointed by the Special Representative. During 2000 UNMIK police and KFOR co-operated in conducting joint security operations; the establishment of a special security task force to combat ethnically motivated political violence, comprising senior UNMIK police and KFOR members, was agreed in June. From January 2001 UNMIK international travel documents were distributed to Kosovars without Yugoslav passports. From early June, in response to ongoing concern at violence between ethnic Albanians and security forces in the former Yugoslav republic of Macedonia (FYRM), UNMIK designated 19 authorized crossing points at Kosovo's international borders with Albania and the FYRM, and its boundaries with Montenegro and Serbia. In mid-May the Special Representative of the Secretary-General signed the Constitutional Framework on Interim Self-Government, providing for the establishment of a Constitutional Assembly. UNMIK undertook efforts to register voters, in particular those from minority ethnic groups, and to continue to facilitate the return of displaced persons to their home communities. The last session of the KTC was held in October, and a general election was conducted, as scheduled, on 17 November. In December the Special Representative of the Secretary-General inaugurated the new 120-member Assembly. However, disagreements ensued among the three main political parties represented in the Assembly concerning the appointment of the positions of President and Prime Minister. In February 2002 the Special Representative negotiated an agreement with the leaders of the main political parties that resolved the deadlock in establishing the Interim Government. Accordingly, in March, the new President, Prime Minister and Interim Government were inaugurated, enabling the commencement of the process of developing self-governing institutions. In November the mission established the UNMIK Administration—Mitrovica, superseding parallel institutions that had operated hitherto in Serb-dominated northern Mitrovica, and thereby extending UNMIK's authority over all Kosovo. During that month a second series of municipal elections took place.

In March 2003 a Transfer Council was established with responsibility for transferring competencies from UNMIK to the provisional institutions of self-government (PISG). In June UNMIK, with UNDP, launched a Rapid Response Returns Facility (RRRF) to assist returnees from inside and outside Kosovo through the provision of housing and socio-economic support. In October the Special Representative of the Secretary-General invited Kosovan and Serb leaders, as well as representatives of the Contact Group, to participate in direct talks. The outcome of the meeting, held in Vienna, Austria, was an agreement to pursue a process of direct dialogue. In March 2004 two working groups, concerned with energy and with missing persons, were established within the framework of direct dialogue; however, the process was suspended following serious ethnic violence which occurred during that month (see below). Also in October 2003 UNMIK established a task force to combat corruption, and concluded with Montenegro a Memorandum of Understanding on Police Co-operation, with the aim of jointly targeting organized crime. In the following month a Memorandum of Understanding was signed with the International Commission on Missing Persons, formalizing co-operation in using DNA technology to identify missing persons.

In December 2003 the Special Representative of the Secretary-General and the Kosovan Prime Minister jointly launched *Standards for Kosovo*, drafted by the UN and partners and detailing eight fundamental democratic standards to be applied in the territory. Leaders of the Serb community declined to participate in the process. At the end of March 2004 the Special Representative and Prime Minister Rexhapi launched the Kosovo Standards Implementation Plan, outlining 109 standards and goals, as a mechanism for reviewing the standards and assessing the progress of the PISG. In mid-March rioting erupted in Kosovska Mitrovica and violent clashes between Serb and Albanian communities occurred throughout the province. After two days of serious incident 19 civilians were reported to have been killed, some 1,000 injured and an estimated 4,100 people from the Kosovan Serb, Roma and Ashkali communities had been displaced. In addition, 730 houses and 36 sites of cultural or religious importance had been damaged or destroyed. UNMIK undertook to restore the confidence of the affected communities, to assist with the reconstruction of damaged infrastructure and to investigate the organizers and main perpetrators of the violence. It also initiated a review of its own operational procedures, as well as the conduct of local politicians. The priority areas for the mission were identified as providing a secure environment, including the protection of minorities, and ensuring the success of the Standards Implementation Plan. In August a newly appointed Special Representative of the UN Secretary-General also re-emphasized the need to stimulate the local economy. In that month UNMIK, with UNDP and the local authorities, launched a youth employment creation project. In September UNMIK established a Financial Information Centre to help to deter money-laundering and other related offences. UNMIK assisted in preparations for legislative elections, to be held in October, and supported efforts to ensure a large and representative voter turn-out. In November the Special Representative met the newly elected political leaders and agreed on the establishment of new ministries for energy and mining, local government, and returns and communities. The inaugural session of the new Assembly was convened in December. In that month the Special Representative and the new Prime Minister, Ramush Haradinaj, concluded an agreement on making the Standards a priority for the Kosovan Government and on action for their implementation. In January 2005 a new UNMIK Senior Adviser on Minority Issues was appointed in order to assist the government's efforts to integrate fully minorities into Kosovan society. In March Haradinaj resigned following notification of his indictment by the International Criminal Tribunal for the former Yugoslavia. UNMIK supported the establishment of a coalition administration, and announced the establishment of a new body to promote political consensus within the province. The first meeting of the so-called Kosovo Forum, to which all political leaders were invited, was convened in June. During March–May meetings of the working groups, convened within the framework of direct dialogue between Serbia and Kosovo, were held, concerned with missing persons, energy and return of displaced persons. In October the UN Secretary-General recommended that political negotiations on the future status of the province commence. A Special Envoy for the Future Status Process, Martii Ahtisaari, was appointed in the following month. In December new UNMIK regulations provided for the establishment of Ministries of Justice and of Internal Affairs.

In March 2006 the Housing and Property Directorate was superseded by the Kosovo Property Agency. In August UNMIK and the Kosovan Ministry of Transport signed a memorandum governing the transfer of responsibility for the humanitarian transportation of minority communities in Kosovo from UNMIK to the Ministry. During that month the Interim Government approved the European Partnership Action Plan, which replaced the Kosovo Standards Implementation Plan during late 2006 as the basic reference document concerning standards. The 109 standards goals enshrined in the Standards Implementation Plan were incorporated into the Action Plan, which was co-ordinated by the Agency for European Integration. Negotiations on the future status of Kosovo were organized by the Special Envoy for the Future Status Process during 2006, and in February 2007 he presented a Settlement Proposal to the relevant parties. The provisional Proposal, which provided for a Kosovan constitution, flag and national anthem and for Kosovo to apply for independent membership of international organizations, while remaining under close international supervision, was rejected by many Kosovan Serbs on the grounds that it appeared to advance the advent of a fully independent Kosovo, and also by extremist Kosovan Albanian elements since it did not guarantee immediate full independence. During violent protests against the proposals organized by radical Kosovo Albanians two protesters were killed by Kosovan and UNMIK police, leading to the resignations of the UNMIK Police Commissioner and the Kosovan Minister of Internal Affairs. The Special Envoy pursued further discussions with all parties, however, in March he declared an end to the negotiation process. A few days later he presented revisions to the Settlement Proposal. In April a delegation of the UN Security Council visited the region to consider the final settlement plans. In July the UN Secretary-General issued a technical assessment of the progress achieved in Kosovo towards implementing the Standards. He also noted ongoing ethnic tensions in the province that were threatening further progress and a low rate of minority returns. A troika of the Contact Group on Kosovo, comprising representatives of the EU, Russia and USA, was established to undertake intensive negotiations to determine a final status for the province. In December, however, the troika reported that no agreement had been reached.

UNMIK monitored the preparation for and conduct of a general election in Kosovo, held in November 2007. In February 2008 the mission appealed for restraint following a declaration of independence from Serbia, announced by the newly-inaugurated Kosovan Assembly. In the following month the mission condemned a violent attack, by Serbian protesters, against a Court in northern Mitrovica, and subsequent clashes with UNMIK and KFOR personnel who regained control of the building.

At 31 December 2007 UNMIK comprised 1,996 civilian police and 39 military observers, supported by 468 international civilian personnel, 1,953 local civilian staff and 137 UN Volunteers. The General Assembly apportioned US $210.68m. to the Special Account for UNMIK to finance the operation during the period 1 July 2007–30 June 2008.

United Nations Interim Force in Lebanon—UNIFIL

Address: Naqoura, Lebanon.

Force Commander and Chief of Mission: Maj.-Gen. CLAUDIO GRAZIANO (Italy).

UNIFIL was established by UN Security Council Resolution 425 in March 1978, following an invasion of Lebanon by Israeli forces. The force was mandated to confirm the withdrawal of Israeli forces, to restore international peace and security, and to assist the Government of Lebanon in ensuring the return of its effective authority in southern Lebanon. UNIFIL also extended humanitarian assistance to the population of the area, particularly following the second Israeli invasion of Lebanon in 1982. UNIFIL has provided civilians with food, water, fuel; medical and dental services; and some veterinary assistance. In April 1992, in accordance with its mandate, UNIFIL completed the transfer of part of its zone of operations to the control of the Lebanese army.

In March 1998 the Israeli Government announced that it recognized Security Council Resolution 425, requiring the unconditional withdrawal of its forces from southern Lebanon. It stipulated, however, that any withdrawal of its troops must be conditional on receiving security guarantees from the Lebanese authorities. A formal decision to this effect, adopted on 1 April, was rejected by the Lebanese and Syrian Governments. In April 2000 the Israeli Government formally notified the UN Secretary-General of its intention to comply forthwith and in full with Resolution 425. Later in that month the UN Secretary-General dispatched a team of experts to study the technical aspects of the impending implementation of Resolution 425, and sent a delegation, led by his Special Co-ordinator for the Middle East Peace Process, Terje Roed-Larsen, and the Commander of UNIFIL, to consult with regional governments and groupings. The withdrawal of Israeli troops commenced in mid-May. Meanwhile, the Security Council endorsed an operational plan to enable UNIFIL to verify the withdrawal. All concerned parties were urged to co-operate with UNIFIL in order to ensure the full implementation of the resolution. In accordance with its mandate, UNIFIL was to be disbanded following the resumption by the Lebanese Government of effective authority and the normal responsibilities of a state throughout the area, including the re-establishment of law and order structures. In mid-June the UN Secretary-General confirmed that Israeli forces had fully evacuated from southern Lebanon. Soon afterwards UNIFIL reported several Israeli violations of the line of withdrawal, the so-called Blue Line. The Israeli Government agreed to rectify these by the end of July, and on 24 July the UN Secretary-General confirmed that no serious violations remained. UNIFIL, reinforced with additional troops, patrolled the area vacated by the Israeli forces, monitored the line of withdrawal, undertook demining activities, and continued to provide humanitarian assistance. From August the Lebanese Government deployed a Joint Security Force to the area and began re-establishing local administrative structures and reintegrating basic services into the rest of the country. However, the authorities declined to deploy military personnel along the border zone, on the grounds that a comprehensive peace agreement with Israel would first need to be achieved. In November, following two serious violations of the Blue Line in the previous month by both Israeli troops and Hezbollah militia, the Security Council urged the Lebanese Government to take effective control of the whole area vacated by Israel and to assume international responsibilities. In January 2001 the UN Secretary-General reported that UNIFIL no longer exercised control over the area of operation, which remained relatively stable. The Security Council endorsed his proposals to reconfigure the Force in order to focus on its remaining mandate of maintaining and observing the cease-fire along the line of withdrawal; this was completed by the end of 2002. In response to an increase from early 2002 in incidents generating tension in the area of UNIFIL's operation, reportedly perpetrated by Hezbollah and other militants, and continuous Israeli air violations of the Blue Line, Terje Roed-Larsen and the Secretary-General's Personal Representative for Southern Lebanon undertook diplomatic efforts aimed at restoring stability, and, despite restrictions on its movements, UNIFIL increased its patrols. In January 2003 the UN Secretary-General reported that the number of ground violations of the Blue Line had decreased significantly. From August, however, the number of reported violent incidents increased. Nonetheless, UNIFIL continued to work to clear areas of land of anti-personnel devices and to assist the integration of the formerly occupied zone into the rest of the country. In July 2004 UNIFIL representatives, with other UN officials, worked to defuse tensions following an alleged Hezbollah sniper attack against Israeli forces and subsequent Israeli violations of Lebanese airspace. At the end of that year the UN expressed concern at further repeated violations of the Blue Line from both sides. A serious breach of the cease-fire occurred in May 2005. In late June UNIFIL reported attacks on Israeli troop positions by Hezbollah militia and a forceful response by the Israeli Defence Force. In November UNIFIL brokered a cease-fire following further hostilities across the Blue Line, initiated by Hezbollah; however there were reports of a missile attack on Israeli positions in the following month. The Security Council subsequently urged all parties to end violations of the Blue Line and for the Lebanese Government to maintain order and exert greater authority throughout its territory.

In mid-July 2006 a full-scale conflict erupted between the Israeli armed forces and Hezbollah, following the capture by Hezbollah of two Israeli soldiers, and killing of three others, on 12 July. An estimated 1,000 Lebanese civilians were killed and 900,000 displaced from their homes during the unrest. A cease-fire between Hezbollah and Israel entered into effect on 14 August, following the adoption by the UN Security Council on 11 August of Resolution 1701, which demanded 'the immediate cessation by Hezbollah of all attacks and the immediate cessation by Israel of all offensive military operations' in Lebanon; welcomed a recent decision of the Lebanese Government to deploy 15,000 armed troops in southern Lebanon; and increased the Force's authorized troop strength to a maximum of 15,000, and expanded its mandate to include monitoring the cease-fire, supporting the Lebanese troop deployment in southern Lebanon, facilitating humanitarian access to civilian communities, and assisting voluntary and safe returns of people displaced by the conflict. In September 2006 a new Strategic Military Cell (SMC), reporting to the Under-Secretary-General for Peacekeeping Operations, was established to provide military guidance to UNIFIL. In the following month a Maritime Task Force was established, the first in a UN peacekeeping operation, to patrol the waters off the Lebanese coast in order to counter illegal trade in arms. In June 2007 six soldiers serving under UNIFIL were killed in a car bomb attack in south-eastern Lebanon.

At 31 January 2008 the Force comprised 12,455 military personnel; at 31 December 2007 there were some 910 international and local civilian staff. The General Assembly appropriation for the operation for the period 1 July 2007–30 June 2008 amounted to US $713.6m.

United Nations Military Observer Group in India and Pakistan—UNMOGIP

Address: Rawalpindi, Pakistan (November–April), Srinagar, India (May–October).

Chief Military Observer: Col JARMO HELENIUS (Finland) (acting).

The Group was established in 1948 by UN Security Council resolutions aiming to restore peace in the region of Jammu and Kashmir, the status of which had become a matter of dispute between the Governments of India and Pakistan. Following a cease-fire which came into effect in January 1949, the military observers of UNMOGIP were deployed to assist in its observance. There is no periodic review of UNMOGIP's mandate. In 1971, following the signature of a new cease-fire agreement, India claimed that UNMOGIP's mandate had lapsed, since it was originally intended to monitor the agreement reached in 1949. Pakistan, however, regarded UNMOGIP's mission as unchanged, and the Group's activities have continued, although they have been somewhat restricted on the Indian side of the 'line of control', which was agreed by India and Pakistan in 1972.

At 31 January 2008 there were 43 military observers deployed on both sides of the 'line of control'; it is supported by 74 international and local civilian personnel. The approved budget for the operation for the period 2006–07 was US $15.8m.

United Nations Mission for the Referendum in Western Sahara—MINURSO

Address: el-Aaiún, Western Sahara.

Special Representative of the UN Secretary-General and Chief of Mission: JULIAN HARSTON (United Kingdom).

Force Commander: Gen. ZHAO JINGMIN (People's Republic of China).

In April 1991 the UN Security Council endorsed the establishment of MINURSO to verify a cease-fire in the disputed territory of Western Sahara, which came into effect in September 1991, and to implement a settlement plan, involving the repatriation of Western Saharan refugees (in co-ordination with UNHCR), the release of all Sahrawi political prisoners, and the organization of a referendum on the future of the territory. Western Sahara is claimed by Morocco, the administering power since 1975, and by the Algerian-supported Frente Popular para la Liberación de Saguia el Hamra y Río de Oro—Frente Polisario. Although originally envisaged for January 1992, the referendum was postponed indefinitely. In 1992 and 1993 the UN Secretary-General's Special Representative organized negotiations between the Frente Polisario and the Moroccan Government, who were in serious disagreement regarding criteria for eligibility to vote in the plebiscite. In March 1993 the Security Council advocated that further efforts should be made to compile a satisfactory electoral list and to resolve the outstanding differences on procedural issues. An Identification Commission was established to begin the process of voter registration, although this was obstructed by the failure of the Moroccan Government and the Frente Polisario to pursue political dialogue. The identification and registration operation was formally initiated in August 1994. In December 1995 the UN Secretary-General reported that the identification of voters had stalled, owing to persistent obstruction of the process on the part of the Moroccan and Frente Polisario authorities. In May 1996 the Security Council endorsed a recommendation of the Secretary-General to suspend the identification process until all sides demonstrate their willingness to co-operate with the mission. The Council decided that MINURSO's operational capacity should be reduced by 20%, with sufficient troops retained to monitor and verify the cease-fire.

In early 1997 the Secretary-General of the UN attempted to revive the possibility of an imminent resolution of the dispute, amid increasing concerns that the opposing authorities were preparing for a resumption of hostilities in the event of a collapse of the existing cease-fire, and appointed James Baker, a former US Secretary of State, as his Personal Envoy to the region. In June Baker obtained the support of Morocco and the Frente Polisario, as well as Algeria and Mauritania (which border the disputed territory), to conduct further negotiations in order to advance the referendum process. Direct talks between senior representatives of the Moroccan Government and the Frente Polisario authorities were initiated later in that month, in Lisbon, Portugal, under the auspices of the UN, and attended by Algeria and Mauritania in an observer capacity. In September the two sides concluded an agreement which aimed to resolve the outstanding issues of contention and enable the referendum to be conducted in late 1998. The agreement included a commitment by both parties to identify eligible Sahrawi voters on an individual basis, in accordance with the results of the last official census in 1974, and a code of conduct to ensure the impartiality of the poll. In October 1997 the Security Council endorsed a recommendation of the Secretary-General to increase the strength of the mission, to enable it to supervise nine identification centres. The process of voter identification resumed in December.

In January 1998 the Security Council approved the deployment of an engineering unit to support MINURSO's de-mining activities. By early September of that year the initial identification process had been completed. However, the controversial issue of the eligibility of 65,000 members of three Saharan tribal groups remained unresolved. In October the Security Council endorsed a series of measures proposed by the UN Secretary-General to advance the referendum, including a strengthened Identification Commission to consider requests from any applicant from the three disputed tribal groups on an individual basis. The proposals also incorporated the need for an agreement by both sides with UNHCR with regard to arrangements for the repatriation of refugees. In November, following a visit to the region by the Secretary-General, the Frente Polisario accepted the proposals, and in March 1999 the Moroccan Government signed an agreement with the UN to secure the legal basis of the MINURSO operation. In May the Moroccan Government and the Frente Polisario agreed in principle to a draft plan of action for cross-border confidence measures. In July 1999 the UN published the first part of a provisional list of qualified voters. An appeals process then commenced, in accordance with the settlement plan. In late November almost 200 Moroccan prisoners of war were released by the Frente Polisario, following a series of negotiations led by the Special Representative of the UN Secretary-General. The identification of applicants from the three disputed Saharan tribal groups was completed at the end of December. In January 2000 the second, final part of the provisional list of qualified voters was issued, and a six-week appeals process ensued. In December 1999 the Security Council acknowledged that persisting disagreements obstructing the implementation of the settlement plan (mainly concerning the processing and analysis of appeals, the release of remaining prisoners and the repatriation of refugees) precluded any possibility of conducting the planned referendum before 2002.

In June 2001 the Personal Envoy of the UN Secretary-General elaborated a draft Framework Agreement on the Status of Western Sahara as an alternative to the settlement plan. The draft Agreement envisaged the disputed area remaining part of Morocco, but with substantial devolution of authority. Any referendum would be postponed. The Security Council authorized Baker to discuss the proposals with all concerned parties. However, the Frente Polisario and Algeria rejected the draft Agreement. In November the Security Council, at the insistence of the Frente Polisario, requested the opinion of the UN Legal Counsel regarding the legality of two short-term reconnaissance licences granted by Morocco to international petroleum companies for operation in Western Sahara. In January 2002 the Secretary-General's Personal Envoy visited the region and met with leaders of both sides. He welcomed the release by the Frente Polisario of a further 115 Moroccan prisoners, but urged both sides to release all long-term detainees. In July the Frente Polisario released a further 101 Moroccan prisoners, leaving a total of 1,260 long-term detainees, of whom 816 had been held for more than 20 years. During February–November 2003 the Frente Polisario released 643 more prisoners. Morocco continued to detain 150 Sahrawi prisoners. In January the Secretary-General's Personal Envoy presented to both sides and to the Governments of neighbouring states a new arrangement for a political settlement, providing for self-determination, that had been requested by Resolution 1429 of the Security Council. In July the Frente Polisario accepted the so-called Peace Plan for Self-Determination of the People of Western Sahara. In April 2004, however, it was rejected by the Moroccan Government.

In March 2004 MINURSO co-operated with UNHCR to implement a family visits programme, providing for exchange of contacts of relatives divided by the dispute. MINURSO provided transport and other logistical support for the scheme, which was intended to be part of a series of confidence-building measures. In June James Baker resigned as Personal Envoy of the Secretary-General. In September the Special Representative of the Secretary-General, who had assumed responsibility for pursuing a political solution, held his first series of formal meetings with all parties to the dispute. In April 2005 the Secretary-General advised that MINURSO's force strength be maintained given the lack of progress in negotiating a political settlement. In July the Secretary-General appointed a new Personal Envoy for the Western Sahara, Peter van Walsum, who undertook his first visit to heads of state in the region in October in an attempt to review the 2003 Peace Plan. In August 2005 the Frente Polisario released all remaining Moroccan prisoners.

In early 2006 Morocco established a Royal Advisory Council for Saharan Affairs that comprised Moroccan political parties and Sahrawi leaders, but not the Frente Polisario. In February a ministerial delegation of the Moroccan Government presented the member states of the Group of Friends of Western Sahara (France, Russia, Spain, the UK and the USA), as well as Germany and the UN Secretary-General, with the basics of a possible future plan for granting extended autonomy to Western Sahara. In April 2007 the UN Security Council reiterated a strong request that both parties enter into discussions without preconditions. In June direct talks between representatives of the Moroccan Government and the Frente Polisario, attended by representatives of Algeria and Mauritania, were held under the auspices of the Personal Envoy of the UN Secretary-General in Manhasset, New York, USA. Further negotiations were conducted in August. Both sides were reported to have agreed that the process should continue and that the current status quo in Western Sahara was unacceptable. The third and fourth rounds of discussions between the two sides were held in January and March 2008, respectively.

The mission has headquarters in the north and south of the disputed territory. There is a liaison office in Tindouf, Algeria, which was established in order to maintain contact with the Frente Polisario (which is based in Algeria) and the Algerian Government.

At 31 January 2008 MINURSO comprised 189 military observers, 27 troops and six police; at 31 December 2007 it was supported by 244 international and local civilian personnel and 23 UN Volunteers. The General Assembly appropriation to cover the cost of the mission for the period 1 July 2007–30 June 2008 amounted to US $47.6m.

United Nations Mission in Ethiopia and Eritrea—UNMEE

Address: Asmara, Eritrea; Addis Ababa, Ethiopia.

Acting Special Representative of the UN Secretary-General and Head of Mission: AZOUZ ENNIFAR (Tunisia).

Force Commander: Maj.-Gen. MOHAMMAD TASIR MASADEH (Jordan).

In July 2000 the Security Council authorized the establishment of UNMEE to facilitate compliance with and verify a cease-fire agreement that had been signed by the Governments of Eritrea and Ethiopia in mid-June (having been mediated by the Organization of African Unity—OAU, now African Union—AU), with a view to settling a long-standing border conflict between the two countries. In September the Security Council authorized the deployment of up to 4,200 military personnel to the operation, which was given an initial six-month mandate. The Security Council emphasized that UNMEE's mandate would be terminated on completion of the process to delimit and demarcate the Eritrea–Ethiopia border. In December the Eritrean and Ethiopian authorities concluded a full peace accord, providing for the establishment of a Boundary Commission mandated to delimit the border on the basis of relevant colonial treaties and international law. The eventual decision of the Commission was to be accepted by both parties as 'final and binding'. In February 2001 the Military Co-ordination Commission (which had been established jointly by the UN and the OAU in accordance with the cease-fire accord to address military and technical aspects of the peace process, and had met for the first time in December 2000) agreed a timetable to enable Eritrean and Ethiopian forces, monitored by UNMEE, to redeploy in order to establish a 25km temporary security zone (TSZ) in the border area; the security zone was declared operational in April 2001. UNMEE was subsequently to continue to monitor both forces, to co-ordinate and provide technical assistance for de-mining activities in the vacated and adjacent areas, and to co-ordinate local humanitarian and human rights activities by UN and other agencies. From mid-2001 UNMEE repeatedly protested against alleged restrictions placed on its freedom of movement by the Eritrean authorities in areas adjoining the TSZ, as these impeded the mission's capability to monitor the redeployment of that country's forces. In January 2002 the Security Council urged that UNMEE be allowed full freedom of movement and requested that the Eritrean Government disclose details of an alleged continuing military and police presence within the TSZ. In mid-April the Boundary Commission published its decision on the delimitation of the two countries' common border. The Secretary-General urged Eritrea and Ethiopia to implement the decision without delay. UNMEE was to monitor the next phase of the peace process, involving the border's physical demarcation. During late April and early May the Ethiopian Government temporarily closed the Ethiopian border to UNMEE personnel, claiming that UNMEE had not consulted sufficiently with it regarding the mission's logistical support for, and the transfer of personnel to, the Boundary Commission's field office; that the Commission had not established its field presence on the Ethiopian side of the border; and that UNMEE had inappropriately permitted journalists to visit a border village. In August the Security Council adjusted the mission's mandate to support the implementation of decisions adopted by the Boundary Commission. During 2002–03 UNMEE personnel undertook various humanitarian projects including the provision of medical assistance, rebuilding and extending water supplies, constructing shelters for the internally displaced population, and rehabilitating roads. In July 2002 two outreach centres were opened in the Ethiopian and Eritrean capitals (respectively, Addis Ababa and Asmara) to provide information to the public about the peace process. In 2003 and early 2004 the Secretary-General noted that the movements of UNMEE personnel were being restricted by both the Eritrean and Ethiopian authorities. In January 2004 the Secretary-General appointed a new Special Envoy on Ethiopia and Eritrea, Lloyd Axworthy, who was mandated to consult with the Eritrean and Ethiopian authorities with a view to accelerating the implementation of the December 2000 peace accord. Axworthy held consultations with the Ethiopian authorities in February 2004; the Eritrean leadership, however, refused to receive him. In May the Security Council urged both sides to co-operate more fully with UNMEE and expressed concern at ongoing restrictions on the movement of UN troops. In 2004 UNMEE undertook awareness and training programmes in aspects of de-mining, HIV/AIDS and human rights. Little political progress was achieved during the year; in November, however, the Ethiopian Government presented a new five-point peace plan, which was welcomed by the UN Secretary-General.

In July 2005 the UN Security Council expressed concern at the continued lack of progress in implementing the decision of the Boundary Commission, as well as new restrictions on UNMEE police officers in the Eritrean capital, Asmara, and the suspension of direct flights between the capitals of the two countries. The Council also reiterated concern at worsening food security in both countries. Nonetheless, UNMEE reported that the military situation in the border area remained stable and that ongoing de-mining activities were benefiting the local population and encouraging the return of displaced persons. In September the Security Council again urged Ethiopia to accept the decision of the Boundary Commission, both governments to implement the decision fully and without delay, and Eritrea to remove all existing restrictions on UN movements. In October, however, the Eritrean Government imposed a ban on helicopter flights by UNMEE in its airspace. UNMEE subsequently suspended its mine clearance activities, owing to safety concerns, and evacuated personnel from 18 remote observation posts in the TSZ. In late November the Security Council passed a resolution demanding a reversal of Eritrea's constraints on UNMEE operations, Ethiopia's acceptance of the Boundary Commission decision, and a return to troop deployment levels in the TSZ to those of December 2004, owing to a concern at a build-up of troops on both sides. The resolution provided for the possible imposition of punitive measures if the conditions were not met. A few days later, at a meeting chaired by UNMEE's Force Commander, representatives of both sides agreed not to escalate further tensions in the border region. In December 2005 the UN condemned a request by the Eritrean authorities that all UNMEE personnel from Canada, Russia, the USA and European countries leave the country within 10 days. The UN Secretary-General immediately dispatched two senior officials to the region to review the situation and defuse the escalating political crisis. In mid-December the Security Council reiterated its immediate condemnation of Eritrea's decision and approved the temporary relocation of some 87 military and civilian staff from that country to Ethiopia. At the end of December UNMEE reported that Ethiopian troops had begun to retreat from the border, but expressed concerns at ongoing heightened tensions in the zone.

In October 2006 the UN Security Council expressed concern at the large-scale movement of Eritrean troops within the TSZ and urged their immediate withdrawal. In November the Boundary Commission granted both parties a further 12 months to complete the boundary demarcation process. In January 2007 the UN Secretary-General reported that non-co-operation by Eritrea with his acting Special Representative and continuing obstructions imposed upon UNMEE's movements were severely restricting the operations of the mission and that Ethiopia's continuing refusal to implement the decision of the Boundary Commission was contributing to continued stalemate. The humanitarian situation in the region remained of considerable concern. In March UNMEE expressed concern at further restrictions imposed on its cease-fire monitoring role by the Eritrean authorities and criticised the ordered expulsion of the manager of the mission's Mine Action Co-ordination Centre. In May the UN Security Council urged both countries to refrain from violence, given the increasing tension in the region, violations of the TSZ and lack of progress in resolving the dispute.

From early December 2007 the Eritrea Government terminated the delivery of fuel supplies to UNMEE (citing a 'technical matter'), thereby forcing the mission to reduce significantly its operations in the TSZ. At the beginning of February 2008 the UN Secretary-General sent the Eritrean President an ultimatum, stating that he would instruct UNMEE to start relocating its personnel and equipment from Eritrea within one week failing the resumption of fuel deliveries. In addition the Secretary-General dispatched a technical mission to the area to assess the situation; the Eritrean authorities, however, denied the mission permission to enter Eritrea. With assistance from the UN technical mission, UNMEE devised an emergency relocation plan, providing for the movement from the TSZ into Ethiopia of 1,375 personnel and their equipment. The Eritrean authorities refused to assist with the relocation operation, claiming it to be at variance with the provisions of the December 2000 peace accord. An alternative contingency plan involving the movement and regrouping of the stranded personnel and equipment into Asmara and Assab was implemented in mid-February 2008 despite hindrance from the Eritrean defence forces. In late February the UN Secretariat addressed a note verbale to Eritrea, requesting that it reconsider its position, resume the supply of fuel to UNMEE, lift all restrictions against the mission, and permit the mission to exercise its mandate. The Eritrean authorities did not respond. In late March the Secretary-General declared the restrictions imposed on UNMEE by the Eritrean authorities to be in breach of the fundamental principles of peace-keeping, instructed UNMEE to make arrangements to repatriate the regrouped military personnel to their home countries, pending further developments, and urged that the decisions of the Boundary Commission be implemented.

At 31 January 2008 UNMEE comprised 1,463 troops and 211 military observers, supported by 350 international and local civilian personnel and 62 UN Volunteers. The General Assembly appropriation to cover the cost of the mission for the period 1 July 2007–30 June 2008 amounted to US $113.5m., to be financed by a Special Account.

United Nations Mission in Liberia—UNMIL

Address: Monrovia, Liberia.

Special Representative of the UN Secretary-General and Head of Mission: ELLEN MARGRETHE LØJ (Denmark).

Force Commander: Lt-Gen. CHIKADIBIA OBIAKOR (Nigeria).

UNMIL was authorized by the UN Security Council in September 2003 to support the implementation of the cease-fire accord agreed in June and the Comprehensive Peace Agreement concluded in August by the parties to the conflict in Liberia. UNMIL was mandated to assist with the development of an action plan for the disarmament, demobilization, reintegration and, where appropriate, repatriation of all armed groups and to undertake a programme of voluntary disarmament; to protect civilians and UN personnel, equipment and facilities; to support humanitarian and human rights activities; to support the implementation of national security reforms; and, in co-operation with ECOWAS and other partners, to assist the National Transitional Government (inaugurated in mid-October) with the training of a national police force and the restructuring of the military. Troops were also to assist with the rehabilitation of damaged physical infrastructure, in particular the road network. On 1 October UNMIL assumed authority from an ECOWAS-led multinational force in Liberia (the ECOWAS Mission in Liberia—ECOMIL) which had been endorsed by the Security Council in August; ECOMIL's 3,600 troops were reassigned to UNMIL, which had an authorized maximum strength of 15,000 military personnel. In 2004 UNMIL's civil affairs component assessed the functional capacities of public administration structures, including government ministries, in order to assist the National Transitional Government in re-establishing authority throughout Liberia. UNMIL was to support the National Transitional Government in preparing the country for national elections, which were expected to be held in October 2005. In December 2003 the programme for disarmament, demobilization, rehabilitation and reintegration (DDRR) officially commenced when the first cantonment site was opened. However, the process was disrupted by an unexpectedly large influx of former combatants and a few days later the process was temporarily suspended. In mid-January 2004 an agreement was concluded by all parties on necessary prerequisites to proceeding with the programme, including the launch of an information campaign, which was to be co-ordinated and organized by UNMIL, and the construction of new reception centres and cantonment sites. The DDRR process resumed, under UNMIL command, in mid-April. A training programme for the country's new police service was inaugurated in July and the first UN-trained police officers were deployed at the end of the year. By July 2007 some 3,500 officers had graduated from the UN training programme. In August 2004 UNMIL launched a further vocational training scheme for some 640 former combatants to learn building skills. By the end of October, when the disarmament phase of the DDRR programme was officially terminated, more than 96,000 former combatants, including 10,000 child soldiers, had handed over their weapons. Some 7,200 commenced formal education. At the same time, however, UNMIL troops were deployed throughout the country to restore order, after an outbreak of sectarian hostilities prompted widespread looting and destruction of property and businesses. In early December the Special Representative of the UN Secretary-General hosted a meeting of the heads of all West African peace-keeping and political missions, in order to initiate a more integrated approach to achieving stability and peace throughout the region.

During 2005 UNMIL continued to work to integrate ex-combatants into society through vocational training schemes, and to support community rehabilitation efforts, in particular through the funding of Quick Impact Projects. By August an estimated 78,000 former combatants had participated in rehabilitation and reintegration schemes, funded bilaterally and by a Trust Fund administered by the UN Development Programme. A programme to enrol 20,000 disarmed combatants in formal education was initiated in November. UNMIL provided technical assistance to the National Elections Commission, which, in April, initiated a process of voter registration in preparation for presidential and legislative elections. UNMIL was also concerned with maintaining a peaceful and secure environment for the electoral campaigns and polling days and undertook a large-scale civic education campaign in support of the democratic election process. In October UNMIL, with the Transitional Government, established a Joint National Security Operations Centre. The elections were held, as scheduled, in October, with a second-round presidential poll in November. The new president and administration were inaugurated in January 2006. UNMIL determined to strengthen its focus on the rule of law, economic recovery and good governance. It also pledged to support the government in efforts to remove UN sanctions against sales of rough diamonds and to become a member of the Kimberley Process Certification Scheme by providing air support for surveillance and mapping activities in mining areas. Throughout 2006 and 2007 UNMIL personnel undertook projects to rehabilitate and construct roads and bridges, police stations, courtrooms and educational facilities. The mission also initiated, with the support of other UN agencies, a scheme to create employment throughout the country. In March 2007 UNMIL initiated a Sports for Peace programme to promote national reconciliation. In late April the UN Security Council removed the embargo against sales of diamonds from Liberia, and in the following month UNMIL transferred control of the regional diamond certification office to the national authorities.

In September 2005 the UN Security Council authorized a temporary increase in the mission's military strength in order to compensate for the dispatch of 250 troops, with effect from 1 January 2006, to provide protection at the Special Court in Sierra Leone, following the termination of the UN mission in that country.

In September 2006 the UN Security Council endorsed a recommendation by the Secretary-General that a consolidation, drawdown and withdrawal plan for UNMIL should be developed and implemented; the consolidation phase was completed in December 2007, and the final withdrawal of the mission was scheduled for 2010. In August 2007 the UN Secretary-General recognized the efforts of the new government in consolidating peace and promoting economic recovery in the country.

At 31 January 2008 UNMIL comprised 13,291 troops, 1,205 police and 194 military observers, supported by 507 international personnel, 944 local civilian staff and 223 UN Volunteers. The General Assembly appropriation to the Special Account for UNMIL amounted to US $688.4m. for the period 1 July 2007–30 June 2008.

United Nations Mission in Sudan—UNMIS

Address: Khartoum, Sudan.

Special Representative of the UN Secretary-General and Head of Mission: ASHRAF JEHANGIR QAZI (Pakistan).

Force Commander: Lt-Gen. JASBIR SINGH LIDDER (India).

In June 2004 the Security Council agreed to establish an Advance Team in Sudan, as a special political mission, in order to support efforts towards achieving a peaceful settlement of the conflict in that country. The Council also expressed concern at the situation of an estimated 2m. people in Darfur, western Sudan, who had been displaced by civil conflict and suffered extensive attacks by militia groups. In July the newly-appointed Special Representative of the UN Secretary-General, Jan Pronk, visited Darfur under the auspices of a Joint Implementation Mechanism, established earlier in that month by the UN and Sudanese Government to work towards alleviating the humanitarian crisis. At the end of that month the Security Council resolved to impose an arms embargo against rebel groups in Darfur, and endorsed efforts of the African Union (AU) in mediating a political solution. In mid-November the Security Council met in special session in Nairobi, Kenya, to assess the situation in Sudan and to address the problems in Darfur. The Council witnessed the signing of a Memorandum of Understanding between the Sudanese Government and Sudan People's Liberation Movement/Army (SPLM/A) to end the conflict in southern Sudan, and pledged to support any lasting settlement. In January 2005 both sides signed a Comprehensive Peace Agreement. The UN Mission in Sudan was formally established under Resolution 1590, which was adopted by the Security Council in March. Its mandate was to support implementation of the Comprehensive Peace Agreement, for example by monitoring the cease-fire arrangements and investigating any violations, assisting in the establishment of a disarmament, demobilization and reintegration programme, supporting a restructuring of the police service, and implementing a public information campaign in support of the peace process. In addition, the mission was to facilitate and co-ordinate the voluntary return of refugees and internally displaced persons, to provide de-mining assistance and technical advice, and to contribute to international efforts to protect and promote human rights in Sudan. UNMIS was to work closely with the AU's Mission in Sudan (AMIS) to foster peace and reinforce stability in Darfur.

In May 2005 the UNMIS Force Commander chaired the first meeting of a Cease-fire Joint Military Committee (CJMC), comprising representatives of the Sudanese Government, the SPLM/A and the UN. In accordance with the Comprehensive Peace Agreement the Committee was to monitor troop locations and strength, the stocks of weapons and ammunition and co-ordinate the clearance of anti-personnel mines, as well as undertake other military tasks assigned under the Agreement. In May and early June UNMIS reported repeated outbreaks of violence, mainly in southern Darfur. The Special Representative of the UN Secretary-General urged an immediate end to hostilities between rebel factions. In July a preliminary agreement was signed by the Government and rebel movements to end the conflict in Darfur. Later in that month a Government of National Unity was inaugurated. A new Interim National Assembly was inaugurated at the end of August. In September the first Area Joint Military Committee meetings were held—in Kadugli and Juba—as subsidiary bodies of the CJMC to oversee the cease-fire process at area sector level. In that month UNMIS expressed its concern for the future of the cease-fire in Darfur and UN humanitarian activities in the region given an escalation of violence. At the end of September an Interim Legislative Council of Southern Sudan was inaugurated, comprising representatives of all political and military factions. Nonetheless, security remained a major concern of UNMIS. In November UNMIS arbitrated a meeting between the leaders of two conflicting groups in Abyei, southern Sudan, in order to build confidence and initiate a reconciliation between the sides. During the second half of 2005 UNMIS personnel assisted in the rehabilitation of infrastructure in southern Sudan, including the construction of two bridges and the reopening of the Juba–Yei road. Its Human Rights Unit organized technical workshops on harmonizing Sudanese law with international humanitarian standards and on the role of parliamentarians in upholding human rights. Other UNMIS activities included training for HIV/AIDS education and measures to strengthen the country's police force. In August 2007 UNMIS officials held the first of regular consultations with the Government of Southern Sudan, agreed in June, on implementation of the January 2005 Comprehensive Peace Agreement. In early 2008 the UN Secretary-General was undertaking a comprehensive strategic assessment of the mandate of UNMIS.

In August 2006 the UN Security Council expanded the mandate of UNMIS to provide for its deployment to Darfur, in order to enforce a cease-fire and support the implementation of the Darfur Peace Agreement (DPA), which had been signed in early May by the Sudanese Government and the SPLM/A. Under its expanded mandate UNMIS was to monitor and verify the implementation by the parties to the cease-fire agreement and DPA; to observe and monitor the movements of armed groups and deployment of government forces by ground and aerial means; to investigate violations of the agreements; to monitor transborder activities of armed groups along the Sudanese borders with Chad and the Central African Republic; and to promote human rights, civilian protection and monitoring activities, including particular attention to the needs of women and children. The Council also authorized that the mission should be strengthened by up to 17,300 military personnel, up to 3,300 civilian police personnel, and up to 16 police units. Furthermore, the Council requested the Secretary-General to devise jointly with the AU, in consultation with the parties to the DPA, a plan and schedule for a transition from AMIS to a sole UN operation in Darfur. The Sudanese Government, however, initially rejected the concept of an expanded UN peace-keeping mission, on the grounds that it would compromise national sovereignty. In late December the UN, AU and Sudanese Government established a tripartite mechanism which was to facilitate the implementation of a UN-formulated three-phase approach, endorsed by the AU Peace and Security Council in November, that would culminate in a hybrid AU/UN mission in Darfur. In January 2007 UNMIS provided AMIS with supplies and extra personnel under the first ('light support') phase. In April the Sudanese Government endorsed the proposed second ('heavy') phase, which was to involve the delivery of force enablers, police units, civilian personnel and mission support items. From early 2007 UNMIS undertook to engage the non-signatories of the DPA in the political process in Darfur. In June the Sudanese Government agreed to support unconditionally the deployment of a Hybrid AU/UN Operation in Darfur (UNAMID), following a meeting with a delegation from the UN Security Council. UNAMID was authorized by the Security Council in July. UNMIS was to provide logistical support to UNAMID. In December 2007 UNMIS, UNAMID and the AU-UN Joint Mediation Support Team for Darfur (JMST) formed a joint task force to recommend policies and mechanisms for enhancing co-operation.

At 31 January 2008 UNMIS comprised 8,715 troops, 537 military observers and 639 police officers, supported by 866 international and 2,400 local staff and 262 UN Volunteers. The General Assembly appropriation to cover the cost of the mission for the period 1 July 2007–30 June 2008 amounted to US $846.3m.

United Nations Mission in the Central African Republic and Chad—MINURCAT

Address: N'Djamena, Chad.

Special Representative of the UN Secretary-General: VICTOR DA SILVA ANGELO (Portugal).

The mission was established in September 2007 as part of a multi-dimensional presence, authorized by Resolution 1778 of the UN Security Council, to create a secure environment in northeastern CAR and eastern Chad for the voluntary and sustainable return of refugees and displaced persons, as well as to enhance the existing humanitarian situation, and to help create favourable conditions for the reconstruction and economic and social development of these areas. The UN mission was mandated to work with other organizations for the security and protection of civilians, including the relocation of refugees camps close to the border and providing training and other technical advice on the establishment of a specialized Chadian humanitarian protection force. The mission was also mandated to monitor and promote human rights and the rule of law, and to strengthen the capacities of the governments and civil society to uphold international human rights standards. A military force of the European Union, EUFOR Chad/CAR, was also authorized by Resolution 1778 to work alongside the UN mission; EUFOR Chad/CAR was inaugurated in January 2008.

MINURCAT has an authorized strength of 300 police officers and 50 military liaison officers. The mission's operational strength at 31 January 2008 comprised seven military advisors and 52 police personnel. The budget for MINURCAT amounted to US $182.4m. for the period 1 July 2007–30 June 2008, funded from a Special Account comprising assessed contributions from UN member states.

United Nations Mission in the Democratic Republic of the Congo—MONUC

Address: Kinshasa, Democratic Republic of the Congo.

Liaison offices are situated in Bujumbura (Burundi); Addis Ababa (Ethiopia); Windhoek (Namibia); Kigali (Rwanda); Kampala (Uganda); Lusaka (Zambia); and Harare (Zimbabwe).

Special Representative of the UN Secretary-General and Chief of Mission: ALAN DOSS (United Kingdom).

Force Commander: Lt-Gen. BABACAR GAYE (Senegal).

Police Commissioner: SUDESH KUMAR (India).

In August 1999 the UN Security Council authorized the deployment of up to 90 military liaison personnel to support implementation of a cease-fire agreement for the Democratic Republic of the Congo (DRC) which had been signed in Lusaka, Zambia, in July, by the heads of state of the DRC, Angola, Namibia, Rwanda, Uganda and Zimbabwe. The Council approved the establishment of MONUC in late November. The mission was mandated, in co-operation with a Joint Military Commission comprising representatives of the parties to the conflict, to oversee the implementation of the agreement, including monitoring the cease-fire and the disengagement of forces; to facilitate the delivery of humanitarian assistance; and to develop a mine action plan and undertake emergency de-mining activities. In February 2000 the Security Council authorized the expansion of the mission to comprise up to 5,537 military personnel, including up to 500 military observers who were to be dispatched to the DRC to monitor and verify the cease-fire and disengagement of forces. In April a sub-plan on military disengagement and redeployment was agreed in Kampala, Uganda, by the parties to the conflict and, in December, a revised sub-plan was adopted in Harare, Zimbabwe. However, by early 2001 the Lusaka cease-fire accord and Kampala and Harare sub-plans remained to be implemented and only a small contingent of MONUC observers had been deployed in the DRC. In mid-February the Security Council demanded that the parties to the conflict commence the phased disengagement and redeployment of their forces by mid-March and stipulated that plans for the full withdrawal of foreign troops and the disarmament, demobilization and resettlement of militia must be prepared and adopted by mid-May. The resolution raised the maximum number of military observers to 550, to be stationed around four regional headquarters; the deployment of up to 1,900 armed security personnel to protect these bases was also authorized. River boat units were to be deployed to assist with the transportation of observers and supplies and to reinforce the mission's presence; it was hoped that commercial activity along river routes would thus also be supported. Small contingents of MONUC troops were deployed in the DRC from March, including, in the following month, to the strategic rebel-occupied north-eastern town of Kisangani. In June the Security Council approved a revised concept of operations for MONUC, entailing the establishment of a civilian police element, enhancing the mission's presence in Kisangani and strengthening its logistic support capabilities. In October 2002 the UN Secretary-General reported that 90 teams of military observers were stationed at 50 sites in the DRC. Preparations were under way for the implementation of the mission's third phase of operations (authorized at the end of 2001), which was to entail the deployment of a full peace-keeping force to oversee the complete withdrawal of foreign troops from DRC territory and the disarmament, demobilization and reintegration of rebel forces. In December 2002 the UN Security Council authorized the expansion of the mission to co-ordinate this process.

In July 2001 MONUC launched a Quick Impact Projects programme, which focuses on the areas of education; health; environment; agriculture; public infrastructure rehabilitation; income generating activities; and support for vulnerable groups.

Some progress towards the implementation of the Lusaka cease-fire accord was achieved at the Inter-Congolese Dialogue held in Sun City, South Africa, from February–April 2002, when a bilateral power-sharing agreement was concluded between the DRC Government and Mouvement de libération du Congo—MLC rebels supported by the Ugandan Government. In mid-May a failed mutiny attempt by dissident rebels in Kisangani led to an outbreak of violence that resulted in at least 50 civilian fatalities. MONUC conducted patrols of the city and provided protection to a number of individuals who considered their lives to be at risk. Subsequently the Rwandan-backed Rassemblement congolais pour la démocratie (RCD)-Goma rebels controlling Kisangani accused the Special Representative of the Secretary-General of displaying a pro-Government bias and announced that he and several mission personnel were 'banned' from the area occupied by the grouping. A resolution of the Security Council in early June demanded that the RCD-Goma rebels cease their obstruction of the mission's activities in Kisangani immediately.

Following the adoption in July and August 2002, respectively, of the so-called Pretoria agreement between the DRC and Rwandan Governments, and Luanda agreement between the DRC and Ugandan Governments, nearly all Rwandan and Ugandan forces were withdrawn before the end of that year. Meanwhile, troop withdrawals, under MONUC observation, were also initiated by Angola, Burundi, Namibia and Zimbabwe. In December the Security Council adopted a resolution expanding the mission's authorized military strength to 8,700, to consist mainly of two intervention forces, which were to be deployed gradually. During that month the All-Inclusive Agreement on the Transition in the DRC, providing for the eventual staging of elections in the DRC, was signed by the participants in the Inter-Congolese Dialogue, in Pretoria, South Africa.

In response to continuing armed conflict and human rights violations in Bunia, north-eastern DRC, resulting in the deaths of more than 400 civilians in May 2003, a UN-backed temporary Interim Emergency Multinational Force (IEMF) was deployed to stabilize the situation there from June. In July the Security Council adopted a resolution increasing MONUC's authorized strength to 10,800 troops and extending the mission's mandate. The resolution authorized MONUC to take necessary measures to protect civilians and humanitarian workers under imminent threat of physical violence and to protect UN personnel and facilities, and imposed an arms embargo against all DRC and foreign armed groups in the east of the country. MONUC supported the IEMF during mid-2003, prior to resuming full responsibility for maintaining security in Bunia and thus replacing the Force in mid-September. At the end of June a DRC Transitional Government was established, in accordance with the December 2002 All-Inclusive Agreement on the Transition in the DRC. MONUC retained a presence in the capital, Kinshasa, to provide security for the new administration. An electoral assistance unit was created within the mission to support the preparations for the national elections scheduled under the Agreement to take place within two years. In July 2003 the Security Council adopted a resolution imposing an arms embargo on rebel groups and foreign troops operating in the Kivu and Ituri regions of eastern DRC and mandating MONUC to monitor the flow of arms there.

In May 2004 MONUC attempted to negotiate a cease-fire after fighting occurred in Bukavu, eastern DRC, between troops of the transitional government and forces loyal to two dissident military leaders. At the start of June, however, the dissident forces seized control of Bukavu, in order, it was claimed, to prevent further alleged killings of the minority Congolese Tutsi (Banyamulenge) population. Many properties, including UN warehouses, were looted. In other areas of the country there were violent protests against MONUC for failing to intervene in the situation. A few days later the dissident troops withdrew. In mid-June a MONUC team of human rights investigators determined that there was no evidence of any atrocities having been perpetrated against the Banyamulenge. In July thousands more people living in the eastern Lake Kivu district were displaced as a result of further clashes between government and dissident troops. In August a Burundian Hutu rebel group, the National Liberation Forces (FNL), claimed responsibility for the deaths of more than 160 Banyamulenge at a UN refugee camp in Gatumba, Burundi, close to the DRC border. The UN Security Council met in emergency session following the incident, amid concern at the escalation of tensions in the region. MONUC and UN forces in Burundi determined to reinforce security along the border. A Joint Verification Commission was established, in September, by the DRC and Rwandan authorities to address border security issues and to improve bilateral relations, for which MONUC was to serve as its secretariat. In October the Security Council agreed to expand MONUC to some 16,700 troops (although less than the force strength recommended by the UN Secretary-General) in order to reinforce its operational capabilities and avert further deterioration in the stability of the country. The Council also identified new responsibilities for the mission, including the protection of civilians 'under immediate threat of violence', inspection of air cargo in eastern regions to ensure that the ban on arms trading is upheld, and reporting on the presence of foreign troops and relevant troop movements, as well as tasks in support of the consolidation of the Transitional Government. In November MONUC undertook a joint operation with the Congolese army to protect the eastern Walungu area from rebel troops and deployed an additional brigade to North Kivu to provide additional security in the region. At the same time it established a new operations centre to monitor the disarmament of combatants and the retreat of foreign forces. Efforts to stabilize those parts of the country, however, were undermined from late November by reports from the Rwandan Government that it was prepared to attack former rebels living in the DRC who were perceived to be an ongoing threat to Rwandan security. The Security Council urged all states to refrain from any action that affected regional security or contravened international law, and, specifically, demanded the withdrawal of any Rwandan forces from the DRC and the disarmament of any rebel militia. An escalation of inter-factional hostilities in North Kivu province prompted an estimated 30,000 to leave their homes. MONUC troops established a temporary buffer zone in the worst affected areas in order to facilitate the delivery of humanitarian aid. In late February 2005 nine MONUC peace-keeping soldiers were killed during a patrol of a suspected militia camp in the Ituri district. With effect from early April MONUC declared Ituri an 'Arms Free District', prohibiting the possession of weapons.

In July 2005 MONUC initiated a series of operations in South Kivu province to pursue members of the Forces démocratiques pour la liberation du Rwanda (FDLR), who had reportedly been attacking the local civilian population, and to reinforce security in the eastern region of the country. In October MONUC provided military support for a new government operation to dislodge Rwandan Hutu rebels and to restore security, and in November deployed additional troops close to the border with Uganda to deter ongoing attacks in that region. In December the UN Security Council imposed a deadline of 15 January 2006 for foreign combatants in the DRC to disarm. In early January eight MONUC soldiers were killed by suspected Ugandan rebels in Garamba Park, close to the Sudanese border. At that time an estimated 20,000 civilians fled into western Uganda owing to an escalation in hostilities between the national army and rebel troops and several thousand others were also displaced. In February MONUC supported the army in a new operation against Hutu rebels in Ituri district; this was suspended in March, however, to allow for further training and preparation of the Congolese troops. In late May a MONUC soldier was killed by rebel forces in Ituri and five MONUC soldiers were taken hostage; they were released in July. Ongoing fighting in north-eastern provinces between government troops and rebel militias caused several thousand people to leave their homes. Provisional disarmament, demobilization and reintegration agreements were concluded with three Ituri rebel groups during 2006.

In mid-2005, following the adoption in May of a new draft constitution by the transitional National Assembly, MONUC's electoral assistance unit worked with the DRC Independent Electoral Commission to provide voter registration centres, train registration personnel and initiate the voter registration process in advance of a national referendum on the draft constitution that was initially scheduled to be held in November. Voter registration in Kinshasa was concluded at the end of July, and in early September the UN Security Council authorized US $103m. to provide additional logistical support to the nationwide registration process. The Council also approved a temporary increase in the strength of the mission by 841, including additional police personnel and five formed police units each of 125 officers. A temporary expansion in the military strength of the mission, by 300 troops, was approved in October. MONUC provided extensive technical and logistical assistance during the constitutional referendum, which was conducted, peacefully, in December. In 2006 an extensive electoral support operation was undertaken by the mission to prepare for presidential and legislative elections. In March the UN Secretary-General, Kofi Annan, visited the country to promote the democratic process. In April the UN Security Council authorized a temporary redeployment of an infantry battalion and some 50 military observers from the UN mission in Burundi to strengthen MONUC's security and monitoring capabilities in advance of the elections. MONUC reported the voting, conducted in July, to have been successful and largely peaceful; in August, however, there were violent clashes between supporters of the two leading presidential candidates. MONUC undertook to negotiate between both candidates and promoted confidence-building measures, including investigating allegations of electoral violations. A new National Assembly was inaugurated in September. In October MONUC initiated joint patrols, with European and national security forces, in the capital, Kinshasa, to uncover illegally-held firearms prior to the second round of the presidential election scheduled to be held at the end of that month. MONUC condemned violent demonstrations that followed the provisional release of results. The new President, Joseph Kabila, was inaugurated in December. In early 2007 MONUC appealed for an end to the violence that had erupted in the western Bas-Congo province following the release of local election results, and immediately deployed a multi-disciplinary team to enforce order and investigate the unrest in which an estimated 134 people had died. MONUC troops continued to patrol areas in eastern DRC to maintain stability, and undertook negotiations with a local militia leader to surrender and disarm his troops. In March MONUC condemned intense fighting that had occurred in the capital, Kinshasa, between government troops and forces loyal to the defeated former Vice-President, Jean-Pierre Bemba. MONUC aimed to assist civilians affected by the violence and determined to conduct an inquiry into the events. In June MONUC increased its patrols in North and South Kivu Provinces in order to strengthen security against the continuing military activity of armed groups. In August MONUC dispatched some 200 additional troops to Katale, in North Kivu, to help to control an escalation in hostilities there. MONUC troops supported DRC government forces in the capture of a rebel leader in North Kivu in October. During 2008 MONUC was to continue to focus on protecting and providing humanitarian support to civilians in Ituri, North and South Kivu, and Katanga, while also supporting the capacity development of the national police throughout the DRC.

MONUC works closely with the Multi-Country Demobilization and Reintegration Programme, administered by the World Bank, and with UNDP, the lead agency for reintegration in the DRC. By November 2007 165,687 former combatants had been disarmed and, of these, 62,929 had been integrated into the government forces while 102,758 had been demobilized. More than 15,000 foreign rebels had been disarmed and repatriated by that time.

At 31 January 2008 MONUC comprised 16,612 troops, 737 military observers and 1,036 police officers; it is assisted by 924 international staff, 2,088 local civilian personnel and 546 UN Volunteers. The budget for the mission amounted to US $1,115.7m for the period 1 July 2007–30 June 2008, funded from a Special Account comprising assessed contributions from UN member states.

United Nations Observer Mission in Georgia—UNOMIG

Address: Sukhumi, Georgia.

Special Representative of the UN Secretary-General and Head of Mission: JEAN ARNAULT (France).

Chief Military Observer: Maj.-Gen. NIAZ MUHAMMAD KHAN KHATTAK (Pakistan).

UNOMIG was established in August 1993 to verify compliance with a cease-fire agreement, signed in July between the Government of Georgia and the Abkhazian separatist movement. The mission was the UN's first undertaking in the former USSR. In October the UN Secretary-General stated that a breakdown in the cease-fire agreement had invalidated UNOMIG's mandate. He proposed, however, to maintain, for information purposes, the eight-strong UNOMIG team in the city of Sukhumi, which had been seized by Abkhazian forces in late September. In December the Security Council authorized the deployment of additional military observers in response to the signing of a memorandum of understanding by the conflicting parties earlier that month. Further peace negotiations, which were conducted in January–March 1994 under the authority of the UN Secretary-General's Special Envoy, achieved no political consensus. In July the Security Council endorsed the establishment of a Commonwealth of Independent States (CIS) peace-keeping force to verify a cease-fire agreement that had been signed in May. At the same time the Security Council increased UNOMIG's authorized strength and expanded the mission's mandate to incorporate the following tasks: to monitor and verify the implementation of the agreement and to investigate reported violations; to observe the operation of the CIS peace-keeping force; to verify that troops and heavy military equipment remain outside the security zone and the restricted weapons zone; to monitor the storage of the military equipment withdrawn from the restricted zones; to monitor the withdrawal of Georgian troops from the Kodori Gorge region to locations beyond the Abkhazian frontiers; and to patrol regularly the Kodori Gorge. Peace negotiations were pursued in 1995, despite periodic outbreaks of violence in Abkhazia. In October 1996 the UN Security Council established a human rights office as part of UNOMIG. In May 1997 the Security Council endorsed a proposal of the UN Secretary-General to strengthen the political element of UNOMIG in order to enable the mission to assume a more active role in furthering a negotiated settlement. In July direct discussions between representatives of the Georgian and Abkhazian authorities, the first in more than two years, were held under UN auspices. In December a new Abkhaz-Georgian Co-ordinating Council was inaugurated. In early 1998 the security situation in Abkhazia deteriorated. Following an outbreak of violence in May the conflicting parties signed a cease-fire accord, which incorporated an agreement that UNOMIG and CIS forces would continue to work to create a secure environment to allow for the return of displaced persons to the Gali region of Abkhazia. In addition, the UN Security Council urged both parties to establish a protection unit to ensure the safety of UN military observers. In December 2000, following a series of detentions and hostage-takings of mission personnel in the Kodori Gorge during late 1999 and 2000, UNOMIG suspended patrols of that area. Reviewing the operation in January 2001 the UN Secretary-General expressed concern at the recent recurrent abductions and urged the Abkhazian side to cease imposing restrictions on the mission's freedom of movement. A Programme of Action on confidence-building measures was concluded in March; however, the negotiation process was interrupted from April, owing to increasing insecurity in the conflict zone and the ongoing activities of illegal armed groups. In October a UNOMIG helicopter was shot down in the Kodori Gorge, resulting in the deaths of nine people. UNOMIG suspended its patrols of the area. Meetings of the Abkhaz-Georgian Co-ordinating Council were suspended in 2001. In January 2002 a protocol was signed between the conflicting parties providing for the withdrawal of Georgian troops from the upper Kodori valley and the resumption of UN ground patrols. Further discussion on implementation of the protocol resulted in the first joint patrol being conducted in late

March. In April a protocol was concluded by both sides for a final withdrawal of Georgian troops and the resumption of regular UNOMIG/CIS patrols. Renewed diplomatic efforts to secure a political agreement on the future status of Abkhazia initially focused on a paper of Basic Principles for the Distribution of Competences between Tbilisi and Sukhumi, which had been prepared by the Special Representative of the UN Secretary-General. The document was rejected as a basis for negotiations by the Abkhazian leadership; however, discussions were held between the leadership of the two sides to consider measures to stabilize further the situation in the Kodori Gorge. Meeting in Geneva, Switzerland, in February and July 2003 the UN Secretary General's so-called 'Group of Friends on Georgia', comprising France, Germany, Russia, the United Kingdom and the USA, identified co-operation in economic, political and security matters and the return of refugees and internally displaced persons as being of key importance for the advancement of the peace process and therefore also priority focus areas for UNOMIG. From November a new civilian police component of UNOMIG became operational, although objections by certain Abkhaz groups prevented their deployment in the Gali sector. UNOMIG's Engineering Section continued to undertake small-scale reconstruction projects, in particular of roads and bridges, in order to facilitate communications. In October 2003 UNOMIG and the CIS peace-keeping force signed a protocol entailing closer co-operation in combating crime and improving security. In May 2004 the Special Representative chaired a meeting with regard to security guarantees, held in accordance with recommendations of the UN Group of Friends on Georgia and with agreements reached at a previous meeting convened in February. No further substantive dialogue was held during the year, although in December the UN hosted a high-level meeting of the Group of Friends which reviewed the main challenges and determined to meet both sides in order to consider the resumption of negotiations. Georgian and Abkhazian representatives participated in a meeting of the Group of Friends held in April 2005, and, in the following month, a meeting on security issues that was organized by the Secretary-General's Special Representative and attended by representatives of the two sides and of UNOMIG and the CIS peace-keeping mission, adopted a protocol aimed at strengthening the implementation of the cease-fire agreement signed in May 1994 and other security commitments. In July 2005 UNOMIG hosted a high-level meeting on security aspects of the proposed rehabilitation of the Sochi–Tbilisi railway. In August, at a meeting chaired by the Special Representative, both sides renewed their commitment to a peaceful settlement of the conflict and for a safe return of all refugees and internally displaced persons. Efforts to formulate joint documents on the non-use of force and the return of all displaced persons were to be pursued through the good offices of the Special Representative. In early 2006 UNOMIG, acting under its humanitarian mandate, initiated a project with the European Commission and UNDP to rehabilitate electricity, public health facilities and agriculture in four districts. On 1 March the mission inaugurated a free bus service connecting the Georgian and Abkhazian sides across the Inguri river bridge. During May meetings of the Co-ordinating Council, inaugurated in 1997 and suspended in 2001, were resumed.

Abkhaz–Georgian relations deteriorated in July 2006, following the adoption by the Georgian legislature of a resolution urging the suspension and withdrawal of the CIS peace-keeping mission from Georgian territory. In late July a Georgian special military operation aimed at restoring law and order in the upper Kodori valley, in contravention of the May 1994 cease-fire agreement, raised tensions further. Consequently, UNOMIG established two temporary observation points to monitor movements in the upper Kodori valley area. UNOMIG resumed patrolling the area in December 2006. In October the UN Security Council adopted a resolution which urged both sides to honour all previous agreements concluded regarding non-violence and confidence-building measures and emphasized the importance of effective co-operation between UNOMIG and the CIS mission. In January 2007 UNOMIG increased its maritime patrols, following allegations by the Abkhaz regime of provocative Georgian activities in Abkhazian coastal waters. In early March UNOMIG sent a fact-finding team to investigate an exchange of firebetween Abkhaz militia and Georgian security forces near the Inguri river bridge, arising from an unofficial Georgian protest demonstration against the staging in February and March by the Abkhaz regime of local and parliamentary elections. (The polls were declared illegitimate by several international organizations, including the European Union, NATO and the OSCE, and were not observed by UNOMIG.) In mid-March the Georgian Government informed UNOMIG that two villages in the upper Kodori valley had come under aerial attack. Allegations by the Georgian Government of Russian involvement were refuted by the Abkhaz and Russian authorities. An UNOMIG-led quadripartite joint fact-finding group, comprising UNOMIG, the CIS mission and representatives of the Abkhaz and Georgian sides, was subsequently appointed to investigate the incident. At a meeting in late June of senior representatives of the UN Group of Friends and representatives of the Abkhaz and Georgian sides, convened under the chairmanship of the UN Under-Secretary-General for Peace-keeping Operations, in Bonn, Germany, the two sides determined to advance their dialogue on security matters and to co-operate in implementing humanitarian initiatives, including the European Commission/UNDP-sponsored rehabilitation project initiated in 2006. In October 2007 UNOMIG facilitated a meeting between the Georgian minister on conflict resolution and the Abkhaz de facto minister for foreign affairs. The two sides reached a preliminary understanding on convening meetings on security issues. The Georgian ministers also agreed to release seven Abkhaz prisoners, who had been detained during an armed clash between both sides, outside of the conflict zone, in September. The men were handed over later in that month under UNOMIG observation.

At 31 January 2008 UNOMIG comprised 131 military observers and 18 civilian police; at 31 December 2008 it was supported by 281 international and local civilian personnel and one UN Volunteer. The General Assembly budget appropriation to the Special Account for the mission amounted to US $35.0m. for the period 1 July 2007–30 June 2008.

United Nations Operation in Côte d'Ivoire—UNOCI

Address: Abidjan, Côte d'Ivoire.

Special Representative of the Secretary-General and Head of Mission: CHOI YOUNG-JIN (Republic of Korea).

Force Commander: Maj.-Gen. FERNAND MARCEL AMOUSSOU (Benin).

UNOCI was authorized by the UN Security Council in February 2004 and began operations in early April. It was mandated to observe and monitor the implementation of the Linas-Marcoussis Agreement, signed by the parties to the conflict in Côte d'Ivoire in January 2003, and hitherto supported by the UN Mission in Côte d'Ivoire (MINUCI), forces of the Economic Community of West African States—ECOWAS and French peace-keeping troops. UNOCI was authorized also to assist with the disarmament, demobilization and reintegration of rebel groups, to protect civilians and UN personnel, institutions and equipment, and to support ongoing humanitarian and human rights activities. With a contingent of the French 'Licorne' peace-keeping force, UNOCI was to monitor a so-called Zone of Confidence separating the two areas of the country under government and rebel control. In July all parties, attending a meeting of West African heads of state that had been convened by the UN Secretary-General and the President of Ghana, endorsed the Accra III Agreement identifying means of implementing the Linas-Marcoussis Accord. UNOCI was to participate in a tripartite monitoring group, together with ECOWAS and the African Union, to oversee progress in implementing the agreement. In mid-August UNOCI launched a radio station, in accordance with its mandate, to assist the process of national reunification and in the following month established some secure transit routes between the areas under government and rebel control in order to facilitate travel and enable family reunions. None the less, by October UNOCI officials expressed concern at ongoing violations of human rights and a deterioration in security, as well as a lack of progress in implementing provisions of the peace accords.

In early November 2004 government troops violated the cease-fire and the Zone of Confidence by launching attacks against rebel Forces Nouvelles in the north of the country. An emergency session of the UN Security Council, convened following an escalation of the hostilities and a fatal air strike on a French peace-keeping unit, urged both sides to refrain from further violence. Security further deteriorated in the south of the country when French troops destroyed the government air force prompting rioting in the capital, Abidjan, and violence directed towards foreign nationals. UNOCI assisted with the evacuation of foreign workers and their families and provided secure refuge for other personnel. In mid-November the Security Council imposed an immediate embargo on the sale or supply of armaments to Côte d'Ivoire and demanded a cessation of hostilities and of the use of media broadcasts to incite hatred and violence against foreigners. UNOCI was to monitor the terms of the resolution and to broadcast its own messages of support for the peace process. By the end of that month reports indicated that the security situation had improved and that some of the estimated 19,000 who fled the country to Liberia had started to return. In addition, conditions in the northern city of Bouaké were improving as water and electricity supplies were restored. In December UNOCI funded three Quick Impact Projects, in order to highlight the humanitarian aspect of the mission, and commenced joint patrols with government forces to uphold security in Abidjan.

In February 2005 the UN Security Council demanded that all parties co-operate with UNOCI in compiling a comprehensive list of armaments under their control as preparation for implementing a programme of disarmament, demobilization and reintegration. In March UNOCI increased its presence in western regions of the country owing to an increase in reported violent incidents. In the following month UNOCI troops were deployed to the border regions with Liberia and Ghana in order to support implementation of the UN-imposed arms embargo. UNOCI troops also monitored the withdrawal of heavy weaponry by both Government forces and the Forces Nouvelles. In June UN representatives condemned the massacre of almost 60 civilians in Duékoué, in the west of the country, and urged that an inquiry be held into the incident. UNOCI reinforcements were sent to restore stability in the area and undertook joint patrols with local forces. Later in that month the UN Security Council authorized an increase in UNOCI's military and civilian police components, as well as the redeployment of troops from other missions in the region in order to restore security in the country. In July UN troops, investigating reports of violent attacks by rebel groups, were prevented from entering two towns north of Abidjan. UNOCI later complained at further reported obstruction of human rights and civilian police teams. In spite of persisting concerns regarding the political and human rights situation in the country, UNOCI continued to provide logistical and technical assistance to the independent national electoral commission in preparations for elections, scheduled to be held in October; however, these were later postponed. A transitional government of national unity was formed in late December. In early 2006 UN property and personnel were subjected to hostile attacks during a period of unrest by groups protesting against a report of an International Working Group, co-chaired by the Special Representative of the UN Secretary-General, that had recommended the dissolution of the national assembly (the mandate of which had already expired). Several hundred humanitarian personnel were evacuated from the country. In the following month the Security Council imposed 12-month sanctions and travel bans against three leaders deemed to be responsible for directing the disturbances. In January the Council agreed to review UNOCI's authorized strength, but did not authorize a recommendation of the Secretary-General to expand the mission by an additional 3,400 troops and 475 police officers. At the end of February UNOCI initiated a large-scale operation to provide security for school examinations, to be held in the north of the country for the first time in three years. In June the Security Council authorized an increase in the mission's force strength by 1,025 military personnel and 475 police officers needed to strengthen security throughout the country and undertake disarmament operations. In October UNOCI conducted joint border patrols with UN forces in Liberia to monitor movements of combatants and weapons. In January 2007 the Security Council formally enlarged UNOCI's mandate to co-ordinate with UNMIL to monitor the arms embargo and to conduct a voluntary repatriation and resettlement programme for foreign ex-combatants. The Council's resolution also defined UNOCI's mandate as being to monitor the cessation of hostilities and movements of armed groups; to assist programmes for the disarmament, demobilization and reintegration of all combatants; to disarm and dismantle militias; to support population identification and voter registration programmes; to assist the reform of the security sector and other activities to uphold law and order; to support humanitarian assistance and the promotion of human rights; and to provide technical support for the conduct of free and fair elections no later than 31 October. A new political agreement to work towards national reconciliation was signed by leaders of the opposing parties in Ouagadougou, Burkina Faso, in March. According to the agreement the Zone of Confidence was to be dismantled and replaced by a UN-monitored 'green line'. UNOCI organized a series of meetings to ensure the support of traditional leaders for the peace process. In June UNOCI condemned a rocket attack on a plane carrying the country's Prime Minister. The process of disarmament was officially launched on 30 July; it was, however, hindered by the absence of an agreement on arrangements for the reintegration of former militia members. The redeployment of UNOCI troops from the former Zone of Confidence was ongoing in early 2008.

At 31 January 2008 UNOCI had an operational strength of 7,840 troops, 187 military observers and 1,111 police officers, supported by 407 international and 573 local civilian personnel and 285 UN Volunteers. The General Assembly appropriated US $470.8m. to finance the mission during the period 1 July 2007–30 June 2008.

United Nations Peace-keeping Force in Cyprus—UNFICYP

Address: Nicosia, Cyprus.
Special Representative of the UN Secretary-General and Chief of Mission: MICHAEL MØLLER (Denmark).
Force Commander: Maj.-Gen. RAFAEL JOSÉ BARNI (Argentina).

UNFICYP was established in March 1964 by a UN Security Council resolution (initially for a three-month duration) to prevent a recurrence of fighting between the Greek and Turkish Cypriot communities, and to contribute to the maintenance of law and order and a return to normal conditions. The Force controls a 180-km buffer zone, established (following the Turkish intervention in 1974) between the cease-fire lines of the Turkish forces and the Cyprus National Guard. It is mandated to investigate and act upon all violations of the cease-fire and buffer zone. The Force also performs humanitarian functions, such as facilitating the supply of electricity and water across the cease-fire lines, and offering emergency medical services. In August 1996 serious hostilities between elements of the two communities in the UN-controlled buffer zone resulted in the deaths of two people and injuries to many others, including 12 UN personnel. Following further intercommunal violence, UNFICYP advocated the prohibition of all weapons and military posts along the length of the buffer zone. The Force also proposed additional humanitarian measures to improve the conditions of minority groups living in the two parts of the island. In July 1997 a series of direct negotiations between the leaders of the two communities was initiated, in the presence of the UN Secretary-General's Special Adviser; however, the talks were suspended at the end of that year. In November 1999 the Greek Cypriot and Turkish Cypriot leaders agreed to participate in proximity negotiations, to be mediated by the UN. Consequently, five rounds of these took place during the period December 1999–November 2000. In January 2002 a new series of direct talks between the leaders of the two communities commenced, under the auspices of the Secretary-General's Special Adviser. In May the Secretary-General visited Cyprus and met the two leaders. Further meetings between the Secretary-General and the two leaders took place in September (in Paris) and October (New York). In November he submitted to them for consideration a document providing the basis for a comprehensive settlement agreement; a revised version of the document was released in the following month. A further revised version of the draft settlement plan document was presented to the leaders of the two communities during a visit by the Secretary-General to Cyprus in late February 2003. He urged that both sides put this to separate simultaneous referendums at the end of March, in the hope that, were the settlement plan approved, Cyprus would be able to accede to the European Union (EU) in a reunited state on 1 May 2004. Progress stalled, however, at a meeting between the two sides held in early March 2003 in The Hague, Netherlands. In April the Security Council adopted a resolution calling upon both parties to continue to work towards a settlement using the Secretary-General's plan as the unique basis for future negotiations. In reports to the Security Council the UN Secretary-General has consistently recognized UNFICYP as being indispensable to maintaining calm on the island and to creating the best conditions for his good offices. In November 2003 he noted that a number of restrictions placed on UNFICYP's activities during 2000 by the Turkish Cypriot authorities and Turkish forces remained in place. In February 2004 the Greek Cypriot and Turkish Cypriot leaders committed themselves to the Secretary-General's settlement plan. Negotiations on settling outstanding differences were chaired by the Secretary-General's Special Adviser for Cyprus throughout March. Despite a lack of agreement when the two sides met with the Secretary-General in late March, a finalized text was presented at the end of that month. The proposed Foundation Agreement was subsequently put to referendums in both sectors in April when it was approved by two-thirds of Turkish Cypriot voters, but rejected by some 75% of Greek Cypriot voters. In June the Secretary-General determined to undertake a comprehensive review of UNFICYP's mandate and force levels, in view of the political developments on the island, and announced his decision not to resume his good offices. In October the Security Council endorsed the recommendations of the Secretary-General's review team, which included a reduction in the mission's authorized strength from 1,230 to 860 military personnel, to include 40 military observers and liaison officers, and an increase in the deployment of civilian police officers from 44 to 69. In November UNFICYP troops initiated an EU-funded project to remove anti-personnel landmines from the buffer zone separating the two communities. A second phase of the project was launched in August 2005 and completed in November 2006.

In July 2006 the Turkish Cypriot leader and the Greek Cypriot President met, in the presence of the Special Representative of the UN's Under-Secretary-General for Political Affairs. The leadesr agreed on a set of principles and decisions aimed at reinstating the negotiating process. In early 2007 UNFICYP conducted an intercommunal survey of public opinion on the presence of the UN in the country. In September UNFICYP hosted a second meeting of the leaders of the two communities. They agreed on a need to initiate a settlement process and confirmed that they would continue a bi-communal dialogue under UN auspices. A new Greek Cypriot President was elected in February 2008. In the following month the Special Representative of the UN Secretary-General convened a meeting of the two leaders, who agreed to the establishment of technical committees and working groups in preparation for detailed political negotiations.

At 31 January 2008 UNFICYP had an operational strength of 859 troops and 66 civilian police officers; at 31 December 2007 it was supported by 143 international and local civilian staff. The General

Assembly appropriated US $48.06m. to the Special Account for UNFICYP to finance the period 1 July 2007–30 June 2008, of which one-third was to be funded by voluntary contributions from the Government of Cyprus and $6.5m. to be donated by the Government of Greece.

United Nations Stabilization Mission in Haiti—MINUSTAH

Address: Port-au-Prince, Haiti.

Special Representative of the UN Secretary-General: HÉDI ANNABI (Tunisia).

Principal Deputy Special Representative of the UN Secretary-General: LUIZ CARLOS DA COSTA (Brazil).

Force Commander: Maj.-Gen. CARLOS ALBERTO DOS SANTOS CRUZ (Brazil).

In early 2004 political tensions within Haiti escalated as opposition groups demanded political reforms and the resignation of President Jean-Bertrand Aristide. Increasingly violent public demonstrations took place throughout the country, in spite of diplomatic efforts by regional organizations to resolve the crisis, and in February armed opposition forces seized control of several northern cities. At the end of that month, with opposition troops poised to march on the capital and growing pressure from the international community, President Aristide tendered his resignation and fled the country. On that same day the UN Security Council, acting upon a request by the interim President, authorized the establishment of a Multinational Interim Force (MIF) to help to secure law and order in Haiti. The Council also declared its readiness to establish a follow-on UN mission. In late April the Security Council agreed to establish MINUSTAH, which was to assume authority from the MIF with effect from 1 June. MINUSTAH was mandated to create a stable and secure environment, to support the transitional government in institutional development and organizing and monitoring elections, and to monitor the human rights situation. Among its declared objectives was the improvement of living conditions of the population through security measures, humanitarian actions and economic development. In September MINUSTAH worked closely with other UN agencies and non-governmental organizations to distribute food and other essential services to thousands of people affected by a severe tropical storm. By the end of 2004 MINUSTAH's priority continued to be the security situation in the country. The following civil units were also fully operational: electoral assistance; child protection; gender; civil affairs; human rights; and HIV/AIDS. In January 2005 MINUSTAH, with the UN Development Programme, the Haitian Government and the Provisional Electoral Council, signed an agreement on the organization of local, parliamentary and presidential elections, to be held later in that year. In May the UN Secretary-General expressed concern at the security environment with respect to achieving political transition. In the following month the Security Council approved a temporary reinforcement of MINUSTAH to provide increased security in advance of the elections. The military component was to comprise up to 7,500 troops (an additional strength of 750 troops) and the civilian police force up to 1,897 officers. The Council requested that the Secretary-General devise a strategy for the progressive reduction of MINUSTAH force levels in the post-election period. From mid-2005 MINUSTAH forces worked to improve security in the country, in particular to reduce the criminal activities of armed groups in poorer urban areas. In November MINUSTAH deployed experts to train electoral agents and supervisors; however, the electoral timetable was delayed. Presidential and legislative elections were conducted in early February 2006. MINUSTAH officers provided security during the voting and maintained order as the results were being clarified. The mission subsequently pledged to support a post-election process of national dialogue and reconciliation and measures to strengthen the country's police force in order to re-establish law and order in areas of the capital, Port-au-Prince. A second round of voting in the legislative election was conducted in April. In August the UN Security Council, in extending MINUSTAH's mandate, determined that the mission strengthen its role in preventing crime and reducing community violence, in particular kidnappings and other activities by local armed groups. In February 2007 MINUSTAH launched a large-scale operation in part of the Cité Soleil quarter of the capital, Port-au-Prince, to extend its security presence in the most vulnerable locations and to counter the activities of criminal gangs. At the same time UN personnel helped to rehabilitate education, youth and medical facilities in those areas. In April MINUSTAH provided security and logistical support during the conduct of local municipal and mayoral elections. By November an estimated 9,000 local police officers had graduated from MINUSTAH training institutes. Efforts to control gang violence and uphold security in the poorest urban areas were ongoing in 2007/08. In February 2008 MINUSTAH announced that it was to fund six local infrastructure improvement projects to generate temporary employment for 7,000 people in the Cité Soleil and Martissant districts of Port-au-Prince.

At 31 January 2008 MINUSTAH comprised 7,066 troops and 1,927 civilian police; there is a support team of 498 international civilian staff, 1,140 local civilian staff and 197 UN Volunteers (as at 31 December 2007). The mission is financed by assessments in respect of a Special Account. The approved budget for the period 1 July 2007–30 June 2008 amounted to US $535.4m.

United Nations Truce Supervision Organization—UNTSO

Address: Government House, Jerusalem.

Chief-of-Staff: Maj.-Gen. IAN CAMPBELL GORDON (Australia).

UNTSO was established initially to supervise the truce called by the UN Security Council in Palestine in May 1948 and has assisted in the application of the 1949 Armistice Agreements. Its activities have evolved over the years, in response to developments in the Middle East and in accordance with the relevant resolutions of the Security Council. There is no periodic renewal procedure for UNTSO's mandate.

UNTSO observers assist UN peace-keeping forces in the Middle East, at present UNIFIL and UNDOF. The mission maintains offices in Beirut, Lebanon and Damascus, Syria. In addition, UNTSO operates a number of outposts in the Sinai region of Egypt to maintain a UN presence there. UNTSO observers have been available at short notice to form the nucleus of new peace-keeping operations.

In late July 2006 the UN Secretary-General strongly condemned the killing by Israeli fire of four members of UNTSO who had been supporting the UN Interim Force in Lebanon (UNIFIL) during the full-scale conflict that erupted in that month between the Israeli armed forces and Hezbollah.

The operational strength of UNTSO at 31 January 2008 was 153 military observers; it is supported by 226 international and local civilian staff. UNTSO expenditures are covered by the regular budget of the United Nations. The appropriation for the two year period 2006–07 was US $62.27m.

United Nations Peace-building

Address: Department of Political Affairs, United Nations, New York, NY 10017, USA.
Telephone: (212) 963-1234; **fax:** (212) 963-4879; **internet:** www.un.org/Depts/dpa/.

The Department of Political Affairs provides support and guidance to UN peace-building operations and political missions working in the field to prevent and resolve conflicts or to promote enduring peace in post-conflict societies. The UN Assistance Mission in Afghanistan, UN Integrated Office in Sierra Leone and UN Integrated Office in Burundi are directed by the Department of Peace-keeping Operations.

The World Summit of UN heads of state held in September 2005 approved recommendations made by the UN Secretary-General in his March 2005 report entitled 'In Larger Freedom: Towards Development, Security and Human Rights for All' for the creation of an intergovernmental advisory Peace-building Commission. In December the UN Security Council and General Assembly authorized the establishment of the Commission; it was inaugurated, as a special subsidiary body of both the Council and Assembly, in June 2006. A multi-year standing peace-building fund, financed by voluntary contributions from member states and mandated to support post-conflict peace-building activities, was established in October 2006. A Peace-building Support Office was established within the UN Secretariat to administer the fund, as well as to support the Commission. In early 2008 the Peace-building Commission was actively concerned with the situation in three African countries: Burundi, Liberia, and Guinea-Bissau.

Office of the Special Representative of the UN Secretary-General for West Africa—UNOWA

Address: BP 23851 Dakar-Ponty, 5 ave Carde, Immeuble Caisse de sécurité sociale, Dakar, Senegal.
Telephone: (221) 849-07-29; **fax:** (221) 842-50-95; **internet:** www.un.org/unowa.
Special Representative of the UN Secretary-General: LAMINE CISSÉ (Senegal).

UNOWA was established, with an initial three-year mandate, from January 2002, to elaborate an integrated approach by the United Nations to the prevention and management of conflict in West Africa; and to promote peace, security and development in the sub-region. (UNOWA's mandate has subsequently been renewed, most recently for a further three years until December 2010.) In pursuit of these objectives the Special Representative of the Secretary-General (SRSG) meets regularly with the leaders of UN regional and political offices in West Africa. UNOWA projects have included an initiative to address cross-border challenges, such as mercenaries, child-soldiers and small arms proliferation. UNOWA was also involved in monitoring the crisis in Côte d'Ivoire. UNOWA takes part in a joint work programme with the Economic Community of West African States (ECOWAS), whose projects embrace security-sector reform—identified as a key priority for the sub-region—small arms, transborder co-operation, etc. A trilateral partnership between UNOWA, the European Union and ECOWAS has also been established. UNOWA is involved too in the development of a regional harmonized approach to disarmament, demobilization and reintegration in West Africa. UNOWA has launched an initiative to address economic, political, security and humanitarian problems that confront in particular the populations of certain border areas in West Africa. Integrated, multi-agency strategies are to be developed in respect of four border clusters: Guinea/Côte d'Ivoire/Liberia/Sierra Leone (Guinea Forestière); Mali/Burkina Faso/Côte d'Ivoire/Ghana; Mauritania/Mali/Niger; and Senegal/The Gambia/Guinea-Bissau. UNOWA conducts regional good offices missions. One of its major concerns is to help minimize instability arising from elections or the transfer of power. The SRSG serves additionally as chairman of the Cameroon-Nigeria Mixed Commission, which has met regularly since December 2002.

At 30 November 2007 UNOWA comprised six international civilian and nine local civilian personnel.

Office of the United Nations Special Co-ordinator for Lebanon—UNSCOL

Address: UN House, Riad es-Solh Sq., POB 11, 8577 Beirut, Lebanon.
Special Co-ordinator for Lebanon: GEIR O. PEDERSEN (Norway).

The Office of the United Nations Special Co-ordinator for Lebanon was established in February 2007, replacing the Office of the Personal Representative of the UN Secretary-General for southern Lebanon (established in August 2000). The Office co-ordinates the UN presence in Lebanon and works closely with the expanded UN peacekeeping mission in Lebanon, UNIFIL.

At 30 November 2007 UNSCO comprised 12 international civilian and 13 local civilian personnel.

Office of the United Nations Special Co-ordinator for the Middle East Peace Process—UNSCO

Address: Gaza, Jerusalem, Ramallah.
Special Co-ordinator for the Middle East Peace Process: ROBERT R. SERRY (Netherlands).

The Office of the United Nations Special Co-ordinator for the Middle East (UNSCO) was established in June 1994 after the conclusion of the Declaration of Principles on Interim (Palestinian) Self-Government Arrangements—the 'Oslo Accord'. UNSCO was to seek, during the transition process envisaged by the Declaration, to ensure 'an adequate response to the needs of the Palestinian people and to mobilise financial, technical, economic and other assistance'. In 1995 UNSCO's mandate was reconfigured as the Office of the Special Co-ordinator for the Middle East Peace Process and Personal Representative of the Secretary-General to the Palestine Liberation Organization and the Palestine (National) Authority (PA). The Office has been mandated to assist in all issues related to the humanitarian situation facing the Palestinian people, and supports negotiations and the implementation of political agreements. The Regional Affairs Unit (RAU) of the Office assists in the fulfilment of that part of the Office's mandate that requires it to co-ordinate its work and to co-operate closely with all of the parties to the Middle East peace process, including the governments of Israel, Lebanon, Syria, Jordan and Egypt, the PA, Palestinian civil society, the Arab League and individual Arab states that have assumed a key role in facilitating the peace process. The Special Co-ordinator also collaborates closely with key international actors, in particular those which, together with the United Nations, constitute the Middle East Quartet, i.e. the European Union, Russia and the USA, and serves as the Envoy of the UN Secretary-General to the Quartet. In addition to the RAU, UNSCO maintains a Media Office and a Research Unit.

At 30 November 2007 UNSCO comprised 25 international civilian and 26 local civilian personnel.

United Nations Assistance Mission in Afghanistan—UNAMA

Address: POB 5858, Grand Central Station, New York, NY 10163-5858, USA.
Telephone: (813) 246000; **fax:** (831) 246069; **e-mail:** spokesperson-unama@un.org; **internet:** www.unama-afg.org.
Special Representative of the UN Secretary-General: KAI EIDE (Norway).

The United Nations Assistance Mission in Afghanistan (UNAMA) was established by the UN Security Council in March 2002. UNAMA's mandate has subsequently been renewed annually. The Mission was initially authorized to fulfil tasks assigned to the UN under the December 2001 Bonn Agreement on provisional arrangements for Afghanistan. Following the termination in September 2005 of the process determined by the Bonn Agreement, and the adoption of the Afghanistan Compact by the London Conference on Afghanistan, co-chaired by the UN and Afghanistan from 31 January–1 February 2006, UNAMA is responsible for assisting Afghanistan's Government with the implementation of the Afghanistan Compact. The Compact represents a framework for co-operation between the Afghan authorities, the UN and the international community until end-2010. The Compact identifies three key and interdependent pillars of activity for its term: security; governance, rule of law and human rights; and economic and social development. In addition, the Compact will also focus on the elimination of Afghanistan's narcotics industry. The Mission is also mandated to provide political and strategic advice for the peace process; provide good offices; promote human rights; provide technical assistance; and, in co-operation with the Afghan authorities, to manage all UN humanitarian relief, recovery, reconstruction and development activities. Peace-building tasks that fall under UNAMA's political mandate include the prevention and resolution of conflicts; building confidence and the promotion of national reconciliation; monitoring the political and human rights situation; and investigating human rights violations. As appropriate, UNAMA is charged with recommending corrective actions; maintaining dialogue with Afghan leaders, political parties, civil society groups, institutions and representatives of the central authorities; and undertaking good offices to foster the peace process. The implementation of the Bonn Agreement during the transitional period included the following institutional measures: emergency Loya Jirga (2002); constitutional Loya Jirga (2004); presidential elections (2004); legislative elections (2005). Nineteen UN agencies work together with their Afghan government counterparts and with national and international NGO partners. UNAMA co-ordinates all of the activities of the UN system, whose programme of work is determined by Afghan needs and priorities.

At 30 November 2007 UNAMA comprised 217 international civilian and 1,027 local civilian personnel, 15 military observers, three civilian police and 31 UN Volunteers. In time, as part of its pursuit of strong, sustainable Afghan institutions, UNAMA aims to appoint Afghan nationals to posts that have traditionally been occupied by expatriates.

United Nations Assistance Mission for Iraq—UNAMI

Address: Amman, Jordan.
Telephone: (6) 5504700; **fax:** (6) 5504705; **e-mail:** jarrar@un.org; **internet:** www.uniraq.org.
Special Representative of the UN Secretary-General for Iraq: STAFFAN DE MISTURA (Sweden).

The United Nations Assistance Mission for Iraq (UNAMI) was initially established by UN Security Council Resolution 1500 (14 August 2003) as a one-year mission to co-ordinate and support humanitarian efforts in post-conflict Iraq. Later in August, however, terrorist attacks on the UNAMI headquarters in Baghdad killed the newly appointed Special Representative of the UN Secretary-General for Iraq (and UN High Commissioner for Human Rights), Sergio Vieira de Mello, and 21 other UN personnel. UN international staff were subsequently withdrawn from Iraq and, until the formation of the Iraqi Interim Government at the end of June 2004, UNAMI operated primarily from outside Iraq (from Cyprus, Jordan and Kuwait). Meanwhile, political and security concerns were urgently reviewed by the UN Secretary-General. UNAMI consists of two pillars—political and reconstruction and development—and a Human Rights Office (HRO) which maintains links with the Office of the Higher Commissioner for Human Rights. Generally, the work of the political pillar is carried out in support of the good offices and facilitation role of the Special Representative of the Secretary-General (SRSG). The political office also supports, as necessary, the HRO and the reconstruction and development pillar. In April–May 2004 the UN helped to establish the Independent Electoral Commission of Iraq (IECI). In accordance with the mandate accorded to it under UN Security Council Resolution 1546 (June 2004), UNAMI assisted in the convening of an Iraqi national conference in August, including in the selection of a Consultative Council. In January 2005 elections were held in Iraq to choose a Transitional National Assembly that would be charged with drafting a permanent constitution. These elections also formed the basis for the establishment of a Transitional Government and presidency. UNAMI's electoral unit assisted and advised the IECI, which was responsible for the organization and conduct of these elections. From May until 15 October 2005, in response to requests for assistance from the Transitional Government, UNAMI provided support and advice to the constitution-making process.

UNAMI endorsed the International Compact for Iraq, a five-year framework for co-operation between Iraq and the international community jointly chaired by the Iraqi Government and the UN Secretariat, that was launched in May 2007. In August the UN Security Council expanded UNAMI's mandate, incorporating a responsibility to promote, support and facilitate the implementation of the International Compact, as well as the co-ordination and delivery of humanitarian assistance, and to support and advise on national reconciliation efforts.

With regard to reconstruction and development, the work of UNAMI is organized into seven 'clusters': agriculture, food security, environment and natural resources management; education and culture; governance and human development; health and nutrition; infrastructure rehabilitation; refugees, internally displaced persons and durable solutions; and support to the electoral process. UNAMI's objectives in respect of these include: to address the long-term challenge of achieving sustainable food security; to strengthen the overall quality of education and service delivery at all levels; to support policy development, and preserve and conserve the tangible and intangible Iraqi cultural heritage; to improve the human development situation in Iraq and promote good governance by strengthening institutional capacity, contributing to the creation of employment opportunities and providing policy advice; to support the national health strategy of the Iraqi Ministry of Health in meeting basic health needs; to formulate and implement programmes on institutional/policy reform, capacity-building, and service provision necessary to rehabilitate and develop the infrastructure of human settlements; to support the Iraqi authorities in providing adequate assistance and effective protection to uprooted populations in Iraq, and to assist them in preventing new displacement as well as in achieving durable solutions; and to provide technical support and capacity-building to the IECI.

UNAMI is mandated, under Resolution 1546, 'to promote the protection of human rights, national reconciliation, and judicial and legal reform in order to strengthen the rule of law in Iraq'. Through two units the HRO monitors and reports on the human rights situation and addresses the reconstruction of Iraqi national human rights institutions. HRO activities, accomplished, proceeding or planned, include providing technical support to the ministries of justice and human rights; the establishment of a national centre for missing and disappeared person in Iraq; and the establishment of a national human rights institution.

At 30 November 2007 UNAMI personnel (based in Iraq, Jordan and Kuwait) comprised 276 international civilian and 351 local civilian staff. There were, in addition, 223 troops and seven military observers.

United Nations Integrated Office in Burundi—BINUB

Address: Bujumbura, Burundi.
Executive Representative of the Secretary-General: YOUSSEF MAHMOUD (Tunisia).

The United Nations Integrated Office in Burundi (Bureau Intégré des Nations Unies au Burundi—BINUB) was established on 1 January 2007, replacing the United Nations Operation in Burundi, which was terminated in December 2006. BINUB is mandated to support the Burundi Government in its efforts to achieve long-term peace and security, with a particular focus on strengthening the conflict-prevention capacities of national institutions and civil society; supporting public institutions with strengthening good governance and accountability; promoting freedom of the press; consolidating the rule of law; supporting the Dar-es-Salaam Comprehensive Cease-fire Agreement concluded in September 2006; supporting the development of a national plan for reform of the security sector; supporting the completion of the ongoing national programme for the demobilization and reintegration of former combatants; supporting efforts to combat the proliferation of small arms; promoting human rights; assisting with the establishment of transitional justice mechanisms, including a truth and reconciliation commission; strengthening the partnership and co-ordination between the Government and international donors; and ensuring effective co-ordination among UN agencies in Burundi. A Government of National Unity was established in November 2007. In the following month the UN Security Council extended BINUB's mandate until 31 December 2008.

At 30 November 2007 BINUB comprised 116 international civilian and 217 local civilian personnel, as well as eight military observers, 12 police and 46 UN Volunteers. A budget of US $33.1m. was approved for the Office in 2007.

United Nations Integrated Office in Sierra Leone—UNIOSIL

Address: Freetown, Sierra Leone.
Officer-in-Charge: GEBREMEDHIN HAGOSS (Ethiopia).

The United Nations Integrated Office in Sierra Leone (UNIOSIL) was established on 1 January 2006 in accordance with UN Security Council Resolution 1620 (31 August 2005). UNIOSIL is the successor mission to the large UN peace-keeping operation in Sierra Leone, UNAMSIL, whose mandate was completed in December 2005. The key elements of UNIOSIL's mandate, as set out, with an initial term of one year, in Resolution 1620, are that it should assist the government of Sierra Leone: to build the capacity of national institutions to tackle the root causes of the country's conflict, supply basic services and hasten progress towards attainment of the Millennium Developments Goals through poverty reduction and sustainable economic growth; to develop a national action plan for human rights and establishing the national human rights commission; to build the capacity of the National Electoral Commission to conduct, free, fair and credible legislative elections in 2007; to enhance good governance; to strengthen the rule of law; to strengthen the Sierra Leonean security sector; and to promote a culture of peace, dialogue and participation in critical national issues. UNIOSIL is further mandated to liaise with the Sierra Leonean security sector and other partners; to co-ordinate with UN missions and offices and regional organizations in West Africa in tackling cross-border challenges; and to co-ordinate with the Special Court for Sierra Leone. The head of UNIOSIL, the Executive Representative of the Secretary-General, also serves as the Resident Representative of the UN Development Programme and as the UN Resident and Humanitarian Co-ordinator. UNIOSIL comprises five sections that focus respectively on the key areas of its mandate: good governance and peace consolidation; human rights and the rule of law; civilian police and military assistance; development; and public information. Parliamentary and presidential elections were successfully conducted in August/September 2007. In December the UN's Peace-building Commission signed a co-operation framework agreement with the Sierra Leone government further to consolidate security in the country. Later in that month the UN Security Council approved an extension of UNIOSIL's mandate for a final period until 30 September 2008.

At 30 November 2007 UNIOSIL comprised 75 international and 199 local personnel, assisted by 23 UN Volunteers. There were, in addition, 14 military observers and 21 police officers.

United Nations Mission in Nepal—UNMIN

Address: UN House, Pulchowk POB 107, Kathmandu, Nepal.
Telephone: (1) 5548553; **fax:** (1) 5548597; **e-mail:** ocha-nepal@un.org.
Special Representative of the UN Secretary-General and Head of Office: IAN MARTIN (United Kingdom).

The United Nations Mission in Nepal (UNMIN), authorized by a resolution of the UN Security Council in January 2007, is mandated to monitor the cease-fire and assist, through technical support and monitoring activities, with the election of a Constituent Assembly as provided for under the Comprehensive Peace Agreement concluded between the Nepalese Government and the Communist Party of Nepal (Maoist) in November 2006. UNMIN also chairs the Joint Monitoring Co-ordinating Committee, comprising members of the Nepalese armed forces and Maoist forces, which is the mechanism for co-ordinating decisions related to monitoring the management of arms and armed personnel. Arms monitors maintain a presence at the main Maoist army cantonment sites and at the main Nepalese army barracks. During 2007 UNMIN arms monitors also completed the verification and registration of Maoist armed personnel. Mine experts advise on the safe storage and destruction of anti-personnel devices. Civil affairs officers are mandated to assist the process of re-establishment of local governance and public security, and encourage local dialogue to promote peace-building. Specialized officers in each region have been appointed to monitor and advise upon child protection and to encourage the inclusion of women and other marginalized groups in the democratic process. UNMIN works closely with the UN's Office of the United Nations High Commissioner for Human Rights to monitor the human rights situation in the country. The election of a Constituent Assembly was postponed twice in 2007, having first been scheduled to be held in June, and later in November. A new date, of 10 April 2008, was agreed upon by the main political parties in December 2007. UNMIN undertook fully to deploy electoral advisors throughout the regions and to monitor compliance with the cease-fire code of conduct. In early March 10 people were killed when an UNMIN helicopter crashed in eastern Nepal.

At January 2008 UNMIN comprised 871 personnel, including 144 arms monitors, six police advisers, 126 UN Volunteers, 208 international staff and 387 national staff. A budget of US $88.8m. was approved for the Mission in 2007.

United Nations Peace-building Office in the Central African Republic—BONUCA

Address: POB 4661, Grand Central Station, New York, NY 10163-4661, USA.
Telephone: (212) 963-9718; **fax:** (212) 963-0794.
Special Representative of the UN Secretary-General and Head of Office: Gen. LAMINE CISSÉ (Senegal).

The United Nations Peace-building Office in the Central African Republic (BONUCA) was established in February 2000 following the withdrawal of the UN Peace-keeping Mission in the Central African Republic (MINURCA). BONUCA has contributed good offices and other assistance to the restoration of constitutional order in the Central African Republic following elections in 2005. BONUCA's work has focused on, *inter alia*, electoral assistance, military reform, human rights, training civilian police and the disarmament, demobilization and reintegration of former combatants.

At 30 November 2007 BONUCA comprised 24 international civilian and 53 local civilian personnel. There were, in addition, five military advisers, six police and three UN Volunteers.

United Nations Peace-building Support Office in Guinea-Bissau—UNOGBIS

Address: UN Bldg, CP 179, Rua Rui Djassi, Bissau, Guinea-Bissau.
Telephone: 20-36-18; **fax:** 20-36-13.
Special Representative of the UN Secretary-General and Head of Office: SHOLA OMOREGIE (Nigeria).

Established to assist Guinea-Bissau in its peace-building efforts, including the electoral process, the United Nations Peace-building Support Office in Guinea-Bissau (UNOGBIS) first became operational in June 1999. Unlike other UN peace-building missions, UNOGBIS was not preceded by a UN peace-keeping mission. The intensification of persistent political violence and uncertainty in 2004 led the UN Security Council to assume authority for the mandate in that year. UN Security Council Resolution 1580 (2004) extended and revised the mandate of UNOGBIS. Since 2003 the work of UNOGBIS has focused on transition to civilian rule in the aftermath of a military coup that took place in that year. UNOGBIS is mandated by the Security Council to promote national reconciliation, respect for human rights and the rule of law; to support national capacity for conflict prevention; to encourage reform of the security sector and stable civil-military relations; to encourage government efforts to suppress trafficking in small arms; and to collaborate with a 'comprehensive peace-building strategy' to strengthen state institutions and mobilize international resources. In December 2007 the UN Security Council agreed to extend UNOGBIS for a further 12-month period and authorized a revised mandate to support efforts by the Guinea-Bissau authorities to counter illegal drugs-trafficking.

At 30 November 2007 UNOGBIS comprised 12 international civilian and 10 local civilian personnel, two military advisers, one police adviser, and one UN Volunteer.

United Nations Political Office for Somalia—UNPOS

Address: POB 48246-00100, Nairobi, Kenya.
Telephone: (20) 7622131; **fax:** (20) 7622697.
Special Representative of the UN Secretary-General and Head of Office: AHMEDOU OULD-ABDALLAH (Mauritania).

The United Nations Political Office for Somalia (UNPOS) was established in 1995 with the objective of assisting the Secretary-General to advance peace and reconciliation in the country by utilizing its contacts with Somali leaders and civic organizations. Owing to the security situation in that country, UNPOS operates from offices in Nairobi, Kenya. UNPOS provides good offices, co-ordinates international political support and financial assistance to peace and reconciliation initiatives and monitors and reports on developments in the country. In 2002–04 UNPOS supported the Somali National Reconciliation Conference that was organized in Nairobi under the auspices of the Inter-governmental Authority on Development, and worked with international partners to facilitate agreement among Somali leaders on a transitional administration. By early 2005 the Conference had established a broad-based Transitional Federal Government which was able to relocate to Somalia from its temporary base in Kenya. The UN Security Council consequently authorized UNPOS to promote reconciliation through dialogue between Somali parties; to assist efforts to address the 'Somaliland' issue; to co-ordinate the support of Somalia's neighbours and other international partners for the country's peace process; and to assume a leading political role in peace-building initiatives. In spite of an outbreak of hostilities in May 2006 the Transitional Federal Institutions continued to function during that year and to co-operate with the UN's Special Representative to pursue peace negotiations. In 2007 the Special Representative worked to support efforts to achieve national reconciliation.

At 30 November 2007 UNPOS comprised 16 international civilian and 10 local civilian personnel.

United Nations Population Fund—UNFPA

Address: 220 East 42nd St, New York, NY 10017, USA.
Telephone: (212) 297-5000; **fax:** (212) 297-4911; **internet:** www.unfpa.org.

Created in 1967 as the Trust Fund for Population Activities, the UN Fund for Population Activities (UNFPA) was established as a Fund of the UN General Assembly in 1972 and was made a subsidiary organ of the UN General Assembly in 1979, with the UNDP Governing Council (now the Executive Board) designated as its governing body. In 1987 UNFPA's name was changed to the United Nations Population Fund (retaining the same acronym).

Organization

(March 2008)

EXECUTIVE DIRECTOR

The Executive Director, who has the rank of Under-Secretary-General of the UN, is responsible for the overall direction of the Fund, working closely with governments, other United Nations bodies and agencies, and non-governmental and international organizations to ensure the most effective programming and use of resources in population activities.

Executive Director: THORAYA A. OBAID (Saudi Arabia).

EXECUTING AGENCIES

UNFPA provides financial and technical assistance to developing countries and countries with economies in transition, at their request. In many projects assistance is extended through member organizations of the UN system (in particular, FAO, ILO, UNESCO, WHO), although projects are executed increasingly by national governments themselves. The Fund may also call on the services of international, regional and national non-governmental and training organizations, as well as research institutions. In addition, nine UNFPA regional technical services teams, composed of experts from the UN, its specialized agencies and non-governmental organizations, assist countries at all stages of project/programme development and implementation.

FIELD ORGANIZATION

UNFPA operates field offices, each headed by an UNFPA Representative, in some 112 countries. In other countries UNFPA uses UNDP's field structure of Resident Representatives as the main mechanism for performing its work. The field offices assist governments in formulating requests for aid and co-ordinate the work of the executing agencies in any given country or area. UNFPA has nine regional technical services teams (see above). In accordance with a new strategic plan for the period 2008–11, UNFPA aimed to establish five regional and six sub-regional offices.

Activities

UNFPA aims to promote health, in particular reproductive health, and gender equality as essential elements of long-term sustainable development. It aims to assist countries, at their request, to formulate policies and strategies to reduce poverty and support development and to collect and analyse population data to support better understanding of their needs. UNFPA's activities are broadly defined by the Programme of Action adopted by the International Conference on Population and Development (ICPD), which was held in Cairo, Egypt, in September 1994. The Programme's objectives envisaged universal access to reproductive health and family planning services, a reduction in infant, child and maternal mortality, a reduction in the rate of HIV infection, improving life expectancy at birth, and universal access to primary education for all children by 2015. The Programme also emphasized the necessity of empowering and educating women, in order to achieve successful sustainable human development. A special session of the UN General Assembly (entitled ICPD + 5, and attended by delegates from 177 countries) was held in June–July 1999 to assess progress in achieving the objectives of the Cairo Conference and to identify priorities for future action. ICPD + 5 adopted several key actions for further implementation of the Programme of Action. These included advancing understanding of the connections between poverty, gender inequalities, health, education, the environment, financial and human resources, and development; focusing on the economic and social implications of demographic change; greater incorporation of gender issues into social and development policies and greater involvement of women in decision-making processes; greater support for HIV/AIDS prevention activities; and strengthened political commitment to the reproductive health of adolescents. Several new objectives were adopted by the special session, including the achievement of 60% availability of contraceptives and reproductive health care services by 2005, 80% by 2010, with universal availability by 2015. The ICPD objectives were been incorporated into the Millennium Development Goals (MDGs), agreed in September 2000 by a summit of UN heads of state or government, and, increasingly, are included in national development frameworks and poverty reduction strategies. The overall objective for UNFPA's strategic plan for the period 2008–11 was to accelerate the progress and national ownership of the ICPD Programme of Action, in order to help countries to achieve the MDGs.

REPRODUCTIVE HEALTH AND RIGHTS

UNFPA recognizes that improving reproductive health is an essential requirement for improving the general welfare of the population and the basis for empowering women and achieving sustainable social and economic development. The ICPD succeeded in raising the political prominence of reproductive health issues and stimulating consideration by governments of measures to strengthen and restructure their health services and policies. In October 2007 the UN General Assembly officially incorporated the aim of achieving, by 2015, universal access to reproductive health into the target for Goal 5 of the MDGs. UNFPA encourages the integration of family planning into all maternal, child and other reproductive health care. Its efforts to improve the quality of these services include support for the training of health-care personnel and promoting greater accessibility to education and services. Many reproductive health projects focus on the reduction of maternal mortality (i.e. those related to pregnancy), which was included as a central objective of the ICPD Programme, and recognized as a legitimate element of international human rights instruments concerning the right to life/survival. Projects to reduce maternal deaths, which amount to about 500,000 each year, have focused on improving accessibility to essential obstetric care and ensuring the provision of skilled attendance to women in labour. The ICPD reported that a major cause of maternal deaths was unsafe abortions, and urged governments to confront the issue as a major public health concern. UNFPA is concerned with reducing the use of abortion (i.e. its use as a means of family planning). UNFPA an active member of a core planning group of international organizations and partnerships that organized the first Women Deliver conference, held in London, United Kingdom, in October 2007. Participants, including government ministers and representatives of organizations, private sector foundations and non-government bodies, endorsed a final commitment to increase investment in women's health and to make improving maternal health a development priority. In February 2008 UNFPA appealed for donations to a new fund, with a target figure of US $465m., to support efforts in 75 developing countries to improve maternal health care. In addition to maternal deaths, an estimated 10m.-15m. women suffer serious or long-lasting illnesses or disabilities as a result of inadequate care in pregnancy and childbirth. In 2003 UNFPA launched a Global Campaign to End Fistula, which aims to improve the prevention and treatment of this obstetric condition in 30 countries in Africa and Asia and to achieve its elimination by 2015. UNFPA supports research into contraceptives and training in contraceptive technology. UNFPA organizes in-depth studies on national contraceptive requirements and aims to ensure an adequate supply of contraceptives and reproductive health supplies to developing countries. In the early 2000s the Fund and other partners developed a Reproductive Health Commodity Strategy (RHCS), which aimed to improve developing countries' self-sufficiency in the management and provision of reproductive health commodities. UNFPA encourages partnerships between private-sector interests and the governments of developing nations, with a view to making affordable commercial contraceptive products more easily available to consumers and thereby enabling governments to direct subsidies at the poorest sectors of society.

UNFPA is a co-sponsor of the Joint UN Programme on HIV/AIDS (UNAIDS), and is the UNAIDS convening agency with responsibility for young people and for condom programming, as well as taking a leading role in the UNAIDS inter-agency task team on gender and HIV/AIDS. The Fund, in co-operation with the other participants in UNAIDS, aims to strengthen the global response to the HIV/AIDS epidemic, and is also concerned to reduce levels of other sexually-transmitted infections (STIs) and reproductive tract infections (RTIs), and of infertility. UNFPA gives special attention to the specific needs of adolescents, for example through education and counselling initiatives, and to women in emergency situations. The Fund maintains that meeting the reproductive health needs of adolescents is an urgent priority in combating poverty and HIV/AIDS. Through the joint Adolescent Girls Initiative, UNFPA, UNICEF and WHO promote policy dialogues in 11 countries.

UNFPA takes a lead role in an emergency situation, following natural disaster or conflict, in providing supplies and services to protect reproductive health, in particular in the most vulnerable groups i.e. young girls and pregnant women. It also supports counselling, education and training activities, and the construction of clinics and other health facilities, following humanitarian crises. In December 2007 UNFPA supplied emergency health kits for safe delivery to areas affected by a cyclone in Bangladesh. In January 2008 UNFPA provided medical equipment and supplies to communities displaced by civil unrest in Kenya and, in particular, worked to assist those affected by an increase in sexual violence. At the end of 2007 UNFPA appealed for US $34m. to provide humanitarian assistance to 24 countries, including maternal health services in Somalia, treating victims of sexual violence in Darfur, Sudan, and efforts to prevent the spread of HIV infection among women and girls in Zimbabwe.

POPULATION AND DEVELOPMENT

UNFPA promotes work on population as a central component of the goals of the international community to eradicate poverty and achieve sustainable development. UNFPA helps countries to formulate and implement comprehensive population policies as a part of any sustainable development strategies, and aims to ensure that the needs and concerns of women are incorporated into development and population policies. Research, educational and advocacy activities are undertaken to focus on specific aspects of development and population concern, for example migration, ageing and environmental sustainability. UNFPA provides assistance and training for national statistical offices in undertaking basic data collection, for example censuses and demographic surveys. UNFPA also provides assistance for analysis of demographic and socio-economic data, for research on population trends and for the formulation of government policies. A *State of World Population* report is published annually. UNFPA supports a programme of fellowships in demographic analysis, data processing and cartography.

GENDER EQUALITY

A fundamental aspect of UNFPA's mission is to achieve gender equality, in order to promote the basic human rights of women and, through the empowerment of women, to support the elimination of poverty. Incorporated into all UNFPA activities are efforts to improve the welfare of women, in particular by providing reproductive choice, to eradicate gender discrimination, and to protect women from sexual and domestic violence and coercion. The Fund aims to encourage the participation of women at all levels of decision- and policy-making and supports programmes that improve the access of all girls and women to education and grant women equal access to land, credit and employment opportunities. UNFPA aims to eradicate traditional practices that harm women. In 1997 UNFPA appointed a special ambassador to generate international awareness of the dangers of female genital mutilation. Other activities are directed at particular issues concerning girls and adolescents and projects to involve men in reproductive health care initiatives.

Finance

UNFPA is supported entirely by voluntary contributions from donor countries. In 2006 the Fund's regular income totalled US $360.5m., contributed by a record 180 countries. Total expenditure in that year totalled some $537.2m. Of total programme expenditure about 60.3% was allocated to reproductive health care and family planning, and about 20.7% to population and development. In that year the regional distribution of the Fund's assistance was as follows: sub-Saharan Africa 34.1%, Asia and the Pacific 30.4%, the Arab States and Europe 13.2%, and Latin America and the Caribbean 9.0%, while inter-regional and global programmes received 13.2% of total assistance.

Publications

Adding it Up: The Benefits of Investing in Sexual and Reproductive Health Care (in English, published jointly with the Alan Guttmacher Institute).
Annual Report.
Dispatches (every two months, in Arabic, English, French and Spanish).
Frontlines: News from the Field (electronic newsletter).
Preventing HIV Infection, Promoting Reproductive Health: UNFPA Response (annually, in English, French and Spanish).
State of World Population (annually, in Arabic, English, French, Russian and Spanish).
Reports, technical publications, guide-lines and manuals.

United Nations Relief and Works Agency for Palestine Refugees in the Near East—UNRWA

Address: Gamal Abd an-Nasser St, Gaza City.
Telephone: (8) 6777333; **fax:** (8) 6777555.
Address: Bayader Wadi Seer, POB 140157, Amman 11814, Jordan.
Telephone: (6) 5826171; **fax:** (6) 5826177; **e-mail:** unrwa-pio@unrwa.org; **internet:** www.un.org/unrwa.

UNRWA was established by the UN General Assembly to provide relief, health, education and welfare services for Palestine refugees in the Near East, initially on a short-term basis. UNRWA began operations in May 1950 and, in the absence of a solution to the refugee problem, its mandate has subsequently been extended by the General Assembly.

Organization
(March 2008)

UNRWA employs an international staff of about 120 and more than 24,200 local staff, mainly Palestine refugees. The Commissioner-General is the head of all UNRWA operations and reports directly to the UN General Assembly. UNRWA has no governing body, but its activities are reviewed annually by an Advisory Commission. In November 2005 the UN General Assembly approved an expansion of the Commission from 10 members to 21, reflecting the funding commitments in recent years of the governments concerned. It also authorized the Palestinian authorities, the European Community and the League of Arab States to attend as observers.

Commissioner-General: KAREN KONING ABUZAYD (USA).

FIELD OFFICES

Each field office is headed by a director and has departments responsible for education, health and relief and social services programmes, finance, administration, supply and transport, legal affairs and public information. Operational support officers work in Gaza and the West Bank to monitor and report on the humanitarian situation and facilitate UNRWA field activities.

Gaza: POB 61; Al Azhar Rd, Rimal Quarter, Gaza City; tel. (8) 6777333; fax (8) 6777555.
Jordan: POB 484, 11118 Amman; Al Zubeidi Bldg No. 16, Mustafa Bin Abdullah St, Barakeh, Tla'a Al-Ali, Amman; tel. (6) 5609100; fax (6) 5609112.
Lebanon: POB 11-0947, Beirut 1107 2060; Bir Hassan, Beirut; tel. (1) 840490; fax (1) 840466; e-mail lebanon@unrwa.org.
Syria: POB 4313; UN Compound, Mezzah Highway/Beirut Rd, Damascus; tel. (11) 6133035; fax (11) 6133047.
West Bank: POB 19149, Jerusalem; Sheik Jarrah Qtr, East Jerusalem; tel. (2) 5890400; fax (2) 5890744.

LIAISON OFFICES

Egypt: 2 Dar-el-Shifa St, Garden City, POB 227, Cairo; tel. (2) 794-8502; fax (2) 794-8504.
Switzerland: Rm 92–94 Annexe Le Bocage, Palais des Nations, 1211 Geneva; tel. 229171166; fax 229170956.
USA: 1 United Nations Plaza, Room DC1–1265, New York, NY 10017; tel. (212) 963-2255; fax (212) 935-7899.

Activities

ASSISTANCE ACTIVITIES

Since 1950 UNRWA has been the main provider of relief, health, education and social services for Palestine refugees in Lebanon, Syria, Jordan, the West Bank and the Gaza Strip. For UNRWA's purposes, a Palestine refugee is one whose normal residence was in Palestine for a minimum of two years before the 1948 conflict and who, as a result of the Arab–Israeli hostilities, lost his or her home and means of livelihood. To be eligible for assistance, a refugee must reside in one of the five areas in which UNRWA operates and be in need. A refugee's descendants who fulfil certain criteria are also eligible for UNRWA assistance. After the renewal of Arab–Israeli hostilities in the Middle East in June 1967, hundreds of thousands of people fled from the fighting and from Israeli-occupied areas to east Jordan, Syria and Egypt. UNRWA provided emergency relief for displaced refugees and was additionally empowered by a UN General Assembly resolution to provide 'humanitarian assistance, as far as practicable, on an emergency basis and as a temporary measure' for those persons other than Palestine refugees who were newly displaced and in urgent need. In practice, UNRWA lacked the funds to aid the other displaced persons and the main burden of supporting them devolved on the Arab governments concerned. The Agency, as requested by the Government of Jordan in 1967 and on that Government's behalf, distributes rations to displaced persons in Jordan who are not registered refugees of 1948.

In June 2004 UNRWA and the Swiss Government hosted an international conference to address the humanitarian needs of the

Palestinian refugees. The conference, which was convened in Geneva, Switzerland, was attended by representatives of 67 countries and 34 international organizations. The recommendations of the conference contributed to a new medium-term plan, covering 2005–09, which was presented in February 2005. The plan focused on the following four main objectives for the agency: to ensure parity of UNRWA's services with the host authority and international standards; to address the needs of vulnerable refugees; to maximize the economic potential of refugees; and to build capacity within UNRWA.

At 31 December 2006 UNRWA was providing essential services to 4,448,429 registered refugees. Of these, an estimated 1,327,772 (30%) were living in 58 camps serviced by the Agency, while the remaining refugees had settled in local towns and villages of the host countries. UNRWA's three principal areas of activity are education, health, and relief and social services. Some 82% of the Agency's 2007 general fund budget was devoted to these three operational programmes.

Education accounted for 55% of UNRWA's 2007 budget. In the 2006/07 school year there were 484,781 pupils enrolled in 666 UNRWA schools, and 20,973 educational staff. UNRWA also operated eight vocational and teacher-training centres, which provided a total of 5,669 training places, and three other educational sciences faculties. Technical co-operation for the Agency's education programme is provided by UNESCO.

Health services accounted for 19% of UNRWA's 2007 general fund budget. At December 2006 there were 127 primary health care units providing outpatient medical care, disease prevention and control, maternal and child health care and family planning services, of which 96 also offered dental care and 102 had laboratory services. At that time the number of health staff totalled 4,762. UNRWA also operates a hospital in the West Bank and offers assistance towards emergency and other secondary treatment, mainly through contractual agreements with non-governmental and private hospitals. Technical assistance for the health programme is provided by WHO. UNRWA employs more than 100 school and mental health counsellors in schools, clinics and community centres under its Pyscho-Social Support programme to assist refugees, in particular children, experiencing psychological stress. UNRWA aims to provide essential environmental health services. By the end of 2006 all camp shelters were connected to water networks, and 84% were connected to sewerage networks.

Relief and social services accounted for 9% of UNRWA's general fund budget for 2007. These services comprise the distribution of food rations, the provision of emergency shelter and the organization of welfare programmes for the poorest refugees (at 31 December 2006 250,010 refugees, or 6% of the total registered refugee population, were eligible to receive special hardship assistance). In 2006 UNRWA provided technical and financial support to 65 women's programme centres and 39 community-based rehabilitation centres.

In order to encourage Palestinian self-reliance the Agency issues grants to ailing businesses and loans to families who qualify as special hardship cases. In 1991 UNRWA launched an income generation programme, which provides capital loans to small businesses and micro-enterprises with the objective of creating sustainable employment and eliminating poverty, particularly in the Occupied Territories. The programme was extended to Palestinian refugees in the West Bank in 1996 and in Jordan and Syria in 2003. By 31 December 2006 126,474 loans, with a total estimated value of US $131.09m., had been awarded under the programme.

RECENT EMERGENCIES

UNRWA's emergency humanitarian support activities for Palestinian refugees include the provision of basic food and medical supplies; the implementation of a programme of emergency workdays, which aims to provide employment and income for labourers with dependents, while improving the local infrastructure; the provision of extra schooling days to make up for those missed because of the conflict, trauma counselling for children, and post-injury rehabilitation; and the reconstruction of shelters. In November 2000 UNRWA launched an emergency humanitarian appeal for US $39m. in additional funds to assist Palestinian refugees affected by the most recent escalation of violence in the region and the Israeli-imposed blockade on PA-controlled territory. UNRWA became the lead agency with responsibility for the co-ordination and delivery of emergency assistance, as well as for monitoring the immediate needs of the local populations. A second appeal was made by the Agency in April 2001, for some $37m., and a third emergency appeal, for $77m., was issued in June. In mid-January 2002 UNRWA provided emergency supplies, including tents, blankets, mats and food following the demolition of 54 shelters by Israeli forces. A fourth emergency appeal, for some $117m., was launched at the end of January to provide food aid, medical care, shelter reconstruction and emergency work programmes for refugees in the affected areas. In February the Commissioner-General protested at the Israeli bombing of Gaza City and at the damage caused by Israeli security forces in the Palestinian towns of Jenin and Nablus. In March the Commissioner-General expressed deep concern at the worsening humanitarian situation in the Palestinian territories, as well as his outrage at the death of an UNRWA staff member during an Israeli incursion into Tulkarem camp. Later in that month UNRWA assessed that the damage inflicted against UNRWA infrastructure during March amounted to $3.8m. In early April UNRWA efforts to deliver emergency food and medical supplies to Ramallah hospital and other areas in the West Bank were hindered by attacks and threats by Israeli troops. The Commissioner-General expressed concern at the deteriorating security and humanitarian situation and for the welfare of detained and besieged UN workers. In mid-April UNRWA was permitted limited access to Jenin refugee camp, which had experienced extensive fighting during a two-week period of occupation by Israeli forces. UNRWA delivered food and water and attempted to co-ordinate international efforts to send search and rescue teams into the camp. It also undertook to reintroduce essential services and to initiate the reconstruction of refugee homes. At the same time UNRWA noted with concern the entry restrictions imposed by Israel against the Gaza Strip, which were causing extreme food shortages. In May UNRWA organized a conference of 28 countries to highlight the need for an additional $70m. to meet the humanitarian requirements resulting from the Israeli incursions. Some $56m. in additional aid was requested in July. During that month the United Arab Emirates Red Crescent Society agreed to provide UNRWA with $27m. in funding towards a two-year programme to rehabilitate the Jenin camp.

In December 2002 UNRWA launched an appeal for US $93.7m. to fund emergency relief efforts in the first six months of 2003; by February 2003, however, only a small proportion of the requested funds had been pledged and none received, necessitating a retrenchment of the Agency's assistance activities. Following a renewed appeal by UNRWA's Commissioner-General in that month, a total of $41.3m. had been pledged by the termination of the appeal period at 30 June. In May UNRWA protested strongly at the imposition by the Israeli authorities of a ban on movement by UN international staff within Gaza that was severely impeding the Agency's activities. In June the Agency announced its sixth emergency appeal, requesting $102.9m. to cover its emergency relief efforts during the period 1 July–31 December. During 2003 the demolition of homes in Gaza and the West Bank by Israeli military forces escalated significantly; it was reported that during the period November 2000–December 2003 more than 15,000 people had thus been rendered homeless, and that more than 16,000 temporary shelters had been damaged. Throughout 2003 UNRWA expressed concern at the construction by Israel of the West Bank 'security fence', or 'barrier', which was estimated to affect some 200,000 people through loss of land, water, agricultural resources and education, and hindered UNRWA's ability to provide and distribute humanitarian assistance. UNRWA has continued to monitor closely the construction and impact of the barrier. A seventh Emergency Appeal, amounting to $195.6m., was issued in December 2003 to finance UNRWA's emergency relief activities in 2004, of which some $62m. was to be allocated to the emergency workdays programme and some $55m. to the provision of basic food commodities for 222,000 severely impoverished refugee families. In May 2004 a Supplementary Appeal, for $15.8m., was launched following large-scale incursions by Israeli forces into densely populated areas of Rafah, Gaza Strip, as a result of which some 60 people were reported to have died and 298 buildings, housing more than 700 people, had been destroyed or irreparably damaged. The additional funds requested were to meet the immediate needs of those affected, the majority of whom were UNRWA registered refugees, including the provision of food, financial support and emergency housing. In mid-July UNRWA organized a supply convoy to deliver some 370 metric tons of food to an estimated 20,000 people in the northern town of Beit Hanoun, which had been besieged by the Israeli military since the end of June. A further incursion by the Israeli Defence Force into northern Gaza Strip was initiated at the end of September, isolating some 36,000 people. UNRWA delivered emergency food aid to 1,000 families affected by the operation, and undertook an assessment of its impact when Israeli troops withdrew in mid-October. In December UNRWA launched an appeal for $185.8m. to fund emergency relief operations in 2005. During 2005 UNRWA noted a considerable decline in violence and the destruction of property. From June–September a process of Israeli disengagement was successfully undertaken from the Gaza Strip and four small settlements in northern West Bank. Nonetheless, UNRWA advised that the humanitarian situation of the majority of refugees had not improved and, in launching its ninth emergency appeal in December, requested continued assistance from the international community. The appeal, amounting to $95.5m., was to be directed to funding temporary employment opportunities, in order to provide a source of income for many households, emergency food distribution, the provision of emergency cash subsidies and a mobile health programme in the West Bank.

Following the victory by the militant Islamic Resistance Movement (Hamas) at legislative elections held in the Palestinian Autonomous Territories in January 2006 and installation of a Hamas-led administration there in March, the EU and USA announced that they would withhold direct aid to the PA, but would increase their contributions to humanitarian organizations engaged in the region. During 2006 UNRWA protested repeatedly that its activities in Gaza were being severely disrupted owing to the constant closure of the Karni crossing between Gaza and Israel. In late August the Agency reported that its operations in Gaza were nearly stalled and that the difficulties with access to the area had resulted in acute shortages of food, fuel and construction supplies. In July of that year UNRWA appealed for US $7.2m. to fund emergency humanitarian assistance for Palestinian refugees based in Lebanon and Syria who had been affected as a consequence of the conflict that erupted in that month between the Israeli armed forces and the militant Shi'a organization Hezbollah. The Agency was also assisting Lebanese civilians displaced by the conflict who had sought shelter in UNRWA schools. By the end of 2006 UNRWA reported its extreme concern at the socio-economic crisis affecting the Palestinian people, caused partly by the withholding of official donor assistance and ongoing restrictions on access and movement of people and goods. It launched an appeal for $246.2m. in emergency funding, mostly to meet basic humanitarian requirements, in 2007. In July 2007 UNRWA announced it had suspended all public works rehabilitation and construction projects in Gaza owing to a lack of basic supplies resulting from the border closures.

In May 2007 an outbreak of sectarian violence in northern Lebanon disrupted UNRWA's supply of humanitarian assistance and forced an estimated 27,000 people to leave their homes. In June UNRWA issued a 'flash appeal' for US $12.7m. to meet the immediate needs of the displaced refugees and to improve the conditions at Beddawi camp, which was providing temporary shelter to the majority of those fleeing the fighting. In September UNRWA issued an emergency appeal for northern Lebanon, amounting to $54.8m. for the period 1 September 2007–31 August 2008, to meet the needs of the affected population and to support the rehabilitation of the Nahr el-Bared camp, which had been extensively damaged by the fighting.

In December 2007 UNRWA issued an emergency appeal in support of its activities in 2008 amounting to US $237.7m., including $80.4m. for direct hire employment, $79.4m. to provide food assistance and $46.1m. for emergency cash assistance.

Statistics

REFUGEES REGISTERED WITH UNRWA
(31 December 2006)

Country	Number	% of total
Jordan	1,858,362	42
Gaza Strip	1,016,964	23
West Bank	722,302	16
Syria	442,363	10
Lebanon	408,438	9
Total	4,448,429	100

Finance

UNRWA is financed almost entirely by voluntary contributions from governments and the European Union, the remainder being provided by UN bodies, non-governmental organizations, business corporations and private sources, which also contribute to extra-budgetary activities. UNRWA's general fund budget for 2007 amounted to US $505.67m. The budget for the two-year period 2008–09 amounted to $1,207.7m.

Publication

Annual Report of the Commissioner-General of UNRWA.

United Nations Training and Research Institutes

United Nations Institute for Disarmament Research—UNIDIR

Address: Palais des Nations, 1211 Geneva 10, Switzerland.
Telephone: 229173186; **fax:** 229170176; **e-mail:** unidir@unog.ch; **internet:** www.unidir.org.

UNIDIR is an autonomous institution within the United Nations. It was established by the General Assembly in 1980 for the purpose of undertaking independent research on disarmament and related problems, particularly international security issues. UNIDIR's statute became effective on 1 January 1985.

The work of the Institute is based on the following objectives: to provide the international community with more diversified and complete data on problems relating to international security, the armaments race and disarmament in all fields, so as to facilitate progress towards greater global security and towards economic and social development for all peoples; to promote informed participation by all states in disarmament efforts; to assist ongoing negotiations on disarmament, and continuing efforts to ensure greater international security at a progressively lower level of armaments, in particular nuclear weapons, by means of objective studies and analyses; and to conduct long-term research on disarmament in order to provide a general insight into the problems involved and to stimulate new initiatives for negotiations. UNIDIR's activities are divided into the following three areas: global security and disarmament, regional security and disarmament, and human security and disarmament.

The work programme of UNIDIR is reviewed annually and is subject to approval by its Board of Trustees. During 2007 UNIDIR organized conferences, seminars and consultations on a range of issues, including: humanitarian impacts of and international responses to cluster munitions; preventing the spread of weapons to non-state armed groups; and means of engaging armed non-state actors to respect humanitarian law and human rights law. Examples of ongoing research projects in 2008 included: verification in all its aspects, including the role of the UN in verification; creating a new dynamic for public-private partnerships for peaceful and sustainable development; international assistance for implementing the UN Programme of Action on the Illicit Trade in Small Arms and Light Weapons; EU and UN planning for crisis management and peace-building; transfers of small arms, light weapons and ammunition within West Africa and their consequences on disarmament and conflict prevention initiatives; preventing biological weapons proliferation; and analysing states' views on developing an arms trade treaty. Research projects are conducted within the Institute, or commissioned to individual experts or research organizations. For some major studies, multinational groups of experts are established. The Institute offers a research fellowship programme focusing on topics relating to regional security. UNIDIR maintains a database on research institutes (DATARIs) in the field of international security (accessible at dataris.sipri.org). The Institute organizes an ongoing discussion series, the so-called Geneva Forum, as a means of sharing expertise on a broad range of issues among government and non-governmental officials, UN personnel, media representatives and academics. The Geneva Forum publishes the *Media Guide to Disarmament and Arms Control*.

The Institute is financed mainly by voluntary contributions from governments and public or private organizations. A contribution to the costs of the Director and staff may be provided from the UN regular budget.

The Director of UNIDIR reports annually to the General Assembly on the activities of the Institute. The UN Secretary-General's Advisory Board on Disarmament Studies functions as UNIDIR's Board of Trustees.

Director: PATRICIA LEWIS (United Kingdom).
Publications: *Disarmament Forum* (quarterly), *UNIDIR Highlights*, research reports (6 a year), research papers (irregular).

United Nations Institute for Training and Research—UNITAR

Address: Palais des Nations, 1211 Geneva 10, Switzerland.
Telephone: 229178455; **fax:** 229178047; **e-mail:** info@unitar.org; **internet:** www.unitar.org.

UNITAR was established in 1963, as an autonomous body within the United Nations, in order to enhance the effectiveness of the latter body in achieving its major objectives. In recent years the main focus of the Institute has shifted to training and capacity-building, with basic research being conducted only if extra-budgetary funds are made available. Training is provided at various levels for personnel on assignments under the United Nations and its specialized agencies or under organizations operating in related fields. It is focused on two main areas of concern: diplomacy and international affairs; and economic and social development. In 2008 UNITAR programmes included courses on peace-keeping training; peace-making and conflict prevention; environmental law; international affairs; chemicals and waste management; environmental governance; climate change; finance and trade; decentralized co-operation; and UNOSAT (the UN Operational Satellite Applications Programme, aimed at crisis response, sustainable recovery, vulnerability reduction, and local capacity building). Most training programmes are designed and conducted in Geneva. UNITAR's New York office, established in 1996, organizes the training of delegates at United Nations headquarters. The International Training Center for Local Actors (CIFAL), inaugurated in 2001 in partnership with UNOPS, in Divonne-les-Bains, France, assists with UN crisis situation management activities and focuses on the role of local communities in emergency humanitarian responses; and the Hiroshima Office, established in 2003, focuses on management and conservation of World Heritage sites; sea and human security; biodiversity; international economics and finance; and post-conflict reconstruction.

UNITAR offers a fellowship programme in peace-making and preventive diplomacy to provide advanced training for international and national civil servants in conflict analysis and mediation. It also organizes, jointly with the UN Office for Legal Affairs, an annual fellowship programme in international law.

UNITAR is financed by voluntary contributions from UN member states, by donations from foundations and other non-governmental sources, and by income generated by its Reserve Fund.

Executive Director: CARLOS LOPES (Guinea Bissau).

United Nations International Research and Training Institute for the Advancement of Women—INSTRAW

Address: Calle César Nicolás Pensón 102-A, POB 21747, Santo Domingo, Dominican Republic.
Telephone: (809) 685-2111; **fax:** (809) 685-2117; **e-mail:** comments@un-instraw.org; **internet:** www.un-instraw.org.

The Institute was established by ECOSOC, and endorsed by the General Assembly, in 1976, following a recommendation of the World Conference on the International Women's Year (1975). INSTRAW provides training, conducts research and collects and disseminates relevant information in order to stimulate and to assist the advancement of women and their integration in the development process, both as participants and beneficiaries. Research areas in 2008 focused on gender, peace and security; gender, remittances and development; gender, governance and women's political participation; and financing for development.

INSTRAW was created as an autonomous body of the UN, funded by voluntary contributions. However, in December 2002 the UN General Assembly endorsed a number of recommendations on the future operation of the Institute presented by a working party appointed in December 2001; these included: abolishing the autonomous status of the Institute; abolishing its Board of Trustees; linking the Institute to the UN Secretariat's Department of Political and Social Affairs, under the direct authority of the Department's Under-Secretary-General; and allocating INSTRAW US $500,000 annually from the UN regular budget. Accordingly, in August 2003 ECOSOC adopted a resolution that amended INSTRAW's statute to replace the Board of Trustees with a 10-member Executive Board (comprising two representatives from each of the UN's five regional groupings elected by ECOSOC for a three-year term of office). In 2007 INSTRAW, the UN Foundation and UNFIP signed an agreement establishing the Fund for UN-INSTRAW, which was to help finance the Institute's activities. INSTRAW's operating budget for 2008 amounted to $1.5m.

Director: CARMEN MORENO (Mexico).
Publications: *INSTRAW News*, training materials, research studies.

United Nations Interregional Crime and Justice Research Institute—UNICRI

Address: Viale Maestri del Lavoro 10, 10127 Turin, Italy.
Telephone: (011) 6537111; **fax:** (011) 6313368; **e-mail:** information@unicri.it; **internet:** www.unicri.it.

The Institute was established in 1968 as the United Nations Social Defence Research Institute. Its present name was adopted by a resolution of ECOSOC in 1989. The Institute undertakes research, training and information activities in the fields of crime prevention and criminal justice, at international, regional and national levels.

In collaboration with national governments, UNICRI aims to establish a reliable base of knowledge and information on organized crime; to identify strategies for the prevention and control of crime, within the framework of contributing to socio-economic development and protecting human rights; and to design systems to support policy formulation, implementation and evaluation. UNICRI organizes workshops and conferences, and promotes the exchange of information through its international documentation centre on criminology. Main areas of activity during 2008 included post-graduate education; analysis; global programmes on security/counter-terrorism, against trafficking in human beings, and on emerging crimes (including money-laundering in Serbia); and country justice reform programmes in Albania, Angola, Mozambique and the Andean countries. The UNICRI Terrorism Prevention Unit, mandated to combat international terrorism through technical co-operation activities, works closely with law enforcement agencies world-wide.

UNICRI is funded by the United Nations Crime Prevention and Criminal Justice Fund, which is financed by voluntary contributions from UN member states, non-governmental organizations, academic institutions and other concerned bodies.

Director: SANDRO CALVANI (Italy).
Publications: *UNICRI Journal* (2 a year), training materials, research studies.

United Nations Research Institute for Social Development—UNRISD

Address: Palais des Nations, 1211 Geneva 10, Switzerland.
Telephone: 229173020; **fax:** 229170650; **e-mail:** info@unrisd.org; **internet:** www.unrisd.org.

UNRISD was established in 1963 as an autonomous body within the United Nations, to conduct multi-disciplinary research into the social dimensions of contemporary problems affecting development.

The Institute aims to provide governments, development agencies, grass-roots organizations and scholars with a better understanding of how development policies and processes of economic, social and environmental change affect different social groups.

UNRISD research is undertaken in collaboration with a network of national research teams drawn from local universities and research institutions. UNRISD aims to promote and strengthen research capacities in developing countries. Its main focus areas are the eradication of poverty; the promotion of democracy and human rights; environmental sustainability; gender equality; and the effects of globalization. In March 2005 UNRISD presented a major policy report on gender and development in the 10 years since the Beijing fourth World Conference on Women. In 2008 UNRISD's main programme areas and areas of research were: social policy and development; democracy, governance and well-being; civil society and social movements; markets, business and regulation; identities, conflict and cohesion; and gender and development. During 2007–08 the Institute convened a series of seminars on 'Identity, Power and Rights of the Indigenous Peoples'.

The Institute is supported by voluntary grants from governments, and also receives financing from other UN organizations, and from various other national and international agencies.

Director: THANDIKA MKANDAWIRE (Malawi).
Publications: *Conference News, UNRISD Informa* (1–2 a year), *UNRISD News* (1–2 a year), discussion papers and monographs, special reports, programme and occasional papers.

United Nations System Staff College

Address: Viale Maestri del Lavoro 10, 10127 Turin, Italy.
Telephone: (011) 6535911; **fax:** (011) 6535902; **e-mail:** unscp@itcilo.it; **internet:** www.unssc.org.

In July 2001 the UN General Assembly approved a statute for the UN System Staff College (UNSSC), which, it envisaged, would provide knowledge management, training and continuous learning opportunities for all UN personnel, with a view to developing UN system-wide co-operation and operational effectiveness. The inaugural meeting of the Board of Governors was held in November, and the College formally began operations on 1 January 2002. It aims to promote the exchange of knowledge and shared learning, to administer learning and training workshops, as well as distance learning opportunities, to provide support and expert advice, and to act as a clearing house for learning activities. In 2008 the College's activities were organized on the following programme clusters: UN System Learning and Training Services; Management and Leadership; Peace and Security; and Development Co-operation.

The UNSSC is financed by a combination of course fees, voluntary grants from governments and contributions in kind from various UN organizations in the form of staff secondments.

Director: CARLOS LOPES (Guinea-Bissau) (acting).

United Nations University—UNU

Address: 53–70, Jingumae 5-chome, Shibuya-ku, Tokyo 150-8925, Japan.
Telephone: (3) 3499-2811; **fax:** (3) 3499-2828; **e-mail:** mbox@hq.unu.edu; **internet:** www.unu.edu.

The University is sponsored jointly by the United Nations and UNESCO. It is an autonomous institution within the United Nations, guaranteed academic freedom by a charter approved by the General Assembly in 1973. It is governed by a 28-member University Council of scholars and scientists, of whom 24 are appointed by the Secretary-General of the UN and the Director-General of UNESCO (who, together with the Executive Director of UNITAR, are *ex-officio* members of the Council; the Rector is also on the Council). The University is not traditional in the sense of having students or awarding degrees, but works through networks of collaborating institutions and individuals. These include Associated Institutions (universities and research institutes linked with the UNU under general agreements of co-operation). The UNU undertakes multi-disciplinary research on problems that are the concern of the United Nations and its agencies, and works to strengthen research and training capabilities in developing countries. It provides post-graduate fellowships for scientists and scholars from developing countries, and conducts various training activities in association with its programme. Its main thematic programme areas are peace; governance; development; science, technology and society; and environment.

The UNU's research and training centres and programmes include the UNU Institute for Environment and Human Security (UNU-EHS), based in Bonn, Germany; the World Institute for Development Economics Research (UNU/WIDER) in Helsinki, Finland; the Economic and Social Research and Training Centre on Innovation and Technology (UNU-MERIT) in Maastricht, Netherlands; the International Institute for Software Technology (UNU/IIST) in Macao; the UNU Institute for Natural Resources in Africa (UNU-INRA) in Accra, Ghana (with a mineral resources unit in Lusaka, Zambia); the UNU Programme for Biotechnology in Latin America and the Caribbean (UNU/BIOLAC), based in Caracas, Venezuela; the International Leadership Institute (UNU/ILI) in Amman, Jordan; the Institute of Advanced Studies (UNU/IAS), based in Yokohama, Japan; the UNU International Network on Water, Environment and Health (UNU/INWEH) in Hamilton, Canada; the UNU Programme on Comparative Regional Integration Studies (UNU/CRIS), in Bruges, Belgium; the UNU Food and Nutrition Programme for Human and Social Development (UNU-FNP), based at Cornell University, USA; the UNU International Institute for Global Health (UNU-IIGH), based in Kuala Lumpur, Malaysia; and the UNU Geothermal Training Programme (UNU/GTP) and UNU Fisheries Training Programme (UNU/FTP), both based in Iceland. An Initiative on Conflict Resolution and Ethnicity (INCORE), is jointly managed by UNU and the University of Ulster.

The UNU is financed by voluntary contributions from UN member states.

Rector: Prof. Dr KONRAD OSTERWALDER (Switzerland).
Publications: *UNU Nexions* (2 a year), *Work In Progress* (1–2 a year), *WIDERAngle* (2 a year), *Africa Research* (irregular), regular journals, abstracts, research papers.

University for Peace

Address: POB 138-6100, San José, Costa Rica.
Telephone: 205-9000; **fax:** 249-1929; **e-mail:** info@upeace.org; **internet:** www.upeace.org.

The University for Peace was established by the United Nations in 1980 to conduct research on, *inter alia*, disarmament, mediation, the resolution of conflicts, the preservation of the environment, international relations, peace education and human rights. The Council of the University (the governing body, comprising 17 members) was reconstituted in March 1999, meeting for the first time since 1994. In May 1999 the Council initiated a programme of extensive reforms and expansion. A programme of short courses for advanced international training was reintroduced in 2001. In 2000 a University for Peace Centre and Policy Institute was established in Geneva, Switzerland, and an Institute for Media, Peace and Security was inaugurated, with administrative headquarters in Paris, France. In 2001 the World Centre for Research and Training in Conflict Resolution was established in Bogotá, Colombia. By 2008 Masters degrees were available in Environmental Security and Peace; Gender and Peace-Building; International Law and Human Rights; International Law and the Settlement of Disputes; International Peace Studies; Media, Conflict and Peace Studies; Natural Resources and Peace; Natural Resources and Sustainable Development; and Peace Education. The University aims to develop a global network of partner institutions. A Central Asia Programme, concerned with education in peace-building and conflict prevention in the former Soviet Central Asia, was initiated in 2000. In January 2002 the University launched an Africa Programme, which aims to build African capacity for education, training and research on matters related to peace and security. A University for Peace Academic Advisory Council, mandated to improve the organization of the University's academic programme and build partnerships and networks with other academic institutions for collaboration in the areas of both teaching and research, was inaugurated in May 2003. In December 2006 the University for Peace launched the UPEACE Human Rights Centre, which aims to provide education and training on human rights issues and to ensure that, in the practice of human rights activities, careful consideration is paid to theoretical aspects.

Rector: JOHN J. MARESCA (USA).

World Food Programme—WFP

Address: Via Cesare Giulio Viola 68, Parco dei Medici, 00148 Rome, Italy.
Telephone: (06) 65131; **fax:** (06) 6513-2840; **e-mail:** wfpinfo@wfp.org; **internet:** www.wfp.org.

WFP, the principal food aid organization of the United Nations, became operational in 1963. It aims to alleviate acute hunger by providing emergency relief following natural or man-made humanitarian disasters, and supplies food aid to people in developing countries to eradicate chronic undernourishment, to support social development and to promote self-reliant communities.

Organization

(March 2008)

EXECUTIVE BOARD

The governing body of WFP is the Executive Board, comprising 36 members, 18 of whom are elected by the UN Economic and Social Council (ECOSOC) and 18 by the Council of the Food and Agriculture Organization (FAO). The Board meets four times each year at WFP headquarters.

SECRETARIAT

WFP's Executive Director is appointed jointly by the UN Secretary-General and the Director-General of FAO and is responsible for the management and administration of the Programme. In 2006 there were 10,587 staff members, of whom nearly 92% were working in the field. WFP administers some 87 country offices, in order to provide operational, financial and management support at a more local level, and maintains six regional bureaux, located in Bangkok, Thailand (for Asia), Cairo, Egypt (for the Middle East, Central Asia and Eastern Europe), Panama City, Panama (for Latin America and the Caribbean), Johannesburg, South Africa (for Southern Africa), Kampala, Uganda (for Central and Eastern Africa), and Dakar, Senegal (for West Africa).

Executive Director: JOSETTE SHEERAN (USA).

Activities

WFP is the only multilateral organization with a mandate to use food aid as a resource. It is the second largest source of assistance in the UN, after the World Bank group, in terms of actual transfers of resources, and the largest source of grant aid in the UN system. WFP handles more than one-third of the world's food aid. WFP is also the largest contributor to South–South trade within the UN system, through the purchase of food and services from developing countries. WFP's mission is to provide food aid to save lives in refugee and other emergency situations, to improve the nutrition and quality of life of vulnerable groups and to help to develop assets and promote the self-reliance of poor families and communities. WFP aims to focus its efforts on the world's poorest countries and to provide at least 90% of its total assistance to those designated as 'low-income food-deficit'. At the World Food Summit, held in November 1996, WFP endorsed the commitment to reduce by 50% the number of undernourished people, no later than 2015. During 2006 WFP food assistance benefited some 87.8m. people (including 58.8m. children) in 78 countries, of whom 24.3m. received aid through development projects, 16.4m. through emergency operations, and 47.0m. through Protracted Relief and Recovery Operations. Total food deliveries in 2006 amounted to 4.0m. metric tons. WFP rations comprise basic food items (cereals, oil and pulses), and, where possible, additional complementary items (such as meat or fish, vegetables, fruit, fortified cereal blends, sugar and condiments).

WFP aims to address the causes of chronic malnourishment, which it identifies as poverty and lack of opportunity. It emphasizes the role played by women in combating hunger, and endeavours to address the specific nutritional needs of women, to increase their access to food and development resources, and to promote girls' education. It also focuses resources on supporting the food security of households and communities affected by HIV/AIDS and on promoting food security as a means of mitigating extreme poverty and vulnerability and thereby combating the spread and impact of HIV/AIDS. In February 2003 WFP and the Joint UN Programme on HIV/AIDS (UNAIDS) concluded an agreement to address jointly the relationship between HIV/AIDS, regional food shortages and chronic hunger, with a particular focus on Africa, South-East Asia and the Caribbean. In October of that year WFP became a co-sponsor of UNAIDS. WFP urges the development of new food aid strategies as a means of redressing global inequalities and thereby combating the threat of conflict and international terrorism.

WFP food donations must meet internationally-agreed standards applicable to trade in food products. In May 2003 WFP's Executive Board approved a new policy on donations of genetically modified (GM) foods and other foods derived from biotechnology, determining that the Programme would continue to accept donations of GM/biotech food and that, when distributing it, relevant national standards would be respected.

Since the 1990s WFP has developed a range of mechanisms to enhance its preparedness for emergency situations (such as conflict, drought and other natural disasters) and to improve its capacity for responding effectively to crises as they arise. A new programme of emergency response training was inaugurated in 2000, while security concerns for personnel was incorporated as a new element into all general planning and training activities. Through its Vulnerability Analysis and Mapping (VAM) project, WFP aims to identify potentially vulnerable groups by providing information on food security and the capacity of different groups for coping with shortages, and to enhance emergency contingency-planning and long-term assistance objectives. In 2008 VAM field units were operational in more than 50 countries. WFP also co-operates with other UN agencies including UNICEF (the largest partner in 2006), FAO, IFAD, WHO and UNHCR. Since 2003 WFP has been mandated to provide aviation transport services to the wider humanitarian community. The key elements of WFP's emergency response capacity are its strategic stores of food and logistics equipment, stand-by arrangements to enable the rapid deployment of personnel, communications and other essential equipment, and the Augmented Logistics Intervention Team for Emergencies (ALITE), which undertakes capacity assessments and contingency-planning. During 2000 WFP led efforts, undertaken with other UN humanitarian agencies, for the design and application of local UN Joint Logistics Centre facilities, which aimed to co-ordinate resources in an emergency situation. In 2001 a UN Humanitarian Response Depot was opened in Brindisi, Italy, under the direction of WFP experts, for the storage of essential rapid response equipment. In that year the Programme published a set of guide-lines on contingency planning.

During 2005 the UN's Inter-Agency Standing Committee (IASC), concerned with co-ordinating the international response to humanitarian disasters, developed a concept of organizing agency assistance to IDPs through the institutionalization of a 'Cluster Approach', currently comprising 11 core areas of activity. WFP was designated the lead agency for the clusters on Emergency Telecommunications (jointly with OCHA and UNICEF) and Logistics.

Through its development activities, WFP aims to alleviate poverty in developing countries by promoting self-reliant families and communities. Food is supplied, for example, as an incentive in development self-help schemes and as part-wages in labour-intensive projects of many kinds. In all its projects WFP aims to assist the most vulnerable groups and to ensure that beneficiaries have an adequate and balanced diet. Activities supported by the Programme include the settlement and resettlement of groups and communities; land reclamation and improvement; irrigation; the development of forestry and dairy farming; road construction; training of hospital staff; community development; and human resources development such as feeding expectant or nursing mothers and school children, and support for education, training and health programmes. No individual country is permitted to receive more than 10% of the Programme's available development resources. During 2001 WFP initiated a new Global School Feeding Campaign to strengthen international co-operation to expand educational opportunities for poor children and to improve the quality of the teaching environment. In 2003 WFP launched a *19-Cents-a-day* campaign to encourage donors to support its school feeding activities (19 US cents being the estimated cost of one school lunch). During 2006 school feeding projects benefited 20.2m. children.

Following a comprehensive evaluation of its activities, WFP is increasingly focused on linking its relief and development activities to provide a continuum between short-term relief and longer-term rehabilitation and development. In order to achieve this objective, WFP aims to integrate elements that strengthen disaster mitigation into development projects, including soil conservation, reafforestation, irrigation infrastructure, and transport construction and rehabilitation; and to promote capacity-building elements within relief operations, e.g. training, income-generating activities and environmental protection measures. In 1999 WFP adopted a new Food Aid and Development policy, which aims to use food assistance both to cover immediate requirements and to create conditions conducive to enhancing the long-term food security of vulnerable populations. During that year WFP began implementing Protracted Relief and Recovery Operations (PRROs), where the emphasis is on fostering stability, rehabilitation and long-term development for victims of natural disasters, displaced persons and refugees. PRROs are introduced no later than 18 months after the initial emergency operation and last no more than three years. When undertaken in collaboration with UNHCR and other international agencies, WFP has responsibility for mobilizing basic food commodities and for related transport, handling and storage costs. Some 18 new PRROs were approved in 2006.

In 2006 WFP operational expenditure in Europe and the CIS amounted to US $32.0m. (1% of total operational expenditure in that year), including $5.9m. for emergency relief operations and $26.1m. for PRROs.

In 2006 WFP operational expenditure in Latin America and the Caribbean amounted to US $72.0m. Of the total regional expenditure in 2006 $46.3m. was for emergency relief operations, $24.4m. for agricultural, rural and human resource development projects, and $1.2m. for special operations. WFP estimates that some 46% of Haiti's population is malnourished and has supported vulnerable people in that country who have been affected by the political and civil unrest, as well as natural disasters, through education, nutrition and health, and disaster mitigation activities. A two-year PRRO covering the period May 2005–April 2007 aimed to support 550,000 Haitians. In October 2005 WFP provided immediate emergency food aid to some 87,000 families in Guatemala, in response to devastation caused by Hurricane 'Stan'. In June 2007 WFP launched a two-year regional PRRO to strengthen natural disaster preparedness and mitigation among marginalized populations in El Salvador, Guatemala, Honduras and Nicaragua. A joint needs assessment of IDPs in Colombia, conducted by WFP and the ICRC in 2004, concluded that some 366,000 displaced people there were insufficiently nourished. In April 2005, taking into consideration the findings of the needs assessment, WFP launched a US $40.2m. two-year PRRO which aimed to assist 499,000 vulnerable Colombian IDPs. During August–October 2007 WFP implemented an emergency operation in Cordoba and Sucre, Colombia, to assist 55,000 vulnerable people in rural communities whose livelihoods had been affected by flooding.

In 2006 the main regional focus of WFP relief activities was sub-Saharan Africa, which received 62% of global food aid deliveries. Operational expenditure in the region amounted to US $1,761.9m. (66% of total operational expenditure in that year), including $635.8m. for emergency relief operations, $882.1m. for PRROs, and $112.4m. for agricultural, rural and human resource development projects. In 2007 WFP undertook operations to feed some 54m. people suffering severe food insecurity in five regions of sub-Saharan Africa.

A US $621m. PRRO was implemented during 2005–07 in Lesotho, Malawi, Mozambique, Swaziland and Zambia, following on from emergency feeding activities initiated in those countries and Zimbabwe in 2001. The ongoing humanitarian crisis in that sub-region has been attributed to the combined effects of drought, flooding and often weak government capacity to deliver basic social services, aggravated by the effects of the regional epidemic of HIV/AIDS. (It is estimated that one-half of all HIV/AIDS sufferers in southern Africa are employed in farming.) In view of the effects on crop production of flooding in south-eastern Africa in February 2007, followed by a devastating drought, WFP warned in August that nearly 5m. people there might require food assistance by early 2008, including some 4m. in Zimbabwe, which was suffering a severe economic crisis. A PRRO was being implemented in Angola during April 2006–March 2009 to provide food assistance for education in conflict-affected communities. In mid-2004 WFP appealed for $200m. to assist an estimated 2m. people were in urgent need of food aid in Darfur, western Sudan, owing to ongoing ethnic conflict, and a further $30m. to distribute food to an estimated 192,500 people from Darfur who had fled to camps in Chad. During 2005 WFP expanded its presence in Darfur to cover more than 400 sites (compared with 167 sites at the end of 2004) and initiated a school-feeding project in the region. From May 2006, owing to insufficient funding for the operation in Darfur, WFP significantly reduced food supplies there, lowering the daily ration from 2,100 kilocalories (considered an adequate daily requirement) to 1,050 kilocalories. A total of 400 metric tons of food aid were distributed by the Fund in Sudan in that year. A one-year emergency operation in Sudan for 2007 aimed to provide 682,136 metric tons of food aid to 5.5m. beneficiaries (mainly women and children) at a cost of $685.4m. Since late 2004 WFP has been supporting malnourished people in Niger affected by the devastation caused to cereal production by both severe drought and locust infestation; nearly 3m. people from Niger received food assistance from WFP and its partners in 2005, with required funding for the operation estimated in August at $57.6m. Food distribution continued in 2007. Drought-affected communities in the Horn of Africa were a particular focus of WFP activities in sub-Saharan Africa in that year. A PRRO to provide food assistance to vulnerable groups and refugees in Djibouti was being undertaken during the period April 2007–March 2009. A two-year PRRO was being implemented during 2007–08 to provide food assistance to Eritrean, Somali and Sudanese refugees in Ethiopia. A five-year country programme for Ethiopia, covering 2007–11, was to support 2.2m. beneficiaries. A PRRO to provide food assistance to Somali and Sudanese refugees in Kenya was to be implemented during the period 1 October 2007–30 September 2009, and a PRRO to provide food aid for relief and the protection of livelihoods in Somalia was being implemented during the two-year period 1 August 2006–31 July 2008. A PRRO to assist refugees encamped in north-western Tanzania was being undertaken during 2007–08. In January 2008 WFP distributed food aid through the Kenyan Red Cross and provided trucks for the transportation of food in support of people affected by the aftermath of ethnic conflict that erupted following a disputed presidential election in December 2007. During January 2008 WFP approved a $2m. special operation in support of further humanitarian efforts. The first component of the operation was to cover road transport and warehousing for non-food items for humanitarian agencies; and the second component was to cover aerial assessments and transport.

In 2006 WFP operational expenditure in the Middle East and North Africa amounted to US $91.3m. (3% of total operational expenditure in that year), including $9.9m. for emergency relief operations, $51.2m. for PRROs, and $10.1m. for agricultural, rural and human resource development projects. In March 2003 WFP appealed for donations totalling $1,300m. to finance its food aid operations in Iraq, as part of a larger United Nations 'flash appeal' for $2,218m. in humanitarian support for that country during April–October. WFP undertook a massive logistics operation to distribute food aid throughout the country with an intended total of 26m. beneficiaries; some 2m. metric tons of food aid were delivered to Iraq over that period, representing WFP's largest ever single emergency assistance operation. WFP has subsequently remained engaged in preventing hunger in Iraq, undertaking activities including surveying food security, strengthening national capacity, assisting a newly-established distribution system, and supporting a government-administered school-feeding programme. In June 2007 WFP initiated a new operation, costing some $107m., to provide food assistance to 665,000 Palestinians in the West Bank and Gaza Strip over the two-year period September 2007–August 2009. In December 2007 WFP undertook a Rapid Food Security Needs Assessment of the situation in the Palestinian territories.

In July 2006 WFP launched a three-month emergency operation that provided nearly 13m. metric tons of food assistance to 824,000 Lebanese civilians who had been displaced by Israeli military strikes against the bases in southern Lebanon of the militant Shi'a organization Hezbollah; some 50,000 of the Lebanese recipients of WFP food assistance had sought shelter in Syria. As the lead agency in the UN's Logistics cluster, WFP was designated as the UN agency responsible for the logistics of transporting humanitarian aid to and within Lebanon.

In 2006 WFP operational expenditure in Asia amounted to US $474.1 (18% of total operational expenditure in that year), including $56.1m. for emergency relief operations, $218.5m. for PRROs and $94.3m. for agricultural, rural and human resource development projects.

WFP has been active in Afghanistan, where severe drought and conflict have caused massive food insecurity and population displacement. A PRRO covering the period 1 January 2006–31 December 2008, and extending to an estimated 6.6m. Afghans, followed on from a previous PRRO covering April 2003–December 2005. The operation aimed to provide rations to vulnerable Afghans (e.g. IDPs, TB patients and their families, school children, teachers and illiterate people) in food-insecure areas, through food-for-work, food-for-training and food-for-education activities, in partnership with the Afghanistan Government and with other organizations. Capacity-building support to national agencies was to be incorporated into the PRRO. During March–June 2008 WFP aimed to distribute emergency food assistance to some 2.5m. people in rural and urban areas of Afghanistan who were suffering the effects of soaring commodity prices. Following a severe earthquake in northern Pakistan and bordering areas of India and Afghanistan in October 2005, WFP appealed to the international community for US $56m. to provide food to 1m. survivors for an initial six-month period. WFP distributed emergency food assistance in response to severe flooding that devastated areas of Bangladesh, northern India, Nepal and Pakistan in July–August 2007.

The food situation in the Democratic People's Republic of Korea (DPRK) has required substantial levels of emergency food supplies in recent years, owing to natural disasters and consistently poor harvests. During 1995–99 an estimated 1.5m.–3.5m. people died of starvation in the DPRK. In February 2006 WFP approved a $102.2m. PRRO for the DPRK, covering the period 1 April 2006–31 March 2008, which followed on from 10 successive emergency operations that had achieved some progress in reducing rates of malnutrition in that country. In August 2005 the DPRK Government had requested WFP to shift its focus from emergency relief to development activities. The two-year PRRO aimed to provide 150,000 metric tons of food aid to 1.9m. people, and to support the Government's strategy to achieve long-term food security. Vitamin- and mineral-enriched domestically-produced foods were to be distributed to young children and women of child-bearing age, and cereal rations were to be given to underemployed communities to enable them to build and rehabilitate agricultural and other community assets. A short-term emergency operation to assist 215,000 people affected by floods that struck the DPRK in August 2007 was implemented during August–November of that year. An emergency operation to provide relief and recovery assistance to 500,000 victims of Typhoon Durian, which devastated the Bicol region of the Philippines in December 2006, was implemented during February–September 2007. During the two-year period 1 April 2007–31 March 2009 WFP was undertaking a PRRO in Laos to assist 272,000 people in food-insecure households affected by recent crop losses. A PRRO to assist vulnerable families in Myanmar was being implemented during the three-year period 1 January 2007–31 December 2009. In late September 2007 WFP urged the Myanmar authorities to ease restrictions on the movement of food supplies that had been imposed owing to unrest in the country, as these were inhibiting WFP's implementation of its relief activities.

Following a massive earthquake in the Indian Ocean in December 2004, which caused a series of tidal waves, or tsunamis, that devastated coastal regions in 14 countries in South and South-East Asia and East Africa, initial WFP emergency operations were funded from the Immediate Response Account (see below). In January 2005 WFP requested emergency funding of US $256m., of which $185m. was to support an initial six-month programme to provide food aid to 2m. people affected by the natural disaster, mainly in Sri Lanka, the Maldives and Indonesia, and $72m. was for three Special Operations, concerned with logistics augmentation, air support and the establishment of a UN Joint Logistics Centre for Inter-Agency Co-ordination, of which WFP was the lead agency. In Indonesia (close to the epicentre of the earthquake) WFP established new field offices and an Emergency Operations Centre in the capital, Jakarta. From mid-2005 WFP focused its activities, increasingly, on recovery and rebuilding communities.

Finance

The Programme is funded by voluntary contributions from donor countries, intergovernmental bodies such as the European Commission, and the private sector. Contributions are made in the form of commodities, finance and services (particularly shipping). Commitments to the International Emergency Food Reserve (IEFR), from which WFP provides the majority of its food supplies, and to the Immediate Response Account of the IEFR (IRA), are also made on a voluntary basis by donors. WFP's operational expenditures in 2006 amounted to some US $2,665m. Contributions by donors in that year totalled $2,705m.

Publications

Annual Report.
Food and Nutrition Handbook.
School Feeding Handbook.
World Hunger Series.

Statistics

OPERATIONAL EXPENDITURE IN 2006 BY REGION AND TYPE*
(US $ '000)

Region	Development	Relief	Special operations
Sub-Saharan Africa	130,139	1,517,868	112,399
Asia	94,317	274,646	99,285
Latin America and the Caribbean	24,442	46,339	1,202
North Africa and the Middle East	10,090	61,150	15,783
Europe and the CIS	—	32,044	—
Total†	268,210	1,962,307	236,336

* Excludes programme support and administrative costs.
† Includes operational expenditures such as trust fund expenditures that cannot be apportioned by project/operation.

SPECIALIZED AGENCIES WITHIN THE UN SYSTEM

Food and Agriculture Organization of the United Nations—FAO

Address: Viale delle Terme di Caracalla, 00100 Rome, Italy.
Telephone: (06) 5705-1; **fax:** (06) 5705-3152; **e-mail:** fao-hq@fao.org; **internet:** www.fao.org.

FAO, the first specialized agency of the UN to be founded after the Second World War, aims to alleviate malnutrition and hunger, and serves as a co-ordinating agency for development programmes in the whole range of food and agriculture, including forestry and fisheries. It helps developing countries to promote educational and training facilities and to create appropriate institutions.

MEMBERS

FAO has 191 member nations; the European Community is a member organization.

Organization
(March 2008)

CONFERENCE

The governing body is the FAO Conference of member nations. It meets every two years, formulates policy, determines the organization's programme and budget on a biennial basis, and elects new members. It also elects the Director-General of the Secretariat and the Independent Chairman of the Council. Regional conferences are also held each year.

COUNCIL

The FAO Council is composed of representatives of 49 member nations, elected by the Conference for rotating three-year terms. It is the interim governing body of FAO between sessions of the Conference. There are eight main Governing Committees of the Council: the Finance and Programme Committees, and the Committees on Commodity Problems, Fisheries, Agriculture, Forestry, World Food Security, and Constitutional and Legal Matters.

SECRETARIAT

There are some 3,600 FAO staff, of whom about one-half are based at headquarters. FAO maintains five regional offices (see below), nine sub-regional offices, five liaison offices (in Yokohama, Japan; Washington, DC, USA, liaison with North America; Geneva, Switzerland and New York, USA, with the UN; and Brussels, Belgium, with the European Union), and some 74 country offices. Work is undertaken by the following departments: Agriculture and Consumer Protection; Economic and Social Development; Fisheries and Aquaculture; Forestry; Human, Financial and Physical Resources; Knowledge and Communication; Natural Resource Management and Environment; and Technical Co-operation.

Director-General: JACQUES DIOUF (Senegal).

REGIONAL OFFICES

Africa: POB 1628, Accra, Ghana; tel. (21) 675000; fax (21) 668427; e-mail fao-raf@fao.org; internet www.fao.org/world/regional/raf; Regional Rep. OLOCHE ANEBI EDACHE.

Asia and the Pacific: Maliwan Mansion, 39 Phra Atit Rd, Bangkok 10200, Thailand; tel. (2) 697-4000; fax (2) 697-4445; e-mail fao-rap@fao.org; internet www.fao.org/world/regional/rap/; Regional Rep. HE CHANGCHUI.

Europe: Viale delle Terme di Caracalla, Room A-304, 00100 Rome, Italy; tel. (06) 57051; fax (06) 5705-3152; e-mail reud-regrep@fao.org; internet www.fao.org/world/regional/reu; Regional Rep. JUTTA KRAUSE.

Latin America and the Caribbean: Avda Dag Hammarskjöld 3241, Casilla 10095, Vitacura, Santiago, Chile; tel. (2) 337-2100; fax (2) 337-2101; e-mail fao-rlc@field.fao.org; internet www.rlc.fao.org; Regional Rep. JOSÉ GRAZIANO DA SILVA.

Near East: 11 El-Eslah el-Zerai St, Dokki, POB 2223, Cairo, Egypt; tel. (2) 3316000; fax (2) 7495981; e-mail fao-rne@fao.org; internet www.fao.org/world/regional/rne; Regional Rep. MOHAMED ALBRAITHEN.

Activities

FAO aims to raise levels of nutrition and standards of living by improving the production and distribution of food and other commodities derived from farms, fisheries and forests. FAO's ultimate objective is the achievement of world food security, 'Food for All'. The organization provides technical information, advice and assistance by disseminating information; acting as a neutral forum for discussion of food and agricultural issues; advising governments on policy and planning; and developing capacity directly in the field.

In November 1996 FAO hosted the World Food Summit, which was held in Rome and was attended by heads of state and senior government representatives of 186 countries. Participants approved the Rome Declaration on World Food Security and the World Food Summit Plan of Action, with the aim of halving the number of people afflicted by undernutrition, at that time estimated to total 828m. world-wide, by no later than 2015. A review conference to assess progress in achieving the goals of the summit, entitled World Food Summit: Five Years Later, held in June 2002, reaffirmed commitment to this objective, which is also incorporated into the UN Millennium Development Goals (MDGs). During that month FAO announced the formulation of a global 'Anti-Hunger Programme', which aimed to promote investment in the agricultural sector and rural development, with a particular focus on small-scale farmers, and to enhance food access for those most in need, for example through the provision of school meals, schemes to feed pregnant and nursing mothers and food-for-work programmes. FAO hosts the UN System Network on Rural Development and Food Security, comprising some 20 UN bodies, which was established in 1997 as an interagency mechanism to follow-up the World Food Summits.

In November 1999 the FAO Conference approved a long-term Strategic Framework for the period 2000–15, which emphasized national and international co-operation in pursuing the goals of the 1996 World Food Summit. The Framework promoted interdisciplinarity and partnership, and defined three main global objectives: constant access by all people to sufficient, nutritionally adequate and safe food to ensure that levels of undernourishment were reduced by 50% by 2015 (see above); the continued contribution of sustainable agriculture and rural development to economic and social progress and well-being; and the conservation, improvement and sustainable use of natural resources. It identified five corporate strategies (each supported by several strategic objectives), covering the following areas: reducing food insecurity and rural poverty; ensuring enabling policy and regulatory frameworks for food, agriculture, fisheries and forestry; creating sustainable increases in the supply and availability of agricultural, fisheries and forestry products; conserving and enhancing sustainable use of the natural resource base; and generating knowledge. In October 2007 the findings of an Independent External Evaluation into the role and functions of FAO were published. The report recommended that FAO elaborate an immediate action plan for reform to ensure its continued efficiency and effectiveness.

World Food Day, commemorating the foundation of FAO, is held annually on 16 October.

AGRICULTURE AND CONSUMER PROTECTION

FAO's overall objective is to lead international efforts to counter hunger and to improve levels of nutrition. Within this context FAO is concerned to improve crop and grassland productivity and to develop sustainable agricultural systems to provide for enhanced food security and economic development. It provides member countries with technical advice for plant improvement, the application of plant biotechnology, the development of integrated production systems and rational grassland management. There are groups concerned with the main field cereal crops, i.e. rice, maize and wheat, which *inter alia* identify means of enhancing production, collect and analyse relevant data and promote collaboration between research institutions, government bodies and other farm management organizations. In 1985 and 1990 FAO's International Rice Commission endorsed the use of hybrid rice, which had been developed in the People's Republic of China, as a means of meeting growing demand for the crop, in particular in the Far East, and has subsequently assisted member countries to acquire the necessary technology and training to develop hybrid rice production. In Africa FAO has collaborated with the West African Rice Development Association to promote and facilitate the use of new rice varieties and crop management practices. FAO is the lead agency for the International Year of the Potato (2008), which aims to highlight the importance of the potato in combating world hunger.

FAO is also concerned with the development and diversification of horticultural and industrial crops, for example oil seeds, fibres and medicinal plants. FAO collects and disseminates data regarding crop trials and new technologies. It has developed an information processing site, Ecocrop, to help farmers identify appropriate crops and environmental requirements. FAO works to protect and support the sustainable development of grasslands and pasture, which contribute to the livelihoods of an estimated 800m. people world-wide.

FAO's plant protection service incorporates a range of programmes concerned with the control of pests and the use of pesticides. In February 2001 FAO warned that some 30% of pesticides sold in developing countries did not meet internationally accepted quality standards. In November 2002 FAO adopted a revised International Code of Conduct on the Distribution and Use of Pesticides (first adopted in 1985) to reduce the inappropriate distribution and use of pesticides and other toxic compounds, particularly in developing countries. In September 1998 a new legally-binding treaty on trade in hazardous chemicals and pesticides was adopted at an international conference held in Rotterdam, Netherlands. The so-called Rotterdam Convention required that hazardous chemicals and pesticides banned or severely restricted in at least two countries should not be exported unless explicitly agreed by the importing country. It also identified certain pesticide formulations as too dangerous to be used by farmers in developing countries, and incorporated an obligation that countries halt national production of those hazardous compounds. The treaty entered into force in February 2004. FAO was co-operating with UNEP to provide an interim secretariat for the Convention. FAO has promoted the use of Integrated Pest Management (IPM) initiatives to encourage the use, at local level, of safer and more effective methods of pest control, such as biological control methods and natural predators.

FAO hosts the secretariat of the International Plant Protection Convention (first adopted in 1951, revised in 1997) which aims to prevent the spread of plant pests and to promote effective control measures. The secretariat helps to define phytosanitary standards, promote the exchange of information and extend technical assistance to contracting parties (166 at October 2007).

FAO is concerned with the conservation and sustainable use of plant and animal genetic resources. It works with regional and international associations to develop seed networks, to encourage the use of improved seed production systems, to elaborate quality control and certification mechanisms and to co-ordinate seed security activities, in particular in areas prone to natural or man-made disasters. FAO has developed a World Information and Early Warning System (WIEWS) to gather and disseminate information concerning plant genetic resources for food and agriculture and to undertake periodic assessments of the state of those resources. FAO is also developing, as part of the WIEWS, a Seed Information Service to extend information to member states on seeds, planting and new technologies. In June 1996 representatives of more than 150 governments convened in Leipzig, Germany, at an International Technical Conference organized by FAO to consider the use and conservation of plant genetic resources as an essential means of enhancing food security. The meeting adopted a Global Plan of Action, which included measures to strengthen the development of plant varieties and to promote the use and availability of local varieties and locally adapted crops to farmers, in particular following a natural disaster, war or civil conflict. In November 2001 the FAO Conference adopted the International Treaty on Plant Genetic Resources for Food and Agriculture, which was to provide a framework to ensure access to plant genetic resources and to related knowledge, technologies and funding. The Treaty entered into force in June 2004, having received the required number of ratifications, and the first meeting of the Treaty's Governing Body was convened in June 2006. At mid-2007 some 52 states had acceded to the Treaty.

FAO's Animal Production and Health Division is concerned with the control and management of major animal diseases, and, in recent years, with safeguarding humans from livestock diseases. Other programmes are concerned with the contribution of livestock to poverty alleviation, the efficient use of natural resources in livestock production, the management of animal genetic resources, promoting the exchange of information and mapping the distribution of livestock around the world. In 2001 FAO established a Pro-Poor Livestock Policy Initiative to support the formulation and implementation of livestock-related policies to improve the livelihood and nutrition of the world's rural poor, with an initial focus on the Andean region, the Horn of Africa, West Africa, South Asia and the Mekong.

The Emergency Prevention System for Transboundary Animal and Plant Pests and Diseases (EMPRES) was established in 1994 to strengthen FAO's activities in the prevention, early warning, control and, where possible, eradication of pests and highly contagious livestock diseases (which the system categorizes as epidemic diseases of strategic importance, such as rinderpest or foot-and-mouth; diseases requiring tactical attention at international or regional level, e.g. Rift Valley fever; and emerging diseases, e.g. bovine spongiform encephalopathy—BSE). EMPRES has a desert locust component, and has published guide-lines on all aspects of desert locust monitoring. FAO has assumed responsibility for technical leadership and co-ordination of the Global Rinderpest Eradication Programme (GREP), which has the objective of eliminating the disease by 2010. In November 1997 FAO initiated a Programme Against African Trypanosomiasis, which aimed to counter the disease affecting cattle in almost one-third of Africa. In November 2004 FAO established a specialized Emergency Centre for Transboundary Animal Disease Operations (ECTAD) to enhance FAO's role in assisting member states to combat animal disease outbreaks and in co-ordinating international efforts to research, monitor and control transboundary disease crises. In May 2004 FAO and the World Organisation for Animal Health (OIE) signed an agreement to clarify their respective areas of competence and improve co-operation, in response to an increase in contagious transboundary animal diseases (such as foot-and-mouth disease and avian influenza, see below). The two bodies agreed to establish a global framework on the control of transboundary animal diseases, entailing improved international collaboration and circulation of information. In early 2006 the Global Early Warning and Response System for Major Animal Diseases, including Zoonoses (GLEWS), was established by FAO, OIE and the World Health Organization (WHO) to strengthen their joint capacity to detect, monitor and respond to animal disease threats.

In September 2004 FAO and WHO declared an ongoing epidemic in certain east Asian countries of the H5N1 strain of highly pathogenic avian influenza (HPAI) to be a 'crisis of global importance': the disease was spreading rapidly through bird populations and was also transmitting to human populations through contact with diseased birds (mainly poultry). In that month FAO published *Recommendations for the Prevention, Control and Eradication of Highly Pathogenic Avian Influenza in Asia*. In April 2005 FAO and OIE established an international network of laboratories and scientists (OFFLU) to exchange data and provide expert technical advise on avian influenza. In the following month FAO, with WHO and OIE, launched a global strategy for the progressive control of the disease. In November a conference on Avian Influenza and Human Pandemic Influenza, jointly organized by FAO, WHO and OIE and the World Bank, issued a plan of action identifying a number of responses, including: supporting the development of integrated national plans for H5N1 containment and human pandemic influenza preparedness and response; assisting countries with the aggressive control of H5N1 and with establishing a more detailed understanding of the role of wild birds in virus transmission; nominating rapid response teams of experts to support epidemiological field investigations; expanding national and regional capacity in surveillance, diagnosis, and alert and response systems; expanding the network of influenza laboratories; establishing multi-country networks for the control or prevention of animal transboundary diseases; expanding the global antiviral stockpile; strengthening veterinary infrastructures; and mapping a global strategy and work plan for co-ordinating antiviral and influenza vaccine research and development. In June 2006 FAO and OIE convened a scientific conference on the spread of H5N1 that advocated as a basis for H5N1 management early detection of the disease in wild birds, improved biosecurity and hygiene in the poultry trade, rapid response to disease outbreaks, and the establishment of a global tracking and monitoring facility involving participation by all relevant organizations, as well as by scientific centres, farmers' groupings, bird-watchers and hunters, and wildlife and wild bird habitat conservation bodies. The conference also urged investment in telemetry/satellite technology to improve tracking capabilities. International conference and pledging meetings on the disease have been convened in Beijing, People's Republic of China (PRC), in January 2006, Bamako, Mali, in December and in New Delhi, India, in December 2007. In January 2008 FAO warned that the virus remained a global threat with recent outbreaks confirmed in Bangladesh, Benin, PRC, Egypt, Germany, India, Indonesia, Iran, Israel, Myanmar, Poland, Russia, Ukraine, Turkey and Viet Nam.

In December 1992 FAO, with WHO, organized an International Conference on Nutrition, which approved a World Declaration on Nutrition and a Plan of Action, aimed at promoting efforts to combat malnutrition as a development priority. Since the conference, more than 100 countries have formulated national plans of action for nutrition, many of which were based on existing development plans such as comprehensive food security initiatives, national poverty alleviation programmes and action plans to attain the targets set by the World Summit for Children in September 1990. FAO promotes other efforts, at household and community level, to improve nutrition and food security, for example a programme to support home gardens. It aims to assist the identification of food insecure and vulnerable populations, both through its *State of Food Insecurity in the World* reports and taking a lead role in the development of Food Insecurity and Vulnerability Information and Mapping Systems (FIVIMS), a recommendation of the World Food Summit. In 1999 FAO signed a memorandum of understanding with UNAIDS on strengthening co-operation to combat the threat posed by the HIV/AIDS epidemic to food security, nutrition and rural livelihoods. FAO is committed to incorporating HIV/AIDS into food security and livelihood projects, to strengthening community care and to highlighting the importance of nutrition in the care of those living with HIV/AIDS.

FAO is committed to promoting food quality and safety in all different stages of food production and processing. It supports the development of integrated food control systems by member states, which incorporate aspects of food control management, inspection, risk analysis and quality assurance. The joint FAO/WHO Codex Alimentarius Commission, established in 1962, aims to protect the health of consumers, ensure fair trade practices and promote the co-ordination of food standards activities at an international level. In January 2001 a joint team of FAO and WHO experts issued a report concerning the allergenicity of foods derived from biotechnology (i.e. genetically modified—GM—foods). In July the Codex Alimentarius Commission agreed the first global principles for assessing the safety of GM foods, and approved a series of maximum levels of environmental contaminants in food. In June 2004 FAO published guidelines for assessing possible risks posed to plants by living modified organisms (LMOs). In July 2001 the Codex Alimentarius Commission adopted guide-lines on organic livestock production, covering organic breeding methods, the elimination of growth hormones and certain chemicals in veterinary medicines, and the use of good quality organic feed with no meat or bone meal content. In January 2003 FAO organized a technical consultation on biological risk management in food and agriculture which recognized the need for a more integrated approach to so-called biosecurity, i.e. the prevention, control and management of risks to animal, human and plant life and health. FAO has subsequently developed a *Toolkit*, which was published in 2007, to help countries to develop and implement national biosecurity systems and to enhance biosecurity capacity. In October 2006 FAO inaugurated a new Crisis Management Centre (CMC) to co-ordinate the organization's response to outbreaks of H5N1 and other major emergencies related to animal or food health.

FAO aims to assist member states to enhance the efficiency, competitiveness and profitability of their agricultural and food enterprises. FAO extends assistance in training, capacity building and the formulation of agribusiness development strategies. It promotes the development of effective 'value chains' connecting primary producers with consumers and supports other linkages within the agribusiness industry. Similarly, FAO aims to strengthen marketing systems, links between producers and retailers and training in agricultural marketing and works to improve the regulatory framework for agricultural marketing. FAO promotes the use of new machinery and technologies to increase agricultural production and extends a range of services to support mechanization, including training, maintenance, testing and the promotion of labour saving technologies. Other programmes are focused on farm management, post-harvest management, food and non-food processing, rural finance, and rural infrastructure. FAO helps reduce immediate post-harvest losses, with the introduction of improved processing methods and storage systems. FAO participates in PhAction, a forum of 12 agencies that was established in 1999 to promote post-harvest research and the development of effective post-harvest services and infrastructure.

FAO's Joint Division with the International Atomic Energy Agency (IAEA) is concerned with the use of nuclear techniques in food and agriculture. It co-ordinates research projects, provides scientific and technical support to technical co-operation projects and administers training courses. A joint laboratory in Seibersdorf, Austria, is concerned with testing biotechnologies and in developing non-toxic fertilizers (especially those that are locally available) and improved strains of food crops (especially from indigenous varieties). In the area of animal production and health, the Joint Division has developed progesterone-measuring and disease diagnostic kits. Other sub-programmes of the Joint Division are concerned with soil and water, plant breeding and nutrition, insect pest control and food and environmental protection.

NATURAL RESOURCES MANAGEMENT AND ENVIRONMENT

FAO is committed to promoting the responsible and sustainable management of natural resources and other activities to protect the environment. FAO assists member states to mitigate the impact of climate change on agriculture, to adapt and enhance the resilience of agricultural systems to climate change, and to promote practices to reduce the emission of greenhouse gases from the agricultural sector. In recent years FAO has strengthened its work in the area of using natural biomass resources as fuel, both at grassroots level and industrial processing of cash crops. In 2006 FAO established the International Bioenergy Platform to serve as a focal point for research, data collection, capacity-building and strategy formulation by local, regional and international bodies concerned with bioenergy. FAO also serves as the secretariat for the Global Bioenergy Partnership, which was inaugurated in May 2006 to facilitate the collaboration between governments, international agencies and representatives of the private sector and civil society in the sustainable development of bioenergy. In June 2008 FAO was scheduled to host, with the International Fund for Agricultural Development (IFAD) and the World Food Programme (WFP), a High Level Conference on World Food Security and the Challenges of Climate Change and Bioenergy.

FAO aims to enhance the sustainability of land and water systems, and as a result to secure agricultural productivity, through the improved tenure, management, development and conservation of those natural resources. The organization promotes equitable access to land and water resources and supports integrated land and water management, including river basin management and improved irrigation systems. FAO has developed AQUASTAT as a global information system concerned with water and agricultural issues, comprising databases, country and regional profiles, surveys and maps.

Within the FAO's Natural Resources Management and Environment Department is a Research and Extension Division, which provides advisory and technical services to support national capacity-building, research, communication and education activities. It maintains several databases which support and facilitate the dissemination of information, for example relating to proven transferable technologies and biotechnologies in use in developing countries. The Division advises countries on communication strategies to strengthen agricultural and rural development, and has actively supported the use of rural radio. FAO is the UN lead agency of an initiative, 'Education for Rural People', which aims to improve the quality of and access to basic education for people living in rural areas and to raise awareness of the issue as an essential element of achieving the MDGs. The Research and Extension Division hosts the secretariat of the Global Forum on Agricultural Research, which was established in October 1996 as a collaboration of research centres, non-governmental and private sector organizations and development agencies. The Forum aims to strengthen research and promote knowledge partnerships concerned with the alleviation of poverty, the increase in food security and the sustainable use of natural resources. The Division also hosts the secretariat of the Science Council of the Consultative Group on International Agricultural Research (CGIAR), which, specifically, aims to enhance and promote the quality, relevance and impact of science within the network of CGIAR research centres and to mobilize global scientific expertise.

FISHERIES AND AQUACULTURE

FAO aims to facilitate and secure the long-term sustainable development of fisheries and aquaculture, in both inland and marine waters, and to promote its contribution to world food security. In March 1995 a ministerial meeting of fisheries adopted the Rome Consensus on World Fisheries, which identified a need for immediate action to eliminate overfishing and to rebuild and enhance depleting fish stocks. In November the FAO Conference adopted a Code of Conduct for Responsible Fishing, which incorporated many global fisheries and aquaculture issues (including fisheries resource conservation and development, fish catches, seafood and fish processing, commercialization, trade and research) to promote the sustainable development of the sector. In February 1999 the FAO Committee on Fisheries adopted new international measures, within the framework of the Code of Conduct, in order to reduce over-exploitation of the world's fish resources, as well as plans of action for the conservation and management of sharks and the reduction in the incidental catch of seabirds in longline fisheries. The voluntary measures were endorsed at a ministerial meeting, held in March and attended by representatives of some 126 countries, which issued a declaration to promote the implementation of the Code of Conduct and to achieve sustainable management of fisheries and aquaculture. In March 2001 FAO adopted an international plan of action to address the continuing problem of so-called illegal, unreported and unregulated fishing (IUU). In that year FAO estimated that about one-half of major marine fish stocks were fully exploited, one-quarter under-exploited, at least 15% over-exploited, and 10% depleted or recovering from depletion. IUU was estimated to account for up to 30% of total catches in certain fisheries. In October FAO and the Icelandic Government jointly organized the Reykjavik Conference on Responsible Fisheries in the Marine Ecosystem, which adopted a declaration on pursuing responsible and sustainable fishing activities in the context of ecosystem-based fisheries management (EBFM). EBFM involves determining the boundaries of individual marine ecosystems, and maintaining or rebuilding the habitats and biodiversity of each of these so that all species will be supported at levels of maximum production. In March 2005 FAO's Committee of Fisheries adopted voluntary guide-lines for the so-called eco-labelling and certification of fish and fish products, i.e. based on information regarding capture management and the sustainable use of resources.

FAO undertakes extensive monitoring, publishing every two years *The State of World Fisheries and Aquaculture*, and collates and maintains relevant databases. It formulates country and regional profiles and has developed a specific information network for the fisheries sector, GLOBEFISH, which gathers and disseminates information regarding market trends, tariffs and other industry issues. FAO aims to extend technical support to member states with regard to the management and conservation of aquatic resources, and other measures to improve the utilization and trade of products, including the reduction of post-harvest losses, preservation marketing and quality assurance. FAO promotes aquaculture (which contributes almost one-third of annual global fish landings) as a valuable source of animal protein and income-generating activity for rural communities. It has undertaken to develop an ecosystem approach to aquaculture (EAA) and works to integrate aquaculture with agricultural and irrigation systems. In February 2000 FAO and the Network of Aquaculture Centres in Asia and the Pacific (NACA) jointly convened a Conference on Aquaculture in the Third Millennium, which was held in Bangkok, Thailand, and attended by participants representing more than 200 governmental and non-governmental organizations. The Conference debated global trends in aquaculture and future policy measures to ensure the sustainable development of the sector. It adopted the Bangkok Declaration and Strategy for Aquaculture Beyond 2000.

FORESTRY

FAO is committed to the sustainable management of trees, forests and forestry resources. It aims to address the critical balance of ensuring the conservation of forests and forestry resources while maximising their potential to contribute to food security and social and economic development. FAO's Strategic Plan for Forestry was approved in March 1999; its main objectives were to maintain the environmental diversity of forests, to realize the economic potential of forests and trees within a sustainable framework, and to expand access to information on forestry. In March 2007 the Committee on Forestry requested that a consultative process be initiated to develop a new strategic plan, with the intention that it be presented for discussion at the next meeting of the Committee to be held in March 2009. Regional forestry commissions were to consider the strategy at their meetings to be convened throughout 2008.

FAO assists member countries to formulate, implement and monitor national forestry programmes, and encourages the participation of all stakeholders in developing plans for the sustainable management of tree and forest resources. FAO also helps to implement national assessments of those programmes and of other forestry activities. At a global level FAO undertakes surveillance of the state of the world's forests and publishes a report every two years. A separate Forest Resources Assessment is published every five years, the latest (for 2010) was initiated in March 2008. FAO is committed to collecting and disseminating accurate information and data on forests. It maintains the Forestry Information System (FORIS) to make relevant information and forest-related databases widely accessible.

FAO is a member of the Collaborative Partnership on Forests, which was established in April 2004 on the recommendation of the UN's Economic and Social Council. FAO organizes a World Forestry Congress, generally held every six years; the next was to be convened in Buenos Aires, Argentina, in October 2009.

ECONOMIC AND SOCIAL DEVELOPMENT

FAO provides a focal point for economic research and policy analysis relating to food security and sustainable development. It produces studies and reports on agricultural development, the impact of development programmes and projects, and the world food situation, as well as on commodity prices, trade and medium-term projections. It supports the development of methodologies and guide-lines to improve research into food and agriculture and the integration of wider concepts, such as social welfare, environmental factors and nutrition, into research projects. In November 2004 the FAO Council adopted a set of voluntary Right to Food Guidelines, and established a dedicated administrative unit, that aimed to 'support the progressive realization of the right to adequate food in the context of national food security' by providing practical guidance to countries in support of their efforts to achieve the 1996 World Food Summit commitment and UN MDG relating to hunger reduction. FAO's Statistical Division assembles, analyses and disseminates statistical data on world food and agriculture and aims to ensure the consistency, broad coverage and quality of available data. The Division advises member countries on enhancing their statistical capabilities. It maintains FAOSTAT as a core database of statistical information relating to nutrition, fisheries, forestry, food production, land use, population etc. In 2004 FAO developed a new statistical framework to provide for the organization and integration of statistical data and metadata from sources within a particular country. CountrySTAT was piloted in Kenya, Kyrgyzstan and Ghana in 2005 and in 15 more developing countries in 2006/07. FAO's internet-based interactive World Agricultural Information Centre (WAICENT) offers access to agricultural publications, technical documentation, codes of conduct, data, statistics and multimedia resources. FAO compiles and co-ordinates an extensive range of international databases on agriculture, fisheries, forestry, food and statistics, the most important of these being AGRIS (the International Information System for the Agricultural Sciences and Technology) and CARIS (the Current Agricultural Research Information System). In June 2000 FAO organized a high-level Consultation on Agricultural Information Management (COAIM), which aimed to increase access to and use of agricultural information by policy-makers and others. The second COAIM was held in September 2002 and the third meeting was convened in June 2007.

FAO's Global Information and Early Warning System (GIEWS), which become operational in 1975, maintains a database on and monitors the crop and food outlook at global, regional, national and sub-national levels in order to detect emerging food supply difficulties and disasters and to ensure rapid intervention in countries experiencing food supply shortages. It publishes regular reports on the weather conditions and crop prospects in sub-Saharan Africa and in the Sahel region, issues special alerts which describe the situation in countries or sub-regions experiencing food difficulties, and recommends an appropriate international response. FAO has also supported the development and implementation of Food Insecurity and Vulnerability Information and Mapping Systems (FIVIMS) and hosts the secretariat of the inter-agency working group on development of the FIVIMS. In October 2007 FAO inaugurated an online Global Forum on Food Security and Nutrition, to contribute to the compilation and dissemination of information relating to food security and nutrition throughout the world.

TECHNICAL CO-OPERATION

The Technical Co-operation Department has responsibility for FAO's operational activities, including policy development assistance to member countries; the mobilization of resources; investment support; field operations; emergency operations and rehabilitation; and the Technical Co-operation Programme.

FAO provides policy advice to support the formulation, implementation and evaluation of agriculture, rural development and food security strategies in member countries. It administers a project to assist developing countries to strengthen their technical negotiating skills, in respect to agricultural trade issues. FAO also aims to co-ordinate and facilitate the mobilization of extrabudgetary funds from donors and governments for particular projects. It administers a range of trust funds, including a Trust Fund for Food Security and Food Safety, established in 2002 to generate resources for projects to combat hunger, and the Government Co-operative Programme. FAO's Investment Centre, established in 1964, aims to promote greater external investment in agriculture and rural development by assisting member countries to formulate effective and sustainable projects and programmes. The Centre collaborates with international financing institutions and bilateral donors in the preparation of projects, and administers cost-sharing arrangements, with, typically, FAO funding 40% of a project. The Centre is a co-chair (with the German government) of the Global Donor Platform for Rural Development, which was established in 2004, comprising multilateral, donor and international agencies, development banks and research institutions, to improve the co-ordination and effectiveness of rural development assistance.

FAO's Technical Co-operation Programme, which was inaugurated in 1976, provides technical expertise and funding for small-scale projects to address specific issues within a country's agriculture, fisheries or forestry sectors. An Associate Professional Officers programme co-ordinates the sponsorship and placement of young professionals to gain experience working in an aspect of rural or agricultural development.

In 1994 FAO initiated the Special Programme for Food Security (SPFS), designed to assist low-income countries with a food deficit to increase food production and productivity as rapidly as possible, primarily through the widespread adoption by farmers of improved production technologies, with emphasis on areas of high potential. Within the SPFS framework are national and regional food security initiatives, all of which aim towards the MDG objective of reducing the incidence of hunger by 50% by 2015. In 2007 the SPFS was operational in 102 countries, of which 82 were categorized as 'low-income food-deficit'. The Programme promotes South-South co-operation to improve food security and the exchange of knowledge and experience. By 2007 38 bilateral co-operation agreements were in force, for example, between Egypt and Cameroon, and Viet Nam and Benin.

FAO provided technical assistance to the New Partnership for Africa's Development (NEPAD) in the formulation of its Comprehensive African Agriculture Development Programme which was endorsed at an FAO regional conference in July 2002 and adopted by African governments in July 2003. The objectives of the SPFS were incorporated into the Programme. FAO's Investment Centre has assisted some 51 countries formulate National Medium Term Investment Programmes, under the auspices of NEPAD.

FAO organizes an annual series of fund-raising events, 'TeleFood', some of which are broadcast on television and the internet, in order to raise public awareness of the problems of hunger and malnutrition. Since its inception in 1997 public donations to TeleFood have reached some US $20m., financing more than 2,500 'grass-roots' projects in 130 countries. The projects have provided tools, seeds and other essential supplies directly to small-scale farmers, and have been especially aimed at helping women.

The Technical Co-operation Division co-ordinates FAO's emergency operations, concerned with all aspects of disaster and risk prevention, mitigation, reduction and emergency relief and rehabilitation, with a particular emphasis on food security and rural populations. FAO works with governments to develop and implement disaster prevention policies and practices. It aims to strengthen the capacity of local institutions to manage and mitigate risk and provides technical assistance to improve access to land for displaced populations in countries following conflict or a natural disaster. Other disaster prevention and reduction efforts include dissemination of information from the various early-warning systems and support for adaptation to climate variability and change, for example by the use of drought-resistance crops or the adoption of conservation agriculture techniques. Following an emergency FAO works with governments and other development and humanitarian partners to assess the immediate and longer-term agriculture and food security needs of the affected population. It has developed an Integrated Food Security and Humanitarian Phase Classification Scheme to determine the appropriate response to a disaster situation. Emergency co-ordination units may be established to manage the local response to an emergency and to facilitate and co-ordinate the delivery of inter-agency assistance. In order to rehabilitate agricultural production following a natural or man-made disaster FAO provides emergency seed, tools, other materials and technical and training assistance. During 2005 the UN's Inter-Agency Standing Committee, concerned with co-ordinating the international response to humanitarian disasters, developed a concept of providing assistance through a 'cluster' approach, comprising core areas of activity. FAO was designated the lead agency for the Agriculture cluster. FAO also contributes the agricultural relief and rehabilitation component of the UN's Consolidated Appeals Process, which aims to co-ordinate and enhance the effectiveness of the international community's response to an emergency. In April 2004 FAO established a Special Fund for Emergency and Rehabilitation Activities to enable it to response promptly to a humanitarian crisis before making an emergency appeal for additional resources.

FAO Statutory Bodies

(based at the Rome headquarters, unless otherwise indicated)

African Commission on Agricultural Statistics: c/o FAO Regional Office for Africa, POB 1628, Accra, Ghana; f. 1961 to advise member countries on the development and standardization of food and agricultural statistics; 37 member states.

African Forestry and Wildlife Commission: f. 1959 to advise on the formulation of forest policy and to review and co-ordinate its implementation on a regional level; to exchange information and advise on technical problems; 42 member states.

Agriculture, Land and Water Use Commission: c/o FAO Regional Office, POB 2223, Cairo, Egypt; f. 2000 by merger of the Near East Regional Commission on Agriculture and the Regional Commission on Land and Water Use in the Near East; 23 member states.

Animal Production and Health Commission for Asia and the Pacific: c/o FAO Regional Office, Maliwan Mansion, 39 Phra Atit Rd, Bangkok 10200, Thailand; f. 1975 to support national and regional livestock production and research; 17 member states.

Asia and Pacific Commission on Agricultural Statistics: c/o FAO Regional Office, Maliwan Mansion, 39 Phra Atit Rd, Bangkok 10200, Thailand; f. 1962 to review the state of food and agricultural statistics in the region and to advise member countries on the development and standardization of agricultural statistics; 25 member states.

Asia and Pacific Plant Protection Commission: c/o FAO Regional Office, Maliwan Mansion, Phra Atit Rd, Bangkok 10200, Thailand; f. 1956 (new title 1983) to strengthen international co-operation in plant protection to prevent the introduction and spread of destructive plant diseases and pests; 25 member states.

Asia-Pacific Fishery Commission: c/o FAO Regional Office, Maliwan Mansion, 39 Phra Atit Rd, Bangkok 10200, Thailand; f. 1948 to develop fisheries, encourage and co-ordinate research, disseminate information, recommend projects to governments, propose standards in technique and management measures; 20 member states.

Asia-Pacific Forestry Commission: internet www.apfcweb.org; f. 1949 to advise on the formulation of forest policy, and review and co-ordinate its implementation throughout the region; to exchange information and advise on technical problems; 29 member states.

Caribbean Plant Protection Commission: f. 1967 to preserve the existing plant resources of the area; 13 member states.

Codex Alimentarius Commission (Joint FAO/WHO Food Standards Programme): e-mail codex@fao.org; internet www.codexalimentarius.net; f. 1962 to make proposals for the co-ordination of all international food standards work and to publish a code of international food standards; established Intergovernmental Task Force on Foods Derived from Biotechnology in 1999; Trust Fund to support participation by least-developed countries was inaugurated in 2003; there are numerous specialized Codex committees, e.g. for food labelling, hygiene and additives, pesticide residues, milk and milk products, and processed fruits and vegetables; 165 member states.

Commission for Controlling the Desert Locust in Southwest Asia: f. 1964 to carry out all possible measures to control plagues of the desert locust in Afghanistan, India, Iran and Pakistan.

Commission for Controlling the Desert Locust in the Central Region: c/o FAO Regional Office for the Near East, POB 2223, Cairo, Egypt; 16 member states.

Commission for Controlling the Desert Locust in Northwest Africa: f. 1971 to promote research on control of the desert locust in NW Africa.

Commission for Inland Fisheries of Latin America: Avda Dag Hammarskjöld 3241, Casilla 10095, Vitacura, Santiago, Chile; f. 1976 to promote, co-ordinate and assist national and regional fishery and limnological surveys and programmes of research and development leading to the rational utilization of inland fishery resources; 21 member states.

Commission on Genetic Resources for Food and Agriculture: internet www.fao.org/ag/cgrfa/default.htm; f. 1983 as the Commission on Plant Genetic Resources, renamed in 1995; provides a forum for negotiation on the conservation and sustainable utilization of genetic resources for food and agriculture, and the equitable sharing of benefits derived from their use; 164 member states.

Commission on Livestock Development for Latin America and the Caribbean: Avda Dag Hammarskjöld 3241, Casilla 10095, Vitacura, Santiago, Chile; f. 1986; 24 member states.

Commission on Phytosanitary Measures: f. 1997 as the governing body of the revised International Plant Protection Commission.

Committee for Inland Fisheries of Africa: f. 1971 to promote improvements in inland fisheries and aquaculture in Africa.

European Commission on Agriculture: f. 1949 to encourage and facilitate action and co-operation in technological agricultural problems among member states and between international organizations concerned with agricultural technology in Europe.

European Commission for the Control of Foot-and-Mouth Disease: internet www.fao.org/ag/againfo/commissions/en/eufmd/eufmd.html; f. 1953 to promote national and international action for the control of the disease in Europe and its final eradication.

European Forestry Commission: f. 1947 to advise on the formulation of forest policy and to review and co-ordinate its implementation on a regional level; to exchange information and to make recommendations; 27 member states.

European Inland Fisheries Advisory Commission: internet www.fao.org/fi/body/eifac/eifac.asp; f. 1957 to promote improvements in inland fisheries and to advise member governments and FAO on inland fishery matters; 34 member states.

Fishery Committee for the Eastern Central Atlantic: f. 1967.

General Fisheries Council for the Mediterranean—GFCM: internet www.fao.org/fi/body/rfb/index.htm; f. 1952 to develop aquatic resources, to encourage and co-ordinate research in the fishing and allied industries, to assemble and publish information, and to recommend the standardization of equipment, techniques and nomenclature.

Indian Ocean Fishery Commission: f. 1967 to promote national programmes, research and development activities, and to examine management problems; 41 member states.

International Poplar Commission: f. 1947 to study scientific, technical, social and economic aspects of poplar and willow cultivation; to promote the exchange of ideas and material between research workers, producers and users; to arrange joint research programmes, congresses, study tours; to make recommendations to the FAO Conference and to National Poplar Commissions.

International Rice Commission: internet www.fao.org/ag/AGP/AGPC/doc/field/commrice/welcome.htm; f. 1949 to promote national and international action on production, conservation, distribution and consumption of rice, except matters relating to international trade; supports the International Task Force on Hybrid Rice, the Working Group on Advanced Rice Breeding in Latin America and the Caribbean, the Inter-regional Collaborative Research Network on Rice in the Mediterranean Climate Areas, and the Technical Co-operation Network on Wetland Development and Management/Inland Valley Swamps; 60 member states.

Latin American and Caribbean Forestry Commission: f. 1948 to advise on formulation of forest policy and review and co-ordinate its implementation throughout the region; to exchange information and advise on technical problems; meets every two years; 31 member states.

Near East Forestry Commission: f. 1953 to advise on formulation of forest policy and review and co-ordinate its implementation throughout the region; to exchange information and advise on technical problems; 20 member states.

North American Forestry Commission: f. 1959 to advise on the formulation and co-ordination of national forest policies in Canada, Mexico and the USA; to exchange information and to advise on technical problems; three member states.

South West Indian Ocean Fisheries Commission: f. 2005 to promote the sustainable development and utilization of coastal fishery resources of East Africa and island states in that sub-region; 14 member states.

Western Central Atlantic Fishery Commission: f. 1973 to assist international co-operation for the conservation, development and utilization of the living resources, especially shrimps, of the Western Central Atlantic.

Finance

FAO's Regular Programme, which is financed by contributions from member governments, covers the cost of FAO's Secretariat, its Technical Co-operation Programme (TCP) and part of the cost of several special action programmes. The budget for the two-year period 2008–09 totalled US $929.8m. Much of FAO's technical assistance programme is funded from extra-budgetary sources, predominantly by trust funds that come mainly from donor countries and international financing institutions.

Publications

Commodity Review and Outlook (annually).
Ethical Issues in Food and Agriculture.
FAO Statistical Yearbook (annually).
FAOSTAT Statistical Database (on-line).
Food Crops and Shortages (6 a year).
Food Outlook (5 a year).
Food Safety and Quality Update (monthly; electronic bulletin).
Forest Resources Assessment.
The State of Agricultural Commodity Markets (every 2 years).
The State of Food and Agriculture (annually).
The State of Food Insecurity in the World (annually).
The State of World Fisheries and Aquaculture (every 2 years).
The State of the World's Forests (every 2 years).
Unasylva (quarterly, also on-line).
Yearbook of Fishery Statistics.
Yearbook of Forest Products.
Commodity reviews; studies, manuals. A complete catalogue of publications is available at www.fao.org/icatalog/inter-e.htm.

International Atomic Energy Agency—IAEA

Address: POB 100, Wagramerstrasse 5, 1400 Vienna, Austria.
Telephone: (1) 26000; **fax:** (1) 26007; **e-mail:** official.mail@iaea.org; **internet:** www.iaea.org.

The International Atomic Energy Agency (IAEA) is an intergovernmental organization, established in 1957 in accordance with a decision of the General Assembly of the United Nations. Although it is autonomous, the IAEA is administratively a member of the United Nations, and reports on its activities once a year to the UN General Assembly. Its main objectives are to enlarge the contribution of atomic energy to peace, health and prosperity throughout the world and to ensure, so far as it is able, that assistance provided by it or at its request or under its supervision or control is not used in such a way as to further any military purpose. The 2005 Nobel Peace Prize was awarded, in two equal parts, to the IAEA and to the Agency's Director-General.

MEMBERS

IAEA has 143 members. Some 67 intergovernmental and non-governmental organizations have formal agreements with the IAEA.

Organization
(March 2008)

GENERAL CONFERENCE

The Conference, comprising representatives of all member states, convenes each year for general debate on the Agency's policy, budget and programme. It elects members to the Board of Governors, and approves the appointment of the Director-General; it admits new member states.

BOARD OF GOVERNORS

The Board of Governors consists of 35 member states elected by the General Conference. It is the principal policy-making body of the Agency and is responsible to the General Conference. Under its own authority, the Board approves all safeguards agreements, important projects and safety standards.

SECRETARIAT

The Secretariat, comprising about 2,307 staff, is headed by the Director-General, who is assisted by six Deputy Directors-General. The Secretariat is divided into six departments: Technical Co-operation; Nuclear Energy; Nuclear Safety and Security; Nuclear Sciences and Applications; Safeguards; and Management. A Standing Advisory Group on Safeguards Implementation advises the Director-General on technical aspects of safeguards.

Director-General: Dr MOHAMED EL-BARADEI (Egypt).

Activities

In recent years the IAEA has implemented several reforms of its management structure and operations. The three pillars supporting the Agency's activities are: safety and security, science and technology (assisting research on and practical application of atomic energy for peaceful uses), and safeguards and verification (ensuring that special fissionable and other materials, services, equipment and information made available by the Agency or at its request or under its supervision are not used for any non-peaceful purpose).

TECHNICAL CO-OPERATION AND TRAINING

The IAEA provides assistance in the form of experts, training and equipment to technical co-operation projects and applications worldwide, with an emphasis on radiation protection and safety-related activities. Training is provided to scientists, and experts and lecturers are assigned to provide specialized help on specific nuclear applications. The IAEA supported the foundation in September 2003 of the World Nuclear University, comprising a world-wide network of institutions that aim to strengthen international co-operation in promoting the safe use of nuclear power in energy production, and in the application of nuclear science and technology in areas including sustainable agriculture and nutrition, medicine, fresh water resources management and environmental protection.

FOOD AND AGRICULTURE

In co-operation with FAO, the Agency conducts programmes of applied research on the use of radiation and isotopes in fields including: efficiency in the use of water and fertilizers; improvement of food crops by induced mutations; eradication or control of destructive insects by the introduction of sterilized insects (radiation-based Sterile Insect Technique); improvement of livestock nutrition and health; studies on improving efficacy and reducing residues of pesticides, and increasing utilization of agricultural wastes; and food preservation by irradiation. The programmes are implemented by the Joint FAO/IAEA Division of Nuclear Techniques in Food and Agriculture and by the FAO/IAEA Agriculture and Biotechnology Laboratory, based at IAEA's laboratory complex in Seibersdorf, Austria. A Training and Reference Centre for Food and Pesticide Control, based at Seibersdorf, supports the implementation of national legislation and trade agreements ensuring the quality and safety of food products in international trade.

LIFE SCIENCES

In co-operation with the World Health Organization (WHO), the IAEA promotes the use of nuclear techniques in medicine, biology and health-related environmental research, provides training, and conducts research on techniques for improving the accuracy of radiation dosimetry.

The IAEA/WHO Network of Secondary Standard Dosimetry Laboratories (SSDLs) comprises 81 laboratories in 62 member states. The Agency's Dosimetry Laboratory in Seibersdorf performs dose inter-comparisons for both SSDLs and radiotherapy centres. The IAEA undertakes maintenance plans for nuclear laboratories; national programmes of quality control for nuclear medicine instruments; quality control of radioimmunoassay techniques; radiation sterilization of medical supplies; and improvement of cancer therapy.

PHYSICAL AND CHEMICAL SCIENCES

The Agency's programme in physical sciences includes industrial applications of isotopes and radiation technology; application of nuclear techniques to mineral exploration and exploitation; radiopharmaceuticals; and hydrology, involving the use of isotope techniques for assessment of water resources. Nuclear data services are provided, and training is given for nuclear scientists from developing countries. The Physics, Chemistry and Instrumentation Laboratory at Seibersdorf supports the Agency's research in human health, industry, water resources and environment.

NUCLEAR POWER

At December 2006 there were 435 nuclear power plants in operation and 29 reactors under construction world-wide (of which 17 were located in developing countries). Nuclear power accounted for about 16% of total electrical energy generated during 2006. The IAEA helps developing member states to introduce nuclear-powered electricity-generating plants through assistance with planning, feasibility studies, surveys of manpower and infrastructure, and safety measures. The Agency also assesses life extension and decommissioning strategies for ageing nuclear power plants. It publishes books on numerous aspects of nuclear power, and provides training courses on safety in nuclear power plants and other topics. An energy data bank collects and disseminates information on nuclear technology, and a power-reactor information system monitors the technical performance of nuclear power plants. There is increasing interest in the use of nuclear reactors for seawater desalination and radiation hydrology techniques to provide potable water. In July 1992 the EC, Japan, Russia and the USA signed an agreement to co-operate in the engineering design of an International Thermonuclear Experimental Reactor (ITER). The project aimed to demonstrate the scientific and technological feasibility of fusion energy, with the aim of providing a source of clean, abundant energy in the 21st century. An Extension Agreement, signed in 1998, provided for the continuation of the project. Negotiations on the the Joint Implementation of ITER commenced in June 2001. The People's Republic of China and the Republic of Korea also participate in the process. In May 2001 the International Project on Innovative Nuclear Reactors and Fuel Cycles (INPRO) was inaugurated. INPRO, which has 28 members, aims to promote nuclear energy as a means of meeting future sustainable energy requirements and to facilitate the exchange of information by member states to advance innovations in nuclear technology. The IAEA is a permanent observer at the Generation IV International Forum (GIF), which was inaugurated in 2000 and aims to establish a number of international collaborative nuclear research and development agreements.

RADIOACTIVE WASTE MANAGEMENT

The Agency provides practical help to member states in the management of radioactive waste. The Waste Management Advisory Programme (WAMAP) was established in 1987, and undertakes advisory missions in member states. A code of practice to prevent the illegal dumping of radioactive waste was drafted in 1989, and another on the international transboundary movement of waste was drafted in 1990. A ban on the dumping of radioactive waste at sea came into effect in 1994, under the Convention on the Prevention of Marine Pollution by Dumping of Wastes and Other Matters. The IAEA was to determine radioactive levels, for purposes of the Convention, and provide assistance to countries for the safe disposal of radioactive wastes. A new category of radioactive waste—very low level waste (VLLW)—was introduced in the early 2000s in some countries. A VLLW repository, at Morvilliers, France, became fully operational in 2004. The Agency has issued modal regulations for the air, sea and land transportation of all radioactive materials.

In September 1997 the IAEA adopted a Joint Convention on the Safety of Spent Fuel Management and on the Safety of Radioactive Waste Management. The first internationally binding legal device to address such issues, the Convention was to ensure the safe storage and disposal of nuclear and radioactive waste, during both the construction and operation of a nuclear power plant, as well as following its closure. The Convention entered into force in June 2001, and had been ratified by 46 parties at March 2008.

NUCLEAR SAFETY

The IAEA's nuclear safety programme encourages international co-operation in the exchange of information, promoting implementation of its safety standards and providing advisory safety services. It includes the IAEA International Nuclear Event Scale (INES), which measures the severity of nuclear events, incidents and accidents; the Incident Reporting System; an emergency preparedness programme (which maintains an Emergency Response Centre, located in Vienna, Austria); operational safety review teams; the International Nuclear Safety Group (INSAG); the Radiation Protection Advisory Team; and a safety research co-ordination programme. The safety review teams provide member states with advice on achieving and maintaining a high level of safety in the operation of nuclear power plants, while research programmes establish risk criteria for the nuclear fuel cycle and identify cost-effective means to reduce risks in energy systems. A new version of the INES, to be issued by the end of 2008, was to incorporate revisions aimed at providing more detailed ratings of activities including human exposure to sources of radiation and the transportation of radioactive materials.

The nuclear safety programme promotes a global safety regime, which aims to ensure the protection of people and the environment from the effects of ionizing radiation and the minimization of the likelihood of potential nuclear accidents, etc. Through the Commission on Safety Standards (which has sub-committees on nuclear safety standards, radiation safety standards, transport safety standards and waste safety standards) the programme establishes IAEA safety standards and provides for their application. In September 2006 the IAEA published a new primary safety standard, the Fundamental Safety Principles, representing a unified philosophy of nuclear safety and protection that was to provide the conceptual basis for the Agency's entire safety standards agenda. The IAEA's Safety Glossary Terminology Used in Nuclear Safety and Radiation Protection is updated regularly.

The Convention on the Physical Protection of Nuclear Material was signed in 1980, which committed contracting states to ensuring the protection of nuclear material during transportation within their territory or on board their ships or aircraft. In July 2005 delegates from 89 states party adopted a number of amendments aimed at strengthening the Convention.

Following a serious accident at the Chornobyl (Chernobyl) nuclear power plant in Ukraine (then part of the USSR) in April 1986, two conventions were formulated by the IAEA and entered into force in October. The first, the Convention on Early Notification of a Nuclear Accident, commits parties to provide information about nuclear accidents with possible transboundary effects at the earliest opportunity (it had 102 parties by March 2008); and the second, the Convention on Assistance in the Case of a Nuclear Accident or Radiological Emergency, commits parties to endeavour to provide assistance in the event of a nuclear accident or radiological emergency (this had 100 parties by March 2008). During 1990 the IAEA organized an assessment of the consequences of the Chernobyl accident, undertaken by an international team of experts, who reported to an international conference on the effects of the accident, convened at the IAEA headquarters in Vienna in May 1991. In February 1993 INSAG published an updated report on the Chernobyl incident, which emphasized the role of design factors in the accident, and the need to implement safety measures in the RBMK-type reactor. In March 1994 an IAEA expert mission visited Chernobyl and reported continuing serious deficiencies in safety at the defunct reactor and the units remaining in operation. An international conference reviewing the radiological consequences of the accident, 10 years after the event, was held in April 1996, co-sponsored by the IAEA, WHO and the European Commission. The last of the Chernobyl plant's three operating units was officially closed in December

2000. During the 2000s the IAEA was offering a wide range of assistance with the decommissioning of Chernobyl.

In September 1999 the IAEA activated its Emergency Response Centre, following a serious incident at a fuel conversion facility in Tokaimura, Japan. The Centre was used to process information from the Japanese authorities and to ensure accurate reporting of the event. In October a three-member IAEA team of experts visited the site to undertake a preliminary investigation into the causes and consequences of the accident.

An International Convention on Nuclear Safety was adopted at an IAEA conference in June 1994. The Convention applies to land-based civil nuclear power plants: adherents commit themselves to fundamental principles of safety, and maintain legislative frameworks governing nuclear safety. The Convention entered into force in October 1996 and had been ratified by 61 states by March 2008.

In September 1997 more than 80 member states adopted a protocol to revise the 1963 Vienna Convention on Civil Liability for Nuclear Damage, fixing the minimum unit limit of liability for the operator of a nuclear reactor at 300m. Special Drawing Rights (SDRs, the accounting units of the IMF) in the event of an accident. The amended protocol also extended the length of time during which claims may be brought for loss of life or injury. It entered into force in October 2003. The International Expert Group on Nuclear Liability (INLEX) was established in the same year. A Convention on Supplementary Compensation for Nuclear Damage established a further compensatory fund to provide for the payment of damages following an accident; contributions to the Fund were to be calculated on the basis of the nuclear capacity of each member state. The Convention had three contracting states by March 2008.

In July 1996 the IAEA co-ordinated a study on the radiological situation at the Mururoa and Fangatauta atolls, following the French nuclear test programmes in the South Pacific. Results published in May 1998 concluded there was no radiological health risk and that neither remedial action nor continued environmental monitoring was necessary.

The IAEA is developing a training course on measurement methods and risk analysis relating to the presence of depleted uranium (which can be used in ammunition) in post-conflict areas. In November 2000 IAEA specialists participated in a fact-finding mission organized by UNEP in Kosovo and Metohija, which aimed to assess the environmental and health consequences of the use of depleted uranium in ammunition by NATO during its 1999 aerial offensive against the then Federal Republic of Yugoslavia. (A report on the situation was published by UNEP in March 2001.) In June 2003 the Agency published the results of an assessment undertaken in 2002 of the possible long-term radiological impact of depleted uranium residues, derived from the 1991 Gulf War, at several locations in Kuwait; it determined that the residues did not pose a health threat to local populations.

In May 2001 the IAEA convened an international conference to address the protection of nuclear material and radioactive sources from illegal trafficking. In September, in view of the perpetration of major terrorist attacks against targets in the USA during that month, the IAEA General Conference addressed the potential for nuclear-related terrorism. It adopted a resolution that emphasized the importance of the physical protection of nuclear material in preventing its illicit use or the sabotage of nuclear facilities and nuclear materials. Three main potential threats were identified: the acquisition by a terrorist group of a nuclear weapon; acquisition of nuclear material to construct a nuclear weapon or cause a radiological hazard; and violent acts against nuclear facilities to cause a radiological hazard. In March 2002 the Board of Governors approved in principle an action plan to improve global protection against acts of terrorism involving nuclear and other radioactive materials. The plan addressed the physical protection of nuclear materials and facilities; the detection of malicious activities involving radioactive materials; strengthening national control systems; the security of radioactive sources; evaluation of security and safety at nuclear facilities; emergency response to malicious acts or threats involving radioactive materials; ensuring adherence to international guidelines and agreements; and improvement of programme co-ordination and information management. It was estimated that the Agency's upgraded nuclear security activities would require significant additional annual funding. In March 2003 the IAEA organized an International Conference on Security of Radioactive Sources, held in Vienna. In 2006, a total of 149 incidents were reported by 95 states to the Illicit Trafficking Database (ITDB); this represented the highest number of incidents registered on the ITDB since 1993.

In June 2004 the Board of Governors approved an action plan on the decommissioning of nuclear facilities. In 2006 the IAEA provided decommissioning support in the form of technical co-operation projects to 12 member states.

DISSEMINATION OF INFORMATION

The International Nuclear Information System (INIS), which was established in 1970, provides a computerized indexing and abstracting service. Information on the peaceful uses of atomic energy is collected by member states and international organizations and sent to the IAEA for processing and dissemination (see list of publications below). The IAEA also co-operates with FAO in an information system for agriculture (AGRIS) and with the World Federation of Nuclear Medicine and Biology, and the non-profit Cochrane Collaboration, in maintaining an electronic database of best practice in nuclear medicine. The IAEA Nuclear Data Section provides cost-free data centre services and co-operates with other national and regional nuclear and atomic data centres in the systematic world-wide collection, compilation, dissemination and exchange of nuclear reaction data, nuclear structure and decay data, and atomic and molecular data for fusion.

SAFEGUARDS

The Treaty on the Non-Proliferation of Nuclear Weapons (known also as the Non-Proliferation Treaty or NPT), which entered into force in 1970, requires each 'non-nuclear-weapon state' (one which had not manufactured and exploded a nuclear weapon or other nuclear explosive device prior to 1 January 1967) which is a party to the Treaty to conclude a safeguards agreement with the IAEA. Under such an agreement, the state undertakes to accept IAEA safeguards on all nuclear material in all its peaceful nuclear activities for the purpose of verifying that such material is not diverted to nuclear weapons or other nuclear explosive devices. In May 1995 the Review and Extension Conference of parties to the NPT agreed to extend the NPT indefinitely, and reaffirmed support for the IAEA's role in verification and the transfer of peaceful nuclear technologies. At the next review conference, held in April–May 2000, the five 'nuclear-weapon states'—the PRC, France, Russia, the United Kingdom and the USA—issued a joint statement pledging their commitment to the ultimate goal of complete nuclear disarmament under effective international controls. A further review conference was convened in May 2005. By March 2008 185 non-nuclear-weapon states and the five nuclear-weapon states were parties to the Treaty. A number of non-nuclear-weapon states, however, had not complied, within the prescribed time-limit, with their obligations under the Treaty regarding the conclusion of the relevant safeguards agreement with the Agency.

The five nuclear-weapon states have concluded safeguards agreements with the Agency that permit the application of IAEA safeguards to all their nuclear activities, excluding those with 'direct national significance'. A Comprehensive Nuclear Test Ban Treaty (CTBT) was opened for signature in September 1996, having been adopted by the UN General Assembly. The Treaty was to enter into international law upon ratification by all 44 nations with known nuclear capabilities. A separate verification organization was to be established, based in Vienna. A Preparatory Commission for the treaty organization became operational in 1997. By March 2008 177 countries had signed the CTBT and 142 had ratified it, including 34 of the 44 states with known nuclear capabilities. However, the US Senate rejected ratification of the CTBT in October 1999.

Several regional nuclear weapons treaties require their member states to conclude comprehensive safeguards agreements with the IAEA, including the Treaty for the prohibition of Nuclear Weapons in Latin America (Tlatelolco Treaty, with 33 states party at March 2008); the South Pacific Nuclear-Free Zone Treaty (Rarotonga Treaty, 13 states party at March 2008); the Treaty in the South-East Asia Nuclear-Weapon Free Zone (Treaty of Bangkok, adopted in 1995, 10 states party at March 2008); and the African Nuclear-Weapon Free Zone Treaty (Pelindaba Treaty, adopted in 1996, with 24 states party at March 2008). In September 2006 experts from Kazakhstan, Kyrgyzstan, Tajikistan, Turkmenistan and Uzbekistan, adopted a treaty on establishing a Central Asian Nuclear Weapon Free Zone (CANWFZ); the treaty had been ratified by Kyrgyzstan and Uzbekistan at March 2008. At the end of 2006 a total of 237 IAEA safeguards agreements were in force with 162 states, covering 925 nuclear facilities. During that year the Agency conducted 2,142 inspections. Expenditure on the Safeguards Regular Budget for 2006 was US $92.0m., and extra-budgetary programme expenditure amounted to $8.4m. The IAEA maintains an imagery database of nuclear sites, and is installing digital surveillance systems (including unattended and remote monitoring capabilities) to replace obsolete analogue systems.

In June 1995 the Board of Governors approved measures to strengthen the safeguards system, including allowing inspection teams greater access to suspected nuclear sites and to information on nuclear activities in member states, reducing the notice time for inspections by removing visa requirements for inspectors and using environmental monitoring (i.e. soil, water and air samples) to test for signs of radioactivity. In April 1996 the IAEA initiated a programme to prevent and combat illicit trafficking of nuclear weapons, and in May 1998 the IAEA and the World Customs Organization signed a Memorandum of Understanding to enhance co-operation in the prevention of illicit nuclear trafficking. In May 1997 the Board of Governors adopted a model additional protocol approving measures to strengthen safeguards further, in order to ensure the compliance of non-nuclear-weapon states with IAEA commitments. The new protocol compelled member states to provide inspection teams with improved access to information concerning existing and planned nuclear activities, and to allow access to locations other than known nuclear sites within that country's territory. By December 2006 75 states had ratified additional protocols to their safeguards agreements.

IAEA's Safeguards Analytical Laboratory analyses nuclear fuel-cycle samples collected by IAEA safeguards inspectors. The Agency's Marine Environment Laboratory, in Monaco, studies radionuclides and other ocean pollutants.

In April 1992 the Democratic People's Republic of Korea (DPRK) ratified a safeguards agreement with the IAEA. In late 1992 and early 1993, however, the IAEA unsuccessfully requested access to two non-declared sites in the DPRK, where it was suspected that material capable of being used for the manufacture of nuclear weapons was stored. In March 1993 the DPRK announced its intention of withdrawing from the NPT: it suspended its withdrawal in June, but continued to refuse full access to its nuclear facilities for IAEA inspectors. In May 1994 the DPRK began to refuel an experimental nuclear power reactor at Yongbyon, but refused to allow the IAEA to analyse the spent fuel rods in order to ascertain whether plutonium had been obtained from the reactor for possible military use. In June the IAEA Board of Governors halted IAEA technical assistance to the DPRK (except medical assistance) because of continuous violation of the NPT safeguards agreements. In the same month the DPRK withdrew from the IAEA (though not from the NPT); however, it allowed IAEA inspectors to remain at the Yongbyon site to conduct safeguards activities. In October the Governments of the DPRK and the USA concluded an agreement whereby the former agreed to halt construction of two new nuclear reactors, on condition that it received international aid for the construction of two 'light water' reactors (which could not produce materials for the manufacture of nuclear weapons). The DPRK also agreed to allow IAEA inspections of all its nuclear sites, but only after the installation of one of the light water reactors had been completed (entailing a significant time lapse). In November IAEA inspectors visited the DPRK to initiate verification of the suspension of the country's nuclear programme, in accordance with the agreement concluded in the previous month. From 1995 the IAEA pursued technical discussions with the DPRK authorities as part of the Agency's efforts to achieve the full compliance of the DPRK with the IAEA safeguards agreement. By the end of 1999 the canning of spent fuel rods from the Yongbyon nuclear power reactor was completed. However, little overall progress had been achieved, owing to the obstruction of inspectors by the authorities in that country, including their refusal to provide samples for analysis. The IAEA was unable to verify the suspension of the nuclear programme and declared that the DPRK continued to be in non-compliance with its NPT safeguards agreement. In accordance with a decision of the General Conference in September 2001, IAEA inspectors subsequently resumed a continuous presence in the DPRK. The DPRK authorities permitted low-level inspections of the Yongbyon site by an IAEA technical team in January and May 2002. It was envisaged at that time that the new 'light water' reactors would become operational by 2008. However, in December 2002, following repeated requests by the IAEA that the DPRK verify the accuracy of reports that it was implementing an undeclared uranium enrichment programme, the DPRK authorities disabled IAEA safeguards surveillance equipment placed at three facilities in Yongbyon and took measures to restart reprocessing capabilities at the site, requesting the immediate withdrawal of the Agency's inspectors. (The inspectors were withdrawn at the end of the month.) In early January 2003 the IAEA Board of Governors adopted a resolution deploring the DPRK's non-co-operation and urging its immediate and full compliance with the Agency. Shortly afterwards, however, the DPRK announced its withdrawal from the NPT, while stating that it would limit its nuclear activities to peaceful purposes. In February the IAEA found the DPRK to be in further non-compliance with its safeguards agreement, and condemned the reported successful reactivation of the Yongbyon reactor. In August a series of six-party talks on the situation was launched, involving the DPRK, the PRC, Japan, the Republic of Korea, Russia and the USA, under the auspices of the PRC Government. In September 2004 the General Conference adopted a resolution that urged the DPRK to dismantle promptly and completely any nuclear weapons programme and to recognize the verification role of the Agency, while strongly encouraging the ongoing diplomatic efforts to achieve a peaceful outcome. In February 2005 the DPRK suspended its participation in the six-party talks, and asserted that it had developed nuclear weapons as a measure of self-defence. The talks resumed during July–September, when the six parties signed a joint statement, in which the DPRK determined to resume its adherence to the NPT and Agency safeguards, and consequently to halt its development of nuclear weapons; the USA and the Republic of Korea affirmed that no US nuclear weapons were deployed on the Korean Peninsula; the five other parties recognized the DPRK's right to use nuclear energy for peaceful purposes, and agreed to consider at a later date the provision of a light water reactor to that country; and all parties undertook to promote co-operation in security and economic affairs. A timetable for future progress was to be established at the next phase of the six-party talks, the first session of which convened briefly in early November; the DPRK, however, subsequently announced that it would only resume the talks pending the release by the USA of recently-frozen DPRK financial assets. In July 2006 the UN Security Council condemned a recent ballistic missile test by the DPRK, noting the potential of such missiles to be used for delivering nuclear, chemical or biological payloads, and urged the DPRK to return immediately to the six-party talks without precondition and work towards the implementation of the September 2005 joint statement. In early 2006 October the IAEA Director-General expressed serious concern in response to an announcement by the DPRK that it had conducted a nuclear test. In mid-October the Security Council adopted Resolution 1718, demanding that the DPRK suspend all activities related to its ballistic missile programme, abandon all nuclear weapons and existing nuclear programmes, abandon all other existing weapons of mass destruction and ballistic missile programmes in a complete, verifiable and irreversible manner, and return to the six-party talks. The Council also imposed sanctions against the DPRK.

The six-party talks were resumed in February 2007, and resulted in an ad hoc agreement by all the participants that the DPRK would shut down and seal—for the purpose of eventual abandonment—the Yongbyon facility, and would invite back IAEA personnel to conduct all necessary monitoring and verifications; that the DPRK would discuss with the other parties a list of all its nuclear programmes; that the DPRK and the USA would enter into negotiations aimed at resolving pending bilateral issues and moving toward full diplomatic relations; that the USA would initiate the process of removing the designation of the DPRK as a state-sponsor of terrorism; that the DPRK and Japan would start negotiations aimed at normalizing their relations; and that the parties would agree to co-operate in security and economic affairs (as detailed under the September 2005 joint statement). In the latter regard, the parties agreed to the provision of emergency energy assistance to the DPRK. In mid-July 2007 an IAEA team visited the DPRK and verified the shutdown of the Yongbyon facility. Upon the resumption of the six-party talks in late September, the participants adopted an agreement wherein the DPRK resolved to disable permanently its nuclear facilities.

In April 1991 the UN Security Council requested the IAEA to conduct investigations into Iraq's capacity to produce nuclear weapons, following the end of the war between Iraq and the UN-authorized, US-led multinational force. The IAEA was to work closely with a UN Special Commission of experts (UNSCOM), established by the Security Council, whose task was to inspect and dismantle Iraq's weapons of mass destruction (including chemical and biological weapons). In July the IAEA declared that Iraq had violated its safeguards agreement with the IAEA by not submitting nuclear material and relevant facilities in its uranium-enrichment programme to the Agency's inspection. This was the first time that a state party to the NPT had been condemned for concealing a programme of this nature. In October the sixth inspection team, composed of UNSCOM and representatives of the IAEA, was reported to have obtained conclusive documentary evidence that Iraq had a programme for developing nuclear weapons. By February 1994 all declared stocks of nuclear-weapons-grade material had been removed from Iraq. Subsequently, the IAEA pursued a programme of long-term surveillance of nuclear activity in Iraq, under a mandate issued by the UN Security Council. In September 1996 Iraq submitted to the IAEA a 'full, final and complete' declaration of its nuclear activities. However, in September–October 1997 the IAEA recommended that Iraq disclose further equipment, materials and information relating to its nuclear programme. In April 1998 IAEA technical experts were part of a special group that entered eight presidential sites in Iraq to collect baseline data, in accordance with a Memorandum of Understanding concluded between the UN Secretary-General and the Iraqi authorities in February. The accord aimed to ensure full Iraqi co-operation with UNSCOM and IAEA personnel. In August, however, Iraq suspended co-operation with UN inspectors, which prevented IAEA from implementing its programme of ongoing monitoring and verification (OMV) activities. Iraq's action was condemned by the IAEA General Conference in September. In October the IAEA reported that while there was no evidence of Iraq having produced nuclear weapons or having retained or obtained a capability for the production of nuclear weapons, the Agency was unable to guarantee that all items had been found. All IAEA inspectors were temporarily relocated from Iraq to Bahrain in November, in accordance with a decision to withdraw UNSCOM personnel owing to Iraq's failure to agree to resume co-operation. In March 2000 UNSCOM was replaced by a new arms inspection body, the UN Monitoring, Verification and Inspection Commission (UNMOVIC). Although the IAEA carried out inventory verifications of nuclear material in Iraq in January 2000,

January 2001 and January 2002, pursuant to Iraq's NPT safeguards agreement, full inspection activities in conjunction with UNMOVIC remained suspended. In September 2002 the US President expressed concern that Iraq was challenging international security owing to its non-compliance with successive UN resolutions relating to the elimination of weapons of mass destruction. In November the UN Security Council adopted Resolution 1441 providing for an enhanced inspection mission and a detailed timetable according to which Iraq would have a final opportunity to comply with its disarmament obligations. Following Iraq's acceptance of the resolution, experts from the IAEA's so-called Iraq Nuclear Verification Office and UNMOVIC resumed inspections on 27 November, with Council authorization to have unrestricted access to all areas and the right to interview Iraqi scientists and weapons experts. In early December Iraq submitted a declaration of all aspects of its weapons programmes, as required under Resolution 1441. In January 2003 Dr Mohamed el-Baradei, the IAEA Director-General, requested an ongoing mandate for his inspectors to clarify the situation regarding nuclear weapons. In mid-March el-Baradei reported that no evidence had been found of nuclear weapons programme activities in Iraq, while also stating that the Agency had not had sufficient time to complete its investigations. Shortly before the initiation of unilateral military action against Iraq by US and allied forces on 19 March IAEA and UNMOVIC personnel were withdrawn from the country. Their field activities were suspended and, following the overthrow in April of the Saddam Hussain regime, responsibility for weapons inspections in Iraq were assumed by a US-led Iraq Survey Group. In late April el-Baradei emphasized the necessity of securing the sites of Iraq's declared nuclear materials from looting and damage. In June 2007 the UN Security Council, noting testimonials that all of Iraq's known weapons of mass destruction had been deactivated and that the Iraqi Government had declared its support for international non-proliferation regimes, voted to terminate the mandates of the IAEA weapons inspectors in Iraq and of UNMOVIC.

In September 2003 the IAEA adopted a resolution demanding that the Iranian Government sign, ratify and fully implement an additional protocol to its safeguards agreement promptly and unconditionally. The Agency also urged Iran to suspend its uranium enrichment and reprocessing activities, pending satisfactory application of the provisions of the additional protocol. Iran issued a declaration of its nuclear activities in October, and, in December, signed an additional protocol and agreed to suspend uranium enrichment processing, as requested. The Agency dispatched inspectors to Iran from October to conduct an intensive verification process. In April 2004 the IAEA Director-General visited Iran and concluded an agreement on a joint action plan to address the outstanding issues of the verification process. Iran provided an initial declaration under the (as yet unratified) additional protocol in May. In June, however, the Director-General expressed his continued concern at the extent of Iranian co-operation with IAEA inspectors. In September the Board of Governors adopted a resolution in which it strongly regretted continuing enrichment-related and reprocessing activities by Iran and requested their immediate suspension. The Director-General announced in late November that the suspension had been verified. In August 2005 the Agency adopted a resolution condemning Iran for resuming uranium conversion. In the following month a further resolution was adopted by the Board of Governors, in support of a motion by the European Union, citing Iran's non-compliance with the NPT and demanding that Iran accelerate its co-operation with the Agency regarding the outstanding issues. In early February 2006 the Board of Governors adopted a resolution that recalled repeated failures by Iran to comply with its obligations under its NPT safeguards agreement, expressed serious concern at the nature of Iran's nuclear programme, and urged that, with a view to building confidence in the exclusively peaceful nature of the programme, Iran should suspend fully all activities related to uranium enrichment (reportedly resumed in January) and reprocessing; ratify and fully implement the additional protocol agreed in 2003; and implement transparency measures extending beyond its formal arrangements with the Agency. The resolution requested the IAEA Director-General to report the steps required of Iran to the UN Security Council and to inform the Security Council of all related IAEA documents and resolutions. In response, the Iranian authorities declared that they would suspend all legally non-binding measures imposed by the IAEA, including containment and surveillance measures provided for under the additional protocol, and that consequently all IAEA seals and cameras should be removed from Iranian sites by mid-February 2006. At the end of July the UN Security Council, having reviewed the relevant information provided by the IAEA Director-General, issued Resolution 1696, in which it demanded that Iran suspend all enrichment-related and reprocessing activities, including research and development, within a period of one month, and stipulated that non-compliance might result in the imposition on Iran of economic and diplomatic sanctions. The resolution requested that the IAEA Director-General submit to the Council at the end of August a report on Iran's response. The report, which was made public in mid-September, found that Iran had not suspended its enrichment-related activities and was still not in compliance with the provisions of the additional protocol. In December the Security Council imposed sanctions against Iran, and in March 2007 the Council imposed a ban on the export of arms from that country.

In June 2007 the IAEA Director-General and the Iranian authorities agreed to develop within 60 days a plan on the modalities for resolving outstanding safeguards implementation issues; accordingly, in August, a work plan on this area (also detailing procedures and timelines) was finalized. At that time the IAEA declared that previous Agency concerns about plutonium reprocessing activities in Iran were now resolved, as its findings had verified earlier statements made by the Iranian authorities. At the end of that month the IAEA Director-General reported that Iran had not yet suspended its uranium enrichment activities. The IAEA Director-General visited Iran in January 2008 to discuss with the Iranian administration means of accelerating the implementation of safeguards and confidence-building measures. It was agreed that remaining verification issues that had been specified in the August 2007 workplan should be resolved by mid-February 2008. In February 2008 the IAEA Board of Governors reported that Iran was still pursuing its uranium enrichment activities, and that the Iranian Government needed to continue to build confidence about the scope and purported peaceful nature of its nuclear programme. Consequently, in the following month, the UN Security Council adopted a new resolution on Iran in which it professed concern for the proliferation risk presented by the Iranian nuclear programme and authorized inspections of any cargo to and from Iran suspected of transporting prohibited equipment; strengthened the monitoring of Iranian financial institutions; and added names to the existing list of individuals and companies subject to asset and travel restrictions.

Following the announcement by Libya in mid-December 2003 that it would conclude an additional protocol to its safeguards agreement with the IAEA, the Agency worked closely with that country to verify the extent of its past undeclared and present nuclear materials and activities. The Libyan authorities signed an additional protocol in March 2004.

While assessing nuclear activities in Iran and Libya from late 2003 the Agency also undertook investigations into the supply routes and sources of the technology and materials used in their past undeclared nuclear programmes, demonstrating evidence of a complex black market. The Agency demanded full co-operation from the source countries involved.

In late 1997 the IAEA began inspections in the USA to verify the conversion for peaceful uses of nuclear material released from the military sector. In 1998 the United Kingdom announced that substantial quantities of nuclear material previously in its military programme would become available for verification under its voluntary offer safeguards agreement.

NUCLEAR FUEL CYCLE

The Agency promotes the exchange of information between member states on technical, safety, environmental, and economic aspects of nuclear fuel cycle technology, including uranium prospecting and the treatment and disposal of radioactive waste; it provides assistance to member states in the planning, implementation and operation of nuclear fuel cycle facilities and assists in the development of advanced nuclear fuel cycle technology. The Agency operates a number of databases and a simulation system related to the nuclear fuel cycle through its Integrated Nuclear Fuel Cycle Information System (iNFCIS). Every two years, in collaboration with OECD, the Agency prepares estimates of world uranium resources, demand and production.

Finance

The Agency is financed by regular and voluntary contributions from member states. Expenditure approved under the regular budget for 2008 amounted to some US $288.8m., and the target for voluntary contributions to finance the IAEA technical assistance and co-operation programme in that year was $80.0m.

Publications

Annual Report.
Atoms for Peace.
Fundamental Safety Principles.
IAEA Bulletin (quarterly).
IAEA Newsbriefs (every 2 months).
IAEA Safety Glossary Terminology Used in Nuclear Safety and Radiation Protection.
IAEA Yearbook.

INTERNATIONAL ORGANIZATIONS — United Nations (Specialized Agencies)

INIS Atomindex (bibliography, 2 a month).
INIS Reference Series.
INSAG Series.
Legal Series.
Meetings on Atomic Energy (quarterly).
The Nuclear Fuel Cycle Information System: A Directory of Nuclear Fuel Cycle Facilities.
Nuclear Fusion (monthly).

Nuclear Safety Review (annually).
Nuclear Technology Review (annually).
Panel Proceedings Series.
Publications Catalogue (annually).
Safety Series.
Technical Directories.
Technical Reports Series.

International Bank for Reconstruction and Development— IBRD (World Bank)

Address: 1818 H St, NW, Washington, DC 20433, USA.
Telephone: (202) 473-1000; **fax:** (202) 477-6391; **e-mail:** pic@worldbank.org; **internet:** www.worldbank.org.

The IBRD was established in December 1945. Initially it was concerned with post-war reconstruction in Europe; since then its aim has been to assist the economic development of member nations by making loans where private capital is not available on reasonable terms to finance productive investments. Loans are made either directly to governments, or to private enterprises with the guarantee of their governments. The World Bank, as it is commonly known, comprises the IBRD and the International Development Association (IDA). The affiliated group of institutions, comprising the IBRD, the IDA, the International Finance Corporation (IFC), the Multilateral Investment Guarantee Agency (MIGA) and the International Centre for Settlement of Investment Disputes (ICSID, see below), is referred to as the World Bank Group.

MEMBERS

There are 185 members. Only members of the International Monetary Fund (IMF) may be considered for membership in the World Bank. Subscriptions to the capital stock of the Bank are based on each member's quota in the IMF, which is designed to reflect the country's relative economic strength. Voting rights are related to shareholdings.

Organization
(March 2008)

Officers and staff of the IBRD serve concurrently as officers and staff in the IDA. The World Bank has offices in New York, Brussels, Paris (for Europe), Frankfurt, London, Geneva and Tokyo, as well as in more than 100 countries of operation. Country Directors are located in some 30 country offices.

BOARD OF GOVERNORS

The Board of Governors consists of one Governor appointed by each member nation. Typically, a Governor is the country's finance minister, central bank governor, or a minister or an official of comparable rank. The Board normally meets once a year.

EXECUTIVE DIRECTORS

With the exception of certain powers specifically reserved to them by the Articles of Agreement, the Governors of the Bank have delegated their powers for the conduct of the general operations of the World Bank to a Board of Executive Directors which performs its duties on a full-time basis at the Bank's headquarters. There are 24 Executive Directors (see table below); each Director selects an Alternate. Five Directors are appointed by the five members having the largest number of shares of capital stock, and the rest are elected by the Governors representing the other members. The President of the Bank is Chairman of the Board.

The Executive Directors fulfil dual responsibilities. First, they represent the interests of their country or groups of countries. Second, they exercise their authority as delegated by the Governors in overseeing the policies of the Bank and evaluating completed projects. Since the Bank operates on the basis of consensus (formal votes are rare), this dual role involves frequent communication and consultations with governments so as to reflect accurately their views in Board discussions.

The Directors consider and decide on Bank policy and on all loan and credit proposals. They are also responsible for presentation to the Board of Governors at its Annual Meetings of an audit of accounts, an administrative budget, the *Annual Report* on the operations and policies of the World Bank, and any other matter that, in their judgement, requires submission to the Board of Governors. Matters may be submitted to the Governors at the Annual Meetings or at any time between Annual Meetings.

PRINCIPAL OFFICERS

The principal officers of the Bank are the President of the Bank, three Managing Directors, three Senior Vice-Presidents and 24 Vice-Presidents.

President and Chairman of Executive Directors: ROBERT B. ZOELLICK (USA).

Managing Directors: JUAN JOSÉ DABOUB (El Salvador), GRAEME WHEELER (New Zealand), Dr NGOZI OKONJO-IWEALA (Nigeria).

Activities

FINANCIAL OPERATIONS

IBRD capital is derived from members' subscriptions to capital shares, the calculation of which is based on their quotas in the IMF. At 30 June 2007 the total subscribed capital of the IBRD was US $189,801m., of which the paid-in portion was $11,486m. (6.1%); the remainder is subject to call if required. Most of the IBRD's lendable funds come from its borrowing, on commercial terms, in world capital markets, and also from its retained earnings and the flow of repayments on its loans. IBRD loans carry a variable interest rate, rather than a rate fixed at the time of borrowing.

IBRD loans usually have a 'grace period' of five years and are repayable over 15 years or fewer. Loans are made to governments, or must be guaranteed by the government concerned, and are normally made for projects likely to offer a commercially viable rate of return. In 1980 the World Bank introduced structural adjustment lending, which (instead of financing specific projects) supports programmes and changes necessary to modify the structure of an economy so that it can restore or maintain its growth and viability in its balance of payments over the medium-term.

The IBRD and IDA together made 301 new lending and investment commitments totalling US $24,695.8m. during the year ending 30 June 2007, compared with 279 (amounting to $23,641.2m.) in the previous year. During 2006/07 the IBRD alone approved commitments totalling $12,828.8m. (compared with $14,135.0m. in the previous year), of which $4,353.3m. (34%) was allocated to Latin America and the Caribbean and $3,340.1m. (26%) to projects in Europe and Central Asia. Disbursements by the IBRD in the year ending 30 June 2007 amounted to $11,055m. (For details of IDA operations, see separate chapter on IDA.)

IBRD operations are supported by medium- and long-term borrowings in international capital markets. During the year ending 30 June 2007 the IBRD's net income amounted to –US $140m.

The World Bank's primary objectives are the achievement of sustainable economic growth and the reduction of poverty in developing countries. In the context of stimulating economic growth the Bank promotes both private sector development and human resource development and has attempted to respond to the growing demands by developing countries for assistance in these areas. In March 1997 the Board of Executive Directors endorsed a 'Strategic Compact' to increase the effectiveness of the Bank in achieving its central objective of poverty reduction. The reforms included greater decentralization of decision-making, and investment in front-line operations, enhancing the administration of loans, and improving access to information and co-ordination of Bank activities through a knowledge management system comprising four thematic networks: the

Human Development Network; the Environmentally and Socially Sustainable Development Network; the Finance, Private Sector and Infrastructure Development Network; and the Poverty Reduction and Economic Management Network. In 2000/01 the Bank adopted a new Strategic Framework which emphasized two essential approaches for Bank support: strengthening the investment climate and prospects for sustainable development in a country, and supporting investment in the poor. In September 2001 the Bank announced that it was to join the UN as a full partner in implementing the so-called Millennium Development Goals (MDGs), and was to make them central to its development agenda. The objectives, which were approved by governments attending a special session of the UN General Assembly in September 2000, represented a new international consensus to achieve determined poverty reduction targets. The Bank was closely involved in preparations for the International Conference on Financing for Development, which was held in Monterrey, Mexico, in March 2002. The meeting adopted the Monterrey Consensus, which outlined measures to support national development efforts and to achieve the MDGs. During 2002/03 the Bank, with the IMF, undertook to develop a monitoring framework to review progress in the MDG agenda. The first *Global Monitoring Report* was issued by the Bank and IMF in April 2004. Other efforts to support a greater emphasis on development results were also undertaken by the Bank during 2003/04 as part of a new strategic action plan, and the Bank has continued closely to monitor its contribution to poverty reduction objectives.

The Bank's efforts to reduce poverty include the compilation of country-specific assessments and the formulation of country assistance strategies (CASs) to review and guide the Bank's country programmes. Since August 1998 the Bank has published CASs, with the approval of the government concerned. A new results-based CAS initiative was piloted in 2003/04. In 1998/99 the Bank's Executive Directors endorsed a Comprehensive Development Framework (CDF) to effect a new approach to development assistance based on partnerships and country responsibility, with an emphasis on the interdependence of the social, structural, human, governmental, economic and environmental elements of development. The Framework, which aimed to enhance the overall effectiveness of development assistance, was formulated after a series of consultative meetings organized by the Bank and attended by representatives of governments, donor agencies, financial institutions, non-governmental organizations, the private sector and academics.

In December 1999 the Bank introduced a new approach to implement the principles of the CDF, as part of its strategy to enhance the debt relief scheme for heavily indebted poor countries (HIPCs, see below). Applicant countries were requested to formulate, in consultation with external partners and other stakeholders, a results-oriented national strategy to reduce poverty, to be presented in the form of a Poverty Reduction Strategy Paper (PRSP). In cases where there might be some delay in issuing a full PRSP, it was permissible for a country to submit a less detailed 'interim' PRSP (I-PRSP) in order to secure the preliminary qualification for debt relief. The approach also requires the publication of annual progress reports. In 2001 the Bank introduced a new Poverty Reduction Support Credit to help low-income countries to implement the policy and institutional reforms outlined in their PRSP. The first credits were approved for Uganda and Viet Nam in May and June respectively. Increasingly, PRSPs have been considered by the international community to be the appropriate country-level framework to assess progress towards achieving the MDGs. A joint review of the poverty reduction strategy approach was undertaken by the Bank and IMF in 2004/05.

In September 1996 the World Bank/IMF Development Committee endorsed a joint initiative to assist HIPCs to reduce their debt burden to a sustainable level, in order to make more resources available for poverty reduction and economic growth. A new Trust Fund was established by the World Bank in November to finance the initiative. The Fund, consisting of an initial allocation of US $500m. from the IBRD surplus and other contributions from multilateral creditors, was to be administered by IDA. Of the 41 HIPCs identified by the Bank, 33 were in sub-Saharan Africa. In April 1997 the World Bank and the IMF announced that Uganda was to be the first beneficiary of the initiative, enabling the Ugandan Government to reduce its external debt by some 20%, or an estimated $338m. In early 1999 the World Bank and IMF initiated a comprehensive review of the HIPC initiative. By April meetings of the Group of Seven industrialized nations (G-7) and of the governing bodies of the Bank and IMF indicated a consensus that the scheme needed to be amended and strengthened, in order to allow more countries to benefit from the initiative, to accelerate the process by which a country may qualify for assistance, and to enhance the effectiveness of debt relief. In June the G-7 and Russia (known as the G-8), meeting in Cologne, Germany, agreed to increase contributions to the HIPC Trust Fund and to cancel substantial amounts of outstanding debt, and proposed more flexible terms for eligibility. In September the Bank and IMF reached an agreement on an enhanced HIPC scheme. During the initial phase of the process to ensure suitability for debt relief, each applicant country should formulate a PRSP, and should demonstrate prudent financial management in the implementation of the strategy for at least one year, with support from the IDA and IMF. At the pivotal 'decision point' of the process, having thus developed and successfully applied the poverty reduction strategy, applicant countries still deemed to have an unsustainable level of debt were to qualify for interim debt relief from the IMF and IDA, as well as relief on highly concessional terms from other official bilateral creditors and multilateral institutions. During the ensuing 'interim period' countries were required successfully to implement further economic and social development reforms, as a final demonstration of suitability for securing full debt relief at the 'completion point' of the scheme. Data produced at the decision point was to form the base for calculating the final debt relief (in contrast to the original initiative, which based its calculations on projections of a country's debt stock at the completion point). In the majority of cases a sustainable level of debt was targeted at 150% of the net present value (NPV) of the debt in relation to total annual exports (compared with 200%–250% under the original initiative). Other countries with a lower debt-to-export ratio were to be eligible for assistance under the scheme, providing that their export earnings were at least 30% of GDP (lowered from 40% under the original initiative) and government revenue at least 15% of GDP (reduced from 20%). In March 2005 the Bank and the IMF implemented a new Debt Sustainability Framework in Low-income Countries to provide guidance on lending to low-income countries and to improve monitoring and prevention of the accumulation of unsustainable debt. In June finance ministers of the G-8 proposed providing additional resources to achieve the full cancellation of debts owed by eligible HIPCs to assist those countries to meet their MDG targets. Countries that had reached their completion point were to qualify for immediate assistance. In July the heads of state and government of G-8 countries requested the Bank to ensure the effective delivery of the additional funds and to provide a framework for performance measurement. In September the Bank's Development Committee and the International Monetary and Financial Committee of the IMF endorsed the proposal, subsequently referred to as the Multilateral Debt Relief Initiative (MDRI). The Committees agreed to protect the financial capability of IDA, as one of the institutions (with the IMF and African Development Bank) which was to meet the additional cancellation commitments, and to develop a monitoring programme. By 31 March 2008 23 countries (Benin, Bolivia, Burkina Faso, Cameroon, Ethiopia, The Gambia, Ghana, Guyana, Honduras, Madagascar, Malawi, Mali, Mauritania, Mozambique, Nicaragua, Niger, Rwanda, São Tomé and Príncipe, Senegal, Sierra Leone, Tanzania, Uganda and Zambia) had reached completion point under the enhanced HIPC initiative, while a further 10 countries had reached their decision point. At the end of 2007 total assistance committed under the HIPC initiative amounted to some $41,900m. in end-2005 NPV terms, or $62,200m. in total estimated nominal debt service relief.

During 2000/01 the World Bank strengthened its efforts to counter the problem of HIV and AIDS in developing countries. In November 2001 the Bank appointed its first Global HIV/AIDS Adviser. In September 2000 a new Multi-Country HIV/AIDS Programme for Africa (MAP) was launched, in collaboration with UNAIDS and other major donor agencies and non-governmental organizations. Some US $500m. was allocated to the initiative and was used to support efforts in seven countries. In February 2002 the Bank approved an additional $500m. for a second phase of MAP, which was envisaged to assist HIV/AIDS schemes in a further 12 countries, as well as regional activities. A MAP initiative for the Caribbean, with a budget of $155m., was launched in 2001. The Bank has undertaken research into the long-term effects of HIV/AIDS, and hosts the Global HIV/AIDS Monitoring and Evaluation Support Team of UNAIDS. In November 2004 the Bank launched an AIDS Media Center to improve access to information regarding HIV/AIDS, in particular to journalists in developing countries.

In March 2007 the Board of Executive Directors approved an action plan to develop further its Clean Energy for Development Investment Framework. The action plan focused on efforts to improve access to clean energy, in particular in sub-Saharan Africa; to support the transition to low carbon-emission development; and to support adaptation to climate change.

In addition to providing financial services, the Bank also undertakes analytical and advisory services, and supports learning and capacity-building, in particular through the World Bank Institute (see below), the Staff Exchange Programme and knowledge-sharing initiatives. The Bank has supported efforts, such as the Global Development Gateway, to disseminate information on development issues and programmes, and, since 1988, has organized the Annual Bank Conference on Development Economics (ABCDE) to provide a forum for the exchange and discussion of development-related ideas and research. In September 1995 the Bank initiated the Information for Development Programme (InfoDev) with the aim of fostering partnerships between governments, multilateral institutions and private-sector experts in order to promote reform and investment in developing countries through improved access to information technology.

TECHNICAL ASSISTANCE

The provision of technical assistance to member countries has become a major component of World Bank activities. The economic and sector work (ESW) undertaken by the Bank is the vehicle for considerable technical assistance and often forms the basis of CASs and other strategic or advisory reports. In addition, project loans and credits may include funds earmarked specifically for feasibility studies, resource surveys, management or planning advice, and training. The Economic Development Institute has become one of the most important of the Bank's activities in technical assistance. It provides training in national economic management and project analysis for government officials at the middle and upper levels of responsibility. It also runs overseas courses aiming to build up local training capability, and administers a graduate scholarship programme.

The Bank serves as an executing agency for projects financed by the UN Development Programme (UNDP). It also administers projects financed by various trust funds.

Technical assistance (usually reimbursable) is also extended to countries that do not need Bank financial support, e.g. for training and transfer of technology. The Bank encourages the use of local consultants to assist with projects and stimulate institutional capability.

The Project Preparation Facility (PPF) was established in 1975 to provide cash advances to prepare projects that may be financed by the Bank. In 1992 the Bank established an Institutional Development Fund (IDF), which became operational on 1 July; the purpose of the Fund was to provide rapid, small-scale financial assistance, to a maximum value of US $500,000, for capacity-building proposals. In 2002 the IDF was reoriented to focus on good governance, in particular financial accountability and system reforms.

ECONOMIC RESEARCH AND STUDIES

In the 1990s the World Bank's research, conducted by its own research staff, was increasingly concerned with providing information to reinforce the Bank's expanding advisory role to developing countries and to improve policy in the Bank's borrowing countries. The principal areas of current research focus on issues such as maintaining sustainable growth while protecting the environment and the poorest sectors of society, encouraging the development of the private sector, and reducing and decentralizing government activities.

Consultative Group on International Agricultural Research (CGIAR): founded in 1971 under the sponsorship of the World Bank, FAO and UNDP. IFAD is also a co-sponsor. The Bank is chairman of the Group (which includes governments, private foundations and multilateral development agencies) and provides its secretariat. The Group was formed to raise financial support for international agricultural research work for improving crops and animal production in the developing countries; it supports 15 research centres. Its work is focused on the following five research areas: increasing productivity; protecting the environment; saving biodiversity; improving policies; and strengthening national research; Dir REN WANG (People's Republic of China).

CO-OPERATION WITH OTHER ORGANIZATIONS

The World Bank co-operates with other international partners with the aim of improving the impact of development efforts. It collaborates with the IMF in implementing the HIPC scheme and the two agencies work closely to achieve a common approach to development initiatives. The Bank has established strong working relationships with many other UN bodies, in particular through a mutual commitment to poverty reduction objectives. In May 2000 the Bank signed a joint statement of co-operation with the OECD. The Bank holds regular consultations with other multilateral development banks and with the European Union with respect to development issues. The Bank-NGO Committee provides an annual forum for discussion with non-governmental organizations (NGOs). Strengthening co-operation with external partners was a fundamental element of the Comprehensive Development Framework, which was adopted in 1998/99 (see above). In 2001/02 a Partnership Approval and Tracking System was implemented to provide information on the Bank's regional and global partnerships.

In 1997 a Partnerships Group was established to strengthen the Bank's work with development institutions, representatives of civil society and the private sector. The Group established a new Development Grant Facility, which became operational in October, to support partnership initiatives and to co-ordinate all of the Bank's grant-making activities. Also in 1997 the Bank, in partnership with the IMF, UNCTAD, UNDP, the World Trade Organization (WTO) and International Trade Commission, established an Integrated Framework for Trade-related Assistance to Least Developed Countries, at the request of the WTO, to assist those countries to integrate into the global trading system and improve basic trading capabilities.

In June 1995 the World Bank joined other international donors (including regional development banks, other UN bodies, Canada, France, the Netherlands and the USA) in establishing a Consultative Group to Assist the Poorest (CGAP), which was to channel funds to the most needy through grass-roots agencies. An initial credit of approximately US $200m. was committed by the donors. The Bank manages the CGAP Secretariat, which is responsible for the administration of external funding and for the evaluation and approval of project financing. The CGAP provides technical assistance, training and strategic advice to microfinance institutions and other relevant bodies. As an implementing agency of the Global Environment Facility (GEF) the Bank assists countries to prepare and supervise GEF projects relating to biological diversity, climate change and other environmental protection measures. It is an example of a partnership in action which addresses a global agenda, complementing Bank country assistance activities. Other funds administered by the Bank include the Global Program to Eradicate Poliomyelitis, launched during the financial year 2002/03, the Least Developed Countries Fund for Climate Change, established in September 2002, an Education for All Fast-Track Initiative Catalytic Trust Fund, established in 2003/04, and a Carbon Finance Assistance Trust Fund, established in 2004/05. In 2006/07 the Bank established a Global Facility for Disaster Reduction and Recovery. In September 2007 the Bank's Executive Directors approved a Carbon Partnership Facility and a Forest Carbon Partnership Facility to support its climate change activities.

The Bank is a lead organization in providing reconstruction assistance following natural disasters or conflicts, usually in collaboration with other UN agencies or international organizations, and through special trust funds. In November 2001 the Bank worked with UNDP and the Asian Development Bank to assess the needs of Afghanistan following the removal of the Taliban authorities in that country. At an International Conference on Reconstruction Assistance to Afghanistan, held in Tokyo, Japan, in January 2002, the Bank's President proposed extending US $500m. in assistance over a 30-month period, and providing an immediate amount of $50m.–$70m. in grants. In May an Afghanistan Reconstruction Trust Fund was established to provide a co-ordinated financing mechanism to support the interim administration in that country. The Bank is the Administrator of the Trust, which is managed jointly by the Bank, Asian Development Bank, Islamic Development Bank and UNDP. In May 2003 a Bank representative participated in an international advisory and monitoring board to assess reconstruction and development needs following international conflict in Iraq and removal of its governing regime. In October the Bank, with the UN Development Group, published a report identifying 14 priority areas for reconstruction, with funding requirements of $36,000m. over the period 2004–07, which was presented to an international donor conference held later in that month. The conference, held in Madrid, Spain, approved the establishment of an International Reconstruction Fund Facility for Iraq to channel international donations and to co-ordinate reconstruction activities. In January 2004 the Bank's Board of Executive Directors authorized the Bank to administer an integral part of the facility, the Iraq Trust Fund (ITF), to finance a programme of emergency projects and technical assistance. By 30 November 2007 international donors had committed about $467.1m. to the ITF (in addition to $1,299.3m. to the Fund administered by the UN's Development Group). The Bank was a partner, with the Iraqi Government, the UN Secretariat, the IMF and other financial institutions, in the International Compact with Iraq, a five-year framework for co-operation that was launched in May 2007. At the end of 2004 the Bank responded immediately to assist countries affected by a massive earthquake and subsequent tsunami which devastated many coastal areas of some 14 countries in the Indian Ocean. Bank staff undertook assessments and other efforts to accelerate recovery planning, mobilize financial support and help to co-ordinate relief and recovery efforts in affected regions. Some $672m. was allocated by the Bank, mainly in grants to be directed to Indonesia, Sri Lanka and the Maldives, for the first phase of reconstruction efforts. By June 2005 the Bank had committed more than $835m. to countries affected by the tsunami, in particular to repair damaged services, to assist the reconstruction of housing and to restore livelihoods. The Bank administers a Multi Donor Trust Fund for Aceh and North Sumatra that was established by the Indonesian Government to manage some $500m. in pledged aid. In October the Bank, with the Asian Development Bank, undertook a preliminary damage and needs assessment following a massive earthquake in north-west Pakistan. The cost of the disaster was estimated at $5,200m., with initial reconstruction funding requirements of $3,500m. An international donors' conference was convened in November. In March 2007 the Bank established a new framework to accelerate the response to a disaster or emergency situation.

The Bank has worked with FAO, WHO and the World Organisation of Animal Health (OIE) to develop strategies to monitor, contain and eradicate the spread of highly pathogenic avian influenza. In

September 2005 the Bank organized a meeting of leading experts on the issue and in November it co-sponsored, with FAO, WHO and the OIE, an international partners conference, focusing on control of the disease and preparedness planning for any future related influenza pandemic in humans. In January 2006 the Bank's Board of Directors approved the establishment of a funding programme, with resources of up to US $500m., to assist countries to combat the disease. Later in that month the Bank co-sponsored, with the European Commission and the People's Republic of China, an International Ministerial Pledging Conference on Avian and Human Pandemic Influenza, convened in Beijing. Participants pledged some $1,900m. to fund disease control and pandemic preparedness activities at global, regional and country levels.

The Bank conducts co-financing and aid co-ordination projects with official aid agencies, export credit institutions, and commercial banks to leverage additional concessional funds for recipient countries. During the year ending 30 June 2007 130 Bank projects leveraged US $6,300m. in co-financing.

EVALUATION

The Independent Evaluation Group is an independent unit within the World Bank. It conducts Country Assistance Evaluations to assess the development effectiveness of a Bank country programme, and studies and publishes the results of projects after a loan has been fully disbursed, so as to identify problems and possible improvements in future activities. In addition, the department reviews the Bank's global programmes and produces the *Annual Review of Development Effectiveness*. In 1996 a Quality Assurance Group was established to monitor the effectiveness of the Bank's operations and performance.

In September 1993 the Bank established an independent Inspection Panel, consistent with the Bank's objective of improving project implementation and accountability. The Panel, which became operational in September 1994, was to conduct independent investigations and report on complaints from local people concerning the design, appraisal and implementation of development projects supported by the Bank. By March 2008 the Panel had received 52 formal requests for inspection.

IBRD INSTITUTIONS

World Bank Institute (WBI): founded in March 1999 by merger of the Bank's Learning and Leadership Centre, previously responsible for internal staff training, and the Economic Development Institute (EDI), which had been established in 1955 to train government officials concerned with development programmes and policies. The new Institute aimed to emphasize the Bank's priority areas through the provision of training courses and seminars relating to poverty, crisis response, good governance and anti-corruption strategies. From 2004 the Institute was to place greater emphasis on individual country needs and on long-term institutional capacity-building. During 2006/07 WBI activities reached more than 75,000 participants world-wide. The Institute has continued to support a Global Knowledge Partnership, which was established in 1997 to promote alliances between governments, companies, other agencies and organizations committed to applying information and communication technologies for development purposes. Under the EDI a World Links for Development programme was also initiated to connect schools in developing countries with partner establishments in industrialized nations via the internet. In 1999 the WBI expanded its programmes through distance learning, a Global Development Network, and use of new technologies. A new initiative, Global Development Learning Network (GDLN), aimed to expand access to information and learning opportunities through the internet, videoconferences and organized exchanges. In 2007 there were some 120 GDLN centres, or affiliates. At that time formal partnership arrangements were in place between WBI and almost 200 learning centres and public, private and non-governmental organizations; a further 250 informal partnerships were also in place; Vice-Pres. RAKESH NANGIA (acting); pubs *Annual Report*, *Development Outreach* (quarterly), other books, working papers, case studies.

International Centre for Settlement of Investment Disputes (ICSID): founded in 1966 under the Convention of the Settlement of Investment Disputes between States and Nationals of Other States. The Convention was designed to encourage the growth of private foreign investment for economic development, by creating the possibility, always subject to the consent of both parties, for a Contracting State and a foreign investor who is a national of another Contracting State to settle any legal dispute that might arise out of such an investment by conciliation and/or arbitration before an impartial, international forum. The governing body of the Centre is its Administrative Council, composed of one representative of each Contracting State, all of whom have equal voting power. The President of the World Bank is (*ex officio*) the non-voting Chairman of the Administrative Council. By mid-2007 144 countries had signed and ratified the Convention to become ICSID Contracting States. At that time 236 cases had been registered with the Centre, of which 26 had been registered in the 2006/07 financial year; Sec.-Gen. NASSIB G. ZIADÉ (Chile/Lebanon) (acting).

Publications

Abstracts of Current Studies: The World Bank Research Program (annually).
African Development Indicators (annually).
Annual Report on Operations Evaluation.
Annual Report on Portfolio Performance.
Annual Review of Development Effectiveness.
Doing Business (annually).
EDI Annual Report.
Global Commodity Markets (quarterly).
Global Development Finance (annually, also on CD-Rom and online).
Global Economic Prospects (annually).
ICSID Annual Report.
ICSID Review—Foreign Investment Law Journal (2 a year).
Joint BIS-IMF-OECD-World Bank Statistics on External Debt (quarterly, also available online).
New Products and Outreach (EDI, annually).
News from ICSID (2 a year).
Poverty Reduction and the World Bank (annually).
Poverty Reduction Strategies Newsletter (quarterly).
Research News (quarterly).
Staff Working Papers.
World Bank Annual Report.
World Bank Atlas (annually).
World Bank Economic Review (3 a year).
The World Bank and the Environment (annually).
World Bank Research Observer.
World Development Indicators (annually, also on CD-Rom and online).
World Development Report (annually, also on CD-Rom).

Statistics

LENDING OPERATIONS, BY SECTOR
(projects approved, year ending 30 June; US $ million)

	2006	2007
Agriculture, fishing and forestry	1,751.9	1,717.4
Education	1,990.6	2,021.8
Energy and mining	3,030.3	1,784.0
Finance	2,319.7	1,613.6
Health and other social services	2,132.3	2,752.5
Industry and trade	1,542.2	1,181.3
Information and communication	81.0	148.8
Law, justice and public administration	5,857.6	5,468.2
Transportation	3,214.6	4,949.0
Water, sanitation and flood protection	1,721.0	3,059.4
Total	23,641.2	24,695.8

IBRD INCOME AND EXPENDITURE
(year ending 30 June; US $ million)

Revenue	2006	2007
Income from loans:		
Interest	4,791	5,391
Commitment charges	73	76
Income from investments and securities	1,057	1,173
Other income	267	268
Total income	6,188	6,908

INTERNATIONAL ORGANIZATIONS   United Nations (Specialized Agencies)

Expenditure	2006	2007
Interest on borrowings	3,836	4,324
Amortization of issuance and prepayment costs	105	92
Administrative expenses	1,058	1,065
Contributions to special programmes	173	171
Provision for loan losses	−724	−405
Other financial expenses	—	2
Total	4,448	5,249
Operating income	1,740	1,659
Effects of adjustment and accounting charge	−4,129	−1,799
Net income	−2,389	−140

IBRD LOANS AND IDA CREDITS APPROVED, BY SECTOR AND REGION
(1 July 2006–30 June 2007; US $ million)

Sector	Africa	East Asia and Pacific	South Asia	Europe and Central Asia	Latin America and the Caribbean	Middle East and North Africa	Total
Agriculture, fishing and forestry	369.7	268.6	733.6	53.4	83.4	208.5	1,717.4
Education	706.6	125.3	724.7	81.9	369.1	14.3	2,021.8
Energy and mining	773.0	118.5	243.7	337.6	19.5	291.6	1,784.0
Finance	26.3	230.1	678.1	353.5	286.4	39.2	1,613.6
Health and other social services	687.3	132.7	1,006.2	192.9	649.1	84.3	2,752.5
Industry and trade	144.2	102.0	292.9	395.5	236.3	10.3	1,181.3
Information and communication	146.0	0.0	2.8	0.0	0.0	0.0	148.8
Law, justice and public administration	1,352.5	887.7	1,165.8	812.6	1,187.8	61.9	5,468.2
Transportation	870.8	1,554.7	559.9	712.3	1,223.9	27.4	4,949.0
Water, sanitation and flood protection	720.5	624.3	223.9	822.4	497.8	170.5	3,059.4
Total	5,796.9	4,043.9	5,631.6	3,762.2	4,553.3	907.9	24,695.8
of which: IBRD	37.5	2,806.6	1,599.5	3,340.1	4,353.3	691.9	12,828.8
IDA	5,759.4	1,237.4	4,032.1	422.1	200.0	216.0	11,866.9

IBRD OPERATIONS AND RESOURCES, 2003–07
(years ending 30 June; US $ million)

	2002/03	2003/04	2004/05	2005/06	2006/07
Loans approved	11,231	11,045	13,611	14,135	12,829
Gross disbursements	11,921	10,109	9,722	11,833	11,055
New medium- to long-term borrowings	17,246	12,062	12,404	10,086	10,209
Net income	5,344	−2,404	3,831	−2,389	−140
Subscribed capital	189,567	189,718	189,718	189,718	189,801
Loans outstanding	116,240	109,610	104,401	103,004	97,805

Source: *World Bank Annual Report 2007*.

INTERNATIONAL ORGANIZATIONS

United Nations (Specialized Agencies)

EXECUTIVE DIRECTORS AND THEIR VOTING POWER
(March 2008)

Executive Director	Casting votes of	IBRD Total votes	IBRD % of total	IDA Total votes	IDA % of total
Appointed:					
E. Whitney Debevoise	USA	265,219	16.41	2,157,988	12.76
Toru Shikibu	Japan	127,250	7.87	1,721,312	10.18
Michael Hofmann	Germany	72,649	4.49	1,136,019	6.72
Ambroise Fayolle	France	69,647	4.31	714,499	4.22
Alex Gibbs	United Kingdom	69,647	4.31	916,353	5.42
Elected:					
Gino Alzetta (Belgium)	Austria, Belarus*, Belgium, Czech Republic, Hungary, Kazakhstan, Luxembourg, Slovakia, Slovenia, Turkey	77,669	4.81	794,064	4.70
Jorge Familiar (Mexico)	Costa Rica, El Salvador, Guatemala, Honduras, Mexico, Nicaragua, Spain, Venezuela*	72,786	4.50	381,723	2.26
Herman Wijffels (Romania)	Armenia, Bosnia and Herzegovina, Bulgaria*, Croatia, Cyprus, Georgia, Israel, the former Yugoslav republic of Macedonia, Moldova, Netherlands, Romania*, Ukraine	72,208	4.47	656,666	3.88
Samy Watson (Canada)	Antigua and Barbuda*, The Bahamas*, Barbados, Belize, Canada, Dominica, Grenada, Guyana, Ireland, Jamaica*, Saint Christopher and Nevis, Saint Lucia, Saint Vincent and the Grenadines	62,217	3.85	740,459	4.38
Rogerio Studart (Brazil)	Brazil, Colombia, Dominican Republic, Ecuador, Haiti, Panama, Philippines, Trinidad and Tobago	57,462	3.56	510,914	3.02
Giovanni Majnoni (Italy)	Albania, Greece, Italy, Malta*, Portugal, San Marino*, Timor-Leste	56,705	3.51	567,437	3.36
James Hagan (Australia)	Australia, Cambodia, Kiribati, Republic of Korea, Marshall Islands, Federated States of Micronesia, Mongolia, New Zealand, Palau, Papua New Guinea, Samoa, Solomon Islands, Vanuatu	55,800	3.45	549,180	3.25
Danendra Kumar (India)	Bangladesh, Bhutan, India, Sri Lanka	54,945	3.40	695,690	4.11
Mulu Ketsela (Ethiopia)	Angola, Botswana, Burundi, Ethiopia, The Gambia, Kenya, Lesotho, Liberia, Malawi, Mozambique, Namibia*, Nigeria, Seychelles*, Sierra Leone, South Africa, Sudan, Swaziland, Tanzania, Uganda, Zambia, Zimbabwe	54,347	3.36	752,993	4.45
Svein Aass (Norway)	Denmark, Estonia*, Finland, Iceland, Latvia, Lithuania*, Norway, Sweden	54,039	3.34	880,435	5.21
Shija Shah (Pakistan)	Afghanistan, Algeria, Ghana, Iran, Morocco, Pakistan, Tunisia	51,544	3.19	365,623	2.16
Michel Mordasini (Switzerland)	Azerbaijan, Kyrgyzstan, Poland, Serbia, Switzerland, Tajikistan, Turkmenistan*, Uzbekistan	49,192	3.04	660,940	3.91
Merza Hasan Hasan (Kuwait)	Bahrain*, Egypt, Iraq, Jordan, Kuwait, Lebanon, Libya, Maldives, Oman, Qatar*, Syria, United Arab Emirates, Yemen	47,042	2.91	371,148	2.19
Jiayi Zou	People's Republic of China	45,049	2.79	332,400	1.97
Abdulrahman M. Almofadhi	Saudi Arabia	45,045	2.79	575,240	3.40
Alexy G. Kvasov	Russia	45,045	2.79	52,501	0.31
Mat Aron Deraman (Malaysia)	Brunei*, Fiji, Indonesia, Laos, Malaysia, Myanmar, Nepal, Singapore, Thailand, Tonga, Viet Nam	41,096	2.54	466,563	2.76
Felix Alberto Camarasa (Argentina)	Argentina, Bolivia, Chile, Paraguay, Peru, Uruguay*	37,499	2.32	267,761	1.58
Louis Philippe Ong Seng (Mauritius)	Benin, Burkina Faso, Cameroon, Cape Verde, Central African Republic, Chad, Comoros, Democratic Republic of the Congo, Republic of the Congo, Côte d'Ivoire, Djibouti, Equatorial Guinea, Gabon, Guinea, Guinea-Bissau, Madagascar, Mali, Mauritania, Mauritius, Niger, Rwanda, São Tomé and Príncipe, Senegal, Togo	32,252	2.00	644,673	3.81

Note: IBRD voting status as at 31 December 2007; IDA as at 29 February 2008. Eritrea (843 votes in IBRD and 31,162 in IDA), Montenegro (938 votes in IBRD and 44,271), Somalia (802 votes in IBRD and 10,506 in IDA) and Suriname (662 votes in IBRD) did not participate in the 2006 regular election of Executive Directors.

* Member of IBRD only (not IDA).

INTERNATIONAL ORGANIZATIONS United Nations (Specialized Agencies)

International Development Association—IDA

Address: 1818 H Street, NW, Washington, DC 20433, USA.
Telephone: (202) 473-1000; **fax:** (202) 477-6391; **internet:** www.worldbank.org/ida.

The International Development Association began operations in November 1960. Affiliated to the IBRD, IDA advances capital to the poorer developing member countries on more flexible terms than those offered by the IBRD.

MEMBERS

IDA has 166 members.

Organization

(March 2008)

Officers and staff of the IBRD serve concurrently as officers and staff of IDA.

President and Chairman of Executive Directors: ROBERT B. ZOELLICK (USA).

Activities

IDA assistance is aimed at the poorer developing countries (i.e. those with an annual GNP per capita of less than US $1,065 were to qualify for assistance in 2007/08) in order to support their poverty reduction strategies. Under IDA lending conditions, credits can be extended to countries whose balance of payments could not sustain the burden of repayment required for IBRD loans. Terms are more favourable than those provided by the IBRD; credits are for a period of 35 or 40 years, with a 'grace period' of 10 years, and carry no interest charges. At mid-2007 80 countries were eligible for IDA assistance, including several small-island economies with a GNP per head greater than $1,065, but which would otherwise have little or no access to Bank funds, and 16 so-called 'blend borrowers' which are entitled to borrow from both the IDA and IBRD.

IDA's total development resources, consisting of members' subscriptions and supplementary resources (additional subscriptions and contributions), are replenished periodically by contributions from the more affluent member countries. An agreement to provide a substantial replenishment of funds, amounting to some US $34,000m. for the period 1 July 2005–30 June 2008, was concluded in February 2005. New contributions pledged by 40 donor countries amounted to $20,700m. of the total replenishment. The agreement incorporated a renewed focus on stimulating economic growth in support of the Millennium Development Goals, with a strengthened monitoring and results-assessment agenda based on poverty reduction objectives. The replenishment programme also placed greater emphasis on the use of grants to address the needs of the poorest countries, in particular those most vulnerable to debt. Negotiations on the 15th replenishment of IDA funds (IDA15) commenced in March 2007, in Paris, France. Participants selected the following 'special themes' for further discussion: the role of IDA in global aid architecture; the effectiveness of IDA assistance at country level; and IDA's role in fragile states. In December an agreement was concluded to replenish IDA resources by some $41,600m., for the period 1 July 2008–30 June 2011, of which $25,100m. was pledged by 45 donor countries.

During the year ending 30 June 2007 new IDA commitments amounted to US $11,867m. for 189 projects, compared with $9,506m. in the previous year. Of total IDA assistance during 2006/07 $5,759.4m. (49%) was for Africa and $4,032.1m. (34%) for South Asia. One-third of lending was for infrastructure projects. An increasing proportion of IDA lending, accounting for some 18% of total financing in 2006/07, is in the form of grants for the poorest or most vulnerable countries.

IDA administers a Trust Fund, which was established in November 1996 as part of a World Bank/IMF initiative to assist heavily indebted poor countries (HIPCs). In September 2005 the World Bank's Development Committee and the International Monetary and Financial Committee of the IMF endorsed a proposal of the Group of Eight (G-8) industrialized countries to cancel the remaining multilateral debt owed by HIPCs that had reached their completion point under the scheme (see IBRD). In December IDA convened a meeting of donor countries to discuss funding to uphold its financial capability upon its contribution to the so-called Multilateral Debt Relief Initiative (MDRI). IDA's participation in the scheme was approved by the Board of Executive Directors in March 2006 and entered into effect on 1 July. By late 2007 23 countries had reached completion point. At the start of that year total debt relief provided by IDA since the HIPC initiative commenced was estimated to be US $53,600m., of which $36,400m. was committed under the MDRI.

Publication

Annual Report.

Statistics

IDA OPERATIONS AND RESOURCES, 2003–07
(years ending 30 June; US $ million)

	2002/03	2003/04	2004/05	2005/06	2006/07
Commitments*	7,282	9,035	8,696	9,506	11,867
Disbursements	7,019	6,936	8,950	8,910	8,579
Number of projects	141	158	165	173	189

* Excluding HIPC development grants.
Source: *World Bank Annual Report 2007.*

International Finance Corporation—IFC

Address: 2121 Pennsylvania Ave, NW, Washington, DC 20433, USA.
Telephone: (202) 473-3800; **fax:** (202) 974-4384; **e-mail:** information@ifc.org; **internet:** www.ifc.org.

IFC was founded in 1956 as a member of the World Bank Group to stimulate economic growth in developing countries by financing private-sector investments, mobilizing capital in international financial markets, and providing technical assistance and advice to governments and businesses.

MEMBERS

IFC has 179 members.

Organization

(March 2008)

IFC is a separate legal entity in the World Bank Group. Executive Directors of the World Bank also serve as Directors of IFC. The

President of the World Bank is *ex officio* Chairman of the IFC Board of Directors, which has appointed him President of IFC. Subject to his overall supervision, the day-to-day operations of IFC are conducted by its staff under the direction of the Executive Vice-President. At the end of June 2007 IFC had 3,134 staff members, of whom 51% were based in field offices.

PRINCIPAL OFFICERS

President: ROBERT B. ZOELLICK (USA).
Executive Vice-President: LARS THUNELL (Sweden).

REGIONAL AND INDUSTRY DEPARTMENTS

Seven Regional Departments cover: sub-Saharan Africa; East Asia and the Pacific; South Asia; Central and Eastern Europe; Southern Europe and Central Asia; Latin America and the Caribbean; and the Middle East and North Africa. These aim to develop strategies for member countries, promote businesses, and strengthen relations with governments and the private sector. The Industry Departments include Agribusiness; Global Financial Markets; Global Information and Communications Technologies (jointly managed with the World Bank); Global Manufacturing and Services; Health and Education; Infrastructure; Oil, Gas, Mining and Chemicals (jointly managed with the World Bank); and Private Equity and Investment Funds.

REGIONAL AND RESIDENT MISSIONS

There are Regional and Resident Missions in Australia, Bangladesh, Brazil, Cambodia, People's Republic of China, Dominican Republic, Egypt, Guyana, Haiti, India, Kazakhstan, Laos, Mongolia, Russia, Serbia, South Africa, Sri Lanka, Trinidad and Tobago, Turkey, United Arab Emirates and Viet Nam. There are also Special Representatives in France, Germany and the United Kingdom (for Europe), an office in Tokyo, Japan, and other programme co-ordinators, managers and investment officers in more than 30 additional countries.

Activities

IFC aims to promote economic development in developing member countries by assisting the growth of private enterprise and effective capital markets. It finances private sector projects, through loans, the purchase of equity, quasi-equity products, and risk management services, and assists governments to create conditions that stimulate the flow of domestic and foreign private savings and investment. IFC may provide finance for a project that is partly state-owned, provided that there is participation by the private sector and that the project is operated on a commercial basis. IFC also mobilizes additional resources from other financial institutions, in particular through syndicated loans, thus providing access to international capital markets. IFC provides a range of advisory services to help to improve the investment climate in developing countries and offers technical assistance to private enterprises and governments. Increasingly IFC is focused on extending assistance to 'frontier' markets, i.e. those designated by the World Bank as low-income or high-risk countries or regions. Other strategic priorities in 2006/07 included building long-term relationships with local companies; ensuring environmental and social sustainability; helping the private sector strengthen infrastructure, from ports and roads to schools and hospitals; and developing local financial markets.

To be eligible for financing projects must be profitable for investors, as well as financially and economically viable; must benefit the economy of the country concerned; and must comply with IFC's environmental and social guide-lines. IFC aims to promote best corporate governance and management methods and sustainable business practices, and encourages partnerships between governments, non-governmental organizations and community groups. In 2001/02 IFC developed a Sustainability Framework to help to assess the longer-term economic, environmental and social impact of projects. The first Sustainability Review was published in mid-2002. In 2002/03 IFC assisted 10 international banks to draft a voluntary set of guide-lines (the Equator Principles), based on IFC's environmental, social and safeguard monitoring policies, to be applied to their global project finance activities. A revised set of Equator Principles was released in July 2006. (By February 2008 59 financial institutions had signed up to the Equator Principles.)

IFC's authorized capital is US $2,450m. At 30 June 2007 paid-in capital was $2,365m. The World Bank was originally the principal source of borrowed funds, but IFC also borrows from private capital markets. IFC's net income amounted to $2,618m. in 2006/07, compared with $1,278m. in the previous year.

In the year ending 30 June 2007 project financing approved by IFC amounted to US $9,995m. for 299 projects in 69 countries (compared with $8,275m. for 284 projects in the previous year). Of the total approved in 2006/07 $8,220m. was for IFC's own account, while $1,775m. was in the form of loan syndications and underwriting of securities issues and investment funds by more than 100 participant banks and institutional investors. Generally, IFC limits its financing to less than 25% of the total cost of a project, but may take up to a 35% stake in a venture (although never as a majority shareholder). Disbursements for IFC's account amounted to $5,841m. in 2006/07 (compared with $4,428m. in the previous year).

In 2006/07 the largest proportion of investment commitments, for IFC's account, was allocated to Latin America and the Caribbean (21.7%). Sub-Saharan Africa received 16.8%, the Middle East and North Africa 13.6%, Southern Europe and Central Asia 12.8%, South Asia 12.4%, East Asia and the Pacific 10.9%, Central and Eastern Europe 8.1%, and global projects 3.8%. In that year 41.2% of total financing committed was for global financial markets. Other commitments included global manufacturing and services (16.5%), infrastructure (12.1%) and oil, gas and mining (10.9%).

IFC's Private Sector Advisory Services (PSAS), jointly managed with the World Bank, advises governments and private enterprises on policy, transaction implementation and foreign direct investment. The Foreign Investment Advisory Service (FIAS), jointly operated and financed with the World Bank and MIGA, provides technical assistance and advice on promoting foreign investment and strengthening the country's investment framework at the request of governments. FIAS completed 83 projects in 2006/07, bringing a total of 760 projects since the Service was established in 1987. Under the Technical Assistance Trust Funds Program (TATF), established in 1988, IFC manages resources contributed by various governments and agencies to provide finance for feasibility studies, project identification studies and other types of technical assistance relating to project preparation. In 2004 a Grassroots Business Initiative was established, with external donor funding, to support businesses that provide economic opportunities for disadvantaged communities in Africa, Latin America, and South and Southeast Asia. Other areas of advisory services include carbon finance, cleaner technologies and sustainable investing.

IFC support for private sector development includes technical assistance and advisory services for small-scale entrepreneurs to assist the development of business proposals and efforts to generate funding for their projects. IFC has established, with the support of external donors, a network of Small and Medium Enterprise (SME) facilities and programmes which aim to provide support services at enterprise level, to assist the development of local private sector support institutions, and to advocate ways to improve the business-enabling environment. At the end of 2007 these included the Private Enterprise Partnership for Africa (PEP-Africa), with headquarters in Johannesburg, South Africa; the Private Enterprise Partnership for the Pacific; the Mekong Private Sector Development Facility (MPDF), which supports the development of SMEs in Cambodia, Laos and Viet Nam; the Private Enterprise Partnership-Southeast Europe; a Private Enterprise Partnership to serve countries in eastern Europe and central Asia; the Private Enterprise Partnership for China (PEP-China), with headquarters in Chengdu, Sichuan Province; the SouthAsia Enterprise Development Facility, based in Dhaka, Bangladesh; the Program for Eastern Indonesian SME Assistance (PENSA), based in Bali, Indonesia; the Technical Assistance Facility for Latin America and the Caribbean; the Private Enterprise Partnership for the Middle East and North Africa (PEP-MENA); the Private Enterprise Partnership for the Philippines (PEP-Philippines), to provide technical assistance to SMEs in that country, in particular in the Mindanao autonomous region; and the Private Enterprise Partnership-Aceh & Nias (PEP-Aceh & Nias), which had a four-year mandate to support the development of SMEs in areas worst affected by the tsunami in late 2004. In November 2004 IFC announced the establishment of a Global Trade Finance Programme, with funding of some US $500m., which aimed to support SME importers and exporters in emerging markets, to facilitate South-South trade in goods and services, and to extend technical assistance and training to local financial institutions.

Publications

Annual Report.
Doing Business (annually).
Emerging Stock Markets Factbook (annually).
Impact (quarterly).
Lessons of Experience (series).
Results on the Ground (series).
Review of Small Businesses (annually).
Sustainability Report (annually).
Discussion papers and technical documents.

Statistics

IFC OPERATIONS AND RESOURCES, 2005–07
(fiscal years ending 30 June; US $ million, unless otherwise stated)

	2005	2006	2007
Approved investments			
Number of new projects	236	284	299
Total commitments signed*	6,449	8,275	9,995
For IFC's own account	5,373	6,703	8,220
Disbursements			
Total financing disbursed	4,011	5,739	7,456
For IFC's own account	3,456	4,428	5,841
Resources and income			
Borrowings	15,359	14,967	15,879
Paid-in capital	2,365	2,364	2,365
Retained earnings	7,433	8,711	11,329
Net income	2,015	1,278	2,618

*Including loan guarantees and risk management products.
Source: *IFC Annual Report 2007*.

Multilateral Investment Guarantee Agency—MIGA

Address: 1818 H Street, NW, Washington, DC 20433, USA.
Telephone: (202) 473-6163; **fax:** (202) 522-2630; **internet:** www.miga.org.

MIGA was founded in 1988 as an affiliate of the World Bank. Its mandate is to encourage the flow of foreign direct investment to, and among, developing member countries, through the provision of political risk insurance and investment marketing services to foreign investors and host governments, respectively.

MEMBERS

MIGA has 171 member countries. Membership is open to all countries that are members of the World Bank.

Organization
(March 2008)

MIGA is legally and financially separate from the World Bank. It is supervised by a Council of Governors (comprising one Governor and one Alternate of each member country) and an elected Board of Directors (of no less than 12 members).

President: ROBERT B. ZOELLICK (USA).

Executive Vice-President: YUKIKO OMURA (Japan).

Activities

The convention establishing MIGA took effect in April 1988. Authorized capital was US $1,082m. In April 1998 the Board of Directors approved an increase in MIGA's capital base. A grant of $150m. was transferred from the IBRD as part of the package, while the capital increase (totalling $700m. callable capital and $150m. paid-in capital) was approved by MIGA's Council of Governors in April 1999. A three-year subscription period then commenced, covering the period April 1999–March 2002 (later extended to March 2003). At 30 June 2007 109 countries had subscribed $745.8m. of the new capital increase. At that time total subscriptions to the capital stock amounted to $1,885.6m., of which $359.7m. was paid-in.

MIGA guarantees eligible investments against losses resulting from non-commercial risks, under four main categories:

(i) transfer risk resulting from host government restrictions on currency conversion and transfer;

(ii) risk of loss resulting from legislative or administrative actions of the host government;

(iii) repudiation by the host government of contracts with investors in cases in which the investor has no access to a competent forum;

(iv) the risk of armed conflict and civil unrest.

Before guaranteeing any investment, MIGA must ensure that it is commercially viable, contributes to the development process and is not harmful to the environment. During the fiscal year 1998/99 MIGA and IFC appointed the first Compliance Advisor and Ombudsman to consider the concerns of local communities directly affected by MIGA- or IFC-sponsored projects. In February 1999 the Board of Directors approved an increase in the amount of political risk insurance available for each project, from US $75m. to $200m.

During the year ending 30 June 2007 MIGA issued 45 investment insurance contracts for 29 projects with a value of US $1,400m. Since 1988 the total investment guarantees issued amounted to some $17,400m., through 884 contracts in support of 556 projects.

MIGA works with local insurers, export credit agencies, development finance institutions and other organizations to promote insurance in a country, to ensure a level of consistency among insurers and to support capacity-building within the insurance industry. MIGA also offers investment marketing services to help to promote foreign investment in developing countries and in transitional economies, and to disseminate information on investment opportunities. In early 2007 MIGA's technical assistance services were amalgamated into the Foreign Advisory Investment Service (FIAS, see IFC), of which MIGA became a lead partner, along with IFC and the World Bank.

In October 1995 MIGA established a new network on investment opportunities, which connected investment promotion agencies (IPAs) throughout the world on an electronic information network. The so-called IPA*net* aimed to encourage further investments among developing countries, to provide access to comprehensive information on investment laws and conditions and to strengthen links between governmental, business and financial associations and investors. A new version of IPA*net* was launched in 1997 (and can be accessed at www.ipanet.net). In June 1998 MIGA initiated a new internet-based facility, 'PrivatizationLink', to provide information on investment opportunities resulting from the privatization of industries in developing economies. In October 2000 a specialized facility within the service was established to facilitate investment in Russia (russia.privatizationlink.com). During 2000/01 an office was established in Paris, France, to promote and co-ordinate European investment in developing countries, in particular in Africa and Eastern Europe. In March 2002 MIGA opened a regional office, based in Johannesburg, South Africa. In September a new regional office was inaugurated in Singapore, in order to facilitate foreign investment in Asia.

In April 2002 MIGA launched a new service, 'FDIXchange', to provide potential investors, advisors and financial institutions with up-to-date market analysis and information on foreign direct investment opportunities in emerging economies (accessible at www.fdixchange.com). An FDIXchange Investor Information Development Programme was launched in January 2003. In January 2004 a new FDI Promotion Centre became available on the internet (www.fdi-promotion.com) to facilitate information exchange and knowledge-sharing among investment promotion professionals, in particular in developing countries. (A Serbian language version was launched in June 2005.) During 2003/04 MIGA established a new fund, the

INTERNATIONAL ORGANIZATIONS

Invest-in-Development Facility, to enhance the role of foreign investment in attaining the Millennium Development Goals. In 2005/06 MIGA supported for the first time a project aimed at selling carbon credits gained by reducing greenhouse gas emissions; it provided US $2m. in guarantee coverage to the El Salvador-based initiative. A new internet service, relating to political risk management and insurance, was launched during 2006/07 (www.pri-center.com).

In July 2004 an Afghanistan Investment Guarantee Facility, to be administered by MIGA, became operational to provide political risk guarantees for foreign investors in that country.

Publications

Annual Report.
MIGA News (online newsletter; every 2 months).
Other guides, brochures and regional briefs.

International Civil Aviation Organization—ICAO

Address: 999 University St, Montréal, QC H3C 5H7, Canada.
Telephone: (514) 954-8219; **fax:** (514) 954-6077; **e-mail:** icaohq@icao.int; **internet:** www.icao.int.

The Convention on International Civil Aviation was signed in Chicago in 1944. As a result, ICAO was founded in 1947 to develop the techniques of international air navigation and to help in the planning and improvement of international air transport.

MEMBERS

ICAO has 190 contracting states.

Organization
(March 2008)

ASSEMBLY

Composed of representatives of all member states, the Assembly is the organization's legislative body and meets at least once every three years. It reviews the work of the organization, sets out the work programme for the next three years, approves the budget and determines members' contributions. The 36th Assembly was held in September 2007.

COUNCIL

Composed of representatives of 36 member states, elected by the Assembly. It is the executive body, and establishes and supervises subsidiary technical committees and makes recommendations to member governments; meets in virtually continuous session; elects the President, appoints the Secretary-General, and administers the finances of the organization. The Council is assisted by the Air Navigation Commission, the Air Transport Committee, the Committee on Joint Support of Air Navigation Services, the Finance Committee, the Committee on Unlawful Interference and the Technical Co-operation Committee. The functions of the Council are:

(i) to adopt international standards and recommended practices and incorporate them as annexes to the Convention on International Civil Aviation;

(ii) to arbitrate between member states on matters concerning aviation and implementation of the Convention;

(iii) to investigate any situation which presents avoidable obstacles to development of international air navigation;

(iv) to take whatever steps are necessary to maintain safety and regularity of operation of international air transport;

(v) to provide technical assistance to the developing countries under the UN Development Programme and other assistance programmes.

President of the Council: ROBERTO KOBEH GONZÁLEZ (Mexico).

SECRETARIAT

The Secretariat, headed by a Secretary-General, is divided into five main divisions: the Air Navigation Bureau, the Air Transport Bureau, the Technical Co-operation Bureau, the Legal Bureau, and the Bureau of Administration and Services.
Secretary-General: TAÏEB CHÉRIF (Algeria).

REGIONAL OFFICES

Asia and Pacific: 252/1 Vibhavadi-Rangsit Rd, Ladyao, Chatuchak, Bangkok 10900, Thailand; tel. (2) 537-8189; fax (2) 537-8199; e-mail icao_apac@bangkok.icao.int; internet www.bangkok.icao.int; Regional Dir MOKHTAR AHMED AWAN.

Eastern and Southern Africa: Limuru Rd, Gigiri, POB 46294, Nairobi, Kenya; tel. (20) 7622395; fax (20) 7623028; e-mail icao@icao.unon.org; internet www.icao.int/esaf; Regional Dir GEOFFREY P. MOSHABESHA.

European and North Atlantic: 3 bis Villa Émile-Bergerat, 92522 Neuilly-sur-Seine Cédex, France; tel. 1-46-41-85-85; fax 1-46-41-85-00; e-mail icaoeurnat@paris.icao.int; internet www.paris.icao.int; Regional Dir KARSTEN THEIL.

Middle East: POB 85, Cairo Airport Post Office Terminal One, Cairo 11776, Egypt; tel. (2) 267-4840; fax (2) 267-4843; e-mail icaomid@cairo.icao.int; internet www.icao.int/mid; Regional Dir MOHAMED R. M. KHONJI.

North America, Central America and the Caribbean: Apdo Postal 5-377, CP 06500, México, DF, Mexico; tel. (55) 5250-3211; fax (55) 5203-2757; e-mail icao_nacc@mexico.icao.int; internet www.icao.int/nacc; Regional Dir L. J. MARTIN.

South America: ave Víctor Andrés Belaúnde 147, San Isidro, Lima, Peru; tel. (1) 611-8686; fax (1) 611-8689; e-mail mail@lima.icao.int; internet www.lima.icao.int; Regional Dir JOSÉ MIGUEL CEPPI.

Western and Central Africa: 15 blvd de la République, BP 2356, Dakar, Senegal; tel. 839-9393; fax 823-6926; e-mail icaodkr@icao.sn; internet www.icao.int/wacaf; Regional Dir A. GUITTEYE.

Activities

ICAO aims to ensure the safe and orderly growth of civil aviation; to encourage skills in aircraft design and operation; to improve airways, airports and air navigation; to prevent the waste of resources in unreasonable competition; to safeguard the rights of each contracting party to operate international air transport; and to prevent discriminatory practices. ICAO collects and publishes statistics relating to civil aviation. In December 2004 the Council adopted the following as strategic objectives for the period 2005–10: to enhance global civil aviation safety; to enhance global civil aviation security; to minimize the adverse effect of global civil aviation on the environment; to enhance the efficiency of aviation operations; to maintain the continuity of aviation operations; and to strengthen law governing international civil aviation.

SAFETY

ICAO aims to ensure and enhance all aspects of air safety and security. A Global Aviation Safety Plan (GASP) was initiated in 1998 to promote new safety measures. ICAO assists member countries to develop appropriate educational and training activities. It also supports programmes to assist the victims of aircraft accidents. The 32nd Assembly, held in September–October 1998, endorsed the establishment of a Universal Safety Oversight Audit Programme (USOAP), to provide for mandatory, systematic and harmonized safety audits regularly to be undertaken in member states in fields including the airworthiness of aircraft, flight operations and personnel licensing. The Programme became operational on 1 January 1999 with the aim of auditing all member states and compiling an Audit Findings and Differences Database over an initial three-year period (subsequently extended). In October 2001 the Assembly approved the concept of an International Financial Facility for Aviation Safety (IFFAS) to provide funds to states to adhere to ICAO safety-related standards. The Facility became effective in 2003. In October 2004 the Assembly recognized the USOAP as having significantly contributed to raising the level of safety oversight world-wide and endorsed its expansion, from 1 January 2005, to incorporate all safety-related provisions of the Annexes to the Chicago Convention. The Assembly also requested ICAO to accelerate the development of standards and guidance under its programme for the prevention of Controlled Flight Into Terrain accidents; urged contracting states strictly to control the movement and storage of man-portable defence systems; and resolved to review standards relating to the health or passengers and crews, as an integral element of safe air travel. In late 2005, following a series of aircraft accidents, ICAO determined to convene a meeting of Directors-General of Civil Aviation in order to assess the current status of aviation safety, to identify way to achieve improvements in safety standards and to develop a new framework of safety measures. The conference, convened in March 2006, endorsed a Global Strategy for Aviation Safety. The declaration issued at the meeting stipulated that, *inter alia,* provisions should be implemented, not later than March 2008, for safety-related information, including results of audits within the USOAP, to be shared among states, the public and other interested parties. Also at the conference, the Directors-General endorsed Part I of a Global Aviation Safety Roadmap, delivered to ICAO in December of 2005 by the Industry Safety Strategy Group. The Roadmap identified mid- and long-term goals related to air-safety oversight and regulation matters. In December 2006 Part II of the Roadmap was finalized, outlining strategies for achieving these objectives. A new Global Aviation Safety Plan, based on the Roadmap, was published in June 2007, identifying safety targets for the period 2008–11. In September 2007 the Assembly endorsed a new Comprehensive Regional Implementation Plan for Aviation Safety in Africa, which had been formulated by African governments, with representatives of the local civil aviation authorities and air industry.

ICAO maintains a Flight Safety Information Exchange (FSIX) website to help to disseminate safety-related information, including safety and security audits, within the aviation community. The main subject areas cover safety oversight information, resolving safety deficiencies, regional regulations and safety management.

SECURITY

In October 1998 a protocol to the Chicago Convention, prohibiting the use of weapons against civil aircraft in flight, entered into effect, having been adopted in 1984 following an attack on a Korean Airlines passenger flight. In 2000 ICAO developed model legislation to cover offences committed on board aircraft by unruly passengers (other than hijacking, sabotage etc., which are already governed by international legislation). Following the terrorist attacks perpetrated against targets in the USA in September 2001, involving the use of hijacked aircraft as weapons, the 33rd Assembly—held in September–October—adopted a Declaration on the Misuse of Civil Aircraft as Weapons of Destruction and Other Terrorist Acts involving Civil Aviation. The Declaration urged a review of ICAO's aviation security programme and consideration of the initiation of a programme to audit airport security arrangements and member states civil aviation security programmes. In October the Council established a Special Group on Aviation War Risk Insurance to make recommendations on the development of a co-ordinated and long-term approach in this area. A proposal by the Special Group concerning the establishment of a Global Scheme on Aviation War Risk Insurance (Globaltime), to be provided by a non-profit entity with initial multilateral government support, was approved in principle by the Council in May 2002. A high-level ministerial conference, convened under ICAO auspices in February of that year to discuss preventing, combating and eradicating acts of terrorism involving civil aviation, and strengthening the organization's role in overseeing the adoption and national implementation of security-related standards and procedures, endorsed a global Aviation Security Plan of Action and reaffirmed the responsibility of states to ensure aviation security on their territories. The Plan provided for development of an effective global response to emerging threats; strengthened security-related provisions of the Convention on International Civil Aviation; and enhanced co-ordination of regional and sub-regional audit programmes. In June a Universal Security Audit Programme was launched, as part of the Aviation Security Plan of Action, to help to identify and correct deficiencies in the implementation of security-related standards. The first mandatory security audit was conducted in November; an initial audit of all contracting states was scheduled to have been completed by the end of 2007. A new Implementation Support and Development Branch was established in June 2007 to support member states with significant safety oversight or security deficiencies and to help to implement correction action plans.

ICAO is developing a globally inter-operable system of Machine Readable Travel Documents (MRTDs), incorporating biometric identification data, in order to enhance airport and international security. ICAO is providing technical assistance to support the efforts of contracting states to develop MRTDs and to achieve the objective that all states issue machine readable passports by 1 April 2010.

NAVIGATION

ICAO's Air Navigation Bureau develops technical studies for the Air Navigation Commission, as well as recommendations for standards and recommended practices relating to the safety, regularity and efficiency of international air navigation. Areas of activity include meteorology, automated data interchange systems, accident investigation and prevention, aviation medicine and air traffic management. In March 1998 the ICAO Council adopted a Global Air Navigation Plan for Communications, Navigation, Surveillance, and Air Traffic Management (CNS/ATM) Systems. In May an international conference was held in Rio de Janeiro, Brazil, to consider implementation of the CNS/ATM systems. The conference urged greater financing and co-operation between states to ensure that the CNS/ATM becomes the basis of a global ATM system. An Air Traffic Management Operational Concept Panel, which was to develop standards and recommend procedures for the development of an integrated ATM system, was convened for the first time in March–April 1999. In October 1998 the Assembly adopted a Charter on the Rights and Obligations of States relating to Global Navigation Satellite Systems (GNSS) to serve as an interim framework on the GNSS. A long-term legal framework on principles governing the GNSS, including a new international convention, remains under consideration. The 11th Air Navigation Conference, convened by ICAO in September–October 2003, in Montréal, endorsed an operational concept for a globally harmonized air navigation system that aimed to enhance safety and reduce airspace and airport congestion. In June 2003 ICAO published measures for preventing the spread by air travel of Severe Acute Respiratory Syndrome (SARS) and other contagious diseases, based on guide-lines issued by the World Health Organization. In 2005 ICAO assisted countries and international organizations to develop preparedness strategies with regard to the threat of a pandemic of highly pathogenic avian influenza.

ENVIRONMENTAL PROTECTION

ICAO activities with respect to the environment are primarily focused on areas that require a co-ordinated international approach, i.e. aircraft noise and engine emissions. International standards and guide-lines for noise certification of aircraft and international provisions for the regulation of aircraft engine emissions have been adopted and published in Annex 16 to the Chicago Convention. ICAO was recognized in the 1997 Kyoto Protocol to the Framework Convention on Climate Change as the global body through which industrialized nations were to pursue the limitation or reduction of so-called greenhouse gas emissions from international aviation. In 1998 ICAO's Committee on Aviation Environmental Protection recommended a reduction of 16% in the permissible levels of nitrogen oxides emitted by aircraft engines. The new limits, to be applicable to new engine designs from 2003, were adopted by the ICAO Council in early 1999. Further reduced limits were approved in 2004. In June 2001 the Council adopted a stricter noise standard (applicable from 1 January 2006) for jet and large propeller-driven aircraft, as well as new noise limits for helicopters and new provisions concerning re-certification. In October the Assembly approved a series of measures developed by the Committee concerning a balanced approach to aircraft noise and based on the following elements: quieter aircraft; land-use planning and management in the vicinity of airports; operational procedures for noise abatement; and operating restrictions.

In September 2007 the ICAO Council determined to establish a new Group on International Aviation and Climate Change, comprising senior government officials, in order to formulate an 'aggressive' programme of action on aviation and climate change, with a framework to help to achieve emissions reductions, for example through fuel efficiency targets and other voluntary measures. The Group held its inaugural meeting in February 2008.

ICAO SPECIFICATIONS

These are contained in annexes to the Chicago Convention, and in three sets of Procedures for Air Navigation Services (PANS Documents). The specifications are periodically revised in keeping with developments in technology and changing requirements. The 18 annexes to the Convention include personnel licensing, rules relating to the conduct of flights, meteorological services, aeronautical charts, air–ground communications, safety specifications, identification, air-traffic control, rescue services, environmental protection, security and the transporting of dangerous goods. Technical Manuals and Circulars are issued to facilitate implementation.

TECHNICAL CO-OPERATION

ICAO's Technical Co-operation Bureau promotes the implementation of ICAO Standards and Recommended Practices, including the CNS/ATM and safety oversight measures, and assists developing countries in the execution of various projects, financed by UNDP and other sources. The TRAINAIR programme helps relevant institutions to develop a standard aviation training package, and promotes international co-operation in training and course development.

ICAO works in close co-operation with other UN bodies, such as the World Meteorological Organization, the International Telecommunication Union, the Universal Postal Union, the World Health Organization and the International Maritime Organization. Non-governmental organizations which also participate in ICAO's work include the International Air Transport Association, the Airports Council International, the International Federation of Air Line Pilots' Associations, and the International Council of Aircraft Owner and Pilot Associations.

Finance

ICAO is financed mainly by contributions from member states. The authorized budget for 2008 and 2009 amounted to US $79.95m. and $80.09m. respectively.

Publications

Annual Report of the Council.
Aviation Training Directory.
Directory of National Civil Aviation Administrations (online database).
ICAO Journal (6 a year, in English, French and Spanish).
World of Civil Aviation.
Conventions, agreements, rules of procedures, regulations, technical publications and manuals.

International Fund for Agricultural Development—IFAD

Address: Via del Serafico 107, 00142 Rome, Italy.
Telephone: (06) 54591; **fax:** (06) 5043463; **e-mail:** ifad@ifad.org; **internet:** www.ifad.org.

IFAD was established in 1977, following a decision by the 1974 UN World Food Conference, with a mandate to combat hunger and eradicate poverty on a sustainable basis in the low-income, food-deficit regions of the world. Funding operations began in January 1978.

MEMBERS

IFAD has 164 members.

Organization

(March 2007)

GOVERNING COUNCIL

Each member state is represented in the Governing Council (the Fund's highest authority) by a Governor and an Alternate. Sessions are held annually with special sessions as required. The Governing Council elects the President of the Fund (who also chairs the Executive Board) by a two-thirds majority for a four-year term. The President is eligible for re-election.

EXECUTIVE BOARD

Consists of 18 members and 18 alternates, elected by the Governing Council, who serve for three years. The Executive Board is responsible for the conduct and general operation of IFAD and approves loans and grants for projects; it holds three regular sessions each year. An independent Office of Evaluation reports directly to the Board.

The governance structure of the Fund is based on the classification of members. Membership of the Executive Board is distributed as follows: eight List A countries (i.e. industrialized donor countries), four List B (petroleum-exporting developing donor countries), and six List C (recipient developing countries), divided equally among the three Sub-List C categories (i.e. for Africa, Europe, Asia and the Pacific, and Latin America and the Caribbean).

President and Chairman of Executive Board: LENNART BÅGE (Sweden).
Vice-President: KANAYO F. F. NWANZE (Nigeria).

DEPARTMENTS

IFAD has three main administrative departments, each headed by an Assistant President: Finance and Administration; Programme Management (with five regional Divisions and a Technical Advisory Division); and External Affairs (including a Policy Division, Communication Division and a Resource Mobilization Unit). Offices of the General Counsel and of Internal Audit report to the Office of the President and Vice-President.

Activities

IFAD provides financing primarily for projects designed to improve food production systems in developing member states and to strengthen related policies, services and institutions. In allocating resources IFAD is guided by: the need to increase food production in the poorest food-deficit countries; the potential for increasing food production in other developing countries; and the importance of improving the nutrition, health and education of the poorest people in developing countries, i.e. small-scale farmers, artisanal fishermen, nomadic pastoralists, indigenous populations, rural women, and the rural landless. All projects emphasize the participation of beneficiaries in development initiatives, both at the local and national level. Issues relating to gender and household food security are incorporated into all aspects of its activities. IFAD is committed to achieving the so-called Millennium Development Goals (MDGs), pledged by governments attending a special session of the UN General Assembly in September 2000, and, in particular, the objective to reduce by 50% the proportion of people living in extreme poverty by 2015. In 2001 the Fund introduced new measures to improve monitoring and impact evaluation, in particular to assess its contribution to achieving the MDGs.

In December 2006 the Executive Board adopted IFAD's Strategic Framework for 2007–10, in which it reiterated its commitment to enabling the rural poor to achieve household food security and to overcome their poverty. Accordingly, the Fund's efforts were to focus on ensuring that poor rural populations have improved and sustainable access to, and sufficiently developed skills to take advantage of: natural resources; better agricultural technologies and production services; a broad range of financial services; transparent competitive agricultural input and produce markets; opportunities for rural off-farm employment and enterprise development; and local and national policy and programming processes. Within this Framework the Fund has also formulated regional strategies for rural poverty reduction, based on a series of regional poverty assessments. In 2003 a new Policy Division was established under the External Affairs Department to co-ordinate policy work at the corporate level. A Policy Forum was launched in 2004, comprising IFAD senior management and staff.

IFAD is a leading repository in the world of knowledge, resources and expertise in the field of rural hunger and poverty alleviation. In 2001 it renewed its commitment to becoming a global knowledge institution for rural poverty-related issues. Through its technical assistance grants, IFAD aims to promote research and capacity-building in the agricultural sector, as well as the development of technologies to increase production and alleviate rural poverty. In recent years IFAD has been increasingly involved in promoting the use of communication technology to facilitate the exchange of information and experience among rural communities, specialized institutions and organizations, and IFAD-sponsored projects. Within the strategic context of knowledge management, IFAD has supported initiatives to support regional electronic networks, such as ENRAP (see below) in Asia and the Pacific and FIDAMERICA in Latin America and the Caribbean, as well as to develop other lines of communication between organizations, local agents and the rural poor.

IFAD is empowered to make both grants and loans. Grants are limited to 7.5% of the resources committed in any one financial year. Loans are available on highly concessionary, intermediate and ordinary terms. Highly concessionary loans carry no interest but have an annual service charge of 0.75% and a repayment period of 40 years, including a 10-year grace period. Intermediate term loans are subject to a variable interest charge, equivalent to 50% of the interest rate charged on World Bank loans, and are repaid over 20 years. Ordinary loans carry a variable interest charge equal to that charged by the World Bank, and are repaid over 15–18 years. In 2006 highly concessionary loans represented some 79% of total lending in that year. In order to increase the impact of its lending resources on food production, the Fund seeks as much as possible to attract other external donors and beneficiary governments as cofinanciers of its projects. In 2006 external cofinancing accounted for some 12% of all project funding, while domestic contributions, i.e. from recipient governments and other local sources, accounted for 31%.

At the end of 2006 total IFAD loans approved since 1978 amounted to US $9,416.6m. for 748 projects. During the same period the Fund approved 1,980 research and technical assistance grants, at a cost of $574.7m. In 2006 total IFAD project loans approved amounted to $515.0m. for 31 projects, as follows: $168.7m. for six operations in Asia and the Pacific (or 32.4% of the total committed in that year), $93.9m. for five projects in Eastern and Southern Africa (18.1%), $77.7m. for four projects in the Near East and North Africa (14.9%), $90.1m. for five projects in Latin America and the Caribbean (17.3%), and $89.6m. for seven projects in Western and Central Africa (17.2%). Technical assistance grants amounting to $41.8m. (for research, training and project preparation and development) were awarded, bringing the total financial assistance approved in 2006 to $556.8m., compared with $515.0m. in the previous year.

IFAD's development projects usually include a number of components, such as infrastructure (e.g. improvement of water supplies, small-scale irrigation and road construction); input supply (e.g. improved seeds, fertilizers and pesticides); institutional support (e.g. research, training and extension services); and producer incentives (e.g. pricing and marketing improvements). IFAD also attempts to enable the landless to acquire income-generating assets: by increasing the provision of credit for the rural poor, it seeks to free them from dependence on the capital market and to generate productive activities.

In addition to its regular efforts to identify projects and programmes, IFAD organizes special programming missions to certain selected countries to undertake a comprehensive review of the constraints affecting the rural poor, and to help countries to design strategies for the removal of these constraints. In general, projects based on the recommendations of these missions tend to focus on institutional improvements at the national and local level to direct inputs and services to small farmers and the landless rural poor. Monitoring and evaluation missions are also sent to check the progress of projects and to assess the impact of poverty reduction efforts.

The Fund supports projects that are concerned with environmental conservation, in an effort to alleviate poverty that results from the deterioration of natural resources. In addition, it extends environmental assessment grants to review the environmental consequences of projects under preparation. In October 1997 IFAD was appointed to administer the Global Mechanism of the Convention to Combat Desertification in those Countries Experiencing Drought and Desertification, particularly in Africa, which entered into force in December 1996. The Mechanism was envisaged as a means of mobilizing and channelling resources for implementation of the Convention. A series of collaborative institutional arrangements were to be concluded between IFAD, UNDP and the World Bank in order to facilitate the effective functioning of the Mechanism. In May 2001 the Global Environmental Facility approved IFAD as an executing agency.

In February 1998 IFAD inaugurated a new Trust Fund to complement the multilateral debt initiative for heavily indebted poor countries (HIPCs). The Fund was intended to assist IFAD's poorest members deemed to be eligible under the initiative to channel resources from debt repayments to communities in need. In February 2000 the Governing Council approved full participation by IFAD in the enhanced HIPC debt initiative agreed by the World Bank and IMF in September 1999.

During 1998 the Executive Board endorsed a policy framework for the Fund's provision of assistance in post-conflict situations, with the aim of achieving a continuum from emergency relief to a secure basis from which to pursue sustainable development. In July 2001 IFAD and UNAIDS signed a memorandum of understanding on developing a co-operation agreement. A meeting of technical experts from IFAD, FAO, WFP and UNAIDS, held in December, addressed means of mitigating the impact of HIV/AIDS on food security and rural livelihoods in affected regions. In January 2005 IFAD announced that it aimed to mobilize some US $100m. to assist countries affected by the devastating tsunami that had struck coastal regions in the Indian Ocean in late December 2004. Following the disaster IFAD also participated in needs assessments in Indonesia, Sri Lanka and the Maldives, which were to provide the basis for longer-term resource allocation and mobilization.

During the late 1990s IFAD established several partnerships within the agribusiness sector, with a view to improving performance at project level, broadening access to capital markets, and encouraging the advancement of new technologies. Since 1996 it has chaired the Support Group of the Global Forum on Agricultural Research (GFAR), which facilitates dialogue between research centres and institutions, farmers' organizations, non-governmental bodies, the private sector and donors. In October 2001 IFAD became a co-sponsor of the Consultative Group on International Agricultural Research (CGIAR). In 2006 IFAD reviewed the work of the International Alliance against Hunger, which was established in 2004 to enhance co-ordination among international agencies and non-governmental organizations concerned with agriculture and rural development, and national alliances against hunger.

Finance

In accordance with the Articles of Agreement establishing IFAD, the Governing Council periodically undertakes a review of the adequacy of resources available to the Fund and may request members to make additional contributions. The seventh replenishment of IFAD funds, covering the period 2007–09, amounted to US $720m. The provisional budget for administrative expenses for 2008 amounted to $74.1m., while some $5.5m. was budgeted in that year to the Fund's Office of Evaluation.

Publications

Annual Report.
IFAD Update (2 a year).
Rural Poverty Report 2001.
Staff Working Papers (series).

International Labour Organization—ILO

Address: 4 route des Morillons, 1211 Geneva 22, Switzerland.
Telephone: (22) 7996111; **fax:** (22) 7988685; **e-mail:** ilo@ilo.org; **internet:** www.ilo.org.

ILO was founded in 1919 to work for social justice as a basis for lasting peace. It carries out this mandate by promoting decent living standards, satisfactory conditions of work and pay and adequate employment opportunities. Methods of action include the creation of international labour standards; the provision of technical co-operation services; and research and publications on social and labour matters. In 1946 ILO became a specialized agency associated with the UN. It was awarded the Nobel Peace Prize in 1969. ILO's tripartite structure gives representation to employers' and workers' organizations alongside governments.

MEMBERS
ILO has 181 members.

Organization
(March 2008)

INTERNATIONAL LABOUR CONFERENCE

The supreme deliberative body of ILO, the Conference meets annually in Geneva, with a session devoted to maritime questions when necessary; it is attended by about 2,000 delegates, advisers and observers. National delegations are composed of two government delegates, one employers' delegate and one workers' delegate. Non-governmental delegates can speak and vote independently of the views of their national government. The conference elects the Governing Body and adopts International Labour Conventions and Recommendations. Every two years the Conference adopts the ILO Budget.

The President and Vice-Presidents hold office for the term of the Conference only.

GOVERNING BODY

ILO's executive council meets three times a year in Geneva to decide policy and programmes. It is composed of 28 government members,

14 employers' members and 14 workers' members. Ten of the titular government seats are held permanently by 'states of chief industrial importance': Brazil, the People's Republic of China, France, Germany, India, Italy, Japan, Russia, the United Kingdom and the USA. The remaining 18 are elected from other countries every three years. Employers' and workers' members are elected as individuals, not as national candidates.

Among the Committees formed by the Governing Body are: the Committee on Freedom of Association; the Programme, Financial and Administrative Committee; the Building Sub-Committee; the Committee on Legal Issues and International Labour Standards; the Sub-Committee on Multinational Enterprises; the Working Party on Policy regarding the Revision of Standards; the Committee on Employment and Social Policy; the Committee on Sectoral and Technical Meetings and Related Issues; the Committee on Technical Co-operation; and the Working Party on the Social Dimension of Globalization.

Chairperson: (2007–08) D. JAYATILLEKA (Sri Lanka).

Employers' Vice-Chairperson: DANIEL FUNES DE RIOJA (Argentina).

Workers' Vice-Chairperson: Sir ROY TROTMAN (Barbados).

INTERNATIONAL LABOUR OFFICE

The International Labour Office is ILO's secretariat, operational headquarters and publishing house. It is staffed in Geneva and in the field by about 2,250 people of some 120 nationalities. Operations are decentralized to regional, area and branch offices in nearly 40 countries.

Director-General: JUAN O. SOMAVÍA (Chile).

REGIONAL OFFICES

Africa: BP 3960, Abidjan 01, Côte d'Ivoire; tel. 20-21-26-39; fax 22-21-28-80; e-mail abidjan@ilo.org.

Latin America and the Caribbean: Apdo Postal 14–124, Lima, Peru; tel. (1) 6150300; fax (1); tel. 6150400; e-mail oit@oit.org.pe.

Arab States: POB 11-4088, Beirut, Lebanon; tel. (1) 752400; fax (1) 752405; e-mail beirut@ilo.org.

Asia and the Pacific: POB 2-349, Bangkok 10200, Thailand; tel. 2881234; fax 2881735; e-mail bangkok@ilo.org.

Europe and Central Asia: 4 route des Morillons, 1211 Geneva 22, Switzerland; tel. 227996666; fax 227996061; e-mail europe@ilo.org.

Activities

ILO pursues the goal of 'Decent Work for All' and, in 1999, adopted a Decent Work Agenda, which has four basic pillars: employment, as the principal route out of poverty; rights, which empower men and women to escape from poverty; social protection, which safeguards against poverty; and tripartism and social dialogue, regarding the participation of employers' and workers' organizations as of key importance in shaping government policy for poverty reduction. Through the Decent Work Agenda ILO supports the UN's Millennium Development Goals, adopted by UN heads of state participating in the Millennium Summit convened in September 2000.

STANDARDS AND FUNDAMENTAL PRINCIPLES AND RIGHTS AT WORK

One of ILO's primary functions is the adoption by the International Labour Conference of conventions and recommendations setting minimum labour standards. Through ratification by member states, conventions create binding obligations to put their provisions into effect. Recommendations provide guidance as to policy and practice. By March 2008 a total of 188 conventions and 199 recommendations had been adopted, ranging over a wide field of social and labour matters, based on the following principles: freedom of association, the abolition of forced and child labour, and the elimination of discrimination in employment promotion, training and the protection of workers. Together they form the International Labour Code. Some 127 countries had ratified all of ILO's fundamental conventions by March 2008. The Committee of Experts on the Application of Conventions and Recommendations and the Conference Committee on the Application of Standards monitor the adoption of international labour standards. In June 1998 a Declaration on Fundamental Principles and Rights at Work, establishing eight fundamental labour standards, was adopted by the Conference. All member states were obliged to observe the four principles upon which these standards were based (see above), whether or not they had ratified the corresponding international conventions.

From 1996 ILO resolved to strengthen its efforts, working closely with UNICEF, to encourage member states to ratify and to implement relevant international standards on child labour. In June 1999 the International Labour Conference adopted the Worst Forms of Child Labour Convention (No. 182); the convention entered into force in November 2000. By March 2008 it had been ratified by 165 states. The Organization helped to organize an International Conference on Child Labour, convened in The Hague, Netherlands, in February 2002. In May ILO issued a global study entitled *A Future without Child Labour*, in which it estimated that one-eighth of the world's children were exposed to the worst forms of child labour. The first World Day against Child Labour, sponsored by ILO, was held on 12 June; it has subsequently been held annually. By March 2008 88 countries were taking part in ILO's International Programme for the Elimination of Child Labour (IPEC, established in 1992), with emphasis placed on the elimination of the most severe forms of labour such as hazardous working conditions and occupations, child prostitution and trafficking of children. In addition, IPEC gives special attention to children who are particularly vulnerable, for example those under 12 years of age. The 96th ILO Conference, convened in June 2007, launched a new initiative aimed at eliminating child labour in agriculture.

In May 2003 ILO issued the first global report on discrimination at work, *Time for Equality at Work*, compiled as a follow-up to the 1998 Declaration on Fundamental Principles and Rights at Work.

EMPLOYMENT AND INCOME

ILO aims to monitor, examine and report on the situation and trends in employment throughout the world, and considers the effects on employment and social justice of economic trade, investment and related phenomena. In January 2008 ILO estimated that some 189.9m. workers world-wide (6% of the global labour force) were unemployed and reported that one-half of the global labour force was in vulnerable employment. In addition, it was reported that 16.4% of all workers were living on less than US $1 a day, with a further 43.5% living on less than US $2 a day. In February 2002 ILO established a World Commission on the Social Dimension of Globalization to consider means of utilizing economic globalization to stimulate economic growth and reduce poverty. The Commission issued its final report, entitled *A Fair Globalization*, in February 2004. It was endorsed by the 92nd International Labour Conference, held in June. In March 2003 ILO adopted the Global Employment Agenda, a comprehensive framework for managing changes to employment derived from the developing global economy, through investment in knowledge and skills, maintaining a healthy labour market and ensuring adequate social safety nets. In November 2007 ILO convened a Forum on Decent Work for a Fair Globalization, in Lisbon, Portugal, comprising some 300 representatives of the ILO tripartite social partners, and other interested parties, to address the possibility of establishing a new Decent Work Movement to overcome growing global inequality.

ILO's programme sector on skills, knowledge and employability supports governments in structuring policies for improved investment in learning and training for enhanced employability, productivity and social inclusion. The programme focuses on promoting access to training and decent work for specific groups, such as youths, the disabled, and workers in the informal economy, and on protecting the rights of the elderly. The Job Creation and Enterprise Development Programme aims to assist governments, employers, workers and other related groups with fostering a successful business environment, for example through the identification and implementation of appropriate policies, legal frameworks and management strategies, the promotion of access to business development and training services, and the promotion of local economic development programmes. It also incorporates a specific programme to promote the development of micro and small enterprises, in co-operation with governments, communities and other social partners. ILO's Gender Promotion Programme aims to promote effective gender mainstreaming and is responsible for a global programme for the creation of more and better jobs for women and men. The programme assists countries to develop and implement National Action Plans to achieve this objective. A programme on crisis response and reconstruction addresses the effect on employment of armed conflicts, natural disasters, social movements or political transitions, and financial and economic disruptions. The impact of current global financial and economic trends on employment creation, poverty alleviation and social exclusion are addressed by ILO's Social Finance Programme. The programme works to reduce vulnerability, to create jobs through enterprise development, and to make financial policies more employment-sensitive, for example by providing information on microfinance and promoting microfinance institutions, and by conducting research on the impact of financial sector liberalization on the poor.

The Multinational Enterprise Programme is responsible for the promotion of and follow-up to the Tripartite Declaration of Principles concerning Multinational Enterprises and Social Policy, which was adopted in 1977 and amended in 2000. The Declaration provides international guide-lines, agreed by governments and employers' and workers' organizations, on investment policy and practice. The programme is also responsible for co-ordinating work on corporate social responsibility, as well as for ILO's participation in the Global Compact, an initiative of the UN Secretary-General, which was inaugurated in 2000 comprising leaders in the fields of business, labour and civil society who undertook to promote human rights, the fundamental principles of ILO, and protection of the environment.

ILO maintains technical relations with the IMF, the World Bank, OECD, the WTO and other international organizations on global economic issues, international and national strategies for employment, structural adjustment, and labour market and training policies. A number of employment policy reviews have been carried out by ILO within the framework of the UN Administrative Committee on Co-ordination Task Force on Full Employment and Sustainable Livelihoods.

SOCIAL PROTECTION

Access to an adequate level of social protection is recognized in ILO's 1944 Declaration of Philadelphia, as well as in a number of international labour standards, as a basic right of all individuals. ILO aims to enable countries to extend social protection to all groups in society and to improve working conditions and safety at work. The fundamental premise of ILO's programme sector on socio-economic security is that basic security for all is essential for productive work and human dignity in the future global economy. The achievement of basic security is deemed to entail the attainment of basic humanitarian needs, including universal access to health services and a decent level of education. The programme aims to address the following concerns: what constitutes socio-economic security and insecurity in member countries; identifying the sources of such insecurity; and identifying economic, labour and social policies that could improve socio-economic security while promoting sustainable economic growth. The programme focuses on the following dimensions of work-based security: the labour market (the provision of adequate employment opportunities); employment (for example, protection against dismissal); occupational security (the opportunity to develop a career); work (protection against accidents, illness and stress at work); skills; income; and representation (the right to collective representation in the labour market, through independent trade unions and employers associations, etc.). ILO's Social Security Policy and Development Branch assists member states and constituents in the design, reform and implementation of social security policies based on the principles embodied in international labour standards, with a special focus on developing strategies to extend social security coverage. The Branch provides general research and analysis of social security issues; extends technical assistance to member states for designing, reforming and expanding social security schemes; provides services to enable community-based organizations to develop their own social security systems; promotes and oversees the implementation of ILO standards on social security; develops training programmes and materials; and disseminates information. The Financial, Actuarial and Statistical Services Branch aims to improve the financial planning, management and governance of national social security schemes and social protection systems. In June 2003 ILO inaugurated a Global Campaign on Social Security and Coverage for All, with a particular focus on the informal economy. ILO estimates that only one-fifth of the world's population has sufficient social security coverage. The key operational tool of the Campaign is ILO's STEP (Strategies and Tools against Social Exclusion and Poverty) Programme which undertakes field work, research, training and the dissemination of knowledge to help to extend social protection and combat social exclusion.

ILO's Programme on Safety and Health at Work and the Environment aims to protect workers in hazardous occupations; to provide protection to vulnerable groups of workers outside the scope of normal protection measures; to improve the capacity of governments and employers' and workers' organizations to address workers' well-being, extend the scope of occupational health care etc.; and to ensure that policy-makers recognize and document the social and economic impact of implementing measures that enhance workers' protection. ILO Guidelines on Occupational Safety and Health Management Systems (ILO-OSH 2001) provides a framework of action at an international, national and organizational level. ILO's Conditions of Work Branch conducts research and provides advocacy, training and technical co-operation to governments and employers' and workers' organizations in areas such as wages, working time, maternity protection and life outside of work. The International Migration Branch focuses on protecting the rights, and promoting the integration, of migrant workers, forging international consensus on the management of migration, and furthering knowledge of international migration. In June 2004 the 92nd International Labour Conference adopted a plan of action providing for the development of a multilateral framework to extend labour protection standards to migrant workers. The framework was to include international guide-lines on labour inspection, the promotion of decent work, recruitment, and hazardous employment. ILO's Global Programme on HIV/AIDS and the World of Work, formally established in November 2000, issued a code of practice in May 2001, focusing on prevention, management and mitigation of the impact of HIV/AIDS on the world of work, support for HIV/AIDS-affected workers, and eliminating discrimination on the basis of perceived HIV status. ILO is a co-sponsor (with UNICEF, UNDP, UNFPA, UNESCO, WHO, the World Bank, WFP, UNODC and UNHCR) of the Joint UN Programme on HIV/AIDS (UNAIDS), which was established on 1 January 1996 to co-ordinate and strengthen world-wide action against HIV/AIDS. In July 2004 an ILO report assessed the financial cost of HIV/AIDS in terms of loss of output and estimated the impact of the epidemic on the global labour force. ILO adopted a Code of Practice on HIV/AIDS and the World of Work in October 2005.

SOCIAL DIALOGUE

This area was identified as one of the four strategic objectives in order to concentrate and reinforce ILO's support for strengthening the process of tripartism, the role and activities of its tripartite constituents (i.e. governments, employers and workers' organizations), and, in particular, their capacity to engage in and to promote the use of social dialogue. ILO recognizes that the enactment of labour laws, and ensuring their effective enforcement, collective bargaining and other forms of co-operation are important means of promoting social justice. It aims to assist governments and employers' and workers' organizations to establish sound labour relations, to adapt labour laws to meet changing economic and social needs, and to improve labour administration.

The Social Dialogue, Labour Law and Labour Administration Department maintains an International Observatory of Labour Law which provides information concerning national labour legislation and facilitates the dissemination of information regarding development in labour law throughout the world. The Department also supports the training and professional development of labour court judges and publishes the proceedings of meetings of European labour court judges.

Successive International Labour Conferences, most recently the 96th Conference, held in June 2007, have focused special attention on reports of ongoing infringements of, and continued failure over several years to implement, the Freedom of Association and Protection of the Right to Organize Convention, 1948 (No. 87) in Belarus and Myanmar. A commission to examine alleged abuses of trade union rights in Myanmar was established in November 2003. A Committee on Freedom of Association examines allegations of abuses committed against trade union organizations and reports to the Governing Body.

INSTITUTES

International Institute for Labour Studies (IILS): 4 route des Morillons, 1211 Geneva 22, Switzerland; tel. 227996128; fax 227998542; e-mail inst@ilo.org; established in 1960 and based at ILO's Geneva headquarters, the Institute promotes the study and discussion of policy issues of concern to ILO and its constituents, i.e. government, employers and workers. The core theme of the Institute's activities is the interaction between labour institutions, development and civil society in a global economy. It identifies emerging social and labour issues by developing new areas for research and action, and encourages dialogue on social policy between the tripartite constituency of ILO and the international academic community and other experts. The Institute maintains research networks, conducts courses, seminars and social policy forums, and supports internships and visiting scholar and internship programmes. The ILO Director-General is Chairman of the Board of the Institute.

International Training Centre of ILO: Corso Unità d'Italia 125, 10127 Turin, Italy; tel. (011) 693-6372; fax (011) 693-6350; internet www.itcilo.it; f. 1964 by ILO to offer advanced training facilities for managers, trainers and social partners, and technical specialists from ILO mem. states; became operational in 1965; since 1991 the Centre has been increasingly used by UN agencies to provide training for improving the management of development and for building national capacities to sustain development programmes; Exec. Dir FRANÇOIS EYRAUD.

Finance

The proposed regular budget for the two years 2006–07 was US $594.3m.

Publications

(in English, French and Spanish unless otherwise indicated)

Bulletin of Labour Statistics (quarterly).

Global Employment Trends.
International Labour Review (quarterly).
International studies, surveys, works of practical guidance or reference (on questions of social policy, manpower, industrial relations, working conditions, social security, training, management development, etc).
Key Indicators of the Labour Market.
Labour Law Documents (selected labour and social security laws and regulations; 3 a year).
Official Bulletin (3 a year).

Reports (for the annual sessions of the International Labour Conference, etc. (also in Arabic, Chinese and Russian).
World Employment Report (every 2–3 years).
World Labour Report (every 2 years).
World of Work (magazine issued in several languages; 5 a year).
Yearbook of Labour Statistics.
Also maintains a database on international labour standards, ILO-LEX, and a database on national labour law, NATLEX, in electronic form.

International Maritime Organization—IMO

Address: 4 Albert Embankment, London, SE1 7SR, United Kingdom.
Telephone: (20) 7735-7611; **fax:** (20) 7587-3210; **e-mail:** info@imo.org; **internet:** www.imo.org.

The Inter-Governmental Maritime Consultative Organization (IMCO) began operations in 1959, as a specialized agency of the UN to facilitate co-operation among governments on technical matters affecting international shipping. Its main functions are the achievement of safe and efficient navigation, and the control of pollution caused by ships and craft operating in the marine environment. IMCO became IMO in 1982.

MEMBERS
IMO has 167 members and three associate members.

Organization
(March 2008)

ASSEMBLY
The Assembly consists of delegates from all member countries, who each have one vote. Associate members and observers from other governments and the international agencies are also present. Regular sessions are held every two years. The Assembly is responsible for the election of members to the Council and approves the appointment of the Secretary-General of the Secretariat. It considers reports from all subsidiary bodies and decides the action to be taken on them; it votes the agency's budget and determines the work programme and financial policy.

The Assembly also recommends to members measures to promote maritime safety and security, and to prevent and control maritime pollution from ships.

COUNCIL
The Council is the governing body of the Organization between the biennial sessions of the Assembly. Its members, representatives of 40 states, are elected by the Assembly for a term of two years. The Council appoints the Secretary-General; transmits reports by the subsidiary bodies, including the Maritime Safety Committee, to the Assembly, and reports on the work of the Organization generally; submits budget estimates and financial statements with comments and recommendations to the Assembly. The Council normally meets twice a year.

Facilitation Committee: Constituted by the Council in May 1972 as a subsidiary body, this Committee deals with measures to facilitate maritime travel and transport and matters arising from the 1965 Facilitation Convention. Membership is open to all IMO member states.

MARITIME SAFETY COMMITTEE
The Maritime Safety Committee is open to all IMO members. The Committee meets at least once a year and submits proposals to the Assembly on technical matters affecting the safety of shipping. In December 2002 a conference of contracting states to the 1974 International Convention on Safety of Life at Sea (see below) adopted a series of security measures relating to the international maritime and port industries that had been formulated by the Safety Committee in view of the major terrorist attacks perpetrated against targets in the USA in September 2001.

SUB-COMMITTEES:
Bulk Liquids and Gases*
Carriage of Dangerous Goods, Solid Cargoes and Containers
Fire Protection
Flag State Implementation*
Radiocommunications and Search and Rescue
Safety of Navigation
Ship Design and Equipment
Stability and Load Lines and Fishing Vessel Safety
Standards of Training and Watchkeeping

* Also sub-committees of the Marine Environment Protection Committee.

LEGAL COMMITTEE
Established by the Council in June 1967 to deal initially with legal issues connected with the loss of the tanker *Torrey Canyon*, and subsequently with any legal problems laid before IMO. Membership open to all IMO member states.

MARINE ENVIRONMENT PROTECTION COMMITTEE
Established by the eighth Assembly (1973) to co-ordinate IMO's work on the prevention and control of marine pollution from ships, and to assist IMO in its consultations with other UN bodies, and with international organizations and expert bodies in the field of marine pollution. Membership is open to all IMO members.

TECHNICAL CO-OPERATION COMMITTEE
Evaluates the implementation of projects for which IMO is the executing agency, and generally reviews IMO's technical assistance programmes. Established in 1965 as a subsidiary body of the Council, and formally institutionalized by means of an amendment to the IMO constitution in 1984. Membership is open to all IMO member states.

SECRETARIAT
The Secretariat consists of the Secretary-General and a staff appointed by the Secretary-General and recruited on as wide a geographical basis as possible. The Secretariat comprises the following divisions: Administrative; Conference; Legal affairs and external relations; Marine environment; Maritime safety; Technical co-operation.

Secretary-General: EFTHIMIOS MITROPOULOS (Greece).

Activities
The 23rd regular session of the Assembly, held in London in November–December 2003 adopted a strategic plan for the Organization covering the six-year period 2004–10. The 24th Assembly was convened in November–December 2005. It adopted a framework and set of procedures for a new Member State Audit Scheme, which aimed to monitor and strengthen the implementation of IMO standards. Other resolutions adopted related to: revised guide-lines for the identification and designation of particularly sensitive sea areas (PSSAs); a request that the UN Security Council consider the issue of piracy and armed robbery against ships in waters off the coast of Somalia; commitment to greater technical co-operation, in particular in support of the UN Millennium Development Goals; the elaboration of a new legally binding instrument on ship recycling; and the convening, in 2007, of a conference to adopt a Wreck Removal Convention.

In June 2006 Chile and Denmark became the first two member states to sign memoranda of co-operation on participation in the Member State Audit Scheme.

CONVENTIONS
(of which IMO is the Depository)

Convention on Facilitation of International Maritime Traffic, 1965: came into force in March 1967.

International Convention on Load Lines, 1966: came into force in July 1968; Protocol, adopted in 1988, came into force in February 2000; numerous other amendments.

International Convention on Tonnage Measurement of Ships, 1969: Convention embodies a universal system for measuring ships' tonnage. Came into force in 1982.

International Convention relating to Intervention on the High Seas in Cases of Oil Pollution Casualties, 1969: came into force in May 1975; a Protocol adopted in 1973 came into force in 1983.

International Convention on Civil Liability for Oil Pollution Damage, 1969: came into force in June 1975; amended by Protocols of 1976, 1984 and 1992 (which was to replace the original Convention); further amendments to the 1992 Protocol, adopted in 2000, came into force in November 2003.

International Convention on the Establishment of an International Fund for Compensation for Oil Pollution Damage, 1971: came into force in October 1978; amended by Protocols of 1976, 1984 and 1992 (which replaced the original Convention).; further amendments to the 1992 Protocol, adopted in 2000, came into force in November 2003; a Protocol to establish a Supplementary Fund was adopted in 2003 and came into force in March 2005.

Convention relating to Civil Liability in the Field of Maritime Carriage of Nuclear Material, 1971: came into force in 1975.

Special Trade Passenger Ships Agreement, 1971: came into force in 1974.

Convention on the International Regulations for Preventing Collisions at Sea, 1972: came into force in July 1977; numerous amendments.

Convention on the Prevention of Marine Pollution by Dumping of Wastes and Other Matter ('London Convention'), 1972: came into force in August 1975; numerous amendments, including, 1993, to incorporate a ban on low-level nuclear waste, which came into force in February 1994; Protocol, which was to replace the original Convention, adopted in 1996.

International Convention for Safe Containers, 1972: came into force in September 1977.

International Convention for the Prevention of Pollution from Ships, 1973: (as modified by the Protocol of 1978, known as MARPOL 73/78); came into force in October 1983; extended to include regulations to prevent air pollution in September 1997; came into force in May 2005.

International Convention for the Safety of Life at Sea (SOLAS), 1974: came into force in May 1980; a Protocol drawn up in 1978 came into force in May 1981; a second Protocol, of 1988, came into force in February 2000; amendments including special measures to enhance maritime safety came into force in July 2004.

Athens Convention relating to the Carriage of Passengers and their Luggage by Sea, 1974: came into force in April 1987.

Convention on the International Maritime Satellite Organization, 1976: came into force in July 1979.

Convention on Limitation of Liability for Maritime Claims, 1976: came into force in December 1986; a Protocol came into force in May 2004.

International Convention for the Safety of Fishing Vessels, Torremolinos, 1977: replaced by a Protocol adopted in 1993; to come into force 12 months after 15 countries with an aggregate fleet of at least 14,000 vessels of 24 metres in length and over have become parties thereto.

International Convention on Standards of Training, Certification and Watchkeeping for Seafarers, 1978: came into force in April 1984; restructured by amendments that entered into force in February 1997; countries deemed to be implementing the Convention fully are recorded on a so-called 'white list'.

International Convention on Maritime Search and Rescue, 1979: came into force in June 1985.

Convention for the Suppression of Unlawful Acts against the Safety of Maritime Navigation, 1988: came into force in March 1992. Further Protocol adopted in October 2005.

Protocol for the Suppression of Unlawful Acts against the Safety of Fixed Platforms located on the Continental Shelf, 1988: came into force in March 1992; further Protocol adopted in October 2005.

International Convention on Salvage, 1989: came into force in July 1996.

International Convention on Oil Pollution, Preparedness, Response and Co-operation, 1990: came into force in May 1995.

International Convention on Maritime Liens and Mortgages, 1992: came into force in September 2004.

International Convention on Liability and Compensation for Damage in Connection with the Carriage of Hazardous and Noxious Substances by Sea, 1996: will come into force 18 months after 12 states of which four have not less than 2m. units of gross tonnage have become parties thereto.

International Convention on Civil Liability for Bunker Oil Pollution Damage, 2001: will come into force 12 months after 18 states of which five have not less than 1m. units of gross tonnage have become parties thereto.

International Convention on the Control of Harmful Antifouling Systems on Ships, 2001: will enter into force 12 months after 25 states representing 25% of the world's merchant shipping tonnage have become parties thereto.

International Convention for the Control and Management of Ships' Ballast Water and Sediments, 2004: will come into force 12 months after 30 states representing not less than 35% of the world's merchant shipping tonnage have become parties thereto.

Nairobi International Convention on the Removal of Wrecks, 2007: will enter into force 12 months after 10 states have become parties thereto.

Port State Control Agreements: Paris Memorandum of Understanding (MOU) on Port State Control, 1982; Viña del Mar Agreement, 1992; Tokyo MOU, 1993; Caribbean MOU, 1996; Mediterranean MOU, 1997; Indian Ocean MOU, 1998; Abuja MOU, 1999; Black Sea, MOU, 2000. An International Ship and Port Facility Security Code was adopted under IMO auspices in December 2002 and entered into force in July 2004.

TRAINING INSTITUTES

IMO International Maritime Law Institute (IMLI): POB 31, Msida, MSD 1000, Malta; tel. 21319343; fax 21343092; e-mail info@imli.org; internet www.imli.org; f. 1988; provides degree courses, other training courses, study and research facilities for specialists in maritime law; promotes the development and dissemination of knowledge and expertise in the international legal regime of merchant shipping and related areas; Dir Prof. DAVID ATTARD; pubs *IMLI News*, *IMLI e-News*, *IMLI Global Directory*.

International Maritime Academy (IMA): via E. Weiss 15, 34127 Trieste, Italy; tel. (040) 350829; fax (040) 350322; e-mail imoima@imoima.org; internet www.imoima.org; f. 1988; provides postgraduate training for seafarers and onshore staff employed in maritime-related fields; Dir Adm. FRANCESCO SPANIO.

World Maritime University (WMU): POB 500, Citadellsvägen 29, 201 24 Malmö, Sweden; tel. (40) 356300; fax (40) 128442; e-mail info@wmu.se; internet www.wmu.se; f. 1983; offers postgraduate courses in maritime disciplines, a master's and doctoral programme and professional development courses; undertakes various research projects; Pres. Dr KARL LAUBSTEIN (Canada); Registrar B. P. BROWNE (USA); pubs *WMU News*, *WMU Handbook*, *WMU Journal of Maritime Affairs* (2 a year), several books on maritime issues.

OTHER AFFILIATED BODIES

Partnership in Environmental Management for the Seas of East Asia (PEMSEA): POB 2502, Quezon City, 1165 Metro Manila, Philippines; tel. (2) 9202211; fax (2) 9269712; e-mail info@pemsea.org; internet www.pemsea.org; administered by IMO in conjunction with UNDP and the Global Environment Facility; supports implementation of Integrated Coastal Management programmes and has prepared a Sustainable Development Strategy for the Seas of East Asia.

Regional Marine Pollution Emergency Response Centre for the Mediterranean Sea (REMPEC): Maritime House, Lascaris Wharf, Valletta VLT 1921, Malta; tel. 21337296; fax 21339951; e-mail rempec@rempec.org; internet www.rempec.org; f. 1976 as the Regional Oil Combating Centre for the Mediterranean Sea; administered by IMO in conjunction with the Regional Seas Programme of the UN Environment Programme; aims to develop measures to prevent and combat pollution from ships in the Mediterranean; responsible for implementing a new EU-funded regional project, initiated in November 2005, for Euro-Mediterranean co-operation on maritime safety and prevention of pollution from ships; Dir FRÉDÉRIC HÉBERT (France).

Regional Marine Pollution Emergency, Information and Training Center for the Wider Caribbean Region: Fokkerweg 26, Willemstad Curaçao, Netherlands Antilles; tel. 461-4012; fax 461-1996; e-mail uneprcuja@cwjamaica.com; f. 1995; aims to help prevent and respond to major pollution incidents in the region's marine environment; administered by IMO in conjunction with the Regional Seas Programme of the UN Environment Programme.

Finance

Contributions are received from the member states. The budget appropriation for the two years 2008–09 amounted to £49.8m.

Publications

IMO News (quarterly).
Numerous specialized publications, including international conventions of which IMO is depositary.

International Monetary Fund—IMF

Address: 700 19th St, NW, Washington, DC 20431, USA.
Telephone: (202) 623-7000; **fax:** (202) 623-4661; **e-mail:** publicaffairs@imf.org; **internet:** www.imf.org.

The IMF was established at the same time as the World Bank in December 1945, to promote international monetary co-operation, to facilitate the expansion and balanced growth of international trade and to promote stability in foreign exchange.

MEMBERS

The IMF has 185 members.

Organization

(March 2008)

Managing Director: DOMINIQUE STRAUSS-KAHN (France).
First Deputy Managing Director: JOHN LIPSKY (USA).
Deputy Managing Directors: TAKATOSHI KATO (Japan), MURILO PORTUGAL (Brazil).

BOARD OF GOVERNORS

The highest authority of the Fund is exercised by the Board of Governors, on which each member country is represented by a Governor and an Alternate Governor. The Board normally meets once a year. The Board of Governors has delegated many of its powers to the Executive Directors. However, the conditions governing the admission of new members, adjustment of quotas and the election of Executive Directors, as well as certain other important powers, remain the sole responsibility of the Board of Governors. The voting power of each member on the Board of Governors is related to its quota in the Fund (see table below).

In September 1999 the Board of Governors adopted a resolution to transform the Interim Committee of the Board of Governors (established in 1974) into the International Monetary and Financial Committee (IMFC). The IMFC, which held its inaugural meeting in April 2000, comprises 24 members, representing the same countries or groups of countries as those on the Board of Executive Directors (see below). It advises and reports to the Board on matters relating to the management and adaptation of the international monetary and financial system, sudden disturbances that might threaten the system and proposals to amend the Articles of Agreement, but has no decision-making authority.

The Development Committee (the Joint Ministerial Committee of the Boards of Governors of the World Bank and the IMF on the Transfer of Real Resources to Developing Countries, created in 1974, with a structure similar to that of the IMFC) reviews development policy issues and financing requirements.

BOARD OF EXECUTIVE DIRECTORS

The 24-member Board of Executive Directors, responsible for the day-to-day operations of the Fund, is in continuous session in Washington, under the chairmanship of the Fund's Managing Director or Deputy Managing Directors. The USA, United Kingdom, Germany, France and Japan each appoint one Executive Director. There is also one Executive Director each from the People's Republic of China, Russia and Saudi Arabia, while the remainder are elected by groups of all other member countries. As in the Board of Governors, the voting power of each member is related to its quota in the Fund, but in practice the Executive Directors normally operate by consensus.

The Managing Director of the Fund serves as head of its staff, which is organized into departments by function and area. At April 2007 the Fund staff employed some 2,714 staff members from 165 countries.

REGIONAL REPRESENTATION

There is a network of regional offices and Resident Representatives in more than 90 member countries. In addition, special information and liaison offices are located in Tokyo, Japan (for Asia and the Pacific), in New York, USA (for the United Nations), and in Europe (Paris, France; Geneva, Switzerland; Belgium, Brussels; and Warsaw, Poland, for Central Europe and the Baltics).

Principal Office in Europe: 64–66 ave d'Iena, 75116 Paris, France; tel. 1-40-69-30-70; fax 1-47-23-40-89; offices are also located in Belgium, Brussels and Geneva, Switzerland; Dir SALEH M. NSOULI.

Regional Office for Asia and the Pacific: 21F Fukoku Seimei Bldg, 2-2-2, Uchisaiwai-cho, Chiyodu-ku, Tokyo 100, Japan; tel. (3) 3597-6700; fax (3) 3597-6705; f. 1997; Dir AKIRA ARIYOSHI.

Regional Office for Central Europe and the Baltics: 00-108 Warsaw, 37c Zielna, Poland; tel. (22) 3386700; fax (22) 3386500; e-mail cee-office@imf.org; f. 2005; Senior Regional Rep. CHRISTOPH B. ROSENBERG.

Activities

The purposes of the IMF, as defined in the Articles of Agreement, are:

(i) To promote international monetary co-operation through a permanent institution which provides the machinery for consultation and collaboration on monetary problems;

(ii) To facilitate the expansion and balanced growth of international trade, and to contribute thereby to the promotion and maintenance of high levels of employment and real income and to the development of members' productive resources;

(iii) To promote exchange stability, to maintain orderly exchange arrangements among members, and to avoid competitive exchange depreciation;

(iv) To assist in the establishment of a multilateral system of payments in respect of current transactions between members and in the elimination of foreign exchange restrictions which hamper the growth of trade;

(v) To give confidence to members by making the general resources of the Fund temporarily available to them, under adequate safeguards, thus providing them with the opportunity to correct maladjustments in their balance of payments, without resorting to measures destructive of national or international prosperity;

(vi) In accordance with the above, to shorten the duration of and lessen the degree of disequilibrium in the international balances of payments of members.

In joining the Fund, each country agrees to co-operate with the above objectives. In accordance with its objective of facilitating the expansion of international trade, the IMF encourages its members to accept the obligations of Article VIII, Sections two, three and four, of the Articles of Agreement. Members that accept Article VIII undertake to refrain from imposing restrictions on the making of payments and transfers for current international transactions and from engaging in discriminatory currency arrangements or multiple currency practices without IMF approval. At the end of 2007 some 90% of members had accepted Article VIII status.

The financial crises of the late 1990s, notably in several Asian countries, Brazil and Russia, contributed to widespread discussions concerning the strengthening of the international monetary system. In April 1998 the Executive Board identified the following fundamental aspects of the debate: reinforcing international and domestic financial systems; strengthening IMF surveillance; promoting greater availability and transparency of information regarding member countries' economic data and policies; emphasizing the central role of the IMF in crisis management; and establishing effective procedures to involve the private sector in forestalling or resolving financial crises. During 1999/2000 the Fund implemented several measures in connection with its ongoing efforts to appraise and reinforce the global financial architecture, including, in March 2000, the adoption by the Executive Board of a strengthened framework to safeguard the use of IMF resources. During 2000 the Fund established the IMF Center, in Washington, DC, which aimed to promote awareness and understanding of its activities. In September the Fund's new Managing Director announced his intention to focus and streamline the principles of conditionality (which links Fund financing with the implementation of specific economic policies by the recipient countries) as part of the wider reform of the international financial system. A comprehensive review was undertaken, during which the issue was considered by public forums and representatives of civil society. New guide-lines on conditionality, which, *inter alia*, aimed to promote national ownership of policy reforms and to introduce specific criteria for the implementation of conditions given different states' circumstances, were approved by the Executive Board in September 2002. In 2000/01 the Fund established an International Capital Markets Department to improve its understanding of financial markets and a separate Consultative Group on capital markets to serve as a forum for regular dialogue between the Fund and representatives of the private sector. In mid-2006 the International Capital Markets Department was merged with the Monetary and Financial Systems Department to create the Monetary and Capital Markets Department, with the intention of strengthening surveillance of global financial transactions and monetary arrangements.

In 2002 a position of Director for Special Operations was created to enhance the Fund's ability to respond to critical situations affecting member countries. In February the newly appointed Director immediately assumed leadership of the staff team working with the authorities in Argentina to help that country to overcome its extreme economic and social difficulties. Detailed consideration ensued of means of orderly resolution of financial crises. In April 2003 the Board of Directors determined that the Fund promote more actively the use of Collective Action Clauses in international bond contracts, as a voluntary measure to facilitate debt restructuring should the need arise.

SPECIAL DRAWING RIGHTS

The special drawing right (SDR) was introduced in 1970 as a substitute for gold in international payments, and was intended eventually to become the principal reserve asset in the international monetary system. SDRs are allocated to members in proportion to their quotas. In October 1996 the Executive Board agreed to a new allocation of SDRs in order to achieve their equitable distribution among member states (i.e. all members would have an equal number of SDRs relative to the size of their quotas). In particular, this was deemed necessary since 38 countries that had joined the Fund since the last allocation of SDRs in 1981 had not yet received any of the units of account. In September 1997 at the annual meeting of the Executive Board, a resolution approving a special allocation of SDR 21,400m. was passed, in order to ensure an SDR to quota ratio of 29.32%, for all member countries. The resolution was to come into effect following its acceptance by 60% of member countries, having 85% of the total voting power. (At November 2006 131 members, holding 77.3% of the voting power, had agreed to the proposal.)

From 1974 to 1980 the SDR was valued on the basis of the market exchange rate for a basket of 16 currencies, belonging to the members with the largest exports of goods and services; since 1981 it has been based on the currencies of the five largest exporters (France, Germany, Japan, the United Kingdom and the USA), although the list of currencies and the weight of each in the SDR valuation basket is revised every five years. In January 1999 the IMF incorporated the new currency of the European Economic and Monetary Union, the euro, into the valuation basket; it replaced the French and German currencies, on the basis of their conversion rates with the euro as agreed by the EU. From 1 January 2006 the relative weights assigned to the currencies in the valuation basket were redistributed. The value of the SDR averaged US $1.58025 during 2007, and at 31 March 2008 stood at $1.64450.

The Second Amendment to the Articles of Agreement (1978) altered and expanded the possible uses of the SDR in transactions with other participants. These 'prescribed holders' of the SDRs have the same degree of freedom as Fund members to buy and sell SDRs and to receive or use them in loans, pledges, swaps, donations or settlement of financial obligations. At 30 April 2007 there were 15 prescribed holders.

QUOTAS

Each member is assigned a quota related to its national income, monetary reserves, trade balance and other economic indicators. A member's subscription is equal to its quota and is payable partly in SDRs and partly in its own currency. The quota determines a member's voting power, which is based on one vote for each SDR 100,000 of its quota *plus* the 250 votes to which each member is entitled. A member's quota also determines its access to the financial resources of the IMF, and its allocation of SDRs.

Quotas are reviewed at intervals of not more than five years, to take into account the state of the world economy and members' different rates of development. Special increases, separate to the general review, may be made in exceptional circumstances. These have been approved by the Fund for the People's Republic of China in 1980 and 2001, for Saudi Arabia in 1981, and for Cambodia in 1984. In June 1990 the Board of Governors authorized proposals for a Ninth General Review of quotas. Total quotas were to be increased by roughly 50% (depending on various factors). At the same time the Board of Governors stipulated that the quota increase could occur only after the Third Amendment of the IMF's Articles of Agreement had come into effect. The amendment provides for the suspension of voting and other related rights of members that do not fulfil their obligations under the Articles. By September 1992 the necessary proportion of IMF members had accepted the amendment, and it entered into force in November. The Tenth General Review of quotas was concluded in December 1994, with the Board recommending no further increase in quotas. However, the Board resolved to monitor closely the Fund's liquidity. In October 1996 the Fund's Managing Director advocated an increase in quotas under the latest review of at least two-thirds in the light of the IMF's reduced liquidity position. (The IMF had extended unprecedentedly large amounts in stand-by arrangements during the period 1995–96, notably to Mexico and Russia.) In January 1998 the Board of Governors adopted a resolution in support of an increase in quotas of 45%, subject to approval by member states constituting 85% of total quotas. Sufficient consent had been granted by January 1999 to enable the Eleventh General Review of Quotas to enter into effect. The Twelfth General Review was initiated in December 2001, and was concluded at the end of January 2003 without an increase in quotas. The Thirteenth General Review was concluded, without an increase in quotas, in January 2008. In September 2006 the Board of Governors adopted a resolution on Quota and Voice Reform in the IMF, representing a two-year reform package aimed at improving the alignment of the quota shares of member states to represent more accurately their relative positions in the global economy and also to enhance the participation and influence of emerging market and low-income countries. An immediate ad hoc quota increase was approved for the People's Republic of China, the Republic of Korea, Mexico and Turkey. In March 2008 the Executive Board approved a second round of ad hoc quota increases as part of the proposed extensive reform of the governance and quota structure, which also committed the Fund to regular, five-yearly realignments of quotas. The proposals required the approval of the Board of Governors and were to come into effect upon being accepted by member states representing 85% of total votes. At 31 March 2008 total quotas in the Fund amounted to SDR 217,372.8m.

RESOURCES

Members' subscriptions form the basic resource of the IMF. They are supplemented by borrowing. Under the General Arrangements to Borrow (GAB), established in 1962, the 'Group of Ten' industrialized nations (G-10—Belgium, Canada, France, Germany, Italy, Japan, the Netherlands, Sweden, the United Kingdom and the USA) and Switzerland (which became a member of the IMF in May 1992 but which had been a full participant in the GAB from April 1984) undertake to lend the Fund as much as SDR 17,000m. in their own currencies to assist in fulfilling the balance of payments requirements of any member of the group, or in response to requests to the Fund from countries with balance of payments problems that could threaten the stability of the international monetary system. In 1983 the Fund entered into an agreement with Saudi Arabia, in association with the GAB, making available SDR 1,500m., and other borrowing arrangements were completed in 1984 with the Bank for International Settlements, the Saudi Arabian Monetary Agency, Belgium and Japan, making available a further SDR 6,000m. In 1986 another borrowing arrangement with Japan made available SDR 3,000m. In May 1996 GAB participants concluded an agreement in principle to expand the resources available for borrowing to SDR 34,000m., by securing the support of 25 countries with the financial capacity to support the international monetary system. The so-called New Arrangements to Borrow (NAB) was approved by the Executive Board in January 1997. It was to enter into force, for an initial five-year period, as soon as the five largest potential creditors participating in NAB had approved the initiative and the total credit arrangement of participants endorsing the scheme had reached at least SDR 28,900m. While the GAB credit arrangement was to remain in effect, the NAB was expected to be the first facility to be activated in the event of the Fund's requiring supplementary resources. In July 1998 the GAB was activated for the first time in more than 20 years in order to provide funds of up to US $6,300m. in support of an IMF emergency assistance package for Russia (the first time the GAB had been used for a non-participant). The NAB became effective in November, and was used for the first time as part of an extensive programme of support for Brazil, which was adopted by the IMF in early December. (In March 1999, however, the activation was cancelled.) In November 2002 NAB participants approved Chile's Central Bank as the 26th participant.

FINANCIAL ASSISTANCE

The Fund makes resources available to eligible members on an essentially short-term and revolving basis to provide members with temporary assistance to contribute to the solution of their payments problems. Before making a purchase, a member must show that its balance of payments or reserve position makes the purchase necessary. Apart from this requirement, reserve tranche purchases (i.e. purchases that do not bring the Fund's holdings of the member's currency to a level above its quota) are permitted unconditionally. Exchange transactions within the Fund take the form of members' purchases (i.e. drawings) from the Fund of the currencies of other members for the equivalent amounts of their own currencies.

With further purchases, however, the Fund's policy of conditionality means that a member requesting assistance must agree to adjust its economic policies, as stipulated by the IMF. All requests other than for use of the reserve tranche are examined by the Executive Board to determine whether the proposed use would be consistent with the Fund's policies, and a member must discuss its proposed adjustment programme (including fiscal, monetary, exchange and trade policies) with IMF staff. Purchases outside the reserve tranche are made in four credit tranches, each equivalent to 25% of the member's quota; a member must reverse the transaction by repurchasing its own currency (with SDRs or currencies specified by the Fund) within a specified time. A credit tranche purchase is usually made under a 'Stand-by Arrangement' with the Fund, or under the Extended Fund Facility. A Stand-by Arrangement is normally of one or two years' duration, and the amount is made available in instalments, subject to the member's observance of 'performance criteria'; repurchases must be made within three-and-a-quarter to five years. An Extended Arrangement is normally of three years' duration, and the member must submit detailed economic programmes and progress reports for each year; repurchases must be made within four-and-a-half to 10 years. A member whose payments imbalance is large in relation to its quota may make use of temporary facilities established by the Fund using borrowed resources, namely the 'enlarged access policy' established in 1981, which helps to finance Stand-by and Extended Arrangements for such a member, up to a limit of between 90% and 110% of the member's quota annually. Repurchases are made within three-and-a-half to seven years. In October 1994 the Executive Board approved a temporary increase in members' access to IMF resources, on the basis of a recommendation by the then Interim Committee. The annual access limit under IMF regular tranche drawings, Stand-by Arrangements and Extended Fund Facility credits was increased from 68% to 100% of a member's quota, with the cumulative access limit remaining at 300% of quota. The arrangements were extended, on a temporary basis, in November 1997.

In addition, special-purpose arrangements have been introduced, all of which are subject to the member's co-operation with the Fund to find an appropriate solution to its difficulties. The Compensatory Financing Facility (CCF) provides compensation to members whose export earnings are reduced as a result of circumstances beyond their control, or which are affected by excess costs of cereal imports. In December 1997 the Executive Board established a new Supplemental Reserve Facility (SRF) to provide short-term assistance to members experiencing exceptional balance of payments difficulties resulting from a sudden loss of market confidence. The SRF was activated immediately to provide SDR 9,950m. to the Republic of Korea, as part of a Stand-by Arrangement amounting to SDR 15,550m. (at that time the largest amount ever committed by the Fund). In July 1998 SDR 4,000m. was made available to Russia under the SRF and, in December, some SDR 9,100m. was extended to Brazil under the SRF as part of a new Stand-by Arrangement. In January 2001 some SDR 2,100m. in SRF resources were approved for Argentina as part of an SDR 5,187m. Stand-by Arrangement augmentation. (In January 2002 the Executive Board approved an extension of one year for Argentina's SRF repayments.) The SDR 22,821m. Stand-by credit approved for Brazil in September 2002 included some SDR 7,600m. committed under the SRF. In April 1999 an additional facility, the Contingent Credit Lines (CCL), was established to provide short-term financing on similar terms to the SRF in order to prevent more stable economies being affected by adverse international financial developments and to maintain investor confidence. No funds were ever committed under the CCL, however, and in November 2003 the Executive Board resolved to allow the facility to terminate, as scheduled, at the end of that month. The Board requested further consideration of other precautionary arrangements to limit the risk of financial crises. In April 2004 the Board approved a new initiative, the Trade Integration Mechanism, to support countries experiencing short-term balance of payments shortfalls as a result of multilateral trade liberalization. Bangladesh, in July, was the first country to obtain assistance in accordance with the Mechanism (in the form of an augmentation of an existing PRGF arrangement).

In October 1995 the Interim Committee of the Board of Governors endorsed recent decisions of the Executive Board to strengthen IMF financial support to members requiring exceptional assistance. An Emergency Financing Mechanism was established to enable the IMF to respond swiftly to potential or actual financial crises, while additional funds were made available for short-term currency stabilization. (The Mechanism was activated for the first time in July 1997, in response to a request by the Philippines Government to reinforce the country's international reserves, and was subsequently used during that year to assist Thailand, Indonesia and the Republic of Korea, and, in July 1998, Russia.) Emergency assistance was also to be available to countries in a post-conflict situation, extending the existing arrangements for countries having been affected by natural disasters, to facilitate the rehabilitation of their economies and to improve their eligibility for further IMF concessional arrangements. Assistance, typically, was to be limited to 25% of a member's quota, although up to 50% would be permitted in certain circumstances. In May 2001 the Executive Board decided to provide a subsidized loan rate for post-conflict emergency assistance for PRGF-eligible countries and an account was established to administer contributions from bilateral donors. In January 2005 the Executive Board decided to extend the subsidized rate for natural disasters. During 2006/07 the Fund approved assistance of SDR 50.8m. for Lebanon under the emergency post-conflict assistance facility.

In November 1999 the Fund's existing facility to provide balance of payments assistance on concessional terms to low-income member countries, the Enhanced Structural Adjustment Facility, was reformulated as the Poverty Reduction and Growth Facility, with greater emphasis on poverty reduction and sustainable development as key elements of growth-orientated economic strategies. Assistance under the PRGF (for which 77 countries were deemed eligible) was to be carefully matched to specific national requirements. Prior to drawing on the facility each recipient country was, in collaboration with representatives of civil society, non-governmental organizations and bilateral and multilateral institutions, to develop a national poverty reduction strategy, which was to be presented in a Poverty Reduction Strategy Paper (PRSP). PRGF loans carry an interest rate of 0.5% per year and are repayable over 10 years, with a five-and-a-half-year grace period; each eligible country is normally permitted to borrow up to 140% of its quota (in exceptional circumstances the maximum access can be raised to 185%). A PRGF Trust replaced the former ESAF Trust. In January 2006 a new Exogenous Shocks Facility was inaugurated to provide concessional assistance on the same terms as those of the PRGF for countries not eligible for funding under the PRGF.

During 2006/07 the IMF approved regular funding commitments for new arrangements amounting to SDR 237.4m. for two new Stand-by Arrangements, compared with a total of SDR 8,336m. in the previous year. Ten new PRGF arrangements, amounting to SDR 401.2m., were approved in 2006/07, together with the augmentation of two existing arrangements (SDR 36.8m.) and the reduction, by SDR 75m., of a further arrangement. During 2006/07 members' purchases from the general resources account amounted to SDR 2,329m., compared with SDR 2,156m. in the previous year. Outstanding IMF credit at 30 April 2007 totalled SDR 11,216m., compared with SDR 23,144m. in the previous year.

The PRGF supports, through long-maturity loans and grants, IMF participation in an initiative to provide exceptional assistance to heavily indebted poor countries (HIPCs), in order to help them to achieve a sustainable level of debt management. The initiative was formally approved at the September 1996 meeting of the Interim Committee, having received the support of the 'Paris Club' of official creditors, which agreed to increase the relief on official debt from 67% to 80%. In all 41 HIPCs were identified, of which 33 were in sub-Saharan Africa. Resources for the HIPC initiative are channelled through the PRGF Trust. In early 1999 the IMF and World Bank initiated a comprehensive review of the HIPC scheme, in order to consider modifications of the initiative and to strengthen the link between debt relief and poverty reduction. A consensus emerged among the financial institutions and leading industrialized nations to enhance the scheme, in order to make it available to more countries, and to accelerate the process of providing debt relief. In September the IMF Board of Governors expressed its commitment to undertaking an off-market transaction of a percentage of the Fund's gold reserves (i.e. a sale, at market prices, to central banks of member countries with repayment obligations to the Fund, which were then to be made in gold), as part of the funding arrangements of the enhanced HIPC scheme; this was undertaken during the period December 1999–April 2000. Under the enhanced initiative it was agreed that countries seeking debt relief should first formulate, and successfully implement for at least one year, a national poverty reduction strategy (see above). In May 2000 Uganda became the first country to qualify for full debt relief under the enhanced scheme. In September 2005 the IMF and World Bank endorsed a proposal of the Group of Eight (G-8) nations to achieve the cancellation by the IMF, IDA and African Development Bank of 100% of debt claims on countries that had reached completion point under the HIPC initiative, in order to help them to achieve their Millennium Development Goals. The debt cancellation was to be undertaken within the framework of a Multilateral Debt Relief Initiative (MDRI). The IMF's Executive Board determined, additionally, to extend MDRI debt relief to all countries with an annual per capita of GDP $380, to be financed by IMF's own resources. Other financing was to be made from existing bilateral contributions to the PRGF Trust Subsidy Account. In December the Executive Board gave final approval to the first group of countries assessed as eligible for 100% debt relief under the MDRI, including 17 of the 18 countries that had reached completion point at that time (i.e. Benin, Bolivia, Burkina Faso, Ethiopia, Ghana, Guyana, Honduras, Madagascar, Mali, Mozambique, Nicaragua, Niger, Rwanda, Senegal, Tanzania, Uganda and Zambia, excluding Mauritania) as well as Cambodia and Tajikistan. The initiative became effective in January 2006 once the final consent of the 43 contributors to the PRGF Trust Subsidy Account had been received. By the end of 2007 a further six countries (Cameroon, The Gambia, Malawi, Mauritania, São Tomé and Príncipe and Sierra Leone) had qualified for and received MDRI relief. At that time the IMF had committed some SDR 2,304m. under the MDRI scheme.

SURVEILLANCE

Under its Articles of Agreement, the Fund is mandated to oversee the effective functioning of the international monetary system. Accordingly, the Fund aims to exercise firm surveillance over the exchange rate policies of member states and to assess whether a country's economic situation and policies are consistent with the objectives of sustainable development and domestic and external stability. The Fund's main tools of surveillance are regular, bilateral consultations with member countries conducted in accordance with Article IV of the Articles of Agreement, which cover fiscal and monetary policies, balance of payments and external debt developments, as well as policies that affect the economic performance of a country, such as the labour market, social and environmental issues and good governance, and aspects of the country's capital accounts, and finance and banking sectors. In April 1997, in an effort to improve the value of surveillance by means of increased transparency, the Executive Board agreed to the voluntary issue of Press Information Notices (PINs) following each member's Article IV consultation with the Board, to those member countries wishing to make public the Fund's views. Other background papers providing information on and analysis of economic developments in individual countries continued to be made available. The Executive Board monitors global economic developments and discusses policy implications from a multilateral perspective, based partly on World Economic Outlook reports and Global Financial Stability Reports. In addition, the IMF studies the regional implications of global developments and policies pursued under regional fiscal arrangements. The Fund's medium-term strategy, initiated in 2006, determined to strengthen its surveillance policies to reflect new challenges of globalization on international financial and macroeconomic stability. In June 2007 the Executive Board approved a Decision on Bilateral Surveillance to update and clarify principles for a member's exchange rate policies and to define best practice for the Fund's bilateral surveillance activities.

In April 1996 the IMF established the Special Data Dissemination Standard (SDDS), which was intended to improve access to reliable economic statistical information for member countries that have, or are seeking, access to international capital markets. In March 1999 the IMF undertook to strengthen the Standard by the introduction of a new reserves data template. By April 2007 64 countries had subscribed to the Standard. The financial crisis in Asia, which became apparent in mid-1997, focused attention on the importance of IMF surveillance of the economies and financial policies of member states and prompted the Fund further to enhance the effectiveness of its surveillance through the development of international standards in order to maintain fiscal transparency. In December 1997 the Executive Board approved a new General Data Dissemination System (GDDS), to encourage all member countries to improve the production and dissemination of core economic data. The operational phase of the GDDS commenced in May 2000. By August 2007 89 countries were participating in the GDDS. The Fund maintains a Dissemination Standards Bulletin Board (accessible at dsbb.imf.org), which aims to ensure that information on SDDS subscribing countries is widely available.

In April 1998 the then Interim Committee adopted a voluntary Code of Good Practices on Fiscal Transparency: Declaration of Principles, which aimed to increase the quality and promptness of official reports on economic indicators, and in September 1999 it adopted a Code of Good Practices on Transparency in Monetary and Financial Policies: Declaration of Principles. The IMF and World Bank jointly established a Financial Sector Assessment Programme (FSAP) in May 1999, initially as a pilot project, which aimed to promote greater global financial security through the preparation of confidential detailed evaluations of the financial sectors of individual countries. It remained under regular review by the Boards of Governors of the Fund and World Bank. During 2006/07 18 FSAP assessments were completed, of which six were updated assessments. As part of the FSAP Fund staff may conclude a Financial System Stability Assessment (FSSA), addressing issues relating to macroeconomic stability and the strength of a country's financial system. A separate component of the FSAP are Reports on the Observance of Standards and Codes (ROSCs), which are compiled after an assessment of a country's implementation and observance of internationally recognized financial standards. By 31 July 2007 516 ROSCs had been published for 133 economies.

In March 2000 the IMF Executive Board adopted a strengthened framework to safeguard the use of IMF resources. All member countries making use of Fund resources were to be required to publish annual central bank statements audited in accordance with internationally accepted standards. It was also agreed that any instance of intentional misreporting of information by a member country should be made public. In the following month the Executive Board approved the establishment of an Independent Evaluation Office (IEO) to conduct objective evaluations of IMF policy and operations. The Office commenced activities in July 2001. In 2006/07 the Office concluded an evaluation on the IMF and Aid to Sub-Saharan Africa.

In April 2001 the Executive Board agreed on measures to enhance international efforts to counter money-laundering, in particular through the Fund's ongoing financial supervision activities and its programme of assessment of offshore financial centres (OFCs). In November the IMFC, in response to the terrorist attacks against targets in the USA, which had occurred in September, resolved, *inter alia*, to strengthen the Fund's focus on surveillance, and, in particular, to extend measures to counter money-laundering to include the funds of terrorist organizations. It determined to accelerate efforts to assess offshore centres and to provide technical support to enable poorer countries to meet international financial standards. In March 2004 the Board of Directors resolved that an anti-money laundering and countering the financing of terrorism (AML/CFT) component be introduced into regular OFC and FSAP assessments conducted by the Fund and the World Bank, following a pilot programme undertaken from November 2002 with the World Bank, the Financial Action Task Force and other regional supervisory bodies. The first phase of the OFC assessment programme was concluded in February 2005, at which time 41 of 44 contacted jurisdictions had been assessed and the reports published.

TECHNICAL ASSISTANCE

Technical assistance is provided by special missions or resident representatives who advise members on every aspect of economic management, while more specialized assistance is provided by the IMF's various departments. In 2000/01 the IMFC determined that technical assistance should be central to the IMF's work in crisis prevention and management, in capacity-building for low-income countries, and in restoring macroeconomic stability in countries following a financial crisis. Technical assistance activities subsequently underwent a process of review and reorganization to align them more closely with IMF policy priorities and other initiatives.

Since 1993 the IMF has delivered some technical assistance, aimed at strengthening local capacity in economic and financial management, through regional centres. The first, established in that year, was a Pacific Financial Technical Assistance Center, located in Fiji. A Caribbean Regional Technical Assistance Centre (CARTAC), located in Barbados, began operations in November 2001. In October 2002 an East African Regional Technical Assistance Centre (East AFRITAC), based in Dar es Salaam, Tanzania, was inaugurated and a second AFRITAC was opened in Bamako, Mali, in May 2003, to cover the West African region. In October 2004 a new technical assistance centre for the Middle East (METAC) was inaugurated, based in Beirut, Lebanon. A regional technical assistance centre for Central Africa, located in Libreville, Gabon, was inaugurated in 2006/07. In September 2002 the IMF signed a memorandum of understanding with the African Capacity Building Foundation to strengthen collaboration, in particular within the context of a new IMF Africa Capacity-Building Initiative.

The IMF Institute, which was established in 1964, trains officials from member countries in macroeconomic management, financial analysis and policy, balance of payments methodology and public finance. The IMF Institute also co-operates with other established regional training centres and institutes in order to refine its delivery of technical assistance and training services. The IMF is a co-sponsor, with UNDP and the Japan administered account, of the Joint Vienna Institute, which was opened in the Austrian capital in October 1992 and which trains officials from former centrally-planned economies in various aspects of economic management and public administration. In May 1998 an IMF—Singapore Regional Training Institute (an affiliate of the IMF Institute) was inaugurated, in collaboration with the Singaporean Government, in order to provide training for officials from the Asia-Pacific region. In January 1999 the IMF, in co-operation with the African Development Bank and the World Bank, announced the establishment of a Joint Africa Institute, in Abidjan, Côte d'Ivoire, which was to offer training to officials from African countries. Also in 1999 a joint Regional Training Programme, administered with the Arab Monetary Fund, was established in the United Arab Emirates. During 2000/01 the Institute established a new training programme with government officials in Liaoning Province, the People's Republic of China. A regional training centre for Latin America became operational in Brasilia, Brazil in 2001. In July 2006 the Joint India-IMF Training Programme was inaugurated in Pune, India

Publications

Annual Report.
Balance of Payments Statistics Yearbook (also on CD-ROM).
Civil Society Newsletter (quarterly).
Direction of Trade Statistics (quarterly and annually).
Emerging Markets Financing (quarterly).
Finance and Development (quarterly).
Financial Statements of the IMF (quarterly).
Global Financial Stability Report (2 a year).
Global Monitoring Report (annually, with the World Bank).
Government Finance Statistics Yearbook.
IMF Commodity Prices (monthly).
IMF Financial Activities (weekly, online).
IMF in Focus (annually).
IMF Research Bulletin (quarterly).
IMF Survey (monthly, and online).
International Financial Statistics (monthly and annually).
Joint BIS-IMF-OECD-World Bank Statistics on External Debt (quarterly).
Quarterly Report on the Assessments of Standards and Codes.
Staff Papers (quarterly).
World Economic Outlook (2 a year).
Other country reports, economic and financial surveys, occasional papers, pamphlets, books.

Statistics

QUOTAS
(SDR million)

	March 2008
Afghanistan	161.9
Albania	48.7
Algeria	1,254.7
Angola	286.3
Antigua and Barbuda	13.5
Argentina	2,117.1
Armenia	92.0
Australia	3,236.4
Austria	1,872.3
Azerbaijan	160.9
Bahamas	130.3
Bahrain	135.0
Bangladesh	533.3
Barbados	67.5
Belarus	386.4
Belgium	4,605.2
Belize	18.8
Benin	61.9
Bhutan	6.3
Bolivia	171.5
Bosnia and Herzegovina	169.1
Botswana	63.0
Brazil	3,036.1
Brunei	215.2
Bulgaria	640.2
Burkina Faso	60.2
Burundi	77.0
Cambodia	87.5
Cameroon	185.7
Canada	6,369.2
Cape Verde	9.6
Central African Republic	55.7
Chad	56.0
Chile	856.1
China, People's Republic	8,090.1

—continued	March 2008
Colombia	774.0
Comoros	8.9
Congo, Democratic Republic	533.0
Congo, Republic	84.6
Costa Rica	164.1
Côte d'Ivoire	325.2
Croatia	365.1
Cyprus	139.6
Czech Republic	819.3
Denmark	1,642.8
Djibouti	15.9
Dominica	8.2
Dominican Republic	218.9
Ecuador	302.3
Egypt	943.7
El Salvador	171.3
Equatorial Guinea	32.6
Eritrea	15.9
Estonia	65.2
Ethiopia	133.7
Fiji	70.3
Finland	1,263.8
France	10,738.5
Gabon	154.3
The Gambia	31.1
Georgia	150.3
Germany	13,008.2
Ghana	369.0
Greece	823.0
Grenada	11.7
Guatemala	210.2
Guinea	107.1
Guinea-Bissau	14.2
Guyana	90.9
Haiti	81.9
Honduras	129.5
Hungary	1,038.4
Iceland	117.6
India	4,158.2
Indonesia	2,079.3
Iran	1,497.2
Iraq	1,188.4
Ireland	838.4
Israel	928.2
Italy	7,055.5
Jamaica	273.5
Japan	13,312.8
Jordan	170.5
Kazakhstan	365.7
Kenya	271.4
Kiribati	5.6
Korea, Republic	2,927.3
Kuwait	1,381.1
Kyrgyzstan	88.8
Laos	52.9
Latvia	126.8
Lebanon	203.0
Lesotho	34.9
Liberia	129.2
Libya	1,123.7
Lithuania	144.2
Luxembourg	279.1
Macedonia, former Yugoslav republic	68.9
Madagascar	122.2
Malawi	69.4
Malaysia	1,486.6
Maldives	8.2
Mali	93.3
Malta	102.0
Marshall Islands	3.5
Mauritania	64.4
Mauritius	101.6
Mexico	2,585.8
Micronesia, Federated States	5.1
Moldova	123.2
Mongolia	51.1
Montenegro	27.5
Morocco	588.2
Mozambique	113.6
Myanmar	258.4
Namibia	136.5
Nepal	71.3
Netherlands	5,162.4
New Zealand	894.6

INTERNATIONAL ORGANIZATIONS — United Nations (Specialized Agencies)

—continued	March 2008
Nicaragua	130.0
Niger	65.8
Nigeria	1,753.2
Norway	1,671.7
Oman	194.0
Pakistan	1,033.7
Palau	3.1
Panama	206.6
Papua New Guinea	131.6
Paraguay	99.9
Peru	638.4
Philippines	879.9
Poland	1,369.0
Portugal	867.4
Qatar	263.8
Romania	1,030.2
Russia	5,945.4
Rwanda	80.1
Saint Christopher and Nevis	8.9
Saint Lucia	15.3
Saint Vincent and the Grenadines	8.3
Samoa	11.6
San Marino	17.0
São Tomé and Príncipe	7.4
Saudi Arabia	6,985.5
Senegal	161.8
Serbia	467.7
Seychelles	8.8
Sierra Leone	103.7
Singapore	862.5
Slovakia	357.5
Slovenia	231.7
Solomon Islands	10.4
Somalia	44.2
South Africa	1,868.5
Spain	3,048.9
Sri Lanka	413.4
Sudan	169.7
Suriname	92.1
Swaziland	50.7
Sweden	2,395.5
Switzerland	3,458.5
Syria	293.6
Tajikistan	87.0
Tanzania	198.9
Thailand	1,081.9
Timor-Leste	8.2
Togo	73.4
Tonga	6.9
Trinidad and Tobago	335.6
Tunisia	286.5
Turkey	1,191.3
Turkmenistan	75.2
Uganda	180.5
Ukraine	1,372.0
United Arab Emirates	611.7
United Kingdom	10,738.5
USA	37,149.3
Uruguay	306.5
Uzbekistan	275.6
Vanuatu	17.0
Venezuela	2,659.1
Viet Nam	329.1
Yemen	243.5
Zambia	489.1
Zimbabwe	353.4

FINANCIAL ACTIVITIES
(SDR million, year ending 30 April)

Type of Transaction	2002	2003	2004	2005	2006	2007
Total disbursements	30,146	23,002	18,695	2,379	2,559	2,806
Purchases by facility (General Resources Account)*	29,194	21,784	17,830	1,608	2,156	2,329
Loans under PRGF arrangements	952	1,218	865	771	403	477
Repurchases and repayments	19,976	8,712	22,528	14,830	35,991	14,678
Repurchases	19,207	7,784	21,638	13,907	32,783	14,166
Trust Fund and SAF/PRGF loan repayments	769	928	890	923	3,208	512
Total outstanding credit provided by Fund (end of year)	58,699	72,879	69,031	56,576	23,144	11,216
Of which:						
General Resources Account	52,081	65,978	62,153	49,854	19,227	7,333
SAF Arrangements	341	137	86	45	9	9
PRGF Arrangements†	6,188	6,676	6,703	6,588	3,819	3,785
Trust Fund	89	89	89	89	89	89

* Including reserve tranche purchases.
† Including Saudi Fund for Development associated loans.
Source: *IMF Annual Report 2007*.

INTERNATIONAL ORGANIZATIONS

United Nations (Specialized Agencies)

BOARD OF EXECUTIVE DIRECTORS
(March 2008)

Director	Casting Votes of	Total Votes	%
Appointed:			
MEG LUNDSAGER	USA	371,743	16.79
DAISUKE KOTEGAWA	Japan	133,378	6.02
KLAUS D. STEIN	Germany	130,332	5.88
AMBROISE FAYOLLE	France	107,635	4.86
ALEX GIBBS	United Kingdom	107,635	4.86
Elected:			
WILLY KIEKENS (Belgium)	Austria, Belarus, Belgium, Czech Republic, Hungary, Kazakhstan, Luxembourg, Slovakia, Slovenia, Turkey	113,969	5.15
AGE F. P. BAKKER (Netherlands)	Armenia, Bosnia and Herzegovina, Bulgaria, Croatia, Cyprus, Georgia, Israel, the former Yugoslav republic of Macedonia, Moldova, Netherlands, Romania, Ukraine	105,412	4.76
JOSE A. ROJAS (Venezuela)	Costa Rica, El Salvador, Guatemala, Honduras, Mexico, Nicaragua, Spain, Venezuela	98,659	4.45
ARRIGO SADUN (Italy)	Albania, Greece, Italy, Malta, Portugal, San Marino, Timor-Leste	90,968	4.10
RICHARD MURRAY (Australia)	Australia, Kiribati, Republic of Korea, Marshall Islands, Federated States of Micronesia, Mongolia, New Zealand, Palau, Papua New Guinea, Philippines, Samoa, Seychelles, Solomon Islands, Vanuatu	85,360	3.85
GE HUAYONG	People's Republic of China	81,151	3.66
JONATHAN FRIED (Canada)	Antigua and Barbuda, The Bahamas, Barbados, Belize, Canada, Dominica, Grenada, Ireland, Jamaica, Saint Christopher and Nevis, Saint Lucia, Saint Vincent and the Grenadines	80,636	3.64
JENS HENRIKSSON (Sweden)	Denmark, Estonia, Finland, Iceland, Latvia, Lithuania, Norway, Sweden	76,276	3.44
A. SHAKOUR SHAALAN (Egypt)	Bahrain, Egypt, Iraq, Jordan, Kuwait, Lebanon, Libya, Maldives, Oman, Qatar, Syria, United Arab Emirates, Yemen	70,852	3.20
ABDALLAH S. AALAZZAZ	Saudi Arabia	70,105	3.16
PERRY WARJIYO (Indonesia)	Brunei, Cambodia, Fiji, Indonesia, Laos, Malaysia, Myanmar, Nepal, Singapore, Thailand, Tonga, Viet Nam	69,019	3.12
PETER GAKUNU (Kenya)	Angola, Botswana, Burundi, Eritrea, Ethiopia, The Gambia, Kenya, Lesotho, Liberia, Malawi, Mozambique, Namibia, Nigeria, Sierra Leone, South Africa, Sudan, Swaziland, Tanzania, Uganda, Zambia	66,763	3.01
THOMAS MOSER (Switzerland)	Azerbaijan, Kyrgyzstan, Poland, Serbia, Switzerland, Tajikistan, Turkmenistan, Uzbekistan	61,827	2.79
ALEKSEI V. MOZHIN	Russia	59,704	2.69
MOHAMMAD JAFAR MOJARRAD (Iran)	Afghanistan, Algeria, Ghana, Iran, Morocco, Pakistan, Tunisia	53,662	2.42
PAULO NOGUEIRA BATISTA, Jr (Brazil)	Brazil, Colombia, Dominican Republic, Ecuador, Guyana, Haiti, Panama, Suriname, Trinidad and Tobago	53,634	2.42
ADARSH KISHORE (India)	Bangladesh, Bhutan, India, Sri Lanka	52,112	2.35
JAVIER SILVA RUETE (Peru)	Argentina, Bolivia, Chile, Paraguay, Peru, Uruguay	43,395	1.96
LAUREAN W. RUTAYISIRE (Rwanda)	Benin, Burkina Faso, Cameroon, Cape Verde, Central African Republic, Chad, Comoros, Democratic Republic of the Congo, Republic of the Congo, Côte d'Ivoire, Djibouti, Equatorial Guinea, Gabon, Guinea, Guinea-Bissau, Madagascar, Mali, Mauritania, Mauritius, Niger, Rwanda, São Tomé and Príncipe, Senegal, Togo	30,749	1.39

Note: The total number of votes does not include the votes of Somalia (0.03% of the total of votes in the General Department and the Special Drawing Rights Department), which did not participate in the 2006 election of Executive Directors, or of Montenegro, which joined the Fund in January 2007. Zimbabwe's voting rights (0.17%) were suspended effective 6 June 2003.

International Telecommunication Union—ITU

Address: Place des Nations, 1211 Geneva 20, Switzerland.
Telephone: 227305111; **fax:** 227337256; **e-mail:** itumail@itu.int; **internet:** www.itu.int.

Founded in 1865, ITU became a specialized agency of the UN in 1947. It acts inter alia to encourage world co-operation for the improvement and national use of telecommunications to promote technical development, to harmonize national policies in the field, and to promote the extension of telecommunications throughout the world.

MEMBERS

ITU has 191 member states. More than 700 scientific and technical companies, public and private operators, broadcasters and other organizations are also ITU members.

Organization
(March 2008)

PLENIPOTENTIARY CONFERENCE

The supreme organ of ITU; normally meets every four years. The main tasks of the Conference are to elect ITU's leadership, establish policies, revise the Constitution and Convention (see below) and approve limits on budgetary spending. The 2006 Conference was held in Doha, Qatar, in March.

WORLD CONFERENCES ON INTERNATIONAL TELECOMMUNICATIONS

The World Conferences on International Telecommunications are held at the request of members and after approval by the Plenipotentiary Conference. The World Conferences are authorized to review and revise the regulations applying to the provision and operation of international telecommunications services. Separate Conferences are held by Union's three sectors (see below): Radiocommunication Conferences (every two or three years); Telecommunication Standardization Assemblies (every four years or at the request of one-quarter of ITU members); and Telecommunication Development Conferences (every four years).

ITU COUNCIL

The Council meets annually in Geneva and is composed of 46 members elected by the Plenipotentiary Conference.

The Council ensures the efficient co-ordination and implementation of the work of the Union in all matters of policy, administration and finance, in the interval between Plenipotentiary Conferences, and approves the annual budget.

GENERAL SECRETARIAT

The Secretary-General is elected by the Plenipotentiary Conference and is assisted by a Co-ordination Committee that also comprises the Deputy Secretary-General and the Directors of the three sector Bureaux. The General Secretariat comprises departments for Administration and Finance; Conferences and Publications; Information Services; Internal Audit; ITU Telecom (conference organization); Legal Affairs; and Strategic Planning and Membership. The Secretariat's staff totals some 800, representing more than 80 nationalities; the official and working languages are Arabic, Chinese, English, French, Russian and Spanish.

Secretary-General: HAMADOUN I. TOURÉ (Mali).
Deputy Secretary-General: HOULIN ZHAO (People's Republic of China).

Constitution and Convention

Between 1865 and 1992 each Plenipotentiary Conference adopted a new Convention of ITU. At the Additional Plenipotentiary Conference held in December 1992, in Geneva, Switzerland, a new Constitution and Convention were signed. They were partially amended by the following two Plenipotentiary Conferences held in Kyoto, Japan, in 1994, and Minneapolis, USA, in 1998. The Constitution contains the fundamental provisions of ITU, whereas the Convention contains other provisions which complement those of the Constitution and which, by their nature, require periodic revision.

The Constitution establishes the purposes and structure of the Union, contains the general provisions relating to telecommunications and special provisions for radio, and deals with relations with the UN and other organizations. The Convention establishes the functioning of the Union and the three sectors, and contains the general provisions regarding conferences and assemblies. Both instruments are further complemented by the *Radio Regulations* and the *International Telecommunications Regulations* (see below).

Activities

In December 1992 an Additional Plenipotentiary Conference, convened in Geneva, Switzerland, determined that the ITU should be restructured into three sectors corresponding to its main functions: standardization; radiocommunication; and development. In October 1994 the ordinary Plenipotentiary Conference, held in Kyoto, Japan, adopted ITU's first strategic plan. A second strategic plan, for the period 1999–2003, adopted by the Plenipotentiary Conference that was convened in Minneapolis, USA, in October–November 1998, recognized new trends and developments in the world telecommunication environment, such as globalization, liberalization, and greater competition, assessed their implications for ITU, and proposed new strategies and priorities to enable the Union to function effectively. The conference approved the active involvement of ITU in governance issues relating to the internet, and recommended that a World Summit on the Information Society (WSIS, see below) be convened, given the rapid developments in that field. In October 2002 the Plenipotentiary Conference, convened in Marrakesh, Morocco, adopted a third strategic plan, for the period 2004–07 which emphasized ITU's role in facilitating universal access to the global information economy and society. ITU was to take a lead role in UN initiatives concerning information and communication technologies and support all efforts to overcome the digital divide. The 2006 Conference, held in November, in Antalya, Turkey, adopted a fourth strategic plan covering the period 2008–11, which established a road map on the future course of the Union, and endorsed ITU's essential role in Bridging the Digital Divide and in leading the multi-stakeholder process for the follow-up and implementation of relevant WSIS objectives. Main thematic areas of focus in 2008 included: the implementation of the Union's Global Cybersecurity Agenda; pursuing the objective of 'connecting the unconnected' by 2015; developing emergency telecommunications as a critical pillar of disaster management; and implementing the Next Generation Network (NGN) Global Standards Initiative.

In October 2007 ITU, jointly with the African Union, World Bank, and the UN Global Alliance for ICT and Development, and in close co-operation with other partners, organized the first Connect Africa summit, convened in Kigali, Rwanda, with the aim of mobilizing the human, financial and technical resources required to close ICT gaps throughout Africa. The summit generated investment commitments in excess of US $5,500m., and agreed to accelerate ICT connectivity goals in the region from 2015 to 2012.

WORLD SUMMIT ON THE INFORMATION SOCIETY

The ITU took a lead role in organizing the WSIS, which was held, under the auspices of the UN Secretary-General, in two phases: the first took place in Geneva in December 2003, and the second in Tunis, Tunisia in November 2005. The Geneva meeting, attended by representatives of 175 countries, recognized the central role of ITU in building an information society and approved a Declaration of Principles and Plan of Action, which urged co-operation by public- and private-sector stakeholders, civil society interests and UN agencies in encouraging new projects and partnerships aimed at bridging the so-called international digital divide. The second meeting adopted the Tunis Agenda for the Information Society, which called upon the UN Secretary-General to establish an Internet Governance Forum (IGF), with a view to establishing a more inclusive dialogue on global internet policy. In March 2006 the UN Secretary-General announced that a small secretariat would be formed to assist with convening the planned Forum, the first session of which was held in Athens, Greece, in October–November. The second IGF session was held in Rio de Janeiro, Brazil, in November 2007, and the third was scheduled to take place in December 2008, in New Delhi, India.

RADIOCOMMUNICATION SECTOR

The role of the sector is globally to manage, and to ensure the equitable and efficient use of, the radio-frequency spectrum by all radiocommunication services, including those that use satellite orbits (the latter being in increasing demand from fixed, mobile, amateur, broadcasting, emergency telecommunications, environmental monitoring and communications services, global positioning systems, meteorology and space research services). The sector also conducts studies, and adopts recommendations on sector issues. The *Radio Regulations*, which first appeared in 1906, include general rules for the assignment and use of frequencies and the associated orbital positions for space stations. They include a Table of Frequency Allocations (governing the use of radio frequency bands between 9 kHz and 400 GHz) for the various radio services (*inter alia* radio broadcasting, television, radio astronomy, navigation aids, point-to-point service, maritime mobile, amateur). They are reviewed and revised by the World Radiocommunication Conferences: the most recent revision was issued in 2004. The technical work on issues to be considered by the conferences is conducted by Radiocommunication Assemblies, on the basis of recommendations made by Study Groups. These groups of experts study technical questions relating to radiocommunications, according to a study programme formulated by the Assemblies. The Assemblies may approve, modify or reject any recommendations of the Study Groups, and are authorized to establish new groups and to abolish others. The procedural rules used in the application of the Radio Regulations may be considered by a Radio Regulations Board, which may also perform duties relating to the allocation and use of frequencies and consider cases of interference.

The administrative work of the sector is the responsibility of the Radiocommunication Bureau, which is headed by an elected Director. The Bureau co-ordinates the work of Study Groups, provides administrative support for the Radio Regulations Board, and works alongside the General Secretariat to prepare conferences and to provide relevant assistance to developing countries. The Director is assisted by an Advisory Group.

Director: VALERY TIMOFEEV (Russia).

TELECOMMUNICATION STANDARDIZATION SECTOR

The Telecommunications Standardization sector studies technical, operational and tariff issues in order to standardize telecommunications throughout the world. The sector's conferences adopt the *International Telecommunications Regulations*, which establish ITU guide-lines to guarantee the effective provision of telecommunication services. Recommendations may be approved outside of the four-year interval between conferences if a sectoral Study Group (comprising private and public sector experts) concludes such action to be urgent. In 2008 Study Groups were engaged in the following areas of interest: operational aspects of service provision, networks and performance; tariff and accounting principles; telecommunication management; protection against electromagnetic environmental effects; outside plant and related indoor installations; integrated broadband cable networks and television and sound transmission; signalling requirements and protocols; performance and quality of service; NGN; optical and other transport network infrastructures; multimedia terminals, systems and applications; security, languages and telecommunications softwares; and mobile telecommunications networks. The Telecommunication Standardization Advisory Group (TSAG) reviews sectoral priorities, programmes, operations and administrative matters, and establishes, organizes and provides guide-lines to the Study Groups. The 2004 World Telecommunication Standardization Assembly (WTSA), convened in October, in Florianópolis, Brazil, adopted an action plan for addressing the global standardization gap. Consequently a Group on Bridging the Standardization Gap was established within the TSAG.

Preparations for conferences and other meetings of the sector are made by the Telecommunication Standardization Bureau (ITU-T). It administers the application of conference decisions, as well as relevant provisions of the International Telecommunications Regulations. ITU-T is headed by an elected Director, who is assisted by an Advisory Group. The Director reports to conferences and to the ITU Council on the activities of the sector. The 2008 WTSA was scheduled to be held in Johannesburg, South Africa, in October; it was to be preceeded by a Global Standards Symposium that was to address means of enabling increased participation by developing countries in the standards making process, as well as addressing challenges to the standards agenda, such as accessibility and climate change.

Director: MALCOLM JOHNSON (United Kingdom).

TELECOMMUNICATION DEVELOPMENT SECTOR

The sector's objectives are to facilitate and enhance telecommunications development by offering, organizing and co-ordinating technical co-operation and assistance activities, to promote the development of telecommunications infrastructure, networks and services in developing countries, to facilitate the transfer of appropriate technologies and the use of resources, and to provide advice on issues specific to telecommunications. The sector implements projects under the UN development system or other funding arrangements. In January 2005 ITU launched an initiative to establish a network of some 100 Multipurpose Community Telecentres in 20 African countries, with the aim of providing broader access to ICTs. A global development initiative entitled 'Connect the World' was introduced by ITU in June, with the aim of providing access to ICTs to 1,000m. people without connectivity. The initiative, involving 22 stakeholders, was developed within the context of the WSIS agenda to encourage new projects and partnerships to bridge the digital divide.

The sector holds conferences regularly to encourage international co-operation in the development of telecommunications, and to determine strategies for development. Conferences consider the result of work undertaken by Study Groups on issues of benefit to developing countries, including development policy, finance, network planning and operation of services. The fourth World Telecommunication Development Conference (WTDC), convened in March 2006, in Doha, Qatar, addressed development priorities in the context of the Digital Divide, and the promotion of international co-operation to strengthen telecommunication infrastructure and institutions in developing countries.

The administrative work of the sector is conducted by the Telecommunication Development Bureau, which may also study specific problems presented by a member state. The Director of the Bureau reports to conferences and the ITU Council, and is assisted by an Advisory Board.

Director: SAMI AL-BASHEER (Saudi Arabia).

Finance

The budget for the two-year period 2006–07 totalled 339.43m. Swiss francs.

Publications

ITU Internet Reports.
ITU News (10 a year, in English, French and Spanish).
Trends in Telecommunication Reform (2007: The Road to NGNs).
World Information Society Report.
Conventions, databases, statistics, regulations, technical documents and manuals, conference documents.

United Nations Educational, Scientific and Cultural Organization—UNESCO

Address: 7 place de Fontenoy, 75352 Paris 07 SP, France.
Telephone: 1-45-68-10-00; **fax:** 1-45-67-16-90; **e-mail:** bpi@unesco.org; **internet:** www.unesco.org.

UNESCO was established in 1946 'for the purpose of advancing, through the educational, scientific and cultural relations of the peoples of the world, the objectives of international peace and the common welfare of mankind'.

MEMBERS
UNESCO has 193 members and six associate members.

Organization
(March 2008)

GENERAL CONFERENCE
The supreme governing body of the Organization, the Conference meets in ordinary session once in two years and is composed of representatives of the member states. It determines policies, approves work programmes and budgets and elects members of the Executive Board.

EXECUTIVE BOARD
The Board, comprising 58 members, prepares the programme to be submitted to the Conference and supervises its execution; it meets two times a year.

SECRETARIAT
The organization is headed by a Director-General, appointed for a four-year term. There are Assistant Directors-General for the main thematic sectors, i.e education, natural sciences, social and human sciences, culture, and communication and information, as well as for the support sectors of external relations and co-operation and of administration.

Director-General: KOÏCHIRO MATSUURA (Japan).

CO-OPERATING BODIES
In accordance with UNESCO's constitution, national Commissions have been set up in most member states. These help to integrate work within the member states and the work of UNESCO. Most member states also have their own permanent delegations to UNESCO. UNESCO aims to develop partnerships with cities and local authorities.

FIELD CO-ORDINATION
UNESCO maintains a network of offices to support a more decentralized approach to its activities and enhance their implementation at field level. Cluster offices provide the main structure of the field co-ordination network. These cover a group of countries and help to co-ordinate between member states and with other UN and partner agencies operating in the area. In 2007 there were 27 cluster offices covering 143 states. In addition 21 national offices serve a single country, including those in post-conflict situations or economic transition and the nine most highly-populated countries. The regional bureaux (see below) provide specialized support at a national level.

REGIONAL BUREAUX

Regional Bureau for Education in Africa: 12 ave L. S. Senghor, BP 3318, Dakar, Senegal; tel. 849-23-23; fax 823-83-23; e-mail dakar@unesco.org; internet www.dakar.unesco.org; Dir LALLA AÏCHA BEN BARKA.

Regional Bureau for Science and Technology in Africa: POB 305920, Nairobi, Kenya; tel. (20) 762-1234; fax (20) 762-2750; e-mail nairobi@unesco.org; internet www.unesco-nairobi.org/; f. 1965 to execute UNESCO's regional science programme, and to assist in the planning and execution of national programmes; Dir JOSEPH M. G. MASSAQUOI.

Regional Bureau for Education in the Arab States: POB 5244, Cité Sportive, Beirut, Lebanon; tel. (1) 850013; fax (1) 834854; e-mail beirut@unesco.org; internet portal.unesco.org/beirut.

Regional Bureau for Sciences in the Arab States: 8 Abdel Rahman Fahmy St, Garden City, Cairo 11511, Egypt; tel. (2) 7945599; fax (2) 7945296; e-mail cairo@unesco.org; internet www.unesco.org.eg; also covers informatics; Dir AWAD ELHASSAN (acting).

Regional Bureau for Science and Culture in Europe: Palazzo Zorzi, 4930 Castello, 30122 Venice, Italy; tel. (041) 260-1511; fax (041) 528-9995; e-mail veniceoffice@unesco.org; internet www.unesco.org/venice; Dir ENGELBERT RUOSS.

Regional Bureau for Culture in Latin America and the Caribbean (ORCALC): Calzada 551, esq. D, Vedado, Havana 4, Cuba; tel. (7) 832-7741; fax (7) 833-3144; e-mail habana@unesco.org.cu; internet www.unesco.org.cu; f. 1950; activities include research and programmes of cultural development and cultural tourism; maintains a documentation centre and a library of 14,500 vols; Dir HERMAN VAN HOFF; publs *Oralidad* (annually), *Boletín Electrónico* (quarterly).

Regional Bureau for Education in Latin America and the Caribbean: Calle Enrique Delpiano 2058, Providencia, Santiago, Chile; Casilla 127, Correo 29, Providencia, Santiago, Chile; tel. (2) 472-4600; fax (2) 655-1046; e-mail unesco@unesco.cl; internet www.unesco.cl; Dir ROSA BLANCO GUIJARRO.

Regional Bureau for Science for Latin America and the Caribbean: Calle Dr Luis Piera 1992, 2°, Casilla 859, 11000 Montevideo, Uruguay; tel. (2) 413-2075; fax (2) 413-2094; e-mail orcyt@unesco.org.uy; internet www.unesco.org.uy; also cluster office for Argentina, Brazil, Chile, Paraguay, Uruguay; Dir JORGE GRANDI.

Regional Bureau for Education in Asia and the Pacific: POB 967, Bangkok 10110, Thailand; tel. (2) 391-0577; fax (2) 391-0866; e-mail bangkok@unescobkk.org; internet www.unescobkk.org; Dir SHELDON SCHAEFFER.

Regional Science Bureau for Asia and the Pacific: UNESCO Office, Jalan Galuh II 5, Kebayoran Baru, Jakarta 12110, Indonesia; tel. (21) 7399818; fax (21) 72796489; e-mail jakarta@unesco.org; internet www.unesco.or.id; Dir HUBERT J. GIJZEN.

Activities

In the implementation of all its activities UNESCO aims to contribute to achieving the UN Millennium Development Goal (MDG) of halving levels of extreme poverty by 2015, as well as other MDGs concerned with education and sustainable development. UNESCO is the lead agency for the International Decade for a Culture of Peace and Non-violence for the Children of the World (2001–10). In November 2007 the General Conference approved a medium-term strategy to guide UNESCO during the period 2008–13. UNESCO's central mission as defined under the strategy was to contribute to building peace, the alleviation of poverty, sustainable development and intercultural dialogue through its core programme sectors (Education; Natural Sciences; Social and Human Sciences; Culture; and Communication and Information). The strategy identified five 'overarching objectives' for UNESCO in 2008–13, within this programme framework: Attaining quality education for all; Mobilizing scientific knowledge and science policy for sustainable development; Addressing emerging ethical challenges; Promoting cultural diversity and intercultural dialogue; and Building inclusive knowledge societies through information and communication.

The 2008–13 medium-term strategy reaffirmed the organization's commitment to prioritising Africa and its development efforts. In particular, it was to extend support to countries in post-conflict and disaster situations and strengthen efforts to achieve international targets and those identified through the New Partnership for Africa's Development (NEPAD, see under African Union). A further priority for UNESCO, to be implemented through all its areas of work, was gender equality. Specific activities were to be pursued in support of the welfare of youth, least developed countries and small island developing states.

EDUCATION

UNESCO recognizes education as an essential human right, and an overarching objective for 2008–13 was to attain quality education for all. Through its work programme UNESCO is committed to achieving the MDGs of eliminating gender disparity at all levels of education and attaining universal primary education in all countries by 2015. The focus of many of UNESCO's education initiatives are the nine most highly-populated developing countries (Bangladesh, Brazil, the People's Republic of China, Egypt, India, Indonesia, Mexico, Nigeria and Pakistan), known collectively as the E-9 ('Education-9') countries.

UNESCO leads and co-ordinates global efforts in support of 'Education for All' (EFA), which was adopted as a guiding principle of UNESCO's contribution to development following a world conference, convened in March 1990. In April 2000 several UN agencies, including UNESCO and UNICEF, and other partners sponsored the World Education Forum, held in Dakar, Senegal, to assess international progress in achieving the goal of Education for All and to adopt a strategy for further action (the 'Dakar Framework'), with the aim of ensuring universal basic education by 2015. The Dakar Framework, incorporating six specific goals, emphasized the role of improved access to education in the reduction of poverty and in diminishing inequalities within and between societies. UNESCO was appointed as the lead agency in the implementation of the Framework, focusing on co-ordination, advocacy, mobilization of resources, and information-sharing at international, regional and national levels. It was to oversee national policy reforms, with a particular focus on the integration of EFA objectives into national education plans. An EFA Global Action Plan was formulated in 2006 to reinvigorate efforts to achieve EFA objectives and, in particular, to provide a framework for international co-operation and better definition of the roles of international partners and of UNESCO in leading the initiative. UNESCO's medium-term strategy for 2008–13 committed the organization to strengthening its role in co-ordinating EFA efforts at global and national levels, promoting monitoring and capacity-building activities to support implementation of EFA objectives, and facilitating mobilization of increased resources for EFA programmes and strategies (for example through the EFA-Fast Track Initiative, launched in 2002 to accelerate technical and financial support to low-income countries).

UNESCO advocates 'Literacy for All' as a key component of Education for All, regarding literacy as essential to basic education and to social and human development. UNESCO is the lead agency of the UN Literacy Decade (2003–12), which aims to formulate an international plan of action to raise literacy standards throughout the world and to assist policy-makers to integrate literacy standards and goals into national education programmes. The Literacy Initiative for Empowerment (LIFE) was developed as an element of the Literacy Decade to accelerate efforts in some 35 countries where illiteracy is a critical challenge to development. UNESCO is also the co-ordinating agency for the UN Decade of Education for Sustainable Development (2005–14), through which it aims to establish a global framework for action and strengthen the capacity of education systems to incorporate the concepts of sustainable development into education programmes. The April 2000 World Education Forum recognized the global HIV/AIDS pandemic to be a significant challenge to the attainment of Education for All'. UNESCO, as a co-sponsor of UNAIDS, takes an active role in promoting formal and non-formal preventive health education. Through a Global Initiative on HIV/AIDS and Education (EDUCAIDS) UNESCO aims to develop comprehensive responses to HIV/AIDS rooted in the education sector, with a particular focus on vulnerable children and young people. An initiative covering the 10-year period 2006–15, the Teacher Training Initiative in sub-Saharan Africa, aims to address the shortage of teachers in that region (owing to HIV/AIDS, armed conflict and other causes) and to improve the quality of teaching.

A key priority area of UNESCO's education programme is to foster quality education for all, through formal and non-formal educational opportunities. It assists members to improve the quality of education provision through curricula content, school management and teacher training. UNESCO aims to expand access to education at all levels and to work to achieve gender equality. In particular, UNESCO aims to strengthen capacity-building and education in natural, social and human sciences and promote the use of new technologies in teaching and learning processes.

The Associated Schools Project (ASPnet—comprising some 7,900 institutions in 176 countries in July 2007) has, since 1953, promoted the principles of peace, human rights, democracy and international co-operation through education. It provides a forum for dialogue and for promoting best practices. At tertiary level UNESCO chairs a University Twinning and Networking (UNITWIN) initiative, which was established in 1992 to establish links between higher education institutions and to foster research, training and programme development. A complementary initiative, Academics Across Borders, was inaugurated in November 2005 to strengthen communication and the sharing of knowledge and expertise among higher education professionals. In October 2002 UNESCO organized the first Global Forum on International Quality Assurance, Accreditation and the Recognition of Qualifications to establish international standards and promote capacity-building for the sustainable development of higher education systems.

Within the UN system UNESCO is responsible for providing technical assistance and educational services in the context of emergency situations. This includes establishing temporary schools, providing education to refugees and displaced persons, as well as assistance for the rehabilitation of national education systems. In Palestine, UNESCO collaborates with UNRWA to assist with the training of teachers, educational planning and rehabilitation of schools.

NATURAL SCIENCES

The World Summit on Sustainable Development, held in August–September 2002, recognised the essential role of science (including mathematics, engineering and technology) as a foundation for achieving the MDGs of eradicating extreme poverty and ensuring environmental sustainability. UNESCO aims to promote this function within the UN system and to assist member states to utilise and foster the benefits of scientific and technical knowledge. A key objective for the medium-term strategy 2008–13 was to mobilize science knowledge and policy for sustainable development. Throughout the natural science programme priority was to be placed on Africa, least developed countries and small island developing states. The Local and Indigenous Knowledge System (LINKS) initiative aims to strengthen dialogue among traditional knowledge holders, natural and social scientists and decision-makers to enhance the conservation of biodiversity, in all disciplines, and to secure an active and equitable role for local communities in the governance of resources.

In November 1999 the General Conference endorsed a Declaration on Science and the Use of Scientific Knowledge and an agenda for action, which had been adopted at the World Conference on Science, held in June–July 1999, in Budapest, Hungary. By leveraging scientific knowledge, and global, regional and country level science networks, UNESCO aims to support sustainable development and the sound management of natural resources. It also advises governments on approaches to natural resource management, in particular the collection of scientific data, documenting and disseminating good practices and integrating social and cultural aspects into management structures and policies. UNESCO's Man and the Biosphere Programme supports a world-wide network of biosphere reserves (comprising 531 sites in 105 countries at March 2008), which aim to promote environmental conservation and research, education and training in biodiversity and problems of land use (including the fertility of tropical soils and the cultivation of sacred sites). The third World Congress of Biosphere Reserves was held in Madrid, Spain, in February 2008. UNESCO also supports a Global Network of National Geoparks (53 in 17 countries at January 2008) which was inaugurated in 2004 to promote collaboration among managed areas of geological significance to exchange knowledge and expertise and raise awareness of the benefits of protecting those environments.

UNESCO promotes and supports international scientific partnerships to monitor, assess and report on the state of Earth systems. With the World Meteorological Organization and the International Council of Science, UNESCO sponsors the World Climate Research Programme, which was established in 1980 to determine the predictability of climate and the effect of human activity on climate. UNESCO hosts the secretariat of the World Water Assessment Programme (WWAP), which prepares the periodic *World Water Development Report*. UNESCO is actively involved in the 10-year project, agreed by more than 60 governments in February 2005, to develop a Global Earth Observation System of Systems (GEOSS). The project aims to link existing and planned observation systems in order to provide for greater understanding of the earth's processes and dissemination of detailed data, for example predicting health epidemics or weather phenomena or concerning the management of ecosystems and natural resources. UNESCO's Intergovernmental Oceanographic Commission serves as the Secretariat of the Global Ocean Observing System. The International Geoscience Programme, undertaken jointly with the International Union of Geological Sciences (IUGS), facilitates the exchange of knowledge and methodology among scientists concerned with geological processes and aims to raise awareness of the links between geoscience and sustainable socio-economic development. The IUGS and UNESCO jointly initiated the International Year of Planet Earth (2008).

UNESCO is committed to contributing to international efforts to enhance disaster preparedness and mitigation. Through education UNESCO aims to reduce the vulnerability of poorer communities to disasters and improve disaster management at local and national levels. It also co-ordinates efforts at an international level to establish monitoring networks and early-warning systems to mitigate natural disasters, in particular in developing tsunami early-warning systems in Africa, the Caribbean, the South Pacific, the Mediterranean Sea and the North East Atlantic similar to those already established for the Indian and Pacific oceans. Other regional partnerships and knowledge networks were to be developed to strengthen capacity-building and the dissemination of information and good practices relating to risk awareness and mitigation and disaster management. Disaster education and awareness were to be incorporated as key elements in the UN Decade on Education for Sustainable Development (see above). UNESCO is also the lead agency for the International Flood Initiative, which was inaugurated in January 2005 at the World Conference on Disaster Reduction, held in Kobe, Japan. The Initiative aimed to promote an integrated approach to flood management in order to minimize the damage and loss of life caused by floods, mainly with a focus on research, training, promoting good governance and providing technical assistance

A priority of the natural science programme for 2008–09 was to promote policies and strengthen human and institutional capacities in science, technology and innovation. At all levels of education UNESCO aimed to enhance teaching quality and content in areas of science and technology and, at regional and sub-regional level, to strengthen co-operation mechanisms and policy networks in training and research. With the International Council of Scientific Unions and the Third World Academy of Sciences, UNESCO operates a short-term fellowship programme in the basic sciences and an exchange programme of visiting lecturers.

UNESCO is the lead agency of the New Partnership for Africa's Development (NEPAD) Science and Technology Cluster and the NEPAD Action Plan for the Environment.

SOCIAL AND HUMAN SCIENCES

UNESCO is mandated to contribute to the world-wide development of the social and human sciences and philosophy, which it regards as of great importance in policy-making and maintaining ethical vigilance. The structure of UNESCO's Social and Human Sciences programme takes into account both an ethical and standard-setting dimension, and research, policy-making, action in the field and future-oriented activities. One of UNESCO's so-called overarching objectives in the period 2008–13 was to address emerging ethical challenges.

A priority area of UNESCO's work programme on Social and Human Sciences for 2008–09 was to promote principles, practices and ethical norms relevant for scientific and technological development. It fosters international co-operation and dialogue on emerging issues, as well as raising awareness and promoting the sharing of knowledge at regional and national levels. UNESCO supports the activities of the International Bioethics Committee (IBC—a group of 36 specialists who meet under UNESCO auspices) and the Intergovernmental Bioethics Committee and hosts the secretariat of the 18-member World Commission on the Ethics of Scientific Knowledge and Technology (COMEST), established in 1999, which aims to serve as a forum for the exchange of information and ideas and to promote dialogue between scientific communities, decision-makers and the public.

The priority Ethics of science and technology element aims to promote intergovernmental discussion and co-operation; to conduct explorative studies on possible UNESCO action on environmental ethics and developing a code of conduct for scientists; to enhance public awareness; to make available teaching expertise and create regional networks of experts; to promote the development of international and national databases on ethical issues; to identify ethical issues related to emerging technologies; to follow up relevant declarations, including the Universal Declaration on the Human Genome and Human Rights (see below); and to support the Global Ethics Observatory, an online world-wide database of information on applied bioethics and other applied science- and technology-related areas (including environmental ethics) that was launched in December 2005 by the IBC.

UNESCO itself provides an interdisciplinary, multicultural and pluralistic forum for reflection on issues relating to the ethical dimension of scientific advances, and promotes the application of international guide-lines. In May 1997 the IBC approved a draft version of a Universal Declaration on the Human Genome and Human Rights, in an attempt to provide ethical guide-lines for developments in human genetics. The Declaration, which identified some 100,000 hereditary genes as 'common heritage', was adopted by the UNESCO General Conference in November and committed states to promoting the dissemination of relevant scientific knowledge and co-operating in genome research. In October 2003 the General Conference adopted an International Declaration on Human Genetic Data, establishing standards for scientists working in that field, and in October 2005 the General Conference adopted the Universal Declaration on Bioethics and Human Rights. At all levels UNESCO aims to raise awareness and foster debate about the ethical implications of scientific and technological developments and promote exchange of experiences and knowledge between governments and research bodies.

UNESCO recognizes that globalization has a broad and significant impact on societies. It is committed to countering negative trends of social transformation by strengthening the links between research and policy formulation by national and local authorities, in particular concerning poverty eradication. In that respect, UNESCO promotes the concept that freedom from poverty is a fundamental human right. In 1994 UNESCO initiated an international social science research programme, the Management of Social Transformations (MOST), to promote capacity-building in social planning at all levels of decision-making. In 2003 the Executive Board approved a continuation of the programme but with a revised strategic objective of strengthening links between research, policy and practice. In 2008–13 UNESCO aimed to promote new collaborative social science research programmes and to support capacity-building in developing countries.

UNESCO aims to monitor emerging social or ethical issues and, through its associated offices and institutes, formulate preventative action to ensure they have minimal impact on the attainment of UNESCO's objectives. As a specific challenge UNESCO is committed to promoting the International Convention against Doping in Sport, which entered into force in 2007. UNESCO also focuses on the educational and cultural dimensions of physical education and sport and their capacity to preserve and improve health.

Fundamental to UNESCO's mission is the rejection of all forms of discrimination. It disseminates information aimed at combating racial prejudice, works to improve the status of women and their access to education, promotes equality between men and women, and raises awareness of discrimination against people affected by HIV/AIDS, in particular among young people. In 2004 UNESCO inaugurated an initiative to enable city authorities to share experiences and collaborate in efforts to counter racism, discrimination, xenophobia and exclusion. As well as the International Coalition of Cities against Racism, regional coalitions were to be formed with more defined programmes of action. An International Youth Clearing House and Information Service (INFOYOUTH) aims to increase and consolidate the information available on the situation of young people in society, and to heighten awareness of their needs, aspirations and potential among public and private decision-makers. Supporting efforts to facilitate dialogue among different cultures and societies and promoting opportunities for reflection and consideration of philosophy and human rights, for example the celebration of World Philosophy Day, are also among UNESCO's fundamental aims.

CULTURE

In undertaking efforts to preserve the world's cultural and natural heritage UNESCO has attempted to emphasize the link between culture and development. In December 1992 UNESCO established the World Commission on Culture and Development, to strengthen links between culture and development and to prepare a report on the issue. The first World Conference on Culture and Development was held in June 1999, in Havana, Cuba. In November 2001 the General Conference adopted the UNESCO Universal Declaration on Cultural Diversity, which affirmed the importance of intercultural dialogue in establishing a climate of peace. UNESCO's medium-term strategy for 2008–13 recognized the need for a more integrated approach to cultural heritage as an area requiring conservation and development and one offering prospects for dialogue, social cohesion and shared knowledge.

A priority element of UNESCO's draft work programme on Culture for 2008–09 was promoting cultural diversity through the safeguarding of heritage and enhancement of cultural expressions. In January 2002 UNESCO inaugurated the Global Alliance on Cultural Diversity, to promote partnerships between governments, non-governmental bodies and the private sector with a view to supporting cultural diversity through the strengthening of cultural industries and the prevention of cultural piracy. In October 2005 the General Conference approved an International Convention on the Protection of the Diversity of Cultural Expressions. It entered into force in March 2007 and the first session of the intergovernmental committee servicing the Convention was convened in Ottawa, Canada, in December.

UNESCO's World Heritage Programme, inaugurated in 1978, aims to protect historic sites and natural landmarks of outstanding universal significance, in accordance with the 1972 UNESCO Convention Concerning the Protection of the World Cultural and Natural Heritage, by providing financial aid for restoration, technical assistance, training and management planning. The medium-term strategy for 2008–13 acknowledged that new global threats may affect natural and cultural heritage. It also reinforced the concept that conservation of sites contributes to social cohesion. At July 2007 the 'World Heritage List' comprised 851 sites in 84 countries, of which 660 had cultural significance, 166 were natural landmarks, and 25 were of 'mixed' importance. Examples include: the Great Barrier Reef (in Australia), the Galapagos Islands (Ecuador), Chartres Cathedral (France), the Taj Mahal at Agra (India), Auschwitz concentration camp (Poland), the historic sanctuary of Machu Picchu (Peru), Robben Island (South Africa), the Serengeti National Park (Tanzania), and the archaeological site of Troy (Turkey). UNESCO also maintains a 'List of World Heritage in Danger', comprising 30 sites at July 2007, in order to attract international attention to sites particularly at risk from the environment or human activities.

UNESCO supports the safeguarding of humanity's non-material 'intangible' heritage, including oral traditions, music, dance and medicine. An Endangered Languages Programme was initiated in 1993. By 2007 the Programme estimated that, of some 6,700 languages spoken world-wide, about one-half were endangered. It works to raise awareness of the issue, for example through publication of the *Atlas of the World's Languages in Danger of Disappearing*, to strengthen local and national capacities to safeguard and document languages and administers a Register of Good Practices in Language Preservation. In October 2003 the UNESCO General Conference adopted a Convention for the Safeguarding of Intangible Cultural Heritage, which provided for the establishment of an intergovernmental committee and for participating states to formulate national inventories of intangible heritage. The Convention entered into force in April 2006 and the intergovernmental committee convened its inaugural session in November. The second session was held in Tokyo, Japan, in September 2007. A List of Intangible Cultural Heritage in Need of Urgent Safeguarding was scheduled to be operational by 2009. In May 2001, November 2003 and November 2005 (i.e. before the Convention entered into effect) UNESCO awarded the title of 'Masterpieces of the Oral and Intangible Heritage of Humanity' to a total of 90 examples of intangible heritage deemed to be of outstanding value. UNESCO's culture programme also aims to safeguard movable cultural heritage and to support and develop museums as a means of preserving heritage and making it accessible to society as a whole.

In November 2001 the General Conference authorized the formulation of a Declaration against the Intentional Destruction of Cultural Heritage. In addition, the Conference adopted the Convention on the Protection of the Underwater Cultural Heritage, covering the protection from commercial exploitation of shipwrecks, submerged historical sites, etc., situated in the territorial waters of signatory states. The Convention was expected to enter into force in November 2007. UNESCO also administers the 1954 Hague Convention on the Protection of Cultural Property in the Event of Armed Conflict and the 1970 Convention on the Means of Prohibiting and Preventing the Illicit Import, Export and Transfer of Ownership of Cultural Property. In 1992 a World Heritage Centre was established to enable rapid mobilization of international technical assistance for the preservation of cultural sites. Through the World Heritage Information Network (WHIN), a world-wide network of more than 800 information providers, UNESCO promotes global awareness and information exchange.

UNESCO aims to support the development of creative industries and or creative expression. Through a variety of projects UNESCO promotes art education, supports the rights of artists, and encourages crafts, design, digital art and performance arts. In October 2004 UNESCO launched a Creative Cities Network to facilitate public and private sector partnerships, international links, and recognition of a city's unique expertise. By mid-2007 nine cities had joined the network. UNESCO is active in preparing and encouraging the enforcement of international legislation on copyright, raising awareness on the need for copyright protection to uphold cultural diversity, and is contributing to the international debate on digital copyright issues and piracy.

Within its ambition of ensuring cultural diversity, UNESCO recognizes the role of culture as a means of promoting peace and dialogue. Several projects have been formulated within a broader concept of Roads of Dialogue. In Central Asia a project on intercultural dialogue follows on from an earlier multi-disciplinary study of the ancient Silk Roads trading routes linking Asia and Europe, which illustrated many examples of common heritage. Other projects include a study of the movement of peoples and cultures during the slave trade, a Mediterranean Programme, the Caucasus Project and the Arabia Plan, which aims to promote world-wide knowledge and understanding of Arab culture. UNESCO has overseen an extensive programme of work to formulate histories of humanity and regions, focused on ideas, civilizations and the evolution of societies and cultures. These have included the *General History of Africa*, *History of Civilizations of Central Asia*, and *History of Humanity*. In 2008–09 UNESCO endeavoured to consider and implement the findings of the Alliance of Civilizations, a high-level group convened by the UN Secretary-General that published a report in November 2006.

COMMUNICATION AND INFORMATION

UNESCO regards information, communication and knowledge as being at the core of human progress and well-being. The Organization advocates the concept of knowledge societies, based on the principles of freedom of expression, universal access to information and knowledge, promotion of cultural diversity, and equal access to quality education. In 2008–13 it determined to consolidate and implement this concept, in accordance with the Declaration of Principles and Plan of Action adopted by the World Summit on the Information Society (WSIS) in November 2005.

A key strategic objective of building inclusive knowledge societies was to be through enhancing universal access to communication and information. At national and global levels UNESCO promotes the rights of freedom of expression and of access to information. It promotes the free flow and broad diffusion of information, knowledge, data and best practices, through the development of communications infrastructures, the elimination of impediments to freedom of expression, and the development of independent and pluralistic media, including through the provision of advisory services on media legislation, particularly in post-conflict countries and in countries in transition. UNESCO recognizes that the so-called global 'digital divide', in addition to other developmental differences between countries, generates exclusion and marginalization, and that increased participation in the democratic process can be attained through strengthening national communication and information capacities. UNESCO promotes policies and mechanisms that enhance provision for marginalized and disadvantaged groups to benefit from information and community opportunities. Activities at local and national level include developing effective 'infostructures', such as libraries and archives and strengthening low-cost community media and information access points, for example through the establishment of Community Multimedia Centres (CMCs). Many of UNESCO's principles and objectives in this area are pursued through the Information for All Programme, which entered into force in 2001. It is administered by an intergovernmental council, the secretariat of which is provided by UNESCO. UNESCO also established, in 1982, the International Programme for the Development of Communication (IPDC), which aims to promote and develop independent and pluralistic media in developing countries, for example by the establishment or modernization of news agencies and newspapers and training media professionals. the promotion of the right to information, and through efforts to harness informatics for development purposes and strengthen member states' capacities in this field.

UNESCO supports cultural and linguistic diversity in information sources to reinforce the principle of universal access. It aims to raise awareness of the issue of equitable access and diversity, encourage good practices and develop policies to strengthen cultural diversity in all media. In 2002 UNESCO established Initiative B@bel as a multidisciplinary programme to promote linguistic diversity, with the aim of enhancing access of under-represented groups to information sources as well as protecting under-used minority languages. UNESCO's Programme for Creative Content supports the development of and access to diverse content in both the electronic and audio-visual media. The Memory of the World project, established in 1992, aims to preserve in digital form, and thereby to promote wide access to, the world's documentary heritage. By July 2007 158 inscriptions had been included on the project's register. UNESCO also supports other efforts to preserve and disseminate digital archives and, in 2003, adopted a Charter for the Preservation of Digital Heritage.

UNESCO promotes freedom of expression, of the press and independence of the media as fundamental human rights and the basis of democracy. It aims to assist member states to formulate policies and legal frameworks to uphold independent and pluralistic media and infostructures and to enhance the capacities of public service broadcasting institutions. In regions affected by conflict UNESCO supports efforts to establish and maintain an independent media service and to use it as a means of consolidating peace. UNESCO also aims to develop media and information systems to respond to and mitigate the impact of disaster situations, and to integrate these objectives into wider UN peace-building or reconstruction initiatives. UNESCO is the co-ordinating agency for 'World Press Freedom Day', which is held annually on 3 May. The theme for 2007 was 'Press freedom, safety of journalists and impunity'. It also awards an annual World Press Freedom Prize. UNESCO maintains an Observatory on the Information Society, which provides up-to-date information on the development of new ICTs, analyses major trends, and aims to raise awareness of related ethical, legal and societal issues. UNESCO promotes the upholding of human rights in the use of cyberspace. In 1997 it organized the first International Congress on Ethical, Legal and Societal Aspects of Digital Information ('INFOethics').

UNESCO promotes the application of information and communication technology for sustainable development. In particular it supports efforts to improve teaching and learning processes through electronic media and to develop innovative literacy and education initiatives, such as the ICT-Enhanced Learning (ICTEL) project. UNESCO also aims to enhance understanding and use of new technologies and support training and ongoing learning opportunities for librarians, archivists and other information providers.

Finance

UNESCO's activities are funded through a regular budget provided by contributions from member states and extrabudgetary funds from other sources, particularly UNDP, the World Bank, regional banks and other bilateral Funds-in-Trust arrangements. UNESCO co-operates with many other UN agencies and international non-governmental organizations.

UNESCO's proposed Regular Programme budget for the two years 2008–09 was US $631m.

Publications

(mostly in English, French and Spanish editions; Arabic, Chinese and Russian versions are also available in many cases)

Atlas of the World's Languages in Danger of Disappearing (online).
Copyright Bulletin (quarterly).
Encyclopedia of Life Support Systems (online).
International Review of Education (quarterly).
International Social Science Journal (quarterly).
Museum International (quarterly).
Nature and Resources (quarterly).
The New Courier (quarterly).
Prospects (quarterly review on education).
UNESCO Sources (monthly).
UNESCO Statistical Yearbook.
World Communication Report.
World Educational Report (every 2 years).
World Heritage Review (quarterly).
World Information Report.
World Science Report (every 2 years).

Books, databases, video and radio documentaries, statistics, scientific maps and atlases.

Specialized Institutes and Centres

Abdus Salam International Centre for Theoretical Physics: Strada Costiera 11, 34014 Trieste, Italy; tel. (040) 2240111; fax (040) 224163; e-mail sci_info@ictp.it; internet www.ictp.it; f. 1964; promotes and enables advanced study and research in physics and mathematical sciences; organizes and sponsors training opportunities, in particular for scientists from developing countries; aims to provide an international forum for the exchange of information and ideas; Dir KATEPALLI R. SREENIVASEN (India).

European Centre for Higher Education (CEPES): Str. Stirbei Vodă 39, 010102 Bucharest, Romania; tel. (1) 313-0839; fax (1) 312-3567; e-mail info@cepes.ro; internet www.cepes.ro; Dir Dr JAN SADLAK.

International Bureau of Education (IBE): POB 199, 1211 Geneva 20, Switzerland; tel. 229177800; fax 229177801; e-mail doc.centre@ibe.unesco.org; internet www.ibe.unesco.org; f. 1925, became an intergovernmental organization in 1929 and was incorporated into UNESCO in 1969; the Council of the IBE is composed of representatives of 28 member states of UNESCO, designated by the General Conference; the Bureau's fundamental mission is to deal with matters concerning educational content, methods, and teaching/learning strategies; an International Conference on Education is held periodically; Dir CLEMENTINA ACEDO (Venezuela); publs *Prospects* (quarterly review), *Educational Innovation* (newsletter), educational practices series, monographs, other reference works.

UNESCO International Centre for Technical and Vocational Education and Training: Görrestr. 15, 53113 Bonn, Germany; tel. (228) 243370; fax (228) 2433777; e-mail info@unevoc.unesco.org; internet www.unevoc.unesco.org; f. 2002; promotes high-quality lifelong technical and vocational education in UNESCO's member states, with a particular focus on young people, girls and women, and the disadvantaged; Dir RUPERT MACLEAN.

UNESCO International Institute for Capacity Building in Africa (UNESCO–IICBA): ECA Compound, Africa Ave, POB 2305, Addis Ababa, Ethiopia; tel. (11) 5445284; fax (11) 514936; e-mail info@unesco-iicba.org; internet www.unesco-iicba.org; f. 1999 to promote capacity building in the following areas: teacher education, curriculum development; educational policy, planning and management, and distance education; Dir JOSEPH NJIMBIDT NGU (Cameroon).

INTERNATIONAL ORGANIZATIONS

UNESCO International Institute for Educational Planning (IIEP): 7–9 rue Eugène Delacroix, 75116 Paris, France; tel. 1-45-03-77-00; fax 1-40-72-83-66; e-mail information@iiep.unesco.org; internet www.unesco.org/iiep; f. 1963; serves as a world centre for advanced training and research in educational planning; aims to help all member states of UNESCO in their social and economic development efforts, by enlarging the fund of knowledge about educational planning and the supply of competent experts in this field; legally and administratively a part of UNESCO, the Institute is autonomous, and its policies and programme are controlled by its own Governing Board, under special statutes voted by the General Conference of UNESCO; a satellite office of the IIEP was opened in Buenos Aires, Argentina, in June 1998; Dir MARK BRAY (United Kingdom).

UNESCO International Institute for Higher Education in Latin America and the Caribbean: Avda Los Chorros con Calle Acueducto, Edif. Asovincar, Altos de Sebucán, Apdo 68394, Caracas 1062-A, Venezuela; tel. (212) 286-0555; fax (212) 286-0527; e-mail prensa@unesco.org.ve; internet www.iesalc.unesco.org.ve; Dir ANA LÚCIA GAZZOLA.

UNESCO Institute for Information Technologies in Education: 8 Kedrova St, 117292 Moscow, Russia; tel. (495) 129-29-90; fax (495) 129-12-25; e-mail info@iite.ru; internet www.iite.ru; the Institute aims to formulate policies regarding the development of, and to support and monitor the use of, information and communication technologies in education; it conducts research and organizes training programmes; Dir Dr VLADIMIR KINELEV.

UNESCO Institute for Life-long Learning: Feldbrunnenstr. 58, 20148 Hamburg, Germany; tel. (40) 448-0410; fax (40) 410-7723; e-mail uil@unesco.org; internet www.unesco.org/education/uil; f. 1951, as the Institute for Education; a research, training, information, documentation and publishing centre, with a particular focus on adult basic and further education and adult literacy; Dir ADAMA OUANE (Mali).

UNESCO Institute for Statistics: CP 6128, Succursale Centre-Ville, Montréal, QC, H3C 3J7, Canada; tel. (514) 343-6880; fax (514) 343-6882; e-mail uis@unesco.org; internet www.uis.unesco.org; f. 2001; collects and analyses national statistics on education, science, technology, culture and communications; Dir HENDRIK VAN DER POL (Netherlands).

UNESCO Institute for Water Education: Westvest 7, 2611 AX Delft, Netherlands; tel. (15) 2151-715; fax (15) 2122-921; e-mail info@unesco-ihe.org; internet www.unesco-ihe.org; f. 2003; activities include advisory and policy-making functions; setting international standards for postgraduate education programmes and professional training in the water sector; education, training and research; and co-ordination of a global network of water sector organizations; Dir Prof. RICHARD A. MEGANCK.

United Nations Industrial Development Organization—UNIDO

Address: Vienna International Centre, Wagramerstr. 5, POB 300, 1400 Vienna, Austria.
Telephone: (1) 260260; **fax:** (1) 2692669; **e-mail:** unido@unido.org; **internet:** www.unido.org.

UNIDO began operations in 1967, as an autonomous organization within the UN Secretariat, and became a specialized agency of the UN in 1985. UNIDO's objective is to promote sustainable industrial development in developing nations and states with economies in transition. It aims to assist such countries to integrate fully into the global economic system by mobilizing knowledge, skills, information and technology to promote productive employment, competitive economies and sound environment.

MEMBERS

UNIDO has 172 members.

Organization

(March 2008)

GENERAL CONFERENCE

The General Conference, which consists of representatives of all member states, meets once every two years. It is the chief policy-making organ of the Organization, and reviews UNIDO's policy concepts, strategies on industrial development and budget. The 12th General Conference was held in Vienna, Austria, in November–December 2007.

INDUSTRIAL DEVELOPMENT BOARD

The Board consists of 53 members elected by the General Conference for a four-year period. It reviews the implementation of the approved work programme, the regular and operational budgets and other General Conference decisions, and, every four years, recommends a candidate for the post of Director-General to the General Conference for appointment.

PROGRAMME AND BUDGET COMMITTEE

The Committee, consisting of 27 members elected by the General Conference for a two-year term, assists the Industrial Development Board in preparing work programmes and budgets.

SECRETARIAT

The Secretariat comprises the office of the Director-General and three divisions, each headed by a Managing Director: Programme Development and Technical Co-operation; Programme Co-ordination and Field Operations; and Administration. In 2006 UNIDO employed 654 staff members at its headquarters and other established offices.

Director-General: KANDEH YUMKELLA (Sierra Leone).

FIELD REPRESENTATION

UNIDO has 16 country offices and 12 regional offices. UNIDO's field activities throughout the world are assisted annually by some 2,100 experts.

Activities

UNIDO bases its assistance on two core functions: serving as a global forum for generating and disseminating industry-related knowledge; and designing and implementing technical co-operation programmes in support of its clients' industrial development efforts. The two core functions are complementary and mutually supportive: policy-makers benefit from experience gained in technical co-operation projects, while, by helping to define priorities, the Organization's analytical work identifies where technical co-operation will have greatest impact. Its assistance is also underpinned by the following three thematic priorities: poverty reduction through productive activities; trade capacity-building; and environment and energy. The comprehensive services provided by UNIDO (which can be used in stand-alone projects or combined under national or regional integrated programmes—IPs or country service frameworks—CSFs) cover:

(i) Industrial governance and statistics;

(ii) Promotion of investment and technology;

(iii) Industrial competitiveness and trade;

(iv) Private-sector development;

(v) Agro-industries;

(vi) Sustainable energy and climate change;

(vii) The Montreal Protocol;

(viii) Environment management.

In December 1997 the seventh session of the General Conference endorsed a Business Plan on the Future Role and Functions of UNIDO, which regrouped the Organization's activities into two main areas—Strengthening of industrial capacities, and Cleaner and sustainable industrial development. According to the Plan, activities were to be concentrated in support of the development and mainstreaming of small and medium-sized enterprises (SMEs, identified as the principal means for achieving equitable and sustainable industrial development), in support of agro-based industries and their integration into national industrial structures, and in least-developed countries (LDCs), in particular in Africa, with emphasis on service provision at regional and sub-regional level. In 2002 the Industrial Development Board adopted a set of strategic guide-lines aimed at improving UNIDO's programme delivery. In December 2005 the 11th session of the General Conference adopted a *Strategic Long-term Vision Statement* covering the period 2005–15, focused on promoting the Organization's three thematic priorities (see above).

UNIDO's investment promotion and institutional capacity-building activities delivers technical co-operation assistance to developing countries and economies in transition. There are seven priority areas: industrial policy formulation and implementation; statistics and information networks; metrology, standardization, certification and accreditation; continuous improvement and quality management; investment and technology promotion; policy framework for SMEs; policy for women's entrepreneurship and entrepreneurship development. New project approvals in 2006 totalled some $113.7m. UNIDO has extended its networking with the private sector while assisting developing countries and economies in transition with capacity-building for sustained industrial growth. Promotion of business partnerships, for example, has been strengthened through the Organization's world-wide network of investment and technology promotion offices, investment promotion units, and subcontracting and partnership exchanges, as well as through the Asia-Africa Investment and Technology Promotion Centre. UNIDO has pursued efforts to overcome the so-called 'digital divide' between and within countries. The Organization has helped to develop electronic and mobile business for SMEs in developing countries and economies in transition. It has also launched an internet-based electronic platform, UNIDO Exchange (accessible at exchange.unido.org) for sharing intelligence and fostering business partnerships. UNIDO's Technology Foresight initiative, launched in 1999, involves the systematic visualization of long-term developments in the areas of science, technology, industry, economy and society, with the aim of identifying technologies capable of providing future economic and social benefits. The initiative is being implemented in Latin America and the Caribbean and in Central and Eastern Europe and the CIS.

Through strategic alliances with international certification and standards organizations UNIDO is assisting enterprises in developing countries to overcome technical barriers while improving product quality and access to international markets. UNIDO's industrial business development services—such as business incubators, rural entrepreneurship development and SME cluster development—for SME support institutions are aimed at enabling SMEs to play a key role in economic growth.

UNIDO provides advice to governmental agencies and industrial institutions to improve the management of human resources. The Organization also undertakes training projects to develop human resources in specific industries, and aims to encourage the full participation of women in economic progress through gender awareness programmes and practical training to improve women's access to employment and business opportunities.

UNIDO participated in the Third United Nations Conference on the Least-Developed Countries (UN-LDCs III), held in Brussels, Belgium, in May 2001. The Organization launched a package of 'deliverables' (special initiatives) in support of the Programme of Action adopted by the Conference, which emphasized the importance of productive capacity in the international development agenda. These related to energy, market access (the enablement of LDCs to participate in international trade), and SME networking and cluster development (with a particular focus on agro-processing and metal-working).

In 2002 UNIDO participated in the International Conference on Financing and Development, held in Monterrey, Mexico, in March, and the World Summit on Sustainable Development (WSSD), held in Johannesburg, South Africa, in August–September. At the Monterrey conference UNIDO launched an initiative designed to facilitate access to international markets for developing countries and countries with transitional economies by assisting them in overcoming barriers to trade. A similar initiative, seeking to promote rural energy for productive use, especially in the poorest countries, was launched at the WSSD.

As a result of the reforms introduced in the 1990s, UNIDO shifted its programming modality from a project-based framework to one with a national scope. Emphasis was given to industrialization in Africa, owing to the prevalence there of LDCs and the necessity to reduce regional inequalities in view of increasing globalization. National IPs emphasize capacity-building for the enhancement of industrial competitiveness and private-sector development, which is regarded as a major priority for the transformation of African economies. The basic philosophy has been to identify, jointly with key stakeholders in major industrial sub-sectors, the basic tools required to determine their national industrial development needs and priorities. This process has facilitated the definition and establishment of comprehensive national medium-term and long-term industrial development agendas. UNIDO has developed national programmes for 24 African countries. In 2001 a West African regional IP was launched, with a special focus on agro-industries in Benin, Burkina Faso, Guinea, Niger, Senegal and Togo. In 1996 UNIDO formally inaugurated the Alliance for Africa's Industrialization, which constituted the industrial sector element of the UN System-wide Special Initiative on Africa. This aimed to promote development of the continent's natural resources, strengthen labour resources and build government capacities in order to exploit new global markets, in particular in the agro-industrial sector. The Organization supported the Conference on Industrial Partnership and Investment in Africa, held in October 1999 in Dakar, Senegal, which aimed to provide a forum for developing industrial partnerships and promote industrial development. UNIDO was to be responsible for the technical implementation of a regional programme on quality management and standardization, covering the member countries of the Union économique et monétaire ouest-africaine (UEMOA), to be undertaken in collaboration with the European Union, that was approved in 2000. In addition, a technical support programme to improve the level of fish exports has been approved.

UNIDO is increasingly involved in general environmental projects. As one of the implementing agencies of the Multilateral Fund for the Implementation of the Montreal Protocol, UNIDO assists developing countries in efforts gradually to reduce the use of ozone-depleting substances. It is also involved in implementing the Kyoto Protocol of the Framework Convention on Climate Change (relating to greenhouse gas emissions) in old factories world-wide. By late 2004 UNIDO had helped to develop 10 national ozone units responsible for designing, monitoring and implementing programmes to phase-out ozone-depleting substances. By June 2007 34 National Cleaner Production Centres had been established world-wide (including one, in Cuba, which was a national network) under a joint UNIDO/UNEP programme that was launched in 1994 to promote the use and development of environmentally sustainable technologies and to build national capacities in cleaner production.

UNIDO also supports collaborative efforts between countries with complementary experience or resources in specific sectors. The investment and technology promotion network publicizes investment opportunities, provides information to investors and promotes business contacts between industrialized and developing countries and economies in transition. UNIDO is increasingly working to achieve investment promotion and transfer of technology and knowledge among developing countries. The Organization has developed several databases, including the Biosafety Information Network Advisory Service (BINAS), the Business Environment Strategic Toolkit (BEST), Industrial Development Abstracts (IDA, providing information on technical co-operation), and the International Referral System on Sources of Information (IRS).

UNIDO has helped to establish and operate the following International Technology Centres: the International Centre for Science and High Technology (based in Trieste, Italy); the International Centre for Advancement of Manufacturing Technology (Bangalore, India); the UNIDO Regional Centre for Small Hydro Power (Trivandum, India); the Centre for the Application of Solar Energy (Perth, Australia); the International Centre of Medicine Biotechnology (Obolensk, Russia); and the International Materials Assessment and Application Centre (in Rio de Janeiro, Brazil). Four others—the International Centre for Materials Technology Promotion, the Shenzhen International Technology Promotion Centre, the Shanghai Information Technology Promotion Centre (all in the People's Republic of China) and the International Centre for Materials Evaluation Technology (Republic of Korea)—were under development in the mid-2000s.

Finance

The provisional regular budget for the two years 2008–09 amounted to €154.6m., financed by assessed contributions payable by member states. There was an operational budget of some €22.1m. for the same period, financed from the reimbursement of support costs pertaining to technical co-operation and other services for the same period. The Organization's technical co-operation expenditure was budgeted at some €204.9m. Technical co-operation activities are financed mainly by voluntary contributions from member countries and donor institutions, and by UNDP, the Multilateral Fund for the Implementation of the Montreal Protocol on Substances that Deplete the Ozone Layer, the Global Environment Facility, and the Common Fund for Commodities. The Industrial Development Fund is used by UNIDO to finance development projects that fall outside the usual systems of multilateral funding.

Publications

Annual Report.

INTERNATIONAL ORGANIZATIONS

Development of Clusters and Networks of SMEs.
Gearing up for a New Development Agenda.
Industry for Growth into the New Millennium.
International Yearbook of Industrial Statistics (annually).
Manual for the Evaluation of Industrial Projects.
Manual for Small Industrial Businesses.
Reforming the UN System—UNIDO's Need-Driven Model.
UNIDOScope (monthly, electronic newsletter).

Using Statistics for Process Control and Improvement: An Introduction to Basic Concepts and Techniques.
World Industrial Development Report.
World Information Directory of Industrial Technology and Investment Support Services.
Several other manuals, guide-lines, numerous working papers and reports.

Universal Postal Union—UPU

Address: Case Postale 13, 3000 Bern 15, Switzerland.
Telephone: 313503111; **fax:** 313503110; **e-mail:** info@upu.int; **internet:** www.upu.int.

The General Postal Union was founded by the Treaty of Berne (1874), beginning operations in July 1875. Three years later its name was changed to the Universal Postal Union. In 1948 the UPU became a specialized agency of the UN. The UPU promotes the sustainable development of high-quality, universal, efficient and accessible postal services.

MEMBERS
The UPU has 191 members.

Organization
(March 2008)

CONGRESS
The supreme body of the Union is the Universal Postal Congress, which meets, in principle, every five years. Congress focuses on general principles and broad policy issues. It is responsible for the Constitution (the basic act of the Union), the General Regulations (which contain provisions relating to the application of the Constitution and the operation of the Union), changes in the provision of the Universal Postal Convention, approval of the strategic plan and budget parameters, formulation of overall policy on technical co-operation, and for elections and appointments. Amendments to the Constitution are recorded in Additional Protocols, of which there are currently six. The 23rd Congress was held in Bucharest, Romania, in September–October 2004. The 24th Congress was scheduled to be held in Nairobi, Kenya. In early 2008, however, it was relocated, to Geneva, Switzerland, owing to concerns regarding security, and was scheduled to take place in July–August 2008.

COUNCIL OF ADMINISTRATION
The Council, created by the Seoul Congress, 1994, to replace the former Executive Council, meets annually at Bern. It is composed of a Chairman and representatives of 41 member countries of the Union elected by the Universal Postal Congress on the basis of an equitable geographical distribution. It is responsible for supervising the affairs of the Union between Congresses. The Council also considers policies that may affect other sectors, such as standardization and quality of service, provides a forum for considering the implications of governmental policies with respect to competition, deregulation and trade-in-service issues for international postal services, and considers intergovernmental aspects of technical co-operation. The Council approves the Union's budget, supervises the activities of the International Bureau and takes decisions regarding UPU contacts with other international agencies and bodies. It is also responsible for promoting and co-ordinating all aspects of technical assistance among member countries.

POSTAL OPERATIONS COUNCIL (POC)
As the technical organ of the UPU, the POC, which holds annual sessions and comprises 40 elected member countries, is responsible for the operational, economic and commercial aspects of international postal services. The POC has the authority to amend and enact the Detailed Regulations of the Universal Postal Convention, on the basis of decisions made at Congress. It promotes the studies undertaken by some postal services and the introduction of new postal products. It also prepares and issues recommendations for member countries concerning uniform standards of practice. On the recommendation of the 1999 Beijing Congress the POC established a Standards Board with responsibility for approving standards relating to telematics, postal technology and Electronic Data Interchange (EDI). The POC aims to assist national postal services to modernize postal products, including letter and parcel post, financial services and expedited mail services.

CONSULTATIVE COMMITTEE
The Consultative Committee was established in September 2004 by the 23rd Congress, meeting in Bucharest, Romania. Membership of the Committee was to be open to private companies and other non-government organizations with an involvement or concern in international postal services. All members were to be extended full observer status in all organs of the Union. The Committee was to convene twice a year, in Bern, to coincide with meetings of the Council of Administration and the Postal Operations Council. The Committee replaced an Advisory Group which had been constituted in 2000 upon recommendation of a high-level group, established at the Beijing Congress to consider the future development of the organization.

INTERNATIONAL BUREAU
The day-to-day administrative work of the UPU is executed through the International Bureau, which provides secretariat and support facilities for the UPU's bodies. It serves as an instrument of liaison, information and consultation for the postal administration of the member countries and promotes technical co-operation among Union members. It also acts as a clearing house for the settlement of accounts between postal administrations for inter-administration charges related to the exchange of postal items and international reply coupons. The Bureau supports the technical assistance programmes of the UPU and serves as an intermediary between the UPU, the UN, its agencies and other international organizations, customer organizations and private delivery services. Increasingly the Bureau has assumed a greater role in certain areas of postal administration, for example, the application of telematics, postal technology and EDI through its Postal Technology Centre, the development of postal markets, and the monitoring of quality of postal services world-wide.

Director-General of the International Bureau: EDOUARD DAYAN (France).

Activities

The essential principles of the Union are the following:

(i) to develop social, cultural and commercial communication between people through the efficient operation of the postal services;

(ii) to guarantee freedom of transit and free circulation of postal items;

(iii) to ensure the organization, development and modernization of the postal services;

(iv) to promote and participate in postal technical assistance between member countries;

(v) to ensure the interoperability of postal networks by implementing a suitable policy of standardization;

(vi) to meet the changing needs of customers;

(vii) to improve the quality of service.

In addition to the Constitution and the General Regulations, the Universal Postal Convention is also a compulsory Act of the UPU (binding on all member countries), in view of its importance in the postal field and historical value. The Convention and its Detailed Regulations contain the common rules applicable to the international postal service and provisions concerning letter- and parcel-post. The Detailed Regulations are agreements concluded by the national postal administrations elected by Congress to the POC. The

POC is empowered to revise and enact these, taking into account decisions made at Congress.

The Postal Payment Services Agreement and its Regulations, adopted by the 1999 Beijing Congress to replace the former Money Orders, Giro and Cash-on-Delivery Agreements, is an optional arrangement. Not all member countries have acceded to this Agreement.

In recent years the UPU has reviewed its activities and has focused on the following factors underlying the modern postal environment: the growing role played by technology; the expanding reach of the effects of globalization; and the need to make the customer the focus of new competitive strategies. The 1999 Beijing Congress authorized the establishment of a high-level group to make recommendations on the future development of the UPU, which proposed the reorganization of the Union around three circles of member interest: (i) governments and state regulatory bodies; (ii) postal operators; and (iii) external stakeholders in postal systems, to be represented on a new Consultative Committee. In October 2002 the UPU organized a strategy conference entitled 'Future Post', at which delegates representing governments and postal services addressed challenges confronting the postal industry. The 23rd Congress, held in September–October 2004, adopted the Bucharest World Postal Strategy, detailing a number of objectives to be pursued by governments, postal administrations and restricted unions, and the UPU permanent bodies, over the period 2005–08. The strategy incorporated the following objectives: to ensure the provision of a good quality, affordable universal post service; to improve the quality and level of efficiency of the international postal network; to facilitate the development of markets to respond to customer needs; to undertake reform of the postal sector in order to ensure the sustainable development of postal services; and to strengthen and broaden co-operation with all stakeholders of the postal sector. The Bucharest Congress also adopted a new package of proposals for so-called terminal dues; a new quality of standards and targets for international mail services; a resolution relating to security, the combating of terrorism and prevention of money-laundering through use of the mail network; and a proposal to amend the UPU Convention to recognize legally the Electronic Postmark as an optional postal service. In June 2007 the first of a series of regional meetings was held to consider the future strategy of the organization. In November the Council adopted a draft strategy for 2009–2012, to be presented to the 24th Congress, scheduled to be held in Geneva, Switzerland, in July–August 2008.

The 1999 Congress approved the establishment of a Quality Service Fund, which was to be financed by industrialized member countries (by a 7.5% increase in dues) in order to support service improvement projects in developing member states. It was anticipated to be a temporary arrangement, to be dissolved at the end of 2008. In 2007 the Fund financed 75 projects in more than 50 countries at a cost of US $15.8m. Other efforts to generate resources available for postal development and reform are undertaken by the Postal Development Action Group, established in 1991.

On 1 October 2003 a new UPU clearing system became operational to enable postal operators to exchange bills electronically. During 2004 the UPU sponsored an application to the Internet Corporation for Assigned Names and Numbers (ICANN) to obtain a top-level internet domain, .post, for use, *inter alia*, by national and other postal operators, postal-related organizations, regional associations, UPU-regulated services, and trademarks and brand names; ICANN granted preliminary approval to the .post domain in September 2005.

Finance

All of the UPU's regular budget expenses are financed by member countries, based on a contribution class system. The UPU's budget for the two-year period 2007–08 totalled 71.4m. Swiss francs.

Publications

Letter Post Compendium.
Postal Statistics.
POST*Info (online newsletter of postal technology centre).
Union Postale (quarterly, in French, German, English, Arabic, Chinese, Spanish and Russian).
UPU EDI Messaging Standards.
UPU Technical Standards.
Other guides and industry reports.

World Health Organization—WHO

Address: Ave Appia 20, 1211 Geneva 27, Switzerland.
Telephone: 227912111; **fax:** 227913111; **e-mail:** info@who.int; **internet:** www.who.int.

WHO, established in 1948, is the lead agency within the UN system concerned with the protection and improvement of public health.

MEMBERS

WHO has 192 members and two associate members.

Organization

(March 2008)

WORLD HEALTH ASSEMBLY

The Assembly meets in Geneva, once a year. It is responsible for policy making and the biennial programme and budget; appoints the Director-General; admits new members; and reviews budget contributions.

EXECUTIVE BOARD

The Board is composed of 32 health experts designated by, but not representing, their governments; they serve for three years, and the World Health Assembly elects 10–12 member states each year to the Board. It meets at least twice a year to review the Director-General's programme, which it forwards to the Assembly with any recommendations that seem necessary. It advises on questions referred to it by the Assembly and is responsible for putting into effect the decisions and policies of the Assembly. It is also empowered to take emergency measures in case of epidemics or disasters.

Chairman: Dr BALAJI SADASIVAN (Singapore).

SECRETARIAT

Director-General: Dr MARGARET CHAN (People's Republic of China).

Deputy Director-General: Dr ANARFI ASAMOA-BAAH (Ghana).

Assistant Directors-General: DENIS AITKEN (United Kingdom) (Representative of the Director-General for Partnership and UN Reform), ALA ALWAN (Iraq) (Health Action in Crises), TIMOTHY G. EVANS (Canada) (Information, Evidence and Research), Dr DAVID L. HEYMANN (USA) (Communicable Diseases and Representative of the Director-General for Polio Eradication), DAISY MAFUBELU (South Africa) (Family and Community Health), HIROKI NAKATANI (Japan) (HIV/AIDS, TB, Malaria and Neglected Tropical Diseases), Dr ANDERS NORDSTRÖM (Sweden) (Health Systems and Services), ANDREY V. PIROGOV (Russia) (Executive Director of the WHO Office at the UN), NAMITA PRADHAM (India) (General Management), SUZANNE WEBER-MOSDORF (Germany) (Representative of the Director-General on European Union Affairs), HOWARD ZUCKER (USA) (Representative of the Director-General), Dr CARISSA F. ETIENNE (designate).

PRINCIPAL OFFICES

Each of WHO's six geographical regions has its own organization, consisting of a regional committee representing relevant member states and associate members, and a regional office staffed by experts in various fields of health.

Africa Office: Cité du Djoue BP 06, Brazzaville, Republic of the Congo; tel. 83-93-08; fax 83-95-06; e-mail regafro@afro.who.int; internet www.afro.who.int/; Dir Dr LUÍS GOMES SAMBO (Angola).

Americas Office: Pan-American Health Organization, 525 23rd St, NW, Washington, DC 20037, USA; tel. (202) 974-3000; fax (202) 974-3663; e-mail director@paho.org; internet www.paho.org; also admin-

INTERNATIONAL ORGANIZATIONS
United Nations (Specialized Agencies)

isters The Caribbean Epidemiology Centre (CAREC); Dir Dr MIRTA ROSES PERIAGO (Argentina).

Eastern Mediterranean Office: POB 7608, Abdul Razzak al Sanhouri St, Cairo (Nasr City) 11371, Egypt; tel. (2) 6702535; fax (2) 6702492; e-mail postmaster@emro.who.int; internet www.emro.who.int; Dir Dr HUSSEIN ABDUL RAZZAQ GEZAIRY (Saudi Arabia).

Europe Office: 8 Scherfigsvej, 2100 Copenhagen Ø, Denmark; tel. 39-17-17-17; fax 39-17-18-18; e-mail postmaster@euro.who.int; internet www.euro.who.int; Dir Dr MARC DANZON (France).

South-East Asia Office: World Health House, Indraprastha Estate, Mahatma Gandhi Rd, New Delhi 110002, India; tel. (11) 23370804; fax (11) 23379507; e-mail registry@searo.who.int; internet www.searo.who.int; Dir Dr SAMLEE PLIANBANGCHANG.

Western Pacific Office: POB 2932, Manila 1000, Philippines; tel. (2) 5288001; fax (2) 5211036; e-mail postmaster@wpro.who.int; internet www.wpro.who.int; Dir Dr SHIGERU OMI (Japan).

WHO Centre for Health Development: I. H. D. Centre Bldg, 9th Floor, 5–1, 1-chome, Wakinohama-Kaigandori, Chuo-ku, Kobe, Japan; tel. (78) 230-3178; fax (78) 230-3178; e-mail wkc@who.or.jp; internet www.who.or.jp; f. 1995 to address health development issues; Dir Dr SOICHIRO IWAO.

WHO European Office for Investment for Health and Development: Palazzo Franchetti, S. Marco 2847, 30124 Venice, Italy; tel. (041) 279-3865; fax (041) 279-3869; e-mail info@ihd.euro.who.int; f. 2003 to develop a systematic approach to the integration of social and economic factors into European countries' development strategies.

WHO Lyon Office for National Epidemic Preparedness and Response: 58 ave Debourg, 69007 Lyon, France; tel. 4-72-71-64-70; fax 4-72-71-64-71; supports global capacity-building for detection of and response to epidemics of infectious diseases; provides bridging role between WHO headquarters, the regional offices and ongoing activities in the field; Dir Dr GUÉNAËL RODIER.

WHO Mediterranean Centre for Vulnerability Reduction (WMC): rue du Lac Windermere, BP 40, 1053 Les Berges du Lac, Tunisia; tel. (71) 964-681; fax (71) 764-4558; e-mail info@wmc.who.int; internet wmc.who.int; f. 1997; advocates globally for appropriate health policies; trains health professionals; supports capacity-building for community action at grassroots level; works closely with WHO's regional offices; Dir Dr ELIL RENGANATHAN.

Activities

WHO's objective is stated in its constitution as 'the attainment by all peoples of the highest possible level of health'. 'Health' is defined as 'a state of complete physical, mental and social well-being and not merely the absence of disease and infirmity'.

WHO has developed a series of international classifications, including the *International Statistical Classification of Disease and Related Health Problems (ICD)*, providing an etiological framework of health conditions, and currently in its 10th edition; and the complementary *International Classification of Functioning, Disability and Health (ICF)*, which describes how people live with their conditions.

WHO acts as the central authority directing international health work, and establishes relations with professional groups and government health authorities on that basis.

It provides, on request from member states, technical and policy assistance in support of programmes to promote health, prevent and control health problems, control or eradicate disease, train health workers best suited to local needs and strengthen national health systems. Aid is provided in emergencies and natural disasters.

A global programme of collaborative research and exchange of scientific information is carried out in co-operation with about 1,200 national institutions. Particular stress is laid on the widespread communicable diseases of the tropics, and the countries directly concerned are assisted in developing their research capabilities.

It keeps diseases and other health problems under constant surveillance, promotes the exchange of prompt and accurate information and of notification of outbreaks of diseases, and administers the International Health Regulations. It sets standards for the quality control of drugs, vaccines and other substances affecting health. It formulates health regulations for international travel.

It collects and disseminates health data and carries out statistical analyses and comparative studies in such diseases as cancer, heart disease and mental illness.

It receives reports on drugs observed to have shown adverse reactions in any country, and transmits the information to other member states.

It promotes improved environmental conditions, including housing, sanitation and working conditions. All available information on effects on human health of the pollutants in the environment is critically reviewed and published.

Co-operation among scientists and professional groups is encouraged. The organization negotiates and sustains national and global partnerships. It may propose international conventions and agreements, and develops and promotes international norms and standards. The organization promotes the development and testing of new technologies, tools and guide-lines. It assists in developing an informed public opinion on matters of health.

WHO's first global strategy for pursuing 'Health for all' was adopted in May 1981 by the 34th World Health Assembly. The objective of 'Health for all' was identified as the attainment by all citizens of the world of a level of health that would permit them to lead a socially and economically productive life, requiring fair distribution of available resources, universal access to essential health care, and the promotion of preventive health care. In May 1998 the 51st World Health Assembly renewed the initiative, adopting a global strategy in support of 'Health for all in the 21st century', to be effected through regional and national health policies. The new approach was to build on the primary health care approach of the initial strategy, but was to strengthen the emphasis on quality of life, equity in health and access to health services. The following have been identified as minimum requirements of 'Health for all':

Safe water in the home or within 15 minutes' walking distance, and adequate sanitary facilities in the home or immediate vicinity;

Immunization against diphtheria, pertussis (whooping cough), tetanus, poliomyelitis, measles and tuberculosis;

Local health care, including availability of essential drugs, within one hour's travel;

Trained personnel to attend childbirth, and to care for pregnant mothers and children up to at least one year old.

In the implementation of all its activities WHO aims to contribute to achieving by 2015 the UN Millennium Development Goals (MDGs) that were agreed by the September 2000 UN Millennium Summit. WHO has particular responsibility for the MDGs of: reducing child mortality, with a target reduction of two-thirds in the mortality rate among children under five; improving maternal health, with a specific goal of reducing by 75% the numbers of women dying in childbirth; and combating HIV/AIDS, malaria and other diseases. In addition, it directly supports the following Millennium 'targets': halving the proportion of people suffering from malnutrition; halving the proportion of people without sustainable access to safe drinking water and basic sanitation; and providing access, in co-operation with pharmaceutical companies, to affordable, essential drugs in developing countries. Furthermore, WHO reports on 17 health-related MDG indicators; co-ordinates, jointly with the World Bank, the High-Level Forum on the Health MDGs, comprising government ministers, senior officials from developing countries, and representatives of bilateral and multilateral agencies, foundations, regional organizations and global partnerships; and undertakes technical and normative work in support of national and regional efforts to reach the MDGs.

The Eleventh General Programme of Work, for the period 2006–15, defined a policy framework for pursuing the principal objectives of building healthy populations and combating ill health. The Programme took into account: increasing understanding of the social, economic, political and cultural factors involved in achieving better health and the role played by better health in poverty reduction; the increasing complexity of health systems; the importance of safeguarding health as a component of humanitarian action; and the need for greater co-ordination among development organizations. It incorporated four interrelated strategic directions: lessening excess mortality, morbidity and disability, especially in poor and marginalized populations; promoting healthy lifestyles and reducing risk factors to human health arising from environmental, economic, social and behavioural causes; developing equitable and financially fair health systems; and establishing an enabling policy and an institutional environment for the health sector and promoting an effective health dimension to social, economic, environmental and development policy. WHO is the sponsoring agency for the Health Workforce Decade (2006–15).

During 2005 the UN's Inter-Agency Standing Committee (IASC), concerned with co-ordinating the international response to humanitarian disasters, developed a concept of organizing agency assistance to IDPs through the institutionalization of a 'Cluster Approach', comprising 11 core areas of activity. WHO was designated the lead agency for the clusters on Health.

COMMUNICABLE DISEASES

WHO identifies infectious and parasitic communicable diseases as a major obstacle to social and economic progress, particularly in developing countries, where, in addition to disabilities and loss of productivity and household earnings, they cause nearly one-half of all deaths. Emerging and re-emerging diseases, those likely to cause epidemics, increasing incidence of zoonoses (diseases or infections passed from vertebrate animals to humans by means of parasites, viruses, bacteria or unconventional agents), attributable to factors such as environmental changes and changes in farming practices, outbreaks of unknown etiology, and the undermining of some drug therapies by the spread of antimicrobial resistance are main areas of concern. In recent years WHO has noted the global spread of communicable diseases through international travel, voluntary human migration and involuntary population displacement.

WHO's Communicable Diseases group works to reduce the impact of infectious diseases world-wide through surveillance and response; prevention, control and eradication strategies; and research and product development. The group seeks to identify new technologies and tools, and to foster national development through strengthening health services and the better use of existing tools. It aims to strengthen global monitoring of important communicable disease problems. The group advocates a functional approach to disease control. It aims to create consensus and consolidate partnerships around targeted diseases and collaborates with other groups at all stages to provide an integrated response. In 2000 WHO and several partner institutions in epidemic surveillance established a Global Outbreak Alert and Response Network (GOARN). Through the Network WHO aims to maintain constant vigilance regarding outbreaks of disease and to link world-wide expertise to provide an immediate response capability. In March 2005 GOARN responded to an outbreak of Marburg haemorrhagic fever in Angola, which, by July, had killed more than 300 people. From March 2003 WHO, through the Network, was co-ordinating the international investigation into the global spread of Severe Acute Respiratory Syndrome (SARS), a previously unknown atypical pneumonia. From the end of that year WHO was monitoring the spread through several Asian countries of the virus H5N1 (a rapidly mutating strain of zoonotic highly pathogenic avian influenza—HPAI) that was transmitting to human populations through contact with diseased birds, mainly poultry. It was feared that H5N1 would mutate into a form transmissable from human to human. In February 2005 WHO issued guide-lines for the global surveillance of the spread of H5N1 infection in human and animal populations. WHO urged all countries to develop influenza pandemic preparedness plans and to stockpile antiviral drugs, and in May, in co-operation with the UN Food and Agriculture Organization (FAO) and the World Organisation for Animal Health (OIE), it launched a Global Strategy for the Progressive Control of Highly Pathogenic Avian Influenza. A conference on Avian Influenza and Human Pandemic Influenza that was jointly organized by WHO, FAO, OIE and the World Bank in November 2005 issued a plan of action identifying a number of responses, including: supporting the development of integrated national plans for H5N1 containment and human pandemic influenza preparedness and response; assisting countries with the aggressive control of H5N1 and with establishing a more detailed understanding of the role of wild birds in virus transmission; nominating rapid response teams of experts to support epidemiological field investigations; expanding national and regional capacity in surveillance, diagnosis, and alert and response systems; expanding the network of influenza laboratories; establishing multi-country networks for the control or prevention of animal trans-boundary diseases; expanding the global antiviral stockpile; strengthening veterinary infrastructures; and mapping a global strategy and work plan for co-ordinating antiviral and influenza vaccine research and development. An International Pledging Conference on Avian and Human Influenza, convened in January 2006 in Beijing, People's Republic of China (PRC), and co-sponsored by the World Bank, European Commission and PRC Government, in co-operation with WHO, FAO and OIE, requested a minimum of US $1,200m. in funding towards combating the spread of the virus. By March 2008 a total of 373 human cases of H5N1 had been laboratory-confirmed, in Azerbaijan, Cambodia, PRC, Djibouti, Egypt, Indonesia, Iraq, Laos, Nigeria, Thailand, Turkey and Viet Nam, resulting in 236 deaths. Cases in poultry had become endemic in parts of Asia, and recent outbreaks in poultry had been reported in some European and Middle Eastern countries, and in some countries in West, Central and Northeast Africa.

One of WHO's major achievements was the eradication of smallpox. Following a massive international campaign of vaccination and surveillance (begun in 1958 and intensified in 1967), the last case was detected in 1977 and the eradication of the disease was declared in 1980. In May 1996 the World Health Assembly resolved that, pending a final endorsement, all remaining stocks of the smallpox virus were to be destroyed on 30 June 1999, although 500,000 doses of smallpox vaccine were to remain, along with a supply of the smallpox vaccine seed virus, in order to ensure that a further supply of the vaccine could be made available if required. In May 1999, however, the Assembly authorized a temporary retention of stocks of the virus until 2002. In late 2001, in response to fears that illegally-held virus stocks could be used in acts of biological terrorism (see below), WHO reassembled a team of technical experts on smallpox. In January 2002 the Executive Board determined that stocks of the virus should continue to be retained, to enable research into more effective treatments and vaccines.

In 1988 the World Health Assembly launched the Global Polio Eradication Initiative (GPEI), which aimed, initially, to eradicate poliomyelitis by the end of 2000; this target was subsequently advanced to 2005, and most recently to 2008 (see below). National Immunization Days (NIDs, facilitated in conflict zones by the negotiation of so-called 'days of tranquility') have been employed in combating the disease, alongside the strengthening of routine immunization services. Vitamin A has also been administered during NIDS in order to reduce nutritional deficiencies in children and thereby boost their immunity. Since the inauguration of the GPEI WHO has declared the following regions 'polio-free': the Americas (1994); Western Pacific (2000); and Europe (2002). In August 1996 WHO, UNICEF and Rotary International, together with other national and international partners, initiated a campaign to 'Kick Polio out of Africa', with the aim of immunizing more than 100m. children in 46 countries against the disease over a three-year period. In January 2004 the ministers of health of six countries then regarded as 'polio-endemic' (Afghanistan, Egypt, India, Niger, Nigeria and Pakistan), and global partners, meeting under the auspices of WHO and UNICEF, adopted the Geneva Declaration on the Eradication of Poliomyelitis, in which they made a commitment to accelerate the drive towards eradication of the disease, by improving the scope of vaccination programmes. Significant progress in eradication of the virus was reported in Asia during that year. In sub-Saharan Africa, however, an outbreak originating in northern Nigeria in mid-2003—caused by a temporary cessation of vaccination activities in response to local opposition to the vaccination programme—had spread, by mid-2004, to 10 previously polio-free countries. These included Côte d'Ivoire and Sudan, where ongoing civil unrest and population displacements impeded control efforts. During 2004–05 some 23 African governments, including those of the affected West and Central African countries, organized, with support from the African Union, a number of co-ordinated mass vaccination drives, which resulted in the vaccination of about 100m. children. By mid-2005 this localized epidemic was declared over; it was estimated that nearly 200 children in the region had been paralyzed by the disease since mid-2003. In January 2004 the GPEI adopted a strategic plan for the eradication of polio covering the period 2004–08, which entailed the following key objectives: securing the world-wide interruption of poliovirus transmission (from 2004); achieving certification of global polio eradication (during 2006–08); developing guide-lines for the Global Oral Polio Vaccine Cessation Phase (2006–08); and mainstreaming the GPEI (from 2009). In May 2005 the World Health Assembly reaffirmed the goal of eradicating polio, urged sustained financial and political support towards this, and received for consideration a framework document on the formulation of a post-certification immunization policy for polio. The number of confirmed polio cases world-wide stood at 1,831 during the period January 2005–January 2006. (In 1988 35,000 cases had been confirmed in 125 countries, with the actual number of cases estimated at around 350,000.) At March 2008 Afghanistan, India, Nigeria and Pakistan were still designated as 'polio-endemic'.

WHO's Onchocerciasis Control Programme in West Africa (OCP), active during 1974–2002, succeeded in eliminating transmission in 10 countries in the region, excepting Sierra Leone, of onchocerciasis ('river blindness', spread by blackflies, and previously a major public health problem and impediment to socio-economic development in West Africa). It was estimated that under the OCP some 18m. people were protected from the disease, 600,000 cases of blindness prevented, and 25m. ha of land were rendered safe for cultivation and settlement. The former headquarters of the OCP, based in Ouagadougou, Burkina Faso, were to be transformed into a Multi-disease Surveillance Centre. In January 1996 a new initiative, the African Programme for Onchocerciasis Control (APOC), covering 19 countries outside West Africa, became operational, with funding co-ordinated by the World Bank and with WHO as the executing agency.

The Onchocerciasis Elimination Programme in the Americas (OEPA), launched in 1992, co-ordinates work to control the disease, which can cause blindness, in six endemic countries of Latin America. In January 1998 a new 20-year programme to eliminate lymphatic filariasis was initiated, with substantial funding and support from two major pharmaceutical companies, and in collaboration with the World Bank, the Arab Fund for Economic and Social Development and the governments of Japan, the United Kingdom and the USA. South American trypanosomiasis ('Chagas disease') is endemic in Central and South America, causing the deaths of some 45,000 people each year and infecting a further 16m.–18m. A regional intergovernmental commission is implementing a programme to eliminate Chagas from the Southern Cone region of Latin America; it is hoped that this goal will be achieved by 2010. The countries of the Andean region of Latin America initiated a plan for the elimination of transmission of Chagas disease in February 1997, and a similar plan was launched by Central American governments in October.

WHO is committed to the elimination of leprosy (the reduction of the prevalence of leprosy to less than one case per 10,000 population). The use of a highly effective combination of three drugs (known as multi-drug therapy—MDT) resulted in a reduction in the number of leprosy cases world-wide from 10m.–12m. in 1988 to 286,063 in January 2005. The number of countries having more than one case of leprosy per 10,000 had declined to nine by that time, compared with 122 in 1985. The country with the highest number of active leprosy cases at January 2005 was India (148,910), while Brazil had the second highest number of cases (30,693). The country with the highest prevalence of leprosy cases was Madagascar, with 2.5 cases per 10,000 population. The Global Alliance for the Elimination of Leprosy, launched in November 1999 by WHO, in collaboration with governments of affected countries and several private partners, including a major pharmaceutical company, aims to support the eradication of the disease through the provision until end-2010 of free MDT treatment. In June 2005 WHO adopted a Strategic Plan for Further Reducing the Leprosy Burden and Sustaining Leprosy Control Activities, covering the period 2006–10 and following on from a previous strategic plan for 2000–05. In 1998 WHO launched the Global Buruli Ulcer Initiative, which aimed to co-ordinate control of and research into Buruli ulcer, another mycobacterial disease. In July of that year the Director-General of WHO and representatives of more than 20 countries, meeting in Yamoussoukro, Côte d'Ivoire, signed a declaration on the control of Buruli ulcer. In May 2004 the World Health Assembly adopted a resolution urging improved research into, and detection and treatment of, Buruli ulcer.

The Special Programme for Research and Training in Tropical Diseases, established in 1975 and sponsored jointly by WHO, UNDP and the World Bank, as well as by contributions from donor countries, involves a world-wide network of some 5,000 scientists working on the development and application of vaccines, new drugs, diagnostic kits and preventive measures, and an applied field research on practical community issues affecting the target diseases.

The objective of providing immunization for all children by 1990 was adopted by the World Health Assembly in 1977. Six diseases (measles, whooping cough, tetanus, poliomyelitis, tuberculosis and diphtheria) became the target of the Expanded Programme on Immunization (EPI), in which WHO, UNICEF and many other organizations collaborated. As a result of massive international and national efforts, the global immunization coverage increased from 20% in the early 1980s to the targeted rate of 80% by the end of 1990. In 1992 the Assembly resolved to reach a new target of 90% immunization coverage with the six EPI vaccines; to introduce hepatitis B as a seventh vaccine; and to introduce the yellow fever vaccine in areas where it occurs endemically.

In June 2000 WHO released a report entitled 'Overcoming Antimicrobial Resistance', in which it warned that the misuse of antibiotics could render some common infectious illnesses unresponsive to treatment. At that time WHO issued guide-lines which aimed to mitigate the risks associated with the use of antimicrobials in livestock reared for human consumption.

HIV/AIDS, TB, MALARIA AND NEGLECTED DISEASES

Combating the human immunodeficiency virus/acquired immunodeficiency syndrome (HIV/AIDS), tuberculosis (TB) and malaria are organization-wide priorities and, as such, are supported not only by their own areas of work but also by activities undertaken in other areas. In July 2000 a meeting of the Group of Seven industrialized nations and Russia (G-8), convened in Genoa, Italy, announced the formation of a new Global Fund to Fight AIDS, TB and Malaria (as previously proposed by the UN Secretary-General and recommended by the World Health Assembly) (see below).

The HIV/AIDS epidemic represents a major threat to human well-being and socio-economic progress. Some 95% of those known to be infected with HIV/AIDS live in developing countries, and AIDS-related illnesses are the leading cause of death in sub-Saharan Africa. It is estimated that more than 25m. people world-wide died of AIDS during 1981–2005. WHO supports governments in developing effective health-sector responses to the HIV/AIDS epidemic through enhancing their planning and managerial capabilities, implementation capacity, and health systems resources. The Joint UN Programme on HIV/AIDS (UNAIDS) became operational on 1 January 1996, sponsored by WHO and other UN agencies; the UNAIDS secretariat is based at WHO headquarters. Sufferers of HIV/AIDS in developing countries have often failed to receive advanced antiretroviral (ARV) treatments that are widely available in industrialized countries, owing to their high cost. (It was estimated in 2005 that only 15% of HIV/AIDS patients were receiving the optimum treatment.) In May 2000 the World Health Assembly adopted a resolution urging WHO member states to improve access to the prevention and treatment of HIV-related illnesses and to increase the availability and affordability of drugs. A WHO-UNAIDS HIV Vaccine Initiative was launched in that year. In June 2001 governments participating in a special session of the UN General Assembly on HIV/AIDS adopted a Declaration of Commitment on HIV/AIDS. WHO, with UNAIDS, UNICEF, UNFPA, the World Bank, and major pharmaceutical companies, participates in the 'Accelerating Access' initiative, which aims to expand access to care, support and ARVs for people with HIV/AIDS. In March 2002, under its 'Access to Quality HIV/AIDS Drugs and Diagnostics' programme, WHO published a comprehensive list of HIV-related medicines deemed to meet standards recommended by the Organization. In April WHO issued the first treatment guide-lines for HIV/AIDS cases in poor communities, and endorsed the inclusion of HIV/AIDS drugs in its *Model List of Essential Medicines* (see below) in order to encourage their wider availability. The secretariat of the International HIV Treatment Access Coalition, founded in December of that year by governments, non-governmental organizations, donors and others to facilitate access to ARVs for people in low- and middle-income countries, is based at WHO headquarters. In 2006 WHO, UNAIDS and partner organizations negotiated a framework approach aimed at achieving universal access to HIV/AIDS prevention, treatment, care and support by 2010. The resulting document was entitled the '2007–10 Strategic Framework for UNAIDS support to countries' efforts to move towards universal access'. WHO supports the following *Three Ones* principles, endorsed in April 2004 by a high-level meeting organized by UNAIDS, the United Kingdom and the USA, with the aim of strengthening national responses to the HIV/AIDS pandemic: for every country there should be one agreed national HIV/AIDS action framework; one national AIDS co-ordinating authority; and one agreed monitoring and evaluation system.

The total number of people world-wide living with HIV/AIDS at December 2006 was estimated at 39.6m., including some 2.3m. children under 15 years of age. It was reported that 4.3m. people were newly infected during that year.

At December 2006 an estimated 24.7m. people in sub-Saharan Africa were estimated to have HIV/AIDS. In 2005 an estimated 5.8m. people were living with HIV/AIDS in South Africa, more people than in any other country world-wide, while in Botswana, Lesotho, Swaziland and Zimbabwe the prevalence rates in pregnant women attending antenatal clinics indicated national adult prevalence rates in excess of 30%.

In 1995 WHO established a Global Tuberculosis Programme to address the challenges of the TB epidemic, which had been declared a global emergency by the Organization in 1993. According to WHO estimates, one-third of the world's population carries the TB bacillus, generating around 9m. active cases and killing around 2m. people each year. The largest concentration of TB cases is in South-East Asia. TB is the principal cause of death for people infected with the HIV virus and an estimated one-third of people living with HIV/AIDS globally are co-infected with TB. WHO provides technical support to all member countries, with special attention given to those with high TB prevalence, to establish effective national tuberculosis control programmes. WHO's strategy for TB control includes the use of the expanded DOTS (direct observation treatment, short-course) regime, involving the following five tenets: sustained political commitment to increase human and financial resources and to make TB control in endemic countries a nation-wide activity and an integral part of the national health system; access to quality-assured TB sputum microscopy; standardized short-course chemotherapy for all cases of TB under proper case-management conditions; uninterrupted supply of quality-assured drugs; and maintaining a recording and reporting system to enable outcome assessment. Simultaneously, WHO is encouraging research with the aim of further advancing DOTS, developing new tools for prevention, diagnosis and treatment, and containing new threats (such as the HIV/TB co-epidemic). Inadequate control of DOTS in some areas, leading to partial and inconsistent treatments, has resulted in the development of drug-resistant and, often, incurable strains of TB. The incidence of so-called Multidrug Resistant TB (MDR-TB) strains, that are unresponsive to at least two of the four most commonly used anti-TB drugs, has risen in recent years, and WHO estimates that, annually, 300,000 new MDR-TB cases are arising world-wide, of which about four-fifths are 'super strains', resistant to at least three of the main anti-TB drugs. WHO has developed DOTS-Plus, a specialized strategy for controlling the spread of MDR-TB in areas of high prevalence. In September 2006 WHO expressed strong concern at the emergence of strains of Extensive Drug Resistant TB (XDR-TB) that are virtually untreatable with most existing anti-TB drugs. XDR-TB is believed to be most prevalent in Eastern Europe and Asia.

The 'Stop TB' partnership, launched by WHO in 1999, in partnership with the World Bank, the US Government and a coalition of non-governmental organizations, co-ordinates the Global Plan to Stop TB, which represents a 'roadmap' for TB control. The current phase of the plan, covering the period 2006–15, aims to facilitate the achievement of the MDG of halting and beginning to reverse by 2015 the incidence of TB by means of access to quality diagnosis and treatment for all; to supply ARVs to 3m. TB patients co-infected with HIV; to treat nearly 1m. people for MDR-TB; to develop a new anti-TB drug by 2010 and a new vaccine by 2015; and to develop rapid and inexpensive diagnostic tests at the point of care. The Global TB Drug

Facility, launched by 'Stop TB' in 2001, aims to increase access to high-quality anti-TB drugs for sufferers in developing countries.

In October 1998 WHO, jointly with UNICEF, the World Bank and UNDP, formally launched the Roll Back Malaria (RBM) programme. The disease acutely affects at least 350m.–500m. people, and kills an estimated 1m. people, every year. Some 90% of all malaria cases occur in sub-Saharan Africa. It is estimated that the disease directly causes 18% of all child deaths in that region. The global RBM Partnership, linking governments, development agencies, and other parties, aims to mobilize resources and support for controlling malaria. The RBM Partnership Global Strategic Plan for the period 2005–15, adopted in November 2005, lists steps required to intensify malaria control interventions with a view to attaining targets set by the Partnership for 2010 and 2015 (the former targets include: ensuring the protection of 80% of people at risk from malaria and the diagnosis and treatment within one day of 80% of malaria patients, and reducing the global malaria burden by one-half compared with 2000 levels; and the latter: achieving a 75% reduction in malaria morbidity and mortality over levels at 2005). WHO recommends a number of guide-lines for malaria control, focusing on the need for prompt, effective antimalarial treatment, and the issue of drug resistance; vector control, including the use of insecticide-treated bednets; malaria in pregnancy; malaria epidemics; and monitoring and evaluation activities. WHO, with several private- and public-sector partners, supports the development of more effective anti-malaria drugs and vaccines through the 'Medicines for Malaria' venture.

Global Fund to Fight AIDS, TB and Malaria: 6–8 chemin Blandonnet, 1214 Vernier-Geneva, Switzerland; tel. 227911700; fax 227911701; e-mail info@theglobalfund.org; internet www.theglobalfund.org; f. 2000 as a partnership between governments, civil society, private-sector interests, UN bodies (including WHO, UNAIDS, the IBRD and UNDP), and other agencies to raise resources for combating AIDS, TB and malaria; the Fund supports but does not implement assistance programmes; US $3,700m. was pledged by international donors at a conference convened in Sept. 2005 to replenish the Fund during 2006–07; by January 2007 the Fund had approved $7,000m. (of which $3,300m. had been disbursed) in respect of nearly 450 grants supporting prevention and treatment programmes in 136 countries; by that time the cumulative allocation of grant funding by region was as follows: Africa (56%), East Asia and the Pacific (14%), the Middle East and North Africa and South Asia (11%), Latin America and the Caribbean (10%), and Eastern Europe and Central Asia (8%); while the distribution by health sector was: HIV/AIDS (58%), malaria (24%), TB (17%) and strengthening of health systems (1%); Exec. Dir Dr MICHEL KAZATCHKINE.

Joint UN Programme on HIV/AIDS (UNAIDS): 20 ave Appia, 1211 Geneva 27, Switzerland; tel. 227913666; fax 227914187; e-mail unaids@unaids.org; internet www.unaids.org; established in 1996 to lead, strengthen and support an expanded response to the global HIV/AIDS pandemic; activities focus on prevention, care and support, reducing vulnerability to infection, and alleviating the socioeconomic and human effects of HIV/AIDS; launched the Global Coalition on Women and AIDS in Feb. 2004; in June 2005 adopted a policy position paper for intensifying HIV prevention; co-sponsors: WHO, UNICEF, UNDP, UNFPA, UNODC, ILO, UNESCO, the World Bank, WFP, UNHCR; Exec. Dir PETER PIOT (Belgium).

NON-COMMUNICABLE DISEASES AND MENTAL HEALTH

The Non-communicable Diseases and Mental Health group comprises departments for the surveillance, prevention and management of uninfectious diseases, such as those arising from an unhealthy diet, and departments for health promotion, disability, injury prevention and rehabilitation, mental health and substance abuse. Surveillance, prevention and management of non-communicable diseases, tobacco, and mental health are organization-wide priorities.

Addressing the social and environmental determinants of health is a main priority of WHO. Tobacco use, unhealthy diet and physical inactivity are regarded as common, preventable risk factors for the four most prominent non-communicable diseases: cardiovascular diseases, cancer, chronic respiratory disease and diabetes. WHO aims to monitor the global epidemiological situation of non-communicable diseases, to co-ordinate multinational research activities concerned with prevention and care, and to analyse determining factors such as gender and poverty. In 1998 the organization adopted a resolution on measures to be taken to combat non-communicable diseases; their prevalence was anticipated to increase, particularly in developing countries, owing to rising life expectancy and changes in lifestyles. For example, between 1995 and 2025 the number of adults affected by diabetes world-wide was projected to increase from 135m. to 300m. In 2001 chronic diseases reportedly accounted for about 59% of the estimated 56.5m. total deaths globally and for 46% of the global burden of disease. In February 1999 WHO initiated a new programme, 'Vision 2020: the Right to Sight', which aimed to eliminate avoidable blindness (estimated to be as much as 80% of all cases) by 2020. Blindness was otherwise predicted to increase by as much as twofold, owing to the increased longevity of the global population. In May 2004 the World Health Assembly endorsed a Global Strategy on Diet, Physical Activity and Health; it was estimated at that time that more than 1,000m. adults world-wide were overweight, and that, of these, some 300,000 were clinically obese. WHO has studied obesity-related issues in co-operation with the International Association for the Study of Obesity (IASO). The International Task Force on Obesity, affiliated to the IASO, aims to encourage the development of new policies for managing obesity. WHO and FAO jointly commissioned an expert report on the relationship of diet, nutrition and physical activity to chronic diseases, which was published in March 2003.

WHO's programmes for diabetes mellitus, chronic rheumatic diseases and asthma assist with the development of national initiatives, based upon goals and targets for the improvement of early detection, care and reduction of long-term complications. WHO's cardiovascular diseases programme aims to prevent and control the major cardiovascular diseases, which are responsible for more than 14m. deaths each year. It is estimated that one-third of these deaths could have been prevented with existing scientific knowledge. The programme on cancer control is concerned with the prevention of cancer, improving its detection and cure, and ensuring care of all cancer patients in need. In May 2004 the World Health Assembly adopted a resolution on cancer prevention and control, recognizing an increase in global cancer cases, particularly in developing countries, and stressing that many cases and related deaths could be prevented. The resolution included a number of recommendations for the improvement of national cancer control programmes. WHO is a co-sponsor of the Global Day Against Pain, which was held for the first time in 2004 and was to take place thereafter annually on 11 October. The Global Day highlights the need for improved pain management and palliative care for sufferers of diseases such as cancer and AIDS, with a particular focus on patients living in low-income countries with minimal access to opioid analgesics, and urges recognition of access to pain relief as a basic human right.

The WHO Human Genetics Programme manages genetic approaches for the prevention and control of common hereditary diseases and of those with a genetic predisposition representing a major health importance. The Programme also concentrates on the further development of genetic approaches suitable for incorporation into health care systems, as well as developing a network of international collaborating programmes.

WHO works to assess the impact of injuries, violence and sensory impairments on health, and formulates guide-lines and protocols for the prevention and management of mental problems. The health promotion division promotes decentralized and community-based health programmes and is concerned with developing new approaches to population ageing and encouraging healthy life-styles and self-care. It also seeks to relieve the negative impact of social changes such as urbanization, migration and changes in family structure upon health. WHO advocates a multi-sectoral approach—involving public health, legal and educational systems—to the prevention of injuries, which represent 16% of the global burden of disease. It aims to support governments in developing suitable strategies to prevent and mitigate the consequences of violence, unintentional injury and disability. Several health promotion projects have been undertaken, in collaboration between WHO regional and country offices and other relevant organizations, including: the Global School Health Initiative, to bridge the sectors of health and education and to promote the health of school-age children; the Global Strategy for Occupational Health, to promote the health of the working population and the control of occupational health risks; Community-based Rehabilitation, aimed at providing a more enabling environment for people with disabilities; and a communication strategy to provide training and support for health communications personnel and initiatives. In 2000 WHO, UNESCO, the World Bank and UNICEF adopted the joint Focusing Resources for Effective School Health (FRESH Start) approach to promoting life skills among adolescents.

In July 1997 the fourth International Conference on Health Promotion (ICHP) was held in Jakarta, Indonesia, where a declaration on 'Health Promotion into the 21st Century' was agreed. The fifth ICHP was convened in June 2000, in Mexico City, Mexico.

Mental health problems, which include unipolar and bipolar affective disorders, psychosis, epilepsy, dementia, Parkinson's disease, multiple sclerosis, drug and alcohol dependency, and neuro-psychiatric disorders such as post-traumatic stress disorder, obsessive compulsive disorder and panic disorder, have been identified by WHO as significant global health problems. Although, overall, physical health has improved, mental, behavioural and social health problems are increasing, owing to extended life expectancy and improved child mortality rates, and factors such as war and poverty. WHO aims to address mental problems by increasing awareness of mental health issues and promoting improved mental health services and primary care.

The Substance Abuse department is concerned with problems of alcohol, drugs and other substance abuse. Within its Programme on Substance Abuse (PSA), which was established in 1990 in response to the global increase in substance abuse, WHO provides technical support to assist countries in formulating policies with regard to the prevention and reduction of the health and social effects of psychoactive substance abuse. PSA's sphere of activity includes epidemiological surveillance and risk assessment, advocacy and the dissemination of information, strengthening national and regional prevention and health promotion techniques and strategies, the development of cost-effective treatment and rehabilitation approaches, and also encompasses regulatory activities as required under the international drugs-control treaties in force.

The Tobacco or Health Programme aims to reduce the use of tobacco, by educating tobacco-users and preventing young people from adopting the habit. In 1996 WHO published its first report on the tobacco situation world-wide. According to WHO, about one-third of the world's population aged over 15 years smoke tobacco, which causes approximately 3.5m. deaths each year (through lung cancer, heart disease, chronic bronchitis and other effects). In 1998 the 'Tobacco Free Initiative', a major global anti-smoking campaign, was established. In May 1999 the World Health Assembly endorsed the formulation of a Framework Convention on Tobacco Control (FCTC) to help to combat the increase in tobacco use (although a number of tobacco growers expressed concerns about the effect of the convention on their livelihoods). The FCTC entered into force in February 2005. The greatest increase in tobacco use is forecast to occur in developing countries.

FAMILY AND COMMUNITY HEALTH

WHO's Family and Community Health group addresses the following areas of work: child and adolescent health, research and programme development in reproductive health, making pregnancy safer and men and women's health. Making pregnancy safer is an organization-wide priority. The group's aim is to improve access to sustainable health care for all by strengthening health systems and fostering individual, family and community development. Activities include newborn care; child health, including promoting and protecting the health and development of the child through such approaches as promotion of breast-feeding and use of the mother-baby package, as well as care of the sick child, including diarrhoeal and acute respiratory disease control, and support to women and children in difficult circumstances; the promotion of safe motherhood and maternal health; adolescent health, including the promotion and development of young people and the prevention of specific health problems; women, health and development, including addressing issues of gender, sexual violence, and harmful traditional practices; and human reproduction, including research related to contraceptive technologies and effective methods. In addition, WHO aims to provide technical leadership and co-ordination on reproductive health and to support countries in their efforts to ensure that people: experience healthy sexual development and maturation; have the capacity for healthy, equitable and responsible relationships; can achieve their reproductive intentions safely and healthily; avoid illnesses, diseases and injury related to sexuality and reproduction; and receive appropriate counselling, care and rehabilitation for diseases and conditions related to sexuality and reproduction.

In September 1997 WHO, in collaboration with UNICEF, formally launched a programme advocating the Integrated Management of Childhood Illness (IMCI), following successful regional trials in more than 20 developing countries during 1996–97. IMCI recognizes that pneumonia, diarrhoea, measles, malaria and malnutrition cause some 70% of the approximately 11m. childhood deaths each year, and recommends screening sick children for all five conditions, to obtain a more accurate diagnosis than may be achieved from the results of a single assessment. WHO's Division of Diarrhoeal and Acute Respiratory Disease Control encourages national programmes aimed at reducing childhood deaths as a result of diarrhoea, particularly through the use of oral rehydration therapy and preventive measures. The Division is also seeking to reduce deaths from pneumonia in infants through the use of a simple case-management strategy involving the recognition of danger signs and treatment with an appropriate antibiotic.

In March 1996 WHO's Centre for Health Development opened at Kobe, Japan. The Centre researches health developments and other determinants to strengthen policy decision-making within the health sector.

SUSTAINABLE DEVELOPMENT AND HEALTHY ENVIRONMENTS

The Sustainable Development and Healthy Environments group focuses on the following areas of work: health in sustainable development; nutrition; health and environment; food safety; and emergency preparedness and response. Food safety is an organization-wide priority.

WHO promotes recognition of good health status as one of the most important assets of the poor. The Sustainable Development and Healthy Environment group seeks to monitor the advantages and disadvantages for health, nutrition, environment and development arising from the process of globalization (i.e. increased global flows of capital, goods and services, people, and knowledge); to integrate the issue of health into poverty reduction programmes; and to promote human rights and equality. Adequate and safe food and nutrition is a priority programme area. WHO collaborates with FAO, the World Food Programme, UNICEF and other UN agencies in pursuing its objectives relating to nutrition and food safety. An estimated 780m. people world-wide cannot meet basic needs for energy and protein, more than 2,000m. people lack essential vitamins and minerals, and 170m. children are estimated to be malnourished. In December 1992 WHO and FAO hosted an international conference on nutrition, at which a World Declaration and Plan of Action on Nutrition was adopted to make the fight against malnutrition a development priority. Following the conference, WHO promoted the elaboration and implementation of national plans of action on nutrition. WHO aims to support the enhancement of member states' capabilities in dealing with their nutrition situations, and addressing scientific issues related to preventing, managing and monitoring protein-energy malnutrition; micronutrient malnutrition, including iodine deficiency disorders, vitamin A deficiency, and nutritional anaemia; and diet-related conditions and non-communicable diseases such as obesity (increasingly affecting children, adolescents and adults, mainly in industrialized countries), cancer and heart disease. In 1990 the World Health Assembly resolved to eliminate iodine deficiency (believed to cause mental retardation); a strategy of universal salt iodization was launched in 1993. In collaboration with other international agencies, WHO is implementing a comprehensive strategy for promoting appropriate infant, young child and maternal nutrition, and for dealing effectively with nutritional emergencies in large populations. Areas of emphasis include promoting healthcare practices that enhance successful breast-feeding; appropriate complementary feeding; refining the use and interpretation of body measurements for assessing nutritional status; relevant information, education and training; and action to give effect to the International Code of Marketing of Breast-milk Substitutes. The food safety programme aims to protect human health against risks associated with biological and chemical contaminants and additives in food. With FAO, WHO establishes food standards (through the work of the Codex Alimentarius Commission and its subsidiary committees) and evaluates food additives, pesticide residues and other contaminants and their implications for health. The programme provides expert advice on such issues as food-borne pathogens (e.g. listeria), production methods (e.g. aquaculture) and food biotechnology (e.g. genetic modification). In July 2001 the Codex Alimentarius Commission adopted the first global principles for assessing the safety of genetically modified (GM) foods. In March 2002 an intergovernmental task force established by the Commission finalized 'principles for the risk analysis of foods derived from biotechnology', which were to provide a framework for assessing the safety of GM foods and plants. In the following month WHO and FAO announced a joint review of their food standards operations. In February 2003 the FAO/WHO Project and Fund for Enhanced Participation in Codex was launched to support the participation of poorer countries in the Commission's activities.

WHO's programme area on environment and health undertakes a wide range of initiatives to tackle the increasing threats to health and well-being from a changing environment, especially in relation to air pollution, water quality, sanitation, protection against radiation, management of hazardous waste, chemical safety and housing hygiene. Some 1,100m. people world-wide have no access to clean drinking water, while a further 2,400m. people are denied suitable sanitation systems. WHO helped launch the Water Supply and Sanitation Council in 1990 and regularly updates its *Guidelines for Drinking Water Quality*. In rural areas the emphasis continues to be on the provision and maintenance of safe and sufficient water supplies and adequate sanitation, the health aspects of rural housing, vector control in water resource management, and the safe use of agrochemicals. In urban areas assistance is provided to identify local environmental health priorities and to improve municipal governments' ability to deal with environmental conditions and health problems in an integrated manner; promotion of the 'Healthy City' approach is a major component of the programme. Other programme activities include environmental health information development and management, human resources development, environmental health planning methods, research and work on problems relating to global environment change, such as UV-radiation. A report considering the implications of climate change on human health, prepared jointly by WHO, WMO and UNEP, was published in July 1996. The WHO Global Strategy for Health and Environment, developed in response to the WHO Commission on Health and Environment which reported to the UN Conference on Environment and Development in June 1992, provides the framework for programme activities. In December 2001 WHO published a report on the relationship between macroeconomics and health.

Through its International EMF Project WHO is compiling a comprehensive assessment of the potential adverse effects on human health deriving from exposure to electromagnetic fields (EMF). In June 2004 WHO organized a workshop on childhood sensitivity to EMF.

WHO's work in the promotion of chemical safety is undertaken in collaboration with ILO and UNEP through the International Programme on Chemical Safety (IPCS), the Central Unit for which is located in WHO. The Programme provides internationally evaluated scientific information on chemicals, promotes the use of such information in national programmes, assists member states in establishment of their own chemical safety measures and programmes, and helps them strengthen their capabilities in chemical emergency preparedness and response and in chemical risk reduction. In 1995 an Inter-organization Programme for the Social Management of Chemicals was established by UNEP, ILO, FAO, WHO, UNIDO and OECD, in order to strengthen international co-operation in the field of chemical safety. In 1998 WHO led an international assessment of the health risk from bendocine disruptors (chemicals which disrupt hormonal activities).

In January 2001 WHO sent a team of experts to Kosovo and Metohija (Serbia) to assess the potential impact on the health of the local population of exposure to depleted uranium, which had been used by NATO in ammunition during its aerial offensive against the FRY in 1999.

In September 2005 a forum comprising representatives of WHO, IAEA, UNDP, UNEP, FAO, OCHA, the World Bank and the UN Scientific Committee on the effects of Atomic Radiation, and the governments of Belarus, Russia and Ukraine, issued an assessment of the long-term health, environmental and socio-economic effects of the 1986 Chornobyl (Chernobyl) nuclear reactor accident.

Since the major terrorist attacks perpetrated against targets in the USA in September 2001, WHO has focused renewed attention on the potential malevolent use of bacteria (such as bacillus anthracis, which causes anthrax), viruses (for example, the variola virus, causing smallpox) or toxins, or of chemical agents, in acts of biological or chemical terrorism. In September 2001 WHO issued draft guidelines entitled 'Health Aspects of Biological and Chemical Weapons'.

Within the UN system, WHO's Department of Emergency and Humanitarian Action co-ordinates the international response to emergencies and natural disasters in the health field, in close co-operation with other agencies and within the framework set out by the UN's Office for the Co-ordination of Humanitarian Affairs. In this context, WHO provides expert advice on epidemiological surveillance, control of communicable diseases, public health information and health emergency training. Its emergency preparedness activities include co-ordination, policy-making and planning, awareness-building, technical advice, training, publication of standards and guide-lines, and research. Its emergency relief activities include organizational support, the provision of emergency drugs and supplies and conducting technical emergency assessment missions. The Division's objective is to strengthen the national capacity of member states to reduce the adverse health consequences of disasters. In responding to emergency situations, WHO always tries to develop projects and activities that will assist the national authorities concerned in rebuilding or strengthening their own capacity to handle the impact of such situations. Under the UN's Consolidated Inter-agency Appeal Process (CAP) for 2008, launched in December 2007, WHO appealed for US $93,906.3m. to fund its emergency humanitarian operations.

In January 2005, following a massive earthquake in the Indian Ocean in December 2004, which caused a series of tidal waves, or tsunamis, that devastated coastal regions in 14 countries in South and South-East Asia and East Africa, WHO requested emergency funding of US $67.1m. to support an initial six-month relief operation. Priorities included the establishment of a local disease surveillance and early warning system; co-ordination of humanitarian health assistance at international and national level; guidance on critical public health matters (such as disease outbreak response, water quality and sanitation, and mental health and pre-existing disease management); ensuring equitable access to essential health care; and ensuring the prompt provision of medical supplies.

HEALTH TECHNOLOGY AND PHARMACEUTICALS

WHO's Health Technology and Pharmaceuticals group, made up of the departments of essential drugs and other medicines, vaccines and other biologicals, and blood safety and clinical technology, covers the following areas of work: essential medicines—access, quality and rational use; immunization and vaccine development; and world-wide co-operation on blood safety and clinical technology. Blood safety and clinical technology are an organization-wide priority.

The Department of Essential Drugs and Other Medicines promotes public health through the development of national drugs policies and global guide-lines and through collaboration with member countries to promote access to essential drugs, the rational use of medicines and compliance with international drug-control requirements. The department comprises four teams: Policy Access and Rational Use; the Drug Action Programme; Quality, Safety and the Regulation of Medicines; and Traditional Medicine.

The Department of Vaccines and Other Biologicals undertakes activities related to quality assurance and safety of biologicals; vaccine development; vaccine assessment and monitoring; access to technologies; and the development of policies and strategies aimed at maximizing the use of vaccines.

The Policy Access and Rational Use team and the Drug Action Programme assist in the development and implementation by member states of pharmaceutical policies, in ensuring a supply of essential drugs of good quality at low cost, and in the rational use of drugs. Other activities include global and national operational research in the pharmaceutical sector, and the development of technical tools for problem solving, management and evaluation. The Policy Access and Rational Use team also has a strong advocacy and information role, promulgated through a periodical, the *Essential Drugs Monitor*, an extensive range of technical publications, and an information dissemination programme targeting developing countries.

The Quality, Safety and Regulation of Medicines team supports national drug-regulatory authorities and drug-procurement agencies and facilitates international pharmaceutical trade through the exchange of technical information and the harmonization of internationally respected norms and standards. In particular, it publishes the *International Pharmacopoeia*, the *Consultative List of International Nonproprietary Names for Pharmaceutical Substances*, and annual and biennial reports of Expert Committees responsible for determining relevant international standards for the manufacture and specification of pharmaceutical and biological products in international commerce. It provides information on the safety and efficacy of drugs, with particular regard to counterfeit and substandard projects, to health agencies and providers of health care, and it maintains the pharmaceuticals section of the UN *Consolidated List of Products whose Consumption and/or Sale have been Banned, Withdrawn, Severely Restricted or Not Approved by Governments*. The *WHO Model List of Essential Medicines* is updated about every two years and is complemented by corresponding model prescribing information; the 15th *Model List* was published in 2007 and identified 312 essential drugs. In September 2002 WHO issued the first *WHO Model Formulary*, which gives detailed information on the safe and effective use of all essential drugs.

The Traditional Medicine team encourages and supports member states in the integration of traditional medicine into national healthcare systems and in the appropriate use of traditional medicine, in particular through the provision of technical guide-lines, standards and methodologies. In May 2002 WHO adopted a strategy on the regulation of traditional medicine and complementary or alternative medicines (TM/CAM)

In January 1999 the Executive Board adopted a resolution on WHO's Revised Drug Strategy which placed emphasis on the inequalities of access to pharmaceuticals, and also covered specific aspects of drugs policy, quality assurance, drug promotion, drug donation, independent drug information and rational drug use. Plans of action involving co-operation with member states and other international organizations were to be developed to monitor and analyse the pharmaceutical and public health implications of international agreements, including trade agreements. In April 2001 experts from WHO and the World Trade Organization participated in a workshop to address ways of lowering the cost of medicines in less developed countries. In the following month the World Health Assembly adopted a resolution urging member states to promote equitable access to essential drugs, noting that this was denied to about one-third of the world's population. WHO participates with other partners in the 'Accelerating Access' initiative, which aims to expand access to antiretroviral drugs for people with HIV/AIDS (see above).

WHO reports that 2m. children die each year of diseases for which common vaccines exist. In September 1991 the Children's Vaccine Initiative (CVI) was launched, jointly sponsored by the Rockefeller Foundation, UNDP, UNICEF, the World Bank and WHO, to facilitate the development and provision of children's vaccines. The CVI has as its ultimate goal the development of a single oral immunization shortly after birth that will protect against all major childhood diseases. An International Vaccine Institute was established in Seoul, Republic of Korea, as part of the CVI, to provide scientific and technical services for the production of vaccines for developing countries. In September 1996 WHO, jointly with UNICEF, published a comprehensive survey, entitled *State of the World's Vaccines and Immunization*. In 1999 WHO, UNICEF, the World Bank and a number of public- and private-sector partners formed the Global Alliance for Vaccines and Immunization (GAVI), which aimed to expand the provision of existing vaccines and to accelerate the development and introduction of new vaccines and technologies, with the ultimate goal of protecting children of all nations and from all socio-economic backgrounds against vaccine-preventable diseases.

WHO supports states in ensuring access to safe blood, blood products, transfusions, injections, and healthcare technologies.

INFORMATION, EVIDENCE AND RESEARCH

The Information, Evidence and Research group addresses the following areas of work: evidence for health policy; health information management and dissemination; and research policy and promotion and organization of health systems. Through the generation and dissemination of evidence the Information, Evidence and Research group aims to assist policy-makers assess health needs, choose intervention strategies, design policy and monitor performance, and thereby improve the performance of national health systems. The group also supports international and national dialogue on health policy.

WHO co-ordinates the Health InterNetwork Access to Research Initiative (HINARI), which was launched in July 2001 to enable relevant authorities in developing countries to access more than 2,000 biomedical journals through the internet at no or greatly reduced cost, in order to improve the world-wide circulation of scientific information; some 28 medical publishers participate in the initiative.

HEALTH DAYS

World Health Day is observed on 7 April every year, and is used to promote awareness of a particular health topic ('Working together for health', in 2006). World Leprosy Day is held every year on 30 January, World TB Day on 24 March, World No Tobacco Day on 31 May, World Heart Day on 24 September, World Mental Health Day on 10 October, World Diabetes Day, in association with the International Diabetes Federation, on 14 November, World AIDS Day on 1 December, and World Asthma Day on 11 December.

ASSOCIATED AGENCY

International Agency for Research on Cancer: 150 Cours Albert Thomas, 69372 Lyon Cédex 08, France; tel. 4-72-73-84-85; fax 4-72-73-85-75; e-mail com@iarc.fr; internet www.iarc.fr; established in 1965 as a self-governing body within the framework of WHO, the Agency organizes international research on cancer. It has its own laboratories and runs a programme of research on the environmental factors causing cancer. Members: Australia, Belgium, Canada, Denmark, Finland, France, Germany, Italy, Japan, Netherlands, Norway, Spain, Sweden, Switzerland, United Kingdom, USA; Dir Dr P. BOYLE (United Kingdom).

Finance

WHO's regular budget is provided by assessment of member states and associate members. An additional fund for specific projects is provided by voluntary contributions from members and other sources, including UNDP and UNFPA.

A total budget of US $3,745.1m. was proposed for the two years 2008–09.

WHO PROPOSED BUDGET APPROPRIATIONS BY REGION, 2008–09

Region	Amount ('000 US dollars)	% of total budget
Africa	992.4	26.5
Americas	255.4	6.8
South-East Asia	407.5	10.9
Europe	250.8	6.7
Eastern Mediterranean	399.3	10.7
Western Pacific	323.8	8.6
Headquarters	1,115.9	29.8
Total	3,745.1	100.0

Publications

Bulletin of the World Health Organization (monthly).
Eastern Mediterranean Health Journal (annually).
International Classification of Functioning, Disability and Health—ICF.
International Statistical Classification of Disease and Related Health Problems.
Model List of Essential Medicines (every two years).
Pan-American Journal of Public Health (annually).
3 By 5 Progress Report.
Toxicological Evaluation of Certain Veterinary Drug Residues in Food (annually).
Weekly Epidemiological Record (in English and French, paper and electronic versions available).
WHO Drug Information (quarterly).
WHO Global Atlas of Traditional, Complementary and Alternative Medicine.
WHO Model Formulary.
World Health Report (annually, in English, French and Spanish).
World Malaria Report (with UNICEF).
Zoonoses and Communicable Diseases Common to Man and Animals.

Technical report series; catalogues of specific scientific, technical and medical fields available.

World Intellectual Property Organization—WIPO

Address: 34 chemin des Colombettes, BP 18, 1211 Geneva 20, Switzerland.
Telephone: 223389111; **fax:** 227335428; **e-mail:** wipo.mail@wipo.int; **internet:** www.wipo.int.

WIPO was established by a Convention signed in Stockholm in 1967, which came into force in 1970. It became a specialized agency of the UN in December 1974.

MEMBERS
WIPO has 184 members.

Organization
(March 2008)

GENERAL ASSEMBLY

The General Assembly is one of the three WIPO governing bodies, and is composed of all states that are party to the WIPO Convention and that are also members of any of the WIPO-administered Unions (see below). The Assembly meets in ordinary session once a year to agree on programmes and budgets. It elects the Director-General, who is the executive head of WIPO.

CONFERENCE
All member states are represented in the Conference, which meets in ordinary session once every two years.

CO-ORDINATION COMMITTEE
Countries belonging to the Committee are elected from among the member states of WIPO, the Paris and Berne Unions, and, *ex officio*, Switzerland. It meets in ordinary session once a year.

INTERNATIONAL BUREAU

The International Bureau, as WIPO's secretariat, prepares the meetings of the various bodies of WIPO and the Unions, mainly through the provision of reports and working documents. It organizes the meetings, and sees that the decisions are communicated to all concerned, and, as far as possible, that they are carried out.

The International Bureau implements projects and initiates new ones to promote international co-operation in the field of intellectual property. It acts as an information service and publishes reviews. It is also the depositary of most of the treaties administered by WIPO.

Director-General: Dr KAMIL IDRIS (Sudan).

More than 170 non-governmental organizations have observer status at WIPO. There are two advisory bodies: the Policy Advisory Commission (comprising eminent politicians, diplomats, lawyers and public officials) and the Industry Advisory Commission (comprising senior business representatives).

Activities

WIPO works to ensure that the rights of creators and owners of intellectual property (IP) are protected throughout the world, with a view to facilitating the advancement of science, technology and the arts and promoting international trade. IP comprises two principal branches: industrial property (patents and other rights in technological inventions, rights in trademarks, industrial designs, appellations of origin, etc.) and copyright and neighbouring rights (in literary, musical, artistic, photographic and audiovisual works).

WIPO administers and encourages member states to sign and enforce international treaties relating to the protection of IP, of which the most fundamental are the Paris Convention for the Protection of Industrial Property (1883), the Berne Convention for the Protection of Literary and Artistic Works (1886), and the Patent Co-operation Treaty (PCT). The strategic goals of WIPO's work programme for 2008–09 were: promoting a balanced IP system and realizing the development potential of IP; strengthening IP infrastructure, institutions and human resources; progressive development of international IP law; delivery of quality services in global IP protection systems; and promoting greater efficiency of management and support processes. WIPO aims to support governments and organizations in establishing policies and structures to harness the potential of IP for development. The organization seeks to simplify and harmonize national IP legislation and procedures (for example through implementation of the Trademark Law Treaty, 1994, and development of the Patent Law Treaty, 2000), provide services for international applications for industrial property rights, provide training and legal and technical assistance to developing countries, facilitate the resolution of private IP disputes, develop the use of information technology for storing, accessing and using valuable IP information, and to provide a forum for informed debate and for the exchange of expertise on IP. In 2005 WIPO founded an Office for Strategic Use of IP for Development, and in 2007 it incorporated proposals related to IP within the WIPO Development Agenda.

The rapid advancement of digital communications networks has posed challenges regarding the protection and enforcement of IP rights. WIPO has undertaken a range of initiatives to address the implications for copyright and industrial property law, and for electronic commerce transcending national jurisdictions. WIPO's Electronic Commerce Section co-ordinates programmes and activities relating to the IP aspects of electronic commerce. In September 1999 WIPO organized the first International Conference on Electronic Commerce and IP; a 'Digital Agenda' was launched by the organization at the Conference. The second International Conference on Electronic Commerce and IP was held in September 2001.

In view of the advances in technology and economic globalization in recent years WIPO has focused increasingly on the relationship between IP and issues such as traditional knowledge, biological diversity, environmental protection and human rights. In 1998–99 WIPO prepared the first ever report on the IP concerns of holders of traditional knowledge. In April 2000 the organization convened its first Meeting on IP and Genetic Resources. A WIPO Intergovernmental Committee on IP and Genetic Resources, Traditional Knowledge and Folklore was established in September. In January 2002 an international forum organized by WIPO adopted the Muscat Declaration on IP and Traditional Knowledge, recognizing the contribution of traditional knowledge to international co-operation.

In September 2001 member states approved the WIPO Patent Agenda, a process of global consultations aimed at creating a blueprint for the development of the international patent system.

In September 2007 WIPO member states adopted a Development Agenda consisting of a series of recommendations that included a set of 45 agreed proposals covering the following clusters of activities: Technical Assistance and Capacity Building; Norm-setting, Flexibilities, Public Policy and Public Knowledge; Technology Transfer, Information and Communication Technology (ICT) and Access to Knowledge; Assessments, Evaluation and Impact Studies; and Institutional Matters including Mandate and Governance.

PROGRESSIVE DEVELOPMENT OF INTERNATIONAL PROPERTY LAW

One of WIPO's major activities is the progressive development and application of international norms and standards. The organization prepares new treaties and undertakes the revision of the existing treaties that it administers. WIPO administers international classifications established by treaties and relating to inventions, marks and industrial designs: periodically it reviews these to ensure their improvement in terms of coverage and precision. WIPO also carries out studies on issues in the field of IP that could be the subject of model laws or guide-lines for implementation at national or international levels. The organization is increasingly active in harmonizing and simplifying procedures in order to make the registration of IP more easily accessible. WIPO aims to keep pace with rapid developments in the IP domain. Standing committees have been formed by member states to examine questions of substantive law or harmonization in the organization's main fields of activity and to ensure that the interests of member states are addressed promptly.

CO-OPERATION FOR DEVELOPMENT

WIPO aims to modernize national IP systems. It offers assistance to increase the capabilities of developing countries to benefit from the international IP framework, with a view to promoting the optimal use of human and other resources and thereby contributing to national prosperity. WIPO supports governments with IP-related institution-building, human resources development, and preparation and implementation of legislation. The WIPO Worldwide Academy, created in 1998, undertakes training, teaching and research on IP matters, focusing particularly on developing countries. The Academy maintains a Distance Learning Centre using on-line facilities, digital multimedia technology and video conferencing. WIPO's Information and Documentation Centre holds extensive reference materials. Under its Digital Agenda WIPO aims to assist the integration of developing countries into the internet environment, particularly through the use of WIPOnet, a global digital network of IP information capable of transmitting confidential data that was launched in January 2001. The organization also manages the IP Digital Libraries database project and maintains the WIPO Collection of Laws for Electronic Access (CLEA) multi-lingual database.

WIPO advises countries on obligations under the World Trade Organization's agreement on Trade-Related Aspects of IP Rights (TRIPS). The two organizations undertook a joint technical co-operation initiative to assist least-developed countries to harmonize their national legislative and administrative structures in compliance with the TRIPS accord by 1 January 2006.

WIPO presented a programme of action to the Third UN Conference on the Least-Developed Countries (UN-LDCs III, held in Brussels, Belgium in May 2001), which was aimed at strengthening LDC's IP systems. In May 2002 WIPO convened a Sino-African IP Forum.

A programme focusing on the IP concerns of small and medium-sized enterprises was approved by the WIPO General Assembly in September 2000. An International Forum on IP and SMEs, organized jointly by WIPO and the Italian Government in Milan, Italy in February 2001, adopted the Milan Plan of Action for helping SMEs to benefit fully from the IP system.

GLOBAL PROTECTION SYSTEMS AND SERVICES

WIPO administers a small number of treaties, covering inventions (patents), trademarks and industrial designs, under which one international registration or filing has effect in any of the relevant signatory states. The services provided by WIPO under such treaties simplify the registration process and reduce the cost of making individual applications or filings in each country in which protection for a given IP right is sought. The most widely used of these treaties is the PCT, under which a single international patent application is valid in all signatory countries selected by the applicant. The PCT system has expanded rapidly in recent years. The PCT-SAFE (Secure Applications Filed Electronically) system became operational in February 2004, safeguarding the electronic filing of patent applications. Through its Information Management for the PCT (IMPACT) project WIPO aims to automate fully the operations of the PCT. The corresponding treaties concerning the international registration of trademarks and industrial designs are, respectively, the Madrid Agreement (and its Protocol), and the Hague Agreement. WIPO's Advisory Committee on Enforcement of Industrial Property Rights assesses best practices and procedures for the effective enforcement of IP rights.

WIPO maintains the following international registration services: **International registration of trademarks:** operating since 1893; during 2006 there were 37,224 registrations and 15,205 renewals of trademarks; publ. *WIPO Gazette of International Marks* (every two weeks).

International deposit of industrial designs: operating since 1928; during 2005 1,135 applications were made for deposits, renewals and prolongations of 6,806 industrial designs; publ. *International Designs Bulletin* (monthly).

International applications for patents: operating since 1978; during 2005 135,602 record copies of international applications for patents under the PCT were received; publ. *PCT Gazette* (weekly).

WIPO also maintains the WIPO Arbitration and Mediation Centre, which became operational in October 1994, to facilitate the settlement of IP disputes between private parties. The Centre also organizes arbitrator and mediator workshops and assists in the development of WIPO model contract clauses and industry-specific resolution schemes. The Centre operates a Domain Name Dispute

Resolution Service, which plays a leading role in reviewing cases of conflict between trademarks and internet domain names, in accordance with the Uniform Domain Name Dispute Resolution Policy that was, on WIPO's recommendation, adopted by the Internet Corporation for Assigned Names and Numbers—ICANN in October 1999. By January 2007 more than 9,700 cases concerning disputes over generic top-level domains had been filed with the Centre. WIPO's first Internet Domain Name Process, a series of international consultations, undertaken in 1999, issued several recommendations for controlling the abuse of trademarks on the internet. A second Internet Domain Name Process, completed in 2001, addressed the improper registration of other identifiers ('cybersquatting'), including standard non-proprietary names for pharmaceutical substances, names and acronyms of intergovernmental organizations, geographical indications and terms, and trade names. WIPO maintains an online database of cybersquatting cases (accessible at arbiter.wipo.int/domains/search).

INTELLECTUAL PROPERTY TREATIES
(define internationally agreed basic standards of IP protection in each member state; status at February 2008, unless otherwise stated)

International Union for the Protection of Industrial Property (Paris Convention): the treaty was signed in Paris in 1883, and last revised in 1967; there were 170 members of the Union's Assembly at February 2008 and two parties to the Convention that were not Assembly members. Member states must accord to nationals and residents of other member states the same advantages under their laws relating to the protection of inventions, trademarks and other subjects of industrial property as they accord to their own nationals.

International Union for the Protection of Literary and Artistic Works (Berne Union): the treaty was signed in Bern in 1886 and last revised in 1971; there were 160 members of the Union's Assembly at February 2008 and three parties to the Convention that were not Assembly members. Members of the Union's Assembly must accord the same protection to the copyright of nationals of other member states as to their own. The treaty also prescribes minimum standards of protection, for example, that copyright protection generally continues throughout the author's life and for 50 years after. It includes special provision for the developing countries.

Madrid Agreement for the Repression of False or Deceptive Indications of Source on Goods: signed 14 April 1891; 35 states party.

Rome Convention for the Protection of Performers, Producers of Phonograms and Broadcasting Organizations: signed 26 October 1961; 86 states party.

Phonograms Convention for the Protection of Producers of Phonograms against Unauthorized Duplication of their Phonograms: signed 29 October 1971; 76 states party.

Brussels Convention Relating to the Distribution of Programme-carrying Signals Transmitted by Satellite: signed 21 May 1974; 31 states party.

Nairobi Treaty on the Protection of the Olympic Symbol: signed 26 September 1981; 46 states party.

Treaty on the International Registration of Audiovisual Works (Film Register Treaty): signed 20 April 1989; 13 states party.

Trademark Law Treaty: signed 27 October 1994; 40 states party.

WIPO Copyright Treaty: signed 20 December 1996; 64 states party.

WIPO Performances and Phonograms Treaty: signed 20 December 1996; 62 states party.

Geneva Act of the Hague Agreement Concerning the International Registration of Industrial Designs, 1999: entered into force 23 December 2003; 19 states party at 31 December 2005.

Patent Law Treaty, 2000: entered into force 28 April 2005; 17 states party.

Singapore Treaty on the Law of Trademarks: signed 28 March 2006, three ratifications.

Washington Treaty on Intellectual Property in Respect of Integrated Circuits: signed 26 May, 1989, three ratifications.

GLOBAL PROTECTION SYSTEM TREATIES
(ensure that one international registration or filing will have effect in any relevant signatory state; status at February 2008)

Madrid Agreement Concerning the International Registration of Marks: signed 14 April 1891; 56 states party.

The Hague Agreement Concerning the International Registration of Industrial Designs: signed 16 November 1925; 47 states party.

Lisbon Agreement for the Protection of Appellations of Origin and their International Registration: signed 31 October 1958; 26 states party.

Patent Co-operation Treaty (PCT): signed 19 June 1970; 138 states party.

Budapest Treaty on the International Recognition of the Deposit of Micro-organisms for the Purposes of Patent Procedure: signed 28 April 1977; 68 states party.

Protocol Relating to the Madrid Agreement Concerning the International Registration of Marks: signed 28 June 1989; 74 contracting states.

CLASSIFICATION TREATIES
(create classification systems that organize information concerning inventions, trademarks and industrial designs; status at February 2008)

Locarno Agreement Establishing an International Classification for Industrial Designs: signed 8 October 1968; 49 states party.

Nice Agreement Concerning the International Classification of Goods and Services for the Purposes of the Registration of Marks: signed 15 June 1957; 82 states party.

Strasbourg Agreement Concerning the International Patent Classification (IPC): signed 24 March 1971; 58 states party.

Vienna Agreement Establishing an International Classification of the Figurative Elements of Marks: signed 12 June 1973; 24 states party.

Finance

The approved budget for the two years 2008–09 amounted to 626m. Swiss francs. Some 86% of WIPO's revenue derives from the international registration systems maintained by the organization; the remainder derives mainly from contributions by member states.

Publications

Les appellations d'origine (annually, in French).
Essential Elements of Intellectual Property.
Industrial Property and Copyright (monthly, in English and French; bimonthly, in Spanish).
Intellectual Property for Small and Medium-sized Enterprises.
Industrial Property Statistics (CD-Rom).
Intellectual Property in Asia and the Pacific (quarterly, in English).
Intellectual Property Profile of the Least-Developed Countries.
International Designs Bulletin (monthly, in English and French).
PCT Gazette (weekly, in English and French).
PCT Newsletter (monthly, in English).
PCT Yearly Review (in English).
WIPO Academy Review.
WIPO Gazette of International Marks (every two weeks, in English and French).
WIPO Magazine (bimonthly, in English, French and Spanish).
WIPO Overview.
WIPO Patent Report—Statistics on Worldwide Patent Activities.
A collection of industrial property and copyright laws and treaties; a selection of publications related to intellectual property.

INTERNATIONAL ORGANIZATIONS — United Nations (Specialized Agencies)

World Meteorological Organization—WMO

Address: 7 bis, ave de la Paix, CP 2300, 1211 Geneva 2, Switzerland.
Telephone: 227308111; **fax:** 227308181; **e-mail:** wmo@wmo.int; **internet:** www.wmo.int.

The WMO was established in 1950 and was recognized as a Specialized Agency of the UN in 1951, operating in the fields of meteorology, climatology, operational hydrology and related fields, as well as their applications.

MEMBERS

WMO has 188 members.

Organization
(March 2008)

WORLD METEOROLOGICAL CONGRESS

The supreme body of the Organization, the Congress, is convened every four years and represents all members; it adopts regulations, and determines policy, programme and budget. Fifteenth Congress: May 2007.

EXECUTIVE COUNCIL

The Council has 37 members and meets at least once a year to prepare studies and recommendations for the Congress; it supervises the implementation of Congress resolutions and regulations, informs members on technical matters and offers advice.

SECRETARIAT

The Secretariat acts as an administrative, documentary and information centre; undertakes special technical studies; produces publications; organizes meetings of WMO constituent bodies; acts as a link between the meteorological and hydrometeorological services of the world, and provides information for the general public. The WMO Secretariat hosts the secretariat of the intergovernmental Group on Earth Observations (GEO), which was founded by participants at the Earth Observation Summit convened in Washington, DC, USA, in July 2003 and held its first meeting in May 2005 (GEO-IV was held in Cape Town, South Africa, in November 2007).

Secretary-General: MICHEL JARRAUD (France).

REGIONAL ASSOCIATIONS

Members are grouped in six Regional Associations (Africa, Asia, Europe, North and Central America, South America and South-West Pacific), whose task is to co-ordinate meteorological activity within their regions and to examine questions referred to them by the Executive Council. Sessions are held at least once every four years.

TECHNICAL COMMISSIONS

The Technical Commissions are composed of experts nominated by the members of the Organization. Sessions are held at least once every four years. The Commissions cover the following areas: Basic Systems; Climatology; Instruments and Methods of Observation; Atmospheric Sciences; Aeronautical Meteorology; Agricultural Meteorology; Hydrology; Oceanography and Marine Meteorology.

WORLD CLIMATE CONFERENCE

The First World Climate Conference was convened in 1979 and the Second World Climate Conference took place in 1990. WMO, in co-operation with other UN agencies, has been undertaking preparations for the third World Climate Conference, scheduled to be hosted by the Swiss Government in Geneva, in February 2009.

Activities

WORLD WEATHER WATCH (WWW) PROGRAMME

Combining facilities and services provided by the members, the Programme's primary purpose is to make available meteorological and related geophysical and environmental information enabling them to maintain efficient meteorological services. Facilities in regions outside any national territory (outer space, ocean areas and Antarctica) are maintained by members on a voluntary basis. In May 2007 the 15th WMO Congress made a number of decisions aimed at improving Weather Watch Programme instruments and observation methods and assisting developing countries to strengthen their operational capacities.

Antarctic Activities: co-ordinates WMO activities related to the Antarctic, in particular the surface and upper-air observing programme, plan the regular exchange of observational data and products needed for operational and research purposes, study problems related to instruments and methods of observation peculiar to the Antarctic, and develop appropriate regional coding practices. Contacts are maintained with scientific bodies dealing with Antarctic research and with other international organizations on aspects of Antarctic meteorology.

Data Management: monitors the integration of the different components of the World Weather Watch (WWW) Programme, with the intention of increasing the efficiency of, in particular, the Global Observing System, the Global Data Processing System and the Global Telecommunication System. The Data Management component of the WWW Programme develops data handling procedures and standards for enhanced forms of data representation, in order to aid member countries in processing large volumes of meteorological data.

Emergency Response Activities: assists national meteorological services to respond effectively to man-made environmental emergencies, particularly nuclear accidents, through the development, co-ordination and implementation of WMO/IAEA established procedures and response mechanisms for the provision and exchange of observational data and specialized transport model products.

Global Data Processing and Forecasting System: consists of World Meteorological Centres (WMCs) in Melbourne (Australia), Moscow (Russia) and Washington, DC (USA); 40 Regional/Specialized Meteorological Centres (RSMCs); and 187 National Meteorological Centres. The WMCs and RSMCs provide analyses, forecasts and warnings for exchange on the Global Telecommunications System. Some centres concentrate on the monitoring and forecasting of environmental quality and special weather phenomena, such as tropical cyclones, monsoons, droughts, etc., which have a major impact on human safety and national economies. These analyses and forecasts are designed to assist the members in making local and specialized forecasts.

Global Observing System: makes simultaneous observations at around 11,000 land stations. Meteorological information is also received from 3,000 aircraft, 7,000 ships, 600 drifting buoys, and nine polar orbiting and six geostationary meteorological satellites. About 160 members operate some 1,300 ground stations equipped to receive picture transmissions from geostationary and polar-orbiting satellites.

Global Telecommunication System: provides telecommunication services for the rapid collection and exchange of meteorological information and related data; consists of: the Main Telecommunication Network (MTN), six Regional Meteorological Telecommunication networks, and the national telecommunication networks. The system operates through 183 National Meteorological Centres, 29 Regional Telecommunications Hubs and the three WMCs.

Instruments and Methods of Observation Programme: promotes the world-wide standardization of meteorological and geophysical instruments and methods of observation and measurement to meet agreed accuracy requirements. It provides related guidance material and training assistance in the use and maintenance of the instruments.

System Support Activity: provides guidance and support to members in the planning, establishment and operation of the WWW. It includes training, technical co-operation support, system and methodology support, operational WWW evaluations, advanced technology support, an operations information service, and the WWW referral catalogue.

Tropical Cyclone Programme: established in response to UN General Assembly Resolution 2733 (XXV), aims to develop national and regionally co-ordinated systems to ensure that the loss of life and damage caused by tropical cyclones and associated floods, landslides and storm surges are reduced to a minimum. The Programme supports the transfer of technology, and includes five regional tropical cyclone bodies covering more than 60 countries, to improve warning systems and for collaboration with other international organizations in activities related to disaster mitigation.

WORLD CLIMATE PROGRAMME

Adopted by the Eighth World Meteorological Congress (1979), the World Climate Programme (WCP) comprises the following components: World Climate Data and Monitoring Programme (WCDMP), World Climate Applications and Climate Information Services (CLIPS) Programme (WCASP), World Climate Impact Assessment and Response Strategies Programme (WCIRP), World Climate Research Programme (WCRP). The WCP is supported by the Global Climate Observing System (GCOS), which provides comprehensive observation of the global climate system, involving a multi-disciplinary range of atmospheric, oceanic, hydrologic, cryospheric and biotic properties and processes. In 1997–98 the GCOS was particularly active in monitoring the impact of the El Niño weather phenomenon on the climate system. The objectives of the WCP are: to use existing climate information to improve economic and social planning; to improve the understanding of climate processes through research, so as to determine the predictability of climate and the extent of man's influence on it; and to detect and warn governments of impending climate variations or changes, either natural or man-made, which may significantly affect critical human activities.

Co-ordination of the overall Programme is the responsibility of the WMO, together with direct management of the WCDMP and WCASP. The UN Environment Programme (UNEP) has accepted responsibility for the WCIRP, while the WCRP is jointly administered by WMO, the International Council for Science (ICSU) and UNESCO's Intergovernmental Oceanographic Commission. Other organizations involved in the Programme include FAO, WHO, and the Consultative Group on International Agricultural Research (CGIAR). In addition, the WCP supports the WMO/UNEP Intergovernmental Panel on Climate Change and the implementation of international agreements, such as the UN Framework Convention on Climate Change (see below); and co-ordinates climate activities within WMO.

World Climate Applications and Climate Information and Services Programme (WCASP): promotes applications of climate knowledge in the areas of food production, water, energy (especially solar and wind energy), urban planning and building, human health, transport, tourism and recreation.

World Climate Data and Monitoring Programme (WCDMP): aims to make available reliable climate data for detecting and monitoring climate change for both practical applications and research purposes. The major projects are: the Climate Change Detection Project (CCDP); development of climate databases; computer systems for climate data management (CLICOM); the World Data and Information Referral Service (INFOCLIMA); the Climate Monitoring System; and the Data Rescue (DARE) project.

World Climate Impact Assessment and Response Strategies Programme (WCIRP): aims to make reliable estimates of the socio-economic impact of climate changes, and to assist in forming national policies accordingly. It concentrates on: study of the impact of climate variations on national food systems; assessment of the impact of man's activities on the climate, especially through increasing the amount of carbon dioxide and other radiatively active gases in the atmosphere; and developing the methodology of climate impact assessments.

World Climate Research Programme (WCRP): organized jointly with the Intergovernmental Oceanographic Commission of UNESCO and the ICSU, to determine to what extent climate can be predicted, and the extent of man's influence on climate. Its three specific objectives are: establishing the physical basis for weather predictions over time ranges of one to two months; understanding and predicting the variability of the global climate over periods of several years; and studying the long-term variations and the response of climate to natural or man-made influence over periods of several decades. Studies include: changes in the atmosphere caused by emissions of carbon dioxide, aerosols and other gases; the effect of cloudiness on the radiation balance; the effect of ground water storage and vegetation on evaporation; the Arctic and Antarctic climate process; and the effects of oceanic circulation changes on the global atmosphere. The 10-year Tropical Ocean and Global Atmosphere Project, which ended in 1994, developed forecasting techniques used to monitor the climate phenomenon, El Niño, in 1997–98.

Global Climate Observing System (GCOS): aims to ensure that data on climate are obtained and made available for: climate system monitoring and climate change detection and attribution; assessing impacts of, and vulnerability to, climate variability and change, e.g. extreme events, terrestrial ecosystems, etc., and analysing options for adaptation; research to improve understanding, modelling and prediction of the climate system; and application to sustainable economic development. The strategy of the GCOS has been to work with its international and regional partners and to engage countries both directly and through international fora such as WMO, other GCOS sponsors and the UN Framework Convention on Climate Change.

ATMOSPHERIC RESEARCH AND ENVIRONMENT PROGRAMME

This major Programme aims to help members to implement research projects; to disseminate relevant scientific information; to draw the attention of members to outstanding research problems of major importance, such as atmospheric composition and environment changes; and to encourage and help members to incorporate the results of research into operational forecasting or other appropriate techniques, particularly when such changes of procedure require international co-ordination and agreement.

Global Atmosphere Watch (GAW): a world-wide system that integrates most monitoring and research activities involving the long-term measurement of atmospheric composition, and is intended to serve as an early warning system to detect further changes in atmospheric concentrations of 'greenhouse' gases, changes in the ozone layer and as associated ultraviolet radiation, and in long-range transport of pollutants, including acidity and toxicity of rain, as well as the atmospheric burden of aerosols. The instruments of these globally standardized observations and related research are a set of 22 global stations in remote areas and, in order to address regional effects, some 200 regional stations measuring specific atmospheric chemistry parameters, such as ozone and acid deposition. GAW is the main contributor of data on chemical composition and surface ultraviolet radiation to the GCOS. Through GAW, WMO has collaborated with the UN Economic Commission for Europe (ECE) and has been responsible for the meteorological part of the Monitoring and Evaluation of the Long-range Transmission of Air Pollutants in Europe. In this respect, WMO has arranged for the establishment of two Meteorological Synthesizing Centres (Oslo, Norway, and Moscow, Russia) which provide daily analysis of the transport of pollution over Europe. GAW also gives attention to atmospheric chemistry studies, prepares scientific assessments and encourages integrated environmental monitoring. Quality Assurance/Science Activity Centres have been established to ensure an overall level of quality in GAW. Atmospheric composition information is maintained by and available through a series of six GAW World Data Centres. GAW operates the GAW Urban Environment Meteorological Research Programme (GURME), which assists National Meteorological and Hydrological Services (NMHSs) in dealing with regional and urban pollution monitoring and forecasting, through the provision of guidelines and information on the requisite measuring and modelling infrastructures, and by bringing together NMHSs, regional and city administrations and health authorities. GURME is being developed in co-operation with the World Health Organization.

WMO and other agencies support UNESCO's International Oceanographic Commission with implementing tsunami warning systems for the Caribbean region, the north-eastern Atlantic, the Mediterranean and connected seas, and the Pacific. An Indian Ocean Tsunami Warning and Mitigation System is under development. In May 2007 the 15th WMO Congress stressed the importance of developing and maintaining tsunami warning systems and ocean forecast/warning systems.

Physics of Clouds and Weather Modification Research Programme: encourages scientific research on cloud physics and chemistry, with special emphasis on interaction between clouds and atmospheric chemistry, as well as weather modification such as precipitation enhancement ('rain-making') and hail suppression. It provides information on world-wide weather modification projects, and guidance in the design and evaluation of experiments. It also studies the chemistry of clouds and their role in the transport, transformation and dispersion of pollution.

Tropical Meteorology Research Programme: aims to promote and co-ordinate members' research efforts into such important problems as monsoons, tropical cyclones, meteorological aspects of droughts in the arid zones of the tropics, rain-producing tropical weather systems, and the interaction between tropical and mid-latitude weather systems. This should lead to a better understanding of tropical systems and forecasting, and thus be of economic benefit to tropical countries.

World Weather Research Programme (WWRP): promotes the development and application of improved weather forecasting techniques. The Programme is primarily concerned with forecasting weather events that have the potential to cause considerable socio-economic dislocation. Advances in forecasting capability are pursued through a combination of improved scientific understanding (gained through field experiments and research), forecast technique development, the demonstration of new forecasting capabilities, and the transfer of these advances to all NMHSs in conjunction with related training through various Research Developments Projects (RDPs) and Forecast Demonstration Projects (FDPs). In particular, THORPEX: a Global Atmospheric Research Programme, is being developed and implemented as part of the WWRP to accelerate improvements in the accuracy of 1–14-day weather forecasts in order to achieve social and economic benefits. The Programme builds upon ongoing advances within the basic research and operational forecasting communities. It aims to make progress by enhancing international collaboration between these communities and with users of forecast products.

APPLICATIONS OF METEOROLOGY PROGRAMME

Public Weather Services Programme: assists members in providing reliable and effective weather and related services for the benefit of the public. The main objectives of the Programme are: to strengthen members' capabilities to meet the needs of the community through the provision of comprehensive weather and related services, with particular emphasis on public safety and welfare; and to foster a better understanding by the public of the capabilities of national meteorological services and how best to use their services.

Agricultural Meteorology Programme: the study of weather and climate as they affect agriculture and forestry, the selection of crops and their protection from disease and deterioration in storage, soil conservation, phenology and physiology of crops and productivity and health of farm animals; the Commission for Agricultural Meteorology supervises the applications projects and also advises the Secretary-General in his efforts to co-ordinate activities in support of food production. There are also special activities in agrometeorology to monitor and combat drought and desertification, to apply climate and real-time weather information in agricultural planning and operations, and to help improve the efficiency of the use of human labour, land, water and energy in agriculture; close co-operation is maintained with FAO, centres of CGIAR and UNEP.

Aeronautical Meteorology Programme: provides operational meteorological information required for safe, regular and efficient air navigation, as well as meteorological assistance to non-real-time activities of the aviation industry. The objective is to ensure the world-wide provision of cost-effective and responsive aviation operations. The Programme is implemented at global, regional and national levels, the Commission for Aeronautical Meteorology (CAeM) playing a major role, taking into account relevant meteorological developments in science and technology, studying aeronautical requirements for meteorological services, promoting international standardization of methods, procedures and techniques, and considering requirements for basic and climatological data as well as aeronautical requirements for meteorological observations and specialized instruments and enhanced understanding and awareness of the impact of aviation on the environment. Activities under this Programme are carried out, where relevant, with the International Civil Aviation Organization (ICAO) and in collaboration with users of services provided to aviation.

Marine Meteorology and Oceanography Programme: undertakes operational monitoring of the oceans and the maritime atmosphere; collection, exchange, archival recording and management of marine data; processing of marine data, and the provision of marine meteorological and oceanographic services in support of the safety of life and property at sea and of the efficient and economic operation of all sea-based activities. The joint WMO/Intergovernmental Oceanographic Commission (IOC) Technical Commission for Oceanography and Marine Meteorology (JCOMM) has broad responsibilities in the overall management of the Programme. Many programme elements are undertaken jointly with the IOC, within the context of JCOMM, and also of the Global Ocean Observing System (GOOS). Close co-operation also occurs with the International Maritime Organization (IMO), as well as with other bodies both within and outside the UN system.

HYDROLOGY AND WATER RESOURCES PROGRAMME

The overall objective of this major Programme is to apply hydrology to meet the needs of sustainable development and use of water and related resources; for the mitigation of water-related disasters; and to ensure effective environment management at national and international levels. The Programme consists of the following mutually supporting component programmes:

Programme on Basic Systems in Hydrology (BSH): provides the basis and framework for the majority of the scientific and technical aspects of WMO activities in hydrology and water resources. The BSH covers the collection, transmission and storage of data, the transfer of operationally proven technology through the Hydrological Operational Multipurpose System (HOMS), and the development of the World Hydrological Cycle Observing System (WHYCOS), with the aim of improving countries' capacity to supply reliable water-related data, and manage and exchange accurate and timely water resources information.

Programme on Forecasting and Applications in Hydrology (FAH): covers aspects of the Hydrology and Water Resources Programme relating to hydrological modelling and forecasting, and to the application of hydrology in studies of global change. The FAH organizes activities in support of water resources development and management, and hazard mitigation, and promotes interdisciplinary co-operation to enhance flood forecasting at the national, regional and global level. The Programme is linked to the World Climate and Tropical Cyclone programmes.

Programme on Sustainable Development of Water Resources (SDW): encourages the full participation of hydrological services in national planning and in the implementation of actions consequent to the relevant recommendations of the United Nations Conference on Environment and Development (UNCED, held in Rio de Janeiro, Brazil, in 1992), and the World Summit on Sustainable Development (WSSD, held in Johannesburg, South Africa, in 2002).

Programme on Capacity Building in Hydrology and Water Resources (CBH): provides a framework under which National Hydrological Services (NHSs) are supported in their institutional development, through education and training activities, development of guidance material, assistance in the preparation of water legislation, reorganization of services and changes in administrative and legal frameworks.

Programme on Water-related Issues (WRI): maintains WMO's important role in international activities relating to water resource assessment and hydrological forecasting. A major aspect of this component programme is the organization's collaboration with other UN agencies.

Other WMO programmes contain hydrological elements, which are closely co-ordinated with the Hydrology and Water Resources Programme. These include the Tropical Cyclone Programme, the World Climate Programme, and the Global Energy and Water Budget Experiment of the World Climate Research Programme.

EDUCATION AND TRAINING PROGRAMME

The overall objective of this Programme is to assist members in developing adequately trained staff to meet their responsibilities for providing meteorological and hydrological information services.

Activities include surveys of the training requirements of member states, the development of appropriate training programmes, the monitoring and improvement of the network of 23 Regional Meteorological Training Centres, the organization of training courses, seminars and conferences and the preparation of training materials. The Programme also arranges individual training programmes and the provision of fellowships. The Panel of Experts on Education and Training was established by the Executive Council to serve as an advisory body on all aspects of technical and scientific education and of training in meteorology and operational hydrology.

TECHNICAL CO-OPERATION PROGRAMME

The objective of the WMO Technical Co-operation Programme is to assist developing countries in improving their meteorological and hydrological services so that they can serve the needs of their people more effectively. This is achieved through improving, *inter alia,* their early warning systems for severe weather; their agricultural-meteorological services, to facilitate more reliable and fruitful food production; and the assessment of climatological factors for economic planning. At a regional level the Programme concentrates on disaster prevention and mitigation. In 2006 a Severe Weather Forecasting Demonstration Project was launched in south-eastern Africa; the 15th WMO Congress convened in May 2007 determined that this should be expanded and implemented throughout Africa and regions.

Programme for the Least Developed Countries: has as its long-term objective enhancement of the capacities of the NMHSs of LDCs so that they can contribute efficiently and in a timely manner to socio-economic development efforts. Priority areas are poverty alleviation and natural disaster preparedness and mitigation. Specific projects will be developed for individual countries and at a subregional level for countries in Africa, Asia and the Pacific.

Voluntary Co-operation Programme (VCP): WMO assists members in implementing the World Weather Watch Programme to develop an integrated observing and forecasting system. Member governments contribute equipment, services and fellowships for training, in addition to cash donations.

WMO also carries out assistance projects under Trust Fund arrangements, financed by national authorities, either for activities in their own country or in a beneficiary country and managed by UNDP, the World Bank, regional development banks, the European Union and others. WMO provides assistance to UNDP in the development of national meteorological and hydrological services, in the application of meteorological and hydrological data to national economic development, and in the training of personnel.

REGIONAL PROGRAMME

WMO's Regional Programme cuts across the other major WMO programmes of relevance to the regions and addresses meteorological, hydrological and other geophysical issues which are unique to and of common concern to a region or group of regions. It provides a framework for the formulation of most of the global WMO Programmes and serves as a mechanism for their implementation at the national, subregional and regional levels. The Programme provides support to the WMO regional associations and contributes to the development of NMHSs through capacity-building and other priority

NATURAL DISASTER PREVENTION AND MITIGATION PROGRAMME

The purpose of this cross-cutting Programme is to ensure the integration of relevant activities being carried out by the various WMO programmes in the area of disaster prevention and mitigation, and to provide for the effective co-ordination of pertinent WMO activities with the related activities of international, regional and national organizations, including civil defence organizations. The Programme should also provide scientific and technical support to WMO actions made in response to disaster situations, and its activities should emphasize pre-disaster preparedness and be based on activities within a number of WMO programmes, including the Public Weather Services and other components of the Applications of Meteorology Programme. The Programme will serve as a vehicle for enabling the delivery of increasingly accurate and reliable warnings of severe events, especially through co-ordinating WMO actions aimed at improving mechanisms and communications for the delivery, use and evaluation of warnings, provision of prompt advice and assistance to members; and at enhancing effective international co-operation and collaboration.

SPACE PROGRAMME

The 14th WMO Congress initiated this new, cross-cutting programme to increase the effectiveness of, and contributions from, satellite systems for WMO programmes. Congress recognized the critical importance of data, products and services provided by the expanded space-based component of the GOS. In recent years the use by WMO members of satellite data, products and services has grown tremendously, to the benefit of almost all WMO programmes and WMO-supported programmes. The 53rd session of the Executive Council adopted a landmark decision to expand the space-based component of the GOS to include appropriate research and development ('R&D') and environmental satellite missions. The Congress agreed that the Commission for Basic Systems should continue to play a leading role, in full consultation with the other technical commissions for the Space Programme. Anticipated benefits from the Programme include an increasing contribution to the development of the GOS, as well as to that of other WMO-supported programmes and associated observing systems, through the provision of continuously improved data, products and services, from both operational and R&D satellites. The Programme also aims to facilitate and promote the wider availability and meaningful utilization world-wide of such improved data.

INTERNATIONAL POLAR YEAR

WMO, jointly with the International Council for Science, jointly sponsored the International Polar Year (IPY), which was observed during March 2007–March 2008, although the full scientific programme associated with the IPY covered two annual cycles over the period March 2007–March 2009. The IPY focused on the Arctic and Antarctic polar regions and involved more than 200 projects addressing a wide range of physical, biological and social areas of research.

CO-OPERATION WITH OTHER BODIES

As a Specialized Agency of the UN, WMO actively participates in the UN system. In addition, WMO has concluded a number of formal agreements and working arrangements with international organizations both within and outside the UN system, at the intergovernmental and non-governmental level. As a result, WMO participates in major international conferences convened under the auspices of the UN or other organizations.

Intergovernmental Panel on Climate Change (IPCC): established in 1988 by WMO and UNEP; comprises some 3,000 scientists as well as other experts and representatives of all UN member governments. Approximately every five years the IPCC assesses all available scientific, technical and socio-economic information on anthropogenic climate change. The IPCC provides, on request, scientific, technical and socio-economic advice to the parties to the Conference of the Parties to the UN Framework Convention on Climate Change (UNFCCC) and to its subsidiary bodies, and compiles reports on specialized topics, such as *Aviation and the Global Atmosphere* and *Regional Impacts of Climate Change*. The IPCC informs and guides, but does not prescribe, policy. In December 1995 the IPCC presented evidence to 120 governments, demonstrating 'a discernible human influence on global climate'. In 2001 the Panel issued its *Third Assessment Report*, in which it confirmed this finding and presented new and strengthened evidence attributing most global climate warming over the past 50 years to human activities. IPCC's *Fourth Assessment Report*, the final instalment of which was issued in November 2007, concluded that increases in global average air and ocean temperatures, widespread melting of snow and ice, and the rising global average sea level demonstrate that the warming of the climate system is unequivocal; that observational evidence from all continents and most oceans indicates that many natural systems are being affected by regional climate changes; that a global assessment of data since 1970 has shown that it is likely that anthropogenic warming has had a discernable influence on many physical and biological systems; and that other effects of regional climate changes are emerging.

Secretariat of the UN Framework Convention on Climate Change: Haus Carstanjen, Martin-Luther-King-Strasse 8, 53175 Bonn, Germany; tel. (228) 815-1000; fax (228) 815-1999; e-mail secretariat@unfccc.int; internet unfccc.int; WMO and UNEP worked together to formulate the Convention, in response to the first report of the IPCC, issued in August 1990, which predicted an increase in the concentration of 'greenhouse' gases (i.e. carbon dioxide and other gases that have a warming effect on the atmosphere) owing to human activity. The UNFCCC was signed in May 1992 and formally adopted at the UN Conference on Environment and Development, held in June. It entered into force in March 1994. It committed countries to submitting reports on measures being taken to reduce the emission of greenhouse gases and recommended stabilizing these emissions at 1990 levels by 2000; however, this was not legally-binding. In July 1996, at the second session of the Conference of the Parties (COP) of the Convention, representatives of developed countries declared their willingness to commit to legally-binding objectives for emission limitations in a specified timetable. Multilateral negotiations ensued to formulate a mandatory treaty on greenhouse gas emissions. At the third COP, held in Kyoto, Japan, in December 1997, 38 industrial nations endorsed mandatory reductions of combined emissions of the six major gases by an average of 5.2% during the five-year period 2008–12, to pre-1990 levels. The so-called Kyoto Protocol was to enter into force on being ratified by at least 55 countries party to the UNFCCC, including industrialized countries with combined emissions of carbon dioxide in 1990 accounting for at least 55% of the total global greenhouse gas emissions by developed nations. Many of the Protocol's operational details, however, remained to be determined. The fourth COP, convened in Buenos Aires, Argentina, in November 1998, adopted a plan of action to promote implementation of the UNFCCC and to finalize the operational details of the Kyoto Protocol. These included the Clean Development Mechanism, by which industrialized countries may obtain credits towards achieving their reduction targets by assisting developing countries to implement emission-reducing measures, and a system of trading emission quotas. The fifth COP, held in Bonn, Germany, in October–November 1999, and the first session of the sixth COP, convened in The Hague, Netherlands, in November 2000, failed to reach agreement on the implementation of the Buenos Aires plan of action, owing to a lack of consensus on several technical matters, including the formulation of an effective mechanism for ascertaining compliance under the Kyoto Protocol, and adequately defining a provision of the Protocol under which industrialized countries may obtain credits towards achieving their reduction targets in respect of the absorption of emissions resulting from activities in the so-called land-use, land-use change and forestry (LULUCF) sector. Further, informal, talks were held in Ottawa, Canada, in early December. Agreement on implementing the Buenos Aires action plan was finally achieved at the second session of the sixth COP, held in Bonn in July 2001. The seventh COP, convened in Marrakech, Morocco, in October–November, formally adopted the decisions reached in July, and elected 15 members to the Executive Board of the Clean Development Mechanism. The eighth COP, convened in New Dehli, India, in October–November 2002, issued the Dehli Declaration, urging states parties that had not done so already to ratify the Kyoto Protocol, and urging the integration of climate change objectives in key areas into national sustainable development strategies. In March the USA (the most prolific national producer of harmful gas emissions) announced that it would not ratify the Kyoto Protocol. A major advance achieved at the ninth COP was agreement on the modalities and scope for carbon-absorbing forest-management projects in the Clean Development Mechanism. The Kyoto Protocol eventually entered into force on 16 February 2005, 90 days after its ratification by Russia. By December 2007 the Protocol had received ratifications from 175 states and the European Community, including ratifications by industrialized nations with combined responsibility for 63.7% of greenhouse gas emissions by developed nations in 1990 (although excluding participation by the USA). Australia ratified the Protocol during December 2007. Negotiations commenced in May 2007 on establishing an international agreement to succeed the Kyoto Protocol after its expiry in 2012.

INTERNATIONAL DAY

World Meteorological Day is observed every year on 23 March. The theme in 2008 was 'Observing our planet for a better future'.

Finance

WMO is financed by contributions from members on a proportional scale of assessment. For the fourteenth financial period, the four years 2004–07, a programme and budget of 253.8m. Swiss francs was approved, of which 249.8m. Swiss francs were to be funded from assessed contributions and 4.0m. Swiss francs would be made available from any cash surplus arising from the previous financial period. Outside this budget, WMO implements a number of projects as executing agency for UNDP or else under trust-fund arrangements.

Publications

Annual Report.
MeteoWorld.
WMO Bulletin (quarterly in English, French, Russian and Spanish).
World Climate News.
Reports, technical regulations, manuals and notes and training publications.

World Tourism Organization

Address: Capitán Haya 42, 28020 Madrid, Spain.
Telephone: (91) 5678100; **fax:** (91) 5713733; **e-mail:** omt@unwto.org; **internet:** www.world-tourism.org.

The World Tourism Organization (UNWTO) was formally established in 1975 following transformation of the International Union of Official Travel Organisations into an intergovernmental body, in accordance with a resolution of the UN General Assembly approved in 1969. The organization became a specialized agency of the UN in December 2003. It aims to promote and develop sustainable tourism, in particular in support of socio-economic growth in developing countries.

MEMBERS

153 member states, seven associate members, 370 affiliate members.

Organization
(March 2008)

GENERAL ASSEMBLY

The General Assembly meets every two years to approve the budget and programme of work of the organization and to consider issues of concern for the tourism sector. It consists of representatives of all full and associate members; affiliate members and representatives of other international organizations participate as observers. The 17th General Assembly was convened in Cartagena, Colombia, in November 2007, and the 18th Assembly was scheduled to be held in Kazakhstan, in 2009.

EXECUTIVE COUNCIL

The Council, comprising 29 members elected by the General Assembly, is the governing body responsible for supervising the activities of the organization. It meets twice a year. The following specialized committees are subsidiary organs of the Council and advise on management and programme content: Programme; Budget and Finance; Statistics and Macroeconomic Analysis of Tourism; Market Intelligence and Promotion; Sustainable Development of Tourism; and Quality Support and Trade. In addition, there is a World Committee on Tourism Ethics and a Sub-committee for the Review of Applications for Affiliate Membership.

REGIONAL COMMISSIONS

There are six regional commissions, comprising all members and associate members from that region, which meet at least once a year to determine the organization's priorities and future activities in the region. The commissions cover Africa, the Americas, East Asia and the Pacific, Europe, the Middle East, and South Asia.

SECRETARIAT

The Secretariat is responsible for implementing the organization's work programme. A regional support office for Asia and the Pacific is based in Osaka, Japan. Six regional representatives, based at the Secretariat, support national tourism authorities, act as a liaison between those authorities and international sources of finance, and represent the body at national and regional events.
Secretary-General: Francesco Frangialli (France).

AFFILIATE MEMBERS

UNWTO is unique as an intergovernmental body in extending membership to operational representatives of the industry and other related sectors, for example transport companies, educational institutions, insurance companies, publishing groups. A UNWTO Education Council aims to support UNWTO's education and human resource development activities. It undertakes research projects, grants awards for innovation and the application of knowledge in tourism, and co-ordinates a tourism labour market observatory project. The UNWTO Business Council groups together the affiliate members from the private sector and aims to promote and facilitate partnerships between the industry and governments. A third group of the affiliate membership is the UNWTO Destinations Council, which acts as an operational body supporting the UNWTO Destination Management programme with particular concern for issues relevant to tourist destinations, for example local tourism marketing, economic measurements and management of congestion.
CEO of UNWTO Affiliate Members: Victoria Marcos (Spain).

Activities

The World Tourism Organization promotes the development of responsible, sustainable and universally accessible tourism within the broad context of contributing to economic development, international prosperity and peace and respect for human rights. As a specialized agency of the UN UNWTO aims to emphasize the role of tourism as a means of supporting socio-economic development and achieve the UN Millennium Development Goals (MDGs). Through its network of affiliated members UNWTO extends its activities and objectives to the private sector, tourism authorities and educational institutions.

DEVELOPMENT ASSISTANCE

UNWTO aims to support member states to develop and promote their tourist industry in order to contribute to socio-economic growth and poverty alleviation in those countries. Activities to transfer technical skills and knowledge to developing countries are fundamental tasks for the organization. It aims to assist member countries to develop tourism plans and strategies and helps to secure and manage specific development projects, for example the formulation of tourism legislation in Syria, hotel classification in Bolivia and statistics development in Botswana. Other aspects of developing tourism concern the involvement of local communities, fostering public-private partnerships and the preservation of cultural and natural heritage. UNWTO maintains a register of specialized consultants and firms to undertake appropriate missions.

In September 2002 at the World Summit on Sustainable Development, held in Johannesburg, South Africa, UNWTO, in collaboration with the UN Conference on Trade and Development (UNCTAD), launched the Sustainable Tourism-Eliminating Poverty (ST-EP) initiative. It aimed to encourage social, economic and ecologically sustainable tourism with the aim of alleviating poverty in the world's poorest countries. In September 2004 UNWTO signed an agreement with the Republic of Korea providing for the establishment of a ST-EP Foundation in the capital, Seoul. UNWTO has conducted a series of capacity-building seminars and other training activities concerning tourism and poverty alleviation, within the framework of the ST-EP initiative. It convenes an annual ST-EP forum, in Berlin, Germany, to involve a range of tourism agencies and companies in the scheme. Project identification missions have been conducted in some 30 developing countries and, from the end of 2005, projects began to be implemented, with a focus on local level tourism development and small-scale entrepreneurial schemes.

MARKET

UNWTO aims to ensure that quality standards and safety and security aspects are incorporated into all tourism products and services. It is also concerned with the social impact of tourism and the regulatory trading framework. UNWTO has formulated international standards for tourism measurement and reporting. It compiles comprehensive tourism statistics and forecasts. A Tourism Satellite Account (TSA) was developed to analyse the economic impact of tourism. It was endorsed by the UN Statistical Commission in 2000 and is recognized as a framework for providing internationally comparable data. The TSA is also considered by UNWTO to be a strategic project within the broader objective of developing a system of tourism statistics. In October 2005 a world conference on TSAs, held in the Iguazu region of Argentina, Brazil and Paraguay, agreed on 10 defined objectives to extend and develop the use of TSAs.

In 1991 UNWTO's General Assembly approved a series of Recommended Measures for Tourism Safety which member states were encouraged to apply. UNWTO has established a Safety and Security in Tourism Network to consider aspects of the recommended measures and to facilitate collaboration between institutions and experts concerned with safety and security issues. The Network publishes national factsheets on safety and security in countries and tourist destinations, compiled by a designated national tourism administration focal point, for use by tourism professionals and the general public. Other essential quality standards promoted by the organization are hygiene and food safety, accessibility, product and pricing transparency and authenticity. UNWTO is also concerned with ensuring that tourist activities are in keeping with the surrounding environment.

UNWTO assists governments and tourist professionals to identify, analyse and forecast tourism trends and to assess the relative performance of each country's tourist industry. The organization also assist member states with tourism promotion through marketing tools and the formulation of tourism development strategies. A Market Intelligence and Promotion Committee was formally established in October 2002. Following the terrorism attacks against targets in the USA in September 2001 a Tourism Recovery Committee was established to monitor events affecting tourism, to help to restore confidence in the industry and to strengthen UNWTO activities concerned with safety and security.

In January 2005 the Executive Council convened its first ever emergency session in response to the devastation of many coastal areas in the Indian Ocean caused by an earthquake and tsunami which affected some 14 countries at the end of 2004. The Council, meeting in Phuket, Thailand, along with other regional organizations, private sector representatives and tourism experts, adopted an action plan to support the recovery of the tourism sector in many of the affected areas, to help to restore tourist confidence in the region and to rehabilitate tourism infrastructure, in particular in Thailand, the Maldives, Indonesia and Sri Lanka. A co-ordinating unit to oversee the longer-term projects was established in February 2005 and its functions were integrated into UNWTO's broader emergency response framework in mid-2006. In 2005 UNWTO pledged its commitment to working with governments and the private sector to incorporate tourism concerns into preparedness programmes relating to the threat of highly pathogenic avian influenza. A Tourism Emergency Response Network was established in April 2006 as a grouping of travel organizations committed to supporting UN efforts to respond to avian influenza and the threat of a potential human pandemic. UNWTO maintains a tourism emergency tracking system, which identifies recent outbreaks of the disease.

UNWTO participates as an observer at the World Trade Organization on issues relating to trade in tourism services, with particular concern to negotiations under the General Agreement on Trade in Services (GATS) for a separate annex on tourism. UNWTO hosts a voluntary working group on liberalization.

In order to generate awareness of tourism among the international community UNWTO sponsors a World Tourism Day, held each year on 27 September. In 2008 the official events were to be hosted by Peru, on the theme 'Responding to the challenge of climate change'.

SUSTAINABLE TOURISM DEVELOPMENT

UNWTO aims to encourage and facilitate the application of sustainable practices within the tourism industry. It publishes guides on sustainable development for use by local authorities as well as compilations for good practices. UNWTO has also published several manuals for tourism planning at regional, national and local level and has organized seminars on planning issues in developing countries. UNWTO actively promotes voluntary initiatives for sustainability including labelling schemes, certification systems and awards.

In 1999 UNWTO was mandated, together with the UN Environment Programme, to assume responsibility for the International Year of Ecotourism which was held in 2002, as well as all preparatory and follow-up activities. A World Ecotourism Summit, which was convened in Québec, Canada in May, was attended by delegates from 132 countries. It resulted in the Québec Declaration containing guide-lines for sustainable ecotourism development and management. UNWTO publishes a series of compilations of good practices for small and medium-sized businesses involved with ecotourism. UNWTO sponsored the first International Conference on Climate Change and Tourism, which was held in Djerba, Tunisia, in April 2003. A final declaration of the conference urged that UNWTO take the lead in focusing international attention on the issue and called upon all parties to continue research efforts, to encourage sustainability in tourism, to generate awareness and to implement defined actions. The second International Conference on Climate Change and Tourism, organized by UNWTO, UNEP and WMO, was convened in Davos, Switzerland, in October 2007. The meeting concluded the Davos Declaration, which urged greater action by the tourism sector to respond to the challenges of climate change, for example by employing new energy efficiency technologies, in order to support the objectives of the UN Millennium Development Goals.

In 1997 a Task Force for the Protection of Children from Sexual Exploitation in Tourism was established by UNWTO as a forum for governments, industry associations and other organizations to work together with the aim of identifying, preventing and eradicating the sexual exploitation of children. In March 2007 the mandate of the Task Force was expanded to include protection of children and young people against all forms of exploitation in tourism, including child labour and trafficking. In 1999 the General Assembly adopted a Global Code of Ethics for Tourism. The Code was endorsed by a special resolution of the UN General Assembly in 2001. The Code aims to protect resources upon which tourism depends and to ensure that the economic benefits of tourism are distributed equitably. A World Committee on Tourism Ethics, established in 2003 to support the implementation of the Code, held its first meeting in Rome, Italy, in February 2004 and subsequently has been convened on an annual basis. In March 2000 UNWTO, with the UN Educational, Scientific and Cultural Organization (UNESCO) and UNEP, established a Tour Operators Initiative to encourage socially responsible tourism development within the industry.

In November 2007 the General Assembly resolved to appoint the organization's first Special Advisor on Women and Tourism.

In 1994 UNWTO, in co-operation with UNESCO, initiated a project to promote tourism, in support of economic development, along the traditional Silk Road trading routes linking Asia and Europe. A fourth international meeting of participants in the project was convened in Bukhara, Uzbekistan, in October 2002. In October 2004 a Silk Road Tourism Office was opened in Samarkand, Uzbekistan. In 1995 UNWTO and UNESCO launched the Slave Route project to stimulate tourism and raise cultural awareness in several West African countries. In October 2007 UNWTO hosted an International Conference on Tourism, Religion and the Dialogue of Cultures, in Córdoba, Spain, to contribute to the discussion and promotion of the UN initiative for an Alliance of Civilizations.

EDUCATION AND KNOWLEDGE MANAGEMENT

UNWTO is committed to supporting education and training within the tourism industry and to developing a network of specialized research and training institutes. Most activities are undertaken by the UNWTO Education Council and the Themis Foundation. A specialized office concerned with human resource development was opened in September 2003, in Andorra.

UNWTO Themis Foundation: Avinguda Dr Vilanova 9, Edif. Thaïs 4c, Andorra la Vella, Andorra; tel. 802600; fax 829955; e-mail wto.themis@andorra.ad; internet www.unwto.org/education-new/english/themis.php; aims to promote quality and efficiency in tourism education and training. Works closely with the human resource development programme of UNWTO and promotes UNWTO's specialized training products and services, in particular the TedQual certification and the practicum programme for tourism officials.

INFORMATION AND COMMUNICATIONS

In January 2004 UNWTO hosted the first World Conference on Tourism Communications. Regular regional conferences have since been organized, within the framework of a Special Programme for Capacity Sharing in International Tourism Communications (TOURCOM), to enhance the capacity of regional and national tourism authorities to apply international standards and best practices to the promotion and communication of tourism.

UNWTO aims to act as a clearing house of information for the tourist industry. A UNWTO Documentation Centre collates extensive information on tourism activities and promotes access to and exchange of information among members states and affiliated partners. The Centres offers access to tourism legislation and other regulatory procedures through its LEXTOUR database on the internet. The Centre also administers a tourism information database (INFODOCTOUR). A Thesaurus on Tourism and Leisure Activities was published in 2001.

INTERNATIONAL ORGANIZATIONS   United Nations (Specialized Agencies)

FINANCE
The budget for the two-year period 2008–09 amounted to €25.1m.

PUBLICATIONS
Compendium of Tourism Statistics.
Tourism Market Trends (annually).
Yearbook of Tourism Statistics.
UNWTO World Tourism Barometer (3 a year).
UNWTOBC Interactive (monthly).
UNWTO News (quarterly, in English, French and Spanish).
Other research or statistical reports, studies, guide-lines and fact-sheets.

AFRICAN DEVELOPMENT BANK—ADB

Address: Headquarters: rue Joseph Anoma, 01 BP 1387, Abidjan 01, Côte d'Ivoire.
Telephone: 20-20-44-44; **fax:** 20-20-49-59; **e-mail:** afdb@afdb.org; **internet:** www.afdb.org.
Address: Temporary relocation agency: 15 ave du Ghana, angle des rues Pierre de Coubertin et Hedi Nouira, BP 323, 1002 Tunis Belvédère, Tunisia.
Telephone: (71) 333-511; **fax:** (71) 351-933.

Established in 1964, the Bank began operations in July 1966, with the aim of financing economic and social development in African countries. The Bank's headquarters are based in Abidjan, Côte d'Ivoire. From February 2003, however, in view of ongoing insecurity in Côte d'Ivoire, the Bank's operations were relocated on a temporary basis to Tunis, Tunisia (see above).

AFRICAN MEMBERS

Algeria	Equatorial Guinea	Namibia
Angola	Eritrea	Niger
Benin	Ethiopia	Nigeria
Botswana	Gabon	Rwanda
Burkina Faso	The Gambia	São Tomé and
Burundi	Ghana	Príncipe
Cameroon	Guinea	Senegal
Cape Verde	Guinea-Bissau	Seychelles
Central African	Kenya	Sierra Leone
Republic	Lesotho	Somalia
Chad	Liberia	South Africa
Comoros	Libya	Sudan
Congo,	Madagascar	Swaziland
Democratic	Malawi	Tanzania
Republic	Mali	Togo
Congo, Republic	Mauritania	Tunisia
Côte d'Ivoire	Mauritius	Uganda
Djibouti	Morocco	Zambia
Egypt	Mozambique	Zimbabwe

There are also 24 non-African members.

Organization
(April 2008)

BOARD OF GOVERNORS

The highest policy-making body of the Bank, which also elects the Board of Directors and the President. Each member country nominates one Governor, usually its Minister of Finance and Economic Affairs, and an alternate Governor or the Governor of its Central Bank. The Board meets once a year; the 2008 meeting was scheduled to be held in Maputo, Mozambique, in May.

BOARD OF DIRECTORS

The Board consists of 18 members (of whom six are non-African), elected by the Board of Governors for a term of three years, renewable once; it is responsible for the general operations of the Bank. The Board meets on a weekly basis.

OFFICERS

The President is responsible for the organization and the day-to-day operations of the Bank under guidance of the Board of Directors. The President is elected for a five-year term and serves as the Chairman of the Board of Directors. A new organizational structure became effective in July 2006, according to which the President oversees the following senior management: Chief Economist; Vice-Presidents of Finance, Corporate Services, Country and Regional Programmes and Policy, Sector Operations, and Infrastructure, Private Sector and Regional Integration; Auditor General; General Counsel; Secretary-General; and Ombudsman.

Executive President and Chairman of Board of Directors: DONALD KABERUKA (Rwanda).
Secretary-General: MODIBO TOURÉ (Mali).

FINANCIAL STRUCTURE

The ADB Group of development financing institutions comprises the African Development Fund (ADF) and the Nigeria Trust Fund (NTF), which provide concessionary loans, and the African Development Bank itself. The group uses a unit of account (UA), which, at December 2006, was valued at US $1.50440.

The capital stock of the Bank was at first exclusively open for subscription by African countries, with each member's subscription consisting of an equal number of paid-up and callable shares. In 1978, however, the Governors agreed to open the capital stock of the Bank to subscription by non-regional states on the basis of nine principles aimed at maintaining the African character of the institution. The decision was finally ratified in May 1982, and the participation of non-regional countries became effective on 30 December. It was agreed that African members should still hold two-thirds of the share capital, that all loan operations should be restricted to African members, and that the Bank's President should always be an African national. In May 1998 the Board of Governors approved an increase in capital of 35%, and resolved that the non-African members' share of the capital be increased from 33.3% to 40%. In 2006 the ADB's authorized capital was US $32,901.23m. At the end of 2006 subscribed capital was $32,786.89m. (of which the paid-up portion was $3,547.05m.).

Activities

At the end of 2006 total loan and grant approvals by the ADB Group since the beginning of its operations amounted to US $59,058.75m. In 2006 the Group approved 122 loans and grants amounting to $3,896.3m., compared with $3,278.2m. for 102 loans and grants in the previous year. Of the total approved in 2006 finance received the largest proportion of assistance (21.5%), while transport received 20.1%, multi-sector activities 17.9%, and agriculture and rural development 10.4%.

In 2002 the Bank's Board of Directors approved a Strategic Plan for 2003–07 incorporating four fundamental principles for Bank activities: country ownership; greater selectivity; participatory approaches; and enhanced co-operation with development partners. Bank operations were to continue to emphasis the central objectives of promoting sustainable economic growth and achieving poverty reduction. In 2006 the Bank established a High Level Panel of eminent personalities to advise on the Bank's future strategic vision; the group commenced work in October.

Since 1996 the Bank has collaborated closely with international partners, in particular the World Bank, in efforts to address the problems of heavily indebted poor countries—HIPCs (see IBRD). Of the 41 countries identified as potentially eligible for assistance under the scheme 33 were in sub-Saharan Africa. Following the introduction of an enhanced framework for the initiative, the Bank has been actively involved in the preparation of Poverty Reduction Strategy Papers, that provide national frameworks for poverty reduction programmes. At the end of 2006 the Bank Group had approved US $5,067m. in HIPC debt relief. In April 2006 the Board of Directors endorsed a new Multilateral Debt Relief Initiative (MDRI) which provided for 100% cancellation of eligible debts from the ADF, IMF and the International Development Association to secure additional resources for countries to help them attain their Millennium Development Goals (MDGs). ADF's participation in the MDRI, which became effective in September, was anticipated to provide some $8,540m. in debt relief for 33 African countries.

The Bank contributed funds for the establishment, in 1986, of the Africa Project Development Facility, which assists the private sector in Africa by providing advisory services and finance for entrepreneurs: it was managed by the International Finance Corporation (IFC), until replaced by the Private Enterprise Partnership for Africa in April 2005. In 1989 the Bank, in co-ordination with IFC and UNDP, created the African Management Services Company (AMSCo) which provides management support and training to private companies in Africa. The Bank is one of three multilateral donors, with the World Bank and UNDP, supporting the African Capacity Building Foundation, which was established in 1991 to strengthen and develop institutional and human capacity in support of sustainable development activities. The Bank was to host the secretariat of a new Africa Investment Consortium, which was inaugurated in October 2005 by several major African institutions and donor countries to accelerate efforts to develop the region's infrastructure. The first African Economic Conference (AEC), organized by the Bank Group, was held in Tunis, Tunisia, in November 2006. A second AEC, on the theme of 'Opportunities and Challenges of Development for Africa in the Global Arena', was convened in Addis Ababa, Ethiopia, in November 2007.

In March 2004 a Rural Water Supply and Sanitation Initiative was approved to accelerate access in member countries to sustainable safe water and basic sanitation, in order to meet the requirements of several MDGs. The Bank was to host the first African Water Week, organized jointly with African ministers responsible for water, in March 2008.

The Bank provides technical assistance to regional member countries in the form of experts' services, pre-investment feasibility studies, and staff training; much of this assistance is financed through bilateral aid funds contributed by non-African member states. The Bank's African Development Institute provides training for officials of regional member countries in order to enhance the management of Bank-financed projects and, more broadly, to strengthen national capacities for promoting sustainable development. The Institute also manages an ADB/Japan Fellowship programme that provides scholarships to African students to pursue further education. In 1990 the ADB established the African Business Round Table (ABR), which is composed of the chief executives of Africa's leading corporations. The ABR aims to strengthen Africa's private sector, promote intra-African trade and investment, and attract foreign investment to Africa. The ABR is chaired by the Bank's Executive President. At its fourth annual meeting, held in Arusha, Tanzania, in March 1994, the ABR resolved to establish an African Investment Bank, in co-operation with the ADB, which was to provide financial services to African companies. In November 1999 a Joint Africa Institute, which had been established by the Bank, the World Bank and the IMF, was formally inaugurated in Abidjan, Côte d'Ivoire. The Institute aimed to enhance training opportunities in economic policy and management and to strengthen capacity-building in the region.

In 1990 a Memorandum of Understanding (MOU) for the Reinforcement of Co-operation between the Organization of African Unity, now African Union, the UN Economic Commission for Africa and the ADB was signed by the three organizations. A joint secretariat supports co-operation activities between the organizations. In 1999 a Co-operation Agreement was formally concluded between the Bank and the Common Market for Eastern and Southern Africa (COMESA). In March 2000 the Bank signed an MOU on its strategic partnership with the World Bank. Other MOUs were signed during that year with the United Nations Industrial Development Organization, the World Food Programme, and the Arab Maghreb Union. The Bank is actively involved in the New Partnership for Africa's Development (NEPAD), established in 2001 to promote sustainable development and eradicate poverty throughout the region.

AFRICAN DEVELOPMENT BANK (ADB)

The Bank makes loans at a variable rate of interest, which is adjusted twice a year, plus a commitment fee of 0.75%. Loan approvals amounted to US $1,572.7m. for 38 loans in 2006, compared with $1,241.7m. for 34 loans in the previous year. Since October 1997 new fixed and floating rate loans have also been made available.

AFRICAN DEVELOPMENT FUND (ADF)

The Fund commenced operations in 1974. It grants interest-free loans to low-income African countries for projects with repayment over 50 years (including a 10-year grace period) and with a service charge of 0.75% per annum. Grants for project feasibility studies are made to the poorest countries.

In May 1994 donor countries withheld any new funds owing to dissatisfaction with the Bank's governance. In May 1996, following the implementation of various institutional reforms to strengthen the Bank's financial management and decision-making capabilities and to reduce its administrative costs, an agreement was concluded on the seventh replenishment of ADF resources. Donor countries pledged some US $2,690m. for the period 1996–98. An additional allocation of $420m. was endorsed at a special donors' meeting held in Osaka, Japan, in June. The seventh replenishment provided for the establishment of an ADF Microfinance Initiative (AMINA), initially for a two-year period, to support small-scale capacity-building projects. In January 1999 negotiations on the eighth replenishment of the Fund were concluded with an agreement to provide additional resources amounting to $3,437m. The replenishment was approved by the Board of Governors in May, and came into effect in December. In September 2002 donor countries pledged $3,500m. for the ninth replenishment of the Fund, covering the period 2002–04. The so-called ADF-X was concluded in December 2004, with an agreement to replenish the Fund by some $5,400m. It was agreed that poverty reduction and the promotion of sustainable growth were to remain the principal objectives of the Fund for the period 2005–07. The first round of ADF-XI discussions was held in March 2007. In December donor countries committed $8,900m. to replenish the Fund for the three-year period 2008–10, during which there was to be a focus on infrastructure, governance and regional integration.

In 2006 84 ADF loans and grants were approved amounting to US $2,323.7m., compared with $2,032.0m. for 65 loans and grants in the previous year.

NIGERIA TRUST FUND (NTF)

The Agreement establishing the Nigeria Trust Fund was signed in February 1976 by the Bank and the Government of Nigeria. The Fund is administered by the Bank and its loans are granted for up to 25 years, including grace periods of up to five years, and carry 0.75% commission charges and 4% interest charges. The loans are intended to provide financing for projects in co-operation with other lending institutions. The Fund also aims to promote the private sector and trade between African countries by providing information on African and international financial institutions able to finance African trade.

Operations under the NTF were suspended in 2006, pending a detailed assessment and consideration of the Fund's activities which commenced in November.

ASSOCIATED INSTITUTIONS

The Bank actively participated in the establishment of five associated institutions:

African Reinsurance Corporation (Africa-Re): Africa Re House, Plot 1679, Karimu Kotun St, Victoria Island, PMB 12765, Lagos, Nigeria; tel. (1) 2626660; fax (1) 2663282; e-mail info@africa-re.com; internet www.africa-re.com; f. 1977; started operations in 1978; its purpose is to foster the development of the insurance and reinsurance industry in Africa and to promote the growth of national and regional underwriting capacities; auth. cap. US $100m., of which the Bank holds 10%; there are 12 directors, one appointed by the Bank; mems: 41 countries, five development finance institutions, and some 110 insurance and reinsurance cos; Man. Dir BAKARY KAMARA; publ. *The African Reinsurer* (annually).

African Export-Import Bank (Afreximbank): POB 404 Gezira, Cairo 11568; World Trade Centre Bldg, 1191 Corniche el-Nil, Cairo 11221, Egypt; tel. (2) 5780282; fax (2) 5780277; e-mail mail@afreximbank.com; internet www.afreximbank.com; f. 1993; aims to increase the volume of African exports and to expand intra-African trade by financing exporters and importers directly and indirectly through trade finance institutions, such as commercial banks; in Nov. 2001, under the auspices of Afreximbank, a Memorandum of General Principles was signed by African bankers for the establishment of an African Bankers Forum; auth. cap. US $750m.; paid-up cap. $149.4m. (Dec. 2005); Pres. JEAN-LOUIS EKRA; publ. *Annual Report*.

Association of African Development Finance Institutions (AADFI): Immeuble AIAFD, blvd Latrille, rue J61, Cocody Deux Plateaux, Abidjan 04, Côte d'Ivoire; tel. 22-52-33-89; fax 22-52-25-84; e-mail adfi@aviso.ci; internet www.aadfi.org; f. 1975; aims to promote co-operation among financial institutions in the region in matters relating to economic and social development, research, project design, financing and the exchange of information; mems: 92 in 43 African and non-African countries; Chair. Sir REMI OMOTOSO (Nigeria); Sec.-Gen. JOSEPH AMIHERE; publs *Annual Report*, *AADFI Information Bulletin* (quarterly), *Finance and Development in Africa* (2 a year).

Shelter-Afrique (Société pour l'habitat et le logement territorial en Afrique): Longonot Rd, POB 41479, Nairobi, Kenya; tel. (20) 2722305; fax (20) 2722024; e-mail info@shelterafrique.org; internet www.shelterafrique.org; f. 1982 to finance housing in mem. countries; auth. share cap. is US $300m., held by 41 African countries, the ADB, Africa-Re and CDC Group plc (formerly the Commonwealth Development Corpn); Man. Dir P. M'BAYE.

Société Internationale Financière pour les Investissements et le Développement en Afrique (SIFIDA): c/o BNP Paribas (Suisse) SA, Case Postale, 1211 Geneva 11, Switzerland; tel. 582122905; fax 582122920; internet www.sifida.com; f. 1970 by 120 financial and industrial institutions, including the ADB and the IFC; following its purchase by BNP/Paribas in 1996 the company was in the process of being liquidated. SIFIDA remains active in the field of structured finance in emerging (primarily African) markets and also provides financial advisory services, notably in the context of project finance, privatization and medium-term structured finance; Man. Dir JACQUES LOEHR.

Publications

Annual Report.
ADB Business Bulletin (10 a year).
ADB Statistics Pocketbook.
ADB Today (every 2 months).
African Development Report (annually).
African Development Review.
African Economic Outlook (annually, with OECD).
African Statistical Journal (2 a year).

Annual Procurement Report.
Compendium of Statistics on Bank Group Operations (annually).
Economic Research Papers.
Gender, Poverty and Environmental Indicators on African Countries (annually).
OPEV Sharing (quarterly newsletter).
Quarterly Operational Summary.
Selected Statistics on African Countries (annually).
Summaries of operations and projects, background documents, Board documents.

Statistics

SUMMARY OF BANK GROUP ACTIVITIES
(US $ million)

	2005	2006	Cumulative total*
ADB loans			
Number	34	38	1,029
Amount approved	1,241.65	1,572.65	33,091.83
Disbursements	850.92	825.07	21,010.92
ADF loans and grants			
Number	65	84	2,129
Amount approved	2,032.02	2,323.65	25,560.17
Disbursements	987.72	1,030.76	13,923.08
NTF loans			
Number	3	—	75
Amount approved	4.56	—	406.76
Disbursements	4.85	8.16	268.21
Group total			
Number	102	122	3,233
Amount approved	3,278.23	3,896.30	59,058.75
Disbursements	1,843.48	1,864.00	35,202.21

* Since the initial operations of the three institutions (1967 for ADB, 1974 for ADF and 1976 for NTF).

GROUP LOAN AND GRANT APPROVALS BY SUB-REGION AND COUNTRY
(millions of UA)

Sub-region/Country	2005	2006	Cumulative total*
Central Africa			
Burundi	12.3	16.3	325.1
Cameroon	25.6	124.8	900.7
Central African Republic	—	3.3	142.7
Chad	37.5	13.0	407.7
Congo, Republic	—	17.4	303.4
Congo, Democratic Republic	87.5	1.9	1,209.5
Equatorial Guinea	—	—	67.2
Gabon	15.4	—	688.8
Rwanda	—	25.0	436.2
São Tomé and Príncipe	—	4.0	103.6
Sub-total	178.2	205.6	4,584.9
East Africa			
Comoros	—	—	64.7
Djibouti	0.3	0.3	114.5
Eritrea	—	—	78.8
Ethiopia	43.6	231.0	1,694.2
Kenya	41.5	57.0	781.3
Madagascar	57.3	35.3	612.9
Mauritius	7.7	—	279.3
Seychelles	0.3	—	89.8
Somalia	0.3	0.3	151.4
Tanzania	—	145.3	1,070.0
Uganda	88.5	53.0	997.4
Sub-total	239.7	522.4	5,934.3
North Africa			
Algeria	—	—	1,889.1
Egypt	284.3	398.5	2,412.4
Mauritania	0.3	9.7	361.2
Morocco	175.7	245.9	4,137.0
Sudan	—	0.3	351.2
Tunisia	181.7	14.7	3,516.5
Sub-total	642.1	669.2	12,667.4
Southern Africa			
Angola	17.5	—	339.4
Botswana	—	—	362.1
Lesotho	—	6.8	307.4
Malawi	15.4	30.0	636.0
Mozambique	9.5	118.9	1,034.0
Namibia	—	—	167.8
South Africa	—	—	511.0
Swaziland	0.4	5.5	300.1
Zambia	0.4	63.9	721.9
Zimbabwe	0.4	—	726.9
Sub-total	43.5	225.1	5,106.5
West Africa			
Benin	59.5	15.0	504.8
Burkina Faso	56.8	15.0	595.2
Cape Verde	—	4.1	170.4
Côte d'Ivoire	—	—	1,143.5
Gambia	5.5	8.0	228.6
Ghana	86.0	66.0	1,020.6
Guinea	22.7	3.5	566.7
Guinea Bissau	1.4	6.1	185.2
Liberia	—	3.0	157.0
Mali	49.9	15.0	649.5
Niger	40.7	16.0	358.4
Nigeria	108.3	111.9	2,418.3
Senegal	83.2	—	669.5
Sierra Leone	39.7	2.0	281.2
Togo	—	2.2	187.4
Sub-total	553.7	267.8	9,136.2
Multinational	85.8	417.9	1,569.8
Total	1,742.9	2,308.1	38,999.3

* Since the initial operation of the three institutions (1967 for ADB, 1974 for ADF and 1976 for NTF).

Source: *Annual Report 2006.*

AFRICAN UNION—AU

Address: POB 3243, Addis Ababa, Ethiopia.
Telephone: (11) 5517700; **fax:** (11) 5517844; **e-mail:** webmaster@africa-union.org; **internet:** www.africa-union.org.

In May 2001 the Constitutive Act of the African Union entered into force. In July 2002 the African Union (AU) became fully operational, replacing the Organization of African Unity (OAU), which had been founded in 1963. The AU aims to support unity, solidarity and peace among African states; to promote and defend African common positions on issues of shared interest; to encourage human rights, democratic principles and good governance; to advance the development of member states by encouraging research and by working to eradicate preventable diseases; and to promote sustainable development and political and socio-economic integration, including co-ordinating and harmonizing policy between the continent's various 'regional economic communities' (see below).

MEMBERS*

Algeria	Eritrea	Nigeria
Angola	Ethiopia	Rwanda
Benin	Gabon	São Tomé and Príncipe
Botswana	The Gambia	
Burkina Faso	Ghana	Senegal
Burundi	Guinea	Seychelles
Cameroon	Guinea-Bissau	Sierra Leone
Cape Verde	Kenya	Somalia
Central African	Lesotho	South Africa

Republic	Liberia	Sudan
Chad	Libya	Swaziland
Comoros	Madagascar	Tanazania
Congo, Democratic Republic	Malawi	Togo
	Mali	Tunisia
Congo, Republic	Mauritania†	Uganda
Côte d'Ivoire	Mauritius	Zambia
Djibouti	Mozambique	Zimbabwe
Egypt	Namibia	
Equatorial Guinea	Niger	

* The Sahrawi Arab Democratic Republic (SADR–Western Sahara) was admitted to the OAU in February 1982, following recognition by more than one-half of the member states, but its membership was disputed by Morocco and other states which claimed that a two-thirds' majority was needed to admit a state whose existence was in question. Morocco withdrew from the OAU with effect from November 1985, and has not applied to join the AU. The SADR ratified the Constitutive Act in December 2000 and is a full member of the AU.

† In August 2005, following the overthrow of its elected Government in a military *coup d'état*, Mauritania's participation in the activities of the AU was suspended.

Note: The Constitutive Act stipulates that member states in which Governments accede to power by unconstitutional means are liable to suspension from participating in the Union's activities and to the imposition of sanctions by the Union.

Organization
(April 2008)

ASSEMBLY

The Assembly, comprising member countries' heads of state and government, is the supreme organ of the Union and meets at least once a year (with alternate sessions held in Addis Ababa, Ethiopia) to determine and monitor the Union's priorities and common policies and to adopt its annual work programme. Resolutions are passed by a two-thirds' majority, procedural matters by a simple majority. Extraordinary sessions may be convened at the request of a member state and on approval by a two-thirds' majority. A chairperson is elected at each meeting from among the members, to hold office for one year. The Assembly ensures compliance by member states with decisions of the Union, adopts the biennial budget, appoints judges of the African Court of Human and Peoples' Rights, and hears and settles disputes between member states. The first regular Assembly meeting was held in Durban, South Africa, in July 2002. A first extraordinary summit meeting of the Assembly was convened in Addis Ababa in February 2003. The 10th ordinary session of the Assembly was convened in Addis Ababa in January–February 2008.

Chairperson: (2008/09) JAKAYA KIKWETE (Pres. of Tanzania).

EXECUTIVE COUNCIL

Consists of ministers of foreign affairs and others and meets at least twice a year (in February and July), with provision for extraordinary sessions. The Council's Chairperson is the minister of foreign affairs (or another competent authority) of the country that has provided the Chairperson of the Assembly. Prepares meetings of, and is responsible to, the Assembly. Determines the issues to be submitted to the Assembly for decision, co-ordinates and harmonizes the policies, activities and initiatives of the Union in areas of common interest to member states, and monitors the implementation of policies and decisions of the Assembly.

PERMANENT REPRESENTATIVES COMMITTEE

The Committee, which comprises Ambassadors accredited to the AU and meets at least once a month. It is responsible to the Executive Council, which it advises, and whose meetings, including matters for the agenda and draft decisions, it prepares.

COMMISSION

The Commission is the permanent secretariat of the organization. It comprises a Chairperson (elected for a four-year term of office by the Assembly), Deputy Chairperson and eight Commissioners (responsible for: peace and security; political affairs; infrastructure and energy; social affairs; human resources, science and technology; trade and industry; rural economy and agriculture; and economic affairs) who are elected on the basis of equal geographical distribution. Members of the Commission serve a term of four years and may stand for re-election for one further term of office. Further support staff assist the smooth functioning of the Commission. The Commission represents the Union under the guidance of, and as mandated by, the Assembly and the Executive Council, and reports to the Executive Council. It deals with administrative issues, implements the decisions of the Union, and acts as the custodian of the Constitutive Act and Protocols, and other agreements. Its work covers the following domains: control of pandemics; disaster management; international crime and terrorism; environmental management; negotiations relating to external trade; negotiations relating to external debt; population, migration, refugees and displaced persons; food security; socio-economic integration; and all other areas where a common position has been established by Union member states. It has responsibility for the co-ordination of AU activities and meetings.

Chairperson: JEAN PING (Gabon).

SPECIALIZED TECHNICAL COMMITTEES

There are specialized committees for monetary and financial affairs; rural economy and agricultural matters; trade, customs and immigration matters; industry, science and technology, energy, natural resources and environment; transport, communications and tourism; health, labour and social affairs; and education, culture and human resources. These have responsibility for implementing the Union's programmes and projects.

PAN-AFRICAN PARLIAMENT

The Pan-African Parliament comprises five deputies (including at least one woman) from each AU member state, presided over by an elected President assisted by four Vice-Presidents. The President and Vice-Presidents must equitably represent the central, northern, eastern, southern and western African states. The Parliament convenes at least twice a year; an extraordinary session may be called by a two-thirds' majority of the members. The Parliament currently has only advisory and consultative powers. Its eventual evolution into an institution with full legislative authority is planned. The Parliament is headquartered at Midrand, South Africa.

President: Dr GERTRUDE MONGELA (Tanzania).

AFRICAN COURT OF JUSTICE

In May 2006 a Protocol to the African Charter on Human and People's Rights was finalized providing for the merger of the African Court on Human and People's Rights (endorsed by the OAU in June 1998) and the proposed African Court of Justice provided for in the Constitutive Act of African Union. In April 2008 a preparatory meeting of experts opened on drafting a Single Legal Instrument on the Merger of the African Court on Human and Peoples' Rights and of the Court of Justice.

PEACE AND SECURITY COUNCIL

The Protocol to the Constitutive Act of the African Union Relating to the Peace and Security Council of the African Union entered into force on 26 December 2003; the 15-member elected Council was formally inaugurated on 25 May 2004. It acts as a decision-making body for the prevention, management and resolution of conflicts.

ECONOMIC, SOCIAL AND CULTURAL COUNCIL

The Economic, Social and Cultural Council (ECOSOCC), inaugurated in March 2005, is to have an advisory function and to comprise representatives of civic, professional and cultural bodies at national, regional and diaspora levels. Its main organs are to be: an elected General Assembly; Standing Committee; Credential Committee; and Sectoral Cluster Communities. It is envisaged that the Council will strengthen the partnership between member governments and African civil society. Following ECOSOCC's inauguration a consultation process was launched for the eventual organization of elections to the planned General Assembly. Prior to the activation of the Assembly an interim elected Standing Committee was to hold office for a two-year period. The Sectoral Cluster Communities were to be established to formulate opinions and influence AU decision-making in the following 10 areas: peace and security; political affairs; infrastructure and energy; social affairs and health; human resources, science and technology; trade and industry; rural economy and agriculture; economic affairs; women and gender; and cross-cutting programmes.

PROPOSED INSTITUTIONS

In April 2008 three financial institutions, for managing the financing of programmes and projects, remained to be established: an African Central Bank, an African Monetary Fund, and an African Investment Bank.

Activities

From the 1950s various attempts were made to establish an inter-African organization. In November 1958 Ghana and Guinea (later joined by Mali) drafted a Charter that was to form the basis of a Union of African States. In January 1961 a conference was held at Casablanca, Morocco, attended by the heads of state of Ghana, Guinea, Mali, Morocco, and representatives of Libya and of the provisional government of the Algerian Republic (GPRA). Tunisia, Nigeria, Liberia and Togo declined the invitation to attend. An African Charter was adopted and it was decided to institute an African Military Command and an African Common Market. Between October 1960 and March 1961 three conferences were held by French-speaking African countries: at Abidjan, Côte d'Ivoire; Brazzaville, Republic of the Congo (ex-French); and Yaoundé, Cameroon. None of the 12 countries that attended these meetings had been present at the Casablanca Conference. These conferences led to the signing, in September 1961, at Tananarive, Madagascar, of a charter establishing the Union africaine et malgache, later the Organisation commune africaine et mauricienne (OCAM). In May 1961 a conference was held at Monrovia, Liberia, attended by the heads of state or representatives of 19 countries: Cameroon, Central African Republic, Chad, Congo Republic (ex-French), Côte d'Ivoire, Dahomey, Ethiopia, Gabon, Liberia, Madagascar, Mauritania, Niger, Nigeria, Senegal, Sierra Leone, Somalia, Togo, Tunisia and Upper Volta. Meeting again (with the exception of Tunisia and with the addition of the ex-Belgian Congo Republic) in January 1962 at Lagos, Nigeria, they established a permanent secretariat and a standing committee of finance ministers, and accepted a draft charter for an Organization of Inter-African and Malagasy States.

It was the Conference of Addis Ababa, convened in 1963, which finally brought together African states despite the regional, political and linguistic differences that divided them. The foreign ministers of 32 African states attended the Preparatory Meeting held in mid-May: Algeria, Burundi, Cameroon, Central African Republic, Chad, Congo (Brazzaville—now Republic of the Congo), Congo (Léopoldville—now Democratic Republic of the Congo), Côte d'Ivoire, Dahomey (now Benin), Ethiopia, Gabon, Ghana, Guinea, Liberia, Libya, Madagascar, Mali, Mauritania, Morocco, Niger, Nigeria, Rwanda, Senegal, Sierra Leone, Somalia, Sudan, Tanganyika (now Tanzania), Togo, Tunisia, Uganda, the United Arab Republic (Egypt) and Upper Volta (now Burkina Faso). The topics discussed by the meeting were: (i) the creation of an Organization of African States; (ii) co-operation among African states in the following fields: economic and social; education, culture and science; collective defence; (iii) decolonization; (iv) apartheid and racial discrimination; (v) the effects of economic grouping on the economic development of Africa; (vi) disarmament; (vii) the creation of a Permanent Conciliation Commission; and (viii) Africa and the United Nations. The Heads of State Conference that opened on 23 May 1963 drew up the Charter of the Organization of African Unity, which was then signed by the heads of 30 states on 25 May. The Charter was essentially functional and reflected a compromise between the concept of a loose association of states favoured by the Monrovia Group and the federal idea supported by the Casablanca Group, in particular by Ghana.

In May 1994 the Abuja Treaty Establishing the African Economic Community (AEC, signed in June 1991) entered into force. The formation of the Community was expected to be a gradual process, to be completed by 2028. An extraordinary summit meeting, convened in September 1999, in Sirte, Libya, at the request of the Libyan leader Col al-Qaddafi, determined to establish an African Union, based on the principles and objectives of the OAU and AEC, but furthering African co-operation, development and integration. Heads of state declared their commitment to accelerating the establishment of regional institutions, including a pan-African parliament, a court of human and peoples' rights and a central bank, as well as the implementation of economic and monetary union, as provided for by the Abuja Treaty Establishing the AEC. In July 2000 at the annual OAU summit meeting, held at Lomé, Togo, 27 heads of state and government signed the draft Constitutive Act of the African Union, which was to enter into force one month after ratification by two-thirds of member states' legislatures; this was achieved on 26 May 2001. The Union was inaugurated, replacing the OAU, on 9 July 2002, at a summit meeting of heads of state and government held in Durban, South Africa, after a transitional period of one year had elapsed since the endorsement of the Act in July 2001. During the transitional year, pending the transfer of all assets and liabilities to the Union, the OAU Charter remained in effect. A review of all OAU treaties was implemented, and those deemed relevant were retained by the AU. The four key organs of the AU were launched in July 2002. Morocco is the only African country that is not a member of the AU. The AU aims to strengthen and advance the process of African political and socio-economic integration initiated by the OAU. The Union operates on the basis of both the Constitutive Act and the Abuja Treaty. It is envisaged that the process of implementing the Abuja Treaty will be accelerated.

The AU has the following areas of interest: peace and security; political affairs; infrastructure and energy; social affairs; human resources, science and technology; trade and industry; rural economy and agriculture; and economic affairs. In July 2001 the OAU adopted a New African Initiative, which was subsequently renamed the New Partnership for Africa's Development (NEPAD, see below). NEPAD, which was officially launched in October, represents a long-term strategy for socio-economic recovery in Africa and aims to promote the strengthening of democracy and economic management in the region. The heads of state of Algeria, Egypt, Nigeria, Senegal and South Africa played leading roles in its preparation and management. In June 2002 NEPAD heads of state and government adopted a Declaration on Democracy, Political, Economic and Corporate Governance and announced the development of an African Peer Review Mechanism (APRM—whose secretariat was to be hosted by the UN Economic Commission for Africa). Meeting during that month the Group of Seven industrialized nations and Russia (the G-8) welcomed the formation of NEPAD and adopted an Africa Action Plan in support of the initiative. NEPAD is ultimately answerable to the AU Assembly. The inaugural summit of the Assembly, held in Durban, South Africa, in July 2002, issued a Declaration on the Implementation of NEPAD, which urged all member states to adopt the Declaration on Democracy, Political, Economic and Corporate Governance and to participate in the peer-review process. By March 2008 some 29 nations had agreed to participate in the APRM. NEPAD focuses on the following sectoral priorities: infrastructure (covering information and communication technologies, energy, transport, water and sanitation), human resources development, agriculture, culture, science and technology, mobilizing resources, market access and the environment. It implements action plans concerned with capacity-building, the environment, and infrastructure. The summit meeting of the AU Assembly convened in Maputo, Mozambique in July 2003 determined that NEPAD should be integrated into AU structures and processes. In March 2007 a special NEPAD summit held in Algiers, Algeria, on the theme *Brainstorming on NEPAD*, issued a 13-point communiqué on the best means of achieving this objective without delay.

The eighth AU Assembly, held in January 2007 in Cairo, Egypt, adopted a decision on the need for a *Grand Debate on the Union Government*, concerned with the possibility of establishing an AU Government as a precursor to the eventual creation of a United States of Africa. The ninth Assembly, convened in July 2007 in Accra, Ghana, adopted the Accra Declaration, in which AU heads of state and government expressed commitment to the formation of a Union Government of Africa and ultimate aim of creating a United States of Africa, and pledged, as a means to this end, to accelerate the economic and political integration of the African continent; to rationalize, strengthen and harmonize the activities of the regional economic communities; to conduct an immediate audit of the organs of the AU ('Audit of the Union'); and to establish a ministerial committee to examine the concept of the Union Government. A panel of eminent persons was subsequently established to conduct the proposed institutional Audit of the Union; the panel became operational at the beginning of September, and presented its review to the 10th Assembly, which was held in January–February 2008 in Addis Ababa. A committee comprising 10 heads of state was appointed to consider the findings detailed in the review and to report on these to the 11th Assembly, scheduled to be held in Cairo in July 2008.

In March 2005 the UN Secretary-General issued a report on the functioning of the United Nations which included a clause urging donor nations to focus particularly on the need for a 10-year plan for capacity-building within the AU.

PEACE AND SECURITY

The Protocol to the Constitutive Act of the African Union Relating to the Establishment of the Peace and Security Council, adopted by the inaugural AU summit of heads of state and government in July 2002, entered into force in December 2003, superseding the 1993 Cairo Declaration on the OAU Mechanism for Conflict Prevention, Management and Resolution. The Protocol provides for the inauguration of an AU collective security and early warning mechanism, comprising a 15-country Peace and Security Council, operational at the levels of heads of state and government, ministers of foreign affairs, and permanent representatives, to be supported by a five-member advisory Panel of the Wise, a Continental Early Warning System, an African Standby Force and a Peace Fund (superseding the OAU Peace Fund, which was established in June 1993). In March 2004 the Executive Council elected 15 member states to serve on the inaugural Peace and Security Council. The activities of the Peace and Security Council were to include the promotion of peace, security and stability; early warning and preventive diplomacy; peace-making mediation; peace support operations and intervention; peace-building activities and post-conflict reconstruction; and humanitarian action and disaster management. The Council was to ensure the common defence policy of the Union, and to ensure the implementation of the 1999 OAU Convention on the Prevention and Combating of Terrorism (which provided for the exchange of information to help counter terrorism and for signatory states to refrain from granting asylum to terrorists). Member states were to set aside standby troop contingents for the planned African Standby Force, which was to be mandated to undertake observation, monitoring and other peace-support missions; to deploy in member states as required to prevent the resurgence or escalation of violence; to intervene in member states as required to restore stability; to conduct post-conflict disarmament and demobilization and other peace-building activities; and to provide emergency humanitarian assistance. The Council was to harmonize and co-ordinate the activities of other regional security mechanisms. An extraordinary AU summit meeting, convened in Sirte, Libya, in February 2004, adopted a declaration approving the establishment of the multinational African Standby Force, which was to comprise five regional brigades and to be fully operational by 2010. A Policy Framework Document on the establishment of the African Standby Force and the Military Staff Committee, adopted in May 2003 by the third meeting of the African chiefs of defence staff, was approved by the third regular summit of AU heads of state, held in July 2004.

The extraordinary OAU summit meeting convened in Sirte, Libya, in September 1999 determined to hold a regular ministerial Conference on Security, Stability, Development and Co-operation in Africa (CSSDCA): the first CSSDCA took place in Abuja, Nigeria, in May 2000. The CSSDCA process provides a forum for the development of policies aimed at advancing the common values of the AU and AEC in the areas of peace, security and co-operation. In December 2000 OAU heads of state and government adopted the Bamako Declaration, concerned with arresting the circulation of small arms on the continent.

In May 2003 the AU, UNDP and UN Office for Project Services agreed a US $6.4m. project entitled 'Support for the Implementation of the Peace and Security Agenda of the African Union'. In June of that year a meeting of the G-8 and NEPAD adopted a Joint Africa/G-8 Plan to enhance African capabilities to undertake Peace Support Operations. Within the framework of the Plan, a consultation between the AU, the NEPAD Secretariat, the G-8, the African regional economic communities, as well as the European Union (EU) and UN and other partners, was convened in Addis Ababa in April 2005. In September 2002 and October 2003 the AU organized high-level intergovernmental meetings on preventing and combating terrorism in Africa. An AU Special Representative on Protection of Civilians in Armed Conflict Situations in Africa was appointed in September 2004.

In January 2005 the African Union Non-Aggression and Common Defence Pact was adopted to promote co-operation in developing a common defence policy and to encourage member states to foster an attitude of non-aggression. The Pact establishes measures aimed at preventing inter-and intra-state conflicts and arriving at peaceful resolutions to conflicts. It also sets out a framework defining, *inter alia*, the terms 'aggression' and 'intervention' and determining those situations in which intervention may be considered an acceptable course of action. As such, the Pact stipulates that an act, or threat, of aggression against an individual member state is to be considered an act, or threat, of aggression against all members states.

In recent years the OAU/AU has been involved in peace-making and peace-building activities in several African countries and regions.

In April 2003 the AU authorized the establishment of a 3,500-member African Mission in Burundi (AMIB) to oversee the implementation of cease-fire accords in that country, support the disarmament and demobilization of former combatants, and ensure favourable conditions for the deployment of a future UN peace-keeping presence. In June 2004 AMIB was terminated and its troops 'rehatted' as participants in the newly-authorized UN Operation in Burundi (ONUB).

The July 2003 Maputo Assembly determined to establish a post-conflict reconstruction ministerial committee on Sudan. The first meeting of the committee, convened in March 2004, resolved to dispatch an AU team of experts to southern Sudan to compile a preliminary assessment of that region's post-conflict requirements; this was undertaken in late June. In early April, meeting in N'Djamena, Chad, the Sudan Government and other Sudanese parties signed, under AU auspices, a Humanitarian Cease-fire Agreement providing for the establishment of an AU-led Cease-fire Commission and for the deployment of an AU military observer mission (the AU Mission in the Sudan—AMIS) to the western Sudanese region of Darfur, where widespread violent unrest (including reportedly systematic attacks on the indigenous civilian population by pro-government militias), resulting in a grave humanitarian crisis, had prevailed since early 2003. Following the adoption in late May 2004 of an accord on the modalities for the implementation of the Humanitarian Cease-fire Agreement (also providing for the future deployment of an armed protection force as an additional component of AMIS, as requested by a recent meeting of the Peace and Security Council), the Cease-fire Commission was inaugurated at the end of that month and, at the beginning of June, the Commission's head-quarters were opened in El-Fasher, Sudan; some 60 AMIS military observers were dispatched to the headquarters during that month. In early July the AU Assembly agreed to increase the strength of AMIS to 80 observers. From mid-2004 the AU mediated negotiations between the parties to the conflict in Darfur on the achievement of a comprehensive peace agreement. AMIS's military component, agreed in May 2004, initially comprising 310 troops from Nigeria and Rwanda and mandated to monitor the cease-fire and protect the Mission, began to be deployed in mid-August. In October the Peace and Security Council decided to expand AMIS into a full peace-keeping operation, eventually to comprise 3,300 troops, police and civilian support staff. The mission's mandate was enhanced to include promoting increased compliance by all parties with the cease-fire agreement and helping with the process of confidence-building; responsibility for monitoring compliance with any subsequent agreements; assisting IDP and refugee returns; and contributing to the improvement of the security situation throughout Darfur. In April 2005 the Peace and Security Council authorized the further enhancement of AMIS to comprise, by the end of September, some 6,171 military personnel, including up to 1,560 civilian police personnel. A pledging conference for the mission, convened in April, resulted in commitments from AU partners and some member states totalling US $291.6m.; the promised funding included $77.4m. from the EU and $50m. from the USA. In March 2006 the Peace and Security Council agreed, in principle, to support the transformation of AMIS into a UN operation. In late March Arab League heads of state agreed to provide funding for the AU force to remain operational and voted to support Sudanese opposition to the deployment of non-African peace-keeping troops. In late April, following talks in Abuja, Nigeria, AU mediators submitted a proposed peace agreement to representatives of the Sudanese Government and rebel groups; the so-called Darfur Peace Agreement (DPA) was signed on 5 May by the Sudanese Government and the main rebel grouping (the Sudan Liberation Movement).

In August 2006 the UN Security Council expanded the mandate of UNMIS to provide for its deployment to Darfur, in order to enforce a cease-fire and support the implementation of DPA. The Council also requested the UN Secretary-General to devise jointly with the AU, in consultation with the parties to the DPA, a plan and schedule for a transition from AMIS to a sole UN operation in Darfur. The Sudanese Government, however, initially rejected the concept of an expanded UN peace-keeping mission, on the grounds that it would compromise national sovereignty. Eventually, in late December, the UN, AU and Sudanese Government established a tripartite mechanism which was to facilitate the implementation of a UN-formulated three-phase approach, endorsed by the AU Peace and Security Council in November, that would culminate in a hybrid AU/UN mission in Darfur. In January 2007 UNMIS provided AMIS with supplies and extra personnel under the first ('light') phase of the approach; the second ('heavy') phase, finalized in that month, was to involve the delivery of force enablers, police units, civilian personnel and mission support items. UNMIS continued to make efforts to engage the non-signatories of the DPA in the political process in Darfur. In June the AU and UN special representatives for Darfur defined a political 'road map' to lead eventually to full negotiations in support of a peaceful settlement to the sub-regional conflict. In August the first AU/UN-chaired 'pre-negotiation' discussions with those rebel groups in Darfur that were not party to the DPA approved an agreement on co-operation in attempting to secure a settlement.

In June 2007 the Sudanese Government agreed to support unconditionally the deployment of the Hybrid UN/AU Operation in Darfur (UNAMID); UNAMID was authorized by the UN Security Council in the following month, with a mandated force ceiling of up to 26,000 troops and police officers, supported by 5,000 international and local civilian staff. UNAMID was scheduled to have its management, command and control structures in place by October and assume command of AMIS at the end of the year. A Joint Support Co-ordination Mechanism (JSCM) in Addis Ababa, comprising liaison officers and equipment, was to ensure effective consultation between UN and AU headquarters. By February 2008 UNAMID had absorbed 1,380 police officers from AMIS. It was reported in that month that the UN and AU were finalizing an exchange of letters defining their partnership with regard to UNAMID. In December 2007 UNAMID, UNMIS and the AU-UN Joint Mediation Support Team for Darfur (JMST) formed a joint task force to recommend policies and mechanisms for enhancing co-operation. UNAMID's operational strength in March 2008 totalled 7,372 troops, 137 military observers and 1,704 police officers. UNAMID was being led by a joint AU/UN envoy, Rodolphe Adada.

Meeting in January 2006 the Peace and Security Council accepted in principle the future deployment of an AU Peace Support Mission in Somalia, with a mandate to support that member country's transitional federal institutions; meanwhile, it was envisaged that an IGAD peace support mission (IGASOM, approved by IGAD in January 2005 and endorsed by that month's AU summit) would be stationed in Somalia. In mid-March 2006 the IGAD Assembly reiterated its support for the deployment of IGASOM, and urged the UN Security Council to grant an exemption to the UN arms embargo applied to Somalia in order to facilitate the regional peace support initiative. At a consultative meeting on the removal of the arms embargo, convened in mid-April, in Nairobi, Kenya, representatives of the Somali transitional federal authorities presented for consideration by the AU and IGAD a draft national security and stabilization plan. It was agreed that a detailed mission plan should be formulated to underpin the proposed AU/IGAD peace missions. In January 2007 the Peace and Security Council authorized the deployment of the AU Mission in Somalia (AMISOM), in place of the proposed IGASOM. AMISOM was to be deployed for an initial period of six months, with a mandate to contribute to the political stabilization of Somalia. It was envisaged that AMISOM would evolve into a UN operation focusing on the post-conflict restoration of Somalia. In the following month the UN Security Council endorsed AMISOM and proposed that it should eventually be superseded by such a UN operation. AMISOM became operational in May 2007.

In February 2008 the AU welcomed the efforts of African leaders, including the outgoing Chairman of the AU Assembly, President Kufuor of Ghana, and the former UN Secretary-General, Kofi Annan, to secure a peaceful outcome to the political crisis and violent unrest that had erupted in Kenya following the disputed outcome of a presidential election staged in December 2007. In March 2008 the Pan-African Parliament sent an observer mission to monitor the legislative and presidential elections that were held concurrently in Zimbabwe.

The EU assists the AU financially in the areas of peace and security; institutional development; governance; and regional economic integration and trade. In June 2004 the European Commission activated for the first time its newly-established Africa Peace Facility (APF), which was endowed with €250m. during 2004–07. The EU replenished the APF with a further €300m. in May 2007 to cover the period 2008–10. Since October 2007 APF and UN funding have jointly financed the deployment of UNAMID.

INFRASTRUCTURE, ENERGY AND THE ENVIRONMENT

Meeting in Lomé, Togo, in July 2001, OAU heads of state and government authorized the establishment of an African Energy Commission (AFREC), with the aim of increasing co-operation in energy matters between Africa and other regions. AFREC was launched in February 2008. It was envisaged at that time that an African Electrotechnical Standardization Commission (AFSEC) would also become operational, as a subsidiary body of AFREC.

In 1964 the OAU adopted a Declaration on the Denuclearization of Africa, and in April 1996 it adopted the African Nuclear Weapons Free Zone Treaty (also known as the 'Pelindaba Treaty'), which identifies Africa as a nuclear weapons-free zone and promotes co-operation in the peaceful uses of nuclear energy.

In 1968 OAU member states adopted the African Convention on the Conservation of Nature and Natural Resources. The Bamako Convention on the Ban of the Import into Africa and the Control of Transboundary Movement and Management of Hazardous Wastes within Africa was adopted by OAU member states in 1991 and entered into force in April 1998.

In February 2007 the first Conference of African Ministers responsible for Maritime Transport was convened to discuss maritime transport policy in the region. A draft declaration was submitted at the Conference, held in Abuja, Nigeria, outlining the AU's vision for a common maritime transport policy aimed at 'linking Africa' and detailing programmes for co-operation on maritime safety and security and the development of an integrated transport infrastructure. The subsequently adopted Abuja Maritime Transport Declaration formally provided for an annual meeting of maritime transport ministers, to be hosted by each region in turn in a rotational basis.

POLITICAL AND SOCIAL AFFAIRS

The African Charter on Human and People's Rights, which was adopted by the OAU in 1981 and entered into force in October 1986, provided for the establishment of an 11-member African Commission on Human and People's Rights, based in Banjul, The Gambia. A Protocol to the Charter, establishing an African Court of People's and Human Rights, was adopted by the OAU Assembly of Heads of State in June 1998 and entered into force in January 2004. In April 2008 a preparatory meeting of experts opened on elaborating a draft Single Legal Instrument on the Merger of the African Court on Human and Peoples' Rights and of the Court of Justice provided for in the Constitutive Act of the AU; a Protocol relating to this merger had been finalized in May 2006. A further Protocol, relating to the Rights of Women, was adopted by the July 2003 Maputo Assembly. The African Charter on the Rights and Welfare of the Child was opened for signature in July 1990 and entered into force in November 1999. A Protocol to the Abuja Treaty Establishing the AEC relating to the Pan-African Parliament, adopted by the OAU in March 2001, entered into force in December 2003. The Parliament was inaugurated in March 2004 and was, initially, to exercise advisory and consultative powers only, although its eventual evolution into an institution with full legislative powers is envisaged. In March 2005 the advisory Economic, Social and Cultural Council was inaugurated.

The July 2002 inaugural summit meeting of AU heads of state and government adopted a Declaration Governing Democratic Elections in Africa, providing guide-lines for the conduct of national elections in member states and outlining the AU's electoral observation and monitoring role. In March an OAU observer team found the Zimbabwean presidential election, held in controversial circumstances during that month, to have been conducted freely and fairly. In April 2003 the AU Commission and the South African Independent Electoral Commission jointly convened an African Conference on Elections, Democracy and Governance, in Pretoria, South Africa. In recent years several large population displacements have occurred in Africa, mainly as a result of violent conflict. In 1969 OAU member states adopted the Convention Governing the Specific Aspects of Refugee Problems in Africa, which entered into force in June 1974 and had been ratified by 45 states at April 2008. The Convention promotes close co-operation with UNHCR. The AU maintains a Special Refugee Contingency Fund to provide relief assistance and to support repatriation activities, education projects, etc., for displaced people in Africa. The AU aims to address pressing health issues affecting member states, including the eradication of endemic parasitic and infectious diseases and improving access to medicines. An African Summit on HIV/AIDS, TB and other related Infectious Diseases was convened, under OAU auspices, in Abuja in March 2001 and, in May 2006, an AU Special Summit on HIV/AIDS. TB and Malaria was convened, also in Abuja, to review the outcomes of the 2000 Summit. The theme of the 2006 Special Summit was Universal Access to HIV/AIDS, TB and Malaria Services by 2010, and it adopted the Abuja Call for Accelerated Action on HIV/AIDS, TB and Malaria. An AU Scientific, Technical and Research Commission is based in Lagos, Nigeria, and a Centre for Linguistic and Historical Studies by Oral Tradition is based in Niamey, Niger.

The seventh AU summit, convened in Banjul, The Gambia, in July 2006, adopted the African Youth Charter, providing for the implementation of youth policies and strategies across Africa, with the aim of encouraging young African people to participate in the development of the region and to take advantage of increasing opportunities in education and employment. The Charter outlined the basic rights and responsibilities of youths, which were divided into four main categories: youth participation; education and skills development; sustainable livelihoods; and health and wellbeing. The Charter also details the obligations of member states towards young people. The AU designated 2008 as the Year of African Youth.

In December 2007 the AU adopted a plan of action on drug control and crime prevention covering the period 2007–12, and determined to establish a follow-up mechanism to monitor and evaluate implementation of the plan.

TRADE, INDUSTRY AND ECONOMIC CO-OPERATION

In October 1999 a conference on Industrial Partnerships and Investment in Africa was held in Dakar, Senegal, jointly organized by the OAU with UNIDO, the ECA, the African Development Bank and the Alliance for Africa's Industrialization. In June 1997 the first meeting between ministers of the OAU and the EU was convened in New York, USA. In April 2000 the first EU–Africa summit of heads of state and government was held in Cairo, under the auspices of the EU and OAU. The summit adopted the Cairo Plan of Action, which addressed areas including economic integration, trade and investment, private-sector development in Africa, human rights and good governance, peace and security, and development issues such as education, health and food security. The second EU–Africa summit meeting was initially to have been held in April 2003 but was postponed, owing to disagreements concerning the participation of President Mugabe of Zimbabwe, against whom the EU had imposed sanctions. More than 200 business representatives participated in an AU Business Summit, convened in July 2002, in Durban, South Africa, alongside the inaugural AU summit of heads of state and government. In February 2007 the EU and the AU began a period of consultation on a joint EU-Africa Strategy, the first to develop a long-term vision of the future partnership between the two parties. The strategy was adopted by the second EU-Africa Summit, which was convened, finally, in December 2007, in Lisbon, Portugal (with participation by President Mugabe).

The AU aims to reduce obstacles to intra-African trade and to reverse the continuing disproportionate level of trade conducted by many African countries with their former colonial powers. In June 2005 an AU conference of Ministers of Trade was convened, in Cairo, to discuss issues relating to the development of Trade in Africa, particularly in the context of the World Trade Organization's (WTO) Doha Work Programme. The outcome of the meeting was the adoption of the Cairo Road-Map on the Doha Work Programme, which addressed several important issues including the import,

INTERNATIONAL ORGANIZATIONS

African Union

export and market access of agricultural and non-agricultural commodities, development issues and trade facilitation.

In June 1991 the OAU Assembly of Heads of State signed the Abuja Treaty Establishing the African Economic Community (AEC). The Treaty was to enter into force after ratification by two-thirds of member states. The Community was to be established by 2028, following a gradual six-phase process involving the co-ordination, harmonization and progressive integration of the activities of all existing and future sub-regional economic unions. (There are 14 so-called 'regional economic communities', or RECs, in Africa, including the following major RECs that are regarded as the five pillars, or building blocks, of the AEC: the Common Market for Eastern and Southern Africa—COMESA, the Communauté économique des états de l'Afrique centrale—CEEAC, the Economic Community of West African States—ECOWAS, the Southern African Development Community—SADC, and the Union of the Arab Maghreb. The subsidiary RECs are: the Communauté économique et monétaire de l'Afrique centrale—CEMAC, the Community of Sahel-Saharan States—CEN-SAD, the East African Community—EAC, the Economic Community of the Great Lakes Countries, the Intergovernmental Authority on Development—IGAD, the Indian Ocean Commission—IOC, the Mano River Union, the Southern African Customs Union, and the Union économique et monétaire ouest-africaine—UEMOA.) The Abuja Treaty entered into force on 12 May 1994, having been ratified by the requisite number of OAU member states. The inaugural meeting of the AEC took place in June 1997. In July 2007 the ninth AU Assembly adopted a Protocol on Relations between the African Union and the RECs, aimed at facilitating the harmonization of policies and ensuring compliance with the schedule of the Abuja Treaty.

In February 2008 the AU Assembly endorsed an action plan on the industrial development of Africa that had been adopted in September 2007 by the first extraordinary session of the Conference of African Ministers of Industry.

RURAL ECONOMY AND AGRICULTURE

In July 2003 the second Assembly of heads of state and government adopted a Declaration on Agriculture and Food Security in Africa, focusing on the need to revitalize the agricultural sector and to combat hunger on the continent by developing food reserves based on African production. The leaders determined to deploy policies and budgetary resources to remove current constraints on agricultural production, trade and rural development; and to implement the Comprehensive Africa Agriculture Programme (CAADP), which had been developed by NEPAD and FAO in 2002–03. The CAADP focused on increasing investment in the areas of water management, rural infrastructure, programmes to increase productivity, and capacity development for market access; and also on means of addressing emergencies, and the advancement of research and technology. The heads of state and government agreed that, by 2008/09, at least 10% of national budgets should be allocated to agriculture and rural development.

In December 2006 AU leaders convened at a Food Security Summit in Abuja adopted a declaration of commitment to increasing intra-African trade by promoting and protecting as strategic commodities at the continental level cotton, legumes, maize, oil palm, rice and beef, dairy, fisheries and poultry products; and promoting and protecting as strategic commodities at the sub-regional level cassava, sorghum and millet. The AU leaders also declared a commitment to initiating the implementation of the NEPAD Home-grown School Feeding Project, the African Regional Nutrition Strategy, the NEPAD African Nutrition Initiative, and the NEPAD 10-Year Strategy for Combating Vitamin and Mineral Deficiency.

The AU's Programme for the Control of Epizootics (PACE) has co-operated with FAO to combat the further spread of the Highly Pathogenic Avian Influenza (H5N1) virus, outbreaks of which were reported in poultry in several West African countries in the mid-2000s; joint activities have included establishing a regional network of laboratories and surveillance teams and organizing regional workshops on H5N1 control.

HUMANITARIAN RESPONSE

In December 2005 a ministerial conference on disaster reduction in Africa, organized by the AU Commission, adopted a programme of action for the implementation of the Africa Regional Strategy for Disaster Risk Reduction (2006–10), formulated in the context of the Hyogo Framework of Action for the period 2005–15 that was agreed by 168 countries at the World Conference on Disaster Reduction held in Kobe, Japan in January 2005.

Finance

The AU inherited more than US $50m. in debts owed by member states to the OAU. Some 75% of the AU's budget is financed by contributions from Algeria, Egypt, Libya, Nigeria and South Africa.

Specialized Agencies

African Accounting Council: POB 11223, Kinshasa, Democratic Republic of the Congo; tel. (12) 33567; f. 1979; provides assistance to institutions in member countries on standardization of accounting; promotes education, further training and research in accountancy and related areas of study; publ. *Information and Liaison Bulletin* (every two months).

African Civil Aviation Commission (AFCAC): 15 blvd de la République, BP 2356, Dakar, Senegal; tel. 893-93-73; fax 823-26-61; e-mail cafac@telecomplus.sn; internet www.afcac-cafac.sn; f. 1969 to co-ordinate civil aviation matters in Africa and to co-operate with ICAO and other relevant civil aviation bodies; promotes the development of the civil aviation industry in Africa in accordance with provisions of the 1991 Abuja Treaty; fosters the application of ICAO Standards and Recommended Practices; examines specific problems that might hinder the development and operation of the African civil aviation industry; 46 mem states; promotes co-ordination and better utilization and development of African air transport systems and the standardization of aircraft, flight equipment and training programmes for pilots and mechanics; organizes working groups and seminars, and compiles statistics; Pres. TSHEPO PEEGE (South Africa); Sec. CHARLES MAURICE DIOP.

African Telecommunications Union (ATU): ATU Secretariat, POB 35282 Nairobi, 00200 Kenya; tel. (20) 4453308; fax (20) 4453359; e-mail sg@atu-uat.org; internet www.atu-uat.org; f. 1999 as successor to Pan-African Telecommunications Union (f. 1977); promotes the rapid development of information communications in Africa, with the aim of making Africa an equal participant in the global information society; works towards universal service and access and full inter-country connectivity; promotes development and adoption of appropriate policies and regulatory frameworks; promotes financing of development; encourages co-operation between members and the exchange of information; advocates the harmonization of telecommunications policies; 46 national mems, 16 associate mems comprising fixed and mobile telecoms operators; Sec.-Gen. AKOSSI AKOSSI.

Pan-African Institution of Education for Development (PIED): 29 ave de la Justice, BP 1764, Kinshasa I, Democratic Republic of the Congo; tel. (12) 34527; e-mail baseeduc@hotmail.com; f. 1973, became specialized agency in 1986, present name adopted 2001; undertakes educational research and training, focuses on co-operation and problem-solving, acts as an observatory for education; publs *Bulletin d'Information* (quarterly), *Revue africaine des sciences de l'éducation* (2 a year), *Répertoire africain des institutions de recherche* (annually).

Pan-African News Agency (PANAPRESS): BP 4056, ave Bourjuiba, Dakar, Senegal; tel. 824-13-95; fax 824-13-90; e-mail marketing@panapress.com; internet www.panapress.com; f. 1979 as PanAfrican News Agency, restructured under current name in 1997; regional headquarters in Khartoum, Sudan; Lusaka, Zambia; Kinshasa, Democratic Republic of the Congo; Lagos, Nigeria; Tripoli, Libya; began operations in May 1983, restructured in late 1990s; receives information from national news agencies and circulates news in Arabic, English, French and Portuguese; Dir-Gen. BABACAR FALL; publs *Press Review*, *In-Focus*.

Pan-African Postal Union (PAPU): POB 6026, Arusha, Tanzania; tel. (27) 2508604; fax (27) 2508606; e-mail sg@papu.co.tz; internet www.upap-papu.org; f. 1980 to extend members' co-operation in the improvement of postal services; 43 mem. countries; Sec.-Gen. JILANI BEN HADDADA; publ. *PAPU News*.

Pan-African Railways Union: BP 687, Kinshasa, Democratic Republic of the Congo; tel. (12) 23861; f. 1972 to standardize, expand, co-ordinate and improve members' railway services; the ultimate aim is to link all systems; main organs: Gen. Assembly, Exec. Bd, Gen. Secr., five tech. cttees; mems in 30 African countries.

Supreme Council for Sports in Africa: BP 1363, Yaoundé, Cameroon; tel. and fax 23-95-80; f. 1965; Sec.-Gen. SONSTONE KASHIBA; publs *SCSA News* (6 a year), *African Sports Movement Directory* (annually).

ASSOCIATED PARTNERSHIP

New Partnership for Africa's Development (NEPAD): POB 1234, Halfway House, Midrand, 1685 South Africa; tel. (11) 313-3716; fax (11) 313-3684; e-mail africam@nepad.org; internet www

.nepad.org; f. 2001 as a long-term strategy to promote socio-economic development in Africa; adopted Declaration on Democracy, Political, Economic and Corporate Governance and the African Peer Review Mechanism in June 2002; heads of state implementation cttee comprises representatives of 20 countries (four from each of the AU's five regions: northern, eastern, southern, western and central); steering cttee, comprising Algeria, Egypt, Nigeria, Senegal and South Africa, meets once a month; the UN allocated US $11.2m. in support of NEPAD under its 2008–09 budget; the July 2003 AU Maputo summit decided that NEPAD should be integrated into AU structures and processes; this process was ongoing in 2008; Exec. Head of Secretariat (vacant).

ANDEAN COMMUNITY OF NATIONS
(COMUNIDAD ANDINA DE NACIONES—CAN)

Address: Paseo de la República 3895, San Isidro, Lima 27; Apdo 18-1177, Lima 18, Peru.
Telephone: (1) 4111400; **fax:** (1) 2213329; **e-mail:** contacto@comunidadandina.org; **internet:** www.comunidadandina.org.

The organization was established in 1969 as the Acuerdo de Cartagena (the Cartagena Agreement), also referred to as the Grupo Andino (Andean Group) or the Pacto Andino (Andean Pact). In March 1996 member countries signed a Reform Protocol of the Cartagena Agreement, in accordance with which the Andean Group was superseded in August 1997 by the Andean Community of Nations (CAN, generally referred to as the Andean Community). The Andean Community was to promote greater economic, commercial and political integration within a new Andean Integration System (Sistema Andino de Integración), comprising the organization's bodies and institutions. The Community covers an area of 4,710,000 sq km, with some 115m. inhabitants.

MEMBERS
Bolivia   Colombia   Ecuador   Peru

Note: Argentina, Brazil, Chile, Paraguay and Uruguay are associate members of the Community. Mexico and Panama have observer status. Venezuela withdrew from the Community in April 2006.

Organization
(April 2008)

ANDEAN PRESIDENTIAL COUNCIL
The presidential summits, which had been held annually since 1989, were formalized under the 1996 Reform Protocol of the Cartagena Agreement as the Andean Presidential Council. The Council is the highest-level body of the Andean Integration System, and provides the political leadership of the Community.

COMMISSION
The Commission consists of a plenipotentiary representative from each member country, with each country holding the presidency in turn. The Commission is the main policy-making organ of the Andean Community, and is responsible for co-ordinating Andean trade policy.

COUNCIL OF FOREIGN MINISTERS
The Council of Foreign Ministers meets annually or whenever it is considered necessary, to formulate common external policy and to co-ordinate the process of integration.

GENERAL SECRETARIAT
In August 1997 the General Secretariat assumed the functions of the Board of the Cartagena Agreement. The General Secretariat is the body charged with implementation of all guide-lines and decisions issued by the bodies listed above. It submits proposals to the Commission for facilitating the fulfilment of the Community's objectives. Members are appointed for a three-year term. Under the reforms agreed in March 1996 the Secretary-General is elected by the Council of Foreign Ministers for a five-year term, and has enhanced powers to adjudicate in disputes arising between member states, as well as to manage the sub-regional integration process. There are three Directors-General.
Secretary-General: Dr FREDDY EHLERS ZURITA (Ecuador).

PARLIAMENT
Parlamento Andino: Avda 13, No. 70–61, Bogotá, Colombia; tel. (1) 217-3357; fax (1) 348-2805; e-mail correo@parlamentoandino.org; internet www.parlamentoandino.org; f. 1979; comprises five members from each country, and meets in each capital city in turn; makes recommendations on regional policy; in April 1997 a new protocol was adopted which provided for the election of members by direct and universal voting; Pres. IVONNE BAKI.

COURT OF JUSTICE
Tribunal de Justicia de la Comunidad Andina: 33-65, Calle Augusto Egas y Bosmediano, Sector Bella-Vista, Quito, Ecuador; tel. (22) 446448; fax (22) 2922462; e-mail tjca@tribunalandino.org.ec; internet www.tribunalandino.org.ec; f. 1979, began operating in 1984; a protocol approved in May 1996 (which came into force in August 1999) modified the Court's functions; its main responsibilities are to resolve disputes among member countries and interpret community legislation; comprises one judge from each member country, appointed for a renewable period of six years; the Presidency is assumed annually by each judge in turn.

Activities

In May 1979, at Cartagena, Colombia, the Presidents of the then five member countries signed the 'Mandate of Cartagena', which envisaged greater economic and political co-operation, including the establishment of more sub-regional development programmes (especially in industry). In May 1989 the Group undertook to revitalize the process of Andean integration, by withdrawing measures that obstructed the programme of trade liberalization, and by complying with tariff reductions that had already been agreed upon. In May 1991, in Caracas, Venezuela, a summit meeting of the Andean Group agreed the framework for the establishment of a free trade area on 1 January 1992 (achieved in February 1993) and for an eventual Andean common market.

In March 1996 heads of state, meeting in Trujillo, Peru, agreed to a substantial restructuring of the Andean Group. The heads of state signed the Reform Protocol of the Cartagena Agreement, providing for the establishment of the Andean Community of Nations, which was to have greater ambitious economic and political objectives. Consequently, in August 1997 the Andean Community was inaugurated, and the Group's Junta was replaced by a new General Secretariat, headed by a Secretary-General with enhanced executive and decision-making powers. The initiation of these reforms was designed to accelerate harmonization in economic matters. In April 1997 the Peruvian Government announced its intention to withdraw from the Cartagena Agreement, owing to disagreements about the terms of Peru's full integration into the Community's trading system. Later in that month the heads of state of the four other members attended a summit meeting, in Sucre, Bolivia, and reiterated their commitment to strengthening regional integration. A high-level group of representatives was established to pursue negotiations with Peru regarding its future relationship with the Community (agreement was reached in June—see below). In January 2002 a special Andean presidential summit, held in Santa Cruz, Bolivia, reiterated the objective of creating a common market and renewing efforts to strengthen sub-regional integration, including the adoption of a common agricultural policy and the standardization of macroeconomic policies.

In June 2002 ministers of defence and of foreign affairs of the Andean Community approved an Andean Charter for Peace and Security, establishing principles and commitments for the formulation of a policy on sub-regional security, the establishment of a zone of peace, joint action in efforts to counter terrorism, and the limitation of external defence spending. Other provisions of the Charter included commitments to eradicate illegal trafficking in firearms, ammunition and explosives, to expand and reinforce confidence-building measures, and to establish verification mechanisms to strengthen dialogue and efforts in those areas. In January 2003 the Community concluded a co-operation agreement with Interpol providing for collaboration in combating national and transnational crime, and in June the presidential summit adopted an Andean Plan for the Prevention, Combating and Eradication of Small, Light

Weapons. The heads of state, convened in Quirama, Colombia, also endorsed a new strategic direction for the Andean integration process based on the following core themes: developing the Andean common market, common foreign policy and social agenda, the physical integration of South America, and sustainable development. In July 2004 the 15th presidential summit, held in Quito, Ecuador, formulated priority objectives for a New Strategic Scheme. A sub-regional workshop to formulate an Andean Plan to Fight Corruption was held in April 2005, organized by the General Secretariat and the European Commission.

In April 2006 the President of Venezuela announced his intention to withdraw that country from the Andean Community, with immediate effect, expressing opposition to the bilateral free trade agreements signed by Colombia and Peru with the USA on the grounds that they would undermine efforts to achieve regional economic integration. The Community countered that Venezuela's commitment to Andean integration had been placed in doubt by its declared allegiance to other regional groupings, in particular Mercosur.

TRADE

A council for customs affairs met for the first time in January 1982, aiming to harmonize national legislation within the group. In December 1984 the member states launched a common currency, the Andean peso, aiming to reduce dependence on the US dollar and to increase regional trade. The new currency was to be supported by special contributions to the Fondo Andino de Reservas (now the Fondo Latinoamericano de Reservas) amounting to US $80m., and was to be 'pegged' to the US dollar, taking the form of financial drafts rather than notes and coins.

The 'Caracas Declaration' of May 1991 provided for the establishment of an Andean free trade area (AFTA), which entered into effect (excluding Peru—see below) in February 1993. Heads of state also agreed in May 1991 to create a common external tariff (CET), to standardize member countries' trade barriers in their dealings with the rest of the world, and envisaged the eventual creation of an Andean common market. In December heads of state defined four main levels of external tariffs (between 5% and 20%). In August 1992 the Group approved a request by Peru for the suspension of its rights and obligations under the Pact, thereby enabling the other members to proceed with hitherto stalled negotiations on the CET. Peru was readmitted as a full member of the Group in 1994, but participated only as an observer in the ongoing negotiations.

In November 1994 ministers of trade and integration, meeting in Quito, Ecuador, concluded a final agreement on a four-tier structure of external tariffs (although Bolivia was to retain a two-level system). The CET agreement came into effect on 1 February 1995. The agreement covered 90% of the region's imports which were to be subject to the following tariff bands: 5% for raw materials; 10%–15% for semi-manufactured goods; and 20% for finished products. In order to reach an agreement, special treatment and exemptions were granted, while Peru, initially, was to remain a 'non-active' member of the accord. In June 1997 an agreement was concluded to ensure Peru's continued membership of the Community, which provided for that country's integration into AFTA. The Peruvian Government determined to eliminate customs duties on some 2,500 products with immediate effect. The process of incorporating Peru into AFTA was completed by January 2006.

In May 1999 the 11th presidential summit agreed to establish the Andean Common Market by 2005; the Community adopted a policy on border integration and development to prepare the border regions of member countries for the envisaged free circulation of people, goods, capital and services, while consolidating sub-regional security. In June 2001 the Community agreed to recognize national identification documents issued by member states as sufficient for tourist travel in the sub-region. Community heads of state, meeting in January 2002 at a special Andean presidential summit, agreed to consolidate and improve the free trade zone by mid-2002 and apply a new CET (with four levels, i.e. 0%, 5%, 10% and 20%). To facilitate this process a common agricultural policy was to be adopted and macro-economic policies were to be harmonized. In June 2002 ministers of foreign affairs approved a schedule of activities relating to the new CET. In October member governments determined the new tariff levels applicable to 62% of products and agreed the criteria for negotiating levels for the remaining 38%. The new CET was to become effective on 1 January 2004. This date was subsequently postponed. In January 2006 ministers of trade approved a working programme to define the Community's common tariff policy, which was to incorporate a flexible CET. The value of intra-Community trade totalled some US $8,900m. in 2005, compared with $7,300m. in the previous year.

EXTERNAL RELATIONS

In September 1995 heads of state of member countries identified the formulation of common positions on foreign relations as an important part of the process of relaunching the integration initiative. A Protocol Amending the Cartagena Agreement was signed in June 1997 to confirm the formulation of a common foreign policy. During 1998 the General Secretariat held consultations with government experts, academics, representatives of the private sector and other interested parties to help formulate a document on guide-lines for a common foreign policy. The guide-lines, establishing the principles, objectives and mechanisms of a common foreign policy, were approved by the Council of Foreign Ministers in 1999. In July 2004 Andean ministers of foreign affairs approved new guide-lines for an Andean common policy on external security, which aimed to prevent and counter new security threats more effectively through co-operation and co-ordination. The ministers, meeting in Quito, Ecuador, also adopted a Declaration on the Establishment of an Andean Peace Zone, free from nuclear, chemical or biological weapons. In April 2005 the Community Secretariat signed a memorandum of understanding with the Organization for the Prohibition of Chemical Weapons, which aimed to consolidate the Andean Peace Zone, assist countries to implement the Chemical Arms Convention and promote further collaboration between the two groupings.

The Community has sought to strengthen relations with the European Union, and a co-operation agreement was signed between the two blocs in April 1993. A Euro-Andean Forum is held periodically to promote mutual co-operation, trade and investment. In February 1998 the Community signed a co-operation and technical assistance agreement with the EU in order to combat drugs trafficking. At the first summit meeting of Latin American and Caribbean (LAC) and EU leaders held in Rio de Janeiro, Brazil, in June 1999, Community-EU discussions were held on strengthening economic, trade and political co-operation and on the possibility of concluding an Association Agreement. In May 2002 the European Union adopted a Regional Strategy for the Andean Community covering the period 2002–06. The second LAC and EU summit meeting, held in May 2002 in Madrid, Spain, welcomed a new initiative to negotiate an accord on political dialogue and co-operation, envisaging that this would strengthen the basis for subsequent bilateral negotiations. Consequently, the Political Dialogue and Co-operation Agreement was negotiated during May–October 2003, and signed in December. In May 2004 a meeting of the two sides held during the third LAC-EU summit, in Guadalajara, Mexico, confirmed that an EU-CAN Association Agreement was a common strategic objective. In January 2005 an ad hoc working group was established in order to undertake a joint appraisal exercise on regional economic integration. The fourth Latin America, Caribbean (LAC) and EU summit meeting, held in Vienna, Austria, in May 2006, approved the establishment of an EU-LAC Parliamentary Assembly; this was inaugurated in November. The meeting also welcomed the proposed EU-CAN Association Agreement. Negotiations on an agreement were formally inaugurated at the meeting of Andean heads of state held in Tarifa, Bolivia, in June 2007, and the first round of negotiations was held in September. A second round was held in Brussels, Belgium, in December.

In March 2000 the Andean Community concluded an agreement to establish a political consultation and co-operation mechanism with the People's Republic of China. At the first ministerial meeting within this framework, which took place in October 2002, it was agreed that consultations would be held thereafter on a biennial basis. The first meeting of the Council of Foreign Ministers with the Chinese Vice-President took place in January 2005. A high-level meeting between senior officials from Community member states and Japan was organized in December 2002; further consultations were to be convened, aimed at cultivating closer relations.

In April 1998, at the 10th Andean presidential summit, an agreement was signed with Panama establishing a framework for negotiations providing for the conclusion of a free trade accord by the end of 1998 and for Panama's eventual associate membership of the Community. A political dialogue and co-operation agreement, a requirement for Panama's associate membership status, was signed by the two sides in September 2007.

Also in April 1998 the Community signed a framework agreement with the Mercado Común del Sur (Mercosur) on the establishment of a free trade accord. Although negotiations between the Community and Mercosur were subsequently delayed, bilateral agreements between the countries of the two groupings were extended. A preferential tariff agreement was concluded between Brazil and the Community in July 1999; the accord entered into effect, for a period of two years, in August. In August 2000 a preferential tariff agreement concluded with Argentina entered into force. The Community commenced negotiations on drafting a preferential tariff agreement with (jointly) El Salvador, Guatemala and Honduras in March of that year. In September leaders of the Community and Mercosur, meeting at a summit of Latin American heads of state, determined to relaunch negotiations, with a view to establishing a free trade area. In July 2001 ministers of foreign affairs of the two groupings approved the establishment of a formal mechanism for political dialogue and co-ordination in order to facilitate negotiations and to enhance economic and social integration. In December 2003 Mercosur and the Andean Community signed an Economic Complementary Agreement providing for free trade provisions, according to which tariffs on 80% of trade between the two groupings were to be phased out by 2014 and tariffs to be removed from the remaining 20% of, initially protected, products by 2019. The entry into force of the accord, scheduled for 1 July 2004, was postponed owing to delays in drafting the tariff reduction schedule. Members of the Latin American Integration Association (Aladi) remaining outside Mercosur and the Andean Community—Cuba, Chile and Mexico—were to be permitted to apply to join the envisaged larger free trade zone. In July 2005 the Community granted Argentina, Brazil, Paraguay and Uruguay associate membership of the grouping, as part of efforts to achieve a reciprocal association agreement. Mexico was invited to assume observer status in September 2004. In November 2006 Mexico and the Andean Community signed an agreement to establish a mechanism for political dialogue and co-operation in areas of mutual interest. The first meeting of the mechanism was held in New York, USA, in September 2007. In December 2004 the Andean Community agreed to grant observer status to Chile, and in September 2006 Chile was formally invited to join the organization as an associate member. In December the first meeting of the CAN-Chile Joint Commission was convened in Cochabamba, Bolivia. An agreement on Chile's full participation in all Community bodies and mechanisms was approved in July 2007.

In March 1998 ministers of trade from 34 countries, meeting in San José, Costa Rica, concluded an agreement on the structure of negotiations for the establishment of a Free Trade Area of the Americas (FTAA). The process was formally initiated by heads of state, meeting in Santiago, Chile, in the following month. The Community negotiated as a bloc to obtain chairmanship of three of the nine negotiating groups: on market access (Colombia), on competition policy (Peru), and on intellectual property (Venezuela). In April 2001, convened in Québec, Canada, leaders of the participating countries determined to conclude negotiations on the FTAA by January 2005. At a special summit of the Americas, held in January 2004 in Monterrey, Mexico, the leaders adopted a declaration committing themselves to its eventual establishment although failed to specify a completion date for the process. Negotiations remained stalled in 2008.

In December 2004 leaders from 12 Latin American countries attending a pan-South American summit, convened in Cusco, Peru, approved in principle the creation of a new South American Community of Nations (SACN). It was envisaged that negotiations on the formation of the new Community, which was to entail the merger of the Andean Community, Mercosur and Aladi (with the participation of Chile, Guyana and Suriname), would be completed within 15 years. In April 2005 a region-wide meeting of ministers of foreign affairs was convened, within the framework of establishing the SACN. The first South American Community meeting of heads of state was held in September, in Brasília, Brazil. The meeting issued mandates to the heads of sub-regional organizations to consider integration processes, the convergence of economic agreements and common plans of action. In April 2007, at the first South American Energy Summit, convened in Margarita Island, Venezuela, heads of state endorsed the establishment of a Union of South American Nations (UNASUR), to replace SACN as the lead organization for regional integration. It was envisaged that UNASUR would have political decision-making functions, supported by a small permanent secretariat, to be located in Quito, Ecuador, and would co-ordinate on economic and trade matters with the Andean Community, Mercosur and Aladi. A summit meeting formally to inaugurate UNASUR, scheduled to be convened in December, was postponed. A rescheduled meeting, to be convened in March 2008, at which a constitutional document formally establishing UNASUR was to be signed, was also postponed, owing to the diplomatic dispute between Ecuador and Colombia. It was later scheduled to be convened in May.

In August 1999 the Secretary-General of the Community visited Guyana in order to promote bilateral trading opportunities and to strengthen relations with the Caribbean Community. The Community held a meeting on trade relations with the Caribbean Community during 2000.

INDUSTRY AND ENERGY

In May 1987 member countries signed the Quito Protocol, modifying the Cartagena Agreement, to amend the strict rules that had formerly been imposed on foreign investors in the region. In March 1991 the Protocol was amended, with the aim of further liberalizing foreign investment and stimulating an inflow of foreign capital and technology. External and regional investors were to be permitted to repatriate their profits (in accordance with the laws of the country concerned) and there was no stipulation that a majority shareholding must eventually be transferred to local investors. A further directive, adopted in March, covered the formation of multinational enterprises in order to ensure that at least two member countries have a shareholding of 15% or more of the capital, including the country where the enterprise was to be based. These enterprises were entitled to participate in sectors otherwise reserved for national enterprises, subject to the same conditions as national enterprises in terms of taxation and export regulations, and to gain access to the markets of all member countries. In September 1999 Colombia, Ecuador and Venezuela signed an accord to facilitate the production and sale of vehicles within the region. The agreement became effective in January 2000, with a duration of 10 years.

In November 1988 member states established a bank, the Banco Intermunicipal Andino, which was to finance public works. In October 2004 a sub-regional committee on small and medium-sized enterprises (SMEs) endorsed efforts by the Community Secretariat to establish an Andean System of SME Guarantees to facilitate their access to credit.

In May 1995 the Group initiated a programme to promote the use of cheap and efficient energy sources and greater co-operation in the energy sector. The programme planned to develop a regional electricity grid. During 2003 efforts were undertaken to establish an Andean Energy Alliance, with the aim of fostering the development of integrated electricity and gas markets, as well as other objectives of developing renewable energy sources, promoting 'energy clusters' and ensuring regional energy security. The first meeting of ministers of energy, electricity, hydrocarbons and mines, convened in Quito, Ecuador, in January 2004, endorsed the Alliance.

TRANSPORT AND COMMUNICATIONS

The Andean Community has pursued efforts to improve infrastructure throughout the region. In 1983 the Commission formulated a plan to assist land-locked Bolivia, particularly through improving roads connecting it with neighbouring countries and the Pacific Ocean. An 'open skies' agreement, giving airlines of member states equal rights to airspace and airport facilities within the grouping, was signed in May 1991. In June 1998 the Commission approved the establishment of an Andean Commission of Land Transportation Authorities, which was to oversee the operation and development of land transportation services. Similarly, an Andean Committee of Water Transportation Authorities has been established to ensure compliance with Community regulations regarding ocean transportation activities. The Community aims to facilitate the movement of goods throughout the region by the use of different modes of transport ('multimodal transport') and to guarantee operational standards. It also intends to harmonize Community transport regulations and standards with those of Mercosur countries. In September 2005 the first summit meeting of the proposed SACN issued a declaration to support and accelerate infrastructure, transport and communications integration throughout the region.

In August 1996 a regulatory framework was approved for the development of a commercial Andean satellite system. In December 1997 the General Secretariat approved regulations for granting authorization for the use of the system; the Commission subsequently granted the first Community authorization to an Andean multinational enterprise (Andesat), comprising 48 companies from all five member states. In 1994 the Community initiated efforts to establish digital technology infrastructure throughout the Community: the resulting Andean Digital Corridor comprises ground, underwater and satellite routes providing a series of cross-border interconnections between the member countries. The Andean Internet System, which aims to provide internet protocol-based services throughout the Community, was operational in Colombia, Ecuador and Venezuela in 2000, and was due to be extended to all five member countries. In May 1999 the Andean Committee of Telecommunications Authorities agreed to remove all restrictions to free trade in telecommunications services (excluding sound broadcasting and television) by 1 January 2002. The Committee also determined to formulate provisions on interconnection and the safeguarding of free competition and principles of transparency within the sector. In November 2006 the Andean Community approved a new regulatory framework for the commercial exploitation of the Andean satellite system belonging to member states.

Asociación de Empresas de Telecomunicaciones de la Comunidad Andina (ASETA): Calle La Pradera 510 y San Salvador, Casilla 17-1106042, Quito, Ecuador; tel. (2) 256-3812; fax (2) 256-2499; e-mail info@aseta.org; internet www.aseta.org; f. 1974; co-ordinates improvements in national telecommunications services, in order to contribute to the further integration of the countries of the Andean Community; Sec.-Gen. MARCELO LÓPEZ ARJONA.

RURAL DEVELOPMENT AND FOOD SECURITY

An Andean Agricultural Development Programme was formulated in 1976 within which 22 resolutions aimed at integrating the Andean agricultural sector were approved. In 1984 the Andean Food Security System was created to develop the agrarian sector, replace imports progressively with local produce, and improve rural living conditions. In April 1998 the Presidential Council instructed the Commission, together with ministers of agriculture, to formulate an Andean Common Agricultural Policy, including measures to harmonize trade policy instruments and legislation on animal and plant health. The

12th Andean presidential summit, held in June 2000, authorized the adoption of the concluded Policy and the enforcement of a plan of action for its implementation. In January 2002, at the special Andean presidential summit, it was agreed that all countries in the bloc would adopt price stabilization mechanisms for agricultural products.

In July 2004 Andean ministers of agriculture approved a series of objectives and priority actions to form the framework of a Regional Food Security Policy, as requested by heads of state in the previous year. Also in July 2004 Andean heads of state endorsed the Andean Rural Development and Agricultural Competitiveness Programme to promote sub-regional efforts in areas such as rural development, food security, production competitiveness, animal health and technological innovation. In October 2005 ministers of trade and of agriculture approved the establishment of a special fund to finance the programme.

ENVIRONMENT

In March–April 2005 the first meeting of an Andean Community Council of Ministers of the Environment and Sustainable Development was convened, in Paracas, Peru. An Andean Environmental Agenda, covering the period 2006–10, aims to strengthen the capacities of member countries with regard to environmental and sustainable development issues, in particular biodiversity, climate change and water resources. In accordance with the Agenda the Community was working to establish an Andean Institute for Biodiversity, and to establish and implement regional strategies on integrated water resource management and on climate change. In June 2007 the Secretariat signed an agreement with Finland to implement a regional biodiversity programme in the Amazon region of Andean member countries (BIOCAN). In October the Secretariat organized Clima Latino, hosted by two city authorities in Ecuador, comprising conferences, workshops and cultural events at which climate change was addressed. The Community represented member countries at the conference of parties to the UN Framework Convention on Climate Change, held in Bali, Indonesia, in December, and demanded greater international political commitment and funding to combat the effects of climate change, in particular to monitor and protect the Amazon rainforest.

In July 2002 an Andean Committee for Disaster Prevention and Relief (CAPRADE) was established to help to mitigate the risk and impact of natural disasters in the sub-region. The Committee was to be responsible for implementing the Andean Strategy for Disaster Prevention and Relief, which was approved by the Council of Foreign Ministers in July 2004.

SOCIAL INTEGRATION

Several formal agreements and institutions have been established within the framework of the Andean Integration System to enhance social development and welfare. The Community aims to incorporate these bodies into the process of enhanced integration and to promote greater involvement of representatives of civil society. In May 1999 the 11th Andean presidential summit adopted a 'multidimensional social agenda' focusing on job creation and on improvements in the fields of education, health and housing throughout the Community. In June 2000 the 12th presidential summit instructed the Andean institutions to prepare individual programmes aimed at consolidating implementation of the Community's integration programme and advancing the development of the social agenda. At a special presidential summit in January 2002, corresponding ministers were directed to meet during the first half of the year to develop a Community strategy to complement national efforts in this area. In June 2003 ministers of foreign affairs and foreign trade adopted 16 legal provisions aimed at giving maximum priority to the social dimension of integration within the Community, including a measure providing for mobility of workers between member countries. A new Andean passport system, which had been approved in 2001, entered into effect in December 2005. In July 2004 Community heads of state declared support for a new Andean Council of Social Development Ministers and a draft Comprehensive Social Development Plan. Other bodies established in 2003/04 included Councils of Ministers of Education and of Ministers responsible for Cultural Policies, and a Consultative Council of Municipal Authorities. At the 13th presidential summit, held in Valencia, Venezuela, in June 2001, heads of state adopted an Andean Co-operation Plan for the Control of Illegal Drugs and Related Offences, which was to promote a united approach to combating these problems. An executive committee was to be established under the accord to oversee implementation of an action plan. In July 2005 the Council of Foreign Ministers approved an Andean Alternative Development Strategy which aimed to support sustainable local development initiatives, including alternatives to the production of illegal drug crops. Also in July heads of state determined to constitute a Social Humanitarian Fund. In June 2007 Community heads of state approved the establishment of a Working Committee on Indigenous People's Rights. In the following month the Community convened the first forum of intellectuals and researchers to strengthen the debate on indigenous issues and their incorporation into the integration process. During that year work was ongoing to develop and implement an Integral Plan for Social Development, first approved by the Council of Foreign Ministers in September 2004.

INSTITUTIONS

Consejo Consultivo Empresarial Andino (Andean Business Advisory Council): Paseo de la República 3895, Lima, Peru; tel. (1) 4111400; fax (1) 2213329; e-mail rsuarez@comunidadandina.org; first meeting held in November 1998; an advisory institution within the framework of the Sistema Andino de Integración; comprises elected representatives of business organizations; advises Community ministers and officials on integration activities affecting the business sector; Chair. LUIS CARLOS VILLEGAS ECHEVERRI.

Consejo Consultivo Laboral Andino (Andean Labour Advisory Council): Paseo de la República 3832, Of. 502, San Isidro, Lima 27, Peru; tel. (1) 4217334; fax (1) 2226124; internet www.ccla.org.pe; an advisory institution within the framework of the Sistema Andino de Integración; comprises elected representatives of labour organizations; advises Community ministers and officers on related labour issues; Chair. CÉRVULO BAUTISTA MATOMA (Colombia).

Convenio Andrés Bello (Andrés Bello Agreement): Avda 13 85–60, Bogotá, Colombia; tel. (1) 644-9292; fax (1) 610-0139; e-mail ecobello@col1.telecom.com.co; internet www.cab.int.co; f. 1970, modified in 1990; aims to promote integration in the educational, technical and cultural sectors; a new Interinstitutional Co-operation Agreement was signed with the Secretariat of the CAN in August 2003; mems: Bolivia, Chile, Colombia, Cuba, Ecuador, Panama, Paraguay, Peru, Spain, Venezuela; Exec. Sec. Dr FRANCISCO HUERTA MONTALVO (Ecuador).

Convenio Hipólito Unanue (Hipólito Unanue Agreement): Edif. Cartagena, Paseo de la República 3832, 3°, San Isidro, Lima, Peru; tel. (1) 2210074; fax (1) 2222663; e-mail postmaster@conhu.org.pe; internet www.orasconhu.org; f. 1971 on the occasion of the first meeting of Andean ministers of health; became part of the institutional structure of the Community in 1998; aims to enhance the development of health services, and to promote regional co-ordination in areas such as environmental health, disaster preparedness and the prevention and control of drug abuse; Exec. Sec. Dr OSCAR FEO ISTURIZ.

Convenio Simón Rodríguez (Simón Rodríguez Agreement): Paseo de la República 3895, esq. Aramburú, San Isidro, Lima 27, Peru; tel. (1) 4111400; fax (1) 2213329; promotes a convergence of social and labour conditions throughout the Community, for example, working hours and conditions, employment and social security policies, and to promote the participation of workers and employers in the sub-regional integration process; Protocol of Modification signed in June 2001; ratification process ongoing.

Corporación Andina de Fomento (CAF) (Andean Development Corporation): Torre CAF, Avda Luis Roche, Altamira, Apdo 5086, Caracas, Venezuela; tel. (212) 2092111; fax (212) 2092444; e-mail infocaf@caf.com; internet www.caf.com; f. 1968, began operations in 1970; aims to encourage the integration of the Andean countries by specialization and an equitable distribution of investments; conducts research to identify investment opportunities, and prepares the resulting investment projects; gives technical and financial assistance; and attracts internal and external credit; auth. cap. US $5,000m.; subscribed or underwritten by the governments of member countries, or by public, semi-public and private-sector institutions authorized by those governments; the Board of Directors comprises representatives of each country at ministerial level; mems: the Andean Community, Argentina, Brazil, Chile, Costa Rica, Jamaica, Mexico, Panama, Paraguay, Spain, Trinidad and Tobago, Uruguay, Venezuela, and 15 private banks in the Andean region; Exec. Pres. ENRIQUE GARCÍA RODRÍGUEZ (Bolivia).

Fondo Latinoamericano de Reservas (FLAR) (Latin American Reserve Fund): Avda 82, 12–18, 7°, POB 241523, Bogotá, Colombia; tel. (1) 634-4360; fax (1) 634-4384; e-mail flar@flar.net; internet www.flar.net; f. 1978 as the Fondo Andino de Reservas to support the balance of payments of member countries, provide credit, guarantee loans, and contribute to the harmonization of monetary and financial policies; adopted present name in 1991, in order to allow the admission of other Latin American countries; in 1992 the Fund began extending credit lines to commercial cos for export financing; it is administered by an Assembly of the ministers of finance and economy of the member countries, and a Board of Directors comprising the Presidents of the central banks of the member states; mems: Bolivia, Colombia, Costa Rica, Ecuador, Peru, Venezuela; subscribed cap. US $2,109.4m.. cap. p.u. $1,465.3m. (1 April 2007); Chair. ANA MARÍA CARRASQUILLA.

Universidad Andina Simón Bolívar (Simón Bolívar Andean University): Calle Real Audiencia 73, Casilla 545, Sucre, Bolivia; tel. (64) 60265; fax (64) 60833; e-mail uasb@uasb.edu.bo; internet www.uasb.edu.bo; f. 1985; institution for postgraduate study and

ARAB FUND FOR ECONOMIC AND SOCIAL DEVELOPMENT—AFESD

Address: POB 21923, Safat, 13080 Kuwait.
Telephone: 4959000; **fax:** 4815760; **e-mail:** hq@arabfund.org; **internet:** www.arabfund.org.

Established in 1968 by the Economic Council of the Arab League, the Fund began its operations in 1974. It participates in the financing of economic and social development projects in the Arab states.

MEMBERSHIP
Twenty-one members (see table of subscriptions below)

Organization
(April 2008)

BOARD OF GOVERNORS
The Board of Governors consists of a Governor and an Alternate Governor appointed by each member of the Fund. The Board of Governors is considered as the General Assembly of the Fund, and has all powers.

BOARD OF DIRECTORS
The Board of Directors is composed of eight Directors elected by the Board of Governors from among Arab citizens of recognized experience and competence. They are elected for a renewable term of two years.
The Board of Directors is charged with all the activities of the Fund and exercises the powers delegated to it by the Board of Governors.
Director-General and Chairman of the Board of Directors: ABDLATIF YOUSUF AL-HAMAD (Kuwait).

FINANCIAL STRUCTURE
In 1982 the authorized capital was increased from 400m. Kuwaiti dinars (KD) to KD 800m., divided into 80,000 shares having a value of KD 10,000 each. At the end of 2006 paid-up capital was KD 663.04m.

SUBSCRIPTIONS*
(KD million, December 2006)

Algeria	64.78	Oman	17.28
Bahrain	2.16	Palestine	1.10
Djibouti	0.02	Qatar	6.75
Egypt	40.50	Saudi Arabia	159.07
Iraq	31.76	Somalia	0.21
Jordan	17.30	Sudan	11.06
Kuwait	169.70	Syria	24.00
Lebanon	2.00	Tunisia	6.16
Libya	59.85	United Arab Emirates	28.00
Mauritania	0.82	Yemen	4.52
Morocco	16.00	**Total**	**663.04**

* 1 Kuwaiti dinar = US $3.5 (December 2006).

Activities
Pursuant to the Agreement Establishing the Fund (as amended in 1997 by the Board of Governors), the purpose of the Fund is to contribute to the financing of economic and social development projects in the Arab states and countries by:

1. Financing economic development projects of an investment character by means of loans granted on concessionary terms to governments and public enterprises and corporations, giving preference to projects which are vital to the Arab entity, as well as to joint Arab projects;

2. Financing private sector projects in member states by providing all forms of loans and guarantees to corporations and enterprises (possessing juridical personality), participating in their equity capital, and providing other forms of financing and the requisite financial, technical and advisory services, in accordance with such regulations and subject to such conditions as may be prescribed by the Board of Directors;

3. Forming or participating in the equity capital of corporations possessing juridical personality, for the implementation and financing of private sector projects in member states, including the provision and financing of technical, advisory and financial services;

4. Establishing and administering special funds with aims compatible with those of the Fund and with resources provided by the Fund or other sources;

5. Encouraging, directly or indirectly, the investment of public and private capital in a manner conducive to the development and growth of the Arab economy;

6. Providing expertise and technical assistance in the various fields of economic development.

LOANS BY SECTOR, 2006

Sector	Amount (KD million)	%
Infrastructure sectors	291.00	84.4
Transport and telecommunications	182.00	52.8
Energy and electricity	69.00	20.0
Water and sewerage	40.00	11.6
Productive sectors	10.00	2.9
Industry and mining	7.00	2.0
Agriculture and rural development	3.00	0.9
Social services	35.00	10.1
Other	9.00	2.6
Total	**345.00**	**100.0**

The Fund co-operates with other Arab organizations such as the Arab Monetary Fund, the League of Arab States and OAPEC in preparing regional studies and conferences, for example in the areas of human resource development, demographic research and private sector financing of infrastructure projects. It also acts as the secretariat of the Co-ordination Group of Arab National and Regional Development Financing Institutions. These organizations also work together to produce a *Joint Arab Economic Report*, which considers economic and social developments in the Arab states.

During 2006 the Fund approved 18 loans, totalling KD 345.0m., to help finance 15 new projects and three ongoing projects in nine member countries. At the end of that year total lending since 1974 amounted to KD 5,449.7m., which helped to finance 431 projects in 17 Arab countries. In 2006 more than 50% of financing was for projects in the transport and telecommunications sector, while 20% was for energy and electricity projects. During the period 1974–2006 31% of project financing was for energy and electricity, 24% for transport and telecommunications, 17% for agriculture and rural development, 11% for water and sewerage, 9% for social services and 7% for industry and mining.

During 2006 the Fund extended 32 new technical assistance grants, totalling KD 13.9m. Three grants, amounting to KD 8m. (or 58% of total grant financing), were for emergency assistance programmes, while KD 3.4m (25%) was for institutional support and training and KD 1.7m. (12%) for feasibility studies and project preparation. The cumulative total grants provided by the end of 2006 was 820, with a value of KD 123.7m.

In December 1997 AFESD initiated an Arab Fund Fellowships Programme, which aimed to provide grants to Arab academics to conduct university teaching or advanced research.

Publications
Reports, working papers, sector documents, council proceedings.

ARAB MONETARY FUND

Address: Arab Monetary Fund Bldg, Corniche Rd, POB 2818, Abu Dhabi, United Arab Emirates.
Telephone: (2) 6171400; **fax:** (2) 6326454; **e-mail:** centralmail@amfad.org.ae; **internet:** www.amf.org.ae.

The Agreement establishing the Arab Monetary Fund was approved by the Economic Council of Arab States in Rabat, Morocco, in April 1976 and entered into force on 2 February 1977.

MEMBERS

Algeria	Morocco
Bahrain	Oman
Comoros	Palestine
Djibouti	Qatar
Egypt	Saudi Arabia
Iraq*	Somalia*
Jordan	Sudan*
Kuwait	Syria
Lebanon	Tunisia
Libya	United Arab Emirates
Mauritania	Yemen

* From July 1993 loans to Iraq, Somalia and Sudan were suspended as a result of non-repayment of debts to the Fund. Sudan was readmitted in April 2000, following a settlement of its arrears; a memorandum of understanding, to incorporate new loan repayments was concluded in September 2001. At 31 December 2006 arrears totalling AAD 167.63m. were owed to the Fund by Comoros, Iraq and Somalia.

CAPITAL SUBSCRIPTIONS
(million Arab Accounting Dinars, 31 December 2006)

Member	Paid-up capital
Algeria	77.90
Bahrain	9.20
Comoros	0.45
Djibouti	0.45
Egypt	58.80
Iraq	77.90
Jordan	9.90
Kuwait	58.80
Lebanon	9.20
Libya	24.69
Mauritania	9.20
Morocco	27.55
Oman	9.20
Palestine	3.96
Qatar	18.40
Saudi Arabia	88.95
Somalia	7.35
Sudan	18.40
Syria	13.25
Tunisia	12.85
United Arab Emirates	35.30
Yemen	28.30
Total*	596.04

* Excluding Palestine's share (AAD 3.96m.), which was deferred by a Board of Governors' resolution in 1978.

Organization
(April 2008)

BOARD OF GOVERNORS

The Board of Governors is the highest authority of the Arab Monetary Fund. It formulates policies on Arab economic integration and liberalization of trade among member states. With certain exceptions, it may delegate to the Board of Executive Directors some of its powers. The Board of Governors is composed of a governor and a deputy governor appointed by each member state for a term of five years. It meets at least once a year; meetings may also be convened at the request of half the members, or of members holding half of the total voting power.

BOARD OF EXECUTIVE DIRECTORS

The Board of Executive Directors exercises all powers vested in it by the Board of Governors and may delegate to the Director-General such powers as it deems fit. It is composed of the Director-General and eight non-resident directors elected by the Board of Governors. Each director holds office for three years and may be re-elected.

DIRECTOR-GENERAL

The Director-General of the Fund is appointed by the Board of Governors for a renewable five-year term, and serves as Chairman of the Board of Executive Directors.

The Director-General supervises Committees on Loans, Investments, and Administration. Other offices include the Economic and Technical Department, the Economic Policy Institute, the Treasury and Investment Department, an Internal Audit Office, and the Finance and Computer Department.

Director-General and Chairman of the Board of Executive Directors: Dr JASSIM ABDULLAH AL-MANNAI.

FINANCE

The Arab Accounting Dinar (AAD) is a unit of account equivalent to three IMF Special Drawing Rights. (The average value of the SDR in 2006 was US $1.50440.)

In April 1983 the authorized capital of the Fund was increased from AAD 288m. to AAD 600m. The new capital stock comprised 12,000 shares, each having the value of AAD 50,000. At the end of 2006 total paid-up capital was AAD 596.04m.

Activities

The creation of the Arab Monetary Fund was seen as a step towards the goal of Arab economic integration. It assists member states in balance of payments difficulties, and also has a broad range of aims.

The Articles of Agreement define the Fund's aims as follows:

(*a*) to correct disequilibria in the balance of payments of member states;

(*b*) to promote the stability of exchange rates among Arab currencies, to render them mutually convertible, and to eliminate restrictions on current payments between member states;

(*c*) to establish policies and modes of monetary co-operation to accelerate Arab economic integration and economic development in the member states;

(*d*) to tender advice on the investment of member states' financial resources in foreign markets, whenever called upon to do so;

(*e*) to promote the development of Arab financial markets;

(*f*) to promote the use of the Arab dinar as a unit of account and to pave the way for the creation of a unified Arab currency;

(*g*) to co-ordinate the positions of member states in dealing with international monetary and economic problems; and

(*h*) to provide a mechanism for the settlement of current payments between member states in order to promote trade among them.

The Arab Monetary Fund functions both as a fund and a bank. It is empowered:

(*a*) to provide short- and medium-term loans to finance balance of payments deficits of member states;

(*b*) to issue guarantees to member states to strengthen their borrowing capabilities;

(*c*) to act as intermediary in the issuance of loans in Arab and international markets for the account of member states and under their guarantees;

(*d*) to co-ordinate the monetary policies of member states;

(*e*) to manage any funds placed under its charge by member states;

(*f*) to hold periodic consultations with member states on their economic conditions; and

(*g*) to provide technical assistance to banking and monetary institutions in member states.

Loans are intended to finance an overall balance of payments deficit and a member may draw up to 75% of its paid-up subscription, in convertible currencies, for this purpose unconditionally (automatic loans). A member may, however, obtain loans in excess of this limit, subject to agreement with the Fund on a programme aimed at reducing its balance of payments deficit (ordinary and extended loans, equivalent to 175% and 250% of its quota respectively). From 1981 a country receiving no extended loans was entitled to a loan under the Inter-Arab Trade Facility (discontinued in 1989) of up to 100% of its quota. In addition, a member has the right to borrow up to 50% of its paid-up capital in order to cope with an unexpected deficit in its balance of payments resulting from a decrease in its exports of goods and services or a large increase in its imports of agricultural products following a poor harvest (compensatory loans).

Automatic and compensatory loans are repayable within three years, while ordinary and extended loans are repayable within five and seven years respectively. Loans are granted at concessionary and uniform rates of interest which increase with the length of the period of the loan. In 1988 the Fund's executive directors agreed to modify their policy on lending, placing an emphasis on the correction of economic imbalances in recipient countries. In 1996 the Fund established the Structural Adjustment Facility, initially providing up to 75% of a member's paid-up subscription and later increased to 175%. This may include a technical assistance component comprising a grant of up to 2% of the total loan.

Over the period 1978–2006 the Fund extended 135 loans amounting to AAD 1,071.9m. During 2006 the Fund approved one loan of AAD 0.35m.

The Fund's technical assistance activities are extended through either the provision of experts to the country concerned or in the form of specialized training of officials of member countries. Technical missions by Fund experts were sent to Yemen, to help prepare for accession to the World Trade Organization, Algeria and Oman during 2006. In view of the increased importance of this type of assistance, the Fund established, in 1988, the Economic Policy Institute (EPI) which offers regular training courses and specialized seminars for middle-level and senior staff, respectively, of financial and monetary institutions of the Arab countries. During 2006 the EPI organized 13 training courses, three workshops, and a seminar on Arab economic growth and institutions. In April 1999 the Fund signed a memorandum of understanding with the International Monetary Fund to establish a joint regional training programme.

AMF collaborates with AFESD, the Arab League and OAPEC in writing and publishing a *Joint Arab Economic Report*. The Fund also co-operates with AFESD, with the technical assistance of the International Monetary Fund and the World Bank, in organizing an annual seminar. The Fund provides the secretariat for the Council of Arab Central Banks, comprising the governors of central banks and the heads of the monetary agencies in Arab countries. In 1991 the Council established the Arab Committee on Banking Supervision. In 2005 the Council inaugurated a second technical grouping—the Arab Committee on Payments and Settlements Systems.

TRADE PROMOTION

Arab Trade Financing Program (ATFP): POB 26799, Arab Monetary Fund Bldg, 7th Floor, Corniche Rd, Abu Dhabi, United Arab Emirates; tel. (2) 6316999; fax (2) 6316793; e-mail finadmin@atfp.ae; internet www.atfp.org.ae; f. 1989 to develop and promote trade between Arab countries and to enhance the competitive ability of Arab exporters; operates by extending lines of credit to Arab exporters and importers through national agencies (some 174 agencies designated by the monetary authorities of 19 Arab and four other countries at Dec. 2006); the Arab Monetary Fund provided 50% of ATFP's authorized capital of US $500m; participation was also invited from private and official Arab financial institutions and joint Arab/foreign institutions; ATFP administers the Inter-Arab Trade Information Network (IATIN), and organizes Buyers-Sellers meetings to promote Arab goods; Chair. and Chief Exec. Dr JASSIM ABDULLAH AL-MANNAI; publ. *Annual Report* (Arabic and English).

Publications

Annual Report.
AMDB Bulletin (quarterly).
Arab Countries: Economic Indicators (annually).
Foreign Trade of the Arab Countries (annually).
Joint Arab Economic Report (annually).
Money and Credit in the Arab Countries.
National Accounts of the Arab Countries (annually).

Reports on commodity structure (by value and quantity) of member countries' imports from and exports to other Arab countries; other studies on economic, social, management and fiscal issues.

Statistics

LOANS APPROVED, 1978–2006

Type of loan	Number of loans	Amount (AAD '000)
Automatic	58	294,109
Ordinary	11	104,567
Compensatory	14	99,085
Extended	23	297,344
Structural Adjustment Facility	18	212,077
Inter-Arab Trade Facility (cancelled in 1989)	11	64,730
Total	135	1,071,912

LOAN APPROVED, 2006

Borrower	Type of loan	Amount (AAD '000)
Djibouti	Structural Adjustment Facility	350

Source: *Annual Report 2006*.

ASIA-PACIFIC ECONOMIC CO-OPERATION—APEC

Address: 35 Heng Mui Keng Terrace, Singapore 119616.
Telephone: 68919600; **fax:** 68919690; **e-mail:** info@apec.org; **internet:** www.apec.org.

Asia-Pacific Economic Co-operation (APEC) was initiated in November 1989, in Canberra, Australia, as an informal consultative forum. Its aim is to promote multilateral economic co-operation on issues of trade and investment.

MEMBERS

Australia	Japan	Philippines
Brunei	Korea, Republic	Russia
Canada	Malaysia	Singapore
Chile	Mexico	Taiwan*
China, People's Republic	New Zealand	Thailand
Hong Kong	Papua New Guinea	USA
Indonesia	Peru	Viet Nam

* Admitted as Chinese Taipei.

Note: APEC has three official observers: the Association of South East Asian Nations Secretariat; the Pacific Economic Co-operation Council; and the Pacific Islands Forum Secretariat. Observers may participate in APEC meetings and have full access to all related documents and information.

Organization

(April 2008)

ECONOMIC LEADERS' MEETINGS

The first meeting of APEC heads of government was convened in November 1993, in Seattle, Washington, USA. Subsequently, each annual meeting of APEC ministers of foreign affairs and of economic affairs has been followed by an informal gathering of the leaders of the APEC economies, at which the policy objectives of the grouping are discussed and defined. The 15th Economic Leaders' Meeting was convened in September 2007, in Sydney, Australia, and the 16th Meeting was scheduled to take place in November 2008 in Lima, Peru.

MINISTERIAL MEETINGS

APEC ministers of foreign affairs and ministers of economic affairs meet annually. These meetings are hosted by the APEC Chair, which rotates each year, although it was agreed, in 1989, that alternate Ministerial Meetings were to be convened in an ASEAN member country. A Senior Officials' Meeting (SOM) convenes regularly between Ministerial Meetings to co-ordinate and administer the budgets and work programmes of APEC's committees and working groups. Other meetings of ministers are held on a regular basis to enhance co-operation in specific areas.

SECRETARIAT

In 1992 the Ministerial Meeting, held in Bangkok, Thailand, agreed to establish a permanent secretariat to support APEC activities. The Secretariat became operational in February 1993. The Executive Director is appointed from the member economy chairing the group and serves a one-year term. A Deputy Executive Director is appointed by the member economy designated to chair APEC in the following year. In 2008 a Policy Support Unit was to be established within the Secretariat and the appointment of an Executive Director with a fixed-term was under consideration.

Executive Director: JUAN CARLOS CAPUÑAY (Peru).

Deputy Executive Director: MICHAEL TAY (Singapore).

COMMITTEES

Budget and Management Committee (BMC): f. 1993 as Budget and Administrative Committee, present name adopted 1998; advises APEC senior officials on budgetary, administrative and managerial issues. The Committee reviews the operational budgets of APEC committees and groups, evaluates their effectiveness and conducts assessments of group projects. In 2005 the APEC Support Fund (ASF) was established under the auspices of the BMC, with the aim of supporting capacity-building programmes for developing economies; by 2007 subsidiary funds of the ASF had been established relating to human security and avian influenza.

Committee on Trade and Investment (CTI): f. 1993 on the basis of a Declaration signed by ministers meeting in Seattle, Washington, USA, in order to facilitate the expansion of trade and the development of a liberalized environment for investment among member countries; undertakes initiatives to improve the flow of goods, services and technology in the region. Supports Industry Dialogues to promote collaboration between public and private sector representatives in the following areas of activity: Automotive; Chemical; Non-ferrous Metal; and Life Sciences Innovation. An Investment Experts' Group was established in 1994, initially to develop non-binding investment principles. In May 1997 an APEC Tariff Database was inaugurated, with sponsorship from the private sector. A Market Access Group was established in 1998 to administer CTI activities concerned with non-tariff measures. In 2001 the CTI finalized a set of nine non-binding Principles on Trade Facilitation, which aimed to help eliminate procedural and administrative impediments to trade and to increase trading opportunities. A Trade Facilitation Action Plan (TFAP) was approved in 2002. In 2003 a Transparency By 2005 strategy was adopted to systematize transparency standards. In 2006 the TFAP was reviewed and a work plan on trade facilitation was formulated as a basis for the development of a second TFAP; the finalized TFAP II was endorsed by the APEC ministers responsible for trade in July 2007 and by APEC leaders in September. In 2007 the Electronic Commerce Steering Group, established in 1999, became aligned to the CTI. A new Friends of the Chair group was established in 2007 to help to develop an Investment Facilitation Action Plan.

Economic Committee (EC): f. 1994 following an agreement, in November, to transform the existing ad hoc group on economic trends and issues into a formal committee; aims to enhance APEC's capacity to analyse economic trends and to research and report on issues affecting economic and technical co-operation in the region. In addition, the Committee is considering the environmental and development implications of expanding population and economic growth. During 2007–10 the EC was undertaking a work plan on the implementation of the Leaders' Agenda to Implement Structural Reform (LAISR), agreed in November 2004 by the 12th Economic Leaders' Meeting, see below).

SOM Steering Committee on ECOTECH (SCE): f. 1998 to assist the SOM with the co-ordination of APEC's economic and technical co-operation programme (ECOTECH); reconstituted in 2006, with an enhanced mandate to undertake greater co-ordination and oversee project proposals of the working groups; monitors and evaluates project implementation and also identifies initiatives designed to strengthen economic and technical co-operation in infrastructure.

ADVISORY COUNCIL

APEC Business Advisory Council (ABAC): Philamlife Tower, 43rd Floor, 8767 Paseo de Roxas, Makati City 1226, Philippines; tel. (2) 8454564; fax (2) 8454832; e-mail abacsec@pfgc.ph; internet www.abaconline.org; an agreement to establish ABAC, comprising up to three senior representatives of the private sector from each APEC member economy, was concluded at the Ministerial Meeting held in November 1995. ABAC is mandated to advise member states on the implementation of APEC's Action Agenda and on other business matters, and to provide business-related information to APEC fora. ABAC meets three or four times each year and holds an annual Business Summit (known until 2007 as the 'CEO Summit') alongside the annual APEC Economic Leaders' Meeting; Exec. Dir ALICIA MACLEAN.

Activities

APEC is focused on furthering objectives in three key areas, or 'pillars': trade and investment liberalization; business facilitation; and economic and technical co-operation. It was initiated in 1989 as a forum for informal discussion between the then six ASEAN members and their six dialogue partners in the Pacific, and, in particular, to promote trade liberalization in the Uruguay Round of negotiations, which were being conducted under the General Agreement on Tariffs and Trade (GATT). The Seoul Declaration, adopted by ministers meeting in the Republic of Korea in November 1991, defined the objectives of APEC.

ASEAN countries were initially reluctant to support any more formal structure of the forum, or to admit new members, owing to concerns that it would undermine ASEAN's standing as a regional grouping and be dominated by powerful non-ASEAN economies. In August 1991 it was agreed to extend membership to the People's Republic of China, Hong Kong and Taiwan (subject to conditions imposed by the People's Republic of China, including that a Taiwanese official of no higher than vice-ministerial level should attend the annual meeting of ministers of foreign affairs). Mexico and Papua New Guinea acceded to the organization in November 1993, and Chile joined in November 1994. The summit meeting held in November 1997 agreed that Peru, Russia and Viet Nam should be admitted to APEC at the 1998 meeting, but imposed a 10-year moratorium on further expansion of the grouping.

In September 1992 APEC ministers agreed to establish a permanent secretariat. In addition, the meeting created an 11-member non-governmental Eminent Persons Group (EPG), which was to assess trade patterns within the region and propose measures to promote co-operation. At the Ministerial Meeting in Seattle, Washington, USA, in November 1993, members agreed on a framework for expanding trade and investment among member countries, and to establish a permanent committee (the CTI, see above) to pursue these objectives.

In August 1994 the EPG proposed the following timetable for the liberalization of all trade across the Asia-Pacific region: negotiations for the elimination of trade barriers were to commence in 2000 and be completed within 10 years in developed countries, 15 years in newly industrialized economies and by 2020 in developing countries. Trade concessions could then be extended on a reciprocal basis to non-members in order to encourage world-wide trade liberalization, rather than isolate APEC as a unique trading bloc. In November 1994 the meeting of APEC heads of government adopted the Bogor Declaration of Common Resolve, which endorsed the EPG's timetable for free and open trade and investment in the region by the year 2020. Other issues incorporated into the Declaration included the implementation of GATT commitments in full and strengthening the multilateral trading system through the forthcoming establishment of the World Trade Organization (WTO), intensifying development co-operation in the Asia-Pacific region and expanding and accelerating trade and investment programmes. In November 1995 the Ministerial Meeting decided to dismantle the EPG, and to establish the APEC Business Advisory Council (ABAC), consisting of private sector representatives.

Meeting in Osaka, Japan, in November 1995, APEC heads of government adopted the Osaka Action Agenda as a framework to achieve the commitments of the Bogor Declaration. Part One of the Agenda identified action areas for the liberalization of trade and investment and the facilitation of business, for example, customs procedures, rules of origin and non-tariff barriers. It incorporated agreements that the process was to be comprehensive, consistent with WTO commitments, comparable among all APEC economies and non-discriminatory. Each member economy was to ensure the transparency of its laws, regulations and procedures affecting the flow of goods, services and capital among APEC economies and to refrain from implementing any trade protection measures. A second part of the Agenda was to provide a framework for further economic and technical co-operation between APEC members in areas such as energy, transport, infrastructure, SMEs and agricultural technology. In order to resolve a disagreement concerning the inclusion of agricultural products in the trade liberalization process, a provision for flexibility was incorporated into the Agenda, taking into account diverse circumstances and different levels of development in APEC member economies. Liberalization measures were to be implemented from January 1997 (i.e. three years earlier than previously agreed). A Trade and Investment Liberalization and Facilitation Special Account was established to finance projects in support of the implementation of the Osaka Action Agenda. Each member economy was to prepare an Individual Action Plan (IAP) on efforts to achieve the trade liberalization measures, that were to be reviewed annually.

In November 1996 the Economic Leaders' Meeting, held in Subic Bay, the Philippines, approved the Manila Action Plan for APEC (MAPA), which had been formulated at the preceding Ministerial Meeting, held in Manila. MAPA incorporated the IAPs and other collective measures aimed at achieving the trade liberalization and co-operation objectives of the Bogor Declaration, as well as the joint activities specified in the second part of the Osaka Agenda. Heads of government also endorsed a US proposal to eliminate tariffs and other barriers to trade in information technology products by 2000 and determined to support efforts to conclude an agreement to this effect at the forthcoming WTO conference; however, they insisted on the provision of an element of flexibility in achieving trade liberalization in this sector.

The 1997 Economic Leaders' Meeting, held in Vancouver, Canada, in November, was dominated by concern at the financial instability that had affected several Asian economies during that year. The final declaration of the summit meeting endorsed a framework of measures that had been agreed by APEC deputy ministers of finance and central bank governors at an emergency meeting convened in the previous week in Manila, the Philippines (the so-called Manila Framework for Enhanced Asian Regional Co-operation to Promote Financial Stability). The meeting, attended by representatives of the IMF, the World Bank and the Asian Development Bank, committed all member economies receiving IMF assistance to undertake specified economic and financial reforms, and supported the establishment of a separate Asian funding facility to supplement international financial assistance (although this was later rejected by the IMF). APEC ministers of finance and governors of central banks were urged to accelerate efforts for the development of the region's financial and capital markets and to liberalize capital flows in the region. Measures were to include strengthening financial market supervision and clearing and settlement infrastructure, the reform of pension systems, and promoting co-operation among export credit agencies and financing institutions. The principal item on the Vancouver summit agenda was an initiative to enhance trade liberalization, which, the grouping insisted, should not be undermined by the financial instability in Asia. The following 15 economic sectors were identified for 'early voluntary sectoral liberalization' ('EVSL'): environmental goods and services; fish and fish products; forest products; medical equipment and instruments; toys; energy; chemicals; gems and jewellery; telecommunications; oilseeds and oilseed products; food; natural and synthetic rubber; fertilizers; automobiles; and civil aircraft. The implementation of EVSL was to encompass market opening, trade facilitation, and economic and technical co-operation activities.

In May 1998 APEC finance ministers met in Canada to consider the ongoing financial and economic crisis in Asia and to review progress in implementing efforts to alleviate the difficulties experienced by several member economies. The ministers agreed to pursue activities in the following three priority areas: capital market development, capital account liberalization and strengthening financial systems (including corporate governance). The region's economic difficulties remained the principal topic of discussion at the Economic Leaders' Meeting held in Kuala Lumpur, Malaysia, in November. A final declaration reiterated their commitment to co-operation in pursuit of sustainable economic recovery and growth, in particular through the restructuring of financial and corporate sectors, promoting and facilitating private sector capital flows, and efforts to strengthen the global financial system. The meeting endorsed a proposal by ABAC to establish a partnership for equitable growth, with the aim of enhancing business involvement in APEC's programme of economic and technical co-operation. Other initiatives approved included an Agenda of APEC Science and Technology Industry Co-operation into the 21st Century (for which the People's Republic of China announced it was to establish a special fund), and an Action Programme on Skills and Development in APEC. Japan's persisting opposition to a reduction of tariffs in the fish and forestry sectors prevented the conclusion of tariff negotiations under the EVSL scheme, and it was therefore agreed that responsibility for managing the tariff reduction element of the initiative should be transferred to the WTO.

In September 1999 political dialogue regarding civil conflict in East Timor (now Timor-Leste) dominated the start of the annual meetings of the grouping, held in Auckland, New Zealand, although the issue remained separate from the official agenda. The Economic Leaders' Meeting considered measures to sustain the economic recovery in Asia and endorsed the APEC Principles to Enhance Competition and Regulatory Reform (for example, transparency, accountability, non-discrimination) as a framework to strengthen APEC markets and to enable further integration and implementation of the IAPs. Also under discussion was the forthcoming round of multilateral trade negotiations, to be initiated by the WTO. The heads of government proposed the objective of completing a single package of trade agreements within three years and endorsed the abolition of export subsidies for agricultural products. The meeting determined to support the efforts of the People's Republic of China, Russia, Taiwan and Viet Nam to accede to WTO membership. An APEC Business Travel Card scheme, to facilitate business travel within the region, was inaugurated in 1999, having been launched on a trial basis in 1997. By early 2008 some 34,000 individuals were registered under the scheme, in which 18 economies were participating.

The Economic Leaders' Meeting for 2000, held in Brunei in November, urged that an agenda for the now-stalled round of multilateral trade negotiations should be formulated without further delay. The meeting endorsed a plan of action to promote the utilization of advances in information and communications technologies in member economies, for the benefit of all citizens. It adopted the aim of tripling the number of people in the region with access to the internet by 2005, and determined to co-operate with business and education sector interests to attract investment and expertise in the pursuit of this goal. A proposal that the Democratic People's Republic of Korea be permitted to participate in APEC working groups was approved at the meeting.

The 2001 Economic Leaders' Meeting, held in October, in Shanghai, People's Republic of China, condemned the terrorist attacks against targets in the USA of the previous month and resolved to take action to combat the threat of international terrorism. The heads of government declared terrorism to be a direct challenge to APEC's vision of free, open and prosperous economies, and concluded that the threat made the continuing move to free trade, with its aim of bolstering economies, increasing prosperity and encouraging integration, even more of a priority. Leaders emphasized the importance of sharing the benefits of globalization. adopted the Shanghai Accord, which identified development goals for APEC during its second decade and clarified measures for achieving the Bogor goals within the agreed timetable. A process of IAP Peer Reviews was initiated. (By late 2005 the process had been concluded for each member economy.) The meeting also outlined the e-APEC Strategy developed by the e-APEC Task Force established after the Brunei Economic Leaders' meeting. Considering issues of entrepreneurship, structural and regulatory reform, competition, intellectual property rights and information security, the strategy aimed to facilitate technological development in the region. Finally, the meeting adopted a strategy document relating to infectious diseases in the Asia Pacific region, which aimed to promote a co-ordinated response to combating HIV/AIDS and other contagious diseases.

In September 2002 a meeting of APEC ministers of finance was held in Los Cabos, Mexico. Ministers discussed the importance of efforts to combat money-laundering and the financing of terrorism. The meeting also focused on ways to strengthen global and regional economic growth, to advance fiscal and financial reforms and to improve the allocation of domestic savings for economic development. The theme of the 2002 Economic Leaders' Meeting, held in the following month in Los Cabos, Mexico, was 'Expanding the Benefits of Co-operation for Economic Growth and Development—Implementing the Vision'. The meeting issued a statement on the implementation of APEC standards of transparency in trade and investment liberalization and facilitation. Leaders also issued a statement on fighting terrorism and promoting growth. In February the first conference to promote the Secure Trade in the APEC Region (STAR) initiative was convened in Bangkok, Thailand, and attended by representatives of all APEC member economies as well as senior officers of private sector companies and relevant international organizations. The second STAR conference was held in March 2004, in Viña del Mar, Chile; the third in Incheon, Republic of Korea, in February 2005; the fourth in Hanoi, Viet Nam, in February 2006; and the fifth in Sydney, Australia, in June 2007.

The 2003 Economic Leaders' Meeting, convened in October, in Bangkok, Thailand, considered means of advancing the WTO's stalled Doha round of trade negotiations, emphasizing the central importance of its development dimension, and noted progress made hitherto in facilitating intra-APEC trade. The meeting also addressed regional security issues, reiterating the Community's commitment to ensuring the resilience of APEC economies against the threat of terrorism. The Leaders adopted the Bangkok Declaration on Partnership for the Future which identified the following areas as priority concerns for the group: the promotion of trade and investment liberalization; enhancing human security; and helping people and societies to benefit from globalization. The Bangkok meeting also issued a statement on health security, which expressed APEC's determination to strengthen infrastructure for the detection and prevention of infectious diseases, as well as the surveillance of other threats to public health, and to ensure a co-ordinated response to public health emergencies, with particular concern to the outbreak, earlier in the year, of Severe Acute Respiratory Syndrome (SARS).

The 12th Economic Leaders' Meeting was held in Santiago, Chile, in November 2004, on the theme 'One Community, Our Future'. The meeting reaffirmed the grouping's commitment to the Doha Development Agenda, and endorsed the package of agreements concluded by the WTO in July. The meeting approved a Santiago Initiative for Expanded Trade in APEC, to promote further trade and investment liberalization in the region and advance trade facilitation measures. Other areas discussed were human security, HIV/AIDS and other emerging infectious diseases, and energy security. Efforts to combat corruption and promote good governance included a Santiago Commitment to Fight Corruption and Ensure Transparency, the APEC Course of Action on Fighting Corruption and Ensuring Transparency, and a Leaders' Agenda to Implement Structural Reform (LAISR). LAISR covers the following five policy areas: regulatory reform, competition policy, public sector governance, corporate governance, and strengthening economic and legal infrastructure.

In September 2005 APEC finance ministers, meeting in Jeju, Republic of Korea, discussed two main issues: the increased importance of capital flows among member economies, particularly those from worker remittances; and the challenge presented by the region's ageing population. The meeting resolved to promote capital account liberalization and to develop resilient and efficient capital markets. It also adopted the 'Jeju Declaration on Enhancing Regional Co-operation against the Challenges of Population Ageing', in which it acknowledged the urgency of such domestic reforms such as creating sustainable pension systems, providing an increased range of savings products and improving financial literacy. In November 2005 the 13th Economic Leaders' Meeting endorsed a Busan Roadmap to the Bogor Goals, based on an assessment of action plans, which outlined key priorities and frameworks. Particular focus was drawn to support for the multilateral trading system, efforts to promote high quality regional trade agreements and free trade agreements, and strengthened collective and individual action plans. It also incorporated a Busan Business Agenda and commitments to a strategic approach to capacity building and to a pathfinder approach to promoting trade and investment in the region, through work on areas such as intellectual property rights, anti-corruption, secure trade and trade facilitation.

The 14th Economic Leaders' Meeting, held in Hanoi, Viet Nam, in November 2006 on the theme 'Towards One Dynamic Community for Sustainable Development and Prosperity', reaffirmed support for the stalled negotiations on the WTO's Doha Development Agenda; adopted the Hanoi Action Plan on the implementation of the Busan Roadmap (endorsed by the 2005 Leaders' Meeting); endorsed the APEC Action Plan on Prevention and Response to Avian and Influenza Pandemics; and expressed strong concern at the nuclear test conducted by the Democratic Republic of Korea in October.

The participants at the 15th Economic Leaders' Meeting, convened in Sydney, Australia, in September 2007, on the theme 'Strengthening our Community, Building a Sustainable Future', adopted a Declaration on Climate Change, Energy Security and Clean Development, wherein they acknowledged the need to ensure energy supplies to support regional economic growth while also preserving the quality of the environment. The Declaration incorporated an Action Agenda and agreements to establish an Asia-Pacific Network for Energy Technology and an Asia-Pacific Network for Sustainable Forest Management and Rehabilitation. The Economic Leaders also issued a statement once again affirming the need successfully to resolve the stalled WTO Doha Development Round; endorsed a report on means of further promoting Asia-Pacific economic integration; agreed to examine the options and prospects for the development of a Free Trade Area of the Asia-Pacific (FTAAP); welcomed efforts by the Economic Committee to enhance the implementation of the LAISR; endorsed the second Trade Facilitation Action Plan, which aimed to achieve a 5% reduction in business and trade transaction costs by 2010; determined to continue to strengthen the protection and enforcement of intellectual property rights in the region; and approved the Anti-corruption Principles for the Public and Private Sectors, and related codes of conduct, that had been adopted in June by the Anti-corruption and Transparency Experts' Task Force and endorsed by the September 2007 Ministerial Meeting.

SPECIAL TASK GROUPS

These may be established by the SOM to identify issues and make recommendations on areas for consideration by the grouping.

Anti-corruption and Transparency Experts' Task Force (ACT): the Ministerial Meeting, held in Santiago, Chile, in November 2004, endorsed the establishment of the ACT to implement an APEC Course of Action on Fighting Corruption and Ensuring Transparency. Activities to be undertaken included the promotion of ratification and implementation of the UN Convention against Corruption, strengthening measures to prevent and combat corruption and to sanction public officials found guilty of corruption, the promotion of public-private partnerships and enhancing co-operation within the region to combat problems of corruption. In June 2007 the ACT approved a Code of Conduct for Business, in collaboration with ABAC, a set of Conduct Principles for Public Officials, and Anti-corruption Principles for the Public and Private Sectors.

Counter Terrorism Task Force (CTTF): the CTTF was established in February 2003 to co-ordinate implementation of the Leaders' Statement on Fighting Terrorism and Promoting Growth, which had been adopted in October 2002. It was subsequently mandated to implement all other APEC initiatives to enhance human security. The CTTF assists member economies to identify and assess counter-terrorism needs and co-ordinates individual Counter Terrorism Action Plans which identify measures required and the level of implementation achieved to secure trade. The mandate of the CTTF was scheduled to expire at the end of 2008.

Cultural Focal Point Network: the Network was established in March 2005 by the SOM in order to enhance intercultural understanding and raise the profile of APEC. Its mandate included the promotion of cultural exchanges among people of the region, the recommendation of measures to build a sense of community in the APEC region and activities to collect and share good practices that promote cultural exchange.

Gender Focal Point Network: in 1996 an SOM Ad Hoc Advisory Group on Gender Integration was established, which worked until 2002 to implement a Framework for the Integration of Women in APEC and to recommend efforts to further gender integration. In October 2002 ministers meeting in Los Cabos, Mexico, endorsed the establishment of the Gender Focal Point Network to pursue this work programme. The Network reports regularly to the SOM and convenes an annual meeting: the fifth meeting was convened in Cairns, Australia, in June 2007. The Network maintains a *Gender Experts List* and a *Register of Best Practices on Gender Integration*.

Social Safety Net Capacity Building Network (SSN-CBN): an Ad Hoc Task Force on Strengthening Social Safety Nets was established in November 2000, which led efforts to establish the SSN-CBN in 2002. The Network promotes information exchange, research and development on social safety net issues, and implements recommendations of APEC finance ministers and the human resources development working group. The following areas have been identified as priority concerns for the Network: pre-crisis social safety net planning and prevention measures; capacity for evaluating effectiveness of policy action; collection of disaggregated data and access to current data; identifying at-risk populations; designing response institutions and financing; strengthening transparency and accountability in social safety net operations.

Task Force for Emergency Preparedness (TFEP): the TFEP was established in March 2005 in response to the devastating natural disaster that had occurred in the Indian Ocean in late December 2004. The TFEP is mandated to co-ordinate efforts throughout APEC to enhance disaster management capacity-building, to strengthen public awareness regarding natural disaster preparedness, prevention and survival, and to compile best practices. An APEC Senior Disaster Management Co-ordinator Seminar, convened in Cairns, Australia, in August 2007, and comprising representatives of APEC member economies and of international humanitarian organizations, determined to support the development of a three–five year TFEP strategic plan. At a meeting of the TFEP, held at the same conference, delegates from member economies agreed that a dialogue on emergency preparedness and risk reduction should take place in 2008 between regional economies, private sector representatives and major regional and international partners.

WORKING GROUPS

APEC's structure of working groups aims to promote practical and technical co-operation in specific areas, and to help implement individual and collective action plans in response to the directives of the Economic Leaders and meetings of relevant ministers.

Agricultural Technical Co-operation (ATCWG): formally established as an APEC expert's group in 1996, and incorporated into the system of working groups in 2000. The ATCWG aims to enhance the role of agriculture in the economic growth of the region and to promote co-operation in the following areas: conservation and utilization of plant and animal genetic resources; research, development and extension of agricultural biotechnology; processing, marketing, distribution and consumption of agricultural products; plant and animal quarantine and pest management; development of an agricultural finance system; sustainable agriculture; and agricultural technology transfer and training. The ATCWG has primary responsibility for undertaking recommendations connected with the implementation of the APEC Food System, which aims to improve the efficiency of food production, supply and trade within member economies. The ATCWG has conducted projects on human resource development in post-harvest technology and on capacity-building, safety assessment and communication in biotechnology. A high level policy dialogue on agricultural biotechnology was initiated in 2002. Following the outbreak of so-called 'avian flu' and its impact on the region's poultry industry, in 2004 it was agreed that the ATCWG would develop the enhanced biosecurity planning and surveillance capacity considered by APEC's member economies as being essential to protect the region's agricultural sector from the effects of future outbreaks of disease.

Energy (EWG): APEC ministers responsible for energy convened for the first time in August 1996 to discuss major energy challenges confronting the region. The main objectives of the EWG, established in 1990, are: the enhancement of regional energy security and improvement of the fuel supply market for the power sector; the development and implementation of programmes of work promoting the adoption of environmentally sound energy technologies and promoting private sector investment in regional power infrastructure; the development of energy efficiency guide-lines; and the standardization of testing facilities and results. The EWG is supported by five expert groups, on: clean fossil energy, efficiency and conservation, energy data and analysis, new and renewable energy technologies, and minerals and energy exploration and development; and by two task forces, on: renewable energy and energy efficiency financing, and biofuels. In March 1999 the EWG resolved to establish a business network to improve relations and communications with the private sector. The first meeting of the network took place in April. In May 2000 APEC energy ministers meeting in San Diego, California, USA, launched the APEC 21st Century Renewable Energy Initiative, which aims to encourage co-operation in and advance the utilization of renewable energy technologies, envisaging the establishment of a Private Sector Renewable Energy Forum. In July 2002 APEC energy ministers, convened in Mexico City, proposed several initiatives, including the cross-border interconnection of natural gas pipelines and improvements in energy security. Meeting in Portland, Oregon, USA, in June 2003 ministers agreed on a framework to implement APEC's Energy Security Initiative. The first meeting of ministers responsible for mining was convened in Santiago, Chile, in June 2004. In 2004, amid challenges to energy security and unusually high oil prices, the EWG was instructed by APEC Economic Leaders to accelerate the implementation of the Energy Security Initiative, a strategy aimed at responding to temporary supply disruptions and at addressing the broader challenges facing the region's energy supply by means of longer-term policy. In October 2005 APEC ministers responsible for energy convened in Gyeongju, Republic of Korea, to address the theme 'Securing APEC's Energy Future: Responding to Today's Challenges for Energy Supply and Demand'. Meeting in May 2007 in Darwin, Australia, under the theme 'Achieving Energy Security and Sustainable Development through Efficiency, Conservation and Diversity', energy ministers directed the EWG to formulate a voluntary Energy Peer Review Mechanism. The ministers welcomed the work of the Asia-Pacific Partnership on Clean Development and Climate, launched in January 2006 by Australia, People's Republic of China, India, Japan, Republic of Korea and the USA. Pursuant to the Osaka Action Agenda adopted by APEC Economic Leaders in 1995, the Asia Pacific Energy Research Centre (APERC) was established in July 1996 in Tokyo, Japan; APERC's mandate and programmes focus on energy sector development in APEC member states. APERC's principal research themes in 2007 were: energy efficiency in APEC economies; economic review of the People's Republic of China; understanding international energy initiatives; and urban transport energy use in the APEC region.

Fisheries (FWG): aims to maximize the economic benefits and sustainability of fisheries resources for all APEC members. Recent concerns include food safety, the quality of fish products and resource management. In 1996 the FWG initiated a four-year study on trade and investment liberalization in the sector, in the areas of tariffs, non-tariff barriers and investment measures and subsidies. In 1997 the FWG organized two technical workshops on seafood inspection systems, and conducted a workshop addressing destructive fishing techniques. The first APEC Aquaculture Forum, which considered the sustainable development of aquaculture in the region and the development of new markets for APEC fish products, was held in Taipei, Taiwan, in June 1998. In May 1999 new guide-lines were adopted to encourage the participation of the private sector in the activities of the FWG. The FWG's first business forum was convened in July 2000. In April 2002 the first ocean-related ministerial meeting, held in Seoul, Republic of Korea, adopted the Seoul Oceans Declaration, detailing recommendations on marine environmental protection and integrated coastal management. In September 2005 the second ocean-related ministerial meeting took place in Bali, Indonesia, at which the Bali Plan of Action 'Towards Healthy Oceans and Coasts for the Sustainable Growth and Prosperity of the Asia Pacific Community' was adopted. Meeting in Sanctuary Cove, Gold Coast, Australia, in April 2007, APEC member economies considered future priority activities in support of the Bali Plan of Action, covering areas such as illegal, unreported and unregulated (IUU) fishing and monitoring, control and surveillance (MCS) measures.

Health: in October 2003 a Health Task Force (HTF) was established, on an ad hoc basis, to implement health-related activities as directed by APEC leaders, ministers and senior officials, including a Health Safety Initiative, and to address health issues perceived as potential threats to the region's economy, trade and security, in particular emerging infectious diseases. The HTF convened for the first time in Taiwan (Chinese Taipei), in April 2004. It was responsible for enhancing APEC's work on preventing, preparing for and mitigating the effects of highly pathogenic avian influenza (avian flu) and any future related human influenza pandemic. APEC organized an intergovernmental meeting on Avian and Pandemic Influenza Preparedness and Response, convened in Brisbane, Australia, in October 2005. In May 2006 a Ministerial Meeting on Avian and Influenza Pandemics, held in Da Nang, Viet Nam, endorsed an APEC Action Plan on the Prevention of and Response to Avian and Influenza Pandemics. In June 2007 APEC ministers of health, meeting in Sydney, Australia, determined to reconstitute the HTF as the Health Working Group. The Group convened for its first official meeting in February 2008, and confirmed that combating the threat of avian flu remained its priority. Other main areas of work were efforts to counter HIV/AIDS, to extend the use of information technology for health benefits, and to prepare for and respond to all other public health threats.

Human Resources Development (HRD): established in 1990, comprising three networks: the Capacity Building Network, with a focus on human capacity-building, including management and technical skills development and corporate governance; the Education Network, promoting effective learning systems and supporting the role of education in advancing individual, social and economic development; and the Labour and Social Protection Network, concerned with promoting social integration through the strengthening of labour markets, the development of labour market information and policy, and improvements in working conditions and social safety net frameworks. The HRD undertakes activities through these networks to implement ministerial and leaders' directives. A voluntary network of APEC study centres links higher education and research institutions in member economies. Private sector participation in the HRD has been strengthened by the establishment of a network of APEC senior executives responsible for human resources management. Recent initiatives have included a cyber-education co-operation project, a workshop on advanced risk management, training on the prevention and resolution of employment and labour disputes, and an educators' exchange programme on the use of information technology in education.

Industrial Science and Technology (ISTWG): aims to contribute to sustainable development in the region, improve the availability of information, enhance human resources development in the sector, improve the business climate, promote policy dialogue and review and facilitate networks and partnerships. Accordingly, the ISTWG has helped to establish an APEC Virtual Centre for Environmental Technology Exchange in Japan; a Science and Technology Industrial Parks Network; an International Molecular Biology Network for the APEC Region; an APEC Centre for Technology Foresight, based in Thailand; and the APEC Science and Technology Web, an online database. During 1997 and 1998 the ISTWG formulated an APEC Action Framework on Emerging Infectious Diseases and developed an Emerging Infections Network (EINet), based at the University of Washington, Seattle, USA. In March 2004 the fourth meeting of science ministers was held in Christchurch, New Zealand, the first since 1998. In September 2004 the ISTWG established the following four new sub-groups to reflect the key policy issues agreed at the ministerial meeting: Human resources development; International science and technology networks; Connecting research and innovation; and Technological co-operation and strategic planning. These four areas remained as priorities in the ISTWG Work Plan for 2008.

Marine Resource Conservation (MRCWG): promotes initiatives within APEC to protect the marine environment and its resources. In 1996 a five-year project was initiated for the management of red tide and harmful algal blooms in the APEC region. An APEC Action Plan for Sustainability of the Marine Environment was adopted by ministers responsible for the environment, meeting in June 1997. The Plan aimed to promote regional co-operation, an integrated approach to coastal management, the prevention, reduction and control of marine pollution, and sustainable development. Efforts were also being undertaken to establish an Ocean Research Network of centres of excellence in the Pacific. Strategies to encourage private sector participation in promoting the sustainable management of marine resources were endorsed by the MRCWG in June 2000. Four main themes were identified for the Action Plan in the 21st century: balancing coastal development and resource protection; ensuring sustainable fisheries and aquaculture; understanding and observing the oceans and seas; and promoting economic and technical co-operation in oceans management. The Seoul Oceans Declaration, endorsed in April 2002 (see above), established the direction of the

MRCWG's future activities. A new strategic framework for the Group was adopted in May 2004, at a meeting held in Puerto Varas, Chile. In October the third integrated Oceans Management Forum took place on Easter Island, Chile. The MRCWG contributed to the policy directions outlined in the Bali Plan of Action, which was adopted by the APEC ocean-related ministerial meeting convened in Bali, Indonesia in September 2005 (see under Fisheries).

Small and Medium Enterprises (SMEWG): established in 1995, as the Ad Hoc Policy Level Group on Small and Medium Enterprises (SMEs), with a temporary mandate to oversee all APEC activities relating to SMEs. It supported the establishment of an APEC Centre for Technical Exchange and Training for Small and Medium Enterprises, which was inaugurated at Los Baños, near Manila, the Philippines, in September 1996. A five-year action plan for SMEs was endorsed in 1998. The group was redesignated as a working group, with permanent status, in 2000. In August 2002 the SMEWG's action plan was revised to include an evaluation framework to assist APEC and member economies in identifying and analysing policy issues. In the same month a sub-group specialising in micro-enterprises was established. The first APEC Incubator Forum was held in July–August 2003, in Taiwan (Chinese Taipei), to promote new businesses and support their early development. During 2003 the SMEWG undertook efforts to develop a special e-APEC Strategy for SMEs. In 2004 the APEC SME Co-ordination Framework was finalized. The 12th APEC SME ministerial meeting was held in Daegu, Republic of Korea, in September 2005. The meeting adopted the 'Daegu Initiative on SME Innovation Action Plan', which provided a framework for member economies to create economic and policy environments more suitable to SME innovation. In 2006 the 'APEC Private Sector Development Agenda' was launched, as well as a work plan aimed at helping government policy-makers to minimize bureaucracy and ease business regulations with a view to facilitating the working environment of SMEs.

Telecommunications and Information (TEL): incorporates four steering groups concerned with different aspects of the development and liberalization of the sector—Liberalization; Business facilitation; Development co-operation; and Human resource development. Activities are guided by directives of ministers responsible for telecommunications, who first met in 1995, in the Republic of Korea, and adopted a Seoul Declaration on Asia Pacific Information Infrastructure (APII). The second ministerial meeting, held in Gold Coast, Australia, in September 1996, adopted more detailed proposals for liberalization of the sector in member economies. In June 1998 ministers, meeting in Singapore, agreed to remove technical barriers to trade in telecommunications equipment (although Chile and New Zealand declined to sign up to the arrangement). At their fourth meeting, convened in May 2000 in Cancún, Mexico, telecommunications ministers approved a programme of action that included measures to bridge the 'digital divide' between developed and developing member economies, and adopted the APEC Principles on International Charging Arrangements for Internet Services and the APEC Principles of Interconnection. The fifth ministerial meeting, held in May 2002, issued a Statement on the Security of Information and Communications Infrastructures; a compendium of IT security standards has been disseminated in support of the Statement. A report entitled Stocktake of Progress Towards the Key Elements of a Fully Liberalized Telecommunications Sector in the APEC Region was completed in 2004. By 2007 a total of 17 out of 21 member economies had committed to Phase 1 of the mutual recognition arrangement for conformity assessment of telecommunications equipment (relating to test reports) and five economies had committed to Phase 2 (concerned with equipment certification). In 2006 the TEL was restructured to incorporate three steering groups on: liberalization; ICT development; and security and prosperity.

Tourism (TWG): established in 1991, with the aim of promoting the long-term sustainability of the tourism industry, in both environmental and social terms. The TWG administers a Tourism Information Network and an APEC International Centre for Sustainable Tourism. In 1998 the TWG initiated a project to assess the impact of the Asian financial crisis on regional tourism and to identify strategies to counter any negative effects. The first meeting of APEC ministers of tourism, held in the Republic of Korea in July 2000, adopted the Seoul Declaration on the APEC Tourism Charter. The TWG's work plan is based on four policy goals inherent in the Seoul Declaration, namely: the removal of impediments to tourism business and investment; increased mobility of visitors and increased demand for tourism goods and services; sustainable management of tourism; and enhanced recognition of tourism as a vehicle for economic and social development. At a meeting of the TWG in April 2001, APEC and the Pacific Asia Travel Association (PATA) adopted a Code for Sustainable Tourism. The Code is designed for adoption and implementation by a variety of tourism companies and government agencies. It urges members to conserve the natural environment, ecosystems and biodiversity; respect local traditions and cultures; conserve energy; reduce pollution and waste; and ensure that regular environmental audits are carried out. In November 2001 the TWG considered the impact on tourism of the September terrorist attacks on the USA. The Group advocated work to improve the quality and timeliness of tourism data, to enable accurate assessment of the situation. In 2004 the TWG published its report on Best Practices in Safety and Security to Safeguard Tourism against Terrorism. In October 2004 the 'Patagonia Declaration on Tourism in the APEC region' was endorsed at the third tourism ministers' meeting in Punta Arenas, Chile. The Declaration set out a strategic plan to ensure the viability of the regional tourism industry by measuring sustainability, safety and security and developing niche projects such as sports and health tourism. The fourth meeting of tourism ministers, held in Hoi An, Viet Nam, in October 2006, adopted the Hoi An Declaration on Tourism, which aimed to promote co-operation in developing sustainable tourism and investment in the region, with a focus on the following areas: encouragement of private sector participation in a new APEC Tourism and Investment Forum, and the promotion of the APEC Tourism Fair, both of which were to be held on the sidelines of tourism sector ministerial meetings; and liberalization of the air routes between the cultural heritage sites of APEC member states. In April 2008 tourism ministers, meeting in Lima, Peru, adopted the 'Pachacamac Declaration on Responsible Tourism'. At that time, the TWG recognized tourism as a vehicle of social development, as well as an economic force.

Transportation (TPTWG): undertakes initiatives to enhance the efficiency and safety of the regional transportation system, in order to facilitate the development of trade. The TPTWG focuses on three main areas: improving the competitiveness of the transportation industry; promoting a safe and environmentally sound regional transportation system; and human resources development, including training, research and education. The TPTWG has published surveys, directories and manuals on all types of transportation systems, and has compiled an inventory on regional co-operation on oil spills preparedness and response arrangements. A Road Transportation Harmonization Project aims to provide the basis for common standards in the automotive industry in the Asia-Pacific region. The TPTWG has established an internet database on ports and the internet-based Virtual Centre for Transportation Research, Development and Education. It plans to develop a regional action plan on the implementation of Global Navigation Satellite Systems, in consultation with the relevant international bodies. In 2003 the TPTWG was involved in discussions on means of enhancing security throughout international and domestic supply chains in the region while facilitating cross-border movement of legitimate commerce. The TPTWG was also responsible for overseeing various projects in respect of counter-terrorism. A Special Task Force was established to assist member economies to implement a new International Ship and Port Facility Security Code, sponsored by the International Maritime Organization, which entered into force on 1 July 2004. In April 2004 an Aviation Safety Experts' Group met for the first time since 2000. In July 2004 the fourth meeting of APEC ministers of transport directed the TPTWG to prepare a strategy document to strengthen its activities in transport liberalization and facilitation. A Seminar on Post Tsunami Reconstruction and Functions of Ports Safety was held in 2005. The fifth APEC Transportation ministerial meeting, held in Adelaide, Australia, in March 2007, issued a joint ministerial statement detailing the following future focus areas for the TPTWG: the formulation of aggressive road safety strategies; the harmonization of region-wide transportation security measures; the formulation of measures to support developing economies in complying with global security requirements; the formulation of systematized mass transit security measures.

Publications

ABAC Report to APEC Leaders (annually).
APEC at a Glance (annually).
APEC Business Travel Handbook.
APEC Economic Outlook (annually).
APEC Economic Policy Report.
APEC Energy Handbook (annually).
APEC Energy Statistics (annually).
APEC Outcomes and Outlook.
Guide to the Investment Regimes of the APEC Member Economies.
Key APEC Documents (annually).
Towards Knowledge-based Economies in APEC.
Trade and Investment Liberalization in APEC.
Working group reports, regional directories, other irregular surveys.

ASIAN DEVELOPMENT BANK—ADB

Address: 6 ADB Ave, Mandaluyong City, 0401 Metro Manila, Philippines; POB 789, 0980 Manila, Philippines.
Telephone: (2) 6324444; **fax:** (2) 6362444; **e-mail:** information@adb.org; **internet:** www.adb.org.

The ADB commenced operations in December 1966. The Bank's principal functions are to provide loans and equity investments for the economic and social advancement of its developing member countries, to give technical assistance for the preparation and implementation of development projects and programmes and advisory services, to promote investment of public and private capital for development purposes, and to respond to requests from developing member countries for assistance in the co-ordination of their development policies and plans.

MEMBERS

There are 48 member countries and territories within the ESCAP region and 19 others (see list of subscriptions below).

Organization
(April 2008)

BOARD OF GOVERNORS

All powers of the Bank are vested in the Board, which may delegate its powers to the Board of Directors except in such matters as admission of new members, changes in the Bank's authorized capital stock, election of Directors and President, and amendment of the Charter. One Governor and one Alternate Governor are appointed by each member country. The Board meets at least once a year. The 40th Bank Annual Meeting was convened in Kyoto, Japan, in May 2007 and the 42nd Annual Meeting was scheduled to be held in Madrid, Spain in May 2008.

BOARD OF DIRECTORS

The Board of Directors is responsible for general direction of operations and exercises all powers delegated by the Board of Governors, which elects it. Of the 12 Directors, eight represent constituency groups of member countries within the ESCAP region (with about 65% of the voting power) and four represent the rest of the member countries. Each Director serves for two years and may be re-elected.

Three specialized committees (the Audit Committee, the Budget Review Committee and the Inspection Committee), each comprising six members, assist the Board of Directors in exercising its authority with regard to supervising the Bank's financial statements, approving the administrative budget, and reviewing and approving policy documents and assistance operations.

The President of the Bank, though not a Director, is Chairman of the Board.

Chairman of Board of Directors and President: HARUHIKO KURODA (Japan).

Vice-Presidents: URSULA SCHÄFER-PREUSS (Germany), LIQUIN JIN (People's Republic of China), BINDU LOHANI (Nepal), C. LAWRENCE GREENWOOD, Jr (USA).

ADMINISTRATION

The Bank had 2,405 staff at 31 December 2006.

Five regional departments cover Central and West Asia, East Asia, the Pacific, South Asia, and Southeast Asia. Other departments and offices include Private Sector Operations, Central Operations Services, Regional and Sustainable Development, Strategy and Policy, Cofinancing Operations, and Economics and Research, as well as other administrative units.

There are Bank Resident Missions in Afghanistan, Azerbaijan, Bangladesh, Cambodia, the People's Republic of China, India, Indonesia, Kazakhstan, Kyrgyzstan, Laos, Mongolia, Nepal, Pakistan, Papua New Guinea, Sri Lanka, Tajikistan, Thailand, Uzbekistan and Viet Nam, all of which report to the head of the regional department. In addition, the Bank maintains a country office in the Philippines, a Special Office in Timor-Leste, a Pacific Liaison and Co-ordination Office in Sydney, Australia, and a South Pacific Regional Mission, based in Vanuatu (with a Sub-regional Office in Fiji). Representative Offices are located in Tokyo, Japan, Frankfurt am Main, Germany (for Europe), and Washington, DC, USA (for North America).

Managing Director-General: RAJAT M. NAG.

INSTITUTE

ADB Institute (ADBI): Kasumigaseki Bldg, 8th Floor, 2–5 Kasumigaseki 3-chome, Chiyoda-ku, Tokyo 100-6008, Japan; tel. (3) 3593-5500; fax (3) 3593-5571; e-mail info@adbi.org; internet www.adbi.org; f. 1997 as a subsidiary body of the ADB to research and analyse long-term development issues and to disseminate development practices through training and other capacity-building activities; Dean Dr MASAHIRO KAWAI (Japan).

FINANCIAL STRUCTURE

The Bank's ordinary capital resources (which are used for loans to the more advanced developing member countries) are held and used entirely separately from its Special Funds resources (see below). A fourth General Capital Increase (GCI IV), amounting to US $26,318m. (or 100%), was authorized in May 1994. At the final deadline for subscription to GCI IV, on 30 September 1996, 55 member countries had subscribed shares amounting to $24,675.4m.

At 31 December 2006 the position of subscriptions to the capital stock was as follows: authorized US $53,169.0m.; 'callable' subscribed $49,429.4m.

The Bank also borrows funds from the world capital markets. Total borrowings during 2006 amounted to US $5,576m. (compared with $4,230m. in 2005). At 31 December 2006 total outstanding borrowings amounted to $65,129m.

In July 1986 the Bank abolished the system of fixed lending rates, under which ordinary operations loans had carried interest rates fixed at the time of loan commitment for the entire life of the loan. Under the new system the lending rate is adjusted every six months, to take into account changing conditions in international financial markets.

Activities

Loans by the ADB are usually aimed at specific projects. In responding to requests from member governments for loans, the Bank's staff assesses the financial and economic viability of projects and the way in which they fit into the economic framework and priorities of development of the country concerned. In 1985 the Bank decided to expand its assistance to the private sector, hitherto comprising loans to development finance institutions, under government guarantee, for lending to small and medium-sized enterprises; a programme was formulated for direct financial assistance, in the form of equity and loans without government guarantee, to private enterprises. In 1992 a Social Dimensions Unit was established as part of the central administrative structure of the Bank, which contributed to the Bank's increasing awareness of the importance of social aspects of development as essential components of sustainable economic growth. During the early 1990s the Bank also aimed to expand its role as project financier by providing assistance for policy formulation and review and promoting regional co-operation, while placing greater emphasis on individual country requirements. During that period the Bank also introduced a commitment to assess development projects for their impact on the local population and to avoid all involuntary resettlement where possible and established a formal procedure for grievances, under which the Board may authorize an inspection of a project by an independent panel of experts, at the request of the affected community or group.

The currency instability and ensuing financial crises affecting many Asian economies in the second half of 1997 and in 1998 prompted the Bank to reflect on its role in the region. The Bank resolved to strengthen its activities as a broad-based development institution, rather than solely as a project financier, through lending policies, dialogue, co-financing and technical assistance. A Task Force on Financial Sector Reform was established to review the causes and effects of the regional financial crisis. The Task Force identified the Bank's initial priorities as being to accelerate banking and capital market reforms in member countries, to promote market efficiency in the financial, trade and industrial sectors, to promote good governance and sound corporate management, and to alleviate the social impact of structural adjustments. In mid-1999 the Bank approved a technical assistance grant to establish an internet-based Asian Recovery Information Centre, within a new Regional Monitoring Unit, which aimed to facilitate access to information regarding the economic and social impact of the Asian financial crisis, analyses of economic needs of countries, reform programmes and monitoring of the economic recovery process. (In April 2005 the Unit was replaced by an Office of Regional Economic Integration, which aimed to promote economic co-operation and integration among developing member countries and to contribute to economic growth within the whole region.)

In November 1999 the Board of Directors approved a new overall strategy objective of poverty reduction, which was to be the principal consideration for all future Bank lending, project financing and technical assistance. The strategy incorporated key aims of supporting sustainable, grass-roots based economic growth, social development and good governance. The Board also approved a health sector policy, to concentrate resources on basic primary healthcare, and initiated reviews of the Bank's private sector strategy and the efficiency of resident missions. During 2000 the Bank began to refocus its country strategies, projects and lending targets to complement the poverty reduction strategy. In addition, it initiated a process of wide-ranging discussions to formulate a long-term strategic framework for the next 15 years, based on the target of reducing by 50% the incidence of extreme poverty by 2015, one of the so-called Millennium Development Goals (MDGs) identified by the UN General Assembly. The framework, establishing the operational priorities and principles for reducing poverty, was approved in March 2001. A review of the poverty reduction strategy, initiated at the end of 2003, concluded that more comprehensive, results-oriented monitoring and evaluation be put in place, with reference to both country strategies and programmes and management systems. It also recommended a closer alignment of Bank operations with national poverty reduction strategies. The review determined to include capacity development as a new overall thematic priority for the Bank, in addition to environmental sustainability, gender and development, private sector development and regional co-operation. In mid-2004 the Bank initiated a separate reform agenda to incorporate the strategy approach 'Managing for development results' throughout the organization. In July 2006 the Bank adopted a strategy to promote regional co-operation and integration in order to combat poverty through collective regional and cross-border activities.

In June 2004 the Bank approved a new policy to provide rehabilitation and reconstruction assistance following disasters or other emergencies. The policy also aimed to assist developing member countries with prevention, preparation and mitigation of the impact of future disasters. At the end of December the Bank announced assistance amounting to US $325m. to finance immediate reconstruction and rehabilitation efforts in Indonesia, the Maldives and Sri Lanka, which had been severely damaged by a series of large waves, or tsunamis, that had spread throughout the Indian Ocean as a result of a massive earthquake that had occurred close to the west coast of Sumatra, Indonesia. Of the total amount $150m. was to be drawn as new lending commitments from the Asian Development Fund. Teams of Bank experts undertook to identify priority operations and initiated efforts, in co-operation with governments and other partner organizations, to prepare for more comprehensive reconstruction activities. In accordance with the 2004 policy initiative, an interdepartmental task force was established to co-ordinate the Bank's response to the disaster. In January 2005, at a Special ASEAN Leaders' Meeting, held in Jakarta, Indonesia, the Bank pledged assistance amounting to $500m.; later in that month the Bank announced its intention to establish a $600m. Multi-donor Asian Tsunami Fund to accelerate the provision of reconstruction and technical assistance to countries most affected by the disaster. In March 2006 the Bank hosted a high-level co-ordination meeting on rehabilitation and reconstruction assistance to tsunami-affected countries. In October the Bank, with representatives of the World Bank, undertook an immediate preliminary damage and needs assessment following a massive earthquake in north-west Pakistan, which also affected remote parts of Afghanistan and India. The report identified relief and reconstruction requirements totalling some $5,200m. The Bank made an initial contribution of $80m. to a Special Fund (see below) and also pledged concessional support of up to $1,000m. for rehabilitation and reconstruction efforts in the affected areas.

In 2006 the Bank approved 80 loans for 67 projects amounting to US $7,396.3m. Loans from ordinary capital resources in 2006 totalled $6,116.9m., while loans from the ADF amounted to $1,279.4m. The largest proportion of assistance, amounting to some 24% of total lending, was allocated to the finance sector. The largest borrowers were the People's Republic of China, India and Pakistan (each with 21% of total lending). Disbursements of loans during 2006 amounted to $5,758m., bringing cumulative disbursements to $84,253m.

In 2006 grants approved for technical assistance (e.g. project preparation, consultant services and training) amounted to US $241.6m. for 260 projects, of which $92.3m. derived from the TASF, $56.8m. from the JSF, and $92.7m. from other bilateral and multilateral sources. The Bank's Operations Evaluation Office prepares reports on completed projects, in order to assess achievements and problems. In April 2000 the Bank announced that, from 2001, some new loans would be denominated in local currencies, in order to ease the repayment burden on recipient economies.

The Bank co-operates with other international organizations active in the region, particularly the World Bank group, the IMF, UNDP and APEC, and participates in meetings of aid donors for developing member countries. In May 2001 the Bank and UNDP signed a memorandum of understanding (MOU) on strategic partnership, in order to strengthen co-operation in the reduction of poverty, for example the preparation of common country assessments and a common database on poverty and other social indicators. Also in 2001 the Bank signed an MOU with the World Bank on administrative arrangements for co-operation, providing a framework for closer co-operation and more efficient use of resources. In May 2004 the Bank signed a revised MOU with ESCAP to enhance co-operation activities to achieve the MDGs. In early 2002 the Bank worked with the World Bank and UNDP to assess the preliminary needs of the interim administration in Afghanistan, in preparation for an International Conference on Reconstruction Assistance to Afghanistan, held in January, in Tokyo. The Bank pledged to work with its member governments to provide highly concessional grants and loans of some US $500m. over two-and-a-half years, with a particular focus on road reconstruction, basic education, and agricultural irrigation rehabilitation. A new policy concerning co-operation with non-governmental organizations (NGOs) was approved by the Bank in 1998. The Bank administers an NGO Center to provide advice and support to NGOs on involvement in country strategies and development programmes.

The Bank has actively supported regional, sub-regional and national initiatives to enhance economic development and promote economic co-operation within the region. The Bank is the main co-ordinator and financier of a Greater Mekong Sub-region (GMS) programme, initiated in 1992 to strengthen co-operation between Cambodia, the People's Republic of China, Laos, Myanmar, Thailand and Viet Nam. Projects undertaken have included transport and other infrastructure links, energy projects and communicable disease control. The first meeting of GMS heads of state was convened in Phnom-Penh, Cambodia, in November 2002. A Core Environment Programme was inaugurated in 2005. Other sub-regional initiatives supported by the Bank include the Central Asian Regional Economic Cooperation (CAREC), South Asia Sub-regional Economic Cooperation (SASEC) initiative, the Indonesia, Malaysia, Thailand Growth Triangle (IMT-GT), and the Brunei, Indonesia, Malaysia, Philippines East ASEAN Growth Area (BIMP-EAGA).

SPECIAL FUNDS

The Bank is authorized to establish and administer Special Funds. The Asian Development Fund (ADF) was established in 1974 in order to provide a systematic mechanism for mobilizing and administering resources for the Bank to lend on concessionary terms to the least-developed member countries. In 1998 the Bank revised the terms of ADF. Since 1 January 1999 all new project loans are repayable within 32 years, including an eight-year grace period, while quick-disbursing programme loans have a 24-year maturity, also including an eight-year grace period. The previous annual service charge was redesignated as an interest charge, including a portion to cover administrative expenses. The new interest charges on all loans are 1%–1.5% per annum. During 2006 45 ADF loans were approved, amounting to US $1,279m. Successive replenishments of the Fund's resources amounted to $809m. for the period 1976–78, $2,150m. for 1979–82, $3,214m. for 1983–86, $3,600m. for 1987–90, $4,200m. for 1992–95, $6,300m. for 1997–2000, and $5,650m. for 2001–04. In May 2004 28 donor countries pledged $3,200m. towards the ADF's eighth replenishment (ADF IX), which totalled $7,000m. to provide resources for the period 2005–08. The first meeting of donors to consider ADF X, a replenishment of the Fund's resources for the period 2009–12, was held in Sydney, Australia, in September 2007.

The Bank provides technical assistance grants from its Technical Assistance Special Fund (TASF). By the end of 2006, the Fund's total resources amounted to US $1,346.9m., of which $1,126.4m. had been utilized or committed. The Japan Special Fund (JSF) was established in 1988 to provide finance for technical assistance by means of grants, in both the public and private sectors. The JSF aims to help developing member countries restructure their economies, enhance the opportunities for attracting new investment, and recycle funds. The Japanese Government had committed a total of 107,600m. yen (equivalent to some $928.7m.) to the JSF by the end of 2006. During 2006 the Bank approved 64 technical assistance projects for the JSF, amounting to $56.6m. An Asian Currency Crisis Support Facility (ACCSF) was operational for the three-year period March 1999–March 2002, as an independent component of the JSF to provide additional technical assistance, interest payment assistance and guarantees to countries most affected by financial instability, i.e. Indonesia, Republic of Korea, Malaysia, Philippines and Thailand. At the end of 2002 the Japanese Government, as the sole financier of the fund, had contributed 27,500m. yen (some $241.0m.) to the

ACCSF. The Bank administers the ADB Institute Special Fund, which was established to finance the ADB Institute's initial operations. By 31 December 2006 cumulative commitments to the Special Fund amounted to 14,400m. yen (or $121.4m.).

In February 2005 the Bank established the Asian Tsunami Fund, with funds of US $600m., to accelerate the provision of reconstruction and technical assistance to countries most affected by the natural disaster that had affected several countries in the region in December 2004. At the end of 2006 the Fund's uncommitted resources amounted to $19.5m. The Pakistan Earthquake Fund was established in November 2005, with a commitment from the Bank of $80m., to help to deliver emergency grant financing and technical assistance required for immediate rehabilitation and reconstruction efforts following the massive earthquake that had occurred in October. Uncommitted resources amounted to $6.0m. at December 2006.

TRUST FUNDS

The Bank also manages and administers several trust funds and other bilateral donor arrangements. The Japanese Government funds the Japan Scholarship Program, under which 2,104 scholarships had been awarded to recipients from 35 member countries between 1988 and 2006. In May 2000 the Japan Fund for Poverty Reduction was established, with an initial contribution of 10,000m. yen (approximately US $92.6m.) by the Japanese Government, to support ADB-financed poverty reduction and social development activities. By the end of 2006 cumulative commitments to the Fund totalled $360.4m. and 90 projects, amounting to $244.3m., had been approved for implementation. A Japan Fund for Information and Communication Technology (ICT) was established in July 2001, for a three-year period (later extended by one year until mid-2005), to promote the advancement and use of ICT in developing member countries. By the end of 2006, when several projects were still being implemented, some $10.4m. had been committed under the Fund. In March 2004 a Japan Fund for Public Policy Training was established, with an initial contribution by the Japanese Government, to enhance capacity-building for public policy management in developing member countries.

The majority of grant funds in support of the Bank's technical assistance activities are provided by bilateral donors under channel financing arrangements (CFAs), the first of which was negotiated in 1980. CFAs may also be processed as a thematic financing tool, for example concerned with renewable energy, water or poverty reduction, enabling more than one donor to contribute. A Co-operation Fund for Regional Trade and Financial Security Initiative was established in July 2004, with contributions by Australia, Japan and the USA, to support efforts to combat money laundering and the financing of terrorism. In 2006 new CFA funds included the ADB-Australia South Asia Development Partnership Facility and the Second Danish Co-operation Fund for Renewable Energy and Energy Efficiency in Rural Areas.

Finance

Internal administrative expenses totalled US $299.4m. in 2006 and were budgeted at $332.9m. for 2007.

Publications

ADB Business Opportunities (monthly).
ADB Institute Newsletter.
ADB Review (6 a year).
Annual Report.
Asia Economic Monitor (2 a year).
Asian Development Outlook (annually).
Asian Development Review (2 a year).
Basic Statistics (annually).
Key Indicators of Developing Asian and Pacific Countries (annually).
Law and Policy Reform Bulletin (annually).
Loan Disbursement Handbook.
Studies and technical assistance reports, information brochures, guide-lines, sample bidding documents, staff papers.

Statistics

SUBSCRIPTIONS AND VOTING POWER
(October 2007)

Country	Voting power (% of total)	Subscribed capital (% of total)
Regional:		
Afghanistan	0.325	0.034
Armenia	0.537	0.298
Australia	4.917	5.773
Azerbaijan	0.653	0.444
Bangladesh	1.114	1.019
Bhutan	0.303	0.006
Brunei	0.580	0.351
Cambodia	0.338	0.049
China, People's Republic	5.442	6.429
Cook Islands	0.301	0.003
Fiji	0.353	0.068
Georgia	0.571	0.341
Hong Kong	0.733	0.543
India	5.352	6.317
Indonesia	4.646	5.434
Japan	12.756	15.571
Kazakhstan	0.942	0.805
Kiribati	0.302	0.004
Korea, Republic	4.320	5.026
Kyrgyzstan	0.537	0.298
Laos	0.310	0.014
Malaysia	2.472	2.717
The Maldives	0.302	0.004
Marshall Islands	0.301	0.003
Micronesia, Federated States	0.302	0.004
Mongolia	0.310	0.015
Myanmar	0.733	0.543
Nauru	0.302	0.004
Nepal	0.416	0.147
New Zealand	1.524	1.532
Pakistan	2.037	2.174
Palau	0.301	0.003
Papua New Guinea	0.373	0.094
Philippines	2.200	2.377
Samoa	0.301	0.003
Singapore	0.570	0.340
Solomon Islands	0.304	0.007
Sri Lanka	0.761	0.579
Taiwan	1.168	1.087
Tajikistan	0.527	0.286
Thailand	1.385	1.358
Timor-Leste	0.306	0.010
Tonga	0.302	0.004
Turkmenistan	0.501	0.253
Tuvalu	0.300	0.001
Uzbekistan	0.836	0.672
Vanuatu	0.304	0.007
Viet Nam	0.571	0.341
Sub-total	65.040	63.390
Non-regional:		
Austria	0.570	0.340
Belgium	0.570	0.340
Canada	4.474	5.219
Denmark	0.570	0.340
Finland	0.570	0.340
France	2.156	2.322
Germany	3.752	4.316
Ireland	0.570	0.340
Italy	1.741	1.803
Luxembourg	0.570	0.340
Netherlands	1.117	1.023
Norway	0.570	0.340
Portugal	0.570	0.340
Spain	0.570	0.340
Sweden	0.570	0.340
Switzerland	0.764	0.582
Turkey	0.570	0.340
United Kingdom	1.929	2.038
USA	12.756	15.571
Sub-total	34.960	36.610
Total	100.000	100.000

LENDING ACTIVITIES BY SECTOR

Sector	2006 Amount (US $ million)	%	1968–2006 %
Agriculture and natural resources	807.17	10.91	13.38
Education	250.90	3.39	4.67
Energy	1,369.50	18.52	20.06
Finance	1,787.00	24.16	12.61
Health, nutrition and social protection	—	—	2.46
Industry and trade	10.00	0.14	4.48
Law, economic management and public policy	220.00	2.97	3.75
Transport and communications	1,433.20	19.38	23.10
Water supply, sanitation and waste management	638.82	8.64	5.28
Multi-sector	879.70	11.89	10.22
Total	7,396.29	100.00	100.00

LENDING ACTIVITIES BY COUNTRY, 2006
(US $ million)

Country	Ordinary Capital	ADF	Total
Afghanistan	40.00	78.20	118.20
Azerbaijan	10.00	—	10.00
Bangladesh	—	255.10	255.10
Bhutan	—	37.60	37.60
Cambodia	—	62.00	62.00
China, People's Republic	1,572.00	—	1,572.00
India	1,535.00	—	1,535.00
Indonesia	675.00	109.80	784.80
Kazakhstan	125.00	—	125.00
Laos	—	35.20	35.20
Mongolia	—	46.20	46.20
Nepal	—	86.00	86.00
Pakistan	1,428.80	107.00	1,535.80
Papua New Guinea	35.00	18.00	53.00
Philippines	650.00	—	650.00
Sri Lanka	13.50	46.50	60.00
Tajikistan	—	5.50	5.50
Uzbekistan	32.60	27.60	60.20
Viet Nam	—	308.19	308.19
Regional	—	56.50	56.50
Total	6,116.90	1,279.39	7,396.29

Source: *ADB Annual Report 2006*.

ASSOCIATION OF SOUTH EAST ASIAN NATIONS—ASEAN

Address: 70A Jalan Sisingamangaraja, POB 2072, Jakarta 12110, Indonesia.
Telephone: (21) 7262991; **fax:** (21) 7398234; **e-mail:** public@aseansec.org; **internet:** www.aseansec.org.

ASEAN was established in August 1967 in Bangkok, Thailand, to accelerate economic progress and to increase the stability of the South-East Asian region. In November 2007 its 10 members signed an ASEAN Charter, which, on entering into force, was formally to accord the grouping with the legal status of an intergovernmental organization.

MEMBERS

Brunei
Cambodia
Indonesia
Laos
Malaysia
Myanmar
Philippines
Singapore
Thailand
Viet Nam

Organization
(April 2008)

SUMMIT MEETING
The highest authority of ASEAN, bringing together the heads of government of member countries. The first meeting was held in Bali, Indonesia, in February 1976. The 13th summit meeting was held in Singapore in November 2007. The new ASEAN Charter specified that summit meetings were to be convened at least twice a year.

MINISTERIAL MEETINGS
The ASEAN Ministerial Meeting (AMM), comprising ministers of foreign affairs of member states, meets annually, in each member country in turn, to formulate policy guide-lines and to co-ordinate ASEAN activities. These meetings are followed by 'post-ministerial conferences' (PMCs), where ASEAN ministers of foreign affairs meet with their counterparts from countries that are 'dialogue partners' as well as with ministers from other countries. Meetings of ASEAN Economic Ministers (AEM) and ASEAN Finance Ministers Meetings are also convened once a year to direct ASEAN co-operation in their respective areas of responsibility. Joint Ministerial Meetings, consisting of ministers of foreign affairs and of economic affairs are convened prior to a summit meeting, and may be held at the request of either group of ministers. Other ministers meet regularly to promote co-operation in different sectors. The ASEAN Charter envisaged that ministers of foreign affairs would form an ASEAN Co-ordinating Council to assist in the preparation of summit meetings, and would also convene as the ASEAN Foreign Ministers Meeting as part of a new ASEAN Political and Security Community Council.

STANDING COMMITTEE
The Standing Committee normally meets every two months. It consists of the minister of foreign affairs of the host country and ambassadors of the other members accredited to the host country. Upon the new ASEAN Charter entering into effect the Standing Committee was to be superseded by a Committee of Permanent Representatives, comprising an ambassador from each member state.

SECRETARIATS
A permanent secretariat was established in Jakarta, Indonesia, in 1976 to form a central co-ordinating body. The Secretariat comprises four bureaux relating to: Economic Integration, Finance and Integration Support, External Relations and Co-ordination, and Resources Development. The Secretary-General holds office for a five-year term and is assisted by two Deputy Secretaries-General, to be increased to four Deputy Secretaries-General when the ASEAN Charter enters into force. In each member country day-to-day work is co-ordinated by an ASEAN National Secretariat.

Secretary-General: Dr SURIN PITSUWAN (Thailand).

Deputy Secretaries-General: Dr SEOUNG RATHCHAVY (Cambodia), NICHOLAS TANDI DAMMEN (Indonesia).

COMMITTEES AND SENIOR OFFICIALS' MEETINGS
Ministerial meetings are serviced by 29 committees of senior officials, supported by 122 technical working groups. There is a network of subsidiary technical bodies comprising sub-committees, expert groups, ad hoc working groups and working parties.

To support the conduct of relations with other countries and international organizations, ASEAN committees (composed of heads of diplomatic missions) have been established in foreign capitals: those of Australia, Belgium, Canada, the People's Republic of China, France, Germany, India, Japan, the Republic of Korea, New Zealand, Pakistan, Russia, Saudi Arabia, Turkey, the United Kingdom and the USA. There are also ASEAN committees in New York (USA) and Geneva (Switzerland).

Activities

ASEAN was established in 1967 with the signing of the ASEAN Declaration, otherwise known as the Bangkok Declaration, by the ministers of foreign affairs of Indonesia, Malaysia, the Philippines, Singapore and Thailand. In February 1976, the first ASEAN summit meeting adopted the Treaty of Amity and Co-operation in South-East Asia and the Declaration of ASEAN Concord. Brunei joined the organization in January 1984, shortly after attaining independence. Viet Nam was admitted as the seventh member of ASEAN in July 1995. Laos and Myanmar joined in July 1997 and Cambodia was formally admitted in April 1999, fulfilling the organization's ambition to incorporate all 10 countries in the sub-region.

In December 1997 ASEAN heads of government agreed upon a series of commitments to determine the development of the grouping into the 21st century. The so-called Vision 2020 envisaged ASEAN as 'a concert of Southeast Asian nations, outward looking, living in peace, stability and prosperity, bonded together in partnership in dynamic development and in a community of caring societies'. In October 2003 ASEAN leaders adopted a declaration known as 'Bali Concord II', which committed signatory states to the creation of an ASEAN Economic Community, an ASEAN Security Community and an ASEAN Socio-Cultural Community. In December 2005 heads of state determined to establish a High Level Task Force to formulate a new ASEAN Charter. The finalized document, codifying the principles and purposes of the grouping and according it the legal status of an intergovernmental organization, was signed in November 2007 by ASEAN heads of government attending the 13th summit meeting, convened in Singapore. It was to enter into force 30 days after being ratified by all 10 member states.

In December 2005 the first East Asia Summit meeting was convened, following the ASEAN leaders' meeting in Kuala Lumpur, Malaysia. It was attended by ASEAN member countries, the People's Republic of China, Japan, the Republic of Korea, India, Australia and New Zealand; Russia participated as an observer. The meeting agreed to pursue co-operation in areas of common interest and determined to meet annually. It concluded a Declaration on Avian Influenza Prevention, Control and Response. At the second East Asia Summit meeting, held in Cebu, the Philippines, in January 2007, a Declaration on East Asian Energy Security was adopted. An inaugural meeting of East Asian ministers of energy was convened in August. The third summit meeting was held in Singapore, in November.

TRADE AND ECONOMIC CO-OPERATION

In January 1992, heads of government, meeting in Singapore, signed an agreement to create an ASEAN Free Trade Area (AFTA) by 2008. In accordance with the agreement, a common effective preferential tariff (CEPT) scheme came into effect in January 1993. The CEPT covered all manufactured products, including capital goods, and processed agricultural products (which together accounted for two-thirds of intra-ASEAN trade), but was to exclude unprocessed agricultural products. Tariffs were to be reduced to a maximum of 20% within a period of five to eight years and to 0%–5% during the subsequent seven to 10 years. Fifteen categories were designated for accelerated tariff reduction. Member states were, however, still to be permitted exclusion for certain 'sensitive' products. In October 1993 ASEAN trade ministers agreed to modify the CEPT, with only Malaysia and Singapore having adhered to the original tariff reduction schedule. The new AFTA programme, under which all member countries except Brunei were scheduled to begin tariff reductions from 1 January 1994, substantially enlarged the number of products to be included in the tariff reduction process (i.e. on the so-called 'inclusion list') and reduced the list of products eligible for protection. In September 1994, ASEAN ministers of economic affairs agreed to accelerate the implementation of AFTA, advancing the deadline for its entry into operation from 2008 to 1 January 2003. Tariffs were to be reduced to 0%–5% within seven to 10 years, or within five to eight years for products designated for accelerated tariff cuts. In July 1995, Viet Nam was admitted as a member of ASEAN and was granted until 2006 to implement the AFTA trade agreements. In December 1995 heads of government, at a meeting convened in Bangkok, Thailand, agreed to extend liberalization to certain service industries, including banking, telecommunications and tourism. In July 1997 Laos and Myanmar became members of ASEAN and were granted a 10-year period, from 1 January 1998, to comply with the AFTA schedule.

In December 1998, meeting in Hanoi, Viet Nam, heads of government approved a Statement on Bold Measures, detailing ASEAN's strategies to deal with the economic crisis that had prevailed in the region since late 1997. These included incentives to attract investors, for example a three-year exemption on corporate taxation, accelerated implementation of the ASEAN Investment Area (AIA, see below), and advancing the AFTA deadline, for the original six members, to 2002, with some 85% of products to be covered by the arrangements by 2000, and 90% by 2001. It was envisaged that the original six members and the new members would achieve the elimination of all tariffs by 2015 and 2018, respectively. The Hanoi Plan of Action, which was also adopted at the meeting as a framework for the development of the organization over the period 1999–2004, incorporated a series of measures aimed at strengthening macroeconomic and financial co-operation and enhancing economic integration. In April 1999 Cambodia, on being admitted as a full member of ASEAN, signed an agreement to implement the tariff reduction programme over a 10-year period, commencing 1 January 2000. Cambodia also signed a declaration endorsing the commitments of the 1998 Statement on Bold Measures. In May 2000 Malaysia was granted a special exemption to postpone implementing tariff reductions on motor vehicles for two years from 1 January 2003. In November 2000 a protocol was approved permitting further temporary exclusion of products from the CEPT scheme for countries experiencing economic difficulties. On 1 January 2002 AFTA was formally realized among the original six signatories (Brunei, Indonesia, Malaysia, the Philippines, Singapore and Thailand), which had achieved the objective of reducing to less than 5% trade restrictions on 96.24% of products on the inclusion list. Some 98.36% of tariff lines for the core six AFTA members were on the inclusion list at that time. Tariffs on trade in products on the inclusion list for these countries averaged less than 2.9% in 2002. By 1 January 2005 tariffs on just under 99% of products on the 2005 CEPT inclusion list had been reduced to the 0–5% range among the original six signatory countries, with the average tariff standing at 1.93%. With regard to Cambodia, Laos, Myanmar and Viet Nam, some 81% of products fell within the 0–5% range.

To complement AFTA in facilitating intra-ASEAN trade, member countries are committed to the removal of non-tariff barriers (such as quotas), the harmonization of standards and conformance measures, and the simplification and harmonization of customs procedures. In June 1996 the Working Group on Customs Procedures completed a draft legal framework for regional co-operation, designed to simplify and harmonize customs procedures, legislation and product classification. The agreement was signed in March 1997 at the inaugural meeting of ASEAN finance ministers. (Laos and Myanmar signed the customs agreement in July and Cambodia assented to it in April 1999.) In 2001 ASEAN finalized its system of harmonized tariff nomenclature, implementation of which commenced in the following year. In November the summit meeting determined to extend ASEAN tariff preferences to ASEAN's newer members from January 2002, under the ASEAN Integration System of Preferences (AISP), thus allowing Cambodia, Laos, Myanmar and Viet Nam tariff-free access to the more developed ASEAN markets earlier than the previously agreed target date of 2010.

In November 2000 heads of government endorsed an Initiative for ASEAN Integration (IAI), which aimed to reduce economic disparities within the region through effective co-operation, in particular, in training and other educational opportunities. In July 2002 the AMM endorsed an IAI Work Plan, which focused on the following priority areas: human resources development; infrastructure; information and communications technology (ICT); and regional economic integration. The Plan was to be implemented over the six-year period 2002–08. Much of the funding for the Initiative came from ASEAN's external partners, including Australia, India, Japan, Norway and the Republic of Korea.

The Bali Concord II, adopted in October 2003, affirmed commitment to existing ASEAN economic co-operation frameworks, including the Hanoi Plan of Action (and any subsequently agreed regional plans of action) and the IAI, and outlined plans for the creation, by 2020, of an integrated ASEAN Economic Community (AEC), entailing: the harmonization of customs procedures and technical regulations by the end of 2004; the removal of non-tariff trade barriers and the establishment of a network of free trade zones by 2005; and the progressive withdrawal of capital controls and strengthening of intellectual property rights. An ASEAN legal unit was to be established to strengthen and enhance existing dispute settlement systems. (A Protocol on Enhanced Dispute Settlement Mechanism was signed in November 2004.) The free movement of professional and skilled workers would be facilitated by standardizing professional requirements and simplifying visa procedures, with the adoption of a single ASEAN visa requirement envisaged by 2005. In 2004 ASEAN economic and trade ministers worked closely, in co-operation with the private sector, to produce a 'road map' for the integration of 11 sectors identified as priority areas in the AEC plan of action. In July the ASEAN Ministerial Meeting reviewed progress in preparing the Vientiane Action Programme (VAP), the proposed successor to the Hanoi Plan of Action. In November the 10th meeting of ASEAN heads of state, held in Vientiane, Laos, endorsed the VAP with commitments to deepen regional integration and narrow the development gap within the grouping. An ASEAN Development Fund was to be established to support the implementation of the VAP and other action programmes. The leaders adopted two plans of action (concerning security and socio-cultural affairs) to further the implementation of the Bali Concord II regarding the establishment of a three-pillared ASEAN Community, which included the AEC. An ASEAN Framework Agreement for Integration of the Priority Sectors and its Protocols was also signed. Import duties (on 85% of products) were to be eliminated by 2007 for the original members (including Brunei) and by 2012 for newer member states on the following 11 sectors, accounting for more than 50% of intra-ASEAN trade in 2003: agro-based products, air travel, automotive, electronics, fisheries, healthcare, information and communications technology, rubber-based products, textiles and apparels, tourism and wood-based products. A Blueprint and Strategic Schedule for realising the AEC by 2015 was approved by ASEAN ministers of economic affairs in August 2007 and was signed by ASEAN heads of state, meeting in November.

In November 1999 an informal meeting of leaders of ASEAN countries, the People's Republic of China, Japan and the Republic of Korea (designating themselves 'ASEAN + 3') issued a Joint Statement on East Asian Co-operation, in which they agreed to strengthen regional unity, and addressed the long-term possibility of establishing an East Asian common market and currency. Meeting in May 2000, in Chiang Mai, Thailand, ASEAN + 3 ministers of economic affairs proposed the establishment of an enhanced currency-swap mechanism, enabling countries to draw on liquidity support to defend their economies during balance of payments difficulties or speculative currency attacks and to prevent future financial crises. In July ASEAN + 3 ministers of foreign affairs convened an inaugural formal summit in Bangkok, Thailand, and in October ASEAN + 3 economic affairs ministers agreed to hold their hitherto twice-yearly informal meetings on an institutionalized basis. In November an informal meeting of ASEAN + 3 leaders approved further co-operation in various sectors and initiated a feasibility study into a proposal to establish a regional free trade area. In May 2001 ASEAN + 3 ministers of economic affairs endorsed a series of projects for co-operation in ICT, environment, small and medium-sized enterprises, Mekong Basin development, and harmonization of standards. In the same month the so-called Chiang Mai Initiative on currency-swap arrangements was formally approved by ASEAN + 3 finance ministers. A meeting of the ASEAN + 3 leaders was held alongside the seventh ASEAN summit in November. In October ASEAN + 3 agriculture and forestry ministers met for the first time, and discussed issues of poverty alleviation, food security, agricultural research and human resource development. The first meeting of ASEAN + 3 tourism ministers was held in January 2002. In July ASEAN + 3 ministers of foreign affairs declared their support for other regional initiatives, namely an Asia Co-operation Dialogue, which was initiated by the Thai Government in June, and an Initiative for Development in East Asia (IDEA), which had been announced by the Japanese Government in January. An IDEA ministerial meeting was convened in Tokyo, in August. ASEAN + 3 ministers of labour convened in May 2003. In August a meeting of ASEAN + 3 finance ministers agreed to establish a Finance Co-operation Fund, to be administered by the ASEAN Secretariat; the Fund was to support ongoing economic reviews relating to projects such as the Chiang Mai Initiative. In September the sixth consultation between ASEAN + 3 ministers of economic affairs was held, at which several new projects were endorsed, including two on e-commerce. During 2004 an ASEAN + 3 Unit was established in the ASEAN Secretariat. The first meeting of ASEAN + 3 energy ministers was held in June. In November the ASEAN summit meeting agreed to convene a meeting of an East Asia grouping, to be developed in parallel with the ASEAN + 3 framework.

POLITICS AND SECURITY

In 1971 ASEAN members endorsed a declaration envisaging the establishment of a Zone of Peace, Freedom and Neutrality (ZOPFAN) in the South-East Asian region. This objective was incorporated in the Declaration of ASEAN Concord, which was adopted at the first summit meeting of the organization, held in Bali, Indonesia, in February 1976. (The Declaration also issued guide-lines for co-operation in economic development and the promotion of social justice and welfare.) Also in February 1976 a Treaty of Amity and Co-operation was signed by heads of state, establishing principles of mutual respect for the independence and sovereignty of all nations, non-interference in the internal affairs of one another and settlement of disputes by peaceful means. The Treaty was amended in December 1987 by a protocol providing for the accession of Papua New Guinea and other non-member countries in the region. In January 1992 ASEAN leaders agreed that there should be greater co-operation on security matters within the grouping, and that ASEAN's post-ministerial conferences (PMCs) should be used as a forum for discussion of questions relating to security with dialogue partners and other countries. In July 1992 Viet Nam and Laos signed ASEAN's Treaty of Amity and Co-operation. Cambodia acceded to the Treaty in January 1995 and Myanmar signed it in July.

In December 1995 ASEAN heads of government, meeting in Bangkok, Thailand, signed a treaty establishing a South-East Asia Nuclear-Weapon Free Zone (SEANWFZ). The treaty was also signed by Cambodia, Myanmar and Laos. It was extended to cover the offshore economic exclusion zones of each country. On ratification by all parties, the treaty was to prohibit the manufacture or storage of nuclear weapons within the region. Individual signatories were to decide whether to allow port visits or transportation of nuclear weapons by foreign powers through territorial waters. The treaty entered into force on 27 March 1997. ASEAN senior officials were mandated to oversee implementation of the treaty, pending the establishment of a permanent monitoring committee. In July 1999 the People's Republic of China and India agreed to observe the terms of the SEANWFZ.

In July 1992 the ASEAN Ministerial Meeting issued a statement calling for a peaceful resolution of the dispute concerning the strategically significant Spratly Islands in the South China Sea, which are claimed, wholly or partly, by the People's Republic of China, Viet Nam, Taiwan, Brunei, Malaysia and the Philippines. In 1999 ASEAN established a special committee to formulate a code of conduct for the South China Sea to be observed by all claimants to the Spratly Islands. A draft code of conduct was approved in November 1999. In November 2002 ASEAN and China's foreign ministers adopted a Declaration on the Conduct of Parties in the South China Sea, agreeing to promote a peaceful environment and durable solutions for the area, to resolve territorial disputes by peaceful means, to refrain from undertaking activities that would aggravate existing tensions (such as settling unpopulated islands and reefs), and to initiate a regular dialogue of defence officials. In December 2004 in Kuala Lumpur, Malaysia, at the first senior officials' meeting between ASEAN and China on the implementation of the Declaration, it was agreed to adopt the Terms of Reference of the newly established joint working group as a step towards enhancing security and stability in the South China Sea.

In July 1997 ASEAN ministers of foreign affairs reiterated their commitment to the principle of non-interference in the internal affairs of other countries. However, the group's efforts in negotiating a political settlement to the internal conflict in Cambodia marked a significant shift in diplomatic policy towards one of 'constructive intervention', which had been proposed by Malaysia's Deputy Prime Minister in recognition of the increasing interdependence of the region. At the Ministerial Meeting in July 1998 Thailand's Minister of Foreign Affairs, supported by his Philippine counterpart, proposed that the grouping formally adopt a policy of 'flexible engagement'. The proposal, based partly on concerns that the continued restrictions imposed by the Myanma authorities on dissident political activists was damaging ASEAN relations with its dialogue partners, was to provide for the discussion of the affairs of other member states when they have an impact on neighbouring countries. While rejecting the proposal, other ASEAN ministers agreed to pursue a more limited version, referred to as 'enhanced interaction', and to maintain open dialogue within the grouping. In September 1999 the unrest prompted by the popular referendum on the future of East Timor (now Timor-Leste) and the resulting humanitarian crisis highlighted the unwillingness of some ASEAN member states to intervene in other member countries and undermined the political unity of the grouping. A compromise agreement, enabling countries to act on an individual basis rather than as representatives of ASEAN, was formulated prior to an emergency meeting of ministers of foreign affairs, held during the APEC meetings in Auckland, New Zealand. Malaysia, the Philippines, Singapore and Thailand declared their support for the establishment of a multinational force to restore peace in East Timor and committed troops to participate in the Australian-led operation. At their informal summit in November 1999 heads of state approved the establishment of an ASEAN Troika, which was to be constituted as an ad hoc body comprising the foreign ministers of the Association's current, previous and future chairmanship with a view to providing a rapid response mechanism in the event of a regional crisis.

On 12 September 2001 ASEAN issued a ministerial statement on international terrorism, condemning the attacks of the previous day in the USA and urging greater international co-operation to counter terrorism. The seventh summit meeting in November issued a Declaration on a Joint Action to Combat Terrorism. This condemned the September attacks, stated that terrorism was a direct challenge to ASEAN's aims, and affirmed the grouping's commitment to strong measures to counter terrorism. The summit encouraged member countries to sign (or ratify) the International Convention for the Suppression of the Financing of Terrorism, to strengthen national mechanisms against terrorism, and to work to deepen co-operation, particularly in the area of intelligence exchange; international conventions to combat terrorism would be studied to see if they could be integrated into the ASEAN structure, while the possibility of developing a regional anti-terrorism convention was discussed. The summit noted the need to strengthen security co-operation to restore investor confidence. In its Declaration and other notes, the summit explicitly rejected any attempt to link terrorism with religion or race, and expressed concern for the suffering of innocent Afghanis during the US military action against the Taliban authorities in Afghanistan. The summit's final Declaration was worded so as to avoid any mention of the US action, to which Muslim ASEAN states such as

Malaysia and Indonesia were strongly opposed. In November 2002 the eighth summit meeting adopted a Declaration on Terrorism, reiterating and strengthening the measures announced in the previous year. In January 2003 ASEAN police chiefs proposed the establishment of a network of national anti-terrorism task forces, to work in close co-operation with one another.

The ASEAN Charter that was signed in November 2007 envisaged the establishment of a new ASEAN human rights body. It was to extend, for the first time in the grouping, a formal structure for the promotion and protection of human rights and fundamental freedoms.

ASEAN Regional Forum (ARF): In July 1993 the meeting of ASEAN ministers of foreign affairs sanctioned the establishment of a forum to discuss and promote co-operation on security issues within the region, and, in particular, to ensure the involvement of the People's Republic of China in regional dialogue. The ARF was informally initiated during that year's PMC, comprising the ASEAN countries, its dialogue partners (at that time Australia, Canada, the EC, Japan, the Republic of Korea, New Zealand and the USA), and the People's Republic of China, Laos, Papua New Guinea, Russia and Viet Nam. The first formal meeting of the ARF was conducted in July 1994, following the Ministerial Meeting held in Bangkok, Thailand, and it was agreed that the ARF would be convened on an annual basis. The 1995 meeting, held in Brunei, in August, attempted to define a framework for the future of the Forum. It was perceived as evolving through three stages: the promotion of confidence-building (including disaster relief and peace-keeping activities); the development of preventive diplomacy; and the elaboration of approaches to conflict. The third ARF, convened in July 1996, which was attended for the first time by India and Myanmar, agreed a set of criteria and guiding principles for the future expansion of the grouping. In particular, it was decided that the ARF would only admit as participants countries that had a direct influence on the peace and security of the East Asia and Pacific region. The ARF held in July 1997 reviewed progress made in developing the first two 'tracks' of the ARF process, through the structure of inter-sessional working groups and meetings. The Forum's consideration of security issues in the region was dominated by concern at the political situation in Cambodia; support was expressed for ASEAN mediation to restore stability within that country. Mongolia was admitted into the ARF at its meeting in July 1998. India rejected a proposal that Pakistan attend the meeting to discuss issues relating to both countries' testing of nuclear weapons. The meeting ultimately condemned the testing of nuclear weapons in the region, but declined to criticize specifically India and Pakistan. In July 1999 the ARF warned the Democratic People's Republic of Korea (DPRK) not to conduct any further testing of missiles over the Pacific. At the seventh meeting of the ARF, convened in Bangkok, Thailand, in July 2000, the DPRK was admitted to the Forum. The meeting considered the positive effects and challenges of globalization, including the possibilities for greater economic interdependence and for a growth in transnational crime. The eighth ARF meeting in July 2001 in Hanoi, Viet Nam, pursued these themes, and also discussed the widening development gap between nations. The meeting agreed to enhance the role of the ARF Chairman, enabling him to issue statements on behalf of ARF participants and to organize events during the year. In March and April 2002 ARF workshops were held on financial measures against terrorism and on the prevention of terrorism, respectively. The ninth ARF meeting, held in Bandar Seri Begawan, Brunei, in July, assessed regional and international security developments, and issued a statement of individual and collective intent to prevent any financing of terrorism. The statement included commitments by participants to freeze the assets of suspected individuals or groups, to implement international financial standards and to enhance co-operation and the exchange of information. In October the Chairman, on behalf of all ARF participants, condemned the terrorist bomb attacks committed against tourist targets in Bali, Indonesia. Pakistan joined the ARF in July 2004. In November the first ARF Security Policy Conference was held in Beijing, People's Republic of China. The Conference recommended developing various aspects of bilateral and multilateral co-operation, including with regard to non-traditional security threats. Timor-Leste and Bangladesh became participants in the ARF in July 2005. In July 2006 the ARF issued statements on 'co-operation in fighting cyber attacks and terrorist misuse of cyber space' and on disaster management and emergency responses, which determined to formulate guide-lines for enhanced co-operation in humanitarian operations. In January 2007 an ARF maritime security shore exercise was conducted, in Singapore. In March the first ARF Defense Ministers Retreat was convened, in Bali, Indonesia. The 14th ARF, held in Manila, Philippines, in July, approved the establishment of a 'Friends of the Chair' mechanism, comprising three ministers, to promote preventive diplomacy and respond rapidly to political crises.

Since 2000 the ARF has published the *Annual Security Outlook*, to which participating countries submit assessments of the security prospects in the region.

INDUSTRY

The ASEAN-Chambers of Commerce and Industry (CCI) aims to enhance ASEAN economic and industrial co-operation and the participation in these activities of the private sector. In March 1996 a permanent ASEAN-CCI secretariat became operational at the ASEAN Secretariat. The first AIA Council-Business Sector Forum was convened in September 2001, with the aim of developing alliances between the public and private sectors. An ASEAN Business Advisory Council held its inaugural meeting in April 2003.

The ASEAN Industrial Co-operation (AICO) scheme, initiated in 1996, encourages companies in the ASEAN region to undertake joint manufacturing activities. Products derived from an AICO arrangement benefit immediately from a preferential tariff rate of 0%–5%. The AICO scheme superseded the ASEAN industrial joint venture scheme, established in 1983. The attractiveness of the scheme is expected slowly to diminish as ASEAN moves towards the full implementation of the CEPT scheme. ASEAN has initiated studies of new methods of industrial co-operation within the grouping, with the aim of achieving further integration. In April 2004 ASEAN economic ministers signed a Protocol to Amend the Basic Agreement on the AICO Scheme, which aimed to maintain its relevance. As from 1 January 2005 the tariff rate for Brunei, Cambodia, Indonesia, Laos, Malaysia and Singapore was 0%; for the Philippines 0–1%, for Thailand 0–3% and for Myanmar and Viet Nam 0–5%.

The ASEAN Consultative Committee on Standards and Quality (ACCSQ) aims to promote the understanding and implementation of quality concepts, considered to be important in strengthening the economic development of a member state and in helping to eliminate trade barriers. ACCSQ comprises three working groups: standards and information; conformance and assessment; and testing and calibration. A Standards and Quality Bulletin is published regularly to disseminate information and promote transparency on standards, technical regulations and conformity assessment procedures. In September 1994 an ad hoc Working Group on Intellectual Property (IP) Co-operation was established, with a mandate to formulate a framework agreement on intellectual property co-operation and to strengthen ASEAN activities in intellectual property protection. An ASEAN Intellectual Property Right (IPR) Action Plan 2004–10 aimed, *inter alia*, to accelerate IP asset creation and to develop and harmonize regional mechanisms for IPR registration, protection and enforcement.

In 1988 the ASEAN Fund was established, with capital of US $150m., to provide finance for portfolio investments in ASEAN countries, in particular for small and medium-sized enterprises (SMEs). The Hanoi Plan of Action, which was adopted by ASEAN heads of state in December 1998, incorporated a series of initiatives to enhance the development of SMEs, including training and technical assistance, co-operation activities and greater access to information. In September 2004 ASEAN economic ministers approved an ASEAN Policy Blueprint for SME Development 2004–14, first proposed by a working group in 2001, which comprised strategic work programmes and policy measures for the development of SMEs in the region.

A Work Programme on Industrial Relations was adopted in March 2005 and covers ASEAN co-operation in this area in the period 2005–10. In January 2007 senior officials concluded a five-year ASEAN plan of action to support the development and implementation of national occupational safety and health frameworks.

FINANCE AND INVESTMENT

In 1987 heads of government agreed to accelerate regional financial co-operation, to support intra-ASEAN trade and investment. They adopted measures to increase the role of ASEAN currencies in regional trade, to assist negotiations on the avoidance of double taxation, and to improve the efficiency of tax and customs administrators. An ASEAN Reinsurance Corporation was established in 1988, with initial authorized capital of US $10m. Other measures to attract greater financial resource flows in the region, including an ASEAN Plan of Action for the Promotion of Foreign Direct Investment and Intra-ASEAN Investment, were implemented during 1996.

In February 1997 ASEAN central bank governors agreed to strengthen efforts to combat currency speculation through the established network of foreign-exchange repurchase agreements. However, from mid-1997 several Asian currencies were undermined by speculative activities. Subsequent unsuccessful attempts to support the foreign-exchange rates contributed to a collapse in the value of financial markets in some countries and to a reversal of the region's economic growth, at least in the short term, while governments undertook macroeconomic structural reforms. In early December ASEAN ministers of finance, meeting in Malaysia, agreed to liberalize markets for financial services and to strengthen surveillance of member country economies, to help prevent further deterioration of the regional economy. The ministers also endorsed a proposal for the establishment of an Asian funding facility to provide emergency assistance in support of international credit and structural reform programmes. At the informal summit meeting held later in December, ASEAN leaders issued a joint statement in which they expressed the need for mutual support to counter the region's financial crisis and urged greater international assistance to help overcome the situation and address the underlying problems.

In October 1998 ministers of economic affairs, meeting in Manila, the Philippines, signed a Framework Agreement on an ASEAN Investment Area (AIA), which was to provide for equal treatment of domestic and other ASEAN direct investment proposals within the grouping by 2010, and of all foreign investors by 2020. The meeting also confirmed that the proposed ASEAN Surveillance Process (ASP), to monitor the economic stability and financial systems of member states, would be implemented with immediate effect, and would require the voluntary submission of economic information by all members to a monitoring committee, to be based in Jakarta, Indonesia. The ASP and the Framework Agreement on the AIA were incorporated into the Hanoi Plan of Action, adopted by heads of state in December 1998. The summit meeting also resolved to accelerate reforms, particularly in the banking and financial sectors, in order to strengthen the region's economies, and to promote the liberalization of the financial services sector.

In March 1999 ASEAN ministers of trade and industry, meeting in Phuket, Thailand, as the AIA Council, agreed to open their manufacturing, agriculture, fisheries, forestry and mining industries to foreign investment. Investment restrictions affecting those industries were to be eliminated by 2003 in most cases, although Laos and Viet Nam were granted until 2010. In addition, ministers adopted a number of measures to encourage investment in the region, including access to three-year corporate income-tax exemptions, and tax allowances of 30% for investors. The AIA agreement formally entered into force in June 1999, having been ratified by all member countries. In September 2001 ministers agreed to accelerate the full realization of the AIA for non-ASEAN investors in manufacturing, agriculture, forestry, fishing and mining sectors. The date for full implementation was advanced to 2010 for the original six ASEAN members and to 2015 for the newer members. In April 2002 ASEAN ministers of economic affairs signed an agreement to facilitate intra-regional trade in electrical and electronic equipment by providing for the mutual recognition of standards (for example, testing and certification). The agreement was also intended to lower the costs of trade in those goods, thereby helping to maintain competitiveness. In August 2007 the AIA Council determined to revise the Framework Agreement on the AIA in order to implement a more comprehensive investment arrangement in support of the establishment of the AEC.

FOOD, AGRICULTURE AND FORESTRY

In October 1983 a ministerial agreement on fisheries co-operation was concluded, providing for the joint management of fish resources, the sharing of technology, and co-operation in marketing. In July 1994 a Conference on Fisheries Management and Development Strategies in the ASEAN region resolved to enhance fish production through the introduction of new technologies, aquaculture development, improvements of product quality and greater involvement by the private sector.

Co-operation in forestry is focused on joint projects, funded by ASEAN's dialogue partners, which include a Forest Tree Seed Centre, an Institute of Forest Management and the ASEAN Timber Technology Centre. In 2005 the Ad Hoc Experts Working Group on International Forest Policy Processes was created, to support the development of ASEAN joint positions and approaches on regional and international forest issues. In November 2007 ASEAN ministers responsible for forestry issued a statement on strengthening forest law enforcement and governance.

ASEAN holds an emergency rice reserve, amounting to 87,000 metric tons, as part of its efforts to ensure food security in the region. There is an established ASEAN programme of training and study exchanges for farm workers, agricultural experts and members of agricultural co-operatives. Other areas of co-operation aim to enhance food security and the international competitiveness of ASEAN food, agriculture and forestry products, to promote the sustainable use and conservation of natural resources, to encourage greater involvement by the private sector in the food and agricultural industry, and to strengthen joint approaches on international and regional issues. An ASEAN Task Force has been formed to harmonize regulations on agricultural products derived from biotechnology. In December 1998 heads of state determined to establish an ASEAN Food Security Information Service to enhance the capacity of member states to forecast and manage food supplies. In 1999 agriculture ministers endorsed guide-lines on assessing risk from genetically modified organisms (GMOs) in agriculture, to ensure a common approach. In 2001 work was undertaken to increase public and professional awareness of GMO issues, through workshops and studies. In October 2004 ministers of agriculture and forestry, meeting in Yangon, Myanmar, endorsed a Strategic Plan of Action on ASEAN Co-operation in Food, Agriculture and Forestry 2005–10. The ministers also approved certain regional food standards, endorsed the establishment of an ASEAN Animal Health Trust Fund, and resolved to establish a Task Force to co-ordinate regional co-operation for the control and eradication of highly pathogenic avian influenza (HPAI). A Regional Strategy for the Progressive Control and Eradication of HPAI, covering the period 2008–10, was endorsed at a meeting of ASEAN ministers of agriculture and forestry held in November 2007. The meeting also determined to establish an ASEAN Network on Aquatic Animal Health Centres to strengthen diagnostic and certification measures of live aquatic animals within the region.

MINERALS AND ENERGY

The ASEAN Centre for Energy (ACE), based in Jakarta, Indonesia, provides an energy information network, promotes the establishment of interconnecting energy structures among ASEAN member countries, supports the development of renewable energy resources and encourages co-operation in energy efficiency and conservation. An ASEAN energy business forum is held annually and attended by representatives of the energy industry in the private and public sectors. In November 1999 a Trans-ASEAN Gas Pipeline Task Force was established and in April 2000 an ASEAN Interconnection Masterplan Study Working Group was established to formulate a study on the power grid. In July 2002 ASEAN ministers of energy signed a Memorandum of Understanding to implement the pipeline project, involving seven interconnections. The meeting also approved initial plans for the implementation of the regional power grid initiative. A Memorandum of Understanding on the ASEAN Power Grid was signed by ministers of energy meeting in August 2007. In early 2005 the Trans-Thai-Malaysia Gas Pipeline became operational. In June 2004 ASEAN ministers of energy adopted the Plan of Action for Energy Co-operation 2004–09. In 2004 a permanent Secretariat of the heads of ASEAN Power Utilities/Authorities was established on a three-year rotation basis, the first Secretariat being hosted by PT PLN (Persero) of Indonesia from 2004–07.

A Framework of Co-operation in Minerals was adopted by an ASEAN working group of experts in August 1993. The group has also developed a programme of action for ASEAN co-operation in the development and utilization of industrial minerals, to promote the exploration and development of mineral resources, the transfer of mining technology and expertise, and the participation of the private sector in industrial mineral production. The programme of action is implemented by an ASEAN Regional Development Centre for Mineral Resources, which also conducts workshops and training programmes relating to the sector. An ASEAN Minerals Co-operation Action Plan for 2005–10 aims to attract investment in the sector while also promoting environmentally and socially sustainable practices.

TRANSPORT

ASEAN objectives for the transport sector include developing multi-modal transport, harmonizing road transport laws and regulations, improving air space management and developing ASEAN legislation for the carriage of dangerous goods and waste by land and sea. The summit meeting of December 1998 agreed to work to develop a trans-ASEAN transportation network by 2000, comprising principal routes for the movement of goods and people. In September 1999 ASEAN ministers of transport and communications adopted a programme of action for development of the sector in 1999–2004. By September 2001, under the action programme, a harmonized road route numbering system had been completed, a road safety implementation work plan agreed, and two pilot courses, on port management and traffic engineering and safety, had been adopted. A Framework Agreement on Facilitation of Goods in Transit entered into force in October 2000. In September 2002 ASEAN transport ministers signed Protocol 9 on Dangerous Goods, one of the implementing protocols under the framework agreement, which provided for the simplification of procedures for the transportation of dangerous goods within the region using internationally accepted rules and guide-lines. In November 2004 the ASEAN Transport Action Plan 2005–10 was adopted. A 'roadmap' to support the development of an integrated and competitive maritime transport sector in the ASEAN region was signed by ministers of transport in November 2007. At the same time an agreement to strengthen co-operation in maritime cargo and passenger transport was signed with the People's Republic of China.

In October 2001 ministers approved the third package of commitments for the air and transport sectors under the ASEAN framework agreement on services (according to which member countries were to liberalize the selling and marketing of air and maritime transport services). A protocol to implement the forth package of commitments was signed by ministers in November 2004. In September 2002 ASEAN senior transport officials signed the Memorandum of Understanding on Air Freight Services, which represented the first stage in full liberalization of air freight services in the region. As one of the priority sectors within the ASEAN Framework Agreement for Integration of the Priority Sectors and its Protocols, air travel in the region was to be fully integrated by 2010. The Action Plan for ASEAN Air Transport Integration and Liberalisation 2005–15 was adopted in November 2004.

TELECOMMUNICATIONS

ASEAN aims to achieve interoperability and interconnectivity in the telecommunications sector. In October 1999 an initiative was launched to promote and co-ordinate e-commerce and internet utilization. In November 2000 ASEAN heads of government approved an e-ASEAN Framework Agreement to further the aims of the initiative. The Agreement incorporated commitments to develop and strengthen ASEAN's information infrastructure, in order to provide for universal and affordable access to communications services. Tariff reduction on information and communication technology (ICT) products was to be accelerated, with the aim of eliminating all tariffs in the sector by 2010. In July 2001 the first meeting of ASEAN ministers responsible for telecommunications was held, in Kuala Lumpur, Malaysia, during which a Ministerial Understanding on ASEAN co-operation in telecommunications and ICT was signed. In September ASEAN ministers of economic affairs approved a list of ICT products eligible for the elimination of duties under the e-ASEAN Framework Agreement. This was to take place in three annual tranches, commencing in 2003 for the six original members of ASEAN and in 2008 for the newer member countries. During 2001 ASEAN continued to develop a reference framework for e-commerce legislation; it aimed to have e-commerce legislation in place in all member states by 2003. In September 2003 the third ASEAN telecommunications ministerial meeting adopted a declaration incorporating commitments to harness ASEAN technological advances, create digital opportunities and enhance ASEAN's competitiveness in the field of ICT. The ministers also endorsed initiatives to enhance cybersecurity, including the establishment of computer emergency response teams in each member state. In August 2004 an ASEAN ICT Fund was established to accelerate implementation of the grouping's ICT objectives. At the fifth meeting of telecommunications ministers, held in Hanoi, Viet Nam, in September 2005, the Hanoi Agenda on Promoting Online Services and Applications was adopted. 'ASEANconnect', a web portal collating all essential information and data regarding ICT activities and initiatives within ASEAN, was also launched. In August 2007 ASEAN telecommunications ministers, convened in Siem Reap, Cambodia, endorsed a commitment to enhance universal access of ICT services within ASEAN, in particular to extend the benefits of ICT to rural communities and remote areas. At the same time ministers met their counterparts from the People's Republic of China, Japan and the Republic of Korea to strengthen co-operation in ICT issues.

SCIENCE AND TECHNOLOGY

ASEAN's Committee on Science and Technology (COST) supports co-operation in food science and technology, meteorology and geophysics, microelectronics and ICT, biotechnology, non-conventional energy research, materials science and technology, space technology applications, science and technology infrastructure and resources development, and marine science. There is an ASEAN Science Fund, used to finance policy studies in science and technology and to support information exchange and dissemination.

The Hanoi Plan of Action, adopted in December 1998, envisaged a series of measures aimed at promoting development in the fields of science and technology, including the establishment of networks of science and technology centres of excellence and academic institutions, the creation of a technology scan mechanism, the promotion of public- and private sector co-operation in scientific and technological (particularly ICT) activities, and an increase in research on strategic technologies. In September 2001 the ASEAN Ministerial Meeting on Science and Technology, convened for its first meeting since 1998, approved a new framework for implementation of ASEAN's Plan of Action on Science and Technology during the period 2001–04. The Plan aimed to help less developed member countries become competitive in the sector and integrate into regional co-operation activities. In September 2003 ASEAN and the People's Republic of China inaugurated a Network of East Asian Think-tanks to promote scientific and technological exchange. In November 2004 a Ministerial Meeting on Science and Technology decided to establish an ASEAN Virtual Institute of Science and Technology with the aim of developing science and technology human resources in the region. In August 2006 an informal Ministerial Meeting on Science and Technology endorsed in principle a Plan of Action on Science and Technology for 2007–11. The document envisaged ASEAN-COST focusing work on the following areas of activity: environment and disaster management; new and renewable energy; open source software system; and food safety and security.

ENVIRONMENT

An ASEAN Agreement on the Conservation of Nature and Natural Resources was signed in July 1985. In April 1994 a ministerial meeting on the environment approved long-term objectives on environmental quality and standards for the ASEAN region, aiming to enhance joint action in addressing environmental concerns. At the same time, ministers adopted standards for air quality and river water to be achieved by all ASEAN member countries by 2010. In June 1995 ministers agreed to co-operate to counter the problems of transboundary pollution. An ASEAN Regional Centre for Biodiversity Conservation (ARCBC) was established in February 1999.

In December 1997 ASEAN heads of state endorsed a Regional Haze Action Plan to address the environmental problems resulting from forest fires, which had afflicted several countries in the region throughout that year. A Haze Technical Task Force undertook to implement the plan, with assistance from the UN Environment Programme. Sub-regional fire-fighting arrangement working groups for Sumatra and Borneo were established in April 1998 and in May the Task Force organized a regional workshop to strengthen ASEAN capacity to prevent and alleviate the haze caused by the extensive fires. A pilot project of aerial surveillance of the areas in the region most at risk of forest fires was initiated in July. In December heads of government resolved to establish an ASEAN Regional Research and Training Centre for Land and Forest Fire Management. In March 2002 members of the working groups on sub-regional fire-fighting arrangements for Sumatra and Borneo agreed to intensify early warning efforts and surveillance activities in order to reduce the risks of forest fires. In June ASEAN ministers of the environment signed an Agreement on Transboundary Haze Pollution, which was intended to provide a legal basis for the Regional Haze Action Plan. The Agreement, which entered into force in November 2003, required member countries to co-operate in the prevention and mitigation of haze pollution, for example, by responding to requests for information by other states and facilitating the transit of personnel and equipment in case of disaster. The Agreement also provided for the establishment of an ASEAN Co-ordination Centre for Transboundary Haze Pollution Control. The first conference of parties to the Agreement was held in November 2004. An ASEAN Specialized Meteorological Centre (ASMC) based in Singapore, plays a primary role in long-range climatological forecasting, early detection and monitoring of fires and haze. In August 2005, guided by the ASEAN Agreement on Transboundary Haze Pollution, member countries activated bilateral and regional mechanisms to exchange information and mobilize resources to deal with severe fires in Sumatra (Indonesia), peninsular Malaysia and southern Thailand. In September 2007 ASEAN ministers agreed to establish a sub-regional Technical Working Group to focus on addressing land and forest fires in the northern part of the region.

The Strategic Plan of Action on the Environment for 1999–2004 focused on issues of coastal and marine erosion, nature conservation and biodiversity, the implementation of multilateral environmental agreements, and forest fires and haze. Other ASEAN environmental objectives include the implementation of a water conservation programme and the formation and adoption of an ASEAN protocol on access to genetic resources. In May 2001 environment ministers launched the ASEAN Environment Education Action Plan (AEEAP), with the aim of promoting public awareness of environmental and sustainable development issues. In November 2003 ASEAN + 3 ministers of environment agreed to prioritize environmental activities in the following areas: environmentally sustainable cities; global environmental issues; land and forest fires and transboundary haze pollution; coastal and marine environment; sustainable forest management; freshwater resources; public awareness and environmental education; promotion of green technologies and cleaner production; and sustainable development monitoring and reporting. The Vientiane Action Plan (see above) incorporated objectives for environmental and natural resource management for the period 2004–10. In September 2005 the ASEAN Centre for Biodiversity, funded jointly by ASEAN and the EU, was inaugurated in La Union, near Manila, the Philippines. In that month ministers of the environment approved an ASEAN Strategic Plan of Action on Water Resources Management. The ASEAN summit meeting convened in November 2007 was held on the theme of 'energy, environment, climate change, and sustainable development'. A final Declaration on Environmental Sustainability incorporated specific commitments to strengthen environmental protection management, to respond to climate change and to work towards the conservation and sustainable management of natural resources.

TRANSNATIONAL CRIME

In June 1999 the first ministerial meeting to consider issues relating to transnational crime was convened. Regular meetings of senior officials and ministers were subsequently held. The third ministerial meeting, in October 2001, considered initiatives to combat transnational crime, which was defined as including terrorism, trafficking in drugs, arms and people, money-laundering, cyber-crime, piracy and economic crime. In May 2002 ministers responsible for transnational crime issues convened a Special Ministerial Meeting on Terrorism, in Kuala Lumpur, Malaysia. The meeting approved a work programme to implement a plan of action to combat transnational crime, including information exchange, the development of legal arrangements for extradition, prosecution and seizure, the enhancement of co-operation in law enforcement, and the development of regional security training programmes. In a separate initiative Indonesia, Malaysia and the Philippines signed an agreement on information exchange and the establishment of communication procedures. Cambodia acceded to the agreement in July. In November 2004 ASEAN leaders adopted an ASEAN Declaration against Trafficking in Persons, Particularly Women and Children, which aimed to strengthen co-operation to prevent and combat trafficking, through, *inter alia*, the establishment of a new regional focal network, information-sharing procedures and standardized immigration controls. The Plan of Action of the ASEAN Security Community (envisaged by the Bali Concord II—see above) had as its five key areas: political development; shaping and sharing of norms; conflict prevention; conflict resolution; and post-conflict peace building. In November 2004 eight member countries, namely Brunei, Cambodia, Indonesia, Malaysia, Laos, the Philippines, Singapore and Viet Nam, signed a Treaty on Mutual Legal Assistance in Criminal Matters in Kuala Lumpur, Malaysia.

In January 2007 ASEAN leaders, meeting in Cebu, the Philippines, signed an ASEAN Convention on Counter Terrorism.

SOCIAL WELFARE AND DEVELOPMENT

ASEAN is concerned with a range of social issues including youth development, the role of women, health and nutrition, education and labour affairs. In December 1993 ASEAN ministers responsible for social affairs adopted a Plan of Action for Children, which provided a framework for regional co-operation for the survival, protection and development of children in member countries. ASEAN supports efforts to combat drug abuse and illegal drugs-trafficking. It aims to promote education and drug-awareness campaigns throughout the region, and administers a project to strengthen the training of personnel involved in combating drug abuse. In October 1994 a meeting of ASEAN Senior Officials on Drug Matters approved a three-year plan of action on drug abuse, providing a framework for co-operation in four priority areas: preventive drug education; treatment and rehabilitation; law enforcement; and research. In July 1998 ASEAN ministers of foreign affairs signed a Joint Declaration for a Drug-Free ASEAN, which envisaged greater co-operation among member states, in particular in information exchange, educational resources and legal procedures, in order to eliminate the illicit production, processing and trafficking of narcotic substances by 2020. (This deadline was subsequently advanced to 2015.)

In December 1998 ASEAN leaders approved a series of measures aimed at mitigating the social impact of the financial and economic crises that had affected many countries in the region. Plans of Action were formulated on issues of rural development and poverty eradication, while Social Safety Nets, which aimed to protect the most vulnerable members of society, were approved. The summit meeting emphasized the need to promote job generation as a key element of strategies for economic recovery and growth. The fourth meeting of ministers of social welfare in August 2001 noted the need for a holistic approach to social problems, integrating social and economic development. The summit meeting in November considered the widening development gap between ASEAN members and concluded that bridging this gap was a priority. The meeting approved an Initiative for ASEAN Integration Work Plan, which identified infrastructure development, human resource development, access to ICT and the promotion of regional economic integration as priority areas of activity, in particular to assist the newer signatory states, i.e. Cambodia, Laos, Myanmar and Viet Nam. The Plan of Action for the ASEAN Socio-Cultural Community (envisaged in the Bali Concord II—see above) was adopted by ASEAN leaders in November 2004. The first ASEAN + 3 Ministerial Meeting for social welfare and development was convened in Bangkok, Thailand, in December, at which it was agreed that the three key areas of co-operation were to be: the promotion of a community of caring societies in the region; developing policies and programmes to address the issue of ageing; and addressing human resource development in the social sector. In July 2005 it was agreed to establish an ASEAN Development Fund, to which each member country would make an initial contribution of US $1m. In November 2006 ASEAN senior officials adopted a Strategic Framework and Plan of Action for Social Welfare, Family and Children in the period 2007–10. The sixth ASEAN Ministerial Meeting for social welfare and development was convened in Hanoi, Viet Nam, in December 2007. It focused on 'mainstreaming persons with disability in development' and discussed overcoming the development gap between member countries as an essential element of an integrated ASEAN community.

The seventh ASEAN summit meeting, held in November 2001, declared work on combating HIV and AIDS to be a priority. The second phase of a work programme to combat AIDS and provide help for sufferers was endorsed at the meeting. Heads of government expressed their readiness to commit the necessary resources for prevention and care, and to attempt to obtain access to cheaper drugs. An ASEAN task force on AIDS has been operational since March 1993. An ASEAN Co-operation Forum on HIV/AIDS was held in February 2003, in Bangkok, Thailand. An East Asia and Pacific Consultation on Children and AIDS was convened in March 2006 and identified nine urgent actions to respond to children affected by HIV/AIDS. In April 2003 a Special ASEAN Leaders' Meeting on Severe Acute Respiratory Syndrome (SARS) endorsed the recommendations of ministers of health, who convened in special session a few days previously, and agreed to establish an ad hoc ministerial-level Joint Task Force to follow-up and monitor implementation of those decisions. Co-operation measures approved included public information and education campaigns, health and immigration control procedures, and the establishment of an early-warning system on emerging infectious diseases. In June 2006 ASEAN ministers responsible for health adopted a declaration entitled 'ASEAN Unity in Health Emergencies'.

In October 2004 ASEAN ministers approved a new framework action plan on rural development and poverty eradication, covering the period 2004–10, to address priorities including the different levels of development among member countries and issues concerning globalization and social protection. In January 2007 the fifth ASEAN Ministerial Meeting on rural development and poverty eradication, convened in Bangkok, Thailand, focused on community empowerment as a means of addressing rural poverty.

In January 1992 the ASEAN summit meeting resolved to establish an ASEAN University Network (AUN) to hasten the development of a regional identity. A draft AUN Charter and Agreement were adopted in 1995. The Network aims to strengthen co-operation within the grouping, develop academic and professional human resources and transmit information and knowledge. The 17 universities linked by the Network carry out collaborative studies and research programmes. Three more universities became members of the AUN in November 2006. At the seventh ASEAN summit in November 2001 heads of government agreed to establish the first ASEAN University, in Malaysia. In August 2005 it was agreed to convene a regular ASEAN Ministerial Meeting on education; the first meeting was convened in March 2006. In March 2007 education ministers determined to restart an ASEAN Student Exchange Programme.

In January 2007 ASEAN heads of government signed a Declaration on the Protection and Promotion of the Rights of Migrant Workers, which mandated countries to promote fair and appropriate employment protection, payment of wages, and adequate access to decent working and living conditions for migrant workers. A Committee on the Implementation of the ASEAN Declaration was established in July.

DISASTER MANAGEMENT

An ASEAN Committee on Disaster Management was established in early 2003 and worked to formulate a framework for co-operation in disaster management and emergency response. In January 2005 a Special ASEAN Leaders' Meeting was convened in Jakarta, Indonesia, to consider the needs of countries affected by an earthquake and devastating tsunami that had occurred in the Indian Ocean in late December 2004. The meeting, which was also attended by the Secretary-General of the United Nations, the President of the World Bank and other senior envoys of donor countries and international organizations, adopted a Declaration on Action to Strengthen Emergency Relief, Rehabilitation, Reconstruction and Prevention on the Aftermath of Earthquake and Tsunami Disaster. In July 2005 an ASEAN Agreement on Disaster Management and Emergency Response was signed in Vientiane, Laos. The Agreement stated as its objective the provision of mechanisms that would effectively reduce the loss of life and damage to the social, economic and environmental assets of the region and the response to disaster emergencies through concerted national efforts and increased regional and international co-operation.

TOURISM

National tourist organizations from ASEAN countries meet regularly to assist in co-ordinating the region's tourist industry, and a Tourism Forum is held annually to promote the sector. (In January 2008 it was held in Bangkok, Thailand.) The first formal meeting of ASEAN ministers of tourism was held in January 1998, in Cebu, the Philippines. The meeting adopted a Plan of Action on ASEAN Co-operation in Tourism, which aimed to promote intra-ASEAN travel, greater investment in the sector, joint marketing of the region as a single tourist destination and environmentally sustainable tourism. In January 1999 the second meeting of ASEAN ministers of tourism agreed to appoint country co-ordinators to implement various initiatives, including the designation of 2002 as 'Visit ASEAN Millennium Year'; research to promote the region as a tourist destination in the

21st century, and to develop a cruise-ship industry; and the establishment of a network of ASEAN Tourism Training Centres to develop new skills and technologies in the tourist industry. The third meeting of tourism ministers, held in Bangkok, Thailand, in January 2000, agreed to reformulate the Visit ASEAN Millennium Year initiative as a long-term Visit ASEAN programme. This was formally launched in January 2001 at the fourth ministerial meeting. The first phase of the programme promoted brand awareness through an intense marketing effort; the second phase, initiated at the fifth meeting of tourism ministers, held in Yogyakarta, Indonesia, in January 2002, was to direct campaigns towards end-consumers. Ministers urged member states to abolish all fiscal and non-fiscal travel barriers to encourage tourism, including intra-ASEAN travel. In November 2002 the eighth summit of heads of state adopted a framework agreement on ASEAN co-operation in tourism, aimed at facilitating domestic and intra-regional travel. ASEAN national tourism organizations signed an implementation plan for the agreement in May 2003, when they also announced a Declaration on Tourism Safety and Security. As one of the sectors included in the ASEAN Framework Agreement for Integration of the Priority Sectors and its Protocols, signed in November 2004, tourism in the region was to be fully integrated by 2010.

CULTURE AND INFORMATION

Regular workshops and festivals are held in visual and performing arts, youth music, radio, television and films, and print and interpersonal media. In addition, ASEAN administers a News Exchange and provides support for the training of editors, journalists and information officers. In 2000 ASEAN adopted new cultural strategies, with the aim of raising awareness of the grouping's objectives and achievements, both regionally and internationally. The strategies included: producing ASEAN cultural and historical educational materials; promoting cultural exchanges; and achieving greater exposure of ASEAN cultural activities and issues in the mass media. An ASEAN Youth Camp was held for the first time in that year, and subsequently has been organized on an annual basis. ASEAN ministers responsible for culture and arts met for the first time in October 2003. The third ministerial meeting was convened in Nay Pyi Taw, Myanmar, in January 2008, coinciding with the third ASEAN Festival of Arts, which focused on the region's puppetry heritage.

In July 1997 ASEAN ministers of foreign affairs endorsed the establishment of an ASEAN Foundation to promote awareness of the organization and greater participation in its activities; this was inaugurated in July 1998 and is based at the ASEAN secretariat building (www.aseanfoundation.org).

EXTERNAL RELATIONS

ASEAN's external relations have been pursued through a dialogue system, initially with the objective of promoting co-operation in economic areas with key trading partners. The system has been expanded in recent years to encompass regional security concerns and co-operation in other areas, such as the environment. The ARF (see above) emerged from the dialogue system, and more recently the formalized discussions of ASEAN with Japan, China and the Republic of Korea (ASEAN + 3) has evolved as a separate process with its own strategic agenda. The second ASEAN-UN Summit took place in New York, USA, in September 2005. In December 2006 the UN General Assembly granted ASEAN permanent observer status at its meetings.

European Union: In March 1980 a co-operation agreement was signed between ASEAN and the European Community (EC, as the EU was known prior to its restructuring on 1 November 1993), which provided for the strengthening of existing trade links and increased co-operation in the scientific and agricultural spheres. A Joint Co-operation Committee met in November (and annually thereafter). An ASEAN-EC Business Council was launched in December 1983, and three European Business Information Councils have since been established, in Malaysia, the Philippines and Thailand, to promote private sector co-operation. The first meeting of ministers of economic affairs from ASEAN and EC member countries took place in October 1985. In December 1990 the Community adopted new guidelines on development co-operation, with an increase in assistance to Asia, and a change in the type of aid given to ASEAN members, emphasizing training, science and technology and venture capital, rather than assistance for rural development. In October 1992 the EC and ASEAN agreed to promote further trade between the regions, as well as bilateral investment, and made a joint declaration in support of human rights. An EU-ASEAN Junior Managers Exchange Programme was initiated in November 1996, as part of efforts to promote co-operation and understanding between the industrial and business sectors in both regions. An ASEAN-EU Business Network was established in Brussels in 2001, to develop political and commercial contacts between the two sides.

In May 1995 ASEAN and EU senior officials endorsed an initiative to strengthen relations between the two economic regions within the framework of an Asia-Europe Meeting of heads of government (ASEM). The first ASEM was convened in Bangkok, Thailand, in March 1996, at which leaders approved a new Asia-Europe Partnership for Greater Growth. The second ASEM summit meeting, held in April 1998, focused heavily on economic concerns. In February 1997 ministers of foreign affairs of countries participating in ASEM met in Singapore. Despite ongoing differences regarding human rights issues, in particular concerning ASEAN's granting of full membership status to Myanmar and the situation in East Timor (which precluded the conclusion of a new co-operation agreement), the Ministerial Meeting issued a final joint declaration, committing both sides to strengthening co-operation and dialogue on economic, international and bilateral trade, security and social issues. The third ASEM summit meeting was convened in Seoul, Korea in October 2000. In December an ASEAN-EU Ministerial Meeting was held in Vientiane, Laos. Both sides agreed to pursue dialogue and co-operation and issued a joint declaration that accorded support for the efforts of the UN Secretary-General's special envoy towards restoring political dialogue in Myanmar. Myanmar agreed to permit an EU delegation to visit the country and political opposition leaders in early 2001. In September 2001 the Joint Co-operation Committee, meeting for the first time since 1999, resolved to strengthen policy dialogue, in particular in areas fostering regional integration. Four new EU delegations were to be established—in Cambodia, Laos, Myanmar and Singapore. At the 14th ASEAN-EU Ministerial Meeting, held in Brussels, Belgium, in January 2003, delegates adopted an ASEAN-EU Joint Declaration on Co-operation to Combat Terrorism. An ASEM seminar on combating terrorism was held in Beijing, the People's Republic of China, in October. In February the EU awarded €4.5m. under the ASEAN-EU Programme on Regional Integration Support (APRIS) to enhance progress towards establishing AFTA. (The first phase of the APRIS programme was concluded in September 2006, and a second three-year phase, APRIS II, was initiated in November with a commitment by the EU of €7.2m.) In April 2003 the EU proposed the creation of a regional framework, the Trans-Regional EU-ASEAN Trade Initiative (TREATI), to address mutual trade facilitation, investment and regulatory issues. It was suggested that the framework might eventually result in a preferential trade agreement. In January 2004 a joint statement was issued announcing a 'road map' for implementing the TREATI and an EU-ASEAN work plan for that year. The fifth ASEM meeting of heads of state and government was held in Hanoi, Viet Nam, in October, attended for the first time by the 10 new members of the EU and by Cambodia, Laos, and Myanmar. At the session of the Joint Co-operation Committee held in February 2005, in Jakarta, Indonesia, it was announced that the European Commission's communication entitled 'A New Partnership with Southeast Asia', issued in July 2003, would form the basis for the development of the EU's relations with ASEAN, along with Bali Concord II and the VAP. Under the new partnership, the TREATI would represent the framework for dialogue on trade and economic issues, whereas the READI (Regional EC ASEAN Dialogue Instrument) would be the focus for non-trade issues. The sixth ASEM, convened in Helsinki, Finland, in September 2006, on the theme '10 Years of ASEM: Global Challenges and Joint Responses', was attended for the first time by the ASEAN Secretariat, Bulgaria, India, Mongolia, Pakistan and Romania. The participants adopted a Declaration on Climate Change, aimed at promoting efforts to reach consensus in international climate negotiations, and the Helsinki Declaration on the Future of ASEM, detailing guide-lines and practical recommendations for developing future ASEM co-operation. A Declaration on an Enhanced Partnership was endorsed in March 2007 and a plan of action to pursue strengthened co-operation was adopted at an ASEAN-EU summit meeting held in November.

People's Republic of China: Efforts to develop consultative relations between ASEAN and the People's Republic of China were initiated in 1993. Joint Committees on economic and trade co-operation and on scientific and technological co-operation were subsequently established. The first formal consultations between senior officials of the two sides were held in April 1995. In July 1996, in spite of ASEAN's continued concern at China's territorial claims to the Spratly Islands in the South China Sea, China was admitted to the PMC as a full dialogue partner. In February 1997 a Joint Co-operation Committee was established to co-ordinate the China-ASEAN dialogue and all aspects of relations between the two sides. Relations were further strengthened by the decision to form a joint business council to promote bilateral trade and investment. China participated in the informal summit meeting held in December, at the end of which both sides issued a joint statement affirming their commitment to resolving regional disputes through peaceful means. A second meeting of the Joint Co-operation Committee was held in March 1999. China was a participant in the first official ASEAN + 3 meeting of foreign ministers, which was convened in July 2000. An ASEAN-China Experts Group was established in November, to consider future economic co-operation and free trade opportunities. The Group held its first meeting in April 2001 and proposed a framework agreement on economic co-operation and the establishment of an ASEAN-China free trade area within 10 years (with differential treatment and flexibility for newer ASEAN members). Both proposals were endorsed at the seventh ASEAN summit meeting in November 2001. In November 2002 an agreement on economic co-operation was concluded by the ASEAN member states and China. The Framework Agreement on Comprehensive Economic Co-operation between ASEAN and China entered into force in July 2003, and envisaged the establishment of an ASEAN-China Free Trade Area (ACFTA) by 2010 (with the target for the newer member countries being 2015). The Agreement provided for strengthened co-operation in key areas including agriculture, information and telecommunications, and human resources development. It was also agreed to implement the consensus of the Special ASEAN-China Leaders' Meeting on SARS, held in April 2003, and to set up an ASEAN + 1 special fund for health co-operation. In October China acceded to the Treaty on Amity and Co-operation and signed a joint declaration with ASEAN on Strategic Partnership for Peace and Prosperity on strengthening co-operation in politics, economy, social affairs, security and regional and international issues. It was also agreed to continue consultations on China's accession to the SEANWFZ and to expedite the implementation of the Joint Statement on Co-operation in the Field of Non-Traditional Security Issues and the Declaration on the Conduct of Parties in the South China Sea. In November 2004 ASEAN and China signed the Agreement on Trade in Goods and the Agreement on Dispute Settlement Mechanism of the Framework Agreement on Comprehensive Economic Co-operation, to be implemented from 1 July 2005. A Plan of Action to Implement ASEAN-China Joint Declaration on Strengthening Strategic Partnership for Peace and Prosperity was also adopted by both parties at that time. In August 2005 ASEAN signed a memorandum of understanding with China on cultural co-operation. An ASEAN-China Agreement on Trade in Services was signed in January 2007, within the Framework Agreement on Comprehensive Economic Co-operation, and entered into force on 1 July. In November the ASEAN-China summit resolved that the environment should be included as a priority area for future co-operation and endorsed agreements concluded earlier in that month to strengthen co-operation in aviation and maritime transport.

Japan: The ASEAN-Japan Forum was established in 1977 to discuss matters of mutual concern in trade, investment, technology transfer and development assistance. The first meeting between the two sides at ministerial level was held in October 1992. At this meeting, and subsequently, ASEAN requested Japan to increase its investment in member countries and to make Japanese markets more accessible to ASEAN products, in order to reduce the trade deficit with Japan. Since 1993 ASEAN-Japanese development and cultural co-operation has expanded under schemes including the Inter-ASEAN Technical Exchange Programme, the Japan-ASEAN Co-operation Promotion Programme and the ASEAN-Japan Friendship Programme. In December 1997 Japan, attending the informal summit meeting in Malaysia, agreed to improve market access for ASEAN products and to provide training opportunities for more than 20,000 young people in order to help develop local economies. In December 1998 ASEAN heads of government welcomed a Japanese initiative, announced in October, to allocate US $30,000m. to promote economic recovery in the region. In mid-2000 a new Japan-ASEAN General Exchange Fund (JAGEF) was established to promote and facilitate the transfer of technology, investment and personnel. In November 1999 Japan, along with the People's Republic of China and the Republic of Korea, attending an informal summit meeting of ASEAN, agreed to strengthen economic and political co-operation with the ASEAN countries, to enhance political and security dialogue, and to implement joint infrastructure and social projects. Japan participated in the first official ASEAN + 3 meeting of foreign ministers, which was convened in July 2000. An ASEAN-Japan Experts Group, similar to that for China, was to be established to consider how economic relations between the two sides can be strengthened. In recent years Japan has provided ICT support to ASEAN countries, and has offered assistance in environmental and health matters and for educational training and human resource development (particularly in engineering). In October 2003 ASEAN and Japan signed a Framework for Comprehensive Partnership. In mid-December Japan concluded a joint action plan with ASEAN with provisions on reinforcing economic integration within ASEAN and enhancing competitiveness, and on addressing terrorism, piracy and other transnational issues. A joint declaration was also issued on starting discussions on the possibility of establishing an ASEAN-Japan FTA by 2012 (with the newer ASEAN countries participating from 2017). Negotiations on a Comprehensive Economic Partnership Agreement were initiated in April 2005 and concluded in November 2007. In July 2004 Japan acceded to the Treaty on Amity and Co-operation. In November the ASEAN-Japan summit meeting adopted the ASEAN-Japan Joint Declaration for Co-operation in the Fight Against International Terrorism.

Australia and New Zealand: In 1999 ASEAN and Australia undertook to establish the ASEAN-Australia Development Co-operation Programme (AADCP), to replace an economic co-operation programme which had begun in 1974. In August 2002 the two sides signed a formal memorandum of understanding on the AADCP. It was to comprise three core elements, with assistance amounting to $A45m.: a Program Stream, to address medium-term issues of economic integration and competitiveness; a Regional Partnerships Scheme for smaller collaborative activities; and the establishment of a Regional Economic Policy Support Facility within the ASEAN Secretariat. Co-operation relations with New Zealand are based on the Inter-Institutional Linkages Programme and the Trade and Investment Promotion Programme, which mainly provide assistance in forestry development, dairy technology, veterinary management and legal aid training. An ASEAN-New Zealand Joint Management Committee was established in November 1993, to oversee the implementation of co-operation projects. New Zealand's English Language Training for Officials Programme is among the most important of these projects. In September 2001 ASEAN ministers of economic affairs signed a Framework for Closer Economic Partnership (CEP) with their counterparts from Australia and New Zealand (the Closer Economic Relations—CER—countries), and agreed to establish a Business Council to involve the business communities of all countries in the CEP. The CEP was perceived as a first step towards the creation of a free trade area between ASEAN and CER countries. The establishment of such an area would strengthen the grouping's bargaining position regionally and multilaterally, and bring benefits such as increased foreign direct investment and the possible relocation of industry. In November 2004 a Commemorative Summit, marking 30 years of dialogue between the nations, took place between ASEAN leaders and those of Australia and New Zealand at which it was agreed to launch negotiations on a free trade agreement. In July 2005 New Zealand signed ASEAN's Treaty of Amity and Co-operation; Australia acceded to the Treaty in December. In August 2007 the Australian and ASEAN ministers of foreign affairs signed a Joint Declaration on a Comprehensive Partnership, and in November agreed upon a plan of action to implement the accord.

South Asia: In July 1993 both India and Pakistan were accepted as sectoral partners, providing for their participation in ASEAN meetings in sectors such as trade, transport and communications and tourism. An ASEAN-India Business Council was established, and met for the first time, in New Delhi, in February 1995. In December 1995 the ASEAN summit meeting agreed to enhance India's status to that of a full dialogue partner; India was formally admitted to the PMC in July 1996. At a meeting of the ASEAN-India Working Group in March 2001 the two sides agreed to pursue co-operation in new areas, such as health and pharmaceuticals, social security and rural development. The fourth meeting of the ASEAN-India Joint Co-operation Committee in January 2002 agreed to strengthen co-operation in these areas and others, including technology. The first ASEAN-India consultation between ministers of economic affairs, which took place in September, resulted in the adoption as a long-term objective, of the ASEAN-India Regional Trade and Investment Area. The first ASEAN-India summit at the level of heads of state was held in Phnom Penh, Cambodia, in November. An ASEAN-Pakistan Joint Business Council met for the first time in February 2000. In early 2001 both sides agreed to co-operate in projects relating to new and renewable energy resources, ICT, agricultural research and transport and communications. In October 2003 India acceded to the Treaty of Amity and Co-operation and signed a joint Framework Agreement on Comprehensive Economic Co-operation, which was to enter into effect in July 2004. The objectives of the Agreement included: strengthening and enhancing economic, trade and investment co-operation; liberalizing and promoting trade in goods and services; and facilitating economic integration within ASEAN. Various initiatives were discussed in the fields of agriculture, biotechnology, and human resources development, and both sides adopted the Joint Declaration for Co-operation to Combat International Terrorism. It was also agreed that negotiations would begin on establishing an ASEAN-India Regional Trade and Investment Area (RTIA), including a free trade area, for Brunei, Indonesia, Malaysia, Singapore and Thailand by 2011 (with the remaining countries joining in 2016). A Partnership for Peace, Progress and Shared Prosperity was signed at the third ASEAN-India summit, held in November 2004. At the sixth summit meeting, held in November 2007, it was noted that annual bilateral ASEAN-India trade had reached US $30,000m.

Pakistan acceded to the Treaty on Amity and Co-operation in July 2004. In January 2007 Timor-Leste acceded to the Treaty; Sri Lanka and Bangladesh acceded in August.

Republic of Korea: In July 1991 the Republic of Korea was accepted as a 'dialogue partner' in ASEAN, and in December a joint ASEAN-Korea Chamber of Commerce was established. In 1995 co-operation projects on human resources development, science and technology, agricultural development and trade and investment policies were implemented. The Republic of Korea participated in ASEAN's informal summit meetings in December 1997 and November 1999 (see above), and took part in the first official ASEAN + 3 meeting of foreign ministers, convened in July 2000. The Republic's assistance in the field of ICT has become particularly valuable in recent years. In March 2001, in a sign of developing co-operation, ASEAN and the Republic of Korea exchanged views on political and security issues in the region for the first time. The Republic of Korea acceded to the Treaty on Amity and Co-operation in November 2004. In that month an ASEAN-Korea summit meeting agreed to initiate negotiations in early 2005 on the establishment of a free trade area between the two sides, with the aim of eliminating tariffs on 80% of products by 2009. In the same month the country. A Framework Agreement on Comprehensive Economic Co-operation, providing for the establishment of an ASEAN-Korea Free Trade Area, was signed in December 2005. In May 2006 governments of both sides (excluding Thailand, owing to a dispute concerning trade in rice) signed an Agreement on Trade in Goods.

Russia: In March 2000 the first ASEAN-Russia business forum opened in Kuala Lumpur, Malaysia. In 2003 an economic co-operation agreement between Russia and ASEAN was under consideration. In July 2004 ASEAN and Russia signed a Joint Declaration to Combat International Terrorism, while in November Russia acceded to the Treaty of Amity and Co-operation. The first ASEAN-Russia summit meeting was held in December 2005. The leaders agreed on a comprehensive programme of action to promote co-operation between both sides in the period 2005–15. This included commitments to co-operate in areas including counter-terrorism, human resources development, finance and economic activities and science and technology.

USA and Canada: The USA gives assistance for the development of small and medium-sized businesses and other projects, and supports a Center for Technology Exchange. In 1990 ASEAN and the USA established an ASEAN-US Joint Working Group, the purpose of which was to review ASEAN's economic relations with the USA and to identify measures by which economic links could be strengthened. In recent years, dialogue has increasingly focused on political and security issues. In August 2002 ASEAN ministers of foreign affairs met with their US counterpart, and signed a Joint Declaration for Co-operation to Combat International Terrorism. At the same time, the USA announced the ASEAN Co-operation Plan, which was to include activities in the fields of ICT, agricultural biotechnology, health, disaster response and training for the ASEAN Secretariat. ASEAN-Canadian co-operation projects include fisheries technology, the telecommunications industry, use of solar energy, and a forest seed centre. A Working Group on the Revitalization of ASEAN-Canada relations met in February 1999. At a meeting in Bangkok, Thailand, in July 2000, the two sides agreed to explore less formal avenues for project implementation. A Work Plan for ASEAN-Canada Co-operation 2007–10 was adopted in August 2007.

Indo-China: In June 1996 ministers of ASEAN countries, and of the People's Republic of China, Cambodia, Laos and Myanmar adopted a framework for ASEAN-Mekong Basin Development Co-operation. The initiative aimed to strengthen the region's cohesiveness, with greater co-operation on issues such as drugs-trafficking, labour migration and terrorism, and to facilitate the process of future expansion of ASEAN. Groups of experts and senior officials were to be convened to consider funding issues and proposals to link the two regions, including a gas pipeline network, rail links and the establishment of a common time zone. In December 1996 the working group on rail links appointed a team of consultants to conduct a feasibility study of the proposals. The completed study was presented at the second ministerial conference on ASEAN-Mekong Basin Development Co-operation, convened in Hanoi, Viet Nam, in July 2000. At the November 2001 summit China pledged US $5m. to assist with navigation along the upper stretches of the Mekong River, while other means by which China could increase its investment in the Mekong Basin area were considered. At the meeting the Republic of Korea was invited to become a core member of the grouping. Other growth regions sponsored by ASEAN include the Brunei, Indonesia, Malaysia, Philippines, East ASEAN Growth Area (BIMP-EAGA), the Indonesia, Malaysia, Singapore Growth Triangle (IMS-GT), and the West-East Corridor within the Mekong Basin Development initiative.

Publications

Annual Report.
Annual Security Report.
ASEAN Investment Report (annually).
ASEAN State of the Environment Report (1st report: 1997; 2nd report: 2000; 3rd report: 2006).
Business ASEAN (quarterly).
Public Information Series, briefing papers, documents series, educational materials.

BANK FOR INTERNATIONAL SETTLEMENTS—BIS

Address: Centralbahnplatz 2, 4002 Basel, Switzerland..
Telephone: 612808080; **fax:** 612809100; **e-mail:** email@bis.org; **internet:** www.bis.org.

The Bank for International Settlements was founded pursuant to the Hague Agreements of 1930 to promote co-operation among national central banks and to provide additional facilities for international financial operations.

Organization
(April 2008)

GENERAL MEETING

The General Meeting is held annually in June and is attended by representatives of the central banks of countries in which shares have been subscribed. The central banks of the following authorities are entitled to attend and vote at General Meetings of the BIS: Algeria, Argentina, Australia, Austria, Belgium, Bosnia and Herzegovina, Brazil, Bulgaria, Canada, Chile, the People's Republic of China, Croatia, the Czech Republic, Denmark, Estonia, Finland, France, Germany, Greece, Hong Kong, Hungary, Iceland, India, Indonesia, Ireland, Israel, Italy, Japan, the Republic of Korea, Latvia, Lithuania, the former Yugoslav republic of Macedonia, Malaysia, Mexico, the Netherlands, New Zealand, Norway, the Philippines, Poland, Portugal, Romania, Russia, Saudi Arabia, Singapore, Slovakia, Slovenia, South Africa, Spain, Sweden, Switzerland, Thailand, Turkey, the United Kingdom and the USA. Following the redefinition in February 2003 of the Federal Republic of Yugoslavia (FRY) as Serbia and Montenegro, with two central banks, the status of the FRY's issue of capital at the BIS remained under review. Serbia and Montenegro divided into separate independent states in 2006. The European Central Bank became a BIS shareholder in December 1999.

BOARD OF DIRECTORS

The Board of Directors is responsible for the conduct of the Bank's operations at the highest level, and comprises the Governors in office of the central banks of Belgium, Canada, France, Germany, Italy, Japan, the Netherlands, Sweden, Switzerland, the United Kingdom and the USA, and also appointed directors from six of these countries. The Bank's statutes also provide for the election to the Board of not more than nine Governors of other member central banks: those of Canada, Japan, the Netherlands, Sweden and Switzerland are elected members of the Board. In June 2005 an extraordinary general meeting amended the statutes to abolish the position of President of the Bank, which had been jointly vested with Chairmanship of the Board since 1948.

Chairman of the Board: JEAN-PIERRE ROTH (Switzerland).

MANAGEMENT

At April 2007 the Bank had a staff of 562 employees, from 49 countries. The main departments are the General Secretariat, the Monetary and Economic Department and the Banking Department. In July 1998 the BIS inaugurated its first overseas administrative unit, the Representative Office for Asia and the Pacific, which is based in Hong Kong. A Regional Treasury dealing room became operational at the Hong Kong office in October 2000, with the aim of improving access for Asian central banks to BIS financial services during their trading hours. In November 2002 a Representative Office for the Americas was inaugurated in Mexico City, Mexico.

General Manager: MALCOLM D. KNIGHT (Canada).

Activities

The BIS is an international financial institution whose role is to promote international monetary and financial co-operation, and to fulfil the function of a 'central banks' bank'. Although it has the legal form of a company limited by shares, it is an international organization governed by international law, and enjoys special privileges and immunities in keeping with its role (a Headquarters Agreement was concluded with Switzerland in 1987). The participating central banks were originally given the option of subscribing the shares themselves or arranging for their subscription in their own countries. In January 2001, however, an extraordinary general meeting amended the Bank's statutes to restrict ownership to central banks. Accordingly, all shares then held by private shareholders (representing 14% of the total share capital) were repurchased at a compensation rate of 16,000 Swiss francs per share. An additional compensation payment was required following a decision by the Hague Arbitral Tribunal (provided for in the 1930 Hague Agreements) in September 2003.

FINANCE

Until the end of the 2002/03 financial year the Bank's unit of account was the gold franc. An extraordinary general meeting in March 2003 amended the Bank's statutes to redenominate the Bank's share capital in Special Drawing Rights (SDRs), the unit of account of the International Monetary Fund, with effect from 1 April 2003, in order to enhance the efficiency and transparency of the Bank's operations. The meeting decided that the nominal value of shares would be rounded down from SDR 5,696 at 31 March 2003 to SDR 5,000, entailing a reduction of 12.2% in the total share capital. The excess of SDR 92.1m. was transferred to the Bank's reserve funds. The authorized capital of the Bank at 31 March 2007 was 1,500m. gold francs (SDR 3,000m.), divided into 600,000 shares of equal value.

STATEMENT OF ACCOUNT
(In SDR millions; 31 March 2007)

Assets		%
Gold and gold deposits	15,457.6	5.7
Cash and on sight a/c with banks .	92.4	0.0
Treasury bills	43,159.3	15.9
Time deposits and advances . .	91,266.0	33.7
Securities	113,437.5	41.9
Miscellaneous	7,512.4	2.8
Total	270,925.2	100.0

Liabilities		%
Deposits (gold)	13,134.9	4.8
Deposits (currencies) . . .	221,790.1	81.9
Accounts payable	19,584.1	7.2
Other liabilities	4,252.5	1.6
Shareholders' equity . . .	12,163.6	4.5
Total	270,925.2	100.0

BANKING OPERATIONS

The BIS assists central banks in managing and investing their monetary reserves: in 2007 some 140 international financial institutions and central banks from all over the world had deposits with the BIS, representing around 6% of world foreign exchange reserves.

The BIS uses the funds deposited with it partly for lending to central banks. Its credit transactions may take the form of swaps against gold; covered credits secured by means of a pledge of gold or marketable short-term securities; credits against gold or currency deposits of the same amount and for the same duration held with the BIS; unsecured credits in the form of advances or deposits; or standby credits, which in individual instances are backed by guarantees given by member central banks.

The BIS also engages in traditional types of investment: funds not required for lending to central banks are placed in the market as deposits with commercial banks and purchases of short-term negotiable paper, including Treasury bills. Such operations constitute a major part of the Bank's business. Increasingly the Bank has developed its own investment services for central banks, including short-term products and longer-term financial instruments.

Central banks' monetary reserves often need to be available at short notice, and need to be placed with the BIS at short term, for fixed periods and with clearly defined repayment terms. The BIS has to match its assets to the maturity structure and nature of its commitments, and must therefore conduct its business with special regard to maintaining a high degree of liquidity.

The Bank's operations must be in conformity with the monetary policy of the central banks of the countries concerned. It is not permitted to make advances to governments or to open current accounts in their name. Real estate transactions are also excluded.

INTERNATIONAL MONETARY CO-OPERATION

Governors of central banks meet for regular discussions at the BIS to co-ordinate international monetary policy and to promote stability in the international financial markets. There is close co-operation with the IMF and the World Bank. The BIS participates in meetings of the so-called Group of 10 (G-10) industrialized nations (see IMF), which has been a major forum for discussion of international monetary issues since its establishment in 1962. Governors of central banks of the G-10 countries convene for regular Basel Monthly Meetings. In 1971 a Standing Committee of the G-10 central banks was established at the BIS to consider aspects of the development of Eurocurrency markets. In February 1999 the G-10 renamed the body the Committee on the Global Financial System, and approved a revised mandate to undertake systematic short-term monitoring of global financial system conditions; longer-term analysis of the functioning of financial markets; and the articulation of policy recommendations aimed at improving market functioning and promoting stability. A Markets Committee (formerly known as the Committee on Gold and Foreign Exchange, established in 1962) comprises senior officials responsible for market operations in the G-10 central banks. It meets regularly to consider developments in foreign exchange and related financial markets, possible future trends and short-run implications of events on market functioning. In 1990 a Committee on Payment and Settlement Systems was established to monitor and analyse developments in domestic payment, settlement and clearing systems, and cross-border and multicurrency systems. It meets three times a year.

In 1974 the Governors of central banks of the G-10 set up the Basel Committee on Banking Supervision (whose secretariat is provided by the BIS) to co-ordinate banking supervision at the international level. The Committee pools information on banking supervisory regulations and surveillance systems, including the supervision of banks' foreign currency business, identifies possible danger areas and proposes measures to safeguard the banks' solvency and liquidity. An International Conference of Banking Supervisors is held every two years. In 1997 the Committee published new guide-lines, entitled Core Principles for Effective Banking Supervision, that were intended to provide a comprehensive set of standards to ensure sound banking. In 1998 the Committee was concerned with the development and implementation of the Core Principles, particularly given the ongoing financial and economic crisis affecting several Asian countries and instability of other major economies. A Financial Stability Institute was established in 1999, jointly by the BIS and Basel Committee, to enhance the capacity of central banks and supervisory bodies to implement aspects of the Core Principles, through the provision of training programmes and other policy workshops. In January 2001 the Committee issued preliminary proposals on capital adequacy rules. In June 2004 the Committee approved a revised framework of the International Convergence of Capital Measurement and Capital Standards (also known as Basel II) which aimed to promote improvements in risk management and strengthen the stability of the financial system. An updated version of the revised framework, as well as a new version of the Amendment to the Capital Accord to incorporate market risks, was issued in November 2005. The updated versions also incorporated a paper concerned with trading activities and the treatment of double default effects prepared by a joint working group of the Committee and the International Organization of Securities Commissions. In October 2006 the International Conference of Banking Supervisors endorsed an enhanced version of the Core Principles (and its associated assessment methodology), incorporating stricter guide-lines to counter money-laundering and to strengthen transparency. The Basel II capital framework began to be implemented by countries and banks from 1 January 2007. The Committee's Accord Implementation Group undertook to promote full implementation of the accord, to provide supervisory guidance and review procedures.

The BIS hosts the secretariat of the Financial Stability Forum, which was established following a meeting in February 1999 of ministers of finance and governors of the central banks of the Group of Seven (G-7) industrialized nations. The Forum aims to strengthen co-operation among the world's largest economies and economic bodies to improve the monitoring of international finance, to reduce the tendency for financial shocks to spread from one economy to another, and thus to prevent a recurrence of economic crises such as those that occurred in 1997 and 1998. Working groups have studied aspects of highly leveraged, or unregulated, institutions, offshore financial centres, short-term capital flows, deposit insurance schemes and measures to promote implementation of international standards. Since 2001 the Forum has convened regular regional meetings with non-member financial authorities in Latin America,

Asia and the Pacific, and Central and Eastern Europe. Switzerland joined the Forum in 2007.

Since January 1998 the BIS has hosted the secretariat of the International Association of Insurance Supervisors, which aims to promote co-operation within the insurance industry with regard to effective supervision and the development of domestic insurance markets. It also hosts the secretariat of the International Association of Deposit Insurers, founded in May 2002.

RESEARCH

The Bank's Monetary and Economic Department conducts research, particularly into monetary and financial questions; collects and publishes data on securities markets and international banking developments; and administers a Data Bank for central banks. Examples of recent research and policy analysis include inflation targeting procedures, structural changes in foreign exchange markets, financial risks and the business cycle, international capital flows, and transmission mechanism of monetary policy. In 2004 the BIS established a Central Bank Research Hub to promote and facilitate the dissemination of economic research published by central banks. A new forum of central bank users and compilers of statistics, the Irving Fisher Committee on Central Bank Statistics, convened for its inaugural meeting in August 2006. Statistics on aspects of the global financial system are published regularly, including details on international banking activities, international and domestic securities markets, derivatives, global foreign exchange markets, external debt, and payment and settlement systems. In September 2006 a three-year Asian research programme was initiated, concerned with monetary policy and exchange rates and analysing financial markets and institutions. The Bank is a co-sponsor, with the UN, Euro Banking Association, Eurostat, OECD, IMF and World Bank, of the Statistical Data and Metadata Exchange initiative, established in June 2002.

AGENCY AND TRUSTEE FUNCTIONS

Throughout its history the BIS has undertaken various duties as Trustee Fiscal Agent or Depository with regard to international loan agreements. In October 2005 the BIS served as an escrow agent role in a loan with the Central Bank of Nigeria; the arrangement was terminated upon the final release of funds in February 2007.

In April 1994 the BIS assumed new functions in connection with the rescheduling of Brazil's external debt, which had been agreed by the Brazilian Government in November 1993. In accordance with two collateral pledge agreements, the BIS acts in the capacity of Collateral Agent to hold and invest collateral for the benefit of the holders of certain US dollar-denominated bonds, maturing in 15 or 30 years, which have been issued by Brazil under the rescheduling arrangements. The Bank acts in a similar capacity for Peru, in accordance with external debt agreements concluded in November 1996 and a collateral agreement signed with the BIS in March 1997, and for Côte d'Ivoire, under a restructuring agreement signed in May 1997 and collateral agreement signed in March 1998.

Publications

Annual Report (in English, French, German, Italian and Spanish).
BIS Consolidated Banking Statistics (every 6 months).
BIS Papers (series).
Central Bank Survey of Foreign Exchange and Derivatives Market Activity (every 3 years).
International Journal of Central Banking (quarterly).
Joint BIS-IMF-OECD-World Bank Statistics on External Debt (quarterly).
Quarterly Review: International Banking and Financial Market Developments.
Regular OTC Derivatives Market Statistics (every 6 months).

CARIBBEAN COMMUNITY AND COMMON MARKET—CARICOM

Address: POB 10827, Georgetown, Guyana.
Telephone: (2) 222-0001; **fax:** (2) 222-0171; **e-mail:** info@caricom.org; **internet:** www.caricom.org.

CARICOM was formed in 1973 by the Treaty of Chaguaramas, signed in Trinidad, as a movement towards unity in the Caribbean; it replaced the Caribbean Free Trade Association (CARIFTA), founded in 1965. A revision of the Treaty of Chaguaramas (by means of nine separate Protocols), in order to institute greater regional integration and to establish a CARICOM Single Market and Economy (CSME), was instigated in the 1990s and completed in July 2001. The single market component of the CSME was formally inaugurated on 1 January 2006.

MEMBERS

Antigua and Barbuda	Jamaica
Bahamas*	Montserrat
Barbados	Saint Christopher and Nevis
Belize	Saint Lucia
Dominica	Saint Vincent and the
Grenada	Grenadines
Guyana	Suriname
Haiti	Trinidad and Tobago

*The Bahamas is a member of the Community but not the Common Market.

ASSOCIATE MEMBERS

Anguilla	Cayman Islands
Bermuda	Turks and Caicos Islands
British Virgin Islands	

Note: Aruba, Colombia, Dominican Republic, Mexico, the Netherlands Antilles, Puerto Rico and Venezuela have observer status with the Community.

Organization
(April 2008)

HEADS OF GOVERNMENT CONFERENCE AND BUREAU

The Conference is the final authority of the Community and determines policy. It is responsible for the conclusion of treaties on behalf of the Community and for entering into relationships between the Community and international organizations and states. Decisions of the Conference are generally taken unanimously. Heads of government meet annually, although inter-sessional meetings may be convened.

At a special meeting of the Conference, held in Trinidad and Tobago in October 1992, participants decided to establish a Heads of Government Bureau, with the capacity to initiate proposals, to update consensus and to secure the implementation of CARICOM decisions. The Bureau became operational in December, comprising the Chairman of the Conference, as Chairman, as well as the incoming and outgoing Chairmen of the Conference, and the Secretary-General of the Conference, in the capacity of Chief Executive Officer.

COMMUNITY COUNCIL OF MINISTERS

In October 1992 CARICOM heads of government agreed that a Caribbean Community Council of Ministers should be established to replace the existing Common Market Council of Ministers as the second highest organ of the Community. Protocol I amending the Treaty of Chaguaramas, to restructure the organs and institutions of the Community, was formally adopted at a meeting of CARICOM heads of government in February 1997 and was signed by all member states in July. The inaugural meeting of the Community Council of Ministers was held in Nassau, Bahamas, in February 1998. The Council consists of ministers responsible for community affairs, as well as other government ministers designated by member states, and is responsible for the development of the Community's strategic planning and co-ordination in the areas of economic integration, functional co-operation and external relations.

COURT OF JUSTICE

Caribbean Court of Justice (CCJ): 134 Henry St, POB 1768, Port of Spain, Trinidad and Tobago; tel. 623-2225; e-mail info@caribbeancourtofjustice.org; internet www.caribbeancourtofjustice.org; inaugurated in April 2005; an agreement establishing the Court was formally signed by 10 member countries in February 2001; in January 2004 a revised agreement on the establishment of the CCJ, which incorporated provision for a Trust Fund, entered into force; serves as a tribunal to enforce rights and to consider disputes relating to the CARICOM Single Market and Economy; intended to replace the Judicial Committee of the Privy Council as the Court of Final Appeal (effective for Barbados and Guyana); Pres. MICHAEL DE LA BASTIDE.

MINISTERIAL COUNCILS

The principal organs of the Community are assisted in their functions by the following bodies, established under Protocol I amending the Treaty of Chaguaramas: the Council for Trade and Economic Development (COTED); the Council for Foreign and Community Relations (COFCOR); the Council for Human and Social Development (COHSOD); and the Council for Finance and Planning (COFAP). The Councils are responsible for formulating policies, promoting their implementation and supervising co-operation in the relevant areas.

SECRETARIAT

The Secretariat is the main administrative body of the Caribbean Community. The functions of the Secretariat are to service meetings of the Community and of its Committees; to take appropriate follow-up action on decisions made at such meetings; to carry out studies on questions of economic and functional co-operation relating to the region as a whole; to provide services to member states at their request in respect of matters relating to the achievement of the objectives of the Community. The Secretariat incorporates Directorates for Regional Trade and Economic Integration; Foreign and Community Relations; and Human and Social Development.

Secretary-General: EDWIN W. CARRINGTON (Trinidad and Tobago).
Deputy Secretary-General: LOLITA APPLEWHAITE (Barbados).

Activities

ECONOMIC CO-OPERATION

The Caribbean Community's main field of activity is economic integration, by means of a Caribbean Common Market. The Secretariat and the Caribbean Development Bank undertake research on the best means of facing economic difficulties, and meetings of the Chief Executives of commercial banks and of central bank officials are also held with the aim of strengthening regional co-operation.

In July 1984 heads of government agreed to establish a common external tariff (CET) on certain products, in order to protect domestic industries. They also urged the necessity of structural adjustment in the economies of the region, including measures to expand production and reduce imports. In 1989 the Conference of Heads of Government agreed to implement, by July 1993, a series of measures to encourage the creation of a single Caribbean market. These included the establishment of a CARICOM Industrial Programming Scheme; the inauguration of the CARICOM Enterprise Regime; facilitation of travel for CARICOM nationals within the region; full implementation of the rules of origin and the revised scheme for the harmonization of fiscal incentives; free movement of skilled workers; removal of all remaining regional barriers to trade; establishment of a regional system of air and sea transport; and the introduction of a scheme for regional capital movement. A CARICOM Export Development Council, established in November 1989, undertook a three-year export development project to stimulate trade within CARICOM and to promote exports outside the region.

In August 1990 CARICOM heads of government mandated the governors of CARICOM members' central banks to begin a study of the means to achieve a monetary union within CARICOM; they also institutionalized meetings of CARICOM ministers of finance and senior finance officials, to take place twice a year.

The initial deadline of 1991 for the establishment of a CET was not achieved. At a special meeting, held in October 1992, CARICOM heads of government agreed to reduce the maximum level of tariffs from 45% to between 30% and 35%, to be in effect by 30 June 1993 (the level was to be further lowered, to 25%–30% by 1995). The Bahamas, however, was not party to these trading arrangements (since it is a member of the Community but not of the Common Market), and Belize was granted an extension for the implementation of the new tariff levels. At the Heads of Government Conference, held in July 1995 in Guyana, Suriname was admitted as a full member of CARICOM and acceded to the treaty establishing the Common Market. It was granted until 1 January 1996 for implementation of the tariff reductions.

The 1995 Heads of Government Conference approved additional measures to promote the single market. The free movement of skilled workers (mainly graduates from recognized regional institutions) was to be permitted from 1 January 1996. At the same time an agreement on the mutual protection and provision of social security benefits was to enter into force. In July 1996 the heads of government decided that CARICOM ministers of finance, central bank governors and planning agencies should meet more frequently to address single market issues and agreed to extend the provisions of free movement to sports men and women, musicians and others working in the arts and media.

In July 1997 the Conference, meeting in Montego Bay, Jamaica, agreed to accelerate economic integration, with the aim of completing a single market by 1999. At the meeting 11 member states signed Protocol II amending the Treaty of Chaguaramas, which constituted a central element of a CARICOM Single Market and Economy (CSME), providing for the right to establish enterprises, the provision of services and the free movement of capital and labour throughout participating countries. A regional collaborative network was established to promote the CSME. In July 1998, at the meeting of heads of government, held in Saint Lucia, an agreement was signed with the Insurance Company of the West Indies to accelerate the establishment of a Caribbean Investment Fund, which was to mobilize foreign currency from extra-regional capital markets for investment in new or existing enterprises in the region. Some 60% of all funds generated were to be used by CARICOM countries and the remainder by non-CARICOM members of the Association of Caribbean States.

In November 2000 a special consultation on the single market and economy was held in Barbados, involving CARICOM and government officials, academics, and representatives of the private sector, labour organizations, the media, and other regional groupings. In February 2001 heads of government agreed to establish a new high-level sub-committee to accelerate the establishment of the CSME and to promote its objectives. The sub-committee was to be supported by a Technical Advisory Council, comprising representatives of the public and private sectors. By June all member states had signed and declared the provisional application of Protocol II. By May 2007 12 countries had completed the fourth phase of the CET.

In October 2001 CARICOM heads of government, meeting in a special emergency meeting, considered the impact on the region's economy of the terrorist attacks perpetrated against targets in the USA in the previous month. The meeting resolved to enhance aviation security, to implement promotion and marketing campaigns in support of the tourist industry, and to approach international institutions to assist with emergency financing. The economic situation, which had been further adversely affected by the reduced access to the EU banana market, the economic downturn in the USA, and the effects on the investment climate of the OECD Harmful Taxation Initiative, was considered at the Heads of Government Conference, held in Guyana, in July 2002. Heads of government agreed to meet in August in special session to elaborate a programme to revive the economy, on the basis of the work of a newly-appointed technical team. A technical committee was also established in July to develop proposals for a regional stabilization programme, and a Stabilization Fund, with initial capital of US $60m. An inter-sessional Heads of Government Conference that was held in March 2004, however, agreed that there was insufficient support for the Fund to be established at that time.

On 1 January 2006 the single market component of the CSME was formally inaugurated, with Barbados, Belize, Guyana, Jamaica, Suriname and Trinidad and Tobago as active participants. Six more countries (Antigua and Barbuda, Dominica, Grenada, Saint Christopher and Nevis, Saint Lucia, Saint Vincent and the Grenadines) formally joined the single market in July. At the same time CARICOM heads of government approved a contribution formula allowing for the establishment of a Regional Development Fund. In February 2007 an inter-sessional meeting of the Conference of Heads of Government, held in Saint Vincent and the Grenadines, approved a timetable for the full implementation of the CSME: phase I (mid-2005–08) for the consolidation of the single market and the initiation of a single economy; phase II (2009–15) for the consolidation and completion of the single economy process, including the harmonization and co-ordination of economic policies in the region and the establishment of new institutions to implement those policies. In July 2007 CARICOM heads of government endorsed the report, *Towards a Single Development Vision and the Role of the Single Economy*, on which the elaboration of the CSME was based. In January 2008 a Caribbean Competition Commission was inaugurated, in Paramaribo, Suriname, to enforce the rules of competition within the CSME. In February Haiti signed the revised Treaty of Chaguaramas.

In December 2007 a special meeting of the Conference of Heads of Government, convened in Georgetown, Guyana, considered issues relating to regional poverty and the rising cost of living in member states. The meeting resolved to establish a technical team to review the CET on essential commodities to determine whether it should be removed or reduced to deter inflationary pressures. The meeting also agreed to review the supply and distribution of food throughout the region, including transportation issues affecting the price of goods and services, and determined to expand agricultural production and agro-processing. Efforts to harness renewable energy sources were to be strengthened to counter rising fuel prices.

REGIONAL INTEGRATION

In 1989 CARICOM heads of government established the 15-member West Indian Commission to study regional political and economic integration. The Commission's final report, submitted in July 1992, recommended that CARICOM should remain a community of sovereign states (rather than a federation), but should strengthen the integration process and expand to include the wider Caribbean region. It recommended the formation of an Association of Caribbean States (ACS), to include all the countries within and surrounding the Caribbean Basin. In November 1997 the Secretaries-General of CARICOM and the ACS signed a Co-operation Agreement to formalize the reciprocal procedures through which the organizations work to enhance and facilitate regional integration. Suriname was admitted to CARICOM in July 1995. In July 1997 the Heads of Government Conference agreed to admit Haiti as a member, although the terms and conditions of its accession to the organization were not finalized until July 1999. In July 2001 the CARICOM Secretary-General formally inaugurated a CARICOM Office in Haiti, which aimed to provide technical assistance in preparation of Haiti's accession to the Community. In January 2002 a CARICOM special mission visited Haiti, following an escalation of the political violence which had started in the previous month. Ministers of foreign affairs emphasized the need for international aid for Haiti when they met their US counterpart in February. Haiti was admitted as the 15th member of CARICOM at the Heads of Government Conference, held in July.

During 1998 CARICOM was concerned by the movement within Nevis to secede from its federation with Saint Christopher. In July heads of government agreed to dispatch a mediation team to the country (postponed until September). The Heads of Government Conference held in March 1999 welcomed the establishment of a Constitutional Task Force by the local authorities to prepare a draft constitution, on the basis of recommendations of a previous constitutional commission and the outcome of a series of public meetings. In July 1998 heads of government expressed concern at the hostility between the Government and opposition groupings in Guyana. The two sides signed an agreement, under CARICOM auspices, and in September a CARICOM mediation mission visited Guyana to promote further dialogue. CARICOM has declared its support for Guyana in its territorial disputes with Venezuela and Suriname. In December 2001 a CARICOM mission observed a general election in Trinidad and Tobago. Following an inconclusive outcome to the election, a delegation from CARICOM visited that country in late January 2002.

In February 1997 Community heads of government signed a new Charter of Civil Society for the Community, which set out principles in the areas of democracy, government, parliament, freedom of the press and human rights. In July 2002 a conference was held, in Liliendaal, Guyana, attended by representatives of civil society and the CARICOM heads of government. The meeting issued a statement of principles on 'Forward Together', recognizing the role of civil society in meeting the challenges to the region. It was agreed to hold regular meetings and to establish a task force to develop a regional strategic framework for pursuing the main recommendations of the conference. In February 2007 an inter-sessional meeting of CARICOM heads of government determined to add security (including crime) as a fourth pillar of regional integration, in addition to those identified: economic integration; co-ordination of foreign policy; and functional co-operation.

CO-ORDINATION OF FOREIGN POLICY

The co-ordination of foreign policies of member states is listed as one of the main objectives of the Community in its founding treaty. Activities include: strengthening of member states' position in international organizations; joint diplomatic action on issues of particular interest to the Caribbean; joint co-operation arrangements with third countries and organizations; and the negotiation of free trade agreements with third countries and other regional groupings.. In April 1997 CARICOM inaugurated a Regional Negotiating Machinery body, based in Kingston, Jamaica, to co-ordinate and strengthen the region's presence at external economic negotiations. The main areas of activity were negotiations to establish a Free Trade Area of the Americas (FTAA—now stalled), ACP relations with the European Union (EU), and multilateral trade negotiations under the World Trade Organization (WTO).

In July 1991 Venezuela applied for membership of CARICOM, and offered a non-reciprocal free trade agreement for CARICOM exports to Venezuela, over an initial five-year period. In October 1993 the newly-established Group of Three (Colombia, Mexico and Venezuela) signed joint agreements with CARICOM and Suriname on combating drugs-trafficking and environmental protection. In June 1994 CARICOM and Colombia concluded an agreement on trade, economic and technical co-operation, which, *inter alia*, gives special treatment to the least-developed CARICOM countries. CARICOM has observer status in the Latin American Rio Group.

In 1992 Cuba applied for observer status within CARICOM, and in July 1993 a joint commission was inaugurated to establish closer ties between CARICOM and Cuba and to provide a mechanism for regular dialogue. In July 1997 the heads of government agreed to pursue consideration of a free trade accord between the Community and Cuba. A Trade and Economic Agreement was signed by the two sides in July 2000, and a CARICOM office was established in Cuba, in February 2001. In July 2004 a meeting of the two sides was held in Havana, Cuba, at ministerial level. In December 2005 a CARICOM-Cuba meeting of heads of state and government was convened in Barbados. Agreements were signed to strengthen co-operation in education, cultural and the environment, access to health care and efforts to counter international terrorism. A second meeting of CARICOM-Cuba ministers of foreign affairs was convened in May 2007.

In February 1992 ministers of foreign affairs from CARICOM and Central American states met to discuss future co-operation, in view of the imminent conclusion of the North American Free Trade Agreement (NAFTA) between the USA, Canada and Mexico. It was agreed that a consultative forum would be established to discuss the possible formation of a Caribbean and Central American free trade zone. In October 1993 CARICOM declared its support for NAFTA, but requested a 'grace period', during which the region's exports would have parity with Mexican products, and in March 1994 requested that it should be considered for early entry into NAFTA.

In July 1996 the heads of government expressed strong concern over the complaint lodged with the WTO by the USA, Ecuador, Guatemala and Honduras regarding the EU's import regime on bananas, which gave preferential access to bananas from the ACP countries (see the European Union). CARICOM requested the US Government to withdraw its complaint and to negotiate a settlement. Nevertheless, WTO panel hearings on the complaint were initiated in September. Banana producers from the ACP countries were granted third-party status. In May 1997 a meeting of CARICOM heads of government and the US President established a partnership for prosperity and security, and arrangements were instituted for annual consultations between the ministers of foreign affairs of CARICOM countries and the US Secretary of State. However, the Community failed to secure a commitment by the USA to grant the region's exports 'NAFTA-parity' status, or to guarantee concessions to the region's banana industry, following a temporary ruling of the WTO, issued in March, upholding the US trade complaint. The WTO ruling was confirmed in May and endorsed by the WTO dispute settlement body in September. The USA's opposition to a new EU banana policy (which was to terminate the import licensing system, extending import quotas to 'dollar' producers, while maintaining a limited duty-free quota for Caribbean producers) was strongly criticized by CARICOM leaders, meeting in July 1998. In March 1999 the Inter-Sessional meeting of the Conference of Heads of Government issued a statement condemning the imposition by the USA of sanctions against a number of EU imports, in protest at the revised EU banana regime, and the consequences of this action on Caribbean economies, and agreed to review its co-operation with the USA under the partnership for prosperity and security.

In August 1998 CARICOM and the Dominican Republic signed a free trade accord, covering trade in goods and services, technical barriers to trade, government procurement, and sanitary and phytosanitary measures and standards. A protocol to the agreement was signed in April 2000, following the resolution of differences concerning exempted items. The accord was ratified by the Dominican Republic in February 2001 and entered partially into force on 1 December. In November the CARICOM Secretary-General formally inaugurated a Caribbean Regional Technical Assistance Centre (CARTAC), in Barbados, to provide technical advice and training to officials from member countries and the Dominican Republic in support of the region's development, with particular focus on fiscal management, financial sector supervision and regulation, and the compilation of statistics. The IMF was to manage the Centre's operations, while UNDP was to provide administrative and logistical support.

In March 2000 heads of government issued a statement supporting the territorial integrity and security of Belize in that country's ongoing border dispute with Guatemala. CARICOM subsequently urged both countries to implement the provisions of an agreement signed in November and has continued regularly to monitor the situation.

In July 2000 the Heads of Government meeting issued a statement strongly opposing the OECD Harmful Tax Initiative, under which punitive measures had been threatened against 35 countries, including CARICOM member states, if they failed to tighten taxation legislation. The meeting also condemned a separate list, issued by the OECD's Financial Action Task Force on Money Laundering (FATF), which identified 15 countries, including five Caribbean states, of failing to counter effectively international money-laundering. The statement reaffirmed CARICOM's commitment to fighting financial crimes and support for any necessary reform of supervisory practices or legislation, but insisted that national taxation jurisdictions, and specifically competitive regimes designed to attract offshore business, was not a matter for OECD concern. CARICOM remained actively involved in efforts to counter the scheme, and in April 2001 presented its case to the US President. In September the FATF issued a revised list of 19 'unco-operative jurisdictions', including Dominica, Grenada, Saint Christopher and Nevis and Saint Vincent and the Grenadines. In early 2002 most Caribbean states concluded a provisional agreement with the OECD to work to improve the transparency and supervision of offshore sectors.

In February 2002 the first meeting of heads of state and of government of CARICOM and the Central American Integration System (SICA) was convened in Belize City, Belize. The meeting aimed to strengthen co-operation between the groupings, in particular in international negotiations, efforts to counter transnational organized crime, and support for the regions' economies. In late 2002 a joint CARICOM-Spain commission was inaugurated to foster greater co-operation between the two parties. In March 2004 CARICOM signed a free trade agreement with Costa Rica.

In January 2004 CARICOM heads of government resolved to address the escalating political crisis in Haiti. Following a visit by a high-level delegation to that country early in the month discussions were held with representatives of opposition political parties and civil society groups. At the end of January several CARICOM leaders met with Haiti's President Aristide and members of his government and announced a Prior Action Plan, incorporating opposition demands for political reform. The Plan, however, was rejected by opposition parties since it permitted Aristide to complete his term-in-office. CARICOM, together with the OAS, continued to pursue diplomatic efforts to secure a peaceful solution to the crisis. On 29 February Aristide resigned and left the country and a provisional president was appointed. In March CARICOM heads of government determined not to allow representatives of the new interim administration to participate in the councils of the Community until constitutional rule had been reinstated. In July heads of government resolved to send a five-member ministerial team to Haiti to discuss developments in that country with the interim authorities. In July 2005 CARICOM heads of government expressed concern at the deterioration of the situation in Haiti, but reiterated their readiness to provide technical assistance for the electoral process, under the auspices of the UN mission. In March 2006 the CARICOM Chairman endorsed the results of the presidential election, which had been conducted in the previous month, and pledged fully to support Haiti's return to democratic rule.

In July 2005 CARICOM heads of government issued a statement protesting against proposals by the European Commission, issued in the previous month, to reform the EU sugar regime. Particular concern was expressed at a proposed price reduction in the cost of refined sugar of 39% over a four-year period. The heads of government insisted that, in accordance with the ACP-EU Cotonou Agreement, any review of the Sugar Protocol was required to be undertaken with the agreement of both parties and with regard to safeguarding benefits. In December CARICOM heads of government held a special meeting to discuss the EU sugar and banana regimes, in advance of a ministerial meeting of the WTO, held in Hong Kong later in that month. The Conference reiterated the potentially devastating effects on regional economies of the sugar price reduction and proposed new banana tariffs, and expressed the need for greater compensation and for the WTO multilateral negotiations to address fairly issues of preferential access. Negotiations between the ACP Caribbean signatory countries (the so-called CARIFORUM) and the EU on an Economic Partnership Agreement to succeed the Cotonou Agreement, which had commenced in April 2004, were concluded in December 2007. In January 2008 CARICOM's Council for Trade and Economic Development resolved to conduct an independent review of the new agreement.

In March 2006 a CARICOM-Mexico Joint Commission signed an agreement to promote future co-operation, in particular in seven priority areas including: disaster management, energy conservation and regional statistics. In February 2007 the Secretaries-General of CARICOM and SICA signed a plan of action on future co-operation between the two groupings. A second CARICOM-SICA meeting of heads of state and of government was convened in May, in Belize. The meeting endorsed the plan of action and, in addition, instructed their ministers of foreign affairs and of trade to pursue efforts to negotiate a free trade agreement, to be based on that signed by CARICOM with Costa Rica (see above). Trade negotiations were formally inaugurated in August.

In March 2006 CARICOM ministers of foreign affairs met with the US Secretary of State and agreed to strengthen co-operation and enhance bilateral relations. In June 2007 a major meeting, the 'Conference on the Caribbean: a 20/20 Vision', was held in Washington, DC, USA. A series of meetings was held to consider issues and challenges relating to CARICOM's development and integration efforts and to the strengthening of relations with other countries in the region and with the USA. An Experts' Forum was hosted by the World Bank, a Private Sector Dialogue was held at the headquarters of the Inter-American Development Bank, and a Diaspora Forum was convened at the Organization of American States. A summit meeting of CARICOM heads of government and the US President, George W. Bush, was held in the context of the Conference, at which issues concerning trade, economic growth and development, security and social investment were discussed. A second Conference on the Caribbean was scheduled to be held in New York, USA, in June 2008.

CRIME AND SECURITY

In December 1996 CARICOM heads of government determined to strengthen comprehensive co-operation and technical assistance to combat illegal drugs-trafficking. The Conference decided to establish a Caribbean Security Task Force to help formulate a single regional agreement on maritime interdiction, incorporating agreements already concluded by individual members. A Regional Drugs Control Programme at the CARICOM Secretariat aims to co-ordinate regional initiatives with the overall objective of reducing the demand and supply of illegal substances. In July 2001 heads of government resolved to establish a task force to be responsible for producing recommendations for a forthcoming meeting of national security advisers. In October heads of government convened an emergency meeting in Nassau, the Bahamas, to consider the impact of the terrorist attacks against the USA which had occurred in September. The meeting determined to convene immediately the so-called Task Force on Crime and Security in order to implement new policy directives. It was agreed to enhance co-ordination and collaboration of security services throughout the region, in particular in intelligence gathering, analysis and sharing in relation to crime, illicit drugs and terrorism, and to strengthen security at airports, seaports and borders. In July 2002 heads of government agreed on a series of initiatives recommended by the Task Force to counter the escalation in crime and violence. These included strengthening border controls, preparing national anti-crime master plans, establishing broad-based National Commissions on law and order and strengthening the exchange of information and intelligence. In July 2005 CARICOM heads of government endorsed a new Management Framework for Crime and Security, which provided for regular meetings of a Council of Ministers responsible for national security and law enforcement, a Security Policy Advisory Committee, and an Implementing Agency for Crime and Security. Several co-ordinated security measures were implemented during the cricket world cup, which was held across the region in early 2007. In July CARICOM heads of government agreed in principle to extend these security efforts, including the introduction of a voluntary CARICOM Travel Card to facilitate the establishment of a single domestic space.

INDUSTRY, ENERGY AND THE ENVIRONMENT

A protocol relating to the CARICOM Industrial Programming Scheme (CIPS), approved in 1988, is the Community's instrument for promoting the co-operative development of industry in the region. Protocol III amending the Treaty of Chaguaramas, with respect to industrial policy, was opened for signature in July 1998. The Secretariat has established a national standards bureau in each member country to harmonize technical standards. In 1999 members agreed to establish a new CARICOM Regional Organisation for Standards and Quality (CROSQ), as a successor to the Caribbean Common Market Standards Council. The agreement to establish CROSQ, to be located in Barbados, was signed in February 2002. By May 2007 the agreement was being provisionally applied in 12 member countries, and was to enter into force upon the signature of Montserrat.

The CARICOM Alternative Energy Systems Project provides training, assesses energy needs and conducts energy audits. Efforts in regional energy development are directed at the collection and analysis of data for national energy policy documents. Implementation of a Caribbean Renewable Energy Development Programme, a project initiated in 1998, commenced in 2004. The Programme aimed to remove barriers to renewable energy development, establish a foundation for a sustainable renewable energy industry, and to create a framework for co-operation among regional and national renewable energy projects. A Caribbean Renewable Energy Fund was to be established to provide equity and development financing for renewable energy projects.

In January 2001 the Council for Trade and Economic Development approved the development of a specialized CARICOM agency to co-ordinate the gathering of information and other activities relating to climate change. The Caribbean Community Climate Change Centre became operational in early 2004 and was formally inaugurated, in Belmopan, Belize, in August 2005. It serves as an official clearing house and repository of data relating to climate change in the Caribbean region, provides advice to governments and other expertise for the development of projects to manage and adapt to climate change, and undertakes training.

TRANSPORT, COMMUNICATIONS AND TOURISM

A Summit of Heads of Government on Tourism, Trade and Transportation was held in Trinidad and Tobago, in August 1995, to which all members of the ACS and regional tourism organizations were invited. In 1997 CARICOM heads of government considered a number of proposals relating to air transportation, tourism, human resource development and capital investment, which had been identified by Community ministers of tourism as critical issues in the sustainable development of the tourist industry. The heads of government requested ministers to meet regularly to develop tourism policies, and in particular to undertake an in-depth study of human resource development issues in early 1998. A regional summit on tourism, in recognition of the importance of the industry to the economic development of the region, was held in the Bahamas, in December 2001. By early 2007 eight member countries had introduced a new Caribbean passport.

A Caribbean Confederation of Shippers' Councils represents the interests of regional exporters and importers. A Multilateral Agreement Concerning the Operations of Air Services within the Caribbean Community entered into force in November 1998, providing a formal framework for the regulation of the air transport industry and enabling CARICOM-owned and -controlled airlines to operate freely within the region. In July 1999 heads of government signed Protocol VI amending the Treaty of Chaguaramas providing for a common transportation policy, with harmonized standards and practices, which was to be an integral component of the development of a single market and economy. In November 2001 representatives of national civil aviation authorities signed a memorandum of understanding, providing for the establishment of a regional body, the Regional Aviation Oversight Safety System.

In 1989 the Caribbean Telecommunications Union was established to oversee developments in regional telecommunications. In July 2006 the Conference of heads of government, convened in Saint Christopher and Nevis, mandated the development of C@ribNET, a project to extend the availability of high speed internet access throughout the region. In May 2007 the inaugural meeting of a Regional Information Communications and Technology Steering Committee was held, in Georgetown, Guyana, to determine areas of activity for future co-operation in support of the establishment of a Caribbean Information Society.

AGRICULTURE AND FISHERIES

In July 1996 the CARICOM summit meeting agreed to undertake wide-ranging measures in order to modernize the agricultural sector and to increase the international competitiveness of Caribbean agricultural produce. The CARICOM Secretariat was to support national programmes with assistance in policy formulation, human resource development and the promotion of research and technology development in the areas of productivity, marketing, agri-business and water resources management. During 1997 CARICOM Governments continued to lobby against a complaint lodged at the WTO with regard to the EU's banana import regime (offering favourable conditions to ACP producers—see above) and to generate awareness of the economic and social importance of the banana industry to the region. Protocol V amending the Treaty of Chaguaramas, which was concerned with agricultural policy, was opened for signature by heads of government in July 1998. In July 2002 heads of government approved an initiative to develop a CARIFORUM Special Programme for Food Security.

In February 2003 the CARICOM Secretariat was mandated to draft a proposal for a common fisheries policy.

HEALTH AND EDUCATION

In 1986 CARICOM and the Pan-American Health Organization launched 'Caribbean Co-operation in Health' with projects to be undertaken in six main areas: environmental protection, including the control of disease-bearing pests; development of human resources; chronic non-communicable diseases and accidents; strengthening health systems; food and nutrition; maternal and child health care; and population activities. In 2001 CARICOM established the Pan-Caribbean Partnership against HIV/AIDS (PANCAP), with the aim of reducing the spread and impact of HIV and AIDS in member countries. In February 2002 PANCAP initiated regional negotiations with pharmaceutical companies to secure reductions in the cost of anti-retroviral drugs. A Caribbean Environmental Health Institute (see below) aims to promote collaboration among member states in all areas of environmental management and human health. In July 2001 heads of government, meeting in the Bahamas, issued the Nassau Declaration on Health, advocating greater regional strategic co-ordination and planning in the health sector and institutional reform, as well as increased resources. In February 2006 PANCAP and UNAIDS organized a regional consultation on the outcomes of country-based assessments of the HIV/AIDS crisis that had been undertaken in the region, and formulated a Regional Roadmap for Universal Access to HIV and AIDS Prevention, Care, Treatment and Support over the period 2006–10. A special meeting of COHSOD, convened in June 2006, in Trinidad and Tobago, issued the Port of Spain Declaration on the Education Sector Response to HIV and AIDS, which committed member states to supporting the Roadmap through education policy. In September 2007 a special regional summit meeting on chronic non-communicable diseases was held in Port of Spain, Trinidad and Tobago.

CARICOM education programmes have included the improvement of reading in schools through assistance for teacher-training and ensuring the availability of low-cost educational material throughout the region. In July 1997 CARICOM heads of government adopted the recommendations of a ministerial committee, which identified priority measures for implementation in the education sector. These included the objective of achieving universal, quality secondary education and the enrolment of 15% of post-secondary students in tertiary education by 2005, as well as improved training in foreign languages and science and technology. In March 2004 CARICOM ministers of education endorsed the establishment of a Caribbean Knowledge and Learning Network to strengthen tertiary education institutions throughout the region and to enhance knowledge sharing. The Network was formally inaugurated in July, in co-operation with the OECS, in Grenada. A Caribbean Vocational Qualification was introduced in 2007.

From the late 1990s youth activities have been increasingly emphasized by the Community. These have included new programmes for disadvantaged youths, a mechanism for youth exchange and the convening of a Caribbean Youth Parliament. CARICOM organizes a biennial Caribbean Festival of Arts (CARIFESTA). CARIFESTA X was scheduled to be staged in Georgetown, Guyana, in August 2008.

EMERGENCY ASSISTANCE

A Caribbean Disaster Emergency Response Agency (CDERA) was established in 1991 to co-ordinate immediate disaster relief, primarily in the event of hurricanes. In January 2005, meeting on the sidelines of the fifth Summit of the Alliance of Small Island States, in Port Louis, Mauritius, the Secretaries-General of CARICOM, the Commonwealth, the Pacific Islands Forum and the Indian Ocean Commission determined to take collective action to strengthen the disaster preparedness and response capabilities of their member countries in the Caribbean, Pacific and Indian Ocean areas. In September 2006 CARICOM, the European Union and the Caribbean ACP states signed a Financing Agreement for Institutional Support and Capacity-Building for Disaster Management in the Caribbean, which aimed to support CDERA by providing €3.4m. to facilitate the implementation of revised legislation, improved co-ordination between countries in the region and the increased use of information and communications technology in emergency planning. A new Caribbean Catastrophe Risk Insurance Facility (CCRIF), a multi-country initiative enabling participating states to draw funds for responding immediately to adverse natural events, such as earthquakes and hurricanes, became operational in June 2007, with support from international donors, including the Caribbean Development Bank and the World Bank.

INSTITUTIONS

The following are among the institutions formally established within the framework of CARICOM:

Assembly of Caribbean Community Parliamentarians: c/o CARICOM Secretariat; an intergovernmental agreement on the establishment of a regional parliament entered into force in August 1994; inaugural meeting held in Barbados, in May 1996. Comprises up to four representatives of the parliaments of each member country, and up to two of each associate member. It aims to provide a forum for wider community involvement in the process of integration and for enhanced deliberation on CARICOM affairs; authorized to issue recommendations for the Conference of Heads of Government and to adopt resolutions on any matter arising under the Treaty of Chaguaramas.

Caribbean Agricultural Research and Development Institute (CARDI): UWI Campus, St Augustine, Trinidad and Tobago; tel. 645-1205; fax 645-1208; e-mail sking@cardi.org; internet www.cardi.org; f. 1975; aims to contribute to the competitiveness and sustainability of Caribbean agriculture by generating and transferring new and appropriate technologies and by developing effective partnerships with regional and international entities; Exec. Dir Dr ARLINGTON CHESNEY; publs *CARDI Weekly*, *CARDI Review*, technical bulletin series.

Caribbean Centre for Development Administration (CARICAD): Weymouth Corporate Centre, 1st Floor, Roebuck St, St Michael, Barbados; tel. 427-8535; fax 436-1709; e-mail caricad@caricad.net; internet www.caricad.net; f. 1980; aims to assist governments in the reform of the public sector and to strengthen their managerial capacities for public administration; promotes the involvement of the private sector, non-governmental organizations and other bodies in all decision-making processes; Exec. Dir JENNIFER ASTAPHAN.

Caribbean Community Climate Change Centre: Lawrence Nicholas Building, 2nd Floor, Ring Road, POB 563, Belmopan, Belize; tel. 822-1094; fax 822-1365; e-mail kleslie1@caribbeanclimate.bz; internet www.caribbeanclimate.bz; f. 2005 to co-ordinate the region's response to climate change; Exec. Dir Dr KENRICK LESLIE.

Caribbean Competition Commission: Paramaribo, Suriname; f. 2008; to enforce the rules of competition of the CARICOM Single Market and Economy; Chair. KUSHA HARAKSINGH (Trinidad and Tobago).

Caribbean Disaster Emergency Response Agency (CDERA): Bldg 1, Manor Lodge, Lodge Hill, St Michael, Barbados; tel. 425-0386; fax 425-8854; e-mail cdera@caribsurf.com; internet www.cdera.org; f. 1991; aims to respond with immediate assistance following a request by a participating state in the event of a natural or man-made disaster; co-ordinates other relief efforts; assists states to establish disaster preparedness and response capabilities; incorporates national disaster organizations, headed by a co-ordinator, in each participating state; Co-ordinator JEREMY COLLYMORE.

Caribbean Environmental Health Institute (CEHI): POB 1111, The Morne, Castries, St Lucia; tel. 4522501; fax 4532721; e-mail cehi@candw.lc; internet www.cehi.org.lc; f. 1980 (began operations in 1982); provides technical and advisory services to member states in formulating environmental health policy legislation and in all areas of environmental management (for example, solid waste management, water supplies, beach and air pollution, and pesticides control); promotes, collates and disseminates relevant research; conducts courses, seminars and workshops throughout the region; Exec. Dir PATRICIA AQUING (acting).

Caribbean Examinations Council: The Garrison, St Michael 20, Barbados; tel. 436-6261; fax 429-5421; e-mail cxcezo@cxc.org; internet www.cxc.org; f. 1972; develops syllabuses and conducts examinations for the Caribbean Advance Proficiency Examination (CAPE), the Caribbean Secondary Education Certificate (CSEC) and the Caribbean Certificate of Secondary Level Competence (CCSLC); mems: govts of 16 English-speaking countries and territories; Chief Exec. Dr DIDICUS JULES.

Caribbean Food and Nutrition Institute (CFNI): UWI Campus, POB 140, St Augustine, Trinidad and Tobago; tel. 645-2917; fax 663-1544; e-mail cfni@cablenett.net; internet www.cfni.paho.org/; f. 1967 to serve the governments and people of the region and to act as a catalyst among persons and organizations concerned with food and nutrition through research and field investigations, training in nutrition, dissemination of information, advisory services and production of educational material; a specialized centre of the Pan American Health Organization; mems: all English-speaking Caribbean territories, including the mainland countries of Belize and Guyana; Dir Dr FITZROY HENRY; publs *CAJANUS* (quarterly), *Nyam News* (monthly), *Nutrient-Cost Tables* (quarterly), educational material.

Caribbean Meteorological Organization (CMO): 67–71 Edward St, POB 461, Port of Spain, Trinidad and Tobago; tel. 624-4481; fax 623-3634; e-mail cmohq@cmo.org.tt; internet www.cmo.org.tt; f. 1951 to co-ordinate regional activities in meteorology, operational hydrology and allied sciences; became a specialized institution of CARICOM in 1973; comprises a Council of Government Ministers, a Headquarters Unit, the Caribbean Meteorological Foundation and the Caribbean Institute for Meteorology and Hydrology, located in Barbados; mems: govts of 16 countries and territories represented by the National Meteorological and Hydrometeorological Services; Co-ordinating Dir TYRONE W. SUTHERLAND.

Caribbean Telecommunications Union (CTU): Victoria Park Suites, 3rd Floor, 14–17 Victoria Sq., Port of Spain, Trinidad and Tobago; tel. 627-0281; fax 623-1523; internet ctu.connectedcaribbean.com/ctu; f. 1989; aims to co-ordinate the planning and development of telecommunications in the region; encourages the development of regional telecommunications standards, the transfer of technology and the exchange of information among national telecommunications administrations; membership includes mems of CARICOM and other countries in the region, private sector orgs and non-governmental orgs; Pres. CLIVE MULLINGS (Jamaica); Sec.-Gen. BERNADETTE LEWIS (Trinidad and Tobago).

CARICOM Implementing Agency for Crime and Security (IMPACS): Sagicor Building, Ground Floor, 16 Queen's Park West, Port of Spain, Trinidad and Tobago; tel. 622-0245; fax 628-9795; e-mail enquiries@caricomimpacs.org; internet www.caricomimpacs.org; f. 2006 as a permanent institution to co-ordinate activities in the region relating to crime and security.

CARICOM Regional Organisation for Standards and Quality: 'The Heritage', 35 Pine Rd Belleville, St Michael, Barbados; tel. 437-8146; fax 437-4569; e-mail crosq.caricom@crosq.org; internet www.crosq.org; f. 2002; aims to enhance and promote the implementation of standards and quality verification throughout the region and liaise with international standards organizations; Exec. Dir KENNETH MULLIN.

Council of Legal Education: POB 323, Tunapuna, Trinidad and Tobago; tel. 662-5860; fax 662-0927; internet www.clecaribbean.com; f. 1971; responsible for the training of members of the legal profession; administers law schools in Jamaica, Trinidad and Tobago, and the Bahamas; mems: govts of 12 countries and territories; Chair. DENNIS C. MORRISON (Jamaica).

ASSOCIATE INSTITUTIONS

Caribbean Development Bank: POB 408, Wildey, St Michael, Barbados; tel. 431-1600; fax 426-7269; e-mail info@caribank.org; internet www.caribank.org; f. 1969 to stimulate regional economic growth through support for agriculture, industry, transport and other infrastructure, tourism, housing and education; subscribed cap. US $705.0m. (April 2007); in 2006 new loans and grants approved totalled $127m.; the Special Development Fund was replenished in 2005; mems: CARICOM states, and Canada, the People's Republic of China, Colombia, Germany, Italy, Mexico, United Kingdom, Venezuela; Pres. Dr. COMPTON BOURNE.

Caribbean Law Institute: University of the West Indies, Cave Hill Campus, POB 64, Bridgetown, Barbados; tel. 417-4560; fax 417-4138; f. 1988 to harmonize and modernize commercial laws in the region; Exec. Dir Dr WINSTON C. ANDERSON.

Other Associate Institutions of CARICOM, in accordance with its constitution, are the University of Guyana, the University of the West Indies and the Secretariat of the Organisation of Eastern Caribbean States.

Publications

CARICOM Perspective (annually).
CARICOM View (6 a year).

CENTRAL AMERICAN INTEGRATION SYSTEM
(SISTEMA DE LA INTEGRACIÓN CENTROAMERICANA—SICA)

Address: Blv. Orden de Malta 470, Urb. Santa Elena, Antiguo Cuscatlán, San Salvador, El Salvador.
Telephone: 2248-8800; **fax:** 2248-8899; **e-mail:** info.sgsica@sica.int; **internet:** www.sica.int.

Founded in December 1991, when the heads of state of six Central American countries signed the Protocol of Tegucigalpa to the agreement establishing the Organization of Central American States (f. 1951), creating a new framework for regional integration. A General Secretariat of the Sistema de la Integración Centroamericana (SICA) was inaugurated in February 1993 to co-ordinate the process of political, economic, social cultural and environmental integration and to promote democracy and respect for human rights throughout the region.

MEMBERS

Belize	Guatemala	Nicaragua
Costa Rica	Honduras	Panama
El Salvador		

ASSOCIATE MEMBER

Dominican Republic

Note: Spain, Taiwan and the USA have observer status with SICA.

Organization
(April 2008)

SUMMIT MEETINGS

The meetings of heads of state of member countries serve as the supreme decision-making organ of SICA.

COUNCIL OF MINISTERS

Ministers of Foreign Affairs of member states meet regularly to provide policy direction for the process of integration.

CONSULTATIVE COMMITTEE

The Committee comprises representatives of business organizations, trade unions, academic institutions and other federations concerned with the process of integration in the region. It is an integral element of the integration system and assists the Secretary-General in determining the policies of the organization.

President: CARLOS MOLINA.

GENERAL SECRETARIAT

The General Secretariat of SICA was established in February 1993 to co-ordinate the process of enhanced regional integration. It comprises the following divisions: inter-institutional relations; research and co-operation; legal and political affairs; economic affairs; and communications and information.

In September 1997 Central American Common Market (CACM) heads of state, meeting in the Nicaraguan capital, signed the Managua Declaration in support of further regional integration and the establishment of a political union. A commission was to be established to consider all aspects of the policy and to formulate a timetable for the integration process. In February 1998 heads of state resolved to establish a Unified General Secretariat to integrate the institutional aspects of the grouping in a single office, to be located in San Salvador. The process was ongoing in 2007.

Secretary-General: ANÍBAL ENRIQUE QUIÑÓNEZ ABARCA.

SPECIALIZED TECHNICAL SECRETARIATS

Secretaría Ejecutiva de la Comisión Centroamericana de Ambiente y Desarrollo (SE-CCAD): Blv. Orden de Malta 470, Santa Elena, Antiguo Cuscatlán, San Salvador, El Salvador; tel. 2248-8800; fax 2248-8894; e-mail info.ccad@sica.int; internet www.ccad.ws; f. 1989 to enhance collaboration in the promotion of sustainable development and environmental protection; Exec. Sec. Dr MARCO ANTONIO GONZÁLEZ PASTORA.

Secretaría General de la Coordinación Educativa y Cultural Centroamericana (SG-CECC): 100m norte de la Nunciatura, Casa 8815, Rohrmoser, San José, Costa Rica; tel. and fax 232-2891; e-mail sgcecc@racsa.co.cr; internet www.cecc.mep.go.cr; f. 1982; promotes development of regional programmes in the fields of education and culture; Sec.-Gen. MARVIN HERRERA ARAYA.

Secretaría de Integración Económica Centroamericana (SIECA): 4 A Avda 10–25, Zona 14, Apdo 1237, 01901 Guatemala City, Guatemala; tel. 2368-2151; fax 2368-1071; e-mail info@sieca.org.gt; internet www.sieca.org.gt; f. 1960 to assist the process of economic integration and the creation of a Central American Common Market (CACM—established by the organization of Central American States under the General Treaty of Central American Economic Integration, signed in December 1960 and ratified by Costa Rica, Guatemala, El Salvador, Honduras and Nicaragua in September 1963); supervises the correct implementation of the legal instruments of economic integration, carries out relevant studies at the request of the CACM, and arranges meetings; comprises departments covering the working of the CACM: negotiations and external trade policy; external co-operation; systems and statistics; finance and administration; also includes a unit for co-operation with the private sector and finance institutions, and a legal consultative committee; Sec.-Gen. HAROLDO RODAS MELGAR; publs *Anuario Estadístico Centroamericano de Comercio Exterior, Carta Informativa* (monthly), *Cuadernos de la SIECA* (2 a year), *Estadísticas Macroeconómicas de Centroamérica* (annually), *Series Estadísticas Seleccionadas de Centroamérica* (annually), *Boletín Informativo* (fortnightly).

Secretaría de la Integración Social Centroamericana (SISCA): Blv. Orden de Malta 470, Santa Elena, Antiguo Cuscatlán, San Salvador, El Salvador; tel. 2248-8857; fax 2248-8896; e-mail info .sisca@sica.int; internet www.sica.int/sisca; f. 1995; Sec. Dr JOSÉ SERMEÑO-LIMA.

OTHER SPECIALIZED SECRETARIATS

Secretaría de Integración Turística Centroamericana (SITCA): Blv. Orden de Malta 470, Santa Elena, Antiguo Cuscatlán, San Salvador, El Salvador; tel. 2248-8837; fax 2248-8897; e-mail csilva@sgsica.org; f. 1965 to develop regional tourism activities; Dir MERCEDES DE MENA.

Secretaría del Consejo Agropecuario Centroamericano (SCAC): Sacretarion Isidro de Coronado, Apdo Postal 55-2200, San José, Costa Rica; tel. 216-0303; fax 216-0285; e-mail coreca@iica.ac.cr; internet www.coreca.org; f. 1991 to determine and co-ordinate regional policies and programmes relating to agriculture and agroindustry; Exec. Sec. RÓGER GUILLÉN BUSTOS.

Secretaría Ejecutiva del Consejo Monetario Centroamericano (SECMCA) (Central American Monetary Council): Ofiplaza del Este, Edif. C, 75m oeste de la Rotonda la Bandera, San Pedro Montes de Oca, Apdo Postal 5438-1000, San José, Costa Rica; tel. 280-9522; fax 524-1062; e-mail achaves@secmca.org; internet www.secmca.org; f. 1964 by the presidents of Central American central banks, to co-ordinate monetary policies; Exec. Sec. JOSÉ ALFREDO BLANCO VALDÉS; publs *Boletín Estadístico* (annually), *Informe Económico* (annually).

Comisión Centroamericana de Transporte Marítimo (COCATRAM): Frente al Costado Oeste del Hotel Mansión Teodolinda, Barrio Bolonia, Apdo Postal 2423, Managua, Nicaragua; tel. 222-2754; fax 222-2759; e-mail drojas@cocatram.org.ni; internet www.cocatram.org.ni; f. 1981; Exec. Dir ALFONSO BREUILLET GALINDO; publ. *Boletín Informativo*.

AD HOC INTERGOVERNMENTAL SECRETARIATS

Consejo Centroamericano de Instituciones de Seguridad Social (COCISS) (Central American Council of Social Security Institutions): Barrio Abajo 555, 10°, Tegucigalpa, Honduras; tel. 222-8412; fax 222-8414; e-mail cociss@ccss.sa.cr; internet www.ccss.sa.cr/cociss/idcociss.htm; f. 1992; Sec. RICHARD ZABLAH.

Comisión para el Desarrollo Científico y Tecnológico de Centroamérica y Panamá (CTCAP) (Committee for the Scientific and Technological Development of Central America and Panama): Antigua base de Clayton, Edif. 213, Panama; tel. 317-0014; fax 317-0026; e-mail espinoza@ns.hondunet.net; f. 1976; Pres. EUGENIA M. FLORES V.

Consejo del Istmo Centroamericano de Deportes y Recreación (CODICADER) (Committee of the Central American Isthmus for Sport and Recreation): Ministerio de Cultura, Artes y Deportes, Contiguo a Migración, Tegucigalpa, Honduras; tel. 221-3877; fax 236-9532; f. 1992; Sec.-Gen. JORGE MEJÍA.

Unidad Técnica del Consejo Centroamericano de Vivienda y Asentamientos Humanos (CCVAH) (Central American Council on Housing and Human Settlements): Blv. Orden de Malta 470, Santa Elena, Antiguo Cuscatlán, San Salvador, El Salvador; tel. 2248-8856; fax 2248-8856; f. 1992.

Secretaría Ejecutiva del Consejo de Electrificación de América Central (CEAC) (Central American Electrification Council): 9A Calle Pte 950, Edif. CEL, Centro de Gobierno, San Salvador, El Salvador; tel. 2211-6175; fax 2211-6239; e-mail jmontesi@cel.gob.sv; f. 1985; Exec. Sec. JULIO ROBERTO ALVAREZ.

Organización Centroamericana y del Caribe de Entidades Fiscalizadores Superiores (OCCEFS): Tribunal Superior de Cuentas de la República de Honduras Centro Cívico Gubernamental, Col. Las Brisas Comayagüela, Honduras; tel. 234-5210; fax 234-5210; internet www.occefs.org; f. 1995 as the Organización Centroamericana de Entidades Fiscalizadores Superiores, within the framework of the Organización Latinoamericana y del Caribe de Entidades Fiscalizadoras Superiores; assumed present name in 1998; Exec. Sec. RENÁN SAGASTUME FERNÁNDEZ.

CORE INSTITUTIONS

SICA Parliament

12 Avda 33-04, Zona 5, Guatemala City, Guatemala 01005; tel. 2424-4600; fax 2424-4610; e-mail guatemala@parlacen.org.gt; internet www.parlacen.org.gt.; officially inaugurated in 1991; comprises representatives of El Salvador, Guatemala, Honduras, Nicaragua and Panama; Pres. CIRO CRUZ ZEPEDA PEÑA (El Salvador); Sec.-Gen. WERNER VARGAS.

SICA Court of Justice

Apdo Postal 907 Managua, Nicaragua; tel. 266-6273; fax 266-4604; e-mail cortecen@ccj.org.ni; internet www.ccj.org.ni.; officially inaugurated in 1994; tribunal authorized to consider disputes relating to treaties agreed within the regional integration system; in February

1998 Central American heads of state agreed to limit the number of magistrates in the Court to one per country; Pres. FRANCISCO DARIO LOBO LARA; Sec.-Gen. Dr ORLANDO GUERRERO MAYORGA.

OTHER REGIONAL INSTITUTIONS

Finance

Banco Centroamericano de Integración Económica (BCIE) (Central American Bank for Economic Integration): Blv. Suyapa, Contigua a Banco de Honduras, Apdo 772, Tegucigalpa, Honduras; tel. 240-2243; fax 240-2185; e-mail MNunez@bcie.org; internet www.bcie.org; f. 1961 to promote the economic integration and balanced economic development of member countries; finances public and private development projects, particularly those related to industrialization and infrastructure; auth. cap. US $2,000m; regional mems: Costa Rica, El Salvador, Guatemala, Honduras, Nicaragua; non-regional mems: Argentina, the People's Republic of China, Colombia, Mexico, Spain; Pres. HARRY E. BRAUTIGAM; publs *Annual Report*, *Revista de la Integración y el Desarrollo de Centroamérica*.

Public Administration

Centro de Coordinación para la Prevención de Desastres Naturales en América Central (CEPREDENAC): Antigua base de Howard, Ave Rencher, Edif. 707, Panamá, Panama; tel. 316-0048; fax 316-0049; e-mail direcciongeneral@sinaproc.gob.pa; internet www.cepredenac.org; f. 1988, integrated into SICA in 1995; aims to strengthen the capacity of the region to reduce its vulnerability to natural disasters; Exec. Sec. DAVID A. SMITH WILTSHIRE.

Instituto Centroamericano de Administración Pública (ICAP) (Central American Institute of Public Administration): Apdo Postal 10025-1000 San José, Costa Rica; tel. 234-1011; fax 225-2049; e-mail info@icap.ac.cr; internet www.icap.ac.cr; f. 1954 by the five Central American Republics and the United Nations, with later participation by Panama; the Institute aims to train the region's public servants, provide technical assistance and carry out research leading to reforms in public administration; Dir Dr HUGO ZELAYA CÁLIX.

Secretaría Ejecutiva de la Comisión Regional de Recursos Hidráulicos (SE-CRRH): Apdo Postal 21–2300, Curridabat, San José, Costa Rica; tel. 231-5791; fax 296-0047; e-mail crrhcr@sol.racsa.co.cr; internet aguayclima.com; f. 1966; mems: Belize, Costa Rica, El Salvador, Guatemala, Honduras, Nicaragua, Panama; Exec. Sec. MAX CAMPOS ORTIZ.

Agriculture and Fisheries

Organismo Internacional Regional de Sanidad Agropecuaria (OIRSA) (International Regional Organization of Plant Protection and Animal Health): Calle Ramón Belloso, Final Pasaje Isolde, Colonia Escalón, Apdo (01) 61, San Salvador, El Salvador; tel. 2263-1123; fax 2263-1128; e-mail oirsa@oirsa.org; internet www.oirsa.org; f. 1953 for the prevention of the introduction of animal and plant pests and diseases unknown in the region; research, control and eradication programmes of the principal pests present in agriculture; technical assistance and advice to the ministries of agriculture and livestock of member countries; education and qualification of personnel; mems: Belize, Costa Rica, Dominican Republic, El Salvador, Guatemala, Honduras, Mexico, Nicaragua, Panama; Exec. Dir JORGE ANÍBAL ESCOBEDO MARTÍNEZ.

Unidad Coordinadora de la Organización del Sector Pesquero y Acuícola del Istmo Centroamericano (OSPESCA): Blv. Orden de Malta 470, Santa Elena, Antiguo Cuscatlán, San Salvador, El Salvador; tel. 2248-8841; fax 2248-8899; e-mail info.ospesca@sica.int; internet www.sica.int/ospesca; f. 1995, incorporated into SICA in 1999; Regional Co-ordinator MARIO GONZÁLEZ RECINOS.

Education and Health

Comité Coordinador Regional de Instituciones de Agua Potable y Saneamiento de Centroamérica, Panamá y República Dominicana (CAPRE): Avda Bo. 1A, El Obelisco Comayagüela, Tegucigalpa, Honduras; tel. 237-8552; fax 237-2575; e-mail capregtz@sol.racsa.co.cr; f. 1979; Dir LILIANA ARCE UMAÑA.

Consejo Superior Universitario Centroamericano (CSUCA) (Central American University Council): Avda Las Américas 1–03, Zona 14, International Club Los Arcos, 01014 Guatemala City, Guatemala; tel. 2367-1833; fax 2367-4517; e-mail sg@listas.csuca.org; internet www.csuca.org; f. 1948 to guarantee academic, administrative and economic autonomy for universities and to encourage regional integration of higher education; maintains libraries and documentation centres; Council of 32 mems; mems: 18 universities, in Belize, Costa Rica (four), the Dominican Republic, El Salvador, Guatemala, Honduras (two), Nicaragua (four) and Panama (four); Sec.-Gen. EFRAÍN MEDINA GUERRA; publs *Estudios Sociales Centroamericanos* (quarterly), *Cuadernos de Investigación* (monthly), *Carta Informativa de la Secretaría General* (monthly).

Instituto de Nutrición de Centroamérica y Panamá (INCAP) (Institute of Nutrition of Central America and Panama): Calzada Roosevelt 6–25, Zona 11, Apdo Postal 1188-01901, Guatemala City, Guatemala; tel. 2472-3762; fax 2473-6529; e-mail info@incap.ops-oms.org; internet www.incap.org.gt; f. 1949 to promote the development of nutritional sciences and their application and to strengthen the technical capacity of member countries to reach food and nutrition security; provides training and technical assistance for nutrition education and planning; conducts applied research; disseminates information; maintains library (including about 600 periodicals); administered by the Pan American Health Organization (PAHO) and the World Health Organization; mems: CACM mems, Belize and Panama; Dir Dr HERNÁN L. DELGADO; publ. *Annual Report*.

Transport and Communications

Comisión de Telecomunicaciones de Centroamérica (COMTELCA) (Commission for Telecommunications in Central America): Col. Palmira, Edif. Alpha 608, Avda Brasil, Apdo 1793, Tegucigalpa, Honduras; tel. 220-6666; fax 220-1197; e-mail sec@comtelca.hn; internet www.comtelca.hn; f. 1966 to co-ordinate and improve the regional telecommunications network; Dir-Gen. HÉCTOR LEONEL RODRÍGUEZ MILLA.

Corporación Centroamericana de Servicios de Navegación Aérea (COCESNA) (Central American Air Navigation Services Corporation): Apdo 660, Aeropuerto de Toncontín, Tegucigalpa, Honduras; tel. 234-3360; fax 234-2550; e-mail sec-interna@cocesna.org; internet www.cocesna.org; f. 1960; offers radar air traffic control services, aeronautical telecommunications services, flight inspections and radio assistance services for air navigation; provides support in the areas of safety, aeronautical training and aeronautical software; Exec. Pres. EDUARDO MARÍN J.

Activities

In June 1990 the presidents of the Central American Common Market (CACM) countries (Costa Rica, El Salvador, Guatemala, Honduras and Nicaragua) signed a declaration welcoming peace initiatives in El Salvador, Guatemala and Nicaragua, and appealing for a revitalization of CACM, as a means of promoting lasting peace in the region. In December the presidents committed themselves to the creation of an effective common market, proposing the opening of negotiations on a comprehensive regional customs and tariffs policy by March 1991, and the introduction of a regional 'anti-dumping' code by December 1991. They requested the support of multilateral lending institutions through investment in regional development, and the cancellation or rescheduling of member countries' debts. In December 1991 the heads of state of the five CACM countries and Panama signed the Protocol of Tegucigalpa, and in February 1993 the General Secretariat of SICA was inaugurated to co-ordinate the integration process in the region.

In February 1993 the European Community (EC, now European Union—EU) signed a new framework co-operation agreement with the CACM member states extending the programme of economic assistance and political dialogue initiated in 1984; a further co-operation agreement with the EU was signed in early 1996.

In October 1993 the presidents of the CACM countries and Panama signed a protocol to the 1960 General Treaty, committing themselves to full economic integration in the region (with a common external tariff of 20% for finished products and 5% for raw materials and capital goods) and creating conditions for increased free trade. The countries agreed to accelerate the removal of internal non-tariff barriers, but no deadline was set. Full implementation of the protocol was to be 'voluntary and gradual', owing to objections on the part of Costa Rica and Panama. In May 1994, however, Costa Rica committed itself to full participation in the protocol. In March 1995 a meeting of the Central American Monetary Council discussed and endorsed a reduction in the tariff levels from 20% to 15% and from 5% to 1%. However, efforts to adopt this as a common policy were hindered by the implementation of these tariff levels by El Salvador on a unilateral basis, from 1 April, and the subsequent modifications by Guatemala and Costa Rica of their external tariffs. In March 2002 Central American leaders adopted the San Salvador Plan of Action for Central American Economic Integration, establishing several objectives as the basis for the future creation of a regional customs union, with a single tariff.

In December 1994 member states and the USA signed a joint declaration (CONCAUSA), covering co-operation in the following areas: conservation of biodiversity, sound management of energy, environmental legislation, and sustainable economic development. In June 2001 both sides signed a renewed and expanded CON-

CAUSA, now also covering co-operation in addressing climate change, and in disaster preparedness. In May 1997 the heads of state of CACM member countries, together with the Prime Minister of Belize, conferred with the then US President, Bill Clinton, in San José, Costa Rica. The leaders resolved to establish a Trade and Investment Council to promote trade relations; however, Clinton failed to endorse a request from CACM members that their products receive preferential access to US markets, on similar terms to those from Mexico agreed under the NAFTA accord. During the 1990s the Central American Governments pursued negotiations to conclude free trade agreements with Mexico, Panama and the members of the Caribbean Community and Common Market (CARICOM). Nicaragua signed a bilateral accord with Mexico in December (Costa Rica already having done so in 1994). El Salvador, Guatemala and Honduras jointly concluded a free trade arrangement with Mexico in May 2000. In November 1997, at a special summit meeting of CACM heads of state, an agreement was reached with the President of the Dominican Republic to initiate a gradual process of incorporating that country into the process of Central American integration, with the aim of promoting sustainable development throughout the region. The first sectors for increased co-operation between the two sides were to be tourism, health, investment promotion and air transport. A free trade accord with the Dominican Republic was concluded in April 1998, and formally signed in November.

In November 1998 Central American heads of state held an emergency summit meeting to consider the devastation in the region caused by 'Hurricane Mitch'. The Presidents urged international creditors to write off the region's estimated debts of US $16,000m. to assist in the economic recovery of the countries worst-affected. They also reiterated requests for preferential treatment for the region's exports within the NAFTA framework. In October 1999 the heads of state adopted a strategic framework for the period 2000–04 to strengthen the capacity for the physical, social, economic and environmental infrastructure of Central American countries to withstand the impact of natural disasters. In particular, programmes for the integrated management and conservation of water resources, and for the prevention of forest fires were to be implemented.

In June 2001 the heads of state and representatives of Belize, Costa, Rica, El Salvador, Guatemala, Honduras, Mexico, Nicaragua and Panama agreed to activate the Puebla-Panamá Plan (PPP) to promote sustainable social and economic development in the region and to reinforce integration efforts among Central America and the southern states of Mexico (referred to as Mesoamerica). The heads of state identified the principal areas for PPP initiatives, including tourism, road integration, telecommunications, energy interconnection, and the prevention and mitigation of disasters. In June 2002 the heads of state of seven countries, and the Vice-President of Panama, convened in Mérida, Mexico during an investment fair to promote the Plan and reiterated their support for the regional initiatives. The meeting was also held within the framework of the Tuxtla dialogue mechanism, so-called after an agreement signed in 1991 between Mexico and Central American countries, to discuss co-ordination between the parties, in particular in social matters, health, education and the environment. Regular 'Tuxtla' summit meetings have subsequently been convened. A Centre for the Promotion of Small and Medium-sized Enterprises was established in June 2001.

In April 2001 Costa Rica concluded a free trade accord with Canada; the other four CACM countries commenced negotiations with Canada in November with the aim of reaching a similar agreement. In February 2002 Central American heads of state convened an extraordinary summit meeting in Managua, Nicaragua, at which they resolved to implement measures to further the political and economic integration of the region. The leaders determined to pursue initial proposals for a free trade accord with the USA during the visit to the region of US President George W. Bush in the following month, and, more generally, to strengthen trading relations with the EU. They also pledged to resolve all regional conflicts by peaceful means. Earlier in February the first meeting of heads of state or government of Central American and CARICOM countries took place in Belize, with the aim of strengthening political and economic relations between the two groupings. The meeting agreed to work towards concluding common negotiating positions, for example in respect of the FTAA and World Trade Organization.

In May 2002 ministers of foreign affairs of Central America and the EU agreed upon a new agenda for a formalized dialogue and on priority areas of action, including environmental protection, democracy and governance, and poverty reduction. The meeting determined to work towards the eventual conclusion of an Association Agreement, including an agreement on free trade, although the latter was to be conditional upon the completion of the Doha Round of multilateral negotiations on trade liberalization (which was suspended in mid-2006) and upon the attainment of a sufficient level of economic integration in Central America. It was agreed that meetings between the two sides, at ministerial level, were to be held each year. In December 2003 a new EU-Central America Political Dialogue and Co-operation Agreement was signed to replace an existing (1993) framework accord. The EU allocated €74.5m. to finance co-operation programmes under its Regional Strategy for Central America covering the period 2002–06; these were to focus on strengthening the role of civil society in the process of regional integration, reducing vulnerability to natural disasters, and environmental improvement. A new Regional Strategy, for 2007–13, was concluded in March 2007, with an allocation of €75.0m. In May 2006 a meeting of EU and Central American heads of state resolved to initiate negotiations to conclude an Association Agreement. The first round of negotiations was concluded in San José, Costa Rica, in October 2007 and the second round in Brussels, Belgium, in February 2008.

The summit meeting of CACM heads of state, convened in December 2002, in Costa Rica, adopted the 'Declaration of San José', supporting the planned establishment of the Central American customs union (see above), and endorsing the initiation of negotiations with the USA on the creation of a new Central American Free Trade Area (CAFTA). The establishment of a new Central American Tourism Agency was also announced at the meeting.

Negotiations on CAFTA between the CACM countries and the USA were initiated in January 2003. An agreement was concluded between the USA and El Salvador, Guatemala, Honduras and Nicaragua in December, and with Costa Rica in January 2004. Under the resulting US-Central America Free Trade Agreement some 80% of US exports of consumer and industrial goods and more than 50% of US agricultural exports to CAFTA countries were to become duty-free immediately upon its entry into force, with remaining tariffs to be eliminated over a 10-year period for consumer and industrial goods and over a 15-year period for agricultural exports. Almost all CAFTA exports of consumer and industrial products to the USA were to be duty-free on the Agreement's entry into force. The Agreement was signed by the US Trade Representative and CACM ministers of trade and economy, convened in Washington, DC, in May 2004. It required ratification by all national legislatures before entering into effect. Negotiations on a US-Dominican Republic free trade agreement, to integrate the Dominican Republic into CAFTA, were concluded in March and the agreement was signed in August. The so-called DR-CAFTA accord was formally ratified by the USA in August 2005. Subsequently the agreement has entered into force with El Salvador on 1 March 2006, Honduras and Nicaragua on 1 April, Guatemala on 1 July, and the Dominican Republic on 1 March 2007. It was endorsed by a popular referendum held in Costa Rica, in October; by April 2008, however, the accord had yet to be ratified by the country's legislative assembly and a seven-month extension was granted for further consideration by the assembly.

A meeting of Central American heads of state, held in December 2004, was concerned with economic and regional security issues. In March 2005 SICA ministers responsible for security, defence and the interior resolved to establish a special regional force to combat crime, drugs and arms trafficking and terrorism. A new regional agricultural and fisheries policy was inaugurated in July.

In June 2006 representatives of SICA and of Colombia, the Dominican Republic and Mexico adopted the Declaration of Romana, wherein they agreed to implement the Mesoamerican Energy Integration Program, aimed at developing regional oil, electricity and natural gas markets, promoting the use of renewable energy, and increasing electricity generation and interconnection capacity across the region. In the following month, at the 8th Tuxtla summit, convened in Panama, SICA member states approved the legal framework for the Central American Electrical Connection System (known as SIEPAC), which was to be co-funded by the Central American Bank for Economic Integration and the Inter-American Development Bank; SIEPAC was due to be operational by 2008.

In January 2007 the Treaty on Payment Systems and the Liquidation of Assets in Central America and the Dominican Republic was presented to the Secretary-General of SICA. The treaty aimed to increase greater financial co-operation and further to develop the financial markets in the region. In February the Secretaries-General of SICA and CARICOM signed a plan of action to foster greater co-operation in areas including foreign policy, international trade relations, security and combating crime, and the environment. Meetings of ministers of foreign affairs and of the economy and foreign trade were convened in the same month at which preparations were initiated for trade negotiations between the two groupings. In May the second Central American-CARICOM summit meeting was convened, in Belize City, Belize. Heads of state and of government endorsed the efforts to enhance co-operation between the organizations and approved the elaboration of a free trade agreement, based on the existing bilateral accord signed between CARICOM and Costa Rica. Formal negotiations were inaugurated at a meeting of ministers of trade in August. A third SICA-CARICOM summit meeting was scheduled to be convened in Nicaragua, in May 2009.

COMMON MARKET FOR EASTERN AND SOUTHERN AFRICA—COMESA

Address: COMESA Secretariat, Ben Bella Rd, POB 30051, 101101 Lusaka, Zambia.
Telephone: (1) 229725; **fax:** (1) 225107; **e-mail:** comesa@comesa.int; **internet:** www.comesa.int.

The COMESA treaty was signed by member states of the Preferential Trade Area for Eastern and Southern Africa (PTA) in November 1993. COMESA formally succeeded the PTA in December 1994. COMESA aims to promote regional economic and social development.

MEMBERS

Angola	Madagascar
Burundi	Malawi
Comoros	Mauritius
Congo, Democratic Republic	Rwanda
Djibouti	Seychelles
Egypt	Sudan
Eritrea	Swaziland
Ethiopia	Uganda
Kenya	Zambia
Libya	Zimbabwe

Organization
(April 2008)

AUTHORITY

The Authority of the Common Market is the supreme policy organ of COMESA, comprising heads of state or of government of member countries. The inaugural meeting of the Authority took place in Lilongwe, Malawi, in December 1994. The 13th summit meeting was scheduled to be convened in Victoria Falls Town, Zimbabwe, in May 2008.

COUNCIL OF MINISTERS

Each member government appoints a minister to participate in the Council. The Council monitors COMESA activities, including supervision of the Secretariat, recommends policy direction and development, and reports to the Authority.

A Committee of Governors of Central Banks advises the Authority and the Council of Ministers on monetary and financial matters.

COURT OF JUSTICE

The inaugural session of the COMESA Court of Justice was held in March 2001. The sub-regional Court is vested with the authority to settle disputes between member states and to adjudicate on matters concerning the interpretation of the COMESA treaty. The Court is composed of seven judges, who serve terms of five years' duration.
President: NZAMBA KITONGA (Kenya).

SECRETARIAT

COMESA's Secretariat comprises the following divisions: Trade, customs and monetary harmonization; Investment promotion and private sector development; Infrastructure development; and Information and networking. The COMESA/SADC task force operates from the secretariats of both organizations.
Secretary-General: J. E. O. (ERASTUS) MWENCHA (Kenya).

Activities

COMESA aims to promote economic and social progress in member states. Since its establishment in 1994 COMESA has pursued efforts to strengthen the process of regional economic integration that was initiated under the PTA, in order to help member states achieve sustainable economic growth. In May 1999 COMESA established a Free-Trade Area (FTA) Committee to facilitate and co-ordinate preparations for the creation of the common market envisaged under the COMESA treaty. An extraordinary summit of COMESA heads of state or government, held in October 2000, inaugurated the FTA, with nine initial members: Djibouti, Egypt, Kenya, Madagascar, Malawi, Mauritius, Sudan, Zambia and Zimbabwe. The final deadline for all states to join was initially 30 April 2002. This was, however, subsequently postponed. Burundi and Rwanda became members of the FTA in January 2004, and Swaziland undertook in April to seek the concurrence of the Southern African Customs Union, of which it is also a member, to allow it to participate in the FTA. Trading practices within the FTA have been fully liberalized, including the elimination of non-tariff barriers, thereby enabling the free internal movement of goods, services and capital. It was envisaged that a regional customs union would be established in May 2005, with a common external tariff (CET) set at 0%, 5%, 15% and 30% for, respectively, capital goods, raw materials, intermediate goods and final goods. This was not achieved, however, and the 10th summit meeting in June decided instead to set a new deadline of December 2008 for its establishment, urging all of those member states that were not participating in the FTA in mid-2005 to proceed to do so in the meantime, in order to enable them to join the eventual customs union. A Protocol establishing the COMESA Fund, aimed at assisting member states address structural imbalances in their economies, came into effect in mid-November 2006. In May 2007 the 12th meeting of heads of state endorsed all technical aspects of the customs union (now with a simplified CET set at 0% for capital goods and raw materials, 10% for intermediate goods and 25% for finished products). COMESA also plans to form an economic community (entailing monetary union and the free movement of people between member states) by 2014. COMESA aims to formulate a common investment procedure to promote domestic, cross-border and direct foreign investment by ensuring the free movement of capital, services and labour. Heads of regional investment agencies, meeting in August 2000, developed a plan of action for the creation of a common investment agency to facilitate the establishment of a COMESA common investment area (CCIA), in accordance with recommendations by the Authority. A draft framework document on the CCIA was submitted for review by member states in December 2004, and was subject to extensive negotiations. The accord to establish the CCIA was adopted at the 12th summit meeting, held in May 2007, and opened for signature. The development of a protocol to the COMESA treaty on the Free Movement of Persons, Labour, Services, the Right of Establishment and Residence was adopted in 2001 at the sixth summit meeting of the Authority, held in Cairo, Egypt.

A clearing house (based in Harare, Zimbabwe) dealing with credit arrangements and balance of payments issues became operational under the PTA in 1984 in order to facilitate intra-regional trade. The role of the clearing house was diminished by the liberalization of foreign exchange markets in the majority of member countries, and it ceased operating in 1996. In the mid-2000s preparations were under way to create a regional payments and settlement system (REPSS). A contract on the implementation of the REPSS—which was to have its headquarters in Lusaka, Zambia—was signed in December 2006. An Automated System of Customs Data (ASYCUDA) has been established to facilitate customs administration in all COMESA member states. Through support for capacity-building activities and the establishment of other specialized institutions (see below) COMESA aims to reinforce its objectives of regional integration. In August 2001 COMESA inaugurated the African Trade Insurance Agency (ATI), based in Nairobi, Kenya. The ATI manages COMESA's Regional Trade Facilitation Project, promoting trade and investment activities throughout the region. The electronic African Commerce Exchange (ACE) was launched by the Authority in 2000.

Co-operation programmes have been implemented by COMESA in the financial, agricultural, transport and communications, industrial, and energy sectors. A regional food security programme aims to ensure continuous adequate food supplies. In 1997 COMESA heads of state advocated that the food sector be supported by the implementation of an irrigation action plan for the region. The organization also supports the establishment of common agricultural standards and phytosanitary regulations throughout the region in order to stimulate trade in food crops. In March 2005 more than 100 standards on quality assurance, covering mainly agricultural products, were adopted. Meeting for the first time in November 2002, COMESA ministers of agriculture determined to formulate a regional policy on genetically modified organisms. At their second meeting, held in October 2004, ministers of agriculture agreed to prioritize agriculture in their development efforts and (in accordance with a Declaration of the African Union) to allocate at least 10% of national budgets to agriculture and rural development by 2008/09. Other organization-wide initiatives include a road customs declaration document, a scheme for third party motor vehicle insurance, a system of regional travellers cheques, and a regional customs bond guarantee scheme. A Trade Information Network co-ordinates information on the production and marketing of goods manufactured and traded in the region. COMESA is implementing the new

COMESA Information Network, which aims to develop the utilization by member states of advanced information and communication technologies. A COMESA Telecommunications Company (COMTEL) was registered in May 2000. In January 2003 the Association of Regulators of Information and Communication for Eastern and Southern Africa was launched, under the auspices of COMESA. The first COMESA economic forum was held in Cairo, Egypt, in February 2000. The inaugural COMESA business summit was convened in June 2004 in Kampala, Uganda, concurrently with the ninth annual meeting of the Authority. A COMESA Business Forum and trade exhibition, and concurrent round-table dialogue between sub-regional business leaders and the COMESA Council of Ministers, were due to take place in early May, on the sidelines of the 13th summit of the Authority. It was envisaged that the 2008 Business Forum and round-table meeting would provide a platform for discussing issues connected with the developing COMESA Customs Union.

In May 1999 the COMESA Authority resolved to establish a Committee on Peace and Security comprising ministers of foreign affairs from member states. It was envisaged that the Committee would convene at least once a year to address matters concerning regional stability. (Instability in certain member states was regarded as a potential threat to the successful implementation of the FTA.) The Committee met for the first time in 2000. It was announced in September 2002 that the COMESA Treaty was to be amended to provide for the establishment of a formal conflict prevention and resolution structure to be governed by member countries' heads of state.

In March 2008 COMESA sent an observer mission to monitor the conduct of the legislative and parliamentary elections held at the end of that month in Zimbabwe.

Since COMESA's establishment there have been concerns on the part of member states, as well as other regional non-member countries, in particular South Africa, of adverse rivalry between COMESA and the Southern African Development Community (SADC) and of a duplication of roles. In 1997 Lesotho and Mozambique terminated their membership of COMESA owing to concerns that their continued participation in the organization was incompatible with their SADC membership. Tanzania withdrew from COMESA in September 2000, reportedly also in view of its dual commitment to that organization and to SADC. The summit meeting of COMESA heads of state or government held in May of that year expressed support for an ongoing programme of co-operation by the secretariats of COMESA and SADC aimed at reducing the duplication of roles between the two organizations, and urged further mutual collaboration. A co-ordinating COMESA/SADC task force was established in 2001. It has subsequently been expanded to incorporate the East African Community in discussions to enhance harmonization between the organizations and their programmes of work. COMESA has co-operated with other sub-regional organizations to finalize a common position on co-operation between African ACP countries and the EU under the Cotonou Agreement (concluded in June 2000, see chapter on the European Union). In June 2003 Namibia announced its withdrawal from COMESA. At the 10th summit meeting of the Authority in June 2005 Libya was admitted as a full member of COMESA.

In October 2001 COMESA concluded a Trade and Investment Framework Agreement with the USA. In August 2007 COMESA appointed a Special Representative to the Middle East to establish partnerships with that region and to promote trade opportunities.

COMESA INSTITUTIONS

African Trade Insurance Agency (ATI): POB 10620, 00100-GPO, Nairobi, Kenya; tel. (20) 2719727; fax (20) 2719701; e-mail info@africa-ECA.com; internet www.ati-aca.com; f. 2001; mems: 12 African countries; CEO PETER MICHAEL JONES.

COMESA Bankers Association: Private Bag 271, Kapeni House, 1st Floor, Blantyre, Malawi; tel. and fax (1) 674236; e-mail info@comesabankers.org; internet www.comesabankers.org; f. 1987 as the PTA Association of Commercial Banks; name changed as above in 1994; aims to strengthen co-operation between banks in the region; organizes training activities; conducts studies to harmonize banking laws and operations; implements a bank fraud prevention programme; mems: 55 commercial banking orgs in Burundi, Egypt, Eritrea, Ethiopia, Kenya, Malawi, Rwanda, Sudan, Swaziland; Exec. Sec. ERIC C. CHINKANDA (acting).

COMESA Leather and Leather Products Institute (LLPI): POB 2358, 1110 Addis Ababa, Ethiopia; tel. (1) 431318; fax (1) 431321; e-mail comesa.llpi@telecom.net.et; internet comesa-llpi.org; f. 1990 as the PTA Leather Institute; mems: 17 COMESA mem. states; Dir Dr GEREMEW DEBELE.

COMESA Metallurgical Industries Association (COMESA-MIA): Kampala, Uganda; f. 1999; aims to advance capabilities in the production, processing and marketing of metals and allied engineering products, and to develop co-operation and networking in the sector; Sec. WILLIAM BALU-TABAARO.

Compagnie de réassurance de la Zone d'échanges préférentiels (ZEP-RE) (PTA Reinsurance Co): ZEP-RE Place, Longonot Rd, Upper Hill, POB 42769, 00100 Nairobi, Kenya; tel. (20) 2738221; fax (20) 2738444; e-mail mail@zep-re.com; internet www.zep-re.com; f. 1992 (began operations on 1 January 1993); provides local reinsurance services and training to personnel in the insurance industry; total assets US $44.0m. (2006); Chair. PETER KENNETH; Man. Dir RAJNI VARIA.

Eastern and Southern African Trade and Development Bank: NSSF Bldg, 22nd/23rd Floor, Bishop's Rd, POB 48596, 00100 Nairobi, Kenya; tel. (20) 2712250; fax (20) 2711510; e-mail official@ptabank.org; internet www.ptabank.co.ke; f. 1983 as PTA Development Bank; aims to mobilize resources and finance COMESA activities to foster regional integration; promotes investment and co-financing within the region; in Jan. 2003 the US dollar replaced the UAPTA (PTA unit of account) as the Bank's reporting currency; shareholders: 15 COMESA mem. states, the People's Republic of China, Somalia, Tanzania and the African Development Bank; subscribed cap. $354.1m., paid-up cap. $117.5m. (Dec. 2006); Pres. Dr MICHAEL M. GONDWE; Chair. Bd of Dirs ABII TSIGE.

Finance

COMESA is financed by member states. The organization's activities have been undermined by delays by some countries in paying membership dues.

Publications

Annual Report of the Council of Ministers.
Asycuda Newsletter.
COMESA Journal.
COMESA Trade Directory (annually).
COMESA Trade Information Newsletter (monthly).
e-comesa (monthly newsletter).
Demand/supply surveys, catalogues and reports.

THE COMMONWEALTH

Address: Commonwealth Secretariat, Marlborough House, Pall Mall, London, SW1Y 5HX, United Kingdom.
Telephone: (20) 7747-6500; **fax:** (20) 7930-0827; **e-mail:** info@commonwealth.int; **internet:** www.thecommonwealth.org.

The Commonwealth is a voluntary association of 53 independent states, comprising about one-quarter of the world's population. It includes the United Kingdom and most of its former dependencies, and former dependencies of Australia and New Zealand (themselves Commonwealth countries).

The evolution of the Commonwealth began with the introduction of self-government in Canada in the 1840s; Australia, New Zealand and South Africa became independent before the First World War. At the Imperial Conference of 1926 the United Kingdom and the Dominions, as they were then called, were described as 'autonomous communities within the British Empire, equal in status', and this change was enacted into law by the Statute of Westminster, in 1931.

The modern Commonwealth began with the entry of India and Pakistan in 1947, and of Sri Lanka (then Ceylon) in 1948. In 1949, when India decided to become a republic, the Commonwealth Heads of Government agreed to replace allegiance to the British Crown with recognition of the British monarch as Head of the Commonwealth, as a condition of membership. This was a precedent for a number of other members (see Heads of State and Heads of Government, below).

INTERNATIONAL ORGANIZATIONS

MEMBERS*

Antigua and Barbuda	Jamaica	Saint Vincent and the Grenadines
Australia	Kenya	Samoa
Bahamas	Kiribati	Seychelles
Bangladesh	Lesotho	Sierra Leone
Barbados	Malawi	Singapore
Belize	Malaysia	Solomon Islands
Botswana	The Maldives	South Africa
Brunei	Malta	Sri Lanka
Cameroon	Mauritius	Swaziland
Canada	Mozambique	Tanzania
Cyprus	Namibia	Tonga
Dominica	Nauru	Trinidad and Tobago
Fiji	New Zealand	Tuvalu
The Gambia	Nigeria	Uganda
Ghana	Pakistan	United Kingdom
Grenada	Papua New Guinea	Vanuatu
Guyana	Saint Christopher and Nevis	Zambia
India	Saint Lucia	

*Ireland, South Africa and Pakistan withdrew from the Commonwealth in 1949, 1961 and 1972 respectively. In October 1987 Fiji's membership was declared to have lapsed (following the proclamation of a republic there). It was readmitted in October 1997, but was suspended from participation in meetings of the Commonwealth in June 2000. Fiji was formally readmitted to Commonwealth meetings in December 2001 following the staging of free and fair legislative elections in August–September. However, following a further military coup in December 2006, Fiji was once again suspended from participation in meetings of the Commonwealth. Pakistan rejoined the Commonwealth in October 1989. However, it was suspended from participation in meetings during the period October 1999–May 2004. Pakistan was suspended from the Councils of the Commonwealth once again in November 2007. South Africa rejoined in June 1994. Nigeria's membership was suspended in November 1995; it formally resumed membership in May 1999, when a new civilian government was inaugurated. Tuvalu, previously a special member of the Commonwealth with the right to participate in all activities except full Meetings of Heads of Government, became a full member in September 2000. Nauru remains a special member.

Note: In March 2002 Zimbabwe was suspended from participation in meetings of the Commonwealth. Zimbabwe announced its withdrawal from the Commonwealth in December 2003.

Australian External Territories

Ashmore and Cartier Islands	Coral Sea Islands Territory
Australian Antarctic Territory	Heard Island and the McDonald Islands
Christmas Island	Norfolk Island
Cocos (Keeling) Islands	

New Zealand Dependent and Associated Territories

Cook Islands	Ross Dependency
Niue	Tokelau

United Kingdom Overseas Territories

Anguilla	Isle of Man
Bermuda	Montserrat
British Antarctic Territory	Pitcairn Islands
British Indian Ocean Territory	St Helena Ascension
British Virgin Islands	Tristan da Cunha
Cayman Islands	South Georgia and the South Sandwich Islands
Channel Islands	
Falkland Islands	Turks and Caicos Islands
Gibraltar	

HEADS OF STATE AND HEADS OF GOVERNMENT

At April 2008 21 member countries were monarchies and 32 were republics. All Commonwealth countries accept Queen Elizabeth II as the symbol of the free association of the independent member nations and as such the Head of the Commonwealth. Of the 32 republics, the offices of Head of State and Head of Government were combined in 21: Botswana, Cameroon, Cyprus, The Gambia, Ghana, Guyana, Kenya, Kiribati, Malawi, The Maldives, Mozambique, Namibia, Nauru, Nigeria, Seychelles, Sierra Leone, South Africa, Sri Lanka, Tanzania, Uganda and Zambia. The two offices were separated in the remaining 11: Bangladesh, Dominica, Fiji, India, Malta, Mauritius, Pakistan, Samoa, Singapore, Trinidad and Tobago and Vanuatu.

Of the monarchies, the Queen is Head of State of the United Kingdom and of 15 others, in each of which she is represented by a Governor-General: Antigua and Barbuda, Australia, the Bahamas, Barbados, Belize, Canada, Grenada, Jamaica, New Zealand, Papua New Guinea, Saint Christopher and Nevis, Saint Lucia, Saint Vincent and the Grenadines, Solomon Islands and Tuvalu. Brunei, Lesotho, Malaysia, Swaziland and Tonga are also monarchies, where the traditional monarch is Head of State.

The Governors-General are appointed by the Queen on the advice of the Prime Ministers of the country concerned. They are wholly independent of the Government of the United Kingdom.

HIGH COMMISSIONERS

Governments of member countries are represented in other Commonwealth countries by High Commissioners, who have a status equivalent to that of Ambassadors.

Organization
(April 2008)

The Commonwealth is not a federation: there is no central government nor are there any rigid contractual obligations such as bind members of the United Nations.

The Commonwealth has no written constitution but its members subscribe to the ideals of the Declaration of Commonwealth Principles unanimously approved by a meeting of heads of government in Singapore in 1971. Members also approved the Gleneagles Agreement concerning apartheid in sport (1977); the Lusaka Declaration on Racism and Racial Prejudice (1979); the Melbourne Declaration on relations between developed and developing countries (1981); the New Delhi Statement on Economic Action (1983); the Goa Declaration on International Security (1983); the Nassau Declaration on World Order (1985); the Commonwealth Accord on Southern Africa (1985); the Vancouver Declaration on World Trade (1987); the Okanagan Statement and Programme of Action on Southern Africa (1987); the Langkawi Declaration on the Environment (1989); the Kuala Lumpur Statement on Southern Africa (1989); the Harare Commonwealth Declaration (1991); the Ottawa Declaration on Women and Structural Adjustment (1991); the Limassol Statement on the Uruguay Round of multilateral trade negotiations (1993); the Millbrook Commonwealth Action Programme on the Harare Declaration (1995); the Edinburgh Commonwealth Economic Declaration (1997); the Fancourt Commonwealth Declaration on Globalization and People-centred Development (1999); the Coolum Declaration on the Commonwealth in the 21st Century: Continuity and Renewal (2002); the Aso Rock Commonwealth Declaration and Statement on Multilateral Trade (2003); the Malta Commonwealth Declaration on Networking for Development (2005); and the Munyonyo Statement on Respect and Understanding (2007).

MEETINGS OF HEADS OF GOVERNMENT

Commonwealth Heads of Government Meetings (CHOGMs) are private and informal and operate not by voting but by consensus. The emphasis is on consultation and exchange of views for co-operation. A communiqué is issued at the end of every meeting. Meetings are normally held every two years in different capitals in the Commonwealth. The 2007 meeting was held in Kampala, Uganda, in November. The next meeting was scheduled to be convened in 2009, in Trinidad and Tobago.

OTHER CONSULTATIONS

Meetings at ministerial and official level are also held regularly. Since 1959 finance ministers have met in a Commonwealth country in the week prior to the annual meetings of the IMF and the World Bank. Meetings on education, legal, women's and youth affairs are held at ministerial level every three years. Ministers of health hold annual meetings, with major meetings every three years, and ministers of agriculture meet every two years. Ministers of finance, trade, labour and employment, industry, science, tourism and the environment also hold periodic meetings.

Senior officials—cabinet secretaries, permanent secretaries to heads of government and others—meet regularly in the year between meetings of heads of government to provide continuity and to exchange views on various developments.

COMMONWEALTH SECRETARIAT

The Secretariat, established by Commonwealth heads of government in 1965, operates as an international organization at the service of all Commonwealth countries. It organizes consultations between governments and runs programmes of co-operation. Meetings of heads of government, ministers and senior officials decide these programmes and provide overall direction. A Board of Governors, on which all eligible member governments are represented, meets annually to review the Secretariat's work and approve its budget. The Board is supported by an Executive Committee which convenes four times a year to monitor implementation of the Secretariat's work programme. The Secretariat is headed by a secretary-general, elected by heads of government.

In 2002 the Secretariat was restructured, with a view to strengthening the effectiveness of the organization to meet the priorities determined by the meeting of heads of government held in Coolum, Australia, in March 2002. Under the reorganization the number of deputy secretaries-general was reduced from three to two. Certain work divisions were amalgamated, while new units or sections, concerned with youth affairs, human rights and good offices, were created to strengthen further activities in those fields. Accordingly, the new divisional structure was as follows: Legal and constitutional affairs; Political affairs; Corporate services; Communications and public affairs; Strategic planning and evaluation; Economic affairs; Governance and institutional development; Social transformation programmes; and Special advisory services. In addition there were units responsible for human rights, youth affairs, and project management and referrals, and an Office of the Secretary-General. In 2004 the youth affairs unit acquired divisional status.

The Secretariat's strategic plan for 2004/05–2007/08 set out two main, long-term objectives for the Commonwealth: to support member countries in preventing or resolving conflicts, to strengthen democracy and the rule of law, and to achieve greater respect for human rights; and to support pro-poor policies for economic growth and sustainable development in member countries. Four programmes were to facilitate the pursuit of the first objective, 'Peace and Democracy': Good Offices for Peace; Democracy and Consensus Building; Rule of Law; and Human Rights. The second objective—'Pro-Poor Growth and Sustainable Development'—was to be achieved through the following nine programmes: International Trade; Investment; Finance and Debt; Public Sector Development; Environmentally Sustainable Development; Small States; Education; Health; and Young People.

Secretary-General: KAMALESH SHARMA (India).

Deputy Secretaries-General: GABAIPONE MMASEKGOA MASIRE-MWAMBA (Botswana), RANSFORD SMITH (Jamaica).

Activities

INTERNATIONAL AFFAIRS

In October 1991 heads of government, meeting in Harare, Zimbabwe, issued the Harare Commonwealth Declaration, in which they reaffirmed their commitment to the Commonwealth Principles declared in 1971, and stressed the need to promote sustainable development and the alleviation of poverty. The Declaration placed emphasis on the promotion of democracy and respect for human rights and resolved to strengthen the Commonwealth's capacity to assist countries in entrenching democratic practices. In November 1995 Commonwealth heads of government, convened in New Zealand, formulated and adopted the Millbrook Commonwealth Action Programme on the Harare Declaration, to promote adherence by member countries to the fundamental principles of democracy and human rights (as proclaimed in the 1991 Declaration). The Programme incorporated a framework of measures to be pursued in support of democratic processes and institutions, and actions to be taken in response to violations of the Harare Declaration principles, in particular the unlawful removal of a democratically-elected government. A Commonwealth Ministerial Action Group on the Harare Declaration (CMAG) was to be established to implement this process and to assist the member country involved to comply with the Harare principles. On the basis of this Programme, the leaders suspended Nigeria from the Commonwealth with immediate effect, following the execution by that country's military Government of nine environmental and human rights protesters and a series of other violations of human rights. The meeting determined to expel Nigeria from the Commonwealth if no 'demonstrable progress' had been made towards the establishment of a democratic authority by the time of the next summit meeting. In addition, the Programme formulated measures to promote sustainable development in member countries, which was considered to be an important element in sustaining democracy, and to facilitate consensus-building within the international community.

In December 1995 CMAG convened for its inaugural meeting in London, United Kingdom. The Group initially comprised the ministers of foreign affairs of Canada, Ghana, Jamaica, Malaysia, New Zealand, South Africa, the United Kingdom and Zimbabwe, and its membership was to be reconstituted periodically (at April 2008 CMAG comprised the ministers of foreign affairs of Canada, Lesotho, Malaysia, Malta, Papua New Guinea, St Lucia, Sri Lanka, Tanzania and the United Kingdom). The inaugural CMAG meeting commenced by considering efforts to restore democratic government in the three Commonwealth countries then under military regimes, i.e. The Gambia, Nigeria and Sierra Leone. At the second meeting of the Group, in April 1996, ministers commended the conduct of presidential and parliamentary elections in Sierra Leone and the announcement by The Gambia's military leaders that there would be a transition to civilian rule. In June a three-member CMAG delegation visited The Gambia to reaffirm Commonwealth support of the transition process in that country and to identify possible areas of further Commonwealth assistance. In August the Gambian authorities issued a decree removing the ban on political activities and parties, although shortly afterwards they prohibited certain parties and candidates involved in political life prior to the military takeover from contesting the elections. CMAG recommended that in such circumstances no Commonwealth observers should be sent to either the presidential or parliamentary elections, which were held in September 1996 and January 1997 respectively. Following the restoration of a civilian Government in early 1997, CMAG requested the Commonwealth Secretary-General to extend technical assistance to The Gambia in order to consolidate the democratic transition process. In April 1996 it was noted that the human rights situation in Nigeria had continued to deteriorate. CMAG, having pursued unsuccessful efforts to initiate dialogue with the Nigerian authorities, outlined a series of punitive and restrictive measures (including visa restrictions on members of the administration, a cessation of sporting contacts and an embargo on the export of armaments) that it would recommend for collective Commonwealth action in order to exert further pressure for reform in Nigeria. Following a meeting of a high-level delegation of the Nigerian Government and CMAG in June, the Group agreed to postpone the implementation of the sanctions, pending progress on the dialogue. (Canada, however, determined, unilaterally, to impose the measures with immediate effect; the United Kingdom did so in accordance with a decision of the European Union to implement limited sanctions against Nigeria.) A proposed CMAG mission to Nigeria was postponed in August, owing to restrictions imposed by the military authorities on access to political detainees and other civilian activists in that country. In September the Group agreed to proceed with the visit (which then took place in November) and to delay further a decision on the implementation of sanction measures. In July 1997 the Group reiterated the Commonwealth Secretary-General's condemnation of a military coup in Sierra Leone in May, and decided that the country's participation in meetings of the Commonwealth should be suspended pending the restoration of a democratic government.

In October 1997 Commonwealth heads of government, meeting in Edinburgh, United Kingdom, endorsed CMAG's recommendation that the imposition of sanctions against Nigeria be held in abeyance pending the scheduled completion of a transition programme towards democracy by October 1998. It was also agreed that CMAG be formally constituted as a permanent organ to investigate abuses of human rights throughout the Commonwealth.

In March 1998 CMAG commended the efforts of the Economic Community of West African States (ECOWAS) in restoring the democratically-elected Government of President Ahmed Tejan Kabbah in Sierra Leone, and agreed to remove all restrictions on Sierra Leone's participation in Commonwealth activities. Later in that month, a representative mission of CMAG visited Sierra Leone to express its support for Kabbah's administration and to consider the country's needs in its process of reconstruction. At the CMAG meeting held in October members agreed that Sierra Leone should no longer be considered under the Group's mandate; however, they urged the Secretary-General to continue to assist that country in the process of national reconciliation and to facilitate negotiations with opposition forces to ensure a lasting cease-fire. A Special Envoy of the Secretary-General was appointed to co-operate with the UN, ECOWAS and the Organization of African Union (OAU, now African Union—AU) in monitoring the implementation of the Sierra Leone peace process, and the Commonwealth has supported the rebuilding of the Sierra Leone police force. In September 2001 CMAG recommended that Sierra Leone be removed from its remit, but that the Secretary-General should continue to monitor developments there.

In April 1998 the Nigerian military leader, Gen. Sani Abacha, announced that a presidential election was to be conducted in August, but indicated that, following an agreement with other political organizations, he was to be the sole candidate. In June, however, Abacha died suddenly. His successor, Gen. Abdulsalam Abubakar, immediately released several prominent political prisoners, and confirmed his intention to abide by the programme for transition to civilian rule. In October CMAG, convened for its 10th formal meeting, acknowledged Abubakar's efforts towards restoring a democratic government and recommended that member states begin to remove sanctions against Nigeria and that it resume participation in certain Commonwealth activities. The Commonwealth Secretary-General subsequently announced a programme of technical assistance to support Nigeria in the planning and conduct of democratic elections. Staff teams from the Commonwealth Secretariat observed local government, and state and governorship elections, held in December and in January 1999, respectively. A Commonwealth Observer Group was also dispatched to Nigeria to monitor preparations and conduct of legislative and presidential elections, held in February. While the Group reported several irregularities in the conduct of the polling, it confirmed that, in general, the conditions had existed for free and fair elections and that the elections were a legitimate basis for the transition of power to a democratic, civilian government. In April CMAG voted to readmit Nigeria to full membership on 29 May, upon the installation of the new civilian administration.

In 1999 the Commonwealth Secretary-General appointed a Special Envoy to broker an agreement in order to end a civil dispute in Honiara, Solomon Islands. An accord was signed in late June, and it was envisaged that the Commonwealth would monitor its implementation. In October a Commonwealth Multinational Police Peace Monitoring Group was stationed in Solomon Islands; this was renamed the Commonwealth Multinational Police Assistance Group in February 2000. Following further internal unrest, however, the Group was disbanded. In June CMAG determined to send a new mission to Solomon Islands in order to facilitate negotiations between the opposing parties, to convey the Commonwealth's concern and to offer assistance. The Commonwealth welcomed the peace accord concluded in Solomon Islands in October, and extended its support to the International Peace Monitoring Team that was established to oversee implementation of the peace accords. CMAG welcomed the conduct of parliamentary elections held in Solomon Islands in December 2001. CMAG removed Solomon Islands from its agenda in December 2003 but was to continue to receive reports from the Secretary-General on future developments.

In mid-October 1999 a special meeting of CMAG was convened to consider the overthrow of the democratically-elected Government in Pakistan in a military coup. The meeting condemned the action as a violation of Commonwealth principles and urged the new authorities to declare a timetable for the return to democratic rule. CMAG also resolved to send a four-member delegation, comprising the ministers of foreign affairs of Barbados, Canada, Ghana and Malaysia, to discuss this future course of action with the military regime. Pakistan was suspended from participation in meetings of the Commonwealth with immediate effect. The suspension, pending the restoration of a democratic government, was endorsed by heads of government, meeting in November, who requested that CMAG keep the situation in Pakistan under review. At the meeting, held in Durban, South Africa, it was agreed that no country would serve for more than two consecutive two-year terms. CMAG was requested to remain actively involved in the post-conflict development and rehabilitation of Sierra Leone and the process of consolidating peace. In addition, it was urged to monitor persistent violations of the Harare Declaration principles in all countries. Heads of government also agreed to establish a new ministerial group on Guyana and to reconvene a ministerial committee on Belize, in order to facilitate dialogue in ongoing territorial disputes with neighbouring countries. The meeting established a 10-member Commonwealth High Level Review Group to evaluate the role and activities of the Commonwealth. In 2000 the Group initiated a programme of consultations to proceed with its mandate and established a working group of experts to consider the Commonwealth's role in supporting information technology capabilities in member countries.

In June 2000, following the overthrow in May of the Fijian Government by a group of armed civilians, and the subsequent illegal detention of members of the elected administration, CMAG suspended Fiji's participation in meetings of the Commonwealth pending the restoration of democratic rule. In September, upon the request of CMAG, the Secretary-General appointed a Special Envoy to support efforts towards political dialogue and a return to democratic rule in Fiji. The Special Envoy undertook his first visit in December. In December 2001, following the staging of democratic legislative elections in August–September, Fiji was readmitted to Commonwealth meetings on the recommendation of CMAG. Fiji was removed from CMAG's agenda in May 2004, although the Group determined to continue to note developments there, as judgments were still pending in the Fiji Supreme Court on unresolved matters concerning the democratic process. In December 2006, following the overthrow of the Fijian Government by the military, an extraordinary meeting of CMAG determined that Fiji should once again be suspended from meetings of the Commonwealth, pending the reinstatement of democratic governance. Political developments in Fiji were considered by CMAG at its next regular meeting, held in New York, USA, in September 2007. The Group urged the Fijian authorities to hold a democratic general election by March 2009 and determined to keep the situation in that country under review.

In March 2001 CMAG resolved to send a ministerial mission to Zimbabwe, in order to relay to the government the Commonwealth's concerns at the ongoing violence and abuses of human rights in that country, as well as to discuss the conduct of parliamentary elections and extend technical assistance. The mission was rejected by the Zimbabwe Government, which queried the basis for CMAG's intervention in the affairs of an elected administration. In September, under the auspices of a group of Commonwealth foreign ministers partly derived from CMAG, the Zimbabwe Government signed the Abuja Agreement, which provided for the cessation of illegal occupations of white-owned farms and the resumption of the rule of law, in return for financial assistance to support the ongoing process of land reform in that country. In January 2002 CMAG expressed strong concern at the continuing violence and political intimidation in Zimbabwe. The summit of Commonwealth heads of government convened in early March (see below) also expressed concern at the situation in Zimbabwe, and, having decided on the principle that CMAG should be permitted to engage with any member Government deemed to be in breach of the organization's core values, mandated a Commonwealth Chairperson's Committee on Zimbabwe to determine appropriate action should an impending presidential election (scheduled to be held during that month) be found not to have been conducted freely and fairly. Following the publication by a Commonwealth observer team of an unfavourable report on the conduct of the election, the Committee decided to suspend Zimbabwe from meetings of the Commonwealth for one year. In March 2003 the Committee concluded that the suspension should remain in force pending consideration by the next summit of heads of government.

In March 2002, meeting in Coolum, near Brisbane, Australia, Commonwealth heads of government adopted the Coolum Declaration on the Commonwealth in the 21st Century: Continuity and Renewal, which reiterated commitment to the organization's principles and values. Leaders at the meeting condemned all forms of terrorism; welcomed the Millennium Development Goals (MDGs) adopted by the UN General Assembly; called on the Secretary-General to constitute a high-level expert group on implementing the objectives of the Fancourt Declaration; pledged continued support for small states; and urged renewed efforts to combat the spread of HIV/AIDS. The meeting adopted a report on the future of the Commonwealth drafted by the High Level Review Group. The document recommended strengthening the Commonwealth's role in conflict prevention and resolution and support of democratic practices; enhancing the good offices role of the Secretary-General; better promoting member states' economic and development needs; strengthening the organization's role in facilitating member states' access to international assistance; and promoting increased access to modern information and communications technologies. The meeting expanded CMAG's mandate to enable the Group to consider action against serious violations of the Commonwealth's core values perpetrated by elected administrations (such as that in Zimbabwe, see above) as well as by military regimes.

A Commonwealth team of observers dispatched to monitor legislative and provincial elections that were held in Pakistan, in October 2002, found them to have been well-organized and conducted in a largely transparent manner. The team made several recommendations on institutional and procedural issues. CMAG subsequently expressed concern over the promulgation of new legislation in Pakistan following the imposition earlier in the year of a number of extra-constitutional measures. CMAG determined that Pakistan should continue to be suspended from meetings of the Commonwealth, pending a review of the role and functioning of its democratic institutions. Pakistan's progress in establishing democratic institutions was welcomed by a meeting of CMAG in May 2003. In November 2002 a Commonwealth Expert Group on Papua New Guinea, established in the previous month to review the electoral process in that country (in view of unsatisfactory legislative elections that were conducted there in July), made several recommendations aimed at enhancing the future management of the electoral process.

In December 2003 the meeting of heads of government, held in Abuja, Nigeria, resolved to maintain the suspension of Pakistan and Zimbabwe from participation in Commonwealth meetings. President Mugabe of Zimbabwe responded by announcing his country's immediate withdrawal from the Commonwealth and alleging a pro-Western bias within the grouping. Support for Zimbabwe's position was declared by a number of members, including South Africa, Mozambique, Namibia and Zambia. A Commonwealth committee, consisting of six heads of government, was established to monitor the situation in Zimbabwe and only when the committee believed sufficient progress had been made towards consolidating democracy and promoting development within Zimbabwe would the Commonwealth be consulted on readmitting the country.

In concluding the 2003 meeting heads of government issued the Aso Rock Commonwealth Declaration, which emphasized their commitment to strengthening development and democracy, and incorporated clear objectives in support of these goals. Priority areas identified included efforts to eradicate poverty and attain the MDGs, to strengthen democratic institutions, empower women, promote the involvement of civil society, combat corruption and recover assets (for which a working group was to be established), facilitate finance for development, address the spread of HIV/AIDS and other diseases, combat the illicit trafficking in human beings, and promote education. The leaders also adopted a separate statement on multilateral trade, in particular in support of the stalled Doha round of World Trade Organization negotiations.

In response to the earthquake and tsunami that devastated coastal areas of several Indian Ocean countries in late December 2004, the Commonwealth Secretary-General appealed for assistance from

Commonwealth Governments for the mobilization of emergency humanitarian relief. In early January 2005 the Secretariat dispatched a Disaster Relief Co-ordinator to the Maldives to assess the needs of that country and to co-ordinate ongoing relief and rehabilitation activities, and later in that month the Secretariat sent emergency medical doctors from other member states to the Maldives. In mid-January, meeting during the fifth Summit of the Alliance of Small Island States, in Port Louis, Mauritius, the Secretaries-General of the Commonwealth, the Caribbean Community and Common Market (CARICOM), the Pacific Islands Forum and the Indian Ocean Commission determined to take collective action to strengthen the disaster-preparedness and response capacities of their member countries in the Caribbean, Pacific and Indian Ocean areas.

In May 2004 Pakistan was readmitted to the Commonwealth. However, CMAG urged the prompt separation of the military and civilian offices held by the President Musharraf, deeming this arrangement to be undemocratic. In February 2005 CMAG expressed serious concern that Musharraf had failed to relinquish the role of chief of army staff. Noting President Musharraf's own undertaking not to continue as chief of army staff beyond 2007, the Group stated its view that the two offices should not be combined in one person beyond the end (in that year) of the current presidential term. CMAG recommended that the Secretary-General should maintain high-level contacts with Pakistan. In September 2005 CMAG urged Pakistan to accelerate its democratic reforms. Meeting in London in early November, following Musharraf's re-election as President of Pakistan in early October, CMAG condemned the recent abrogation of Pakistan's Constitution and the institution there of a non-constitutional state of emergency; expressed grave concern at the recent dismissal of the Chief Justice and several other members of the judiciary and their placement under house arrest, and at other actions taken against lawyers, opposition politicians and civil society leaders, and at the suspension of all private media broadcasts and restrictions on the press; and noted with alarm a recent legislation that retrospectively gave military courts the right to try civilians on charges of 'anti-national activities'. While welcoming an announcement by President Musharraf that parliamentary elections would be staged in early 2008, CMAG maintained that such elections would only be credible if the state of emergency were revoked and constitutional rights restored. CMAG also noted with concern that Musharraf continued to retain the role of chief of army staff. The Group urged the Government of Pakistan to fulfil its obligations in accordance with Commonwealth principles through the implementation of the following measures: immediate repeal of the state of emergency, immediate release of political party leaders, lawyers, journalists and other activists detained under the state of emergency, and full restoration of the Constitution and of the independence of the judiciary; and for President Musharraf to relinquish his role as chief of army staff. Meeting on 22 November CMAG noted that these measures had not been implemented, as a consequence of which Pakistan was once again suspended from the Councils of the Commonwealth 'pending restoration of democracy and rule of law in the country'. President Musharraf relinquished his command of the Pakistan military at the end of November. The Pakistan authorities did not invite the Commonwealth to send an observer mission to monitor the parliamentary elections that were held in that country in February 2008.

The 2007 meeting of Commonwealth heads of government, convened in Kampala, Uganda, in November, issued the Munyonyo Statement on Respect and Understanding, which commended the work of the Commonwealth Commission on Respect and Understanding (established in 2005) and endorsed its recently published report entitled *Civil Paths to Peace* aimed at building tolerance and understanding of diversity.

Political Affairs Division: assists consultation among member governments on international and Commonwealth matters of common interest. In association with host governments, it organizes the meetings of heads of government and senior officials. The Division services committees and special groups set up by heads of government dealing with political matters. The Secretariat has observer status at the United Nations, and the Division manages a joint office in New York to enable small states, which would otherwise be unable to afford facilities there, to maintain a presence at the United Nations. The Division monitors political developments in the Commonwealth and international progress in such matters as disarmament and the Law of the Sea. It also undertakes research on matters of common interest to member governments, and reports back to them. The Division is involved in diplomatic training and consular co-operation.

In 1990 Commonwealth heads of government mandated the Division to support the promotion of democracy by monitoring the preparations for and conduct of parliamentary, presidential or other elections in member countries at the request of national governments. In 2008 (by April) a Commonwealth observer group had been dispatched to observe parliamentary elections in Belize, in February.

Under the reorganization of the Secretariat in 2002 a Good Offices Section was established within the Division to strengthen and support the activities of the Secretary-General in addressing political conflict in member states and in assisting countries to adhere to the principles of the Harare Declaration. The Secretary-General's good offices may be directed to preventing or resolving conflict and assisting other international efforts to promote political stability. At April 2008 Special Envoys of the Secretary-General were active in six member countries: Cameroon, The Gambia, Guyana, Kenya, the Maldives and Tonga.

Human Rights Unit: undertakes activities in support of the Commonwealth's commitment to the promotion and protection of fundamental human rights. It develops programmes, publishes human rights materials, co-operates with other organizations working in the field of human rights, in particular within the UN system, advises the Secretary-General, and organizes seminars and meetings of experts. The Unit aims to integrate human rights standards within all divisions of the Secretariat.

LAW

Legal and Constitutional Affairs Division: promotes and facilitates co-operation and the exchange of information among member governments on legal matters and assists in combating financial and organized crime, in particular transborder criminal activities. It administers, jointly with the Commonwealth of Learning, a distance training programme for legislative draftsmen and assists governments to reform national laws to meet the obligations of international conventions. The Division organizes the triennial meeting of ministers, Attorneys General and senior ministry officials concerned with the legal systems in Commonwealth countries. It has also initiated four Commonwealth schemes for co-operation on extradition, the protection of material cultural heritage, mutual assistance in criminal matters and the transfer of convicted offenders within the Commonwealth. It liaises with the Commonwealth Magistrates' and Judges' Association, the Commonwealth Legal Education Association, the Commonwealth Lawyers' Association (with which it helps to prepare the triennial Commonwealth Law Conference for the practising profession), the Commonwealth Association of Legislative Counsel, and with other international non-governmental organizations. The Division provides in-house legal advice for the Secretariat. The *Commonwealth Law Bulletin*, published four times a year, reports on legal developments in and beyond the Commonwealth. The Division promotes the exchange of information regarding national and international efforts to combat serious commercial crime through its other publications, *Commonwealth Legal Assistance News* and *Crimewatch*.

The heads of government meeting held in Coolum, Australia, in March 2002 endorsed a Plan of Action for combating international terrorism. A Commonwealth Committee on Terrorism, convened at ministerial level, was subsequently established to oversee its implementation.

A new expert group on good governance and the elimination of corruption in economic management convened for its first meeting in May 1998. In November 1999 Commonwealth heads of government endorsed a Framework for Principles for Promoting Good Governance and Combating Corruption, which had been drafted by the group. The conference of heads of government that met in Coolum in March 2002 endorsed a Commonwealth Local Government Good Practice Scheme, to be managed by the Commonwealth Local Government Forum (established in 1995).

ECONOMIC CO-OPERATION

In October 1997 Commonwealth heads of government, meeting in Edinburgh, United Kingdom, signed an Economic Declaration that focused on issues relating to global trade, investment and development and committed all member countries to free-market economic principles. The Declaration also incorporated a provision for the establishment of a Trade and Investment Access Facility within the Secretariat in order to assist developing member states in the process of international trade liberalization and promote intra-Commonwealth trade.

In May 1998 the Commonwealth Secretary-General appealed to the Group of Eight industrialized nations (G-8) to accelerate and expand the initiative to ease the debt burden of the most heavily indebted poor countries (HIPCs—see World Bank and IMF). In October Commonwealth finance ministers, convened in Ottawa, Canada, reiterated their appeal to international financial institutions to accelerate the HIPC initiative. The meeting also issued a Commonwealth Statement on the global economic crisis and endorsed proposals to help to counter the difficulties experienced by several countries. These measures included a mechanism to enable countries to suspend payments on all short-term financial obligations at a time of emergency without defaulting, assistance to governments to attract private capital and to manage capital market volatility, and the development of international codes of conduct regarding financial and monetary policies and corporate governance. In March 1999 the Commonwealth Secretariat hosted a joint IMF-World Bank conference to review the HIPC scheme and initiate a process of reform. In November Commonwealth heads of government, meeting in South Africa, declared their support for measures undertaken by the World Bank and IMF to enhance the HIPC initiative. At the end of an informal retreat the leaders adopted the Fancourt Commonwealth Declaration on Globalization and People-Centred Development, which emphasized the need for a more equitable spread of wealth generated by the process of globalization, and expressed a renewed commitment to the elimination of all forms of discrimination, the promotion of people-centred development and capacity-building, and efforts to ensure that developing countries benefit from future multilateral trade liberalization measures. In June 2002 the Commonwealth Secretary-General urged more generous funding of the HIPC initiative. Meetings of ministers of finance from Commonwealth member countries participating in the HIPC initiative are convened twice a year, as the Commonwealth HIPC Ministerial Forum. The Secretariat aims to assist HIPCs and other small economies through its Debt Recording and Management System (DRMS), which was first used in 1985 and updated in 2002. In mid-2005 the People's Republic of China became the 55th country (and the 12th non-Commonwealth member) to sign up to the System. The first Pan Commonwealth CS-DRMS User Group meeting was convened in June 2006, at which time there were 56 user countries. In July 2005 the Commonwealth Secretary-General welcomed an initiative of the G-8 to eliminate the debt of those HIPCs that had reached their completion point in the process, in addition to a commitment substantially to increase aid to Africa.

In February 1998 the Commonwealth Secretariat hosted the first Inter-Governmental Organizations Meeting to promote co-operation between small island states and the formulation of a unified policy approach to international fora. A second meeting was convened in March 2001, where discussions focused on the forthcoming WTO ministerial meeting and OECD's Harmful Tax Competition Initiative. In September 2000 Commonwealth finance ministers, meeting in Malta, reviewed the OECD initiative and agreed that the measures, affecting many member countries with offshore financial centres, should not be imposed on governments. The ministers mandated the involvement of the Commonwealth Secretariat in efforts to resolve the dispute; a joint working group was subsequently established by the Secretariat with the OECD. In April 2002 a meeting on international co-operation in the financial services sector, attended by representatives of international and regional organizations, donors and senior officials from Commonwealth countries, was held under Commonwealth auspices in Saint Lucia. In September 2005 Commonwealth finance ministers, meeting in Barbados, considered new guide-lines for Public Financial Management Reform.

The first meeting of governors of central banks from Commonwealth countries was held in June 2001 in London, United Kingdom.

The Commonwealth Secretariat was to participate in the €20m. 'Hub and Spokes' project, launched in October 2004 by the European Commission, with the Agence Intergouvernementale de la Francophonie, as a capacity-building initiative in the areas of trade policy formulation, mainstreaming trade in poverty reduction strategies, and participation in international trade negotiations for the African, Caribbean and Pacific (ACP) group of countries. The Secretariat was to manage the project in 55 of the 78 ACP member states.

In November 2005 Commonwealth heads of government issued the Malta Declaration on Networking the Commonwealth for Development, expressing their commitment to making available to all the benefits of new technologies and to using information technology networks to enhance the effectiveness of the Commonwealth in supporting development. The meeting endorsed a new Commonwealth Action Programme for the Digital Divide and approved the establishment of a special fund to enable implementation of the programme's objectives. Accordingly a Commonwealth Connects programme was established in August 2006 to develop partnerships and help to strengthen the use of and access to information technology in all Commonwealth countries. The 2005 Heads of Government Meeting also issued the Valletta Statement on Multilateral Trade, emphasizing their concerns that the Doha Round of WTO negotiations proceed steadily, on a development-oriented agenda, to a successful conclusion and reiterating their objectives of achieving a rules-based and equitable international trading system. A separate statement drew attention to the specific needs and challenges of small states and urged continued financial and technical support, in particular for those affected by natural disasters.

Economic Affairs Division: organizes and services the annual meetings of Commonwealth ministers of finance and the ministerial group on small states and assists in servicing the biennial meetings of heads of government and periodic meetings of environment ministers. It engages in research and analysis on economic issues of interest to member governments and organizes seminars and conferences of government officials and experts. The Division actively supports developing Commonwealth countries to participate in the Doha Round of multilateral trade negotiations and is assisting the ACP group of countries to negotiate economic partnership agreements with the European Union. It continues to help developing countries to strengthen their links with international capital markets and foreign investors. The Division also services groups of experts on economic affairs that have been commissioned by governments to report on, among other things, protectionism; obstacles to the North-South negotiating process; reform of the international financial and trading system; the debt crisis; management of technological change; the impact of change on the development process; environmental issues; women and structural adjustment; and youth unemployment. A separate section within the Division addresses the specific needs of small states and provides technical assistance. The work of the section covers a range of issues including trade, vulnerability, environment, politics and economics. A Secretariat Task Force services a Commonwealth Ministerial Group of Small States which was established in 1993 to provide strategic direction in addressing the concerns of small states and to mobilize support for action and assistance within the international community. The Economic Affairs Division also co-ordinates the Secretariat's environmental work and manages the Iwokrama International Centre for Rainforest Conservation and Development.

The Division played a catalytic role in the establishment of a Commonwealth Equity Fund, initiated in September 1990, to allow developing member countries to improve their access to private institutional investment, and promoted a Caribbean Investment Fund. The Division supported the establishment of a Commonwealth Private Investment Initiative (CPII) to mobilize capital, on a regional basis, for investment in newly-privatized companies and in small and medium-sized businesses in the private sector. The first regional fund under the CPII was launched in July 1996. The Commonwealth Africa Investment Fund (Comafin), was to be managed by the United Kingdom's official development institution, the Commonwealth Development Corporation, to assist businesses in 19 countries in sub-Saharan Africa, with initial resources of US $63.5m. In August 1997 an investment fund for the Pacific Islands was launched, with an initial capital of $15.0m. A successor fund, with financing of some $20m., was launched in October 2005. A $200m. South Asia Regional Fund was established at the heads of government meeting in October 1997. In October 1998 a fund for the Caribbean states was inaugurated, at a meeting of Commonwealth finance ministers. The 2001 summit of Commonwealth heads of government authorized the establishment of a new fund for Africa (Comafin II): this was inaugurated in March 2002, and attracted initial capital in excess of $200m.

SOCIAL WELFARE

Social Transformation Programmes Division: consists of three sections concerned with education, gender and health.

The **Education Section** arranges specialist seminars, workshops and co-operative projects, and commissions studies in areas identified by ministers of education, whose three-yearly meetings it also services. Its present areas of emphasis include improving the quality of and access to basic education; strengthening the culture of science, technology and mathematics education in formal and non-formal areas of education; improving the quality of management in institutions of higher learning and basic education; improving the performance of teachers; strengthening examination assessment systems; and promoting the movement of students between Commonwealth countries. The Section also promotes multi-sectoral strategies to be incorporated in the development of human resources. Emphasis is placed on ensuring a gender balance, the appropriate use of technology, promoting good governance, addressing the problems of scale particular to smaller member countries, and encouraging collaboration between governments, the private sector and other non-governmental organizations.

The **Gender Affairs Section** is responsible for the implementation of the Commonwealth Plan of Action for Gender Equality, covering the period 2005–15, which succeeded the Commonwealth Plan of Action on Gender and Development (adopted in 1995 and updated in 2000). The Plan of Action supports efforts towards achieving the MDGs, and the objectives of gender equality adopted by the 1995 Beijing Declaration and Platform for Action and the follow-up Beijing + 5 review conference held in 2000. Gender equality, poverty eradication, promotion of human rights, and strengthening democracy are recognized as intrinsically inter-related, and the Plan has a particular focus on the advancement of gender mainstreaming in the following areas: democracy, peace and conflict; human rights and law; poverty eradication and economic empowerment; and HIV/AIDS. In February–March 2005 Commonwealth ministers responsible for gender affairs attended the Beijing + 10 review conference.

The **Health Section** organizes ministerial, technical and expert group meetings and workshops, to promote co-operation on health matters, and the exchange of health information and expertise. The

INTERNATIONAL ORGANIZATIONS

The Commonwealth

Section commissions relevant studies and provides professional and technical advice to member countries and to the Secretariat. It also supports the work of regional health organizations and promotes health for all people in Commonwealth countries.

Youth Affairs: A Youth Affairs unit, reporting directly to a Deputy Secretary-General, was established within the Secretariat in 2002. The unit acquired divisional status in 2004.

The Division administers the **Commonwealth Youth Programme (CYP)**, which was initiated in 1973 to promote the involvement of young people in the economic and social development of their countries. The CYP, funded through separate voluntary contributions from governments, was awarded a budget of £2.6m. for 2006/07. The Programme's activities are centred on four key programmes: Youth Enterprise Development; Youth Networks and Governance; Youth Participation; and Youth Work, Education and Training. Regional centres are located in Zambia (for Africa), India (for Asia), Guyana (for the Caribbean), and Solomon Islands (for the Pacific). The Programme administers a Youth Study Fellowship scheme, a Youth Project Fund, a Youth Exchange Programme (in the Caribbean), and a Youth Service Awards Scheme. It also holds conferences and seminars, carries out research and disseminates information. The Commonwealth Youth Credit Initiative, launched in 1995, provides funds, training and advice to young entrepreneurs. A Plan of Action for Youth Empowerment, covering the period 2007-15, was approved by the sixth meeting of Commonwealth ministers responsible for youth affairs, held in Nassau, Bahamas, in May 2006. The first Commonwealth Youth and Sports Congress was scheduled to be held in India, in 2009. The sixth Commonwealth Youth Forum was convened in Entebbe, Uganda, in November 2007.

In March 2002 Commonwealth heads of government approved the Youth for the Future initiative to encourage and use the skills of young people throughout the Commonwealth. It was to comprise four main components: Youth enterprise development; Youth volunteers; Youth mentors; and Youth leadership awards.

TECHNICAL ASSISTANCE

Commonwealth Fund for Technical Co-operation (CFTC): f. 1971 to facilitate the exchange of skills between member countries and to promote economic and social development; it is administered by the Commonwealth Secretariat and financed by voluntary subscriptions from member governments. The CFTC responds to requests from member governments for technical assistance, such as the provision of experts for short- or medium-term projects, advice on economic or legal matters, in particular in the areas of natural resources management and public-sector reform, and training programmes. The CFTC also administers the Langkawi awards for the study of environmental issues, which is funded by the Canadian Government; the proposed CFTC budget for 2006/07 amounted to £25.6m.

CFTC activities are mainly implemented by the following divisions:

Governance and Institutional Development Division: strengthens good governance in member countries, through advice, training and other expertise in order to build capacity in national public institutions. The Division administers the Commonwealth Service Abroad Programme (CSAP), which is funded by the CFTC. The Programme extends short-term technical assistance through highly qualified volunteers. The main objectives of the scheme are to provide expertise, training and exposure to new technologies and practices, to promote technology transfers and sharing of experiences and knowledge, and to support community workshops and other grassroots activities.

Special Advisory Services Division: advises on economic and legal issues, such as debt and financial management, natural resource development, multilateral trade issues, export marketing, trade facilitation, competitiveness and the development of enterprises.

Finance

The Secretariat's proposed budget for 2006/07 was £13.8m. Member governments meet the cost of the Secretariat through subscriptions on a scale related to income and population.

Publications

Commonwealth Currents (quarterly).
International Development Policies (quarterly).
Report of the Commonwealth Secretary-General (every 2 years).
Numerous reports, studies and papers (catalogue available).

Commonwealth Organizations

(in the United Kingdom, unless otherwise stated)

PRINCIPAL BODIES

Commonwealth Business Council: 18 Pall Mall, London, SW1Y 5LU; tel. (20) 7024-8200; fax (20) 7024-8201; e-mail info@cbcglobal.org; internet www.cbcglobal.org; f. 1997 by the Commonwealth Heads of Government Meeting to promote co-operation between governments and the private sector in support of trade, investment and development; the Council aims to identify and promote investment opportunities, in particular in Commonwealth developing countries, to support countries and local businesses to work within the context of globalization, to promote capacity-building and the exchange of skills and knowledge (in particular through its Information Communication Technologies for Development programme), and to encourage co-operation among Commonwealth members; promotes good governance; supports the process of multilateral trade negotiations and other liberalization of trade and services; represents the private sector at government level; Dir-Gen. and CEO Dr MOHAN KAUL.

Commonwealth Foundation: Marlborough House, Pall Mall, London, SW1Y 5HY; tel. (20) 7930-3783; fax (20) 7839-8157; e-mail geninfo@commonwealth.int; internet www.commonwealthfoundation.com; f. 1966; intergovernmental body promoting people-to-people interaction, and collaboration within the non-governmental sector of the Commonwealth; supports non-governmental organizations, professional associations and Commonwealth arts and culture; awards an annual Commonwealth Writers' Prize; funds are provided by Commonwealth govts; Chair. Prof. GUIDO DE MARCO (Malta); Dir Dr MARK COLLINS (United Kingdom); publ. *Commonwealth People* (quarterly).

Commonwealth of Learning (COL): 1055 West Hastings St, Suite 1200, Vancouver, BC V6E 2E9, Canada; tel. (604) 775-8200; fax (604) 775-8210; e-mail info@col.org; internet www.col.org; f. 1987 by Commonwealth Heads of Government to promote the devt and sharing of distance education and open learning resources, including materials, expertise and technologies, throughout the Commonwealth and in other countries; implements and assists with national and regional educational programmes; acts as consultant to international agencies and national governments; conducts seminars and studies on specific educational needs; core financing for COL is provided by Commonwealth governments on a voluntary basis; in 2006 heads of government endorsed an annual budget for COL of C $12m; Pres. and CEO Sir JOHN DANIEL (Canada/UK); publs *Connections*, *EdTech News*.

The following represents a selection of other Commonwealth organizations:

AGRICULTURE AND FORESTRY

Commonwealth Forestry Association: Crib, Dinchope, Craven Arms, Shropshire, SY7 9JJ; tel. (1588) 672868; fax (870) 0116645; e-mail cfa@cfa-international.org; internet www.cfa-international.org; f. 1921; produces, collects and circulates information relating to world forestry and promotes good management, use and conservation of forests and forest lands throughout the world; mems: 1,200; Pres. DAVID BILLS (Australia/UK); publs *International Forestry Review* (quarterly), *Commonwealth Forestry News* (quarterly), *Commonwealth Forestry Handbook* (irregular).

Standing Committee on Commonwealth Forestry: Forestry Commission, 231 Corstorphine Rd, Edinburgh, EH12 7AT; tel. (131) 314-6137; fax (131) 316-4344; e-mail libby.jones@forestry.gsi.gov.uk; f. 1923 to provide continuity between Confs, and to provide a forum for discussion on any forestry matters of common interest to mem. govts which may be brought to the Cttee's notice by any mem. country or organization; 54 mems; 2010 Conference: United Kingdom; Sec. LIBBY JONES; publ. *Newsletter* (quarterly).

COMMONWEALTH STUDIES

Institute of Commonwealth Studies: 28 Russell Sq., London, WC1B 5DS; tel. (20) 7862-8844; fax (20) 7862-8820; e-mail ics@sas.ac.uk; internet commonwealth.sas.ac.uk; f. 1949 to promote advanced study of the Commonwealth; provides a library and meeting place for postgraduate students and academic staff engaged in research in this field; offers postgraduate teaching; Dir Prof. RICHARD CROOK; publs *Annual Report*, *Collected Seminar Papers*, *Newsletter*, *Theses in Progress in Commonwealth Studies*.

COMMUNICATIONS

Commonwealth Telecommunications Organization: 26-28 Hammersmith Grove, London, W6 7BA; tel. (870) 7777697; fax (870) 0345626; e-mail info@cto.int; internet www.cto.int; f. 1967 as an international development partnership between Commonwealth and non-Commonwealth governments, business and civil society organizations; aims to help to bridge the digital divide and to achieve social and economic development by delivering to developing countries knowledge-sharing programmes in the use of information and communication technologies in the specific areas of telecommunications, IT, broadcasting and the internet; CEO Dr EKWOW SPIO-GARBRAH; publs *CTO Update* (quarterly), *Annual Report*, *Research Reports*.

EDUCATION AND CULTURE

Association of Commonwealth Universities (ACU): Woburn House, 20-24 Tavistock Sq., London, WC1H 9HF; tel. (20) 7380-6700; fax (20) 7387-2655; e-mail info@acu.ac.uk; internet www.acu.ac.uk; f. 1913; promotes international co-operation and understanding; provides assistance with staff and student mobility and development programmes; researches and disseminates information about universities and relevant policy issues; organizes major meetings of Commonwealth universities and their representatives; acts as a liaison office and information centre; administers scholarship and fellowship schemes; operates a policy research unit; mems: c. 500 universities in 36 Commonwealth countries or regions; Sec.-Gen. Dr JOHN ROWETT; publs include *Yearly Review*, *Commonwealth Universities Yearbook*, *ACU Bulletin* (quarterly), *Report of the Council of the ACU* (annually), *Who's Who of Executive Heads: Vice-Chancellors, Presidents, Principals and Rectors*, *International Awards*, student information papers (study abroad series).

Commonwealth Association for Education in Journalism and Communication (CAEJAC): c/o Faculty of Law, University of Western Ontario, London, ON N6A 3K7, Canada; tel. (519) 661-3348; fax (519) 661-3790; e-mail caejc@julian.uwo.ca; f. 1985; aims to foster high standards of journalism and communication education and research in Commonwealth countries and to promote co-operation among institutions and professions; c. 700 mems in 32 Commonwealth countries; Pres. Prof. SYED ARABI IDID (Malaysia); Sec. Prof. ROBERT MARTIN (Canada); publ. *CAEJAC Journal* (annually).

Commonwealth Association of Science, Technology and Mathematics Educators (CASTME): 7 Lion Yard, Tremadoc Rd, London, SW4 7NQ; tel. (20) 7819-3932; fax (20) 7720-5403; e-mail mirkka.juntunen@lect.org.uk; internet www.castme.org; f. 1974; special emphasis is given to the social significance of education in these subjects; organizes an Awards Scheme to promote effective teaching and learning in these subjects, and biennial regional seminars; Hon. Sec. Dr LYN HAINES; publ. *CASTME Journal* (quarterly).

Commonwealth Council for Educational Administration and Management: Department of Education, University of Cyprus, POB 20537, 1678 Lefkosia, Cyprus; tel. 22753739; fax 22377950; e-mail edpetros@ucy.ac.cy; internet www.cceam.org; f. 1970; aims to foster quality in professional development and links among educational administrators; holds nat. and regional confs, as well as visits and seminars; mems: 24 affiliated groups representing 3,000 persons; Pres. Dr PETROS PASHIARDIS; publ. *International Studies in Educational Administration* (2 a year).

Commonwealth Education Trust: New Zealand House, 80 Haymarket, London, SW1Y 4TQ; tel. (20) 7024-9822; fax (20) 7024-9833; e-mail info@commonwealth-institute.org; internet www.commonwealth-institute.org; f. 2007 as the successor trust to the Commonwealth Institute; funds the Centre of Commonwealth Education, established in 2004 as part of Cambridge University; supports the Lifestyle of Our Kids (LOOK) project initiated in 2005 by the Commonwealth Institute (Australia).

League for the Exchange of Commonwealth Teachers: 7 Lion Yard, Tremadoc Rd, London, SW4 7NQ; tel. (870) 7702636; fax (870) 7702637; e-mail info@lect.org.uk; internet www.lect.org.uk; f. 1901; promotes educational exchanges between teachers throughout the Commonwealth; Dir ANNA TOMLINSON; publ. *Annual Review*.

HEALTH

Commonwealth Medical Trust (COMMAT): BMA House, Tavistock Sq., London, WC1H 9JP; tel. (20) 7272-8492; fax (1689) 890609; e-mail office@commat.org; internet www.commat.org; f. 1962 (as the Commonwealth Medical Association) for the exchange of information; provision of tech. co-operation and advice; formulation and maintenance of a code of ethics; promotes the Right to Health; liaison with WHO and other UN agencies on health issues; meetings of its Council are held every three years; mems: medical asscns in Commonwealth countries; Dir MARIANNE HASLEGRAVE.

Commonwealth Pharmaceutical Association: 1 Lambeth High St, London, SE1 7JN; tel. (20) 7572-2364; fax (20) 7572-2508; e-mail admin@commonwealthpharmacy.org; internet www.commonwealthpharmacy.org; f. 1970 to promote the interests of pharmaceutical sciences and the profession of pharmacy in the Commonwealth; to maintain high professional standards, encourage links between members and the creation of nat. asscns; and to facilitate the dissemination of information; holds confs (every four years) and regional meetings; mems: pharmaceutical asscns from over 40 Commonwealth countries; Pres. Dr GRACE ALLEN YOUNG; publ. *Quarterly Newsletter*.

Commonwealth Society for the Deaf (Sound Seekers): 34 Buckingham Palace Rd, London, SW1W 0RE; tel. (20) 7233-5700; fax (20) 7233-5805; e-mail sound.seekers@btinternet.com; internet www.sound-seekers.org.uk; f. 1959; undertakes initiatives to establish audiology services in developing Commonwealth countries, including mobile clinics to provide outreach services; aims to educate local communities in aural hygiene and the prevention of ear infection and deafness; provides audiological equipment and organizes the training of audiological maintenance technicians; conducts research into the causes and prevention of deafness; Chief Exec. GARY WILLIAMS; publ. *Annual Report*.

Sightsavers International: Grosvenor Hall, Bolnore Rd, Haywards Heath, West Sussex, RH16 4BX; tel. (1444) 446600; fax (1444) 446688; e-mail info@sightsavers.org; internet www.sightsavers.org; f. 1950 to prevent blindness and restore sight in developing countries, and to provide education and community-based training for incurably blind people; operates in collaboration with local partners in some 30 developing countries, with high priority given to training local staff; Chair. Lord NIGEL CRISP; Chief Exec. Dr CAROLINE HARPER; publ. *Sight Savers News*.

INFORMATION AND THE MEDIA

Commonwealth Broadcasting Association: 17 Fleet St, London, EC4Y 1AA; tel. (20) 7583-5550; fax (20) 7583-5549; e-mail cba@cba.org.uk; internet www.cba.org.uk; f. 1945; gen. confs are held every two years (2008: Bahamas); mems: c. 100 in more than 50 countries; Pres. ABUBAKAR JIJIWA; Sec.-Gen. ELIZABETH SMITH; publs *Commonwealth Broadcaster* (quarterly), *Commonwealth Broadcaster Directory* (annually).

Commonwealth Journalists Association: c/o Canadian Newspaper Association, 890 Yonge St, Suite 200, Toronto, ON M4W 3P4, Canada; tel. (416) 575-5377; fax (416) 923-7206; e-mail bcantley@cna-acj.ca; internet www.cjaweb.com; f. 1978 to promote co-operation between journalists in Commonwealth countries, organize training facilities and confs, and foster understanding among Commonwealth peoples; Exec. Dir BRYAN CANTLEY; publ. *Newsletter* (3 a year).

Commonwealth Press Union (Association of Commonwealth Newspapers, News Agencies and Periodicals): 17 Fleet St, London, EC4Y 1AA; tel. (20) 7583-7733; fax (20) 7583-6868; e-mail lindsay@cpu.org.uk; internet www.cpu.org.uk; f. 1950; promotes the welfare of the Commonwealth press; provides training for journalists and organizes biennial confs; mems: c. 750 newspapers, news agencies, periodicals in 49 Commonwealth countries; Exec. Dir LINDSAY ROSS; publ. *Annual Report*.

LAW

Commonwealth Lawyers' Association: c/o Institute of Commonwealth Studies, 28 Russell Sq., London, WC1B 5DS; tel. (20) 7862-8824; fax (20) 7862-8816; e-mail cla@sas.ac.uk; internet www.commonwealthlawyers.com; f. 1983 (fmrly the Commonwealth Legal Bureau); seeks to maintain and promote the rule of law throughout the Commonwealth, by ensuring that the people of the Commonwealth are served by an independent and efficient legal profession; upholds professional standards and promotes the availability of legal services; organizes the biannual Commonwealth Law Conference; Sec-Gen. CLAIRE MARTIN; publs *The Commonwealth Lawyer*, *Clarion*.

Commonwealth Legal Advisory Service: c/o British Institute of International and Comparative Law, Charles Clore House, 17 Russell Sq., London, WC1B 5DR; tel. (20) 7862-5151; fax (20) 7862-5152; e-mail info@biicl.org; f. 1962; financed by the British Institute and by contributions from Commonwealth govts; provides research facilities for Commonwealth govts and law reform commissions; Chair. Rt Hon. Lord BROWNE-WILKINSON; publ. *New Memoranda* series.

Commonwealth Legal Education Association: c/o Legal and Constitutional Affairs Division, Commonwealth Secretariat, Marlborough House, Pall Mall, London, SW1Y 5HX; tel. (20) 7747-6415; fax (20) 7747-6406; e-mail clea@commonwealth.int; internet www.cleaonline.org; f. 1971 to promote contacts and exchanges and to provide information regarding legal education; Gen. Sec. JOHN HATCHARD; publs *Commonwealth Legal Education Association Newsletter* (3 a year), *Directory of Commonwealth Law Schools* (every 2 years).

Commonwealth Magistrates' and Judges' Association: Uganda House, 58–59 Trafalgar Sq., London, WC2N 5DX; tel. (20) 7976-1007; fax (20) 7976-2394; e-mail info@cmja.org; internet www

.cmja.org; f. 1970 to advance the administration of the law by promoting the independence of the judiciary, to further education in law and crime prevention and to disseminate information; confs and study tours; corporate membership for asscns of the judiciary or courts of limited jurisdiction; assoc. membership for individuals; Pres. Rt Hon. Justice Tan Sri Dato' Siti NORMA YAAKOB; Exec. Vice-Pres. Lord Justice HENRY BROOKE; publs *Commonwealth Judicial Journal* (2 a year), *CMJA News*.

PARLIAMENTARY AFFAIRS

Commonwealth Parliamentary Association: Westminster House, Suite 700, 7 Millbank, London, SW1P 3JA; tel. (20) 7799-1460; fax (20) 7222-6073; e-mail hq.sec@cpahq.org; internet www.cpahq.org; f. 1911 to promote understanding and co-operation between Commonwealth parliamentarians; organization: Exec. Cttee of 35 MPs responsible to annual Gen. Assembly; 175 brs in national, state, provincial and territorial parliaments and legislatures throughout the Commonwealth; holds annual Commonwealth Parliamentary Confs and seminars; also regional confs and seminars; Sec.-Gen. Dr WILLIAM F. SHIJA; publ. *The Parliamentarian* (quarterly).

PROFESSIONAL AND INDUSTRIAL RELATIONS

Commonwealth Association of Architects: POB 508, Edgware, Middx, HA8 9XZ; tel. (20) 8951-0550; fax (20) 8951-0550; e-mail info@comarchitect.org; internet comarchitect.org; f. 1964; an asscn of 38 socs of architects in various Commonwealth countries; objectives: to facilitate the reciprocal recognition of professional qualifications; to provide a clearing house for information on architectural practice; and to encourage collaboration. Plenary confs every three years; regional confs are also held; Exec. Dir TONY GODWIN; publs *Handbook, Objectives and Procedures: CAA Schools Visiting Boards, Architectural Education in the Commonwealth* (annotated bibliography of research), *CAA Newsnet* (2 a year), a survey and list of schools of architecture.

Commonwealth Association for Public Administration and Management (CAPAM): 1075 Bay St, Suite 402, Toronto, ON M5S 2B1, Canada; tel. (416) 920-3337; fax (416) 920-6574; e-mail capam@capam.org; internet www.capam.org; f. 1994; aims to promote sound management of the public sector in Commonwealth countries and to assist those countries undergoing political or financial reforms; an international awards programme to reward innovation within the public sector was introduced in 1997, and is awarded every 2 years; more than 1,200 individual mems and 80 institutional memberships in some 80 countries; Pres. GERALDINE FRASER-MOLEKETI (South Africa); Exec. Dir and CEO DAVID WAUNG.

SCIENCE AND TECHNOLOGY

Commonwealth Engineers' Council: c/o Institution of Civil Engineers, 1 Great George St, London, SW1P 3AA; tel. (20) 7665-2005; fax (20) 7223-1806; e-mail neil.bailey@ice.org.uk; internet www.ice.org.uk/cec; f. 1946; the Council is a virtual organization that links engineering institutions across the Commonwealth, providing them with an opportunity to exchange views on collaboration and mutual support; mems: 46 institutions in 44 countries; Pres. Prof. TONY RIDLEY; Sec.-Gen. TOM FOULKES.

Commonwealth Geological Surveys Forum: c/o Commonwealth Science Council, CSC Earth Sciences Programme, Marlborough House, Pall Mall, London, SW1Y 5HX; tel. (20) 7839-3411; fax (20) 7839-6174; e-mail comsci@gn.apc.org; f. 1948 to promote collaboration in geological, geochemical, geophysical and remote sensing techniques and the exchange of information; Geological Programme Officer Dr SIYAN MALOMO.

SPORT

Commonwealth Games Federation: 2nd Floor, 138 Piccadilly, London, W1J 7NR; tel. (20) 7491-8801; fax (20) 7409-7803; e-mail info@thecgf.com; internet www.thecgf.com; the Games were first held in 1930 and are now held every four years; participation is limited to competitors representing the mem. countries of the Commonwealth; 2010 games: New Delhi, India, in October; mems: 72 affiliated bodies; Pres. MICHAEL FENNELL; CEO MICHAEL HOOPER.

YOUTH

Commonwealth Youth Exchange Council: 7 Lion Yard, Tremadoc Rd, London, SW4 7NQ; tel. (20) 7498-6151; fax (20) 7622-4365; e-mail mail@cyec.org.uk; internet www.cyec.org.uk; f. 1970; promotes contact between groups of young people of the United Kingdom and other Commonwealth countries by means of educational exchange visits, provides information for organizers and allocates grants; provides host governments with technical assistance for delivery of the Commonwealth Youth Forum, held every two years (2007: Uganda); 222 mem. orgs; Chief Exec. V. S. G. CRAGGS; publs *Contact* (handbook), *Exchange* (newsletter), *Final Communiqués* (of the Commonwealth Youth Forums), *Safety and Welfare* (guide-lines for Commonwealth Youth Exchange groups).

Duke of Edinburgh's Award International Association: Award House, 7–11 St Matthew St, London, SW1P 2JT; tel. (20) 7222-4242; fax (20) 7222-4141; e-mail sect@intaward.org; internet www.intaward.org; f. 1956; a self-development programme for young people, comprising Service, an Adventurous Journey, Physical Recreation, and Skills, in which participants set their own goals and measure their progress against them; more than 6m. young people have participated in the scheme; has a presence in more than 125 countries (not confined to the Commonwealth); Sec.-Gen. GILLIAN SHIRAZI; publs *Award World* (2 a year), *Annual Report*, handbooks and guides.

MISCELLANEOUS

Commonwealth Countries League: 7 The Park, London, NW11 7SS; tel. (20) 8451-6711; e-mail info@ccl-int.org.uk; internet www.ccl-int.org.uk; f. 1925 to secure equal opportunities and status between men and women in the Commonwealth, to act as a link between Commonwealth women's orgs, and to promote and finance secondary education of disadvantaged girls of high ability in their own countries, through the CCL Educational Fund; holds meetings with speakers and an annual conf., organizes the annual Commonwealth Fair for fund-raising; individual mems and affiliated socs in the Commonwealth; Sec. STUART HETHERINGTON-BELL; publs *CCL Newsletter* (3 a year), *Annual Report*.

Commonwealth War Graves Commission: 2 Marlow Rd, Maidenhead, Berks, SL6 7DX; tel. (1628) 634221; fax (1628) 771208; internet www.cwgc.org; casualty and cemetery enquiries; e-mail casualty.enq@cwgc.org; f. 1917 (as Imperial War Graves Commission); responsible for the commemoration in perpetuity of the 1.7m. members of the Commonwealth Forces who died during the wars of 1914–18 and 1939–45; provides for the marking and maintenance of war graves and memorials at some 23,000 locations in 150 countries; mems: Australia, Canada, India, New Zealand, South Africa, United Kingdom; Pres. HRH The Duke of KENT; Dir-Gen. RICHARD KELLAWAY.

Council of Commonwealth Societies: c/o Royal Commonwealth Society, 25 Northumberland Ave, London, WC2N 5AP; tel. (20) 7766-9200; fax (20) 7930-9705; e-mail ccs@rcsint.org; internet www.rcsint.org/day; f. 1947; provides a forum for the exchange of information regarding activities of mem. orgs which promote understanding among countries of the Commonwealth; co-ordinates the distribution of the Commonwealth Day message by Queen Elizabeth, organizes the observance of and promotes Commonwealth Day, and produces educational materials relating to the occasion; seeks to raise the profile of the Commonwealth; mems: 30 official and unofficial Commonwealth orgs; Chair. Lord ALAN WATSON; Sec. ALICE KAWOWA.

Royal Commonwealth Ex-Services League: 48 Pall Mall, London, SW1Y 5JG; tel. (20) 7973-7263; fax (20) 7973-7308; e-mail mgordon-roe@commonwealthveterans.org.uk; internet www.commonwealthveterans.org.uk; links the ex-service orgs in the Commonwealth, assists ex-servicemen of the Crown who are resident abroad; holds triennial confs; 56 mem. orgs in 48 countries; Grand Pres. HRH The Duke of EDINBURGH; publ. *Annual Report*.

Royal Commonwealth Society: 25 Northumberland Ave, London, WC2N 5AP; tel. (20) 7930-6733; fax (20) 7930-9705; e-mail info@rcsint.org; internet www.rcsint.org; f. 1868; to promote international understanding of the Commonwealth and its people; organizes meetings and seminars on topical issues, and cultural and social events; library housed by Cambridge University Library; more than 10,000 mems; Chair. Baroness PRASHAR; Dir STUART MOLE; publs *Annual Report, Newsletter* (3 a year), conference reports.

Royal Over-Seas League: Over-Seas House, Park Place, St James's St, London, SW1A 1LR; tel. (20) 7408-0214; fax (20) 7499-6738; e-mail info@rosl.org.uk; internet www.rosl.org.uk; f. 1910 to promote friendship and understanding in the Commonwealth; clubhouses in London and Edinburgh; membership is open to all British subjects and Commonwealth citizens; Dir-Gen. ROBERT F. NEWELL; publ. *Overseas* (quarterly).

Victoria League for Commonwealth Friendship: 55 Leinster Sq., London, W2 4PW; tel. (20) 7243-2633; fax (20) 7229-2994; e-mail victorialeaguehq@btconnect.com; internet www.victorialeague.co.uk; f. 1901; aims to further personal friendship among Commonwealth peoples and to provide hospitality for visitors; maintains Student House, providing accommodation for students from Commonwealth countries; has brs elsewhere in the UK and abroad; Chair. JOHN KELLY; Gen. Sec. JOHN M. W. ALLAN; publ. *Annual Report*.

THE COMMONWEALTH OF INDEPENDENT STATES—CIS

Address: 220000 Minsk, Kirava 17, Belarus.
Telephone: (17) 222-35-17; **fax:** (17) 227-23-39; **e-mail:** postmaster@www.cis.minsk.by; **internet:** www.cis.minsk.by.

The Commonwealth of Independent States is a voluntary association of 11 states, established at the time of the collapse of the USSR in December 1991.

MEMBERS

Armenia	Moldova
Azerbaijan	Russia
Belarus	Tajikistan
Georgia	Ukraine
Kazakhstan	Uzbekistan
Kyrgyzstan	

Note: Azerbaijan signed the Alma-Ata Declaration (see below), but in October 1992 the Azerbaijan legislature voted against ratification of the foundation documents by which the Commonwealth of Independent States had been established in December 1991. Azerbaijan formally became a member of the CIS in September 1993, after the legislature voted in favour of membership. Georgia was admitted to the CIS in December 1993. Turkmenistan has associate membership of the CIS, reduced from full membership in August 2005.

Organization
(April 2008)

COUNCIL OF HEADS OF STATE

This is the supreme body of the CIS, on which all the member states of the Commonwealth are represented at the level of head of state, for discussion of issues relating to the co-ordination of Commonwealth activities and the development of the Minsk Agreement. Decisions of the Council are taken by common consent, with each state having equal voting rights. The Council meets at least once a year. An extraordinary meeting may be convened on the initiative of the majority of Commonwealth heads of state. The chairmanship of the Council is normally rotated among member states.

COUNCIL OF HEADS OF GOVERNMENT

This Council convenes for meetings at least once every three months; an extraordinary sitting may be convened on the initiative of a majority of Commonwealth heads of government. The two Councils may discuss and take necessary decisions on important domestic and external issues, and may hold joint sittings.

Working and auxiliary bodies, composed of authorized representatives of the participating states, may be set up on a permanent or interim basis on the decision of the Council of Heads of State and the Council of Heads of Government.

EXECUTIVE COMMITTEE

The Executive Committee was established by the Council of Heads of State in April 1999 to supersede the existing Secretariat, the Inter-state Economic Committee and other working bodies and committees, in order to improve the efficient functioning of the organization. The Executive Committee co-operates closely with other CIS bodies including the councils of foreign ministers and defence ministers; the Economic Council; Council of Border Troops Commanders; the Collective Security Council; the Secretariat of the Council of the Inter-parliamentary Assembly; and the Inter-state Committee for Statistics.

Executive Secretary and Chairman of the Executive Committee: SERGEY N. LEBEDEV (Russia).

Activities

On 8 December 1991 the heads of state of Belarus, Russia and Ukraine signed the Minsk Agreement, providing for the establishment of a Commonwealth of Independent States. Formal recognition of the dissolution of the USSR was incorporated in a second treaty (the Alma-Ata Declaration), signed by 11 heads of state in the then Kazakh capital, Alma-Ata (Almaty), later in that month.

In March 1992 a meeting of the CIS Council of Heads of Government decided to establish a commission to examine the resolution that 'all CIS member states are the legal successors of the rights and obligations of the former Soviet Union'. Documents relating to the legal succession of the Soviet Union were signed at a meeting of Heads of State in July. In April an agreement establishing an Inter-parliamentary Assembly (IPA), signed by Armenia, Belarus, Kazakhstan, Kyrgyzstan, Russia, Tajikistan and Uzbekistan, was published. The first Assembly was held in Bishkek, Kyrgyzstan, in September, attended by delegates from all these countries, with the exception of Uzbekistan.

A CIS Charter was adopted at the meeting of the heads of state in Minsk, Belarus, in January 1993. The Charter, providing for a defence alliance, an inter-state court and an economic co-ordination committee, was to serve as a framework for closer co-operation and was signed by all of the members except Moldova, Turkmenistan and Ukraine.

In May 1994 the CIS and UNCTAD signed a co-operation accord. A similar agreement was concluded with the UN Economic Commission for Europe in June 1996. Working contacts have also been established with ILO, UNHCR, WHO and the European Union. In June 1998 the IPA approved a decision to sign the European Social Charter (see Council of Europe); a declaration of co-operation between the Assembly and the OSCE Parliamentary Assembly was also signed.

In November 1995, at the Council of Heads of Government meeting, Russia expressed concern at the level of non-payment of debts by CIS members, which was deemed to be hindering further integration. At the meeting of the Council in April 1996 a long-term plan for the integrated development of the CIS, incorporating measures for further socio-economic, military and political co-operation, was approved.

In March 1997 the then Russian President, Boris Yeltsin, admitted that the CIS institutional structure had failed to ameliorate the severe economic situation of certain member states. Nevertheless, support for the CIS as an institution was reaffirmed by the participants during the meeting. At the heads of state meeting held in Chişinău, Moldova, in October, Russia was reportedly criticized by the other country delegations for failing to implement CIS agreements, for hindering development of the organization and for failing to resolve regional conflicts. Russia, for its part, urged all member states to participate more actively in defining, adopting and implementing CIS policies. Meeting in April 1999 the Council of Heads of Government adopted guide-lines for restructuring the CIS and for the future development of the organization. Economic co-operation was to be a priority area of activity, and in particular, the establishment of a free-trade zone. In June 2000 the Councils of Heads of State and Government issued a declaration concerning the maintenance of strategic stability, approved a plan and schedule for pursuing economic integration, and adopted a short-term programme for combating international terrorism (perceived to be a significant threat in central Asia). An informal CIS 10-year 'jubilee' summit, convened in November 2001, adopted a statement identifying the collective pursuit of stable socio-economic development and integration on a global level as the organization's principal objectives. A summit of heads of state convened in January 2003 agreed that the position of Chairman of the Council of Heads of State (hitherto held by consecutive Russian presidents) should be rotated henceforth among member states. Leonid Kuchma, then President of Ukraine, was elected as the new Chairman. (In September 2004, however, Russia's President Vladimir Putin was reappointed temporarily as the Chairman of the Council, owing to a perceived deterioration in the international security situation and a declared need for experienced leadership.) A summit meeting convened in September 2003, in Yalta, Ukraine, focused on measures to combat crime and terrorism, and endorsed an economic plan for 2003–10.

In September 2004 the CIS Council of Heads of State, meeting in Astana, Kazakhstan, was dominated by consideration of measures to combat terrorism and extremist violence, following a month in which Russia, including North Ossetia, had experienced several atrocities committed against civilian targets. As part of a wider consideration of a reorganization of the CIS, the Council resolved to establish a Security Council.

Member states of the CIS have formed alliances of various kinds among themselves, thereby potentially undermining the unity of the Commonwealth. In March 1996 Belarus, Kazakhstan, Kyrgyzstan and Russia signed the Quadripartite Treaty for greater integration. This envisaged the establishment of a 'New Union', based, initially on a common market and customs union, and was to be open to all CIS members and the Baltic states. Consequently these countries (with Tajikistan) became founding members of the Eurasian Economic Community (EURASEC), inaugurated in October 2001. In April 1996 Belarus and Russia signed the Treaty on the Formation of a

Community of Sovereign Republics (CSR), which provided for extensive economic, political and military co-operation. In April 1997 the two countries signed a further Treaty of Union and, in addition, initialled the Charter of the Union, which detailed the procedures and institutions designed to develop a common infrastructure, a single currency and a joint defence policy within the CSR, with the eventual aim of 'voluntary unification of the member states'. The Charter was signed in May and ratified by the respective legislatures the following month. The Union's Parliamentary Assembly, comprising 36 members from the legislature of each country, convened in official session for the first time shortly afterwards. Azerbaijan, Georgia, Moldova and Ukraine co-operated increasingly from the late 1990s as the so-called GUAM group, which envisaged implementing joint economic and transportation initiatives (such developing a Eurasian Trans-Caucasus transportation corridor) and establishing the GUAM Free-Trade Zone. Uzbekistan joined in April 1999, creating GUUAM. The group agreed in September 2000 to convene regular annual summits of member countries' heads of state and to organize meetings of ministers of foreign affairs at least twice a year. In May 2005 Uzbekistan left GUUAM; consequently, the group reverted to the name GUAM. Meeting in Kyiv, Ukraine, in May 2006 the heads of state of Azerbaijan, Georgia, Moldova and Ukraine adopted a charter formally inaugurating GUAM as a full international organization and renaming it Organization for Democracy and Economic Development—GUAM. The heads of state suggested that the GUAM countries might withdraw from the CIS. In April 2003 Armenia, Belarus, Kazakhstan, Kyrgyzstan, Tajikistan and Russia established the Collective Security Treaty Organization (see below). Russia, Armenia, Azerbaijan and Georgia convene regular meetings as the 'Caucasian Group of Four'. In 1994 Kazakhstan, Kyrgyzstan, Tajikistan and Uzbekistan formed the Central Asian Economic Community. In February 2002 those countries relaunched the grouping as the Central Asian Co-operation Organization (CACO), to indicate that co-operation between member states had extended to political and security matters. Russia joined the organization in 2004. In October 2005, at a summit of CACO leaders in St Petersburg, Russia, it was announced that the organization would be merged with EURASEC. This was achieved in January 2006 with the accession to EURASEC of Uzbekistan, which had hitherto been the only member of CACO that did not also belong to the Community.

The CIS regularly sends observer teams to monitor legislative and presidential elections in member states. In March 2005 Ukraine announced that it was to suspend its participation in the CIS Election Monitoring Organization (CIS-EMO, registered as a non-governmental organization in December 2003), owing to discrepancies in the findings of the observers of that body with those of the Organization for Security and Co-operation in Europe (OSCE) during the Ukrainian presidential election that was held in October and December 2004. The CIS-EMO's assessment had failed to concur with that of the OSCE on several previous occasions.

A number of multilateral meetings of senior representatives of CIS member states held during early 2005, including a meeting of foreign ministers convened in mid-March and a meeting of prime ministers in early April, discussed new recommendations for restructuring the organs of the CIS, with a view to increasing the overall efficiency of the organization. The recommendations were presented to the August 2005 summit of the Council of Heads of State, which was held in Kazan, Russia. Several declarations were signed at the Kazan summit, including a document on co-operation in humanitarian projects and combating illegal migration; however, a consensus on far-reaching reform of the organization failed to be reached by CIS leaders at that time.

The heads of state of Armenia, Georgia, Turkmenistan (which had downgraded its full membership of the CIS to associate membership in 2005) and Ukraine did not attend an informal summit of CIS leaders convened in Moscow in July 2006. Heads of state attending the regular summit meeting for 2006, convened in November, in Minsk, Belarus, urged CIS foreign ministers to submit during 2007 proposals for revitalizing the organization.

At the 2007 CIS summit meeting, held in Dushanbe, Tajikistan, in October, CIS heads of state (excluding those of Georgia and Turkmenistan) adopted the 'Concept for Further Development of the CIS' and an action plan for its implementation. Azerbaijan endorsed the document, but reserved the right to abstain from implementing certain clauses. The Concept cited the 'long-term formation of an integrated economic and political association' as a major objective of the Commonwealth, and determined that the multi-sector nature of the organization should be retained and that the harmonized development of its interacting spheres should continue to be promoted. Further goals detailed in the Concept included: supporting regional socio-economic stability and international security; improving the economic competitiveness of member states; supporting the accession of member states to the WTO; improving regional living standards and conditions; promoting inter-parliamentary co-operation; increasing co-operation between national migration agencies; harmonizing national legislation; and standardizing CIS structures and bodies. The state chairing the Council of Heads of State was to have responsibility for co-ordinating the implementation of the Concept. Leaders attending the Dushanbe summit also determined to establish a special body to oversee migration in the region and adopted an agreement aimed at promoting the civil rights of migrants.

ECONOMIC AFFAIRS

At a meeting of the Council of Heads of Government in March 1992 agreement was reached on repayment of the foreign debt of the former USSR. Agreements were also signed on pensions, joint tax policy and the servicing of internal debt. In May an accord on repayment of inter-state debt and the issue of balance-of-payments statements was adopted by the heads of government, meeting in Tashkent, Uzbekistan. In July it was decided to establish an economic court in Minsk.

The CIS Charter, adopted in January 1993, provided for the establishment of an economic co-ordination committee. In February, at a meeting of the heads of foreign economic departments, a foreign economic council was formed. In May all member states, with the exception of Turkmenistan, adopted a declaration of support for increased economic union and, in September, agreement was reached by all states except Ukraine and Turkmenistan on a framework for economic union, including the gradual removal of tariffs and creation of a currency union. Turkmenistan was subsequently admitted as a full member of the economic union in December 1993 and Ukraine as an associate member in April 1994.

At the Council of Heads of Government meeting in September 1994 all member states, except Turkmenistan, agreed to establish an Inter-state Economic Committee to implement economic treaties adopted within the context of an economic union. The establishment of a payments union to improve the settlement of accounts was also agreed. In April 1998 CIS heads of state resolved to incorporate the functions of the Inter-state Economic Committee, along with those of other working bodies and sectional committees, into a new CIS Executive Committee.

In October 1997 seven heads of government signed a document on implementing the 'Concept for the Integrated Economic Development of the CIS'. The development of economic co-operation between the member states was a priority task of the special forum on reform held in June 1998.

Guide-lines adopted by the Council of Heads of State in April 1999 concerning the future development of the CIS identified economic co-operation and the establishment of a free-trade zone (see Trade) as priority areas for action. At the summit meeting held in September 2003 CIS foreign ministers approved a draft plan aimed at improving and enhancing economic co-operation until 2010. Improving the economic competitiveness of member states was a primary focus of the 'Concept for Further Development of the CIS' that was adopted by the organization's October 2007 summit meeting.

TRADE

Agreement was reached on the free movement of goods between republics at a meeting of the Council of Heads of State in February 1992, and in April 1994 an agreement on the creation of a CIS free-trade zone (envisaged as the first stage of economic union) was concluded. In July a council of the heads of customs committees, meeting in Moscow, approved a draft framework for customs legislation in CIS countries, to facilitate the establishment of a free-trade zone. The framework was approved by all the participants, with the exception of Turkmenistan. In April 1999 CIS heads of state signed a protocol to the 1994 free-trade area accord, which aimed to accelerate co-operation. In June 2000 the Council of Heads of State adopted a plan and schedule for the implementation of priority measures related to the creation of the free-trade zone, and at the September 2003 summit meeting Russia, Belarus, Kazakhstan and Ukraine signed the Union of Four agreement establishing the framework for a Common Economic Space (CES, see below).

At the first session of the Inter-state Economic Committee in November 1994 draft legislation regarding a customs union was approved. The development of a customs union and the strengthening of intra-CIS trade were objectives endorsed by all participants, with the exception of Georgia, at the Council of Heads of Government meeting held in March 1997. In March 1998 Russia, Belarus, Kazakhstan and Kyrgyzstan signed an agreement establishing a customs union, which was to be implemented in two stages: firstly, the removal of trade restrictions and the unification of trade and customs regulations; followed by the integration of economic, monetary and trade policies. In February 1999 Tajikistan signed the 1998 agreement to become the fifth member of the customs union. In October 1999 the heads of state of the five member states of the customs union reiterated their political determination to implement the customs union and approved a programme to harmonize national legislation to create a single economic space. In May 2000 the heads of state announced their intention to raise the status of the customs union to that of an inter-state economic organization, and, in October, the leaders signed the founding treaty of EURASEC. Under the new structure member states aimed to formulate a unified foreign economic policy, and, taking into account existing customs agreements, collectively to pursue the creation of the planned single economic space. In the following month the five member governments signed an agreement enabling visa-free travel within the new Community. (Earlier in 2000 Russia had withdrawn from a CIS-wide visa-free travel arrangement agreed in 1992. Kazakhstan, Turkmenistan and Uzbekistan subsequently withdrew from the agreement, and Belarus announced its intention to do so in late 2005.) In December 2000 member states of the Community adopted several documents aimed at facilitating economic co-operation. EURASEC, governed by an inter-state council based in Astana, Kazakhstan, was formally inaugurated in October 2001. In October 2003 the Community was granted observer status at the UN. The Union of Four agreement on establishing the framework for a CES, adopted in September 2003 by the leaders of Belarus, Kazakhstan, Russia and Ukraine, envisaged the creation of a free-trade zone and the gradual harmonization of tariffs, customs and transport legislation. While participation at each stage would remain optional, decisions would be obligatory and certain areas of sovereignty would eventually be ceded to a council of heads of state and a commission. The Union of Four Agreement entered into force in April 2004. Meeting on the sidelines of the CIS summit held in October 2007, EURASEC leaders determined to establish a fully operational customs union by 2011, with Belarus, Kazakhstan and Russia as the founding members, and Kyrgyzstan, Tajikistan and Uzbekistan to join at a later date, once they had achieved the requisite accession conditions. Ukraine, which was also committed to participation in the GUAM Free-Trade Zone, was not at that time participating actively in the negotiating process on the CES. Also in May 2004, at a meeting between the prime ministers of the CIS member states, all participants except Ukraine signed a protocol to abolish all restrictions on trade by 2012. It is envisaged that the CES, which is open to accession by other CIS member states, will form the basis of the planned wider EURASEC economic integration. Despite significant growth in the gross domestic product of the poorer states of the CIS (Armenia, Azerbaijan, Georgia, Kyrgyzstan, Moldova, Tajikistan and Uzbekistan, known as the 'CIS-7'), in April 2005 the IMF called for greater harmonization of trade rules within the CIS, as well as liberalization of transit policies and the removal of non-tariff barriers.

The CIS maintains a 'loose co-ordination' on issues related to applications by member states to join the World Trade Organization (WTO). Supporting the accession of member states to the WTO was a primary focus of the Concept for Further Development of the CIS that was adopted by the October 2007 summit meeting of the Commonwealth.

BANKING AND FINANCE

In February 1992 CIS heads of state agreed to retain the rouble as the common currency for trade between the republics. However, in July 1993, in an attempt to control inflation, notes printed before 1993 were withdrawn from circulation and no new ones were issued until January 1994. Despite various agreements to recreate the 'rouble zone', including a protocol agreement signed in September 1993 by six states, it effectively remained confined to Tajikistan, which joined in January 1994, and Belarus, which joined in April. Both those countries proceeded to introduce national currencies in May 1995. In January 1993, at the signing of the CIS Charter, the member countries endorsed the establishment of an inter-state bank to facilitate payments between the republics and to co-ordinate monetary-credit policy. Russia was to hold 50% of shares in the bank, but decisions were to be made only with a two-thirds majority approval. In December 2000, in accordance with the CSR and Treaty of Union (see above), the Presidents of Belarus and Russia signed an agreement providing for the adoption by Belarus of the Russian currency from 1 January 2005, and for the introduction of a new joint Union currency by 1 January 2008; the adoption by Belarus of the Russian currency was, however, subsequently postponed.

In October 2004 Russia and Kazakhstan announced a proposal to establish a CIS Development Bank, with a capital of €1m.

DEFENCE

An Agreement on Armed Forces and Border Troops was concluded on 30 December 1991, at the same time as the Agreement on Strategic Forces. This confirmed the right of member states to set up their own armed forces and appointed Commanders-in-Chief of the Armed Forces and of the Border Troops, who were to elaborate joint security procedures. In February 1992 an agreement was signed stipulating that the commander of the strategic forces was subordinate to the Council of Heads of States. Eight states agreed on a unified command for general-purpose (i.e. non-strategic) armed forces for a transitional period of two years. Azerbaijan, Moldova and Ukraine resolved to establish independent armed forces.

In January 1992 Commissions on the Black Sea Fleet (control of which was disputed by Russia and Ukraine) and the Caspian Flotilla (the former Soviet naval forces on the Caspian Sea) were established.

The formation of a defence alliance was provided for in the CIS Charter adopted in January 1993; a proposal by Russia to assume control of all nuclear weapons in the former USSR was rejected at the same time.

In June 1993 CIS defence ministers agreed to abolish CIS joint military command and to abandon efforts to maintain a unified defence structure. The existing CIS command was to be replaced, on a provisional basis, by a 'joint staff for co-ordinating military co-operation between the states of the Commonwealth'. It was widely reported that Russia had encouraged the decision to abolish the joint command, owing to concerns at the projected cost of a CIS joint military structure and support within Russia's military leadership of bilateral military agreements with the country's neighbours. In December the Council of Defence Ministers agreed to establish a secretariat to co-ordinate military co-operation as a replacement to the joint military command. In November 1995 the Council of Defence Ministers authorized the establishment of a Joint Air Defence System, to be co-ordinated largely by Russia. A CIS combat duty system was under development in the early 2000s. Russia and Belarus were also developing a joint air-defence unit in the context of the CSR (see above). In February 2006 Georgia withdrew from the Council of Defence Ministers, on the grounds that it intended to join NATO and did not wish to be a member of both groupings.

In September 1996 the first meeting of the inter-state commission for military economic co-operation was held; a draft agreement on the export of military projects and services to third countries was approved. The basic principles of a programme for greater military and technical co-operation were approved by the Council of Defence Ministers in March 1997. In April 1998 the Council proposed drawing up a draft programme for military and technical co-operation between member countries and also discussed procedures advising on the use and maintenance of armaments and military hardware. The programme was approved by CIS heads of state in October 2002. Draft proposals relating to information security for the military were approved by the Council in December. It was remarked that the inadequate funding of the Council was impeding co-operation.

In August 1996 the Council of Defence Ministers condemned what it described as the political, economic and military threat implied in any expansion of NATO. The statement was not signed by Ukraine. The eighth plenary session of the IPA, held in November, urged NATO countries to abandon plans for the organization's expansion. Strategic co-operation between NATO and CIS member states increased from the mid-1990s, particularly with Russia and Ukraine. In the late 1990s the USA established bilateral military assistance programmes for Azerbaijan, Georgia, and Uzbekistan. Uzbekistan and other central Asian CIS states played a support role in the US-led action initiated in late 2001 against the then Taliban-held areas of Afghanistan (see below).

During September 2004 the CIS Council of Heads of State determined to establish a Security Council, comprising the ministers responsible for foreign affairs and for defence, and heads of security and border control.

REGIONAL SECURITY

At a meeting of heads of government in March 1992 agreements on settling inter-state conflicts were signed by all participating states (except Turkmenistan). At the same meeting an agreement on the status of border troops was signed by five states. In May a five-year Collective Security Treaty was signed. In July further documents were signed on collective security and it was agreed to establish joint peace-making forces to intervene in CIS disputes. In April 1999 Armenia, Belarus, Kazakhstan, Kyrgyzstan, Russia and Tajikistan signed a protocol to extend the Collective Security Treaty (while Azerbaijan, Georgia and Uzbekistan withdrew from the agreement).

In September 1993 the Council of Heads of State agreed to establish a Bureau of Organized Crime, to be based in Moscow. A meeting of the Council of Border Troop Commanders in January 1994 prepared a report on the issue of illegal migration and drug trade across the external borders of the CIS; Moldova, Georgia and Tajikistan did not attend. A programme to counter organized crime within the CIS was approved by heads of government, meeting in Moscow, in April 1996. In March 2001 CIS interior ministers agreed to strengthen co-operation in combating transnational organized crime, in view of reportedly mounting levels of illicit drugs trafficking in the region.

The fourth plenary session of the IPA in March 1994 established a commission for the resolution of the conflicts in the secessionist regions of Nagornyi Karabakh (Azerbaijan) and Abkhazia (Georgia) and endorsed the use of CIS peace-keeping forces. In the following month Russia agreed to send peace-keeping forces to Georgia, and the dispatch of peace-keeping forces was approved by the Council of Defence Ministers in October. The subsequent session of the IPA in October adopted a resolution to send groups of military observers to Abkhazia and to Moldova. The inter-parliamentary commission on the conflict between Abkhazia and Georgia proposed initiating direct negotiations with the two sides in order to reach a peaceful settlement.

In December 1994 the Council of Defence Ministers enlarged the mandate of the commander of the CIS collective peace-keeping forces in Tajikistan: when necessary CIS military contingents were permitted to engage in combat operations without the prior consent of individual governments. At the Heads of State meeting in Moscow in January 1996 Georgia's proposal to impose sanctions against Abkhazia was approved, in an attempt to achieve a resolution of the conflict. Provisions on arrangements relating to collective peace-keeping operations were approved at the meeting; the training of military and civilian personnel for these operations was to commence in October. In March 1997 the Council of Defence Ministers agreed to extend the peace-keeping mandates for CIS forces in Tajikistan and Abkhazia (following much disagreement, the peace-keepers' mandate in Abkhazia was further renewed in October). At a meeting of the Council in January 1998 a request from Georgia that the CIS carry out its decisions to settle the conflict with Abkhazia was added to the agenda. The Council discussed the promotion of military co-operation and the improvement of peace-making activities, and declared that there was progress in the formation of the collective security system, although the situation in the North Caucasus remained tense. In April President Yeltsin requested that the Armenian and Azerbaijani presidents sign a document to end the conflict in Nagornyi Karabakh; the two subsequently issued a statement expressing their support for a political settlement of the conflict. A document proposing a settlement of the conflict in Abkhazia was also drawn up, but the resolutions adopted were not accepted by Abkhazia. Against the wishes of the Abkhazian authorities, the mandate for the CIS troops in the region was extended to cover the whole of the Gali district. The mandate expired in July 1998, but the forces remained in the region while its renewal was debated. In April 1999 the Council of Heads of State agreed to a retrospective extension of the operation's mandate; the mandate subsequently continued to be renewed at six-monthly intervals until March 2003 when it was extended indefinitely. The CIS peace-keeping force in Abkhazia works in close co-operation with the UN Observer Mission in Georgia. The two forces have conducted regular joint patrols of the upper Kodori valley since 2002. The mandate of the CIS peace-keeping operation in Tajikistan was terminated in June 2000. In February 2001 it was reported that regulations had been drafted for the institution of a CIS Special Envoy for the Settlement of Conflicts.

In February 1995 a non-binding memorandum on maintaining peace and stability was adopted by heads of state, meeting in Almaty. Signatories were to refrain from applying military, political, economic or other pressure on another member country, to seek the peaceful resolution of border or territorial disputes and not to support or assist separatist movements active in other member countries. In April 1998 the Council of Defence Ministers approved a draft document proposing that coalition forces be provided with technical equipment to enhance collective security.

In June 1998, at a session of the Council of Border Troop Commanders, some 33 documents were signed relating to border co-operation. A framework protocol on the formation and expedient use of a border troops reserve in critical situations was discussed and signed by several participants. A register of work in scientific and engineering research carried out in CIS countries in the interests of border troops was also adopted. A programme aimed at enhancing co-operation between border troops was adopted by heads of state in October 2002. In February 2004 an expert group drafted regulations for the establishment of a common system to register foreign nationals and stateless persons.

In June 1998 CIS interior ministers, meeting in Tashkent, Uzbekistan, adopted a number of co-operation agreements, including a framework for the exchange of information between CIS law-enforcement agencies; it was also decided to maintain contact with Interpol.

An emergency meeting of heads of state in October 1996 discussed the ongoing conflict in nearby Afghanistan and the consequent threat to regional security. The participants requested the UN Security Council to adopt measures to resolve the situation. In May 2000 the six signatory states to the Collective Security Treaty pledged to strengthen military co-operation in view of the perceived threat to their security from the Taliban regime in Afghanistan. In October those countries signed an agreement on the Status of Forces and Means of Collective Security Systems, establishing a joint rapid deployment function. The so-called CIS Collective Rapid Reaction Force was to be assembled to combat insurgencies, with particular reference to trans-border terrorism from Afghanistan, and also to deter trans-border illegal drugs trafficking (see above). In June 2001 a CIS Anti-terrorism Centre was established in Moscow. The centre was to co-ordinate counter-terrorism activities and to compile a database of international terrorist organizations operating in member states. In October, in response to the major terrorist attacks perpetrated in September against targets in the USA—allegedly co-ordinated by militant fundamentalist Islamist leader Osama bin Laden—the parties to the Collective Security Treaty adopted a new anti-terrorism plan. In December 2002 the committee of the Collective Security Treaty member countries adopted a protocol on the exchange of expertise and information on terrorist organizations and their activities. In April 2003 the signatory states determined to establish the Collective Security Treaty Organization (CSTO); ratification of its founding documents was completed by September, when it applied for UN observer status. In early November CSTO co-ordinated an operation targeting drugs traffickers involving some 30,000 law enforcement officers. The signatory countries to the Collective Security Treaty participate in regular so-called 'CIS Southern Shield' joint military exercises. A CSTO joint anti-terrorism exercise, involving some 2,000 troops, was held in Kazakhstan and Kyrgyzstan in August 2004. A summit meeting of CSTO leaders held in October 2007 endorsed documents enabling the future establishment of CSTO joint peace-keeping forces and the creation of a co-ordination council for the heads of member states' emergency response agencies.

In October 2002 a Central Asian subdivision of the CIS anti-terrorism centre was established in Bishkek, Kyrgyzstan. The CIS summit in September 2003 approved draft decisions to control the sale of portable anti-aircraft missiles and to set up a joint co-ordination structure to address illegal immigration.

In November 2003, following a popular uprising against the Georgian regime, an emergency meeting of CIS foreign ministers was convened in Kyiv, Ukraine. The meeting issued a statement reaffirming Georgia's territorial integrity and calling for the restoration of the constitutional and democratic process; a CIS envoy was dispatched to the capital, Tbilisi, to mediate in a handover of power from the deposed President, Eduard Shevardnadze. In early January 2004 a team of some 70 CIS observers was present at elections to choose a new Georgian President.

In September 2004 CIS ministers of the interior, convened in Kyiv, Ukraine, agreed to draft joint programmes to combat crime and drugs trafficking in the period 2005–07. In October CIS directors of security agencies and intelligence services, meeting in Minsk, Belarus, discussed regional counter-terrorism measures, including efforts to exchange information and restrict sources of terrorist finance. The meeting adopted a new CIS programme on combating international terrorism and manifestations of extremism, to cover the period 2005–07.

LEGISLATIVE CO-OPERATION

An agreement on legislative co-operation was signed at an Inter-Parliamentary Conference in January 1992; joint commissions were established to co-ordinate action on economy, law, pensions, housing, energy and ecology. The CIS Charter, formulated in January 1993, provided for the establishment of an inter-state court. In October 1994 a Convention on the rights of minorities was adopted at the meeting of the Heads of State. In May 1995, at the sixth plenary session of the IPA, several acts to improve co-ordination of legislation were approved, relating to migration of labour, consumer rights, and the rights of prisoners of war.

The creation of a Council of Ministers of Internal Affairs was approved at the Heads of State meeting in January 1996; the Council was to promote co-operation between the law-enforcement bodies of member states. The IPA has approved a number of model laws, relating to areas including banking and financial services; charity; defence; the economy; education; ecology; the regulation of refugee problems; and social issues, including obligatory social insurance against production accidents and occupational diseases. In November 2003 IPA approved 12 model laws relating to the economy, defence, social policy and ecology; and a model law on combating terrorism is being formulated.

OTHER ACTIVITIES

The CIS has held a number of discussions relating to the environment. In July 1992 agreements were concluded to establish an Inter-state Ecological Council. It was also agreed in that month to establish *Mir*, an inter-state television and radio company. In October 2002 a decision was made by CIS heads of government to enhance mutual understanding and co-operation between members countries through *Mir* radio and television broadcasts. In February 1995 the IPA established a Council of Heads of News Agencies, in order to promote the concept of a single information area. CIS leaders meeting in Moscow, Russia, in May 2005 agreed to sign a declaration aimed at enhancing co-operation between CIS members in the humanitarian, cultural and scientific spheres.

A CIS Electric Energy Council was established in 1992, and a Petroleum and Gas Council was created at a Heads of Government meeting in March 1993, to guarantee energy supplies and to invest in the Siberian petroleum industry. The Council was to have a secretariat based in Tyumen, Siberia. In October 2002 the Council of Heads of Government signed a co-operation agreement on energy effectiveness and power supply. In the field of civil aviation, the Inter-state Economic Committee agreed in February 1997 to establish an Aviation Alliance to promote co-operation between the countries' civil aviation industries.

CO-OPERATION COUNCIL FOR THE ARAB STATES OF THE GULF

Address: POB 7153, Riyadh 11462, Saudi Arabia.
Telephone: (1) 482-7777; **fax:** (1) 482-9089; **internet:** www.gcc-sg.org.

More generally known as the Gulf Co-operation Council (GCC), the organization was established on 25 May 1981 by six Arab states.

MEMBERS*

Bahrain	Oman	Saudi Arabia
Kuwait	Qatar	United Arab Emirates

*In December 2001 the Supreme Council admitted Yemen (which applied to join the organization as a full member in 1996) as a member of the GCC's Arab Bureau of Education for the Gulf States, as a participant in meetings of GCC ministers of health and of labour and social affairs, and, alongside the GCC member states, as a participant in the biennial Gulf Cup football tournament. Negotiations on Yemen's full accession to the GCC were under way in 2008.

Organization
(April 2008)

SUPREME COUNCIL

The Supreme Council is the highest authority of the GCC. It comprises the heads of member states and meets annually in ordinary session, and in emergency session if demanded by two or more members. The Council also convenes an annual consultative meeting. The Presidency of the Council is undertaken by each state in turn, in alphabetical order. The Supreme Council draws up the overall policy of the organization; it discusses recommendations and laws presented to it by the Ministerial Council and the Secretariat General in preparation for endorsement. The GCC's charter provided for the creation of a commission for the settlement of disputes between member states, to be attached to and appointed by the Supreme Council. The Supreme Council convenes the commission for the settlement of disputes on an ad hoc basis to address altercations between member states as they arise.

MINISTERIAL COUNCIL

The Ministerial Council consists of the foreign ministers of member states (or other ministers acting on their behalf), meeting every three months, and in emergency session if demanded by two or more members. It prepares for the meetings of the Supreme Council, and draws up policies, recommendations, studies and projects aimed at developing co-operation and co-ordination among member states in various spheres. GCC ministerial committees have been established in a number of areas of co-operation; sectoral ministerial meetings are held periodically.

SUPREME DEFENCE COUNCIL

In December 2001 the Supreme Council authorized the establishment of a Supreme Defence Council. This was to be composed of defence ministers meeting on an annual basis to consider security matters and supervise the implementation of the organization's joint defence pact.

CONSULTATIVE COMMISSION

The Consultative Commission, comprising 30 members (five from each member state) nominated for a three-year period, acts as an advisory body, considering matters referred to it by the Supreme Council.

SECRETARIAT GENERAL

The Secretariat assists member states in implementing recommendations by the Supreme and Ministerial Councils, and prepares reports and studies, budgets and accounts. The Secretary-General is appointed by the Supreme Council for a three-year term renewable once. The position is rotated among member states in order to ensure equal representation. The Secretariat comprises the following divisions and departments: Political Affairs; Economic Affairs; Military Affairs; Human and Environmental Affairs; Legal Affairs; the Office of the Secretary-General; Finance and Administrative Affairs; a Patent Bureau; an Administrative Development Unit; an Internal Auditing Unit; an Information Centre; and a Telecommunications Bureau (based in Bahrain). Assistant Secretary-Generals, in charge of Political Affairs, Economic Affairs, and Military Affairs are appointed by the Ministerial Council upon the recommendation of the Secretary-General. All member states contribute in equal proportions towards the budget of the Secretariat. There is a GCC delegation office in Brussels, Belgium.

Secretary-General: ABDUL RAHMAN BIN HAMAD AL-ATTIYA (Qatar).

Activities

The GCC was established following a series of meetings of foreign ministers of the states concerned, culminating in an agreement on the basic details of its charter on 10 March 1981. The Charter was signed by the six heads of state on 25 May. It describes the organization as providing 'the means for realizing co-ordination, integration and co-operation' in all economic, social and cultural affairs.

ECONOMIC CO-OPERATION

In November 1981 GCC ministers drew up a 'unified economic agreement' covering freedom of movement of people and capital, the abolition of customs duties, technical co-operation, harmonization of banking regulations and financial and monetary co-ordination. At the same time GCC heads of state approved the formation of a Gulf Investment Corporation, to be based in Kuwait (see below). In March 1983 customs duties on domestic products of the Gulf states were abolished, and new regulations allowing free movement of workers and vehicles between member states were also introduced. A common minimum customs levy (of between 4% and 20%) on foreign imports was imposed in 1986. In February 1987 the governors of the member states' central banks agreed in principle to co-ordinate their rates of exchange, and this was approved by the Supreme Council in November. It was subsequently agreed to link the Gulf currencies to a 'basket' of other currencies. In April 1993 the Gulf central bank governors decided to allow Kuwait's currency to become part of the GCC monetary system that was established following Iraq's invasion of Kuwait in order to defend the Gulf currencies. In May 1992 GCC trade ministers announced the objective of establishing a GCC common market. Meeting in September GCC ministers reached agreement on the application of a unified system of tariffs by March 1993. A meeting of the Supreme Council, held in December 1992, however, decided to mandate GCC officials to formulate a plan for the introduction of common external tariffs, to be presented to the Council in December 1993. Only the tax on tobacco products was to be standardized from March 1993, at a rate of 50% (later increased to 70%). In April 1994 ministers of finance agreed to pursue a gradual approach to the unification of tariffs. A technical committee, which had been constituted to consider aspects of establishing a customs union, met for the first time in June 1998. In November 1999 the Supreme Council concluded an agreement to establish the customs union by 1 March 2005. However, in December 2001 the Supreme Council, meeting in Muscat, Oman, adopted a new agreement on regional economic union ('Economic Agreement Between the Arab GCC States'), which superseded the 1981 'unified economic agreement'. The new accord brought forward the deadline for the establishment of the proposed customs union to 1 January 2003 and provided for a standard tariff level of 5% for foreign imports (with the exception of 53 essential commodities previously exempted by the Supreme Council). The agreement also provided for the introduction, by 1 January 2010, of a GCC single currency, linked to the US dollar. The Supreme Council also authorized the creation of a new independent authority for overseeing the unification of specifications and standards throughout member states.

The GCC customs union was launched, as planned, on 1 January 2003. In July the GCC entered into negotiations with Yemen on harmonizing economic legislation. In December 2005 the Supreme Council approved standards for the introduction of the planned single currency and urged the prompt completion of the requirements for establishing the long-envisaged common market. The GCC Common Market was inaugurated on 1 January 2008, with monetary union and the introduction of a GCC single currency still scheduled to follow (in accordance with the provisions of the 2001 Economic Agreement Between the Arab GCC States) at the start of 2010.

In April 1993 GCC central bank governors agreed to establish a joint banking supervisory committee, in order to devise rules for GCC banks to operate in other member states. In December 1997 GCC heads of state authorized guide-lines to this effect. These were to apply only to banks established at least 10 years previously with a share capital of more than US $100m.

A GCC Economic Forum has been convened annually since 2002.

TRADE AND INDUSTRY

In 1982 a ministerial committee was formed to co-ordinate trade policies and development in the region. Technical subcommittees were established to oversee a strategic food reserve for the member states, and joint trade exhibitions (which were generally held every year until responsibility was transferred to the private sector in 1996). In 1986 the Supreme Council approved a measure whereby citizens of GCC member states were enabled to undertake certain retail trade activities in any other member state, with effect from 1 March 1987. In September 2000 GCC ministers of commerce agreed to establish a technical committee to promote the development of electronic commerce and trade among member states.

In 1976 the GCC member states formed the Gulf Organization for Industrial Consulting, based in Doha, Qatar, which promotes regional industrial development. In 1985 the Supreme Council endorsed a common industrial strategy for the Gulf states. It approved regulations stipulating that priority should be given to imports of GCC industrial products, and permitting GCC investors to obtain loans from GCC industrial development banks. In November 1986 resolutions were adopted on the protection of industrial products, and on the co-ordination of industrial projects, in order to avoid duplication. In 1989 the Ministerial Council approved the Unified GCC Foreign Capital Investment Regulations, which aimed to attract foreign investment and to co-ordinate investments amongst GCC countries. Further guide-lines to promote foreign investment in the region were formulated during 1997. In December 1999 the Supreme Council amended the conditions determining rules of origin on industrial products in order to promote direct investment and intra-Community trade. In December 1992 the Supreme Council endorsed Patent Regulations for GCC member states to facilitate regional scientific and technological research. A GCC Patent Office for the protection of intellectual property in the region, was established in 1998. In December 2006 the Supreme Council endorsed a system to unify trademarks in GCC states.

In December 1998 the Supreme Council approved a long-term strategy for regional development, covering the period 2000–25, which had been formulated by GCC ministers of planning. The strategy aimed to achieve integrated, sustainable development in all member states and the co-ordination of national development plans. The Supreme Council also approved a framework Gulf population strategy formulated by the ministers of planning. In December 2000 the Supreme Council agreed gradually to limit, by means of the imposition of quotas and deterrent taxation measures, the numbers of foreign workers admitted to member states, in order to redress the current demographic imbalance resulting from the large foreign population resident in the region (believed to comprise more than one-third of the overall population). Unified procedures and measures for facilitating the intra-regional movement of people and commercial traffic were adopted by the Supreme Council in December 2001, as well as unified standards in the areas of education and health care. In August 2003 the GCC adopted new measures permitting nationals of its member states to work in, and to seek loans from financial institutions in, any other member state.

In December 2005 the Supreme Council approved a plan to unify member states' trade policies. The Council adopted further measures aimed at facilitating the movement of people, goods and services between member countries, with consideration given to environmental issues and consumer protection, and agreed to permit GCC citizens to undertake commercial activities in all member states.

AGRICULTURE

A unified agricultural policy for GCC countries was endorsed by the Supreme Council in November 1985. Co-operation in the agricultural sector extends to consideration of the water resources in the region. Between 1983 and 1990 ministers also approved proposals for harmonizing legislation relating to water conservation, veterinary vaccines, insecticides, fertilizers, fisheries and seeds. A permanent committee on fisheries aims to co-ordinate national fisheries policies, to establish designated fishing periods and to undertake surveys of the fishing potential in the Arabian (Persian) Gulf. In February 2001 GCC ministers responsible for water and electricity determined to formulate a common water policy for the region, which experiences annual shortfalls of water. Unified agricultural quarantine laws were adopted by the Supreme Council in December 2001.

TRANSPORT, COMMUNICATIONS AND INFORMATION

During 1985 feasibility studies were undertaken on new rail and road links between member states, and on the establishment of a joint coastal transport company. A scheme to build a 1,700-km railway to link all the member states and Iraq (and thereby the European railway network) was postponed, owing to its high estimated cost. In the mid-2000s, however, a proposal to construct a railway network linking Bahrain, Qatar and Saudi Arabia was reportedly under consideration. In December 2006 the Supreme Council requested that all GCC members conclude studies on the implementation of a GCC rail network. In November 1993 ministers agreed to request assistance from the International Telecommunication Union on the establishment of a joint telecommunications network, which had been approved by ministers in 1986. The region's telecommunications systems were to be integrated through underwater fibre-optic cables and a satellite-based mobile telephone network. In the mid-1990s GCC ministers of information began convening on a regular basis with a view to formulating a joint external information policy. In November 1997 GCC interior ministers approved a simplified passport system to facilitate travel between member countries.

ENERGY AND ENVIRONMENT

In 1982 a ministerial committee was established to co-ordinate hydrocarbons policies and prices. Ministers adopted a petroleum security plan to safeguard individual members against a halt in their production, to form a stockpile of petroleum products, and to organize a boycott of any non-member country when appropriate. In December 1987 the Supreme Council adopted a plan whereby a member state whose petroleum production was disrupted could 'borrow' petroleum from other members, in order to fulfil its export obligations. GCC petroleum ministers hold occasional co-ordination meetings to discuss the agenda and policies of OPEC, to which all six member states belong.

During the early 1990s proposals were formulated to integrate the electricity networks of the six member countries. In the first stage of the plan the networks of Saudi Arabia, Bahrain, Kuwait and Qatar were to be integrated; those of the United Arab Emirates (UAE) and Oman were to be interconnected and finally linked to the others in the second stage. In December 1997 GCC heads of state declared that work should commence on the first stage of the plan, under the management of an independent authority. The estimated cost of the project was more than US $6,000m. However, it was agreed not to invite private developers to participate in construction of the grid, but that the first phase of the project should be financed by member states (to contribute 35% of the estimated $2,000m. required), and by loans from commercial banking and international monetary institutions. The Gulf Council Interconnection Authority was established in 1999, with its headquarters in Dammam, Saudi Arabia.

In December 2006 the Supreme Council declared its intention to pursue the use of nuclear energy technology in the GCC region. The Council commissioned a study to develop a joint nuclear energy programme, but emphasized that any development of this technology would be for peaceful purposes only and fully disclosed to the international community.

In December 2007 the Supreme Council adopted a green environment initiative, aimed at improving the efficiency and performance of environmental institutions in member states.

CULTURAL CO-OPERATION

The GCC Folklore Centre, based in Doha, Qatar, was established in 1983 to collect, document and classify the regional cultural heritage, publish research, sponsor and protect regional folklore, provide a database on Gulf folklore, and to promote traditional culture through education. The December 2005 summit of heads of state adopted the 'Abu Dhabi Declaration', which stressed that member states should place a strong focus on education and on the development of human resources in order better to confront global challenges.

REGIONAL SECURITY

Although no mention of defence or security was made in the original charter, the summit meeting which ratified the charter also issued a statement rejecting any foreign military presence in the region. The Supreme Council meeting in November 1981 agreed to include defence co-operation in the activities of the organization: as a result, defence ministers met in January 1982 to discuss a common security policy, including a joint air defence system and standardization of weapons. In November 1984 member states agreed to form the Peninsula Shield Force for rapid deployment against external aggression, comprising units from the armed forces of each country under a central command to be based in north-eastern Saudi Arabia.

In October 1987 (following an Iranian missile attack on Kuwait, which supported Iraq in its war against Iran) GCC ministers of foreign affairs issued a statement declaring that aggression against one member state was regarded as aggression against them all. In

December the Supreme Council approved a joint pact on regional co-operation in matters of security. In August 1990 the Ministerial Council condemned Iraq's invasion of Kuwait as a violation of sovereignty, and demanded the withdrawal of all Iraqi troops from Kuwait. The Peninsula Shield Force was not sufficiently developed to be deployed in defence of Kuwait. During the crisis and the ensuing war between Iraq and a multinational force which took place in January and February 1991, the GCC developed closer links with Egypt and Syria, which, together with Saudi Arabia, played the most active role among the Arab countries in the anti-Iraqi alliance. In March the six GCC nations, Egypt and Syria formulated the 'Declaration of Damascus', which announced plans to establish a regional peace-keeping force. The Declaration also urged the abolition of all weapons of mass destruction in the area, and recommended the resolution of the Palestinian question by an international conference. In June Egypt and Syria, whose troops were to have formed the largest proportion of the proposed peace-keeping force, announced their withdrawal from the project, reportedly as a result of disagreements with the GCC concerning the composition of the force and the remuneration involved. A meeting of ministers of foreign affairs of the eight countries took place in July, but agreed only to provide mutual military assistance when necessary. In September 1992 the signatories of the Damascus Declaration adopted a joint statement on regional questions, including the Middle East peace process and the dispute between the UAE and Iran (see below), but rejected an Egyptian proposal to establish a series of rapid deployment forces which could be called upon to defend the interests of any of the eight countries. A meeting of GCC ministers of defence in November agreed to maintain the Peninsula Shield Force. In November 1993 GCC ministers of defence approved a proposal for the significant expansion of the Force and for the incorporation of air and naval units. Ministers also agreed to strengthen the defence of the region by developing joint surveillance and early warning systems. A GCC military committee was established, and convened for the first time in April 1994, to discuss the implementation of the proposals. However, the expansion of the Peninsula Shield Force was not implemented. Joint military training exercises were conducted by troops from five GCC states (excluding Qatar) in northern Kuwait in March 1996. In December 1997 the Supreme Council approved plans for linking the region's military telecommunications networks and establishing a common early warning system. In December 2000 GCC leaders adopted a joint defence pact aimed at enhancing the grouping's defence capability. The pact formally committed member states to defending any other member state from external attack, envisaging the expansion of the Peninsula Shield Force from 5,000 to 22,000 troops and the creation of a new rapid deployment function within the Force. In March 2001 the GCC member states inaugurated the first phase of the long-envisaged joint air defence system. In December GCC heads of state authorized the establishment of a supreme defence council, comprising member states' ministers of defence, to address security-related matters and supervise the implementation of the joint defence pact. The council was to convene on an annual basis. Meeting in emergency session in early February 2003 GCC ministers of defence and foreign affairs agreed to deploy the Peninsula Field Force in Kuwait, in view of the then impending US military action against neighbouring Iraq. The full deployment of 3,000 Peninsula Shield troops to Kuwait was completed in early March; the force was withdrawn two months later. At a consultative meeting held in May, following the perpetration of terrorist attacks in Riyadh, Saudi Arabia, the Supreme Council considered the possible development of a regional missile defence system, to be based on its existing early warning and communications network. In December 2005 the Supreme Council, meeting in Abu Dhabi, UAE, agreed that the Peninsula Shield Force should be reconstituted. Proposals to develop the Force were endorsed by the 2006 heads of state summit, held in December, in Riyadh, Saudi Arabia.

In 1992 Iran extended its authority over the island of Abu Musa, which it had administered under a joint arrangement with the UAE since 1971. In September 1992 the GCC Ministerial Council condemned Iran's continued occupation of the island and efforts to consolidate its presence, and reiterated support of UAE sovereignty over Abu Musa, as well as the largely uninhabited Greater and Lesser Tunb islands (also claimed by Iran). All three islands are situated in the approach to the Strait of Hormuz, through which petroleum exports are transported. In December 1994 the GCC supported the UAE's request that the dispute be referred to the International Court of Justice (ICJ).

In September 1992 a rift within the GCC was caused by an incident on the disputed border between Saudi Arabia and Qatar. Qatar's threat to boycott a meeting of the Supreme Council in December was allayed at the last minute as a result of mediation efforts by the Egyptian President. At the meeting, which was held in the UAE, Qatar and Saudi Arabia agreed to establish a joint technical committee to demarcate the disputed border. In November 1994 a security agreement, to counter regional crime and terrorism, was concluded by GCC states. The pact, however, was not signed by Kuwait, which claimed that a clause concerning the extradition of offenders was in contravention of its constitution; Qatar did not attend the meeting, held in Riyadh, owing to its ongoing dispute with Saudi Arabia. During 1995 the deterioration of relations between Qatar and other GCC states threatened to undermine the Council's solidarity. In December Qatar publicly displayed its dissatisfaction at the appointment, without a consensus agreement, of Saudi Arabia's nominee as the new Secretary-General by failing to attend the final session of the Supreme Council, held in Muscat, Oman. However, at a meeting of ministers of foreign affairs in March 1996, Qatar endorsed the new Secretary-General, following an agreement on future appointment procedures, and reasserted its commitment to the organization. In June Saudi Arabia and Qatar agreed to reactivate the joint technical committee in order to finalize the demarcation of their mutual border: border maps drafted by the committee were approved by both sides in December 1999. In December 1996 Qatar hosted the annual GCC summit meeting; however, Bahrain refused to attend, owing to Qatar's 'unfriendly attitude' and a long-standing dispute between the two countries (referred by Qatar to the ICJ in 1991) concerning the sovereignty of the Hawar islands, and of other islands, maritime and border areas. The issue dominated the meeting, which agreed to establish a four-member committee to resolve the conflicting sovereignty claims. In January 1997 the ministers of foreign affairs of Kuwait, Oman, Saudi Arabia and the UAE, meeting in Riyadh, formulated a seven-point memorandum of understanding to ease tensions between Bahrain and Qatar. The two countries refused to sign the agreement; however, in March both sides announced their intention to establish diplomatic relations at ambassadorial level. In March 2001 the ICJ awarded Bahrain sovereignty of the Hawar islands, while supporting Qatar's sovereignty over other disputed territories. The GCC welcomed the judgment, which was accepted by the Governments of both countries.

In May 1997 the Ministerial Council, meeting in Riyadh, expressed concern at Turkey's cross-border military operation in northern Iraq and urged a withdrawal of Turkish troops from Iraqi territory. In December the Supreme Council reaffirmed the need to ensure the sovereignty and territorial integrity of Iraq. At the same time, however, the Council expressed concern at the escalation of tensions in the region, owing to Iraq's failure to co-operate with the UN Special Commission (UNSCOM). The Council also noted the opportunity to strengthen relations with Iran, in view of political developments in that country. In February 1998 the US Defense Secretary visited each of the GCC countries in order to generate regional support for any punitive military action against Iraq, given that country's obstruction of UN weapons inspectors. Kuwait was the only country to declare its support for the use of force (and to permit the use of its bases in military operations against Iraq), while other member states urged a diplomatic solution to the crisis. Qatar pursued a diplomatic initiative to negotiate directly with the Iraqi authorities, and during February, the Qatari Minister of Foreign Affairs became the most senior GCC government official to visit Iraq since 1990. The GCC supported an agreement concluded between the UN Secretary-General and the Iraqi authorities at the end of February 1998, and urged Iraq to co-operate with UNSCOM in order to secure an end to the problem and a removal of the international embargo against the country. This position was subsequently reiterated by the Supreme Council. In December 2000 Kuwait and Saudi Arabia rejected a proposal by the Qatari Government, supported by the UAE, that the GCC should moderate its policy on Iraq and demand the immediate removal of the international embargo against that country. During that month the Supreme Council determined to establish a committee with the function of touring Arab states to explain the GCC's Iraq policy. In September 2002 the US Secretary of State met representatives of the GCC to discuss ongoing US pressure on the UN Security Council to draft a new resolution insisting that Iraq comply with previous UN demands, setting a time frame for such compliance and authorizing the use of force against Iraq in response to non-compliance. In March 2003, in response to the initiation of US-led military action against Iraq for perceived non-compliance with the resulting Security Council resolution (1441, adopted in November 2002), the GCC Secretary-General urged the resumption of negotiations in place of military conflict. He also expressed regret that the Saddam Hussain regime had failed to co-operate sufficiently with the UN, in disregard of the GCC's recommendations. The GCC summit meeting held in Kuwait, in December 2003, issued a statement accepting the USA's policies towards Iraq at that time, emphasizing the importance of UN participation there, condemning ongoing operations by terrorist forces, and denoting the latter as anti-Islamic. In December 2004 the summit meeting, convened in Manama, Bahrain, urged participation by Iraqi citizens in the January 2005 elections to the Iraq Transitional National Assembly; the December 2005 summit meeting welcomed the conduct of the elections and reaffirmed support for reconstruction activities within Iraq. In December 2006 the Supreme Council urged the Iraqi authorities to disband militia groups and facilitate an end to internal tensions. The meeting also requested all countries to refrain from interference in Iraq's internal affairs and respect that country's sovereignty. The December 2007 summit meeting urged the Iraqi authorities to achieve national reconciliation, reiterating its demand that all armed groups should be dissolved, and requesting that constitutional amendments be made conducive to the restoration of security and peace.

The GCC has condemned repeated military exercises conducted by Iran in the waters around the disputed islands of Abu Musa and Greater and Lesser Tunb as a threat to regional security and a violation of the UAE's sovereignty. Nevertheless, member countries have pursued efforts to strengthen relations with Iran. In May 1999 President Khatami undertook a state visit to Qatar, Saudi Arabia and Syria, prompting concern on the part of the UAE that its support within the GCC and the solidarity of the grouping were being undermined. In June a meeting of GCC ministers of foreign affairs was adjourned, owing to reported disagreements between Saudi Arabia and the UAE. Diplomatic efforts secured commitments, issued by both countries later in that month, to co-operate fully within the GCC. In early July the Ministerial Council reasserted GCC support of the UAE's sovereignty claim over the three disputed islands and determined to establish a committee, comprising the ministers of foreign affairs of Oman, Qatar and Saudi Arabia and the GCC Secretary-General, to resolve the dispute. In December the Supreme Council extended the mandate of the committee to establish a mechanism for direct negotiations between the UAE and Iran. Iran, however, refused to co-operate with the committee; consequently, the committee's mandate was terminated in January 2001. In March the Ministerial Council demanded that Iran cease the construction of buildings for settlement on the disputed islands, and reiterated its support for the UAE's sovereignty claim. In December 2004 GCC leaders issued a declaration in support of the UAE's sovereignty claim; this was rejected by Iran. In December 2007 the 28th GCC summit meeting restated support for the UAE's right to regain sovereignty over the three islands (and their continental shelves and territorial waters) and urged Iran to respond positively to the UAE's efforts to address the issue through direct negotiations. The 28th summit meeting also urged Iran to pursue dialogue with the international community with regard to widespread concerns over its controversial nuclear programme.

The December 2005 summit of GCC heads of state issued a statement declaring that the Gulf region should be a zone free of weapons of mass destruction.

EXTERNAL RELATIONS

In June 1988 an agreement was signed by GCC and European Community (EC) ministers on economic co-operation; this took effect from January 1990. Under the accord a joint ministerial council (meeting on an annual basis) was established, and working groups were subsequently created to promote co-operation in several specific areas, including business, energy, the environment and industry. In October 1990 GCC and EC ministers of foreign affairs commenced negotiations on formulating a free-trade agreement. In October 1995 a conference was held in Muscat, Oman, which aimed to strengthen economic co-operation between European Union (EU, as the restructured EC was now known) and GCC member states, and to promote investment in both regions. GCC heads of state, meeting in December 1997, condemned statements issued by the European Parliament, as well as by other organizations, regarding human rights issues in member states and insisted they amounted to interference in GCC judicial systems. In January 2003 the GCC established a customs union (see above), which was a precondition of the proposed GCC-EU free-trade agreement. Negotiations on the agreement were ongoing in 2008. In April 2008 the GCC and the European Free Trade Association (EFTA) finalized negotiations on the conclusion of a bilateral free-trade agreement.

In September 1994 GCC ministers of foreign affairs decided to end the secondary and tertiary embargo on trade with Israel. In February 1995 a ministerial meeting of signatories of the Damascus Declaration adopted a common stand, criticizing Israel for its refusal to renew the nuclear non-proliferation treaty. In December 1996 the foreign ministers of the Damascus Declaration states, convened in Cairo, Egypt, requested the USA to exert financial pressure on Israel to halt the construction of settlements on occupied Arab territory. In December 2001 GCC heads of state issued a statement holding Israeli government policy responsible for the escalating crisis in the Palestinian territories. The consultative meeting of heads of state held in May 2002 declared its support for a Saudi-proposed initiative aimed at achieving a peaceful resolution of the crisis. GCC heads of state summits have repeatedly urged the international community to encourage Israel to sign the Nuclear Non-Proliferation Treaty.

In June 1997 ministers of foreign affairs of the Damascus Declaration states agreed to pursue efforts to establish a free-trade zone throughout the region, which they envisaged as the nucleus of a future Arab common market. Meanwhile, the Greater Arab Free-Trade Area, an initiative of the League of Arab States, entered into effect on 1 January 2005.

The GCC-USA Economic Dialogue, which commenced in 1985, convenes periodically as a government forum to promote co-operation between the GCC economies and the USA. Since the late 1990s private-sector interests have been increasingly represented at sessions of the Dialogue. It was announced in March 2001 that a business forum was to be established under the auspices of the Dialogue, to act as a permanent means of facilitating trade and investment between the GCC countries and the USA. Crown Prince Abdullah of Saudi Arabia withdrew as leader of the Saudi Arabian delegation to the December 2004 GCC summit in protest at the conclusion, in September, of a bilateral free-trade agreement between Bahrain and the USA and also at ongoing negotiations of proposed similar agreements between the USA and Kuwait, Oman, Qatar and the UAE, all of which were perceived by his government to be in contravention of certain existing agreements.

The GCC Secretary-General denounced the major terrorist attacks that were perpetrated in September 2001 against targets in the USA. Meeting in an emergency session in mid-September, in Riyadh, Saudi Arabia, GCC foreign ministers agreed to support the aims of the developing international coalition against terrorism. Meanwhile, however, member states urged parallel international resolve to halt action by the Israeli security forces against Palestinians. In December the Supreme Council declared the organization's full co-operation with the anti-terrorism coalition. In December 2006 the Supreme Council determined to establish a specialized security committee to counter terrorism.

INVESTMENT CORPORATION

Gulf Investment Corporation (GIC): POB 3402, Safat 13035, Kuwait; tel. 2225000; fax 2225010; e-mail gic@gic.com.kw; internet www.gic.com; f. 1983 by the six member states of the GCC, each contributing 16.6% of the total capital; total assets US $8,113m. (Dec. 2006); investment chiefly in the Gulf region, financing industrial projects (including pharmaceuticals, chemicals, steel wire, aircraft engineering, aluminium, dairy produce and chicken-breeding); provides merchant banking and financial advisory services, and in 1992 was appointed to advise the Kuwaiti Government on a programme of privatization; CEO HISHAM ABDULRAZZAK AR-RAZZUQI; publ. *The GIC Gazetteer* (annually).

Gulf International Bank: POB 1017, ad-Dowali Bldg, 3 Palace Ave, Manama 317, Bahrain; tel. 17534000; fax 17522633; e-mail info@gibbah.com; internet www.gibonline.com; f. 1976 by the six GCC states and Iraq; became a wholly-owned subsidiary of the GIC (without Iraqi shareholdings) in 1991; in April 1999 a merger with Saudi Investment Bank was concluded; cap. US $1,500m., total liabilities $27,739m., total assets $29,954m. (Dec. 2007); Chair. EBRAHIM BIN KHALIFA AL-KHALIFA; CEO Dr KHALED M. AL-FAYEZ.

Publications

GCC News (monthly).
At-Ta'awun (periodical).

COUNCIL OF ARAB ECONOMIC UNITY

Address: 1113 Corniche en-Nil, 4th Floor, POB 1 Mohammed Fareed, 11518 Cairo, Egypt.
Telephone: (2) 5755321; **fax:** (2) 5754090; **e-mail:** caeu@idsc.net.eg; **internet:** www.caeu.org.eg.
Established in 1957 by the Economic Council of the League of Arab States. The first meeting of the Council of Arab Economic Unity was held in 1964.

MEMBERS

Egypt	Palestine
Iraq	Somalia
Jordan	Sudan
Libya	Syria
Mauritania	Yemen

Organization
(April 2008)

COUNCIL
The Council consists of representatives of member states, usually ministers of economy, finance and trade. It meets twice a year; meetings are chaired by the representative of each country for one year.

GENERAL SECRETARIAT
Entrusted with the implementation of the Council's decisions and with proposing work plans, including efforts to encourage participation by member states in the Arab Economic Unity Agreement. The Secretariat also compiles statistics, conducts research and publishes studies on Arab economic problems and on the effects of major world economic trends.

General Secretary: Dr AHMED GOWEILI (Egypt).

COMMITTEES
There are seven standing committees: preparatory, follow-up and Arab Common Market development; Permanent Delegates; budget; economic planning; fiscal and monetary matters; customs and trade planning and co-ordination; statistics. There are also seven ad hoc committees, including meetings of experts on tariffs, trade promotion and trade legislation.

Activities

The Council undertakes to co-ordinate measures leading to a customs union subject to a unified administration; conduct market and commodity studies; assist with the unification of statistical terminology and methods of data collection; conduct studies for the formation of new joint Arab companies and federations; and to formulate specific programmes for agricultural and industrial co-ordination and for improving road and railway networks.

ARAB COMMON MARKET
Based on a resolution passed by the Council in August 1964; its implementation was to be supervised by the Council. Customs duties and other taxes on trade between the member countries were to be eliminated in stages prior to the adoption of a full customs union, and ultimately all restrictions on trade between the member countries, including quotas, and restrictions on residence, employment and transport, were to be abolished. In practice little progress was achieved in the development of an Arab common market during 1964–2000. However, the Council's efforts towards liberalizing intra-Arab trade were intensified in 2001. A meeting of Council ministers of economy and trade convened in Baghdad, Iraq, in June, issued the 'Baghdad Declaration' on establishing an, initially, quadripartite free-trade area comprising Egypt, Iraq, Libya and Syria; future participation by other member states was urged by the Council's General Secretary. The initiative was envisaged as a cornerstone of the Greater Arab Free Trade Area (GAFTA), which was being implemented by the Arab League. The meeting also approved an executive programme for developing the common market, determined to establish a compensation fund to support the integration of the least developed Arab states into the regional economy, and agreed to provide technical assistance for Arab states aiming to join the WTO. It was reported in late 2001 that Palestine had also applied to join the sub-regional free-trade area, and that consideration of its application would delay the zone's entry into force. In May Egypt, Jordan, Morocco and Tunisia (all participants in the Euro-Mediterranean Partnership—see European Union), meeting in Agadir, Morocco, had issued the 'Agadir Declaration' in which they determined to establish by 2010 the Mediterranean Arab Free Trade Area (MAFTA) as a cornerstone of a planned larger Arab-Mediterranean free trade area. The so-called Agadir Agreement on MAFTA was signed in February 2004. Other Arab states that had concluded Association Agreements with the EU and were signatories of GAFTA were invited to join MAFTA. In the mid-2000s the Council was considering a draft 20-year general framework for joint Arab economic action in the areas of investment, infrastructure, human resources development, technology, trade and joint ventures (see below). In December 2002 the Secretary-General of the Council announced the finalization of an Arab investment plan detailing some 4,000 investment opportunities; the Council launched a related internet site, www.arabinvestmap.com, in June 2004. Tariff-free trade between the 17 participants in GAFTA entered into force on 1 January 2005. The Council plans to launch an Arab electronic commerce market; it is envisaged that small and medium-sized enterprises in the region would benefit from this facility. In 2007 it was also working to develop and implement an Arab Investor Card scheme to facilitate the movement of investors and business people between member countries.

JOINT VENTURES
A number of multilateral organizations in industry and agriculture have been formed on the principle that faster development and economies of scale may be achieved by combining the efforts of member states. In industries that are new to the member countries Arab Joint Companies are formed, while existing industries are co-ordinated by the setting up of Arab Specialized Unions. The unions are for closer co-operation on problems of production and marketing, and to help companies deal as a group in international markets. The companies are intended to be self-supporting on a purely commercial basis; they may issue shares to citizens of the participating countries. The joint ventures are:

Arab Joint Companies:

Arab Company for Drug Industries and Medical Appliances (ACDIMA): POB 925161, Amman 11190, Jordan; tel. (6) 5821618; fax (6) 5821649; e-mail acdima@go.com.jo; internet www.acdima.com; f. 1976.

Arab Company for Electronic Commerce: f. 2001.

Arab Company for Industrial Investment: POB 3385, Alwiyah, Baghdad, Iraq; tel. (1) 718-9215; fax (1) 718-0710; e-mail aiic@warkaa.net; f. 1978; sponsors and establishes metal and engineering enterprises in the Arab region.

Arab Company for Livestock Development: POB 5305, Damascus, Syria; tel. 666037.

Arab Mining Company: POB 20198, Amman, Jordan; tel. (6) 5663148; fax (6) 5684114; e-mail armico@go.com.jo; f. 1974.

Specialized Arab Unions and Federations:

Arab Co-operative Union: POB 452, Duki, Giza, Egypt; tel. (2) 3442348; fax (2) 3038481; e-mail co_opunion@yahoo.com; f. 1985.

Arab Federation for Paper, Printing and Packaging Industries: POB 5456, Baghdad, Iraq; tel. (1) 887-2384; fax (1) 886-9639; e-mail info@afpppi.com; internet www.afpppi.com; f. 1977; 250 mems.

Arab Federation of Chemical and Petrochemical Industries: POB 941594, Amman 11194, Jordan; tel. (6) 5682350; e-mail info@afcpi.org; internet www.afcpi.org; f. 1998.

Arab Federation of Engineering Industries: POB 509, Baghdad, Iraq; tel. (1) 776-1101; f. 1975.

Arab Federation of Food Industries: POB 13025, Baghdad, Iraq; e-mail g-secretary@arabffi.org; internet www.arabffi.org; f. 1976.

Arab Federation of Leather Industries: POB 2188, Damascus, Syria; f. 1978; activities currently suspended.

Arab Federation of Shipping: POB 1161, Baghdad, Iraq; tel. (1) 717-4540; fax (1) 717-7243; e-mail secretariat@afos-shipping.org; f. 1979; 22 mems.

Arab Federation of Textile Industries: POB 620, Damascus, Syria; f. 1976; activities currently suspended.

Arab Federation of Travel Agents: POB 7090, Amman, Jordan.

Arab Seaports Federation: POB 1309, Basrah, Iraq; tel. (40) 415621; e-mail arabportfed@yahoo.co.uk; internet www.aspf.org.eg; f. 1977.

Arab Steel Union: Algiers, Algeria; f. 1972.

Arab Sugar Federation: POB 195, Khartoum, Sudan; f. 1977; activities currently suspended.

Arab Union for Cement and Building Materials: POB 9015, Damascus, Syria; tel. (11) 6118598; fax (11) 6111318; e-mail aucbm@scs-net.org; internet www.aucbm.org; f. 1977; 22 mem. countries, 103 mem. cos.; publ. *Cement and Building Materials Review* (quarterly).

Arab Union for Information Technology.

Arab Union of Fish Producers: POB 15064, Baghdad, Iraq; tel. (1) 425-2588; f. 1976.

Arab Union of Hotels and Tourism: Beirut, Lebanon; f. 1994.

Arab Union of Land Transport: POB 926324, Amman 11190, Jordan; tel. (6) 5663153; fax (6) 5664232; e-mail ault@go.com.jo; internet www.auolt.net; f. 1978.

Arab Union of the Manufacturers of Pharmaceuticals and Medical Appliances: POB 81150, Amman 11181, Jordan; tel. (6) 4654306; fax (6) 4648141; f. 1986.

Arab Union of the Manufacturers of Tyres and Rubber Products: Alexandria, Egypt; f. 1993.

Arab Union of Railways: POB 6599, Aleppo, Syria; tel. (21) 2667270; fax (21) 2686000; e-mail uacf@scs-net.org; f. 1979.

General Arab Insurance Federation: 8 Kaser en-Nil St, POB 611, 11511 Cairo, Egypt; tel. (2) 5743177; fax (2) 5762310; e-mail info@gaif.org; internet www.gaif.org; f. 1964.

General Union of Arab Agricultural Workers and Co-operatives: Tripoli, Libya; f. 1993.

Union of Arab Contractors: Cairo, Egypt; f. 1995.

Union of Arab Investors: Cairo, Egypt; f. 1995.

Publications

Annual Bulletin for Arab Countries' Foreign Trade Statistics.
Annual Bulletin for Official Exchange Rates of Arab Currencies.
Arab Economic Unity Bulletin (2 a year).
Demographic Yearbook for Arab Countries.
Economic Report of the General Secretary (2 a year).
Guide to Studies prepared by Secretariat.
Progress Report (2 a year).
Statistical Yearbook for Arab Countries.
Yearbook for Intra-Arab Trade Statistics.
Yearbook of National Accounts for Arab Countries.

COUNCIL OF THE BALTIC SEA STATES—CBSS

Address: Strömsborg, POB 2010, 103 11 Stockhölm, Sweden.
Telephone: (8) 440-19-20; **fax:** (8) 440-19-44; **e-mail:** cbss@cbss.org; **internet:** www.cbss.org.

The Council of the Baltic Sea States (CBSS) was established in 1992 to develop co-operation between member states.

MEMBERS

Denmark
Estonia
Finland
Germany
Iceland
Latvia
Lithuania
Norway
Poland
Russia
Sweden

The European Commission also has full membership status.
Observers: France, Italy, Netherlands, Slovakia, Ukraine, United Kingdom, USA.

Organization
(April 2008)

PRESIDENCY

The presidency is occupied by member states for one year, on a rotating basis. Summit meetings of heads of government are convened every two years. The sixth summit meeting was convened in Reykjavik, Iceland in June 2006.

MINISTERIAL COUNCIL

The Council comprises the ministers of foreign affairs of each member state and a representative of the European Commission. The Council meets every two years and aims to serve as a forum for guidance, direction of work and overall co-ordination among participating states. The 14th session of the Council was held in Malmö, Sweden, in June 2007, and the 15th session was scheduled to be held in Riga, Latvia, in June 2008. Chairmanship of the Council rotates annually among member states and is responsible for co-ordinating the Council's activities between ministerial sessions, with assistance from the Committee of Senior Officials. (Other ministers also convene periodically, on an ad hoc basis by their own decision.)

COMMITTEE OF SENIOR OFFICIALS—CSO

The Committee consists of senior officials of the ministries of foreign affairs of the member states and of the European Commission. It serves as a discussion forum for matters relating to the work of the Council and undertakes inter-sessional activities. The Chairman of the Committee, from the same country serving as President of the CBSS, meets regularly with the previous and future Chairmen. The so-called Troika aims to maintain information co-operation, promote better exchange of information, and ensure more effective decision-making. Three Working Groups—on Democratic Institutions, Economic Co-operation, and Nuclear and Radiation Safety—and a Lead Country expert group—for Civil Security—operate under the auspices of the CSO.

SECRETARIAT

In October 1998 the presidency inaugurated a permanent secretariat in Stockholm. The tasks of the secretariat include the preparation of summit meetings, annual sessions of ministers of foreign affairs, and other meetings of high-level officials and experts, the provision of technical support to the presidency regarding the implementation of plans, maintaining contacts with other sub-regional organizations, and strengthening awareness of the Council and its activities. The Secretariat includes an Energy Unit (established in April 2000), Baltic 21 Unit (January 2001) and a Children's Unit (June 2002).

Director: Dr GABRIELE KÖTSCHAU (Germany).

Activities

The CBSS was established in March 1992 as a forum to enhance and strengthen co-operation between countries in the Baltic Sea region. At a meeting of the Council in Kalmar, Sweden, in July 1996, ministers adopted an Action Programme as a guide-line for CBSS activities. The main programme areas covered stable and participatory political development; economic integration and prosperity; and protection of the environment. The third summit meeting of CBSS heads of government, held at Kolding, Denmark, in April 2000, recommended a restructuring of the organization to consolidate regional intergovernmental, multilateral co-operation in all sectors. In June the ninth meeting of the CBSS Council approved the summit's recommendations. The 10th ministerial session, held in Hamburg, Germany, in June 2001, adopted a set of guide-lines regarding the strengthening of the CBSS.

The ministerial session held in May 1994 determined to appoint an independent Commissioner on Democratic Development, concerned with democratic institutions and human rights, to serve a three-year term of office, from October of that year. The Commissioner's mandate was subsequently twice extended for three years, in July 1997 and June 2000, and was terminated in mid-December 2003.

At the first Baltic Sea States summit, held in Visby, Sweden, in May 1996, heads of government agreed to establish a Task Force on Organized Crime to counter drugs-trafficking, strengthen judicial co-operation, increase the dissemination of information, impose regional crime-prevention measures, improve border controls and provide training. In January 1998 the second summit meeting, convened in Riga, Latvia, agreed to extend the mandate of the Task Force until the end of 2000 and to enhance co-operation in the areas of civic security and border control. In April 2000 the third Baltic Sea States summit prolonged the Task Force's mandate further, until the end of 2004, and in June 2004 the fifth summit extended it until end-2008. The 2000 summit also authorized the establishment of a Task Force on Communicable Disease Control, which was mandated to formulate a joint plan aimed at improving disease control throughout the region, and also to strengthen regional co-operation in combating the threat to public health posed by a significant increase in communicable diseases, in particular HIV/AIDS. The Task Force presented its final report to the CBSS summit meeting held in June 2004. It was recognized that some of the structures of the Task Force could be pursued through a Northern Dimension Partnership in Public Health and Social Well-Being, which was established in late 2003. A Task Force against Trafficking in Human Beings with a Focus on Adults was established in November 2006.

The Council has founded a number of working groups, comprising experts in specific fields, which aim to report on and recommend action on issues of concern to the Council. In 2008 there were three working groups operating under the auspices of the CSO: the Working Group on Democratic Institutions; the Working Group on Economic Co-operation; and the Working Group on Nuclear Radiation Safety; and a lead country expert group concerned with civil security, led by Poland.

A CBSS EuroFaculty programme was implemented during 2000–07 at the Immanuel Kant State University in Kaliningrad, Russia. In December 2007 the CBSS launched a EuroFaculty programme aimed at upgrading tertiary business/economics education in the western Russian region of Pskov (bordering Estonia and Latvia).

A Baltic Business Advisory Council was established in 1996 with the aim of facilitating the privatization process in the member states in transition and promoting small and medium-sized enterprises. A Road Map on Investment Promotion, drafted by the Working Group on Economic Co-operation, was approved by the sixth summit meeting of CBSS heads of state, held in Reykjavik, Iceland, in June 2006. A Ministerial Conference on Trade and Economy was held in Stockholm, Sweden, in May 2007.

In January 2001 the CBSS Council agreed to establish a unit in the CBSS secretariat to implement Baltic 21, the regional variant (adopted by the CBSS in 1998) of 'Agenda 21', the programme of action agreed by the UN Conference on Environment and Development, held in Rio de Janeiro, Brazil, in June 1992. Baltic 21 comprised a programme of 30 projects throughout the region, which aim to promote sustainable development in the agriculture, forestry and fisheries, energy, industry, tourism, transport, and spatial planning sectors. The Baltic Sea Region Energy Co-operation (BASREC) has its own secretariat function and council of senior energy officials, administered by the CBSS secretariat. BASREC also has ad hoc groups on electricity markets, gas markets, energy efficiency and climate change. The promotion of the sustainable and balanced spatial development of the region is addressed within the framework of the Visions and Strategies around the Baltic Sea (VASAB) co-operation.

The CBSS contributed to the implementation of the European Union's Northern Dimension Action Plan (NDAP) for 2000–03 through the formulation, in collaboration with other regional groupings, of a 'List of Priorities and Projects'; it also contributed to the implementation of the second phase of NDAP, covering 2004–06. In 2006 the CBSS prepared, and presented to the European Commission, a survey on the future of the Northern Dimension, prior to the adoption of a new policy framework at a summit meeting convened in Helsinki, Finland, in November. In 2000 CBSS heads of government approved a Northern e-Dimension Action Plan (NeDAP) to co-ordinate efforts to strengthen information technologies through the region.

Finance

The Secretariat is financed by contributions of the governments of the Council's 11 member states. Ongoing activities and co-operation projects are funded through voluntary contributions from member states on the basis of special contribution schemes.

Publication

Baltinfo (every two months).

THE COUNCIL OF EUROPE

Address: Ave de l'Europe, 67075 Strasbourg Cédex, France.
Telephone: 3-88-41-20-33; **fax:** 3-88-41-27-45; **e-mail:** infopoint@coe.int; **internet:** www.coe.int.

The Council was founded in May 1949 to achieve a greater unity between its members, to facilitate their social progress and to uphold the principles of parliamentary democracy, respect for human rights and the rule of law. Membership has risen from the original 10 to 47.

MEMBERS*

Albania	Lithuania
Andorra	Luxembourg
Armenia	Macedonia, former Yugoslav republic
Austria	
Azerbaijan	Malta
Belgium	Moldova
Bosnia and Herzegovina	Montenegro†
Bulgaria	Monaco
Croatia	Netherlands
Cyprus	Norway
Czech Republic	Poland
Denmark	Portugal
Estonia	Romania
Finland	Russia
France	San Marino
Georgia	Serbia†
Germany	Slovakia
Greece	Slovenia
Hungary	Spain
Iceland	Sweden
Ireland	Switzerland
Italy	Turkey
Latvia	Ukraine
Liechtenstein	United Kingdom

*Belarus is a state candidate for membership of the Council of Europe. Canada, the Holy See, Japan, Mexico and the USA have observer status with the Committee of Ministers. The parliaments of Canada, Israel and Mexico have observer status with the Parliamentary Assembly.
†Following the division of Serbia and Montenegro into separate sovereign states in June 2006, Serbia retained the seat hitherto held by Serbia and Montenegro. Montenegro was admitted as a member in May 2007.

Organization
(April 2008)

COMMITTEE OF MINISTERS
The Committee consists of the ministers of foreign affairs of all member states (or their deputies, who are usually ministers' permanent diplomatic representatives in Strasbourg); it decides all matters of internal organization, makes recommendations to governments and draws up conventions and agreements with binding effect; it also discusses matters of political concern, such as European co-operation, compliance with member states' commitments, in particular concerning the protection of human rights, and considers possible co-ordination with other institutions, such as the European Union (EU) and the Organization for Security and Co-operation in Europe (OSCE). The Committee meets weekly at deputy ministerial level and once a year (in May or November) at ministerial level. Six two-day meetings are convened each year to supervise the execution of judgments of the European Court of Human Rights (see below).

CONFERENCES OF SPECIALIZED MINISTERS
There are 20 Conferences of specialized ministers, meeting regularly for intergovernmental co-operation in various fields.

PARLIAMENTARY ASSEMBLY
President: LLÚIS MARIA DE PUIG (Spain).
Chairman of the Socialist Group: ANDREAS GROSS (Switzerland).
Chairman of the Group of the European People's Party: LUC VAN DEN BRANDE (Belgium).
Chairman of the Alliance of Liberals and Democrats for Europe: MÁTYÁS EÖRSI (Hungary).
Chairman of the European Democrat Group: MIKHAIL MARGELOV (Russia).
Chairman of the Unified European Left Group: TINY KOX (Netherlands).

Members are elected or appointed by their national parliaments from among the members thereof; political parties in each delegation follow the proportion of their strength in the national parliament. Members do not represent their governments, speaking on their own behalf. At April 2008 the Assembly had 318 members (and 318 substitutes): 18 each for France, Germany, Italy, Russia and the United Kingdom; 12 each for Poland, Spain, Turkey and Ukraine; 10 for Romania; seven each for Belgium, the Czech Republic, Greece, Hungary, the Netherlands, Portugal and Serbia; six each for Austria, Azerbaijan, Bulgaria, Sweden and Switzerland; five each for Bosnia and Herzegovina, Croatia, Denmark, Finland, Georgia, Moldova, Norway and Slovakia; four each for Albania, Armenia, Ireland and Lithuania; three each for Cyprus, Estonia, Iceland, Latvia, Luxembourg, the former Yugoslav republic of Macedonia, Malta, Montenegro and Slovenia; and two each for Andorra, Liechtenstein, Monaco and San Marino. The parliaments of Canada, Israel and Mexico have permanent observer status. (Belarus's special 'guest status' was suspended in January 1997.)

The Assembly meets in ordinary session once a year. The session is divided into four parts, generally held in the last full week of January, April, June and September. The Assembly submits Recommendations to the Committee of Ministers, passes Resolutions, and discusses reports on any matters of common European interest. It is also a consultative body to the Committee of Ministers, and elects the Secretary-General, the Deputy Secretary-General, the Secretary-General of the Assembly, the Council's Commissioner for Human Rights, and the members of the European Court of Human Rights.

Standing Committee: represents the Assembly when it is not in session, and may adopt Recommendations to the Committee of Ministers and Resolutions on behalf of the Assembly. Consists of the President, Vice-Presidents, Chairmen of the Political Groups, Chairmen of the Ordinary Committees and Chairmen of national delegations. Meetings are usually held at least twice a year.

Ordinary Committees: political affairs; legal and human rights; economic affairs and development; social, health and family affairs; culture, science and education; environment, agriculture, and local and regional affairs; migration, refugees and population; rules of procedure and immunities; equal opportunities for women and men; honouring of obligations and commitments by member states of the Council of Europe.

SECRETARIAT

The Secretariat incorporates the Secretariats and Registry of the institutions of the Council. There are Directorates of Communication and Research, Strategic Planning, Protocol and Internal Audit, and the following Directorates General: Political Affairs; Legal Affairs; Human Rights; Social Cohesion; Education, Culture and Heritage, Youth and Sport; and Administration and Logistics.

Secretary-General: TERRY DAVIS (United Kingdom).

Deputy Secretary-General: MAUD DE BOER-BUQUICCHIO (Netherlands).

Secretary-General of the Parliamentary Assembly: MATEO SORINAS BALFEGÓ (Spain).

EUROPEAN COURT OF HUMAN RIGHTS

The Court was established in 1959 under the European Convention on Human Rights. It has compulsory jurisdiction and is competent to consider complaints lodged by states party to the European Convention and by individuals, groups of individuals or non-governmental organizations claiming to be victims of breaches of the Convention's guarantees. The Court comprises one judge for each contracting state. The Court sits in three-member Committees, empowered to declare applications inadmissible in the event of unanimity and where no further examination is necessary, seven-member Chambers, and a 17-member Grand Chamber. Chamber judgments become final three months after delivery, during which period parties may request a rehearing before the Grand Chamber, subject to acceptance by a panel of five judges. Grand Chamber judgments are final. The Court's final judgments are binding on respondent states and their execution is supervised by the Committee of Ministers. Execution of judgments includes payment of any pecuniary just satisfaction awarded by the Court, adoption of specific individual measures to erase the consequences of the violations found (such as striking out of impugned convictions from criminal records, reopening of judicial proceedings, etc.), and general measures to prevent new similar violations (e.g. constitutional and legislative reforms, changes of domestic case-law and administrative practice, etc.). At its meeting in March 2008 the Committee of Ministers supervised the payment of just satisfaction awarded by the Court in 845 cases, the adoption, in 139 cases or groups of cases, of individual measures, and 178 cases or groups of cases requiring the adoption of new general measures. In addition, the Committee started examining 185 new judgments of the Court and draft final resolutions (concerning 121 cases). When the Committee of Ministers considers that the measures taken comply with the respondent state's obligation to give effect to the judgment, a final resolution is adopted that terminates the supervision of the case. In 2007 the Court delivered 1,735 judgments, and some 85,000 cases were pending in April 2008.

President: JEAN-PAUL COSTA (France).

Registrar: ERIK FRIBERGH (Sweden).

CONGRESS OF LOCAL AND REGIONAL AUTHORITIES OF THE COUNCIL OF EUROPE (CLRAE)

The Congress was established in 1994, incorporating the former Standing Conference of Local and Regional Authorities, in order to protect and promote the political, administrative and financial autonomy of local and regional European authorities by encouraging central governments to develop effective local democracy. The Congress comprises two chambers—a Chamber of Local Authorities and a Chamber of Regions—with a total membership of 318 elected representatives (and 318 elected substitutes). Annual sessions are mainly concerned with local government matters, regional planning, protection of the environment, town and country planning, and social and cultural affairs. A Standing Committee, drawn from all national delegations, meets between plenary sessions of the Congress. Four Statutory Committees (Institutional; Sustainable Development; Social Cohesion; Culture and Education) meet twice a year in order to prepare texts for adoption by the Congress.

The Congress advises the Council's Committee of Ministers and the Parliamentary Assembly on all aspects of local and regional policy and co-operates with other national and international organizations representing local government. The Congress monitors implementation of the European Charter of Local Self-Government, which was opened for signature in 1985 and provides common standards for effective local democracy. Other legislative guide-lines for the activities of local authorities and the promotion of democracy at local level include the 1980 European Outline Convention on Transfrontier Co-operation, and its Additional Protocol which was opened for signature in 1995; a Convention on the Participation of Foreigners in Public Life at Local Level (entered into force in 1997); and the European Charter for Regional or Minority Languages (entered into force 1998). In addition, the European Urban Charter (adopted 1992) defines citizens' rights in European towns and cities, for example in the areas of transport, urban architecture, pollution and security; the European Landscape Convention (entered into force in March 2004) details an obligation for public authorities to adopt policies and measures at local, regional, national and international level for the protection, management and planning of landscapes; and the Charter on the Participation of Young People in Municipal and Regional Life (adopted in 1992 and revised in 2003), sets out guide-lines for encouraging the active involvement of young people in the promotion of social change in their municipality or region. In May 2005 the Congress concluded an agreement with the EU Committee of the Regions on co-operation in ensuring local and regional democracy and self-government.

President: HALVDAN SKARD (Norway).

Activities

In an effort to harmonize national laws, to put the citizens of member countries on an equal footing and to pool certain resources and facilities, the Council of Europe has concluded a number of conventions and agreements covering particular aspects of European co-operation. Since 1989 the Council has undertaken to increase co-operation with all countries of the former Eastern bloc and to facilitate their accession to the organization. In October 1997 heads of state or government of member countries convened for only the second time (the first meeting took place in Vienna, in October 1993) with the aim of formulating a new social model to consolidate democracy throughout Europe. The meeting endorsed a Final Declaration and an Action Plan, which established priority areas for future Council activities, including fostering social cohesion; protecting civilian security; promoting human rights; enhancing joint measures to counter cross-border illegal trafficking; and strengthening democracy through education and other cultural activities. In addition, the meeting generated renewed political commitment to the Programme of Action against Corruption, which has become a key element of Council activities. A third meeting of heads of state or government was held in Warsaw, Poland, in May 2005. In a Final Declaration and an Action Plan the meeting defined the principal tasks of the Council in the coming years, i.e. promoting human rights and the rule of law, strengthening the security of European citizens and fostering co-operation with other international and European organizations. The Council's activities have three cross-cutting themes: children, democracy, and combating violence.

HUMAN RIGHTS

The protection of human rights is one of the Council of Europe's basic goals, to be achieved in four main areas: the effective supervision and protection of fundamental rights and freedoms; identification of new threats to human rights and human dignity; development of public awareness of the importance of human rights; and promotion of human rights education and professional training. The most significant treaties in this area include: the European Convention for the Protection of Human Rights and Fundamental Freedoms (European Convention on Human Rights) (which was adopted in 1950 and entered into force in 1953); the European Social Charter; the European Convention for the Prevention of Torture and Inhuman or Degrading Treatment or Punishment; the Framework Convention for the Protection of National Minorities; the European Charter for Regional or Minority Languages; and the Convention on Action against Trafficking in Human Beings.

The Steering Committee for Human Rights is responsible for intergovernmental co-operation in the field of human rights and fundamental freedoms; it works to strengthen the effectiveness of systems for protecting human rights and to identify potential threats and challenges to human rights. The Committee has been responsible for the elaboration of several conventions and other legal instruments including the following protocols to the European Convention on Human Rights: Protocol No. 11, which entered into force in November 1998, resulting in the replacement of the then existing institutions—the European Commission of Human Rights and the European Court of Human Rights—by a single Court, working on a full-time basis; Protocol No. 12, which entered into force in April 2005, enforcing a general prohibition of discrimination; No. 13, which entered into force in July 2003, guaranteeing the abolition of the death penalty in all circumstances (including in time of war); and No. 14, adopted in May 2004, which aimed to enhance the effectiveness of the Court by improving implementation of the European Convention on Human Rights at national level and the processing of applications, and accelerating the execution of the Court's decisions.

The Steering Committee for Human Rights was responsible for the preparation of the European Ministerial Conference on Human Rights, held in Rome in November 2000, to commemorate the 50th anniversary of the adoption of the European Convention on Human Rights. The Conference highlighted, in particular, 'the need to reinforce the effective protection of human rights in domestic legal systems as well as at the European level'.

The Council of Europe Commissioner for Human Rights (whose office was established by a resolution of the Council's Committee of Ministers in May 1999) promotes respect for human rights in member states.

Commissioner for Human Rights: THOMAS HAMMARBERG (Sweden).

European Committee for the Prevention of Torture and Inhuman or Degrading Treatment or Punishment (CPT)

The Committee was established under the 1987 Convention for the Prevention of Torture as an integral part of the Council of Europe's system for the protection of human rights. The Committee, comprising independent experts, aims to examine the treatment of persons deprived of their liberty with a view to strengthening, if necessary, the protection of such persons from torture and from inhuman or degrading treatment or punishment. It conducts periodic visits to police stations, prisons, detention centres, and all other sites where persons are deprived of their liberty by a public authority, in all states parties to the Convention, and may also undertake ad hoc visits when the Committee considers them necessary. After each visit the Committee drafts a report of its findings and any further advice or recommendations, based on dialogue and co-operation. By April 2008 the Committee had published 199 reports and had undertaken 246 visits (151 periodic and 95 ad hoc).

President: MAURO PALMA (Italy).

European Social Charter

The European Social Charter, in force since 1965, is the counterpart of the European Convention on Human Rights, in the field of protection of economic and social rights. A revised Charter, which amended existing guarantees and incorporated new rights, was opened for signature in May 1996, and entered into force on 1 July 1999. By April 2008 27 member states had ratified the Charter and 24 had ratified the revised Charter. Rights guaranteed by the Charter concern all individuals in their daily lives in matters of housing, health, education, employment, social protection, movement of persons and non-discrimination. The European Committee of Social Rights considers reports submitted to it annually by member states. It also considers collective complaints submitted in the framework of an Additional Protocol (1995), providing for a system which entered into force in July 1998, permitting trade unions, employers' organizations and NGOs to lodge complaints on alleged violations of the Charter. The Committee, composed of 15 members, decides on the conformity of national situations with the Charter. When a country does not bring a situation into conformity, the Committee of Ministers may, on the basis of decisions prepared by a Governmental Committee (composed of representatives of each Contracting Party), issue recommendations to the state concerned, inviting it to change its legislation or practice in accordance with the Charter's requirements.

President of the European Committee of Social Rights: POLONCA KONČAR (Slovenia).

FRAMEWORK CONVENTION FOR THE PROTECTION OF NATIONAL MINORITIES

In 1993 the first summit meeting of Council of Europe heads of state and government, held in Vienna, mandated the Committee of Ministers to draft 'a framework convention specifying the principle that States commit themselves to respect in order to assure the protection of national minorities'. A special committee was established to draft the so-called Framework Convention for the Protection of National Minorities, which was then adopted by the Committee in November 1994. The Convention was opened for signature in February 1995, entering into force in February 1998. Contracting parties (39 states at April 2008) are required to submit reports on the implementation of the treaty at regular intervals to an Advisory Committee composed of 18 independent experts. The Advisory Committee adopts an opinion on the implementation of the Framework Convention by the contracting party, on the basis of which the Committee of Ministers adopts a resolution. A Conference entitled 10 Years of Protecting National Minorities and Regional or Minority Languages was convened in March 2008 to review the impacts of, and the role of regional institutions in implementing, both the Framework Convention and the Convention on Minority Languages.

Executive Secretary: ALAIN CHABLAIS (acting).

RACISM AND INTOLERANCE

In October 1993 heads of state and of government, meeting in Vienna, resolved to reinforce a policy to combat all forms of intolerance, in response to the increasing incidence of racial hostility and intolerance towards minorities in European societies. A European Commission against Racism and Intolerance (ECRI) was established by the summit meeting to analyse and assess the effectiveness of legal, policy and other measures taken by member states to combat these problems. It became operational in March 1994. The European conference against racism, held in October 2000, requested that ECRI should be reinforced and, in June 2002, the Committee of Ministers of the Council of Europe adopted a new Statute for ECRI that consolidated its role as an independent human rights monitoring body focusing on issues related to racism and racial discrimination. Members of ECRI are appointed on the basis of their recognized expertise in the field; they are independent and impartial in fulfilling their mandate. ECRI undertakes activities in three programme areas: country-by-country approach; work on general themes; and relations with civil society. In the first area of activity, ECRI analyses the situation regarding racism and intolerance in each of the member states, in order to advise governments on measures to combat these problems. In December 1998 ECRI completed a first round of reports for all Council members. A second series of country reports was completed in December 2002 and a third monitoring cycle, focusing on implementation and 'specific issues', was initiated in 2003; it was envisaged that some 37 reports would have been published under the third cycle by the end of 2008. ECRI's work on general themes includes the preparation of policy recommendations and guide-lines on issues of importance to combating racism and intolerance. ECRI also collects and disseminates examples of good practices relating to these issues. Under the third programme area ECRI aims to disseminate information and raise awareness of the problems of racism and intolerance among the general public.

EQUALITY BETWEEN WOMEN AND MEN

The Steering Committee for Equality between Women and Men (CDEG—an intergovernmental committee of experts) is responsible for encouraging action at both national and Council of Europe level to promote equality of rights and opportunities between the two sexes. Assisted by various specialist groups and committees, the CDEG is mandated to establish analyses, studies and evaluations, to examine national policies and experiences, to devise concerted policy strategies and measures for implementing equality and, as necessary, to prepare appropriate legal and other instruments. It is also responsible for preparing the European Ministerial Conferences on Equality between Women and Men. The main areas of CDEG activities are the comprehensive inclusion of the rights of women (for example, combating violence against women and trafficking in human beings) within the context of human rights; the issue of equality and democracy, including the promotion of the participation of women in political and public life; projects aimed at studying the specific equality problems related to cultural diversity, migration and minorities; positive action in the field of equality between men and women and the mainstreaming of equality into all policies and programmes at all levels of society. In October 1998 the Committee of Ministers adopted a Recommendation to member states on gender mainstreaming; in May 2000 it approved a Recommendation on action against trafficking in human beings for the purpose of sexual exploitation; and in May 2002 it adopted a Recommendation on the protection of women from violence. Following a decision of the meeting of heads of state or government convened in Warsaw in May 2005, a Council of Europe Task Force to Combat Violence against Women, including Domestic Violence (EG-TFV) was established. In June 2006 the Committee of Ministers adopted the Blueprint of the Council of Europe Campaign to Combat Violence against Women, including Domestic Violence, which had been drafted by the EG-TGF.

MEDIA AND COMMUNICATIONS

Article 10 of the European Convention on Human Rights (freedom of expression and information) forms the basis for the Council of Europe's activities in the area of mass media. Implementation of the Council of Europe's work programme concerning the media is undertaken by the Steering Committee on the Media and New Communication Services (CDMC), which comprises senior government officials and representatives of professional organizations, meeting in plenary session twice a year. The CDMC is mandated to devise concerted European policy measures and appropriate legal instruments. Its underlying aims are to further freedom of expression and information in a pluralistic democracy, and to promote the free flow of information and ideas. The CDMC is assisted by various specialist groups and committees. Policy and legal instruments have been developed on subjects including: exclusivity rights; media concentrations and transparency of media ownership; protection of journalists in situations of conflict and tension; independence of public-service broadcasting, protection of rights holders; legal protection of encrypted television services; media and elections; protection of journalists' sources of information; the independence and functions of broadcasting regulatory authorities; and coverage of legal proceedings by the media. These policy and legal instruments (mainly in the form of non-binding recommendations addressed to member governments) are complemented by the publication of studies, analyses and seminar proceedings on topics of media law and policy. The CDMC has also prepared a number of international binding legal instruments, including the European Convention on Transfrontier Television (adopted in 1989 and ratified by 32 countries by April 2008), the European Convention on the Legal Protection of Services Based on or Consisting of Conditional Access (ratified by eight countries at April 2008), and the European Convention Relating to Questions on Copyright Law and Neighbouring Rights in the Context of Transfrontier Broadcasting by Satellite (ratified by two countries at April 2008).

In March 2005 the Council's Committee of Ministers adopted a declaration on freedom of expression and information in the media in the context of the fight against terrorism. A declaration on the independence and functions of regulatory authorities for the broadcasting sector was adopted by the Committee of Ministers in March 2008. In that month the Committee also adopted a Recommendation on the use of Internet Filters aimed at promoting a balance between freedom of expression and the protection of children against harmful material published on the internet.

SOCIAL COHESION

In June 1998 the Committee of Ministers established the European Committee for Social Cohesion (CDCS). The CDCS has the following responsibilities: to co-ordinate, guide and stimulate co-operation between member states with a view to promoting social cohesion in Europe, to develop and promote integrated, multidisciplinary responses to social issues, and to promote the social standards embodied in the European Social Charter and other Council of Europe instruments, including the European Code of Social Security. In 2002 the CDCS published the *Report on Access to Social Rights in Europe*, concerning access to employment, housing and social protection. The Committee supervises an extensive programme of work on children, families and the elderly. In March 2004 the Committee of Ministers approved a revised version of the Council's strategy for social cohesion (adopted in July 2000).

The European Code of Social Security and its Protocol entered into force in 1968; by April 2008 the Code had been ratified by 20 states and the Protocol by seven states. These instruments set minimum standards for medical care and the following benefits: sickness, old-age, unemployment, employment injury, family, maternity, invalidity and survivor's benefit. A revision of these instruments, aiming to provide higher standards and greater flexibility, was completed for signature in 1990 and had been signed by 14 states at April 2008.

The European Convention on Social Security, in force since 1977, currently applies in Austria, Belgium, Italy, Luxembourg, the Netherlands, Portugal, Spain and Turkey; most of the provisions apply automatically, while others are subject to the conclusion of additional multilateral or bilateral agreements. The Convention is concerned with establishing the following four fundamental principles of international law on social security: equality of treatment, unity of applicable legislation, conservation of rights accrued or in course of acquisition, and payment of benefits abroad. In 1994 a Protocol to the Convention, providing for the enlargement of the personal scope of the Convention, was opened for signature; by April 2008 it had been ratified only by Portugal.

HEALTH

Through a series of expert committees, the Council aims to ensure constant co-operation in Europe in a variety of health-related fields, with particular emphasis on health services and patients' rights, for example: equity in access to health care, quality assurance, health services for institutionalized populations (prisoners, elderly in homes), discrimination resulting from health status and education for health. These efforts are supplemented by the training of health personnel. Recommendations adopted by the Committee of Ministers in the area of health cover blood, cancer control, disabilities, health policy development and promotion, health services, the protection of human rights and dignity of persons with mental disorder, the organization of palliative care, the role of patients, transplantation, access to health care by vulnerable groups, and the impact of new information technologies on health care.

A Partial Agreement in the Social and Public Health Field aims to protect the consumer from potential health risks connected with commonplace or domestic products, including asbestos, cosmetics, flavouring substances, pesticides, pharmaceuticals and products which have a direct or indirect impact on the human food chain, pesticides, pharmaceuticals and cosmetics; and also has provisions on the integration of people with disabilities. Two Euroepean treaties have been concluded within the framework of this Partial Agreement: the European Agreement on the Restriction of the use of Certain Detergents in Washing and Cleaning Products, and the Convention on the Elaboration of a European Pharmacopoeia (establishing legally binding standards for medicinal substances, auxiliary substances, pharmaceutical preparations, vaccines for human and veterinary use and other articles). The latter Convention entered into force in eight signatory states in May 1974 and, by April 2008 had been ratified by 37 states and the European Union. WHO and 17 European and non-European states participate as observers in the sessions of the European Pharmacopoeia Commission. In 1994 a procedure on certification of suitability to the European Pharmacopoeia monographs for manufacturers of substances for pharmaceutical use was established. A network of official control laboratories for human and veterinary medicines was established in 1995, open to all signatory countries to the Convention and observers at the Pharmacopoeia Commission. The sixth edition of the European Pharmacopoeia, in force since 1 January 2008, is updated regularly in its electronic version, and includes more than 1,800 harmonized European standards, or 'monographs', 268 general methods of analysis and 2,210 reagents.

The 1992 Recommendation on A Coherent Policy for People with Disabilities contains the policy principles for the rehabilitation and integration of people with disabilities. This model programme recommends that governments of all member states develop comprehensive and co-ordinated national disability policies taking account of prevention, diagnosis, treatment education, vocational guidance and training, employment, social integration, social protection, information and research. It has set benchmarks, both nationally and internationally. The 1995 Charter on the Vocational Assessment of People with Disabilities states that a person's vocational abilities and not disabilities should be assessed and related to specific job requirements. The 2001 Resolution on Universal Design aims to improve accessibility, recommending the inclusion of Universal Design principles in the training for vocations working on the built environment. The 2001 Resolution on New Technologies recommends formulating national strategies to ensure that people with disabilities benefit from new technologies. In April 2006 the Council of Europe Committee of Ministers adopted a Recommendation endorsing a recently-drafted Council of Europe action plan for 2006–15, with the aim of promoting the rights and full participation of people with disabilities in society and of improving the quality of life of people with disabilities in Europe.

In the co-operation group to combat drug abuse and illicit drugs trafficking (Pompidou Group), 35 states work together, through meetings of ministers, officials and experts, to counteract drug abuse. The Group follows a multidisciplinary approach embracing, in particular, legislation, law enforcement, prevention, treatment, rehabilitation and data collection. In January 2007 the Group initiated an online register of ongoing drug research projects; a revised version of the register was launched in April 2008.

Improvement of blood transfusion safety and availability of blood and blood derivatives has been ensured through European Agreements and guide-lines. Advances in this field and in organ transplantation are continuously assessed by expert committees.

In April 1997 the first international convention on biomedicine was opened for signature at a meeting of health ministers of member states, in Oviedo, Spain. The so-called Convention for the Protection of Human Rights and the Dignity of Human Beings with Respect to the Applications of Biology and Medicine incorporated provisions on scientific research, the principle of informed patient consent, organ and tissue transplants and the prohibition of financial gain and disposal of a part of the human body. It entered into force on 1 November 1999 (see below).

POPULATION AND MIGRATION

The European Convention on the Legal Status of Migrant Workers, in force since 1983, has been ratified by Albania, France, Italy, Moldova, the Netherlands, Norway, Portugal, Spain, Sweden, Turkey and the Ukraine. The Convention is based on the principle of equality of treatment for migrant workers and the nationals of the host country as to housing, working conditions, and social security. The Convention also upholds the principle of the right to family reunion. An international consultative committee, representing the parties to the Convention, monitors the application of the Convention.

In 1996 the European Committee on Migration concluded work on a project entitled 'The Integration of Immigrants: Towards Equal Opportunities' and the results were presented at the sixth conference of European ministers responsible for migration affairs, held in Warsaw. At the conference a new project, entitled 'Tensions and Tolerance: Building better integrated communities across Europe' was initiated; it was concluded in 1999. During the period 1977–2005 an ad hoc committee of experts on the Legal Aspects of Territorial Asylum Refugees and Stateless Persons (CAHAR) assisted the Committee on Migration with examining migration issues at the pan-European level. In 2002 CAHAR prepared a Recommendation relating to the detention of asylum seekers. In May 2005 the Committee of Ministers adopted *Twenty Guide-lines on Forced Return of Illegal Residents*, which had been drafted by CAHAR.

The European Committee on Migration was responsible for activities concerning Roma/Gypsies in Europe, in co-ordination with other relevant Council of Europe bodies. In December 2004 a European Roma and Travellers Forum, established in partnership with the Council of Europe, was inaugurated.

In May 2006 the Council of Europe adopted a Convention on the avoidance of statelessness in relation to State succession.

The European Population Committee, an intergovernmental committee of scientists and government officials responsible for population matters, monitors and analyses population trends throughout Europe and informs governments, research centres and the public of demographic developments and their impact on policy decisions. It compiles an annual statistical review of regional demographic developments and publishes the results of studies on population issues.

COUNCIL OF EUROPE DEVELOPMENT BANK

The Council of Europe Development Bank was established in April 1956 by the Committee of Ministers, initially as the Resettlement Fund, and later as the Council of Europe Social Development Fund, and then renamed again in November 1999. It is a multilateral development bank with a social mandate, promoting social development by granting loans for projects with a social purpose. Projects aimed at solving social problems related to the presence of refugees, displaced persons or forced migrants are a priority. In addition, the Bank finances projects in other fields that contribute directly to strengthening social cohesion in Europe: job creation and preservation in small and medium-sized enterprises; social housing; improving urban living conditions; health and education infrastructure, protection of the environment, and rural modernization; protection and rehabilitation of the historic heritage. At December 2007 the Bank had total assets of €18,509m. In 2007 the Bank approved new projects with a value of €2,414m. Its lending activities have been increasingly targeted at central and eastern European countries.

LEGAL AFFAIRS

The European Committee on Legal Co-operation develops co-operation between member states in the field of law, with the objective of harmonizing and modernizing public and private law, including administrative law and the law relating to the judiciary. The Committee is responsible for expert groups which consider issues relating to administrative law, efficiency of justice, family law, nationality, information technology and data protection.

Numerous conventions and Recommendations have been adopted, and followed up by appropriate committees or groups of experts, on matters which include: efficiency of justice, nationality, legal aid, rights of children, data protection, information technology, children born out of wedlock, animal protection, adoption, information on foreign law, and the legal status of non-governmental organizations.

In December 1999 the Convention for the Protection of Human Rights and the Dignity of Human Beings with Respect to the Applications of Biology and Medicine: Convention on Human Rights and Biomedicine entered into force, as the first internationally binding legal text to protect people against the misuse of biological and medical advances. It aims to preserve human dignity and identity, rights and freedoms, through a series of principles and rules. Additional protocols develop the Convention's general provisions by means of specialized texts. A Protocol prohibiting the medical cloning of human beings was approved by Council heads of state and government in 1998 and entered into force on 1 March 2001. A Protocol on the transplantation of human organs and tissue was opened for signature in January 2002 and entered into force in May 2006, and a Protocol concerning biomedical research opened for signature in January 2005 and entered into force in September 2007. Work on draft protocols relating to protection of the human embryo and foetus, and genetics is ongoing. A Recommendation on xenotransplantation was adopted by the Committee of Ministers in 2003.

In 2001 an Additional Protocol to the Convention for the protection of individuals with regard to automatic processing of personal data was adopted. The Protocol, which opened for signature in November, concerned supervisory authorities and transborder data flows. It entered into force in July 2004.

In 2001 the European Committee for Social Cohesion (CDCS) approved three new conventions on contact concerning children, legal aid, and 'Information Society Services'. In 2002 the CDCS approved a Recommendation on mediation on civil matters and a resolution establishing the European Commission for the Efficiency of Justice (CEPEJ). The aims of the CEPEJ are: to improve the efficiency and functioning of the justice system of member states, with a view to ensuring that everyone within their jurisdiction can enforce their legal rights effectively, increasing citizen confidence in the system; and enabling better implementation of the international legal instruments of the Council of Europe concerning efficiency and fairness of justice.

A Convention on Contact concerning Children was adopted in May 2003. It entered into force in September 2005 and by April 2008 had been ratified by five states. A new convention on the Protection of Children against Sexual Exploitation and Sexual Abuse was adopted in July 2007 and had 27 signatures by April 2008.

The Consultative Council of European Judges has prepared a framework global action plan for judges in Europe. In addition, it has contributed to the implementation of this programme by the adoption of opinions on standards concerning the independence of the judiciary and the irremovability of judges, and on the funding and management of courts.

A Committee of Legal Advisers on Public and International Law (CAHDI), comprising the legal advisers of ministers of foreign affairs of member states and of several observer states, is authorized by the Committee of Ministers to examine questions of public international law, and to exchange and, if appropriate, to co-ordinate the views of member states. The CAHDI functions as a European observatory of reservations to international treaties. Recent activities of the CAHDI include the preparation of a Recommendation on reactions to inadmissible reservations to international treaties, the publication of a report on state practice with regard to state succession and recognition, and another on expression of consent of states to be bound by a treaty.

With regard to crime, expert committees and groups operating under the authority of the European Committee on Crime Problems have prepared conventions on such matters as extradition, mutual assistance, recognition and enforcement of foreign judgments, transfer of proceedings, suppression of terrorism, transfer of prisoners, compensation payable to victims of violent crime, money-laundering, confiscation of proceeds from crime and corruption.

A Convention on Cybercrime, adopted in 2001, entered into force in July 2004 and by April 2008 had received 22 ratifications. In 2003 member states concluded an additional Protocol to the Convention relating to the criminalization of acts of a racist and xenophobic nature committed through computer systems; this entered into force in March 2006 and had been ratified by 11 countries at April 2008. A Council of Europe conference on cybercrime, convened in April 2008, with participation by around 200 experts on combating cybercrime, addressed emerging cybercriminal threats and trends, reviewed the effectiveness of legislation on cybercrime, and adopted guide-lines aimed at improving co-operation between crime investigators and internet service providers.

A Multidisciplinary Group on International Action against Terrorism, established in 2001, elaborated a protocol that updated the 1977 European Convention on the Suppression of Terrorism. In 2002 the Council's Committee of Ministers adopted a set of 'Guide-lines on Human Rights and the Fight against Terrorism'. In 2003 a Committee of Experts on Terrorism (CODEXTER) was inaugurated, with a mandate to oversee and co-ordinate the Council's counter-terrorism activities in the legal field. CODEXTER formulated the Council of Europe Convention for the Prevention of Terrorism, which was opened for signature in May 2005 and entered into force in June 2007. By April 2008 the Convention for the Prevention of Terrorism had been ratified by 11 member states. In 2006 the Council of Europe launched a campaign to combat trafficking, which seeks to raise awareness of the extent of trafficking in present-day Europe and to emphasize the measures that can be taken to prevent it. The campaign also promotes participation in the Convention on Action against Trafficking in Human Beings; the Convention entered into force in February 2008 and, by April of that year, had been ratified by 17 countries.

The Group of States Against Corruption (GRECO) became operational in 1999 and became a permanent body of the Council in 2002. At April 2008 it had 46 members (including the USA). A monitoring mechanism, based on mutual evaluation and peer pressure, GRECO assesses members' compliance with Council instruments for combating corruption, including the Criminal Law Convention on Corruption, which entered into force in July 2002 (and by April 2008 had been ratified by 39 states), and its Additional Protocol (which entered into force in February 2005). The evaluation procedure of GRECO is confidential but it has become practice to make reports public after their adoption. GRECO's First Evaluation Round was completed during 2001–02, and the Second Evaluation Round was conducted during 2003–06. The Third Evaluation Round, which was ongoing in 2008, was initiated in January 2007 and covered member states' compliance with, *inter alia*, requirements of the Criminal Law Convention on Corruption and its Additional Protocol, and the area of transparency of political party funding.

The Select Committee of Experts on the Evaluation of Anti-Money Laundering Measures (MONEYVAL) became operational in 1998. It is responsible for mutual evaluation of the anti-money-laundering measures in place in 28 Council of Europe states that are not members of the Financial Action Task Force (FATF). The MONEYVAL mechanism is based on FATF practices and procedures. States are evaluated against the relevant international standards in the legal, financial and law enforcement sectors. In the legal sector this includes evaluation of states' obligations under the Council of Europe Convention on Laundering, Search, Seizure and Confiscation of the Proceeds from Crime and on the Financing of Terrorism, which was to enter into force in May 2008. After the terrorist attacks against targets in the USA on 11 September 2001, the Committee of Ministers adopted revised terms of reference, which specifically include the evaluation of measures to combat the financing of terrorism. MONEYVAL undertook its first round of onsite visits during 1998–2000. Its second round, focusing even more closely on the effectiveness of national systems, began in 2001 and was completed in 2004. MONEYVAL's third evaluation round, covering the period 2005–10, was being conducted in accordance with a comprehensive global methodology agreed with the FATF, FATF-style regional bodies, IMF and World Bank, and was evaluating the effectiveness of enforcement measures in place to combat the financing of terrorism as well as money laundering. The evaluations of MONEYVAL are confidential, but summaries of adopted reports are made public.

A Criminological Scientific Council, composed of specialists in law, psychology, sociology and related sciences, advises the Committee and organizes criminological research conferences and colloquia. A Council for Penological Co-operation organizes regular high-level conferences of directors of prison administration and is responsible for collating statistical information on detention and community sanctions in Europe. The Council prepared the European Prison Rules in 1987 and the European Rules on Community Sanctions (alternatives to imprisonment) in 1992. A council for police matters was established in 2002.

In May 1990 the Committee of Ministers adopted a Partial Agreement to establish the European Commission for Democracy through Law, to be based in Venice, Italy. The so-called Venice Commission was enlarged in February 2002 and in mid–2007 comprised all Council of Europe member states in addition to Kyrgyzstan (which joined in 2004) Chile (joined in 2005), the Republic of Korea (2006), Algeria (2007) and Morocco (also 2007). The Commission is composed of independent legal and political experts, mainly senior academics, supreme or constitutional court judges, members of national parliaments, and senior public officers. Its main activity is constitutional assistance and it may supply opinions upon request, made through the Committee of Ministers, by the Parliamentary Assembly, the Secretary-General or any member states of the Commission. Other states and international organizations may request opinions with the consent of the Committee of Ministers. The Commission is active throughout the constitutional domain, and has worked on issues including legislation on constitutional courts and national minorities, electoral law and other legislation with implications for national democratic institutions. The creation of the Council for Democratic Elections institutionalized co-operation in the area of elections between the Venice Commission, the Parliamentary Assembly of the Council of Europe, and the Congress of Regional and Local Authorities of the Council of Europe. The Commission disseminates its work through the UniDem (University for Democracy) programme of seminars, the CODICES database, and the *Bulletin of Constitutional Case-Law*. In May 2005 Council Heads of State decided to establish a new Forum for the Future of Democracy, with the aim of strengthening democracy and citizens' participation.

The promotion of local and regional democracy and of transfrontier co-operation constitutes a major aim of the Council's intergovernmental programme of activities. The Steering Committee on Local and Regional Democracy (CDLR) serves as a forum for representatives of member states to exchange information and pursue co-operation in order to promote the decentralization of powers, in accordance with the European Charter on Local Self-Government. The CDLR's principal objective is to improve the legal, institutional and financial framework of local democracy and to encourage citizen participation in local and regional communities. In December 2001 the Committee of Ministers adopted a Recommendation on citizens' participation in public life at local level, drafted on the basis of the work conducted by the CDLR. The CDLR publishes comparative studies and national reports, and aims to identify guide-lines for the effective implementation of the principles of subsidiarity and solidarity. Its work also constitutes a basis for the provision of aid to central and eastern European countries in the field of local democracy. The CDLR is responsible for the preparation and follow-up of Conferences of Ministers responsible for local and regional government.

Intergovernmental co-operation with the CDLR is supplemented by specific activities aimed at providing legislative advice, supporting reform and enhancing management capabilities and democratic participation in European member and non-member countries. These activities are specifically focused on the democratic stability of central and eastern European countries. The programmes for democratic stability in the field of local democracy draw inspiration from the European Charter of Local Self-Government, operating at three levels of government: at intergovernmental level, providing assistance in implementing reforms to reinforce local or regional government, in compliance with the Charter; at local or regional level, co-operating with local and regional authorities to build local government capacity; and at community level, co-operating directly with individual authorities to promote pilot initiatives. Working methods include: awareness-raising conferences; legislative opinion involving written opinions, expert round-tables and working groups; and seminars, workshops and training at home and abroad.

In February 2005 the 14th session of the conference of European ministers responsible for local and regional government adopted the Budapest Agenda for Delivering Good Local and Regional Governance in 2005–10, which identified challenges confronting local and regional democracy in Europe and actions to be taken in response to them. In October 2007 the 15th session of the conference adopted the Valencia Declaration, recommitting to the implementation of the Budapest Agenda and endorsing a new Council of Europe Strategy on Innovation and Good Governance at Local Level. The 15th session also determined to draft an additional protocol to the European Charter on Local Self-Government consolidating at European level the right to democratic participation, citizens' right to information, and the duties of authorities relating to these rights.

The policy of the Council of Europe on transfrontier co-operation between territorial communities or authorities is implemented through two committees. The Committee of Experts on Transfrontier Co-operation, working under the supervision of the CDLR, aims to monitor the implementation of the European Outline Convention on Transfrontier Co-operation between Territorial Communities or Authorities; to make proposals for the elimination of obstacles, in particular of a legal nature, to transfrontier and interterritorial co-operation; and to compile 'best practice' examples of transfrontier co-operation in various fields of activity. In 2002 the Committee of Ministers adopted a Recommendation on the mutual aid and assistance between central and local authorities in the event of disasters affecting frontier areas. A Committee of Advisers for the development of transfrontier co-operation in central and eastern Europe is composed of six members appointed or elected by the Secretary-General, the Committee of Ministers and the Congress of Local and Regional Authorities of Europe. Its task is to guide the promotion of transfrontier co-operation in central and eastern European countries, with a view to fostering good neighbourly relations between the frontier populations, especially in particularly sensitive regions. Its programme comprises: conferences and colloquies designed to raise awareness on the Outline Convention; meetings in border regions between representatives of local communities with a view to strengthening mutual trust; and legal assistance to, and restricted meetings with, national and local representatives responsible for preparing the legal texts for ratification and/or implementation of the Outline Convention. The priority areas outlined by the Committee of Advisers include South-East Europe, northern Europe around the Baltic Sea, the external frontiers of an enlarged European Union, and the Caucasus.

EDUCATION, CULTURE AND HERITAGE

The European Cultural Convention covers education, culture, heritage, sport and youth. Programmes on education, higher education, culture and cultural heritage are managed by four steering committees.

The education programme consists of projects on education for democratic citizenship and human rights, history teaching, the European dimension of education and interreligious dialogue, instruments and policies for plurilingualism, equitable education policies responding to new social, economic and technological realities, and bilateral co-operation for education renewal. Other activities include the partial agreement for the European Centre for Modern Languages located in Graz, Austria, the In-Service Educational Staff Training Programme, the Network for School Links and Exchanges, and the European Schools Day competition, organized in co-operation with the European Union. The Council of Europe's main focus in the field of higher education is on the Bologna Process aiming to establish a European Higher Education Area by 2010.

In December 2000 the Committee of Ministers adopted a Declaration on Cultural Diversity, formulated in consultation with other organizations (including the European Union and UNESCO), which created a framework for developing a European approach to valuing cultural diversity. A European Charter for Regional or Minority Languages entered into force in 1998, with the aim of protecting regional or minority languages, which are considered to be a threatened aspect of Europe's cultural heritage. It was intended to promote the use in private and public life of languages traditionally used within a state's territory. The Charter provides for a monitoring system enabling states, the Council of Europe and individuals to observe and follow up its implementation.

The Framework Convention on the Value of Cultural Heritage for Society (known as the Faro Framework Convention), which was adopted in October 2005 and had been ratified by three countries at

April 2008, establishes principles underpinning the use and development of heritage in Europe in the globalization era.

The European Convention for the Protection of Audiovisual Heritage and its Protocol were opened for signature in November 2001; the first document entered into force in January 2008, and had been ratified by five countries at April of that year. The Eurimages support fund, in which 33 member states participate, helps to finance co-production of films. The Convention for the Protection of the Architectural Heritage and the Protection of the Archaeological Heritage provide a legal framework for European co-operation in these areas. The European Heritage Network is being developed to facilitate the work of professionals and state institutions and the dissemination of good practices in more than 30 countries of the states party to the European Cultural Convention.

YOUTH

In 1972 the Council of Europe established the European Youth Centre (EYC) in Strasbourg. A second residential centre was created in Budapest in 1995. The centres, run with and by international non-governmental youth organizations representing a wide range of interests, provide about 50 residential courses a year (study sessions, training courses, symposia). A notable feature of the EYC is its decision-making structure, by which decisions on its programme and general policy matters are taken by a Programming Committee composed of an equal number of youth organizations and government representatives. In May 2005 a European Youth Summit was convened, in Warsaw, to coincide with the summit of heads of state or government.

The European Youth Foundation (EYF) aims to provide financial assistance to European activities of non-governmental youth organizations and began operations in 1973. Since that time more than 300,000 young people have benefited directly from EYF-supported activities. The Steering Committee for Youth conducts research in youth-related matters and prepares for ministerial conferences.

SPORT

The Committee for the Development of Sport, founded in November 1977, oversees sports co-operation and development on a pan-European basis, bringing together all the 49 states party to the European Cultural Convention. Its activities focus on the implementation of the European Sport Charter and Code of Sports Ethics (adopted in 1992 and revised in 2001), the role of sport in society, the provision of assistance in sports reform to new member states in central and eastern Europe, and the practice of both recreational and high level sport. A Charter on Sport for Disabled Persons was adopted in 1986. The Committee also prepares the Conferences of European Ministers responsible for Sport (usually held every four years) and has been responsible for drafting two important conventions to combat negative influences on sport. The European Convention on Spectator Violence and Misbehaviour at Sport Events (1985) provides governments with practical measures to ensure crowd security and safety, particularly at football matches. The Anti-Doping Convention (1989) has been ratified by 49 European countries (as at April 2008), and is also open to non-European states. In October 2004 the ministerial conference, convened in Budapest, Hungary, adopted principles of good governance in sport, and a resolution on European sports co-operation in 2004–08.

ENVIRONMENT AND SUSTAINABLE DEVELOPMENT

In 1995 a pan-European biological and landscape diversity strategy, formulated by the Committee of Ministers, was endorsed at a ministerial conference of the UN Economic Commission for Europe, which was held in Sofia, Bulgaria. The strategy was to be implemented jointly by the Council of Europe and UNEP, in close co-operation with the European Community. In particular, it provided for implementation of the Convention on Biological Diversity.

The Convention on the Conservation of European Wildlife and Natural Habitats (Bern Convention), which was signed in 1979 and entered into force in June 1982, gives total protection to 693 species of plants, 89 mammals, 294 birds, 43 reptiles, 21 amphibians, 115 freshwater fishes, 113 invertebrates and their habitats. The Convention established a network of protected areas known as the 'Emerald Network'. The Council awards the European Diploma for protection of sites of European significance, supervises a network of biogenetic reserves, and co-ordinates conservation action for threatened animals and plants. A European Convention on Landscape, to provide for the management and protection of the natural and cultural landscape in Europe, was adopted by the Committee of Ministers in 2000 and entered into force in July 2004.

Regional disparities constitute a major obstacle to the process of European integration. Conferences of ministers responsible for regional/spatial planning (CEMAT) are held to discuss these issues. In 2000 they adopted guiding principles for sustainable development of the European continent and, in 2001, a resolution detailing a 10-point programme for greater cohesion among the Regions of Europe. In September 2003 the 13th CEMAT, convened in Ljubljana, Slovenia, agreed on strategies to promote the sustainable spatial development of the continent, including greater public participation in decision-making, an initiative to revitalize the countryside and efforts to prevent flooding. The 14th meeting was held in Portugal, in October 2006, and the 15th was to be convened in 2009.

EXTERNAL RELATIONS

Agreements providing for co-operation and exchange of documents and observers have been concluded with the United Nations and its agencies, and with most of the European inter-governmental organizations and the Organization of American States. Relations with non-member states, other organizations and non-governmental organizations are co-ordinated by the Directorate General of Political Affairs. In 2001 the Council and European Commission signed a joint declaration on co-operation and partnership, which provided for the organization and funding of joint programmes.

Israel, Canada and Mexico are represented in the Parliamentary Assembly by observer delegations, and certain European and other non-member countries participate in or send observers to certain meetings of technical committees and specialized conferences at intergovernmental level. Full observer status with the Council was granted to the USA in 1995, to Canada and Japan in 1996 and to Mexico in 1999. The Holy See has had a similar status since 1970.

The European Centre for Global Interdependence and Solidarity (the 'North–South Centre') was established in Lisbon, Portugal, in 1990, in order to provide a framework for European co-operation in this area and to promote pluralist democracy and respect for human rights. The Centre is co-managed by parliamentarians, governments, non-governmental organizations and local and regional authorities. Its activities are divided into three programmes: public information and media relations; education and training for global interdependence; and dialogue for global partnership. The Centre organizes workshops, seminars and training courses on global interdependence and convenes international colloquies on human rights.

During the early 1990s the Council of Europe established a structure of programmes to assist the process of democratic reform in central and eastern European countries that had formerly been under communist rule. In October 1997 the meeting of heads of state or of government of Council members agreed to extend the programmes as the means by which all states are assisted to meet their undertakings as members of the Council. These specific co-operation programmes were mainly concerned with the development of the rule of law; the protection and promotion of human rights; and strengthening local democracy. A scheme of Democratic Leadership Programmes has also been established for the training of political leaders. Within the framework of the co-operation programme 21 information and documentation offices have been established in 18 countries of central and eastern Europe.

Finance

The budget is financed by contributions from members on a proportional scale of assessment (using population and gross domestic product as common indicators). The 2008 budget totalled €201m.

Publications

Activities Report (in English and French).

The Bulletin (newsletter of the CLRAE, quarterly).

Bulletin On Constitutional Case-Law (3–4 times a year, in English and French).

The Council of Europe: 800 million Europeans (introductory booklet).

Education Newsletter (3 a year).

The Europeans (electronic bulletin of the Parliamentary Assembly).

The Fight Against Terrorism, Council of Europe Standards (in English and French).

Human Rights and the Environment (in English, French and Italian).

Human Rights Information Bulletin (3 a year, in English and French).

The Independent (newsletter of the North-South Centre, 3 a year).

Iris (legal observations of the European audiovisual observatory, monthly).

Naturopa (2 a year, in 15 languages).

Penological Information Bulletin (annually, in English and French).

INTERNATIONAL ORGANIZATIONS

The Pompidou Group Newsletter (3 a year).
Recent Demographic Developments in Europe (annually, in English and French).

Social Cohesion Developments (3 a year).
Yearbook of Film, Television and Multimedia in Europe (in English and French).

ECONOMIC COMMUNITY OF WEST AFRICAN STATES—ECOWAS

Address: ECOWAS Executive Secretariat, 60 Yakubu Gowon Crescent, PMB 401, Asokoro, Abuja, Nigeria.
Telephone: (9) 3147647; **fax:** (9) 3147646; **e-mail:** info@ecowas.int; **internet:** www.ecowas.int.

The Treaty of Lagos, establishing ECOWAS, was signed in May 1975 by 15 states, with the object of promoting trade, co-operation and self-reliance in West Africa. Outstanding protocols bringing certain key features of the Treaty into effect were ratified in November 1976. Cape Verde joined in 1977. A revised ECOWAS treaty, designed to accelerate economic integration and to increase political co-operation, was signed in July 1993.

MEMBERS

Benin	Ghana	Niger
Burkina Faso	Guinea	Nigeria
Cape Verde	Guinea-Bissau	Senegal
Côte d'Ivoire	Liberia	Sierra Leone
The Gambia	Mali	Togo

Organization
(April 2008)

AUTHORITY OF HEADS OF STATE AND GOVERNMENT

The Authority is the supreme decision-making organ of the Community, with responsibility for its general development and realization of its objectives. The Chairman is elected annually by the Authority from among the member states. The Authority meets at least once a year in ordinary session.

COUNCIL OF MINISTERS

The Council consists of two representatives from each member country; the chairmanship is held by a minister from the same member state as the Chairman of the Authority. The Council meets at least twice a year, and is responsible for the running of the Community.

ECOWAS COMMISSION

The ECOWAS Commission, formerly the Executive Secretariat, was inaugurated in January 2007, following a decision to implement a process of structural reform taken at the January 2006 summit meeting of the Authority. Comprising a President, a Vice-President and seven Commissioners, the Commission is elected for a four-year term, which may be renewed once only.

President: Dr MOHAMED IBN CHAMBAS (Ghana).

SPECIALIZED TECHNICAL COMMISSIONS

There are eight technical commissions, comprising representatives of each member state, which prepare Community projects and programmes in the following areas:

(i) Food and Agriculture;

(ii) Industry, Science and Technology, and Energy;

(iii) Environment and Natural Resources;

(iv) Transport, Communications, and Tourism;

(v) Trade, Customs, Taxation, Statistics, and Money and Payments;

(vi) Political, Judicial and Legal Affairs, Regional Security, and Immigration;

(vii) Human Resources, Information, and Social and Cultural Affairs; and

(viii) Administration and Finance.

ECOWAS PARLIAMENT

The inaugural session of the 120-member ECOWAS Parliament, based in Abuja, Nigeria, was held in November 2000. The January 2006 summit meeting of the Authority determined to restructure the Parliament, in line with a process of wider institutional reform. The number of seats was reduced from 120 to 115 and each member of the Parliament was to be elected for a four-year term (reduced from five years). The second legislature was inaugurated in November 2006. There is a co-ordinating administrative bureau, comprising a speaker and four deputy speakers, and there are also eight standing committees (reduced in number from 13) covering each of the Parliament's areas of activity.

Speaker: MAHAMANE OUSMANE (Niger).

ECOWAS COURT OF JUSTICE

The Court of Justice, established in January 2001, is based in Abuja, Nigeria, and comprises seven judges who serve a five-year renewable term of office. At the January 2006 summit meeting the Authority approved the creation of a Judicial Council, comprising qualified and experienced persons, to contribute to the establishment of community laws. The Authority also approved the inauguration of an appellate division within the Court. The judges will hold (non-renewable) tenure for four years.

President: AMINATA MALLE SANOGO.

Activities

ECOWAS aims to promote co-operation and development in economic, social and cultural activity, particularly in the fields for which specialized technical commissions (see above) are appointed, to raise the standard of living of the people of the member countries, increase and maintain economic stability, improve relations among member countries and contribute to the progress and development of Africa. ECOWAS is committed to abolishing all obstacles to the free movement of people, services and capital, and to promoting: harmonization of agricultural policies; common projects in marketing, research and the agriculturally-based industries; joint development of economic and industrial policies and elimination of disparities in levels of development; and common monetary policies. The ECOWAS treaty provides for compensation for states whose import duties are reduced through trade liberalization and contains a clause permitting safeguard measures in favour of any country affected by economic disturbances through the application of the treaty.

Initial slow progress in achieving many of ECOWAS' aims was attributed to the reluctance of some governments to implement policies at the national level, their failure to provide the agreed financial resources, and the absence of national links with the Secretariat; to the high cost of compensating loss of customs revenue; and to the existence of numerous other intergovernmental organizations in the region (in particular the Union économique et monétaire ouest-africaine—UEMOA, which replaced the francophone Communauté économique de l'Afrique de l'ouest in 1994). In respect of the latter obstacle to progress, however, ECOWAS and UEMOA resolved in February 2000 to create a single monetary zone (see below). In October ECOWAS and the European Union (EU) held their first joint high-level meeting, at which the EU pledged financial support for ECOWAS' economic integration programme, and, in April 2001 it was announced that the IMF had agreed to provide technical assistance for the programme.

A revised treaty for the Community was drawn up by an ECOWAS Committee of Eminent Persons in 1991–92, and was signed at the ECOWAS summit conference that took place in Cotonou, Benin, in July 1993. The treaty, which was to extend economic and political co-operation among member states, designated the achievement of a common market and a single currency as economic objectives, while in the political sphere it envisaged the establishment of an ECOWAS parliament, an economic and social council, and an ECOWAS court of justice to enforce Community decisions. The treaty also formally assigned the Community with the responsibility of preventing and settling regional conflicts. At a summit meeting held in Abuja, Nigeria, in August 1994, ECOWAS heads of state and government signed a protocol agreement for the establishment of a regional parliament. The meeting also adopted a Convention on Extradition of non-political offenders. The new ECOWAS treaty entered into effect in August 1995, having received the required number of ratifications. A draft protocol providing for the creation of a mechanism for the prevention, management and settlement of conflicts, and for the maintenance of peace in the region, was approved by ECOWAS heads of state and government in December 1999. The protocol establishing the ECOWAS Parliament came into effect in March 2000. The inaugural session of the Parliament was held in Abuja, Nigeria, in November, and in January 2001 the seven judges of the ECOWAS Court of Justice were sworn in. In December Mauritania withdrew from ECOWAS.

In May 2002 the ECOWAS Authority met in Yamoussoukro, Côte d'Ivoire, to develop a regional plan of action for the implementation of the New Partnership for Africa's Development (NEPAD).

In February 2005 ECOWAS briefly suspended Togo's membership of the Community and imposed an arms embargo on that country and a travel ban on its leaders, owing to the unconstitutional installation of a new President; the sanctions against Togo were reversed when the illegal appointment was withdrawn at the end of the month. In May, in response to unrest in Togo following the allegedly fraudulent election there of Faure Gnassingbé as President, ECOWAS organized a 'mini-summit' meeting, attended by Gnassingbé himself and the leader of the opposition Union des forces de changement, at the conclusion of which, in a communiqué, the Community urged the establishment of a government of unity in Togo.

In January 2006 the Authority, meeting in Niamey, Niger, commended the recent establishment of an ECOWAS Project Development and Implementation Unit, aimed at accelerating the implementation of regional infrastructure projects in sectors such as energy, telecommunications and transport. Also at that meeting the Authority approved further amendments to the revised ECOWAS treaty to provide for institutional reform (see above).

Meeting in Abuja, Nigeria, in June 2007, the Authority adopted a long-term ECOWAS Strategic Vision, detailing the proposed establishment by 2020 of a West African region-wide borderless, stateless space and single economic community.

TRADE AND MONETARY UNION

Under the founding ECOWAS treaty elimination of tariffs and other obstructions to trade among member states, and the establishment of a common external tariff, were planned over a transitional period of 15 years, from 1975. At the 1978 Conference of Heads of State and Government it was decided that from May 1979 no member state might increase its customs tariff on goods from another member. This was regarded as the first step towards the abolition of customs duties within the Community. During the first two years import duties on intra-community trade were to be maintained, and then eliminated in phases over the next eight years. Quotas and other restrictions of equivalent effect were to be abolished in the first 10 years. It was envisaged that in the remaining five years all differences between external customs tariffs would be abolished.

In 1980 ECOWAS heads of state and government decided to establish a free-trade area for unprocessed agricultural products and handicrafts from May 1981. Tariffs on industrial products made by specified community enterprises were also to be abolished from that date, but implementation was delayed by difficulties in defining the enterprises. From 1 January 1990 tariffs were eliminated on 25 listed items manufactured in ECOWAS member states. Over the ensuing decade, tariffs on other industrial products were to be eliminated as follows: the 'most-developed' countries of ECOWAS (Côte d'Ivoire, Ghana, Nigeria and Senegal) were to abolish tariffs on 'priority' products within four years and on 'non-priority' products within six years; the second group (Benin, Guinea, Liberia, Sierra Leone and Togo) were to abolish tariffs on 'priority' products within six years, and on 'non-priority' products within eight years; and the 'least-developed' members (Burkina Faso, Cape Verde, The Gambia, Guinea-Bissau, Mali and Niger) were to abolish tariffs on 'priority' products within eight years and on 'non-priority' products within 10 years. By December 2000 only Benin had removed tariffs on all industrial products. During 2008 all 15 ECOWAS member states were participating in the negotiation phase on the implementation of the common external tariff.

In 1990 ECOWAS heads of state and government agreed to adopt measures that would create a single monetary zone and remove barriers to trade in goods that originated in the Community. ECOWAS regards monetary union as necessary to encourage investment in the region, since it would greatly facilitate capital transactions with foreign countries. In September 1992 it was announced that, as part of efforts to enhance monetary co-operation and financial harmonization in the region, the West African Clearing House was to be restructured as the West African Monetary Agency (WAMA). As a specialized agency of ECOWAS, WAMA was to be responsible for administering an ECOWAS exchange rate system (EERS) and for establishing the single monetary zone. A credit guarantee scheme and travellers' cheque system were to be established in association with the EERS. The agreement founding WAMA was signed by the Governors of the central banks of ECOWAS member states, meeting in Banjul, The Gambia, in March 1996. In July the Authority agreed to impose a common value-added tax (VAT) on consumer goods, in order to rationalize indirect taxation and to stimulate greater intra-Community trade. In August 1997 ECOWAS heads of state and government appointed an ad hoc monitoring committee to promote and oversee the implementation of trade liberalization measures and the establishment of a single monetary zone. The meeting also authorized the introduction of the regional travellers' cheque scheme. In October 1998 the travellers' cheque scheme was formally inaugurated at a meeting of ECOWAS heads of state. The cheques were to be issued by WAMA in denominations of a West African Unit of Account and convertible into each local currency at the rate of one Special Drawing Right (SDR—see IMF). The cheques entered into circulation on 1 July 1999. In March 1998 senior customs officials of ECOWAS countries agreed to harmonize customs policies and administrations, in order to facilitate intra-Community trade, and to pursue the objective of establishing a common external tariff by 2000. However, this deadline was not met. In December 1999 the ECOWAS Authority determined to pursue a 'Fast Track Approach' to economic integration, involving a two-track implementation of related measures. In April 2000 seven, predominantly anglophone, ECOWAS member states—Cape Verde, The Gambia, Ghana, Guinea, Liberia, Nigeria and Sierra Leone—issued the 'Accra Declaration', in which they agreed to establish a second West African monetary union (the West African Monetary Zone—WAMZ) to co-exist initially alongside UEMOA, which unites eight, mainly francophone, ECOWAS member states. As preconditions for adopting a single currency and common monetary and exchange rate policy, the member states of the second West African monetary union were to attain a number of convergence criteria, including: a satisfactory level of price stability; sustainable budget deficits; a reduction in inflation; and the maintenance of an adequate level of foreign exchange reserves. The two complementary monetary unions were expected to harmonize their economic programmes, with a view to effecting an eventual merger, as outlined in an action plan adopted by ECOWAS and UEMOA in February 2000. The ECOWAS Authority summit held in December in Bamako, Mali, adopted an Agreement Establishing the WAMZ, approved the establishment of a West African Monetary Institute to prepare for the formation of a West African Central Bank (WACB), and determined that the harmonization of member countries' tariff structures should be accelerated to facilitate the implementation of the planned customs union. In December 2001 the Authority determined that the currency of the WAMZ (and eventually the ECOWAS-wide currency) would be known as the 'eco' and authorized the establishment during 2002 of an exchange rate mechanism. (This was achieved in April.) Meeting in November 2002 the heads of state and government determined that a forum of ministers of finance from the planned second monetary union should be convened on a regular basis to ensure the effective implementation of fiscal policies. In May 2004 ECOWAS and UEMOA signed a co-operation agreement that provided for the establishment of a Joint Technical Secretariat to enhance the co-ordination of their programmes. Owing to slower-than-anticipated progress in achieving the convergence criteria required for monetary union, the deadline for the inauguration of the WAMZ and launch of the 'eco' was most recently set at December 2009, with the WACB to be established in July 2009.

In January 2006 the Authority approved the implementation of a four-band common external tariff that was to align the WAMZ tariff structure with that of UEMOA, as follows: a 0% tariff would be applied to social goods (for example, educational and medical equipment); 5% would be levied on raw materials and most agricultural inputs; 10% on intermediate goods and rice; and 20% on finished consumer products. At the inaugural meeting of the Joint ECOWAS–UEMOA Management Committee of the ECOWAS Common External Tariff, convened in July 2006, members agreed on a roadmap for implementing the uniform tariff system. The roadmap also outline the legal framework for the introduction of the common external tariff.

In December 1992 ECOWAS ministers agreed on the institutionalization of an ECOWAS trade fair, in order to promote trade liberalization and intra-Community trade. The first trade fair was held in Dakar, Senegal, in 1995; the second was staged in Accra, Ghana, in 1999; and the third fair, at which it was decided that, in future, the event should be biennial, took place in Lomé, Togo, in 2003. A fourth fair was held in Lagos, Nigeria, in October 2005, the fifth took place in Ouagadougou, Burkina Faso, in March 2008, and the sixth was scheduled to take place in Abidjan, Côte d'Ivoire, in 2010.

TRAVEL, TRANSPORT AND COMMUNICATIONS

In 1979 ECOWAS heads of state signed a Protocol relating to free circulation of the region's citizens and to rights of residence and establishment of commercial enterprises. The first provision (the right of entry without a visa) came into force in 1980. An optional ECOWAS travel certificate, valid for travel within the Community in place of a national passport, was established in July 1985. The second provision of the 1979 Protocol, allowing unlimited rights of residence, was signed in 1986 (although Nigeria indicated that unskilled workers and certain categories of professionals would not be allowed to stay for an indefinite period) and came into force in 1989. The third provision, concerning the right to establish a commercial enterprise in another member state was signed in 1990. In July 1992 the ECOWAS Authority formulated a Minimum Agenda for Action for the implementation of Community agreements regarding the free movement of goods and people, for example the removal of non-tariff barriers, the simplification of customs and transit procedures and a reduction in the number of control posts on international roads. However, implementation of the Minimum Agenda was slow. In April 1997 Gambian and Senegalese finance and trade officials concluded an agreement on measures to facilitate the export of goods via Senegal to neighbouring countries, in accordance with ECOWAS protocols relating to inter-state road transit arrangements. An Inter-state Road Transit Authority has been established. A Brown Card scheme provides recognized third-party liability insurance throughout the region. In October 2001 an ECOWAS passport was reported to be ready for issuance; the ECOWAS travel certificate was to remain in operation, while national passports were to be gradually eliminated over a period of five years. Senegal and Benin were the first two member states to issue the ECOWAS passport, which was approved by the Community's heads of state and government in January 2003.

In February 1996 ECOWAS and several private-sector partners established ECOAir Ltd, based in Abuja, Nigeria, which was to develop a regional airline. A regional shipping company, ECOMARINE, commenced operations in February 2003.

In August 1996 the initial phase of a programme to improve regional telecommunications was reported to have been completed. A second phase of the programme (INTELCOM II), which aimed to modernize and expand the region's telecommunications services, was initiated by ECOWAS heads of state in August 1997. A West African Telecommunications Regulators' Association was established, under the auspices of ECOWAS, in September 2000. The January 2006 summit meeting of the Authority approved a new Special Fund for Telecommunications to facilitate improvements to cross-border telecommunications connectivity. In May of that year a meeting of ECOWAS ministers of information and telecommunications was convened, during which guide-lines for harmonizing the telecommunications sector were agreed. In January 2007 ECOWAS leaders adopted a regional telecommunications policy and a regulatory framework that covered areas including interconnection to ICT and services networks, license regimes, and radio frequency spectrum management. A common, liberalized ECOWAS telecommunications market is envisaged.

A programme for the development of an integrated regional road network was adopted in 1980. Under the programme, two major trans-regional roads were to be completed: the Trans-Coastal Highway, linking Lagos, Nigeria, with Nouackchott, Mauritania (4,767 km); and the Trans-Sahelian Highway, linking Dakar, Senegal, with N'Djamena, Chad (4,633 km). By the end of 2000 about 83% of the trans-coastal route was reportedly complete, and about 87% of the trans-Sahelian route. In 2003 the African Development Bank agreed to finance a study on interconnection of the region's railways.

ECONOMIC AND INDUSTRIAL DEVELOPMENT

In November 1984 ECOWAS heads of state and government approved the establishment of a private regional investment bank, to be known as Ecobank Transnational Inc. The bank, which was based in Lomé, Togo, opened in March 1988. ECOWAS has a 10% share in the bank.

The West African Industrial Forum, sponsored by ECOWAS, is held every two years to promote regional industrial investment. Community ministers of industry are implementing an action plan on the formulation of a West African Industrial Master Plan identifying strategies for stimulating regional economic development and attracting external investment.

In September 1995 Nigeria, Ghana, Togo and Benin resolved to develop a gas pipeline to connect Nigerian gas supplies to the other countries. In August 1999 the participating countries, together with two petroleum companies operating in Nigeria, signed an agreement on the financing and construction of the 600-km West African Gas Pipeline, which was to extend from the Nigerian capital, Lagos, to Takoradi, Togo. It became operational in late 2007. The implementation of a planned energy exchange scheme, known as the West African Power Pool Project (WAPP), is envisaged as a means of efficiently utilizing the region's hydro-electricity and thermal power capabilities by transferring power from surplus producers to countries unable to meet their energy requirements. In May 2003 the Community decided to initiate the first phase of WAPP, which was to be implemented in Benin, Côte d'Ivoire, Ghana, Niger, Nigeria and Togo at an estimated cost of US $335m. In January 2005 the Authority endorsed a revised masterplan for the implementation of WAPP, which was scheduled to be completed by 2020. In July 2005 the World Bank approved a $350m.-facility to support the implementation of WAPP. ECOWAS is also developing an initiative aimed at promoting the use of renewable energy resources.

REGIONAL SECURITY

In 1990 a Standing Mediation Committee was formed to mediate disputes between member states. Member states reaffirmed their commitment to refrain from aggression against one another at a summit conference in 1991. The revised ECOWAS treaty, signed in July 1993, incorporates a separate provision for regional security, requiring member states to work towards the maintenance of peace, stability and security.

In December 1997 an extraordinary meeting of ECOWAS heads of state and government was convened in Lomé, Togo, to consider the future stability and security of the region. It was agreed that a permanent mechanism should be established for conflict prevention and the maintenance of peace. ECOWAS leaders also reaffirmed their commitment to pursuing dialogue to prevent conflicts, co-operating in the early deployment of peace-keeping forces and implementing measures to counter trans-border crime and the illegal trafficking of armaments and drugs. At the meeting ECOWAS leaders acknowledged the role of the ECOWAS Cease-fire Monitoring Group (ECOMOG) in restoring constitutional order in Liberia and expressed their appreciation of the force's current efforts in Sierra Leone (see below). In March 1998 ECOWAS ministers of foreign affairs, meeting in Yamoussoukro, Côte d'Ivoire, resolved that ECOMOG should become the region's permanent peace-keeping force, and upheld the decision of heads of state regarding the establishment of a new body, which should be used to observe, analyse and monitor the security situation in the West African region. Ministers agreed to undertake a redefinition of the command structure within the organization in order to strengthen decision-making and the legal status of the ECOMOG force.

In July 1998 ECOWAS ministers of defence and of security adopted a draft mechanism for conflict management, peace-keeping and security, which provided for ECOWAS intervention in the internal affairs of member states, where a conflict or military uprising threatened the region's security. In October the ECOWAS Authority determined to implement a renewable three-year moratorium on the import, export or manufacture of small armaments in order to enhance the security of the sub-region. In March 1999 the Programme of Co-ordination and Assistance for Security and Development (PCASED) was launched to complement the moratorium. The moratorium was renewed for a further three years in July 2001. (In 2004 ECOWAS announced its intention to transform the moratorium into a convention and PCASED was decommissioned.) The Authority also issued a declaration on the control and prevention of drug abuse, agreeing to allocate US $150,000 to establish an Eco-Drug Fund to finance regional activities in countering substance abuse. In June 2006 the Authority adopted the ECOWAS Convention on Small Arms and Light Weapons, their Ammunitions and other Materials, with the aim of regulating the importation and manufacture of such weapons. The ECOWAS Small Arms Control Programme (ECOSAP) was launched in that month, aimed at improving the capacity of national and regional institutions to reduce the proliferation of small weapons across the region. Based in Bamako, Mali, the Programme replaced PCASED and was expected to run for five years. A three-year work programme was to be implemented to provide technical support to the ECOWAS member states and the newly inaugurated ECOWAS Small Arms Unit. Representatives from ECOWAS member states met in Ouagadougou, Burkina Faso, in September 2007 to draft a new West African strategy for enhanced drug control.

The summit meeting of ECOWAS heads of state and government held in December 1999 in Lomé, Togo, approved a draft protocol to the organization's treaty, providing for the establishment of a Permanent Mechanism for the Prevention, Management and Settlement of Conflicts and the Maintenance of Peace in the Region, as envisaged at their conference in December 1997, and for the creation in connection with the Mechanism of a Mediation and Security Council, to comprise representatives of 10 member states, elected for two-year terms. The Mediation and Security Council was to be supported by an advisory Council of Elders, comprising 32 eminent statesmen from the region; this was inaugurated in July 2001. ECOMOG was to be transformed from an ad hoc cease-fire monitoring group (see below) into a permanent standby force available for immediate deployment to avert emerging conflicts in the region. During 1999 ECOWAS member states established the Intergovernmental Action Group Against Money Laundering in Africa (GIABA), which was mandated to combat drug-trafficking and money laundering throughout the region; a revised regulation for GIABA adopted by the Authority in January 2006 expanded the Group's mandate to cover regional responsibility for combating terrorism. In December 2006 a Technical Committee of Experts on Political Affairs, Peace and Security was established as a subsidiary body of the Mediation and Security Council.

The development is under way of the ECOWAS Warning and Response Network (ECOWARN), which, once operational, will assess threats to regional security. In June 2004 the Community approved the establishment of a standby unit of 6,500 troops, including a core rapid reaction component—the ECOWAS Task Force—comprising 1,500 soldiers (deployable within 30 days), a reserve of 1,500 troops, and 3,500 additional troops that could, as necessary, augment the numbers of the Task Force to brigade level (deployable with up to 90 days notice). The ECOWAS Defence and Security Commission approved the operational framework for the standby unit in April 2005.

In October 2006 it was reported that ECOWAS planned to introduce a series of initiatives in each of the member states under the Peace and Development Project (PADEP). The Project intended to foster a 'culture of peace' among the member states of ECOWAS, strengthening social cohesion and promoting economic integration, democracy and good governance.

In March 2008 an ECOWAS Network of Electoral Commissions, comprising heads of member states' institutions responsible for managing elections, was established with the aim of ensuring the transparency and integrity of regional elections and helping to entrench a culture of democracy.

Peace-keeping Operations

In August 1990 the ECOMOG cease-fire monitoring group was dispatched to Liberia in an attempt to enforce a cease-fire between conflicting factions there, to restore public order, and to establish an interim government, until elections could be held. In November a temporary cease-fire was agreed by the protagonists in Liberia, and an interim president was installed by ECOMOG. Following the signature of a new cease-fire agreement a national conference, organized by ECOWAS in March 1991, established a temporary government, pending elections to be held in early 1992. In June 1991 ECOWAS established a committee (initially comprising representatives of five member states, later expanded to nine) to co-ordinate the peace negotiations. In September, at a meeting in Yamoussoukro, Côte d'Ivoire, held under the aegis of the ECOWAS committee, two of the rival factions in Liberia agreed to encamp their troops in designated areas and to disarm under ECOMOG supervision. During the period preceding the proposed elections, ECOMOG was to occupy Liberian air and sea ports, and create a 'buffer zone' along the country's border with Sierra Leone. By September 1992, however, ECOMOG had been unable either to effect the disarmament of two of the principal military factions, the National Patriotic Front of Liberia (NPFL) and the United Liberation Movement of Liberia for Democracy (ULIMO), or to occupy positions in substantial areas of the country, as a result of resistance on the part of the NPFL. The proposed elections were consequently postponed indefinitely.

In October 1992 ECOMOG began offensive action against NPFL positions, with a campaign of aerial bombardment. In November ECOWAS imposed a land, sea and air blockade on the NPFL's territory, in response to the Front's refusal to comply with the Yamoussoukro accord of October 1991. In April 1993 ECOMOG announced that the disarmament of ULIMO had been completed, amid widespread accusations that ECOMOG had supported ULIMO against the NPFL, and was no longer a neutral force. An ECOWAS-brokered cease-fire agreement was signed in Cotonou, Benin, in July, and took effect on 1 August. In September a UN observer mission (UNOMIL) was established in Liberia to work alongside ECOMOG in monitoring the process of disarming troops, as well as to verify the impartiality of ECOMOG.

In September 1994 leaders of Liberia's main military factions, having negotiated with representatives of ECOWAS, the Organization of African Unity (OAU, now the African Union—AU) and the UN, signed an amendment to the Cotonou accord in Akosombo, Ghana. This provided for a new five-member Council of State, in the context of a cease-fire, as a replacement to the expired interim executive authority, and established a new timetable for democratic elections. In early 1995 negotiations to secure a peace settlement, conducted under ECOWAS auspices, collapsed, owing to disagreement on the composition of the new Council of State. In May, in an attempt to ease the political deadlock, ECOWAS heads of state and of government met leaders of the six main warring factions. Under continuing pressure from the international community, the leaders of the Liberian factions signed a new peace accord, in Abuja, Nigeria, in August. This political development led to renewed efforts on the part of ECOWAS countries to strengthen ECOMOG, and by October Burkina Faso, Nigeria, Ghana and Guinea had pledged troop contributions to increase the force's strength from 7,268 to 12,000. In accordance with the peace agreement, ECOMOG forces, with UNO-MIL, were to be deployed throughout Liberia and along its borders to prevent the flow of arms into the country and to monitor the disarmament of the warring parties. In December an attack on ECOMOG troops, by a dissident ULIMO faction (ULIMO–J), disrupted the deployment of the multinational forces and the disarmament process, which was scheduled to commence in mid-January 1996. At least 16 members of the peace-keeping force were killed in the fighting that ensued. Clashes between ECOMOG and the ULIMO–J forces continued in the west of the country in late December 1995 and early January 1996, during which time 130 Nigerian members of ECOMOG were held hostage. In April, following a series of violations of the cease-fire, serious hostilities erupted in the Liberian capital, Monrovia, between government forces and dissident troops. An initial agreement to end the fighting, negotiated under ECOWAS auspices, was unsuccessful; however, it secured the release of several civilians and soldiers who had been taken hostage during the civil disruption. Later in April a further cease-fire agreement was concluded, under the aegis of the US Government, the UN and ECOWAS. In May ministers of foreign affairs of the countries constituting the ECOWAS Committee of Nine advocated that all armed factions be withdrawn from Monrovia and that ECOMOG troops be deployed throughout the capital in order to re-establish the city's 'safe-haven' status. According to the Committee's demands, all property, armaments and equipment seized unlawfully from civilians, ECOMOG and other international organizations during the fighting were to be returned, while efforts to disarm the warring factions and to pursue the restoration of democracy in the country were to be resumed. At the end of May the deployment of ECOMOG troops was initiated. In August a new cease-fire accord was signed by the leaders of the principal factions in Liberia, which envisaged the completion of the disarmament process by the end of January 1997, with elections to be held in May. The disarmament process began in November 1996, and by the end of January 1997 ECOMOG confirmed that 23,000 of the targeted 30,000–35,000 soldiers had been disarmed. The deadline for disarmament was extended by seven days, during which time a further 1,500 soldiers were reported to have been disarmed. However, vigilante attacks by remaining armed faction fighters persisted. The Committee of Nine announced in February that presidential and legislative elections would be held in May, later revising the election schedule to mid-July. ECOMOG was to withdraw from Liberia six months after the election date, until which time it had proposed to offer security for the incoming government and to provide training for a new unified Liberian army. The Committee also agreed, in consultation with the Council of State, to replace the existing Electoral Commission with a new Commission comprising seven members, to reflect all aspects of Liberian society. The Chairman would be selected from among the seven, in consultation with ECOWAS, which along with the UN and the OAU, would act as a 'technical adviser' to the Commission. ECOMOG deployed additional troops, who were joined by other international observers in ensuring that the elections were conducted in the necessary conditions of security. In August, following the inauguration of Charles Taylor (formerly leader of the NPFL) as Liberia's democratically-elected President, ECOWAS heads of state agreed that the ECOMOG force in Liberia was to be reconstituted and would henceforth assist in the process of national reconstruction, including the restructuring of the armed and security forces, and the maintenance of security; it was further envisaged that ECOMOG's mandate (officially due to expire in February 1998) would be extended in agreement with the Liberian Government. A Status of Forces Agreement, which defined ECOMOG's post-conflict responsibilities (i.e. capacity-building and maintenance of security) and imposed conditions on the peace-keeping forces remaining in the country, was signed by the Liberian Government and ECOWAS in June 1998. Relations with the Taylor administration, however, deteriorated, owing to accusations that ECOMOG was providing assistance to opposition groupings. The tense political situation, therefore, and the need for greater resources in Sierra Leone, resulted in ECOMOG transferring its headquarters from Monrovia to Freetown in Sierra Leone. The transfer was reported to have been completed by October, with just two ECOMOG battalions remaining in Liberia. The ECOMOG mission in Liberia was effectively terminated in October 1999 when the final declared stocks of rebel armaments were destroyed. In April 2001 the ECOWAS Authority determined to send a Mediation and Security Council mission to Liberia to monitor compliance with a resolution of the UN Security Council imposing sanctions on the Liberian regime. An ECOWAS military team was sent to Liberia in June 2002 to assess continuing unrest in the country. ECOWAS welcomed a Liberian Leadership Forum that was staged in the following month, in Ouagadougou, Burkina Faso, to address means of achieving peace and reconciliation. In September President Taylor lifted the state of emergency in Liberia. In mid-2003, however, rebel groups began to seize territory in south-eastern areas and to launch a siege on Monrovia. In June a cease-fire brokered by ECOWAS was signed, which provided for a transitional government excluding Taylor. One week later, following the President's announcement that he would stay in power until the expiry of his term of office in January 2004, fighting in the capital resumed, resulting in hundreds of civilian casualties. In July 2003 ECOWAS agreed to send a 3,000-strong force to Liberia; later that month, after considerable international pressure, US President George W. Bush agreed to deploy three US warships to the region to support the Community's troops. In early August troops of the ECOWAS Mission in Liberia (ECOMIL) began to arrive in Monrovia, prompting President Taylor to stand down and to leave the country for exile in Nigeria. At the beginning of October authority was transferred from ECOMIL to a newly-inaugurated UN Mission in Liberia (UNMIL), mandated to support the implementation of the cease-fire accord agreed in June and a Comprehensive Peace Agreement concluded by the parties to the conflict in August. ECOMIL's 3,600 troops were reassigned to UNMIL. ECOWAS was to co-operate with UNMIL and other partners to assist the National Transitional Government (inaugurated in mid-October) with the training of a national police force and the restructuring of the military. Through its mediator for the Liberian peace process, ECOWAS has subsequently played an important role in assisting Liberia prepare for presidential and legislative elections, to be held in October 2005. In September 2004 the ECOWAS Court of Justice indicated its readiness to try former Liberian President Taylor in the event that any Liberian or any other national of the sub-region should file an application on his role in the conflict in Liberia and elsewhere in West Africa. In July 2005 an ECOWAS panel was inaugurated to examine the suitability of prospective members of Liberia's Truth and Reconciliation Commission.

In May 1997 the democratically-elected Sierra Leonean leader, President Ahmed Tejan Kabbah, was overthrown by a military coup involving officers of the national army and RUF rebels. Nigerian forces based in Sierra Leone as part of a bilateral defence pact attempted to restore constitutional order. Their numbers were strengthened by the arrival of more than 700 Nigerian soldiers and two naval vessels which had been serving under the ECOMOG mandate in neighbouring Liberia. At the end of June ECOWAS ministers of foreign affairs, convened in Conakry, Guinea, agreed to pursue the objective of restoring a democratic government in Sierra Leone through dialogue and the imposition of economic sanctions. In July a five-member ECOWAS committee, comprising the foreign ministers of Côte d'Ivoire, Ghana, Guinea, Liberia and Nigeria, together with representatives of the OAU, negotiated an agreement with the so-called Armed Forces Revolutionary Council (AFRC) in Sierra Leone to establish an immediate cease-fire and to pursue efforts towards the restoration of constitutional order. In August ECOWAS heads of state reaffirmed the Community's condemnation of the removal of President Kabbah and officially endorsed a series of punitive measures against the AFRC authorities in order to accelerate the restoration of democratic government. The meeting mandated ECOMOG to maintain and monitor the cease-fire and to prevent all goods, excepting essential humanitarian supplies, from entering that country. It was also agreed that the committee on Sierra Leone include Liberia and be convened at the level of heads of state. In October the UN Security Council imposed an embargo on the sale or supply of armaments to Sierra Leone and authorized ECOWAS to ensure implementation of these measures. ECOMOG conducted a number of attacks against commercial and military targets, with the aim of upholding the international sanctions, and clashes occurred between ECOMOG troops and AFRC/RUF soldiers, in particular around the area of Freetown's Lungi international airport which had been seized by ECOMOG. Despite the escalation in hostilities, the ECOWAS Committee of Five pursued negotiations with the military authorities, and at the end of October both sides signed a peace agreement, in Conakry, Guinea, providing for an immediate end to all fighting and the reinstatement of Kabbah's Government by April 1998; all combatants were to be disarmed and demobilized under the supervision of a disarmament committee comprising representatives of ECOMOG, the military authorities and local forces loyal to President Kabbah. In November 1997, however, the peace process was undermined by reports that ECOMOG forces had violated the cease-fire agreement following a series of air raids on Freetown, which ECOMOG claimed to have been in retaliation for attacks by AFRC/RUF-operated anti-aircraft equipment, and a demand by the AFRC authorities that the Nigerian contingent of ECOMOG leave the country. In mid-February 1998, following a series of offensive attacks against forces loyal to the military authorities, ECOMOG assumed control of Freetown and arrested several members of the AFRC/RUC regime. Some 50 AFRC officials were arrested by troops serving under ECOMOG on arrival at James Spriggs Payne Airport in Liberia, prompting protests from the Liberian Government at the Nigerian military intervention. An 11-member supervisory task force, which included the ECOMOG Commander, was established in Sierra Leone to maintain order, pending Kabbah's return from exile. ECOMOG troops subsequently also monitored the removal of the embargo against the use of the airport and port facilities in Freetown. Kabbah returned to Sierra Leone in March and installed a new administration. It was agreed that ECOMOG forces were to remain in the country in order to ensure the full restoration of peace and security, to assist in the restructuring of the armed forces and to help to resolve the problems of the substantial numbers of refugees and internally displaced persons. In early May ECOWAS Chiefs of Staff, meeting in Accra, Ghana, urged member states to provide more troops and logistical support to strengthen the ECOMOG force in Sierra Leone (at that time numbering some 10,000 troops), which was still involved in ongoing clashes with remaining rebel soldiers in eastern regions of the country. The UN established an Observer Mission in Sierra Leone (UNOMSIL) in July, which was to monitor the cease-fire, mainly in areas secured by ECOMOG troops. In October ECOMOG transferred its headquarters to Freetown, in order, partly, to reinforce its presence in the country. In January 1999 rebel soldiers attacked the capital and engaged in heavy fighting with ECOMOG forces, amid reports that the Liberian Government was supporting the rebels. Nigeria dispatched several thousand additional troops to counter the rebel advance and to secure the border with Liberia. In February, however, once ECOMOG had regained control of Freetown, the Nigerian Government expressed its desire to withdraw all of its troops from the peace-keeping force by May, owing to financial restraints. Efforts to negotiate a peace settlement were initiated, with the Chairman of ECOWAS at that time, President Gnassingbé Eyadéma of Togo, actively involved in mediation between the opposing groups, despite persisting reports of fighting between ECOMOG and rebel soldiers in areas east of the capital. A cease-fire agreement was concluded in May, and a political settlement was signed, by Kabbah and the RUF leader, in Lomé, Togo, in July. ECOMOG's mandate in Sierra Leone was adapted to support the consolidation of peace in that country and national reconstruction. In October UNOMSIL was replaced by the UN Mission in Sierra Leone (UNAMSIL), which was to assist with the implementation of the Lomé accord and to assume many of the functions then being performed by ECOMOG, including the provision of security at Lungi international airport and at other key installations, buildings and government institutions in the Freetown area. In consequence the ECOMOG contingent was withdrawn in April 2000. However, following a resurgence of RUF violence in April and May, when as many as 500 members of UNAMSIL (which had not been deployed to full strength) were captured by the rebels, ECOWAS heads of government agreed to reinforce the UN peace-keeping operation with some 3,000 regional troops. A UN Security Council mission to Sierra Leone in September recommended the establishment of a mechanism to co-ordinate the formulation and implementation by the UN, ECOWAS, the Sierra Leone Government and other parties of a unified strategy to resolve the insecurity in Sierra Leone. A new cease-fire accord was agreed by the Sierra Leone Government and the RUF in November, in Abuja, Nigeria, and in January 2002 the process (monitored by UNAMSIL) of disarming, demobilizing and reintegrating former combatants was completed. An ECOWAS observer team was dispatched to monitor legislative and presidential elections that were held in Sierra Leone in May. In April 2001 representatives of the Mediation and Security Council were dispatched to Liberia to monitor, jointly with a UN delegation, the Liberian Government's compliance with a UN Security Council Resolution aimed at ending support for and eradicating RUF activity in that country, and at terminating illicit trading there in Sierra Leonean diamonds.

At the end of September 2002 an extraordinary summit meeting of ECOWAS heads of state and government was convened in Accra, Ghana, to address the violent unrest that had erupted in Côte d'Ivoire during that month, commencing with an attempted *coup d'état* by disloyal elements of the country's armed forces. The summit meeting condemned the attempt to overthrow democratic rule and constitutional order and established a high-level contact group, comprising the heads of state of Ghana, Guinea-Bissau, Mali, Niger, Nigeria and Togo, to prevail upon the rebels to end hostilities, and to negotiate a general framework for the resolution of the crisis. The contact group helped to mediate a cease-fire in the following month; this was to be monitored by an ECOWAS military mission in Côte d'Ivoire (ECOMICI), which was also to be responsible for ensuring safe passage for deliveries of humanitarian assistance. In March 2003, following the conclusion in January by the parties to the conflict of a peace agreement, signed at Marcoussis, France, ECOWAS chiefs of staff endorsed the expansion of ECOMICI from 1,264 to a maximum of 3,411 men, to monitor the implementation of the peace agreement in co-operation with the UN Mission in Côte d'Ivoire (MINUCI), and French forces. In early April 2004 authority was transferred from ECOMICI and MINUCI to the newly-established UN Operation in Côte d'Ivoire (UNOCI). In mid-June ECOWAS heads of state and government convened at a summit to address means of reviving the implementation of the stalled Marcoussis peace accord. A high-level meeting of ECOWAS heads of state and government, other African leaders, the Chairperson of the AU, and the parties to the Côte d'Ivoire conflict, held in Accra in late July, affirmed that a monitoring mechanism, comprising representatives of ECOWAS, the AU, Côte d'Ivoire and the United Nations, should produce regular reports on progress towards peace in Côte d'Ivoire.

In October ECOWAS urged the UN to strengthen its peace-keeping mission in Côte d'Ivoire and called for the amendment of the mission's mandate to allow it to use force to prevent armed belligerents from entering the 'zone of confidence' established in the country.

In May 2000 the ECOWAS Authority authorized the initiation of an inquiry into the link between illicit trading in diamonds and ongoing rebel activity in the region, with a particular focus on Liberia and Sierra Leone.

ENVIRONMENTAL PROTECTION

ECOWAS promotes implementation of the UN Convention on Desertification Control and supports programmes initiated at national and sub-regional level within the framework of the treaty. Together with the Permanent Inter-State Committee on Drought Control in the Sahel—CILSS, ECOWAS has been designated as a project leader for implementing the Convention in West Africa. Other environmental initiatives include a regional meteorological project to enhance meteorological activities and applications, and in particular to contribute to food security and natural resource management in the sub-region. ECOWAS pilot schemes have formed the basis of integrated control projects for the control of floating (or invasive aquatic) weeds in five water basins in West Africa, which had hindered the development of the local fishery sectors. In 2005 the African Development Bank granted ECOWAS US $3.1m. to assist in floating weed control. A rural water supply programme aims to ensure adequate water for rural dwellers in order to improve their living standards. The first phase of the project focused on schemes to develop village and pastoral water points in Burkina Faso, Guinea, Mali, Niger and Senegal, with funds from various multilateral donors.

AGRICULTURE AND FISHING

In November 1995 an agro-industrial forum, jointly organized by ECOWAS and the EU, was held in Dakar, Senegal. The forum aimed to facilitate co-operation between companies in the two regions, to develop the agro-industrial sector in West Africa and to promote business opportunities.

In February 2001 ECOWAS ministers of agriculture adopted an action plan for the formulation of a common agricultural policy, as envisaged under the ECOWAS treaty. A draft of the ECOWAS Regional Agricultural Policy (ECOWAP) was endorsed by the January 2005 Authority summit. In January 2006 the Authority approved an action plan for the implementation of ECOWAP. The Policy was aimed at enhancing regional agricultural productivity with a view to guaranteeing food-sufficiency and standards. The Community enforces a transhumance certification scheme for facilitating the monitoring of animal movement and animal health surveillance and protection in the sub-region.

SOCIAL PROGRAMME

Four organizations have been established within ECOWAS by the Executive Secretariat: the Organization of Trade Unions of West Africa, which held its first meeting in 1984; the West African Youth Association; the West African Universities' Association; and the West Africa Women's Association (whose statutes were approved by a meeting of ministers of social affairs in May 1987). Regional sports competitions are held annually. The West African Health Organization (WAHO) was established in 2000 by merger of the West African Health Community and the Organization for Co-ordination and Co-operation in the Struggle against Endemic Diseases. In December 2001 the ECOWAS summit of heads of state and government adopted a plan of action aimed at combating trafficking in human beings and authorized the establishment of an ECOWAS Criminal Intelligence Bureau.

INFORMATION AND MEDIA

In March 1990 ECOWAS ministers of information formulated a policy on the dissemination of information about ECOWAS throughout the region and the appraisal of attitudes of its population towards the Community. The ministers established a new information commission. In November 1991 a conference on press communication and African integration, organized by ECOWAS, recommended the creation of an ECOWAS press card, judicial safeguards to protect journalists, training programmes for journalists and the establishment of a regional documentation centre and data bank. In November 1994 the commission of social and cultural affairs, meeting in Lagos, Nigeria, endorsed a series of measures to promote West African integration. These included special radio, television and newspaper features, sporting events and other competitions or rallies. In December 2000 the Council of Ministers approved a new policy on the dissemination of information about the Community's activities.

SPECIALIZED AGENCIES

ECOWAS Bank for Investment and Development: BP 2704, 128 blvd du 13 janvier, Lomé, Togo; tel. 216864; fax 218684; e-mail bidc@bidc-ebid.org; internet www.bidc-ebid.org; f. 2001, replacing the former ECOWAS Fund for Co-operation, Compensation and Development; comprises two divisions, a Regional Investment Bank and a Regional Development Fund; Pres. CHRISTIAN ADOVELANDE.

West African Monetary Agency (WAMA): 11–13 ECOWAS St, PMB 218, Freetown, Sierra Leone; tel. 224485; fax 223943; e-mail wama@sierratel.sl; f. 1975 as West African Clearing House; administers transactions between its 10 member central banks in order to promote sub-regional trade and monetary co-operation; administers ECOWAS travellers' cheques scheme. Mems: Banque Centrale des Etats de l'Afrique de l'Ouest (serving Benin, Burkina Faso, Côte d'Ivoire, Guinea-Bissau, Mali, Niger, Senegal, Togo) and the central banks of Cape Verde, The Gambia, Ghana, Guinea, Liberia, Mauritania, Nigeria and Sierra Leone; Dir-Gen. ANTOINE M. F. NDIAYE (Senegal); publ. *Annual Report*.

West African Monetary Institute (WAMI): Premier Towers, 8th/9th Floors, Cantonments 75, Accra, Ghana; tel. (21) 676-901; fax (21) 676-903; e-mail info@wami-imao.org; internet www.wami-imao.org; f. by the ECOWAS Authority summit in December 2000 to prepare for the establishment of a West African Central Bank, currently scheduled for 1 July 2009; Dir-Gen. Dr OKO JOSEPH NNANNA.

West African Health Organization (WAHO): BP 153 Bobo-Dioulasso 01, Burkina Faso; tel. and fax (226) 975772; e-mail wahooas@wahooas.org; internet www.waho.ecowas.int; f. 2000 by merger of the West African Health Community (f. 1978) and the Organization for Co-ordination and Co-operation in the Struggle against Endemic Diseases (f. 1960); aims to harmonize member states' health policies and to promote research, training, the sharing of resources and diffusion of information; Dir-Gen. Dr KABBA T. JOINER; publ. *Bulletin Bibliographique* (quarterly).

Finance

ECOWAS is financed by contributions from member states, although there is a poor record of punctual payment of dues, which has hampered the work of the Secretariat. Under the revised treaty, signed in July 1993, ECOWAS was to receive revenue from a community tax, based on the total value of imports from member countries. In July 1996 the summit meeting approved a protocol on a community levy, providing for the imposition of a 0.5% tax on the value of imports from a third country. In August 1997 the Authority of Heads of State and Government determined that the community levy should replace budgetary contributions as the organization's principal source of finance. The protocol came into force in January 2000, having been ratified by nine member states, with the substantive regime entering into effect on 1 January 2003. The January 2006 meeting of the Authority approved a budget of US $121m. for the operations of the Community in that year.

Publications

Annual Report.
Contact.
ECOWAS National Accounts.
ECOWAS News.
ECOWAS Newsletter.
West African Bulletin.

ECONOMIC CO-OPERATION ORGANIZATION—ECO

Address: 1 Golbou Alley, Kamranieh St, POB 14155-6176, Tehran, Iran.
Telephone: (21) 22831733; **fax:** (21) 22831732; **e-mail:** registry@ecosecretariat.org; **internet:** www.ecosecretariat.org.

The Economic Co-operation Organization (ECO) was established in 1985 as the successor to the Regional Co-operation for Development, founded in 1964.

MEMBERS

Afghanistan
Azerbaijan
Iran
Kazakhstan
Kyrgyzstan
Pakistan
Tajikistan
Turkey
Turkmenistan
Uzbekistan

The 'Turkish Republic of Northern Cyprus' has been granted special guest status.

Organization
(April 2008)

SUMMIT MEETING

The first summit meeting of heads of state and of government of member countries was held in Tehran in February 1992. Summit meetings are generally held at least once every two years. The ninth summit meeting was convened in Baku, Azerbaijan, in May 2006. The 10th summit meeting was scheduled to be held in Islamabad, Pakistan, in October 2008.

COUNCIL OF MINISTERS

The Council of Ministers, comprising ministers of foreign affairs of member states, is the principal policy- and decision-making body of ECO. It meets at least once a year.

REGIONAL PLANNING COUNCIL

The Council, comprising senior planning officials or other representatives of member states, meets at least once a year. It is responsible for reviewing programmes of activity and evaluating results achieved, and for proposing future plans of action to the Council of Ministers.

COUNCIL OF PERMANENT REPRESENTATIVES

Permanent representatives or Ambassadors of member countries accredited to Iran meet regularly to formulate policy for consideration by the Council of Ministers and to promote implementation of decisions reached at ministerial or summit level.

SECRETARIAT

The Secretariat is headed by a Secretary-General, who is supported by two Deputy Secretaries-General. The following Directorates administer and co-ordinate the main areas of ECO activities: Trade and investment; Transport and communications; Energy, minerals and environment; Agriculture, industry and tourism; Project and economic research and statistics; Human resources and sustainable development; and International relations. The Secretariat services regular ministerial meetings held by regional ministers of agriculture; energy and minerals; finance and economy; industry; trade and investment; and transport and communications.

Secretary-General: KHURSHID ANWAR (Pakistan).

Activities

The Regional Co-operation for Development (RCD) was established in 1964 as a tripartite arrangement between Iran, Pakistan and Turkey, which aimed to promote economic co-operation between member states. ECO replaced the RCD in 1985, and seven additional members were admitted to the Organization in November 1992. The main areas of co-operation are transport (including the building of road and rail links, of particular importance as seven member states are landlocked), telecommunications and post, trade and investment, energy (including the interconnection of power grids in the region), minerals, environmental issues, industry, and agriculture. ECO priorities and objectives for each sector are defined in the Quetta Plan of Action and the Istanbul Declaration; an Almaty Outline Plan, which was adopted in 1993, is specifically concerned with the development of regional transport and communication infrastructure. The period 1998–2007 was designated as the ECO Decade of Transport and Communications. Meeting in October 2005, in Astana, Kazakhstan, the ECO Council of Ministers adopted a document entitled *ECO Vision 2015*, detailing basic policy guidelines for the organization's activities during 2006–15, and setting a number of targets to be achieved in the various areas of regional co-operation.

In 1990 an ECO College of Insurance was inaugurated. A joint Chamber of Commerce and Industry was established in 1993. The third ECO summit meeting, held in Islamabad, Pakistan, in March 1995, concluded formal agreements on the establishment of several other regional institutes and agencies: an ECO Trade and Development Bank, in İstanbul, Turkey (with main branches in Tehran, Iran, and Islamabad, Pakistan); a joint shipping company, airline, and an ECO Cultural Institute, all to be based in Iran; and an ECO Reinsurance Company and an ECO Science Foundation, with headquarters in Pakistan. In addition, heads of state and of government endorsed the creation of an ECO eminent persons group and signed the following two agreements in order to enhance and facilitate trade throughout the region: the Transit Trade Agreement (which entered into force in December 1997) and the Agreement on the Simplification of Visa Procedures for Businessmen of ECO Countries (which came into effect in March 1998). The sixth ECO summit meeting, held in June 2000 in Tehran, urged the completion of the necessary formalities for the creation of the planned ECO Trade and Development Bank and ECO Reinsurance Company. The ECO Cultural Institute was inaugurated in that year. The Shipping Company is now also operational. In May 2001 the Council of Ministers agreed to terminate the ECO airline project, owing to its unsustainable cost, and to replace it with a framework agreement on co-operation in the field of air transport. The ECO Trade and Development Bank was inaugurated in late 2006, and was scheduled to commence operations during 2008. In May 2007 the draft articles of agreement for the establishment of the planned ECO Reinsurance Company were finalized.

In September 1996, at an extraordinary meeting of the ECO Council of Ministers, held in İzmir, Turkey, member countries signed a revised Treaty of İzmir, the Organization's founding charter. An extraordinary summit meeting, held in Ashgabat, Turkmenistan, in May 1997, adopted the Ashgabat Declaration, emphasizing the importance of the development of the transport and communications infrastructure and the network of transnational petroleum and gas pipelines through bilateral and regional arrangements in the ECO area. In May 1998, at the fifth summit meeting, held in Almaty, Kazakhstan, ECO heads of state and of government signed a Transit Transport Framework Agreement (TTFA) and a memorandum of understanding to help combat the cross-border trafficking of illegal goods. (The TTFA entered into force in May 2006.) The meeting also agreed to establish an ECO Educational Institute in Ankara, Turkey. In June 2000 the sixth ECO summit encouraged member states to participate in the development of information and communication technologies through the establishment of a database of regional educational and training institutions specializing in that field. ECO heads of state and government also reconfirmed their commitment to the Ashgabat Declaration. In December 2001 ECO organized its first workshop on energy conservation and efficiency in Ankara. The seventh ECO summit, held in İstanbul, Turkey, in October 2002, adopted the İstanbul Declaration, which outlined a strengthened and more proactive economic orientation for the Organization.

Convening in conference for the first time in March 2000, ECO ministers of trade signed a Framework Agreement on ECO Trade Co-operation (ECOFAT), which established a basis for the expansion of intra-regional trade. The Framework Agreement envisaged the eventual adoption of an accord providing for the gradual elimination of regional tariff and non-tariff barriers between member states. The so-called ECO Trade Agreement (ECOTA) was endorsed at the eighth ECO summit meeting, held in Dushanbe, Tajikistan, in September 2004. Heads of state and government urged member states to ratify ECOTA at the earliest opportunity, in order to achieve their vision of an ECO free-trade area by 2015. The meeting also requested members to ratify and implement the Transit Transport Framework Agreement (see above), to support economic co-operation throughout the region.

ECO ministers of agriculture, convened in July 2002, in Islamabad, adopted a declaration on co-operation in the agricultural sector, which specified that member states would contribute to agricultural rehabilitation in Afghanistan, and considered instigating a mechanism for the regional exchange of agricultural and cattle products. In December 2004, meeting in Antalya, Turkey, agriculture ministers approved the Antalya Declaration on ECO Co-operation in Agriculture and adopted an ECO plan of action on drought management and mitigation. In March 2007, meeting in Tehran, ECO ministers of agriculture approved the concept of an ECO Permanent Commission for Prevention and Control of Animal Diseases and Control of Animal Origin Food-Borne Diseases (ECO-PCPCAD). In April 2007 an ECO experts' group convened to develop a work plan on biodiversity in the ECO region with the aim of promoting co-operation towards achieving a set of agreed biodiversity targets over the period 2007–15. An ECO Seminar on Ecotourism was held in Kastamonu Province, Turkey, in the following month. In September 2007 the ECO Regional Center for Risk Management of Natural Disasters was inaugurated in Mashhad, Iran; the Center was to promote co-operation in drought monitoring and early warning. An ECO International Conference on Disaster Risk Management was convened in the following month, in Islamabad, Pakistan. In February 2006 a high-level group of experts on health was formed; its first meeting, held in the following month, focused on the spread of avian influenza in the region.

A meeting of ministers of industry, convened in November 2005, approved an ECO plan of action on privatization, envisaging enhanced technical co-operation between member states, and a number of measures for increasing cross-country investments; and adopted a declaration on industrial co-operation. The first meeting of the heads of ECO member states' national statistics offices, convened in January 2008 in Tehran, adopted the ECO Framework of Co-operation in Statistics and a related plan of action. An ECO Trade Fair was scheduled to be staged in Pakistan, in July 2008. The Organization maintains ECO TradeNet, an internet-based repository of regional trade information.

ECO has co-operation agreements with several UN agencies and other international organizations in development-related activities. An ECO-UNODC Project on Drug Control and Co-ordination Unit commenced operations in Tehran in July 1999. In December 2007 the ECO Secretary-General welcomed, as a means of promoting regional peace and security, the inauguration of the UN Regional Centre for Preventive Diplomacy in Central Asia (UNRCCA), based in Ashgabat, Turkmenistan. In that month ECO and the Shanghai Co-operation Organization signed a memorandum of understanding on mutual co-operation in areas including trade and transportation, energy and environment, and tourism. ECO has been granted observer status at the UN, OIC and WTO.

In November 2001 the UN Secretary-General requested ECO to take an active role in efforts to restore stability in Afghanistan and to co-operate closely with his special representative in that country. In June 2002 the ECO Secretary-General participated in a tripartite ministerial conference on co-operation for development in Afghanistan that was convened under the auspices of the UN Development Programme and attended by representatives from Afghanistan, Iran and Pakistan. The ECO summit meeting in October authorized the establishment of a special fund to provide financial assistance for reconstruction activities in Afghanistan. Projects to be implemented by the fund were reviewed during the first mission of the ECO Secretariat to Afghanistan, led by the Secretary-General in June 2005.

Finance

Member states contribute to a centralized administrative budget.

Publications

ECO Annual Economic Report.
ECO Bulletin (quarterly).
ECO Environment Bulletin.

EUROPEAN BANK FOR RECONSTRUCTION AND DEVELOPMENT—EBRD

Address: One Exchange Square, 175 Bishopsgate, London, EC2A 2JN, United Kingdom.
Telephone: (20) 7338-6000; **fax:** (20) 7338-6100; **e-mail:** generalenquiries@ebrd.com; **internet:** www.ebrd.com.

The EBRD was founded in May 1990 and inaugurated in April 1991. Its object is to contribute to the progress and the economic reconstruction of the countries of central and eastern Europe which undertake to respect and put into practice the principles of multiparty democracy, pluralism, the rule of law, respect for human rights and a market economy.

MEMBERS

Countries of Operations:

Albania	Macedonia, former Yugoslav republic
Armenia	Moldova
Azerbaijan	Mongolia
Belarus	Montenegro
Bosnia and Herzegovina	Poland
Bulgaria	Romania
Croatia	Russia
Czech Republic	Serbia
Estonia	Slovakia
Georgia	Slovenia
Hungary	Tajikistan
Kazakhstan	Turkmenistan
Kyrgyzstan	Ukraine
Latvia	Uzbekistan
Lithuania	

Other EU members*:

Austria	Italy
Belgium	Luxembourg
Cyprus	Malta
Denmark	Netherlands
Finland	Portugal
France	Spain
Germany	Sweden
Greece	United Kingdom
Ireland	

EFTA members:

Iceland	Norway
Liechtenstein	Switzerland

Other countries:

Australia	Mexico
Canada	Morocco
Egypt	New Zealand
Israel	Turkey
Japan	USA
Republic of Korea	

* The European Community and the European Investment Bank are also shareholder members in their own right.

Organization

(April 2008)

BOARD OF GOVERNORS

The Board of Governors, to which each member appoints a Governor (normally the minister of finance of that country) and an alternate, is the highest authority of the EBRD. It elects the President of the Bank. The Board meets each year. The 2008 Annual Meeting was scheduled to be convened in Kyiv, Ukraine, in May.

BOARD OF DIRECTORS

The Board, comprising 23 directors, elected by the Board of Governors for a three-year term, is responsible for the organization and operations of the EBRD.

ADMINISTRATION

The EBRD's operations are conducted by its Banking Department, headed by the First Vice-President. The other departments are: Finance; Risk Management; Human Resources and Administration; Internal Audit; Communications; and Offices of the President, the Secretary-General, the General Counsel, the Chief Economist and the Chief Compliance Officer. A structure of country teams, industry teams and operations support units oversee the implementation of projects. The EBRD has 33 local offices in 29 countries. At December

2006 there were 1,018 staff at the Bank's headquarters and 261 staff in the Resident Offices.
President: JEAN LEMIERRE (France).
First Vice-President: VAREL FREEMAN (USA).

Activities

In April 1996 EBRD shareholders, meeting in Sofia, Bulgaria, agreed to increase the Bank's capital from ECU 10,000m. to ECU 20,000m., to enable the Bank to continue, and to enhance, its lending programme (the ECU was replaced by the euro, with an equivalent value, from 1 January 1999). It was agreed that 22.5% of the new resources was to be paid-up, with the remainder as 'callable' shares. Contributions were to be paid over a 13-year period from April 1998. At 31 December 2006 paid-up capital amounted to €5,198m.

The Bank aims to assist the transition of the economies of central Europe, southern and eastern Europe and the Caucasus, and central Asia and Russia towards a market economy system, and to encourage private enterprise. The Agreement establishing the EBRD specifies that 60% of its lending should be for the private sector, and that its operations do not displace commercial sources of finance. The Bank helps the beneficiaries to undertake structural and sectoral reforms, including the dismantling of monopolies, decentralization, and privatization of state enterprises, to enable these countries to become fully integrated in the international economy. To this end, the Bank promotes the establishment and improvement of activities of a productive, competitive and private nature, particularly small and medium-sized enterprises (SMEs), and works to strengthen financial institutions. It mobilizes national and foreign capital, together with experienced management teams, and helps to develop an appropriate legal framework to support a market-orientated economy. The Bank provides extensive financial services, including loans, equity and guarantees, and aims to develop new forms of financing and investment in accordance with the requirements of the transition process. In 2006 the Bank formally began to implement a strategy to withdraw, by 2010, from countries where the transition to a market economy was nearing completion, i.e. those now members of the European Union (see below), and strengthen its focus on and resources to Russia, the Caucasus and central Asia. Mongolia and Montenegro became new countries of operations in 2006.

In the year ending 31 December 2006 the EBRD approved 301 operations, involving funds of €4,936m., compared with €4,277m. for 276 operations in the previous year. During 2006 some 45% of all project financing committed was allocated to the financial sector, including loans to SMEs through financial intermediaries. By the end of 2006 the Bank had approved 2,268 projects since it commenced operations, for which financing of €33,348m. had been approved. In addition, the Bank had mobilized resources amounting to an estimated €69,571m.

The economic crisis in Russia, in August 1998, undermined the viability of many proposed projects and adversely affected the Bank's large portfolio of Russian investments. In March 1999, partly in response to the region's economic difficulties, the Board of Directors approved a new medium-term strategy for 2000–03, which focused on advancing the process of transition. Key aspects of the strategy were to develop a sound financial sector and investment climate in its countries of operations; to provide leadership for the development of SMEs; to promote infrastructure development; and to ensure a balanced and focused project portfolio. Since 2002 EBRD, together with the World Bank, IMF and Asian Development Bank, has sponsored the CIS-7 initiative which aimed to generate awareness of the difficulties of transition for seven low-income countries of the Commonwealth of Independent States (Armenia, Azerbaijan, Georgia, Kyrgyzstan, Moldova, Tajikistan, Uzbekistan), strengthen international and regional co-operation, and promote reforms to achieve economic growth. A review of the scheme was published in April 2004. In that month a new initiative was launched to increase activities in those CIS states, designated 'Early Transition Countries' (ETCs), in particular to stimulate private sector business development, market activity and financing of small-scale projects. In November the Bank established a multi-donor ETC Fund to administer donor pledges and grant financing in support of EBRD projects in those countries. In 2006 Mongolia was incorporated into the ETC grouping.

During 1999 the Bank participated in international efforts to secure economic and political stability in the Balkans, following the conflict in Kosovo. Subsequently the Bank has promoted the objectives of the Stability Pact for South-Eastern Europe by expanding its commitments in the region and by taking a lead role among international financial institutions in promoting private sector development. In July 2000 a US/EBRD SME Financing Facility was established for South East Europe and other early transition countries. In April 1999 the Bank and the European Commission launched a new EU/EBRD SME Finance Facility, to provide equity and loan financing for SMEs in countries seeking accession to the EU. The Facility was also to extend technical assistance in areas including financial regulation, competition policy and telecommunications. During 2003 an EU/EBRD Municipal Finance Facility became operational, with funds of €120m., to assist small municipalities to undertake infrastructure projects to meet EU standards. Following the accession of eight Central European and Baltic countries to the EU in May 2004 the Bank envisaged continuing to provide support in restructuring, encouraging private sector investment and the expansion of local businesses. A Trade Facilitation Programme extends bank guarantees in order to promote trading capabilities in the region, in particular for small and medium-sized businesses. By the end of 2006 105 issuing banks in the region, together with 630 confirming banks in countries world-wide, were participating in the Programme. During 2006 the Bank financed 1,134 trade transactions under the Programme, with a value of some €707m. In October 2001 the Bank developed an Action Plan for Central Asia in order to accelerate development and economic stability in the countries neighbouring Afghanistan, as part of a wider objective of securing peace in the region. From 2002 the EBRD was involved in activities concerning the construction of a Baku–Tbilisi–Ceyhan (BTC) oil pipeline.

A high priority is given to attracting external finance for Bank-sponsored projects, in particular in countries at advanced stages of transition, from government agencies, international financial institutions, commercial banks and export credit agencies. The EBRD's Technical Co-operation Funds Programme (TCFP) aims to facilitate access to the Bank's capital resources for countries of operations by providing support for project preparation, project implementation and institutional development. Resources for technical co-operation originate from regular TCFP contributions, specific agreements and contributions to Special Funds. The Baltic Investment Programme, which is administered by Nordic countries, consists of two special funds to co-finance investment and technical assistance projects in the private sectors of Baltic states. The Funds are open to contributions from all EBRD member states. The Russia Small Business Fund (RSBF) was established in 1994 to support local SMEs through similar investment and technical co-operation activities. By the end of 2006 the Fund had disbursed more than 364,000 loans, with funding of some €2,900m. Other financing mechanisms that the EBRD uses to address the needs of the region include Regional Venture Funds, which invest equity in privatized companies, in particular in Russia, and provide relevant management assistance, and the Central European Agency Lines, which disburse lines of credit to small-scale projects through local intermediaries. A Turn-Around Management Programme (TAM) provides practical assistance to senior managers of industrial enterprises to facilitate the expansion of businesses in a market economy. A Business Advisory Services programme complements TAM by undertaking projects to improve competitiveness, strategic planning, marketing and financial management in SMEs. During 2006 115 TAM and 1,050 BAS projects were initiated. In 2001 the EBRD collaborated with other donor institutions and partners to initiate a Northern Dimension Environmental Partnership (NDEP) to strengthen and co-ordinate environmental projects in northern Europe; the Partnership, which became operational in November 2002, includes a 'nuclear window' to address the nuclear legacy of the Russian Northern Fleet. The Bank manages the NDEP Support Fund. At the end of 2006 donor funding to the NDEP amounted to €241m.

The Bank administers a number of other funds specifically to support the promotion of nuclear safety. By the end of 2006 donor countries and the EU had pledged more than €2,000m. to funds including the Nuclear Safety Account (NSA), a multilateral programme of action established in 1993, the Chornobyl (Chernobyl) Shelter Fund (CSF), established in 1997, and International Decommissioning Support Funds (IDSFs). The funds have enabled the closure of nuclear plants for safety reasons in countries where this would otherwise have been prohibitively costly. In December 2000 Chornobyl Unit 3 was closed, and in 2002 two units were closed in Bulgaria. The closure of a further two units in Bulgaria and one in Slovakia was achieved by the end of December 2006; two units in Lithuania were expected to be shut down by 2009. The NSA was also financing the construction of two major pre-decommissioning facilities in Ukraine, and a review of a safety report for a Russian first-generation reactor.

In 1997 the G-7, together with the European Community and Ukraine, endorsed the creation of the CSF-financed Chornobyl Unit 4 Shelter Implementation Plan (SIP) to assist Ukraine in stabilizing the protective sarcophagus covering the damaged Chornobyl reactor. The plan also provides for the construction of a new confinement structure safely to enclose the building. Construction work commenced in December 2004 and was scheduled to be completed in 2008. The first-stage Unit 4 shelter was completed in December 2006. In 1995 the G-7 requested that the Bank fund the completion of two new nuclear reactors in Ukraine, to provide alternative energy sources to the Chornobyl power-station. A study questioning the financial viability of the proposed reactors threatened funding in early 1997; a second survey, however, carried out by the EBRD, pronounced the plan viable, although environmental groups continued to dispute the proposals.

The EBRD's founding Agreement specifies that all operations are to be undertaken in the context of promoting environmentally sound and sustainable development. It undertakes environmental audits and impact assessments in areas of particular concern, which enable the Bank to incorporate environmental action plans into any project approved for funding. An Environment Advisory Council assists with the development of policy and strategy in this area. In May 2006 the Bank launched a Sustainable Energy Initiative, which commits the Bank to doubling investments in energy efficiency and renewable energy projects to some €1,500m. within three years. As part of the Initiative a Multilateral Carbon Credit Fund was established, in December 2006, in co-operation with the European Investment Bank, providing a means by which countries may obtain carbon credits from emission-related projects.

Publications

Annual Report.
Economics of Transition (quarterly).
Law in Transition (2 a year).
Sustainability Report (annually).
Technical Co-operation—Donors Report (annually).
Transition Report (annually).
Voices of Change (annually).
Working papers, fact sheets.

Statistics

PROJECT FINANCING COMMITTED BY SECTOR
(€ million)

	2005	2006
Financial institutions		
Bank equity	94.6	321.5
Bank lending	796.7	1,078.8
Equity funds	284.4	199.6
Non-bank financial institutions	196.1	333.6
Small business finance	55.7	274.3
Energy		
Natural resources	196.2	11.8
Power and energy	528.4	389.8

—continued	2005	2006
Infrastructure		
Municipal infrastructure	297.5	307.1
Transport	668.0	529.2
Corporate sector		
Agribusiness	480.7	426.2
Manufacturing	392.7	714.7
Property and tourism	163.5	200.3
Telecommunications and new media	123.0	149.3
Total	4,277.5	4,936.2

PROJECT FINANCING COMMITTED BY COUNTRY
(in € million)

	2006	Cumulative to 31 Dec. 2006
Albania	48.2	335.7
Armenia	40.4	144.5
Azerbaijan	134.4	737.7
Belarus	23.7	203.3
Bosnia and Herzegovina	133.0	584.2
Bulgaria	155.0	1,369.4
Croatia	302.7	1,576.4
Czech Republic	47.0	1,107.5
Estonia	0.2	470.5
Georgia	114.0	398.8
Hungary	50.5	1,850.5
Kazakhstan	242.0	1,379.9
Kyrgyzstan	18.8	172.0
Latvia	0.0	322.0
Lithuania	20.5	460.9
Macedonia, former Yugoslav republic	35.1	430.2
Moldova	19.8	196.4
Montenegro	0.1	38.5
Poland	259.2	3,659.9
Romania	254.7	3,330.2
Russia	1,863.7	8,206.7
Serbia	327.3	1,107.7
Slovakia	19.0	1,069.4
Slovenia	2.0	658.1
Tajikistan	19.0	56.2
Turkmenistan	0.0	116.7
Ukraine	797.0	2,862.6
Uzbekistan	5.3	492.1

Note: Operations may be counted as fractional numbers if multiple sub-loans are grouped under one framework agreement.

Source: *EBRD Annual Report 2006.*

EUROPEAN SPACE AGENCY—ESA

Address: 8–10 rue Mario Nikis, 75738 Paris Cédex 15, France.
Telephone: 1-53-69-76-54; **fax:** 1-53-69-75-60; **e-mail:** contactesa@esa.int; **internet:** www.esa.int.

ESA was established in 1975 to provide for, and to promote, European co-operation in space research and technology, and their applications, for exclusively peaceful purposes. It replaced the European Space Research Organisation (ESRO) and the European Launcher Development Organisation (both founded in 1962).

MEMBERS*

Austria	Luxembourg
Belgium	Netherlands
Denmark	Norway
Finland	Portugal
France	Spain
Germany	Sweden
Greece	Switzerland
Ireland	United Kingdom
Italy	

* Canada has signed an agreement for close co-operation with ESA, including representation on the ESA Council.

Organization
(April 2008)

COUNCIL

The Council is composed of representatives of all member states. It is responsible for formulating policy and meets at ministerial or delegate level.

ADMINISTRATION

ESA's activities are divided into the following nine Directorates, each headed by a Director: Earth Observation Programmes; Technical and Quality Management; Launcher Programmes; Human Spaceflight, Microgravity and Exploration Programmes; Resources Management; External Relations; Science Programmes; EU and Industrial Programmes; Operations; and Infrastructure. The heads of each Directorate report directly to the Director General.

Director-General: JEAN-JACQUES DORDAIN (France).

ESA CENTRES

European Astronaut Centre (EAC): Köln, Germany. As a subsidiary of the Directorate of Human Spaceflight, manages all European astronaut activities and trains European and international partner astronauts on the European elements of the International Space Station. The Centre employs 16 European astronauts.

European Space Astronomy Centre (ESAC): Villafranca del Castillo, Spain. A centre of excellence for space science and a base for ESA astrophysics and solar system missions. Hosts a virtual observatory.

European Space Operations Centre (ESOC): Darmstadt, Germany. Responsible for all satellite operations and the corresponding ground facilities and communications networks.

European Space Research and Technology Centre (ESTEC): Noordwijk, Netherlands. ESA's principal technical establishment, at which the majority of project teams are based, together with the space science department and the technological research and support engineers; provides the appropriate testing and laboratory facilities.

European Space Research Institute (ESRIN): Frascati, Italy. Responsible for the corporate exploitation of Earth observation data from space.

ESA has liaison offices in Brussels, Belgium, Moscow, Russia and Washington, DC, USA, as well as offices in Houston, USA to support International Space Station activities and in Kourou, French Guyana, for the Ariane launchers.

Activities

ESA's tasks are to define and put into effect a long-term European space policy of scientific research and technological development and to encourage all members to co-ordinate their national programmes with those of ESA to ensure that Europe maintains a competitive position in the field of space technology. ESA's basic activities cover studies on future projects; technological research; and shared technical investments, information systems and training programmes. These, and the science programme, are mandatory activities to which all members must contribute; other programmes are optional and members may determine their own level of participation. In November 2000 the ESA Council and the Council of the European Union adopted parallel resolutions endorsing a European strategy for space. The strategy, which had been jointly prepared in 1999 and was entitled *Europe and Space: A New Chapter*, aimed to strengthen the foundation for European space activities; advance scientific knowledge; and to use the technical capabilities developed in connection with space activities to secure wider economic and social benefits. ESA collaborated with the European Commission in the preparation of a Green Paper on EU Space Policy, which assessed Europe's strengths and weaknesses in the sector. The Green Paper, which addressed such issues as the EU's independent access to space, international co-operation and environmental and security issues, was released in January 2003 as the basis for a period of consultation, involving national and international organizations, the EU space industry, the scientific community and citizens. Meanwhile, in March 2001, ESA and the European Commission had established a Joint Task Force to implement the European strategy for space. In November 2003 negotiations on a framework agreement for structured co-operation between ESA and the European Community were concluded. The framework agreement aimed to facilitate the coherent and progressive development of an overall European space policy; and to establish a common basis and appropriate practical arrangements for efficient and mutually beneficial co-operation between ESA and the EU. Immediately prior to the conclusion of the framework agreement the European Commission had adopted a White Paper on space policy that had been drafted with ESA's support. The White Paper incorporated an action plan for implementing an enlarged European space policy, and included proposals for joint ESA-EU space programmes that took as their basis the framework agreement.

ESA is committed to pursuing international co-operation to achieve its objective of developing the peaceful applications of space technology. ESA works closely with both the US National Aeronautics and Space Administration (NASA) and the Russian Aviation and Space Agency (Rosaviakosmos). In 2003 ESA and the Russian Government signed an Agreement on Co-operation and Partnership in the Exploration and Use of Outer Space for Peaceful Purposes (to be implemented by Rosaviakosmos), succeeding a similar agreement concluded with the USSR in 1990. In recent years ESA has developed a co-operative relationship with Japan, in particular in data relay satellites and the exchange of materials for the International Space Station. ESA has also concluded co-operation agreements with the Czech Republic, Greece, Hungary, Poland and Romania, providing for technical training and joint projects in the fields of space science, Earth observation and telecommunications. In 2003 ESA and Hungary concluded a 'European Co-operating State Agreement', a legal instrument designed to replace existing co-operation agreements between ESA and European states seeking closer relations with the Agency. ESA assists other transitional and developing countries to expand their space activities. It works closely with other international organizations, in particular the European Union and EUMETSAT. ESA has observer status with the UN Committee on the Peaceful Uses of Outer Space and co-operates closely with the UN's Office of Outer Space Affairs, in particular through the organization of a training and fellowship programme.

SCIENCE

The first European scientific space programmes were undertaken under the aegis of ESRO, which launched seven satellites during 1968–72. The Science Programme is a mandatory activity of the Agency and forms the basis of co-operation between member states. Among the most successful scientific satellites and probes subsequently launched by ESA are the Giotto probe, launched in 1985 to study the composition of Halley's comet and reactivated in 1990 to observe the Grigg-Skjellerup comet in July 1992; and Hipparcos, which, between 1989 and 1993, determined the precise astronomic positions and distances of more than 1m. stars. In November 1995 ESA launched the Infrared Space Observatory, which has successfully conducted pre-planned scientific studies providing data on galaxy and star formation and on interstellar matter. ESA has collaborated with NASA in the Ulysses space project (a solar polar mission;); the Solar and Helispheric Observatory (SOHO), launched in 1995 to study the internal structure of the sun; and the Hubble Space Telescope. In October 1997 the Huygens space probe was launched under the framework of a joint NASA–ESA project (the Cassini/Huygens mission) to study the planet Saturn and its largest moon, Titan, where it landed in January 2005. In December 1999 the X-Ray Multimirror Mission (XMM–Newton) was launched from Kourou, French Guyana. It was envisaged that XMM–Newton, the most powerful x-ray telescope ever placed in orbit, would investigate the origin of galaxies, the formation of black holes, etc. Four cluster satellites, launched from Baikonur, Russia, in July–August 2000, were, in association with SOHO, to explore the interaction between the Earth's magnetic field and electrically-charged particles transported on the solar wind. In October 2002 INTEGRAL (International Gamma-Ray Astrophysical Laboratory) was successfully launched by a Russian Proton vehicle, to study the most violent events perceptible in the Universe.

ESA's space missions are an integral part of its long-term science programme, Horizon 2000, which was initiated in 1984. In 1994 a new set of missions was defined, to enable the inclusion of projects using new technologies and participation in future international space activities, which formed the Horizon 2000 Plus extension covering the period 2005–16. Together they were called Horizons 2000.

In May 2002 the Science Programme Committee initiated a new programme, COSMIC VISION, covering the period 2002–12. Under the programme three main projects—Astrophysics, Solar System Science, and Fundamental Physics—were to be developed in production groups, missions within each to be built synergistically, where possible using common technologies and engineering teams:

Astrophysics: Production Group 2: Herschel, exploring the infrared and microwave Universe; Planck, studying the cosmic microwave background; Eddington, searching for extra-solar planets and studying the stellar seismology. (These missions were to be launched during 2007–08.) Group 3: GAIA, the ultimate galaxy mapper (to be launched no later than 2012).

Solar System Science: Group 1: Rosetta, launched in March 2004, to 'rendez-vous' and land on a comet); Mars Express, a Mars orbiter carrying the Beagle2 lander (launched in 2003; however, contact with Beagle2 was lost in January 2004); Venus Express, a Venus orbiter (2005, entered into orbit around Venus in April 2006). Group 2: SMART-1, which was to demonstrate solar propulsion technology while on course to the Moon (2003); BepiColombo, a mission to Mercury; Solar Orbiter, which was to take a closer look at the Sun. (These missions were to be launched in 2011–12.)

Fundamental Physics: SMART 2, a technology demonstration mission; LISA, a joint mission with NASA, searching for gravitational waves (2011).

In addition, the Agency is committed to co-operation with NASA on JWST (James Webb Space Telescope), the successor of the Hubble Space telescope, scheduled to be launched in 2010. The Herschel Space Observatory, designed to investigate the formation of stars and galaxies, was scheduled to be launched in late 2008.

EARTH OBSERVATION

ESA has contributed to the understanding and monitoring of the Earth's environment through its satellite projects. Since 1977 ESA has launched seven Meteosat spacecraft into geosynchronous orbit, which have provided continuous meteorological data, mainly for the purposes of weather forecasting. The Meteosat systems are financed and owned by EUMETSAT, but were operated by ESA until December 1995. ESA and EUMETSAT have collaborated on the development of a successor to the Meteosat weather satellites (Meteosat Second Generation—MSG) to provide enhanced geostationary data coverage. The first satellite, MSG-1, was launched in August 2002. ESA and EUMETSAT have also begun development of the METOP/ EPS (EUMETSAT Polar System) programme, to provide observations from polar orbit. The first METOP satellite was launched in October 2006.

In 1991 ESA launched the ERS-1 satellite, which carried sophisticated instruments to measure the Earth's surface and its atmosphere. A second ERS satellite was launched in April 1995 with the specific purpose of measuring the stratospheric and tropospheric ozone. ENVISAT, the largest and most advanced European-built observation satellite, was launched in February 2002 from Kourou, French Guyana. ENVISAT aims to provide a detailed assessment of the impact of human activities on the Earth's atmosphere, and land and coastal processes, and to monitor exceptional natural events, such as volcanic eruptions.

In June 1998 the ESA Council approved the initiation of activities related to the Living Planet Programme, designed to increase understanding of environmental issues. In May 1999 the Council committed funds for a research mission, CryoSat, to be undertaken, in order to study the impact of global warming on polar ice caps. However, the launch of CryoSat was aborted in October 2005. A CryoSat recovery plan, completed in February 2006, envisaged the launch, in March 2009, of a CryoSat-2 mission, with the same objectives. Future missions also include the Gravity Field and Steady-State Ocean Circulation Explorer (GOCE), scheduled to be launched in 2008; the GOCE mission was to use a unique measurement technique to recover geodetic precision data on the Earth's gravity field. ESA is responsible for the space component of the European Commission's Global Monitoring for Environment and Security (GMES) programme and aimed to launch an earth observation satellite, Sentinel-2, specifically to monitor the land environment, in 2012.

As part of the Treaty Enforcement Services using Earth Observation (TESEO) initiative, agreed in 2001, ESA satellites provide data for a wide range of environmental activities including monitoring wetlands, ensuring compliance with Kyoto Protocol emission targets and combating desertification. Similarly, ESA has agreements with UNESCO to protect wildlife and sites of historic interest, in support of the Convention Concerning the Protection of the World Cultural and Natural Heritage.

TELECOMMUNICATIONS

ESA commenced the development of communications satellites in 1968. These have since become the largest markets for space use and have transformed global communications, with more than 100 satellites circling the Earth for the purposes of telecommunications. The main series of operational satellites developed by ESA are the European Communications Satellites (ECS), based on the original orbital test satellite and used by EUTELSAT, and the Maritime Communications Satellites (MARECS), which have been leased for operations to INMARSAT

In 1989 ESA launched an experimental civilian telecommunications satellite, Olympus, to develop and demonstrate new broadcasting services. Its mission terminated in 1993, however, after it ran out of fuel. An Advanced Relay and Technology Mission Satellite (ARTEMIS) has been developed by ESA to test and operate new telecommunications techniques, and in particular to enable the relay of information directly between satellites. ARTEMIS was launched in July 2001. In 1998 ESA, together with the EU and EUROCONTROL continued to implement a satellite-based navigation system to be used for civilian aircraft and maritime services, similar to the two existing systems operational for military use. ESA was also working with the EU and representatives of the private sector to enhance the region's role in the development of electronic media infrastructure to meet the expanding global demand. In May 1999 the Council approved funding for a satellite multimedia programme, Artes 3, which aimed to support the development of satellite systems and services for delivering information through high-speed internet access. Within the Artes framework ESA, together with the French national centre for space studies, initiated a project to develop a multipurpose geostationary communications platform, Alphabus, substantially to expand Europe's telecommunications capabilities.

NAVIGATION

ESA, in co-operation with the European Commission and Eurocontrol, is implementing the EGNOS System. EGNOS is the European contribution to the Global Navigation Satellite System phase 1 (GNSS-1) and will provide an improved navigation and positioning service for all users of the (American) GPS and (Russian) GLONASS systems. It is envisaged that EGNOS will serve as a major regional component of a seamless, world-wide augmentation system for navigation, aimed at meeting the demanding requirements for aircraft navigation, and comprising (in addition to EGNOS in Europe): WAAS in the USA, MSAS in Japan and GAGAN in India. ESA and the European Commission are also collaborating to design and develop a European satellite and navigation system, *Galileo*. The project will consist of about 30 satellites, a global network of tracking stations, and central control facilities in Europe. The satellites were due to be launched during 2005–08. The GNSS aims to use the *Galileo*, GPS and GLONASS systems to provide an integrated satellite navigation service of unprecedented accuracy and global coverage under civilian control.

LAUNCHERS

The European requirement for independent access to space first manifested itself in the early 1970s against the background of strategic and commercial interests in telecommunications and Earth observation. As a consequence, and based on knowledge gained through national programmes, ESA began development of a space launcher. The resulting Ariane rocket was first launched in December 1979. The project, which incorporated four different launchers; Ariane-1 to Ariane-4, subsequently became an essential element of ESA's programme activities and, furthermore, developed a successful commercial role in placing satellites into orbit. The last flight of Ariane-4 took place in February 2003. From 1985 ESA worked to develop the more powerful Ariane-5 launcher, which has been in commercial operation since 1999, launched from the ESA facility at the Guyana Space Centre. In December 2000 the ESA Council approved the Vega Small Launcher Development and the P80 Advanced Solid Propulsion Stage programmes. The first Vega launch was due to take place in late 2008. A Future Launcher Preparatory Programme is being defined.

HUMAN SPACEFLIGHT

Europe has gained access to human space technology and operations through Spacelab, which ESA developed as the European contribution to the US Space Shuttle Programme, and through the two joint Euromir missions on the Russian space station, Mir. Spacelab has flown into space 25 times and, with the Euromir projects, has enabled ESA to conduct, using its own astronauts, research into life and physical sciences under microgravity conditions. Since the mid-1980s ESA has supported space research in the life and physical sciences through its microgravity programmes. A considerable scientific output has been achieved in key areas such as crystal growth, solidification physics, fluid sciences, thermophysical properties, molecular and cell biology, developmental biology, exobiology and human physiology. The latest microgravity programme, approved in November 2001, is the ESA Programme in Life and Physical Sciences and Applications (ELIPS). ESA is a partner in the International Space Station (ISS), which was initiated by the US Government in 1984, and subsequently developed as a joint project between five partners-Canada, Europe, Japan, Russia and the USA. ESA's main contributions to the ISS are the Columbus Laboratory (launched in February 2008); and the 'Jules Verne' Automated Transfer Vehicle—ATV (launched by Ariane-5 in March 2008), which was designed to provide logistical support to the Space Station. The Columbus laboratory accommodates European multi-user research facilities: Biolab; Fluid Science Laboratory, European Physiology Modules, Material Science Laboratory (all developed within the Microgravity Facilities for the Columbus Programme); and European Drawer Rack and European Stowage Rack (both within the ISS Utilization Programme). In the framework of the ISS agreements with the USA, ESA is allocated 51% usage of Columbus, the remainder being allocated to NASA. In addition to the experiment accommodation capabilities on Columbus, the European Zero-G Airbus, operated under ESA contract by Novespace, provides European researchers short-duration access to microgravity conditions for a wide variety of experiments, ranging from precursor experiments for the ISS to student experiments. Drop-towers and sounding rockets provide additional short-duration opportunities. The ESA Directorate of Human Spaceflight also provides European researchers with flight opportunities on unmanned Russian Foton and Bion capsules.

Finance

All member states contribute to ESA's mandatory programme activities (studies on future projects; technological research; shared technical investments, information systems and training programmes; and the science programme) on a scale based on their national income, and are free to decide on their level of commitment in optional programmes. The total budget for 2006 amounted to about €2,903.9m., of which 18.3% was allocated to launchers (an optional programme), 14.3% to earth observation (optional), 12.6% to human spaceflight (optional), 11.7% to navigation (optional), and 11.6% to space science (mandatory).

INTERNATIONAL ORGANIZATIONS

Publications

ESA Annual Report.
ESA Bulletin (quarterly).
PFF—Preparing for the Future.
CONNECT.
Eurocomp (newsletter).
ECSL News.
Monographs and conference proceedings.

EUROPEAN UNION—EU

The European Coal and Steel Community (ECSC) was created by a treaty signed in Paris on 18 April 1951 (effective from 25 July 1952) to pool the coal and steel production of the six original members. It was seen as a first step towards a united Europe. The European Economic Community (EEC) and European Atomic Energy Community (Euratom) were established by separate treaties signed in Rome on 25 March 1957 (effective from 1 January 1958), the former to create a common market and to approximate economic policies, the latter to promote growth in nuclear industries. The common institutions of the three Communities were established by a treaty signed in Brussels on 8 April 1965 (effective from 1 July 1967).

The EEC was formally changed to the European Community (EC) under the Treaty on European Union (effective from 1 November 1993), although in practice the term EC had been used for several years to describe the three Communities together. The new Treaty established a European Union (EU), which introduced citizenship thereof and aimed to increase intergovernmental co-operation in economic and monetary affairs; to establish a common foreign and security policy; and to introduce co-operation in justice and home affairs. The EU was placed under the supervision of the European Council (comprising heads of state or of government of member countries), while the EC continued to exist, having competence in matters relating to the Treaty of Rome and its amendments.

The Treaty of Paris establishing the ECSC expired on 23 July 2002. A series of events and ceremonies were held to mark the occasion, including a symposium on the history and future of the EU. Upon expiry of the Treaty, which resulted in the termination of the ECSC legal regime and procedures and the dissolution of the ECSC Consultative Committee, the ECSC's assets and liabilities were transferred to the overall EU budget, while rights and obligations arising from international agreements drawn up between the ECSC and third countries were devolved to the EC.

Meetings of the principal organs take place in Brussels, Luxembourg and Strasbourg.

Presidency of the Council of the European Union: Slovenia (January–June 2008); France (July–December 2008).

Secretary-General of the Council of the European Union and High Representative for the Common Foreign and Security Policy: JAVIER SOLANA MADARIAGA (Spain).

President of the European Commission: JOSÉ MANUEL DURÃO BARROSO (Portugal).

President of the European Parliament: HANS-GERT PÖTTERING (Germany).

MEMBERS

Austria	Germany*	Netherlands*
Belgium*	Greece	Poland
Bulgaria	Hungary	Portugal
Cyprus	Ireland	Romania
Czech Republic	Italy*	Slovakia
Denmark	Latvia	Slovenia
Estonia	Lithuania	Spain
Finland	Luxembourg*	Sweden
France*	Malta	United Kingdom

* Original members.

ENLARGEMENT

The six original members (Belgium, France, Germany, Italy, Luxembourg and the Netherlands) were joined in the European Communities (later the European Union—EU) on 1 January 1973 by Denmark, Ireland and the United Kingdom, and on 1 January 1981 by Greece. In a referendum held in February 1982, the inhabitants of Greenland voted to end their membership of the Community, entered into when under full Danish rule. Greenland's withdrawal took effect from 1 February 1985. Portugal and Spain became members on 1 January 1986. Following the reunification of Germany in October 1990, the former German Democratic Republic immediately became part of the Community, although a transitional period was allowed before certain Community legislation took effect there. Austria, Finland and Sweden became members on 1 January 1995.

At the Copenhagen summit on 13 December 2002, an historic agreement was reached when the European Council agreed that 10 candidate countries, comprising eight in Central and Eastern Europe (the Czech Republic, Estonia, Hungary, Latvia, Lithuania, Poland, Slovakia and Slovenia) and Malta and Cyprus, should join the EU on 1 May 2004. The leaders of the 10 new member states signed the accession treaty in Athens on 16 April 2003. The Treaty of Athens had to be ratified by all 25 states prior to accession on 1 May 2004. The 15 existing member states opted to ratify the Treaty in parliament whereas the future member states, except Cyprus (the Cypriot Parliament unanimously approved accession to the EU on 14 July 2003), adopted the Treaty by referendum. A referendum took place in Malta on 8 March 2003, Slovenia on 23 March, Hungary on 12 April, Lithuania on 10 and 11 May, Slovakia on 16 and 17 May, Poland on 7 and 8 June, the Czech Republic on 15 and 16 June, Estonia on 14 September and Latvia on 20 September; each poll recorded a majority in favour of accession. Under the terms of the Treaty, only the Greek Cypriot sector of Cyprus was to be admitted to the EU in the absence of a settlement on the divided status of the island, although the EU made clear its preference for the accession of a united Cyprus. Negotiations in pursuit of a settlement regarding the reunification of Cyprus continued in early 2004. In April, however, in a referendum held only a few days before Cyprus was scheduled to join the EU, some 76% of Greek Cypriot voters rejected a reunification settlement proposed by the UN. At the same time, some 65% of Turkish Cypriot voters endorsed the settlement. Both communities would have had to approve the proposed reunification in order for Cyprus to commence its membership of the EU undivided. The results of the referendums meant that only the Greek sector of the island assumed EU membership from 1 May.

Romania submitted its formal application for EU membership on 22 June 1995, while Bulgaria applied for membership on 14 December. Following the Helsinki European Council's decision in December 1999, accession negotiations started with Romania and Bulgaria in February 2000. The Commission concluded in November 2003 that Bulgaria had a functioning market economy and would be able to perform within the EU in the near future provided it continued to implement its reform programme. In October 2004 a report by the European Commission described Romania as a functioning market economy for the first time, although it confirmed that endemic corruption, ethnic minority rights and human trafficking remained, *inter alia*, areas of concern in both countries. In the same strategy document, the Commission proposed a new clause in accession treaties under which membership negotiations could be suspended if candidate countries failed to fulfil the economic and political criteria established in Copenhagen in December 2002, according to which a prospective member must: be a stable democracy, respecting human rights, the rule of law, and the protection of minorities; have a functioning market economy; and adopt the common rules, standards and policies that make up the body of EU law. Bulgaria and Romania provisionally completed formal negotiations in June and December 2004, respectively, and this was confirmed at the Brussels European Council meeting of 17 December. The Commission formally approved the accession applications of Romania and Bulgaria on 22 February 2005. Bulgaria and Romania signed a joint accession treaty on 25 April, which would enter into force in January 2007. In September 2006 the Commission recommended that Romania and Bulgaria should accede to the EU as planned; both countries formally became members of the Union on 1 January 2007.

Turkey, which had signed an association agreement with the EC in 1963 (although this was suspended between 1980 and 1986, following a military coup), applied for membership of the EU on 14 April 1987. As a populous, predominantly Muslim nation, with a poor record on human rights and low average income levels, Turkey encountered objections to its prospective membership, which opponents claimed would disturb the balance of power within the EU and place an intolerable strain on the organization's finances. The Helsinki European Council of 1999, however, granted Turkey applicant status and encouraged it to undertake the requisite political and economic reforms for eventual membership. By accelerating the pace of reforms, Turkey had made significant progress towards achieving compliance with the Copenhagen criteria by 2004, including far-reaching reforms of the Constitution and the penal code. Turkish ambitions for EU membership were adversely affected in April 2004 by the failure of the UN plan for the reunification of Cyprus, which was rejected in a referendum by the Greek Cypriots in the south of the island (see above). Cyprus has been divided since 1974 when Turkey invaded the northern third of the country in response to a Greek-sponsored coup aiming to unite the island with Greece. Turkey refuses to recognize the Greek Cypriot Government and is the only country to recognize the Government of the northern section of the country, known as the 'Turkish Republic of Northern Cyprus', where it has 30,000 troops deployed. The requirement for the successful resolution of all territorial disputes with members of the EU meant that failure to reach a settlement in Cyprus remained a significant impediment to Turkey's accession to the EU, although the Turkish authorities had expressed strong support for the peace plan. In December 2004, however, the EU agreed to begin accession talks with Turkey on 3 October 2005, although it specified a number of conditions, including the right to impose 'permanent safeguard' clauses in any accession accord. The safeguard clauses had regard to the freedom of movement of Turkish citizens within the EU (seeking to allay fears about large numbers of low-paid Turkish workers entering other EU member states) and restrictions on the level of subsidy available to Turkey for its infrastructure development or agriculture. The EU warned that negotiations could last between 10 and 15 years and that eventual membership was not guaranteed. Turkey was also obliged to sign a protocol to update its association agreement with the EU prior to accession negotiations in October, to cover the 10 new members that had joined the organization in May 2004, including Cyprus. The Turkish Government had previously refused to grant effective recognition to the Greek Cypriot Government and, although it signed the protocol at the end of July 2005, it still insisted that the extension of the association agreement did not constitute formal recognition. In a report issued in November 2006, the Commission criticized the speed of reforms in Turkey and demanded that Turkey open its ports to Cypriot ships by mid-December, in compliance with its agreement to extend its customs union to the 10 new member states in 2005. Turkey announced that there could be no progress on this issue until the EU implemented a regulation drafted in 2004 to end the economic isolation of the 'Turkish Republic of Northern Cyprus', the adoption of which had been blocked by Cyprus. In December 2006, therefore, the EU suspended talks in eight policy areas. New rounds of negotiations were opened in March and June 2007, although none of the 35 policy areas could be officially completed prior to the resolution of the issues relating to Cyprus.

Croatia submitted its application for membership of the EU on 21 February 2003. Croatia is preparing for membership on the basis of an association agreement signed on 29 October 2001 and an interim agreement, which entered into force in March 2002. In April 2004 the European Commission declared that Croatia had fulfilled the political and economic criteria needed to begin EU membership negotiations, and was deemed to be co-operating fully with the International Criminal Tribunal for the former Yugoslavia (ICTY). After the election of Ivo Sanader to the premiership of Croatia in November 2003, considerable progress had been made in the transfer of suspects to the ICTY (based in The Hague, the Netherlands). Accession talks were suspended the day before they were due to commence, on 17 March 2005, on the grounds that Croatia had failed to co-operate fully with the ICTY, owing to its failure to arrest Gotovina. Accession talks were finally opened with Croatia in October, immediately after a declaration by Chief Prosecutor at the ICTY that co-operation had improved. Gotovina, who had been located in Spain by Croatian officials in September, was arrested there in December. Croatia hoped to accede to full membership of the EU in 2009.

At a summit of EU leaders in Brussels in December 2005, the former Yugoslav Republic of Macedonia was granted candidate status, joining Croatia and Turkey. However, no date was established for the initiation of accession negotiations.

INSTITUTIONAL REFORM

In February 2002 a Convention on the Future of Europe was opened in Brussels, chaired by former French President Valéry Giscard d'Estaing. The Convention, which had been agreed upon at the Laeken summit in December 2001, when the European Council adopted the Declaration on the Future of the European Union, included in its remit 60 or more topics aimed at reforming EU institutions to ensure the smooth functioning of the Union after enlargement. The full text of the draft constitutional treaty was submitted to the Council of the European Union on 18 July 2003. The draft was discussed at the Intergovernmental Conference (IGC), which was composed of the representatives of the member states and the accession countries, from October to December.

At an EU summit in Brussels on 12–13 December 2003, under the chairmanship of the Italian Prime Minister, Silvio Berlusconi, the heads of state and of government failed to reach agreement on the final text of the constitution. Although agreement was reached in many policy areas, the summit collapsed over the issue of voting rights. Poland, supported by Spain, resisted the loss of voting rights promised at the Nice summit three years previously. Under the complex voting arrangements agreed under the Treaty of Nice (which, failing agreement on a new constitution, were not due to lapse until 2009), Poland and Spain were both awarded 27 votes on the Council of the European Union (almost as many as the 29 accorded to Germany, France, Italy and the United Kingdom). The German Government, which represents a population almost twice the size of that of Poland and makes the largest contribution to the EU budget, was particularly concerned to redress this imbalance. The IGC continued to discuss the draft constitution during the first half of 2004. At a summit meeting held in Brussels on 18 June 2004, the heads of state and of government of the 25 EU member states finally approved the draft constitutional treaty. A compromise reached over voting rights, whereby measures would require the support of at least 55% of EU states, representing at least 65% of the total population, meant that smaller member states—particularly the new Eastern European members—could not be simply overruled by a small but powerful group of senior members, such as France, Germany and the United Kingdom. The draft constitutional treaty was formally signed in Rome on 29 October by the heads of state or of government of the 25 member states and the three candidate countries of Bulgaria, Romania and Turkey, although it remained subject to ratification by each member nation (either by a vote in the national legislature or by a popular referendum) by the end of October 2006. On 12 January 2005 the European Parliament endorsed the constitution by 500 votes to 137 (there were 40 abstentions). However, the future of the constitutional treaty became uncertain following its rejection in national referendums in France and the Netherlands. At the legally binding referendum in France, which took place on 29 May 2005, 54.8% of the votes cast opposed ratification of the treaty. In the Netherlands ratification was rejected by 61.6% of the votes at a plebiscite held on 1 June. At a meeting in Brussels in June, the leaders of the member states agreed to extend the deadline for ratification of the treaty until at least mid-2007. Seven countries (the United Kingdom, Denmark, Ireland, the Czech Republic, Sweden, Finland and Portugal) announced plans to postpone a national referendum.

Efforts to revive the institutional reform process were renewed in the first half of 2007 under the German Presidency of the Council of the European Union. In June, at a summit in Brussels, the European Council agreed to convene an IGC to draft a new treaty to replace the constitutional treaty. Agreement was reached on the final text of the resulting Draft Treaty amending the Treaty on European Union and the Treaty establishing the European Community (also known as the Reform Treaty or the Treaty of Lisbon) during an informal summit of the European Council in Lisbon on 18–19 October. The treaty was signed in Lisbon on 13 December by the heads of state or of government of the 27 member states. It was hoped that, following ratification by each individual member state, the Treaty of Lisbon would enter into force before elections to the European Parliament due in June 2009. Most countries intended to hold a parliamentary vote on the ratification of the Lisbon Treaty, which amended existing treaties rather than replacing them, although it retained much of the content of the constitutional treaty. However, Ireland was constitutionally bound to conduct a popular referendum on the issue. By mid-April 2008 nine countries had ratified the treaty by parliamentary vote.

Principal Elements of the Treaty of Lisbon

The draft Treaty of Lisbon (formally known as the Treaty of Lisbon amending the Treaty on European Union and the Treaty establishing the European Community) seeks to redefine the functions and procedures of the institutions of the EU. It provides for the creation of a High Representative of the Union for Foreign Affairs and Security Policy (who would be appointed by the European Council by qualified majority with the agreement of the President of the Commission) to represent the EU internationally, combining the roles of EU commissioner responsible for external relations and EU High Representative for the Common Foreign and Security Policy (although foreign policy would still be subject to a national veto). The High Representative of the Union for Foreign Affairs and Security Policy would be mandated by the Council, but would also be one of the Vice-Presidents of the Commission and would chair the External Relations Council. The Lisbon Treaty also envisages the creation of a new permanent president of the European Council, elected by the European Council for a period of two and one-half years, renewable once, to replace the current system of a six-month rotating presidency. However, the system of a six-month rotating presidency would be retained for the different Council formations (except for the External Relations Council, which would be chaired by the new High Representative of the Union for Foreign Affairs and Security Policy), although it would comprise a 'team presidency' of three countries.

The system of qualified majority voting in the Council of the European Union would be extended and redefined, ending the system of national veto in a number of new areas. From November 2014 a qualified majority would be defined as at least 55% of the members of the Council, composed of at least 15 of them and representing member states comprising at least 65% of the EU's population (although a blocking minority would have to include at least four member states). The Lisbon Treaty also includes a provision that the European Council could agree, by unanimity and subject to prior unanimous approval by national legislatures, to introduce qualified majority voting in an area currently requiring unanimity (except in the area of defence), thus obviating the need for treaty change. The European Parliament's legislative powers are consolidated in the Treaty of Lisbon, which grants the Parliament the right of co-decision with the Council of the European Union in an increased number of policy areas, giving it a more prominent role in framing legislation. The maximum number of seats in the European Parliament was raised to 750, with member states accorded a minimum of six and a maximum of 96 seats on a proportional basis. The European Commission was to retain its current composition of one commissioner for each member state until November 2014; thereafter the Commission would comprise a number of commissioners corresponding to two-thirds of the member states, according to a system of equal rotation. The Treaty establishing the European Community (also known as the Treaty of Rome) was to be renamed the Treaty on the Functioning of the Union, with all references to the European Community changed to European Union. The Lisbon Treaty attempts to improve democracy and transparency within the Union, introducing the right for EU citizens to petition the Commission to introduce new legislation and enshrining the principles of subsidiarity (that the EU should only act when an objective can be better achieved at the supranational level, implying that national powers are the norm) and proportionality (that the action should be proportional to the desired objective). National parliaments were to be given the opportunity to examine EU legislation to ensure that it was within the EU's remit and to return legislation to the Commission for reconsideration if one-third of member states found that a proposed law breached these principles. The Treaty of Lisbon provides a legal basis for the EU defence force, with a mutual defence clause, and includes the stipulation that the EU has the power to sign treaties and sit on international bodies as a legal body in its own right. The document also provides for the establishment of a European public prosecutor's office to combat EU fraud and cross-border crime, the right to dual citizenship (i.e. of the EU as well as of a member state) and includes arrangements for the formal withdrawal of a member state from the EU.

Diplomatic Representation

PERMANENT REPRESENTATIVES OF MEMBER STATES

Austria: Hans-Dietmar Schweisgut; 30 ave de Cortenberg, 1040 Brussels; tel. (2) 234-51-00; fax (2) 235-63-00; e-mail bruessel-ov@bmeia.gv.at.

Belgium: Jean De Ruyt; 61–63 rue de la Loi, 1040 Brussels; tel. (2) 233-21-11; fax (2) 231-10-75; e-mail dispatch.belgoeurop@diplobel.fed.be.

Bulgaria: Boyko Vassilev Kotzev; 49 place Marie-Louise, 1000 Brussels; tel. (2) 235-83-00; fax (2) 374-91-88; e-mail info@bg-permrep.eu; internet www.bg-permrep.eu.

Cyprus: Nicos Emiliou; 61 ave de Cortenberg, 1000 Brussels; tel. (2) 735-35-10; fax (2) 735-45-52; e-mail cy.perm.rep@mfa.gov.cy.

Czech Republic: Milena Vicenová; 15 rue Caroly, 1050 Brussels; tel. (2) 213-91-11; fax (2) 213-91-85; e-mail eu.brussels@embassy.mzv.cz; internet www.czechrep.be.

Denmark: Claus Grube; 73 rue d'Arlon, 1040 Brussels; tel. (2) 233-08-11; fax (2) 230-93-84; e-mail brurep@um.dk.

Estonia: Raul Mälk; 11–13 rue Guimard, 1040 Brussels; tel. (2) 227-39-10; fax (2) 227-39-25; e-mail permrep.eu@mfa.ee; internet www.eu.estemb.be.

Finland: Eikka Kosonen; 100 rue de Trèves, 1040 Brussels; tel. (2) 287-84-11; fax (2) 287-84-00; e-mail sanomat.eue@formin.fi; internet www.finland.eu.

France: Pierre Sellal; 14 place de Louvain, 1000 Brussels; tel. (2) 229-82-11; fax (2) 229-82-82; e-mail bruxelles-dfra@diplomatie.gouv.fr.

Germany: Dr Edmund Duckwitz; 8–14 rue Jacques de Lalaing, 1040 Brussels; tel. (2) 787-10-00; fax (2) 787-20-00; e-mail eurogerma.eu@bruessel.auswaertiges-amt.de; internet www.eu-vertretung.de.

Greece: Vassilis Kaskarelis; rue Jacques de Lalaing 19–21, 1040 Brussels; tel. (2) 551-56-11; fax (2) 551-56-51; e-mail mea.bruxelles@rp-grece.be.

Hungary: Tibor Kiss; 92–98 rue de Trèves, 1040 Brussels; tel. (2) 234-12-00; fax (2) 372-07-84; e-mail sec.beu@kum.hu; internet www.hunrep.be.

Ireland: Bobby McDonagh; 89–93 rue Froissart, 1040 Brussels; tel. (2) 230-85-80; fax (2) 230-32-03; e-mail irlprb@iveagh.gov.ie.

Italy: Rocco Antonio Cangelosi; 9 rue du Marteau, 1000 Brussels; tel. (2) 220-04-11; fax (2) 219-34-49; e-mail rpue@rpue.it.

Latvia: Normunds Popens; 39–41 rue d'Arlon, 1000 Brussels; tel. (2) 238-31-00; fax (2) 238-32-50; e-mail permrep.eu@mfa.gov.lv; internet www.am.gov.lv/en/brussels.

Lithuania: Rytis Martikonis; 41–43 rue Belliard, 1040 Brussels; tel. (2) 771-01-40; fax (2) 771-45-97; e-mail office@eurep.mfa.lt; internet www.eurep.mfa.lt.

Luxembourg: Martine Schommer; 75 ave de Cortenberg, 1000 Brussels; tel. (2) 737-56-00; fax (2) 737-56-10; e-mail forename.surname@rpue.etat.lu.

Malta: Richard Cachia Caruana; 25 rue d'Archimède, 1000 Brussels; tel. (2) 343-01-95; fax (2) 343-01-06; e-mail maltarep@gov.mt.

Netherlands: Thom de Bruijn; 48 ave Herrmann Debroux, 1160 Brussels; tel. (2) 679-15-11; fax (2) 679-17-75; e-mail bre@minbuza.nl; internet www.mfa.nl/bre-uk.

Poland: Jan Tombiński; 282–284 ave de Tervueren, 1150 Brussels; tel. (2) 777-72-00; fax (2) 777-72-97; e-mail mail@polrepeu.be; internet www.polrepeu.be.

Portugal: Álvaro Mendonça e Moura; 12 ave de Cortenberg, 1040 Brussels; tel. (2) 286-42-11; fax (2) 231-00-26; e-mail reper@reper-portugal.be; internet www.reper-portugal.be.

Romania: Lazăr Comănescu; 12 rue Montoyer, 1000 Brussels; tel. (2) 700-06-40; fax (2) 700-06-41; e-mail bru@roumisue.org; internet www.ue.mae.ro.

Slovakia: Maroš Šefčovič; 79 ave de Cortenberg, 1000 Brussels; tel. (2) 743-68-11; fax (2) 743-68-88; e-mail slovakmission@pmsreu.be; internet www.eubrussels.mfa.sk.

Slovenia: Igor Senčar; 44 rue du Commerce, 1000 Brussels; tel. (2) 213-63-00; fax (2) 213-63-01; e-mail spbr@gov.si; internet bruselj.predstavnistvo.si/index.php?id=636&L=1.

Spain: Carlos Bastarreche Sagües; 52–54 blvd du Régent, 1000 Brussels; tel. (2) 509-86-11; fax (2) 511-19-40; e-mail forename.surname@reper.mae.es; internet www.es-ue.org/default.asp?lg=1.

Sweden: Sven-Olof Petersson; 30 place de Meeûs, 1000 Brussels; 6 Rond-Point Schuman; tel. (2) 289-56-11; fax (2) 289-56-00; e-mail representationen.bryssel@foreign.ministry.se; internet www.sweden.gov.se/sb/d/2250.

United Kingdom: Kim Darroch; 10 ave d'Auderghem, 1040 Brussels; tel. (2) 287-82-11; fax (2) 287-83-98; e-mail firstname.lastname@fco.gov.uk; internet www.ukrep.be.

PERMANENT MISSIONS TO THE EUROPEAN UNION

Afghanistan: 61 ave de Wolvendael, 1180 Brussels; tel. (2) 761-31-66; fax (2) 761-31-67; e-mail ambassade.afghanistan@skynet.be; Ambassador Zia Nezam.

Albania: 30 rue Tenbosch, 1000 Brussels; tel. (2) 640-35-44; fax (2) 640-31-77; e-mail albanian.ec@skynet.be; Ambassador Mimoza Halimi.

Algeria: 209 ave Molière, 1050 Brussels; tel. (2) 343-50-78; fax (2) 343-51-68; e-mail info@algerian-embassy.be; Ambassador Halim Benattallah.

Andorra: 10 rue de la Montagne, 1000 Brussels; tel. (2) 513-28-06; fax (2) 513-07-41; e-mail ambassade@andorra.be; internet www.andorra.be; Ambassador Imma Tor Faus.

Angola: 182 rue Franz Merjay, 1050 Brussels; tel. (2) 346-18-72; fax (2) 344-08-94; e-mail angola.embassy.brussels@skynet.be; Ambassador Toko Diakengo Serão.

Argentina: 225 ave Louise, 1050 Brussels; tel. (2) 648-93-71; fax (2) 648-08-04; e-mail info@eembargentina.be; Ambassador Guillermo Marcos Jacovella.

Armenia: 28 rue Montoyer, 1000 Brussels; tel. and fax (2) 348-44-00; fax (2) 348-44-08; e-mail armembel@skynet.be; internet www.armembassy.be; Ambassador Viguen Tchitetchian.

Australia: Guimard Centre, 6–8 rue Guimard, 1040 Brussels; tel. (2) 286-05-00; fax (2) 231-07-88; e-mail austemb.brussels@dfat.gov.au; internet www.eu.mission.gov.au; Ambassador Alan Thomas.

Azerbaijan: 464 ave Molière, 1050 Brussels; tel. (2) 345-26-60; fax (2) 345-91-58; e-mail office@azembassy.be; internet www.azembassy.be; Ambassador Emin Eyyubov.

Bahamas: 10 Chesterfield St, London, W1J 5JI, United Kingdom; tel. (20) 7408-4488; fax (20) 7499-9937; e-mail info@bahamashclondon.net; Ambassador Basil G. O'Brien.

Bahrain: 3 bis place des Etats-Unis, 75016 Paris, France; tel. 1-47-23-48-68; Ambassador Shaikha Haya bint Rashid al-Khalifa.

Bangladesh: 29–31 rue Jacques Jordaens, 1000 Brussels; tel. (2) 640-55-00; fax (2) 646-59-98; e-mail bdootbrussels@skynet.be; internet www.bangladeshembassy.be; Ambassador A. H. M. MONIR-UZZAMAN.

Barbados: 100 ave F. D. Roosevelt, 1050 Brussels; tel. (2) 732-17-37; fax (2) 732-32-66; e-mail brussels@foreign.gov.bb; Ambassador ERROL L. HUMPHREY.

Belarus: 192 ave Molière, 1050 Brussels; tel. (2) 340-02-70; fax (2) 340-02-87; e-mail embbel@skynet.be; internet www.belembassy.org/belgium/eng; Ambassador VLADIMIR L. SENKO.

Belize: 136 blvd Brand Whitlock, 1200 Brussels; tel. (2) 732-62-04; fax (2) 732-62-46; e-mail embelize@skynet.be; Ambassador ALEXIS ROSADO.

Benin: 5 ave de l'Observatoire, 1180 Brussels; tel. (2) 375-06-74; fax (2) 375-83-26; e-mail ambabenin_benelux@yahoo.fr; internet www.ambassade_benin.be; Ambassador CHARLES BORROMÉE TODJINOU.

Bhutan: 17–19 chemin du Champ d'Anier, 1209 Geneva, Switzerland; tel. (22) 799-08-90; fax (22) 799-08-99; e-mail mission.bhutan@ties.itu.int; Ambassador SONAM TOBDEN RABGYE.

Bolivia: 176 ave Louise, 1050 Brussels; tel. (2) 627-00-10; fax (2) 647-47-82; e-mail embajada.bolivia@embolbrus.be; Ambassador CRISTIAN MANUEL INCHAUSTE SANDOVAL.

Bosnia and Herzegovina: 15–17 rue Belliard, 7e étage, 1040 Brussels; tel. (2) 502-01-88; fax (2) 644-32-54; e-mail info@bh-embassy-belgium.org; internet www.bh-embassy-belgium.org; Ambassador NIKOLA RADOVANOVIĆ.

Botswana: 169 ave de Tervueren, 1150 Brussels; tel. (2) 735-20-70; fax (2) 735-63-18; e-mail botswana@brutele.be; Ambassador CLAURINAH TSHENOLO MODISE.

Brazil: 30 ave F. D. Roosevelt, 1050 Brussels; tel. (2) 640-20-40; fax (2) 648-80-40; e-mail missao@braseuropa.be; Ambassador ALMIR FRANCO DE SÁ BARBUDA.

Brunei: 238 ave F. D. Roosevelt, 1050 Brussels; tel. (2) 675-08-78; fax (2) 672-93-58; e-mail kedutaan-brunei.brussels@skynet.be; Ambassador PENGIRAN HAJI ALIHASHIM BIN PENGIRAN HAJI YUSUF.

Burkina Faso: 16 place Guy d'Arezzo, 1180 Brussels; tel. (2) 345-99-12; fax (2) 345-06-12; e-mail ambassade.burkina@skynet.be; Ambassador KADRÉ DÉSIRÉ OUEDRAOGO.

Burundi: 46 square Marie-Louise, 1040 Brussels; tel. (2) 230-45-35; fax (2) 230-78-83; e-mail ambassade.burundi@skynet.be; internet www.amb-burundi.be; Ambassador LAURENT KAVAKURE.

Cambodia: 264 ave de Tervueren, 1150 Brussels; tel. (2) 772-03-76; fax (2) 770-89-99; e-mail amcambel@skynet.be; Ambassador SUN SAPHOEUN.

Cameroon: 131–133 ave Brugmann, 1190 Brussels; tel. (2) 345-18-70; fax (2) 344-57-35; Chargé d'affaires a.i. JACQUES ALFRED NDOUMBE EBOULÉ.

Canada: 2 ave de Tervueren, 1040 Brussels; tel. (2) 741-06-60; fax (2) 741-06-29; e-mail breu@international.gc.ca; internet www.international.gc.ca; Ambassador ROSS HORNBY.

Cape Verde: 29 ave Jeanne, 1050 Brussels; tel. (2) 643-62-70; fax (2) 646-33-85; e-mail emb.caboverde@skynet.be; Ambassador FERNANDO JORGE WAHNON FERREIRA.

Central African Republic: 416 blvd Lambermont, 1030 Brussels; tel. (2) 242-28-80; fax (2) 215-13-11; e-mail ambassade.centreafrique@skynet.be; Ambassador ARMAND-GUY ZOUNGUERE-SOKAMBI.

Chad: 52 blvd Lambermont, 1030 Brussels; tel. (2) 215-19-75; fax (2) 216-35-26; e-mail ambassade.tchad@skynet.be; Ambassador MAÏTINE DJOUMBE.

Chile: 106 rue des Aduatiques, 1040 Brussels; tel. (2) 743-36-60; fax (2) 736-49-94; e-mail embachile@embachile.be; internet www.embachile.be; Ambassador JUAN SALAZAR SPARKS.

China, People's Republic: 443–445 ave de Tervueren, 1150 Brussels; tel. (2) 771-33-09; fax (2) 772-37-45; e-mail chinaemb-be@mfa.gov.cn; Ambassador SONG ZHE.

Colombia: 96A ave F. D. Roosevelt, 1050 Brussels; tel. (2) 649-56-79; fax (2) 646-54-91; e-mail colombia@emcolbru.org; internet www.emcolbru.org; Ambassador NICOLÁS ECHAVARRÍA MESA.

Comoros: 63 rue Berthelot, 1190 Brussels; tel. and fax (2) 779-58-38; e-mail ambacom.bxl@skynet.be; Ambassador SULTAN CHOUZOUR.

Congo, Democratic Republic: 30 rue Marie de Bourgogne, 1000 Brussels; tel. (2) 375-47-96; fax (2) 372-23-48; e-mail ambauebruxelles@minaffecirdc.cd; Ambassador JEAN-PIERRE MUTAMBA TSHAMPANGA.

Congo, Republic: 16–18 ave F. D. Roosevelt, 1050 Brussels; tel. (2) 648-38-56; fax (2) 648-42-13; Ambassador JACQUES OBIA.

Cook Islands: 10 rue Berckmans, 1060 Brussels; tel. (2) 543-10-00; fax (2) 543-10-01; e-mail cookislands@prmltd.com; Ambassador TODD MCCLAY.

Costa Rica: 489 ave Louise, 1050 Brussels; tel. (2) 640-55-41; fax (2) 648-31-92; e-mail embcrbel@coditel.net; Ambassador ROBERTO ECHANDI.

Côte d'Ivoire: 234 ave F. D. Roosevelt, 1050 Brussels; tel. (2) 672-23-57; fax (2) 672-04-91; e-mail mailbox@ambacibnl.be; internet www.ambacibnl.be; Ambassador MARIE GOSSET.

Croatia: 50 ave des Arts, 1000 Brussels; tel. (2) 507-54-11; fax (2) 646-56-64; e-mail cromiss.eu@mvp.hr; internet eu.mfa.hr; Ambassador BRANKO BARIČEVIĆ.

Cuba: 77 rue Robert Jones, 1180 Brussels; tel. (2) 343-00-20; fax (2) 344-96-91; e-mail consejero@embacuba.be; Ambassador RODRIGO MALMIERCA DÍAZ.

Djibouti: 204 ave F. D. Roosevelt, 1050 Brussels; tel. (2) 347-69-67; fax (2) 347-69-63; e-mail amb_djib@yahoo.fr; Ambassador MOHAMED MOUSSA CHEHEM.

Dominica: 42 rue de Livourne, 1000 Brussels; tel. (2) 534-26-11; fax (2) 539-40-09; e-mail ecs.embassies@skynet.be; Chargé d'affaires Dr ARNOLD THOMAS.

Dominican Republic: 12 ave Bel Air, 1180 Brussels; tel. (2) 346-49-35; fax (2) 346-51-52; e-mail embajada@dominicana.be; Ambassador FEDERICO ALBERTO CUELLO CAMILO.

Ecuador: 363 ave Louise, 1050 Brussels; tel. (2) 644-30-50; fax (2) 644-28-13; e-mail amb.equateur@skynet.be; internet www.ecuador.be; Ambassador FERNANDO YÉPEZ LASSO.

Egypt: 19 ave de l'Uruguay, 1000 Brussels; tel. (2) 663-58-00; fax (2) 675-58-88; e-mail embassy.egypt@skynet.be; Ambassador Dr MAHMOUD KAREM MAHMOUD.

El Salvador: 171 ave de Tervueren, 1150 Brussels; tel. (2) 733-04-85; fax (2) 735-02-11; e-mail amb.elsalvador@brutele.be; Ambassador HÉCTOR GONZÁLEZ URRUTIA.

Equatorial Guinea: 6 place Guy d'Arezzo, 1180 Brussels; tel. (2) 346-25-09; fax (2) 346-33-09; e-mail guineaecuatorial.brux@skynet.be; Ambassador VITORINO NKA OBIANG MAYE.

Eritrea: 15–17 ave de Wolvendael, 1180 Brussels; tel. (2) 374-44-34; fax (2) 372-07-30; e-mail eri_emba_brus@hotmail.com; Ambassador GIRMA ASMERON TESFAY.

Ethiopia: 231 ave de Tervueren, Brussels; tel. (2) 771-32-94; fax (2) 771-49-14; e-mail etebru@brutele.be; Ambassador BERHANE GEBRE CHRISTOS.

Fiji: 92–94 square Plasky, 1030 Brussels; tel. (2) 736-90-50; fax (2) 736-14-58; e-mail info@fijiembassy.be; internet www.fijiembassy.be; Ambassador SEMERAIA TUINOSORI CAVAILATI.

Gabon: 112 ave Winston Churchill, 1180 Brussels; tel. (2) 340-62-10; fax (2) 346-46-69; e-mail bs.175335@skynet.be; Ambassador RENÉ MAKONGO.

The Gambia: 126 ave F. D. Roosevelt, 1050 Brussels; tel. (2) 640-10-49; fax (2) 646-32-77; e-mail info@gambiaembassy.be; internet www.gambiaembassy.be; Chargé d'affaires a.i. AMIE NYAN-ALABOSON.

Georgia: 62 ave de Tervuren, 1040 Brussels; tel. (2) 761-11-90; fax (2) 732-85-47; e-mail info@georgia-embassy.be; internet www.belgium.mfa.gov.ge; Ambassador SALOME SAMADASHVILI.

Ghana: 7 blvd Général Wahis, 1030 Brussels; tel. (2) 705-82-20; fax (2) 705-66-53; e-mail ghanaemb@chello.be; internet www.ghanaembassy.be; Ambassador NANA BEMA KUMI.

Grenada: 123 rue de Laeken, 1000 Brussels; tel. (2) 223-73-03; fax (2) 223-73-07; Ambassador JOAN-MARIE COUTAIN.

Guatemala: 185 ave Winston Churchill, 1180 Brussels; tel. (2) 345-90-58; fax (2) 344-64-99; e-mail ambaguate.belgica@skynet.be; Ambassador ANTONIO FERNANDO ARENALES FORNO.

Guinea: 108 blvd Auguste Reyers, 1030 Brussels; tel. (2) 771-01-26; fax (2) 762-60-36; e-mail ambassadeguinee.bel@skynet.be; Ambassador AHMED TIDIANE SAKHO.

Guinea-Bissau: 70 ave F. D. Roosevelt, 1050 Brussels; tel. (2) 647-08-90; fax (2) 640-43-12; Ambassador HENRIQUE ADRIANO DA SILVA.

Guyana: 12 ave du Brésil, 1000 Brussels; tel. (2) 675-62-16; fax (2) 675-55-98; e-mail embassy.guyana@skynet.be; Ambassador PATRICK IGNATIUS GOMES.

Haiti: 139 chaussée de Charleroi, 1060 Brussels; tel. (2) 649-73-81; fax (2) 640-60-80; e-mail amb.haiti@brutele.be; Ambassador RAYMOND LAFONTANT.

Holy See: 289 ave Brugmann, 1180 Brussels; tel. (2) 340-77-00; fax (2) 340-77-04; e-mail nonciature.ue.chancellerie@scarlet.be; Apostolic Nuncio ANDRÉ DUPUY.

Honduras: 3 ave des Gaulois, 1040 Brussels; tel. (2) 734-00-00; fax (2) 735-26-26; e-mail ambassade@honduras.be; internet www.honduras.be; Ambassador SONIA CARPIO MENDOZA.

INTERNATIONAL ORGANIZATIONS

Iceland: 11 rond-point Schuman, 1040 Brussels; tel. (2) 238-50-00; fax (2) 230-69-38; e-mail icemb.brussel@utn.stjr.is; internet www.iceland.org/be; Ambassador STEFAN HAUKUR JOHANNESSON.

India: 217 chaussée de Vleurgat, 1050 Brussels; tel. (2) 640-91-40; fax (2) 648-96-38; e-mail admin@indembassy.be; internet www.indembassy.be; Ambassador DIPAK CHATTERJEE.

Indonesia: 38 blvd de la Woluwe, 1200 Brussels; tel. (2) 775-01-20; fax (2) 772-82-10; e-mail primebxl@skynet.be; internet www.embassyofindonesia.eu; Ambassador NADJIB RIPHAT KESOEMA.

Iran: 15 ave F. D. Roosevelt, 1050 Brussels; tel. (2) 627-03-50; fax (2) 762-39-15; e-mail embassy@iranembassy.be; internet www.iranembassy.be; Ambassador ALIASGHAR KHAGI.

Iraq: 115 ave F. D. Roosevelt, 1050 Brussels; tel. (2) 374-59-92; fax (2) 374-76-15; e-mail ambassade.irak@skynet.be; Ambassador MUHAMMAD JAWAN AD-DOREKY.

Israel: 40 ave de l'Observatoire, 1180 Brussels; tel. (2) 373-55-24; fax (2) 373-56-77; e-mail isr.mis.eu@online.be; internet www.israeli-mission.org; Ambassador RAN CURIEL.

Jamaica: 77 ave Hansen Soulie, 1040 Brussels; tel. (2) 230-11-70; fax (2) 234-69-69; e-mail emb.jam.brussels@skynet.br; Ambassador MARCIA GILBERT-ROBERTS.

Japan: 5–6 square de Meeûs, 1000 Brussels; tel. (2) 500-77-11; fax (2) 513-32-41; e-mail infomationdesk@scarlet.be; internet www.eu.emb-japan.go.jp; Ambassador TAKEKAZU KAWAMURA.

Jordan: 104 ave F. D. Roosevelt, 1050 Brussels; tel. (2) 640-77-55; fax (2) 640-27-96; e-mail jordan.embassy@skynet.be; Ambassador DR AHMAD MASA'DEH.

Kazakhstan: 30 ave Van Bever, 1180 Brussels; tel. (2) 374-95-62; fax (2) 374-50-91; e-mail kazakstan.embassy@swing.be; internet www.kazakhstanembassy.be/DisplayPage.asp?PageId=30; Ambassador KONSTANTIN V. ZHIGALOV.

Kenya: 208 ave Winston Churchill, 1180 Brussels; tel. (2) 340-10-40; fax (2) 340-10-50; e-mail info@kenyabrussels.com; internet www.kenyabrussels.com; Ambassador MARX G. N. KAHENDE.

Korea, Democratic People's Republic: Glinkastr. 5/7, 1017 Berlin, Germany; tel. (30) 2293189; fax (30) 2293191.

Korea, Republic: 173–175 chaussée de la Hulpe, 1170 Brussels; tel. (2) 675-57-77; fax (2) 675-52-21; e-mail eukorea@skynet.be; Ambassador CHONG WOO-SEONG.

Kuwait: 43 ave F. D. Roosevelt, 1050 Brussels; tel. (2) 647-79-50; fax (2) 646-12-98; e-mail embassy.kwt@euronet.be; Ambassador NABILA ABDULLA AL-MULLA.

Kyrgyzstan: 47 rue de l'Abbaye, 1050 Brussels; tel. (2) 640-18-68; fax (2) 640-01-31; e-mail kyrgyz.embassy@skynet.be; Ambassador CHINGUIZ AITMATOV.

Laos: 19–21 ave de la Brabançonne, 1000 Brussels; tel. (2) 740-09-50; fax (2) 734-16-66; e-mail ambalaobx@yucom.be; Ambassador THONGPHACHANH SONNASINH.

Lebanon: 2 rue Guillaume Stocq, 1050 Brussels; tel. (2) 645-77-65; fax (2) 645-77-69; e-mail ambassade.liban@brutele.be; Chargé d'affaires a.i. ADNAN MANSOUR.

Lesotho: 45 blvd Général Wahis, 1030 Brussels; tel. (2) 705-39-76; fax (2) 705-67-79; e-mail lesothobrussels@hotmail.com; Ambassador MAMORUTI TIHELI.

Liberia: 50 ave du Château, 1081 Brussels; tel. (2) 411-01-12; fax (2) 411-09-12; e-mail liberia.embassy@pro.tiscali.be; Ambassador YOUNGOR S. TELEWODA.

Libya: 28 ave Victoria, 1000 Brussels; tel. (2) 649-37-37; fax (2) 640-90-76; e-mail libyan_bureau_br@yahoo.com; Ambassador YOUSUF SIFAW HAFIANI.

Liechtenstein: 1 place du Congrès, 1000 Brussels; tel. (2) 229-39-00; fax (2) 219-35-45; e-mail ambassade.liechtenstein@bbru.llv.li; Ambassador HSH Prince NIKOLAUS OF LIECHTENSTEIN.

Macedonia, former Yugoslav republic: 38 rue de la Loi, 1000 Brussels; tel. (2) 732-91-08; fax (2) 732-91-11; e-mail mk.mission@skynet.be; Ambassador BLERIM REKA.

Madagascar: 276 ave de Tervueren, 1150 Brussels; tel. (2) 770-17-26; fax (2) 772-37-31; e-mail info@madagascar-embassy.eu; internet www.madagascar-embassy.eu; Ambassador JEANNOT RAKOTOMALALA.

Malawi: 15 rue de la Loi, 1040 Brussels; tel. (2) 231-09-80; fax (2) 231-10-66; e-mail embassy.malawi@skynet.be; internet www.embassymalawi.be; Ambassador BRAVE NDISALE.

Malaysia: 414a ave de Tervueren, 1150 Brussels; tel. (2) 776-03-40; fax (2) 762-50-49; e-mail mwbrusel@euronet.be; Ambassador Dato MUHAMMAD KAMAL BIN YAN YAHAYA.

Maldives: 22 Nottingham Pl., London, W1U 5NJ, United Kingdom; tel. (20) 7224-2135; fax (20) 7224-2157; e-mail maldives.high.commission@virgin.net; Ambassador HASSAN SOBIR.

Mali: 487 ave Molière, 1050 Brussels; tel. (2) 345-74-32; fax (2) 344-57-00; e-mail ambamali@skynet.be; Ambassador IBRAHIM BOCAR BA.

Mauritania: 6 ave de la Colombie, 1000 Brussels; tel. (2) 672-18-02; fax (2) 672-20-51; e-mail info@amb-mauritania.be; Ambassador MOULAYE OULD MUHAMMAD LAGHDAF.

Mauritius: 68 rue des Bollandistes, 1040 Brussels; tel. (2) 733-99-88; fax (2) 734-40-21; e-mail ambmaur@skynet.be; Ambassador SUTIAWAN GUNESSEE.

Mexico: 94 ave F. D. Roosevelt, 1050 Brussels; tel. (2) 629-07-11; fax (2) 644-08-19; e-mail embamex@embamex.eu; internet www.embamex.eu; Ambassador SANDRA FUENTES-BERAIN.

Moldova: 54 rue Tenbosch, 1050 Brussels; tel. (2) 732-96-59; fax (2) 732-96-60; e-mail bruxelles@mfa.md; Ambassador VICTOR GAICIUC.

Monaco: 17 place Guy d'Arezzo, 1180 Brussels; tel. (2) 347-49-87; fax (2) 343-49-20; e-mail ambassade.monaco@skynet.be; Ambassador JOSÉ BADIA.

Mongolia: 18 ave Besme, 1190 Brussels; tel. (2) 344-69-74; fax (2) 344-32-15; e-mail brussels.mn.embassy@chello.be; Ambassador AVIRMEDIIN BATTÖR.

Montenegro: 34 rue Marie Thérèse, 1210 Brussels; tel. (2) 223-55-61; fax (2) 223-60-28; e-mail office@montenegrinmission.be; Ambassador SLAVICA MILAČIĆ.

Morocco: 275 ave Louise, 1050 Brussels; tel. (2) 626-34-10; fax (2) 626-34-34; e-mail sifamabruxe@euronet.be; Ambassador MUSTAPHA SALAHDINE.

Mozambique: 97 blvd Saint-Michel, 1040 Brussels; tel. (2) 736-25-64; fax (2) 735-62-07; e-mail embamoc.bru@skynet.be; internet www.mozambiqueembassy.be; Ambassador MARIA MANUELA DOS SANTOS LUCAS.

Myanmar: 60 rue de Courcelles, 75008 Paris, France; tel. 1-56-88-15-90; fax 1-45-62-13-30; e-mail me-paris@wanadoo.fr; Ambassador U SAW HLA MIN MIN.

Namibia: 454 ave de Tervueren, 1150 Brussels; tel. (2) 771-14-10; fax (2) 771-96-89; e-mail info@namibiaembassy.be; internet www.namibiaembassy.be; Ambassador HANNO BURKHARD RUMPF.

Nepal: 210 ave Brugmann, 1180 Brussels; tel. (2) 346-26-58; fax (2) 344-13-61; e-mail embn@skynet.be; internet www.nepalembassy.be; Chargé d'affaires a.i. AMBIKA D. LUINTEL.

New Zealand: 1 place de Meeûs, 1000 Brussels; tel. (2) 512-10-40; fax (2) 513-48-56; e-mail nzemb.brussels@skynet.be; internet www.nzembassy.com/belgium; Ambassador PETER KENNEDY.

Nicaragua: 55 ave de Wolvendael, 1180 Brussels; tel. (2) 375-65-00; fax (2) 375-71-88; e-mail sky77706@skynet.be; Chargé d'affaires a.i. SANTIAGO URBINA GUERRERO.

Niger: 78 ave F. D. Roosevelt, 1050 Brussels; tel. (2) 648-61-40; fax (2) 648-27-84; e-mail ambnigerbxl@advalvas.be; Ambassador ABDOU AGBARRY.

Nigeria: 288 ave de Tervueren, 1150 Brussels; tel. (2) 762-52-00; fax (2) 762-37-63; e-mail nigeriaembassy@belgacom.net; internet www.nigeriabrussels.be; Ambassador ADEKUNLE OLADOKUN ADEYANJU.

Niue: 10 rue Berckmans, 1060 Brussels, Belgium; tel. (2) 543-10-02; fax (2) 543-10-01; e-mail niue@prmltd.com; Ambassador TODD MCCLAY.

Norway: 17 rue Archimèdes, 1000 Brussels; tel. (2) 234-11-11; fax (2) 234-11-50; e-mail eu.brussels@mfa.no; internet www.eu-norway.org; Ambassador ODA HELEN SLETNES.

Oman: 27 Koninginnegracht, 2514 AB The Hague, Netherlands; tel. (70) 361-58-00; fax (70) 360-53-64; e-mail embassyoman@wanadoo.nl; Ambassador KHADIJA BINT HASSAN SALMAN AL-LAWATI.

Pakistan: 57 ave Delleur, 1170 Brussels; tel. (2) 673-80-07; fax (2) 675-83-94; e-mail parepbrussels@skynet.be; internet www.embassyofpakistan.be; Ambassador SAEED KHALID.

Panama: 390–392 ave Louise, 1050 Brussels; tel. (2) 649-07-29; fax (2) 648-92-16; e-mail embajada.panama@skynet.be; Ambassador PABLO GARRIDO ARAÚZ.

Papua New Guinea: 430 ave de Tervueren, 1150 Brussels; tel. (2) 779-06-09; fax (2) 772-70-88; e-mail kundu.brussels@skynet.be; Ambassador ISAAC B. LUPARI.

Paraguay: 475 ave Louise, 1050 Brussels; tel. (2) 649-90-55; fax (2) 647-42-48; e-mail embapar@skynet.be; Chargé d'affaires a.i. RAÚL JOSÉ VERA BOGADO.

Peru: 179 ave de Tervueren, 1150 Brussels; tel. (2) 733-33-19; fax (2) 733-48-19; e-mail comunicaciones@embassy-of-peru.be; internet www.embaperu.be; Ambassador JORGE VALDEZ.

Philippines: 297 ave Molière, 1050 Brussels; tel. (2) 340-33-77; fax (2) 345-64-25; e-mail brussels@philembassy.be; Ambassador CRISTINA G. ORTEGA.

INTERNATIONAL ORGANIZATIONS

Qatar: 51 rue de la Vallée, 1050 Brussels; tel. (2) 223-11-55; fax (2) 223-11-66; internet www.qatarembassy.be; Ambassador Sheikh MESHAL BIN HAMAD ATH-THANI.

Russia: 31–33 blvd du Régent, 1000 Brussels; tel. (2) 502-18-55; fax (2) 513-76-49; e-mail misrusce1@coditel.net; internet www.russiaeu.mid.ru; Ambassador VLADIMIR CHIZHOV.

Rwanda: 1 ave des Fleurs, 1150 Brussels; tel. (2) 763-07-21; fax (2) 763-07-53; e-mail ambarwanda.@skynet.be; internet www.ambarwanda.be; Ambassador JOSEPH BONESHA.

Saint Christopher and Nevis: 42 rue de Livourne, 1000 Brussels; tel. (2) 534-26-11; fax (2) 539-40-09; e-mail ecs.embassies@skynet.be; Chargé d'affaires Dr ARNOLD THOMAS.

Saint Lucia: 42 rue de Livourne, 1000 Brussels; tel. (2) 534-26-11; fax (2) 539-40-09; e-mail ecs.embassies@skynet.be; Chargé d'affaires Dr ARNOLD THOMAS.

Saint Vincent and the Grenadines: 42 rue de Livourne, 1000 Brussels; tel. (2) 534-26-11; fax (2) 539-40-09; e-mail ecs.embassies@skynet.be; Chargé d'affaires Dr ARNOLD THOMAS.

Samoa: 20 ave de l'Orée, 1000 Brussels; tel. (2) 660-84-54; fax (2) 675-03-36; e-mail samoaembassy@skynet.be; Ambassador TUALA FALANI CHAN TUNG.

San Marino: 62 ave F. D. Roosevelt, 1050 Brussels; tel. (2) 644-22-24; fax (2) 644-20-57; e-mail ambrsm.bxl@coditel.net; Ambassador GIAN NICOLA FILIPPI BALESTRA.

São Tomé and Príncipe: 175 ave de Tervueren, 1150 Brussels; tel. and fax (2) 734-88-15; e-mail ambassade.sao.tome@skynet.be; Chargé d'affaires a.i. ARMINDO BRITO FERNANDES.

Saudi Arabia: 45 ave F. D. Roosevelt, 1050 Brussels; tel. (2) 649-20-44; fax (2) 647-24-92; e-mail beemb@mofa.gov.sa; Ambassador ABDULLAH BIN YAHYUA AL-MOUALLIMI.

Senegal: 196 ave F. D. Roosevelt, 1050 Brussels; tel. (2) 673-00-97; fax (2) 675-04-60; e-mail senegal.ambassade@coditel.net; Ambassador (vacant).

Serbia: 19 ave Emile de Mot, 1000 Brussels; tel. (2) 649-82-42; fax (2) 649-08-78; e-mail mission.serbia.eu@mfa.gov.yu; Ambassador ROKSANDA NINČIĆ.

Seychelles: 51 ave Mozart, 75016 Paris, France; tel. 1-42-30-57-47; fax 1-42-30-57-40; e-mail ambsey@aol.com; Ambassador CALLIXTE FRANÇOIS-XAVIER D'OFFAY.

Sierra Leone: 410 ave de Tervueren, 1150 Brussels; tel. (2) 771-00-53; fax (2) 771-82-30; e-mail sierraleoneembassy@brutele.be; Ambassador FODE MACLEAN DABOR.

Singapore: 198 ave F. D. Roosevelt, 1050 Brussels; tel. (2) 660-29-79; fax (2) 660-86-85; e-mail singemb_bru@sgmfa.gov.sg; internet www.mfa.gov.sg/brussels; Ambassador ANIL KUMAR NAYAR.

Solomon Islands: 17 ave Edouard Lacomblé, 1040 Brussels; tel. (2) 732-70-85; fax (2) 732-68-85; e-mail siembassy@compuserve.com; internet www.commerce.gov.sb; Ambassador JOSEPH MA'AHANUA.

South Africa: 17–19 rue Montoyer, 1040 Brussels; tel. (2) 285-44-00; fax (2) 285-44-02; e-mail embassy@southafrica.be; internet www.southafrica.be; Ambassador Dr ANIL SOUKLAL.

Sri Lanka: 27 rue Jules Lejeune, 1050 Brussels; tel. (2) 344-53-94; fax (2) 344-67-37; e-mail sri.lanka@tiscali.be; Ambassador K. J. WEERASINGHE.

Sudan: 124 ave F. D. Roosevelt, 1050 Brussels; tel. (2) 647-94-94; fax (2) 648-34-99; e-mail sudanbx@yahoo.com; Ambassador NAJEIB EL-KHEIR ABDELWAHAB.

Suriname: 379 ave Louise, 1050 Brussels; tel. (2) 640-11-72; fax (2) 646-39-62; e-mail sur.amb.bru@online.be; Ambassador GERARD O. HIWAT.

Swaziland: 188 ave Winston Churchill, 1180 Brussels; tel. (2) 347-47-71; fax (2) 347-46-23; Ambassador Dr THEMBAYENA ANNASTASIA DLAMINI.

Switzerland: 1 place du Luxembourg, 1050 Brussels; tel. (2) 286-13-11; fax (2) 230-45-09; e-mail brm.vertretung@eda.admin.ch; internet www.eda.admin.ch/mission_eu; Ambassador JACQUES DE WATTEVILLE.

Syria: 1 ave F. D. Roosevelt, 1050 Brussels; tel. (2) 554-19-21; fax (2) 648-14-85; e-mail syria.mission@skynet.be; Chargé d'affaires a.i. TAMIM MADANI.

Tajikistan: 363–365 ave Louise, BP 14, 1050 Brussels; tel. (2) 640-69-33; fax (2) 649-01-95; e-mail tajemb-belgium@skynet.be; internet www.taj-emb.be; Ambassador SAIMUMIN S. YATIMOV.

Tanzania: 72 ave F. D. Roosevelt, 1050 Brussels; tel. (2) 640-65-00; fax (2) 640-80-26; e-mail tanzanie@skynet.be; Ambassador SIMON U. R. MLAY.

Thailand: 2 square du Val de la Cambre, 1050 Brussels; tel. (2) 640-68-10; fax (2) 648-30-66; e-mail thaibxl@thaiembassy.be; internet www.thaiembassy.be; Ambassador PISAN MANAWAPAT.

Timor-Leste: 12 ave de Cortenberg, 1000 Brussels; tel. (2) 280-00-96; fax (2) 280-02-77; Ambassador JOSÉ ANTONIO AMORIM DIAS.

Togo: 264 ave de Tervueren, 1150 Brussels; tel. (2) 770-17-91; fax (2) 771-50-75; e-mail e-ambassade.togo@skynet.be; Ambassador FÉLIX KODJO SAGBO.

Tonga: 36 Molyneux St, London, W1H 5BQ, United Kingdom; tel. (20) 7724-5828; fax (20) 7723-9074; e-mail fetu@btinternet.com; Ambassador Col FETU'UTOLU TUPOU.

Trinidad and Tobago: 14 ave de la Faisanderie, 1150 Brussels; tel. (2) 762-94-00; fax (2) 772-27-83; e-mail info@embtrinbago.be; Chargé d'affaires a.i. KEITH DE FREITAS.

Tunisia: 278 ave de Tervueren, 1150 Brussels; tel. (2) 771-73-95; fax (2) 771-94-33; e-mail amb.detunisie@brutele.be; Ambassador ABDESSALEM HETIRA.

Turkey: 4 rue Montoyer, 1000 Brussels; tel. (2) 289-62-40; fax (2) 511-04-50; e-mail info@turkdeleg.org; Ambassador VOLKAN BOZKIR.

Turkmenistan: 106 ave F. D. Roosevelt, 1050 Brussels; tel. (2) 648-18-74; fax (2) 648-19-06; e-mail turkmenistan@skynet.be; Ambassador KAKADJAN MOMMADOV.

Uganda: 317 ave de Tervueren, 1150 Brussels; tel. (2) 762-58-25; fax (2) 763-04-38; e-mail ugembrus@brutele.be; Ambassador STEPHEN T. K. KATENTA-APULI.

Ukraine: 99–101 ave Louis Lepoutre, 1180 Brussels; tel. (2) 340-98-60; fax (2) 340-98-79; e-mail pr_ec@mfa.gov.ua; internet www.ukraine-eu.mfa.gov.ua; Ambassador ROMAN SHPEK.

United Arab Emirates: 73 ave F. D. Roosevelt, 1050 Brussels; tel. (2) 640-60-00; fax (2) 646-24-73; e-mail uae_embassy@skynet.be; Ambassador ABDEL HADI ABDEL WAHID AL-KHAJA.

USA: 13 rue Zinner, 1000 Brussels; tel. (2) 508-22-22; fax (2) 512-57-20; e-mail useupa@state.gov; internet useu.usmission.gov; Ambassador C. BOYDEN GRAY.

Uruguay: 22 ave F. D. Roosevelt, 1050 Brussels; tel. (2) 640-11-69; fax (2) 648-29-09; e-mail uruemb@skynet.be; internet www.mrree.gub.uy; Ambassador LUIS ALFREDO SICA BERGARA.

Uzbekistan: 99 ave F. D. Roosevelt, 1050 Brussels; tel. (2) 672-88-44; fax (2) 672-39-46; e-mail ambassador@uzbekistan.be; Ambassador VLADIMIR NOROV.

Vanuatu: 380 ave de Tervuren, 1150 Brussels; tel. and fax (2) 771-74-94; e-mail info@embassyvanuatu.net; Ambassador ROY MICKEY JOY.

Venezuela: 10 ave F. D. Roosevelt, 1050 Brussels; tel. (2) 639-03-40; fax (2) 647-88-20; e-mail embajada@venezuela-eu.org; Ambassador Dr ALEJANDRO ANTONIO FLEMING CABRERA.

Viet Nam: 1 blvd Général Jacques, 1050 Brussels; tel. (2) 379-27-37; fax (2) 374-93-76; e-mail vnem.brussels@skynet.be; Ambassador PHAN THUY THANH.

Yemen: 114 ave F. D. Roosevelt, 1050 Brussels; tel. (2) 646-52-90; fax (2) 646-29-11; e-mail yemen.embassy@skynet.be; Ambassador Dr JAFFER MOHAMED JAFFER.

Zambia: 469 ave Molière, 1050 Brussels; tel. (2) 343-56-49; fax (2) 347-43-33; e-mail zambians_brussels@brutele.be; Chargé d'affaires a.i. MIYAMBO SIPANGULE.

Zimbabwe: 11 square Joséphine Charlotte, 1200 Brussels; tel. (2) 762-58-08; fax (2) 762-96-05; e-mail zimbrussels@skynet.be; Ambassador GIFT PUNUNGWE.

Union Institutions

The EU provides an information service, Europe Direct; assistance with navigating the EU website is available at the internet address europa.eu.int/europedirect/web_assistance_en.htm, while further queries can be made by telephone on 00 800 67891011 from within the 25 member states (mostly without charge) and from the chargeable number 00 32 2 299-96-96 from other countries.

EUROPEAN COMMISSION

Address: 200 rue de la Loi, 1049 Brussels, Belgium.
Telephone: (2) 299-11-11; **fax:** (2) 295-01-38; **e-mail:** forename.surname@ec.europa.eu; **internet:** ec.europa.eu./index-en.htm.

Please note: in an e-mail address, when the forename and/or the surname are composed of more than one word, the different words are linked by a hyphen. If help is needed, you may send a message to address-information@ec.europa.eu requesting the correct e-mail address of the correspondent.

MEMBERS OF THE COMMISSION
(2004–2009)

President: José Manuel Durão Barroso (Portugal).

Vice President, responsible for Institutional Relations and Communication Strategy: Margot Wallström (Sweden).

Vice President, responsible for Enterprise and Industry: Günter Verheugen (Germany).

Vice President, responsible for Transport: Jacques Barrot (France).

Vice President, responsible for Administrative Affairs, Audit and Anti-fraud: Siim Kallas (Estonia).

Vice President, responsible for Justice, Freedom and Security: Franco Frattini (Italy).

Commissioner, responsible for Information Society and Media: Viviane Reding (Luxembourg).

Commissioner, responsible for the Environment: Stavros Dimas (Greece).

Commissioner, responsible for Economic and Monetary Affairs: Joaquín Almunia (Spain).

Commissioner, responsible for Regional Policy: Danuta Hübner (Poland).

Commissioner, responsible for Fisheries and Maritime Affairs: Joe Borg (Malta).

Commissioner, responsible for Financial Programming and the Budget: Dalia Grybauskaitė (Lithuania).

Commissioner, responsible for Science and Research: Janez Potočnik (Slovenia).

Commissioner, responsible for Education, Training, Culture and Youth: Ján Figel (Slovakia).

Commissioner, responsible for Health: Markos Kyprianou (Cyprus).

Commissioner, responsible for Enlargement: Olli Rehn (Finland).

Commissioner, responsible for Development and Humanitarian Aid: Louis Michel (Belgium).

Commissioner, responsible for Taxation and Customs Union: László Kovács (Hungary).

Commissioner, responsible for Competition: Neelie Kroes (Netherlands).

Commissioner, responsible for Agriculture and Rural Development: Mariann Fischer Boel (Denmark).

Commissioner, responsible for External Relations and European Neighbourhood Policy: Benita Ferrero-Waldner (Austria).

Commissioner, responsible for the Internal Market and Services: Charlie McCreevy (Ireland).

Commissioner, responsible for Employment, Social Affairs and Equal Opportunities: Vladimír Špidla (Czech Republic).

Commissioner, responsible for Trade: Peter Mandelson (United Kingdom).

Commissioner, responsible for Energy: Andris Piebalgs (Latvia).

Commissioner, responsible for Consumer Protection: Meglena Kuneva (Bulgaria).

Commissioner, responsible for Multilingualism: Leonard Orban (Romania).

The European Commission, like the European Parliament and Council of the European Union, was established in the 1950s under the EU's founding Treaties. The functions of the Commission are four-fold: to propose legislation to the European Parliament and the Council of the European Union; to implement EU policies and programmes adopted by the European Parliament and to manage and implement the budget; to enforce European law, in conjunction with the Court of Justice, in all the member states; and to represent the EU in international affairs and to negotiate agreements between the EU and other organizations or countries.

A new Commission is appointed for a five-year term, within six months of the elections to the European Parliament. The Governments of the member states agree on an individual to designate as the new Commission President. The President-designate then selects the other members of the Commission, following discussions with the member state Governments. In the performance of their duties, the members of the Commission are forbidden to seek or accept instructions from any government or other body, or to engage in any other paid or unpaid professional activity. The nominated President and other members of the Commission must be approved as a body by the European Parliament before they can take office. Once approved, the Commission may nominate a number of its members as Vice President. Any member of the Commission, if he or she no longer fulfils the conditions required for the performance of his or her duties, or commits a serious offence, may be declared removed from office by the Court of Justice. The Court may furthermore, on the petition of the Council of the European Union or of the Commission itself, provisionally suspend any member of the Commission from his or her duties. The European Parliament has the authority to dismiss the entire Commission by adopting a motion of censure. The number of members of the Commission may be amended by a unanimous vote of the Council of the European Union.

The members of the Commission, also known as the College, meet once a week and a collective decision is made on policy following a presentation by the relevant Commissioner. The Commission's staff is organized into 38 departments, known as Directorates-General and Services. The Directorates-General are each responsible for a particular policy area and they devise and draft the Commission's legislative proposals, which become official when adopted by the Commission at the weekly meeting.

In January 1999 Commissioners accused of mismanagement and corruption retained their positions following a vote of censure by Parliament. However, Parliament appointed a five-member Committee of Independent Experts to investigate allegations of fraud, mismanagement and nepotism within the Commission. In early March two new codes of conduct for Commissioners were announced. On 15 March the Committee published a report that criticized the Commission's failure to control the administration of the budget and other measures implemented by each department. The report also identified individual Commissioners as guilty of nepotism and mismanagement and proposed the establishment of a new independent unit to investigate fraud. As a consequence of the report the Commission agreed, collectively, to resign, although Commissioners retained their positions, and exercised limited duties, until their successors were appointed. In late March EU heads of state and of government nominated Romano Prodi, the former Italian Prime Minister, as the next President of the Commission. His appointment, and that of the team of Commissioners that he had appointed in the interim, were duly ratified by Parliament in September, subject to conditions that formed the foundation of a future inter-institutional agreement between Parliament and the Commission. The Commission did not lose any of its powers, but undertook to be more open in its dealings with the Parliament.

On 1 May 2004, following the accession of 10 new member states, the 20 existing members of the Commission were joined by 10 new members (one from each new member state). For the first six months of their term of office, although considered full members, they worked alongside existing Commissioners and were not allocated their own departments. From 1 November, when a new Commission was to begin its mandate, there were to be 25 members of the Commission, one from each member state as stipulated by the Treaty of Nice (prior to 1 May, large countries had been permitted two Commissioners, while smaller countries had one). In late October, however, the incoming President of the European Commission, José Manuel Durão Barroso, was forced to withdraw his proposed team of commissioners and to reconsider the composition of the Commission in order to avoid an unprecedented defeat in the scheduled parliamentary investiture vote in the European Parliament on 27 October. The reconstituted Commission (two members were replaced and one was allocated a new portfolio) was approved by the European Parliament and took office on 22 November. In January 2007, following the accession of Bulgaria and Romania, the number of Commissioners increased to 27. However, with respect to further enlargement, as it is feared that too large an increase in the number of Commissioners would be prejudicial to collective responsibility, from 2014 the number is to be reduced to a level determined by the Council. The draft Treaty of Lisbon would provide for the number of Commissioners to be limited to two-thirds of the number of member states from 2014, in accordance with a system of rotation.

In January 2004 the Commission launched legal proceedings against the Economic and Financial Council of Ministers (ECOFIN—which comprises the national ministers responsible for finance), one of the formats of the Council of the European Union. The Commission was seeking a ruling from the European Court of Justice on the legality of ECOFIN's decision to suspend disciplinary procedures against France and Germany, both of which were intending to exceed the budget deficit limit of 3% of gross domestic product (GDP), imposed under the Stability and Growth Pact, for the third consecutive year. In July the European Court of Justice ruled that ECOFIN's intervention was not compatible with EU legislation but that ministers retained ultimate control over the implementation of the pact. In November 2005, in response to diminishing public confidence in the institutions of the European Union, the Commission launched the European Transparency Initiative, with the aim of strengthening ethical rules for EU policy-makers, increasing the transparency of lobbying and ensuring the openness of the institutions.

DIRECTORATES-GENERAL AND SERVICES

Policies

Directorate-General for Agriculture and Rural Development: 130 rue de la Loi, 1040 Brussels; tel. (2) 295-32-40; fax (2) 295-01-30; e-mail agri-library@ec.europa.eu; internet ec.europa.eu/dgs/agriculture/index_en.htm; Dir-Gen. JEAN-LUC DEMARTY.

Directorate-General for Competition: 70 rue Joseph II, 1049 Brussels; tel. (2) 299-11-11; fax (2) 295-01-28; e-mail infocomp@ec.europa.eu; internet ec.europa.eu/competition/index_en.html; f. 1958; Dir-Gen. PHILIP LOWE.

Directorate-General for Economic and Financial Affairs: 1 ave de Beaulieu, 1160 Brussels; tel. (2) 299-11-11; fax (2) 296-94-28; e-mail staffdir@ec.europa.eu; internet ec.europa.eu/economy_finance/index_en.htm; Dir-Gen. KLAUS REGLING.

Directorate-General for Education and Culture: 200 rue de la Loi, 1049 Brussels; tel. (2) 299-11-11; fax (2) 295-60-85; e-mail eac-info@ec.europa.eu; internet ec.europa.eu/dgs/education_culture/index_en.htm; Dir-Gen. ODILE QUINTIN.

Directorate-General for Employment, Social Affairs and Equal Opportunities: 27 and 37 rue Joseph II, 1000 Brussels; tel. (2) 299-11-11; fax (2) 296-23-93; e-mail empl-info@ec.europa.eu; internet ec.europa.eu/dgs/employment_social/index_en.htm; Dir-Gen. NIKOLAUS VAN DER PAS.

Directorate-General for Energy and Transport: 24–28 rue Demot, 1040 Brussels; tel. (2) 299-11-11; fax (2) 295-01-50; e-mail tren-info@ec.europa.eu; internet ec.europa.eu/dgs/energy_transport/index_en.html; Dir-Gen. MATTHIAS RUETE.

Directorate-General for Fisheries and Maritime Affairs: 99 rue de Joseph II, 1000 Brussels; tel. (2) 299-11-11; fax (2) 299-30-40; e-mail fisheries-info@ec.europa.eu; internet ec.europa.eu/fisheries/index_en.htm; Dir-Gen. FOKION FOTIADIS.

Directorate-General for Internal Market and Services: 107 ave de Cortenberg, 1049 Brussels; tel. (2) 299-11-11; fax (2) 295-65-00; e-mail markt-info@ec.europa.eu; internet ec.europa.eu/dgs/internal_market/index_en.htm; Dir-Gen. JÖRGEN HOLMQUIST.

Directorate-General for Justice, Freedom and Security: 46 rue du Luxembourg, 1050 Brussels; tel. (2) 299-11-11; fax (2) 296-74-81; e-mail forename.surname@ec.europa.eu; internet ec.europa.eu/dgs/justice_home/index_en.htm; Dir-Gen. JONATHAN FAULL.

Directorate-General for Regional Policy: 23 rue Père de Deken, 1040 Brussels; tel. (2) 296-06-34; fax (2) 296-60-03; e-mail regio-info@ec.europa.eu; internet ec.europa.eu/dgs/regional_policy/index_en.htm; Dir-Gen. DIRK AHNER.

Enterprise and Industry Directorate-General: 45 ave d'Auderghem, 1049 Brussels; tel. (2) 299-11-11; fax (2) 296-99-30; e-mail info-enterprises@ec.europa.eu; internet ec.europa.eu/enterprise/index_en.htm; Dir-Gen. HEINZ ZOUREK.

Environment Directorate-General: 5 ave de Beaulieu, 1160 Brussels; tel. (2) 299-11-11; fax (2) 299-11-05; e-mail envinfo@ec.europa.eu; internet ec.europa.eu/environment/index_en.htm; Dir-Gen. MOGENS PETER CARL.

Health and Consumer Protection Directorate-General: 4 rue Breydel, 1040 Brussels; tel. (2) 299-11-11; fax (2) 296-62-98; e-mail sanco-mailbox@ec.europa.eu; internet ec.europa.eu/dgs/health_consumer/index_en.htm; Dir-Gen. ROBERT MADELIN.

Information Society and Media Directorate-General: 24 ave de Beaulieu, 1049 Brussels; tel. (2) 299-93-99; fax (2) 299-94-99; e-mail infso-desk@ec.europa.eu; internet ec.europa.eu/dgs/information_society/index_en.htm; Dir-Gen. FABIO COLASANTI.

Joint Research Centre (JRC): 200 rue de la Loi, 1049 Brussels; tel. (2) 299-11-11; fax (2) 295-05-46; e-mail jrc-info@ec.europa.eu; internet www.jrc.cec.eu.int; Dir-Gen. ROLAND SCHENKEL.

Research Directorate-General: 21 rue de Champ de Mars, 1050 Brussels; tel. (2) 299-11-11; fax (2) 295-82-20; e-mail research@cec.eu.int; internet ec.europa.eu/dgs/research/index_en.html; Dir-Gen. JOSÉ MANUEL SILVA RODRÍGUEZ.

Taxation and the Customs Union Directorate-General: 59 rue Montoyer, 1000 Brussels; tel. (2) 299-11-11; fax (2) 295-07-56; e-mail librarian-information@ec.europa.eu; internet ec.europa.eu/dgs/taxation_customs/index_en.htm; Dir-Gen. ROBERT VERRUE.

External Relations

Directorate-General for Development (DG DEV): 15 rue de la Science, 1040 Brussels; tel. (2) 299-21-43; fax (2) 296-49-26; e-mail development@ec.europa.eu; internet ec.europa.eu/development/AboutGen_en.cfm; Dir-Gen. STEFANO MANSERVISI.

Directorate-General for Enlargement: 200 rue de la Loi, 1049 Brussels; tel. (2) 299-96-96; fax (2) 296-84-90; e-mail elarg-info@ec.europa.eu; internet ec.europa.eu/dgs/enlargement/index_en.htm; Dir-Gen. MICHAEL LEIGH.

Directorate-General for Trade (DG Trade): 200 rue de la Loi, 1049 Brussels; tel. (2) 299-11-11; fax (2) 299-10-29; e-mail trade-unit3@ec.europa.eu; internet ec.europa.eu/dgs/trade/index_en.htm; Dir-Gen. DAVID O'SULLIVAN.

EuropeAid Co-operation Office: 41 rue de la Loi, 1040 Brussels; tel. (2) 299-32-71; fax (2) 296-94-89; e-mail europeaid-info@ec.europa.eu; internet ec.europa.eu/europeaid/index_en.htm; Dir-Gen. JACOBUS RICHELLE.

External Relations Directorate-General: 170 rue de la Loi, 1040 Brussels; tel. (2) 299-11-11; fax (2) 299-65-29; e-mail relex-feedback@ec.europa.eu; internet ec.europa.eu/dgs/external_relations/index_en.htm; Dir-Gen. ENEKO LANDABURU.

Humanitarian Aid Office (ECHO): 88 rue d'Arlon, 1040 Brussels; tel. (2) 299-11-11; fax (2) 295-45-78; e-mail echo-info@ec.europa.eu; internet ec.europa.eu/echo/contact_en.htm; Dir ANTÓNIO SERVINHO CAVACO.

General Services

Directorate-General Communication: 45 ave d'Auderghem, SDME 2/2, 1049 Brussels; tel. (2) 299-11-11; fax (2) 295-01-43; e-mail comm-web@ec.europa.eu; internet ec.europa.eu/dgs/communication/index_en.htm; Dir-Gen. JORGE DE OLIVEIRA E SOUSA.

European Anti-Fraud Office: 30 rue Joseph II, 1000 Brussels; tel. (2) 296-29-76; fax (2) 296-08-53; e-mail olaf-courrier@ec.europa.eu; internet ec.europa.eu/dgs/olaf/index_en.html; Dir-Gen. FRANZ-HERMANN BRÜNER.

Eurostat (Statistical Office of the European Communities): Bâtiment Jean Monnet, rue Alcide de Gasperi, 2920 Luxembourg Offices; Bâtiment Joseph Bech, 5 Rue Alphonse Weicker, 2721 Luxembourg; tel. 43-01-33-444; fax 43-01-35-349; e-mail eurostat-pressoffice@ec.europa.eu; internet epp.eurostat.ec.europa.eu; Dir-Gen. HERVÉ CARRÉ.

Office for Official Publications of the European Communities (Publications Office): 2 rue Mercier, 2985 Luxembourg; tel. 29-291; fax 29-29-44-619; e-mail info@publications.europa.eu; internet www.publications.eu.int; Dir-Gen. MARTINE REICHERTS.

Secretariat-General: 45 ave d'Auderghem, 1049 Brussels; tel. (2) 299-11-11; fax (2) 296-05-54; e-mail sg-info@ec.europa.eu; internet ec.europa.eu/dgs/secretariat_general/index_en.htm; Sec.-Gen. CATHERINE DAY.

Internal Services

Bureau of European Policy Advisers (BEPA): 200 rue de la Loi, 1049 Brussels; tel. (2) 299-11-11; fax (2) 295-23-05; e-mail BEPA-Info@ec.europa.eu; internet ec.europa.eu/dgs/policy_advisers/index_en.htm; Dir-Gen. VITOR GASPAR.

Directorate-General for the Budget: 45 ave d'Auderghem, 1049 Brussels; tel. (2) 299-11-11; fax (2) 295-95-85; e-mail budget@ec.europa.eu; internet ec.europa.eu/dgs/budget/index_en.htm; Dir-Gen. LUIS ROMERO REQUENA.

Directorate-General for Informatics: rue Alcide de Gasperi, 2920 Luxembourg; e-mail digit-europa@ec.europa.eu; internet ec.europa.eu/dgs/informatics/index_en.htm; Dir-Gen. FRANCISCO GARCÍA MORÁN.

Directorate-General for Interpretation: 200 rue de la Loi, 1040 Brussels; tel. (2) 299-11-11; e-mail scic-euroscic@ec.europa.eu; internet scic.ec.europa.eu/europa/jcms/j_8/home; Head of Service MARCO BENEDETTI.

Directorate-General for Personnel and Administration: 200 rue de la Loi, 1040 Brussels; tel. (2) 299-11-11; fax (2) 299-62-76; e-mail forename.surname@ec.europa.eu; internet ec.europa.eu/dgs/personnel_administration/index_en.htm; Dir-Gen. CLAUDE CHÊNE.

Directorate-General for Translation (DGT): 200 rue de la Loi, 1040 Brussels; rue de Genève, 1140 Bruxelles; tel. (2) 299-11-11; fax (2) 296-97-69; e-mail dgt-webmaster@ec.europa.eu; internet ec.europa.eu/dgs/translation; Dir-Gen. KARL-JOHAN LÖNNROTH.

Office for Infrastructure and Logistics (OIB): Garderie Wilson, 16 rue Wilson, 1040 Brussels; fax (2) 295-76-41; e-mail oil-cad@ec.europa.eu; internet ec.europa.eu/oib/index_en.htm; Dir GÁBOR ZUPKÓ.

Internal Audit Service (IAS): 200 rue de la Loi, 1049 Brussels; tel. (2) 299-11-11; fax (2) 295-41-40; e-mail ias-europa@ec.europa.eu; internet ec.europa.eu/dgs/internal_audit/index_en.htm; Dir-Gen. WALTER DEFFAA.

Legal Service: 85 ave des Nerviens, 1049 Brussels; tel. (2) 299-11-11; fax (2) 296-30-86; e-mail oib-info@ec.europa.eu; internet ec.europa.eu/dgs/legal_service/index_en.htm; Dir-Gen. CLAIRE-FRANÇOISE DURAND.

EUROPEAN COUNCIL

The European Council is the name used to describe summit meetings of the heads of state or of government of the EU member states, their foreign ministers, and senior officials of the European Commission. The Council meets at least twice a year, in the member state that currently exercises the Presidency of the Council of the European Union, or in Brussels.

Until 1975, summit meetings were held less frequently, on an ad hoc basis, usually to adopt major policy decisions regarding the future development of the Community. In answer to the evident need for more frequent consultation at the highest level, it was decided at the summit meeting held in Paris in December 1974 to convene the meetings on a regular basis, under the rubric of the European Council. There was no provision made for the existence of the European Council in the Treaty of Rome, but its position was acknowledged and regularized in the Single European Act (1987). Its role was further strengthened in the Treaty on European Union, which entered into force on 1 November 1993. As a result of the Treaty, the European Council became directly responsible for common policies within the fields of common foreign and security policy and justice and home affairs.

When policy decisions are taken by the European Council that conform to the constitutional requirements of the founding treaties, they have the force of EC legislation. More generally, however, European Council agreements are framed as general principles or a broad consensus on future action, which are subsequently transferred to the European Commission and the Council of the European Union for further investigation, discussion and possible adoption.

COUNCIL OF THE EUROPEAN UNION

Address: Justus Lipsius Bldg, 175 rue de la Loi, 1048 Brussels, Belgium.

Telephone: (2) 281-61-11; **fax:** (2) 281-69-34; **e-mail:** press.office@consilium.europa.eu; **internet:** www.consilium.europa.eu.

The Council of the European Union (until November 1993 known formally as the Council of Ministers of the European Communities and still frequently referred to as the Council of Ministers) is the only institution that directly represents the member states. It is the Community's principal decision-making body, acting, as a rule, only on proposals made by the Commission, and has six main responsibilities: to pass EC legislation (in many fields it legislates jointly with the European Parliament); to co-ordinate the broad economic policies of the member states; to conclude international agreements between the EU and one or more states or international organizations; to approve the EU budget (in conjunction with the European Parliament); to develop the EU's Common Foreign and Security Policy (CFSP), on the basis of guide-lines drawn up by the European Council; and to co-ordinate co-operation between the national courts and police forces in criminal matters. The Council is composed of representatives of the member states, each Government delegating to it one of its members, according to the subject to be discussed (the Council has nine different configurations). These meetings are generally referred to as the Agriculture and Fisheries Council, the Transport, Telecommunications and Energy Council, etc. The General Affairs and External Relations Council, the Economic and Financial Affairs Council (ECOFIN) and the Agriculture and Fisheries Council each normally meet once a month. The Presidency is exercised for a term of six months by each member of the Council in rotation (January–June 2008 Slovenia; July–December 2008 France; January–June 2009 the Czech Republic; July–December 2009 Sweden). The foreign minister of the state holding the Presidency (which coincides with that of the European Council) becomes President of the Council and is responsible during those six months for organizing the business of the Council, in conjunction with the General Secretariat. Meetings of the Council are convened and chaired by the President, acting on his or her own initiative or at the request of a member or of the Commission.

The Treaty of Rome prescribed three types of voting (depending on the issue under discussion): simple majority, qualified majority and unanimity. During negotiations regarding the impending enlargement of the EU, an agreement was reached, in March 1994, on new rules regulating voting procedures in the expanded Council, in response to concerns on the part of Spain and the United Kingdom that their individual influence would be diminished after the accession of 10 new members on 1 May 2004. Under the 'Ioannina compromise' (named after the Greek town where the agreement was concluded), 23–25 opposing votes ensured the continued debate of legislation for a 'reasonable period' until a consensus decision was reached. Amendments to the Treaty of Rome (the Single European Act), effective from July 1987, restricted the right of veto, and were expected to accelerate the development of a genuine common market: they allowed proposals relating to the dismantling of barriers to the free movement of goods, persons, services and capital to be approved by a majority vote in the Council, rather than by a unanimous vote. Unanimity would still be required, however, for certain areas, including harmonization of indirect taxes, legislation on health and safety, veterinary controls, and environmental protection; individual states would also retain control over immigration rules and the prevention of terrorism and of drugs-trafficking. The Treaty of Amsterdam, which came into force on 1 May 1999, extended the use of qualified majority voting (QMV) to a number of areas previously subject to unanimous decision. Under the terms of the Treaty of Nice, which came into force on 1 February 2003, a further range of areas (mostly minor in nature and relating to appointments to various EU institutions) that had previously been subject to national vetoes became subject to QMV. With the expansion of the EU to 25 members in 2004, and subsequently to 27 members in 2007, and the consequent decreased likelihood of Council decisions being unanimous, the use of QMV in an even broader range of decisions was expected to minimize so-called 'policy drag'.

The Single European Act introduced a 'co-operation procedure' whereby a proposal adopted by a qualified majority in the Council must be submitted to the European Parliament for approval: if the Parliament rejects the Council's common position, unanimity shall be required for the Council to act on a second reading, and if the Parliament suggests amendments, the Commission must re-examine the proposal and forward it to the Council again. A 'co-decision procedure' was introduced in 1993 by the Treaty on European Union. The procedure allows a proposal to be submitted for a third reading by a so-called 'Conciliation Committee', composed equally of Council representatives and members of the European Parliament. The Treaty of Amsterdam simplified the co-decision procedure, and extended it to matters previously resolved under the co-operation procedure, although the latter remained in place for matters concerning economic and monetary union.

Under the Treaty of Amsterdam, the Secretary-General of the Council also took the role of 'High Representative', responsible for the co-ordination of the common foreign and security policy. The Secretary-General is supported by a policy planning and early warning unit. In June 1999 Javier Solana Madariaga, at that time Secretary-General of the North Atlantic Treaty Organization (NATO), was designated as the first Secretary-General of the Council.

The Treaty of Nice, which came into force in February 2003, addresses institutional issues that remained outstanding under the Treaty of Amsterdam and that had to be settled before the enlargement of the EU in 2004, and various other issues not directly connected with enlargement. The main focus of the Treaty is the establishment of principles governing the new distribution of seats in the European Parliament, the new composition of the Commission and a new definition of QMV within the Council of the European Union. From 1 May 2004 (when the 10 accession states joined the EU) until 31 October, there were transitional arrangements for changing the weighting of votes in the Council. In accordance with the provisions incorporated in the Treaty of Nice, from 1 November the new weighting system was as follows: France, Germany, Italy and the United Kingdom 29 votes each; Poland and Spain 27 votes each; the Netherlands 13 votes; Belgium, the Czech Republic, Greece, Hungary and Portugal 12 votes each; Austria and Sweden 10 votes each; Denmark, Finland, Ireland, Lithuania and Slovakia seven votes each; Cyprus, Estonia, Latvia, Luxembourg and Slovenia four votes each; and Malta three votes. A qualified majority is to be reached if a majority of member states (in some cases a two-thirds' majority) approve and if a minimum of 232 votes out of a total of 321 is cast in favour (which is 72.3% of the total—approximately the same share as under the previous system). In addition, a member state may request confirmation that the votes in favour represent at least 62% of the total population of the EU. Should this not be the case, the decision will not be adopted by the Council. The number of weighted votes required for the adoption of a decision (referred to as the 'qualified majority threshold') was to be reassessed on the accession of any additional new member state. Accordingly, in January 2007, with the accession of Romania and Bulgaria, which were allocated, respectively, 14 and 10 votes, the 'qualified majority threshold' was increased to 255 votes, which represented 73.9% of the new total of 345 votes. It was widely held that the voting system according to the Treaty of Nice was overly complicated and that it gave undue power to certain less populous countries, notably Spain and Poland (which both held 27 votes each, compared with Germany, which, with a population of at least twice the size of those in Spain and Poland, controlled 29 votes). Accordingly, the draft treaty establishing a constitution for the EU, which was published by the Convention on the Future of Europe in mid-2003, proposed a simpler system of voting for the Council—a vote could be passed when it had the support of 50% of the member states representing at least 60% of the EU's population. Spain and Poland rejected these proposals (which would entail a considerable diminution of their voting strength), and the European Council summit meeting that was held in Brussels in December to discuss the draft constitution collapsed as a result of the impasse. A compromise was eventually achieved under the auspices of the incumbent President of the Council of the European Union, the

INTERNATIONAL ORGANIZATIONS   *European Union*

Irish Prime Minister, Bertie Ahern, and the text of the proposed constitution was approved by the European Council at a summit meeting in Brussels on 18 June 2004. The compromise reached over voting rights meant that measures would require the support of at least 55% of EU states, representing at least 65% of the total population, so that smaller member states—particularly the new Eastern European members—could not be simply overruled by a small but powerful group of long-standing members, such as France, Germany and the United Kingdom. However, the future of the constitutional treaty became uncertain following its rejection in national referendums in France and the Netherlands in May–June 2005. Efforts to revive the institutional reform process resulted, in October 2007, in agreement on the final text of a new Draft Treaty amending the Treaty on European Union and the Treaty establishing the European Community (also known as the Reform Treaty or the Treaty of Lisbon). The treaty was signed in Lisbon, Portugal, on 13 December by the heads of state or of government of the 27 member states. The system of qualified majority voting in the Council of the European Union was to be extended and redefined, ending the system of national vetoes in a number of new areas. From November 2014 a qualified majority would be defined as at least 55% of the members of the Council, composed of at least 15 of them and representing member states comprising at least 65% of the EU's population (although a blocking minority would have to include at least four member states). The draft Lisbon Treaty includes a provision that the European Council could agree, by unanimity and subject to prior unanimous approval by national legislatures, to introduce qualified majority voting in an area currently requiring unanimity (except in the area of defence), thus obviating the need for treaty change. The Lisbon Treaty also envisages the creation of a new permanent president of the European Council, elected by the European Council for a period of two and one-half years, renewable once, to replace the current system of a six-month rotating presidency. However, the system of a six-month rotating presidency would be retained for the different Council formations (except for the External Relations Council, which would be chaired by the new High Representative of the Union for Foreign Affairs and Security Policy), although it would comprise a 'team presidency' of three countries.

PERMANENT REPRESENTATIVES

Preparation and co-ordination of the Council's work (with the exception of agricultural issues, which are handled by the Special Committee on Agriculture) is entrusted to a Committee of Permanent Representatives (COREPER), which meets in Brussels on a weekly basis and which consists of the permanent representatives of the member countries to the Union (who have senior ambassadorial status). A staff of national civil servants assists each ambassador.

GENERAL SECRETARIAT

Secretary-General and High Representative for Common Foreign and Security Policy: JAVIER SOLANA MADARIAGA.
Deputy Secretary-General: PIERRE DE BOISSIEU.
Secretary-General's Private Office: Dir, High Representative and Head of Cabinet ENRIQUE MORA.
Legal Service: Dir-Gen./Legal Adviser JEAN-CLAUDE PIRIS.
Directorates-General:
A (Personnel and Administration): Dir-Gen. VITTORIO GRIFFO.
B (Agriculture and Fisheries): Dir-Gen. ÁNGEL BOIXAREU CARRERA.
C (Internal Market; Competitiveness; Industry; Research; Energy; Transport; Information Society): Dir-Gen. KLAUS GRETSCHMANN.
E (External Economic Relations; Politico-Military Affairs)*: Dir-Gen. ROBERT COOPER.
F (Press, Communication and Protocol): Dir-Gen./Head of Protocol MARC LEPOIVRE.
G (Economic and Social Affairs): Dir-Gen. GRÉGOIRE BROUHNS.
H (Justice and Home Affairs): Dir-Gen. IVAN BIZJAK.
I (Protection of the Environment and Consumers; Civil Protection; Health; Foodstuffs; Education; Youth; Culture; Audiovisual): Dir-Gen. KERSTIN NIBLAEUS.

* Directorate-General D no longer exists.

EUROPEAN PARLIAMENT

Address: Centre Européen, Plateau du Kirchberg, BP 1601, 2929 Luxembourg.
Telephone: 4300-1; **fax:** 4300-29494; **internet:** www.europarl.europa.eu.

PRESIDENT AND MEMBERS

President: HANS-GERT PÖTTERING (Germany).
Members: In accordance with the Treaty of Nice, which came into force in February 2003, the Parliament elected in June 2004 (following the accession of the 10 new member states in May) was composed of 732 members and the distribution of seats among the 25 members was as follows: Germany 99 members; France, Italy and the United Kingdom 78 members each; Spain and Poland 54; the Netherlands 27; Belgium, Greece, Portugal, the Czech Republic and Hungary 24 each; Sweden 19; Austria 18; Denmark, Finland and Slovakia 14 each; Ireland and Lithuania 13; Latvia nine; Slovenia seven; Luxembourg, Cyprus and Estonia six each; and Malta five. Members are elected for a five-year term by direct universal suffrage and proportional representation by the citizens of the member states. Members sit in the Chamber in transnational political, not national, groups. On 1 January 2007, with the accession of Bulgaria and Romania, which were allocated, respectively, 18 and 35 seats, the total number of seats was temporarily increased to 785 to accommodate those countries. The proposed Treaty of Lisbon, signed in Lisbon, Portugal, on 13 December by the heads of state or of government of the 27 member states and subject to ratification by a vote in the national legislatures of member states or by referendum, provided for a maximum number of seats of 750, with each member state being entitled to a minimum of six and a maximum of 96 seats, on a proportional basis.

The European Parliament has three main roles: sharing with the Council of the European Union the power to legislate; holding authority over the annual Union budget (again, jointly with the Council), including the power to adopt or reject it in its entirety; and exercising a measure of democratic control over the executive organs of the European Communities, the Commission and the Council. Notably, it has the power to dismiss the European Commission as a whole by a vote of censure (requiring a two-thirds' majority of the votes cast, which must also be a majority of the total parliamentary membership). The Parliament does not exercise the authority, however, to dismiss individual Commissioners. Increases in parliamentary powers have been brought about through amendments to the Treaty of Rome. The Single European Act, which entered into force on 1 July 1987, introduced, in certain circumstances where the Council normally adopts legislation through majority voting, a co-operation procedure involving a second parliamentary reading, enabling the Parliament to amend legislation. Community agreements with third countries require parliamentary approval. The Treaty on European Union, which came into force in November 1993, introduced the co-decision procedure, permitting a third parliamentary reading (see the Council of the European Union). The Treaty also gives the Parliament the right potentially to veto legislation, and allows it to approve or reject the nomination of Commissioners (including the President of the Commission). The Parliament appoints the European Ombudsman from among its members, who investigates reports of maladministration in Community institutions. The Treaty of Amsterdam, which entered into force in May 1999, expanded and simplified the Parliament's legislative role. The co-decision procedure between the Parliament and the Council was extended into a wider range of policy areas. The Treaty also stipulated that the President of the Commission must be formally approved by the Parliament. In addition, international agreements, treaty decisions and the accession of new member states all require the assent of the Parliament. The Treaty of Nice, which came into force in February 2003, further extended the use of co-decision and introduced a new distribution of seats in the Parliament, which took effect at the elections in June 2004, following the accession of the new member states on 1 May.

Political Groups

	Distribution of seats (April 2008)
Group of the European People's Party (Christian Democrats) and European Democrats (PPE-ED)	288
Socialist Group in the European Parliament (PSE)	215
Group of the Alliance of Liberals and Democrats for Europe (ALDE)	101
Union for Europe of the Nations Group (UEN)	44
Group of the Greens/European Free Alliance (Verts/ALE)	43
Confederal Group of the European United Left/Nordic Green Left (GUE/NGL)	41
Independence/Democracy Group (IND/DEM)	24
Non-affiliated (NI)	29
Total	**785**

INTERNATIONAL ORGANIZATIONS

Since 1 January 2007 the minimum number of members required to form a political group under the Parliament's rules of procedure has been fixed at 20, from a minimum of six member states (previously 29 members were required if they came from one member state; 23 from two; 18 from three; and 14 from four).

The Parliament has an annual session, divided into around 12 one-week meetings, attended by all members and normally held in Strasbourg, France. The session opens with the March meeting. Committee meetings, political group meetings and additional plenary sittings of the Parliament are held in Brussels, while the parliamentary administrative offices are based in Luxembourg.

The budgetary powers of the Parliament (which, together with the Council of the European Union, forms the Budgetary Authority of the Communities) were increased to their present status by a treaty of 22 July 1975. Under this treaty the Parliament can amend non-agricultural spending and reject the draft budget, acting by a majority of its members and two-thirds of the votes cast. The Parliament debates the draft budget in two successive readings, and it does not come into force until it has been signed by the President of the Parliament. The Parliament's Committee on Budgetary Control (COCOBU) monitors how the budget is spent, and each year the Parliament decides whether to approve the Commission's handling of the budget for the previous financial year (a process technically known as 'granting a discharge').

The Parliament is run by a Bureau comprising the President, 14 Vice-Presidents elected from its members by secret ballot to serve for two-and-a-half years, and the five members of the College of Quaestors. The Conference of Presidents is the political governing body of the Parliament, with responsibility for formulating the agenda for plenary sessions and the timetable for the work of parliamentary bodies, and for establishing the terms of reference and the size of committees and delegations. It comprises the President of the Parliament and the Chairmen of the political groups.

The majority of the Parliament's work is conducted by 24 Standing Parliamentary Committees, which correspond to different policy areas and various European Commission agencies: Foreign Affairs; Development; International Trade; Budgets; Budgetary Control; Economic and Monetary Affairs; Employment and Social Affairs; Environment, Public Health and Food Safety; Industry, Research and Energy; Internal Market and Consumer Protection; Transport and Tourism; Regional Development; Agriculture and Rural Development; Fisheries; Culture and Education; Legal Affairs; Civil Liberties, Justice and Home Affairs; Constitutional Affairs; Women's Rights and Gender Equality; Petitions; Human Rights; Security and Defence; Collapse of the Equitable Life Assurance Society and Alleged Use of European Countries by the CIA for the Transport and Illegal Detention of Prisoners.

The first direct elections to the European Parliament took place in June 1979, and Parliament met for the first time in July. The second elections were held in June 1984 (with separate elections held in Portugal and Spain in 1987, following the accession of these two countries to the Community), the third in June 1989, and the fourth in June 1994. Direct elections to the European Parliament were held in Sweden in September 1995, and in Austria and Finland in October 1996. The fifth European Parliament was elected in June 1999. Elections to the sixth European Parliament were held on 10–13 June 2004, following the accession of the 10 new member states in May. The rate of participation by the electorate was 45.3%; among the 10 new member states public apathy was particularly notable, with the rate of participation averaging just 26.4%.

EUROPEAN OMBUDSMAN

Address: 1 ave du Président Robert Schuman, BP 30403, 67001 Strasbourg Cédex, France.
Telephone: 3-88-17-23-13; **fax:** 3-88-17-90-62; **e-mail:** euro-ombudsman@europarl.eu.int; **internet:** ombudsman.europa.eu/home/en/default.htm.

The position was created by the Treaty on European Union (the Maastricht Treaty), and the first Ombudsman took office in July 1995. The Ombudsman is appointed by the European Parliament (from among its own members) for a renewable five-year term. He is authorized to receive complaints (from EU citizens, businesses and institutions, and from anyone residing or having their legal domicile in an EU member state) regarding maladministration in Community institutions and bodies (except in the Court of Justice and Court of First Instance), to make recommendations, and to refer any matters to the Parliament. The Ombudsman submits an annual report on his activities to the European Parliament.

European Ombudsman: Prof. Nikiforos Diamandouros (Greece).

COURT OF JUSTICE OF THE EUROPEAN COMMUNITIES

Address: Cour de justice des Communautés européennes, 2925 Luxembourg.
Telephone: 4303-1; **fax:** 4303-2600; **e-mail:** info@curia.europa.eu; **internet:** curia.europa.eu/en/transitpage.htm.

As the European Union's judicial institution, the Court of Justice acts as a safeguard of EU legislation (technically known as Community law) and has jurisdiction over cases concerning member states, EU institutions, undertakings or individuals. The Court ensures uniform interpretation and application of Community law throughout the EU. The 27 Judges and the eight Advocates-General are each appointed for a term of six years, after which they may be re-appointed for one or two further periods of three years. The role of the Advocates-General is—publicly and impartially—to deliver reasoned opinions on the cases brought before the Court. There is normally one Judge per member state, whose name is put forward by the Government of that member state. These proposed appointments are then subject to a vote in the Council of the European Union. For the sake of efficiency, when the Court holds a plenary session only 13 Judges—sitting as a 'Grand Chamber'—have to attend. The President of the Court, who has overall charge of the Court's work and presides at hearings and deliberations, is elected by the Judges from among their number for a renewable term of three years. The majority of cases are dealt with by one of the eight chambers, each of which consists of a President of Chamber and three or five Judges. The Court may sit in plenary session in cases of particular importance or when a member state or Community institution that is a party to the proceedings so requests. Judgments are reached by a majority vote and are signed by all Judges involved in the case, irrespective of how they voted. The Court has jurisdiction to award damages. It may review the legality of acts (other than recommendations or opinions) of the Council, the Commission or the European Central Bank, of acts adopted jointly by the European Parliament and the Council, and of Acts adopted by the Parliament and intended to produce legal effects vis-à-vis third parties. It is also competent to give judgment on actions by a member state, the Council or the Commission on grounds of lack of competence, of infringement of an essential procedural requirement, of infringement of a Treaty or of any legal rule relating to its application, or of misuse of power. The Court of Justice may hear appeals, on a point of law only, from the Court of First Instance.

The Court is empowered to hear certain other cases concerning the contractual and non-contractual liability of the Communities and disputes between member states in connection with the objects of the Treaties. It also gives preliminary rulings at the request of national courts on the interpretation of the Treaties, of Union legislation, and of the Brussels Convention on Jurisdiction and the Enforcement of Judgments in Civil and Commercial Matters.

COMPOSITION OF THE COURT
(in order of precedence)

President of the Court of Justice: Vassilios Skouris (Greece).
President of the First Chamber: Peter Jann (Austria).
President of the Second Chamber: Christiaan Willem Anton Timmermans (Netherlands).
President of the Third Chamber: Allan Rosas (Finland).
President of the Fourth Chamber: Koen Lenaerts (Belgium).
First Advocate-General: Luís Miguel Poiares Pessoa Maduro (Portugal).
President of the Fifth Chamber: Antonio Tizzano (Italy).
President of the Eighth Chamber: George Arestis (Cyprus).
President of the Seventh Chamber: Uno Lõhmus (Estonia).
President of the Sixth Chamber: Lars Bay Larsen (Denmark).
Advocate-General: Dámaso Ruiz-Jarabo Colomer (Spain).
Judge: José Narciso da Cunha Rodrigues (Portugal).
Judge: Rosario Silva de Lapuerta (Portugal).
Advocate-General: Juliane Kokott (Germany).
Judge: Sir Konrad Hermann Theodor Schiemann (United Kingdom).
Judge: Jerzy Makarczyk (Poland).
Judge: Pranas Kūris (Lithuania).
Judge: Endre Juhász (Hungary).
Judge: Anthony Borg Barthet (Malta).
Judge: Marko Ilešič (Slovenia).
Judge: Jiří Malenovský (Czech Republic).
Judge: Ján Klučka (Slovakia).
Judge: Egils Levits (Latvia).

INTERNATIONAL ORGANIZATIONS   *European Union*

Judge: AINDRIAS Ó CAOIMH (Ireland).
Advocate-General: ELEANOR SHARPSTON (United Kingdom).
Advocate-General: PAOLO MENGOZZI (Italy).
Judge: PERNILLA LINDH (Sweden).
Advocate-General: YVES BOT (France).
Advocate-General: JÁN MAZÁK (Slovakia).
Judge: JEAN-CLAUDE BONICHOT (France).
Judge: THOMAS VON DANWITZ (Germany).
Advocate-General: VERICA TRSTENJAK (Slovenia).
Judge: ALEXANDER ARABADJIEV (Bulgaria).
Judge: CAMELIA TOADER (Romania).
Judge: JEAN-JACQUES KASEL (Luxembourg).
Registrar: ROGER GRASS (France).

COURT OF FIRST INSTANCE OF THE EUROPEAN COMMUNITIES

Address: Cour de justice des Communautés européennes, 2925 Luxembourg.
Telephone: 4303-1; **fax:** 4303-2600; **internet:** curia.europa.eu/en/transitpage.htm.

In order to help the Court of Justice deal with the thousands of cases brought before it and to offer citizens better legal protection, the Court of First Instance was established by the European Council by a decision of October 1988, and began operations in 1989. Since 1994, the Court (which, although independent, is attached to the Court of Justice) has dealt with cases brought by individuals, legal entities and member states against the actions of EU institutions. The decisions of the Court of First Instance may be subject to appeal to the Court of Justice, on issues of law, within two months. As with the Court of Justice, the composition of the Court of First Instance is based on 27 Judges (one from each member state, appointed for a renewable term of six years), one President (elected from among the 27 Judges for a renewable period of three years) and eight chambers. The Court of First Instance has no permanent Advocates-General.

Within the framework of the Treaty of Nice, which provided for the creation of additional judicial panels in specific areas, in November 2004 the Council decided to establish the Civil Service Tribunal in order to reduce the number of cases brought before the Tribunal of First Instance. The specialized tribunal, which had been fully constituted by December 2005, exercises jurisdiction in the first instance in disputes between the EU and its staff. Its decisions are subject to appeal on questions of law only to the Court of First Instance and, in exceptional cases, to review by the European Court of Justice. The Council appoints the tribunal's seven Judges for a period of six years, and the President is elected by the Judges from among their number for a period of three years. The Council is charged with ensuring that as many member states as possible are represented in the tribunal.

COMPOSITION OF THE COURT OF FIRST INSTANCE
(in order of precedence, from 20 September 2007–31 August 2008)

President of the Court of First Instance: MARC JAEGER (Luxembourg).
President of Chamber: VIRPI TIILI (Finland).
President of Chamber: JOSEF AZIZI (Austria).
President of Chamber: ARJEN W. H. MEIJ (Netherlands).
President of Chamber: MIHALIS VILARAS (Greece).
President of Chamber: NICHOLAS J. FORWOOD (United Kingdom).
President of Chamber: MARIA EUGÉNIA MARTINS DE NAZARÉ RIBEIRO (Portugal).
President of Chamber: OTTÓ CZÚCZ (Hungary).
President of Chamber: IRENA PELIKÁNOVÁ (Czech Republic).
Judge: JOHN D. COOKE (Ireland).
Judge: FRANKLIN DEHOUSSE (France).
Judge: ENA CREMONA (Malta).
Judge: IRENA WISZNIEWSKA-BIALECKA (Poland).
Judge: DANIEL ŠVÁBY (Slovakia).
Judge: VILENAS VADAPALAS (Lithuania).
Judge: KÜLLIKE JÜRIMÄE (Estonia).
Judge: INGRIDA LABUCKA (Latvia).
Judge: SAVVAS S. PAPASAVVAS (Cyprus).
Judge: ENZO MOAVERO MILANESI (Italy).
Judge: NILS WAHL (Sweden).
Judge: MIRO PREK (Slovenia).
Judge: TEODOR TCHIPEV (Bulgaria).

Judge: VALERIU CIUCĂ (Romania).
Judge: ALFRED DITTRICH (Germany).
Judge: SANTIAGO SOLDEVILA FRAGOSO (Spain).
Judge: LAUREN TRUCHOT (France).
Judge: STEN FRIMODT NIELSEN (Denmark).
Registrar: EMMANUEL COULON (France).

COMPOSITION OF THE CIVIL SERVICE TRIBUNAL

President: PAUL MAHONEY (United Kingdom).
President of Chamber: HORSTPETER KREPPEL (Germany).
President of Chamber: SEAN VAN RAEPENBUSCH (Belgium).
Judge: IRENA BORUTA (Poland).
Judge: HEIDI KANNINEN (Finland).
Judge: HARIS TAGARAS (Greece).
Judge: STÉPHANE GERVASONI (France).
Registrar: WALTRAUD HAKENBERG (Germany).

EUROPEAN COURT OF AUDITORS

Address: 12 rue Alcide de Gasperi, 1615 Luxembourg.
Telephone: 4398-45410; **fax:** 4398-46430; **e-mail:** euraud@eca.europa.eu; **internet:** www.eca.europa.eu.

The European Court of Auditors (ECA) was created by the Treaty of Brussels, which was signed on 22 July 1975, and commenced its duties in late 1977. It was given the status of an institution on a par with the Commission, the Council, the Court of Justice and the Parliament by the Treaty on European Union. It is the institution responsible for the external audit of the resources managed by the European Communities and the EU. It consists of 27 members (one from each member state) who are appointed for renewable six-year terms (under a qualified majority voting system) by the Council of the European Union, after consultation with the European Parliament (in practice, however, the Council simply endorses the candidates put forward by the member states). The members elect the President of the Court from among their number for a renewable term of three years.

The Court is organized and acts as a collegiate body. It adopts its decisions by a majority of its members. Each member, however, has a direct responsibility for the audit of certain sectors of Union activities.

The Court examines the accounts of all expenditure and revenue of the European Communities and of any body created by them in so far as the relevant constituent instrument does not preclude such examination. It examines whether all revenue has been received and all expenditure incurred in a lawful and regular manner and whether the financial management has been sound. The audit is based on records, and if necessary is performed directly in the institutions of the Communities, in the member states and in other countries. In the member states the audit is carried out in co-operation with the national audit bodies. The Court of Auditors draws up an annual report after the close of each financial year. The Court provides the Parliament and the Council with a statement of assurance as to the reliability of the accounts, and the legality and regularity of the underlying transactions. It may also, at any time, submit observations on specific questions (usually in the form of special reports) and deliver opinions at the request of one of the institutions of the Communities. It assists the European Parliament and the Council in exercising their powers of control over the implementation of the budget, in particular in the framework of the annual discharge procedure, and gives its prior opinion on the financial regulations, on the methods and procedure whereby the budgetary revenue is made available to the Commission, and on the formulation of rules concerning the responsibility of authorizing officers and accounting officers and concerning appropriate arrangements for inspection.

President: VÍTOR MANUEL SILVA CALDEIRA (Portugal).
Members: HENRI GRETHEN (Luxembourg), MAARTEN B. ENGWIRDA (Netherlands), MICHEL CRETIN (France), MÁIRE GEOGHEGAN-QUINN (Ireland), HUBERT WEBER (Austria), HARALD NOACK (Germany), DAVID BOSTOCK (United Kingdom), MORTEN LOUIS LEVYSOHN (Denmark), IOANNIS SARMAS (Greece), JÚLIUS MOLNÁR (Slovakia), VOJKO ANTON ANTONČIČ (Slovenia), GEJZA ZSOLT HALÁSZ (Hungary), JACEK UCZKIEWICZ (Poland), JOSEF BONNICI (Malta), IRENA PETRUŠKEVIČIENE (Lithuania), IGORS LUDBORŽS (Latvia), JAN KINŠT (Czech Republic), KERSTI KALJULAID (Estonia), KIKIS KAZAMIAS (Cyprus), MASSIMO VARI (Italy), JUAN RAMALLO MASSANET (Spain), OLAVI ALA-NISSILÄ (Finland), LARS HEIKENSTEN (Sweden), KAREL PINXTEN (Belgium), NADEZHDA SANDOLOVA (Bulgaria), OVIDIU ISPIR (Romania).
Secretary-General: MICHEL HERVÉ (France).

EUROPEAN CENTRAL BANK

Address: Kaiserstr. 29, 60311 Frankfurt am Main, Germany; Postfach 160319, 60066 Frankfurt am Main, Germany.
Telephone: (69) 13440; **fax:** (69) 13446000; **e-mail:** info@ecb.europa.eu; **internet:** www.ecb.eu/home/html/index.en.html.

The European Central Bank (ECB) was formally established on 1 June 1998, replacing the European Monetary Institute, which had been operational since January 1994. The Bank has the authority to issue the single currency, the euro, which replaced the European Currency Unit (ECU) on 1 January 1999, at the beginning of Stage III of Economic and Monetary Union (EMU), in accordance with the provisions of the Treaty on European Union (the Maastricht Treaty). One of the ECB's main tasks is to maintain price stability in the euro area (i.e. in those member states that have adopted the euro as their national currency)—this is achieved primarily by controlling the money supply and by monitoring price trends. The Bank's leadership is provided by a six-member Executive Board, appointed by common agreement of the presidents or prime ministers of the euro area countries (Austria, Belgium, Finland, France, Germany, Greece, Ireland, Italy, Luxembourg, the Netherlands, Portugal and Spain) for a non-renewable term of eight years (it should be noted that the Statute of the European System of Central Banks—ESCB—provides for a system of staggered appointments to the first Executive Board for members other than the President in order to ensure continuity). The Executive Board is responsible for the preparation of meetings of the Governing Council, the implementation of monetary policy in accordance with the guide-lines and decisions laid down by the Governing Council and for the current business of the ECB. The ECB and the national central banks of all EU member states together comprise the ESCB. The Governing Council, which is the ECB's highest decision-making body and which consists of the six members of the Executive Board and the governors of the central banks of countries participating in EMU, meets twice a month. The prime mission of the Governing Council is to define the monetary policy of the euro area, and, in particular, to fix the interest rates at which the commercial banks can obtain money from the ECB. The General Council is the ECB's third decision-making body; it comprises the ECB's President, the Vice-President and the governors of the central banks of all EU member states.

President: JEAN-CLAUDE TRICHET (France).
Vice-President: LUCAS D. PAPADEMOS (Greece).
Executive Board: JOSÉ MANUEL GONZÁLEZ-PÁRAMO (Spain), GERTRUDE TUMPEL-GUGERELL (Austria), JÜRGEN STARK (Germany), LORENZO BINI SMAGHI (Italy).

EUROPEAN INVESTMENT BANK

Address: 100 blvd Konrad Adenauer, 2950 Luxembourg.
Telephone: 4379-1; **fax:** 4377-04; **e-mail:** info@eib.org; **internet:** www.eib.org.

The European Investment Bank (EIB) is the EU's international financing institution, and was created in 1958 by the six founder member states of the European Economic Community. The shareholders are the member states of the EU, which have all subscribed to the bank's capital. The bulk of the EIB's resources comes from borrowings, principally public bond issues or private placements on capital markets inside and outside the Union.

The EIB's principal task, defined by the Treaty of Rome, is to work on a non-profit basis, making or guaranteeing loans for investment projects which contribute to the balanced and steady development of EU member states. Throughout the Bank's history, priority has been given to financing investment projects which further regional development within the Community. The EIB also finances projects that improve communications, protect and improve the environment, promote urban development, strengthen the competitive position of industry and encourage industrial integration within the Union, support the activities of small and medium-sized enterprises (SMEs), and help ensure the security of energy supplies. Following a recommendation of the Lisbon European Council in March 2000 for greater support for SMEs, the Board of Governors set up the EIB Group, consisting of the EIB and the European Investment Fund. The EIB also provides finance for developing countries in Africa, the Caribbean and the Pacific, under the terms of the Cotonou Agreement (see p. 301), the successor agreement to the Lomé Convention; for countries in the Mediterranean region, under a new Euro-Mediterranean investment facility established in 2002; and for accession countries in Central and Eastern Europe. Lending outside the EU is usually based on Community agreements, but exceptions have been made for specific projects in certain countries, such as Russia.

The Board of Governors of the EIB, which usually meets once a year, lays down general directives on credit policy, approves the annual report and accounts and decides on capital increases. The Board of Directors meets once a month, and has sole power to take decisions in respect of loans, guarantees and borrowings. The Bank's President presides over meetings of the Board of Directors. The day-to-day management of operations is the responsibility of the Management Committee, which is the EIB's collegiate executive body and recommends decisions to the Board of Directors. The Audit Committee, which reports to the Board of Governors regarding the management of operations and the maintenance of the Bank's accounts, is an independent body comprising three members who are appointed by the Board of Governors for a renewable three-year term.

Board of Governors: The Board of Governors comprises one minister (usually the minister with responsibility for finance or economic affairs) from each member state.
Chair: TOMMASO PADOA-SCHIOPPA (Italy).
Board of Directors: The Board of Directors consists of 28 directors, appointed for a renewable five-year term, with one director appointed by each member state and one by the European Commission. There are 16 alternates, also appointed for a renewable five-year term, meaning that some of these positions will be shared by groupings of countries. Since 1 May 2004 decisions have been taken by a majority consisting of at least one-third of members entitled to vote and representing at least 50% of the subscribed capital.
Management Committee: The President and seven Vice-Presidents, nominated for a renewable six-year term by the Board of Directors and approved by the Board of Governors. The President presides over the meetings of the Management Committee but does not vote.
President: PHILIPPE MAYSTADT (Belgium).
Vice-Presidents: MATTHIAS KOLLATZ-AHNEN (Germany), SIMON BROOKS (United Kingdom), EVA SREJBER (Sweden), CARLOS DA SILVA COSTA (Portugal), PHILIPPE DE FONTAINE VIVE CURTAZ (France), TORSTEN GERSFELT (Denmark), MARTA GAJĘCKA (Poland), DARIO SCANNAPIECO (Italy).
Audit Committee: The Audit Committee is composed of three members and three observers, appointed by the Governors for a term of office of three years.
Chair: MAURIZIO DALLOCCHIO (Italy).

EUROPEAN INVESTMENT FUND

Address: 43 ave J. F. Kennedy, 2968 Luxembourg.
Telephone: 4266-881; **fax:** 4266-88200; **e-mail:** info@eif.org; **internet:** www.eif.org.

The European Investment Fund was founded in 1994 as a specialized financial institution to support the growth of small and medium-sized enterprises (SMEs). Its operations are focused on the provision of venture capital, through investment in funds that support SMEs, and on guarantee activities to facilitate access to finance for SMEs. In all its activities the Fund aims to maintain a commercial approach to investment, and to apply risk-sharing principles. The Fund manages the SME Guarantee Facility. The Joint European Resources for Micro to Medium Enterprises (JEREMIE) initiative, which was launched in May 2006, enables EU member countries and regions to use part of their allocation of structural funds to obtain financing that is specifically targeted to support SMEs. The European Investment Fund is operational in the member states of the EU and in the accession countries.

Chief Executive: FRANCIS CARPENTER (United Kingdom).

EUROPEAN ECONOMIC AND SOCIAL COMMITTEE

Address: 99 rue Belliard, 1040 Brussels.
Telephone: (2) 546-90-11; **fax:** (2) 513-48-93; **e-mail:** info@esc.europa.eu; **internet:** eesc.europa.eu/index_en.asp.

The Committee was set up by the 1957 Rome Treaties. It is advisory and is consulted by the Council of the European Union or by the European Commission, particularly with regard to agriculture, free movement of workers, harmonization of laws and transport, as well as legislation adopted under the Euratom Treaty. In certain cases consultation of the Committee by the Commission or the Council is mandatory. In addition, the Committee has the power to deliver opinions on its own initiative.

The Committee has a tripartite structure with members belonging to one of three groupings: the Employers' Group, the Employees' Group and the Various Interests' Group, which includes representatives of social, occupational, economic and cultural organizations. The Committee is appointed for a renewable term of four years by the unanimous vote of the Council of the European Union. The 344 members are nominated by national governments, but are appointed in their personal capacity and are not bound by any mandatory instructions. Germany, France, Italy and the United Kingdom have 24 members each, Spain and Poland have 21, Romania 15, Belgium,

Bulgaria, Greece, the Netherlands, Portugal, Austria, Sweden, the Czech Republic and Hungary 12, Denmark, Ireland, Finland, Lithuania and Slovakia nine, Estonia, Latvia and Slovenia seven, Luxembourg and Cyprus six and Malta five. The Committee is served by a permanent and independent General Secretariat, headed by the Secretary-General.

President: DIMITRIS DIMITRIADIS (Greece) (Employers').

Vice-Presidents: JILLIAN VAN TURNHOUT (Ireland) (Various Interests'), ALEXANDER-MICHAEL GRAF VON SCHWERIN (Germany) (Employees').

Secretary-General: PATRICK VENTURINI (France).

COMMITTEE OF THE REGIONS

Address: 101 rue Belliard, 1040 Brussels.
Telephone: (2) 282-22-11; **fax:** (2) 282-23-25; **e-mail:** info@cor.europa.eu; **internet:** www.cor.europa.eu.

The Treaty on European Union provided for a committee to be established, with advisory status, comprising representatives of regional and local bodies throughout the EU. The first meeting of the Committee was held in March 1994. It may be consulted on EU proposals concerning economic and social cohesion, trans-European networks, public health, education and culture, and may issue an opinion on any issue with regional implications. The Committee meets in plenary session five times a year.

The number of members of the Committee is equal to that of the European Economic and Social Committee. Members are appointed for a renewable term of four years by the Council, acting unanimously on the proposals from the respective member states. The Committee elects its principal officers from among its members for a two-year term.

President: LUC VAN DEN BRANDE (Belgium).
Vice-President: MICHEL DELEBARRE (France).

AGENCIES

Community Fisheries Control Agency—CFCA
European Commission, rue de la Loi, 1049 Brussels; tel. 2-296-00-09; e-mail fisheries-cfca@ec.europa.eu; internet www.cfca.europa.eu.

Established in April 2005 to improve compliance with regulations under the 2002 reform of the Common Fisheries Policy. The CFCA aims to ensure the effectiveness of enforcement by sharing EU and national methods of fisheries' control, monitoring resources and co-ordinating activities. The Agency was to relocate to Vigo, Spain, in 2008.

Executive Director: HARM KOSTER (Netherlands).

Community Plant Variety Office—CPVO
POB 10121, 49101 Angers Cédex 2, France; 3 blvd Maréchal Foch, 49000 Angers, France; tel. 2-41-25-64-00; fax 2-41-25-64-10; e-mail cpvo@cpvo.europa.eu; internet www.cpvo.europa.eu.

Began operations in April 1995, with responsibility for granting intellectual property rights for plant varieties. Supervised by an Administrative Council, and managed by a President, appointed by the Council of the European Union. A Board of Appeal has been established to consider appeals against certain technical decisions taken by the Office. Publishes an annual report listing valid Community plant variety rights, their owners and their expiry date.

President: BART P. KIEWIET (Netherlands).

European Agency for the Management of Operational Co-operation at the External Borders of the European Union—FRONTEX
Rondo ONZ 1, 00-124 Warsaw, Poland; tel. (22) 5449500; fax (22) 5449501; e-mail frontex@frontex.europa.eu; internet www.frontex.europa.eu.

Established by a regulation of the European Parliament in October 2004, the Agency's primary responsibility is the creation of an integrated border management system, in order to ensure a high and uniform level of control and surveillance. The Agency began operations on 1 May 2005.

Executive Director: Col ILKKA LAITINEN (Finland).

European Agency for Reconstruction—EAR
Egnatia 4, 546 26 Thessaloníki, Greece; POB 10177, 541 10 Thessaloníki, Greece; tel. (2310) 505100; fax (2310) 505172; e-mail info@ear.europa.eu; internet www.ear.europa.eu.

Established in February 2000 (by a Council regulation of November 1999) to assume the responsibilities of the European Commission's Task Force for the Reconstruction of Kosovo (which had become operational in July 1999 following the end of hostilities in the southern Serbian province of Kosovo). The Agency is responsible for the management of the main assistance programmes in Montenegro and Serbia (including Kosovo) and the former Yugoslav republic of Macedonia (FYRM). The Agency has operational centres in Belgrade (Serbia), Priština (Kosovo), Podgorica (Montenegro) and Skopje (FYRM).

Director: RICHARD ZINK (Germany).

European Agency for Safety and Health at Work—EU-OSHA
Gran Vía 33, 48009 Bilbao, Spain; tel. (94) 4794360; fax (94) 4794383; e-mail information@osha.europa.eu; internet osha.europa.eu.

Began operations in 1996. Aims to encourage improvements in the working environment, and to make available all necessary technical, scientific and economic information for use in the field of health and safety at work. The Agency supports a network of Focal Points in the member states of the EU, in the member states of the European Free Trade Association (EFTA) and in the candidate states of the EU.

Director: JUKKA TAKALA (Denmark).

European Aviation Safety Agency—EASA
Postfach 101253, 50452 Köln, Germany; Ottoplatz 1, 50679 Köln, Germany; tel. (221) 89990000; fax (221) 89990999; e-mail info@easa.europa.eu; internet www.easa.eu.int.

Established by a regulation of the European Parliament in July 2002; the mission of the agency is to establish and maintain a high, uniform level of civil aviation safety and environmental protection in Europe. The Agency commenced full operations in September 2003, and moved to its permanent seat, in Köln, Germany, in November 2004.

Executive Director: PATRICK GOUDOU (France).

European Centre for the Development of Vocational Training—Cedefop
POB 22427, 551 02 Thessaloníki, Greece; Evropis 123, 570 01 Thessaloníki, Greece; tel. (30) 2310490111; fax (30) 2310490049; e-mail info@cedefop.europa.eu; internet www.cedefop.europa.eu.

Established in 1975, Cedefop assists policy-makers and other officials in member states and partner organizations in issues relating to vocational training policies, and assists the European Commission in the development of these policies. Manages a European Training Village internet site (www.trainingvillage.gr/etv/default.asp).

Director: AVIANA BULGARELLI (Italy).

European Centre for Disease Prevention and Control—ECDC
17183 Stockholm, Sweden; Tomtebodavägen 11A, Solna, Sweden; tel. (8) 586-01000; fax (8) 586-01001; e-mail info@ecdc.europa.eu; internet ecdc.europa.eu.

Founded in 2005 to strengthen European defences against infectious diseases. It works with national health protection bodies to develop disease surveillance and early-warning systems across Europe.

Director: ZSUZSANNA JAKAB (Hungary).

European Chemicals Agency—ECHA
Annankatu 18, Helsinki, Finland; POB 400, 00121 Helsinki, Finland; tel. (9) 686180; e-mail press@echa.europa.eu; internet echa.europa.eu.

The European Chemicals Agency (ECHA) was established by regulations of the European Parliament and the European Council in 2006, and was expected to be fully operational by June 2008. The objective of the ECHA is to supervise and undertake the technical, scientific and administrative aspects of the Registration, Evaluation, Authorization and Restriction of Chemicals (REACH) throughout the EU and in Iceland, Liechtenstein and Norway. It also supports and runs a national helpdesk, and disseminates information on chemicals to the public.

Exec. Dir: GEERT DANCET (Finland).

European Defence Agency—EDA
17–23 rue des Drapiers, 1050 Brussels, Belgium; tel. (2) 504-28-00; fax (2) 504-28-15; e-mail info@eda.europa.eu; internet www.eda.europa.eu.

Founded in July 2004 and became operational in 2005; aims to help member states to improve their defence capabilities for crisis management under the European Security and Defence Policy. The Steering Board is composed of the ministers responsible for defence of 26 member states (all states except Denmark).

Head of the Agency and Chairman of the Steering Board: JAVIER SOLANA MADARIAGA (Spain).
Chief Executive: ALEXANDER WEIS (Germany).

European Environment Agency—EEA
6 Kongens Nytorv, 1050 Copenhagen K, Denmark; tel. 33-36-71-00; fax 33-36-71-99; e-mail eea@eea.europa.eu; internet www.eea.europa.eu.

Became operational in 1994, having been approved in 1990, to gather and supply information to assist the drafting and implementation of

INTERNATIONAL ORGANIZATIONS
European Union

EU policy on environmental protection and improvement. Iceland, Liechtenstein, Norway, Switzerland and Turkey are also members of the Agency. The Agency publishes frequent reports on the state of the environment and on environmental trends.

Executive Director: Prof. JACQUELINE MCGLADE (United Kingdom).

European Food Safety Authority—EFSA

Largo N. Palli 5/A, 43100 Parma, Italy; tel. (39-0521) 036111; fax (39-0521) 036110; e-mail info@efsa.europa.eu; internet www.efsa.europa.eu.

Established by a regulation of the European Parliament in February 2002 and began operations in May 2003; the primary responsibility of the Authority is to provide independent scientific advice on all matters with a direct or indirect impact on food safety. The Authority will carry out assessments of risks to the food chain and scientific assessment on any matter that may have a direct or indirect effect on the safety of the food supply, including matters relating to animal health, animal welfare and plant health. The Authority will also give scientific advice on genetically modified organisms (GMOs), and on nutrition in relation to Community legislation.

Executive Director: CATHERINE GESLAIN-LANÉELLE (France).

European Foundation for the Improvement of Living and Working Conditions—Eurofound

Wyattville Rd, Loughlinstown, Dublin 18, Ireland; tel. (1) 2043100; fax (1) 2826456; e-mail postmaster@eurofound.europa.eu; internet www.eurofound.europa.eu.

Established in 1975, the Foundation aims to provide information and advice on European living and working conditions, industrial relations and the management of change to employers, policy-makers, governments and trade unions, by means of comparative data, research and analysis. In 2001 the Foundation established the European Monitoring Centre on Change (EMCC) to help disseminate information and ideas on the management and anticipation of change in industry and enterprise.

Director: JORMA KARPPINEN (Finland).
Deputy Director: WILLY BUSCHAK (Germany).

European GNSS Supervisory Authority—GSA

56 Rue de la Loi, 1049 Brussels, Belgium; tel. (2) 297-16-16; fax (2) 296-72-38; e-mail news@gsa.europa.eu; internet www.gsa.europa.eu

The European GNSS Supervisory Authority (GSA) was established in July 2004, to oversee all public interests relating to European Global Navigation Satellite System (GNSS) programmes. On 1 January 2007 the GSA officially took over the tasks previously assigned to the Galileo Joint Undertaking (GJU), which had been established in May 2002 by the EU and the European Space Agency to manage the development phase of the Galileo programme (see Research and Innovation). The strategic objectives of the GSA include the achievement of a fully operational Galileo system, capable of becoming the world's leading civilian satellite navigation system, and Europe's only GNSS.

Exec. Dir: PEDRO PEDREIRA (Portugal).

European Joint Undertaking for ITER and the Development of Fusion Energy—Fusion for Energy

2 Josep Pla, Torres Diagonal Litoral, Edificio B3, 08019 Barcelona Spain; tel. (93) 320-18-00; fax (93) 320-18-51; e-mail info@f4e.europa.eu; internet fusionforenergy.europa.eu/index_en.htm.

The Agency was established in April 2007, as a Joint Undertaking under the European Atomic Energy Community (Euratom) Treaty, by a decision of the Council of the European Union (see Energy). Its members comprise the EU member states and Euratom; Switzerland was expected to join as a third country.

Dir: DIDIER GAMBIER (France).

European Judicial Co-operation Unit—EUROJUST

Maanweg 174, 2516 The Hague, the Netherlands; tel. (70) 4125000; fax (70) 4125505; e-mail info@eurojust.europa.eu; internet www.eurojust.europa.eu.

Established in 2002 to improve co-operation and co-ordination between member states in the investigation and prosecution of serious cross-border and organized crime. The Eurojust College is composed of one member (a senior prosecutor or judge) nominated by each member state.

President of the College: JOSÉ LUIS LOPES DA MOTA (Portugal).
Administrative Director: ERNST MERZ (Germany).

European Maritime Safety Agency—EMSA

Av. Dom João 11, Lote 1.06.2.5, 1998-001 Lisbon, Portugal; tel. (21) 1209200; fax (21) 1209210; e-mail information@emsa.europa.eu.int; internet www.emsa.europa.eu.

Established by a regulation of the European Parliament in June 2002; the primary responsibility of the Agency is to provide technical and scientific advice to the Commission in the field of maritime safety and prevention of pollution by ships. The Agency held its inaugural meeting in December 2002, and in December 2003 it was decided that the permanent seat of the Agency would be Lisbon, Portugal. Norway and Iceland are also members of EMSA.

Executive Director: WILLEM DE RUITER (Netherlands).

European Medicines Agency—EMEA

7 Westferry Circus, Canary Wharf, London, E14 4HB, United Kingdom; tel. (20) 7418-8400; e-mail mail@emea.europa.eu; internet www.emea.europa.eu.

Established in 1995 for the evaluation, authorization and supervision of medicinal products for human and veterinary use.

Executive Director: THOMAS LÖNNGREN (Sweden).

European Monitoring Centre for Drugs and Drug Addiction—EMCDDA

Rua da Cruz de Sta. Apolónia 23–25, 1149-045 Lisbon, Portugal; tel. (21) 8113000; fax (21) 8111711; e-mail info@emcdda.europa.eu; internet www.emcdda.europa.eu.

Founded in 1993 and became fully operational at the end of 1995, with the aim of providing member states with objective, reliable and comparable information on drugs and drug addiction in order to assist in combating the problem. The Centre co-operates with other European and international organizations and non-Community countries. The Centre publishes an *Annual Report on the State of the Drugs Problem in Europe*. A newsletter, *Drugnet Europe*, is published quarterly.

Executive Director: WOLFGANG GÖTZ (Germany).

European Network and Information Security Agency—ENISA

POB 1309, 710 01 Heraklion, Crete, Greece; Science and Technology Park of Crete, Vassilika Vouton, 700 13 Heraklion, Crete, Greece; tel. (2810) 391280; fax (2810) 391410; e-mail info@enisa.europa.eu; internet www.enisa.europa.eu.

Established by a regulation of the European Parliament in March 2004; commenced operations in 2005. The primary responsibilities of the Agency are to promote closer European co-ordination on the security of communications networks and information systems and to provide assistance in the application of EU measures in this field. The agency publishes a quarterly magazine.

Executive Director: ANDREA PIROTTI (Italy).

European Police College—CEPOL

CEPOL House, Bramshill Hook, Hampshire, RG27 0JW, United Kingdom; tel. (1256) 60-26-68; fax (1256) 60-29-96; e-mail secretariat@cepol.europa.eu; internet www.cepol.europa.eu.

Founded in 2005 to help create a network of senior police-officers throughout Europe, to encourage cross-border co-operation in combating crime, and to improve public security and law and order through the organization of training activities and research.

Director: ULF GÖRANSSON (Sweden).

European Police Office—EUROPOL

POB 90850, 2509 The Hague, the Netherlands; Raamweg 47, The Hague, Netherlands; tel. (70) 3025000; fax (70) 3025896; e-mail info@europol.europa.eu; internet www.europol.europa.eu.

Established in 1992, Europol is a law-enforcement organization that aims to aid EU member states to combat organized crime, by handling criminal intelligence throughout Europe and promoting co-operation between the law-enforcement bodies of member countries.

Director: MAX-PETER RATZEL (Germany).

European Railway Agency—ERA

BP 20392, 59307 Valenciennes Cedex, France; 160 blvd Henri Harpignies, 59300 Valenciennes, France; tel. 3-27-09-65-00; fax 3-27-33-40-65; e-mail press-info@era.europa.eu; internet www.era.europa.eu.

Established by a regulation of the European Parliament in April 2004; the primary responsibility of the Agency is to reinforce the safety and interoperability of railways in the EU. The Agency held its inaugural meeting in July 2004 and was fully operational by mid-2006.

Executive Director: MARCEL VERSLYPE (Belgium).

European Training Foundation—ETF

Villa Gualino, Viale Settimio Severo 65, 10133 Turin, Italy; tel. (011) 630-22-22; fax (011) 630-22-00; e-mail info@etf.europa.eu; internet www.etf.europa.eu.

The Foundation, which was established in 1990 and became operational in 1994, provides policy advice to the European Commission and to the EU's partner countries, to support vocational education and training reform. The ETF works in the countries surrounding the EU, which are involved either in the European Neighbourhood Partnership Instrument, or in the enlargement process under the Instrument for Pre-accession Assistance. The ETF also works in a number of other countries from Central Asia. The ETF also gives technical assistance to the European Commission for the implementation of the Trans-European Mobility Scheme for University Studies (TEMPUS), which focuses on the reform of higher education systems in partner countries.

Director: Dr MURIEL DUNBAR (United Kingdom).

European Union Agency for Fundamental Rights—FRA

Rahlgasse 3, 1060 Vienna, Austria; tel. (1) 580300; fax (1) 5803093; e-mail information@eumc.europa.eu; internet www.eumc.europa.eu

Founded in March 2007, replacing the European Monitoring Centre on Racism and Xenophobia (EUMC). The Agency aims to provide assistance to EU member states on fundamental rights matters during the application of Community law. The FRA continues the work of the EUMC on racism, xenophobia, anti-Semitism and related intolerance, and utilizes its experience of data-collection methods and co-operation with governments and international organizations. In addition, the FRA gives significant emphasis to increasing public awareness of rights issues and to co-operation with civil society.

Director: (vacant).

European Union Institute for Security Studies—EUISS

43 ave du Président Wilson, 75775 Paris Cédex 16; tel. 1-56-89-19-30; fax 1-56-89-19-31; e-mail institute@iss.europa.eu; internet www.iss.europa.eu.

Established by a Council Joint Action in July 2001, and inaugurated in January 2002. The Institute aims to help implement and develop the EU's Common Foreign and Security Policy (CFSP), and carries out political analysis and forecasting. The Institute produces several publications: the Chaillot Papers, Occasional Papers and a quarterly Newsletter, as well as books containing in-depth studies of specialized topics.

Director: NICOLE GNESOTTO (France).

European Union Satellite Centre—EUSC

Apdo. de Correos 511, Torréjon de Ardoz, 28850 Madrid, Spain; tel. (91) 6786000; fax (91) 6786006; e-mail info@eusc.europa.eu; internet www.eusc.europa.eu.

Established by a Council Joint Action in July 2001 and operational from 1 January 2002. The Agency is dedicated to providing material derived from the analysis of satellite imagery in support of the Common Foreign and Security Policy. The Institute produces several publications: the Chaillot Papers, Occasional Papers and a quarterly newsletter, as well as books containing in-depth studies of specialized topics.

Director: FRANK ASBECK (Germany).

Office for Harmonization in the Internal Market (Trade Marks and Designs)—OHIM

Apdo. de Correos 77, 03080 Alicante, Spain; Avda de Europa 4, 03008 Alicante, Spain; tel. (96) 513-91-00; fax (96) 513-91-73; e-mail information@oami.europa.eu; internet www.oami.europa.eu.

Established in 1993 to promote and control trade marks and designs throughout the EU.

President: WUBBO DE BOER (Netherlands).

Translation Centre for the Bodies of the European Union—CdT

Bâtiment Nouvel Hémicycle, 1 rue du Fort Thüngen, 1499 Luxembourg; tel. 4217-11-1; fax 4217-11-220; e-mail cdt@cdt.europa.eu; internet www.cdt.europa.eu.

Established in 1994 to meet the translation needs of other decentralized Community agencies.

Director: GAILÉ DAGILIENÉ (Lithuania).

Activities of the Community

AGRICULTURE

Agriculture (including rural development) is by far the largest single item on the Community budget, accounting for 46% of annual expenditure in 2007, although this represented a significant reduction compared with 1984, when agriculture accounted for 70% of annual expenditure. Expenditure on agriculture and rural development in 2008 was budgeted at €53,702m., equivalent to some 45% of the total budget.

Co-operation in the Community has traditionally been at its most highly organized in the area of agriculture. The Common Agricultural Policy (CAP), which took effect from 1962, was originally devised to ensure food self-sufficiency for Europe following the food shortages of the post-war period and to ensure a fair standard of living for the agricultural community. Its objectives are described in the Treaty of Rome. The markets for agricultural products have been progressively organized following three basic principles: unity of the market (products must be able to circulate freely within the Community and markets must be organized according to common rules); Community preference (products must be protected from low-cost imports and from fluctuations on the world market); common financial responsibility: the European Agricultural Guarantee Fund (which replaced the European Agricultural Guidance and Guarantee Fund in 2007) finances the export of agricultural products to third countries, intervention measures to regulate agricultural markets and direct payments to farmers.

Agricultural prices are, in theory, fixed each year at a common level for the Community as a whole, taking into account the rate of inflation and the need to discourage surplus production of certain commodities. Export subsidies are paid to enable farmers to sell produce at the lower world market prices without loss. When market prices of certain cereals, sugar, some fruits and vegetables, dairy produce and meat fall below a designated level the Community intervenes, and buys a quantity, which is then stored until prices recover.

Serious reform of the CAP began in 1992, following strong criticism of the EC's agricultural and export subsidies during the 'Uruguay Round' of negotiations on the General Agreement on Tariffs and Trade (GATT, see World Trade Organization—WTO) in 1990. In May 1992 ministers adopted a number of reforms, which aimed to transfer the Community's agricultural support from upholding prices to maintaining farmers' incomes, thereby removing the incentive to over-produce. Intervention prices were reduced and farmers were compensated by receiving additional grants, which, in the case of crops, took the form of a subsidy per hectare of land planted. To qualify for these subsidies, arable farmers (except for those with the smallest farms) were obliged to remove 15% of their land from cultivation (the 'set-aside' scheme). Incentives were given for alternative uses of the withdrawn land (e.g. forestry).

In March 1999, at the Berlin European Council, the EU Heads of Government concluded an agreement on a programme, Agenda 2000, which aimed to reinforce Community policies and to restructure the financial framework of the EU with a view to enlargement. In terms of agriculture, it was decided to continue the process of agricultural reform begun in 1992 with particular emphasis on environmental concerns, safeguarding a fair income for farmers, streamlining legislation and decentralizing its application. A further element of reform was the increased emphasis on rural development, which was described as the 'second pillar' of the CAP in Agenda 2000. The objective was to restore and increase the competitiveness of rural areas, through supporting employment, diversification and population growth. In addition, producers were to be rewarded for the preservation of rural heritage. Forestry was recognized as an integral part of rural development (previous treaties of the EU had made no provision for a comprehensive common forestry policy).

The accession of 10 new states to the EU in May 2004 was expected to have major implications for the CAP, in that the enlargement would double the EU's arable land area and its farming population. In October 2002 it was agreed that the enlargement process would be part-funded by a deal to maintain farm subsidies at 2006 levels until 2013, with a 1% annual correction for inflation, and that the new members would be offered direct farm payments at 25% of the level paid to existing member states, rising in stages to 100% over 10 years.

In July 2002 the Commissioner responsible for Agriculture, Rural Development and Fisheries, Franz Fischler, proposed directing more funds towards the rural development policy and severing the link between direct payments to farmers and production (a policy styled 'decoupling'). The latter proposals were partly aimed at preparing for the next meeting of the Doha Development Round of the WTO negotiations, which began in November 2001, where the EU was under pressure to reduce policies that distorted world trade; production-linked subsidies promoted over-production and thus high levels of export subsidies and the dumping of surplus foodstuffs in the markets of developing countries, harming both their export capacity and their domestic market. The reforms suggested by the Commission were, however, vigorously opposed by the main beneficiaries of the current system, notably France. Fischler was obliged to submit a revised plan which restored the link between subsidies and production for certain products while still adhering to the principle of decoupling.

The compromise deal for CAP reform was agreed on 26 June 2003 and the agreement was ratified by the Council of the European Union and the accession states on 29 September. Production-linked subsidies were to be replaced by a Single Farm Payment, which was to be calculated from the subsidies received in the years 2000–02, rather than tied to current production levels, and was also to be linked to environmental, food safety and animal welfare standards. Obligatory decoupling was only partial for beef, cereal and mutton, with production still accounting for as much as 25% of payments for cereals and as much as 40% for beef. Overall, however, 90% of payments would no longer be linked to production. Reforms to the dairy sector were to be delayed until 2008. The agreement contained a commitment to reduce all payments above €5,000 a year by 3% in 2005, by 4% in 2006 and by 5% in 2007. Increased resources were to be directed towards rural development projects, protecting the environment and improvements to food quality; organic farmers and those offering high-quality produce with special guarantees were to receive grants of up to €3,000 a year for five years. Under the principle of 'modulation', an increasing percentage of direct farm subsidies was to be retained by individual member states to finance rural development measures. Funds were to be collected at a rate of 3% in 2005, 4% in 2006 and 5% in 2007, a level at which they would remain for subsequent years; the equivalent of at least 80% of the funds gathered in each member state (90% in Germany) should be spent in that country.

In April 2004 the EU Council of Ministers of Agriculture reached agreement for CAP reform of the olive oil, cotton, hops and tobacco sectors. The principle of decoupling aid from production was to be extended to these commodities. A significant share of the current production-linked payments was to be transferred to the Single Farm Payment (which was provided independently of production), although production-linked subsidies were permitted of up to 60% for tobacco, 40% for olive oil, 35% for cotton and 25% for hops. Moreover, full decoupling in the tobacco sector was to be introduced progressively over the four years to 2010 and rural development aid was to finance conversion to other crops in tobacco-producing areas. The remaining production aid for olive oil was to be directed at maintaining olive groves with environmental or social value. The reforms were criticized by some non-governmental organizations (NGOs) on the grounds that the partial decoupling of cotton was insufficient to act as an incentive to farmers to convert to other crops and would thus fail to alleviate the problems of cotton-exporting developing countries. In September 2006 the European Court of Justice annulled the CAP provisions on cotton on the grounds that the Commission had failed to conduct an impact assessment, to consider direct labour costs in the evaluation and decision process, and to take account of the new regime's impact on the ginning industry. The Commission therefore proposed a slightly revised reform of the support scheme for cotton in November 2007. The new proposal maintained the support arrangements agreed in 2004 (i.e. production-linked subsidies of up to 35%), which had not been questioned by the Court, but provided for additional funding for support measures in cotton-producing regions and the creation of a 'label of origin' to enhance the promotion of EU cotton.

The EU finally agreed on reforms to the sugar industry in November 2005, following a WTO ruling earlier in the year (after an action brought by Brazil, Australia and Thailand) that the current level of subsidy breached legal limits. In 2005 the EU sugar sector was still characterized by large subsidies, high internal prices and imports by African, Caribbean and Pacific (ACP) countries on favourable terms under quotas. The EU produced large surpluses of sugar, which were disposed of on the world market to the detriment of more competitive producers, notably developing countries. The reforms, which were implemented from July 2006, included the gradual reduction of the internal EU market price (which was three times the international price for the commodity in 2005) by 36% by 2009, and direct aid payments of €6,300m. over the four years of the phased introduction of the reforms to EU sugar producers as compensation. The proposals were criticized by NGOs, as they would not help create a sustainable international sugar market, and by ACP countries, which claimed the measures would have a severe adverse affect on ACP economies. Compensation for the ACP countries was set at a total of €40m. for 2006. A key element in the reform of the EU sugar sector was the establishment of a restructuring fund, financed by sugar producers, to ease the transition to greater competitiveness. The objective was to remove a total of some 6m. metric tons of sugar quota during the four-year reform period. However, about 1.5m. tons of sugar quota were renounced under the restructuring scheme for the marketing year 2006/07 and only 0.7m. tons for 2007/08, far less than anticipated. Amendments to the sugar-restructuring scheme were adopted in October 2007 in an attempt to encourage greater participation.

Implementation of the CAP reforms agreed in June 2003 commenced on 1 January 2005. By 2009 all EU member states were to be obliged to participate.

Under the new budget agreement for the period 2007–13, announced in December 2005, the United Kingdom negotiated a wide-ranging budget review, to take place in 2008–09, which included expenditure on the CAP, although spending levels on the CAP had previously been agreed until 2013. The budget also provided no new funds to finance farm subsidies to Romania and Bulgaria on their accession to the EU in 2007, which would inevitably lead to a reduction in payments to the existing 25 member states.

At the Doha round of the WTO in Hong Kong in December 2005, agreement was reached on the elimination of export subsidies on farm goods by the end of 2013. This represented a concession by the EU but was three years later than the date sought by the USA and developing countries.

A new regulation laying down specific rules concerning the fruit and vegetables sector was adopted in September 2007 and entered into force in January 2008. Notable reforms included: the integration of the sector into the Single Farm Payment scheme; the requirement that producer organizations allocate at least 10% of their annual expenditure to environmental concerns; an increase in EU funding for the promotion of fruit and vegetable consumption and for organic production; and the abolition of export subsidies for fruit and vegetables. In December 2007 agriculture ministers reached political agreement on proposals for the reform of the wine sector. If formally adopted, the new regulation would provide for the inclusion of the sector in the Single Farm Payment scheme, while distillation subsidies would be phased out, releasing funds for measures such as wine promotion in third countries and the modernization of vineyards and cellars. In addition, a voluntary, three-year scheme would be introduced, under which wine producers would receive subsidies to uproot up to 175,000 ha of vineyards, with the aim of removing surplus and uncompetitive wine from the market.

In November 2007 the European Commission presented a blueprint for further reform of the CAP, launching a six-month consultation following which it intended to propose new legislation. The so-called 'health check' of the CAP was to focus on addressing three main areas: making the direct aid system simpler and more effective; adjusting market support instruments to make them more appropriate for an EU of 27 states; and confronting new challenges, such as climate change, biofuels, water management and the protection of biodiversity. Specific suggestions for consideration included raising the rate of decoupling in those countries that opted to maintain the link between subsidy and production in a number of farm sectors; the abolition of the set-aside scheme; and a gradual increase in the reduction of payments to individual farmers above €5,000 a year from the current 5% to 13% in 2013, with the funds saved to be transferred to the rural development budget.

Food safety has become an issue of increasing significance in the EU, especially since the first case of bovine spongiform encephalopathy (BSE), a transmissible disease that causes the brain tissue to degenerate, was diagnosed in cattle in the United Kingdom in 1986. The use of meat and bone meal (MBM) in animal feed was identified as possibly responsible for the emergence of the disease, and was banned for use in cattle feed in the United Kingdom in 1988. MBM was banned throughout the EU from 1994 for ruminants and in December 2000 for all animals. The possible link between BSE and new variant Creutzfeldt-Jakob disease (v-CJD), a degenerative brain disease that affects humans, led to a collapse in consumer confidence in the European beef market in early 1996. By December 2005 153 people had died of v-CJD in the United Kingdom, the location of the vast majority of cases (France had recorded nine deaths by January 2005, Ireland two and Italy one), although the number of deaths per year in the United Kingdom had declined to nine in 2004 from a peak of 28 in 2000.

In July 1997 agriculture ministers voted to introduce a complete ban on the use for any purpose of 'specified risk materials' (SRMs— i.e. those parts and organs most likely to carry the BSE prion disease agent) from cattle, sheep and goats. The introduction of the ban was postponed until January 1999, as a result of opposition from a number of EU member states, particularly Germany, as well as the USA. The scope of legislation on undesirable substances in animal feed was extended in May 2002, to cover additives, with the aim of enhancing the safety of animal feed.

In October 1998 Portugal was banned from exporting beef and live cattle, following a two-fold increase in reported cases of BSE in the country. In July 1999 the United Kingdom was deemed to have met all of the conditions pertaining to the lifting of the ban on its beef exports, which had been imposed in March 1996; the European Commission announced that limited exports would be permitted to resume from 1 August in the framework of the Date-based Exportation System, under which animals were tracked by an official monitoring system. The French Government finally lifted its ban on imports of British beef in October 2002, following a ruling by the European Court of Justice in December 2001 ordering it to revoke its unilateral ban.

In May 2001 new legislation was adopted by the European Parliament and the Agriculture Council that consolidated much of the existing legislation on BSE and other transmissible spongiform encephalopathies (TSEs) in bovine, ovine and caprine animals. The new TSE Regulation, which replaced previous emergency legislation and clarified the rules for the prevention, control and eradication of TSEs, came into force on 1 July 2001. It comprised two main elements: the passive surveillance of animals manifesting clinical symptoms compatible with BSE, which was introduced from 1998 at EU level, and active monitoring based on the use of rapid post mortem tests, which was introduced from January 2001. The post mortem screening was obligatory for all cattle subject to emergency slaughtering, all bovine animals aged more than 30 months slaughtered in normal conditions and intended for human consumption, all bovine animals found dead or slaughtered during transport but not for human consumption, and all sheep and goats slaughtered aged at more than 18 months. All of the new member states that joined the EU in May 2004 were fully committed to complying with EU legislation on combating BSE, and prior to accession were already removing SRMs from the food chain and testing healthy cattle aged more than 30 months.

EU member states, with the exception of France, agreed to lift the ban on Portuguese beef exports in September 2004. Portugal recorded 92 instances of the disease in 2004, while Spain detected 137 cases. Although the United Kingdom had many more individual cases, the incidence of the disease in 2004 was highest in Portugal, where there were 94.9 BSE cases per million head of cattle compared with 68.8 in the United Kingdom. In November 2005 a nine-year ban on the sale of British beef for human consumption from cattle aged over 30 months was replaced by a system under which, in order to enter the food chain, older cattle were required to test negative under a BSE testing regime. Owing to the continuing decline in the incidence of BSE, in March 2006 further restrictions on the export of British beef were lifted from the beginning of May, allowing for the export of live cattle born after 1 August 1996 and of beef from cattle slaughtered after 15 June 2005 (in line with other EU countries).

In December 2003 the Commission announced that the testing of sheep and goats for BSE-like diseases was to be reduced following the failure of widespread testing to reveal any evidence of infection. However, in January 2005 BSE was detected in an animal other than a cow for the first time when a goat slaughtered in France in 2002 tested positive for the disease. Monitoring of the EU goat population was therefore extended. Increased testing of sheep was introduced in July 2006 after it was revealed in March that routine testing under the TSE monitoring programme had identified unusual molecular profiles in the brain tissue of three sheep (two from France and one from Cyprus).

Following an outbreak of foot-and-mouth disease on farms in the United Kingdom in February 2001, the EU imposed a temporary ban on imports of British livestock products. Cases of foot-and-mouth disease were also noted in the Netherlands, France and Ireland. These three countries were declared free of the disease in September. During the outbreak, the USA and other third countries imposed import restrictions on fresh meat and livestock from the EU. In January 2002 the United Kingdom regained 'clear' status, without recourse to vaccination. In September 2003 the Council of agriculture ministers adopted new legislation on measures to control foot-and-mouth disease in the EU in the light of the outbreak in the United Kingdom. The new regulations included the use of emergency vaccination as a preventative option in the event of any future outbreak and the introduction of measures to ensure a high level of preparedness against a potential outbreak, including contingency planning and vaccine banks. Member states had to comply with the provisions by the end of June 2004. In response to an outbreak of foot-and-mouth disease in the United Kingdom in August 2007, the EU imposed a ban on imports of British livestock susceptible to the disease (cattle, sheep, goats and pigs) and of products from these animals; further cases were confirmed later in August and in September. The ban was lifted at the end of December as no new outbreaks had occurred in the preceding three months. Meanwhile, an outbreak of foot-and-mouth disease in Cyprus in November led to a ban on trade in livestock and meat from that country. The restrictions were eased in mid-January 2008.

In October 2007, in response to a recent increase in outbreaks within Europe of bluetongue disease (a non-contagious, insect-transmitted, viral disease affecting ruminants, particularly sheep), including in areas not previously considered to be at risk, the Standing Committee on the Food Chain and Animal Health (SCFCAH) endorsed a Commission proposal to amend EU legislation on the monitoring and control of the disease and the restrictions to be applied in the case of an outbreak. By this time more than 23,500 outbreaks of the BTV-8 strain of the virus had been confirmed in EU member states since the beginning of the year. In January 2008 the Commission announced that it would co-finance an emergency mass vaccination campaign against bluetongue in the EU that year.

In October 2003 the European Commission announced that it was strengthening a ban on beef from cattle treated with artificial growth hormones, which was originally imposed in 1988, on the grounds that it was dangerous to human health. The USA and Canada, the principal exporters of hormone-treated beef, filed a suit against the ban in 1996 within the WTO, which ruled in 1998 that the ban was illegal as the scientific studies demonstrating the harmfulness of the hormones were inadequate. The EU refused to repeal the ban by the May 1999 deadline set by the WTO, which then granted the USA and Canada leave to impose retaliatory sanctions of US $116.8m. and C $11m., respectively, for each year that the ban was in place. The EU subsequently conducted further scientific studies on the alleged harmful effects of the six types of hormones, reporting that one was a proven carcinogen while the others posed an undetermined risk to consumers. The EU claimed in October 2003 that the new scientific studies together with fresh EU legislation meant that the ban complied with WTO regulations and urged the USA and Canada to lift the punitive trade sanctions on European goods. In January 2005 the EU requested a WTO panel to review the trade sanctions. A panel was duly established in February. At the end of March 2008 the panel ruled that scientific evidence did not support the imposition of the import ban by the EU; Canada and the USA were also criticized for their failure to repeal their retaliatory measures against the EU.

The EU's Food and Veterinary Office was established in April 1997 to ensure that the laws on food safety, animal health and welfare and plant health are applied in all member states. The office carries out audits and checks on food safety in member states and in third countries exporting agricultural produce to the EU. Legislation establishing the European Food Safety Authority (EFSA) was signed in January 2002; the new body was to provide independent scientific advice and support on matters with a direct or indirect impact on food safety. It was to have no regulatory or judicial power, but would co-operate closely with similar bodies in the member states. The first meeting of the EFSA management board took place in September 2002, while its Advisory Forum was convened for the first time in March 2003. In September 2007 the European Commission adopted a communication setting out the EU's animal health strategy for 2007–13. The aims of the new strategy were: to ensure a high level of public health and food safety by reducing the risks posed to humans by problems with animal health; to promote animal health by preventing or reducing the incidence of animal diseases, thus also protecting farming and the rural economy; to improve economic growth, cohesion and competitiveness in animal-related sectors; and to promote farming and animal welfare practices that prevent threats to animal health and minimize the environmental impact of raising animals.

The EU has also adopted a number of protective measures to prevent the introduction of organisms harmful to plants and plant products. Regulations governing the deliberate release of genetically modified organisms (GMOs) into the environment have been in force since October 1991, with an approval process based on a case-by-case analysis of the risks to human health and the environment. A total of 18 GMOs were authorized for use in the EU under this directive. An updated directive took effect in October 2002, which introduced principles for risk assessment, long-term monitoring requirements and full labelling and traceability obligations for food and feed containing more than 0.9% GM ingredients. Labelling was not to be limited to foods containing genetically modified DNA or proteins but would also be extended to foods and food ingredients produced from GMOs but containing no detectable GM material, thus providing the consumer with the ability to choose whether or not to consume food derived from GMOs. A new regulation adopted by the Commission in January 2004, which specified a system precisely to identify and trace each GMO product used in the production of all food and animal feeds, completed the EU's regulatory framework on the authorization, labelling and traceability of GMOs. In May 2003 the USA filed a case at the WTO, with the support of Argentina and Canada, demanding that Europe repeal a de facto moratorium on new GM food product approvals, which had been in place since 1998, owing to widespread public concern about the technology. The EU claimed that the new rules on the release of GMOs would be sufficiently stringent to allow the issue of marketing permits for new GM products, with EFSA producing risk assessments and participating in the authorization process. Some of the 10 member states that acceded in 2004, notably Poland, had been cultivating GM crops for several years. Although by early 2004 all of the accession states had adopted EU regulations on GM products, many had inadequate testing facilities and fears were raised by environmental groups that they would be unable to implement labelling procedures effectively. However, the moratorium was lifted in May and in September the Commission approved for use across the EU a GM variety of maize that had been endorsed by the Governments of Spain and France in 1998. None the less, the USA continued to pursue its case at the WTO. In November 2006 the WTO's Dispute Settlement Body adopted a ruling that the EU moratorium on the authorization of GM products between 1998 and 2004 had contravened world trade regulations. The EU was obliged to implement the recommendations of the WTO by an initial deadline of 21 November 2007, which was subsequently extended until 11 January 2008. However, the EU failed to meet this deadline, as Austria refused to lift restrictions on two GM strains of maize. A few days after the expiry of the January deadline the USA announced its decision to suspend temporarily its right to impose sanctions on EU goods.

In 2004 the Commission, with support from the Council, presented a European action plan for organic food and farming, comprising 21 measures, aimed at promoting the development of organic farming in the EU. The Council also adopted a regulation improving legal protection for organic farming methods and established a programme on the conservation, collection and utilization of genetic resources in agriculture. In 2005 the Commission adopted a proposal for new regulations defining objectives and principles for organic production, clarifying labelling rules and regulating imports. The new regulation on production and labelling was adopted in June 2007 and was to be applied from January 2009, while the new rules concerning imports of organic foods were approved in December 2006 and were to be introduced from the beginning of 2007.

In June 1995 the Agriculture Council agreed to new rules on the welfare of livestock during transport. The agreement, which came into effect in 1996, limited transport of livestock to a maximum of eight hours in any 24-hour period, and stipulated higher standards for their accommodation and care while in transit. In January 1996 the Commission proposed a ban on veal crates, which came into effect from January 1998. In April 2001 the Commission adopted new rules for long-distance animal transport, setting out the required standards of ventilation, temperature and humidity control. A new regulation aimed at further enhancing the welfare of animals during transport was adopted in December 2004. To ensure improved enforcement of the rules, a satellite navigation system was to be introduced from January 2007 to track vehicles carrying livestock. In June 1999 EU agriculture ministers agreed to end battery egg production within the EU by 2012; in December 2000 a regulation was adopted requiring EU producers to indicate the rearing method on eggs and egg-packaging. A new directive laying out minimum standards for the protection of pigs, including provisions banning the use of individual stalls for pregnant sows and gilts, increasing their living space and allowing them to have permanent access to materials for rooting, was applicable from January 2003 to holdings newly built or rebuilt and from January 2013 to all holdings. A similar directive was adopted in June 2007 for the protection of chickens kept for meat production, laying out minimum standards in areas such as stocking density, lighting, litter and ventilation; it was to be implemented by member states within three years. Following 13 years of negotiations, in November 2002 agreement was finally reached between the European Parliament and the member states to ban the sale of virtually all animal-tested cosmetic products in the EU from 2009 and to halt all animal testing for cosmetics, ending a system under which about 38,000 animals were used and killed every year.

In April 2005 the Commission proposed a new directive for Community measures for the control of avian influenza. The decision was adopted in December, superseding legislation that had been in force since 1992. Meanwhile, in October 2005 the EU had banned imports of captive live birds from third countries to reduce the threat of a lethal strain of the highly contagious strain of avian influenza, H5N1, which had begun to spread from South-East Asia in 2003. (By early 2006 H5N1 had reached Turkey, Croatia and Romania.) The avian disease was also transmissible to humans and other animals, usually following direct contact with infected birds. In February 2006, having received the approval of the SCFCAH, the Commission adopted two decisions on measures to be taken by member states in the case of an outbreak of H5N1 in wild birds and in commercial poultry on their territory. The first decision detailed measures to be implemented by member states in the event of suspected or confirmed cases of H5N1 in wild birds. *Inter alia*, protection zones 3 km in radius, and surveillance zones of at least 10 km in radius, were to be established around affected areas. In both zones, all poultry and captive birds were to be kept indoors, on-farm biosecurity measures were to be applied, and restrictions were imposed on the movement of poultry and other captive birds both within and from the affected zones. The second decision related to outbreaks or suspected outbreaks of H5N1 in domestic poultry, setting forth provisions for the establishment of protection and surveillance zones, the culling of infected birds and birds on holdings in their immediate vicinity, and the confinement of poultry indoors, among other measures. In May the Commission and the Community Reference Laboratory for Avian Influenza published the results of surveillance for avian influenza carried out in the EU over the previous 10 months, reporting that, since February, the H5N1 virus had been detected in more than 700 wild birds in 13 member states. It was noted at the same time, however, that there had been a decline in the incidence of the disease in recent weeks. In July the SCFCAH approved a number of draft Commission decisions that introduced new measures, and amended and prolonged existing measures, to protect the EU against avian influenza. Among the measures approved at this time were a prolongation, until 31 December 2006, of the ban on imports of captive live birds and the restriction on the movement of pet birds entering the EU from third countries. A ban on imports of poultry products from the People's Republic of China, Malaysia and Thailand was to remain in place until 31 December 2007 owing to the continued prevalence of H5N1 in South-East Asia. In December 2006 the ban on all imports of captive live birds was extended for three months, until 31 March 2007. The ban was subsequently extended until 30 June. From 1 July a new regulation came into force, banning the import of birds caught in the wild but allowing the import of captive birds from specific countries and regions that had already been approved to export live commercial poultry. Under the new rules, member states would be required to provide more detailed information on such imports.

In January 2007 the Hungarian authorities informed the Commission that an outbreak of highly pathogenic avian influenza had been detected in south-east Hungary—the first incidence of highly pathogenic avian influenza in the EU since August 2006. Tests subsequently established that the virus responsible for the outbreak was H5N1. In February an outbreak of avian influenza, subsequently confirmed to have been caused by H5N1, was reported on a turkey farm in Suffolk, United Kingdom. Following the outbreaks of H5N1 in Hungary and the United Kingdom, the Commission urged all member states to maintain heightened surveillance and biosecurity, and to review the measures they were currently applying. Advice was issued that in areas identified to be at high risk of outbreaks of H5N1, poultry should be kept indoors. Later in February the Commission announced that an emergency team of veterinary experts was to be established to respond to outbreaks of animal diseases at the request of member states or third countries. Further outbreaks of H5NI occurred at a turkey farm in the Czech Republic in June, at a duck farm in Germany in August, at two turkey farms in the United Kingdom in November and at turkey farms in Poland in December, while a number of wild birds were also infected in these three countries as well as in Austria and France. The eradication and control measures required by EU legislation were implemented in response to each outbreak.

FISHERIES

The Common Fisheries Policy (CFP) came into effect in January 1983 after seven years of negotiations, particularly concerning the problem of access to fishing grounds. In 1973 a 10-year agreement had been reached, whereby member states could have exclusive access to waters up to six nautical miles (11.1 km) or, in some cases, 12 miles from their shores; 'historic rights' were reserved in certain cases for foreign fishermen who had traditionally fished within a country's waters. In 1977 the Community set up a 200-mile (370-km) fishing zone around its coastline (excluding the Mediterranean) within which all members would have access to fishing. The 1983 agreement confirmed the 200-mile zone and allowed exclusive national zones of six miles with access between six and 12 miles from the shore for other countries according to specified historic rights. Rules furthering conservation (e.g. standards for fishing tackle) were imposed under the policy, with checks by a Community fisheries inspectorate. Total allowable catches (TACs) were fixed annually by species and were divided into national quotas (prior to 2003 these targets were set under the renewable Multiannual Guidance Programme—MAGP). A body of inspectors answerable to the Commission monitored compliance with the quotas and TACs and with technical measures in Community and some international waters.

In 1990 it was reported that stocks of certain species of fish in EC waters had seriously diminished. Consequently a reduction in quotas was agreed, together with the imposition of a compulsory eight-day period in each month during which fishermen in certain areas (chiefly the North Sea) would stay in port, with exemptions for fishermen using nets with larger meshes that would allow immature fish to escape. In 1992 the compulsory non-fishing period was increased to 135 days between February and December (with similar exemptions).

In December 1992 EC ministers agreed to extend the CFP for a further 10-year period. Two years later ministers concluded a final agreement on the revised CFP, allowing Spain and Portugal to be integrated into the policy by 1 January 1996. A compromise accord was reached regarding access to waters around Ireland and off southwest Great Britain (referred to as the 'Irish box'), by means of which up to 40 Spanish vessels were granted access to 80,000 sq miles of the 90,000 sq mile area. However, the accord was strongly opposed by Irish and British fishermen. In April 1995 seven Spanish vessels were seized by the Irish navy, allegedly for fishing illegally in the Irish Sea. In October fisheries ministers agreed a regime to control fishing in the 'Irish box', introducing stricter controls and instituting new surveillance measures.

The organization of fish marketing involves common rules on size, weight, quality and packing and a system of guide prices established annually by the Council of the European Union. Fish are withdrawn from the market if prices fall too far below the guide price, and compensation may then be paid to the fishermen. Export subsidies are paid to enable the export of fish onto the lower-priced world market and import levies are imposed to prevent competition from low-priced imports. A new import regime took effect from May 1993. This enabled regional fishermen's associations to increase prices to a maximum of 10% over the Community's reference price, although this applied to both EU and imported fish.

Initially, structural assistance actions for fisheries were financed by the European Agricultural Guidance and Guarantee Fund (which was replaced by the European Agricultural Guarantee Fund in 2007). Following the reform of the structural funds in 1993, a separate fund, the Financial Instrument for Fisheries Guidance (FIFG), was set up. The instrument's principal responsibilities included the decommissioning of vessels and the creation, with foreign investors, of joint ventures designed to reduce the fishing effort in EU waters. The fund also supported the building and modernizing of vessels, developments in the aquaculture sector and the creation of protected coastal areas. In addition, it financed contributions to redundancy payments.

The proposals put forward in May 1996 by the European Commission for the fourth MAGP, covering 1997–2002, envisaged catch reductions of up to 40% for species most at risk, and set targets and detailed rules for restructuring fishing fleets in the EU. However, the draft MAGP IV failed to gain approval at the meeting of fisheries ministers held in November 1996. The British Government, in October, insisted that it would not accept additional limits on catches without action to stop 'quota-hopping', in which boats registered in the United Kingdom were bought by operators in other EU countries (mainly Spain and the Netherlands), which were thus able to gain part of the British fishing quotas. (In mid-1998 the British Government received approval from the Commission to introduce new licensing conditions from 1 January 1999 that would compel the owners of boats involved in 'quota-hopping' to establish economic links with the United Kingdom.) In April 1997, following a number of concessions by the Commission, ministers approved MAGP IV. The programme fixed catch reductions at 30% for species most at risk and at 20% for other over-fished species.

In June 1998 the Council of the European Union overcame long-standing objections from a number of member states and adopted a ban on the use of drift nets in the Atlantic Ocean and the Mediterranean Sea, in an attempt to prevent the unnecessary deaths of marine life such as dolphins and sharks. The ban, which was introduced in January 2002, partially implemented a 1992 UN resolution demanding a complete cessation of drift-net fishing. A series of compensatory measures aimed to rectify any short-term detrimental impact on EU fishing fleets. In July 2003 the Commission proposed the implementation of a total ban on the use of drift nets in the Baltic Sea within four years, and the use of acoustic warning devices on fishing nets throughout most EU waters to prevent dolphins and porpoises from becoming fatally entangled in the nets. These proposals were welcomed by animal welfare organizations and the ban was adopted in March 2004.

With concern over stocks continuing to mount, an emergency 11-week ban on deep-sea cod fishing over 40,000 sq miles of the North Sea was introduced in February 2001. In March similar emergency measures for the west of Scotland entered into effect, while emergency measures for the northern hake catch were adopted in June. Measures for the Irish Sea had been instituted in 2000. In December 2001 the Fisheries Council fixed TACs for 2002, incorporating further substantial reductions, with the aim of achieving 'biologically acceptable' levels of stocks. In June 2002 the Commission presented its long-term recovery plans for cod and hake. Under the plans, the Commission proposed establishing a procedure for setting TACs so as to achieve a significant increase in mature fish stocks, with limits on the fishing effort fixed in accordance with the TACs. The plans also provided for the temporary closure of areas where endangered species had congregated, and allowed for more generous EU aid for the decommissioning of vessels (aid for the modernization of vessels, which tends to increase the fishing catch, was to be reduced). By 2002 the Commission had also been alerted to the critical depletion of deep-sea species, the commercialization of which had become increasingly attractive in the 1990s as other species became less abundant. For the first time, in December 2002, the Commission introduced catch limits for deep-water fish species for the period 2003–04, complemented by a system of deep-sea fishing permits. In 2004 the Commission extended TACs to other fish stocks and introduced a number of closed areas for heavily depleted species.

Radical reform of the CFP, aimed at ensuring the sustainable development of the industry, was announced during 2002. The Commission proposed a new multi-annual framework for the efficient conservation of resources and the management of fisheries, incorporating environmental concerns. Under the new framework—which was to replace the MAGP system—a long-term approach to attaining/maintaining fish stocks was to be adopted which was designed to give greater responsibility to member states to achieve a better balance between the fishing capacity of their fleets and the available resources (the erstwhile short-term approach, which had focused mainly on annual objectives, had prevented fishermen from planning ahead and, more seriously, had failed to conserve fish stocks). Under the terms of the new framework, quotas for catches of cod, whiting and haddock were substantially reduced, fishermen were to be guaranteed only nine days a month at sea (with a degree of leeway to extend this to 15 days in some circumstances) and public funding for the renewal or modernization of fishing boats was to be abolished after 2004 (although the provision of aid to improve security and working conditions on board was to be maintained). In addition, it was announced that measures were to be taken to develop co-operation among the various fisheries authorities concerned and to strengthen the uniformity of control and sanctions throughout the EU. The powers of the Commission inspectors were to be extended to ensure the equity and effectiveness of the enforcement of EU regulations. Regional advisory councils (RACs) were also to be established to enable scientists, fishermen and other interested parties to work together to identify modes of achieving sustainable fisheries in the region concerned. In an attempt to compensate for the ongoing decline of the EU fishing fleet, a number of socioeconomic measures were introduced, including the provision of aid from member states to fishermen and vessel owners who had temporarily to halt their fishing activities and the granting of aid to fishermen to help them retrain to convert to professional activities outside the fisheries sector, while permitting them to continue fishing on a part-time basis. The new measures were instigated on 1 January 2003. They replaced the basic rules governing the CFP since 1993 and substantially amended the regulation on structural assistance in the fisheries sector through the FIFG. A new regulation setting up an emergency fund to encourage the decommissioning of vessels (known as the 'Scrapping Fund') was also adopted.

In December 2003 the EU fisheries ministers and the European Commission reached an agreement on quotas for 2004 that aimed to balance conserving stocks with protecting the industry. Quotas for cod and hake catches in the North Sea were frozen at the levels set for 2003, while the North Sea fishing fleet was permitted to catch 30% more prawns and 53% more haddock, compared with the previous year, owing to flourishing stocks of these species. However, many scientists claimed that unless a complete ban were imposed cod stocks could disappear completely. It was calculated that in the early 2000s cod stocks in the North Sea had fallen to one-10th of their level at 1970. In addition to the setting of annual quotas, longer-term recovery programmes for cod and hake were also agreed, in an effort to establish sustainable conservation measures to avoid the need to retain the existing annual bartering system. In a further attempt to ease stocks, restrictions on the number of days fishermen were permitted to spend at sea were maintained for 2004 and the area covered by these restrictions was extended. Furthermore, the Commission proposed the imposition of stricter controls to combat illegal fishing.

In July 2004 the Council adopted a common framework on the establishment of RACs as part of the 2002 reform. In November 2004 the first RAC, for the North Sea, was instituted in Edinburgh, Scotland. The Pelagic RAC and the North Western Waters RAC, based, respectively, in Amsterdam, the Netherlands, and Dublin, Ireland, were created in August and September 2005. A Baltic Sea RAC, based in Copenhagen, Denmark, was set up in March 2006. The RAC for Long Distance Waters and the RAC for the South Western Waters were established in March and April 2007, while the remaining proposed RAC (for the Mediterranean Waters) was to commence operations in the near future.

In December 2004, in line with the recommendations of the North East Atlantic Fisheries Commission (NEAFC), the Commission proposed a 30% reduction in TACs for deep-sea species. In order to alleviate its socioeconomic impact, however, it was subsequently decided that the proposed reduction should be replaced by one of 20%, to be implemented in two annual phases, each of 10%, in 2005–06.

In December 2005 the Agriculture and Fisheries Council reached agreement on national fishing quotas for the following year. Overall, as agreed in December 2004, TACs for deep-sea species were to be reduced by 10% (rather than the 20% proposed by the Commission), while the number of days at sea for cod fleets was cut by 5%, instead of the 15% recommended by the Commission. A ban on anchovy fishing in the Bay of Biscay, in place since July 2005, was lifted with effect from March 2006, but was reimposed in July amid continued concern over depleted stocks. For the first time, TACs and quotas for the Baltic Sea were discussed separately from those covering other Community waters. The Council's decision to increase the TAC for cod in the eastern part of the Baltic by some 17% was severely criticized by Sweden, which abstained from voting.

Meanwhile, in March 2005 the European Commission announced its decision to initiate a consultation process on a new integrated EU maritime policy aimed at developing the potential of the maritime economy in an environmentally sustainable manner. In October 2007 the Commission presented a communication on its vision for the integrated maritime policy, which was endorsed by the Council in December. An accompanying action plan included fisheries-related initiatives such as a scheme to strengthen international co-operation against destructive deep-sea fishing practices and measures to halt imports of illegal fisheries products.

In July 2005 the European Court of Justice ordered France to pay a fine of €20m. and a periodic six-monthly penalty of €57.8m. for continued non-compliance with a 1991 ruling on its failure effectively to enforce CFP measures, particularly regarding the landing and sale of undersized fish. The case was the first in which a financial penalty had been imposed on a member state for flouting fisheries regulations, although a further 81 fisheries infringement procedures were pending against member states, mostly related to over-fishing. In November 2006 the Commission ruled that France had met its legal obligations and would not incur a second penalty payment. In October 2005, in response to proposals from the European Commission, the Agriculture and Fisheries Council adopted a long-term recovery plan for southern hake and Norway lobster off the northern and western coasts of the Iberian peninsula, stocks of which were severely depleted.

In April 2005, in order to improve further compliance with the CFP as reformed in 2002, the Council of Ministers agreed to establish a Community Fisheries Control Agency. The Agency was to strengthen the uniformity and effectiveness of enforcement of fisheries regulations by pooling EU and individual countries' means of control and monitoring and by co-ordinating enforcement activities. In October 2006 the Agency adopted its work programme for 2007. It gave priority to the implementation of recovery plans for cod stocks, protection of bluefin tuna and the fight against illegal, destructive fishing practices. The first joint deployment plan was implemented in 2007, with the participation of seven member states, and related to the recovery of cod stocks in the North Sea, Kattegat, Skagerrak and Eastern Channel. A joint inspection and surveillance scheme covering cod stocks in the Baltic was also initiated in 2007 as a precursor to a future joint deployment plan.

In July 2006, in order to facilitate, within the framework of the CFP, a sustainable European fishing and aquaculture industry, the Agriculture and Fisheries Council adopted a regulation on the establishment of a European Fisheries Fund (EFF). The EFF replaced the FIFG on 1 January 2007. The Fund was to support the industry as it adapted its fleet in order to make it more competitive; and to promote measures to protect the environment. It was also to assist the communities that were most affected by the resulting changes to diversify their economic base. The EFF was to remain in place for seven years, with a total budget of some €3,800m. The regulation also set forth detailed rules and arrangements regarding structural assistance, including an obligation on all member states to draw up a national strategic plan for their fisheries sectors. Assistance was henceforth to be channelled through a single national EFF programme.

In December 2006 the Agriculture and Fisheries Council reached a compromise agreement on fish quotas for 2007. The fixing of TACs was informed by the relative success of recovery plans for at-risk species, but stopped short of following scientific advice to the effect that fishing for cod and some other species should be suspended entirely in the North and Irish Seas. TACs were reduced a further 20% for cod stocks in the west of Scotland and the Celtic Sea, and by 15% for the other stocks covered by recovery plans, except for the North Sea, where the reduction was to be 14%, as agreed with Norway, and the Kattegat, where a reduction of 14% was also to be implemented. Cod was to be further protected by a reduction in the number of days vessels could spend at sea. The Commission acknowledged that the cod recovery plan for 2004 had not produced the improvement in stocks that it had anticipated. Conversely, the relative success of recovery plans for northern hake and sole in the Bay of Biscay led to increases of 20% in the TAC for northern hake and 12% in that for Bay of Biscay sole. In response to increased pressure from scientists and environmental groups for a total ban on fishing for deep-sea species, the Commission adopted cuts ranging from 10% to 25% for five deep-sea species for the period 2007–08, while quotas for another four were rolled over from 2005. Fisheries ministers also adopted new regulations to protect biodiversity in the Mediterranean.

In February 2007, in response to the results of an inquiry conducted by the British authorities that revealed the extent of fishing for herring and mackerel in excess of quota by the United Kingdom and Ireland in 2001–05, the Commission decided to reduce the corresponding TACs for these countries for the period 2007–12. In order to attenuate negative socio-economic consequences, the reductions were to be implemented over a number of years.

The European Commission adopted a communication in March 2007 on reducing unwanted catches and eliminating 'discards' (unwanted fish or other marine organisms that are dumped overboard, having been caught unintentionally). The adoption of a progressive fishery-by-fishery discard ban was envisaged, as well as the setting of standards for maximum acceptable by-catch. The Commission aimed to provide an incentive for the fishing industry to devise ways of meeting the by-catch targets.

Recovery plans were adopted in mid-2007 for sole in the western part of the English Channel and for sole and plaice in the North Sea. Meanwhile, a regulation establishing conservation measures for highly migratory species, such as tuna, marlin and swordfish, was approved. A revision of the cod recovery plan for the Atlantic was also initiated in that year.

In December 2007 the Agriculture and Fisheries Council reached political agreement on TACs and national fishing quotas for the following year. The TAC for cod in the North Sea was increased by 11%, as agreed with Norway, following some improvement in stocks in that area, although the number of days vessels could spend at sea was reduced by 10% and accompanying measures aimed at reducing discards were approved. A 15% increase in the TAC for southern hake was also approved as a result of the success of the recovery plan for that species. However, the TACs for mackerel, blue whiting and sole in the North Sea were reduced by 41%, 37% and 15%, respectively, while those for cod in the Irish Sea and west of Scotland were reduced by 18% and 9%, respectively. The ban on anchovy fishing in the Bay of Biscay was to remain in place, pending a re-examination of stocks. In addition, the Council adopted a regulation establishing a 15-year recovery plan for bluefin tuna, as recommended by the International Commission for the Conservation of Atlantic Tunas. Meanwhile, TACs for the Baltic Sea were set in October. Most notably, in accordance with a recovery plan for Baltic cod adopted in September, the TACs for that species were reduced by 28% in the western part of the Baltic and 5% in the eastern part.

Bilateral fisheries agreements have been signed with other countries (Norway, Iceland and the Faroe Islands) allowing limited reciprocal fishing rights and other advantages ('reciprocity agreements'), and with some African and Indian Ocean countries and Pacific Islands that receive technical and financial assistance in strengthening their fishing industries in return for allowing EU boats to fish in their waters ('fisheries partnership agreements'). Following the withdrawal of Greenland from the Community in February 1985, Community vessels retained fishing rights in Greenland waters, in exchange for financial compensation. In recent years, however, owing to growing competition for scarce fish resources, it has become increasingly difficult for the EU to conclude bilateral fisheries agreements giving its fleets access to surplus fish stocks in the waters of third countries.

Of the 10 new states that joined the EU in 2004, only four had sizeable fishing industries (Poland, Estonia, Latvia and Lithuania); the combined total annual catch of these four states in the early 2000s was equivalent to less than 7% of the EU total. Prior to their membership, the accession states were obliged to establish the necessary administrative capacity for applying the obligations arising from the CFP, including the modernization and renewal of old fishing vessels, the joint conservation of resources, the training of fisheries inspectors, the implementation and monitoring of common marketing standards, the introduction of EU health and hygiene standards, the management of structural policy in fisheries and aquaculture, and the compilation of a register of fishing vessels. In December 2005 the International Baltic Sea Fishery Commission (IBSFC) ceased its activities. Following the accession of Estonia, Latvia, Lithuania and Poland to the EU in 2004, membership of the IBSFC had been reduced to only two parties, the EU and Russia, and the negotiations that had formerly been conducted within its framework could now be undertaken bilaterally.

RESEARCH AND INNOVATION

In the amendments to the Treaty of Rome, effective from July 1987, a section on research and technology (subsequently restyled 'research and innovation') was included for the first time, defining the extent of Community co-operation in this area. Most of the funds allocated to research and innovation are granted to companies or institutions that apply to participate in EU research programmes.

In January 2000 the Commission launched an initiative to establish a European Research Area (ERA). The aim was to promote the more effective use of scientific resources within a single area, in order to enhance the EU's competitiveness and create jobs. The ERA was to provide venture capital and tax concessions for research and high-technology start-up companies. The creation of the ERA was to be supported through the Sixth Framework Programme for research and technological development (FP6), which was launched in 2002. Covering the period 2002–06, the programme, which had a budget of €17,500m. (€16,270m. allocated to the European Community and €1,230m. to the European Atomic Energy Community), aimed to integrate research capacities in Europe (for example by establishing networks of excellence and jointly implemented national programmes), and to concentrate on priority areas such as genomics, sustainable development, aeronautics and space, information technology and food safety.

During 2003–04 plans were discussed regarding the proposed establishment of a European Research Council (ERC), which, as an independent funding body for science, would play a vital role in ERA. Many observers claimed that, unless such a body were set up, hundreds of European scientists would relocate to the USA and parts of Asia, where research funding was substantially greater than in Europe. The FP6 funding system was widely criticized as being overly bureaucratic, biased towards large, complex collaborations and subject to political pressures. More detailed plans for the creation of the ERC were included in the Commission's proposals for the Seventh Framework Programme for research, technological development and demonstration activities (FP7, covering 2007–13), which were published in April 2005 together with the Seventh Framework Programme of the European Atomic Energy Community for nuclear research and training activities (which covered the period 2007–11, but could be renewed for 2012–13) and a new Competitiveness and Innovation Framework Programme (CIP, also covering 2007–13), which was to be closely co-ordinated with FP7. A Scientific Council was to assume responsibility for determining the scientific strategy of the ERC and defining methods of peer review and proposal evaluation. The 22 founding members of the Council were announced in July and held their inaugural meeting in October, subsequently publishing an outline strategy for the launch of the

ERC. Also in October, the Commission adopted an action plan comprising 19 measures aimed at increasing investment in research and development and innovation, particularly from the private sector, in an attempt to reach the target of 3% of gross domestic product (GDP) invested in research by 2010. In December 2006, having been adopted by the European Parliament, the ERC and its budget of €7,500m. were approved by the Council of the European Union. The ERC commenced operations in February 2007. CIP, with a budget of €3,200m., received the formal approval of the Council of the European Union in October 2006. In December the Council adopted decisions establishing FP7 and the Seventh Framework Programme of the European Atomic Energy Community. A budget of €48,770m. was approved for the four specific programmes into which FP7 had been structured: co-operation (€32,413m.); ideas (to be implemented by the ERC—€7,510m.); people (€4,750m.); and capacities (€4,097m.). Some €1,751m. was allocated for the non-nuclear actions of the Joint Research Centre of the European Commission. A budget of €2,702m. was approved by the Council for the Seventh Framework Programme of the European Atomic Energy Community. Joint technology initiatives (JTIs), in which industry, research organizations and public authorities would form public-private partnerships to pursue common research objectives, were to be a major new element of FP7. Several JTIs were proposed in 2007, including ARTEMIS, involving research into embedded systems (specialized computer components dedicated to a specific task that are part of a larger system), and the Innovative Medicines Initiative (IMI). In April 2007 the European Commission initiated a consultation process on the creation of ERA with the adoption of a Green Paper. Following the completion of the consultation in August, the Commission began preparing initiatives for proposal.

The European Strategic Programme for Research and Development in Information Technology (ESPRIT) was inaugurated in 1984 and concentrated on five areas: advanced micro-electronics; software technology; advanced information processing; office automation; and computer integrated manufacturing. One-half of the programme was financed by the EU and one-half by the participating research institutes, universities and industrial companies. In 1998 ESPRIT was integrated into the EU's Information Society Technologies (IST) initiative under the Fifth Framework Programme (FP5, 1998–2002). The IST initiative was designed to accelerate the emergence of an information society in Europe by promoting the development of high-quality, affordable services. The development of information and communication technologies remained a priority for the European Commission in FP7, as part of the co-operation programme, and was allocated €9,050m. in the budget for 2007–13.

In July 1997 the European Parliament approved the Life Patent Directive, a proposal aiming to harmonize European rules on gene patenting in order to promote research into genetic diseases, despite objections over the ethical implications. In December 2000 the EU agreed to establish a parliamentary committee to examine new developments in human genetics. In late 2001 the Commission set up a website to encourage debate on embryonic stem cell research (which could help in the treatment of diseases such as diabetes and Parkinson's), aiming to create a dialogue between experts and the public. The EU is also participating actively in the international human genome project, which seeks to characterize the genomes of humans and other organisms, through mapping and sequencing of their DNA. Despite condemnation from a number of campaign groups, in November 2003 the European Parliament voted to allow EU funds to be spent on controversial stem cell research; in the following month, however, at a meeting of the Council of the European Union, Germany, Austria and Italy reiterated their strong opposition to EU funding of embryo research; the proposal was blocked and the moratorium on central funding was extended indefinitely, although the Commission remained free to approve stem cell research projects on a case-by-case basis and in accordance with strict ethical guidelines. In 2000 the European Group on Ethics in Science and New Technologies (EGE) had published an opinion document which constituted the basis of the strict ethical guidelines governing human embryonic stem cell research under FP6. Under FP7, as under FP6, funding for embryonic stem cell research projects was to be granted on a case-by-case basis. Certain areas, such as human cloning for reproductive purposes, would continue to receive no funding. Research projects proposed under FP7 would remain subject to ethical scrutiny and the national rules of the member states involved would be observed. In June 2007 the EGE adopted an opinion recommending guidelines for reviewing the ethics of FP7 research projects using human embryonic stem cells.

The EU is making efforts to integrate space science into its research activities, and is increasingly collaborating with the European Space Agency (ESA). In September 2000 the EU and ESA adopted a joint European strategy for space, and in the following year the two bodies established a joint task force. In November 2001 the European Commission and ESA agreed to introduce a Global Monitoring for Environment and Security (GMES) programme—based on a combination of *in situ* (land, sea and air) and space-based monitoring—which was expected to be fully operational by 2008; the pilot phase of the initiative was launched in November 2005. Meanwhile, in March 2002 the EU approved the development of the 'Galileo' civil satellite navigation and positioning system, which was to be based on a network of 30 orbiting satellites and which was to be compatible and interoperable with the global positioning system (GPS) currently operated by the US military and with the Russian Glonass system. Galileo was to be financed jointly by ESA and the EU, and the development phase, costing some €1,500m., was to be managed by the Galileo Joint Undertaking (GJU). Galileo Industries was to be located in Germany, which was also to take charge of the space sector, while a second base was to be located in Rome, with Italy in charge of systems engineering. In October 2003, despite objections from the USA, it was announced that the People's Republic of China and India both intended to invest considerable sums of money in the Galileo project. In December 2004 the Council of the European Union approved the deployment phase of Galileo, covering the construction and launch of satellites and the building of ground receiving stations. This phase of the project was to be undertaken by Galileo Industries (renamed European Satellite Navigation Industries in 2007) at an estimated cost of some €2,100m., with the system expected to require €220m. a year for maintenance from the date of its launch. Galileo, which was expected to lead to the creation of about 150,000 jobs, was projected to improve greatly the accuracy and reliability of navigation and timing signals received across the planet. The system was to have many practical applications: e.g. traffic management, direct information for the emergency services, and the prevention of natural disasters such as floods and fires. In December 2005 GIOVE-A, the first of two test GIOVE (Galileo in-orbit validation element) satellites, was launched. The launch of the second, GIOVE-B, initially planned for early 2006, was scheduled for late April 2008, having been repeatedly delayed mainly owing to technical problems. Meanwhile, in March 2007 ESA awarded a contract for the construction of an additional satellite, GIOVE-A2, which was to be ready for launch in the second half of 2008. GIOVE-A was expected to reach the end of its service life in 2008. The first four operational satellites were expected to be launched in 2009, with the whole constellation of 30 projected to be in orbit by 2013, several years later than originally envisaged. In June 2005 the GJU announced that it had commenced negotiations on a contract for managing the deployment and operational phases with a joint consortium of Eurely and iNavSat. In January 2007 the European GNSS (Global Navigation Satellite Systems) Supervisory Authority assumed responsibility for Galileo from the GJU, which had been dissolved. Talks with Eurely/iNavSat collapsed later that year, creating uncertainty regarding the future management and funding of the project, while escalating costs were also of concern. In November the Council and Parliament reached agreement on a proposal by the Commission that the deployment phase of Galileo be funded entirely from the European Community budget, at a cost of €3,400m. over 2007–13, in order to ensure the continuation of the project. Meanwhile, the EU had concluded agreements on participation in the Galileo programme with China, Israel, Ukraine, India, the Republic of Korea and Morocco. Discussions on co-operation had also been initiated with Argentina, Australia, Brazil, Canada, Chile, Malaysia, Mexico, Norway and Russia.

In January 2005, following four years of negotiations, ESA and Russia signed an agreement to allow closer co-operation over the use of facilities and exchange of information. Russia was accorded special status in ESA and was to be permitted to use the Agency's space port in Kourou, French Guiana, for rocket launches. The construction site of the launch base for the Russian Soyuz craft was officially opened in Kourou in February 2007, with the first launch scheduled for late 2008.

In February 2000 the European Parliament urged action to be taken to combat the under-representation of women in science. The Commission is working towards a target of 40% participation by women at all levels in the implementation and management of research programmes. The Helsinki Group on Women and Science, established by the Commission in 1999 and composed of national representatives from all the EU member states and countries associated to the Framework Programmes, meets twice a year to discuss measures aimed at encouraging the participation of women in scientific careers and research. In a report on gender equality in science published in 2006, the European Commission noted that women made up only 29% of those employed as scientists and engineers in 2004 and that, across the EU, only 18% of researchers in the business and enterprise sector were women. Furthermore, women still only constituted 15% of senior academics, and the imbalance was markedly acute in engineering and technology, where women accounted for only 5.8% of those at the highest academic grade.

In February 2006 the Commission recommended the establishment of a European Institute of Technology (EIT), designed to promote excellence in higher education, research and innovation. The EIT was to be based on a Europe-wide network of 'knowledge and innovation communities' (partnerships comprising higher education institutions, research organizations, companies and other interested parties). The EU's contribution to the EIT was forecast at €308.7m. during 2008–13. The European Parliament approved a regulation on the EIT in September 2007, changing the Institute's name to the European Institute of Innovation and Technology. A directive on the establishment of the EIT came into force in April 2008.

The Joint Research Centre (JRC) was established under the European Atomic Energy Community. Directed by the European Commission, but relying for much of its funding on individual contracts, the JRC is a collection of seven institutes, based at five different sites around Europe—Ispra (Italy), Geel (Belgium), Karlsruhe (Germany), Seville (Spain) and Petten (Netherlands). The Institutional and Scientific Relations Directorate—based in Brussels—co-ordinates the research undertaken at the seven institutes and serves as a link between the institutes and European policy-makers. While nuclear research and development remain major concerns of the institutes, their research efforts have diversified substantially over the years. The JRC identified seven priority areas to be addressed under FP7: food safety; biotechnology, chemicals and health; the environment (including climate change and natural disasters); energy and transport; nuclear energy, safety and security; the Lisbon Strategy (see Economic Co-operation), information society and rural development; and internal and external security, anti-fraud measures and development aid. Nuclear work accounts for about one-quarter of all JRC activities, with the share accounted for by non-nuclear work increasing. The JRC also provides technical assistance to applicant countries. The JRC's budget for the FP7 period was €1,751m. for non-nuclear activities and €517m. for nuclear activities.

The EU also co-operates with non-member countries (particularly states belonging to the European Free Trade Association) in bilateral research projects. The Commission and 37 (mainly European) countries—including the members of the EU as individuals—participate, as full members, in the EUREKA programme of research and development in market-orientated industrial technology, which was launched in 1985; in addition to the full members, Morocco is designated a EUREKA associated country, and a number of other countries participate in EUREKA projects through a network of National Information Points (NIPs). EUREKA (the acronym of the European Research Co-ordination Agency), sponsors projects focusing on robotics, engineering, information technology and environmental science, allows resources to be pooled and promotes collaboration. Most of EUREKA's funding is provided by private sources. The Community research and development information service (CORDIS) disseminates findings in the field of advanced technology, with 10 searchable databases containing more than 300,000 individual records. In 1994 a European Technology Assessment Network (ETAN) was developed to improve the dissemination of technological research findings; under FP5 this was replaced by the Strategic Analysis of Specific Political Issues (STRATA) programme, which aims to promote dialogue between researchers and policy-makers on general science, technology and innovation policy issues of European relevance. The programme supports the establishment of networks and expert groups to improve the development of science and technology policies at all levels and to aid interaction with other policy fields.

ENERGY

The treaty establishing the European Atomic Energy Community (Euratom) came into force on 1 January 1958. This was designed to encourage the growth of the nuclear energy industry in the Community by conducting research, providing access to information, supplying nuclear fuels, building reactors and establishing common laws and procedures. A common market for nuclear materials was introduced in 1959 and there is a common insurance scheme against nuclear risks. In 1977 the Commission began granting loans on behalf of Euratom to finance investment in nuclear power stations and the enrichment of fissile materials. An agreement with the International Atomic Energy Agency (IAEA) entered into force in the same year, to facilitate co-operation in research on nuclear safeguards and controls. The EU's Joint Research Centre (JRC, see Research and Innovation) conducts research on nuclear safety and the management of radioactive waste.

The Joint European Torus (JET) is an experimental thermonuclear machine designed to pioneer new processes of nuclear fusion, using the 'Tokamak' system of magnetic confinement to heat gases to very high temperatures and bring about the fusion of tritium and deuterium nuclei. Fusion powers stars and is viewed as a 'cleaner' approach to energy production than nuclear fission and fossil fuels. Switzerland is also a member of the JET project (formally inaugurated in 1984), which is based at Culham in the United Kingdom and which is funded by the European Commission. (Romania was already a member of the JET project before it acceeded to the EU in 2007.) The project is a collaboration between all European fusion organizations, and involves technology and physics research from the global scientific and engineering community. In 1991 JET became the first fusion facility in the world to achieve significant production of controlled fusion power. The European Fusion Development Agreement (EFDA), which entered into force in March 1999, and a new JET implementing agreement, which came into force in January 2000, provide the framework for the collective use of the JET facilities. In 1988 work began with representatives of Japan, the former USSR and the USA on the joint design of an International Thermonuclear Experimental Reactor (Iter), based on JET but with twice its capacity. The aim of Iter was to demonstrate the scientific and technical capacities of fusion energy for peaceful, commercial purposes. By 2005 Iter had become very much an international project, with participant teams from the People's Republic of China, the EU (represented by Euratom), Japan, the Republic of Korea, Russia and the USA, under the auspices of the IAEA. In mid-2005 the six participant teams agreed that the vast trial reactor would be located in Cadarache, in southern France, after Japan withdrew a rival bid to host the facility in return for guarantees regarding its future involvement in Iter. In late 2005 India became a full partner in the project. The main aim of Iter is to demonstrate that fusion could be used to generate electrical power (Iter would be the first fusion experiment with a net output of power) as well as to collect the data required to design and operate the first electricity-producing plant. The construction of the project was expected to take until 2016, after which the reactor would remain operational for 20 years, at a total estimated cost of €10,000m., of which the EU was to contribute about 50%. In April 2006 the management team was designated. The preparation of the Iter site commenced in January 2007; the construction phase was scheduled to begin in 2008. In March 2007 the Council established the European Joint Undertaking for Iter and the Development of Fusion Energy (Fusion for Energy) to manage the EU's contribution to Iter. Overall responsibility for Iter was formally assumed by the newly established Iter International Fusion Energy Organization in October, following the ratification of a joint implementation agreement by all seven participants in the project.

Legislation on the completion of the 'internal energy market', adopted in 1990, aimed to encourage the sale of electricity and gas across national borders in the Community by opening national networks to foreign supplies, obliging suppliers to publish their prices and co-ordinating investment in energy. Energy ministers reached agreement in June 1996 on rules for the progressive liberalization of the electricity market. In December 1997 the Council agreed rules to allow the gas market to be opened up in three stages, over a 10-year period.

In 2001 the Commission amended the timetable for liberalizing the electricity and gas markets: by 2003 all non-domestic consumers were to have the freedom to choose their electricity supplier; by 2004 non-domestic consumers were to have the freedom to choose their gas supplier; and by 2005 all consumers, domestic and non-domestic, would be able to choose both suppliers. The Commission further proposed that the management of transmission and distribution grids should be legally separated from production and sales activities (except for small-scale distribution companies). It was suggested that network access tariffs should be published and approved by national regulators before entering into force, and that a regulator should be established for each member state. To create a genuine single market, the Commission proposed the adoption of rules on tariff-setting across borders, developing a European infrastructure plan for electricity and gas, and the negotiation of reciprocal agreements on the opening of electricity markets with the EU's neighbours. In June 2002 the European Council confirmed amended target dates for the complete two-stage liberalization of the markets: opening up by July 2004 for non-domestic users and by July 2007 for domestic users. The European Regulators Group for electricity and gas (ERGEG) was established in November 2003 to act as an advisory group of independent national regulatory authorities to assist the European Commission in consolidating the internal market for electricity and gas. In early 2006 the ERGEG launched a regional initiative which created three gas and seven electricity zones within the EU. The initiative focused on removing barriers to market integration at a regional level, in order to facilitate the creation of a single competitive market.

In October 2005 the EU signed a treaty establishing an energy community with Albania, Bosnia and Herzegovina, Bulgaria, Croatia, the former Yugoslav republic of Macedonia, Romania and Serbia and Montenegro, which entered into force in July 2006. In November Turkey, Ukraine, Moldova and Norway were admitted as observers. The treaty, which was intended to advance the aim to create an integrated pan-European market for electricity and gas, required the signatories to adopt EU energy regulations. The liberalization of the electricity and gas markets within the participating countries was expected to be completed by 2008 for non-domestic users and by 2015 for domestic users. The World Bank estimated that this planned extension of the single European market for electricity and gas would lead to investment of €21,000m. in energy infrastructure in South-Eastern Europe in the following 15 years. In a report on progress in creating the internal EU electricity and gas market, issued in November 2005, the European Commission concluded that member states needed to implement more effectively the liberalization measures required under the Union's gas and electricity directives. Six member states (Estonia, Greece, Ireland, Luxembourg, Portugal and Spain) were being brought before the European Court of Justice for failing to incorporate the directives into their national legislation, while others had been slow to do so. The Commission identified the lack of integration between national markets as being of major concern, citing an absence of price convergence across the EU and a low level of cross-border trade. Furthermore, the preliminary findings of an ongoing inquiry into competition in the energy sector, which was launched by the Commission in June 2005, confirmed that EU energy markets were not functioning on a competitive basis. In March 2006 the Commission adopted a Green Paper on developing a common European energy policy, which included recommendations on the appointment of a single energy regulator, the creation of an integrated European power grid and the negotiation of a new long-term pact with Russia on energy supplies. In December the Commission issued a final warning ('reasoned opinion') to 16 member states, including Germany, the United Kingdom, Spain, France and Italy, for having failed to open up sufficiently their energy markets. The final report of the competition inquiry, published in January 2007, identified high levels of market concentration, vertical integration of supply, production and infrastructure and collusion between operators to share markets as the main obstacles to the effective integration of the energy market. To address these issues, the Commission recommended the more stringent enforcement of regulations within an improved regulatory framework for energy liberalization. Having received the endorsement of the Council in March, in September the Commission adopted a number of legislative proposals, including new rules to ensure the separation of the operation of transmission networks from production and supply activities; measures to reinforce and harmonize the powers of national regulators; the creation of an Agency for the Co-operation of National Energy Regulators to facilitate cross-border trade in energy products; and the establishment of a new European Network for Transmission System Operators, with the aim of promoting the development of common standards of practice and the co-ordination of EU-level investment in the sector. In addition, a charter on the rights of energy consumers was to be launched in 2008.

The Commission has consistently urged the formation of an effective overall energy policy. The five-year programmes, SAVE and SAVE II, introduced respectively in 1991 and 1995, aimed to establish energy efficiency (e.g. reduction in the energy consumption of vehicles and the use of renewable energy) as a criterion for all EU projects. SAVE was integrated into the 'Energy, Environment and Sustainable Development—EESD' thematic programme initiated under the Fifth Framework Programme (FP5) for 1998–2002 and subsequently incorporated into a new, more encompassing umbrella programme, 'Intelligent Energy for Europe' (EIE), which was to supersede EESD and which was adopted by the Commission for the period 2003–06 as part of the Sixth Framework Programme (FP6). The aim of EIE, which was to receive funding totalling €200m. (rising to around €250m. on the enlargement of the EU in May 2004), was to strengthen the security of supply and to promote energy efficiency and renewable energy sources (RES) such as wind, solar, biomass and small-scale hydropower. A new campaign, the Campaign for Sustainable Energy (2004–07), was launched in mid-2004 to succeed the Campaign for Take-Off (1999–2003). The Renewable Energy Partnership scheme was used in both campaigns to involve public and private partners in supporting RES and energy efficiency. In April 2005 the European Commission proposed that the EIE be continued and expanded under a new Competitiveness and Innovation Framework Programme (CIP), which was to run in conjunction with the Seventh Framework Programme (FP7) for research during 2007–13. Under CIP, the EIE was to incorporate three separate elements: energy efficiency (SAVE); RES for the production of electricity and heat (ALTENER); and the energy aspects of transport (STEER) and was allocated a budget of €730m. for that period.

In order to help the EU to meet its joint commitment under the Kyoto Protocol to reduce greenhouse gas emissions by 8% from 1990 levels by 2012, and to encourage the use of more efficient energy technologies, in July 2003 the Council established the Emissions Trading Scheme (ETS). Under the scheme, which came into force in January 2005, individual companies were allocated a free greenhouse gas emission allowance by national governments. If they reduced emissions beyond their allocated quota, they would be allowed to sell their credits on the open market. In the first phase, covering the period 2005–07, ETS was only applied to large industrial and energy undertakings in certain sectors and only covered carbon dioxide emissions. Several member states opted to extend the scope of ETS for the second trading period (2008–12) by including installations or emissions that were excluded from the first phase. In November 2006 the Commission initiated a review of ETS, proposing an expansion of its coverage to new sectors and emissions. Any changes would take effect from 2013, at the beginning of the third trading period.

In January 2007 the Commission attempted to initiate a more coherent integration of the EU energy and climate policies by incorporating in its proposals a comprehensive series of measures addressing the issue of climate change, while emphasizing the interdependency between security of supply and the promotion of sustainable energy sources. The measures included the establishment of a biennial Strategic Energy Review (SEER) that would monitor progress and identify new challenges in all aspects of energy policy, and was to constitute the basis for future action plans to be adopted by the Council and the Parliament. The Council endorsed the proposals in March 2007; it also stated that its strategic objective was to limit the increase in the average global temperature to no more than 2°C above pre-industrial levels. The EU was to commit itself to reducing its greenhouse gas emissions by 20% (compared to their 1990 levels) by 2020, and by 30% should the USA, China and India make a similar commitment. At the same time, the renewable energy sector was to supply 20% of EU energy by 2020, compared with 6.6% in 1990, and the share of biofuels in overall consumption of energy by the transport sector was to increase by 10%, also by 2020. New legislation was to facilitate the market penetration of renewable energy sources, while individual member states were to decide whether or not to develop their nuclear electricity sectors. The proposals incorporated an energy-efficiency action plan—launched by the Commission in October 2006—which contained a package of priority measures covering a wide range of cost-effective energy efficiency initiatives, to be implemented in the following six years in order to support the goal of reducing energy consumption by 20% by 2020. The development of a European strategic energy technology plan was agreed. It was to be instrumental in increasing research into sustainable technologies (including low-carbon technology) by 50% by 2014. In November 2007 the Commission duly launched the European Strategic Energy Technology Plan (SET-Plan), in which it outlined plans to initiate six new industrial initiatives, focusing on wind power; solar power; biofuels; carbon dioxide capture, transport and storage; the electricity grid (including the creation of a centre to implement a research programme on the European transmission network); and sustainable nuclear fission.

Energy ministers from the EU member states and 12 Mediterranean countries agreed at a meeting held in June 1996 in Trieste, Italy, to develop a Euro-Mediterranean gas and electricity network. The first Euro-Med Energy Forum was held in May 1997, and an action plan (covering the years 1998–2002) to develop an integrated network was adopted in May 1998. In May 2003 the energy ministers of the Euro-Med partnership (including the ministers from the 10 accession states) adopted a declaration launching the Second Regional Energy Plan (2003–06). The Energy Forum's objectives, which promoted massive projects for the creation of North-South and South-South transmission infrastructures, were criticized by environmentalist groups in respect of both environmental and financial concerns. The Energy Forum that took place in September 2006, to agree on priorities for the period 2007–10, advocated the continued integration of Euro-Med energy markets, the development of energy projects of common interest and of sustainable energy. The fifth Euro-Med ministerial conference on energy, held in Cyprus in December 2007, endorsed an action plan for further energy co-operation, covering the period 2008–13, which was to receive funding of €12,400m. from the European Investment Bank. Priorities included: the harmonization of regional energy markets and legislation; the promotion of sustainable development in the energy sector; and the development of initiatives of common interest in areas such as infrastructure, investment financing and research and development.

In 1997 the Community agreed to help a number of newly independent Eastern European countries to overcome energy problems by means of the Interstate Oil and Gas Transport to Europe programme (INOGATE). The overall aim of this programme was to improve the security of Europe's energy supply by promoting the regional integration of the oil and gas pipeline systems both within Eastern Europe itself and towards the export markets of Europe and the West in general, while acting as a catalyst for attracting private investors and international financial institutions to these pipeline projects. INOGATE originally formed part of the TACIS (Technical Assistance to the Commonwealth of Independent States) programme (see External Relations). However, under the Umbrella Agreement of INOGATE, which officially came into force as an international treaty in February 2001, the programme is now open to all interested countries (regardless of their individual status as an oil- and gas-producing country or as a transit country). By late 2007 the Agreement had been signed by 21 states of Central Asia, the Caucasus, Eastern Europe and the EU, and had entered into force in 13 of these countries. In November 2006, as a continuation of the Baku initiative inaugurated in November 2004 under the umbrella of INOGATE, the EU and the governments of countries in the Caspian and Black Sea regions adopted a new Energy Road Map, which established a long-term plan of action. The road map provided for enhanced energy co-operation between all of the partners involved in such areas as the integration of energy markets on the basis of the EU internal energy market; the improvement of energy security by addressing issues of energy exports/imports; supply diversification; energy transit; sustainable energy development; and the securing of investment for projects of common interest.

At the sixth EU-Russia summit, held in Paris in October 2000, the two sides agreed to institute an energy dialogue on a regular basis with a view to establishing a strategic EU-Russia energy partnership. The dialogue was subsequently structured around joint thematic research groups to analyse issues of common interest, notably in the areas of energy strategies and balances, investment, technology transfers, energy infrastructures and energy efficiency and the environment. From 2001 annual progress reports were presented to EU-Russia summit meetings. However, following the disruption in January 2006 of Russian gas supplies to the EU that transited Ukraine, showing the extent of the EU's dependency on Russian gas (about one-quarter of gas supplied to the EU is from Russia), a European Parliament resolution emphasized that there was an urgent need to secure a more stable, reciprocal and transparent EU-Russia energy framework. Cuts in crude oil supplies from Russia to the EU in early 2007, resulting from a dispute between Russia and the transit country, Belarus, led to further demands for measures to enhance the security of the Union's energy supply. In April a restructuring of the thematic groups of the EU-Russia energy dialogue was agreed, to cover energy strategies, forecasts and scenarios; market developments; and energy efficiency. At an EU-Russia summit meeting held in Mafra, Portugal, in October it was agreed to establish a system to provide early warning of threats to the supply of natural gas and petroleum to the EU.

In addition, the EU promotes trans-European networks (TENs, see also Transport), with the aim of developing European energy, telecommunications and transport through the interconnection and opening-up of national networks. Over the years, progress on the development of EU energy networks has proved slow, partly owing to difficulties in co-operation and co-ordination between member states regarding cross-border issues. The TEN-Energy (TEN-E) programme commenced in 1995, with an annual budget of €20m. In 2003 a revision of the guidelines for TEN-E was undertaken to take into account the priorities of the enlarged EU, in particular the competitive operation of the internal energy market and the improvement of the energy supply for the new member states. An important target, therefore, was to integrate fully the new member states in these guidelines and lists of projects. The revised guidelines, adopted by the Council in July 2006, were as follows: to enhance the security of energy supplies in Europe; to strengthen the internal energy market of the enlarged EU; to support the modernization of energy systems in partner countries; to increase the share of renewable energies, in particular in electricity generation; and to facilitate the realization of major new energy infastructure projects. The TEN-E networks policy, in particular, aimed to secure and diversify additional gas import capacity from sources in Russia, the Caspian Basin, northern Africa and the Middle East. The budget agreed for the TEN-E programme for 2007–13 totalled €155m. Priority projects supported by contract under the budget included the controversial North European Gas Pipeline between north-west Russia and Germany, scheduled for completion in 2010 (work began in December 2005), and the construction of the Nabucco gas pipeline between Turkey and Austria, due to take place in 2008–11.

In November 1999 the Commission indicated the need to strengthen the EU's 'Northern Dimension' energy policy (covering Scandinavia, the Baltic states and north-west Russia) through the reinforcement of international co-operation, the opening-up of markets, the promotion of competition and the improvement of nuclear safety. In a communication in September 2000, the Commission set out a new EU strategy on nuclear safety in Central and Eastern Europe and the former Soviet states. The strategy entailed supporting those countries in their efforts to improve operating safety, strengthening their regulatory frameworks, and closing reactors that could not be upgraded to an acceptable standard. The fifth enlargement of the EU, completed in January 2007 with the accession of Bulgaria and Romania, had implications for nuclear safety, since seven of the 12 new member states had nuclear reactors, mostly of the old Soviet design. The closure of two ageing reactors was one of the preconditions for Bulgaria's accession to the EU.

In November 2000 the Commission adopted a Green Paper on the security of energy supply, which was aimed at launching a broad debate on the role of each energy source, with regard to the security of supply, sustainable development, questions of enlargement, and action needed to combat climate change. Security of supply was of vital importance as the EU met around 50% of its energy requirements through imports in 2000 and this figure was expected to increase substantially over the following decade. The final report, published in June 2002, recommended that efforts should be directed towards containing demand rather than increasing supply, by such measures as improving energy efficiency, adopting energy taxes and encouraging the production and market penetration of renewable energy sources. However, noting that the EU's efforts in these areas had been inconsistent and had not produced the desired results, the report also recommended an improved dialogue between the EU and oil-producing countries, the creation of strategic gas stocks, the exploration of nuclear options, and the effective integration of the gas and electricity markets. The Green Paper of March 2006, entitled 'Towards a European strategy for the security of energy supply', re-emphasized the links between security of supply, the creation of a liberalized, integrated EU energy market and the development of sustainable energy. To protect energy supplies against the risk of natural catastrophes, terrorist threats, political risks and rising oil and gas prices, it recommended the following measures: the development of smart electricity networks; the establishment of a European Energy Supply observatory to monitor supply and demand patterns in EU energy markets; improved network security through increased collaboration and exchange of information between transmission system operators under an over-arching European centre of energy networks; a solidarity mechanism to ensure rapid assistance to any member state confronted by damage to its essential infrastructure; and common standards to protect infrastructure and the development of a common European voice to promote partnerships with third countries. In December 2006 the Council agreed to establish a network of energy security correspondents, whose role would be to provide early warnings and thus enhance the Community's ability to react to pressure on external energy security. In March 2007 the Council incorporated into its integrated action plan the need to promote a common European voice in the development of partnerships with neighbouring countries and the other main energy-producing/consuming nations.

ENTERPRISE AND INDUSTRY

Industrial co-operation was the earliest activity of the Community. The treaty establishing the European Coal and Steel Community (ECSC) came into force in July 1952, and by the end of 1954 nearly all barriers to trade in coal, coke, steel, pig-iron and scrap iron had been removed. The ECSC treaty expired in July 2002, and the provisions of the ECSC treaty were incorporated in the EEC treaty, on the grounds that it was no longer appropriate to treat the coal and steel sectors separately.

In the late 1970s and 1980s measures were adopted radically to restructure the steel industry in response to a dramatic reduction in world demand for steel. These included production capacity quotas, a reduction in state subsidies and financial compensation for job losses (in the mid-1970s the European steel industry employed around 774,000 workers). During the 1990s, however, new technologies and modern production processes were introduced, and the European steel sector showed signs of substantial recovery. Privatization and cross-border mergers also improved the industry's competitive performance and by the early 2000s Europe was very much a world leader in high-quality steel production and a competitive global exporter. At that time, the European steel industry generated about €90,000m.–€100,000m. per year, and it directly employed more than 250,000 EU citizens (with several times this number employed in the steel-processing, usage and recycling industries). In 2006 the industry produced almost 200m. metric tons of steel, compared with some 160m. tons in the early 2000s. In 1996 the European Commission adopted a new code on steel aid, for the period 1997–2002. The new code stipulated the conditions under which member states could grant aid to steel companies, namely for research and development, environmental protection, and for full or partial closures of capacity. In March 2004 the European Commission and major stakeholders in the European steel industry launched the European Steel Technology Platform. This high-level group included research institutes in the steel industry, key stakeholders, trade unions, national regulators, universities, etc. The long-term aim of the Platform was to help the sector meet the challenges of the global marketplace, changing supply and demand patterns, environmental objectives (e.g. a reduction in harmful emissions), and the streamlining of EU and national legislation and regulation in this field. In addition, the May 2004 enlargement of the EU increased the need for extensive restructuring of the steel industries. The steel industry played a relatively larger role in the 10 new member states, compared with the existing 15 members. In 2002 the Commission adopted a report on state aid to the coal industry, and in particular the results of restructuring, rationalization and modernization in the member states that still produce coal.

The European textile and clothing industry has been seriously affected by overseas competition over an extended period. From 1974 the Community participated in the Multi-fibre Arrangement (MFA, see WTO), to limit imports from low-cost suppliers overseas. However, as a result of the Uruguay Round of GATT (General Agreement on Tariffs and Trade) trade negotiations, the quotas that existed under the MFA were progressively eliminated during 1994–2004 in accordance with an Agreement on Textiles and Clothing. An action plan for the European textile and clothing industry was drawn up in 1997. This was designed to improve competitiveness, facilitate structural adjustment in the industry and improve conditions of employment and training. A report published by the Commission in

2000 established future priorities for the sector, focusing on preparations for the enlargement of the EU and systems for co-operation in the 'new economy'. Particular importance was attached to ensuring a smooth transition to the quota-free world environment (from 1 January 2005), to enable third countries currently exporting to the EU to maintain their competitive position, and to secure for EU textile and clothing industries in third countries market-access conditions similar to those offered by the EU. A high-level group on textiles and clothing, established by the Commission in order to encourage debate on initiatives to facilitate the sectors' adjustment to major challenges, and to improve their competitiveness, published its first report in 2004, addressing, in the context of competitiveness, such issues as trade policy and national co-operation.

In May 2005, in response to a dramatic increase in clothing exports from the People's Republic of China since 1 January, the EU imposed limits on textile imports from that country. In June the EU and the Chinese Government agreed import quotas on 10 clothing and textile categories until 2008, but by August several of the quotas for 2005 had already been breached. In September the dispute was resolved when it was agreed that one-half of the estimated 80m. Chinese garments that had been impounded at European ports would be released and the remainder counted against the quotas for 2006. In September 2006 the high-level group on textiles and clothing published its second report, which sought, *inter alia*, to chart the likely development of the sectors up to 2020. With regard to the quota-free environment for textiles and clothing that had been introduced at the beginning of 2005, the report noted that a Commission statement released in mid-2006 had indicated that the disruptive impact of liberalization of Chinese textile exports to the EU had been confined to a fairly restricted range of product categories. None the less, China's share of exports to the EU of products in the liberalized categories had risen markedly, to the detriment of traditional EU suppliers. Overall, however, only a modest increase in EU imports of textiles and clothing (in both the liberalized categories and in total) had occurred. According to the Commission statement, in 2005 exports of Chinese textiles and clothing to the EU increased by 42% in terms of volume and by 36% in terms of value. In the liberalized categories, China's market share grew by 130% in terms of volume and by 82% in terms of value. During the first quarter of 2006, however, as a result of the quantitative restrictions imposed from mid-2005, an overall decline of 12% in Chinese exports of textiles and clothing to the EU had been recorded. The statement noted, too, that China was becoming a principal growth market for exports of textiles and clothing from the EU. In October 2007 the Commission and China agreed that, following the expiry in 2008 of the agreement on import quotas, a monitoring system would be introduced to track, but not limit, the issuing of export licences in China and the import of goods into the EU for eight clothing and textile categories. (Export volumes of the two other categories covered by the existing quota arrangement were deemed to be too low to require monitoring.)

Production in EU member states' shipyards has fallen drastically since the 1970s, mainly as a result of competition from shipbuilders in the Far East. In the first half of the 1980s a Council directive allowed for subsidies to help reorganize the shipbuilding industry and to increase efficiency, but subsequently rigorous curbs on state aid to the industry were introduced. In July 1994 the EU signed an accord with Japan, the USA, the Republic of Korea and the Nordic countries to end subsidies to the shipbuilding industry from 1996, subject to ratification by member states. However, owing to the USA's failure to ratify it, the accord never entered into force. State aid was eventually phased out in early 2001. In 2000 the EU and the Republic of Korea concluded an agreement ('Agreed Minutes') with the aim of preventing trade disputes in the shipbuilding sector. Included in the agreement were a number of obligations in respect of subsidization, financial transparency and unfair pricing. However, the Republic of Korea subsequently refused to implement the agreement's provisions. In April 2002 the Commission adopted its fifth report on the state of world shipbuilding. It confirmed previous observations that, in the absence of an international agreement, the market was in crisis, owing to the extremely low prices offered by South Korean shipyards. In May the EU agreed to launch WTO procedures against South Korea, and to establish a 'temporary defensive mechanism' (TDM) of state subsidies to protect European shipbuilding against unfair South Korean practices. In 2003 a report entitled 'LeaderSHIP 2015' was presented by the Commission and a high-level group of shipping experts, which included 30 recommendations for the future development of the EU shipbuilding and ship repair sector. The report indicated that the strength of the European shipbuilding industry lay in the construction of sophisticated vessels, and consequently suggested that aid should be diverted from production aid to development aid. It also stated that the shipyards of Europe should promote safer and more 'environmentally friendly' ships. In 2004 the TDM, which had been due to expire on 31 March of that year, was extended for one year. In response, the Republic of Korea initiated WTO procedures against the EU. In April 2005 (by which time the TDM had in any case expired) a WTO panel concluded that with the TDM the EU had failed to fulfil its obligation to use exclusively WTO dispute settlement procedures to resolve its dispute with the Republic of Korea over that country's subsidization of its shipyards. Also in April, with regard to WTO procedures initiated by the EU against the Republic of Korea, a WTO panel found that the Republic of Korea had indeed provided export subsidies that were explicitly forbidden by the WTO Subsidies and Countervailing Measures Agreement. However, the panel did not support a claim that the Republic of Korea had granted restructuring subsidies to its shipyards. The Republic of Korea was obliged to withdraw its export subsidies within 90 days. In 2000–05 orders placed with Japanese, Korean and, especially, Chinese shipbuilders increased substantially, while the number of orders placed with EU (and other) shipbuilders declined. By late 2005, however, there were indications that the EU's shipbuilding sector was recovering somewhat.

Harmonization of national company law to form a common legal structure within the Community has led to the adoption of directives on disclosure of information, company capital, internal mergers, the accounts of companies and of financial institutions, the division of companies, the qualification of auditors, single-member private limited companies, mergers, take-over bids and the formation of joint ventures. In September 2004 the Commission launched a broad strategy to prevent financial and corporate malpractice. The strategy recommended timely and effective implementation of the Financial Services Action Plan and the Action Plan for Company Law and Corporate Governance, and its key elements were enhanced transparency, improved traceability and better co-ordinated enforcement. In October a 15-member European Corporate Governance Forum was established to monitor corporate governance practices throughout the EU with a view to bringing them closer together. In May 2006 stringent new rules for auditors were adopted in an attempt to prevent accounting scandals; the new directive stated that all companies listed on the stock market would be obliged to have independent audit committees that would recommend an auditor for shareholder approval.

The European Patent Convention was signed in 1973 and entered into force in 1977. Revisions to the Convention were agreed in November 2000, and a revised European Patent Convention entered into force on 13 December 2007. In June 1997 the Commission published proposals to simplify the European patent system through the introduction of a unitary Community patent, which would remove the need to file patent applications with individual member states. The Commission hoped to have the patent in place by the end of 2001, but disagreements between member states resulted in this deadline being missed and the patent had not been introduced by late 2007 (one of the main obstacles was the issue of the translation of the claims in the patent). The unitary Community patent was one of the main focuses of a public consulation launched by the Commission in early 2006 to consider future action in patent policy. In March 2007 the Commission adopted a communication, 'Enhancing the patent system in Europe', based on the results of the consultation, in which it reiterated its commitment to the introduction of a single Community patent. If established, the Community patent would be issued by the European Patent Office (EPO), based in Munich, Germany.

An Office for Harmonization in the Internal Market (OHIM), based in Alicante, Spain, was established in December 1993, and is responsible for the registration of Community trademarks and for ensuring that these receive uniform protection throughout the EU. Numerous directives have been adopted on the technical harmonization and standardization of products (e.g. on safety devices in motor vehicles, labelling of foodstuffs and of dangerous substances, and classification of medicines).

The liberalization of Community public procurement has played an important role in the establishment of the internal market. A directive on public supplies contracts (effective from January 1989, or from March 1992 in Greece, Portugal and Spain) stipulated that major purchases of supplies by public authorities should be offered for tender throughout the Community. Public contracts for construction or civil engineering works in excess of ECU 5m. were to be offered for tender throughout the EC from July 1990 (March 1992 for Greece, Portugal and Spain). From January 1993 the liberalization of procurement was extended to include public utilities in the previously excluded sectors of energy, transport, drinking-water and telecommunications. In 1996 the Commission launched the Système d'information pour les marchés publics (SIMAP) programme, which gives information on rules, procedures and opportunities in the public procurement market, and aims to encourage the optimum use of information technology in public procurement. During 2002 the European Parliament adopted a regulation aimed at simplifying the rules on procurement of contract notices, by introducing a single system for classifying public procurement, to be used by all public authorities; a regulation updating the classification system was adopted in November 2007. The European Public Procurement Network was established in January 2003. The objective of this network, which comprises all EU member states, EU candidate countries, EEA members, Switzerland and other European countries, was to strengthen the application of public procurement rules through a mutual exchange of experience. Reforms to the EU's public procurement directives were adopted in 2004 in an attempt to make the often complex rules more transparent, efficient and comprehensible. In November 2007 a directive was adopted with the aim of improving the effectiveness of review procedures concerning the award of public contracts.

In 1990 the European Council adopted two directives with the aim of removing the tax obstacles faced by companies operating across borders: the Merger Directive was designed to reduce tax measures that could hamper business reorganization and the Parent-Subsidiary Directive abolished double taxation of profit distributed between parent companies in one member state and their subsidiaries in others. In October 2001 the Commission presented a strategy for company taxation in the EU, suggesting the introduction of a single consolidated tax base, to eliminate the large variations in effective company tax rates across the EU. The Commission noted that a new approach was needed, in view of increasing globalization and economic integration in the internal market as well as developments such as economic and monetary union (EMU, see Economic Co-operation). In that month the European Council also adopted two legislative instruments enabling companies to form a European Company (known as a Societas Europaea—SE). A vital element of the internal market, the legislation gave companies operating in more than one member state the option of establishing themselves as single companies, thereby able to function throughout the EU under one set of rules and through a unified management system; companies might be merged to establish an SE. The legislation was aimed at making cross-border enterprise management more flexible and less bureaucratic, and at helping to improve competitiveness. In July 2003 the Council adopted similar legislation enabling co-operatives to form a European Co-operative Society (Societas Cooperativa Europaea—SCE). The Commission launched public consultations in 2003 on two initiatives aimed at establishing a common tax base: one concerned the possibility of using the International Accounting Standards as a starting point to develop an EU-wide consolidated tax base for companies, and the other involved a 'Home State Taxation' pilot project for small and medium-sized enterprises (SMEs). At a meeting of the EU's finance ministers held in the Netherlands in September 2004, there were wide divergences of opinion expressed over the proposals to co-ordinate tax policy throughout the Union; the United Kingdom and Ireland were among those member states that rejected any centralized interference in domestic taxation. None the less, later that year the Commission established a working group to progress the development of a common consolidated corporate tax base (CCCTB); it was anticipated that a formal proposal on the CCCTB would be made in 2008. In February 2005 the Council approved an amendment to the Merger Directive of 1990, extending its provisions to cover a wider range of companies, including SEs and SCEs. A directive aimed at facilitating cross-border mergers of limited liability companies was adopted by the European Parliament and the Council in October 2005. This new directive was expected particularly to assist SMEs that wished to operate in more than one member state, but not throughout Europe, and were not able to seek incorporation under the European Company statute. In February 2007 the European Parliament adopted a resolution requesting that the European Commission draw up a European Private Company statute specifically aimed at SMEs; a public consultation on the development of such a statute was conducted later that year.

In September 1995 a Commission report outlined proposals to improve the business environment for SMEs in particular, by improving fiscal policies and access to finance, and introducing measures aimed at reducing delays in payments and lowering the costs of international transactions. In March 1996 the Commission agreed new guidelines for state aid to SMEs. Aid for the acquisition of patent rights, licences, expertise, etc., was to be allowed at the same level as that for tangible investment. In July 1997 the I-TEC scheme was inaugurated to encourage SMEs to invest in new technology. The Business Environment Simplification Task Force (BEST) was established in 1997 to consider ways of improving legislation and of removing hindrances to the development of businesses, especially SMEs. BEST presented its final report in 1998; the subsequent action plan, designed to improve the overall environment for business, was endorsed in April 1999. A Charter for Small Enterprises, approved in June 2000, aimed to support SMEs in areas such as education and training, the development of regulations, and taxation and financial matters, and to increase representation of the interests of small businesses at national and EU level. In 2007 there were some 23m. SMEs in the EU, accounting for 99% of all EU enterprises and employing around 75m. people. The EU has repeatedly stated that it views small businesses as a vital source of economic growth and employment creation. In January 2005 the Commission launched a €36m. programme to provide finance to SMEs through local banks and other credit institutions, with particular emphasis on the EU's new member states. In November of that year the Commission launched a new policy framework for SMEs, proposing specific actions in five areas: promoting entrepreneurship and skills; improving SMEs' access to markets; simplifying regulations; improving SMEs' growth potential; and strengthening dialogue and consultation with SME stakeholders. In January 2007 the Commission launched an action programme aimed at reducing unnecessary administrative burdens on companies, primarily SMEs, by one-quarter by 2012, focusing on 13 priority areas, including company law, employment relations, taxation, agriculture and transport. In addition, 10 'fast-track' measures were identified, which, it was estimated, would reduce the burden on businesses by €1,300m. per year. A high-level group of experts was appointed in November to advise the Commission on the implementation of the action programme, which had been endorsed by the Council in March.

The European Investment Bank (see p.) provides finance for small businesses by means of 'global loans' to financial intermediaries. A mechanism providing small businesses with subsidized loans was approved by ministers in April 1992. In 2001, noting that SMEs were gradually switching from loan finance to other instruments, including equity, the EU began an initiative to develop European venture capital markets.

A network of 39 Euro Info Centres (EICs), aimed particularly at small businesses, began work in 1987. A total of 241 EICs and 24 associate members were in operation in 30 countries (the 27 EU member states, as well as Iceland, Norway and Turkey) in late 2007, with a further 17 Euro Info Correspondence Centres located in other non-EU countries. The EU's other information services for business include the Community Research and Development Information Service (CORDIS, see Research and Innovation) and the internet-based Your Europe: Business, which brings together advice and data from various sources. A network of Innovation Relay Centres (IRCs), also primarily targeting SMEs, was established in 1995 to facilitate the transfer of technologies throughout Europe; by 2007 a total of 71 IRCs had been set up in 33 countries (Chile, Iceland, Israel, Norway, Switzerland and Turkey, in addition to the 27 EU member states). In addition, around 160 Business and Innovation Centres (BICs) had been established in 21 countries by 2007, with a mission to promote entrepreneurship and the creation of innovative businesses, and to assist existing companies to enhance their prospects through innovation. The EICs, IRCs and BICs were allied under the 'b2europe' initiative, which aimed to establish close links between the various business support networks involved and to ensure the quality of their services.

Meeting in Lisbon, in March 2000, the European Council set the EU the new strategic goal of transforming itself into the most competitive and dynamic economy in the world over the following decade. In January 2000 the EU's Directorates-General for Industry and SMEs and for Innovation were transformed into one Directorate-General for Enterprise Policy (subsequently restyled the Enterprise and Industry Directorate-General). The Commission subsequently adopted a multiannual programme for enterprise and entrepreneurship (MAP) covering the period 2001–05, aimed particularly at SMEs. It was noted that business start-ups should be made easier and the cost of doing business in Europe lowered. Stronger measures were proposed for the protection of intellectual property rights (IPRs), and the harmonization of legislation on IPRs was advocated (differences between national laws in this respect could constitute protectionist barriers to the EU's principle of free movement of goods and services). The programme's overall objective was to create a dynamic, sustainable, innovation-based environment for EU businesses and to develop a climate of confidence among investors. In January 2007 the MAP, which had been extended until the end of 2006, was succeeded by an Entrepreneurship and Innovation Programme under a wider Competitiveness and Innovation Framework Programme for 2007–13, with a budget of some €3,600m. In January 2003 the Commission presented a draft directive on the enforcement of IPRs, which aimed to make it considerably easier to enforce copyrights, patents and trademarks in the EU and to punish those who tampered with technical mechanisms designed to prevent copying or counterfeiting. The proposals were welcomed by the music, film and fashion industries, but were strongly opposed by sections of the telecommunications and information technology industries, which viewed the draft directive as a threat to competition and freedom. The directive was approved in April 2004. In July 2005 the Commission proposed a second directive on the enforcement of IPRs, which would impose criminal penalties for infringements, to supplement the civil and administrative measures contained in the 2004 directive; the draft directive was still under consideration in 2007. Meanwhile, in November 2004 the Commission announced plans to commence monitoring certain countries (particularly the People's Republic of China, Ukraine and Russia) to check that they were making genuine efforts to put a stop to the production of counterfeit goods. The Commission estimated that between 1998 and 2002 the number of counterfeit goods intercepted at the EU's external borders had increased by more than 800%. In October 2005 the Commission launched a new industrial policy, proposing eight new initiatives or actions targeted at specific sectors, including pharmaceuticals, defence and information and communication technologies, as well as seven cross-sectoral initiatives on: competitiveness; energy and the environment; IPRs; improved regulation; research and innovation; market access; skills; and managing structural change. In July 2007 the Commission presented a generally favourable review of EU industrial policy since 2005, although it identified climate change, globalization and technological development as significant ongoing challenges confronting European businesses.

In order to analyse the EU's performance, the Commission uses a set of performance indicators (evaluating, for example, home internet access, high technology patents, public research and development, ICT expenditure as a proportion of GDP, employment in high-technology manufacturing, etc.) to draw up a so-called European Innovation Scoreboard (EIS). The EIS for 2004 noted that the EU's general innovation performance continued to lag behind that of the USA; the USA led Europe in nine of the 11 comparable indicators. The innovation performance of the EU was found to have been relatively constant since 1996, whereas that of the USA and of Japan had improved, widening the innovation gap. In order to challenge the USA the EU had to address weaknesses in patenting, its less well-qualified work-force and lower levels of expenditure on research and development. The EIS for 2007 observed that significant national variations remained in respect of innovation policy. Sweden, Finland, Denmark, Germany and the United Kingdom were the leading EU member states in terms of innovation, and ahead of the USA. However, the EU as a whole continued to fall behind the USA and Japan in terms of innovation. Three of the countries that joined the EU in 2004, the Czech Republic, Estonia and Lithuania, were expected to reach the EU average for innovation within 10 years.

The European Business Angels Network (EBAN) provides a means of introduction between SMEs and investors and encourages the exchange of expertise. The Commission also promotes inter-industry co-operation between enterprises in the EU and in third countries through the Working Party on Euro-Mediterranean Industrial Co-operation, the TransAtlantic Business Dialogue (TABD), the EU-Japan Centre for Industrial Co-operation, the Mercosur-EU Business Forum (MEBF), the EU-Russia Industrialists' Round Table, the EU-India Business Dialogue and the EU-Israel Business Dialogue.

COMPETITION

The Treaty of Rome establishing the European Economic Community provided for the creation of a common market based on the free movement of goods, persons, services and capital. The EU's competition policy aims to guarantee the unity of this internal market, by providing access to a range of high-quality goods and services, at competitive prices. It seeks to prevent anti-competitive practices by companies or national authorities, and to outlaw monopolization, protective agreements and abuses of dominant positions. Overall, it aims to create a climate favourable to innovation, while protecting the interests of consumers.

The Commission has wide investigative powers in the area of competition policy. It may act on its own initiative, or after a complaint from a member state, firm or individual, or after being notified of agreements or planned state aid. Before taking a decision, the Commission organizes hearings; its decisions can be challenged before the Court of First Instance and the Court of Justice, or in national courts.

State aid—which ranges from discrimination in favour of public enterprises to the granting of aid to private sector companies—is contrary to the principles of competition policy. The EU does not attempt to ban state aid completely, but encourages a reduction in its overall level and works to ensure that all aid granted is compatible with the principles of the common market. The procedural rules on state aid were consolidated and clarified in a regulation in 1999. There are several exemptions, notably regarding the provision of aid to small and medium-sized enterprises (SMEs) and for training. The EU has drawn up 'regional aid maps' designed to concentrate aid in those regions with the most severe development problems. In June the European Commission published a State Aid Action Plan (SAAP) for consultation, in which it outlined proposals for a comprehensive five-year reform of state aid policy focusing on promoting growth and creating jobs. The Commission also aimed to simplify procedures and to accelerate decision-making. The first measures to be implemented under the Plan were adopted in the following month. Notably, state compensation paid to companies with an annual turnover of less than €100m. for the provision of public services no longer had to be notified in advance to the Commission if amounting to less than €30m. per year. Overall, the consultation revealed extensive support for the four pillars for reform envisaged by the SAAP: less and better targeted state aid; a refined economic approach; more effective procedures, better enforcement, higher predictability and enhanced transparency; and shared responsibility between the Commission and member states. Since 2001 the Commission has analysed state aid granted by member states in its State Aid Scoreboard. According to the Scoreboard released in late 2005, the first to include comparable figures for all 25 member states, the total amount of state aid granted in the EU in 2004 was an estimated €61,600m., equivalent to 0.60% of the EU's GDP. According to the Scoreboard published in late 2006, state aid granted by member states in 2005 totalled an estimated €63,800m., equivalent to 0.59% of GDP. The Scoreboard released in late 2007 revealed that state aid granted in the EU in 2006 amounted to an estimated €66,700m., equivalent to 0.58% of GDP. State aid granted to industry and services declined from an average of €53,100m. per year (the equivalent of 0.50% of GDP) in 2001–03 to an average of €47,600m. (0.43% of GDP) in 2004–06. (Aid extended to agriculture, fisheries and transport is excluded from this comparison owing to a change in the method used to collect data for agriculture in 2004.) This downward trend was attributed to a significant decrease in rescue and restucturing aid and a continued reduction in aid granted to the coal sector. Aid awarded for environmental objectives had risen significantly, while aid allocated for all other purposes had remained relatively stable. A particularly marked decline in overall state aid was noted in the 10 countries that had acceded to the EU in 2004.

The Treaty of Rome prohibits agreements and concerted practices between firms resulting in the prevention, restriction or distortion of competition within the common market. This ban applies both to horizontal agreements (between firms at the same stage of the production process) and vertical agreements (between firms at different stages). The type of agreements and practices that are prohibited include: price-fixing; imposing conditions on sale; seeking to isolate market segments; imposing production or delivery quotas; agreements on investments; establishing joint sales offices; market-sharing agreements; creating exclusive collective markets; agreements leading to discrimination against other trading parties; collective boycotting; and voluntary restraints on competitive behaviour. Certain types of co-operation considered to be positive, such as agreements promoting technical and economic progress, may be exempt.

In addition, mergers that would significantly impede competition in the common market are banned. The Commission examines prospective mergers in order to decide whether they are compatible with competition principles. In July 2001 the EU blocked a merger between two US companies for the first time, on the grounds that EU companies would be adversely affected. In December the Commission launched a review of its handling of mergers and acquisitions, focusing on the speed of decisions and on bringing European competition standards in line with those in the USA and elsewhere. A new merger regulation was adopted in January 2004 and came into force in May, introducing some flexibility into the timeframe for investigations into proposed mergers.

The Commission is attempting to abolish monopolies in the networks supplying basic services to member states. In June 2002 the Council adopted a directive on the opening up of postal services. Liberalization has also been pursued in the gas and electricity, telecommunications and transport sectors. In July 2002 the Commission approved a plan to open the car industry to greater competition, by applying new Europe-wide rules for car sales, giving car dealers the freedom to operate anywhere in the EU. The reforms, which were strongly opposed by car manufacturers and by the French and German Governments, came into effect in October 2005. In June the Commission launched inquiries into competition in the electricity and gas markets and in the retail banking and business insurance sectors. In January 2007 the Commission adopted the final report of the inquiry into the gas and electricity markets, concluding that consumers and businesses were disadvantaged by inefficiency and expense. Particular problems that were identified by the final report were high levels of market concentration; vertical integration of supply, generation and infrastructure, leading to a lack of equal access to and insufficient investment in infrastructure; and possible collusion between incumbent operators to share markets. The Commission announced its intention to pursue action in individual cases, within the framework of anti-trust, merger control and state aid regulations, and to act to improve the regulatory framework for energy liberalization. The adoption of the final report was accompanied by the adoption of a comprehensive package of measures to establish a New Energy Policy for Europe, with the aim of combating climate change and boosting energy security and competitiveness within the EU. The final report of the inquiry into the retail banking sector, published in January 2007, indicated a number of concerns in the markets for payment cards, payments systems and retail banking products. In particular, the report noted that there were large variations in merchant and interchange fees for payment cards, barriers to entry into the markets for payment systems and credit registers, impediments to customer mobility and product tying. In response to these findings, the Commission announced that it would use its powers, within the framework of competition regulations and in close collaboration with national authorities, to combat serious abuses. The final report of the inquiry into the business insurance sector, published in September, raised concerns about the widespread practice of premium alignment in the reinsurance and coinsurance markets when more than one insurer is involved in covering a single risk and about lack of transparency in the remuneration of insurance brokers, as well as the risk of conflicts of interest jeopardizing the objectivity of brokers' advice to their clients.

In February 2006, in a first reading, the European Parliament adopted a draft directive aimed at opening up the services sector to cross-border competition. The directive had proved controversial, with opponents fearing it would lead to lower wages, lower standards of social and environmental protection and an influx of foreign workers. The Parliament notably amended the directive so that a company offering services in another country would be governed by the rules and regulations of the country in which the service was being provided (rather than those of the company's home country, as the Commission had favoured). The Parliament excluded a number of areas from the future directive's scope, including broadcasting, audiovisual services, legal services, social services, gambling and public health, and also agreed a list of legitimate reasons that a country could cite for restricting the activities of foreign service providers, such as national security, public health and environmental protection. Those in favour of the directive claimed that it had been severely weakened by the Parliament. In December, having been approved by the Parliament at its second reading earlier in that month, the directive was adopted by the Parliament and the Council of the European Union and entered into force.

In 2003 the Commission worked to establish detailed provisions for a modernized framework for anti-trust and merger control in advance of the enlargement of the EU in May 2004. In that month major changes to EU competition law and policy (including substantive and procedural reform of the European Community Merger Regulation) entered into force. As part of the reforms, national competition authorities, acting as a network, and national courts were expected to become much more involved in the enforcement of competition rules, and companies were to be required to conduct more self-assessment of their commercial activities. In March the US Department of Justice had criticized the EU's anti-trust action against the US computer software company Microsoft. The European Commission imposed a fine of €497m. and instructed the company to disclose key elements of its programming (within 120 days) to facilitate the development of competitive products. Microsoft appealed against the decision in the Court of First Instance in Luxembourg in June and the EU penalties were temporarily suspended. In December, however, the court rejected Microsoft's appeal to delay the implementation of the EU sanctions pending the final outcome of the company's main appeal against the Commission's anti-trust decision. Microsoft lodged a further appeal with the Court of First Instance in September 2005, against the Commission's decision to force the company to reveal details of its server programmes. A further appeal by Microsoft against the 2004 ruling was heard at the Court of First Instance in April 2006. In July the Commission imposed a fine of €280.5m. on Microsoft, and threatened to impose heavier penalties on the company in future, for its failure to comply with the EU's demand that it should provide complete and accurate information to permit interoperability between its Windows operating system and rivals' work-group servers. The Commission was also legally entitled to impose a further daily fine of €0.5m., backdated to December 2005, on the company if the royalty fees it charged for the use of its technical information were found to be excessive. Microsoft indicated that it would launch a further legal appeal in response to the latest fine. In March 2007 the Commission communicated a statement of objection to Microsoft, stating its preliminary view that there was no significant innovation in submissions made by the company from December 2005 in respect of compliance with the Commission's anti-trust action of March 2004, and that the royalty fees proposed were therefore unreasonable. Microsoft replied to the statement of objection in the following month. In September 2007 the Court of First Instance rejected Microsoft's appeal against the 2004 anti-trust decision. Microsoft announced in October that it would accept the Court's ruling and comply with the Commission's demands. In October 2004 the USA initiated dispute procedures at the WTO in protest at alleged massive state subsidies to the civil aircraft manufacturer Airbus. However, the EU took retaliatory action regarding state subsidies to the US aircraft manufacturer Boeing. An attempt, from January 2005, to settle the dispute through bilateral talks failed, and both sides renewed their cases at the WTO in May. In July the WTO agreed to establish two panels to examine the complaints of the USA and the EU; members of the panels were appointed in October. In November 2006 the US case against Airbus was formally presented; hearings on this case were held in March and July 2007. The case of the EU against Boeing was presented in March 2007, and a first hearing took place in September.

The international affairs unit of the Directorate-General for Competition co-operates with foreign competition authorities and promotes competition instruments in applicant countries, where it also provides technical assistance. The unit works within the framework of international organizations such as the WTO, the Organisation for Economic Co-operation and Development (OECD) and the United Nations Conference on Trade and Development (UNCTAD). Dedicated co-operation agreements on competition policy have been signed with the USA, Canada and Japan, while other forms of bilateral co-operation on competition issues exist with a number of other countries and regions. In addition, in 2001 the European Commission was a founding member of the International Competition Network, an informal forum for competition authorities from around the world.

TELECOMMUNICATIONS, INFORMATION TECHNOLOGY AND BROADCASTING

In 1990 proposals were adopted by the European Council on the co-ordinated introduction of a European public paging system and of cellular digital land-based mobile communications. In 1991 the Council adopted a directive requiring member states to liberalize their rules on the supply of telecommunications terminal equipment, thus ending the monopolies of national telecommunications authorities. In the same year, the Council adopted a plan for the gradual introduction of a competitive market in satellite communications; a directive relating to the liberalization of satellite telecommunications equipment and services came into force in late 1994, but allowed for deferment until 1 January 1996. In October 1995 the Commission adopted a directive liberalizing the use of cable telecommunications, requiring member states to permit a wide range of services, in addition to television broadcasts, on such networks. The EU market for mobile telephone networks was opened to full competition as a result of a directive adopted by the Commission in January 1996, according to which member states were to abolish all exclusive and special rights in this area, and establish open and fair licensing procedures for digital services. The telecommunications market was to be fully deregulated by 1998, although extensions to the deregulation schedule were agreed for a number of member states. In October 1997 the Commission announced plans to commence legal proceedings against those member states that had not yet adopted the legislation necessary to permit the liberalization of the telecommunications market. Spain agreed to bring forward the full deregulation of its telecommunications market from January 2003 to 1998, which meant that all the major EU telecommunications markets were, in principle, open to competition from 1998.

In July 1998 the Commission identified 14 cases of unfair pricing after commencing an investigation into the charges imposed by telecommunications companies for interconnection between fixed and mobile telephone networks. In December the Commission suspended some of its investigations, after a number of companies introduced price reductions. In February 2000 the Commission requested that national competition authorities, telecommunications regulators, mobile network operators and service providers give information on conditions and price structures for national and international mobile services. In response to concerns regarding the high cost for EU citizens of using a mobile telephone when travelling in another EU country, a new regulation fixing a maximum rate for such charges was adopted and entered into force in June 2007. In order to enhance the transparency of retail prices, mobile telephony providers were also required to inform their customers of the charges applicable to them when making and receiving calls in another member state. A study carried out by national telecom regulators in collaboration with the European Commission, which was released in October, indicated that charges for those using a mobile telephone abroad had been reduced by up to 60% as a result of the new 'Eurotariff'.

In July 2000 a comprehensive reform of the regulatory framework for telecommunications—the so-called 'telecoms package'—was launched. The reform aimed to update EU regulations to take account of changes in the telecommunications, media and information technology (IT) sectors. Noting the continuing convergence of these sectors, the Commission aimed to develop a single regulatory framework for all transmission networks and associated services, in order to exploit the full potential for growth, competition and job creation. The Commission recommended, as a priority, the introduction of a regulation on unbundled access to the local loop (the final connection of telephone wires into the home). The lack of competition in this part of the network was considered a significant obstacle to the widespread provision of low-cost internet access. The regulation obliged incumbent operators to permit shared and full access to the local loop by the end of 2000. In December 2001 the European Parliament voted to adopt a compromise telecoms package. This gave the Commission powers to oversee national regulatory regimes and, in some cases, to overrule national regulatory authorities. It was designed to reduce the dominant market position of monopolies and to open the market to competition. The package included a framework directive and three specific directives (covering issues of authorization, access and interconnection, universal service and users' rights) and measures to ensure harmonized conditions in radio spectrum policy. By the end of 2003 the EU regulatory framework for electronic communications had been completely implemented; during subsequent years, however, the Commission initiated legal proceedings against a number of member states for either their failure fully to transpose the new rules of competition in their national laws or for incorrect implementation of the framework. A report published by the Commission in December 2004 stated that broadband and mobile telephone services in the newly enlarged EU were benefiting from intensifying competition and strong growth. In November 2007 the Commission adopted proposals for a reform of the EU's telecommunications rules, with the aim of strengthening consumer rights; giving consumers more choice by reinforcing competition between operators; promoting investment in new communication infrastructures, notably by freeing radio spectrum for wireless broadband services; and making communication networks more reliable and more secure, for example by introducing new measures to combat unsolicited e-mail, viruses, etc. To improve regulation and to reinforce co-operation between national telecommunications regulators in an attempt to facilitate the creation of pan-European services, the Commission advocated the establishment of a European Telecom Market Authority, which would combine the functions of the European Regulators Group (comprising the national regulators of the member states) and the European Network and Information Security Agency (ENISA—see below).

The EU is undertaking efforts to make the internet more user-friendly, with targeted online services, technical support and IT training. At the European Council meeting held in January 2000 the Commission agreed to put all remaining e-commerce legislation in place by the end of the year. In December the Commission's programme on European digital content was adopted. Recognizing that a large proportion of the content on the internet originated in the USA, this sought to develop the regional potential in this area. During 2002 the European Council approved a new eEurope 2005 action plan, following on from the earlier eEurope 2002 plan. The new plan aimed to create a dynamic electronic business environment (eBusiness) favourable to private investment and job creation, to modernize—in electronic terms—public services (notably government—eGovernment, hospitals—eHealth and schools—eLearning) and to give everyone the opportunity to participate in the global information society. Particular emphasis was placed on the widespread availability and use of broadband networks (at competitive prices) by 2005. Some success was achieved in this area, and by July 2005 there were 48.4m. subscribers to broadband services in the EU (equivalent to 10.6% of the population), an increase of 60% over the previous year. (By July 2007 the number of broadband subscribers was estimated to have risen to 90.2m.) A new initiative, entitled i2010, was adopted by the European Commission in June 2005 to replace the eEurope 2005 plan, which expired at the end of the year. The three main focuses of the new plan were the promotion of a borderless European 'information space' with the aim of establishing an internal market for electronic communications and digital services; the stimulation of innovation through investment in research and the encouragement of industrial application; and the continuation of the policy of making the EU information society as inclusive and accessible as possible. The '.eu' top-level domain name, aimed at giving individuals, organizations and companies the option of having a pan-European identity for their internet presence, was launched in December 2005, when registration commenced for applicants with prior rights, such as trademark holders and public bodies; registration was open to all from April 2006. By late 2007 2.6m. '.eu' domain names had been registered. More than 90% of all providers of public services in the EU had an internet presence by late 2007.

Information and communication technologies (ICT) was one of the main themes of the co-operation programme of the Seventh Framework Programme for research, technological development and demonstration activities (FP7, covering 2007–13)—see Research and Innovation. The development of ICT was allocated €9,050m. in the budget for 2007–13. Aims included strengthening Europe's scientific and technology base in ICTs; stimulating innovation through ICT use; and ensuring that progress in ICTs is rapidly transformed into benefits for citizens, businesses, industry and governments. The Interchange of Data between Administrations (IDA) initiative supported the rapid electronic exchange of information between EU administrations—in January 2005 the IDA was renamed the Interoperable Delivery of pan-European eGovernment Services to Public Administrations, Businesses and Citizens (IDAbc) programme. An action plan promoting safer use of the internet, extended in March 2002 until December 2004, aimed to combat illegal and harmful content on global networks. In December 2004 the EU approved a new programme, called Safer Internet plus (2005–08), to promote safer use of the internet and new online technologies and to combat illegal and harmful content (particularly child pornography and violent and racist material).

In 1992 a White Paper proposed the establishment of trans-European networks (TENs) in telecommunications, energy and transport, in order to improve infrastructure and assist in the development of the common market. Following the liberalization of the telecommunications market in 1998, efforts in this area were concentrated on support (through the eTEN programme) for the development of broadband networks and multimedia applications. The eTen programme, which expired in 2006, focused strongly on public services and its objectives were based on the EU's stated aim of 'an information society for all'. The ICT Policy Support Programme (ICT PSP), part of the wider Competitiveness and Innovation Framework Programme (CIP, covering 2007–13), was designed to build on the former eTEN programme by stimulating innovation and competitiveness through the wider uptake and best use of ICT by citizens, governments and businesses. A budget of €728m. was allocated to the ICT PSP for 2007–13.

In October 2003 new digital privacy legislation aimed at combating unwanted commercial e-mails (known collectively as 'spam') came into force across the EU. The new rules required companies to gain consent before sending e-mails and introduced a ban on the use of 'spam' throughout the EU. The Commission claimed that unwanted e-mails cost European business almost US $3,000m. in lost productivity in 2002 and accounted for more than one-half of all e-mail traffic. It was widely recognized, however, that concerted international action was required, since most of the 'spam' entering Europe originated from abroad (particularly from the USA). None the less, in February 2005 13 European countries agreed to share information and pursue complaints across borders in an effort to combat unsolicited e-mails. A European Network and Information Security Agency (ENISA) became fully operational in October 2004. The main aims of the Agency, which is based in Heraklion, Greece, are to promote closer European co-ordination on information security and to provide assistance in the application of EU measures in this field.

In 1991 a controversial directive ('Television without Frontiers') came into force, establishing minimum standards for television programmes to be broadcast freely throughout the Community: limits were placed on the amount of time devoted to advertisements, a majority of programmes broadcast were to be from the Community, where practicable, and governments were allowed to forbid the transmission of programmes considered morally harmful. In November 2002 the Commission adopted a communication on the promotion and distribution of television programmes. In July 2003 the Commission reiterated proposals (originally presented at the Lisbon summit in March 2000) to help film and audiovisual production companies to have access to external funding from banks and other financial institutions by covering some of the costs of the guarantees demanded by these institutions and/or part of the cost of a loan ('discount contract loan') for financing the production of their works. In May 2005 the Commission urged EU member states to accelerate the changeover from analogue to digital broadcasting, setting a target of 2012 for shutting down analogue services. Digital television offers better picture quality, sound and reception than analogue, as well as more channels and information services, and also uses spectrum more efficiently, thus freeing up capacity for other uses, such as new services combining broadcasting and mobile telephony. In December 2005 the Commission proposed a modernization of the 'Television without Frontiers' directive in view of rapid technological and market developments in the audiovisual sector. A reduction in the regulatory burden on providers of television and similar services was envisaged, as well as the introduction of more flexible rules on advertising. National rules on protection of minors, against incitement to hatred and against surreptitious advertising would be replaced with an EU-wide minimum standard of protection. The proposals distinguished between so-called 'linear' services (e.g. scheduled broadcasting via traditional television, the internet or mobile cellular telephones) and 'non-linear' services, such as on-demand films or news, which would be subject only to a basic set of minimum principles. The modernized 'Television without Frontiers' directive, renamed the 'Audiovisual Media Services without Frontiers' directive, was adopted by the European Parliament in a second reading in November 2007, having been approved by the Council in October. The legislation was to be implemented by member states by the end of 2009. In July 2007 the Commission adopted a strategy urging member states and industry to facilitate and accelerate the introduction of mobile television (the transmission of traditional and on-demand audiovisual content to a mobile device), encouraging the use of DVB-H (Digital Video Broadcasting for Handhelds) technology as the single European standard. This strategy was endorsed by the Council in November.

The 'Media' programme was introduced in 1991 to provide financial support to the television and film industry. 'Media III' (2001–05), which aimed to strengthen further the competitiveness of the European audiovisual industry through pre- and post-production support, incorporated two major initiatives—Media Plus, which, while taking account of the new regulatory environment, aimed to encourage the development, distribution and marketing of European audiovisual material; and Media Training, which basically involved the implementation of a training programme for professionals working in the audiovisual industry. During 2002 the scope of the Media programme was extended to include nine candidate countries, and in 2004 the programme was extended until the end of 2006. In July 2004 the Commission presented its proposals for a successor programme, Media 2007, which would run from 2007 until 2013. In November 2006 Media 2007 was formally adopted by the European Parliament and the Council, with a budget of €755m. The programme was characterized by a radical rethink of its priorities and structure in response to the consequences for the European audiovisual market of the digital revolution and the enlargement of the EU. Media 2007's principal objectives were: to preserve and enhance European cultural diversity and its cinematographic and audiovisual heritage, and to guarantee Europeans' access to it and foster intercultural dialogue; to increase the circulation of European audiovisual works both within and outside the EU; and to reinforce the competitiveness of the European audiovisual sector within the framework of an open and competitive market.

TRANSPORT

The establishment of a common transport policy is stipulated in the Treaty of Rome, with the aim of gradually standardizing the national regulations that hinder the free movement of traffic within the Community, such as the varying safety and licensing rules, diverse restrictions on the size of lorries, and frontier-crossing formalities. A White Paper in 1992 set out a common transport policy for the EU. The paper proposed the establishment of trans-European networks (TENs) to improve transport, telecommunications and energy infrastructure throughout the Community, as well as the integration of transport systems and measures to protect the environment and improve safety. Significant progress has been made on the trans-European transport network (TEN-T), through harmonization and liberalization; however, it must be noted that work has not advanced as rapidly as expected (owing partly to deficiencies in funding resources and partly to the complexities arising from the 2004 enlargement). The overall aim of the EU's TEN-T policy, which included so-called intelligent transport systems and services, was to unite the various national networks into a single European network, by eliminating bottlenecks and adding missing links. The 2000–06 budget for the 14 priority TEN-T projects totalled €4,600m., funded in part by the European Regional Development Fund, the European Investment Bank and the European Investment Fund. In addition, efforts are being made to increase private sector involvement in financing TEN-T, through the development of public-private partnerships (PPPs). The majority of the financial backing, however, is provided by individual member states. As a result of the accession of 10 new member states in 2004, a further 16 TEN-T projects were identified as being priorities for the enlarged Union. The Commission estimated that these projects, together with the 14 adopted earlier, would require investment of €225,000m. for completion by 2020, of which around €140,000m. would be required in 2007–13. The Commission proposed a trans-European network budget of €20,000m. for 2007–13 and the establishment of a Trans-European Transport Network Executive Agency to manage the priority projects. The total cost of completing the TEN-T was estimated at €600,000m. In July 2005 the Commission nominated six co-ordinators to facilitate dialogue between member states on transnational TEN-T projects in an attempt to accelerate their completion. Member states subsequently rejected the Commission's proposed trans-European network budget of €20,000m. in favour of one totalling only €8,000m. The Trans-European Transport Network Executive Agency was established in November 2006, and from 2007 was to manage an annual budget of some €1,000m. In March 2007 the Commission presented a communication on the development of an integrated approach to the three TENs. It was anticipated that the interconnection of the networks, for example by constructing combined infrastructures, would reduce both their cost and their environmental impact.

In recent years the EU has focused on integrating environmental issues and questions of sustainable development into transport policy. In September 2001 the Commission adopted a White Paper on Transport Policy for 2010. This set out a framework designed to accommodate the forecast strong growth in demand for transport on a sustainable basis. The new policy aimed to shift the balance between modes of transport by 2010, by revitalizing railways, promoting maritime and inland waterway transport systems, and by linking up different kinds of transport. The paper proposed an action plan and a strategy designed gradually to break the link between economic and transport growth, with the aim of reducing pressure on the environment and relieving congestion. It was estimated that the completion of TEN-T would reduce transport-generated carbon dioxide emissions by 6.3m. metric tons per year by 2020.

In 1986 transport ministers agreed on a system of Community-wide permits for commercial vehicles, to facilitate the crossing of frontiers, and in 1993 they agreed on measures concerning road haulage. A common tax system for trucks using EC roads led to the full liberalization of road 'cabotage' (whereby road hauliers may provide services in the domestic market of another member state) by July 1998. In May 1998 transport ministers approved legislation compelling member governments to clear serious obstructions, such as truck blockades, that hinder the free movement of goods. The White Paper on Transport Policy adopted in September 2001 proposed the harmonization of petrol taxes across the EU.

In 1991 directives were adopted by the Council on the compulsory use of safety belts in vehicles weighing less than 3.5 metric tons. Further regulations applying to minibuses and coaches were introduced in 1996. In June 2000 the Commission issued a communication setting out measures to improve the safety and efficiency of road transport and to ensure fair competition. These included road traffic monitoring, the regulation of employed drivers' working time, and regularity of employment conditions. In November 2002 the European Parliament adopted a directive on speed limitation devices for certain categories of motor vehicles, including haulage vehicles and passenger vehicles carrying more than eight passengers. In March 2006 the European Parliament and Council adopted a regulation reducing maximum driving times and increasing obligatory rest periods for professional drivers and a directive increasing the number of checks on lorries; the new legislation entered into force in April 2007. In May the Commission proposed three regulations aimed at reforming the rules governing admission to the occupation of road transport operator and access to the road transport market. The Commission adopted a consultation document on urban transport in September.

In the late 1980s ministers of transport approved measures to contribute to the liberalization of air transport within the Community. In 1990 ministers agreed to make further reductions in guaranteed quotas for a country's airlines on routes to another country, and to liberalize air cargo services. In 1992 they approved an 'open-skies' arrangement that would allow any EC airline to operate domestic flights within another member state (with effect from 1 April 1997). In November 2002 the European Court of Justice ruled that bilateral 'open-skies' treaties, or Air Services Agreements (ASAs), between countries were illegal if they discriminated against airlines from other member states; the ruling was in response to a case brought by the Commission against eight member states that had concluded such agreements with the USA. In response to the ruling, in June 2003 the Commission and member states identified two ways of resolving the issues raised by the Court's ruling: either bilateral negotiations between each member state concerned and its partners, amending each bilateral ASA separately, or single 'horizontal' agreements negotiated by the Commission on behalf of the member states. Each horizontal agreement aims to amend the relevant provisions of all existing bilateral ASAs in the context of a single negotiation with one third country. By May 2006 separate bilateral negotiations had led to changes with 39 partner states, representing the correction of 69 bilateral agreements, while by December 2007 horizontal negotiations had led to changes with 32 partner states. In 2004–05 the Commission initiated infringement proceedings against a number of member states that were persisting in maintaining discriminatory bilateral air agreements with the USA. At the same time the Commission was conducting negotiations with the USA in an attempt to conclude an overall 'open-skies' agreement, under which a common aviation area would be created. In November 2005 a preliminary agreement was concluded with the USA, and in early March 2007 EU and US negotiators concluded a draft accord. The EU-US aviation agreement, encompassing some 60% of global air traffic, was approved by EU transport ministers later in March and formally signed in April. In March 2005 the Commission requested mandates from the Council to negotiate air transport agreements with both the People's Republic of China and Russia. An EU-China aviation summit, intended to enhance co-operation in the sector, was held in the Chinese capital, Beijing, in mid-2005, and in December negotiations on an EU-China 'horizontal agreement', undertaken with the aim of restoring legal certainty to bilateral air services agreements, were initiated. In November 2006 the EU and Russia concluded an agreement on Siberian overflight payments, which had been disputed by the two sides for some 20 years. Prior to the agreement, which was approved by EU transport ministers in March 2007 and was regarded as an important measure towards the normalization of EU-Russian relations in the sphere of aviation, EU airlines had been obliged to pay royalties to the Russian airline Aeroflot in exchange for the right to fly over Russian territory *en route* to Japan, China and the Republic of Korea. In December 2005 the Commission completed negotiations with eight South-East European partners, Norway and Iceland on the creation of a European Common Aviation Area (ECAA), which would entail the harmonization of standards and regulations on safety, security, competition policy, social policy and consumer rights, as well as the establishment of a single market for aviation; the political agreement on the creation of the ECAA was signed in June 2006. In December the EU and Morocco concluded an innovative aviation agreement that, in addition to replacing all of the bilateral agreements between member states and Morocco, included a number of fundamental market regulation objectives. Notably, unlike conventional 'open-skies' agreements, the accord with Morocco allowed for cross-investment between European and Moroccan companies. In November 2007 the EU initiated negotiations with Canada on a comprehensive aviation agreement; the Commission has also proposed a separate agreement to align all existing bilateral agreements between EU member states and Canada with EU legislation. Also in November the Commission adopted a communication on developing a common aviation area with Israel and requested a mandate from the Council to negotiate a comprehensive aviation agreement with that country. Talks on the creation of a common aviation area with Ukraine commenced in the following month. The Commission was also seeking to enhance co-operation on aviation issues with Australia, Chile, India and New Zealand.

In July 1994, despite EU recommendations for tighter controls on subsidies awarded to airlines, as part of efforts to increase competitiveness within the industry, the Commission approved substantial subsidies that had been granted by the French and Greek governments to their respective national airlines. Subsequently, the Commission specified that state assistance could be granted to airlines 'in exceptional, unforeseen circumstances, outside the control of the company'. Following the terrorist attacks perpetrated against targets in the USA in September 2001, and the consequent difficulties suffered by the air transport sector, the EU ruled that a degree of aid or compensation was permissible, but stressed that this must not lead to distortion of competition. In 2005 the Commission authorized state aid to be granted for the restructuring of the national airlines of Cyprus and Italy, but declared that aid granted by the Greek Government to Olympic Airways and Olympic Airlines since December 2002 had been illegal. In April 2006 the Commission sent a reasoned opinion to the Greek authorities for failure to recover €161m. of state aid granted to Olympic Airways between 1998 and 2002, which the European Court of Justice had ruled to be illegal, and decided to refer Greece to the Court for failure to quantify and recover all the unlawfully granted aid to Olympic Airways and Olympic Airlines since December 2002. In December 2007 the Commission also initiated a formal investigation into financial transfers made to Olympic Airways Services and Olympic Airlines since 2005. Meanwhile, in March 2007, following a year-long investigation, the Commission concluded that a restructuring plan for Cyprus Airways was compatible with European law, while several investigations were launched that year into potential state aid granted to airlines using various German, Finnish and Italian airports.

In early 1999 a dispute arose between the EU and the USA over the introduction of new EU legislation to curb aircraft noise. Initially, the EU proposed to prevent aircraft fitted with 'hush kits' from flying in the EU after 1 April 2002 unless they were already operating there before 1 April 1999 (aircraft fitted with hush kits create more noise than newer aircraft, use more fuel and cause more pollution). The legislation was subsequently amended to avert the threat of a temporary boycott of some European flights by the US authorities, and a new directive on the use of a 'balanced approach' to noise management around airports was adopted in March 2002.

In July 2002 the European Parliament adopted a regulation creating a European Aviation Safety Agency (EASA). The EASA (which officially opened its permanent seat in Köln, Germany, in December 2004) was to cover all aircraft registered in member states, unless agreed otherwise. The Commission has also formulated ground rules for inquiries into civil air incidents and has issued proposals for assessing the safety of aircraft registered outside the EU. In October 2001 the Commission proposed establishing common rules in the field of civil aviation security, to strengthen public confidence in air transport following the terrorist attacks on the USA. Issues addressed included securing cockpits, improving airground communications and using video cameras in aircraft. Member states also agreed to incorporate into Community law co-operation arrangements on security measures. These measures covered control of access to sensitive areas of airports and aircraft, control of passengers and hand luggage, control and monitoring of hold luggage, and training of ground staff. In October 2006 the Commission adopted a regulation restricting the liquids that air passengers were allowed to carry beyond certain screening points at airports and onto aircraft. The new regulation, introduced in response to the threat posed to civil aviation security by home-made liquid explosives, was to be applied to all flights departing from member states' airports. In November 2005 the Commission adopted a proposal to extend the responsibilities of the EASA, notably concerning control over pilots' licences and the regulation of airlines based in third countries operating in the EU; the Commission's proposal was still under consideration in early 2008. In December 2005 EU transport ministers approved a regulation introducing a Europe-wide 'blacklist' of unsafe airlines and granting passengers the right to advance information about the identity of the air carrier operating their flight.

In December 1999 the Commission presented a communication on streamlining air traffic control to create a Single European Sky, of which the overall aim was to restructure the EU's airspace on the basis of traffic, rather than national frontiers. In December 2002 EU transport ministers agreed on a package of measures under which the separate European air traffic control providers would be regulated as a single entity, and EU airspace over 28,500 ft (approximately 8,690 m) would be under unified control. In November 2005 the European Commission launched SESAR, a Single European Sky industrial and technological programme to develop a new air traffic management system. The project consisted of three phases: the definition phase (2005–07), costing €60m. (co-funded by the Commission and the European Organisation for the Safety of Air Navigation—EUROCONTROL); the development phase (2008–13), estimated to cost around €300m. per year (co-funded by the Commission, EUROCONTROL and the industry); and the deployment phase (2014–20), to be financed by the industry. Partner states were to be invited to join the SESAR Joint Undertaking, a public-private entity that was to be established to manage the development stage of the project. A regulation creating the SESAR Joint Undertaking was formally approved by the Council and Parliament in February 2007. Meanwhile, in April 2006 a directive was adopted on the introduction of a Community air traffic controller licence, with the aim of raising safety standards and improving the operation of the air traffic control system.

In 1986 progress was made towards the establishment of a common maritime transport policy, with the adoption of regulations on unfair pricing practices, safeguard of access to cargoes, application of competition rules and the eventual elimination of unilateral cargo reservation and discriminatory cargo-sharing arrangements. In December 1990 the Council approved, in principle, the freedom for shipping companies to provide maritime transport anywhere within the Community. Cabotage by sea began to be introduced from January 1993 and was virtually complete by January 1999. Cabotage was also introduced in the inland waterways transport sector in 1993. By January 2000 the inland waterways market had been liberalized, although obstacles to the functioning of the single market subsequently persisted, including differing technical regulations among member states. In March 2005 the European Commission launched a consultation process on a new integrated EU maritime policy aimed at developing the potential of the maritime economy in an environmentally sustainable manner. The commissioners responsible for sea-related policies were charged with preparing a consultation paper addressing all economic and recreational maritime activities, such as shipping, fishing, oil and gas extraction, use of wind and tidal power, shipbuilding, tourism and marine research. The resultant Green Paper was adopted by the Commission in June 2006. Following the conclusion of a consultation process based on the document, in October 2007 the Commission presented a communication on its vision for the integrated maritime policy, which was endorsed by the Council in December. An accompanying action plan included initiatives such as a European strategy for marine research; national integrated maritime policies; an integrated network for maritime surveillance; a European marine observation and data network; and a strategy to mitigate the effects of climate change on coastal regions.

In March 2000 the Commission adopted a communication on the safety of the seaborne oil trade. It proposed the introduction of a first package of short-term measures to strengthen controls, including the right to refuse access to substandard ships, more stringent inspections and a generalization of the ban on single-hull oil tankers. In May the Commission adopted a proposal to harmonize procedures between bulk carriers and terminals, in order to reduce the risk of accidents caused by incorrect loading and unloading. In the same month the Commission signed a memorandum of understanding with several countries on the establishment of the Equasis database, intended to provide information on the safety and quality of ships. In December the Commission set out a second package of safety measures, broad agreement was reached on the first package, and the EU agreed to accelerate the gradual introduction of double-hull tankers (single-hull tankers were to be completely phased out by 2010). In June 2002 the European Parliament established by regulation the European Maritime Safety Agency (the permanent seat of which was to be located in Lisbon, Portugal); its tasks were to include preparing legislation in the field of maritime safety, co-ordination of investigations following accidents at sea, assisting member states in implementing maritime safety measures, and providing assistance to candidate countries. In March 2004 the Agency was given additional responsibility for combating pollution caused by ships. In November 2005 the Commission proposed a third package of maritime safety measures, including a requirement that member states ensure that ships flying their flags comply with international standards; an improvement in the quality and effectiveness of ship inspections, with increased targeting of vessels deemed to pose the greatest risk and less frequent inspections of high-quality ships; and an obligation that member states designate an independent authority responsible for the prior identification of places of refuge for ships in distress. The Commission noted that the EU had become a major maritime power, accounting for some 25% of the world's fleet, particularly with the accession of Malta and Cyprus.

In April 1998 the Commission published a report on railway policy, with the aim of achieving greater harmonization, the regulation of state subsidies and the progressive liberalization of the rail-freight market. In October 1999 EU transport ministers concluded an agreement that was regarded as a precursor to the full liberalization and revitalization of the rail-freight market. Rail transport's share of the total freight market had declined substantially since the 1970s, but it was widely recognized that, in terms of environmental protection and safety, transport of freight by rail was greatly preferable to road haulage. The agreement provided for the extension of access to a planned core Trans-European Rail Freight Network (TERFN, covering some 50,000 km), with a charging system designed to ensure optimum competitiveness. During 2000–04 the EU adopted three 'railway packages', which dealt with the progressive deregulation of the rail market. However, a number of EU member states vehemently opposed granting full access to their national railway networks. Other measures incorporated in the packages included developing a common approach to rail safety; upholding principles of interoperability; and setting up a European Railway Agency (ERA). The ERA was established by a regulation of the European Parliament in April 2004. The main aim of the Agency, the permanent seat of which was inaugurated in Lille/Valenciennes, France, in June 2005, was to reinforce the safety and interoperability of railways in the EU. In March 2005 the European Commission and representatives of the rail industry signed a memorandum of understanding on the deployment of a European Rail Traffic Management System (ERTMS) on a major part of the European network. The ERTMS, a single European rail signalling system, was intended to enhance safety and reduce infrastructure costs in the longer term; existing national systems were to be gradually withdrawn within 10–12 years. In December 2006 the Commission presented a communication proposing measures to remove technical and operational barriers to international rail activities, with the aim of making the rail industry more competitive, particularly in relation to road and air transport; the simplification of procedures for the approval of locomotives for operational service across the EU; and the extension of the powers of the ERA.

The Marco Polo programme (2003–06), which succeeded the earlier PACT (pilot action for combined transport) scheme, aimed to reduce road congestion and to improve the environmental performance of the freight transport system within the Community and to enhance intermodality, thereby contributing to an efficient and sustainable transport system. To achieve this objective, the programme supported actions in the freight transport, logistics and other relevant markets. These actions were aimed at maintaining the distribution of freight between various modes of transport at 1998 levels by helping to shift the expected aggregate increase in road freight traffic to short sea shipping, rail and inland waterways or to a combination of modes of transport in which road journeys were as short as possible. The programme, which had a budget of €100m., was also supported by non-EU countries such as Norway, Iceland and Liechtenstein. In October 2006 the European Parliament and the Council adopted a regulation providing for the establishment of a significantly expanded Marco Polo II programme, which would run from 2007–13. The budget for Marco Polo II was fixed at €400m. and the scope of the programme was extended to countries bordering the EU.

A directive adopted in April 2004 aimed to establish an electronic toll collection system across the EU that would apply to roads, tunnels, bridges, ferries and urban congestion-charging schemes. Notably, all new electronic toll systems brought into service from 1 January 2007 were required to use at least one of three prescribed existing technologies.

JUSTICE, FREEDOM AND SECURITY

Under the Treaty on European Union, EU member states undertook to co-operate in the areas of justice and home affairs, particularly in relation to the free movement of people between member states. Issues of common interest were defined as asylum policy; border controls; immigration; drug addiction; fraud; judicial co-operation in civil and criminal matters; customs co-operation; and police co-operation for the purposes of combating terrorism, drugs-trafficking and other serious forms of international crime. In view of the sensitivity of many of the issues involved in this sphere, the EU affords great weight to the positions and opinions of individual states. There tends to be a greater degree of flexibility than in other areas, and requirements are frequently less stringent.

In November 2004 the EU agreed an ambitious five-year programme, known as the Hague programme, which was aimed at making the EU an area of common 'freedom, justice and security'. The programme incorporated many new policies, including a common European asylum system, a common repatriation policy for illegal immigrants, an EU diplomatic corps, common issuing of visas, harmonization of divorce and family laws to help to settle cross-border disputes, mutual recognition of court judgments, complete sharing of police information, and a European criminal record. In May 2005 the Commission presented an action plan for implementing the Hague programme, identifying 10 specific priorities: (i) ensuring the development of policies enhancing citizenship and promoting respect for fundamental rights; (ii) strengthening member states' capabilities to combat terrorism; (iii) developing a common immigration policy; (iv) developing an integrated approach to the management of external borders and a common visa policy; (v) establishing a common asylum area; (vi) adopting measures to help member states improve their policies on the integration of migrants; (vii) balancing privacy and security in the sharing of information among law enforcement and judicial authorities; (viii) developing a strategy to tackle organized crime at EU level; (ix) ensuring effective access to justice and the enforcement of judgments; and (x) giving meaning to notions of shared responsibility and solidarity between member states in efforts to meet the objectives of freedom, justice and security. In June 2006 the Commission published its first political assessment of progress made in the implementation of the Hague programme. The assessment concluded that, in respect of the inter-institutional adoption process, the level of achievement in 2005 had been satisfactory and that most of the actions due in that year as part of the Hague action plan had either been, or were in the process of being, achieved. However, among other areas of concern, the Commission noted that the principle of unanimous voting, when applicable, had delayed the adoption of Hague programme priority measures, one example being the common asylum area. The adoption process in police and criminal justice matters remained especially problematic, unanimous voting having retarded the adoption of key measures, such as the European evidence warrant and the framework decision on 'procedural rights' in criminal proceedings. A second assessment, published in July 2007, reiterated many of the concerns expressed in the first report and indicated that less had been accomplished during 2006 (with only 53% of planned measures achieved) than in 2005 (just over 65%). This was largely attributed to continued slow progress in the areas of police co-operation, prevention of organized crime and judicial co-operation in criminal matters, with, for example, the Council still unable to reach a consensus on the framework decision on 'procedural rights'. In addition, the Commission criticized delays by member states in the implementation of previously agreed initiatives. None the less, satisfactory progress was recorded in areas such as fundamental rights, citizenship, civil justice, the European strategy on drugs, asylum and migration, visa and border policies, and counter-terrorism.

A European Police Office (Europol), facilitating the exchange of information between police forces, operates from The Hague, Netherlands. A special Europol unit dealing with the trafficking of illicit drugs and nuclear and radioactive materials began work in 1994. Europol's mandate has been extended to cover illegal immigrants, stolen vehicles, paedophilia and terrorist activities, money-laundering and counterfeiting of the euro and other means of payment.

The EU convention on extradition, signed by ministers of justice in September 1996 prior to ratification by national governments, simplified and accelerated procedures in this area, reduced the number of cases where extradition could be refused, and made it easier to extradite members of criminal organizations. In November 1997 the Commission proposed an extension to European law to allow civil and commercial judgments made in the courts of member states to be enforced throughout the whole of the EU. A regulation on the mutual recognition and enforcement of such judgments came into force in March 2001 across the EU, with the exception of Denmark. In 2000 a convention on mutual assistance in criminal matters (such as criminal hearings by video and telephone conference and cross-border investigations) was adopted.

The Grotius-Civil programme of incentives and exchanges for legal practitioners was established in 1996. It was designed to aid judicial co-operation between member states by improving reciprocal knowledge of legal and judicial systems. The successor programme, Grotius II, focused on general and criminal law. In February 2002 the EU established a 'Eurojust' unit, composed of prosecutors, magistrates and police-officers from member states, to help co-ordinate prosecutions and support investigations into incidences of serious organized crime. A European Police College (CEPOL) has also been created, initially consisting of a network of existing national training institutes; in December 2003, however, the European Council decided that a permanent CEPOL institution would be established at Bramshill in the United Kingdom. CEPOL was formally established as an EU agency in 2005.

In March 2000 an action programme entitled 'The prevention and control of organized crime: a European strategy' was adopted. A European crime prevention network was formally established in May 2001. There are also agreements within the EU on co-operation between financial intelligence units and between police forces for the purposes of combating child pornography. In addition, the EU has a common strategy designed to help Russia combat organized crime. The EU ran the FALCONE programme—a series of incentives, training opportunities and exchanges for those responsible for the fight against organized crime in individual member states. The STOP (sexual treatment of persons) programme operated a similar system for those responsible for combating trade in humans and the sexual exploitation of children. Several programmes, including Grotius II, STOP and FALCONE, were merged into a single framework programme, called AGIS, in January 2003. AGIS covered police and judicial co-operation in criminal matters, initially in 2003–07. In 2006, however, AGIS was terminated, one year early, in order to allow it to be succeeded by new programmes focusing on internal security and criminal justice, which were adopted by the Council in February 2007 and were to operate in 2007–13. The new programmes comprised, under the framework programme 'Security and Safeguarding Liberties', the new specific programmes 'Prevention of and Fight Against Crime' and 'Prevention, Preparedness and Consequence Management of Terrorism and other Security Related Risks', which had an overall budget of €745m. for 2007–13; and, under the framework programme 'Fundamental Rights and Justice', the new specific programme 'Criminal Justice', with an overall budget of some €196m. for 2007–13.

In September 2001 member states harmonized their definitions of human trafficking and set common minimum prison sentences. In January 2005 the European Commission adopted a proposal for a framework decision on the fight against organized crime, in which it sought to harmonize the definition of what constitutes a criminal organization. A White Paper on exchanges of information on criminal convictions in the EU was also adopted, proposing, notably, that a computerized mechanism be established to allow the criminal record offices of the member states to share information. In June, in a communication on developing a 'strategic concept' on tackling organized crime, the Commission recommended the development of common methodologies among national and EU bodies involved in combating organized crime, as well as an EU crime statistics system.

The European Monitoring Centre for Drugs and Drug Addiction (EMCDDA) is based in Lisbon, Portugal. In 2000 Norway became the first non-EU state to be admitted to EMCDDA. The EU is working with other third countries to tackle issues of drugs demand and supply. In December 2004 the European Council endorsed an EU strategy on drugs (2005–12), which set out the framework, objectives and priorities for two consecutive four-year action plans. In February 2005 the Commission adopted the first of these, covering 2005–08, which aimed significantly to reduce the prevalence of drugs use and to combat the trade in illicit drugs. A 'Drug Prevention and Information Programme' was adopted in September 2007, under the framework programme 'Fundamental Rights and Justice'. With a budget of €21m. for the period 2007–13, the Programme's general objectives were to prevent and reduce drugs use and dependence; to enhance information on the effects of drug use; and to support the implementation of the EU drugs strategy and action plans.

The EU's draft Charter of Fundamental Rights, which was signed in December 2000, outlines the rights and freedoms recognized by the EU. It includes civil, political, economic and social rights, with each based on a previous charter, convention, treaty or jurisprudence. The charter may be used to challenge decisions taken by the Community institutions and by member states when implementing EU law. A reference to the charter, making it legally binding, was included in the Treaty of Lisbon amending the Treaty on European Union and the Treaty establishing the European Community (previously known as the Reform Treaty), which was signed in December 2007 and was awaiting ratification by member states in 2008. A protocol to the Treaty of Lisbon limited the application of the charter in the United Kingdom and Poland to rights recognized by national legislation in those countries. In June 2005 the European Commission adopted a proposal for a regulation establishing an EU Agency for Fundamental Rights. The regulation was adopted in its final form in February 2007, allowing the establishment of the Agency, as the successor to the European Monitoring Centre on Racism and Xenophobia, on 1 March. In April the specific programme 'Fundamental Rights and Citizenship' was established under the framework programme 'Fundamental Rights and Justice'. With a budget of €94m. for 2007–13, the Programme aimed to promote the development of a European society based on respect for fundamental rights; to strengthen civil society organizations and to encourage a dialogue with them regarding fundamental rights; to combat racism, xenophobia and anti-semitism; and to improve contacts between legal, judicial and administrative authorities and the legal professions.

The Justice and Home Affairs Council held an emergency meeting in September 2001 following the terrorist attacks on the USA. It determined a number of measures to be taken to improve security in the Community. First, the Council sought to reach a common definition of acts of terrorism, and to establish higher penalties for such acts. The new definition included cyber and environmental attacks. The Council decided that, for the perpetrators of terrorist attacks, as well as those involved in other serious crimes (including trafficking in arms, people and drugs and money-laundering), the process of extradition would ultimately be replaced by a procedure for hand-over based on a European arrest warrant. In the mean time, member states were urged to implement the necessary measures to allow the existing conventions on extradition to enter into force. The member states reached agreement on the arrest warrant in December; under the agreement, covering 32 serious offences, EU countries may no longer refuse to extradite their own nationals. The warrant entered into force in eight of the then 15 EU member states on 1 January 2004 (the seven other member states having failed to meet the implementation deadline of 31 December 2003). The European arrest warrant had been implemented in all 25 member states by mid-2005. The Council also determined to accelerate the implementation of the convention on mutual assistance in criminal matters and to establish a joint investigation team. Member states were encouraged to ratify the convention on combating the financing of terrorism and to exercise greater rigour in the issuing of travel documents. The heads of the security and intelligence services of member states met in October 2001, in the first EU-wide meeting of this kind, to discuss the co-ordinated action to be taken to curb terrorism. They were to meet in regular sessions thereafter. A team of counter-terrorist specialists, established within Europol, was to produce an assessment of terrorist threats to EU states, indicating the likely nature and location of any such attacks. Rapid links were forged with US counterparts—in December Europol signed a co-operation agreement on the exchange of strategic information (excluding personal data) with the USA; in December 2002 the agreement was extended to include the exchange of personal data. The heads of the EU's anti-terrorist units also held a meeting following the September 2001 attacks, to discuss issues such as joint training exercises, equipment sharing, the joint procurement of equipment and possible joint operations. Prior to these emergency meetings, intelligence and security information had been shared bilaterally and on a small scale, impeding Europol's effectiveness. Terrorist bombings in Madrid, Spain, in March 2004 injected a greater sense of urgency into EU counter-terrorism efforts, and gave added impetus to EU initiatives aimed at improving travel-document security and impeding the cross-border movements of terrorists. Following the attacks, the EU created the new position of Counter-terrorist Co-ordinator, whose main task would be to tackle ongoing challenges encountered by the EU as it sought to translate its various counter-terrorist initiatives into effective law-enforcement tools. Among the Co-ordinator's principal responsibilities would be enhancing intelligence-sharing among EU members and promoting the implementation of already-agreed EU anti-terrorism measures, some of which had been impeded by the legislative processes of individual member states. The Justice and Home Affairs Council held an extraordinary meeting following the terrorist attacks in London, United Kingdom, in July 2005, at which ministers pledged to accelerate the adoption and implementation of enhanced counter-terrorism measures, focusing on issues such as the financing of terrorism, information-sharing by law-enforcement authorities, police co-operation and the retention of telecommunications data by service providers. In December the Council adopted a new EU counter-terrorism strategy focused on preventing people embracing terrorism, protecting citizens and infrastructure, pursuing and investigating suspects, and responding to the consequences of an attack. A specific strategy for combating radicalization and the recruitment of terrorists was approved at the same time. Despite concerns over privacy rights, the Council also reached agreement on a draft directive on the retention of telecommunications data for a period of between six months and two years for use in anti-terrorism investigations. Police would have access to information about telephone calls, text messages and internet data, but not to the exact content. The directive was approved by the European Parliament later that month. In November 2007 the Commission adopted a series of proposals on the criminalization of terrorist training, recruitment and public provocation to commit terrorist offences, on the prevention of the use of explosives by terrorists and on the use of airline passenger information in law-enforcement investigations.

Measures related to the abolition of customs formalities at intra-community frontiers were completed by mid-1991, and entered into force in January 1993. In June 1990 Belgium, France, Germany, Luxembourg and the Netherlands, meeting in Schengen, Luxembourg, signed a convention to implement an earlier agreement (concluded in 1985 at the same location), abolishing frontier controls on the free movement of persons from 1993. Delay in the establishment of the Schengen Information System (SIS), providing a computer network on suspect persons or cargo for use by the police forces of signatory states, resulted in the postponement of the implementation of the new agreement. Seven countries (Belgium, France, Germany, Luxembourg, the Netherlands, Portugal and Spain) agreed to implement the agreement with effect from March 1995. Frontier controls at airports on those travelling between the seven countries were dismantled during a three-month transition period, which ended on 1 July 1995. However, after that date the French Government announced that it would retain land-border controls for a further six months, claiming that drugs-trafficking and illegal immigration had increased as a result of the agreement. In March 1996 France decided to lift its border controls with Spain and Germany while maintaining controls on borders with the Benelux countries, mainly owing to fears concerning the transportation of illicit drugs from the Netherlands via Belgium and Luxembourg. Italy joined the 'Schengen Group' in October 1997, and Austria in December. Border controls for both countries were removed in 1998. Denmark, Finland and Sweden (and non-EU members Norway and Iceland) were admitted as observers of the accord from 1 May 1996, and all five countries joined the 'Schengen Group' in March 2001. Meanwhile, in March 1999 signatories of the Schengen accords on visa-free border crossings began to waive visa requirements with Estonia, Latvia and Lithuania. The Treaty of Amsterdam, which came into effect on 1 May, incorporated the so-called Schengen 'acquis' (comprising the 1985 agreement, 1990 convention and additional accession protocols and executive decisions), in order to integrate it into the framework of the EU. The Treaty permitted the United Kingdom and Ireland to maintain permanent jurisdiction over their borders and rules of asylum and immigration. Countries acceding to the EU after 2000 were automatically to adhere to the Schengen arrangements. In February 2002 the Council approved Ireland's participation in some of the provisions of the Schengen *acquis*.

Following the enlargement of the EU in May 2004, border controls between the 15 existing members and the 10 new members remained in force until 2007. Although the 10 new states technically belonged to the Schengen agreement, the Commission decided that the SIS computer network was not large enough to incorporate data from 10 more countries. Work on a new computerized information system, SIS II, began in 2002 but suffered delays and was not expected to be completed until 2009. Pending deployment of SIS II, a modified version of SIS, named SISone4ALL, was intoduced to allow the extension of the Schengen area to proceed. In December 2007 the provisions of the Schengen agreement were applied to the land and sea borders of nine of the 10 countries that joined the EU in 2004, with controls at airports to be removed in March 2008. The inclusion of Cyprus in the Schengen area was to be delayed for at least a further year, while Bulgaria and Romania hoped to be ready for full implementation of the agreement by 2011. Switzerland, a non-EU member, was scheduled to join the Schengen area in late 2008.

The need to develop a common EU policy on immigration became increasingly important in the late 1990s, with the number of immigrants forecast to rise considerably in the near future. In November 2000 the Commission adopted a communication outlining a common asylum procedure and providing for a uniform status, valid throughout the EU, for persons granted asylum. In March 2001 a common list of countries whose citizens required visas to enter the EU was finally adopted. The EU has also developed the so-called 'Eurodac' database for co-ordinating information on the movements of asylum seekers; Eurodac allows for the comparison of fingerprints of refugees. In September 2001 the Commission proposed a directive establishing a common European definition of a refugee, aimed at curtailing movement from state to state until one is reached that is prepared to give protection; the directive was adopted in April 2004. An action programme, entitled ARGO, covering the period 2002–06, advocated EU administrative co-operation in the fields of asylum, visas, immigration and external borders. In February 2002 the European Council adopted a comprehensive plan to combat illegal immigration. Priority areas included visa policy, readmission and repatriation policies, the monitoring of borders, the role of Europol and penalties. A European Agency for the Management of Operational Co-operation at the External Borders of the European Union (FRONTEX) was established by a regulation of the European Parliament in October 2004, the primary responsibility of which would be the creation of an integrated border management system, which would ensure a high and uniform level of control and surveillance. The Agency commenced operations on 1 May 2005, with its seat at Warsaw, Poland. In June 2004 the Council adopted a decision concerning the development of a system for the exchange of visa data between member states, the Visa Information System (VIS). In June 2007 the Parliament and the Council approved a regulation allowing consulates and other competent authorities to use the VIS when processing visa applications and to check visas and a decision allowing police and law-enforcement authorities to consult the data under certain conditions. The VIS, which was not expected to become operational before the end of 2008, was intended to enhance the internal security of member states and contribute to the fight against illegal immigration. In September 2005, in line with the objectives of the Hague programme, the Commission presented a package of measures on asylum and immigration. The proposals included the application of common standards to the return of illegal immigrants, the adoption of a more coherent approach to the integration of migrants, the encouragement of migrants to contribute to the development of their home countries, and the introduction of Regional Protection Programmes to assist refugees remaining in their regions of origin and their host countries. In December, in a move towards the creation of a common European asylum system, the Justice and Home Affairs Council adopted a directive on asylum procedures, setting minimum standards for granting and withdrawing refugee status, as well as an action plan on preventing human trafficking. A new framework programme entitled 'Solidarity and Management of Migration Flows' was adopted in December 2006 with the aim of improving management of migratory flows at EU level. Allocated an overall budget of €4,020m. for 2007–13, the programme was divided into four specific policy areas, each with its own financial instrument: the control and surveillance of external borders (External Borders Fund, €1,820m.); the return of third-country nationals residing illegally in the EU (European Return Fund, €676m.); the integration of legally resident third-country nationals (European Integration Fund, €825m.); and asylum (European Refugee Fund—first established in 2000—€699m.). In May 2007 the Commission proposed a directive on the introduction and enforcement of sanctions against employers engaging illegal immigrants.

All 15 of the existing members of the EU, except the United Kingdom, Ireland and Sweden, had planned to impose at least a two-year period of restriction on immigrants from the eight former communist countries (the Czech Republic, Estonia, Hungary, Latvia, Lithuania, Poland, Slovenia and Slovakia) after their accession to the EU in May 2004, to prevent their labour markets being saturated with inexpensive labour. Workers from the new member states Malta and Cyprus were allowed into existing EU countries without any restrictions. By January 2007, in addition to the United Kingdom, Ireland and Sweden, Spain, Finland, Greece, Portugal and Italy had opened their markets to workers from the member states that joined in 2004, while Belgium, France, Denmark, the Netherlands and Luxembourg had adopted a flexible approach in respect of either the labour market as a whole (Denmark) or sectors/professions in which shortages existed (Belgium, France, Netherlands, Luxembourg). Germany and Austria had both maintained employment restrictions. Austria, Germany, Greece, Ireland, Portugal, Spain and the United Kingdom imposed employment restrictions on workers from Bulgaria and Romania following their accession to the EU on 1 January 2007, while Belgium, France, Denmark, Italy, Luxembourg and the Netherlands adopted the same flexible approach that they were applying to the states that joined in 2004.

EDUCATION, TRAINING AND CULTURE

The Treaty of Rome, although not covering education directly, gave the Community the role of establishing general principles for implementing a common vocational training policy. The Treaty on European Union urged greater co-operation on education policy, including encouraging exchanges and mobility for students and teachers, distance learning and the development of European studies. In July 2000 the EU's Economic and Social Committee adopted a report on education in Europe. The Committee considered the development of a more integrated education strategy for Europe and advocated the study of new approaches to schooling, including differing structures and wider objectives, more diverse fields of learning and greater use of modern technologies.

The postgraduate European University Institute (EUI) was founded in Florence, Italy, in 1972, with departments of history and civilization, economics, law, and political and social sciences. The EUI is also the depository for the historical archives of the EC institutions. Approximately 140 new research students enrol at the Institute each year. An Academy of European Law was founded within the EUI in 1990, and in 1992 the Robert Schuman Centre for Advanced Studies was established to develop inter-disciplinary and comparative postdoctoral research. The establishment of 25 Jean Monnet European Centres of Excellence was approved in 1998; by 2006 the number of these Centres had risen to 112. The Jean Monnet programme, which supports institutions and activities in the field of European integration, also finances the establishment of Jean Monnet chairs at universities world-wide; there were 720 such chairs by 2006. The Jean Monnet programme targets disciplines in which Community developments are an increasingly important part of the subject studied—e.g. Community law, European economic and political integration, and the history of the European construction process.

In 1980 an educational information network, 'Eurydice', began operations, with a central unit in Brussels and national units providing data on the widely varying systems of education within member states. In 1987 the Council adopted a European Action Scheme for the Mobility of University Students ('Erasmus'). The scheme was expanded to include EFTA member states from 1992. The 'Lingua' programme promoted the learning and teaching of foreign languages in the Community. From 1 January 1995 the Erasmus and Lingua schemes were incorporated into a new Community programme, 'Socrates'. A second phase of the Socrates programme ran during 2000–06. As well as the Erasmus and Lingua initiatives, Socrates included actions on school education ('Comenius') and adult education ('Grundtvig'). The programme prioritized the learning of EU languages; the promotion of mobility in education (for example, through educational exchanges); innovation in educational practices (particularly focusing on information and communications technologies); and lifelong learning. In November 2006 the Council and the Parliament approved the establishment of an integrated action programme in the field of lifelong learning for 2007–13 (with an overall budget of €6,970m.), which incorporated the existing four sectoral initiatives—Comenius, Erasmus, Grundtvig and the 'Leonardo da Vinci' programme (see below)—as well as the Jean Monnet programme, and introduced a new transversal programme to facilitate activities involving more than one area of education, such as language learning and innovation in information and communication technologies.

In November 2005 the Commission presented a new framework strategy for multilingualism, urging member states to further the teaching, learning and use of languages and proposing the adoption of national action plans to promote multilingualism. A separate portfolio was created for multilingualism within the Commission in January 2007. In September a high-level group of experts on multilingualism, established one year earlier, published its final report, which concentrated on several areas: the need to raise awareness of, and enhance motivation for, language learning; the potential of the media in evoking and sustaining motivation for language learning; languages for business; interpretation and translation issues; regional and minority languages; and research into multilingualism.

The Trans-European Mobility Programme for University Studies (TEMPUS) was launched in 1990 to foster co-operation between institutions of higher education and their counterparts in Central and Eastern Europe, as part of the wider aid programme to those countries. Under the second phase of the scheme (TEMPUS II, covering 1994–98), the former Soviet republics were eligible to participate. Under TEMPUS III (2000–06), the programme widened its remit to incorporate certain non-academic institutions, as well as extending geographical coverage to include Mediterranean non-member countries. The next phase of the programme, TEMPUS IV, was to cover the period 2007–13. The European Training Foundation (ETF), which was established in Turin, Italy, in 1995, supports TEMPUS projects as part of its general assistance for the development of vocational training and retraining in EU partner countries. The Foundation deals with those countries supported by the EU's Instrument for Pre-accession Assistance and European Neighbourhood and Partnership Instrument (see External Relations), as well as the Central Asian republics of Kazakhstan, Kyrgyzstan, Tajikistan and Uzbekistan. After the accession to the EU of the eight new central and eastern European countries in 2004, the ETF sustained its involvement in human-resources development in Romania and Bulgaria (until their accession in January 2007), and increased its activities in Croatia, Turkey and the former Yugoslav Republic of Macedonia.

In 1975 a European Centre for the Development of Vocational Training (Centre Européen pour le Développement de la Formation Professionnelle—CEDEFOP) was established in Berlin, Germany. The centre relocated to Thessaloníki, Greece, in 1995. Much of CEDEFOP's recent work has focused on the employment problems encountered by women, especially those who wish to return to work after a long absence, on encouraging the participation of older workers in vocational training, and on addressing the needs of low-skilled people. The Leonardo da Vinci programme was introduced in 1994 to help European citizens to enhance their skills and to improve the quality and accessibility of vocational training. The programme supports lifelong learning policies and promotes transnational projects in an effort to increase mobility and foster innovation in European vocational education and training. In January 2000 a programme for the promotion of European pathways for work-linked training, including apprenticeship, came into force. (According to the Commission, European pathways for training referred to any period of vocational training completed by a person undergoing work-linked training as part of their training in another member state, complying with a number of quality criteria.) The programme involved the introduction of the new EU 'EUROPASS Training' document, which attested to periods of training completed in another member state. The EUROPASS programme, which was officially launched in February 2005 and which brought into a single framework several existing tools for the transparency of diplomas, certificates and competences, was aimed at promoting both occupational mobility, between countries as well as across sectors, and mobility for learning purposes. In September 2006 the Commission proposed the establishment of a European qualifications framework (EQF), based on eight reference levels of qualifications, with the aim of further promoting mobility and lifelong learning. Member states would be required to relate their own qualifications systems to the EQF by 2010, and by 2012 every new qualification issued in the EU would have a reference to the appropriate EQF level. The EQF was formally adopted in April 2008.

In April 2000 the EU's 'Youth' community action programme for 2000–06 was adopted, with a budget of €520m. This incorporated all the previous youth programmes and related activities, including Youth for Europe, which covered the period 1995–99, and the European Voluntary Service programmes. The overall objective of the new programme was to help young people (aged between 15 and 25 years) to contribute to the building of Europe and to foster a spirit of initiative. From the outset, Youth included applicant countries and also ran a Euro-Med partnership programme. In October 2004 a successor programme, entitled 'Youth in Action', was formally adopted to cover the period 2007–13. With a total budget of €885m., its aims were to foster a sense of citizenship, solidarity and mutual understanding within young people, to enhance the quality of support systems for youth activities and to promote European co-operation in youth policy. In March 2005 the Council adopted a European Pact for Youth, which focused on improving the education, training, mobility, vocational integration and social inclusion of young Europeans, while facilitating the reconciliation of family life and working life.

The EU's Culture 2000 framework programme (2000–06) replaced the Raphael, Kaleidoscope and Ariane programmes. The programme (which in 2003 included the participation of all 10 accession states, as well as Romania and Bulgaria) focused on the following themes: legislation of benefit to cultural projects; the cultural aspects of existing support policies; and the incorporation of culture into the field of external relations. Its main aim was to promote a 'common cultural area' inclusive of cultural diversity and common cultural heritage; this objective provoked a certain amount of opposition on the grounds that it could lead to transnational cultural conformity and that it could damage national and regional cultural diversity. However, as part of the so-called Cardiff process of integration of environmental and sustainable development issues (see Environment), the Commission is bound to make efforts to preserve cultural heritage in the formulation of other policies. In July 2004 the Commission presented its proposals for the Culture 2007 programme (2007–13), focusing on three priorities: the mobility of those working in the cultural sector; the transnational circulation of works of art; and intercultural dialogue. The Culture 2007 programme was formally adopted in December 2006, with a total budget of some €400m. for 2007–13. In the same month the Parliament and Council adopted a proposal from the Commission that 2008 be designated European Year of Intercultural Dialogue; 27 national projects and seven pan-European projects were planned. In May 2007, for the first time, the European Commission proposed a European strategy for culture policy, identifying three main objectives: the promotion of cultural diversity and intercultural dialogue; the promotion of culture as a catalyst for creativity in the framework of the Lisbon Strategy; and the promotion of culture as a vital element in the EU's international relations. The culture strategy was endorsed by the Council in November.

The European City of Culture initiative was launched in 1985 (and renamed the European Capital of Culture initiative in 1999). Member states nominate one or more cities in turn, according to an agreed chronological order. The capitals of culture are then formally selected by the Council on the recommendation of the Commission, taking into account the view of a selection panel. From 2007 the selection panel comprised 13 members, six appointed by the member state concerned and the remaining seven by the European institutions. From 2009 there were to be two capitals of culture from member states each year, one of which would be from the 10 countries that joined the Union in May 2004, plus a maximum of one city from European non-member countries. The following cities were selected as capitals of culture for the late 2000s: Luxembourg and Sibiu (Romania) for 2007, Liverpool (United Kingdom) and Stavanger (Norway) for 2008, Linz (Austria) and Vilnius (Lithuania) for 2009, and Essen (Germany), Pécs (Hungary) and İstanbul (Turkey) for 2010.

SOCIAL AFFAIRS AND EMPLOYMENT

The Single European Act, which entered into force in 1987, added to the original Treaty of Rome articles that emphasized the need for 'economic and social cohesion' in the Community, i.e. the reduction of disparities between the various regions. This was to be achieved principally through the existing 'structural funds' (see p. 304)—the European Regional Development Fund, the European Social Fund, and the Guidance Section of the European Agricultural Guidance and Guarantee Fund, which was replaced by the European Fund for Agricultural Development in 2007. In 1988 the Council declared that Community operations through the structural funds, the European Investment Bank and other financial instruments should have five priority objectives: (i) promoting the development and structural adjustment of the less-developed regions (where gross domestic product per head was less than 75% of the Community average); (ii) converting the regions, frontier regions or parts of regions seriously affected by industrial decline; (iii) combating long-term unemployment among people above the age of 25; (iv) providing employment for young people (aged under 25); and (v) with a view to the reform of the common agricultural policy (CAP), speeding up the adjustment of agricultural structures and promoting the development of rural areas.

In 1989 the Commission proposed a Charter of Fundamental Social Rights of Workers (later known as the Social Charter), covering freedom of movement, fair remuneration, improvement of working conditions, the right to social security, freedom of association and collective wage agreements, the development of participation by workers in management, and sexual equality. The Charter was approved (with some modifications) by the heads of government of all Community member states, except the United Kingdom, in December. On the insistence of the United Kingdom, the chapter on social affairs of the Treaty on European Union, negotiated in December 1991, was omitted from the Treaty to form a separate protocol (the so-called Social Chapter, complete with an opt-out arrangement for the United Kingdom).

In September 1994 ministers adopted the first directive to be approved under the Social Charter, concerning the establishment of mandatory works councils in multinational companies. After lengthy negotiations, it was agreed that the legislation was to apply to companies employing more than 1,000 people, of whom 150 worked in at least two EU member states. The United Kingdom was excluded from the directive; however, British companies operating in other European countries were to participate in the scheme (although without counting United Kingdom-based employees towards the applicability thresholds). The directive came into force in September 1996. In April 1996 the Commission proposed that part-time, fixed-term and temporary employees should receive comparable treatment to permanent, full-time employees. A directive ensuring equal treatment for part-time employees was adopted by the Council in December 1997. A directive on parental leave, the second directive to be adopted under the Social Charter, provided for a statutory minimum of three months' unpaid leave to allow parents to care for young children, and was adopted in June 1996.

In May 1997 the new Labour Government of the United Kingdom approved the Social Charter, which was to be incorporated into the Treaty of Amsterdam. The Treaty, which entered into force in May 1999, consequently removed the opt-out clause and incorporated the Social Chapter in the revised Treaty of Rome. In December 1999 the Council adopted amendments extending the two directives adopted under the Charter to include the United Kingdom.

The Treaty of Amsterdam authorized the European Council to take action against all types of discrimination. Several directives and programmes on gender equality and equal opportunities have been approved and the Commission has initiated legal proceedings against a number of member states before the European Court of Justice for infringements. In December 2006 the Council and Parliament approved the establishment of a European Institute for Gender Equality, which was to be located in Vilnius, Lithuania. In June 2000 the Council adopted a directive implementing the principle of equal treatment regardless of racial or ethnic origin in employment, education, social security, health care and access to goods and services. This was followed in November by a directive establishing a framework for equal treatment regardless of religion or belief, disability, age or sexual orientation. The European Monitoring Centre on Racism and Xenophobia (EUMC), which was established in Vienna, Austria, in 1997, maintained an information network (the European Information Network on Racism and Xenophobia—RAXEN) and database. In February 2004 the Commission held a joint seminar with the European Jewish Congress in Brussels to discuss the concerns of the Jewish community that anti-Semitism was increasing in Europe; Jewish leaders accused the EU authorities of inaction and indifference in the face of a rise in anti-Semitic incidents (some violent) in Europe. In June 2005 the Commission presented a framework strategy on non-discrimination and equal opportunities, aimed at ensuring the full implementation and enforcement by member states of anti-discrimination legislation, and designated 2007 as 'European Year of Equal Opportunities for All'. In March 2007 the EUMC was converted into the European Union Agency for Fundamental Rights (FRA), which immediately assumed the mandate of the EUMC in the fields of racism and xenophobia and, in respect of other fundamental rights, was gradually to develop knowledge, expertise and work programmes.

Numerous directives on health and safety in the workplace have been adopted by the Community. The Major Accident Hazards Bureau (MAHB), which was established in 1996 and is based at the Joint Research Centre at Ispra, Italy, helps to prevent and to mitigate industrial accidents in the EU. To this end, MAHB maintains a Major Accident Reporting System database and a Community Documentation Centre on Industrial Risk. There is also a European Agency for Health and Safety at Work, which was established in 1995 in Bilbao, Spain. The Agency has a health and safety information network composed of 'focal points' in each member state, in the candidate countries and in the four EFTA states. In February 2007 the Commission adopted a new five-year strategy for health and safety at work aimed at reducing work-related illness and accidents by 25% by 2012. Under the previous strategy (2002–06) fatal accidents had been reduced by 17% and accidents resulting in absence from work for three days or more by 20%.

In June 1993 the Working Time Directive (WTD) was approved, restricting the working week to a maximum duration of 48 hours, except where overtime arrangements are agreed with trade unions. The WTD also prescribed minimum rest periods and a minimum of four weeks' paid holiday a year. However, certain categories of employee were exempt from the maximum 48-hour week rule, including those in the transport sector, those employed in offshore oil extraction, fishermen and junior hospital doctors. In April 2000 agreement was reached on extending some or all of the rights of the WTD to cover most excluded workers; this extension was to be phased in under transitional arrangements. A Road Transport Directive, which applies to mobile workers who participate in road transport activities covered by EU drivers' hours rules, was adopted in March 2002 and took effect in March 2005. In January 2004 the Commission launched a review of the WTD following an increase in the use of the opt-out clause by a number of member states. In September the Commission recommended that the opt-out clause be retained, instead proposing the introduction of stricter conditions to make it more difficult for employers to persuade staff to work more than 48 hours per week against their will. The Commission also proposed that the 'inactive' part of on-call time not be counted as working time and that member states be allowed to calculate average working hours over a full year, rather than the current period of four months. In May 2005, however, in a first reading, the European Parliament voted in favour of proposals to phase out the opt-out clause (except for the police, army and emergency services, and chief executive officers and senior managers) and to count all on-call time as working time, although members agreed with the Commission regarding the use of a one-year reference period for calculating the average working week. Nevertheless, any change to the WTD would require the approval of the Council of the European Union, which was deeply divided over the issue; no agreement had been reached by early 2008. Meanwhile, the Commission indicated that it was likely to initiate legal proceedings against member states that failed to incorporate into their national legislation recent judgments by the European Court of Justice to the effect that time spent asleep but on-call by hospital doctors should count as working time.

The European Foundation for the Improvement of Living and Working Conditions, which was established in Dublin, Ireland, in 1975, undertakes four-year research and development programmes in the fields of employment, sustainable development, equal opportunities, social cohesion, health and well-being, and participation. Prior to the EU's enlargement in May 2004, the Foundation made available wide-ranging new data and analysis on living and working conditions in the existing member states and in the accession and candidate states. A Quality of Life in Europe survey, which was conducted during 2003 in 28 countries, was published in 2004. The survey, which was the first of its kind, focused on employment, economic resources, family life, community life, health and education. A second survey was conducted during 2007 in all 27 EU member states, Croatia and Turkey (both candidate countries), and Norway; first results were expected to be published in the second half of 2008.

The European Confidence Pact for Employment was launched by the Commission in 1996 as a comprehensive strategy to combat unemployment, involving a common approach by public authorities, employers and employees. An employment body, European Employment Services (EURES), launched in 1994, operates as a network of more than 700 specialist advisers across Europe, who (with the co-operation of national public employment services, trade unions, employers' organizations, local authorities, etc., and with access to a detailed database) provide the three basic EURES services of information, guidance and placement to both job-seekers and employers interested in the European job market. EURES has a particularly effective role to play in cross-border regions where there are significant degrees of cross-border commuting by employees. EURES, which covers the countries of the European Economic Area (EEA) and Switzerland, also provides a public database of employment vacancies and a database through which job-seekers can make their curricula vitae available to a wide range of employers.

An employment summit held in Luxembourg in November 1997 committed member governments to providing training or work placements for unemployed young people within six months, and for the long-term unemployed within 12 months. Member states also agreed to reduce taxation on labour-intensive service industries from 1 July 1998 and to produce national action plans (known as national reform programmes from 2005) for employment. Under the European employment strategy, initiated in 1997 and incorporated in the Treaty of Amsterdam, an Employment Committee was established in 2000 to oversee the co-ordination of the employment strategies of the member states and an employment package was to be presented (as a joint effort by the Council of the European Union and the Commission) each year. The package contains reports on member states' performances, individual recommendations and policy guidelines for the future. The overall EU employment rate for the population aged 15–64 averaged 64.3% in 2006 (71.6% for men; 57.1% for women), considerably short of the overall target rate of 70% set for 2010. Rates ranged from 54.5% in Poland to 77.4% in Denmark. The EU employment rate for older people (aged 55–64) averaged 43.5% (52.6% for men; 34.8% for women). In December 2007 EU ministers responsible for employment and social affairs adopted a set of common principles of 'flexicurity' (a combination of flexibility and security) that member states should follow when developing labour market policies. This new approach was based on four components: effective labour market policies; flexible and reliable contractual arrangements; comprehensive lifelong learning strategies; and modern and adequate social protection systems.

A European Social Protection Committee was established in June 2000. In addition, the EU administers MISSOC—the Mutual Information System on Social Protection in the EU member states and the EEA. Switzerland is also included in MISSOC. In February 2005 the

European Commission launched its new Social Agenda (2005–10) for modernizing the EU's social model. The new Agenda focused on providing jobs and equal opportunities for all and ensuring that the benefits of the EU's growth and employment-creation schemes reached all levels of society. By modernizing labour markets and social protection systems, it was hoped that the Agenda would help people to seize the opportunities created by international competition, technological advances and changing population patterns, while protecting the most vulnerable in society. The Agenda had three priorities: employment, the fight against poverty and the promotion of equal opportunities. A new programme for employment and social solidarity (PROGRESS) was subsequently established to provide financial support for the implementation of the objectives set out in the Social Agenda. With an overall budget of €743m. for 2007–13, PROGRESS replaced four previous programmes that had expired in 2006 and was to cover the policy areas of social protection and inclusion, employment, non-discrimination, gender equality and working conditions.

The Charter of Fundamental Rights (CFR) was proclaimed at the Nice Summit of the European Council in December 2000. The text of the CFR consists of seven chapters, covering dignity, freedoms, equality, solidarity, citizens' rights, justice and general provisions. No new rights were actually created as part of the CFR; rather, it presents in a single document the existing rights and freedoms enjoyed by EU citizens through the European Convention on Human Rights, the Charter of Fundamental Social Rights of Workers and various other EU treaties. Despite the fact that it contained nothing new, the member states were not initially willing to make the CFR a legally binding document. However, a reference to the CFR, making it legally binding, was included in the Treaty of Lisbon amending the Treaty on European Union and the Treaty establishing the European Community, which was signed in December 2007 and was awaiting ratification by member states in 2008. (A protocol limited the application of the CFR in the United Kingdom and Poland.)

The EU disability strategy has three main focuses: co-operation between the Commission and the member states; the full participation of people with disabilities; and the mainstreaming of disability in policy formulation (particularly with regard to employment). EU activities relating to disability include dialogue with the European Disability Forum and a 'European Day of Disabled People', which takes place in December each year. Following the designation of 2003 as 'European Year of People with Disabilities', a disability action plan for 2004–10 was formulated with the aim of enhancing the economic and social integration of people with disabilities. The plan's three main objectives were to implement fully the directive on equal treatment in employment and occupation adopted in November 2000 (see above); to reinforce the incorporation of disability issues into the relevant Community policies; and to improve accessibility for all.

CONSUMER PROTECTION AND HEALTH

Consumer protection is one of the stated priorities of EU policy, and has been implemented via a series of action programmes covering areas such as safety of products and services (e.g. food additives, safety of toys and childcare articles, packaging and labelling of goods), protecting consumers' economic and legal interests, and promoting consumer representation. A number of measures have been taken to strengthen consumer power, by promoting consumer associations and drawing up a requirement for fair commercial practices.

In February 1997 the Commission extended the function of its directorate-general on consumer policy to incorporate consumer health protection. This decision (which followed widespread consumer concerns regarding the bovine spongiform encephalopathy (BSE) crisis—see Agriculture) was designed to ensure that sufficient importance was given to food safety. In November a Scientific Steering Committee was established to provide advice on consumer health issues. Eight sectoral steering committees were formed at the same time, covering a range of public health and consumer protection issues. Five of the committees were devoted to food safety, one to cosmetic and non-food products, one to medicinal products and medical devices, and one to issues of toxicity and the environment. The Scientific Steering Committee held its final meeting in April 2003, a new European Food Safety Authority (see Agriculture) having been established to assume responsibility for providing the Commission with scientific advice on food safety. With a wide brief to cover all stages of food production and supply right through to consumers, the Authority has been based in Parma, Italy, since June 2005. In March 2004 the Commission adopted a decision to establish three new scientific steering committees in the fields of consumer products, health and environmental risks, and emerging and newly identified health risks. The new committees were to replace the existing committees for consumer products and non-food products intended for consumers, for toxicity, ecotoxicity and the environment, and for medicinal products and medical devices. Meanwhile, in July 1998 an Institute for Health and Consumer Protection (IHCP), attached to the Commission's Joint Research Centre, was established to improve research in this field.

In January 2000 the Commission adopted a White Paper on food safety, proposing a comprehensive, integrated approach covering foodstuffs from 'farm to table'. The paper envisaged a programme of measures, including legislation on the responsibilities of food and feedstuff manufacturers, the welfare of animals during transport and the traceability of products. Stringent rules and appropriate checks at all stages of the production chain were to be introduced and the importance of clear labelling, presentation and advertising was emphasized. The paper proposed that certain substances recognized scientifically as being sources of allergies should be included in lists of ingredients on labels. From October 1999 food products labelled as 'GM-free' in the EU were permitted to contain up to 1% of genetically modified (GM) material. In July 2001 the Commission developed its rules on the labelling and tracing of GM organisms (GMOs, see Agriculture). During 2004 a framework was developed for the creation of international guidelines on the measurement of chemical and biological elements in food and other products. The system would facilitate the detection of GMOs and the measurement of sulphur content in motor fuels. New legislation on the safety of food and animal feed came into force in January 2005. Business operators were required to ensure the safety of their products and apply appropriate systems and procedures to establish the traceability of food, feed, food-producing animals and all substances incorporated into foodstuffs at all stages of production, processing and distribution. An Advisory Group on the Food Chain and Animal and Plant Health was established by the Commission in March and held its inaugural meeting in July. A Community Register of Feed Additives was first published in November, in accordance with a regulation on additives for use in animal nutrition. In January 2006 new regulations on food and animal feed hygiene, which were to apply to every stage of the food chain, entered into force. At the same time, an EU-wide ban on the use of antibiotics in animal feed to stimulate growth took effect, as part of efforts to reduce the non-essential use of antibiotics in order to address the problem of micro-organisms becoming resistant to traditional medical treatments. A stringent regulation requiring that all health claims on food, drinks or food supplements be substantiated by independent experts was adopted in December 2006.

In May 2002 the Commission presented its new strategy for consumer policy for 2002–06. Specific measures agreed included a proposal for a harmonization of rules for consumer credit, as well as a resolution on labelling of video and computer games, aimed at ensuring their suitability for young people. In the same year, the monitoring of certain foodstuffs was extended to include labelling of irradiated foods, authorization of two new sweeteners, and labelling and marketing of food supplements. In October 2004 the European Parliament and the Council adopted a regulation on the establishment of a network of public authorities responsible for enforcing legislation to protect the interests of consumers in the event of cross-border disputes. The network of enforcement agencies, the Consumer Protection Co-operation Network (CPC), commenced operations at the end of 2006 and was officially launched in February 2007. The first joint enforcement investigation was conducted in September, into misleading advertising and unfair practices on airline ticket-selling websites, and in November it was revealed that irregularities had been discovered on more than 50% of the sites checked. Companies failing to change their practices were warned that they could face legal action leading to fines or closure of their websites. Meanwhile, a European Consumer Centres Network (ECC-Net) was established in January 2005 to provide a single point of contact in each member state for consumers to obtain information about their rights and assistance in pursuing complaints, particularly in cases concerning cross-border purchases. Legislation increasing the compensation rights of air travellers took effect in February 2005. New rights to compensation and assistance in the event of cancellations or long delays were introduced, compensation was increased for passengers unable to board a flight owing to overbooking by the airline and cover was extended to passengers travelling on charter or domestic flights. In March 2007 the Commission adopted a new consumer policy strategy for 2007–13. Subtitled 'Empowering consumers, enhancing their welfare, effectively protecting them', the strategy's principal objectives were: to ensure a high level of consumer protection, in particular by means of improved information on consumer-related data, improved consultation and improved representation of consumers' interests; and to ensure the effective application of consumer protection rules, in particular through co-operation between authorities and bodies charged with implementing consumer legislation, information, education and dispute resolution with reference to consumer complaints.

In February 2005 the European Parliament approved a new directive to harmonize the framework across the EU for banning unfair commercial practices. The new legislation, which clarified consumers' rights, banned pressure selling and misleading marketing and facilitated cross-border trade, took effect in December 2007, although only 14 member states had implemented the directive by that time. In February 2003 the Commission adopted an action plan for a more coherent and standardized European contract law. A communication outlining the next stage of the plan was adopted in October 2004, and substantive work on the issue commenced in March 2005 and continued in 2006–07. The long-term aim was to develop a 'Common Frame of Reference', which would contain clear definitions of legal terms, fundamental principles and coherent model rules of contract law.

In September 2002 the European Parliament adopted a programme of Community action in the field of public health for the period 2003–08, with a budget of €312m. The three basic objectives of the programme were: to improve health-related information; to encourage swift and co-ordinated responses to threats to health; and to promote health and prevent diseases. A second programme of Community action in the field of health, for the period 2008–13, was adopted in October 2007, with a budget of €321.5m. Its three general objectives were: to improve citizens' health security; to promote health, including the reduction of health inequalities; and to generate and disseminate health information and knowledge. Meanwhile, the Commission adopted a new health strategy for the same period with the aims of fostering good health in an ageing Europe, protecting citizens from health threats, and supporting dynamic health systems and new technologies.

Various epidemiological surveillance systems are in operation, covering major communicable diseases. An early warning and response system to help member states deal with outbreaks of diseases was in place by the end of 2000. Partly in response to the outbreak of severe acute respiratory syndrome (SARS) in the Far East in 2003 and the outbreak of avian influenza in the Netherlands in early 2003 and in Viet Nam in early 2004, in April 2004 the European Parliament and the Council adopted a regulation establishing a European Centre for Disease Prevention and Control, to enable the EU to share its disease-control expertise more effectively and to allow multinational investigation teams to be drawn up quickly and efficiently. The Centre, based in Sweden, became operational in May 2005. A report prepared by the Centre for the Commission and published in February 2007 concluded that, while the EU and member states had made substantial progress in preparing for an influenza pandemic, additional efforts needed to be made in such areas as, among others, co-ordination at the European level, implementation at the local level and research on influenza. The detection of the lethal H5N1 strain of avian influenza in Turkey, Romania and Croatia in October 2005 led to EU bans on imports of live birds and other poultry products from these countries, and reinforced measures to reduce the risk of introducing the disease into EU poultry farms were adopted; similar bans already applied to several other, mainly East Asian, countries. The disease is transmissible to other animals and humans, usually through direct contact with infected birds. In December a new directive establishing updated EU measures on the control of avian influenza was adopted, based on information received as a result of recent outbreaks of the disease and new scientific knowledge about how the disease spreads and potential risks to human health. In January 2006 the EU prohibited the import of poultry from the six countries bordering eastern Turkey (where four people had died from the disease). By May 13 EU countries had reported cases of the H5N1 virus being detected in wild birds; no cases had been reported in humans. Following outbreaks of H5N1 in Hungary and the United Kingdom in January–February 2007, the Commission urged all member states to maintain heightened surveillance and biosecurity, and to review the measures they were currently applying. Advice was issued that in areas identified to be at high risk of outbreaks of H5N1, poultry should be confined indoors. Later in February the Commission announced that an emergency team of veterinary experts was to be established to respond to outbreaks of animal diseases at the request of member states or third countries. Further outbreaks of H5NI occurred at a farm in the Czech Republic in June, in Germany in August, in the United Kingdom in November and in Poland in December, while a number of wild birds were also infected in these three countries as well as in Austria and France. The eradication and control measures dictated by EU legislation on avian influenza were implemented in response to each outbreak. From 1 July a new regulation came into force, superseding the ban on imports of captive live birds, which had been extended a number of times. Under the new rules, the import of birds caught in the wild remained banned, but the import of captive birds from specific countries and regions that had already been approved to export live commercial poultry was to be permitted. The EU implements a number of individual action plans, including one to combat cancer. In November 2005 the Commission adopted two new health plans: the first was intended to strengthen Europe's preparedness to cope with cross-border public health emergencies (such as SARS and bioterrorism), and the second, on strategies to respond to a possible influenza pandemic, updated an existing plan drawn up in March 2004. Under the Treaty on European Union, the EU assumed responsibility for the problem of drug addiction; a European Monitoring Centre for Drugs and Drug Addiction (EMCDDA, see Justice, Freedom and Security) was established in Lisbon, Portugal, in 1995.

A new, €72m. anti-smoking campaign was launched in March 2005, aimed at children and young adults. The campaign, which followed a previous three-year, €18m. programme that ended in December 2004, was to last four years and was to include a series of television and cinema advertisements across the EU. The commissioner responsible for health urged member states to ban smoking in public places. Also in March an EU Platform for Action on Diet, Physical Activity and Health was launched, as part of an overall strategy on nutrition and physical activity being developed by the Commission to address rising levels of obesity. The Commission initiated a public consultation in December on how to reduce obesity levels and the prevalence of associated chronic diseases in the EU. In July an EU directive came into effect that prohibited tobacco advertising in the print media, on radio and over the internet, as well as the sponsorship by tobacco companies of cross-border cultural and sporting events. The directive applied only to advertising and sponsorship with a cross-border dimension. Tobacco advertising on television had already been banned in the EU in the early 1990s. In the first half of 2007 the Commission conducted an extensive public consultation on the optimum means of promoting smoke-free environments in the EU. In May the Commission adopted a White Paper on nutrition- and obesity-related health issues, in which it urged food manufacturers to reduce levels of salt, fat and sugar in their products and emphasized the need to encourage Europeans to undertake more physical activity. A European Alcohol and Health Forum, comprising more than 40 businesses and non-governmental organizations, was formed in June 2007 to focus on initiatives to protect European citizens from the harmful use of alcohol. In October 2006 the Commission had adopted a communication setting out an EU strategy to support member states in reducing alcohol-related harm.

The Food Supplements Directive, which was approved in 2002 and was designed to strengthen controls on the sale of natural remedies, vitamin supplements and mineral plant extracts, came into effect in August 2005. Under the legislation, only vitamins and minerals on an approved list could be used in supplements and restrictions were to be placed on the upper limits of vitamin doses. In July 2005 the European Court of Justice had confirmed the validity of the directive, which had been challenged by a group of consumers' and retail associations in the United Kingdom.

In October 2005 the European Commission launched a public consultation on mental health, noting that more than 27% of adults in the EU suffered from some form of mental illness every year. The Commission intended to propose an EU-wide mental health strategy following the completion of the consultation process in May 2006.

The enlargement of the EU in May 2004 to incorporate 10 new member states was expected to cause a number of problems for the EU with regard to public health policy given that, in general, the health status indicators of the majority of the accession states compared poorly with the EU average. Some of the new member states, which (with only one or two exceptions) had few resources to spend on health, faced serious problems with communicable diseases (particularly HIV/AIDS), and the health systems of most were in need of improvement. In December 2005 the Commission adopted a communication on plans for combating HIV/AIDS within the EU and neighbouring countries during 2006–09, emphasizing the need for a greater focus on prevention in view of recent data indicating that the number of people newly diagnosed with HIV in Europe was continuing to increase steadily.

ENVIRONMENT

Environmental action by the EU was initiated in 1972. Successive action programmes were complemented by a variety of legislation, including regulations on air and water pollution (e.g. 'acid rain', pollution by fertilizers and pesticides, and emissions from vehicles), directives on the transport of hazardous waste across national boundaries, measures on waste treatment, noise abatement and the protection of natural resources, and legislation to guarantee freedom of access to information on the environment held by public authorities. The Maastricht Treaty on European Union, which entered into force in November 1993, gave environmental action policy status, and the Treaty of Amsterdam identified sustainable development as one of the Community's overall aims.

The Community's fifth environmental action programme (1993–2000), entitled 'Towards Sustainability', aimed to address the root causes of environmental degradation, by raising public awareness and working to change the behaviour of authorities, enterprises and the general public. The programme focused on anticipating, as well as addressing, environmental problems. A 1998 communication on the so-called 'Cardiff Process' of integrating environmental considerations into all EU policies confirmed this programme's broad approach. The Commission recognized that full integration was a long-term aim. For the short term, it identified two priority objectives: the fulfilment of the environmental measures contained in the Agenda 2000 action programme (relating, for example, to the reform of the Common Agricultural Policy and to EU enlargement), and the implementation of the Kyoto Protocol (see below). The programme listed several initiatives that were to be pursued, including better resource management by industry, the curbing of consumer demand for products that generate pollution, the development of more 'environmentally friendly' agriculture and a more effective management of mass tourism.

The EU's sixth environmental action programme (2002–12), entitled 'Environment 2010: Our Future, Our Choice', was adopted by the European Parliament in July 2002, and emphasized the continuing importance of the integration of environmental considerations into other EU policies, focusing on four priority areas: climate change, nature and biodiversity, environment, health and quality of life, and the management of natural resources and waste. The programme also identified explicitly the measures required to implement successfully the EU's sustainable development strategy. In addition, it encouraged an extended dialogue with the administrations of all the applicant states (10 of which joined the EU in May 2004, followed by Bulgaria and Romania in January 2007), and sought to encourage greater public participation in environmental debates. A mid-term review of the programme, presented in April 2007, concluded that, although the EU was on track with adopting the policy measures outlined in the programme, global emissions of greenhouse gases were rising, the loss of biodiversity was accelerating, pollution continued to harm public health and the volume of waste produced in member states was increasing. The report also noted only limited progress in efforts to integrate environmental concerns into other policy areas and to improve the enforcement of EU environmental legislation.

The EU's programme of research on the environment, carried out on a shared-cost basis by various scientific institutions, covers the economic and social aspects of environmental issues and the Union's participation in global change programmes. The environment (including climate change) was one of the 10 themes of the 'co-operation' specific programme of the Seventh Framework Programme for research, technological development and demonstration activities covering 2007–13 (see Research and Innovation). With a budget of €1,900m., a wide range of environmental research activities were to be funded under FP7, grouped into four areas: climate change, pollution and risks; sustainable management of resources; environmental technologies; and earth observation and assessment tools for sustainable development. The Institute for Environment and Sustainability, located in Ispra, Italy, was created in 2001 as part of the Joint Research Centre to provide research-based support to the development and implementation of European environmental policies.

In 1990 the EC established the European Environment Agency (EEA, see p. 257) to monitor environmental issues and provide advice. The agency, which is located in Copenhagen, Denmark, and which became operational in November 1994, also provides targeted information to policy-makers and the public and disseminates comparable environmental data. The agency is open to non-EU countries and it was the first EU body to have members from the accession states. In February 2004 the Commission and the EEA launched the European Pollutant Emission Register (EPER), the first Europe-wide register of industrial emissions into air and water, reporting on 50 substances emitted to air and water from 56 industrial activities. In 2009 the EPER was scheduled to be replaced by a European Pollutant Release and Transfer Register, which was to provide more comprehensive information on industrial pollution, reporting on more than 91 substances released to air, water and land from 65 activities. The European Parliament approved legislation in April 2004 that made firms causing pollution liable for the costs of repairing the damage caused to natural habitats, water resources and wildlife. However, only the Governments of Italy, Latvia and Lithuania had introduced the law at national level by April 2007, as required, prompting the Commission to warn other member states that it would initiate legal proceedings if they failed to incorporate the law. In December the Commission proposed a new directive on reducing industrial emissions, which was to replace seven existing directives. The draft directive was intended, *inter alia*, to tighten emission limits in certain industrial sectors, to introduce minimum standards for environmental inspections of industrial installations and to extend the scope of legislation to cover other polluting activities, such as medium-sized combustion plants.

In 1992 the LIFE programme was established as a financial instrument to promote the development and implementation of environmental policy, funding priority activities in EU member states and providing technical assistance to countries in Central and Eastern Europe and the Mediterranean. The LIFE programme was subdivided into LIFE-Environment; LIFE-Nature; and LIFE-Third Countries. In May 2007 the Council and Parliament adopted a new funding programme, LIFE+, which was to be the EU's single financial instrument targeting only the environment. With a budget of €2,143m. for the period 2007–13, LIFE+ consisted of three thematic components: nature and biodiversity; environment policy and governance; and information and communication.

In 1985 the Community (and a number of individual member states) ratified the Vienna Convention for the Protection of the Ozone Layer, and in 1987 the Community signed a protocol to the treaty, controlling the production of chlorofluorocarbons (CFCs). In 1990 ministers of the environment undertook to ban the production of CFCs by mid-1997 (the introduction of the ban was later brought forward to 1996), and in 1998 the Commission proposed committing EU countries to the progressive elimination of remaining ozone-depleting substances, by introducing a ban on the sale and use of CFCs and imposing production limits on hydrochlorofluorocarbons (HCFCs), which were originally introduced to replace CFCs. In 1990 ministers agreed to stabilize emissions of carbon dioxide, believed to be responsible for 'global warming', at 1990 levels by 2000 (2005 for the United Kingdom). In December 1997, at the third conference of parties to the UN Framework Convention on Climate Change (UNFCCC), agreement was reached on the Kyoto Protocol, under which emissions of six greenhouse gases were to be reduced by 8% between 2008 and 2012, in comparison with 1990 levels. In June 1998 ministers of the environment agreed upon individual emission targets for each EU member state. The Kyoto Protocol was formally approved by the European Council in April 2002 and entered into force in February 2005.

In March 2000 the Commission noted that emissions were actually rising in relation to 1990 levels. The European Climate Change Programme (ECCP) was adopted in 2000. This outlined the strategy needed to meet commitments under the Kyoto Protocol and aimed to incorporate climate change concerns into various EU policies. In January 2000 the EU's Theseo 2000-Solve experiment was launched; this was the largest experiment ever undertaken to study the ozone layer above northern Europe. The EU Greenhouse Gas Emissions Trading Scheme (ETS), which was launched in January 2005, obliges companies that exceed their allocation of carbon dioxide emissions to buy extra allowances from more efficient companies or incur considerable fines. However, experts criticized certain EU Governments, notably Italy and Austria, for allowing industry to increase emissions through generous permit limits. In December 2006 the Commission proposed a directive on including the aviation sector in ETS; the Council reached political agreement on the draft directive in December 2007. In November 2006 the Commission initiated a review of ETS, proposing an expansion of its coverage to new sectors and emissions and the further harmonization of its application between member states. A working group under the ECCP, comprising representatives of member states, industry, non-governmental organizations and academic and research bodies, discussed the reform of the system during the first half of 2007; any changes would take effect from 2013. In October 2007 the European Commission announced that it had reached an agreement with the three countries of the European Economic Area on linking their respective emissions trading systems. In the same month the Commission and nine individual EU member states were founding members, together with New Zealand, Norway and several US states and Canadian provinces, of the International Carbon Action Partnership, which was intended to provide an international forum for countries and regions with mandatory emissions capping and trading systems.

In 2005 the EU began considering priorities for its policy on climate change after 2012, when the current commitments under the Kyoto Protocol were due to expire. Recommendations of the Commission, presented in February 2005, included broader international participation in reducing emissions, the inclusion of more sectors, notably aviation, maritime transport and forestry, and increased innovation in the development of climate-friendly technologies. In March EU ministers responsible for the environment proposed setting targets for industrialized countries to reduce their greenhouse gas emissions by 15%–30% by 2020 and by 60%–80% by 2050, compared with 1990 levels. In September 2005 the EU reached separate agreements with the People's Republic of China and India on strengthening co-operation in the field of climate change. A second phase of the ECCP, ECCP II, was launched in October, with the aim of reviewing the progress of individual member states towards achieving their individual targets on reducing emissions and developing a framework for EU climate change policy beyond 2012. Transport was identified as an area of particular concern, with emissions in the sector reported to be some 20% higher than in 1990. More than 30 measures had been implemented under the first phase of the ECCP since its establishment in 2000. In January 2007, in a communication ('Limiting Global Climate Change to 2° Celcius: The Way Ahead for 2020 and Beyond'), the Commission set out its proposals for climate change management, which were aimed at limiting the increase in the average global temperature to no more than 2°C above pre-industrial levels. In March, at a summit meeting, EU leaders set a number of joint targets as part of the continued effort to combat the effects of 'global warming', which, together, it was claimed, constituted the Union's first-ever comprehensive agreement on climate and energy policy. The fundamental element of the new strategy was a unilateral pledge by the EU to reduce emissions of carbon dioxide by 20% (compared with emission levels in 1990) by 2020. The measures agreed allowed, furthermore, for a possible increase in the targeted reduction to 30%, if the USA, China, India and other industrialized nations were to match that commitment. A target was also set to raise the contribution of renewable energy sources to 20% by 2020, compared with its existing contribution of 6.5%. However, it was widely acknowledged, by both observers and those, including the German Chancellor, Angela Merkel, who had been instrumental in the agreement, that political negotiations between the Commission and the individual member states in pursuit of these targets were likely to be long and difficult. The Commission issued a Green Paper in June 2007 on the need to adapt to current and future climate change in order to lessen potential adverse effects on people, the economy and the environment. In September the Commission proposed the establishment of a Global Climate Change Alliance, through which the EU would provide financial support for adaptation and mitigation efforts in the most vulnerable developing countries. The Commission's annual report on progress towards meeting the Kyoto objectives, presented in November and based on projections by member states, indicated that the EU was likely to achieve its 8% reduction target by 2012. At the UN Climate Change Conference held in Bali, Indonesia, in December, it was agreed to negotiate a new international accord to replace the Kyoto Protocol of the UNFCCC following its expiry in 2012. The 'Bali Roadmap' set out an agenda for these negotiations, which were to be concluded by the end of 2009, as demanded by the EU, although specific emissions targets were not included in the agreement.

In June 1996 the Commission agreed a strategy, drawn up in collaboration with the European petroleum and car industries and known as the Auto-Oil Programme, for reducing harmful emissions from road vehicles by between 60% and 70% by 2010 in an effort to reduce air pollution. The programme committed member states to the progressive elimination of leaded petrol by 2000 (with limited exemptions until 2005). From 2000 petrol-powered road vehicles were to be fitted with 'on-board diagnostic' (OBD) systems to monitor emissions. Diesel vehicles were to be installed with OBD systems by 2005. Under Auto-Oil II, the directive was revised in 2003, establishing specifications to come into force on 1 January 2005, with new limits on sulphur content of both petrol and diesel. Moreover, even lower limits would come into force for all fuel marketed from December 2009, although there would be limited availability from 2005. In July 1998 the Commission announced plans to reduce pollution from nuclear power stations by lowering emissions of sulphur dioxides, nitrogen oxides and dust by one-half. A new directive limiting the sulphur content of marine fuel came into force in August 2005. In February 2007 the Commission adopted a communication that set forth a comprehensive new strategy to reduce emissions of carbon dioxide from new cars and vans sold in the EU. The new strategy was to be combined with revised quality standards for vehicle fuels, which had been proposed in January, and would enable the EU to achieve its aim of limiting carbon dioxide emissions from new cars to no more than 120g per km by 2012—a reduction of about one-quarter compared with current levels. The draft directive, which was proposed by the Commission in December, defined a range of permitted emissions of carbon dioxide for new cars according to the mass of the vehicle, which was designed to ensure an average of 130g of emissions per km. Complementary measures (including improvements in the efficiency of car components, such as tyres and air conditioning systems, and a greater use of biofuels) were to contribute the additional required reduction of 10g per km. Additionally, in order to foster among car manufacturers competition on the basis of fuel economy, rather than on size and power, the Commission extended an invitation to car-makers to sign an EU code of good practice on car marketing and advertising.

In September 2005 the European Commission presented a thematic strategy on air pollution, prepared under the auspices of Clean Air for Europe (CAFE), a programme of technical analysis and policy development launched in March 2001. While covering all major pollutants, the new air-quality policy focused particularly on particulates and ground-level ozone pollution, which were known to pose the greatest risk to human health. The strategy aimed to cut the annual number of premature deaths from pollution-related diseases by almost 40% by 2020, compared with the 2000 level, and also to reduce the area of forests and other ecosystems suffering damage from airborne pollutants. The Commission envisaged merging all existing legislation on air quality into a single directive. In October 2005 the Commission proposed a strategy to protect the marine environment, which aimed to ensure that all EU marine waters were environmentally healthy by 2021. This was the second of seven thematic strategies to be adopted under the sixth environmental action programme (2002–12). The Commission proposed strategies on the prevention and recycling of waste and the sustainable use of natural resources in December 2005, and on the urban environment in January 2006. In July 2006 the Commission proposed a directive aimed at establishing a framework for achieving a more sustainable use of pesticides by reducing the risks posed by pesticides to human health and the environment (its sixth thematic strategy). In September the Commission adopted a comprehensive strategy dedicated to soil protection, including a proposal for a directive setting forth common principles for soil protection across the EU. A directive on the assessment and management of flood risks entered into force in November 2007, requiring member states to conduct preliminary assessments by 2011 to identify river basins and associated coastal areas at risk of flooding, to develop flood-risk maps by 2013 for areas deemed to be at risk, and to establish flood-risk management plans for these areas by 2015.

In September 2000 the EU adopted a directive on end-of-life vehicles (ELVs), containing measures for the collection, treatment, recovery and disposal of such waste. The ruling forced manufacturers to pay for the disposal of new cars from July 2002 and of old cars from January 2007. The directive set recycling and recovery targets, restricted the use of heavy metals in new cars from 2003, and specified that ELVs might only be dismantled by authorized agencies. EU directives on waste electronic and electrical equipment and the restriction of the use of certain hazardous substances in electronic and electrical equipment came into force in February 2003. The directives were based on the premise of producer responsibility and aimed to persuade producers to improve product design in order to facilitate recycling and disposal. Increased recycling of electrical and electronic equipment would limit the total quantity of waste going to final disposal. Under the legislation consumers would be able to return equipment free of charge from August 2005. In order to prevent the generation of hazardous waste, the second directive required the substitution of various heavy metals (lead, mercury, cadmium, and hexavalent chromium) and brominated flame retardants in new electrical and electronic equipment marketed from July 2006. In January 2005 the Commission adopted a new strategy on reducing mercury pollution, which was endorsed by EU ministers of the environment in June. A regulation banning mercury exports from the EU by 2011 was proposed by the Commission in October 2006. In September 2007 a directive was adopted on phasing out, by April 2009, the use of toxic mercury in measuring devices in cases where it could be substituted by safer alternatives; this was expected to lead to an annual reduction of 33 metric tons in mercury emissions in the EU.

A regulation revising EU laws on trade in wild animals and plants was adopted by ministers of the environment in December 1996. This aimed to tighten controls and improve the enforcement of restrictions on trade in endangered species. A series of directives adopted in 2002 formulated new EU policy on the conservation of wild birds, fishing and protection for certain species of whales. Every three years the Commission publishes an official report on the conservation of wild birds; a report, in March 2002, identified a decline of almost 25% in wild bird species in Europe, despite efforts made over the last 20 years. A report published by Birdlife International in November 2004 claimed that 226 bird species (43% of the total in Europe) were threatened by intensive agriculture and changes in climate. The EU has pledged to attempt to halt the decline of wildlife in Europe by 2010.

As part of the EU's efforts to promote awareness of environmental issues and to encourage companies to do likewise, the voluntary Eco-Management and Audit Scheme (EMAS) was launched in April 1995. Under the scheme, participating industrial companies undergo an independent audit of their environmental performance. In addition, the EU awards 'eco-labels' for products that limit harmful effects on the environment (including foodstuffs, beverages and pharmaceutical products, among others). The criteria to be met are set by the EU Eco-Labelling Board (EUEB).

In October 2003 the Commission presented a new environmental policy—the Registration, Evaluation and Authorisation of Chemicals system (REACH)—which was originally intended to collate crucial safety information on tens of thousands of potentially dangerous chemicals used in consumer goods industries. However, following intensive lobbying by the chemical industry sector, the scope of REACH was reduced (for example, the number of chemicals to be tested was cut and the number of chemicals that would require licences was also substantially curtailed). The European Parliament approved the proposed legislation in a first reading in November 2005, and in December the Council reached a political agreement on REACH. Environmentalists criticized ministers for weakening the legislation by relaxing the conditions set by the Parliament for authorization of the most dangerous chemicals. The REACH regulation was formally adopted in December 2006. A new European Chemicals Agency, which was to be responsible for managing REACH, commenced operations in Helsinki, Finland, at the beginning of June 2007. Later that month the Commission proposed a regulation to align the current EU system of classification of chemical substances and mixtures to the UN Globally Harmonized System of Classification and Labelling of Chemicals.

SECURITY AND DEFENCE

Under the Single European Act, which came into force on 1 July 1987 (amending the Treaty of Rome), it was formally stipulated for the first time that member states should inform and consult each other on foreign policy matters (as was already, in practice, often the case).

In June 1992 the Petersberg Declaration of Western European Union (WEU) defined the role of WEU as the defence component of the EU and outlined the 'Petersberg tasks' relating to crisis management, including humanitarian, peace-keeping and peace-making operations, which could be carried out under WEU authority (now EU authority). In 1992 France and Germany established a joint force called Eurocorps, based in Strasbourg, France, which was later joined by Belgium, Spain and Luxembourg. An agreement was signed in January 1993 that specified that Eurocorps troops could serve under the command of the North Atlantic Treaty Organization (NATO), thus relieving concern, particularly from the United Kingdom and the USA, that the Eurocorps would undermine NATO's role in Europe. In May member states of the Eurocorps agreed to make the Eurocorps available to WEU. WEU also ratified in May 1995 the decision by Spain, France, Italy and Portugal to establish land and sea forces, the European Operational Rapid Force (EUROFOR) and the European Maritime Force (EUROMARFOR) respectively, which were also to undertake the Petersberg tasks under the auspices of WEU. Several other multinational forces also belonged to Forces Answerable to the WEU (FAWEU). At the EU summit in Köln, Germany, in June 1999, EU member states accepted a proposal for the Eurocorps to be placed at the disposal of the EU for crisis response operations. At the end of that year Eurocorps member states agreed to transform the Eurocorps into a rapid reaction corps headquarters available both to the EU and NATO. In 2002 NATO certified the Eurocorps as a NATO high readiness force, which required the headquarters to be open to all NATO members as well as those from the EU; thus representatives from Austria, Canada, Finland, Greece, Italy, the Netherlands, Poland, Turkey and the United Kingdom are integrated into the headquarters.

The Maastricht Treaty on European Union, which came into force on 1 November 1993, provided for joint action by member governments in matters of common foreign and security policy (CFSP), and envisaged the eventual formation of a European security and defence policy (ESDP), with the possibility of a common defence force, although existing commitments to NATO were to be honoured. The Treaty raised WEU to the rank of an 'integral part of the development of the Union', while preserving its institutional autonomy, and gave it the task of elaborating and implementing decisions and actions with defence implications.

The Treaty of Amsterdam, which entered into force in May 1999, aimed to strengthen the concept of a CFSP within the Union and incorporated a process of common strategies to co-ordinate external relations with a third party. Under the Amsterdam Treaty, WEU was to provide the EU with access to operational capability for undertaking the so-called 'Petersberg tasks'. In late March 1999 representatives of the Commission and NATO held a joint meeting, for the first time, to discuss the conflict in the southern Serbian province of Kosovo and Metohija. In April a meeting of NATO Heads of State and of Government determined that NATO's equipment, personnel and infrastructure would be available to any future EU military operation. In June the European Council, meeting in Köln, determined to strengthen the ESDP, stating that the EU needed a capacity for autonomous action, without prejudice to actions by NATO and acknowledging the supreme prerogatives of the UN Security Council. The European Council initiated a process of assuming direct responsibility for the Petersberg tasks, which were placed at the core of the ESDP process. In December, following consultation with NATO, the European Council, meeting in Helsinki, Finland, adopted the European Defence Initiative, comprising the following goal: by 2003 the EU should be able to deploy within 60 days and for a period of up to one year a rapid reaction force, comprising up to 60,000 national troops from member states, capable of implementing the full range of Petersberg tasks. At the Helsinki meeting, the establishment of three permanent military institutions was proposed: a Political and Security Committee (PSC), a Military Committee and a Military Staff. The PSC, which was fully established by 2001, monitors the international situation, helps define policies and assess their implementation, encourages dialogue and, under the auspices of the Council, takes responsibility for the political direction of capability development. In the event of a crisis situation, it oversees the strategic direction of any military response, proposes political objectives and supervises their enactment. The Military Committee gives military advice to the PSC, and comprises the chiefs of defence of member states, represented by military delegates. It serves as a forum for military consultation and co-operation and deals with risk assessment, the development of crisis management and military relations with non-EU European NATO members, accession countries, and NATO itself. Meanwhile, the Military Staff, comprising experts seconded by the member states, provides the EU with an early-warning capability, takes responsibility for strategic planning for the Petersberg tasks and implements the Military Committee's policies. Permanent arrangements have been agreed for EU-NATO consultation and co-operation in this area. The process of transferring the crisis management responsibilities of WEU to the EU was finalized by July 2001. From January 2007 a new EU Operations Centre (OpsCentre), located in Brussels, was available as a third option for commanding EU crisis management missions. Hitherto autonomous EU operations were commanded either with recourse to NATO's command structure or from the national operational headquarters of one of five member states (France, Germany, Greece, Italy and the United Kingdom). Although the EU OpsCentre was to have a permanent staff of only eight core officers, it was envisaged that a total of 89 officers and civilians would be able to begin planning an operation within five days of the Council deciding to activate the centre, achieving full capability to command the operation within 20 days.

In December 2001 the EU announced that the rapid reaction force was, theoretically, ready, although only as yet capable of undertaking small-scale crisis management tasks. A deal was agreed at the Copenhagen summit in December 2002 about sharing planning resources with NATO, in theory clearing the way for the beginning of EU military operations. In January 2003 EU forces were deployed for the first time in an international peace-keeping role, when 500 police-officers were dispatched to Bosnia and Herzegovina to take over policing duties from the existing UN force. In March the European Parliament voted to approve the EU's first military mission, allowing 450 lightly armed EU troops to take over from NATO peace-keepers in the former Yugoslav republic of Macedonia. The EU announced in June its first military operation outside the continent of Europe, agreeing to send 1,400 peace-keepers to attempt to curb the ethnic violence in the Democratic Republic of the Congo (DRC). In July 2004 ministers responsible for foreign affairs agreed that EU-led military forces would take over from NATO in Bosnia and Herzegovina by the end of 2004. The EU duly assumed control of operations in December; 7,000 troops (EUFOR) were deployed under EU command with a mission (Operation Althea) to ensure stability in the country. In February 2007 a transition plan for EUFOR-Althea was announced whereby the force's size was to be reduced to under 2,500 troops. The reconfigured EUFOR-Althea continued to fulfil its peace-keeping mandate, while retaining the capacity to reverse the effects of the reduction in its strength and to re-establish a more robust military presence if necessary. A second EUFOR deployment, to the DRC, was approved in April 2006; EU forces supported the UN mission in the country while presidential and legislative elections were conducted and concluded their operations in November of that year. In October 2007 the Council approved a EUFOR operation to support a UN mission in eastern Chad and north-eastern Central African Republic in efforts to improve security in those regions, where more than 200,000 people from the Darfur region of western Sudan had sought refuge from violence in their own country. The force began deployment in early 2008. Following the unilateral declaration of independence by the Serbian province of Kosovo in February, an EU Rule of Law Mission (EULEX Kosovo), comprising some 1,900 foreign personnel and 1,100 local staff, was to be deployed in Kosovo, with an initial mandate of two years, to support the authorities in maintaining public order; the UN Interim Administration Mission in Kosovo (UNMIK) was to be withdrawn. However, it was reported that Kosovo Serb reluctance to accept the EULEX mission presented an impediment to UNMIK's withdrawal.

At a meeting in Brussels in November 2004, EU ministers responsible for defence agreed to create up to 13 battle groups for deployment to crisis areas by 2007. Battle groups were to comprise between 1,000 and 1,500 troops and were to be capable of being deployed within 10 days of a unanimous decision from EU member states and the creation of a battle plan and would be equipped to stay in an area for up to four months. Each group was to be commanded by a 'lead nation' and associated with a force headquarters. The battle groups reached initial operational capacity in January 2005, meaning that at least one battle group was on standby every six months. France, Italy, Spain and the United Kingdom set up their own battlegroups. The creation of the battle groups was partly to compensate for the inadequacies of the rapid reaction force of 60,000 troops, which, while theoretically declared ready for action in May 2003, in practice was adversely affected by shortfalls in equipment, owing to a lack of investment in procurement and research and a failure to co-ordinate purchases among member states. In November 2005 it was announced that the number of battle groups to be created was to be increased to 15 and additional groups were subsequently proposed. In January 2007 the battle groups reached full operational capacity, meaning that two battle group operations could be undertaken concurrently.

In June 2004 the European Council approved the creation of a European Defence Agency. A Council Joint Action on the establishment of the Agency was adopted in July, and it commenced operations later that year. The new European Defence Agency was to be responsible for improving the EU's defence capabilities in relation to crisis management and for promoting co-operation on research and procurement, strengthening the European defence industrial and technological base and developing a competitive European defence equipment market. In November 2007 EU ministers responsible for defence adopted a framework for a joint strategy on defence research and technology.

The ESDP, now known as the common security and defence policy (CSDP), was to remain an integral part of the CFSP under the draft Treaty of Lisbon, which was signed on 13 December 2007 by the heads of state or of government of the 27 member states. According to the Treaty, the progressive framing of a common defence policy was intended to lead to a common defence, following a unanimous decision of the European Council. A mutual defence clause and a solidarity clause (in the event of a member state becoming the victim of terrorist attack or natural or man-made disaster) were included, and joint disarmament operations, military advice and assistance, conflict prevention and post-conflict stabilization were added to the Petersberg tasks.

In June 2000 the EU established a civilian crisis management committee. In the same month the European Council defined four priority areas for civilian crisis management: developing the role of the police; strengthening the rule of law; strengthening civilian administrations; and improving civil protection. As part of the general rapid reaction force (see above), the EU aimed to be able to deploy up to 5,000 police-officers for international missions by 2003. In February 2001 the Council adopted a regulation creating a rapid reaction mechanism (RRM) to improve the EU's civilian capacity to respond to crises. The mechanism bypassed cumbersome decision-making processes, to enable civilian experts in fields such as mine clearance, customs, police training, election-monitoring, institution-building, media support, rehabilitation and mediation to be mobilized speedily. In November 2006 the Council and Parliament adopted a regulation establishing an Instrument for Stability for 2007–13 to replace the RRM. In 2005 the EU established a number of operations in third countries, including police missions in the DRC and the Palestinian territories, and border assistance missions at the Rafah crossing point between Gaza and Egypt and at the frontier between Moldova and Ukraine. An integrated EU rule-of-law mission for Iraq also commenced operations in July of that year, with a mandate to train senior officials and executive staff from the judiciary, the police and the penitentiary, while a monitoring mission was deployed in the province of Aceh, Indonesia, between September 2005 and December 2006 to monitor the implementation of a peace agreement between the Indonesian Government and a separatist movement. Operations mounted in 2006 included measures undertaken, in two phases, in support of the Benghazi AIDS Action Plan in Libya, initially launched in 2004. An EU police mission commenced a three-year assignment to Afghanistan in June 2007.

In September 2004 five European ministers responsible for defence signed an agreement in Noordwijk, the Netherlands, to establish a police force, which could be deployed internationally for post-conflict peace-keeping duties and maintaining public order. The European Gendarmerie Force, which was officially inaugurated at its headquarters in Vicenza, north-eastern Italy, in January 2006, was initially to comprise members from France, Italy, Spain, Portugal and the Netherlands. The Force was to be capable of deploying a mission of up to 800 gendarmes within 30 days, which could be reinforced.

In October 2002 an extraordinary session of the Brussels European Council adopted a European action plan to combat terrorism, which aimed to contribute to a global anti-terrorism strategy. Its priority objectives included deepening political dialogue with third countries, strengthening arrangements for shared intelligence and using military or civilian capabilities to protect civilian populations in the event of terrorist attack. In December EU ministers of justice agreed to allow the exchange of information on crime and terrorist suspects between European and US agencies. In the wake of the bomb attacks carried out by suspected Islamist extremists in Madrid, Spain, in March 2004, the leaders of the EU agreed to implement a series of counter-terrorism measures, including monitoring data from mobile telephone calls and the internet; introducing a single EU-wide arrest warrant; harmonizing penalties for terrorist crimes; 'freezing' assets held by outlawed groups; and appointing a senior counter-terrorism co-ordinator to help efforts to pool intelligence across Europe. The draft EU constitutional treaty includes a solidarity clause, under which member states would act jointly in the event of a terrorist attack, natural disaster or a man-made catastrophe. In May 2004, despite challenges to the legality of the move by the European Parliament on the grounds that it infringed civil liberties, the EU agreed to pass airline passenger data to US security agencies to enhance its capacity to fight terrorism. Following terrorist attacks in London, United Kingdom, in July 2005, EU ministers of justice and home affairs agreed to accelerate the implementation of counter-terrorism measures. In December the Council adopted a new EU counter-terrorism strategy (see Justice, Freedom and Security).

Under the European code of conduct on arms exports, the EU publishes an annual report on defence exports based on confidential information provided by each member state. EU member states must withhold export licences to countries where it is deemed that arms sales might lead to political repression or external aggression. The Community funds projects aimed at the collection and destruction of weapons in countries emerging from conflict. The EU is strongly committed to nuclear non-proliferation. Under its programme of co-operation with Russia, the Union works to dismantle or destroy nuclear, chemical and biological weapons and weapons of mass destruction.

FINANCIAL SERVICES AND CAPITAL MOVEMENTS

Freedom of capital movement and the creation of a uniform financial area were regarded as vital for the completion of the EU's internal market by 1992. In 1987, as part of the liberalization of the flow of capital, a Council directive came into force whereby member states were obliged to remove restrictions on three categories of transactions: long-term credits related to commercial transactions; acquisition of securities; and the admission of securities to capital markets. In June 1988 the Council of Ministers approved a directive whereby all restrictions on capital movements (financial loans and credits, current and deposit account operations, transactions in securities and other instruments normally dealt in on the money market) were to be removed by 1 July 1990. A number of countries were permitted to exercise certain restrictions until the end of 1992, and further extensions were then granted to Portugal and Greece. With the entry into force of the Maastricht Treaty in November 1993, the principle of full freedom of capital movements was incorporated into the structure of the EU.

The EU worked to develop a single market in financial services throughout the 1990s. In October 1998 the Commission drew up a framework for action in the financial services sector. This communication was followed by a Financial Services Action Plan (FSAP) in May 1999, with three strategic objectives: to establish a single market in wholesale financial services; to make retail markets open and secure; and to strengthen the rules on prudential supervision in order to keep pace with new sources of financial risk. The prudential supervision of financial conglomerates (entities offering a range of financial services in areas such as banking, insurance and securities), which were developing rapidly, was identified as an area of particular importance. During 2002 a directive was drawn up on the supplementary supervision of such businesses, in recognition of the increasing consolidation in the financial sector and the emergence of cross-sector financial groups. Individual targets specified in the 1999 FSAP included removing the outstanding barriers to raising capital within the EU; creating a coherent legal framework for supplementary pension funds; and providing greater legal certainty in cross-border securities trading.

During 2003 several important steps were taken regarding the FSAP. In November the Commission adopted a package of seven measures aiming to establish a new organizational architecture in all financial services sectors. The Commission stressed that this initiative was required urgently if the FSAP was to be implemented and enforced effectively. The deadline of 2005 for the adoption of the FSAP measures was largely met, with 98% of the measures having been completed, and their implementation by member states was being closely monitored by the Commission. In December 2005 the Commission presented its financial services policy for 2005–10, identifying five priorities: to consolidate progress and ensure effective implementation and enforcement of existing rules; to extend the 'better regulation principles' (i.e. transparency, wide consultation and thorough evaluation) to all policy-making; to enhance supervisory co-operation and convergence; to create greater competition between service providers, especially those active in retail markets; and to expand the EU's external influence in globalizing capital markets.

In July 2001 progress towards the creation of a single financial market was impeded by the European Parliament's rejection of a proposed takeover directive that had been under negotiation for 12 years. The directive had aimed to ensure that shareholders were treated in the same way throughout the EU after takeover bids, and had sought to create a single Community framework governing takeovers. The proposed directive was eventually approved by the European Parliament (with a number of strategic amendments) in December 2003. The Council gave its final approval to the directive in March 2004, and it came into force in May. The takeover directive was due to be incorporated into member states' national laws by 20 May 2006. In February 2007 a report by the Commission on the implementation of the takeover directive indicated that the continued use by a large number of member states of exemptions from the directive's main provisions (which were not mandatory) might bring about new barriers in the EU takeover market, rather than eliminate existing ones. A directive enhancing the rights of shareholders of listed companies was adopted in June; member states were to implement the directive within two years.

A directive on Community banking, adopted in 1977, laid down common prudential criteria for the establishment and operation of banks in member states. A second banking directive, adopted in 1989, aimed to create a single community licence for banking, thereby permitting a bank established in one member country to open branches in any other. The directive entered into force on 1 January 1993. Related measures were subsequently adopted, with the aim of ensuring the capital adequacy of credit institutions and the prevention of money-laundering by criminals. In September 1993 ministers approved a directive on a bank deposit scheme to protect account-holders. These directives were consolidated into one overall banking directive in March 2000. Non-bank institutions may be granted a 'European passport' once they have complied with the principles laid down in the EU's first banking directive on the mutual recognition of licences, prudential supervision and supervision by the home member state. Non-bank institutions must also comply with the directive on money-laundering. In May 2001 a directive on the reorganization and closure of failed credit institutions with branches in more than one member state was agreed; it entered into force in May 2004. The capital requirements directive, which was adopted in June 2006, provided for the introduction of a supervisory framework on capital measurement and capital standards in accordance with the Basel II rules agreed by the Basel Committe on Banking Supervision (see Bank for International Settlements). The new framework aimed to enhance consumer protection and strengthen the stability of the financial system by fostering improved risk management among financial institutions.

In September 2000 a directive was issued governing the actions of non-bank institutions with regard to the issuance of 'electronic money' (money stored on an electronic device, for example a chip card or in a computer memory). The directive authorized non-bank institutions to issue electronic money on a non-professional basis, with the aim of promoting a 'level playing field' with other credit institutions. Other regulations oblige the institutions to redeem electronic money at par value in coins and bank notes, or by transfer without charge. A review of this directive, prompted by various market developments since its introduction, such as the use of pre-paid telephone cards, which some member states considered as electronic money and others did not, was proposed by the Commission in July 2006 and was to follow the approval of the directive on payment services. The directive on payment services, which was adopted in November 2007, provided the legal framework for the creation of the Single Euro Payments Area (SEPA), an initiative designed to make all electronic payments across the euro area, for example by credit card, debit card, bank transfer or direct debit, as straightforward, efficient and secure as domestic payments within a single member state. Non-bank institutions would also be permitted to provide payment services under the new directive, thus opening the market to competition. The provisions of the directive were to be implemented by all member states by November 2009.

In July 1994 the third insurance co-ordination directives, relating to life assurance and non-life insurance, came into effect, creating a framework for an integrated Community insurance market. The directive on the reorganization and winding-up of insurance undertakings was adopted by the EU in February 2001 and came into force in April 2003. The main aim of the directive was to provide greater consumer protection and it formed part of a wider drive to achieve a consistent approach to insolvency proceedings across the EU. A new directive on life assurance was adopted in November 2002, superseding all previous directives in this field. In May 2005 the EU adopted a fifth motor insurance directive, which considerably increased the minimum amounts payable for personal injuries and damage to property and designated pedestrians and cyclists as specific categories of victims who are entitled to compensation. A directive on reinsurance was adopted in November; companies specializing in this area had not previously been specifically regulated by EU legislation. In July 2007 the Commission proposed a thorough reform of EU insurance legislation, which was designed to improve consumer protection, modernize supervision, deepen market integration and increase the international competitiveness of European insurers. The new system, known as 'Solvency II', would introduce more extensive solvency requirements for insurers, in order to guarantee that they have sufficient capital to withstand adverse events, covering not only traditional insurance risks, but also economic risks, including market risk (such as a fall in the value of an insurer's investments), credit risk (for example when debt obligations are not met) and operational risk (such as malpractice or system failure). In addition, insurers would be compelled to devote significant resources to the identification, measurement and proactive management of risks. The Commission hoped to secure adoption of the proposed directive on Solvency II (which would replace 14 existing directives) by 2009, in order to have the new system in operation in 2012. The European Insurance and Occupational Pensions Committee works to improve co-operation with national supervisory authorities.

In September 2007 the Council and Parliament adopted a directive designed to harmonize procedural rules and assessment criteria throughout the Community with regard to acquisitions and increases of shareholdings in the banking, insurance and securities sectors. A directive aimed at modernizing and simplifying rules on value-added tax (VAT) for financial and insurance services was proposed by the Commission in November. It was noted that although these services were generally exempt from VAT, the exemption was not being applied uniformly by member states and that a clear definition of exempt services was therefore required.

In May 1993 ministers adopted a directive on investment services, which (with effect from 1 January 1996) allowed credit institutions to offer investment services in any member state, on the basis of a licence held in one state. The 1999 FSAP aimed to achieve the further convergence of national approaches to investment, in order to increase the effectiveness of the 1993 directive. The directive on the market in financial services, which was adopted in April 2004 to replace the 1993 directive, aimed to allow investment firms to operate throughout the EU on the basis of authorization in their home member state and to ensure that investors enjoyed a high level of protection when employing investment firms, regardless of their location in the EU. The directive was originally to be implemented by April 2006, but this deadline was extended owing to the complexity of the measures required. As a result, the directive was to be incorporated into member states' national laws by January 2007, and entered into force in November of that year.

In late 1999 the Commission put forward proposals to remove tax barriers and investment restrictions affecting cross-border pension schemes, as variations among member states in the tax liability of contributions to supplementary pension schemes were obstructing the transfer of pension rights from one state to another, contradicting the Treaty of Rome's principles of free movement. In October 2000 a specific legal framework for institutions for occupational retirement provision (IORPs) was proposed. This seeks to abolish barriers to investment by pension funds and would permit the cross-border management of IORP pension schemes, with mutual recognition of the supervisory methods in force. In September 2003 the occupational pensions directive (IORP directive), which was designed to allow workers of multinational companies to have access to cross-border employer pension schemes, became EU law. It was to be implemented by member states within two years.

In November 1997 the Commission adopted proposals to co-ordinate tax policy among member states. The measures aimed to simplify the transfer of royalty and interest payments between member states and to prevent the withholding of taxes. In February 1999 the European Parliament endorsed a proposal by the Commission to harmonize taxation further, through the co-ordination of savings taxes. In November 2000 finance ministers agreed on a proposed savings tax directive, the details of which were endorsed in July 2001. This directive set out rules on the exchange of information on savings accounts of individuals resident in one EU country and receiving interest in another. However, in December Austria, Luxembourg and Belgium abandoned the agreement, insisting that they would only comply if other tax havens in Europe, such as Monaco, Liechtenstein and Switzerland, were compelled to amend their banking secrecy laws.

Two other proposed directives were issued in November 2000, the first relating to interest and royalties and the second concerning the code of conduct for business taxation. Together with the savings tax directive, these were known as the EU tax package. The EU finance ministers finally reached agreement on the terms of the package in June 2003. The package consisted of a political code of conduct to eliminate harmful business tax regimes; a legislative measure to ensure an effective minimum level of taxation of savings income; and a legislative measure to eliminate source taxes on cross-border payments of interest and royalties between associated companies. The Council of the EU reached agreement on the controversial savings tax directive (after 15 years of negotiation) in June 2004; the directive entered into force on 1 July 2005. The aim of the directive was to prevent EU citizens from avoiding taxes on savings by keeping their money in foreign bank accounts. Under the directive, each member state would ultimately be expected to provide information to other member states on interest paid from that member state to individual savers resident in those other member states. For a transitional period, Belgium, Luxembourg and Austria were to be allowed to apply a withholding tax instead, at a rate of 15% for the first three years (2005–07), 20% for the subsequent three years (2008–10) and 35% from 1 July 2011. Negotiations had been concluded with Switzerland, Liechtenstein, Monaco, Andorra and San Marino to ensure the adoption of equivalent measures in those countries to allow effective taxation of savings income paid to EU residents.

The May 2000 convention on mutual assistance in criminal matters (see Justice, Freedom and Security) committed member states to co-operation in combating economic and financial crime. In May 2001 the Council adopted a framework decision on preventing fraud and counterfeiting in non-cash means of payment, recognizing this as a criminal offence. An EU conference in Paris, France, in February 2002 (which was also attended by representatives of seven candidate countries and Russia) agreed to tackle money-laundering by setting minimum secrecy levels and compelling internet service providers to identify operators of suspect financial deals. Following the terrorist attacks on the USA in September 2001, the EU attempted to accelerate the adoption of the convention combating the financing of terrorism, and began work on a new directive on 'freezing' assets or evidence related to terrorist crimes. In October 2005 a regulation on the compulsory declaration at EU borders of large amounts (i.e. more than €10,000) of cash (including banknotes and cheques) entered into force. The aim of this measure, which applied only to the external borders of the Union, was to prevent the entry into the EU of untraceable money, which could then be used to fund criminal or terrorist activities. A third money-laundering directive (which was extended to cover terrorist financing as well as money-laundering) was also adopted in that month. In November 2006 the Council and Parliament adopted a regulation aimed at ensuring that law-enforcement authorities have access to basic information on the payer of transfers of funds in the context of investigating terrorists and tracing their assets.

In February 2001 the Commission launched a complaints network for out-of-court settlements in the financial sector (FIN-NET), to help consumers find amicable solutions in cases where the supplier is in another member state. A directive establishing harmonized rules on the cross-border distance-selling of financial services was adopted in June 2002. The first meeting took place in June 2006 of the Financial Services Consumer Group, a permanent committee, comprising representatives of consumer organizations from each of the member states as well as those active at EU level, established by the Commission to discuss financial services policies and proposals of particular relevance to consumers. In December 2007 the Commission published a White Paper proposing measures to improve the competitiveness and efficiency of European residential mortgage markets by facilitating the cross-border supply and funding of mortgage credit and by increasing the diversity of products available.

ECONOMIC CO-OPERATION

A review of the economic situation is presented annually by the Commission, analysing recent developments and short- and medium-term prospects. Economic policy guidelines for the following year are adopted annually by the Council.

The following objectives for the end of 1973 were agreed by the Council in 1971, as the first of three stages towards European economic and monetary union: the narrowing of exchange-rate margins to 2.25%; creation of a medium-term pool of reserves; co-ordination of short- and medium-term economic and budgetary policies; a joint position on international monetary issues; harmonization of taxes; creation of the European Monetary Co-operation Fund (EMCF); and creation of the European Regional Development Fund.

The narrowing of exchange margins (the 'snake') came into effect in 1972; however, Denmark, France, Ireland, Italy and the United Kingdom later floated their currencies, with only Denmark permanently returning to the arrangement. Sweden and Norway also linked their currencies to the 'snake', but Sweden withdrew from the arrangement in August 1977, and Norway withdrew in December 1978.

The European Monetary System (EMS) came into force in March 1979, with the aim of creating closer monetary co-operation, leading to a zone of monetary stability in Europe, principally through an Exchange Rate Mechanism (ERM), supervised by the ministries of finance and the central banks of member states. Not all Community members participated in the ERM: Greece did not join, Spain joined only in June 1989, the United Kingdom in October 1990 and Portugal in April 1992. To prevent wide fluctuations in the value of members' currencies against each other, the ERM fixed for each currency a central rate in European Currency Units (ECUs, see below), based on a 'basket' of national currencies; a reference rate in relation to other currencies was fixed for each currency, with established fluctuation margins. Central banks of the participating states intervened by buying or selling currencies when the agreed margin was likely to be exceeded. Each member placed 20% of its gold reserves and dollar reserves, respectively, into the EMCF, and received a supply of ECUs to regulate central bank interventions. Short- and medium-term credit facilities were given to support the balance of payments of member countries. The EMS was initially put under strain by the wide fluctuations in the exchange rates of non-Community currencies and by the differences in economic development among members, which led to nine realignments of currencies in 1979–83. Subsequently, greater stability was achieved, with only two realignments of currencies between 1984 and 1988. In 1992–93, however, there was great pressure on currency markets, necessitating further realignments; in September 1992 Italian and British membership of the ERM was suspended. In late July 1993, as a result of intensive currency speculation on European financial markets (forcing the weaker currencies to the very edge of their permitted margins), the ERM almost collapsed. In response to the crisis, EC finance ministers decided to widen the fluctuation margins allowed for each currency, except in the cases of Germany and the Netherlands, which agreed to maintain their currencies within the original limits. The new margins were regarded as allowing for so much fluctuation in exchange rates as to represent a virtual suspension of the ERM, although some countries, notably France and Belgium, expressed their determination to adhere as far as possible to the original 'bands' in order to fulfil the conditions for eventual monetary union. In practice, most currencies remained within the former narrower bands during 1994. Austria became a member of the EMS in January 1995, and its currency was subject to ERM conditions. While Sweden decided to remain outside the EMS, Finland joined in October 1996. In November of that year the Italian lira was readmitted to the ERM.

In September 1988 a committee (chaired by Jacques Delors, then President of the European Commission, and comprising the governors of member countries' central banks, representatives of the European Commission and outside experts) was established to discuss European monetary union. The resulting 'Delors plan' was presented to heads of government in June 1989, who agreed to begin the first stage of the process of monetary union—the drafting of a treaty on the subject—in 1990. The Intergovernmental Conference on Economic and Monetary Union was initiated in December 1990, and continued to work (in parallel with the Intergovernmental Conference on Political Union) throughout 1991. The Intergovernmental Conference was responsible for the drafting of the economic and monetary provisions of the Treaty on European Union, which was agreed by the European Council in December 1991 and which came into force on 1 November 1993. The principal feature of the Treaty's provisions on Economic and Monetary Union (EMU) was the gradual introduction of a single currency, to be administered by a single central bank. During the remainder of Stage I member states were to adopt programmes for the 'convergence' of their economies and ensure the complete liberalization of capital movements. Stage II began on 1 January 1994, and included the establishment of a European Monetary Institute (EMI), replacing the EMCF and comprising governors of central banks and a president appointed by heads of government. Heads of government were to decide, not later than 31 December 1996, whether a majority of member states fulfilled the necessary conditions for the adoption of a single currency: if so, they were to establish a date for the beginning of Stage III. If no date had been set by the end of 1997, Stage III was to begin on 1 January 1999, and was to be confined to those members that did fulfil the necessary conditions. After the establishment of a starting date for Stage III, the European Central Bank (ECB) and a European System of Central Banks were to be set up to replace the EMI. During Stage III exchange rates were to be irrevocably fixed, and a single currency introduced. Member states that had not fulfilled the necessary conditions for the adoption of a single currency would be exempt from participating. The United Kingdom was to be allowed to make a later, separate decision on whether to proceed to Stage III, while Denmark reserved the right to submit its participation in Stage III to a referendum. The near-collapse of the ERM in July 1993 cast serious doubts on the agreed timetable for monetary union, although in October the EC heads of government reaffirmed their commitment to the objective.

In December 1995 the European Council confirmed that Stage III of EMU was to begin on 1 January 1999, and confirmed that the proposed single currency would be officially known as the euro. The economic conditions for member states wishing to enter Stage III (including an annual budget deficit of no more than 3% of annual gross domestic product—GDP—and total public debt of no more than 60% of annual GDP) were also confirmed. Participants in EMU were to be selected in early 1998, on the basis of economic performance during 1997. In October 1996 the Commission issued a draft regulation on a proposed Stability and Growth Pact (SGP), intended to ensure that member countries maintained strict budgetary discipline during Stage III of monetary union. Another draft regulation formed the legal framework for the euro, confirming that it would be the single currency of participating countries from 1 January 1999. During a transitional period of up to three years national currencies would remain in circulation, having equivalent legal status to the euro. The communication outlined the main features of a new ERM, which would act as a 'waiting room' for countries preparing to join the single currency. Member countries remaining outside the monetary system, whether or not by choice, would remain part of the single market.

Although all of the then 15 members of the EU endorsed the principle of monetary union, with France and Germany the most ardent supporters, some countries had political doubts about joining. In October 1997 both the United Kingdom and Sweden confirmed that they would not participate in EMU from 1999. Denmark was also to remain outside the single currency.

Technical preparations for the euro were confirmed during a meeting of the European Council in Dublin, Ireland, in December 1996. The heads of government endorsed the new ERM and the legal framework for the euro and agreed to the proposed SGP. In March 1998 the Commission and the European Investment Bank (EIB) published reports on the progress made by member states towards the fulfilment of convergence criteria. The Commission concluded that Greece alone failed to satisfy the necessary conditions. In March Greece was admitted to the ERM, causing a 14% devaluation of its national currency. In May heads of state and of government confirmed that Greece failed to fulfil the conditions required for the adoption of a single currency from 1999. The meeting agreed that existing ERM central rates were to be used to determine the final rates of exchange between national currencies and the euro, which would be adopted on 1 January 1999. A European Central Bank (ECB) was established in June 1998, which was to be accountable to a European Forum, comprising members of the European Parliament (MEPs) and chairmen of the finance committees of the national parliaments of EU member countries.

On 31 December the ECOFIN Council adopted the conversion rates for the national currencies of the countries participating in the single currency. The euro was formally launched on 1 January 1999. ERM-II, the successor to the ERM, was launched on the same day. Both Greece and Denmark joined ERM-II, but in September 2000 some 53% of Danish voters participating in a national referendum rejected the adoption of the euro. On 1 January 2001 Greece became the 12th EU member state to adopt the euro. In September 2003 the majority of Swedish voters—some 56%—participating in a national referendum chose to reject Sweden's adoption of the euro.

The SGP, which was designed to sustain confidence in the euro, is seen as the cornerstone of monetary union. Under its original terms, member states were obliged to keep budget deficits within 3% of GDP, and to bring their budgets close to balance by 2004. However, during 2002 the Pact was heavily criticized for being inflexible, when a number of countries (including Portugal and Germany) could not meet its requirements. In September 2002 the 2004 deadline for reaching a balanced budget was extended by two years (benefiting France, Germany, Italy and Portugal), although the 3% limit for budgetary deficit remained, while some concessionary provision was introduced to allow countries with low levels of long-term debt, such as the United Kingdom and Ireland, to increase investment spending by running larger short-term budget deficits.

In November 2003 France and Germany, which were both likely to breach the budget deficit limit of 3% of GDP for a third consecutive year, persuaded the EU ministers responsible for finance to suspend the disciplinary procedure under which they could have faced punitive fines. The two countries had argued that further fiscal austerity could have precipitated a recession in their economies. Under compromise agreements, Germany and France were to reduce their budget deficits by 0.6% and 0.8% of GDP, respectively, in 2004 and by 0.5% and 0.6%, respectively, in 2005. However, even these reductions would not be required if growth rates in the French and German economies were unexpectedly low. The refusal of France and Germany to restrict their expenditure provoked anger among some smaller EU countries that had implemented strict austerity programmes in order to comply with the Pact. In January 2004 the European Commission launched a legal action against the Council of Finance Ministers in the European Court of Justice. The Court ruled in July that the Council had acted illegally in temporarily suspending the budget rules. However, prior to this ruling, in June, the economic affairs commissioner had announced a review of the SGP in order to clarify the rules of the Pact. Critics of the SGP, notably Germany, complained that the Pact was too inflexible and prevented countries from increasing public investment to stimulate the economy in an economic downturn. Amendments to the SGP were finally agreed by EU finance ministers in March 2005, and formally adopted by the Council in June. Although the existing limits on budget deficits and total public debt (of 3% and 60% of GDP, respectively) were retained, the reforms allowed for countries to be exempt from disciplinary action if they breached the deficit limit temporarily as a result of exceptional circumstances, such as a severe economic downturn, and extended the deadline for correcting a deficit deemed excessive. Germany secured agreement that costs related to its unification in 1990 be excluded from deficit calculations, while allowance was also to be made when assessing deficits for costs incurred in implementing major structural reforms, such as pension system reform.

All 10 countries that joined the EU on 1 May 2004 (Cyprus, the Czech Republic, Estonia, Hungary, Latvia, Lithuania, Malta, Poland, Slovakia and Slovenia) were obliged to participate in EMU; however, adoption of the euro was dependent on the fulfilment of the same Maastricht convergence criteria as the initial entrants, which comprised conditions regarding inflation, debt, budget deficit, long-term interest rates and exchange-rate stability. The exchange-rate criteria included the requirement to spend at least two years in ERM-II. Although the currency was permitted to fluctuate 15% either side of a central rate or, by common agreement, within a narrower band, the ECB specified that the limit of 2.25% would be applied when judging whether countries had achieved sufficient stability to join the euro area. The entry into the euro area of the new member states was not expected to affect the ECB's monetary policy, as the new member states only accounted for about 5% of the GDP of the enlarged EU. Although many of the new member countries were keen to adopt the euro as soon as possible, the ECB warned of the risks associated with early membership of ERM-II, sharing widespread concerns that the required fiscal austerity and loss of flexibility over exchange-rate policy would stifle economic growth in the accession countries. Moreover, currencies would also become vulnerable to speculative attacks once they entered ERM-II. Owing to differences in the economies of the new member states, progress towards adoption of the euro was likely to vary significantly. On 28 June 2004 Estonia, Lithuania and Slovenia joined ERM-II. In May 2006, in a specific convergence report drawn up at the request of Slovenia and Lithuania to assess their readiness to adopt the euro, the Commission concluded that Slovenia met all of the conditions for admission to the euro area, while Lithuania should retain its current status as a member state with a derogation. Slovenia duly adopted the euro on 1 January 2007. In December 2006, in a regular assessment, Estonia was judged to have not yet fulfilled all of the conditions for admission to the euro area. Cyprus, Latvia and Malta joined ERM-II on 2 May 2005, followed by Slovakia on 28 November. Cyprus and Malta were admitted to the euro area on 1 January 2008, increasing the number of countries in the euro area to 15. Slovakia was seeking to adopt the euro in January 2009.

In September 2004 revised figures released by Greece revealed previous gross under-reporting of the country's national budgetary deficit and debt figures. It was subsequently established that Greece had not complied with membership rules for the single currency in 2000, the year in which it qualified to join. Greece received a formal warning from the Commission in December for publishing inaccurate data concerning its public finances for 1997–2003. Five member states succeeded in reducing their deficits sufficiently to allow the closure of excessive deficit procedures against them in 2007: France in January, Germany, Greece and Malta in June, and the United Kingdom in October. The Czech Republic, Hungary, Italy, Poland, Portugal and Slovakia remained subject to excessive deficit procedures in early 2008.

In November 2004 the former Dutch Prime Minister, Wim Kok, published a report on the progress of the EU states toward the objectives established at a meeting in Lisbon, Portugal, in 2000, known as the Lisbon Strategy. The Lisbon Strategy urged EU governments to implement economic and social changes, including tax reductions, health-care and pension-system reform and the introduction of more flexible employment systems, in order to outperform the US economy by 2010. Kok's report concluded that the Strategy had been too broad and that many targets would be missed, and recommended a future focus on 14 main indicators with an emphasis on job creation and economic growth. In March 2005 heads of state and government endorsed a revision of the Lisbon Strategy proposed by the Commission. As recommended by Kok, the renewed Strategy focused more clearly on measures to promote job creation and economic growth. In addition, simplified governance arrangements were approved in July, with the introduction of one set of integrated policy guidelines to address macroeconomic, microeconomic and employment issues. On the basis of the new guidelines, member states submitted three-year national reform programmes in October.

In January 2006 the Commission published its annual progress report on the Lisbon Strategy, in which it analysed member states' national reform programmes and identified four priorities for further action: increasing investment in education, research and innovation; reducing administrative burdens on businesses; encouraging people of all ages to find employment; and guaranteeing a secure and sustainable energy supply. The annual assessment of the Strategy carried out in December 2006 concluded that *inter alia* important progress had been made towards reinforcing financial sustainability, although achieving sound finances in the medium to long term remained a significant challenge; that weak competition in many markets was problematic; and that the EU needed to tackle the twin problems of inflexible labour markets and of 'segmentation' between workers on permanent contracts with high employment protection and those working on fixed-term contracts with little or no security. The main conclusion of the annual progress report presented in December 2007 was that the Lisbon Strategy was contributing to recent improvements in the performance of the EU economy and that structural reforms were raising the long-term prospects for prosperity, but that further reforms would be required in 2008–13 to sustain economic growth, amid growing uncertainty in the global economy. Particular concern was expressed regarding the low level of investment in the EU in both information and communication technologies and research and development, the continued segmentation of many labour markets and a lack of worker mobility. It was also noted that the pace of reform had been uneven among member states. The Commission proposed a series of new policy initiatives, including national action plans on reducing early school-leaving and improving basic reading skills, national broadband strategies to increase high-speed internet usage, new legislation aimed at fostering the development and growth of small and medium-sized enterprises, further measures to integrate EU financial services markets, the completion of the internal market for energy and the creation of an affordable patent system.

The Euro

With the creation of the European Monetary System (EMS) in 1999, a new monetary unit, the European Currency Unit (ECU), was adopted. Its value and composition were identical to those of the

European Unit of Account (EUA) already used in the administrative fields of the Community. The ECU was a composite monetary unit, in which the relative value of each currency was determined by the gross national product and the volume of trade of each country.

The ECU, which was assigned the function of the unit of account used by the European Monetary Co-operation Fund (EMCF), was also used as the denominator for the Exchange Rate Mechanism (ERM); as the denominator for operations in both the intervention and the credit mechanisms; and as a means of settlement between monetary authorities of the European Community. From April 1979 the ECU was also used as the unit of account for the purposes of the Common Agricultural Policy (CAP). From 1981 it replaced the EUA in the general budget of the Community; the activities of the European Development Fund (EDF) under the Lomé Convention; the balance sheets and loan operations of the European Investment Bank (EIB); and the activities of the European Coal and Steel Community (ECSC). In June 1985 measures were adopted by the governors of the Community's central banks, aiming to strengthen the EMS by expanding the use of the ECU, for example, by allowing international monetary institutions and the central banks of non-member countries to become 'other holders' of ECUs.

In June 1989 it was announced that, with effect from 20 September, the Portuguese and Spanish currencies were to be included in the composition of the ECU. From that date the amounts of the national currencies included in the composition of the ECU were 'weighted' as follows (in percentages): Belgian franc 7.6; Danish krone 2.5; French franc 19.0; Deutsche Mark 30.1; Greek drachma 0.8; Irish pound 1.1; Italian lira 10.2; Luxembourg franc 0.3; Netherlands guilder 9.4; Portuguese escudo 0.8; Spanish peseta 5.3; and the United Kingdom pound sterling 13.0. The composition of the ECU 'basket' of currencies was 'frozen' with the entry into force of the Treaty on European Union on 1 November 1993. This was not affected by the accession to the EU of Austria, Finland and Sweden; consequently those countries' currencies were not represented in the ECU 'basket'.

As part of Stage III of the process of Economic and Monetary Union (EMU), the ECU was replaced by a single currency, the euro (€), on 1 January 1999, at a conversion rate of 1:1.

A payments settlement system, known as TARGET (Trans-European Automated Real-time Gross Settlement Express Transfer), was introduced for countries participating in EMU on 4 January 1999. By 2002 TARGET had become one of the world's largest payment systems, and was considered to be making a considerable contribution to the integration of the euro money market and the smooth implementation of the single monetary policy. An upgraded version of the system, TARGET2, was launched in November 2007. The Single Euro Payments Area (SEPA), which was to be introduced gradually during 2008–10, was designed to enable all electronic payments across the euro area to be made as efficiently and securely as domestic payments within a single member state.

On 1 January 2002 the euro entered into circulation in the 12 participating countries. By the end of February the former national currencies of all of the participating countries had been withdrawn. The introduction of the new currency took place without major problems, and even ahead of the official phasing-out of national currencies the changeover was functioning smoothly; by the beginning of February the euro was used in more than 95% of cash transactions.

The euro's value in national currencies is calculated and published daily. By mid-1999 the value of the euro had declined by some 12% against the US dollar compared with its value on introduction. Its decline was attributed to the relatively high degree of economic growth taking place in the USA compared with rates in the euro zone. The euro dropped below parity level with the dollar in December. The ECB raised interest rates four times during the six months to May 2000, in an attempt to combat the failure in confidence. In September 2000 the monetary authorities of the USA and Japan, concerned about the impact of the weakness of the euro on the world economy, intervened jointly with the ECB in exchange markets. In November 2000 the currency reached its lowest recorded level. The euro rallied briefly in early 2001, but by June its value was declining once again. The ECB lowered interest rates four times during 2001 (including in September, as part of a joint effort by central banks to counteract the economic effects of the terrorist attacks on the USA). By November the currency had lost about one-fifth of its value against the US dollar since its launch in 1999.

Immediately following the introduction of the euro in the 12 participating countries in January 2002, its value rose significantly; during 2002 it continued to appreciate against other currencies, reaching parity with the US dollar in June, a stage which marked its highest level since February 2000. The euro continued to appreciate sharply against the dollar, by 20% in 2003, largely as a result of the large US current-account deficit and its financing requirements. In early 2004 the euro weakened slightly against the dollar, although it appreciated sharply in subsequent months, reaching its highest ever rate of €1 = US $1.37 in December. However, the ECB resisted pressure to lower interest rates; the previous change in interest rates had been in early June 2003, when the ECB reduced its key refinancing rate to 2.0%. Although the high value of the euro had an adverse effect on exports, it had a favourable impact on imports, keeping imported inflation low and partially protecting the euro area from the negative effects of high petroleum prices. During the first four months of 2005 the exchange rate remained stable, at about €1 = US $1.30, but the euro's value against the dollar weakened thereafter, reaching a low of around €1 = US $1.17 in November. This depreciation was attributed to slow economic growth and political uncertainty following the rejection of the EU constitutional treaty by voters in referendums in France and the Netherlands. In December 2005 the ECB raised interest rates for the first time since October 2000, increasing the refinancing rate to 2.25%, amid concerns over rising inflation, fuelled by high petroleum prices, and indications of stronger economic growth in the euro zone. By early February 2006 the euro had recovered in value to a rate of €1 = US $1.21. In March the ECB raised interest rates for a second time, to 2.5%. By the end of April the euro had increased in value to €1 = US $1.24, but it declined somewhat between May and August. In June the refinancing rate was increased to 2.75%, and further increases to, respectively, 3.00% and 3.25%, were effected in August and October. On each day from 24 November until 10 January 2007, the value of the euro was greater than €1 = US $1.30. In December 2006 the refinancing rate was raised again, to 3.50%. Further increases to, respectively, 3.75% and 4.00%, were effected in March and June 2007. Meanwhile, the value of the euro against the dollar continued to strengthen throughout 2007 and into 2008, reaching €1 = US $1.59 in late April 2008.

External Relations

CENTRAL AND EASTERN EUROPE

During the late 1980s the extensive political changes and reforms in Eastern European countries led to a strengthening of links with the EC. Agreements on trade and economic co-operation were concluded with several countries. Community heads of government agreed in December 1989 to establish a European Bank for Reconstruction and Development—EBRD, with participation by member states of the Organisation for Economic Co-operation and Development—OECD and the Council for Mutual Economic Assistance, to promote investment in Eastern Europe; the EBRD began operations in April 1991. In the 1990s 'Europe Agreements' were signed with Czechoslovakia, Hungary and Poland (1991), Bulgaria and Romania (1993), Estonia, Latvia and Lithuania (1995) and Slovenia (1996), which led to formal applications for membership of the EU. On 1 May 2004 the Czech Republic, Estonia, Hungary, Latvia, Lithuania, Poland, Slovakia and Slovenia acceded to the EU. Bulgaria and Romania formally joined the EU on 1 January 2007.

Originally created by the EC in 1989 to co-ordinate aid from member states of the OECD to Hungary and Poland, in 2005 the PHARE (Poland/Hungary Aid for Restructuring of Economies) programme covered the eight new member states from Central and Eastern Europe, as well as the candidate countries Bulgaria and Romania. The programme's aim was to assist these countries in their preparations for joining the EU. Although eight of the 10 countries eligible for PHARE joined the Union on 1 May 2004, payments for projects continued to be disbursed until 2006. In addition, the new member states received financial assistance under a 'transition facility' until the end of 2006, to strengthen their institutional capacity. Meanwhile, pre-accession aid was increased substantially for Bulgaria and Romania, which were together allocated some €4,500m. for 2004–06. In July 2006 an Instrument for Pre-Accession Assistance (IPA) was adopted by the Council, which replaced PHARE and other such programmes (Instrument for Structural Policies for Pre-Accession—ISPA; Special Accession Programme for Agriculture and Rural Development—SAPARD; Community Assistance for Reconstruction, Development and Stabilisation, with reference to the Western Balkans—CARDS; and the Turkey instrument) from January 2007. The IPA aims to provide targeted assistance to candidate countries (Croatia, the former Yugoslav republic of Macedonia and Turkey in early 2008) or those that are potential candidates (e.g. Albania, Bosnia and Herzegovina, Montenegro and Serbia) for membership of the EU, and was to allocate funds totalling some €11,468m. in 2007–13. There were also programmes under a post-accession Transition Facility for Bulgaria and Romania in 2007.

In 1991 the EC established the Technical Assistance to the Commonwealth of Independent States (TACIS) programme, to promote the development of successful market economies and foster democracy in the countries of the former USSR through the provision of expertise and training. (TACIS initially extended assistance to the Baltic states. In 1992, however, these became eligible for assistance under PHARE and withdrew from TACIS.) The TACIS/EBRD Bangkok Facility provides EU financing to assist in the preparation for, and implementation of, EBRD investment in the CIS region. (Mongolia was eligible for TACIS assistance in 1991–2003, but was subsequently covered by the Asia Latin America—ALA programme.) The TACIS programme's budget for 2000–06 was €3,138m.

In March 2003 the European Commission launched a European Neighbourhood Policy (ENP) with the aim of enhancing co-operation with countries adjacent to the enlarged Union. A new European Neighbourhood and Partnership Instrument (ENPI) replaced TACIS and MEDA (which was concerned with EU co-operation with Mediterranean countries) from 2007. All countries covered by the ENP (Armenia, Azerbaijan, Belarus, Georgia, Moldova, Ukraine and several Mediterranean countries) were to be eligible for support under the ENPI. Russia was not covered by the ENP, and the relationship between Russia and the EU was described as a Strategic Partnership, which was also to be funded by the ENPI. In accordance with the ENP, in December 2004 the EU agreed 'Action Plans' with Moldova and Ukraine, establishing targets for political and economic co-operation. These Plans were adopted by EU foreign ministers and the two countries concerned in February 2005. ENP Action Plans for Armenia, Azerbaijan and Georgia were developed in 2005 and published in late 2006. The EU did not enter into discussions on a Plan with Belarus, stating that it first required the country to hold free and fair elections in order to establish a democratic form of government (see below). The eventual conclusion of more ambitious relationships with partner countries achieving sufficient progress in meeting the priorities set out in the Action Plans (through the negotiation of European Neighbourhood Agreements) was envisaged.

In 1992 EU heads of government decided to replace an agreement on trade and economic co-operation that had been concluded with the USSR in 1989 with new Partnership and Co-operation Agreements (PCAs), providing a framework for closer political, cultural and economic relations between the EU and the former republics of the USSR. The PCAs were preceded by preliminary Interim Agreements, and an Interim Agreement with Russia on trade concessions came into effect in February 1996. In December 1997 a PCA with Russia entered into force. The first meeting of the Co-operation Council for the EU-Russia PCA took place in January 1998. In June 1999 the EU adopted a Common Strategy on Russia, which applied until June 2004. This aimed to promote the consolidation of democracy and rule of law in the country; the integration of Russia into the common European economic and social space; and regional stability and security. At the sixth EU-Russia summit in October 2000 the two sides agreed to initiate a regular energy dialogue, with the aim of establishing an EU-Russia Energy Partnership. However, the status of Kaliningrad, a Russian enclave situated between Poland and Lithuania, became an increasing source of contention as the EU prepared to admit those two countries. Despite opposition from Russia, the EU insisted that residents of Kaliningrad would need a visa to cross EU territory. In November 2002, at an EU-Russia summit meeting held in Brussels, a compromise agreement was reached, according to which residents of the enclave were to be issued with multiple-transit travel documentation; the new regulations took effect in July 2003. Also in November 2002, the EU granted Russian exporters market economy status, in recognition of the progress made by Russia to liberalize its economy. At a summit held in St Petersburg, Russia, in May 2003, the EU and Russia agreed to improve their co-operation by creating four 'common spaces' within the framework of the PCA. The two sides agreed to establish a common economic space; a common space for freedom, security and justice; a space for co-operation on external security; and for research, education and culture. However, relations between the EU and Russia remained strained by Russia's opposition to EU enlargement, partly owing to fears of a detrimental effect on the Russian economy, as some of its neighbouring countries (significant markets for Russian goods) were obliged to introduce EU quotas and tariffs. In February 2004 the European Commission made proposals to improve the efficacy of EU-Russia relations, given their increased dependence, the enlargement due to take place in May, and unresolved territorial conflicts in a number of countries close to the Russian and EU borders (Azerbaijan, Georgia and Moldova). In May, at a bilateral summit held in the Russian capital, Moscow, the EU agreed to support Russia's membership of the World Trade Organization (WTO), following Russia's extension in April of its PCA with the EU to the 10 accession states. The Russian President, Vladimir Putin, signed legislation ratifying the Kyoto Protocol of the UN Convention on Climate Change in November, following EU criticism of the country's failure to do so. The Kyoto Protocol entered into force in February 2005. Consultations on human rights took place between the EU and Russia for the first time in March of that year, in Luxembourg. At a summit held in Moscow in May the two sides adopted a single package of 'road maps', to facilitate the creation of the four common spaces in the medium term. A further summit, which took place in London, the United Kingdom, in October, focused on the practical implementation of the road maps. As part of the common space on freedom and justice, agreements on visa facilitation (simplifying the procedures for issuing short-stay visas) and on readmission (setting out procedures for the return of people found to be illegally resident in the territory of the other party) were reached in that month, and were signed at the EU-Russia summit held in Sochi, Russia, in May 2006. In July the Commission approved draft negotiating directives for a new EU-Russia Agreement to replace the PCA, which was to come to the end of its initial 10-year period in December 2007. The PCA remained in force pending the conclusion of a new agreement. In March 2007 the Commission published a Country Strategy Paper for EU-Russia relations in 2007–13. Associated with the paper was a National Indicative Programme for Russia for 2007–10, which envisaged that financial allocations from the EU to Russia during that period would amount to €30m. annually. Financial co-operation was intended to focus on the common spaces and the package of road maps for their creation. At an EU-Russia summit meeting held in Mafra, Portugal, in October 2007 it was agreed to establish a system to provide early warning of threats to the supply of natural gas and petroleum to the EU, following the serious disruption of supplies to EU countries from Russia, via Belarus, in previous years.

In February 1994 the EU Council of Ministers agreed to pursue closer economic and political relations with Ukraine, following an agreement by that country to renounce control of nuclear weapons on its territory. A PCA was signed by the two sides in June. In December EU ministers of finance approved a loan totalling ECU 85m., conditional on Ukraine's implementation of a strategy to close the Chernobyl (Chornobyl) nuclear power plant. An Interim Trade Agreement with Ukraine came into force in February 1996; this was replaced by a PCA in March 1998. In December 1999, the EU adopted a Common Strategy on Ukraine, aimed at developing a strategic partnership on the basis of the PCA. The Chernobyl plant closed in December 2000. The EU has provided funding to cover the interim period prior to the completion of two new reactors (supported by the EBRD and the European Atomic Energy Community— Euratom) to replace the plant's generating capacity. The EU welcomed the inauguration as President of the pro-Western candidate, Viktor Yushchenko, in January 2005, and the EU action plan for Ukraine adopted in the following month envisaged enhanced co-operation in many areas. At a summit held in the Ukrainian capital, Kyiv, in December, the EU and Ukraine signed agreements on aviation and on Ukraine's participation in the EU's 'Galileo' civil satellite navigation and positioning system (see Research and Innovation) and a memorandum of understanding on increased co-operation in the energy sector. Ukraine reiterated its strategic goal to be integrated fully into the EU, and the EU pledged support for Ukraine's bid to join the WTO. It was also announced at the summit that Ukraine had been granted market economy status. Meanwhile, an EU mission to monitor Ukraine's border with Moldova was deployed for an initial period of two years, at the request of both countries' Governments. It was hoped that the mission would help prevent trafficking in people, the smuggling of goods, the proliferation of weapons and customs fraud. A dispute between Russia and Ukraine over gas prices in January 2006 was of considerable concern to the EU, which relied on Russia for some 25% of its gas (with some member states entirely dependent on imports from Russia), most of which passed through Ukraine. In March 2007 negotiations began on an enhanced agreement between the EU and Ukraine, which was intended to supersede the PCA. In the same month it was announced that the EU was to increase substantially the amount of aid allocated to Ukraine for the implementation of the EU action plan. A total of €494m. was to be made available to Ukraine in 2007–10. In mid-February 2008 EU ministers of foreign affairs attended a conference on the EU's Black Sea Synergy programme, held in Kyiv, Ukraine. Following the accession to the EU of the littoral states Bulgaria and Romania, the programme aims to improve co-operation between countries bordering the Black Sea, as well as between members of the Black Sea region and the EU.

An Interim Agreement with Belarus was signed in March 1996. However, in February 1997 the EU suspended negotiations for the conclusion of the Interim Agreement and for a PCA in view of serious reverses to the development of democracy in that country. EU technical assistance programmes were suspended, with the exception of aid programmes and those considered directly beneficial to the democratic process. In 1999 the EU announced that the punitive measures would be withdrawn gradually upon the attainment of certain benchmarks. By July 1999 PCAs had entered into force with all of the CIS states except for Belarus, Tajikistan and Turkmenistan. In 2000 the EU criticized the Government of Belarus for failing to accept its recommendations on the conduct of the legislative elections held in October. In November 2002 the EU member states imposed a travel ban on President Alyaksandr Lukashenka of Belarus and other senior Belarusian officials, in protest against the lack of democracy and the declining human rights situation in the country; the ban was lifted in April 2003. Unlike Russia and Ukraine, Belarus was reluctant to negotiate with the EU about border concerns, as the new EU member states introduced a visa regime. In September 2004 the European Parliament condemned Lukashenka's attempt to gain a third term of office by scheduling a referendum to change the country's Constitution, which permitted a maximum of two terms. The EU subsequently imposed a travel ban on officials responsible for the allegedly fraudulent legislative elections and the referendum held in Belarus in October, which abolished limits on the number of terms that the President was permitted to serve. The Council, nevertheless, reiterated the EU's willingness to develop closer relations with Belarus, including within the ENP, if President Lukashenka and his Government were to embark on fundamental democratic and economic reforms. In January 2005 the EU condemned the imprisonment of a former opposition presidential candidate on allegedly politically motivated charges. As part of efforts to support civil society and democratization, in September the European Commission initiated a €2m. project to increase access in Belarus to independent sources of news and information. In April 2006, following President Lukashenka's re-election in the previous month, the EU extended the travel ban imposed in 2004 to include Lukashenka and 30 government ministers and other officials, owing to concerns about electoral standards. In November 2006, in a communication to the Belarusian authorities, the EU detailed the benefits that Belarus could expect to gain, within the framework of the European Neighbourhood Policy, were the country to embark on a process of democratization and to show due respect for human rights and the rule of law.

In March 1997 the EU sent two advisory delegations to Albania to help to restore order after violent unrest and political instability erupted in that country. A request by the Albanian Government for the deployment of EU peace-keeping troops was refused, but it was announced in early April that the EU was to provide humanitarian aid of some ECU 2m., to be used for emergency relief. In September 2002 the European Parliament voted in support of opening negotiations for a SAA with Albania, following satisfactory progress in that country, with regard to presidential elections and electoral reform. In November 2005 the Commission urged Albania to increase its efforts to combat organized crime and corruption, to enhance media freedom and to conduct further electoral reform. In the following month the Council adopted a revised European Partnership for Albania, identifying priorities for the country to address. Negotiations on the signature of a SAA with Albania, which officially commenced at the end of January 2003, were completed in February 2006 and the SAA was formally signed in June. In September 2007 a visa facilitation agreement was signed between the EU and Albania, which entered into force at the beginning of 2008. (An agreement on readmission had come into force in May 2006.)

A co-operation agreement was signed with Yugoslavia in 1980 (but not ratified until April 1983), allowing tariff-free imports and Community loans. New financial protocols were signed in 1987 and 1991. However, EC aid was suspended in July 1991, following the declarations of independence by the Yugoslav republics of Croatia and Slovenia, and the subsequent outbreak of civil conflict. Efforts were made in the ensuing months by EC ministers of foreign affairs to negotiate a peaceful settlement between the Croatian and Serbian factions, and a team of EC observers was maintained in Yugoslavia from July, to monitor successive cease-fire agreements. In October the EC proposed a plan for an association of independent states, to replace the Yugoslav federation: this was accepted by all of the Yugoslav republics except Serbia, which demanded a redefinition of boundaries to accommodate within Serbia all predominantly Serbian areas. In November the application of the Community's co-operation agreements with Yugoslavia was suspended (with exemptions for the republics which co-operated in the peace negotiations). In January 1992 the Community granted diplomatic recognition to the former Yugoslav republics of Croatia and Slovenia, and in April it recognized Bosnia and Herzegovina, while withholding recognition from Macedonia (owing to pressure from the Greek Government, which feared that the existence of an independent Macedonia would imply a claim on the Greek province of the same name). In May EC ambassadors were withdrawn from the Yugoslav capital, Belgrade, in protest at Serbia's support for aggression by Bosnian Serbs against other ethnic groups in Bosnia and Herzegovina, and in the same month the Community imposed a trade embargo on Serbia and Montenegro.

New proposals for a settlement of the Bosnian conflict, submitted by EC and UN mediators in 1993, were accepted by the Bosnian Croats and by the Bosnian Government in March, but rejected by the Bosnian Serbs. In June the European Council pledged more rigorous enforcement of sanctions against Serbia. In July, at UN/EC talks in Geneva, all three parties to the Bosnian war agreed on a plan to divide Bosnia and Herzegovina into three separate republics; however, the Bosnian Government rejected the proposals for the share of territory to be allotted to the Muslim community.

In April 1994, following a request from EU ministers of foreign affairs, a Contact Group, consisting of France, Germany, the United Kingdom, the USA and Russia, was initiated to undertake peace negotiations. In the following month ministers of foreign affairs of the USA, Russia and the EU (represented by five member states) jointly endorsed a proposal to divide Bosnia and Herzegovina in proportions of 49% to the Bosnian Serbs and 51% to the newly established Federation of Muslims and Croats. The proposal was rejected by the Bosnian Serb assembly in July and had to be abandoned after the Muslim-Croat Federation withdrew its support subsequent to the Bosnian Serb vote. In July the EU formally assumed political control of Mostar, in southern Bosnia and Herzegovina, in order to restore the city's administrative infrastructure and secure peace.

Despite some criticism of US policy towards the former Yugoslavia, in September 1995 the EU supported US-led negotiations in Geneva to devise a plan to end the conflict in Bosnia and Herzegovina. The plan closely resembled the previous proposals of the Contact Group: two self-governing entities were to be created within Bosnia and Herzegovina, with 51% of territory being allocated to the Muslim-Croat Federation and 49% to Bosnian Serbs. The proposals were finally agreed after negotiations in Dayton, USA, in November 1995, and an accord was signed in Paris in December.

In January 1996 the EU announced its intention to recognize Yugoslavia (Serbia and Montenegro), despite the opposition of the USA. During 1996–99 the EU allocated ECU 1,000m. for the repatriation of refugees, restructuring the economy and technical assistance, in addition to ECU 1,000m. in humanitarian aid provided since the beginning of the conflict in the former Yugoslavia. During 1991–2000 Bosnia and Herzegovina received a total of €1,032m. in assistance from the EU.

In 2000 the EU published a road map for Bosnia and Herzegovina, outlining measures that must be undertaken by the Government prior to the initiation of a feasibility study on the formulation of a Stabilization and Association Agreement (SAA). In September 2002 the Commission reported that Bosnia and Herzegovina had essentially adhered to the terms of the road map. In January 2003 a new EU Police Mission (EUPM) took over from the UN peace-keeping force in Bosnia and Herzegovina. This was the first operation under the common European Security and Defence Policy. The EUPM was re-established in 2006, and aimed to support the police-reform process and continue to help to combat organized crime. Meanwhile, on 28 January 2004 the Bosnian Government issued a decree, providing for the reunification of Mostar (divided between Croat- and Bosnian-controlled municipalities since 1993) into a single administration, thereby fulfilling one of the major preconditions for signature of a SAA with the EU. In December 2004 a 7,000-member EU Force (EUFOR) assumed control of military operations in Bosnia and Herzegovina from a Stabilization Force (SFOR) led by the North Atlantic Treaty Organization (NATO). Negotiations on a SAA officially commenced in November 2005. In January 2006, as part of the ongoing negotiations, an EU-Bosnia and Herzegovina Consultative Task Force that had been established in 1998 was formally restyled Reform Process Monitoring. In February 2007 a transition plan for EUFOR was announced, whereby the force's size was to be reduced to some 2,500 troops. The reconfigured EUFOR would continue to fulfil its peace-keeping mandate, while retaining the capacity to reverse the effects of the reduction in its strength and to re-establish a more robust military presence if necessary. On 4 December 2007 a SAA with the EU was initialled (with its official signature dependent on further political reforms). A visa facilitation and readmission agreement between Bosnia and Herzegovina and the EU came into force at the beginning of 2008.

A SAA was signed with Croatia in October 2001. In February 2003 Croatia submitted a formal application for membership of the EU. In December 2004 the European Council announced that negotiations on membership would commence in mid-March 2005, provided that Croatia co-operated fully with the ICTY. The SAA entered into force in February 2005. In early 2005 the only outstanding issue between Croatia and the ICTY was the need for the arrest and transfer to The Hague of the retired Gen. Ante Gotovina, who went into hiding in 2001 when the ICTY charged him with war crimes against ethnic Serbs during a military operation in 1995. The planned accession talks with Croatia were postponed in March 2005, following an official report by the Chief Prosecutor at the ICTY, Carla Del Ponte, which stated that the Croatian authorities had failed to demonstrate full co-operation with the ICTY. However, in early October Del Ponte issued an assessment stating that Croatia's co-operation with the ICTY had improved, and negotiations were initiated. In December Gotovina was apprehended in the Canary Islands, Spain, reportedly as a result of information received by ICTY investigators from the Croatian authorities; his arrest was perceived as removing the main obstacle to EU membership.

In December 1993 six member states of the EU formally recognized the former Yugoslav republic of Macedonia (FYRM) as an independent state, but in February 1994 Greece imposed a commercial embargo against the FYRM, on the grounds that the use of the name and symbols (e.g. on the state flag) of 'Macedonia' was a threat to Greek national security. In March, however, ministers of foreign affairs of the EU decided that the embargo was in contravention of EU law, and in April the Commission commenced legal proceedings in the European Court of Justice against Greece. In September 1995 Greece and the FYRM began a process of normalizing relations, after the FYRM agreed to change the design of its state flag. In October Greece ended its economic blockade of the FYRM. A trade and co-operation agreement with the FYRM entered into force in January 1998. In April 2001 a SAA was signed with the FYRM. At the same time, an interim agreement was adopted, allowing for trade-related matters of the SAA to enter into effect in June, without the need for formal ratification by the national parliaments of the EU member states. (The SAA provided for the EU to open its markets to 95% of exports from the FYRM.) However, the Macedonian Government was informed that it would be required to deliver concessions to the ethnic Albanian minority population prior to entering into the agreement. In 2002 the remit of the European Agency for Reconstruction, which had been originally established to implement aid programmes in Kosovo, was extended to include the FYRM. The SAA entered into force in April 2004. A formal application for membership of the EU was submitted in March of that year, and the FYRM was granted candidate status in December 2005. A visa facilitation and readmission agreement between the FYRM and the EU came into force at the beginning of 2008.

On 31 March 2003 a NATO contingent in the FYRM was replaced by an EU-led mission, entitled Operation Concordia, comprising 350 military personnel. It was replaced in December 2003 by a 200-member EU police mission, Operation Proxima, which, in addition to maintaining security and combating organized crime in the country, was to advise the Macedonian police forces. Operation Proxima's mandate expired at the end of 2005.

In 1998 the escalation of violence in the Serbian province of Kosovo (Federal Republic of Yugoslavia), between Serbs and the ethnic Albanian majority, prompted the imposition of sanctions by EU ministers of foreign affairs. In March ministers agreed to impose an arms embargo, to halt export credit guarantees to Yugoslavia and to restrict visas for Serbian officials. A ban on new investment in the region was imposed in June. In the same month, military observers from the EU, Russia and the USA were deployed to Kosovo. During October the Yugoslav Government allowed a team of international experts to investigate atrocities in the region, under an EU mandate. Several EU countries participated in the NATO military offensive against Yugoslavia, which was initiated in March 1999 owing to the continued repression of ethnic Albanians in Kosovo by Serbian forces. Ministers approved a new series of punitive measures in April, including an embargo on the sale or supply of petroleum to the Yugoslav authorities and an extension of a travel ban on Serbian officials and business executives. Humanitarian assistance was extended to provide relief for the substantial numbers of refugees who fled Kosovo amid the escalating violence, in particular to assist the Governments of Albania and the FYRM.

In September 1999 EU foreign ministers agreed to ease sanctions in force against Kosovo and Montenegro. In October the EU began to implement an 'Energy for Democracy' initiative, with the objective of supplying some €5m.-worth of heating oil to Serbian towns controlled by groups in opposition to the Yugoslav President, Slobodan Milošević. In February 2000 the EU suspended its ban on the Yugoslav national airline. However, the restrictions on visas for Serbian officials were reinforced. Kosovo received a total of €474.7m. under EU programmes in 2000 and the EU was the largest financial contributor to the province in 2001.

In May 2000 the EU agreed an emergency aid package to support Montenegro against destabilization by Serbia. Following the election of a new administration in the FRY in late 2000, the EU immediately withdrew all remaining sanctions, with the exception of those directed against Milošević and his associates, and pledged financial support of €200m. The FRY was welcomed as a full participant in the stabilization and association process (see below). It was announced that a Consultative Task Force would be set up when conditions permitted. The EU insisted that the FRY must co-operate fully with the International Criminal Tribunal for the former Yugoslavia (ICTY). Following the arrest of Milošević by the FRY authorities in April 2001, the first part of the EU's aid package for that year (amounting to €240m.) was released. During 2002 EU humanitarian aid to Serbia totalled €37.5m., to assist the large numbers of refugees and displaced persons. Negotiations on a SAA between the State Union of Serbia and Montenegro (as the FRY became known in February 2003) and the EU commenced in November 2005. However, owing to the country's failure fully to co-operate with the ICTY, the Commission decided to terminate these negotiations in May 2006, while emphasizing its willingness to resume talks as soon as full co-operation with the ICTY had been achieved. Following Montenegro's declaration of independence on 3 June 2006, the Narodna skupština Republike Srbije (National Assembly of the Republic of Serbia) confirmed that Serbia was the official successor state of the State Union of Serbia and Montenegro. On 12 June the EU recognized Montenegrin independence, and the Serbian Government officially recognized Montenegro as an independent state three days later. At the end of September the Narodna skupština adopted a new Constitution, which was confirmed by referendum in late October. In early June 2007 the President of the European Commission invited Serbia to resume negotiations on a SAA, following the arrest, within Serbia, of Zdravko Tolimir, a former Bosnian Serb army officer; the continuation of negotiations remained conditional on Serbia's full co-operation with the ICTY. A visa facilitation and readmission agreement between Serbia and the EU came into force at the beginning of 2008. In late February the EU suspended negotiations with Serbia on a SAA, after violence broke out in Belgrade following the declaration of independence by Kosovo (see below).

Meanwhile, following the declaration of independence by Montenegro in June 2006, the EU Council pledged to develop the relationship of the EU with Montenegro as a sovereign state. The first Enhanced Permanent Dialogue meeting between Montenegro and the EU was held in the Montenegrin capital, Podgorica, in late July. On the same day, the Council adopted a mandate for the negotiation of a SAA with Montenegro (based on the previous mandate for negotiations with the State Union of Serbia and Montenegro). Negotiations on a SAA were initiated in September. In November the Commission published a dedicated Annual Progress Report on Montenegro, together with a new European Partnership for Montenegro. On 15 March 2007 the SAA with the EU was initialled (with its official signature dependent on further political reforms). A visa facilitation and readmission agreement between Montenegro and the EU came into force at the beginning of 2008.

On 17 February 2008 the Assembly of Kosovo endorsed a declaration establishing the province as a sovereign state, independent from Serbia. Serbia immediately protested that the declaration of independence contravened international law and demanded that it be annulled. The USA extended recognition to Kosovo on the following day, and a large number of EU member nations announced their intention to do so. A supervisory EU mission in Kosovo (to be known as EULEX), initially comprising some 1,800 foreign personnel, was due to become operational after a 120-day transition period. Meanwhile, the UN Mission in Kosovo was to transfer its responsibilities to the Kosovo authorities. Several EU member states (Cyprus, Romania, Slovakia and Spain) announced their intention to withhold recognition of Kosovo as an independent state. In late February the EU condemned attacks on foreign embassies in Belgrade by Serb protesters.

In June 1999 the EU, in conjunction with the Group of Seven industrialized nations and Russia (the G-8), regional governments and other organizations concerned with the stability of the region, launched the Stability Pact for South Eastern Europe, a comprehensive conflict-prevention strategy, which was placed under the auspices of the Organization for Security and Co-operation in Europe (OSCE). The Stability Pact aimed to strengthen the efforts of the countries of South East Europe in fostering peace, democracy, respect for human rights and economic prosperity. For its part, the EU proposed to offer customized SAAs to Albania, Bosnia, Croatia, the FYRM and, eventually, the FRY, provided that they fulfilled certain conditions (see above). The FRY (renamed Serbia and Montenegro in February 2003) was excluded from the Pact until October 2000, following the staging there of democratic presidential elections. Since the establishment of the Pact, the heads of state and government of the member countries have met regularly in the framework of the South East Europe Co-operation Process (SEECP). In 2001–07 aid aimed at supporting the participation of the countries of the Western Balkans in the SAA process was provided through the CARDS programme. In January 2007 CARDS was replaced by the new IPA, which was to cover the period 2007–13. In November 2006, at the same time as it adopted Enlargement Strategy and Progress Reports, the Commission adopted the IPA Multi-Annual Financial Framework for 2008–10 (including figures for 2007). Under the Financial Framework, Croatia was to receive a total of €589.9m. in 2007–10; the FYRM €302.8m.; Serbia €771.1m.; Montenegro €131.3m.; Kosovo €261.4m.; Bosnia and Herzegovina €332.0m.; and Albania €306.1m. (Funds were also to be allocated to Turkey under the Financial Framework.) An additional allocation of €559.1m. for regional and horizontal programmes was also envisaged.

An EU-Western Balkans summit was held in June 2004 to continue the progress made at the Thessaloníki European Council meeting of June 2003. A joint declaration was adopted confirming EU support for the future of the Balkan countries in the EU under the SAA process and the Thessaloníki agenda was published, which provided a framework for progress towards European integration for the Balkans. It was announced that in future meetings would take place between ministers responsible for foreign affairs, justice and home affairs as well as heads of state.

OTHER EUROPEAN COUNTRIES

The members of the European Free Trade Association (EFTA) concluded bilateral free-trade agreements with the EEC and the ECSC during the 1970s. On 1 January 1984 the last tariff barriers were eliminated, thus establishing full free trade for industrial products between the Community and EFTA members. Some EFTA members subsequently applied for membership of the EC: Austria in 1989, Sweden in 1991, and Finland, Switzerland and Norway in 1992. Formal negotiations on the creation of a 'European Economic Area' (EEA), a single market for goods, services, capital and labour among EC and EFTA members, began in June 1990, and were concluded in October 1991. The agreement was signed in May

1992 (after a delay caused by a ruling of the Court of Justice of the EC that a proposed joint EC-EFTA court, for adjudication in disputes, was incompatible with the Treaty of Rome; EFTA members then agreed to concede jurisdiction to the Court of Justice on cases of competition involving both EC and EFTA members, and to establish a special joint committee for other disputes). In a referendum in December, Swiss voters rejected ratification of the agreement, and the remaining 18 countries signed an adjustment protocol in March 1993, allowing the EEA to be established without Switzerland (which was to have observer status). The EEA entered into force on 1 January 1994. Despite the rejection of the EEA by the Swiss electorate, the Swiss Government declared its intention to continue to pursue its application for membership of the EU. Formal negotiations on the accession to the EU of Austria, Finland and Sweden began on 1 February, and those on Norway's membership started on 1 April. Negotiations were concluded in March 1994. Heads of government of the four countries signed treaties of accession to the EU in June, which were to come into effect from 1995, subject to approval by a national referendum in each country. Accession to the EU was endorsed by the electorates of Austria, Finland and Sweden in June, October and November 1994, respectively. Norway's accession, however, was rejected in a national referendum (by 52.4% of voters) conducted at the end of November. The success of the campaign opposing Norway's entry to the EU was attributed to several factors: in particular, fears were expressed by farmers that the influx of cheaper agricultural goods from the EU would lead to bankruptcies and unemployment in the agricultural sector, and by workers in the fishing industry that stocks of fish would be severely depleted if EU boats were granted increased access to Norwegian waters. There was also widespread concern that national sovereignty would be compromised by the transfer to the EU of certain executive responsibilities. Since the 1994 referendum, Norway's relations with the EU have been based on full participation in the EEA as well as involvement (at non-signatory level) in the EU's Schengen Agreement. Austria, Finland and Sweden became members of the EU on 1 January 1995. Liechtenstein, which became a full member of EFTA in September 1991, joined the EEA on 1 May 1995. Negotiations conducted with Switzerland from 1992 on the formulation of a new bilateral economic arrangement proceeded slowly. The main obstacles to an agreement concerned Switzerland's work permit quotas for EU citizens, and the weight limit on trucks passing through its territory. In April 1996 the Swiss Government approved the Neue Eisenbahn-Alpen-Transversale (NEAT) project to construct two new Alpine tunnels in order to expedite international freight transport by rail; it was announced that this was to be financed mainly by levying a weight and distance toll on heavy goods vehicles crossing Swiss territory. Agreement was reached in December 1996 to gradually withdraw Swiss work permit quotas for citizens of EU member states within six years of an economic treaty being signed between the EU and Switzerland. In December 1998 political agreement was reached with Switzerland to abolish the weight limit and instead impose road-haulage charges on trucks weighing 40 metric tons or more. Later that month an interim EU-Swiss trade agreement was concluded. By February 2000 the Swiss Government had negotiated seven bilateral free-trade agreements with the EU. The accords included the gradual elimination of immigration controls between Switzerland and the EU over a 12-year period in order to allay popular anxiety regarding the possibility of EU workers depriving the Swiss of employment. Following the submission of a petition by pro-EU lobbyists, a referendum was held in March 2001 on whether to begin 'fast-track' accession negotiations with the EU; participation in the ballot was unusually high and the motion was rejected by a large majority, 77% of the voters. The Swiss Government, however, announced that the vote did not represent a rejection of the EU, but rather reflected the desire to move towards membership at a slower pace, and that its plans for eventual membership of the EU remained unchanged. The first EU-Switzerland summit meeting took place in Brussels in May 2004, after which nine new sectoral agreements (covering areas such as savings tax, fraud, the Schengen Agreement on border controls and the environment) were signed by the two parties. The participation of Switzerland in the Schengen area and the extension of the agreement on the free movement of persons to the 10 states that joined the EU in May 2004 were approved by Swiss voters in public referendums in June and September 2005. A protocol on these measures and on the nine sectoral agreements was signed in October 2004 and entered into force in April 2006. In February 2006 a memorandum of understanding (MOU) on Switzerland's agreement to contribute €125m. annually over five years to selected projects supporting social and economic cohesion in the enlarged EU was signed. This financial commitment, made in recognition of Switzerland's privileged access, via numerous bilateral agreements, to the enlarged internal market of the EU was approved by Swiss voters in a public referendum in November. It was recognized in early 2007 that both the agreement on the free movement of persons and the MOU on Switzerland's financial contribution to cohesion would have to be adapted to take into account Bulgaria and Romania's accession to the EU. In mid-2006 the Swiss Government published a report on bilateral relations with the EU—the first such document it had released since 1999. The so-called Europe Report concluded, *inter alia*, that the bilateral approach would remain the country's only viable option in the short and medium terms, but stated nevertheless that Switzerland's application for EU membership should be maintained in case such an approach should become difficult or impossible to pursue.

Despite the fact that Iceland joined EFTA in 1970 and ratified the EEA in 1993 (although the extension of the single market legislation excluded agriculture and fisheries management, as in Norway and Liechtenstein), it did not thereafter apply for EU membership. Although opposition to Iceland's joining the EU persisted at government level in the first half of the 2000s, relations between the EU and Iceland had generally developed smoothly since 1993—notably Iceland negotiated participation in the Schengen Agreement (although, as a signatory, it was not involved in decision-making within the agreement).

A trade agreement with Andorra entered into force on 1 January 1991, establishing a customs union for industrial products, and allowing duty-free access to the EC for certain Andorran agricultural products. A co-operation agreement with Andorra (covering a wide range of issues) and an agreement on the taxation of savings income were signed in November 2004 and entered into force in July 2005. Similar agreements on the taxation of savings income also took effect in Liechtenstein, Monaco and San Marino in July 2005. Negotiations on a co-operation and customs union agreement between the EC and San Marino were concluded in December 1991; the agreement, however, did not enter into force until May 2002. The euro became the sole currency in circulation in Andorra, Monaco, San Marino and the Vatican City at the beginning of 2002.

THE MIDDLE EAST AND THE MEDITERRANEAN

A scheme to negotiate a series of parallel trade and co-operation agreements encompassing almost all of the non-member states on the coast of the Mediterranean was formulated by the EC in 1972. Association Agreements, intended to lead to customs union or the eventual full accession of the country concerned, had been signed with Greece (which eventually became a member of the Community in 1981) in 1962, Turkey in 1964 and Malta in 1971; a fourth agreement was signed with Cyprus in 1972. (Malta and Cyprus became members of the EU in May 2004.) These established free access to the Community market for most industrial products and tariff reductions for most agricultural products. Annexed were financial protocols under which the Community was to provide concessional finance. During the 1970s a series of agreements covering trade and economic co-operation were concluded with the Arab Mediterranean countries and Israel, all establishing free access to EC markets for most industrial products. Access for agricultural products was facilitated, although some tariffs remained. In 1982 the Commission formulated an integrated plan for the development of its own Mediterranean regions and recommended the adoption of a new policy towards the non-Community countries of the Mediterranean. This was to include greater efforts towards diversifying agriculture, in order to avoid surpluses of items such as citrus fruits, olive oil and wine (which the Mediterranean countries all wished to export to the Community) and to reduce these countries' dependence on imported food. From 1 January 1993 the majority of agricultural exports from Mediterranean non-Community countries were granted exemption from customs duties.

In June 1995 the European Council endorsed a proposal by the Commission to reform and strengthen the Mediterranean policy of the EU. The initiative envisaged the eventual establishment of a Euro-Mediterranean Economic Area (EMEA), to be preceded by a gradual liberalization of trade within the region through bilateral and regional free-trade arrangements, and the adoption of financial and technical measures to support the implementation of structural reforms in Mediterranean partner countries. In November a conference of foreign affairs ministers of the EU member states, 11 Mediterranean non-member countries (excluding Libya) and the Palestinian authorities was convened in Barcelona, Spain. The conference endorsed the agreement on the EMEA and resolved to establish a permanent Euro-Mediterranean ministerial dialogue. It issued the 'Barcelona Declaration', endorsing commitments to uphold democratic principles and to pursue greater co-operation in the control of international crime, drugs-trafficking and illegal migration. The Declaration set the objective of establishing a Euro-Mediterranean free-trade area by 2010. The process of co-operation and dialogue under this agreement became known as the Euro-Mediterranean Partnership (or 'Barcelona Process'). In September 1998 the Commission proposed measures to extend the single market to the Mediterranean countries and sought to formulate common rules on customs and taxation, free movement of goods, public procurement, intellectual property, financial services, data protection and accounting.

In April 1997 the second Euro-Mediterranean Conference of ministers of foreign affairs was held, in Malta, to review implementation of the partnership strategy. Euro-Mediterranean foreign ministers convened for a third conference in April 1999, in Stuttgart, Germany. The Stuttgart conference agreed that Libya could eventually become a partner in the process, following the removal of UN sanctions on that country (which took place in September 2003) and acceptance of the full terms of the Barcelona Declaration. Libya subsequently attended meetings as an observer. A fourth conference, convened in November 2000, in Marseilles, France, focused on the adoption of a new common strategy for the Mediterranean, aimed at strengthening the Barcelona Process. With economic, financial, social and cultural components, the new approach involved increased political dialogue with partnership countries as well as further efforts to improve security, democracy and human rights. The fifth Euro-Mediterranean Conference, in Valencia, Spain, in April 2002, reaffirmed the principles of the Barcelona Declaration and adopted an action plan covering different fields of the partnership.

The sixth Euro-Mediterranean Conference, held in December 2003, in Naples, Italy, was the last such meeting before the enlargement of the EU in May 2004, and, as such, stressed the political importance of the partnership and emphasized the potential for closer integration between Europe and Mediterranean countries (as offered by the EU's 'Wider Europe' policy, which covered areas such as transport, energy and telecommunications). At the conference agreement was reached on the establishment of a Euro-Mediterranean Parliamentary Assembly, to allow partners to meet on a more formal basis; a reinforced lending facility by the European Investment Bank (EIB, see p. 256) was agreed, in order to stimulate growth in the private sector; and, finally, it was agreed that a Euro-Mediterranean Foundation for the Dialogue of Cultures would be set up, which would aim to increase dialogue and promote exchanges, co-operation and mobility between people at all levels (with particular focus on young people). The inaugural meeting of the Euro-Mediterranean Parliamentary Assembly took place in Athens, Greece, in March 2004. The Assembly replaced the Euro-Mediterranean Parliamentary Forum, which had been established in 1998. The seventh Euro-Mediterranean Conference, which was held in Luxembourg in May 2005, discussed recent European Commission proposals to strengthen EU relations with the Mediterranean, notably in the areas of economic reform, education, and human rights and democracy. In late November of that year an extraordinary Euro-Mediterranean summit of heads of government and state took place in Barcelona to mark the 10th anniversary of the Euro-Mediterranean Partnership. However, the only non-EU leaders to attend were the President of the Palestinian National Authority and the Prime Minister of Turkey, with lower-level delegations representing the other non-member countries. A code of conduct on countering terrorism and a five-year work programme on the further development of the Partnership were adopted at the talks. The eighth Euro-Mediterranean Conference, held in Tampere, Finland, in November 2006, culminated in the unanimous adoption of the so-called Tampere conclusions. Notable among the conclusions was the commitment expressed to strengthening the role of civil society in Mediterranean partner countries, with particular emphasis on democracy, political pluralism, expanded participation in political life, public affairs and decision-making, further strengthening the role of women in society, and enhanced respect for and promotion of human rights and fundamental freedoms. The ninth Euro-Mediterranean conference was held in Lisbon, Portugal, in November 2007, and implementation of the five-year work programme and the Tampere conclusions was reviewed. The political objectives of the Barcelona process were supported by a budget of some €3,300m. for the period 2007–10.

In March 2003 the European Commission launched a new European Neighbourhood Policy (ENP) with the aim of enhancing co-operation with countries that would neighbour the EU following its enlargement. Algeria, Egypt, Israel, Jordan, Lebanon, Libya, Morocco, the Palestinian Autonomous Areas, Syria and Tunisia were covered by the ENP, which was intended to complement the Barcelona Process, in addition to several countries to the east of the Union. Under the ENP, the EU intended to negotiate individual 'Action Plans' with neighbouring countries, establishing targets for further political and economic co-operation. The Action Plans were to build on existing contractual relationships between the partner country and the EU (for example, Association Agreements or Partnership and Co-operation Agreements). The eventual conclusion of more ambitious relationships with partner countries achieving sufficient progress in meeting the priorities set out in the Action Plans (through the negotiation of European Neighbourhood Agreements) was envisaged. The first Action Plans—for, in the Mediterranean region, Israel, Jordan, Morocco, the Palestinian Authority and Tunisia—were launched in December 2004.

The EU's primary financial instrument for the implementation of the Euro-Mediterranean Partnership has been the MEDA programme, providing support for the reform of economic and social structures within partnership countries. The legal basis of the MEDA programme was the MEDA Regulation, adopted in July 1996. In 1999 the MEDA Regulation was reviewed and revised.

The amended programme was named MEDA II. Covering the period 2000–06, MEDA II was granted a budget of €5,350m. In 2007 a new European Neighbourhood and Partnership Instrument (ENPI) replaced MEDA and the Technical Assistance to the Commonwealth of Independent States (TACIS) programme (which was concerned with EU co-operation with the countries of the former USSR). ENPI was conceived as a flexible, policy-orientated instrument to target sustainable development and conformity with EU policies and standards. In 2007–13 some €12,000m. was to be made available, within its framework, to support ENP Action Plans and the Strategic Partnership with Russia. An ENPI cross-border co-operation programme was to cover activities across the external borders of the EU in the south and the east, supported by funds totalling €1,180m. in 2007–13.

The first Euro-Mediterranean Energy Forum was convened in May 1997 and a second Energy Forum was held in May 1998; a number of other sectoral conferences have been organized (covering industry, the environment, water, the information society and agriculture). The first Euro-Mediterranean ministerial conference on trade was convened in May 2001, in Brussels; further meetings within this framework were held regularly thereafter.

Turkey, which had signed an Association Agreement with the EC in 1963 (although this was suspended between 1980 and 1986 following a military coup), applied for membership of the EU in April 1987. Accession talks began in October 2005 (see Enlargement).

Co-operation agreements concluded in the 1970s with the Maghreb countries (Algeria, Morocco and Tunisia), the Mashreq countries (Egypt, Jordan, Lebanon and Syria) and Israel covered free access to the Community market for industrial products, customs preferences for certain agricultural products, and financial aid in the form of grants and loans from the EIB. A co-operation agreement negotiated with the Republic of Yemen was non-preferential. In June 1992 the EC approved a proposal to conclude new bilateral agreements with the Maghreb countries, incorporating the following components: political dialogue; financial, economic, technical and cultural co-operation; and the eventual establishment of a free-trade area. A Euro-Mediterranean Association Agreement with Tunisia was signed in July 1995 and entered into force in March 1998. A similar agreement with Morocco (concluded in 1996) entered into force in March 2000. (In July 1987 Morocco applied to join the Community, but its application was rejected on the grounds that it is not a European country.) The EU's relations with Algeria have been affected by political and civil instability in that country and by concerns regarding the Government's respect for human rights and democratic principles. In March 1997 negotiations were initiated between the European Commission and representatives of the Algerian Government on a Euro-Mediterranean Association Agreement that would incorporate political commitments relating to democracy and human rights; this was signed in December 2001 and entered into force in September 2005. An Association Agreement with Jordan was signed in November 1997 and entered into force in May 2002. A Euro-Mediterranean Association Agreement with Egypt (which has been a major beneficiary of EU financial co-operation since the 1970s) was signed in June 2001 and was fully ratified in June 2004. In May 2001 Egypt, together with Jordan, Morocco and Tunisia, issued the Agadir Declaration, providing for the establishment of a Mediterranean Arab Free Trade Area (MAFTA), as a cornerstone of the planned Euro-Mediterranean free-trade area. The agreement entered into force in July 2006. Meanwhile, an interim Association Agreement with Lebanon was signed in June 2002, and entered into force in April 2006. Protracted negotiations on an Association Agreement with Syria were eventually concluded in October 2004, but the Agreement had not been signed by early 2008. In late 2004 the EU agreed ENP Action Plans with Jordan, Morocco and Tunisia; these were adopted by the EU in February 2005 and approved by Jordan in January and by Morocco and Tunisia in July. Action Plans for Lebanon and Egypt were adopted, respectively, in January and March 2007.

In January 1989 the EC and Israel eliminated the last tariff barriers to full free trade for industrial products. A Euro-Mediterranean Association Agreement with Israel was signed in 1995, providing further trade concessions and establishing an institutional political dialogue between the two parties. The agreement entered into force in June 2000. In late 2004 an ENP Action Plan on further co-operation was agreed by the EU and Israel; it was adopted by the EU in February 2005 and by the Israeli authorities in April of that year. Following the signing of the September 1993 Israeli-Palestine Liberation Organization (PLO) peace agreement, the EC committed substantial funds in humanitarian assistance for the Palestinians. A Euro-Mediterranean Interim Association Agreement on Trade and Co-operation was signed with the PLO in February 1997 and entered into force in July. The agreement confirmed existing trade concessions offered to the Palestinians since 1986 and provided for free trade to be introduced during an initial five-year period. In April 1998 the EU and the Palestinian (National) Authority (PA) signed a security co-operation agreement, which provided for regular meetings to promote joint efforts on security issues, in particular on combating terrorism. In April 1999 the European Parliament demanded an investigation into the handling of Commission funds to Palestinian-controlled areas of the West Bank and Gaza. At that time the EU was reported to be the largest donor to the PA. The escalation of violence between Israel and the Palestinians from September 2000 resulted in a significant deterioration in EU-Israel relations. During 2002 the EU criticized Israel for its policy of restricting the movements of Yasser Arafat, the Palestinian President, and in May of that year Israel alleged that EU funding to the PA was being diverted for terrorist activities, although the EU insisted that its aid was closely monitored by the IMF. The EU formed part of the Quartet (alongside the UN, the USA and Russia), which was established in July 2002 to monitor and aid the implementation of Palestinian civil reforms, and to guide the international donor community in its support of the Palestinian reform agenda. In September the Quartet put forward a three-stage peace plan (the so-called road-map, which was published in April 2003), including provision for free elections for the Palestinian people, the creation of a Palestinian state and negotiations between Israel and Palestine, aiming at a final settlement by 2005–06. In late 2004 the EU agreed an Action Plan with the PA; it was adopted by the EU in February 2005 and by the PA in May. In 2005 the European Commission allocated funds of around €280m. to support further steps towards the creation of a viable Palestinian state. The Commission stressed that it considered the following to be the priority areas for Palestinian reform: a well-functioning judiciary, a democratic and independent election process, and public financial transparency. In November 2005, on the basis of an agreement reached by Israel and the PA following Israel's withdrawal from Gaza and the northern West Bank, the EU established an EU Border Assistance Mission (EU BAM Rafah) to monitor operations at the Rafah border crossing between Egypt and the Gaza Strip, which reopened under PA control in that month. With an initial duration of 12 months, the mission was to comprise approximately 75 police-officers. Meanwhile, an EU Police Mission for the Palestinian Territories commenced operations in January 2006, with a three-year mandate to support the PA in establishing sustainable and effective policing arrangements. (At January 2008 the mission comprised 32 unarmed personnel.) EU observation missions monitored Palestinian presidential and legislative elections in January 2005 and January 2006, respectively; EU support to the Palestinian electoral process amounted to €18.5m. In February 2006 the EU announced the disbursement of some €120m. in emergency aid to the PA, which was suffering a financial crisis following Israel's decision to halt monthly payments of some US $50m. in tax revenues, in response to the victory of the militant Islamist group Hamas in the Palestinian legislative elections. In April, however, the EU decided to suspend direct aid to the Hamas-led Palestinian Government formed in late March, owing to the new administration's failure to commit itself to non-violence, to recognition of the right of Israel to exist and to existing peace agreements. In June EU member states and the European Commission established the Temporary International Mechanism (TIM), an emergency assistance mechanism to provide support directly to the Palestinian people, without government contact. The mandate of EU BAM Rafah was extended for a period of one year in May 2007, although operations were suspended in mid-June after Hamas militants seized control of the Gaza Strip, prompting President Mahmud Abbas to dissolve the 'national unity' coalition administration of Hamas and Abbas' Fatah movement. After the formation of new, interim Government under Dr Salam Fayyad, the EU renewed co-operation with, and assistance to, the PA. Hamas refused to recognize the legitimacy of the interim administration. On 27 November a conference was convened in Annapolis, MD, the USA, which culminated in a Statement of Joint Understanding on renewed negotiations on a final settlement. On 17 December France co-hosted a donor conference, at which the EU pledged some US $3,400m. for 2008–10 in support of the PA's Palestinian Reform and Development Plan (PRDP). On 1 February 2008 the European Commission launched a new mechanism, known as PEGASE, to support the PRDP, with a wider remit than the TIM, which had always been intended as a temporary measure. PEGASE aimed to support activities in four principal areas: governance (including fiscal reform, security and the rule of law), social development (including social protection, health and education), economic and private-sector development, and development of public infrastructure (in areas such as water, the environment and energy).

Following successful negotiations during 1997, a new, expanded co-operation agreement with Yemen, incorporating a political element (i.e. commitments to democratic principles and respect for human rights), and providing for 'most favoured nation' treatment, entered into force in July 1998. In 2003 bilateral relations between the EU and Yemen were strengthened through the decision to launch a political dialogue. The establishment of the political dialogue was announced at the Joint Co-operation Committee in October 2003. A first meeting took place in July 2004 and focused on democracy, human rights, democratization and co-operation in the fight against terrorism. The political dialogue was continued at a second meeting in September 2005, at which it was agreed that EU ambassadors in the Yemeni capital, Sana'a, would meet senior Yemeni government representatives on a quarterly basis to discuss, in particular, Yemen's political and economic development. A third political dialogue meeting took place in November 2006.

Talks were held with Iran in April 1992 on the establishment of a co-operation accord. In December the Council of Ministers recommended that a 'critical dialogue' be undertaken with Iran, owing to the country's significance to regional security. In April 1997 the 'critical dialogue' was suspended and ambassadors were recalled from Iran, following a German court ruling that found the Iranian authorities responsible for having ordered the murder of four Kurdish dissidents in Berlin in 1992. Later in that month ministers of foreign affairs resolved to restore diplomatic relations with Iran, in order to protect the strong trading partnership. In November 2000 an EU-Iran Working Group on Trade and Investment met for the first time to discuss the possibility of increasing and diversifying trade and investment. By November 2003 four such meetings had taken place. During 2002 attempts were made to improve relations with Iran, as negotiations began in preparation for a Trade and Co-operation Agreement. An eventual trade deal was to be linked to progress in political issues, including human rights, weapons proliferation and counter-terrorism. In mid-2003 the EU (in conformity with US policy) warned Iran to accept stringent new nuclear inspections, and threatened the country with economic repercussions (including the abandonment of the proposed trade agreement) unless it restored international trust in its nuclear programme. A 'comprehensive dialogue' between the EU and Iran (which replaced the 'critical dialogue' in 1998) was suspended by Iran in December 2003. In January 2005 the EU resumed trade talks with Iran after the Iranian authorities agreed to suspend uranium enrichment. However, these talks were halted by the Commission in August, following Iran's resumption of uranium conversion to gas (the stage before enrichment). In November the General Affairs and External Relations Council expressed concern at human rights violations in Iran, urging the country to resume discussions with the EU in the framework of the EU-Iran human rights dialogue, the last such talks having been held in June 2004. The Council also condemned recent statements by Iran's President, Mahmoud Ahmadinejad, in which he called for the destruction of the state of Israel. Following Iran's removal of international seals from a nuclear research facility in January 2006, the EU supported moves to refer Iran to the UN Security Council. In mid-2006, during a visit to Tehran, the High Representative of the Common Foreign and Security Policy and Secretary-General of the Council of the European Union and of the Western European Union, Javier Solana, presented to the Iranian authorities new proposals by the international community on how negotiations on Iran's nuclear programme could be initiated. In December in a declaration on Iran that was included in the conclusions of the presidency of the European Council, the Council criticized the country's failure to implement measures required by both the International Atomic Energy Agency and the UN Security Council in respect of its nuclear programme, and expressed regret at Iran's decision to cancel discussions in the framework of the EU-Iran human rights dialogue.

A co-operation agreement between the EC and the countries of the Gulf Co-operation Council (GCC), which entered into force in January 1990, provided for co-operation in industry, energy, technology and other fields. Negotiations on a full free-trade pact began in October, but it was expected that any agreement would involve transition periods of some 12 years for the reduction of European tariffs on 'sensitive products' (i.e. petrochemicals). In November 1999 the GCC Supreme Council agreed to establish a customs union (a precondition of the proposed EU-GCC free-trade agreement) by March 2005. In December 2001 the GCC countries decided to advance the introduction of the customs union by two years; the union was consequently established in January 2003. Free-trade negotiations between the EU and the GCC countries continued throughout 2002–07.

Contacts with the Arab world in general take place within the framework of the 'Euro-Arab Dialogue', established in 1973 to provide a forum for discussion of economic issues through working groups on specific topics. Following a decision in 1989 to reactivate the Dialogue, meetings were suspended in 1990 as a result of Iraq's invasion of Kuwait. In April 1992 senior EC and Arab officials agreed to resume the process.

The increased tension in the Middle East prior to the US-led military action in Iraq in March 2003 placed considerable strain on relations between member states of the EU, and exposed the lack of a common EU policy on Iraq. A summit of EU foreign ministers in Denmark in August 2002 emphasized the EU's support for the UN weapons inspectors in Iraq, and in January 2003 the EU warned the USA that only the UN Security Council could determine whether military action was justified. In the same month (in which the six-month Greek presidency of the EU began) an EU diplomatic mission led by the Greek foreign minister visited seven Arab states in an effort to avert war. Divisions remained between member states, with the United Kingdom, Spain, Italy, Portugal and Denmark supporting the US policy, while France and Germany led the other members in opposing the impending conflict, or, at the least, in insisting on a second UN resolution. In February 2003 the European Council held an extraordinary meeting to discuss the crisis in Iraq, and issued a statement reconfirming its commitment to the UN. In April, however, the EU leaders reluctantly accepted a dominant role for the USA and the United Kingdom in post-war Iraq, and Denmark, Spain and the Netherlands announced plans to send peace-keeping troops to the country. At the Madrid Donors' Conference for Iraq in October the EU and its accession states pledged more than €1,250m. (mainly in grants) for Iraq's reconstruction. Of this total, €200m. was pledged for 2003–04 (in addition to the €100m. in humanitarian assistance that the EU had already set aside for Iraq in 2003). In March 2004 the Commission adopted a programme setting three priorities for reconstruction assistance to Iraq in that year: restoring the delivery of principal public services; increasing employment and reducing poverty; and strengthening governance, civil society and human rights. The EU welcomed the handover of power by the Coalition Provisional Authority to the Iraqi Interim Government in June 2004 and supported the holding of elections to the Transitional National Assembly in Iraq in January 2005. An EU integrated rule-of-law mission for Iraq, which was to provide training in management and criminal investigation to staff and senior officials from the judiciary, the police and the penitentiary, commenced operations in July 2005, with an initial mandate of 12 months. The EU provided a further €200m. towards Iraq's reconstruction and recovery during 2005, including €30m. towards the organization of legislative elections in December of that year, following the approval of a new Constitution in October. In December an agreement was signed on the establishment of a European Commission delegation office in the Iraqi capital, Baghdad. Under the Commission's Iraq Assistance Programme for 2006, which comprised four main elements—furthering democracy, promoting good governance, improving the quality of life of Iraqis and a reserve to allow for a flexible approach to new government priorities—€200m. was pledged to the development of a secure, stable and democratic Iraq; €40m. was to be allocated to the furthering democracy component of the programme, €40m. to the promotion of good governance, €110m. to improving the quality of life of Iraqis and €10m. to the reserve. In June 2006, in response to the formation of a new Iraqi Government, the Commission set forth its proposals for an EU-wide strategy to govern EU relations with Iraq. The strategy comprised five objectives: overcoming divisions within Iraq and building democracy; promoting the rule of law and human rights; supporting the Iraqi authorities in the delivery of basic services; supporting the reform of public administration; and promoting economic reform. In November negotiations commenced on a trade and co-operation agreement with Iraq; second and third rounds of negotiations took place in June and November 2007.

LATIN AMERICA

A non-preferential trade agreement was signed with Uruguay in 1974, and economic and commercial co-operation agreements with Mexico in 1975 and with Brazil in 1980. A five-year co-operation agreement with the members of the Central American Common Market and with Panama entered into force in 1987, as did a similar agreement with the member countries of the Andean Group (now the Andean Community—Bolivia, Colombia, Ecuador, Peru and Venezuela). Co-operation agreements were signed with Argentina and Chile in 1990, and in that year, tariff preferences were approved for Bolivia, Colombia, Ecuador and Peru, in support of those countries' efforts to combat drugs-trafficking. In May 1992 an interinstitutional co-operation agreement was signed with the Southern Common Market (Mercosur); in the following month the EC and the member states of the Andean Group initialled a new co-operation agreement, which was to broaden the scope of economic and development co-operation and enhance trade relations, and a new co-operation agreement was signed with Brazil. In July 1993 the EC introduced a tariff regime to limit the import of bananas from Latin America, in order to protect the banana-producing countries of the ACP group, then linked to the EC by the Lomé Convention. From 1996 the EU forged closer links with Latin America, by means of strengthened political ties, an increase in economic integration and free trade, and co-operation in other areas. In April 1997 the EU extended further trade benefits to the countries of the Andean Community.

The first ministerial conference between the EC and the then 11 Latin American states of the Rio Group took place in April 1991; since then high-level joint ministerial meetings have been held every two years. The last ministerial conference between the EU and the 19 Rio Group states took place in Santo Domingo, the Dominican Republic, in April 2007. The next meeting is due to take place in Prague, the Czech Republic, in 2009. The first summit meeting of all EU and Latin American and Caribbean heads of state or government was held in Rio de Janeiro, Brazil, in June 1999, when a strategic partnership was launched. A second EU-Latin America/Caribbean (EU-LAC) summit took place in Madrid, Spain, in May 2002, and covered co-operation in political, economic, social and cultural fields. A political dialogue and co-operation agreement with the Andean Community and its member states was signed in December 2003. At the third EU-LAC summit meeting, held in Guadalajara, Mexico, in May 2004 it was agreed by the two parties that an association agreement, which included a free-trade area, was a common objective. In December 2005 the European Commission proposed a renewed strategy for strengthening the strategic partnership with Latin America, ahead of the fourth EU-LAC summit in May 2006. Its proposals included increasing political dialogue between the two regions, stimulating economic and commercial exchanges, encouraging regional integration, addressing inequality and adapting the EU's development and aid policy to correspond more closely to conditions in Latin America. At the fourth EU-LAC summit, held in Vienna, Austria, it was decided that negotiations for association agreements with Central America and with the Andean Community (now comprising Bolivia, Colombia, Ecuador and Peru) should be initiated. The summit also endorsed a proposal to establish an EU-Latin America parliamentary assembly. The assembly met for the first time in November. In April 2007 the EU and the Andean Community announced plans to initiate negotiations on an Association Agreement; negotiations were launched in June in Tarija, Bolivia. Talks on an Association Agreement between the EU and the countries of Central America (Costa Rica, El Salvador, Guatemala, Honduras and Nicaragua) commenced in Costa Rica in October. A second round of negotiations took place in February 2008 in Brussels, Belgium. The fifth EU-LAC summit was scheduled to take place in Lima, Peru, in May 2008, and was to concentrate on the themes of poverty, inequality and inclusion, and sustainable development (climate change, the environment, and energy).

In late December 1994 the EU and Mercosur signed a joint declaration that aimed to promote trade liberalization and greater political co-operation. In September 1995, at a meeting in Montevideo, Uruguay, a framework agreement on the establishment of a free-trade regime between the two organizations was initialled. The agreement was formally signed in December. In July 1998 the Commission voted to commence negotiations towards an interregional association agreement with Mercosur and Chile, which would strengthen existing co-operation agreements. Negotiations were initiated in April 2000.

In July 1997 the EU and Mexico concluded an Economic Partnership, Political Co-ordination and Co-operation Agreement and an interim agreement on trade. The accords were signed in December. The main part of the interim agreement entered into effect in July 2000 and the co-operation agreement entered into force in October. In November 1999 the EU and Mexico concluded a free-trade agreement, which provided for the removal of all tariffs on bilateral trade in industrial products by 2007. The first meeting of the Joint Council established by the Economic Partnership, Political Co-ordination and Co-operation Agreement between the EU and Mexico was held in February 2001; further meetings have since been held on a regular basis.

In June 1996 the EU and Chile signed a framework agreement on political and economic co-operation, which provided for a process of bilateral trade liberalization, as well as co-operation in other industrial and financial areas. An EU-Chile Joint Council was established. In November 1999 the EU and Chile commenced practical negotiations on developing closer political and economic co-operation, within the framework of a proposed association agreement. In November 2002 the EU and Chile signed an association and free-trade agreement, which entered into force in March 2005; it provided for the liberalization of trade within seven years for industrial products and 10 years for agricultural products. The first meeting of the Association Council set up by the agreement took place in Athens, Greece, in March 2003, and the second was held in Luxembourg in May 2005. Representatives of civil society met within the framework of the association agreement for the first time in late 2006.

In May 2007 the European Commission proposed launching a strategic partnership with Brazil, in recognition of its increasing international prominence and strong bilateral ties with Europe. The first EU-Brazil summit was held in Lisbon, Portugal, in July.

Cuba remained the only Latin American country that did not have a formal economic co-operation agreement with the EU. In June 1995 a Commission communication advocated greater economic co-operation with Cuba. This policy was strongly supported by a resolution of the European Parliament in January 1996, but was criticized by the US Government, which continued to maintain an economic embargo against Cuba. Later that year the EU agreed to make the extent of economic co-operation with Cuba (which was a one-party state) contingent on progress towards democracy. In 2000 Cuba withdrew its application to join the successor to the Lomé Convention, the Cotonou Agreement, following criticism by some European governments of its human rights record. However, improvements in bilateral relations between Cuba and the EU led to the opening of an EU legation office in the Cuban capital, Havana, in March 2003 and support for Cuba's renewed application to join the Cotonou

Agreement. However, human rights abuses perpetrated by the Cuban regime in April (the imprisonment of a large number of dissidents) led to the downgrading of diplomatic relations with Cuba by the EU, the instigation of an EU policy of inviting dissidents to embassy receptions in Havana (the so-called cocktail wars) and the indefinite postponement of Cuba's application to join the Cotonou Agreement. In May Cuba withdrew its application for membership and in July the Cuban President, Fidel Castro, announced that the Government would not accept aid from the EU and would terminate all political contact with the organization. In December 2004 the EU proposed a compromise—namely not to invite any Cubans, whether government ministers or dissidents, to future embassy receptions—but reiterated its demand that Cuba unconditionally release all political prisoners who remained in detention (several dissidents had already been released). In response, Cuba announced in January 2005 that it was restoring diplomatic ties with all EU states. At the end of that month the EU temporarily suspended the diplomatic sanctions imposed on Cuba in mid-2003 and announced its intention to resume a 'constructive dialogue' with the Cuban authorities. In March 2005 the European Commissioner responsible for Development and Humanitarian Aid, Louis Michel, visited Cuba, where he held meetings with the Cuban President, as well as several dissidents. The EU extended the temporary suspension of diplomatic sanctions against Cuba for one year in June, and again in mid-2006 and mid-2007, in the hope that constructive dialogue would bring about reform in the areas of human rights and democratization and the release of further political prisoners.

ASIA AND AUSTRALASIA

Relations between the EU and the Association of South-East Asian Nations (ASEAN) are based on the Co-operation Agreement of 1980. Under this agreement, joint committee meetings are held approximately every 18 months. There are also regular ministerial meetings and post-ministerial conferences. In addition, the EU is a member of the ASEAN Regional Forum (ARF), a security grouping designed to promote peace and stability, established in 1994. In December of that year the European Council endorsed a new strategy for Asia, which recognized the region's increasing economic and political importance and pledged to strengthen bilateral and regional dialogue. In May 1995 ASEAN and EU senior officials endorsed an initiative to convene an Asia-Europe Meeting of heads of government (ASEM). The first ASEM summit was held in March 1996 in Bangkok, Thailand. It was agreed to launch an Asia-Europe Partnership for Greater Growth, in order to expand trade, investment and technology transfer. An Asia-Business Forum was to be formed, as well as an Asia-Europe Foundation in Singapore to promote educational and cultural exchanges. The second ASEM summit, convened in the United Kingdom in April 1998, was dominated by economic and financial concerns, and both sides' declared intention to prevent a return to protectionist trading policies. The meeting established an ASEM Trust Fund, under the auspices of the World Bank, to alleviate the social impact of financial crisis. Other initiatives adopted by ASEM were an Asia-Europe Co-operation Framework to co-ordinate political, economic and financial co-operation, a Trade Facilitation Action Plan, and an Investment Promotion Action Plan, which incorporated a new Investment Experts Group. ASEM heads of government convened for the third time in Seoul, Republic of Korea, in October 2000. ASEM III welcomed the ongoing rapprochement between the two Korean nations, declared a commitment to the promotion of human rights, and endorsed several initiatives related to globalization and information technology. The meeting established a new Asia-Europe Co-operation Framework (AECF), identifying ASEM's principles and priorities for the next 10 years. ASEM IV took place in Copenhagen, Denmark, in September 2002. Statements were subsequently adopted on co-operation in the fight against international terrorism, and on the situation in the Korean peninsula. Economic issues were also discussed, in particular the need to continue the 'Doha' negotiating round of the World Trade Organization (WTO). At the same time, the first EU-Korea summit was held; discussion centred on a reduction in customs barriers and aid to shipbuilding. ASEM V took place in Hanoi, Viet Nam, in October 2004; at the meeting regional developments in Europe and Asia, including the recent EU enlargement and the human rights situation in Myanmar, were addressed. ASEM VI, convened in Helsinki, Finland, in September 2006, addressed the theme '10 Years of ASEM: Global Challenges and Joint Responses'. The participants adopted a Declaration on Climate Change, aimed at promoting efforts to reach consensus in international climate negotiations, and the Helsinki Declaration on the Future of ASEM, detailing practical recommendations for developing future ASEM co-operation.

In September 2001 the EU adopted a new Communication on relations with Asia for the coming decade, which focused on strengthened partnership, particularly in the areas of politics, security, trade and investment. It aimed to reduce poverty and to promote democracy, good governance and the rule of law throughout the region. A fundamental aim was to strengthen the EU's presence in Asia, promoting mutual awareness and knowledge on both sides.

Bilateral non-preferential co-operation agreements were signed with Bangladesh, India, Pakistan and Sri Lanka between 1973 and 1976. A further agreement with India, extended to include co-operation in trade, industry, energy, science and finance, came into force in December 1981. A third agreement, which entered into effect in August 1994, included commitments to develop co-operation between the two sides and improve market access, as well as to the observance of human rights and democratic principles. The first EU-India summit meeting was held in Lisbon, Portugal, in June 2000. In November 2003 the EU urged India to reciprocate the EU's open market stance towards India by lowering its import tariffs on European products. In November 2004 the EU and India signed a 'strategic partnership' agreement; as a result of the agreement India became a special EU partner, alongside the USA, Canada, the People's Republic of China (PRC) and Russia. The sixth EU-India summit meeting, held in New Delhi, India, in September 2005, adopted a joint action plan to implement the strategic partnership. It was agreed to establish a dialogue on security issues, disarmament and non-proliferation, to increase co-operation in efforts to combat terrorism, and to create a high-level trade group to examine ways of strengthening economic relations. An agreement on India's participation in the EU's 'Galileo' civil satellite navigation and positioning system was also signed. In February 2007, in a country strategy paper for India covering the period 2007–13, the Commission proposed that €470m. should be made available to support the joint action plan for India. In addition, it was proposed that co-operation should focus on assisting India to achieve its millennium development goals in the health and education sectors. A new and extended agreement with Pakistan on commercial and economic co-operation entered into force in May 1986; in May 1992 an agreement was signed on measures to stimulate private investment in Pakistan. A new accord with Sri Lanka, designed to promote co-operation in areas such as trade, investment and protection of the environment, entered into force in April 1995. A similar agreement with Nepal entered into force in June 1996. In July 1996 EU Governments authorized the European Commission to conclude similar agreements with Bangladesh and Pakistan. A draft co-operation agreement was initialled with Pakistan in April 1998. However, following the military coup in Pakistan in October 1999, the agreement was suspended. Political dialogue with Pakistan recommenced on an ad hoc basis in November 2000, and the co-operation agreement was signed in Islamabad in November 2001; Pakistan reiterated its firm commitment to return to democratic government. The co-operation agreement with Pakistan entered into force in April 2004. In January 2007 the Commission proposed an assistance package for Pakistan in 2007–11 that amounted to €200m., compared with €125m. in development co-operation funding granted in 2002–06. Financial assistance until 2011 was to be concentrated on rural development in Pakistan's North West Frontier Province and in Baluchistan; and on the development of education and human resources. The new co-operation accord with Bangladesh (which replaced the 1976 commercial co-operation agreement) was signed in May 2000 and came into force in March 2001. In 2002–06, within the framework of a country strategy paper, assistance granted to Bangladesh totalled €290m., including €60m. for trade and economic co-operation, the largest such allocation made by the EU for that purpose world-wide.

A trade agreement was signed with the PRC in 1978 and renewed in May 1985. In June 1989, following the violent repression of the Chinese pro-democracy movement by the PRC Government, the EC imposed economic sanctions and an embargo on arms sales to that country. In October 1990 it was decided that relations with the PRC should be 'progressively normalized'. The EU has supported the PRC's increased involvement in the international community and, in particular, supported its application for membership of the WTO. The first EU-PRC meeting of heads of government was convened in April 1998. In November the President of the Commission made an official visit to the PRC and urged that country to remove trade restrictions imposed on European products. In the same month the EU and Hong Kong signed a co-operation agreement to combat drugs-trafficking and copyright piracy. A bilateral trade agreement between the EU and the PRC was concluded in May 2000, removing a major barrier to the PRC's accession to the WTO; this was approved in November 2001. In March 2002 the European Commission approved a strategy document setting out a framework for co-operation between the EU and the PRC in 2002–06. At the sixth EU-PRC summit, held in the Chinese capital, Beijing, in October 2003, two agreements were signed establishing a new dialogue on industrial policy and confirming the PRC's participation in the 'Galileo' project. At the seventh EU-PRC summit, which took place in The Hague, Netherlands, in December 2004, the two sides further strengthened their strategic partnership. The EU raised the topics of human rights and the fight against illegal migration, and discussions also focused on economic issues, including the Doha Development Round, textiles and other trade concerns. A joint declaration was signed on nuclear non-proliferation and arms control, and agreements were also concluded on customs co-operation, and science and technology. The eighth summit, held in Beijing in September 2005, marked the 30th anniversary of the establishment of EU-PRC diplomatic relations. During the meeting, the establishment of an EU-PRC partnership on climate change was confirmed. The ninth EU-PRC summit, convened in September 2006, agreed that negotiations should be initiated on a comprehensive Partnership and Co-operation Agreement (PCA), which would also update the 1985 trade and economic co-operation agreement. In October 2006, in a strategy communication, the Commission set forth details of a new agenda for EU-PRC relations, the priorities of which included support for the PRC's transition towards greater openness and political pluralism and co-operation on climate change. In a separate policy paper, the Commission detailed a new strategy for expanding EU-PRC relations in the areas of trade and investment. Negotiations for a comprehensive PCA were launched in January 2007. The 10th EU-PRC summit took place in Beijing in November. At the meeting, heads of state and of government witnessed the signature of a €500m. framework loan from the European Investment Bank to support efforts to tackle climate change. In addition, the Chinese side urged the EU to lift the arms embargo imposed against the PRC, and both sides agreed to increase co-operation in order to facilitate the holding of the 2008 Summer Olympic Games in Beijing.

A framework agreement on trade and co-operation between the EU and the Republic of Korea was signed in 1996 and entered into force in April 2001. In October 1997 the EU and the Republic of Korea signed an agreement regarding a reciprocal opening of markets for telecommunications equipment, following a protracted dispute. In September 2006 an agreement was concluded on the Republic of Korea's participation in the EU's 'Galileo' programme. In April 2007 the Council authorized the Commission to commence negotiations with the Republic of Korea towards the conclusion of a free-trade agreement.

In September 1997 the EU joined the Korean Peninsula Energy Development Organization, an initiative founded in 1995 to increase nuclear safety and reduce the risk of nuclear proliferation from the energy programme of the Democratic People's Republic of Korea (DPRK). In September 1999, for the first time, ministerial-level discussions took place between the EU and the DPRK at the UN General Assembly. In May 2001 the EU announced that it was to establish diplomatic relations with the DPRK to facilitate the Union's efforts in support of reconciliation in the Korean Peninsula and, in particular, in support of economic reform and the easing of the acute food and health problems in the DPRK. In October 2002 the EU expressed its deep concern after the DPRK admitted that it had conducted a clandestine nuclear weapons programme, in serious breach of the country's international non-proliferation commitments. In the following month the EU stated that failure to resolve the nuclear issue would jeopardize the future development of EU-DPRK relations. In response to the DPRK's announcement in October 2006 that it had conducted a nuclear test, the EU strongly condemned the 'provocative' action and urged the DPRK to abandon its nuclear programme.

In June 1992 the EC signed trade and co-operation agreements with both Mongolia and Macao. The 10th EU-Mongolia joint committee met in Brussels in September 2007, and focused on political and economic issues. The meeting concluded that negotiations would be initiated on a Partnership and Co-operation Agreement. An agreement on aviation was also reached, as a result of which legal certainty was to be restored to 11 air-service agreements between Mongolia and individual EU member states. The 13th EU-Macao joint committee met in Brussels in December.

A co-operation accord was formally signed with Viet Nam in July 1995, under which the EU agreed to increase quotas for Vietnamese textile products, to support the country's efforts to join the WTO and to provide aid for environmental and public management projects. The agreement entered into force in June 1996. Meanwhile, a permanent EU mission to Viet Nam had been established in February. In October 2004 the EU and Viet Nam concluded a bilateral agreement on market access in preparation for Viet Nam's accession to the WTO, which took place in January 2007. In addition, an agreement signed in December lifted all EU quantitative restrictions for Vietnamese textiles with effect from 1 January 2005. In May 2007 the EU and Viet Nam agreed to initiate negotiations on a new Partnership and Co-operation Agreement, to replace that of 1995.

In October 1996 the EU imposed strict limits on entry visas for Myanma officials, because of Myanmar's refusal to allow the Commission to send a mission to the country to investigate allegations of forced labour. In March 1997 EU ministers of foreign affairs agreed to revoke Myanmar's special trade privileges under the Generalized System of Preferences (GSP). The EU has successively extended its ban on arms exports to Myanmar and its prohibition on the issuing of visas. In April 2003 a new 'Common Position' was adopted by the EU, which consolidated and extended the scope of existing sanctions against Myanmar and strengthened the arms embargo; EU sanctions were further extended in April 2004 in view of the military regime's failure to make any significant progress in normalizing the administration of the country and addressing the EU's concerns with regard to human rights. EU foreign ministers agreed to Myanmar's participation in ASEM V in October at a level below head of government. Following the summit, however, the EU revised the Common Position, further broadening sanctions against Myanmar, as the military regime had failed to comply with certain demands, including the release from house arrest of the opposition leader Aung San Suu Kyi. The Common Position was renewed in April 2006 and November 2007. Non-preferential co-operation agreements were signed with Laos and Cambodia in April 1997. The agreement with Laos (which emphasized development assistance and economic co-operation) entered into force on 1 December; the agreement with Cambodia was postponed owing to adverse political developments in that country. The EU concluded a textiles agreement with Laos, which provisionally entered into force in December 1998; as a result of the agreement, exports of textiles to the EU from Laos increased significantly. In 1998 the EU provided financial assistance to support preparations for a general election in Cambodia, and dispatched observers to monitor the election, which was held in July. The EU co-operation agreement with Cambodia entered into force in November 1999. EU-Cambodia relations were further enhanced with the opening of an EU delegation in Phnom-Penh in early 2002 and a Cambodian embassy in Brussels in late 2004. In September 1999 the EU briefly imposed an arms embargo against Indonesia, which was at that time refusing to permit the deployment of an international peace-keeping force in East Timor (now Timor-Leste). In April 2005 the EU extended preferential trade conditions to Indonesia, which meant that the country would benefit from lower customs duties in certain sectors. From September of that year the EU, together with contributing countries from ASEAN, as well as Norway and Switzerland, deployed a monitoring mission in the Indonesian province of Aceh to supervise the implementation of a peace agreement between the Government of Indonesia and the separatist Gerakan Aceh Merdeka (Free Aceh Movement). The mission's initial mandate of six months was extended in February, June and September 2006, and concluded in December.

Textiles exports by Asian countries have caused concern in the EU, owing to the depressed state of its textiles industry. In 1982 bilateral negotiations were held with Asian producers, notably Hong Kong, the Republic of Korea and Macao. Agreements were eventually reached involving reductions in clothing quotas and 'anti-surge' clauses to prevent flooding of European markets. In 1986 new bilateral negotiations were held and agreements were reached with the principal Asian textiles exporters for 1987–91 (later extended to December 1993, when the 'Uruguay Round' of GATT negotiations was finally concluded): in most cases a slight increase in quotas was permitted. Under the conclusions of the Uruguay Round, the MFA was replaced by an Agreement on Textiles and Clothing (ATC), which provided for the progressive elimination of the quotas that existed under the MFA during 1994–2004. In January 1995 bilateral textiles agreements, signed by the EU with India, Pakistan and the PRC, specified certain trade liberalization measures to be undertaken, including an increase of the PRC's silk export quota and a removal of trade barriers on small-business and handloom textile products from India, while including commitments from the Asian countries for greater efforts to combat textile and design fraud. In March 1998 the Commission signed an agreement on textile products with Nepal, in order to secure an orderly and equitable development of trade in these products. In March 2001 the EU and Sri Lanka signed an agreement to open their mutual textiles markets. The agreement lifted all textiles quotas with Sri Lanka in exchange for tariff reductions by Sri Lanka and the binding of all its tariffs for the textiles and clothing sector at the WTO. In May 2005 the EU imposed limits on textiles imports from the PRC, in response to a dramatic increase in Chinese clothing exports since the expiry of the ATC on 1 January. In June the EU and the PRC Government agreed import quotas on 10 clothing and textile categories until 2008, but by August several of the quotas for 2005 had already been breached. In September the dispute was resolved when it was agreed that one-half of the estimated 80m. Chinese garments that had been impounded at European ports would be released and the remainder counted against the quotas for 2006. Also in September a report published by the high-level group on textiles and clothing—established by the Commission in 2003—sought, *inter alia*, to chart the likely development of the sectors up to 2020. With regard to the quota-free environment for textiles and clothing that had been introduced at the beginning of 2005, the report noted that a Commission statement released in mid-2006 had indicated that the disruptive impact of liberalization of Chinese textile exports to the EU had been confined to a fairly restricted range of product categories. None the less, the PRC's share of exports to the EU of products in the liberalized categories had risen markedly, to the detriment of traditional EU suppliers. Overall, however, only a modest increase in EU imports of textiles and clothing (in both the liberalized categories and in total) had occurred. According to the Commission statement, in 2005 exports of Chinese textiles and clothing to the EU increased by

42% in terms of volume and by 36% in terms of value. In the liberalized categories, the PRC's market share grew by 130% in terms of volume and by 82% in terms of value. During the first quarter of 2006, however, as a result of the quantitative restrictions imposed from mid-2005, an overall decline of 12% in Chinese exports of textiles and clothing to the EU had been recorded. The statement noted, too, that the PRC was becoming an important growth market for exports of textiles and clothing from the EU.

Numerous discussions have been held since 1981 on the Community's increasing trade deficit with Japan, and on the failure of the Japanese market to accept more European exports. In July 1991, the heads of government of Japan and of the EC signed a joint declaration on closer co-operation in both economic and political matters. The European office of the EU-Japan Industrial Co-operation Centre was opened in Brussels in June 1996; the Centre, which was established in 1987 as a joint venture between the Japanese Government and the European Commission, sought to increase industrial co-operation between the EU and Japan. In January 1998 an EU-Japan summit meeting was held, followed by a meeting at ministerial level in October. Subsequent summits (the 16th was held in Berlin, Germany, in June 2007) have aimed to strengthen dialogue.

The EU pledged assistance for the reconstruction of Afghanistan following the removal of the Taliban regime in late 2001, and in 2002 announced development aid of €1,000m. for the period 2002–06, in addition to humanitarian aid. (By the end of 2006 the total of €1,000m. had been exceeded.) In March 2003 the European Commission hosted, along with the World Bank, the Afghanistan High Level Strategic Forum. The Government of Afghanistan convened the meeting to discuss with its partners, donors and multilateral organizations the progress and future vision for state-building in Afghanistan, as well as the long-term funding requirements for reconstruction. In 2004–05 the EU provided substantial support for the election process in Afghanistan, dispatching a Democracy and Election Support Mission to assess aspects of the presidential election, which was held in October 2004, and a full Election Observation Mission to monitor legislative and provincial elections, which took place in September 2005. In November the EU and Afghanistan adopted a joint declaration on a new partnership aimed at promoting Afghanistan's political and economic development and strengthening EU-Afghan relations. Increased co-operation was envisaged in areas such as political and economic governance, judicial reform, counter-narcotics measures and human rights, and the declaration also provided for a regular political dialogue, in the form of annual meetings at ministerial level. The EU welcomed the launch by the UN-sponsored London Conference on Afghanistan, held on 31 January–1 February 2006, of the Afghanistan Compact, representing a framework for co-operation between the government of Afghanistan, the UN and the international community for a five-year period terminating at the end of 2010. In January 2007 the Commission proposed a package of financial support for Afghanistan in 2007–10, totalling €600m. Reform of Afghanistan's justice system, rural development, in particular the promotion of alternatives to poppy cultivation, and the health sector were identified as the priority areas on which EU assistance should focus. In May 2007 the Council adopted a Joint Action on a proposed EU police mission to Afghanistan; EUPOL, comprising some 160 police-officers, was officially launched on 15 June, and aimed to help develop a police force in Afghanistan that would work to respect human rights and operate within the framework of the rule of law, and to address the issue of police reform at central, regional and provincial levels. In addition, a programme of judicial reform was launched.

In 2000 the EU contributed €19m. to a Trust Fund established by the World Bank to finance reconstruction activities in East Timor. In December the EU hosted the third multilateral conference of donors to the territory. The European Commission contributed €187.7m. in aid to Timor-Leste between 1999 and early 2005, mainly for emergency and rehabilitation needs. The EU's long-term assistance strategy for Timor-Leste was focused on two sectors: basic health services provision and rural development.

Regular consultations are held with Australia at ministerial and senior official level. In January 1996 the Commission proposed a framework agreement to formalize the EU's trade and political relationship with that country. In September, however, after the Australian Government had objected to the human rights clause contained in all EU international agreements, negotiations were suspended. In June 1997 a joint declaration was signed, committing both sides to greater political, cultural and economic co-operation. In 2001 a National Europe Centre, based at the Australian National University in Canberra, was established jointly by the EU and the University to consolidate EU-Australia relations. The EU-Australia ministerial consultations convened in Melbourne, Australia, in April 2003, adopted an Agenda for Co-operation, which detailed seven priority areas for co-operation over the next five years: security and strategic issues; trade; education, science and technology; transport; environment; development co-operation; and migration and asylum. A joint declaration detailing areas of co-operation and establishing a consultative framework to facilitate their development was signed between the EU and New Zealand in May 1999. Mutual recognition agreements were also signed with Australia and New Zealand in 1999, with the aim of facilitating bilateral trade in industrial products. In March 2004 an action plan identifying priorities for future co-operation was agreed. In September 2007 a new joint declaration on relations and co-operation was adopted by the EU and New Zealand, replacing the 1999 joint declaration and 2004 action plan.

THE USA AND CANADA

A framework agreement for commercial and economic co-operation between the Community and Canada was signed in Ottawa in 1976. It was superseded in 1990 by a Declaration on EC-Canada Relations. In February 1996 the Commission proposed closer ties with Canada and an action plan including early warning to avoid trade disputes, elimination of trade barriers, and promotion of business contacts. An action plan and joint political declaration were signed in December.

Canadian and EU leaders meet regularly at bilateral summits. At a summit held in Ottawa in December 2002 the Canadian Government and the EU decided to initiate a review of bilateral relations and to develop a Trade and Investment Enhancement Agreement (TIEA). Negotiations on the TIEA, which would aim to reduce the impediments to trade and investment flows, were initiated in May 2005. An important aspect of the proposed accord was to promote the mutual recognition of professional qualifications and quality standards, in order to facilitate investment. Meanwhile, at the Ottawa summit meeting held in March 2004, Canada and the EU adopted a Partnership Agenda to promote political and economic co-operation. In October 2005 the EU and Canada signed an agreement on the transfer of air passenger data. Under the agreement, airlines flying from the EU to Canada were to transfer selected passenger data to the Canadian authorities to help identify passengers who could be a security threat. In the following month, an agreement establishing a framework for the participation of Canada in EU crisis management operations was signed.

A number of specific agreements have been concluded between the Community and the USA: a co-operation agreement on the peaceful use of atomic energy entered into force in 1959, and agreements on environmental matters and on fisheries came into force in 1974 and 1984, respectively. Additional agreements provide for co-operation in other fields of scientific research and development, while bilateral contacts take place in many areas not covered by a formal agreement. A Transatlantic Declaration on EC-US relations was concluded in November 1990: the two parties agreed to consult each other on important matters of common interest, and to increase formal contacts. A new Transatlantic Agenda for EU-US relations was signed by the US President and the Presidents of the European Commission and the European Council at a meeting in Madrid, Spain, in December 1995. In May 1998, at an EU-US summit held in London, United Kingdom, a new transatlantic economic partnership (TEP) was launched. In June 2005 an EU-US economic summit reached agreement on an initiative to enhance transatlantic economic integration and growth, which covered co-operation in diverse areas in order to promote economic integration and increase the potential for economic growth. The first informal EU-US economic ministerial meeting took place in Brussels in November. A joint work programme for the implementation of the economic initiative adopted at the June summit was agreed, while further discussions focused on the protection of intellectual property rights, regulatory co-operation, trade and security issues and improving innovation. In January 2006 the Commission hosted the first high-level EU-US Regulatory Co-operation Forum, which aimed to minimize barriers to bilateral trade.

The USA has frequently criticized the Common Agricultural Policy, which it regards as creating unfair competition for US exports by its system of export refunds and preferential agreements. In 1998 the WTO upheld a US complaint about the EU ban on imports of hormone-treated beef, which had led to a retaliatory US ban on meat imports from the EU. Following the EU's refusal to repeal the ban by the deadline of May 1999, the WTO authorized the imposition by the USA and Canada of retaliatory sanctions of US $116.8m. and C $11m., respectively, for each year that the ban was in place. The USA rejected claims by the EU in October 2003 that new scientific studies and EU legislation meant that the ban now complied with WTO regulations, and that the sanctions should therefore be lifted. In early 2005 the EU requested a WTO panel to review the trade sanctions. In March 2008 the panel ruled that scientific evidence did not support the imposition of the import ban by the EU; Canada and the USA were also criticized for their failure to repeal their retaliatory measures against the EU. In June 2003, at a US-EU summit in Washington, DC, it was acknowledged that agriculture remained a major obstacle to agreement in the Doha round of the WTO. In May the USA had further strained relations by filing a WTO complaint, supported by Argentina and Canada, to end the EU's *de facto* moratorium on genetically modified food, which began in 1998 and was based on European safety concerns, on the grounds that it was an unfair trade barrier. Another issue of contention between the USA and the EU was the EU's banana import regime (see EU-ACP Partnership). At a WTO Ministerial Conference held in Hong Kong in December 2005 to advance the Doha round of negotiations, agreement was reached on the elimination of export subsidies on agricultural goods by the end of 2013. The EU had rejected a deadline of 2010 proposed by the USA.

In October 1996 EU ministers of foreign affairs agreed to pursue in the WTO a complaint regarding the effects on European businesses of the USA's trade embargo against Cuba, formulated in the Helms-Burton Act. In April 1997 the EU and the USA approved a temporary resolution of the Helms-Burton dispute, whereby the US Administration was to limit the application of sanctions in return for a formal suspension of the WTO case. In mid-1996 the US Congress had adopted legislation imposing an additional trade embargo (threatening sanctions against any foreign company investing more than US $40m. in energy projects in a number of prescribed states, including Iran and Libya), the presence of which further complicated the EU-US debate in September 1997, when a French petroleum company, Total, provoked US anger, owing to its proposed investment in an Iranian natural gas project. In May 1998 an EU-US summit meeting reached agreement on a 'Transatlantic Economic Partnership' (TEP), to remove technical trade barriers, eliminate industrial tariffs, establish a free-trade area in services, and further liberalize measures relating to government procurement, intellectual property and investment. The agricultural and audiovisual sectors were to be excluded from the agreement. The USA agreed to exempt European companies from the trade embargo on Iran and Libya, and to seek congressional approval for an indefinite waiver for the Helms-Burton Act, thereby removing the threat of sanctions from Total. The EU had allowed the WTO case to lapse in April, but it warned that a new WTO panel would be established if the USA took action against European companies trading with Cuba. In return, the EU agreed to increase co-operation in combating terrorism and the proliferation of weapons of mass destruction and to discourage investment in expropriated property. Following approval by the Council in November, it was agreed that implementation of the TEP would begin in advance of an EU-US summit meeting in December.

In July 1997 the EU became involved in intensive negotiations with the US aircraft company Boeing over fears that its planned merger with McDonnell Douglas would harm European interests. In late July the EU approved the merger, after Boeing accepted concessions including an agreement to dispense with exclusivity clauses for 20-year supply contracts and to maintain McDonnell Douglas as a separate company for a period of 10 years. In June the EU and the USA agreed to introduce a mutual recognition agreement, which was to enable goods (including medicines, pharmaceutical products, telecommunications equipment and electrical apparatus) undergoing tests in Europe to be marketed in the USA or Canada without the need for further testing. In August 2004 a fresh trade dispute erupted between the USA and the EU over the subsidies that the two sides paid to their respective aircraft industries. The USA claimed that the financial support European governments provided to aircraft manufacturer Airbus was in breach of world trade rules, while the EU stated that the same was true of the US Administration's subsidies for Boeing. The USA made a formal complaint to the WTO over the EU's support for Airbus in October; the EU immediately responded in kind by filing a complaint regarding the US financial assistance to Boeing. Following the failure of bilateral talks to resolve the dispute, in July 2005 the WTO agreed to establish two panels to examine the complaints of the USA and the EU; members of the panels were appointed in October. In November 2006 the US case against Airbus was formally presented; hearings were held in March and July 2007. The case of the EU against Boeing was presented in March 2007, and a first hearing took place in September.

In July 2002 the Commission submitted a complaint to the WTO regarding tax exemptions granted to US companies exporting goods via subsidiaries established in tax-free countries (foreign sales corporations). The WTO found in favour of the Commission and authorized the EU to levy punitive tariffs of up to US $4,000m. in compensation for the US tax exemptions, which benefited large companies, including Boeing and Microsoft, and which the WTO ruled were discriminatory and should be abolished. In February 2003 the EU released a final list of about 50,000 goods that would be subjected to tariffs of 100%, but postponed implementation of the sanctions, pending the progress of a bill to amend the tax law in the US Congress. In March 2004, however, the legislation remained in place and the EU began the phased imposition of duties (initially at 5%, but increasing by 1% every month) on a range of US exports, including jewellery, toys, honey, refrigerators, paper, nuclear reactors and roller skates. This represented the first time that the EU had taken retaliatory action against the USA in a trade dispute. In October the US President, George W. Bush, signed legislation that repealed the tax exemptions from 1 January 2005 but contained transitional provisions allowing for exemptions to be maintained for some exporters until the end of 2006 and for an indefinite period on certain binding contracts. The EU appealed to the WTO regarding the transitional provisions, suspending sanctions from January 2005 pending a ruling. In September the WTO panel examining the dispute concluded that, despite the changes to its legislation, the USA had not yet fully abided by the Organization's previous rulings and that the tax exemptions maintained under transitional provisions violated WTO rules. In February 2006 the WTO upheld this ruling, rejecting an appeal from the USA. The USA amended its legislation in May and EU sanctions were terminated in the same month.

From 1 May 2005 the EU imposed an additional 15% duty on a range of US goods (including paper, farm goods, textiles and machinery) as punishment for the failure of the USA to revoke a clause in its anti-dumping legislation, known as the Byrd Amendment. The Byrd Amendment, which was promulgated in October 2000, made provision for funds accruing from the payment of anti-dumping and anti-subsidy duties to be paid to the US companies that filed the complaint. The WTO ruled the Amendment illegal in 2002, but the USA failed to repeal the legislation by the deadline of December 2003. In February 2006 the European Commission welcomed the enactment in the USA of legislation repealing the Byrd Amendment, while expressing regret that it would not take effect immediately (under a transition clause, duties imposed on goods imported into the USA until 30 September 2007 were to be distributed after their collection, which, under US practice, could take place several years after the import).

In December 2003 President Bush announced his decision to repeal US tariffs of up to 30% on imports of steel, which had been imposed in March 2002. The decision followed a ruling by the WTO in January that the imposition of tariffs by the USA was illegal.

In political matters, some member states criticized the USA's objections to the establishment of the International Criminal Court (which came into effect in The Hague, Netherlands, in 2003), while there was also criticism of the USA's strategy towards Iraq in early 2003 (see the Middle East and the Mediterranean), as the EU emphasized that only the UN Security Council could determine whether military action in Iraq was justified. The EU-US annual summit held in June, however, emphasized the need for transatlantic co-operation following the overthrow by a US-led coalition force of Saddam Hussain's regime in Iraq, stressing the need to unite against global terrorism and the proliferation of weapons of mass destruction. In February 2005 President Bush made a 'goodwill' tour of Europe in an attempt to improve strained relations; although there were claims on both sides of a new spirit of co-operation, many issues of contention remained (for example Iraq, EU plans to consider lifting its arms embargo on China and Bush's continued refusal to sign the Kyoto Protocol on climate change).

A visit to several European countries by the US Secretary of State, Condoleezza Rice, in early December 2005 was largely overshadowed by allegations, published in November, that the USA's Central Intelligence Agency (CIA) had used European airports to transport suspected Islamist militants to secret detention centres in Eastern Europe for interrogation in an illegal programme of so-called 'extraordinary rendition'. Rice acknowledged the practice of rendition, but denied that prisoners were tortured and refused to comment on the alleged existence of CIA prisons in Eastern Europe. In late November the EU requested clarification from the USA about the alleged secret prisons and transfer flights, while the Council of Europe established an inquiry into the matter. Meanwhile, the European Parliament formed its own 46-member committee to investigate the allegations. The final report of the Parliament's inquiry, published in February 2007, rejected extraordinary rendition as an illegal instrument used by the USA in the fight against terrorism. The report noted that secret detention facilities may have been located at US military bases in Europe, and deplored the acquiescence of some member states in illegal CIA operations and the failure of the EU Council of Ministers to co-operate with the inquiry.

AFRICAN, CARIBBEAN AND PACIFIC (ACP) COUNTRIES

In June 2000, meeting in Cotonou, Benin, heads of state and of government of the EU and African, Caribbean and Pacific (ACP) countries concluded a new 20-year partnership accord between the EU and ACP states. The EU-ACP Partnership Agreement, known as the Cotonou Agreement, entered into force on 1 April 2003 (although many of its provisions had been applicable for a transitional period since August 2000), following ratification by the then 15 EU member states and more than the requisite two-thirds of the ACP countries. Previously, the principal means of co-operation between the Community and developing countries were the Lomé Conventions. The First Lomé Convention (Lomé I), which was concluded at Lomé, Togo, in February 1975 and came into force on 1 April 1976, replaced the Yaoundé Conventions and the Arusha Agreement. Lomé I was designed to provide a new framework of co-operation, taking into account the varying needs of developing ACP countries. The Second Lomé Convention entered into force on 1 January 1981 and the Third Lomé Convention on 1 March 1985 (trade provisions) and 1 May 1986 (aid). The Fourth Lomé Convention, which had a 10-year commitment period, was signed in December 1989: its trade provisions entered into force on 1 March 1990, and the remainder entered into force in September 1991.

The Cotonou Agreement was to cover a 20-year period from 2000 and was subject to revision every five years. A financial protocol was attached to the Agreement which indicated the funds available to the ACP through the European Development Fund (EDF), the main instrument for Community aid for development co-operation in ACP countries. The ninth EDF, covering the initial five-year period from March 2000, provided a total budget of €13,500m., of which €1,300m. was allocated to regional co-operation and €2,200m. was for the new investment facility for the development of the private sector. In addition, uncommitted balances from previous EDFs amounted to a further €2,500m. The new Agreement envisaged a more participatory approach with more effective political co-operation to encourage good governance and democracy, increased flexibility in the provision of aid to reward performance and a new framework for economic and trade co-operation. Its objectives were to alleviate poverty, contribute to sustainable development and integrate the ACP economies into the global economy. Negotiations to revise the Cotonou agreement were initiated in May 2004 and concluded in February 2005. The political dimension of the Agreement was broadly strengthened and a reference to co-operation in counter-terrorism and the prevention of the proliferation of weapons of mass destruction was included.

Under the provisions of the new accord, the EU was to negotiate free-trade arrangements (replacing the previous non-reciprocal trade preferences) with the most developed ACP countries during 2000–08; these would be structured around a system of six regional free-trade zones, and would be designed to ensure full compatibility with World Trade Organization (WTO) provisions. Once in force, the agreements would be subject to revision every five years. The first general stage of negotiations for the Economic Partnership Agreements (EPA), involving discussions with all ACP countries regarding common procedures, began in September 2002. The regional phase of EPA negotiations to establish a new framework for trade and investment commenced in October 2003. Negotiations had been scheduled for completion in mid-2007 to allow for ratification by 2008, when the WTO exception for existing arrangements expired. However, the negotiation period was subsequently extended. By March 2008 15 ACP states had initialled full EPAs. Another 20 countries had reached partial agreements, covering the liberalization of goods and agricultural products. The EPAs attracted some criticism for their focus on trade liberalization and their perceived failure to recognize the widespread poverty of ACP countries. Meanwhile, the EU had launched an initiative to allow free access to the products of the least-developed ACP nations by 2005. Stabex and Sysmin, instruments under the Lomé Conventions designed to stabilize export prices for agricultural and mining commodities, respectively, were replaced by a system called FLEX, introduced in 2000, to compensate ACP countries for short-term fluctuations in export earnings. In February 2001 the EU agreed to phase out trade barriers on imports of everything but military weapons from the world's 48 least-developed countries, 39 of which were in the ACP group. Duties on sugar, rice, bananas and some other products were to remain until 2009. In May 2001 the EU announced that it would cancel all outstanding debts arising from its trade accords with former colonies of member states.

One major new programme set up on behalf of the ACP countries and financed by the EDF was Pro€Invest, which was launched in 2002, with funding of €110m. over a seven-year period. In October 2003 the Commission proposed to incorporate the EDF into the EU budget (it had previously been a fund outside the EU budget, to which the EU member states made direct voluntary contributions). The cost-sharing formula for the 25 member states would automatically apply, obviating the need for negotiations about contributions for the 10th EDF. The Commission proposal was endorsed by the European Parliament in April 2004. Despite the fears of ACP countries that the enlargement of the EU could jeopardize funding, the 10th EDF was agreed in December 2005 by the European Council and provided funds of €22,682m. for the period 2008–13.

On 1 July 1993 the EC introduced a regime to allow the preferential import into the Community of bananas from former French and British colonies in the Caribbean. This was designed to protect the banana industries of ACP countries from the availability of cheaper bananas, produced by countries in Latin America. Latin American and later US producers brought a series of complaints before the WTO, claiming that the EU banana import regime was in contravention of free-trade principles. The WTO upheld their complaints on each occasion leading to adjustments of the complex quota and tariffs systems in place. Following the WTO authorization of punitive US trade sanctions, in April 2001 the EU reached agreement with the USA and Ecuador on a new banana regime. Under the new accord, the EU was granted the so-called Cotonou waiver, which allowed it to maintain preferential access for ACP banana exports, in return for the adoption of a new tariff-only system for bananas from Latin American countries from 1 January 2006. The Latin American producers were guaranteed total market access under the agreement and were permitted to seek arbitration if dissatisfied with the EU's proposed tariff levels. Following the WTO rejection of EU proposals for tariff levels of €230 and €187 per metric ton (in comparison with existing rates of €75 for a quota of 2.2m. tons and €680 thereafter), in November 2005 the EU announced that a tariff of €176, with a duty-free quota of 775,000 metric tons for ACP producers, would be implemented on 1 January 2006. In late 2006 Ecuador initiated a challenge to the EU's proposals at the WTO. Twelve other countries subsequently initiated third-party challenges to the proposals at the WTO, in support of the challenge by Ecuador. In April 2008 the WTO upheld the challenge initiated by Ecuador, and ordered the EU to bring its tariffs into conformity with WTO regulations.

Following a WTO ruling at the request of Brazil, Australia and Thailand in 2005 that the EU's subsidized exports of sugar breached legal limits, reform of the EU's sugar regime was required by May 2006. Previously, the EU purchased fixed quotas of sugar from ACP producers at two or three times the world price, the same price that it paid to sugar growers in the EU. In November 2005 the EU agreed to reform the sugar industry through a phased reduction of its prices for white sugar of 36% by 2009 (which was still double the market price in 2005). Compensation to EU producers was generous, amounting to €6,300m. over the four years beginning in January 2006, but compensation to ACP producers was worth just €40m. in 2006. Development campaigners and impoverished ACP countries, notably Jamaica and Guyana, condemned the plans.

In June 1995 negotiations opened with a view to concluding a wide-ranging trade and co-operation agreement with South Africa, including the eventual creation of a free-trade area (FTA). The accord was approved by heads of state and of government in March 1999, after agreement was reached to eliminate progressively, over a 12-year period, the use of the terms 'port' and 'sherry' to describe South African fortified wines. The accord provided for the removal of duties from about 99% of South Africa's industrial exports and some 75% of its agricultural products within 10 years, while South Africa was to liberalize its market for some 86% of EU industrial goods (with protection for the motor vehicle and textiles industries), within a 12-year period. The accord also introduced increased development assistance for South Africa after 1999. The long-delayed agreement was finally signed in January 2002, allowing South African wines freer access to the European market. Under the terms of the agreement, South Africa was allowed to export 42m. litres of wine a year duty-free to the EU, in exchange for abandoning the use of names such as 'sherry', 'port', 'ouzo' or 'grappa'. In March 1997 the Commission approved a Special Protocol for South Africa's accession to the Lomé Convention, and in April South Africa attained partial membership. Full membership was withheld, as South Africa was not regarded as, in all respects, a developing country, and was therefore not entitled to aid provisions.

In May 2003 Timor-Leste joined the ACP and the ACP-EC Council of Ministers approved its accession to the ACP-EC Partnership Agreement. Cuba, which had been admitted to the ACP in December 2000, was granted observer status. Cuba withdrew its application to join the Cotonou Agreement in July 2003.

Article 96 of the Cotonou Agreement, which provides for suspension of the Agreement in specific countries in the event of violation of one of its essential elements (respect for human rights, democratic principles and the rule of law) was invoked against Haiti in 2001 and this was extended annually to December 2004. However, relations with Haiti were in the process of normalization from September of that year. A decision was taken to normalize relations with Guinea-Bissau, following positive measures taken by the Government there. Sanctions were applied to Côte d'Ivoire in December 2004. During 2002 the European Council condemned the worsening human rights situation in Zimbabwe, describing the elections held there in 2002 as deeply flawed, and imposed a range of targeted sanctions, including a travel ban on and freezing of the assets of certain members of the leadership, an arms embargo, and the suspension of development aid. In February 2003 it was announced that the second Europe-Africa summit, scheduled to take place in Lisbon, Portugal, in April, had been postponed indefinitely when EU leaders decided that they could not find a way to exclude the Zimbabwean leader, Robert Mugabe. At the same time the EU sanctions against Zimbabwe were renewed for a further year. The number of senior administration officials subject to a travel ban was increased from 79 to 95 in February 2004 as EU sanctions against Zimbabwe were extended for a further year. The EU claimed that the elections held in Zimbabwe in February 2005 were fraudulent and non-democratic, and consequently extended its sanctions for a further year. Sanctions were subsequently extended on an annual basis. The comprehensive Liberian peace agreement signed in Accra, Ghana, led to the lifting in 2003 of certain restrictions imposed on Liberia in 2002 in order to liberate funds to finance peace-keeping operations and promote the restoration of democracy. Outstanding sanctions against Liberia were lifted in January 2006.

INTERNATIONAL ORGANIZATIONS

European Union

ACP-EU Institutions

The three institutions of the Cotonou Agreement are the Council of Ministers, the Committee of Ambassadors and the Joint Parliamentary Assembly.

Council of Ministers: comprises the members of the Council of the European Union and members of the EU Commission and a member of the Government of each ACP signatory to the Cotonou Agreement; meets annually.

Committee of Ambassadors: comprises the Permanent Representative of each member state to the European Union and a representative of the EU Commission and the Head of Mission (ambassador) of each ACP state accredited to the EU; assists the Council of Ministers and meets regularly, in particular to prepare the session of the Council of Ministers.

Joint Parliamentary Assembly: EU and ACP are equally represented; attended by parliamentary delegates from each of the ACP countries and an equal number of members of the European Parliament; two co-presidents are elected by the Assembly from each of the two groups; meets twice a year; 24 vice-presidents (12 EU and 12 ACP) are also elected by the Assembly and with the co-presidents constitute the Bureau of the Joint Parliamentary Assembly, which meets several times a year; Co-Pres GLENYS KINNOCK, RENÉ RADEMBINO-CONIQUET.

Secretariat of the ACP-EC Council of Ministers: 175 rue de la Loi, 1048 Brussels; tel. (2) 281-61-11; fax (2) 281-69-34; Co-Secretaries PAUL CULLEY, JEAN ROBERT GOULONGANA.

Centre for the Development of Enterprise (CDE): 52 ave Herrmann Debroux, 1160 Brussels, Belgium; tel. (2) 679-18-11; fax (2) 679-26-03; e-mail info@cde.int; internet www.cde.int/index.aspx; f. 1977 to encourage and support the creation, expansion and restructuring of industrial companies (mainly in the fields of manufacturing and agro-industry) in the ACP states by promoting co-operation between ACP and European companies, in the form of financial, technical or commercial partnership, management contracts, licensing or franchise agreements, sub-contracts, etc.; manages the Pro€Invest programme; Dir FERNANDO MATOS ROSA.

Technical Centre for Agricultural and Rural Co-operation (CTA): Postbus 380, 6700 AJ Wageningen, Netherlands; tel. (317) 467100; fax (317) 460067; e-mail cta@cta.int; internet www.agricta.org; f. 1983 to provide ACP states with better access to information, research, training and innovations in agricultural development and extension; Dir Dr HANSJÖRG NEUN.

ACP Institutions

ACP Council of Ministers: composed of a member of Government for each ACP state or a government-designated representative; the principal decision-making body for the ACP group; meets twice annually; ministerial sectoral meetings are held regularly.

ACP Committee of Ambassadors: the second decision-making body of the ACP Group; it acts on behalf of the Council of Ministers between ministerial sessions and is composed of the ambassadors or one representative from every ACP State.

ACP Secretariat: ACP House, 451 ave Georges Henri, Brussels, Belgium; tel. (2) 743-06-00; fax (2) 735-55-73; e-mail info@acpsec.org; internet www.acpsec.org; Sec.-Gen. Sir JOHN KAPUTIN (Papua New Guinea).

On 15 April 2005 27 APC countries signed a charter creating the ACP Consultative Assembly, which formalized the existing inter-parliamentary co-operation between the ACP member states.

The ACP States

Angola
Antigua and Barbuda
Bahamas
Barbados
Belize
Benin
Botswana
Burkina Faso
Burundi
Cameroon
Cape Verde
Central African Republic
Chad
Comoros
Congo, Democratic Republic
Congo, Republic
Cook Islands
Côte d'Ivoire
Cuba
Djibouti
Dominica
Dominican Republic
Equatorial Guinea
Eritrea
Ethiopia
Fiji
Gabon
The Gambia
Ghana
Grenada
Guinea
Guinea-Bissau
Guyana
Haiti
Jamaica
Kenya
Kiribati
Lesotho
Liberia
Madagascar
Malawi
Mali
Marshall Islands
Mauritania
Mauritius
Federated States of Micronesia
Mozambique
Namibia
Nauru
Niger
Nigeria
Niue
Palau
Papua New Guinea
Rwanda
Saint Christopher and Nevis
Saint Lucia
Saint Vincent and the Grenadines
Samoa
São Tomé and Príncipe
Senegal
Seychelles
Sierra Leone
Solomon Islands
Somalia
South Africa
Sudan
Suriname
Swaziland
Tanzania
Timor-Leste
Togo
Tonga
Trinidad and Tobago
Tuvalu
Uganda
Vanuatu
Zambia
Zimbabwe

GENERALIZED PREFERENCES

In July 1971 the Community introduced a generalized system of preferences (GSP) for tariffs in favour of developing countries, ensuring duty-free entry to the EC of all manufactured and semi-manufactured industrial products, including textiles—but subject in certain circumstances to preferential limits. Preferences, usually in the form of a tariff reduction, are also offered on some agricultural products. In 1980 the Council agreed to the extension of the scheme for a second decade (1981–90): at the same time it adopted an operational framework for industrial products, which gives individual preferential limits based on the degree of competitiveness of the developing country concerned. From the end of 1990 an interim scheme was in operation, pending the introduction of a revised scheme based on the outcome of the 'Uruguay Round' of GATT negotiations on international trade (which were finally concluded in December 1993). Since 1977 the Community has progressively liberalized GSP access for the least-developed countries by according them duty-free entry on all products and by exempting them from virtually all preferential limits. In 1992–93 the GSP was extended to Albania, the Baltic states, the CIS and Georgia; in September 1994 it was extended to South Africa.

In December 1994 the European Council adopted a revised GSP to operate during 1995–98. It provided additional trade benefits to encourage the introduction by governments of environmentally sound policies and of internationally recognized labour standards. Conversely, a country's preferential entitlement could be withdrawn, for example, if it permitted forced labour. Under the new scheme, preferential tariffs amounted to 85% of the common customs duty for very sensitive products (for example, most textile products), and 70% or 35% for products classified as sensitive (for example, chemicals and electrical goods). The common customs duty was suspended for non-sensitive products (for example, paper, books and cosmetics). In accordance with the EU's foreign policy objective of focusing on the development of the world's poorest countries, duties were eliminated in their entirety (with the exception of arms and ammunition) for 49 least-developed countries. Duties were also suspended for a further five Latin American countries, conditional on the implementation of campaigns against the production and trade of illegal drugs.

A new GSP for 1999–2001 largely extended the existing scheme unchanged. The next GSP regulation, for 2002–04 (subsequently extended until the end of 2005), was revised to expand product coverage and improve preferential margins. In May 2003 new regulations were adopted enabling certain countries to be exempted from the abolition of tariff preferences on export of their products to the EU if that sector was judged to be in crisis. Under a new GSP for 2006–08, the coverage of the general arrangement was extended to a further 300 products, mostly in the agriculture and fishery sectors, bringing the total number of products covered to some 7,200. The focus of the new regime was on developing countries most in need. Additional preferences were granted under a new 'GSP+' incentive scheme to particularly vulnerable countries pursuing good governance and sustainable development policies (judged by their ratification and implementation of relevant international conventions). Bolivia, Colombia, Costa Rica, Ecuador, El Salvador, Georgia, Guatemala, Honduras, Moldova, Mongolia, Nicaragua, Panama, Peru, Sri Lanka and Venezuela were declared eligible for GSP+, which took effect, exceptionally, on 1 July 2005, replacing the special arrangements to combat drugs production and trafficking in force under the previous GSP.

AID TO DEVELOPING AND NON-EU COUNTRIES

The main channels for Community aid to developing countries are the Cotonou Agreement and the Mediterranean Financial Protocols, but technical and financial aid and assistance for refugees, training, trade promotion and co-operation in industry, energy, science and technology are also provided to about 30 countries in Asia and Latin America. The European Community Humanitarian Office (ECHO) was established in 1991 with a mandate to co-ordinate emergency humanitarian assistance and food aid provided by the Community, and became fully operational in early 1993. ECHO, which is based in Brussels, finances operations conducted by non-governmental organizations and international agencies, with which it works in partnership. Relations between ECHO and its partners are governed by Framework Partnership Agreements (FPAs), the purpose of which is to define roles and responsibilities in the implementation of humanitarian operations financed by the European Community. In December 2003 ECHO signed an FPA with the International Committee of the Red Cross, the International Federation of Red Cross and Red Crescent Societies, and the national Red Cross societies of the EU member states and Norway. A new FPA with non-governmental organizations entered into force on 1 January 2004; this agreement expired on 30 December 2007, and a revised FPA came into force on 1 January 2008. ECHO's relations with UN agencies are covered by a Financial and Administrative Framework Agreement signed in April 2003. ECHO aims to meet the immediate needs of victims of natural and man-made disasters world-wide, in such areas as assisting displaced persons, health, sanitary and mine-clearing programmes. In 2007 ECHO committed funds totalling €768.5m. to humanitarian assistance; the ACP countries accounted for 55% of expenditure in that year. Sudan received the largest proportion of ACP funding (€110.5m.), followed by the Democratic Republic of the Congo (some €50m.). Significant funding was also made available to: Chad (€30.5m.); Zimbabwe (€30.2m.); the Sahel region (€25.5m.); Uganda (€24.0m.); and Ethiopia (€20.0m.). ECHO also provided some €20.8m. to aid victims of conflict in the separatist Russian republic of Chechnya, and aid worth more than €88m. to help the humanitarian situation in the Palestinian-controlled territories in the Middle East. Funds were also made available to the Asia region, most notably some €27m. for those affected by the crisis in Afghanistan and environmental hazards in Afghanistan, Iran and Pakistan.

Finance

THE COMMUNITY BUDGET

The EU budget, which funds EU policies and finances all the EU institutions, is limited by agreement of all the member states. The Commission puts forward spending proposals, which have to be approved by the European Parliament and the Council of the European Union. The Parliament signs the agreed budget into law. Revenue for the budget comes from customs duties, sugar levies, payments based on value-added tax (VAT) and contributions from the member states based on their gross national income (GNI). The Commission is accountable each year to the European Parliament for its use of EU funds. External audits are carried out by the European Court of Auditors. To combat fraud, the European Anti-Fraud Office (OLAF) was established in June 1999.

The general budget contains the expenditures of the six main Community institutions—the Commission, the Council, Parliament, the Court of Justice, the Court of Auditors, and the Economic and Social Committee and the Committee of the Regions—of which Commission expenditure (covering administrative costs and expenditure on operations) forms the largest proportion. Expenditure is divided into two categories: that necessarily resulting from the Treaties (compulsory expenditure) and other (non-compulsory) expenditure. The budgetary process is aided by the establishment of Financial Perspectives, which are spending plans covering a number of years, thus guaranteeing the security of long-term EU projects and activities. Although the Financial Perspective limits expenditure in each policy area for each of the years covered, a more detailed annual budget still has to be agreed each year. The Commission presents the preliminary draft annual budget in late April or early May of the preceding year and the adopted budget is published in February of the relevant year. Since 2004 the budget has been structured according to policy areas. If the budget has not been adopted by the beginning of the financial year, monthly expenditure may amount to one-12th of the appropriations adopted for the previous year's budget. The Commission may (even late in the year during which the budget is being executed) revise estimates of revenue and expenditure, by presenting supplementary and/or amending budgets. Expenditure under the general budget is financed by 'own resources', comprising agricultural duties (on imports of agricultural produce from non-member states), customs duties, application of VAT on goods and services, and (since 1988) a levy based on the GNI of member states. Member states are obliged to collect 'own resources' on the Community's behalf.

In January 2006 the European Commission proposed an action plan to simplify the audit system, following the Court of Auditors' failure to approve the EU's accounts for the 11th consecutive year. The Commission criticized member states, which supervise about 80% of EU spending, and suggested the harmonization of audit systems across the 25 countries.

In May 2006 a new financial framework for the enlarged EU was formally adopted, when the European Parliament, the Council and the Commission signed an inter-institutional agreement on budgetary discipline and sound financial management, which entered into force at the beginning of January 2007. According to the framework, the EU was to focus on three main priority areas in 2007–13: integrating the single market to achieve sustainable growth by promoting competitiveness, cohesion and the preservation and management of natural resources; promoting the concept of European citizenship by prioritizing freedom, justice and security, and ensuring access to basic public goods and services; and establishing a strong global influence for Europe through its regional responsibilities, through emphasizing sustainable development, and by contributing to security. According to the agreement, which was amended in December 2007, the annual average upper limit on payment appropriations for 2007–13 amounted to 1.03% of the GNI of the 27 member states. Meanwhile, in mid-December 2006 the Council adopted new financial regulations, which aimed to improve the management of EU expenditure; the regulations demanded the publication of a list of all those receiving EU funds. All provisions of the Financial Regulation and its Implementing Rules had entered into force by 1 May 2007.

The 2007 EU budget provided for payment appropriations of €115,500m. (representing 0.99% of the member states' GNI), and commitment appropriations of €126,500m. (1.08% of GNI). The EU budget for 2008 was adopted by the European Parliament in December 2007, and provided for payment appropriations of €120,300m., equivalent to 0.96% of the 27 member states' GNI, and for commitment appropriations of €129,100m., equivalent to 1.03% of GNI. The largest proportion of spending, some 45%, was to be allocated to increased economic competitiveness and greater cohesion between the 27 member states.

STRUCTURAL FUNDS

The Community's 'structural funds' comprise the Guidance Section of the European Agricultural Guidance and Guarantee Fund, the European Regional Development Fund, the European Social Fund and the Cohesion Fund. There is also a financial instrument for fisheries guidance (the Financial Instrument for Fisheries Guidance—FIFG—which was established in 1993). In accordance with the Single European Act (1987), reforms of the Community's structural funds were adopted by the Council with effect from 1 January 1989, with the aim of more accurate identification of priority targets, and greater selectivity to enable action to be concentrated in the least-favoured regions (see Social Policy). Agenda 2000, which was approved by the Council in March 1999, provided for the reform of the structural funds to make available some €213,000m. for 2000–06, at 1999 prices. During 2002 the European Council established a new European Union Solidarity Fund, designed as a disaster relief fund in response to the flooding that affected Germany, Austria and several candidate countries during the summer of that year. A budget of €1,000m. per year was agreed for the Fund in November 2002.

In July 2006 the Council and the European Parliament adopted five new regulations that were to constitute the legal basis for the pursuit of cohesion objectives in 2007–13. A general regulation indicated common principles and standards for the implementation of the three cohesion mechanisms, the European Regional Development Fund (ERDF—see below), the European Social Fund (ESF—see below) and the Cohesion Fund (see below). The regulation on the ERDF defined the scope of its interventions, among them the promotion of private and public investments assisting in the reduction of regional disparities across the EU. Funding priorities were identified as research, innovation, environmental protection and risk prevention. The regulation concerning the ESF determined that it should be implemented in accordance with European employment strategy in 2007–13, and that it should focus on increasing the flexibility of workers and enterprises, enhancing access to and participation in the labour market, reinforcing social inclusion—by such means as combating discrimination—and promoting partnership for reform in the areas of employment and inclusion. In view of its application to member states with a gross national income (GNI) of less than 90% of the Community average, the new regulation concerning the Cohesion Fund extended eligibility for it to the new member states, in addition to Greece and Portugal. Spain was also to qualify for the Cohesion Fund, but on a transitional basis. A fifth regulation established a European Grouping of Territorial Co-operation, whose aim was to facilitate cross-border and transnational/inter-regional co-operation between regional and local authorities.

In 2007–13 the ERDF, the ESF and the Cohesion Fund were to contribute to three objectives: convergence (ERDF, ESF and the Cohesion Fund); regional competitiveness and employment (ERDF and ESF); and European territorial co-operation (ERDF). The con-

INTERNATIONAL ORGANIZATIONS

vergence objective was to concern 84 regions in 17 of the 27 member states and, on a 'phasing-out' basis, a further 16 regions where per caput gross domestic product was only slightly more than the threshold of 75% of the Community average. Indicative allocations for the convergence objective in 2007–13 (expressed in 2004 prices) were to total €251,100m. The regional competitiveness and employment objective was to apply to 168 regions in the 27 member states, 13 of which were so-called 'phasing-in' regions, eligible for special financial allocations in view of their former status as Objective 1 regions. Indicative allocations for the regional competitiveness and employment objective were to total €49,100m., including €10,400m. for the phasing-in regions. A total of €7,750m. was to be made available for the European territorial co-operation objective in 2007–13.

Cohesion Fund

The Treaty on European Union and its protocol on economic and social cohesion provided for the establishment of a 'Cohesion Fund', which began operating on 1 April 1993, with a budget of ECU 1,500m. for the first year. This was to subsidize projects in the fields of the environment and trans-European energy and communications networks in member states with a per caput gross national income of less than 90% of the Community average (in practice, this was to mean Greece, Ireland, Portugal and Spain). Commitments under the Fund in the budget appropriations for 2005 amounted to €5,132m. The Fund's total budget for the period 2000–06 was €18,000m. This was increased to €61,590m. for 2007–13.

European Agricultural Guarantee Fund—EAGF

This fund was created in September 2005 to replace the Guarantee Section of the European Agricultural Guidance and Guarantee Fund, the fund that finances the Common Agricultural Policy (CAP). It came into operation at the beginning of 2007 and *inter alia* provides finance for the export of agricultural products to third countries, intervention measures to regulate agricultural markets and direct payments to farmers.

European Fund for Agricultural Development—EAFRD

This fund was created in September 2005 and came into operation at the beginning of 2007. It replaced the Guidance Section of the European Agricultural Guidance and Guarantee Fund and the rural development measures previously financed under the Guarantee section. It is responsible for the single financial contribution from the EU to rural development programmes.

European Regional Development Fund—ERDF

Payments began in 1975. The Fund is intended to compensate for the unequal rate of development in different regions of the Community. It finances investment leading to the creation or maintenance of jobs, improvements in infrastructure, local development initiatives and the business activities of small and medium-sized enterprises in 'least favoured regions'.

European Social Fund—ESF

The Fund (established in 1960) provides resources with the aim of combating long-term unemployment and facilitating the integration into the labour market of young people and the socially disadvantaged. It also supports schemes to help workers to adapt to industrial changes.

Financial Instrument for Fisheries Guidance—FIFG

The FIFG was set up in 1993, following the reform of the structural funds. The FIFG aims to contribute to achieving a sustainable balance between fishery resources and their exploitation. It also seeks to strengthen the competitiveness of the sector and the development of areas dependent upon it.

BUDGET EXPENDITURE APPROPRIATIONS FOR THE ACTIVITIES OF THE EUROPEAN COMMISSION
(€ million)

	2006	2007
Economic and financial affairs	455.4	494.9
Enterprise	371.7	510.0
Competition	68.4	71.7
Employment and social affairs	11,910.8	11,439.3
Agriculture and rural development	54,547.4	54,509.7
Energy and transport	1,437.4	1,808.9
Environment	326.3	353.5
Research	3,497.1	3,564.7
Information society	1,405.8	1,434.7
Direct research	329.6	348.5

—continued	2006	2007
Fisheries	1,062.0	955.2
Internal market	56.5	56.4
Regional policy	28,720.6	34,834.9
Taxation and customs union	107.1	110.0
Education and culture	989.5	1,222.7
Press and communication	179.9	201.0
Health and consumer protection	529.6	544.7
Area of freedom, security and justice	592.0	671.5
External relations	3,439.6	3,574.7
Trade	64.8	71.5
Development and relations with African, Caribbean and Pacific (ACP) States	1,081.9	1,243.6
Enlargement	2,318.0	1,064.6
Humanitarian aid	719.0	749.7
Fight against fraud	63.6	72.5
Commission's policy co-ordination and legal advice	159.7	168.7
Administration	886.5	987.5
Budget	1,141.8	519.5
Audit	9.7	9.2
Statistics	117.2	121.4
Pensions	945.2	997.5
Language services	346.6	358.9
Reserves	229.0	734.5
Total Commission	118,109.7	123,806.0
Other institutions (excl. pensions)	2,460.1	2,577.2
Grand total	**120,569.8**	**126,383.2**

Source: European Commission, *General Report on the Activities of the European Union* (2007).

REVENUE
(€ million)

Source of revenue	2006	2007
Agricultural and sugar levies	1,014.00	1,449.10
Customs duties	13,874.90	15,083.80
VAT-based resource	17,200.28	18,517.23
GNI-based resource	68,921.21	71,153.08
Miscellaneous plus surplus from the previous year	6,368.08	7,642.61
Total	**107,378.47**	**113,845.82**

Source: European Commission, *General Report on the Activities of the European Union* (2007).

NATIONAL CONTRIBUTION TO THE EU BUDGET*

Country	Contribution for 2006	% of total
Austria	2,013.9	2.3
Belgium	2,635.2	3.0
Cyprus	120.7	0.1
Czech Republic	886.3	1.0
Denmark	1,869.7	2.1
Estonia	111.0	0.1
Finland	1,429.6	1.6
France	15,353.2	17.6
Germany	17,573.3	20.1
Greece	1,629.7	1.9
Hungary	678.3	0.8
Ireland	1,279.7	1.5
Italy	11,933.5	13.7
Latvia	132.7	0.2
Lithuania	195.8	0.2
Luxembourg	198.3	0.2
Malta	39.4	0.0
Netherlands	4,487.1	5.1
Poland	2,174.6	2.5
Portugal	1,260.7	1.4
Slovenia	243.8	0.3
Slovakia	346.5	0.4
Spain	8,601.9	9.9
Sweden	2,297.7	2.6
United Kingdom	9,830.2	11.3
Total	**87,322.9**	**100.0**

*Excluding traditional own resources (TOR) payments, comprising agricultural duties, sugar levies and customs duties, which totalled €15,028.3m. in 2006.
Source: European Commission, *EU Budget 2006 Financial Report*.

Publications*

Bulletin of the European Union (10 a year).
The Courier ACP-EU (every 2 months, in English, French, Portuguese and Spanish on ACP-EU affairs).
European Economy Research Letter (3 a year).
General Report on the Activities of the European Union (annually).

Official Journal of the European Union (website on which all contracts from the public sector that are valued above a certain threshold must be published; internet www.ojec.com).
Publications of the European Communities (quarterly).
EUR-Lex Website (treaties, legislation and judgments; internet europa.eu.int/eur-lex/lex/).
Information sheets, background reports and statistical documents.

*Most publications are available in all of the official languages of the Union and are available free of charge online. They can be obtained from the Office for Official Publications of the European Communities (Publications Office), 2 rue Mercier, 2985 Luxembourg; tel. 29291; fax 495719; email info@publications.europa.eu; internet publications.europa.eu/index_en.htm.

THE FRANC ZONE

Address: Direction des Relations Internationales et Européennes (Service de la Zone Franc), Banque de France, 39 rue Croix-des-Petits-Champs, 75049, Paris Cédex 01, France.
Telephone: 1-42-92-31-46; **fax:** 1-42-92-39-88; **e-mail:** comozof@banque-france.fr; **internet:** www.banque-france.fr/fr/eurosys/zonefr/page2.htm.

MEMBERS*

Benin	French Overseas
Burkina Faso	Territories
Cameroon	Gabon
Central African Republic	Guinea-Bissau
Chad	Mali
Comoros	Niger
Republic of the Congo	Senegal
Côte d'Ivoire	Togo
Equatorial Guinea	

*Prior to 1 January 2002, when the transition to a single European currency (euro) was finalized (see below), the Franc Zone also included Metropolitan France, the French Overseas Departments (French Guiana, Guadeloupe, Martinique and Réunion), the French Overseas Collectivité Départementale (Mayotte) and the French Overseas Collectivité Territoriale (St Pierre and Miquelon). The French Overseas Territory (French Polynesia) and the French Overseas Countries (New Caledonia and the Wallis and Futuna Islands) have continued to use the franc CFP (franc des Comptoirs français du Pacifique, 'French Pacific franc').

Apart from Guinea and Mauritania (see below), all of the countries that formerly comprised French West and Equatorial Africa are members of the Franc Zone. The former West and Equatorial African territories are still grouped within the two currency areas that existed before independence, each group having its own variant on the CFA, issued by a central bank: the franc de la Communauté Financière d'Afrique ('franc CFA de l'Ouest'), issued by the Banque centrale des états de l'Afrique de l'ouest—BCEAO, and the franc Coopération financière en Afrique centrale ('franc CFA central'), issued by the Banque des états de l'Afrique centrale—BEAC.

The following states withdrew from the Franc Zone during the period 1958–73: Guinea, Tunisia, Morocco, Algeria, Mauritania and Madagascar. Equatorial Guinea, formerly a Spanish territory, joined the Franc Zone in January 1985, and Guinea-Bissau, a former Portuguese territory, joined in May 1997.

The Comoros, formerly a French Overseas Territory, did not join the Franc Zone following its unilateral declaration of independence in 1975. However, the franc CFA was used as the currency of the new state and the Institut d'émission des Comores continued to function as a Franc Zone organization. In 1976 the Comoros formally assumed membership. In July 1981 the Banque centrale des Comores replaced the Institut d'émission des Comores, establishing its own currency, the Comoros franc.

The Franc Zone operates on the basis of agreements concluded between France and each group of member countries, and the Comoros. The currencies in the Franc Zone were formerly linked with the French franc at a fixed rate of exchange. However, following the introduction of the euro (European single currency) in January 1999, within the framework of European economic and monetary union, in which France was a participant, the Franc Zone currencies were effectively linked at fixed parity to the euro (i.e. parity was based on the fixed conversion rate for the French franc and the euro). From 1 January 2002, when European economic and monetary union was finalized and the French franc withdrawn from circulation, the franc CFA, Comoros franc and franc CFP became officially pegged to the euro, at a fixed rate of exchange. (In accordance with Protocol 13 on France, appended to the 1993 Maastricht Treaty on European Union, France was permitted to continue issuing currencies in its Overseas Territories—i.e. the franc CFP—following the completion of European economic and monetary union.) All the convertability arrangements previously concluded between France and the Franc Zone remained in force. Therefore Franc Zone currencies are freely convertible into euros, at the fixed exchange rate, guaranteed by the French Treasury. Each group of member countries, and the Comoros, has its own central issuing bank, with overdraft facilities provided by the French Treasury. (The issuing authority for the French Overseas Territories is the Institut d'émission d'outre-mer, based in Paris.) Monetary reserves are held mainly in the form of euros. The BCEAO and the BEAC are authorized to hold up to 35% of their foreign exchange holdings in currencies other than the euro. Franc Zone ministers of finance normally meet twice a year to review economic and monetary co-operation. The meeting is normally attended by the French Minister of Co-operation and Francophony.

During the late 1980s and early 1990s the economies of the African Franc Zone countries were adversely affected by increasing foreign debt and by a decline in the prices paid for their principal export commodities. The French Government, however, refused to devalue the franc CFA, as recommended by the IMF. In 1990 the Franc Zone governments agreed to develop economic union, with integrated public finances and common commercial legislation. In April 1992, at a meeting of Franc Zone ministers, a treaty on the insurance industry was adopted, providing for the establishment of a regulatory body for the industry, the Conférence Intrafricaine des Marchés d'Assurances (CIMA), and for the creation of a council of Franc Zone ministers responsible for the insurance industry, with its secretariat in Libreville, Gabon. (A code of conduct for members of CIMA entered into force in February 1995.) At the meeting held in April 1992 ministers also agreed that a further council of ministers was to be created with the task of monitoring the social security systems in Franc Zone countries. A programme drawn up by Franc Zone finance ministers concerning the harmonization of commercial legislation in member states through the establishment of l'Organisation pour l'Harmonisation du Droit des Affaires en Afrique (OHADA) was approved by the Franco-African summit in October. A treaty to align corporate and investment regulations was signed by 11 member countries in October 1993.

In August 1993, in view of financial turmoil related to the continuing weakness of the French franc and the abandonment of the European exchange rate mechanism, the BCEAO and the BEAC determined to suspend repurchasing of francs CFA outside the Franc Zone. Effectively this signified the temporary withdrawal of guaranteed convertibility of the franc CFA with the French franc. Devaluations of the franc CFA and the Comoros franc (by 50% and 33.3%, respectively) were implemented in January 1994. Following the devaluation the CFA countries embarked on programmes of economic adjustment, including restrictive fiscal and wage policies and other monetary, structural and social measures, designed to stimulate growth and to ensure eligibility for development assistance from international financial institutions. France established a special development fund of FFr 300m. to alleviate the immediate social consequences of the devaluation, and announced substantial debt cancellations. In April the French Government announced assistance amounting to FFr 10,000m. over three years to Franc Zone countries undertaking structural adjustment programmes. The IMF, which had strongly advocated a devaluation of the franc CFA, and the World Bank approved immediate soft-credit loans, technical assistance and cancellations or rescheduling of debts. In June 1994 heads of state (or representatives) of African Franc Zone countries convened in Libreville, Gabon, to review the effects of the currency realignment. The final communiqué of the meeting urged further international support for the countries' economic development efforts. In April 1995 Franc Zone finance ministers, meeting in Paris, recognized the positive impact of the devaluation on agricultural export sectors, in particular in west African countries. In January 1996 Afristat, a research and training institution based in Bamako, Mali, commenced activities, having been established in accordance with a decision by the Franc Zone member countries and the French Government made in September 1993. Afristat aims to support national statistical organizations in participating states in order to strengthen their economic management capabilities. The IMF and the World Bank have continued to support economic development efforts in the Franc Zone. France provides debt relief to Franc Zone member states eligible under the World Bank's HIPC. In April 2001 the African Franc Zone member states determined jointly to develop anti-money laundering legislation.

In February 2000 UEMOA and ECOWAS adopted an action plan for the creation of a single West African Monetary Zone and consequent replacement of the franc Communauté financière africaine by a single West African currency (see below).

CURRENCIES OF THE FRANC ZONE

1 franc CFA = €0.00152. CFA stands for Communauté financière africaine in the West African area and for Coopération financière en Afrique centrale in the Central African area. Used in the monetary areas of West and Central Africa respectively.

1 Comoros franc = €0.00201. Used in the Comoros, where it replaced the franc CFA in 1981.

1 franc CFP = €0.00839. CFP stands for Comptoirs français du Pacifique. Used in New Caledonia, French Polynesia and the Wallis and Futuna Islands.

WEST AFRICA

Union économique et monétaire ouest-africaine (UEMOA): BP 543, Ouagadougou 01, Burkina Faso; tel. 31-88-73; fax 31-88-72; e-mail commission@uemoa.int; internet www.uemoa.int; f. 1994; promotes regional monetary and economic convergence, and envisages the eventual creation of a sub-regional common market. A preferential tariff scheme, eliminating duties on most local products and reducing by 30% import duties on many Union-produced industrial goods, became operational on 1 July 1996; in addition, from 1 July, a community solidarity tax of 0.5% was imposed on all goods from third countries sold within the Union, in order to strengthen UEMOA's capacity to promote economic integration. (This was increased to 1% in December 1999.) In June 1997 UEMOA heads of state and government agreed to reduce import duties on industrial products originating in the Union by a further 30%. An inter-parliamentary committee, recognized as the predecessor of a UEMOA legislature, was inaugurated in Mali in March 1998. In September Côte d'Ivoire's stock exchange was transformed into the Bourse regionale des valeurs mobilières, a regional stock exchange serving the Union, in order to further economic integration. On 1 January 2000 internal tariffs were eliminated on all local products (including industrial goods) and a joint external tariff system, reportedly in five bands of between 0% and 20%, was imposed on goods deriving from outside the new customs union. Guinea-Bissau was excluded from the arrangement owing to its unstable political situation. The UEMOA member countries also belong to ECOWAS and, in accordance with a decision taken in April 2000, aim to harmonize UEMOA's economic programme with that of a planned second West African monetary union (the West African Monetary Zone—WAMZ), to be established by the remaining—mainly anglophone—ECOWAS member states in 2009 (as currently scheduled). A merger of the two complementary monetary unions, and the replacement of the franc Communauté financière africaine by a new single West African currency (the 'eco', initially to to be adopted by the WAMZ), is eventually envisaged. In January 2003 member states adopted a treaty on the establishment of a UEMOA parliament. During 2006–10 UEMOA was implementing a regional economic programme aimed at developing regional infrastructures. Mems: Benin, Burkina Faso, Côte d'Ivoire, Guinea-Bissau, Mali, Niger, Senegal and Togo; Pres. SOUMAILA CISSE (Mali)

Union monétaire ouest-africaine (UMOA) (West African Monetary Union): established by Treaty of November 1973, entered into force 1974; in 1990 the UMOA Banking Commission was established, which is responsible for supervising the activities of banks and financial institutions in the region, with the authority to prohibit the operation of a banking institution. UMOA constitutes an integral part of UEMOA.

Banque centrale des états de l'Afrique de l'ouest (BCEAO): ave Abdoulaye Fadiga, BP 3108, Dakar, Senegal; tel. 839-05-00; fax 823-93-35; e-mail webmaster@bceao.int; internet www.bceao.int; f. 1962; central bank of issue for the mems of UEMOA; total assets 5,099,908m. francs CFA (31 Dec. 2005); mems: Benin, Burkina Faso, Côte d'Ivoire, Guinea-Bissau, Mali, Niger, Senegal and Togo; Gov. HENRI PHILIPPE DAKOURY TABLEY; Sec.-Gen. MODIENNE GUISSE; publs *Annual Report, Notes d'Information et Statistiques* (monthly), *Annuaire des banques, Bilan des banques et établissements financiers* (annually).

Banque ouest-africaine de développement (BOAD): 68 ave de la Libération, BP 1172, Lomé, Togo; tel. 221-42-44; fax 221-52-67; e-mail boadsiege@boad.org; internet www.boad.org; f. 1973 to promote the balanced development of mem. states and the economic integration of West Africa; a Guarantee Fund for Private Investment in West Africa, established jtly by BOAD and the European Investment Bank in Dec. 1994, aims to guarantee medium- and long-term credits to private sector businesses in the region; mems: Benin, Burkina Faso, Côte d'Ivoire, Guinea-Bissau, Mali, Niger, Senegal, Togo; Pres. ABDOULAYE BIO TCHANÉ (Benin); Vice-Pres. ISSA COULIBALY; publs *Rapport Annuel, BOAD en Bref* (quarterly).

Bourse Régionale des Valeurs Mobilières (BRVM): 18 ave Joseph Anoma, BP 3802, Abidjan 01, Côte d'Ivoire; tel. 20-32-66-85; fax 20-32-66-84; e-mail brvm@brvm.org; internet www.brvm.org; f. 1998; Dir-Gen. JEAN-PAUL GILLET.

CENTRAL AFRICA

Communauté économique et monétaire de l'Afrique centrale (CEMAC): BP 969, Bangui, Central African Republic; tel. and fax 61-21-79; fax 61-21-35; e-mail secemac@cemac.cf; internet www.cemac.cf; f. 1998; formally inaugurated as the successor to the Union douanière et économique de l'Afrique centrale (UDEAC, f. 1966) at a meeting of heads of state held in Malabo, Equatorial Guinea, in June 1999; aims to promote the process of sub-regional integration within the framework of an economic union and a monetary union; CEMAC was also to comprise a parliament and sub-regional tribunal; UDEAC established a common external tariff for imports from other countries and administered a common code for investment policy and a Solidarity Fund to counteract regional disparities of wealth and economic development; mems: Cameroon, Central African Republic, Chad, Republic of the Congo, Equatorial Guinea, Gabon; Pres ANTOINE NTSIMI.

At a summit meeting in December 1981, UDEAC leaders agreed in principle to form an economic community of Central African states (Communauté économique des états de l'Afrique centrale—CEEAC), to include UDEAC members and Burundi, Rwanda, São Tomé and Príncipe and Zaire (now Democratic Republic of the Congo). CEEAC began operations in 1985.

Banque de développement des états de l'Afrique centrale (BDEAC): place du Gouvernement, BP 1177, Brazzaville, Republic of the Congo; tel. 81-18-85; fax 81-18-80; e-mail bdeac@bdeac.org; internet www.bdeac.org; f. 1975; total assets 53,306m. francs CFA (31 Dec. 2006); shareholders: Cameroon, Central African Republic, Chad, Republic of the Congo, Gabon, Equatorial Guinea, ADB, BEAC, France, Germany and Kuwait; Pres. ANICET GEORGES DOLOGUÉLÉ.

Banque des états de l'Afrique centrale (BEAC): 736 ave Mgr François Xavier Vogt, BP 1917, Yaoundé, Cameroon; tel. 223-40-30; fax 223-33-29; e-mail beac@beac.int; internet www.beac.int; f. 1973 as the central bank of issue of Cameroon, the Central African Republic, Chad, Republic of the Congo, Equatorial Guinea and Gabon; a monetary market, incorporating all national financial institutions of the BEAC countries, came into effect on 1 July 1994; total assets 2,667,412m. francs CFA (31 Dec. 2004); Gov. JEAN-FÉLIX MAMALEPOT; publs *Rapport annuel, Etudes et statistiques* (monthly).

CENTRAL ISSUING BANKS

Banque centrale des Comores: place de France, BP 405, Moroni, Comoros; tel. (73) 1814; fax (73) 0349; e-mail bancecom@comorestelecom.km; internet www.bancecom.com; f. 1981; Gov. AHAMADI ABDOUBASTOI.

Banque centrale des états de l'Afrique de l'ouest: see above.

Banque des états de l'Afrique centrale: see above.

Institut d'émission d'outre-mer (IEOM): 5 rue Roland Barthes, 75012 Paris Cédex 12, France; tel. 1-53-44-41-41; fax 1-43-47-51-34; e-mail direction@iedom-ieom.fr; internet www.ieom.fr; f. 1966; issuing authority for the French Overseas Territories; Dir-Gen. YVES BARROUX; Dir PATRICK BESSE.

FRENCH ECONOMIC AID

France's connection with the African Franc Zone countries involves not only monetary arrangements, but also includes comprehensive French assistance in the forms of budget support, foreign aid, technical assistance and subsidies on commodity exports.

Official French financial aid and technical assistance to developing countries is administered by the following agencies:

Agence française de développement (AFD): 5 rue Roland Barthes, 75598 Paris Cédex 12, France; tel. 1-53-44-31-31; fax 1-44-87-99-39; e-mail com@afd.fr; internet www.afd.fr/; f. 1941; fmrly the Caisse française de développement—CFD; French development bank which lends money to member states and former member states of the Franc Zone and several other states, and executes the financial operations of the FSP (see below). Following the devaluation of the franc CFA in January 1994, the French Government cancelled some FFr 25,000m. in debt arrears owed by member states to the CFD. The CFD established a Special Fund for Development and the Exceptional Facility for Short-term Financing to help alleviate the immediate difficulties resulting from the devaluation. Serves as the secretariat for the Fonds français pour l'environnement mondial (f. 1994). Since 2000 the AFD has been implementing France's support of the World Bank's HIPC initiative; Pres. PIERRE-ANDRÉ WILTZER; Dir-Gen. JEAN-MICHEL SEVERINO.

Fonds de Solidarité Prioritaire (FSP): c/o Ministry of Foreign and European Affairs, 37 quai d'Orsay, 75351 Paris; tel. 1-43-17-53-53; fax 1-43-17-52-03; internet www.diplomatie.gouv.fr; f. 2000, taking over from the Fonds d'aide et de coopération (f. 1959) the administration of subsidies from the French Government to 54 countries of the Zone de solidarité prioritaire; FSP is administered by the French Ministry of Foreign and European Affairs, which allocates budgetary funds to it.

INTER-AMERICAN DEVELOPMENT BANK—IDB

Address: 1300 New York Ave, NW, Washington, DC 20577, USA.
Telephone: (202) 623-1000; **fax:** (202) 623-3096; **e-mail:** pic@iadb.org; **internet:** www.iadb.org.

The Bank was founded in 1959 to promote the individual and collective development of Latin American and Caribbean countries through the financing of economic and social development projects and the provision of technical assistance. From 1976 membership was extended to include countries outside the region.

MEMBERS

Argentina
Austria
Bahamas
Barbados
Belgium
Belize
Bolivia
Brazil
Canada
Chile
Colombia
Costa Rica
Croatia
Denmark
Dominican Republic
Ecuador
El Salvador
Finland
France
Germany
Guatemala
Guyana
Haiti
Honduras
Israel
Italy
Jamaica
Japan
Republic of Korea
Mexico
Netherlands
Nicaragua
Norway
Panama
Paraguay
Peru
Portugal
Slovenia
Spain
Suriname
Sweden
Switzerland
Trinidad and Tobago
United Kingdom
USA
Uruguay
Venezuela

Organization

(April 2008)

BOARD OF GOVERNORS

All the powers of the Bank are vested in a Board of Governors, consisting of one Governor and one alternate appointed by each member country (usually ministers of finance or presidents of central banks). The Board meets annually, with special meetings when necessary. The 48th annual meeting of the Board of Governors took place in Guatemala City, Guatemala, in March 2007, and the 49th meeting was held in Miami, USA, in April 2008.

BOARD OF EXECUTIVE DIRECTORS

The Board of Executive Directors is responsible for the operations of the Bank. It establishes the Bank's policies, approves loan and technical co-operation proposals that are submitted by the President of the Bank, and authorizes the Bank's borrowings on capital markets.

There are 14 executive directors and 14 alternates. Each Director is elected by a group of two or more countries, except the Directors representing Canada and the USA. The USA holds 30% of votes on the Board, in respect of its contribution to the Bank's capital. The Board has five permanent committees, relating to: Policy and evaluation; Organization, human resources and board matters; Budget, financial policies and audit; Programming; and a Steering Committee.

ADMINISTRATION

In December 2006 the Board of Executive Directors approved a new structure which aimed to strengthen the Bank's country focus and improve its operational efficiency. Three new positions of Vice-Presidents were created. Accordingly the executive structure comprised the President, Executive Vice-President and Vice-Presidents for Countries (with responsibility for four region departments); Sectors and Knowledge; Private Sector and Non-sovereign Guaranteed Operations; and Finance and Administration. The principal Offices were of the Auditor-General, Outreach and Partnerships, External Relations, Risk Management, and Strategic Planning and Development Effectiveness. The Bank has country offices in each of its borrowing member states, and special offices in Paris, France and in Tokyo, Japan. At the end of 2006 there were 1,834 Bank staff (excluding the Board of Executive Directors and the Evaluation Office), of whom 518 were based in country offices. The administrative expenses for 2006 amounted to US $446m.

President: LUIS ALBERTO MORENO (Colombia).
Executive Vice-President: DANIEL M. ZELIKOW (USA).

Activities

Loans are made to governments and to public and private entities for specific economic and social development projects and for sectoral reforms. These loans are repayable in the currencies lent and their terms range from 12 to 40 years. Total lending authorized by the Bank by the end of 2006 amounted to US $145,020m. During 2006 the Bank approved loans totalling $6,381m., compared with $7,148m. in 2005. Disbursements on authorized loans amounted to $6,489m. in 2006, compared with $5,328m. in the previous year. In April 2005 the Board of Governors approved a new lending framework for the period 2005–08. The framework, which amended the limits on investment and policy-based loans, aimed to strengthen the country focus in lending programmes, to assess and meet more closely the needs of borrowing countries, and to harmonize procedures with other multilateral lending operations.

The subscribed ordinary capital stock, including inter-regional capital, which was merged into it in 1987, totalled US $100,953m. at the end of 2006, of which $4,340m. was paid-in and $96,613m. was callable. The callable capital constitutes, in effect, a guarantee of the securities which the Bank issues in the capital markets in order to increase its resources available for lending. In July 1995 the eighth general increase of the Bank's authorized capital was ratified by member countries: the Bank's resources were to be increased by $41,000m. to $102,000m.

In 2006 the Bank borrowed the equivalent of US $5,419m. on the international capital markets, bringing total borrowings outstanding to $46,396m. at the end of the year. In 2006 net income amounted to $243m., compared to $762m. in 2005.

The Fund for Special Operations enables the Bank to make concessional loans for economic and social projects where circumstances call for special treatment, such as lower interest rates and longer repayment terms than those applied to loans from the ordinary resources. The Board of Governors approved US $200m. in new contributions to the Fund in 1990, and in 1995 authorized $1,000m. in extra resources for the Fund. During 2006 the Fund made 23 loans totalling $602m., bringing the cumulative total of Fund lending to $18,300m. for 1,197 loans. Assistance may be provided to countries adversely affected by economic crises or natural disasters through an Emergency Lending Program.

In 1998 the Bank agreed to participate in an initiative of the International Monetary Fund and the World Bank to assist heavily indebted poor countries (HIPCs) to maintain a sustainable level of debt. Four member countries were eligible for assistance under the initiative (Bolivia, Guyana, Honduras and Nicaragua). Also in 1998, following projections of reduced resources for the Fund for Special Operations, borrowing member countries agreed to convert about US $2,400m. in local currencies held by the Bank, in order to maintain a convertible concessional Fund for poorer countries, and to help to reduce the debt-servicing payments under the HIPC initiative. In mid-2000 a committee of the Board of Governors endorsed a financial framework for the Bank's participation in an enhanced HIPC initiative, which aimed to broaden the eligibility criteria and accelerate the process of debt reduction. The Bank was to provide $896m. (in net present value), in addition to $204m. committed under the original scheme, of which $307m. was for Bolivia, $65m. for Guyana, $391m. for Nicaragua and $133m. for Honduras. The Bank assisted the preparation of national Poverty Reduction Strategy Papers, a condition of reaching the 'completion point' of the process. In 2006 the Bank considered its role in the Multilateral Debt Relief Initiative (MDRI), which had been approved by the World Bank and IMF in 2005 as a means of achieving 100% cancellation of debts for eligible HIPCs. An agreement to join the MDRI was concluded in January 2007 and confirmed by the Bank's President in March. Under the initiative, for which the Bank's participation was to be retrospective from 1 January, the four eligible completion point countries were to receive additional debt relief amounting to some $3,370m., to be financed by the Bank's Fund for Special Operations. In June 2006 the Bank inaugurated a new initiative, Opportunities for the Majority, to improve conditions for low-income populations throughout the region.

The Bank supports a range of consultative groups, in order to strengthen donor co-operation with countries in the Latin America and Caribbean region. In December 1998 the Bank established an emergency Consultative Group for the Reconstruction and Transformation of Central America to co-ordinate assistance to countries that had suffered extensive damage as a result of Hurricane Mitch. The Bank hosted the first meeting of the group in the same month, which was attended by government officials, representatives of donor agencies and non-governmental organizations and academics. A total of US $6,200m. was pledged in the form of emergency aid, longer-term financing and debt relief. A second meeting of the group was held in May 1999, in Stockholm, Sweden, at which the assistance package was increased to some $9,000m., of which the Bank and World Bank committed $5,300m. In March 2001 the group convened, in Madrid, Spain, to promote integration and foreign investment in Central America. The meeting, organized by the Bank, was also used to generate $1,300m. in commitments from international donors to assist emergency relief and reconstruction efforts in El Salvador following an earthquake earlier in the year. In October the Bank organized a consultative group meeting in support of a Social Welfare and Alternative Preventive Development Programme for Ecuador, to which donor countries committed $266m. Other consultative efforts co-ordinated by the Bank include groups to support the peace process in Colombia and in Guatemala. In November 2001 the Bank hosted the first meeting of a Network for the Prevention and Mitigation of Natural Disasters in Latin America and the Caribbean, which was part of a regional policy dialogue, sponsored by the Bank to promote broad debate on strategic issues. In July 2004 the Bank co-hosted an international donor conference, together with the World Bank, the European Union and the United Nations, to consider the immediate and medium-term needs for Haiti following a period of political unrest. Some $1,080m. was pledged at the conference, of which the Bank's contribution was $260m. In April 2006 the Bank established the Disaster Prevention Fund, financed through ordinary capital, to help countries to improve their disaster preparedness and reduce their vulnerability to natural hazards. A separate Multidonor Disaster Prevention Trust Fund was established at the end of 2006 to finance technical assistance and investment in preparedness projects.

An increasing number of donor countries have placed funds under the Bank's administration for assistance to Latin America, outside the framework of the Ordinary Resources and the Bank's Special Operations. These include the Social Progress Trust Fund (set up by the USA in 1961); the Venezuelan Trust Fund (set up in 1975); the Japan Special Fund (1988); and other funds administered on behalf of Austria, Belgium, Canada, Denmark, Finland, France, Israel, Italy, Japan, the Netherlands, Norway, Portugal, Spain, Sweden, Switzerland, the United Kingdom and the EU. A Program for the Development of Technical Co-operation was established in 1991, which is financed by European countries and the EU. During 2006 cofinancing by bilateral and multilateral sources amounted to US $3,641.1m., which helped to finance some 38 projects in 18 countries, including a regional operation for Central America. In 2005 the Bank inaugurated a Trade Finance Facilitation Program to support economic growth in the region by expanding the financing available for international trade activities. The programme was given permanent status in November 2006. By April 2008 31 issuing banks from 14 Latin American and Caribbean countries were participating in the programme.

The Bank provides technical co-operation to help member countries to identify and prepare new projects, to improve loan execution, to strengthen the institutional capacity of public and private agencies, to address extreme conditions of poverty and to promote small- and micro-enterprise development. The Bank has established a special co-operation programme to facilitate the transfer of experience and technology among regional programmes. In 2006 the Bank approved 442 technical co-operation operations, totalling US $103.4m., mainly financed by income from the Fund for Special Operations and donor trust funds. The Bank supports the efforts of the countries of the region to achieve economic integration and has provided extensive technical support for the formulation of integration strategies in the Andean, Central American and Southern Cone regions. In 2001 the Bank took a lead role in a Central American regional initiative, the Puebla-Panamá Plan, which aimed to consolidate integration and support for social and economic development. The Bank is also a member of the technical co-ordinating committee of the Integration of Regional Infrastructure in South America initiative, which aimed to promote multinational development projects, capacity-building and integration in that region. In April 2006 the Bank established a new fund to support the preparation of infrastructure projects and promote public-private partnerships.

AFFILIATES

Inter-American Investment Corporation (IIC): 1350 New York Ave, NW, Washington, DC 20577, USA; tel. (202) 623-3900; fax (202) 623-2360; e-mail iicmail@iadb.org; internet www.iadb.org/iic; f. 1986 as a legally autonomous affiliate of the Inter-American Development Bank, to promote the economic development of the region; commenced operations in 1989; initial capital stock was US $200m., of which 55% was contributed by developing member nations, 25.3% by the USA, and the remainder by non-regional members; in total, the IIC has 42 shareholders (26 Latin American and Caribbean countries, 13 European countries, Israel, Japan and the USA); in 2001 the Board of Governors of the IADB agreed to increase the IIC's capital to $500m; places emphasis on investment in small and medium-sized enterprises without access to other suitable sources of equity or long-term loans; in 2006 the IIC approved 46 operations amounting to $510.7m., of which $337.7m. was from its own resources and $173.0m. mobilized by IIC from other sources; Gen. Man. JACQUES ROGOZINSKI; publ. *Annual Report* (in English, French, Portuguese and Spanish).

Multilateral Investment Fund (MIF): 1300 New York Ave, NW, Washington, DC 20577, USA; tel. (202) 942-8211; fax (202) 942-8100; e-mail mifcontact@iadb.org; internet www.iadb.org/mif; f. 1993 as an autonomous fund administered by the Bank, to promote private sector development in the region; the 21 Bank members who signed the initial draft agreement in 1992 to establish the Fund pledged to contribute US $1,200m.; the Fund's activities are undertaken through three separate facilities concerned with technical co-operation, human resources development and small enterprise development; in 2000 a specialist working group, established to consider MIF operations, recommended that it target its resources on the following core areas of activity: small business development; market functioning; and financial and capital markets; in June 2002 the Fund approved $1.2m. to assist the financial intelligence units in eight South American countries in their efforts to counter money laundering; the Bank's Social Entrepreneurship Program makes available credit to individuals or groups without access to commercial or development loans; some $10m. is awarded under the programme to fund projects in 26 countries; in April 2005 38 donor countries agreed to establish MIF II, and replenish the Fund's resources with commitments totalling $502m.; MIF II came into effect in March 2007; Man. DONALD F. TERRY.

INSTITUTIONS

Instituto para la Integración de América Latina y el Caribe (Institute for the Integration of Latin America and the Caribbean): Esmeralda 130, 17°, 1035 Buenos Aires, Argentina; tel. (11) 4320-1850; fax (11) 4320-1865; e-mail int/inl@iadb.org; internet www.iadb.org/intal; f. 1965 under the auspices of the Inter-American Development Bank; forms part of the Bank's Integration and Regional Programmes Department; undertakes research on all aspects of regional integration and co-operation and issues related to international trade, hemispheric integration and relations with other regions and countries of the world; activities come under four main headings: regional and national technical co-operation projects on integration; policy fora; integration fora; and journals and information; hosts the secretariat of the Integration of Regional Infrastructure in South America (IIRSA) initiative; maintains an extensive Documentation Center and various statistical databases; Dir RICARDO CARCIOFI; publs *Integración y Comercio / Integration and Trade* (2 a year), *Intal Monthly Newsletter*, *Informe Andino / Andean Report*, *CARICOM Report*, *Informe Centroamericano / Central American Report*, *Informe Mercosur / Mercosur Report* (2 a year).

Inter-American Institute for Social Development (INDES): 1350 New York Ave, NW, Washington, DC 20057, USA; fax (202) 623-2008; e-mail indes@iadb.org; internet www.iadb.org/indes; commenced operations in 1995; aims to support the training of senior officials from public sector institutions and organizations involved with social policies and social services; organizes specialized sub-regional courses and seminars and national training programmes;

produces teaching materials and also serves as a forum for the exchange of ideas on social reform; Co-ordinator KAREN MOKATE.

Publications

Annual Report (in English, French, Portuguese and Spanish).
Annual Report on Oversight and Evaluation.
Equidad (quarterly).
Ethics and Development (weekly).
IDBamérica (monthly, English and Spanish).
IDB Projects (10 a year, in English).
Infrastructure and Financial Markets Review (quarterly).
Latin American Economic Policies (quarterly).
Micro Enterprise Américas (annually).
Microenterprise Development Review (2 a year).
Social Development Newsletter (2 a year).
Brochure series, occasional papers, working papers, reports.

Statistics

DISTRIBUTION OF LOANS AND GUARANTEES
(US $ million)

Sector	2006	%	1961–2006	%
Competitiveness				
Energy	1,044.4	16.4	20,077.3	13.8
Transportation and communication	717.3	11.2	15,777.0	10.9
Agriculture and fisheries	62.1	1.0	13,612.2	9.4
Industry, mining and tourism	5.0	0.1	12,750.3	8.8
Multisector credit and preinvestment	0.0	0.0	3,638.6	2.5
Science and technology	331.5	5.2	1,936.1	1.3
Trade financing	252.9	4.0	2,345.1	1.6
Productive infrastructure	333.3	5.2	1,175.9	0.8
Capital markets	443.6	7.0	533.9	0.4

Sector—*continued*	2006	%	1961–2006	%
Social Sector Reform				
Social investment	994.5	15.6	19,867.6	13.7
Water and sanitation	370.0	5.8	9,473.4	6.5
Urban development	74.4	1.2	7,446.1	5.1
Education	60.5	0.9	5,579.9	3.8
Health	140.0	2.2	2,981.5	2.1
Environment	84.8	1.3	2,753.0	1.9
Microenterprise	2.9	0.0	492.3	0.3
Reform and Modernization of the State				
Reform and public sector support	24.3	0.4	11,383.5	7.8
Financial sector reform	801.0	12.6	7,406.3	5.1
Fiscal reform	177.0	2.8	4,040.7	2.8
Decentralization policies	353.0	5.5	1,072.5	0.7
Modernization and administration of justice	54.0	0.8	368.9	0.3
Planning and state reform	26.4	0.4	143.1	0.1
Parliamentary modernization	0.0	0.0	71.9	0.0
Civil society	0.0	0.0	22.0	0.0
Trade policy support	0.0	0.0	27.4	0.0
E-government	28.0	0.4	43.3	0.0
Total	6,380.9	100.0	145,020.0	100.0

YEARLY AND CUMULATIVE LOANS AND GUARANTEES, 1961–2006
(US $ million; after cancellations and exchange adjustments)

Country	Total Amount 2006	Total Amount 1961–2006	Ordinary Capital* 1961–2006	Fund for Special Operations 1961–2006	Funds in Administration 1961–2006
Argentina	1,625.7	22,657.4	21,963.4	644.9	49.1
Bahamas	8.8	380.4	378.4	—	2.0
Barbados	0.7	420.3	361.1	40.2	19.0
Belize	25.0	112.3	112.3	—	—
Bolivia	153.0	3,735.8	1,235.4	2,427.1	73.3
Brazil	515.7	28,675.4	26,986.2	1,556.0	133.2
Chile	213.3	5,426.8	5,178.7	204.2	43.9
Colombia	620.0	12,809.8	11,982.7	762.8	64.3
Costa Rica	70.0	2,488.5	1,992.9	357.5	138.1
Dominican Republic	181.0	3,028.0	2,204.3	736.1	87.6
Ecuador	326.9	4,573.7	3,527.3	956.3	90.1
El Salvador	102.5	3,287.3	2,361.3	778.2	147.8
Guatemala	239.0	2,918.2	2,197.9	650.1	70.2
Guyana	116.7	1,085.2	115.9	962.4	6.9
Haiti	100.4	1,280.9	—	1,274.5	6.4
Honduras	125.9	2,877.8	564.4	2,247.9	65.5
Jamaica	5.0	1,774.0	1,407.4	168.5	198.9
Mexico	387.0	19,486.9	18,870.0	559.0	57.9
Nicaragua	132.5	2,478.2	280.6	2,131.6	66.0
Panama	304.7	2,434.5	2,101.6	290.2	42.7
Paraguay	257.2	2,160.3	1,544.8	602.5	13.0
Peru	565.0	7,737.8	7,084.6	432.0	221.2
Suriname	—	104.7	102.7	2.0	—
Trinidad and Tobago	28.0	1,070.5	1,014.7	30.6	25.2
Uruguay	190.9	4,197.9	4,051.9	104.2	41.8
Venezuela	26.0	4,848.4	4,674.1	101.4	72.9
Regional	60.0	2,968.2	2,717.8	236.7	13.7
Total	6,380.9	145,020.0	125,012.4	18,256.9	1,750.7

* Includes non-sovereign guaranteed loans, net of participations.
Source: IADB *Annual Report, 2006.*

INTERGOVERNMENTAL AUTHORITY ON DEVELOPMENT—IGAD

Address: BP 2653, Djibouti.
Telephone: 354050; **fax:** 356994; **e-mail:** igad@igad.org; **internet:** www.igad.org.

The Intergovernmental Authority on Development (IGAD), established in 1996 to supersede the Intergovernmental Authority on Drought and Development (IGADD, founded in 1986), aims to co-ordinate the sustainable socio-economic development of member countries, to combat the effects of drought and desertification, and to promote regional food security.

MEMBERS*

Djibouti
Eritrea*
Ethiopia
Kenya
Somalia
Sudan
Uganda

*Eritrea announced its impending withdrawal from IGAD in April 2007.

Organization
(April 2008)

ASSEMBLY

The Assembly, consisting of heads of state and of government of member states, is the supreme policy-making organ of the Authority. It holds a summit meeting at least once a year. The chairmanship of the Assembly rotates among the member countries on an annual basis.

Chairman: MWAI KIBAKI (Kenya).

COUNCIL OF MINISTERS

The Council of Ministers is composed of the minister of foreign affairs and one other minister from each member state. It meets at least twice a year and approves the work programme and the annual budget of the Secretariat.

COMMITTEE OF AMBASSADORS

The Committee of Ambassadors comprises the ambassadors or plenipotentiaries of member states to Djibouti. It convenes as regularly as required to advise and assist the Executive Secretary concerning the interpretation of policies and guide-lines and the realization of the annual work programme.

SECRETARIAT

The Secretariat, the executive body of IGAD, is headed by the Executive Secretary, who is appointed by the Assembly for a term of four years, renewable once. In addition to the Office of the Executive Secretary, the Secretariat comprises the following three divisions: Agriculture and Environment; Economic Co-operation; and Political and Humanitarian Affairs, each headed by a director.

Executive Secretary: Dr ATTALLA HAMAD BASHIR (Sudan).

Activities

IGADD was established in 1986 by Djibouti, Ethiopia, Kenya, Somalia, Sudan and Uganda, to combat the effects of aridity and desertification arising from the severe drought and famine that has periodically affected the Horn of Africa. Eritrea became a member of IGADD in September 1993, following its proclamation as an independent state. In April 1995, at an extraordinary summit meeting held in Addis Ababa, Ethiopia, heads of state and of government resolved to reorganize and expand the Authority. In March 1996 IGAD was endorsed to supersede IGADD, at a second extraordinary summit meeting of heads of state and of government, held in Nairobi, Kenya. The meeting led to the adoption of an agreement for a new organizational structure and the approval of an extended mandate to co-ordinate and harmonize policy in the areas of economic co-operation and political and humanitarian affairs, in addition to its existing responsibilities for food security and environmental protection.

IGAD aims to achieve regional co-operation and economic integration. To facilitate this IGAD assists the governments of member states to maximize resources and co-ordinates efforts to initiate and implement regional development programmes and projects. In this context, IGAD promotes the harmonization of policies relating to agriculture and natural resources, communications, customs, trade and transport; the implementation of pro-grammes in the fields of social sciences, research, science and technology; and effective participation in the global economy. Meetings between IGAD foreign affairs ministers and the IGAD Joint Partners' Forum, comprising the grouping's donors, are convened periodically to discuss issues such as food security and humanitarian affairs. In October 2001 delegates from IGAD and representatives of government and civil society in member states initiated a process to establish an IGAD-Civil Society Forum; the founding assembly of the Forum was convened in Nairobi, Kenya in July 2003.

In October 2003 the 10th IGAD summit meeting ratified a decision of the eighth summit, held in November 2000, to absorb the Harare, Zimbabwe- and Nairobi-based Drought Monitoring Centre (an initiative of 24 eastern and southern African states inaugurated in 1989 under the auspices of the UNDP and World Meteorological Organization) as a specialized institution of IGAD and to rename it the IGAD Climate Prediction and Applications Centre (ICPAC).

In November 2000 the eighth IGAD summit approved the establishment of an IGAD Inter-parliamentary Union. A draft protocol on the Union, finalized in May 2003, was signed by the participants in the first meeting of regional speakers of parliament in February 2004; the meeting also determined that the headquarters of the Union should be based in Addis Ababa, Ethiopia.

In January 2008 the IGAD Regional AIDS Partnership Program was launched: jointly with the World Bank the IGAD Secretariat is developing a mechanism for monitoring the occurrence of HIV/AIDS in member states.

In June 2006 IGAD launched the IGAD Capacity-building Program Against Terrorism (ICPAT), a four-year programme based in Addis Ababa, Ethiopia, which aimed to combat the reach of international terrorism through the enhancement of judicial measures and interdepartmental co-operation, improving border control activities, supporting training and information-sharing, and promoting strategic co-operation.

A draft framework for an IGAD Gender Peer Review Mechanism is under consideration; it is envisaged that the Mechanism would be a means of addressing the issue of violence against women in the region as well as other matters relating to women's progress.

FOOD SECURITY AND ENVIRONMENTAL PROTECTION

IGAD seeks to achieve regional food security, the sustainable development of natural resources and environmental protection, and to encourage and assist member states in their efforts to combat the consequences of drought and other natural and man-made disasters. The region suffers from recurrent droughts, which severely impede crop and livestock production. Natural and man-made disasters increase the strain on resources, resulting in annual food deficits. About 80% of the IGAD sub-region is classified as arid or semi-arid, and some 40% of the region is unproductive, owing to severe environmental degradation. Activities to improve food security and preserve natural resources have included: the introduction of remote-sensing services; the development of a Marketing Information System and of a Regional Integrated Information System (RIIS); the establishment of training and credit schemes for fishermen; research into the sustainable production of drought-resistant, high-yielding crop varieties; transboundary livestock disease control and vaccine production; the control of environmental pollution; the promotion of alternative sources of energy in the home; the management of integrated water resources; the promotion of community-based land husbandry; training programmes in grain marketing; and the implementation of the International Convention to Combat Desertification. IGAD's Livestock Marketing Information System (LMIS) aims to Our objective is to improve food security in the sub-region.

ECONOMIC CO-OPERATION

The Economic Co-operation division concentrates on the development of a co-ordinated infrastructure for the region, in particular in the areas of transport and communications, to promote foreign, cross-border and domestic trade and investment opportunities. IGAD seeks to harmonize national transport and trade policy and thereby facilitate the free movement of people, goods and services. The improvements to infrastructure also aim to facilitate more timely interventions in conflicts, disasters and emergencies in the sub-region. Projects under way in the early 2000s included: the construction of missing segments of the Trans-African Highway and the Pan African Telecommunications Network; the removal of barriers to trade and communications; improvements to ports and inland container terminals; and the modernization of railway and telecommunications services. In November 2000 the IGAD Assembly determined to establish an integrated rail network connecting all member countries. In addition, the heads of state and government considered the possibility of drafting legislation to facilitate the expansion of intra-IGAD trade. The development of economic co-operation has been impeded by persisting conflicts in the sub-region (see below). An IGAD Business Forum was to be established in Asmara, Eritrea.

POLITICAL AND HUMANITARIAN AFFAIRS

The field of political and humanitarian affairs focuses on conflict prevention, management and resolution through dialogue. The division's primary aim is to restore peace and stability to member countries affected by conflict, in order that resources may be diverted for development purposes. Efforts have been pursued to strengthen capacity for conflict prevention and to relieve humanitarian crises. The ninth IGAD summit meeting, held in Khartoum in January 2002, adopted a protocol to IGAD's founding agreement establishing a conflict early warning and response mechanism (CEWARN). CEWARN, which was to be based in Addis Ababa, Ethiopia, was to collect and analyse information for the preparation of periodic early warning reports concerning the potential outbreak of violent conflicts in the region. The inaugural meeting of CEWARN was held in June. In February 2006 IGAD convened a ministerial conference on refugees, returnees and internally displaced persons, to consider means of addressing the burden posed by population displacement in member states; at that time it was estimated that 11m. people had been forcibly displaced from their homes in the region.

The Executive Secretary of IGAD participated in the first summit meeting of all East African heads of state and government, convened in April 2005 in Addis Ababa, Ethiopia; the meeting approved a memorandum of understanding on the establishment of the Eastern African Standby Brigade (EASBRIG), which was to form the regional component of the African Union (AU) African Standby Force.

In September 1995 negotiations between the Sudanese Government and opposition leaders were initiated, under the auspices of IGAD, with the aim of resolving the conflict in southern Sudan; these were subsequently reconvened periodically. In March 2001 IGAD's mediation committee on southern Sudan, chaired by President Daniel arap Moi of Kenya, publicized a seven-point plan for a peaceful settlement of the conflict. In early June, at a regional summit on the situation in Sudan convened by IGAD, it was agreed that a permanent negotiating forum comprising representatives of the parties to the conflict would be established at the Authority's secretariat. In mid-July 2002 the Sudanese Government and the main rebel grouping in that country signed, under IGAD auspices, in Machakos, Kenya, a protocol providing for a six-year period of autonomy for southern Sudan to be followed by a referendum on self-determination, and establishing that northern Sudan would be governed in accordance with *Shari'a* law and southern Sudan by a secular judicial system. Peace negotiations subsequently continued under IGAD auspices. A cease-fire agreement was concluded by the parties to the conflict in October, to which an addendum was adopted in February 2003, recommending the deployment of an IGAD verification and monitoring team to oversee compliance with the agreement. In September of that year the parties to the conflict signed an accord on interim security arrangements. During 2003–04 IGAD mediated several further accords that paved the way for the conclusion, in January 2005, of a final, comprehensive peace agreement.

In May–August 2000 a conference aimed at securing peace in Somalia was convened in Arta, Djibouti, under the auspices of IGAD. The conference appointed a transitional Somali legislature, which then elected a transitional national president. The eighth summit of IGAD heads of state and government, held in Khartoum, Sudan, in November, welcomed the conclusion in September of an agreement on reconciliation between the new Somali transitional administration and a prominent opposition alliance, and determined that those member countries that neighboured Somalia (the 'frontline states' of Djibouti, Ethiopia and Kenya) should co-operate in assisting the process of reconstruction and reconciliation in that country. The summit appointed a special envoy to implement IGAD's directives concerning the Somali situation. In January 2002 the ninth IGAD summit meeting determined that a new conference for promoting reconciliation in Somalia (where insecurity continued to prevail) should be convened, under IGAD's auspices. The leaders also issued a statement condemning international terrorism and urged Somalia, in particular, to make a firm commitment to eradicating terrorism. The second Somalia reconciliation conference, initiated in October, in Eldoret, Kenya, under IGAD auspices, issued a Declaration on Cessation of Hostilities, Structures and Principles of the Somalia National Reconciliation Process, as a basis for the pursuit of a peace settlement. In February 2003 the conference was relocated to Nairobi. In July delegates at the ongoing Nairobi conference reached a provisional agreement on the formation of a Somali interim government; however, this was rejected by the president of the transitional government. Progress at the conference stalled further in early October, owing to disagreement between participating groups concerning the adoption of a federal system for the country; later in that month Djibouti withdrew its support from the negotiations, owing to a perceived lack of neutrality on the part of the IGAD technical committee. The Nairobi conference resumed in January 2004 and, later in that month, determined to establish a new parliament; this was inaugurated in August. In January 2005 IGAD heads of state and government authorized the deployment of a Peace Support Mission to Somalia (IGASOM) to assist the transitional federal authorities there, pending the subsequent deployment of an AU peace force; this arrangement was endorsed in the same month by the AU. In mid-March 2006 the IGAD Assembly reiterated its support for the planned deployment of IGASOM, and urged the UN Security Council to grant an exemption to the UN arms embargo applied to Somalia in order to facilitate the regional peace support initiative. At a consultative meeting on the removal of the arms embargo, convened in mid-April, in Nairobi, Kenya, representatives of the Somali transitional federal authorities presented for consideration by IGAD and the AU a draft national security and stabilization plan. It was agreed that a detailed mission plan should be formulated to underpin the proposed IGAD/AU peace missions. In January 2007 the AU Peace and Security Council authorized the deployment of the AU Mission in Somalia (AMISOM) in place of the proposed IGASOM.

Following the violent escalation of a border dispute between Eritrea and Ethiopia in mid-1998 IGAD supported efforts by the Organization of African Unity (now AU) to mediate a cease-fire between the two sides. This was achieved in mid-2000.

At the beginning of February 2008 IGAD heads of state and government convened in Addis Ababa, on the sidelines of the 10th Assembly of the AU, to discuss the violent unrest that had erupted in Kenya following that country's December 2007 disputed general election; following the meeting an IGAD ministerial delegation was dispatched to Kenya as a gesture of regional solidarity with the Kenyan people and with the ongoing peace initiative led by the former UN Secretary-General, Kofi Annan.

Publications

Annual Report.
IGAD News (2 a year).
Proceedings of the Summit of Heads of State and Government; Reports of the Council of Ministers' Meetings.

INTERNATIONAL CHAMBER OF COMMERCE—ICC

Address: 38 cours Albert 1er, 75008 Paris, France.
Telephone: 1-49-53-28-28; **fax:** 1-49-53-28-59; **e-mail:** webmaster@iccwbo.org; **internet:** www.iccwbo.org.

The ICC, founded in 1919, is the primary world business organization, representing enterprises world-wide from all business sectors. The ICC aims to promote cross-border trade and investment and to support enterprises in meeting the challenges and opportunities presented by globalization. the ICC regards trade as a force for peace and prosperity. In the 2000s the ICC was undergoing an extensive process of reform.

MEMBERS

ICC membership comprises corporations, national professional and sectoral associations, business and employer federations, chambers of commerce, and individuals involved in international business from more than 130 countries. National Committees or Groups have been formed in some 85 countries and territories to co-ordinate ICC objectives and functions at the national level.

Organization
(April 2008)

ICC WORLD COUNCIL

The ICC World Council is the governing body of the organization. It meets twice a year and is composed of members nominated by the National Committees. Ten direct members, from countries where no National Committee exists, may also be invited to participate. The Council elects the Chairman and Vice-Chairman for terms of two years. Ten 'direct' members originating in countries that do not have a national committee may also be invited to participate in the meetings of the World Council.

Chairman: MARCUS WALLENBERG (Sweden).

EXECUTIVE BOARD

The Executive Board consists of up to 30 business leaders and *ex-officio* members appointed by the ICC World Council upon recommendation of the Chairman. Members serve for a three-year term, one-third of the members retiring at the end of each year. It ensures the strategic direction of ICC activities and the implementation of its policies, and meets at least three times each year.

INTERNATIONAL SECRETARIAT

The ICC International Secretariat, based in Paris, is the operational arm of the ICC. It implements the work programme approved by the ICC World Council, providing intergovernmental organizations with commercial views on issues that directly affect business operations. The International Secretariat is led by the Secretary-General, who is appointed by the World Council on the recommendation of the Executive Board.

Secretary-General: GUY SEBBAN (France).

NATIONAL COMMITTEES AND GROUPS

Each affiliate is composed of leading business organizations and individual companies. It has its own secretariat, monitors issues of concern to its national constituents, and draws public and government attention to ICC policies.

WORLD CHAMBERS CONGRESS

The ICC's World Chambers Federation (WCF) organizes the ICC's supreme World Chambers Congress every two years; the sixth was to be convened in Kuala Lumpur, Malaysia, in June 2009.

CONFERENCES

Regular ICC topical conferences and seminars, organized by ICC Events, disseminate ICC expertise in various fields including international arbitration, trade, banking and commercial practice.

COMMISSIONS

Policy Commissions:

Commission on Anti-Corruption;

Commission on Arbitration;

Commission on Banking Technique and Practice;

Commission on Business in Society;

Commission on Commercial Law and Practice;

Commission on Competition;

Commission on Customs and Trade Regulations;

Commission on E-business, IT and Telecoms;

Commission on Environment and Energy;

Commission on Financial Services and Insurance;

Commission on Intellectual Property;

Commission on Marketing and Advertising;

Commission on Taxation;

Commission on Trade and Investment Policy;

Commission on Transport and Logistics

ADVISORY GROUP

Corporate Economist Advisory Group.

OTHER BODIES

ICC Commercial Crime Services;

ICC Services (incorporates ICC Events and ICC Publications);

ICC World Chambers Federation.

ICC Commercial Crime Services Divisions:

International Maritime Bureau (IMB): a Piracy Reporting Centre provides the most accurate and up-to-date information to shippers regarding pirate activity on the world's oceans.

Financial Investigation Bureau (FIB): works to detect financial fraud before it occurs by allowing banks and other financial institutions access to a database of shared information.

Counterfeiting Intelligence Bureau (CIB): runs a number of initiatives to protect against counterfeiting including Counterforce, Countertech and Countersearch international networks, the Counterfeit Pharmaceutical Initiative, the IHMA's Hologram Image Register and the Universal Hologram Scanner.

Activities

The ICC's main activities are setting voluntary rules guiding the conduct of international trade, arbitrating trade disputes, and establishing policy.

The various Commissions of the ICC (listed above) are composed of approximately 1,000 practising business executives and experts from all sectors of economic life, nominated by National Committees. ICC recommendations must be adopted by a Commission following consultation with National Committees, and then approved by the ICC World Council or Executive Board, before they can be regarded as official ICC policies. Meetings of Commissions are generally held twice a year. Task Forces are frequently constituted by Commissions to undertake specific projects and report back to their parent body. The Commissions produce a wide array of specific codes and guidelines of direct use to the world business community; formulate statements and initiatives for presentation to governments and international bodies; and comment constructively and in detail on proposed actions by intergovernmental organizations and governments that are likely to affect business.

The ICC works closely with other international organizations. It has undertaken a broad range of activities with the UN, the World Trade Organization (WTO), the European Union (EU) and many other intergovernmental bodies. The ICC presidency meets annually with the leader of the country hosting the G-8 summit to discuss business aspects of the meeting.

The ICC plays a part in combating international crime connected with commerce through its Commercial Crime Services (CCS). Based in London, United Kingdom, the CCS operates according to two basic principles: to prevent and investigate commercial crime and to facilitate the prosecution of criminals involved in such crimes.

The ICC provides a framework for settling international commercial disputes. The Commission on Arbitration acts as a forum for experts and also reviews the ICC's dispute settlement services, for example regarding the deployment of new technologies. In 2007 the ICC International Court of Arbitration, which was established in 1923, received 599 requests for arbitration, and more than 15,000 cases have been filed by the Court since its inception. Other ICC services for dispute resolution include its Rules of Arbitration, its Alternative Dispute Resolution, and the International Centre for Expertise, which administers ICC Rules of Expertise and Rules for Documentary Credit and Dispute Resolution Expertise (DOCDEX).

The ICC's World Chambers Federation (WCF), a global network of chambers of commerce, acts as a platform for interaction and exchange of best practice. It is responsible for the ATA Carnet temporary export document system. The WCF also organizes the biennial World Chambers Federation Congresses. In June 2008, in Stockholm, Sweden, the ICC aimed to launch the first annual ICC World Business Summit, a forum for business decision makers in government and in the private sector. The first ICC World Business Summit was to have the theme 'world economy at a crossroads', and was to address two main topics: global rules for an interdependent world economy, and waging war on fakes and IP theft.

The ICC has developed rules and guide-lines relating to electronic transactions, including guide-lines for ethical advertising on the internet and for data protection. The ICC has devised a system of standard trade definitions most commonly used in international sales contracts ('Incoterms') and the Uniform Customs and Practice (UCP) for Documentary Credits, used by banks to finance international trade. The Incoterms were being updated in 2008, and the UCP for Documentary Credits were most recently updated in 2007. There are also ICC voluntary codes for eliminating extortion and bribery, and for promoting sound environmental management practices.

Following the launch of the ICC's Business Action to Stop Counterfeiting and Piracy (BASCAP) initiative in November 2004, more than 150 companies and trade associations have become actively engaged in a set of projects designed to combat counterfeiting and piracy and increase awareness of the economic and social harm such activities cause. In March 2008 chief executive officers and senior corporate executives participating in BASCAP convened in New York with representatives of the World Customs Organization, World Intellectual Property Organization and US Government to discuss means of co-operation in addressing counterfeiting and piracy. The BASCAP delegates urged the prompt negotiation of an Anti-Counterfeiting Trade Agreement (ACTA). The ICC issues an annual Intellectual Property Roadmap.

Finance

The International Chamber of Commerce is a private, non-profit-making organization financed partly by contributions from National Committees and other members, according to the economic importance of the country which each represents, and partly by revenue from fees for various services and from sales of publications.

Publications

Annual Report.
Documentary Credits Insight (quarterly).
ICC International Court of Arbitration Bulletin.
Intellectual Property Roadmap (annually).
Publications on general and technical business and trade-related subjects are also available online.

INTERNATIONAL CRIMINAL COURT

Address: Maanweg 174, 2516 AB The Hague, Netherlands.
Telephone: (70) 515-8097; **fax:** (70) 515-8376; **e-mail:** asp@asp.icc-cpi.int; **internet:** www.icc-cpi.int.

The International Criminal Court (ICC) was established by the Rome Statute of the International Criminal Court, adopted by 120 states participating in a United Nations Diplomatic Conference in July 1998. The Rome Statute (and therefore the temporal jurisdiction of the ICC) entered into force on 1 July 2002, 60 days after ratification by the requisite 60th signatory state in April. The ICC is a permanent, independent body, in relationship with the United Nations, that aims to promote the rule of law and punish the most serious international crimes. The Rome Statute reaffirmed the principles of the UN Charter and stated that the relationship between the Court and the United Nations system should be determined by a framework relationship agreement between the states parties to the Rome Statute and the UN General Assembly: under the so-called negotiated relationship agreement, which entered into force in October 2004, upon signature by the Court's President and the Secretary-General of the United Nations, there was to be mutual exchange of information and documentation to the fullest extent and co-operation and consultation on practical matters, and it was stipulated that the Court might, if deemed appropriate, submit reports on its activities to the UN Secretary-General and propose to the Secretary-General items for consideration by the United Nations.

The Court comprises the Presidency (consisting of a President and first and second Vice-Presidents), Chambers (including a Pre-Trial Division, Trial Division and Appeals Division) with 18 permanent judges, Office of the Prosecutor (comprising the Chief Prosecutor and up to two Deputy Prosecutors), and Registry. The judges must each have a different nationality and equitably represent the major legal systems of the world, a fair geographical distribution, and a fair proportion of men and women. They are elected by the Assembly of States Parties to the Rome Statute from two lists, the first comprising candidates with established competence in criminal law and procedures and the second comprising candidates with established competence in relevant areas of international law, to terms of office of three, six or nine years. The President and Vice-Presidents are elected by an absolute majority of the judges for renewable three-year terms of office. The Chief Prosecutor is elected by an absolute majority of states parties to the Rome Statute to an unrenewable nine-year term of office. The first judges were elected to the Court in February 2003, the first Presidency in March, and the first Chief Prosecutor in April.

The Court has established a Victims Trust Fund to finance compensation, restitution or rehabilitation for victims of crimes (individuals or groups of individuals). The Fund is administered by the Registry and supervised by an independent board of directors.

By 2008 three cases were being pursued by the Court that had been referred to it by states party to the Rome Statute, and one case was being pursued that had been referred by the UN Security Council (see below). Some six warrants for arrest were in force at that time, and three indictees were in the custody of the Court.

Situation in Uganda: referred to the Court in January 2004 by the Ugandan Government; the Chief Prosecutor agreed to open an investigation into the situation in July 2004; relates to the long-term unrest in the north of the country; in October 2005 the Court unsealed warrants for arrest (issued under seal in July) against five commanders of the Ugandan Lord's Resistance Army (LRA), including the LRA leader, Joseph Kony; in July 2007 the Court proceeding against one of the named commanders were terminated on the grounds that he had been killed during LRA rebel activities in August 2006.

Situation in the Democratic Republic of the Congo (DRC): referred in April 2004 by the DRC Government; the Chief Prosecutor agreed to open an investigation into the situation in June 2004; relates to alleged war crimes; in March 2006 Thomas Lubanga Dyilo, a DRC militia leader, was arrested by the Congolese authorities and transferred to the Court, thereby becoming the first ICC indictee to be captured; Dyilo was charged with conscripting child soldiers, a sealed warrant for his arrest having been issued in February; in July 2007 warrants of arrest were issued for the DRC rebel commanders Germain Katanga and Mathieu Ngudjolo Chui; Katanga was transferred into the custody of the Court in October 2007 and Ngudjolo Chui in February 2008.

Situation in the Central African Republic (CAR): referred in January 2005 by the CAR Government; the Chief Prosecutor agreed to open an investigation into the situation in May 2005; relates to war crimes and crimes against humanity allegedly committed during the period October 2002–March 2003.

Situation in Darfur, Sudan: referred to the Court in March 2005 by the UN Security Council on the basis of the recently-issued report of an International Commission of Inquiry on Darfur; the Chief Prosecutor agreed to open an investigation into the situation in June 2005; relates to the situation prevailing in Darfur since 1 July 2002; the UN Secretary-General handed the Chief Prosecutor a sealed list of 51 names of people identified in the report as having committed crimes under international law; in April 2007 the Court issued warrants for the arrests of Ahmad Harun, a former Sudanese government minister, and Ali Kushayb, a leader of the Sudanese Janjaweed militia, who were both accused of perpetrating war crimes and crimes against humanity.

The Office of the Prosecutor also receives communications from civilian individuals and organizations relating to alleged crimes that come under the Court's jurisdiction; during the period 2002–06 some 1,732 such communications were received.

In April 2006 the International Criminal Court and the Special Court for Sierra Leone concluded a memorandum of understanding in accordance with which the Special Court was to use the courtroom and detention facilities of the International Criminal Court for the trial of Charles Taylor, the former president of Liberia, on charges of crimes against humanity. In June Taylor was transferred to the Criminal Court's detention centre in The Hague; his trial commenced in June 2007.

By February 2008 105 states had ratified the Rome Statute.

THE JUDGES
(April 2008)

	Term
President: Philippe Kirsch (Canada)	6 years
First Vice-President: Akua Kuenyehia (Ghana)	3 years
Second Vice President: René Blattmann (Bolivia)	6 years
Georghios N. Pikis (Cyprus)	6 years
Elizabeth Odio Benito (Costa Rica)	9 years
Claude Jorda (France)	6 years
Navanethem Pillay (South Africa)	6 years
Sang-Hyun Song (Republic of Korea)	3 years
Hans-Peter Kaul (Germany)	3 years
Mauro Politi (Italy)	6 years
Maureen Harding Clark (Ireland)	9 years
Erkki Kourula (Finland)	3 years

—continued	Term
Fatoumata Dembele Diarra (Mali)	9 years
Anita Ušacka (Latvia)	3 years
Sir Adrian Fulford (United Kingdom)	9 years
Sylvia de Figueiredo Steiner (Brazil)	9 years
Ekaterina Trendafilova (Bulgaria)	9 years
Daniel Ntanda Nsereko (Uganda)	51 months*
Fumiko Saiga (Japan)	15 months*
Bruno Cotte (France)	51 months*

* Elected for partial terms to fill vacancies.

Chief Prosecutor: Luis Moreno Ocampo (Argentina).
Registrar: Silvana Arbia (Italy).

Finance

The proposed budget for the International Criminal Court for 2008 amounted to €97.8m.

INTERNATIONAL OLYMPIC COMMITTEE

Address: Château de Vidy, 1007 Lausanne, Switzerland.
Telephone: 216216111; **fax:** 216216216; **internet:** www.olympic.org.

The International Olympic Committee was founded in 1894 to ensure the regular celebration of the Olympic Games.

Organization
(April 2008)

INTERNATIONAL OLYMPIC COMMITTEE

The International Olympic Committee (IOC) is a non-governmental international organization comprising 115 members—who are representatives of the IOC in their countries and not their countries' delegates to the IOC, and include 15 active Olympic athletes, 15 National Olympic Committee presidents, 15 International Sports Federation presidents, and 70 other individuals—as well as 24 Honorary members and three Honor members. The members meet in session at least once a year. A Nomination Commission examines and reports to the Executive Board on each candidate for membership of the IOC.

The IOC is the final authority on all questions concerning the Olympic Games and the Olympic movement. There are 203 recognized National Olympic Committees, which are the sole authorities responsible for the representation of their respective countries at the Olympic Games. The IOC may give recognition to International Federations which undertake to adhere to the Olympic Charter, and which govern sports that comply with the IOC's criteria.

An International Council of Arbitration for Sport (ICAS) has been established. ICAS administers the Court of Arbitration for Sport which hears cases brought by competitors.

EXECUTIVE BOARD

The session of the IOC delegates to the Executive Board the authority to manage the IOC's affairs. The President of the Board is elected for an eight-year term, and is eligible for re-election once for an additional term of four years. The Vice-Presidents are elected for four-year terms, and may be re-elected after a minimum interval of four years. Members of the Board are elected to hold office for four years. The Executive Board generally meets four to five times per year.

President: Dr Jacques Rogge (Belgium).
Vice-Presidents: Gunilla Lindberg (Sweden), Lambis V. Nikolaou (Greece), Chiharu Igaya (Japan), Thomas Bach (Germany).
Members of the Board: Gerhard Heiberg (Norway), Denis Oswald (Switzerland), Mario Vázquez Raña (Mexico), Ottavio Cinquanta (Italy), Sergei Bubka (Ukraine), Zaiqing Yu (People's Republic of China), Richard L. Carrión (Puerto Rico), Ser Miang Ng (Singapore), Mario Pescante (Italy), Sam Ramsamy (South Africa).

IOC COMMISSIONS

Athletes' Commission: f. 1981; comprising active and retired athletes, represents their interests; may issue recommendations to the Executive Board.

Commission for Culture and Olympic Education: f. 2000 by merger of the Culture Commission (f. 1968) and the IOC Commission for the International Olympic Academy and Olympic Education (f. 1961).

Ethics Commission: f. 1999 to develop and monitor rules and principles to guide the selection of hosts for the Olympic Games, and the organization and execution of the Games; the activities of the Ethics Commission are funded by the Foundation for Universal Olympic Ethics, inaugurated in 2001.

Finance Commission: aims to ensure the efficient management of the IOC's financial resources.

International Relations Commission: f. 2002 to promote a positive relationship between the Olympic Movement and national governments and public authorities..

Juridicial Commission: f. 1974 to provide legal opinions and perform other tasks of a legal nature.

Marketing Commission: helps to perpetuate the work of the Olympic Movement through the provision of financial resources and programmes aimed at protecting and enhancing the Olympic image and Olympic values.

Medical Commission: f. 1967; concerned with the protection of the health of athletes, respect for medical and sport ethics, and equality for all competing athletes.

Nominations Commission: f. 1999 to institute a procedure for electing and re-electing IOC members.

Olympic Philately, Numismatic and Memorabilia Commission: f. 1993; aims to increase awareness of Olympic commemorative paraphenalia.

Olympic Programme Commission: reviews, and analyses the Olympic programme of sports, disciplines and events; develops recommendations on the principles and structure of the programme.

Olympic Solidarity Commission: f. 1961; assists National Olympic Committees (NOCs); responsible for managing and administering the share of television rights allocated to NOCs.

Press Commission: advises Olympic Games organizing committees on the provision of optimum working conditions for the written and photographic media.

Radio and Television Commission: advises Olympic Games organizing committees and national broadcasting organizations on the provision of the optimum working conditions for the broadcast media.

Sport and Environment Commission: f. 1995 to promote environmental protection and sustainable development.

Sport and Law Commission: f. 1996 to act as a forum for discussion of legal issues concerning the Olympic Movement.

Sport for All Commission: f. 1983 to encourage and support the principles of Sport for All.

TV and New Media Commission: prepares and implements overall IOC strategy for future broadcast rights negotiations.

Women and Sport Commission: f. 2004 (by transformation of a working group, f. 1995 to advise the Executive Board on policies to promote women in sport).

In addition, co-ordination commissions for specific Olympic Games are founded after the election of a host city to oversee and assist the organizing committee in the planning and management of the Games: in early 2008 co-ordination commissions were in force for Beijing 2008; Vancouver 2010; London 2012; and Sochi 2014.

ADMINISTRATION

The administration of the IOC is under the authority of the Director-General, who is appointed by the Executive Board, on the proposal of the President, and is assisted by Directors responsible for the following administrative sectors: international co-operation; Olympic Games co-ordination; finance, marketing and legal affairs; technology; control and co-ordination of operations; communications; and medical.

Director-General: Urs Lacotte.

Activities

The fundamental principles of the Olympic movement are:

Olympism is a philosophy of life, exalting and combining, in a balanced whole, the qualities of body, will and mind. Blending sport with culture, education and respect for the environment, Olympism seeks to create a way of life based on the joy found in effort, the educational value of good example and respect for universal fundamental ethical principles.

Under the supreme authority of the IOC, the Olympic movement encompasses organizations, athletes and other persons who agree to be guided by the Olympic Charter. The criterion for belonging to the Olympic movement is recognition by the IOC.

The goal of the Olympic movement is to contribute to building a peaceful and better world by educating youth through sport practised without discrimination of any kind and in the Olympic spirit, which requires mutual understanding with a spirit of friendship, solidarity and fair-play.

The activity of the Olympic movement is permanent and universal. It reaches its peak with the bringing together of the athletes of the world at the great sport festival, the Olympic Games.

The Olympic Charter is the codification of the fundamental principles, rules and bye-laws adopted by the IOC. It governs the organization and operation of the Olympic movement and stipulates the conditions for the celebration of the Olympic Games. In March 1998, at a meeting organized with other international sports governing bodies, it was agreed to form a working group to defend the principle of self-regulation in international sports organizations. In March 1999, following the publication in January of the results of an investigation into allegations of corruption and bribery, an extraordinary session of the IOC was convened, at which the six Committee members were expelled for violating rules relating to Salt Lake City's bid to host the Olympic Winter Games in 2002; four other members had already resigned, while an Executive Board member had received disciplinary action. The President of the IOC retained his position after receiving a vote of confidence. The session approved a number of reform measures, including the establishment of a new independent Ethics Commission to oversee cities' bids to host the Olympic Games, and the establishment of a commission mandated to recommend far-reaching reforms to the internal structure of the organization and to the bidding process. In December 1999, having considered the recommendations of the commission, the IOC adopted 50 reforms aimed at creating a more open, responsive and accountable organization. These included a new permanent procedure for the elimination of member visits to bid cities, the application of terms of office, limiting the expansion of the Summer Games, and the election of 15 active athletes to the IOC membership.

In response to ongoing concern at drugs abuse in sport an independent World Anti-Doping Agency (WADA) was established by the IOC in November 1999 and, on 1 January 2000, an Anti-Doping Code entered into effect. Participants attending the World Conference on Doping in Sport, held in Copenhagen, Denmark, in March 2003, adopted the Copenhagen Declaration on Doping in Sport and promoted the World Anti-Doping Code, formulated by WADA, as the basis for combating such abuses.

In July 2000 the International Olympic Committee established a subsidiary International Olympic Truce Foundation, and an International Olympic Truce Centre, based in Athens, Greece, with the aim of promoting a culture of peace through the pursuit of sport and the Olympic ideals. In early 2002 the Olympic Games Study Commission was established to address means of reducing the cost and complexity of the Games. The Commission presented a full report of its findings, incorporating several recommendations for the future organization of the Games, to the 115th Session of the IOC, held in Prague, Czech Republic, in July 2003. The Commission was subsequently dissolved. In November 2002 the Olympic Programme Commission made a full review of the sports programme for the first time since 1936. It decided to cap the number of sports at 28, the number of events at 300, and the number of participating athletes at 10,500.

In July 2007 the IOC determined to establish Summer and Winter Youth Olympic Games (YOG); the first Summer YOG were to be held in 2010 in Singapore, and the first Winter YOG in 2012.

ASSOCIATED AGENCY

World Anti-Doping Agency—WADA: Stock Exchange Tower, Suite 1700, 800 Place Victoria, POB 120 Montréal, QC H4Z 1B7, Canada; tel. (514) 904-9232; fax (514) 904-8650; e-mail info@wada-ama.org; internet www.wada-ama.org; f. 1999 to promote and co-ordinate efforts to achieve drug-free sport; has five committees: Ethics and Education; Finance and Administration; Health, Medical and Research; Legal; Standards and Harmonization; Chair. JOHN FAHEY; Dir Gen. DAVID HOWMAN.

THE GAMES OF THE OLYMPIAD

The Olympic Summer Games take place during the first year of the Olympiad (period of four years) which they are to celebrate. They are the exclusive property of the IOC, which entrusts their organization to a host city seven years in advance.

1896 Athens	1964 Tokyo
1900 Paris	1968 Mexico City
1904 St Louis	1972 Munich
1908 London	1976 Montreal
1912 Stockholm	1980 Moscow
1920 Antwerp	1984 Los Angeles
1924 Paris	1988 Seoul
1928 Amsterdam	1992 Barcelona
1932 Los Angeles	1996 Atlanta
1936 Berlin	2000 Sydney
1948 London	2004 Athens
1952 Helsinki	2008 Beijing
1956 Melbourne	2012 London
1960 Rome	

The programme of the Games must include at least 15 of the total number of Olympic sports (sports governed by recognized International Federations and admitted to the Olympic programme by decision of the IOC at least seven years before the Games). The Olympic summer sports are: aquatics (including swimming, diving and water polo), archery, athletics, badminton, baseball, basketball, boxing, canoeing, cycling, equestrian sports, fencing, football, gymnastics, handball, field hockey, judo, modern pentathlon, rowing, sailing, shooting, softball, table tennis, tae kwondo, tennis, triathlon, volleyball, weight-lifting, wrestling.

OLYMPIC WINTER GAMES

The Olympic Winter Games comprise competitions in sports practised on snow and ice. Since 1994 they have been held in the second calendar year following that in which the Games of the Olympiad take place.

1924 Chamonix	1976 Innsbruck
1928 St Moritz	1980 Lake Placid
1932 Lake Placid	1984 Sarajevo
1936 Garmisch-Partenkirchen	1988 Calgary
1948 St Moritz	1992 Albertville
1952 Oslo	1994 Lillehammer
1956 Cortina d'Ampezzo	1998 Nagano
1960 Squaw Valley	2002 Salt Lake City
1964 Innsbruck	2006 Turin
1968 Grenoble	2010 Vancouver
1972 Sapporo	2014 Sochi

The Winter Games may include biathlon, bobsleigh, curling, ice hockey, luge, skating and skiing.

Finance

The International Olympic Committee derives marketing revenue from the sale of broadcast rights, the Olympic Partners sponsorship Programme, local sponsorship, ticketing, and licensing. Some 8% of this is retained for the Committee's operational budget, with the remainder allocated to Olympic organizing committees, National Olympic Committees and teams, and international sports federations.

Publication

Olympic Review (quarterly).

INTERNATIONAL ORGANIZATION FOR MIGRATION—IOM

Address: 17 route des Morillons, CP 71, 1211 Geneva 19, Switzerland.
Telephone: 227179111; **fax:** 227986150; **e-mail:** info@iom.int; **internet:** www.iom.int.

The Intergovernmental Committee for Migration (ICM) was founded in 1951 as a non-political and humanitarian organization with a predominantly operational mandate, including the handling of orderly and planned migration to meet specific needs of emigration and immigration countries; and the processing and movement of refugees, displaced persons and other individuals in need of international migration services to countries offering them resettlement opportunities. In 1989 ICM's name was changed to the International Organization for Migration (IOM). IOM was admitted as an observer to the UN General Assembly in 1992.

MEMBERS

Afghanistan
Albania
Algeria
Angola
Argentina
Armenia
Australia
Austria
Azerbaijan
Bahamas
Bangladesh
Belarus
Belgium
Belize
Benin
Bolivia
Bosnia and Herzegovina
Brazil
Bulgaria
Burkina Faso
Cambodia
Cameroon
Canada
Cape Verde
Chile
Colombia
Congo, Democratic Republic
Congo, Republic
Costa Rica
Côte d'Ivoire
Croatia
Cyprus
Czech Republic
Denmark
Dominican Republic
Ecuador
Egypt
El Salvador
Estonia
Finland
France
Gabon
The Gambia
Georgia
Germany
Ghana
Greece
Guatemala
Guinea
Guinea-Bissau
Haiti
Honduras
Hungary
Iran
Ireland
Israel
Italy
Jamaica
Japan
Jordan
Kazakhstan
Kenya
Korea, Republic
Kyrgyzstan
Latvia
Liberia
Libya
Lithuania
Luxembourg
Madagascar
Mali
Malta
Mauritania
Mauritius
Mexico
Moldova
Montenegro
Morocco
Nepal
Netherlands
New Zealand
Nicaragua
Niger
Nigeria
Norway
Pakistan
Panama
Paraguay
Peru
Philippines
Poland
Portugal
Romania
Rwanda
Senegal
Serbia
Sierra Leone
Slovakia
Slovenia
South Africa
Sri Lanka
Sudan
Sweden
Switzerland
Tajikistan
Tanzania
Thailand
Togo
Tunisia
Turkey
Uganda
Ukraine
United Kingdom
USA
Uruguay
Venezuela
Yemen
Zambia
Zimbabwe

Observers: Bhutan, Burundi, People's Republic of China, Cuba, Ethiopia, Guyana, Holy See, India, Indonesia, former Yugoslav republic of Macedonia, Mozambique, Namibia, Papua New Guinea, Qatar, Russia, San Marino, São Tomé and Príncipe, Somalia, Turkmenistan and Viet Nam. In addition, more than 70 international, governmental and non-governmental organizations hold observer status with IOM.

Organization
(April 2008)

IOM is governed by a Council which is composed of representatives of all member governments, and has the responsibility for making final decisions on policy, programmes and financing. An Executive Committee of nine member governments elected by the Council examines and reviews the Organization's work; considers and reports on any matter specifically referred to it by the Council; advises the Director-General on any matters which he may refer to it; makes, between sessions of the Council, any urgent decisions on matters falling within the competence of the Council, which are then submitted for approval by the Council; and presents advice or proposals to the Council or the Director-General on its own initiative. The Director-General is responsible to the Council and the Executive Committee. Alongside the Director-General's Office there are offices of International Migration Law and Legal Affairs; Management Co-ordination; Information Technology and Communications; and Gender Co-ordination. In recent years IOM has transferred some administrative functions from its headquarters to two administrative centres, located in Manila, Philippines, and Ciudad del Saber, Panama.

Director-General: BRUNSON MCKINLEY (USA).
Deputy Director-General: NDIORO NDIAYE (Senegal).

Activities

IOM aims to provide assistance to member governments in meeting the operational challenges of migration, to advance understanding of migration issues, to encourage social and economic development through migration and to work towards effective respect of the human dignity and well-being of migrants. It provides a full range of migration assistance to, and sometimes *de facto* protection of, migrants, refugees, displaced persons and other individuals in need of international migration services. This includes recruitment, selection, processing, medical examinations (of which some 1.5m. had been performed globally by 2008), and language and cultural orientation courses, placement, activities to facilitate reception and integration and other advisory services. IOM co-ordinates its refugee activities with the UN High Commissioner for Refugees (UNHCR) and with governmental and non-governmental partners. In May 1997 IOM and UNHCR signed a memorandum of understanding which aimed to facilitate co-operation between the two organizations. Since it commenced operations in February 1952 IOM is estimated to have provided assistance to more than 12m. migrants. IOM estimates that migrants comprise some 3% of the global population, and that some 15%–20% of migrant movements are unregulated.

IOM's International Migration Law (IML) and Legal Affairs Department promotes awareness and knowledge of the legal instruments that govern migration at national, regional and international level; provides training and capacity-building services connected with IML; and researches IML. IOM maintains an international database of IML.

IOM provides information and advice to support the efforts of governments and other stakeholders to formulate effective national, regional and global migration management policies and strategies; and conducts research, aimed at guiding migration policy and practice, in areas including migration trends and data, IML, migration and development, health and migration, counter-trafficking, labour migration, trade, remittances, irregular migration, integration and return migration.

IOM was a founder member with other international organizations of the inter-agency Global Migration Group (GMG, established as the Geneva Migration Group in April 2003 and renamed in 2006). The GMG provides a framework for discussion among the heads of member organizations on the application of decisions and norms relating to migration, and for stronger leadership in addressing related issues.

In October 2005 IOM's Director-General inaugurated a new Business Advisory Board, comprising 13 business leaders representing a cross-section of global concerns. It was envisaged that the initiative would promote an effective partnership between the Organization and the private sector aimed at supporting the planning, development and implementation of improved mobility policies and practices. During that month IOM welcomed the issue of a report by the Global Commission on International Migration, an initiative launched by the UN Secretary-General in December 2003 to address global migration issues.

IOM operates within the framework of the main service areas outlined below.

MIGRATION AND DEVELOPMENT

IOM places a strategic focus on advancing a positive relationship between migration and development; on fostering a deeper understanding of the linkages between migration and development; and on enhancing the benefits that well-managed migration can have for the development, growth and prosperity of migrants' countries of origin and of destination, as well as for the migrants personally. IOM's activities in this area include strengthening the capacity of governments and other stakeholders to engage expatriate migrant communities in development processes in their countries of origin; promoting economic and community development in places from which there is a high level of emigration; enhancing the development impact of remittances; and facilitating the return and reintegration of qualified nationals. There are two main branches of Migration and Development programming: Migration and Economic/Community Development; and Capacity-building Through Qualified Human Resources and Experts.

IOM's Migration and Economic/Community Development programme area covers three principal fields of activity. Firstly, IOM seeks to maximize the positive potential from migration for the development of countries of origin and destination, promoting an increase in more development-oriented migration policies, and implementing initiatives aimed at building the capacity of governments and other stakeholders in countries of origin to involve their migrant populations in home country development projects. Secondly, IOM aims to address the root causes of economically motivated migration by assisting governments and other actors with the strategic focusing of development activities to expand economic opportunities and improve social services and infrastructures in regions experiencing outward or returning migration. Thirdly, IOM promotes data collection, policy dialogue and dissemination of good practices, and pilot project implementation, in the area of remittances (funds send home by migrant workers, mainly in the form of private money transfers), with the aim of improving the development impact of remittances.

IOM's Capacity-building Through Qualified Human Resources and Experts programme area focuses on the return from abroad and socio-economic reintegration of skilled and qualified nationals. Return and Reintegration of Qualified Nationals (RQN) and similar projects include recruitment, job placement, transport and limited employment support services, and aim to influence the economic and social environment in countries of origin in a manner conducive to further returns. IOM also focuses on the recruitment and selection of highly-trained workers and professionals to fill positions in priority sectors of the economy in developing countries for which qualified persons are not available locally, taking into account national development priorities as well as the needs and concerns of receiving communities.

In November 1996 IOM established a RQN programme to facilitate the employment of refugees returning to Bosnia and Herzegovina. By December 1999, when the programme was terminated, more than 750 professionals had been placed in jobs in that country. In 2001 IOM initiated a Programme for the Return of Judiciary and Prosecutors to Minority Areas in Bosnia and Herzegovina. A programme to encourage the Return and Reintegration of Qualified Afghan Nationals (RQAFN), co-funded by the European Commission, is ongoing, and assisted 604 Afghans during December 2001–July 2004. In 2005 IOM, the United Nations Volunteers (UNV) and the Iraqi Government established an ongoing RQN–Transfer of Knowledge Through Expatriate Nationals (TOKTEN) programme for Iraq, known as *Iraqis Rebuilding Iraq*, with funding from the International Reconstruction Fund Facility for Iraq. In addition, IOM operates the Migration for Development in Africa (MIDA) capacity-building programme, which was introduced in 2001 to follow on from a previous Return of Qualified African Nationals scheme that assisted 690 Africans during the period 1983–99. IOM and the EU jointly fund a scheme to support Rwandan students abroad and encourage their return to Rwanda.

In April 2006 IOM and the Netherlands Government initiated the Temporary Return of Qualified Nationals (TRQN) project, with the aim of supporting reconstruction and development efforts in Afghanistan, Bosnia and Herzegovina, Kosovo, Montenegro, Serbia, Sierra Leone and Sudan. Under the TRQN, IOM provides logistical and financial assistance to experts originating in any of the target countries who are also nationals of or have residence in the Netherlands, to help them participate in projects aimed at enriching the target countries.

FACILITATING MIGRATION

Integrated world markets, transnational business networks and the rapid growth of ICTs have contributed to large-scale movements of workers, students, family members, and other migrants. IOM implements programmes that assist governments and migrants with recruitment, language training, pre-departure cultural orientation, pre-consular support services, arrival reception, and integration, and has introduced initiatives in areas including document verification, migrant information, interviews, applicant testing and logistical support. There are three main branches of Facilitating Migration programming: Labour Migration; Migrant Processing and Assistance; and Migrant Integration.

Through it Labour Migration activities IOM aims to promote regulated orderly labour migration while combating illegal, often clandestine, migration; and and to foster the economic and social development of countries of origin, transit and destination. Jointly with governments and other agencies, IOM has developed specific labour migration programmes that include elements such as capacity-building; pre-departure training; return and reintegration support; and regional dialogue and planning.

Through its Migrant Processing and Assistance activities IOM provides assistance to facilitate migration under organized and regular migration schemes that are tailored to meet specific programme needs and cover the different stages of the migration process: information and application, interview and approval, and post-approval (including pre-departure counselling and cultural orientation). Similar assistance is also provided to experts participating in international technical co-operation activities, to students studying abroad and, in some cases, to their dependents.

IOM's Migration Integration activities promote strategies aimed at enabling migrants to adjust easily to new environments abroad and focus on the dissemination of information on the rights and obligations of migrants and refugees in home and in host countries, the provision of advisory and counselling services, and the reinforcement of their skills. In addition IOM promotes awareness-raising activities in host societies that highlight the positive contributions that migrants can make, with a view to reducing the risks of discrimination and xenophobia.

REGULATING MIGRATION

IOM aims to counter the growing problem of smuggling and trafficking in migrants, which has resulted in several million people being exploited by criminal agents and employers. IOM aims to provide shelter and assistance for victims of trafficking; to provide legal and medical assistance to migrants uncovered in transit or in the receiving country; and to offer voluntary return and reintegration assistance. The Organization maintains a counter-trafficking module database which aims to facilitate the management of assistance for victims of trafficking. IOM organizes mass information campaigns in countries of origin, in order to highlight the risks of smuggling and trafficking, and aims to raise general awareness of the problem. The most common countries of origin covered in the database are Belarus, Bulgaria, the Dominican Republic, Moldova, Romania and Ukraine. IOM also provides training to increase the capacity of governments and other organizations to counter irregular migration. Since 1996 IOM has worked in Cambodia and Thailand to help victims of trafficking to return home. A transit centre has been established on the border between the two countries, where assessments are carried out, advice is given, and the process of tracing families is undertaken. IOM has campaigned for the prevention of trafficking in women from the Baltic states. IOM launched a series of new training modules in November 2006, designed to enhance the knowledge and understanding of the issues of human trafficking. In February 2007 IOM signed a counter-trafficking agreement with Norway and Denmark to provide assistance to an IOM humanitarian project in Bangladesh. The three-year Prevention and Protection of Victims of Human Trafficking in Bangladesh project, costing approximately US $3.2m., incorporates capacity-building initiatives and community involvement in promoting human rights and tackling human trafficking in 22 of the country's districts.

IOM offers Assisted Voluntary Return (AVR) services to migrants and governments, with the aim of facilitating the efficient and humane return and reintegration of migrants who wish to repatriate voluntarily to their countries of origin. Pre-departure, transportation and post-arrival assistance is provided to unsuccessful asylum seekers, migrants in irregular situations, migrants stranded in transit, stranded students, etc. AVR services can be tailored to the particular needs of specific groups, such as vulnerable migrants. IOM established a Stranded Migrant Facility in 2005.

Through its Technical Co-operation on Migration Division IOM offers advisory services on to governments on the optimum administrative structures, policy, legislation, operational systems and human resource systems required to regulate migration. IOM technical co-operation also focuses on capacity-building projects such as training courses for government migration officials, and analysis of and suggestions for solving emerging migration problems. Throughout these activities IOM aims to maintain an emphasis on the rights and well-being of migrants, and in particular to ensure that the specific needs of migrant women are incorporated into programmes and policies.

In 2001 IOM introduced the so-called 1035 Facility, which supports developing member states and member states with economies in transition with the implementation of migration management capacity-building projects. By April 2008 in excess of 200 projects in more than 85 member states had been supported by the Facility.

MOVEMENT, EMERGENCY AND POST-CRISIS RESPONSE

IOM provides services to assist with the resettlement of individuals accepted under regular national immigration programmes; these include: supporting the processing of relevant documentation; medical screening; arranging safe transportation; and, in some cases, the provision of language training and cultural orientation. IOM also assists with the voluntary repatriation of refugees, mainly in support of UNHCR's voluntary repatriation activities.

In emergency situations IOM provides transportation and humanitarian assistance to individuals requiring evacuation, as well as providing support to countries of temporary protection. IOM supports internally displaced populations through the provision of emergency shelter and relief materials. Post-emergency movement assistance for returning displaced populations is also provided (mainly IDPs, demobilized soldiers and persons affected by natural disasters). In post-crisis situations it actively supports governments in the reconstruction and rehabilitation of affected communities and offers short-term community and micro-enterprise development programmes. In such situations IOM's activities may include health-sector assistance and counter-trafficking awareness activities, psycho-social support, capacity-building for disaster transportation and logistics; and registration and information management of affected populations.

During 2005 the UN developed a concept of organizing humanitarian agency assistance to IDPs through the institutionalization of a 'Cluster Approach', currently comprising 11 core areas of activity. IOM was designated the lead humanitarian agency for the cluster on Camp Co-ordination and Management in natural disaster situations (UNHCR was to lead that cluster in conflict situations).

Since April 2003, following the launching in March of US-led military action against the Saddam Hussain regime in Iraq, IOM has been lead organization for emergency distributions of food and non-food items for the displaced population inside Iraq, and has co-ordinated the assessment and monitoring of Iraqi IDPs, including providing data on their numbers, locations and needs. IOM works to restore essential services, including the provision of drinking water, good sanitation, health, and education, in central and southern Iraq. In February 2008 IOM requested US $13.5m. under the Consolidated Inter-agency Appeal Process organized by the UN, in order to finance seven projects (related to food, protection and shelter) being implemented in support of IDPs, returnees and host communities in Iraq. In early 2008 IOM was assisting voluntary returns and tracking the numbers of spontaneous returns (416,966 during November 2005–January 2008) to southern Sudan. During 2006 IOM personnel in Darfur, Sudan, verified 36,775 IDP relocations, 6,475 IDP returns and 1,973 refugee repatriations, aiming to ensure that movements were conducted voluntarily and safely. During the conflict in Lebanon in mid-2006 IOM provided food, medical care and advice to some 10,000 migrants stranded in that country. By August of that year IOM had assisted in the evacuation or repatriation of more than 5,000 people from Lebanon and Syria. In May 2004 IOM launched the Haiti Transition Initiative, which aimed to rebuild communities and infrastructures devastated by conflict in that country. In 2006 IOM facilitated a number of inter-ministerial workshops aimed at encouraging Haiti to adopt a stance of greater co-operation with regard to international migration. These took place prior to a UN High-level Dialogue on International Migration and Development, held in New York, USA, in September 2006.

CLAIMS PROGRAMMES

IOM was designated as one of the implementing organizations of the settlement agreement concluded between survivors of the Nazi holocaust and Swiss banks. IOM established the Holocaust Victim Assets Programme (HVAP) to process claims made by certain target groups. A German Forced Labour Compensation Programme (GFLCP) was founded to process applications for claims of forced labour and personal injury and for property loss. By September 2005 IOM had recommended payment of 18,431 of a total of 49,371 claims received under the HVAP, while claims received under the GFLCP included 332,307 for slave and forced labour, 41,837 for personal injury and 34,997 for property loss. Under the terms of the settlement agreement, with regard to 'looted assets', IOM was mandated to distribute $20.5m. to humanitarian programmes, specifically to assist elderly Roma and Sinti, Jehovah's Witnesses, disabled and homosexual victims and targets of Nazi persecution. The HVAP and GFLCP were terminated in December 2006.

IOM provides assistance and advice to the Commission for Resolution of Real Property Disputes (CRRPD), an independent agency of the Government of Iraq that was established in March 2006 to resolve claims on property in Iraq relating to the period from 17 July 1968–9 April 2003.

MIGRATION HEALTH

IOM's Migration Health Department aims to ensure that migrants are fit to travel, do not pose a danger to those travelling with them, and that they receive medical attention and care when necessary. IOM also undertakes research and other technical support and policy development activities in the field of health care. Medical screening of prospective migrants is routinely conducted, along with immunizations and specific counselling, e.g. for HIV/AIDS. IOM administers programmes for disabled refugees and undertakes medical evacuation of people affected by conflict. Under its programmes for health assistance and advice, IOM conducts health education programmes, training for health professionals in post-conflict regions, and assessments of availability and access to health care for migrant populations. IOM provides assistance for post-emergency returning populations, through the rehabilitation of health infrastructures; provision of medical supplies; mental health programmes, including psychosocial support; and training of personnel.

IOM collaborates with government health authorities and relevant intergovernmental and non-governmental organizations. In September 1999 IOM and UNAIDS signed a co-operation framework to promote awareness on HIV/AIDS issues relating to displaced populations, and to ensure the needs of migrants are incorporated into national and regional AIDS strategies. In October IOM and WHO signed an agreement to strengthen collaborative efforts to improve the health care of migrants. IOM maintains a database of its tuberculosis diagnostic and treatment programmes, which facilitates the management of the disease. An information system on immigration medical screening data was being developed to help to analyse disease trends among migrants.

International Centre for Migration and Health
11 route du Nant-d'Avril, 1214 Geneva, Vernier, Switzerland; tel. 227831080; fax 227831087; e-mail admin@icmh.ch; internet www.icmh.ch.

Established in March 1995, by IOM and the University of Geneva, with the support of WHO, to respond to the growing needs for information, documentation, research, training and policy development in migration health; designated as a WHO collaborating centre for health-related issues among people displaced by disasters.
Executive Director: Dr MANUEL CARBALLO.

Finance

IOM's operational budget for 2007 totalled US $747m.

Publications

Global Eye on Human Trafficking (quarterly).
International Migration (quarterly).
IOM Harare Newsletter.
IOM News (quarterly, in English, French and Spanish).
Migration (2 a year).
Migration and Climate Change.
Migration Health Annual Report.
Report by the Director-General (in English, French and Spanish).
Trafficking in Migrants (quarterly).
World Migration Report (annually).
Research reports, *IOM Info Sheets* surveys and studies.

INTERNATIONAL RED CROSS AND RED CRESCENT MOVEMENT

The International Red Cross and Red Crescent Movement is a world-wide independent humanitarian organization, comprising three components: the International Committee of the Red Cross (ICRC), founded in 1863; the International Federation of Red Cross and Red Crescent Societies (the Federation), founded in 1919; National Red Cross and Red Crescent Societies in 185 countries; and Magen David Adom, an Israeli society equivalent to the Red Cross and Red Crescent Societies. In 1997 all constituent parts of the

Movement adopted the Seville Agreement on co-operation in the undertaking of international relief activities. The Agreement excludes activities that are entrusted to individual components by the statutes of the Movement or the Geneva Conventions.

between the Movement's bodies, clearly defining the distribution of tasks between agencies. In particular, the Agreement aimed to ensure continuity between international operations carried out in a crisis situation and those developed in its aftermath.

Organization

INTERNATIONAL CONFERENCE

The supreme deliberative body of the Movement, the Conference comprises delegations from the ICRC, the Federation and the National Societies, and of representatives of States Parties to the Geneva Conventions (see below). The Conference's function is to determine the general policy of the Movement and to ensure unity in the work of the various bodies. It usually meets every four to five years, and is hosted by the National Society of the country in which it is held.

The 29th International Conference was held in Geneva, Switzerland, in June 2006. The meeting approved membership of the Palestinian Red Crescent Society and the Israeli society Magen David Adom. A Third Additional Protocol (Protocol III—see below) to the Geneva Conventions was adopted in December 2005 and entered into force in January 2007. Protocol III recognizes as third emblem of the Movement a red crystal, which is deemed to be a neutral symbol devoid of political or religious connotations.

STANDING COMMISSION

The Commission meets at least twice a year in ordinary session. It promotes harmony in the work of the Movement, and examines matters which concern the Movement as a whole. It is formed of two representatives of the ICRC, two of the Federation, and five members of National Societies elected by the Conference.

COUNCIL OF DELEGATES

The Council comprises delegations from the National Societies, from the ICRC and from the Federation. The Council is the body where the representatives of all the components of the Movement meet to discuss matters that concern the Movement as a whole.

In November 1997 the Council adopted an Agreement on the organization of the activities of the Movement's components. The Agreement aimed to promote increased co-operation and partnership

Fundamental Principles of the Movement

Humanity: The International Red Cross and Red Crescent Movement, born of a desire to bring assistance without discrimination to the wounded on the battlefield, endeavours, in its international and national capacity, to prevent and alleviate human suffering wherever it may be found. Its purpose is to protect life and health and to ensure respect for the human being. It promotes mutual understanding, friendship, co-operation and lasting peace amongst all peoples.

Impartiality: It makes no discrimination as to nationality, race, religious beliefs, class or political opinions. It endeavours to relieve the suffering of individuals, being guided solely by their needs, and to give priority to the most urgent cases of distress.

Neutrality: In order to continue to enjoy the confidence of all, the Movement may not take sides in hostilities or engage in controversies of a political, racial, religious or ideological nature.

Independence: The Movement is independent. The National Societies, while auxiliaries in the humanitarian services of their governments and subject to national laws, must retain their autonomy so that they may always be able to act in accordance with the principles of the Movement.

Voluntary Service: It is a voluntary relief movement not prompted by desire for gain.

Unity: There can be only one Red Cross or Red Crescent Society in any one country. It must be open to all. It must carry on its humanitarian work throughout the territory.

Universality: The International Red Cross and Red Crescent Movement, in which all National Societies have equal status and share equal responsibilities and duties in helping each other, is world-wide.

International Committee of the Red Cross—ICRC

Address: 19 ave de la Paix, 1202 Geneva, Switzerland.
Telephone: 227346001; **fax:** 227332057; **e-mail:** press.gva@icrc.org; **internet:** www.icrc.org.

Founded in 1863, the ICRC is at the origin of the Red Cross and Red Crescent Movement, and co-ordinates all international humanitarian activities conducted by the Movement in situations of conflict. New statutes of the ICRC, incorporating a revised institutional structure, entered into force in July 1998.

The ICRC is an independent institution of a private character composed exclusively of Swiss nationals. Members are co-opted, and their total number may not exceed 25. The international character of the ICRC is based on its mission and not on its composition.

Organization
(April 2008)

ASSEMBLY

The Assembly is the supreme governing body of the ICRC. It formulates policy, defines the Committee's general objectives and strategies, oversees its activities, and approves its budget and accounts. The Assembly is composed of the members of the ICRC, and is collegial in character. The President and Vice-Presidents of the ICRC hold the same offices in the Assembly.

President: JAKOB KELLENBERGER.
Vice-Presidents: OLIVIER VODOZ, CHRISTINE BEERLI.

ASSEMBLY COUNCIL

The Council (formerly the Executive Board) is a subsidiary body of the Assembly, to which the latter delegates certain of its responsibilities. It prepares the Assembly's activities and takes decisions on matters within its competence. The Council is composed of five members elected by the Assembly and is chaired by the President of the ICRC.

Members: JAKOB KELLENBERGER, CHRISTINE BEERLI, JEAN ABT, JEAN DE COURTEN, JACQUES MOREILLON.

DIRECTORATE

The Directorate is the executive body of the ICRC, overseeing the efficient running of the organization and responsible for the application of the general objectives and institutional strategies decided by the Assembly. Members are appointed by the Assembly to serve a four-year term.

Director-General: ANGELO GNAEDINGER.
Members: PIERRE KRAEHENBUEL (Director of Operations), JACQUES STROUN (Director of Human Resources), DORIS PFISTER (Director of Resources and Operational Support), YVES DACCORD (Director of Communication), PHILIP SPOERRI (Director for International Law and Co-operation within the Movement).

Activities

The International Committee of the Red Cross was founded in 1863 in Geneva, by Henry Dunant and four of his friends. The original purpose of the Committee was to promote the foundation, in every country, of a voluntary relief society to assist wounded soldiers on the battlefield (the origin of the National Societies of the Red Cross or Red Crescent), as well as the adoption of a treaty protecting wounded soldiers and all those who come to their rescue. The mission of the ICRC was progressively extended through the Geneva Conventions (see below). The present activities of the ICRC consist in giving legal protection and material assistance to military and civilian victims of wars (international wars, internal strife and disturbances) and in promoting and monitoring the application of international humanitarian law. The ICRC takes into account the legal standards and the specific cultural, ethical and religious features of the environment in which it operates. It aims to influence the conduct of all actual and potential perpetrators of violence by seeking direct dialogue with combatants. In 1990 the ICRC was granted observer status at the United Nations General Assembly. The ICRC overall programme of activities covers the following areas:

The protection of vulnerable individuals and groups under international humanitarian law, including activities related to ensuring respect for detainees (monitoring prison conditions), respect for civilians, reuniting relatives separated in conflict situations and restoring family links, and tracing missing persons;

The implementation of assistance activities, aimed at restoring a sufficient standard of living to victims of armed conflict, including the provision of medical aid and emergency food supplies, initiatives to improve water supply, basic infrastructure and access to health care, and physical rehabilitation assistance (for example to assist civilians injured by land-mines);

Preventive action, including the development and implementation of international humanitarian law and dissemination of humanitarian principles, with a view to protecting non-combatants from violence;

The use of humanitarian diplomacy to raise awareness of humanitarian issues among states and within international organizations;

Building private sector relations;

Co-operation with National Societies.

The ICRC Advisory Service, established in 1996, offers legal and technical assistance to national authorities with incorporating international humanitarian law (IHL) into their national legislation, assists them in their implementation of IHL, maintains a database on IHL, and publishes specialist documents. A Documentation Centre has also been established for exchanging information on national measures and activities aimed at promoting humanitarian law in countries. The Centre is open to all states and National Societies, as well as to interested institutions and the general public.

In April 1998 the Assembly endorsed a plan of action, based on the following four priorities identified by the 'Avenir' project to define the organization's future role, that had been launched in 1996: improving the status of international humanitarian action and knowledge of and respect for IHL; carrying out humanitarian action in closer proximity to victims, with long-term plans and identified priorities; strengthening dialogue with all parties (including launching joint appeals with other organizations if necessary); and increasing the ICRC's efficiency. In December 2003 the 28th International Conference of the Red Cross and Red Crescent adopted an Agenda for Humanitarian Action. The main components of the Agenda, which had the overall theme 'protecting human dignity', were: respecting and restoring the dignity of persons and families missing as a result of conflict situations; strengthening controls on weapons development, proliferation and use; lessening the impact of disasters through the implementation of disaster risk reduction measures and improving preparedness and response mechanisms; and reducing vulnerability to the effects of disease associated with lack of access to comprehensive prevention, care and treatment.

The ICRC's Institutional Strategy covering the period 2007–10 stressed the Committee's resolve to adopt an approach to meeting humanitarian needs resulting from conflict situations while placing special emphasis on further developing professional expertise in the areas of protection and health. The ICRC has noted in recent years that, while some conflicts remain underpinned by territorial or ideological disputes, increasing numbers of conflicts and so-called 'situations of violence' are being fuelled by pressure to secure control over natural resources, and that there is evidence of increasing activity by economically predatory armed elements. Fragile humanitarian situations are complicated by other factors, including weapon proliferation; environmental degradation; mass migration to cities and increased urban violence; and acts of terrorism and anti-terrorism operations. The ICRC has identified two principal challenges to the neutral and independent implementation of its humanitarian activities: developing a refined understanding of the diversity and specificity of armed conflicts and other situations of violence; and addressing meaningfully the many needs of affected civilian populations.

The ICRC consistently reviews the 1980 UN Convention on prohibitions or restrictions on the use of certain conventional weapons which may be deemed to be excessively injurious or to have indiscriminate effects and its protocols. In September 1997 the ICRC participated in an international conference, held in Oslo, Norway, which adopted the Convention on the Prohibition of the Use, Stockpiling, Production and Transfer of Anti-personnel Mines and on their Destruction. The Convention entered into force on 1 March 1999. In April 1998 the Swiss Government established a Geneva International Centre for Humanitarian Demining, in co-operation with the United Nations and the ICRC, to co-ordinate the destruction of landmines world-wide.

In 1995 the ICRC adopted a 'Plan of Action concerning Children in Armed Conflicts', to promote the principle of non-recruitment and non-participation in armed conflict of children under the age of 18 years. A co-ordinating group was established, with representatives of the individual National Societies and the International Federation of Red Cross and Red Crescent Societies. The ICRC participated in drafting the Optional Protocol to the Convention on the Rights of the Child, which was adopted by the UN General Assembly in May 2000 and entered into force in February 2002, raising from 15 to 18 years the minimum age for recruitment in armed conflict.

The ICRC's presence in the field is organized under the following three categories: responsive action, aimed at addressing the immediate effects of crises; remedial action, with an emphasis on rehabilitation; and environment-building activities, aimed at creating political, institutional, humanitarian and economic situations that are suitable for generating respect for human rights. ICRC operational delegations focus on responsive action and remedial action, while environment-building is undertaken by ICRC regional delegations. The regional delegations undertake humanitarian diplomacy efforts (e.g. networking, promoting international humanitarian law and distributing information), logistical support to operational delegations, and their own operations; they also have an early warning function, alerting the ICRC to developing conflict situations. The ICRC targets its activities at the following groups: 'victims', comprising civilians affected by violent crises, people deprived of their freedom, and the wounded and sick; and institutions and individuals with influence, i.e. national and local authorities, security forces, representatives of civil society, and ICRC National Societies. Children, women, internally displaced people and missing persons are of particular concern to the ICRC.

The ICRC's 'FamilyLinks' internet pages (accessible at www.familylinks.icrc.org/) aim to reunite family members separated by conflict or disaster situations. In February 2003 the ICRC launched 'The Missing', a major initiative that aimed to raise awareness of the issue of persons unaccounted for owing to armed conflict or internal violence. The ICRC assisted with the preparation of the International Convention for the Protection of all Persons from Enforced Disappearance, adopted by the UN General Assembly in December 2006, and representing the first international treaty to prohibit practices facilitating enforced disappearance.

During 2006 ICRC representatives visited some 478,299 prisoners held in 2,577 places of detention in 71 countries world-wide. A total of 633,961 messages were collected from or distributed to family members separated by conflict, and 11,569 persons reported as missing were traced. Regular substantial assistance was provided to 193 hospitals and 303 other health-care facilities world-wide, benefiting about 2.4m. people. During the year the ICRC participated in orthopaedic projects assisting 141,961 patients world-wide, including through the manufacturing and fitting of artificial limbs. In 2008 the ICRC was actively concerned with around 80 conflicts and was undertaking major operations in (in order of budgetary priority): Iraq (provisionally allocated 107.3m. Swiss francs), Sudan (provisionally allocated 106.4m. Swiss francs), Israel and the Palestinian territories (68.2m. Swiss francs), Afghanistan (60.3m.), the Democratic Republic of the Congo (37.1m.), Colombia (34.2m.), Somalia (30.2m.), Chad (27.9m.), Sri Lanka (26.7m.) and Uganda (23.2m.). In 2008 operations in sub-Saharan Africa were allocated the highest proportion of the total field budget (some 43%), followed by the Middle East and North Africa (24%), Asia and the Pacific (19%) and Europe and the Americas (14%).

In 2008 some 587 ICRC personnel were deployed in Iraq. The ICRC's activities in Iraq in 2007 included discovering the situations of 93 recently missing Iraqis and of 12 Iraqis missing since the 1990–91 Gulf War; visiting about 5,000 Iraqi detainees in 21 places of detention and collecting and distributing an estimated 76,000 messages between Iraqi detainees and their families, and providing travel allowances enabling 31,000 family members to visit 11,600 detained relatives. In that year the ICRC also distributed relief items to 140,000 Iraqi IDPs and to 60,000 needy persons; provided 16 Iraqi Red Crescent branches with relief items for distribution; and assisted more than 6,000 Iraqi households through micro-economic projects. Some 28 Iraqi hospitals were provided with medical supplies and drugs.

Some 1,584 ICRC personnel were deployed in Sudan in 2008. The ICRC provides for the basic material and health welfare needs of more than 120,000 IDPs accommodated in the Gereida camp in South Darfur. In 2007 the ICRC's activities in Darfur also included reuniting families, supporting six health clinics providing primary care to an estimated 252,000 people, and the maintenance of mobile medical teams providing preventive and curative care to civilians in remote areas of the province.

THE GENEVA CONVENTIONS

In 1864, one year after its foundation, the ICRC submitted to the states called to a Diplomatic Conference in Geneva a draft international treaty for 'the Amelioration of the Condition of the Wounded in Armies in the Field'. This treaty was adopted and signed by 12 states, which thereby bound themselves to respect as neutral wounded soldiers and those assisting them. This was the first Geneva Convention.

With the development of technology and weapons, the introduction of new means of waging war, and the manifestation of certain phenomena (the great number of prisoners of war during World War I; the enormous number of displaced persons and refugees during World War II; the internationalization of internal conflicts in recent years), the necessity was felt of having other international treaties to protect new categories of war victims. The ICRC, for more than 134 years, has been the leader of a movement to improve and complement international humanitarian law.

There are now four Geneva Conventions, adopted on 12 August 1949: I—to protect wounded and sick in armed forces on land, as well as medical personnel; II—to protect the same categories of people at sea, as well as the shipwrecked; III—concerning the treatment of prisoners of war; IV—for the protection of civilians in time of war. Two Additional Protocols were adopted on 8 June 1977, for the protection of victims in international armed conflicts (Protocol I) and in non-international armed conflicts (Protocol II). A Third Additional Protocol (Protocol III), endorsing the red crystal as an additional emblem of the Movement, was adopted on 8 December 2005 and entered into force on 14 January 2007.

By April 2008 194 states were parties to the Geneva Conventions; 167 were parties to Protocol I, 163 to Protocol II and 28 to Protocol III.

Finance

The ICRC's work is financed by a voluntary annual grant from governments parties to the Geneva Conventions, the European Commission, voluntary contributions from National Red Cross and Red Crescent Societies and by gifts and legacies from private donors. The ICRC's provisional budget for 2008 amounted to approximately 932.6m. Swiss francs, of which 771.1m. Swiss francs were allocated to field operations.

In October 2005, as part of a long-term strategy to diversify funding sources, the ICRC launched a Corporate Support Group in partnership with seven Swiss-based companies, which had been selected in accordance with ethical guide-lines based on ICRC's mandate and on the principles and statutes of the International Red Cross and Red Crescent Movement. The Corporate Support Group Partners pledged to donate a minimum of 3m. Swiss francs over a six-year period.

Publications

Annual Report (editions in English, French and Spanish).
FORUM series.
The Geneva Conventions (texts and commentaries).
ICRC News (weekly, English, French, German and Spanish editions).
International Review of the Red Cross (quarterly in English and French; annually in Arabic, Russian and Spanish).
The Additional Protocols (texts and commentaries).
Various publications on subjects of Red Cross interest (medical studies, international humanitarian law, etc.), some in electronic form.

International Federation of Red Cross and Red Crescent Societies

Address: 17 chemin des Crêts, Petit-Saconnex, CP 372, 1211 Geneva 19, Switzerland.
Telephone: 227304222; **fax:** 227330395; **e-mail:** secretariat@ifrc.org; **internet:** www.ifrc.org.

The Federation was founded in 1919 (as the League of Red Cross Societies). It works on the basis of the Principles of the Red Cross and Red Crescent Movement to inspire, facilitate and promote all forms of humanitarian activities by the National Societies, with a view to the prevention and alleviation of human suffering, and thereby contribute to the maintenance and promotion of peace in the world. The Federation acts as the official representative of its member societies in the field. The Federation maintains close relations with many inter-governmental organizations, the United Nations and its Specialized Agencies, and with non-governmental organizations. It has permanent observer status with the United Nations.

MEMBERS

National Red Cross and Red Crescent Societies in 185 countries, and Magen David Adom, Israel's equivalent of the Red Cross Society, in April 2008.

Organization
(April 2008)

GENERAL ASSEMBLY

The General Assembly is the highest authority of the Federation and meets every two years in commission sessions (for development, disaster relief, health and community services, and youth) and plenary sessions. It is composed of representatives from all National Societies that are members of the Federation.

GOVERNING BOARD

The Board (formerly the Executive Council) meets every six months and is composed of the President of the Federation, nine Vice-Presidents, representatives of 16 National Societies elected by the Assembly, and the Chairman of the Finance Commission. Its functions include the implementation of decisions of the General Assembly; it also has powers to act between meetings of the Assembly.

President: Juan Manuel Suárez del Toro Rivero (Spain).

COMMISSIONS

Development Commission;
Disaster Relief Commission;
Finance Commission;
Health and Community Services Commission;
Youth Commission.

The Commissions meet, in principle, twice a year, before the Governing Board meeting. Members are elected by the Assembly under a system that ensures each Society a seat on one Commission.

SECRETARIAT

The Secretariat assumes the statutory responsibilities of the Federation in the field of relief to victims of natural disasters, refugees and civilian populations who may be displaced or exposed to abnormal hardship. In addition, the Secretariat promotes and co-ordinates assistance to National Societies in developing their basic structure and their services to the community. The Secretariat has the following main departments: co-operation and governance support and risk management and audit; and the following divisions: support services, co-ordination and programmes, and policy and communications. The Secretary-General nominates honorary and special envoys for specific situations.

Secretary-General: Markku Niskala (Finland).

Activities

In October 1999 the Assembly adopted Strategy 2010, outlining the Federation's objectives and strategies for the next 10 years, in order to address new demands placed on it, for example by the proliferation of other humanitarian groups, restricted finance, and pressure from donors for efficiency, transparency and results. The Strategy involved a significant restructuring of the organization. In November

2005 the Assembly adopted a Global Agenda, comprising the following objectives which aimed to contribute to the attainment of the UN Millennium Development Goals: to reduce the deaths, injuries and impact of disasters on peoples' lives; to improve methods of dealing with public health crises; to combat intolerance and discrimination; and to build Red Cross and Red Crescent capacity at the community level to prepare for and cope with threats to lives and livelihoods.

DISASTER RESPONSE

The Federation supports the establishment of emergency response units, which aim to act effectively and independently to meet the needs of victims of natural or man-made disasters. The units cover basic health care provision, referral hospitals, water sanitation, logistics, telecommunications and information units. The Federation advises National Societies in relief health. In the event of a disaster the following areas are covered: communicable disease alleviation and vaccination; psychological support and stress management; health education; the provision of medicines; and the organization of mobile clinics and nursing care. The Societies also distribute food and clothing to those in need and assist in the provision of shelter and adequate sanitation facilities and in the management of refugee camps. The 2005 Global Agenda provided for a significant increase in Federation activities, in particular in the provision of emergency shelter, following natural disasters.

During 2005 the UN's Inter-Agency Standing Committee (IASC), concerned with co-ordinating the international response to humanitarian disasters, developed a concept of organizing agency assistance to IDPs through the institutionalization of a 'Cluster Approach', comprising nine core areas of activity. The Federation was designated the lead agency for the Emergency Protection (in natural disasters) cluster.

DEVELOPMENT

The Federation undertakes capacity-building activities with the National Societies to train and develop staff and volunteers and to improve management structures and processes, in particular in the area of disaster-preparedness. Blood donor programmes are often undertaken by National Societies, sometimes in conjunction with WHO. The Federation supports the promotion of these programmes and the implementation of quality standards. Other activities in the health sector aim to strengthen existing health services and promote community-based health care and first aid; the prevention of HIV/AIDS and substance abuse; and health education and family planning initiatives. The Federation also promotes the establishment and development of education and service programmes for children and for other more vulnerable members of society, including the elderly and disabled. Education projects support the promotion of humanitarian values.

Finance

The permanent Secretariat of the Federation is financed by the contributions of member Societies on a pro-rata basis. Each relief action is financed by separate, voluntary contributions, and development programme projects are also financed on a voluntary basis.

Publications

Annual Report.
Handbook of the International Red Cross and Red Crescent Movement (with the ICRC).
Red Cross, Red Crescent Magazine (quarterly, English, French and Spanish).
Weekly News.
World Disasters Report (annually).
Newsletters on several topics; various guides and manuals for Red Cross and Red Crescent activities.

INTERNATIONAL SEABED AUTHORITY

Address: 14–20 Port Royal St, Kingston, Jamaica.
Telephone: 922-9105; **fax:** 922-0195; **e-mail:** webmaster@isa.org.jm; **internet:** www.isa.org.jm.

The Authority is an autonomous international organization established in accordance with the 1982 United Nations Convention on the Law of the Sea and 1994 Agreement Relating to the Implementation of Part XI of the Convention. The Authority was founded in November 1994 and became fully operational in June 1996.

Organization
(April 2008)

ASSEMBLY

The Assembly is the supreme organ of the Authority, consisting of representatives of all member states. In conjunction with the Council, it formulates the Authority's general policies. It elects Council members and members of the Finance Committee. It also approves the budget, submitted by the Council on the recommendation of the Finance Committee. The 13th session of the Assembly was held in July 2007.

COUNCIL

The Council, elected by the Assembly for four-year terms, acts as the executive organ of the Authority. It consists of 36 members, comprising the four states that are the largest importers or consumers of seabed minerals, the four largest investors in seabed minerals, the four major exporters of seabed minerals, six developing countries representing special interests, and 18 members covering all the geographical regions.

LEGAL AND TECHNICAL COMMISSION

The Legal and Technical Commission, comprising 25 experts elected for five-year terms, assists the Council by making recommendations concerning sea-bed activities, assessing the environmental implications of activities in the area, proposing measures to protect the marine environment, and reviewing the execution of exploration contracts.

FINANCE COMMITTEE

The Committee, comprising 15 experts, was established to make recommendations to the Assembly and the Council on all financial and budgetary issues.

SECRETARIAT

The Secretariat provides administrative services to all the bodies of the Authority and implements the relevant work programmes. It comprises the Office of the Secretary-General, Offices of Resources and Environmental Monitoring, Legal Affairs, and Administration and Management. Under the terms of the 1994 Agreement Relating to the Implementation of Part XI of the Convention, the Secretariat is performing the functions of the Enterprise, the organ through which the Authority carries out deep sea-bed mining operations (directly or through joint ventures). It is envisaged that the Enterprise will eventually operate independently of the Secretariat.

Secretary-General: Satya N. Nandan (Fiji).

Activities

The Authority, functioning as an autonomous international organization in relationship with the UN, implements the Convention on the Law of the Sea (which was adopted in April 1982 and entered into force in November 1994). All states party to the Convention (155 at March 2008) are members. The Convention covers the uses of ocean space: navigation and overflight, resource exploration and exploitation, conservation and pollution, and fishing and shipping; as well as governing conduct on the oceans; defining maritime zones; establishing rules for delineating sea boundaries; assigning legal rights, duties and responsibilities to states; and providing machinery for the settlement of disputes. Its main provisions are as follows:

Coastal states are allowed sovereignty over their territorial waters of up to 12 nautical miles in breadth; foreign vessels are to be allowed 'innocent passage' through these waters;

Ships and aircraft of all states, including landlocked states, are allowed 'transit passage' through straits used for international navigation; states bordering these straits can regulate navigation and other aspects of passage;

Archipelagic states (composed of islands and interconnecting waters) have sovereignty over a sea area enclosed by straight lines drawn between the outermost points of the islands;

Coastal states and inhabited islands are entitled to proclaim a 200-mile exclusive economic zone (EEZ) with respect to natural resources and jurisdiction over certain activities (such as protection and preservation of the environment), and rights over the adjacent continental shelf, up to 350 miles from the shore under specified circumstances;

All states have freedom of navigation, overflight, scientific research and fishing within the EEZ, in addition to the right to lay submarine cables and pipelines, but must co-operate in measures to conserve living resources;

A 'parallel system' is to be established for exploiting the international seabed, where all activities are to be supervised by the International Seabed Authority; landlocked and geographically disadvantaged states have the right to participate, on an equitable basis, in the exploitation of an appropriate part of the surplus of living resources of the EEZs of coastal states of the same region or sub-region;

Coastal states have sovereign rights over the continental shelf (the national area of the seabed, which can extend up to 200 nautical miles from the shore) for exploring and exploiting its natural resources; the UN Commission on the Limits of the Continental Shelf shall make recommendations to states on the shelf's outer boundaries when it extends beyond 200 miles;

All states party to the Convention share, through the Authority, the revenue generated from exploiting non-living resources from any part of the continental shelf extending beyond 200 miles; the distribution of revenue is determined according to equitable sharing criteria, taking into account the interests and needs of developing and landlocked states;

States are bound to control pollution and co-operate in forming preventive rules, and incur penalties for failing to combat pollution; states bordering enclosed, or semi-enclosed, waters are bound to co-operate in managing living resources, environmental policies and research activities;

Marine scientific research in the zones under national jurisdiction is subject to the prior consent of the coastal state, but consent may be denied only under specific circumstances;

States are bound to co-operate in the development and transfer of marine technology 'on fair and reasonable terms and conditions' and with proper regard for all legitimate interests;

States are obliged to settle by peaceful means disputes on the application and interpretation of the Convention; disputes must be submitted to a compulsory procedure entailing decisions binding on all parties.

The Convention provides for the establishment of an International Tribunal for the Law of the Sea (see below), which has exclusive jurisdiction over disputes relating to the international seabed area. In July 1994 the UN General Assembly adopted the Agreement Relating to the Implementation of Part XI of the Convention. At March 2008 there were 131 states party to the Agreement. The original Part XI, concerning the exploitation of the international ocean bed, and particularly the minerals to be found there (chiefly manganese, cobalt, copper and nickel), envisaged as the 'common heritage of mankind', had not been supported by the USA and other industrialized nations on the grounds that countries possessing adequate technology for deep-sea mining would be insufficiently represented in the Authority; that the operations of private mining consortia would be unacceptably limited by the stipulations that their technology should be shared with the Authority's 'Enterprise'; and that production should be limited in order to protect land-based mineral producers. Under the 1994 Agreement there was to be no mandatory transfer of technology, the Enterprise was to operate according to commercial principles; and there were to be no production limits, although a compensation fund was to assist land-based producers adversely affected by seabed mining. Several industrial nations then ratified the Convention and Agreement (which entered into force in July 1996), although the USA had not yet ratified either by March 2008. An agreement on the implementation of the provisions of the Convention relating to the conservation and management of straddling and highly migratory fish stocks was opened for signature in December 1995 and entered into force in December 2001; by March 2008 it had been ratified by 68 states.

In July 2000 the Authority adopted the Regulations for Prospecting and Exploration for Polymetallic Nodules in the Area. Pursuant to the Regulations, eight exploration contracts have been signed: the first seven contracts were signed, between 2001–02, with registered pioneer investors who had submitted plans of work for deep seabed exploration; the eighth was signed, in July 2006, with the Federal Institute for Geosciences and Natural Resources of the Federal Republic of Germany. The Authority maintains a database on polymetallic nodules (POLYDAT) and a central data repository (CDR) for all marine minerals in the seabed. In February 2008 the Authority, jointly with the Indian Government, convened a workshop on polymetallic nodule mining technology: current status and challenges ahead.

In February 2008 the Authority launched a new endowment fund aimed at promoting and supporting collaborative marine scientific research in the international seabed area.

Finance

The Authority's budget is adopted by the Assembly on the recommendations of both the Council and the Finance Committee. The budget for the Authority for the biennium 2007–08 was US $11.8m. The administrative expenses of the Authority are met by assessed contributions of its members.

Publications

Basic Texts of the ISA (in English, French and Spanish).
Handbook (annually).
The Law of the Sea: Compendium of Basic Documents.
Selected decisions of sessions of the Authority, consultations, documents, rules of procedure, technical reports and studies, etc.

Associated Institutions

The following were also established under the terms of the Convention:

Commission on the Limits of the Continental Shelf: Division for Ocean Affairs and the Law of the Sea, Room DC2-0450, United Nations, New York, NY 10017, USA; tel. (212) 963-3966; fax (212) 963-5847; e-mail doalos@un.org; internet www.un.org/Depts/los/clcs_new/clcs_home.htm; 21 members, serving a five-year term (the most recent election of members took place in June 2007); responsible for making recommendations regarding the establishment of the outer limits of the continental shelf of a coastal state, where the limit extends beyond 200 nautical miles (370 km).

International Tribunal for the Law of the Sea: Am internationalen Seegerichtshof 1, 22609 Hamburg, Germany; tel. (40) 356070; fax (40) 35607245; e-mail itlos@itlos.org; internet www.itlos.org; inaugurated in 1996; 21 judges; responsible for interpreting the Convention and ruling on disputes brought by states parties to the Convention on matters within its jurisdiction; Registrar PHILIPPE GAUTIER (Belgium).

International Trade Union Confederation—ITUC

Address: 5 blvd du Roi Albert II, bte 1, 1210 Brussels, Belgium.
Telephone: (2) 224-02-10; **fax:** (2) 201-58-15; **e-mail:** info@ituc-csi.org; **internet:** www.ituc-csi.org.

ITUC was established in November 2006 by the merger of the International Confederation of Free Trade Unions (ICFTU, founded in 1949 by trade union federations that had withdrawn from the World Federation of Trade Unions), the World Confederation of Labour (WCL, founded in 1920 as the International Federation of Christian Trade Unions and reconstituted and renamed in 1968), and eight national trade union organizations. ITUC aims to defend and promote the rights of working people by encouraging co-operation between trade unions, and through global campaigning and advocacy. The principal areas of activity are: trade union and human rights; the economy, society and the workplace; equality and non-discrimination; and international solidarity. The principles of trade union democracy and independence are enshrined in ITUC's Constitution. In November 2006, following its establishment, ITUC ratified an agreement with the so-called Global Unions (global trade union federations, see list below) and the Trade Union Advisory Committee to the OECD (TUAC) to form a Council of Global Unions, with the aims of promoting trade union membership and advancing common trade union interests world-wide.

MEMBERS

311 organizations in 155 countries and territories with 168m. members.

Organization
(April 2008)

WORLD CONGRESS

The Congress, the highest authority of ITUC, meets in ordinary session at least once every four years. The first Congress was held in Vienna, Austria, in November 2006.

Delegations from national federations vary in size on the basis of their paying membership. The Congress examines past activities and financial reports of the Confederation; reports on the activities of ITUC's regional organizations and on the Council of Global Unions (the structured partnership with the global union federations and TUAC); addresses general policy questions; maps out future plans; considers proposals for amendments to the Constitution and any other proposals submitted by member organizations; and elects the General Council, the General Secretary and the Confederation's three auditors. The General Secretary leads the Secretariat and is an *ex officio* member of the General Council and of the Executive Bureau.

GENERAL COUNCIL

The General Council comprises 70 members, of whom 24 represent Europe; 18 represent the Americas; 15 represent the Asia-Pacific region; 11 represent Africa; and two have 'open' membership. The Council meets at least once a year and acts as the supreme authority of the Confederation between World Congresses, with responsibility for directing the activities of the Confederation and effecting decisions and recommendations of the Congress. The Council's agenda is prepared by the General Secretary.

The General Council appoints a Women's Committee and a Youth Committee. It may also establish a Human and Trade Union Rights Committee and other committees as it deems appropriate.

The General Secretary is supported by two Deputy General Secretaries.

EXECUTIVE BUREAU

At its first meeting after the regular World Congress the General Council elects an Executive Bureau, comprising the President, the General Secretary and up the 25 members of the General Council. The Executive Bureau is authorized to address questions of urgency that arise between meetings of the General Council, or which are entrusted to it by the General Council. The Bureau meets at least twice a year.

President: SHARAN BURROW (Australia).

PERMANENT COMMITTEES

Women's Committee.
Youth Committee.

SECRETARIAT

General Secretary: GUY RYDER (United Kingdom).

BRANCH OFFICES

ITUC Amman Office: POB 925875, Amman 11190, Jordan; tel. (6) 5603181; fax (6) 5603185; e-mail icftuamm@go.com.jo; Co-ordinator NEZAM QAHOUSH.

ITUC Geneva Office: 46 ave Blanc, 1202 Geneva, Switzerland; tel. 227384202; fax 227381082; e-mail ituc.geneva@ituc-csi.org; Dir ANNA BIONDI.

ITUC Moscow Office: 2142, Leninsky Prospekt 42, 117119 Moscow, Russia; tel. (495) 938-7356; fax (495) 938-7304; e-mail icftumos@cq.ru; Dir ANDREI MROST.

ITUC South East European Office: 71000 Sarajevo, Koturova 8, Bosnia and Herzegovina; tel. (33) 238976; fax (33) 238984; e-mail icftubux@bih.net.ba; Rep. JASMIN RADZEPOVIC.

ITUC United Nations Office: 211 East 43rd St, Suite 710, New York, NY 10017, USA; tel. (212) 370-0180; fax (212) 370-0188; e-mail icftuny@igc.org; Perm. Rep. GEMMA ADABA.

There are also Permanent Representatives accredited to FAO (Rome), IMO (London), UNIDO and IAEA (Vienna), and to UNEP and UN-Habitat (Nairobi).

REGIONAL ORGANIZATIONS

African Regional Organisation of ITUC (ITUC-Africa): POB 67273, Nairobi, Kenya; tel. (20) 244336; fax (20) 215072; e-mail info@ituc-africa.org; internet www.ituc-africa.org; f. Nov. 2007; Gen. Sec. KWASI ADU-AMANKWAH.

ITUC Regional Organisation for Asia-Pacific (ITUC-AP): 9th Floor, NTUC Centre, One Marina Blvd, Singapore 018989; tel. 63273590; fax 63273576; e-mail gs@ituc-ap.org; internet www.ituc-ap.org; f. Sept. 2007; Gen. Sec. NORIYUKI SUZUKI.

Trade Union Confederation of the Americas (TUCA): Rua Formosa 367, Centro CEP 01049-000, São Paulo, Brazil; tel. (11) 21040750; fax (11) 21040751; e-mail sede@cioslorit.org; internet www.cioslorit.org; f. March 2008; Gen. Sec. VICTOR BAEZ.

Membership of the European Trade Union Confederation includes European ITUC-affiliated organizations.

Finance

Affiliated federations pay a standard fee—€185.85 (2008), €191.45 (2009), €197.20 (2010)—or its equivalent in other currencies, per 1,000 members per annum, which finances the activities of the Confederation.

A Solidarity Fund, financed by contributions from affiliated organizations, supports the development and practice of democratic trade unionism world-wide and assists workers and trade unionists victimized by repressive political measures.

Associated Global Union Secretariats

Building and Wood Workers International (BWI): 54 route des Acacias, 1227 Carouge, Switzerland; tel. 228273777; fax 228273770; e-mail info@bwint.org; internet www.bwint.org; f. 2005 by merger of International Federation of Building and Woodworkers (f. 1934) and World Federation of Building and Wood Workers (f. 1936); mems: 313 national unions with a membership of more than 12m. workers in 127 countries; organization: Congress, World Council, World Board; Pres. KLAUS WIESEHÜGEL (Germany); Sec.-Gen. ANITA NORMARK (Sweden); publ. *BWI Online on the web* (daily).

Education International (EI): 5 blvd du Roi Albert II, 1210 Brussels, Belgium; tel. (2) 224-06-06; fax (2) 224-06-06; e-mail info@ei-ie.org; internet www.ei-ie.org; f. 1993; the fmr World Confederation of Teachers (f. 1962) merged with EI in 2006; aims to represent the causes of teachers and education employees and to promote the development of education; mems: 348 organizations representing 29m. teachers and education workers in 166 countries; Pres. THULUS NXESI (South Africa); Gen. Sec. FRED VAN LEEUWEN (Netherlands).

International Federation of Chemical, Energy, Mine and General Workers' Unions (ICEM): 109 ave Emile de Béco, B-1050 Brussels, Belgium; tel. (2) 626-20-20; fax (2) 648-43-16; e-mail info@icem.org; internet www.icem.org; f. 1995 by merger of the International Federation of Chemical, Energy and General Workers' Unions (f. 1907) and the Miners' International Federation (f. 1890); mems: 389 trade unions covering approximately 20m. workers in 122 countries; main sectors cover energy industries; chemicals; pharmaceuticals and biotechnology; mining and extraction; pulp and paper; rubber; ceramics; glass; building materials; and environmental services; Pres. SENZENI ZOKWANA; Gen. Sec. FRED HIGGS (until 31 Dec. 2007), MANFRED WARDA (Germany) (designate); publs *ICEM Info* (quarterly), *ICEM Focus on Health, Safety and Environment* (2 a year), *ICEM Update* Irregular.

International Federation of Journalists (IFJ): International Press Centre, 155 rue de la Loi, 1040 Brussels, Belgium; tel. (2) 235-22-00; fax (2) 235-22-19; e-mail ifj@ifj.org; internet www.ifj.org; f. 1952 to link national unions of professional journalists dedicated to the freedom of the press, to defend the rights of journalists, and to raise professional standards; it conducts surveys, assists in trade union training programmes, organizes seminars and provides information; it arranges fact-finding missions in countries where press freedom is under pressure, and issues protests against the persecution and detention of journalists and the censorship of the mass media; holds Congress every three years (May–June 2007: Moscow, Russia); mems: 147 unions in 106 countries, comprising 450,000 individuals; Pres. CHRISTOPHER WARREN (Australia); Gen. Sec. AIDAN WHITE (United Kingdom); publ. *IFJ Direct Line* every two months.

International Metalworkers' Federation (IMF): 54 bis, route des Acacias, CP 1516, 1227 Geneva, Switzerland; tel. 223085050; fax 223085055; e-mail info@imfmetal.org; internet www.imfmetal.org; f. 1893; mems: national orgs covering 24.8m. workers in 207 unions in 101 countries; holds Congress every four years; has six regional offices; seven industrial departments; World Company Councils for unions in multinational corporations; Pres. JÜRGEN PETERS (Germany); Gen. Sec. MARCELLO MALENTACCHI; publs *IMF News Briefs* (weekly), *Metal World* (quarterly).

International Textile, Garment and Leather Workers' Federation (ITGLWF): rue Joseph Stevens 8 (boîte 4), 1000 Brussels, Belgium; tel. (2) 512-26-06; fax (2) 511-09-04; e-mail office@itglwf.org; internet www.itglwf.org; f. 1970; mems: 220 unions covering 10m. workers in 110 countries; holds Congress every four years: (Oct. 2004: Istanbul, Turkey); Pres. MANFRED SCHALLMEYER (Germany); Gen. Sec. NEIL KEARNEY (Ireland); publ. *ITGLWF Newsletter* (quarterly).

International Transport Workers' Federation (ITF): 49–60 Borough Rd, London, SE1 1DR, United Kingdom; tel. (20) 7403-2733; fax (20) 7357-7871; e-mail mail@itf.org.uk; internet www.itfglobal.org; f. 1896; mems: national trade unions covering 5m. workers in 604 unions in 137 countries; holds Congress every four years; has eight Industrial Sections; Pres. RANDALL HOWARD (USA); Gen. Sec. DAVID COCKROFT (United Kingdom); publ. *Transport International* (quarterly).

International Union of Food, Agricultural, Hotel, Restaurant, Catering, Tobacco and Allied Workers' Associations (IUF): 8 rampe du Pont-Rouge, 1213 Petit-Lancy, Switzerland; tel. 227932233; fax 227932238; e-mail iuf@iuf.org; internet www.iuf.org; f. 1920; mems: 336 affiliated organizations covering about 12m. workers in 120 countries; holds Congress every five years; Pres. GARY NEBEKER (USA); Gen. Sec. TOMOJI MISATO; publs bi-monthly bulletins.

Public Services International (PSI): 45 ave Voltaire, BP9, 01211 Ferney-Voltaire Cédex, France; tel. 4-50-40-64-64; fax 4-50-40-73-20; e-mail psi@world-psi.org; internet www.world-psi.org; f. 1907; mems: 620 unions and professional associations covering 20m. workers in 154 countries; holds Congress every five years (Sept. 2007: Vienna, Austria); Pres. YLVA THÖRN (Sweden); Gen. Sec. PETER WALDORFF (Denmark); publ. *Focus* (quarterly).

Union Network International (UNI): ave Reverdil 8–10, 1260 Nyon, Switzerland; tel. 223652100; fax 223652121; e-mail contact@union-network.org; internet www.union-network.org; f. 2000 by merger of Communications International (CI), the International Federation of Commercial, Clerical, Professional and Technical Employees (FIET), the International Graphical Federation (IGF), and Media and Entertainment International (MEI); mems: 900 unions in more than 140 countries, representing 15.5m. people; activities cover the following 12 sectors: commerce; electricity; finance; graphical; hair and beauty; professional and information technology staff; media, entertainment and the arts; postal; property services; social insurance and private health care; telecommunications; and tourism; first World Congress convened in Berlin, Germany, in September 2001; third World Congress scheduled to be held in Nagasaki, Japan in 2010; Pres. JOE HANSEN (USA); Gen. Sec. PHILIP J. JENNINGS (United Kingdom); publs *UNIinfo* (quarterly), *UNInet News* (monthly).

INTER-PARLIAMENTARY UNION—IPU

Address: 5 chemin du Pommier, CP 330, 1218 Le Grand Saconnex/Geneva, Switzerland.
Telephone: 229194150; **fax:** 229194160; **e-mail:** postbox@mail.ipu.org; **internet:** www.ipu.org.

Founded in 1889, the IPU aims to promote peace, co-operation and representative democracy by providing a forum for multilateral political debate between representatives of national parliaments.

MEMBERS

National parliaments of 146 sovereign states; seven international parliamentary associations (associate members). Most member states are affiliated to one of six geopolitical groupings, known as the African, Arab, Asia-Pacific, Eurasia, Latin American and '12-Plus' (European) groups.

Organization
(April 2008)

ASSEMBLY

The Assembly (formerly known as the Inter-Parliamentary Conference and renamed in April 2003) is the main statutory body of the IPU, comprising eight to 10 representatives from each member parliament. It meets twice a year to discuss current issues in world affairs and to make political recommendations. Other specialized meetings of parliamentarians may also be held, on a global or regional basis. The Assembly is assisted by the following three plenary Standing Committees: on Peace and International Security; Sustainable Development, Finance and Trade; and Democracy and Human Rights.

GOVERNING COUNCIL

The Governing Council (formerly the Inter-Parliamentary Council, renamed in April 2003) comprises two representatives of each member parliament, usually from different political groups. It is responsible for approving membership and the annual programme and budget of the IPU, and for electing the Secretary-General. The Council may consider substantive issues and adopt resolutions and policy statements, in particular on the basis of recommendations from its subsidiary bodies.

President: PIER FERDINANDO CASINI (Italy).

MEETING OF WOMEN PARLIAMENTARIANS

The Meeting is a mechanism for co-ordination between women parliamentarians. Since 1975 the Meeting has been convened twice a year, on the occasion of IPU statutory meetings, to discuss subjects of common interest, to formulate strategies to develop the IPU's women's programme, to strengthen their influence within the organization and to ensure that women are elected to key positions. The Meeting is assisted by a Co-ordinating Committee.

SUBSIDIARY BODIES

In addition to the thematic Standing Committees of the IPU Assembly, various other committees and groups undertake and co-ordinate IPU activities in specific areas. The following bodies are subsidiary to the IPU Council:

Standing Committee on Peace and International Security;

Standing Committee on Sustainable Development, Finance and Trade;

Standing Committee on Democracy and Human Rights;

Committee on the Human Rights of Parliamentarians;

Committee on Middle East Questions;

Committee on United Nations Affairs;

Group of Facilitators for Cyprus;

Ad Hoc Committee to Promote Respect for International Humanitarian Law;

Co-ordinating Committee of the Meeting of Women MPs;

Gender Partnership Group.

The Association of Secretaries-General of Parliaments (ASGP), an autonomous, self-managing body that meets during the IPU Assembly, has consultative status at the IPU.

EXECUTIVE COMMITTEE

The Committee, comprising 17 members and presided over by the President of the Council, oversees the administration of the IPU and advises the Council on membership, policy and programme, and any other matters referred to it.

SECRETARIAT

Secretary-General: ANDERS B. JOHNSSON (Sweden).

Activities

PROMOTION OF REPRESENTATIVE DEMOCRACY

This is one of the IPU's core areas of activity, and covers a wide range of concerns, such as democracy, gender issues, human rights and ethnic diversity, parliamentary action to combat corruption, and links between democracy and economic growth. The IPU sets standards and guide-lines, provides technical assistance for strengthening national representative institutions, promotes human rights and the protection of members of parliament, supports partnership between men and women in politics, and promotes knowledge of the functioning of national parliaments. In September 1997 the Council adopted a Universal Declaration on Democracy. The IPU subsequently published a study entitled *Democracy: Its Principles and Achievements*. The IPU aims to establish a Parliamentary Resource Centre at its headquarters.

The IPU aims to improve knowledge of the functioning of national parliaments by gathering and disseminating information on their constitutional powers and responsibilities, structure, and membership, and on the electoral systems used. The IPU also organizes international seminars and gatherings for parliamentarians, officials, academics and other experts to study the functioning of parliamentary institutions. A Technical Co-operation Programme aims to mobilize international support in order to improve the capabilities, infrastructure and technical facilities of national parliaments and enhance their effectiveness. Under the Programme, the IPU may provide expert advice on the structure of legislative bodies, staff training, and parliamentary working procedures, and provide technical equipment and other resources.

In 1993 the Council resolved that the IPU be present at all national elections organized, supervised or verified by the United Nations. The IPU has reported on the rights and responsibilities of election observers and issued guide-lines on the holding of free and fair elections. These include the 1994 *Declaration on Criteria for Free and Fair Elections*, a study entitled *Free and Fair Elections* (initially published in 1994, and re-issued in a new, expanded version in 2006), and Codes of Conduct for Elections. In November 2004, to commemorate the 10th anniversary of the *Declaration*, the IPU organized an international round table on electoral standards. In January 2005 IPU observers world-wide monitored the expatriate vote in the elections for the Transitional National Assembly in Iraq.

The IPU maintains a special database (PARLINE) on parliaments of the world, giving access to information on the structure and functioning of all existing parliaments, and on national elections. It conducts regular world studies on matters regarding the structure and functioning of parliaments. It also maintains a separate database (PARLIT) comprising literature from around the world on constitutional, electoral and parliamentary matters.

In August–September 2000 the IPU organized the first international conference of presiding officers of national parliaments. The second speakers' conference took place in September 2005.

INTERNATIONAL PEACE AND SECURITY

The IPU aims to promote conflict resolution and international security through political discussion. Certain areas of conflict are monitored by the Union on an ongoing basis (for example, Cyprus and the Middle East), while others are considered as they arise. In the 1990s the IPU was particularly concerned with the situation in the former Yugoslavia, and condemned incidents of violations of humanitarian law and supported efforts to improve the lives of those affected by the conflict. A meeting in July 2003 of Israeli and Palestinian parliamentarians agreed to establish an Israeli-Palestinian parliamentary working group on co-operation. In April 2003 the 108th Inter-Parliamentary Conference adopted a resolution urging an end to the unilateral military action against Iraq launched in March by a US-led coalition. The resolution also emphasized the importance of international law and urged full co-operation with the United Nations. In October 2004 the Assembly discussed an emergency item on the need for parliamentary action to restore peace and security in Iraq. An extensive programme of activities is undertaken by the IPU with regard to the Mediterranean region. In June 1992 the first Conference on Security and Co-operation in the Mediterranean (CSCM) took place; the objectives outlined at the Conference were integrated as a structured process of the IPU. A second CSCM was held in Valletta, Malta, in November 1995, and a third was convened at Marseilles, France, in March–April 2000. In February 2005 participants attending the fourth CSCM, held in Nafplion, Greece, agreed to terminate the process and establish in its place a Parliamentary Assembly of the Mediterranean. The IPU was to provide secretariat support to the new Parliamentary Assembly pending the establishment of its headquarters. The inaugural session of the Assembly was convened in Amman, Jordan in September 2006.

The IPU has worked constantly to promote international and regional efforts towards disarmament, as part of the process of enhancing peace and security. Issues that have been discussed by the Assembly include nuclear non-proliferation, a ban on testing of nuclear weapons, and a global register of arms transfers.

SUSTAINABLE DEVELOPMENT

The Standing Committee for Sustainable Development, Finance and Trade guides the IPU's work in this area, with a broad approach of linking economic growth with social, democratic, human welfare and environmental considerations. Issues of world economic and social development on which the IPU has approved recommendations include employment in a globalizing world, the globalization of economy and liberalization of trade, Third World debt and its impact on the integration of those countries affected into the process of globalization, international mass migration and other demographic problems, and the right to food. The IPU co-operates with programmes and agencies of the UN, in particular in the preparation of major socio-economic conferences, including the World Summit for Social Development, which was held in Copenhagen, Denmark, in March 1995, the Fourth World Conference on Women, held in Beijing, People's Republic of China, in September 1995, and the World Food Summit, held in Rome, Italy, in November 1996. In September 1996 a tripartite meeting of parliamentary, governmental and inter-governmental representatives, convened at the UN headquarters in New York, considered legislative measures to pursue the objectives of the World Summit for Social Development; a follow-up meeting was held in March 1999. In November–December 1998 the IPU, in co-operation with FAO, organized an Inter-Parliamentary Conference concerned with 'Attaining the World Food Summit's Objectives through a Sustainable Development Strategy'. The IPU assisted with preparations for the World Food Summit: Five Years Later, held in Rome, Italy, in June 2002. The IPU and the European Parliament jointly organize an annual parliamentary conference on the WTO, which addresses issues including access to markets, the development dimension of the multilateral trading system, agriculture and subsidies. The conference aims to add a parliamentary dimension to multilateral co-operation on trade matters and thereby to enhance the transparency of the WTO's activities and to strengthen democracy at international level. The most recent session was held in Geneva, Switzerland, in December 2006.

Activities to protect the environment are undertaken within the framework of sustainable development. In 1984 the first Inter-Parliamentary Conference on the Environment, convened in Nairobi, Kenya, advocated the inclusion of environmental considerations into the development process. The IPU was actively involved in the preparation of the UN Conference on Environment and Development (UNCED), which was held in Rio de Janeiro, Brazil, in June 1992. Subsequently the IPU's environment programme has focused on implementing the recommendations of UNCED, and identifying measures to be taken at parliamentary level to facilitate that process. The IPU also monitors the actual measures taken by national parliaments to pursue the objective of sustainable development, as well as emerging environmental problems. In 1997 the IPU published the *World Directory of Parliamentary Bodies for Environment*. In April 2005 the Assembly held an emergency debate on the role of parliaments in the prevention of natural disasters and the protection of vulnerable groups.

In November 2007 the IPU, in co-operation with UNDP, UNAIDS and the Philippines legislature, convened the first Global Parliamentary Meeting on HIV/AIDS, at which participating parliamentary representatives addressed the role of national legislatures in responding to the HIV/AIDS pandemic.

The IPU and UNDP concluded a comprehensive MOU in November 2007 aimed at expanding mutual co-operation in support of world-wide democratic governance; future areas of co-operation were to cover national budgetary processes; and parliamentary activities aimed at advancing the achievement of the UN Millennium Goals and at implementing UN treaties and conventions, and strategies aimed at poverty reduction and the empowerment of women.

HUMAN RIGHTS AND HUMANITARIAN LAW

The IPU aims to incorporate human rights concerns, including employment, the rights of minorities, and gender issues, in all areas of activity. The Assembly and specialized meetings of parliamentarians frequently consider and make relevant recommendations on human rights issues. A five-member Committee on the Human Rights of Parliamentarians is responsible for the consideration of complaints relating to alleged violations of the human rights of members of parliament, for example state harassment, arbitrary arrest and detention, unfair trail and violation of parliamentary immunity, based on a procedure adopted by the IPU in 1976, when the Committee was established. The Committee conducts hearings and site missions to investigate a complaint and communicates with the authorities of the country concerned. If no settlement is reached at that stage, the Committee may then publish a report for the Governing Council and submit recommendations on specific measures to be adopted. In early 2008 the Committee was addressing 34 cases of allegations of human rights violations against 200 current or former members of parliament.

The IPU works closely with the International Committee of the Red Cross to uphold respect for international humanitarian law (IHL). It supports the implementation of the Geneva Conventions and their Additional Protocols, and the adoption of appropriate national legislation. In 1995 the Council adopted a special resolution to establish a reporting mechanism at the parliamentary level to ensure respect for IHL. Consequently IPU initiated a world survey on legislative action regarding the application of IHL, as well as efforts to ban anti-personnel land-mines. In April and September 1998 the Council adopted special resolutions on parliamentary action to secure the entry into force and implementation of the Convention on the Prohibition of the Use, Stockpiling, Production and Transfer of Anti-personnel Mines and on their Destruction, which was signed by representatives of some 120 countries meeting in Ottawa, Canada, in December 1997. Further resolutions to that effect were adopted by the Inter-Parliamentary Conference in October 1999 and in April 2001.

In February 2008 the IPU and UNODC jointly organized a Parliamentary Forum on Human Trafficking, convened in Vienna, Austria, in the context of the global Vienna Forum to Fight Human Trafficking.

In 2004 the IPU published the most recent edition of its *World Directory of Parliamentary Human Rights Bodies*.

WOMEN IN POLITICS

The IPU aims to promote the participation of women in the political and parliamentary decision-making processes, and, more generally, in all aspects of society. It organizes debates and events on these issues and maintains an online statistical database on women in politics, compiled by regular world surveys, as well as a women in politics bibliographic database. The IPU also actively addresses wider issues of concern to women, such as literacy and education, women in armed conflicts, women's contribution to development, and women in the electoral process. The eradication of violence against women was the subject of a special resolution adopted by the Conference in 1991. The Meeting of Women MPs has monitored efforts by national authorities to implement the recommendations outlined in the resolution. In 1996 the IPU promoted the Framework for Model Legislation on Domestic Violence, formulated by the UN Special Rapporteur on the issue, which aimed to assist national parliaments in preparing legislation to safeguard women. At the Fourth World Conference on Women, held in Beijing, in September 1995, the IPU organized several events to bring together parliamentarians and other leading experts, diplomats and officials to promote the rights of women and of children. In February 1997 the IPU organized a Specialized Inter-Parliamentary Conference, in New Delhi, India, entitled 'Towards partnership between men and women in politics'. Following the Conference the IPU established a Gender Partnership Group, comprising two men and two women, within the Executive Committee, to ensure that IPU activities and decisions serve the interests and needs of all members of the population. The Group was authorized to report to the IPU Council.

The IPU aims to promote the importance of women's role in economic and social development and their participation in politics as a democratic necessity, and recognizes the crucial role of the media in presenting the image of women. Within the context of the 1997 New Delhi Conference, the IPU organized a second Round Table on the Image of Women Politicians in the Media (the first having been convened in November 1989). The debate urged fair and equal representation of women politicians by the media and for governments to revise their communications policies to advance the image of female parliamentarians.

In March 2007 IPU, jointly with UNDP, UNIFEM and other partners, launched the International Knowledge Network of Women in Politics (iKNOW Politics), an online workspace aimed at supporting government officials, researchers, etc., in achieving the objective of advancing female participation in politics.

EDUCATION, SCIENCE AND CULTURE

Activities in these sectors are often subject to consideration by statutory meetings of the Assembly. Assembly resolutions have focused on the implementation of educational and cultural policies designed to foster greater respect for demographic values, adopted in April 1993; on bioethics and its implications world-wide for human rights protection, adopted in April 1995; and on the importance of education and culture as prerequisites for securing sustainable development (with particular emphasis on the education of women and the application of new information technologies), necessitating their high priority status in national budgets, adopted in April 2001. Specialized meetings organized by the IPU have included the Asia and Pacific Inter-Parliamentary Conference on 'Science and technology for regional sustainable development', held in Tokyo, Japan, in June 1994, and the Inter-Parliamentary Conference on 'Education, science, culture and communication on the threshold of the 21st century', organized jointly with UNESCO, and held in Paris, France, in June 1996. In October 2003 the IPU and UNESCO launched a network of national focal points linking the IPU's member parliaments and UNESCO, with the aim of circulating information and improving co-operation in the area of education, science, culture and communications.

In November 2006, the IPU and the UN Department of Economic and Social Affairs inaugurated the Rome, Italy-based Global Centre for Information and Communication Technologies in Parliament. The Centre, whose establishment was endorsed at the World Summit of the Information Society held in November 2005 in Tunis, Tunisia, is mandated to act as a clearing house for information, research, innovation, technology and technical assistance, and to promote a structured dialogue among parliaments, centres of excellence, international organizations, civil society, private sector interests, and international donors.

In October 2007 IPU, in conjunction with the UN Department for Economic and Social Affairs and the Association of Secretaries-General of Parliament, with support from the Global Centre for ICT in Parliament, convened the first World e-Parliament Conference, with participation by members of parliament, parliamentary officials, academics, and representatives of international organizations and of civil society. The e-Conference aimed to identify best practices in the use of new technologies to modernize parliamentary processes and communications. In February 2008 the IPU issued the first World e-Parliament Report.

Finance

The IPU is financed by its members from public funds. The 2007 annual budget totalled 17.5m. Swiss francs. In addition external financial support, primarily from UNDP, is received for some special activities.

Publications

Activities of the Inter-Parliamentary Union (annually).
Chronicle of Parliamentary Elections (annually).
Free and Fair Elections.
IPU Information Brochure (annually).
World Directory of Parliamentary Human Rights Bodies.
World Directory of Parliaments (annually).
World e-Parliament Report.
The World of Parliaments (quarterly).
Other handbooks, reports and surveys, documents, proceedings of the Assembly.

ISLAMIC DEVELOPMENT BANK

Address: POB 5925, Jeddah 21432, Saudi Arabia.
Telephone: (2) 6361400; **fax:** (2) 6366871; **e-mail:** idbarchives@isdb.org; **internet:** www.isdb.org.

The Bank was established following a conference of Ministers of Finance of member countries of the Organization of the Islamic Conference (OIC), held in Jeddah in December 1973. Its aim is to encourage the economic development and social progress of member countries and of Muslim communities in non-member countries, in accordance with the principles of the Islamic *Shari'a* (sacred law). The Bank formally opened in October 1975. The Bank and its associated entities—the Islamic Research and Training Institute, the Islamic Corporation for the Development of the Private Sector, the Islamic Corporation for the Insurance of Investment and Export Credit, and the International Islamic Trade Finance Corporation—constitute the Islamic Development Bank Group.

MEMBERS

There are 56 members.

Organization

(April 2008)

BOARD OF GOVERNORS

Each member country is represented by a governor, usually its Minister of Finance, and an alternate. The Board of Governors is the supreme authority of the Bank, and meets annually. The 32nd meeting was convened in Dakar, Senegal, in May 2007.

BOARD OF EXECUTIVE DIRECTORS

The Board consists of 14 members, seven of whom are appointed by the seven largest subscribers to the capital stock of the Bank; the remaining seven are elected by Governors representing the other subscribers. Members of the Board of Executive Directors are elected for three-year terms. The Board is responsible for the direction of the general operations of the Bank.

ADMINISTRATION

In addition to the President of the Bank, there are three Vice-Presidents, responsible for Operations, Trade and Policy, and Corporate Resources and Services.

President of the Bank and Chairman of the Board of Executive Directors: Dr AHMAD MOHAMED ALI (Saudi Arabia).

Vice-President Operations: Dr AMADOU BOUBACAR CISSE (Niger).

Vice-President Trade and Policy: Dr SYED JAAFAR AZNAN (Malaysia).

Vice-President Corporate Resources and Services: Dr SYED JAAFAR AZNAN (Malaysia) (acting).

REGIONAL OFFICES

Kazakhstan: 050000 Almaty, Aiteki Bi Street 67; tel. (727) 272-70-00; fax (727) 250-13-02; e-mail idb_roa@nursat.kz; Dir NIK ZEINAL ABIDIN.

Malaysia: Menara Bank Pembangunan Bandar Wawasan, Level 13, Jalan Sultan Ismail, 50250 Kuala Lumpur; tel. (3) 26946627; fax (3) 26946626; e-mail ROKL@isdb.org; Dir AHMAD SALEH HARIRI.

Morocco: Km 6.4, Ave Imam Malik Route des Zaers, POB 5003, Rabat; tel. (37) 757191; fax (37) 775726; Dir SIDI MOHAMED OULD TALEB.

FINANCIAL STRUCTURE

The Bank's unit of account is the Islamic Dinar (ID), which is equivalent to the value of one Special Drawing Right (SDR) of the IMF (average value in 2006 SDR 1 = US $1.50440). In May 2006 the Bank's Board of Governors approved an increase in the authorized capital from ID 15,000m. to ID 30,000m. At January 2007 total subscriptions amounted to ID 13,217.68m.

SUBSCRIPTIONS

(million Islamic Dinars, as at 19 January 2007)

Country	Amount	Country	Amount
Afghanistan	9.93	Maldives	4.96
Albania	9.24	Mali	18.19
Algeria	459.22	Mauritania	9.77
Azerbaijan	9.77	Morocco	91.69
Bahrain	25.88	Mozambique	9.23
Bangladesh	182.16	Niger	24.63
Benin	18.19	Nigeria	4.65
Brunei	24.63	Oman	50.92
Burkina Faso	24.63	Pakistan	459.21
Cameroon	45.85	Palestine	19.55
Chad	9.77	Qatar	97.73
Comoros	2.50	Saudi Arabia	3,685.13
Côte d'Ivoire	4.65	Senegal	45.89
Djibouti	4.96	Sierra Leone	4.96
Egypt	686.84	Somalia	4.96
Gabon	54.58	Sudan	72.77
The Gambia	9.24	Suriname	4.96
Guinea	45.85	Syria	18.49
Guinea-Bissau	4.96	Tajikistan	4.96
Indonesia	406.49	Togo	4.96
Iran	1,293.34	Tunisia	19.55
Iraq	25.91	Turkey	1,165.86
Jordan	73.50	Turkmenistan	4.96
Kazakhstan	19.28	Uganda	187.75
Kuwait	985.88	United Arab Emirates	882.84
Kyrgyzstan	4.96	Uzbekistan	2.50
Lebanon	9.77	Yemen	92.38
Libya	1,478.24		
Malaysia	294.01		

Activities

The Bank adheres to the Islamic principle forbidding usury, and does not grant loans or credits for interest. Instead, its methods of project financing are: provision of interest-free loans, mainly for infrastructural projects which are expected to have a marked impact on long-term socio-economic development; provision of technical assistance (e.g. for feasibility studies); equity participation in industrial and agricultural projects; leasing operations, involving the leasing of equipment such as ships, and instalment sale financing; and profit-sharing operations. Funds not immediately needed for projects are used for foreign trade financing. Under the Import Trade Financing Operations (ITFO) scheme, funds are used for importing commodities for development purposes (i.e. raw materials and intermediate industrial goods, rather than consumer goods), with priority given to the import of goods from other member countries. The Export Financing Scheme (EFS), established as the Longer-term Trade Financing Scheme in 1987/88, aims to provide financing for the export of non-traditional and capital goods. A special programme under the EFS became operational in AH 1419, on the basis of a memorandum of understanding signed between the Bank and the Arab Bank for Economic Development in Africa (BADEA), to finance Arab exports to non-Arab League members of the OAU (now African Union). In AH 1424 the Bank adopted a new group strategic framework, which identified three principal objectives: the promotion of Islamic financial industry and institutions; poverty alleviation; and the promotion of co-operation among member countries. To achieve these objectives, the Bank determined the following as priority areas of activity: human development; agricultural development and food security; infrastructure development; intra-trade among member countries; private sector development; and research and development in Islamic economics, banking and finance.

The Bank's Special Assistance Programme was initiated in AH 1400 to support the economic and social development of Muslim communities in non-member countries, in particular in the education and health sectors. It also aimed to provide emergency aid in times of natural disasters, and to assist Muslim refugees throughout the world. Operations undertaken by the Bank are financed by the Waqf Fund (formerly the Special Assistance Account). By the end of AH 1427 some US $615m. had been approved under the Waqf Fund Special Assistance Programme for 1,129 operations, of which 439 were in member countries and 690 were for Muslim organizations and communities in non-member countries. Other assistance activities include scholarship programmes, technical co-operation projects and the sacrificial meat utilization project. In January 2005 the Bank allocated $500m. to assist the survivors of the Indian

Ocean earthquake and tsunami which struck coastal areas in 14 countries in late December 2004. The Bank dispatched missions to provide emergency relief to Indonesia, the Maldives and Sri Lanka, and planned to send further teams to assess the requirements for reconstruction. The Bank approved an assistance programme amounting to $501.6m. following a massive earthquake in north-west Pakistan that occurred in October 2005. The funds aimed to support recovery, rehabilitation and reconstruction efforts. The Bank increasingly has worked to assist post-conflict member countries in rehabilitation and reconstruction. It is a member of the management committee of the Afghanistan Reconstruction Trust Fund, which was established in 2001; during 2003 the Bank approved an operation to assist Afghan refugees. In December 2003 the Bank approved a Programme for Reconstruction of Iraq, with funding of ID 365.5m. ($500m.) to be implemented over a five-year period. In October 2002 the Bank's Board of Governors, meeting in Burkina Faso, adopted the Ouagadougou Declaration on the co-operation between the Bank group and Africa, which identified priority areas for Bank activities, for example education and the private sector. The Bank pledged $2,000m. to finance implementation of the Declaration over the five years 2004–08.

By 19 January 2007 the Bank had approved a total of ID 13,162.4m. for project financing and technical assistance since operations began in 1976, ID 20,254.1m. for foreign trade financing, and ID 484.0m. for special assistance operations, excluding amounts for cancelled operations. During the Islamic year 1427 (31 January 2006 to 19 January 2007) the Bank approved a net total of ID 3,508.3m., for 361 operations.

The Bank approved 40 loans in the Islamic Year 1427, amounting to ID 280.8m. These loans supported projects concerned with the education and health sectors, infrastructural improvements, and agricultural developments. During that year the Bank's total disbursements totalled ID 1,589.1m., bringing the total cumulative disbursements since the Bank began operations to ID 23,613.7m. The Bank approved 62 technical assistance operations during that year in the form of grants and loans, amounting to ID 10.8m.

Import trade financing approved during the Islamic year 1427 amounted to ID 1,435.0m. for 75 operations. By the end of that year cumulative import trade financing amounted to ID 15,950.9m., of which 39% was for imports of crude petroleum, 25% for intermediate industrial goods and 9% for refined petroleum products. During AH 1427 the Bank's export financing scheme was formally dissolved, although continued to fund projects pending the commencement of operations of the International Islamic Trade Finance Corporation (ITFC, see below). At the end of that year total export financing approved under the scheme amounted to ID 1,183.4m. for 217 operations. The Bank also finances other trade financing operations, including the Islamic Corporation for the Development of the Private Sector (see below), the Awqaf Properties Investment Fund and the Treasury Department. In addition, a Trade Co-operation and Promotion Programme supports efforts to enhance trade among OIC member countries. In June 2005 the Board of Governors approved the establishment of the ITFC as an autonomous trade promotion and financing institution within the Bank Group. The inaugural meeting of the ITFC was held in February 2007. In May 2006 the Board of Governors approved a new fund to reduce poverty and support efforts to achieve the UN Millennium Development Goals, in accordance with a proposal of the Organization of the Islamic Conference. It was inaugurated, as the Islamic Solidarity Fund for Development, in May 2007; at that time 28 countries had pledged $1,600m. to the Fund. The Fund became operational in early 2008.

In AH 1407 (1986–87) the Bank established an Islamic Bank's Portfolio for Investment and Development (IBP) in order to promote the development and diversification of Islamic financial markets and to mobilize the liquidity available to banks and financial institutions. During AH 1427 the IBP approved eight operations amounting to ID 135.8m. The Bank's Unit Investment Fund (UIF) became operational in 1990, with the aim of mobilizing additional resources and providing a profitable channel for investments conforming to *Shari'a*. The initial issue of the UIF was US $100m., which has subsequently been increased to $325m. The Fund finances mainly private-sector industrial projects in middle-income countries and also finances short-term trade operations. In October 1998 the Bank announced the establishment of a new fund to invest in infrastructure projects in member states. The Bank committed $250m. to the fund, which was to comprise $1,000m. equity capital and a $500m. Islamic financing facility. In November 2001 the Bank signed an agreement with Malaysia, Bahrain, Indonesia and Sudan for the establishment of an Islamic financial market. In April 2002 the Bank, jointly with governors of central banks and the Accounting and Auditing Organization for Islamic Financial Institutions, concluded an agreement, under the auspices of the IMF, for the establishment of an Islamic Financial Services Board. The Board, which was to be located in Kuala Lumpur, Malaysia, was intended to elaborate and harmonize standards for best practices in the regulation and supervision of the Islamic financial services industry. In August 2003 the Bank mobilized some $400m. from the international financial markets through the issue of the International Islamic Sukuk bond.

In AH 1404 (1983–84) the Bank established a scholarship programme for Muslim communities in non-member countries to provide opportunities for students to pursue further education or other professional training. The programme also assists nine member countries on an exceptional basis. By the end of the Islamic year 1427 the programme had benefited some 7,450 students, at a cost of ID 46.52m., from 58 countries. The Merit Scholarship Programme, initiated in AH 1412 (1991–92), aims to develop scientific, technological and research capacities in member countries through advanced studies and/or research. A total of 346 scholarships had been awarded, at a cost of ID 10.0m., by the end of AH 1427. In AH 1419 (1998–99) a Scholarship Programme in Science and Technology for IDB Least Developed Member Countries became operational for students in 20 eligible countries. By the end of AH 1427 183 students had been selected under the programme to study in other Bank member countries. of whom 77 had graduated under the Programme.

The Bank's Programme for Technical Co-operation aims to mobilize technical capabilities among member countries and to promote the exchange of expertise, experience and skills through expert missions, training, seminars and workshops. In December 1999 the Board of Executive Directors approved two technical assistance grants to support a programme for the eradication of illiteracy in the Islamic world, and one for self-sufficiency in human vaccine production. The Bank also undertakes the distribution of meat sacrificed by Muslim pilgrims. The Bank was the principal source of funding of the International Center for Biosaline Agriculture, which was established in Dubai, UAE, in September 1999.

BANK GROUP ENTITIES

International Islamic Trade Finance Corporation: Jeddah, Saudia Arabia; f. 2007; aims to promote trade and trade financing in Bank member countries, to facilitate access to public and private capital, and to promote investment opportunities; auth. cap. US $3,000m.; subs. cap. $750m.; CEO Dr WALID AL WOHAIB.

Islamic Corporation for the Development of the Private Sector: POB 54069, Jeddah 21514, Saudi Arabia; tel. (2) 6441644; fax (2) 6444427; e-mail icd@isdb.org; internet www.icd-idb.org; f. 1999; to identify opportunities in the private sector, provide financial products and services compatible with Islamic law, mobilize additional resources for the private sector in member countries, and encourage the development of Islamic financing and capital markets; the Bank's share of the capital is 50%, member countries 30% and public financial institutions of member countries 20%; p.u. cap. US $282.2m. (Jan. 2006); mems: 44 countries, the Bank, and five public financial institutions (a further seven countries have signed the Articles of Agreement and are in the process of ratification); CEO and Gen. Man. KHALID M. AL-ABOODI.

Islamic Corporation for the Insurance of Investment and Export Credit (ICIEC): POB 15722, Jeddah 21454, Saudi Arabia; tel. (2) 6445666; fax (2) 6379504; e-mail idb.iciec@isdb.org.sa; internet www.iciec.com; f. 1994; aims to promote trade and the flow of investments among member countries of the OIC through the provision of export credit and investment insurance services; auth. cap. ID 100m., subscribed cap. ID 97.24m., p.u. cap. ID 72.74m. (Jan. 2007); mems: 35 member states and the Islamic Development Bank (which contributes 50% of its capital); Gen. Man. Dr ABDEL RAHMAN A. TAHA.

Islamic Research and Training Institute: POB 9201, Jeddah 21413, Saudi Arabia; tel. (2) 6361400; fax (2) 6378927; e-mail irti@isdb.org; internet www.irti.org; f. 1982 to undertake research enabling economic, financial and banking activities to conform to Islamic law, and to provide training for staff involved in development activities in the Bank's member countries; the Institute also organizes seminars and workshops, and holds training courses aimed at furthering the expertise of government and financial officials in Islamic developing countries; Acting Dir BASHIR ALI KHALLAT; publs *Annual Report*, *Islamic Economic Studies* (2 a year), various research studies, monographs, reports.

Publication

Annual Report.

Statistics

OPERATIONS APPROVED, ISLAMIC YEAR 1427
(31 January 2006–19 January 2007)

Type of operation	Number of operations	Total amount (million Islamic Dinars)
Total project financing	181	1,490.0
Project financing	119	1,479.3
Technical assistance	62	10.8
Trade financing operations*	133	2,005.6
Special assistance operations	47	12.6
Total†	361	3,508.3

* Including ITFO, the EFS, the Islamic Bank's Portfolio, the UIF, and the Awqaf Properties Investment Fund.
† Excluding cancelled operations.

DISTRIBUTION OF PROJECT FINANCING AND TECHNICAL ASSISTANCE BY SECTOR, ISLAMIC YEAR 1427
(31 January 2006–19 January 2007)

Sector	Number of operations	Amount (million Islamic Dinars)	%
Agriculture and agro-industry	19	87.2	7.7
Industry and mining	6	145.4	12.9
Transport and communications	19	306.4	27.1
Public utilities	26	328.7	29.1
Social sectors	49	252.5	22.4
Financial services/Other	21	9.3	0.8
Total†	140	1,129.4	100.0

† Excluding cancelled operations.

LATIN AMERICAN INTEGRATION ASSOCIATION—LAIA
(ASOCIACIÓN LATINOAMERICANA DE INTEGRACIÓN—ALADI)

Address: Cebollatí 1461, Casilla 20.005, 11200 Montevideo, Uruguay.
Telephone: (2) 410-1121; **fax:** (2) 419-0649; **e-mail:** sgaladi@aladi.org; **internet:** www.aladi.org.

The Latin American Integration Association was established in August 1980 to replace the Latin American Free Trade Association, founded in February 1960.

MEMBERS

Argentina	Colombia	Paraguay
Bolivia	Cuba	Peru
Brazil	Ecuador	Uruguay
Chile	Mexico	Venezuela

Observers: People's Republic of China, Costa Rica, Dominican Republic, El Salvador, Guatemala, Honduras, Italy, Japan, Republic of Korea, Nicaragua, Panama, Portugal, Romania, Russia, Spain, Switzerland and Ukraine; also the UN Economic Commission for Latin America and the Caribbean (ECLAC), the UN Development Programme (UNDP), the European Union, the Inter-American Development Bank, the Organization of American States, the Andean Development Corporation, the Inter-American Institute for Co-operation on Agriculture, the Latin American Economic System, and the Pan American Health Organization/World Health Organization.

Organization
(April 2008)

COUNCIL OF MINISTERS

The Council of Ministers of Foreign Affairs is responsible for the adoption of the Association's policies. It meets when convened by the Committee of Representatives.

CONFERENCE OF EVALUATION AND CONVERGENCE

The Conference, comprising plenipotentiaries of the member governments, assesses the integration process and encourages negotiations between members. It also promotes the convergence of agreements and other actions on economic integration. The Conference meets when convened by the Committee of Representatives.

COMMITTEE OF REPRESENTATIVES

The Committee, the permanent political body of the Association, comprises a permanent and a deputy representative from each member country. Permanent observers have been accredited by 15 countries and eight international organizations (see above). The Committee is the main forum for the negotiation of ALADI's initiatives and is responsible for the correct implementation of the Treaty and its supplementary regulations. There are the following auxiliary bodies:

Advisory Commission for Financial and Monetary Affairs.
Advisory Commission on Customs Valuation.
Advisory Council for Enterprises.
Advisory Council for Export Financing.
Advisory Council for Customs Matters.
Budget Commission.
Commission for Technical Support and Co-operation.
Council for Financial and Monetary Affairs: comprises the Presidents of member states' central banks, who examine all aspects of financial, monetary and exchange co-operation.
Council of National Customs Directors.
Council on Transport for Trade Facilitation.
Labour Advisory Council.
Nomenclature Advisory Commission.
Sectoral Councils.
Tourism Council.

GENERAL SECRETARIAT

The General Secretariat is the technical body of the Association; it submits proposals for action, carries out research and evaluates activities. The Secretary-General is elected for a three-year term, which is renewable. There are two Assistant Secretaries-General.

Secretary-General: JOSÉ RIVERA BANUET (Mexico) (acting).

Activities

The Latin American Free Trade Association (LAFTA) was an intergovernmental organization, created by the Treaty of Montevideo in February 1960 with the object of increasing trade between the Contracting Parties and of promoting regional integration, thus contributing to the economic and social development of the member countries. The Treaty provided for the gradual establishment of a free trade area, which would form the basis for a Latin American Common Market. Reduction of tariff and other trade barriers was to be carried out gradually until 1980.

By 1980, however, only 14% of annual trade among members could be attributed to LAFTA agreements. In June it was decided that LAFTA should be replaced by a less ambitious and more flexible organization, the Latin American Integration Association (Asociación Latinoamericana de Integración—ALADI), established by the 1980 Montevideo Treaty, which came into force in March 1981, and was fully ratified in March 1982. The Treaty envisaged an area of economic preferences, comprising a regional tariff preference for goods originating in member states (in effect from 1 July 1984) and regional and partial scope agreements (on economic complementation, trade promotion, trade in agricultural goods, scientific and technical co-operation, the environment, tourism, and other matters), taking into account the different stages of development of the members, and with no definite timetable for the establishment of a full common market.

The members of ALADI are divided into three categories: most developed (Argentina, Brazil and Mexico); intermediate (Chile, Colombia, Peru, Uruguay and Venezuela); and least developed (Bolivia, Cuba—which joined the Association in August 1999—Ecuador and Paraguay), enjoying a special preferential system. By 2007 intra-ALADI exports were estimated to total US $94,410m., an increase of almost 20% compared with the previous year.

Certain LAFTA institutions were retained and adapted by ALADI, e.g. the Reciprocal Payments and Credits Agreement (1965, modified in 1982) and the Multilateral Credit Agreement to Alleviate Temporary Shortages of Liquidity, known as the Santo Domingo Agreement (1969, extended in 1981 to include mechanisms for counteracting global balance of payments difficulties and for assisting in times of natural disaster).

By August 1998 98 agreements had entered into force. Seven were 'regional agreements' (in which all member countries participate). These agreements included a regional tariff preference agreement, whereby members allow imports from other member states to enter with tariffs 20% lower than those imposed on imports from other countries, and a Market Opening Lists agreement in favour of the three least developed member states, which provides for the total elimination of duties and other restrictions on imports of certain products. The remaining 91 agreements were 'partial scope agreements' (in which two or more member states participate), including: renegotiation agreements (pertaining to tariff cuts under LAFTA); trade agreements covering particular industrial sectors; the agreements establishing the Southern Common Market (Mercosur) and the Group of Three (G3); and agreements covering agriculture, gas supply, tourism, environmental protection, books, transport, sanitation and trade facilitation. A new system of tariff nomenclature, based on the 'harmonized system', was adopted from 1 January 1990 as a basis for common trade negotiations and statistics. General regimes on safeguards and rules of origin entered into force in 1987.

The Secretariat convenes meetings of entrepreneurs in various private industrial sectors, to encourage regional trade and co-operation. In early 2001 ALADI conducted a survey on small and medium-sized enterprises in order to advise the Secretary-General in formulating a programme to assist those businesses and enhance their competitiveness.

ALADI has worked to establish multilateral links or agreements with Latin American non-member countries or integration organizations, and with other developing countries or economic groups outside the continent. In February 1994 the Council of Ministers of Foreign Affairs urged that ALADI should become the co-ordinating body for the various bilateral, multilateral and regional accords (with the Andean Community, Mercosur and G3, etc.), with the aim of eventually forming a region-wide common market. The General Secretariat initiated studies in preparation for a programme to undertake this co-ordinating work. At the same meeting in February there was a serious disagreement regarding the proposed adoption of a protocol to the Montevideo Treaty to enable Mexico to participate in the North American Free Trade Agreement (NAFTA), while remaining a member of ALADI. Brazil, in particular, opposed such a solution. However, in June the first Interpretative Protocol to the Montevideo Treaty was signed by the Ministers of Foreign Affairs: the Protocol allows member states to establish preferential trade agreements with developed nations, with a temporary waiver of the most-favoured nation clause, subject to the negotiation of unilateral compensation.

Mercosur (comprising Argentina, Brazil, Paraguay and Uruguay) aims to conclude free trade agreements with the other members of ALADI. In March 2001 ALADI signed a co-operation agreement with the Andean Community to facilitate the exchange of information and consolidate regional and subregional integration. In December 2003 Mercosur and the Andean Community signed an Economic Complementary Agreement, and in April 2004 concluded a free trade agreement, to come into effect on 1 July 2004 (although later postponed). Those ALADI member states remaining outside Mercosur and the Andean Community—Cuba, Chile and Mexico—would be permitted to apply to join the envisaged larger free trade zone. In December 2004 leaders from 12 Latin American countries attending a pan-South American summit, convened in Cusco, Peru, approved in principle the creation of a new South American Community of Nations (SACN). In April 2005 the ALADI Secretary-General attended the first joint meeting of ministers of foreign affairs convened within the framework of establishing the SACN. In April 2007, at the first South American Energy Summit, convened in Margarita Island, Venezuela, heads of state endorsed the establishment of a Union of South American Nations (UNASUR), to replace SACN as the lead organization for regional integration. UNASUR was anticipated to have political decision-making functions, supported by a small permanent secretariat, to be located in Quito, Ecuador, and was to co-ordinate on economic and trade matters with Mercosur, the Andean Community and ALADI.

Publications

Empresarios en la Integración (monthly, in Spanish).
Noticias ALADI (monthly, in Spanish).
Estadísticas y Comercio (quarterly, in Spanish).
Reports, studies, brochures, texts of agreements.

LEAGUE OF ARAB STATES

Address: POB 11642, Arab League Bldg, Tahrir Sq., Cairo, Egypt.
Telephone: (2) 575-0511; **fax:** (2) 574-0331; **internet:** www.arableagueonline.org/.

The League of Arab States (more generally known as the Arab League) is a voluntary association of sovereign Arab states, designed to strengthen the close ties linking them and to co-ordinate their policies and activities and direct them towards the common good of all the Arab countries. It was founded in March 1945.

MEMBERS

Algeria	Lebanon	Somalia
Bahrain	Libya*	Sudan
Comoros	Mauritania	Syria
Djibouti	Morocco	Tunisia
Egypt	Oman	United Arab
Iraq	Palestine†	Emirates
Jordan	Qatar	Yemen
Kuwait	Saudi Arabia	

* In October 2002 Libya announced that it was to withdraw from the League.
† Palestine is considered an independent state, and therefore a full member of the League.

Organization
(April 2008)

COUNCIL

The supreme organ of the Arab League, the Council consists of representatives of the member states, each of which has one vote, and a representative for Palestine. The Council meets ordinarily every March, normally at the League headquarters, at the level of heads of state ('kings, heads of state and emirs'), and in March and September at the level of foreign ministers. The summit-level meeting reviews all issues related to Arab national security strategies, co-ordinates supreme policies of the Arab states towards regional and international issues, reviews recommendations and reports submitted to it by meetings at foreign minister level, appoints the Secretary-General of the League, and is mandated to amend the League's Charter. Decisions of the summit-level Council are passed on a consensus basis. Foreign ministers' meetings assess the implementation of summit resolutions, prepare relevant reports, and make arrangements for subsequent summits. Committees comprising a smaller group of foreign ministers may be appointed to follow up closely summit resolutions. Extraordinary summit-level meetings may be held at the request of one member state or the Secretary-General, if approved by a two-thirds' majority of member states. Extraordinary sessions of ministers of foreign affairs may be held at the request of two member states or of the Secretary-General. The presidency of ordinary meetings is rotated in accordance with the alphabetical order of the League's member states. Unanimous decisions of the Council are binding upon all member states of the League; majority decisions are binding only on those states which have accepted them.

The Council is supported by technical and specialized committees advising on financial and administrative affairs, information affairs and legal affairs. In addition, specialized ministerial councils have been established to formulate common policies for the regulation and the advancement of co-operation in the following sectors: communications; electricity; environment; health; housing and construction; information; interior; justice; social affairs; tourism; transportation; and youth and sports.

GENERAL SECRETARIAT

The administrative and financial offices of the League. The Secretariat carries out the decisions of the Council, and provides financial and administrative services for the personnel of the League. General departments comprise: the Bureau of the Secretary-General, Arab Affairs, Economic Affairs, Information Affairs, Legal Affairs, Palestine Affairs, Political International Affairs, Military Affairs, Social Affairs, Administrative and Financial Affairs, and Internal Audit. In addition, there is a Documentation and Information Centre, an Arab League Centre in Tunis, Tunisia, an Arab Fund for Technical Assistance in African States, a Higher Arab Institute for Translation in Algiers, Algeria, a Music Academy in Baghdad, Iraq, and a Special Bureau for Boycotting Israel, based in Damascus, Syria (see below). The following bodies have also been established: an administrative court, an investment arbitration board and a higher auditing board.

The Secretary-General is appointed at summit meetings of the Council by a two-thirds' majority of the member states, for a five-year, renewable term. He appoints the Assistant Secretaries-General and principal officials, with the approval of the Council. He has the rank of ambassador, and the Assistant Secretaries-General have the rank of ministers plenipotentiary.

Secretary-General: AMR MUHAMMAD MOUSSA (Egypt).

DEFENCE AND ECONOMIC CO-OPERATION

Groups established under the Treaty of Joint Defence and Economic Co-operation, concluded in 1950 to complement the Charter of the League.

Arab Unified Military Command: f. 1964 to co-ordinate military policies for the liberation of Palestine.

Economic and Social Council: compares and co-ordinates the economic policies of the member states; supervises the activities of the Arab League's specialized agencies. The Council is composed of ministers of economic affairs or their deputies; decisions are taken by majority vote. The first meeting was held in 1953. In February 1997 the Economic and Social Council adopted the Executive Programme of the League's (1981) Agreement to Facilitate and Develop Trade Among Arab Countries, with a view to establishing a Greater Arab Free Trade Area (see below).

Joint Defence Council: supervises implementation of those aspects of the treaty concerned with common defence. Composed of foreign and defence ministers; decisions by a two-thirds' majority vote of members are binding on all.

Permanent Military Commission: f. 1950; composed of representatives of army general staffs; main purpose: to draw up plans of joint defence for submission to the Joint Defence Council.

ARAB DETERRENT FORCE

Created in June 1976 by the Arab League Council to supervise successive attempts to cease hostilities in Lebanon, and afterwards to maintain the peace. The mandate of the Force has been successively renewed. The Arab League summit conference in October 1976 agreed that costs were to be paid in the following percentage contributions: Saudi Arabia and Kuwait 20% each, the United Arab Emirates 15%, Qatar 10% and other Arab states 35%.

PARLIAMENT

Inaugurated in December 2005, in Cairo, the Parliament comprises 88 members (four delegates from each Arab state, including some representing non-elected bodies). It has no legislative function and aims to encourage co-operation between member states.

OTHER INSTITUTIONS OF THE LEAGUE

Other bodies established by resolutions adopted by the Council of the League:

Administrative Tribunal of the Arab League: f. 1964; began operations 1966.

Arab Fund for Technical Assistance to African Countries: f. 1975 to provide technical assistance for development projects by providing African and Arab experts, grants for scholarships and training, and finance for technical studies.

Higher Auditing Board: comprises representatives of seven member states, elected every three years; undertakes financial and administrative auditing duties.

Investment Arbitration Board: examines disputes between member states relating to capital investments.

Special Bureau for Boycotting Israel: POB 437, Damascus, Syria; f. 1951 to prevent trade between Arab countries and Israel, and to enforce a boycott by Arab countries of companies outside the region that conduct trade with Israel.

SPECIALIZED AGENCIES

All member states of the Arab League are also members of the Specialized Agencies, which constitute an integral part of the Arab League. (See also entries on Arab Fund for Economic and Social Development, the Arab Monetary Fund, Council of Arab Economic Unity and the Organization of Arab Petroleum Exporting Countries.)

Arab Academy for Science, Technology and Maritime Transport (AASTMT): POB 1029, Alexandria, Egypt; tel. (3) 5622388; fax (3) 5622366; internet www.aast.edu; f. 1975 as Arab Maritime Transport Academy; provides specialized training in marine transport, engineering, technology and management; Pres. MOHAMED FARGHALY; publs *Maritime Research Bulletin* (monthly), *Journal of the Arab Academy for Science, Technology and Maritime Transport* (2 a year).

Arab Administrative Development Organization (ARADO): 2 El Hegaz St, POB 2692 al-Horreia, Heliopolis, Cairo, Egypt; tel. (2) 22580006; fax (2) 22580077; e-mail arado@arado.org.eg; internet www.arado.org.eg; f. 1961 (as Arab Organization of Administrative Sciences), became operational in 1969; administration development, training, consultancy, research and studies, information, documentation; promotes Arab and international co-operation in administrative sciences; includes Arab Network of Administrative Information; 20 Arab state members; library of 26,000 volumes, 400 periodicals; Dir-Gen. Prof. REFAT ABDELHALIM ALFAOURI; publs *Arab Journal of Administration* (biannual), *Management Newsletter* (quarterly), research series, training manuals.

Arab Atomic Energy Agency (AAEA): POB 402, al-Manzah 1004, 1004 Tunis, Tunisia; tel. (71) 800099; fax (71) 781820; e-mail aaea@gnet.tn; f. 1988 to co-ordinate research into the peaceful uses of atomic energy; Dir-Gen. Prof. Dr MAHMOUD NASREDDIN (Lebanon); publs *The Atom and Development* (quarterly), other publs in the field of nuclear sciences and their applications in industry, biology, medicine, agriculture, food irradiation and seawater desalination.

Arab Bank for Economic Development in Africa (Banque arabe pour le développement économique en Afrique—BADEA): Sayed Abd ar-Rahman el-Mahdi St, POB 2640, Khartoum 11111, Sudan; tel. (1) 83773646; fax (1) 83770600; e-mail badea@badea.org; internet www.badea.org; f. 1973 by Arab League; provides loans and grants to African countries to finance development projects; paid-up cap. US $2,200m. (Dec. 2006); in 2006 the Bank approved loans and grants totalling $163.8m. and technical assistance for feasibility studies and institutional support amounting to $6.3m.; by the end of 2006, total loan and grant commitments approved since funding activities began in 1975 amounted to $2,960.3m.; subscribing countries: all countries of Arab League, except the Comoros, Djibouti, Somalia and Yemen; recipient countries: all countries of the African Union, except those belonging to the Arab League; Chair. AHMAD ABDALLAH AL-AKEIL (Saudi Arabia); Dir-Gen. ABDELAZIZ KHELEF (Algeria); publs *Annual Report Co-operation for Development* (quarterly), studies on Afro-Arab co-operation, periodic brochures.

Arab Centre for the Study of Arid Zones and Dry Lands (ACSAD): POB 2440, Damascus, Syria; tel. (11) 5743039; fax (11) 5743063; e-mail email@acsad.org; internet www.acsad.org; f. 1968 to conduct regional research and development programmes related to water and soil resources, plant and animal production, agro-meteorology, and socio-economic studies of arid zones; the Centre holds conferences and training courses and encourages the exchange of information by Arab scientists; Dir-Gen. NOURA IMAM.

Arab Industrial Development and Mining Organization: rue France, Zanagat al-Khatawat, POB 8019, Rabat, Morocco; tel. (37) 772600; fax (37) 772188; e-mail aidmo@arifonet.org.ma; internet www.arifonet.org.ma; f. 1990 by merger of Arab Industrial Development Organization, Arab Organization for Mineral Resources and Arab Organization for Standardization and Metrology; comprises a 13-member Executive Council, a High Consultative Committee of Standardization, a High Committee of Mineral Resources and a Co-ordination Committee for Arab Industrial Research Centres; a Council of ministers of member states responsible for industry meets every two years; Dir-Gen. TALA'AT BEN DAFER; publs *Arab Industrial Development* (monthly and quarterly newsletters).

Arab Labour Organization: POB 814, Cairo, Egypt; tel. (2) 3362721; fax (2) 3484902; internet www.alolabor.org; f. 1965 for co-operation between member states in labour problems; unification of labour legislation and general conditions of work wherever possible; research; technical assistance; social insurance; training, etc; the organization has a tripartite structure: governments, employers and workers; Dir-Gen. IBRAHIM GUDIR; publs *ALO Bulletin* (monthly), *Arab Labour Review* (quarterly), *Legislative Bulletin* (annually), series of research reports and studies concerned with economic and social development issues in the Arab world.

Arab League Educational, Cultural and Scientific Organization (ALECSO): ave Mohamed V, POB 1120, Tunis, Tunisia; tel. (71) 784-466; fax (71) 784-496; e-mail alecso@email.ati.tn; internet www.alecso.org.tn; f. 1970 to promote and co-ordinate educational, cultural and scientific activities in the Arab region; 21 mem. states; regional units: Arab Centre for Arabization, Translation, Authorship, and Publication—Damascus, Syria; Institute of Arab Manuscripts—Cairo, Egypt; Institute of Arab Research and Studies—Cairo, Egypt; Khartoum International Institute for Arabic Language—Khartoum, Sudan; and the Arabization Co-ordination Bureau—Rabat, Morocco; Dir-Gen. Dr MONGI BOUSNINA; publs *Arab Journal of Culture* (2 a year), *Arab Journal of Education* (2 a year), *Arab Journal of Science and Information* (2 a year), *Arab Bulletin of Publications* (annually), *ALECSO Newsletter* (monthly).

Arab Organization for Agricultural Development (AOAD): 7 al-Amarat St, POB 474, Khartoum 11111, Sudan; tel. (1) 83472176; fax (1) 83471402; e-mail info@aoad.org; internet www.aoad.org; f. 1970; began operations in 1972 to contribute to co-operation in agricultural activities, and in the development of natural and human resources for agriculture; compiles data, conducts studies, training and food security programmes; includes Information and Documentation Centre, Arab Centre for Studies and Projects, and Arab Institute of Forestry and Biodiversity; Dir-Gen. Dr SALEM AL-LOZI; publs *Agricultural Statistics Yearbook*, *Annual Report on Agricultural Development*, *The State of Arab Food Security* (annually), *Agriculture and Development in the Arab World* (quarterly), *Accession Bulletin* (every 2 months), *AOAD Newsletter* (monthly), *Arab Agricultural Research Journal*, *Arab Journal for Irrigation Water Management* (2 a year).

Arab Satellite Communications Organization (ARABSAT): POB 1038, Diplomatic Quarter, Riyadh 11431, Saudi Arabia; tel. (1) 4820000; fax (1) 4887999; e-mail info@arabsat.com; internet www.arabsat.com; f. 1976; regional satellite telecommunications organization providing television, telephone and data exchange services to members and private users; operates five satellites, which cover all Arab and Western European countries; Dir-Gen. KHALID AHMED BALKHEYOUR.

Arab States Broadcasting Union (ASBU): POB 250, 1080 Tunis Cedex; 6 rue des Entrepreneurs, zone industrielle Charguia 2, Ariana Aéroport, Tunisia; tel. (71) 849000; fax (71) 843054; e-mail asbu@asbu.intl.tn; internet www.asbu.net; f. 1969 to promote Arab fraternity, co-ordinate and study broadcasting subjects, to exchange expertise and technical co-operation in broadcasting; conducts training and audience research; 21 active mems, four participating mems, five assoc. mems; Pres. of Exec. Council HAMRAWI HABIB CHAWKI (Algeria); publ. *Arab Broadcasters* (quarterly).

Inter-Arab Investment Guarantee Corporation: POB 23568, Safat 13096, Kuwait; tel. 4959000; fax 4841240; e-mail info@iai.org.kw; internet www.iaigc.org; f. 1975; insures Arab investors for non-commercial risks, and export credits for commercial and non-commercial risks; undertakes research and other activities to promote inter-Arab trade and investment; cap. p.u. c. US $150m., res $146m. (Aug. 2006); mems: all Arab countries except the Comoros; Dir-Gen. FAHAD RASHID AL-IBRAHIM; publs *News Bulletin* (quarterly), *Arab Investment Climate Report* (annually).

ARAB LEAGUE OFFICES AND INFORMATION CENTRES ABROAD

Established by the Arab League to co-ordinate work at all levels among Arab embassies abroad.

Austria: Schwarzenbergplatz 6, 1030 Vienna; tel. (1) 5130767; fax (1) 5126644; e-mail arab.league.vienna@aon.at; Head of Mission MECHAIL WAHBA.

Belgium: 28 ave de l'Uruguay, 1000 Brussels; tel. (2) 675-88-22; fax (2) 660-36-25; e-mail ligue.etats.arabes@skynet.be; Head of Mission MOHAMMED EZ-ZAAF.

China, People's Republic: 1-14-2 Lian Ma He Nan, Tayuan Diplomatic Building, Beijing 100600; tel. (10) 65324083; fax (10) 65324082; e-mail lasj@a-1.net.cn; Head of Mission Dr MOHAMMED FOUAD SRRRI.

Ethiopia: Permanent Mission of the League of Arab States to the African Union and the Economic Commission for Africa, POB 5768, Addis Ababa; tel. (11) 52635350; fax (11) 635181; e-mail last@ethionet.et; Head of Mission MOHAMED MAHMOUD WEDDADY.

France: 36 rue Fortuny, 75017 Paris; tel. 1-43-80-61-50; fax 1-48-88-91-71; e-mail leap@pelnet.com; Head of Mission Dr NASSIF HETTI.

Germany: Markgrafenstr. 25, Ecke Schutzenstr., 10117 Berlin; tel. (30) 20622890; fax (30) 20455672; Ambassador SALEM EL-QUATEEN.

India: D-47 Anand Niketan, New Delhi 110021; tel. (11) 24675672; fax (11) 24675582; e-mail leagueofarab@hotmail.com; Head of Mission ZABYAH EL-MEHERY.

Italy: Via Nomentana 133, 00161 Rome; tel. (06) 44249994; fax (06) 4404482; e-mail arshif@legaaraba.org; Head of Mission Mohamed el-Hassan SHABBO.

Russia: 123242 Moscow, ul. Konyushkovskaya 28; tel. (495) 253-92-70; fax (495) 253-99-60; e-mail medgasmi2002@yahoo.fr; Head of Mission JUMAA IBRAHIM AL-FARJANI.

Spain: Paseo de la Castellana 180, 60°, 28046 Madrid; tel. (91) 3507516; fax (91) 3507910; e-mail liga.arabe@terra.es; Head of Mission MOHAMMED AN-NASSERY.

Switzerland: 9 rue du Valais, 1202 Geneva; tel. 227323030; fax 227316947; e-mail saad.alfarargi@ties.itu.int; Ambassador SAAD AL-FARARGI.

United Kingdom: 52 Green St, London, W1K 6RS; tel. (20) 7629-0044; fax (20) 7493-7943; e-mail las@jamia-uk.demon.co.uk; Head of Mission Dr ADEL BABESAIL.

USA: 1100 17th St, NW, Suite 602, Washington, DC 20036; 747 Third Ave, 35th Floor, New York, NY 10017 (UN Office); tel. (202) 2653210; fax (202) 3311525; tel. (212) 8388700; fax (212) 3553909; e-mail arableague@aol.com; Ambassador HUSSEIN HASSONA.

Activities

The League of Arab States was founded in 1945 with the signing of the Pact of the Arab League. A Cultural Treaty was signed in the following year. In 1952, agreements were concluded on extradition, writs, letters of request and the nationality of Arabs outside their country of origin, and in the following year a Convention was adopted on the privileges and immunities of the League. In 1954, a Nationality Agreement was concluded. At an emergency summit meeting held in 1985, two commissions were established to mediate in disagreements between Arab states (between Jordan and Syria, Iraq and Syria, Iraq and Libya, and Libya and the Palestine Liberation Organization (PLO). The League's headquarters, which had been transferred from Cairo, Egypt, to Tunis, Tunisia, in 1979, were relocated to Cairo in 1990. In 1993, the Council of the League admitted the Comoros as the League's 22nd member. At a meeting of the Council held in September 2000, foreign ministers of member states adopted an Appendix to the League's Charter that provided for the Council to meet ordinarily every March at the level of a summit conference of heads of state ('kings, heads of state and emirs'). The Council was to continue to meet at foreign ministerial level every March and September. In 2001 Amr Moussa, hitherto Egypt's minister of foreign affairs, was appointed as the League's new Secretary-General. In October 2002 Libya announced plans to withdraw from the League, although these were subsequently suspended. In April 2003 Libya reiterated its decision to terminate its membership, citing the organization's failure to take 'a firm and strong position' over the war in Iraq. (Libya's move, however, did not yet represent an official demand, one year after which, under the terms of the League's Charter, its withdrawal would become effective.) In July the Egyptian Government unveiled a series of measures aimed at strengthening the League. The proposed reforms included the adoption of majority voting and the establishment of a body to resolve conflicts in the region (previously agreed at the 1996 summit and sanctioned by member states' foreign ministers in 2000). The plan, which was supported by Saudi Arabia and Jordan, was to be presented to the next summit conference. The 2004 summit meeting of Arab League heads of state, scheduled to be held in Tunis in late March, was postponed by the Tunisian Government two days in advance following disagreements among member states over a number of issues on the summit's agenda, including democratic reforms in Arab states and the proposed reforms to the League. The meeting, which was eventually held in May in Tunis, approved a *Pledge of Accord and Solidarity* that committed the League heads of state to implementing in full decisions of the League. The Arab leaders also stated their commitment to conducting political, economic and social reforms, respect for human rights, and to strengthening the role of women, despite continuing opposition from several member states. The 2005 heads of state summit meeting, convened in Algiers, Algeria, in mid-March, commemorated the 60th anniversary of the League's foundation. The 2006 summit, convened in Khartoum, Sudan, in late March, extended Amr Moussa's term of office as Secretary-General for a further five years. The summit meeting of heads of state held in Riyadh, Saudi Arabia, in March 2007, determined that in future Arab consultative summits should be convoked when deemed necessary to address specific issues.

SECURITY

In 1950 Arab League member states concluded a Joint Defence and Economic Co-operation Treaty. In 1995 the Council discussed plans for a regional court of justice and for an Arab Code of Honour to prevent the use of force in disputes between Arab states. In April 1998 Arab League ministers of the interior and of justice adopted the Arab Convention for the Suppression of Terrorism, which incorporated security and judicial measures, such as extradition arrangements and the exchange of evidence. The agreement was to enter into effect 30 days after being ratified by at least seven member countries. (This was achieved in May 2000.) In August 1998 the League denounced terrorist bomb attacks against the US embassies in Kenya and Tanzania. Nevertheless, it condemned US retaliatory military action, a few days later, against suspected terrorist targets in Afghanistan and Sudan, and endorsed a request by the Sudanese Government that the Security Council investigate the incident. An emergency meeting of the League's Council, convened in mid-September 2001 in response to major terrorist attacks on the USA, perpetrated by militant Islamist fundamentalists, condemned the atrocities, while urging respect for the rights of Arab and Muslim US citizens. The Secretary-General subsequently emphasized the need for co-ordinated global anti-terrorist action to have clearly defined goals and to be based on sufficient consultations and secure evidence. He also deplored anti-Islamic prejudice, stated that US-led action against any Arab state would not be supported and that Israeli participation in an international anti-terrorism alliance would be unacceptable. A meeting of League foreign ministers in Doha, Qatar, in early October condemned international terrorism but did not express support for retaliatory military action by the USA and its allies. In December a further emergency meeting of League foreign affairs ministers was held to discuss the deepening Middle East crisis. In January 2002 the League appointed a commissioner responsible for promoting dialogue between civilizations. The commissioner was mandated to encourage understanding in Western countries of Arab and Muslim civilization and viewpoints, with the aim of redressing perceived negative stereotypes (especially in view of the Islamist fundamentalist connection to the September 2001 terrorist atrocities). In early April 2003 the Secretary-General expressed his regret that the Arab states had failed to prevent the ongoing war in Iraq, and urged the development of a new regional security order. In November the UN Secretary-General, Kofi Annan, appointed the Secretary-General of the League to serve as the Arab region's representative on the UN High-Level Panel on Threats, Challenges and Change. In March 2007 the League's summit meeting resolved to establish an expert-level task force to consider national security issues.

TRADE AND ECONOMIC CO-OPERATION

In 1953 Arab League member states formed an Economic and Social Council. In 1956 an agreement was concluded on the adoption of a Common Tariff Nomenclature. In 1962 an Arab Economic Unity Agreement was concluded. The first meeting of the Council of Arab Economic Unity took place in June 1964. An Arab Common Market Agreement was endorsed by the Council in August. In February 1997 the Economic and Social Council adopted the Executive Programme of the (1981) Agreement to Facilitate and Develop Trade Among Arab Countries, with a view to creating a Greater Arab Free Trade Area (GAFTA), which aimed to facilitate and develop trade among participating countries through the reduction and eventual elimination of customs duties over a 10-year period (at a rate of 10% per year), with effect from January 1998. In February 2002 the Economic and Social Council agreed to bring forward the inauguration of GAFTA to 1 January 2005. Consequently customs duties, which, according to schedule, had been reduced by 50% from January 1998–January 2002, were further reduced by 10% by January 2003, 20% by January 2004, and a final 20% by January 2005. GAFTA entered into force, as planned, with 17 participating countries (accounting for about 94% of the total volume of intra-Arab trade). The Council agreed to supervise the implementation of the free-trade agenda and formally to review its progress twice a year.

WATER RESOURCES

In April 1993 the Council approved the creation of a committee to consider the political and security aspects of water supply in Arab countries. In March 1996, following protests by Syria and Iraq that extensive construction work in southern Turkey was restricting water supply in the region, the Council determined that the waters of the Euphrates and Tigris rivers be shared equitably between the three countries. In April an emergency meeting of the Council issued a further endorsement of Syria's position in the dispute with Turkey.

ARAB–ISRAELI AFFAIRS

In 1964 the second summit conference of Arab heads of state welcomed the establishment of the PLO. The fifth summit conference, held in 1969, issued a call for the mobilization of all Arab nations against Israel. In 1977, by the so-called Tripoli Declaration, Algeria, Iraq, Libya and the People's Democratic Republic of Yemen decided to boycott meetings of the Arab League held in Egypt in response to a visit by President Sadat of Egypt to Israel. In 1979 a meeting of the League's Council resolved to withdraw Arab ambassadors from Egypt; to recommend severance of political and diplomatic relations with Egypt; to suspend Egypt's membership of the League on the date of the signing of its formal peace treaty with Israel (26 March); to transfer the headquarters of the League to Tunis; to condemn US policy regarding its role in concluding the Camp David agreements (in September 1978) and the peace treaty; to halt all bank loans, deposits, guarantees or facilities, as well as all financial or technical contributions and aid to Egypt; and to prohibit trade exchanges with the Egyptian state and with private establishments dealing with Israel.

In November 1981 the 12th summit conference of the Arab League was suspended owing to disagreement over a Saudi Arabian proposal, known as the Fahd Plan, which included not only the Arab demands on behalf of the Palestinians, as approved by the UN General Assembly, but also an implied *de facto* recognition of Israel. In September 1982 the 12th summit conference was reconvened. It adopted a peace plan, which demanded Israel's withdrawal from territories occupied in 1967, and removal of Israeli settlements in these areas; freedom of worship for all religions in the sacred places; the right of the Palestinian people to self-determination, under the leadership of the PLO; temporary supervision for the West Bank and the Gaza Strip; the creation of an independent Palestinian state, with Jerusalem as its capital; and a guarantee of peace for the states of the region by the UN Security Council.

In 1983 a summit meeting of the League due to be held in November was postponed owing to members' differences of opinion concerning Syria's opposition to Yasser Arafat's chairmanship of the PLO, and Syrian support for Iran in the war against Iraq. In July 1986 King Hassan of Morocco announced that he was resigning as chairman of the next League summit conference, after criticism by several Arab leaders of his meeting with the Israeli Prime Minister earlier that month. A ministerial meeting held in October condemned any attempt at direct negotiation with Israel. In November 1987 an extraordinary summit conference stated, *inter alia*, that the resumption of diplomatic relations with Egypt was a matter to be decided by individual states. In June 1988 a summit conference agreed to provide finance for the PLO to continue the Palestinian uprising in Israeli-occupied territories. It reiterated a demand for a peaceful settlement in the Middle East (thereby implicitly rejecting recent proposals by the US Government for a conference that would exclude the PLO). At a summit conference held in May 1989 Egypt was readmitted to the League. The conference expressed support for the then chairman of the PLO, Yasser Arafat, in his recent peace proposals made before the UN General Assembly, and reiterated the League's support for proposals that an international conference should be convened to discuss the rights of Palestinians: in so doing, it accepted UN Security Council Resolutions 242 and 338 on a peaceful settlement in the Middle East and thus gave tacit recognition to the State of Israel. The meeting also supported Arafat in rejecting Israeli proposals for elections in the Israeli-occupied territories of the West Bank and the Gaza Strip.

In September 1991, in spite of deep divisions between Arab League member states, it was agreed that a committee should be formed to co-ordinate Arab positions in preparation for the US-sponsored peace talks between Arab countries and Israel. (In the event an ad hoc meeting, attended by Egypt, Jordan, Syria, the PLO, Saudi Arabia—representing the Gulf Co-operation Council (GCC)—and Morocco—representing the Union of the Arab Maghreb—was held in October, prior to the start of the talks.) In April 1993 the League pledged its commitment to the Middle East peace talks. Following the signing of the Israeli-PLO peace accord in September the Council convened in emergency session, at which it approved the agreement, despite opposition from some members, notably Syria. In November it was announced that the League's boycott of commercial activity with Israel was to be maintained. In 1994 the League condemned a decision of the GCC, announced in late September, to end the secondary and tertiary trade embargo against Israel, by which member states refuse to trade with international companies that have investments in Israel. A statement issued by the League insisted that the embargo could be removed only on the decision of the Council.

In March 1995 Arab ministers of foreign affairs approved a resolution urging Israel to renew the Nuclear Non-Proliferation Treaty (NPT). The resolution stipulated that failure by Israel to do so would cause Arab states to seek to protect legitimate Arab interests by alternative means. In May an extraordinary session of the Council condemned a decision by Israel to confiscate Arab-owned land in East Jerusalem for resettlement. The Israeli Government announced the suspension of its expropriation plans. In April 1996 an emergency meeting of the Council was convened at the request of Palestine, in order to attract international attention to the problem of radiation from an Israeli nuclear reactor. The Council requested an immediate technical inspection of the site by the UN, and further demanded that Israel be obliged to sign the NPT to ensure the eradication of its nuclear weaponry.

In June 1996 an extraordinary summit conference of Arab League heads of state was convened, the first since 1990, in order to formulate a united Arab response to the election, in May, of a new government in Israel and to the prospects for peace in the Middle East. The conference (from which Iraq was excluded from the meeting in order to ensure the attendance of the Gulf member states) urged Israel to honour its undertaking to withdraw from the Occupied Territories, including Jerusalem, and to respect the establishment of an independent Palestinian state, in order to ensure the success of the peace process. A final communiqué of the meeting warned that Israeli co-operation was essential to prevent Arab states from reconsidering their participation in the peace process and the re-emergence of regional tensions. In September the League met in emergency session following an escalation of civil unrest in Jerusalem and the Occupied Territories. The League urged the UN Security Council to prevent further alleged Israeli aggression against the Palestinians. In November the League criticized Israel's settlement policy, and at the beginning of December convened in emergency session to consider measures to end any expansion of the Jewish population in the West Bank and Gaza. In March 1997 the Council met in emergency session in response to the Israeli Government's decision to proceed with construction of a new settlement at Har Homa (Jabal Abu-Ghunaim) in East Jerusalem. The Council pledged its commitment to seeking a reversal of the decision and urged the international community to support this aim. At the end of March ministers of foreign affairs of Arab League states agreed to end all efforts to secure normal diplomatic relations with Israel (although binding agreements already in force with Egypt, Jordan and Palestine were exempt) and to close diplomatic offices and missions while construction work continued in East Jerusalem. In September 1997 ministers of foreign affairs of member states voted to pursue the decision, adopted in March, not to strengthen relations with Israel. Several countries urged a formal boycott of the forthcoming Middle East and North Africa conference, in protest at the lack of progress in the peace process (for which the League blamed Israel, which was due to participate in the conference). However, the meeting upheld a request by the Qatari Government, the host of the conference, that each member should decide individually whether to attend. In the event, only seven Arab League member countries participated in the conference, which was held in Doha in mid-November, while the Secretary-General of the League decided not to attend as the organization's official representative.

A meeting of the Council in March 1998, attended by ministers of foreign affairs of 16 of the League's member states, rejected Israel's proposal to withdraw from southern Lebanon, which was conditional on the deployment by the Lebanese Government of extra troops to secure Israeli territory from attack, and, additionally, urged international support to secure Israel's withdrawal from the Golan Heights. Among items concluded by the Council at its meeting in September were condemnation of Turkey's military co-operation with Israel and a request that the UN dispatch a fact-finding mission to examine conditions in the Israeli-occupied territories and alleged violations of Palestinian property rights.

In March 1999 a meeting of the League's Council expressed support for a UN resolution convening an international conference to facilitate the implementation of agreements applying to Israel and the Occupied Territories, condemned Israel's refusal to withdraw from the Occupied Territories without a majority vote in favour from its legislature, as well as its refusal to resume the peace negotiations with Lebanon and Syria that had ended in 1996, and advocated the publication of evidence of Israeli violence against Palestinians. The Council considered other issues, including the need to prevent further Israeli expansion in Jerusalem and the problem of Palestinian refugees, and reiterated demands for international support to secure Israel's withdrawal from the Golan Heights. In June the League condemned an Israeli aerial attack on Beirut and southern Lebanon. In October 1999 the Secretary-General of the League condemned the Mauritanian authorities for concluding an agreement with Israel to establish diplomatic relations. In November the League demanded that Israel compensate Palestinians for alleged losses incurred by their enforced use of the Israeli currency. In late December, prior to a short-lived resumption of Israeli-Syrian peace negotiations, the League reaffirmed its full support for Syria's position.

In February 2000 the League strongly condemned an Israeli aerial attack on southern Lebanon; the League's Council changed the venue of its next meeting, in March, from the League's Cairo headquarters to Beirut as a gesture of solidarity with Lebanon. The League welcomed the withdrawal of Israeli forces from southern Lebanon in May, although it subsequently condemned continuing territorial violations by the Israeli military. At a meeting of the Council in early September resolutions were passed urging international bodies to avoid participating in conferences in Jerusalem, reiterating a threatened boycott of a US chain of restaurants which was accused of operating a franchise in an Israeli settlement in the West Bank, and opposing an Israeli initiative for a Jewish emblem to be included as a symbol of the International Red Cross and Red Crescent Movement. At an emergency summit meeting convened in late October in response to mounting insecurity in Jerusalem and the Occupied Territories, 15 Arab heads of state, senior officials from six countries and Yasser Arafat, the then Palestinian National Authority (PA) leader, strongly rebuked Israel, which was accused of inciting the ongoing violent disturbances by stalling the progress of the peace process. The summit determined to 'freeze' co-operation with Israel, requested the formation of an international committee to conduct an impartial assessment of the situation, urged the UN Security Council to establish a mechanism to bring alleged Israeli 'war criminals' to trial, and requested the UN to approve the creation of an international force to protect Palestinians residing in the Occupied Territories. The summit also endorsed the establishment of an 'al-Aqsa Fund', with a value of US $800m., which was to finance initiatives aimed at promoting the Arab and Islamic identity of Jerusalem, and a smaller 'Jerusalem Intifada Fund' to support the families of Palestinians killed in the unrest. A follow-up committee was subsequently established to implement the resolutions adopted by the emergency summit.

In early January 2001 a meeting of Arab League foreign ministers reviewed a proposed framework agreement, presented by outgoing US President Clinton, which aimed to resolve the continuing extreme tension between the Israeli and Palestinian authorities. The meeting agreed that the issues dominating the stalled Middle East peace process should not be redefined, strongly objecting to a proposal that, in exchange for Palestinian assumption of control over Muslim holy sites in Jerusalem, Palestinians exiled at the time of the foundation of the Israeli state in 1948 should forgo their claimed right to return to their former homes. In March 2001 the League's first ordinary annual summit-level Council was convened, in Amman, Jordan. The summit issued the Amman Declaration, which emphasized the promotion of Arab unity, and demanded the reversal of Israel's 1967 occupation of Arab territories. Heads of state attending the summit requested that the League consider means of reactivating the now relaxed Arab economic boycott of Israel. In May 2001 a meeting of League ministers of foreign affairs determined that all political contacts with Israel should be suspended in protest at aerial attacks by Israel on Palestinian targets in the West Bank. In July representatives of 13 member countries met in Damascus, Syria, under the auspices of the Special Bureau for Boycotting Israel. The meeting declared unanimous support for reactivated trade measures against Israeli companies and foreign businesses dealing with Israel. In August an emergency meeting of ministers of foreign affairs of the member states was convened at the request of the Palestinian authorities to address the recent escalation of hostilities and Israel's seizure of institutions in East Jerusalem. The meeting, which was attended by the League's Secretary-General and the leader of the PA, Yasser Arafat, aimed to formulate a unified Arab response to the situation.

In early March 2002 a meeting of League foreign ministers agreed to support an initiative proposed by Crown Prince Abdullah of Saudi Arabia aimed at brokering a peaceful settlement to the, by then, critical Palestinian–Israeli crisis. The Saudi-backed plan—entailing the restoration of 'normal' Arab relations with Israel and acceptance of its right to exist in peace and security, in exchange for a full Israeli withdrawal from the Occupied Territories, the establishment of an independent Palestinian state with East Jerusalem at its capital, and the return of refugees—was unanimously endorsed, as the first-ever pan-Arab Palestinian-Israeli peace initiative, by the summit-level Council held in Beirut in late March. The plan urged compliance with UN Security Council Resolution 194 concerning the return of Palestinian refugees to Israel, or appropriate compensation for their property; however, precise details of eligibility criteria for the proposed return, a contentious issue owing the potentially huge numbers of refugees and descendants of refugees involved, were not elaborated. Conditions imposed by Israel on Yasser Arafat's freedom of movement deterred him from attending the summit. At the end of March the League's Secretary-General condemned the Israeli military's siege of Arafat's presidential compound in Ramallah (initiated in retaliation against a succession of Palestinian bomb attacks on Israeli civilians). In April an extraordinary Council meeting, held at the request of Palestine to consider the 'unprecedented deterioration' of the situation in the Palestinian territories, accused certain states (notably the USA) of implementing a pro-Israeli bias that enabled Israel to act outside the scope of international law and to ignore relevant UN resolutions, and accused Israel of undermining international co-operation in combating terrorism by attempting to equate its actions towards the Palestinian people with recent anti-terrorism activities conducted by the USA. A meeting organized by the Special Bureau for Boycotting Israel at the end of April agreed to expand boycott measures and assessed the status of 17 companies believed to have interests in Israel. Israel's termination of its siege of Arafat's Ramallah compound in early May was welcomed by the Secretary-General. A meeting of Arab information ministers in mid-

June launched a US $22.5m. campaign to combat Israel's Palestine policy through the international media. Following an aerial raid by the Israeli military on targets in Gaza in late July, the League urged a halt to the export of weaponry, particularly F-16 military aircraft, to Israel. A Council meeting held in early September agreed to intensify Arab efforts to expose Israeli atrocities against the Palestinians and urged the international community to provide protection and reparations for Palestinians. The Council authorized the establishment of a committee to address the welfare of imprisoned Palestinians and urged the USA and the United Kingdom to reconsider their policies on exporting weaponry to Israel, while issuing a resolution concerning the danger posed by Israel's possession of weapons of mass destruction. In early October the Secretary-General expressed concern at new US legislation aimed at securing the relocation of the USA's embassy in Israel from Tel-Aviv to Jerusalem, stating that this represented a symbolic acceptance of Jerusalem as the Israeli capital, in contravention of relevant UN resolutions.

In November 2003 the League welcomed the adoption by the UN Security Council of a resolution endorsing the adoption in April by the so-called 'Quartet', comprising envoys from the UN, European Union, Russia and the USA, of a 'performance-based roadmap to a permanent two-state solution to the Israeli–Palestinian conflict'. In January 2004 the International Court of Justice (ICJ) authorized the participation of the League in proceedings relating to a request for an advisory opinion on the *Legal Consequences of the Construction of a Wall in the Occupied Palestinian Territory*, referred to the ICJ by the UN General Assembly in late 2003; the League welcomed the ICJ's conclusions on the case, published in July 2004. The 2004 summit meeting of Arab League heads of state, held in Tunis in May, condemned contraventions of international law by the Israeli Government, in particular continuing settlement activities and the use of unjudicial killings and other violence, and focused on the humanitarian situation of Palestinians recently displaced by large-scale house demolitions in Rafah, Gaza. In January 2005 the League welcomed the election of Mahmud Abbas as the new Executive President of the PA, following the death in November 2004 of Yasser Arafat. The 2005 heads of state summit meeting, held in Algiers in March, renewed support for the initiative proposed by Crown Prince Abdullah of Saudi Arabia in March 2002, although this had been rejected by the Israeli authorities. In June 2005 the Secretary-General expressed concern that a forthcoming Israeli disengagement from Gaza and northern areas of the West Bank might serve to divert attention from the threat to a solution of the Israeli–Palestinian conflict that was posed by developments regarding settlements, outposts and the security barrier ('wall') under construction in the West Bank.

In March 2007 the annual summit meeting of the League reaffirmed the League's support for the 2002 peace initiative and urged the Israeli authorities to resume direct negotiations based on the principles of the initiative. In July 2007 the foreign ministers of Egypt and Jordan, representing the League, visited Israel to promote the 2002 initiative. Support for the peace initiative was reiterated at the March 2008 summit meeting.

CONFLICT IN THE PERSIAN (ARABIAN) GULF

In March 1984 an emergency meeting established an Arab League committee to encourage international efforts to bring about a negotiated settlement of the Iran–Iraq War. In May ministers of foreign affairs adopted a resolution urging Iran to stop attacking non-belligerent ships and installations in the Gulf region; similar attacks by Iraq were not mentioned. An extraordinary summit conference was held in November 1987, mainly to discuss the war between Iran and Iraq. Contrary to expectations, the participants unanimously agreed on a statement expressing support for Iraq in its defence of its legitimate rights, and criticizing Iran for its procrastination in accepting UN Security Council Resolution 598 of July, which had recommended a cease-fire and negotiations on a settlement of the conflict. In March 2001 the League's Council accused Iran of threatening regional security by conducting military manoeuvres on the three disputed islands—Abu Musa and the Greater and Lesser Tunb—in the Persian (Arabian) Gulf that were also claimed by the United Arab Emirates (UAE). In September 1992 the League's Council issued a condemnation of Iran's alleged occupation of the three islands and decided to refer the issue to the UN.

In May 1990 a summit conference, held in Baghdad, Iraq (which was boycotted by Syria and Lebanon), criticized recent efforts by Western governments to prevent the development of advanced weapons technology in Iraq. In August an emergency summit conference was held to discuss the invasion and annexation of Kuwait by Iraq. Twelve members (Bahrain, Djibouti, Egypt, Kuwait, Lebanon, Morocco, Oman, Qatar, Saudi Arabia, Somalia, Syria and the UAE) approved a resolution condemning Iraq's action, and demanding the withdrawal of Iraqi forces from Kuwait and the reinstatement of the Government. The 12 states expressed support for the Saudi Arabian Government's invitation to the USA to send forces to defend Saudi Arabia; they also agreed to impose economic sanctions on Iraq, and to provide troops for an Arab defensive force in Saudi Arabia. The remaining member states, however, condemned the presence of foreign troops in Saudi Arabia, and their ministers of foreign affairs refused to attend a meeting, held at the end of August, to discuss possible solutions to the crisis. In November King Hassan of Morocco urged the convening of an Arab summit conference, in an attempt to find an 'Arab solution' to Iraq's annexation of Kuwait. However, the divisions in the Arab world over the issue meant that conditions for such a meeting could not be agreed.

In September 1996 the League condemned US missile attacks against Iraq as an infringement of that country's sovereignty. In addition, it expressed concern at the impact on Iraqi territorial integrity of Turkish intervention in the north of Iraq. In June 1997 the League condemned Turkey's military incursion into northern Iraq and demanded a withdrawal of Turkish troops from Iraqi territory. In November 1997 the League expressed concern at the tensions arising from Iraq's decision not to co-operate fully with UN weapons inspectors, and held several meetings with representatives of the Iraqi administration in an effort to secure a peaceful conclusion to the impasse.

In early 1998 the Secretary-General of the League condemned the use or threat of force against Iraq and continued to undertake diplomatic efforts to secure Iraq's compliance with UN Security Council resolutions. The League endorsed the agreement concluded between the UN Secretary-General and the Iraqi authorities in late February, and reaffirmed its commitment to facilitating the eventual removal of the international embargo against Iraq. In November, following an escalation of tensions between the Iraqi authorities and UN weapons inspectors, the Secretary-General reiterated the League's opposition to the use of force against Iraq, but urged Iraq to maintain a flexible approach in its relations with the UN. The League condemned the subsequent bombing of strategic targets in Iraq, conducted by US and British military aircraft from mid-December, and offered immediate medical assistance to victims of the attacks. An emergency meeting of ministers of foreign affairs, held in late January 1999 to formulate a unified Arab response to the aerial attacks on targets in Iraq, expressed concern at the military response to the stand-off between Iraq and the UN, and agreed to establish a seven-member ad hoc committee to consider the removal of punitive measures against Iraq within the framework of UN resolutions. However, the Iraqi delegation withdrew from the meeting in protest at the final statement, which included a request that Iraq recognize Kuwait's territorial integrity.

During March 2000 the Secretary-General of the League expressed regret over Iraq's failure to join the ad hoc committee established in early 1999 and also over Iraq's refusal to co-operate with the recently established UN Monitoring, Verification and Inspection Commission (UNMOVIC).

In March 2001 the League, convened at the level of heads of state in Amman, Jordan, demanded the removal of the UN sanctions against Iraq. At the summit-level Council, held in Beirut in March 2002, a *rapprochement* occurred between Iraq and Kuwait when the Iraqi envoy representing Saddam Hussain declared Iraq's respect for Kuwait's sovereignty and security. In August the Secretary-General expressed strong concern at US threats to attack Iraq in view of its failure to implement UN resolutions, stating that such action would seriously undermine regional stability. A Council meeting held in early September reiterated its complete opposition to the threat of aggression against any Arab country, including Iraq, and demanded the withdrawal of the sanctions against that country. In mid-September, following an ultimatum by the USA that military action against Iraq would ensue were the UN to fail within a short time limit to ensure the elimination of any Iraqi-held weapons of mass destruction, the League urged Iraq to negotiate the return of UN weapons inspectors with a view to avoiding confrontation. Soon afterwards, following tripartite consultations between the Secretary-General of the League, the UN Secretary-General and the Iraqi foreign minister concerning the implementation of UN resolutions and eventual withdrawal of UN sanctions, Iraq agreed to admit UNMOVIC personnel. An emergency meeting of the Council, convened in early November, reviewed the recent adoption by the UN Security Council of Resolution 1441, establishing a strict time frame for Iraqi compliance with UN demands and authorizing the use of force against Iraq in response to non-compliance. The Council urged Iraq to co-operate with UNMOVIC and IAEA inspection teams, requested the inclusion of Arab weapons inspectors in the teams, and urged that the resolution should not be used as a pretext to launch a war against Iraq, emphasizing the importance of a peaceful resolution of the situation.

In March 2003 a meeting of heads of state, convened in Sharm esh-Sheikh, Egypt, issued a final communiqué rejecting threatened aggression against Iraq, reiterating that the Saddam Hussain regime should co-operate with UN weapons inspectors, urging that the inspectors be given enough time to complete their work, and declaring that the League would form a committee of diplomats to explain its position to concerned international parties. In late March, following the initiation of US-led military action against the

Saddam Hussain regime, the League participated in a joint meeting of Arab organizations convened to consider means of assisting the Iraqi people. In March 2006 the League determined to establish a mission in Iraq to contribute to that country's rehabilitation and national reconciliation.

LIBYA AND THE INTERNATIONAL COMMUNITY

In December 1991 the League expressed solidarity with Libya, which was under international pressure to extradite two government agents who were suspected of involvement in the explosion which destroyed a US passenger aircraft over Lockerbie, United Kingdom, in December 1988. In March 1992 the League appointed a committee to seek to resolve the disputes between Libya and the USA, the United Kingdom and France over the Lockerbie bomb and the explosion which destroyed a French passenger aircraft over Niger in September 1989. The League condemned the UN's decision, at the end of March, to impose sanctions against Libya, and appealed for a negotiated solution. In September 1997 Arab League ministers of foreign affairs advocated a gradual removal of international sanctions against Libya, and agreed that member countries should permit international flights to leave Libya for specific humanitarian and religious purposes and when used for the purpose of transporting foreign nationals. In August 1998 the USA and United Kingdom accepted a proposal of the Libyan Government, supported by the Arab League, that the suspects in the Lockerbie case be tried in The Hague, Netherlands, under Scottish law. In March 1999 the League's Council determined that member states would suspend sanctions imposed against Libya, once arrangements for the trial of the suspects in the Lockerbie case had been finalized. (The suspects were transferred to a detention centre in the Netherlands in early April, whereupon the UN Security Council suspended its sanctions against Libya.) At the end of January 2001, following the completion of the trial in The Hague of the two Libyans accused of complicity in the Lockerbie case (one of whom was found guilty and one of whom was acquitted), the Secretary-General of the League urged the UN Security Council fully to terminate the sanctions against Libya that had been suspended in 1999. Meeting in mid-March, the League's Council pledged that member states would not consider themselves bound by the (inactive) UN sanctions. In early September 2002 the Council deplored the USA's continuing active imposition of sanctions against Libya and endorsed Libya's right to claim compensation in respect of these.

LEBANON

In January 1989 an Arab League group, comprising six ministers of foreign affairs, began discussions with the two rival Lebanese governments on the possibility of a political settlement in Lebanon. In May a new mediation committee was established, with a six-month mandate to negotiate a cease-fire in Lebanon, and to reconvene the Lebanese legislature with the aim of holding a presidential election and restoring constitutional government in Lebanon. In September the principal factions in Lebanon agreed to observe a cease-fire, and the surviving members of the Lebanese legislature (originally elected in 1972) met at Ta'if, in Saudi Arabia, in October, and approved the League's proposed 'charter of national reconciliation'. The Arab League welcomed the withdrawal (made in response to international pressure after the assassination of former Lebanese Prime Minister, Rafik al-Hariri, in February 2005) of Syrian armed forces and intelligence officials from Lebanon in mid-2005 as a fulfilment of the Taif Agreement that had been concluded in 1989. In August 2006 the League established a human rights investigation committee to consider the recent military action that had occurred following the kidnapping, by a Lebanese militia group, of an Israeli soldier. The committee reported in December that Israel had violated humanitarian law. In October the League's Economic and Social Council formulated a plan to support Lebanon in its reconstruction and economic development efforts. In March 2007 the summit meeting condemned all Israeli violations of Lebanese territorial sovereignty and, in particular, the destruction of civilian infrastructure. In January 2008 Arab League foreign ministers adopted a three-point plan aimed at resolving the ongoing political crisis in Lebanon. Lebanon did not participate in, and Algeria, Egypt, Jordan, Morocco and Saudi Arabia sent low-level delegations to, the March 2008 summit meeting, held in Damascus, Syria, in protest at the alleged role of Syria and Iran in the Lebanese crisis.

CONFLICT IN SUB-SAHARAN AFRICA

In November 1997 the League criticized the decision of the US Government to impose economic sanctions against Sudan. In March 2001 the Council reiterated the League's opposition to the economic sanctions maintained by the USA against Sudan. In early September 2002 the Council established a committee to encourage peace efforts in Sudan.

In 1992 the League attempted to mediate between the warring factions in Somalia. In early June 2002 the League appointed a special representative to Somalia to assist with the ongoing reconciliation efforts in that country.

In May 1999 the League expressed its concern at the political situation in the Comoros, following the removal of the government and the establishment of a new military regime in that country at the end of April. In March 2001 the Council welcomed the political *rapprochement* achieved in the Comoros in February.

In May 2004 representatives of the League participated in an African Union fact-finding mission to assess the ongoing humanitarian crisis in Darfur, Sudan. In August an emergency meeting of League foreign ministers, convened to address the situation in Darfur, declared support for the Sudanese Government's measures to disarm Arab militias and punish human rights violations there. In November the League was asked to join a panel appointed to monitor the cease-fire agreement that had been adopted in April by the parties to the Darfur conflict. In March 2006 the meeting of heads of state agreed to offer financial support to the African Union Mission in Sudan, deployed to the Darfur region of that country. The summit meeting in March 2007 expressed continued support for all peace accords signed between conflicting parties in Sudan.

Finance

In March 2008 the Council approved a budget of US $46m. for the Secretariat in 2009.

Publications

Arab Perspectives—Sh'oun Arabiyya (monthly).
Journal of Arab Affairs (monthly).
Bulletins of treaties and agreements concluded among the member states, essays, regular publications circulated by regional offices.

NORTH AMERICAN FREE TRADE AGREEMENT—NAFTA

Address: *(Canadian section)* Royal Bank Centre, 90 Sparks St, Suite 705, Ottawa, ON K1P 5B4.
Telephone: (613) 992-9388; **fax:** (613) 992-9392; **e-mail:** canada@nafta-sec-alena.org; **internet:** www.nafta-sec-alena.org/canada.
Address: *(Mexican section)* Blvd Adolfo López Mateos 3025, 2°, Col Héroes de Padierna, 10700 México, DF.
Telephone: (55) 629-9630; **fax:** (55) 629-9637; **e-mail:** mexico@nafta-sec-alena.org.
Address: *(US section)* 14th St and Constitution Ave, NW, Room 2061, Washington, DC 20230.
Telephone: (202) 482-5438; **fax:** (202) 482-0148; **e-mail:** usa@nafta-sec-alena.org; **internet:** www.nafta-sec-alena.org.

The North American Free Trade Agreement (NAFTA) grew out of the free-trade agreement between the USA and Canada that was signed in January 1988 and came into effect on 1 January 1989. Negotiations on the terms of NAFTA, which includes Mexico in the free-trade area, were concluded in October 1992 and the Agreement was signed in December. The accord was ratified in November 1993 and entered into force on 1 January 1994. The NAFTA Secretariat is composed of national sections in each member country.

MEMBERS

Canada   Mexico   USA

MAIN PROVISIONS OF THE AGREEMENT

Under NAFTA almost all restrictions on trade and investment between Canada, Mexico and the USA were to be gradually removed over a 15-year period. Most tariffs were eliminated immediately on agricultural trade between the USA and Mexico, with tariffs on 6% of agricultural products (including corn, sugar, and some fruits and vegetables) to be abolished over the 15 years. Tariffs on automobiles and textiles were to be phased out over 10 years in all three countries. Mexico was to open its financial sector to US and Canadian investment, with all restrictions to be removed within 14 years. Barriers to investment were removed in most sectors, with exemptions for petroleum in Mexico, culture in Canada and airlines and radio communications in the USA. Mexico was to liberalize government procurement, removing preferential treatment for domestic companies over a 10-year period. In transport, heavy goods vehicles were to have complete freedom of movement between the three countries by 2000. An interim measure, whereby transport companies could apply for special licences to travel further within the borders of each country than the existing limit of 20 miles (32 km), was postponed in December 1995, shortly before it was scheduled to come into effect. The postponement was due to concerns, on the part of the US Government, relating to the implementation of adequate safety standards by Mexican truck-drivers. The 2000 deadline for the free circulation of heavy goods vehicles was not met, owing to the persistence of these concerns. In February 2001 a five-member NAFTA panel of experts appointed to adjudicate on the dispute ruled that the USA was violating the Agreement. In December the US Senate approved legislation entitling Mexican long-haul trucks to operate anywhere in the USA following compliance with rigorous safety checks to be enforced by US inspectors. In April 1998 the fifth meeting of the three-member ministerial Free Trade Commission (see below), held in Paris, France, agreed to remove tariffs on some 600 goods, including certain chemicals, pharmaceuticals, steel and wire products, textiles, toys, and watches, from 1 August. As a result of the agreement, a number of tariffs were eliminated as much as 10 years earlier than had been originally planned.

In April 2003 the Mexican Government announced that, in order to protect the livelihoods of local producers, it was planning to renegotiate provisions of the Agreement that would permit, with effect from January 2008, the tariff-free importation of maize and beans from Canada and the USA.

In the case of a sudden influx of goods from one country to another that adversely affects a domestic industry, the Agreement makes provision for the imposition of short-term 'snap-back' tariffs.

Disputes are to be settled in the first instance by intergovernmental consultation. If a dispute is not resolved within 30 to 40 days, a government may call a meeting of the Free Trade Commission. In October 1994 the Commission established an Advisory Committee on Private Commercial Disputes to recommend procedures for the resolution of such disputes. If the Commission is unable to settle the issue a panel of experts in the relevant field is appointed to adjudicate. In June 1996 Canada and Mexico announced their decision to refer the newly-enacted US 'Helms-Burton' legislation on trade with Cuba to the Commission. They claimed that the legislation, which provides for punitive measures against foreign companies that engage in trade with Cuba, imposed undue restrictions on Canadian and Mexican companies and was, therefore, in contravention of NAFTA. However, at the beginning of 1997 certain controversial provisions of the Helms-Burton legislation were suspended for a period of six months by the US administration. In April these were again suspended, as part of a compromise agreement with the European Union. The relevant provisions continued to be suspended at six-monthly intervals, and remained suspended in 2008. An Advisory Committee on Private Commercial Disputes Regarding Agricultural Goods was formed in 1998.

In December 1994 NAFTA members issued a formal invitation to Chile to seek membership of the Agreement. Formal discussions on Chile's entry began in June 1995, but were stalled in December when the US Congress failed to approve 'fast-track' negotiating authority for the US Government, which was to have allowed the latter to negotiate a trade agreement with Chile, without risk of incurring a line-by-line veto from the US Congress. In February 1996 Chile began high-level negotiations with Canada on a wide-ranging bilateral free-trade agreement. Chile, which already had extensive bilateral trade agreements with Mexico, was regarded as advancing its position with regard to NAFTA membership by means of the proposed accord with Canada. The bilateral agreement, which provided for the extensive elimination of customs duties by 2002, was signed in November 1996 and ratified by Chile in July 1997. However, in November 1997 the US Government was obliged to request the removal of the 'fast-track' proposal from the legislative agenda, owing to insufficient support within Congress.

In April 1998 heads of state of 34 countries, meeting in Santiago, Chile, agreed formally to initiate the negotiating process to establish a Free Trade Area of the Americas (FTAA). The US Government had originally proposed creating the FTAA through the gradual extension of NAFTA trading privileges on a bilateral basis. However, the framework agreed upon by ministers of trade of the 34 countries, meeting in March, provided for countries to negotiate and accept FTAA provisions on an individual basis and as part of a sub-regional economic bloc. It was envisaged that the FTAA would exist alongside the sub-regional associations, including NAFTA. In April 2001, meeting in Québec, Canada, leaders of the participating countries agreed to conclude the negotiations on the FTAA by January 2005 and implement it by the end of that year. At a special summit of the Americas, held in January 2004 in Monterrey, Mexico, however, the leaders did not specify a completion date for the negotiations, although they adopted a declaration committing themselves to its eventual establishment. Negotiations were suspended in March and remained stalled in early 2008.

ADDITIONAL AGREEMENTS

During 1993, as a result of domestic pressure, the new US Government negotiated two 'side agreements' with its NAFTA partners, which were to provide safeguards for workers' rights and the environment. A Commission for Labour Co-operation was established under the North American Agreement on Labour Co-operation (NAALC) to monitor implementation of labour accords and to foster co-operation in that area. The North American Commission for Environmental Co-operation (NACEC) was initiated to combat pollution, to ensure that economic development was not environmentally damaging and to monitor compliance with national and NAFTA environmental regulations. Panels of experts, with representatives from each country, were established to adjudicate in cases of alleged infringement of workers' rights or environmental damage. The panels were given the power to impose fines and trade sanctions, but only with regard to the USA and Mexico; Canada, which was opposed to such measures, was to enforce compliance with NAFTA by means of its own legal system. In 1995 the North American Fund for Environmental Co-operation (NAFEC) was established. NAFEC, which is financed by the NACEC, supports community environmental projects.

In February 1996 the NACEC consented for the first time to investigate a complaint brought by environmentalists regarding non-compliance with domestic legislation on the environment. Mexican environmentalists claimed that a company that was planning to build a pier for tourist ships (a project that was to involve damage to a coral reef) had not been required to supply adequate environmental impact studies. The NACEC was limited to presenting its findings in such a case, as it could only make a ruling in the case of complaints brought by one NAFTA government against another. The NACEC allocates the bulk of its resources to research undertaken to support compliance with legislation and agreements on the environment. However, in October 1997 the council of NAFTA ministers of the environment, meeting in Montréal, Canada, approved a new structure for the NACEC's activities. The NACEC's main objective was to be the provision of advice concerning the environmental impact of trade issues. It was also agreed that the Commission was further to promote trade in environmentally-sound products and to encourage private-sector investment in environmental trade issues.

With regard to the NAALC, National Administration Offices have been established in each of the three NAFTA countries in order to monitor labour issues and to address complaints about non-compliance with domestic labour legislation. However, punitive measures in the form of trade sanctions or fines (up to US $20m.) may only be imposed in the specific instances of contravention of national legislation regarding child labour, a minimum wage or health and safety standards. A Commission for Labour Co-operation has been established (see below) and incorporates a council of ministers of labour of the three countries.

In August 1993 the USA and Mexico agreed to establish a Border Environmental Co-operation Commission (BECC) to assist with the co-ordination of projects for the improvement of infrastructure and to monitor the environmental impact of the Agreement on the US–Mexican border area, where industrial activity was expected to intensify. The Commission is located in Ciudad Juárez, Mexico. By April 2008 the BECC had certified 137 projects, at a cost of US $2,923m. In October 1993 the USA and Mexico concluded an agreement to establish the North American Development Bank (NADB or NADBank), which was mandated to finance environmental and infrastructure projects along the US–Mexican border.

Commission for Labour Co-operation: 1211 Connecticut Ave, NW Suite 200, Washington, DC 20036, USA; tel. (202) 464-1100; fax (202) 464-9487; e-mail info@naalc.org; internet www.naalc.org; f. 1994; Exec. Dir DANIEL BERNIER (Canada); publ. Annual Report.

North American Commission for Environmental Co-operation (NACEC): 393 rue St Jacques Ouest, Bureau 200, Montréal, QC H2Y 1N9, Canada; tel. (514) 350-4300; fax (514) 350-4314; e-mail info@ccemtl.org; internet www.cec.org; f. 1994; Exec. Dir FELIPE ADRIÁN VÁZQUEZ; publs Annual Report, Taking Stock (annually), industry reports, policy studies.

North American Development Bank (NADB/NADBank): 203 South St Mary's, Suite 300, San Antonio, TX 78205, USA; tel. (210) 231-8000; fax (210) 231-6232; internet www.nadbank.org; at 31 January 2008 the NADB had authorized capital of US $3,000m., subscribed equally by Mexico and the USA, of which $390m. was paid-up; Man. Dir JORGE C. GARCÉS (USA); publs Annual Report, NADBank News.

NORTH ATLANTIC TREATY ORGANIZATION—NATO

Address: blvd Léopold III, 1110 Brussels, Belgium.
Telephone: (2) 707-41-11; **fax:** (2) 707-45-79; **e-mail:** natodoc@hq.nato.int; **internet:** www.nato.int.

The Atlantic Alliance was established on the basis of the 1949 North Atlantic Treaty as a defensive political and military alliance of a group of European states (then numbering 10) and the USA and Canada. The Alliance aims to provide common security for its members through co-operation and consultation in political, military and economic fields, as well as scientific, environmental, and other non-military aspects. The objectives of the Alliance are implemented by NATO. Since the collapse of the communist governments in Central and Eastern Europe, from 1989 onwards, and the dissolution, in 1991, of the Warsaw Treaty of Friendship, Co-operation and Mutual Assistance (the Warsaw Pact), which had hitherto been regarded as the Alliance's principal adversary, NATO has undertaken a fundamental transformation of its structures and policies to meet the new security challenges in Europe.

MEMBERS*

Belgium	Hungary	Portugal
Bulgaria	Iceland	Romania
Canada	Italy	Slovakia
Czech Republic	Latvia	Slovenia
Denmark	Lithuania	Spain
Estonia	Luxembourg	Turkey
France	Netherlands	United Kingdom
Germany	Norway	USA
Greece	Poland	

* Greece and Turkey acceded to the Treaty in 1952, and the Federal Republic of Germany in 1955. France withdrew from the integrated military structure of NATO in 1966, although remaining a member of the Atlantic Alliance; in 1996 France resumed participation in some, but not all, of the military organs of NATO. Spain acceded to the Treaty in 1982, but remained outside the Alliance's integrated military structure until 1999. The Czech Republic, Hungary and Poland were formally admitted as members of NATO in March 1999. In March 2003 protocols of accession, amending the North Atlantic Treaty, were adopted by the 19 NATO member states with a view to admitting Bulgaria, Estonia, Latvia, Lithuania, Romania, Slovakia and Slovenia to the Alliance. In March 2004, the protocols of accession having been ratified by all of the member states, those seven countries were formally invited to join NATO and, on 29 March, they acceded to the Treaty.

Organization
(April 2008)

NORTH ATLANTIC COUNCIL

The Council, the highest authority of the Alliance, is composed of representatives of the 26 member states. It meets at the level of Permanent Representatives, ministers of foreign affairs, or heads of state and government, and, at all levels, has effective political and decision-making authority. Ministerial meetings are held at least twice a year. Occasional meetings of defence ministers are also held. At the level of Permanent Representatives the Council meets at least once a week.

The Secretary-General of NATO is Chairman of the Council, and each year a minister of foreign affairs of a member state is nominated honorary President, following the English alphabetical order of countries.

Decisions are taken by common consent and not by majority vote. The Council is a forum for wide consultation between member governments on major issues, including political, military, economic and other subjects, and is supported by the Senior or regular Political Committee, the Military Committee and other subordinate bodies.

PERMANENT REPRESENTATIVES

Belgium: Franciskus van Daele.
Bulgaria: Lubomir Ivanov.
Canada: Dr Robert McRae.
Czech Republic: Štefan Füle.
Denmark: Per Poulsen-Hansen.
Estonia: Jüri Luik.
France: Richard Duqué.
Germany: Ulrich Brandenburg.
Greece: Thrassyvoulos-Terry Stamatopoulos.
Hungary: Zoltán Martinusz.
Iceland: Gunnar Gunnarsson.
Italy: Stefano Stefanini.
Latvia: Jānis Eichmanis.
Lithuania: Linas Linkevičius.
Luxembourg: Alphonse Berns.
Netherlands: Herman Schaper.
Norway: Kim Traavik.
Poland: Bogusław W. Winid.
Portugal: Manuel Tomás Fernandes Pereira.
Romania: Sorin Dumitru Ducaru.
Slovakia: Igor Slobodník.
Slovenia: Dr Božo Cerar.
Spain: Pablo Benavides Orgaz.
Turkey: Tacan Ildem.
United Kingdom: Stewart Eldon.
USA: Victoria Nuland.

Note: NATO partner countries are represented by heads of diplomatic missions or liaison officers located at NATO headquarters.

DEFENCE PLANNING COMMITTEE

Most defence matters are dealt with in the Defence Planning Committee, composed of representatives of all member countries except France. The Committee provides guidance to NATO's military authorities and, within the field of its responsibilities, has the same functions and authority as the Council. Like the Council, it meets regularly at ambassadorial level and assembles twice a year in ministerial sessions, when member countries are represented by their ministers of defence.

NUCLEAR PLANNING GROUP

Defence ministers of countries participating in the Defence Planning Committee meet regularly in the Nuclear Planning Group (NPG) to discuss specific policy issues relating to nuclear forces, such as safety, deployment issues, nuclear arms control and proliferation. The NPG is supported by a Staff Group, composed of representatives of all members participating in the NPG, which meets at least once a week. The NPG High Level Group, chaired by the USA and comprising national policy-makers and experts, exists as a senior advisory body to the NPG in respect of nuclear policy and planning issues.

OTHER COMMITTEES

There are also committees for political affairs, economics, military medical services, armaments, defence review, science, infrastructure, logistics, communications, civil emergency planning, information and cultural relations, and civil and military budgets. In addition, other committees consider specialized subjects such as NATO pipelines, air traffic management, etc. Since 1992 most of these committees have consulted on a regular basis with representatives from central and eastern European countries.

INTERNATIONAL SECRETARIAT

The Secretary-General is Chairman of the North Atlantic Council, the Defence Planning Committee and the Nuclear Planning Group. He is the head of the International Secretariat, with staff drawn from the member countries. He proposes items for NATO consultation and is generally responsible for promoting consultation and co-operation in accordance with the provisions of the North Atlantic Treaty. He is empowered to offer his help informally in cases of disputes between member countries, to facilitate procedures for settlement.

Secretary-General: Jakob Gijsbert (Jaap) de Hoop Scheffer (Netherlands).
Deputy Secretary-General: Claudio Bisogniero (Italy).

There is an Assistant Secretary-General for each of the operational divisions listed below.

PRINCIPAL DIVISIONS

Division of Defence Investment: responsible for enhancing NATO's defence capacity (including armaments planning, air defence and security investment) by developing and investing in the Alliance's assets and capabilities; Asst Sec.-Gen. Peter C. W. Flory (USA).

Division of Defence Policy and Planning: responsible for defence planning, nuclear policy and defence against weapons of mass destruction; Asst Sec.-Gen. Jiří Šedivý (Czech Republic).

Division of Political Affairs and Security Policy: is concerned with regional, economic and security affairs and relations with other international organizations and partner countries; Asst Sec.-Gen. MARTIN ERDMANN (Germany).

Division of Public Diplomacy: responsible for dissemination of information on NATO's activities and policies through the media, the official website and print publications as well as seminars and conferences; Asst Sec.-Gen. JEAN-FRANÇOIS BUREAU (France).

Executive Management Division: ensures the efficient running of the International Secretariat and provides support to elements such as conference services, information management and human and financial resources; Asst Sec.-Gen. DOUGLAS DEMPSTER (Canada).

Operations Division: responsible for the Alliance's crisis management and peace-keeping activities and civil emergency planning and exercises; Asst Sec.-Gen. MARTIN HOWARD (United Kingdom).

Military Organization

MILITARY COMMITTEE

Composed of the allied Chiefs-of-Staff, or their representatives, of all member countries: the highest military body in NATO under the authority of the Council. Meets at least twice a year at Chiefs-of-Staff level and remains in permanent session with Permanent Military Representatives. It is responsible for making recommendations to the Council and Defence Planning Committee and Nuclear Planning Group on military matters and for supplying guidance on military questions to Supreme Allied Commanders and subordinate military authorities. The Committee is supported by an International Military Staff.

In December 1995 France agreed to rejoin the Military Committee, which it had formally left in 1966.

Chairman: Gen. RAYMOND HENAULT (Canada).

COMMANDS

Allied Command Operations: Casteau, Belgium—Supreme Headquarters Allied Powers Europe—SHAPE; Supreme Allied Commander Europe—SACEUR Gen. JOHN. CRADDOCK (USA).

Allied Command Transformation: Norfolk, Virginia, USA; Supreme Allied Commander Transformation—SACT Lt-Gen. JAMES N. MATTIS (USA).

Activities

The common security policy of the members of the North Atlantic Alliance is to safeguard peace through the maintenance of political solidarity and adequate defence at the lowest level of military forces needed to deter all possible forms of aggression. Each year, member countries take part in a Defence Review, designed to assess their contribution to the common defence in relation to their respective capabilities and constraints. Allied defence policy is reviewed periodically by ministers of defence.

Political consultations within the Alliance take place on a permanent basis, under the auspices of the North Atlantic Council (NAC), on all matters affecting the common security interests of the member countries, as well as events outside the North Atlantic Treaty area.

Co-operation in environmental, scientific and technological fields takes place in the NATO Science Committee and in its Committee on the Challenges of Modern Society. Both these bodies operate an expanding international programme of science fellowships, advance study institutes and research grants. NATO has also pursued co-operation in relation to civil emergency planning. These activities represent NATO's 'Third Dimension'.

Since the 1980s the Alliance has been actively involved in co-ordinating policies with regard to arms control and disarmament issues designed to bring about negotiated reductions in conventional forces, intermediate and short-range nuclear forces and strategic nuclear forces. A Verification Co-ordinating Committee was established in 1990. In April 1999 the summit meeting determined to improve co-ordination on issues relating to weapons of mass destruction through the establishment of a separate centre at NATO headquarters. At a summit meeting of the Conference on Security and Co-operation in Europe (CSCE), now renamed the Organization for Security and Co-operation in Europe (OSCE), in November 1990 the member countries of NATO and the Warsaw Pact signed an agreement limiting Conventional Armed Forces in Europe (CFE), whereby conventional arms would be reduced to within a common upper limit in each zone. The two groups also issued a Joint Declaration, stating that they were no longer adversaries and that none of their weapons would ever be used 'except in self-defence'. In March 1992, under the auspices of the CSCE, the ministers of foreign affairs of the NATO and of the former Warsaw Pact countries (with Russia, Belarus, Ukraine and Georgia taking the place of the USSR) signed the 'Open Skies' treaty. Under this treaty, aerial reconnaissance missions by one country over another were to be permitted, subject to regulation. The eight former Soviet republics with territory in the area of application of the CFE Treaty committed themselves to honouring its obligations in June. At the summit meeting of the OSCE in December 1996 the signatories of the CFE Treaty agreed to begin negotiations on a revised treaty governing conventional weapons in Europe. In July 1997 the CFE signatories concluded an agreement on Certain Basic Elements for Treaty Adaptation, which provided for substantial reductions in the maximum levels of conventional military equipment at national and territorial level, replacing the previous bloc-to-bloc structure of the Treaty. In accordance with a series of agreements or Commitments, approved at an OSCE meeting held in Istanbul, Turkey, in November 1999, Russia was required to withdraw forces from and reduce levels of military equipment in Georgia and Moldova, a process being monitored by NATO. In April 2007 NATO ministers of foreign affairs held immediate discussions following an announcement by Russia's President that it intended to suspend unilaterally its implementation of CFE obligations. An extraordinary conference of parties to the CFE was convened in June to consider Russia's security concerns relating to the final document on adaptation of the Treaty. In July NATO expressed its concern following an announcement by the Russian Government that it was to suspend obligations under the Treaty, with effect from mid-December. In April 2008 NATO heads of state and government urged Russia to resume its implementation of the Treaty.

An extensive review of NATO's structures was initiated in June 1990, in response to the fundamental changes taking place in Central and Eastern Europe. In November 1991 NATO heads of government, convened in Rome, recommended a radical restructuring of the organization in order to meet the demands of the new security environment, which was to include further reductions in military forces in Europe, active involvement in international peace-keeping operations, increased co-operation with other international institutions and close co-operation with its former adversaries, the USSR and the countries of Eastern Europe. The basis for NATO's new force structure was incorporated into a new Strategic Concept, which was adopted in the Rome Declaration issuing from the summit meeting. The concept provided for the maintenance of a collective defence capability, with a reduced dependence on nuclear weapons. Substantial reductions in the size and levels of readiness of NATO forces were undertaken, in order to reflect the Alliance's strictly defensive nature, and forces were reorganized within a streamlined integrated command structure. Forces were categorized into immediate and rapid reaction forces (including the ACE Rapid Reaction Corps—ARRC, which was inaugurated in October 1992), main defence forces and augmentation forces, which may be used to reinforce any NATO region or maritime areas for deterrence, crisis management or defence. During 1998 work was undertaken on the formulation of a new Strategic Concept, reflecting the changing security environment and defining NATO's future role and objectives, which recognized a broader sphere of influence of NATO in the 21st century and confirmed NATO to be the principal generator of security in the Euro-Atlantic area. It emphasized NATO's role in crisis management and a renewed commitment to partnership and dialogue. The document was approved at a special summit meeting, convened in Washington, DC, USA, in April 1999, to commemorate the 50th anniversary of the Alliance. A separate initiative was approved to assist member states to adapt their defence capabilities to meet changing security requirements, for example improving the means of troop deployment and equipping and protecting forces.

In January 1994 NATO heads of state and government welcomed the entry into force of the Maastricht Treaty, establishing the European Union (EU, superseding the EC). The Treaty included an agreement on the development of a common foreign and security policy, which was intended to be a mechanism to strengthen the European pillar of the Alliance. NATO subsequently co-operated with Western European Union (WEU) in support of the development of a European Security and Defence Identity. In June 1996 NATO ministers of foreign affairs reached agreement on the implementation of a 'Combined Joint Task Force (CJTF) concept'. Measures were to be taken to establish the 'nuclei' of these task forces at certain NATO headquarters, which would provide the basis for missions that could be activated at short notice for specific purposes such as crisis management and peace-keeping. It was also agreed to make CJTFs available for operations undertaken by WEU. In conjunction with this, WEU was to be permitted to make use of Alliance hardware and capabilities (in practice, mostly belonging to the USA) subject to the endorsement of the NAC. The summit meeting held in April 1999 confirmed NATO's willingness to establish a direct NATO-EU relationship. The first formal meeting of the Military Committees of the EU and NATO took place in June 2001 to exchange information relating to the development of EU-NATO security co-operation. In

November 2003 NATO and the EU conducted a joint crisis management exercise for the first time. In order to support an integrated security structure in Europe, NATO also co-operates with the OSCE and has provided assistance for the development of the latter's conflict prevention and crisis management activities.

In January 2001 NATO established an ad hoc working committee in response to concerns expressed by several member governments regarding the health implications of the use of depleted uranium munitions during the Alliance's military intervention in the Balkans. The committee was to co-ordinate the compilation of information regarding the use of depleted uranium and to co-operate with the Yugoslav authorities in the rehabilitation of the local environment. An extraordinary meeting of chiefs of military medical services, including surgeons-general and medical experts, was also convened to consider the issue.

On 12 September 2001 the NAC agreed to invoke, for the first time, Article 5 of the North Atlantic Treaty, providing for collective self-defence, in response to terrorist attacks against targets in the USA that had taken place on the previous day. The measure was formally implemented in early October after the US authorities presented evidence substantiating claims that the attacks had been directed from abroad. The NAC endorsed eight specific US requests for logistical and military support in its efforts to counter terrorism, including enhanced sharing of intelligence and full access to airfields and ports in member states. It also agreed to dispatch five surveillance aircraft to help to patrol US airspace and directed the standing naval force to the Eastern Mediterranean (see 'Operation Active Endeavour', below). In December NATO ministers of defence initiated a review of military capabilities and defences with a view to strengthening its ability to counter international terrorism.

In November 2002 NATO heads of state and government, convened in Prague, Czech Republic, approved a comprehensive reform of the Alliance's capabilities in order to reflect a new operational outlook and enable the transition to smaller, more flexible forces. The command structure was to be reduced and redefined, under operational and functional strategic commands, while a NATO Response Force (NRF), comprising a flexible and interoperable force of readily deployable land, sea and air elements, was to be established. The meeting agreed on further measures to strengthen NATO's capabilities to defend against terrorism and approved a broader commitment to improve and develop modern warfare capabilities. The Prague Summit initiatives were endorsed by a meeting of NATO defence ministers in June 2003. In March 2005 the NAC approved a charter formally to establish an organization to manage an Active Layered Theatre Ballistic Missile Defence programme, which aimed to establish a new collective defence capability. The NRF was inaugurated in October 2003, with a force strength of 9,500 troops. It was intended to enable NATO to react swiftly and efficiently in new areas of operation, such as evacuations, disaster management and counter terrorism. By October 2004 the NRF had reached its initial operating capacity, comprising some 17,000 troops. It reached its full capacity, of 25,000 troops, in November 2006. A summit meeting convened in Istanbul, Turkey in June 2004, evaluated progress made in transforming the Alliance's capabilities. In November 2006 NATO heads of state and government, meeting in Riga, Latvia, endorsed and made public a Comprehensive Political Guidance document which aimed to provide a framework and direction for the Alliance in the next 10–15 years. In particular, it identified the likely capability requirements of future operations, the need to respond to new threats and challenges, such as terrorism and the spread of weapons of mass destruction, and the development of relations with non-NATO countries. In June 2007 NATO ministers of defence, meeting to review the transformation of the Alliance's operational capabilities, agreed to assess, by February 2008, the political and military implications of a possible redeployment of US missile defences in Europe.

In April 2003 an agreement was signed by six member states—the Czech Republic, Denmark, Germany, the Netherlands, Norway and Poland—formally establishing the Civil-Military Co-operation Group North. The group was to be based at Budel, Netherlands and was intended to provide NATO commanders with a co-ordinated approach to civil-military co-operation during crises and in post-conflict areas.

PARTNERSHIPS

In May 1997 a Euro-Atlantic Partnership Council (EAPC) was inaugurated as a successor to the North Atlantic Co-operation Council (NACC), that had been established in December 1991 to provide a forum for consultation on political and security matters with the countries of central and eastern Europe, including the former Soviet republics. An EAPC Council was to meet monthly at ambassadorial level and twice a year at ministerial level. It was to be supported in its work by a steering committee and a political committee. The EAPC was to pursue the NACC Work Plan for Dialogue, Partnership and Co-operation and incorporate it into a new Work Plan, which was to include an expanded political dimension of consultation and co-operation among participating states. The Partnership for Peace (PfP) programme, which was established in January 1994 within the framework of the NACC, was to remain an integral element of the new co-operative mechanism. The PfP incorporated practical military and defence-related co-operation activities that had originally been part of the NACC Work Plan. Participation in the PfP requires an initial signature of a framework agreement, establishing the common principles and objectives of the partnership, the submission of a presentation document, indicating the political and military aspects of the partnership and the nature of future co-operation activities and the development of individual partnership programmes establishing country-specific objectives. In June 1994 Russia, which had previously opposed the strategy as being the basis for future enlargement of NATO, signed the PfP framework document, which included a declaration envisaging an 'enhanced dialogue' between the two sides. Despite its continuing opposition to any enlargement of NATO, in May 1995 Russia agreed to sign a PfP Individual Partnership Programme, as well as a framework document for NATO-Russian dialogue and co-operation beyond the PfP. During 1994 a Partnership Co-ordination Cell (PCC), incorporating representatives of all partnership countries, became operational in Mons, Belgium. The PCC, under the authority of the NAC, aims to co-ordinate joint military activities and planning in order to implement PfP programmes. The first joint military exercises with countries of the former Warsaw Pact were conducted in September. NATO began formulating a PfP Status of Forces Agreement (SOFA) to define the legal status of Allies' and partners' forces when they are present on each other's territory; the PfP SOFA was opened for signature in June 1995. The new EAPC was to provide a framework for the development of an enhanced PfP programme, which NATO envisaged would become an essential element of the overall European security structure. Accordingly, the military activities of the PfP were to be expanded to include all Alliance missions and incorporate all NATO committees into the PfP process, thus providing for greater co-operation in crisis management, civil emergency planning and training activities. In addition, all PfP member countries were to participate in the CJTF concept through a structure of Partners Staff Elements, working at all levels of the Alliance military structure. Defence ministers of NATO and the 27 partner countries were to meet regularly to provide the political guidance for the enhanced Planning and Review Process of the PfP. In December 1997 NATO ministers of foreign affairs approved the establishment of a Euro-Atlantic Disaster Response Co-ordination Centre (EADRCC), and a non-permanent Euro-Atlantic Disaster Response Unit. The EADRCC was inaugurated in June 1998 and immediately commenced operations to provide relief to ethnic Albanian refugees fleeing the conflict in the Serbian province of Kosovo. In November the NAC approved the establishment of a network of PfP training centres, the first of which was inaugurated in Ankara, Turkey. The centres were a key element of a Training and Education Programme, which was endorsed at the summit meeting in April 1999. A policy of establishing individual PfP Trust Funds was approved in September 2000. These aimed to provide support for military reform and demilitarization activities in partners countries, in particular the destruction of anti-personnel landmines. In November 2002 heads of state and government, meeting in Prague, Czech Republic, endorsed a new initiative to formulate Individual Partnership Action Plans (IPAPs) designed to strengthen bilateral relations with a partner country, improve the effectiveness of NATO assistance in that country, and provide for intensified political dialogue. The Istanbul summit meeting in June 2004 agreed to strengthen co-operation with partner countries in the Caucasus and Central Asia. A Special Representative of the Secretary-General to the two regions was appointed in September. In October the first IPAP was signed with Georgia, with the aim of defining national security and defence objectives, reforms and country-specific NATO assistance. IPAPs were concluded with Azerbaijan in May 2005, Armenia in December, Kazakhstan in January 2006 and with Moldova in May. In 2008 Bosnia and Herzegovina and the former Yugoslav republic of Macedonia determined to develop IPAPs.

The enlargement of NATO, through the admission of new members from the former USSR and Central and Eastern European countries, was considered to be a progressive means of contributing to the enhanced stability and security of the Euro-Atlantic area. In December 1996 NATO ministers of foreign affairs announced that invitations to join the Alliance would be issued to some former eastern bloc countries during 1997. The NATO Secretary-General and member governments subsequently began intensive diplomatic efforts to secure Russia's tolerance of these developments. It was agreed that no nuclear weapons or large numbers of troops would be deployed on the territory of any new member country in the former Eastern bloc. In May 1997 NATO and Russia signed the Founding Act on Mutual Relations, Co-operation and Security, which provided for enhanced Russian participation in all NATO decision-making activities, equal status in peace-keeping operations and representation at the Alliance headquarters at ambassadorial level, as part of a recognized shared political commitment to maintaining stability and security throughout the Euro-Atlantic region. A NATO-Russian Permanent Joint Council (PJC) was established under the Founding Act, and met for the first time in July; the Council provided each side the opportunity for consultation and participation in the other's security decisions, but without a right of veto. In March 1999 Russia condemned NATO's military action against the Federal Republic of Yugoslavia and announced the suspension of all relations within the framework of the Founding Act, as well as negotiations on the establishment of a NATO mission in Moscow. The PJC convened once more in May 2000, and subsequent meetings were held in June and December. In February 2001 the NATO Secretary-General agreed with the then acting Russian President a joint statement of commitment to pursuing dialogue and co-operation. A NATO information office was opened in Moscow in that month. In December an agreement was concluded by NATO ministers of foreign affairs and their Russian counterpart to establish an eventual successor body to the PJC. The new NATO-Russia Council, in which NATO member states and Russia were to have equal status in decision-making, was inaugurated in May 2002. The Council aimed to strengthen co-operation in issues including counter-terrorism, crisis management, nuclear non-proliferation, and arms control. The third NATO-Russia conference on the role of the military in combating terrorism was convened in April 2004. In September the Council issued a joint statement condemning atrocities committed against civilians in North Ossetia and other parts of the Russian Federation. In April 2005, at an informal meeting of the ministers of foreign affairs of the NATO-Russia Council, Russia signed the PfP Status of Forces Agreement that provides a legal framework for the movement to and from Allied countries, partner countries and Russia of military personnel and support staff. In June a meeting of the Council endorsed Political-Military Guidance towards Enhanced Interoperability between Russian and NATO forces, thereby facilitating the preparation of those forces for possible joint operations. In April 2006 an informal meeting of the Council's ministers of foreign affairs reviewed NATO-Russia co-operation to date and adopted recommendations identifying interoperability, a pilot Afghanistan counter-narcotics project, a co-operative airspace initiative (CAI) and intensified political dialogue as the priority areas for future co-operation. In April 2008 the NRC, meeting at the level of heads of state, determined to extend on a permanent basis the joint project on counter-narcotics training of Afghan and Central Asian personnel and to accelerate the CAI project to ensure it reaches full operational capability by the end of 2009.

In May 1997 NATO ministers of foreign affairs, meeting in Sintra, Portugal, concluded an agreement with Ukraine providing for enhanced co-operation between the two sides; the so-called Charter on a Distinctive Relationship was signed at the NATO summit meeting held in Madrid, Spain, in July. In May 1998 NATO agreed to appoint a permanent liaison officer in Ukraine to enhance co-operation between the two sides and assist Ukraine to formulate a programme of joint military exercises. The first NATO-Ukraine meeting at the level of heads of state took place in April 1999. A NATO-Ukraine Commission met for the first time in March 2000. In February 2005, at a NATO-Ukraine summit meeting, NATO leaders expressed support for Ukraine's reform agenda and agreed to strengthen co-operation with the country. In view of its commitment to strengthened co-operation, NATO announced that it would launch a project, the largest of its kind ever undertaken, to assist Ukraine in the decommissioning of old ammunitions, small arms and light weapons stockpiles. In April NATO invited Ukraine to begin an 'Intensified Dialogue' on its aspirations to NATO membership and on the necessary relevant reforms that it would be required to undertake. In the same month NATO and Ukraine effected an exchange of letters preparing the way for Ukraine to support 'Operation Active Endeavour' (see below). In June talks held between NATO ministers of defence and their Ukrainian counterpart focused on NATO's assistance to Ukraine in the reform of its defence and security sectors. In October the NATO-Ukraine Commission held its first meeting within the framework of the Intensified Dialogue initiated in April. A meeting of the ministers of defence of the NATO-Ukraine Commission held in June 2006 discussed Ukraine's defence policy and the ongoing transformation of the Ukrainian armed forces. In this context, ministers confirmed that the NATO-Ukraine Joint Working Group on Defence Reform should remain a key mechanism. In April 2008 NATO heads of state and government approved, in principle, Ukraine's future membership of the Alliance.

The Madrid summit meeting in July 1997 endorsed the establishment of a Mediterranean Co-operation Group to enhance NATO relations with Egypt, Israel, Jordan, Mauritania, Morocco and Tunisia. The Group was to provide a forum for regular political dialogue between the two groupings and to promote co-operation in training, scientific research and information exchange. In April 1999 NATO heads of state endorsed measures to strengthen the so-called Mediterranean Dialogue. Algeria joined the Mediterranean Dialogue in February 2000. The June 2004 summit meeting determined to enhance the Mediterranean Dialogue and launched a new 'Istanbul Co-operation Initiative' aimed at promoting broader co-operation with the Middle East. By April 2007 Bahrain, Kuwait, Qatar and the UAE had joined the Istanbul Co-operation Initiative. In February 2006 NATO and Mediterranean Dialogue partner countries convened their first meeting at the level of ministers of defence. In April, under the chairmanship of NATO's Deputy Secretary-General, the NAC and representatives of the seven Mediterranean Dialogue countries met in Rabat, Morocco, in order to review their co-operation to date and to discuss its future prospects. All countries were encouraged to formulate Individual Co-operation Programmes as a framework for future co-operation. In November NATO heads of state and government, meeting in Riga, Latvia, inaugurated a NATO Training Co-operation Initiative to extend defence and specialist training and expertise with Mediterranean Dialogue and Istanbul Co-operation Initiative partner countries. The Initiative aimed to help those countries to strengthen their defence structures and enhance the interoperability of their armed forces with those of the Alliance.

In July 1997 heads of state and government formally invited the Czech Republic, Hungary and Poland to begin accession negotiations. Accession Protocols for the admission of those countries were signed in December and required ratification by all member states. The three countries formally became members of NATO in March 1999. In April the NATO summit meeting, held in Washington, DC, USA, initiated a new Membership Action Plan (MAP) to extend practical support to aspirant member countries and to formalize a process of reviewing applications. In March 2003 protocols of accession, amending the North Atlantic Treaty, were adopted by the then 19 NATO member states with a view to admitting Bulgaria, Estonia, Latvia, Lithuania, Romania, Slovakia and Slovenia to the Alliance. In March 2004, the protocols of accession having been ratified by all of the member states, those seven countries were formally invited to join NATO and, on 29 March, they acceded to the Treaty. In April 2008 NATO heads of state and government, meeting in Bucharest, Romania, invited Albania and Croatia to commence accession negotiations and declared support for Georgia and Ukraine to apply for MAP status.

OPERATIONS

During the 1990s NATO increasingly developed its role as a mechanism for peace-keeping and crisis management. In June 1992 NATO ministers of foreign affairs, meeting in Oslo, Norway, announced the Alliance's readiness to support peace-keeping operations under the aegis of the CSCE on a case-by-case basis: NATO would make both military resources and expertise available to such operations. In July NATO, in co-operation with WEU, undertook a maritime operation in the Adriatic Sea to monitor compliance with the UN Security Council's resolutions imposing sanctions against the Yugoslav republics of Serbia and Montenegro. In October NATO was requested to provide staff and finance the military headquarters of the United Nations peace-keeping force in Bosnia and Herzegovina, the UN Protection Force in Yugoslavia (UNPROFOR). In December NATO ministers of foreign affairs expressed the Alliance's readiness to support peace-keeping operations under the authority of the UN Security Council. From April 1993 NATO fighter and reconnaissance aircraft began patrolling airspace over Bosnia and Herzegovina in order to enforce the UN prohibition of military aerial activity over the country. In addition, from July NATO aircraft provided protective cover for UNPROFOR troops operating in the 'safe areas' established by the UN Security Council. In February 1994 NATO conducted the first of several aerial strikes against artillery positions that were violating heavy-weapons exclusion zones imposed around 'safe areas' and threatening the civilian populations. Throughout the conflict the Alliance also provided transport, communications and logistics to support UN humanitarian assistance in the region.

The peace accord for the former Yugoslavia, which was initialled in Dayton, USA, in November 1995, and signed in Paris in December, provided for the establishment of a NATO-led Implementation Force (IFOR) to ensure compliance with the treaty, in accordance with a strictly defined timetable and under the authority of a UN Security Council mandate. In December a joint meeting of allied foreign and defence ministers endorsed the military structure for the peace mission, entitled 'Operation Joint Endeavour', which was to involve approximately 60,000 troops from 31 NATO and non-NATO countries. IFOR, which constituted NATO's largest military operation ever, formally assumed responsibility for peace-keeping in Bosnia and Herzegovina from the UN on 20 December.

By mid-1996 the military aspects of the Dayton peace agreement had largely been implemented under IFOR supervision. Substantial progress was achieved in the demobilization of soldiers and militia and in the cantonment of heavy weaponry. During 1996 IFOR personnel undertook many activities relating to the civilian reconstruction of Bosnia and Herzegovina, including the repair of roads, railways and bridges, reconstruction of schools and hospitals, delivery of emergency food and water supplies, and emergency medical transportation. IFOR also co-operated with, and provided logistical support for, the Office of the High Representative of the International Community in Bosnia and Herzegovina, which was charged with overseeing implementation of the civilian aspects of the Bosnian peace accord. IFOR assisted the OSCE in preparing for and overseeing the all-Bosnia legislative elections that were held in September, and provided security for displaced Bosnians who crossed the inter-entity boundary in order to vote in their towns of origin. In December NATO ministers of foreign affairs approved a follow-on operation, with an 18-month mandate, to be known as the Stabilization Force (SFOR). SFOR was to be about one-half the size of IFOR, but was to retain 'the same unity of command and robust rules of engagement' as the previous force. Its principal objective was to maintain a safe environment at a military level to ensure that the civil aspects of the Dayton peace accord could be fully implemented, including the completion of the de-mining process, the repatriation of refugees, rehabilitation of local infrastructure and preparations for municipal elections. In December 1997 NATO ministers of defence confirmed that SFOR would be maintained at its current strength of some 31,000 troops, subject to the periodic six-monthly reviews. In February 1998 NATO resolved to establish within SFOR a specialized unit to respond to civil unrest and uphold public security. At the same time the NAC initiated a series of security co-operation activities to promote the development of democratic practices and defence mechanisms in Bosnia and Herzegovina. In October 1999 the NAC formally agreed to implement a reduction in SFOR's strength to some 20,000 troops, as well as a revision of its command structure, in response to the improved security situation in Bosnia and Herzegovina. In May 2002 NATO determined to reduce SFOR to 12,000 troops by the end of that year, and in December 2003 NATO defence ministers undertook to reduce NATO's presence to some 7,000 troops by mid-2004. The June 2004 summit meeting determined to terminate SFOR's mandate at the end of 2004, and endorsed an EU initiative to establish a new mission, EUFOR, in Bosnia and Herzegovina. NATO maintains a military headquarters in Sarajevo, in order to continue to assist the authorities in Bosnia and Herzegovina in matters of defence reform.

In March 1998 an emergency session of the NAC was convened at the request of the Albanian Government, which was concerned at the deteriorating security of its border region with the Serbian province of Kosovo and Metohija. In June NATO defence ministers authorized the formulation of plans for airstrikes against Serbian targets. A few days later some 80 aircraft dispatched from 15 NATO bases flew close to Albania's border with Kosovo, in an attempt to demonstrate the Alliance's determination to prevent further reprisals against the ethnic Albanian population. Plans for NATO airstrikes were finalized in early October. However, the Russian Government remained strongly opposed to the use of force and there was concern among some member states over whether there was sufficient legal basis for NATO action without further UN authorization. Nevertheless, in mid-October, following Security Council condemnation of the humanitarian situation in Kosovo, the NAC agreed on limited airstrikes against Serbian targets, with a 96-hour delay on the 'activation order'. At the same time the US envoy to the region, Richard Holbrooke, concluded an agreement with President Milošević to implement the conditions of a UN resolution (1199). A 2,000-member international observer force, under the auspices of the OSCE, was to be established to monitor compliance with the agreement, supported by a NATO Co-ordination Unit, based in the former Yugoslav republic of Macedonia (FYRM), to assist with aerial surveillance. In mid-November NATO ambassadors approved the establishment of a 1,200–1,800 strong multinational force, under French command, to assist in any necessary evacuation of OSCE monitors. A NATO Kosovo Verification Command Centre was established in Kumanovo, north-east FYRM, later in that month. In January 1999 NATO ambassadors convened in an emergency session following the discovery of the bodies of 45 ethnic Albanians in the Kosovan village of Racak. Intensive diplomatic efforts, co-ordinated by the six-country 'Contact Group' on the former Yugoslavia, succeeded in bringing both sides in the dispute to talks on the future of Kosovo. President Milošević, however, continued to oppose the establishment of a NATO force in Kosovo and declined to endorse a political agreement in accordance with a deadline imposed by the Contact Group. Amid reports of renewed Serbian violence against Albanian civilians in Kosovo, the NAC subsequently reconfirmed its support for NATO military intervention.

On 24 March 1999 an aerial offensive against the Federal Republic of Yugoslavia (which was renamed 'Serbia and Montenegro' in 2003 and divided into separate states of Montenegro and Serbia in 2006) was initiated by NATO, with the declared aim of reducing that country's capacity to commit attacks on the Albanian population. The first phase of the allied operation was directed against defence facilities, followed, a few days later, by the second phase which permitted direct attacks on artillery positions, command centres and other military targets in a declared exclusion zone south of the 44th parallel. The escalation of the conflict prompted thousands of Albanians to flee Kosovo, while others were reportedly forced from their homes by Serbian security personnel, creating massive refugee populations in neighbouring countries. In early April NATO ambassadors agreed to dispatch some 8,000 troops, as an ACE Mobile Force Land operation (entitled 'Operation Allied Harbour'), to provide humanitarian assistance to the estimated 300,000 refugees in Albania at that time and to provide transportation to relieve overcrowded camps, in particular in border areas. Refugees in the FYRM were to be assisted by the existing NATO contingent (numbering some 12,000 troops by early April), which was permitted by the authorities in that country to construct new camps for some 100,000 displaced Kosovans. An additional 1,000 troops were transferred from the FYRM to Albania in mid-May in order to construct a camp to provide for a further 65,000 refugees. NATO's 50th anniversary summit meeting, held in Washington, DC, USA, in late April, was dominated by consideration of the conflict and of the future stability of the region. A joint statement declared the determination of all Alliance members to increase economic and military pressure on President Milošević to withdraw forces from Kosovo. In particular, the meeting agreed to prevent shipments of petroleum reaching Serbia through Montenegro, to complement the embargo imposed by the EU and a new focus of the bombing campaign which aimed to destroy the fuel supply within Serbia. However, there was concern on the part of several NATO governments with regard to the legal and political aspects of implementing the embargo. The meeting failed to adopt a unified position on the use of ground forces. Following further intensive diplomatic efforts to secure a cease-fire in Kosovo, on 9 June a Military Technical Agreement was signed between NATO and the Federal Republic of Yugoslavia, incorporating a timetable for the withdrawal of all Serbian security personnel. On the following day the UN Security Council adopted Resolution 1244, which authorized an international security presence in Kosovo, under NATO, the Kosovo Peace Implementation Force (KFOR), and an international civilian presence, the UN Interim Administration Mission in Kosovo (UNMIK). The NAC subsequently suspended the airstrike campaign, which, by that time, had involved some 38,000 sorties. An initial 20,000 KFOR troops entered Kosovo on 12 June. A few days later an agreement was concluded with Russia, whose troops had also entered Kosovo and taken control of Pristina airport, which provided for the joint responsibility of the airstrip with a NATO contingent and for the participation of some 3,600 Russian troops in KFOR, reporting to the country command in each sector. On 20 June the withdrawal of Yugoslav troops from Kosovo was completed, providing for the formal ending of NATO's air campaign. KFOR's immediate responsibility was to provide a secure environment to facilitate the safe return of refugees, and, pending the full deployment of UNMIK, to assist the reconstruction of infrastructure and civil and political institutions. In addition, NATO troops were to assist personnel of the international tribunal to investigate sites of alleged violations of human rights and mass graves. In January 2000 NATO agreed that the Eurocorps defence force would assume command of KFOR headquarters in April. At that time KFOR's main concerns were to protect the minority populations, maintain security and reintegrate members of the KLA into civilian life. KFOR was also to continue to work closely with UNMIK in the provision of humanitarian aid, the rehabilitation of infrastructure and the development of civil administration. In February an emergency meeting of the NAC was convened to review the situation in the divided town of Titova Mitrovica, northern Kosovo, where violent clashes had occurred between the ethnic populations and five people had died during attempts by KFOR to impose order. The NAC expressed its determination to reinforce KFOR's troop levels. In October KFOR worked with OSCE and UN personnel to maintain a secure environment and provide logistical assistance for the holding of municipal elections in Kosovo. During the year KFOR attempted to prevent the movement and stockpiling of illegal armaments in the region. In November there was a marked deterioration in the security situation in Kosovo, and KFOR attempted to halt several outbreaks of cross-border violence. A Weapons Destruction Programme was successfully conducted by KFOR between April 2000–December 2001; a second programme was initiated in March 2002, while an Ammunition Destruction Programme commenced in January. In May the NAC approved a modification of KFOR's mission that was designed to facilitate the introduction of a more regional approach to operations and permit a reduction in KFOR's strength from 38,000 troops to some 33,200 by the end of the year. In July 2003, in view of progress made in the security situation, the withdrawal of the Russian contingent from KFOR was effected. In March 2004, in response to renewed inter-ethnic violence in Kosovo, NATO deployed additional troops from previously designated operational and strategic reserve forces in order to support operations undertaken by KFOR (whose strength totalled some 18,500 troops at this time) to protect Kosovar Serbs and other ethnic minorities in addition to ethnic Albanians. In mid-2005 NATO ministers of defence announced that KFOR would retain its full operational capability while the UN conducted a review of Kosovo's compliance with international standards, as a prelude, possibly, to the initiation of negotiations on Kosovo's final status. In February 2006 direct, UN-led talks between Serbian and Kosovo Albanian officials commenced in Vienna, Austria. Several more rounds of direct talks, as well as other expert missions, were conducted during 2006. A draft comprehensive proposal for a status settlement was presented to both sides in February 2007 and to the UN Security Council, for its consideration, in March. By the end of that year, however, the two sides, under the direction of the EU, Russia and USA 'troika', had failed to reach agreement on the future status of Kosovo. NATO's ministers of foreign affairs, meeting in December 2007, agreed that KFOR would remain in the province, at current troop levels, unless the UN Security Council decides otherwise. They also expressed NATO's readiness to implement any future security arrangement and to co-operate with all parties. In February 2008 Kosovo's governing authorities issued a unilateral declaration of independence from Serbia, supported by many EU countries. NATO's Secretary-General and NAC reaffirmed the commitment to maintain a force in Kosovo and to support any future arrangements. In March KFOR and UN personnel were injured during violent demonstration in north Mitrovica.

In March 2001 Albanian separatists in the FYRM escalated their campaign in the north of that country prompting thousands of Albanians to flee into Kosovo. KFOR troops attempted to prevent Kosovo Albanians from supporting the rebels, fighting as the National Liberation Army (NLA), in order to avert further violence and instability. NATO dispatched military and political missions to meet with the Macedonian authorities, and agreed that Serbian troops were to be permitted to enter the ground safety zone in the Presevo valley (bordering on Kosovo and the FYRM) to strengthen security and prevent it becoming a safe haven for the rebel fighters. In June NATO troops supervised the withdrawal of some 300 armed Albanian rebels who had been besieged in a town neighbouring Skopje, the Macedonian capital. A cease-fire agreement, mediated by NATO, was concluded by the Macedonian authorities and Albanian militants in early July. In mid-July, however, ethnic Albanian insurgents in the Tetovo area were reportedly violating the cease-fire accord. An agreement regarding disarmament and conditions for ethnic minorities, as well as for the immediate withdrawal of troops, was concluded in August. Some 3,800 NATO troops were deployed at the end of that month, under so-called 'Operation Essential Harvest'. At the end of the operation's 30-day mandate almost 4,300 guns had been surrendered, together with 400,000 mines, grenades and ammunition rounds. The NLA formally disbanded, in accordance with the peace agreement. The NAC approved a successor mission, 'Task Force Fox', comprising 700 troops, to protect the civilian observers of the accord (to be deployed by the EU and OSCE). In June 2002 a team from NATO headquarters met with the Macedonian authorities to discuss measures to enhance the country's co-operation with the Alliance. In November, as the expiry of the extended mandate of Task Force Fox approached, NATO agreed, at the request of the FYRM authorities, to deploy a new peace-keeping mission, 'Operation Allied Harmony', from December in order to afford continued protection to the civilian observers of the cease-fire accord and to assist the Macedonian authorities to assume responsibility for security. On 31 March 2003 NATO's peace-keeping mission in the FYRM was succeeded by an EU-led operation.

In September 2001, following the terrorist attacks against targets in the USA and the decision to invoke Article 5 of the North Atlantic Treaty, NATO redirected the standing naval force to provide an immediate Alliance presence in the Eastern Mediterranean. In the following month 'Operation Active Endeavour' was formally launched, to undertake surveillance and monitoring of maritime trade in the region and to detect and deter terrorist activity, including illegal trafficking. In February 2003 the NAC agreed to extend the operation to escort non-military vessels through the Strait of Gibraltar; this aspect of the mission was suspended in May 2004. In March 2004 the NAC determined to expand the operation to the whole of the Mediterranean and to seek the support of this extension, through their active participation in the operation, by participants in the EAPC and the PfP programme. An Exchange of Letters between NATO and Russia, concluded in December 2004, facilitated the implementation from February 2006 of joint training activities. In September 2006 NATO authorized the participation of a Russian naval ship in the operation. The NAC approved the active involvement of a Ukrainian ship in the operation in May 2007. By early 2008 more than 75,000 vessels had been monitored under the operation, and some 100 compliant boardings had taken place.

In August 2003 NATO undertook its first mission outside of the Euro-Atlantic area when it assumed command of the UN-mandated International Security Assistance Force (ISAF) in Afghanistan. In October the office of a Senior Civilian Representative was established to liaise with the national government and representatives of the international community and advance NATO's politico-military objectives in the country. In December NATO ministers of defence agreed progressively to extend ISAF's mission in Afghanistan beyond the capital, Kabul. The transfer of command of the Kunduz Provincial Reconstruction Team (PRT) to NATO in January 2004 represented the first step of that expansion. In June the summit meeting, held in Istanbul, Turkey, determined to expand the ISAF in order to assist the Afghan authorities to extend and exercise authority across the country. A first phase of the mission's expansion, involving the establishment of PRTs in Baghlan, Feyzabad, Mazar-e-Sharif and Meymana, had been completed by October of that year. In December the NAC authorized a second expansionary phase, which envisaged the establishment of four PRTs in western provinces of Afghanistan. This was undertaken in 2005. In September an additional 2,000 NATO troops were temporarily deployed to Afghanistan to provide security during provincial and parliamentary elections, held in that month. In December NATO ministers of foreign affairs endorsed a revised operational plan to incorporate a Stage 3 and Stage 4 Expansion of ISAF. The Stage 3 and Stage 4 Expansions, achieved, respectively, in July and October 2006, entailed extending operations to cover the entire country and establishing 15 additional PRTs, five regional commands and two forward support bases (in Kandahar and Khost). Additional ISAF officers were dispatched to mentor and liaise with national army units, support government programmes to disarm rebel groups and support government and international programmes to counter illicit narcotic production. NATO continued to emphasize immediate reconstruction and development activities, through its civil military co-operation units, working closely with government and local and community leaders, and co-operated with the Pakistani military and Afghan National Army through a Tripartite Commission and a Joint Intelligence and Operations Centre. By early 2008 NATO was commanding some 47,000 troops (including National Support Elements) from 40 countries and 26 PRTs. In September 2006 NATO's Secretary-General signed a declaration with the Afghan President establishing a Framework for Enduring Co-operation in Partnership, committing NATO to long-term support for the country's efforts to secure democratic government and territorial integrity.

In June 2004 NATO heads of state and government, meeting in Istanbul, Turkey, agreed to offer assistance to the newly-inaugurated Iraqi Interim Government with the training of its security forces. The meeting also endorsed a new NATO Policy on Combating Trafficking in Human Beings, with the aim of supporting the efforts of countries and international organizations to counter the problem. In July a NATO Training Implementation Mission was initiated to undertake the training commitments in Iraq. In December the NAC authorized an expansion of the Mission, of up to 300 personnel, and the establishment of an Iraq Training, Education and Doctrine Centre. The expanded operation was to be called the NATO Training Mission–Iraq. By April 2008 it had trained more than 10,000 members of the Iraqi security forces, and had an extended mandate until 2009. In September 2005 an Iraqi Joint Staff College was inaugurated.

In April 2005 the African Union (AU) requested NATO assistance to support its peace-keeping mission in Darfur, western Sudan, where civil conflict had caused a severe humanitarian crisis. In May the NAC provisionally agreed to provide logistical support for the mission. Further consultations were held with the AU, UN and EU. In June the NAC confirmed that it would assist in the expansion of the AU mission (AMIS) by airlifting supplementary AU peace-keepers into the region. No NATO combat troops were to be deployed to Darfur. The first airlifts were undertaken in July and in August NATO agreed to transport civilian police officers. NATO established a Senior Military Liaison Officer team, in Addis Ababa, Ethiopia, to liaise with the AU. In June 2006 the AU requested enhanced NATO assistance for its peace-keeping mission in Darfur, including the certification of troops allocated to the peace-keeping force, assistance with lessons learned and support in the establishment of a joint operations centre. NATO undertook staff training to further the mission's capacity-building activities. In November NATO ministers extended its support for proposals by the AU and UN to undertake a hybrid peace-keeping mission in Darfur. NATO support to AMIS was concluded on 31 December 2007 when the mission was transferred to the UN/AU operation. In June 2007 NATO agreed to support an AU mission in Somalia by providing strategic airlifts for deployment of personnel and equipment.

From October 2005 until 1 February 2006 NATO undertook a mission to provide relief to areas of north-west Pakistan severely damaged and isolated by a massive earthquake. NATO airlifted relief supplies into the region, transported civilians and official personnel, and deployed some 1,200 engineers and troops to assist with road clearance and the construction of shelters and other local infrastructure.

NATO Agencies

Civilian production and logistics organizations responsible to the NAC:

Central Europe Pipeline Management Agency (CEPMA): BP 552, 78005 Versailles Cédex, France; tel. 1-39-24-49-00; fax 1-39-55-65-39; f. 1957; responsible for the 24-hour operation of the Central Europe Pipeline System and its storage and distribution facilities.

NATO Air Command and Control System Management Agency (NACMA): Bâtiment Z, 140 ave du Bourget, 1110 Brussels, Belgium; tel. (2) 707-41-11; fax (2) 707-87-77; internet www.nacma.nato.int; conducts planning, system engineering, implementation and configuration management for NATO's ACCS programme.

NATO Airborne Early Warning and Control Programme Management Organisation (NAPMO): Akerstraat 7, 6445 CL Brunssum, Netherlands; fax (45) 5254373; f. 1978; responsible for the management and implementation of the NATO Airborne Early Warning and Control Programme.

NATO Consultation, Command and Control Agency (NC3A): 1110 Brussels, Belgium; tel. (2) 707-41-11; fax (2) 707-87-70; internet www.nc3a.nato.int; works within the framework of the NATO C3 Organization (f. 1996 by restructuring of the NATO Communications and Information Systems Organization and the Tri-Service Group on Communications and Electronics, incorporating the former Allied Data Systems Interoperability Agency, the Allied Naval Communications Agency and the Allied Tactical Communications Agency); provides scientific advice and assistance to NATO military and political authorities; helps to develop, procure and implement cost-effective system capabilities to support political consultations and military command and control functions; also maintains offices in The Hague.

NATO CIS Operating and Support Agency (NACOSA): maintains NATO's communications and information system (CIS); supervised by the NC3 Board.

NATO Communications and Information Systems (NCISS) School: 04010 Borgo Piave, Latina, Italy; tel. (0773) 6771; fax (0773) 662467; e-mail tc@nciss.nato.it; internet www.nciss.nato.it; f. 1959; provides advanced training to civilian and military personnel in the operation and maintenance of NATO's communications and information systems; conducts orientation courses for partner countries.

NATO EF 2000 and Tornado Development, Production and Logistics Management Agency (NETMA): Insel Kammerstrasse 12–14, Postfach 1302, 82008 Unterhaching, Germany; tel. (89) 666800; fax (89) 66680555; replaced the NATO Multirole Combat Aircraft (MRCA) Development and Production Management Agency (f. 1969) and the NATO European Fighter (EF) Aircraft Development, Production and Logistics Management Agency (f. 1987); responsible for the joint development and production of the European Fighter Aircraft and the MRCA (Tornado).

NATO HAWK Management Office: 26 rue Galliéni, 92500 Rueil-Malmaison, France; tel. 1-47-08-75-00; fax 1-47-52-10-99; e-mail bgohnhmo@csi.com; f. 1959 to supervise the multinational production and upgrading programmes of the HAWK surface-to-air missile system in Europe; Gen. Man. A. BOCCHI.

NATO Helicopter Design and Development Production and Logistics Management Agency (NAHEMA): Le Quatuor, Bâtiment A, 42 route de Galice, 13082 Aix-en-Provence Cédex 2, France; tel. 4-42-95-92-00; fax 4-42-64-30-50.

NATO Maintenance and Supply Agency (NAMSA): 11 rue de la Gare, 8325 Capellen, Luxembourg; tel. 30-631; fax 30-87-21; e-mail CONTACT@namsa.nato.int; internet www.namsa.nato.int; f. 1958; provides logistics services to NATO and NATO nations; Gen. Man. KARL-HEINZ MÜNZNER.

Responsible to the Military Committee:

NATO Civil/Military Frequency Management Sub-Committee (Civ./Mil. FMSC): 1110 Brussels, Belgium; tel. (2) 707-55-28; e-mail chsmb@hq.nato.int; replaced the Allied Radio Frequency Agency (f. 1951); the Civ./Mil. FMSC is the frequency authority of the Alliance and establishes and co-ordinates in close co-operation with civil Authorities all policy concerned with the military use of the radio frequency spectrum; Branch Chief JOACHIM-S. STRICK.

NATO Defense College (NDC): Via Giorgio Pelosi 1, 00143 Rome Cecchignola, Italy; tel. (06) 5052591; fax (06) 50525799; internet www.ndc.nato.int; f. 1951 to train officials for posts in NATO organizations or in national ministries; organizes international research seminars; Commandant Lt-Gen. MARC VANKEIRSBILCK (Belgium).

NATO Standardisation Agency (NSA): 1110 Brussels, Belgium; tel. (2) 707-55-76; fax (2) 707-57-18; e-mail NSA@hq.nato.int; lead agent for the development, co-ordination and assessment of operational standardization, in order to enhance interoperability; initiates, co-ordinates, supports and administers standardization activities conducted under the authority of the NATO Committee for Standardisation.

Research and Technology Organisation (RTO): BP 25, 7 rue Ancelle, 92201 Neuilly-sur-Seine Cédex, France; tel. 1-55-61-22-00; fax 1-55-61-22-99; e-mail mailbox@rta.nato.int; internet www.rta.nato.int; f. 1998 by merger of the Advisory Group for Aerospace Research and Development and the Defence Research Group; brings together scientists and engineers from member countries for exchange of information and research co-operation (formally established 1998); provides scientific and technical advice for the Military Committee, for other NATO bodies and for member nations; comprises a Research and Technology Board and a Research and Technology Agency, responsible for implementing RTO's work programme.

Responsible to Supreme Allied Commander Europe (SACEUR):

NATO (SHAPE) School: Am Rainenbichl 54, 82487 Oberammergau, Germany; tel. (8822) 94811052; fax (8822) 94811396; e-mail pao@natoschool.nato.int; internet www.natoschool.nato.int; f. 1975; acts as a centre for training military and civilian personnel of NATO countries, and, since 1991, for officials from partner countries, in support of NATO policies, operations and objectives; Commandant Col JAMES J. TABAK.

Responsible to Supreme Allied Commander Transformation:

NATO Undersea Research Centre (NURC): Viale San Bartolomeo 400, 19126 La Spezia, Italy; tel. (0187) 5271; fax (0187) 527700; e-mail pio@nurc.nato.int; internet www.nurc.nato.int; f. 1959; conducts maritime research in response to NATO's operational and transformational requirements, in particular through its science programme; focuses on the undersea domain and on solutions to maritime security problems; brings researchers together through rotational scientific staffing and through extensive partnering with NATO mem. states; Dir Dr FRANÇOIS-RÉGIS MARTIN-LAUZER.

Finance

As NATO is an international, not a supra-national, organization, its member countries themselves decide the amount to be devoted to their defence effort and the form which the latter will assume. Thus, the aim of NATO's defence planning is to develop realistic military plans for the defence of the Alliance at reasonable cost. Under the annual defence planning process, political, military and economic factors are considered in relation to strategy, force requirements and available resources. The procedure for the co-ordination of military plans and defence expenditures rests on the detailed and comparative analysis of the capabilities of member countries. All installations for the use of international forces are financed under a common-funded infrastructure programme. In accordance with the terms of the Partnership for Peace strategy, partner countries undertake to make available the necessary personnel, assets, facilities and capabilities to participate in the programme. The countries also share the financial cost of military exercises in which they participate.

Publications

NATO publications (in English and French, with some editions in other languages) include:

NATO Basic Texts.
NATO Handbook.
NATO in the 21st Century.
NATO Ministerial Communiqués.
NATO Review (quarterly, in 24 languages).
NATO Update (monthly, electronic version only).
Economic and scientific publications.

ORGANISATION FOR ECONOMIC CO-OPERATION AND DEVELOPMENT—OECD

Address: 2 rue André-Pascal, 75775 Paris Cédex 16, France.
Telephone: 1-45-24-82-00; **fax:** 1-45-24-85-00; **e-mail:** webmaster@oecd.org; **internet:** www.oecd.org.

OECD was founded in 1961, replacing the Organisation for European Economic Co-operation (OEEC) which had been established in 1948 in connection with the Marshall Plan. It constitutes a forum for governments to discuss, develop and attempt to co-ordinate their economic and social policies. The organization aims to promote policies designed to achieve the highest level of sustainable economic growth, employment and increase in the standard of living, while maintaining financial stability and democratic government, and to contribute to economic expansion in member and non-member states and to the expansion of world trade.

MEMBERS

Australia
Austria
Belgium
Canada
Czech Republic
Denmark
Finland
France
Germany
Greece
Hungary
Iceland
Ireland
Italy
Japan
Republic of Korea
Luxembourg
Mexico
Netherlands
New Zealand
Norway
Poland
Portugal
Slovakia
Spain
Sweden
Switzerland
Turkey
United Kingdom
USA

The European Commission also takes part in OECD's work.

Organization
(April 2008)

COUNCIL

The governing body of OECD is the Council, at which each member country is represented. The Council meets from time to time (usually once a year) at the level of government ministers, with the chairmanship rotated among member states. It also meets regularly at official level, when it comprises the Secretary-General and the Permanent Representatives of member states to OECD. It is responsible for all questions of general policy and may establish subsidiary bodies as required, to achieve the aims of the organization. Decisions and recommendations of the Council are adopted by mutual agreement of all its members.

Heads of Permanent Delegations
(with ambassadorial rank)

Australia: Christopher Langman.
Austria: Wolfgang Petritsch.
Belgium: Chris Hoornaert.
Canada: Paul-Henri Lapointe.
Czech Republic: Karel Dyba.
Denmark: (vacant).
Finland: Pertti Majanen.
France: Philippe Marland.
Germany: Dr Matei Ion Hoffman.
Greece: Anthony Nikolaos Tatsos.
Hungary: Péter Gottfried.
Iceland: Tómas Ingi Olrich.
Ireland: Paul Murray.
Italy: Bruno Cabras.
Japan: Norio Hattori.
Republic of Korea: Tae-shin Kwon.
Luxembourg: Georges Santer.
Mexico: Augustin García-López Loaeza.
Netherlands: Joan Boer.
New Zealand: Sarah Dennis.
Norway: Harald Neple.
Poland: Jan Woroniecki.
Portugal: Eduardo Ferro Rodrigues.
Slovakia: Jana Kotová.
Spain: (vacant).
Sweden: Mats Ringborg.
Switzerland: Eric Martin.
Turkey: Ahmet Erozan.
United Kingdom: David Lyscom.
USA: Christopher Egan.
European Commission: Laurence Argimon-Pistre.

EXECUTIVE COMMITTEE

The Executive Committee prepares the work of the Council. It is also called upon to carry out specific tasks where necessary. In addition to its regular meetings, the Committee meets occasionally in special sessions attended by senior government officials.

SECRETARIAT

The Council, the committees and other bodies in OECD are assisted by an independent international secretariat headed by the Secretary-General. An Executive Director is responsible for the management of administrative support services. There are OECD Centres in Berlin, Germany; Mexico City, Mexico; Tokyo, Japan; and Washington, DC, USA.

Secretary-General: José Ángel Gurría Treviño (Mexico).
Deputy Secretaries-General: Aart Jan de Geus (Netherlands), Thelma J. Askey (USA), Pier Carlo Padoan (Italy), Mari Amano (Japan).

AUTONOMOUS AND SEMI-AUTONOMOUS BODIES

African Partnership Forum.
Centre for Educational Research and Innovation (CERI).
Development Centre.
Financial Action Task Force.
International Energy Agency.
International Transport Forum.
Nuclear Energy Agency.
Sahel and West Africa Club.

Activities

The greater part of the work of OECD, which covers all aspects of economic and social policy, is prepared and carried out in about 200 specialized bodies (committees, working parties, etc); all members are normally represented on these bodies, except on those of a restricted nature.

OECD administers a support unit to the Heiligendamm Process, which was inaugurated in June 2007 with the aim of strengthening relations between the Group of Seven industrialized nations and Russia (the G-8) and the main emerging economies, so-called Outreach economies, i.e. Brazil, the People's Republic of China, India, Mexico and South Africa. The dialogue was to be pursued, initially for two years, within the following thematic framework: cross border investment; innovation and intellectual property; energy and climate change; and development, in particular in Africa.

ECONOMIC POLICY

OECD aims to promote stable macroeconomic environments in member and non-member countries. The Economics Department works to identify priority concerns for governments and to assess the economic implications of a broad range of structural issues, such as ageing, labour market policies, migration, public expenditure and financial market developments. *Economic Outlook*, analysing the major trends in short-term economic prospects and key policy issues, is published twice a year. The main organ for the consideration and direction of economic policy is the Economic Policy Committee, which comprises governments' chief economic advisers and central bankers, and meets two or three times a year. It has several working parties and groups, including Working Party No. 1 on Macro-Economic and Structural Policy Analysis, Working Party No. 3 on Policies for the Promotion of Better International Payments Equilibrium, and the Working Party on Short-Term Economic Prospects.

The Economic and Development Review Committee, comprising all member countries, is responsible for surveys of the economic situation and macroeconomic and structural policies of each member country. A report, including specific policy recommendations, is issued every 12 to 18 months on each country, after an examination carried out by the Committee.

STATISTICS

Statistical data and related methodological information are collected from member governments and, where possible, consolidated, or converted into an internationally comparable form. The Statistics Directorate maintains and makes available data required for macro-economic forecasting, i.e. national accounts, the labour force, foreign trade, prices, output, and monetary, financial, industrial and other short-term statistics. Work is also undertaken to develop new statistics and new statistical standards and systems in areas of emerging policy interest (such as sustainable development). In addition, the Directorate passes on to non-member countries member states' experience in compiling statistics. In the early 2000s a new Statistical Information System, incorporating new technical infrastructure, was developed which aimed to improve the efficiency of data collection, processing, storage etc, to improve the quality of OECD statistics, and to enhance accessibility to the data. In April 2004 a new Experts Group on Statistical and Metadata Exchange began work to foster dialogue with external partners on strategic issues relating to the development and practical implementation of new technologies and procedures for statistical data exchange. The first World Forum on Statistics, Knowledge and Policy was held in November, in Palermo, Italy. The second Forum, on the theme of Measuring and Fostering the Progress of Societies, was convened in Istanbul, Turkey, in June 2007.

DEVELOPMENT CO-OPERATION

The Development Assistance Committee (DAC) is the principal body through which OECD deals with issues relating to co-operation with developing countries and is one of the key forums in which the major bilateral donors work together to increase their effectiveness in support of sustainable development. The DAC is supported by the Development Co-operation Directorate, which monitors aid programmes and resource flows, compiles statistics and seeks to establish codes of practice in aid. There are also working parties on statistics, on aid evaluation, on gender equality and on development co-operation and environment; and networks on poverty reduction, on good governance and capacity development, and on conflict, peace and development co-operation.

Guided by the Development Partnerships Strategy formulated in 1996, the DAC's mission is to foster co-ordinated, integrated, effective and adequately financed international efforts in support of sustainable economic and social development. Recognizing that developing countries themselves are ultimately responsible for their own development, the DAC concentrates on how international co-operation can contribute to the population's ability to overcome poverty and participate fully in society. Principal activities include: adopting authoritative policy guide-lines; conducting periodic critical reviews of members' programmes of development co-operation; providing a forum for dialogue, exchange of experience and the building of international consensus on policy and management issues; and publishing statistics and reports on aid and other resource flows to developing countries and countries in transition. A working set of indicators of development progress has been established by the DAC, in collaboration with experts from UN agencies (including the World Bank) and from developing countries.

The DAC holds an annual high-level meeting of ministers responsible for international aid, and heads of aid agencies from member governments, with senior officials from the World Bank, IMF and UNDP. In February–March 2005 OECD/DAC co-sponsored a High-Level Forum on Aid Effectiveness, held in Paris, France. The key issues arising from the Forum were considered at the DAC high level meeting, convened in mid-March. In addition, the meeting reviewed OECD's contribution to achieving the UN Millennium Development Goals, issues relating to development, peace and security, and a report commissioned by heads of state participating in the New Partnership for Africa's Development (NEPAD) entitled *Mutual Review of Development Effectiveness in the NEPAD context*.

Development Centre: f. 1962; acts as a forum for dialogue and undertakes research and policy analysis in order to assist the development of policy to stimulate economic and social growth in developing and emerging economies; membership open to both OECD and non-OECD countries.

Sahel and West Africa Club: f. 1976, initially to support countries affected by drought in the Sahel region of Africa; expanded to include other countries in West Africa in 2001; acts as an informal discussion grouping between some 17 African countries and OECD members.

African Partnership Forum: f. 2003, following G-8 meeting of heads of state in Evian, France; comprises representatives of G-8 countries, NEPAD and major bilateral and multilateral development partners; meets twice a year; aims to strengthen efforts in support of Africa's development.

PUBLIC GOVERNANCE AND TERRITORIAL DEVELOPMENT

The Public Governance and Territorial Development Directorate is concerned with identifying changing needs in society and in markets, and with helping countries to adapt their governmental systems and territorial policies. One of the Directorate's primary functions is to provide a forum for exchanging ideas on how to meet the challenges countries face in the area of governance. It is concerned with improving public sector governance through comparative data and analysis, the setting and promotion of standards, and the facilitation of transparency and peer review, as well as to encourage the participation of civil society in public governance. The Public Management Committee (PUMA) serves as a forum for senior officials responsible for the central management systems of government, providing information, analysis and recommendations on public management and governing capacity. A Working Party of Senior Budget Officials is the principal international forum for issues concerning international budgeting. In November 2004 the Global Forum on Governance considered methods of preventing and detecting corruption in public procurement. In 1992 a joint initiative of OECD and the European Union (EU), operating within OECD, was established to support good governance in the countries of Central and Eastern Europe that were to accede to, or were candidates for either accession to or association with, the EU. The so-called Support for Improvement in Governance and Management (SIGMA) programme assists in the reform and modernization of public institutions in those countries and assesses their progress in those areas.

In October 2007 OECD, with UNDP, the Organization of American States and the Inter-American Development Bank, inaugurated the Partnership for Democratic Governance, to assist developing countries to improve governance and strengthen their accountability and effectiveness. OECD hosts an advisory unit of the initiative.

The Territorial Development Policy Committee assists central governments with the design and implementation of more effective, area-based strategies, encourages the emergence of locally driven initiatives for economic development, and promotes better integration of local and national approaches. Generally, the Committee's work programme emphasizes the need for innovative policy initiatives and exchange of knowledge in a wide range of policies, such as entrepreneurship and technology diffusion and issues of social exclusion and urban deprivation. National and regional territorial reviews are undertaken to analyse economic and social trends and highlight governance issues.

INTERNATIONAL TRADE

The OECD Trade Committee, supports the continued liberalization and efficient operation of the multilateral trading system, with the aim of contributing to the expansion of world trade on a non-discriminatory basis. Its activities include examination of issues concerning trade relations among member countries as well as relations with non-member countries, and consideration and discussion of trade measures taken by a member country which adversely affect another's interests. Through its working parties, the Committee analyses trade issues relating to, for example, the environment and agriculture. It holds regular consultations with civil society organizations.

A Working Party on Export Credits and Credit Guarantees serves as a forum for the discussion and co-ordination of export credit policies. OECD maintains an Export Credit Arrangement, which provides a framework for the use of officially supported export credits, stipulating the most generous financial terms and conditions available. Governments participating in the Arrangement meet regularly. In 2000 the Working Party agreed an Action Statement on Bribery and Officially Supported Export Credits; this was strengthened and converted into an OECD Recommendation in December 2006. In June 2007 the OECD Council adopted a Revised Recommendation on Common Approaches to the Environment and Officially Supported Export Credits (updated from 2003).

The Trade Committee considers the challenges that are presented to the existing international trading system by financial or economic instability, the process of globalization of production and markets and the ensuing deeper integration of national economies. Following the entry into force of the World Trade Organization (WTO) agreements in 1995, OECD continued to study and assess aspects of the international trade agenda. In November 1999 OECD published a report on the impact of further trade liberalization on developing countries, in preparation for the next round of multilateral trade negotiations (which was launched by WTO in November 2001). OECD is committed to the Doha Development Agenda, the framework for the multilateral trade negotiations currently under way in WTO. OECD and WTO have established a joint database that provides information about trade-related technical assistance and capacity-building in respect of trade policy and regulation; trade development; and infrastructure. In accordance with the Doha Agenda OECD is undertaking analysis of the implications on business of the growing number of regional trade agreements and the relationship between those agreements and the multilateral system.

ENTREPRENEURSHIP AND LOCAL DEVELOPMENT

In June 2000 OECD convened a Ministerial Conference on Small and Medium-sized Enterprises (SMEs), in Bologna, Italy, and initiated a process to promote SMEs and entrepreneurship policies. A second Ministerial Conference was held in Istanbul, Turkey, in June 2004. Within the context of the so-called Bologna Process, an OECD Global Conference on SME and Entrepreneurship Funding was held in late March 2006, in Brasilia, Brazil. In July 2004 OECD established a Centre for Entrepreneurship, SMEs and Local Development. It was to be responsible for promoting OECD work on entrepreneurship and for bringing together experts in the field. In addition, it was to disseminate best practices on the design, implementation and evaluation of initiatives to promote entrepreneurship, SMEs and local economic and employment development.

FINANCIAL AND ENTERPRISE AFFAIRS

Promoting the efficient functioning of markets and enterprises and strengthening the multilateral framework for trade and investment is the responsibility of the main OECD committees and working groups supported by the Directorate for Financial and Enterprise Affairs. The Directorate analyses emerging trends, provides policy guide-lines and recommendations, gives examples of best practice and maintains benchmarks to measure progress.

The Committee on Capital Movements and Invisible Transactions monitors the implementation of the Codes of Liberalization of Invisible Transactions and of Current Invisible Operations as legally binding norms for all member countries. The Committee on International Investment and Multinational Enterprises monitors the OECD Guide-lines for Multinational Enterprises, a corporate Code of Conduct recommended by OECD member governments, business and labour units. A Declaration on International Investment and Multinational Enterprises, while non-binding, contains commitments on the conduct and treatment of foreign-owned enterprises established in member countries. A comprehensive review of the Declaration was completed in 2000. Negotiations on a Multilateral Agreement on Investment (MAI), initiated by OECD ministers in 1995 to provide a legal framework for international investment, broke down in October 1998, although 'informal consultation' on the issue was subsequently pursued.

The Committee on Competition Law and Policy promotes the harmonization of national competition policies, co-operation in competition law enforcement, common merger reporting rules and pro-competitive regulatory reform, the development of competition laws and institutions, and efforts to change policies that restrain competition. The Committee on Financial Markets exercises surveillance over recent developments, reform measures and structural and regulatory conditions in financial markets. It aims to promote international trade in financial services, to encourage the integration of non-member countries into the global financial system, and to improve financial statistics. The Insurance Committee monitors structural changes and reform measures in insurance markets, for example the liberalization of insurance markets, financial insolvency, co-operation on insurance and reinsurance policy, the monitoring and analysis of regulatory and structural developments, and private pensions and health insurance. A working party on private pensions meets twice a year. In 2002 OECD member governments approved guide-lines for the administration of private pension funds, the first initiative they had taken to set international standards for the governance and supervision of collective pension funds. Specialized work on public debt is undertaken by the Working Party on Government Debt Management. An OECD Global Forum on Public Debt Management and Emerging Government Securities Markets is convened each year.

In May 1997 the OECD Council endorsed plans to introduce a global ban on the corporate bribery of public officials; the OECD Convention on Bribery of Foreign Public Officials in International Business Transactions entered into force in February 1999. By January 2005 the Convention had been ratified by all 30 OECD member states and six non–member countries, of which total 35 had undergone a 'phase I' review of legislation conformity with anti-bribery standards. In May 1999 ministers endorsed a set of OECD Principles for Corporate Governance, covering ownership and control of corporate entities, the rights of shareholders, the role of stakeholders, transparency, disclosure and the responsibilities of boards. In 2000 these became one of the 12 core standards of global financial stability, and they are used as a benchmark by other international financial institutions. In 2002 OECD mandated a Steering Group on Corporate Governance to review and update the Principles. The revised set of Principles was published in 2004. OECD collaborates with the World Bank and other organizations to promote good governance world-wide, for example through regional round tables and the Global Corporate Governance Forum. OECD provides the secretariat for the Financial Action Task Force on Money Laundering (FATF), which develops and promotes policies to combat money-laundering.

TAXATION

OECD promotes internationally-accepted standards and practices of taxation, and provides a forum for the exchange of information and experience of tax policy and administration. The Committee on Fiscal Affairs is concerned with promoting the removal of tax barriers, monitoring the implementation and impact of major tax reforms, developing a neutral tax framework for electronic commerce, and studying the tax implications of the globalization of national economies. A Centre for Tax Policy and Administration supports the work of the Committee. Other activities include the publication of comparable statistics on taxation and guide-lines on transfer pricing, and the study of tax evasion and tax and electronic commerce. OECD is a sponsor, with the IMF and World Bank, of an International Tax Dialogue. OECD also convenes a Global Forum on Taxation to promote co-operation and dialogue with non-member countries. OECD administers a network of Multilateral Tax Centres that provide workshops and a venue for exchanges between national officials and OECD experts.

Since 1998 OECD has promoted co-ordinated action for the elimination of so-called 'harmful' tax practices, designed to reduce the incidence of international money-laundering, and the level of potential tax revenue lost by OECD members. In mid-2000 OECD launched an initiative to abolish 'harmful tax systems', identifying a number of offshore jurisdictions as 'tax havens' lacking financial transparency, and inviting these to co-operate with by amending national financial legislation. Several of the countries and territories named agreed to follow a timetable for reform, with the aim of eliminating such practices by the end of 2005. Others, however, were reluctant to participate. (The USA also strongly opposed the initiative.) In April 2002 OECD announced that co-ordinated defensive measures would be implemented against non-complying jurisdictions ('un-co-operative tax havens') from early 2003. OECD has also highlighted examples of preferential tax regimes in member countries. In February 2004 the Committee on Fiscal Affairs published a Progress Report on the elimination of harmful tax practices. By early 2008 only Andorra, Liechtenstein and Monaco remained on the list of un-co-operative tax havens.

FOOD, AGRICULTURE AND FISHERIES

OECD undertakes analysis of relevant issues and advises governments, in particular in relation to policy reform, trade liberalization and sustainable agriculture and fisheries. OECD is also a focal point for global efforts in the certification and standardization of products, packaging and testing procedures, though its agricultural codes and schemes. A Committee for Agriculture reviews major developments in agricultural policies, deals with the adaptation of agriculture to changing economic conditions, elaborates forecasts of production and market prospects for the major commodities, identifies best practices for limiting the impact of agricultural production on the environment, promotes the use of sustainable practices in the sector and considers questions of agricultural development in emerging and transition economies. A separate Fisheries Committee carries out similar tasks in its sector, and, in particular, analyses the consequences of policy measures with a view to promoting responsible and sustainable fisheries. The Directorate administers a Biological Resources in Agriculture programme, which sponsors research fellowships as well as workshops and conferences, to enhance international co-operation in priority areas of agro-food research.

ENVIRONMENT

The OECD Environment Directorate works in support of the Environment Policy Committee (EPOC) on environmental issues. EPOC assesses performance; encourages co-operation on environmental policy; promotes the integration of environmental and economic policies; works to develop principles, guide-lines and strategies for effective environmental management; provides a forum for member states to address common problems and share data and experience; and promotes the sharing of information with non-member states. The Directorate conducts peer reviews of environmental conditions and progress. A first cycle of 32 Environmental Performance Reviews of member and selected non-member countries was completed in 2000, and a second cycle commenced in 2001. The Directorate aims to improve understanding of past and future trends through the collection and dissemination of environmental data.

OECD programmes and working parties on the environment consider a range of issues, including the harmonization of biotechnology regulation, the environmental impact of production and consumption, natural resource management, trade and investment and the environment, and chemical safety. In some cases working parties collaborate with other Directorates (for example, the Working Parties on Trade and Environment and on Agriculture and Environment). An Experts Group on Climate Change, based in the

Environment Directorate, undertakes studies related to international agreements on climate change. In 1995 the BioTrack Online programme was developed to disseminate information relating to the regulatory oversight of biotechnology, with particular emphasis on environmental and food safety.

In May 2001 OECD ministers of the environment, convened in Paris, France, adopted the OECD Environmental Strategy for the 21st Century, containing recommendations for future work. The Strategy, which was to be implemented by 2010, focused on fostering sustainable development, and strengthening co-operation with non-member countries and partnerships with the private sector and civil society. Fundamental objectives included the efficient use of renewable and non-renewable resources; the avoidance of irreversible damage; the maintenance of ecosystems; and separating environmental pressures from economic growth. The strategy identified several issues requiring urgent action, such as the generation of municipal waste, increased car and air travel, greenhouse gas emissions, groundwater pollution, and the exploitation of marine fisheries. The meeting endorsed guide-lines for the provision of environmentally sustainable transport, as well as the use of a set of key environmental indicators. A review of the key indicators was presented to a meeting of environment ministers, convened in April 2004. The OECD Forum in 2008 was to be convened, in June, on the theme of Climate Change, Growth and Stability.

SCIENCE, TECHNOLOGY AND INDUSTRY

The Directorate for Science, Technology and Industry aims to assist member countries in formulating, adapting and implementing policies that optimize the contribution of science, technology, industrial development and structural change to economic growth, employment and social development. It provides indicators and analysis on emerging trends in these fields, identifies and promotes best practices, and offers a forum for dialogue.

Areas considered by the Committee for Scientific and Technological Policy include the management of public research, technology and innovation, and intellectual property rights. A Working Party on Biotechnology was established in 1993 to pursue study of biotechnology and its applications, including issues such as scientific and technological infrastructure, and the relation of biotechnology to sustainable industrial development. Statistical work on biotechnology is undertaken by a Working Party of National Experts on Science and Technology Indicators. In 1992 a megascience forum was established to bring together senior science policy officials to identify and pursue opportunities for international co-operation in scientific research. It was succeeded, in 1999, by the Global Science Forum. In 2000 multilateral negotiations on establishing a Global Biodiversity Information Facility (GBIF) were concluded. The GBIF began operations in 2001 to connect global biodiversity databases in order to make available a wide range of data online.

The Committee for Information, Computer and Communications Policy monitors developments in telecommunications and information technology and their impact on competitiveness and productivity, with a new emphasis on technological and regulatory convergence. It also promotes the development of new rules (e.g. guide-lines on information security) and analyses trade and liberalization issues. The Committee maintains a database of communications indicators and telecommunications tariffs. A Working Party on Information Security and Privacy promotes a co-ordinated approach to efforts to enhance trust in the use of electronic commerce. In August 2004 an OECD Task Force was established to co-ordinate efforts to counter unsolicited e-mail ('spam'). OECD supports the Digital Opportunities Task Force (Dot.force) which was established in June 2000 by the G-8 to recommend action with a view to eliminating the so-called 'digital divide' between developed and less developed countries and between different population sectors within nations. OECD's Global Conference on Telecommunications Policy for the Digital Environment, held in January 2002, emphasized the importance of competition in the sector and the need for regulatory reform. A ministerial meeting on the Future of the Internet Economy was to be held in Seoul, Republic of Korea, in June 2008.

The Committee on Industry and the Business Environment focuses on industrial production; business performance; innovation and competitiveness in industrial and services sectors; and policies for private sector development in member and selected non-member economies. In recent years the Committee has addressed issues connected with globalization, regulatory reform, SMEs, and the role of industry in sustainable development. Business and industry policy fora explore a variety of issues with the private sector and develop recommendations. Issues addressed recently include environmental strategies for industry and new technologies. A working party on SMEs conducts an ongoing review of the contribution of SMEs to growth and employment and carries out a comparative assessment of best practice policies. (See also Bologna Process, above.)

The Transport Division of the Directorate for Science, Technology and Industry considers aviation, maritime, shipbuilding, road and intermodal transport issues. Maritime Transport and Steel Committees aim to promote multilateral solutions to sectoral friction and instability based on the definition and monitoring of rules. The Working Party on Shipbuilding seeks to establish normal competitive conditions in that sector, especially through dialogue with non-OECD countries. The Tourism Committee promotes sustained growth in the tourism sector and encourages the integration of tourism issues into other policy areas. On 1 January 2004 a new Transport Research Centre was established by merger of OECD's road transport and intermodal linkages research programme and the economic research activities of the European Conference of Ministers of Transport. In May 2006 the European Conference of Ministers of Transport agreed to establish and become integrated into a new International Transport Forum. The inaugural meeting of the Forum was scheduled to be held in May 2008.

EMPLOYMENT, LABOUR AND SOCIAL AFFAIRS

The Employment, Labour and Social Affairs Committee is concerned with the development of the labour market and selective employment policies to ensure the utilization of human capital at the highest possible level and to improve the quality and flexibility of working life, as well as the effectiveness of social policies; it plays a central role in addressing OECD's concern to reduce high and persistent unemployment through the creation of high-quality jobs. The Committee's work covers such issues as the role of women in the economy, industrial relations, measurements of unemployment, and the development of an extensive social database. The Committee also carries out single-country and thematic reviews of labour-market policies and social assistance systems. It has assigned a high priority to work on the policy implications of an ageing population and on indicators of human capital investment.

OECD undertakes analysis of health care and health expenditure issues, and reviews the organization and performance of health systems. In 2001 a three-year OECD Health Project was launched with the aim of evaluating and analysing the performance of healthcare systems in member countries and the factors affecting their performance. In May 2004 OECD ministers responsible for health convened for the first time to consider the completed Project. Upon their recommendation a new Group on Health was established in January 2005 to direct a further programme of work, to be supported by a new Health Division within the Directorate of Employment, Labour and Social Affairs. Social policy areas of concern include benefits and wages, family-friendly policies, and the social effects of population ageing.

A Non-Member Economies and International Migration Division works on social policy issues in emerging economies and economies in transition, especially relating to education and labour market reforms and to the economic and social aspects of migration. The Directorate undertakes regular analysis of trends in international migration, including consideration of its economic and social impact, the integration of immigrants, and international co-operation in the control of migrant flows.

EDUCATION

In 2002 a new Directorate for Education was created in order to raise the profile of OECD's work, which is conducted in the context of its view of education as a lifelong activity. The Directorate comprises Divisions on Education and Training, Indicators and Analysis, Education Management, and Infrastructure. Programmes undertaken by the Directorate include a Programme for Co-operation with non-member Economies, the Programme of International Student Assessments (PISA), the Programme on Institutional Management in Higher Education and the Programme on Education Building, as well as regular peer reviews of education systems. A Programme for the International Assessment of Adult Competencies (PIAAC) was under development in 2008 and was expected to be administered for the first time in 2011.

Centre for Educational Research and Innovation (CERI): f. 1968; an independently-funded programme within the Directorate for Education; promotes the development of research activities in education, together with experiments of an advanced nature, designed to test innovations in educational systems and to stimulate research and development.

CO-OPERATION WITH NON-MEMBER ECONOMIES

The Centre for Co-operation with Non-Members (CCNM) was established in January 1998, by merger of the Centre for Co-operation with Economies in Transition (founded in 1990) and the Liaison and Co-ordination Unit. It serves as the focal point for the development of policy dialogue with non-member economies, managing multi-country, thematic, regional and country programmes. These include a Baltic Regional Programme, Programmes for Russia and for Brazil, an Emerging Asian Economies Programme and the OECD Programme of Dialogue and Co-operation with China. The Centre also manages OECD's various Global Forums, which discuss a wide range of specific issues that defy resolution in a single country or region, for example international investment, sustainable development, biotechnology, and trade. The Centre co-ordinates and maintains OECD's relations with other international organizations. An integral part of the CCNM is the joint venture with the EU, the Support for Improvement in Governance and Management (SIGMA) programme (see above), which is directed towards the transition economies of Central and Eastern Europe.

Non-member economies are invited by the CCNM, on a selective basis, to participate in or observe the work of certain OECD committees and working parties. The Centre also provides a limited range of training activities in support of policy implementation and institution building. In 1994 the OECD Centre for Private Sector Development, based in Istanbul, Turkey, commenced operations as a joint project between the OECD and the Turkish Government to provide policy advice and training to administrators from transitional economies in Eastern Europe, Central Asia and Transcaucasus. Subsequently, the Centre has evolved into a regional forum for policy dialogue and co-operation with regard to issues of interest to transitional economies. The CCNM is also a sponsor of the Joint Vienna Institute, which offers a variety of administrative, economic and financial management courses to participants from transition economies. In May 2007 OECD invited Chile, Estonia, Israel, Russia and Slovenia to initiate discussions with a view to future membership of the organization. So-called 'road maps' for accession negotiations were agreed with those five countries in December.

In November 2006 OECD's Trade Union Advisory Committee (TUAC) ratified an agreement with the International Trade Union Confederation and the so-called 'Global Unions' (global trade union federations) to form a Council of Global Unions, with the aims of promoting trade union membership and advancing common trade union interests world-wide.

Finance

OECD's total budget for 2008 amounted to €342.9m.

Publications

Activities of OECD (Secretary-General's Annual Report).
Agricultural Outlook (annually).
Development Co-operation Report (annually).
Economic Policy Reforms (annually).
Education at a Glance (annually).
Energy Balances (quarterly).
Energy Prices and Taxes (quarterly).
Financial Market Trends (3 a year).
Financial Statistics (Part 1 (domestic markets): monthly; Part 2 (international markets): monthly; Part 3 (OECD member countries): 25 a year).
Foreign Trade Statistics (monthly).
Higher Education Management and Policy (3 a year).
Indicators of Industry and Services Activity (quarterly).
International Migration Outlook (annually).
International Trade by Commodities Statistics (5 a year).
Joint BIS-IMF-OECD-World Bank Statistics on External Debt (quarterly).
Main Developments in Trade (annually).
Main Economic Indicators (monthly).
Monthly Statistics of International Trade.
National Accounts Quarterly.
OECD Economic Outlook (2 a year).
OECD Economic Studies (2 a year).
OECD Economic Surveys (every 12 to 18 months for each country).
OECD Employment Outlook (annually).
OECD Environmental Outlook.
OECD Factbook (annually).
OECD Journal of Competition Law and Policy (quarterly).
OECD Observer (every 2 months).
Oil, Gas, Coal and Electricity Statistics (quarterly).
Review of Fisheries (annually).
Short-term Economic Indicators: Transition Economies (quarterly).
What's New @ OECD (monthly).

Numerous specialized reports, working papers, books and statistics on economic and social subjects are also published.

INTERNATIONAL ENERGY AGENCY—IEA

Address: 9 rue de la Fédération, 75739 Paris Cédex 15, France.
Telephone: 1-40-57-65-00; **fax:** 1-40-57-65-59; **e-mail:** info@iea.org; **internet:** www.iea.org.

The Agency was established by the OECD Council Decision Establishing an International Energy Agency to develop co-operation on energy questions among participating countries.

MEMBERS

Australia	Greece	Norway*
Austria	Hungary	Portugal
Belgium	Ireland	Slovakia
Canada	Italy	Spain
Czech Republic	Japan	Sweden
Denmark	Republic of Korea	Switzerland
Finland	Luxembourg	Turkey
France	Netherlands	United Kingdom
Germany	New Zealand	USA

*Norway participates in the IEA under a special Agreement.
Note: The European Commission also takes part in the IEA's work as an observer.

In October 2007 Poland was invited to become a member of the IEA.

Organization

(April 2008)

GOVERNING BOARD

Composed of ministers or senior officials of the member governments. Meetings are held every two years at ministerial level and five times a year at senior official level. Decisions may be taken by a special weighted majority on a number of specified subjects, particularly concerning emergency measures and emergency reserve commitments; a simple weighted majority is required for procedural decisions and decisions implementing specific obligations in the agreement. Unanimity is required only if new obligations, not already specified in the agreement, are to be undertaken.

SECRETARIAT

The Secretariat comprises the following offices: Energy Statistics; Energy Technology and Research and Development; Global Energy Dialogue; Oil Markets and Emergency Preparedness; and Long-term Co-operation and Policy Analysis. There are also the following Standing Groups and Committees: Standing Group on Long-Term Co-operation; Standing Group on the Oil Market; Standing Group on Emergency Questions; Committee on Energy Research and Technology (with working parties); and the Standing Group on Global Energy Dialogue.

Executive Director: NOBUO TANAKA (Japan).

Activities

The Agreement on an International Energy Programme was signed in November 1974 and formally entered into force in January 1976. The Agreement commits the participating countries of the International Energy Agency to share petroleum in certain emergencies, to strengthen their long-term co-operation in order to reduce dependence on petroleum imports, to increase the availability of information on the petroleum market, to co-operate in the development and co-ordination of energy policies, and to develop relations with the petroleum-producing and other petroleum-consuming countries.

The IEA collects, processes and disseminates statistical data and information on all aspects of the energy sector, including production, trade, consumption, prices and greenhouse gas emissions. The IEA aims to promote co-operation among policy-makers and energy experts to discuss common energy issues, to enhance energy technology and research and development, in particular projects concerned with energy efficiency, conservation and protection of the environment, and to engage major energy producing and consuming non-member countries.

The IEA has developed a system of emergency measures to be used in the event of a reduction in petroleum supplies. Under the International Energy Programme, member states are required to stock crude oil equivalent to 90 days of the previous year's net imports. These measures, which also include demand restraint, were to take effect in disruptions exceeding 7% of the IEA or individual country average daily rate of consumption. A more flexible system of response to oil supply disruption has also been developed under the Co-ordinated Energy Response Measures in 1984. In September 2005 member countries agreed on collective action to make available to the market an addition 60m. barrels of crude oil and oil products, in response to concerns at interruptions to the oil supply from the Gulf of Mexico following extensive hurricane damage. The action was terminated in December. The IEA undertakes emergency response reviews and workshops, and publishes an Emergency Management Manual to facilitate a co-ordinated response to a severe disruption in petroleum supplies. The Oil Markets and Emergency Preparedness Office monitors and reports on short-term developments in the petroleum market. It also considers other related issues, including international crude petroleum pricing, petroleum trade and stock developments and investments by major petroleum-producing countries.

Through its Energy Technology Office the IEA promotes international collaboration in this field and the participation of energy industries to facilitate the application of new technologies, through effective transfer of knowledge, technology innovation and training. Member states have initiated over 40 Implementing Agreements, which provide a framework for international collaboration and information exchange in specific areas, including renewable energy, fossil fuels, end-use technologies and fusion power. OECD member states, non-member states, the energy producers and suppliers are encouraged to participate in these Agreements. The Committee on Energy Research and Technology, which supports international collaboration, is serviced by four expert bodies: Working Parties on Fossil Fuels, Renewable Energy Technologies and Energy End-Use Technologies and a Fusion Power Co-ordinating Committee.

The IEA Long-Term Co-operation Programme is designed to strengthen the security of energy supplies and promote stability in world energy markets. It provides for co-operative efforts to conserve energy, to accelerate the development of alternative energy sources by means of both specific and general measures, to strengthen research and development of new energy technologies and to remove legislative and administrative obstacles to increased energy supplies. Regular reviews of member countries' efforts in the fields of energy conservation and accelerated development of alternative energy sources assess the effectiveness of national programmes in relation to the objectives of the Agency.

The IEA actively promotes co-operation and dialogue with non-members and international organizations in order to promote global energy security, environmental protection and economic development. The IEA holds bilateral and regional technical meetings and conducts surveys and reviews of the energy situation in non-member countries.. Co-operation agreements with key energy-consuming countries, including India and the People's Republic of China, are a priority. The Agency also has co-operation agreements with Russia and the Ukraine and works closely with the petroleum-producing countries of the Middle East. In the latter states the IEA has provided technical assistance for the development of national energy legislation, regulatory reform and energy efficiency projects. The IEA is represented on the Executive Committee of the International Energy Forum (formerly the Oil Producer-Consumer Dialogue) to promote greater co-operation and understanding between petroleum producing and consuming countries. It is also active in the Joint Oil Data Initiative (JODI), a collaborative initiative of seven international organisations to improve oil data transparency.

In recent years the IEA has increased its focus on issues related to the environment and sustainable development. It supports analysis of actions to mitigate climate change, studies of the implications of the Kyoto Protocol to the UN Framework Convention on Climate Change, and analysis of policies designed to reduce greenhouse gas emissions, including emissions trading. It is a partner in the Global Bioenergy Partnership and is active in the Renewable Energy and Efficiency Partnership (REEEP). Since 2001 IEA has organized, with the International Emissions Trading Association and the Electric Power Research Institute, an annual workshop of greenhouse gas emissions trading. The Agency also analyses the regulation and reform of energy markets, especially for electricity and gas. The IEA Regulatory Forum held in February 2002 considered the implications for security of supply and public service of competition in energy markets.

Publications

CO^2 *Emissions from Fuel Combustion* (annually).
Coal Information (annually).
Electricity Information (annually).
Energy Balances and Energy Statistics of OECD and non-OECD Countries (annually).
Energy Policies of IEA Countries (annually).
Key World Energy Statistics.
Natural Gas Information (annually).
Natural Gas Market Review (annually).
Oil Information (annually).
Oil Market Report (monthly).
Renewables Information (annually).
World Energy Outlook (annually).
Other reports, studies, statistics, country reviews.

OECD NUCLEAR ENERGY AGENCY—NEA

Address: Le Seine Saint-Germain, 12 blvd des Îles, 92130 Issy-les-Moulineaux, France.
Telephone: 1-45-24-10-10; **fax:** 1-45-24-11-10; **e-mail:** nea@nea.fr; **internet:** www.nea.fr.

The NEA was established in 1958 to further the peaceful uses of nuclear energy. Originally a European agency, it has since admitted OECD members outside Europe.

MEMBERS

All members of OECD (except New Zealand and Poland).

Organization
(April 2008)

STEERING COMMITTEE FOR NUCLEAR ENERGY

Meets twice a year. Comprises senior representatives of member governments, presided over by a chairman. Reports directly to the OECD Council.

SECRETARIAT

Director-General: LUIS ENRIQUE ECHÁVARRI (Spain).

MAIN COMMITTEES

Committee on Nuclear Regulatory Activities.
Committee on Radiation Protection.
Committee on the Safety of Nuclear Installations.
Committee for Technical and Economic Studies on Nuclear Development and the Fuel Cycle (Nuclear Development Committee).
Nuclear Law Committee.
Nuclear Science Committee.
Radioactive Waste Management Committee.

NEA DATA BANK

The Data Bank was established in 1978, as a successor to the Computer Programme Library and the Neutron Data Compilation Centre. The Data Bank develops and supplies data and computer programmes for nuclear technology applications to users in laboratories, industry, universities and other areas of interest. Under the supervision of the Nuclear Science Committee, the Data Bank collates integral experimental data, and functions as part of a network of data centres to provide direct data services. It was responsible for co-ordinating the development of the Joint Evaluation Fission and Fusion (JEFF) data reference library, and works with the Radioactive Waste Management Division of the NEA on the Thermonuclear Database project (see below).

Activities

The NEA's mission is to assist its member countries in maintaining and further developing, through international co-operation, the scientific, technological and legal bases required for the safe, environmentally-friendly and economical use of nuclear energy for peaceful purposes. It maintains a continual survey with the co-operation of other organizations, notably the International Atomic Energy Agency (IAEA), of world uranium resources, production and demand, and of economic and technical aspects of the nuclear fuel cycle.

A major part of the Agency's work is devoted to the safety and regulation of nuclear power, including co-operative studies and projects related to the prevention of nuclear accidents and the long-term safety of radioactive waste disposal systems. The Committee on Nuclear Regulatory Activities contributes to developing a consistent and effective regulatory response to current and future challenges. These challenges include operational experience feedback, increased public expectations concerning safety in the use of nuclear energy, industry initiatives to improve economics and inspection practices, the necessity to ensure safety over a plant's entire life cycle, and new reactors and technology. The Committee on the Safety of Nuclear Installations contributes to maintaining a high level of safety performance and safety competence by identifying emerging safety issues through the analysis of operating experience and research results, contributing to their resolution and, when needed, establishing international research projects. The Radioactive Waste Management Committee assists member countries in the management of radioactive waste and materials, focusing on the development of strategies for the safe, sustainable and broadly acceptable management of all types of radioactive waste, in particular long-lived waste and spent fuel. The Committee on Radiation Protection and Public Health, comprising regulators and protection experts, aims to identify new and emerging issues, analyse their impact and recommend action to address issues and to enhance protection regulation and implementation. It is served by various expert groups and a working party on nuclear emergency matters. The Nuclear Development Committee supports member countries in formulating nuclear energy policy, addressing issues of relevance for governments and the industry at a time of nuclear technology renaissance and sustained government interest in ensuring long-term security of energy supply, reducing the risk of global climate change and pursuing sustainable development. The aim of the NEA nuclear science programme is to help member countries identify, share, develop and disseminate basic scientific and technical knowledge used to ensure safe and reliable operation of current nuclear systems, as well as to develop next-generation technologies. The main areas covered are reactor physics, fuel behaviour, fuel cycle physics and chemistry, critical safety and radiation shielding. The Nuclear Law Committee (NLC) promotes the harmonization of nuclear legislation governing the peaceful uses of nuclear energy in member countries and in selected non-member countries. It supports the modernization and strengthening of national and international nuclear liability regimes. Under the supervision of the NLC, the NEA also compiles, analyses and disseminates information on nuclear law through a regular publications programme and organizes the International School of Nuclear Law educational programme. The NEA also co-operates with non-member countries of Central and Eastern Europe and the CIS in areas such as nuclear safety, radiation protection and nuclear law.

In January 2005 a policy group of the Generation IV International Forum (GIF) confirmed arrangements under which the NEA would provide technical secretariat support to the GIF, including the funding of this activity by GIF members through voluntary contributions. The GIF is a major international initiative aimed at developing the next generation of nuclear energy systems. In September 2006 the NEA was selected to perform the technical secretariat functions for Stage 2 of a Multinational Design Evaluation Programme (MDEP), which had been established to share the resources and knowledge accumulated by national nuclear regulatory authorities during their assessment of new reactor designs, with the aim of improving both the efficiency and the effectiveness of the process.

JOINT PROJECTS

Joint projects and information exchange programmes enable interested countries to share the costs of pursuing research or the sharing of data, relating to particular areas or problems, with the support of the NEA.

Nuclear Safety

OECD Halden Reactor Project: Halden, Norway; experimental boiling heavy water reactor, which became an OECD project in 1958; from 1964, under successive agreements with participating countries, the reactor has been used for long-term testing of water reactor fuels and for research into automatic computer-based control of nuclear power stations; the main focus is on nuclear fuel safety and man-machine interface; some 100 nuclear energy research institutions and authorities in 20 countries support the project.

OECD/NEA Behaviour of Iodine (BIP) Project: initiated, for a three-year period, in July 2007; aims to provide separate effects and modelling studies of iodine behaviour in a nuclear reactor containment building following a severe accident; participating orgs and agencies from 13 countries.

OECD/NEA Cabri Water Loop Project: revised eight-year programme initiated in 2000; conducted at the Institute for Protection and Nuclear Safety (IPSN), based in France; investigates the capacity of high burn-up fuel to withstand sharp power peaks that may occur in power reactors owing to rapid reactivity insertion in the reactor core (i.e. reactivity-initiated accidents); 19 participating orgs.

OECD/NEA COMPSIS Project: initiated, for a three-year period, in 2005; aims to improve safety management and the quality of risk analysis by collecting and analysing operating experience on computer-based control systems important to safety; 12 participants.

OECD/NEA Fire Incidents Records Exchange Project: initiated in 2002; aims to encourage multilateral co-operation in the collection and analysis of data relating to fire events in nuclear environments, on an international scale; 12 participants.

OECD/NEA Fire Propagation in Elementary, Multi-rooms Scenarios (PRISME) Project: initiated for a five-year period in Jan. 2006; aims to support the qualification of fire codes and the development of fire protection strategies; 10 participating countries.

OECD/NEA International Common Cause Failure Data Exchange (ICDE) Project: initiated in 1994 and formally operated by the NEA since April 1998; encourages multilateral co-operation in the collection and analysis of data on common cause failure (CCF) events occurring at nuclear power plants, with the aim of enabling greater understanding and prevention of such events; 11 participating countries.

OECD/NEA Melt Coolability and Concrete Interaction (MCCI) Project: initiated 2002; conducted at the Argonne National Laboratory, USA; aims to provide experimental data on severe accident molten core coolability and interaction with containment concrete, contributing to improved accident management; 13 participating countries.

OECD/NEA Piping Failure Data Exchange Project (OPDE): initiated in June 2002; aims to collect and analyse piping failure event data with the aim of generating qualitative insights into the root causes of such events; 12 participating countries.

OECD/NEA PKL-2 Project: three-year project initiated in Jan. 2004; to investigate pressurised water reactor safety issues, in particular boron dilution events after small-break, loss of coolant accidents accidents and loss of residual heat removal in mid-loop operation with a closed reactor coolant system in context with boron dilution; 14 participating countries.

OECD/NEA PSB-VVER Project: covers the period Feb. 2003–June 2008; conducted at a large-scale, thermal-hydraulics facility located at the Electrogorsk Research and Engineering Centre in Russia; is intended to provide the experimental data needed for the validation of thermal-hydraulic codes and to support refinements to safety assessment tools for Russian-designed VVER-1000 reactors; participating orgs from seven countries.

OECD/NEA Rig of Safety Assessment (ROSA) Project: initiated April 2005, with a mandate until Dec. 2009; aims to resolve issues in thermal-hydraulics analyses relevant to light water reactor safety using the Japanese rig-of-safety assessment large-scale test facility (ROSA/LSTF); participants from 13 countries.

OECD/NEA SESAR Thermal-hydraulics (SETH-2) Project: follow-up testing project, to cover the period 2007–2010; research on important thermal-hydraulic phenomena in support of accident management; conducted at the Paul Scherrer Institute PANDA facility, based in Switzerland, and the Commissariat à l'énergie atomique MISTRA facilities in France; participating orgs from 10 countries.

OECD/NEA Steam Explosion Resolution for Nuclear Applications (SERENA) Project: covers the period 2007–2010; established to further the findings of a programme to assess the capabilities of the current generation of fuel-coolant interaction computer codes to predict steam explosion-induced loads in reactor situations; 10 participating countries.

OECD/NEA Stress Corrosion Cracking and Cable Ageing (SCAP) Project: four-year project initiated in June 2006; to establish information and knowledge databases with regard to major ageing phenomena for stress corrosion cracking and degradation of cable insulation; 14 participating countries.

OECD/NEA Studsvik Cladding Integrity Project: five-year project initiated in July 2004; aims to utilise the hot cell facilities and expertise available at the Swedish Studsvik establishment in order to assess material properties and to determine conditions that can lead to fuel failures; 11 participating countries.

OECD/NEA Thermal-hydraulics, Hydrogen, Aerosols, Iodine (ThAI) Project: initiated, for a three-year period, in Jan. 2007; aims to provide further data relating to the distribution of combustible hydrogen and the behaviour of fission products; participating orgs from eight countries.

Radioactive Waste Management

International Co-operative Programme on Decommissioning: initiated in 1985; promotes exchange of technical information and experience for ensuring that safe, economic and optimum environmental options for decommissioning are used; 12 participating countries.

Thermonuclear Database (TDB Project): aims to develop a quality-assured, comprehensive thermodynamic database of selected chemical elements for use in the safety assessment of radioactive waste repositories; data are selected by review teams; phase II commenced in 1998 and is ongoing; phase III commenced in Feb. 2003 focusing on new reviews of inorganic species and compounds of other elements; 12 participating countries and 17 participating organizations.

Radiation Protection

Information System on Occupational Exposure (ISOE): initiated in 1992 and co-sponsored by the IAEA; maintains largest database world-wide on occupational exposure to ionizing radiation at nuclear power plants; participants: 461 reactors (some of which are either defunct or actively decommissioning) in 29 countries.

Finance

The Agency's annual budget amounts to some €10.0m., while funding of €2.8m. is made available for the Data Bank. These sums may be supplemented by members' voluntary contributions.

Publications

Annual Report.
NEA News (2 a year).
Nuclear Energy Data (annually).
Nuclear Law Bulletin (2 a year).
Publications on a range of issues relating to nuclear energy, reports and proceedings.

ORGANIZATION FOR SECURITY AND CO-OPERATION IN EUROPE—OSCE

Address: 1010 Vienna, Kärntner Ring 5–7, Austria.
Telephone: (1) 514-36-0; **fax:** (1) 514-36-96; **e-mail:** info@osce.org; **internet:** www.osce.org.

The OSCE was established in 1972 as the Conference on Security and Co-operation in Europe (CSCE), providing a multilateral forum for dialogue and negotiation. It produced the Helsinki Final Act of 1975 on East–West relations (see below). The areas of competence of the CSCE were expanded by the Charter of Paris for a New Europe (1990), which transformed the CSCE from an ad hoc forum into an organization with permanent institutions, and the Helsinki Document 1992 (see 'Activities'). In December 1994 the summit conference adopted the new name of OSCE, in order to reflect the Organization's changing political role and strengthened secretariat.

PARTICIPATING STATES

Albania	Greece	Portugal
Andorra	Hungary	Romania
Armenia	Iceland	Russia
Austria	Ireland	San Marino
Azerbaijan	Italy	Serbia
Belarus	Kazakhstan	Slovakia
Belgium	Kyrgyzstan	Slovenia
Bosnia and Herzegovina	Latvia	Spain
	Liechtenstein	Sweden
Bulgaria	Lithuania	Switzerland
Canada	Luxembourg	Tajikistan
Croatia	Macedonia, former Yugoslav republic	Turkey
Cyprus		Turkmenistan
Czech Republic	Malta	Ukraine
Denmark	Moldova	United Kingdom
Estonia	Monaco	USA
Finland	Montenegro	Uzbekistan
France	Netherlands	Vatican City (Holy See)
Georgia	Norway	
Germany	Poland	

Organization

(April 2008)

SUMMIT CONFERENCES

Heads of state or government of OSCE participating states convene periodically to set priorities and political orientation of the Organization. The most recent conference was held in İstanbul, Turkey, in November 1999.

MINISTERIAL COUNCIL

The Ministerial Council (formerly the Council of Foreign Ministers) comprises ministers of foreign affairs of member states. It is the central decision-making and governing body of the OSCE and meets every year in which no summit conference is held.

PERMANENT COUNCIL

The Council, which is based in Vienna, is responsible for day-to-day operational tasks. Members of the Council, comprising the permanent representatives of member states to the OSCE, convene weekly. The Council is the regular body for political consultation and decision-making, and may be convened for emergency purposes.

FORUM FOR SECURITY CO-OPERATION (FSC)

The FSC, comprising representatives of delegations of member states, meets weekly in Vienna to negotiate and consult on measures aimed at strengthening security and stability throughout Europe. Its main objectives are negotiations on arms control, disarmament, and confidence- and security-building; regular consultations and intensive co-operation on matters related to security; and the further reduction of the risks of conflict. The FSC is also responsible for the implementation of confidence- and security-building measures (CSBMs); the preparation of seminars on military doctrine; the holding of annual implementation assessment meetings; and the provision of a forum for the discussion and clarification of information exchanged under agreed CSBMs.

CHAIRMAN-IN-OFFICE (CIO)

The CIO is vested with overall responsibility for executive action. The position is held by a minister of foreign affairs of a member state for a one-year term. The CIO may be assisted by a troika, consisting of the preceding, current and succeeding chairpersons; ad hoc steering groups; or personal representatives, who are appointed by the CIO with a clear and precise mandate to assist the CIO in dealing with a crisis or conflict.

Chairman-in-Office: ILKKA KANERVA (Finland) (2008).

SECRETARIAT

The Secretariat comprises the following principal units: the Conflict Prevention Centre, the Action against Terrorism Unit, the Anti-trafficking Assistance Unit, the Office of the Co-ordinator of OSCE Economic and Environmental Activities, External Co-operation, the

Strategic Police Matters Unit, the Training Section, a Department of Human Resources, and the Department of Management and Finance, responsible for technical and administrative support activities. The OSCE maintains an office in Prague, Czech Republic, which assists with documentation and information activities.

The position of Secretary-General was established in December 1992 and the first appointment to the position was made in June 1993. The Secretary-General is appointed by the Ministerial Council for a three-year term of office. The Secretary-General is the representative of the CIO and is responsible for the management of OSCE structures and operations.

Secretary-General: MARC PERRIN DE BRICHAMBAUT (France).
Co-ordinator of OSCE Economic and Environmental Activities: BERNARD SNOY (Belgium).
Director of Conflict Prevention Centre: HERBERT SALBER (Germany).
Special Representative and Co-ordinator for Combating Trafficking in Human Beings: EVA BIAUDET (Finland).

OSCE Specialized Bodies

High Commissioner on National Minorities
POB 20062, 2500 EB The Hague, Netherlands; tel. (70) 3125500; fax (70) 3635910; e-mail hcnm@hcnm.org; internet www.osce.org/hcnm.
The office of High Commissioner on National Minorities was established in December 1992, with the first High Commissioner appointed in January 1993. The High Commissioner is an instrument for conflict prevention, tasked with identifying ethnic tensions that have the potential to develop into conflict, thereby endangering peace, stability or relations between OSCE participating states, and to promote their early resolution. The High Commissioner works in confidence and provides strictly confidential reports to the OSCE CIO. The High Commissioner is appointed by the Ministerial Council, on the recommendation of the Senior Council, for a three-year term.
High Commissioner: KNUT VOLLEBAEK (Norway).

Office for Democratic Institutions and Human Rights (ODIHR)
Aleje Ujazdowskie 19, 00-557 Warsaw, Poland; tel. (22) 520-06-00; fax (22) 520-06-05; e-mail office@odihr.pl; internet www.osce.org/odihr.
Established in July 1999, the ODIHR has responsibility for promoting human rights, democracy and the rule of law. The Office provides a framework for the exchange of information on and the promotion of democracy-building, respect for human rights and elections within OSCE states. In addition, it co-ordinates the monitoring of elections and provides expertise and training on constitutional and legal matters.
Director: CHRISTIAN STROHAL (Austria).

Office of the Representative on Freedom of the Media
Kärntner Ring 5–7, 1010 Vienna, Austria; tel. (1) 512-21-450; fax (1) 512-21-459; e-mail pm-fom@osce.org; internet www.osce.org/fom.
The office was founded in 1998 to strengthen the implementation of OSCE commitments regarding free, independent and pluralistic media.
Representative: MIKLÓS HARASZTI (Hungary).

Parliamentary Assembly
Radhusstraede 1, 1466 Copenhagen K, Denmark; tel. 33-37-80-40; fax 33-37-80-30; e-mail osce@oscepa.dk; internet www.oscepa.org.
The OSCE Parliamentary Assembly, which is composed of 320 parliamentarians from the 56 participating countries, was inaugurated in July 1992, and meets annually. The Assembly comprises a Standing Committee, a Bureau and three General Committees and is supported by a Secretariat in Copenhagen, Denmark.
President: GÖRAN LENNMARKER (Sweden).
Secretary-General: R. SPENCER OLIVER (USA).

OSCE Related Bodies

COURT OF CONCILIATION AND ARBITRATION
Villa Rive-Belle, 266 route de Lausanne, 1292 Chambésy, Geneva, Switzerland; tel. 227580025; fax 227582510; e-mail cca.osce@bluewin.ch; internet www.osce.org/cca.
An OSCE Convention on Conciliation and Arbitration, providing for the establishment of the Court, was concluded in 1992 and entered into effect in December 1994. The first meeting of the Court was convened in May 1995. OSCE states that have ratified the Convention may submit a dispute to the Court for settlement by the Arbitral Tribunal or the Conciliation Commission.
President: ROBERT BADINTER (France).

JOINT CONSULTATIVE GROUP (JCG)
The states that are party to the Treaty on Conventional Armed Forces in Europe (CFE), which was concluded within the CSCE framework in 1990, established the Joint Consultative Group (JCG). The JCG, which meets in Vienna, addresses questions relating to compliance with the Treaty; enhancement of the effectiveness of the Treaty; technical aspects of the Treaty's implementation; and disputes arising out of its implementation. There are currently 30 states participating in the JCG.

OPEN SKIES CONSULTATIVE COMMISSION
The Commission represents all states parties to the 1992 Treaty on Open Skies, and promotes its implementation. Its regular meetings are serviced by the OSCE secretariat.

Activities

In July 1990 heads of government of the member countries of the North Atlantic Treaty Organization (NATO) proposed to increase the role of the CSCE 'to provide a forum for wider political dialogue in a more united Europe'. The Charter of Paris for a New Europe, which undertook to strengthen pluralist democracy and observance of human rights, and to settle disputes between participating states by peaceful means, was signed in November. At the summit meeting the Treaty on Conventional Armed Forces in Europe (CFE), which had been negotiated within the framework of the CSCE, was signed by the member states of NATO and of the Warsaw Pact. The Treaty limits non-nuclear air and ground armaments in the signatory countries. In April 1991 parliamentarians from the CSCE countries agreed on the creation of a pan-European parliamentary assembly. Its first session was held in Budapest, Hungary, in July 1992.

The Council of Foreign Ministers met for the first time in Berlin, Germany, in June 1991. The meeting adopted a mechanism for consultation and co-operation in the case of emergency situations, to be implemented by the Council of Senior Officials (CSO; subsequently renamed the Senior Council, which was dissolved in 2006, with all functions transferred to the Permanent Council). A separate mechanism regarding the prevention of the outbreak of conflict was also adopted, whereby a country can demand an explanation of 'unusual military activity' in a neighbouring country. These mechanisms were utilized in July in relation to the armed conflict in Yugoslavia between the Republic of Croatia and the Yugoslav Government. In mid-August a meeting of the CSO resolved to reinforce considerably the CSCE's mission in Yugoslavia and in September the CSO agreed to impose an embargo on the export of armaments to Yugoslavia. In October the CSO resolved to establish an observer mission to monitor the observance of human rights in Yugoslavia.

In January 1992 the Council of Foreign Ministers agreed that the Conference's rule of decision-making by consensus was to be altered to allow the CSO to take appropriate action against a participating state 'in cases of clear and gross violation of CSCE commitments'. This development was precipitated by the conflict in Yugoslavia, where the Yugoslav Government was held responsible by the majority of CSCE states for the continuation of hostilities and was suspended from the grouping. It was also agreed at the meeting that the CSCE should undertake fact-finding and conciliation missions to areas of tension, with the first such mission to be sent to Nagornyi Karabakh, the largely Armenian-populated enclave in Azerbaijan.

In March 1992 CSCE participating states reached agreement on a number of confidence-building measures, including commitments to exchange technical data on new weapons systems; to report activation of military units; and to prohibit military activity involving very large numbers of troops or tanks. Later in that month at a meeting of the Council of Foreign Ministers, which opened the Helsinki Follow-up Conference, the members of NATO and the former members of the Warsaw Pact (with Russia, Belarus, Ukraine and Georgia taking the place of the USSR) signed the Open Skies Treaty. Under the treaty, aerial reconnaissance missions by one country over another were permitted, subject to regulation. An Open Skies Consultative Commission was subsequently established (see above).

The summit meeting of heads of state and government that took place in Helsinki, Finland, in July 1992, adopted the Helsinki Document, in which participating states defined the terms of future CSCE peace-keeping activities. Conforming broadly to UN practice, peace-keeping operations would be undertaken only with the full consent of the parties involved in any conflict and only if an effective cease-fire were in place. The CSCE may request the use of the military resources of NATO, the CIS, the EU, Western European Union (WEU) or other international bodies. The Helsinki Document declared the CSCE a 'regional arrangement' in the sense of Chapter VIII of the UN's Charter, which states that such a regional grouping should attempt to resolve a conflict in the region before referring it to the Security Council. In 1993 the First Implementation Meeting on Human Dimension Issues (the CSCE term used with regard to issues concerning human rights and welfare) took place. The Meeting, for which the ODIHR serves as a secretariat, provides a now annual forum for the exchange of news regarding OSCE commitments in the fields of human rights and democracy. Also in 1993 the first annual Economic Forum was convened to focus on the transition to and development of free-market economies as an essential aspect of democracy-building. It was renamed the Economic and Environment Forum in 2007 to incorporate consideration of environmental security matters.

In December 1993 a Permanent Committee (now renamed the Permanent Council) was established in Vienna, providing for greater political consultation and dialogue through its weekly meetings. In December 1994 the summit conference redesignated the CSCE as the Organization for Security and Co-operation in Europe (OSCE) and endorsed the role of the Organization as the primary instrument for early warning, conflict prevention and crisis management in the region. The conference adopted a 'Code of Conduct on Politico-Military Aspects of Security', which set out principles to guide the role of the armed forces in democratic societies. The summit conference that was held in Lisbon, Portugal, in December 1996 agreed to adapt the CFE Treaty, in order to further arms-reduction negotiations on a national and territorial basis. The conference also adopted the 'Lisbon Declaration on a Common and Comprehensive Security Model for Europe for the 21st Century', committing all parties to pursuing measures to ensure regional security. A Security Model Committee was established and began to meet regularly during 1997 to consider aspects of the Declaration, including the identification of risks and challenges to future European security; enhancing means of joint co-operative action within the OSCE framework in the event of non-compliance with OSCE commitments by participating states; considering other new arrangements within the OSCE framework that could reinforce security and stability in Europe; and defining a basis of co-operation between the OSCE and other relevant organizations to co-ordinate security enforcement. In November 1997 the Office of the Representative on Freedom of the Media was established in Vienna, to support the OSCE's activities in this field. In the same month a new position of Co-ordinator of OSCE Economic and Environmental Activities was created.

In November 1999 OSCE heads of state and of government, convened in Istanbul, Turkey, signed a new Charter for European Security, which aimed to formalize existing norms regarding the observance of human rights and to strengthen co-operation with other organizations and institutions concerned with international security. The Charter focused on measures to improve the operational capabilities of the OSCE in early warning, conflict prevention, crisis management and post-conflict rehabilitation. Accordingly, Rapid Expert Assistance and Co-operation (REACT) teams were to be established to enable the Organization to respond rapidly to requests from participating states for assistance in crisis situations. The REACT programme became operational in April 2001. The 1999 summit meeting also adopted a Platform for Co-operative Security as a framework for co-operation with other organizations and institutions concerned with maintaining security in the OSCE area. At the Istanbul meeting a revised CFE Treaty was signed, providing for a stricter system of limitations and increased transparency, which was to be open to other OSCE states not currently signatories. The US and EU governments determined to delay ratification of the Agreement of the Adaptation of the Treaty until Russian troop levels in the Caucasus had been reduced.

In April 2000 the OSCE High Commissioner on National Minorities issued a report reviewing the problems confronting Roma and Sinti populations in OSCE member states. In April 2001 the ODIHR launched a programme of assistance for the Roma communities of south-eastern Europe. The OSCE and the then UN Office for Drug Control and Crime Prevention (ODCCP) jointly organized a conference in October 2000, supported by the Governments of Kazakhstan, Kyrgyzstan, Tajikistan, Turkmenistan and Uzbekistan and attended by representatives of 67 states and 44 international organizations, which aimed to promote co-operation, democratization, security and stability in Central Asia and to address the threat of drugs-trafficking, organized crime and terrorism in the sub-region. In November an OSCE Document on Small Arms and Light Weapons was adopted, aimed at curtailing the spread of armaments in member states. A workshop on implementation of the Document was held in February 2002. In mid-November 2000 the Office of the Representative on Freedom of the Media organized a conference, staged in Dushanbe, Tajikistan, of journalists from Kazakhstan, Kyrgyzstan, Tajikistan and Uzbekistan. In February 2001 the ODIHR established an Anti-Trafficking Project Fund to help to finance its efforts to combat trafficking in human beings. In July the OSCE Parliamentary Assembly adopted a resolution concerned with strengthening transparency and accountability within the Organization.

In September 2001 the Secretary-General condemned terrorist attacks perpetrated against targets in the USA, allegedly by militant Islamist fundamentalists. In early October OSCE member states unanimously adopted a statement in support of the developing US-led global coalition against international terrorism. In December the Ministerial Council, meeting in Romania, approved the 'Bucharest Action Plan' outlining the Organization's contribution to countering terrorism. A Personal Representative for Terrorism was appointed by the CIO in January 2002 to co-ordinate the implementation of the initiatives. Later in December 2001 the OSCE sponsored, with the ODCCP, an International Conference on Security and Stability in Central Asia, held in Bishkek, Kyrgyzstan. The meeting, which was attended by representatives of more than 60 countries and organizations, was concerned with strengthening efforts to counter terrorism and providing effective support to the Central Asian states. In October 2002 the ODIHR and the Government of Azerbaijan organized an international conference on religious freedom and combating terrorism. At a Ministerial Council meeting held in Porto, Portugal, in December, the OSCE issued a Charter on Preventing Terrorism, which condemned terrorism 'in all its forms and manifestations' and called upon member states to work together to counter, investigate and prosecute terrorist acts. The charter also acknowledged the links between terrorism, organized crime and trafficking in human beings. At the same time, a political declaration entitled 'Responding to Change' was adopted, in which member states pledged their commitment to mutual co-operation in combating threats to security. At the OSCE's first Annual Security Review Conference, held in Vienna, in July 2003, a range of practical options for addressing the new threats and challenges to security were set out. These included the introduction of common security features on travel documentation, stricter controls on manual portable air defence systems and the improvement of border security and policing methods. Security issues were also the subject of the Rotterdam Declaration, adopted by some 300 members of the Parliamentary Assembly in July, which stated that it was imperative for the OSCE to maintain a strong field presence and for field missions to be provided with sufficient funding and highly trained staff. It also recommended that the OSCE assume a role in unarmed peace-keeping operations.

During July 2003 the first OSCE conference on the effects of globalization was convened in Vienna, attended by some 200 representatives from international organizations. Participants called for the advancement of good governance in the public and private sectors, the development of democratic institutions and the creation of conditions that would enable populations to benefit from the global economy. At a meeting of the Ministerial Council, convened in Maastricht, Netherlands, in December, member states endorsed a document that aimed to address risks to regional security and stability arising from stockpiles of conventional ammunition through, *inter alia*, detailing practical steps for their destruction. In December 2004 the Ministerial Council, held in Sofia, Bulgaria, condemned terrorist attacks that had been committed during the year, including in Madrid, Spain, in March, and in Beslan, Russia, in September. The meeting issued a statement expressing determination to pursue all measures to prevent and combat international terrorism, while continuing to protect and uphold human rights. In order to consider OSCE's capacity to address new security challenges, and to provide a new strategic vision for the organization, the Council resolved to establish a Panel of Eminent Persons on Strengthening the Effectiveness of the OSCE. The Panel presented its report, comprising some 70 recommendations, to the Permanent Council in June 2005.

In July 2003 the Permanent Council adopted a new Action Plan to Combat Trafficking in Human Beings. The Plan was endorsed by the Ministerial Council, held in Maastricht, Netherlands, in December. The Council approved the appointment of a Special Representative on Combating Trafficking in Human Beings, mandated to raise awareness of the issues and to ensure member governments comply with international procedures and conventions, and the establishment of a special unit within the secretariat. In July 2004 the Special Representative organized an international conference to consider issues relating to human trafficking, including human rights, labour, migration, organized crime, and minors. Participants agreed to establish an Alliance against Trafficking in Persons, which aimed to consolidate co-operation among international and non-governmental organizations.

OSCE provides technical assistance to the Southeast European Co-operative Initiative.

OSCE MISSIONS AND FIELD ACTIVITIES

In 2008 there were OSCE missions in Bosnia and Herzegovina, Georgia, Kosovo, the former Yugoslav republic of Macedonia, Moldova, Montenegro and Serbia. The OSCE was also undertaking field activities in Albania, Armenia, Azerbaijan, Belarus, Croatia, Kazakhstan, Kyrgyzstan, Tajikistan, Turkmenistan and Uzbekistan. The OSCE has institutionalized structures to assist in the implementation of certain bilateral agreements. In 2008 there was also an OSCE representative to the Russian-Latvian Joint Commission on Military Pensioners. During 1994–2006 the OSCE sent a representative to the Estonian Government Commission on Military Pensioners (terminated in September 2006).

In August 1995 the CIO appointed a Personal Representative concerned with the conflict between Armenia and Azerbaijan in the Nagornyi Karabakh region. The OSCE provided a framework for discussions between the two countries through its 11-nation Minsk Group. In October 1997 Armenia and Azerbaijan reached agreement on OSCE proposals for a political settlement; however, the concessions granted by the Armenian President, Levon Ter-Petrossian, which included the withdrawal of troops from certain strategic areas of Nagornyi Karabakh, precipitated his resignation in February 1998. The proposals were rejected by his successor, Robert Kocharian. Nevertheless, meetings of the Minsk Group continued in 1998 and both countries expressed their willingness to recommence negotiations. The then CIO, Bronisław Geremek, met with the leaders of both countries in November and persuaded them to exchange prisoners of war. In 2005/06 the Minsk Group undertook intensive negotiations to formulate a set of basic principles for a peaceful settlement of the Nagornyi Karabakh conflict, including proposals for the redeployment of Armenian troops, demilitarization of formally occupied territories and a popular referendum to determine the final legal status of the region. In spite of continued diplomatic efforts, in July 2007 the co-Chair of the Minsk Group expressed concern at the lack of agreement on the basic principles. In July 1999 the OSCE Permanent Council approved the establishment of an Office in Yerevan (Armenia), which began operations in February 2000. The Office works independently of the Minsk Group to promote OSCE principles within the country in order to support political and economic stability. It aims to contribute to the development of democratic institutions and to the strengthening of civil society. An Office in Baku (Azerbaijan) opened in July 2000 with a mandate to undertake activities in democratization, human rights, economy and the environment, and media. In November 2001 the Office in Yerevan presented a report on trafficking in human beings in Armenia, which had been compiled as a joint effort by the OSCE, IOM and UNICEF. In March 2002 the CIO visited the region to discuss prospects for peace, and the OSCE's role in the process. In that year a programme on military and security issues was initiated in Armenia which was to enhance the OSCE's role in police-related activities in conflict prevention, crisis management and post-conflict rehabilitation. In July 2003 the Armenian police service signed a Memorandum of Understanding with the OSCE, launching a major police assistance programme. The first phase of the programme, the renovation of a police training centre, was initiated in March 2005; the centre opened, in Yerevan, in March 2007. In February 2005 the OSCE and Azerbaijani authorities agreed to increase co-operation in judicial and legal reform, after consideration of a report on trial monitoring compiled by the Office in Baku and ODIHR in 2003 and 2004. Other activities undertaken by the Office in 2006 and 2007 included assisting the establishment of public environmental information centres and supporting the development of small and medium-sized enterprises. In February 2007 a national voter register was inaugurated, having been established with the support of the Office. A public anti-corruption centre was opened in the capital, in April, and two regional centres were established in Martuni and Stepanavan in May. In that month an OSCE/ODIHR election observation mission noted considerable progress in democratic processes during the recently-conducted legislative elections.

The OSCE Mission to Georgia was established in 1992 to work towards a political settlement between disputing factions within the country. Since 1994 the Mission has contributed to efforts to define the political status of South Ossetia and has supported UN peacekeeping and human rights activities in Abkhazia. In December 1999 the Permanent Council, at the request of the Government of Georgia expanded the mandate of the existing OSCE Mission to Georgia to include monitoring that country's border with the Chechen Republic of Ichkeriya (Chechnya). The first permanent observation post opened in February 2000 and the monitoring team was fully deployed by July. In December 2001 the Permanent Council approved an expansion in the border monitoring mission to cover the border between Georgia and Ingushetia. A further expansion, to include monitoring Georgia's border with Dagestan, was effected from January 2003. A special envoy of the OSCE Chairman visited Georgia in July 2004 following a deterioration in the security situation. In November the Mission assisted the Georgian Government to develop an Action Plan to combat trafficking in human beings. In the same month the Mission helped to organize a national workshop on combating money-laundering and suppressing the financing of terrorism. In April 2005 the OSCE Permanent Council established a Training Assistance Programme for some 800 Georgian border guards. In June 2006 OSCE participating states pledged more than €10m. in support of projects for social and economic rehabilitation in the zone of the Georgian–Ossetian conflict. The donors' conference was the first of its kind to be organized by the OSCE. During 2007 the Mission continued to support activities concerned with police reform, human rights monitoring and education, munitions disposal, border control and management, counter-trafficking, and strengthening local democracy.

In September 1997 the Permanent Council determined to establish an OSCE Advisory and Monitoring Group in Belarus to assist with the process of democratization; the Group commenced operations in February 1998. It was subsequently active in strengthening civil society, organizing training seminars and workshops in electoral practices, monitoring the human rights situation, including the registration of political parties and the development of an independent media, and in mediating between the President and opposition parties. The OSCE/ODIHR declared legislative elections staged in Belarus in October 2000 not to have been conducted freely and fairly, and pronounced that presidential elections held in September 2001 had not met the standards required by the Organization. In December 2002 the decision was taken to terminate the Group and to establish in its place an OSCE Office in Minsk with a mandate to promote institution-building, strengthen relations with civil society and development economic and environmental activities. The Office was opened in January 2003. In September the ODIHR entered into dialogue with the Belarus authorities on reforming electoral legislation. In the same month the Minsk Office expressed its concern at the recent closure of non-governmental organizations in Belarus for alleged violations of the law. In October 2004 some 270 observers from 38 countries participated in a joint mission of the ODIHR and the OSCE Parliamentary Assembly to monitor parliamentary elections in Belarus. The mission concluded that several fundamental democratic principles had not been adhered to during the electoral process. In June 2005 the Minsk Office expressed concern at sentences of 'restricted freedom' passed on two prominent Belarusian opposition figure after they had been charged with organizing group activities which violated public order. In December the Office likewise voiced its disquiet at the adoption by the House of Representatives of the Belarusian National Assembly of legal amendments 'that could deal a serious blow to civil society and individuals'. In late March 2006 the OSCE CIO expressed his profound concern over detentions and arbitrary court proceedings that had occurred in the aftermath of a presidential election held earlier in the month, urging the Belarusian authorities 'immediately to put an end to the persecution of their opponents'. In April the CIO criticized a prison sentence passed on Belarus's principal opposition leader, Alyaksandr Milinkevich, and called for his immediate release. In July the CIO condemned the five-and-half-years prison sentence passed on anotheropposition candidate in the presidential election, after he had been arraigned on charges of 'hooliganism' and 'organizing and participating in group activities that gravely violated public order'. In August the CIO expressed concern at sentences passed on four members of a local organization charged with intending to act as observers in the March election.

An OSCE Mission to Moldova was established in February 1993, in order to assist conflicting parties in that country to pursue negotiations on a political settlement, as well as to observe the military situation in the region and to provide advice on issues of human and minority rights, democratization and the repatriation of refugees. In December 1999 the Permanent Council, with the approval of the Russian Government, authorized an expansion of the Mission's mandate to ensure the full removal and destruction of Russian ammunition and armaments and to co-ordinate financial and technical assistance for the withdrawal of foreign troops and the destruction of weapons. In June 2001 the Mission established a tripartite working group, with representatives of the Russian Ministry of Defence and the local authorities in Transnistria to assist and support the process of disposal of munitions. Destruction of heavy weapons began in mid-2002, under the supervision of the Mission. In 2005 observers from the ODIHR and OSCE Parliamentary Assembly participated in international missions to monitor parliamentary and local elections in Moldova, conducted in March and July, respectively. In March 2006 the OSCE Mission to Moldova initiated a Trial Monitoring Programme to observe court proceedings and judicial processes. In May 2003 a seminar on federalism, organized by the OSCE Parliamentary Assembly, was held further to promote negotiations between Moldova and the Transnistrian region on the development of a new Moldovan constitution, based on the principles of federalism. A second parliamentary conference on federalism was convened in September. In September 2004 the OSCE Mission financed a workshop as part of a two-year project concerned with 'strengthening protection and assistance to victims of trafficking, adults and minors'. During 2005 the OSCE Mission hosted negotiations which resulted in the Transnistrian authorities extending permanent registration to four Moldovan schools. In March 2006 the OSCE CIO expressed concern at the situation along the Transnistrian section of the Moldovan–Ukrainian state border and instructed the Mission to pursue a solution by consulting with all relevant parties. During a visit to Moldova in May the CIO urged all parties to the Transnistrian issue to resume negotiations. In January 2007 representatives of the OSCE, Russia and Ukraine met, with observers from the European Union and USA, to consider the future of the settlement process and invited chief negotiators from the Moldovan and Transnistrian authorities to initiate mediated discussions in the following month.

In 1999 an OSCE Project Co-ordinator in Ukraine was established, following the successful conclusion of the OSCE Mission to Ukraine (which had been established in November 1994). The Project Co-ordinator is responsible for pursuing co-operation between Ukraine and the OSCE and providing technical assistance in areas including legal reform, freedom of the media, trafficking in human beings, and the work of the human rights Ombudsman. In April 2002 an ODIHR Election Observation Mission monitored parliamentary elections held in Ukraine. In July 2003 the Project Co-ordinator and the Ukrainian defence ministry launched a joint programme to assist former military personnel to adapt to civilian life. In September 2004 an ODIHR mission was deployed to observe forthcoming presidential elections. More than 300 short-term observers monitored the first and second round polls, which were held in October and November respectively. In December the country's Supreme Court ruled that, owing to electoral irregularities, the second round voting should be re-run at the end of that month. The OSCE/ODIHR mission remained in the country to observe the process, and produced preliminary recommendations on the conduct of the re-run. In late January 2005 the CIO attended the inauguration of the newly-elected President, Viktor Yuschchenko. During 2005 activities of the Project Co-ordinator included supporting the establishment of a new investment promotion agency, organizing a conference on gender equality and law enforcement, training courses for judges in the new court system, a seminar to draft a national programme to combat human trafficking and a forum on media and election law, and hosting an international conference on strengthening the rule of law in the country. In June 2006, during a visit to Ukraine, the OSCE CIO expressed his support for the Ukrainian authorities' active engagement in negotiations with Moldova over the so-called Transnistrian border question. In a meeting with Ukraine's President and the country's foreign minister the CIO commended 'democratic advances' that had been made in parliamentary elections held in March. In 2007 the OSCE organized workshops and other initiatives to strengthen efforts to counter trafficking in humans among government officials, judges, consular officials and non-governmental organizations. In September the OSCE led an international election observation mission to oversee the conduct of parliamentary elections.

In March 1997 the OSCE dispatched a fact-finding mission to Albania to help restore political and civil stability, which had been undermined by the collapse of national pyramid saving schemes at the start of the year. An agreement was negotiated between Albania's President Sali Berisha and opposition parties to hold elections in mid-1997 and to establish a government of national reconciliation. In March the Permanent Council agreed to establish an OSCE Presence in Albania, and confirmed that the organization should provide the framework for co-ordinating other international efforts in the country. OSCE efforts focused on reaching a political consensus on new legislation for the conduct of the forthcoming elections to establish a government of national reconciliation. Voting took place in June–July, with 500 OSCE observers providing technical electoral assistance and helping to monitor the voting. In March 1998 the OSCE Presence was mandated to monitor the country's borders with the Kosovan region of southern Serbia and to prevent any spillover effects from the escalating crisis. (This role was reduced following the political settlement for Kosovo and Metohija concluded in mid-1999.) In June 1998 the OSCE observed local elections in Albania. It became the Co-Chair, with the EU, of the Friends of Albania group, which then brought together countries and international bodies concerned with the situation in Albania for the first time in September. In October the Permanent Council determined to enhance the Presence's role in border-monitoring activities. With other organizations, the OSCE was involved in the preparation of the country's draft constitution, finalized in October, and an ODIHR Election Observation Mission was established to observe the referendum on the constitution held in November. The OSCE Presence in Albania has subsequently provided advice and support to the Albanian Government regarding democratization, the rule of law, the media, human rights, anti-trafficking, election preparation and monitoring, and the development of civil society. It supports an Economics and Environment Unit and an Elections Unit, which, since the parliamentary elections of 2001, has facilitated the process of electoral reform. The Presence also monitors the Government's weapons collection programme. OSCE/ODIHR election observation missions were deployed in 2005 to monitor voting in local elections in March and parliamentary elections in July. In early 2006 the Presence supported a training course for 100 police officers in the use of border surveillance equipment. In April, during a visit to Albania, the OSCE CIO urged the country's leaders to resume the process of electoral reform and to implement recommendations made by the ODIHR following the legislative elections held in 2005. An environmental information centre was opened in December 2006. In January 2007 the OSCE, with the European Commission, launched a joint scheme to assist the Albanian government to modernize the address and civil registration systems.

The OSCE Mission to Bosnia and Herzegovina was established in December 1995 to achieve the objectives of the peace accords for the former Yugoslavia, in particular to oversee the process of democratization. The OSCE's efforts to organize and oversee the Bosnian national elections, which were held in September 1996, was the largest-ever electoral operation undertaken by the organization, with some 1,200 electoral observers deployed. The OSCE subsequently monitored municipal elections, held in September 1997, and the elections to the National Assembly of the Serb Republic and to the Bosnian Serb presidency in November. In 1998 the mission was charged with organizing the second post-war general elections in Bosnia and Herzegovina. The mission assisted with the registration of voters and, in September, was responsible for the supervision of the elections at polling stations within and outside the country. The final results of the election to the Bosnian Serb presidency were delayed, owing to the unexpected victory of an extreme nationalist, which, it was feared, could jeopardize the peace process. The OSCE immediately emphasized the necessity of maintaining the process. It also insisted on the need to transfer responsibility for the electoral process to the national authorities for future elections. In March 1999 the OSCE initiated an educational campaign relating to new election laws. However, a permanent electoral legal framework had not been approved by the time of legislative elections held in November 2000; the OSCE was therefore active in both preparing and monitoring these. The Mission's responsibility for elections in the country ended in November 2001 when a new permanent Election Commission was inaugurated. However, it was to continue to provide support for the Commission's secretariat. Other key areas of Mission activity are the promotion of democratic values, monitoring and promoting respect for human rights, strengthening the legal system, assisting with the creation of a modernized, non-discriminatory education system and establishing democratic control over the armed forces. An Agreement on Regional Arms Control was signed in 1995, providing for confidence- and security-building measures and a reduction in excess armaments. The Mission has established consultative commissions to promote dialogue among military personnel from different entities within the country. In late 2002 an OSCE-sponsored audit of several public enterprises and government ministries in Bosnia and Herzegovina was initiated. The results of the audits of three utility companies and of the Ministry of Social Policy, Displaced Persons and Refugees were published in March 2003. In January–August 2004 the Mission undertook monitoring of the criminal justice system. A report, concerned with the implementation of new procedural codes, was presented in December. In September the agreement on confidence- and security-building measures, mandated under the Dayton peace accords, was suspended in acknowledgement of the country's extensive political reforms. In December the Mission transferred its co-chairmanship of the country's Defence Reform Commission (DRC) to the new NATO headquarters in Sarajevo, although representatives of the Mission continued to be involved in work of the DRC. The Mission's work in 2005 was, increasingly, to be focused on ensuring peoples' rights to social welfare, healthcare and adequate housing. In April 2006 the OSCE CIO expressed his support for constitutional amendments adopted by the constitutional and legal affairs committee of the House of Representatives.

An OSCE Mission to Croatia was established in April 1996 to provide assistance and expertise in the field of human and minority rights, and to assist in the implementation of legislation and the development of democratic institutions. The Mission's mandate was extended in June 1997 in order to enhance its capacity to protect human rights, in particular the rights of minorities, to monitor freedom of the media and the return and treatment of refugees and displaced persons, and to make specific recommendations to the Croatian authorities. The Mission conducts extensive field monitoring to facilitate the return of refugees and displaced persons. In October 1998 the Mission assumed the responsibilities of the United Nations Police Support Group (UNPSG). The OSCE Police Monitoring Group, comprising a maximum of 120 unarmed OSCE civilian police monitors, was deployed in the region, representing the organization's first police-monitoring role. The Group was terminated in October 2000, although the OSCE has continued to advise on and monitor police activities in Croatia. The OSCE was also to be responsible for monitoring the border regions, with particular concern for customs activities. The OSCE/ODIHR monitored legislative and presidential elections held in Croatia in January 2000. The OSCE welcomed the adoption of the Constitutional Law on National Minorities adopted in December 2002 and urged ethnic minorities to participate in elections for minority self-government that took place in May 2003, in respect of which the OSCE funded a public information campaign. The OSCE likewise urged the Government to facilitate the participation of expatriate refugee voters in legislative elections held in November. In June the Mission initiated an 18-month public awareness campaign to promote reconciliation and the sustainable return of refugees and has subsequently produced regular reports on the situation. In October 2005 the Mission organized a conference on the rights of national minorities. In June 2006 an OSCE review recognized that many local democratic institutions had made considerable progress towards self-sustainability and determined that the Mission had met its international commitments in respect of police reform, civil society development, freedom of the media, and political affairs; these areas of activity were consequently terminated by December. The Mission was terminated in December 2007 and replaced, on 1 January 2008, by an OSCE Office in Zagreb.

In mid-1998 the OSCE was involved in the mediation effort to resolve the conflict between the Serbian authorities and ethnic Albanian separatists in the formerly autonomous province of Kosovo and Metohija. In October, following months of diplomatic effort and the threat of NATO air strikes, Yugoslav President Slobodan Milošević agreed to comply with UN Security Council Resolution 1199, which required an immediate cease-fire, Serbian troop withdrawals, the commencement of meaningful peace negotiations, the safe return of refugees and unrestricted access for humanitarian aid. Under a peace plan proposed by the US special envoy, Richard Holbrooke, President Milošević agreed to the formation of a 2,000-member OSCE Kosovo Verification Mission (KVM) to monitor compliance, in addition to surveillance flights by unarmed NATO aircraft. The Mission's mandate was formally established in October 1998 for a period of one year. Upon achievement of a political settlement defining the area's self-government, and its subsequent implementation, the KVM was to be responsible for supervising elections in Kosovo, assisting in the establishment of democratic institutions and developing a Kosovo police force. The long-term mission was accepted in return for the eventual removal of Yugoslavia's suspension from the OSCE. However, sporadic fighting continued in the province, and the monitoring force began unofficially to assume a peace-keeping role. In January 1999 the KVM successfully negotiated for the release of eight Yugoslav soldiers held hostage by the separatist forces. Later in that month, following the KVM's denunciation of the killing of some 45 ethnic Albanians by Serbian security forces in the village of Racak, President Milošević ordered the head of the mission, William Walker, to leave the region. The order was later revoked. Meanwhile, OSCE monitors were forced to withdraw from Racak under fire from Serbian troops. An emergency meeting of the OSCE in Vienna agreed to maintain the mission. However, in March, following the failure of negotiations to resolve the crisis, the CIO decided to evacuate the 1,380 unarmed monitors, owing to the deteriorating security situation in Kosovo. In early April the CIO condemned the mass expulsion of ethnic Albanians from Kosovo and other violations of human rights committed by Serbian forces. Within the framework of a political settlement for Kosovo, which was formally concluded in June, the OSCE was to be responsible for democracy- and institution-building under the auspices of the UN Interim Administration Mission for Kosovo (UNMIK). The OSCE Mission in Kosovo, mandated to comprise 1,300 personnel, was established on 1 July. OSCE monitors were deployed to assess the human rights situation throughout the region, and in August a new OSCE-administered police training school was inaugurated. (By October 2004 6,925 police-officers had trained under the OSCE police education programme.) In December 1999 the OSCE published a report on the situation in Kosovo, which confirmed that Serbian forces had conducted systematic abuses of human rights but also raised suspicion against the Kosovo Liberation Army (KLA) for organizing retribution attacks against Serbian civilians later in the year. In February 2000 the OSCE Mission established an Institute for Civil Administration to train public officials in principles of democratic governance. A Kosovo Law Centre was established in June to provide technical assistance to the legal community, with a view to promoting democratic principles and human rights. In the following month the Department for Democratic Governance and Civil Society was established by UNMIK, and was to be administered by the OSCE Mission. In August an Ombudsperson, nominated by the OSCE, was appointed to a new Office of the Ombudsperson, which became operational in November: the role of the Ombudsperson was to investigate and mediate claims of human rights violations arising within Kosovo. The OSCE was responsible for registering about 1m. voters prior to municipal elections that were held in Kosovo in October. During 2001 the Mission assisted the registration process for voting in a general election, and supervised the polling which took place in November. In early 2002 the Mission initiated training sessions for members of the new Kosovo Assembly. At that time the Mission was restructured, consolidating the number of field offices from 21 to nine. Among the priorities of the Mission were work on the sustainability of institutions created; developing the capacity of Kosovars to administer their own institutions (through the Kosovo Institute of Public Administration) and ensure that they adhere to democratic standards; and the promotion of reconciliation and tolerance and of the right to return. In June 2004 the Mission initiated an Out-of-Kosovo voting scheme to update the voter registration for upcoming Assembly elections. Following the election in October, the Mission, with other partner organizations co-ordinated under an Assembly Support Initiative, again undertook an induction programme for newly-elected members. In early 2005 the Mission commended the signing of a new Press Code and determined to facilitate the establishment of a Press Council. A commitment to strengthen the human rights infrastructure within the provisional institutions of the Kosovan administration was signed in early 2006. In February, during a visit to Kosovo, the OSCE CIO urged political leaders to initiate processes of decentralization and implementation of standards concurrently with ongoing status discussions. In January a new Youth and Education Support Unit was established within the Mission's Department of Democratization. In 2006 and 2007 the Mission assisted the Assembly to draft new legislation on the regulation of the security industry, and conducted a survey on the private security sector. In May 2007 an OSCE-funded Kosovo Media Institute, was inaugurated to provide professional training to journalists and media technicians. In 2008 the Mission remained OSCE's largest field operation.

In November 2000 the Federal Republic of Yugoslavia (FRY) was admitted into the OSCE. The FRY was renamed 'Serbia and Montenegro' in February 2003, and split into separate sovereign states of Montenegro and Serbia in June 2006. An OSCE Mission to the FRY was inaugurated in March 2001 (and, consequently, renamed the OSCE Mission to Serbia and Montenegro in 2003 and divided into two separate Missions in June 2006.) The initial mandate of the Mission was to assist in the areas of democracy and protection of human rights and in the restructuring and training of law enforcement agencies and the judiciary, to provide advice to government authorities with regard to reform of the media, and, in close co-operation with the United Nations High Commissioner for Refugees, to facilitate the return of refugees to and from neighbouring countries as well as within the FRY. In March 2002 the Mission facilitated the census process in southern Serbia. In June 2003 the Mission announced the launch of an Outreach Campaign, to ensure regular visits by Mission representatives to more remote municipalities. At the same time the Mission undertook a border-policing project in an effort to reduce human trafficking and organized crime in Serbia and Montenegro. ODIHR deployed election observation missions for presidential and parliamentary elections held in Serbia and Montenegro in late 2003. An ODIHR team observed a presidential election in the Serb Republic, conducted in June 2004. In September the Mission financed monitoring of municipal elections by a local non-governmental organization. During 2005 the Mission organized an international conference on combating human trafficking (convened in May), a regional conference on combating organized crime and trade in illegal drugs (in June), a conference on energy security (September), and the first regional conference on police education and training (November). In 2006 the Mission initiated dialogue between the Serbian police and the Roma community. In December ODIHR deployed an observation mission to oversee parliamentary elections that were conducted in the following month. The President of the OSCE Parliamentary Assembly subsequently declared the elections to have been 'free and fair'. New OSCE police training centres were inaugurated in May 2007.

Following its establishment in June 2006 the OSCE Mission to Montenegro has assisted that country to formulate a new constitution and has organized several conferences and high-level debates concerning constitutional guarantees, the role of the constitutional court and the independence of the judiciary. Other areas of activity have been concerned with establishing a prison monitoring mechanism to uphold human rights and strengthening standards in the media.

The OSCE Spillover Monitor Mission to Skopje was established in September 1992 to help to prevent the conflict in the former Yugoslavia from destabilizing the former Yugoslav republic of Macedonia (FYRM). Its initial mandate was to monitor the border region, as well as monitoring human rights and promoting the development of democratic institutions, including an independent media. The Mission is also concerned with mediating between interethnic groups in the country, and has provided support for implementation of the Ohrid framework political agreement, signed in August 2001, through the deployment of international confidence-building monitors and police advisers. In December OSCE monitors accompanied multi-ethnic police officers to areas of early conflict, as part of the August agreement. In March 2002 OSCE signed its first memorandum of understanding with the European Commission, in respect of policing operations in FYRM. The Mission supports a Police Academy and ongoing police training programmes. In September 2002 the OSCE participated in monitoring parliamentary elections in FYRM. In mid-2003 the Mission initiated a trial observation programme, by a coalition of non-governmental organizations, in order to restore confidence in the country's legal system. ODIHR led international election observation missions to monitor a popular referendum, held in November in relation to legislation to establish municipal boundaries; and to observe local elections, held in March 2005. In March 2006 the OSCE CIO expressed support for President Branko Crvenkovski's initiative to organize discussions on ways of improving the conduct of elections. Since 2002 the Mission has supported the Office of the Ombudsman, and in June 2007 initiated a second phase of the support project.

In March 2000 the OSCE adopted a Regional Strategy for South-Eastern Europe, aimed at enhancing co-operation amongst its presences in the region. The OSCE was actively involved in co-ordinating the Stability Pact for South-Eastern Europe, which was initiated, in June 1999, as a collaborative plan of action by the EU, Group of Seven industrialized nations and Russia (the G-8), regional governments and other organizations concerned with the stability of the region. (This can be accessed at www.stabilitypact.org.) A meeting of participants in the Pact was convened to coincide with the OSCE summit meeting, held in November. In October 2001 the OSCE organized a Stability Pact regional conference, held in Bucharest, Romania. A memorandum of understanding between the OSCE Mission to the FRY and the Stability Pact was signed in December. By 2008 the OSCE was continuing to work closely in support of the Stability Pact, providing country-specific expertise, capacity-building and training activities.

The OSCE Mission to Tajikistan was established in December 1993, and began operations in February 1994. The Mission worked with the UN Mission of Observers to Tajikistan (UNMOT) to promote a peace process in that country, and was a guarantor of the peace agreement concluded in June 1997. The Mission remained actively concerned with promoting respect for human rights, assisting the development of the local media, locating missing persons, and the fair distribution of humanitarian aid. Following multi-party parliamentary elections, held in February 2000, the Mission's focus was to be on post-conflict rehabilitation. In October 2002 the Permanent Council, taking into account the progress made in Tajikistan since the end of the civil conflict, decided to adapt the OSCE's mandate in the country and to replace the mission with a Centre in Dushanbe, with effect from the beginning of November. On 1 January 2004 the Centre initiated a two-year Mine Action Programme. In February 2005 an ODIHR mission observed parliamentary elections in Tajikistan, and reported a failure to meet certain OSCE commitments and other international standards. In November the Centre opened an explosive ordinance disposal training centre and demolition ground as the first stage in implementing a programme on small arms and light weapons and conventional ammunition. The activities of the Centre in 2006 included facilitating conferences and meetings on the establishment of a national human rights institution in Tajikistan and on democratic principles in the country's electoral process.

In December 2000 the Permanent Council renamed the OSCE Liaison Office in Central Asia the OSCE Centre in Tashkent. The Centre aimed to promote OSCE principles within Uzbekistan; it also functioned as an information exchange between OSCE bodies and participating Central Asian states and as a means of liaising with OSCE presences in the region. In July 1998 the Permanent Council determined to establish OSCE Centres in Bishkek (Kyrgyzstan), Almaty (Kazakhstan), and Ashgabad (Turkmenistan), all of which opened in January 1999. In general the Centres were to encourage each country's integration into the OSCE, and implementation of its principles, and to focus on the economic, environmental, human and political aspects of security. In January 2000, for the first time, the OSCE refused to dispatch official observers to monitor presidential elections in a member state, owing to concerns about the legitimacy of elections held in Kazakhstan. Subsequently the Centre in Almaty, with the ODIHR and the OSCE Parliamentary Assembly, initiated a roundtable-on-elections project to improve electoral legislation, thus strengthening the political system. The project concluded in January 2002, when participants presented a list of recommendations to the national parliament. In September 2004 an OSCE mission observed parliamentary elections held in Kazakhstan. In a joint statement with a parliamentary delegation of the Council of Europe, the mission declared concern at procedural standards in relation to election legislation in that country. In mid-October the OSCE Centres in Bishkek and Almaty organized a roundtable concerned with the electoral processes in Kazakhstan and Kyrgyzstan attended by participants from state institutions and civil society organizations. A joint ODIHR and OSCE Parliamentary Assembly mission observed legislative elections held in Kyrgyzstan in February and March 2005. The mission reported many procedural and democratic shortcomings in the election process. Following an escalation of civil and political tensions after the polls, the Centre in Bishkek offered to provide a forum for dialogue between the authorities and opposition groups. Some improvements to the electoral process were reported by the ODIHR misson that monitored an early presidential election in July. During 2005 the Centre in Bishkek supported a police assistance programme, an election assistance programme, good governance projects, economic development initiatives, and conflict prevention activities. In that year the Centre in Almaty assisted the Kazakh authorities to develop a national action plan on combating human trafficking, to implement efforts to control small arms and lights weapons, to develop a pollution control register, and to combat money-laundering and other illegal financial activities. Some 450 international observers participated in a mission to monitor a presidential election, held in December. The ODIHR subsequently reported a failure to meet certain OSCE and international standards. In March 2006 the Centre in Almaty organized a roundtable discussion of draft Kazakh legislation to combat money-laundering and terrorism. In the same month, on the occasion of talks with President Niyazov of Turkmenistan in Ashgabad, the OSCE CIO emphasized the importance of political reforms and democratization. In June the Centre in Bishkek organized a meeting to review progress made towards OSCE commitments during presidential and local elections in 2005 and parliamentary elections in 2006. In November the OSCE Centre in Almaty organized an international conference on the development of democratic processes in Kazakhstan. (In June 2007 the Centre was renamed the OSCE Centre in Astana.) In July 2006 an OSCE Project Co-ordinator was established in Uzbekistan as a new form of co-operation between the OSCE and that country.

By 2004 all five Central Asian OSCE Centres launched a Central Asian Youth Network to promote collaboration among the region's students and study of OSCE's fundamental principles. An OSCE Academy in Bishkek was inaugurated in December 2002 as a regional centre for training, research and dialogue, in particular in security-related issues.

Japan, the Republic of Korea, Thailand and Afghanistan have the status of 'partners for co-operation' with the OSCE, while Algeria, Egypt, Israel, Jordan, Morocco and Tunisia are 'Mediterranean partners for co-operation'. Regular consultations are held with these countries in order to discuss security issues of common concern. In October 2004 OSCE deployed a team of observers to monitor the presidential election in Afghanistan, representing the Organization's first election mission in a partner country.

Finance

All activities of the institutions, negotiations, ad hoc meetings and missions are financed by contributions from member states. The budget for 2008 amounted to €164.2m.

Publications

Annual Report of the Secretary-General.
The Caucasus: In Defence of the Future.
Decision Manual (annually).
OSCE Handbook.
OSCE Newsletter (monthly, in English and Russian).
Factsheets on OSCE missions, institutions and other structures are published regularly.

ORGANIZATION OF AMERICAN STATES—OAS

(ORGANIZACIÓN DE LOS ESTADOS AMERICANOS—OEA)

Address: 17th St and Constitution Ave, NW, Washington, DC 20006, USA.
Telephone: (202) 458-3000; **fax:** (202) 458-6319; **e-mail:** pi@oas.org; **internet:** www.oas.org.

The ninth International Conference of American States (held in Bogotá, Colombia, in 1948) established the Organization of American States (OAS) by adopting the Charter of the Organization of American States; the OAS succeeded the Commercial Bureau of American

INTERNATIONAL ORGANIZATIONS

Organization of American States

Republics, founded in 1890, and the Pan-American Union. The Charter was subsequently amended by the Protocol of Buenos Aires (creating the annual General Assembly), signed in 1967 and enacted in 1970; by the Protocol of Cartagena de Indias, which was signed in 1985 and enacted in 1988; and by the Protocol of Washington, signed in 1992 and enacted in 1997. The purpose of the OAS is to strengthen the peace and security of the continent; to promote human rights and to promote and consolidate representative democracy, with due respect for the principle of non-intervention; to prevent possible causes of difficulties and to ensure the peaceful settlement of disputes that may arise among the member states; to provide for common action in the event of aggression; to seek the solution of political, juridical and economic problems that may arise among the member states; to promote, by co-operative action, their economic, social and cultural development; to achieve an effective limitation of conventional weapons; to devote the largest amount of resources to the economic and social development of the member states; and to confront shared problems such as poverty, terrorism, the trade in illegal drugs, and corruption. The OAS is the principal regional multilateral forum. It plays a leading role in implementing mandates established by the hemisphere's leaders through the Summits of the Americas.

MEMBERS

Antigua and Barbuda
Argentina
Bahamas
Barbados
Belize
Bolivia
Brazil
Canada
Chile
Colombia
Costa Rica
Cuba*
Dominica
Dominican Republic
Ecuador
El Salvador
Grenada
Guatemala
Guyana
Haiti
Honduras
Jamaica
Mexico
Nicaragua
Panama
Paraguay
Peru
Saint Christopher and Nevis
Saint Lucia
Saint Vincent and the Grenadines
Suriname
Trinidad and Tobago
USA
Uruguay
Venezuela

*The Cuban Government was suspended from OAS activities in 1962.

Permanent Observers: Algeria, Angola, Armenia, Austria, Azerbaijan, Belgium, Bosnia and Herzegovina, Bulgaria, People's Republic of China, Croatia, Cyprus, Czech Republic, Denmark, Egypt, Equatorial Guinea, Estonia, Finland, France, Georgia, Germany, Ghana, Greece, Holy See, Hungary, India, Ireland, Israel, Italy, Japan, Kazakhstan, Republic of Korea, Latvia, Lebanon, Luxembourg, Morocco, Netherlands, Nigeria, Norway, Pakistan, Philippines, Poland, Portugal, Qatar, Romania, Russia, Saudi Arabia, Serbia, Slovakia, Slovenia, Spain, Sri Lanka, Sweden, Switzerland, Thailand, Tunisia, Turkey, Ukraine, United Kingdom, Yemen and the European Union.

Organization
(April 2008)

GENERAL ASSEMBLY

The Assembly meets annually and may also hold special sessions when convoked by the Permanent Council. As the highest decision-making body of the OAS, it decides general action and policy. The 37th regular session of the General Assembly was held in Panama in June 2007; the 38th General Assembly was scheduled to be convened in Medellín, Colombia, in June 2008.

MEETINGS OF CONSULTATION OF MINISTERS OF FOREIGN AFFAIRS

Meetings are convened, at the request of any member state, to consider problems of an urgent nature and of common interest to member states, or to serve as an organ of consultation in cases of armed attack or other threats to international peace and security. The Permanent Council determines whether a meeting should be convened and acts as a provisional organ of consultation until ministers are able to assemble.

PERMANENT COUNCIL

The Council meets regularly throughout the year at OAS headquarters. It is composed of one representative of each member state with the rank of ambassador; each government may accredit alternate representatives and advisers and when necessary appoint an interim representative. The office of Chairman is held in turn by each of the representatives, following alphabetical order according to the names of the countries in Spanish. The Vice-Chairman is determined in the same way, following reverse alphabetical order. Their terms of office are three months.

The Council guides ongoing policies and actions and oversees the maintenance of friendly relations between members. It supervises the work of the OAS and promotes co-operation with a variety of other international bodies including the United Nations. It comprises a General Committee and Committees on Juridical and Political Affairs, Hemispheric Security, Inter-American Summits Management and Civil Society Participation in OAS Activities, and Administrative and Budgetary Affairs. There are also ad hoc working groups. The official languages are English, French, Portuguese and Spanish.

INTER-AMERICAN COUNCIL FOR INTEGRAL DEVELOPMENT (CIDI)

The Council was established in 1996, replacing the Inter-American Economic and Social Council and the Inter-American Council for Education, Science and Culture. Its aim is to promote co-operation among the countries of the region, in order to accelerate economic and social development. An Executive Secretariat for Integral Development provides CIDI with technical and secretarial services. Technical co-operation and training programmes are managed by a subsidiary body of the Council, the Inter-American Agency for Co-operation and Development, which was established in 1999.

Executive Secretary: ALFONSO QUIÑÓNEZ.

INTER-AMERICAN JURIDICAL COMMITTEE (IAJC)

The Committee's purposes are: to serve as an advisory body to the OAS on juridical matters; to promote the progressive development and codification of international law; and to study juridical problems relating to the integration of the developing countries in the hemisphere, and, in so far as may appear desirable, the possibility of attaining uniformity in legislation. It comprises 11 jurists, nationals of different member states, elected for a period of four years, with the possibility of re-election.

President: JEAN-PAUL HUBERT (Canada); Av. Marechal Floriano 196, 3° andar, Palácio Itamaraty, Centro, 20080-002, Rio de Janeiro, RJ, Brazil; tel. (21) 2206-9903; fax (21) 2203-2090; e-mail cjioea.trp@terra.com.br.

GENERAL SECRETARIAT

The Secretariat, the central and permanent organ of the Organization, performs the duties entrusted to it by the General Assembly, Meetings of Consultation of Ministers of Foreign Affairs and the Councils. There is an Administrative Tribunal, comprising six elected members, to settle staffing disputes.

Secretary-General: JOSÉ MIGUEL INSULZA (Chile).
Assistant Secretary-General: ALBERT R. RAMDIN (Suriname).

INTER-AMERICAN COMMITTEES AND COMMISSIONS

Inter-American Commission on Human Rights (Comisión Interamericana de Derechos Humanos): 1889 F St, NW, Washington, DC 20006, USA; tel. (202) 458-6002; fax (202) 458-3992; e-mail cidhoea@oas.org; internet www.cidh.oas.org; f. 1960; comprises seven commissioners; promotes the observance and protection of human rights in the member states of the OAS; examines and reports on the human rights situation in member countries; considers individual petitions relating to alleged human rights violations by member states; in February 2005 established a Special Rapporteurship on the Rights of People of Afro-Descendants, and against Racial Discrimination; other rapporteurs analyse and report on the rights of children, women, indigenous peoples, migrant workers, prisoners and displaced persons, and on freedom of expression; the Commission also has a special unit on human rights defenders; Chair. PAOLO CAROZZA (USA); Exec. Sec. SANTIAGO A. CANTON.

Inter-American Committee on Ports (Comisión Interamericana de Puertos—CIP): 1889 F St, NW, Washington, DC 20006, USA; tel. (202) 458-3871; fax (202) 458-3517; e-mail cip@oas.org; internet www.oas.org/cip; f. 1998; serves as the permanent inter-American forum to strengthen co-operation on port-related issues among the member states, with the active participation of the private sector; the Committee, comprising 34 mem. states, meets every two years; its Executive Board, which executes policy decisions, meets annually; four technical advisory groups have been established to advise on port operations, port security, navigation control, and environmental protection; Sec. CARLOS M. GALLEGOS.

Inter-American Court of Human Rights (IACHR) (Corte Interamericana de Derechos Humanos): Apdo Postal 6906-1000, San José, Costa Rica; tel. (506) 234-0581; fax (506) 234-0584; e-mail corteidh@corteidh.or.cr; internet www.corteidh.or.cr; f. 1978 as an autonomous judicial institution whose purpose is to apply and interpret the American Convention on Human Rights (which entered into force in 1978: in 2007 the Convention had been ratified by 24 OAS member states, of which 21 had accepted the competence of the Court); comprises seven jurists from OAS member states; Pres. CECILIA MEDINA QUIROGA (Chile); Sec. PABLO SAAVEDRA-ALESSANDRI (Chile); publ. *Annual Report*.

Inter-American Drug Abuse Control Commission (Comisión Interamericana para el Control del Abuso de Drogas—CICAD): 1889 F St, NW, Washington, DC 20006, USA; tel. (202) 458-3178; fax (202) 458-3658; e-mail oidcicad@oas.org; internet www.cicad.oas.org; f. 1986 by the OAS to promote and facilitate multilateral co-operation in the control and prevention of the trafficking, production and use of illegal drugs, and related crimes; reports regularly, through the Multilateral Evaluation Mechanism, on progress against illegal drugs in each member state and region-wide; mems: 34 countries; Exec. Sec. JAMES F. MACK; publs *Statistical Survey* (annually), *Directory of Governmental Institutions Charged with the Fight Against the Illicit Production, Trafficking, Use and Abuse of Narcotic Drugs and Psychotropic Substances*, *Evaluation of Progress in Drug Control*, *Progress Report on Drug Control—Implementation and Recommendations* (twice a year).

Inter-American Telecommunication Commission (Comisión Interamericana de Telecomunicaciones—CITEL): 1889 F St, NW, Washington, DC 20006, USA; tel. (202) 458-3004; fax (202) 458-6854; e-mail citel@oas.org; internet www.citel.oas.org; f. 1993 to promote the development and harmonization of telecommunications in the region, in co-operation with governments and the private sector; CITEL has more than 200 associate members representing private associations or companies, permanent observers, and international organizations; under its Permanent Executive Committee specialized consultative committees focus on telecommunication standardization and radiocommunication, including broadcasting; mems: 35 countries; Exec. Sec. CLOVIS JOSÉ BAPTISTA NETO.

Activities

STRENGTHENING DEMOCRACY

The OAS promotes and supports good governance in its member states through various activities, including electoral observations, crisis-prevention missions, and programmes to strengthen government institutions and to support a regional culture of democracy. In September 2001 the member states adopted the Inter-American Democratic Charter, which details the essential elements of representative democracy, including free and fair elections; respect for human rights and fundamental freedoms; the exercise of power in accordance with the rule of law; a pluralistic political party system; and the separation and independence of the branches of government. Transparency and responsible administration by governments, respect for social rights, freedom of expression and citizen participation are among other elements deemed by the Charter to define democracy.

The observation of elections is one of the most important tasks of the OAS. During 1990–2007 the OAS deployed nearly 100 observer missions at the invitation of member states. Depending on the specific situation and the particular needs of each country, missions vary from a few technical experts sent for a limited time to a large country-wide team of monitors dispatched to observe the full electoral process for an extended period commencing with the political parties' campaigns. The missions present their observations to the OAS Permanent Council, along with recommendations for how each country's electoral process might be strengthened. Mission conducted in 2007 included observation of legislative elections in Ecuador, held in September, a general election in Jamaica (September), a referendum in Costa Rica (October), municipal elections in Colombia (October) and a presidential election in Guatemala (held in September and November).

The OAS has responded to numerous political crises in the region. In some cases, at the request of member states, it has sent special missions to provide critical support to the democratic process. During 2005–06 the OAS was particularly active in Nicaragua. In June 2005, responding to issues raised by the Government of President Enrique Bolaños, the OAS General Assembly expressed concern about developments that posed a threat to the separation and independence of branches of government. Citing the Inter-American Democratic Charter and the OAS Charter, the General Assembly authorized an OAS mission to help establish a broad national dialogue in that country; accordingly, the OAS Secretary-General subsequently led a high-level mission to Nicaragua to support efforts to find democratic solutions to the situation, and also appointed a special envoy to facilitate dialogue there. In October 2005 the Government and opposition forged an agreement aimed at enhancing stability and promoting national dialogue. The OAS Special Mission to Accompany the Democratic and Electoral Process in Nicaragua continued to follow the political situation in 2006, monitoring regional elections in March and general elections in November, in which Daniel Ortega won the presidency. In a subsequent report to the OAS Permanent Council, the Chief-of-Mission noted that Nicaragua had made significant steps forward in its democratic development and that its elections were 'increasingly clean and competitive'.

In 2005, acting on instructions from the OAS political bodies, the General Secretariat also sent special missions to assist with the resolution of political conflicts in Bolivia and Ecuador. Following an institutional crisis in Ecuador in that year the OAS offered support for the establishment of an impartial, independent Supreme Court of Justice and the OAS Secretary-General appointed two distinguished jurists as his special representatives to observe the selection process; members of Ecuador's new Supreme Court were sworn in during November. The OAS also played a role in Bolivia in 2005, following the resignation in June of President Carlos Mesa. The OAS Secretary-General appointed a special representative to facilitate political dialogue and to head the OAS observation mission on the electoral process that resulted in Evo Morales winning the presidency.

In August 2000 the OAS Secretary-General undertook the first of several high-level missions to negotiate with the authorities in Haiti in order to resolve the political crisis resulting from a disputed general election in May. In January 2001, following a meeting with the Haitian Prime Minister, the Assistant Secretary-General recommended that the OAS renew its efforts to establish a dialogue between the government, opposition parties and representatives of civil society in that country. In May the OAS and CARICOM undertook a joint mission to Haiti in order to assess prospects for a democratic resolution to the political uncertainties, and in June the OAS General Assembly issued a resolution urging all parties in Haiti to respect democratic order. At the end of that month the OAS Secretary-General led a visit of the joint mission to Haiti, during which further progress was achieved on the establishment of a new electoral council. Following political and social unrest in Haiti in December 2001, the OAS and CARICOM pledged to conduct an independent investigation into the violence, and in March 2002 an agreement to establish a Special OAS Mission for Strengthening Democracy in Haiti was signed in the capital, Port-au-Prince. The independent commission of inquiry reported to the OAS at the beginning of July, and listed a set of recommendations relating to law reform, security and other confidence-building measures to help to secure democracy in Haiti. In January 2004 the OAS Special Mission condemned the escalation of political violence in Haiti and in February took a lead in drafting a plan of action to implement a CARICOM-brokered action plan to resolve the crisis. In late February the Permanent Council met in special session, and urged the United Nations to take necessary and appropriate action to address the deteriorating situation in Haiti. On 29 February President Aristide resigned and left the country; amidst ongoing civil unrest, a provisional president was sworn in. The OAS Mission continued to attempt to maintain law and order, in co-operation with a UN-authorized Multinational Interim Force, and facilitated political discussions on the establishment of a transitional government. From March the Special Mission participated in the process to develop an Interim Co-operation Framework, identifying the urgent and medium-term needs of Haiti, which was presented to a meeting of international donors held in July. In June the OAS General Assembly adopted a resolution instructing the Permanent Council to undertake all necessary diplomatic initiatives to foster the restoration of democracy in Haiti, and called upon the Special Mission to work with the new UN Stabilization Mission in Haiti in preparing, organizing and monitoring future elections. During 2005 OAS technical experts, together with UN counterparts, assisted Haiti's Provisional Electoral Council (PEC) with the process of voter registration for legislative and presidential elections scheduled for later in that year, as well as to formulate an electronic vote tabulation system; this was to serve as the basis for a permanent civil registry. In July the newly-elected OAS Secretary-General visited Haiti and expressed his support for the PEC and the ongoing electoral process. In January 2006 the OAS Permanent Council declared its grave concern at a further postponement of the elections. In the following month, however, the Council expressed its satisfaction that polling taken place in a free and fair manner. The Secretary-General visited Haiti to meet with officials and offer his support for the declared president-elect, René Préval. The OAS has continued to extend support to the country and to co-ordinate international assistance, mainly through its Haiti Task Force, chaired by the Assistant Secretary-General. In February 2008 a special mission of the Permanent Council visited Haiti to assess priorities for future support.

In April 2002 a special session of the General Assembly was convened to discuss the ongoing political instability in Venezuela. The Assembly applied its authority granted under the Inter-American Democratic Charter to condemn the alteration of the constitutional order in Venezuela which forced the temporary eviction of President Hugo Chávez from office. In January 2003 the OAS announced the establishment of a Group of Friends, composed of representatives from Brazil, Chile, Mexico, Spain, Portugal and the USA, to support its efforts to resolve the ongoing crisis in Venezuela. In March the OAS Secretary-General was invited by Venezuelan opposition groupings to mediate negotiations with the Government. The talks culminated in May with the signing of an OAS-brokered agreement which, it was hoped, would lead to mid-term referendums on elected officials, including the presidency. The OAS, with the Carter Center, subsequently oversaw and verified the collection of signatures to determine whether referendums should be held. Following the staging of a recall referendum on the Venezuelan presidency in August 2004, OAS member states urged that there should be a process of reconciliation in that country.

In special situations, when both or all member states involved in a dispute ask for its assistance, the OAS plays a longer-term role in supporting countries to resolve bilateral or multilateral issues. In September 2005 Belize and Guatemala signed an agreement at the OAS establishing a framework for negotiations and confidence-building measures to help maintain good bilateral relations while they sought a permanent solution to a long-standing territorial dispute. In April 2006 another OAS-supported effort was concluded successfully when El Salvador and Honduras signed an accord settling differences over the demarcation of their common border. In March 2008 a Meeting of Consultation of OAS ministers of foreign affairs was convened following an escalation of diplomatic tension between Colombia and Ecuador resulting from a violation of Ecuador's borders by Colombian soldiers in pursuit of opposition insurgents. The meeting approved a resolution to establish a mechanism to restore confidence between the two countries and to negotiate an appropriate settlement to the dispute.

The OAS places a high priority on combating corruption in recognition of the undermining effect this has on democratic institutions. In 1996 the OAS member states adopted the Inter-American Convention against Corruption, which at early 2007 had been ratified by 33 member states. In 2002 the treaty's signatory states initiated a peer review process to examine their compliance with the treaty's key provisions. The Follow-Up Mechanism for the Implementation of the Inter-American Convention against Corruption assesses progress and recommends concrete measures that the states parties can implement to improve compliance. Representatives of civil society organizations are also given the opportunity to meet with experts and present information for their consideration. A second round of the review process commenced in 2006. All participating countries have been assessed at least once and the completed progress reports are available to the public. The OAS has also held seminars and training sessions in the region on such matters as improving transparency in government and drafting model anti-corruption legislation.

In recent years, the OAS has expanded its outreach to civil society. By 2007 210 non-governmental organizations (NGOs) had registered to take part in OAS activities. Civil society groups are encouraged to participate in workshops and round-tables in advance of the OAS General Assembly to prepare proposals and recommendations to present to the member states. This is also the case with Summits of the Americas and the periodic ministerial meetings, such as those on education, labour, culture, and science and technology. NGOs contributed ideas to the development of the Inter-American Democratic Charter and have participated in follow-up work on hemispheric treaties against corruption and terrorism.

The OAS has also focused on strengthening ties with the private sector. In 2006 it concluded a co-operation agreement with the business forum Private Sector of the Americas which aimed to promote dialogue and to support public–private alliances with a view to creating jobs, combating poverty and strengthening development. Business leaders from the region develop proposals and recommendations to present to the OAS General Assembly and to the Summits of the Americas.

Under the Democratic Charter a 'respect for human rights and fundamental freedoms' is deemed to be an essential element of a democracy. The Inter-American Commission on Human Rights and the Inter-American Court of Human Rights are the pillars of a system designed to protect individuals in the Americas who have suffered violations of their rights. A key function of the Commission is to consider petitions from individuals who claim that a state has violated a protected right and that they have been unable to find justice. The Commission brings together the petitioner and the state to explore a 'friendly settlement'. If such an outcome is not possible, the Commission may recommend specific measures to be carried out by the state to remedy the violation. If a state does not follow the recommendations the Commission has the option to publish its report or take the case to the Inter-American Court of Human Rights, as long as the state involved has accepted the Court's compulsory jurisdiction. The Commission convenes for six weeks each year.

In addition to hearing cases the Court may exercise its advisory jurisdiction to interpret the human rights treaties in effect in the region. The Commission, for its part, may conduct an on-site visit to a country, at the invitation of its Government, to analyse and report on the human rights situation. The Commission has also created rapporteurships focusing on particular human rights issues. In 2005 it created a rapporteurship on the rights of persons of African descent and against racial discrimination. Other rapporteurs analyse and report on the rights of children, women, indigenous peoples migrant workers, prisoners and displaced persons, and on freedom of expression. The Commission also has a special unit on human rights defenders. The OAS also works beyond the inter-American human rights system to promote the rights of vulnerable groups. The member states are in the process of negotiating the draft American Declaration on the Rights of Indigenous Peoples, which is intended to promote and protect a range of rights covering such areas as family, spirituality, work, culture, health, the environment, and systems of knowledge, language and communication. A special fund was established for voluntary contributions by member states and permanent observers in order to help cover the costs involved in broadening indigenous participation. The OAS also works to promote and protect women's rights. The Inter-American Commission of Women (CIM), established in 1928, has had an impact on shaping laws and policies in many countries. One of its key initiatives led to the adoption of the Inter-American Convention on the Prevention, Punishment and Eradication of Violence against Women, also known as the Convention of Belém do Pará, which was adopted in 1994 by the OAS General Assembly and, by 2007, had been ratified by 32 OAS member states. Since 2005 parties to the Belém do Pará Convention have been participating in a follow-up mechanism designed to determine how the countries are complying with the treaty and progress achieved in preventing and punishing violence against women. In 2006 the CIM also initiated an examination of strategies for reversing the spread of HIV/AIDS among women in the region. The Commission has urged greater efforts to integrate a gender perspective into every aspect of the OAS agenda.

SOCIAL AND ECONOMIC DEVELOPMENT

Combating poverty and promoting social equity and economic development are priority concerns of the OAS. In 2007 the member states were negotiating the text of a new Social Charter of the Americas. The OAS works on a number of fronts to combat poverty and promote development, in partnership with regional and global agencies, the private sector and the international community. In 2006 the OAS General Assembly approved a new Strategic Plan for Partnership for Integral Development 2006–09, which was to to guide OAS actions in this area. OAS development policies and priorities are determined by the organization's political bodies, including the General Assembly, the Permanent Council and the Inter-American Council for Integral Development (CIDI), with direction from the Summits of the Americas. The OAS Executive Secretariat for Integral Development (SEDI) implements the policies through projects and programmes. Specialized departments within SEDI focus on education, culture, science and technology; sustainable development; trade, tourism and competitiveness; and social development and employment. SEDI also supports the regional ministerial meetings on topics such as culture, education, labour and sustainable development that are held periodically as part of the Summit of the Americas process. These regional meetings foster dialogue and strengthen co-operation in specific sectors and ensure that Summit policies are implemented at the national level. The OAS convenes the ministerial meetings, prepares documents for discussion and tracks the implementation of Summit mandates. In November 2006 regional ministers of culture met in Montréal, Canada, to address the contribution of the cultural sector towards promoting development and combating poverty, and in the following month regional ministers of the environment met in Santa Cruz de la Sierra, Bolivia, to define strategies and goals related to sustainable development, environmental protection, the management of resources and the mitigation of natural disasters.

The OAS Department of Sustainable Development assists member states with formulating policies and executing projects that are aimed at integrating environmental protection with rural development and poverty alleviation, and that ensure high levels of transparency, public participation and gender equity. Its projects, which receive substantial outside funding, focus on several key areas.

Water resource management projects include initiatives that support member states in managing transboundary water resources in the major river basins of South and Central America, in partnership with the UNEP, the World Bank and the Global Environment Facility (GEF). The OAS is also active in various international fora that address water-related issues.

Projects focusing on natural disasters and climate adaptation include a new programme, launched in April 2006, which is aimed at assisting member countries to reduce the risk of natural disasters, particularly those related to climatic variations that have been linked to rises in sea levels. The OAS also works with CARICOM on the Main-streaming Adaptation to Climate Change project. Activities include incorporating risk reduction into development and economic planning; supporting good governance in such areas as the use of appropriate building codes and standards for public and residential buildings; supporting innovative financial instruments related to risk transfer; and supporting regional collaboration with different agencies and organizations.

The OAS serves as the technical secretariat for the Renewable Energy in the Americas initiative, which offers governments access to information on renewable energy and energy-efficient technologies, and facilitates contacts between the private sector and state energy entities in the Americas. The OAS also provides technical assistance for developing renewable energy projects and facilitating their funding.

Various OAS-supported activities help member countries to improve the management of biological diversity. The Inter-American Biodiversity Information Network (IABIN), which has been supported since 2004 by the GEF, World Bank and other sources, is a principal focus of OAS biodiversity efforts. The Department of Sustainable Development also supports the work of national conservation authorities in areas such as migratory species and biodiversity corridors. It co-operates with the private sector to support innovative financing through payment for ecological services, and maintains a unique on-line portal regarding land tenure and land title, which is used throughout the Americas.

In the areas of environmental law, policy and economics the OAS conducts environmental and sustainability assessments to help member states to identify key environmental issues that impact trade. Efforts include working with countries to develop priorities for capacity-building in such areas as domestic laws, regulations and standards affecting market access of goods and services. Other initiatives include supporting countries in water and renewable energy legislation; supporting efforts towards the more effective enforcement of domestic laws; and facilitating natural disaster risk reduction and relief.

In mid-2006 the OAS launched a programme aimed at supporting countries with managing pesticides and industrial chemicals. The programme was to co-ordinate its work closely with UNEP Chemicals, the UN Stockholm Convention and other entities.

The OAS supports member states at national, bilateral and multilateral level to cope with trade expansion and economic integration. Through its Department of Trade, Tourism and Competitiveness the OAS General Secretariat provides support in strengthening human and institutional capacities; and in enhancing trade opportunities and competitiveness, particularly for micro, small and medium-sized enterprises. One of the Department's key responsibilities is to help member states (especially smaller economies) to develop the capacity they need to negotiate, implement and administer trade agreements and to take advantage of the benefits offered by free trade and expanded markets. Many member states seek assistance from the OAS to meet successfully the challenges posed by increasing globalization and the need to pursue multiple trade agendas. Through its Foreign Trade Information System (SICE) the OAS also acts as a repository for information about trade and trade-related issues in the region, including the texts of trade agreements, information on trade disciplines, data, and national legislation.

The OAS has provided support to the Free Trade Area of the Americas (FTAA) process, endorsed by the First Summit of the Americas, held in December 1994 (see below), as well as supporting sub-regional and bilateral trade agreements. A trade unit was established in 1995 in order to strengthen the organization's involvement in trade issues and the process of economic integration, which became a priority area following the First Summit of the Americas. The trade unit provided technical assistance in support of the establishment of the FTAA and co-ordinated activities between regional and sub-regional integration organizations. At the Special Summit of the Americas, held in January 2004 in Monterrey, Mexico, the leaders failed to specify a completion date for the negotiations, although they adopted a declaration committing themselves to its eventual establishment. Negotiations on the FTAA subsequently stalled. The unit also supports a Hemispheric Co-operation Programme, which was established by ministers of trade of the Americas, meeting in November 2002, to assist smaller economies to gain greater access to resources and technical assistance. The OAS also administers an Inter-American Foreign Trade Information System (SICE) which facilitates the exchange of information on trade and trade-related issues.

MULTIDIMENSIONAL SECURITY

The promotion of hemispheric security is a fundamental purpose of the OAS. In October 2003, at a Special Conference on Security convened in Mexico City, the member states established a 'multidimensional' approach that recognized both traditional security concerns and newer threats such as international terrorism, drug trafficking, money-laundering, illegal arms dealing, trafficking in persons, institutional corruption and organized crime. In some countries problems such as poverty, disease, environmental degradation and natural disasters increase vulnerability and undermine human security. In March 2006, during a special session of the OAS General Assembly, the member states paved the way for closer co-operation on defence issues by formally designating the Inter-American Defense Board (IADB) as an OAS agency. Under its new mandate the operations and structure of the IADB were to be in keeping with the OAS Charter and the Inter-American Democratic Charter, including 'the principles of civilian oversight and the subordination of military institutions to civilian authority'. The IADB provides technical and educational advice and consultancy services to the OAS and its member states on military and defence matters.

Following the 11 September 2001 terrorist attacks perpetrated against targets in the USA the OAS member states strengthened their co-operation against the threat of terrorism. The Inter-American Convention against Terrorism, which seeks to prevent the financing of terrorist activities, strengthen border controls and increase co-operation among law enforcement authorities in different countries, was opened for signature in June 2002 and entered into force in July 2003. At mid-2007 it had been signed by all 34 active member states and ratified by 23. The Inter-American Committee against Terrorism (CICTE) offers technical assistance and specialized training in key counter-terrorism areas including port security, airport security, customs and border security, and legislation and legal assistance. In 2006 CICTE provided training to security officials in the Caribbean countries that were preparing to host the 2007 Cricket World Cup. Through CICTE member countries have also improved co-operation in improving the quality of identification and travel documents, strengthening cyber-security and adopting financial controls to prevent money-laundering and the funding of terrorist activities.

The Inter-American Drug Abuse Control Commission (CICAD) seeks to reduce the supply of and demand for illegal drugs, building on the 1996 Anti-Drug Strategy in the Hemisphere. The CICAD Executive Secretariat implements programmes aimed at preventing and treating substance abuse; reducing the supply and availability of illicit drugs; strengthening national drug-control institutions; improving practices to control firearms and money laundering; developing alternate sources of income for growers of coca, poppy and marijuana; and helping member governments to improve the gathering and analysis of data. The Multilateral Evaluation Mechanism (MEM) measures drug-control progress in the member states and the hemisphere as a whole, based on a series of objective indicators. The national reports on the third evaluation round, completed in 2006, included 506 specific recommendations designed to help countries strengthen their policies to combat drugs-related activities, and to increase multilateral co-operation. Following each evaluation round the MEM process examines how countries are carrying out the recommendations.

In 1997 the member states adopted the Inter-American Convention against the Illicit Manufacturing of and Trafficking in Firearms, Ammunition, Explosives, and other Related Materials (known as CIFTA), which by 2007 had been ratified by 26 member states. These countries have strengthened co-operation and information-sharing on CIFTA-related issues. In 2005 the OAS convened the first meeting of national authorities that make operational decisions on granting export, import and transit licenses for firearms, with a view to creating an information-exchange network to prevent illegal manufacturing and trafficking.

Since the 1990s the OAS has co-ordinated a comprehensive international programme to remove many thousands of antipersonnel landmines posing a threat to civilians in countries that have been affected by conflict. By the end of 2005 four member states—Costa Rica, Guatemala, Honduras and Suriname—had completed their mine-clearance programmes and had been declared landmine-safe. In 2007 humanitarian demining operations were continuing in Nicaragua, Colombia, Ecuador and Peru. The OAS co-ordinates activities, identifying, obtaining and delivering the necessary resources, including funds, equipment and personnel; the IADB oversees technical demining operations, working with field supervisors from various countries; and the actual demining is executed by teams of trained soldiers, security forces or other personnel from the affected country. In addition to supporting landmine clearance the OAS Mine Action Program helps with mine risk education; victim assistance and the socio-economic reintegration of formerly mined zones; the establishment of a mine action database; and support for a ban on the production, use, sale, transfer and stockpiling of antipersonnel landmines. It has also helped to destroy more than 1m. stockpiled mines in Argentina, Colombia, Chile, Ecuador, Honduras, Nicaragua and Peru.

The OAS Trafficking in Persons Section organizes seminars and training workshops for law-enforcement officials and others to raise awareness on human trafficking, which includes human exploitation, smuggling and other human rights violations. In March 2006 the Venezuelan Government hosted a Meeting of National Authorities on Trafficking in Persons in order to study ways to strengthen co-operation and to develop regional policies and strategies to prevent human trafficking. Gang violence is another growing public security concern in the region.

SUMMITS OF THE AMERICAS

Since December 1994, when the First Summit of the Americas was convened in Miami, USA (see below), the leaders of the region's 34 democracies have met periodically to examine political, economic and social development priorities and to determine common goals and forge a common agenda. This process has increasingly shaped OAS policies and priorities and many OAS achievements, for example the adoption of the Inter-American Democratic Charter and the creation of mechanisms to measure progress against illicit drugs and corruption, have been attained as a result of Summit mandates. The Summits of the Americas have provided direction for the OAS in the areas of human rights, hemispheric security, trade, poverty reduction, gender equity and greater civil society participation. The OAS serves as the institutional memory and technical secretariat to the Summit process. It supports the countries in follow-up and planning, and provides technical, logistical and administrative support. The OAS Summits Secretariat co-ordinates the implementation of mandates assigned to the OAS and chairs the Joint Summit Working Group, which includes the institutions of the inter-American system. The OAS also has responsibility for strengthening outreach to civil society to ensure that nongovernmental organizations, academic institutions, the private sector and other interests can contribute ideas and help to monitor and implement Summit initiatives.

In December 1994 the First Summit of the Americas was convened in Miami, USA. The meeting endorsed the concept of a Free Trade Area of the Americas (FTAA), and also approved a Plan of Action to strengthen democracy, eradicate poverty and promote sustainable development throughout the region. The OAS subsequently embarked on an extensive process of reform and modernization to strengthen its capacity to undertake a lead role in implementing the Plan. The organization realigned its priorities in order to respond to the mandates emerging from the Summit and developed a new institutional framework for technical assistance and co-operation, although many activities continued to be undertaken by the specialized or associated organizations of the OAS (see below). In 1996 the OAS member states participated in the interim Summit of the Americas on Sustainable Development, convened in Santa Cruz de la Sierra, Bolivia, which established sustainable development goals that incorporated economic, social and environmental concerns. The Second Summit of the Americas, which took place in 1998 in Santiago, Chile, focused on education, as well as such issues as strengthening democracy, justice and human rights; promoting integration and free trade; and eradicating poverty and discrimination. In 1998, following the Second Summit, the OAS established an Office of Summit Follow-Up, in order to strengthen its servicing of the meetings, and to co-ordinate tasks assigned to it. The Third Summit, convened in Québec, Canada, in April 2001, reaffirmed the central role of the OAS in implementing decisions of the summit meetings and instructed the organization to pursue the process of reform in order to enhance its operational capabilities, in particular in the areas of human rights, combating trade in illegal drugs, and enforcement of democratic values. The Summit declaration stated that commitment to democracy was a requirement for a country's participation in the summit process. The Third Summit urged the development of an Inter-American Democratic Charter to reinforce OAS instruments for defending and promoting democracy; the Democratic Charter was adopted in September of that year. The Third Summit also determined that the OAS was to be the technical secretariat for the summit process, assuming many of the responsibilities previously incumbent on the host country. Further to its mandate, the OAS established a Summits of the Americas Secretariat, which assists countries in planning and follow-up and provides technical, logistical and administrative support for the Summit Implementation Review Group and the summit process. An interim Special Summit of the Americas was held in January 2004, in Monterrey, Mexico, to reaffirm commitment to the process; the Special Summit established a range of concrete goals on three main issues: achieving economic growth to reduce poverty; promoting social development; and strengthening democratic governance. The Fourth Summit of the Americas was convened in Mar del Plata, Argentina, in November 2005, on the theme 'creating jobs to fight poverty and strengthen democracy'. The meeting approved a plan of action, incorporating both hemispheric co-operation and national commitments, to achieve employment growth and security. The Fifth Summit was scheduled to take place in Port of Spain, Trinidad and Tobago, in April 2009.

TOURISM AND CULTURE

A specialized unit for tourism was established in 1996 in order to strengthen and co-ordinate activities for the sustainable development of the tourism industry in the Americas. The unit supports regional and subregional conferences and workshops, as well as the Inter-American Travel Congress, which was convened for the first time in 1993 to serve as a forum to formulate region-wide tourism policies. The unit also undertakes research and analysis of the industry.

In 1998 the OAS approved an Inter-American Programme of Culture to support efforts being undertaken by member states and to promote co-operation in areas such as cultural diversity; protection of cultural heritage; training and dissemination of information; and the promotion of cultural tourism. The OAS also assists with the preparation of national and multilateral cultural projects, and co-operates with the private sector to protect and promote cultural assets and events in the region. In July 2002 the first Inter-American meeting of ministers of culture approved the establishment of an Inter-American Committee on Culture, within the framework of the Council for Integral Development (CIDI), to co-ordinate high-level dialogue and co-operation on cultural issues. In April 2006 the OAS, the Caribbean Tourism Organization and the Caribbean Hotel Association signed an agreement on the provision of training and assistance aimed at improving the capacity of the Caribbean tourism industry.

Finance

The OAS programme budget for 2008, approved by the General Assembly in mid-2007, amounted to US $93.5m., of which $87.5m. was to come from the regular fund, and $6.0m. from the Special Multilateral Fund ('Voluntary Fund') of the Inter-American Council for Integral Development (FEMCIDI). Expenditure from Special Funds was to amount to $93.5m. In 2009 the total proposed budget amounted to $186.1m.

Publications

(in English and Spanish)

Américas (6 a year).
Annual Report.
Numerous cultural, legal and scientific reports and studies.

Specialized Organizations and Associated Agencies

Inter-American Children's Institute (Instituto Americano del Niño, la Niña y Adolescentes—IIN): Avda 8 de Octubre 2904, POB 16212, Montevideo 11600, Uruguay; tel. (2) 487-2150; fax (2) 487-3242; e-mail iin@oas.org; internet www.iin.oea.org; f. 1927; promotes the regional implementation of the Convention on the Rights of the Child, assists in the development of child-oriented public policies; promotes co-operation between states; and aims to develop awareness of problems affecting children and young people in the region. The Institute organizes workshops, seminars, courses, training programmes and conferences on issues relating to children, including, for example, the rights of children, children with disabilities, and the child welfare system. It also provides advisory services, statistical data and other relevant information to authorities and experts throughout the region; Dir-Gen. MARIA DE LOS DOLORES AGUILAR MARMOLEJO; publ. *iinfancia*(annually).

Inter-American Commission of Women (Comisión Interamericana de Mujeres—CIM): 1889 F St, NW, Suite 350 Washington, DC 20006, USA; tel. (202) 458-6084; fax (202) 458-6094; e-mail spcim@oas.org; internet www.oas.org/cim; f. 1928 as the first ever official intergovernmental agency created expressly to ensure recognition of the civil and political rights of women; the CIM is the principal forum for generating hemispheric policy to advance women's rights and gender equality; comprises 34 principal delegates; the Assembly of Delegates, convened every two years, is the highest authority of the Commission, establishing policies and a plan of action for each biennium and electing the seven-member Executive Committee; Pres. JACQUI QUINN-LEANDRO (Antigua and Barbuda); Exec. Sec. CARMEN LOMELLIN (USA).

Inter-American Committee Against Terrorism (Comité Interamericano Contra el Terrorismo—CICTE): 1889 F St, NW, Washington, DC 20006, USA; tel. (202) 458-6960; fax (202) 458-3857; e-mail cicte@oas.org; internet www.cicte.oas.org; f. 1999 to enhance the exchange of information via national authorities, formulate proposals to assist member states in drafting counter-terrorism legislation in all states, compile bilateral, sub-regional, regional and multilateral treaties and agreements signed by member states and promote universal adherence to international counter-terrorism conventions, strengthen border co-operation and travel documentation security measures, and develop activities for training and crisis management; Exec. Sec. CAROL FULLER (USA).

Inter-American Defense Board (Junta Interamericana de Defensa—JID): 2600 16th St, NW, Washington, DC 20441, USA; tel. (202) 939-6041; fax (202) 387-2880; e-mail iadc-registrar@jid.org; internet www.jid.org; promotes co-operative security interests in the Western Hemisphere; new statutes adopted in 2006 formally designated the Board as an OAS agency; works on issues such as humanitarian demining, disaster assistance and confidence-building measures directly suporting the hemispheric security goals of the OAS and of regional ministers of defence; also provides a senior-level academic programme in security studies for military, national police and civilian leaders at the Inter-American Defense College; Dir-Gen. Brig. ANCIL W. ANTOINE (Trinidad and Tobago).

Inter-American Indigenous Institute (Instituto Indigenista Interamericano—III): Avda de las Fuentes 106, Col. Jardines del Pedregal, Delegación Álvaro Obregón, 01900 México, DF, Mexico; tel. (55) 5595-8410; fax (55) 5595-4324; e-mail ininin@data.net.mx; internet www.indigenista.org; f. 1940; conducts research on the situation of the indigenous peoples of America; assists the exchange of information; promotes indigenous policies in member states aimed at the elimination of poverty and development within Indian communities, and to secure their position as ethnic groups within a democratic society; Hon. Dir Dr GUILLERMO ESPINOSA VELASCO (Mexico); publs *América Indígena* (quarterly), *Anuario Indigenista*.

Inter-American Institute for Co-operation on Agriculture (IICA) (Instituto Interamericano de Cooperación para la Agricultura): Apdo Postal 55–2200 San Isidro de Coronado, San José, Costa Rica; tel. (506) 216-0222; fax (506) 216-0233; e-mail iicahq@iica.ac.cr; internet www.iica.int; f. 1942 (as the Inter-American Institute of Agricultural Sciences, present name adopted 1980); supports the efforts of member states to improve agricultural development and rural well-being; encourages co-operation between regional organizations, and provides a forum for the exchange of experience; Dir-Gen. Dr CHELSTON W. D. BRATHWAITE (Barbados).

Justice Studies Center of the Americas (Centro de Estudios de Justicia de las Américas): Holanda 2023, Providencia, Santiago, Chile; tel. (2) 2742933; fax (2) 3415769; e-mail info@cejamericas.org; internet www.cejamericas.org; f. 1999; aims to support the modernization of justice systems in the region; Exec. Dir CRISTIÁN RIEGO RAMÍREZ.

Pan American Development Foundation (PADF) (Fundación Panamericana para el Desarrollo): 1889 F St, NW, Washington, DC 20006, USA; tel. (202) 458-3969; fax (202) 458-6316; e-mail padf-dc@padf.org; internet www.padf.org; f. 1962 to promote and facilitate economic and social development in Latin America and the Caribbean by means of innovative partnerships and integrated involvement of the public and private sectors; provides low-interest credit for small-scale entrepreneurs, vocational training, improved health care, agricultural development and reafforestation, and strengthening local non-governmental organizations; provides emergency disaster relief and reconstruction assistance; Exec. Dir JOHN SANBRAILO; Sec. PHILIPPE R. ARMAND.

Pan American Health Organization (PAHO) (Organización Panamericana de la Salud): 525 23rd St, NW, Washington, DC 20037, USA; tel. (202) 974-3000; fax (202) 974-3663; e-mail webmaster@paho.org; internet www.paho.org; f. 1902; co-ordinates regional efforts to improve health; maintains close relations with national health organizations and serves as the Regional Office for the Americas of the World Health Organization; Dir Dr MIRTA ROSES PERIAGO (Argentina).

Pan-American Institute of Geography and History (PAIGH) (Instituto Panamericano de Geografía e Historia–IPGH): Ex-Arzobispado 29, 11860 México, DF, Mexico; tel. (55) 5277-5888; fax (55) 5271-6172; e-mail secretariageneral@ipgh.org; internet www.ipgh.org.mx; f. 1928; co-ordinates and promotes the study of cartography, geophysics, geography and history; provides technical assistance, conducts training at research centres, distributes publications, and organizes technical meetings; Sec.-Gen. SANTIAGO BORRERO MUTIS (Colombia); Publs *Revista Cartográfica* (2 a year), *Revista Geográfica* (2 a year), *Revista de Historia de América* (2 a year), *Revista Geofísica* (2 a year), *Revista de Arqueología Americana* (annually), *Folklore Americano* (annually), *Boletín de Antropología Americana* (annually).

ORGANIZATION OF ARAB PETROLEUM EXPORTING COUNTRIES—OAPEC

Address: POB 20501, Safat 13066, Kuwait.
Telephone: 4959000; **fax:** 4959755; **e-mail:** oapec@oapecorg.org; **internet:** www.oapecorg.org.

OAPEC was established in 1968 to safeguard the interests of members and to determine ways and means for their co-operation in various forms of economic activity in the petroleum industry. OAPEC member states contributed 29.8% of total world petroleum production in 2006 and 11.9% of total global marketed natural gas in 2005. At the end of 2006 OAPEC member states accounted for an estimated 56.4% of total global oil reserves and 28.6% of total global reserves of natural gas.

MEMBERS

Algeria	Kuwait	Saudi Arabia
Bahrain	Libya	Syria
Egypt	Qatar	United Arab Emirates
Iraq		

Organization

(April 2008)

MINISTERIAL COUNCIL

The Council consists normally of the ministers of petroleum of the member states, and forms the supreme authority of the Organization, responsible for drawing up its general policy, directing its activities and laying down its governing rules. It meets twice yearly, and may hold extraordinary sessions. Chairmanship is on an annual rotation basis.

EXECUTIVE BUREAU

Assists the Council to direct the management of the Organization, approves staff regulations, reviews the budget, and refers it to the Council, considers matters relating to the Organization's agreements and activities and draws up the agenda for the Council. The Bureau comprises one senior official from each member state. Chairmanship is by rotation on an annual basis, following the same order as the Ministerial Council chairmanship. The Bureau convenes at least three times a year.

GENERAL SECRETARIAT

Secretary-General: ABDUL AZIZ A. AL-TURKI (Saudi Arabia).

Besides the Office of the Secretary-General, there are four departments: Finance and Administrative Affairs, Information and Library, Technical Affairs, and Economics. The last two form the Arab Centre for Energy Studies (which was established in 1983).

JUDICIAL TRIBUNAL

The Tribunal comprises seven judges from Arab countries. Its task is to settle differences in interpretation and application of the OAPEC Agreement, arising between members and also between OAPEC and its affiliates; disputes among member countries on petroleum activities falling within OAPEC's jurisdiction and not under the sovereignty of member countries; and disputes that the Ministerial Council decides to submit to the Tribunal.

President: Dr MOUSTAFA ABDUL HAYY AL-SAYED.

Activities

OAPEC co-ordinates different aspects of the Arab petroleum industry through the joint undertakings described below. It co-operates with the League of Arab States and other Arab organizations, and attempts to link petroleum research institutes in the Arab states. It organizes or participates in conferences and seminars, many of which are held jointly with non-Arab organizations in order to enhance Arab and international co-operation. OAPEC collaborates with AFESD, the Arab Monetary Fund and the League of Arab States in compiling the annual *Joint Arab Economic Report*, which is issued by the Arab Monetary Fund.

OAPEC provides training in technical matters and in documentation and information. The General Secretariat also conducts technical and feasibility studies and carries out market reviews. It provides information through a library, 'databank' and the publications listed below.

In association with AFESD, OAPEC organizes the Arab Energy Conference every four years. The conference is attended by OAPEC ministers of petroleum and energy, senior officials from other Arab states, and representatives of invited institutions and organizations concerned with energy issues. The eighth Arab Energy Conference, focusing on the same theme, was held in Amman, Jordan, in May 2006. OAPEC, with other Arab organizations, participates in the Higher Co-ordination Committee for Higher Arab Action.

In December 2003 a delegation of the then Iraq Interim Cabinet briefed government representatives from other OAPEC member states on the planned reactivation of the Baghdad-based Arab Well Logging Company and Arab Petroleum Training Institute (see below), which had both suspended operations in 1990.

Finance

The combined General Secretariat and Judicial Tribunal budget for 2007 was 1.76m. Kuwaiti dinars (KD).

Publications

Annual Statistical Report.
Energy Resources Monitor (quarterly, Arabic).
OAPEC Monthly Bulletin (Arabic and English editions).
Oil and Arab Co-operation (quarterly, Arabic).
Secretary-General's Annual Report (Arabic and English editions).
Papers, studies, conference proceedings.

OAPEC-Sponsored Ventures

Arab Maritime Petroleum Transport Company (AMPTC): POB 22525, Safat 13086, Kuwait; tel. 4844500; fax 4842996; e-mail amptc.kuwait@amptc.net; internet www.amptc.net; f. 1973 to undertake transport of crude petroleum, gas, refined products and petro-chemicals, and thus to increase Arab participation in the tanker transport industry; owns and operates a fleet of oil tankers and other carriers; auth. cap. US $200m.; Gen. Man. SULAYMAN AL-BASSAM.

Arab Petroleum Investments Corporation (APICORP): POB 9599, Dammam 31423, Saudi Arabia; tel. (3) 847-0444; fax (3) 847-0022; e-mail apicorp@apicorp-arabia.com; internet www.apicorp-arabia.com; f. 1975 to finance investments in petroleum and petrochemicals projects and related industries in the Arab world and in developing countries, with priority being given to Arab joint ventures; projects financed include gas liquefaction plants, petrochemicals, tankers, oil refineries, pipelines, exploration, detergents, fertilizers and process control instrumentation; auth. cap. US $1,200m.; paid-up cap. $550m.; shareholders: Kuwait, Saudi Arabia and United Arab Emirates (17% each), Libya (15%), Iraq and Qatar (10% each), Algeria (5%), Bahrain, Egypt and Syria (3% each); Chair. ABDULLAH A. AL-ZAID (Saudi Arabia); Gen. Man. and CEO AHMAD BIN HAMAD AL-NUAIMI.

Arab Detergent Chemicals Company (ARADET): POB 27864, el-Monsour, Baghdad, Iraq; tel. (1) 541-9893; fax (1) 543-0265; e-mail info@aradetco.com; internet www.aradetco.com; f. 1981; produces and markets linear alkyl benzene; construction of a sodium multiphosphate plant is under way; APICORP holds 32% of shares in the co; auth. cap. 72m. Iraqi dinars; subs. cap. 60m. Iraqi dinars.

Arab Petroleum Services Company (APSCO): POB 12925, Tripoli, Libya; tel. (21) 45861; fax (21) 3331930; f. 1977 to provide petroleum services through the establishment of companies specializing in various activities, and to train specialized personnel; auth. cap. 100m. Libyan dinars; subs. cap. 15m. Libyan dinars; Chair. AYAD HUSSEIN AD-DALI; Gen. Man. ISMAIL AL-KORAITLI.

Arab Drilling and Workover Company: POB 680, Suani Rd, km 3.5, Tripoli, Libya; tel. (21) 800064; fax (21) 805945; f. 1980; 40% owned by APSCO; auth. cap. 12m. Libyan dinars; Gen. Man. MUHAMMAD AHMAD ATTIGA.

Arab Geophysical Exploration Services Company (AGESCO): POB 84224, Airport Rd, Tripoli, Libya; tel. (21) 4804863; fax (21) 4803199; f. 1985; 40%-owned by APSCO; auth. cap. 12m. Libyan dinars; subs. cap. 4m. Libyan dinars; Gen. Man. AYAD HUSSEIN AD-DALI.

Arab Well Logging Company (AWLCO): POB 6225, Baghdad, Iraq; tel. (1) 541-8259; f. 1983 to provide well-logging services and data interpretation; wholly-owned subsidiary of APSCO; auth. cap. 7m. Iraqi dinars.

Arab Petroleum Training Institute (APTI): POB 6037, Al-Tajeyat, Baghdad, Iraq; tel. (1) 523-4100; fax (1) 521-0526; f. 1978 to provide instruction in many technical and managerial aspects of the oil industry.

Arab Shipbuilding and Repair Yard Company (ASRY): POB 50110, Hidd, Bahrain; tel. 671111; fax 670236; e-mail asryco@batelco.com.bh; internet www.asry.net; f. 1974 to undertake repairs and servicing of vessels; operates a 500,000 dwt dry dock in Bahrain; two floating docks operational since 1992; has recently diversified it activities, e.g. into building specialized service boats and upgrading oil rigs; cap. (auth. and subs.) US $170m.; Chair. EID ABDULLA YOUSIF (Bahrain); Chief Exec. MOHAMED M. AL-KHATEEB.

ORGANIZATION OF THE BLACK SEA ECONOMIC CO-OPERATION—BSEC

Address: Sakıp Sabancı Cad., Müşir Fuad Paşa Yalısı, Eski Tersane 34460 İstinye-İstanbul, Turkey.
Telephone: (212) 229-63-30; **fax:** (212) 229-63-36; **e-mail:** info@bsec-organization.org; **internet:** www.bsec-organization.org.

The Black Sea Economic Co-operation (BSEC) was established in 1992 to strengthen regional co-operation, particularly in the field of economic development. In June 1998, at a summit meeting held in Yalta, Ukraine, participating countries signed the BSEC Charter, thereby officially elevating BSEC to regional organization status. The Charter entered into force on 1 May 1999, at which time BSEC formally became the Organization of the Black Sea Economic Co-operation, retaining the same acronym.

MEMBERS

Albania	Georgia	Russia
Armenia	Greece	Serbia
Azerbaijan	Moldova	Turkey
Bulgaria	Romania	Ukraine

Note: Observer status has been granted to Austria, Belarus, Croatia, Czech Republic, Egypt, France, Germany, Israel, Italy, Poland, Slovakia, Tunisia and the USA. The Black Sea Commission, the BSEC Business Council, the European Commission, the International Black Sea Club, and the Energy Charter Conference also have observer status. Iran, the former Yugoslav republic of Macedonia, Montenegro and Uzbekistan have applied for full membership.

Organization

(April 2008)

PRESIDENTIAL SUMMIT

The Presidential Summit, comprising heads of state or government of member states, represents the highest authority of the body.

COUNCIL

The Council of Ministers of Foreign Affairs is BSEC's principal decision-making organ. Ministers meet twice a year to review progress and to define new objectives. Chairmanship of the Council rotates among members; the Chairman-in-Office co-ordinates the activities undertaken by BSEC. The Council is supported by a Committee of Senior Officials. Upon request of the Chairman-in-Office a Troika, comprising the current, most recent and next Chairman-in-Office, or their representatives, is convened to consider BSEC's ongoing and planned activities.

PERMANENT INTERNATIONAL SECRETARIAT

The Secretariat's tasks are, primarily, of an administrative and technical nature, and include the maintenance of archives, and the preparation and distribution of documentation. Much of the organization's activities are undertaken by 15 working groups, each headed by an Executive Manager, and by various ad hoc groups and meetings of experts.

Secretary-General: LEONIDAS CHRYSANTHOPOULOS (Greece).

Activities

In June 1992, at a summit meeting held in İstanbul, heads of state and of government signed the summit declaration on BSEC, and adopted the Bosphorus statement, which established a regional structure for economic co-operation. The grouping attained regional organization status in May 1999 (see above). The Organization's main areas of co-operation include transport; communications; trade and economic development; banking and finance; energy; tourism; agriculture and agro-industry; health care and pharmaceuticals; environmental protection; science and technology; the exchange of statistical data and economic information; collaboration between customs authorities; and combating organized crime, drugs-trafficking, trade in illegal weapons and radioactive materials, and terrorism. In order to promote regional co-operation, the Organization also aims to strengthen the business environment by providing support for small and medium-sized enterprises; facilitating closer contacts between businesses in member countries; progressively eliminating obstacles to the expansion of trade; creating appropriate conditions for investment and industrial co-operation, in particular through the avoidance of double taxation and the promotion and protection of investments; encouraging the dissemination of information concerning international tenders organized by member states; and promoting economic co-operation in free-trade zones. A Working Group on Culture was established in November 2006 to promote and protect the cultural identity of the region.

A BSEC Business Council was established in İstanbul in December 1992 by the business communities of member states. It has observer status at the BSEC, and aims to identify private and public investment projects, maintain business contacts and develop programmes in various sectors. A Black Sea Trade and Development Bank has been established, in Thessaloníki, Greece, as the Organization's main funding institution, to finance and implement joint regional projects. It began operations on 1 July 1999 (see below). A BSEC Co-ordination Centre, located in Ankara, Turkey, aims to promote the exchange of statistical and economic information. An International Centre for Black Sea Studies (ICBSS) was established in Athens, Greece, in March 1998, in order to undertake research concerning the BSEC, in the fields of economics, industry and technology.

In recent years BSEC has undergone a process of reform aimed at developing a more project-based orientation. In April 2001 the Council adopted the so-called BSEC Economic Agenda for the Future Towards a More Consolidated, Effective and Viable BSEC Partnership, which provided a roadmap for charting the implementation of the Organization's goals. In 2002 a Project Development Fund was established and a regional programme of governance and institutional renewal was launched. Under the new orientation the roles of BSEC's Committee of Senior Officials and network of country co-ordinators were to be enhanced. In April 2008 the BSEC Council inaugurated a new €1m. BSEC Hellenic Development Fund. The Council also adopted the modalities for BSEC fast-track co-operation, aimed at enabling small groups of member states to proceed with policies that other member states were unwilling or unable to pursue.

BSEC aims to foster relations with other international and regional organizations, and has been granted observer status at the UN General Assembly. In 1999 BSEC agreed upon a Platform of Co-operation for future structured relations with the European Union. The main areas in which BSEC determined to develop co-operation with the EU were transport, energy and telecommunications infrastructure; trade and the promotion of foreign direct investment; sustainable development and environmental protection, including nuclear safety; science and technology; and combating terrorism and organized crime. BSEC supports the Stability Pact for South-Eastern Europe, initiated in June 1999 as a collaborative plan of action by the EU, the Group of Seven industrialized nations and Russia (the G-8), regional governments and other organizations concerned with the stability of the region. The Declaration issued by BSEC's decennial anniversary summit, held in İstanbul in June 2002, urged that collaboration with the EU should be enhanced. In April 2005 representatives of BSEC and the EU met in Brussels, Belgium, to address possibilities for such co-operation, focusing in particular on the EU's policy in the Black Sea region and on the development of regional transport and energy networks (see Alexandroupolis Declaration, below). In June 2007 BSEC heads of state confirmed their commitment to an enhanced relationship with the EU, based on a communication of the European Commission, published in April, entitled 'Black Sea Synergy—a New Regional Co-operation Initiative'. In November 2006 BSEC signed a Memorandum of Understanding with the International Road Federation.

BSEC has supported implementation of the Bucharest Convention on the Protection of the Black Sea Against Pollution, adopted by Bulgaria, Georgia, Romania, Russia, Turkey and Ukraine in April 1992. In October 1996 those countries adopted the Strategic Action Plan for the Rehabilitation and Protection of the Black Sea (BSSAP), to be implemented by the Commission of the Bucharest Convention. In March 2001 the transport ministers of BSEC member states adopted a Transport Action Plan, which envisaged reducing the disparities in regional transport systems and integrating the BSEC regional transport infrastructure with wider international networks and projects. In April 2007 BSEC governments signed an agreement for the co-ordinated development of a 7,000 km-long Black Sea Ring Highway. A memorandum of understanding relating to the development of 'Motorways of the Sea' was also signed. In March 2005 ministers of BSEC member states responsible for energy adopted the Alexandroupolis Declaration, approving a common framework for future collaboration on the creation of a regional energy market, and urging the liberalization of electricity and natural gas markets in accordance with EU directives as a basis for this.

Finance

BSEC is financed by annual contributions from member states on the following scale: Greece, Russia, Turkey and Ukraine each contribute 15% of the budget; Bulgaria, Romania and Serbia contribute 7.5%; the remaining members each contribute 3.5%.

Publication

Black Sea News (quarterly).

Related Bodies

Parliamentary Assembly of the Black Sea: 1 Hareket Kösku, Dolmabahçe Sarayi, Besiktas, 80680 İstanbul, Turkey; tel. (212) 227-6070; fax (212) 227-6080; e-mail pabsec@pabsec.org; internet www.pabsec.org; f. 1993; the Assembly, consisting of the representatives of the national parliaments of member states, aims to provide a legal basis for the implementation of decisions within the BSEC framework; comprises three committees concerning economic, commercial, technological and environmental affairs; legal and political affairs; and cultural, educational and social affairs; the presidency rotates every six months; Sec.-Gen. ALEXEY KUDRIAVTSEV.

Black Sea Trade and Development Bank: 1 Komninon str., 54624 Thessaloniki, Greece; tel. (2310) 290400; fax (2310) 221796; e-mail info@bstdb.org; internet www.bstdb.org; f. 1999; the Bank supports economic development and regional co-operation by providing trade and project financing, guarantees, and equity for development projects supporting both public and private enterprises in its member countries; auth. cap. SDR 1,000m.; Sec.-Gen. GEORGE KOTTAS.

BSEC Business Council: Müsir Fuad Pasa Yalisi, Eski Tersane, 80860 Istinye, İstanbul, Turkey; tel. (212) 229-1144; fax (212) 229-0332; e-mail info@bsec-business.org; internet www.bsec-business.org; f. 1992; aims to secure greater economic integration and to promote investment in the region; Sec.-Gen. Dr COSTAS MASMANIDIS.

International Centre for Black Sea Studies: 4 Xenophontos Str., 10557 Athens, Greece; tel. (210) 3242321; fax (210) 3242244; e-mail icbss@icbss.org; internet www.icbss.org; f. 1998; aims to foster co-operation and promote research and knowledge-sharing among BSEC mems and partner countries; administers a Black Sea Research Network; convenes an Annual Conference and Annual Lecture; Dir Gen. Dr DIMITRIOS TRIANTAPHYLLOU; publs *Black Sea Monitor* (quarterly), Policy Briefs.

ORGANIZATION OF THE ISLAMIC CONFERENCE—OIC

Address: Kilo 6, Mecca Rd, POB 178, Jeddah 21411, Saudi Arabia.
Telephone: (2) 690-0001; **fax:** (2) 275-1953; **e-mail:** info@oic-oic.org; **internet:** www.oic-oci.org.

The Organization was formally established in May 1971, when its Secretariat became operational, following a summit meeting of Muslim heads of state at Rabat, Morocco, in September 1969, and the Islamic Foreign Ministers' Conference in Jeddah in March 1970, and in Karachi, Pakistan, in December 1970.

MEMBERS

Afghanistan	Indonesia	Qatar
Albania	Iran	Saudi Arabia
Algeria	Iraq	Senegal
Azerbaijan	Jordan	Sierra Leone
Bahrain	Kazakhstan	Somalia
Bangladesh	Kuwait	Sudan
Benin	Kyrgyzstan	Suriname
Brunei	Lebanon	Syria
Burkina Faso	Libya	Tajikistan
Cameroon	Malaysia	Togo
Chad	The Maldives	Tunisia
Comoros	Mali	Turkey
Côte d'Ivoire	Mauritania	Turkmenistan
Djibouti	Morocco	Uganda
Egypt	Mozambique	United Arab Emirates
Gabon	Niger	
The Gambia	Nigeria	Uzbekistan
Guinea	Oman	Yemen
Guinea-Bissau	Pakistan	
Guyana	Palestine	

Note: Observer status has been granted to Bosnia and Herzegovina, the Central African Republic, Russia, Thailand, the Muslim community of the 'Turkish Republic of Northern Cyprus', the Moro National Liberation Front (MNLF) of the southern Philippines, the United Nations, the African Union, the Non-Aligned Movement, the League of Arab States, the Economic Co-operation Organization, the Union of the Arab Maghreb and the Co-operation Council for the Arab States of the Gulf. The revised OIC Charter, endorsed in March 2008, made future applications for OIC membership and observer status conditional upon Muslim demographic majority and membership of the UN.

Organization
(April 2008)

SUMMIT CONFERENCES

The supreme body of the Organization is the Conference of Heads of State, which met in 1969 at Rabat, Morocco, in 1974 at Lahore, Pakistan, and in January 1981 at Mecca, Saudi Arabia, when it was decided that ordinary summit conferences would normally be held every three years in future. An extraordinary summit conference was convened in Doha, Qatar, in March 2003, to consider the situation in Iraq. A further extraordinary conference, held in December 2005, in Mecca, Saudi Arabia, determined to restructure the OIC. The 11th ordinary Conference was held in Dakar, Senegal, in March 2008. The summit conference troika comprises member countries equally representing OIC's African, Arab and Asian membership.

CONFERENCE OF MINISTERS OF FOREIGN AFFAIRS

Conferences take place annually, to consider the means for implementing the general policy of the Organization, although they may also be convened for extraordinary sessions. The ministerial conference troika comprises member countries equally representing OIC's African, Arab and Asian membership.

SECRETARIAT

The executive organ of the Organization, headed by a Secretary-General (who is elected by the Conference of Ministers of Foreign Affairs for a five-year term, renewable only once) and four Assistant Secretaries-General (similarly appointed).
Secretary-General: Prof. Dr EKMELEDDIN IHSANOGLU (Turkey).

At the summit conference in January 1981 it was decided that an International Islamic Court of Justice should be established to adjudicate in disputes between Muslim countries. Experts met in January 1983 to draw up a constitution for the court; however, by 2008 it was not yet in operation.

EXECUTIVE COMMITTEE

The third extraordinary conference of the OIC, convened in Mecca, Saudi Arabia, in December 2005, mandated the establishment of the Executive Committee, comprising the summit conference and ministerial conference troikas, the OIC host country, and the OIC Secretariat, as a mechanism for following-up resolutions of the Conference.

STANDING COMMITTEES

Al-Quds Committee: f. 1975 to implement the resolutions of the Islamic Conference on the status of Jerusalem (Al-Quds); it meets at the level of foreign ministers; maintains the Al-Quds Fund; Chair. King MUHAMMAD VI OF MOROCCO.

Standing Committee for Economic and Commercial Co-operation (COMCEC): f. 1981; Chair. ABDULLAH GÜL (Pres. of Turkey).

Standing Committee for Information and Cultural Affairs (COMIAC): f. 1981; Chair. ABDOULAYE WADE (Pres. of Senegal).

Standing Committee for Scientific and Technological Co-operation (COMSTECH): f. 1981; Chair. Gen. PERVEZ MUSHARRAF (Pres. of Pakistan).

Other committees comprise the Islamic Peace Committee, the Permanent Finance Committee, the Committee of Islamic Solidarity with the Peoples of the Sahel, the Eight-Member Committee on the Situation of Muslims in the Philippines, the Six-Member Committee on Palestine, the Committee on United Nations reform, and the ad hoc Committee on Afghanistan. In addition, there is an Islamic Commission for Economic, Cultural and Social Affairs, and there are OIC contact groups on Bosnia and Herzegovina, Kosovo, Jammu and Kashmir, Sierra Leone, and Somalia. A Commission of Eminent Persons was inaugurated in 2005.

Activities

The Organization's aims, as proclaimed in the Charter (adopted in 1972, with revisions endorsed in 1990 and 2008), are:

(i) To promote Islamic solidarity among member states;

(ii) To consolidate co-operation among member states in the economic, social, cultural, scientific and other vital fields, and to arrange consultations among member states belonging to international organizations;

(iii) To endeavour to eliminate racial segregation and discrimination and to eradicate colonialism in all its forms;

(iv) To take necessary measures to support international peace and security founded on justice;

(v) To co-ordinate all efforts for the safeguard of the Holy Places and support of the struggle of the people of Palestine, and help them to regain their rights and liberate their land;

(vi) To strengthen the struggle of all Muslim people with a view to safeguarding their dignity, independence and national rights;

(vii) To create a suitable atmosphere for the promotion of co-operation and understanding among member states and other countries.

The first summit conference of Islamic leaders (representing 24 states) took place in 1969 following the burning of the Al Aqsa Mosque in Jerusalem. At this conference it was decided that Islamic governments should 'consult together with a view to promoting close co-operation and mutual assistance in the economic, scientific, cultural and spiritual fields, inspired by the immortal teachings of Islam'. Thereafter the foreign ministers of the countries concerned met annually, and adopted the Charter of the Organization of the Islamic Conference in 1972.

At the second Islamic summit conference (Lahore, Pakistan, 1974), the Islamic Solidarity Fund was established, together with a committee of representatives which later evolved into the Islamic Commission for Economic, Cultural and Social Affairs. Subsequently, numerous other subsidiary bodies have been set up (see below).

ECONOMIC CO-OPERATION

A general agreement for economic, technical and commercial co-operation came into force in 1981, providing for the establishment of joint investment projects and trade co-ordination. This was followed by an agreement on promotion, protection and guarantee of investments among member states. A plan of action to strengthen economic co-operation was adopted at the third Islamic summit conference in

1981, aiming to promote collective self-reliance and the development of joint ventures in all sectors. In 1994 the 1981 plan of action was revised; the reformulated plan placed greater emphasis on private-sector participation in its implementation. Although several meetings of experts were subsequently held to discuss some of the 10 priority focus areas of the plan, little progress was achieved in implementing it during the 1990s and early 2000s. In October 2003 a meeting of COMCEC endorsed measures aimed at accelerating the implementation of the plan of action.

The fifth summit conference, held in 1987, approved proposals for joint development of modern technology, and for improving scientific and technical skills in the less developed Islamic countries. The first international Islamic trade fair was held in Jeddah, Saudi Arabia, in March 2001.

In 1991 22 OIC member states signed a Framework Agreement on a Trade Preferential System (TPS-OIC) among the OIC Member States; this entered into force in 2003, following the requisite ratification by more than 10 member states, and was envisaged as representing the first step towards the eventual establishment of an Islamic common market. A Trade Negotiating Committee (TNC) was established following the entry into force of the Framework Agreement. The first round of trade negotiations on the establishment of the TPS-OIC, concerning finalizing tariff-reduction modalities and an implementation schedule for the Agreement, was held during April 2004–April 2005. In November 2006, at the launch of the second round of negotiations, ministers adopted a road-map for establishing the TPS-OIC by 1 January 2009. In June 2007 the TNC adopted rules of origin for the TPS-OIC.

The first OIC Anti-Corruption and Enhancing Integrity Forum was convened in August 2006 in Kuala Lumpur, Malaysia.

CULTURAL CO-OPERATION

The Organization supports education in Muslim communities throughout the world, and was instrumental in the establishment of Islamic universities in Niger and Uganda. It organizes seminars on various aspects of Islam, and encourages dialogue with the other monotheistic religions. Support is given to publications on Islam both in Muslim and Western countries. The OIC organizes meetings at ministerial level to consider aspects of information policy and new technologies.

HUMANITARIAN ASSISTANCE

Assistance is given to Muslim communities affected by wars and natural disasters, in co-operation with UN organizations, particularly UNHCR. A resolution on the status of refugees in the Muslim world that was adopted by the 10th OIC summit meeting, held in October 2003, urged all member states to accede to the 1951 UN Convention on the Status of Refugees. In March 2008 a conference of OIC leaders and Islamic non-governmental organizations determined to establish an OIC centre for the analysis of humanitarian requirements in OIC member states. The countries of the Sahel region (Burkina Faso, Cape Verde, Chad, The Gambia, Guinea, Guinea-Bissau, Mali, Mauritania, Niger and Senegal) receive particular attention as victims of drought. OIC member states have provided humanitarian assistance to the Muslim population affected by the conflict in Chechnya, and to Darfur, southern Sudan. In 2008 the OIC and Islamic Development Bank were planning an international conference on the rehabilitation and reconstruction of Darfur. The OIC has established trust funds to assist vulnerable people in Afghanistan, Bosnia and Herzegovina, and Sierra Leone. In March 2008 the OIC launched a humanitarian support operation for Palestinians in Gaza; an initial 'assistance caravan' transported medical supplies and equipment to the area.

POLITICAL CO-OPERATION

Since its inception the OIC has called for vacation of Arab territories by Israel, recognition of the rights of Palestinians and of the Palestine Liberation Organization (PLO) as their sole legitimate representative, and the restoration of Jerusalem to Arab rule. The 1981 summit conference called for a *jihad* (holy war—though not necessarily in a military sense) 'for the liberation of Jerusalem and the occupied territories'; this was to include an Islamic economic boycott of Israel. In 1982 Islamic ministers of foreign affairs decided to establish Islamic offices for boycotting Israel and for military co-operation with the PLO. The 1984 summit conference agreed to reinstate Egypt (suspended following the peace treaty signed with Israel in 1979) as a member of the OIC, although the resolution was opposed by seven states.

In August 1990 a majority of ministers of foreign affairs condemned Iraq's recent invasion of Kuwait, and demanded the withdrawal of Iraqi forces. In August 1991 the Conference of Ministers of Foreign Affairs obstructed Iraq's attempt to propose a resolution demanding the repeal of economic sanctions against the country. The sixth summit conference, held in Senegal in December, reflected the divisions in the Arab world that resulted from Iraq's invasion of Kuwait and the ensuing war. Twelve heads of state did not attend, reportedly to register protest at the presence of Jordan and the PLO at the conference, both of which had given support to Iraq. Disagreement also arose between the PLO and the majority of other OIC members when a proposal was adopted to cease the OIC's support for the PLO's *jihad* in the Arab territories occupied by Israel, in an attempt to further the Middle East peace negotiations.

In August 1992 the UN General Assembly approved a non-binding resolution, introduced by the OIC, that requested the UN Security Council to take increased action, including the use of force, in order to defend the non-Serbian population of Bosnia and Herzegovina (some 43% of Bosnians being Muslims) from Serbian aggression, and to restore its 'territorial integrity'. The OIC Conference of Ministers of Foreign Affairs, which was held in December, demanded anew that the UN Security Council take all necessary measures against Serbia and Montenegro, including military intervention, in order to protect the Bosnian Muslims.

A report by an OIC fact-finding mission, which in February 1993 visited Azad Kashmir while investigating allegations of repression of the largely Muslim population of the Indian state of Jammu and Kashmir by the Indian armed forces, was presented to the 1993 Conference. The meeting urged member states to take the necessary measures to persuade India to cease the 'massive human rights violations' in Jammu and Kashmir and to allow the Indian Kashmiris to 'exercise their inalienable right to self-determination'. In September 1994 ministers of foreign affairs, meeting in Islamabad, Pakistan, agreed to establish a contact group on Jammu and Kashmir, which was to provide a mechanism for promoting international awareness of the situation in that region and for seeking a peaceful solution to the dispute. In December OIC heads of state approved a resolution condemning reported human rights abuses by Indian security forces in Kashmir.

In July 1994 the OIC Secretary-General visited Afghanistan and proposed the establishment of a preparatory mechanism to promote national reconciliation in that country. In mid-1995 Saudi Arabia, acting as a representative of the OIC, pursued a peace initiative for Afghanistan and issued an invitation for leaders of the different factions to hold negotiations in Jeddah.

A special ministerial meeting on Bosnia and Herzegovina was held in July 1993, at which seven OIC countries committed themselves to making available up to 17,000 troops to serve in the UN Protection Force in the former Yugoslavia (UNPROFOR). The meeting also decided to dispatch immediately a ministerial mission to persuade influential governments to support the OIC's demands for the removal of the arms embargo on Bosnian Muslims and the convening of a restructured international conference to bring about a political solution to the conflict. In December 1994 OIC heads of state, convened in Morocco, proclaimed that the UN arms embargo on Bosnia and Herzegovina could not be applied to the Muslim authorities of that Republic. The Conference also resolved to review economic relations between OIC member states and any country that supported Serbian activities. An aid fund was established, to which member states were requested to contribute between US $500,000 and $5m., in order to provide further humanitarian and economic assistance to Bosnian Muslims. In relation to wider concerns the conference adopted a Code of Conduct for Combating International Terrorism, in an attempt to control Muslim extremist groups. The code commits states to ensuring that militant groups do not use their territory for planning or executing terrorist activity against other states, in addition to states refraining from direct support or participation in acts of terrorism. In a further resolution the OIC supported the decision by Iraq to recognize Kuwait, but advocated that Iraq comply with all UN Security Council decisions.

In July 1995 the OIC contact group on Bosnia and Herzegovina (at that time comprising Egypt, Iran, Malaysia, Morocco, Pakistan, Saudi Arabia, Senegal and Turkey), meeting in Geneva, declared the UN arms embargo against Bosnia and Herzegovina to be 'invalid'. Several Governments subsequently announced their willingness officially to supply weapons and other military assistance to the Bosnian Muslim forces. In September a meeting of all OIC ministers of defence and foreign affairs endorsed the establishment of an 'assistance mobilization group' which was to supply military, economic, legal and other assistance to Bosnia and Herzegovina. In a joint declaration the ministers also demanded the return of all territory seized by Bosnian Serb forces, the continued NATO bombing of Serb military targets, and that the city of Sarajevo be preserved under a Muslim-led Bosnian Government. In November the OIC Secretary-General endorsed the peace accord for the former Yugoslavia, which was concluded, in Dayton, USA, by leaders of all the conflicting factions, and reaffirmed the commitment of Islamic states to participate in efforts to implement the accord. In the following month the OIC Conference of Ministers of Foreign Affairs, convened in Conakry, Guinea, requested the full support of the international community to reconstruct Bosnia and Herzegovina through humanitarian aid as well as economic and technical co-operation. Ministers declared that Palestine and the establishment of fully-autonomous Palestinian control of Jerusalem were issues of central importance for the Muslim world. The Conference urged the removal of all aspects of occupation and the cessation of the construction of Israeli settlements in the occupied territories. In addition, the final statement of the meeting condemned Armenian aggression against Azerbaijan, registered concern at the persisting civil conflict in Afghanistan, demanded the elimination of all weapons of mass destruction and pledged support for Libya (affected by the US trade embargo). Ministers determined that an intergovernmental group of experts should be established in 1996 to address the situation of minority Muslim communities residing in non-OIC states.

In December 1996 OIC ministers of foreign affairs, meeting in Jakarta, Indonesia, urged the international community to apply pressure on Israel in order to ensure its implementation of the terms of the Middle East peace process. The ministers reaffirmed the importance of ensuring that the provisions of the Dayton Peace Agreement for the former Yugoslavia were fully implemented, called for a peaceful settlement of the Kashmir issue, demanded that Iraq fulfil its obligations for the establishment of security, peace and stability in the region and proposed that an international conference on peace and national reconciliation in Somalia be convened. In March 1997, at an extraordinary summit held in Pakistan, OIC heads of state and of government reiterated the organization's objective of increasing international pressure on Israel to ensure the full implementation of the terms of the Middle East peace process. An 'Islamabad Declaration' was also adopted, which pledged to increase co-operation between members of the OIC. In June the OIC condemned the decision by the US House of Representatives to recognize Jerusalem as the Israeli capital. The Secretary-General of the OIC issued a statement rejecting the US decision as counter to the role of the USA as sponsor of the Middle East peace plan.

In early 1998 the OIC appealed for an end to the threat of US-led military action against Iraq arising from a dispute regarding access granted to international weapons inspectors. The crisis was averted by an agreement concluded between the Iraqi authorities and the UN Secretary-General in February. In March OIC ministers of foreign affairs, meeting in Doha, Qatar, requested an end to the international sanctions against Iraq. Additionally, the ministers urged all states to end the process of restoring normal trading and diplomatic relations with Israel pending that country's withdrawal from the occupied territories and acceptance of an independent Palestinian state. In April the OIC, jointly with the UN, sponsored new peace negotiations between the main disputing factions in Afghanistan, which were conducted in Islamabad, Pakistan. In early May, however, the talks collapsed and were postponed indefinitely. In September the Secretaries-General of the OIC and UN agreed to establish a joint mission to counter the deteriorating security situation along the Afghan–Iranian border, following the large-scale deployment of Taliban troops in the region and consequent military manoeuvres by the Iranian authorities. They also reiterated the need to proceed with negotiations to conclude a peaceful settlement in Afghanistan. In December the OIC appealed for a diplomatic solution to the tensions arising from Iraq's withdrawal of co-operation with UN weapons inspectors, and criticized subsequent military airstrikes, led by the USA, as having been conducted without renewed UN authority. An OIC Convention on Combating International Terrorism was adopted in 1998. An OIC committee of experts responsible for formulating a plan of action for safeguarding the rights of Muslim communities and minorities met for the first time in 1998.

In early April 1999 ministers of foreign affairs of the countries comprising OIC's contact group met to consider the crisis in Kosovo. The meeting condemned Serbian atrocities being committed against the local Albanian population and urged the provision of international assistance for the thousands of people displaced by the conflict. The group resolved to establish a committee to co-ordinate relief aid provided by member states. The ministers also expressed their willingness to help to formulate a peaceful settlement and to participate in any subsequent implementation force. In June an OIC Parliamentary Union was inaugurated; its founding conference was convened in Tehran, Iran.

In early March 2000 the OIC mediated contacts between the parties to the conflict in Afghanistan, with a view to reviving peace negotiations. Talks, held under OIC auspices, ensued in May. In November OIC heads of state attended the ninth summit conference, held in Doha, Qatar. In view of the significant deterioration in relations between Israel and the Palestinian (National) Authority (PA) during late 2000, the summit issued a Declaration pledging solidarity with the Palestinian cause and accusing the Israeli authorities of implementing large-scale systematic violations of human rights against Palestinians. The summit also issued the Doha Declaration, which reaffirmed commitment to the OIC Charter and undertook to modernize the organization's organs and mechanisms. Both the elected Government of Afghanistan and the Taliban sent delegations to the Doha conference. The summit determined that Afghanistan's official participation in the OIC, suspended in 1996, should not yet be reinstated. In early 2001 a high-level delegation from the OIC visited Afghanistan in an attempt to prevent further destruction of ancient statues by Taliban supporters.

In May 2001 the OIC convened an emergency meeting, following an escalation of Israeli–Palestinian violence. The meeting resolved to halt all diplomatic and political contacts with the Israeli government, while restrictions remained in force against Palestinian-controlled territories. In June the OIC condemned attacks and ongoing discrimination against the Muslim Community in Myanmar. In the same month the OIC Secretary-General undertook a tour of six African countries—Burkina Faso, The Gambia, Guinea, Mali, Niger and Senegal—to promote co-operation and to consider further OIC support for those states. In August the Secretary-General condemned Israel's seizure of several Palestinian institutions in East Jerusalem and aerial attacks against Palestinian settlements. The OIC initiated high-level diplomatic efforts to convene a meeting of the UN Security Council in order to discuss the situation.

In September 2001 the OIC Secretary-General strongly condemned major terrorist attacks perpetrated against targets in the USA. Soon afterwards the US authorities rejected a proposal by the Taliban regime that an OIC observer mission be deployed to monitor the activities of the Saudi Arabian-born exiled militant Islamist fundamentalist leader Osama bin Laden, who was accused by the US Government of having co-ordinated the attacks from alleged terrorist bases in the Taliban-administered area of Afghanistan. An extraordinary meeting of OIC ministers of foreign affairs, convened in early October, in Doha, Qatar, to consider the implications of the terrorist atrocities, condemned the attacks and declared its support for combating all manifestations of terrorism within the framework of a proposed collective initiative co-ordinated under the auspices of the UN. The meeting, which did not pronounce directly on the recently-initiated US-led military retaliation against targets in Afghanistan, urged that no Arab or Muslim state should be targeted under the pretext of eliminating terrorism. It determined to establish a fund to assist Afghan civilians. In February 2002 the Secretary-General expressed concern at statements of the US administration describing Iran and Iraq (as well as the Democratic People's Republic of Korea) as belonging to an 'axis of evil' involved in international terrorism and the development of weapons of mass destruction. In early April OIC foreign ministers convened an extraordinary session on terrorism, in Kuala Lumpur, Malaysia. The meeting issued the 'Kuala Lumpur Declaration', which reiterated member states' collective resolve to combat terrorism, recalling the organization's 1994 code of conduct and 1998 convention to this effect; condemned attempts to associate terrorist activities with Islamists or any other particular creed, civilization or nationality, and rejected attempts to associate Islamic states or the Palestinian struggle with terrorism; rejected the implementation of international action against any Muslim state on the pretext of combating terrorism; urged the organization of a global conference on international terrorism; and urged an examination of the root causes of international terrorism. In addition, the meeting strongly condemned Israel's ongoing military intervention in areas controlled by the PA. The meeting adopted a plan of action on addressing the issues raised in the declaration. Its implementation was to be co-ordinated by a 13-member committee on international terrorism. Member states were encouraged to sign and ratify the Convention on Combating International Terrorism in order to accelerate its implementation. In June 2002 ministers of foreign affairs, meeting in Khartoum, Sudan, issued a declaration reiterating the OIC call for an international conference to be convened, under UN auspices, in order clearly to define terrorism and to agree on the international procedures and mechanisms for combating terrorism through the UN. The conference also repeated demands for the international community to exert pressure on Israel to withdraw from all Palestinian-controlled territories and for the establishment of an independent Palestinian state. It endorsed the peace plan for the region that had been adopted by the summit meeting of the League of Arab States in March.

In June 2002 the OIC Secretary-General expressed his concern at the escalation of tensions between Pakistan and India regarding Kashmir. He urged both sides to withdraw their troops and to refrain from the use of force. In the following month the OIC pledged its support for Morocco in a territorial dispute with Spain over the small island of Perejil, but called for a negotiated settlement to resolve the issue.

An extraordinary summit conference of Islamic leaders convened in Doha, Qatar, in early March 2003, to consider the ongoing Iraq crisis welcomed the Saddam Hussain regime's acceptance of UN Security Council Resolution 1441 and consequent co-operation with UN weapons inspectors, and emphatically rejected any military strike against Iraq or threat to the security of any other Islamic state. The conference also urged progress towards the elimination of all weapons of mass destruction in the Middle East, including those held by Israel. In May the 30th session of the Conference of Ministers of Foreign Affairs, entitled 'Unity and Dignity', issued the Tehran Declaration, in which it resolved to combat terrorism and to contribute to preserving peace and security in Islamic countries. The Declaration also pledged its full support for the Palestinian cause and rejected the labelling as 'terrorist' of those Muslim states deemed to be resisting foreign aggression and occupation. The 10th OIC summit meeting, held in October, in Putrajaya, Malaysia, issued the Putrajaya Declaration, in which Islamic leaders resolved to enhance Islamic states' role and influence in international affairs. The leaders adopted a plan of action that entailed: reviewing and strengthening OIC positions on international issues; enhancing dialogue among Muslim thinkers and policy-makers through relevant OIC insitutions; promoting constructive dialogue with other cultures and civilizations; completing an ongoing review of the structure and efficacy of the OIC Secretariat; establishing a working group to address means of enhancing the role of Islamic education; promoting among member states the development of science and technology, discussion of ecological issues, and the role of information communication technology in development; improving mechanisms to assist member states in post-conflict situations; and advancing trade and investment through data-sharing and encouraging access to markets for products from poorer member states.

In mid-May 2004 the OIC Secretary-General urged combat forces in Iraq to respect the inviolability of that country's holy places. Shortly afterwards he condemned the ongoing destruction of Palestinian homes by Israeli forces, and consequent population displacement, particularly in Rafah, Gaza. He urged international organizations to condemn Israel's actions and appealed to the UN Security Council to intervene promptly in the situation and to compel Israel to respect international law. In June the Secretary-General welcomed progress achieved by a round of expert-level talks on nuclear confidence-building measures conducted during that month by India and Pakistan. An observer mission dispatched by the OIC to monitor presidential elections held in the Palestinian territories in early January 2005, at the request of the PA, was rejected by Israel. Later in that month the inaugural meeting of an OIC Commission of Eminent Persons was convened in Putrajaya, Malaysia. The Commission was mandated to finalize recommendations in the following areas: the preparation of a strategy and plan of action enabling the Islamic community to meet the challenges of the 21st century; the preparation of a comprehensive plan for promoting enlightened moderation, both within Islamic societies and universally; and the preparation of proposals for the future reform and restructuring of the OIC system. An OIC Digital Solidarity Fund was inaugurated in May 2005. In December the third extraordinary OIC summit, convened in Mecca, Saudi Arabia, adopted a 'Ten-Year Programme of Action to Meet the Challenges Facing the Umma in the 21st Century', a related Mecca Declaration and a report by the Commission of Eminent Persons. The summit determined to restructure the OIC, and mandated the establishment of an Executive Committee, comprising the summit conference and ministerial conference troikas (equally reflecting the African, Arab and Asian member states), the OIC host country, and the OIC Secretariat, as a mechanism for following-up Conference resolutions.

In January 2006 the OIC strongly condemned the publication in a Norwegian newspaper of a series of caricatures of the Prophet Muhammad that had originally appeared in a Danish publication in September 2005 and had caused considerable offence to Islamists. In August 2006 the OIC convened a meeting of humanitarian bodies in Istanbul, Turkey, to address means of collecting donations for and delivering assistance to victims of the ongoing crises in Lebanon and the Palestinian territories. Shortly afterwards a meeting of the newly-formed Executive Committee, held in Kuala Lumpur, Malaysia, agreed to form a Contact Group for Lebanon, to be co-ordinated by Malaysia. In October a meeting of Iraqi Islamic scholars from all denominations issued the Makkah Declaration on the Iraqi situation, in which they urged unity between different Islamic factions in that country. The first OIC Conference on Women was held in the following month, on the theme 'the role of women in the development of OIC member states'.

The 11th OIC heads of state summit meeting, held in Dakar, Senegal, in March 2008, endorsed a revised OIC Charter. The summit welcomed recent contacts between the Israeli and Palestinian leaders. Participation by OIC member states in the OIC Digital Solidarity Fund was promoted, and the meeting also requested each member state to establish a board to monitor national implementation of the Tunis Declaration on the Information Society, adopted by the November 2005 World Summit on the Information Society. In view of a reported rise in anti-Islamic attacks in western nations, OIC leaders denounced stereotyping, profiling and discrimination, and urged the promotion of Islam by Islamic states as a 'moderate, peaceful and tolerant religion'.

Finance

The OIC's activities are financed by mandatory contributions from member states.

Subsidiary Organs

Islamic Centre for the Development of Trade: Complexe Commercial des Habous, ave des FAR, BP 13545, Casablanca, Morocco; tel. (2) 314974; fax (2) 310110; e-mail icdt@icdt.org; internet www.icdt.org; f. 1983 to encourage regular commercial contacts, harmonize policies and promote investments among OIC mems; Dir-Gen. ALLAL RACHDI; publs *Tijaris: International and Inter-Islamic Trade Magazine* (bi-monthly), *Inter-Islamic Trade Report* (annually).

Islamic Jurisprudence (Fiqh) Academy: POB 13917, Jeddah, Saudi Arabia; tel. (2) 667-1664; fax (2) 667-0873; internet www.fiqhacademy.org.sa; f. 1982; Sec.-Gen. Sheikh MOHAMED HABIB IBN AL-KHODHA.

Islamic Solidarity Fund: c/o OIC Secretariat, POB 178, Jeddah 21411, Saudi Arabia; tel. (2) 680-0800; fax (2) 687-3568; f. 1974 to meet the needs of Islamic communities by providing emergency aid and the finance to build mosques, Islamic centres, hospitals, schools and universities; Chair. Sheikh NASIR ABDULLAH BIN HAMDAN; Exec. Dir ABDULLAH HERSI.

Islamic University in Uganda: POB 2555, Mbale, Uganda; tel. (45) 33502; fax (45) 34452; e-mail iuiu@info.com.co.ug; internet www.iuiu-mbale.com; f. 1988 to meet the educational needs of Muslim populations in English-speaking African countries; second campus in Kampala; mainly financed by OIC; Rector Dr AHMAD KAWESA SENGENDO.

Islamic University of Niger: BP 11507, Niamey, Niger; tel. 723903; fax 733796; internet www.universite_say.ne/; f. 1984; provides courses of study in *Shari'a* (Islamic law) and Arabic language and literature; also offers courses in pedagogy and teacher training; receives grants from Islamic Solidarity Fund and contributions from OIC member states; Rector Prof. ABDELALI OUDHRIRI.

Islamic University of Technology (IUT): Board Bazar, Gazipur 1704, Dhaka, Bangladesh; tel. (2) 980-0960; fax (2) 980-0970; e-mail vc@iut-dhaka.edu; internet www.iutoic-dhaka.edu; f. 1981 as the Islamic Centre for Technical and Vocational Training and Resources, named changed to Islamic Institute of Technology in 1994, current name adopted in June 2001; aims to develop human resources in OIC mem. states, with special reference to engineering, technology, tech. and vocational education and research; 135 staff and 646 students; library of 26,500 vols; Vice-Chancellor Prof. Dr IMTIAZ HOSSAIN; publs *News Bulletin* (annually), *Journal of Engineering and Technology* (2 a year), annual calendar and announcement for admission, reports, human resources development series.

Research Centre for Islamic History, Art and Culture (IRCICA): POB 24, Beşiktaş 80692, İstanbul, Turkey; tel. (212) 2591742; fax (212) 2584365; e-mail ircica@ircica.org; internet www.ircica.org; f. 1980; library of 60,000 vols; Dir-Gen. Prof. Dr HALIT EREN; publs *Newsletter* (3 a year), monographical studies.

Statistical, Economic and Social Research and Training Centre for the Islamic Countries: Attar Sok 4, GOP 06700, Ankara, Turkey; tel. (312) 4686172; fax (312) 4673458; e-mail oicankara@sesrtcic.org; internet www.sesrtcic.org; f. 1978; Dir-Gen. S. ALPAY; publs *Journal of Economic Co-operation among Islamic Countries* (quarterly), *InfoReport* (quarterly), *Statistical Yearbook* (annually).

Specialized Institutions

International Islamic News Agency (IINA): King Khalid Palace, Madinah Rd, POB 5054, Jeddah 21422, Saudi Arabia; tel. (2) 665-8561; fax (2) 665-9358; e-mail iina@islamicnews.org.sa; internet www.islamicnews.org.sa; f. 1972; distributes news and reports daily on events in the Islamic world, in Arabic, English and French; Dir-Gen. ERDEM KOK.

Islamic Educational, Scientific and Cultural Organization (ISESCO): BP 2275 Rabat 10104, Morocco; tel. (37) 772433; fax (37) 772058; e-mail cid@isesco.org.ma; internet www.isesco.org.ma; f. 1982; Dir-Gen. Dr ABDULAZIZ BIN OTHMAN ALTWAIJRI; publs *ISESCO Newsletter* (quarterly), *Islam Today* (2 a year), *ISESCO Triennial*.

Islamic States Broadcasting Union (ISBU): POB 6351, Jeddah 21442, Saudi Arabia; tel. (2) 672-1121; fax (2) 672-2600; internet www.isboo.org; f. 1975; Sec.-Gen. HUSSEIN AL-ASKARY.

Affiliated Institutions

International Association of Islamic Banks (IAIB): King Abdulaziz St, Queen's Bldg, 23rd Floor, Al-Balad Dist, POB 9707, Jeddah 21423, Saudi Arabia; tel. (2) 651-6900; fax (2) 651-6552; f. 1977 to link financial institutions operating on Islamic banking principles; activities include training and research; mems: 192 banks and other financial institutions in 34 countries; Sec.-Gen. SAMIR A. SHAIKH.

Islamic Chamber of Commerce and Industry: POB 3831, Clifton, Karachi 75600, Pakistan; tel. (21) 5874756; fax (21) 5870765; e-mail icci@icci-oic.org; internet icci-oic.org; f. 1979 to promote trade and industry among member states; comprises nat. chambers or feds of chambers of commerce and industry; Sec.-Gen. AQEEL AHMAD AL-JASSEM.

Islamic Committee for the International Crescent: POB 17434, Benghazi, Libya; tel. (61) 95823; fax (61) 95829; f. 1979 to attempt to alleviate the suffering caused by natural disasters and war; Sec.-Gen. Dr AHMAD ABDALLAH CHERIF.

Islamic Solidarity Sports Federation: POB 5844, Riyadh 11442, Saudi Arabia; tel. and fax (1) 482-2145; f. 1981; Sec.-Gen. Dr MOHAMMAD SALEH GAZDAR.

Organization of Islamic Capitals and Cities (OICC): POB 13621, Jeddah 21414, Saudi Arabia; tel. (2) 698-1953; fax (2) 698-1053; e-mail webmaster@oicc.org; internet www.oicc.org; f. 1980 to preserve the identity and heritage of Islamic capitals and cities; aims to advance sustainable development in Islamic capitals and cities; to develop comprehensive urban norms, systems and plans with a view to promoting optimum cultural, environmental, urban, economic and social conditions therein; and to support co-operation between member cities; comprises 145 capitals and cities as active members, eight observer members and 15 associate members, in Asia, Africa, Europe and South America; Sec.-Gen. OMAR ABDULLAH KADI.

Organization of the Islamic Shipowners' Association: POB 14900, Jeddah 21434, Saudi Arabia; tel. (2) 663-7882; fax (2) 660-4920; e-mail oisa@sbm.net.sa; f. 1981 to promote co-operation among maritime cos in Islamic countries; in 1998 mems approved the establishment of a new commercial venture, the Bakkah Shipping Company, to enhance sea transport in the region; Sec.-Gen. Dr ABDULLATIF A. SULTAN.

World Federation of Arab-Islamic Schools: POB 3446, Jeddah, Saudi Arabia; tel. (2) 670-0019; fax (2) 671-0823; f. 1976; supports Arab-Islamic schools world-wide and encourages co-operation between the institutions; promotes the dissemination of the Arabic language and Islamic culture; supports the training of personnel.

ORGANIZATION OF THE PETROLEUM EXPORTING COUNTRIES—OPEC

Address: Obere Donaustrasse 93, 1020 Vienna, Austria.
Telephone: (1) 211-12-279; **fax:** (1) 214-98-27; **e-mail:** prid@opec.org; **internet:** www.opec.org.

OPEC was established in 1960 to link countries whose main source of export earnings is petroleum; it aims to unify and co-ordinate members' petroleum policies and to safeguard their interests generally. In 1976 OPEC member states established the OPEC Fund for International Development.

OPEC's share of world petroleum production was 44.5% in 2006 (compared with 54.7% in 1974). OPEC members were estimated to possess 77.2% of the world's known reserves of crude petroleum in 2006. In that year OPEC members possessed about 49.3% of known reserves of natural gas, and accounted for 17.8% of total production of marketed natural gas.

MEMBERS

Algeria
Angola
Indonesia
Iran
Iraq
Kuwait
Libya
Nigeria
Qatar
Saudi Arabia
United Arab Emirates
Venezuela

Organization
(April 2008)

CONFERENCE

The Conference is the supreme authority of the Organization, responsible for the formulation of its general policy. It consists of representatives of member countries, who examine reports and recommendations submitted by the Board of Governors. It approves the appointment of Governors from each country and elects the Chairman of the Board of Governors. It works on the unanimity principle, and meets at least twice a year. In September 2000 the Conference agreed that regular meetings of heads of state or government should be convened every five years.

BOARD OF GOVERNORS

The Board directs the management of the Organization; it implements resolutions of the Conference and draws up an annual budget. It consists of one governor for each member country, and meets at least twice a year.

MINISTERIAL MONITORING COMMITTEE

The Committee (f. 1982) is responsible for monitoring price evolution and ensuring the stability of the world petroleum market. As such, it is charged with the preparation of long-term strategies, including the allocation of quotas to be presented to the Conference. The Committee consists of all national representatives, and is normally convened four times a year. A Ministerial Monitoring Sub-committee, reporting to the Committee on production and supply figures, was established in 1993.

ECONOMIC COMMISSION

A specialized body operating within the framework of the Secretariat, with a view to assisting the Organization in promoting stability in international prices for petroleum at equitable levels; consists of a Board, national representatives and a commission staff; meets at least twice a year.

SECRETARIAT

Secretary-General: ABDULLA SALEM EL-BADRI (Libya).

Research Division: comprises the Data Services Department; the Energy Studies Department; and the Petroleum Market Analysis Department; Dir Dr HASAN M. QABAZARD.

Administration and Human Resources Department: Responsible for all organization methods, provision of administrative services for all meetings, personnel matters, budgets, accounting and internal control; reviews general administrative policies and industrial relations practised throughout the oil industry; Head ALEJANDRO RODRIGUEZ RIVAS.

Public Relations and Information Department: Concerned with communicating OPEC objectives, decisions and actions; produces and distributes a number of publications, films, slides and tapes; and disseminates news of general interest regarding the Organization and member countries on energy and other related issues. Operates a daily on-line news service, the OPEC News Agency (OPECNA). An OPEC Library contains an extensive collection of energy-related publications; Head Dr OMAR F. IBRAHIM.

Legal Office: Provides legal advice, supervises the Secretariat's legal commitments, evaluates legal issues of concern to the Organization and member countries, and recommends appropriate action; Senior Legal Counsel Dr IBIBIA L. WORIKA.

Office of the Secretary-General: Provides the Secretary-General with executive assistance in maintaining contacts with governments, organizations and delegations, in matters of protocol and in the preparation for and co-ordination of meetings; Head ABDULLAH AL-SHAMERI.

Activities

OPEC's principal objectives, according to its Statute, are: to co-ordinate and unify the petroleum policies of member countries and to determine the best means for safeguarding their individual and collective interests; to seek ways and means of ensuring the stabilization of prices in international oil markets, with a view to eliminating harmful and unnecessary fluctuations; and to provide a steady income to the producing countries, an efficient, economic and regular supply of petroleum to consuming nations, and a fair return on capital to those investing in the petroleum industry.

The first OPEC conference was held in Baghdad, Iraq, in September 1960. It was attended by representatives from Iran, Iraq, Kuwait, Saudi Arabia and Venezuela, the founder members. These were joined by Qatar in the following year, when a Board of Governors was formed and statutes agreed. Indonesia and Libya were admitted to membership in 1962, Abu Dhabi in 1967, Algeria in 1969, Nigeria in 1971, Ecuador in 1973 and Gabon in 1975; Abu Dhabi's membership was transferred to the United Arab Emirates (UAE) in 1974. Ecuador resigned from OPEC in 1992 and Gabon did so in 1996. Angola became a member in 2007, and Ecuador rejoined the organization in the same year.

PRICES AND PRODUCTION

OPEC's five original members first met following the imposition of price reductions by petroleum companies in the previous month (August 1960). During the 1960s members sought to assert their rights in an international petroleum market that was dominated by multinational companies. Between 1965 and 1967 a two-year joint production programme limited annual growth in output so as to secure adequate prices. During the 1970s member states increased their control over their domestic petroleum industries, and over the pricing of crude petroleum on world markets. In 1971 the five-year 'Tehran Agreement' on pricing was concluded between the six producing countries from the Arabian Gulf region and 23 petroleum companies. In January 1972 petroleum companies agreed to adjust the petroleum revenues of the largest producers after changes in currency exchange rates (Geneva Agreement), and in 1973 OPEC and the petroleum companies agreed to raise posted prices of crude petroleum by 11.9% and installed a mechanism to make monthly adjustments to prices in future (Second Geneva Agreement). In October of that year a pricing crisis occurred when Arab member states refused to supply petroleum to nations that had supported Israel in its conflict with Egypt and Syria earlier in that month. Negotiations on the revision of the Tehran Agreement failed in the same month, and the Gulf states unilaterally declared increases of 70% in posted prices, from US $3.01 to $5.11 per barrel. In December the OPEC Conference decided to increase the posted price to $11.65 per barrel from the beginning of 1974 (despite Saudi Arabian opposition): almost a fourfold increase in three months. During 1974 royalties and taxes imposed on petroleum companies were increased in all member states except Saudi Arabia. OPEC's first summit meeting of heads of state or government was held in March 1975, and in September a ministerial meeting agreed to increase prices by 10% for the period to June 1976. During 1976 and 1977 disagreements between 'moderate' members (principally Saudi Arabia and Iran) and 'radical' members (led by Algeria, Iraq and Libya) caused discrepancies in pricing: a 10% increase was agreed by 11 member states as of 1 January 1977, but Saudi Arabia and the UAE decided to limit their increase to 5%. A further increase of 5% by Saudi Arabia and the UAE in July restored a single level of pricing, but in December the Conference was unable to agree on a new increase, and prices remained stable until the end of 1978, when it was agreed that during 1979 prices should increase by an average of 10% in four instalments over the year, to compensate for the effects of the depreciation of the US dollar. The overthrow of the Iranian Government in early 1979, however, led to a new steep increase in petroleum prices.

In June 1980 the Conference decided to set the price for a 'marker' crude at US $32 per barrel, and stipulated that the value differentials which could be added to this (on account of quality and geographical location) should not exceed $5 per barrel. Prices continued to vary, however, and in May 1981 Saudi Arabia refused to increase its price of $32 per barrel unless the higher prices charged by other members were lowered. Members agreed to reduce surplus production during the year, and in October the marker price was increased to $34 per barrel, with a 'ceiling' price of $38 per barrel. In March 1982 an emergency meeting of ministers of petroleum agreed (for the first time in OPEC's history) to defend the Organization's price structure by imposing an overall production ceiling of 18m. barrels per day (b/d), reducing this to 17.5m. b/d at the beginning of 1983, although ministers initially failed to agree on production quotas for individual members, or on adjustments to the differentials in prices charged for the high-quality crude petroleum produced by Algeria, Libya and Nigeria compared with that produced by the Gulf States. In February 1983 Nigeria reduced its price to $30 per barrel, and to avoid a 'price war' OPEC set the official price of marker crude at $29 per barrel. Quotas were allocated for each member country except Saudi Arabia, which was to act as a 'swing producer' to supply the balancing quantities to meet market requirements. In October 1984 the production ceiling was lowered to 16m. b/d, and in December price differentials for light (more expensive) and heavy (cheaper) crudes were altered in an attempt to counteract price-cutting by non-OPEC producers, particularly Norway and the United Kingdom. During 1985, however, most members effectively abandoned the marker price system, and production in excess of quotas, unofficial discounts and barter deals by members, and price cuts by non-members (such as Mexico, which had hitherto kept its prices in line with those of OPEC) contributed to a weakening of the market. During the first half of 1986 petroleum prices dropped to below $10 per barrel. Discussions were held with non-member producing countries (Angola, Egypt, Malaysia, Mexico and Oman) which agreed to co-operate in limiting production, although the United Kingdom declined. In August all members except Iraq agreed upon a return to production quotas (Iraq declined to co-operate after its request to be allocated the same quota as Iran had been refused): total production was to be limited to 14.8m. b/d (16.8m. b/d including Iraq). This measure resulted in an increase in prices to about $15 per barrel. In December members (except Iraq) agreed to return to a fixed pricing system at a level of $18 per barrel as the OPEC reference price (based on a 'basket' of seven crudes, not, as hitherto, on a 'marker' crude, Arabian Light) with effect from 1 February 1987, setting a total production limit of 15.8m. b/d for the first half of the year. OPEC's role of actually setting crude oil prices had come to an end, however, and from the late 1980s prices were determined by movements in the international markets, with OPEC's role being to increase or restrain production in order to prevent harmful fluctuations in prices. In June 1987, with prices having stabilized, the Conference decided to limit production to 16.6m. b/d (including Iraq's output) for the rest of the year. In April 1988, following a further reduction in prices below $15 per barrel, non-OPEC producers offered to reduce the volume of their petroleum exports by 5% if OPEC members would do the same. Saudi Arabia insisted that existing quotas should be more strictly observed before it would reduce its production. The production limit was increased to 18.5m. b/d for the first half of 1989 and, after prices had recovered to about $18 per barrel, to 19.5m. b/d for the second half of 1989, and to 22m. b/d for the first half of 1990.

In May 1990 members resolved to adhere more strictly to the agreed production quotas, in response to a decline in prices, which stood at about US $14 per barrel in June. In August Iraq invaded Kuwait (which it had accused, among other grievances, of violating production quotas). Petroleum exports by the two countries were halted by an international embargo, and petroleum prices immediately increased to exceed $25 per barrel. OPEC ministers promptly allowed a temporary increase in production by other members, of between 3m. and 3.5m. b/d (mostly by Saudi Arabia, the UAE and Venezuela), to stabilize prices, and notwithstanding some fluctuations later in the year, this was achieved. During 1991 and 1992 ministers attempted to reach a minimum reference price of $21 per barrel by imposing production limits that varied between 22.3m. b/d and 24.2m. b/d. Kuwait, which resumed production in 1992 after extensive damage had been inflicted on its oil-wells during the conflict with Iraq, was granted a special dispensation to produce without a fixed quota until the following year. Ecuador withdrew from OPEC in November 1992, citing the high cost of membership and the organization's refusal to increase Ecuador's production quota. In 1993 a Ministerial Monitoring Sub-committee was established to supervise compliance with quotas, because of members' persistent over-production. A production ceiling of 24.46m. b/d was set for the first quarter of 1993 and was reduced to 23.5m. b/d from 1 March (including a fixed quota for Kuwait for the first time since the Iraqi invasion). In July discussions between Iraq and the UN on the possible supervised resumption of Iraqi petroleum exports depressed petroleum prices to below $16 per barrel, and at the end of the year prices fell below $14, after the Conference rejected any further reduction in the current limit (imposed from 1 October) of 24.52m. b/d, which remained in force during 1994 and 1995, although actual output continued to be well in excess of quotas. In March 1996 prices reached $21 per barrel (largely owing to unusually cold weather in the northern hemisphere). In May the UN and Iraq concluded an agreement allowing Iraq to resume exports of petroleum in order to fund humanitarian relief efforts within Iraq, and OPEC's overall production ceiling was accordingly raised to 25.03m. b/d from June, remaining at this level until the end of 1997. Gabon withdrew from OPEC in June 1996, citing difficulties in meeting its budgetary contribution. Prices declined during the first half of 1997, falling to a low point of $16.7 per barrel in April, owing to the resumption of Iraqi exports, depressed world demand and continuing over-production: an escalation in political tension in the Gulf region, however, and in particular Iraq's reluctance to co-operate with UN weapons inspectors, prompted a price increase to about $21.2 per barrel in October. The overall production ceiling was raised by about 10%, to 27.5m. b/d, with effect from the beginning of 1998, but during that year prices declined, falling below $12 per barrel from August (demand having been affected by the current economic difficulties in south-east Asia), and OPEC imposed a succession of reductions in output, down to 24.387m. b/d from 1 July. Non-member countries (chiefly Mexico) also concluded agreements with OPEC to limit their production in that year, and in March 1999 Mexico, Norway, Oman and Russia agreed to decrease production by a total of 388,000 b/d, while OPEC's own production limit was reduced to 22.976m. b/d. Evidence of almost 90% compliance with the new production quotas contributed to market confidence that stockpiles of petroleum would be reduced, and resulted in sustained price increases during the second half of the year: the reference price for petroleum rose above $24 per barrel in September.

By March 2000 petroleum prices had reached their highest level since 1990, briefly exceeding US $34 per barrel. In that month OPEC ministers agreed to raise output by 1.45m. b/d, in order to ease supply shortages, and introduced an informal price band mechanism that was to signal the need for adjustments in production should prices deviate for more than 20 days from an average bracket of $22–$28 per barrel. Further increases in production, totalling 1.8m. b/d, took effect in the second half of the year (with five non-OPEC members, Angola, Mexico, Norway, Oman and Russia also agreeing to raise their output), but prices remained high and there was intense international pressure on OPEC to resolve the situation: in September both the Group of Seven industrialized countries (G-7) and the IMF issued warnings about the potential economic and social consequences of sustained high petroleum prices. In that month OPEC heads of state and government, convened in their first summit meeting since 1975, responded by issuing the 'Caracas Declaration', in which they resolved (among other things) to promote market stability through their policies on pricing and production, to increase co-operation with other petroleum exporters, and to improve communication with consumer countries. During the first half of 2001, with a view to stabilizing prices that by January had fallen back to around $25 per barrel, the Conference agreed to implement reductions in output totalling 2.5m. b/d, thereby limiting overall production to 24.2m. b/d, with a further reduction of 1m. b/d from 1 September. Terrorist attacks on targets in the USA in September gave rise to market uncertainty, and prices declined further, averaging $17–$18 per barrel in November and December. In September the Conference announced the establishment of a working group of experts from OPEC and non-OPEC petroleum-producing countries, to evaluate future market developments and advance dialogue and co-operation. In December the Conference announced a further reduction in output by 1.5m. b/d (to 21.7m. b/d) from 1 January 2002, provided that non-OPEC producers also reduced their output, which they agreed to do by 462,500 b/d. This output limit was maintained throughout 2002, and the reference basket price averaged $24.4 per barrel during the year, with temporary increases caused partly by a one-month suspension of Iraq's exports in April (in protest at Israeli military intervention in Palestinian-controlled areas), and by a strike in the Venezuelan petroleum industry. From 1 January 2003 the production ceiling was raised to 23m. b/d, but stricter compliance with individual quotas meant a reduction in actual output, and prices rose above the target range, with the reference basket price reaching $32 per barrel in February, as a result of the continued interruption of the Venezuelan supply, together with the market's reaction to the likelihood of US-led military action against Iraq. In January the Conference agreed to raise the production ceiling to 24.5m. b/d from 1 February, and in March (when Venezuelan production had resumed) members agreed to make up from their available excess capacities any shortfall that might result following military action against Iraq. In the event the war on Iraq that commenced later in that month led to such a rapid overthrow of Saddam Hussain's regime that there were fears that a petroleum surplus, driving down prices, would result, and a production ceiling of 25.4m. b/d was set with effect from the beginning of June: although higher than the previous limit, it represented a 2m. b/d reduction in actual output at that time. The production ceiling of 24.5m. b/d was reinstated from 1 November, in view of the gradual revival of Iraqi exports. The OPEC reference basket price averaged $28.1 per barrel in 2003. In 2004, however, petroleum prices increased considerably, with the reference basket price averaging $36 per barrel over the year, despite OPEC's raising its production ceiling (excluding Iraq's output), in several stages, from the 23.5m. b/d limit imposed from 1 April to 27m. b/d with effect from 1 November. In January 2005 the Conference suspended the $22–$28 price band mechanism, acknowledging this to be unrealistic at the present time. The production ceiling was increased to 27.5m. b/d in March and to 28m. b/d in June, but the OPEC reference basket price nevertheless averaged $50.6 per barrel over the year. The March Conference attributed the continuing rise in prices to expectations of strong demand, speculation on the futures markets, and geopolitical tensions; it expressed particular concern that a shortage of effective global refining capacity was also contributing to higher prices by causing 'bottlenecks' in the downstream sector, and announced that members had accelerated the implementation of existing capacity expansion plans. In June the Conference approved an increase in the composition of the OPEC reference basket from seven to 11 crudes, representing the main export crudes of all member countries, weighted according to production and exports to the main markets: the new composition was intended to reflect more accurately the average quality of crude petroleum in OPEC's member states. In September the Conference adopted a 'Long-Term Strategy' for OPEC, setting objectives concerning members' long-term petroleum revenues, fair and stable prices, the role of petroleum in meeting future energy demand, the stability of the world oil market, and the security of regular supplies to consumers. During 2006 petroleum prices continued to rise, with the OPEC reference basket price averaging $61.08 per barrel for the year. The rise was partly attributable to uncertainty about Iran's future output (since there was speculation that international sanctions might be imposed on that country as a penalty for continuing its nuclear development programme), and to a reduction in Nigeria's production as a result of internal unrest. Existing production targets were maintained until November, when the production ceiling was lowered to 26.3m. b/d, and a further reduction of 500,000 b/d was announced in December. In March 2007 the Conference agreed to maintain the current level of production. Concern over fuel supplies and distribution contributed to steadily rising prices, in spite of OPEC's statements estimating that there were sufficient stock levels to meet demand. In September the reference basket price (expanded to include 12 crude oils in that month) reached a monthly average of $74.18 per barrel, increasing to monthly averages of $79.36 in October and $88.99 in November, despite an increase in OPEC's output by 500,000 b/d from 1 November. In October OPEC's Secretary-General reiterated that the market was well supplied, and attributed the rising prices chiefly to market speculators, with persistent refinery bottlenecks, seasonal maintenance work, ongoing geopolitical problems in the Middle East and fluctuations in the US dollar also continuing to play a role in driving oil prices higher. In November the third OPEC summit meeting of heads of state and government agreed on principles concerning the stability of global energy markets, the role of energy in sustainable development, and the relationship between energy and environmental concerns. In December the Conference observed that, despite the current volatility of prices, the petroleum market continued to be well supplied, with stocks at comfortable levels, and decided to leave the production ceiling unchanged for the time being. Meeting in March 2008, the Conference again determined to maintain the current production ceiling.

ENERGY DIALOGUES

Annual 'workshops' began in 2003 as a joint activity by OPEC and the International Energy Agency, bringing together experts, analysts and government officials to discuss aspects of energy supply and demand.

The first formal meeting of the European Union-OPEC Energy Dialogue took place in June 2005, at ministerial level, with the aim of exchanging views on energy issues of common interest, including petroleum market developments, and thus contributing to stability, transparency and predictability in the market. A 'roundtable' meeting was held in November to discuss recent petroleum market developments and future prospects, and a conference was held in 2006 to discuss energy technologies, with a particular focus on carbon capture and storage.

Russia (a major producer of petroleum) was given OPEC observer status in 1992, and was subsequently represented at a number of ministerial and other meetings. A formal Energy Dialogue was established in December 2005: it was planned that annual ministerial meetings would be held, together with technical exchanges, seminars and joint research, on such subjects as petroleum market developments and prospects, data flow, investments across the supply chain, and energy policies.

In March 2005 the Chinese Government proposed the creation of an official dialogue between OPEC and the People's Republic of China (a major customer of OPEC members) and this was formally established in December, with the aim of exchanging views on energy issues, particularly security of supply and demand, through annual ministerial meetings, technical exchanges and energy 'roundtables'.

ENVIRONMENTAL CONCERNS

OPEC has frequently expressed its concern that any measures adopted to avert climate change by reducing the emission of carbon dioxide caused by the consumption of fossil fuels would seriously affect its members' income. In 1998, for example, OPEC representatives attending a conference of the parties to the UN Framework Convention on Climate Change warned that OPEC would claim compensation for any lost revenue resulting from initiatives to limit petroleum consumption, and at subsequent sessions, while expressing support for the fundamental principles of the Convention, OPEC urged that developing countries whose economies were dependent on the export of fossil fuels should not be unfairly treated. In June 2007 OPEC's Secretary-General criticized the industrialized nations' efforts to increase production of biofuel (derived from agricultural commodities) in order to reduce consumption of fossil fuels: he warned that OPEC might reduce its future investment in petroleum production accordingly. In November the third summit meeting of OPEC heads of state and government acknowledged the long-term challenge of climate change, but emphasized the continuing need for stable petroleum supplies to support global economic growth and development, and urged that policies aimed at combating climate change should be balanced, taking into account their impact on developing countries, including countries heavily dependent on the production and export of fossil fuels. The meeting stressed the importance of cleaner and more efficient petroleum technologies, and the development of technologies such as carbon capture and storage.

INTERNATIONAL ORGANIZATIONS

Finance

Total budgetary expenditure in 2007 amounted to €19.8m.

Publications

Annual Report.
Annual Statistical Bulletin.
Environmental Newsletter (quarterly).
Monthly Oil Market Report.
OPEC Bulletin (10 a year).
OPEC Review (quarterly).
World Oil Outlook (annually).
Reports, information papers, press releases.

OPEC FUND FOR INTERNATIONAL DEVELOPMENT

Address: POB 995, 1011 Vienna, Austria.
Telephone: (1) 515-64-0; **fax:** (1) 513-92-38; **e-mail:** info@opecfund.org; **internet:** www.opecfund.org.

The Fund was established by OPEC member countries in 1976.

MEMBERS

Member countries of OPEC.

Organization

(April 2008)

ADMINISTRATION

The Fund is administered by a Ministerial Council and a Governing Board. Each member country is represented on the Council by its minister of finance. The Board consists of one representative and one alternate for each member country.

Chairman, Ministerial Council: Dr IBRAHIM AL-ASSAF (Saudi Arabia).
Chairman, Governing Board: JAMAL NASSER LOOTAH (UAE).
Director-General of the Fund: SULEIMAN JASIR AL-HERBISH (Saudi Arabia).

FINANCIAL STRUCTURE

The resources of the Fund, whose unit of account is the US dollar, consist of contributions by OPEC member countries, and income received from operations or otherwise accruing to the Fund.

The initial endowment of the Fund amounted to US $800m. Its resources have been replenished three times, and have been further increased by the profits accruing to seven OPEC member countries through the sales of gold held by the International Monetary Fund. The pledged contributions to the OPEC Fund amounted to $3,435.0m. at the end of 2006, and paid-in contributions totalled some $2,952.1m.

Activities

The OPEC Fund for International Development is a multilateral agency for financial co-operation and assistance. Its objective is to reinforce financial co-operation between OPEC member countries and other developing countries through the provision of financial support to the latter on appropriate terms, to assist them in their economic and social development. The Fund was conceived as a collective financial facility which would consolidate the assistance extended by its member countries; its resources are additional to those already made available through other bilateral and multilateral aid agencies of OPEC members. It is empowered to:

(i) Provide concessional loans for balance-of-payments support;

(ii) Provide concessional loans for the implementation of development projects and programmes;

(iii) Make contributions and/or provide loans to eligible international agencies; and

(iv) Finance technical assistance and research through grants.

The eligible beneficiaries of the Fund's assistance are the governments of developing countries other than OPEC member countries, and international development agencies whose beneficiaries are developing countries. The Fund gives priority to the countries with the lowest income.

The Fund may undertake technical, economic and financial appraisal of a project submitted to it, or entrust such an appraisal to an appropriate international development agency, the executing national agency of a member country, or any other qualified agency. Most projects financed by the Fund have been co-financed by other development finance agencies. In each such case, one of the co-financing agencies may be appointed to administer the Fund's loan in association with its own. This practice has enabled the Fund to extend its lending activities to more than 100 countries over a short period of time and in a simple way, with the aim of avoiding duplication and complications. As its experience grew, the Fund increasingly resorted to parallel, rather than joint financing, taking up separate project components to be financed according to its rules and policies. In addition, it started to finance some projects completely on its own. These trends necessitated the issuance in 1982 of guide-lines for the procurement of goods and services under the Fund's loans, allowing for a margin of preference for goods and services of local origin or originating in other developing countries: the general principle of competitive bidding is, however, followed by the Fund. The loans are not tied to procurement from Fund member countries or from any other countries. The margin of preference for goods and services obtainable in developing countries is allowed on the request of the borrower and within defined limits. Fund assistance in the form of programme loans has a broader coverage than project lending. Programme loans are used to stimulate an economic sector or sub-sector, and assist recipient countries in obtaining inputs, equipment and spare parts. Besides extending loans for project and programme financing and balance of payments support, the Fund also undertakes other operations, including grants in support of technical assistance and other activities (mainly research), and financial contributions to other international institutions. In 1998 the Fund began to extend lines of credit to support private sector activities in beneficiary countries. The so-called Private Sector Facility aims to encourage the growth of private enterprises, in particular small and medium-sized enterprises, and to support the development of local capital markets. A new Trade Finance Facility, to provide loans, lines of credit and guarantees in support of international trade operations in developing countries, was launched in December 2006.

By the end of December 2006 the Fund had approved 1,113 public sector loans since operations began in 1976, totalling US $6,726.7m., of which $5,396.4m. (or 80%) was for project financing, $724.2m. (11%) was for balance-of-payments support, $314.8m. (5%) was for programme financing and $241.3m. (4%) was allocated as financing for the Heavily Indebted Poor Countries (HIPC) initiative (see World Bank). Private sector financing totalled $518.1m. for 96 operations granted in the same period. At that time total disbursements amounted to $4,139m. The Fund's 16th lending programme, approved for a three-year period, became effective on 1 January 2005.

Direct loans are supplemented by grants to support technical assistance, food aid and research. By the end of December 2006 842 grants, amounting to US $379.6m., had been committed, including $83.6m. to the Common Fund for Commodities (established by the UN Conference on Trade and Development—UNCTAD), $52.6m. in support of emergency relief operations, $118.0m. in technical assistance, often in co-operation with UN agencies or other development organizations, and a special contribution of $20m. to the International Fund for Agricultural Development (IFAD). In addition, the OPEC Fund had committed $971.8m. to other international institutions by the end of 2006, comprising OPEC members' contributions to the resources of IFAD, and irrevocable transfers in the name of its members to the IMF Trust Fund. A Special Grant Account for Palestine and an HIV/AIDS Special Account became operational in 2002; by the end of 2006 grants approved under these accounts amounted to $33.0m. and $43.1m. respectively. At that time $20.0m. had been approved under a new Food Aid Special Grant Account, which was established in 2003 to combat famine in Africa. In June

2005 a Special Account for Emergency Relief Operations was established.

During the year ending 31 December 2006 the Fund's total commitments amounted to US $699.7m. These commitments included 44 public sector project loans, amounting to $524.2m. The largest proportion of project loans (amounting to $182.6m., 34.8% of the total) was for the energy sector, including the strengthening of electricity transmission capacity and the national grid systems in Bolivia, Tajikistan and Zambia; upgrading power plants in Senegal and Egypt; rehabilitation of the electricity system in the Cuban capital, Havana; and implementation of an Arab Gas Pipeline project in Syria. Transportation projects accounted for $157.7m., or 30.1% of the total, in nine countries. Some $66.0m. (12.6%) was approved for the agriculture and agro-industry sector in Cuba, Haiti, Syria and Sudan, while five loans, amounting to $36.0m. (6.9%) were for water supply and sewerage projects in Bangladesh, Eritrea, Mauritius, Rwanda and Zambia. Multi-sector loans (9.3%) supported rural development projects in Albania, Bosnia and Herzegovina, the Republic of Congo, Niger and Viet Nam; urban development in the east coast of Seychelles; and small-scale social projects in Nicaragua. The remainder of lending distribution was for health (5.3%), and education projects (1.0%). Private sector operations in 2006 amounted to $100.2m., of which 40% was allocated to industry, 17% to infrastructure projects, and 14% to microfinance projects. In 2003, following the completion of a five-year review of the Fund's Private Sector Facility, the Ministerial Council pledged significant additional funding in support of the increasing demand from developing countries for risk capital and long-term financing.

During 2006 the Fund approved US $30.96m. for 78 grants, of which $3.60m. was for eight technical assistance projects, $1.06m. for 17 research projects and other related activities and $3.45m. for seven emergency assistance operations. Some $8.85m. was allocated to the HIV/AIDS Special Account and $14.0m. was for the Special Grant Account for Palestine, to fund relief and rehabilitation projects.

Publications

Annual Report (in Arabic, English, French and Spanish).
OPEC Fund Newsletter (3 a year).
Occasional papers and documents.

Statistics

OPEC FUND COMMITMENTS AND DISBURSEMENTS IN 2006
(US $ million)

	Commitments	Disbursements
Public-sector lending operations:	558.57	236.18
Project financing	524.17	199.83
Programme financing	—	3.35
HIPC initiative financing*	34.40	33.00
Trade Finance Facility	10.00	—
Private-sector lending operations	100.20	41.41
Grant programme:	30.96	27.22
Technical assistance	3.60	3.93
Research and other activities	1.06	1.23
Emergency aid	3.45	3.86
HIV/AIDS Special Account	8.85	5.04
Special Grant Account for Palestine	14.00	6.48
Food Aid Special Grant Account	—	2.18
Common Fund for Commodities	—	4.50
Total	699.73	304.81

* Heavily Indebted Poor Countries initiative, jointly administered by the International Monetary Fund and World Bank.

PUBLIC SECTOR PROJECT LOANS APPROVED IN 2006
(US $ million)

	Loans approved
Sector:	
Agriculture and agro-industry	65.99
Education	5.25
Energy	182.60
Health	27.75
Transportation	157.70
Water supply and sewerage	36.00
Multisectoral	48.88
Total	524.17
Region:	
Africa	248.91
Asia	202.75
Latin America and the Caribbean	47.04
Europe	25.47

Source: *OPEC Fund Annual Report 2006*.

PACIFIC COMMUNITY

Address: BP D5, 98848 Nouméa Cédex, New Caledonia.
Telephone: 26-20-00; **fax:** 26-38-18; **e-mail:** spc@spc.int; **internet:** www.spc.int.

In February 1947 the Governments of Australia, France, the Netherlands, New Zealand, the United Kingdom, and the USA signed the Canberra Agreement establishing the South Pacific Commission, which came into effect in July 1948. (The Netherlands withdrew from the Commission in 1962, when it ceased to administer the former colony of Dutch New Guinea, now Papua, formerly known as Irian Jaya, part of Indonesia.) In October 1997 the 37th South Pacific Conference, convened in Canberra, Australia, agreed to rename the organization the Pacific Community, with effect from 6 February 1998. The Secretariat of the Pacific Community (SPC) services the Community, and provides research, technical advice, training and assistance in economic, social and cultural development to 22 countries and territories of the Pacific region. It serves a population of about 6.8m., scattered over some 30m. sq km, more than 98% of which is sea.

MEMBERS

American Samoa	Niue
Australia	Northern Mariana Islands
Cook Islands	Palau
Fiji	Papua New Guinea
France	Pitcairn Islands
French Polynesia	Samoa
Guam	Solomon Islands
Kiribati	Tokelau
Marshall Islands	Tonga
Federated States of Micronesia	Tuvalu
	United Kingdom
Nauru	USA
New Caledonia	Vanuatu
New Zealand	Wallis and Futuna Islands

INTERNATIONAL ORGANIZATIONS — Pacific Community

Organization
(April 2008)

CONFERENCE OF THE PACIFIC COMMUNITY

The Conference is the governing body of the Community (replacing the former South Pacific Conference) and is composed of representatives of all member countries and territories. The main responsibilities of the Conference, which meets every two years, are to appoint the Director-General, to determine major national or regional policy issues in the areas of competence of the organization and to note changes to the Financial and Staff Regulations approved by the Committee of Representatives of Governments and Administrations (CRGA). The fifth Pacific Community Conference was convened in November 2007 in Apia, Samoa, and the sixth was to be held in Tonga in 2009.

COMMITTEE OF REPRESENTATIVES OF GOVERNMENTS AND ADMINISTRATIONS (CRGA)

This Committee comprises representatives of all member states and territories, having equal voting rights. It meets annually to consider the work programme evaluation conducted by the Secretariat and to discuss any changes proposed by the Secretariat in the context of regional priorities; to consider and approve any policy issues for the organization presented by the Secretariat or by member countries and territories; to consider applicants and make recommendations for the post of Director-General; to approve the administrative and work programme budgets; to approve amendments to the Financial and Staff Regulations; and to conduct annual performance evaluations of the Director-General.

SECRETARIAT

The Secretariat of the Pacific Community (SPC) is headed by a Director-General, a Senior Deputy Director-General and a Deputy Director-General, based in Suva, Fiji. Three administrative Divisions cover Land Resources, Marine Resources and Social Resources. The Secretariat also provides information services, including library facilities, publications, translation and computer services. The organization has about 250 staff members.

Director-General: Dr JIMMIE RODGERS (Solomon Islands).

North Pacific Regional Office: POB 2299, Botanical Garden 2, Kolonia, Pohnpei, Federated States of Micronesia; tel. (691) 3207523; fax (697) 3205854.

Suva Regional Office: Private Mail Bag, Suva, Fiji; tel. 3370733; fax 3370021; e-mail spcsuva@spc.org.fj.

Activities

The SPC provides, on request of its member countries, technical assistance, advisory services, information and clearing-house services aimed at developing the technical, professional, scientific, research, planning and management capabilities of the regional population. The SPC also conducts regional conferences and technical meetings, as well as training courses, workshops and seminars at the regional or country level. It provides small grants-in-aid and awards to meet specific requests and needs of members. In November 1996 the Conference agreed to establish a specific Small Islands States fund to provide technical services, training and other relevant activities. The organization's three programme divisions are: land resources, marine resources and social resources. The Pacific Community oversees the maritime programme and telecommunications policy activities of the Pacific Islands Forum Secretariat.

The 1999 Conference, held in Tahiti in December, adopted the 'Déclaration de Tahiti Nui', a mandate that detailed the operational policies and mechanisms of the Pacific Community, taking into account operational changes not covered by the founding Canberra Agreement. The Déclaration was regarded as a 'living document' that would be periodically revised to record subsequent modifications of operational policy.

The SPC has signed memoranda of understanding with WHO, the Forum Fisheries Agency, the South Pacific Regional Environment Programme (SPREP), and several other partners. The organization participates in meetings of the Council of Regional Organizations in the Pacific (CROP). Representatives of the SPC, SPREP and the South Pacific Applied Geoscience Commission hold periodic 'troika' meetings to develop regional technical co-operation and harmonization of work programmes.

The SPC is lead agency in six, and co-lead agency in a further five, of the 30 initiatives intended for implementation during 2006–08 under the Pacific Plan for Strengthening Regional Co-operation and Integration that was endorsed by the October 2005 Pacific Islands Forum.

LAND RESOURCES

The Land Resources Division (LRD) comprises three major programmes: the sustainable management of integrated forest and agriculture systems programme; the biosecurity and trade support programme; and the food security and health programme. The LRD strategic plan for 2005–08 focused on two primary objectives: achieving sustainable management of integrated forest and agricultural systems; and improving biosecurity and trade facilitation. Under the plan, crop production was to be supported through an emphasis on soil fertility improvement, mitigation of water shortages, and improving the efficiency of agricultural laboratories; the national capacity of Pacific Island countries and territories (PICTs) to implement sustainable forest management policies was to be strengthened; the development of the livestock sector was to be given higher priority; and the public health implications of animal diseases, particularly zoonoses that pass from animals to humans, were to be addressed. PICTs were to be supported in the preparation of draft national biosecurity legislation and in developing and updating agriculture and forestry emergency response plans. The LRD has increasingly decentralized the delivery of its services, which are co-ordinated at the country level by personnel within national agricultural systems. The LRD aims to develop the capacity of PICTs in initiatives such as policy analysis and advice, and support for agricultural science and technology. In March 1999 the LRD inaugurated the Regional Germplasm Centre, which assists PICTs in efforts to conserve and access regional genetic resources. In 2001 the Pacific Community endorsed the Pacific Agricultural Plant Genetic Resources Network (PAPGREN), which is implemented by the LRD and other partners. The Pacific Animal Health Information System (PAHIS) provides data on regional livestock numbers and the regional status of animal diseases, and the Pacific Islands Pest List Database provides a register of regional agriculture, forestry and environmental pests. In 2003 an EU-funded Development of Sustainable Agriculture in the Pacific (DSAP) project was initiated to assist 10 member countries to implement sustainable agriculture measures and to improve food production and security. A further six Pacific countries joined the programme in 2004.

MARINE RESOURCES

The Marine Resources Division (MRD) aims to support and co-ordinate the sustainable development and management of inshore fisheries resources in the region, to undertake scientific research in order to provide member governments with relevant information for the sustainable development and management of tuna and billfish resources in and adjacent to the South Pacific region, and to provide data and analytical services to national fisheries departments. The principal programmes under the MRD are the Coastal Fisheries Programme (CFP), the Oceanic Fisheries Programme (OFP), and the Regional Maritime Programme (RMP). The development and advisory activities of the CFP are focused within the near territorial and archipelagic waters of the PICTs. The CFP is divided into the following sections: the Reef Fisheries Observatory; sustainable fisheries development; fisheries management; fisheries training; and aqualculture. The SPC administers the Pacific Island Aquaculture Network, a forum for promoting regional aquaculture development. During 2007 a Pacific Regional Aquatic Biosecurity Initiative was initiated. In contrast to the CFP, the OFP focuses it activities within 200-mile exclusive economic zones and surrounding waters, and is mandated to equip PICTs with the necessary scientific information and advice for rationally managing and exploiting the regional resources of tuna, billfish and related species. The OFP consists of the following three sections: statistics and monitoring; tuna ecology and biology; and stock assessment and modelling. The statistics and monitoring section maintains a database of industrial tuna fisheries in the region. The OFP contributed research and statistical information for the formulation of the Convention for the Conservation and Management of Highly Migratory Fish Stocks in the Western and Central Pacific, which entered into force in June 2004 and aims to establish a regime for the sustainable management of tuna reserves. In March 2002 the SPC and European Commission launched a Pacific Regional Oceanic and Coastal Fisheries Project (PROCFISH). The oceanic component of the project aimed to assist the OFP with advancing knowledge of tuna fisheries ecosystems, while the coastal element was to produce the first comparative regional baseline assessment of reef fisheries. The RMP's principal areas of focus are advising member governments on maritime issues; the provision of technical capacity support; and training in the areas of maritime administration, institutions, ports, shipping and seafaring. In 2002 the RMP launched the model Pacific Islands Maritime Legislation and Regulations as a framework for the development of national maritime legislation. The RMP's priorities during 2006–10 were: supporting PICTs in retaining/gaining status on the International Maritime Organization's 'white list' of nations deemed to be implementing fully the International Convention on Standards of Training, Certification and Watchkeeping for Seafarers; supporting further regional compliance with the international security regime;

and advancing regional professional peer networks. The inaugural regional meeting of ministers responsible for maritime transport was convened in April 2007. The theme of the fifth Pacific Community Conference, convened in November 2007, was 'The future of Pacific fisheries'; a set of recommendations on managing the regional fisheries were endorsed by the Conference.

The SPC hosts the Pacific Office of the WorldFish Center (the International Centre for Living Aquatic Resources Management—ICLARM); the SPC and the WorldFish Center have jointly implemented a number of projects. The SPC also hosts the Co-ordination Unit of the Coral Reef Initiative for the South Pacific (CRISP), which was launched in January 2005 to address the protection and management of the region's coral reefs.

SOCIAL RESOURCES

The Social Resources Division comprises the Human Development Programme, the Public Health Programme, the Regional Media Centre, and the Statistics and Demography Programmes.

The Human Development Programme (HDP) focuses on the areas of gender; youth; culture; and community education. The HDP's Pacific Women's Bureau (PWB) aims to promote the social, economic and cultural advancement of women in the region by assisting governments and regional organizations to include women in the development planning process. The PWB also provides technical and advisory services, advocacy and management support training to groups concerned with women in development and gender and development, and administers the Pacific Women's Information Network (PACWIN). The Pacific Youth Bureau (PYB) co-ordinates the implementation of the Pacific Youth Strategy 2010, which aims to develop opportunities for young people to play an active role in society. The PYB provides non-formal education and support for youth, community workers and young adults in community development subjects and provides grants to help young people find employment. It also advises and assists the Pacific Youth Council in promoting a regional youth identity. At the first Pacific Youth Festival, held in Tahiti in July 2006, a Pacific Youth Charter was formulated, to be incorporated into the Pacific Youth Strategy 2010. A Pacific Youth Mapping Exercise (PYME) was undertaken in 2007, with the aim of establishing a complete picture of youth programmes being implemented across the region. The HDP works to preserve and promote the cultural heritage of the Pacific Islands. The Programme assists with the training of librarians, archivists and researchers and promotes instruction in local languages, history and art at schools in the PICTs. The SPC acts as the secretariat of the Council of Pacific Arts, which organizes the Festival of Pacific Arts on a four-yearly basis. The ninth Festival was held in July 2004, in Palau, and the 10th Festival was scheduled to be staged in July–August 2008, in American Samoa. In November 2006 the HDP published *Guidelines for developing national legislation for the protection of traditional knowledge and expressions of culture*, with the aim of protecting indigenous Pacific knowledge and cultures. The SPC regional office in Suva, Fiji, administers a Community Education Training Centre (CETC), which conducts a seven-month training course for up to 40 women community workers annually, with the objective of training women in methods of community development so that they can help others to achieve better living conditions for island families and communities.

The Public Health Programme (PHP) aims to implement health promotion programmes; to assist regional authorities to strengthen health information systems and to promote the use of new technology for health information development and disease control; to promote efficient health services management; and to help all Pacific Islanders to attain a level of health and quality of life that will enable them to contribute to the development of their communities. The three main areas of focus of the PHP are: noncommunicable diseases (such as heart disease, cerebrovascular disease and diabetes, which are prevalent in parts of the region); communicable diseases (such as HIV/AIDS, other sexually-tranmitted infections—STIs, TB, and vector-borne diseases such as malaria and dengue fever); and public health policy. A Healthy Pacific Lifestyle section aims to assist member countries to improve and sustain health, in particular through advice on nutrition, physical activity and the damaging effects of alcohol and tobacco. The Public Health Surveillance and Communicable Disease Control section is the focal point of the Pacific Public Health Surveillance Network (PPHSN), a regional framework established in 1996 jointly by the SPC and WHO, with the aim of sustainably advancing regional public health surveillance and response. The SPC operates a project (mainly funded by Australia and New Zealand), to prevent AIDS and STIs among young people through peer education and awareness. In August 2004 a new grants scheme was launched to fund the development and implementation of national HIV/AIDS and STI strategic plans. The SPC is the lead regional agency for co-ordinating and monitoring the implementation of the Pacific Regional Strategy on HIV/AIDS, which was endorsed by both the Community and the Pacific Islands Forum in 2004, and covers the period 2004–08. In March 2007 the Pacific Community launched the Oceania Society for Sexual Health and HIV Medicine, a new Pacific network aimed at ensuring access to best practice prevention, treatment, care and support services in the area of sexual health and HIV/AIDS. The SPC and WHO jointly organize regular meetings aimed at strengthening TB control in the region. In February 2006 the SPC established a Pacific Regional Infection Control Network, based in Fiji, to improve communication and access to expert technical advice on all aspects of infectious diseases and control. During 2006 the SPC, in partnership with FAO, WHO and the World Organisation for Animal Health, established the Pacific Regional Influenza Pandemic Preparedness Project (PRIPPP), with the aim of supporting the PICTs in elaborateing plans to prepare for outbreaks of avian influenza or other rapidly contagious diseases. A Pacific Community Pandemic Task Force, established under the PRIPPP and comprising human and animal health experts from Pacific governments and international and regional organizations, met for the first time in March 2007 at the Pacific Community headquarters.

The Regional Media Centre provides training, technical assistance and production materials in all areas of the media for member countries and territories, community work programmes, donor projects and regional non-governmental organizations. The Centre comprises a radio broadcast unit, a graphic design and publication unit and a TV and video unit. In 2000 the SPC's Information Technology and Communication Unit launched ComET, a satellite communications project aimed at linking more closely the organization's headquarters in New Caledonia and regional office in Fiji. The Information and Communications Programme is developing the use of modern communication technology as an invaluable resource for problem-solving, regional networking, and uniting the Community's scattered, often physically isolated, island member states. In conjunction with the Secretariat of the Pacific Islands Forum the SPC convened the first regional meeting of Information and Communication Technology workers, researchers and policy-makers in August 2001.

The Statistics Programme assists governments and administrations in the region to provide effective and efficient national statistical services through the provision of training activities, a statistical information service and other advisory services. A Regional Meeting of Heads of Statistics facilitates the integration and co-ordination of statistical services throughout the region, while the Pacific Regional Information System (PRISM), initiated by the National Statistics Office of the Pacific Islands and developed with British funding, provides statistical information about member countries and territories.

The Demography Programme provides technical support in population, demographic and development issues to member governments, other SPC programmes, and organizations active in the region. The Programme aims to assist governments effectively to analyse data and utilize it into the formulation of national development policies and programmes. The Programme organizes national workshops in population and development planning, provides short-term professional attachments, undertakes demographic research and analysis, and disseminates information.

Finance

The SPC's 2008 budget totalled US $49m., to be funded jointly by Community member states and international donors.

Publications

Annual Report.
Fisheries Newsletter (quarterly).
Pacific Aids Alert Bulletin (quarterly).
Pacific Island Nutrition (quarterly).
Regional Tuna Bulletin (quarterly).
Report of the Conference of the Pacific Community.
Women's Newsletter (quarterly).
Technical publications, statistical bulletins, advisory leaflets and reports.

PACIFIC ISLANDS FORUM

Address: Private Mail Bag, Suva, Fiji.
Telephone: 3312600; **fax:** 3301102; **e-mail:** info@forumsec.org.fj; **internet:** www.forumsec.org.

The Pacific Islands Forum (which in October 2000 changed its name from South Pacific Forum, in order to reflect the expansion of its membership since its establishment) was founded as the gathering of Heads of Government of the independent and self-governing states of the South Pacific; the first annual Forum meeting was held on 5 August 1971, in Wellington, New Zealand. The Pacific Islands Forum Secretariat was established (as the South Pacific Bureau for Economic Co-operation—SPEC) by an agreement signed on 17 April 1973, at the third Forum meeting, in Apia, Western Samoa (now Samoa). SPEC was redesignated as the South Pacific Forum Secretariat in 1988, and the present name was adopted in October 2000. The Secretariat aims to enhance the economic and social well-being of the Pacific Islands peoples, in support of the efforts of national governments. In October 2005 the 36th Forum adopted an Agreement Establishing the Pacific Islands Forum, which aimed to formalize the grouping's status as a full intergovernmental organization.

MEMBERS

Australia
Cook Islands
Fiji
Kiribati
Marshall Islands
Federated States of Micronesia
Nauru
New Zealand
Niue
Palau
Papua New Guinea
Samoa
Solomon Islands
Tonga
Tuvalu
Vanuatu

Note: French Polynesia and New Caledonia were admitted to the Forum as associate members in 2006. The Asian Development Bank, the Commonwealth, the UN, Tokelau, and Wallis and Futuna are observers. The 2007 Forum offered observer status to the Western and Central Pacific Fisheries Commission. Timor-Leste has 'special observer' status (granted in 2002).

Organization
(April 2008)

FORUM OFFICIALS COMMITTEE
The Forum Officials Committee is the Secretariat's executive board, overseeing its activities. It comprises representatives and senior officials from all member countries. It meets twice a year, immediately before the meetings of the Pacific Islands Forum and at the end of the year, to discuss in detail the Secretariat's work programme and annual budget.

FORUM MEETING
Each annual leaders' Forum is chaired by the Head of Government of the country hosting the meeting, who remains as Forum Chairperson until the next Forum. The Forum has no written constitution or international agreement governing its activities nor any formal rules relating to its purpose, membership or conduct of meeting. Decisions are always reached by consensus, it never having been found necessary or desirable to vote formally on issues. In October 1994 the Forum was granted observer status by the General Assembly of the United Nations. The 38th Forum took place in Nuku'alofa, Tonga, in October 2007.

DIALOGUE PLENARY MEETING
From 1989–2006 each annual Pacific Islands Forum meeting was followed by individual dialogues with representatives of selected countries considered to have a long-term interest in the region. A review of the post-Forum dialogues, undertaken in August 2006, recommended that the individual dialogues should be replaced by a new single Post-Forum Dialogue Plenary Meeting, to enable structured communication at ministerial level between Forum and Dialogue countries; and that 'core' dialogue partners, with a special engagement in and commitment to the region, should be identified. The findings of the review were approved in October 2006 by the 37th Forum meeting, and the new post-Forum dialogue structure was initiated following the 38th Forum. In 2008 Canada, the People's Republic of China, France, India, Indonesia, Italy, Japan, the Republic of Korea, Malaysia, Philippines, Thailand, the United Kingdom, the USA, and the European Union had dialogue partner status. A separate post-Forum session is convened between the Republic of China (Taiwan) and six of the Forum member states.

SECRETARIAT
The Secretariat acts as the administrative arm of the Forum. It is headed by a Secretary-General, with a staff of some 70 people drawn from the member countries. The Secretariat comprises the following four Divisions: Corporate Services; Development and Economic Policy; Trade and Investment; and Political, International and Legal Affairs. The Secretariat's Pacific Plan Office services the Pacific Plan Action Committee and supports the overall implementation of the Pacific Plan. A Pacific ACP/EU Co-operation unit assists member states and regional organizations with submitting projects to the EU. A Smaller Island States unit was established within the Secretariat in 2006. The Secretariat chairs the Council of Regional Organizations in the Pacific (CROP), an ad hoc committee comprising the heads of 11 regional organizations, which aims to discuss and co-ordinate the policies and work programmes of the various agencies in order to avoid duplication of or omissions in their services to member countries.

Secretary-General: GREGORY (GREG) URWIN (Australia).
Deputy Secretary-General: FELETI TE'O (Tuvalu).

Activities

The Pacific Islands Forum provides an opportunity for informal discussions to be held on a wide range of common issues and problems and meets annually or when issues require urgent attention.

The Pacific Islands Forum Secretariat organizes Forum-related events, implements decisions by the Leaders, facilitates the delivery of development assistance to member states, and undertakes the political and legal mandates of Forum meetings.

In August 2003 regional leaders attending the 34th Forum, held in Auckland, New Zealand, determined that a review of the activities of the Forum and its Secretariat should be undertaken, and established an Eminent Persons Group to initiate that process.

In February 2007 a Regional Institutional Framework (RIF) Taskforce, comprising representatives of the member states of the Council of Regional Organizations in the Pacific agencies, convened for the first time, under Secretariat auspices. The RIF Taskforce was mandated by the October 2006 Forum to develop an appropriate institutional framework for supporting the implementation of the Pacific Plan. It was envisaged that the Pacific regional institutions would be reorganized under the following three pillars: a political and general policy institution; an activity sector-focused technical institution; and academic/training organizations. Lourdes Pangelinan, a former Director-General of the Pacific Community, was given responsibility for overseeing the development of the RIF.

PACIFIC PLAN
In April 2004 a Special Leaders' Retreat convened in Auckland, New Zealand, in order to consider the future activities and direction of the Forum, mandated the development of a new 'Pacific Plan on Strengthening Regional Co-operation and Integration' as a means of addressing the challenges confronting the Pacific Island states. Consequently a Pacific Plan Task Force, managed by the Forum Secretary-General in consultation with a core leaders' group, undertook work to formulate the document. The finalized Pacific Plan, which was endorsed by the October 2005 Forum, incorporates development initiatives that are focused around the four 'pillars' of economic growth; sustainable development; good governance; and security. It also recognizes the specific needs of Smaller Island States. The Pacific Plan is regarded as a 'living document', which can be amended and updated continuously to accommodate emerging priorities. The Pacific Plan Action Committee (PPAC), comprising representatives of the Forum member states and chaired by the Forum Chairperson, has met regularly since January 2006. Regional organizations, working in partnership with national governments and other partners, are responsible for co-ordinating the implementation of—and compiling reports on—many of the specific Pacific Plan initiatives, some 30 of which are intended for 'immediate implementation' during 2006–08. The 37th Forum leaders' meeting in October 2006 adopted the Nadi Decisions on the Pacific Plan, prioritizing several key commitments in the four pillar areas; these were consequently incorporated into the ('living') Plan during 2007. In October 2007 the 38th Forum adopted a further set of key commitments, the Vava'U Decisions on the Pacific Plan.

POLITICAL AND SOCIAL AFFAIRS AND REGIONAL SECURITY
The Political, International and Legal Affairs Division of the Secretariat organizes and services the meetings of the Forum, dissemin-

ates its views, administers the Forum's observer office at the United Nations, and aims to strengthen relations with other regional and international organizations, in particular APEC and ASEAN. The Division's other main concern is to promote regional co-operation in law enforcement and legal affairs, and it provides technical support for the drafting of legal documents and for law enforcement capacity-building.

In recent years the Forum Secretariat has been concerned with assessing the legislative reforms and other commitments needed to ensure implementation of the 1992 Honiara Declaration on Law Enforcement Co-operation. The Secretariat assists member countries to ratify and implement the 1988 UN Convention against Illicit Trafficking in Narcotic Drugs and Psychotropic Substances. At the end of 2001 a conference of Forum immigration ministers expressed concern at rising levels of human-trafficking and illegal immigration in the region, and recommended that member states become parties to the 2000 UN Convention Against Transnational Organized Crime. A Pacific Transnational Crime Co-ordination Centre was established in Suva, Fiji, in 2004, to enhance and gather law enforcement intelligence. In September 2006 the Forum, in co-operation with the USA and the UN Global Programme Against Money Laundering (administered by the UN Office on Drugs and Crime), launched the Pacific Anti-Money Laundering Programme (PALP). PALP provides technical assistance to member states for the development of their national anti-money laundering and counter-terrorism financing regimes, in accordance with the Pacific Plan's development priority of regional security. Under the Pacific Plan, the Forum Secretariat requested the establishment of a Pacific Islands Regional Security Technical Co-operation Unit to support legislative efforts regarding, *inter alia*, transnational organized crime, counter-terrorism and financial intelligence.

The South Pacific Nuclear-Free Zone Treaty (Treaty of Rarotonga), prohibiting the acquisition, stationing or testing of nuclear weapons in the region, came into effect in December 1986, following ratification by eight states. The USSR signed the protocols to the treaty (whereby states possessing nuclear weapons agree not to use or threaten to use nuclear explosive devices against any non-nuclear party to the Treaty) in December 1987 and ratified them in April 1988; the People's Republic of China did likewise in December 1987 and October 1988 respectively. In July 1993 the Forum petitioned the USA, the United Kingdom and France, asking them to reconsider their past refusal to sign the Treaty in the light of the end of the 'Cold War'. In July 1995, following the decision of the French Government to resume testing of nuclear weapons in French Polynesia, members of the Forum resolved to increase diplomatic pressure on the three Governments to sign the Treaty. In October the United Kingdom, the USA and France announced their intention to accede to the Treaty, by mid-1996. Following France's decision, announced in January 1996, to end the programme four months earlier than scheduled, representatives of the Governments of the three countries signed the Treaty in March. In view of its resumption of nuclear testing in 1995–96, France's 'dialogue partner' status was suspended by the Forum Government during October 1995–September 1996.

Since 2001 the Forum has sent election observer groups to monitor elections taking place in member states, and, since 2004, joint election observer missions have been undertaken with the Commonwealth. During 2007 Forum election observer teams were dispatched to observe parliamentary elections held in Nauru in August and in the Marshall Islands in November; and a joint mission, comprising Forum representatives and officials from the Commonwealth Secretariat, observed legislative elections staged during June–August in Papua New Guinea.

In October 2000 leaders attending the 31st Forum, convened in Tarawa, Kiribati, adopted the Biketawa Declaration, which outlined a mechanism for responding to any security crises that might occur in the region, while also urging members to undertake efforts to address the fundamental causes of potential instability. In August 2003 regional leaders convened at the 34th Forum commended the swift response by member countries and territories in deploying a Regional Assistance Mission in Solomon Islands (RAMSI), which had been approved by Forum ministers of foreign affairs at a meeting held in Sydney, Australia, in June, in accordance with the Biketawa Declaration; RAMSI was still operative in early 2008.

The 33rd Forum, held in Suva, Fiji, in August 2002, adopted the Nasonini Declaration on Regional Security, which recognized the need for immediate and sustained regional action to combat international terrorism and transnational crime, in view of the perceived increased threat to global and regional security following the major terrorist attacks perpetrated against targets in the USA in September 2001.

In August 2003 regional leaders attending the 34th Forum adopted a set of Forum Principles of Good Leadership, establishing key requirements for good governance, including respect for law and the system of government, and respect for cultural values, customs and traditions, and for freedom of religion.

In August 2004 the 35th Forum approved an HIV/AIDS Regional Strategy and requested its implementation with immediate effect. In October 2005 the 36th Forum welcomed the development of a new Pacific Regional Influenza Pandemic Preparedness Project.

TRADE, ECONOMIC CO-OPERATION AND SUSTAINABLE DEVELOPMENT

The Secretariat's Trade and Investment Division extends advice and technical assistance to member countries in policy, development, export marketing, and information dissemination. Trade policy activities are mainly concerned with improving private sector policies, for example investment promotion, assisting integration into the world economy (including the provision of information and technical assistance to member states on WTO-related matters and supporting Pacific Island ACP states with preparations for negotiations on trade partnership with the EU under the Cotonou Agreement), and the development of businesses. During 2004–09 the Secretariat was supported in these activities through PACREIP (see below). The Secretariat aims to assist both island governments and private sector companies to enhance their capacity in the development and exploitation of export markets, product identification and product development. A regional trade and investment database is being developed. The Secretariat co-ordinates the activities of the regional trade offices located in Australia, New Zealand and Japan (see below). A representative trade office in Beijing, People's Republic of China, opened in January 2002. A Forum office was opened in Geneva, Switzerland, in 2004 to represent member countries at the WTO. In April 2005 the Pacific Islands Private Sector Organisation (PIPSO), representing regional private sector interests, was established. The PIPSO Secretariat, hosted by the Forum Secretariat, was inaugurated in April 2007. In August of that year PIPSO organized the first Pacific Islands Business Forum, convened in Nadi, Fiji.

In 1981 the South Pacific Regional Trade and Economic Co-operation Agreement (SPARTECA) came into force. SPARTECA aimed to redress the trade deficit of the Pacific Island countries with Australia and New Zealand. It is a non-reciprocal trade agreement under which Australia and New Zealand offer duty-free and unrestricted access or concessional access for specified products originating from the developing island member countries of the Forum. In 1985 Australia agreed to further liberalization of trade by abolishing (from the beginning of 1987) duties and quotas on all Pacific products except steel, cars, sugar, footwear and garments. In August 1994 New Zealand expanded its import criteria under the agreement by reducing the rule of origin requirement for garment products from 50% to 45% of local content. In response to requests from Fiji, Australia agreed to widen its interpretation of the agreement by accepting as being of local content manufactured products that consist of goods and components of 50% Australian content. A new Fiji/Australia Trade and Economic Relations Agreement (AFTERA) was concluded in March 1999 to complement SPARTECA and compensate for certain trade benefits that were in the process of being withdrawn.

In July 1997 the inaugural meeting of Forum economy ministers was convened in Cairns, Australia. It formulated an Action Plan to encourage the flow of foreign investment into the region by committing members to economic reforms, good governance and the implementation of multilateral trade and tariff policies.

Two major regional trade accords signed by Forum heads of state in August 2001 entered into force in April 2003 and October 2002, respectively: the Pacific Island Countries Trade Agreement (PICTA), providing for the establishment of a Pacific Island free trade area (FTA); and the related Pacific Agreement on Closer Economic Relations (PACER), incorporating trade and economic co-operation measures and envisaging the phased establishment of a regional single market comprising the PICTA FTA and Australia and New Zealand. The FTA was to be implemented over a period of eight years for developing member countries and 10 years for smaller island states and least developed countries. It was envisaged that negotiations on free trade agreements between Pacific Island states and Australia and New Zealand, with a view to establishing the larger regional single market envisaged by PACER, would commence within eight years of PICTA's entry into force. SPARTECA (see above) would remain operative pending the establishment of the larger single market, into which it would be subsumed. Under the provisions of PACER, Australia and New Zealand were to provide technical and financial assistance to PICTA signatory states in pursuing the objectives of PACER. In August 2003 regional leaders attending the 34th Forum agreed, in principle, that the USA and France should become parties to both PICTA and PACER. In September 2004 Forum trade officials adopted a Regional Trade Facilitation Programme (RTFP), within the framework of PACER, which included measures concerned with customs procedures, quarantine, standards and other activities to harmonize and facilitate trade between Pacific Island states and Australia and New Zealand, as well as with other international trading partners. It was announced in August 2007 that a review of the RTFP was to be undertaken.

In April 2001 the Secretariat convened a meeting of seven member island states—the Cook Islands, the Marshall Islands, Nauru, Niue, Samoa, Tonga and Vanuatu—as well as representatives from Australia and New Zealand, to address the regional implications of the OECD's Harmful Tax Competition Initiative. (OECD had identified the Cook Islands, the Marshall Islands, Nauru and Niue as so-called 'tax havens' lacking financial transparency and had demanded that they impose stricter legislation to address the incidence of international money-laundering on their territories.) The meeting requested the OECD to engage in conciliatory negotiations with the listed Pacific Island states. The August 2001 Forum reiterated this stance, proclaiming the sovereign right of nations to establish individual tax regimes, and supporting the development of a new co-operative framework to address financial transparency concerns. In December the Secretariat hosted a workshop for officials from nine member states concerned with combating financial crime. The workshop was attended and sponsored by several partner organizations and bodies, including the IMF.

The Development and Economic Policy Division of the Secretariat aims to co-ordinate and promote co-operation in development activities and programmes throughout the region. The Division administers a Short Term Advisory Service, which provides consultancy services to help member countries meet economic development priorities, and a Fellowship Scheme to provide practical training in a range of technical and income-generating activities. A Small Island Development Fund aims to assist the economic development of the SIS sub-group of member countries (see below) through project financing. A separate fellowship has also been established to provide training to the Kanak population of New Caledonia, to assist in their social, economic and political development. In 2004 the Secretariat formulated a Pacific Regional Assistance to Nauru (PRAN) initiative, that had been endorsed by Forum leaders in August. The Division aims to assist regional organizations to identify development priorities and to provide advice to national governments on economic analysis, planning and structural reforms.

The Secretariat services the Pacific Group Council of ACP states receiving assistance from the EU, and in 1993 a joint unit was established within the Secretariat headquarters to assist Pacific ACP countries and regional organizations in submitting projects to the EU for funding. The Pacific Regional Economic Integration Programme (PACREIP), launched in February 2004 as the largest programme under EU-Pacific co-operation, and covering the period 2004–09, focuses on building the capacity of the Pacific ACP states to advance regional economic integration through the implementation of PICTA, to negotiate effectively at the WTO, and to conduct negotiations on the conclusion of an EU-Pacific Economic Co-operation Agreement (EPA). A draft EPA was published in August 2007. PACREIP also aims to support regional private sector development, trade facilitation, biosecurity, the development of an environmental impact assessment, financial sector and fiscal reforms, and tourism sector development.

In October 1999 heads of state and government attending the 30th Forum, held in Koror, Palau, adopted a Forum Vision for the Pacific Information Economy, which recognized the importance of information technology infrastructure for the region's economic and social development and the possibilities for enhanced co-operation in investment, job creation, education, training and cultural exchange. In October 2000 the 31st Forum endorsed a proposal to establish a Regional Financial Information Sharing Facility and national financial intelligence units.

ENVIRONMENT

The Forum actively promotes the development of effective international legislation to reduce emissions by industrialized countries of so-called 'greenhouse gases'. Such gases contribute to the warming of the earth's atmosphere (the 'greenhouse effect') and to related increases in global sea-levels, and have therefore been regarded as a major threat to low-lying islands in the region. The Secretariat has played an active role in supporting regional participation at meetings of the Conference of the Parties to the UN Framework Convention on Climate Change (UNFCCC), and helps to co-ordinate Forum policy on the environment. With support from the Australian Government, it administers a network of stations to monitor sea-levels and climate change throughout the Pacific region. The 29th Forum, held in Pohnpei, Federated States of Micronesia, in August 1998, adopted a Statement on Climate Change, which urged all countries to ratify and implement the gas emission reductions agreed upon by UN member states in December 1997 (the so-called Kyoto Protocol of the UNFCCC), and emphasized the Forum's commitment to further measures for verifying and enforcing emission limitation. In October 2005 the 36th Forum approved the Pacific Islands Framework for Action on Climate Change 2006–15, and noted the need to implement national action plans to address climate change issues. In October 2007 leaders attending the 38th Forum reiterated deep concern over the economic, social and environmental impact of climate change, noting the recent findings of the IPCC's *Fourth Assessment Report*

and the importance of negotiating a comprehensive international framework to tackle climate change after the expiry of the Kyoto Protocol in 2012.

In September 1995 the 26th Forum, held in Madang, Papua New Guinea, endorsed a draft Code of Conduct on the management and monitoring of indigenous forest resources in selected South Pacific countries, which had been initiated at the 25th Forum; however, while the six countries concerned committed themselves to implementing the Code through national legislation, its signing was deferred, owing to an initial unwillingness on the part of Papua New Guinea and Solomon Islands.

In August 2002 regional leaders attending the 33rd Forum approved a Pacific Island Regional Ocean Policy, which aimed to ensure the future sustainable use of the ocean and its resources by Pacific Island communities and external partners. A Declaration on Deep Sea Bottom Trawling to Protect Biodiversity on the High Seas was adopted in October 2005 by the 36th Forum. In October 2007 leaders attending the 38th Forum urged increased efforts among Forum members to foster a long-term strategic approach to ensuring the effective management of fish stocks, with a particular focus on tuna, and adopted a related Declaration on Pacific Fisheries Resources.

In September 1995 the 26th Forum adopted the Waigani Convention, banning the import into the region of all radioactive and other hazardous wastes, and providing controls for the transboundary movement and management of these wastes. Forum leaders have frequently reiterated protests against the shipment of radioactive materials through the region.

In January 2005, meeting on the fringes of the fifth Summit of the Alliance of Small Island States, in Port Louis, Mauritius, the Secretaries-General of the Pacific Islands Forum Secretariat, the Commonwealth, CARICOM, and the Indian Ocean Commission determined to take collective action to strengthen the disaster preparedness and response capacities of their member countries in the Pacific, Caribbean and Indian Ocean areas. In October 2005 the 36th Forum endorsed the Pacific Regional Framework for Action for Building the Resilience of Nations and Communities to Disasters during 2005–15.

TRANSPORT

The Forum established the Pacific Forum Line and the Association of South Pacific Airlines (see below), as part of its efforts to promote co-operation in regional transport. On 1 January 1997 the work of the Forum Maritime Programme, which included assistance for regional maritime training and for the development of regional maritime administrations and legislation, was transferred to the regional office of the South Pacific Commission (renamed the Pacific Community from February 1998) at Suva. Telecommunications policy activities were also transferred to the then South Pacific Commission at the start of 1997. In May 1998 ministers responsible for aviation in member states approved a new regional civil aviation policy, which envisaged liberalization of air services, common safety and security standards and provisions for shared revenue.

In August 2004 the 35th Forum adopted a set of Principles on Regional Transport Services, based on the results of a study requested by the 34th Forum, 'to improve the efficiency, effectiveness and sustainability of air and shipping services'.

The Pacific Islands Air Services Agreement (PIASA) was opened for signature in August 2003, and entered into effect in October 2007, having been ratified by six Pacific Island countries. In August 2004 the Pacific Islands Civil Aviation and Security Treaty (PICASST) was opened for signature, and, in June 2005 PICASST entered into force, establishing a Port Vila, Vanuatu-based Pacific Aviation Security Office. In accordance with the Principles on Regional Transport Services, which were adopted by Forum Leaders in August 2004, the Secretariat was to support efforts to enhance air and shipping services, as well as develop a regional digital strategy.

SMALLER ISLAND STATES

In 1990 the Cook Islands, Kiribati, Nauru, Niue and Tuvalu, amongst the Forum's smallest island member states, formed the Smaller Island States (SIS) economic sub-group, which meets regularly to address their specific smaller island concerns. These include, in particular, economic disadvantages resulting from a poor resource base, absence of a skilled work-force and lack of involvement in world markets. Small island member states have also been particularly concerned about the phenomenon of global warming and its potentially damaging effects on the region. In September 1997 the Marshall Islands was admitted as the sixth member of SIS, and Palau was subsequently admitted as the seventh member. In February 1998 senior Forum officials, for the first time, met with representatives of the Caribbean Community and the Indian Ocean Commission, as well as other major international organizations, to discuss means to enhance consideration and promotion of the interests of small island states. An SIS unit, established within the Forum Secretariat in 2006, aims to enable high-profile representation of the SIS perspective, particularly in the development of the Pacific Plan, and to enable the small island member states to benefit fully from the implementation of the Plan.

Recent Meetings of the Pacific Islands Forum

The 35th Forum was held in August 2004, in Apia, Samoa. Leaders commended the work being undertaken by the Pacific Plan Task Force, and anticipated a substantial document to be presented to the 36th Forum. Leaders adopted new Principles on Regional Transport Services; and reiterated the importance of fisheries to the region's economy and population, resolving to pursue an increase in sustainable returns through greater participation of resource-owning countries in the fishing industry. Furthermore, Forum leaders approved an HIV/AIDS Regional Strategy; resolved to support a request from the Government of Nauru for economic and technical assistance in accordance with the Biketawa Declaration (2000); and determined to review the region's response to national disasters and other emergencies, with particular concern given to the recovery efforts of Niue following a devastating cyclone which struck the territory in January.

Leaders attending the 36th Forum, convened in Papua New Guinea in late October 2005, endorsed the newly-formulated Pacific Plan, and adopted an Agreement Establishing the Pacific Islands Forum, which aimed to formalize the grouping's status as a full intergovernmental organization. Leaders also approved the Pacific Islands Framework for Action on Climate Change 2006–15 and endorsed the Pacific Regional Framework for Action for Building the Resilience of Nations and Communities to Disasters during 2005–15. The 36th Forum urged the adoption of national and regional avian influenza preparedness measures and considered a proposal to establish a Pacific Health Fund to address issues such as avian influenza, HIV/AIDS, malaria, and non-communicable diseases.

The 37th Forum, held in Nadi, Fiji in October 2006, approved the Nadi Decisions, a series of key commitments aimed at advancing the implementation of the Pacific Plan in the Plan's four 'pillar' areas of economic growth, sustainable development, good governance, and regional security and partnerships. Leaders attending the 37th Forum also determined that a taskforce should be established to develop a new regional institutional framework for its member states. In addition they adopted a Declaration on Deep Sea Bottom Trawling to Protect Biodiversity on the High Seas; welcomed the development of the Pacific Regional Influenza Pandemic Preparedness Project; agreed to establish a task force to review RAMSI; and determined to develop a Regional Co-operation for Counter-Terrorism Assistance and Response model.

The 38th Forum, convened in Nuku'alofa, Tonga, in October 2007, noted that considerable progress had been achieved in the implementation of initiatives across all four of the pillars of the Pacific Plan and agreed on several key commitments (the Vava'U Decisions) in order to move the Plan forwards. Leaders attending the Forum adopted a Declaration on Pacific Fisheries Resources; and noted the importance of negotiating a comprehensive post-2012 framework to tackle climate change. Leaders commended the work of RAMSI, and noted that a consultative mechanism between the Government of Solomon Islands, RAMSI and the Pacific Islands Forum had been established, and also the findings of the task force on RAMSI. They also noted the continuing work of the Pacific Regional Assistance to Nauru initiative.

Finance

The Governments of Australia and New Zealand each contribute some one-third of the annual budget and the remaining amount is shared by the other member Governments. Extra-budgetary funding is contributed mainly by Australia, New Zealand, Japan, the EU and France. The Forum's 2006 budget amounted to approximately $F36.0m. During the 36th Forum it was proposed that a fund be established for the implementation of the Pacific Plan, to be managed by the Pacific Plan Action Committee.

Publications

Annual Report.
Forum News (quarterly).
Forum Trends.
Forum Secretariat Directory of Aid Agencies.
Pacific Plan Progress Report.
South Pacific Trade Directory.
SPARTECA (guide for Pacific island exporters).
Reports of meetings; profiles of Forum member countries.

Overseas Agencies and Affiliated Organizations

Association of South Pacific Airlines (ASPA): POB 9817, Nadi Airport, Nadi, Fiji; tel. 6723526; fax 6720196; f. 1979 at a meeting of airlines in the South Pacific, convened to promote co-operation among the member airlines for the development of regular, safe and economical commercial aviation within, to and from the South Pacific; mems: 16 regional airlines, two associates; Chair. JOHN CAMPBELL; Sec.-Gen. GEORGE E. FAKTAUFON.

Forum Fisheries Agency (FFA): POB 629, Honiara, Solomon Islands; tel. (677) 21124; fax (677) 23995; e-mail info@ffa.int; internet www.ffa.int; f. 1979 to promote co-operation in fisheries among coastal states in the region; collects and disseminates information and advice on the living marine resources of the region, including the management, exploitation and development of these resources; provides assistance in the areas of law (treaty negotiations, drafting legislation, and co-ordinating surveillance and enforcement), fisheries development, research, economics, computers, and information management; the FFA was closely involved in the legal process relating to the establishment of a Western and Central Pacific Fisheries Commission, which was inaugurated in 2004; a Vessel Monitoring System, to provide automated data collection and analysis of fishing vessel activities throughout the region, was inaugurated by the FFA in 1998; on behalf of its 16 member countries, the FFA administers a multilateral fisheries treaty, under which vessels from the USA operate in the region, in exchange for an annual payment; the FFA is implementing the FFA Strategic Plan 2005–20, detailing the medium-term direction of the Agency; Dir DAN SUA; publs *FFA News Digest* (every two months), *FFA Reports*, *MCS Newsletter* (quarterly), *Tuna Market Newsletter* (monthly).

Pacific Forum Line: POB 105-612, Auckland 1143, New Zealand; tel. (9) 356-2333; fax (9) 356-2330; e-mail info@pflnz.co.nz; internet www.pflnz.co.nz; f. 1977 as a joint venture by South Pacific countries, to provide shipping services to meet the special requirements of the region; operates three container vessels; conducts shipping agency services in Australia, Fiji, New Zealand and Samoa, and stevedoring in Samoa; Chair. A. VOCEA; CEO W. J. MACLENNAN.

Pacific Islands Centre (PIC): Sotobori Sky Bldg, 5th Floor, 2-11 Ichigayahonmura-cho, Shinjuku-ku, Tokyo 162-0845, Japan; tel. (3) 3268-8419; fax (3) 3268-6311; e-mail info@pic.or.jp; internet www.pic.or.jp; f. 1996 to promote and to facilitate trade, investment and tourism among Forum members and Japan; Dir KEIICHI HASEGAWA.

Pacific Islands Forum Trade Office: 5-1-3-1 Tayuan Diplomatic Compound, 1 Xin Dong Lu, Chaoyang District, Beijing 100600, People's Republic of China; tel. (10) 6532-6622; fax (10) 6532-6360; e-mail answers@pifto.org.cn; internet www.pifto.org.cn; f. 2001.

Pacific Islands Private Sector Organization (PIPSO): c/o Pacific Islands Forum Secretariat, Private Mail Bag, Suva, Fiji; tel. 3312600; fax 3301102; e-mail info@forumsec.org.fj; internet www.pipso.org; f. 2005 to represent regional private-sector interests; organizes Pacific Islands Business Forum; Exec. Dir HENRY SANDAY.

Pacific Islands Trade and Investment Commission (Sydney): Level 11, 171 Clarence St, Sydney, NSW 20010, Australia; tel. (2) 9290-2133; fax (2) 9299-2151; e-mail info@pitic.org.au; internet www.pitic.org.au; f. 1979; assists Pacific Island Governments and business communities to identify market opportunities in Australia and promotes investment in the Pacific Island countries; Trade Commr AIVU TAUVASA (Papua New Guinea).

Pacific Islands Trade and Investment Commission (New Zealand): POB 109-395, 5 Short St, Level 3, Newmarket, Auckland, New Zealand; tel. (9) 5295165; fax (9) 5231284; e-mail info@pitic.org.nz; internet www.pitic.org.nz; Trade Commr CHRISTOPHER ROY COCKER.

SOUTH ASIAN ASSOCIATION FOR REGIONAL CO-OPERATION—SAARC

Address: POB 4222, Tridevi Marg, Kathmandu, Nepal.
Telephone: (1) 4221785; **fax:** (1) 4227033; **e-mail:** saarc@saarc-sec.org; **internet:** www.saarc-sec.org.

The South Asian Association for Regional Co-operation (SAARC) was formally established in 1985 in order to strengthen and accelerate regional co-operation, particularly in economic development.

MEMBERS

Afghanistan	Maldives
Bangladesh	Nepal
Bhutan	Pakistan
India	Sri Lanka

Observers: People's Republic of China, Iran, Japan, Republic of Korea, the European Union.

Organization
(April 2008)

SUMMIT MEETING

Heads of state and of government of member states represent the body's highest authority, and a summit meeting is normally held annually. The 14th summit meeting was convened in New Delhi, India, in April 2007. The 15th summit meeting was scheduled to be held in Colombo, Sri Lanka, in July–August 2008.

COUNCIL OF MINISTERS

The Council of Ministers comprises the ministers of foreign affairs of member countries, who meet twice a year. The Council may also meet in extraordinary session at the request of member states. The responsibilities of the Council include formulation of policies, assessing progress and confirming new areas of co-operation.

STANDING COMMITTEE

The Committee consists of the secretaries of foreign affairs of member states. It has overall responsibility for the monitoring and co-ordination of programmes and financing, and determines priorities, mobilizes resources and identifies areas of co-operation. It usually meets twice a year, and submits its reports to the Council of Ministers. The Committee is supported by an ad hoc Programming Committee made up of senior officials, who meet to examine the budget of the Secretariat, confirm the Calendar of Activities and resolve matters assigned to it by the Standing Committee.

TECHNICAL COMMITTEES

SAARC's Integrated Programme of Action is implemented by seven Technical Committees covering: Agriculture and rural development; Energy; Environment, meteorology and forestry; Human resource development; Science and technology; Social development; and Transport and communications. Each committee is headed by a representative of a member state and meets annually.

SECRETARIAT

The Secretariat was established in 1987 to co-ordinate and oversee SAARC activities. It comprises the Secretary-General and a Director from each member country. The Secretary-General is appointed by the Council of Ministers, after being nominated by a member state, and serves a three-year term of office. The Director is nominated by member states and appointed by the Secretary-General for a term of three years, although this may be increased in special circumstances.

Secretary-General: Dr SHEEL KANT SHARMA (India).

Activities

The first summit meeting of SAARC heads of state and government, held in Dhaka, Bangladesh, in December 1985, resulted in the signing of the Charter of the South Asian Association for Regional Co-operation (SAARC). In August 1993 ministers of foreign affairs of seven countries, meeting in New Delhi, India, adopted a Declaration on South Asian Regional Co-operation and launched an Integrated Programme of Action (IPA), which identified the main areas for regional co-operation. The ninth summit meeting, held in May 1997, authorized the establishment of a Group of Eminent Persons to review the functioning of the IPA. On the basis of the group's recommendations a reconstituted IPA, to be administered by a more efficient arrangement of Technical Committees, was initiated in June 2000.

SAARC is committed to improving quality of life in the region by accelerating economic growth, social progress and cultural development; promoting self-reliance; encouraging mutual assistance; increasing co-operation with other developing countries; and co-operating with other regional and international organizations. The SAARC Charter stipulates that decisions should be made unanimously, and that 'bilateral and contentious issues' should not be discussed. Regular meetings, at all levels, are held to further co-operation in areas covered by the Technical Committees (see above). A priority objective is the eradication of poverty in the region, and in 1993 SAARC endorsed an Agenda of Action to help achieve this. A framework for exchanging information on poverty eradication has also, since, been established. The 11th SAARC summit meeting, held in Kathmandu, Nepal, in January 2002, adopted a convention on regional arrangements for the promotion of child welfare in South Asia. The 11th summit also determined to reinvigorate regional poverty reduction activities in the context of the UN General Assembly's Millennium Development Goal of halving extreme poverty by 2015, and of other internationally-agreed commitments. The meeting reconstituted the Independent South Asian Commission on Poverty Alleviation—ISACPA, which had been established in 1991. ISACPA reported to the 12th summit meeting of heads of state, held in Islamabad, Pakistan, in January 2004. The 12th summit meeting, held in Islamabad, Pakistan, in January 2004, declared poverty alleviation to be the overarching goal of all SAARC activities and requested ISACPA to continue its work in an advocacy role and to prepare a set of SAARC Development Goals (SDGs) for future consideration. At the meeting heads of state endorsed a Plan of Action on Poverty Alleviation, and also adopted a SAARC Social Charter that had been drafted by with assistance from representatives of civil society, academia, non-governmental organizations and government, under the auspices of an inter-governmental expert group, and incorporated objectives in areas including poverty alleviation, promotion of health and nutrition, food security, water supply and sanitation, children's development and rights, participation by women, and human resources development. The 13th SAARC summit meeting, held in Dhaka, Bangladesh, in November 2005, declared the SAARC Decade of Poverty Alleviation covering the period 2006–15 and determined to replace SAARC's Three-tier Mechanism on Poverty Alleviation (established in 1995) with a Two-tier Mechanism on Poverty Alleviation, comprising ministers and secretaries responsible for poverty alleviation at national level. The 14th summit meeting, held in New Delhi, India, in April 2007, acknowledged ISACPA's efforts in elaborating the SDGs and entrusted the Two-tier Mechanism with monitoring progress towards the achievement of these.

The 2002 summit urged the development of a regional strategy for preventing and combating HIV/AIDS and other communicable diseases; the SAARC Tuberculosis Centre (see below) was to play a co-ordinating role in this area. In April 2003 SAARC ministers of health convened an emergency meeting to consider the regional implications of the spread of Severe Acute Respiratory Syndrome (SARS), a previously unknown atypical pneumonia. In November of that year SAARC ministers of health determined to establish a regional surveillance and rapid reaction system for managing health crises and natural disasters. An emergency meeting of health and agriculture and livestock ministers was convened in New Delhi, India, in January 2004 to address the spread of Avian Influenza.

In January 1996 the first SAARC Trade Fair was held, in New Delhi, India, to promote intra-SAARC commerce. At the same time SAARC ministers of commerce convened for their first meeting to discuss regional economic co-operation. The sixth trade fair was held in New Delhi, India, in January 2005. A group on customs co-operation was established in 1996 to harmonize trading rules and regulations within the grouping, to simplify trade procedures and to upgrade facilities. In 1999 a regional action plan to harmonize national standards, quality control and measurements came into effect. In August 2001 SAARC commerce ministers met, in New Delhi, to discuss a co-ordinated approach to the World Trade Organization (WTO) negotiations.

A Committee on Economic Co-operation (CEC), comprising senior trade officials of member states, was established in July 1991 to monitor progress concerning trade and economic co-operation issues. In the same year the summit meeting approved the creation of an inter-governmental group to establish a framework for the promotion of specific trade liberalization measures. A SAARC Chamber of Commerce (SCCI) became operational in 1992, with headquarters in Karachi, Pakistan. (The SCCI headquarters were subsequently transferred to Islamabad, Pakistan.) In April 1993 ministers signed a SAARC Preferential Trading Arrangement (SAPTA), which came into effect in December 1995. The 10th summit meeting proposed a series of measures to accelerate progress in the next round of SAPTA trade negotiations, including a reduction in the domestic content requirements of SAPTA's rules of origin, greater tariff concessions on products being actively traded and the removal of certain discriminatory and non-tariff barriers. In December 1995 the Council resolved that the ultimate objective for member states should be the establishment of a South Asian Free Trade Area (SAFTA), superseding SAPTA. An Agreement on SAFTA was signed in January 2004, at the 12th summit, and on 1 January 2006 it entered into force, providing for the phased elimination of tariffs: these were to be reduced to 30% in least developed member countries and to 20% in the others over an initial two-year period, and subsequently to 0–5% over a period of five years. The Agreement established a mechanism for administering SAFTA and for settling disputes at ministerial level.

A SAARC Youth Volunteers Programme (SYVOP) enables young people to work in other member countries in the agriculture and forestry sectors. The Programme is part of a series of initiatives designed to promote intra-regional exchanges and contact. A Youth Awards Scheme to reward outstanding achievements by young people was inaugurated in 1996. Founded in 1987, the SAARC Audio-visual Exchange Programme (SAVE) broadcasts radio and television programmes on social and cultural affairs to all member countries, twice a month, in order to disseminate information about SAARC and its members. SAVE organizes an annual SAARC Telefilm festival. The SAARC Consortium of Open and Distance Learning was established in 2000. A Visa Exemption Scheme, exempting 21 specified categories of person from visa requirements, with the aim of promoting closer regional contact, became operational in March 1992. A SAARC citizens forum promotes interaction among the people of South Asia. In addition, SAARC operates a fellowships, scholarships and chairs scheme and a scheme for the promotion of organized tourism. The 12th SAARC summit meeting designated 2006 as South Asia Tourism Year.

In June 2005 SAARC ministers of the environment met in special session to consider the impact of the devastating earthquake and subsequent massive ocean movements, or tsunamis, that struck in the Indian Ocean at the end of 2004. The meeting reviewed an assessment of the extent of loss and damage in each country, and of the relief and rehabilitation measures being undertaken. Ministers resolved to strengthen early warning and disaster management capabilities in the region, and determined to support the rehabilitation of members' economies, in particular through the promotion of the tourism sector.

From October 2004 SAARC implemented, under supervision from the ADB, a Regional Multimodal Transport Study; this was extended in 2007 to cover Afghanistan. The first South Asia Energy dialogue was convened in March 2007 in New Delhi, India.

At the third SAARC summit, held in Kathmandu in November 1987, member states signed a regional convention on measures to counteract terrorism. The convention, which entered into force in August 1988, commits signatory countries to the extradition or prosecution of alleged terrorists and to the implementation of preventative measures to combat terrorism. Monitoring desks for terrorist and drugs offences have been established to process information relating to those activities. The first SAARC conference on co-operation in police affairs, attended by the heads of the police forces of member states, was held in Colombo in July 1996. The conference discussed the issues of terrorism, organized crime, the extradition of criminals, drugs-trafficking and drug abuse. A convention on narcotic drugs and psychotropic substances was signed during the fifth SAARC summit meeting, held in Malé in 1990. The convention entered into force in September 1993, following its ratification by member states. It is implemented by a co-ordination group of drug law enforcement agencies. At the 11th SAARC summit member states adopted a convention on the prevention of trafficking of women and children for prostitution. The 12th summit adopted an Additional Protocol on Suppression of Terrorism with a view to preventing the financing of terrorist activities.

There is a wide network of SAARC Regional Centres. In 1998 an Agricultural Information Centre was established, in Dhaka, Bangladesh, to serve as a central institution for the dissemination of knowledge and information in the agricultural sector. It maintains a network of centres in each member state, which provide for the efficient exchange of technical information and for strengthening agricultural research. An agreement establishing a Food Security Reserve to meet emergency food requirements was signed in November 1987, and entered into force in August 1988. In 2004 the 12th summit meeting determined to establish a Food Bank incorporating a Food Reserve comprising 241,580 metric tons of wheat and/or rice;

the Food Bank was to act as a regional food security reserve during times of normal food shortages as well as during emergencies. The Intergovernmental Agreement establishing the SAARC Food Bank was signed by leaders attending the 14th summit meeting in April 2007. Other regional institutions include the SAARC Tuberculosis Centre in Thimi, Nepal, which opened in July 1992 with the aim of preventing and reducing the prevalence of the disease in the region through the co-ordination of tuberculosis control programmes, research and training; a SAARC Documentation Centre, established in New Delhi in May 1994; and a SAARC Meteorological Research Centre which opened in Dhaka in January 1995. A Human Resources Development Centre was established in Islamabad, Pakistan in 1999. In January 2004 the summit meeting endorsed the establishment of a Cultural Centre, to be based in Sri Lanka, a Coastal Zone Management Centre, in the Maldives, and an Information Centre in Nepal. In July the Council of Ministers approved the establishment of additional regional centres for forestry, to be based in Bhutan, and for energy, to be located in Pakistan. Regional funds include a SAARC-Japan Special Fund established in September 1993. One-half of the fund's resources, provided by the Japanese Government, was to be used to finance projects identified by Japan, including workshops and cultural events, and one-half was to be used to finance projects identified by SAARC member states. The eighth SAARC summit meeting, held in New Delhi in May 1996, established a South Asian Development Fund, comprising a Fund for Regional Projects, a Regional Fund and a fund for social development and infrastructure building. A meeting of SAARC financial experts, held in September 2005, submitted for further consideration by the Association proposals that the South Asian Development Fund should be replaced by a new SAARC Development Fund (SDF), comprising a Social Window (to finance poverty alleviation projects), an Infrastructure Window (for infrastructure development) and an Economic Window (for non-infrastructure commercial programmes). The meeting also considered the possibility of establishing a South Asian Development Bank. A roadmap for the establishment of the SDF was endorsed by the SAARC Council of Ministers in August 2006, and the first meeting of a newly-constituted SDF Board was convened in February 2007.

SAARC co-operates with other regional and international organizations. In February 1993 SAARC signed a memorandum of understanding with UNCTAD whereby both parties agreed to exchange information on trade control measures, in order to increase transparency and thereby facilitate trade. In February 1994 SAARC signed a framework co-operation agreement with ESCAP to enhance co-operation on development issues through a framework of joint studies, workshops and information exchange. A memorandum of understanding with the European Commission was signed in July 1996. SAARC has also signed co-operation agreements with UNICEF (in 1993), the Asia Pacific Telecommunity (1994), UNDP (1995), UN Drug Progamme (1995), the International Telecommunication Union (1997), the Canadian International Development Agency (1997), WHO (2000), and UNIFEM (2001). An informal dialogue at ministerial level has been conducted with ASEAN and the European Union since 1998. SAARC and WIPO hold regular consultations concerning regional co-operation on intellectual property rights, and regular consultations are convened with the WTO. During 2004 memorandums of understanding were signed with the Joint UN Programme on HIV/AIDS (in April), the UN Population Fund (UNFPA, in June), and with the South Asia Co-operative Environment Programme (SACEP, in July). In September 2005 SAARC hosted the 10th Consultative meeting of executive heads of sub-regional organizations of Asia and the Pacific. SAARC, with ESCAP, was to lead a new joint working group on disaster management.

Finance

The national budgets of member countries provide the resources to finance SAARC activities. The Secretariat's annual budget is shared among member states according to a specified formula.

Publications

SAARC News (3/4 a year).
Other official documents, regional studies, reports.

Regional Apex Bodies

Association of Persons of the Legal Communities of the SAARC Countries (SAARCLAW) : 495 HSIDC, Udyog Vihar Phase V, N. H. 8, Gurgaon 122016, National Capital Region, India;

tel. (124) 4040193; fax (124) 4040194; e-mail info@saarclaw.com; internet www.saarclaw.com; f. 1991; recognized as a SAARC regional apex body in July 1994; aims to enhance exchanges and co-operation amongst the legal communities of the sub-region and to promote the development of law; Pres. Dr ABHISHEK M. SINGHVI; Sec.-Gen. TANIA AMIR.

SAARC Chamber of Commerce and Industry (SCCI): House 397, St 64, I-8/3, Islamabad, Pakistan; tel. (51) 4860611; fax (51) 4860610; e-mail info@saarcchamber.com; internet www.saarcchamber.com; f. 1992; promotes economic and trade co-operation throughout the sub-region and greater interaction between the business communities of member countries; organizes SAARC Economic Co-operation Conferences and Trade Fairs; Pres. TARIQ SAYEED; Dir WAQAR AHMAD.

South Asian Federation of Accountants (SAFA): c/o Institute of Chartered Accountants of India, ICAI Bhavan, POB 7100, Indraprastha Marg, New Delhi 110002, India; tel. (11) 23370195; fax (11) 23379334; e-mail safa@icai.org; internet www.esafa.org; f. 1984; recognized as a SAARC regional apex body in Jan. 2002; aims to develop regional co-ordination for the accountancy profession; Pres. SYED SHABBAR ZAIDI; Sec.-Gen. Dr ASHOK HALDIA.

Other recognized regional bodies include the South Asian Association for Regional Co-operation of Architects, the Association of Management Development Institutions, the SAARC Federation of University Women, the SAARC Association of Town Planners, the SAARC Cardiac Society, the Association of SAARC Speakers and Parliamentarians, the Federation of State Insurance Organizations of SAARC Countries, the Federation of State Insurance Organizations of SAARC Countries, the SAARC Diploma Engineers Forum, the Radiological Society of SAARC Countries, the SAARC Teachers' Federation, the SAARC Surgical Care Society and the Foundation of SAARC Writers and Literature.

SOUTHERN AFRICAN DEVELOPMENT COMMUNITY—SADC

Address: SADC House, Government Enclave, Private Bag 0095, Gaborone, Botswana.

Telephone: 3951863; **fax:** 3972848; **e-mail:** registry@sadc.int; **internet:** www.sadc.int.

The first Southern African Development Co-ordination Conference (SADCC) was held at Arusha, Tanzania, in July 1979, to harmonize development plans and to reduce the region's economic dependence on South Africa. In August 1992 the 10 member countries of the SADCC signed a treaty establishing the Southern African Development Community (SADC), which replaced SADCC. The treaty places binding obligations on member countries, with the aim of promoting economic integration towards a fully developed common market. A tribunal was to be established to arbitrate in the case of disputes between member states arising from the treaty. By September 1993 all of the member states had ratified the treaty; it came into effect in early October. A protocol on the establishment of the long-envisaged SADC tribunal was adopted in 2000. The Protocol on Politics, Defence and Security Co-operation, regulating the structure, operations and functions of the Organ on Politics, Defence and Security, established in June 1996 (see under Regional Security), entered into force in March 2004. A troika system, comprising the current, incoming and outgoing SADC chairmanship, operates at the level of the Summit, Council of Ministers and Standing Committee of Officials, and co-ordinates the Organ on Politics, Defence and Security. Other member states may be co-opted into the troika as required. A system of SADC national committees, comprising representatives of government, civil society and the private sector, oversees the implementation of regional programmes at country level and helps to formulate new regional strategies. In recent years SADC institutions have been undergoing a process of intensive restructuring.

MEMBERS

Angola	Malawi	South Africa
Botswana	Mauritius	Swaziland
Congo, Democratic Republic	Mozambique	Tanzania
	Namibia	Zambia
Lesotho	Seychelles*	Zimbabwe
Madagascar		

* Seychelles, which withdrew from SADC in July 2004, was readmitted to the organization in August 2007.

Organization

(April 2008)

SUMMIT MEETING

The meeting is held at least once a year and is attended by heads of state and government or their representatives. It is the supreme policy-making organ of SADC and is responsible for the appointment of the Executive Secretary. A report on the restructuring of SADC, adopted by an extraordinary summit held in Windhoek, Namibia, in March 2001, recommended that biannual summit meetings should be convened. The most recent summit meeting of heads of state and government was held in Lusaka, Zambia, in August 2007.

COUNCIL OF MINISTERS

Representatives of SADC member countries at ministerial level meet at least once a year.

INTEGRATED COMMITTEE OF MINISTERS

The Integrated Committee of Ministers (ICM), comprising at least two ministers from each member state and responsible to the Council of Ministers, oversees the four priority areas of integration (trade, industry, finance and investment; infrastructure and services; food, agriculture and natural resources; and social and human development and special programmes) and monitors the Directorates that administer these; facilitates the co-ordination and harmonization of cross-sectoral activities; and provides policy guidance to the Secretariat. The ICM also supervises the implementation of the Regional Indicative Strategic Development Plan (RISDP—see below).

STANDING COMMITTEE OF OFFICIALS

The Committee, comprising senior officials, usually from the ministry responsible for economic planning or finance, acts as the technical advisory body to the Council. It meets at least once a year. Members of the Committee also act as a national contact point for matters relating to SADC.

SECRETARIAT

Executive Secretary: TOMÁS AUGUSTO SALOMÃO (Mozambique).

The extraordinary summit held in March 2001 determined that the mandate and resources of the Secretariat should be strengthened. A Department of Strategic Planning, Gender and Development and Policy Harmonization was established, comprising permanently-staffed Directorates covering the four priority areas of integration (see above).

Activities

In July 1979 the first Southern African Development Co-ordination Conference was attended by delegations from Angola, Botswana, Mozambique, Tanzania and Zambia, with representatives from donor governments and international agencies. In April 1980 a regional economic summit conference was held in Lusaka, Zambia, and the Lusaka Declaration, a statement of strategy entitled 'Southern Africa: Towards Economic Liberation', was approved. The members aimed to reduce their dependence on South Africa for rail and air links and port facilities, imports of raw materials and manufactured goods, and the supply of electric power. In 1985, however, an SADCC report noted that since 1980 the region had become still more dependent on South Africa for its trade outlets, and the 1986 summit meeting, although it recommended the adoption of economic sanctions against South Africa, failed to establish a timetable for doing so.

In January 1992 a meeting of the SADCC Council of Ministers approved proposals to transform the organization (by then expanded to include Lesotho, Malawi, Namibia and Swaziland) into a fully integrated economic community, and in August the treaty establishing SADC was signed. An SADC Programme of Action (SPA) was to combine the strategies and objectives of the organization's sectoral programmes. South Africa became a member of SADC in August

1994, thus strengthening the objective of regional co-operation and economic integration. Mauritius became a member in August 1995. In September 1997 SADC heads of state agreed to admit the Democratic Republic of the Congo (DRC) and Seychelles as members of the Community; Seychelles withdrew in July 2004. In August 2005 Madagascar was admitted as a member by SADC heads of state.

A possible merger between SADC and the Preferential Trade Area for Eastern and Southern African States (PTA), which consisted of all the members of SADC apart from Botswana and had similar aims of enhancing economic co-operation, was rejected by SADC's Executive Secretary in January 1993. He denied that the two organizations were duplicating each other's work, as had been suggested. However, concerns of regional rivalry with the PTA's successor, the Common Market for Eastern and Southern Africa (COMESA), persisted. In August 1996 an SADC–COMESA ministerial meeting advocated the continued separate functioning of the two organizations. A programme of co-operation between the secretariats of SADC and COMESA, aimed at reducing all duplication of roles between the two organizations, is under way. A co-ordinating SADC/COMESA task force was established in 2001.

In September 1994 the first conference of ministers of foreign affairs of SADC and the European Union (EU) was held in Berlin, Germany. The two sides agreed to establish working groups to promote closer trade, political, regional and economic co-operation. In particular, a declaration issued from the meeting specified joint objectives, including a reduction of exports of weapons to southern Africa and of the arms trade within the region, promotion of investment in the region's manufacturing sector and support for democracy at all levels. A consultative meeting between representatives of SADC and the EU was held in February 1995, in Lilongwe, Malawi, at which both groupings resolved to strengthen security in the southern African region. A second SADC–EU ministerial conference, held in Namibia in October 1996, endorsed a Regional Indicative Programme (RIP) to enhance co-operation between the two organizations over the next five years. The third ministerial conference took place in Vienna, Austria, in November 1998. In September 1999 SADC signed a co-operation agreement with the US Government, which incorporated measures to promote US investment in the region, and commitments to support HIV/AIDS assessment and prevention programmes and to assist member states to develop environmental protection capabilities. The fourth SADC–EU ministerial conference, convened in Gaborone, Botswana, in November 2000, adopted a joint declaration on the control of small arms and light weapons in the SADC region. The meeting also emphasized that the termination of illicit trading in diamonds would be a major contributory factor in resolving the ongoing conflicts in Angola and the DRC (see below). The fifth SADC–EU ministerial conference was held in Maputo, Mozambique, in November 2002. In July SADC and the EU approved a road map to guide future co-operation, and in October of that year an EU–SADC ministerial 'double troika' meeting took place in The Hague, Netherlands, to mark 10 years of dialogue between the two organizations. At the meeting both SADC and the EU reaffirmed their commitment to reinforcing co-operation with regard to peace and security in Africa. It was agreed to pursue the revitalization within the SADC region of training for peace-keeping, possibly with the support of the RIP and the European Programme for Reconstruction and Development in South Africa.

In July 1996 the SADC Parliamentary Forum was inaugurated, with the aim of promoting democracy, human rights and good governance throughout the region. Membership of the Forum, which is headquartered in Windhoek, Namibia, is open to national parliaments of all SADC countries, and offers fair representation for women. Representatives serve for a period of five years. The Forum receives funds from member parliaments, governments and charitable and international organizations. In September 1997 SADC heads of state endorsed the establishment of the Forum as an autonomous institution. The Forum frequently deploys missions to monitor parliamentary and presidential elections in the region. A regional women's parliamentary caucus was inaugurated in April 2002. In 2005 a training arm of the Forum, the SADC Parliamentary Leadership Centre, was established.

The August 2004 summit meeting of heads of state and government, held in Grand Baie, Mauritius, adopted a new Protocol on Principles and Guide-lines Governing Democratic Elections, which advocated: full participation by citizens in the political process; freedom of association; political tolerance; elections at regular intervals; equal access to the state media for all political parties; equal opportunity to exercise the right to vote and be voted for; independence of the judiciary; impartiality of the electoral institutions; the right to voter education; the respect of election results proclaimed to be free and fair by a competent national electoral authority; and the right to challenge election results as provided for in the law.

At the summit meeting of heads of state and government held in Maseru, Lesotho, in August 2006 a new Protocol on Finance and Investment was adopted. Amendments to SADC protocols on the Tribunal, trade, immunities and privileges, transport, communications and meteorology, energy and mining, combating illicit drugs and education and training were also approved at the meeting. The summit emphasized the need to scale up implementation of the SADC's agenda for integration, identifying the RISDP (see below) and the Strategic Indicative Plan for the Organ (SIPO) as the principal instruments for achieving this objective. In pursuit of this aim, the summit established a task force—comprising ministers responsible for finance, investment, economic development, trade and industry—charged with defining the measures necessary for the eradication of poverty and how their implementation might be accelerated.

The extraordinary summit meeting convened in March 2001 adopted a report detailing recommendations on the restructuring of SADC's institutions, with a view to facilitating the effective application of the objectives of the organization's treaty and of the SPA. During 2001–03 the Community's former system comprising 21 sectors was, accordingly, reorganized under four new directorates: trade, industry, finance and investment; infrastructure and services; food, agriculture and natural resources; and social and human development and special programmes. The directorates are administered from the secretariat in Gaborone, in order to ensure greater efficiency (the previous sectoral system had been decentralized). The report adopted in March 2001 outlined a Common Agenda for the organization, which covered the promotion of poverty reduction measures and of sustainable and equitable socio-economic development, promotion of democratic political values and systems, and the consolidation of peace and security. The extraordinary summit meeting also authorized the establishment of an integrated committee of ministers mandated to formulate a five-year Regional Indicative Strategic Development Plan (RISDP), intended as the key policy framework for managing the SADC Common Agenda. A draft of the RISDP, adopted by the SADC Council of Ministers in March 2003, was approved by the summit meeting convened in Dar es Salaam, Tanzania, in August. In April 2006 SADC adopted the Windhoek Declaration on a new relationship between the Community and its international co-operating partners. The declaration provides a framework for co-operation and dialogue between the SADC and international partners, facilitating the implementation of the SADC Common Agenda.

In 2000s SADC, with other African regional economic communities, was considering a draft protocol on relations between them and the African Union (AU). A high-level meeting concerned with integrating the objectives of the New Partnership for Africa's Development (NEPAD) into SADC's regional programme activities was convened in August 2004. The summit meeting of heads of state and government held in Maseru, Lesotho, in August 2006 determined that an extraordinary session of the SADC Council of Ministers should be convened to develop a common approach towards the issue of Union government. In November of that year, at an EU–SADC ministerial 'double troika' meeting held in Maseru, Lesotho, SADC representatives agreed to the development of institutional support to the member states through the establishment of a Human Rights Commission and a new SADC Electoral Advisory Council (SEAC).

REGIONAL SECURITY

In November 1994 SADC ministers of defence, meeting in Arusha, Tanzania, approved the establishment of a regional rapid-deployment peace-keeping force, which could be used to contain regional conflicts or civil unrest in member states. In April 1997 a training programme was organized in Zimbabwe, which aimed to inform troops from nine SADC countries of UN peace-keeping doctrines, procedures and strategies. A peace-keeping exercise involving 4,000 troops was held in South Africa, in April 1999. A further SADC peace-keeping exercise was conducted in February 2002 in Tanzania, jointly with Tanzanian and Ugandan forces. An SADC Mine Action Committee has been established to monitor and co-ordinate the process of removing anti-personnel land devices from countries in the region. The summit meeting of heads of state and government held in August 2007 authorized the establishment of the SADC Standby Brigade (SADCBRIG), with the aim of ensuring collective regional security and stability.

In June 1996 SADC heads of state and government, meeting in Gaborone, Botswana, inaugurated an Organ on Politics, Defence and Security (OPDS), with the aim of enhancing co-ordination of national policies and activities in these areas. The stated objectives of the body were, *inter alia*, to safeguard the people and development of the region against instability arising from civil disorder, inter-state conflict and external aggression; to undertake conflict prevention, management and resolution activities, by mediating in inter-state and intra-state disputes and conflicts, pre-empting conflicts through an early-warning system and using diplomacy and peace-keeping to achieve sustainable peace; to promote the development of a common foreign policy, in areas of mutual interest, and the evolution of common political institutions; to develop close co-operation between the police and security services of the region; and to encourage the observance of universal human rights, as provided for in the charters of the UN and the Organization of African Unity (OAU—now AU). In August 2000 proposals were announced (strongly supported by South Africa) to develop the OPDS as a substructure of SADC, with subdivisions for defence and international diplomacy, to be chaired by a member country's head of state, working within a troika system; these were approved at the extraordinary summit held in March 2001. A Protocol on Politics, Defence and Security Co-operation—to be implemented by an Inter-state Politics and Diplomacy Committee—regulating the structure, operations and functions of the Organ, was adopted and opened for signature in August and entered into force in March 2004.

The March 2001 extraordinary SADC summit adopted a Declaration on Small Arms, promoting the curtailment of the proliferation of and illicit trafficking in light weapons in the region. A Protocol on the Control of Firearms, Ammunition and Other Related Materials was adopted in August of that year. In July SADC ministers of defence approved a draft regional defence pact, providing for a mechanism to prevent conflict involving member countries and for member countries to unite against outside aggression. In January 2002 an extraordinary summit of SADC heads of state, held in Blantyre, Malawi, adopted a Declaration against Terrorism.

In September 1998 SADC chiefs of staff agreed that the Community should assist the Angolan Government to eliminate the UNITA movement, owing to its adverse impact on the region's security. In August 2001 SADC heads of state resolved to support the continuing imposition of sanctions by the UN Security Council against the UNITA rebels in Angola; it was agreed to promote the international certification system for illicit trade in rough diamonds (believed to finance UNITA's activities), to install mobile radar systems that would detect illegal cross-border flights in the region, and to establish a body to compile information and to devise a strategy for terminating the supply of petroleum products to UNITA. SADC welcomed the cease-fire that was signed by the Angolan Government and UNITA in April 2002; all UN sanctions against UNITA were withdrawn by December.

From 1998 SADC member states were concerned with the political situation and escalation of civil conflict in the DRC and the threat to regional security posed by the presence of Rwandan and Ugandan troops in that country assisting anti-government forces. In August, following a request from then President Laurent Kabila of the DRC for SADC assistance, the ministers of defence of Angola, Namibia and Zimbabwe, meeting in Harare, Zimbabwe, determined actively to support the DRC administration by immediately sending troops and military equipment to that country. Subsequently, Rwandan and allied rebel forces withdrew to eastern DRC, maintaining control over large areas of that region. In mid-September the SADC summit of heads of state and government issued a communiqué that recognized the legitimacy of the pro-Kabila intervention. Meanwhile, SADC member states, with the OAU and UN, participated in negotiations on resolving the conflict. In June 1999 SADC ministers of defence and of foreign affairs convened in Lusaka, Zambia, with the aim of securing a cease-fire agreement. An accord was finally signed in July between President Kabila of the DRC, leaders of the rebel forces, and foreign allies of both sides. All foreign troops were to be withdrawn within nine months according to a schedule to be drawn up by the UN, OAU and a Joint Military Commission, and a UN peace-keeping force was to be deployed to the DRC (consequently, in November, the UN Security Council authorized the establishment of the UN Mission in the Democratic Republic of the Congo—MONUC). However, the disengagement and redeployment of troops from front-line positions did not commence until February 2001. In October 2001 the Inter-Congolese Dialogue on negotiating a peaceful outcome to conflict began in Addis Ababa, Ethiopia, under the auspices of former President Ketumile Masire of Botswana; the Dialogue was reconvened during February–April 2002 and in October–December of that year, in South Africa. The Pretoria Accord, an inclusive powersharing agreement, was signed by the participants in the Dialogue in mid-December, and was ratified by all parties in April 2003. Rwandan troops were officially withdrawn from the DRC in October 2002; the Angolan, Namibian, and Zimbabwean troops were withdrawn by the end of December; and the Ugandan forces by May 2003. President Joseph Kabila of the DRC (who had superseded his father upon the assassination of the latter in January 2001) established a transitional government in July 2003. Despite the official cease-fire, conflict remained endemic during the mid-2000s in eastern DRC, where Rwandan Hutu militiamen and rival Rwanda- and Uganda-supported rebel groups continued to operate illegally. In June 2004 SADC sent a fact-finding mission to the DRC to investigate the continuing armed military activities. SADC Parliamentary Forum observers monitored the legislative and a first stage of presidential elections that were held in the DRC in July 2006 and the second stage of presidential elections, held in October; following the latter, Joseph Kabila was inaugurated as elected President in December.

An extraordinary SADC summit meeting convened in March 2007, in Dar es Salaam, Tanzania, mandated the OPDS to assess the political and security situations in the DRC and Lesotho (see below). The ministerial committee of the OPDS troika stressed to the summit the need for SADC support to the post-conflict-reconstruction process in the DRC. An extraordinary meeting of the ministerial committee of the OPDS troika convened in October of that year resolved to mobilize humanitarian assistance for eastern areas of the DRC in view of a recent escalation in violent unrest there, with a particular focus on assisting internally displaced civilians.

In September 1998 SADC representatives attempted to mediate between government and opposition parties in Lesotho amidst a deteriorating security situation in that country. At the end of the month, following an attempt by the Lesotho military to seize power, South Africa, together with Botswana, sent troops into Lesotho to restore civil order. The operation, which was declared to have been conducted under SADC auspices, prompted widespread criticism owing to the troops' involvement in heavy fighting with opposition forces. A committee was established by SADC to secure a cease-fire in Lesotho. In October an SADC ministerial team, comprising representatives of South Africa, Botswana, Mozambique and Zimbabwe, negotiated an accord between the opposing sides in Lesotho providing for the conduct of democratic elections. The withdrawal of foreign troops from Lesotho was initiated at the end of April 1999, and was reported to have been completed by mid-May.

In April 2007 the OPDS ministerial troika, in respect of a mandate issued by the extraordinary SADC summit convened in Dar es Salaam in the previous month, issued an assessment report on the *impasse* between the ruling party, opposition parties and other stakeholders following unsatisfactory legislative elections held in February of that year. In mid-June an eminent person mission aimed at facilitating the post-electoral political dialogue in Lesotho was inaugurated, on the recommendation of the assessment report.

In August 2001 SADC established a task force, comprising representatives of five member countries, to address the ongoing political crisis in Zimbabwe. The Community sent two separate observer teams to monitor the controversial presidential election held in Zimbabwe in March 2002; the SADC Council of Ministers team found the election to have been conducted freely and fairly, while the Parliamentary Forum group was reluctant to endorse the poll. Having evaluated both reports, the Community approved the election. An SADC Council of Ministers group was convened to observe the parliamentary elections held in Zimbabwe in March 2005; however, the Zimbabwean Government refused to invite a delegation from the SADC Parliamentary Forum. The Zimbabwean Government claimed to have enacted electoral legislation in accordance with the provisions of the August 2004 SADC Protocol on Principles and Guide-lines Governing Democratic Elections (see above). The extraordinary summit meeting of SADC heads of state and government, convened in Dar es Salaam, Tanzania, in March 2007, to address the political, economic, and security situation in the region, declared 'solidarity with the government and people of Zimbabwe' and mandated President Thabo Mbeki of South Africa to facilitate dialogue between the Zimbabwean government and opposition. Mbeki reported to the ordinary SADC summit held in August of that year that restoring Zimbabwe's capacity to generate foreign exchange through balance-of-payments support would be of pivotal importance in promoting economic recovery and that the SADC should assist Zimbabwe with addressing the issue of international sanctions.

In early March 2008 an SADC election observer team was sent to monitor preparations for and the conduct of presidential and national and local legislative elections that were staged in Zimbabwe at the end of that month. In mid-April, at which time the Zimbabwe Electoral Commission had failed to declare the results of the presidential election, prompting widespread international criticism, the SADC convened an extraordinary summit to address the electoral outcome. The OPDS presented to the summit a report by the observer team on the presidential and legislative elections which claimed that the electoral process had been acceptable to all parties. The summit urged the Zimbabwe Electoral Commission to verify and release the results of the elections without further delay and requested President Mbeki of South Africa to continue in his role as facilitator of dialogue with the Zimbabwe authorities.

TRADE, INDUSTRY AND INVESTMENT

Under the treaty establishing SADC, efforts were to be undertaken to achieve regional economic integration. The Directorate of Trade, Industry, Finance and Investment aims to facilitate such integration, and poverty eradication, through the creation of an enabling investment and trade environment in SADC countries. Objectives include the establishment of a single regional market; the progressive removal of barriers to the movement of goods, services and people; and the promotion of cross-border investment. SADC supports programmes for industrial research and development and standardization and quality assurance, and aims to mobilize industrial investment resources and to co-ordinate economic policies and the development of the financial sector. In August 1996, at a summit meeting held in Lesotho, SADC member states signed the Protocol on Trade, providing for the establishment of a regional Free Trade Area, through the gradual elimination of tariff barriers (with an eight-year implementation schedule envisaged at that time). (Angola and the DRC are not signatories to the Protocol.) In October 1999 representatives of the private sector in SADC member states established the Association of SADC Chambers of Commerce, based in Mauritius. The Protocol on Trade entered into force in January 2000, and an Amendment Protocol on Trade came into force in August, incorporating renegotiated technical details on the gradual elimination of tariffs, rules of origin, customs co-operation, special industry arrangements and dispute settlement procedures. The implementation phase of the Protocol on Trade commenced in September. In accordance with a revised schedule, some 85% of intra-SADC trade tariffs were withdrawn by 1 January 2008, when the SADC Free Trade Area entered into force. The remaining intra-SADC trade tariffs were to be removed by 2012. According to the schedule, reaffirmed at the EU–SADC ministerial meeting in 2006, an SADC customs union was to be implemented by 2010, a common market by 2015, monetary union by 2016, and a single currency was to be introduced by 2018. Annual meetings are convened to review the work of expert teams in the areas of standards, quality, assurance, accreditation and metrology. At an SADC Extraordinary Summit convened in October 2006 it was determined that a roadmap was to be developed to facilitate the process of establishing a customs union.

The mining sector contributes about 10% of the SADC region's annual GDP. The principal objective of SADC's programme of action on mining is to stimulate increased local and foreign investment in the sector, through the assimilation and dissemination of data, prospecting activities, and participation in promotional fora. In December 1994 SADC held a mining forum, jointly with the EU, in Lusaka, Zambia, with the aim of demonstrating to potential investors and promoters the possibilities of mining exploration in the region. A second mining investment forum was held in Lusaka in December 1998; and a third ('Mines 2000'), also in Lusaka, in October 2000. Subsequently a Mines 2000 follow-up programme has been implemented. Other objectives of the mining sector are the improvement of industry training, increasing the contribution of small-scale mining, reducing the illicit trade in gemstones and gold, increasing co-operation in mineral exploration and processing, and minimizing the adverse impact of mining operations on the environment. In February 2000 a Protocol on Mining entered into force, providing for the harmonization of policies and programmes relating to the development and exploitation of mineral resources in the region. SADC supports the Kimberley Process Certification Scheme aimed at preventing illicit trade in illegally mined rough diamonds. (The illicit trade in so-called 'conflict diamonds' and other minerals is believed to have motivated and financed many incidences of rebel activity in the continent, for example in Angola and the DRC.)

In July 1998 a Banking Association was officially constituted by representatives of SADC member states. The Association was to establish international banking standards and regional payments systems, organize training and harmonize banking legislation in the region. In April 1999 governors of SADC central banks determined to strengthen and harmonize banking procedures and technology in order to facilitate the financial integration of the region. Efforts to harmonize stock exchanges in the region were also initiated in 1999.

The summit meeting of heads of state and government held in Maseru, Lesotho, in August 2006 adopted a new Protocol on Finance and Investment. The document, regarded as constituting the main framework for economic integration in southern Africa, outlined, *inter alia*, how the region intends to proceed towards monetary union by 2010 and was intended to complement the ongoing implementation of the SADC Protocol on Trade and targets contained in the RISDP.

INFRASTRUCTURE AND SERVICES

The Directorate of Infrastructure and Services focuses on transport, communications and meteorology, energy, tourism and water. At SADC's inception transport was regarded as the most important area to be developed, on the grounds that, as the Lusaka Declaration noted, without the establishment of an adequate regional transport and communications system, other areas of co-operation become impractical. Priority was to be given to the improvement of road and railway services into Mozambique, so that the land-locked countries of the region could transport their goods through Mozambican ports instead of South African ones. The Southern African Transport and Communications Commission (SATCC) was established, in Maputo, Mozambique, in order to undertake SADC's activities in this sector. During 1995 the SATCC undertook a study of regional transport and communications to provide a comprehensive framework and strategy for future courses of action. A task force was also established to identify measures to simplify procedures at border crossings throughout southern Africa. In 1996 the SATCC Road Network Management and Financing Task Force was established. An SADC Transport Investment Forum was convened in Windhoek, Namibia, in April 2001. In March the Association of Southern African National Road Agencies (ASANRA) was established to foster the development of an integrated regional transportation system. Eleven railways in the region form the Interconnected Regional Rail Network (IRRN), comprising nearly 34,000 km of route track.

SADC development projects have aimed to address missing links and over-stretched sections of the regional network, as well as to improve efficiency, operational co-ordination and human resource development, such as management training projects. Other objectives have been to ensure the compatibility of technical systems within the region and to promote the harmonization of regulations relating to intra-regional traffic and trade. In 1997 Namibia announced plans, supported by SADC, to establish a rail link with Angola in order to form a trade route similar to that created in Mozambique, on the western side of southern Africa. In March 1998 the final stage of the trans-Kalahari highway, linking ports on the east and west coasts of southern Africa, was officially opened. In July 1999 a 317-km rail link between Bulawayo, Zimbabwe, and the border town of Beitbridge, administered by SADC as its first build-operate-transfer project, was opened. SADC promotes greater co-operation in the civil aviation sector, in order to improve efficiency and to reverse a steady decline in the region's airline industries. Within the telecommunications sector efforts have been made to increase the capacity of direct exchange lines and international subscriber dialling (ISD) services. In January 1997 the Southern African Telecommunications Regional Authority (SATRA), a regulatory authority, was established.

The SADC's road network, whose length totals more than 1m. km, constitutes the regions's principal mode of transport for both freight and passengers and is thus vital to the economy. Unsurfaced, low-volume roads account for a substantial proportion of the network and many of these are being upgraded to a sealed standard as part of a wider strategy that focuses on the alleviation of poverty and the pursuit of economic growth and development.

SADC policy guide-lines on 'making information and communications technology a priority in turning SADC into an information-based economy' were adopted in November 2001. Policy guide-lines and model regulations on tariffs for telecommunications services have also been adopted. An SADC Expedited Mail Service operates in the postal services sector.

The SADC Drought Monitoring Centre organizes an annual Southern African Regional Climate Outlook Forum (SARCOF), which assesses seasonal weather prospects.

Areas of activity in the energy sector include: joint petroleum exploration, training programmes for the petroleum sector and studies for strategic fuel storage facilities; promotion of the use of coal; development of hydroelectric power and the co-ordination of SADC generation and transmission capacities; new and renewable sources of energy, including pilot projects in solar energy; assessment of the environmental and socio-economic impact of wood-fuel scarcity and relevant education programmes; and energy conservation. In July 1995 SADC energy ministers approved the establishment of the Southern African Power Pool, whereby all member states were to be linked into a single electricity grid. (Several grids are already integrated and others are being rehabilitated.) At the same time, ministers endorsed a protocol to promote greater co-operation in energy development within SADC, providing for the establishment of an Energy Commission, responsible for 'demand-side' management, pricing, ensuring private-sector involvement and competition, training and research, collecting information, etc.; the protocol entered into force in September 1998. SADC implements a Petroleum Exploration Programme. In September 1997 heads of state endorsed an Energy Action Plan to proceed with the implementation of co-operative policies and strategies in four key areas of energy: trade, information exchange, training and organizational capacity-building, and investment and financing. A technical unit of the Energy Commission was to be responsible for implementation of the Action Plan. Two major regional energy supply projects were under development in the mid-2000s: utilities from Angola, Botswana, the DRC, Namibia and South Africa were participating in the Western Power Corridor project, approved in October 2002, and a feasibility study was initiated in 2003 for a planned Zambia–Tanzania Inter-connector Project.

The tourism sector operates within the context of national and regional socio-economic development objectives. It comprises four components: tourism product development; tourism marketing and research; tourism services; and human resources development and training. SADC has promoted tourism for the region at trade fairs in Europe, and has initiated a project to provide a range of promotional material and a regional tourism directory. In 1993 the Council approved the implementation of a project to design a standard grading classification system for tourist accommodation in the region, which had been completed with the assistance of the World Tourism Organization. In September 1997 the legal charter for the establishment of a new Regional Tourism Organization for Southern Africa (RETOSA), to be administered jointly by SADC officials and private-sector operators, was signed by ministers of tourism. RETOSA assists member states to formulate tourism promotion policies and strategies. During 1999 a feasibility study on the development of the Upper Zambezi basin as a site for eco-tourism was initiated. Consultations are under way on the development of a common visa (UNIVISA) system to promote tourism in the region. By February 2007 several countries, including Mozambique, South Africa and Swaziland, had abolished visa requirements for citizens of other SADC member states. Preparations for the introduction of the UNIVISA were being undertaken across the region; it was anticipated that the common visa would be in place by 2008, in advance of the 2010 FIFA World Cup, to be hosted by South Africa.

SADC aims to promote equitable distribution and effective management of water resources. A Protocol on Shared Watercourse Systems entered into force in April 1998, and a Revised Protocol on Shared Watercourses came into force in September 2003. A regional strategic action plan for integrated water resources development and management in the SADC region was launched in 1999.

FOOD, AGRICULTURE AND NATURAL RESOURCES

The Directorate of Food, Agriculture and Natural Resources aims to develop, co-ordinate and harmonize policies and programmes on agriculture and natural resources with a focus on sustainability. The Directorate covers the following sectors: agricultural research and training; inland fisheries; forestry; wildlife; marine fisheries and resources; food security; livestock production and animal disease control; and environment and land management. According to SADC figures, agriculture contributes one-third of the region's GNP, accounts for about one-quarter of total earnings of foreign exchange and employs some 80% of the labour force. The principal objectives in this field are regional food security, agricultural development and natural resource development.

The Southern African Centre for Co-operation in Agricultural Research (SACCAR), was established in Gaborone, Botswana, in 1985. It aims to strengthen national agricultural research systems, in order to improve management, increase productivity, promote the development and transfer of technology to assist local farmers, and improve training. Examples of activity include: a sorghum and millet improvement programme; a land and water management research programme; a root crop research network; agroforestry research, implemented in Malawi, Tanzania, Zambia and Zimbabwe; and a grain legume improvement programme, comprising separate research units for groundnuts, beans and cowpeas. SADC's Plant Genetic Resources Centre, based near Lusaka, Zambia, aims to collect, conserve and utilize indigenous and exotic plant genetic resources and to develop appropriate management practices. In 2003 an SADC fact-finding mission on genetically modified organisms (GMOs) visited Belgium and the USA and made a number of recommendations for consideration by a newly-established advisory committee on biosafety and biotechnology based at the SADC Secretariat; the recommendations were endorsed by senior officials of ministries of agriculture in June. SADC member states were to develop national legislation on GMOs by the end of 2004.

SADC aims to promote inland and marine fisheries as an important, sustainable source of animal protein. Marine fisheries are also considered to be a potential source of income of foreign exchange. In May 1993 the first formal meeting of SADC ministers of marine fisheries convened in Namibia, and it was agreed to hold annual meetings. Meeting in May 2002 marine fisheries ministers expressed concern about alleged ongoing illegal, unregulated and unreported (IUU) fisheries activities in regional waters. The development of fresh water fisheries is focused on aquaculture projects, and their integration into rural community activities. The SADC Fisheries Protocol entered into force in September 2003. Environment and land management activities have an emphasis on sustainability as an essential quality of development. SADC aims to protect and improve the health, environment and livelihoods of people living in the southern African region; to preserve the natural heritage and biodiversity of the region; and to support regional economic development on a sustainable basis. There is also a focus on capacity-building, training, regional co-operation and the exchange of information in all areas related to the environment and land management. SADC operates an Environmental Exchange Network and implements a Land Degradation and Desertification Control Programme. Projects on the conservation and sustainable development of forestry and wildlife are under implementation. An SADC Protocol on Forestry was signed in October 2002, and in November 2003 the Protocol on Wildlife Conservation and Law Enforcement entered into force.

Under the food security programme, the Regional Early Warning Unit aims to anticipate and prevent food shortages through the provision of information relating to the food security situation in member states. As a result of frequent drought crises, SADC member states have agreed to inform the food security sector of their food and non-food requirements on a regular basis, in order to assess the needs of the region as a whole. A Regional Food Reserve Facility is to be developed. A programme on irrigation development and water management aims to reduce regional dependency on rain-fed agricultural production, while a programme on the promotion of agricultural trade and food safety aims to increase intra-regional and inter-regional trade with a view to improving agriculture growth and rural incomes. An SADC extraordinary summit on agriculture and food security, held in May 2004 in Dar es Salaam, Tanzania, considered strategies for accelerating development in the agricultural sector and thereby securing food security and reducing poverty in the region.

The sector for livestock production and animal disease control has aimed to improve breeding methods in the region through the Management of Farm Animal Genetic Research Programme. It also seeks to control diseases such as contagious bovine pleuropneumonia, foot-and-mouth disease and African swine fever through diagnosis, monitoring and vaccination programmes. An *Animal Health Mortality Bulletin* is published, as is a monthly *Animal Disease Situation Bulletin*, which alerts member states to outbreaks of disease in the region. An SADC regional foot-and-mouth disease policy was being formulated in the mid-2000s.

SOCIAL AND HUMAN DEVELOPMENT AND SPECIAL PROGRAMMES

SADC helps to supply the region's requirements in skilled manpower by providing training in the following categories: high-level managerial personnel; agricultural managers; high- and medium-level technicians; artisans; and instructors. The Technical Committee on Accreditation and Certification aims to harmonize and strengthen the education and training systems in SADC through initiatives such as the standardization of curricula and examinations. Human resources development activities focus on determining active labour market information systems and institutions in the region, improving education policy analysis and formulation, and addressing issues of teaching and learning materials in the region. SADC administers an Intra-regional Skills Development Programme. SADC has initiated a programme of distance education to enable greater access to education, and operates a scholarship and training awards programme. In September 1997 heads of state, meeting in Blantyre, Malawi, endorsed the establishment of a Gender Department within the Secretariat to promote the advancement and education of women. A Declaration on Gender and Development was adopted. At the same time representatives of all member countries (except Angola) signed a Protocol on Education and Training, which was to provide a legal framework for co-operation in this sector; this entered into force in July 2000. In 2001 a gender audit study of aspects of the SADC SPA was finalized. An SADC regional human development report for 2000 was published in 2001 by UNDP and the Southern African Regional Institute for Policy Studies. An SADC Protocol on Combating Illicit Drugs entered into force in March 1999. In October 2000 an SADC Epidemiological Network on Drug Use was established to enable the systematic collection of narcotics-related data. SADC operates a regional drugs control programme, funded by the EU. In February 2007 a task force was mandated to investigate measures for improving employment conditions in member countries. The formulation of an SADC Protocol on Gender Equality has been under development.

In August 1999 an SADC Protocol on Health was adopted. SADC has adopted a strategic framework (most recently covering the period 2004–07) and programme of action for tackling HIV/AIDS, which are endemic in the region. In December 1999 a multisectoral subcommittee on HIV/AIDS was established. In August 2000 SADC adopted a set of guide-lines to underpin any future negotiations with major pharmaceutical companies on improving access to and reducing the cost of drugs to combat HIV/AIDS. In July 2003 an SADC special summit on HIV/AIDS, convened in Maseru, Lesotho, and attended by representatives of the World Bank, UNAIDS and WHO, issued the Maseru Declaration on HIV/AIDS, identifying priority areas for action, including prevention, access to testing and treatment, and social mobilization. The implementation of the strategic framework and Maseru Declaration were to be co-ordinated through an SADC Business Plan on HIV/AIDS, which was to focus on harmonizing regional guide-lines on mother-to-child transmission and anti-retroviral therapy; and to address issues relating to access to affordable essential drugs, including bulk procurement and regional production. A Forum for the directors of the SADC national AIDS authorities and an SADC Regional HIV/AIDS Partnership Forum meet regularly to address the regional HIV/AIDS situation. An SADC Protocol on Sexually Transmitted Infections Treatment and a regional policy on Orphans and Vulnerable Children have been under development. SADC is implementing a Southern African Tuberculosis Control Initiative (SATCI); the office of SATCI TB/HIV Co-ordinator was inaugurated in February 2001. In May 2000 an SADC Malaria Task Force was established.

SADC seeks to promote employment and harmonize legislation concerning labour and social protection. Activities include: the implementation of International Labour Standards, the improvement of health and safety standards in the workplace, combating child labour and the establishment of a statistical database for employment and labour issues.

Following the ratification of the treaty establishing the Community, regional socio-cultural development was to be emphasized as part of the process of greater integration. The SADC Press Trust was established, in Harare, Zimbabwe, to disseminate information about SADC and to articulate the concerns and priorities of the region. Public education initiatives have commenced to encourage the involvement of people in the process of regional integration and development, as well as to promote democratic and human rights' values. In 1994 the SADC Festival on Arts and Culture project was initiated. Interdisciplinary and monodisciplinary festivals are alternated on a two-yearly basis. The following monodisciplinary festivals are planned: theatre (in 2008) and visual arts (2012). An SADC Cultural Fund was established in 1996. A draft SADC protocol on piracy and protection of copyright and neighbouring rights has been prepared.

Finance

SADC's administrative budget for 2007/08 amounted to US $18.9m., to be financed mainly by contributions from member states.

Publications

Quarterly Food Security Bulletin.
SACCAR Newsletter (quarterly).
SADC Annual Report.
SADC Energy Bulletin.
SADC Today (six a year).
SATCC Bulletin (quarterly).
SKILLS.
SPLASH.

SOUTHERN COMMON MARKET—MERCOSUR/MERCOSUL

(MERCADO COMÚN DEL SUR/MERCADO COMUM DO SUL)

Address: Edif. Mercosur, Luis Piera 1992, 1°, 11200 Montevideo, Uruguay.
Telephone: (2) 412-9024; **fax:** (2) 418-0557; **e-mail:** secretaria@mercosur.org.uy; **internet:** www.mercosur.int/msweb.

Mercosur (known as Mercosul in Portuguese) was established in March 1991 by the heads of state of Argentina, Brazil, Paraguay and Uruguay with the signature of the Treaty of Asunción. The primary objective of the Treaty is to achieve the economic integration of member states by means of a free flow of goods and services between member states, the establishment of a common external tariff, the adoption of common commercial policy, and the co-ordination of macroeconomic and sectoral policies. The Ouro Preto Protocol, which was signed in December 1994, conferred on Mercosur the status of an international legal entity with the authority to sign agreements with third countries, groups of countries and international organizations.

MEMBERS

Argentina   Brazil   Paraguay   Uruguay

Note: Venezuela was admitted as a full member of Mercosur in July 2006, pending ratification by each country's legislature. Bolivia, Chile, Colombia, Ecuador and Peru are associate members.

Organization

(April 2008)

COMMON MARKET COUNCIL

The Common Market Council (Consejo del Mercado Común) is the highest organ of Mercosur and is responsible for leading the integration process and for taking decisions in order to achieve the objectives of the Asunción Treaty.

COMMON MARKET GROUP

The Common Market Group (Grupo Mercado Común) is the executive body of Mercosur and is responsible for implementing concrete measures to further the integration process.

TRADE COMMISSION

The Trade Commission (Comisión de Comercio del Mercosur) has competence for the area of joint commercial policy and, in particular, is responsible for monitoring the operation of the common external tariff (see below). The Brasília Protocol may be referred to for the resolution of trade disputes between member states.

JOINT PARLIAMENTARY COMMISSION

The Joint Parliamentary Commission (Comisión Parlamentaria Conjunta) is made up of parliamentarians from the member states and is charged with accelerating internal national procedures to implement Mercosur decisions, including the harmonization of country legislation.

CONSULTATIVE ECONOMIC AND SOCIAL FORUM

The Consultative Economic and Social Forum (Foro Consultivo Económico-Social) comprises representatives from the business community and trade unions in the member countries and has a consultative role in relation to Mercosur.

ADMINISTRATIVE SECRETARIAT

Director: Dr José Manuel Quijano (Uruguay).

Activities

Mercosur's free trade zone entered into effect on 1 January 1995, with tariffs removed from 85% of intra-regional trade. A regime of gradual removal of duties on a list of special products was agreed, with Argentina and Brazil given four years to complete this process while Paraguay and Uruguay were allowed five years. Regimes governing intra-zonal trade in the automobile and sugar sectors remained to be negotiated. Mercosur's customs union also came into force at the start of 1995, comprising a common external tariff (CET) of 0%–20%. A list of exceptions from the CET was also agreed; these products were to lose their special status and were to be subject to the general tariff system concerning foreign goods by 2006.

In December 1995 Mercosur presidents affirmed the consolidation of free trade as Mercosur's 'permanent and most urgent goal'. To this end they agreed to prepare norms of application for Mercosur's customs code, accelerate paper procedures and increase the connections between national computerized systems. It was also agreed to increase co-operation in the areas of agriculture, industry, mining, energy, communications, transport and tourism, and finance. At this meeting Argentina and Brazil reached an accord aimed at overcoming their dispute regarding the trade in automobiles between the two countries. They agreed that cars should have a minimum of 60% domestic components and that Argentina should be allowed to complete its balance of exports of cars to Brazil, which had earlier imposed a unilateral quota on the import of Argentine cars. In June 1995 Mercosur ministers responsible for the environment agreed to harmonize environmental legislation and to form a permanent sub-group of Mercosur

In May 1996 Mercosur parliamentarians met with the aim of harmonizing legislation on patents in member countries. In December Mercosur heads of state, meeting in Fortaleza, Brazil, approved agreements on harmonizing competition practices (by 2001), integrating educational opportunities for post-graduates and human resources training, standardizing trading safeguards applied against third-country products (by 2001) and providing for intra-regional cultural exchanges. An Accord on Sub-regional Air Services was signed at the meeting (including by the heads of state of Bolivia and Chile) to liberalize civil transport throughout the region. In addition, the heads of state endorsed texts on consumer rights that were to be incorporated into a Mercosur Consumers' Defence Code.

In June 1996 the Joint Parliamentary Commission agreed that Mercosur should endorse a 'Democratic Guarantee Clause', whereby a country would be prevented from participation in Mercosur unless democratic, accountable institutions were in place. The clause was adopted by Mercosur heads of state at the summit meeting held in San Luis de Mendoza, Argentina, later in the month. The presidents approved the entry into Mercosur of Bolivia and Chile as associate members. An Economic Complementation Accord with Bolivia, which includes Bolivia in Mercosur's free trade zone, but not in the customs union, was signed in December 1995 and was to come into force on 1 January 1997. In December 1996 the Accord was extended until 30 April 1997, when a free trade zone between Bolivia and Mercosur was to become operational. Measures of the free trade agreement, which was signed in October 1996, were to be implemented over a transitional period commencing on 28 February 1997 (revised from 1 January). Chile's Economic Complementation Accord with Mercosur entered into effect on 1 October 1996, with duties on most products to be removed over a 10-year period (Chile's most sensitive products were given 18 years for complete tariff elimination). Chile was also to remain outside the customs union, but was to be involved in other integration projects, in particular infrastructure projects designed to give Mercosur countries access to both the Atlantic and Pacific Oceans (Chile's Pacific coast was regarded as Mercosur's potential link to the economies of the Far East).

In June 1997 the first meeting of tax administrators and customs officials of Mercosur member countries was held, with the aim of enhancing information exchange and promoting joint customs inspections. During 1997 Mercosur's efforts towards regional economic integration were threatened by Brazil's adverse external trade balance and its Government's measures to counter the deficit, which included the imposition of import duties on certain products. In November the Brazilian Government announced that it was to increase its import tariff by 3%, in a further effort to improve its external balance. The measure was endorsed by Argentina as a means of maintaining regional fiscal stability. The new external tariff, which was to remain in effect until 31 December 2000, was formally adopted by Mercosur heads of state at a meeting held in Montevideo, Uruguay, in December 1997. At the summit meeting a separate Protocol was signed providing for the liberalization of trade in services and government purchases over a 10-year period. In order to strengthen economic integration throughout the region, Mercosur leaders agreed that Chile, while still not a full member of the organization, should be integrated into the Mercosur political structure, with equal voting rights. In December 1998 Mercosur heads of state agreed on the establishment of an arbitration mechanism for disputes between members, and on measures to standardize human, animal and plant health and safety regulations throughout the grouping. In March 1998 the ministers of the interior of Mercosur countries, together with representatives of the Governments of Chile and Bolivia, agreed to implement a joint security arrangement for the border region linking Argentina, Paraguay and Brazil. In particular, the initiative aimed to counter drugs-trafficking, money-laundering and other illegal activities in the area.

Tensions within Mercosur were compounded in January 1999 owing to economic instability in Brazil and its Government's decision effectively to devalue the national currency, the real. In March the grouping's efforts at integration were further undermined by political instability in Paraguay. As a consequence of the devaluation of its currency, Brazil's important automotive industry became increasingly competitive, to the detriment of that of Argentina. Argentina imposed tariffs on imports of Brazilian steel and demanded some form of temporary safeguards on certain products as compensation for their perceived loss of competitiveness resulting from the devalued real. An extraordinary meeting of the Common Market Council was convened, at Brazil's request, in August, in order to discuss the dispute, as well as measures to mitigate the effects of economic recession throughout the sub-region. However, little progress was made and the bilateral trade dispute continued to undermine Mercosur's integration objectives. Argentina imposed new restrictions on textiles and footwear, while, in September, Brazil withdrew all automatic import licences for Argentine products, which were consequently to be subject to the same quality control, sanitary measures and accounting checks applied to imports from non-Mercosur countries. In January 2000, however, the Argentine and Brazilian Governments agreed to refrain from adopting potentially divisive unilateral measures and resolved to accelerate negotiations on the resolution of ongoing differences. In March Mercosur determined to promote and monitor private accords to cover the various areas of contention, and also established a timetable for executing a convergence of regional macroeconomic policies. In June Argentina and Brazil signed a bilateral automobile agreement. The motor vehicle agreement, incorporating new tariffs and a nationalization index, was endorsed by all Mercosur leaders at a meeting convened in Florianopolis, Brazil, in December. The significant outcome of that meeting was the approval of criteria, formulated by Mercosur finance ministers and central bank governors, determining monetary and fiscal targets to achieve economic convergence. Annual inflation rates were to be no higher than 5% in 2002–05, and reduced to 4% in 2006 and 3% from 2007 (with an exception for Paraguay). Public debt was to be reduced to 40% of gross domestic product (GDP) by 2010, and fiscal deficits were to be reduced to no more than 3% of GDP by 2002. The targets aimed to promote economic stability throughout the region, as well as to reduce competitive disparities affecting the unity of the grouping. The Florianopolis summit meeting also recommended the formulation of social indicators to facilitate achieving targets in the reduction of poverty and the elimination of child labour. However, political debate surrounding the meeting was dominated by the Chilean Government's announcement that it had initiated bilateral free trade discussions with the USA, which was considered, in particular by the Brazilian authorities, to undermine Mercosur's unified position at multilateral free trade negotiations. Procedures to incorporate Chile as a full member of Mercosur were suspended. (Chile and the USA concluded negotiations on a bilateral free trade agreement in December 2002.)

In early 2001 Argentina imposed several emergency measures to strengthen its domestic economy, in contradiction of Mercosur's external tariffs. In March Brazil was reported to have accepted the measures, which included an elimination of tariffs on capital goods and an increase in import duties on consumer goods, as an exceptional temporary trade regime; this position was reversed by mid-2001 following Argentina's decision to exempt certain countries from import tariffs. In February 2002, at a third extraordinary meeting of the Common Market Council, held in Buenos Aires, Argentina, Mercosur heads of state expressed their support for Argentina's application to receive international financial assistance, in the wake of that country's economic crisis. Although there were fears that the crisis might curb trade and stall economic growth across the region, Argentina's adoption of a floating currency made the prospect of currency harmonization between Mercosur member countries appear more viable. The summit meeting held in July in Buenos Aires, Argentina, adopted an agreement providing for reduced tariffs and increased quotas in the grouping's automotive sector, with a view to establishing a fully liberalized automotive market by 2006. In December 2002 Mercosur ministers of justice signed an agreement permitting citizens of Mercosur member and associate member states to reside in any other Mercosur state, initially for a two-year period. At a summit convened in June 2003, in Asunción, Paraguay, heads of state of the four member countries agreed to strengthen integration of the bloc and to harmonize all import tariffs by 2006, thus creating the basis for a single market. They also agreed to establish a directly-elected Mercosur legislature by 2006. The July 2004 summit of Mercosur heads of state announced that an Asunción-based five-member tribunal (comprising one legal representative from each of Mercosur's four member countries, plus one 'consensus' member) responsible for ruling on appeals in cases of disputes between member countries was to become operational in the following month. In June 2005 Mercosur heads of state announced a US $100m. structural convergence fund to support education, job creation and infrastructure projects in the poorest regions, in particular in Paraguay and Uruguay, in order to remove some economic disparities within the grouping. The meeting also endorsed a multilateral energy project to link gasfields in Camisea, Peru, to existing supply pipelines in Argentina, Brazil and Uruguay, via Tocopilla, Chile. The so-called Mercosur parliament, which initially was to serve as an advisory committee, held its inaugural session in Montevideo, Uruguay, in May 2007.

EXTERNAL RELATIONS

In December 1995 Mercosur and the European Union (EU) signed a framework agreement for commercial and economic co-operation, which provided for co-operation in the economic, trade, industrial, scientific, institutional and cultural fields and the promotion of wider political dialogue on issues of mutual interest. In June 1997 Mercosur heads of state, convened in Asunción, reaffirmed the group's intention to pursue trade negotiations with the EU, Mexico and the Andean Community, as well as to negotiate as a single economic bloc in discussions with regard to the establishment of a Free Trade Area of the Americas (FTAA). Chile and Bolivia were to be incorporated into these negotiations. Negotiations between Mercosur and the EU on the conclusion of an Interregional Association Agreement commenced in 1999. Specific discussion of tariff reductions and market access commenced at the fifth round of negotiations, held in July 2001, at which the EU proposed a gradual elimination of tariffs on industrial imports over a 10-year period and an extension of access quotas for agricultural products; however, negotiations stalled in 2005 owing to differences regarding farm subsidies. During 1997 negotiations to establish a free trade accord with the Andean Community were hindered by differences regarding schedules for tariff elimination and Mercosur's insistence on a local content of 60% to qualify for rules of origin preferences. However, in April 1998 the two groupings signed an accord that committed them to the establishment of a free trade area by January 2000. Negotiations in early 1999 failed to conclude an agreement on preferential tariffs between the two blocs, and the existing arrangements were extended on a bilateral basis. In March the Andean Community agreed to initiate free trade negotiations with Brazil; a preferential tariff agreement was concluded in July. In August 2000 a similar agreement between the Community and Argentina entered into force. In September leaders of Mercosur and the Andean Community, meeting at a summit of Latin American heads of state, determined to relaunch negotiations. The establishment of a mechanism to support political dialogue and co-ordination between the two groupings, which aimed to enhance the integration process, was approved at the first joint meeting of ministers of foreign affairs in July 2001. In April 2004 Mercosur and the Andean Community signed a free trade accord, providing for tariffs on 80% of trade between the two groupings to be phased out by 2014 and for tariffs to be removed from the remaining 20% of, initially protected, products by 2019. The entry into force of the accord, scheduled for 1 July 2004, was postponed owing to delays in drafting the tariff reduction schedule. Peru became an associate member of Mercosur in December 2003, and Colombia and Ecuador were granted associate membership in December 2004. In July 2004 Mexico was invited to attend all meetings of the organization with a view to future accession to associate membership. Bilateral negotiations on a free trade agreement between Mexico and Mercosur were initiated in 2001. In 2005 Mercosur and the Andean Community formulated a reciprocal association agreement, to extend associate membership to all member states of both groupings. In December Mercosur heads of state agreed to a request by Venezuela (which had been granted associate membership in December 2004) to become a member with full voting rights. The leaders signed a protocol, in July 2006, formally to admit Venezuela to the group. The accord, however, required ratification by each country's legislature; at early 2008 the parliaments of Brazil and Paraguay had yet to endorse the protocol. Also in December 2005 Bolivia was invited to join as a full member. At the summit meeting of heads of state held in January 2007 in Rio de Janeiro, Brazil, Bolivia stated two conditions on which its membership would be dependent: continued membership of the Andean Community and exemption from Mercosur's common external tariff.

In March 2003 Argentina and Brazil, with the support of other Mercosur member states, formed the Southern Agricultural Council (CAS), which was to represent the interests of the grouping as a whole in negotiations with third countries. In December 2004 leaders from 12 Latin American countries (excluding Argentina, Ecuador, Paraguay and Uruguay) attending a pan-South American summit, convened in Cusco, Peru, approved in principle the creation of a new South American Community of Nations (SACN). It was envisaged that negotiations on the formation of the new Community, which was to entail the merger of Mercosur, the Andean Community and the Latin American Integration Association (ALADI), would be completed within 15 years. In April 2005 a region-wide meeting of ministers of foreign affairs was convened within the framework of establishing the SACN. A joint SACN communiqué was released, expressing concern at the deterioration of constitutional rule and democratic institutions in Ecuador and announcing its intention to send a ministerial mission to that country. The first SACN summit meeting was convened in September, in Brasília, Brazil. In April 2007, at the first South American Energy Summit, convened in Margarita Island, Venezuela, heads of state endorsed the establishment of a Union of South American Nations (UNASUR), to replace SACN as the lead organization for regional integration. UNASUR was to have political decision-making functions, supported by a small permanent secretariat, to be located in Quito, Ecuador, and was to co-ordinate on economic and trade matters with Mercosur, the Andean Community and ALADI. A summit meeting formally to inaugurate UNASUR, scheduled to be convened in December, was postponed. A rescheduled meeting, to be convened in March 2008, at which a constitutional document formally establishing UNASUR was to be signed, was also postponed, owing to a diplomatic dispute between Ecuador and Colombia. It was later scheduled to be convened in May.

In March 1998 ministers of trade of 34 countries agreed a detailed framework for negotiations on the establishment of the FTAA. Mercosur secured support for its request that a separate negotiating group be established to consider issues relating to agriculture, as one of nine key sectors to be discussed. The FTAA negotiating process was formally initiated by heads of state of the 34 countries meeting in Santiago, Chile, in April 1998. In June Mercosur and Canada signed a Trade and Investment Co-operation Arrangement, which aimed to remove obstacles to trade and to increase economic co-operation between the two signatories. The summit meeting held in December 2000 was attended by the President of South Africa, and it was agreed that Mercosur would initiate free trade negotiations with that country. (These commenced in October 2001.) In June 2001 Mercosur leaders agreed to pursue efforts to conclude a bilateral trade agreement with the USA, an objective previously opposed by the Brazilian authorities, while reaffirming their commitment to the FTAA process. Leaders attending a special summit of the Americas, convened in January 2004 in Monterrey, Mexico, failed to specify a completion date for the FTAA process, although they adopted a declaration committing themselves to its eventual establishment. However, negotiations were suspended in March, and remained stalled in 2008. In December 2007 Mercosur signed a free trade accord with Israel.

Finance

The annual budget for the secretariat is contributed by the five full member states.

Publication

Boletín Oficial del Mercosur (quarterly).

WORLD COUNCIL OF CHURCHES—WCC

Address: 150 route de Ferney, POB 2100, 1211 Geneva 2, Switzerland.
Telephone: 227916111; **fax:** 227910361; **e-mail:** infowcc@wcc-coe.org; **internet:** www.wcc-coe.org.

The Council was founded in 1948 to promote co-operation between Christian Churches and to prepare for a clearer manifestation of the unity of the Church.

MEMBERS

There are 347 member Churches in more than 120 countries. Chief denominations: Anglican, Baptist, Congregational, Lutheran, Methodist, Moravian, Old Catholic, Orthodox, Presbyterian, Reformed and Society of Friends. The Roman Catholic Church is not a member but sends official observers to meetings.

Organization
(April 2008)

ASSEMBLY

The governing body of the World Council, consisting of delegates of the member Churches, it meets every seven or eight years to frame policy and consider some main themes. It elects the Presidents of the Council, who serve as members of the Central Committee. The ninth Assembly was held in Porto Alegre, Brazil, in February 2006.

Presidium: ABUNE PAULOS (Ethiopia), Rev. Dr SIMON DOSSOU (Benin), Rev. Dr SORITUA NABABAN (Indonesia), Rev. Dr OFELIA ORTEGA (Cuba), Rev. Dr BERNICE POWELL JACKSON (USA), JOHN TAROANUI DOOM, Archbishop Dr ANASTASIOS OF TIRANA AND ALL ALBANIA, Dr MARY TANNER (United Kingdom).

CENTRAL COMMITTEE

Appointed by the Assembly to carry out its policies and decisions, the Committee consists of 150 members chosen from Assembly delegates. It meets every 12 to 18 months.

The Central Committee comprises the Programme Committee and the Finance Committee. Within the Programme Committee there are advisory groups on issues relating to communication, women, justice, peace and creation, youth, ecumenical relations, and inter-religious relations. There are also five commissions and boards.

Moderator: Rev. Dr WALTER ALTMANN (Armenian Apostolic Church, Lebanon).

Vice-Moderators: Prof. Dr GENNADIOS OF SASSIMA (Turkey), Rev. Dr MARGARETHA M. HENDRIKS-RIRIMASSE (Indonesia).

EXECUTIVE COMMITTEE

Consists of the Presidents, the Officers and 20 members chosen by the Central Committee from its membership to prepare its agenda, expedite its decisions and supervise the work of the Council between meetings of the Central Committee. Meets every six months.

CONSULTATIVE BODIES

Various bodies, including advisory groups, commissions and reference groups, comprising members from WCC governing bodies and member churches, advise the secretariat on policy direction, implementation and evaluation. The main bodies are the Commissions on Faith and Order (plenary and standing bodies), on World Mission and Evangelism, on Education and Ecumenical Formation, of the Churches on International Affairs, and the Echos Commission on Youth in the Ecumenical Movement (inaugurated in May 2007).

GENERAL SECRETARIAT

The General Secretariat implements the policies laid down by the WCC and co-ordinates the Council's work. The General Secretariat is also responsible for an Ecumenical Institute, at Bossey, Switzerland, which provides training in ecumenical leadership.

General Secretary: Rev. Dr SAMUEL KOBIA (Kenya).

Activities

The ninth WCC Assembly, held in February 2006, approved a reorganization of the WCC's work programme, to be based on six key areas of activity. It also recommitted the WCC to the Decade to Overcome Violence (2001–10).

THE WCC AND THE ECUMENICAL MOVEMENT IN THE 21ST CENTURY

The WCC aims to support co-operation among member churches and their involvement in the activities of the organization. It also works to enhance partnerships with other regional and international ecumenical organizations to support the ecumenical movement as a whole, and aims to facilitate communication and consultation among relevant bodies with regard to the future of the ecumenical movement. The WCC supported the development of a Global Christian Forum, which initiated regional consultations among churches in 2004 and convened its first global meeting in November 2007. Within this work programme was a commitment to promote the active participation of young adults in the life of churches and the ecumenical movement, for example through an internship programme at the WCC secretariat, and to ensure that women are and specific issues concerning them are fully considered and represented.

UNITY, MISSION, EVANGELISM AND SPIRITUALITY

This work programme is directed and supported by the Commissions on Faith and Order and on World Mission and Evangelism. It aims to promote a 'visible unity' among member churches and to encourage them to address potentially divisive issues and develop mutually acceptable positions. The WCC produces materials to share among churches information on worship and spiritual life practices and to co-ordinate and promote the annual Week of Prayer for Christian Unity. Other activities aim to confront and overcome any discrimination against ethnic minorities, people with disabilities or other excluded groups within the church and society as a whole. A project to study how to hold commitment to unity together with mission and evangelism was being undertaken within the work programme.

PUBLIC WITNESS: ADDRESSING POWER, AFFIRMING PEACE

The Public Witness programme aims to ensure that the Council's concerns relating to violence, war, human rights, economic injustice, poverty and exclusion are raised and addressed at an international level, including at meetings of UN or other inter-governmental bodies. At a regional and local level the Council aims to accompany churches in critical situations in their efforts to defend human rights and dignity, overcome impunity, achieve accountability and build just and peaceful societies. An Ecumenical Accompaniment Programme in Palestine and Israel (EAPPI) was inaugurated in August 2002 to provide for individuals to support and protect vulnerable groups in the Occupied Territories and to accompany the Israeli Peace movement. The WCC has established an Israeli/Palestine Ecumenical Forum to bring together churches in the region to develop unified policy positions in support of peace and justice. The WCC supports a range of activities within the framework of its Decade to Overcome Violence (2001–10). An International Day of Prayer for Peace is held each year on 21 September. In February 2006 the Council agreed that the Decade would culminate in an International Ecumenical Peace Convocation, to be held in May 2011.

JUSTICE, DIAKONIA AND RESPONSIBILITY FOR CREATION

The Council supports its members efforts to combat injustice and meet human needs. It aims to strengthen churches' organizational capacities and to strengthen and monitor accountability (and greater understanding) between donors and recipients of resources. It is also committed to strengthening the role of churches in the fields of health and healing, in particular in HIV/AIDS and mental health related issues. The Council undertakes networking and advocacy activities at an international level and promotes dialogue among church health networks and those of civil society. In 2002 the Council inaugurated the Ecumenical HIV and AIDS Initiative in Africa (EHAIA) to inform and assist churches in Africa in their efforts to support communities affected by HIV/AIDS. A new Ecumenical Solidarity Fund (ESF) provides grants in support of capacity-building efforts, activities to combat racism and other strategic initiatives. The Council aims to strengthen activities relating to migration and racism and to develop new advocacy strategies. The Council provides a forum for discussion and exchange of information on the use of science and new technologies, for example genetically modified seeds and stem cell research. As part of a wider concern for challenges facing the planet, the WCC has formulated a public campaign to raise awareness of climate change, its impact and the need to address the related problems. It hosts the secretariat of the Ecumenical Water Network, which aims to highlight issues relating to the scarcity of water resources in many parts of the work and to advocate community-based initiatives to manage resources more effectively.

EDUCATION AND ECUMENICAL FORMATION

The WCC is committed to supporting ecumenical and faith formation, as well as providing educational opportunities itself. The Ecumenical Institute, in Bossey, Switzerland, offers academic courses, research opportunities and residential programmes, including one for the promotion of inter-faith dialogue. The WCC organizes seminars and workshops to promote good practices in ecumenical formation and leadership training. The Council aims to strengthen theological education through accreditation standards, exchange programmes and modifying curricula. It administers a sponsorship programme to provide opportunities for ecumenical learning in different cultures.

INTER-RELIGIOUS DIALOGUE AND CO-OPERATION

This work programme aims to promote peaceful co-existence of different faiths and communities within society. It supports interfaith dialogue and opportunities to develop mutual trust and respect, in particular among women and young people of different faiths. A new website promoting best practices in inter-religious dialogue and co-operation was under development in late 2007. The Council encourages reflection on Christianity in an inter-faith society. In 2006 it inaugurated, with the Roman Catholic Church, a process of consultations on religious freedom, to result in the definition of a code of conduct on religious conversion. The Council supports churches in conflict situations to counter religious intolerance or discrimination. It undertakes research, field visits, advocacy work and capacity-building in support of churches or communities affected by conflict.

Finance

The main contributors to the WCC's budget are the churches and their agencies, with funds for certain projects contributed by other organizations. The 2006 budget amounted to 41m. Swiss francs.

Publications

Catalogue of periodicals, books and audio-visuals.
Current Dialogue (2 a year).
Ecumenical News International (weekly).
Ecumenical Review (quarterly).
EEF-NET (2 a year).
International Review of Mission (quarterly).
Ministerial Formation (quarterly).
WCC News (quarterly).
WCC Yearbook.

WORLD FEDERATION OF TRADE UNIONS—WFTU

Address: 40 Zan Moreas St, 11745 Athens, Greece.
Telephone: (21) 09236700; **fax:** (21) 09214517; **e-mail:** info@wftucentral.org; **internet:** www.wftucentral.org.

The Federation was founded in 1945, on a world-wide basis. A number of members withdrew from the Federation in 1949 to establish the International Confederation of Free Trade Unions (now the International Trade Union Confederation).

MEMBERS

Affiliated or associated national federations (including the six Trade Unions Internationals) in 126 countries representing some 135m. individuals.

Organization
(April 2008)

WORLD TRADE UNION CONGRESS

The Congress meets every five years. It reviews WFTU's work, endorses reports from the executives, and elects the General Council. The size of the delegations is based on the total membership of national federations. The Congress is also open to participation by non-affiliated organizations. The 15th Congress, convened in Havana, Cuba, in December 2005, marked the 60th anniversary of the founding of the organization.

GENERAL COUNCIL

The General Council meets three times between Congresses, and comprises members and deputies elected by Congress from nominees of national federations. Every affiliated or associated organization and Trade Unions International has one member and one deputy member.

The Council receives reports from the Presidential Council, approves the plan and budget and elects officers.

PRESIDENTIAL COUNCIL

The Presidential Council meets twice a year and conducts most of the executive work of WFTU. It comprises a President, elected each year from among its members, the General Secretary and 18 Vice-Presidents.

SECRETARIAT

The Secretariat consists of the General Secretary, and six Deputy General Secretaries. It is appointed by the General Council and is responsible for general co-ordination, regional activities, national trade union liaison, press and information, administration and finance.

WFTU has regional offices in New Delhi, India (for the Asia-Pacific region), Havana, Cuba (covering the Americas), Dakar, Senegal (for Africa), Damascus, Syria (for the Middle East) and in Moscow, Russia (covering the CIS countries).

General Secretary: GEORGE MAVRIKOS (Greece).

Finance

Income is derived from affiliation dues, which are based on the number of members in each trade union federation.

Publication

Flashes from the Trade Unions (fortnightly, in English, French and Spanish; monthly in Arabic and Russian).

Trade Unions Internationals

The following autonomous Trade Unions Internationals (TUIs) are associated with WFTU:

Trade Unions International of Agriculture, Food, Commerce, Textile and Allied Workers: 263 rue de Paris, 93514 Montreuil, France; tel. 1-48-18-83-27; fax 1-48-51-57-49; e-mail uis@fnaf.cgt.fr; f. 1997 by merger of the TUI of Agricultural, Forestry and Plantation Workers (f. 1949), the TUI of Food, Tobacco, Hotel and Allied Industries Workers (f. 1949), the TUI of Workers in Commerce (f. 1959) and the TUI of Textile, Clothing, Leather and Fur Workers (f. 1949); Pres. FREDDY HUCK (France); Gen. Sec. DMITRII DOZORIN (Russia).

Trade Unions International of Public and Allied Employees: off 10A Shankharitola St, Kolkata 700014, India; tel. (33) 2217-7721; fax (33) 2265-9450; e-mail aisgef@dataone.in; internet www.tradeunionindia.org; f. 1949; mems: 34m. in 152 unions in 54 countries; Branch Commissions: State, Municipal, Postal and Telecommunications, Health, Banks and Insurance; Pres. LULAMILE SOTAKA (South Africa); Gen. Sec. SUKOMAL SEN (India); publ. *Information Bulletin* (in three languages).

Trade Unions International of Transport Workers: Tengerszem U. 21/B, 1142 Budapest, Hungary; tel. and fax (1) 2851593; f. 1949; holds International Trade Conference (every 4 years) and General Council (annually); mems: 95 unions from 37 countries; Pres. NASR ZARIF MOUHREZ (Syria); Gen. Sec. JÓZSEF TÓTH (Hungary); publ. *TUI Reporter* (every 2 months, in English and Spanish).

Trade Unions International of Workers of the Building, Wood and Building Materials Industries (Union Internationale des Syndicats des Travailleurs du Bâtiment, du Bois et des Matériaux de Construction—UITBB): Box 281, 00101 Helsinki, Finland; tel. (9) 693-1130; fax (9) 693-1020; e-mail rguitbb@kaapeli.fi; internet www.uitbb.org; f. 1949; mems: unions in 50 countries, grouping 2m. workers; Sec.-Gen. JOSÉ DINIS (Portugal); publ. *Bulletin*.

Trade Unions International of Workers in the Energy, Metal, Chemical, Oil and Related Industries: c/o 3A Calle Maestro Antonio Caso 45, Col. Tabacalera, 06470 Mexico City, Mexico; tel. and fax (55) 5546-3200; e-mail uis-temqpia@sme.org; f. 1998 by merger of the TUI of Chemical, Oil and Allied Workers (f. 1950), the TUI of Energy Workers (f. 1949) and the TUI of Workers in the Metal Industry (f. 1949); Gen. Sec. MARTIN ESPARZA FLORES (Mexico); publ. *Bulletin*.

World Federation of Teachers' Unions: 6/6 Kalicharan Ghosh Rd, Kolkata 700 050, India; tel. (33) 2528-4786; fax (33) 2557-1293; f. 1946; mems: 132 national unions of teachers and educational and scientific workers in 78 countries, representing over 24m. individuals; Pres. LESTURUGE ARIYAWANSA (Sri Lanka); Gen. Sec. MRINMOY BHATTACHARYYA (India); publ. *Teachers of the World* (quarterly, in English).

INTERNATIONAL ORGANIZATIONS World Trade Organization

WORLD TRADE ORGANIZATION—WTO

Address: Centre William Rappard, rue de Lausanne 154, 1211 Geneva, Switzerland.
Telephone: (22) 7395111; **fax:** (22) 7314206; **e-mail:** enquiries@wto.org; **internet:** www.wto.org.

The WTO is the legal and institutional foundation of the multilateral trading system. It was established on 1 January 1995, as the successor to the General Agreement on Tariffs and Trade (GATT).

MEMBERS*

Albania
Angola
Antigua and Barbuda
Argentina
Armenia
Australia
Austria
Bahrain
Bangladesh
Barbados
Belgium
Belize
Benin
Bolivia
Botswana
Brazil
Brunei
Bulgaria
Burkina Faso
Burundi
Cambodia
Cameroon
Canada
Cape Verde
Central African Republic
Chad
Chile
China, People's Republic
China, Republic†
Colombia
Congo, Democratic Republic
Congo, Republic
Costa Rica
Côte d'Ivoire
Croatia
Cuba
Cyprus
Czech Republic
Denmark
Djibouti
Dominica
Dominican Republic
Ecuador
Egypt
El Salvador
Estonia
Fiji
Finland
France
Gabon
The Gambia
Georgia
Germany
Ghana
Greece
Grenada
Guatemala
Guinea
Guinea-Bissau
Guyana
Haiti
Honduras
Hong Kong
Hungary
Iceland
India
Indonesia
Ireland
Israel
Italy
Jamaica
Japan
Jordan
Kenya
Korea, Republic
Kuwait
Kyrgyzstan
Latvia
Lesotho
Liechtenstein
Lithuania
Luxembourg
Macau
Macedonia, former Yugoslav republic
Madagascar
Malawi
Malaysia
Maldives
Mali
Malta
Mauritania
Mauritius
Mexico
Moldova
Mongolia
Morocco
Mozambique
Myanmar
Namibia
Nepal
Netherlands
New Zealand
Nicaragua
Niger
Nigeria
Norway
Oman
Pakistan
Panama
Papua New Guinea
Paraguay
Peru
Philippines
Poland
Portugal
Qatar
Romania
Rwanda
Saint Christopher and Nevis
Saint Lucia
Saint Vincent and the Grenadines
Saudi Arabia
Senegal
Sierra Leone
Singapore
Slovakia
Slovenia
Solomon Islands
South Africa
Spain
Sri Lanka
Suriname
Swaziland
Sweden
Switzerland
Tanzania
Thailand
Togo
Trinidad and Tobago
Tunisia
Turkey
Uganda
United Arab Emirates
United Kingdom
USA
Uruguay
Vanuatu
Viet Nam
Venezuela
Zambia
Zimbabwe

*The European Community also has membership status.
†Admitted as the Separate Customs Territory of Taiwan, Penghu, Kinmen and Matsu (referred to as Chinese Taipei).

Note: At April 2008 28 applications to join the WTO were either under consideration or awaiting consideration by accession working parties. The application of Ukraine had been approved in February and, pending ratification by its legislature, it was envisaged that Ukraine would accede to the WTO in August. In addition, an accession request had also been received from Syria (in 2001); however, no decision had been reached to commence negotiations.

Organization
(April 2008)

MINISTERIAL CONFERENCE

The Ministerial Conference is the highest authority of the WTO. It is composed of representatives of all WTO members at ministerial level, and may take decisions on all matters under any of the multilateral trade agreements. The Conference is normally required to meet at least every two years. The sixth Conference took place in Hong Kong in December 2005; the seventh Conference was postponed owing to the delayed conclusion of the Doha Development Round.

GENERAL COUNCIL

The General Council, which is also composed of representatives of all WTO members, is required to report to the Ministerial Conference and conducts much of the day-to-day work of the WTO. The Council convenes as the Dispute Settlement Body, to oversee the trade dispute settlement procedures, and as the Trade Policy Review Body, to conduct regular reviews of the trade policies of WTO members. The Council delegates responsibility to three other major Councils: for trade-related aspects of intellectual property rights, for trade in goods and for trade in services.

TRADE NEGOTIATIONS COMMITTEE

The Committee was established in November 2001 by the Declaration of the fourth Ministerial Conference, held in Doha, Qatar, to supervise the agreed agenda of trade negotiations. It operates under the authority of the General Council and was mandated to establish negotiating mechanisms and subsidiary bodies for each subject under consideration. A structure of negotiating groups and a declaration of principles and practices for the negotiations were formulated by the Committee in February 2002.

SECRETARIAT

The WTO Secretariat comprises some 635 staff. Its responsibilities include the servicing of WTO delegate bodies, with respect to negotiations and the implementation of agreements, undertaking accession negotiations for new members and providing technical support and expertise to developing countries.

The WTO Institute for Training and Technical Co-operation, based at the Secretariat, offers courses on trade policy; introduction to the WTO for least-developed countries; WTO dispute settlement rules and procedures; and other specialized topics. Other programmes include training-of-trainers schemes and distance-learning services.

Director-General: Pascal Lamy (France).
Deputy Directors-General: Alejandro Jara (Chile), Valentine Sendanyoye Rugwabiza (Rwanda), Harsha Vardhana Singh (India), Rufus Yerxa (USA).

Activities

The Final Act of the Uruguay Round of GATT multilateral trade negotiations, which were concluded in December 1993, provided for extensive trade liberalization measures and for the establishment of a permanent structure to oversee international trading procedures. The Final Act was signed in April 1994, in Marrakesh, Morocco. At the same time a separate accord, the Marrakesh Declaration, was signed by the majority of GATT contracting states, endorsing the establishment of the WTO. The essential functions of the WTO are: to administer and facilitate the implementation of the results of the Uruguay Round; to provide a forum for multilateral trade negotiations; to administer the trade dispute settlement procedures; to review national trade policies; and to co-operate with other international institutions, in particular the IMF and World Bank, in order to achieve greater coherence in global economic policy-making.

The WTO Agreement contains some 29 individual legal texts and more than 25 additional Ministerial declarations, decisions and understandings, which cover obligations and commitments for member states. All these instruments are based on a few fundamental principles, which form the basis of the WTO Agreement. An integral part of the Agreement is 'GATT 1994', an amended and updated version of the original GATT Agreement of 1947, which was formally concluded at the end of 1995. Under the 'most-favoured nation' (MFN) clause, members are bound to grant to each other's products treatment no less favourable than that accorded to the products of any third parties. A number of exceptions apply, principally for customs unions and free-trade areas and for measures in favour of and among developing countries. The principle of 'national treatment' requires goods, having entered a market, to be treated no less favourably than the equivalent domestically-produced goods. Secure and predictable market access, to encourage trade, investment and job creation, may be determined by 'binding' tariffs, or customs duties. This process means that a tariff level for a particular product becomes a commitment by a member state, and cannot be increased without compensation negotiations with its main trading partners. Other WTO agreements also contribute to predictable trading conditions by demanding commitments from member countries and greater transparency of domestic laws and national trade policies. By permitting tariffs, whilst adhering to the guide-lines of being non-discriminatory, the WTO aims to promote open, fair and undistorted competition.

The WTO aims to encourage development and economic reform among the increasing number of developing countries and countries with economies in transition participating in the international trading system. These countries, particularly the least-developed states, have been granted transition periods and greater flexibility to implement certain WTO provisions. Industrial member countries are encouraged to assist developing nations by their trading conditions and by not expecting reciprocity in trade concession negotiations. In addition, the WTO operates a limited number of technical assistance programmes, mostly relating to training and the provision of information technology.

Finally, the WTO Agreement recognizes the need to protect the environment and to promote sustainable development. A Committee on Trade and Environment examines the relationship between trade policies, environmental measures and sustainable development and to recommend any appropriate modifications of the multilateral trading provisions.

At the 1996 Conference representatives of some 28 countries signed a draft Information Technology Agreement (ITA), which aimed to eliminate tariffs on the significant global trade in IT products by 2000. By February 1997 some 39 countries, representing the required 90% share of the world's IT trade, had consented to implement the ITA. It was signed in March, and was to cover the following main product categories: computers; telecommunications products; semiconductors or manufacturing equipment; software; and scientific instruments. Tariff reductions in these sectors were to be undertaken in four stages, commencing in July, and subsequently on 1 January each year, providing for the elimination of all tariffs by the start of 2000. By April 2008 there were 70 participants in the ITA, representing some 97% of world trade in IT products. In February 1999 the WTO announced plans to investigate methods of removing non-tariff barriers to trade in IT products, such as those resulting from non-standardization of technical regulations. A work programme on non-tariff measures was approved by the Committee of Participants on the Expansion of Trade in IT Products in November 2000.

At the end of the Uruguay Round a 'built-in' programme of work for the WTO was developed. In addition, the Ministerial Conferences in December 1996 and May 1998 addressed a range of issues. The final declaration issued from the Ministerial Conference in December 1996 incorporated a text on the contentious issue of core labour standards, although it was emphasized that the relationship between trade and labour standards was not part of the WTO agenda. The text recognized the International Labour Organization's competence in establishing and dealing with core labour standards and endorsed future WTO/ILO co-operation. The declaration also included a plan of action on measures in favour of the world's least-developed countries, to assist these countries in enhancing their trading opportunities. The second Conference, convened in May 1998, decided against imposing customs duties on international electronic transactions, and agreed to establish a comprehensive work programme to address the issues of electronic commerce. The Conference also supported the creation of a framework of international rules to protect intellectual property rights and provide security and privacy in transactions. Developing countries were assured that their needs in this area would be taken into account. Members agreed to begin preparations for the launch of comprehensive talks on global trade liberalization. In addition, following repeated mass public demonstrations against free trade, it was agreed to try to increase the transparency of the WTO and improve public understanding of the benefits of open global markets.

Formal negotiations on the agenda of a new multilateral trade 'round', which was initially scheduled to be launched at the third Ministerial Conference, to be held in Seattle, USA, in late November–December 1999, commenced in September 1998. While it was confirmed that further liberalization of agriculture and services was to be considered, no consensus was reached (in particular between the Cairns Group of countries and the USA, and the European Union (EU), supported by Japan) on the terms of reference or procedures for these negotiations prior to the start of the Conference. In addition, developing countries criticized renewed efforts, mainly by the USA, to link trade and labour standards and to incorporate environmental considerations into the discussions. Efforts by the EU to broaden the talks to include investment and competition policy were also resisted by the USA. The conduct of the Ministerial Conference was severely disrupted by public demonstrations by a diverse range of interest groups concerned with the impact of WTO accords on the environment, workers' rights and developing countries. The differences between member states with regard to a formal agenda failed to be resolved during extensive negotiations, and the Conference was suspended. At a meeting of the General Council, convened later in December, member countries reached an informal understanding that any agreements concluding on 31 December would be extended. Meanwhile, the Director-General attempted to maintain a momentum for proceeding with a new round of trade negotiations. In February 2000 the General Council agreed to resume talks with regard to agriculture and services, and to consider difficulties in implementing the Uruguay Accord, which was a main concern of developing member states. The Council also urged industrialized nations to pursue an earlier initiative to grant duty-free access to the exports of least-developed countries. In May the Council resolved to initiate a series of Special Sessions to consider implementation of existing trade agreements, and approved more flexible provisions for implementation of TRIPS (see below), as part of ongoing efforts to address the needs of developing member states and strengthen their confidence in the multilateral trading system.

During 2001 negotiations were undertaken to reach agreement on further trade liberalization. A draft accord was approved by the General Council in October. The fourth Ministerial Conference, held in Doha, Qatar, in November, adopted a final declaration providing a mandate for a three-year agenda for negotiations on a range of subjects, commencing on 1 January 2002. Most of the negotiations were initially scheduled to be concluded, on 1 January 2005, as a single undertaking, i.e. requiring universal agreement on all matters under consideration. (The deadline was subsequently advanced to end-2006, and in July 2006 was postponed indefinitely—see below.) A new Trade Negotiations Committee was established to supervise the process, referred to as the Doha Development Round. Several aspects of existing agreements were to be negotiated, while new issues included: WTO rules, such as subsidies, regional trade agreements and anti-dumping measures, and market access. The Declaration incorporated a commitment to negotiate issues relating to trade and the environment, including fisheries subsidies, environmental labelling requirements, and the relationship between trade obligations of multilateral environment agreements and WTO rules. The Conference approved a separate decision on implementation-related issues, to address the concerns of developing countries in meeting their WTO commitments. Several implementation issues were agreed at the meeting, while others were incorporated into the Development Agenda. Specific reference was made in the Declaration to providing greater technical co-operation and capacity-building assistance to WTO developing country members. A Doha Development Agenda Global Trust Fund was established in late 2001, with a core budget of CHF 15m., to help finance technical support for trade liberalization in less developed member states. In September 2002 the WTO Director-General announced that, in support of the ongoing trade negotiations, the following four pillars of the Organization should be strengthened: beneficial use of the legal framework binding together the multilateral system; technical and capacity-building assistance to least-developed and developing countries; greater coherence in international economic policy-making; and the WTO's functioning as an institution.

The fifth Ministerial Conference, however, convened in Cancún, Mexico, in September 2003 to advance the Doha Development Round, failed to achieve consensus on a number of issues, in particular investment and competition policy. Senior officials from member states convened in December to discuss the future of the Doha Round, but no major breakthrough was achieved. Members did, however, indicate their willingness to recommence work in negotiating groups, which had been suspended after the Cancún conference. The General Council, meanwhile, was to continue working to explore the possibilities of agreements on a multilateral approach on trade facilitation and transparency in government procurement.

In July 2004 the General Council presented for consideration and revision by WTO member states a new draft Doha Agenda Work Programme (the so-called 'July Package' of framework trade agreements) aimed at reviving the stalled Doha Development Round. Following intensive negotiations, the finalized July Package was adopted by the General Council at the beginning of August. The Package included an interim accord on agricultural subsidies that established guide-lines for future Doha Round negotiations, entailing a key commitment by rich developed nations eventually to eliminate all agricultural export subsidies. Although no deadline was set for the completion of this process, it was agreed that maximum permitted subsidies would be reduced by 20% in the first year of the implementation of the new regime. The EU would remove some US $360m. of annual export subsidies, with similar concessions also to be made by the USA. However, the EU's subsidies to its milk and sugar producers and the USA's subsidies to its cotton farmers were withdrawn from the Package and were to be addressed by separate negotiations. Under the July Package proposals all countries were to be required to reduce tariffs on agricultural imports, but the poorest countries would be set lower reduction targets and longer periods for their implementation.

The sixth Ministerial Conference, convened in Hong Kong, in December 2005, set a deadline of 30 April 2006 for finalizing details of modalities for agriculture and industrial goods, with a view to concluding the Doha Round at the end of 2006. It was also agreed that duty- and quota-free access for at least 97% of least-developed countries' exports should be achieved by 2008. However, in July 2006 the Doha Development Round of negotiations was suspended across all sectors, with all related deadlines postponed, owing to failure by the participating countries to reach a satisfactory final agreement on agricultural trade, and, in particular, deadlock on the issues of reductions in market access restrictions and domestic support mechanisms in the agriculture sector. Participants were urged by the WTO Director-General to reconsider their negotiating positions. In February 2007 the Director-General announced that negotiations across all sectors had been resumed. In June discussions between the EU, USA, India and Brazil, which were aimed at bridging the gaps in their negotiating positions and had been regarded as a basis for advancing the wider negotiations, failed to reach any agreement on the main areas of dispute i.e. farm subsidies and market access. In July the WTO Director-General endorsed compromise texts that had been negotiated for trade in agriculture and for non-agricultural market access.

Addressing the IMF in April 2008, the WTO Director-General urged WTO member governments to agree at ministerial level by the end of May a framework for cutting agricultural tariffs, agricultural subsidies and industrial tariffs, as a means of facilitating the completion of the Doha Round by the end of 2008. He stressed the role of the WTO's rules-based trading system as a source of economic stability for governments, businesses and consumers, and indicated that the prompt finalization of the Doha Round would provide reassurance to international markets given the emerging climate of increased global financial uncertainty.

AGRICULTURE

The Final Act of the Uruguay Round extended previous GATT arrangements for trade in agricultural products through new rules and commitments to ensure more predictable and fair competition in the sector. All quantitive measures limiting market access for agricultural products were to be replaced by tariffs (i.e. a process of 'tariffication'), enabling more equal protection and access opportunities. All tariffs on agricultural items were to be reduced by 36% by developed countries, over a period of six years, and by 24% by developing countries (excluding least-developed member states) over 10 years. A special treatment clause applied to 'sensitive' products (mainly rice) in four countries, for which limited import restrictions could be maintained. Efforts to reduce domestic support measures for agricultural products were to be based on calculations of total aggregate measurements of support (Total AMS) by each member state. A 20% reduction in Total AMS was required by developed countries over six years, and 13% over 10 years by developing countries. No reduction was required of least-developed countries. Developed member countries were required to reduce the value and quantity of direct export subsidies by 36% and 21% respectively (on 1986–90 levels) over six years. For developing countries these reductions were to be two-thirds those of developed nations, over 10 years. A specific concern of least-developed and net-food importing developing countries, which had previously relied on subsidized food products, was to be addressed through other food aid mechanisms and assistance for agricultural development. The situation was to be monitored by WTO's Committee on Agriculture. Negotiations on the further liberalization of agricultural markets were part of the WTO 'built-in' programme for 2000 or earlier, but remained a major area of contention. In March 2000 negotiations on market access in the agricultural sector commenced, under an interim chairman owing to a disagreement among participating states. The Doha Declaration, approved in that month, established a timetable for further negotiations on agriculture, which were initially scheduled to be concluded as part of the single undertaking on 1 January 2005. (The deadline was subsequently postponed indefinitely.) A compromise agreement was reached with the EU to commit to a reduction in export subsidies, with a view to phasing them out (without a firm deadline for their elimination). Member states agreed to aim for further reductions in market access restrictions and domestic support mechanisms, and to incorporate non-trade concerns, including environmental protection, food security and rural development, into the negotiations. In December 2005 the sixth Ministerial Conference set a deadline of 2013 for the elimination of agricultural export subsidies, with significant progress to have been achieved by 2010; a deadline of end-2006 was established for the elimination of export subsidies for cotton by developed countries. However, the Doha Round of negotiations and all associated deadlines were suspended in July. In February 2007 it was announced that negotiations had resumed. In July the WTO Director-General endorsed compromise texts that had been negotiated for trade in agriculture and for non-agricultural market access.

The Agreement on the Application of Sanitary and Phytosanitary Measures aims to regulate world-wide standards of food safety and animal and plant health in order to encourage the mutual recognition of standards and conformity, so as to facilitate trade in these products. The Agreement includes provisions on control inspection and approval procedures. In September 1997, in the first case to be brought under the Agreement, a dispute panel of the WTO ruled that the EU's ban on imports of hormone-treated beef and beef products from the USA and Canada was in breach of international trading rules. In January 1998 the Appellate Body upheld the panel's ruling, but expressed its support for restrictions to ensure food standards if there was adequate scientific evidence of risks to human health. The EU maintained the ban, against resistance from the USA, while it carried out scientific risk assessments.

TEXTILES AND CLOTHING

From 1974–1994 the former Multi-Fibre Arrangement (MFA) provided the basis of international trade concerning textiles and clothing, enabling the major importers to establish quotas and protect their domestic industries, through bilateral agreements, against more competitive low-cost goods from developing countries. MFA restrictions that were in place on 31 December 1994 were carried over into a new transitional 10-year Agreement on Textiles and Clothing (ATC) and were phased out through integration into GATT 1994, in four planned stages: products accounting for 16% of the total volume of textiles and clothing imports (at 1990 levels) to be integrated from 1 January 1995; a further 17% on 1 January 1998; not less than a further 18% on 1 January 2002; and all remaining products by 1 January 2005. Since the expiry on that date of the ATC, international trade in clothing and textiles has, as envisaged, been governed by general rules and disciplines embodied in the multilateral trading system.

TRADE IN SERVICES

The General Agreement on Trade in Services (GATS), which was negotiated during the GATT Uruguay Round, is the first set of multilaterally-agreed and legally-enforceable rules and disciplines ever negotiated to cover international trade in services. The GATS comprises a framework of general rules and disciplines, annexes addressing special conditions relating to individual sectors and national schedules of market access commitments. A Council for Trade in Services oversees the operation of the agreement.

The GATS framework consists of 29 articles, including the following set of basic obligations: total coverage of all internationally-traded services; national treatment, i.e. according services and service suppliers of other members no less favourable treatment than that accorded to domestic services and suppliers; MFN treatment (see above), with any specific exemptions to be recorded prior to the implementation of the GATS, with a limit of 10 years duration; transparency, requiring publication of all relevant national laws and legislations; bilateral agreements on recognition of standards and qualifications to be open to other members who wish to negotiate accession; no restrictions on international payments and transfers; progressive liberalization to be pursued; and market access and national treatment commitments to be bound and recorded in national schedules. These schedules, which include exemptions to the MFN principles, contain the negotiated and guaranteed conditions under which trade in services is conducted and are an integral part of the GATS.

Annexes to the GATS cover the movement of natural persons, permitting governments to negotiate specific commitments regarding the temporary stay of people for the purpose of providing a service; the right of governments to take measures in order to ensure the integrity and stability of the financial system; the role of telecommunications as a distinct sector of economic activity and as a means of supplying other economic activities; and air transport services, excluding certain activities relating to traffic rights.

At the end of the Uruguay Round governments agreed to continue negotiations in the following areas: basic telecommunications, maritime transport, movement of natural persons and financial services. The Protocol to the GATS relating to movement of natural persons was concluded in July 1995. In May 1996 the USA withdrew from negotiations to conclude an agreement on maritime transport services. At the end of June the participating countries agreed to suspend the discussions and to recommence negotiations in 2000 (see below).

In July 1995 some 29 members signed an interim agreement to grant greater access to the banking, insurance, investment and securities sectors from August 1996. Negotiations to strengthen the agreement and to extend it to new signatories (including the USA, which had declined to sign the agreement, claiming lack of reciprocity by some Asian countries) commenced in April 1997. A final agreement was successfully concluded in December: 102 countries endorsed the elimination of restrictions on access to the financial services sectors from 1 March 1999, and agreed to subject those services to legally-binding rules and disciplines. In late January 1999 some 35 signatory states had yet to ratify the financial services agreement, and its entry into force was postponed. Negotiations on trade in basic telecommunications began in May 1994 and were scheduled to conclude in April 1996. Before the final deadline, however, the negotiations were suspended, owing to US concerns, which included greater access to satellite telecommunications markets in Asia and greater control over foreign companies operating from the domestic markets. An agreement was finally concluded by the new deadline of 15 February 1997. Accordingly the largest telecommunications markets, i.e. the USA, the EU and Japan, were to eliminate all remaining restrictions on domestic and foreign competition in the industry by 1 January 1998 (although delays were granted to Spain, until December 1998, Ireland, until 2000, and Greece and Portugal, until 2003). The majority of the 69 signatories to the accord also agreed on common rules to ensure that fair competition could be enforced by the WTO disputes settlement mechanism, and pledged their commitment to establishing a regulatory system for the telecommunications sector and guaranteeing transparency in government licensing. The agreement entered into force on 5 February 1998, having been rescheduled, owing to the delay on the part of some signatory countries (then totalling 72 states) in ratifying the accord and incorporating the principles of industry regulation into national legislation.

The negotiations to liberalize trade in services, suspended in 1996, were formally reopened in January 2000, with new guide-lines and procedures for the negotiations approved in March 2001. The negotiations were incorporated into the Doha Agenda and were to be concluded as part of a single undertaking, initially by 1 January 2005, although the deadline was subsequently postponed.

INTELLECTUAL PROPERTY RIGHTS

The WTO Agreement on Trade-Related Aspects of Intellectual Property Rights (TRIPS), which entered into force on 1 January 1995, recognizes that widely varying standards in the protection and enforcement of intellectual property rights and the lack of multilateral disciplines dealing with international trade in counterfeit goods have been a growing source of tension in international economic relations. The TRIPS agreement aims to ensure that nationals of member states receive equally favourable treatment with regard to the protection of intellectual property and that adequate standards of intellectual property protection exist in all WTO member countries. These standards are largely based on the obligations of the Paris and Berne Conventions of WIPO, however, and the agreement aims to expand and enhance these where necessary, for example: computer programmes, to be protected as literary works for copyright purposes; definition of trade marks eligible for protection; stricter rules of geographical indications of consumer products; a 10-year protection period for industrial designs; a 20-year patent protection available for all inventions; tighter protection of layout design of integrated circuits; and protection for trade secrets and 'know-how' with a commercial value.

Under the agreement member governments are obliged to provide procedures and remedies to ensure the effective enforcement of intellectual property rights. Civil and administrative procedures outlined in the TRIPS include provisions on evidence, injunctions, judicial authority to order the disposal of infringing goods, and criminal procedures and penalties, in particular for trademark counterfeiting and copyright piracy. A one-year period from TRIPS' entry into force was envisaged for developed countries to bring their legislation and practices into conformity with the agreement. Developing countries were to do so in five years (or 10 years if an area of technology did not already have patent protection) and least-developed countries in 11 years. A Council for Trade-Related Property Rights monitors the compliance of governments with the agreement and its operation. During 2000 the implementation of TRIPS was one the key areas of contention among WTO members. In November WTO initiated a review of TRIPS, although this was expected to consider alteration of the regime rather than of its implementation. At that time some 70 developing countries were failing to apply TRIPS rules. In November 2001 the Doha Ministerial Conference sought to resolve the ongoing dispute regarding the implementation of TRIPS in respect of pharmaceutical patents in developing countries. A separate declaration aimed to clarify a flexible interpretation of TRIPS in order for governments to meet urgent public health priorities. The deadline for some of the poorest countries to apply provisions on pharmaceutical patents was extended to 1 January 2016. The TRIPS Council was mandated to undertake further consideration of problems concerning compulsory licensing. The Doha Declaration also committed the Council to concluding, by the next (2003) Ministerial Conference, negotiations on a multilateral registration system for geographical indications for wines and spirits; however, this deadline was not achieved, and was subsequently postponed indefinitely. In November 2005 the original deadline of 1 January 2006 for least-developed countries to bring their legislation and practices into conformity with TRIPS was extended by the Council for Trade-Related Property Rights to 1 July 2013; the Council also determined that technical assistance to support the application of the agreement in those member countries should be enhanced.

LEGAL FRAMEWORK

In addition to the binding agreements mentioned above, WTO aims to provide a comprehensive legal framework for the international trading system. Under GATT 1994 'anti-dumping' measures were permitted against imports of a product with an export price below its normal value, if these imports were likely to cause damage to a domestic industry. The WTO agreement provides for greater clarity and more-detailed rules determining the application of these measures and determines settlement procedures in disputes relating to anti-dumping actions taken by WTO members. In general, anti-dumping measures were to be limited to five years. WTO's Agreement on Subsidies and Countervailing Measures is intended to expand on existing GATT agreements. It classifies subsidies into three categories: prohibited, which may be determined by the Dispute Settlement Body and must be immediately withdrawn; actionable, which must be withdrawn or altered if the subsidy is found to cause adverse effects on the interests of other members; and non-actionable, for example subsidies involving assistance to industrial research, assistance to disadvantaged regions or adaptation of facilities to meet new environmental requirements; non-actionable subsidies, however, were terminated in 1999. The Agreement also contains provisions on the use of duties to offset the effect of a subsidy (so-called countervailing measures) and establishes procedures for the initiation and conduct of investigations into this action. Countervailing measures must generally be terminated within five years of their imposition. Least-developed countries, and developing countries with gross national product per capita of less than US $1,000, are exempt from disciplines on prohibited export subsidies; however, it was envisaged that these would be eliminated by 2003 in all other developing countries and by 2002 in countries with economies in transition. In November 2001 the Doha Ministerial Conference agreed to permit developing countries individually to request an extension of the interim period prior to elimination; consequently, a number of such member countries were granted extensions.

WTO members may take safeguard actions to protect a specific domestic industry from a damaging increase of imported products. However, the WTO agreement aims to clarify criteria for imposing safeguards, their duration (normally to be no longer than four years, which may be extended to eight years) and consultations on trade compensation for the exporting countries. At 1 December 1995 50 member states had notified the Committee on Safeguards of the WTO Secretariat of their existing domestic safeguard legislations, as required under the agreement. Any measures to protect domestic industries through voluntary export restraints or other market-sharing devices were to be phased out by the end of 1998, or a year later for one specific safeguard measure, subject to mutual agreement of the members directly concerned. Safeguard measures are not applicable to products from developing countries as long as their share of imports of the product concerned does not exceed 3%.

Further legal arrangements act to ensure the following: that technical regulations and standards (including testing and certification procedures) do not create unnecessary obstacles to trade; that import licensing procedures are transparent and predictable; that the valuation of goods for customs purposes are fair and uniform; that GATT principles and obligations apply to import preshipment inspection activities; the fair and transparent administration of rules of origin; and that no investment measures which may restrict or distort trade may be applied. A Working Group on Notification Obligations and Procedures aims to ensure that members fulfil their notification requirements, which facilitate the transparency and surveillance of the trading rules.

PLURILATERAL AGREEMENT

The majority of GATT agreements became multilateral obligations when the WTO became operational in 1995; however, four agreements, which had a selective group of signatories, remained in effect. These so-called plurilateral agreements, the Agreement on Trade in Civil Aircraft, the Agreement on Government Procurement, the International Dairy Agreement and the International Bovine Meat Agreement, aimed to increase international co-operation and fair and open trade and competition in these areas. The bovine meat and dairy agreements were terminated in 1997. The remaining two plurilateral agreements establish their own management bodies, which are required to report to the General Council.

TRADE POLICY REVIEW MECHANISM

The mechanism, which was established provisionally in 1989, was given a permanent role in the WTO. Through regular monitoring and surveillance of national trade policies the mechanism aims to increase the transparency and understanding of trade policies and practices and to enable assessment of the effects of policies on the world trading system. In addition, it records efforts made by governments to bring domestic trade legislation into conformity with WTO provisions and to implement WTO commitments. Reviews are conducted in the Trade Policy Review Body on the basis of a policy statement of the government under review and an independent report prepared by the WTO Secretariat. Under the mechanism the world's four largest traders, the EU, the USA, Japan and Canada, were to be reviewed every two years. Special groups were established to examine new regional free-trade arrangements and the trade policies of acceding countries. In February 1996 a single Committee on Regional Trade Agreements was established, superseding these separate working parties. The Committee aimed to ensure that these groupings contributed to the process of global trade liberalization and to study the implications of these arrangements on the multilateral system. At the Ministerial Conference held in December 1996 it was agreed to establish a new working group to conduct a study of transparency in government procurement practices.

SETTLEMENT OF DISPUTES

A separate annex to the WTO agreement determines a unified set of rules and procedures to govern the settlement of all WTO disputes, substantially reinforcing the GATT procedures. WTO members are committed not to undertake unilateral action against perceived violations of the trade rules, but to seek recourse in the dispute settlement mechanism and abide by its findings.

The first stage of the process requires bilateral consultations between the members concerned in an attempt to conclude a mutually-acceptable solution to the issue. These may be undertaken through the good offices and mediation efforts of the Director-General. Only after a consultation period of 60 days may the complainant ask the General Council, convened as the Dispute Settlement Body (DSB), to establish an independent panel to examine the case, which then does so within the terms of reference of the agreement cited. Each party to the dispute submits its arguments and then presents its case before the panel. Third parties which notify their interest in the dispute may also present views at the first substantive meeting of the panel. At this stage an expert review group may be appointed to provide specific scientific or technical advice. The panel submits sections and then a full interim report of its findings to the parties, who may then request a further review involving additional meetings. A final report should be submitted to the parties by the panel within six months of its establishment, or within three months in cases of urgency, including those related to perishable goods. Final reports are normally adopted by the DSB within 60 days of issuance. In the case of a measure being found to be inconsistent with the relevant WTO agreement, the panel recommends ways in which the member may bring the measure into conformity with the agreement. However, under the WTO mechanism either party has the right to appeal against the decision and must notify the DSB of its intentions before adoption of the final report. Appeal proceedings, which are limited to issues of law and the legal interpretation covered by the panel report, are undertaken by three members of the Appellate Body within a maximum period of 90 days. The report of the Appellate Body must be unconditionally accepted by the parties to the dispute (unless there is a consensus within the DSB against its adoption). If the recommendations of the panel or appeal report are not implemented immediately, or within a 'reasonable period' as determined by the DSB, the parties are obliged to negotiate mutually-acceptable compensation pending full implementation. Failure to agree compensation may result in the DSB authorizing the complainant to suspend concessions or obligations against the other party. In any case the DSB monitors the implementation of adopted recommendations or rulings, while any outstanding cases remain on its agenda until the issue is resolved. By July 2005 332 trade complaints had been notified to the WTO since 1995, on more than 180 different issues.

In late 1997 the DSB initiated a review of the WTO's understanding on dispute settlement, as required by the Marrakesh Agreement. The Doha Declaration, which was adopted in November 2001, mandated further negotiations to be conducted on the review and on additional proposals to amend the dispute procedure as a separate undertaking from the rest of the work programme. Negotiations were to be concluded by May 2003. In July of that year, however, the General Council acknowledged that the special session on dispute procedure required more time to conclude its work.

CO-OPERATION WITH OTHER ORGANIZATIONS

WTO is mandated to pursue co-operation with the IMF and the World Bank, as well as with other multilateral organizations, in order to achieve greater coherence in global economic policy-making. In November 1994 the preparatory committee of the WTO resolved not to incorporate the new organization into the UN structure as a specialized agency. Instead, co-operation arrangements with the IMF and World Bank were to be developed. In addition, efforts were pursued to enhance co-operation with UNCTAD in research, trade and technical issues. The Directors-General of the two organizations agreed to meet at least twice a year in order to develop the working relationship. In particular, co-operation was to be undertaken in WTO's special programme of activities for Africa, which aimed to help African countries expand and diversify their trade and benefit from the global trading system. Since 1997 WTO has co-operated with the IMF, ITC, UNCTAD, UNDP and World Bank in an Integrated Framework for trade-related technical assistance to least developed countries. An enhanced Integrated Framework (EIF) was adopted in May 2007. Every April WTO, the IMF, World Bank, UNCTAD and ECOSOC participate in high-level consultations.

International Trade Centre (UNCTAD/WTO): Palais des Nations, 1211 Geneva 10, Switzerland; tel. 227300111; fax 227334439; e-mail itcreg@intracen.org; internet www.intracen.org; f. 1964 by GATT; jointly operated with the UN (through UNCTAD) since 1968; ITC works with developing countries in product and market development, the development of trade support services, trade information, human resource development, international purchasing and supply management, and needs assessment and programme design for trade promotion; publs *International Trade Forum* (quarterly), market studies, handbooks, etc.

Executive Director: J. PATRICIA FRANCIS (Jamaica).

Finance

The WTO's 2007 budget amounted to 182m. Swiss francs, financed mainly by contributions from members in proportion to their share of total trading conducted by WTO members.

Publications

Annual Report (2 volumes).
Annual Report of the Appellate Body.
International Trade Statistics (annually).
World Trade Report (annually).
World Trade Review (3 a year).
World Trade Report (annually).
WTO Focus (monthly).

OTHER INTERNATIONAL ORGANIZATIONS

Agriculture, Food, Forestry and Fisheries	page 402	Press, Radio and Television	439
Arts and Culture	405	Religion	441
Commodities	407	Science	444
Development and Economic Co-operation	410	Social Sciences	450
Economics and Finance	415	Social Welfare and Human Rights	453
Education	417	Sport and Recreations	457
Environmental Conservation	421	Technology	459
Government and Politics	422	Tourism	463
Industrial and Professional Relations	427	Trade and Industry	464
Law	429	Transport	468
Medicine and Health	432	Youth and Students	470
Posts and Telecommunications	439	**Index at end of volume**	

OTHER INTERNATIONAL ORGANIZATIONS

Agriculture, Food, Forestry and Fisheries

(for organizations concerned with agricultural commodities, see Commodities)

African Timber Organization (ATO): BP 1077, Libreville, Gabon; tel. 732928; fax 734030; e-mail oab-gabon@internetgabon.com; f. 1976 to enable members to study and co-ordinate ways of ensuring the optimum utilization and conservation of their forests; mems: 13 African countries; publs *ATO Information Bulletin* (quarterly), *International Magazine of African Timber* (2 a year).

Arab Authority for Agricultural Investment and Development (AAAID): POB 2102, Khartoum, Sudan; tel. (11) 780777; fax (11) 772600; e-mail info@aaaid.org; internet www.aaaid.org; f. 1976 to accelerate agricultural development in the Arab world and to ensure food security; acts principally by equity participation in agricultural projects in member countries; AAAID has adopted new programmes to help raise productivity of food agricultural products and introduced zero-tillage farming technology for developing the rain-fed sector, which achieved a substantial increase in the yields of grown crops, including sorghum, cotton, sesame, and sunflower; mems: 19 countries; Pres. and Chair. ABDUL KAREEM MOHAMMAD AL-AMRI; publs *Journal of Agricultural Investment* (English and Arabic), *Extension and Investment Bulletins*, *Annual Report* (Arabic and English), *AAAID Newsletter* (quarterly).

Asian Vegetable Research and Development Center (AVRDC): POB 42, Shanhua, Tainan 74199, Taiwan; tel. (6) 5837801; fax (6) 5830009; e-mail avrdcbox@avrdc.org; internet www.avrdc.org; f. 1971; aims to enhance the nutritional well-being and raise the incomes of the poor in rural and urban areas of developing countries, through improved varieties and methods of vegetable production, marketing and distribution; runs an experimental farm, laboratories, gene-bank, greenhouses, quarantine house, insectarium, library and weather station; provides training for research and production specialists in tropical vegetables; exchanges and disseminates vegetable germplasm through regional centres in the developing world; serves as a clearing-house for vegetable research information; and undertakes scientific publishing; mems: Australia, France, Germany, Japan, Republic of Korea, Philippines, Taiwan, Thailand, USA; Dir-Gen. Dr THOMAS A. LUMPKIN; publs *Annual Report*, *Technical Bulletin*, *Proceedings*, *Centerpoint* (quarterly).

Association of Agricultural Research Institutions in the Near East and North Africa: POB 950764, 11195 Amman, Jordan; tel. (6) 5525750; fax (6) 5525930; e-mail icarda-jordan@cgiar.org; internet www.aarinena.org; f. 1985; aims to strengthen co-operation among national, regional and international research institutions; is developing a Regional Agricultural Information System; Exec. Sec. IBRAHIM YUSUF HAMDAN (Jordan).

CAB International (CABI): Nosworthy Way, Wallingford, Oxon, OX10 8DE, United Kingdom; tel. (1491) 832111; fax (1491) 833508; e-mail corporate@cabi.org; internet www.cabi.org; f. 1929 as the Imperial Agricultural Bureaux (later Commonwealth Agricultural Bureaux), current name adopted in 1985; aims to improve human welfare world-wide through the generation, dissemination and application of scientific knowledge in support of sustainable development; places particular emphasis on sustainable agriculture, forestry, human health and the management of natural resources, with priority given to the needs of developing countries; compiles and publishes extensive information (in a variety of print and electronic forms) on aspects of agriculture, forestry, veterinary medicine, the environment and natural resources, and Third World rural development; maintains regional centres in the People's Republic of China, India, Kenya, Malaysia, Pakistan, Switzerland, Trinidad and Tobago, and the United Kingdom; mems: 45 countries and territories; Chair. Dr JOHN REGAZZI.

CABI Bioscience: Bakeham Lane, Egham, Surrey, TW20 9TY, United Kingdom; tel. (1491) 829080; fax (1491) 829100; e-mail bioscience.egham@cabi.org; internet www.cabi-bioscience.org; f. 1998 by integration of the following four CABI scientific institutions: International Institute of Biological Control; International Institute of Entomology; International Institute of Parasitology; International Mycological Institute; undertakes research, consultancy, training, capacity-building and institutional development measures in sustainable pest management, biosystematics and molecular biology, ecological applications and environmental and industrial microbiology; maintains centres in Kenya, Malaysia, Pakistan, Switzerland, Trinidad and Tobago, and the United Kingdom; Dir Dr JOAN KELLEY.

Collaborative International Pesticides Analytical Council Ltd (CIPAC): c/o Dr M. D. Müller, Swiss Federal Res. Station, 8820 Wädenswil, Switzerland; tel. 17836412; fax 17836439; e-mail markus.mueller@faw.admin.ch; internet www.cipac.org; f. 1957 to organize international collaborative work on methods of analysis for pesticides used in crop protection; 24 mems, 7 hon. life mems; Chair. Dr MARKUS D. MÜLLER (Switzerland); Sec. Dr LÁZLÓ BURA (Hungary).

Desert Locust Control Organization for Eastern Africa (DLCOEA): POB 4255, Addis Ababa, Ethiopia; tel. (1) 461477; fax (1) 460296; e-mail dlc@ethionet.et; internet www.dlcoea.org.et; f. 1962 to promote effective control of desert locust in the region and to conduct research into the locust's environment and behaviour; also assists member states in the monitoring, forecasting and extermination of other migratory pests; mems: Djibouti, Eritrea, Ethiopia, Kenya, Somalia, Sudan, Tanzania, Uganda; Dir PETER O. ODIYO; Co-ordinator J. M. GATIMU; publs *Desert Locust Situation Reports* (monthly), *Annual Report*, technical reports.

European and Mediterranean Plant Protection Organization (EPPO): 1 rue Le Nôtre, 75016 Paris, France; tel. 1-45-20-77-94; fax 1-42-24-89-43; e-mail hq@eppo.fr; internet www.eppo.org; f. 1951, present name adopted in 1955; aims to promote international co-operation between government plant protection services to prevent the introduction and spread of pests and diseases of plants and plant products; mems: governments of 49 countries and territories; Chair. ARNITIS RINGOLDS; Dir-Gen. NICOLAAS ARIE VAN OPSTAL; publs *EPPO Bulletin*, *Data Sheets on Quarantine Organisms*, *Guidelines for the Efficacy Evaluation of Pesticides*, *Crop Growth Stage Keys*, *Summary of the Phytosanitary Regulations of EPPO Member Countries*, *Reporting Service*.

European Association for Animal Production (EAAP) (Fédération européenne de zootechnie): Via Tomassetti 3 A/1, 00161 Rome, Italy; tel. (06) 44202639; fax (06) 86329263; e-mail eaap@eaap.org; internet www.eaap.org; f. 1949 to help improve the conditions of animal production and meet consumer demand; holds annual meetings; mems: asscns in 38 countries; Pres. JIM FLANAGAN (Ireland); publ. *Animal Journal*.

European Association for Research on Plant Breeding (EUCARPIA): c/o Instituto Valenciano de Investigaciones Agrarias, Apdo Oficial, E-46113 Moncada, Valencia, Spain; tel. (9634) 24049; fax (9634) 24106; e-mail eucarpia.secretariat@ivia.es; internet www.eucarpia.org; f. 1956 to promote scientific and technical co-operation in the plant breeding field; mems: 1,100 individuals, 65 corporate mems; Pres. Prof. JAIME PROHENS-TOMÁS (Spain); Sec.-Gen. Dr MARIA LUISA BADENES (Spain); publ. *EUCARPIA Bulletin*.

European Grassland Federation: c/o Dr Willy Kessler, Agroscope Reckenholz-Tänikon Research Station ART, Reckenholzstr. 191, 8046, Zürich, Switzerland; tel. 443777376; fax 443770201; e-mail fedsecretary@europeangrassland.org; internet www.europeangrassland.org; f. 1963 to facilitate and maintain liaison between European grassland organizations and to promote the interchange of scientific and practical knowledge and experience; holds General Meeting every two years and symposia at other times; mems: 30 full and five corresponding mem. countries in Europe; Pres. Dr. GÖRAN DALIN; Sec. Dr WILLY KESSLER (Switzerland); publ. *Grassland Science in Europe*.

European Livestock and Meat Trading Union (UECBV): 81A rue de la Loi, 1040 Brussels, Belgium; tel. (2) 230-46-03; fax (2) 230-94-00; e-mail uecbv@pophost.eunet.be; f. 1952 to study problems of the European livestock and meat trade and inform members of all relevant legislation; acts as an international arbitration commission; conducts research on agricultural markets, quality of livestock, and veterinary regulations; mems: national organizations in 23 countries, and the European Association of Livestock Markets; Pres. LAURENT SPANGHERO; Sec.-Gen. JEAN-LUC MERIAUX.

Inter-American Association of Agricultural Librarians, Documentalists and Information Specialists (Asociación Interamericana de Bibliotecarios, Documentalistas y Especialistas en Información Agrícolas—AIBDA): c/o IICA-CIDIA, Apdo 55-2200 Coronado, Costa Rica; tel. 216-0222; fax 216-0291; e-mail aibda@iica.int; internet www.iica.int/AIBDA; f. 1953 to promote professional improvement through technical publications and meetings, and to promote improvement of library services in agricultural sciences; mems: 653 in 31 countries and territories; Pres. RUBÉN URBIZAGÁSTEGUI (Peru); publs *Boletín Informativo* (3 a year), *Boletín Especial* (irregular), *Revista AIBDA* (2 a year), *AIBDA Actualidades* (4 or 5 a year).

Inter-American Tropical Tuna Commission (IATTC): 8604 La Jolla Shores Drive, La Jolla, CA 92037-1508, USA; tel. (858) 546-7100; fax (858) 546-7133; e-mail info@iattc.org; internet www.iattc.org; f. 1950; administers two programmes, the Tuna-Billfish Programme and the Tuna-Dolphin Programme. The principal

INTERNATIONAL ORGANIZATIONS — Agriculture, Food, Forestry and Fisheries

responsibilities of the Tuna-Billfish Programme are: to study the biology of the tunas and related species of the eastern Pacific Ocean to estimate the effects of fishing and natural factors on their abundance; to recommend appropriate conservation measures in order to maintain stocks at levels which will afford maximum sustainable catches; and to collect information on compliance with Commission resolutions. The principal functions of the Tuna-Dolphin Programme are: to monitor the abundance of dolphins and their mortality incidental to purse-seine fishing in the eastern Pacific Ocean; to study the causes of mortality of dolphins during fishing operations and promote the use of fishing techniques and equipment that minimize these mortalities; to study the effects of different fishing methods on the various fish and other animals of the pelagic ecosystem; and to provide a secretariat for the International Dolphin Conservation Programme; mems: Costa Rica, Ecuador, El Salvador, France, Guatemala, Japan, Mexico, Nicaragua, Panama, Peru, Republic of Korea, Spain, USA, Vanuatu, Venezuela; Dir ROBIN ALLEN; publs *Bulletin* (irregular), *Annual Report, Fishery Status Report, Stock Assessment Report* (annually), *Special Report* (irregular).

International Association for Cereal Science and Technology (ICC): Marxergasse 2, 1030 Vienna, Austria; tel. (1) 707-72-020; fax (1) 707-72-040; e-mail office@icc.or.at; internet www.icc.or.at; f. 1955 (as the International Association for Cereal Chemistry, name changed 1986); aims to promote international co-operation in the field of cereal science and technology through the dissemination of information and the development of standard methods of testing and analysing products; mems: 49 mem. and six observer mem. states; Pres. Dr CONCHA COLLAR (Spain); Sec.-Gen. Dr ROLAND POMS (Austria).

International Association for Vegetation Science (IAVS): Alterra, Green World Research, POB 47, 6700 AA Wageningen, Netherlands; tel. (317) 477914; fax (317) 424988; e-mail Joop .Schaminee@wur.nl; internet www.iavs.org; f. 1938; mems: 1,500 in 70 countries; Pres. Prof. Dr E. O. BOX; Gen Sec. Dr J. H. J. SCHAMINÉE (Netherlands); publs *Phytocoenologia, Journal of Vegetation Science, Applied Vegetation Science.*

International Association of Agricultural Economists (IAAE): c/o Farm Foundation, 1211 West 22nd St, Suite 216, Oak Brook, IL 60523-2197, USA; tel. (630) 571-9393; fax (630) 571-9580; e-mail iaae@farmfoundation.org; internet www.iaae-agecon.org; f. 1929 to foster development of agricultural economic sciences; aims to further the application of research into agricultural processes; works to improve economic and social conditions for agricultural and rural life; mems: in 83 countries; Pres. PRABHU PINGALI (Italy); Sec. and Treas. WALTER J. ARMBRUSTER (USA); publs *Agricultural Economics* (8 a year), *IAAE Newsletter* (2 a year).

International Association of Agricultural Information Specialists: c/o Toni Greider, POB 63, Lexington, KY 40588-0063, USA; tel. (859) 254-0752; fax (859) 257-8379; e-mail info@iaald.org; internet www.iaald.org; f. 1955 to provide educational and networking opportunities for agricultural information professionals worldwide; aims to enable its members to create, capture, access and disseminate information to achieve a more productive and sustainable use of the world's land, water, and renewable natural resources and to contribute to improved livelihoods of rural communities through educational programmes, conferences, and networking opportunities; affiliated to INFITA; mems: 400 in 84 countries; Pres. PETER BALLANTYNE (Netherlands); Sec.-Treas. TONI GREIDER (USA); publ. *Agricultural Information Worldwide.*

International Association of Horticultural Producers (IAHP): Louis Pasteurlaan 6, POB 280, 2700 AG Zoetermeer, Netherlands; tel. (79) 3470701; fax (79) 3470405; e-mail aiph@tuinbouw.nl; internet www.aiph.org; f. 1948; represents the common interests of commercial horticultural producers in the international field; authorizes international horticultural exhibitions; mems: national asscns in 25 countries; Pres. DOEKE FABER (Netherlands); publ. *Yearbook of International Horticultural Statistics.*

International Bee Research Association (IBRA): 18 North Rd, Cardiff, CF10 3DT, United Kingdom; tel. (29) 2037-2409; fax (29) 2066-5522; e-mail mail@ibra.org.uk; internet www.ibra.org.uk; f. 1949 to further bee research and provide an information service for bee scientists and bee-keepers world-wide; mems: 1,200 in 130 countries; Chair Dr WILLIAM KIRK; publs *Bee World* (quarterly), *Apicultural Abstracts* (quarterly), *Journal of Apicultural Research* (quarterly), *Buzz Extra* (quarterly).

International Centre for Tropical Agriculture (Centro Internacional de Agricultura Tropical—CIAT): Apdo Aéreo 6713, Cali, Colombia; tel. (2) 445-0000; fax (2) 445-0073; e-mail ciat@cgiar.org; internet www.ciat.cgiar.org; f. 1967 to contribute to the alleviation of hunger and poverty in tropical developing countries by using new techniques in agriculture research and training; focuses on production problems in field beans, cassava, rice and tropical pastures in the tropics; Dir-Gen. Dr JOACHIM VOSS; publs *Annual Report, Growing Affinities* (2 a year), *Pasturas Tropicales* (3 a year), catalogue of publications.

International Commission for the Conservation of Atlantic Tunas (ICCAT): Calle Corazón de Maria 8, 28002 Madrid, Spain; tel. (91) 4165600; fax (91) 4152612; e-mail info@iccat.es; internet www.iccat.es; f. 1969 under the provisions of the International Convention for the Conservation of Atlantic Tunas (1966) to maintain the populations of tuna and tuna-like species in the Atlantic Ocean and adjacent seas at levels that permit the maximum sustainable catch; collects statistics; conducts studies; mems: 40 contracting parties; Chair. Dr BILL HOGARTH (USA); Exec. Sec. DRISS MESKI (Morocco); publs *ICCAT Biennial Report, ICCAT Collective Vol. of Scientific Papers, Statistical Bulletin* (annually), *Data Record* (annually).

International Commission of Sugar Technology (Commission Internationale Technique de Sucrerie—CITS): Marktbreiter Str. 74, 97199 Ochsenfurt, Germany; tel. (9331) 91450; fax (9331) 91462; f. 1949 to discuss investigations and promote scientific and technical research work; Pres. LÉON SUÉ (Belgium); Hon. Sec.-Gen. ROBERT PIECK.

International Committee for Animal Recording (ICAR): Via Tomassetti 3-1/A, 00161, Rome, Italy; tel. (06) 44202639; fax (06) 86329263; e-mail icar@eaap.org; internet www.icar.org; f. 1951 to extend and improve the work of recording and to standardize methods; mems: in 58 countries; Pres. JARMO JUGA (Finland).

International Crops Research Institute for the Semi-Arid Tropics (ICRISAT): Patancheru, Andhra Pradesh 502 324, India; tel. (40) 30713222; fax (40) 30713072; e-mail icrisat@cgiar.org; internet www.icrisat.org; f. 1972 to promote the genetic improvement of crops and for research on the management of resources in the world's semi-arid tropics, with the aim of reducing poverty and protecting the environment; research covers all physical and socio-economic aspects of improving farming systems on unirrigated land; Dir-Gen. Dr WILLIAM D. DAR (Philippines); publs *ICRISAT Report* (annually), *SAT News* (2 a year), *International Chickpea and Pigeonpea Newsletter, International Arachis Newsletter, International Sorghum and Millet Newsletter* (annually), information and research bulletins.

International Dairy Federation (IDF): Diamant Bldg, 80 blvd Auguste Reyers, 1030 Brussels, Belgium; tel. (2) 733-98-88; fax (2) 733-04-13; e-mail info@fil-idf.org; internet www.fil-idf.org; f. 1903 to link all dairy asscns, in order to encourage the solution of scientific, technical and economic problems affecting the dairy industry; mems: national cttees in 53 countries; Dir-Gen. CHRISTIAN ROBERT; publs *Bulletin of IDF, IDF-ISO Standard Methods of Analysis.*

International Federation of Agricultural Producers (IFAP): 60 rue St-Lazare, 75009 Paris, France; tel. 1-45-26-05-53; fax 1-48-74-72-12; e-mail ifap@ifap.org; internet www.ifap.org; f. 1946 to represent, in the international field, the interests of agricultural producers; encourages the exchange of information and ideas; works to develop understanding of world problems and their effects upon agricultural producers; encourages sustainable patterns of agricultural development; holds conference every two years; mems: national farmers' organizations and agricultural co-operatives of 83 countries; Pres. JACK WILKINSON (Canada); Sec.-Gen. DAVID KING; publs *The World Farmer* (monthly), *Proceedings of General Conferences.*

International Federation of Beekeepers' Associations (APIMONDIA): Corso Vittorio Emanuele II 101, 00186 Rome, Italy; tel. and fax (06) 6852286; e-mail apimondia@mclink.it; internet www.apimondia.org; f. 1949; collects and brings up to date documentation on international beekeeping; carries out studies into the particular problems of beekeeping; organizes international congresses, seminars, symposia and meetings; co-operates with other international organizations interested in beekeeping, in particular, with the FAO; mems: 65 asscns from 56 countries; Pres. ASGER SØGAARD JØRGENSEN (Denmark); Sec.-Gen. RICCARDO JANNONI-SEBASTIANINI (Italy); publs *Apiacta* (quarterly, in English, French, German and Spanish), *Dictionary of Beekeeping Terms, AGROVOC* (thesaurus of agricultural terms), studies.

International Food Policy Research Institute (IFPRI): 2033 K St, NW, Washington, DC 20006, USA; tel. (202) 862-5600; fax (202) 467-4439; e-mail ifpri@cgiar.org; internet www.ifpri.org; f. 1975; co-operates with academic and other institutions in further research; develops policies for cutting hunger and malnutrition; committed to increasing public awareness of food policies; Chair. Dr ROSS GARNAUT (Australia); Dir Gen. JOACHIM VON BRAUN (Germany).

International Service for National Agricultural Research (ISNAR): IFPRI, ISNAR Division, ILRI, POB 5689, Addis Ababa, Ethiopia; tel. (11) 646-3215; fax (11) 646-2927; e-mail ifpri-addisababa@cgiar.org; fmrly based in The Hague, Netherlands, the ISNAR Program relocated to Addis Ababa in 2004, under the governance of IFPRI; Dir Dr WILBERFORCE KISAMBA-MUGERWA.

International Hop Growers' Convention: Malgajeva 18, 3000 Celje, Slovenia; tel. (63) 712-16-18; fax (63) 712-16-20; e-mail martin.pavlovic@guest.arnes.si; internet www.hmelj-giz.si/ihgc; f. 1950; acts as a centre for the collection of data and reports on hop production, beer exports and imports and sales, estimates the world crop and promotes scientific research; mems: national asscns in 20 countries, four hop trading companies; Pres. BERNARD INGWILLER (France); Sec.-Gen. Dr MARTIN PAVLOVIĆ.

International Institute for Beet Research (IIRB): rue Washington 40, 1050 Brussels, Belgium; Holtenser Landstr. 77, 37079 Göttingen, Germany; tel. (551) 500-65-84; fax (551) 500-65-85; e-mail mail@iirb.org; internet www.iirb.org; f. 1932 to promote research and the exchange of information; organizes meetings and study groups; mems: 500 in 27 countries; Pres. PAOLA PEDRONI (Italy); Sec.-Gen. HELMUT TESCHEMACHER (Germany).

International Institute of Tropical Agriculture (IITA): Oyo Rd, PMB 5320, Ibadan, Oyo State, Nigeria; tel. (2) 2412626; fax (2) 2412221; e-mail iita@cgiar.org; internet www.iita.org; f. 1967; principal financing arranged by the Consultative Group on International Agricultural Research—CGIAR, co-sponsored by the FAO, the IBRD and the UNDP; research programmes comprise crop management, improvement of crops and plant protection and health; conducts a training programme for researchers in tropical agriculture; maintains a library of 75,000 vols and a database; administers six agro-ecological research stations; Dir-Gen. Dr PETER HARTMAN (USA); publs *Annual Report*, *IITA Research* (quarterly), technical bulletins, research reports.

International Livestock Research Institute (ILRI): POB 30709, Nairobi 00100, Kenya; tel. (20) 4223000; fax (20) 4223001; e-mail ilri-kenya@cgiar.org; internet www.ilri.org; f. 1995 to supersede the International Laboratory for Research on Animal Diseases and the International Livestock Centre for Africa; conducts laboratory and field research on animal health and other livestock issues; carries out training programmes for scientists and technicians; maintains a specialized science library; Dir Dr CARLOS SERÉ; publs *Annual Report*, *Livestock Research for Development* (newsletter, 2 a year).

International Maize and Wheat Improvement Centre (CIMMYT): Apdo Postal 6-641, 06600 México, DF, Mexico; tel. (55) 5804-7502; fax (55) 5804-7558; e-mail cimmyt@cgiar.org; internet www.cimmyt.org; conducts world-wide research programme for sustainable maize and wheat cropping systems to help the poor in developing countries; Dir-Gen. Dr MASARU IWANAGA.

International Organization for Biological Control of Noxious Animals and Plants: IOBC Permanent Secretariat, AGROPOLIS, ave Agropolis, 34394 Montpellier Cédex 5, France; e-mail iobc@agropolis.fr; internet www.unipa.it/iobc/; f. 1955 to promote and co-ordinate research on the more effective biological control of harmful organisms; re-organized in 1971 as a central council with world-wide affiliations and six largely autonomous regional sections; Pres. Prof. Dr JOOP C. VAN LENTEREN (Netherlands); Gen. Sec. Prof. Dr STEFANO COLAZZA (Italy); publs *BioControl*, *Newsletter*.

International Organization of Citrus Virologists (IOCV): c/o C. N. Roistacher, Dept of Plant Pathology, Univ. of California, Riverside, CA 92521-0122, USA; tel. (909) 684-0934; fax (909) 684-4324; e-mail chester.r@worldnet.att.net; f. 1957 to promote research on citrus virus diseases at international level by standardizing diagnostic techniques and exchanging information; mems: 250; Chair. PEDRO MORENO; Sec. CHESTER N. ROISTACHER.

International Red Locust Control Organization for Central and Southern Africa (IRLCO-CSA): POB 240252, Ndola, Zambia; tel. (2) 651251; fax (2) 650117; e-mail locust@zamnet.zm; internet www.irlcocsa.com; f. 1971 to control locusts in eastern, central and southern Africa; also assists in the control of African army-worm and quelea-quelea; mems: six countries; Dir MOSES M. OKHOBA; publs *Annual Report*, *Quarterly Report*, *Monthly Report*, scientific reports.

International Rice Research Institute (IRRI): Los Baños, Laguna, DAPO Box 7777, Metro Manila, Philippines; tel. (2) 5805600; fax (2) 5805699; e-mail irri@cgiar.org; internet www.irri.org; f. 1960; conducts research on rice, with the aim of developing technologies of environmental, social and economic benefit; works to enhance national rice research systems and offers training; operates Riceworld, a museum and learning centre about rice; maintains a library of technical rice literature; organizes international conferences and workshops; Dir-Gen. Dr ROBERT S. ZEIGLER; publs *Rice Literature Update*, *Hotline*, *Facts about IRRI*, *News about Rice and People*, *International Rice Research Notes*.

International Seed Testing Association (ISTA): Zürichstrasse 50, Postfach 308, 8303 Bassersdorf, Switzerland; tel. 448386000; fax 448386001; e-mail ista.office@ista.ch; internet www.seedtest.org; f. 1924 to promote uniformity and accurate methods of seed testing and evaluation in order to facilitate efficiency in production, processing, distribution and utilization of seeds; organizes meetings, workshops, symposia, training courses and triennial congresses; mems: 76 countries; Pres. KATALIN ERTSEY (Hungary); Sec.-Gen. Dr MICHAEL MUSCHICK; publs *Seed Science and Technology* (3 a year), *Seed Testing International (ISTA News Bulletin)* (2 a year), *International Rules for Seed Testing* (annually).

International Sericultural Commission (ISC): 25 quai Jean-Jacques Rousseau, 69350 La Mulatière, France; tel. 4-78-50-41-98; fax 4-78-86-09-57; e-mail info@inserco.org; internet www.inserco.org; f. 1948 to encourage the development of silk production; mems: governments of Brazil, Egypt, France, Greece, India, Indonesia, Iran, Japan, Madagascar, Romania, Syria, Thailand, Tunisia; Sec.-Gen. Dr GÉRARD CHAVANCY (France); publ. *Sericologia* (quarterly).

International Society for Horticultural Science (ISHS): Decroylaan 42 (01.21), POB 500, 3001 Leuven 1, Belgium; tel. (16) 22-94-27; fax (16) 22-94-50; e-mail info@ishs.org; internet www.ishs.org; f. 1959 to promote co-operation in horticultural science research; mems: 54 mem. countries, 300 organizations, 6,000 individuals; Pres. Dr NORMAN E. LOONEY (Canada); Exec. Dir Ir JOZEF VAN ASSCHE (Belgium); publs *Chronica Horticulturae* (quarterly), *Acta Horticulturae*, *Horticultural Research International*.

International Union for the Protection of New Varieties of Plant (Union internationale pour la protection des obtentions végétales—UPOV): 34 chemin des Colombettes, 1211 Geneva 20, Switzerland; tel. 223389111; fax 227330336; e-mail upov.mail@upov.int; internet www.upov.int; f. 1961 by the International Convention for the Protection of New Varieties of Plants (entered into force 1968, revised in 1972, 1978 and 1991); aims to encourage the development of new plant varieties and provide an effective system of intellectual property protection for plant breeders. Admin. support provided by WIPO; mems: 65 states; Pres. of the Council DOUG WATERHOUSE; Sec.-Gen. Dr KAMIL IDRIS.

International Union of Forest Research Organizations (IUFRO): Mariabrunn (BFW), Hauptstrasse 7, 1140 Vienna, Austria; tel. (1) 877-01-51-0; fax (1) 877-01-51-50; e-mail office@iufro.org; internet www.iufro.org; f. 1892; aims to promote global co-operation in forest-related research and enhance the understanding of the ecological, economic and social aspects of forests and trees; disseminates scientific knowledge to stakeholders and decision-makers and aims to contribute to forest policy and on-the-ground forest management; mems: 700 orgs in more than 110 countries, involving some 15,000 scientists; Pres. Prof. DON KOO LEE (Republic of Korea); Exec. Dir PETER MAYER (Austria); publs *Annual Report*, *IUFRO News* (10 a year, electronic format only), *IUFRO World Series*, *IUFRO Occasional Paper Series*, *IUFRO Research Series*.

International Union of Soil Sciences: c/o Department of Soil Science, University of Reading, POB 233, Reading, RG6 6DW, United Kingdom; tel. (118) 378-6559; fax (118) 378-6666; e-mail iuss@rdg.ac.uk; internet www.iuss.org; f. 1924; mems: national academies or national soil science societies from 143 countries; Pres. Prof. ROGER SWIFT (Australia); Sec.-Gen. Prof. STEPHEN NORTCLIFF (United Kingdom); publ. *Bulletin* (2 a year).

International Whaling Commission (IWC): The Red House, 135 Station Rd, Impington, Cambridge, CB4 9NP, United Kingdom; tel. (1223) 233971; fax (1223) 232876; e-mail secretariat@iwcoffice.com; internet www.iwcoffice.org; f. 1946 under the International Convention for the Regulation of Whaling, for the conservation of world whale stocks; reviews the regulations covering whaling operations; encourages research; collects, analyses and disseminates statistical and other information on whaling. A ban on commercial whaling was passed by the Commission in July 1982, to take effect three years subsequently (in some cases, a phased reduction of commercial operations was not completed until 1988). A revised whale-management procedure was adopted in 1992, to be implemented after the development of a complete whale management scheme; mems: governments of 78 countries; Sec. Dr NICOLA GRANDY; publs *Annual Report*, *Journal of Cetacean Research and Management*.

North Pacific Anadromous Fish Commission: 889 W. Pender St, Suite 502, Vancouver, BC V6C 3B2, Canada; tel. (604) 775-5550; fax (604) 775-5577; e-mail secretariat@npafc.org; internet www.npafc.org; f. 1993; mems: Canada, Japan, Republic of Korea, Russia, USA; Pres. DOHYUNG KOO; publs *Annual Report*, *Newsletter* (2 a year), *Statistical Yearbook*, *Scientific Bulletin*, *Technical Report*.

Northwest Atlantic Fisheries Organization (NAFO): 2 Morris Drive, POB 638, Dartmouth, NS B2Y 3Y9, Canada; tel. (902) 468-5590; fax (902) 468-5538; e-mail info@nafo.int; internet www.nafo.int; f. 1979 (fmrly International Commission for the Northwest Atlantic Fisheries); aims at optimum use, management and conservation of resources; promotes research and compiles statistics; Pres. DAVID BEVAN (Canada); Exec. Sec. Dr JOHANNE FISCHER; publs *Annual Report* (electronic format only), *Statistical Bulletin*, *Journal of Northwest Atlantic Fishery Science* (in electronic and print formats), *Scientific Council Reports*, *Scientific Council Studies*, *Sampling Yearbook*, *Meeting Proceedings*.

INTERNATIONAL ORGANIZATIONS

Western and Central Pacific Fisheries Commission: Kaselehie St, POB 2356, Kolonia, Pohnpei State 96941, Federated States of Micronesia; tel. 3201992; fax 3201108; e-mail contact@wcpfc.org; internet www.wcpfc.org; f. 2004 under the Convention for the Conservation and Management of Highly Migratory Fish Stocks in the Western and Central Pacific, which entered into force in June of that year, six months after the deposit of the 13th ratification; inaugural session convened in December, in Pohnpei, Federated States of Micronesia; mems: 31 countries and the European Community; Exec. Dir ANDREW WRIGHT.

World Association for Animal Production (WAAP): Via Tomassetti 3A/1, 00161 Rome, Italy; tel. (06) 44202639; fax (06) 86329263; e-mail waap@waap.it; internet www.waap.it; f. 1965; holds world conference on animal production every five years; encourages, sponsors and participates in regional meetings, seminars and symposia; mems: 17 mem. organizations; Pres. ASSEFAW TEWOLDE (Costa Rica); Sec.-Gen. ANDREA ROSATI; publ. *WAAP Newsletter*.

World Association of Veterinary Food Hygienists (WAVFH): Federal Institute for Health Protection of Consumers and Veterinary Medicine (BgVV), Diedersdorfer Weg 1, 12277 Berlin, Germany; tel. (30) 8412-2101; fax (30) 8412-2951; e-mail p.teufel@bgvv.de; f. 1955 to promote hygienic food control and discuss research; mems: national asscns in 40 countries; Pres. Prof. PAUL TEUFEL; Sec. Treas. Dr L. ELLERBROEK.

World Association of Veterinary Microbiologists, Immunologists and Specialists in Infectious Diseases: Ecole Nationale Vétérinaire d'Alfort, 7 ave du Général de Gaulle, 94704 Maisons-Alfort Cédex, France; tel. 1-43-96-70-21; fax 1-43-96-70-22; f. 1967 to facilitate international contacts in the fields of microbiology, immunology and animal infectious diseases; Pres. Prof. C. PILET (France); publs *Comparative Immunology, Microbiology and Infectious Diseases*.

WorldFish Center (International Centre for Living Aquatic Resources Management—ICLARM): Jalan Batu Maung, Batu Maung, 11960 Bayan Lepas, Penang, Malaysia; POB 500, GPO, 10670 Penang; tel. (4) 626-1606; fax (4) 626-5530; e-mail worldfishcenter@cgiar.org; internet www.worldfishcenter.org; f. 1973; became a mem. of the Consultative Group on International Agricultural Research (CGIAR) in 1992; aims to contribute to food security and poverty eradication in developing countries through the sustainable development and use of living aquatic resources; carries out research and promotes partnerships; Dir-Gen. Dr STEPHEN J. HALL; publ. *NAGA* (quarterly newsletter).

World Organisation of Animal Health: 12 rue de Prony, 75017 Paris, France; tel. 1-44-15-18-88; fax 1-42-67-09-87; e-mail oie@oie.int; internet www.oie.int; f. 1924 as Office International des Epizooties (OIE); objectives include promoting international transparency of animal diseases; collecting, analysing and disseminating scientific veterinary information; providing expertise and promoting international co-operation in the control of animal diseases; promoting veterinary services; providing new scientific guide-lines on animal production, food safety and animal welfare; launched in May 2005, jointly with FAO and WHO, a Global Strategy for the Progressive Control of Highly Pathogenic Avian Influenza (H5N1), and, in partnership with other organizations, has convened conferences on avian influenza; experts in a network of 156 collaborating centres and reference laboratories; 167 mems; Dir-Gen. BERNARD VALLAT; publs *Disease Information* (weekly), *World Animal Health* (annually), *Scientific and Technical Review* (3 a year), other manuals, codes etc.

World Ploughing Organization (WPO): Grolweg 2, 6964 BL HALL, Netherlands; tel. (313) 619634; fax (313) 619735; e-mail hans.spieker@worldploughing.org; internet www.worldploughing.org; f. 1952 to promote the World Ploughing Contest in a different country each year, to improve techniques and promote better understanding of soil cultivation practices through research and practical demonstrations; arranges tillage clinics world-wide; mems: affiliates in 30 countries; Gen. Sec. HANS SPIEKER; publ. *WPO Handbook* (annually).

World's Poultry Science Association (WPSA): c/o Dr P. C. M. Simons, POB 31, 7360 AA Beekbergen, Netherlands; tel. (55) 506-3250; fax (55) 506-4858; e-mail piet.simons@wur.nl; internet www.wpsa.com; f. 1912 (as the International Asscn of Poultry Instructors); aims to advance and exchange knowledge relating to poultry science and the poultry industry; organizes World Poultry Congress every four years (2008: Brisbane, Australia); mems: 7,300 individuals in more than 100 countries, branches in 73 countries; Pres. Prof. Dr RÜVEYDE AKBAY (Turkey); Sec.-Gen. Dr PIET C. M. SIMONS (Netherlands); publ. *The World's Poultry Science Journal* (quarterly).

World Veterinary Association: Emdrupvej 28A, 2100 Copenhagen Ø, Denmark; tel. 38-71-01-56; fax 38-71-03-22; e-mail wva@ddd.dk; internet www.worldvet.org; f. 1959 as a continuation of the International Veterinary Congresses; organizes quadrennial congress; mems: organizations in more than 80 countries, 19 organizations of veterinary specialists as associate members; Pres. Prof. LEON RUSSELL; Exec. Sec. Dr LARS HOLSAAE.

Arts and Culture

Europa Nostra—Pan-European Federation for Cultural Heritage: Lange Voorhout 35, 2514 EC The Hague, Netherlands; tel. (70) 3024057; fax (70) 3617865; e-mail office@europanostra.org; internet www.europanostra.org; f. 1963; groups, organizations and individuals concerned with the protection and enhancement of the European architectural and natural heritage and of the European environment; has consultative status with the Council of Europe; mems: 220 mem. orgs, around 170 supporting bodies, more than 1,200 individual mems; Pres. HRH The Prince Consort of Denmark; Exec. Pres. OTTO VON DER GABLENTZ (Germany); Sec.-Gen. SNESKA QUAEDVLIEG-MIHAILOVIĆ.

European Association of Conservatoires, Music Academies and Music High Schools: POB 805, 3500 AV Utrecht, Netherlands; tel. (30) 2361242; fax (30) 2361290; e-mail aecinfo@aecinfo.org; internet www.aecinfo.org; f. 1953; aims to establish and foster contacts and exchanges between and represent the interests of members; initiates and supports international collaboration through research projects, congresses and seminars; mems: 226 member institutions in 53 countries; Pres. JOHANNES JOHANSSON; Gen. Sec. GEORGE CAIRD; publs e-mail newsletters (2–3 a year), project newsletters (3 a year), conference proceedings, research findings, various other publs and websites.

European Cultural Foundation: Jan van Goyenkade 5, 1075 HN Amsterdam, Netherlands; tel. (20) 5733868; fax (20) 6752231; e-mail eurocult@eurocult.org; internet www.eurocult.org; f. 1954 as a non-governmental organization, supported by private sources, to promote activities of mutual interest to European countries on aspects of culture; maintains national committees in 23 countries and a transnational network of institutes and centres: European Institute of Education and Social Policy, Paris; Institute for European Environmental Policy, London, Madrid and Berlin; Association for Innovative Co-operation in Europe (AICE), Brussels; EURYDICE Central Unit (the Education Information Network of the European Community), Brussels; European Institute for the Media, Düsseldorf; European Foundation Centre, Brussels; Fund for Central and East European Book Projects, Amsterdam; Institute for Human Sciences, Vienna; East West Parliamentary Practice Project, Amsterdam; and Centre Européen de la Culture, Geneva; also manages a grants programme for European co-operation projects; Chair. Dr KATHINKA DITTRICH VAN WERINGH (Germany); Dir GOTTFRIED WAGNER; publs *Annual Report*, *Newsletter* (monthly).

European Society of Culture: Guidecca 54 P (Calle Michelangelo, Villa Hériot), 30133 Venice, Italy; tel. (041) 5230210; fax (041) 5231033; e-mail info@societaeuropeacultura.it; internet www.societaeuropeacultura.it; f. 1950 to unite artists, poets, scientists, philosophers and others through mutual interests and friendship in order to safeguard and improve the conditions required for creative activity; maintains a library of 10,000 volumes; mems: national and local centres, and 2,000 individuals, in 60 countries; Pres. Prof. VINCENZO CAPPELLETTI (Italy); Gen. Sec. Dott. MICHELLE CAMPAGNOLO-BOUVIER.

Inter-American Music Council (Consejo Interamericano de Música—CIDEM): 2511 P St NW, Washington, DC 20007, USA; f. 1956 to promote the exchange of works, performances and information in all fields of music, to study problems relative to music education, to encourage activity in the field of musicology, to promote folklore research and music creation, and to establish distribution centres for music material of the composers of the Americas; mems: national music societies of 33 American countries; Sec.-Gen. EFRAÍN PAESKY.

International Association of Art (IAA): Maison de l'UNESCO, 1 rue Miollis, 75732 Paris Cédex 15, France; tel. 1-45-68-44-53; fax 1-45-67-22-87; f. 1954; mems: 104 national committees; Pres. UNA WALKER; Sec.-Gen. J. C. DE SALINS; publ. *IAA Newsletter* (quarterly).

International Association of Art Critics: 32 rue Yves Toudic, 75010 Paris, France; tel. 1-47-70-17-42; fax 1-47-70-17-81; e-mail office.paris@aica-int.org; internet www.aica-int.org; f. 1949 to increase co-operation in plastic arts, promote international cultural exchanges and protect the interests of mems; mems: 4,062 in 77 countries; Pres. HENRY MEYRIC HUGHES (United Kingdom); Sec.-Gen. RAMON TIO BELLIDO (France); publs *Annuaire*, *Newsletter* (quarterly).

International Association of Bibliophiles: Réserve des livres rares, Quai François Mauriac, 75706 Cédex 13, France; fax 1-53-79-54-60; f. 1963 to create contacts between bibliophiles and encourage book-collecting in different countries; organizes meetings and encourages congresses, meetings, exhibitions and the award of scholarships; mems: 450; Pres. T. KIMBALL BROOKER (USA); Sec.-Gen. JEAN-MARC

CHATELAIN (France); publs *Le Bulletin du Bibliophile* (2 a year), yearbooks.

International Association of Film and Television Schools (Centre international de liaison des écoles de cinéma et de télévision—CILECT): 8 rue Thérésienne, 1000 Brussels, Belgium; tel. (49) 16099189654; fax (49) 6519952584; e-mail secretariat@cilect.org; internet www.cilect.org; f. 1955 to link higher teaching and research institutes and improve education of makers of films and television programmes; organizes conferences and student film festivals; runs a training programme for developing countries; mems: 122 institutions in 56 countries; Pres. CATERINA D'AMICO (Italy); Exec. Sec. HENRY VERHASSELT (Belgium); publ. *Newsletter*.

International Association of Literary Critics: 38 rue du Faubourg St-Jacques, 75014 Paris, France; tel. 1-40-51-33-00; fax 1-43-54-92-99; internet www.aicl.org; f. 1969; national centres in 34 countries; organizes congresses; Pres. NERIA DE GIOVANNI; publ. *Revue* (2 a year).

International Board on Books for Young People (IBBY): Nonnenweg 12, Postfach, 4003 Basel, Switzerland; tel. 612722917; fax 612722757; e-mail ibby@ibby.org; internet www.ibby.org; f. 1953 to support and link bodies in all countries connected with children's book work; encourages the distribution of good children's books; promotes scientific investigation into problems of juvenile books; presents the Hans Christian Andersen Award every two years to a living author and a living illustrator whose work is an outstanding contribution to juvenile literature; presents the IBBY-Asahi Reading Promotion Award (every two years) to an organization that has made a significant contribution towards the encouragement of reading; sponsors International Children's Book Day (2 April); mems: national sections and individuals in more than 70 countries; Pres. PATRICIA ALDANA (Canada); Dir LIZ PAGE; publs *Bookbird* (quarterly, in English), *Congress Papers*, *IBBY Honour List* (every 2 years), special bibliographies.

International Centre for the Study of the Preservation and Restoration of Cultural Property (ICCROM): Via di San Michele 13, 00153 Rome, Italy; tel. (06) 585531; fax (06) 58553349; e-mail iccrom@iccrom.org; internet www.iccrom.org; f. 1959; assembles documents on the preservation and restoration of cultural property; stimulates research and proffers advice; organizes missions of experts; undertakes training of specialists; mems: 117 countries; Dir-Gen. Dr MOUNIR BOUCHENAKI (Algeria); publ. *Newsletter* (annually, in Arabic, English, French and Spanish).

International Centre of Films for Children and Young People (Centre international du film pour l'enfance et la jeunesse—CIFEJ): 3774 rue Saint-Denis, Bureau 200, Montréal, QC H2W 2M1, Canada; tel. (514) 284-9388; fax (514) 284-0168; e-mail info@cifej.com; internet www.cifej.com; f. 1955; serves as a clearing house for information about: entertainment films (cinema and television) for children and young people, the influence of films on the young, and the regulations in force for the protection and education of young people; promotes production and distribution of suitable films and their appreciation; awards the CIFEJ prize at selected film festivals; mems: 150 mems in 55 countries; Exec. Dir JO-ANNE BLOUIN; publ. *CIFEJ Info* (monthly).

International Committee for the Diffusion of Arts and Literature through the Cinema (Comité international pour la diffusion des arts et des lettres par le cinéma—CIDALC): 24 blvd Poissonnière, 75009 Paris, France; tel. 1-42-46-13-60; f. 1930 to promote the creation and release of educational, cultural and documentary films and other films of educational value, in order to contribute to closer understanding between peoples; awards medals and prizes for films of exceptional merit; mems: national committees in 19 countries; Sec.-Gen. MARIO VERDONE (Italy); publs *Annuaire CIDALC*, *Cinéma éducatif et culturel*.

International Comparative Literature Association (ICLA) (Association Internationale de Littérature Comparée): c/o Steven P. Sondrup, Brigham Young University HRCB, Provo, UT 84604-4538, USA; tel. (801) 422-5598; fax (801) 422-0307; e-mail ailc.icla@gmail.com; internet icla.byu.edu/www/; f. 1954 to work for the development of the comparative study of literature in modern languages; mems: 35 regional associations; Pres. MANFRED SCHMELING; publs *ICLA Bulletin* (annually), *Literary Research* (2 a year).

International Confederation of Societies of Authors and Composers—World Congress of Authors and Composers: 20–26 blvd du Parc, 92200 Neuilly-sur-Seine, France; tel. 1-55-62-08-50; fax 1-55-62-08-60; e-mail cisac@cisac.org; internet www.cisac.org; f. 1926 to protect the rights of authors and composers; organizes biennial congress; mems: 210 mem. societies from 109 countries; Dir Gen. ERIC BAPTISTE.

International Council of Museums (ICOM): Maison de l'UNESCO, 1 rue Miollis, 75732 Paris Cédex 15, France; tel. 1-47-34-05-00; fax 1-43-06-78-62; e-mail secretariat@icom.museum; internet icom.museum; f. 1946; committed to the conservation and communication to society of the world's natural and cultural heritage; achieves its major objectives through its 30 int. committees, each devoted to the study of a particular type of museum or to a specific museum-related discipline; maintains with UNESCO the organization's documentation centre; mems: 21,000 individuals and institutions in 140 countries; Pres. ALISSANDRA CUMMINS (Barbados); publ. *ICOM News—Nouvelles de l'ICOM—Noticias del ICOM* (quarterly).

International Committee of Museums and Collections of Arms and Military History (ICOMAM): Parc du Cinquantenaire 3, 1000 Brussels, Belgium; tel. (2) 737-79-00; e-mail chairman@icomam.icom.museum; internet www.klm-mra.be/icomam/; f. 1957 as International Association of Museums of Arms and Military History (IAMAM); present name assumed in 2004; links museums and other scientific institutions with public collections of arms and armour and military equipment, uniforms, etc; holds triennial conferences and occasional specialist symposia; mems: over 260 institutions in more than 60 countries; Pres. GUY M. WILSON (United Kingdom); Sec.-Gen. JAN PIET PUYPE (Netherlands); publ. *The Mohonk Courier*.

International Council on Monuments and Sites (ICOMOS): 49–51 rue de la Fédération, 75015 Paris, France; tel. 1-45-67-67-70; fax 1-45-66-06-22; e-mail secretariat@icomos.org; internet www.international.icomos.org; f. 1965 to promote the study and preservation of monuments and sites and to arouse and cultivate the interest of public authorities and people of every country in their cultural heritage; disseminates the results of research into the technical, social and administrative problems connected with the conservation of the architectural heritage; holds triennial General Assembly and Symposium; mems: 7,700, 24 international committees, 110 national committees; Pres. Dr MICHAEL PETZET (Germany); Sec.-Gen. DINU BUMBARU (Canada); publs *ICOMOS Newsletter* (quarterly), *Scientific Journal* (quarterly).

International Federation for Theatre Research (IFTR) (Fédération Internationale pour la Recherche Théâtrale): c/o Dean of Arts & Humanities, Lancaster University, Lancaster, LA1 4YN, United Kingdom; e-mail d.whitton@lancaster.ac.uk; internet www.firt-iftr.org; f. 1955 by 21 countries at the International Conference on Theatre History, London; Pres. BRIAN SINGLETON (Ireland); Joint Secs-Gen. Prof. DAVID WHITTON (United Kingdom), Prof. FRÉDÉRIC MAURIN (Canada); publ. *Theatre Research International* (in association with Cambridge University Press, 3 a year).

International Federation of Film Archives (Fédération Internationale des Archives du Film—FIAF): 1 rue Defacqz, 1000 Brussels, Belgium; tel. (2) 538-30-65; fax (2) 534-47-74; e-mail info@fiafnet.org; internet www.fiafnet.org; f. 1938 to encourage the creation of audio-visual archives for the collection and conservation of the moving image heritage of every country; facilitates co-operation and exchanges between film archives; promotes public interest in the art of the cinema; aids and conducts research; compiles new documentation; holds annual congress; mems: in 65 countries; Pres. EVA ORBANZ (Germany); Sec.-Gen. MEG LABRUM (Australia); publs *Journal of Film Preservation* (2 a year), *FIAF International Film Archive Database* (2 a year).

International Federation of Film Producers' Associations (Fédération Internationale des associations de Producteurs de Films—FIAPF): 9 rue de l'Echelle, 75001 Paris, France; tel. 1-44-77-97-50; fax 1-42-56-16-55; e-mail info@fiapf.org; internet www.fiapf.org; f. 1933 to represent film production internationally, to defend its general interests and promote its development; studies all cultural, legal, economic, technical and social problems related to film production; mems: 31 producers' organizations in 25 countries; Pres. ANDRÉS VICENTE GOMEZ (Spain); Dir-Gen. VALÉRIE LÉPINE (France).

International Institute for Children's Literature and Reading Research (Internationales Institut für Jugendliteratur und Leseforschung): Mayerhofgasse 6, 1040 Vienna, Austria; tel. (1) 505-03-59; fax (1) 50503-5917; e-mail office@jugendliteratur.net; internet www.jugendliteratur.net; f. 1965 as an international documentation, research and advisory centre of juvenile literature and reading; maintains specialized library; arranges conferences and exhibitions; compiles recommendation lists; mems: individual and group members in 28 countries; Pres. Dr HILDE HAWLICEK; Dir KARIN HALLER; publ. *1000 & 1 Buch* (quarterly).

International Institute for Conservation of Historic and Artistic Works: 6 Buckingham St, London, WC2N 6BA, United Kingdom; tel. (20) 7839-5975; fax (20) 7976-1564; e-mail iic@iiconservation.org; internet www.iiconservation.org; f. 1950; mems: 2,400 individual, 400 institutional mems; Pres. JERRY PODANY; Exec. Sec. GRAHAM VOCE; publs *Studies in Conservation* (quarterly), *Reviews in Conservation* (annually), *News in Conservation* (every 2 months), *Congress Preprints* (every 2 years).

International Music Council (IMC): Maison de l'UNESCO, 1 rue Miollis, 75732 Paris Cédex 15, France; tel. 1-45-68-48-50; fax 1-43-06-87-98; e-mail imc@unesco.org; internet www.unesco.org/imc; f. 1949 to promote musical diversity and cultural rights for all;

mems: national councils in 73 countries and more than 50 international and regional music organizations, as well as independent organizations in the field of arts and culture; Pres. Richard Letts (Australia); Exec. Officer Silja Fischer.

Members of IMC include:

European Festivals Association: Kastel Borluut, Kleine Gentstraat 46, 9051 Ghent, Belgium; tel. (9) 241-80-804; fax (9) 241-80-89; e-mail info@efa-aef.org; internet www.efa-aef.org; f. 1952 to maintain high artistic standards and the representative character of art festivals; holds annual General Assembly; a Eurofest Research and Training Centre is based in Coppet, Switzerland; mems: more than 100 regular international performing arts festivals in 38 countries; Pres. Darko Brlek; publ. *Festivals* (annually).

International Association of Music Libraries, Archives and Documentation Centres (IAML): c/o Music Room, National Library of New Zealand, POB 1467, Wellington, New Zealand; tel. (4) 474-3039; fax (4) 474-3035; e-mail roger.flury@natlib.govt.nz; internet www.iaml.info; f. 1951; mems: 1,925 institutions and individuals in 49 countries; Pres. Martie Severt (Netherlands); Sec.-Gen. Roger Flury (New Zealand); publ. *Fontes artis musicae* (quarterly).

International Council for Traditional Music (ICTM): ICTM Secretariat, School of Music, Australian National University, Bldg 100, Canberra, ACT 0200, Australia; tel. (2) 6125-1449; fax (2) 6125-9775; e-mail secretariat@ictmusic.org; internet www.ictmusic.org; f. 1947 (as International Folk Music Council) to further the study, practice, documentation, preservation and dissemination of traditional music of all countries; holds ICTM World Conference every two years; mems: 1,885; Pres. Dr Adrienne L. Kaeppler (USA); Sec.-Gen. Dr Stephen Wild (Australia); publs *Yearbook for Traditional Music*, *ICTM Bulletin* (2 a year), *Directory of Traditional Music* (every 2 years).

International Federation of Musicians: 21 bis rue Victor Massé, 75009 Paris, France; tel. 1-45-26-31-23; fax 1-45-26-31-57; e-mail office@fim-musicians.com; internet www.fim-musicians.com/; f. 1948 to promote and protect the interests of musicians in affiliated unions; mems: 75 unions in 64 countries; Pres. John F. Smith (United Kingdom); Gen. Sec. Benoît Machuel (France).

International Music and Media Centre (Internationales Musik + Medienzentrum): Stiftgasse 29, 1070 Vienna, Austria; tel. (1) 889 03-15; fax (1) 889 03-1577; e-mail office@imz.at; internet www.imz.at; f. 1961 for the study and dissemination of music through technical media (film, television, radio, gramophone); organizes congresses, seminars and screenings on music in audio-visual media; holds courses and competitions designed to strengthen the relationship between performing artists and audio-visual media; mems: 180 ordinary mems and 30 associate mems in 35 countries, including 50 broadcasting orgs; Pres. Chris Hunt (United Kingdom); Sec.-Gen. Franz A. Patay (Austria).

International Society for Contemporary Music (ISCM): c/o Gaudeamus, Swammerdamstraat 38, 1091 RV Amsterdam, Netherlands; tel. (20) 5191800; fax (20) 5191801; e-mail info@iscm.nl; internet www.iscm.nl; f. 1922 to promote the development of contemporary music; organizes annual World Music Day; mems: organizations in 50 countries; Pres. Richard Tsang; Sec.-Gen. Henk Heuvelmans.

Jeunesses Musicales International (JMI): Palais des Beaux-Arts, 13 rue Baron Horta, 1000 Brussels, Belgium; tel. (2) 513-97-74; fax (2) 514-47-55; e-mail mail@jmi.net; internet www.jmi.net; f. 1945 to enable young people to develop, through music, and to stimulate contacts between member countries; mems: orgs in 40 countries; Sec.-Gen. Dag Franzén; publ. *JMI News* (6 a year).

World Federation of International Music Competitions (WFIMC): 104 rue de Carouge, 1205 Geneva, Switzerland; tel. 223213620; fax 227811418; e-mail info@wfimc.org; internet www.wfimc.org; f. 1957 to co-ordinate the arrangements for affiliated competitions and to exchange experience; holds General Assembly annually; mems: 120; Pres. Marianne Granvig; Sec.-Gen. Renate Ronnefeld.

International PEN (World Association of Writers): Brownlow House, 50–51 High Holborn, London, WC1V 6ER, United Kingdom; tel. (20) 7405-0338; fax (20) 7405-0339; e-mail executivedirector@internationalpen.org.uk; internet www.internationalpen.org.uk; f. 1921 to promote co-operation between writers; mems: c. 14,000, 141 centres world-wide; International Pres. Jiří Gruša; International Sec. Joanne Leedom-Ackerman; publ. *PEN International* (2 a year, in English, French and Spanish, with the assistance of UNESCO).

International Theatre Institute (ITI): Maison de l'UNESCO, 1 rue Miollis, 75732 Paris Cédex 15, France; tel. 1-45-68-48-80; fax 1-45-66-50-40; e-mail iti@unesco.org; internet iti-worldwide.org; f. 1948 to facilitate cultural exchanges and international understanding in the domain of the theatre and performing arts; promotes performing arts/theatre on a national and international level and facilitates international collaboration; mems: more than 90 mem. nations, each with an ITI national centre; Pres. Manfred Beilharz (Germany); Sec.-Gen. Tobias Biancone (Switzerland/France); publs *ITI News* (3 times a year in English and French), *World Theatre Directory* (every 2 years), *The World of Theatre* (every 2 years).

Nordic Cultural Fund (Nordisk Kulturfond): c/o Nordic Council/Nordic Council of Ministers, Store Strandstræde 18, 1255 Copenhagen K; tel. 3396-0246; fax 3332-5636; e-mail mj@norden.org; internet www.nordiskkulturfond.org; f. 1967; administered by the secretariat of the Nordic Council and Nordic Council of Ministers; considers applications from the Nordic region for assistance for research, education and general cultural activities; grants may also be awarded for the dissemination of information concerning Nordic culture within and outside the region; Dir Mats Jönsson.

Organization of World Heritage Cities: 15 rue Saint-Nicolas, Québec, QC G1K 1M8, Canada; tel. (418) 692-0000; fax (418) 692-5558; e-mail secretariat@ovpm.org; internet www.ovpm.org; f. 1993 to assist cities inscribed on the UNESCO World Heritage List to implement the Convention concerning the Protection of the World Cultural and Natural Heritage (1972); promotes co-operation between city authorities, in particular in the management and sustainable development of historic sites; holds an annual General Assembly, comprising the mayors of member cities; mems: 218 cities world-wide; Sec.-Gen. Lee Minaidis (interim); publ. *OWHC Newsletter* (2 a year, in English, French and Spanish).

Pan-African Writers' Association (PAWA): PAWA House, Roman Ridge, POB C456, Cantonments, Accra, Ghana; tel. (21) 773-062; fax (21) 773-042; e-mail pawa@ghana.com; f. 1989 to link African creative writers, defend the rights of authors and promote awareness of literature; mems: 52 national writers' associations on the continent; Sec.-Gen. Atukwei Okai (Ghana).

Royal Asiatic Society of Great Britain and Ireland: 14 Stephenson Way, London, NW1 2HD, United Kingdom; tel. (20) 7388-4539; fax (20) 7391-9429; e-mail info@royalasiaticsociety.org; internet www.royalasiaticsociety.org; f. 1823 for the study of history and cultures of the East; mems: c. 700, branch societies in Asia; Pres. Prof. Anthony Stockwell; Dir Dr A. Powell; publ. *Journal* (3 a year).

United World Federation of United Cities: 41 rue de la République, 93200 Saint Denis, France; tel. 1-55-84-23-50; fax 1-55-84-23-51; e-mail contact@fmcu-uto.org; internet www.fmcu-uto.org; f. 1957, as the United Towns Organization, by Le Monde Bilingue (f. 1951); aims to set up permanent links between towns throughout the world, leading to social, cultural, economic and other exchanges favouring world peace, understanding and development; involved in sustainable development and environmental activities at municipal level; mem. of the Habitat II follow-up group; mems: 4,000 local and regional authorities throughout the world; World Pres. Mercedes Bresso; Sec.-Gen. Paolo Morello; publs *Cités Unies* (quarterly, in French, English and Spanish), *Newsletter* (3 a year in English, French, Italian and Spanish).

World Crafts Council International (WCCI): El Comendador 1916, Providencia, Santiago, Chile; tel. (2) 354-5636; fax (2) 232-5811; e-mail wis@wccwis.cl; internet www.wccwis.cl; f. 1964; aims to strengthen the status of crafts as a vital part of cultural and economic life, to link crafts people around the world, and to foster wider recognition of their work; mems: national organizations in more than 89 countries; Pres. Maria Celina Rodriguez Olea (Chile).

Commodities

African Groundnut Council (AGC): C43, Wase Satelite Town, Rjiyar Zaki, Kano, Kano State, Nigeria; tel. (1) 8970605; e-mail info@afgroundnutcouncil.org; internet www.afgroundnutcouncil.org; f. 1964 to advise producing countries on marketing policies; mems: Gambia, Mali, Niger, Nigeria, Senegal, Sudan; Exec. Sec. Elhadj Mour Mamadou Samb (Senegal); publ. *Groundnut Review*.

African Oil Palm Development Association (AFOPDA): 15 BP 341, Abidjan 15, Côte d'Ivoire; tel. 21-25-15-18; fax 20-21-97-06; f. 1985; seeks to increase production of, and investment in, palm oil; mems: Benin, Cameroon, Democratic Republic of the Congo, Côte d'Ivoire, Ghana, Guinea, Nigeria, Togo; Exec. Sec. Baudelaire Hounsinou Sourou.

African Petroleum Producers' Association (APPA): POB 1097, Brazzaville, Republic of the Congo; tel. 665-38-57; fax 669-99-38; e-mail appa@africanpetroleumproducers.org; f. 1987 by African petroleum-producing countries to reinforce co-operation among regional producers and to stabilize prices; council of ministers responsible for the hydrocarbons sector meets twice a year; holds annual Congress and Exhibition: Cotonou, Benin (June 2007); mems:

Algeria, Angola, Benin, Cameroon, Democratic Republic of the Congo, Republic of the Congo, Côte d'Ivoire, Egypt, Equatorial Guinea, Gabon, Libya, Nigeria; Exec. Sec. MAXIME OBIANG-NZE; publ. *APPA Bulletin* (2 a year).

Asian and Pacific Coconut Community (APCC): 3rd Floor, Lina Bldg, Jalan H. R. Rasuna Said Kav. B7, Kuningan, Jakarta 12920, Indonesia; POB 1343, Jakarta 10013; tel. (21) 5221712; fax (21) 5221714; e-mail apcc@indo.net.id; internet www.apccsec.org; f. 1969 to promote and co-ordinate all activities of the coconut industry, to achieve higher production and better processing, marketing and research; organizes annual Coconut Technical Meeting (COCO-TECH); mems: Fiji, India, Indonesia, Kiribati, Malaysia, Marshall Islands, Federated States of Micronesia, Papua New Guinea, Philippines, Samoa, Solomon Islands, Sri Lanka, Thailand, Vanuatu, Viet Nam; Chair. OSCAR GARIN; Exec. Dir ROMULO N. ARANCON, Jr ; publs *Cocomunity* (monthly), *CORD* (2 a year), *CocoInfo International* (2 a year), *Coconut Statistical Yearbook*, guide-lines and other ad hoc publications.

Association of Natural Rubber Producing Countries (ANRPC): Bangunan Getah Asli, 148 Jalan Ampang, 7th Floor, 50450 Kuala Lumpur, Malaysia; tel. (3) 2611900; fax (3) 2613014; e-mail anrpc@capo.jaring.my; f. 1970 to co-ordinate the production and marketing of natural rubber, to promote technical co-operation amongst members and to bring about fair and stable prices for natural rubber; holds seminars, meetings and training courses on technical and statistical subjects; a joint regional marketing system has been agreed in principle; mems: India, Indonesia, Malaysia, Papua New Guinea, Singapore, Sri Lanka, Thailand, Viet Nam; Sec.-Gen. G. W. S. K. DE SILVA; publs *ANRPC Statistical Bulletin* (quarterly), *ANRPC Newsletter*.

Cocoa Producers' Alliance (CPA): National Assembly Complex, Tafawa Balewa Sq., POB 1718, Lagos, Nigeria; tel. (1) 2635574; fax (1) 2635684; e-mail info@copal-cpa.com; internet www.copal-cpa.org; f. 1962 to exchange technical and scientific information, to discuss problems of mutual concern to producers, to ensure adequate supplies at remunerative prices and to promote consumption; mems: Brazil, Cameroon, Côte d'Ivoire, Dominican Republic, Gabon, Ghana, Malaysia, Nigeria, São Tomé and Príncipe, Togo; Sec.-Gen. HOPE SONA EBAI.

Common Fund for Commodities: POB 74658, 1070 BR, Amsterdam, Netherlands; tel. (20) 5754949; fax (20) 6760231; e-mail managing.director@common-fund.org; internet www.common-fund.org; f. 1989 as the result of an UNCTAD negotiation conference; finances commodity development measures including research, marketing, productivity improvements and vertical diversification, with the aim of increasing the long-term competitiveness of particular commodities; paid-in capital US $165m; mems: 106 countries and the AU, EC and COMESA; Man. Dir (also Chief Exec.) ALI MCHUMO.

European Aluminium Association (EEA): 12 ave de Broqueville, 1150 Brussels, Belgium; tel. (2) 775-63-63; fax (2) 779-05-31; e-mail eaa@eaa.be; internet www.eaa.net; f. 1981 to encourage studies, research and technical co-operation, to make representations to international bodies and to assist national asscns in dealing with national authorities; mems: individual producers of primary aluminium, 18 national groups for wrought producers, the Organization of European Aluminium Smelters, representing producers of recycled aluminium, and the European Aluminium Foil Association, representing foil rollers and converters; Chair. C. BORIES; Sec.-Gen. PATRICK DE SCHRYNMAKERS; publs *Annual Report*, *EAA Quarterly Report*.

European Association for the Trade in Jute and Related Products: Adriaan Goekooplaan 5, POB 29822, 2502 LV, The Hague, Netherlands; tel. (70) 3384659; fax (70) 3512777; e-mail info@eurojute.com; internet www.eurojute.com; f. 1970 to maintain contacts between national asscns, permit the exchange of information and represent the interests of the trade; carries out scientific research; mems: enterprises in nine European countries; Sec.-Gen. H. J. J. KRUIPER.

European Committee of Sugar Manufacturers: 182 ave de Tervuren, 1150 Brussels, Belgium; tel. (2) 762-07-60; fax (2) 771-00-26; e-mail cefs@cefs.org; internet www.cefs.org; f. 1954 to collect statistics and information, conduct research and promote co-operation between national organizations; mems: national asscns in 22 European countries and other associate members worldwide; Pres. JOHANN MARIHART; Dir-Gen. J. L. BARJOL.

Inter-African Coffee Organization (IACO) (Organisation internationale du café—OIAC): BP V210, Abidjan, Côte d'Ivoire; tel. 20-21-61-31; fax 20-21-62-12; e-mail oiac-iaco@aviso.ci; f. 1960 to adopt a common policy on the marketing and consumption of coffee; aims to foster greater collaboration in research technology transfer through the African Coffee Research Network (ACRN); seeks to improve the quality of coffee exports, and implement poverty reduction programmes focusing on value added product (VAP) and the manufacturing of green coffee; mems: 25 coffee-producing countries in Africa; Chair. AMADOU SOUMAHORO (Côte d'Ivoire); Sec.-Gen. JOSEFA LEONEL CORREIA SACKO (Angola).

International Cadmium Association: 168 ave Tervueren, 1150 Brussels, Belgium; tel. (2) 777-05-60; fax (2) 777-06-65; e-mail info@cadmium.org; f. 1976; covers all aspects of the production and use of cadmium and its compounds; includes almost all producers and users of cadmium; Chair. DAVID SINCLAIR (USA).

International Cocoa Organization (ICCO): Commonwealth House, 1–19 New Oxford St, London, WC1A 1NU, United Kingdom; tel. (20) 7400-5050; fax (20) 7421-5500; e-mail info@icco.org; internet www.icco.org; f. 1973 under the first International Cocoa Agreement, 1972; the ICCO supervises the implementation of the agreements, and provides member governments with up-to-date information on the world cocoa economy; the sixth International Cocoa Agreement (2001) entered into force in October 2003; mems: 13 exporting countries and 28 importing countries; and the European Union; Exec. Dir Dr JAN VINGERHOETS (Netherlands); publs *Quarterly Bulletin of Cocoa Statistics*, *Annual Report*, *World Cocoa Directory*, *Cocoa Newsletter*, studies on the world cocoa economy.

International Coffee Organization (ICO): 22 Berners St, London, W1T 3DD, United Kingdom; tel. (20) 7612-0600; fax (20) 7612-0630; e-mail info@ico.org; internet www.ico.org; f. 1963 under the International Coffee Agreement, 1962, which was renegotiated in 1968, 1976, 1983, 1994 (extended in 1999) and 2001; aims to improve international co-operation and provide a forum for intergovernmental consultations on coffee matters; to facilitate international trade in coffee by the collection, analysis and dissemination of statistics; to act as a centre for the collection, exchange and publication of coffee information; to promote studies in the field of coffee; and to encourage an increase in coffee consumption; mems: 45 exporting and 32 importing countries; Chair. of Council MAURO OREFICE (Italy); Exec. Dir NÉSTOR OSORIO (Colombia).

International Confederation of European Sugar Beet Growers (Confédération internationale des betteraviers européens—CIBE): 29 rue du Général Foy, 75008 Paris, France; tel. 1-44-69-39-00; fax 1-42-93-28-93; f. 1925 to act as a centre for the co-ordination and dissemination of information about beet sugar production and the industry; to represent the interests of sugar beet growers at an international level; mems: asscns in Austria, Belgium, Czech Republic, Denmark, Finland, France, Germany, Greece, Hungary, Ireland, Italy, Latvia, Lithuania, Netherlands, Poland, Portugal, Romania, Slovakia, Slovenia, Spain, Sweden, Switzerland, Turkey, United Kingdom; Pres. OTTO VON ARNOLD (Sweden); Sec.-Gen. H. CHAVANES (France).

International Cotton Advisory Committee (ICAC): 1629 K St, NW, Suite 702, Washington, DC 20006-1636, USA; tel. (202) 463-6660; fax (202) 463-6950; e-mail secretariat@icac.org; internet www.icac.org; f. 1939 to observe developments in world cotton; to collect and disseminate statistics; to suggest measures for the furtherance of international collaboration in maintaining and developing a sound world cotton economy; and to provide a forum for international discussions on cotton prices; mems: 44 countries; Exec. Dir Dr TERRY TOWNSEND (USA); publs *Cotton This Week!* (internet/e-mail only), *Cotton This Month*, *Cotton: Review of the World Situation* (every 2 months), *Cotton: World Statistics* (annually), *The ICAC Recorder*, *World Textile Demand* (annually), other surveys, studies, trade analyses and technical publications.

International Gas Union (IGU): POB 550, c/o Dong Energy A/S, Agern Allé 24–26, 2970 Hoersholm, Denmark; tel. 45-17-12-00; fax 45-17-19-00; e-mail secr.igu@dong.dk; internet www.igu.org; f. 1931; represents the gas industry world-wide; mems: 68 Charter mems, 28 Associate mems; Pres. ERNESTO A. LOPEZ ANADÓN (Argentina); Sec.-Gen. PETER K. STORM (Denmark).

International Grains Council (IGC): 1 Canada Sq., Canary Wharf, London, E14 5AE, United Kingdom; tel. (20) 7513-1122; fax (20) 7513-0630; e-mail igc@igc.org.uk; internet www.igc.org.uk; f. 1949 as International Wheat Council, present name adopted in 1995; responsible for the administration of the International Grains Agreement, 1995, comprising the Grains Trade Convention (GTC) and the Food Aid Convention (FAC, under which donors pledge specified minimum annual amounts of food aid for developing countries in the form of grain and other eligible products); aims to further international co-operation in all aspects of trade in grains, to promote international trade in grains, and to achieve a free flow of this trade, particularly in developing member countries; seeks to contribute to the stability of the international grain market; acts as a forum for consultations between members; provides comprehensive information on the international grain market; mems: 25 countries and the EU; Exec. Dir ETSUO KITAHARA; publs *World Grain Statistics* (annually), *Wheat and Coarse Grain Shipments* (annually), *Report for the Fiscal Year* (annually), *Grain Market Report* (monthly), *IGC Grain Market Indicators* (weekly).

International Jute Study Group (IJSG): 145 Monipuriparu, Tejgaon, Dhaka 1215, Bangladesh; POB 6073, Gulshan, Dhaka; tel. (2) 9125581; fax (2) 9125248; e-mail info@jute.org; internet www.jute.org; f. 2002 as successor to International Jute Organization (f. 1984 in accordance with an agreement made by 48 producing and consuming countries in 1982, under the auspices of UNCTAD); aims to improve the jute economy and the quality of jute and jute products through research and development projects and market promotion; Sec.-Gen SUDRIPTA ROY.

International Lead and Zinc Study Group (ILZSG): Rua Almirante Barroso 38, 5th Floor, Lisbon 1000-013, Portugal; tel. (21) 3592420; fax (21) 3592429; e-mail root@ilzsg.org; internet www.ilzsg.org; f. 1959 for intergovernmental consultation on world trade in lead and zinc; conducts studies and provides information on trends in supply and demand; mems: 27 countries and the European Commission; Chair. V. K. THAKRAL (India); Sec.-Gen. DON SMALE; publ. *Lead and Zinc Statistics* (monthly).

International Molybdenum Association (IMOA): 245 rue Pere Eudore Devroye, 1150 Brussels, Belgium; tel. (2) 770-88-78; fax (2) 770-88-98; e-mail info@imoa.info; internet www.imoa.info; f. 1989; collates statistics; promotes the use of molybdenum; monitors health and environmental issues in the molybdenum industry; mems: 70; Pres. VICTOR PEREZ; Sec.-Gen. MICHAEL MABY.

International Olive Council: Príncipe de Vergara 154, 28002 Madrid, Spain; tel. (91) 5903638; fax (91) 5631263; e-mail iooc@internationaloliveoil.org; internet www.internationaloliveoil.org; f. 1959 to administer the International Agreement on Olive Oil and Table Olives, which aims to promote international co-operation in connection with problems of the world economy for olive products; works to prevent unfair competition, to encourage the production and consumption of, and international trade in, olive products, and to reduce the disadvantages caused by fluctuations of supplies on the market; also takes action to foster a better understanding of the nutritional, therapeutic and other properties of olive products, to foster international co-operation for the integrated, sustainable development of world olive growing, to encourage research and development, to foster the transfer of technology and training activities in the olive products sector, and to improve the interaction between olive growing and the environment; mems: of the International Agreement on Olive Oil and Table Olives, 2005 (fifth Agreement, in force until 31 Dec. 2014): 14 countries, and the European Community; Exec. Dir MOHAMMED OUHMAD SBITRI; publ. *OLIVAE* (2 a year, in English, French, Italian and Spanish).

International Organisation of Vine and Wine (Organisation Internationale de la Vigne et du Vin—OIV): 18 rue d'Aguesseau, 75008 Paris, France; tel. 1-44-94-80-80; fax 1-42-66-90-63; e-mail contact@oiv.int; internet www.oiv.int; f. 2001 (agreement establishing an International Wine Office signed Nov. 1924, name changed to International Vine and Wine Office in 1958); researches vine and vine product issues in the scientific, technical, economic and social areas, disseminates knowledge, and facilitates contacts between researchers; mems: 41 countries and five countries with observer status; Dir-Gen. FEDERICO CASTELLUCCI (Italy); publs *Bulletin de l'OIV* (every 2 months), *Lexique de la Vigne et du Vin*, *Recueil des méthodes internationales d'analyse des vins*, *Code international des Pratiques oenologiques*, *Codex oenologique international*, numerous scientific publications.

International Organization of Spice Trading Associations (IOSTA): c/o American Spice Trade Association, 2025 M St, NW, Suite 800, Washington, DC 20036, USA; tel. (202) 367-1127; fax (202) 367-2127; e-mail info@astaspice.org; f. 1999; mems: eight national and regional spice organizations.

International Pepper Community (IPC): 4th Floor, Lina Bldg, Jalan H. R. Rasuna Said, Kav. B7, Kuningan, Jakarta 12920, Indonesia; tel. (21) 5224902; fax (21) 5224905; e-mail ipc@indo.net.id; internet www.ipcnet.org; f. 1972 for promoting, co-ordinating and harmonizing all activities relating to the pepper economy; mems: Brazil, India, Indonesia, Malaysia, Federated States of Micronesia, Papua New Guinea, Sri Lanka, Thailand; Exec. Dir ANANDAN ABDULLAH; publs *Pepper Statistical Yearbook*, *International Pepper News Bulletin* (quarterly), *Directory of Pepper Exporters*, *Directory of Pepper Importers*, *Weekly Prices Bulletin*, *Pepper Market Review*.

International Platinum Association: Kroegerstr. 5, Frankfurt-am-Main, 60313, Germany; tel. (69) 287941; fax (69) 283601; e-mail info@platinuminfo.net; internet www.platinuminfo.net; links principal producers and fabricators of platinum; Pres. IAN FARMER; Man. Dir GABRIELE RANDLSHOFER.

International Rubber Study Group: Heron House, 109–115 Wembley Hill Rd, Wembley, HA9 8DA, United Kingdom; tel. (20) 8900-5400; fax (20) 8903-2848; e-mail irsg@rubberstudy.com; internet www.rubberstudy.com; f. 1944 to provide a forum for the discussion of problems affecting synthetic and natural rubber and to provide statistical and other general information on rubber; mems: 17 governments; Sec.-Gen. Dr HIDDE P. SMIT (Netherlands); publs *Rubber Statistical Bulletin* (every 2 months), *Rubber Industry Report* (every 2 months), *Proceedings of International Rubber Forums* (annually), *World Rubber Statistics Handbook*, *Key Rubber Indicators*, *Rubber Statistics Yearbook*, *Outlook for Elastomers* (annually).

International Silk Association: 34 rue de la Charité, 69002 Lyon, France; tel. 4-78-42-10-79; fax 4-78-37-56-72; e-mail isa-silk.ais-sole@wanadoo.fr; f. 1949 to promote closer collaboration between all branches of the silk industry and trade, develop the consumption of silk, and foster scientific research; collects and disseminates information and statistics relating to the trade and industry; organizes biennial congresses; mems: employers' and technical organizations in 40 countries; Gen. Sec. X. LAVERGNE; publs *ISA Newsletter* (monthly), congress reports, standards, trade rules, etc.

International Sugar Organization: 1 Canada Sq., Canary Wharf, London, E14 5AA, United Kingdom; tel. (20) 7513-1144; fax (20) 7513-1146; e-mail exdir@isosugar.org; internet www.isosugar.org; administers the International Sugar Agreement (1992), with the objectives of stimulating co-operation, facilitating trade and encouraging demand; aims to improve conditions in the sugar market through debate, analysis and studies; serves as a forum for discussion; holds annual seminars and workshops; sponsors projects from developing countries; mems: 81 countries producing some 83% of total world sugar; Exec. Dir Dr PETER BARON; publs *Sugar Year Book*, *Monthly Statistical Bulletin*, *Market Report and Press Summary*, *Quarterly Market Outlook*, seminar proceedings.

International Tea Committee Ltd (ITC): 1 Carlton House Terrace, London, SW1Y 5DB, United Kingdom; tel. (20) 7839-5090; e-mail inteacom@globalnet.co.uk; internet www.inttea.com; f. 1933 to administer the International Tea Agreement; now serves as a statistical and information centre; in 1979 membership was extended to include consuming countries; producer mems: national tea boards or asscns in Bangladesh, People's Republic of China, India, Indonesia, Kenya, Malawi, Sri Lanka; consumer mems: United Kingdom Tea Asscn, Tea Asscn of the USA Inc., Irish Tea Trade Asscn, Netherland Coffee Roasters and Tea Packers' Asscn, and the Tea Asscn of Canada; assoc. mems: Netherlands and UK ministries of agriculture, and national tea boards/asscns in eight producing countries; Chief Exec. MANUJA PEIRIS; publs *Annual Bulletin of Statistics*, *Monthly Statistical Summary*.

International Tea Promotion Association (ITPA): c/o Tea Board of Kenya, POB 20064, City Sq., 00200 Nairobi, Kenya; tel. (20) 572421; fax (20) 562120; e-mail teaboardk@kenyaweb.com; internet www.teaboard.or.ke; f. 1979; mems: eight countries; Chair. NICHOLAS NGANGA; publ. *International Tea Journal* (2 a year).

International Tobacco Growers' Association (ITGA): Av. Gen. Humberto Delgado 30-A, 6001-081 Castelo Branco, Portugal; tel. (272) 325901; fax (272) 325906; e-mail itga@tobaccoleaf.org; internet www.tobaccoleaf.org; f. 1984 to provide a forum for the exchange of views and information of interest to tobacco producers; mems: 20 countries producing over 80% of the world's internationally traded tobacco; Chief Exec. ANTÓNIO ABRUNHOSA (Portugal); publs *Tobacco Courier* (quarterly), *Tobacco Briefing*.

International Tropical Timber Organization (ITTO): International Organizations Center, 5th Floor, Pacifico-Yokohama, 1-1-1, Minato-Mirai, Nishi-ku, Yokohama 220-0012, Japan; tel. (45) 223-1110; fax (45) 223-1111; e-mail itto@itto.or.jp; internet www.itto.or.jp; f. 1985 under the International Tropical Timber Agreement (1983); a new treaty, ITTA 1994, came into force in 1997; provides a forum for consultation and co-operation between countries that produce and consume tropical timber, and is dedicated to the sustainable development and conservation of tropical forests; facilitates progress towards 'Objective 2000', which aims to move as rapidly as possible towards achieving exports of tropical timber and timber products from sustainably managed resources; encourages, through policy and project work, forest management, conservation and restoration, the further processing of tropical timber in producing countries, and the gathering and analysis of market intelligence and economic information; mems: 33 producing and 26 consuming countries and the EU; Exec. Dir EMMANUEL ZE MEKA (Cameroon); publs *Annual Review and Assessment of the World Timber Situation*, *Tropical Timber Market Information Service* (every 2 weeks), *Tropical Forest Update* (quarterly).

International Tungsten Industry Association (ITIA): rue Père Eudore, Deveroye 245, 1150 Brussels, Belgium; tel. (2) 770-88-78; fax (2) 770-88-98; e-mail info@itia.info; internet www.itia.info; f. 1988 (fmrly Primary Tungsten Asscn, f. 1975); promotes use of tungsten; collates statistics; prepares market reports; monitors health and environmental issues in the tungsten industry; mems from 17 countries; Pres. BURGHARD ZEILER; Sec.-Gen. MICHAEL MABY.

International Zinc Association: 168 ave de Tervueren, Box 4, 1150 Brussels, Belgium; tel. (2) 776-00-70; fax (2) 776-00-89; e-mail info@iza.com; internet www.izincworld.com; f. 1990 to represent the world zinc industry; provide a forum for senior executives to address global issues requiring industry-wide action; consider new applications for zinc and zinc products; foster understanding of zinc's role in the environment; build a sustainable development policy; mems: 33

zinc-producing countries; Exec. Dir STEPHEN R. WILKINSON; publ. *Zinc Protects* (quarterly).

Lead Development Association International: 17A Welbeck Way, London, W1G 9YJ, United Kingdom; tel. (20) 7499-8422; fax (20) 7493-1555; e-mail enq@ldaint.org; internet www.ldaint.org; f. 1956; provides authoritative information on the use of lead and its compounds; financed by lead producers and users in the United Kingdom, Europe and elsewhere; Dir Dr D. N. WILSON (United Kingdom).

Petrocaribe: f. June 2005; an initiative of the Venezuelan Government to enhance the access of countries in the Caribbean region to petroleum on preferential payment terms; aims to co-ordinate the development of energy policies and plans regarding natural resources among signatory countries; 4th summit meeting held in Cienfuegos, Cuba, in December 2007; mems: Antigua and Barbuda, Belize, Cuba, Dominica, Dominican Republic, Grenada, Guyana, Haiti, Honduras, Jamaica, Nicaragua, Saint Christopher and Nevis, Saint Lucia, Saint Vincent and the Grenadines, Suriname, Venezuela.

Regional Association of Oil and Natural Gas Companies in Latin America and the Caribbean (Asociación Regional de Empresas de Petróleo y Gas Natural en Latinoamérica y el Caribe—ARPEL): Javier de Viana 2345, Casilla de correo 1006, 11200 Montevideo, Uruguay; tel. (2) 4106993; fax (2) 4109207; e-mail arpel@arpel.org.uy; internet www.arpel.org; f. 1965 as the Mutual Assistance of the Latin American Oil Companies; aims to initiate and implement activities for the development of the oil and natural gas industry in Latin America and the Caribbean; promotes the expansion of business opportunities and the improvement of the competitive advantages of its members; promotes guide-lines in support of competition in the sector; and supports the efficient and sustainable exploitation of hydrocarbon resources and the supply of products and services. Works in co-operation with international organizations, governments, regulatory agencies, technical institutions, universities and non-governmental organizations; mems: 28 state-owned enterprises, representing more than 90% of regional operations, in Argentina, Bolivia, Brazil, Canada, Chile, Colombia, Costa Rica, Cuba, Ecuador, Jamaica, Mexico, Nicaragua, Paraguay, Peru, Suriname, Trinidad and Tobago, Uruguay, Venezuela; Exec. Sec. JOSÉ FÉLIX GARCÍA GARCÍA; publ. *Boletín Técnico*.

Sugar Association of the Caribbean (Inc.): c/o Caroni (1975) Ltd, Brechin Castle, Conva, Trinidad and Tobago; tel. 636-2449; fax 636-2847; f. 1942; mems: national sugar cos of Barbados, Belize, Guyana, Jamaica and Trinidad and Tobago, and Sugar Assen of St Kitts–Nevis–Anguilla; CEO Dr IAN MCDONALD; publs *SAC Handbook*, *SAC Annual Report*, *Proceedings of Meetings of WI Sugar Technologists*.

Union of Banana-Exporting Countries (Unión de Paises Exportadores de Banano—UPEB): Apdo 4273, Bank of America, 7°, Panamá 5, Panama; tel. 263-6266; fax 264-8355; e-mail iicapan@pan.gbm.net; f. 1974 as an intergovernmental agency to assist in the cultivation and marketing of bananas and to secure prices; collects statistics; mems: Colombia, Costa Rica, Guatemala, Honduras, Nicaragua, Panama, Venezuela; publs *Informe UPEB*, *Fax UPEB*, *Anuario de Estadísticas*, bibliographies.

West Africa Rice Development Association (WARDA): 01 BP 2031, Cotonou, Benin; tel. 21-35-01-88; fax 21-35-05-56; e-mail warda@cgiar.org; internet www.cgiar.org/warda; f. 1971 as a mem. of the network of agricultural research centres supported by the Consultative Group on International Agricultural Research (CGIAR); aims to contribute to food security and poverty eradication in poor rural and urban populations, particularly in West and Central Africa, through research, partnerships, capacity strengthening and policy support on rice-based systems; promotes sustainable agricultural development based on environmentally-sound management of natural resources; maintains research stations in Côte d'Ivoire, Nigeria and Senegal; provides training and consulting services; mems: 17 west African countries; Dir-Gen. Dr PAPA ABDOULAYE SECK (Senegal); publs *Program Report* (annually), *Participatory Varietal Selection* (annually), *Rice Interspecific Hybridization Project Research Highlights* (annually), *Biennial WARDA/National Experts Committee Meeting Reports*, *Inland Valley Newsletter*, *ROCARIZ Newsletter*, training series, proceedings, leaflets.

West Indian Sea Island Cotton Association (Inc.): c/o Barbados Agricultural Development Corporation, Fairy Valley, Christ Church, Barbados; mems: organizations in Antigua and Barbuda, Barbados, Jamaica, Montserrat and St Christopher and Nevis; Pres. LEROY ROACH; Sec. MICHAEL I. EDGHILL.

World Association of Beet and Cane Growers (WABCG): c/o IFAP, 60 rue St Lazare, 75009 Paris, France; tel. 1-45-26-05-53; fax 1-48-74-72-12; e-mail wabcg@ifap.org; internet www.ifap.org/wabcg; f. 1983 (formal adoption of Constitution, 1984); groups national organizations of independent sugar beet and cane growers; aims to boost the economic, technical and social development of the beet- and cane-growing sector; works to strengthen professional representation in international and national fora; serves as a forum for discussion and exchange of information; mems: 21 beet-growing organizations, 14 cane-growing organizations, from 30 countries; Pres. ROGER STEWART (South Africa); Sec. HUGUES BEYLER; publs *World Sugar Farmer News* (quarterly), *World Sugar Farmer Fax Sheet*, *WABCG InfoFlash*, study reports.

World Federation of Diamond Bourses: 62 Pelikaanstraat, 2018 Antwerp, Belgium; tel. (3) 234-91-21; fax (3) 226-40-73; e-mail info@worldfed.com; internet www.worldfed.com; f. 1947 to protect the interests of affiliated bourses and their individual members and to settle disputes through international arbitration; mems: 25 bourses world-wide; Pres. ERNIE BLOM (South Africa); Sec.-Gen. MICHAEL H. VAUGHAN (Belgium).

World Gold Council: 55 Old Broad St, London, EC2M 1RX, United Kingdom; tel. (20) 7826-4700; fax (20) 7826-4799; internet www.gold.org; f. 1987 as world-wide international assen of gold producers, to promote the demand for gold; Chair. PIERRE LASSONDE; Chief Exec. JAMES E. BURTON.

World Petroleum Council: 1 Duchess St, 4th Floor, Suite 1, London, W1N 3DE, United Kingdom; tel. (20) 7637-4958; fax (20) 7637-4965; e-mail pierce@world-petroleum.org; internet www.world-petroleum.org; f. 1933 to serve as a forum for petroleum science, technology, economics and management; undertakes related information and liaison activities; 2008 Congress: Madrid, Spain; mems: Permanent Council includes 61 mem. countries; Pres. Dr RANDY GOSSEN (Canada); Dir-Gen. Dr PIERCE W. F. RIEMER (United Kingdom).

World Sugar Research Organisation (WSRO): POB 50134, London, SW1V 3XR, United Kingdom; tel. (20) 7821-6800; fax (20) 7834-4137; e-mail wsro@wsro.org; internet www.wsro.org; an alliance of sugar producers, processors, marketers and users; monitors and communicates research on role of sugar and other carbohydrates in nutrition and health; organizes conferences and symposia; operates a database of information; serves as a forum for exchange of views; mems: 67 orgs in 30 countries; Dir-Gen. Dr RICHARD COTTRELL; publs *WSRO Research Bulletin* (online, monthly), *WSRO Newsletter*, papers and conference proceedings.

Development and Economic Co-operation

African Capacity Building Foundation (ACBF): Intermarket Life Towers, 7th and 15th Floors, cnr Jason Moyo Ave/Sam Nujoma St, POB 1562, Harare, Zimbabwe; tel. (4) 790398; fax (4) 702915; e-mail root@acbf-pact.org; internet www.acbf-pact.org; f. 1991 by the World Bank, UNDP, the African Development Bank, African and non-African governments; assists African countries to strengthen and build local capacity in economic policy analysis and development management. Implementing agency for the Partnership for Capacity Building in Africa (PACT, established in 1999); Exec. Sec. Dr SOUMANA SAKO.

African Training and Research Centre in Administration for Development (Centre Africain de Formation et de Recherche Administratives pour le Développement—CAFRAD): blvd Pavillon International, BP 310, Tangier, 90001 Morocco; tel. (61) 306269; fax (39) 325785; e-mail cafrad@cafrad.org; internet www.cafrad.org; f. 1964 by agreement between Morocco and UNESCO; undertakes research into administrative problems in Africa and documents results; provides a consultation service for governments and organizations; holds workshops to train senior civil servants; prepares the Biennial Pan-African Conference of Ministers of the Civil Service; mems: 37 African countries; Chair. MOHAMED BOUSSAID; Dir-Gen. Dr SIMON MAMOSI LELO; publs *African Administrative Studies* (2 a year), *Research Studies*, *Newsletter* (internet), *Collection: Etudes et Documents*, *Répertoires des Consultants et des institutions de formation en Afrique*.

Afro-Asian Rural Development Organization (AARDO): No. 2, State Guest Houses Complex, Chanakyapuri, New Delhi 110 021, India; tel. (11) 24100475; fax (11) 24672045; e-mail aardohq@nde.vsnl.net.in; internet www.aardo.org; f. 1962 to act as a catalyst for the co-operative restructuring of rural life in Africa and Asia and to explore opportunities for the co-ordination of efforts to promote rural welfare and to eradicate hunger, thirst, disease, illiteracy and poverty; carries out collaborative research on development issues; organizes training; encourages the exchange of information; holds international conferences and seminars; awards 150 individual training fellowships at nine institutes in Egypt, India, Japan, the Republic of Korea, Malaysia and Taiwan; mems: 15 African countries, 14 Asian countries, one African associate; Sec.-Gen. ABDALLA YAHIA ADAM (Sudan); publs *Afro-Asian Journal of Rural Development* (2 a year), *Annual Report*, *AARDO Newsletter* (2 a year).

INTERNATIONAL ORGANIZATIONS

Development and Economic Co-operation

Amazon Co-operation Treaty Organization: SHIS-QI 05, Conjunto 16, casa 21, Lago Sul, Brasília, DF 71615-160, Brasil; tel. (61) 3248-4119; fax (61) 3248-4238; internet www.acto.info/; f. 1978, permanent secretariat established 1995; aims to promote the co-ordinated and sustainable development of the Amazonian territories; there are regular meetings of ministers of foreign affairs; there are specialized co-ordinators of environment, health, science technology and education, infrastructure, tourism, transport and communications, and of indigenous affairs; mems: Bolivia, Brazil, Colombia, Ecuador, Guyana, Peru, Suriname, Venezuela; Sec.-Gen. Francisco Ruiz (acting).

Arab Gulf Programme for the United Nations Development Organizations (AGFUND): POB 18371, Riyadh 11415, Saudi Arabia; tel. (1) 4418888; fax (1) 4412962; e-mail info@agfund.org; internet www.agfund.org; f. 1981 to provide grants for projects in mother and child care carried out by United Nations organizations, Arab non-governmental organizations and other international bodies, and to co-ordinate assistance by the nations of the Gulf; financing comes mainly from member states, all of which are members of OPEC; mems: Bahrain, Kuwait, Oman, Qatar, Saudi Arabia, UAE; Pres. HRH Prince Talal bin Abdal-Aziz.

Arctic Council: c/o Ministry of Foreign Affairs, Smolenskaya–Sennaya pl. 32/34, 119200, Moscow G-200, Russia; tel. (495) 244-1239; fax (495) 244-2559; e-mail e-mail: ac-chair@mid.ru; internet www.arctic-council.org; f. 1996 to promote co-ordination of activities in the Arctic region, in particular in the areas of education, development and environmental protection; mems: Canada, Denmark, Finland, Iceland, Norway, Russia, Sweden, USA; chairmanship of the Council rotates on a two-yearly basis (Nov. 2006–Nov. 2008: Norway).

Association of Caribbean States (ACS): 5–7 Sweet Briar Rd, St Clair, POB 660, Port of Spain, Trinidad and Tobago; tel. 622-9575; fax 622-1653; e-mail communications@acs-aec.org; internet www.acs-aec.org; f. 1994 by the Governments of the 13 CARICOM countries and Colombia, Costa Rica, Cuba, Dominican Republic, El Salvador, Guatemala, Haiti, Honduras, Mexico, Nicaragua, Suriname and Venezuela; aims to promote economic integration, sustainable development and co-operation in the region; to preserve the environmental integrity of the Caribbean Sea which is regarded as the common patrimony of the peoples of the region; to undertake concerted action to protect the environment, particularly the Caribbean Sea; and to co-operate in the areas of trade, transport, sustainable tourism, and natural disasters. Policy is determined by a Ministerial Council and implemented by a Secretariat based in Port of Spain. In December 2001 a third Summit of Heads of State and Government was convened in Venezuela, where a Plan of Action focusing on issues of sustainable tourism, trade, transport and natural disasters was agreed. The fourth ACS Summit was held in Panama, in July 2005. A final Declaration included resolutions to strengthen co-operation mechanisms with the EU and to promote a strategy for the Caribbean Sea Zone to be recognized as a special area for the purposes of sustainable development programmes, support for a strengthened social agenda and efforts to achieve the Millennium Development Goals, and calls for member states to sign or ratify the following accords: an ACS Agreement for Regional Co-operation in the area of Natural Disasters; a Convention Establishing the Sustainable Tourism Zone of the Caribbean; and an ACS Air Transport Agreement; mems: 25 signatory states, four associate mems, 19 observers, six founding observer countries; Sec.-Gen. Dr Rubén Arturo Silié Valdez.

Association of Development Financing Institutions in Asia and the Pacific (ADFIAP): Skyland Plaza, 2nd Floor, Sen. Gil J. Puyat Ave, Makati City, Metro Manila, 1200 Philippines; tel. (2) 8161672; fax (2) 8176498; e-mail inquires@adfiap.org; internet www.adfiap.org; f. 1976 to promote the interests and economic development of the respective countries of its member institutions, through development financing; mems: 66 institutions in 32 countries; Chair. Isoa Kaloumaira (Fiji); Sec.-Gen. Octavio B. Peralta; publs *Asian Banking Digest*, *Journal of Development Finance* (2 a year), *ADFIAP Newsletter*, *ADFIAP Accompli*, *DevTrade Finance*.

Benelux Economic Union: 39 rue de la Régence, 1000 Brussels, Belgium; tel. (2) 519-38-11; fax (2) 513-42-06; e-mail info@benelux.be; internet www.benelux.be; f. 1960 to bring about the economic union of Belgium, Luxembourg and the Netherlands; aims to introduce common policies in the field of cross-border co-operation and harmonize standards and intellectual property legislation; structure comprises: Committee of Ministers; Council; Court of Justice; Consultative Inter-Parliamentary Council; the Economic and Social Advisory Council; and the General Secretariat; Sec.-Gen. Dr B. M. J. Hennekam (Netherlands); publs *Benelux Newsletter*, *Bulletin Benelux*.

Caribbean-Britain Business Council: 2 Belgrave Sq., London, SW1X 8PJ, United Kingdom; tel. (20) 7235-9484; fax (20) 7823-1370; e-mail admin@caribbean-council.org; internet www.caribbean-council.org; f. 2001; promotes trade and investment development between the United Kingdom, the Caribbean and the European Union; Chair. Barry Humphreys; Exec. Dir David Jessop; publ. *Caribbean Briefing* (weekly).

Caritas Internationalis (International Confederation of Catholic Organizations for charitable and social action): Palazzo San Calisto, 00120 Città del Vaticano; tel. (06) 6987-9799; fax (06) 6988-7237; e-mail caritas.internationalis@caritas.va; internet www.caritas.org; f. 1950 to study problems arising from poverty, their causes and possible solutions; national mem. organizations undertake assistance and development activities. The Confederation co-ordinates emergency relief and development projects, and represents mems at international level; mems: 162 national orgs; Pres. Denis Viénot (France); Sec.-Gen. Duncan MacLaren; publs *Caritas Matters* (quarterly), *Emergency Calling* (2 a year).

Central Asia Regional Economic Co-operation (CAREC): CAREC Unit, ADB, POB 789, 0980 Manila, Philippines; tel. (2) 6325857; fax (2) 6362387; internet www.adb.org/Carec; f. 1997; a sub-regional alliance supported by several multilateral institutions (Asian Development Bank, European Bank for Reconstruction and Development, International Monetary Fund, Islamic Development Bank, United Nations Development Programme, and World Bank) to promote economic co-operation and development; supports projects in the following priority areas: transport, energy, trade policy, trade facilitation; mems: Afghanistan, Azerbaijan, Kazakhstan, Kyrgyzstan, Mongolia, Tajikistan, Uzbekistan, Xinjiang Uygur Autonomous Region (of the People's Republic of China).

Central European Free Trade Association: internet www.cefta.org; f. 1992, Central European Free Trade Agreement (CEFTA) entered into force 1993; enlarged CEFTA signed 19 Dec. 2006; free trade agreement covering a number of sectors; mems: Albania, Bosnia and Herzegovina, Croatia, Macedonia, Moldova, Montenegro, Serbia, UNMIK (representing Kosovo).

Colombo Plan: Bank of Ceylon Merchant Tower, 13th Floor, 28 St Michael's Rd, Colombo 03, Sri Lanka; tel. (11) 2564448; fax (11) 2564531; e-mail info@colombo-plan.org; internet www.colombo-plan.org; f. 1950, as the Colombo Plan for Co-operative Economic and Social Development in Asia and the Pacific, by seven Commonwealth countries, to encourage economic and social development in that region, based on principles of partnership and collective effort; the Plan comprises four training programmes: the Drug Advisory Programme, to enhance the capabilities of officials, in government and non-governmental organizations, involved in drug abuse prevention and control; the Programme for Public Administration, to develop human capital in the public sector; the Programme for Private Sector Development, which implements skill development programmes in the area of small and medium-sized enterprises and related issues; and the Staff College for Technician Education (see below); all training programmes are voluntarily funded, while administrative costs of the organization are shared equally by all member countries; developing countries are encouraged to become donors and to participate in economic and technical co-operation activities; mems: 25 countries; Sec.-Gen. Kittipan Kanjanapipatkul (Thailand); publs *Annual Report*, *Colombo Plan Focus* (quarterly), *Consultative Committee Proceedings and Conclusions* (every 2 years).

Colombo Plan Staff College for Technician Education: POB 7500, Domestic Airport Post Office, NAIA, Pasay City 1300, Philippines; tel. (2) 6310991; fax (2) 6310996; e-mail cpsc@skyinet.net; internet www.cpsc.org.ph; f. 1973 with the support of member governments of the Colombo Plan; aims to enhance the development of technician education systems in developing mem. countries; Dir Man-Gon Park; publ. *CPSC Quarterly*.

Communauté économique des états de l'Afrique centrale (CEEAC) (Economic Community of Central African States): BP 2112, Libreville, Gabon; tel. 73-35-48; internet www.ceeac.org; f. 1983, operational 1 January 1985; aims to promote co-operation between member states by abolishing trade restrictions, establishing a common external customs tariff, linking commercial banks, and setting up a development fund, over a period of 12 years; works to combat drug abuse and to promote regional security; mems: 10 African countries; Sec.-Gen. Louis-Sylvain Goma.

Community of Sahel-Saharan States (Communauté des états Sahelo-Sahariens—CEN-SAD): POB 4041, Aljazeera Sq., Tripoli, Libya; tel. (21) 333-2347; fax (21) 444-0076; e-mail censad_sg@yahoo.com; internet www.cen-sad.org; f. 1998; fmrly known as COMESSA; aims to strengthen co-operation between signatory states in order to promote their economic, social and cultural integration and to facilitate conflict resolution and poverty alleviation; partnership agreements concluded with many orgs, including the AU, the UN and ECOWAS; mems: Benin, Burkina Faso, Central African Republic, Chad, Côte d'Ivoire, Djibouti, Egypt, Eritrea, The Gambia, Ghana, Guinea-Bissau, Liberia, Libya, Mali, Morocco, Niger, Nigeria, Senegal, Sierra Leone, Somalia, Sudan, Togo, Tunisia; Sec.-Gen. Dr Mohammed al-Madani al-Azhari (Libya).

Conseil de l'Entente (Entente Council): 01 BP 3734, angle ave Verdier/rue de Tessières, Abidjan 01, Côte d'Ivoire; tel. 20-33-28-35; fax 20-33-11-49; e-mail fegece@conseil-entente.org; f. 1959 to promote economic development in the region; the Council's Mutual Aid and Loan Guarantee Fund (Fonds d' entraide et de garantie des emprunts) finances development projects, including agricultural projects, support for small and medium-sized enterprises, vocational training centres, research into new sources of energy and building of hotels to encourage tourism. A Convention of Assistance and Co-operation was signed in Feb. 1996. Holds annual summit; mems: Benin, Burkina Faso, Côte d'Ivoire, Niger, Togo; Sec.-Gen. OUSMANE TAMIMOU; publ. *Rapport d'activité* (annually).

Communauté économique du bétail et de la viande (CEBV) du Conseil de l'Entente (Livestock and Meat Economic Community of the Entente Council): 01 BP 638 Ouagadougou, Burkina Faso; tel. 21-30-62-67; fax 21-30-62-68; e-mail cebv@cenatrin.bf; internet www.cenatrin.bf/cebv; f. 1970 to promote the production, processing and marketing of livestock and meat; negotiates between members and with third countries on technical and financial co-operation and co-ordinated legislation; attempts to co-ordinate measures to combat drought and cattle diseases; mems: states belonging to the Conseil de l'Entente; Exec. Sec. Dr ELIE LADIKPO (Togo).

Council of American Development Foundations (Consejo de Fundaciones Americanas de Desarrollo—SOLIDARIOS): Calle 6 No. 10 Paraíso, Apdo Postal 620, Santo Domingo, Dominican Republic; tel. 549-5111; fax 544-0550; e-mail solidarios@codetel.net.do; f. 1972; exchanges information and experience, arranges technical assistance, raises funds to organize training programmes and scholarships; administers development fund to finance programmes carried out by members through a loan guarantee programme; provides consultancy services. Mem. foundations provide technical and financial assistance to low-income groups for rural, housing and microenterprise development projects; mems: 18 institutional mems in 14 Latin American and Caribbean countries; Pres. MERCEDES P. DE CANALDA; Sec.-Gen. ISABEL C. ARANGO; publs *Solidarios* (quarterly), *Annual Report*.

Developing Eight (D-8): Müşir Fuad Paşa Yalısı (Eski Tersane), Sakıp Sabancı Cad. 90, Istinye 80860 İstanbul, Turkey; tel. (212) 2775513; fax (212) 2775519; e-mail developing-8@mfa.gov.tr; internet www.mfa.gov.tr/d-8/; inaugurated at a meeting of heads of state in June 1997; aims to foster economic co-operation between member states and to strengthen the role of developing countries in the global economy; project areas include trade and industry, agriculture, human resources, telecommunications, rural development, finance (including banking and privatization), energy, environment, and health; fifth Summit meeting: convened in Bali, Indonesia, May 2006; mems: Bangladesh, Egypt, Indonesia, Iran, Malaysia, Nigeria, Pakistan, Turkey; Exec. Dir AYHAN KAMEL.

Earth Council: POB 319-6100, San José, Costa Rica; tel. 205-1600; fax 249-3500; e-mail ecouncil@ecouncil.ac.cr; internet www.ecouncil.ac.cr; f. 1992, following the UN Conference on Environment and Development; aims to promote and support sustainable development; supported the establishment of National Councils for Sustainable Development (NCSDs) and administers a programme to promote co-operation and dialogue and to facilitate capacity-building and training, with NCSDs; works, with other partner organizations, to generate support for an Earth Charter. The Earth Council Institute, comprising 18 members, functions as an advisory board to the Council; Chair. MAURICE STRONG (Canada); Pres. and CEO of Earth Council Institute FRANS VAN HAREN (Netherlands).

East African Community (EAC): AICC Bldg, Kilimanjaro Wing, 5th Floor, POB 1096, Arusha, Tanzania; tel. (27) 2504253; fax (27) 2504255; e-mail eac@eachq.org; internet www.eac.int; f. 2001, following the adoption of a treaty on political and economic integration (signed in November 1999) by the heads of state of Kenya, Tanzania and Uganda, replacing the Permanent Tripartite Commission for East African Co-operation (f. 1993) and reviving the former East African Community (f. 1967; dissolved 1977); initial areas for co-operation were to be trade and industry, security, immigration, transport and communications, and promotion of investment; further objectives were the elimination of trade barriers and ensuring the free movement of people and capital within the grouping; a customs union came into effect on 1 Jan. 2005; a Court of Justice and a Legislative Assembly have been established; in April 2006 heads of state agreed that negotiations on a common market would commence in July and were to be concluded by Dec. 2008; Rwanda and Burundi formally became members of the Community on 1 July 2007; Sec.-Gen. JUMA VOLTER MWAPACHU (Tanzania).

Economic Community of the Great Lakes Countries (Communauté économique des pays des Grands Lacs—CEPGL): POB 58, Gisenyi, Rwanda; tel. 61309; fax 61319; f. 1976 main organs: annual Conference of Heads of State, Council of Ministers of Foreign Affairs, Permanent Executive Secretariat, Consultative Commission, Security Commission, three Specialized Technical Commissions; there are four specialized agencies: a development bank, the Banque de Développement des Etats des Grands Lacs (BDEGL) at Goma, Democratic Republic of the Congo; an energy centre at Bujumbura, Burundi; the Institute of Agronomic and Zootechnical Research, Gitega, Burundi; and a regional electricity company (SINELAC) at Bukavu, Democratic Republic of the Congo; mems: Burundi, the Democratic Republic of the Congo, Rwanda; publs *Grands Lacs* (quarterly review), *Journal* (annually).

Eurasian Economic Community (EURASEC): 105066 Moscow, 1-i Basmannyi per. 6/4, Russia; tel. (495) 223-90-00; fax (495) 223-90-24; e-mail evrazes@evrazes.ru; internet www.evrazes.com; f. 2000; formerly a Customs Union agreed between Belarus, Kazakhstan, Kyrgyzstan, Russia and Tajikistan in 1999; the merger of EURASEC with the Central Asian Co-operation Organization (CACO) was agreed in Oct. 2005, and achieved in Jan. 2006 with the accession to EURASEC of Uzbekistan, which had hitherto been the only mem. of CACO that did not also belong to EURASEC; aims to create a common economic space with a single currency; a free trade zone was established at the end of 2002; in Oct. 2007 EURASEC leaders approved the legal basis for establishing a new customs union, initially to comprise Belarus, Kazakhstan and Russia, with Kyrgyzstan, Tajikistan and Uzbekistan expected to join by 2011; mems co-operate on issues including customs tariff harmonization, migration, border security and negotiating admission to the WTO; Armenia, Moldova and Ukraine have observer status; Sec.-Gen. TAIR A. MANSUROV.

European Free Trade Association (EFTA): 9–11 rue de Varembé, 1211 Geneva 20, Switzerland; tel. 223322600; fax 223322677; e-mail mail.gva@efta.int; internet www.efta.int; f. 1960 to bring about free trade in industrial goods and to contribute to the liberalization and expansion of world trade; EFTA states (except Switzerland) participate in the European Economic Area (EEA) with the 27 member countries of the European Union; has concluded free trade agreements with *inter alia* Canada, Chile, Croatia, Egypt, Israel, Jordan, Republic of Korea, Lebanon, Macedonia, Mexico, Mercosur, Morocco, Palestinian Authority, Singapore, Southern African Customs Union (SACU), Tunisia and Turkey; mems: Iceland, Liechtenstein, Norway, Switzerland; Sec.-Gen. KÅRE BRYN (Norway); publs *EFTA Annual Report*, *EFTA Bulletin*.

Food Aid Committee: c/o International Grains Council, 1 Canada Sq., Canary Wharf, London, E14 5AE, United Kingdom; tel. (20) 7513-1122; fax (20) 7513-0630; e-mail igc-fac@igc.org.uk; internet www.igc.org.uk; f. 1967; responsible for administration of the Food Aid Convention—FAC (1999), a constituent element of the International Grains Agreement (1995); aims to make appropriate levels of food aid available on a consistent basis to maximize the impact and effectiveness of such assistance; provides a framework for co-operation, co-ordination and information-sharing among members on matters related to food aid. The 23 donor members pledge to supply a minimum of 5m. metric tons of food annually to developing countries and territories, mostly as gifts: in practice aid has usually exceeded 8m. tons annually. Secretariat support is provided by the International Grains Council; Exec. Dir G. DENIS; publ. *Report on shipments* (annually).

Gambia River Basin Development Organization (Organisation pour la mise en valeur du fleuve Gambie—OMVG): BP 2353, 13 passage Leblanc, Dakar, Senegal; tel. 822-31-59; fax 822-59-26; e-mail omvg@omvg.sn; f. 1978 by Senegal and The Gambia; Guinea joined in 1981 and Guinea-Bissau in 1983. A masterplan for the integrated development of the Kayanga/Geba and Koliba/Corubal river basins has been developed, encompassing a projected natural resources management project; a hydraulic development plan for the Gambia river was formulated during 1996–98; a pre-feasibility study on connecting the national electric grids of the four member states has been completed, and a feasibility study for the construction of the proposed Sambangalou hydroelectric dam, was undertaken in the early 2000s; maintains documentation centre; Exec. Sec. JUSTINO VIEIRA.

Group of Three (G3): c/o Secretaría de Relaciones Exteriores, 1 Tlatelolco, Del. Cuauhtémoc, 06995 México, DF, Mexico; e-mail gtres@sre.gob.mx; f. 1990 by Colombia, Mexico and Venezuela to remove restrictions on trade between the three countries; the trade agreement covers market access, rules of origin, intellectual property, trade in services, and government purchases, and entered into force in early 1994. Tariffs on trade between member states were to be removed on a phased basis. Co-operation was also envisaged in employment creation, the energy sector and the fight against cholera. The secretariat function rotates between the three countries on a two-yearly basis. In May 2006 Venezuela announced its intention to withdraw from the Group, which it formally submitted in November.

Indian Ocean Commission (IOC) (Commission de l'Océan Indien—COI): Q4, Ave Sir Guy Forget, BP 7, Quatre Bornes, Mauritius; tel. 425-9564; fax 425-2709; e-mail coi7@intnet.mu; internet www.coi-info.org; f. 1982 to promote regional co-operation, particularly in economic development; projects include tuna-fishing development, protection and management of environmental resources and strengthening of meteorological services; tariff reduction is also envisaged; organizes an annual regional trade fair; mems: Comoros, France (representing the French Overseas Department of Réunion), Madagascar, Mauritius, Seychelles; Sec.-Gen. MONIQUE ANDREAS-ESOAVELOMANDROSO; publ. *La Lettre de l'Océan Indien*.

Indian Ocean Rim Association for Regional Co-operation (IOR–ARC): Sorèze House, Wilson Ave, Vacoas, Mauritius; tel. 698-3979; fax 698-5390; e-mail iorarchq@intnet.mu; the first intergovernmental meeting of countries in the region to promote an Indian Ocean Rim initiative was convened in March 1995; charter to establish the Asscn was signed at a ministerial meeting in March 1997; aims to promote the sustained growth and balanced devt of the region and of its mem. states and to create common ground for regional economic co-operation, *inter alia* through trade, investment, infrastructure, tourism, and science and technology; seventh meeting of Council of Ministers held in Tehran, Iran, March 2007; mems: Australia, Bangladesh, India, Indonesia, Iran, Kenya, Madagascar, Malaysia, Mauritius, Mozambique, Oman, Singapore, South Africa, Sri Lanka, Tanzania, Thailand, United Arab Emirates and Yemen. Dialogue Partner countries: People's Republic of China, Egypt, France, Japan, United Kingdom. Observer: Indian Ocean Tourism Org; Chair. LAKSHMAN KADIRGAMAR (Sri Lanka); Exec. Dir TUAN ZAROOK A. SAMSUDEEN (Sri Lanka).

Inter-American Planning Society (Sociedad Interamericana de Planificación—SIAP): c/o Revista Interamericana de Planificación, Casilla 01-05-1978, Cuenca, Ecuador; tel. (7) 823860; fax (7) 823949; e-mail siap1@siap.org.ec; f. 1956 to promote development of comprehensive planning; mems: institutions and individuals in 46 countries; Exec. Sec. LUIS E. CAMACHO (Colombia); publs *Correo Informativo* (quarterly), *Inter-American Journal of Planning* (quarterly).

International Co-operation for Development and Solidarity (Co-opération Internationale pour le Développement et la Solidarité—CIDSE): 16 rue Stévin, 1000 Brussels, Belgium; tel. (2) 230-77-22; fax (2) 230-70-82; e-mail postmaster@cidse.org; internet www.cidse.org; f. 1967 as a network of Catholic development organizations in Europe and North America working in the field of development and North-South solidarity; promotes co-operation and the development of common strategies on advocacy work, development projects and programmes and development education; mems: 15 Catholic agencies in 14 countries and territories; Pres. PAUL CHITNIS; Sec.-Gen. CHRISTIANE OVERKAMP.

Inuit Circumpolar Conference: 170 Laurier Ave West, Suite 504, Ottawa, ON K1P 5V5, Canada; tel. (613) 563-2642; fax (613) 565-3089; e-mail icc@magma.ca; internet www.inuit.org; f. 1977 to protect the indigenous culture, environment and rights of the Inuit people (Eskimoes), and to encourage co-operation among the Inuit; conferences held every four years; mems: Inuit communities in Canada, Greenland, Alaska and Russia; Pres. AQQALUK LYNGE; Exec. Dir HJALMAR DAHL; publ. *Silarjualiriniq*.

Lake Chad Basin Commission (LCBC): BP 727, N'Djamena, Chad; tel. 52-41-45; fax 52-41-37; e-mail lcbc@intnet.td; f. 1964 to encourage co-operation in developing the Lake Chad region and to promote the settlement of regional disputes; work programmes emphasize the regulation of the utilization of water and other natural resources in the basin; the co-ordination of natural resources development projects and research; holds annual summit of heads of state; mems: Cameroon, Central African Republic, Chad, Niger, Nigeria; Exec. Sec. MUHAMMAD SANI ADAMU; publ. *Bibliographie générale de la cblt* (2 a year).

Latin American Association of Development Financing Institutions (Asociación Latinoamericana de Instituciones Financieras para el Desarrollo—ALIDE): Apdo Postal 3988, Paseo de la República 3211, Lima 100, Peru; tel. (1) 4422400; fax (1) 4428105; e-mail sg@alide.org.pe; internet www.alide.org.pe; f. 1968 to promote co-operation among regional development financing bodies; programmes: technical assistance; training; studies and research; technical meetings; information; projects and investment promotion; mems: 67 active, 3 assoc. and 5 collaborating (banks and financing institutions and development organizations in 22 Latin American countries, Slovenia and Spain); Sec.-Gen. ROMMEL ACEVEDO; publs *ALIDE Bulletin* (6 a year), *ALIDENOTICIAS Newsletter* (monthly), *Annual Report*, *Latin American Directory of Development Financing Institutions*.

Latin American Economic System (Sistema Económico Latinoamericano—SELA): Torre Europa, 4°, Urb. Campo Alegre, Avda Francisco de Miranda, Caracas 1060, Venezuela; Apdo 17035, Caracas 1010-A, Venezuela; tel. (212) 955-7111; fax (212) 951-5292; e-mail difusion@sela.org; internet www.sela.org; f. 1975 in accordance with the Panama Convention; aims to foster co-operation and integration among the countries of Latin America and the Caribbean, and to provide a permanent system of consultation and co-ordination in economic and social matters; conducts studies and other analysis and research; extends technical assistance to sub-regional and regional co-ordination bodies; provides library, information service and data bases on regional co-operation. The Latin American Council, the principal decision-making body of the System, meets annually at ministerial level and high-level regional consultation and co-ordination meetings are held; there is also a Permanent Secretariat; mems: 28 countries; Perm. Sec. ROBERTO GUARNIERI (Venezuela); publs *Capítulos del SELA* (3 a year), *Bulletin on Latin America and Caribbean Integration* (monthly), *SELA Antenna in the United States* (quarterly).

Liptako-Gourma Integrated Development Authority (LGA): POB 619, ave M. Thevenond, Ouagadougou, Burkina Faso; tel. (3) 30-61-48; f. 1972; scope of activities includes water infrastructure, telecommunications and construction of roads and railways; in 1986 undertook study on development of water resources in the basin of the Niger river (for hydroelectricity and irrigation); mems: Burkina Faso, Mali, Niger; Dir-Gen. GISANGA DEMBÉLÉ (Mali).

Mano River Union: Private Mail Bag 133, Delco House, Lightfoot Boston St, Freetown, Sierra Leone; tel. (22) 226883; f. 1973 to establish a customs and economic union between member states to accelerate development via integration; a common external tariff was instituted in 1977. Intra-union free trade was officially introduced in May 1981, as the first stage in progress towards a customs union. A non-aggression treaty was signed by heads of state in 1986. The Union was inactive for three years until mid-1994, owing to regional conflict and disagreements regarding funding. In January 1995 a Mano River Centre for Peace and Development was established, which was to be temporarily based in London. The Centre aims to provide a permanent mechanism for conflict prevention and resolution, and monitoring of human rights violations, and to promote sustainable peace and development. A new security structure was approved in 2000. In Aug. 2001 ministers of foreign affairs, security, internal affairs, and justice, meeting as the Joint Security Committee, resolved to deploy joint border security and confidence-building units, and to work to re-establish the free movement of people and goods; mems: Guinea, Liberia, Sierra Leone; Dir Dr ABDOULAYE DIALLO.

Mekong River Commission (MRC): POB 6101, Vientiane, Laos; tel. (21) 263263; fax (21) 263264; e-mail mrcs@mrcmekong.org; internet www.mrcmekong.org; f. 1995 as successor to the Committee for Co-ordination of Investigations of the Lower Mekong Basin ('Mekong Committee' f. 1957); aims to promote and co-ordinate the sustainable development and use of the water and related resources of the Mekong River Basin for navigational and non-navigational purposes, in order to assist the social and economic development of member states and preserve the ecological balance of the basin; provides scientific information and policy advice; supports the implementation of strategic programmes and activities; organizes an annual donor consultative group meeting; maintains regular dialogue with Myanmar and the People's Republic of China; mems: Cambodia, Laos, Thailand, Viet Nam; CEO JEREMY BIRD; publs *Annual Report*, *Catch and Culture* (3 a year), *Mekong News* (quarterly).

Niger Basin Authority (Autorité du Bassin du Niger): BP 729, Niamey, Niger; tel. 723102; fax 724208; e-mail abnsec@intnet.ne; internet www.abn.ne; f. 1964 (as River Niger Commission; name changed 1980) to harmonize national programmes concerned with the River Niger Basin and to execute an integrated development plan; compiles statistics; regulates navigation; runs projects on hydrological forecasting, environmental control; infrastructure and agro-pastoral development; mems: Benin, Burkina Faso, Cameroon, Chad, Côte d'Ivoire, Guinea, Mali, Niger, Nigeria; Exec. Sec. MOHAMMED BELLO TUGA (Nigeria); publ. *NBA-INFO* (quarterly).

Nile Basin Initiative: POB 192, Entebbe, Uganda; tel. (41) 321329; fax (41) 320971; e-mail nbisec@nilebasin.org; internet www.nilebasin.org; f. 1999; aims to achieve sustainable socio-economic development through the equitable use and benefits of the Nile Basin water resources and to create an enabling environment for the implementation of programmes with a shared vision. Highest authority is the Nile Basin Council of Ministers (Nile-COM); other activities undertaken by a Nile Basin Technical Advisory Committee (Nile-TAC); mems: Burundi, Democratic Republic of the Congo, Egypt, Eritrea, Ethiopia, Kenya, Rwanda, Sudan, Tanzania, Uganda; Exec. Dir PATRICK KAHANGIRE.

Nordic Development Fund: POB 185, 00171 Helsinki, Finland; tel. (10) 618-002; fax (9) 622-1491; e-mail info.ndf@ndf.fi; internet www.ndf.fi; f. 1989; supports activities by national administrations for overseas development, with resources amounting to €330m; Man. Dir HELGE SEMB.

Organization for the Development of the Senegal River (Organisation pour la mise en valeur du fleuve Sénégal—OMVS): c/o Haut-Commissariat, 46 rue Carnot, BP 3152, Dakar, Senegal; tel. 823-45-30; fax 822-01-63; e-mail omvsphc@sentoo.sn; internet www.omvs.org; f. 1972 to promote the use of the Senegal river for hydroelectricity, irrigation and navigation; the Djama dam in

Senegal provides a barrage to prevent salt water from moving upstream, and the Manantali dam in Mali is intended to provide a reservoir for irrigation of about 375,000 ha of land and for production of hydroelectricity and provision of year-round navigation for ocean-going vessels. In 1997 two companies were formed to manage the dams: Société de gestion de l'énergie de Manantali (SOGEM) and Société de gestion et d'exploitation du barrage de Djama (SOGED); mems: Mali, Mauritania, Senegal; Guinea has observer status; Pres. ABOUBACARY COULIBALY (Mali).

Organization for the Management and Development of the Kagera River Basin (Organisation pour l'aménagement et le développement du bassin de la rivière Kagera—OBK): BP 297, Kigali, Rwanda; tel. (7) 84665; fax (7) 82172; f. 1978; envisages joint development and management of resources, including the construction of an 80-MW hydroelectric dam at Rusumo Falls, on the Rwanda-Tanzania border, a 2,000-km railway network between the four member countries, road construction (914 km), and a telecommunications network between member states; mems: Burundi, Rwanda, Tanzania, Uganda; Exec. Sec. JEAN-BOSCO BALINDA.

Organization of the Co-operatives of America (Organización de las Cooperativas de América): Apdo Postal 241263, Carrera 11, No 86-32, Of. 101, Bogotá, Colombia; tel. (1) 6103296; fax (1) 6101912; f. 1963 for improving socio-economic, cultural and moral conditions through the use of the co-operatives system; works in every country of the continent; regional offices sponsor plans and activities based on the most pressing needs and special conditions of individual countries; mems: national or local orgs in 23 countries and territories; Exec. Sec. Dr CARLOS JULIO PINEDA SUÁREZ; publs *América Cooperativa* (monthly), *OCA News* (monthly).

Pacific Basin Economic Council (PBEC): 900 Fort St, Suite 1080, Honolulu, HI 96813, USA; tel. (808) 521-9044; fax (808) 521-8530; e-mail info@pbec.org; internet www.pbec.org; f. 1967; an asscn of business representatives aiming to promote business opportunities in the region, in order to enhance overall economic development; advises governments and serves as a liaison between business leaders and government officials; encourages business relationships and co-operation among members; holds business symposia; mems: 20 economies (Australia, Canada, Chile, People's Republic of China, Colombia, Ecuador, Hong Kong, Indonesia, Japan, Republic of Korea, Malaysia, Mexico, New Zealand, Peru, Philippines, Russia, Singapore, Taiwan, Thailand, USA); Pres. and CEO ROBERT LEES; Pres. STEPHEN OLSEN; publs *Pacific Journal* (quarterly), *Executive Summary* (annual conference report).

Pacific Economic Co-operation Council (PECC): 29 Heng Mui Keng Terrace, Singapore 119620; tel. 67379823; fax 67379824; e-mail info@pecc.org; internet www.pecc.org; f. 1980; an independent, policy-orientated organization of senior research, government and business representatives from 25 economies in the Asia-Pacific region; aims to foster economic development in the region by providing a forum for discussion and co-operation in a wide range of economic areas; PECC is an official observer to APEC; holds a General Meeting annually; mems: Australia, Brunei, Canada, Chile, the People's Republic of China, Colombia, Ecuador, Hong Kong, Indonesia, Japan, the Republic of Korea, Malaysia, Mexico, New Zealand, Peru, Philippines, Russia, Singapore, Taiwan, Thailand, USA, Viet Nam and the Pacific Islands Forum; assoc. mems: French Pacific Territories and Mongolia; Sec. Gen. EDUARDO PEDROSA; publs *Issues PECC* (quarterly), *Pacific Economic Outlook* (annually), *Pacific Food Outlook* (annually).

Pan-African Institute for Development (PAID): BP 4056, Douala, Cameroon; tel. and fax 342-80-30; e-mail ipd.sg@camnet.cm; f. 1964; gives training to people from African countries involved with development at grassroots, intermediate and senior levels; emphasis is given to: development management and financing; agriculture and rural development; issues of gender and development; promotion of small and medium-sized enterprises; training policies and systems; environment, health and community development; research, support and consultancy services; and specialized training. There are four regional institutes: Central Africa (Douala, Cameroon), Sahel (Ouagadougou, Burkina Faso), West Africa (Buéa, Cameroon), Eastern and Southern Africa (Kabwe, Zambia) and a European office in Geneva; Pres. of the Governing Council Dr MBUKI V. MWAMUFIYA; publs *Newsletter* (2 a year), *Annual Progress Report*, *PAID Report* (quarterly).

Partners in Population and Development: IPH Bldg, 2nd Floor, Mohakhali, Dhaka 1212, Bangladesh; tel. (2) 988-1882; fax (2) 882-9387; e-mail partners@ppdsec.org; internet www.south-south-ppd.org; f. 1994; aims to implement the decisions of the International Conference on Population and Development, held in Cairo, Egypt in 1994, in order to expand and improve South-South collaboration in the fields of family planning and reproductive health; administers a Visionary Leadership Programme, a Global Leadership Programme, and other training and technical advisory services; mems: 21 developing countries; Exec. Dir SANGEET HARRY JOOSEERY.

Permanent Interstate Committee on Drought Control in the Sahel (Comité permanent inter états de lutte contre la sécheresse au Sahel—CILSS): POB 7049, Ouagadougou 03, Burkina Faso; tel. 50-37-41-25; fax 50-37-41-32; e-mail cilss@cilss.bf; internet www.cilssnet.org; f. 1973; works in co-operation with UNDP Drylands Development Centre; aims to combat the effects of chronic drought in the Sahel region, by improving irrigation and food production, halting deforestation and creating food reserves; initiated a series of projects to improve food security and to counter poverty, entitled Sahel 21; the heads of state of all members had signed a convention for the establishment of a Fondation pour le Développement Durable du Sahel; maintains Institut du Sahel at Bamako (Mali) and centre at Niamey (Niger); mems: Burkina Faso, Cape Verde, Chad, The Gambia, Guinea-Bissau, Mali, Mauritania, Niger, Senegal; Pres. AMADOU TOUMANI TOURÉ (Mali); Exec. Sec. MUSA S. MBENGA (The Gambia); publ. *Reflets Sahéliens* (quarterly).

Population Council: 1 Dag Hammarskjöld Plaza, New York, NY 10017, USA; tel. (212) 339-0500; fax (212) 755-6052; e-mail pubinfo@popcouncil.org; internet www.popcouncil.org; f. 1952; the council is organized into three programmes: HIV and AIDS; Poverty, Gender, and Youth; and Reproductive Health; aims to improve reproductive health and achieve a balance between people and resources; analyses demographic trends; conducts biomedical research to develop new contraceptives; works with private and public agencies to improve the quality and scope of family planning and reproductive health services; helps governments to design and implement population policies; communicates results of research. Four regional offices, in India, Mexico, Egypt and Ghana, and 18 country offices, with programmes in more than 60 countries. Additional office in Washington, DC, USA, carries out world-wide operational research and activities for reproductive health and the prevention of HIV and AIDS; Pres. PETER DONALDSON; publs *Momentum* (2 a year), *Studies in Family Planning* (quarterly), *Population and Development Review* (quarterly), *Population Briefs* (3 a year).

Puebla-Panamá Plan (PPP): Torre Roble, 8°, San Salvador, El Salvador; tel. 2261-5444; fax 2260-9175; e-mail c.trinidad@planpuebla-panama.org; internet www.planpuebla-panama.org; f. 2001; relaunched with formal institutionalized structure in 2004; aims to promote economic development and reduce poverty in member countries; eight key areas of activity: energy, transport, telecommunications, tourism, trade environment and competitiveness, human development, sustainable development, prevention and mitigation of natural disasters; administers the Mesoamerica Biological Corridor initiative to enhance the management of the region's biodiversity; mems: Belize, Colombia, Costa Rica, El Salvador, Guatemala, Honduras, Mexico, Nicaragua, Panama; Exec. Dir MARÍA TERESA ORELLANA DE RENDÓN.

Society for International Development: Via Panisperna 207, 00184 Rome, Italy; tel. (06) 4872172; fax (06) 4872170; e-mail info@sidint.org; internet www.sidint.org; f. 1957; a global network of individuals and institutions wishing to promote participative, pluralistic and sustainable development; builds partnerships with civil society groups and other sectors; fosters local initiatives and new forms of social experimentation; mems: 3,000 individual mems and 55 institutional mems in 125 countries, 65 local chapters; Pres. ENRIQUE IGLESIAS; Sec.-Gen. ROBERTO SAVIO; publs *Development* (quarterly), *Bridges* (newsletter, every 2 months).

South Centre: Chemin du Champ-d'Anier 17–19, CP 228, 1211 Geneva 19, Switzerland; tel. 227918050; fax 227988531; e-mail south@southcentre.org; internet www.southcentre.org; f. 1990 as a follow-up mechanism of the South Commission (f. 1987); in 1995 established as an intergovernmental body to promote South-South solidarity and co-operation by generating ideas and action-oriented proposals on major policy issues; mems: 50 mem. countries; Chair. Prof. YASH TANDON (Uganda); publs *South Bulletin* (every 2 weeks), *Policy Brief* (monthly).

Southeast European Co-operative Initiative (SECI): Heldenplatz 1, Vienna 1010; tel. (1) 531-37-422; fax (1) 531-37-420; e-mail seci@osce.org; internet www.secinet.info; f. 1996 in order to encourage co-operation among countries of the sub-region and to facilitate their integration into European structures; receives technical support from the ECE and OSCE; ad hoc Project Groups have been established to undertake preparations for the following selected projects: commercial arbitration and mediation; co-operation between the Danube countries; electricity grids; energy efficiency; environmental recovery; combating organized crime; regional road transport; securities markets; trade and transport facilitation; and transport infrastructure; activities are overseen by a SECI Agenda Committee and a SECI Business Advisory Council; mems: Albania, Bosnia and Herzegovina, Bulgaria, Croatia, Greece, Hungary, former Yugoslav Republic of Macedonia, Moldova, Romania, Serbia, Slovenia, Turkey; Co-ordinator ERHARD BUSEK.

Union of the Arab Maghreb (Union du Maghreb arabe—UMA): 14 rue Zalagh, Agdal, Rabat, Morocco; tel. (37) 671-274; fax (37) 671-253; e-mail sg.uma@maghrebarabe.org; internet www.maghrebarabe

.org; f. 1989; aims to encourage joint ventures and to create a single market; structure comprises a council of heads of state (meeting annually), a council of ministers of foreign affairs, a follow-up committee, a consultative council of 30 delegates from each country, a UMA judicial court, and four specialized ministerial commissions. Chairmanship rotates annually between heads of state. A Maghreb Investment and Foreign Trade Bank, funding joint agricultural and industrial projects, has been established and a customs union created; mems: Algeria, Mauritania, Morocco, Tunisia; Sec.-Gen. HABIB BEN YAHIA (Tunisia).

Vienna Institute for International Dialogue and Co-operation (Wiener Institut für internationalen Dialog und Zusammenarbeit): Möllwaldplatz 5/3, 1040 Vienna, Austria; tel. (1) 713-35-94; fax (1) 713-35-94/73; e-mail office@vidc.org; internet www.vidc.org; f. 1987 (as Vienna Institute for Development and Co-operation; fmrly Vienna Institute for Development, f. 1964); manages development policy research on sectoral, regional and cross-cutting issues (for example, gender issues); arranges cultural exchanges between Austria and countries from Africa, Asia and Latin America; deals with conception and organization of anti-racist and integrative measures in sport, in particular football; Pres. BARBARA PRAMMER; Dir WALTER POSCH; publs *Report Series*, *Echo*.

World Economic Forum: 91–93 route de la Capite, 1223 Cologny/Geneva, Switzerland; tel. 228691212; fax 227862744; e-mail contact@weforum.org; internet www.weforum.org; f. 1971; the Forum comprises commercial interests gathered on a non-partisan basis, under the stewardship of the Swiss Government, with the aim of improving society through economic development; convenes an annual meeting in Davos, Switzerland; organizes the following programmes: Technology Pioneers; Women Leaders; and Young Global Leaders; and aims to mobilize the resources of the global business community in the implementation of the following initiatives: the Global Health Initiative; the Disaster Relief Network; the West-Islamic World Dialogue; and the G-20/International Monetary Reform Project; the Forum is governed by a guiding Foundation Board; an advisory International Business Council; and an administrative Managing Board; regular mems: representatives of 1,000 leading commercial companies world-wide; selected mem. companies taking a leading role in the movement's activities are known as 'partners'.

Economics and Finance

African Centre for Monetary Studies (ACMS): 15 blvd Franklin Roosevelt, BP 4128, Dakar, Senegal; tel. 821-93-80; fax 822-73-43; e-mail caem@syfed.refer.sn; began operations 1978; aims to promote better understanding of banking and monetary matters; studies monetary problems of African countries and the effect on them of international monetary developments; seeks to enable African countries to co-ordinate strategies in international monetary affairs; established as an organ of the Association of African Central Banks (AACB) following a decision by the OAU Heads of State and Government; mems: all mems of the AACB; Chair. Dr PAUL A. OGWUMA (Nigeria); Dir MAMADOU SIDIBE.

African Insurance Organization (AIO): 30 ave de Gaulle, BP 5860, Douala, Cameroon; tel. 33-42-47-58; fax 33-43-20-08; e-mail info@africaninsurance.org; internet www.africaninsurance.org; f. 1972 to promote the expansion of the insurance and reinsurance industry in Africa, and to increase regional co-operation; holds annual conference, periodic seminars and workshops, and arranges meetings for reinsurers, brokers, consultant and regulators in Africa; has established African insurance 'pools' for aviation, petroleum and fire risks, and created asscns of African insurance educators, supervisory authorities and insurance brokers and consultants; Pres. STEFFEN GILBERT; Sec.-Gen. ROLAND RASAMOELY (Cameroon) (acting); publ. *African Insurance Annual Review*.

Asian Clearing Union (ACU): 207/1 Pasdaran Ave, POB 15875/7177, 16646 Tehran, Iran; tel. (21) 22842076; fax (21) 22847677; e-mail acusecret@cbi.ir; internet www.asianclearingunion.org; f. 1974 to provide clearing arrangements, whereby members settle payments for intra-regional transactions among the participating central banks, on a multilateral basis, in order to economize on the use of foreign exchange and promote the use of domestic currencies in trade transactions among developing countries; part of ESCAP's Asian trade expansion programme; the Central Bank of Iran is the Union's agent; from Jan. 1996 the value of one Asian Monetary Unit (also referred to as an ACU Dollar) was aligned with that of one US dollar; mems: central banks of Bangladesh, Bhutan, India, Iran, Myanmar, Nepal, Pakistan, Sri Lanka; Sec.-Gen. LIDA BORHAN-AZAD; publs *Annual Report*, monthly newsletter.

Asian Reinsurance Corporation: 17th Floor, Tower B, Chamnan Phenjati Business Center, 65 Rama 9 Rd, Huaykwang, Bangkok 10320, Thailand; tel. (2) 245-2169; fax (2) 248-1377; e-mail asianre@asianrecorp.com; internet www.asianrecorp.com; f. 1979 by ESCAP with UNCTAD, to operate as a professional reinsurer, giving priority in retrocessions to national insurance and reinsurance markets of member countries, and as a development organization providing technical assistance to countries in the Asia-Pacific region; cap. (auth.) US $15m., (p.u.) $9m.; mems: Afghanistan, Bangladesh, Bhutan, People's Republic of China, India, Iran, Republic of Korea, Philippines, Sri Lanka, Thailand; Gen. Man. S. A. KUMAR.

Association of African Central Banks (AACB): 15 blvd Franklin Roosevelt, BP 4128, Dakar, Senegal; tel. 821-93-80; fax 822-73-43; f. 1968 to promote contacts in the monetary and financial sphere, in order to increase co-operation and trade among member states; aims to strengthen monetary and financial stability on the African continent; mems: 40 African central banks representing 47 states; Chair. FARHAT O. BENGDARA (Libya).

Association of African Tax Administrators (AATA): POB 13255, Yaoundé, Cameroon; tel. 22-41-57; fax 23-18-55; f. 1980 to promote co-operation in the field of taxation policy, legislation and administration among African countries; mems: 20 states; Exec. Sec. OWONA PASCAL-BAYLON.

Association of Asian Confederations of Credit Unions (AACCU): 24 Soi 60 Ramkanheang Rd, Bangkapi, Bangkok 10240, Thailand; tel. (2) 374-3170; fax (2) 374-5321; e-mail accu@aaccu.coop; internet www.aaccu.net; links and promotes credit unions and co-operatives in Asia, provides research facilities and training programmes; mems: in credit union leagues and federations in 24 Asian countries; Pres. OH-MAN KWON; CEO RANJITH HETTIARACHCHI (Thailand); publs *ACCU News* (every 3 months), *Annual Report*, *ACCU Directory*.

Association of European Institutes of Economic Research (AIECE) (Association d'instituts européens de conjoncture économique): 3 place Montesquieu, 1348 Louvain-la-Neuve, Belgium; tel. (10) 47-34-26; fax (10) 47-39-45; e-mail olbrechts@aiece.org; internet www.aiece.org; f. 1957; provides a means of contact between member institutes; organizes two meetings annually, at which discussions are held on the economic situation and on a special theoretical subject; mems: 43 institutes in 20 European countries and five int. orgs; Admin. Sec. PAUL OLBRECHTS.

Banco del Sur (South American Bank): Caracas, Venezuela; f. Dec. 2007; aims to provide financing for social and investment projects in South America; auth. cap. US $7,000m.; mems: Argentina, Brazil, Bolivia, Ecuador, Paraguay, Uruguay, Venezuela.

Centre for Latin American Monetary Studies (Centro de Estudios Monetarios Latinoamericanos—CEMLA): Durango 54, Col. Roma, Del. Cuauhtémoc, 06700 México, DF, Mexico; tel. (55) 5533-0300; fax (55) 5525-4432; e-mail estudios@cemla.org; internet www.cemla.org; f. 1952; organizes technical training programmes on monetary policy, development finance, etc; runs applied research programmes on monetary and central banking policies and procedures; holds regional meetings of banking officials; mems: 30 associated members (Central Banks of Latin America and the Caribbean), 20 co-operating members (supervisory institutions of the region and non-Latin American Central Banks); Dir-Gen. KENNETH GILMORE COATES SPRY; publs *Bulletin* (every 2 months), *Monetaria* (quarterly), *Money Affairs* (2 a year).

Comité Européen des Assurances (CEA): 26 blvd Haussmann, 75009 Paris, France; tel. 1-44-83-11-83; fax 1-47-70-03-75; internet www.cea.assur.org; f. 1953 to represent the interests of European insurers, to encourage co-operation between members, to allow the exchange of information and to conduct studies; mems: national insurance asscns of 30 full mems, 25 EU mem. states; Pres. GÉRARD DE LA MARTINIÈRE (France); Dir-Gen. MICHAELA KOLLER (Germany); publs *CEA Executive Update* (monthly newsletter), *European Insurance in Figures* (annually), *The European Life Insurance Market* (annually).

East African Development Bank: 4 Nile Ave, POB 7128, Kampala, Uganda; tel. (41) 230021; fax (41) 259763; e-mail dg@eadb.org; internet www.eadb.org; f. 1967 by the former East African Community to promote development within Kenya, Tanzania and Uganda, which each hold 24.07% of the equity capital; the remaining equity is held by the African Development Bank and other institutional investors; Chair. Dr EZRA SURUMA; Dir-Gen. GODFREY TUMUSIIME.

Eastern Caribbean Central Bank (ECCB): POB 89, Basseterre, St Christopher and Nevis; tel. 465-2537; fax 465-9562; e-mail info@eccb-centralbank.org; internet www.eccb-centralbank.org; f. 1983 by OECS governments; maintains regional currency (Eastern Caribbean dollar) and advises on the economic development of member states; mems: Anguilla, Antigua and Barbuda, Dominica, Grenada, Montserrat, Saint Christopher and Nevis, Saint Lucia, Saint Vincent and the Grenadines; Gov. Sir K. DWIGHT VENNER.

Econometric Society: Dept of Economics, New York University, 19 West Fourth St, 6th Floor, New York, NY 10012, USA; tel. (212) 998-3820; fax (212) 995-4487; e-mail sashi@econometricsociety.org;

INTERNATIONAL ORGANIZATIONS — Economics and Finance

internet www.econometricsociety.org; f. 1930 to promote studies aiming at a unification of the theoretical-quantitative and the empirical-quantitative approaches to economic problems; mems: c. 7,000; Gen. Man. CLAIRE SASHI; publ. *Econometrica* (6 a year).

European Federation of Finance House Associations (Eurofinas): 267 ave de Tervueren, 1150 Brussels, Belgium; tel. (2) 778-05-60; fax (2) 778-05-79; internet www.eurofinas.org; f. 1959 to study the development of instalment credit financing in Europe, to collate and publish instalment credit statistics, and to promote research into instalment credit practice; mems: finance houses and professional asscns in 13 European countries; Chair. ERIC SPIELREIN (France); publs *Eurofinas Newsletter* (monthly), *Annual Report*, *Study Reports*.

European Federation of Financial Analysts Societies (EFFAS): Einsteinstr. 5, 63303 Dreieich, Frankfurt-am-Main, Germany; tel. (6103) 583348; fax (6103) 583335; e-mail claudia.stinnes@effas.com; internet www.effas.com; f. 1962 to co-ordinate the activities of European asscns of financial analysts; aims to raise the standard of financial analysis and improve the quality of information given to investors; encourages unification of national rules and draws up rules of profession; holds biennial congress; mems: asscns in 25 European countries; Chair. FRITZ H. RAU; Gen. Sec. CLAUDIA STINNES.

European Financial Management and Marketing Association (EFMA): 16 rue d'Aguesseau, 75008 Paris, France; tel. 1-47-42-52-72; fax 1-47-42-56-76; e-mail info@efma.com; internet www.efma.com; f. 1971 to link financial institutions by organizing seminars, conferences and training sessions and an annual Congress and World Convention, and by providing information services; mems: more than 2,400 financial institutions world-wide; Chair. LARS G NORDSTRÖM; Sec.-Gen. PATRICK DESMARÈS; publ. *Newsletter*.

European Private Equity and Venture Capital Association (EVCA): 4 Minervastraat, 1930 Zaventem, Belgium; tel. (2) 715-00-20; fax (2) 725-07-04; e-mail evca@evca.com; internet www.evca.com; f. 1983 to link private equity and venture capital companies within Europe; provides information services; supports networking; organizes lobbies and campaigns; works to promote the asset class in Europe and world-wide; holds three conferences each year as well as seminars, organizes EVCA Institute training courses; mems: over 950; Chair. Sir DAVID COOKSEY (United Kingdom); Sec.-Gen. JAVIER ECHARRI; publs *Yearbook*, research and special papers, legal documents, industry guide-lines.

Financial Action Task Force (FATF) (Groupe d'action financière—GAFI): 2 rue André-Pascal, 75775 Paris Cédex 16, France; tel. 1-45-24-79-45; fax 1-44-30-61-37; e-mail contact@fatf-gafi.org; internet www.fatf-gafi.org; f. 1989, on the recommendation of the Group of Seven industrialized nations (G-7), to develop and promote policies to combat money laundering and the financing of terrorism; formulated a set of recommendations (40+9) for countries world-wide to implement; established partnerships with regional task forces in the Caribbean, Asia-Pacific, Central Asia, Europe, East and South Africa, the Middle East and North Africa and South America; mems: 34 state jurisdictions, the European Commission, and the Co-operation Council for the Arab States of the Gulf; observer: India, Republic of Korea; Pres. JAMES SASSOON (United Kingdom); Exec. Sec. ALAIN DAMAIS; publs *Annual Report*, *e-Bulletin*.

Financial Stability Forum: c/o BIS, Centralbahnplatz 2, 4002 Basel, Switzerland; tel. 612808298; fax 612809100; e-mail fsforum@bis.org; internet www.fsforum.org; f. 1999; brings together senior representatives of national financial authorities, international financial institutions, international regulatory and supervisory groupings and committees of central bank experts and the European Central Bank; aims to promote international financial stability and strengthen the functioning of the financial markets; Chair. MARIO DRAGHI.

Fonds Africain de Garantie et de Co-opération Economique (FAGACE) (African Guarantee and Economic Co-operation Fund): 01 BP 2045 RP, Cotonou, Benin; tel. 30-03-76; fax 30-02-84; e-mail fagace@intnet.bj; internet www.fagace.org; commenced operations in 1981; guarantees loans for development projects, provides loans and grants for specific operations and supports national and regional enterprises; mems: nine African countries; Dir-Gen. LIBASSE SAMB.

International Accounting Standards Board (IASB): 30 Cannon St, London, EC4M 6XH, United Kingdom; tel. (20) 7246-6410; fax (20) 7246-6411; e-mail iasb@iasb.org.uk; internet www.iasb.org.uk; f. 1973 as International Accounting Standards Committee, reorganized and present name adopted 2001; aims to develop, in the public interest, a single set of high-quality, uniform, clear and enforceable global accounting standards requiring the submission of high-quality, transparent and comparable information in financial statements and other financial reporting, in order to assist participants in world-wide capital markets and other end-users to make informed decisions on economic matters; aims also to promote the use and rigorous application of these global accounting standards, and to bring about the convergence of these with national accounting standards; Chair. and CEO Sir DAVID TWEEDIE; publs *IASB Insight* (quarterly), *Bound Volume of International Accounting Standards* (annually), *Interpretations of International Accounting Standards*.

International Association for Research in Income and Wealth: 111 Sparks Street, Suite 500, Ottawa, Ontario, K1P 5B5, Canada; tel. (613) 233-8891; fax (613) 233-8250; e-mail info@iariw.org; internet www.iariw.org; f. 1947 to further research in the general field of national income and wealth and related topics by the organization of biennial conferences and other means; mems: approx. 400; Exec. Dir ANDREW SHARPE (Canada); publ. *Review of Income and Wealth* (quarterly).

International Association of Deposit Insurers: c/o BIS, Centralbahnplatz 2, 4002 Basel, Switzerland; tel. 612809933; fax 612809554; e-mail info@iadi.org; internet www.iadi.org; f. 2002; aims to contribute to the stability of the international financial system by promoting co-operation among deposit insurers and establishing effective systems; Chair. JEAN PIERRE SABOURIN; Sec. JOHN RAYMOND LABROSSE.

International Association of Insurance Supervisors: c/o BIS, Centralbahnplatz 2, 4002 Basel, Switzerland; tel. 612257300; fax 612809151; e-mail iais@bis.org; internet www.iaisweb.org; f. 1994 to improve supervision of the insurance industry and promote global financial stability; Chair. MICHEL FLAMÉE; Sec.-Gen. YOSHIHIRO KAWAI.

International Bureau of Fiscal Documentation (IBFD): H. J. E. Wenckebachweg 210, POB 20237, 1000 HE Amsterdam, Netherlands; tel. (20) 5540100; fax (20) 6228658; e-mail info@ibfd.org; internet www.ibfd.org; f. 1938 to supply information on fiscal law and its application; maintains library on international taxation; Chair. Prof. Dr G. MAISTO; CEO W. FALTER; publs *Bulletin for International Fiscal Documentation*, *Asia Pacific Tax Bulletin*, *Derivatives and Financial Instruments*, *European Taxation*, *International VAT Monitor*, *International Transfer Pricing Journal*, *Supplementary Service to European Taxation* (all monthly), *Tax News Service* (weekly); studies, data bases, regional tax guides.

International Capital Market Association (ICMA): Rigistr. 60, POB, 8033 Zürich, Switzerland; tel. 443634222; fax 443637772; e-mail info@icma-group.org; internet www.icma-group.org; f. 2005 by merger of International Primary Market Association (IPMA) and International Securities Association (ISMA), f. 1969; maintains and develops an efficient and cost-effective market for capital; mems: 400 banks and major financial institutions in 48 countries; Exec. Pres. RENÉ KARSENTI (Netherlands); publs reports and market surveys.

International Centre for Local Credit: Koninginnegracht 2, 2514 AA The Hague, Netherlands; tel. (70) 3750850; fax (70) 3454743; e-mail centre@bng.nl; f. 1958 to promote local authority credit by gathering, exchanging and distributing information and advice on member institutions and on local authority credit and related subjects; studies important subjects in the field of local authority credit; mems: 22 financial institutions in 16 countries; Sec.-Gen. P. P. VAN BESOUW (Netherlands); publs *Bulletin*, *Newsletter* (quarterly).

International Economic Association: 23 rue Campagne Première, 75014 Paris, France; tel. 1-43-27-91-44; fax 1-42-79-92-16; e-mail iea@iea-world.org; internet www.iea-world.com; f. 1949 to promote international collaboration for the advancement of economic knowledge and develop personal contacts between economists, and to encourage the provision of means for the dissemination of economic knowledge; mems: asscns in 59 countries; Pres. Prof. GUILLERMO A. CALVO (Argentina); Sec.-Gen. Prof. JEAN-PAUL FITOUSSI (France).

International Federation of Accountants: 545 Fifth Ave, 14th Floor, New York, NY 10017, USA; tel. (212) 286-9344; fax (212) 286-9570; e-mail julissaguevara@ifac.org; internet www.ifac.org; f. 1977 to develop a co-ordinated world-wide accounting profession with harmonized standards; mems: over 160 accountancy bodies in 120 countries; Pres. GRAHAM WARD; Chief Exec. IAN BALL; publ. *International Standards on Auditing*.

International Fiscal Association (IFA): World Trade Center, POB 30215, 3001 DE Rotterdam, Netherlands; tel. (10) 4052990; fax (10) 4055031; e-mail n.gensecr@ifa.nl; internet www.ifa.nl; f. 1938 to study international and comparative public finance and fiscal law, especially taxation; holds annual congresses; mems in 91 countries and branches in 51 countries; Pres. Dr M. DESAX (Switzerland); Sec.-Gen. M. J. ELLIS (Netherlands); publs *Cahiers de Droit Fiscal International*, *Yearbook of the International Fiscal Association*, *IFA Congress Seminar Series*.

International Institute of Public Finance: University of Saarland, PO Box 151150, 66041 Saarbrücken, Germany; tel. (681) 302-3653; fax (681) 302-4369; e-mail schneider@iipf.net; internet www.iipf.org; f. 1937; a private scientific organization aiming to establish contacts between people of every nationality, whose main or supplementary activity consists in the study of public finance; holds one meeting a year devoted to a specific scientific subject; Pres. MICHAEL KEEN (United Kingdom); Exec. Sec. BIRGIT SCHNEIDER.

International Organization of Securities Commissions (IOSCO): Calle Oquendo 12, 28006 Madrid, Spain; tel. (91) 417-5549; fax (91) 555-9368; e-mail mail@oicv.iosco.org; internet www.iosco.org; f. 1983 to facilitate co-operation between securities and futures regulatory bodies at the international level; in 1998 adopted the Objectives and Principles of Securities Regulation (the IOSCO Principles); mems: 188 agencies; Chair. JANE DIPLOCK (New Zealand); Sec.-Gen. GREG TANZER (Australia); publs *Annual Report*, *IOSCO News* (3 a year).

International Union for Housing Finance: York House, 23 Kingsway, London WC2B 6UJ, United Kingdom; tel. +44 (20) 7440-2210; fax (20) 7836-4176; e-mail info.iuhf@housingfinance.org; internet www.housingfinance.org; f. 1914 to foster world-wide interest in savings and home-ownership and co-operation among members; encourages comparative study of methods and practice in housing finance; promotes development of appropriate legislation on housing finance; mems: 152 in over 60 countries; Sec.-Gen. ADRIAN COLES; publs *Housing Finance International* (quarterly), *IUHF Newsletter* (3 a year).

Latin American Banking Federation (Federación Latino-americana de Bancos—FELABAN): Cra 11A No. 93-67 Of. 202 A.A 091959, Bogotá, Colombia; tel. (1) 6218617; fax (1) 6217659; internet www.latinbanking.com; f. 1965 to co-ordinate efforts towards wide and accelerated economic development in Latin American countries; mems: 19 Latin American national banking asscns; Pres. JUAN ANTONIO NIÑO (Panama); Sec.-Gen. MARICIELO GLEN DE TOBÓN (Colombia).

Nordic Investment Bank (NIB) (Nordiska Investeringsbanken): Fabianinkatu 34, POB 249, 00171 Helsinki, Finland; tel. (10) 618001; fax (10) 6180725; e-mail info@nib.int; internet www.nib.int; f. 1975; provides finance and guarantees for the implementation of investment projects and exports in the Nordic and Baltic regions; the main sectors of the Bank's activities are energy, infrastructure development, transport and communications, and manufacturing; also manages an Environmental Loan Facility which facilitates environmental investments in the Nordic Adjacent Areas (north-west Russia); mems: Governments of Denmark, Estonia, Finland, Iceland, Latvia, Lithuania, Norway and Sweden; Pres. and CEO JOHNNY ÅKERHOLM.

Nordic Project Fund (NoPef): POB 241, 00171 Helsinki, Finland; tel. (9) 180-0350; e-mail ib.sonnerstad@nopef.com; internet www.nopef.com; f. 1982; aims to strengthen the international competitiveness of Nordic exporting cos, and to promote industrial co-operation in international projects (e.g. in environmental protection); grants loans to Nordic cos for feasibility expenses relating to projects; with effect from 1 Jan. 2008 NoPef's geographical target area expanded to include Bulgaria, Romania and countries outside the EU and EFTA; Man. Dir IB SØNNERSTAD.

Union of Arab Banks (UAB): POB 11-2416, Riad El-Solh 1107 2210, Beirut, Lebanon; tel. (1) 785711; fax (1) 867925; e-mail uab@uabonline.org; internet www.uabonline.org; f. 1972; aims to foster co-operation between Arab banks and to increase their efficiency; prepares feasibility studies for projects; 2007 Arab Banking Conference: Tripoli, Libya; mems: more than 300 Arab banks and financial institutions; Chair. Dr JOSEPH TORBEY (Lebanon).

World Council of Credit Unions (WOCCU): POB 2982, 5710 Mineral Point Rd, Madison, WI 53705-4493, USA; tel. (608) 231-7130; fax (608) 238-8020; e-mail mail@woccu.org; internet www.woccu.org; f. 1970 to link credit unions and similar co-operative financial institutions and assist them in expanding and improving their services; provides technical and financial assistance to credit union asscns in developing countries; mems: 42,616 credit unions in 92 countries; CEO PETE CREAR; publs *WOCCU Annual Report*, *Credit Union World* (3 a year), *Spotlights On Development*; technical monographs and brochures.

World Federation of Exchanges: 176 rue de Rivoli, 75001 Paris, France; tel. 1-58-62-54-00; fax 1-58-62-50-48; e-mail secretariat@world-exchanges.org; internet www.world-exchanges.org; f. 1961; fmrly Fédération Internationale des Bourses de Valeurs—FIBV; central reference point for the securities industry; offers member exchanges guidance in business strategies, and improvement and harmonization of management practices; works with public financial authorities to promote increased use of regulated securities and derivatives exchanges; mems: 57 full mems, 21 affiliates and 34 corresponding exchanges; Pres. MASSIMO CAPUANO; Sec-Gen. THOMAS KRANTZ.

World Savings Banks Institute: 11 rue Marie Thérèse, 1000 Brussels, Belgium; tel. (2) 211-11-11; fax (2) 211-11-99; e-mail info@savings-banks.com; internet www.savings-banks.com; f. 1924 as International Savings Banks Institute, present name and structure adopted in 1994; promotes co-operation among members and the development of savings banks world-wide; mems: 104 banks and asscns in 86 countries; Pres. Dr HOLGER BERNDT (Germany); publs *Annual Report*, *International Savings Banks Directory*, *Perspectives* (4–5 a year).

Education

Agence Universitaire de la Francophonie (AUF): BP 400, succ. Côte-des-Neiges, Montréal, QC H3S 2S7, Canada; tel. (514) 343-6630; fax (514) 343-5783; e-mail rectorat@auf.org; internet www.auf.org; f. 1961; aims to develop a francophone university community, through building partnerships with students, teachers, institutions and governments; mems: 617 institutions; Pres. Prof. CHARLES GOMBÉ MBALAWA (Congo); Dir-Gen. and Rector MICHÈLE GENDREAU-MASSALOUX (France); publ. *Le Français à l'Université* (quarterly).

AMSE-AMCE-WAER (Association mondiale des sciences de l'éducation) (Asociación mundial de ciencias de la educación) (World Association for Educational Research): c/o Yves Lenoir, Faculty of Education, Sherbrooke Univ., 2500 blvd de l'Université Sherbrooke, QC J1K 2R1, Canada; tel. (819) 821-8000; fax (819) 829-5343; e-mail amseamcewaer@usherbrooke.ca; internet amseamcewaer.educ.usherbrooke.ca; f. 1953, present title adopted 2004; aims to encourage research in educational sciences by organizing congresses, issuing publications and supporting the exchange of information; international conference scheduled to be held in 2008, in Morocco; mems: individual members in 32 countries; Pres. Prof. Dr YVES LENOIR; Gen. Sec. and Treas. ABDELKRIM HASNI; publ. *Educational Research around the World*.

Asian South Pacific Bureau of Adult Education (ASPBAE): c/o MAAPL, Eucharistic Congress Bldg No. 3, 9th Floor, 5 Convent St, Colaba, Mumbai 400 039, India; tel. (22) 22021391; fax (22) 22832217; e-mail aspbae@vsnl.com; internet www.aspbae.org; f. 1964 to assist non-formal education and adult literacy; organizes training courses and seminars; provides material and advice relating to adult education; mems in 31 countries and territories; Sec.-Gen. MARIA-LOURDES ALMAZAN-KHAN; publ. *ASPBAE News* (3 a year).

Asian Confederation of Teachers: c/o FIT, 55 Abhinav Apt, Mahturas Rd Extn, Kandivli, Mumbai 400 067, India; tel. (22) 8085437; fax (22) 6240578; e-mail vsir@hotmail.com; f. 1990; mems in 10 countries and territories; Pres. MUHAMMAD MUSTAPHA; Sec.-Gen. VINAYAK SIRDESAI.

Association for Childhood Education International: 17904 Georgia Ave, Suite 215, Olney, MD 20832, USA; tel. (301) 570-2111; fax (301) 570-2212; e-mail headquarters@acei.org; internet www.acei.org; f. 1892 to work for the education of children (from infancy through early adolescence) by promoting desirable conditions in schools, raising the standard of teaching, co-operating with all groups concerned with children, informing the public of the needs of children; mems: 12,000; Pres. JEANNIE BURNETT; Exec. Dir GERALD C. ODLAND; publs *Childhood Education* (6 a year), *Professional Focus Newsletters*, *Journal of Research in Childhood Education* (quarterly), books on current educational subjects.

Association Montessori Internationale: Koninginneweg 161, 1075 CN Amsterdam, Netherlands; tel. (20) 6798932; fax (20) 6767341; e-mail info@montessori-ami.org; internet www.montessori-ami.org; f. 1929 to propagate the ideals and educational methods of Dr Maria Montessori on child development, without racial, religious or political prejudice; organizes training courses for teachers in 15 countries; world congress held every four years (2009: Chennai, India); Pres. ANDRÉ ROBERFROID; publ. *Communications* (2 a year), *AMI Bulletin*.

Association of African Universities (AAU) (Association des universités africaines): POB 5744, Accra-North, Ghana; tel. (21) 774495; fax (21) 774821; e-mail info@aau.org; internet www.aau.org; f. 1967 to promote exchanges, contact and co-operation among African university institutions and to collect and disseminate information on research and higher education in Africa; mems: 113 mems in 30 countries; Sec.-Gen. Prof. AKILAGPA SAWYERR (Ghana); publs *AAU Newsletter* (3 a year), *Directory of African Universities* (every 2 years).

Association of Arab Universities: POB 401, Jubeyha, Amman, Jordan 11941; tel. (6) 5345131; fax (6) 5332994; e-mail secgen@aaru.edu.jo; internet www.aaru.edu.jo; f. 1964; a scientific conference is held every 3 years; council meetings held annually; mems: 163 universities; Sec.-Gen. Prof. Dr SALEH HASHEM; publ. *AARU Bulletin* (annually and quarterly, in Arabic).

Association of Caribbean University and Research Institutional Libraries (ACURIL): Apdo postal 23317, San Juan 00931-3317, Puerto Rico; tel. 790-8054; fax 764-2311; e-mail acurilsec@yahoo.com; internet acuril.uprrp.edu; f. 1968 to foster contact and collaboration between mem. universities and institutes; holds conferences, meetings and seminars; circulates information through newsletters and bulletins; facilitates co-operation and the pooling of resources in research; encourages exchange of staff and students; mems: 250; Pres. PEDRO ADELE MERRITT BERNARD PADILLA (Puerto Rico/Jamaica) (2007–08); Exec.-Sec. ONEIDA R. ORTIZ (Puerto Rico); publ. *Cybernotes*.

Association of European Research Libraries (Ligue des Bibliothèques Européennes de Recherche—LIBER): c/o LIBER Secretariat, Susan Vejlsgaard, Det Kongelige Bibliotek, POB 2149, 1016 Copenhagen K, Denmark; tel. 33-93-62-22; fax 33-91-95-96; e-mail sv@kb.dk; internet www.kb.dk/liber; f. 1971 to encourage collaboration between the general research libraries of Europe, and national and university libraries in particular; gives assistance in finding practical ways of improving the quality of the services provided; mems: 366 libraries and individuals in 41 countries; Pres. HANS GELEIJNSE (Netherlands); Gen.-Sec. ANN MATHESON (United Kingdom); publ. *LIBER Quarterly*.

Association of South-East Asian Institutions of Higher Learning (ASAIHL): Secretariat, Rm 113, Jamjuree 1 Bldg, Chulalongkorn University, Phyathai Rd, Bangkok 10330, Thailand; tel. (2) 251-6966; fax (2) 253-7909; e-mail oninnat@chula.ac.th; internet www.seameo.org/asaihl; f. 1956 to promote the economic, cultural and social welfare of the people of South-East Asia by means of educational co-operation and research programmes; and to cultivate a sense of regional identity and interdependence; collects and disseminates information, organizes discussions; mems: 160 university institutions in 16 countries; Pres. DATO DZULKIFLI ABDUL RAZAK; Sec.-Gen. Dr NINNAT OLANVORAVUTH; publs *Newsletter*, *Handbook* (every 3 years).

Catholic International Education Office: 60 rue des Eburons, 1000 Brussels, Belgium; tel. (2) 230-72-52; fax (2) 230-97-45; e-mail oiec@pophost.eunet.be; internet www3.planalfa.es/oiec; f. 1952 for the study of the problems of Catholic education throughout the world; co-ordinates the activities of members; represents Catholic education at international bodies; mems: 102 countries, 18 assoc. mems, 13 collaborating mems, 6 corresponding mems; Pres. Mgr CESARE NOSIGLIA; Sec.-Gen. ANDRÉS DELGADO HERNÁNDEZ; publs *OIEC Bulletin* (every 3 months, in English, French and Spanish), *OIEC Tracts on Education*.

Comparative Education Society in Europe (CESE): Institut für Augemeine Pädagogik, Humboldt-Universität zu Berlin, Unter den Linden 6, 10099 Berlin, Germany; tel. (30) 20934094; fax (30) 20931006; e-mail juergen.schriewer@educat.hu-berlin.de; internet www.cese-europe.org; f. 1961 to promote teaching and research in comparative and international education; organizes conferences and promotes literature; mems: in 49 countries; Pres. Prof. ROBERT COWEN (United Kingdom); Sec. and Treas. Prof. HANS-GEORG KOTTHOFF (Germany); publ. *Newsletter* (quarterly).

Council of Legal Education (CLE): c/o Registrar, POB 323, Tunapuna, Trinidad and Tobago; tel. 662-5860; fax 662-0927; f. 1971; responsible for the training of members of the legal profession; mems: govts of 12 countries and territories.

Education Action: 3 Dufferin St, London, EC1Y 8NA, United Kingdom; tel. (20) 7426-5800; e-mail info@education-action.org; internet www.education-action.org; f. 1920, as European Student Relief (renamed in 1950 World University Service); focuses on improving the lives of people in war torn countries, from Africa and the Middle East, and refugees from war living in the UK through education and employment training; Chief Exec. ALLAN WELLS (United Kingdom).

European Association for Education of Adults (EAEA): 60 rue de la Concorde, 1050 Brussels, Belgium; tel. (2) 513-52-05; fax (2) 513-57-34; e-mail gina.ebner@eaea.org; internet www.eaea.org; f. 1953; aims to create a 'learning society' by encouraging demand for learning, particularly from women and excluded sectors of society; seeks to improve response of providers of learning opportunities and authorities and agencies; mems: 114 orgs in 41 countries; Pres. JÁNOS TÓTH; Gen. Sec. GINA EBNER; publs *EAEA Monograph Series*, newsletter.

European Federation for Catholic Adult Education (Federation Européene pour l'Éducation Catholique des Adultes—FEECA): 221 ave de Tervueren, 1150, Brussels, Belgium; tel. (2) 738-07-90; fax (2) 738-07-95; e-mail office@cathyouthadult.org; f. 1963 to strengthen international contact between mems and to assist with international research and practical projects in adult education; holds conference every two years; Pres. ERICA SCHUSTER (Austria); Sec. SIMONE KAUFHOLD.

European Foundation for Management Development (EFMD): 88 rue Gachard, 1050 Brussels, Belgium; tel. (2) 629-08-10; fax (2) 629-08-11; e-mail info@efmd.be; internet www.efmd.be; f. 1971 through merger of European Association of Management Training Centres and International University Contact for Management Education; aims to help improve the quality of management development, disseminate information within the economic, social and cultural context of Europe and promote international co-operation; mems: over 500 institutions in 65 countries world-wide (28 in Europe); Pres. GERARD VAN SCHAIK; Dir-Gen. ERIC CORNUEL; publs *Forum* (3 a year), *The Bulletin* (3 a year), *Guide to European Business Schools and Management Centres* (annually).

European Union of Arabic and Islamic Scholars (Union Européenne des Arabisants et Islamisants—UEAI): c/o Bernadette Martel-Thoumian, Université de Grenoble, BP 47, 38040 Grenoble, Cedex 9, France; e-mail Bernadette.Martel-Thoumian@upmf-grenoble.fr; f. 1964 to organize congresses of Arabic and Islamic Studies; holds congress every two years; mems: 300 in 28 countries; Pres. Prof. SILVIA NAEF (Switzerland); Sec. Prof. BERNADETTE MARTEL-THOUMIAN (France).

European University Association (EUA): 13 rue d'Egmont, 1000 Brussels, Belgium; tel. (2) 230-55-44; fax (2) 230-57-51; e-mail info@eua.be; internet www.eua.be; f. 2001 by merger of the Association of European Universities and the Confederation of EU Rectors' Conferences; represents European universities and national rectors' conferences; promotes the development of a coherent system of European higher education and research through projects and membership services; provides support and guidance to mems. mems: 775 in 45 countries; Pres. GEORG WINCKLER; Sec.-Gen. LESLEY WILSON; publs *Thema*, *Directory*, *Annual Report*.

Graduate Institute of International Studies (Institut universitaire de hautes études internationales—HEI): POB 36, 132 rue de Lausanne, 1211 Geneva 21, Switzerland; tel. 229085700; fax 229085710; e-mail info@hei.unige.ch; internet hei.unige.ch; f. 1927 to establish a centre for advanced studies in international relations of the present day; maintains a library of 147,000 vols; Dir Prof. PHILIPPE BURRIN.

Inter-American Centre for Research and Documentation on Vocational Training (Centro Interamericano de Investigación y Documentación sobre Formación Profesional—CINTERFOR): Avda Uruguay 1238, Casilla de correo 1761, Montevideo, Uruguay; tel. (2) 9020557; fax (2) 9021305; e-mail dirmvd@cinterfor.org.uy; internet www.ilo.org/public/english/region/ampro/cinterfor; f. 1964 by the International Labour Organization for mutual help among the Latin American and Caribbean countries in planning vocational training; services are provided in documentation, research, exchange of experience; holds seminars and courses; Dir PEDRO DANIEL WEINBERG; publs *Bulletin CINTERFOR/OIT Heramientas para la transformación, Trazos de la formación*, studies, monographs and technical papers.

Inter-American Confederation for Catholic Education (Confederación Interamericana de Educación Católica—CIEC): Calle 78 No 12–16 (of. 101), Apdo Aéreo 90036, Bogotá 8 DE, Colombia; tel. (1) 255-3676; fax (1) 255-0513; e-mail secretariageneral@ciec.to; internet www.ciec.to; f. 1945 to defend and extend the principles and rules of Catholic education, freedom of education, and human rights; organizes congress every three years; Pres. WALTER DE JESÚS GUILLÉN SOTO (Panama); Sec.-Gen. RAMÓN EMILIO RIVAS TORRES; publ. *Educación Hoy*.

Inter-American Organization for Higher Education (IOHE): 333 Grande Allée Est, bureau 230, Québec, QC G1R 2H8, Canada; tel. (418) 650-1515; fax (418) 650-1519; e-mail secretariat@oui-iohe.qc.ca; internet www.oui-iohe.qc.ca; f. 1980 to promote co-operation among universities of the Americas and the development of higher education; mems: some 400 institutions and 20 national and regional higher education asscns; Exec. Dir MARCEL HAMELIN.

International Association for Educational and Vocational Guidance (IAEVG): c/o Linda Taylor, South London Connexions Ltd Canius House, 1 Scarbrook Rd, Croydon, Surrey, CR0 1SQ, United Kingdom; tel. (20) 8929-4707; fax (20) 8929-4763; e-mail lindataylor@connexions-southlondon.org.uk; internet www.iaevg.org; f. 1951 to contribute to the development of vocational guidance and promote contact between persons associated with it; mems: 40,000 from 60 countries; Pres. Dr BERNHARD JENSCHKE (Germany); Sec.-Gen. LINDA TAYLOR (United Kingdom); publs *Bulletin* (2 a year), *Newsletter* (3 a year).

International Association for the Development of Documentation, Libraries and Archives in Africa: Villa 2547 Dieuppeul II, BP 375, Dakar, Senegal; tel. 824-09-54; f. 1957 to organize and develop documentation and archives in all African countries; mems: national asscns, institutions and individuals in 48 countries; Sec.-Gen. ZACHEUS SUNDAY ALI (Nigeria).

International Association of Educators for World Peace: POB 3282, Mastin Lake Station, Huntsville, AL 35810-0282, USA; tel. (256) 534-5501; fax (256) 536-1018; e-mail mercieca@knology.net; internet www.iaewp.org; f. 1969 to develop education designed to contribute to the promotion of peaceful relations at personal, community and international levels; aims to communicate and clarify controversial views in order to achieve maximum understanding; organizes annual World Peace Conferences; helps put into practice the Universal Declaration of Human Rights; mems: 45,000 in 80 countries; Pres. Dr CHARLES MERCIECA (USA); Sec.-Gen. NENAD

JAVORNIK (Croatia); publs *Diplomacy Journal* (quarterly), *Peace Education Journal* (annually).

International Association of Papyrologists (Association Internationale de Papyrologues): Association Egyptologique Reine Elisabeth, Parc du Cinquantenaire 10, 1000 Brussels, Belgium; tel. (2) 741-73-64; e-mail amartin@ulb.ac.be; internet www.ulb.ac.be/assoc/aip; f. 1947; links all those interested in Graeco-Roman Egypt, especially Greek texts; mem. of the International Federation of the Societies of Classical Studies; mems: about 400; Pres. Prof. DOROTHY J. THOMPSON (United Kingdom); Sec. Prof. ALAIN MARTIN (Belgium).

International Association of Physical Education in Higher Education (Association Internationale des Ecoles Supérieures d'Éducation Physique—AIESEP): Department of Sport Sciences, University of Liège, Allée des Sports, 4 Bât B-21 B-4000 Liège, Belgium; tel. (4) 366-38-80; fax (4) 366-29-01; e-mail Marc.Cloes@ulg.ac.be; internet www.aiesep.org; f. 1962; organizes congresses, exchanges, and research in physical education; mems: institutions in 51 countries; Sec.-Gen. Dr MARC CLOES.

International Association of Universities (IAU)/ International Universities Bureau (IUB): 1 rue Miollis, 75732 Paris cédex 15, France; tel. 1-45-68-48-00; fax 1-47-34-76-05; e-mail iau@unesco.org; internet www.unesco.org/iau/; f. 1948 to allow co-operation at the international level among universities and other institutions of higher education; provides clearing-house services and operates the joint IAU/UNESCO Information Centre on Higher Education; conducts meetings and research on issues concerning higher education; mems: 600 institutions of higher education and other organizations concerned with higher education in some 160 countries; Pres. GOOLAM MOHAMEDBHAI; Sec.-Gen. and Exec. Dir EVA EGRON-POLAK; publs *Higher Education Policy* (quarterly), *IAU Horizons* (every 2 months), *International Handbook of Universities* (every 2 years), *Issues in Higher Education* (monographs), *World Higher Education Database* (CD-ROM, annually).

International Association of University Professors and Lecturers (IAUPL) (Association Internationale des Professeurs et Maîtres de Conférence Universitaires): 87 rue de Rome, 75017 Paris, France; tel. 1-44-90-01-01; fax 1-44-90-08-87; e-mail autonomesup@aol.com; f. 1945 for the development of academic fraternity amongst university teachers and research workers; the protection of independence and freedom of teaching and research; the furtherance of the interests of all university teachers; and the consideration of academic problems; mems: federations in 13 countries and territories.

International Baccalaureate Organization (IBO): Route des Morillons 15, Grand-Saconnex 1218, Geneva, Switzerland; tel. 227917740; fax 227910277; e-mail ibhq@ibo.org; internet www.ibo.org; f. 1968 to plan curricula and an international university entrance examination, the International Baccalaureate diploma, recognized by major universities world-wide; offers the Primary Years Programme for children aged 3–12, the Middle Years Programme for students in the 11–16 age range, and the Diploma Programme for 17–18 year olds; mems: 2,217 participating schools in 125 countries; Pres. of Bd of Governors MONIQUE SEEFRIED (France/USA); Dir-Gen. JEFF BEARD.

International Catholic Federation for Physical and Sports Education (Fédération Internationale Catholique d'Education Physique et Sportive—FICEP): 22 rue Oberkampf, 75011 Paris, France; tel. 1-43-38-50-57; fax 1-43-14-06-65; e-mail info@ficep.org; internet www.ficep.org; f. 1911 to group Catholic asscns for physical education and sport of different countries and to develop the principles and precepts of Christian morality by fostering meetings, study and international co-operation; mems: 14 affiliated national federations representing about 3.5m. members; Pres. CLÉMENT SCHERTZINGER (France); Sec.-Gen. FRITZ SMOLY (Austria).

International Congress of African Studies: c/o International African Institute, Thornhaugh St, London, WC1H 0XG, United Kingdom; tel. (20) 7898-4420; fax (20) 7898-4419; e-mail iai@soas.ac.uk; f. 1962 to encourage co-operation and research in African studies; Congress convened approx. every five years; publ. *Proceedings*.

International Council for Adult Education (ICAE): Ave. 18 de Julio 2095/301, CP 11200, Montevideo, Uruguay; tel. and fax (2) 4097982; e-mail secretariat@icae.org.uy; internet www.icae.org.uy; f. 1973 as a partnership of adult learners, teachers and organizations; General Assembly meets every four years; mems: seven regional organizations and over 700 literacy, adult and lifelong learning asscns in more than 50 countries; Pres. PAUL BÉLANGER; publs *Convergence*, *ICAE News*.

International Council for Open and Distance Education (ICDE): Lilleakerveien 23, 0283 Oslo, Norway; tel. 22-06-26-30; fax 22-06-26-31; e-mail icde@icde.no; internet www.icde.org; f. 1938 (name changed 1982); furthers distance (correspondence) education by promoting research, encouraging regional links, providing information and organizing conferences; mems: institutions, corporations and individuals in 120 countries; Sec.-Gen.and CEO ANA PERONA FJELDSTAD (Norway) (acting); publ. *Open Praxis* (2 a year).

International Federation for Parent Education (IFPE) (Fédération internationale pour l'éducation des parents—FIEP): 1 ave Léon Journault, 92318 Sèvres Cédex, France; tel. 1-45-07-21-64; fax 1-46-26-69-27; e-mail fiep@videotron.ca; f. 1964 to gather in congresses and colloquia experts from different scientific fields and those responsible for family education in their own countries and to encourage the establishment of family education where it does not exist; mems: 60 nat. and local mem. orgs, 35 individual mems and 4 int. or regional orgs; Pres. MONEEF GUITOUNI (Canada); publ. *Lettre de la FIEP* (2 a year).

International Federation of Catholic Universities (Fédération internationale d'universités catholiques—FIUC): 21 rue d'Assas, 75270 Paris Cédex 06, France; tel. 1-44-39-52-26; fax 1-44-39-52-28; e-mail sgfiuc@bureau.fiuc.org; internet www.fiuc.org/; f. 1948; aims to ensure a strong bond of mutual assistance among all Catholic universities in the search for truth; to help to solve problems of growth and development, and to co-operate with other international organizations; mems: some 200 in 53 countries; Pres. Rev. JAN PETERS (Netherlands); Sec.-Gen. GUY-RÉAL THIVIERGE (Canada); publ. *Monthly Newsletter*.

International Federation of Library Associations and Institutions (IFLA): POB 95312, 2509 CH The Hague, Netherlands; tel. (70) 3140884; fax (70) 3834827; e-mail ifla@ifla.org; internet www.ifla.org; f. 1927 to promote international co-operation in librarianship and bibliography; mems: over 1,700 members in 150 countries; Pres. CLAUDIA LUX (2007–09); Sec.-Gen. PETER LOR; publs *IFLA Annual Report*, *IFLA Directory*, *IFLA Journal*, *International Cataloguing and Bibliographic Control* (quarterly), *IFLA Professional Reports*.

International Federation of Organizations for School-Correspondence and Exchange: Via Torino 256, 10015 Ivrea, Italy; tel. (0125) 234433; e-mail fioces@ipfs.org; internet ipfs.org/fioces.htm; f. 1929; aims to contribute to the knowledge of foreign languages and civilizations and to bring together young people of all nations by furthering international scholastic correspondence; mems: 78 national bureaux of scholastic correspondence and exchange in 21 countries; Pres. ALBERT V. RUTTER (Malta); Gen. Sec. LIVIO TONSO (Italy).

International Federation of Physical Education (Fédération internationale d'éducation physique—FIEP): c/o Prof. Robert Decker, 7–9 rue du X Octobre, 7243 Bereldange, Luxembourg; tel. and fax 33-94-81; e-mail robert.decker@education.lu; f. 1923; studies physical education on scientific, pedagogic and aesthetic bases, with the aim of stimulating health, harmonious development or preservation, healthy recreation, and the best adaptation of the individual to the general needs of social life; organizes international congresses and courses; awards research prize; mems: from 112 countries; Vice-Pres. (Europe) Prof. ROBERT DECKER; publ. *FIEP Bulletin* (3 a year, in English, French, and Spanish).

International Federation of Teachers of Modern Languages (Fédération des Professeurs de Langues Vivantes): POB 216, Belgrave 3160, Australia; tel. (6139) 754-4714; fax (6139) 416-9899; e-mail djc@netspace.net.au; internet www.fiplv.org; f. 1931; holds meetings on every aspect of foreign-language teaching; has consultative status with UNESCO; mems: 28 national and regional language asscns and nine international unilingual asscns (teachers of English, Esperanto, French, German, Portuguese, Russian); Pres. DENIS CUNNINGHAM; Sec.-Gen. EYNAR LEUPOLD; publ. *FIPLV World News* (2 a year, in English, French, German and Spanish).

International Federation of University Women (IFUW): 10 rue du Lac, 1207 Geneva, Switzerland; tel. 227312380; fax 227380440; e-mail lbr@ifuw.org; internet www.ifuw.org; f. 1919; to promote lifelong learning; to work for improvement of the status of women and girls; to encourage and enable women as leaders and decision-makers; Affiliates: 79 national asscns; Pres. LOUISE CROOT (New Zealand); Sec.-Gen. LEIGH BRADFORD RATTEREE; publ. *triennial report*.

International Federation of Workers' Education Associations: Surcon House, 11a Copson Street, Manchester, M20 3HE, United Kingdom; tel. (161) 445-9272; fax (161) 445-3625; e-mail dave.spooner@ifwea.org; internet www.ifwea.org; f. 1947 to promote co-operation between non-governmental bodies concerned with workers' education; organizes clearing-house services; promotes exchange of information; holds international seminars, conferences and summer schools; Pres. JOÃO PROENCA (Portugal); Gen. Sec. DAVE SPOONER (United Kingdom); publ. *Worker's Education* (quarterly).

International Institute for Adult Education Methods: POB 19395/6194, 5th Floor, Golfam St, 19156 Tehran, Iran; tel. (21) 2220313; f. 1968 by UNESCO and the Government of Iran, to collect, analyse and distribute information on activities concerning methods of literacy training and adult education; sponsors seminars; maintains documentation service and library on literacy and adult education; Dir Dr MOHAMMAD REZA HAMIDIZADE; publs *Selection of Adult Education Issues* (monthly), *Adult Education and Development* (quarterly), *New Library Holdings* (quarterly).

International Institute of Philosophy (IIP) (Institut international de philosophie): 8 rue Jean-Calvin, 75005 Paris, France; tel. 1-43-36-39-11; e-mail inst.intern.philo@wanadoo.fr; f. 1937 to clarify fundamental issues of contemporary philosophy and to promote mutual understanding among thinkers of different backgrounds and traditions; mems: 105 in 43 countries; Pres. H. LENK (Germany); Sec.-Gen. P. AUBENQUE (France); publs *Bibliography of Philosophy* (quarterly), *Proceedings of annual meetings, Chroniques, Philosophy and World Community* (series), *Philosophical Problems Today, Open Problems*.

International Reading Association: 800 Barksdale Rd, POB 8139, Newark, DE 19714-8139, USA; tel. (302) 731-1600; fax (302) 731-1057; e-mail pubinfo@reading.org; internet www.reading.org; f. 1956 to improve the quality of reading instruction at all levels, to promote the habit of lifelong reading, and to develop every reader's proficiency; mems: 85,000 in 118 countries; Pres. LINDA GAMBRELL; publs *The Reading Teacher* (8 a year), *Journal of Adolescent and Adult Literacy* (8 a year), *Reading Research Quarterly, Lectura y Vida* (quarterly), *Reading Today* (6 a year).

International Schools Association (ISA): 10333 Diego Drive South, Boca Raton, FL 33428, USA; tel. (561) 883-3854; fax (561) 483-2004; e-mail info@isaschools.org; internet www.isaschools.org; f. 1951 to co-ordinate work in international schools and to promote their development; convenes biennial Conferences and annual Youth Leadership Seminars on topics of global concern, and organizes specialist seminars on internationalism and international-mindedness; has consultative status at ECOSOC; mems: 100 schools throughout the world; Pres. CLIVE CARTHEW; publs *Newsletter* (online, 3 a year), *Internationalism in Schools—a Self Study Guide*, other occasional reports/studies.

International Society for Business Education: POB 2083 Marion, IN 46952, USA; tel. (765) 664-7753; fax (765) 651-3110; e-mail secretary@siec-isbe.org; internet www.siec-isbe.org; f. 1901; encourages international exchange of information; organizes international courses and congresses on business education; mems: 2,200 national organizations and individuals in 23 countries; Pres. Dr HANS WEBER (Switzerland); Gen. Sec. Dr JOHN LIGHTLE (USA); publ. *International Review for Business Education*.

International Society for Education through Art (INSEA): c/o Peter Hermans, Citogroep, POB 1109, 6801 BC Arnhem, Netherlands; fax (26) 3521202; e-mail insea@citogroep.nl; internet www.insea.org; f. 1951 to unite art teachers throughout the world, to exchange information and to co-ordinate research into art education; organizes international congresses and exhibitions of children's art; Pres. ANN CHENG SHIANG KUO (Taiwan); Sec. Dr MICHAEL DAY (USA); publ. *INSEA News* (3 a year).

International Society for Music Education (ISME): POB 909, Nedlands, WA 6909, Australia; tel. (8) 9386-2654; fax (8) 9386-2658; e-mail isme@isme.org; internet www.isme.org; f. 1953 to organize international conferences, seminars and publications on matters pertaining to music education; acts as advisory body to UNESCO in matters of music education; mems: national committees and individuals in more than 70 countries; Pres. HÅKAN LUNDSTRÖM (Sweden) (2008-2010); Sec.-Gen. JUDY THÖNELL (Australia); publs *ISME Newsletter, International Journal of Music Education*.

International Society for the Study of Medieval Philosophy: Collège Mercier, 14 place du Cardinal Mercier, 1348 Louvain-la-Neuve, Belgium; tel. (10) 47-48-07; fax (10) 47-82-85; e-mail siepm@isp.vcp.ac.be; f. 1958 to promote the study of medieval thought and the collaboration between individuals and institutions in this field; organizes international congresses; mems: 576; Pres. Prof. DAVID LUSCOMBE (United Kingdom); Sec. Prof. JACQUELINE HAMESSE (Belgium); publ. *Bulletin de Philosophie Médiévale* (annually).

International Youth Library (Internationale Jugendbibliothek): Schloss Blutenburg, 81247 Munich, Germany; tel. (89) 8912110; fax (89) 8117553; e-mail bib@ijb.de; internet www.ijb.de; f. 1949, since 1953 an associated project of UNESCO; promotes the international exchange of children's literature; provides study opportunities for specialists in childrens' books; maintains a library of 540,000 volumes in about 130 languages; Dir Dr BARBARA SCHARIOTH; publs *The White Ravens, IJB Report*, catalogues.

Organization of Ibero-American States for Education, Science and Culture (Organización de Estados Iberoamericanos para la Educación, la Ciencia y la Cultura—OEI): Centro de Recursos Documentales e Informáticos, Calle Bravo Murillo 38, 28015 Madrid, Spain; tel. (91) 594-43-82; fax (91) 594-32-86; e-mail oeimad@oei.es; internet www.oei.es; f. 1949 (as the Ibero-American Bureau of Education); promotes peace and solidarity between member countries, through education, science, technology and culture; provides information, encourages exchanges and organizes training courses; the General Assembly (at ministerial level) meets every four years;

mems: govts of 20 countries; Sec.-Gen. FRANCISCO JOSÉ PIÑÓN; publ. *Revista Iberoamericana de Educación* (quarterly).

Organization of the Catholic Universities of Latin America (Organización de Universidades Católicas de América Latina—ODUCAL): c/o Dr J. A. Tobías, Universidad del Salvador, Viamonte 1856, CP 1056, Buenos Aires, Argentina; tel. (11) 4813-1408; fax (11) 4812-4625; e-mail udes-rect@salvador.edu.ar; f. 1953 to assist the social, economic and cultural development of Latin America through the promotion of Catholic higher education in the continent; mems: 43 Catholic universities in 15 Latin American countries; Pres. Dr JUAN ALEJANDRO TOBÍAS (Argentina); publs *Anuario, Sapientia, Universitas*.

Pan-African Association for Literacy and Adult Education: c/o ANAFA, BP 10358, Dakar, Senegal; tel. 825-48-50; fax 824-44-13; e-mail anafa@metissacana.sn; f. 2000 to succeed African Asscn for Literacy and Adult Education (f. 1984); Co-ordinator Dr LAMINE KANE.

Southeast Asian Ministers of Education Organization (SEAMEO): M. L. Pin Malakul Bldg, 920 Sukhumvit Rd, Bangkok 10110, Thailand; tel. (2) 391-0144; fax (2) 381-2587; e-mail secretariat@seameo.org; internet www.seameo.org; f. 1965 to promote co-operation among the Southeast Asian nations through projects in education, science and culture; SEAMEO has 15 regional centres including: BIOTROP for tropical biology, in Bogor, Indonesia; INNOTECH for educational innovation and technology, in Philippines; SEAMOLEC, an open-learning centre, in Indonesia; RECSAM for education in science and mathematics, in Penang, Malaysia; RELC for languages, in Singapore; RIHED for higher education development, in Bangkok, Thailand; SEARCA for graduate study and research in agriculture, in Los Baños, Philippines; SPAFA for archaeology and fine arts, in Bangkok, Thailand; TROPMED for tropical medicine and public health, with regional centres in Indonesia, Malaysia, Philippines and Thailand and a central office in Bangkok; VOCTECH for vocational and technical education; RETRAC, a training centre, in Ho Chi Minh City, Viet Nam; and the SEAMEO Regional Centre for History and Tradition (CHAT) in Yangon, Myanmar; mems: Brunei, Cambodia, Indonesia, Laos, Malaysia, Philippines, Singapore, Thailand, Timor-Leste and Viet Nam; assoc. mems: Australia, Canada, France, Germany, Netherlands, New Zealand, Norway and Spain; Pres. BAMBANG SUDIBYO; Dir Dr EDILBERTO C. DE JESUS (Philippines); publs *Annual Report, SEAMEO Education Agenda*.

Union of Universities of Latin America and the Caribbean (Unión de Universidades de América Latina y el Caribe—UDUAL): Edificio UDUAL, Apdo postal 70-232, Ciudad Universitaria, Del. Coyoacán, 04510 México, DF, Mexico; tel. (55) 5622-0091; fax (55) 5622-0092; e-mail contacto@udual.org; internet www.udual.org; f. 1949 to organize exchanges between professors, students, research fellows and graduates and generally encourage good relations between the Latin American universities; arranges conferences; conducts statistical research; maintains centre for university documentation; mems: 159 universities and eight university networks; Pres. Dr GUSTAVO GARCÍA DE PAREDES (Panama); Sec.-Gen. Dr RAFAEL CORDERA CAMPOS (Mexico); publs *Universidades* (2 a year), *Gaceta UDUAL* (quarterly), *Censo* (every 2 years).

World Education Fellowship: 54 Fox Lane, London, N13 4AL, United Kingdom; tel. (20) 8245-4561; e-mail laura.cusack@iinet.net.au; internet www.wef.org.au; f. 1921 to promote education for international understanding, and the exchange and practice of ideas, together with research into progressive educational theories and methods; mems: sections and groups in 20 countries; Pres. Prof. COLIN POWER (Australia); Chair. CHRISTINE WYKES (United Kingdom); Gen. Sec. GUADALUPE G. DE TURNER (United Kingdom); publ. *The New Era in Education* (3 a year).

World Esperanto Association (Universala Esperanto-Asocio): Nieuwe Binnenweg 176, 3015 BJ Rotterdam, Netherlands; tel. (10) 4361044; fax (10) 4361751; e-mail uea@co.uea.org; internet www.uea.org; f. 1908 to assist the spread of the international language, Esperanto, and to facilitate the practical use of the language; mems: 6,066 individual mems in 117 countries; 11,732 individual affiliated mems in 67 countries; Pres. RENATO CORSETTI (Italy); Gen. Sec. ULLA LUIN (Sweden); publs *Esperanto* (monthly), *Kontakto* (every 2 months), *Jarlibro* (annually), *Esperanto Documents*.

World Union of Catholic Teachers (Union mondiale des enseignants catholiques—UMEC): Piazza San Calisto 16, 00120 Città del Vaticano; tel. (06) 69887286; f. 1951; encourages the grouping of Catholic teachers for the greater effectiveness of Catholic schools, distributes documentation on Catholic doctrine with regard to education, and facilitates personal contacts through congresses, and seminars, etc; nationally and internationally, mems: 32 organizations in 29 countries; Pres. ARNOLD BACKX (Netherlands); Sec.-Gen. MICHAEL EMM (United Kingdom); publ. *Nouvelles de l'UMEC*.

Environmental Conservation

BirdLife International: Wellbrook Ct, Girton Rd, Cambridge, CB3 0NA, United Kingdom; tel. (1223) 277318; fax (1223) 277200; e-mail birdlife@birdlife.org; internet www.birdlife.org; f. 1922 as the International Council for Bird Preservation; a global partnership of organizations that determines status of bird species throughout the world and compiles data on all endangered species; identifies conservation problems and priorities; initiates and co-ordinates conservation projects and international conventions; mems: partners or representatives in more than 100 countries; Chair. PETER JOHAN SCHEI; Dir Dr MICHAEL RANDS (United Kingdom); publs *Bird Red Data Book*, *World Birdwatch* (quarterly), *Bird Conservation Series*, study reports.

Caspian Environment Programme: 63 Golestan Alley, Valiasr Ave, 1966733413 Tehran, Iran; tel. (21) 22042285; fax (21) 22051850; e-mail cep.pcu@undp.org; internet www.caspianenvironment.org; f. 1998 by Azerbaijan, Iran, Kazakhstan, Russia and Turkmenistan with the aim of halting the deterioration of environmental conditions in the area of the Caspian Sea and also with a view to promoting sustainable development in the region.

Coalition Clean Baltic (CCB): Östra Ågatan 53, SE-753 22 Uppsala, Sweden; tel. and fax (18) 71-11-55; e-mail secretariat@ccb.se; f. 1990, network of 25 environmental non-governmental organizations from all countries bordering the Baltic Sea; Exec. Sec. GUNNAR NORÉN.

Commission for the Conservation of Antarctic Marine Living Resources (CCAMLR): POB 213, North Hobart, Tasmania 7002, Australia; tel. (3) 6210-1111; fax (3) 6224-8744; e-mail ccamlr@ccamlr.org; internet www.ccamlr.org; established under the 1982 Convention on the Conservation of Antarctic Marine Living Resources to manage marine resources in the Antarctic region; Exec. Sec. DENZIL G. M. MILLER.

Commission on the Protection of the Black Sea Against Pollution: Dolmabahçe Saray II. Hareket Köxkü, 34353 Bexiktax, Istanbul, Turkey; tel. (212) 2279927; fax (212) 2279933; e-mail ahmet.kideys@blacksea-commission.org; internet www.blacksea-commission.org; established under the 1992 Convention on the Protection of the Black Sea Against Pollution (Bucharest Convention) to implement the Convention and its Protocols; also oversees the 1996 Strategic Action Plan for the Rehabilitation and Protection of the Black Sea; Exec. Dir Prof. AHMET KIDEYS.

Consortium for Oceanographic Research and Education (CORE): 1201 New York Ave, NW, Suite 420, Washington, DC 20005, USA; tel. (202) 332-0063; fax (202) 332-9751; e-mail core@coreocean.org; internet www.comlsecretariat.org; f. 1999 to launch and host the International Steering Committee and Secretariat for the Census of Marine Life, a 10-year initiative to assess the diversity, distribution and abundance of marine life being implemented by a network of researchers from more than 70 countries; aims to promote, support and advance the science of oceanography; Pres. RICHARD WEST.

Friends of the Earth International: Prins Hendrikkade 48, POB 19199, 1000 GD Amsterdam, Netherlands; tel. (20) 6221369; fax (20) 6392181; internet www.foei.org; f. 1971 to promote the conservation, restoration and rational use of the environment and natural resources through public education and campaigning; mems: 68 national groups; Chair. MEENA RAMAN; publ. *Link* (quarterly).

Global Coral Reef Monitoring Network: POB 772, Townsville MC 4810, Australia; tel. (7) 4729-8452; fax (7) 4729-8449; e-mail c.wilkinson@aims.gov.au; internet www.gcrmn.org; f. 1994, as an operating unit of the International Coral Reef Initiative; aims include improving the management and sustainable conservation of coral reefs, strengthening links between regional organizations and ecological and socioeconomic monitoring networks, and disseminating information to assist the formulation of conservation plans; Global Co-ordinator Dr CLIVE WILKINSON (Australia).

Greencross International: 160A route de Florissant, 1231 Conches/Geneva, Switzerland; tel. 227891662; fax 227891695; e-mail gcinternational@gci.ch; internet www.greencrossinternational.net; f. 1993; aims to promote Earth Charter, to mitigate the environmental legacy of conflicts, to deter conflict in water-stressed regions, to combat desertification, to promote new energy consumption patterns, and to promote international conferences on and awareness of environmental issues; Pres. and CEO ALEXANDER LIKHOTAL (Russia) (*ex officio*).

Greenpeace International: Ottho Heldringstraat 5, 1066 AZ Amsterdam, Netherlands; tel. (20) 7182000; fax (20) 5148151; e-mail supporter.services@int.greenpeace.org; internet www.greenpeace.org; f. 1971 to campaign for the protection of the environment; aims to bear witness to environmental destruction, and to demonstrate solutions for positive change; mems: offices in 41 countries; Chair. ANNE SUMMERS (Australia); Exec. Dir GERD LEIPOLD (Germany).

International Commission for the Protection of the Rhine: Postfach 200253, 56002 Koblenz; Hohenzollernstrasse 18, 56068 Koblenz, Germany; tel. (261) 94252; fax (261) 94252; e-mail sekretariat@iksr.de; internet www.iksr.org; f. 1950; prepares and commissions research on the nature of the pollution of the Rhine; proposes protection, ecological rehabilitation and flood prevention measures; mems: 23 delegates from France, Germany, Luxembourg, Netherlands, Switzerland and the EU; Pres. Dr FRITZ HOLZWARTH; Sec. J. H. OTERDOOM; publ. *Annual Report*.

International Coral Reef Initiative: internet www.icriforum.org; f. 1994 at the first Conference of the Parties of the Convention on Biological Diversity; a partnership of governments, non-governmental organizations, scientific bodies and the private sector; aims to highlight the degradation of coral reefs and provide a focus for action to ensure the sustainable management and conservation of these and related marine ecosystems; in 1995 issued a Call to Action and a Framework for Action; Co-Chair. (2007–09) ROBERT GUDNEY (Mexico), STEPHANIE CASWELL (USA).

International Emissions Trading Association: 24 rue Merle d'Aubigné, 1207 Geneva, Switzerland; tel. 227370500; fax 227370508; e-mail info@ieta.org; internet www.ieta.org; f. 1999 to establish a functional international framework for trading greenhouse gas emissions, in accordance with the objectives of the UN Framework Convention on Climate Change; serves as a specialized information centre on emissions trading and the greenhouse gas market; mems: 179 international companies; Pres. and CEO HENRY DERWENT.

IUCN—The World Conservation Union: 28 rue Mauverney, 1196 Gland, Switzerland; tel. 229990000; fax 229990002; e-mail webmaster@iucn.org; internet www.iucn.org; f. 1948, as the International Union for Conservation of Nature and Natural Resources; supports partnerships and practical field activities to promote the conservation of natural resources, to secure the conservation of biological diversity as an essential foundation for the future; to ensure wise use of the earth's natural resources in an equitable and sustainable way; and to guide the development of human communities towards ways of life in enduring harmony with other components of the biosphere, developing programmes to protect and sustain the most important and threatened species and ecosystems and assisting governments to devise and carry out national conservation strategies; incorporates the Species Survival Commission (SSC), a science-based network of volunteer experts aiming to ensure conservation of present levels of biodiversity; compiles annually-updated Red List of Threatened Species, comprising in 2007 some 41,415 species, of which 16,306 were threatened with extinction and 65 only found in captivity or in cultivation; maintains a conservation library and documentation centre and units for monitoring traffic in wildlife; mems: more than 1,000 states, government agencies, non-governmental organizations and affiliates in some 140 countries; Pres. MOHAMMED VALLI MOOSA (South Africa); Dir-Gen. JULIA MARTON-LEFÈVRE (USA); publs *World Conservation Strategy*, *Caring for the Earth*, *Red List of Threatened Plants*, *Red List of Threatened Species*, *United Nations List of National Parks and Protected Areas*, *World Conservation* (quarterly), *IUCN Today*.

Nordic Environment Finance Corpn (NEFCO): Fabianinkatu 34, POB 249, 00171 Helsinki, Finland; tel. (9) 18001; fax (9) 630976; e-mail info@nefco.fi; internet www.nefco.org; f. 1990; finances environmentally beneficial projects in Central and Eastern Europe with transboundary effects that also benefit the Nordic region; MAGNUS RYSTEDT.

Permanent Commission of the South Pacific (Comisión Permanente del Pacífico Sur): Av. Carlos Julio Arosemena, Km. 3 Edificio Inmaral, Guayaquil, Ecuador; e-mail cpps_pse@cpps-int.org; internet www.cpps-int.org; f. 1952 to consolidate the presence of the zonal coastal states; Sec.-Gen. Dr GONZALO PEREIRA.

Secretariat of the Pacific Regional Environment Programme (SPREP): POB 240, Apia, Samoa; tel. 21929; fax 20231; e-mail sprep@sprep.org; internet www.sprep.org; f. 1978 by the South Pacific Commission (where it was based, now Pacific Community), the South Pacific (now Pacific Islands) Forum, ESCAP and UNEP; formally established as an independent institution in 1993; aims to promote regional co-operation in environmental matters, to assist members to protect and improve their shared environment, and to help members work towards sustainable development; mems: 21 Pacific islands, Australia, France, New Zealand, USA; Dir ASTERIO TAKESY (Federated States of Micronesia); publs *SPREP Newsletter* (quarterly), *CASOLink* (quarterly), *La lettre de l'environnement* (quarterly), *South Pacific Sea Level and Climate Change Newsletter* (quarterly).

South Asia Co-operative Environment Programme (SACEP): 10 Anderson Rd, Colombo 05, Sri Lanka; tel. (11) 2589787; fax (11) 2589369; e-mail info@sacep.org; internet www.sacep.org; f. 1982;

aims to promote regional co-operation in the protection and management of the environment, in particular in the context of sustainable economic and social development; works closely with governmental and non-governmental national, regional and international institutions in conservation and management efforts; Governing Council meets regularly; working to establish a South Asia Biodiversity Clearing House Mechanism; also actively developing specific projects: the conservation and integrated management of marine turtles and their habitats in the South Asia Seas region; reef-based corals management; accelerated penetration of cost effective renewable energy technologies; the establishment of a Basel Convention Sub-regional Centre for South Asia; protected areas management of world heritage sites and implementation of the Ramsar Strategic Plan at a sub-regional level; mems: Afghanistan, Bangladesh, Bhutan, India, Maldives, Nepal, Pakistan, Sri Lanka; Dir-Gen. Dr A. A. BOAZ; publs *SACEP Newsletter*, *South Asia Environmental and Education Action Plan*, other reports.

Wetlands International: POB 471, 6700 AL Wageningen, Netherlands; tel. (317) 478854; fax (317) 478850; e-mail post@wetlands.org; internet www.wetlands.org; f. 1995 by merger of several regional wetlands organizations; aims to protect and restore wetlands, their resources and biodiversity through research, information exchange and conservation activities; promotes implementation of the 1971 Ramsar Convention on Wetlands; Chair. MAX FINLAYSON; CEO JANE MADGWICK.

World Ocean Observatory: c/o Open Space Institute, 1350 Broadway, Rm 201, New York, NY 10018, USA; tel. (212) 356-4295; e-mail info@thew2o.net; internet www.thew2o.net; f. 2004; recommendation of the final report of the Independent World Commission on the Oceans; serves as a focal point for ocean-related information from governments, non-governmental organizations and other networks; aims to enhance public awareness of the importance of oceans and facilitate the dissemination of information; maintains an online radio station and organizes other online events; Dir PETER NEILL; publ. *World Ocean Observer* (monthly).

World Society for the Protection of Animals (WSPA): 89 Albert Embankment, London, SE1 7TP, United Kingdom; tel. (20) 7587-5000; fax (20) 7793-0208; e-mail wspa@wspa-international.org; internet www.wspa-international.org; f. 1981, incorporating the World Federation for the Protection of Animals (f. 1950) and the International Society for the Protection of Animals (f. 1959); promotes animal welfare and conservation by humane education, practical field projects, international lobbying and legislative work; mems: over 850 member societies in 150 countries; Pres. RANALD MONRO; Dir-Gen. Maj.-Gen. PETER DAVIES.

World Water Council: Espace Gaymard, 2–4 pl. d'Arvieux, 13002 Marseille, France; tel. 4-91-99-41-00; fax 4-91-99-41-01; internet www.worldwatercouncil.org; f. 1996; aims to facilitate the efficient conservation, protection, development, planning, management and use of water resources on an environmentally sustainable basis; organizes a World Water Forum held every three years since 1997 (2006: Mexico City); Exec. Dir DANIEL ZIMMER (*ex officio*).

WWF International: 27 ave du Mont-Blanc, 1196 Gland, Switzerland; tel. 223649111; fax 223648836; e-mail info@wwfint.org; internet www.panda.org; f. 1961 (as World Wildlife Fund), name changed to World Wide Fund for Nature in 1986, current nomenclature adopted 2001; aims to stop the degradation of natural environments, conserve bio-diversity, ensure the sustainable use of renewable resources, and promote the reduction of both pollution and wasteful consumption; addresses six priority issues: forests, freshwater, marine, species, climate change, and toxics; has identified, and focuses its activities in, 200 'ecoregions' (the 'Global 200'), believed to contain the best part of the world's remaining biological diversity; actively supports and operates conservation programmes in more than 90 countries; mems: 54 offices, five associate orgs, c. 5m. individual mems world-wide; Pres. Chief EMEKA ANYAOKU (Nigeria); Dir-Gen. JAMES P. LEAPE; publs *Annual Report*, *Living Planet Report*.

Government and Politics

African Association for Public Administration and Management (AAPAM): Britak Centre, Ragati and Mara Rds, POB 48677, 00100 GPO, Nairobi, Kenya; tel. (20) 2730555; fax (20) 2731153; e-mail aapam@aapam.org; internet www.aapam.org; f. 1971 to promote good practices, excellence and professionalism in public administration through training, seminars, research, publications; convenes regular conferences to share learning experiences among members, and an annual Roundtable Conference; funded by membership contributions, government and donor grants; mems: 500 individual, 50 corporate; Pres. JOHN MITALA (Uganda); Sec.-Gen. Dr YOLAMA R. BARONGO (Uganda); publs *Newsletter* (quarterly), *Annual Seminar Report*, *Newsletter* (quarterly), *African Journal of Public Administration and Management* (2 a year), studies.

Afro-Asian Peoples' Solidarity Organization (AAPSO): 89 Abdel Aziz Al-Saoud St, POB 11559-61 Manial El-Roda, Cairo, Egypt; tel. (2) 3636081; fax (2) 3637361; e-mail aapso@idsc.net.eg; internet www.aapso.fg2o.org; f. 1958; acts among and for the peoples of Africa and Asia in their struggle for genuine independence, sovereignty, socio-economic development, peace and disarmament; mems: national committees and affiliated organizations in 66 countries and territories, assoc. mems in 15 European countries; Sec.-Gen. NOURI ABDEL RAZZAK HUSSEIN (Iraq); publs *Solidarity Bulletin* (monthly), *Socio-Economic Development* (3 a year).

Agency for the Prohibition of Nuclear Weapons in Latin America and the Caribbean (Organismo para la Proscripción de las Armas Nucleares en la América Latina y el Caribe—OPANAL): Schiller 326, 5°, Col. Chapultepec Morales, 11570 México, DF, Mexico; tel. (55) 5255-2914; fax (55) 5255-3748; e-mail info@opanal.org; internet www.opanal.org; f. 1969 to ensure compliance with the Treaty for the Prohibition of Nuclear Weapons in Latin America (Treaty of Tlatelolco), 1967; to ensure the absence of all nuclear weapons in the application zone of the Treaty; to contribute to the movement against proliferation of nuclear weapons; to promote general and complete disarmament; to prohibit all testing, use, manufacture, acquisition, storage, installation and any form of possession, by any means, of nuclear weapons; the organs of the Agency comprise the General Conference, meeting every two years, the Council, meeting every two months, and the secretariat; a General Conference is held every two years; mems: 33 states that have fully ratified the Treaty; the Treaty has two additional Protocols: the first signed and ratified by France, the Netherlands, the United Kingdom and the USA, the second signed and ratified by China, the USA, France, the United Kingdom and Russia; Sec.-Gen. EDMUNDO VARGAS CARREÑO (Chile).

Alliance of Small Island States (AOSIS): c/o 800 Second Ave, Suite 910, New York, NY 10017, USA; tel. (212) 697-9361; fax (212) 599-0505; e-mail slumission@aol.com; internet www.sidsne.org/aosis; f. 1990 as an ad hoc intergovernmental grouping to focus on the special problems of small islands and low-lying coastal developing states; mems: 43 island nations; Chair. JULIAN R. HUNTE (Saint Lucia); publ. *Small Islands, Big Issues*.

ANZUS: c/o Dept of Foreign Affairs and Trade, R. G. Casey Bldg, John McEwen Crescent, Barton, ACT 0221, Australia; tel. (2) 6261-1111; fax (2) 6271-3111; internet www.dfat.gov.au; the ANZUS Security Treaty was signed in 1951 by Australia, New Zealand and the USA, and ratified in 1952 to co-ordinate partners' efforts for collective defence for the preservation of peace and security in the Pacific area, through the exchange of technical information and strategic intelligence, and a programme of exercises, exchanges and visits. In 1984 New Zealand refused to allow visits by US naval vessels that were either nuclear-propelled or potentially nuclear-armed, and this led to the cancellation of joint ANZUS military exercises: in 1986 the USA formally announced the suspension of its security commitment to New Zealand under ANZUS. Instead of the annual ANZUS Council meetings, bilateral talks were subsequently held every year between Australia and the USA. ANZUS continued to govern security relations between Australia and the USA, and between Australia and New Zealand; security relations between New Zealand and the USA were the only aspect of the treaty to be suspended. Senior-level contacts between New Zealand and the USA resumed in 1994. The Australian Govt invoked the Anzus Security Treaty for the first time following the international terrorist attacks against targets in the USA that were perpetrated in September 2001.

Association of Pacific Islands Legislatures (APIL): Carl Rose Bldg, Suite 207, 181 E. Marine Corps Drive, Hagatna, Guam; tel. (671) 477-2719; fax (671) 473-3004; e-mail apil@kuentos.guam.net; internet www.guam.net/pub/apil/index.htm; f. 1981 to provide a permanent structure of mutual assistance for representatives of the people of the Pacific Islands; comprises legislative representatives from 12 Pacific Island Govts; Sec.-Gen. WALDEN K. C. WEILBACHER.

Association of Secretaries General of Parliaments: c/o Committee Office, House of Commons, London, SW1, United Kingdom; tel. (20) 7219-8195; e-mail phillipsris@parliament.uk; internet www.asgp.info; f. 1938; studies the law, practice and working methods of different Parliaments; proposes measures for improving those methods and for securing co-operation between the services of different Parliaments; operates as a consultative body to the Inter-Parliamentary Union, and assists the Union on subjects within the scope of the Association; mems: c. 200 representing 145 countries; five assoc. institutions; Pres. ANDERS FORSBERG (Sweden); Jt Secs FRÉDÉRIC SLAMA (France), ROGER PHILLIPS (United Kingdom); publ. *Constitutional and Parliamentary Information* (2 a year).

Atlantic Treaty Association: Quartier Prince Albert, 20 rue des Petits Carmes, 1000 Brussels, Belgium; tel. (2) 502-31-60; fax (2) 502-48-77; e-mail info@ata-sec.org; internet www.ata-sec.org; f. 1954 to inform public opinion on the North Atlantic Alliance and to promote the solidarity of the peoples of the North Atlantic; holds annual assemblies, seminars, study conferences for teachers and young politicians; mems: national asscns in 26 member countries of NATO; 12 assoc. mems from central and eastern Europe, two observer mems; Pres. ROBERT E. HUNTER (USA); Sec.-Gen. TROELS FRØLING (Denmark).

Baltic Council: f. 1993 by the Baltic Assembly, comprising 60 parliamentarians from Estonia, Latvia and Lithuania; the Council of Ministers of the three Baltic countries co-ordinates policy in the areas of foreign policy, justice, the environment, education and science.

Celtic League: 11 Cleiy Rhennee, Kirk Michael, Isle of Man, IM6 1HT, United Kingdom; tel. (1624) 877918; e-mail b.moffatt@advsys.co.im; internet www.manxman.co.im/cleague; f. 1961 to foster co-operation between the six Celtic nations (Ireland, Scotland, Man, Wales, Cornwall and Brittany), especially those actively working for political autonomy by non-violent means; campaigns politically on issues affecting the Celtic countries; monitors military activity in the Celtic countries; co-operates with national cultural organizations to promote the languages and culture of the Celts; mems: approx. 1,400 individuals in the Celtic communities and elsewhere; Chair. CATHAL O LUAIN; Gen. Sec. BERNARD MOFFAT; publ. *Carn* (quarterly).

Central European Initiative (CEI): CEI Executive Secretariat, Via Genova 9, 34121 Trieste, Italy; tel. (040) 7786777; fax (040) 360640; e-mail cei-es@cei-es.org; internet www.ceinet.org; f. 1989 as 'Quadragonal' co-operation between Austria, Italy, Hungary and Yugoslavia, became 'Pentagonal' in 1990 with the admission of Czechoslovakia, and 'Hexagonal' with the admission of Poland in 1991, present name adopted in 1992, when Bosnia and Herzegovina, Croatia and Slovenia were admitted; the Czech Republic and Slovakia became separate mems in January 1993, and Macedonia also joined in that year; Albania, Belarus, Bulgaria, Romania and Ukraine joined the CEI in 1995 and Moldova in 1996; the Federal Republic of Yugoslavia (now the separate sovereign states of Montenegro and Serbia) admitted in 2000; encourages regional political and economic co-operation; Dir-Gen. Dr HARALD KREID; publ. *Newsletter* (monthly).

Centrist Democrat International: 67 rue d'Arlon, 1040 Brussels, Belgium; tel. (2) 285-41-60; fax (2) 285-41-66; e-mail idc@idc-cdi.org; internet www.idc-cdi.org; f. 1961 (as Christian Democrat and Peoples' Parties International); serves as an asscn of political groups adhering to Christian humanist and democratic theology; mems: parties in 64 countries (of which 47 in Europe); Exec. Sec. ANTONIO LÓPEZ ISTURIZ; publs *DC-Info* (quarterly), *Human Rights* (5 a year), *Documents* (quarterly).

Collective Security Treaty Organization (CSTO): 103012 Moscow, Varvarka 7, Russia; tel. (495) 606-97-71; fax (495) 625-76-20; e-mail odkb@gov.ru; internet www.dkb.gov.ru; f. 2003 by signatories to the Treaty on Collective Security (signed Tashkent, Uzbekistan, May 1992); aims to co-ordinate and strengthen military and political co-operation and to promote regional and national security; maintains a joint rapid deployment force; the Oct. 2007 leaders' summit endorsed documents enabling the establishment of CSTO joint peace-keeping forces and the creation of a co-ordination council for the heads of member states' emergency response agencies; became an observer in the UN General Assembly in 2004; in April 2006 signed a protocol with the UN Office on Drugs and Crime to develop joint projects to combat drugs-trafficking, terrorism and transborder crime; mems: Armenia, Belarus, Kazakhstan, Kyrgyzstan, Russia, Tajikistan, Uzbekistan; Sec.-Gen. NIKOLAY BORDYUZHA.

Comunidade dos Países de Língua Portuguesa (CPLP) (Community of Portuguese-Speaking Countries): rua S. Caetano 32, 1200-829 Lisbon, Portugal; tel. (21) 392-8560; fax (21) 392-8588; e-mail comunicacao@cplp.org; internet www.cplp.org; f. 1996; aims to produce close political, economic, diplomatic and cultural links between Portuguese-speaking countries and to strengthen the influence of the Lusophone commonwealth within the international community; dispatched an observer mission to oversee presidential elections held in Timor-Leste in May 2007; mems: Angola, Brazil, Cape Verde, Guinea-Bissau, Mozambique, Portugal, São Tomé and Príncipe, Timor-Leste; Exec. Sec. LUÍS DE MATOS DE MONTEIRO DA FONSECA (Cape Verde).

Eastern Regional Organization for Public Administration (EROPA): National College of Public Administration, Univ. of the Philippines, Diliman, Quezon City 1101, Philippines; tel. and fax (2) 9297789; e-mail eropa.secretariat@gmail.com; internet www.eropa.org.ph; f. 1960 to promote regional co-operation in improving knowledge, systems and practices of governmental administration, to help accelerate economic and social development; organizes regional conferences, seminars, special studies, surveys and training programmes; accredited, in 2000, as an online regional centre of the UN Public Administration Network for the Asia and Pacific region; there are three regional centres: Training Centre (New Delhi), Local Government Centre (Tokyo), Development Management Centre (Seoul); mems: 11 countries, 74 groups, 394 individuals; Sec.-Gen. PATRICIA A. STO TOMAS (Philippines); publs *EROPA Bulletin* (quarterly), *Asian Review of Public Administration* (2 a year).

European Movement: 25 sq. de Meeûs, 1000 Brussels, Belgium; tel. (2) 508-30-88; fax (2) 508-30-89; e-mail secretariat@europeanmovement.eu; internet www.europeanmovement.eu; f. 1947 by a liaison committee of representatives from European organizations, to study the political, economic and technical problems of a European Union and suggest how they could be solved and to inform and lead public opinion in the promotion of integration; Conferences have led to the creation of the Council of Europe, College of Europe, etc; mems: national councils and committees in 43 European countries, and several international social and economic orgs, 24 assoc. mems; Pres. PAT COX; Sec.-Gen. HENRIK H. KRÖNER.

European Union of Women (EUW): 2 Pittakou St, 105 58 Athens, Greece; tel. (1) 3314847; fax (1) 3314817; e-mail fpetralia@parliament.gr; f. 1955 to increase the influence of women in the political and civic life of their country and of Europe; mems: national organizations in 21 countries; Chair. FANNY PALLI PETRALIA; Sec.-Gen. VASSO KOLLIA.

Global Elders: POB 49785, London WC2H 7WQ, United Kingdom; e-mail info@theelders.org; internet www.theelders.org; f. 2001; aims to alleviate human suffering world-wide by offering a catalyst for the peaceful resolution of conflicts, seeking new approaches to unresolved global issues, and sharing wisdom; comprises: Kofi Annan (Ghana), Ela Bhatt (India), Lakhdar Brahimi (Algeria), Gro Brundtland (Norway), Jimmy Carter (USA), Fernando H Cardoso (Brazil), Graça Machel (Mozambique), Nelson Mandela (South Africa), Desmond Tutu (South Africa), Mary Robinson (Ireland), Aung San Suu Kyi (Myanmar), Muhammad Yunus (Bangladesh), Li Zhaoxing (People's Republic of China).

Gulf of Guinea Commission (Commission du Golfe de Guinée—CGG): f. 2001 to promote co-operation among mem; countries and the peaceful and sustainable development of natural resources in the sub-region; mems: Angola, Cameroon, the Repub. of the Congo, Equatorial Guinea, Gabon, Nigeria, São Tomé and Príncipe.

Hansard Society: 40–43 Chancery Lane, London, WC2A 1JA, United Kingdom; tel. (20) 7438-1222; fax (20) 7438-1229; e-mail hansard@hansard.lse.ac.uk; internet www.hansardsociety.org.uk; f. 1944 as Hansard Society for Parliamentary Government; aims to promote political education and research and the informed discussion of all aspects of modern parliamentary government; Dir CLARE ETTINGHAUSEN; publ. *Parliamentary Affairs* (quarterly).

Ibero-American General Secretariat (Secretaría General Iberoamericana—SEGIB): Calle Serrano 187, 28002 Madrid, Spain; tel. (91) 590-19-80; e-mail info@segib.org; internet www.segib.org; f. 2003; aims to provide institutional and technical support to the annual Iberoamerican summit meetings, to monitor programmes agreed at the meetings and to strengthen the Ibero-American community; meetings of Ibero-American heads of state and government (the first of which was convened in Guadalajara, Mexico in 1991) aim to promote political, economic and cultural co-operation among the 19 Spanish- and Portuguese-speaking Latin American countries and three European countries; Sec.-Gen. ENRIQUE IGLESIAS (Uruguay).

International Alliance of Women (Alliance Internationale des Femmes): c/o Lenaustr. 5/2/12, 4053 Haid bei Ansfelden, Austria; tel. (7229) 876-34; e-mail iawsec@womenalliance.org; internet www.womenalliance.org; f. 1904 to obtain equality for women in all fields and to encourage women to assume decision-making responsibilities at all levels of society; lobbies at international organizations; mems: 58 national affiliates and associates; Pres. ROSY WEISS; Sec.-Gen. LENE PIND; publs *International Women's News* (3 a year), electronic newsletter (monthly).

International Association for Community Development (IACD): POB 23680, Edinburgh, EH6 6XX, United Kingdom; e-mail info@iacdglobal.org; internet www.iacdglobal.org; promotes community development across international policies and programmes, supports community development practitioners and encourages the exchange of research and information; membership open to individuals and organizations working in or supporting community development across eight world regions; organizes annual international colloquium for community-based organizations; Pres. Elect ALEX RUHUNDA (Uganda); publs *IACD Newsletter* (2 a year), monthly e-bulletins.

International Commission for the History of Representative and Parliamentary Institutions (CHRPI): c/o Dr David Dean, Dept of History, Carleton Univ., 400 Peterson Hall, 1125 Colonel By Drive, Ottawa, ON KIS 5116, Canada; tel. (613) 520-2828; fax (613) 520-2819; internet www.univie.ac.at/ichrpi; f. 1936; promotes research into the origin and development of representative and parliamentary institutions world-wide; encourages wide and comparative study of such institutions, both current and historical; facilitates the exchange of information; mems: 300 individuals in 31 countries; Pres. WILHELM BRAUNEDER (Austria); Sec.-Gen. Dr DAVID DEAN (Canada); publs *Parliaments, Estates and Representation* (annually), studies.

INTERNATIONAL ORGANIZATIONS

International Conference on the Great Lakes Region, Secretariat: Bujumbura, Burundi; f. 2006 following the signing of the Security, Stability and Development Pact for the Great Lakes Region at the second summit meeting of the International Conference on the Great Lakes Region, held in December, in Nairobi, Kenya; the UN Security Council proposed the organization of a Great Lakes Conference to initiate a process that would bring together regional leaders to pursue agreement on a set of principles and to articulate programmes of action to help end the cycle of regional conflict and establish durable peace, stability, security, democracy and development in the whole region; the first summit meeting of the Conference was convened in Dar es Salaam, Tanzania, in November 2004; mems: Angola, Burundi, the Central African Republic, the Democratic Republic of the Congo, the Republic of the Congo, Kenya, Rwanda, Sudan, Tanzania, Uganda, Zambia; Exec. Sec. LIBERATA MULAMALA.

International Democrat Union: POB 1536, Vika, 0117 Oslo, Norway; tel. 22-82-90-00; fax 22-82-90-80; e-mail secretariat@idu.org; internet www.idu.org; f. 1983 as a group of centre and centre-right political parties; facilitates the exchange of information and views; promotes networking; organizes campaigning seminars for politicians and party workers; holds Party Leaders' meetings every three years, also executive meetings and a Young Leaders' Forum; mems: political parties in some 60 countries, 46 assoc. mems in regions; Exec. Sec. EIRIK MOEN.

International Federation of Resistance Movements (FIR): Lassallestr. 40/2/2/6, 1020 Vienna, Austria; tel. (1) 726-30-91; f. 1951; supports the medical and social welfare of former victims of fascism; works for peace, disarmament and human rights, and against fascism and neo-fascism; mems: 76 national organizations; Pres. MICHEL VANDERBORGHT; Sec.-Gen. OSKAR WIESFLECKER (Austria).

International Institute for Democracy and Electoral Assistance (IDEA): Strömsborg, 103 34 Stockholm, Sweden; tel. (8) 698-3700; fax (8) 20-2422; e-mail info@idea.int; internet www.idea.int; f. 1995; aims to promote sustainable democracy in new and established democracies; provides world-wide electoral assistance and focuses on broader democratic issues in Africa, the Caucasus and Latin America; 23 mem. states; Sec.-Gen. VIDAR HELGESEN (Norway).

International Institute for Peace: Möllwaldplatz 5, 1040 Vienna, Austria; tel. (1) 504-64-37; fax (1) 505-32-36; e-mail secretariat@iip.at; internet www.iip.at; f. 1957; non-governmental organization with consultative status at ECOSOC and UNESCO; studies conflict prevention; new structures in international law; security issues in Europe and world-wide; mems: individuals and corporate bodies invited by the executive board; Pres. ERWIN LANC (Austria); Dir PETER STANIA (Austria); publ. *Peace and Security* (quarterly).

International Institute for Strategic Studies (IISS): Arundel House, 13–15 Arundel St, London, WC2R 3DX, United Kingdom; tel. (20) 7379-7676; fax (20) 7836-3108; e-mail iiss@iiss.org; internet www.iiss.org; f. 1958; concerned with the study of the role of force in international relations, including problems of international strategy, the ethnic, political and social sources of conflict, disarmament and arms control, peace-keeping and intervention, defence economics, etc; independent of any government; mems: c. 3,000; Dir-Gen. Dr JOHN M. W. CHIPMAN; publs *Survival* (quarterly), *The Military Balance* (annually), *Strategic Survey* (annually), *Adelphi Papers* (10 a year), *Strategic Comments* (10 a year).

International Lesbian and Gay Association (ILGA): 34 ave des Villas, 1060 Brussels, Belgium; tel. and fax (2) 502-24-71; e-mail ilga@ilga.org; internet www.ilga.org; f. 1978; works to abolish legal, social and economic discrimination against homosexual and bisexual women and men, and transexuals, throughout the world; co-ordinates political action at an international level; co-operates with other supportive movements; 2007 world conference: Geneva, Switzerland; mems: 350 national and regional asscns in 80 countries; Co-Secs-Gen. PHILIPP BRAUN, ROSANNA FLAMER-CALDERA; publs *ILGA Bulletin* (quarterly), *GBLT Human Rights Annual Report*.

International Peace Bureau (IPB): 41 rue de Zürich, 1201 Geneva, Switzerland; tel. 227316429; fax 227389419; e-mail mailbox@ipb.org; internet www.ipb.org; f. 1891; promotes international co-operation for general and complete disarmament and the non-violent solution of international conflicts; co-ordinates and represents peace movements at the UN; conducts projects on Disarmament for Development and the abolition of nuclear weapons; mems: 300 peace orgs and 150 individual mems in 70 countries; Pres. TOMAS MAGNUSSON; Sec.-Gen. COLIN ARCHER (United Kingdom); publs *IPB News* (every 2 weeks, by email), *IPB Geneva News*.

International Political Science Association (IPSA) (Association Internationale de Science Politique—AISP): c/o Concordia Univ., 331 ave Docteur Penfield, Montréal, QC H3G 1C5, Canada; tel. (514) 848-8717; fax (514) 848-4095; e-mail info@ipsa.com; internet www.ipsa.ca; f. 1949; aims to promote the development of political science; organizes World Congress (July 2006: Fukuoka, Japan, 'Is Democracy Working?'; 2009: Santiago, Chile); mems: 41 national asscns, 100 institutions, 1,350 individual mems; Pres. LOURDES SOLA (Brazil); Sec.-Gen. GUY LACHAPELLE (Canada); publs *Participation* (3 a year), *International Political Science Abstracts* (6 a year), *International Political Science Review* (quarterly).

International Union of Young Christian Democrats (IUYCD): 16 rue de la Victoire, 1060 Brussels, Belgium; tel. (2) 537-13-22; fax (2) 537-93-48; f. 1962; mems: national organizations in 59 countries and territories; Sec.-Gen. MARCOS VILLASMIL (Venezuela); publs *IUYCD Newsletter* (fortnightly), *Debate* (quarterly).

Jewish Agency for Israel (JAFI): 34 Ben Yehuda St., City Tower, 14th Floor, Jerusalem, Israel; tel. (2) 6202251; fax (2) 6202577; e-mail barbaram@jafi.org; internet www.jafi.org.il; f. 1929; reconstituted 1971 as an instrument through which world Jewry can work to develop a national home; constituents are: World Zionist Organization, United Israel Appeal, Inc. (USA), and Keren Hayesod; Chair. Exec. ZEEV BIELSKI; Chair. Bd. CAROLE SOLOMON; Dir-Gen. MOSHE VIGDOR.

Latin American Parliament (Parlamento Latinoamericano): Avda Auro Soares de Moura Andrade 564, São Paulo, Brazil; tel. (11) 3824-6325; fax (11) 3824-0621; internet www.parlatino.org.br; f. 1965; permanent democratic institution, representative of all existing political trends within the national legislative bodies of Latin America; aims to promote the movement towards economic, political and cultural integration of the Latin American republics, and to uphold human rights, peace and security; Sec.-Gen. RAFAEL CORREA FLORES; publs *Acuerdos, Resoluciones de las Asambleas Ordinarias* (annually), *Parlamento Latinoamericano–Actividades de los Órganos, Revista Patria Grande* (annually), statements and agreements.

Liberal International: 1 Whitehall Pl., London, SW1A 2HD, United Kingdom; tel. (20) 7839-5905; fax (20) 7925-2685; e-mail all@liberal-international.org; internet www.liberal-international.org; f. 1947; co-ordinates foreign policy work of member parties, and promotes freedom, tolerance, democracy, international understanding, protection of human rights and market-based economics; has consultative status at ECOSOC of United Nations and the Council of Europe; mems: 101 member parties and (10) co-operating organizations in 63 countries; Pres. Lord JOHN ALDERDICE; Sec.-Gen. JASPER VEEN; publ. *Liberal Aerogramme* (quarterly).

NATO Parliamentary Assembly: 3 place du Petit Sablon, 1000 Brussels, Belgium; tel. (2) 513-28-65; fax (2) 514-18-47; internet www.nato-pa.int; f. 1955 as the NATO Parliamentarians' Conference; name changed 1966 to North Atlantic Assembly; renamed as above 1999; the inter-parliamentary assembly of the North Atlantic Alliance; holds two plenary sessions a year and meetings of committees (Political, Defence and Security, Economics and Security, Civil Dimension of Security, Science and Technology) to facilitate parliamentary awareness and understanding of key Alliance security issues, to provide the Alliance governments with a collective parliamentary voice, to contribute to a greater degree of transparency of NATO policies, and to strengthen the transatlantic dialogue; Pres. JOSÉ LELLO (Portugal); Sec.-Gen. SIMON LUNN (United Kingdom).

Non-aligned Movement (NAM): c/o Permanent Representative of Malaysia to the UN, 313 East 43rd St, New York, NY 10016, USA (no permanent secretariat); tel. (212) 986-6310; fax (212) 490-8576; e-mail malaysia@un.int; internet www.namkl.org.my; f. 1961 by a meeting of 25 Heads of State, with the aim of linking countries that had refused to adhere to the main East/West military and political blocs; co-ordination bureau established in 1973; works for the establishment of a new international economic order, and especially for better terms for countries producing raw materials; maintains special funds for agricultural development, improvement of food production and the financing of buffer stocks; South Commission promotes co-operation between developing countries; seeks changes in the United Nations to give developing countries greater decision-making power; holds summit conference every three years; 14th conference (September 2006): Havana, Cuba; mems: 116 countries.

Nordic Council/Nordic Council of Ministers: Store Strandstraede 18, 1255 Copenhagen, Denmark; tel. 33-96-040-0; fax 33-11-18-70; e-mail nordisk-rad@norden.org; internet www.norden.org; f. 1952 for co-operation between the Nordic parliaments and governments; the Nordic Council of Ministers co-ordinates the activities of the governments of the Nordic countries when decisions are to be implemented; co-operation with adjacent areas includes the Baltic States, where Nordic governments are committed to furthering democracy, security and sustainable development, to contribute to peace, security and stability in Europe; the Nordic–Baltic Scholarship Scheme awards grants to students, teachers, scientists, civil servants and parliamentarians; Dir FRIDA NOKKEN; Sec.-Gen. of the Council of Ministers HALLDÓR ÁSGRÍMSSON (Iceland); publs *Norden the Top of Europe* (monthly newsletter in English and Russian), *Norden this week* (weekly newsletter).

Northern Forum: 716 W 4th Ave, Suite 100, Anchorage, Alaska, USA; tel. (907) 561-3280; fax (907) 561-6645; e-mail NForum@northernforum.org; internet www.northernforum.org; f. 1991; aims to improve the quality of life of Northern peoples through support for sustainable development and socio-economic co-operation throughout the region; Exec. Dir PRISCILLA P. WOHL.

Organisation for the Prohibition of Chemical Weapons (OPCW): Johan de Wittlaan 32, 2517JR The Hague, Netherlands; tel. (70) 4163300; fax (70) 3063535; e-mail media@opcw.org; internet www.opcw.org; f. April 1997, on the entry into force of the Chemical Weapons Convention (CWC)—an international, multilateral disarmament treaty banning the development, production, stockpiling, transfer and use of chemical weapons—to oversee its implementation; verifies the irreversible destruction of declared chemical weapons stockpiles, as well as the elimination of all declared chemical weapons production facilities; OPCW member states undertake to provide protection and assistance if chemical weapons have been used against a state party, or if such weapons threaten a state party, and together with OPCW inspectors, monitor the non-diversion of chemicals for activities prohibited under the CWC and verify the consistency of industrial chemical declarations; CWC states parties are obligated to declare any chemical weapons-related activities, to secure and destroy any stockpiles of chemical weapons within the stipulated deadlines, as well as to inactivate and eliminate any chemical weapons production capacity within their jurisdiction; mems: states party to the Convention (183 at Jan. 2008); 2008 budget: €75m; Dir-Gen. ROGELIO PFIRTER.

Organisation Internationale de la Francophonie (La Francophonie): 28 rue de Bourgogne, 75007 Paris, France; tel. 1-44-11-12-50; fax 1-44-11-12-76; e-mail oif@francophonie.org; internet www.francophonie.org; f. 1970 as l'Agence de coopération culturelle et technique; promotes co-operation among French-speaking countries in the areas of education, culture, peace and democracy, and technology; implements decisions of the Sommet francophone; technical and financial assistance has been given to projects in every member country, mainly to aid rural people; mems: 55 states and govts; 13 countries with observer status; Sec. Gen. ABDOU DIOUF (Senegal); publ. *Journal de l'Agence de la Francophonie* (quarterly).

Organisation of Eastern Caribbean States (OECS): Morne Fortune, POB 179, Castries, Saint Lucia; tel. 452-2537; fax 453-1628; e-mail oesec@oecs.org; internet www.oecs.org; f. 1981 by the seven states which formerly belonged to the West Indies Associated States (f. 1966); aims to promote the harmonized development of trade and industry in member states; single market created on 1 January 1988; principal institutions are: the Authority of Heads of Government (the supreme policy-making body), the Foreign Affairs Committee, the Defence and Security Committee, and the Economic Affairs Committee; there is also an Export Development and Agricultural Diversification Unit—EDADU (based in Dominica); an OECS Technical Mission to the World Trade Organization in Geneva, Switzerland, was inaugurated in June 2005; mems: Antigua and Barbuda, Dominica, Grenada, Montserrat, Saint Christopher and Nevis, Saint Lucia, Saint Vincent and the Grenadines; assoc. mems: Anguilla, British Virgin Islands; Dir-Gen. Dr LEN ISHMAEL.

Organization for Democracy and Economic Development—GUAM: vul. Melnykova 36/1, 04119 Kyiv, Ukraine; tel. (44) 4837457; fax (44) 4837457; e-mail office@guam.org.ua; internet www.guam.org; f. 1997 as a consultative alliance of Georgia, Ukraine, Azerbaijan and Moldova (GUAM); Uzbekistan joined the grouping in April 1999, when it became known as GUUAM, but withdrew in May 2005, causing the grouping's name to revert to GUAM; formally inaugurated as a full international organization and current name adopted by heads of state at a summit held in Kyiv in May 2006; objectives include the promotion of a regional space of democracy, security, and stable economic and social development; strengthening relations with the EU and NATO; developing a database on terrorism, organized crime, drugs-trafficking, and related activities; establishing a GUAM energy security council; creating the GUAM Free-Trade Zone, in accordance with an agreement signed by heads of state at a meeting in Yalta, Ukraine, in July 2002; further economic development, including the creation of an East–West trade corridor and transportation routes for petroleum; and participation in conflict resolution and peace-keeping activities, with the establishment of peace-keeping forces and civilian police units under consideration; Sec.-Gen. VALERI CHECHELASHVILI (Georgia).

Organization of Solidarity of the Peoples of Africa, Asia and Latin America (OSPAAAL) (Organización de Solidaridad de los Pueblos de Africa, Asia y América Latina): Apdo 4224, Calle C No 670 esq. 29, Vedado, Havana 10400, Cuba; tel. (7) 830-5136; fax (7) 833-3985; e-mail ospaal1966@enet.cu; internet www.tricontinental.cubaweb.info; f. 1966 at the first Conference of Solidarity of the Peoples of Africa, Asia and Latin America, to unite, co-ordinate and encourage national liberation movements in the three continents, to oppose foreign intervention in the affairs of sovereign states, colonial and neo-colonial practices, and to fight against racialism and all forms of racial discrimination; favours the establishment of a new international economic order; mems: 56 organizations in 46 countries; Sec.-Gen. ALFONSO FRAGA PEREZ; publ. *Tricontinental* (quarterly).

Parliamentary Association for Euro-Arab Co-operation (PAEAC): 475 ave Louise, 1050 Brussels, Belgium; tel. (2) 231-13-00; fax (2) 231-06-46; e-mail info@medea.be; internet www.medea.be; f. 1974 as an assen of 650 parliamentarians of all parties from the national parliaments of the Council of Europe countries and from the European Parliament, to promote friendship and co-operation between Europe and the Arab world; Executive Committee holds annual joint meetings with Arab Inter-Parliamentary Union; represented in Council of Europe, Western European Union and European Parliament; works for the progress of the Euro-Arab Dialogue and a settlement in the Middle East that takes into account the national rights of the Palestinian people; Jt Chair. MICHAEL LANIGAN (Ireland), ROY PERRY (United Kingdom); Sec.-Gen. POL MARCK (Belgium); publs *Information Bulletin* (quarterly), *Euro-Arab and Mediterranean Political Fact Sheets* (2 a year), conference notes.

Party of European Socialists (PES): 98 rue du Trône, 1050 Brussels, Belgium; tel. (2) 548-90-80; fax (2) 230-17-66; e-mail info@pes.org; internet www.pes.org; f. 1992 to replace the Confederation of the Socialist Parties of the EC (f. 1974); affiliated to Socialist International; mems: 32 member parties, six associate parties and seven observer parties; four mem. orgs, three associate mem. orgs and 9 observer mem. orgs; Pres. POUL N. RASMUSSEN; Sec.-Gen. PHILIP CORDERY; publs various, including statutes, manifestos and Congress documents.

Rio Group: f. 1987 at a meeting in Acapulco, Mexico, of eight Latin American government leaders, who agreed to establish a 'permanent mechanism for joint political action'; additional countries subsequently joined the Group (see below); holds annual summit meetings at presidential level. At the ninth presidential summit (Quito, Ecuador, September 1995) a 'Declaration of Quito' was adopted, which set out joint political objectives, including the strengthening of democracy; combating corruption, drugs-production and -trafficking and 'money-laundering'; and the creation of a Latin American and Caribbean free trade area (supporting the efforts of the various regional groupings). Opposes US legislation (the 'Helms-Burton' Act), which provides for sanctions against foreign companies that trade with Cuba; also concerned with promoting sustainable development in the region, the elimination of poverty, and economic and financial stability. The Rio Group holds regular ministerial conferences with the European Union (13th meeting held in April 2007); mems: Argentina, Bolivia, Brazil, Chile, Colombia, Costa Rica, Dominican Republic, Ecuador, El Salvador, Guatemala, Guyana, Honduras, Mexico, Nicaragua, Panama, Paraguay, Peru, Uruguay, Venezuela.

Shanghai Co-operation Organization (SCO): 41, Liangmaqiao Road, Chaoyang District, Beijing, People's Republic of China; tel. (10) 65329806; fax (10) 65329808; e-mail sco@sectsco.org; internet www.sectsco.org; f. 2001, replacing the Shanghai Five (f. 1996 to address border disputes); comprises People's Republic of China, Kazakhstan, Kyrgyzstan, Russia, Tajikistan and Uzbekistan; aims to achieve security through mutual co-operation: promotes economic co-operation and measures to eliminate terrorism and drugs-trafficking; agreement on combating terrorism signed June 2001; a Convention on the Fight against Terrorism, Separatism and Extremism signed June 2002; Treaty on Long-term Good Neighbourliness, Friendship and Co-operation was signed August 2007; maintains an SCO anti-terrorism centre in Tashkent, Uzbekistan; holds annual summit meeting (Aug. 2007: Bishkek, Kyrgyzstan); Sec.-Gen. BOLAT NURGALIYEV (Kazakhstan).

Socialist International: Maritime House, Clapham, London, SW4 0JW, United Kingdom; tel. (20) 7627-4449; fax (20) 7720-4448; e-mail secretariat@socialistinternational.org; internet www.socialistinternational.org; f. 1864; re-established in 1951; the world's oldest and largest assen of political parties, grouping democratic socialist, labour and social democratic parties from every continent; provides a forum for political action, policy discussion and the exchange of ideas; works with many international organizations and trades unions (particularly members of ITUC; holds Congress every three years; the Council meets twice a year, and regular conferences and meetings of party leaders are also held; committees and councils on a variety of subjects and in different regions meet frequently; mems: 103 full member, 30 consultative and 14 observer parties in 122 countries; there are three fraternal organizations and nine associated orgs, including: the Party of European Socialists (PES), the Group of the PES at the European Parliament and the International Federation of the Socialist and Democratic Press; Pres. GEORGE A. PAPANDREOU (Greece); Gen. Sec. LUIS AYALA (Chile); publ. *Socialist Affairs* (quarterly).

International Falcon Movement—Socialist Educational International: 98 rue du Trône, 2nd Floor, 1050 Brussels, Belgium; tel. (2) 215-79-27; fax (2) 245-00-83; e-mail contact@ifm-sei.org; internet www.ifm-sei.org; f. 1924 to help children and adolescents develop international understanding and a sense of social responsibility and to prepare them for democratic life; co-operates with several institutions concerned with children, youth and education; mems: 57 mems world-wide; Pres. ÖSTEN LÖUGREN (Sweden); Sec.-Gen. UWE OSTENDORFF (Germany); publs *IFM-SEI Bulletin* (quarterly), *IFM-SEI World News*, *EFN Newsletter* (6 a year), *Asian Regional Bulletin*, *Latin American Regional Bulletin*.

International Union of Socialist Youth (IUSY): Amtshausgasse 4, 1050 Vienna, Austria; tel. (1) 523-12-67; fax (1) 523-12-679; e-mail iusy@iusy.org; internet www.iusy.org; f. 1907 as Socialist Youth International (present name adopted 1946), to educate young people in the principles of free and democratic socialism and further the co-operation of democratic socialist youth organizations; conducts international meetings, symposia, etc; mems: 143 youth and student organizations in 100 countries; Pres. FIKILE MBALULA; Gen. Sec. YVONNE O'CALLAGHAN (Ireland); publs *IUSY Newsletter*, *FWG News*, *IUSY—You see us in Action*.

Socialist International Women: Maritime House, Old Town, Clapham, London, SW4 0JW, United Kingdom; tel. (20) 7627-4449; fax (20) 7720-4448; e-mail socintwomen@gn.apc.org; internet www.socintwomen.org.uk; f. 1907 to promote the understanding among women of the aims of democratic socialism; to facilitate the exchange of experience and views; to promote programmes opposing discrimination in society; and to work for human rights in general and for development and peace; mems: 152 organizations; Pres. PIA LOCATELLI; Sec.-Gen. MARLÈNE HAAS; publ. *Women and Politics* (quarterly).

Stockholm International Peace Research Institute (SIPRI): Signalistgatan 9, 169 70 Solna, Sweden; tel. (8) 655-97-00; fax (8) 655-97-33; e-mail sipri@sipri.org; internet www.sipri.org; f. 1966; carries out studies on international security and arms control issues, including on conflict and crisis management, peace-keeping and regional security, and chemical and biological warfare; mems: about 50 staff mems, half of whom are researchers; Dir Dr GILL BATES (USA); publs *SIPRI Yearbook: Armaments, Disarmament and International Security*, monographs and research reports.

Transparency International: Alt Moabit 96, 10559 Berlin, Germany; tel. (30) 3438200; fax (30) 34703912; e-mail ti@transparency.org; internet www.transparency.org; f. 1993; aims to promote governmental adoption of anti-corruption practices and accountability at all levels of the public sector; works to ensure that international business transactions are conducted with integrity and without resort to corrupt practices; raises awareness of the damaging effects of corruption; produces an annual Corruption Perceptions Index, a Bribe Payers Index, a Global Corruption Barometer and an annual Global Corruption Report; holds International Anti-Corruption Conference every two years; some 90 chapters world-wide; Chair. Dr HUGUETTE LABELLE.

Trilateral Commission: 1156 15th St, NW, Washington, DC 20005, USA; tel. (202) 467-5410; fax (202) 467-5415; e-mail contactus@trilateral.org; internet www.trilateral.org; also offices in Paris and Tokyo; f. 1973 by private citizens of western Europe, Japan and North America, to encourage closer co-operation among these regions on matters of common concern; through analysis of major issues the Commission seeks to improve public understanding of problems, to develop and support proposals for handling them jointly, and to nurture the habit of working together in the 'trilateral' area. The Commission issues 'task force' reports on such subjects as monetary affairs, political co-operation, trade issues, the energy crisis and reform of international institutions; mems: about 335 individuals eminent in academic life, industry, finance, labour, etc.; those currently engaged as senior government officials are excluded; Chair. THOMAS S. FOLEY, YOTARO KOBYASHI, PETER SUTHERLAND; Dirs MICHAEL J. O'NEIL, TADASHI YAMAMOTO, PAUL RÉVAY; publs *Task Force Reports*, *Triangle Papers*.

Union of International Associations (UIA): 40 rue Washington, 1050 Brussels, Belgium; tel. (2) 640-18-08; fax (2) 643-61-99; e-mail uia@uia.be; internet www.uia.org; f. 1907, present title adopted 1910; aims to facilitate the evolution of the activities of the world-wide network of non-profit organizations, especially non-governmental and voluntary asscns; collects and disseminates information on such organizations; promotes research on the legal, administrative and other problems common to these asscns; mems: 109 individuals in 35 countries; Gen. Sec. JACQUES DE MEVIUS; publs *International Congress Calendar* (quarterly), *Yearbook of International Organizations*, *International Organization Participation* (annually), *Global Action Network* (annually), *Encyclopedia of World Problems and Human Potential*, *Documents for the Study of International Non-Governmental Relations*, *International Congress Science* series, *International Association Statutes* series, *Who's Who in International Organizations*.

Union of South American Nations (UNASUR): in Dec. 2004 leaders from 12 Latin American countries attending a pan-South American summit, convened in Cusco, Peru, approved in principle the creation of a new South American Community of Nations (SACN), to entail the merger of the Andean Community, Mercosur and Aladi (with the participation of Chile, Guyana and Suriname); the first South American Community meeting of heads of state was held in September, in Brasília, Brazil; in April 2007, at the first South American Energy Summit, convened in Margarita Island, Venezuela, heads of state endorsed the establishment of a Union of South American Nations (UNASUR), to replace SACN as the lead organization for regional integration; it was envisaged that UNASUR would have political decision-making functions, supported by a small permanent secretariat, to be located in Quito, Ecuador, and would co-ordinate on economic and trade matters with the Andean Community, Mercosur and Aladi; summit meetings formally to inaugurate UNASUR were scheduled to be held in December 2007, then March 2008; both were postponed; ministers of foreign affairs of the 12 member countries, meeting in Cartagena, Colombia, endorsed a draft constitutional treaty in January 2008; Sec.-Gen. RODRIGO BORJA CEVALLOS (designate).

United Cities and Local Governments (UCLG): Carrer Avinyó 15, 08002 Barcelona, Spain; tel. (93) 3428750; fax (93) 3428760; e-mail info@cities-localgovernments.org; internet www.cities-localgovernments.org; f. 2004 by merger of the Int. Union of Local Authorities and the World Federation of United Cities; aims to increase the role and influence of local governments, promotes democratic local governance, and facilitates partnerships and networks among cities and local authorities; initiated a Millennium Towns and Cities Campaign to encourage civic authorities to support implementation of the MDGs; launched the Global Observatory on Local Democracy and Decntralisation (GOLD) to provide information on the situation and evolution of decentralisation, self-government and local government across the world; mems: 112 local government asscns, more than 1,000 mem. cities in 95 countries; Sec.-Gen. ELISABETH GATEAU; publ. *Global Report on Decentralisation and Local Democracy*.

Unrepresented Nations and Peoples Organization (UNPO): POB 85878, 2508 CN The Hague, Netherlands; tel. (70) 3646504; fax (70) 3646608; e-mail unpo@unpo.org; internet www.unpo.org; f. 1991; an international, nonviolent, and democratic membership organization representing indigenous peoples, minorities, and unrecognised or occupied territories united in the aim of protecting and promoting their human and cultural rights, preserving their environments, and finding nonviolent solutions to conflicts that affect them; mems: 60 orgs representing occupied nations, indigenous peoples and minorities; Gen. Sec. MARINO BUSDACHIN; publ. *UNPO Yearbook*.

War Resisters' International: 5 Caledonian Rd, London, N1 9DX, United Kingdom; tel. (20) 7278-4040; fax (20) 7278-0444; e-mail info@wri-irg.org; internet www.wri-irg.org; f. 1921; encourages refusal to participate in or support wars or military service, collaborates with movements that work for peace and non-violent social change; mems: approx. 150,000; Chair. HOWARD CLARK; Co-ordinator ANDREAS SPECK; publ. *The Broken Rifle* (quarterly), *Peace News* (quarterly), *warprofiteers-news*.

Western European Union (WEU): 15 rue de l'Association, 1000 Brussels, Belgium; tel. (2) 500-44-12; fax (2) 500-44-70; e-mail secretariatgeneral@weu.int; internet www.weu.int; f. 1955, within the terms of the Brussels Treaty (1948), as the main organization for European co-operation in the field of defence and security; in December 1991 WEU agreed that the organization be developed as the defence component of the EU and as the means of strengthening the European pillar of the Atlantic Alliance; in June 1992 ministers agreed upon an operational role for WEU, by supporting international humanitarian, peace-keeping and crisis management missions ('Petersburg Tasks'); mid-1992–mid-1996 undertook a joint monitoring operation with NATO in the Adriatic sea; May 1997–May 2001 maintained a Multinational Advisory Police Element (MAPE) in Albania; greater co-operation with the EU and possible integration of WEU into the EU was incorporated into the Amsterdam Treaty (1997); WEU's crisis management responsibilities were transferred to the EU by July 2001; mems: Belgium, France, Germany, Greece, Italy, Luxembourg, Netherlands, Portugal, Spain, United Kingdom; six Associate Members, seven Associate Partners and five Observers; Sec.-Gen. JAVIER SOLANA MADARIAGA (Spain)

Assembly of Western European Union: 43 ave du Président Wilson, 75775 Paris Cédex 16, France; tel. 1-53-67-22-00; fax 1-53-67-22-01; e-mail info@assembly.weu.int; internet www.assembly-weu.org; composed of the representatives of the Brussels Treaty powers to the Parliamentary Assembly of the Council of Europe; it meets at least twice a year, and may proceed on any matter regarding the application of the Brussels Treaty and on any matter submitted to the Assembly for an opinion by the Council; may adopt resolutions or recommendations, which can be transmitted to international organizations, governments and national parliaments; since 2000 has acted as the Interparliamentary European Security and Defence Assembly, focusing on the development of a European Security and Defence Policy and the EU's civil and military crisis-management capabilities; Pres. JEAN-PIERRE MASERET (France).

Women's International Democratic Federation (WIDF) (Fédération Démocratique Internationale des Femmes—FDIF): c/o 'Femmes solidaires', 25 rue du Charolais, 75012 Paris, France; tel. 1-40-01-90-90; fax 1-40-01-90-81; e-mail fdif@fdif.eu.org; f. 1945 to unite women regardless of nationality, race, religion or political opinion; to enable them to work together to win and defend their rights as citizens, mothers and workers; to protect children; and to ensure peace and progress, democracy and national independence; structure: Congress, Secretariat and Executive Committee; mems: 629 organizations in 104 countries; Pres. SYLVIE JAN (France); publs *Women of the Whole World* (6 a year), *Newsletter*.

World Disarmament Campaign: POB 28209, Edinburgh, EH9 1ZR, United Kingdom; tel. (131) 447-4004; f. 1980 to encourage governments to take positive and decisive action to end the arms race, acting on the four main commitments called for in the Final Document of the UN's First Special Session on Disarmament; aims to mobilize people of every country in a demand for multilateral disarmament, to encourage consideration of alternatives to the nuclear deterrent for ensuring world security, and to campaign for a strengthened role for the UN in these matters; publ. *World Disarm!* (6 a year).

World Federalist Movement: 708 Third Ave, 24th Floor, New York, NY 10017, USA; tel. (212) 599-1320; fax (212) 599-1332; e-mail info@wfm-igp.org; internet www.wfm-igp.org; f. 1947; aims to acquire for the UN the authority to make and enforce laws for the peaceful settlement of disputes, and to raise revenue under limited taxing powers; to establish better international co-operation in the areas of environment, development and disarmament; and to promote federalism throughout the world; an Institute for Global Policy was established in 1983 as the research and policy analysis mechanism of the WFM; Congress meetings held every five years (Aug. 2007: Geneva, Switzerland); mems: 20 member organizations and 16 assoc. organizations; Pres. LOIS WILSON; Exec. Dir WILLIAM R. PACE; publs *World Federalist News* (quarterly), *International Criminal Court Monitor* (quarterly).

World Federation of United Nations Associations (WFUNA) (Fédération Mondiale des Associations Pour les Nations Unies—FMANU): c/o Palais des Nations, Rm E4-2A, 1211 Geneva 10, Switzerland; tel. 229173239; fax 229170185; e-mail wfuna@unog.ch; internet www.wfuna.org; f. 1946 to encourage popular interest and participation in United Nations programmes, discussion of the role and future of the UN, and education for international understanding; Plenary Assembly meets every two years; WFUNA has founded International Youth and Student Movement for the United Nations; mems: national asscns in more than 100 countries; Pres. Dr HANS BLIX (Sweden); Sec.-Gen. PERA WELLS; publ. *WFUNA News*.

World Peace Council: Othonos 10, Athens 10557, Greece; tel. (210) 331-6326; fax (210) 322-4302; e-mail info@wpc-in.org; internet www.wpc-in.org; f. 1950 at the Second World Peace Congress, Warsaw; principles: the prevention of nuclear war; the peaceful co-existence of the various socio-economic systems in the world; settlement of differences between nations by negotiation and agreement; complete disarmament; elimination of colonialism and racial discrimination; and respect for the right of peoples to sovereignty and independence; mems: representatives of national organizations, groups and individuals from 140 countries, and of 30 international organizations; Executive Committee of 40 mems elected by world assembly held every three years; Exec. Sec. ATHANASSIOS PAFILIS; publ. *Peace Courier* (monthly).

Youth of the European People's Party (YEPP): 10 Rue du Commerce, 1000 Brussels, Belgium; tel. (2) 285-41-63; fax (2) 285-41-65; e-mail yepp@epp-eu.org; internet www.yepp-eu.org; f. 1997 to unite national youth organizations of member parties of European Young Christian Democrats and Democrat Youth Community of Europe; aims to develop contacts between youth movements and advance general political debate among young people; mems: 54 organizations in some 35 European countries; Pres. YANNIS SMYRLIS (Greece); Sec.-Gen. MARTIN HUMER (Austria).

Industrial and Professional Relations

Arab Federation of Petroleum, Mining and Chemicals Workers: POB 5339, Tripoli, Libya; tel. (21) 444-7597; fax (21) 444-9139; f. 1961 to establish industrial relations policies and procedures for the guidance of affiliated unions; promotes establishment of trade unions in the relevant industries in countries where they do not exist; publs *Arab Petroleum* (monthly), specialized publications and statistics.

European Association for Personnel Management (EAPM): c/o ANDRH, 91 rue de Miromesnil, 75008 Paris, France; tel. 1-56-88-18-33; fax 1-56-88-18-29; e-mail webmaster@eapm.org; internet www.eapm.org; f. 1962 to disseminate knowledge and information concerning the personnel function of management, to establish and maintain professional standards, to define the specific nature of personnel management within industry, commerce and the public services, and to assist in the development of national asscns; mems: 27 national asscns; Pres. RUDOLF THURNER (Austria); Sec.-Gen. PIERRE YVES POULAIN (France).

European Cities Marketing: 99 rue de Talant, 21000 Dijon, France; tel. 3-80-56-02-04; fax 3-80-56-02-05; e-mail service-centre@europeancitiesmarketing.com; internet www.europeancitiesmarketing.com; European Cities Marketing is the network of City Tourist Offices and Convention Bureaus; aims to strengthen city tourism by providing sales and marketing opportunities, communicating information, sharing knowledge and expertise, educating and working together on an operational level; Pres. FRANK MAGEE (Ireland).

European Civil Service Federation (ECSF) (Fédération de la Fonction Publique Européenne—FFPE): 200 rue de la Loi, L 102 6/14,1049 Brussels, Belgium; e-mail secretariat.politique@ffpe.org; internet www.ffpe.org; f. 1962 to foster the idea of a European civil service of staff of international organizations operating in western Europe or pursuing regional objectives; upholds the interests of civil service members; mems: local cttees in 12 European countries and individuals in 66 countries; Sec.-Gen. L. RIJNOUDT; publ. *Eurechos*.

European Construction Industry Federation (Fédération de l'Industrie Européenne de la Construction—FIEC): 66 ave Louise, 1050 Brussels, Belgium; tel. (2) 514-55-35; fax (2) 511-02-76; e-mail info@fiec.org; internet www.fiec.org; f. 1905 as International European Construction Federation, present name adopted 1999; mems: 33 national employers' organizations in 27 countries; Pres. WILHELM KÜCHLER (Germany); Dir-Gen. ULRICH PAETZOLD; publs *FIEC News* (2 a year), *Annual Report*, *Construction Activity in Europe*.

European Federation of Lobbying and Public Affairs (Fédération européenne du lobbying et public afairs—FELPA): 61 rue du Trône, 1050 Brussels, Belgium; tel. (2) 511-74-30; fax (2) 511-12-84; aims to enhance the development and reputation of the industry; encourages professionals active in the industry to sign a code of conduct outlining the ethics and responsibilities of people involved in lobbying or public relations work with the institutions of the EU; Pres. Y. DE LESPINAY.

European Industrial Research Management Association (EIRMA): 46 rue Lauriston, 75116 Paris, France; tel. 1-53-23-83-10; fax 1-47-20-05-30; e-mail info@eirma.asso.fr; internet www.eirma.asso.fr; f. 1966 under auspices of the OECD; a permanent body in which European science and technology firms meet to consider approaches to industrial innovation, support research and development, and take joint action to improve performance in their various fields; mems: 150 in 21 countries; Pres. LEIF KJAERGAARD; Sec.-Gen. Dr ANDREW DEARING; publs *Annual Report*, *Conference Reports*, *Working Group Reports*, *Workshop Reports*.

European Trade Union Confederation (ETUC) (Confédération européenne des syndicats): 5 blvd du Roi Albert II, 1210 Brussels, Belgium; tel. (2) 224-04-11; fax (2) 224-04-54; e-mail etuc@etuc.org; internet www.etuc.org; f. 1973; comprises 82 national trade union confederations and 12 European industrial federations in 36 European countries, representing 60m. workers; co-operates closely with the International Trade Union Confederation; Pres. WANJA LUNDBY-WEDIN (Sweden); Gen. Sec. JOHN MONKS (United Kingdom).

Federation of International Civil Servants' Associations (FICSA): Palais des Nations, Office BOC 74, 1211 Geneva 10, Switzerland; tel. 229173150; fax 229170660; e-mail ficsa@unog.ch; internet www.ficsa.org; f. 1952 to co-ordinate policies and activities of member asscns and unions, to represent staff interests before inter-agency and legislative organs of the UN and to promote the development of an international civil service; mems: 27 asscns and unions consisting of staff of UN orgs, 10 associate mems from non-UN organizations, 17 consultative asscns and 26 inter-organizational federations with observer status; Pres. EDMOND MOBIO; Gen. Sec. VALÉRIE SEGUIN; publs *Annual Report*, *FICSA Newsletter*, *FICSA Update*, *FICSA circulars*.

INSOL International: 2–3 Philpot Lane, London, EC3M 8AQ, United Kingdom; tel. (20) 7929-6679; fax (20) 7929-6678; e-mail pennyr@insol.ision.co.uk; internet www.insol.org; f. 1982 as International Federation of Insolvency Professionals; comprises national asscns of accountants and lawyers specializing in corporate turn-around and insolvency; holds on day seminars, an annual conference and congress every four years; mems: 36 asscns, with more than 9,500 individual members in 60 countries; Pres. ROBERT SANDERSON (Canada); Exec. Dir CLAIRE BROUGHTON; publs *INSOL World* (quarterly newsletter), *International Insolvency Review* (2 a year).

International Association of Conference Interpreters: 10 ave de Sécheron, 1202 Geneva, Switzerland; tel. 229081540; fax 227934151; e-mail info@aiic.net; internet www.aiic.net; f. 1953 to represent professional conference interpreters, ensure the highest possible standards and protect the legitimate interests of mems; establishes criteria designed to improve the standards of training; recognizes schools meeting the required standards; has consultative status with the UN and several of its agencies; mems: 2,779 in 90 countries; Pres. BENOÎT KREMER (Switzerland); Exec. Sec. JOSYANE CRISTINA; publs *Code of Professional Conduct*, *Yearbook* (listing interpreters), etc.

International Association of Conference Translators: 15 route des Morillons, 1218 Le Grand-Saconnex, Geneva, Switzerland; tel. 227910666; fax 227885644; e-mail secretariat@aitc.ch; internet www.aitc.ch; f. 1962; represents revisers, translators, précis writers and editors working for international conferences and organizations; aims to protect the interests of those in the profession and help maintain high standards; establishes links with international organizations and conference organizers; mems: c. 450 in 33 countries; Pres. MICHEL FOURNIER; Exec. Sec. MICHEL BOUSSOMMIER; publs *Directory*, *Bulletin*.

International Association of Crafts and Small and Medium-Sized Enterprises (IACME): c/o Centre patronal, CP 1215, 1001 Lausanne, Switzerland; tel. 217963326; fax 217963390; e-mail iacme@centrepatronal.ch; f. 1947 to defend undertakings and the freedom of enterprise within private economy, to develop training, to encourage the creation of national organizations of independent enterprises and promote international collaboration, to represent the common interests of members and to institute exchange of ideas and information; mems: organizations in 26 countries; Chair. FRANCO MUSCARA; Gen. Sec. JACQUES DESGRAZ.

International Association of Mutual Insurance Companies (AISAM) (Association internationale des sociétés d'assurance mutuelle): 22B/16 sq. de Meeûs, 1050, Brussels, Belgium; tel. (2) 503-38-78; fax (2) 503-30-55; e-mail aisam@aisam.org; internet www.aisam.org; f. 1963 for the establishment of good relations between members and the protection of the general interests of private insurance based on the principle of mutuality; mems: over 140 in 25 countries; Pres. PEUGEOT PATRICK (France); Sec.-Gen. LIEVE LOWET; publs *Mutuality* (2 a year), *AISAM Directory*, *Newsletter*.

International Federation of Actors (Fédération internationale des acteurs—FIA): Guild House, Upper St Martin's Lane, London, WC2H 9EG, United Kingdom; tel. (20) 7379-0900; fax (20) 7379-8260; e-mail info@fia-actors.com; internet www.fia-actors.com; f. 1952; Exec. Cttee meets annually, Congress convened every four years; mems: 100 performers' unions in 75 countries; Pres. TOMAS BOLME (Sweden); Gen. Sec. DOMINICK LUQUER.

International Federation of Air Line Pilots' Associations (IFALPA): Interpilot House, Gogmore Lane, Chertsey, Surrey, KT16 9AP, United Kingdom; tel. (1932) 571711; fax (1932) 570920; e-mail ifalpa@ifalpa.org; internet www.ifalpa.org; f. 1948 to represent pilots at the ICAO and other industry fora and organizations, especially in technical and safety matters; establishes standards for air safety world-wide; seeks to ensure fair conditions of employment for pilots; mems: 95 asscns, over 100,000 pilots; Pres. Capt. TED MURPHY; publs *Interpilot* (2 a year), safety bulletins and news-sheets.

International Federation of Biomedical Laboratory Science (IFBLS): Office POB 2830, Hamilton, Ontario, ON L8N 3N8, Canada; tel. (905) 528-8642; fax (905) 528-4968; e-mail office@ifbls.org; internet www.ifbls.org; f. 1954 to allow discussion of matters of common professional interest; fmrly the International Association of Medical Laboratory Technologists (f. 1954); aims to promote globally the highest standards in the delivery of care, of professional training, and ethical and professional practices; develops and promotes active professional partnerships in health care at the international level; promotes and encourages participation of members in international activities; holds international congress every second year; mems: 180,000 in 37 countries; Pres. RUTH PIERCE (Canada); publ. *Biomedical Laboratory Science International* (quarterly).

International Federation of Business and Professional Women: POB 568, Horsham RH13 9ZP, United Kingdom; tel. (1403) 739343; fax (1403) 734432; e-mail members@bpw-international.org.uk; internet www.bpwi.org; f. 1930 to promote interests of business and professional women and secure combined action by such women; mems: national federations, associate clubs and individual associates, totalling more than 100,000 mems in over 100 countries; Pres. Dr CHONCHANOK VIRAVAN (Thailand); Exec. Sec. FREDA MIRIKLIS (Australia); publ. *BPW News International* (every 2 months).

International Graphical Federation (Fédération graphique internationale): 17 rue des Fripiers, Galerie du Centre, bloc 2, 1000 Brussels, Belgium; tel. (2) 223-02-20; fax (2) 223-18-14; e-mail igf-fgi@enter.org; f. 1925; mems: national federations in 15 countries, covering 100,000 workers; Pres. L. VAN HAUDT (Belgium); Sec.-Gen. R. E. VAN KESTEREN (Netherlands).

International Industrial Relations Association (IIRA): c/o International Labour Office, 1211 Geneva 22, Switzerland; tel. 227996841; fax 227998541; e-mail iira@ilo.org; internet www.ilo.org/iira; f. 1966 to encourage development of national asscns of specialists, facilitate the spread of information, organize conferences, and promote internationally planned research, through study groups and regional meetings; a World Congress is held every three years; mems: 39 asscns, 47 institutions and 1,100 individuals; Pres. Prof. LUIS APARICIO VALDEZ; Sec. Prof. TAYO FASHOYIN; publs *IIRA Bulletin* (3 a year), *IIRA Membership Directory*, *IIRA Congress proceedings*.

International Organisation of Employers (IOE): 26 chemin de Joinville, BP 68, 1216 Cointrin/Geneva, Switzerland; tel. 229290000; fax 229290001; e-mail ioe@ioe-emp.org; internet www.ioe-emp.org; f. 1920; aims to establish and maintain contacts between mems and to represent their interests at the international level; works to promote free enterprise; and to assist the development of employers' organizations; General Council meets annually; there is a Management Board and a General Secretariat; mems: 143 federations in 137 countries; Pres. ABRAHAM KATZ (USA); Sec.-Gen. ANTONIO PEÑALOSA (Spain); publ. *IOE.net*.

International Organization of Experts (ORDINEX): 19 blvd Sébastopol, 75001 Paris, France; tel. 1-40-28-06-06; fax 1-40-28-03-13; e-mail contact@ordinex.org; internet www.ordinex.org; f. 1961 to establish co-operation between experts on an international level; mems: 600; Pres. FRANZ SCHREINER (Austria); Sec.-Gen. PIERRE ROYER (France); publ. *General Yearbook*.

International Public Relations Association (IPRA): 12 Dunley Hill Court, Ranmore Common, Dorking, Surrey RH5 6SX, United Kingdom; tel. (1483) 280130; fax (1483) 280131; e-mail info@ipra.org; internet www.ipra.org; f. 1955 to provide an exchange of ideas, technical knowledge and professional experience among those engaged in public relations, and to foster the highest standards of professional competence; mems: 1,000 in 98 countries; CEO JAMES HOLT; publs *Frontline* (every 2 months), *Directory of Members* (annually).

International Society of City and Regional Planners (ISoCaRP): POB 983, 2501 CZ, The Hague, Netherlands; tel. (70) 3462654; fax (70) 3617909; e-mail isocarp@isocarp.org; internet www.isocarp.org; f. 1965 to promote better planning practice through the exchange of knowledge; holds annual international congress (2007: Antwerp, Belgium); mems: 480 in 70 countries; Exec. Dir JUDY VAN HEMERT; publs *Newsletter* (3 a year), *ISoCaRP REVIEW* (annually), seminar and congress reports.

International Union of Architects (Union internationale des architectes—UIA): 51 rue Raynouard, 75016 Paris, France; tel. 1-45-24-36-88; fax 1-45-24-02-78; e-mail uia@uia-architectes.org; internet www.uia-architectes.org; f. 1948; holds triennial congress; mems: 106 countries; Pres. GAÉTAN SIEW (Mauritius); Gen. Sec. JORDI FARRANDO (Spain); publ. *Lettre d'informations* (monthly).

Latin American Federation of Agricultural Workers (Federación Latinoamericana de Trabajadores Agrícolas, Pecuarios y Afines—FELTRA): Antiguo Local Conadi, B° La Granja, Comayaguela, Tegucigalpa, Honduras; tel. 2252526; fax 2252525; e-mail feltra@123.hn; internet www.acmoti.org; f. 1999 by reorganization of FELTACA (f. 1961) to represent the interests of workers in agricultural and related industries in Latin America; mems: national unions in 28 countries and territories; Sec.-Gen. MARCIAL REYES CABALLERO; publ. *Boletín Luchemos* (quarterly).

Nordic Industrial Fund—Centre for Innovation and Development (Nordisk InnovationsCenter): Stensberggt. 25, 0170 Oslo, Norway; tel. 47-61-44-00; e-mail k.storvik@nordicinnovation.net; internet www.nordicinnovation.net; f. 1973; provides grants, subsidies and loans for industrial research and development projects of interest to Nordic countries; Man. Dir KJETIL STORVIK.

Nordic Industry Workers' Federation (Nordiska Industriarbetare-Federationen—NIF): Olof Palmes gata 11, 5th Floor, Box 1114, 111 81 Stockholm, Sweden; tel. (8) 7868500; fax (8) 105968; e-mail kent.karrlander.nif@industrifacket.se; internet www.nordif.org; f. 1901; promotes collaboration between affiliates representing workers in the chemicals, energy, garment, manufacturing, mining, paper and textile sectors in Denmark, Finland, Iceland, Norway and Sweden; supports sister unions economically and in other ways in labour market conflicts; mems: c. 350,000 in 16 unions; Pres. LEIF OHLSSON; Sec. KENT KÄRRLANDER.

Organisation of African Trade Union Unity (OATUU): POB M386, Accra, Ghana; tel. (21) 508855; fax (21) 508851; e-mail oatuu@ighmail.com; f. 1973 as a single continental trade union org., independent of international trade union organizations; has affiliates from all African trade unions. Congress, the supreme policy-making body, is composed of four delegates per country from affiliated national trade union centres, and meets at least every four years; the General Council, composed of one representative from each affiliated trade union, meets annually to implement Congress decisions and to approve the annual budget; mems: trade union movements in 53 independent African countries; Sec.-Gen. Gen. HASSAN A. SUNMONU (Nigeria); publ. *The African Worker*.

Pan-African Employers' Confederation (PEC): c/o Mauritius Employers' Federation, Cerné House, 13 La Chaussée, Port Louis, Mauritius; tel. 212-1599; fax 212-6725; e-mail info@mef-online.org; f. 1986 to link African employers' organizations and represent them at the AU, UN and ILO; mems: representation in 39 countries on the continent; Sec.-Gen. AZAD JEETUN (Mauritius).

World Movement of Christian Workers (WMCW): 124 blvd du Jubilé, 1080 Brussels, Belgium; tel. (2) 421-58-40; fax (2) 421-58-49; e-mail mmtc@skynet.be; f. 1961 to unite national movements that advance the spiritual and collective well-being of workers; holds General Assembly every four years; mems: 47 affiliated movements in 39 countries; Sec.-Gen. NORBERT KLEIN; publ. *Infor-WMCW*.

World Federation of Scientific Workers (WFSW) (Fédération mondiale des travailleurs scientifiques—FMTS): Case 404, 263 rue de Paris, 93516 Montreuil Cédex, France; tel. 1-48-18-81-75; fax 1-48-18-80-03; e-mail fmts@fmts-wfsw.org; internet www.fmts-wfsw.org; f. 1946 to improve the position of science and scientists, to assist in promoting international scientific co-operation and to promote the use of science for beneficial ends; studies and publicizes problems of general, nuclear, biological and chemical disarmament; surveys the position and activities of scientists; mems: organizations in 28 countries; Pres. ANDRÉ JAEGLÉ (France); Sec.-Gen. PASCAL JANOTS (France).

World Union of Professions (Union mondiale des professions libérales): 38 rue Boissière, 75116 Paris, France; tel. 1-44-05-90-15; fax 1-44-05-90-17; e-mail info@umpl.com; internet www.umpl.com; f. 1987 to represent and link members of the liberal professions; mems: 27 national inter-professional organizations, two regional groups and 12 international federations; Chair. Dr CHRISTIAN RONDEAU.

Law

African Bar Association: 29/31 Obafemi Awolowo Way, Ikeja, Lagos, Nigeria (temporary address); tel. (1) 4936907; fax (1) 7752202; f. 1972; aims to uphold the rule of law, maintain the independence of the judiciary, and improve legal services; Pres. PETER ALA ADJETY (Ghana); Sec.-Gen. FEMI FELANA (Nigeria).

African Society of International and Comparative Law (ASICL): 402 Holloway Rd, London, N7 6PZ, United Kingdom; tel. (20) 7609-3800; fax (20) 7609-5400; e-mail asicl@compuserve.com; f. 1986; promotes public education on law and civil liberties; aims to provide a legal aid and advice system in each African country, and to facilitate the exchange of information on civil liberties in Africa; Pres. MOHAMED BEDJAOUI; Sec. EMILE YAKPO (Ghana); publs *Newsletter* (every 2 months), *African Journal of International and Comparative Law* (quarterly).

Asian-African Legal Consultative Organization (AALCO): E-66, Vasant Marg, Vasant Vihar, New Delhi 110057, India; tel. (11) 26152251; fax (11) 26152041; e-mail mail@aalco.int; internet www.aalco.int; f. 1956 to consider legal problems referred to it by member countries and to serve as a forum for Afro-Asian co-operation in international law, including international trade law, and economic relations; provides background material for conferences, prepares standard/model contract forms suited to the needs of the region; promotes arbitration as a means of settling international commercial disputes; trains officers of member states; has permanent UN observer status; has established four International Commercial Arbitration Centres in Kuala Lumpur, Malaysia, Cairo, Egypt, Lagos, Nigeria and Tehran, Iran; mems: 47 countries; Pres. BRIGITTE MABANDLA (South Africa); Sec.-Gen. Dr WAFIK ZAHER KAMIL (Egypt).

Centre for International Environmental Law (CIEL): 1367 Connecticut Ave, NW, Suite 300, Washington, DC 20036, USA; tel. (202) 785-8700; fax (202) 785-8701; e-mail info@ciel.org; internet www.ciel.org; f. 1989; aims to solve environmental problems and promote sustainable societies through use of law; works to strengthen international and comparative environmental law and policy and to incorporate fundamental ecological principles into international law; provides a range of environmental legal services; educates and trains environmental lawyers; Pres. DANIEL B. MAGRAW, Jr.

Comité maritime international (CMI): Mechelsesteenweg 196, 2018 Antwerp, Belgium; tel. (3) 227-35-26; fax (3) 227-35-28; e-mail admin@cmi-imc.org; internet www.comitemaritime.org; f. 1897 to contribute to the unification of maritime law and to encourage the creation of national asscns; work includes drafting of conventions on collisions at sea, salvage and assistance at sea, limitation of shipowners' liability, maritime mortgages, etc; mems: national asscns in more than 59 countries; Pres. JEAN-SERGE ROHART (France);

Sec. Gen. NIGEL FRAWLEY (Canada); publs *CMI Newsletter*, *Year Book*.

Council of the Bars and Law Societies of Europe (CCBE): 1–5 ave de la Joyeuse Entrée, 1040 Brussels, Belgium; tel. (2) 234-65-10; fax (2) 234-65-11; e-mail ccbe@ccbe.org; internet www.ccbe.org; f. 1960; the officially recognized representative organization for the legal profession in the European Union and European Economic Area; liaises between the bars and law societies of member states and represents them before the European institutions; also maintains contact with other international organizations of lawyers; principal objective is to study all questions affecting the legal profession in member states and to harmonize professional practice; mems: 31 delegations (representing more than 700,000 European lawyers), and observer/associate delegations from six countries; Pres. PÉTER KÖVES; Sec.-Gen. JONATHAN GOLDSMITH.

Hague Conference on Private International Law: Scheveningseweg 6, 2517 KT, The Hague, Netherlands; tel. (70) 3633303; fax (70) 3604867; e-mail secretariat@hcch.net; internet www.hcch.net; f. 1893 to work for the unification of the rules of private international law; Permanent Bureau f. 1955; mems: 68 (incl. the European Community); Sec.-Gen. J. H. A. VAN LOON; publs *Proceedings of Diplomatic Sessions* (every 4 years), *Collection of Conventions*, *The Judges' Newsletter on International Child Protection*.

Institute of International Law (Institut de Droit international): The Graduate, 132 rue de Lausanne, CP 136, 1211 Geneva 21, Switzerland; tel. 229085720; fax 229086277; e-mail gerardi@hei.unige.ch; internet www.idi-iil.org; f. 1873 to promote the development of international law through the formulation of general principles, in accordance with civilized ethical standards; provides assistance for the gradual and progressive codification of international law; mems: limited to 132 members and associates world-wide; Sec.-Gen. JOE VERHOEVEN (Belgium); publ. *Annuaire de l'Institut de Droit international*.

Inter-African Union of Lawyers (IAUL) (Union interafricaine des avocats): BP14409, Libreville, Gabon; tel. 76-41-44; fax 74-54-01; f. 1980; holds congress every three years; Pres. ABDELAZIZ BENZAKOUR (Morocco); Sec.-Gen. FRANÇOIS XAVIER AGONDJO-OKAWE (Gabon); publ. *L'avocat africain* (2 a year).

Inter-American Bar Association (IABA): 1211 Connecticut Ave, NW, Suite 202, Washington, DC 20036, USA; tel. (202) 466-5944; fax (202) 466-5946; e-mail iaba@iaba.org; internet www.iaba.org; f. 1940 to promote the rule of law and to establish and maintain relations between asscns and organizations of lawyers in the Americas; mems: 90 asscns and 3,500 individuals in 27 countries; Sec.-Gen. HARRY A. INMAN (USA); publs *Newsletter* (quarterly), *Conference Proceedings*.

Intergovernmental Committee of the Universal Copyright Convention: Division of Arts and Cultural Enterprise, UNESCO, 1 rue Miollis, 75700 Paris, France; tel. 1-45-68-47-45; fax 1-45-68-55-89; e-mail e.glele@unesco.org; established to study the application and operation of the Universal Copyright Convention and to make preparations for periodic revisions of this Convention; studies other problems concerning the international protection of copyright, in co-operation with various international organizations; mems: 18 states; Legal Officer PETYA TOTCHAROVA; publ. *Copyright Bulletin* (quarterly: digital format in English, French and Spanish; print format in Chinese and Russian).

International Association for the Protection of Industrial Property (AIPPI): Tödistrasse 16, 8027 Zürich 27, Switzerland; tel. 442805880; fax 442805885; e-mail mail@aippi.org; internet www.aippi.org; f. 1897 to encourage the development of legislation on the international protection of industrial property and the development and extension of international conventions, and to make comparative studies of existing legislation with a view to its improvement and unification; holds triennial congress; mems: 8,200 (national and regional groups and individual mems) in 108 countries; Pres. RONALD E. MYRICK (2007–08); Sec.-Gen. MICHAEL BRUNNER; publs *Yearbook*, reports.

International Association of Democratic Lawyers: 21 rue Brialmont, 1210 Brussels, Belgium; tel. and fax and fax (2) 223-33-10; e-mail jsharma@vsnl.com; internet www.iadllaw.org; f. 1946 to facilitate contacts and exchange between lawyers, encourage study of legal science and international law and support the democratic principles favourable to the maintenance of peace and co-operation between nations; promotes the preservation of the environment; conducts research on labour law, private international law, agrarian law, etc; has consultative status with UN; mems: in 96 countries; Pres. JITENDRA SHARMA (India); Sec.-Gen. JEANNE MIRER (USA); publ. *International Review of Contemporary Law* (2 a year, in French, English and Spanish).

International Association of Youth and Family Judges and Magistrates (IAYFJM): Lagergasse 6–8, 1030 Vienna, Austria; tel. (1) 713-18-25; fax (1) 58801-134-99; e-mail nesrinlushta@yahoo.com; internet www.judgesandmagistrates.org; f. 1928 to support the protection of youth and family, and criminal behaviour and juvenile maladjustment; members exercise functions as juvenile and family court judges or within professional services linked to youth and family justice and welfare; organizes study groups, meetings and an international congress every four years (Aug.–Sept. 2006: Belfast, Northern Ireland); mems: 12 national asscns and mems in more than 80 countries; Pres. RENATE WINTER (Austria); Sec.-Gen. NESRIN LUSHTA.

International Association of Law Libraries (IALL): POB 5709, Washington, DC 20016-1309, USA; e-mail ann.morrison@dal.ca; internet www.iall.org; f. 1959 to encourage and facilitate the work of librarians and others concerned with the bibliographic processing and administration of legal materials; mems: over 600 from more than 50 countries (personal and institutional); Pres. JULES WINTERTON (United Kingdom); Sec. ANN MORRISON (Canada); publ. *International Journal of Legal Information* (3 a year).

International Association of Legal Sciences (IALS) (Association internationale des sciences juridiques): c/o CISS, 1 rue Miollis, 75015 Paris, France; tel. 1-45-68-25-59; fax 1-45-66-76-03; f. 1950 to promote the mutual knowledge and understanding of nations and the increase of learning by encouraging throughout the world the study of foreign legal systems and the use of the comparative method in legal science; governed by a president and an executive committee of 11 members known as the International Committee of Comparative Law; sponsored by UNESCO; mems: national committees in 47 countries; Pres. Prof. WLADIMIR TOUMANOV (Russia); Sec.-Gen. M. LEKER (Israel).

International Association of Penal Law: 41 rue Bonado, 64000 Pau, France; tel. 5-59-98-08-24; fax 5-59-27-24-56; e-mail info@penal.org; internet www.penal.org; f. 1924 to promote collaboration between those from different countries working in penal law, studying criminology, or promoting the theoretical and practical development of international penal law; mems: 1,800; Pres. Prof. JOSÉ LUIS DE LA CUESTA; Sec.-Gen. Dr HELMUT EPP; publs *Revue Internationale de Droit Pénal* (2 a year), *Nouvelles Etudes Penales*.

International Bar Association (IBA): 1 Stephen St, 10th Floor, London W1T 1AT, United Kingdom; tel. (20) 7691-6868; fax (20) 7691-6544; e-mail iba@int-bar.org; internet www.ibanet.org; f. 1947; a non-political federation of national bar asscns and law societies; aims to discuss problems of professional organization and status; to advance the science of jurisprudence; to promote uniformity and definition in appropriate fields of law; to promote administration of justice under law among peoples of the world; to promote in their legal aspects the principles and aims of the United Nations; mems: 154 member organizations in 164 countries, 17,500 individual members in 173 countries; Pres. FRANCIS NEATE (United Kingdom); Sec. Gen. FERNANDO PELAEZ-PIER (Venezuela); publs *International Business Lawyer* (11 a year), *International Bar News* (3 a year), *International Legal Practitioner* (quarterly), *Journal of Energy and Natural Resources Law* (quarterly).

International Commission of Jurists (ICJ): POB 91, 33 rue des Bains, 1211 Geneva 8, Switzerland; tel. 229793800; fax 229793801; e-mail info@icj.org; internet www.icj.org; f. 1952 to promote the implementation of international law and principles that advance human rights; provides legal expertise to ensure that developments in international law adhere to human rights principles and that international standards are implemented at the national level; disseminates reports and other legal documents through the ICJ Legal Resource Centre; maintains Centre for the Independence of Judges and Lawyers (f. 1978); in Oct. 2005 established an Eminent Jurists' Panel on Terrorism, Counter-terrorism and Human Rights; mems: 82 sections and affiliated orgs in 62 countries; Sec.-Gen. NICHOLAS HOWEN; publs special reports.

International Commission on Civil Status: 3 place Arnold, 67000 Strasbourg, France; e-mail ciec-sg@ciec1.org; internet www.ciec1.org; f. 1950 for the establishment and presentation of legislative documentation relating to the rights of individuals; carries out research on means of simplifying the judicial and technical administration with respect to civil status; mems: governments of Austria, Belgium, Croatia, France, Germany, Greece, Hungary, Italy, Luxembourg, Netherlands, Poland, Portugal, Spain, Switzerland, Turkey, United Kingdom; Pres. ROSELINE DEMOUSTIER (Belgium); Sec.-Gen. PAUL LAGARDE (France); publs *Guide Pratique international de l'état civil* (available online), various studies on civil status.

International Copyright Society (Internationale Gesellschaft für Urheberrecht e. V.—INTERGU): Rosenheimer Strasse 11, 81667 Munich, Germany; tel. (89) 48003-00; fax (89) 48003-969; f. 1954 to enquire scientifically into the natural rights of the author and to put the knowledge obtained to practical application worldwide, in particular in the field of legislation; mems: 187 individuals and corresponding organizations in 37 countries; CEO Prof. REINHOLD KREILE; publs *Schriftenreihe* (61 vols), *Yearbook*.

International Council for Commercial Arbitration (ICCA): c/o International Centre for Settlement of Investment Disputes, 1818 H St, NW, Washington, DC 20433, USA; tel. (202) 744-8801; fax (202) 522-2615; e-mail arparra@earthlink.net; internet www.arbitration-icca.org; promotes international arbitration and other forms of dispute resolution; convenes Congresses and Conferences for discussion and the presentation of papers; mems: 42 mems, 17 advisory mems; Pres. Dr GEROLD HERRMANN (Austria); Sec.-Gen. ANTONIO R. PARRA (USA); publs *Yearbook on Commercial Arbitration, International Handbook on Commercial Arbitration, ICCA Congress Series*.

International Council of Environmental Law: Godesberger Allee 108–112, 53175 Bonn, Germany; tel. (228) 2692-240; fax (228) 2692-251; e-mail icel@intlawpol.org; internet www.i-c-e-l.org/indexen.html; f. 1969 to exchange information and expertise on legal, administrative and policy aspects of environmental questions; Exec. Governors Dr WOLFGANG E. BURHENNE (Germany), AMADO TOLENTINO, Jr (Philippines); publs *Directory, References, Environmental Policy and Law, International Environmental Law—Multilateral Treaties*, etc.

International Criminal Police Organization (INTERPOL): 200 quai Charles de Gaulle, 69006 Lyon, France; fax 4-72-44-71-63; e-mail cp@interpol.int; internet www.interpol.int; f. 1923, reconstituted 1946; aims to promote and ensure mutual assistance between police forces in different countries; co-ordinates activities of police authorities of member states in international affairs; works to establish and develop institutions with the aim of preventing transnational crimes; centralizes records and information on international criminals; operates a global police communications network linking all member countries; holds General Assembly annually; mems: 186 countries; Sec.-Gen. RONALD K. NOBLE (USA); publs *International Criminal Police Review, International Crime Statistics, Stolen Works of Art* (CD-Rom), *Interpol Guide to Vehicle Registration Documents* (annually).

International Customs Tariffs Bureau: 38 rue de l'Association, 1000 Brussels, Belgium; tel. (2) 501-87-74; fax (2) 218-30-25; e-mail dir@bitd.org; internet www.bitd.org; f. 1890; serves as the executive instrument of the International Union for the Publication of Customs Tariffs; translates and publishes all customs tariffs in five languages—English, French, German, Italian, Spanish; mems: 52 mem. countries; Pres. JAN GRAULS (Belgium); Dir MARC DE SCHOUTHEETE; publs *International Customs Journal, Annual Report*.

International Development Law Organization (IDLO): Via San Sebastianello 16, 00187 Rome, Italy; tel. (06) 6979261; fax (06) 6781946; e-mail idlo@idlo.int; internet www.idlo.int; f. 1983; aims to promote the rule of law and good governance in developing countries, transition economies and nations emerging from conflict and to assist countries to establish effective infrastructure to achieve sustainable economic growth, security and access to justice; activities include Policy Dialogues, Technical Assistance, Global Network of Alumni and Partners, Training Programs, Research and Publications; maintains Regional Offices in Cairo, Egypt, covering Arabic-speaking countries and in Sydney, Australia, covering the Asia Pacific area; also operates Project Offices in Afghanistan, Indonesia, Sudan and Kyrgyzstan; mems: 18 mem states; Chair. LUIGI BIAMONTI; Dir-Gen. WILLIAM T. LORIS.

International Federation for European Law (Fédération Internationale pour le Droit Européen—FIDE): 113 ave Louise, 1050 Brussels, Belgium; tel. (2) 534-71-63; fax (2) 534-28-58; e-mail fide2008@jku.at; f. 1961 to advance studies on European law among members of the European Community by co-ordinating activities of member societies; organizes conferences every two years; mems: 12 national asscns; Pres. Prof. HERIBERT FRANZ KOECK; Sec.-Gen. Prof. MARGIT MARIA KAROLLUS.

International Federation of Senior Police Officers (Federation Internationale des Fonctionnaires Superieures de Police—FIFSP): FIFSP, Ministère de l'Intérieur, 127 rue Faubourg Saint Honoré, 75008 Paris, France; tel. 1-49-27-40-67; fax 1-45-62-48-52; f. 1950 to unite policemen of different nationalities, adopting the general principle that prevention should prevail over repression, and that the citizen should be convinced of the protective role of the police; established International Centre of Crime and Accident Prevention, 1976 and International Association against Counterfeiting, 1994; mems: 34 national organizations; Pres. JUAN GARCÍA LLOVERA; Sec.-Gen. JEAN-PIERRE HAVRIN (France); publ. *International Police Information* (quarterly, in English, French and German).

International Institute for the Unification of Private Law (UNIDROIT): Via Panisperna 28, 00184 Rome, Italy; tel. (06) 696211; fax (06) 69941394; e-mail info@unidroit.org; internet www.unidroit.org; f. 1926 to undertake studies of comparative law, to prepare for the establishment of uniform legislation, to prepare drafts of international agreements on private law and to organize conferences and publish works on such subjects; holds international congresses on private law and meetings of organizations concerned with the unification of law; maintains a library of 215,000 vols; mems:

govts of 60 countries; Pres. Prof. BERARDINO LIBONATI (Italy); Sec.-Gen. Prof. HERBERT KRONKE (Germany); publs *Uniform Law Review* (quarterly), *Digest of Legal Activities of International Organizations*, etc.

International Institute of Space Law (IISL): 8–10 rue Mario Nikis, 75015 Paris, France; tel. 1-45-67-42-60; fax 1-42-73-21-20; e-mail president@iafastro-iisl.com; internet www.iafastro-iisl.com; f. 1959 at the XI Congress of the International Astronautical Federation; organizes annual Space Law colloquium; studies juridical and sociological aspects of astronautics; makes awards; Pres. Dr NANDASIRI JASENTULIYANA (USA); publs *Proceedings of Annual Colloquium on Space Law, Survey of Teaching of Space Law in the World*.

International Juridical Institute (IJI): Permanent Office for the Supply of International Legal Information, Spui 186, 2511 BW, The Hague, Netherlands; tel. (70) 3460974; fax (70) 3625235; e-mail iji@worldonline.nl; internet www.iji.nl; f. 1918 to supply information on any non-secret matter of international interest, respecting international, municipal and foreign law and the application thereof; Pres. A. V. M. STRUYCKEN; Dir A. L. G. A. STILLE.

International Law Association (ILA): Charles Clore House, 17 Russell Sq., London, WC1B 5DR, United Kingdom; tel. (20) 7323-2978; fax (20) 7323-3580; e-mail info@ila-hq.org; internet www.ila-hq.org; f. 1873 for the study and advancement of international law, both public and private and the promotion of international understanding and goodwill; mems: 3,700 in 50 regional branches; 25 international cttees; Pres. MILOS BARUTCISKI (Canada); Chair. Exec. Council Lord SLYNN OF HADLEY (United Kingdom); Sec.-Gen. DAVID J. C. WYLD (United Kingdom).

International Nuclear Law Association (INLA): 29 sq. de Meeûs, 1000 Brussels, Belgium; tel. (2) 547-58-41; fax (2) 503-04-40; e-mail info@aidn-inla.be; internet www.aidn-inla.be; f. 1972 to promote international studies of legal problems related to the peaceful use of nuclear energy; holds conference every two years; mems: 460 in 38 countries; Sec.-Gen. PATRICK REYNERS; publs *Congress reports*, *Une Histoire de 25 ans*.

International Penal and Penitentiary Foundation (IPPF) (Fondation internationale pénale et pénitentiaire—FIPP): c/o Prof. Tak, Radboud University, 6500 Nijmegen, Netherlands; tel. (24) 3613095; fax (24) 3611695; e-mail P.Tak@jur.ru.nl; f. 1951 to encourage studies in the field of prevention of crime and treatment of delinquents; mems in 23 countries (membership limited to three people from each country) and corresponding mems; Pres. GEORGE KELLENS (Belgium); Sec.-Gen. PETER TAK (Netherlands).

International Police Association (IPA): Arthur Troop House, 1 Fox Rd, West Bridgford, Nottingham, NG2 6AJ, United Kingdom; tel. (115) 945-5985; fax (115) 982-2578; e-mail isg@ipa-iac.org; internet www.ipa-iac.org; f. 1950 to permit the exchange of professional information, create ties of friendship between all sections of the police service and organize group travel and studies; mems: 380,000 in more than 61 countries; International Pres. MICHAEL ODYSSEOS; International Sec.-Gen. JOHN WAUMSLEY.

International Society for Labour and Social Security Law (ISLSSL): CP 500, CH-1211 Geneva 22, Switzerland; tel. 227996961; fax 227998749; e-mail sidtss@ilo.org; internet www.asociacion.org.ar/ISLLSS; f. 1958 to encourage collaboration between labour law and social security specialists; holds World Congress every three years, as well as irregular regional congresses (Europe, Africa, Asia and Americas); mems: 66 national asscns of labour law officers; Pres. KAZUO SUGENO (Japan); Sec.-Gen. ARTURO BRONSTEIN (Argentina).

International Union of Latin Notaries (Union Internationale du Notariat Latin—UINL): Alsina 2280, 2°, 1090 Buenos Aires, Argentina; tel. (11) 4952-8848; fax (11) 4952-7094; e-mail onpiuinl@onpi.org.ar; internet www.uinl.org; f. 1948 to study and standardize notarial legislation and promote the progress, stability and advancement of the Latin notarial system; mems: organizations and individuals in 76 countries; Pres. Dr EDUARDO GALLINO; publs *Revista Internacional del Notariado* (quarterly), *Notarius International*.

Law Association for Asia and the Pacific (LAWASIA): LAWASIA Secretariat, GPO Box 980, Brisbane, Qld 4001, Australia; tel. (7) 3222-5888; fax (7) 3222-5850; internet www.lawasia.asn.au; f. 1966; provides an international, professional network for lawyers to update, reform and develop law within the region; comprises six Sections and 21 Standing Committees in Business Law and General Practice areas, which organize speciality conferences; also holds a biennial conference (2007: Hong Kong); mems: national orgs in 23 countries; 1,500 mems in 55 countries; Pres. MAH WENG KWAI (Malaysia); publs *Directory* (annually), *Journal* (annually), *LAWASIA Update* (3 times a year: April, Aug., Dec.).

Permanent Court of Arbitration: Peace Palace, Carnegieplein 2, 2517 KJ, The Hague, Netherlands; tel. (70) 3024165; fax (70) 3024167; e-mail bureau@pca-cpa.org; internet www.pca-cpa.org; f. by the Convention for the Pacific Settlement of International Disputes (1899, 1907); provides for the resolution of disputes involving combinations of states, private parties and intergovernmental organizations, under its own rules of procedure, by means of arbitration, conciliation and fact-finding; operates a secretariat, the International Bureau, which provides registry services and legal support to ad hoc tribunals and commissions; draws up lists of adjudicators with specific expertise; and maintains documentation on mass claims settlement processes; mems: governments of 107 countries; Sec.-Gen. TJACO VAN DEN HOUT (Netherlands); publs *Kluwer Law International Database* (ed), *Journal of International Arbitration* (ed), *World Trade and Arbitration Materials* (ed), *Peace Palace Papers* (ed), *International Law Seminars* (annually).

SECI Center: calea 13 Septembrie 3–5, Sector 5, 050711 Bucharest, Romania; tel. (21) 303-60-09; fax (21) 303-60-77; internet www.secicenter.org; f. 2000 by the Southeast European Co-operative Initiative; an operative collaboration of customs and police officials working under the guidance of recommendations and directives from INTERPOL and the World Customs Organization; Task Force on Illegal Human Beings Trafficking established May 2000, Task Force on Illegal Drugs Trafficking established July 2000, Task Force on Commercial Fraud established February 2001; mems: Albania, Bosnia and Herzegovina, Bulgaria, Croatia, Greece, Hungary, former Yugoslav Republic of Macedonia, Moldova, Romania, Serbia, Slovenia, Turkey.

Society of Comparative Legislation: 28 rue Saint-Guillaume, 75007 Paris, France; tel. 1-44-39-86-23; fax 1-44-39-86-28; e-mail slc@legiscompare.com; internet www.legiscompare.com; f. 1869 to study and compare laws of different countries, and to investigate practical means of improving the various branches of legislation; mems: 600 in 48 countries; Pres. JEAN-LOUIS DEWOST (France); Sec.-Gen. BÉNÉDICTE FAUVARQUE-COSSON (France); publ. *Revue Internationale de Droit Comparé* (quarterly).

Union Internationale des Avocats (International Association of Lawyers): 25 rue du Jour, 75001 Paris, France; tel. 1-44-88-55-66; fax 1-44-88-55-77; e-mail uiacentre@uianet.org; internet www.uianet.org; f. 1927 to promote the independence and freedom of lawyers, and defend their ethical and material interests on an international level; aims to contribute to the development of international order based on law; mems: over 200 asscns and 3,000 lawyers in over 110 countries; Pres. DELOS N. LUTTON; Exec. Dir MARIE-PIERRE RICHARD.

Union of Arab Jurists (UAJ): POB 6026, Al-Mansour, Baghdad, Iraq; tel. (1) 537-2371; fax (1) 537-2369; f. 1975 to facilitate contacts between Arab lawyers, to safeguard the Arab legislative and judicial heritage, to encourage the study of Islamic jurisprudence; and to defend human rights; mems: national jurists asscns in 15 countries; Sec.-Gen. SHIBIB LAZIM AL-MALIKI; publ. *Al-Hukuki al-Arabi* (Arab Jurist).

World Jurist Association (WJA): 7910 Woodmont Ave, Suite 1440, Bethesda, Maryland 20814, USA; tel. (202) 466-5428; fax (202) 452-8540; e-mail wja@worldjurist.org; internet www.worldjurist.org; f. 1963; promotes the continued development of international law and the legal maintenance of world order; holds biennial world conferences, World Law Day and demonstration trials; organizes research programmes; mems: lawyers, jurists and legal scholars in 155 countries; Pres. RONALD M. GREENBERG; Exec. Vice-Pres. MARGARETHA M. HENNEBERRY (USA); publs *The World Jurist* (6 a year), Research Reports, *Law and Judicial Systems of Nations*, 4th revised edn (directory), *World Legal Directory*, *Law/Technology* (quarterly), *World Law Review* Vols I–V (World Conference Proceedings), *The Chief Justices and Judges of the Supreme Courts of Nations* (directory), work papers, newsletters and journals.

World Association of Judges (WJA): 7910 Woodmont Ave, Suite 1440, Bethesda, Maryland 20814, USA; tel. (202) 466-5428; fax (202) 452-8540; e-mail wja@worldjurist.org; f. 1966 to advance the administration of judicial justice through co-operation and communication among ranking jurists of all countries; Pres. Prince BOLA AJIBOLA (Nigeria).

World Association of Law Professors (WALP): 7910 Woodmont Ave, Suite 1440, Bethesda, Maryland 20814, USA; tel. (202) 466-5428; fax (202) 452-8540; e-mail wja@worldjurist.org; internet www.worldjurist.org; f. 1975 to improve scholarship and education in matters related to international law; Pres. HILARIO G. DAVIDE, Jr (Philippines).

World Association of Lawyers (WAL): 7910 Woodmont Ave, Suite 1440, Bethesda, Maryland 20814, USA; tel. (202) 466-5428; fax (202) 452-8540; e-mail wja@worldjurist.org; internet www.worldjurist.org; f. 1975 to develop international law and improve lawyers' effectiveness in this field; Pres. ALEXANDER BELOHLAVEK (Czech Republic).

Medicine and Health

Aerospace Medical Association (AsMA): 320 S. Henry St, Alexandria, VA 22314-3579, USA; tel. (703) 739-2240; fax (703) 739-9652; e-mail info@asma.org; internet www.asma.org; f. 1929 as Aero Medical Association; aims to advance the science and art of aviation and space medicine; establishes and maintains co-operation between medical and allied sciences concerned with aerospace medicine; works to promote, protect, and maintain safety in aviation and astronautics; mems: individual, constituent and corporate in 75 countries; Pres. Dr RICHARD T. JENNINGS; Exec. Dir RUSSELL B. RAYMAN (USA); publ. *Aviation Space and Environmental Medicine* (monthly).

Asia-Pacific Academy of Ophthalmology (APAO): c/o Dept of Ophthalmology and Visual Sciences, Chinese University of Hong Kong, 3/F 147 K Argyle St, Kowloon, Hong Kong; tel. 27623171; fax 27159490; e-mail secretariat@apaophth.org; internet www.apaophth.org; f. 1956; holds Congress annually since 2006 (previously every two years); mems: 17 mem. orgs; Pres. YASUO TANO; Sec.-Gen. DENNIS LAM.

Asia Pacific Dental Federation (APDF): c/o Dr J. Annan, 16 The Terrace, Wellington, New Zealand; tel. (4) 472-5516; fax (4) 476-088; e-mail jannan@apdf.info; internet www.apdf.info; f. 1955 to establish closer relationships among dental asscns in Asian and Pacific countries and to encourage research on dental health in the region; holds congress every year; mems: 27 national dental asscns; Pres. Dr JEFFREY Y. S. TSANG; Sec.-Gen. Dr JEFF ANNAN.

Association for Paediatric Education in Europe (APEE) (Association pour l'Enseignement de la Pédatrie en Europe): c/o Dr Claude Billeaud, Dept Néonatal Médicine, Maternité-CHU Pellegrin, 33076 Bordeaux Cédex, France; tel. 5-56-79-55-39; fax 5-56-79-61-56; e-mail claude.billeaud@neonata.u-bordeaux2.fr; internet www.atinternet.com/apee; f. 1970 to promote research and practice in educational methodology in paediatrics; mems: 120 in 20 European countries; Pres. Dr JUAN BRINES (Spain); Sec.-Gen. Dr CLAUDE BILLEAUD (France).

Association of National European and Mediterranean Societies of Gastroenterology (ASNEMGE): Hollandstr. 14/Mezzanine, 1020 Vienna, Austria; tel. (1) 219-91-80; fax (1) 219-91-80-29; e-mail info@asnemge.org; internet www.asnemge.org; f. 1947 to facilitate the exchange of ideas between gastroenterologists and to disseminate knowledge; organizes International Congress of Gastroenterology every four years; mems: in 43 countries, national societies and sections of national medical societies; Pres. Prof. C. J. HAWKEY (United Kingdom); Gen. Sec. Prof. ROLF HULTCRANTZ (Sweden).

Balkan Medical Union (Uniunii Medicale Balcanice—UMB): POB 149, 1 rue G. Clémenceau, 70148 Bucharest, Romania; tel. (1) 3137857; fax (1) 3121570; f. 1932; studies medical problems, particularly ailments specific to the Balkan region; promotes a regional programme of public health; facilitates the exchange of information between doctors in the region; organizes research programmes and congresses; mems: doctors and specialists from Albania, Bulgaria, Cyprus, Greece, Moldova, Romania, Turkey and the countries of the former Yugoslavia; Pres. Prof. H. CIOBANU (Moldova); publs *Archives de l'union médicale Balkanique* (quarterly), *Bulletin de l'union médicale Balkanique* (6 a year), *Annuaire*.

Council for International Organizations of Medical Sciences (CIOMS): c/o WHO, ave Appia, 1211 Geneva 27, Switzerland; tel. 227913467; fax 227914286; e-mail cioms@who.int; internet www.cioms.ch; f. 1949 to serve the scientific interests of the international biomedical community; aims to facilitate and promote activities in biomedical sciences; runs long-term programmes on bioethics, health policy, ethics and values, drug development and use, and the international nomenclature of diseases; maintains collaborative relations with the UN; holds a general assembly every three years; mems: 66 organizations; Pres. Prof. MICHEL B. VALLOTTON; Sec.-Gen. Prof. J. E. IDÄNPÄÄN-HEIKKILÄ; publs *Reports on Drug Development and Use*, *Proceedings of CIOMS Conferences*, *International Nomenclature of Diseases*, *International Ethical Guide-lines for Biomedical Research Involving Human Subjects*.

Cystic Fibrosis Worldwide: POB 677, 5600 AR Eindhoven, Netherlands; tel. (40) 2592760; fax (40) 2592701; e-mail info@cfww.org; internet www.cfww.org; f. 2003 by merger of the International Association of Cystic Fibrosis Adults and International Cystic Fibrosis (Muscoviscidosis) Association (f. 1964); promotes the development of lay organizations and the advancement of knowledge among medical, scientific and health professionals in underdeveloped areas; convenes annual conference; Pres. MITCH MESSER (Australia); Exec. Dir CHRISTINE NOKE (USA); publs *Annual Report*, *CFW Newsletter* (quarterly), *Joseph Levy Lecture*, booklet on physiotherapy.

European Association for Cancer Research (EACR): c/o The School of Pharmacy, Univ. of Nottingham, University Park, Nottingham, NG7 2RD, United Kingdom; tel. (115) 9515114; fax (115) 9515115; e-mail eacr@nottingham.ac.uk; internet www.eacr.org; f. 1968 to facilitate contact between cancer research workers and to organize scientific meetings in Europe; operates a number of fellowship and award programmes; mems: more than 6,000 in 76 countries world-wide, incl. six national societies in France, Germany, Hungary, Italy, Spain and the United Kingdom; Pres. MARCO A. PIEROTTI; Sec.-Gen. RICHARD MARAIS (United Kingdom).

European Association for the Study of Diabetes (EASD): Rheindorfer Weg 3, 40591 Düsseldorf, Germany Germany; tel. and fax (211) 75-84-69; e-mail secretariat@easd.org; internet www.easd.org; f. 1965 to support research in the field of diabetes, to promote the rapid diffusion of acquired knowledge and its application; holds annual scientific meetings within Europe; mems: 6,000 in 101 European and other countries; Pres. E. FERRANNINI (Italy); Exec. Dir Dr VIKTOR JÖRGENS (Germany); publ. *Diabetologia* (13 a year).

European Association of Social Medicine: Corso Bramante 83, 10126 Turin, Italy; f. 1953 to provide co-operation between national asscns of preventive medicine and public health; mems: asscns in 14 countries; Pres. Dr JEAN-PAUL FOURNIER (France); Sec.-Gen. Prof. Dr ENRICO BELLI (Italy).

European Brain and Behaviour Society (EBSS): c/o University of St Andrews School of Psychology, Fife, KY16 9JU, United Kingdom; tel. (1334) 462050; fax (1334) 463042; e-mail vjb@st-and.ac.uk; internet www.ebbs-science.org; f. 1969; holds an annual conference and organizes workshops; Pres. GIORGIO INNOCENTI; Sec.-Gen. VERITY BROWN (United Kingdom); publ. *Newsletter* (annually).

European Federation of Internal Medicine (EFIM): c/o Dr J. W. F. Elte, Dept of Internal Medicine, St Franciscus Gasthuis, 3004 BA Rotterdam, Netherlands; tel. (10) 4616094; fax (10) 4612692; e-mail j.elte@sfg.nl; internet www.efim.org; f. 1969 as European Asscn of Internal Medicine (present name adopted 1996); aims to bring together European specialists, and establish communication between them, to promote internal medicine; organizes congresses and meetings; provides information; mems: 32 European societies of internal medicine; Pres. Prof. STEFAN LINDGREN (Sweden); Sec. Dr JAN WILLEM ELTE; publ. *European Journal of Internal Medicine* (8 a year).

European Health Management Association (EHMA): 4 rue de la Science, 1000 Brussels, Belgium; tel. (2) 502-65-25; e-mail info@ehma.org; internet www.ehma.org; f. 1966; aims to improve health care in Europe by raising standards of managerial performance in the health sector; fosters co-operation between managers, academia, policy makers and educators to understand health management in different European contexts and to influence both service delivery and the policy agenda in Europe; mems: 225 institutions in 30 countries; Pres. Dr NAOMI CHAMBERS; Dir JENNIFER BREMNER; publs *Newsletter*, *Eurobriefing* (quarterly).

European League against Rheumatism (EULAR): Seestrasse 240, 8802 Kilchberg-Zurich, Switzerland; tel. 447163030; fax 447163039; e-mail secretariat@eular.org; internet www.eular.org; f. 1947 to co-ordinate research and treatment of rheumatic complaints; holds an annual Congress in Rheumatology; mems: in 41 countries; Exec. Dir F. WYSS; publ. *Annals of the Rheumatic Diseases*.

European Organization for Caries Research (ORCA): c/o Lutz Stösser, Dept of Oral Microbiology, Academic Centre for Dentistry Amsterdam (ACTA), vd Boechorststr 7, 1081 BT Amsterdam, Netherlands; tel. (361) 7411205; e-mail stoesser@zmkh.ef.uni-jena.de; internet www.orca-caries-research.org; f. 1953 to promote and undertake research on dental health, encourage international contacts, and make the public aware of the importance of care of the teeth; mems: research workers in 23 countries; Pres. Prof. ADRIAN S. LUSSI (Italy); Sec.-Gen. Dr J. J. DE SOET (Netherlands); publ. *Caries Research*.

European Orthodontic Society (EOS): Flat 20, 49 Hallam St, London, W1W 6JN, United Kingdom; tel. (20) 7935-2795; fax (20) 7323-0410; e-mail eoslondon@compuserve.com; internet www.eoseurope.org; f. 1907 (name changed in 1935), to advance the science of orthodontics and its relations with the collateral arts and sciences; mems: 2,725 in 85 countries; Pres. Prof. HANS-PETER BANTLEON; publ. *European Journal of Orthodontics* (6 a year).

European Society of Radiology: c/o ESR Office, Neutorgasse 9/2A, Vienna, Austria; e-mail communications@myesr.org; internet www.myesr.org; f. 2005 by merger of European Society of Radiology (f. 1962) and European Congress of Radiology; aims to harmonize and improve training programmes throughout Europe and develop a new research institute; organizes an Annual Congress; mems: some 29,300 individual mems; Pres. Prof. ANDREAS ADAM (United Kingdom).

European Union of Medical Specialists (Union Européenne des Médecins Spécialistes—UEMS): 20 ave de la Couronne, Kroonlaan, Brussels 1050, Belgium; tel. (2) 649-51-64; fax (2) 640-37-30; e-mail uems@skynet.be; internet www.uems.net; f. 1958 to harmonize and improve the quality of medical specialist practices in the EU and safeguard the interests of medical specialists; seeks formulation of common training policy; mems: 27 full mems: seven assoc. mems; Pres. Dr ZLATKO FRAS (Slovenia); Sec.-Gen. Dr BERNARD MAILLET (Belgium).

Eurotransplant International Foundation: POB 2304, 2301 CH Leiden, Netherlands; tel. (71) 5795795; fax (71) 5790057; e-mail mfranzen@eurotransplant.nl; internet www.eurotransplant.nl; f. 1967; co-ordinates the exchange of organs for transplants in Austria, Belgium, Croatia, Germany, Luxembourg, Netherlands and Slovenia; keeps register of c. 15,000 patients with all necessary information for matching with suitable donors in the shortest possible time; organizes transport of the organ and transplantation; collaborates with similar organizations in western and eastern Europe; Dirs A. OOSTERLEE, Dr A. RAMMEL, W. G. VAN ZWET.

FDI World Dental Federation: L'Avant Centre, 13 chemin du Levant, 01210 Ferney Voltaire, France; tel. and fax 4-50-40-55-55; e-mail info@fdiworldental.org; internet www.fdiworldental.org; f. 1900; mems: 163 national dental asscns and 36 affiliates; Pres. Dr MICHÈLE AERDEN (Belgium); Exec. Dir Dr J. T. BARNARD (South Africa); publ. *International Dental Journal* (every 2 months).

Federation of French-Language Obstetricians and Gynaecologists (Fedération des gynécologues et obstetriciens de langue française—FGOLF): Clinique Baudelocque, 123 blvd de Port-Royal, 75674 Paris Cédex 14, France; tel. 1-42-34-11-43; fax 1-42-34-12-31; f. 1920 for the scientific study of phenomena having reference to obstetrics, gynaecology and reproduction in general; mems: 1,500 in 50 countries; Pres. Prof. H. RUF (France); Gen. Sec. Prof. J. R. ZORN (France); publ. *Journal de Gynécologie Obstétrique et Biologie de la Reproduction* (8 a year).

Federation of the European Dental Industry (Fédération de l'Industrie Dentaire en Europe—FIDE): Aachener Str. 1053–1055, 50858 Cologne, Germany; tel. (221) 50068712; fax (221) 50068721; e-mail shelton@fide-online.org; internet www.fide-online.org; f. 1957 to promote the interests of dental industry manufacturers; mems: national asscns in 13 European countries; Pres. and Chair. Dr JUERGEN EBERLEIN (Germany); Sec. Dr MARKUS HEIBACH (Germany).

General Association of Municipal Health and Technical Experts: 83 ave Foch, BP 3916, 75761 Paris Cédex 16, France; tel. 1-53-70-13-53; fax 1-53-70-13-40; e-mail aghtm@aghtm.org; internet www.aghtm.org; f. 1905 to study all questions related to urban and rural health; mems: in 35 countries; Dir-Gen. ALAIN LASALMONIE (France); publ. *TSM-Techniques, Sciences, Méthodes* (monthly).

ICDDR, B: Centre for Health and Population Research: GPO Box 128, Dhaka 1212, Bangladesh; tel. (2) 8860523; fax (2) 8823116; e-mail info@icddrb.org; internet www.icddrb.org; f. 1960 as Pakistan-SEATO Cholera Research Laboratory, international health research institute (International Centre for Diarrhoeal Disease Research, Bangladesh—ICDDR, B since 1978); undertakes research, training and information dissemination on diarrhoeal diseases, child health, nutrition, emerging infectious diseases, environmental health, sexually transmitted diseases, HIV/AIDS, poverty and health, vaccine evaluation and case management, with particular reference to developing countries; supported by 55 governments and international orgs; Exec. Dir Prof. DAVID A. SACK; publs *Annual Report, Journal of Health, Population and Nutrition* (quarterly), *Glimpse* (quarterly), *Shasthya Sanglap* (3 a year), *Health and Science Bulletin* (quarterly), *SUZY* (newsletter, 2 a year), scientific reports, working papers, monographs, special publications.

Inter-American Association of Sanitary and Environmental Engineering (Asociación Interamericana de Ingeniería Sanitaria y Ambiental—AIDIS): Rua Nicolau Gagliardi 354, 05429-010 São Paulo, SP, Brazil; tel. (11) 3812-4080; fax (11) 3814-2441; e-mail aidis@aidis.org.br; internet www.aidis.org.br; f. 1948 to assist in the development of water supply and sanitation; mems: 32 countries; Pres. ALEX CHECHILNITZKY (Chile); Exec. Dir LUIZ AUGUSTO DE LIMA PONTES (Brazil); publs *Revista Ingeniería Sanitaria* (quarterly), *Desafío* (quarterly).

International Academy of Aviation and Space Medicine (IAASM): c/o Dr C. Thibeault, 502-8500 pl. St Charles, Brossard, QC J4X2Z8, Canada; tel. (450) 923-6826; fax (450) 923-1236; e-mail ctebo@videotron.ca; internet www.iaasm.org; f. 1955 to facilitate international co-operation in research and teaching in the fields of aviation and space medicine; mems: in 45 countries; Pres. Dr FRANK PETTYJOHN (USA); Sec.-Gen. Dr CLAUDE THIBEAULT (Canada).

International Academy of Cytology: Burgunderstr. 1, 79104 Freiburg, Germany; tel. (761) 292-3801; fax (761) 292-3802; e-mail centraloffice@cytology-iac.org; internet www.cytology-iac.org; f. 1957 to facilitate the international exchange of information on specialized problems of clinical cytology, to stimulate research and to standardize terminology; mems: 2,400; Pres. (2007–10) Prof. ALAIN P. VERHEST (Belgium); Sec. Gen. VOLKER SCHNEIDER; publs *Acta Cytologica, Analytical and Quantitative Cytology and Histology* (both every 2 months).

International Agency for the Prevention of Blindness (IAPB): L. V. Prasad Eye Institute, L. V. Prasad Marg, Banjara Hills, Hyderabad 500 034, India; tel. (40) 2354-5389; fax (40) 2354-8271; e-mail iapb@lvpei.org; internet www.iapb.org; f. 1975; promotes advocacy and information sharing on the prevention of blindness; aims to encourage the formation of national prevention of blindness committees and programmes; has an official relationship with WHO; Pres. Dr GULLAPALLI N. RAO (India); Sec.-Gen. Dr LOUIS PIZZARELLO (USA); publ. *IAPB News*.

International Anatomical Congress: c/o Prof. Dr Wolfgang Kühnel, Institut für Anatomie, Medizinische Universität zu Lübeck, Ratzeburger Allee 160, 23538 Lübeck, Germany; tel. (451) 500-4030; fax (451) 500-4034; e-mail buchuel@anet.mu-luebeck.de; f. 1903; runs international congresses for anatomists to discuss research, teaching methods and terminology in the fields of gross and microscopical anatomy, histology, cytology, etc.; Pres. J. ESPERENCA-PINE (Portugal); Sec.-Gen. Prof. Dr WOLFGANG KÜHNEL (Germany); publ. *Annals of Anatomy*.

International Association for Child and Adolescent Psychiatry and Allied Professions (IACAPAP): c/o Dr P.-A. Rydelius, Astrid Lindgren Children's Hospital, 171 76 Stockholm, Sweden; tel. (8) 5177-72-05; fax (8) 5177-72-14; e-mail per-anders.rydelius@ki.se; internet www.iacapap.org; f. 1937; aims to promote the study, treatment, care and prevention of mental and emotional disorders and disabilities of children, adolescents and their families. The emphasis is on practice and research through collaboration between child psychiatrists and the allied professions of psychology, social work, pediatrics, public health, nursing, education, social sciences and other relevant fields; IACAPAP developed the guidelines and principles of Ethics in Child and Adolescent Mental Health; IACAPAP also develops and adopts other Declarations, Statements and Position Papers of help to mental health professionals in their work, for example the Melbourne Declaration 2006 'Nurturing Diversity', the IACAPAP Ethics 2006 and the Position Paper on a Rights-Based and Evidence-Based Approach to the Care of Persons with ASD adopted in Oslo, Norway, in Sept. 2007; mems: national asscns and individuals in 45 countries; Pres. Dr PER-ANDERS RYDELIUS; Sec.-Gen. Dr LUIS A. ROHDE; publs *The Child in the Family* (Yearbook of the IACAPAP), *Newsletter (IACAPAP Bulletin)*, Monographs.

International Association for Dental Research (IADR): 1619 Duke St, Alexandria, VA 22314-3406, USA; tel. (703) 548-0066; fax (703) 548-1883; e-mail research@iadr.com; internet www.dentalresearch.org; f. 1920 to encourage research in dentistry and related fields; holds annual meetings, triennial conferences and divisional meetings; Pres. Dr TAKAYUKI KURODA; Exec. Dir Dr CHRISTOPHER H. FOX.

International Association for Group Psychotherapy and Group Processes (IAGP): IAGP, POB 745, Bukit Merah Central Post Office, Singapore 911539, Singapore; tel. 67373663; fax 67387466; e-mail office@iagp.com; internet www.iagp.com; f. 1973; holds a congress every three years and regional congresses at more frequent intervals; mems: in 49 countries; Pres. FRANCES BONDS-WHITE (USA); Sec. KATE BRADSHAW TAUVON (Sweden); publs *The Forum, Globeletter* (2 a year).

International Association for the Study of Obesity (IASO): 231 North Gower St, London, NW1 2NR, United Kingdom; e-mail enquiries@iaso.org; internet www.iaso.org; f. 1986; supports research into the prevention and management of obesity throughout the world and disseminates inormation regarding disease and accompanying health and social issues; incorporates the International Obesity Task Force; international congress every four years (2006: Sydney, Australia); Exec. Dir CAROLINE SMALL.

International Association of Agricultural Medicine and Rural Health (IAAMRH): OALI (NIPCH), Budapest 1135, Szabolcs u. 33-35, Hungary; tel. and fax (1) 450-1768; fax (1) 439-0473; e-mail ipszilard@t-email.hu; internet www.iaamrh.org; f. 1961 to study the problems of medicine in agriculture in all countries and to prevent the diseases caused by the conditions of work in agriculture; mems: 405; Pres. Dr ASHOK PATIL (India); Gen. Sec. Dr ISTVAN SZILARD (Hungary).

International Association of Applied Psychology (IAAP): c/o Prof. José M. Prieto, Colegio Oficial de Psicólogos, Cuesta de San Vicente 4–5, 28008 Spain; tel. (91) 394-3236; fax (91) 351-0091; e-mail iaap@psi.ucm.es; internet www.iaapsy.org; f. 1920, present title adopted in 1955; aims to establish contacts between those carrying out scientific work on applied psychology, to promote research and to encourage the adoption of measures contributing to this work; organizes International Congress of Applied Psychology every four years (2006: Athens, Greece) and co-sponsors International Congress of Psychology every two years (2008: Berlin, Germany); mems: 2,200 in 94 countries; Pres. Prof. MIKE KNOWLES (Australia); Sec.-Gen. Prof. JOSÉ M. PRIETO (Spain); publ. *Applied Psychology: An International Review* (quarterly).

INTERNATIONAL ORGANIZATIONS — Medicine and Health

International Association of Asthmology (INTERASMA): c/o Prof. Hugo Neffen, Irigoyen Freyre 2670, 3000 Santa Fé, Argentina; tel. (42) 453-7638; fax (42) 456-9773; internet www.interasma.org; f. 1954 to advance medical knowledge of bronchial asthma and allied disorders; mems: 1,100 in 54 countries; Pres. Prof. HUGO NEFFEN (Argentina); Sec./Treas. Prof. IGNACIO J. ANSOTEGUI (Spain); publs *Interasma News, Journal of Investigative Allergology and Clinical Immunology* (every 2 months), *Allergy and Clinical Immunology International* (every 2 months).

International Association of Bioethics: POB 280, University of the Philippines, Diliman, Quezon City 1101, Philippines; tel. (2) 436-8873; fax (2) 426-9590; e-mail bioethics-international@kssp.upd.edu.ph; internet www.bioethics-international.org; f. 1992; aims to facilitate contact and to promote exchange of information among people working in the bioethics field; aims to promote the development of research and training in bioethics; organizes international conferences (8th World Congress of Bioethics: Aug. 2006, Beijing, People's Republic of China); mems: over 1,000 individuals and institutions in more than 40 countries; Pres. Prof. MATTI HAYRI (United Kingdom); Sec. Prof. DEBORA DINIZ (Brazil); publ. *Bioethics Journal*.

International Association of Gerontology and Geriatrics (IAGG): Rua Hilário de Gouveia 66, 1102 Copacabana, 22040-020 Rio de Janeiro, RJ, Brazil; tel. and fax (21) 2235-1510; e-mail iagg@iagg.com.br; internet www.iagg.com.br; f. 1950 as the International Association of Gerontological Societies to promote research and training in all fields of gerontology and to protect the interests of gerontologic societies and institutions; assumed current name in 2005, with the aim of promoting and developing Geriatrics as a medical specialism; holds World Congress every four years; mems: 46,000 in over 60 countries; Pres. Dr RENATO MAIA GUIMARÃES (Brazil); Sec.-Gen. CLAUDIA BURLÁ (Brazil); publ. *IAGG Newsletter* (annually).

International Association of Hydatidology: Florida 460, 3°, 1005 Buenos Aires, Argentina; tel. (11) 4322-2030; fax (11) 4325-8231; f. 1941; mems: 1,200 in 41 countries; Pres. Dr RAÚL MARTÍN MENDY; Sec.-Gen. Dr JORGE ALFREDO IRIARTE (Argentina); publs *Archivos Internacionales de la Hidatidosis* (every 2 years), *Boletín de Hidatidosis* (quarterly).

International Association of Logopedics and Phoniatrics (IALP): Tilweg 1, 9971 Ulrum, Netherlands; e-mail mbehlau@uol.com.br; internet www.ialp.info; f. 1924 to promote standards of training and research in human communication disorders, to establish information centres and communicate with kindred organizations; 29th International Congress on Logopedics and Phoniatrics to be held in Athens, Greece, in Aug. 2008; mems: 125,000 in 56 societies from 30 countries; Pres. Dr MARA BEHLAU (Brazil); Sec. Dr HELEN GRECH (Malta); publ. *Folia Phoniatrica et Logopedica* (6 a year).

International Association of Medicine and Biology of the Environment (IAMBE): c/o 115 rue de la Pompe, 75116 Paris, France; tel. 1-45-53-45-04; fax 1-45-53-41-75; e-mail aimbe.world@free.fr; f. 1971 with assistance from the UN Environment Programme; aims to contribute to the solution of problems caused by human influence on the environment; structure includes 13 technical commissions; mems: individuals and orgs in 79 countries; Hon. Pres. Prof. R. DUBOS; Pres. Dr R. ABBOU.

International Association of Oral and Maxillofacial Surgeons (IAOMS): 17 W 220, 22nd St, Suite 420, Oakbrook Terrace, IL 60181, USA; tel. (630) 833-0945; fax (630) 833-1382; e-mail info@iaoms.org; internet www.iaoms.org; f. 1963 to advance the science and art of oral and maxillofacial surgery; organizes biennial international conference; mems: over 3,000; Pres. Dr JOHN WILLIAMS (United Kingdom); Exec. Dir Dr JOHN F. HELFRICK (USA); publs *International Journal of Oral and Maxillofacial Surgery* (2 a year), *Newsletter*.

International Brain Research Organization (IBRO): 255 rue St Honoré, 75001 Paris, France; tel. 1-46-47-92-92; fax 1-45-20-60-06; e-mail admin@ibro.info; internet www.ibro.org; f. 1960 to further all aspects of brain research; mems: 45 corporate, 16 academic and 51,000 individual; Pres. Prof. A. J. AGUAYO (Canada); Sec.-Gen. Prof. J. S. LUND (USA); publs *IBRO News, Neuroscience* (bi-monthly).

International Bronchoesophagological Society: Mayo Clinic Arizona, 13400 E. Shea Blvd, Scottsdale, AZ 85259, USA; e-mail helmers.richard@mayo.edu; f. 1951 to promote the progress of bronchoesophagology and to provide a forum for discussion among bronchoesophagologists with various medical and surgical specialities; holds Congress every two years; mems: 600 in 37 countries; Exec. Sec./Treas. Dr RICHARD A. HELMERS.

International Bureau for Epilepsy (IBE): 11 Priory Hall, Stillorgan, Dublin 18, Ireland; tel. (1) 2108850; fax (1) 2108450; e-mail ibedublin@eircom.net; internet www.ibe-epilepsy.org; f. 1961; collects and disseminates information about social and medical care for people with epilepsy; organizes international and regional meetings; advises and answers questions on social aspects of epilepsy; has special consultative status with ECOSOC; mems: 118 national epilepsy orgs; Pres. SUSANNE LUND; Exec. Dir ANN LITTLE; publ. *International Epilepsy News* (quarterly).

International Catholic Committee of Nurses and Medico-Social Assistants (Comité International Catholique des Infirmières et Assistantes Médico-Sociales—CICIAMS): Sr. Mary's Bloomfield Ave, Donnybrook, Dublin 4 Ireland; tel. (1) 668-9150; e-mail ciciams@eircom.net; internet www.ciciams.org; f. 1933 to group professional Catholic nursing asscns; to represent Christian thought in the general professional field at international level; to co-operate in the general development of the profession and to promote social welfare; mems: 49 full, 20 corresponding mems; Pres. MARYLEE MEEHAN; Gen. Sec. GERALDINE MCSWEENEY; publ. *Nouvelles/News/Nachrichten* (3 a year).

International Cell Research Organization (ICRO) (Organisation Internationale de Recherche sur la Cellule): c/o UNESCO, SC/BES/LSC, 1 rue Miollis, 75732 Paris, France; fax 1-45-68-58-16; e-mail icro@unesco.org; internet www.unesco.org/icro; f. 1962 to create, encourage and promote co-operation between scientists of different disciplines throughout the world for the advancement of fundamental knowledge of the cell, normal and abnormal; organizes international laboratory courses on modern topics of cell and molecular biology and biotechnology for young research scientists; mems: 400; Pres. Prof. QI-SHUI LIN (People's Republic of China); Exec. Sec. Prof. GEORGES N. COHEN (France).

International Chiropractors' Association: 1110 North Glebe Rd, Suite 650, Arlington, VA 22201, USA; tel. (703) 528-5000; fax (703) 528-5023; e-mail chiro@chiropractic.org; internet www.chiropractic.org; f. 1926 to promote advancement of the art and science of chiropractors; mems: 7,000 individuals, and affiliated asscns; Pres. Dr JOHN MALTBY; Exec. Dir RONALD M. HENDRICKSON; publs *International Review of Chiropractic* (every 2 months), *ICA Today* (every 2 months).

International College of Surgeons (ICS): 1516 N. Lake Shore Drive, Chicago, IL 60610, USA; tel. (312) 642-3555; fax (312) 787-1624; e-mail info@icsglobal.org; internet www.icsglobal.org; f. 1935, as a world-wide federation of surgeons and surgical specialists for the advancement of the art and science of surgery; aims to create a common bond among the surgeons of all nations and promote the highest standards of surgery, without regard to nationality, creed, or colour; sends teams of surgeons to developing countries to teach local surgeons; provides research and scholarship grants, organizes surgical congresses around the world; manages the International Museum of Surgical Science in Chicago; mems: c. 6,000 in 112 countries; Pres. FIDEL RUIZ-HEALY (Mexico); Exec. Dir MAX C. DOWNHAM (USA); publ. *International Surgery* (every 2 months).

International Commission on Occupational Health (ICOH): c/o National Institute for Occupational Safety and Prevention, Via Fontana Candida 1, 1-00040 Monteporzio Catone (Rome), Italy; e-mail icoh@iol.it; internet www.icohweb.org; f. 1906, present name adopted 1985; aims to study and prevent pathological conditions arising from industrial work; arranges congresses on occupational medicine and the protection of workers' health; provides information for public authorities and learned societies; mems: 1,800 in 94 countries; Pres. Prof. JORMA RANTANEN (Finland); Sec.-Gen. Dr SERGIO IAVICOLI (Italy); publ. *Newsletter* (electronic version).

International Commission on Radiological Protection (ICRP): 17116 Stockholm, Sweden; tel. (8) 729-72-75; fax (8) 729-72-98; e-mail jack.valentin@ssi.se; internet www.icrp.org; f. 1928 to provide technical guidance and promote international co-operation in the field of radiation protection; committees on Radiation Effects, Doses from Radiation Exposure, Protection in Medicine, Application of Recommendations, and Radiological Protection of the Environment; mems: c. 85; Chair. Dr LARS-ERIK HOLM (Sweden); Scientific Sec. Dr J. VALENTIN (Sweden); publ. *Annals of the ICRP*.

International Committee of Military Medicine (ICMM) (Comité international de médecine militaire—CIMM): Hôpital Militaire Reine Astrid, rue Bruyn, 1120 Brussels, Belgium; tel. (2) 264-43-48; fax (2) 264-43-67; e-mail info@cimm-icmm.org; internet www.cimm-icmm.org; f. 1921 as Permanent Committee of the International Congresses of Military Medicine and Pharmacy; name changed 1990; aims to increase co-operation and promote activities in the field of military medicine; considers issues relating to mass medicine, dentistry, military pharmacy, veterinary sciences and the administration and organization of medical care missions, among others; mems: official delegates from 100 countries; Chair. Col-Gen. IGOR BYKOV (Russia); Sec.-Gen. Col Dr JACQUES SANABRIA (Belgium); publ. *Revue Internationale des Services de Santé des Forces Armées* (quarterly).

International Council for Laboratory Animal Science (ICLAS): Fundació UAB, Edifici Blanc, Campus de la UAB, 08193 Bellaterra, Spain; e-mail administration@iclas.org; internet www.iclas.org; f. 1956; promotes the ethical care and use of laboratory animals in research, with the aim of advancing human and animal health; establishes standards and provides support resources; encourages international collaboration to develop knowledge; Pres. Dr GILLES DEMERS (Canada); Sec.-Gen. Dr CECILIAI CARBONE (Argentina).

International Council for Physical Activity and Fitness Research (ICPAFR): c/o Prof. F. G. Viviani, Faculty of Psychology, Univ. of Padua, via Venezia 8, 35131 Padua, Italy; tel. (049) 827-6632; fax (049) 827-6600; e-mail franco.viviani@unipd.it; internet www.medicina.unipd.it/Servizi/ICPAFR/ICPAFR.htm; f. 1964 to construct international standardized physical fitness tests, to encourage research based upon the standardized tests and to enhance participation in physical activity; organizes biennial symposiums on topics related to physical activity and fitness; mems: some 35 countries; Pres. Prof. FRANCO G. VIVIANI (Italy); Sec./Treas. ALISON MACMANUS; publs *International Guide to Fitness and Health*, proceedings of seminars and symposia, other fitness and health publs.

International Council of Nurses (ICN): 3 place Jean-Marteau, 1201 Geneva, Switzerland; tel. 229080100; fax 229080101; e-mail icn@icn.ch; internet www.icn.ch; f. 1899 to allow national asscns of nurses to work together to develop the contribution of nursing to the promotion of health; holds quadrennial Congresses; mems: 129 national nurses' asscns; Pres. HIROKO MINAMI (Japan); Exec. Dir JUDITH OULTON; publ. *The International Nursing Review* (quarterly).

International Diabetes Federation (IDF): 19 ave Emile de Mot, 1000 Brussels, Belgium; tel. (2) 538-55-11; fax (2) 538-51-14; e-mail info@idf.org; internet www.idf.org; f. 1949 to help in the collection and dissemination of information on diabetes and to improve the welfare of people suffering from diabetes; mems: 200 asscns in 158 countries; Exec. Dir LUC HENDRICKX; publs *Diabetes Voice*, *Bulletin of the IDF* (quarterly).

International Epidemiological Association (IEA): 38 Ismailah St, Apt 201, Mostafa Kamal, Alexandria, Egypt; tel. and fax (3) 5467576; e-mail IEAsecretariat@link.net; internet www.IEAweb.org; f. 1954; mems: 1,500; promotes epidemiology and organizes international scientific meetings and region-specific meetings; Pres. Prof. JORN OLSEN (USA); Sec. Prof. AHMED MANDIL (Egypt); publ. *International Journal of Epidemiology* (6 a year).

International Federation for Medical and Biological Engineering (IFMBE): 10000 Zagreb, Unska 3, Faculty of Electrical Engineering and Computing, Univ. of Zagreb, Croatia; tel. (1) 6129938; fax (1) 6129652; e-mail office@ifmbe.org; internet www.ifmbe.org; f. 1959; mems: 58 societies; Pres. Prof. MAKOTO KIKUCHI; Sec.-Gen. RATKO MAGJAREVIC (Croatia).

International Federation for Medical Psychotherapy (IFMP): c/o Prof. E. Heim, Tannackstr. 3, 3653 Oberhofen, Switzerland; tel. and fax 332431141; e-mail senf-blum@t-online.de; f. 1946 to further research and teaching of psychotherapy; organizes international congresses; mems: c. 6,000 psychotherapists from around 40 countries, 36 societies; Pres. Dr EDGAR HEIM (Switzerland); Sec.-Gen. Prof. Dr WOLFGANG SENE (Germany).

International Federation of Clinical Chemistry and Laboratory Medicine (IFCC): via Carlo Farini 81, 20159 Milan, Italy; tel. (02) 6680-9912; fax (02) 6078-1846; e-mail ifcc@ifcc.org; internet www.ifcc.org; f. 1952; mems: 78 national societies (about 33,000 individuals) and 33 corporate mems; Pres. Prof. JOCELYN M. B. HICKS (USA); Sec. Dr PÄIVI LAITINEN (Finland); publs *Journal* (electronic version), *Annual Report*.

International Federation of Clinical Neurophysiology: c/o Concorde Administration Ltd, 42 Canham Rd, London, W3 7SR, United Kingdom; tel. (20) 8743-3106; fax (20) 8743-1010; e-mail ifcn@ifcn.info; internet www.ifcn.info; f. 1949 to attain the highest level of knowledge in the field of electro-encephalography and clinical neurophysiology in all the countries of the world; mems in 58 countries; Pres. Prof. FRANÇOIS MAUGUIÈRE (France); Sec. Prof. G. F. A. HARDING (United Kingdom); publs *Clinical Neurophysiology* (monthly), *Evoked Potentials* (every 2 months), *EMG and Motor Control* (every 2 months).

International Federation of Fertility Societies (IFFS): 19 Mantua Rd, Mount Royal, NJ 08061, USA; tel. (856) 0423-7222; fax (856) 423-3420; e-mail secretariat@iffs-reproduction.org; internet www.iffs-reproduction.org; f. 1951 to study problems of fertility and sterility; mems: approx. 40,000 world-wide; Pres. Prof. BERNARD HEDON; Sec.-Gen. GAMAL I. SEROUR; publ. *Newsletter* (2 a year).

International Federation of Gynecology and Obstetrics (FIGO): FIGO House, Suite 3, Waterloo Court, 10 Theed St, London, SE1 8ST, United Kingdom; tel. (20) 7928-1166; fax (20) 7928-7099; e-mail figo@figo.org; internet www.figo.org; f. 1954; aims to improve standards in gynaecology and obstetrics, promote better health care for women, facilitate the exchange of information, and perfect methods of teaching; mems in 108 mem. socs; Pres. Dr DOROTHY SHAW (Canada); Hon. Sec. Prof. IAN FRASER (Australia); publ. *International Journal of Obstetrics and Gynecology*.

International Federation of Ophthalmological Societies: c/o Dr Bruce E. Spivey, 945 Green St, San Francisco, CA 94133, USA; tel. (415) 409-8410; fax (415) 409-8403; e-mail info@icoph.org; internet www.icoph.org; f. 1933; works to support and develop ophthalmology, especially in developing countries; carries out education and assessment programmes; promotes clinical standards; holds World Ophthalmology Congress every two years; Pres. Prof. G. O. H. NAUMANN (Germany); Sec.-Gen. Dr BRUCE E. SPIVEY.

International Federation of Oto-Rhino-Laryngological Societies (IFOS): POB 115, 2300 AC Leiden, Netherlands; fax (71) 5803221; e-mail info@ifosworld.org; internet www.ifosworld.org; f. 1965 to initiate and support programmes to protect hearing and prevent hearing impairment; holds Congresses every four years; Pres. Dr DESIDERIO PASSALI (Italy); Sec.-Gen. JAN J. GROTE (Netherlands); publ. *IFOS Newsletter* (quarterly).

International Federation of Surgical Colleges: c/o Royal College of Surgeons in Ireland, 123 St Stephen's Green, Dublin 2, Ireland; tel. (1) 4022707; e-mail swagunn@swissonline.ch; internet www.ifsc-net.org; f. 1958 to encourage high standards in surgical training; accepts volunteers to serve as surgical teachers in developing countries and co-operates with WHO in these countries; provides journals and text books for needy medical schools; conducts international symposia; offers grants; mems: colleges or asscns in 77 countries, 420 individual associates; Pres. Prof. ALBRECHT ENCKE (Germany); Hon. Sec. Prof. S. WILLIAM. A. GUNN (Switzerland); publ. *IFSC News*.

International Hospital Federation (IHF) (Fédération Internationale des Hôpitaux—FIH): 13 chemin du Levant, 01210 Ferney Voltaire, France; tel. 4-50-42-60-00; fax 4-50-42-60-01; e-mail info@ihf-fih.org; internet www.ihf-fih.org; f. 1947 for information exchange and education in hospital and health service matters; represents institutional health care in discussions with WHO; conducts conferences and courses on management and policy issues; mems in five categories: national hospital and health service organizations; professional asscns, regional organizations and individual hospitals; individual mems; professional and industrial mems; honorary mems; Dir-Gen. Prof. PER-GUNNAR SVENSSON; publs *World Hospitals and Health Services* (quarterly), *Hospitals International* (quarterly), *Hospital Management International* (Yearbook 1), *New World Health* (Yearbook 2).

International League against Epilepsy (ILAE): 204 ave Marcel Thiry, 1200 Brussels, Belgium; tel. (2) 774-95-47; fax (2) 774-96-90; e-mail ndevolder@ilae.org; internet www.ilae-epilepsy.org; f. 1909 to link national professional asscns and to encourage research, including classification and the development of anti-epileptic drugs; collaborates with the International Bureau for Epilepsy and with WHO; mems: 96 chapters; Pres. PETER WOLF; Sec.-Gen. Dr SOLOMON MOSHE.

International League of Associations for Rheumatology (ILAR): c/o Prof. von Feldt, Univ. of Pennsylvania, Division of Rheumatology, 5 Maloney, Suite 504, Philadelphia, PA 19104-4283, USA; tel. (215) 662-4659; fax (215) 662-4500; internet www.ilar.org; f. 1927 to promote international co-operation for the study and control of rheumatic diseases; to encourage the foundation of national leagues against rheumatism; to organize regular international congresses and to act as a connecting link between national leagues and international organizations; mems: 13,000; Pres. Prof. ABRAHAM GARCIA KUTZBACH (Guatemala); Sec.-Gen. Prof. JOAN VON FELDT (USA); publs *Annals of the Rheumatic Diseases* (in the United Kingdom), *Revue du Rhumatisme* (in France), *Reumatismo* (in Italy), *Arthritis and Rheumatism* (in the USA), etc.

International Leprosy Association (ILA): c/o Univ. of Oxford, International Leprosy Association Global Project on the History of Leprosy, Wellcome Unit for The History of Medicine, 45–47 Banbury Rd, Oxford, OX2 6PE, United Kingdom; tel. (1865) 284627; fax (1865) 274095; f. 1931 to promote international co-operation in work on leprosy; holds congress every five years (2008: Hyderabad, India); Pres. Dr S. K. NOORDEEN; Sec. Dr C. S. WALTER; publ. *International Journal of Leprosy and Other Mycobacterial Diseases* (quarterly).

International Narcotics Control Board (INCB): 1400 Vienna, POB 500, Austria; tel. (1) 260-60-0; fax (1) 260-60-58-67; e-mail secretariat@incb.org; internet www.incb.org; f. 1961 by the Single Convention on Narcotic Drugs, to supervise implementation of drug control treaties by governments; mems: 13 individuals; Pres. PHILIP EMAFO (Nigeria); Sec. KOLI KOUAME; publ. *Annual Report* (with three technical supplements).

International Opticians' Association: c/o Association of British Dispensing Opticians, 199 Gloucester Terrace, London, W2 6LD, United Kingdom; tel. (020) 7298-5100; fax (020) 7298-5111; e-mail bdoris@abdo.org.uk; internet www.abdo.org.uk; f. 1951 to promote the science of opthalmic dispensing, and to maintain and advance standards and effect co-operation in optical dispensing; Pres. DAVID KIRK; Gen. Sec. Sir ANTHONY GARRETT.

INTERNATIONAL ORGANIZATIONS

International Organization for Medical Physics (IOMP): Fairmount House, 230 Tadcaster Rd, York, YO24 1ES, United Kingdom; tel. (0) 7787563913; e-mail peter.smith@mpa.n-i.nhs.uk; internet www.iomp.org; f. 1963; aims to advance medical physics practice world-wide by disseminating scientific and technical information, fostering the educational and professional development of medical physicists, and promoting the highest quality medical services for patients; mems: represents more than 16,000 medical physicists worldwide and 75 adhering national organisations of medical physics; Pres. Prof. BARRY ALLEN (Australia); Sec.-Gen. Dr PETER SMITH (United Kingdom); publ. *Medical Physics World*.

International Pediatric Association (IPA): c/o Tufts-New England Medical Center, 750 Washington St, Box 8683, Boston, MA 02111, USA; tel. (617) 636-8683; fax (617) 636-8388; internet www.ipa-world.org; f. 1912; holds triennial congresses and regional and national workshops; mems: national paediatric societies in 136 countries, 10 regional affiliate societies, 11 paediatric specialty societies; Pres. ADENIKE GRANGE (Nigeria); Exec. Dir Dr JANE G. SCHALLER (USA); publ. *International Child Health* (quarterly).

International Pharmaceutical Federation (Fédération Internationale Pharmaceutique—FIP): POB 84200, 2508 AE, The Hague, Netherlands; tel. (70) 302-1970; fax (70) 302-1999; e-mail fip@fip.org; internet www.fip.org; f. 1912; aims to represent and serve pharmacy and pharmaceutical sciences world-wide and to improve access to medecines; holds World Congress of Pharmacy and Pharmaceutical Sciences annually; mems: 86 national pharmaceutical organizations in 62 countries, 55 associate, supportive and collective mems, 4,000 individuals; Gen. Sec. A. J. M. (TON) HOEK (Netherlands); publ. *International Pharmacy Journal* (2 a year).

International Psychoanalytical Association (IPA): Broomhills, Woodside Lane, London, N12 8UD, United Kingdom; tel. (20) 8446-8324; fax (20) 8445-4729; e-mail ipa@ipa.org.uk; internet www.ipa.org.uk; f. 1908; aims to assure the continued vigour and development of psychoanalysis; acts as a forum for scientific discussions; controls and regulates training; contributes to the interdisciplinary area common to the behavioural sciences; mems: 11,500 in 34 countries; Pres. Prof. CLÁUDIO EIZIRIK; Sec.-Gen. MÓNICA SIEDMANN DE ARMESTO; publs *Bulletin*, *Newsletter*.

International Rhinologic Society: c/o Prof. Clement, ENT-Dept, AZ-VUB, Laarbeeklaan 101, 1090 Brussels, Belgium; tel. (2) 477-68-89; fax (2) 477-68-80; e-mail knoctp@az.vub.ac.be; f. 1965; holds congress every four years; Pres. IN-YONG PARK (Republic of Korea); Sec. Prof. P. A. R. CLEMENT (Belgium); publ. *Rhinology*.

International Society for Vascular Surgery: 900 Cummings Center, Suite 221-U, Beverly, MA 01915, USA; tel. (978) 927-8330; fax (978) 524-8890; e-mail iscvs@prri.com; internet www.vascularweb.org; f. 1950 as the International Society for Cardiovascular Surgery (ISCVS) to stimulate research on the diagnosis and therapy of cardiovascular diseases and to exchange ideas on an international basis; present name adopted in 2005; Pres. Dr LAZAR J. GREENFIELD (USA); Sec.-Gen. Dr ANTHONY WHITTEMORE (USA).

International Society for Oneiric Mental Imagery Techniques: c/o Odile Dorkel, 56 rue Sedaine, 75011 Paris, France; tel. 1-47-00-16-63; e-mail odile.orkel@wanadoo.fr; links a group of research workers, technicians and psychotherapists using oneirism techniques under waking conditions, with the belief that a healing action cannot be dissociated from the restoration of creativity; mems: in 17 countries; Pres. ODILE DORKEL (France); Sec.-Gen. JEAN-FRANÇOIS CESARO (France).

International Society for the Psychopathology of Expression and Art Therapy (SIPE): c/o M. Sudres, Université Toulouse-Mirail, U.F.R. Psychologie, 5 allée Antonio Machado, 31058 Toulouse Cédex 9, France; e-mail sudres@univ_tlse2.fr; internet online-art-therapy.com; f. 1959 to bring together specialists interested in the problems of expression and artistic activities in connection with psychiatric, sociological and psychological research; mems: 625; Pres. L. SCHMITT (France); Sec.-Gen. J. L. SUDRES (France); publ. *Newsletter* (quarterly).

International Society of Audiology: University Hospital Rotterdam, Audiological Centre, 3015 CE Rotterdam, Netherlands; tel. (10) 4639222; fax (10) 4634240; e-mail info@isa-audiology.org; internet www.isa-audiology.org; f. 1952 to facilitate the knowledge, protection and rehabilitation of human hearing and to represent the interests of audiology professionals and of the hearing-impaired; organizes biannual Congress and workshops and seminars; mems: 500 individuals; Pres. Prof. G. TAVARTKILADZE; Gen. Sec. Dr J. VERSCHUURE; publ. *International Journal of Audiology* (monthly).

International Society of Blood Transfusion (ISBT): c/o Eurocongres Conference Management, Jan van Goyenkade 11, 1075 HP Amsterdam, Netherlands; tel. (20) 6794311; fax (20) 6737306; e-mail info@isbt-web.org; internet www.isbt-web.org; f. 1937; mems: c. 1,000 in over 85 countries; Pres. FRANCINE DÉCARY; Sec.-Gen. Dr P. T. W. STRENGERS; publ. *Transfusion Today* (quarterly).

International Society of Dermatopathology (ISVD): c/o Mill House Veterinary Surgery, Kings Lynn, Norfolk, United Kingdom; tel. (1553) 771457; e-mail vets@vetcutis.freeserve.co.uk; internet www.vetcutis.freeserve.co.uk/vetcutis.freeserve.co.uk; f. 1958; groups professionals interested in the microscopic interpretation of skin diseases; aims to advance veterinary and comparative dermatopathology; encourages the development of technologies for the diagnosis of skin diseases in animals; promotes professional training; Pres. Dr THELMA LEE GROSS (USA); Sec. Dr DAVID H. SHEARER (United Kingdom).

International Society of Developmental Biologists: c/o Dr Stefan Schulte-Merker, Hubrecht Laboratorium/Netherlands Institute for Developmental Biology, Uppsalalaan 8, 3584 CT, Utrecht, Netherlands; tel. (30) 2510211; e-mail schulte@niob.knaw.nl; internet www.niob.knaw.nl/isdb/; f. 1911 as International Institute of Embryology; aims to promote the study of developmental biology and to encourage international co-operation among investigators in the field; mems: 850 in 33 countries; Pres. Prof. MASATOSHI TAKEICHI (Japan); International Sec. Prof. SARAH HAKE (USA); publ. *Mechanisms of Development* and *Gene Expression Patterns*.

International Society of Internal Medicine: Dept. of Medicine, Spital Netz Bern Hospitals, Zieglerspital, 3001 Bern, Switzerland; tel. 319707178; fax 319707763; e-mail hanspeter.kohler@spitalnetzbern.ch; internet www.acponline.org/isim; f. 1948 to encourage research and education in internal medicine; mems: 61 national societies; 2008 congress: Buenos Aires, Argentina; Pres. Prof. ROLF STREULI (Switzerland); Sec.-Gen. Prof. HANS PETER KOHLER (Switzerland).

International Society of Lymphology: Room 4406, University of Arizona, 1501 North Campbell Ave, POB 245200, Tucson, AZ 85724-5063, USA; tel. (520) 626-6118; fax (520) 626-0822; e-mail lymph@u.arizona.edu; internet www.u.arizona.edu/~witte/ISL.htm; f. 1966 to further progress in lymphology through personal contacts and the exchange of ideas; mems: 375 in 42 countries; Pres. M. ANDRADE (Brazil); Sec.-Gen. M. H. WITTE (USA); publ. *Lymphology* (quarterly).

International Society of Neuropathology: c/o Dr Seth Love, Dept of Neuropathology, Institute of Clinical Sciences, Frenchay Hospital, Bristol, BS16 1LE, United Kingdom; fax (117) 9753765; e-mail ISN@sethlove.co.uk; internet www.intsocneuropathol.com; f. 1950 as The International Committee of Neuropathology; renamed as above in 1967; Pres. Dr BERNARDINO GHETTI (USA); Sec.-Gen. Dr SETH LOVE (United Kingdom).

International Society of Orthopaedic Surgery and Traumatology (Société Internationale de Chirurgie Orthopédique et de Traumatologie): 40 rue Washington, bte 9, 1050 Brussels, Belgium; tel. (2) 648-68-23; fax (2) 649-86-01; e-mail hq@sicot.org; internet www.sicot.org; f. 1929; convenes an annual conference and world congresses every three years; mems: 102 countries, 3,000 individuals; Pres. Prof. CHADWICK F. SMITH; Sec.-Gen. MAURICE HINSENKAMP; publ. *Newsletter* (every 2 months).

International Society of Physical and Rehabilitation Medicine (ISPRM): ISPRM Central Office, Werner van Cleemputte, Medicongress, 28–34 Waalpoel, 9960 Assenede, Belgium; tel. (9) 344-39-59; fax (9) 344-40-10; e-mail info@isprm.org; internet www.isprm.org; f. 1999 by merger of International Federation of Physical Medicine and Rehabilitation (f. 1952) and International Rehabilitation Medicine Association (f. 1968); mems: in 68 countries; fourth international congress: Seoul, Republic of Korea (June 2007); Pres. CHANG IL PARK (Republic of Korea); Sec. Dr MARTA IMAMURA (Brazil).

International Society of Radiology (ISR): 7910 Woodmont Ave, Suite 800, Bethesda, Maryland 20814, USA; tel. (301) 657-2652; fax (301) 907-8768; e-mail secretary@isradiology.org; internet www.isradiology.org; f. 1953 to promote radiology world-wide; International Commissions on Radiation Units and Measurements (ICRUM), on Radiation Protection (ICRP), and on Radiological Education (ICRE); organizes biannual International Congress of Radiology; collaborates with WHO; mems: more than 50 national radiological societies; Pres. CLAUDE MANELFE; Sec.-Gen. NICKOLAS C. GOURTSOYIANNIS; Exec. Dir OTHA W. LINTON; publ. *Newsletter*.

International Society of Surgery (ISS): Netzibodenstr. 34, POB 1527, 4133 Pratteln, Switzerland; tel. 618159666; fax 618114775; e-mail surgery@iss-sic.ch; internet www.iss-sic.ch; f. 1902 to promote understanding between surgical disciplines; groups surgeons to address issues of interest to all surgical specialists; supports general surgery as a training base for abdominal surgery, surgery with integuments and endocrine surgery; organizes congresses, 43rd World Congress of Surgery: Adelaide, Australia (September 2009); mems: 4,000; Pres. MICHAEL G. SARR; Sec.-Gen. Prof. FELIX HARDER; publ. *World Journal of Surgery* (monthly).

International Spinal Cord Society (ISCoS): National Spinal Injuries Centre, Stoke Mandeville Hospital, Aylesbury, Bucks, HP21 8AL, United Kingdom; tel. (1296) 315866; fax (1296) 315870; e-mail admin@iscos.org.uk; internet www.iscos.org.uk; f. 1961; formerly the International Medical Society of Paraplegia (f. 1961); studies all problems relating to traumatic and non-traumatic lesions of the spinal cord, including causes, prevention, research and rehabilitation; promotes the exchange of information; assists in efforts to guide and co-ordinate research; Pres. Prof. W. DONOVAN; publ. *Spinal Cord*.

International Union against Cancer (Union internationale contre le cancer—UICC): 62 route de Frontenex, 1207 Geneva, Switzerland; tel. 228091811; fax 228091810; e-mail info@uicc.org; internet www.uicc.org; f. 1933 to promote the campaign against cancer on an international level; organizes International Cancer Congress every two years; administers the American Cancer Society UICC International Fellowships for Beginning Investigators (ACSBI), the Astrazeneca and Novartis UICC Transnational Cancer Research Fellowships (TCRF), the UICC International Cancer Technology Transfer Fellowships (ICRETT), the Yamagiwa-Yoshida Memorial UICC International Cancer Study Grants (YY), the Trish Greene UICC International Oncology Nursing Fellowships (IONF), the UICC Asia-Pacific Cancer Society Training Grants (APCASOT), and the Latin America UICC COPES Training and Education Fellowship (LACTEF); conducts worldwide programmes of campaign organization; public and professional education; and patient support, detection and diagnosis; and programmes on epidemiology and prevention; tobacco and cancer; the treatment of cancer; and tumour biology; mems: voluntary national organizations, cancer research and treatment organizations, institutes and governmental agencies in more than 80 countries; Pres. Dr FRANCO CAVALLI (Switzerland); Exec. Dir ISABEL MORTARA (Switzerland); publs *International Journal of Cancer* (36 a year), *UICC News* (quarterly), *International Calendar of Meetings on Cancer* (2 a year).

International Union against Tuberculosis and Lung Disease (IUATLD): 68 blvd St Michel, 75006 Paris, France; tel. 1-44-32-03-60; fax 1-43-29-90-87; e-mail union@iuatld.org; internet www.iuatld.org; f. 1920 to co-ordinate the efforts of anti-tuberculosis and respiratory disease asscns, to mobilize public interest, to assist control programmes and research around the world, to collaborate with governments and WHO and to promote conferences; mems: asscns in 165 countries, 3,000 individual mems; Pres. Prof. ASMA EL-SONY; Exec. Dir Dr NILS BILLO; publs *The International Journal of Tuberculosis and Lung Disease* (in English, with summaries in French and Spanish; incl. conference proceedings), *Newsletter*.

International Union for Health Promotion and Education (IUHPE): 42 blvd de la Libération, 93203 St Denis Cedex, France; tel. 1-48-13-71-20; fax 1-48-09-17-67; e-mail mclamarre@iuhpe.org; internet www.iuhpe.org; f. 1951; provides an international network for the exchange of practical information on developments in health promotion and education; promotes research; encourages professional training for health workers, teachers, social workers and others; holds a World Conference on Health Promotion and Health Education every three years; organizes regional conferences and seminars; mems: in more than 90 countries; Pres. Prof. MAURICE MITTELMARK (Norway); Exec. Dir MARIE-CLAUDE LAMARRE (France); publs. *Health Promotion International*, *Promotion and Education* (quarterly, in English, French and Spanish).

Latin American Association of National Academies of Medicine: Carrera 7, Bogotá, Colombia; tel. and fax (1) 2493122; e-mail alanam_colombia@hotmail.com; f. 1967; mems: 11 national Academies; Exec. Sec. Dr ZOÍLO CUÉLLAR-MONTOYA (Colombia).

Medical Women's International Association (MWIA): 7555 Morley Drive, Burnaby, B.C., V5E 3Y2, Canada; tel. (604) 439-8993; fax (604) 439-8994; e-mail secretariat@mwia.net; internet www.mwia.net; f. 1919 to facilitate contacts between women in medicine and to encourage co-operation in matters connected with international health problems; mems: national asscns in 47 countries, and individuals; Pres. Dr ATSUKO HESHIKI (Japan); Sec.-Gen. Dr SHELLEY ROSS (Canada); publ. *MWIA UPDATE* (3 a year).

Middle East Neurosurgical Society: c/o Dr Gamal Azab, 20 Amine Fikri St, Ramleh Station, Alexandria, Egypt; f. 1958 to promote clinical advances and scientific research among its members and to spread knowledge of neurosurgery and related fields among all members of the medical profession in the Middle East; mems: 684 in nine countries; Pres. Dr GAMAL AZAB; Hon. Sec. IZAT SHERIF.

Multiple Sclerosis International Federation (MSIF): 3rd Floor, Skyline House, 200 Union St, London, SE1 0LX, United Kingdom; tel. (20) 7620-1911; fax (20) 7620-1922; e-mail info@msif.org; internet www.msif.org; f. 1967; promotes shared scientific research into multiple sclerosis and related neurological diseases; stimulates the active exchange of information; provides support for new and existing multiple sclerosis societies; Pres. SARAH PHILLIPS; Chief Exec. CHRISTINE PURDY; publs *MSIF Annual Review* (annually), *MS: The Guide to Treatment and Management* (every 2 years), *MS in Focus* (2 a year), *MSIF Directory* (annually), *How To* series (annually).

Organisation panafricaine de lutte contre le SIDA (OPALS): 15/21 rue de L'Ecole de Médecine, 75006 Paris, France; tel. 1-43-26-72-28; fax 1-43-29-70-93; e-mail opals@croix-rouge.fr; f. 1988; disseminates information relating to the treatment and prevention of AIDS; provides training of medical personnel; promotes co-operation between African medical centres and specialized centres in the USA and Europe; Pres. Prof. MARC GENTILINI; publ. *OPALS Liaison*.

Organization for Co-ordination in the Struggle against Endemic Diseases in Central Africa (Organisation de coordination pour la lutte contre les endémies en Afrique Centrale—OCEAC): BP 288, Yaoundé, Cameroon; tel. 23-22-32; fax 23-00-61; e-mail oceac@camnet.cm; internet www.cm.refer.org/site_oceac; f. 1965 to standardize methods of controlling endemic diseases, to co-ordinate national action, and to negotiate programmes of assistance and training on a regional scale; mems: Cameroon, Central African Republic, Chad, Republic of the Congo, Equatorial Guinea, Gabon; Sec.-Gen. Dr AUGUSTE BILONGO-MANÉNÉ; publ. *Bulletin de Liaison et de Documentation* (quarterly).

Pan-American Association of Ophthalmology (PAAO): 1301 South Bowen Rd, Suite 365, Arlington, TX 76013, USA; tel. (817) 275-7553; fax (817) 275-3961; e-mail info@paao.org; internet www.paao.org; f. 1939 to promote friendship within the profession and the dissemination of scientific information; holds biennial Congress (2009: San Francisco, USA); mems: national ophthalmological societies and other bodies in 39 countries; Pres. Dr RICHARD L. ABBOTT; Exec. Dir TERESA BRADSHAW; publ. *Vision Panamerica* (quarterly).

Pan-Pacific Surgical Association: 1212 Punahou St, Suite 3506, Honolulu, HI 96826, Hawaii, USA; tel. (808) 941-1010; fax (808) 951-7004; e-mail ppsa.info@panpacificsurgical.org; internet www.panpacificsurgical.org; f. 1929 to bring together surgeons to exchange scientific knowledge relating to surgery and medicine, and to promote the improvement and standardization of hospitals and their services and facilities; congresses are held every two years; mems: 2,716 regular, associate and senior mems from 44 countries; Pres. Dr JEROME C. GOLDSTEIN; Chair. THOMAS KOSASA.

Rehabilitation International: 25 East 21st St, New York, NY 10010, USA; tel. (212) 420-1500; fax (212) 505-0871; e-mail ri@riglobal.org; internet www.riglobal.org; f. 1922 to improve the lives of people with disabilities through the exchange of information and research on equipment and methods of assistance; functions as a global network of disabled people, service providers, researchers and government agencies; advocates promoting and implementing the rights, inclusion and rehabilitation of people with disabilities; organizes international conferences and co-operates with UN agencies and other international organizations; mems: organizations in 90 countries; Pres. MICHAEL FOX; Sec.-Gen. TOMAS LAGERWALL; publs *International Rehabilitation Review* (annually), *Rehabilitación* (2 or 3 a year).

Society of French-speaking Neuro-Surgeons (Société de neurochirurgie de langue française—SNLF): c/o Prof. C. Raftopoulos, ave Hippocrate 10, 1200, Brussels, Belgium; tel. (2) 764-10-88; fax (2) 764-89-61; e-mail Raftopoulos@chir.ucl.ac.be; internet www.snclf.com; f. 1949; holds annual convention and congress; mems: 700; Pres. Prof. JEAN CHAZAL (France); Sec. Prof. CHRISTIAN RAFTOPOULOS (Belgium); publ. *Neurochirurgie* (6 a year).

Transplantation Society (Société de Transplantation): Central Business Office, Édifice Place du Quartier, 1111 St Urbain St, Suite 108, Montreal, QC H2Z 1Y6, Canada; tel. (514) 874-1717; fax (514) 874-1716; e-mail info@transplantation-soc.org; internet www.transplantation-soc.org; f. 1966; over 3,000 members in 65 countries; Pres. Dr KATHRYN WOOD; Exec. Sec. PHILIP DOMBROSKI.

World Allergy Organization (IAACI): 555 East Wells St, Suite 1100, Milwaukee, WI 53202-3823, USA; tel. (414) 276-1791; fax (414) 276-3349; e-mail info@worldallergy.org; internet www.worldallergy.org; f. 1945, as International Association of Allergology and Clinical Immunology, to further work in the educational, research and practical medical aspects of allergic and immunological diseases; 2007 Congress: Bangkok, Thailand; mems: 74 national and regional societies; Pres. Prof. MICHAEL A. KALINER (USA); Sec.-Gen. Prof. CONNIE KATELARIS (Australia); publ. *Allergy and Clinical Immunology International* (6 a year).

World Association for Disaster and Emergency Medicine (WADEM): International Office, POB 55158, Madison, WI 53705-8958, USA; e-mail mlb@medicine.wisc.edu; internet wadem.medicine.wisc.edu; f. 1976 to improve the world-wide delivery of emergency and humanitarian care in mass casualty and disaster situations, through training, symposia, and publications; mems: 600 in 62 countries; Pres. MARVIN L. BIRNBAUM (USA); Sec. EDITA STOK (Slovenia); publ. *Prehospital and Disaster Medicine*.

World Association of Societies of Pathology and Laboratory Medicine (WASPaLM): c/o Japanese Society of Laboratory Medicine (JSLM), 5F Takahashi Bldg 1-7-1, Sarugakucho Chiyoda-ku, Tokyo, 101-0064, Japan; tel. (3) 3295-0351; fax (3) 3295-0352; e-mail waspalm@jscp.org; internet www.waspalm.org; f. 1947 to link national societies and co-ordinate their scientific and technical means of action; promotes the development of anatomic and clinical pathology, especially by convening conferences, congresses and meetings, and through the interchange of publications and personnel; mems: 54 national asscns; Pres. Dr MARILENE MELO (Brazil); Sec.-Treas. Dr MICHAEL OELLERICH (Germany); publ. Newsletter (quarterly).

World Confederation for Physical Therapy (WCPT): Kensington Charity Centre, 4th Floor, Charles House, 375 Kensington High St, London, W14 8QH, United Kingdom; tel. (20) 7471-6765; fax (20) 7471-6766; e-mail info@wcpt.org; internet www.wcpt.org; f. 1951; represents physical therapy internationally; encourages high standards of physical therapy education and practice; promotes exchange of information among members, and the development of a scientific professional base through research; aims to contribute to the development of informed public opinion regarding physical therapy; holds seminars and workshops and quadrennial scientific congress showcasing advancements in physical therapy research, practice and education (June 2007: Vancouver, Canada); mems: 101 national physical therapy orgs; Pres. MARILYN MOFFAT; Sec.-Gen. BRENDA J. MYERS; publ. WCPT News (quarterly).

World Council of Optometry (WCO): 8360 Old York, 4th Floor West, Elkins Park, PA 19027, USA; tel. (215) 780-1320; fax (215) 780-1325; e-mail wco@pco.edu; internet www.worldoptometry.org; f. 1927 to co-ordinate efforts to provide a good standard of ophthalmic optical (optometric) care throughout the world; enables exchange of ideas between different countries; focuses on optometric education; gives advice on standards of qualification; considers optometry legislation throughout the world; mems: 70 optometric organizations in 50 countries and four regional groups; Pres. Dr VIC CONNORS (USA); Exec. Dir Dr ANTONY DI STEFANO (USA); publ. Interoptics (quarterly).

World Federation for Medical Education (WFME) (Fédération mondiale pour l'enseignement de la medicine): Univ. of Copenhagen Faculty of Health Sciences, Blegdamsvej 3, 2200 Copenhagen N, Denmark; tel. (353) 27103; fax (353) 27070; e-mail wfme@wfme.org; internet www.wfme.org; f. 1972; aims to promote and integrate medical education world-wide; links regional and international asscns; has official relations with WHO, UNICEF, UNESCO, UNDP and the World Bank; Pres. Dr HANS KARLE; Exec. Dir ULRIK MEYER.

World Federation for Mental Health (WFMH): 6564 Loisdale Court, Suite 301, Springfield, VA 22150-1812, USA; tel. (703) 313-8680; fax (703) 313-8683; e-mail info@wfmh.com; internet www.wfmh.org; f. 1948 to promote the highest standards of mental health; works with agencies of the United Nations in promoting mental health; assists other voluntary asscns in improving mental health services; voting, affiliate and individual members in more than 100 countries; Sec.-Gen. and CEO PRESTON J. GARRISON; publs Newsletter (quarterly), Annual Report.

World Federation of Associations of Paediatric Surgeons (WOFAPS): c/o Prof. J. Boix-Ochoa, Clinica Infantil 'Vall d'Hebron', Departamento de Cirugía Pediátrica, Valle de Hebron 119–129, Barcelona 08035, Spain; internet www.wofaps.co.za; f. 1974; mems: 80 asscns; Pres. Prof. ARNOLD G. CORAN; Sec.-Gen./Treas. Prof. PEPE BOIX-OCHOA.

World Federation of Associations of Poison Centres and Clinical Toxicology Centres: c/o Prof. Louis Roche, CIRC, 150 cours Albert-Thomas, 69372 Lyon, Cédex 2, France; tel. 4-78-74-16-74; f. 1975 as World Federation of Associations of Clinical Toxicology Centres and Poison Control Centres; mems: 37; Pres. Dr HANS PERSSON (Sweden); Sec.-Gen. Prof. LOUIS ROCHE; publ. Bulletin of the World Federation (quarterly).

World Federation of Hydrotherapy and Climatotherapy: Cattedra di Terapia Med. E Medic. Termal, Università degli Studi, via Cicognara 7, 20129 Milan, Italy; tel. (02) 50318456; fax (02) 50318461; e-mail umberto.solimene@unimi.it; internet www.femteconline.com; f. 1947 as International Federation of Thermalism and Climatism; recognized by WHO in 1986; present name adopted 1999; mems: in 44 countries; Pres. M. NIKOLAI A. STOROZHENKO (Russia); Gen. Sec. Prof. UMBERTO SOLIMENE (Italy).

World Federation of Neurology (WFN): 12 Chandos St, London, W1G 9DR, United Kingdom; tel. (20) 7323-4011; fax (20) 7323-4012; e-mail wfnlondon@aol.com; internet www.wfneurology.org; f. 1955 as International Neurological Congress, present title adopted 1957; aims to assemble members of various congresses associated with neurology and promote co-operation among neurological researchers. Organizes Congress every four years; mems: 23,000 in 102 countries; Pres. JOHAN AARLI (Norway); Sec.-Treas. Dr RAAD SHAKIR (United Kingdom); publs Journal of the Neurological Sciences, World Neurology (quarterly).

World Federation of Neurosurgical Societies (WFNS): c/o Prof. Edward R. Laws, Dept. of Neurological Surgery, Univ. of Virginia, Box 212, Health Science Center, Charlottesville, VA 22908, USA; tel. (804) 924-2650; fax (804) 924-5894; internet www.wfns.ne; f. 1957 to assist in the development of neurosurgery and to help the formation of asscns; facilitates the exchange of information and encourages research; mems: 57 societies in 56 countries; Pres. Dr JACQUES BROTCHI; Sec. Prof. EDWARD R. LAWS, Jr .

World Federation of Occupational Therapists (WFOT): POB 30, Forrestfield, Western Australia 6058, Australia; e-mail wfot@multiline.com.au; internet www.wfot.org; f. 1952 to further the rehabilitation of the physically and mentally disabled by promoting the development of occupational therapy in all countries; facilitates the exchange of information and publications; promotes research in occupational therapy; holds international congresses every four years; mems: national professional asscns in 65 countries, with total membership of c. 100,000; Pres. KIT SINCLAIR (Hong Kong); Exec. Dir MARILYN PATTISON (Australia); publ. Bulletin (2 a year).

World Federation of Public Health Associations: c/o APHA, 800 I St, NW, Washington, DC 20001-3710, USA; tel. (202) 777-2490; fax (202) 777-2533; e-mail stacey.succop@apha.org; internet www.wfpha.org; f. 1967; brings together researchers, teachers, health service providers and workers in a multidisciplinary environment of professional exchange, studies and action; endeavours to influence policies and to set priorities to prevent disease and promote health; holds a triennial Congress: Istanbul, Turkey (2009); mems: 68 national public health asscns and five regional asscns; Sec.-Gen. BARBARA HATCHER (USA); publs WFPHA Report (in English), and occasional technical papers.

World Federation of Societies of Anaesthesiologists (WFSA): 21 Portland Place, London, W1B 1PY, United Kingdom; tel. (20) 7631-8880; fax (20) 7631-8882; e-mail wfsahq@anaesthesiologists.org; internet www.anaesthesiologists.org; f. 1955; aims to make available the highest standards of anaesthesia, pain treatment, trauma management and resuscitation to all peoples of the world; mems: 120 national societies; Pres. Prof. A. E. E. MEURSING (Netherlands); Hon. Sec. Prof. JOHN MOYERS (USA); publs Update in Anaesthesia (2 a year), Annual Report.

World Gastroenterology Organization (Organisation mondiale de gastro-entérologie—OMGE): c/o Bridget Barbieri, Medconnect GmbH, Brünnsteinstr. 10, 81541 München, Germany; tel. (89) 41419240; fax (89) 41419245; e-mail omge@worldgastroenterology.org; internet www.worldgastroenterology.org; f. 1958 to promote clinical and academic gastroenterological practice throughout the world, and to ensure high ethical standards; focuses on the improvement of standards in gastroenterology training and education on a global scale; a WGO Foundation, incorporated in 2007, is dedicated to raising funds to support WGO educational programs and activities; mems: 103 national societies, four regional asscns; Pres. Prof. EAMON M.M. QUIGLEY; Sec.-Gen. Dr HENRY COHEN.

World Heart Federation: 7, rue des Battoir, 1211 Geneva 4, Switzerland; tel. 228070320; fax 228070339; e-mail admin@worldheart.org; internet www.worldheart.org; f. 1978 as International Society and Federation of Cardiology, name changed as above 1998; aims to help people to achieve a longer and better life through prevention and control of heart disease and stroke, with a focus on low and middle income countries; mems: 197 orgs in more than 100 countries; Pres. Dr SHAHRYAR SHEIKH (Pakistan); CEO JANET VOÛTE (Switzerland); publs Nature Clinical Practice Cardiovascular Journal, Prevention and Control.

World Medical Association (WMA): 13 chemin du Levant, CIB-Bâtiment A, 01210 Ferney-Voltaire, France; tel. 4-50-40-75-75; fax 4-50-40-59-37; e-mail wma@wma.net; internet www.wma.net; f. 1947 to achieve the highest international standards in all aspects of medical education and practice, to promote closer ties among doctors and national medical asscns by personal contact and all other means, to study problems confronting the medical profession, and to present its views to appropriate bodies; holds an annual General Assembly; mems: 83 national medical asscns; Pres. Dr KGOSI LETLAPE (South Africa); Sec.-Gen. Dr OTMAR KLOIBER (Germany); publ. The World Medical Journal (quarterly).

World Psychiatric Association (WPA): Psychiatric Hospital 2, chemin du Petit-Bel-Air 1225, Chêne-Bourg, Switzerland; tel. 223055730; fax 223055735; e-mail wpasecretariat@wpanet.org; internet www.wpanet.org; f. 1961 for the exchange of information on problems of mental illness and to strengthen relations between psychiatrists in all countries; organizes World Psychiatric Congresses and regional and inter-regional scientific meetings; mems: 150,000 psychiatrists in 100 countries; Pres. JUAN E. MEZZICH (USA); Sec.-Gen. JOHN COX (United Kingdom).

World Self-Medication Industry (WSMI): 13 chemin du Levant, 01210 Ferney-Voltaire, France; tel. 4-50-28-47-28; fax 4-50-28-40-24; e-mail admin@wsmi.org; internet www.wsmi.org; Dir-Gen. Dr DAVID E. WEBBER.

INTERNATIONAL ORGANIZATIONS

Posts and Telecommunications

Arab Permanent Postal Commission: c/o Arab League Bldg, Tahrir Sq., Cairo, Egypt; tel. (2) 5750511; fax (2) 5775626; f. 1952; aims to establish stricter postal relations between the Arab countries than those laid down by the Universal Postal Union, and to pursue the development and modernization of postal services in member countries; publs *APU Bulletin* (monthly), *APU Review* (quarterly), *APU News* (annually).

Arab Telecommunications Union: POB 2397, Baghdad, Iraq; tel. (1) 555-0642; f. 1953 to co-ordinate and develop telecommunications between member countries; to exchange technical aid and encourage research; promotes establishment of new cable telecommunications networks in the region; Sec.-Gen. ABDUL JAFFAR HASSAN KHALAF IBRAHIM AL-ANI; publs *Arab Telecommunications Union Journal* (2 a year), *Economic and Technical Studies*.

Asia-Pacific Telecommunity (APT): No. 12/49, Soi 5, Chaengwattana Rd, Thungsonghong, Bangkok 10210, Thailand; tel. (2) 573-0044; fax (2) 573-7479; e-mail aptmail@apt.org; internet www.apt.org; f. 1979 to cover all matters relating to telecommunications in the region; serves as the focal organization for ICT in the Asia-Pacific region; contributes, through its various programmes and activities, to the growth of the ICT sector in the region and assists members in their preparation for global telecommunications conferences, as well as promoting regional harmonization for such events; mems: Afghanistan, Australia, Bangladesh, Bhutan, Brunei, People's Republic of China, Fiji, India, Indonesia, Iran, Japan, Korea, Democratic Republic of Korea, Republic of Korea, Laos, Malaysia, Maldives, Marshall Islands, Federated States of Micronesia, Mongolia, Myanmar, Nauru, Nepal, New Zealand, Pakistan, Palau, Papua New Guinea, Philippines, Samoa, Singapore, Sri Lanka, Thailand, Tonga, Viet Nam; assoc. mems: Republic of China, Cook Islands, Hong Kong, Macao, Niue; 101 affiliated mems; Exec. Dir AMARENDRA NARAYAN.

Asian-Pacific Postal Union: APPU Bureau, POB 1, Laksi Post Office, 111 Chaeng Wattana Rd, Bangkok 10210, Thailand; tel. (2) 573-7282; fax (2) 573-1161; e-mail admin@appu-bureau.org; internet www.appu-bureau.org; f. 1962 to extend, facilitate and improve the postal relations between the member countries and to promote co-operation in the field of postal services; holds Congress every five years; mems: postal administrations in 30 countries; Dir SOMCHAI REOPANICHKUL; publs *Annual Report, Exchange Program of Postal Officials, APPU Newsletter*.

European Conference of Postal and Telecommunications Administrations: Federal Ministry of Economics and Labour, Scharnhorststr. 34–37, 10115 Berlin, Germany; e-mail kai.ulrich@bmwa.bund.de; internet www.cept.org; f. 1959 to strengthen relations between member administrations and to harmonize and improve their technical services; set up Eurodata Foundation, for research and publishing; mems: 26 countries; Sec. KAI ULRICH; publ. *Bulletin*.

European Telecommunications Satellite Organization (EUTELSAT): 70 rue Balard, 75502, Paris Cédex 15, France; tel. 1-53-98-47-47; fax 1-53-98-37-00; internet www.eutelsat.com; f. 1977 to operate satellites for fixed and mobile communications in Europe; EUTELSAT's in-orbit resource comprises 18 satellites; commercialises capacity in three satellites operated by other companies; mems: public and private telecommunications operations in 47 countries; Chair. and CEO GIULIANO BERRETTA.

INMARSAT (International Mobile Satellite Organization): 99 City Rd, London, EC1Y 1AX, United Kingdom; tel. (20) 7728-1000; fax (20) 7728-1044; internet www.inmarsat.org; f. 1979, as International Maritime Satellite Organization, to provide (from February 1982) global communications for shipping via satellites on a commercial basis; satellites in geo-stationary orbit over the Atlantic, Indian and Pacific Oceans provide telephone, telex, facsimile, telegram, low to high speed data services and distress and safety communications for ships of all nations and structures such as oil rigs; in 1985 the operating agreement was amended to include aeronautical communications, and in 1988 amendments were approved which allow provision of global land-mobile communications; in April 1999 INMARSAT was transferred to the private sector and became a limited company; an intergovernmental secretariat was to be maintained to monitor INMARSAT's public service obligations; mems: 86 countries; Chair. and CEO ANDY SUKAWATY.

International Telecommunications Satellite Organization (INTELSAT): 3400 International Drive, NW, Washington, DC 20008-3098, USA; tel. (202) 944-6800; fax (202) 944-8125; internet www.intelsat.com; f. 1964 to establish a global commercial satellite communications system; Assembly of Parties attended by representatives of member governments, meets every two years to consider policy and long-term aims and matters of interest to members as sovereign states; meeting of Signatories to the Operating Agreement held annually; 24 INTELSAT satellites in geosynchronous orbit provide a global communications service; provides most of the world's overseas traffic; in 1998 INTELSAT agreed to establish a private enterprise, incorporated in the Netherlands, to administer six satellite services; mems: 143 governments; CEO DAVID MCGLADE (USA).

Internet Corporation for Assigned Names and Numbers (ICANN): 4676 Admiralty Way, Suite 330, Marina del Rey, CA 90292-6601, USA; tel. (310) 823-9358; fax (310) 823-8649; e-mail icann@icann.org; internet www.icann.org; f. 1998; non-profit, private-sector body; aims to co-ordinate the technical management and policy development of the internet; comprises three Supporting Organizations to assist, review and develop recommendations on internet policy and structure relating to addresses, domain names, and protocol; Pres. and CEO PAUL TWOMEY (Australia).

Pacific Telecommunications Council (PTC): 2454 S. Beretania St, 302 Honolulu, HI 96826-1596, USA; tel. (808) 941-3789; fax (808) 944-4874; e-mail info@ptc.org; internet www.ptc.org; f. 1980 to promote the development, understanding and beneficial use of telecommunications and information systems/services throughout the Pacific region; provides forum for users and providers of communications services; sponsors annual conference and seminars; mems: 650 (corporate, government, academic and individual); Pres. DAVID LASSNER (USA).

Postal Union of the Americas, Spain and Portugal (Unión Postal de las Américas, España y Portugal): Cebollatí 1468/70, 1°, Casilla de Correos 20.042, Montevideo, Uruguay; tel. (2) 4100070; fax (2) 4105046; e-mail secretaría@upaep.com.uy; internet www.upaep.com.uy; f. 1911 to extend, facilitate and study the postal relationships of member countries; mems: 27 countries; Sec.-Gen. SERRANA BASSINI.

Press, Radio and Television

African Union of Broadcasting (AUB): 101 rue Carnot, BP 3237, Dakar, Senegal; tel. 821-16-25; fax 822-51-13; e-mail urtnadkr@sentoo.sn; f. 1962 as Union of National Radio and Television Organizations of Africa (URTNA), new org. f. Nov. 2006; co-ordinates radio and television services, including monitoring and frequency allocation, the exchange of information and coverage of national and international events among African countries; mems: 48 orgs and six associate members; CEO a.i. LAWRENCE ATIASE.

Asia-Pacific Broadcasting Union (ABU): POB 1164, 59700 Kuala Lumpur, Malaysia; tel. (3) 22823592; fax (3) 22844382; e-mail info@abu.org.my; internet www.abu.org.my; f. 1964 to foster and co-ordinate the development of broadcasting in the Asia-Pacific area, to develop means of establishing closer collaboration and co-operation among broadcasting orgs, and to serve the professional needs of broadcasters in Asia and the Pacific; holds annual General Assembly; mems: 146 in 55 countries and territories; Sec.-Gen. DAVID ASTLEY (Australia); publs *ABU News* (every 2 months), *ABU Technical Review* (every 2 months).

Association for the Promotion of International Press Distribution (DISTRIPRESS): Beethovenstrasse 20, 8002 Zürich, Switzerland; tel. 442024121; fax 442021025; e-mail info@distripress.net; internet www.distripress.net; f. 1955 to assist in the promotion of the freedom of the press throughout the world, supporting and aiding UNESCO in promoting the free flow of ideas; organizes meetings of publishers and distributors of newspapers, periodicals and paperback books, to promote the exchange of information and experience among members; mems: 470 in 96 countries; Pres. JOHN KAYSER (USA); Man. Dir Dr PETER EMÖD (Switzerland); publs *Distripress Gazette, Who's Who*.

Association of European Journalists (AEJ): 145 ave Baron Albert d'Huart, 1950 Kraainem, Belgium; tel. (2) 646-78-65; fax (2) 644-39-34; e-mail npkramer@skynet.be; internet www.aej.org; f. 1963 to participate actively in the development of a European consciousness; to promote deeper knowledge of European problems and secure appreciation by the general public of the work of European institutions; to facilitate members' access to sources of European information; and to defend freedom of the press; mems: 2,100 individuals and national assens in 25 countries; Pres. DIEGO CARCEDO (Spain); Sec.-Gen. N. PETER KRAMER (Belgium); publ. *Newsletter*.

Association of Private European Cable Operators: 1 blvd Anspach, boîte 25, 1000 Brussels, Belgium; tel. (2) 223-25-91; fax (2) 223-06-96; f. 1995 to promote the interests of independent cable operators and to ensure exchange of information on cable and telecommunications; carries out research on relevant technical and legal questions; mems: 27 orgs in 19 countries; Pres. M. DE SUTTER.

European Alliance of News Agencies: Norrbackagatan 23, 11341 Stockholm, Sweden; tel. and fax (8) 301-324; e-mail erik-n@telia.com;

INTERNATIONAL ORGANIZATIONS — Press, Radio and Television

internet www.pressalliance.com; f. 1957 as European Alliance of Press Agencies (name changed 2002); aims to promote co-operation among members and to study and protect their common interests; annual assembly; mems: in 30 countries; Man. Dir. PAUL TESSELAAR; Sec.-Gen. ERIK NYLÉN.

European Broadcasting Union (EBU): CP 45, 17A Ancienne-Route, 1218 Grand-Saconnex, Geneva, Switzerland; tel. 227172111; fax 227474000; e-mail ebu@ebu.ch; internet www.ebu.ch; f. 1950 in succession to the International Broadcasting Union; a professional asscn of broadcasting organizations, supporting the interests of members and assisting the development of broadcasting in all its forms; activities include the Eurovision news and programme exchanges and the Euroradio music exchanges; mems: 74 active (European) in 54 countries, 48 associate mems; Pres. FRITZ PLEITGEN; Sec.-Gen. JEAN RÉVEILLON (France); publs *EBU Technical Review* (annually), *Dossiers* (2 a year).

IFRA: Washingtonplatz 1, 64287 Darmstadt, Germany; tel. (6151) 7336; fax (6151) 733800; e-mail info@ifra.com; internet www.ifra.com; f. 1961; IFRA is the world-wide research and service organization for the news publishing industry; acts as the platform for decision-makers from the newspaper industry; mems: more than 3,100 (newspapers and suppliers) in nearly 80 countries; Pres. Dr HORST PIRKER; CEO REINER MITTELBACH; publ. *IFRA Magazine* (monthly, and online).

Inter-American Press Association (IAPA) (Sociedad Interamericana de Prensa): Jules Dubois Bldg, 1801 SW 3rd Ave, Miami, FL 33129, USA; tel. (305) 634-2465; fax (305) 635-2272; e-mail info@sipiapa.org; internet www.sipiapa.org; f. 1942 to guard the freedom of the press in the Americas; to promote and maintain the dignity, rights and responsibilities of the profession of journalism; to foster a wider knowledge and greater interchange among the peoples of the Americas; mems: 1,400; Exec. Dir JULIO E. MUÑOZ; publ. *IAPA News* (monthly).

International Amateur Radio Union: POB 310905, Newington, CT 06131-0905, USA; tel. (860) 594-0200; fax (860) 594-0259; internet www.iaru.org; f. 1925 to link national amateur radio societies and represent the interests of two-way amateur radio communication; mems: 159 national amateur radio societies; Pres. LARRY E. PRICE; Sec. DAVID SUMNER.

International Association of Broadcasting (Asociación Internacional de Radiodifusión—AIR): Carlos Quijano 1264, 1110 Montevideo, Uruguay; tel. (2) 9011319; fax (2) 9080458; e-mail airiab@distrinet.com.uy; internet www.airiab.com; f. 1946 to preserve free and private broadcasting; to promote co-operation between the corporations and public authorities; to defend freedom of expression; mems: national asscns of broadcasters; Pres. ALFONSO RUIZ DE ASSIN; Dir-Gen. Dr HÉCTOR OSCAR AMENGUAL; publ. *La Gaceta de AIR* (every 2 months).

International Association of Sound and Audiovisual Archives: c/o Gunnel Jönsson, SRF Radio Archive, SE 105 10 Stockholm, Sweden; tel. (8) 784-1535; fax (8) 784-2285; e-mail gunnel.jonsson@srf.se; internet www.iasa-web.org; f. 1969; supports the professional exchange of sound and audiovisual documents, and fosters international co-operation between audiovisual archives in all fields, in particular in the areas of acquisition, documentation, access, exploitation copyright, and preservation; holds annual conference; mems: 400 individuals and institutions in 64 countries; Sec.-Gen. GUNNEL JÖNSSON (Sweden); publs *IASA Journal* (2 a year), *IASA Information Bulletin* (2 a year), *eBulletin* (2 a year).

International Catholic Union of the Press (Union catholique internationale de la presse—UCIP): 37–39 rue de Vermont, CP 197, 1211 Geneva 20, Switzerland; tel. 227340071; fax 227340053; e-mail helo@ucip.ch; internet www.ucip.ch; f. 1927 to link all Catholics who influence public opinion through the press, to inspire a high standard of professional conscience and to represent the interest of the Catholic press at international organizations; mems: Federation of Catholic Press Agencies, Federation of Catholic Journalists, Federation of Catholic Dailies, Federation of Catholic Periodicals, Federation of Teachers in the Science and Technics of Information, Federation of Church Press Associations, Federation of Book Publishers, eight regional asscns; Pres. ISMAR DE OLIVEIRA SOARES; Sec.-Gen. JOSEPH CHITTILAPPILLY (India); publ. *UCIP-Information*.

International Council for Film, Television and Audiovisual Communication (Conseil international du cinema de la television et de la communication audiovisuelle): 1 rue Miollis, 75732 Paris Cédex 15, France; tel. 1-45-68-48-55; fax 1-45-67-28-40; e-mail cict@unesco.org; internet www.unesco.org/iftc; f. 1958 to support collaboration between UNESCO and professionals engaged in cinema, television and audiovisual communications; mems: 36 international film and television organizations; Pres. HISANORI ISOMURA; Gen. Sec. GUILIO C. GIORDANO; publ. *Letter of Information* (monthly).

International Council of French-speaking Radio and Television Organizations (Conseil international des radios-télévisions d'expression française): 52 blvd Auguste-Reyers, 1044 Brussels, Belgium; tel. (2) 732-45-85; fax (2) 732-62-40; e-mail cirtef@rtbf.be; internet www.cirtef.org; f. 1978 to establish links between French-speaking radio and television organizations; mems: 46 orgs; Pres. TORIDEN CHELLAPERMAL (Mauritius); Sec.-Gen. GUILA THIAM (Senegal).

International Federation of Film Critics (Fédération Internationale de la Presse Cinématographique—FIPRESCI): Schleissheimerstr. 83, 80797 Munich, Germany; tel. (89) 182303; fax (89) 184766; e-mail info@fipresci.org; internet www.fipresci.org; f. 1930 to develop the cinematographic press and promote cinema as an art; organizes international meetings and juries in film festivals; mems: national organizations or corresponding members in 68 countries; Pres. ANDREI PLAKHOV (Russia); Gen. Sec. KLAUS EDER (Germany).

International Federation of Press Cutting Agencies: Streulistr. 19, POB 8030 Zürich, Switzerland; tel. 443888200; fax 443888201; e-mail fibep@bluewin.ch; f. 1953 to improve the standing of the profession, prevent infringements, illegal practices and unfair competition; and to develop business and friendly relations among press cuttings agencies throughout the world; mems: 81 agencies; Pres. CARLOS BEGAS (Israel); Gen. Sec. THOMAS HENNE (Switzerland).

International Federation of the Periodical Press (FIPP): Queen's House, 55/56 Lincoln's Inn Fields, London, WC2A 3LJ, United Kingdom; tel. (20) 7404-4169; fax (20) 7404-4170; e-mail info@fipp.com; internet www.fipp.com; f. 1925; works for the benefit of magazine publishers around the world by promoting the common editorial, cultural and economic interests of consumer and business-to-business publishers, both in print and electronic media; fosters formal and informal alliances between magazine publishers and industry suppliers; mems: one regional asscn (for Latin America), 47 national asscns, 172 publishing cos, 60 assoc. mems and six individual mems; Pres. and CEO DONALD KUMMERFELD; publ. *Magazine World* (quarterly).

International Federation of the Socialist and Democratic Press: CP 737, 1-2021 Milan, Italy; tel. (02) 8050105; f. 1953 to promote co-operation between editors and publishers of socialist newspapers; affiliated to the Socialist International; mems: about 100; Sec. UMBERTO GIOVINE.

International Institute of Communications: Regent House, 24/25 Nutford Place, London, W1H 5YN, United Kingdom; tel. (20) 7725-7040; fax (20) 7725-7092; e-mail enquiries@iicom.org; internet www.iicom.org; f. 1969 (as the International Broadcast Institute) to link all working in the field of communications, including policy makers, broadcasters, industrialists and engineers; holds local, regional and international meetings; undertakes research; mems: over 1,000 corporate, institutional and individual; Pres. ARNE WESSBERG (Finland); Dir-Gen. BRIAN QUINN; publs *Intermedia* (quarterly).

International Maritime Radio Association: South Bank House, Black Prince Rd, London, SE1 7SJ, United Kingdom; tel. (20) 7587-1245; fax (20) 7587-1436; e-mail secgen@cirm.org; internet www.cirm.org; f. 1928 to study and develop means of improving marine radio communications and radio aids to marine navigation; mems: some 75 organizations and companies from 21 maritime nations involved in marine electronics in the areas of radio communications and navigation; Pres. BRUNO MUSELLA (Italy); Sec.-Gen. and Chair. of Technical Cttee MICHAEL RAMBAUT.

International Press Institute (IPI): Spiegelgasse 2, 1010 Vienna, Austria; tel. (1) 5129011; fax (1) 5129014; e-mail ipi@freemedia.at; internet www.freemedia.at; f. 1951 as a non-governmental organization of editors, publishers and news broadcasters supporting the principles of a free and responsible press; aims to defend press freedom; conducts research; maintains a library; holds regional meetings and an annual World Congress; mems: about 2,000 from 120 countries; Chair. PIOTR NIEMCZYCKI (Poland); Dir DAVID DADGE (Austria); publs *IPI Congress Report* (annually), *World Press Freedom Review* (annually).

International Press Telecommunications Council (IPTC): 20 Garrick Street, London, WC2E 9BT, United Kingdom; tel. (20) 3178-4922; fax (20) 7664-7878; e-mail office@iptc.org; internet www.iptc.org; f. 1965 to safeguard the telecommunications interests of the world press; keeps its members informed of current and future telecommunications developments; acts as the news industry's formal standards body; meets three times a year and maintains three committees and 10 working parties; mems: 69 press asscns, news agencies, newspapers and industry vendors; Chair. STÉPHANE GUÉRILLOT; Man. Dir MICHAEL STEIDL; publs *IPTC Spectrum* (annually), *IPTC Mirror* (monthly).

Latin-American Catholic Press Union: Apdo Postal 17-21-178, Quito, Ecuador; tel. (2) 548-046; fax (2) 501-658; f. 1959 to coordinate, promote and improve the Catholic press in Latin America; mems: national asscns and local groups in most Latin American countries; Pres. ISMAR DE OLIVEIRA SOARES (Brazil); Sec. CARLOS EDUARDO CORTÉS (Colombia).

INTERNATIONAL ORGANIZATIONS

Organization of Asia-Pacific News Agencies (OANA): c/o Bernama News Agency, 38 Jalan 1/65A, 50400 Kuala Lumpur, Malaysia; tel. (3) 26939933; fax (3) 26981102; internet www.oananews.org; f. 1961 to promote co-operation in professional matters and mutual exchange of news, features, etc. among the news agencies of Asia and the Pacific via the Asia-Pacific News Network (ANN); 13th General Assembly: Bangkok, Thailand, 2007; mems: 40 news agencies in 33 countries; Pres. SYED JAMIL JAAFAR (Malaysia); Sec.-Gen. AZMAN UJANG.

Press Foundation of Asia: POB 1843, S & L Bldg, 3rd Floor, 1500 Roxas Blvd, Manila, Philippines; tel. (2) 5233223; fax (2) 5224365; e-mail pfa@pressasia.org; f. 1967; an independent, non-profit-making organization governed by its newspaper members; acts as a professional forum for about 200 newspapers in Asia; aims to reduce cost of newspapers to potential readers, to improve editorial and management techniques through research and training programmes and to encourage the growth of the Asian press; operates *Depthnews* feature service; mems: 200 newspapers; Exec. Chair. MAZLAN NORDIN (Malaysia); Chief Exec. MOCHTAR LUBIS (Indonesia); publs *Pressasia* (quarterly), *Asian Women* (quarterly).

Reporters sans Frontières: 5 rue Geoffroy Marie, 75009 Paris, France; tel. 1-44-83-84-84; fax 1-45-23-11-51; e-mail rsf@rsf.org; internet www.rsf.org; f. 1985 to defend press freedom throughout the world; generates awareness of violations of press freedoms and supports journalists under threat or imprisoned as a result of their work; mems in 77 countries; Dir ROBERT MÉNARD; publs *Annual Report*, *La Lettre de Reporters sans Frontières* (6 a year).

World Association for Christian Communication (WACC): 308 Main St, Toronto, ON M4C 4X7, Canada; tel. (416) 691-1999; fax (416) 691-1997; e-mail wacc@wacc.org.uk; internet www.waccglobal.org/wacc; f. 1975 to promote human dignity, justice and peace through freedom of expression and the democratization of communication; offers professional guidance on communication policies; interprets developments in and the consequences of global communication methods; works towards the empowerment of women; assists the training of Christian communicators; mems:corporate and personal mems in 120 countries, organized in eight regional asscns; Pres. Dr MUSIMBI KANYORO; Gen.-Sec. R. L. NAYLOR (Canada); publs *Action*, *Newsletter* (10 a year), *Media Development* (quarterly), *Communication Resource*, *Media and Gender Monitor* (both occasional).

World Association of Newspapers (WAN): 7 rue Geoffroy Saint Hilaire, 75005 Paris, France; tel. 1-47-42-85-00; fax 1-47-42-49-48; e-mail tbalding@wan.asso.fr; internet www.wan-press.org; f. 1948 to defend the freedom of the press, to safeguard the ethical and economic interests of newspapers and to study all questions of interest to newspapers at international level; mems: 76 national newspaper asscns, individual newspaper executives in 102 countries, 10 news agencies and 10 regional and world-wide press groups; Pres. GAVIN O'REILLY (Ireland); CEO TIMOTHY BALDING; publ. *Newsletter*.

Religion

Agudath Israel World Organisation: Hacherut Sq., POB 326, Jerusalem 91002, Israel; tel. (2) 5384357; fax (2) 5383634; f. 1912 to help solve the problems facing Jewish people all over the world in the spirit of the Jewish tradition; holds World Congress (every five years) and an annual Central Council; mems: over 500,000 in 25 countries; Chair. J. M. ABRAMOWITZ (Jerusalem); Secs Rabbi MOSHE GEWIRTZ, Rabbi CHAIM WEINSTOCK; publs *Hamodia* (Jerusalem, daily, in Hebrew; New York, daily, in English; Paris, weekly, in French), *Jedion* (Hebrew, monthly), *Jewish Tribune* (London, weekly), *Jewish Observer* (New York, monthly), *Dos Yiddishe Vort* (New York, monthly), *Coalition* (New York), *Perspectives* (Toronto, monthly), *La Voz Judia* (Buenos Aires, monthly), *Jüdische Stimme* (Zürich, weekly).

All Africa Conference of Churches (AACC): Waiyaki Way, POB 14205, 00800 Westlands, Nairobi, Kenya; tel. (20) 4441483; fax (20) 4443241; e-mail secretariat@aacc-ceta.org; internet www.aacc-ceta.org; f. 1963; an organ of co-operation and continuing fellowship among Protestant, Orthodox and independent churches and Christian Councils in Africa; 2008 Assembly: Maputu, Mozambique; mems: 169 churches and affiliated Christian councils in 39 African countries; Pres. The Right Rev. Dr NYANSAKO-NI-NKU (Cameroon); Gen. Sec. Rev. Dr MVUME DANDALA (South Africa); publs *ACIS/APS Bulletin*, *Tam Tam*.

Alliance Israélite Universelle (AIU): 45 rue La Bruyère, 75428 Paris Cédex 09, France; tel. 1-53-32-88-55; fax 1-48-74-51-33; e-mail info@aiu.org; internet www.aiu.org; f. 1860 to work for the emancipation and moral progress of the Jews; maintains 40 schools in eight countries; library of 120,000 vols; mems: 8,000 in 16 countries; Pres. ADY STEG; Dir Gen. JEAN-JACQUES WAHL (France); publs *Les Cahiers de l'Alliance Israélite Universelle* (3 a year, in French), *Les Cahiers du Judaïsme*, *The Alliance Review* (in English).

Bahá'í International Community: Bahá'í World Centre, POB 155, 31001 Haifa, Israel; tel. (4) 8358394; fax (4) 8313312; e-mail opi@bwc.org; internet www.bahai.org; f. 1844; the aim of the Bahá'í International Community is to promote the unity of mankind and world peace through the teachings of the Bahá'í religion, including the equality of men and women and the elimination of all forms of prejudice; maintains schools for children and adults world-wide, operates educational and cultural radio stations in the USA, Asia and Latin America; and works to promote health education in many countries around the world; has 33 publishing trusts throughout the world, which have translated literature into 802 languages; governing body: Universal House of Justice (nine mems elected by 183 National Spiritual Assemblies); mems: in 101,969 local communities, 2,112 different indigenous tribes, races and ethnic groups (in 191 countries and 47 dependent territories or overseas departments); Sec.-Gen. ALBERT LINCOLN (USA); publs *Bahá'í World* (annually), *One Country* (quarterly, in 6 languages).

Baptist World Alliance: 405 North Washington St, Falls Church, VA 22046, USA; tel. (703) 790-8980; fax (703) 893-5160; e-mail bwa@bwanet.org; internet www.bwanet.org; f. 1905; aims to unite Baptists, lead in evangelism, respond to people in need and defend human rights; mems: 37m. individuals and more than 200 Baptist unions and conventions representing about 110m. people worldwide; Pres. DAVID COFFEY (United Kingdom); Gen. Sec. NEVILLE CALLAM (Jamaica); publ. *The Baptist World* (quarterly).

Caribbean Conference of Churches: POB 876, Port of Spain, Trinidad and Tobago; tel. 662-3064; fax 662-1303; e-mail ccchq@tstt.net.tt; internet www.cc-caribe.org; f. 1973; governed by a General Assembly which meets every 5 years and appoints a 15-member Continuation Committee (board of management) to establish policies and direct the work of the organization between Assemblies; maintains three sub-regional offices in Antigua, Jamaica and Trinidad with responsibility for programme implementation in various territories; mems: 33 member churches in 34 territories in the Dutch-, English-, French-, and Spanish-speaking territories of the region; Gen. Sec. GERARD GRANADO; publ. *Ecuscope Caribbean*.

Christian Conference of Asia (CCA): c/o Payap Univ. Muang, Chiang Mai 50000, Thailand; tel. (53) 243906; fax (53) 247303; e-mail cca@cca.org.hk; internet www.cca.org.hk; f. 1957 (present name adopted 1973) to promote co-operation and joint study in matters of common concern among the Churches of the region and to encourage interaction with other regional Conferences and the World Council of Churches; planned relocation to Chiang Mai, Thailand, pending; mems: more than 100 churches and councils of churches from 18 Asian countries; Gen. Sec. Dr PRAWATE KHID-ARN; publ. *CCA News* (quarterly).

Christian Peace Conference: POB 136, Prokopova 4, 130 00 Prague 3, Czech Republic; tel. 222781800; fax 222781801; e-mail christianpeace@volny.cz; internet www.volny.cz/christianpeace; f. 1958 as an international movement of theologians, clergy and lay-people, aiming to bring Christendom to recognize its share of guilt in both world wars and to dedicate itself to the service of friendship, reconciliation and peaceful co-operation of nations, to concentrate on united action for peace and justice, and to co-ordinate peace groups in individual churches and facilitate their effective participation in the peaceful development of society; works through five continental asscns, regional groups and member churches in many countries; Moderator Dr SERGIO ARCE MARTÍNEZ; Co-ordinator Rev. BRIAN G. COOPER; publs *CPC Information* (8 a year, in English and German), occasional *Study Volume*.

Conference of European Churches (CEC): POB 2100, 150 route de Ferney, 1211 Geneva 2, Switzerland; tel. 227916111; fax 227916227; e-mail cec@cec-kek.org; internet www.cec-kek.org; f. 1959 as a regional ecumenical organization for Europe and a meeting-place for European churches, including members and non-members of the World Council of Churches; holds assemblies every six years; mems: 125 Protestant, Anglican, Orthodox and Old Catholic churches in all European countries; Gen. Sec. The Ven. COLIN WILLIAMS; publs *Monitor* (quarterly), CEC communiqués, reports.

Conference of International Catholic Organizations: 37–39 rue de Vermont, 1202 Geneva, Switzerland; tel. 227338392; e-mail daniel.vanespen@signis.net; internet www.oic-ico.org; f. 1927 to encourage collaboration and agreement between the different Catholic international organizations in their common interests, and to contribute to international understanding; organizes international assemblies and meetings to study specific problems; permanent commissions deal with human rights, the new international economic order, social problems, the family health, education, etc; mems: some 40 Catholic international organizations; Pres. ERNEST KOENIG.

Consultative Council of Jewish Organizations (CCJO): 420 Lexington Ave, New York, NY 10170, USA; tel. (212) 808-5437;

f. 1946 to co-operate and consult with the UN and other international bodies directly concerned with human rights and to defend the cultural, political and religious rights of Jews throughout the world; Sec.-Gen. WARREN GREEN (USA).

European Baptist Federation (EBF): Nad Habrovkou 3, Jeneralka, 164 00 Prague 6, Czech Republic; tel. 296392250; fax 296392254; e-mail office@ebf.org; internet www.ebf.org; f. 1949 to promote fellowship and co-operation among Baptists in Europe; to further the aims and objects of the Baptist World Alliance; to stimulate and co-ordinate evangelism in Europe; to provide for consultation and planning of missionary work in Europe and elsewhere in the world; mems: 51 Baptist Unions in European countries and the Middle East; Pres. HELARI PUU (Estonia); Gen. Sec. TONY PECK (United Kingdom).

European Evangelical Alliance: 186 Kennington Park Rd, London, SE11 4BT, United Kingdom; tel. (20) 7582-7276; fax (20) 7582-2043; e-mail info@europeanea.org; internet www.europeanea.org; f. 1953 to promote understanding and co-operation among evangelical Christians in Europe and to stimulate evangelism; mems: 15m. in 35 European countries; Pres. Rev. NIKOLAY MEDELCHEV (Bulgaria); Sec. GORDON SHOWELL-ROGERS.

Federation of Jewish Communities of the CIS: 127055 Moscow, 5A 2nd Vysheslavtzev Pereulok, Russia; tel. (495) 737-82-75; fax (495) 783-84-71; e-mail info@fjc.ru; internet www.fjc.ru; f. 1998 to restore Jewish society, culture and religion throughout the countries of the fmr Soviet Union through the provision of professional assistance, educational support and funding to member communities; Pres. LEV LEVIEV.

Friends World Committee for Consultation: 173 Euston Road, London NW1 2AX, United Kingdom; tel. (20) 7663-1199; fax (20) 7663-1189; e-mail world@fwcc.quaker.org; internet www.fwccworld.org; f. 1937 to encourage and strengthen the spiritual life within the Religious Society of Friends (Quakers); to help Friends to a better understanding of their vocation in the world; and to promote consultation among Friends of all countries; representation at the United Nations as a non-governmental organization with general consultative status; mems: appointed representatives and individuals from 70 countries; Gen. Sec. NANCY IRVING; publs *Friends World News* (2 a year), *Calendar of Yearly Meetings* (annually), *Quakers around the World* (handbook).

Global Christian Forum: POB 306, 1290 Versoix, Switzerland; tel. 227554546; fax 227550108; e-mail gcforum@freesurf.ch; internet www.globalchristianforum.net; established, initially, in 1998 by the World Council of Churches as an autonomous Continuation Committee, and later as an International Consultation, to provide opportunities for church movements and organizations to consider common questions and to foster mutual respect; a series of regional meetings was held 2004–07 and the first global forum was convened in November 2007 in Nairobi, Kenya; Sec. Gen. HUBERT VAN BEEK.

International Association for Religious Freedom (IARF): 2 Market St, Oxford, OX1 3ET, United Kingdom; tel. (1865) 202744; fax (1865) 202746; e-mail hq@iarf.net; internet www.iarf.net; f. 1900 as a world community of religions, subscribing to the principle of openness and upholding the United Nation's Universal Declaration on freedom of religion or belief; conducts religious freedom programmes, focusing on inter-religious harmony; holds regional conferences and triennial congress; mems: 100 groups in 27 countries; Pres. Rev. ABHI JANAMANCHI (USA); Sec. JEFFREY TEAGLE.

International Association of Buddhist Studies (IABS): c/o Prof. T. J. F. Tillemans, Section des langues et civilisations orientales, Université de Lausanne, 1015 Lausanne, Switzerland; fax 216923045; e-mail mail@iabsinfo.org; internet www.iabsinfo.org; f. 1976; supports studies of Buddhist religion, philosophy and literature; holds international conference every three or four years; Gen. Sec. TOM J. F. TILLEMANS; publ. *Journal* (2 a year).

International Council of Christians and Jews (ICCJ): Martin Buber House, POB 1129, 64629 Heppenheim, Germany; tel. (6252) 93120; fax (6252) 68331; e-mail info@iccj-buberhouse.de; internet www.iccj.org; f. 1947 to promote mutual respect and co-operation; holds annual international colloquium, seminars, meetings for young people and for women; maintains a forum for Jewish–Christian–Muslim relations; mems: 38 national councils world-wide; Pres. Rev. Prof. Dr JOHN T. PAWLIKOWSKI; publs *ICCJ History*, *ICCJ Brochure*, conference documents.

International Council of Jewish Women: Shaked 363, Zur Hadassah 99875, Israel; tel. and fax (2) 5336955; e-mail president@icjw.org; internet www.icjw.org; f. 1912 to promote friendly relations and understanding among Jewish women throughout the world; campaigns for human and women's rights, exchanges information on community welfare activities, promotes volunteer leadership, sponsors field work in social welfare, co-sponsors the International Jewish Women's Human Rights Watch and fosters Jewish education; mems: over 2m. mems in 52 orgs across 47 countries; Pres. LEAH AHARONOV; publs *Newsletter*, *Links around the World* (2 a year, English and Spanish), *International Jewish Women's Human Rights Watch* (2 a year).

International Fellowship of Reconciliation (IFOR): Spoorstraat 38, 1815 BK Alkmaar, Netherlands; tel. (72) 512-30-14; fax (72) 515-11-02; e-mail office@ifor.org; internet www.ifor.org; f. 1919; international, spiritually-based movement committed to active non-violence as a way of life and as a means of building a culture of peace and non-violence; maintains over 65 branches, affiliates and groups in more than 40 countries; Pres. JONATHAN SISSON (Switzerland); publs *IFOR in Action* (quarterly), *Patterns in Reconciliation* (2 a year), *International Reconciliation* (3–4 times a year), *Cross the Lines* (3 a year, in Arabic, English, French, Russian and Spanish), occasional paper series.

International Humanist and Ethical Union (IHEU): 1 Gower Street, London, WC1E 6HD, United Kingdom; tel. (870) 288-7631; fax (870) 288-7631; e-mail iheu-office@iheu.org; internet www.iheu.org; f. 1952 to bring into asscn all those interested in promoting ethical and scientific humanism and human rights; mems: national organizations and individuals in 37 countries; Pres. SONIA EGGERICKX; Exec. Dir BABU R. R. GOGINENI; publ. *International Humanist News* (quarterly).

International Organization for the Study of the Old Testament: Dolnicarjeva 1, 1000 Ljubljana, Slovenia; tel. (1) 4340198; fax (1) 4330405; f. 1950; holds triennial congresses; Pres. Prof. JOŽE KRAŠOVEC; publ. *Vetus Testamentum* (quarterly).

Latin American Council of Churches (Consejo Latinoamericano de Iglesias—CLAI): Casilla 17-08-8522, Calle Inglaterra N.32–113 y Mariana de Jesús, Quito, Ecuador; tel. (2) 255-9933; fax (2) 256-8373; e-mail israel@clai.org.ec; internet www.clai.org.ec; f. 1982; mems: 147 churches in 19 countries; Gen. Sec. Rev. ISRAEL BATISTA; publs *Nuevo Siglo* (monthly, in Spanish), other quarterly newspapers and magazines in English and Spanish.

Latin American Episcopal Council (Consejo Episcopal Latinoamericano—CELAM): Carrera 5A 11831, Apartado Aéreo 51086, Bogotá, Colombia; tel. (1) 6578330; fax (1) 6121929; e-mail celam@celam.org; internet www.celam.org; f. 1955 to co-ordinate Church activities in and with the Latin American and the Caribbean Catholic Bishops' Conferences; mems: 22 Episcopal Conferences of Central and South America and the Caribbean; Pres. Cardinal FRANCISCO JAVIER ERRÁZURIZ OSSA; publ. *Boletín* (6 a year).

Lutheran World Federation: 150 route de Ferney, POB 2100, 1211 Geneva 2, Switzerland; tel. 227916111; fax 227916630; e-mail info@lutheranworld.org; internet www.lutheranworld.org; f. 1947; groups 138 Lutheran Churches in 77 countries; provides inter-church aid and relief work in various areas of the globe; gives service to refugees, including resettlement; carries out theological research, conferences and exchanges; grants scholarship aid in various fields of church life; conducts inter-confessional dialogue with Roman Catholic, Seventh-day Adventist, Anglican and Orthodox churches; mems: 66.2m. worldwide; Pres. Bishop MARK S. HANSON (USA); Gen. Sec. Rev. Dr ISHMAEL NOKO (Zimbabwe); publs *Lutheran World Information* (English and German, daily e-mail news service and monthly print edition), *LWF Today* and *LWF Documentation* (both irregular).

Middle East Council of Churches: POB 5376, Beirut, Lebanon; tel. (1) 344896; fax (1) 344894; internet www.mec-churches.org; f. 1974; mems: 28 churches; Pres Pope SHENOUDAH III, Patriarch PETROS IV, Rev. Dr SAFWAT AL-BAYADI, Archbishop ANBA YUHANNA QOLTA; Gen. Sec. GIRGIS IBRAHIM SALIH; publs *MECC News Report* (monthly), *Al Montada News Bulletin* (quarterly, in Arabic), *Courrier oecuménique du Moyen-Orient* (quarterly), *MECC Perspectives* (3 a year).

Muslim World League (MWL) (Rabitat al-Alam al-Islami): POB 537, Makkah, Saudi Arabia; tel. (2) 5600919; fax (2) 5601319; e-mail info@themwl.org; internet www.themwl.org; f. 1962; aims to advance Islamic unity and solidarity, and to promote world peace and respect for human rights; provides financial assistance for education, medical care and relief work; has 45 offices throughout the world; Sec.-Gen. Prof. Dr ABDULLAH BIN ABDUL MOHSIN AL-TURKI; publs *Al-Aalam al Islami* (weekly, Arabic), *Dawat al-Haq* (monthly, Arabic), *Muslim World League Journal* (monthly, English), *Muslim World League Journal* (quarterly, Arabic).

Opus Dei (Prelature of the Holy Cross and Opus Dei): Viale Bruno Buozzi 73, 00197 Rome, Italy; tel. (06) 808961; e-mail newyork@opusdei.org; internet www.opusdei.org; f. 1928 by St Josemaría Escrivá de Balaguer to spread, at every level of society, an increased awareness of the universal call to sanctity and apostolate in the exercise of one's work; mems: 84,541 Catholic laypeople and 1,875 priests; Prelate Most Rev. JAVIER ECHEVARRÍA; publ. *Romana (Bulletin of the Prelature)* (2 a year).

Pacific Conference of Churches: POB 208, 4 Thurston St, Suva, Fiji; tel. 3311277; fax 3303205; e-mail pacific@is.com.fj; f. 1961; organizes assembly every five years, as well as regular workshops, meetings and training seminars throughout the region; mems: 36

churches and councils; Moderator Pastor REUBEN MAGEKON; Gen. Sec. Rev. VALAMOTU PALU.

Pax Romana International Catholic Movement for Intellectual and Cultural Affairs (ICMICA); and International Movement of Catholic Students (IMCS): 15 rue du Grand-Bureau, POB 374, 1211 Geneva 4, Switzerland; tel. 228230707; fax 228230708; e-mail international_secretariat@paxromana.org; internet www.paxromana.org; f. 1921 (IMCS), 1947 (ICMICA), to encourage in members an awareness of their responsibilities as people and Christians in the student and intellectual milieux; to promote contacts between students and graduates throughout the world and co-ordinate the contribution of Catholic intellectual circles to international life; mems: 80 student and 60 intellectual orgs in 80 countries; ICMICA—Pres. JEAN NSONJIBA LOKENGA (Uganda); Gen. Sec. PAUL ORTEGA (Spain); IMCS—Pres. KEVIN AHERN (USA).

Salvation Army: International HQ, 101 Queen Victoria St, London, EC4P 4EP, United Kingdom; tel. (20) 7332-0101; fax (20) 7236-4981; internet www.salvationarmy.org; f. 1865 to spread the Christian gospel and relieve poverty; emphasis is placed on the need for personal discipleship, and to make its evangelism effective it adopts a quasi-military form of organization. Social, medical and educational work is also performed in the 109 countries where the Army operates; Pres. Gen. JOHN LARSSON; Chief of Staff Commissioner ISRAEL L. GAITHER; publ. *The War Cry* (weekly).

Theosophical Society: Adyar, Chennai 600 020, India; tel. (44) 24915552; fax (44) 4902706; e-mail intl.hq@ts-adyar.org; internet www.ts-adyar.org; f. 1875; aims at universal brotherhood, without distinction of race, creed, sex, caste or colour; study of comparative religion, philosophy and science; investigation of unexplained laws of nature and powers latent in man; mems: 32,000 in 70 countries; Pres. RADHA S. BURNIER; Int. Sec. MARY ANDERSON; publs *The Theosophist* (monthly), *Adyar News Letter* (quarterly), *Brahmavidya* (annually).

United Bible Societies: World Service Centre, Reading Bridge House, Reading, RG1 8PJ, United Kingdom; tel. (118) 950-0200; fax (118) 950-0857; e-mail comms@ubs-wsc.org; internet www.biblesociety.org; f. 1946; co-ordinates the translation, production and distribution of the Bible by Bible Societies world-wide; works with national Bible Societies to develop religious programmes; mems: 141 Bible Societies in more than 200 countries; Pres. Dr George BARTON (New Zealand); Gen. Sec. Rev. Dr MILLER MILLOY (United Kingdom); publs *The Bible Translator* (quarterly), *Publishing World* (3 a year), *Prayer Booklet* (annually), *World Report* (monthly).

Watch Tower Bible and Tract Society: 25 Columbia Heights, Brooklyn, NY 11201–2483, USA; tel. (718) 560-5600; fax (718) 560-8850; internet www.watchtower.org; f. 1881; 113 branches; serves as legal agency for Jehovah's Witnesses; publ. *The Watchtower* (semimonthly in 167 languages).

World Alliance of Reformed Churches (Presbyterian and Congregational): Box 2100, 150 route de Ferney, 1211 Geneva 2, Switzerland; tel. 227916240; fax 227916505; e-mail warc@warc.ch; internet www.warc.ch; f. 1970 by merger of WARC (Presbyterian) (f.1875) with International Congregational Council (f. 1891) to promote fellowship among Reformed, Presbyterian and Congregational churches; mems: 216 churches in 107 countries; Pres. CLIFTON KIRKPATRICK (USA); Gen. Sec. Rev. Dr SETRI NYOMI (Ghana); publs *Reformed World* (quarterly), *Up-Date*.

World Christian Life Community: Borgo Santo Spirito 8, 00193 Rome, Italy; tel. (06) 6868079; fax (06) 68132497; e-mail exsec@cvx-clc.net; internet www.cvx-clc.net; f. 1953 as World Federation of the Sodalities of our Lady (first group f.1563) as a lay organization based on the teachings of Ignatius Loyola, to integrate Christian faith and daily living; mems: groups in 55 countries representing about 100,000 individuals; Pres. DANIELA FRANK; Exec. Sec. GUY MAGINZI; publ. *Progressio* (in English, French and Spanish).

World Conference of Religions for Peace: 777 United Nations Plaza, New York, NY 10017, USA; tel. (212) 687-2163; fax (212) 983-0566; e-mail info@wcrp.org; internet www.religionsforpeace.org; f. 1970 to co-ordinate action of various world religions for world peace; mems: more than 80 inter-religious councils in Africa, Asia, Europe and Latin America; Sec.-Gen. Dr WILLIAM VENDLEY.

World Congress of Faiths: London Inter Faith Centre, 125 Salusbury Rd, London, NW6 6RG, United Kingdom; tel. (20) 8959-3129; fax (20) 7604-3052; e-mail enquiries@worldfaiths.org; internet www.worldfaiths.org; f. 1936 to promote a spirit of fellowship among mankind through an understanding of one another's religions, to bring together people of all nationalities, backgrounds and creeds in mutual respect and tolerance, to encourage the study and understanding of issues arising out of multi-faith societies, and to promote welfare and peace; sponsors lectures, conferences, retreats, etc; works with other interfaith organizations; mems: about 400; Pres. Rev. MARCUS BRAYBROOKE; Chair. Rabbi JACQUELINE TABICK; publ. *Interreligious Insight* (quarterly), *One Family*.

World Evangelical Alliance: 600 Alden Rd, Suite 300, Markham, ON L3R 0E7, Canada; tel. (905) 752-2164; fax (905) 479-4742; e-mail info@worldevangelical.org; internet www.worldevangelical.org; f. 1951 as World Evangelical Fellowship, on reorganization of World Evangelical Alliance (f. 1846), reverted to original name Jan. 2002; an int. grouping of national and regional bodies of evangelical Christians; encourages the organization of national fellowships and assists national mems in planning their activities; mems: national evangelical asscns in 127 countries; International Dir GEOFF TUNNICLIFFE; publs *Evangelical World* (monthly), *Evangelical Review of Theology* (quarterly).

World Fellowship of Buddhists: 616 Benjasiri Pk, Soi Medhinivet off Soi Sukhumvit 24, Bangkok 10110, Thailand; tel. (2) 661-1284; fax (2) 661-0555; e-mail wfb-hq@asianet.co.th; internet www.wfb-hq.org; f. 1950 to promote strict observance and practice of the teachings of the Buddha; holds General Conference every 2 years; 146 regional centres in 37 countries; Pres. PHAN WANNAMETHEE; Hon. Sec.-Gen. PHALLOP THAIARRY; publs *WFB Journal* (6 a year), *WFB Review* (quarterly), *WFB Newsletter* (monthly), documents, booklets.

World Hindu Federation: c/o Dr Jogendra Jha, Pashupati Kshetra, Kathmandu, Nepal; tel. (1) 470182; fax (1) 470131; e-mail hem@karki.com.np; f. 1981 to promote and preserve Hindu philosophy and culture and to protect the rights of Hindus, particularly the right to worship; executive board meets annually; mems: in 45 countries and territories; Sec.-Gen. Dr JOGENDRA JHA (Nepal); publ. *Vishwa Hindu* (monthly).

World Jewish Congress: 501 Madison Ave, New York, NY 10022, USA; tel. (212) 755-5770; fax (212) 755-5883; internet www.worldjewishcongress.org; f. 1936 as a voluntary asscn of representative Jewish communities and organizations throughout the world; aims to foster the unity of the Jewish people and ensure the continuity and development of their heritage; mems: Jewish communities in 80 countries; Pres. RONALD LAUDER (USA); Sec.-Gen. STEPHEN E. HERBITS; publs *Dispatches*, *Jerusalem Review*, regular updates, policy studies.

World Methodist Council: International Headquarters, POB 518, Lake Junaluska, NC 28745, USA; tel. (828) 456-9432; fax (828) 456-9433; e-mail georgefreeman@mindspring.com; internet www.worldmethodistcouncil.org; f. 1881 to deepen the fellowship of the Methodist peoples, encourage evangelism, foster Methodist participation in the ecumenical movement and promote the unity of Methodist witness and service; mems: 76 churches in 132 countries, comprising 38m. individuals; Gen. Sec. GEORGE H. FREEMAN (USA); publ. *World Parish* (quarterly).

World Sephardi Federation: 13 rue Marignac, 1206 Geneva, Switzerland; tel. 223473313; fax 223472839; e-mail office@wsf.org.il; internet www.jafi.org.il/wsf; f. 1951 to strengthen the unity of Jewry and Judaism among Sephardi and Oriental Jews, to defend and foster religious and cultural activities of all Sephardi and Oriental Jewish communities and preserve their spiritual heritage, to provide moral and material assistance where necessary and to co-operate with other similar organizations; mems: 50 communities and organizations in 33 countries; Pres. NESSIM D. GAON; Sec.-Gen. SHIMON DERY.

World Student Christian Federation (WSCF): Ecumenical Centre, POB 2100, 1211 Geneva 2, Switzerland; tel. 227916358; fax 227916152; e-mail wscf@wscf.ch; internet www.wscfglobal.org; f. 1895; aims to proclaim Jesus Christ as Lord and Saviour in the academic community, and to present students with the claims of the Christian faith over their whole life; has consultative status with the UN and advisory status at the World Council of Churches; holds General Assembly every four years; mems: more than 100 national Student Christian Movements, and six regional officers; Chair. Dr KEN GUEST (USA); Gen. Sec. MICHAEL WALLACE (Switzerland).

World Union for Progressive Judaism: 13 King David St, Jerusalem 94101, Israel; tel. (2) 6203447; fax (2) 6203525; e-mail wupjis@wupj.org.il; internet wupj.org.il; f. 1926; promotes and co-ordinates efforts of Reform, Liberal, Progressive and Reconstructionist congregations throughout the world; supports new congregations; assigns and employs rabbis; sponsors seminaries and schools; organizes international conferences; maintains a youth section; mems: orgs and individuals in around 40 countries; Pres. Rabbi URI REGEV; Exec. Dir Rabbi RICHARD G. HIRSCH (Israel); publs *News Updates*, *International Conference Reports*, *European Judaism*.

World Union of Catholic Women's Organisations: 37 rue Notre-Dame-des-Champs, 75006 Paris, France; tel. 1-45-44-27-65; fax 1-42-84-04-80; e-mail wucwoparis@wanadoo.fr; internet www.wucwo.org; f. 1910 to promote and co-ordinate the contribution of Catholic women in international life, in social, civic, cultural and religious matters; mems: 5m.; Pres. KAREN M. HURLEY (USA); Sec.-Gen. GILLIAN BADCOCK (United Kingdom); publ. *Women's Voice* (quarterly, in four languages).

Science

Association for the Taxonomic Study of the Flora of Tropical Africa: National Botanic Garden of Belgium, Domein van Bouchout, 1860 Meise, Belgium; tel. (2) 260-09-28; fax (2) 260-08-45; e-mail rammeloo@br.fgov.be; f. 1950 to facilitate co-operation and liaison between botanists engaged in the study of the flora of tropical Africa south of the Sahara including Madagascar; maintains a library; mems: c. 800 botanists in 63 countries; Sec.-Gen. Prof. J. RAMMELOO; publs *AETFAT Bulletin* (annually), *Proceedings*.

Association of Geoscientists for International Development (AGID): c/o 15 Malvern Rd, Mapperley, Nottingham, NG3 5GZ, United Kingdom; tel. (115) 818-4206; fax (115) 210-4958; e-mail kmellito@usp.br; internet agid.igc.usp.br; f. 1974 to encourage communication and the exchange of knowledge between those interested in the application of the geosciences to international development; contributes to the funding of geoscience development projects; provides postgraduate scholarships; mems: 2,000 individual and institutional mems in over 120 countries; Pres. AFIA AKHTAR (Bangladesh) (2004–08); Sec. Dr A. J. REEDMAN (United Kingdom); publs *Geoscience and Developments* (2 or 3 a year), reports on geoscience and development issues.

Council for the International Congresses of Entomology: c/o FAO, POB 3700 MCPO, 1277 Makati, Philippines; tel. (2) 8134229; fax (2) 8127725; e-mail joliver@gasou.edu; f. 1910 to act as a link between quadrennial congresses and to arrange the venue for each congress; the committee is also the entomology section of the International Union of Biological Sciences; Chair. Dr M. J. WHITTAM (Australia); Sec. Dr J. OLIVER (USA).

European Association of Geoscientists and Engineers (EAGE): POB 59, 3990 DB Houten, Netherlands; tel. (30) 6354055; fax (30) 6343524; e-mail eage@eage.org; internet www.eage.org; f. 1997 by merger of European Asscn of Exploration Geophysicists and Engineers (f. 1951) and the European Asscn of Petroleum Geoscientists and Engineers (f. 1988); these two organizations have become, respectively, the Geophysical and the Petroleum Divisions of the EAGE; aims to promote the applications of geoscience and related subjects and to foster co-operation between those working or studying in the fields; organizes conferences, workshops, education programmes and exhibitions; seeks global co-operation with organizations with similar objectives; mems: approx. 8,500 in more than 100 countries; Exec. Dir A. VAN GERWEN; publs *Geophysical Prospecting* (6 a year), *First Break* (monthly), *Petroleum Geoscience* (quarterly).

European Atomic Forum (FORATOM): 57 rue de la Loi, 1040 Brussels, Belgium; tel. (2) 502-45-95; fax (2) 502-39-02; e-mail foratom@foratom.org; internet www.foratom.org; f. 1960; promotes the peaceful use of nuclear energy; provides information on nuclear energy issues to the EU, the media and the public; represents the nuclear industry within the EU institutions; holds periodical conferences; mems: atomic forums in 16 countries; Dir Gen. SANTIAGO SAN ANTONIO.

European Molecular Biology Organization (EMBO): Meyerhofstr. 1, Postfach 1022.40, 69012 Heidelberg, Germany; tel. (6221) 8891-0; fax (6221) 8891-200; e-mail embo@embo.org; internet www.embo.org; f. 1962 to promote collaboration in the field of molecular biology and to establish fellowships for training and research; has established the European Molecular Biology Laboratory where a majority of the disciplines comprising the subject are represented; mems: 1,100 elected mems in Europe, 60 assoc. mems worldwide; Exec. Dir Prof. FRANK GANNON; publs *Annual Report*, *EMBO Journal* (24 a year), *EMBO Reports* (monthly).

European Organization for Nuclear Research (CERN): 1211 Geneva 23, Switzerland; tel. 227676111; fax 227676555; e-mail cern.reception@cern.ch; internet www.cern.ch; f. 1954 to provide for collaboration among European states in nuclear research of a pure scientific and fundamental character, for peaceful purposes only; Council comprises two representatives of each member state; major experimental facilities: Proton Synchrotron (of 25–28 GeV), and Super Proton Synchrotron (of 450 GeV); mems: 20 European countries; observers: Israel, Japan, Russia, Turkey, USA, European Commission, UNESCO; Dir-Gen. Dr ROBERT AYMAR; publs *CERN Courier* (monthly), *Annual Report*, *Scientific Reports*.

European-Mediterranean Seismological Centre: c/o LDG, BP 12, 91680 Bruyères-le-Châtel, France; tel. 1-69-26-78-14; fax 1-69-26-70-00; e-mail csem@emsc-csem.org; internet www.emsc-csem.org; f. 1976 for rapid determination of seismic hypocentres in the region; maintains data base; mems: institutions in 45 countries; Pres. C. BROWITT; Sec.-Gen. R. BOSSU; publ. *Newsletter* (2 a year).

Federation of Arab Scientific Research Councils: POB 13027, Al Karkh/Karadat Mariam, Baghdad, Iraq; tel. (1) 888-1709; fax (1) 886-6346; f. 1976 to encourage co-operation in scientific research, promote the establishment of new institutions and plan joint regional research projects; mems: national science bodies in 15 countries; Sec.-Gen. Dr TAHA AL-NUEIMI; publs *Journal of Computer Research*, *Journal of Environmental and Sustained Development*, *Journal of Biotechnology*.

Federation of Asian Scientific Academies and Societies (FASAS): c/o Academy of Sciences Malaysia, 902 Jalan Tun Ismail, 50480 Kuala Lumpur, Malaysia; tel. (3) 26949898; fax (3) 26945858; e-mail admin@akademisains.gov.my; f. 1984 to stimulate regional co-operation and promote national and regional self-reliance in science and technology, by organizing meetings, training and research programmes and encouraging the exchange of scientists and of scientific information; mems: national scientific academies and societies from Afghanistan, Australia, Bangladesh, People's Republic of China, India, Republic of Korea, Malaysia, Nepal, New Zealand, Pakistan, Philippines, Singapore, Sri Lanka, Thailand; Pres. Tan Sri Datuk Dr OMAR ABDUL RAHMAN (Malaysia); Sec. Dato' IR LEE YEE CHEONG (Malaysia).

Federation of European Biochemical Societies: c/o Institute of Cancer Biology and Danish Centre for Human Genome Research, Danish Cancer Society, Strandboulevarden 49, 2100 Copenhagen Ø, Denmark; tel. 35-25-73-64; fax 35-25-73-76; e-mail secretariat@febs.org; internet www.febs.org; f. 1964 to promote the science of biochemistry through meetings of European biochemists, advanced courses and the provision of fellowships; mems: approx. 40,000 in 36 societies; Chair. Prof. JOLANTA BARANSKA; Sec.-Gen. Prof. JULIO E. CELIS; publs *The FEBS Journal*, *FEBS News*, *FEBS Letters*, *FEBS Newsletter*.

Foundation for International Scientific Co-ordination (Fondation 'Pour la science', Centre international de synthèse): Caphés-CNRS ENS, 45 rue d'Ulm, 75005 Paris, France; tel. 1-44-32-26-54; fax 1-44-32-26-56; e-mail revuedesynthese@ens.fr; internet www.ehess.fr/acta/synthese/; f. 1925; Dir ERIC BRIAN; publs *Revue de Synthèse*, *Revue d'Histoire des Sciences*, *Semaines de Synthèse*, *L'Evolution de l'Humanité*.

Institute of General Semantics: 2260 College Ave, Fort Worth, TX 76110, USA; tel. (817) 922-9950; fax (817) 922-9903; e-mail isgs@time-binding.org; internet www.generalsemantics.org; f. 1943 as the International Society for General Semantics to advance knowledge of and inquiry into non-Aristotelian systems and general semantics; merged with Institute of General Semantics (f. 1938) in 2004; mems: approx. 700 (100 int.); Pres. CHARLES RUSSELL, Jr (USA); Exec. Dir STEVE STOCKDALE (USA).

Intergovernmental Oceanographic Commission: UNESCO, 1 rue Miollis, 75015 Paris Cedex 15, France; tel. 1-45-68-39-84; fax 1-45-68-58-10; e-mail b.aliaga@unesco.org; internet ioc.unesco.org/iocweb; f. 1960 to promote scientific investigation of the nature and resources of the oceans through the concerted action of its members; mems: 129 govts; Chair. Dr DAVID T. PUGH (United Kingdom); Exec. Sec. Dr PATRICIO BERNAL; publs *IOC Technical Series* (irregular), *IOC Manuals and Guides* (irregular), *IOC Workshop Reports* (irregular) and *IOC Training Course Reports* (irregular), annual reports.

International Academy of Astronautics (IAA): 6 rue Galilee, POB 1268–16, 75766 Paris Cédex 16, France; tel. 1-47-23-82-15; fax 1-47-23-82-16; internet www.iaaweb.org; f. 1960; fosters the development of astronautics for peaceful purposes, holds scientific meetings and makes scientific studies, reports, awards and book awards; maintains 19 scientific cttees and a multilingual terminology data base (20 languages); mems: 1,213 active mems, 5 hon. mems, in 75 countries; Sec.-Gen. Dr JEAN-MICHEL CONTANT; publ. *Acta Astronautica* (monthly).

International Association for Biologicals (IABS): 8 chemin de la Gravière, 1227 Acacias, Geneva, Switzerland; tel. 223011036; fax 223011037; e-mail iabs@iabs.org; internet www.iabs.org; f. 1955 to connect producers and controllers of immunological products (sera, vaccines, etc.), for the study and development of methods of standardization; supports international organizations in their efforts to solve problems of standardization; mems: c. 400; Pres. A. ESHKOL (Switzerland); Sec. D. GAUDRY (France); publs *Newsletter* (quarterly), *Biologicals* (quarterly).

International Association for Earthquake Engineering: Ken chiku-kaikan Bldg, 3rd Floor, 5-26-20, Shiba, Minato-ku, Tokyo 108-0014, Japan; tel. (3) 3453-1281; fax (3) 3453-0428; e-mail secretary@iaee.or.jp; internet www.iaee.or.jp; f. 1963 to promote international co-operation among scientists and engineers in the field of earthquake engineering through exchange of knowledge, ideas and results of research and practical experience; mems: national cttees in 49 countries; Pres. Prof. LUIS ESTEVA (Mexico); Sec.-Gen. HIROKAZU IEMURA.

International Association for Ecology (INTECOL): c/o College of Forest Science, Department of Forest Resources, Kookmin Univ., Songbuk-gu, Seoul 136-702, Republic of Korea; e-mail kimeuns@kookmin.ac.kr; internet www.intecol.net; f. 1967 to provide opportunities for communication between ecologists world-wide; to co-operate with organizations and individuals having related aims and interests; to encourage studies in the different fields of ecology;

affiliated to the International Union of Biological Sciences; mems: 35 national and international ecological societies, and 1,000 individuals; Pres. JOHN A. LEE (United Kingdom); Sec.-Gen. EUN-SHIK KIM (Korea).

International Association for Mathematical Geology (IAMG): 4 Cataraqui St., Suite 310 Kingston ON K7K 1Z7 Canada; tel. (613) 544-6878; fax (613) 531-0626; e-mail office@iamg.org; internet www.iamg.org; f. 1968 for the preparation and elaboration of mathematical models of geological processes; the introduction of mathematical methods in geological sciences and technology; assistance in the development of mathematical investigation in geological sciences; the organization of international collaboration in mathematical geology through various forums and publications; educational programmes for mathematical geology; affiliated to the International Union of Geological Sciences; mems: c. 600; Pres. FRITS P. AGTERBERG (Canada); Sec.-Gen. CLAYTON V. DEUTSCH (Canada); publs *Mathematical Geology* (8 a year), *Computers and Geosciences* (10 a year), *Natural Resources Research* (quarterly), *Newsletter* (2 a year).

International Association for Mathematics and Computers in Simulation: c/o Free University of Brussels, Automatic Control, CP 165/84, 50 ave F. D. Roosevelt, 1050 Brussels, Belgium; tel. (2) 650-20-85; fax (2) 650-45-34; e-mail Robert.Beauwens@ulb.ac.be; internet www.research.rutgers.edu/~imacs/; f. 1955 to further the study of mathematical tools and computer software and hardware, analogue, digital or hybrid computers for simulation of soft or hard systems; mems: 1,100 and 27 assoc. mems; Pres. ROBERT BEAUWENS (Belgium); Treas. ERNEST H. MUND; publs *Mathematics and Computers in Simulation* (6 a year), *Applied Numerical Mathematics* (6 a year), *Journal of Computational Acoustics*.

International Association for the Physical Sciences of the Ocean (IAPSO): Johan Rodhe, POB 460, 40530 Göteborg, Sweden; e-mail johan.rodhe@gu.se; internet www.olympus.net/IAPSO; f. 1919 to promote the study of scientific problems relating to the oceans and interactions occurring at its boundaries, chiefly in so far as such study may be carried out by the aid of mathematics, physics and chemistry;; to initiate, facilitate and co-ordinate research; and to provide for discussion, comparison and publication; affiliated to the International Union of Geodesy and Geophysics; mems: 81 member states; Pres. Prof. LAWRENCE MYSAK; Sec.-Gen. Prof JOHAN RODHE (Sweden); publ. *Publications Scientifiques* (irregular).

International Association for Plant Physiology (IAPP): c/o Dr D. Graham, Div. of Food Science and Technology, CSIRO, POB 52, North Ryde, NSW, Australia 2113; tel. (2) 9490-8333; fax (2) 9490-3107; e-mail douglasgraham@dfst.csiro.au; f. 1955 to promote the development of plant physiology at the international level through congresses, symposia and workshops, by maintaining communication with national societies and by encouraging interaction between plant physiologists in developing and developed countries; affiliated to the International Union of Biological Sciences; Pres. Prof. S. MIYACHI; Sec.-Treas. Dr D. GRAHAM.

International Association for Plant Taxonomy (IAPT): Institute of Botany, University of Vienna, Rennweg 14, 1030 Vienna, Austria; tel. (1) 4277-54098; fax (1) 4277-54099; e-mail office@iapt-taxon.org; internet www.botanik.univie.ac.at/iapt; f. 1950 to promote the development of plant taxonomy and encourage contacts between people and institutes interested in this work; maintains the International Bureau for Plant Taxonomy and Nomenclature; affiliated to the International Union of Biological Sciences; mems: institutes and individuals in 85 countries; Exec. Sec. Dr ALESSANDRA RICCIUTI LAMONEA; publs *Taxon* (quarterly), *Regnum vegetabile* (irregular).

International Association of Botanic Gardens (IABG): c/o Prof. J. E. Hernández-Bermejo, Córdoba Botanic Garden, Apdo 3048, 14071 Córdoba, Spain; tel. (957) 200355; fax (957) 295333; e-mail jardinbotcord@cod.servicom.es; f. 1954 to promote co-operation between scientific collections of living plants, including the exchange of information and specimens; to promote the study of the taxonomy of cultivated plants; and to encourage the conservation of rare plants and their habitats; affiliated to the International Union of Biological Sciences; Pres. Prof. H. E. SHANAN (People's Republic of China); Sec. Prof. J. ESTEBAN HERNÁNDEZ-BERMEJO (Spain).

International Association of Geodesy: Niels Bohr Institute, Juliane Maries Vej 30, 2100 Copenhagen Oe, Denmark; tel. 35-32-05-82; fax 35-36-53-57; e-mail cct@gfy.ku.dk; internet www.iag-aig.org; f. 1922 to promote the study of all scientific problems of geodesy and encourage geodetic research; to promote and co-ordinate international co-operation in this field; to publish results; affiliated to the International Union of Geodesy and Geophysics; mems: national committees in 73 countries; Pres. G. BEUTLER (Germany); Sec.-Gen. C. C. TSCHERNING (Denmark); publs *Journal of Geodesy*, *Travaux de l'AIG*.

International Association of Geomagnetism and Aeronomy (IAGA): c/o Prof. Bengt Hultqvist, Swedish Institute of Space Physics, POB 812, 98128, Kiruna, Sweden; tel. (980) 84340; e-mail hultqv@irf.se; f. 1919 for the study of questions relating to geomagnetism and aeronomy and the encouragement of research; holds General and Scientific Assemblies every two years; affiliated to the International Union of Geodesy and Geophysics; mems: countries that adhere to the IUGG; Pres. CHARLES E. BARTON (Australia); Sec.-Gen. Prof. BENGT HULTQVIST (Sweden); publs *IAGA Bulletin*, *IAGA News*, *IAGA Guides*.

International Association of Hydrological Sciences: Ecole des Mines de Paris, 35 rue Saint Honoré, 77305 Fontainebleau, France; tel. 1-64-69-47-40; fax 1-64-69-47-03; e-mail iahs@ensmp.fr; internet www.cig.ensmp.fr/~iahs/; f. 1922 to promote co-operation in the study of hydrology and water resources; Pres. Dr ARTHUR ASKEW (Switzerland); Sec.-Gen. Dr PIERRE HUBERT (France); publs *Journal* (every 2 months), *Newsletter* (3 a year).

International Association of Meteorology and Atmospheric Sciences (IAMAS): Dept of Physics, Univ. of Toronto, Toronto, ON M5S 1A7, Canada; tel. (416) 978-2982; fax (416) 978-8905; e-mail list@atmosp.physics.utoronto.ca; internet www.iamas.org; f. 1919; maintains permanent commissions on atmospheric ozone, radiation, atmospheric chemistry and global pollution, dynamic meteorology, polar meteorology, clouds and precipitation, climate, atmospheric electricity, planetary atmospheres and their evolution, and meteorology of the upper atmosphere; holds general assemblies every four years, special assemblies between general assemblies; affiliated to the International Union of Geodesy and Geophysics; Pres. Dr MICHAEL MACCRACKEN (USA); Sec.-Gen. Prof. R. LIST (Canada).

International Association of Sedimentologists: c/o Prof. José-Pedro Calvo, Departamento de Petrología y Geoquímica, Facultad CC Geológicas, Universidad Complutense, 28040 Madrid, Spain; tel. (91) 394-4905; fax (91) 544-2535; e-mail info@iasnet.org; internet www.iasnet.org; f. 1952; affiliated to the International Union of Geological Sciences; mems: 2,200; Pres. Prof. J. A. MCKENZIE (Switzerland); Gen. Sec. Prof. JOSÉ-PEDRO CALVO (Spain); publ. *Sedimentology* (every 2 months).

International Association of Volcanology and Chemistry of the Earth's Interior (IAVCEI): Institute of Earth Sciences 'Jaume Almera', CSIC, Lluis Sole Sabaris s/n, 08028 Barcelona, Spain; tel. (93) 4095410; fax (93) 4110012; e-mail joan.marti@ija.csic.es; internet www.iavcei.org; f. 1919 to examine scientifically all aspects of volcanology; affiliated to the International Union of Geodesy and Geophysics; Pres. Prof. SETSUYA NAKADA (Japan); Sec.-Gen. Prof. JOAN MARTI (Spain); publs *Bulletin of Volcanology*, *Catalogue of the Active Volcanoes of the World*, *Proceedings in Volcanology*.

International Association of Wood Anatomists: USDA Forest Service, Forest Products Laboratory, 1 Gifford Pinchot Dr., Madison WI 53726-2398, USA; tel. (608) 231-9200; fax (608) 231-9508; e-mail rmiller1@facstaff.wisc.edu; internet www.iawa-website.org; f. 1931 for the purpose of study, documentation and exchange of information on the structure of wood; holds annual conference; mems: 650 in 68 countries; Exec. Sec. REGIS B. MILLER; publ. *IAWA Journal*.

International Astronautical Federation (IAF): 94 bis ave du Suffren, 75015 Paris, France; tel. 1-45-67-42-60; fax 1-42-73-21-20; e-mail secretariat.iaf@iafastro.org; internet www.iafastro.com; f. 1950 to foster the development of astronautics for peaceful purposes at national and international levels; encourages the advancement of knowledge about space and the development and application of space assets for the benefit of humanity; organizes an annual International Astronautical Congress in conjunction with its associates, the International Academy of Astronautics (IAA) and the International Institute of Space Law (IISL); mems: 165 national astronautical societies in 45 countries; Pres. JAMES V. ZIMMERMAN (USA); Exec. Dir. PHILIPPE WILLEKENS.

International Astronomical Union (IAU): 98 bis blvd d'Arago, 75014 Paris, France; tel. 1-43-25-83-58; fax 1-43-25-26-16; e-mail iau@iap.fr; internet www.iau.org; f. 1919 to facilitate co-operation between the astronomers of various countries and to further the study of astronomy in all its branches; organizes colloquia every two months; mems: organizations in 65 countries, and 9,000 individual mems; Pres. RONALD EKERS (Australia); Gen. Sec. ODDBJORN ENGVOLD (Norway); publs *IAU Information Bulletin* (2 a year), *Symposia Series* (6 a year), *Highlights* (every 3 years).

International Biometric Society: International Business Office, 1444 I St, NW, Suite 700 Washington, DC 20005, USA; tel. (202) 712-9049; fax (202) 216-9646; e-mail ibs@bostrom.com; internet www.tibs.org; f. 1947 for the advancement of quantitative biological science through the development of quantitative theories and the application, development and dissemination of effective mathematical and statistical techniques; the Society has 16 regional organizations and 17 national groups, is affiliated with the International Statistical Institute and WHO, and constitutes the Section of Biometry of the International Union of Biological Sciences; mems: over 6,000 in more than 70 countries; Pres. THOMAS A. LOUIS; Sec. ASHWINI MATHUR; publs *Biometrics* (quarterly), *Biometric Bulletin* (quarterly), *Journal of Agricultural, Biological and Environmental Statistics* (quarterly).

International Botanical Congress: c/o Dr Josef Greimler, Botany, Univ. of Vienna, Rennweg 14, 1030 Vienna, Austria; e-mail office@ibc2005.ac.at; f. 1864 to inform botanists of recent progress in the plant sciences; the Nomenclature Section of the Congress attempts to provide a uniform terminology and methodology for the naming of plants; other Divisions deal with developmental, metabolic, structural, systematic and evolutionary, ecological botany; genetics and plant breeding; 2005 Congress: Vienna, Austria; 2011 Congress: Melbourne, Australia; affiliated to the International Union of Biological Sciences; Sec. Dr JOSEF GREIMLER.

International Bureau of Weights and Measures (Bureau international des poids et mesures—BIPM): Pavillon de Breteuil, 92312 Sèvres Cédex, France; tel. 1-45-07-70-70; fax 1-45-34-20-21; e-mail info@bipm.org; internet www.bipm.org; f. 1875 works to ensure the international unification of measurements and their traceability to the International System of Unification; carries out research and calibration; organizes international comparisons of national measurement standards; mems: 51 member states and 10 associates; Pres. J. KOVALEVSKY (France); Sec. R. KAARLS (Netherlands); publs *Le Système International d'Unités* (in English and French), *Metrologia* (6 a year), scientific articles, reports and monographs, committee reports.

International Cartographic Association: 136 bis rue de Grenelle, 75700 Paris 07 SP, France; tel. 1-43-98-82-95; fax 1-43-98-84-00; e-mail konecny@geogr.muni.cz; internet www.icaci.org; f. 1959 for the advancement, instigation and co-ordination of cartographic research involving co-operation between different nations; particularly concerned with furtherance of training in cartography, study of source material, compilation, graphic design, drawing, scribing and reproduction techniques of maps; organizes international conferences, symposia, meetings, exhibitions; mems: 80 countries; Pres. MILAN KONECNY; publ. *ICA Newsletter* (2 a year).

International Centre of Insect Physiology and Ecology: POB 30772, Nairobi, Kenya; tel. (20) 861680; fax (20) 803360; e-mail icipe@africaonline.co.ke; internet www.icipe.org; f. 1970; specializes in research and development of environmentally sustainable and affordable methods of managing tropical arthropod plant pests and disease vectors, and in the conservation and utilization of biodiversity of insects of commercial and ecological importance; organizes training programmes; Dir-Gen. Dr HANS RUDOLPH HERREN; publs *Insect Science and its Application* (quarterly), *Annual Report*, training manuals, technical bulletins, newsletter.

International Commission for Optics (ICO): Departamento de Optica, Facultad de Ciencias Fisicas, Universidad Complutense de Madrid, Ciudad Universitaria s/n, 28040 Madrid, Spain; tel. (91) 394-4684; fax (91) 394-4683; e-mail icosec@fis.ucm.es; internet www.ico-optics.org; f. 1948 to contribute to the progress of theoretical and instrumental optics, to assist in research and to promote international agreement on specifications; holds Gen. Assembly every three years; mems: committees in 50 territories, and six international societies; Pres. Prof. ARI T. FRIBERG; Sec.-Gen. Prof. MARIA L. CALVO (Spain); publ. *ICO Newsletter*.

International Commission for Plant-Bee Relationships: c/o Prof. I. Williams, Plant and Invertebrate Ecology Division, Rothamsted Research, Harpenden, Herts, AL5 2JQ, United Kingdom; e-mail ingrid.williams@bbsrc.ac.uk; f. 1950 to promote research and its application in the field of bee botany, and collect and spread information; to organize meetings, etc., and collaborate with scientific organizations; affiliated to the International Union of Biological Sciences; mems: 240 in 41 countries; Pres. Prof. INGRID WILLIAMS; Sec. Dr J. L. OSBORNE.

International Commission for the Scientific Exploration of the Mediterranean Sea (Commission internationale pour l'exploration scientifique de la mer Méditerranée—CIESM): 16 blvd de Suisse, 98000 Monaco; tel. 93-30-38-79; fax 92-16-11-95; e-mail fbriand@ciesm.org; internet www.ciesm.org; f. 1919 for scientific exploration of the Mediterranean Sea; organizes multilateral research investigations, workshops, congresses; includes 6 scientific committees; mems: 23 member countries, 3,200 scientists; Pres. SAS Prince ALBERT II of MONACO; Sec.-Gen. Prof. F. DOUMENGE; Dir-Gen. Prof. F. BRIAND; publs Congress reports, science and workshop series.

International Commission on Physics Education: e-mail elm@physics.unoquelph.ca; f. 1960 to encourage and develop international collaboration in the improvement and extension of the methods and scope of physics education at all levels; collaborates with UNESCO and organizes international conferences; mems: appointed triennially by the International Union of Pure and Applied Physics; Sec. E. L. MCFARLAND.

International Commission on Radiation Units and Measurements, Inc (ICRU): 7910 Woodmont Ave, Suite 400, Bethesda, MD 20814-3095, USA; tel. (301) 657-2652; fax (301) 907-8768; e-mail icru@icru.org; internet www.icru.org; f. 1925 to develop internationally acceptable recommendations regarding: (1) quantities and units of radiation and radioactivity, (2) procedures suitable for the measurement and application of these quantities in clinical radiology and radiobiology, (3) physical data needed in the application of these procedures; makes recommendations on quantities and units for radiation protection (see International Radiation Protection Association); mems: from about 18 countries; Chair. A. WAMBERSIE; Sec. S. SELTZER; publs reports.

International Commission on Zoological Nomenclature: c/o Natural History Museum, Cromwell Rd, London, SW7 5BD, United Kingdom; tel. (20) 7942-5653; e-mail iczn@nhm.ac.uk; internet www.iczn.org; f. 1895; has judicial powers to determine all matters relating to the interpretation of the International Code of Zoological Nomenclature and also plenary powers to suspend the operation of the Code where the strict application of the Code would lead to confusion and instability of nomenclature; also responsible for maintaining and developing the Official Lists and Official Indexes of Names and Works in Zoology; affiliated to the International Union of Biological Sciences; Pres. Prof. D. J. BROTHERS (South Africa); Exec. Sec. Dr E. MICHEL (United Kingdom); publs *Bulletin of Zoological Nomenclature* (quarterly), *International Code of Zoological Nomenclature*, *Official Lists and Indexes of Names and Works in Zoology*, *Towards Stability in the Names of Animals*.

International Council for Science (ICSU): 51 blvd de Montmorency, 75016 Paris, France; tel. 1-45-25-03-29; fax 1-42-88-94-31; e-mail secretariat@icsu.org; internet www.icsu.org; f. 1919 as International Research Council; present name adopted 1931; new statutes adopted 1996; to co-ordinate international co-operation in theoretical and applied sciences and to promote national scientific research through the intermediary of affiliated national organizations; General Assembly of representatives of national and scientific members meets every three years to formulate policy. The following committees have been established: Cttee on Science for Food Security, Scientific Cttee on Antarctic Research, Scientific Cttee on Oceanic Research, Cttee on Space Research, Scientific Cttee on Water Research, Scientific Cttee on Solar-Terrestrial Physics, Cttee on Science and Technology in Developing Countries, Cttee on Data for Science and Technology, Programme on Capacity Building in Science, Scientific Cttee on Problems of the Environment, Steering Cttee on Genetics and Biotechnology and Scientific Cttee on International Geosphere-Biosphere Programme. The following services and Inter-Union Committees and Commissions have been established: Federation of Astronomical and Geophysical Data Analysis Services, Inter-Union Commission on Frequency Allocations for Radio Astronomy and Space Science, Inter-Union Commission on Radio Meteorology, Inter-Union Commission on Spectroscopy, Inter-Union Commission on Lithosphere; national mems: academies or research councils in 98 countries; Scientific mems and assocs: 105 nat. scientific bodies and 29 int. scientific unions; Pres. GOVERDHAN MEHTA; Exec. Sec. THOMAS ROSSWALL; publs *ICSU Yearbook*, *Science International* (quarterly), *Annual Report*.

International Council for Scientific and Technical Information: 51 blvd de Montmorency, 75016 Paris, France; tel. 1-45-25-65-92; fax 1-42-15-12-62; e-mail icsti@icsti.org; internet www.icsti.org; f. 1984 as the successor to the International Council of Scientific Unions Abstracting Board (f. 1952); aims to increase accessibility to scientific and technical information; fosters communication and interaction among all participants in the information transfer chain; mems: 48 organizations; Pres. GÉRARD GIROUD (Netherlands); Gen. Sec. ELLIOT SIEGEL (USA).

International Council for the Exploration of the Sea (ICES): H. C. Andersens Blvd 44–46, 1553 Copenhagen V, Denmark; tel. 33-38-67-00; fax 33-93-42-15; e-mail info@ices.dk; internet www.ices.dk; f. 1902 to encourage and facilitate research on the utilization and conservation of living resources and the environment in the North Atlantic Ocean and its adjacent seas; publishes and disseminate results of research; advises member countries and regulatory commissions; mems: 20 mem. countries and five countries or bodies with observer status; Gen. Sec. GERD HUBOLD; publs *ICES Journal of Marine Science*, *ICES Marine Science Symposia*, *ICES Fisheries Statistics*, *ICES Cooperative Research Reports*, *ICES Oceanographic Data Lists and Inventories*, *ICES Techniques in Marine Environmental Sciences*, *ICES Identification Leaflets for Plankton*, *ICES Identification Leaflets for Diseases and Parasites of Fish and Shellfish*, *ICES/CIEM Information*.

International Council of Psychologists: 8302 York Road, B-45 Elkin Park, PA 19027, USA; tel. (512) 245-7605; fax (512) 245-3153; e-mail mattikg@comcast.net; internet icpsych.tripod.com/; f. 1941 to advance psychology and the application of its scientific findings throughout the world; holds annual conventions; mems: 1,200 qualified psychologists; Sec.-Gen. Dr MATTI K. GERSHENFELD; publs *International Psychologist* (quarterly), *World Psychology* (quarterly).

International Council of the Aeronautical Sciences (ICAS): c/o FOI, SE-16490 Stockholm, Sweden; tel. (8) 55503151; e-mail secr.exec@icas.org; internet www.icas.org; f. 1957 to encourage free interchange of information on aeronautical science and technology; holds biennial Congresses (2008: USA); mems: national asscns in more than 30 countries; Pres. FRED ABBINK (Netherlands); Exec. Sec. ANDERS GUSTAFSSON (Sweden).

International Earth Rotation and Reference Systems Service: Central Bureau, c/o Bundesamt für Kartographie und Geodäsie (BKG), Richard-Strauss-Allee 11, 60598 Frankfurt am Main, Germany; tel. (69) 6333273; fax (69) 6333425; e-mail central_bureau@iers.org; internet www.iers.org; f. 1988 (fmrly International Polar Motion Service and Bureau International de l'Heure); maintained by the International Astronomical Union and the International Union of Geodesy and Geophysics; defines and maintains the international terrestrial and celestial reference systems; determines earth orientation parameters (terrestrial and celestial co-ordinates of the pole and universal time) connecting these systems; monitors global geophysical fluids; organizes collection, analysis and dissemination of data; Chair. Directing Bd Prof. CHOPO MA.

International Federation of Cell Biology (IFCB): c/o Dr Denys Wheatley, Dept of Cell Pathology, Univ. of Aberdeen, Hilton Campus, Hilton Place, Aberdeen, AB24 4FA, United Kingdom; tel. (1467) 670280; fax (1467) 629123; e-mail wheatley@abdn.ac.uk; internet www.ifcbiol.org; f. 1972 to foster international co-operation, and organize conferences; Pres. Dr CHENG-WEN WU; Sec.-Gen. Dr DENYS WHEATLEY; publs *Cell Biology International* (monthly), reports.

International Federation of Operational Research Societies (IFORS): c/o Mary Magrogan, 901 Elkridge Landing Rd, Suite 400, Linthicum, MD 21090, USA; tel. (410) 691-7858; fax (410) 691-6127; e-mail secretary@ifors.org; internet www.ifors.org; f. 1959 for development of operational research as a unified science and its advancement in all nations of the world; mems: c. 30,000 individuals, 48 national societies, five kindred societies; Pres. Dr THOMAS L. MAGNANTI (USA); Sec. MARY MAGROGAN; publs *International Abstracts in Operational Research*, *IFORS Bulletin*, *International Transactions in Operational Research*.

International Federation of Science Editors: School for Scientific Communication, Abruzzo Science Park, Via Antica Arischia 1, 67100 L'Aquila, Italy; tel. (0862) 3475308; fax (0862) 3475213; e-mail miriam.balaban@aquila.infn.it; f. 1978; links editors in different branches of science with the aim of improving scientific writing, editing, ethics and communication internationally; Pres. MIRIAM BALABAN (Italy).

International Federation of Societies for Microscopy (IFSM): c/o Dept of Chem., Mater. and Bio. Eng., 191 Auditorium Rd, Unit 3222, University of Connecticut, Storrs, CT 06269-3222, USA; tel. (860) 486-4020; fax (860) 486-2959; internet www.ifsm.umn.edu; f. 1955 to contribute to the advancement of all aspects of electron microscopy; promotes and co-ordinates research; sponsors meetings and conferences; holds International Congress every four years; mems: representative organizations of 40 countries; Pres. Prof. DAVID J. H. COCKAYNE (United Kingdom); Gen.-Sec. C. BARRY CARTER (USA).

International Food Information Service (IFIS): UK Office (IFIS Publishing), Lane End House, Shinfield Rd, Shinfield, Reading, RG2 9BB, United Kingdom; tel. (118) 988-3895; fax (118) 988-5065; e-mail ifis@ifis.org; internet www.foodsciencecentral.com; f. 1968; board of governors comprises two members each from CAB-International (United Kingdom), Bundesministerium für Landwirtschaft, Ernährung und Forsten (represented by Deutsche Landwirtschafts-Gesellschaft e.V.) (Germany), and the Institute of Food Technologists (USA); collects and disseminates information on all disciplines relevant to food science, food technology and nutrition; Man. Dir Prof. J. D. SELMAN; publ. *Food Science and Technology Abstracts* (monthly, also available online).

International Foundation of the High-Altitude Research Stations Jungfraujoch and Gornergrat: Sidlerstrasse 5, 3012 Bern, Switzerland; tel. 316314052; fax 316314405; e-mail louise.wilson@phim.unibe.ch; internet www.ifjungo.ch; f. 1931; international research centre which enables scientists from many scientific fields to carry out experiments at high altitudes. Six countries contribute to support the station: Austria, Belgium, Germany, Italy, Switzerland, United Kingdom; Pres. Prof. E. FLÜCKIGER.

International Geographical Union (IGU): Dept of Geography, Seoul Nat. Univ., 56-1, Shillim-dong, Kwanak-gu, Seoul 151-742, Republic of Korea; tel. (2) 880-5008; fax (2) 873-4987; e-mail yuik@snu.ac.kr; internet www.igu-net.org; f. 1922 to encourage the study of problems relating to geography, to promote and co-ordinate research requiring international co-operation, and to organize international congresses and commissions; mems: 83 countries, 11 associates; Pres. Prof. JOSÉ PALACIO-PRIETO (Mexico); Sec.-Gen. Prof. YU WOO-IK (Republic of Korea); publ. *IGU Bulletin* (2 a year).

International Glaciological Society: Scott Polar Research Institute, Lensfield Rd, Cambridge, CB2 1ER, United Kingdom; tel. (1223) 355974; fax (1223) 354931; e-mail igsoc@igsoc.org; internet www.igsoc.org; f. 1936; aims to stimulate interest in and encourage research into the scientific and technical problems associated with snow and ice; mems: 850 in 30 countries; Pres. Professor ATSUMU OHMURA; Sec.-Gen. MAGNÚS MÁR MAGNÚSSON; publs *Journal of Glaciology* (quarterly), *Ice* (News Bulletin, 3 a year), *Annals of Glaciology*.

International Hydrographic Organization (IHO): 4 quai Antoine 1er, BP 445, 98000 Monaco; tel. 93-10-81-00; fax 93-10-81-40; e-mail info@ihb.mc; internet www.iho.shom.fr; f. 1921 to link the hydrographic offices of member governments and co-ordinate their work, with a view to rendering navigation easier and safer; seeks to obtain, as far as possible, uniformity in charts and hydrographic documents; fosters the development of electronic chart navigation; encourages adoption of the best methods of conducting hydrographic surveys; encourages surveying in those parts of the world where accurate charts are lacking; provides IHO Data Centre for Digital Bathymetry; and organizes quinquennial conference; mems: 76 states; Directing Committee: Pres. Vice Adm. A. MARATOS (Greece); Dirs Rear Adm. K. BARBOR (USA), Capt. H. GORZIGLIA (Chile); publs *International Hydrographic Bulletin*, *IHO Yearbook*, other documents (available on the IHO website).

International Institute of Refrigeration: 177 blvd Malesherbes, 75017 Paris, France; tel. 1-42-27-32-35; fax 1-47-63-17-98; e-mail iifiir@iifiir.org; internet www.iifiir.org; f. 1908 to further the science of refrigeration and its applications on a world-wide scale; to investigate, discuss and recommend any aspects leading to improvements in the field of refrigeration; maintains FRIDOC database (available via internet); mems: 61 national, 1,500 associates; Dir DIDIER COULOMB (France); publs *Bulletin* (every 2 months), *International Journal of Refrigeration* (8 a year), *Newsletter* (quarterly), books, proceedings, recommendations.

International Mathematical Union (IMU): c/o Zuse Institute Berlin Takustr. 7, 14195 Berlin, Germany; e-mail secretary@mathunion.org; fax (30) 84185-269; internet www.mathunion.org; f. 1952 to support and assist the International Congress of Mathematicians and other international scientific meetings or conferences and to encourage and support other international mathematical activities considered likely to contribute to the development of mathematical science—pure, applied or educational; mems: 63 countries; Pres. L. LOVÁSZ (Hungary); Sec.-Gen. MARTIN GRÖTSCHEL (Germany).

International Mineralogical Association: c/o Maryse Ohnenstetter, 15 rue Notre Dame des Pauvres, BP 20, 54501 Vandoeuvre-les-Nancy Cedex, France; tel. 3-83-59-42-46; fax 3-83-51-17-98; e-mail mohnen@crpg.cnrs-nancy.fr; internet www.ima-mineralogy.org; f. 1958 to further international co-operation in the science of mineralogy; affiliated to the International Union of Geological Sciences; mems: national societies in 39 countries; Sec. MARYSE OHNENSTETTER.

International Organization of Legal Metrology: 11 rue Turgot, 75009 Paris, France; tel. 1-48-78-12-82; fax 1-42-82-17-27; e-mail biml@oiml.org; internet www.oiml.org; f. 1955 to serve as documentation and information centre on the verification, checking, construction and use of measuring instruments, to determine characteristics and standards to which measuring instruments must conform for their use to be recommended internationally, and to determine the general principles of legal metrology; mems: governments of 59 countries; Pres. ALAN E. JOHNSTON (Canada); publ. *Bulletin* (quarterly).

International Palaeontological Association: c/o Paleontological Institute, 1475 Jayhawk Blvd, Rm 121, Lindley Hall, University of Kansas, Lawrence, KS 66045, USA; tel. (785) 864-3338; fax (785) 864-5276; e-mail rmaddocks@uh.edu; internet ipa.geo.ku.edu; f. 1933; affiliated to the International Union of Geological Sciences and the International Union of Biological Sciences; Pres. Dr DAVID A. T. HARPER (Denmark); Sec.-Gen. Prof. ROSALIE F. MADDOCKS (USA); publs *Lethaia* (quarterly), *Directory of Paleontologists of the World*, *Directory of Fossil Collectors of the World*.

International Peat Society: Vapaudenkatu 12, 40100 Jyväskylä, Finland; tel. (14) 3385440; fax (14) 3385410; e-mail ips@peatsociety.fi; internet www.peatsociety.fi; f. 1968 to encourage co-operation in the study and use of mires, peatlands, peat and related material, through international meetings, research groups and the exchange of information; mems: 21 National Cttees, research institutes and other organizations, and individuals from 37 countries; Pres. MARKKU MÄKELÄ (Finland); Sec.-Gen. JAAKKO SILPOLA (Finland); publs *Peat News* (monthly electronic newsletter), *International Peat Journal* (annually), *Peatlands International* (2 a year).

International Phonetic Association (IPA): Department of Theoretical and Applied Linguistics, School of English, Aristotle University of Thessaloniki, Thessaloniki 54124, Greece; tel. (2310) 997429; fax (2310) 997432; e-mail knicol@enl.auth.gr; internet www.arts.gla.ac.uk/ipa/ipa.html; f. 1886 to promote the scientific study of phonetics and its applications; organizes International Congress of Phonetic Sciences every four years (2007: Saarbrücken, Germany); mems: 550; Pres. Prof. JOHN C. WELLS (United Kingdom); Sec. Dr KATERINA NICOLAIDIS; publs *Journal of the International*

Phonetic Association (3 a year), *Handbook of the International Phonetic Association.*

International Phycological Society: c/o Department of Biological Science, Florida State Univ., Tallahassee, FL 32306-1100, USA; fax (850) 644-9829; e-mail prasad@bio.fsu.edu; internet www.intphycsoc .org; f. 1961 to promote the study of algae, the distribution of information, and international co-operation in this field; mems: about 1,000; Pres. C. A. Maggs; Sec. A. K. S. K. Prasad; publ. *Phycologia* (every 2 months).

International Primatological Society: c/o Library and Information Service, National Primate Research Center, Univ. of Wisconsin-Madison, 1220 Capitol Court, Madison, WI 53715-1299, USA; tel. (608) 263-3512; fax (608) 265-2067; e-mail library@primate.wisc.edu; internet pin.primate.wisc.edu/ips/; f. 1964 to promote primatological science in all fields; mems: about 1,500; Pres. Dr D. Fragaszy; Sec.-Gen. Dr J. A. R. A. M. van Hooff; publs *Bulletin*, *International Journal of Primatology*, *Codes of Practice.*

International Radiation Protection Association (IRPA): c/o Jacques Lochard, CEPN, 28 rue de la Redoute, Fontenay-aux-Roses 92260, France; tel. 1-55-52-19-20; fax 1-55-52-19-21; internet www .irpa.net; f. 1966 to link individuals and societies throughout the world concerned with protection against ionizing radiations and allied effects, and to represent doctors, health physicists, radiological protection officers and others engaged in radiological protection, radiation safety, nuclear safety, legal, medical and veterinary aspects and in radiation research and other allied activities; mems: 16,000 in 42 societies; Pres. Philip E. Metcalf (South Africa); Exec. Officer Jacques Lochard (France); publ. *IRPA Bulletin*.

International Society for Human and Animal Mycology (ISHAM): Dept of Bacteriology and Immunology, Haartman Institute, Univ. of Helsinki, Haartmaninkatu 3, POB 21, 00014 Helsinki, Finland; tel. (9) 19126894; fax (9) 26382; e-mail malcolm .richardson@helsinki.fi; internet www.isham.org; f. 1954 to pursue the study of fungi pathogenic for man and animals; holds congresses (2006: Paris, France); mems: 1,100 in 70 countries; Pres. Dr David W. Warnock; Gen. Sec. Dr Malcolm Richardson; publ. *Medical Mycology* (6 a year).

International Society for Rock Mechanics: c/o Laboratório Nacional de Engenharia Civil, 101 Av. do Brasil, 1700-066 Lisboa, Portugal; tel. (21) 8443419; fax (21) 8443021; e-mail secretariat .isrm@lnec.pt; internet www.isrm.net; f. 1962 to encourage and co-ordinate international co-operation in the science of rock mechanics; assists individuals and local organizations in forming national bodies; maintains liaison with organizations representing related sciences, including geology, geophysics, soil mechanics, mining engineering, petroleum engineering and civil engineering; organizes international meetings; encourages the publication of research; mems: c. 5,000 mems and 46 nat. groups; Pres. Nielen van der Merwe; Sec.-Gen. Dr Luís Lamas; publ. *News Journal* (3 a year).

International Society for Stereology: c/o CMM—Ecole des Mines de Paris, 35, rue Saint Honoré, 77300 Fontainebleau, France; tel. 1-64-69-47-06; fax 1-64-69-47-07; e-mail iss@cmm.ensmp.fr; internet www.stereologysociety.org; f. 1961; an interdisciplinary society gathering scientists from metallurgy, geology, mineralogy and biology to exchange ideas on three-dimensional interpretation of two-dimensional samples (sections, projections) of their material by means of stereological principles; mems: 300; Pres. Prof. Dominique Jeulin; Treas./Sec. Dr Etienne Decencière.

International Society for Tropical Ecology: c/o Botany Dept, Banaras Hindu University, Varanasi, 221 005 India; tel. (542) 368399; fax (542) 368174; e-mail tropecol@banaras.ernet.in; f. 1956 to promote and develop the science of ecology in the tropics in the service of humanity; to publish a journal to aid ecologists in the tropics in communication of their findings; and to hold symposia from time to time to summarize the state of knowledge in particular or general fields of tropical ecology; mems: 500; Sec. Prof. J. S. Singh (India); Editor Prof. K. P. Singh; publ. *Tropical Ecology* (2 a year).

International Society of Biometeorology (IBS): c/o Dr Scott Greene, Dept of Geography, Univ. of Oklahoma, Norman, OK 73071, USA; tel. (405) 325-4319; fax (405) 447-8412; e-mail jgreene@ou.edu; internet www.biometeorology.org; f. 1956 to unite all biometeorologists working in the fields of agricultural, botanical, cosmic, entomological, forest, human, medical, veterinarian, zoological and other branches of biometeorology; mems: 250 individuals, nationals of 46 countries; Pres. Dr Larry Kalkstein (USA); Sec. Dr Scott Greene (USA); publs *Biometeorology* (Proceedings of the Congress of ISB), *International Journal of Biometeorology* (quarterly), *Biomeorology Bulletin*.

International Society of Criminology (Société internationale de criminologie): 4 rue Ferrus, 75014 Paris, France; tel. 1-45-88-00-23; fax 1-45-88-96-40; e-mail crim.sic@wanadoo.fr; f. 1934 to promote the development of the sciences in their application to the criminal phenomenon; mems: in 63 countries; Sec.-Gen. Georges Picca; publ. *Annales internationales de Criminologie.*

International Society of Limnology (Societas Internationalis Limnologiae—SIL): University of North Carolina at Chapel Hill, SPH, ESE, CB# 7431, Rosenau Hall, Chapel Hill, NC 27599-7431, USA; tel. (336) 376-9362; fax (336) 376-8825; e-mail msondergaard@ bi.ku.dk; internet www.limnology.org; f. 1922 (as the International Assen of Theoretical and Applied Limnology, name changed 2007) for the study of physical, chemical and biological phenomena of lakes and rivers; affiliated to the International Union of Biological Sciences; mems: c. 3,200; Pres. Brian Moss (United Kingdom); Gen. Sec. and Treas. Morten Søndergaard (Denmark).

International Union for Physical and Engineering Sciences in Medicine (IUPESM): c/o Dr Heikki Terio, Karolinska Univ. Hospital, Dept of Biomedical Engineering, 14186 Stockholm, Sweden; tel. (8) 58580852; fax (8) 58586290; e-mail heikki.terio@ karolinska.se; internet www.iupesm.org; f. 1980 by its two constituent orgs (International Federation for Medical and Biological Engineering, and International Organization for Medical Physics); promotes international co-operation in health care science and technology and represents the professional interests of members; organizes seminars, workshops, scientific conferences; holds World Congress every three years (2009: Munich, Germany); Pres. Prof. Joachim Nagel (Germany); Sec.-Gen. Dr Heikki Terio (Sweden); publs *IUPESM Newsletter* (2 a year), Congress proceedings.

International Union for Pure and Applied Biophysics (IUPAB): School of Biochemistry and Molecular Biology, University of Leeds, Leeds, LS2 9JT, United Kingdom; tel. (113) 2333023; fax (113) 2333167; e-mail a.c.t.north@leeds.ac.uk; internet www.iupab .org; f. 1961 to organize international co-operation in biophysics and promote communication between biophysics and allied subjects, to encourage national co-operation between biophysical societies, and to contribute to the advancement of biophysical knowledge; mems: 50 adhering bodies; Pres. I. Pecht (Israel); Sec.-Gen. Prof. A. C. T. North (United Kingdom); publ. *Quarterly Reviews of Biophysics.*

International Union for Quaternary Research (INQUA): Dept of Geography, Museum Building, Trinity College, Dublin 2, Ireland; tel. (1) 6081213; e-mail pcoxon@tcd.ie; internet www.inqua.tcd.ie; f. 1928 to co-ordinate research on the Quaternary geological era throughout the world; holds congress every four years (2003: Reno, USA); mems: in 46 countries and states; Sec.-Gen. Prof. Peter Coxon (Ireland); publs *Quaternary International*, *Quaternary Perspectives.*

International Union of Biochemistry and Molecular Biology (IUBMB): Institut de Botanique, 28 rue Goethe, 67083 Strasbourg Cedex, France; tel. 3-90-24-18-32; e-mail Jacques-Henry.Weil@ ibmp-ulp.u-strasbg.fr; internet www.iubmb.unibe.ch; f. 1955 to sponsor the International Congresses of Biochemistry, to co-ordinate research and discussion, to organize co-operation between the societies of biochemistry and molecular biology, to promote high standards of biochemistry and molecular biology throughout the world and to contribute to the advancement of biochemistry and molecular biology in all its international aspects; mems: 76 bodies; Pres. Prof. Mary Osborn (USA); Gen. Sec. Prof. Jacques-Henry Weil (France).

International Union of Biological Sciences (IUBS): Bat 442, Université Paris-Sud 11, 91405 Orsay cédex, France; tel. 1-69-15-50-27; fax 1-69-15-79-47; e-mail secretariat@iubs.org; internet www .iubs.org; f. 1919; serves as an international forum for the promotion of biology; administers scientific programmes on biodiversity, integrative biology (of ageing, bioenergy, and climate change), biological education, bioethics, bio-energy, and Darwin 200 (in 2009); carries out international collaborative research programmes; convenes General Assembly every 3 years; mems: 44 national bodies, 80 scientific bodies; Exec. Dir Dr Talal Younes; publs *Biology International* (quarterly), *IUBS Monographs, IUBS Methodology, Manual Series.*

International Union of Crystallography: c/o M. H. Dacombe, 2 Abbey Sq., Chester, CH1 2HU, United Kingdom; tel. (1244) 345431; fax (1244) 344843; internet www.iucr.org; f. 1947 to facilitate the international standardization of methods, units, nomenclature and symbols used in crystallography; and to form a focus for the relations of crystallography to other sciences; mems: in 40 countries; Pres. Prof. Y. Ohashi (Japan); Gen. Sec. S. Lidin (Sweden); publs *IUCR Newsletter, Acta Crystallographica, Journal of Applied Crystallography, Journal of Synchroton Radiation, International Tables for Crystallography, World Directory of Crystallographers, IUCr/OUP Crystallographic Symposia, IUCr/OUP Monographs on Crystallography, IUCr/OUP Texts on Crystallography.*

International Union of Food Science and Technology: POB 61021, 511 Maplegrove Rd, Oakville, ON L6J 6X0, Canada; tel. (905) 815-1926; fax (905) 815-1574; e-mail secretariat@iufost.org; internet www.iufost.org; f. 1970; sponsors international symposia and congresses; mems: 60 national groups; Pres. Alan Mortimer (Australia); Sec.-Gen. Judith Meech (Canada); publs *IUFOST Newsline* (3 a year), *International Review of Food Science and Technology.*

International Union of Geodesy and Geophysics (IUGG): c/o Dr Alik Ismail-Zadeh, University of Karlsruhe, Geophysical Institute, Hertzstr. 16, Geb. 06.36, 76187 Karlsruhe, Germany; tel. (721) 6084610; fax (721) 71173; e-mail alik.ismail-zadeh@gpi.uka.de; internet www.iugg.org; f. 1919; federation of eight asscns representing Cryospheric Sciences, Geodesy, Seismology and Physics of the Earth's Interior, Physical Sciences of the Ocean, Volcanology and Chemistry of the Earth's Interior, Hydrological Sciences, Meteorology and Atmospheric Physics, Geomagnetism and Aeronomy, which meet in committees and at the General Assemblies of the Union; organizes scientific meetings and sponsors various permanent services to collect, analyse and publish geophysical data; mems: in 67 countries; Pres. Dr. TOM BEER (Australia); Sec.-Gen. Dr ALIK ISMAIL-ZADEH (Germany); publs *IUGG Yearbook, Journal of Geodesy* (quarterly), *IASPEI Newsletter* (irregular), *Bulletin Volcanologique* (2 a year), *Hydrological Sciences Journal* (quarterly), *Bulletin de l'Association Internationale d'Hydrologie Scientifique* (quarterly), *IAMAP News Bulletin* (irregular).

International Union of Geological Sciences (IUGS): c/o Geological Survey of Canada, 601 Booth St, Ottawa, ON K1A 0E8, Canada; tel. (613) 947-0333; fax (613) 992-0190; e-mail pbobrows@nrcan.gc.ca; internet www.iugs.org/; f. 1961 to encourage the study of geoscientific problems, facilitate international and inter-disciplinary co-operation in geology and related sciences, and support the quadrennial International Geological Congress; organizes international meetings and co-sponsors joint programmes, including the International Geological Correlation Programme (with UNESCO); mems: in 85 countries; Pres. Prof. ZHANG HONGREN (People's Republic of China); Sec.-Gen. Dr PETER T. BOBROWSKY (Canada).

International Union of Immunological Societies (IUIS): Executive Manager, IUIS Central Office, c/o Vienna Academy of Postgraduate Medical Education and Research, Alser Strasse 4, 1090 Vienna, Austria; tel. (1) 405-13-83-13; fax (1) 405-13-83-23; e-mail iuis-central-office@medacad.org; internet www.iuisonline.org; f. 1969; holds triennial international congress; mems: national societies in 57 countries and territories; Pres. ROLF ZINKERNAGEL; Sec.-Gen. Dr MOHAMED R. DAHA; Exec. Man. SYLVIA TRITTINGER.

International Union of Microbiological Societies (IUMS): c/o Dr Robert A. Samson, Centraalbureau voor Schimmelcultures Fungal Biodiversity Centre, POB 85167, 3508 AD, Utrecht, Netherlands; tel. (30) 2122600; fax (30) 2512097; e-mail samson@cbs.knaw.nl; internet www.iums.org; f. 1930; mems: 106 national microbiological societies; Pres. KARL HEINZ SCHLEIFER (Germany); Sec.-Gen. ROBERT A. SAMSON; publs *International Journal of Systematic Bacteriology* (quarterly), *International Journal of Food Microbiology* (every 2 months), *Advances in Microbial Ecology* (annually), *Archives of Virology*.

International Union of Nutritional Sciences (IUNS): c/o Dr Galal, UCLA School of Public Health, Community Health Sciences, POB 951772, Los Angeles, CA 90095-1772, USA.; tel. (310) 206-9639; fax (310) 794-1805; e-mail info@iuns.org; internet www.iuns.org; f. 1946 to promote advancement in nutrition science, research and development through international co-operation at the global level; aims to encourage communication and collaboration among nutrition scientists as well as to disseminate information in nutritional sciences through modern communication technology; mems: 80 adhering bodies; Pres. Dr RICARDO UAUY; Sec.-Gen. Dr OSMAN GALAL; publs *Annual Report, IUNS Directory, Newsletter*.

International Union of Pharmacology: c/o Lindsay Hart, Dept of Pharmacology, College of Medicine, Univ. of California, Irvine, CA 92697, USA; tel. (949) 824-1178; fax (949) 824-4855; e-mail l.hart@iuphar.org; internet www.iuphar.org; f. 1963 to promote co-ordination of research, discussion and publication in the field of pharmacology, including clinical pharmacology, drug metabolism and toxicology; co-operates with WHO in all matters concerning drugs and drug research; holds international congresses; mems: 51 national societies, 12 assoc. mem. societies, three corporate mems; Pres. PAUL M. VANHOUTTE (France); Sec.-Gen. Prof. SUE PIPER DUCKLES; publ. *PI (Pharmacology International)*.

International Union of Photobiology: c/o Dennis Valenzeno, Univ. of Alaska Anchorage, 3211 Providence Drive, Anchorage, AK 99508, USA; tel. (907) 786-4789; fax (907) 786-4700; e-mail dvalenze@kumc.edu; internet www.iupb.org; f. 1928 (frmly International Photobiology Asscn); stimulation of scientific research concerning the physics, chemistry and climatology of non-ionizing radiations (ultra-violet, visible and infra-red) in relation to their biological efffects and their applications in biology and medicine; 18 national committees represented; affiliated to the International Union of Biological Sciences. International Congresses held every four years; Pres. MASAMITSU WADA; Sec.-Gen. DENNIS VALENZENO.

International Union of Physiological Sciences (IUPS): IUPS Secretariat, LGN, Bâtiment CERVI, Hôpital de la Pitié-Salpêtrière, 83 blvd de l'Hôpital, 75013 Paris, France; tel. 1-42-17-75-37; fax 1-42-17-75-75; e-mail rsoni@chups.jussieu.fr; internet www.iups.org; f. 1955; mems: 50 national, six asscn, four regional, two affiliated and 14 special mems; Pres. Prof. AKIMICHI KANEKO (Japan); Sec. Prof. OLE PETERSEN.

International Union of Psychological Science: c/o Prof. P. L.-J. Ritchie, Ecole de psychologie, Université d'Ottawa, 145 Jean-Jacques-Lussier, CP 450, Succ. A, Ottawa, ON KIN 6N5, Canada; tel. (613) 562-5800; fax (613) 562-5169; e-mail pritchie@uottawa.ca; internet www.iupsys.org; f. 1951 to contribute to the development of intellectual exchange and scientific relations between psychologists of different countries; mems: 68 national and 12 affiliate orgs; Pres. Prof. BRUCE OVERMIER (USA); Sec.-Gen. Prof. P. L.-J. RITCHIE (Canada); publs *International Journal of Psychology* (quarterly), *The IUPsyS Directory* (irregular), *Psychology CD Rom Resource File* (annually).

International Union of Pure and Applied Chemistry (IUPAC): Bldg 19, 104 T. W. Alexander Dr., Research Triangle Park, POB 13757, NC 27709-3757, USA; tel. (919) 485-8700; fax (919) 485-8706; e-mail secretariat@iupac.org; internet www.iupac.org; f. 1919 to organize permanent co-operation between chemical asscns in the member countries, to study topics of international importance requiring standardization or codification, to co-operate with other international organizations in the field of chemistry and to contribute to the advancement of all aspects of chemistry; holds a biennial General Assembly; mems: in 49 countries; Pres. Prof. BRYAN HENRY (Canada); Sec.-Gen. Dr DAVID BLACK (Australia).

International Union of Pure and Applied Physics (IUPAP): c/o One Physics Ellipse, College Park, MD 20740–3844, USA; tel. and fax (301) 209-3270; e-mail franz@aps.org; internet www.iupap.org; f. 1922 to promote and encourage international co-operation in physics and facilitate the world-wide development of science; mems: in 53 countries; Pres. ALAN ASTBURY; Sec.-Gen. JUDY R. FRANZ.

International Union of Radio Science: c/o INTEC, Ghent University, Sint-Pietersnieuwstraat 41, 9000 Ghent, Belgium; tel. (9) 264-3320; fax (9) 264-4288; e-mail info@ursi.org; internet www.ursi.org; f. 1919 to stimulate and co-ordinate, on an international basis, studies, research, applications, scientific exchange and communication in the field of radio science; aims to encourage the adoption of common methods of measurement and the standardization of measuring instruments used in scientific work; represents radio science at national and international levels; there are 44 national committees; Pres. Prof. F. LEFEUVRE (France); Sec.-Gen. Prof. P. LAGASSE (Belgium); publs *The Radio Science Bulletin* (quarterly), *Records of General Assemblies* (every 3 years).

International Union of the History and Philosophy of Science: Division of the History of Science and Technology (DHS): National Hellenic Research Foundation, 48 Vas. Constantinou av., 11635 Athens, Greece; e-mail e.nicolaïdis@dhstweb.org; Division of the History of Logic, Methodology and Philosophy of Science (DLMPS): 161 rue Ada, 34392 Montpellier, France; f. 1956 to promote research into the history and philosophy of science; DHST has 50 national committees and DLMPS has 35 committees; DHST: Pres. Prof. RONALD NUMBERS (USA); Sec.-Gen. Prof. EFTHYMIOS NICOLAÏDES (Greece); DLMPS Council: Pres. Prof. M. RABIN (Israel); Sec.-Gen. Prof. D. WESTERSTAHL (Sweden).

International Union of Theoretical and Applied Mechanics: c/o Prof. Dick H. van Campen, Dept of Mechanical Engineering, Eindhoven University of Technology, POB 513, 5600 Eindhoven, Netherlands; tel. (40) 2472768; fax (40) 2461418; e-mail sg@iutam.net; internet www.iutam.net; f. 1947 to form links between those engaged in scientific work (theoretical or experimental) in mechanics or related sciences; organizes international congresses of theoretical and applied mechanics, through a standing Congress Committee, and other international meetings; engages in other activities designed to promote the development of mechanics as a science; mems: from 49 countries; Pres. Prof. L. B. FREUND (USA); Sec.-Gen. Prof. D. H. VAN CAMPEN (Netherlands); publs *Annual Report, Newsletter*.

International Union of Toxicology: IUTOX Headquarters, 1821 Michael Faraday Dr., Suite 300, Reston, VA 20190, USA; tel. (703) 438-3103; fax (703) 438-3113; e-mail iutoxhq@iutox.org; internet www.iutox.org; f. 1980 to foster international co-operation among toxicologists and promote world-wide acquisition, dissemination and utilization of knowledge in the field; sponsors International Congresses and other education programmes; mems: 47 national societies; Sec.-Gen. A. WALLACE HAYES; publs *IUTOX Newsletter*, Congress proceedings.

International Water Association (IWA): Alliance House, 12 Caxton St, London SW1H OQS, United Kingdom; tel. (20) 7654-5500; fax (20) 7654-5555; e-mail water@iwahq.org.uk; internet www.iwahq.org; f. 1999 by merger of the International Water Services Association and the International Association on Water Quality; aims to encourage international communication, co-operative effort, and exchange of information on water quality management, through conferences, electronic media and publication of research reports; mems: c. 9,000 in 130 countries; Pres. Prof. LÁSZLÓ SOMLYÓDY (Hungary); Exec. Dir PAUL REITER (USA); publs *Water Research* (monthly), *Water Science and Technology* (24 a year), *Water 21* (6 a year), *Yearbook, Scientific and Technical Reports.*

Pacific Science Association: 1525 Bernice St, Honolulu, HI 96817, USA; tel. (808) 848-4124; fax (808) 847-8252; e-mail info@pacificscience.org; internet www.pacificscience.org; f. 1920; a regional non-governmental organization that seeks to advance science, technology, and sustainable development in and of the Asia-Pacific region, by actively promoting interdisciplinary and international research and collaboration; sponsors Pacific Science Congresses and Inter-Congresses and scientific working groups and facilitates research initiatives on critical emerging issues for the region; 20th Congress: Okinawa, Japan, 2007; 11th Inter-Congress: Tahiti, French Polynesia, 2009; mems: institutional representatives from 35 areas, scientific societies, individual scientists; Pres. Prof. CONGBIN FU (People's Republic of China); Exec. Sec. JOHN BURKE BURNETT; publs *Pacific Science* (quarterly), *Information Bulletin* (2 a year).

Pan-African Union of Science and Technology: POB 2339, Brazzaville, Republic of the Congo; tel. 832265; fax 832185; f. 1987 to promote the use of science and technology in furthering the development of Africa; organizes triennial congress; Pres. Prof. EDWARD AYENSU; Sec.-Gen. Prof. LÉVY MAKANY.

Pugwash Conferences on Science and World Affairs: Ground Floor Flat, 63A Great Russell St, London, WC1B 3BJ, United Kingdom; tel. (20) 7405-6661; fax (20) 7831-5651; e-mail pugwash@mac.com; internet www.pugwash.org; f. 1957 to organize international conferences of scientists to discuss problems arising from the development of science, particularly the dangers to mankind from weapons of mass destruction; mems: national Pugwash groups in 38 countries; Pres. Prof. M. S. SWAMINATHAN; Sec.-Gen. Prof. PAOLO COTTA-RAMUSINO; publs *Pugwash Newsletter* (2 a year), occasional papers, monographs.

Scientific, Technical and Research Commission (STRC): Nigerian Ports Authority Bldg, PMB 2359, Marina, Lagos, Nigeria; tel. (1) 2633430; fax (1) 2636093; e-mail oaustrcl@hyperia.com; f. 1965 to succeed the Commission for Technical Co-operation in Africa (f. 1954); implements priority programmes of the African Union relating to science and technology for development; supervises the Inter-African Bureau for Animal Resources (Nairobi, Kenya), the Inter-African Bureau for Soils (Lagos, Nigeria) and the Inter-African Phytosanitary Commission (Yaoundé, Cameroon) and several joint research projects; provides training in agricultural man., and conducts pest control programmes; services various inter-African committees of experts, including the Scientific Council for Africa; publishes and distributes specialized scientific books and documents of original value to Africa; organizes training courses, seminars, symposia, workshops and technical meetings.

Unitas Malacologica (Malacological Union): c/o Dr P. B. Mordan, The Natural History Museum, Science Depts, Zoology: Mollusca, Cromwell Rd, London, SW7 5BD, United Kingdom; tel. (20) 7938-9359; fax (20) 7938-8754; e-mail p.mordan@nhm.ac.uk; f. 1962 to further the study of molluscs; affiliated to the International Union of Biological Sciences; holds triennial congress; mems: 400 in over 30 countries; Pres. Dr F. WELLS (Australia); Sec. Dr PETER B. MORDAN (United Kingdom); publ. *UM Newsletter* (2 a year).

World Organisation of Systems and Cybernetics (WOSC) (Organisation Mondiale pour la Systémique et la Cybernétique): c/o Dr Alex M. Andrew, 95 Finch Rd, Earley, Reading, Berkshire RG6 7JX, United Kingdom; tel. and fax (118) 926-9328; e-mail alexandrew@britishlibrary.net; internet www.cybsoc.org/wosc/; f. 1969 to act as clearing-house for all societies concerned with cybernetics and systems, to aim for the recognition of cybernetics as fundamental science, to organize and sponsor international exhibitions of automation and computer equipment, congresses and symposia, and to promote and co-ordinate research in systems and cybernetics; sponsors an honorary fellowship and awards a Norbert Wiener memorial gold medal; mems: national and international societies in 30 countries; Pres. Prof. R. VALLÉE (France); Dir-Gen. Dr ALEX M. ANDREW; publs *Kybernetes, the International Journal of Cybernetics and Systems.*

Social Sciences

African Social and Environmental Studies Programme: Box 4477, Nairobi, Kenya; tel. (20) 747960; fax (20) 747960; f. 1968; develops and disseminates educational material on social and environmental studies in eastern and southern Africa; mems: 18 African countries; Chair. Prof. WILLIAM SENTEZA-KAJUBI; Exec. Dir Prof. PETER MUYANDA MUTEBI; publs *African Social and Environmental Studies Forum* (2 a year), teaching guides.

Arab Towns Organization (ATO): POB 68160, Kaifan 71962, Kuwait; tel. 4849705; fax 4849322; e-mail ato@ato.net; internet www.ato.net; f. 1967; aims to promote co-operation and the exchange of expertise with regard to urban administration; works to improve the standard of municipal services and utilities in Arab towns and to preserve the character and heritage of Arab towns. Administers an Institute for Urban Development (AUDI), based in Riyadh, Saudi Arabia, which provides training and research for municipal officers; the Arab Towns Development Fund, to help member towns implement projects; and the ATO Award, to encourage the preservation of Arab architecture; mems: 413 towns; Dir-Gen. MOHAMMED ABDUL HAMID AL-SAQR; Sec.-Gen. ABD AL-AZIZ Y. AL-ADASANI; publ. *Al-Madinah Al-Arabiyah* (every 2 months).

Association for the Study of the World Refugee Problem (AWR): internet www.awr-int.de; f. 1951 to promote and co-ordinate scholarly research on refugee problems; Pres. RAINER WIESTNER (Italy); Gen. Sec. Dr JENS LÖCHER; publs *AWR Bulletin* (quarterly, in English, French, Italian and German), treatises on refugee problems (17 vols).

Council for Research in Values and Philosophy (CRVP): POB 261, Cardinal Station, Washington, DC 20064, USA; tel. and fax (202) 319-6089; e-mail cua-rvp@cua.edu; internet www.crvp.org; organizes conferences and an annual 10-week seminar; mems: 70 teams from 60 countries; Pres. Prof. KENNETH L. SCHMITZ (Canada); Sec.-Treas. Prof. GEORGE F. MCLEAN (USA); publs *Cultural Heritage and Contemporary Change* series (190 titles).

Council for the Development of Social Science Research in Africa (CODESRIA): Ave Cheikh, Anta Diop x Canal IV, BP 3304, CP 18524, Dakar, Senegal; tel. 824-03-74; fax 824-57-95; e-mail codesria@codesria.sn; internet www.codesria.org; f. 1973; promotes research, organizes conferences, working groups and information services; mems: research institutes and university faculties and researchers in African countries; Exec. Sec. ADEBAYO OLUKOSHI; publs *Africa Development* (quarterly), *CODESRIA Bulletin* (quarterly), *Index of African Social Science Periodical Articles* (annually), *African Journal of International Affairs* (2 a year), *African Sociological Review* (2 a year), *Afrika Zameni* (annually), *Identity, Culture and Politics* (2 a year), *Afro Arab Selections for Social Sciences* (annually), directories of research.

Eastern Regional Organisation for Planning and Housing: POB 10867, 50726 Kuala Lumpur, Malaysia; tel. (3) 20925217; fax (3) 20924217; e-mail info@earoph.net; internet www.earoph.net; f. 1958 to promote and co-ordinate the study and practice of housing and regional town and country planning; maintains offices in Japan, India and Indonesia; mems: 57 organizations and 213 individuals in 28 countries; Pres. CANDY BROAD (Australia); Sec.-Gen. KHAIRIAH TALHA; publs *EAROPH News and Notes* (monthly), *Town and Country Planning* (bibliography).

English-Speaking Union: Dartmouth House, 37 Charles St, Berkeley Sq., London, W1J 5ED, United Kingdom; tel. (20) 7529-1550; fax (20) 7495-6108; e-mail esu@esu.org; internet www.esu.org; f. 1918 to promote international understanding between Britain, the Commonwealth, the United States and Europe, in conjunction with the ESU of the USA; mems: 70,000 (incl. USA); Chair. Lord HUNT OF WIRRAL; Dir-Gen. VALERIE MITCHELL; publ. *Concord.*

European Association for Population Studies (EAPS): POB 11676, 2502 AR The Hague, Netherlands; tel. (70) 3565200; fax (70) 3647187; e-mail contact@eaps.nl; internet www.eaps.nl; f. 1983 to foster research and provide information on European population problems; organizes conferences, seminars and workshops; mems: demographers from 40 countries; Exec. Sec. GYS BEETS; publ. *European Journal of Population/Revue Européenne de Démographie* (quarterly).

European Society for Rural Sociology: c/o M. Lehtola, Swedish School of Social Science, POB 16, Univ. of Helsinki, Finland; tel. (9) 19128483; fax (9) 19128485; e-mail minna.lehtola@sockom.helsinki.fi; internet esrs.hu/execom03.htm; f. 1957 to further research in, and co-ordination of, rural sociology and provide a centre for documentation of information; mems: 300 individuals, institutions and asscns in 29 European countries and nine countries outside Europe; Pres. Dr IMRE KOVÁCH (Hungary); Sec. MINNA LEHTOLA (Finland); publ. *Sociologia Ruralis* (quarterly).

Federation EIL: POB 6141, Brattleboro, VT 05302, USA; tel. (802) 258-3467; fax (802) 258-3427; e-mail federation@experiment.org; internet www.experiment.org; f. 1932 as Experiment in International Living; an international federation of non-profit educational and cultural exchange institutions; works to create mutual understanding and respect among people of different nations, as a means of furthering peace; mems: organizations in more than 20 countries; Dir ILENE TODD.

Fédération internationale des associations vexillologiques (International Federation of Vexillological Associations): 504 Branard St, Houston, TX 77006-5018, USA; tel. (713) 529-2545; fax (713) 752-2304; e-mail sec.gen@fiav.org; internet www.fiav.org; f. 1969; unites associations and institutions throughout the world whose object is the pursuit of vexillology, i.e. the creation and development of a body of knowledge about flags of all types, their forms and functions, and of scientific theories and principles based on that knowledge; sponsors International Congresses of Vexillology every two years (2009: Yokohama, Japan); mems: 52 institutions and asscns world-wide; Pres. Prof. MICHEL LUPANT (Belgium); Sec.-Gen. CHARLES A. SPAIN, Jr (USA); publ. *Info FIAV* (annually).

International African Institute (IAI): School of Oriental and African Studies, Thornhaugh St, Russell Sq., London, WC1H 0XG, United Kingdom; tel. (20) 7898-4420; fax (20) 7898-4419; e-mail iai@soas.ac.uk; internet www.iaionthe.net; f. 1926 to promote the study of African peoples, their languages, cultures and social life in their traditional and modern settings; organizes an international seminar programme bringing together scholars from Africa and elsewhere; links scholars in order to facilitate research projects, especially in the social sciences; Chair. Prof. V. Y. MUDIMBE; Hon. Dir Prof. PHILIP BURNHAM; publs *Africa* (quarterly), *Africa Bibliography* (annually).

International Association for Media and Communication Research: c/o Ole Prehn, Aalborg University, Kroghstr. 3, 9220 Aalborg East, Denmark; tel. 96-35-90-38; fax 98-15-68-69; e-mail prehn@hum.aau.dk; internet www.iamcr.net; f. 1957 (fmrly International Asscn for Mass Communication Research) to stimulate interest in mass communication research and the dissemination of information about research and research needs, to improve communication practice, policy and research and training for journalism, and to provide a forum for researchers and others involved in mass communication to meet and exchange information; mems: over 2,300 in c. 70 countries; Pres. ROBIN MANSELL; Sec.-Gen. OLE PREHN; publ. *Newsletter*.

International Association for the History of Religions (IAHR): c/o Prof. Tim Jensen, Institute of Philosophy, Education and the Study of Religion, Dept of the Study of Religions, Univ. of Southern Denmark, Odense, Campusvej 55, 5230 Odense M, Denmark; tel. 65-50-33-15; fax 65-50-26-68; e-mail t.jensen@ifpr.sdu.dk; internet www.iahr.dk; f. 1950 to promote international collaboration of scholars, to organize congresses and to stimulate research; mems: 37 nat. and five regional assocs; Pres. Prof. ROSALIND I. J. HACKETT; Gen. Sec. Prof. TIM JENSEN.

International Association of Applied Linguistics (Association internationale de linguistique appliquée—AILA): Angewandte Linguistik, Universität Erfurt, Postfach 900221, 99105 Erfurt, Germany; tel. (361) 737-4320; fax (361) 737-4329; e-mail aila@uni-erfurt.de; internet www.aila.info; f. 1964; organizes seminars on applied linguistics, and a World Congress every three years (2008: Essen, Germany); mems: more than 8,000; Pres. SUSAN M. GASS (USA); Sec.-Gen. Prof. KARLFRIED KNAPP (Germany); publs *AILA Review* (annually), *AILA News* (2 a year).

International Association of Metropolitan City Libraries (INTAMEL): c/o Frans Meijer, Bibliotheek Rotterdam, Hoogstraat 110, 3011 PV Rotterdam, Netherlands; tel. (10) 2816140; fax (10) 2816221; e-mail f.meijer@bibliotheek.rotterdam.nl; f. 1967; serves as a platform for libraries in cities of over 400,000 inhabitants or serving a wide and diverse geographical area; promotes the exchange of ideas and information on a range of topics including library networks, automation, press relations and research; mems: 98 libraries in 28 countries; Pres. FRANS MEIJER (Netherlands); publs *INTAMEL Metro* (2 a year), conference reports.

International Committee for Social Sciences Information and Documentation: c/o Clacso, Callao 875, 3rd Floor, Buenos Aires 1023, Argentina; e-mail saugy@clacso.edu.ar; internet www.unesco.org/most/icssd.htm; f. 1950 to collect and disseminate information on documentation services in social sciences, to help improve documentation, to advise societies on problems of documentation and to draw up rules likely to improve the presentation of documents; mems: from international asscns specializing in social sciences or in documentation, and from other specialized fields; Sec.-Gen. CATALINA SAUGY (Argentina); publs *International Bibliography of the Social Sciences* (annually), *Newsletter* (2 a year).

International Committee for the History of Art: c/o Prof. Dr P. J. Schneemann, Institut für Kunstgeschichte, Hodlerstr. 8, 3011 Bern, Switzerland; tel. 316314741; fax 316318669; e-mail schneemann@ikg.unibe.ch; internet www.esteticas.unam.mx/ciha; f. 1930 by the 12th International Congress on the History of Art, for collaboration in the scientific study of the history of art; holds international congress every four years, and at least two colloquia between congresses; mems: National Committees in 34 countries; Pres. Prof. RUTH PHILLIPS (Canada); Sec. Prof. Dr PETER JOHANNES SCHNEEMANN (Switzerland); publ. *Bibliographie d'Histoire de l'Art—Bibliography of the History of Art* (quarterly).

International Committee of Historical Sciences: Département d'histoire, UQAM, CP 8888, Succursale Centre-ville, Montréal, QC H3C 3P8, Canada; e-mail cish@uqam.ca; internet www.cish.org; f. 1926 to work for the advancement of historical sciences by means of international co-ordination; holds international congress every five years, 2005: Sydney, Australia; mems: 54 national committees, 28 affiliated international orgs and 12 internal commissions; Pres. Prof. JOSÉ LUIS PESET (Spain); Sec.-Gen. Prof. JEAN-CLAUDE ROBERT (Canada); publ. *Bulletin d'Information du CISH*.

International Council for Philosophy and Humanistic Studies (ICPHS): Maison de l'UNESCO, 1 rue Miollis, 75732 Paris Cédex 15, France; tel. 1-45-68-48-85; fax 1-40-65-94-80; e-mail cipsh@unesco.org; internet www.unesco.org/cipsh; f. 1949 under the auspices of UNESCO to encourage respect for cultural autonomy by the comparative study of civilization and to contribute towards international understanding through a better knowledge of humanity; works to develop international co-operation in philosophy, humanistic and kindred studies; encourages the setting up of international organizations; promotes the dissemination of information in these fields; sponsors works of learning, etc; mems: 13 orgs representing 145 countries; Pres. IN SUK CHA; Sec.-Gen. MAURICE AYMARD; publs *Bulletin of Information* (biennially), *Diogenes* (quarterly).

International Council on Archives (ICA): 60 rue des Francs-Bourgeois, 75003 Paris, France; tel. 1-40-27-63-06; fax 1-42-72-20-65; e-mail ica@ica.org; internet www.ica.org; f. 1948 to develop relationships between archivists in different countries; aims to protect and enhance archives, to ensure preservation of archival heritage; facilitates training of archivists and conservators; promotes implementation of a professional code of conduct; encourages ease of access to archives; has 13 regional branches; mems: more than 1,400 in 190 countries; Pres. LORENZ MIKOLETZKY (Austria); Sec.-Gen. JOAN VAN ALBADA; publs *Comma* (quarterly), *Flash Newsletter* (3 a year), annual CD-Rom.

International Ergonomics Association (IEA): 1515 Engineering Drive, 3126 Engineering Centers Building, Madison, WI 53706, USA; tel. (608) 265-0503; fax (608) 263-1425; e-mail carayon@engr.wisc.edu; internet www.iea.cc; f. 1957 to bring together organizations and persons interested in the scientific study of human work and its environment; to establish international contacts among those specializing in this field, to co-operate with employers' asscns and trade unions in order to encourage the practical application of ergonomic sciences in industries, and to promote scientific research in this field; mems: 42 federated societies; Pres. DAVID CAPLE (Australia); Sec.-Gen. Prof. PASCALE CARAYON; publ. *Ergonomics* (monthly).

International Federation for Housing and Planning (IFHP): Wassenaarseweg 43, 2596 CG The Hague, Netherlands; tel. (70) 3244557; fax (70) 3282085; e-mail info@ifhp.org; internet www.ifhp.org; f. 1913 to study and promote the improvement of housing and the theory and practice of town planning; holds an annual World Congress (2008: San Juan, Puerto Rico, in Oct.); mems: 200 orgs and 300 individuals in 65 countries; Pres. FRANCESC X. VENTURA I TEIXIDOR (Spain); Sec.-Gen. DEREK MARTIN; publ. *Newsletter* (quarterly).

International Federation for Modern Languages and Literatures: c/o A. Pettersson, Dept of Scandinavian Languages and Comparative Literature, Umea University, 901 87 Umea, Sweden; tel. (90) 786-5797; fax (90) 786-7790; e-mail anders.pettersson@littvet.umu.se; internet www.fillm.ulg.ac.be; f. 1928 to establish permanent contact between historians of literature, to develop or perfect facilities for their work and to promote the study of modern languages and literature; holds Congress every three years; mems: 19 asscns, with individual mems in 98 countries; Sec.-Gen. ANDERS PETTERSSON (Sweden).

International Federation of Institutes for Socio-religious Research: 1/13 pl. Montesquieu, 1348 Louvain-la-neuve, Belgium; e-mail social.compass@anso.ucl.ac.be; f. 1958; federates centres engaged in scientific research in order to analyse and discover the social and religious phenomena at work in contemporary society; mems: institutes in 26 countries; Pres. Canon Fr A. BASTENIER (Belgium); Sec. C. POLAIN; publ. *Social Compass (International Review of Sociology of Religion)* (quarterly, in English and French).

International Federation of Philosophical Societies (FISP): c/o P. Kemp, Dept of Philosophy of Education, the Danish Univ. of Education, Tuborgvej 164, 2400 Copenhagen NV, Denmark; tel. 88-88-94-53; fax 88-88-97-24; e-mail kemp@dpu.dk; internet www.fisp.org; f. 1948 under the auspices of UNESCO, to encourage international co-operation in the field of philosophy; holds World Congress of Philosophy every five years (2008: Seoul, Republic of Korea); mems: 100 societies from 50 countries; 27 international societies; Pres. PETER KEMP (Denmark); Sec.-Gen. WILLIAM MCBRIDE (USA); publs *Newsletter*, *International Bibliography of Philosophy*, *Chroniques de Philosophie*, *Contemporary Philosophy*, *Philosophical Problems Today*, *Philosophy and Cultural Development*, *Ideas Underlying World Problems*, *The Idea of Values*.

International Federation of Social Science Organizations (IFSSO): Institute of Law, nardoni 18, 110 000 Prague 1, Czech Republic; tel. 224913858; fax 224913858; f. 1979 to assist research and teaching in the social sciences, and to facilitate co-operation and enlist mutual assistance in the planning and evaluation of programmes of major importance to members; mems: 31 national councils or academies in 29 countries; Pres. Prof. CARMENCITA T. AGUILAR; Sec.-Gen. Prof. J. BLAHOZ; publs *IFSSO Newsletter* (2 a year), *International Directory of Social Science Organizations*.

International Federation of Societies of Classical Studies: c/o Prof. P. Schubert, 7 rue des Beaux-Arts, 2000 Neuchatel, Switzerland; tel. 223797035; fax 223797932; e-mail paul.schubert@lettres .unige.ch; internet www.fiecnet.org; f. 1948 under the auspices of UNESCO; mems: 80 societies in 44 countries; Pres. HEINRICH VON STADEN (USA); Sec.-Gen. Prof. PAUL SCHUBERT (Switzerland); publs *L'Année Philologique, Thesaurus linguae Latinae*.

International Institute for Ligurian Studies: Via Romana 39, 18012 Bordighera, Italy; tel. (0184) 263601; fax (0184) 266421; e-mail istituto@üsl.it; f. 1947 to conduct research on ancient monuments and regional traditions in the north-west arc of the Mediterranean (France and Italy); maintains library of 80,000 vols; mems: in France, Italy, Spain, Switzerland; Dir Prof. CARLO VARALDO (Italy).

International Institute of Administrative Sciences (IIAS): 1 rue Defacqz, 1000 Brussels, Belgium; tel. (2) 536-08-80; fax (2) 537-97-02; e-mail iias@iiasiisa.be; internet www.iiasiisa.be; f. 1930 for the comparative examination of administrative experience; carries out research and programmes designed to improve administrative law and practices; maintains library of 15,000 vols; has consultative status with UN, UNESCO and ILO; organizes international congresses, annual conferences, working groups; mems: 46 mem. states, 55 national sections, nine international governmental orgs, 51 corporate mems, 13 individual members; Pres. FRANZ STREHL (Austria); Dir-Gen. ROLET LORETAN (Switzerland); publs *International Review of Administrative Sciences* (quarterly), *Newsletter* (3 a year).

International Institute of Sociology (IIS): c/o The Swedish Collegium for Advanced Study, Götavägen 4, 75236 Uppsala, Sweden; tel. (18) 55-70-85; e-mail info.iis@swedishcollegium.se; internet www.iisoc.org; f. 1893 to enable sociologists to meet and to study sociological questions; mems: c. 300 in 47 countries; Pres. BJÖRN WITTROCK (Sweden); Sec.-Gen. PETER HEDSTRÖM; publ. *The Annals of the IIS*.

International Musicological Society (IMS): CP 1561, 4001 Basel, Switzerland; fax 449231027; e-mail dorothea.baumann@ ims-online.ch; internet www.ims-online.ch; f. 1927; holds international congresses every five years (July 2007: Zürich, Switzerland); mems: c. 1,000 in 48 countries; Pres. DAVID FALLOWS, TIMAN SEEBAS (Austria); Sec.-Gen. Dr DOROTHEA BAUMANN (Switzerland); publ. *Acta Musicologica* (2 a year).

International Numismatic Commission: Cabinet des Médailles de la Bibliothèque nationale de France, 58 rue de Richelieu, 75084 Paris Cédex 02, France; tel. 1-53-79-83-63; fax 1-53-79-89-47; e-mail michel.amandry@bnf.fr; internet www.inc-cin.org; f. 1936; facilitates co-operation between scholars studying coins and medals; mems: numismatic orgs in 36 countries; Pres. MICHEL AMANDRY; Sec. CARMEN ARNOLD-BIUCCHI.

International Peace Academy (IPA): 777 United Nations Plaza, New York, NY 10017-3521, USA; tel. (212) 687-4300; fax (212) 983-8246; e-mail ipa@ipacademy.org; internet www.ipacademy.org; f. 1970 to promote the prevention and settlement of armed conflicts between and within states through policy research and development; educates government officials in the procedures needed for conflict resolution, peace-keeping, mediation and negotiation, through international training seminars and publications; off-the-record meetings are also conducted to gain complete understanding of a specific conflict; Chair. RITA E. HAUSER; Pres. TERJE ROD-LARSEN.

International Peace Research Association (IPRA): c/o K. Kodama, Mie University, Dept of Humanities, Kamihama, Tsu 514, Japan; tel. and fax (592) 319156; e-mail kkodama@human .mie-u.ac.jp; internet www.human.mie-u.ac.jp/~peace/; f. 1964 to encourage interdisciplinary research on the conditions of peace and the causes of war; mems: 150 corporate, five regional branches, 1,000 individuals, in 93 countries; Sec.-Gen. KATSUYA KODAMA (Japan); publ. *IPRA Newsletter* (quarterly).

International Social Science Council (ISSC): Maison de l'UNESCO, 1 rue Miollis, 75732 Paris Cédex 15, France; tel. 1-45-68-48-60; fax 1-45-66-76-03; e-mail issc@unesco.org; internet www .unesco.org/ngo/issc; f. 1952; aims to promote the advancement of the social sciences throughout the world and their application to the major problems of the world; encourages co-operation at an international level between specialists in the social sciences; comprises programmes on International Human Dimensions of Global Environmental Change (IHDP), Gender, Globalization and Democratization, and Comparative Research on Poverty (CROP); mems: International Association of Legal Sciences, International Economic Association, International Federation of Social Science Organizations, International Geographical Union, International Institute of Administrative Sciences, International Peace Research Association, International Political Science Association, International Sociological Association, International Union for the Scientific Study of Population, International Union of Anthropological and Ethnological Sciences, International Union of Psychological Science, World Association for Public Opinion Research, World Federation for Mental Health; 28 national orgs; 16 associate members; Pres. Prof. GUDMUND HERNES (Norway); Sec.-Gen. Dr HEIDE HACKMANN (France).

International Society of Social Defence and Humane Criminal Policy (ISSD): c/o Centro nazionale di prevenzione e difesa sociale, Piazza Castello 3, 20121 Milan, Italy; tel. (02) 86460714; fax (02) 72008431; e-mail cnpds.ispac@cnpds.it; internet www.cnpds.it; f. 1945 to combat crime, to protect society and to prevent citizens from being tempted to commit criminal actions; mems: in 43 countries; Pres. SIMONE ROZÈS (France); Sec.-Gen. EDMONDO BRUTI LIBERATI (Italy); publ. *Cahiers de défense sociale* (annually).

International Sociological Association: c/o Faculty of Political Sciences and Sociology, Universidad Complutense, 28223 Madrid, Spain; tel. (91) 3527650; fax (91) 3524945; e-mail isa@isa-sociology .org; internet www.isa-sociology.org; f. 1949 to promote sociological knowledge, facilitate contacts between sociologists, encourage the dissemination and exchange of information and facilities and stimulate research; has 53 research committees on various aspects of sociology; holds World Congresses every four years (17th Congress: Göteborg, Sweden, July 2010); Exec. Sec. IZABELA BARLINSKA; publs *Current Sociology* (6 a year), *International Sociology* (6 a year), *Sage Studies in International Sociology* (based on World Congress).

International Statistical Institute (ISI): POB 950, Prinses Beatrixlaan 428, 2270 AZ Voorburg, Netherlands; tel. (70) 3375737; fax (70) 3860025; e-mail isi@cbs.nl; internet www.isi.cbs.nl; f. 1885; devoted to the development and improvement of statistical methods and their application throughout the world; executes international research programmes; mems: 2,000 ordinary mems, 11 hon. mems, 166 *ex-officio* mems, 69 corporate mems, 45 affiliated organizations, 32 national statistical societies; Pres. NIELS KEIDING (Denmark); Dir Permanent Office DANIEL BERZE; publs *Bulletin of the International Statistical Institute* (proceedings of biennial sessions), *International Statistical Review* (3 a year), *Short Book Reviews* (3 a year), *Statistical Theory and Method Abstracts–Z* (available on CD-Rom and online), *ISI Newsletter* (3 a year), *Membership Directory* (available online).

International Studies Association (ISA): Social Science 324, Univ. of Arizona, Tucson, AZ 85721, USA; tel. (520) 621-7715; fax (520) 621-5780; e-mail isa@u.arizona.edu; internet www.isanet.org; f. 1959; links those whose professional concerns extend beyond their own national boundaries (government officials, representatives of business and industry, and scholars); mems: 3,500 in 60 countries; Pres. ANN TICKNER; Exec. Dir THOMAS J. VOLGY; publs *International Studies Quarterly*, *International Studies Perspectives*, *International Studies Review*, *ISA Newsletter*.

International Union for the Scientific Study of Population (IUSSP): 3–5 rue Nicolas, 75980 Paris Cedex 20, France; tel. 1-56-06-21-73; fax 1-56-06-22-04; e-mail iussp@iussp.org; internet www .iussp.org; f. 1928 to advance the progress of quantitative and qualitative demography as a science; mems: 1,917 in 121 countries; Pres. JACQUES VALLIN; publs *IUSSP Bulletin* and books on population.

International Union of Academies (IUA) (Union académique internationale—UAI): Palais des Académies, 1 rue Ducale, 1000 Brussels, Belgium; tel. (2) 550-22-00; fax (2) 550-22-05; e-mail info@ uai-iua.org; internet www.uai-iua.org; f. 1919 to promote international co-operation through collective research in philology, archaeology, art history, history and social sciences; mems: academic institutions in 61 countries; Pres. AGOSTINO PARAVICINI BAGLIANI (Switzerland); Secs LÉO HOUZIAUX, JEAN-LUC DE PAEPE.

International Union of Anthropological and Ethnological Sciences (IUAES): c/o Dr P. J. M. Nas, Faculty of Social Sciences, Univ. of Leiden, Wassenaarseweg 52, POB 9555, 2300 RB Leiden, Netherlands; tel. (71) 5273992; fax (71) 5273619; e-mail nas@fsw .leidenuniv.nl; internet www.leidenuniv.nl/fsw/iuaes/; f. 1948 under the auspices of UNESCO, to enhance exchange and communication between scientists and institutions in the fields of anthropology and ethnology; aims to promote harmony between nature and culture; organizes 22 international research commissions; mems: institutions and individuals in 100 countries; Pres. Prof. LUIS ALBERTO VARGAS (Mexico); Sec.-Gen. Dr PETER J. M. NAS (Netherlands); publ. *IUAES Newsletter* (3 a year).

International Union of Prehistoric and Protohistoric Sciences: c/o Prof. J. Bourgeois, Dept of Archaeology and Ancient History of Europe, Univ. of Ghent, Blandijnberg 2, 9000 Ghent, Belgium; tel. (9) 264-41-06; fax (9) 264-41-73; e-mail jean.bourgeois@ rug.ac.be; internet www.geocities.com/athens/ithaca/7152; f. 1931 to promote congresses and scientific work in the fields of pre- and protohistory; mems: 120 countries; Pres. Prof. P. BONENFANT (Belgium); Sec.-Gen. Prof. J. BOURGEOIS (Belgium).

Mensa International: 15 The Ivories, 6–8 Northampton St, London, N1 2HY, United Kingdom; tel. (20) 7226-6891; fax (20) 7226-7059; internet www.mensa.org; f. 1946 to identify and foster intelligence for the benefit of humanity; mems: individuals who score higher than 98% of people in general in a recognized intelligence test may become mems; there are 100,000 mems world-wide; Exec. Dir MICHAEL FEENAN (United Kingdom); publ. *Mensa International Journal* (monthly).

Permanent International Committee of Linguists: Postbus 9515, 2300 RA Leiden, Netherlands; tel. (71) 5141648; fax (71) 5272115; e-mail sterkenburg@inl.nl; internet www.ciplnet.com; f. 1928; aims to further linguistic research, to co-ordinate activities undertaken for the advancement of linguistics, and to make the results of linguistic research known internationally; holds Congress every five years; mems: 34 countries and two international linguistic organizations; Pres. F. KIEFER (Hungary); Sec.-Gen. P. G. J. VAN STERKENBURG (Netherlands); publ. *Linguistic Bibliography* (annually).

Third World Forum: 39 Dokki St, POB 43, Orman Giza, Cairo, Egypt; tel. (2) 7488092; fax (2) 7480668; e-mail 20sabry2@gega.net; internet www.forumtiersmonde.net; f. 1973 to link social scientists and others from the developing countries, to discuss alternative development policies and encourage research; maintains regional offices in Egypt, Mexico, Senegal and Sri Lanka; mems: individuals in more than 50 countries.

World Association for Public Opinion Research: c/o Univ. of Nebraska-Lincoln, UNL Gallup Research Center, 200 N 11th St, Lincoln, NE 68588-0242, USA; tel. (402) 458-2030; fax (402) 458-2038; e-mail wapor@unl.edu; internet www.wapor.org; f. 1947 to establish and promote contacts between persons in the field of survey research on opinions, attitudes and behaviour of people in the various countries of the world; works to further the use of objective, scientific survey research in national and international affairs; mems: 450 from 72 countries; Pres. Prof. ESTEBAN LÓPEZ-ESCOBAR; Gen. Sec. Prof. Dr ALLAN MCCUTCHEON; publs *WAPOR Newsletter* (quarterly), *International Journal of Public Opinion* (quarterly).

World Society for Ekistics: c/o Athens Center of Ekistics, 24 Strat. Syndesmou St, 106 73 Athens, Greece; tel. (210) 3623216; fax (210) 3629337; e-mail ekistics@otenet.gr; internet www.ekistics.org; f. 1965; aims to promote knowledge and ideas concerning human settlements through research, publications and conferences; encourages the development and expansion of education in ekistics; aims to recognize the benefits and necessity of an inter-disciplinary approach to the needs of human settlements; mems: 187 individuals; Pres. Dr RUŞEN KELEŞ; Sec.-Gen. P. PSOMOPOULOS.

Social Welfare and Human Rights

African Commission on Human and Peoples' Rights: 48 Kairaba Ave, POB 673, Banjul, The Gambia; tel. 4392962; fax 4390764; e-mail achpr@achpr.org; internet www.achpr.org; f. 1987; mandated to monitor compliance with the African Charter on Human and People's Rights (ratified in 1986); investigates claims of human rights abuses perpetrated by govts that have ratified the Charter (claims may be brought by other African govts, the victims themselves, or by a third party); meets twice a year for 15 days in March and Oct; mems: 11; Sec. Dr MARY MABOREKE.

Aid to Displaced Persons and its European Villages: 35 rue du Marché, 4500 Huy, Belgium; tel. (85) 21-34-81; fax (85) 23-01-47; e-mail aidepersdepl.huy@proximedia.be; f. 1957 to carry on and develop work begun by the Belgian asscn Aid to Displaced Persons; aims to provide material and moral aid for refugees; European Villages established at Aachen, Bregenz, Augsburg, Berchem-Ste-Agathe, Spiesen, Euskirchen, Wuppertal as centres for refugees; Pres. LUC DENYS (Belgium).

Amnesty International: 1 Easton St, London, WC1X 0DW, United Kingdom; tel. (20) 7413-5500; fax (20) 7956-1157; e-mail amnestyis@amnesty.org; internet www.amnesty.org; f. 1961; an independent, democratic, self-governing world-wide movement of people who campaign for internationally recognized human rights, such as those enshrined in the Universal Declaration of Human Rights; undertakes research and action focused on preventing and ending grave abuses of the rights to physical and mental integrity, freedom of conscience and expression, and freedom from discrimination, within the context of its work impartially to promote and protect all human rights; mems: more than 1.8m. represented by 7,800 local, youth, student and other specialist groups, in more than 150 countries and territories; nationally organized sections in 58 countries and presection co-ordinating structures in another 22 countries; major policy decisions are taken by an International Council comprising representatives from all national sections; financed by donations; no funds are sought or accepted from governments; Sec.-Gen. IRENE KHAN (Bangladesh); publs *International Newsletter* (monthly), *Annual Report*, other country reports.

Anti-Slavery International: Thomas Clarkson House, The Stableyard, Broomgrove Rd, London, SW9 9TL, United Kingdom; tel. (20) 7501-8920; fax (20) 7738-4110; e-mail info@antislavery.org; internet www.antislavery.org; f. 1839; aims to eliminate all forms of slavery by exposing manifestations of it around the world and campaigning against it; supports initiatives by local organizations to release people from slavery, and develops rehabilitation programmes aimed at preventing people from re-entering slavery; pressures governments to implement international laws prohibiting slavery and to develop and enforce similar national legislation; mems: c. 2,000 world-wide; Chair. DEE SULLIVAN; Dir MARY CUNNEEN; publs *Annual Review* (quarterly), *Reporter* (quarterly), special reports and research documentation.

Associated Country Women of the World (ACWW): Mary Sumner House, 24 Tufton St, London, SW1P 3RB, United Kingdom; tel. (20) 7799-3875; fax (20) 7340-9950; e-mail info@acww.org.uk; internet www.acww.org.uk; f. 1933; aims to aid the economic and social development of countrywomen and home-makers of all nations, to promote international goodwill and understanding, to work to alleviate poverty, and promote good health and education; Gen. Sec. IAN MCCONCHIE; publ. *The Countrywoman* (quarterly).

Association Internationale de la Mutualité (AIM) (International Association of Mutual Health Funds): 50 rue d'Arlon, Fifth Floor, 1000 Brussels, Belgium; tel. (2) 234-57-00; fax (2) 234-57-08; e-mail aim.secretariat@aim-mutual.org; internet www.aim-mutual.org; f. 1950 as a grouping of autonomous health insurance and social protection bodies; aims to promote and reinforce access to health care by developing the sound management of mutualities; serves as a forum for exchange of information and debate; mems: 45 national federations in 32 countries; Pres. MAURICE DURANTON (France); Gen. Dir MARCEL J. G. SMEETS (Netherlands); publs *AIMS* (newsletter), reports on health issues.

Aviation sans Frontières (ASF): Brussels National Airport, Brucargo 706, POB 60, 1931 Brucargo, Belgium; tel. (2) 753-24-70; fax (2) 753-24-71; e-mail office@asfbelgium.org; internet www.asfbelgium.org; f. 1983 to make available the resources of the aviation industry to humanitarian organizations, for carrying supplies and equipment at minimum cost, both on long-distance flights and locally; Pres. JEAN-CLAUDE GÉRIN; Gen. Man. XAVIER FLAMENT.

Co-ordinating Committee for International Voluntary Service (CCIVS): Maison de l'UNESCO, 1 rue Miollis, 75732 Paris Cédex 15, France; tel. 1-45-68-49-36; fax 1-42-73-05-21; e-mail ccivs@unesco.org; internet www.unesco.org/ccivs; f. 1948 to co-ordinate youth voluntary service organizations world-wide; Organizes seminars and conferences; publishes relevant literature; undertakes planning and execution of projects in collaboration with UNESCO, the UN, the EU etc; Affiliated mems: 350 orgs in more than 100 countries; Pres. JINSU YOM; Dir S. COSTANZO-SOW; publs *News from CCIVS* (3 a year), *The Volunteer's Handbook*, other guides, handbooks and directories.

Co-ordinator of the Indigenous Organizations of the Amazon Basin (COICA): Calle Sevilla 24–358 y Guipuzcoa, La Floresta, Quito, Ecuador; e-mail com@coica.org; internet www.coica.org; f. 1984; aims to co-ordinate the activities of national organizations concerned with the indigenous people and environment of the Amazon basin, and promotes respect for human rights and the self-determination of the indigenous populations; nine member orgs; Co-ordinator-Gen. JOCELYN ROGER THERESE; publ. *Nuestra Amazonia* (quarterly, in English, Spanish, French and Portuguese).

EIRENE (International Christian Service for Peace): 56503 Neuwied, Postfach 1322, Germany; tel. (2631) 83790; fax (2631) 837990; e-mail eirene-int@eirene.org; internet www.eirene.org; f. 1957; carries out professional training, apprenticeship programmes, agricultural work and support co-operatives in Africa and Latin America; runs volunteer programmes in co-operation with peace groups in Europe and the USA; Gen. Sec. ANGELA KÖNIG.

European Federation of Older Persons (EURAG): Wielandgasse 9, 8010 Graz, Austria; tel. and fax (316) 81-4608; e-mail office@eurag-europe.org; internet www.eurag-europe.org; f. 1962 as the European Federation for the Welfare of the Elderly (present name adopted 2002); serves as a forum for the exchange of experience and practical co-operation among member organizations; represents the interests of members before international organizations; promotes understanding and co-operation in matters of social welfare; draws attention to the problems of old age; mems: orgs in 33 countries; Pres. ULLA HERFORT-WÖRNDLE; Dir Mag. GERHARD TEISSEL (Austria); publ. (in English, French, German and Italian) *EURAG Information* (monthly).

Federation of Asia-Pacific Women's Associations (FAWA): Centro Escolar University, 9 Mendiola St, San Miguel, Manila, Philippines; tel. (2) 741-0446; e-mail zmaustria@ceu.edu.ph;

f. 1959 to provide closer relations, and bring about joint efforts among Asians, particularly women, through mutual appreciation of cultural, moral and socio-economic values; mems: 415,000; Pres. Susy Chia-Isai (Singapore); Sec. Woo Choon Mei (Singapore); publ. *FAWA News Bulletin* (quarterly).

Global Commission on International Migration (GCIM): 1 rue Richard-Wagner, 1202 Geneva, Switzerland; tel. 227484850; fax 227484851; internet www.gcim.org; f. 2003 to place international migration issues on the global agenda, to analyse migration policy, to examine links with other fields, and to present recommendations for consideration by the UN Secretary-General, governments and other parties; Commission ceased active operations on 31 Dec. 2005; publ. *Migration in an Interconnected World: New Directions for Action.*

Global Humanitarian Forum: ave de la Paix 9, 1202 Geneva, Switzerland; tel. 229197500; fax 229197519; e-mail ghf-geneva@ghf-geneva.org; internet www./www.ghf-geneva.org; f. 2007 to support dialogue and encourage partnerships to focus international attention on and generate increased investment towards addressing key humanitarian concerns; also seeks to place international migration issues on the global agenda; CEO Walter Fust (Switzerland).

Global Migration Group (GMG): f. 2003, as the Geneva Migration Group; renamed as above in 2006; mems: ILO, IOM, UNCTAD, UNDP, United Nations Department of Economic and Social Affairs (UNDESA), UNFPA, OHCHR, UNHCR, UNODC, and the World Bank; holds regular meetings to discuss issues relating to int. migration, chaired by mem. orgs on a six-month rotational basis.

Inclusion Europe: Galeries de la Toison d'Or, 29 ch. d'Ixelles, bte 393/32, 1050 Brussels, Belgium; tel. (2) 502-28-15; fax (2) 502-80-10; e-mail secretariat@inclusion-europe.org; internet www.inclusion-europe.org; f. 1988 to advance the human rights and defend the interests of people with learning or intellectual disabilities, and their families, in Europe; mems: 46 societies in 34 European countries; Pres. Ingrid Körner; Dir Geert Freyhoff; publs *INCLUDE* (in English and French), *Information Letter* (weekly online, in English and French), *Human Rights Observer* (in English and French), *Enlargement Update* (on-line every 2 weeks, in English and French), other papers and publs.

Initiatives of Change International: POB 3, 1211 Geneva 20, Switzerland; tel. 227491620; fax 227330267; e-mail iofc-international@iofc.org; internet www.iofc.org; f. 1921; an international network specializing in conflict resolution that is open to people of all cultures, nationalities, religions and beliefs, and works towards change, both locally and globally, commencing at the personal level; has special consultative status with ECOSOC and participatory status with the Council of Europe; supports and publicizes the grassroots work of the National Societies of Initiatives of Change; works in 60 countries; fmrly the Moral Rearmament (MRA) movement; current name adopted in 2001; Pres. Mohamed Sahnoun; publs *Changer International* (French, 6 a year), *For a Change* (English, 6 a year), *Caux Information* (German, monthly).

Inter-American Conference on Social Security (Conferencia Interamericano de Seguridad Social—CISS): c/o F. Flores, Instituto Mexicano del Seguro Social, Paseo de la Reforma 476, 1°, Col. Juarez, Del. Cuauhtemoc, CP 06600, México, DF, Mexico; tel. (55) 5211-4853; fax (55) 5211-2623; e-mail ciss@ciss.org.mx; internet www.ciss.org.mx; f. 1942 to contribute to the development of social security in the countries of the Americas and to co-operate with social security institutions; CISS bodies are: the General Assembly, the Permanent Inter-American Committee on Social Security, the Secretariat General, six American Commissions of Social Security and the Inter-American Center for Social Security Studies; mems: 66 social security institutions in 36 countries; Pres. Fernando Flores (Mexico); Sec.-Gen. Dr Gabriel Martínez González (Mexico); publs *Social Security Journal / Seguridad Social* (every 2 months), *The Americas Social Security Report* (annually), *Social Security Bulleting* (monthly, online), monographs, study series.

International Abolitionist Federation: 11 rue des Savoies, 1205 Geneva, Switzerland; tel. 227813060; fax 227813133; e-mail iaf@iaf-online.org; f. 1875; aims to abolish traffic in persons, the exploitation of the prostitution of others, state regulation of prostitution, degradation, humiliation and marginalizing of women and children, all forms of discrimination based on gender, and all contemporary forms of slavery and slavery-like practices; holds international congress every three years and organizes regional conferences to raise awareness of the cultural, religious and traditional practices that affect adversely the lives of women and children; affiliated orgs in 17 countries, corresponding mems in 40 countries; publ. *IAF Information* (1-2 a year).

International Association for Education to a Life without Drugs (Internationaler Verband für Erziehung zu suchtmittelfreiem Leben—IVES): c/o Uljas Syväniemi, Haiharankatu 15 G 64, 33710 Tampere, Finland; e-mail uljas.syvaniemi@koti.tpo.ti; f. 1954 (as the International Association for Temperance Education) to promote international co-operation in education on the dangers of alcohol and drugs; collects and distributes information on drugs; maintains regular contact with national and international organizations active in these fields; holds conferences; mems: 77,000 in 10 countries; Pres. Uljas Syväniemi; Sec. Dag Magne Johannessen.

International Association for Suicide Prevention: c/o Ms M. Campos, IASP Central Administrative Office, Le Barade, 32330 Gondrin, France; tel. 5-62-29-19-47; fax 5-62-29-19-47; e-mail iasp1960@aol.com; internet www.med.uio.no/iasp/; f. 1960; serves as a common platform for interchange of acquired experience, literature and information about suicide; disseminates information; arranges special training; encourages and carries out research; organizes the Biennial International Congress for Suicide Prevention; mems: 340 individuals and societies, in 55 countries of all continents; Pres. Prof. Brian Mishara; publ. *Crisis* (quarterly).

International Association of Children's International Summer Villages (CISV International Ltd): Mea House, Ellison Pl., Newcastle upon Tyne, NE1 8XS, United Kingdom; tel. (191) 232-4998; fax (191) 261-4710; e-mail international@cisv.org; internet www.cisv.org; f. 1950 to promote peace, education and cross-cultural friendship; conducts International Camps for children and young people mainly between the ages of 11 and 19; mems: c. 49,000; International Pres. Cathy Knoop; Sec.-Gen. Gabrielle Mandell; publs *CISV News*, *Annual Review*, *Local Work Magazine*, *Interspectives* (all annually).

International Association of Schools of Social Work: c/o A. Tasse, Graduate School of Social Work, Univ. of Addis Ababa, POB 1176, Ethiopia; tel. (1) 231084; fax (1) 239768; e-mail abye.tasse@ids.fr; internet www.iassw-aiets.org; f. 1928 to provide international leadership and encourage high standards in social work education; mems: 1,600 schools of social work in 70 countries, and 25 national asscns of schools; Pres. Prof. Dr Abye Tasse (Ethiopia); Sec. Lynne Healy; publs *Newsletters* (in English, French and Spanish), *Directory of Schools of Social Work*, *Journal of International Social Work*, reports and case studies.

International Association of Social Educators (AIEJI): Galgebakken Soender 5-4, DK-2620 Albertslund, Denmark; tel. 40457844; fax 33259844; e-mail steinov@enghaven.dk; internet www.aieji.net; f. 1951 (as International Asscn of Workers for Troubled Children and Youth); provides a centre of information about child welfare; encourages co-operation between members; 2009 Congress: Copenhagen, Denmark; mems: national and regional public or private asscns from 22 countries and individual members in many other countries; Pres. Benny Andersen (Denmark); Gen. Sec. Lars Steinov (Denmark).

International Catholic Migration Commission: 37–39 rue de Vermont, CP 96, 1211 Geneva 20, Switzerland; tel. 229191020; fax 229191048; e-mail icmc@icmc.net; internet www.icmc.net; f. 1951; offers migration aid programmes; grants interest-free travel loans; assists refugees on a world-wide basis, helping with social and technical problems; mems: in 65 countries; Pres. Prof. Stefano Zamagni (Italy); Sec. Rev. Fr Neil Karunaratne (Sri Lanka); publ. *Annual Report.*

International Christian Federation for the Prevention of Alcoholism and Drug Addiction: 20a Ancienne Route, Apt. No 42, 1218 Grand-Saconnex, Geneva, Switzerland; tel. 227888158; fax 227888136; e-mail jonathan@iprolink.ch; f. 1960, reconstituted 1980 to promote world-wide education and remedial work through the churches and to co-ordinate Christian concern about alcohol and drug abuse, in co-operation with the World Council of Churches and WHO; Chair. Karin Israelsson (Sweden); Gen. Sec. Jonathan N. Gnanadason.

International Civil Defence Organization (ICDO) (Organisation internationale de protection civile—OIPC): POB 172, 10–12 chemin de Surville, 1213 Petit-Lancy, Geneva, Switzerland; tel. 228796969; fax 228796979; e-mail info@icdo.org; internet www.icdo.org; f. 1931, present statutes in force 1972; aims to contribute to the development of structures ensuring the protection of populations and the safeguarding of property and the environment in the face of natural and man-made disasters; promotes co-operation between civil defence organizations in member countries; Sec.-Gen. Nawaf B. S. Al Sleibi (Jordan); publ. *International Civil Defence Journal* (quarterly, in Arabic, English, French, Russian and Spanish).

International Commission for the Prevention of Alcoholism and Drug Dependency: 12501 Old Columbia Pike, Silver Spring, MD 20904-6600, USA; tel. (301) 680-6719; fax (301) 680-6707; e-mail the_icpa@hotmail.com; f. 1952 to encourage scientific research on intoxication by alcohol, its physiological, mental and moral effects on the individual, and its effect on the community; mems: individuals in 120 countries; Exec. Dir Dr Peter N. Landless; publ. *ICPA Reporter*.

International Council of Voluntary Agencies (ICVA): 26–28 Ave Guiseppe Motta, 1202 Geneva, Switzerland; tel. 229509600; fax 229509609; e-mail secretariat@icva.ch; internet www.icva.ch; f. 1962 as a global network of human rights and humanitarian and development NGOs; focuses on information exchange and advocacy,

INTERNATIONAL ORGANIZATIONS

Social Welfare and Human Rights

primarily in the areas of humanitarian affairs and refugee issues; mems: 78 non-governmental orgs; Chair. THOMAS GETMAN; Co-ordinator ED SCHENKENBERG VAN MIEROP; publ. *Talk Back* (newsletter, available online).

International Council of Women (ICW) (Conseil International des Femmes—CIF): 13 rue Caumartin, 75009 Paris, France; tel. 1-47-42-19-40; fax 1-42-66-26-23; e-mail icw-cif@wanadoo.fr; internet www.icw-cif.org; f. 1888 to bring together in international affiliation Nat. Councils of Women from all continents, for consultation and joint action; promotes equal rights for men and women and the integration of women in development and decision-making; has five standing committees; mems: 65 national councils; Pres. ANAMAH TAN; Sec.-Gen. RADOSVETA BRUZAUD; publ. *Newsletter*.

International Council on Alcohol and Addictions (ICAA): CP 189, 1001 Lausanne, Switzerland; tel. 213209865; fax 213209817; e-mail secretariat@icaa.ch; internet www.icaa.de; f. 1907; provides an international forum for all those concerned with the prevention of harm resulting from the use of alcohol and other drugs; offers advice and guidance in development of policies and programmes; organizes training courses, congresses, symposia and seminars in different countries; mems: affiliated organizations in 74 countries, as well as individual members; Pres. Dr PETER A. VAMOS (Canada); Exec. Dir Dr JÖRG SPIELDENNER (Germany); publs *ICAA News, Alcoholism* (2 a year).

International Council on Jewish Social and Welfare Services (INTERCO): World Jewish Relief, The Forum, 74–80 Camden St, London, NW1 OEG, United Kingdom; tel. (20) 7691-1771; fax (20) 7691-1780; e-mail info@wjr.org.uk; internet www.worldjewishrelief.org.uk; f. 1961; functions include the exchange of views and information among member agencies concerning the problems of Jewish social and welfare services; represents views to governments and international organizations. mems: organizations in France, Switzerland, United Kingdom and the USA; Exec. Sec. VIVIENNE LEWIS.

International Council on Social Welfare (ICSW): c/o MOVISIE, POB 19129, 3501 DC Utrecht, Netherlands; tel. (30) 7892226; fax (30) 7892111; e-mail icsw@icsw.org; internet www.icsw.org; f. 1928 to provide an international forum for the discussion of social work and related issues and to promote interest in social welfare; holds international conference every two years; provides documentation and information services; mems: 31 national committees, 9 international orgs, 46 other orgs; Pres. SOLVEIG ASKJEM; Exec. Dir DENYS CORRELL; publ.*Global Cooperation Newsletter Monthly*.

International Dachau Committee: 2 rue Chauchat, 75009 Paris, France; tel. 1-45-23-39-99; fax 1-48-00-06-73; f. 1958 to perpetuate the memory of the political prisoners of Dachau; to manifest the friendship and solidarity of former prisoners whatever their beliefs or nationality; to maintain the ideals of their resistance, liberty, tolerance and respect for persons and nations; and to maintain the former concentration camp at Dachau as a museum and international memorial; mems: national asscns in 20 countries; Pres. Gen. ANDRÉ DELPECH; Sec.-Gen. JEAN SAMUEL; publ. *Bulletin Officiel du Comité International de Dachau* (2 a year).

International Federation for Human Rights Leagues (FIDH): 17 passage de la Main d'Or, 75011 Paris, France; tel. 1-43-55-25-18; fax 1-43-55-18-80; e-mail fidh@fidh.org; internet www.fidh.org; f. 1922; promotes the implementation of the Universal Declaration of Human Rights and other instruments of human rights protection; aims to raise awareness and alert public opinion to issues of human rights violations; undertakes investigation and observation missions; carries out training; uses its consultative and observer status to lobby international authorities; mems: 141 national leagues in over 100 countries; Pres. SIDIKI KABA; publs *Lettre* (2 a month), mission reports.

International Federation of the Blue Cross: CP 6813, 3001 Bern, Switzerland; tel. 313005860; fax 313005869; e-mail i.abderhalden@ifbc.info; internet www.ifbc.info; f. 1877 to aid the victims of intemperance and drug addiction, and to take part in the general movement against alcoholism; Pres. Pastor RAYMOND BASSIN (Switzerland); Co-Secs-Gen IRENE ABDERHALDEN, MARK MOSER.

International Federation of Educative Communities (FICE): c/o Monika Niederle, Hasengasse 60/14, 1100 Vienna, Austria; tel. (1) 33134-20391; fax (1) 33134-99-20391; e-mail monikaniederle@hotmail.com; internet www.fice-inter.org; f. 1948 under the auspices of UNESCO to co-ordinate the work of national asscns, and to promote the international exchange of knowledge and experience in the field of childcare; Congress held every 2 years (2008: Helsinki, Finland, in June); mems: national asscns from 21 European countries, India, Israel, Canada, Morocco, the USA and South Africa; Pres. MONIKA NIEDERLE (Austria); Gen. Sec. ANDREW HOSIE (United Kingdom); publ. *Bulletin* (2 a year).

International Federation of Persons with Physical Disability (FIMITIC): Plittersdorfer Str. 103, 53173 Bonn, Germany; tel. (228) 9359-191; fax (228) 9359-192; e-mail fimitic@t-online.de; internet www.fimitic.org; f. 1953; an international, humanitarian, non-profit, politically and religiously neutral non-governmental umbrella federation of persons with physical disability under the guidance of the disabled themselves; focuses activities on ensuring the equalization of opportunities and full participation of persons with physical disabilities in society and fights against any kind of discrimination against persons with disabilities; mems: national groups from 28 European countries; Pres. NIGEL BRANDER (Ireland); Sec.-Gen. MARIJA-LIDIJA STIGLIC; publs *Bulletin, Nouvelles*.

International Federation of Social Workers (IFSW): POB 6875, Schwarztorstrasse 22, 3001 Bern, Switzerland; tel. 313826015; fax 313811222; e-mail global@ifsw.org; internet www.ifsw.org; f. 1928 as International Permanent Secretariat of Social Workers; present name adopted 1956; aims to promote social work as a profession through international co-operation on standards, training, ethics and working conditions; organizes international conferences; represents the profession at the UN and other international bodies; supports national asscns of social workers; mems: national asscns in 85 countries; Pres. DAVID N. JONES (United Kingdom); Sec.-Gen. TOM JOHANNESEN (Switzerland); publs *IFSW update* (available online), policy statements and manifestos.

International League against Racism and Antisemitism: Paris-Siège national, 42 rue du Louvre, 75001 Paris, France; tel. 1-45-08-08-08; fax 1-45-08-18-18; e-mail licra@licra.org; internet www.licra.ch; f. 1927; mems in 17 countries; Pres. PATRICK GAUBERT.

International League for Human Rights: 228 East 45th St, 5th Floor, New York, NY 10017, USA; tel. (212) 661-0480; fax (212) 661-0416; e-mail info@ilhr.org; internet www.ilhr.org; f. 1942 to implement political, civil, social, economic and cultural rights contained in the Universal Declaration of Human Rights adopted by the United Nations and to support and protect defenders of human rights world-wide; mems: individuals, national affiliates and correspondents throughout the world; Pres. ROBERT ARSENAULT; Exec. Dir DAVID TAM-BARYOH; publs various human rights reports.

International Planned Parenthood Federation (IPPF): 4 Newhams Row, London, SE1 3UZ, United Kingdom; tel. (20) 7939-8200; fax (20) 7939-8300; e-mail info@ippf.org; internet www.ippf.org; f. 1952; aims to promote and support sexual and reproductive health rights and choices world-wide, with a particular focus on the needs of young people; works to bring relevant issues to the attention of the media, parliamentarians, academics, governmental and non-governmental organizations, and the general public; mobilizes financial resources to fund programmes and information materials; offers technical assistance and training; collaborates with other international organizations. The International Medical Panel of the IPPF formulates guide-lines and statements on current medical and scientific advice and best practices; mems: independent family planning asscns in over 151 countries; Pres. Dr JACQUIE SHARPE; Dir-Gen. Dr STEVEN SINDING.

International Prisoners' Aid Association: POB 7333, Arlington, VA 22207, USA; tel. (703) 836-0024; fax (703) 516-9735; e-mail desifl@aol.com; f. 1950; works to improve prisoners' aid services, with the aim of promoting the rehabilitation of the individual and increasing the protection of society; mems: national federations in 29 countries; Pres. Dr WOLFGANG DOLEISCH (Austria); Exec. Dir Dr BADR-EL-DIN ALI; publ. *Newsletter* (3 a year).

International Social Security Association (ISSA): 4 route des Morillons, CP 1, 1211 Geneva 22, Switzerland; tel. 227996617; fax 227998509; e-mail issa@ilo.org; internet www.issa.int; f. 1927 to promote the development of social security throughout the world, mainly through the improvement of techniques and administration, in order to advance social and economic conditions on the basis of social equality; collects and disseminates information on social security programmes throughout the world; undertakes research and policy analysis on the social security issues and distributes their results; encourages mutual assistance between member organizations; facilitates good practice collection and exchange; co-operates with other international or regional organizations exercising activities related to the field; communicates with its constituency and media and promotes social security through advocacy and information; and forges partnerships between the ISSA and other international organizations active in the area of social security to advance common strategies, including the ILO, the OECD and the World Bank; organizes a World Social Security Forum and General Assembly every three years (2010: Cape Town, South Africa) and four Regional Social Security Forums (in Africa, the Americas, Asia/Pacific and Europe); convenes topic-related technical seminars in various regions; hosts international conferences, for example on information and communication technology in social security, social security actuaries and statisticians, and international policy research; co-organizes the World Congress on Occupational Safety and Health every three years; mems: 365 institutions in 154 countries; Pres. CORAZON DE LA PAZ-BERNARDO (Philippines); Sec.-Gen. HANS-HORST KONKOLEWSKY; publs *International Social Security Review* (quarterly, in English, French, German, Spanish), *Social*

Security Observer (quarterly, in English, French, German, Spanish), *Social Security Worldwide*, internet databases.

International Social Service (Service social international—SSI): 32 quai du Seujet, 1201 Geneva, Switzerland; tel. 229067700; fax 229067701; e-mail info@iss-ssi.org; internet www.iss-ssi.org; f. 1921 to aid families and individuals whose problems require services beyond the boundaries of the country in which they live, and where the solution of these problems depends upon co-ordinated action on the part of social workers in two or more countries; studies from an international standpoint the conditions and consequences of emigration in their effect on individual, family, and social life; operates on a non-sectarian and non-political basis; mems: branches in 14 countries, five affiliated offices, and correspondents in some 100 other countries; Pres. ROLF WIDMER (Switzerland); Sec.-Gen. JEAN AYOUB; publs *ISS Reports*, *Newsletter* (available online).

International Union of Family Organisations: 28 place Saint-Georges, 75009 Paris, France; tel. 1-48-78-07-59; fax 1-42-82-95-24; f. 1947 to bring together all organizations throughout the world working for family welfare; maintains commissions and working groups on issues including standards of living, housing, marriage guidance, rural families, etc; there are six regional organizations: the Pan-African Family Organisation (Rabat, Morocco), the North America organization (Montréal, Canada), the Arab Family Organisation (Tunis, Tunisia), the Asian Union of Family Organisations (New Delhi, India), the European regional organization (Berne, Switzerland) and the Latin American Secretariat (Curitiba, Brazil); mems: national asscns, groups and governmental departments in over 55 countries; Pres. MARIA TERESA DA COSTA MACEDO (Portugal).

International Union of Tenants: Box 7514, 10392 Stockholm, Sweden; tel. (8) 7910200; fax (8) 204344; e-mail info@iut.nu; internet www.iut.nu; f. 1955 to collaborate in safeguarding the interests of tenants; participates in activities of UN-Habitat; has working groups for EC matters, eastern Europe, developing countries and for future development; holds annual council meeting and triennial congress; mems: national tenant orgs in 29 European countries, and Australia, Benin, Canada, India, Japan, New Zealand, Nigeria, South Africa, Tanzania Togo, Uganda, and USA; Chair. SVEN CARLSSON; Sec.-Gen. MAGNUS HAMMAR; publ. *The Global Tenant* (quarterly).

Inter-University European Institute on Social Welfare (IEISW): 179 rue du Débarcadère, 6001 Marcinelle, Belgium; tel. (71) 44-72-67; fax (71) 47-27-44; e-mail ieiasmayence@hotmail.com; f. 1970 to promote, carry out and publicize scientific research on social welfare and community work; Pres. JOSEPH GILLAIN; Gen. Dir SERGE MAYENCE; publ. *COMM*.

Lions Clubs International: 300 West 22nd St, Oak Brook, IL 60523-8842, USA; tel. (630) 571-5466; fax (630) 571-8890; e-mail lions@lionsclubs.org; internet www.lionsclubs.org; f. 1917 to foster understanding among people of the world; to promote principles of good government and citizenship and an interest in civic, cultural, social and moral welfare and to encourage service-minded people to serve their community without financial reward; mems: 1.35m. in over 45,000 clubs in 197 countries and geographic areas; Int. Pres. JIMMY M. ROSS; publ. *The Lion* (10 a year, in 20 languages).

Médecins sans frontières (MSF): 78 rue de Lausanne, CP 116, 1211 Geneva 21, Switzerland; tel. 228498400; fax 228498404; internet www.msf.org; f. 1971; independent medical humanitarian org. composed of physicians and other members of the medical profession; aims to provide medical assistance to victims of war and natural disasters; operates longer-term programmes of nutrition, immunization, sanitation, public health, and rehabilitation of hospitals and dispensaries; awarded the Nobel peace prize in 1999; mems: national sections in 21 countries in Europe, Asia and North America; Pres. Dr CHRISTOPHE FOURNIER; publ. *Activity Report* (annually).

Pan-Pacific and South East Asia Women's Association (PPSEAWA): POB 119, Nuku'alofa, Tonga; tel. 24003; fax 41404; e-mail info@ppseawa.org; internet www.ppseawa.org; f. 1928 to foster better understanding and friendship among women in the region, and to promote co-operation for the study and improvement of social conditions; holds international conference every three years; mems: 19 national member organizations; Pres. Dr VIOPAPA ANNANDALE; publ. *PPSEAWA Bulletin* (2 a year).

Rotary International: 1560 Sherman Ave, Evanston, IL 60201, USA; tel. (847) 866-3000; fax (847) 866-8237; e-mail ers@rotary.org; internet www.rotary.org; f. 1905 to carry out activities for the service of humanity, to promote high ethical standards in business and professions and to further international understanding, goodwill and peace; mems: 1.2m. in more than 32,000 Rotary Clubs in more than 200 countries; Pres. WILFRID J. WILKINSON; Gen. Sec. EDWIN H. FUTA (USA); publs *The Rotarian* (monthly, English), *Rotary World* (5 a year, in 9 languages).

Service Civil International (SCI): St-Jacobsmarkt 82, 2000 Antwerp, Belgium; tel. (3) 226-57-27; fax (3) 232-03-44; e-mail info@sciint.org; internet www.sciint.org; f. 1920 to promote peace and understanding through voluntary service projects; more than 3,000 volunteers participate in SCI workcamps world-wide each year; SCI also organizes seminars, training activities, campaigns and other peace activities; mems: 14,000 in 36 countries; Pres. MIHAI CRISAN (acting); publ. *Action* (quarterly).

Society of Saint Vincent de Paul: 6 rue du Londres, 75009 Paris, France; tel. 1-53-45-87-53; fax 1-42-61-72-56; e-mail cgi.information@ozanet.org; internet www.ozanet.org; f. 1833 to conduct charitable activities such as childcare, youth work, work with immigrants, adult literacy programmes, residential care for the sick, handicapped and elderly, social counselling and work with prisoners and the unemployed, through personal contact; mems: over 600,000 in 130 countries; Pres. JOSÉ RAMÓN DÍAZ-TORREMOCHA; Sec.-Gen. ERICH SCHMITZ; publ. *Vincentpaul* (quarterly, in English, French, Portuguese and Spanish).

SOLIDAR: 22 rue de Commerce, 1000 Brussels, Belgium; tel. (2) 500-10-20; fax (2) 500-10-30; e-mail solidar@skynet.be; internet www.solidar.org; f. 1951 (fmrly International Workers' Aid); an asscn of independent development and social welfare agencies based in Europe, linked to the labour and democratic socialist movements; aims to contribute to the creation of radical models of economic and social development, and to advance practical solutions that enable people to have increased control over their future; mems: 42 agencies in 20 countries; Sec.-Gen. CONNY REUTER.

Soroptimist International: 87 Glisson Rd, Cambridge, CB1 2HG, United Kingdom; tel. (1223) 311833; fax (1223) 467951; e-mail hq@soroptimistinternational.org; internet www.soroptimistinternational.org/; f. 1921 to strive for the advancement of the status of women, high ethical standards, human rights for all, equality and development of peace through international goodwill, understanding and friendship; convention held every four years (2007: Glasgow, United Kingdom); mems: 90,000 in 3,000 clubs in 125 countries and territories; International Pres. LYNN DUNNING; Exec. Officer ROSIE COUTTS; publ. *International Soroptimist* (quarterly).

World Blind Union: Calle Almansa 66, 28039 Madrid, Spain; tel. (91) 4365366; fax (91) 5894749; e-mail umc@once.es; internet www.worldblindunion.org; f. 1984 (amalgamating the World Council for the Welfare of the Blind and the International Federation of the Blind) to work for the prevention of blindness and the welfare of blind and visually-impaired people; encourages development of braille, talking book programmes and other media for the blind; organizes rehabilitation, training and employment; works on the prevention and cure of blindness in co-operation with the International Agency for the Prevention of Blindness; co-ordinates aid to the blind in developing countries; maintains the Louis Braille birth-place as an international museum; mems: in 158 countries; Pres. Dr WILLIAM ROWLAND (South Africa); Sec.-Gen. ENRIQUE PÉREZ (Spain); publ. *World Blind* (2 a year, in English, English Braille and on cassette, in Spanish and Spanish Braille and on cassette, and in French).

World Federation of the Deaf (WFD): POB 65, 00401 Helsinki, Finland; tel. (9) 5803573; fax (9) 5803572; e-mail Info@wfdeaf.org; internet www.wfdeaf.org; f. 1951 to serve the interests of deaf people and their national organizations and represent these in international fora; works towards the goal of full participation by deaf people in society; encourages deaf people to set up and run their own organizations; priority is given to the promotion of the recognition and use of national sign languages, the education of deaf people and deaf people in the developing world; mems: 129 member countries; Pres. MARKKU JOKINEN; publ. *WFD News* (2–3 a year).

World ORT: ORT House, 126 Albert St, London, NW1 7NE, United Kingdom; tel. (20) 7446-8500; fax (20) 7446-8650; e-mail wo@ort.org; internet www.ort.org; f. 1880 for the development of industrial, agricultural and artisanal skills among Jews; conducts vocational training programmes for children and adults, including instructors' and teachers' education and apprenticeship training; implements technical assistance programmes in co-operation with interested governments; manages global network of schools, colleges, training centres and programmes; has assisted more than 3m. people; mems: committees in more than 40 countries; Dir-Gen. ROBERT SINGER; publs *Annual Report*, *World ORT Times*.

World Social Forum (WSF): Support Office: Rua General Jardim 660, 7th Floor, São Paulo, Brazil 01223-010; e-mail forumsocialmundial.org.br; internet www.forumsocialmundial.org; f. 2001 as an annual global meeting of civil society bodies; the first WSF was held in Porto Alegre, Brazil, in Jan. 2001; a Charter of Principles was adopted in June 2002; the WSF is a permanent global process which aims to pursue alternatives to neo-liberal policies and commercial globalization; its objectives include the development and promotion of democratic international systems and institutions serving social justice, equality and the sovereignty of peoples, based on respect for the universal human rights of citizens of all nations and for the environment; the sixth (2006) Forum was polycentric, held in Bamako (Mali), Caracas (Venezuela), and Karachi (Pakistan), and the seventh (2007) Forum was convened in Nairobi, Kenya; an

INTERNATIONAL ORGANIZATIONS

International Council, comprising 129 civil society organizations and commissions, guides the Forum and considers general political questions and methodology; the Support Office in São Paulo, Brazil, provides administrative assistance to the Forum process, to the International Council and to the specific organizing committees for each annual event; mems: civil society organizations and movements world-wide.

World Veterans Federation: 17 rue Nicolo, 75116 Paris, France; tel. 1-40-72-61-00; fax 1-40-72-80-58; e-mail wvf@wvf-fmac.org; internet www.wvf-fmac.org; f. 1950 to maintain international peace and security by the application of the San Francisco Charter and work to help implement the Universal Declaration of Human Rights and related international conventions; aims to defend the spiritual and material interests of war veterans and war victims; promotes practical international co-operation in disarmament, legislation concerning war veterans and war victims, and development of international humanitarian law, etc; maintains regional committees for Africa, Asia and the Pacific, and Europe and a Standing Committee on Women; mems: 173 national orgs in 90 countries, representing about 27m. war veterans and war victims; Pres. ABDUL HAMID IBRAHIM; Sec.-Gen. MOHAMMED BENJELLOUN; publ. *WVF News*.

Zonta International: 557 W Randolph St, Chicago, IL 60661-2206, USA; tel. (312) 930-5848; fax (312) 930-0951; e-mail zontaintl@zonta.org; internet www.zonta.org; f. 1919; links executives in business and the professions, with the aim of advancing the status of women world-wide; carries out local and international projects; supports women's education and leadership; makes fellowship awards in various fields; mems: 33,000 in 68 countries and areas; Pres. MARY ELLEN BITTNER; Exec. Dir JANET HALSTEAD; publ. *The Zontian* (quarterly).

Sport and Recreations

Arab Sports Confederation: POB 62997, Riyadh 11595, Saudi Arabia; tel. (1) 482-4927; fax (1) 482-1944; f. 1976 to encourage regional co-operation in sport; mems: 21 Arab national Olympic Committees, 53 Arab sports federations; Sec.-Gen. OTHMAN M. AL-SAAD; publ. *Annual Report*.

Fédération Aéronautique Internationale (FAI) (World Air Sports Federation): 24 ave Mon Repos, 1005 Lausanne, Switzerland; tel. 213451070; fax 213451077; e-mail sec@fai.org; internet www.fai.org; f. 1905 to promote all aeronautical sports; organizes world championships; develops rules through Air Sports Commissions; endorses world aeronautical and astronautical records; mems: in 100 countries and territories; Pres. PIERRE PORTMANN; Sec.-Gen. MAX BISHOP; publ. *Air Sports International*.

Fédération Internationale de Philatélie (International Philatelic Federation): Biberlinstrasse 6, 8032 Zürich, Switzerland; tel. 444223839; fax 444223843; e-mail heiri@f-i-p.ch; internet www.f-i-p.ch/; f. 1926 to promote philately internationally; Pres. JOSEPH WOLFF (Luxembourg); Sec.-Gen. MARIE-LOUISE HEIRI; publ. quarterly journal.

General Association of International Sports Federations (GAISF) (Association Générale de Fédérations Internationales de Sports): 4 blvd du Jardin Exotique, 98000 Monte Carlo, Monaco; tel. 97-97-65-10; fax 93-25-28-73; e-mail info@agfisonline.com; internet www.agfisonline.com; f. 1967 to act as a forum for the exchange of ideas and discussion of common problems in sport; collects and circulates information; and provides secretarial, translation, documentation and consultancy services for members; mems: 104 international sports orgs; Pres. HEIN VERBRUGGEN (Netherlands); Dir-Gen. CHRISTINE DOMINGUEZ (France); publs *GAISF Calendar* (online), *Sports Insider* (weekly, electronic bulletin), *Sports Insider Magazine* (annually).

International Amateur Athletic Federation: 17 rue Princesse Florestine, BP 359, 98007 Monte Carlo Cédex, Monaco; tel. 93-10-88-88; fax 93-15-95-15; e-mail headquarters@iaaf.org; f. 1912 to ensure co-operation and fairness and to combat discrimination in athletics; compiles athletic competition rules and organizes championships at all levels; frames regulations for the establishment of World, Olympic and other athletic records; settles disputes between members; conducts a programme of development consisting of coaching, judging courses, etc; and affiliates national governing bodies; mems: national asscns in 211 countries and territories; Gen. Sec. ISTVÁN GYULAI (Hungary); publs *IAAF Handbook* (every 2 years), *IAAF Review* (quarterly), *IAAF Directory* (annually), *New Studies in Athletics* (quarterly).

International Amateur Boxing Association (AIBA): 10 ave de la Gare, CP 55, 1001 Lausanne, Switzerland; tel. 213212777; fax 213212772; e-mail info@aiba.org; internet www.aiba.net; f. 1946 as the world body controlling amateur boxing for the Olympic Games, continental, regional and inter-nation championships and tournaments in every part of the world; mems: 191 national asscns; Pres.

Sport and Recreations

Prof. A. CHOWDHRY (Pakistan); Sec.-Gen. CANER DOGANELI (Turkey); publ. *World Amateur Boxing Magazine* (quarterly).

International Archery Federation (Fédération internationale de tir à l'arc—FITA): 54 ave de Rhodanie, 1007 Lausanne, Switzerland; tel. 216143050; fax 216143055; e-mail info@archery.org; internet www.archery.org; f. 1931 to promote international archery; organizes world championships and Olympic tournaments; holds Biennial Congress (2007: Leipzig, Germany); mems: national amateur asscns in 138 countries; Pres. UGUR EDENER; Sec.-Gen. TOM DIELEN (Switzerland); publs *Information FITA* (monthly), *The Target* (2 a year).

International Automobile Federation (Fédération Internationale de l'Automobile—FIA): 2 chemin de Blandonnet, CP 296, 1215 Geneva, Switzerland; tel. 225444400; fax 225444450; internet www.fia.com; f. 1904; manages world motor sport and organizes international championships; mems: 213 national automobile clubs and asscns in 120 countries; Pres. MAX MOSLEY; Sec.-Gen. (Sport) PIERRE DE CONINCK; Sec.-Gen. (Mobility) PETER DOGGWILER.

International Badminton Federation (IBF): Batu 3, 1/2 Jalan Cheras, 56000 Kuala Lumpur, Malaysia; tel. (3) 92837155; fax (3) 92847155; e-mail ibf@internationalbadminton.org; internet www.internationalbadminton.org; f. 1934 to oversee the sport of badminton world-wide; mems: affiliated national organizations in 156 countries and territories; Pres. Dr KANG YOUNG JOONG; Chief Operating Officer ANDREW RYAN; publs *World Badminton* (available on-line), *Statute Book* (annually).

International Basketball Federation (Fédération Internationale de Basketball): 53 ave Louis Casaï, 1216 Cointrin/Geneva, Switzerland; tel. 225450000; fax 225450099; e-mail info@fiba.com; internet www.fiba.com; f. 1932, as International Amateur Basketball Federation (present name adopted 1989); world governing body for basketball; mems: 213 affiliated national federations; Sec.-Gen. PATRICK BAUMANN (Switzerland); publ. *FIBA Assist* (monthly).

International Canoe Federation: ave de Thodanie 54, 1007, Lausanne, Switzerland; tel. (21) 612-02-90; fax (21) 612-02-91; internet www.canoeicf.com; f. 1924; administers canoeing at the Olympic Games; promotes canoe/kayak activity in general; mems: 114 national federations; Pres. ULRICH FELDHOFF; Sec.-Gen. SIMON TOULSON.

International Council for Health, Physical Education, Recreation, Sport and Dance (ICHPERSD): 1900 Association Drive, Reston, VA 20191, USA; tel. (800) 213-7193; e-mail ichper@aaperd.org; internet www.ichpersd.org; f. 1958 to encourage the development of programmes in health, physical education, recreation, sport and dance throughout the world, by linking teaching professionals in these fields; publ. *Journal* (quarterly).

International Cricket Council: POB 500070; Al Thuraya Tower 1, 11th Floor, Dubai Media City, Dubai, UAE; tel. (4) 368-8088; fax (4) 368-8080; internet www.icc-cricket.com; f. 1909 as the governing body for international cricket; holds an annual conference; mems: Australia, England, India, New Zealand, Pakistan, South Africa, Sri Lanka, West Indies, Zimbabwe, and 23 associate and 13 affiliate mems; CEO MALCOM SPEED.

International Cycling Union (UCI): 1860 Aigle, Switzerland; tel. 244685811; fax 244685812; e-mail admin@uci.ch; internet www.uci.ch; f. 1900 to develop, regulate and control all forms of cycling as a sport; mems: 160 federations; Pres. PATRICK MCQUAID (Ireland); publs *International Calendar* (annually), *Velo World* (6 a year).

International Equestrian Federation: CP 157, ave Mon-Repos 24, 1005 Lausanne, Switzerland; tel. 213104747; fax 213104760; e-mail info@horsesport.org; internet www.horsesport.org; f. 1921; international governing body of equestrian sport recognized by the International Olympic Committee; establishes rules and regulations for conduct of international equestrian events, including on the health and welfare of horses; mems: 135 mem. countries; Sec.-Gen. MICHAEL STONE.

International Federation of Associated Wrestling Styles: 17 ave Juste-Olivier, 1006 Lausanne, Switzerland; tel. 213128426; fax 213236073; e-mail filalausanne@bluewin.ch; internet www.fila-wrestling.com; f. 1912 to encourage the development of amateur wrestling and promote the sport in countries where it is not yet practised and to further friendly relations between all members; mems: 146 federations; Pres. RAPHAËL MARTINETTI; Sec.-Gen. MICHEL DUSSON; publs *News Bulletin, Wrestling Revue*.

International Federation of Association Football (Fédération internationale de football association—FIFA): FIFA-Str. 20, POB 8044, Zürich, Switzerland; tel. 432227777; fax 432227878; e-mail media@fifa.org; internet www.fifa.com; f. 1904 to promote the game of association football and foster friendly relations among players and national asscns; to control football and uphold the laws of the game as laid down by the International Football Association Board; to prevent discrimination of any kind between players; and to provide arbitration in disputes between national asscns; organizes World Cup competition every four years; mems: 204 national asscns, six

INTERNATIONAL ORGANIZATIONS

Sport and Recreations

continental confederations; Pres. JOSEPH S. BLATTER (Switzerland); Gen. Sec. URS LINSI; publs *FIFA News* (monthly), *FIFA Magazine* (every 2 months) (both in English, French, German and Spanish), *FIFA Directory* (annually), *Laws of the Game* (annually), *Competitions' Regulations* and *Technical Reports* (before and after FIFA competitions).

International Federation of Park and Recreation Administration (IFPRA): Globe House, Crispin Close, Caversham, Reading, Berks, RG4 7JS, United Kingdom; tel. and fax (118) 946-1680; fax (118) 946-1680; e-mail ifpraworld@aol.com; internet www.ifpra.org; f. 1957 to provide a world centre for members of government departments, local authorities, and all organizations concerned with recreational and environmental services to discuss relevant matters; mems: 550 in over 50 countries; Gen. Sec. ALAN SMITH (United Kingdom); publ. *IFPRA World*.

International Fencing Federation (Fédération internationale d'escrime—FIE): Maison du Sport International, 54 ave de Rhodanie, 1007 Lausanne, Switzerland; tel. 213203115; fax 213203116; e-mail info@fie.ch; internet www.fie.ch; f. 1913; promotes development and co-operation between amateur fencers; determines rules for international events; organizes World Championships; mems: 121 national federations; Pres. RENÉ ROCH.

International Gymnastic Federation (Fédération internationale de Gymnastique): 10 rue des Oeuches, CP 359, 2740 Moutier 1, Switzerland; tel. 324946410; fax 324946419; e-mail info@fig-gymnastics.org; internet www.fig-gymnastics.com; f. 1881 to promote the exchange of official documents and publications on gymnastics; mems: 129 affiliated Federations; Pres. BRUNO GRANDI; Gen. Sec. ANDRÉ GUEISBUHLER; publs *FIG Bulletin* (3 a year), *World of Gymnastics* (3 a year).

International Hockey Federation: 61 rue du Valentin, Lausanne, Switzerland; tel. 216410606; fax 216410607; e-mail info@worldhockey.org; internet www.worldhockey.org; f. 1924; mems: 122 national asscns; Pres. ELS VAN BREDA VRIESMAN (Netherlands); Hon. Sec.-Gen. PETER L. COHEN (Australia).

International Judo Federation: Maison des Federations Sportives, ave Mohamed Ali Akid 1003, Tunis, Tunisia; tel. (71) 750-105; fax (71) 743-424; e-mail sgfij@gnet.tn; internet www.ijf.org; f. 1951 to promote cordial and friendly relations between members; to protect the interests of judo throughout the world; to organize World Championships and the judo events of the Olympic Games; to develop and spread the techniques and spirit of judo throughout the world; and to establish international judo regulations; Pres. YONG SUNG PARK (Republic of Korea); Gen. Sec. Dr HEDI DHOUIB (Tunisia).

International Paralympic Committee (IPC): Adenauerallee 212–214, 53113 Bonn, Germany; tel. (228) 2097200; fax (228) 2097209; e-mail info@paralympic.org; internet www.paralympic.org; f. 1989 as the international governing body of sports for athletes with a disability; supervises and co-ordinates the Paralympic summer and winter games (held every four years) and other multi-disability competitions, including the World and Regional Championships; mems: 160 national paralympic committees and four disability-specific international sports federations; Pres. Sir PHILIP CRAVEN (United Kingdom); CEO XAVIER GONZALEZ (Spain); publ. *The Paralympian* (quarterly).

International Rowing Federation (Fédération internationale des sociétés d'aviron—FISA): MSI, 54 ave de Rhodanie, 1007 Lausanne, Switzerland; tel. 216178373; fax 216178375; e-mail info@fisa.org; internet www.worldrowing.com; f. 1892; serves as the world controlling body of the sport of rowing; mems: 128 national federations; Pres. DENIS OSWALD; Sec.-Gen. and Exec. Dir MATT SMITH; publs *World Rowing Directory* (annually), *World Rowing E-Magazine* (quarterly), *FISA Bulletins* (annually).

International Sailing Federation (ISAF): Ariadne House, Town Quay, Southampton, Hants, SO14 2AQ, United Kingdom; tel. (2380) 635111; fax (2380) 635789; e-mail secretariat@isaf.co.uk; internet www.sailing.org; f. 1907; world governing body for the sport of sailing; establishes and amends Racing Rules of Sailing; organizes the Olympic Sailing Regatta, the ISAF Sailing World Championships and other events; mems: 125 member national authorities, 89 classes, nine affiliated members; Pres. GÖRAN PETERSSON; Sec.-Gen. JEROME PELS; publ. *Making Waves*.

International Shooting Sport Federation (ISSF): 80336 Munich, Bavariaring 21, Germany; tel. (89) 5443550; fax (89) 54435544; e-mail munich@issf-sports.org; internet www.issf-sports.org; f. 1907 to promote and guide the development of amateur shooting sports; organizes World Championships and controls the organization of continental and regional championships; supervises the shooting events of the Olympic and Continental Games under the auspices of the International Olympic Committee; mems: 157 nat. federations from 137 affiliated countries; Pres. OLEGARIO VÁZQUEZ RAÑA (Mexico); Sec.-Gen. HORST G. SCHREIBER (Germany); publs *ISSF News*, *International Shooting Sport* (6 a year).

International Skating Union (ISU): 2 chemin de Primerose, 1007 Lausanne, Switzerland; tel. 216126666; fax 216126677; e-mail info@isu.ch; internet www.isu.org; f. 1892; holds regular conferences; mems: 78 national federations in 61 countries; Pres. OTTAVIO CINQUANTA; Gen.-Sec. FREDI SCHMID; publs Judges' manuals, referees' handbooks, general and special regulations.

International Ski Federation (Fédération Internationale de Ski—FIS): Marc Hodler House, Blochstr. 2, 3653 Oberhofen am Thunersee, Switzerland; tel. 332446161; fax 332446171; e-mail mail@fisski.ch; internet www.fis-ski.com; f. 1924 to further the sport of skiing; to prevent discrimination in skiing matters on racial, religious or political grounds; to organize World Ski Championships and regional championships and, as supreme international skiing authority, to establish the international competition calendar and rules for all ski competitions approved by the FIS, and to arbitrate in any disputes; mems: 108 national ski asscns; Pres. GIAN FRANCO KASPER (Switzerland); Sec.-Gen. SARAH LEWIS (United Kingdom); publs *Weekly Newsflash*, *FIS Bulletin* (2 a year).

International Swimming Federation (Fédération internationale de natation—FINA): POB 4, ave de l'Avant, 1005 Lausanne, Switzerland; tel. 213104710; fax 213126610; internet www.fina.org; f. 1908 to promote amateur swimming and swimming sports internationally; administers rules for swimming sports, competitions and for establishing records; organizes world championships and FINA events; runs a development programme to increase the popularity and quality of aquatic sports; mems: 180 federations; Pres. MUSTAPHA LARFAOUI (Algeria); Exec. Dir CORNEL MARCULESCU; publs *Handbook* (every 4 years), *FINA News* (monthly), *World of Swimming* (quarterly).

International Table Tennis Federation: 11 chemin de la Roche, 1020 Renens/Lausanne, Switzerland; tel. 213407090; fax 213407099; e-mail ittf@ittf.com; internet www.ittf.com; f. 1926; Pres. ADHAM SHARARA; Exec. Dir JORDI SERRA; publs *Table Tennis Illustrated*, *Table Tennis News* (both bimonthly), *Table Tennis Legends*, *Table Tennis Fascination*, *Table Tennis: The Early Years*.

International Tennis Federation: Bank Lane, Roehampton, London, SW15 5XZ, United Kingdom; tel. (20) 8878-6464; fax (20) 8878-4744; e-mail communications@itftennis.com; internet www.itftennis.com; f. 1913 to govern the game of tennis throughout the world, promote its teaching and preserve its independence of outside authority; produces the Rules of Tennis; organizes and promotes the Davis Cup Competition for men, the Fed. Cup for women, the Olympic Games Tennis Event, wheelchair tennis, 16 cups for veterans, the ITF Sunshine Cup and the ITF Continental Connelly Cup for players of 18 years old and under, the World Youth Cup for players of 16 years old and under, and the World Junior Tennis Tournament for players of 14 years old and under; organizes entry-level professional tournaments as well as junior and senior circuits; mems: 141 full and 57 associate; Pres. FRANCESCO RICCI BITTI; publs *World of Tennis* (annually), *Davis Cup Yearbook*, *ITF World* (quarterly), *ITF This Week* (weekly).

International Volleyball Federation (Fédération internationale de volleyball—FIVB): 12 ave de la Gare, 1000 Lausanne 1, Switzerland; tel. 213453535; fax 213453545; e-mail info@fivb.org; internet www.fivb.org; f. 1947 to encourage, organize and supervise the playing of volleyball, beach volleyball, and park volley; organizes biennial congress; mems: 218 national federations; Pres. Dr RUBÉN ACOSTA HERNÁNDEZ; Gen. Man. JEAN-PIERRE SEPPEY; publs *Volley-World* (every 2 months), *X-Press* (monthly).

International Weightlifting Federation (IWF): 1146 Budapest, Istvanmezei út 1–3, Hungary; tel. (1) 3530530; fax (1) 3530199; e-mail iwf@iwfnet.net; internet www.iwf.net; f. 1905 to control international weightlifting; draws up technical rules; trains referees; supervises World Championships, Olympic Games, regional games and international contests of all kinds; registers world records; mems: 167 national organizations; Pres. Dr THOMÁS AJAN (Hungary); Gen. Sec. YANNIS SGOUROS (Greece); publs *IWF Constitution and Rules* (every 4 years), *World Weightlifting* (quarterly).

International World Games Association: 10 Lake Circle, Colorado Springs, CO 80906, USA; tel. (719) 471-8096; fax (719) 471-810545; e-mail info@worldgames-iwga.org; internet www.worldgames-iwga.org; f. 1980; organizes World Games every four years (2009: Kaohsiung, People's Republic of China), comprising 32 sports that are not included in the Olympic Games; Pres. RON FROEHLICH; Sec.-Gen. J. A. P. KOREN.

Olympic Council of Asia: POB 6706, Hawalli, 32042 Kuwait City, Kuwait; tel. 5734972; fax 5734973; e-mail info@ocasia.org; internet www.ocasia.org; f. 1981; organizes Asian Games and Asian Winter Games (held every 4 years), and Asian Indoor Games and Asian Beach Games (held every 2 years); mems: 45 national Olympic committees; Dir Gen. HUSAIN AL-MUSALLAM.

Union of European Football Associations (UEFA): 46 route de Genève, 1260 Nyon 2, Switzerland; tel. 848002727; fax 848012727; e-mail info@uefa.com; internet www.uefa.com; f. 1954; works on behalf of Europe's national football asscns to promote football; aims to foster unity and solidarity between national asscns; mems: 53 national asscns; Pres. MICHEL PLATINI (France); Gen. Sec. DAVID TAYLOR; publ. *Magazine* (available online).

World Boxing Organization: First Federal Bldg, 1056 Muñoz Rivera Ave, Suite 711–714, San Juan, PR 00927, Puerto Rico; tel. (787) 765-4444; fax (787) 758-9053; e-mail boxing@wbo-int.com; internet www.wbo-int.com; f. 1962; regulates professional boxing; Pres. FRANCISCO VALCARCEL; Sec. ARNALDO SANCHEZ-RECIO.

World Bridge Federation: 56 route de Vandoeuvres, 1253 Geneva, Switzerland; tel. 227501541; fax 227501620; internet www.worldbridge.org; f. 1958 to promote the game of contract bridge throughout the world; federates national bridge asscns in all countries; conducts world championships competitions; establishes standard bridge laws; mems: 89 countries; Pres. JOSE DAMIANI (France); publ. *World Bridge News* (quarterly).

World Chess Federation (Fédération internationale des echecs—FIDE): 9 Syggrou Ave, Athens 11743, Greece; tel. (210) 9212047; fax (210) 9212859; e-mail office@fide.com; internet www.fide.com; f. 1924; controls chess competitions of world importance and awards international chess titles; mems: national orgs in more than 160 countries; Pres. KIRSAN ILYUMZHINOV; publ. *International Rating List* (2 a year).

World Squash Federation Ltd: 6 Havelock Rd, Hastings, East Sussex, TN34 1BP, United Kingdom; tel. (1424) 429245; fax (1424) 429250; e-mail lorraine@worldsquash.org; internet www.worldsquash.org; f. 1966 to maintain quality and reputation of squash and increase its popularity; monitors rules and makes recommendations for change; trains, accredits and assesses international and world referees; sets standards for all technical aspects of squash; co-ordinates coaching training and awards; runs World Championships; mems: 125 national orgs; Pres. JAHANGIR KHAN; Sec.-Gen. CHRISTIAN LEIGHTON.

World Underwater Federation: Viale Tiziano 74, 00196 Rome, Italy; tel. (06) 32110594; fax (06) 32110595; e-mail cmas@cmas.org; internet www.cmas2000.org; f. 1959 to develop underwater activities; to form bodies to instruct in the techniques of underwater diving; to perfect existing equipment, encourage inventions and experiment with newly marketed products; and to organize international competitions; mems: orgs in 100 countries; Pres. ACHILLE FERRERO (Italy); Sec. PIERRE DERNIER (Belgium); publs *International Year Book of CMAS*, *Scientific Diving: A Code of Practice*, manuals.

Technology

African Organization of Cartography and Remote Sensing: 5 Route de Bedjarah, BP 102, Hussein Dey, Algiers, Algeria; tel. (2) 77-79-34; fax (2) 77-79-34; e-mail oact@wissal.dz; f. 1988 by amalgamation of African Association of Cartography and African Council for Remote Sensing; aims to encourage the development of cartography and of remote sensing by satellites; organizes conferences and other meetings, promotes establishment of training institutions; maintains four regional training centres (in Burkina Faso, Kenya, Nigeria and Tunisia); mems: national cartographic institutions of 24 African countries; Sec.-Gen. UNIS MUFTAH.

African Regional Centre for Technology: Imm. Fahd, 17th Floor, blvd Djilly Mbaye, BP 2435, Dakar, Senegal; tel. 823-77-12; fax 823-77-13; e-mail arct@sonatel.senet.net; f. 1977 to encourage the development of indigenous technology and to improve the terms of access to imported technology; assists the establishment of national centres; mems: govts of 31 countries; Exec. Dir Dr OUSMANE KANE; publs *African Technodevelopment*, *Alert Africa*.

AIIM International: 1100 Wayne Ave, Suite 1100, Silver Spring, Maryland 20910, USA; tel. (301) 587-8202; fax (301) 587-2711; e-mail aiim@aiim.org; internet www.aiim.org; f. 1999 by merger of the Association for Information and Image Management (f. 1943) and the International Information Management Congress (f. 1962); serves as the international body of the document technologies industry; Chair. DON MCMAHAN; Treas. JOHN REINHART.

Bureau International de la Recupération et du Recyclage (Bureau of International Recycling): 24 ave Franklin Roosevelt, 1050 Brussels, Belgium; tel. (2) 627-57-70; fax (2) 627-57-73; e-mail bir@bir.org; internet www.bir.org; f. 1948 as the world federation of the reclamation and recycling industries; promotes international trade in scrap iron and steel, non-ferrous metals, paper, textiles, plastics and glass; mems: asscns in 24 countries; Dir-Gen. FERNANDO DURANTI.

Ecma International: 114 rue de Rhône, 1204 Geneva, Switzerland; tel. 228496000; fax 228496001; e-mail istvan@ecma-international.org; internet www.ecma-international.org; f. 1961 to develop standards and technical reports, in co-operation with the appropriate national, European and international organizations, in order to facilitate and standardize the use of information processing and telecommunications systems; promulgates various standards applicable to the functional design and use of these systems; mems: 23 ordinary mems, 15 associate mems, 13 small and medium-sized enterprises, 29 not-for-profit mems, four small private company mems; Sec.-Gen. Dr ISTVAN SEBESTYEN; publs *Ecma Standards*, *Ecma Memento*, *Ecma Technical Reports*.

EUREKA: 107 rue Neerveld, bte 5, 1200 Brussels, Belgium; tel. (2) 777-09-50; fax (2) 770-74-95; e-mail eureka.secretariat@es.eureka.be; internet www.eureka.be; f. 1985; aims to promote industrial collaboration between member countries on non-military research and development activities; enables joint development of technology; supports innovation and systematic use of standardization in new technology sectors; mems: 126 in 38 countries; Sec.-Gen. Dr HEIKKI KOTILAINEN; publs *Annual Report*, *Eureka Bulletin*.

European Convention for Constructional Steelwork (ECCS): 32-36 ave des Ombrages, bte 20, 1200 Brussels, Belgium; tel. (2) 762-04-29; fax (2) 762-09-35; e-mail eccs@steelconstruct.com; internet www.steelconstruct.com; f. 1955 for the consideration of problems involved in metallic construction; mems: 20 full mems, six assoc. mems, three int. mems and two supporting mems; Sec.-Gen. V. DEHAN; publs Information sheets and documents, symposia reports, model codes.

European Federation of Chemical Engineering: c/o Institution of Chemical Engineers, Davis Bldg, 165–189 Railway Terrace, Rugby, Warwickshire, CV21 3HQ, United Kingdom; tel. (1788) 578214; fax (1788) 560833; e-mail pr@icheme.org; internet www.icheme.org; f. 1953 to encourage co-operation between non-profit-making scientific and technical societies, for the advancement of chemical engineering and its application in the processing industries; mems: 65 societies in 25 European countries, 15 corresponding societies in other countries; Chief Exec. Dr T. J. EVANS.

European Federation of Corrosion: 1 Carlton House Terrace, London, SW1Y 5DB, United Kingdom; tel. (20) 7451-7336; fax (20) 8392-2289; e-mail paul.mcintyre@iom3.org; internet www.materials.org; f. 1955 to encourage co-operation in research on corrosion and methods of combating this; mems: societies in 25 countries; Pres. M. SCHÜTZE (Germany).

European Federation of National Engineering Associations (Fédération européenne d'associations nationales d'ingénieurs—FEANI): 18 ave R. Vandendriessche, 1150 Brussels, Belgium; tel. (2) 639-03-90; fax (2) 639-03-99; e-mail secretariat.general@feani.org; internet www.feani.org; f. 1951 to affirm the professional identity of the engineers of Europe and to strive for the unity of the engineering profession in Europe; mems: 29 mem. countries; Pres. Dr (Ing.) WILLI FUCHS (Germany); Sec.-Gen. PHILIPPE WAUTERS (Belgium); publs *FEANI News*, *INDEX*.

European Metal Union: Einsteinbaan 1, POB 2600, 3430 GA Nieuwegein, Netherlands; tel. (30) 6053344; fax (30) 6053115; e-mail info@metaalunie.nl; f. 1954 as International Union of Metal; liaises between national craft organizations and small and medium-sized enterprises in the metal industry; represents members' interests at a European level; provides for the exchange of information and ideas; mems: national federations from Austria, Germany, Hungary, Luxembourg, Netherlands and Switzerland; Pres. PIET TOLSMA (Netherlands); Sec. HARM-JAN KEIJER (Netherlands).

European Organisation for the Exploitation of Meteorological Satellites (EUMETSAT): 64295 Darmstadt, Am Kavalleriesand 31, Germany; tel. (6151) 807345; fax (6151) 807555; e-mail press@eumetsat.de; internet www.eumetsat.de; f. 1986; establishes, maintains and exploits European systems of operational meteorological satellites; projects include a second generation Meteosat programme for gathering weather data and satellite application facilities; mems: 20 European countries and 10 co-operating states; Dir-Gen. Dr LARS PRAHM; publs *Annual Report*, *IMAGE Newsletter* (2 a year), brochures, conference and workshop proceedings.

European Organization for Civil Aviation Equipment (EURO-CAE): 102 rue Etienne Dolet, 4th Floor, 92240 Malakoff, France; tel. 1-40-92-79-30; fax 1-46-55-62-65; e-mail eurocae@eurocae.com; internet www.eurocae.org; f. 1963; studies and advises on problems related to the equipment used in aeronautics; assists international bodies in the establishment of international standards; mems: 92 manufacturers, and regulatory and research bodies; Pres. TERRENCE KNIBB; Sec.-Gen. FRANCIS GRIMAL; publs Reports, documents and specifications on civil aviation equipment.

Eurospace: 15-17 ave de Ségur, 75005 Paris, France; tel. 1-44-42-00-70; fax 1-44-42-00-79; e-mail letterbox@eurospace.org; internet www.eurospace.org; f. 1961 as an asscn of European aerospace industrial companies responsible for promotion of European Space activity; carries out studies on the legal, economic, technical and financial aspects of space activity; acts as an industrial adviser to the European Space Agency, in particular with regard to future space programmes and industrial policy matters; mems: 60 in 13 European countries; Pres. PASCALE SOURISSE (France); Sec.-Gen. ALAIN GAUBERT.

International Academy for Production Engineering Research: 9 rue Mayran, 75009 Paris, France; tel. 1-45-26-21-80; fax 1-45-26-92-15; e-mail cirp@cirp.net; internet www.cirp.net; f. 1951, as International Institution for Production Engineering Research, to promote by scientific research the study of the mechanical processing of all solid materials; mems: 530 in 40 countries; Pres. LEO ALTING (Denmark); Sec.-Gen. DIDIER DUMUR (France); publ. *Annals* (2 a year).

International Association for Bridge and Structural Engineering (IABSE): ETH—Hönggerberg, 8093 Zürich, Switzerland; tel. 446332647; fax 446331241; e-mail secretariat@iabse.org; internet www.iabse.org; f. 1929 to exchange knowledge and advance the practice of structural engineering world-wide; mems: 4,000 government departments, local authorities, universities, institutes, firms and individuals in over 100 countries; Pres. MANFRED HIRT (Switzerland); Exec. Dir UELI BRUNNER; publs *Structural Engineering International* (quarterly), *Structural Engineering Documents*, *IABSE Report*, e-newsletter.

International Association for Cybernetics (Association internationale de cybernétique): Palais des Expositions, ave Sergent Vrithoff 2, 5000 Namur, Belgium; tel. (81) 71-71-71; fax (81) 71-71-00; e-mail cyb@info.fundp.ac.be; internet pespmc1.vub.ac.be/iac.html; f. 1957 to ensure liaison between research workers engaged in various sectors of cybernetics; promotes the development of the science and its applications; disseminates information; mems: firms and individuals in 42 countries; Chair. J. RAMAEKERS; Gen. Sec. CARINE AIGRET; publ. *Cybernetica* (quarterly).

International Association of Hydraulic Engineering and Research (IAHR): Paseo Bajo Virgen del Puerto 3, 28005 Madrid, Spain; tel. (91) 3357908; fax (91) 3357935; e-mail iahr@iahr.org; internet www.iahr.org; f. 1935; promotes advancement and exchange of knowledge on hydraulic engineering; holds biennial congresses and symposia; mems: 1,850 individual, 300 corporate; Exec. Dir CHRISTOPHER GEORGE; publs *Journal of Hydraulic Research and Journal of River Basin Management*, *IAHR Newsletter*, *Journal of Hydraulic Research*, *Proceedings of Biennial Conferences*, *Fluvial Processes Monograph*, *Fluvial Processes Solutions Manual*, *Hydraulicians in Europe 1800–2000*.

International Association of Marine Aids to Navigation and Lighthouse Authorities: 20 ter rue Schnapper, 78100 St Germain en Laye, France; tel. 1-34-51-70-01; fax 1-34-51-82-05; e-mail iala-aism@wanadoo.fr; internet www.iala-aism.org; f. 1957; holds technical conference every four years; working groups study special problems and formulate technical recommendations, guide-lines and manuals; mems in 80 countries; Sec.-Gen. TORSTEN KRUUSE; publ. *Bulletin* (quarterly).

International Association of Technological University Libraries (IATUL): c/o Paul Sheehan, Dublin City Univ. Library, Dublin 9, Republic of Ireland; e-mail paul.sheehan@dcu.ie; internet www.iatul.org; f. 1955 to promote co-operation between member libraries and stimulate research on library problems; mems: 238 university libraries in 41 countries; Pres. MARIA HEIJNE (Netherlands); Sec. PAUL SHEEHAN (Ireland); publs *IATUL Proceedings*, *IATUL Newsletter* (electronic version only).

International Bridge, Tunnel and Turnpike Association: 1146 19th St, NW, Suite 800, Washington, DC 20036-3725, USA; tel. (202) 659-4620; fax (202) 659-0500; e-mail info@ibtta.org; internet www.ibtta.org; f. 1932 to serve as a forum for sharing knowledge, with the aim of promoting toll-financed transportation services; mems: 280 mems in 25 countries; Exec. Dir. PATRICK D. JONES; publ. *Tollways* (monthly).

International Cargo Handling Co-ordination Association (ICHCA): Suite 2, 85 Western Rd, Romford, Essex RM1 3LS, United Kingdom; tel. (1708) 735295; fax (1708) 735225; e-mail info@ichcainternational.co.uk; internet www.ichcainternational.co.uk; f. 1952 to foster economy and efficiency in the movement of goods from origin to destination; mems: 2,000 in 90 countries; Dir PETER BOSMANS; Exec. Dir ROSEMARY NEILSON; publs *Cargo Tomorrow: Cargo Handling News* (every 2 months), *World of Cargo Handling* (annually), *Who's Who in Cargo Handling* (annually), technical publs and reviews.

International Colour Association: c/o Javier Romero, Universidad de Granada, Facultad de Ciencias, Dept de Óptica, Campus Fuentenueva S/N, 18071 Granada, Spain; e-mail jromero@ugr.es; internet www.aic-colour.org; f. 1967 to encourage research in colour in all its aspects, disseminate the knowledge gained from this research and promote its application to the solution of problems in the fields of science, art and industry; holds international congresses and symposia; mems: organizations in 25 countries; Pres. JOSÉ LUIS CAIVANO (Argentina); Sec. and Treas. Prof. Dr JAVIER ROMERO (Spain).

International Commission of Agricultural Engineering (CIGR): Univ. of Tsukuba, Graduate School of Life and Environmental Sciences, Tennodai 1-1-1, Tsukuba, Ibaraki 305-8572, Japan; tel. (29) 853-6989; fax (29) 853-7496; e-mail biopro@sakura.cc.tsukuba.ac.jp; internet www.cigr.org; f. 1930; aims to stimulate development of science and technology in agricultural engineering; encourages education, training and mobility of professionals; facilitates exchange of research; represents profession at international level; mems: asscns from 92 countries; Pres. Prof. IRENILZA NÄÄS (Brazil); Sec.-Gen. Prof. Emeritus TAKAAKI MAEKAWA (Japan); publs *Bulletin de la CIGR*, *Newsletter* (quarterly), technical reports.

International Commission on Glass: Stazione Sperimentale del Vetro, Via Briati 10, 30141 Murano, Venice, Italy; tel. (041) 739422; fax (041) 739420; e-mail spevetro@ve-nettuno.it; internet www.icg.group.shef.ac.uk; f. 1933 to co-ordinate research in glass and allied products, exchange information and organize conferences; mems: 30 organizations; Pres. A. YARAMAN; Sec.-Gen. F. NICOLETTI.

International Commission on Illumination (CIE): Kegelgasse 27, 1030 Vienna, Austria; tel. (1) 714-31-87-0; fax (1) 714-31-87-18; e-mail ciecb@ping.at; internet www.cie.co.at; f. 1900 as International Commission on Photometry, present name adopted 1913; aims to provide an international forum for all matters relating to the science and art of light and lighting; serves as a forum for the exchange of information; develops and publishes international standards and provides guidance in their application; mems: 38 national committees; Gen. Sec. C. HERMANN; publs standards, technical reports.

International Commission on Irrigation and Drainage (ICID) (Commission Internationale des Irrigations et du Drainage): 48 Nyaya Marg, Chanakyapuri, New Delhi 110 021, India; tel. (11) 26115679; fax (11) 26115962; e-mail icid@icid.org; internet www.icid.org; f. 1950; aims to enhance the world-wide supply of food and fibre by improving the productivity of irrigated and drained lands through the appropriate management of water and application of irrigation, drainage and flood management techniques; promotes the development and application of the arts, sciences and techniques of engineering, agriculture, economics, ecological and social sciences in managing water and land resources for irrigation, drainage and flood management and for river training applications; holds triennial congresses; mems: 105 national committees; Pres. PETER S. LEE (United Kingdom); Sec.-Gen. ER. M. GOPALAKRISHNAN (India); publs *Ir* (quarterly), *World Irrigation*, *Multilingual Technical Dictionary*, *Historical Dams*, *Indus Basin*, *Danube Valley*, *Application of Geosynthetics in Irrigation and Drainage Projects*, technical books.

International Commission on Large Dams: 151 blvd Haussmann, 75008 Paris, France; tel. 1-53-75-16-22; fax 1-40-42-60-71; e-mail secretaire.general@icold-cigb.org; internet www.icold-cigb.org/; f. 1928; mems: in 85 countries; Pres. LLUIS BERGA (Spain); Sec.-Gen. MICHEL DE VIVO; publs *Technical Bulletin* (3 or 4 a year), *World Register of Dams*, *World Register of Mine and Industrial Wastes*, *Technical Dictionary on Dams*, studies.

International Committee on Aeronautical Fatigue (ICAF): c/o Prof. O. Buxbaum, Fraunhofer-Institut für Betriebsfestigkeit LBF, 64289 Darmstadt, Bartningstrasse 47, Germany; tel. (6151) 7051; fax (6151) 705214; f. 1951 for collaboration between aeronautical bodies and laboratories on questions of fatigue of aeronautical structures; organizes periodical conferences; mems: national centres in 13 countries; Sec. Prof. O. BUXBAUM (Germany).

International Council on Large High-Voltage Electric Systems (Conseil international des grands réseaux électriques—CIGRE): 21 rue d'Artois, 75008 Paris, France; tel. 1-53-89-12-90; fax 1-53-89-12-99; e-mail secretary-general@cigre.org; internet www.cigre.org; f. 1921 to facilitate and promote the exchange of technical knowledge and information in the general field of electrical generation and transmission at high voltages; holds general sessions (every 2 years) and symposia; mems: 5,157 in over 80 countries; Pres. D. CROFT (Australia); Sec.-Gen. J. KOWAL (France); publ. *Electra* (every 2 months).

International Council for Research and Innovation in Building and Construction: Postbox 1837, 3000 BV Rotterdam, Netherlands; tel. (10) 4110240; fax (10) 4334372; e-mail secretariat@cibworld.nl; internet www.cibworld.nl; f. 1953 to encourage and facilitate co-operation in building research, studies and documentation in all aspects; mems: governmental and industrial organizations and qualified individuals in 70 countries; Pres. RODNEY MILFORD (South Africa); Sec.-Gen. W. J. P. BAKENS; publs *Information Bulletin* (bi-monthly), conference proceedings and technical, best practice and other reports.

International Electrotechnical Commission (IEC): 3 rue de Varembé, POB 131, 1211 Geneva 20, Switzerland; tel. 229190211; fax 229190300; e-mail info@iec.ch; internet www.iec.ch; f. 1906 as the authority for world standards for electrical and electronic engineering: its standards are used as the basis for regional and national standards, and are used in the preparation of specifications for international trade; mems: national committees representing all branches of electrical and electronic activities in some 60 countries;

CEO and Gen.-Sec. A. AMIT; publs *International Standards and Reports, IEC Bulletin, Annual Report, Catalogue of Publications.*

International Federation for Information and Documentation: POB 90402, 2509 LK The Hague, Netherlands; tel. (70) 3140671; fax (70) 3140667; e-mail fid@fid.nl; f. 1895; aims to promote, and improve, through international co-operation, research in and development of information science, information management and documentation; maintains regional commissions for Latin America, North America and the Caribbean, Asia and Oceania, Western, Eastern and Southern Africa, North Africa and the Near East, and for Europe; mems: 62 national, five international, 330 institutional and individual mems; Pres. K. BRUNNSTEIN; Exec. Dir J. STEPHEN PARKER; publs *FID Review* (every 2 months), *FID Directory* (every 2 years).

International Federation for Information Processing (IFIP): Hofstrasse 3, 2361 Laxenburg, Austria; tel. (2236) 73616; fax (2236) 736169; e-mail ifip@ifip.org; internet www.ifip.org; f. 1960 to promote information science and technology; encourages research, development and application of information processing in science and human activities; furthers the dissemination and exchange of information on information processing; mems: 56 orgs, 3 corresponding mems, 5 hon. mems and 9 affiliate mems; Pres. KLAUS BRUNNSTEIN (Germany); Sec. ROGER JOHNSON.

International Federation for the Promotion of Machine and Mechanism Science: Laboratory of Robotics and Mechatronics, Univ. of Cassino, via di Biasio 43, 03043 Cassino, Italy; tel. (0776) 299-3663; fax (0776) 299-3711; e-mail ceccarelli@unicas.it; internet www.iftomm.org; f. 1969 to study mechanisms, robots, man-machine systems, etc.; promotes research and development in the field of machines and mechanisms by theoretical and experimental methods and practical application; Pres. K. WALDRON; Sec.-Gen. M. CECCARELLI; publs *Mechanism and Machine Theory, Journal of Applied Mechanics, Journal of Gearing and Transmissions, Electronic Journal on Computational Kinematics.*

International Federation of Airworthiness (IFA): 14 Railway Approach, East Grinstead, West Sussex, RH19 1BP, United Kingdom; tel. (1342) 301788; fax (1342) 317808; e-mail sec@ifairworthy.org; internet www.ifairworthy.org; f. 1964 to provide a forum for the exchange of international experience in maintenance, design and operations; holds annual conference; awards international aviation scholarship annually; mems include 23 airlines, 10 airworthiness authorities, 11 aerospace manufacturing companies, 14 service and repair organizations, two consultancies, five professional societies, two aviation insurance companies, one aircraft leasing company, and the Flight Safety Foundation (USA); Pres. JOHN K LAUBER (USA); Exec. Dir J. W. SAULL (United Kingdom); publ. *IFA News* (quarterly).

International Federation of Automatic Control (IFAC): 2361 Laxenburg, Schlossplatz 12, Austria; tel. (2236) 71447; fax (2236) 72859; e-mail secr@ifac.co.at; internet www.ifac-control.org; f. 1957 to serve those concerned with the theory and application of automatic control and systems engineering; mems: 50 national asscns; Pres. Prof. WOOK-HYUN KWON (Republic of Korea); Sec. KURT SCHLACHER; publs *Annual Reviews in Control, Automatica, Control Engineering Practice, Journal of Process Control, Newsletter, Engineering Applications of AI,* IFAC journals and affiliated journals.

International Federation of Automotive Engineering Societies (FISITA): 30 Percy Street, London, W1T 2DB, United Kingdom; tel. (20) 7299-6630; fax (20) 7299-6633; e-mail info@fisita.com; internet www.fisita.com; f. 1948 to promote the technical and sustainable development of all forms of automotive transportation; maintains electronic job centre for automotive engineers (www.fisitajobs.com); holds congresses every two years; mems: national orgs in 38 countries; Chief Exec. IAN DICKIE; publ. *AutoTechnology.*

International Federation of Consulting Engineers (Fédération internationale des ingénieurs-conseils—FIDIC): POB 311, 1215 Geneva 15, Switzerland; tel. 227994900; fax 227994901; e-mail fidic@fidic.org; internet www.fidic.org; f. 1913 to encourage international co-operation and the establishment of standards for consulting engineers; mems: 74 national asscns worldwide, comprising some 500,000 design professionals; Pres. JORGE DÍAZ PADILLA; publs *FIDIC Report, Annual Survey, Annual Review.*

International Federation of Hospital Engineering: 2 Abingdon House, Cumberland Business Centre, Northumberland Rd, Portsmouth, PO5 1DS, United Kingdom; tel. (2392) 823186; fax (2392) 815927; e-mail iheem@btconnect.com; internet www.ifhc.info; f. 1970 to promote internationally standards of hospital engineering and to provide for the exchange of knowledge and experience in the areas of hospital and healthcare facility design, construction, engineering, commissioning, maintenance and estate management; mems: 50, in more than 30 countries; Pres. STEVE DRINKROW (South Africa); Gen. Sec. BERNARD SHAPIRO (South Africa); publ. *Hospital Engineering* (quarterly).

International Institute of Seismology and Earthquake Engineering (IISEE): Building Research Institute, 1 Tatehara, Tsukuba City, Ibaraki 305-0802, Japan; tel. (298) 79-0677; fax (298) 64-6777; e-mail iisee@kenken.go.jp; internet iisee.kenken.go.jp; f. 1962 to work on seismology and earthquake engineering for the purpose of reducing earthquake damage in the world; trains seismologists and earthquake engineers from the earthquake-prone countries; undertakes surveys, research, guidance and analysis of information on earthquakes and related matters; mems: 75 countries; Dir NOBUO HURUKAWA; publs *Year Book, Bulletin* (annually), *Individual Studies* (annually).

International Institute of Welding: 90 rue des Vanesses, ZI Paris Nord II, 93420 Villepinte, France; tel. 1-49-90-36-08; fax 1-49-90-36-80; e-mail iiwceo@wanadoo.fr; internet www.iiw-iis.org; f. 1948; mems: 48 mem Societies; Pres. C. SMALLBONE (Australia); Chief Exec. D. BEAUFILS (France); publ. *Welding in the World* (7 a year).

International Iron and Steel Institute (IISI): 120 rue Col Bourg, 1140 Brussels, Belgium; tel. (2) 702-89-00; fax (2) 702-88-99; e-mail info@iisi.be; internet www.worldsteel.org; f. 1967 to promote the welfare and interests of the world's steel industries; undertakes research into all aspects of steel industries; serves as a forum for exchange of knowledge and discussion of problems relating to steel industries; collects, disseminates and maintains statistics and information; serves as a liaison body between international and national steel organizations; mems: in over 50 countries; Sec.-Gen. IAN CHRISTMAS; publs *Worldsteel Newsletter,* policy statements and reports.

International Measurement Confederation (IMEKO): POB 457, 1371 Budapest 5, Hungary; tel. and fax (1) 353-1562; e-mail imeko.ime@mtesz.hu; internet www.imeko.org; f. 1958 as a federation of member organizations concerned with the advancement of measurement technology; aims to promote exchange of scientific and technical information in field of measurement and instrumentation and to enhance co-operation between scientists and engineers; holds World Congress every three years (2009: Lisbon, Portugul, in September); mems: 37 orgs; Pres. Prof. ANTONIO M. DA CRUZ SERRA (Portugal); Sec.-Gen. Prof. MLADEN BORSIC (Croatia); publs *Acta IMEKO* (proceedings of World Congresses), *IMEKO TC Events Series, Measurement* (quarterly), *IMEKO Bulletin* (2 a year).

International Organization for Standardization: POB 56, 1 rue de Varembé, 1211 Geneva 20, Switzerland; tel. 227490111; fax 227333430; e-mail central@iso.org; internet www.iso.org; f. 1947 to reach international agreement on industrial and commercial standards; mems: national standards bodies of 157 countries; Pres. MASAMI TANAKA (Japan); Sec.-Gen. ALAN BRYDEN; publs *ISO International Standards, ISO Memento* (annually), *ISO Management Systems* (6 a year), *ISO Focus* (11 a year), *ISO Catalogue* (annually, updated regularly online), *ISO Annual Report.*

International Research Group on Wood Protection: Drottning Kristinas väg 33A, Stockholm, Sweden; tel. (8) 10-14-53; fax (8) 10-80-81; e-mail irg@sp.se; internet www.irg-wp.com; f. 1965 as Wood Preservation Group by OECD; independent since 1969; consists of five sections; holds plenary annual meeting; mems: 344 in 50 countries; Pres. Dr JEFFREY MORRELL (USA); Sec.-Gen. JÖRAN JERMER (Sweden); publs technical documents.

International Rubber Research and Development Board (IRRDB): POB 10150, 50908 Kuala Lumpur, Malaysia; fax (3) 21620414; e-mail draziz@pop.jaring.my; internet www.irrdb.com; f. 1937; mems: 15 research institutes; Sec. Datuk Dr A. AZIZ.

International Society for Photogrammetry and Remote Sensing (ISPRS): c/o Orhan Altan, Istanbul Technical Univ., Faculty of Civil Engineering, Dept of Geodesy and Photogrammetry, 34469 Ayazaga-Istanbul, Turkey; tel. (212) 285-3810; fax (212) 285-6587; e-mail oaltan@itu.edu.tr; internet www.isprs.org/; f. 1910; holds congress every four years, and technical symposia; mems: 103 countries; Pres. IAN DOWMAN (United Kingdom); Sec.-Gen. ORHAN ALTAN (Turkey); publs *Journal of Photogrammetry and Remote Sensing* (6 a year), *ISPRS Highlights* (quarterly), *International Archives of Photogrammetry and Remote Sensing* (every 2 years).

International Society for Soil Mechanics and Geotechnical Engineering: City University, Northampton Sq., London, EC1V 0HB, United Kingdom; tel. (20) 7040-8154; fax (20) 7040-8832; e-mail secretariat@issmge.org; internet www.issmge.org; f. 1936 to promote international co-operation among scientists and engineers in the field of geotechnics and its engineering applications; maintains 30 technical committees; holds quadrennial international conference, regional conferences and specialist conferences; mems: 17,000 individuals, 81 national societies, 20 corporate members; Pres. Prof. P. SÊCO E PINTO; Sec.-Gen. Prof. R. N. TAYLOR; publs *ISSMGE Bulletin* (quarterly), *Lexicon of Soil Mechanics Terms* (in eight languages).

International Solar Energy Society: Villa Tannheim, Wiesentalstrasse 50, 79115 Freiburg, Germany; tel. (761) 459060; fax (761) 4590699; e-mail hq@ises.org; internet www.ises.org; f. 1954; addresses all aspects of renewable energy, including characteristics, effects and methods of use; undertakes projects in several countries on various aspects of renewable energy technology and implementation; organizes major international, regional and national congresses; mems: c. 30,000 in some 100 countries; Pres. MONICA OLIPHANT (Australia); Sec. DIETER HOLM (South Africa); publs *Solar Energy Journal* (monthly), *Renewable Energy Focus* (6 a year).

International Solid Waste Association (ISWA): Vesterbrogade 74, 3rd floor, 1620 Copenhagen V, Denmark; tel. 32-96-15-88; fax 32-96-15-84; e-mail iswa@iswa.dk; internet www.iswa.org; f. 1970 to promote the exchange of information and experience in solid waste management, in order to protect human health and the environment; promotes research and development activities; provides advice; organizes conferences; Pres. N. C. VASUKI (USA); Man. Dir SUZANNE ARUP VELTZÉ (Denmark); publs *Waste Management World*, *Waste Management and Research* (6 a year).

International Special Committee on Radio Interference: British Electrotechnical Committee, British Standards Institution, 389 Chiswick High Rd, London, W4 4AL, United Kingdom; tel. (20) 8996-9000; fax (20) 8996-7400; e-mail chris_beckley@electricity.org.uk; f. 1934; special committee of the IEC, promoting international agreement on the protection of radio reception from interference by equipment other than authorized transmitters; recommends limits of such interference and specifies equipment and methods of measurement; mems: national committees of IEC and seven other international orgs; Sec. CHRISTOPHER BECKLEY.

International Union for Electricity Applications: 5 rue Chante-Coq, 92808 Puteaux Cédex, France; tel. 1-41-26-56-48; fax 1-41-26-56-49; e-mail uie@uie.org; internet www.uie.org; f. 1953, present title adopted 1994; aims to study all questions relative to electricity applications, except commercial questions; links national groups and organizes international congresses on electricity applications; mems: national committees, corporate associated and individual members in 18 countries; Pres. RONNIE BELMANS (Belgium); Gen. Sec. Prof. MICHEL MACHIELS; publ. UIE proceedings.

International Union for Vacuum Science, Technique and Applications (IUVSTA): c/o Dr R. J. Reid, 84 Oldfield Drive, Vicars Cross, Chester, CH3 5LW, United Kingdom; tel. (1244) 342-675; e-mail iuvsta.secretary.general@ronreid.me.uk; internet www.iuvsta.org; f. 1958; collaborates with the International Standards Organization in defining and adopting technical standards; holds triennial International Vacuum Congress, European Vacuum Conference, triennial International Conference on Thin Films, and International Conference on Solid Surfaces; administers the Welch Foundation scholarship for postgraduate research in vacuum science and technology; mems: orgs in 30 countries; Pres. Prof. UGO VALBUSA (Italy); Sec.-Gen. Dr R. J. REID (United Kingdom); publ. *News Bulletin* (2 a year—electronic version).

International Union of Air Pollution Prevention and Environmental Protection Associations: 44 Grand Parade, Brighton, BN2 9QA, United Kingdom; tel. (1273) 878770; fax (1273) 606626; e-mail iuappa@nsca.org.uk; internet www.iuappa.com; f. 1963; organizes triennial World Clean Air Congress and regional conferences for developing countries (several a year); undertakes policy development and research programmes on international environmental issues; World Congress: Brisbane, Australia (Sept. 2007); Pres. GAVIN FISHER (New Zealand); Dir-Gen. RICHARD MILLS; publs *IUAPPA Newsletter* (quarterly), *Clean Air around the World*.

International Union of Technical Associations and Organizations (Union internationale des associations et organismes techniques—UATI): UNESCO House, 1 rue Miollis, 75732 Paris Cédex 15, France; tel. 1-45-68-48-29; fax 1-43-06-29-27; e-mail uati@unesco.org; internet www.unesco.org/uati; f. 1951 (fmrly Union of International Technical Associations) under the auspices of UNESCO; aims to promote and co-ordinate activities of member organizations and represent their interests; facilitates relations with international organizations, notably UN agencies; receives proposals and makes recommendations on the establishment of new international technical asscns; mems: 25 orgs; Pres. JACQUES ROUSSET (France); Sec.-Gen. FABIENNE MEYER; publ. *Convergence* (3 a year).

International Union of Testing and Research Laboratories for Materials and Structures: Ecole Normale Supérieure, 61 ave du Président Wilson, 94235 Cachan Cédex, France; tel. 1-47-40-23-97; fax 1-47-40-01-13; e-mail sg@rilem.ens-cachan.fr; f. 1947 for the exchange of information and the promotion of co-operation on experimental research concerning structures and materials; studies research methods with a view to improvement and standardization; mems: laboratories and individuals in 73 countries; Pres. Dr JACQUES BRESSON (France); Sec.-Gen. M. BRUSIN (France); publ. *Materials and Structures—Testing and Research* (10 a year).

International Water Resources Association (IWRA): University of New Mexico, 1915 Roma NE, Albuquerque, NM 87131-1436, USA; tel. (505) 277-9400; fax (505) 277-9405; e-mail iwra@unm.edu; internet www.iwra.siu.edu; f. 1972 to promote collaboration in and support for international water resources programmes; holds conferences; conducts training in water resources management; Pres. GLENN E. STOUT (USA); Sec.-Gen. VICTOR DE KOSINSKY (Belgium); publ. *Water International* (quarterly).

Latin-American Energy Organization (Organización Latinoamericana de Energía—OLADE): Avda Mariscal Antonio José de Sucre, No N58–63 y Fernándes Salvador, Edif. OLADE, Sector San Carlos, POB 17-11-6413 CCI, Quito, Ecuador; tel. (2) 2598-122; fax (2) 2531-691; e-mail oladel@olade.org.ec; internet www.olade.org.ec; f. 1973 to act as an instrument of co-operation in using and conserving the energy resources of the region; mems: 26 Latin-American and Caribbean countries; Exec. Sec. ALVARO RÍOS ROCA; publ. *Energy Magazine*.

Latin-American Iron and Steel Institute: Benjamín 2944, 5°, Las Condes, Santiago, Chile; tel. (2) 233-0545; fax (2) 233-0768; e-mail ilafa@ilafa.org; internet www.ilafa.org; f. 1959 to help achieve the harmonious development of iron and steel production, manufacture and marketing in Latin America; conducts economic surveys on the steel sector; organizes technical conventions and meetings; disseminates industrial processes suited to regional conditions; prepares and maintains statistics on production, end uses, etc., of raw materials and steel products within this area; mems: 18 hon. mems; 49 active mems; 36 assoc. mems; Chair. ROBERTO DE ANDRACA; Sec.-Gen. GUILLERMO MORENO; publs *Acero Latinoamericano* (every 2 months), *Statistical Year Book*, *Directory of Latin American Iron and Steel Companies* (every 2 years).

NORDTEST: Stensberggt. 25, 0170 Oslo, Norway; tel. 47-61-44-00; fax 22-56-55-65; e-mail info@nordicinnovation.net; internet www.nordicinnovation.net; f. 1973; inter-Nordic agency for technical testing and standardization of methods and of laboratory accreditation; Sec. ULLA ELISABETH HERHEIM.

PIANC (International Navigation Association): 20 blvd Roi Albert II, bte 3, 1000 Brussels, Belgium; tel. (2) 553-71-61; fax (2) 553-71-55; e-mail info@pianc-aipcn.org; internet www.pianc-aipcn.org; f. 1885; fmrly Permanent International Asscn of Navigation Congresses; fosters progress in the construction, maintenance and operation of inland and maritime waterways, of inland and maritime ports and of coastal areas; holds International Navigation Congress every four years (2010: Liverpool, United Kingdom); mems: 31 governments, 3,400 others; Pres. E. VAN DEN EEDE; Sec.-Gen. L. VAN SCHEL; publs *On Course* (quarterly), *Illustrated Technical Dictionary* (in 6 languages), *Sailing Ahead* (electronic newsletter), technical reports, Congress papers.

Regional Centre for Mapping of Resources for Development (RCMRD): POB 632, 00618 Ruaraka, Nairobi, Kenya; tel. (20) 8560227; fax (20) 8561673; e-mail rcmrd@rcmrd.org; internet www.rcmrd.org; f. 1975; present name adopted 1997; provides services for the professional techniques of map-making and the application of satellite and remote sensing data in resource analysis and development planning; undertakes research and provides advisory services to African governments; mems: 15 signatory and 10 non-signatory governments; Dir-Gen. Dr WILBER K. OTTICHILO.

Regional Centre for Training in Aerospace Surveys (RECTAS) (Centre Regional de Formations aux Techniques des leves aerospatiaux): PMB 5545, Ile-Ife, Nigeria; tel. (803) 384-0581; e-mail info@rectas.org; internet www.rectas.org; f. 1972; provides training, research and advisory services in aerospace surveys and geoinformatics; administered by the ECA; mems: eight governments; Exec. Dir Dr OLAJIDE KUFONIYI.

Regional Council of Co-ordination of Central and East European Engineering Organizations: c/o MTESZ, 1055 Budapest, Kossuth Lajos tér 6–8, Hungary; tel. (1) 353-4795; fax (1) 353-0317; e-mail mtesz@mtesz.hu; f. 1992; Hon. Pres. JÁNOS TÓTH.

Union of the Electricity Industry (EURELECTRIC): 66 blvd de l'Impératrice, Box 2, 1000 Brussels, Belgium; tel. (2) 515-10-00; fax (2) 515-10-10; e-mail eurelectric@eurelectric.org; internet www.eurelectric.org; f. 1999 by merger of International Union of Producers and Distributors of Electrical Energy (UNIPEDE, f. 1925) and European Grouping of the Electricity Industry (EEIG, f. 1989); aims to study all questions relating to the production, transmission and distribution of electrical energy, and to promote the image of and defend the interests of the electricity supply industry; Pres. RAFAEL MIRANDA ROBREDO; Sec.-Gen. PAUL BULTEEL; publ. *Watt's New* (newsletter).

World Association of Industrial and Technological Research Organizations (WAITRO): c/o SIRIM Berhad, 1 Persiaran Dato' Menteri, Section 2, POB 7035, 40911 Shah Alam, Malaysia; tel. 55446635; fax 55446735; e-mail info@waitro.sirim.my; internet www.waitro.org; f. 1970 by the UN Industrial Development Organization to organize co-operation in industrial and technological research; provides financial assistance for training and joint activities; arranges international seminars; facilitates the exchange of information; mems: 161 research institutes in 75 countries; Pres. Dr DIETER R. FUCHS (Germany); Sec.-Gen. Dr ROHANI HASHIM; publ. *WAITRO News* (quarterly).

INTERNATIONAL ORGANIZATIONS

World Association of Nuclear Operators (WANO): Cavendish Court, First Floor, 11–15 Wigmore St, London, W1U 1PF, United Kingdom; tel. (20) 7478-9200; fax (20) 7495-4502; internet www.wano.org.uk; f. 1989 by operators of nuclear power plants; aims to improve the safety and reliability of nuclear power plants through the exchange of information; operates four regional centres (in Paris, France; Tokyo, Japan; Moscow, Russia; and Atlanta, USA) and a Co-ordinating Centre in the United Kingdom; mems: in 35 countries; Man. Dir LUCAS MAMPAEY.

World Bureau of Metal Statistics: 27A High St, Ware, Herts, SG12 9BA, United Kingdom; tel. (1920) 461274; fax (1920) 464258; e-mail wbms@world-bureau.co.uk; internet www.world-bureau.com; f. 1949; produces statistics of production, consumption, stocks, prices and international trade in copper, lead, zinc, tin, nickel, aluminium and several other minor metals; Man. Dir S. M. EALES; publs *World Metal Statistics* (monthly), *World Tin Statistics* (monthly), *World Nickel Statistics* (monthly), *World Metal Statistics Yearbook*, *World Metal Statistics Quarterly Summary*, *World Stainless Steel Statistics* (annually), *Metallstatistik* (annually).

World Energy Council: 5th Floor, Regency House, 1–4 Warwick St, London, W1B 5LT, United Kingdom; tel. (20) 7734-5996; fax (20) 7734-5926; e-mail info@worldenergy.org; internet www.worldenergy.org; f. 1924 to link all branches of energy and resources technology and maintain liaison between world experts; holds congresses every three years; mems: committees in over 90 countries; Chair. ANDRÉ CAILLÉ (Canada); Sec.-Gen. GERALD DOUCET (Canada); publs *Annual Report*, energy supply and demand projections, resources surveys, technical assessments, reports.

World Federation of Engineering Organizations (WFEO): Maison de l'UNESCO, 1 rue Miollis, 75732 Paris, Cedex 15, France; tel. 1-45-68-48-47; fax 1-45-68-48-47; e-mail tl.fmoi@unesco.org; internet www.unesco.org/wfeo; f. 1968 to advance engineering as a profession; fosters co-operation between engineering organizations throughout the world; undertakes special projects in co-operation with other international bodies; mems: 80 national mems, nine international mems; Pres. JOSÉ MEDEM SANJUAN (Spain); Exec. Dir TAHANI LEFEBURE (France); publ. *WFEO Newsletter* (2 a year).

World Foundrymen Organization (WFO): National Metalforming Centre, 47 Birmingham Rd, West Bromwich, B70 6PY, United Kingdom; tel. (121) 601-6976; fax (1544) 340-332; e-mail secretary@thewfo.com; internet www.thewfo.com; f. 1927; 2008 Congress: India; Pres. Dr GOTTHARD WOLF; Gen. Sec. Eng. ANDREW TURNER.

World Road Association (PIARC): La Grande Arche, Paroi Nord, Niveau 5, 92055 La Défense Cédex, France; tel. 1-47-96-81-21; fax 1-49-00-02-02; e-mail piarc@wanadoo.fr; internet www.piarc.org; f. 1909 as the Permanent International Association of Road Congresses; aims to promote the construction, improvement, maintenance, use and economic development of roads; organizes technical committee and study sessions; mems: 113 governments; public bodies, orgs and private individuals in 142 countries; Pres. COLIN JORDAN (Australia); Sec.-Gen. JEAN-FRANÇOIS CORTÉ (France); publs *Bulletin*, *Technical Dictionary*, *Lexicon*, technical reports.

Tourism

Alliance Internationale de Tourisme: 2 Chemin de Blandonnet, CP 111, 1215 Geneva 15, Switzerland; tel. 225444500; fax 225444550; e-mail ait@aitfia.ch; internet www.aitgva.ch; f. 1898, present title adopted 1919; represents motoring organizations and touring clubs around the world; aims to study all questions relating to international touring and to suggest reforms; mems: 140 asscns with 100m. members in 101 countries; Pres. WERNER KRAUS (Austria); Dir-Gen. PETER DOGGWILER (Switzerland); publ. *AIT News*.

Caribbean Tourism Organization: One Financial Pl., Collymore Rock, St Michael, Barbados; tel. 427-5242; fax 429-3065; e-mail ctobar@caribsurf.com; internet www.onecaribbean.org; f. 1989, by merger of the Caribbean Tourism Association (f. 1951) and the Caribbean Tourism Research and Development Centre (f. 1974); aims to encourage tourism in the Caribbean region; organizes annual Caribbean Tourism Conference, Sustainable Tourism Development Conference and Tourism Investment Conference; conducts training and other workshops on request; maintains offices in New York, Canada and London; mems: 34 Caribbean governments, 400 allied mems; Sec.-Gen. VINCENT VANDERPOOL-WALLACE (Bahamas); publs *Caribbean Tourism Statistical News* (quarterly), *Caribbean Tourism Statistical Report* (annually).

European Travel Commission: 19A ave Marnix, bte 25, 1000 Brussels, Belgium; tel. (2) 548-90-00; fax (2) 514-18-43; e-mail info@visiteurope.com; internet www.visiteurope.com; f. 1948 to promote tourism in and to Europe, to foster co-operation and the exchange of information, and to organize research; mems: national tourist organizations in 37 European countries; Exec. Dir ROB FRANKLIN (United Kingdom).

International Association of Scientific Experts in Tourism: Dufourstr. 40A, 9000 St Gallen, Switzerland; tel. 712242530; fax 712242536; e-mail aiest@unisg.ch; internet www.aiest.org; f. 1949 to encourage scientific activity in tourism, to support tourist institutions of a scientific nature and to organize conventions; mems: 300 from 44 countries; Pres. Prof. Dr PETER KELLER (Switzerland); Gen. Sec. Prof. Dr THOMAS BIEGER (Switzerland); publ. *The Tourism Review* (quarterly).

International Congress and Convention Association (ICCA): Toren A, De Entree 57, 1101 BH Amsterdam, Netherlands; tel. (20) 3981919; fax (20) 6990781; e-mail icca@icca.nl; internet www.iccaworld.com; f. 1963 to establish world-wide co-operation between all involved in organizing congresses, conventions and exhibitions; mems: more than 850 from more than 80 countries; CEO MARTIN SIRK.

International Hotel and Restaurant Association: rue de Montbrillant 87, 1202 Geneva, Switzerland; tel. 227348041; fax 227348056; e-mail info@ih-ra.ch; internet www.ih-ra.com; f. 1946 to act as the authority on matters affecting the international hotel and restaurant industry, to promote its interests and to contribute to its growth, profitability and quality; membership extended to restaurants in 1996; mems: 120 national hospitality asscns, 100 national and international hotel and restaurant chains; Dir Gen. ABRAHAM ROSENTAL; publs *Hotels* (monthly), *Yearbook and Directory* (annually).

Latin-American Confederation of Tourist Organizations (Confederación de Organizaciones Turísticas de la América Latino—COTAL): Viamonte 640, 8°, 1053 Buenos Aires, Argentina; tel. (11) 4322-4003; fax (11) 4393-5696; e-mail cotal@cotal.org.ar; internet www.cotal.org.ar; f. 1957 to link Latin American national asscns of travel agents and their members with other tourist bodies around the world; mems: in 20 countries; Pres. Dr JUAN CARLOS SUAREZ; publ. *Revista COTAL* (every 2 months).

Pacific Asia Travel Association (PATA): Unit B1, 28th Floor, Siam Tower, 989 Rama 1 Rd, Pratumwan, Bangkok 10330, Thailand; tel. (2) 658-2000; fax (2) 658-2010; e-mail patabkk@pata.org; internet www.pata.org; f. 1951; aims to enhance the growth, value and quality of Pacific Asia travel and tourism for the benefit of PATA members; holds annual conference and travel fair; divisional offices in Germany (Frankfurt), Australia (Sydney), USA (Oakland, CA) and the People's Republic of China (Beijing); mems: more than 1,200 governments, carriers, tour operators, travel agents and hotels; Pres. and CEO PETER DE JONG (Netherlands); Sec. and Treas. HIRAN COORAY (Sri Lanka); publs *PATA Compass* (every 2 months), *Statistical Report* (quarterly), *Forecasts Book*, research reports, directories, newsletters.

south-pacific.travel: POB 13119, Suva, Fiji; tel. 3304177; fax 3301995; e-mail info@spto.org; internet www.spto.org; fmrly the Tourism Council of the South Pacific, then the South Pacific Tourism Association; present name adopted in 2007; aims to foster regional co-operation in the development, marketing and promotion of tourism in the island nations of the South Pacific; receives EU funding and undertakes sustainable activities; mems: 13 countries in the South Pacific; Chair. PETER VINCENT (PNG); Chief Exec. ANTHONY EVERITT; publ. *Weekly Newsletter*.

United Federation of Travel Agents' Associations (UFTAA): 1 ave des Castelans, Stade Louis II-Entrée H, 98000 Monaco; tel. 92-05-28-29; fax 92-05-29-87; e-mail uftaa@uftaa.org; internet www.uftaa.org; f. 1966 to unite travel agents' asscns; represents the interests of travel agents at the international level; helps in international legal differences; issues literature on travel; mems: regional federations representing some 80 national asscns; Chair. JOE BORG OLIVIER; Senior Advisor BIRGER BÄCKMAN.

World Association of Travel Agencies (WATA): 11 rue du Boiron, 1260 Nyon, Switzerland; tel. 229951545; fax 223620753; e-mail wata@wata.net; internet www.wata.net; f. 1949 to foster the development of tourism, to help the rational organization of tourism in all countries, to collect and disseminate information and to participate in commercial and financial operations to foster the development of tourism; mems: more than 100 individual travel agencies in some 50 countries; Sec.-Gen. CHRISTINE FOURNIER (Switzerland); publ. *WATA News* (online).

World Travel and Tourism Council (WTTC): 1–2 Queen Victoria Terrace, Sovereign Court, London, E1W 3HA, United Kingdom; tel. (20) 7481-8007; fax (20) 7488-1008; e-mail enquiries@wttc.org; internet www.wttc.org; f. 1989; promotes the development of the travel/tourism industry; analyses impact of tourism on employment levels and local economies and promotes greater expenditure on tourism infrastructure; administers a 'Green Globe' certification programme to enhance environmental management throughout the industry; mems: reps from 100 cos world-wide; Pres. JEAN-CLAUDE BAUMGARTEN; publs *WTTC Backgrounder*, *Travel and Tourism Review*, *Viewpoint* (quarterly), *Blueprint for New Tourism*, regional and country reports.

Trade and Industry

African Regional Organization for Standardization: POB 57363-00200, Nairobi, Kenya; tel. (20) 224561; fax (20) 218792; e-mail arso@bidii.com; internet www.arso-oran.org; f. 1977 to promote standardization, quality control, certification and metrology in the African region, to formulate regional standards, and to co-ordinate participation in international standardization activities; mems: 28 states; Sec.-Gen. DAMIAN UDENNA AGBANELO; publs *ARSO Bulletin* (2 a year), *ARSO Catalogue of Regional Standards* (annually), *ARSO Annual Report*.

Arab Iron and Steel Union (AISU): BP 4, Chéraga, Algiers, Algeria; tel. (21) 37-15-80; fax (21) 37-19-75; e-mail relex@solbarab.com; internet www.arabsteel.info; f. 1972 to develop commercial and technical aspects of Arab steel production by helping member asscns commercialize their production in Arab markets, guaranteeing them high quality materials and intermediary products, informing them of recent developments in the industry and organizing training sessions; also arranges two annual symposia; mems: 80 companies in 15 Arab countries; Gen. Sec. MUHAMMAD LAID LACHGAR; publs *Arab Steel Review* (monthly), *Information Bulletin*, *News Steel World* (2 a month), *Directory* (annually).

Asian Productivity Organization: Hirakawacho Daiichi Seimei Bldg 2F, 1-2-10 Hirakawa-cho, Chiyoda-ku, Tokyo 102—0093, Japan; tel. (3) 5226-3920; fax (3) 5226-3950; e-mail apo@apo-tokyo.org; internet www.apo-tokyo.org; f. 1961 as non-political, non-profit making, non-discriminatory regional intergovernmental organization with the aim of contributing to the socio-economic development of Asia and the Pacific through productivity promotion; activities cover industry, agriculture and service sectors, with the primary focus on human resources development; five key areas are incorporated into its activities: knowledge management, green productivity, strengthening small and medium enterprises, integrated community development and development of national productivity organizations; serves its members as a think tank, catalyst, regional adviser, institution builder and clearing house; mems: 20 countries; Sec.-Gen. SHIGEO TAKENAKA; publs *APO News* (monthly), *Annual Report*, *APO Asia-Pacific Productivity Data and Analysis*, other books and monographs.

Association of African Trade Promotion Organizations (AATPO): blvd Muhammad V, Pavillion International, BP 23, 90 000 Tangier, Morocco; tel. (3) 943730; fax (3) 9325275; e-mail aoapc@oaoapc.org; internet www.aoapc.org; f. 1975 under the auspices of the OAU (now AU) and the ECA to foster regular contact between African states in trade matters and to assist in the harmonization of their commercial policies, in order to promote intra-African trade; conducts research and training; organizes meetings and trade information missions; mems: 26 states; Sec.-Gen. Prof. ADEYINKA W. ORIMALADE; publs *FLASH: African Trade* (monthly), *Directory of African Consultants and Experts in Trade Promotion*, *Directory of Trade Information Contacts in Africa*, *Directory of Trade Information Sources in Africa*, *Directory of State Trading Organizations*, *Directory of Importers and Exporters of Food Products in Africa*, *Basic Information on Africa*, studies.

Association of European Chambers of Commerce and Industry (EUROCHAMBRES): The Chamber House, 19 ave des Arts, 1000 Brussels, Belgium; tel. (2) 282-08-50; fax (2) 230-00-38; e-mail eurochambres@eurochambres.be; internet www.eurochambres.eu; f. 1958 to promote the exchange of experience and information among its members and to bring their joint opinions to the attention of the institutions of the European Union; conducts studies and seminars; co-ordinates EU projects; mems: 44 nat. asscns of Chambers of Commerce and Industry, 2,000 regional and local Chambers and 18m. mem. enterprises in Europe; Pres. JÖRG MITTELSTEN SCHEID (Germany); Sec.-Gen. ARNALDO ABRUZZINI (Italy).

BusinessEurope: 168 ave de Cortenbergh, 1000 Brussels, Belgium; tel. (2) 237-65-11; fax (2) 231-14-45; e-mail main@unice.be; internet www.unice.org; f. 1958 as Union of Industrial and Employers' Confederations of Europe (UNICE); name changed, as above, Jan. 2007; aims to ensure that European Union policy-making takes account of the views of European business; committees and working groups develop joint positions in fields of interest to business and submit these to the Community institutions concerned; the Council of Presidents (of member federations) lays down general policy; the Executive Committee (of Directors-General of member federations) is the managing body; and the Committee of Permanent Delegates, consisting of federation representatives in Brussels, ensures permanent liaison with mems; mems: 39 industrial and employers' federations from 33 countries; Pres. ERNEST-ANTOINE SEILLIÈRE (France).

CAEF—The European Foundry Association: Sohnstrasse 70, 40237 Düsseldorf, Germany; tel. (211) 6871217; fax (211) 6871205; e-mail info@caef.org; internet www.caef.org; f. 1953 to safeguard the common interests of European foundry industries and to collect and exchange information; mems: asscns in 19 countries; Sec.-Gen. Dr KLAUS URBAT; publ. *The European Foundry Industry* (annually).

Cairns Group: (no permanent secretariat); e-mail agriculture.negotiations@dfat.gov.au; internet www.cairnsgroup.org; f. 1986 by major agricultural exporting countries; aims to bring about reforms in international agricultural trade, including reductions in export subsidies, in barriers to access and in internal support measures; represents members' interests in WTO negotiations; mems: Argentina, Australia, Bolivia, Brazil, Canada, Chile, Colombia, Costa Rica, Fiji, Guatemala, Indonesia, Malaysia, New Zealand, Pakistan, Paraguay, Peru, Philippines, South Africa, Thailand, Uruguay; Chair. SIMON CREAN (Australia).

Caribbean Association of Industry and Commerce (CAIC): Ground Floor, 27A Saddle Rd, Maraval, Trinidad and Tobago; tel. 628-9859; fax 622-7810; e-mail info@caic.org.tt; internet www.caic.org.tt; f. 1955; aims to encourage economic development through the private sector; undertakes research and training and gives assistance to small enterprises; encourages export promotion; mems: chambers of commerce and enterprises in 20 countries and territories; Pres. JAMES MOSS-SOLOMON; publ. *Caribbean Investor* (quarterly).

Committee for European Construction Equipment (CECE): Diamant Bldg, blvd Reyers 80, 1030 Brussels, Belgium; tel. (2) 706-82-25; fax (2) 706-82-10; e-mail info@cece-eu.org; internet www.cece-eu.org; f. 1959 to further contact between manufacturers, to improve market conditions and productivity and to conduct research into techniques; mems: representatives from 12 European countries; Sec.-Gen. RALF WEZEL.

Confederation of Asia-Pacific Chambers of Commerce and Industry (CACCI): 13th Floor, 3 Sungshou Rd, Taipei 110, Taiwan; tel. (2) 27255663; fax (2) 27255665; e-mail cacci@ttn.net; internet www.cacci.org.tw; f. 1966; holds biennial conferences to examine regional co-operation, and an annual Council meeting; liaises with governments to promote laws conducive to regional co-operation; serves as a centre for compiling and disseminating trade and business information; encourages contacts between businesses; conducts training and research; mems: 26 national chambers of commerce and industry the region, also affiliate and special mems; Pres. HARVEY CHANG; Dir-Gen. Dr WEBSTER KIANG; publs *CACCI Profile* (monthly), *CACCI Journal of Commerce and Industry* (2 a year).

Consumers International: 24 Highbury Cres., London, N5 1RX, United Kingdom; tel. (20) 7226-6663; fax (20) 7354-0607; e-mail consint@consint.org; internet www.consumersinternational.org; f. 1960 as International Organization of Consumers' Unions—IOCU; links consumer groups world-wide through information networks and international seminars; supports new consumer groups and represents consumers' interests at the international level; maintains four regional offices; mems: 250 asscns in 115 countries; Dir-Gen. RICHARD LLOYD; publs *The African Consumer/Le Consommateur African* (3 a year, English and French), *Asia Pacific Consumer* (online, quarterly), *Consumer 21* (online, quarterly, in English, French and Russian), *Consumidores y Desarollo* (quarterly).

CropLife International: 143 ave Louise, 1050 Brussels, Belgium; tel. (2) 542-04-10; fax (2) 542-04-19; e-mail croplife@croplife.org; internet www.croplife.org; f. 1960 as European Group of National Asscns of Pesticide Manufacturers, international body since 1967, present name adopted in 2001, evolving from Global Crop Protection Federation; represents the plant science industry, with the aim of promoting sustainable agricultural methods; aims to harmonize national and international regulations concerning crop protection products and agricultural biotechnology; promotes observation of the FAO Code of Conduct on the Distribution and Use of Pesticides; holds an annual General Assembly; mems: 6 regional bodies and national asscns in 85 countries; Dir-Gen. CHRISTIAN VERSCHUEREN.

Energy Charter Secretariat: 56 blvd de la Woluwe, 1200 Brussels, Belgium; tel. (2) 775-98-00; fax (2) 775-98-01; e-mail info@encharter.org; internet www.encharter.org; f. 1995 under the provisions of the Energy Charter Treaty (1994); provides a legal framework for promotion of trade and investment across Eurasia in the energy industries; mems: 52 signatory states; Sec.-Gen. ANDRE MERNIER (Belgium); publs *Putting a Price on Energy: International Pricing Mechanisms for Oil and Gas*, *The Energy Charter Treaty—A Reader's Guide*, reports.

ESOMAR—World Association of Opinion and Marketing Research Professionals: Vondelstraat 172, 1054 GV Amsterdam, Netherlands; tel. (20) 6642141; fax (20) 6642922; e-mail customerservice@esomar.org; internet www.esomar.org; f. 1948 (as European Society for Opinion and Marketing Research); aims to further professional interests and encourage high technical standards in the industry; creates and manages a comprehensive programme of industry-specific and thematic conferences, publications and communications, as well as actively advocating self-regulation and the worldwide code of practice; mems: over 4,500 in

100 countries; Pres. FRITS SPANGENBERG (Netherlands); publs *Research World* (monthly), *ESOMAR Directory* (annually).

European Association of Communications Agencies (EACA): 152 blvd Brand Whitlock, 1200 Brussels, Belgium; tel. (2) 740-07-11; fax (2) 740-07-17; e-mail dominic.lyle@eaca.be; internet www.eaca.eu; f. 1959 (as European Association of Advertising Agencies) to maintain and raise the standards of service of all European advertising, media and sales promotions agencies; aims to promote honest, effective advertising, high professional standards, and awareness of the contribution of advertising in a free market economy and to encourage close co-operation between agencies, advertisers and media in European advertising bodies; mems: 30 national advertising agency asscns and 23 multinational agency groups; Pres. GARY LEIH (United Kingdom); Dir-Gen. DOMINIC LYLE.

European Association of Electrical Contractors (AIE): 1 J. Chantraineplantsoen, 3070 Kortenberg, Belgium; tel. (2) 253-42-22; fax (2) 253-67-63; e-mail info@aie-elec.org; internet www.aie-elec.org; mems: national asscns in 21 countries and territories; Gen. Sec. EVELYNE SCHELLEHEUS; publ. *AIE Brochure* (every 2 years).

European Association of Manufacturers of Radiators (EURORAD): Konradstr. 9, 8023 Zürich, Switzerland; tel. 442719090; fax 442719292; f. 1966 to represent the national asscns of manufacturers of radiators made of steel and cast iron, intended to be attached to central heating plants and which convey heat by natural convection and radiation without the need for casing; mems: in 15 countries; Pres. Dr H. GASSER (Belgium); Gen. Sec. K. EGLI (Switzerland).

European Association of National Productivity Centres (EANPC): 60 rue de la Concorde, 1050 Brussels, Belgium; tel. (2) 511-71-00; fax (2) 511-24-01; e-mail eanpc@skynet.be; internet www.eanpc.org; f. 1966 to enable members to pool knowledge about their policies and activities; mems: 19 European centres; Pres. PETER REHNSTRÖM; publs *EPI* (quarterly), *Annual Report*.

European Brewery Convention: POB 510, 2380 BB Zoeterwoude, Netherlands; tel. (71) 5456047; fax (71) 5410013; e-mail secretariat@ebc-nl.com; internet www.ebc-nl.com; f. 1947, present name adopted 1948; aims to promote scientific co-ordination in malting and brewing; mems: national asscns in 20 European countries; Pres. HILARY JONES (United Kingdom); Sec.-Gen. MARJOLEIN VAN WIJNGAARDEN (Netherlands); publs *Analytica*, *Thesaurus*, *Dictionary of Brewing*, monographs, conference proceedings, manuals of good practice.

European Chemical Industry Council: 4 ave van Nieuwenhuyse, Box 1, 1160 Brussels, Belgium; tel. (2) 676-72-11; fax (2) 676-73-00; e-mail mail@cefic.be; internet www.cefic.org; f. 1972; represents and defends the interests of the chemical industry in legal and trade policy, internal market, environmental and technical matters; liaises with intergovernmental organizations; provides secretariat for some 100 product sector groups; mems: 25 national federations, incl. three assoc. mem. feds; Dir-Gen. ALAIN PERROY; Exec. Dir and Gen. Counsel JEAN-CLAUDE LAHAUT.

European Committee for Standardization (Comité européen de normalisation—CEN): 36 rue de Stassart, 1050 Brussels, Belgium; tel. (2) 550-08-11; fax (2) 550-08-19; e-mail infodesk@cenorm.be; internet www.cenorm.be; f. 1961 to promote European standardization; works to eliminate obstacles caused by technical requirements, in order to facilitate the exchange of goods and services; mems: 29 national standards bodies, eight associated and five affiliated bodies in central and eastern Europe and seven partnership standardization bodies; Sec.-Gen. GASTON MICHAUD; publs *Catalogue of European Standards* (2 a year), *CEN Networking* (newsletter, every 2 months), *Bulletin* (quarterly), *Directives and related standards* (in English, French and German), *Directions European Standardization in a Global Context*, *The Benefits of Standards*, *Marking of Products and System Certification* (English only).

European Committee of Associations of Manufacturers of Agricultural Machinery: 80 bld A. Reyers, 1030 Brussels, Belgium; tel. (2) 706-82-16; e-mail ralf.wezel@cema-agri.org; internet www.cema-agri.org; f. 1959 to study economic and technical problems in field of agricultural machinery manufacture, to protect members' interests and to disseminate information; mems: 11 mem. countries; Pres. FEDERICO CORRADINI (Italy); Sec.-Gen. RALF WEZEL (Germany).

European Committee of Textile Machinery Manufacturers (CEMATEX): POB 190, 2700 AD Zoetermeer, Netherlands; tel. (79) 531100; fax (79) 531365; f. 1952; promotes general interests of the industry; mems: orgs in eight European countries; Pres. Dr F. PAETZOLD (Germany); Gen. Sec. R. BICKER CAARTEN.

European Confederation of Iron and Steel Industries (EUROFER): 211 rue du Noyer, 1000 Brussels, Belgium; tel. (2) 738-79-20; fax (2) 736-30-01; e-mail mail@eurofer.be; internet www.eurofer.org; f. 1976 as a confederation of national federations and companies in the European steel industry; aims to foster co-operation between the member federations and companies and to represent their common interests to the EU and other international organizations; mems: in 13 European countries, assoc. mems from central and eastern European countries; Dir-Gen. D. VON HÜLSEN.

European Confederation of Woodworking Industries: 24 rue Montoyer 24, box 20, 1000 Brussels, Belgium; tel. (2) 556-25-85; fax (2) 287-08-75; e-mail info@cei-bois.org; internet www.cei-bois.org; f. 1952 to liaise between national organizations, undertake research and defend the interests of the industry; mems: national federations in 25 European countries, eight branch federations; Chair. MIKAEL ELIASSON (Sweden); Sec.-Gen. FILIP DE JAEGER; publ. *Brochure*.

European Council of Paint, Printing Ink and Artists' Colours Industry: 6 ave E. van Nieuwenhuyse, 1160 Brussels, Belgium; tel. (2) 676-74-80; fax (2) 676-74-90; e-mail secretariat@cepe.org; internet www.cepe.org; f. 1951 to study questions relating to the paint and printing ink industries, to take or recommend measures for the development of these industries or to support their interests, and to exchange information; mems: company mems of national asscns in 23 European countries; Chair. PIERRE-MARIE DE LEENER; Man. Dir JAN VAN DER MEULEN; publs *Annual Review*, guidance documents.

European Federation of Associations of Insulation Enterprises: c/o HDB, Kurfuerstenstr. 129, 10785 Berlin, Germany; tel. (30) 21286163; fax (30) 21286297; e-mail bfa.wksb@bauindustrie.de; f. 1970; groups organizations in Europe representing insulation firms; aims to facilitate contacts between member asscns; studies problems of interest to the profession; works to safeguard the interests of the profession and represent it in international fora; mems: professional orgs in 16 European countries; Sec.-Gen. JUERGEN SCHMOLDT.

European Federation of Insurance Intermediaries (BIPAR): 40 ave Albert-Elisabeth, 1200 Brussels, Belgium; tel. (2) 735-60-48; fax (2) 732-14-18; e-mail bipar@skynet.be; internet www.biparweb.org; f. 1937; represents, promotes and defends the interests of national asscns of professional insurance agents and brokers at the European and international level; works to co-ordinate members' activities; mems: 48 asscns from 30 countries, representing approx. 250,000 brokers and agents; Pres. ALAIN DE MIOMANDRE; publ. *BIPAR Press* (quarterly).

European Federation of Management Consultancies' Associations: 3–5 ave des Arts, 1210 Brussels, Belgium; tel. (2) 250-06-50; fax (2) 250-06-51; e-mail feaco@feaco.org; internet www.feaco.org; f. 1960; aims to promote networking within the management consultancy sector and its interests and promote a high standard of professional competence, by encouraging discussions of, and research into, problems of common professional interest; mems: 24 asscns; Chairman ANTOINE BEUVE-MERY; Sec.-Gen. ELSE GROEN; publs *FEACO Newsletter* (quarterly), *Annual Survey of the European Management Consultancy Market*.

European Federation of Marketing Research Organisations (EFAMRO): Hoek van Hollandlaan 13, 2554 EA Den Haag, Netherlands; tel. (70) 3238820; e-mail efamro@orange.nl; internet www.efamro.com; f. 1965 (frmly known as FEMRA) to facilitate contacts between researchers; maintains specialist divisions on European chemical marketing research, European technological forecasting, paper and related industries, industrial materials, automotives, textiles, methodology, and information technology; mems: nat. asscns in 12 countries; Dir Gen. Dr A. J. OLIVIER.

European Federation of Materials Handling and Storage Equipment: Diamant Bldg, 80 blvd A. Reyers, 1030 Brussels, Belgium; tel. (2) 706-82-37; fax (2) 706-82-53; e-mail stephanie.uny@orgalime.org; internet www.fem-eur.com; f. 1953 to represent the technical, economic and political interests of one of the largest industrial sectors of the European mechanical engineering industry; mems: orgs in 12 European countries; Pres. AMBROGIO BOLLINI; Sec.-Gen. STÉPHANIE UNY.

European Federation of the Plywood Industry (FEIC): 24 rue Montoyer, 1000 Brussels, Belgium; tel. (2) 556-25-84; fax (2) 287-08-75; e-mail info@europanels.org; internet www.europlywood.org; f. 1957 to organize co-operation between members of the industry at the international level; mems: asscns in 18 European countries; Pres. ULDIS BIKIS; Sec.-Gen. K. WYNENDAELE.

European Federation of Tile and Brick Manufacturers: c/o Cérame-Unie, 18–24 rue des Colonies, BP 17, 1000 Brussels, Belgium; tel. (2) 511-30-12; fax (2) 511-51-74; e-mail sec@cerameunie.net; internet www.cerameunie.net; f. 1952 to co-ordinate research between members of the industry, improve technical knowledge and encourage professional training; mems: asscns in 23 European and east European countries; Sec.-Gen. ROGIER CHORUS.

European Furniture Manufacturers Federation (Union européenne de l'ameublement—UEA): 163 rue Royale, Koningsstraat, 1210 Brussels, Belgium; tel. (2) 218-18-89; fax (2) 219-27-01; e-mail secretariat@uea.be; internet www.ueanet.com; f. 1950 to determine and support the general interests of the European furniture industry and facilitate contacts between members of the industry; mems: organizations in 25 European countries; Pres. CALIXTO VALENTI; Sec.-

Gen. B. DE TURCK; publs *UEA Newsletter* (bi-monthly), *Focus on Issues*, *Strategy Survey*.

European General Galvanizers Association (EGGA): Maybrook House, Godstone Rd, Caterham, Surrey, CR3 6RE, United Kingdom; tel. (1883) 331277; fax (1883) 331287; e-mail mail@egga.com; internet www.egga.com; f. 1955 to promote co-operation between members of the industry, especially in improving processes and finding new uses for galvanized products; mems: asscns in 18 European countries; Dir MURRAY COOK (United Kingdom).

European Organization for Quality (EOQ): 3 rue de Luxembourg, 1000 Brussels, Belgium; tel. (2) 501-07-35; fax (2) 501-07-36; e-mail bjouslin@compuserve.com; internet www.eoq.org; f. 1956 to encourage the use and application of quality management, with the aim of improving quality, lowering costs and increasing productivity; organizes the exchange of information and documentation; mems: organizations in 34 European countries; Sec.-Gen. BERTRAND JOUSLIN DE NORAY; publs *European Quality* (6 a year), *Annual Report*.

European Packaging Federation: c/o Institut Français de l'Emballage et du Conditionnement IFEC, 33 rue Louis Blanc, 93582 St-Ouen Cédex, France; tel. 1-40-11-22-12; fax 1-40-11-01-06; e-mail info@ifecpromotion.tm.fr; f. 1953 to encourage the exchange of information between national packaging institutes and to promote technical and economic progress; mems: organizations in 12 European countries; Pres. J. P. POTHET (France); Sec.-Gen. A. FREIDINGER-LEGAY (France).

European Panel Federation: 24 rue Montoyer, box 20, 1000 Brussels, Belgium; tel. (2) 556-25-89; fax (2) 287-08-75; e-mail info@europanels.org; internet www.europanels.org; f. 1958 as European Federation of Associations of Particle Board Manufacturers; present name adopted 1999; works to develop and encourage international co-operation in the particle board and MDF industry; Pres. L. DÖRY; Sec.-Gen. K. WIJNENDALE (Belgium); publ. *Annual Report*.

European Patent Office (EPO): Erhardtstr. 27, 80469 Munich, Germany; tel. (89) 2399-0; fax (89) 2399-4560; e-mail info@epo.org; internet www.epo.org; f. 1977 as the executive branch of the European Patent Organisation, established under the Munich convention of 1973; conducts searches and examination of European patent applications; grants European patents; mems: 32 European countries; Pres. Prof. ALAIN POMPIDOU (France); Chair. Admin. Council ROLAND GROSSENBACHER (Switzerland).

European Union of the Natural Gas Industry (EUROGAS): 4 ave Palmerston, 1000 Brussels, Belgium; tel. (2) 237-11-11; fax (2) 230-62-91; e-mail eurogas@eurogas.org; internet www.eurogas.org; mems: orgs, federations and companies in 25 European countries; Pres. WILLY BOSMANS (Belgium); Sec.-Gen. JEAN-MARIE DEVOS (Belgium).

Fairtrade Labelling Organizations International: Bonner Talweg 177 53129 Bonn, Germany; tel. (228) 949230; fax (228) 2421713; e-mail info@fairtrade.net; internet www.fairtrade.net; world-wide fairtrade standards and certification organization; works with other orgs in the fairtrade movement to contribute to sustainable development and to support the rights of producers and workers; Man.-Dir LUUK ZONNEVELD.

Federación de Cámaras de Comercio del Istmo Centroamericano (Federation of Central American Chambers of Commerce): 10A Calle 3-80, Zona 1, 01001 Guatemala City, Guatemala; tel. 2326-8840; fax 2220-9393; e-mail aechevarria@fecamco.com; internet www.fecamco.com; f. 1961; plans and co-ordinates industrial and commercial exchanges and exhibitions; Exec. Dir ALEJANDRA ECHEVARRIA VALENZUELA.

General Union of Chambers of Commerce, Industry and Agriculture for Arab Countries: POB 11-2837, Beirut, Lebanon; tel. (1) 814269; fax (1) 862841; e-mail gucciaac@destination.com.lb; internet www.gucciaac.org.lb; f. 1951 to enhance Arab economic development, integration and security through the co-ordination of industrial, agricultural and trade policies and legislation; mems: chambers of commerce, industry and agriculture in 22 Arab countries; Sec. Gen. Dr ELIAS GHANTOUS; publs *Arab Economic Report*, *Al-Omran Al-Arabi* (every 2 months), economic papers, proceedings.

Gulf Organization for Industrial Consulting (GOIC): POB 5114, Doha, Qatar; tel. 4858888; fax 4831465; e-mail goic@goic.org.qa; internet www.goic.org.qa; f. 1976 by the Gulf Arab states to encourage industrial co-operation among Gulf Arab states, to pool industrial expertise and to encourage joint development of projects; undertakes feasibility studies, market diagnosis, assistance in policy-making, legal consultancies, project promotion, promotion of small and medium industrial investment profiles and technical training; maintains industrial data bank; mems: mem. states of the Co-operation Council for the Arab States of the Gulf; Sec.-Gen. AHMED KHALIL AL-MUTAWA; publs *GOIC Monthly Bulletin* (in Arabic), *Al Ta'awon al Sina'e* (quarterly, in Arabic and English).

Instituto Centroamericano de Administración de Empresas (INCAE) (Central American Institute for Business Administration): Apdo 960, 4050 Alajuela, Costa Rica; tel. 443-9908; fax 433-9983; e-mail costarica@incae.edu; internet www.incae.ac.cr; f. 1964; provides a postgraduate programme in business administration; runs executive training programmes; carries out management research and consulting; maintains a second campus in Nicaragua; libraries of 85,000 vols; Rector Dr ROBERTO ARTAVIA; publs *Alumni Journal* (in Spanish), *Bulletin* (quarterly), books and case studies.

Inter-American Commercial Arbitration Commission: OAS Administration Bldg, Rm 211, 19th and Constitution Ave, NW, Washington, DC 20006, USA; tel. (202) 458-3249; fax (202) 458-3293; f. 1934 to establish an inter-American system of arbitration for the settlement of commercial disputes by means of tribunals; mems: national committees, commercial firms and individuals in 22 countries; Dir-Gen. Dr ADRIANA POLANIA.

International Advertising Association Inc: 521 Fifth Ave, Suite 1807, New York, NY 10175, USA; tel. (212) 557-1133; fax (212) 983-0455; e-mail iaa@iaaglobal.org; internet www.iaaglobal.org; f. 1938 as a global partnership of advertisers, agencies, the media and other marketing communications professionals; aims to protect freedom of commercial speech and consumer choice; holds World Congress every 2 years (2008: Washington, DC, USA; 2010: Moscow, Russia); mems: 4,000 in 76 countries; World Pres. INDRA ABIDIN (Indonesia); Exec. Dir MICHAEL LEE (USA); publs *IAA Membership Directory*, *Annual Report*.

International Association of Buying and Marketing Groups: Vorgebirgsstr. 43, 53119 Bonn, Germany; tel. (228) 9858420; fax (228) 9858410; e-mail g.olesch@zgv-online.de; f. 1951 to research, document and compile statistics; holds annual conference; mems: 300 buying groups in 13 countries; Sec.-Gen. Dr GÜNTER OLESCH.

International Association of Department Stores: 11-13 rue Guersant, 75017 Paris, France; tel. 1-42-94-02-02; fax 1-42-94-02-04; e-mail iads@iads.org; internet www.iads.org; f. 1928 to conduct research and exchange information and statistics on management, organization and technical problems; maintains a documentation centre; mems: department stores in 18 countries; Pres. HANNU PENTTILÄ (Finland); Gen. Sec. MAARTEN DE GROOT VAN EMBDEN (Netherlands).

International Association of Scholarly Publishers: c/o Michael Huter, Berggasse 5, 1090 Vienna, Austria; tel. (1) 3105356; fax (1) 3197050; e-mail huter@wuv.co.at; f. 1970 for the exchange of information and experience on scholarly and academic publishing by universities and others; assists in the transfer of publishing skills to developing countries; mems: over 140 in 38 countries; Pres. MICHAEL HUTER (Austria); publs *IASP Newsletter* (every 2 months), *International Directory of Scholarly Publishers*.

International Association of the Soap, Detergent and Maintenance Products Industry (AISE) (Association internationale de la savonnerie, de la détergence et des produits d'entretien): 15 A ave Herrmann Debroux, 3rd Floor, 1160 Brussels, Belgium; tel. (2) 679-62-60; fax (2) 679-62-79; e-mail aise.main@aise-net.org; internet www.aise-net.org; f. 1967 to promote the manufacture and use of a wide range of cleaning products, polishes, bleaches, disinfectants and insecticides, to develop the exchange of statistical information and to study technical, scientific, economic and social problems of interest to its members; mems: 35 national asscns; Dir M. G. LABBERTON; publs *Annual Review*, technical documents and reports.

International Booksellers Federation (IBF): 10 rue de la science, 1000 Brussels, Belgium; tel. (2) 223-49-40; fax (2) 223-49-38; e-mail ibf.booksellers@skynet.be; internet www.ibf-booksellers.org; f. 1956 to promote the book trade and the exchange of information, and to protect the interests of booksellers when dealing with other international organizations; sprice maintenance, book market research, advertising, customs and tariffs, the problems of young booksellers, etc; mems: 200 in 22 countries; Pres. KARL PUS; Dir FRANÇOISE DUBRUILLE.

International Bureau for the Standardization of Man-Made Fibres (BISFA): 4 ave van Nieuwenhuyse, 1160 Brussels, Belgium; tel. (2) 676-74-55; fax (2) 676-74-54; e-mail spi@cirfs.org; internet www.bisfa.org; f. 1928 to examine and establish rules for the standardization, classification and naming of various categories of man-made fibres; mems: 44; Sec.-Gen. J. SPIJKERS.

International Butchers' Confederation: bte 10, 4 rue Jacques de Lalaing, 1040 Brussels, Belgium; tel. (2) 230-38-76; fax (2) 230-34-51; e-mail info@cibc.be; f. 1907; aims to defend the interests of small and medium-sized enterprises in the meat trading and catering industry; Pres. EUGEN NAGEL; Sec.-Gen. MARTIN FUCHS.

International Confederation for Printing and Allied Industries (INTERGRAF): 7 pl. E. Flagey, Bte 5, 1050 Brussels, Belgium; tel. (2) 230-86-46; fax (2) 231-14-64; e-mail intergraf@intergraf.org; internet www.intergraf.org; f. 1983 to defend the common interests of the printing and allied interests in mem. countries; mems:

federations in 26 countries; Pres. ROB HODGSON; Sec.-Gen. BEATRICE KLOSE.

International Confederation of Art and Antique Dealers (CINOA): 33 rue Ernest-Allard, 1000 Brussels, Belgium; tel. (2) 502-26-92; e-mail information@cinoa.org; internet www.cinoa.org; f. 1936 to co-ordinate the work of asscns of dealers in works of art and paintings and to contribute to artistic and economic expansion; mems: asscns in 30 countries; Pres. BO KNUTSSON; Sec.-Gen. ERIKA BOCHEREAU.

International Co-operative Alliance (ICA): 15 route des Morillons, 1218 Grand-Saconnex, Geneva, Switzerland; tel. 229298888; fax 227984122; e-mail ica@ica.coop; internet www.ica.coop; f. 1895 for the pursuit of co-operative aims; a General Assembly and four Regional Assemblies meet every two years, on an alternating basis; a 20-member ICA Board controls the affairs of the organization between meetings of the General Assembly; sectoral organisations and thematic committees have been established to promote co-operative activities in the following fields: agriculture, banking, fisheries, consumer affairs, tourism, communications, co-operative research, health, human resource development, housing, insurance, gender issues and industrial, artisanal and worker co-operatives; mems: 226 affiliated national orgs, with a total membership of more than 800m. individuals in 87 countries, and four int. orgs; Pres. IVANO BARBERINI (Italy); Dir-Gen. IAIN MACDONALD (United Kingdom); publs *Review of International Co-operation* (quarterly), *ICA Digest* (electronic newsletter, 2 a month), *Co-op Dialogue* (2 a year).

International Council of Graphic Design Associations (ICOGRADA): 455 St Antoine Ouest, Suite SS 10, Montréal, QC H2Z 1J1, Canada; tel. (514) 448-4949; fax (514) 448-4948; e-mail secretariat@icograda.org; internet www.icograda.org; f. 1963; aims to raise standards of communication design; promotes the exchange of information; organizes congresses; maintains archive; mems: 11 int. affiliated mems, 63 professional mems, 19 assoc. mems, 76 educational mems; Pres. DON RYUN CHANG (Republic of Korea); Sec.-Gen. LISE VEJSE KLINT (Denmark); publs *Newsletter* (quarterly), *Regulations and Guidelines governing International Design Competitions*, *Model Code of Professional Conduct*, other professional documents.

International Council of Societies of Industrial Design (ICSID): 455 St-Antoine W, Suite SS10, Montréal, Québec H2Z 1J1, Canada; tel. (514) 4484949; fax (514) 4484948; e-mail office@icsid.org; internet www.icsid.org; f. 1957 to encourage the development of high standards in the practice of industrial design; works to improve and expand the contribution of industrial design throughout the world; mems: 150 in 53 countries; Pres. Prof. Dr PETER ZEC (Germany); Sec.-Gen. DILI DE SILVA; publs *ICSID News*, *World Directory of Design Schools*.

International Council of Tanners: Leather Trade House, Kings Park Rd, Moulton Park, Northampton, NN3 6JD, United Kingdom; tel. (1604) 679917; fax (1604) 679998; e-mail sec@tannerscouncilct.org; internet www.tannerscouncilct.org; f. 1926 to study all questions relating to the leather industry and maintain contact with national asscns; mems: national tanners' organizations in 33 countries; Pres. MICHAEL PARSONS (United Kingdom); Sec. PAUL PEARSON (United Kingdom).

International Council on Mining and Metals (ICMM): 6th Floor, 35 Portman Sq., London, W1H 6LR, United Kingdom; tel. (20) 7467-5070; fax (20) 7467-5071; e-mail info@icmm.com; internet www.icmm.com; f. 1991 (as the International Council on Metals and the Environment, present name adopted 2002); aims to promote sustainable development practices and policies in the mining, use, recycling and disposal of minerals and metals; mems: 13 cos, 24 asscns; Chair. DAVID KERR (Canada); Sec.-Gen. PAUL MITCHELL (United Kingdom); publ. *ICMM Newsletter* (quarterly).

International Exhibitions Bureau: 34 ave d'Iéna, 75116 Paris, France; tel. 1-45-00-38-63; fax 1-45-00-96-15; e-mail bie@bie-paris.org; internet www.bie-paris.org; f. 1931, revised by Protocol 1972, for the authorization and registration of international exhibitions falling under the 1928 Convention; mems: 98 states; Pres. JIANMIN WU; Sec.-Gen. VICENTE GONZALES LOSCERTALES.

International Fair Trade Association: Prijssestraat 24, 4101 CR, Culemborg, Netherlands; tel. (34) 5535914; fax (84) 7474401; e-mail info@ifat.org; internet www.ifat.org; f. 1989; coalition of trading and producer organizations; supports the market development of fair-trade products and conducts monitoring and advocacy; mems: 70 alternative trade organizations from 30 countries; Dir STEFAN DURWAEL.

International Federation of Associations of Textile Chemists and Colourists (IFATCC): Postfach 403, 4153 Reinach 1, Switzerland; tel. 612991795; e-mail markus_krayer@huntsman.com; f. 1930 for liaison on professional matters between members and the furtherance of scientific and technical collaboration in the development of the textile finishing industry and the colouring of materials;

mems: in 20 countries; Pres. Prof. J.M. CANAL (Spain); Sec. MARKUS KRAYER (Switzerland).

International Federation of Grocers' Associations (IFGA): Vakcentrum, Woerden, Netherlands; tel. (348) 419771; fax (348) 421801; f. 1927; initiates special studies and works to further the interests of members, with special regard to conditions resulting from European integration and developments in consuming and distribution; mems: 30 asscns representing 125,000 sales outlets.

International Federation of Pharmaceutical Manufacturers and Associations (IFPMA): 15 chemin Louis-Dunant, POB 195, 1211 Geneva 20, Switzerland; tel. 223383200; fax 223383299; e-mail info@ifpma.org; internet www.ifpma.org; f. 1968 for the exchange of information and international co-operation in all questions of interest to the pharmaceutical industry, particularly in the field of health legislation, science and research; represents the research-based pharmaceutical, biotech and vaccine sectors; develops ethical principles and practices and co-operates with national and international orgs; mems: 25 international companies and 45 national and regional industry asscns; Pres. FRED HASSAN (USA); Dir-Gen. Dr HARVEY E. BALE, Jr (USA); publs *IFPMA Code of Pharmaceutical Marketing Practices*, action papers, occasional publications.

International Federation of the Phonographic Industry (IFPI): 54 Regent St, London, W1B 5RE, United Kingdom; tel. (20) 7878-7900; fax (20) 7878-7950; e-mail info@ifpi.org; internet www.ifpi.org; f. 1933; represents the interests of record producers by campaigning for the introduction, improvement and enforcement of copyright and related rights legislation; co-ordinates the recording industry's anti-piracy activities; mems: 1,476 in 73 countries; Chair. and Chief Exec. JASON BERMAN.

International Fertilizer Industry Association: 28 rue Marbeuf, 75008 Paris, France; tel. 1-53-93-05-00; fax 1-53-93-05-45; e-mail ifa@fertilizer.org; internet www.fertilizer.org; f. 1927; represents companies involved in all aspects of the global fertilizer industry, including the production and distribution of fertilizers, their raw materials and intermediates; also represents organizations involved in agronomic research and training with regard to crop nutrition; mems: some 450 in more than 80 countries; Pres. SIHAI WU; Dir-Gen. L. M. MAENE.

International Fragrance Association (IFRA): 6 ave des Arts, 1210 Brussels, Belgium; tel. (2) 214-20-60; fax (2) 214-20-69; e-mail secretariat@ifraorg.org; internet www.ifraorg.org; f. 1973 to develop and advance the fragrance industry, to collect and study scientific data on fragrance materials and to make recommendations on their safe use; mems: 16 ordinary mems and 3 observer mems in 18 countries; Pres. THOMAN DAMAS; Dir-Gen. J.-P. HOURI; publs *Code of Practice*, *Information Letters*.

International Fur Trade Federation: POB 495, Weybridge, Surrey, KT12 8WD, United Kingdom; e-mail info@iftf.com; internet www.iftf.com; f. 1949 to promote and organize joint action by fur trade organizations in order to develop and protect the trade in fur skins and the processing of skins; mems: 36 orgs in 30 countries; Exec. Dir J. BAILEY.

International Meat Secretariat (Office international de la viande): 6 rue de la Victoire, 75009 Paris, France; tel. 1-45-26-68-97; fax 1-45-26-68-98; e-mail info@meat-ims.org; internet www.meat-ims.org; f. 1974; organizes World Meat Congress every two years (2008: Cape Town, South Africa, in September); Pres. PATRICK MOORE; Sec.-Gen. LAURENCE WRIXON.

International Organization of Motor Manufacturers (Organisation internationale des constructeurs d'automobiles—OICA): 4 rue de Berri, 75008 Paris, France; tel. 1-43-59-00-13; fax 1-45-63-84-41; e-mail oica@oica.net; internet www.oica.net; f. 1919 to co-ordinate and further the interests of the automobile industry, to promote the study of economic and other matters affecting automobile construction, and to control automobile manufacturers' participation in international exhibitions in Europe; mems: manufacturers' asscns of 16 European countries, China, Japan, the Republic of Korea and the USA; 43 assoc. mems; Gen. Sec. Y. VAN DER SRAATEN; publ. *Yearbook of the World's Motor Industry*.

International Organization of the Flavour Industry (IOFI): 5 chemin de la Parfumerie, 1214 Vernier, Geneva, Switzerland; tel. 224318250; fax 224318806; e-mail secretariat@iofiorg.org; internet www.iofi.org; f. 1969 to support and promote the flavour industry; active in the fields of safety evaluation and regulation of flavouring substances; mems: national asscns in 22 countries; Exec. Dir JOS STELDER; publs *Documentation Bulletin*, *Information Letters*, *Code of Practice*.

International Publishers' Association: 3 ave de Miremont, 1206 Geneva, Switzerland; tel. 223463018; fax 223475717; e-mail secretariat@internationalpublishers.org; internet www.internationalpublishers.org; f. 1896 to defend the freedom of publishers, promote their interests and foster international co-operation; promotes the international trade in books; carries out work on international copyright; mems: 66 professional book publishers' organizations in 55 countries; Pres. ANA MARIA CABANELLAS; Sec.-Gen. JENS BAMMEL.

International Rayon and Synthetic Fibres Committee (Comité international de la rayonne et des fibres synthétiques—CIRFS): 6 ave van Nieuwenhuyse, 1160 Brussels, Belgium; tel. (2) 676-74-55; fax (2) 676-74-54; e-mail secretariat@cirfs.org; internet www.cirfs.org; f. 1950 to improve the quality and promote the use of man-made fibres and products made from fibres; mems: individual producers in 24 countries; Pres. OMER SABANCI; Dir-Gen. COLIN PURVIS (United Kingdom); publs *Statistical Booklet* (annually), market reports, technical test methods.

International Shopfitting Organisation: Gladbachstr. 80, 8044 Zürich, Switzerland; tel. 442678100; fax 442678150; e-mail petra.isenberg@vssm.ch; internet www.shopfitting.org; f. 1959 to promote the interchange of ideas between individuals and firms concerned with shopfitting; mems: companies in 14 countries; Pres. MORTEN GRØN-HANSEN; Sec. PETRA ISENBERG.

International Textile Manufacturers Federation (ITMF): Wiedingstrasse 9, 8055 Zürich, Switzerland; tel. 442836380; fax 442836389; e-mail secretariat@itmf.org; internet www.itmf.org; f. 1904, present title adopted 1978; aims to protect and promote the interests of its members, disseminate information, and encourage co-operation; mems: national textile trade asscns and companies in some 50 countries; Pres. WALTER SIMEONI (South Africa); Dir-Gen. Dr CHRISTIAN P. SCHINDLER (Germany); publs *State of Trade Report* (quarterly), *Country Statements*, *Annual Conference Report*, *Directory*, various statistics, sectoral reports and guidelines.

International Union of Marine Insurance (IUMI): C.F. Meyer-Str. 14, POB 4288, 8022 Zurich, Switzerland; tel. 442082870; fax 442082838; e-mail mail@iumi.com; internet www.iumi.com; f. 1873 to collect and distribute information on marine insurance on a worldwide basis; mems: 54 asscns; Pres. PATRICK DE LA MORINERIE (France); Gen. Sec. FRITZ STABINGER.

International Wool Textile Organisation (IWTO) (Fédération lanière internationale—FLI): 4 rue de l'Industrie, 1000 Brussels, Belgium; tel. (2) 505-40-11; fax (2) 503-47-85; e-mail info@iwto.org; internet www.iwto.org; f. 1929 to link wool textile organizations in member-countries and represent their interests; holds annual Congress (2008: Beijing, People's Republic of China); mems: in 25 countries; Pres. GÜNTHER BEIER (Germany); Gen. Man. HENRIK KUFFNER (Germany); publs *Wool Statistics* (annually), *Global Wool Supplies and Wool Textile Manufacturing Activity* (annually), *Blue Book*, *Red Book*.

International Wrought Copper Council: 55 Bryanston St, London, W1H 7AJ, United Kingdom; tel. (20) 7868-8930; fax (20) 7868-8819; e-mail iwcc@coppercouncil.org; internet www.coppercouncil.org; f. 1953 to link and represent copper fabricating industries and represent the views of copper consumers to raw material producers; organizes specialist activities on technical work and the development of copper; mems: 17 national groups in Europe, Australia, Japan and Malaysia, 13 corporate mems; Chair. THIERRY CENTNER; Sec.-Gen. SIMON PAYTON; publs *Annual Report*, surveys.

Orgalime (European Engineering Industries Association): Diamant Bldg, 80 blvd A Reyers, 1030 Brussels, Belgium; tel. (2) 706-82-35; fax (2) 706-82-50; e-mail secretariat@orgalime.org; internet www.orgalime.org; f. 1954 to provide a permanent liaison between the mechanical, electrical and electronic engineering, and metalworking industries of member countries; mems: 34 national trade asscns in 23 European countries; Pres. Prof. Dr EDWARD G. KRUBASIK (Germany) (designate); Sec.-Gen. ADRIAN HARRIS.

Southern African Customs Union: c/o Dept of Trade and Industry, Private Bag X84, Pretoria, South Africa; tel. (12) 3109393; fax (12) 3220298; f. 1969; provides common pool of customs, excise and sales duties, according to the relative volume of trade and production in each country; goods are traded within the union free of duty and quotas, subject to certain protective measures for less developed mems; the South African rand is legal tender in Lesotho and Swaziland; the Customs Union Commission meets annually in each of the mems' capital cities in turn; mems: Botswana, Lesotho, Namibia, South Africa, Swaziland.

UFI (Global Association of the Exhibition Industry): 35 bis, rue Jouffroy d'Abbans, 75017 Paris, France; tel. 1-42-67-99-12; fax 1-42-27-19-29; e-mail info@ufi.org; internet www.ufi.org; f. 1925 as Union des Foires Internationales; works to increase co-operation between international trade fairs/exhibitions, safeguard their interests and extend their operations; imposes exhibition quality criteria and defines standards; approves 805 events; mems: 498, including 37 asscns, in 85 countries; Pres. CLIFF WALLACE; Man. Dir VINCENT GÉRARD.

Union of European Beverages Associations (UNESDA): 79 blvd St Michel, 1040 Brussels, Belgium; tel. (2) 743-40-50; fax (2) 732-51-02; e-mail mail@unesda.org; internet www.unesda.org; f. 1951, as Confederation of International Soft Drinks Associations; aims to promote co-operation among the national asscns of non-alcoholic drinks manufacturers on all industrial and commercial matters, to stimulate the sales and consumption of soft drinks, to deal with matters of interest to all member asscns and to represent the common interests of member asscns; holds a congress every year; Sec.-Gen. ALAIN BEAUMONT.

World Customs Organization (WCO): 30 rue du Marché, 1210 Brussels, Belgium; tel. (2) 209-92-11; fax (2) 209-92-62; e-mail communication@wcoomd.org; internet www.wcoomd.org; f. 1952 as Customs Co-operation Council (CCC); aims to enhance the effectiveness and efficiency of customs administrations in the areas relating to ensuring compliance with trade regulations, the protection of society and strengthening revenue collection; mems: customs administrations of 171 countries; Chair. TAPANI ERLING (Finland); Sec.-Gen. MICHEL DANET (France); publ. *WCO News* (3 a year).

World Federation of Advertisers: 120 ave Louise, Box 6, 1050 Brussels; tel. (2) 502-57-40; fax (2) 502-56-66; e-mail info@wfanet.org; internet www.wfanet.org; f. 1953; promotes and studies advertising and its related problems; mems: asscns in 55 countries and more than 40 international companies; Pres. BERNHARD GLOCK; Man. Dir STEPHAN LOERKE; publ. *EU Brief* (weekly).

World Packaging Organisation: c/o STFI-Packforsk, POB 5604, 114 86 Stockholm, Sweden; tel. (8) 676-7000; fax (8) 411-5518; e-mail carl.olsmats@stfi.se; internet www.worldpacking.org; f. 1968 to provide a forum for the exchange of knowledge of packaging technology and, in general, to create conditions for the conservation, preservation and distribution of world food production; holds annual congress and competition; mems: Asian, North American, Latin American, European and African packaging federations; Pres. KEITH PEARSON; Gen. Sec. CARL OLSMATS (Sweden).

World Trade Centers Association: 60 East 42nd St, Suite 1901, New York, NY 10165, USA; tel. (212) 432-2626; fax (212) 488-0064; e-mail wtca@wtca.org; internet www.wtca.org; f. 1968 to promote trade through the establishment of world trade centres, including education facilities, information services and exhibition facilities; operates an electronic trading and communication system (WTC On-Line); mems: trade centres, chambers of commerce and other organizations in more than 95 countries; Pres. GUY F. TOZZOLI; Chair. HUGH BRYAN GREVILLE MONTGOMERY; publ. *WTCA News* (monthly).

Transport

African Airlines Association: POB 20116, Nairobi 00200, Kenya; tel. (20) 604855; fax (20) 601173; e-mail afraa@afraa.org; internet www.afraa.org; f. 1968 to give African air companies expert advice in technical, financial, juridical and market matters; to improve air transport in Africa through inter-carrier co-operation; and to develop manpower resources; mems: 34 national carriers; Sec.-Gen. CHRISTIAN E. FOLLY-KOSSI; publs *Newsletter*, reports.

Airports Council International (ACI): POB 16, 1215 Geneva 15-Airport, Switzerland; tel. 227178585; fax 227178888; e-mail aci@aci.aero; internet www.airports.org; f. 1991, following merger of Airport Operators Council International and International Civil Airports Association; aims to represent and develop co-operation among airports of the world; mems: 554 mems operating more than 1,400 airports in 170 countries and territories; Chair. A. GHANEM AL-HAJRI; Dir-Gen. ROBERT J. AARONSON; publs *World Report* (6 a year), *Airport World Magazine*, *Policy Handbook*, reports.

Arab Air Carriers' Organization (AACO): POB 13-5468, Beirut, Lebanon; tel. (1) 861297; fax (1) 863168; e-mail info@aaco.org; internet www.aaco.org; f. 1965 to promote co-operation in the activities of Arab airline companies; mems: 22 Arab air carriers; Pres. Capt. ABDULKALEK AL-KADI (Yemen); Sec.-Gen. ABDUL WAHAB TEFFAHA; publs bulletins, reports and research documents.

Association of Asia Pacific Airlines: Kompleks Antarabangsa, 9th Floor, Jalan Sultan Ismail, 50250 Kuala Lumpur, Malaysia; tel. (3) 21455600; fax (3) 21452500; e-mail aapahdq@aapa.org.my; internet www.aapairlines.org; f. 1966 as Orient Airlines Asscn; present name adopted in 1997; as the trade association of the region's airlines, the AAPA aims to represent their interests and to provide a forum for all members to exchange information and views on matters of common concern; maintains international representation in Brussels, Belgium, and in Washington, DC, USA; mems: 17 scheduled international airlines (carrying approx. one-fifth of global passenger traffic and one-third of global cargo traffic); Dir-Gen. ANDREW J. HERDMAN; publs *Annual Report*, *Annual Statistical Report*, *Monthly International Statistics*, *Orient Aviation* (10 a year).

Association of European Airlines: 350 ave Louise, bte 4, 1050 Brussels, Belgium; tel. (2) 639-89-89; fax (2) 639-89-99; e-mail aea.secretariat@aca.be; internet www.aea.be; f. 1954 to carry out research on political, commercial, economic and technical aspects

INTERNATIONAL ORGANIZATIONS

of air transport; maintains statistical data bank; mems: 37 airlines; Chair. WOLFGANG MAYRHUBER (Germany); Sec.-Gen. ULRICH SCHULTE-STRATHAUS (Germany).

Baltic and International Maritime Council (BIMCO): Bagsvaerdvej 161, 2880 Bagsvaerd, Denmark; tel. 44-36-68-00; fax 44-36-68-68; e-mail mailbox@bimco.org; internet www.bimco.org; f. 1905 to unite shipowners and other persons and organizations connected with the shipping industry; mems: 2,500 in 123 countries, representing over 65% of world merchant tonnage; Pres. KNUD PONTOPPIDAN (Denmark); Sec.-Gen. CARSTEN MELCHIORS; publs *BIMCO Review* (annually), *BIMCO Bulletin* (6 a year), *Vessel* (CD-Rom), manuals.

Central Commission for the Navigation of the Rhine: Palais du Rhin, Place de la République, 67082 Strasbourg, France; tel. and fax 3-88-52-20-10; e-mail ccnr@ccr-zkr.org; internet www.ccr-zkr.org; f. 1815 to ensure free movement of traffic and standard river facilities for ships of all nations; draws up navigational rules; standardizes customs regulations; arbitrates in disputes involving river traffic; approves plans for river maintenance work; there is an administrative centre for social security for boatmen; mems: Belgium, France, Germany, Netherlands, Switzerland; Sec.-Gen. JEAN-MARIE WOEHRLING (France); publs guides, rules and directives (in French and German).

Danube Commission: Benczúr utca 25, 1068 Budapest, Hungary; tel. (1) 352-1835; fax (1) 352-1839; e-mail secretariat@danubecom-intern.org; internet www.danubecom-intern.org; f. 1948; supervises implementation of the Belgrade Convention on the Regime of Navigation on the Danube; approves projects for river maintenance; supervises a uniform system of traffic regulations on the whole navigable portion of the Danube and on river inspection; mems: Austria, Bulgaria, Croatia, Germany, Hungary, Moldova, Montenegro, Romania, Russia, Serbia, Slovakia, Ukraine; Pres. MILOVAN BOŽINOVIĆ; Dir-Gen. Dr ISTVÁN VALKÁR; publs *Basic Regulations for Navigation on the Danube*, *Hydrological Yearbook*, *Statistical Yearbook*, proceedings of sessions.

European Civil Aviation Conference (ECAC): 3 bis Villa Emile-Bergerat, 92522 Neuilly-sur-Seine Cédex, France; tel. 1-46-41-85-44; fax 1-46-24-18-18; e-mail secretariat@ecac-ceac.org; internet www.ecac-ceac.org; f. 1955; aims to promote the continued development of a safe, efficient and sustainable European air transport system; mems: 42 European states; Pres. LUIS FONSECA DE ALMEIDA; Exec. Sec. RAYMOND BENJAMIN.

European Organisation for the Safety of Air Navigation (EUROCONTROL): 96 rue de la Fusée, 1130 Brussels, Belgium; tel. (2) 729-90-11; fax (2) 729-90-44; e-mail epic@eurocontrol.int; internet www.eurocontrol.int; f. 1960; aims to develop a coherent and co-ordinated air traffic control system in Europe. A revised Convention was signed in June 1997, incorporating the following institutional structure: a General Assembly (known as the Commission in the transitional period), a Council (known as the Provisional Council) and an Agency under the supervision of the Director-General; there are directorates, covering human resources and finance matters and a general secretariat. A special organizational structure covers the management of the European Air Traffic Management Programme. EUROCONTROL also operates the Experimental Centre (at Brétigny-sur-Orge, France), the Institute of Air Navigation Services (in Luxembourg), the Central Route Charges Office, the Central Flow Management Unit (both in Brussels) and the Upper Area Control Centre (in Maastricht, Netherlands); mems: 36 European countries; Dir-Gen. DAVID MCMILLAN (United Kingdom).

Forum Train Europe FTE: Schanzenstrasse 5, 3000 Bern 65, Switzerland; fax 512201242; e-mail mailbox@forumtraineurope.org; internet www.forumtraineurope.org; f. 1923 as the European Passenger Train Time-Table Conference to arrange international passenger connections by rail and water; since 1997 concerned also with rail freight; mems: 95 mems from 35 European countries; Pres. HANS-JÜRG SPILLMANN; Sec.-Gen. PETER JÄGGY.

Institute of Air Transport: 103 rue la Boétie, 75008 Paris, France; tel. 1-43-59-38-68; fax 1-43-59-47-37; e-mail contac@ita-paris.com; internet www.ita-paris.com; f. 1945 as an international centre of research on economic, technical and policy aspects of air transport, and on the economy and sociology of transport and tourism; acts as economic and technical consultant in research requested by members on specific subjects; maintains a data bank, a library and a consultation and advice service; organizes training courses on air transport economics; mems: orgs involved in air transport, production and equipment, universities, banks, insurance companies, private individuals and government agencies in 79 countries; Dir-Gen. JACQUES PAVAUX; publs (in French and English), *ITA Press* (2 a month), *ITA Studies and Reports* (quarterly), *Aviation Industry Barometer* (quarterly).

Intergovernmental Organization for International Carriage by Rail: Gryphenhübeliweg 30, 3006 Bern, Switzerland; tel. 313591010; fax 313591011; e-mail info@otif.org; internet www.otif.org; f. 1893 as Central Office for International Carriage by Rail, present name adopted 1985; aims to establish and develop a uniform system of law governing the international carriage of passengers and goods by rail in member states; mems: 42 states; Sec.-Gen. STEFAN SCHIMMING; publ. *Bulletin des Transports Internationaux ferroviaires* (quarterly, in English, French and German).

International Air Transport Association (IATA): 33 route de l'Aéroport, CP 416, 1215 Geneva 15, Switzerland; tel. 227702525; fax 227983553; e-mail information@iata.org; internet www.iata.org; f. 1945 to represent and serve the airline industry; aims to promote safe, reliable and secure air services; to assist the industry to attain adequate levels of profitability while developing cost-effective operational standards; to promote the importance of the industry in global social and economic development; and to identify common concerns and represent the industry in addressing these at regional and international level; maintains regional offices in Amman, Brussels, Dakar, London, Nairobi, Santiago, Singapore and Washington, DC; mems: c. 270 airline companies; Dir-Gen. and CEO GIOVANNI BISIGNANI; publ. *Airlines International* (every 2 months).

IVR: Vasteland 12E, 3011 BL Rotterdam (POB 23210, 3001 KE Rotterdam), Netherlands; tel. (10) 4116070; fax (10) 4129091; e-mail info@ivr.nl; internet www.ivr.nl; f. 1947 for the classification of Rhine ships, the organization and publication of a Rhine ships register, the unification of general average rules, and the harmonization of European inland navigation law; mems: shipowners and asscns, insurers and asscns, shipbuilding engineers, average adjusters and others interested in Rhine traffic; Gen. Sec. T. K. HACKSTEINER.

International Association of Ports and Harbors (IAPH): 7F, New Pier Takeshiba South Tower, Minato-ku, Tokyo 105-0022, Japan; tel. (3) 5403-2770; fax (3) 5403-7651; e-mail info@iaphworldports.org; internet www.iaphworldports.org; f. 1955 to increase the efficiency of ports and harbours through the dissemination of information on port organization, management, administration, operation, development and promotion; encourages the growth of water-borne commerce; holds conference every two years; mems: 350 in 90 states; Pres. O. C. PHANG (Malaysia); Sec.-Gen. SATOSHI INOUE (Japan); publs *Ports and Harbors* (10 a year), *Membership Directory* (annually).

International Association of Public Transport: rue Sainte-Marie 6, Quai de Charbonnages, 1080 Brussels, Belgium; tel. (2) 673-61-00; fax (2) 660-10-72; e-mail hans.rat@uitp.com; internet www.uitp.com; f. 1885 to study all problems connected with the urban and regional public passenger transport industry; mems: 2,700 in 90 countries; Pres. ROBERTO CAVALIERI (Italy); Sec.-Gen. HANS RAT; publs *Public Transport International* (every 2 months), *EUExpress*, *Mobility News* (monthly, electronic), statistics reports.

International Chamber of Shipping: Carthusian Court, 12 Carthusian St, London, EC1M 6EZ, United Kingdom; tel. (20) 7417-8844; fax (20) 7417-8877; e-mail ics@marisec.org; internet www.marisec.org; f. 1921 to co-ordinate the views of the international shipping industry on matters of common interest, in the policy-making, technical and legal fields of shipping operations; mems: national asscns representing free-enterprise shipowners and operators in 32 countries; Sec.-Gen. A. J. MASON.

International Container Bureau: 167 rue de Courcelles, 75017 Paris, France; tel. 1-47-66-03-90; fax 1-47-66-08-91; e-mail bis@bic-code.org; internet www.bic-code.org; f. 1933 to group representatives of all means of transport and activities concerning containers, to promote combined door-to-door transport by the successive use of several means of transport, to examine and bring into effect administrative, technical and customs advances, and to centralize data on behalf of mems; mems: 1,200; Sec.-Gen. JEAN REY; publs *Containers Bulletin*, *Containers Bic-Code* (annually).

International Federation of Freight Forwarders Associations (FIATA): Schaffhauserstr. 104, 8152 Glattbrugg, Switzerland; tel. 432116500; fax 432116565; e-mail info@fiata.com; internet www.fiata.com; f. 1926 to protect and represent its members at international level; mems: 94 organizations and nearly 5,000 individual members in 150 countries; Pres. MANFRED BOES (Germany); Dir MARCO A. SANGALETTI; publ. *FIATA Review* (every 2 months).

International Rail Transport Committee (Comité international des transports ferroviaires—CIT): Weltpoststr. 20, 3015 Bern, Switzerland; tel. 313500190; fax 313500199; e-mail info@cit-rail.org; internet www.cit-rail.org; f. 1902 for the development of international law relating to railway transport, on the basis of the Convention concerning International Carriage by Rail (COTIF) and its Appendices (CIV, CIM), and for the adoption of standard rules on other questions relating to international transport law; mems: 102 transport undertakings in 37 countries; Pres. Prof. RAINER FREISE; Sec. THOMAS LEIMGRUBER (Switzerland).

INTERNATIONAL ORGANIZATIONS

International Railway Congress Association: Section 10, 85 rue de France, 1060 Brussels, Belgium; tel. (2) 520-78-31; fax (2) 525-40-84; e-mail secretariat@aiccf.org; internet www.aiccf.org; f. 1885 to facilitate the progress and development of railways; mems: governments, railway administrations, national and international organizations; Pres. E. SCHOUPPE; Sec.-Gen. A. MARTENS; publ. *Rail International* (monthly).

International Road Federation (IRF): Madison Place, 500 Montgomery St, 5th Floor, Alexandria, Virginia 22314, USA; Geneva Office: 2 chemin de Blandonnet 1214, Vernier, Geneva, Switzerland; tel. (Virginia) (703) 535-1001; fax (Virginia) (703) 535-1007; e-mail info@irfnet.org; internet www.irfnet.org; tel. (Geneva) 223060260; fax (Geneva) 223060270; f. 1948 to encourage the development and improvement of highways and highway transportation; organizes IRF world and regional meetings; mems: 70 national road asscns and 500 individual firms and industrial asscns; Dir-Gen. (Washington) C. PATRICK SANKEY; Dir-Gen. (Geneva) TONY PEARCE; publs *World Road Statistics* (annually), *World Highways* (8 a year).

International Road Safety Organization (La prevention routière internationale—PRI): Estrada da Luz, 90-1°, 1600-160 Lisbon, Portugal; tel. (21) 7222230; fax (21) 7222232; e-mail info@lapri.org; internet www.lapri.org; f. 1959 for exchange of ideas and material on road safety; organizes international action and congresses; assists non-member countries; mems: 74 national organizations; Pres. JOSÉ MIGUEL TRIGOSO (Portugal); Sec.-Gen. MARTINE PETERS; publ. *Newsletter* (6 a year).

International Road Transport Union (IRU): Centre International, 3 rue de Varembé, BP 44, 1211 Geneva 20, Switzerland; tel. 229182700; fax 229182741; e-mail iru@iru.org; internet www.iru.org; f. 1948 to study all problems of road transport, to advocate harmonisation and simplification of regulations relating to road transport, and to promote the use of road transport for passengers and goods; represents, promotes and upholds the interests of the road transport industry at an international level; mems: 180 national asscns in 70 countries; Sec.-Gen. MARTIN MARMY.

International Shipping Federation: Carthusian Court, 12 Carthusian St, London, EC1M 6EZ, United Kingdom; tel. (20) 7417-8844; fax (20) 7417-8877; e-mail isf@marisec.org; internet www.marisec.org; f. 1909 to consider all personnel questions affecting the interests of shipowners; responsible for Shipowners' Group at conferences of the International Labour Organisation; represents shipowners at International Maritime Organization; mems: national shipowners' organizations in 32 countries; Pres. R. WESTFAL-LARSON (Norway); Sec.-Gen. J. C. S. HORROCKS; publs conference papers, guidelines and training records.

International Transport Forum: 2 rue André Pascal, 75775 Paris Cédex 16, France; tel. 1-45-24-97-10; fax 1-45-24-97-42; e-mail itf.contact@oecd.org; internet www.internationaltransportforum.org; f. 2006 by a decision of the European Conference of Ministers of Transport (f. 1953) to broaden membership of the org; aims to create a safe, sustainable, efficient, integrated transport system; provides an annual Forum in Liepzig, Germany; holds round tables, seminars and symposia; shares Secretariat staff with OECD; mems: 51 member countries; Sec.-Gen. JACK SHORT; publs *Annual Report*, various statistical publications and surveys.

International Union for Inland Navigation: 7 quai du Général Koenig, 67085 Strasbourg Cédex, France; tel. 3-88-36-28-44; fax 3-88-37-04-82; f. 1952 to promote the interests of inland waterways carriers; mems: national waterways organizations of Austria, Belgium, France, Germany, Italy, Luxembourg, Netherlands, Switzerland; Pres. P. GRULOIS (Belgium); Sec. M. RUSCHER; publs annual and occasional reports.

International Union of Railways (Union internationale des chemins de fer—UIC): 16 rue Jean-Rey, 75015 Paris, France; tel. 1-44-49-20-20; fax 1-44-49-20-29; e-mail communication@uic.asso.fr; internet www.uic.asso.fr; f. 1922 for the harmonization of railway operations and the development of international rail transport; aims to ensure international interoperability of the rail system; compiles information on economic, management and technical aspects of railways; co-ordinates research and collaborates with industry and the EU; organizes international conferences; mems: 191 railways in 87 countries; Pres. K. C. JENA; Chief Exec. LUC ALIADIÈRE; publs *International Railway Statistics* (annually), *Activities Reports*, *UIC News* (newsletter).

Northern Shipowners' Defence Club (Nordisk Skibsrederforening): Kristinelundv. 22, POB 3033, Elisenberg, 0207 Oslo, Norway; tel. 22-13-56-00; fax 22-43-00-35; e-mail post@nordisk.no; internet www.nordisk.no; f. 1889 to assist members in disputes over charter parties, contracts and sale and purchase, taking the necessary legal steps on behalf of members and bearing the cost of such claims; mems: mainly Finnish, Swedish and Norwegian and some non-Scandinavian shipowners, representing about 1,800 ships and drilling rigs with gross tonnage of about 50m.; Man. Dir GEORG SCHEEL; Chair. NILS P. DYVIK; publ. *A Law Report of Scandinavian Maritime Cases* (annually).

Organisation for the Collaboration of Railways: Hozà 63–67, 00681 Warsaw, Poland; tel. (22) 6573654; fax (22) 6219417; e-mail osjd@osjd.org.pl; internet www.osjd.org; f. 1956; aims to improve standards and co-operation in railway traffic between countries of Europe and Asia; promotes co-operation on issues relating to traffic policy and economic and environmental aspects of railway traffic; ensures enforcement of a number of rail agreements; aims to elaborate and standardize general principles for international transport law. Conference of Ministers of mem. countries meets annually; Conference of Gen. Dirs of Railways meets at least once a year; mems: ministries of transport of 27 countries world-wide; Chair. TADEUSZ SZOZDA; publ. *OSShD Journal* (every 2 months, in Chinese, German and Russian).

Pan American Railway Congress Association (Asociación del Congreso Panamericano de Ferrocarriles): Av. Dr. José María Ramos Mejía 1302, Planta Baja, 1104 Buenos Aires, Argentina; tel. (11) 4315-3445; fax (11) 4312-3834; e-mail acpf@acpf.com.ar; internet www.acpf.com.ar; f. 1907, present title adopted 1941; aims to promote the development and progress of railways in the American continent; holds Congresses every three years; mems: government representatives, railway enterprises and individuals in 21 countries; Pres. LORENZO PEPE; Gen. Sec. FRANCISCO E. STRUZKAI; publ. *Boletín ACPF* (5 a year).

Union of European Railway Industries (UNIFE): POB 11, 221 ave Louise, 1050 Brussels, Belgium; tel. (2) 626-12-60; fax (2) 626-12-61; e-mail mail@unife.org; internet www.unife.org; f. 1975 to represent companies concerned in the manufacture of railway equipment in Europe to European and international organizations; mems: 140 companies in 14 countries; Chair. PHILIPPE MELLIER; Dir-Gen. DREWIN NIEUWENHUIS.

World Airlines Clubs Association (WACA): c/o IATA, 800 Pl. Victoria, POB 113, Montréal, Québec, QC H4Z 1M1, Canada; tel. (514) 874-0202; fax (514) 874-1753; e-mail info@waca.org; internet www.waca.org; f. 1966; holds a General Assembly annually, regional meetings, international events and sports tournaments; mems: clubs in 38 countries; Man. KEITH MILLER; publs *WACA Contact*, *WACA World News*, *Annual Report*.

Youth and Students

AIESEC International: Teilingerstraat 126, 3032 Rotterdam, Netherlands; tel. (10) 4434383; fax (10) 2651386; e-mail info@ai.aiesec.org; internet www.aiesec.org; f. 1948 as International Association of Students in Economics and Management; works to develop leadership skills and socio-economic and international understanding among young people, through exchange programmes and related educational activities; mems: 50,000 students in more than 800 higher education institutions in c. 90 countries and territories; Pres. BRODIE BOLAND; publ. *Annual Report*.

Asia Students Association: 353 Shanghai St, 14/F, Kowloon, Hong Kong; tel. 23880515; fax 27825535; e-mail asasec@netvigator.com; f. 1969; aims to promote students' solidarity in struggling for democracy, self-determination, peace, justice and liberation; conducts campaigns, training of activists, and workshops on human rights and other issues of importance; there are Student Commissions for Peace, Education and Human Rights; mems: 40 national or regional student unions in 25 countries and territories; Secretariat LINA CABAERO (Philippines), STEVEN GAN (Malaysia), CHOW WING-HANG (Hong Kong); publs *Movement News* (monthly), *ASA News* (quarterly).

Council on International Educational Exchange (CIEE): 7 Custom House St, 3rd Floor, Portland, ME 04101, USA; tel. (207) 553-7600; fax (207) 553-7699; e-mail info@ciee.org; internet www.ciee.org; f. 1947; issues International Student Identity Card entitling holders to discounts and basic insurance; arranges overseas work and study programmes for students; co-ordinates summer work programme in the USA for foreign students; administers programmes for teachers and other professionals and sponsors conferences on educational exchange; operates a voluntary service programme; mems: 307 colleges, universities and international educational organizations; Chair. CHARLES PING; publs include *Work, Study, Travel Abroad: The Whole World Handbook*, *Update*, *Volunteer!*, *High-School Student's Guide to Study, Travel and Adventure Abroad*.

European Law Students' Association (ELSA): 239 blvd Général Jacques, 1050 Brussels, Belgium; tel. (2) 646-26-26; fax (2) 646-29-23; e-mail elsa@brutele.be; internet www.elsa.org; f. 1981 to foster mutual understanding and promote social responsibility of law students and young laywers; mems: c. 30,000 students and lawyers in more that 200 law faculties in 35 countries; publs *ELSA Law Review*, *Legal Studies in Europe*.

European Students' Forum (Association des Etats Généraux des Etudiants de l'Europe—AEGEE): 15 rue Nestor de Tière, 1030

INTERNATIONAL ORGANIZATIONS
Youth and Students

Schaarbeek/Brussels, Belgium; tel. (2) 245-23-00; fax (2) 245-62-60; e-mail headoffice@aegee.org; internet www.karl.aegee.org; promotes cross-border communication, co-operation and integration between students; fosters inter-cultural exchange; holds specialized conferences; mems: 17,000 students in 260 university cities in 42 countries; Sec.-Gen. BOJANA BRANKOV.

European Youth Forum: 120 rue Joseph II, 1000 Brussels, Belgium; tel. (2) 230-64-90; fax (2) 230-21-23; e-mail youthforum@youthforum.org; internet www.youthforum.org; f. 1996; represents and advocates for the needs and interests of all young people in Europe; promotes their active participation in democratic processes, as well as understanding and respect for human rights; consults with international organizations and governments on issues relevant to young people; mems: 90 national youth councils and international non-governmental youth orgs; Pres. BETTINA SCHWARZMAYR; Sec.-Gen. DIOGO PINTO.

International Association for the Exchange of Students for Technical Experience (IAESTE): e-mail info@iaeste.org; internet www.iaeste.org; f. 1948; mems: 63 national committees; publs *Activity Report, Annual Report*.

International Association of Dental Students (IADS): c/o FDI World Dental Federation, 13 chemin du Levant l'Avent Centre, 01210 Ferney-Voltaire, France; tel. 4-50-40-50-50; fax 4-50-40-55-55; e-mail taylanakca@hotmail.com; internet www.iads-web.org; f. 1951 to represent dental students and their opinions internationally, to promote dental student exchanges and international congresses; mems: 60,000 students in 45 countries, 15,000 corresponding mems; Pres. ANDREA VEITOVA (Czech Republic); Sec. TAYLAN AKÇA (Turkey); publ. *IADS Newsletter* (3 a year).

International Federation of Medical Students' Associations (IFMSA): c/o WMA, BP 63, 01212 Ferney-Voltaire Cedex, France; fax 4-50-40-59-37; e-mail gs@ifmsa.org; internet www.ifmsa.org; f. 1951 to promote international co-operation in professional treatment and the achievement of humanitarian ideals; provides forum for medical students; maintains standing committees on professional exchange, electives exchange, medical education, public health, refugees and AIDS; organizes annual General Assembly; mems: 94 asscns; Sec.-Gen. ANAS EID; publ. *IFMSA Newsletter* (quarterly).

International Pharmaceutical Students' Federation (IPSF): POB 84200, 2508 AE The Hague, Netherlands; tel. (70) 3021992; fax (70) 3021999; e-mail ipsf@ipsf.org; internet www.ipsf.org; f. 1949 to study and promote the interests of pharmaceutical students and to encourage international co-operation; mems: 46 full mems from national organizations and 27 mems in assoc. from national or local organizations; Pres. KATJA HAKKARAINEN; Sec.-Gen. GEORGINA GÁL; publ. *IPSF News Bulletin* (2 a year).

International Scout and Guide Fellowship (ISGF): 38 ave de la Porte de Hal, 1060 Brussels, Belgium; tel. and fax (2) 511-46-95; e-mail isgf-aisg@skynet.be; internet www.isgf.org; f. 1953 to help adult scouts and guides to keep alive the spirit of the Scout and Guide Promise and Laws in their own lives and to bring that spirit into the communities in which they live and work; promotes liaison and co-operation between national organizations for adult scouts and guides; encourages the founding of an organization in any country where no such organization exists; mems: 90,000 in 59 mem. states; Chair. of Cttee MARTINE LEVY; Sec.-Gen. FAOUZIA KCHOUK.

International Union of Students: POB 58, 17th November St, 110 01 Prague 01, Czech Republic; tel. and fax 271731257; e-mail ius@cfs-fcee.ca; internet www.stud.uni-hannover.de/gruppen/ius; f. 1946 to defend the rights and interests of students and strive for peace, disarmament, the eradication of illiteracy and of all forms of discrimination; operates research centre, sports and cultural centre and student travel bureau; activities include conferences, meetings, solidarity campaigns, relief projects; awards 30–40 scholarships annually; mems: 152 orgs from 114 countries; Pres. JOSEF SKALA; Vice-Pres. MARTA HUBIČKOVÁ; Gen. Sec. GIORGOS MICHAELIDES (Cyprus); publs *World Student News* (quarterly), *IUS Newsletter*, *Student Life* (quarterly), *DE—Democratization of Education* (quarterly).

International Young Christian Workers: 4 ave G. Rodenbach, 1030 Brussels, Belgium; tel. (2) 242-18-11; fax (2) 242-48-00; e-mail postmaster@jociycw.net; internet www.jociycw.net; f. 1925, on the inspiration of the Priest-Cardinal Joseph Cardijn; aims to educate young workers to take on present and future responsibilities in their commitment to the working class, and to gain personal fulfilment through their actions; Pres. JOSÉE DESROSIERS (Canada); Sec.-Gen. ANNA CIROCCO (Australia); publs *International INFO* (3 a year), *IYCW Bulletin* (quarterly).

International Youth Hostel Federation: Gate House, 2nd Floor, Fretherne Rd, Welwyn Garden City, Herts., AL8 6RD, United Kingdom; tel. (1707) 324170; fax (1707) 323980; e-mail iyhf@hihostels.com; internet www.hihostels.com; f. 1932; facilitates international travel by members of the various youth hostel asscns;

advises and helps in the formation of youth hostel asscns in countries where no such organizations exist; records over 35m. overnight stays annually in around 4,000 youth hostels; mems: 60 national asscns with over 3.2m. national members and 1m. international guest members; 12 associated national orgns; Pres. Dr HARISH SAXENA (India); Sec.-Gen. ULRICH BUNJES (Germany); publs *Annual Report, Guidebook on World Hostels* (annually), *Manual, News Bulletin*.

Junior Chamber International (JCI), Inc.: 15645 Olive blvd, Chesterfield, MO 63017, USA; tel. (636) 449-3100; fax (636) 449-3107; e-mail ekodama@jci.cc; internet www.jci.cc; f. 1944 to encourage and advance international understanding and goodwill; aims to solve civic problems by arousing civic consciousness; Junior Chamber organizations throughout the world provide opportunities for leadership training and for the discussion of social, economic and cultural questions; mems: 200,000 in more than 100 countries; Sec.-Gen. EDSON KODAMA (Brazil); publ. *JCI News* (quarterly, in English and more than six other languages).

Latin American and Caribbean Confederation of Young Men's Christian Associations (Confederación Latinoamericana y del Caribe de Asociaciones Cristianas de Jóvenes): Culpina 272, 1406 Buenos Aires, Argentina; tel. (11) 4373-4156; fax (11) 4374-4408; e-mail clacj@wamani.apc.org; f. 1914; aims to encourage the moral, spiritual, intellectual, social and physical development of young men; to strengthen the work of national Asscns and to sponsor the establishment of new Asscns; mems: affiliated YMCAs in 25 countries (comprising 350,000 individuals); Pres. GERARDO VITUREIRA (Uruguay); Gen. Sec. MARCO ANTONIO HOCHSCHEIT (Brazil); publs *Diecisiete/21* (bulletin), *Carta Abierta, Brief*, technical articles and other studies.

Pan-African Youth Movement (Mouvement pan-africain de la jeunesse): 19 rue Debbih Chérif, BP 72, Didouch Mourad, 16000 Algiers, Algeria; tel. and fax (2) 71-64-71; f. 1962; aims to encourage the participation of African youth in socio-economic and political development and democratization; organizes conferences and seminars, youth exchanges and youth festivals; mems: youth groups in 52 African countries and liberation movements; publ. *MPJ News* (quarterly).

WFUNA Youth: c/o WFUNA, 1 United Nations Plaza, Room DC1-1177, New York, NY 10017, USA; tel. (212) 963-5610; fax (212) 963-0447; e-mail coordinating.committee@gmail.com; internet www.wfuna-youth.org; f. 1948 by the World Federation of United Nations Associations (WFUNA) as the International Youth and Student Movement for the United Nations (ISMUN), independent since 1949; an international non-governmental organization of students and young people dedicated especially to supporting the principles embodied in the United Nations Charter and Universal Declaration of Human Rights; encourages constructive action in building economic, social and cultural equality and in working for national independence, social justice and human rights on a world-wide scale; maintains regional offices in Austria, France, Ghana, Panama and the USA; mems: asscns in over 100 mem. states of the UN.

World Alliance of Young Men's Christian Associations: 12 Clos. Belmont, 1208 Geneva, Switzerland; tel. 228495100; fax 228495110; e-mail office@ymca.int; internet www.ymca.int; f. 1855; mems: federation of YMCAs in 124 countries with a membership of over 45 m.; Pres. MARTIN MEIßNER (Germany) (2006–10); Sec.-Gen. Dr SHAHA BARTHOLOMEW; publ. *YMCA World* (quarterly).

World Assembly of Youth: World Youth Complex, Lebuh Ayer Keroh, Ayer Keroh, 75450 Melaka, Malaysia; tel. (6) 2321871; fax (6) 2327271; e-mail info@way.org.my; internet www.way.org.my; f. 1949 as co-ordinating body for youth councils and organizations; organizes conferences, training courses and practical development projects; has consultative status with the UN Economic and Social Council; mems: 120 mem. orgs; Pres. Datuk ALI RUSTAM; Sec.-Gen. EDIOLA PASHOLLARI; publs *WAY Information* (every 2 months), *Youth Roundup* (monthly), *WAY Forum* (quarterly).

World Association of Girl Guides and Girl Scouts (WAGGGS): World Bureau, Olave Centre, 12C Lyndhurst Rd, London, NW3 5PQ, United Kingdom; tel. (20) 7794-1181; fax (20) 7431-3764; e-mail wagggs@wagggsworld.org; internet www.wagggsworld.org; f. 1928 to enable girls and young women to develop their full potential as responsible citizens, and to support friendship and mutual understanding among girls and young women world-wide; World Conference meets every three years; mems: about 10m. individuals in 144 orgs; Chair. World Board ELSPETH HENDERSON; Dir World Bureau MARY MCPHAIL; publs *Triennial Review, Annual Report, Trefoil Round the World* (every 3 years), *Our World News* (quarterly).

World Council of Service Clubs: c/o Miguel Grullón, ave Abraham Lincoln 295, Edif. Alico, 3rd Floor, Santo Domingo, Dominican Republic; e-mail mgrullon@usa.net; internet www.woco.info; f. 1946 to provide a means for the exchange of information and news, with the aim of furthering international understanding and co-operation; aims to create in young people a sense of civic responsibility; works to facilitate the extension of service clubs; mems: over 3,000 clubs in 83 countries; Chair. MIGUEL GRULLÓN.

World Federation of Democratic Youth (WFDY): 1139 Budapest, Frangepán u. 16, Hungary; tel. (1) 350-2202; fax (1) 350-1204; e-mail wfdy@wfdy.org; internet www.wfdy.org; f. 1945; promotes the unity, co-operation, organized action, solidarity and exchange of information and experiences of work and struggle among the progressive youth forces; campaigns against imperialism, fascism, colonialism, exploitation and war and for peace, internationalist solidarity, social progress and youth rights under the slogans Youth unite! and Forward for lasting peace!; mems: 152 members in 102 countries; publ. *World Youth.*

World Organization of the Scout Movement: CP 91, 1211 Geneva 4 Plainpalais, Switzerland; tel. 227051010; fax 227051020; e-mail worldbureau@world.scout.org; internet www.scout.org; f. 1922 to promote unity and understanding of scouting throughout the world; to develop good citizenship among young people by forming their characters for service, co-operation and leadership; and to provide aid and advice to members and potential member asscns. The World Scout Bureau (Geneva) has regional offices in Chile, Egypt, Kenya, the Philippines, Russia, Senegal, South Africa and Ukraine (the European Region has its offices in Brussels and Geneva); mems: over 28m. in 215 countries and territories; Sec.-Gen. EDUARDO MISSONI (Italy); publ. *Worldinfo Triennial Report.*

World Union of Jewish Students (WUJS): POB 7114, 58 King George St, Jerusalem 91070, Israel; tel. (2) 6251682; fax (2) 6251688; e-mail office@wujs.org.il; internet www.wujs.org.il; f. 1924 (with Albert Einstein as its first President); promotes dialogue and co-operation amongst Jewish university students world-wide; divided into six regions; organizes Congress every year; mems: 52 national unions representing over 1.5m. students; Chair. TAMAR SHCHORY; publs *The Student Activist Yearbook, Heritage and History, Forum, WUJS Report.*

World Young Women's Christian Association (World YWCA): 16 Ancienne Route, 1218 Grand-Saconnex, Geneva, Switzerland; tel. 229296040; fax 229296044; e-mail worldoffice@worldywca.org; internet www.worldywca.org; f. 1894; global movement which aims to empower women and girls to change their lives and communities; works to achieve social and economic justice through grassroots development and global advocacy; addresses critical issues affecting women, such as HIV and AIDS and violence; promotes the sharing of human and financial resources among member asscns; mems: in 122 countries; Pres. SUSAN BRENNAN; Gen. Sec. NYARADZAI GUMBONZVANDA; publs *Annual Report, Common Concern, Week of Prayer* (booklet), other reports.

Youth for Development and Co-operation (YDC): Rijswijkstrasse 141, 1062 HN Amsterdam, Netherlands; tel. (20) 6142510; fax (20) 6175545; e-mail ydc@geo2.geonet.de; aims to strengthen youth structures promoting co-operation between young people in the industrialized and developing worlds, in order to achieve development that is environmentally sustainable and socially just; holds seminars, conferences and campaigns on issues related to youth and development; mems: 51 orgs; Sec.-Gen. B. AUER; publ. *FLASH Newsletter* (irregular).

PART TWO
Afghanistan–Jordan

PART TWO

Afghanistan, Jordan

AFGHANISTAN

Introductory Survey

Location, Climate, Language, Religion, Flag, Capital

The Islamic Republic of Afghanistan is a land-locked country in south-western Asia. It is bordered by Turkmenistan, Uzbekistan and Tajikistan to the north, Iran to the west, the People's Republic of China to the north-east and Pakistan to the east and south. The climate varies sharply between the highlands and lowlands; the temperature in the south-west in summer reaches 49°C (120°F), but in the winter, in the Hindu Kush mountains of the north-east, it falls to −26°C (−15°F). Of the many languages spoken in Afghanistan, the principal two are Pashto (Pakhto) and Dari (a dialect of Farsi or Iranian). The majority of Afghans are Muslims of the Sunni sect; there are also minority groups of Shi'a Muslims, Hindus, Sikhs and Jews. The state flag (proportions 1 by 2) has three equal vertical stripes from hoist to fly of black, red and green, bearing in the centre in white and red the state arms and an inscription reading 'There is no God but Allah, and Muhammad is his Prophet, and Allah is Great', in Arabic. The Islamic date 1298 appears under the inscription. The flag was first introduced in 1928, modified in 1964, and banned following the coup in 1978. The only difference featured in the current flag, which was introduced in June 2002 following the collapse of the Taliban, is the inscription bearing the word 'Afghanistan'. The capital is Kabul.

Recent History

The last King of Afghanistan, Mohammad Zahir Shah, reigned from 1933 to 1973. His country was neutral during both World Wars and became a staunch advocate of non-alignment. In 1953 the King's cousin, Lt-Gen. Sardar Mohammad Daoud Khan, was appointed Prime Minister and, securing aid from the USSR, initiated a series of economic plans for the modernization of the country. In 1963 Gen. Daoud resigned and Dr Mohammad Yusuf became the first Prime Minister not of royal birth. Dr Yusuf introduced a new democratic Constitution in the following year, which combined Western ideas with Islamic religious and political beliefs; the King, however, did not permit political parties to operate. Afghanistan made little progress under succeeding Prime Ministers.

In July 1973, while King Zahir was in Italy, the monarchy was overthrown by a coup, in which the main figure was the former Prime Minister, Gen. Daoud. The 1964 Constitution was abolished and Afghanistan was declared a republic. Daoud renounced his royal titles and took office as Head of State, Prime Minister and Minister of Foreign Affairs and Defence.

A Loya Jirga (Grand National Council), appointed from among tribal elders by provincial governors, was convened in January 1977 and adopted a new Constitution, providing for presidential government and a one-party state. Daoud was elected to continue as President for six years and the Loya Jirga was then dissolved. In March President Daoud formed a new civilian Government, nominally ending military rule. However, during 1977 there was growing discontent with Daoud, especially within the armed forces, and in April 1978 a coup, known (from the month) as the 'Saur Revolution', ousted the President, who was killed with several members of his family. Nur Mohammad Taraki, the imprisoned leader of the formerly banned People's Democratic Party of Afghanistan (PDPA), was released and installed as President of the Revolutionary Council and Prime Minister. The country was renamed the Democratic Republic of Afghanistan, the year-old Constitution was abolished and no political parties other than the communist PDPA were allowed to function. Afghanistan's already close relations with the USSR were further strengthened. However, opposition to the new regime led to armed insurrection, particularly by fiercely traditionalist Islamist rebel tribesmen (known, collectively, as the *mujahidin*), in almost all provinces, and the flight of thousands of refugees to Pakistan and Iran. In spite of purges of the army and civil service, Taraki's position became increasingly insecure, and in September 1979 he was ousted by Hafizullah Amin, an erstwhile Deputy Prime Minister and Minister of Foreign Affairs. Amin's imposition of rigorous communist policies proved unsuccessful and unpopular. In December he was killed in a coup, which was supported by the entry into Afghanistan of about 80,000 combat troops from the USSR. This incursion by Soviet armed forces into a traditionally non-aligned neighbouring country aroused world-wide condemnation. Babrak Karmal, a former Deputy Prime Minister under Taraki, was installed as the new Head of State, having been flown into Kabul by a Soviet aircraft from virtual exile in Eastern Europe.

Riots, strikes and inter-factional strife and purges continued into 1980 and 1981. Sultan Ali Keshtmand, hitherto a Deputy Prime Minister, replaced Karmal as Prime Minister in June 1981. In the same month the regime launched the National Fatherland Front (NFF), incorporating the PDPA and other organizations, with the aim of promoting national unity. Despite a series of government reorganizations carried out in the early 1980s, the PDPA regime failed to win widespread popular support. Consequently, the Government attempted to broaden the base of its support: in April 1985 it summoned a Loya Jirga, which ratified a new Constitution for Afghanistan, and during the second half of 1985 and the first half of 1986 elections were held for new local government organs (it was claimed that 60% of those elected were non-party members) and several non-party members were appointed to high-ranking government posts (including the chairmanship of the NFF).

In May 1986 Dr Najibullah (the former head of the state security service, KHAD) succeeded Karmal as General Secretary of the PDPA. Karmal retained the lesser post of President of the Revolutionary Council. In the same month Najibullah announced the formation of a collective leadership comprising himself, Karmal and Prime Minister Keshtmand. In November, however, Karmal was relieved of all party and government posts. Haji Muhammad Chamkani, formerly First Vice-President (and a non-PDPA member), became Acting President of the Revolutionary Council, pending the introduction of a new constitution and the establishment of a permanent legislature.

In December 1986 an extraordinary plenum of the PDPA Central Committee approved a policy of national reconciliation, involving negotiations with opposition groups, and the proposed formation of a coalition government of national unity. In early January 1987 a Supreme Extraordinary Commission for National Reconciliation, led by Abd ar-Rahim Hatif (the Chairman of the National Committee of the NFF), was formed to conduct the negotiations. The NFF was renamed the National Front (NF), and became a separate organization from the PDPA. The new policy of reconciliation won some support from former opponents, but the seven-party *mujahidin* alliance (Ittehad-i-Islami Afghan Mujahidin, Islamic Union of Afghan Mujahidin—IUAM), which was based in Peshawar, Pakistan, refused to observe the cease-fire or to participate in negotiations, while continuing to demand a complete and unconditional Soviet withdrawal from Afghanistan.

In July 1987, as part of the process of national reconciliation, several important developments occurred: a law permitting the formation of other political parties (according to certain provisions) was introduced; Najibullah announced that the PDPA would be prepared to share power with representatives of opposition groups in the event of the formation of a coalition government of national unity; and the draft of a new Constitution was approved by the Presidium of the Revolutionary Council. The main innovations incorporated in the draft Constitution were: the formation of a multi-party political system, under the auspices of the NF; the formation of a bicameral legislature, called the Meli Shura (National Assembly), composed of a Sena (Senate) and a Wolasi Jirga (House of Representatives); the granting of a permanent constitutional status to the PDPA; the bestowal of unlimited power on the President, who was to hold office for seven years; and the reversion of the name of the country from the Democratic Republic to the Republic of Afghanistan. A Loya Jirga ratified the new Constitution in November.

Meanwhile, a considerable proportion of the successful candidates in local elections held throughout the country in August 1987 were reported to be non-PDPA members. On 30 September Najibullah was unanimously elected as President of the Revolutionary Council, and Haji Muhammad Chamkani resumed his former post as First Vice-President. In order to strengthen his position, Najibullah ousted all the remaining supporters of former President Karmal from the Central Committee and Politburo of the PDPA in October. In the following month a Loya Jirga unanimously elected Najibullah as President of the State.

In April 1988 elections were held to both houses of the new National Assembly, which replaced the Revolutionary Council. Although the elections were boycotted by the *mujahidin*, the Government left vacant 50 of the 234 seats in the House of Representatives, and a small number of seats in the Senate, in the hope that the guerrillas would abandon their armed struggle and present their own representatives to participate in the new administration. The PDPA itself won only 46 seats in the House of Representatives, but was guaranteed support from the NF, which secured 45, and from the various newly recognized left-wing parties, which won a total of 24 seats. In May Dr Muhammad Hasan Sharq (a non-PDPA member and a Deputy Prime Minister since June 1987) replaced Keshtmand as Prime Minister, and in June a new Council of Ministers was appointed.

On 18 February 1989, following the completion of the withdrawal of Soviet troops from Afghanistan (see below), Najibullah implemented a government reorganization, involving the replacement of non-communist ministers with loyal PDPA members. On the same day, Prime Minister Sharq (who had been one of the main promoters of the policy of national reconciliation) resigned from his post and was replaced by Keshtmand. Following the declaration of a state of emergency by Najibullah (citing allegations of repeated violations of the Geneva accords by Pakistan and the USA—see below) on 19 February, a PDPA-dominated 20-member Supreme Council for the Defence of the Homeland was established. The Council, which was headed by President Najibullah and was composed of ministers, members of the PDPA Politburo and high-ranking military figures, assumed full responsibility for the country's economic, political and military policies (although the Council of Ministers continued to function).

In early March 1990 the Minister of Defence, Lt-Gen. Shahnawaz Tanay, with the alleged support of the air force and some divisions of the army, led an unsuccessful coup attempt against Najibullah's Government. Najibullah subsequently enacted thorough purges of PDPA and army leaders and decided to revert rapidly to some form of constitutional civilian government. On 20 May the state of emergency was lifted; the Supreme Council for the Defence of the Homeland was disbanded; and a new Council of Ministers, under the premiership of Fazle Haq Khalikyar, was appointed. At the end of the month a Loya Jirga was convened in Kabul, which ratified constitutional amendments, greatly reducing Afghanistan's socialist orientation; ending the PDPA's and the NF's monopoly over executive power and paving the way for fully democratic elections; introducing greater political and press freedom; encouraging the development of the private sector and further foreign investment; and lessening the role of the State and affording greater prominence to Islam. The extensive powers of the presidency were, however, retained. In addition, in late June the PDPA changed its name to the Homeland Party (HP—Hizb-i Watan), and dissolved the Politburo and the Central Committee, replacing them with an Executive Board and a Central Council, respectively. The party adopted a new programme, of which the hallmark was hostility to ideology. Najibullah was unanimously elected as Chairman of the HP. An important factor in Najibullah's decision to continue with, and to extend, the process of national reconciliation was the fact that the USSR's own internal problems meant that the Soviet administration was unwilling to sustain, for much longer, the supplies of weapons, goods and credits that were helping to support the Kabul regime.

Fighting between the *mujahidin* and Afghan army units had begun in the eastern provinces after the 1978 coup and was aggravated by the implementation of unpopular social and economic reforms by the new administrations. The Afghan army relied heavily upon Soviet military aid in the form of weapons, equipment and expertise, but morale and resources were severely affected by defections to the rebels' ranks: numbers fell from around 80,000 men in 1978 to about 40,000 in 1985. During 1984–89 the guerrilla groups, which had been poorly armed at first, received ever-increasing support (both military and financial) from abroad, notably from the USA (which began to supply them with sophisticated anti-aircraft weapons in 1986), the United Kingdom and the People's Republic of China. Despite the Government's decision to seal the border with Pakistan, announced in September 1985, and the strong presence of Soviet forces there, foreign weapons continued to reach the guerrillas via Pakistan. Many of the guerrillas established bases in the North-West Frontier Province of Pakistan (notably in the provincial capital, Peshawar). From 1985 the fighting intensified, especially in areas close to the border between Afghanistan and Pakistan. There were many violations of the border, involving shelling, bombing and incursions into neighbouring airspace. The general pattern of the war, however, remained the same: the regime held the main towns and a few strategic bases, and relied on bombing of both military and civilian targets, and occasional attacks in force, together with conciliatory measures such as the provision of funds for local development, while the rebel forces dominated rural areas and were able to cause serious disruption.

The civil war brought famine to parts of Afghanistan, and there was a mass movement of population from the countryside to Kabul, and of refugees to Pakistan and Iran. In mid-1988 the office of the UN High Commissioner for Refugees (UNHCR) estimated the number of Afghan refugees in Pakistan at 3.15m., and the number in Iran at 2.35m. Supply convoys were often prevented from reaching the cities, owing to the repeated severing of major road links by the guerrillas. Kabul, in particular, began to suffer from severe shortages of food and fuel, which were only partially alleviated by airlifts of emergency aid supplies.

From 1980 extensive international negotiations took place to try to achieve the complete withdrawal of Soviet forces from Afghanistan. Between June 1982 and September 1987 seven rounds of indirect talks took place between the Afghan and Pakistani Ministers of Foreign Affairs in Geneva, Switzerland, under the auspices of the UN. In October 1986 the USSR made a token withdrawal of six regiments (6,000–8,000 men) from Afghanistan. As a result of the discussions in Geneva, an agreement was finally signed on 14 April 1988. The Geneva accords consisted of five documents: detailed undertakings by Afghanistan and Pakistan, relating to non-intervention and non-interference in each other's affairs; international guarantees of Afghan neutrality (with the USA and the USSR as the principal guarantors); arrangements for the voluntary and safe return of Afghan refugees; a document linking the preceding documents with a timetable for a Soviet withdrawal; and the establishment of a UN monitoring force, which was to oversee both the Soviet troop departures and the return of the refugees. The withdrawal of Soviet troops commenced on 15 May.

Neither the *mujahidin* nor Iran played any role in the formulation of the Geneva accords, and, in spite of protests by Pakistan, no agreement was incorporated regarding the composition of an interim coalition government in Afghanistan, or the 'symmetrical' cessation of Soviet aid to Najibullah's regime and US aid to the *mujahidin*. Therefore, despite the withdrawal of the Soviet troops, the supply of weapons to both sides was not halted, and the fighting continued. Pakistan repeatedly denied accusations that it had violated the accords by continuing to harbour Afghan guerrillas and to act as a conduit for the supply of weapons. At the end of November 1988 Soviet officials held direct talks with representatives of the *mujahidin* in Peshawar, the first such meeting since the start of the 10-year conflict. High-level discussions were held in early December in Saudi Arabia between Prof. Burhanuddin Rabbani, the Chairman of the IUAM, and the Soviet ambassador to Afghanistan. These discussions collapsed, however, when the *mujahidin* leaders reiterated their demand that no members of Najibullah's regime should be incorporated in any future Afghan government, while the Soviet officials continued to insist on a government role for the PDPA. In spite of the unabated violence, the USSR, adhering to the condition specified in the Geneva accords, had withdrawn all of its troops from Afghanistan by mid-February 1989.

In mid-1988 the *mujahidin* had intensified their military activities, attacking small provincial centres and launching missiles against major cities. By the end of 1990, however, the *mujahidin* had failed to achieve any significant military successes and their control was confined to rural areas. The guerrillas also failed to make any important advances on the political front. Talks between the IUAM and the Iranian-based Hizb-i Wahadat-i Islami (Islamic Unity Party), an alliance of eight Shi'a Afghan resistance groups, repeatedly failed to reach any agreement as to the composition of a broadly based interim government. Consequently, in February 1989 the IUAM convened its own *shura* (council) in Rawalpindi, Pakistan, at which an interim government-in-exile (known as the Afghan Interim Government, AIG) was elected. The AIG, however, was officially recognized by only four countries. It also failed to gain any substantial support or recognition from the guerrilla commanders, who were beginning to establish their own unofficial alliances inside the country. In March, however, the AIG received a form of diplomatic recognition when it was granted membership of the Organization of the Islamic Conference (OIC). In addition, in June the US Government appointed a special envoy to the *mujahidin*, with the rank of personal ambassador. In mid-1989 the unity of the *mujahidin* forces was seriously weakened by an increase in internecine violence among the various guerrilla groups, while the AIG was riven by disputes between moderates and fundamentalists. The USA, Saudi Arabia and Pakistan began to reduce financial aid and military supplies to the IUAM in Peshawar, and to undertake the difficult task of delivering weapons and money directly to guerrilla commanders and tribal leaders inside Afghanistan.

Following extensive negotiations with the regional powers involved in the crisis, the UN Secretary-General made a declaration in May 1991, setting out five principles for a settlement, the main points of which were: recognition of the national sovereignty of Afghanistan; the right of the Afghan people to choose their own government and political system; the establishment of an independent and authorized mechanism to oversee free and fair elections to a broadly based government; a UN-monitored cease-fire; and the donation of sufficient financial aid to facilitate the return of the refugees and internal reconstruction. The declaration received the approval of the Afghan and Pakistani Governments, but was rejected by the AIG.

Reflecting its disenchantment with the guerrilla cause, the US Government substantially reduced its aid to the *mujahidin* in 1991. New military campaigns had been launched by the *mujahidin* in the second half of 1990 in an attempt to impress their international supporters, disrupt the return of refugees and obstruct contacts between the Government and moderate guerrillas. At the end of March 1991, following more than two weeks of heavy fighting, the south-eastern city of Khost was captured by the *mujahidin*, representing the most severe reversal sustained by the Government since the Soviet withdrawal.

An unexpected breakthrough towards resolving the Afghan crisis occurred in mid-September 1991, when the USA and the USSR announced that they would stop supplying arms to the warring factions, and would encourage other countries (namely Pakistan, Saudi Arabia and Iran) to do likewise. Although both the Afghan Government and the *mujahidin* welcomed this pledge, neither side showed any sign of implementing the proposed cease-fire, and, indeed, the fighting intensified around Kabul. In February 1992, however, the peace process was given a major boost when Pakistan made it clear that, rather than continuing actively to encourage the *mujahidin*, through arms supplies and training, it was urging all the guerrilla factions to support the five-point UN peace plan. In doing so, Pakistan was effectively abandoning its insistence on the installation of a fundamentalist government in Kabul. There were growing fears, none the less, that the peace process might be placed in jeopardy by an increase in ethnic divisions within both the government forces and a number of *mujahidin* groups, between the majority Pashtuns and minority groups such as the Tajiks and Uzbeks. As a result of a mutiny staged by Uzbek militia forces in the Afghan army, under the command of Gen. Abdul Rashid Dostam, the northern town of Mazar-i-Sharif was captured by the *mujahidin* in March.

On 16 April 1992 events took an unexpected turn when Najibullah was forced to resign by his own ruling party, following the capture of the strategically important Bagram airbase and the nearby town of Charikar, only about 50 km north of Kabul, by the Jamiat-i Islami guerrilla group under the command of the Tajik general, Ahmad Shah Masoud. Najibullah went into hiding in the capital, under UN protection, while one of the Vice-Presidents, Abd ar-Rahim Hatif, assumed the post of acting President. Within a few days of Najibullah's downfall, every major town in Afghanistan was under the control of different coalitions of *mujahidin* groups co-operating with disaffected army commanders. Masoud was given orders by the guerrilla leaders in Peshawar to secure Kabul. On 25 April the forces of both Masoud and of Gulbuddin Hekmatyar, the leader of a rival guerrilla group, the Pashtun-dominated Hizb-i Islami (Islamic Party), whose men were massed to the south of the capital, entered Kabul. The army surrendered its key positions, and immediately the city was riven by *mujahidin* faction-fighting. The military council that had, a few days earlier, replaced the Government relinquished power to the *mujahidin*. Having discarded the UN's proposal to form a neutral body, the guerrilla leaders in Peshawar agreed to establish a 51-member interim Islamic Jihad Council, composed of military and religious leaders, which was to assume power in Kabul. The leader of the small, moderate Jebha-i-Nejat-i-Melli (National Liberation Front), Prof. Sibghatullah Mojaddedi, was to chair the Islamic Jihad Council for two months, after which period a 10-member Leadership Council, comprising *mujahidin* chiefs and presided over by the head of the Jamiat-i Islami, Prof. Burhanuddin Rabbani, would be set up for a period of four months. Within the six months a special council was to meet to designate an interim administration, which was to hold power for up to a year pending elections.

Mojaddedi arrived in Kabul on 28 April 1992 as the President of the new interim administration. The Islamic Jihad Council was not, however, supported by Hekmatyar, whose radical stance differed substantially from Mojaddedi's more tolerant outlook. At the end of the month Hekmatyar's forces lost control of their last stronghold in the centre of Kabul. Within a few weeks the Government of the newly proclaimed Islamic State of Afghanistan had won almost universal diplomatic recognition, and by early May about one-half of the Islamic Jihad Council had arrived in the capital. An acting Council of Ministers was formed, in which Masoud was given the post of Minister of Defence and the premiership was set aside for Ustad Abdol Sabur Farid, a Tajik commander from the Hizb-i Islami (Hekmatyar declined to accept the post). As part of the process of 'Islamization', the death penalty was introduced, alcohol and narcotics were banned and the wearing of strict Islamic dress by all women was enforced. Despite Mojaddedi's repeated pleas to Hekmatyar and his followers to lay down their arms, Hekmatyar, who was particularly angered by the presence of Gen. Dostam's Uzbek forces in the capital, continued to bombard Kabul with artillery and indiscriminate rocket launches from various strongholds around the city, killing and wounding scores of citizens.

On 28 June 1992 Mojaddedi surrendered power to the Leadership Council, which immediately offered Burhanuddin Rabbani the presidency of the country and the concomitant responsibility for the interim Council of Ministers for four months, as set forth in the Peshawar Agreement (see above). In early July Farid assumed the premiership, which had been held open for him since late April. On assuming the presidency Rabbani announced the adoption of a new Islamic flag, the establishment of an economic council, which was to address the country's severe economic problems, and the appointment of a commission to draw up a new constitution. A Deputy President was appointed in late July. In early August the withdrawal of the members of the Hizb-i Islami faction led by Maulvi Muhammad Yunus Khalis from the Leadership Council revealed serious rifts within the Government. A further problem was the continuing inter-*mujahidin* violence in Kabul. Within days the violence had escalated into a full-scale ground offensive, launched by Hekmatyar's forces against the capital. The airport was closed, hundreds of people were killed or wounded, and tens of thousands of civilians fled the city. In response, President Rabbani expelled Hekmatyar from the Leadership Council and dismissed Prime Minister Farid. Hekmatyar demanded the expulsion of the 75,000 Uzbek militia from Kabul as a precondition to peace talks, alleging that Gen. Dostam was still closely allied to former members of the communist regime. At the end of the month a cease-fire agreement was reached between Rabbani and Hekmatyar and, after a few days of relative calm, the airport was reopened. Sporadic fighting involving various *mujahidin* and militia groups (notably Gen. Dostam's Uzbek forces) continued, however, in Kabul itself and in the provinces throughout the remainder of the year. At the end of October the Leadership Council agreed to extend Rabbani's tenure of the presidency by two months. On 30 December a special advisory council, known as the Resolution and Settlement Council (Shura-e Ahl-e Hal wa Aqd), which was composed of 1,335 tribal leaders, was convened in Kabul. The Council elected Rabbani, who was the sole candidate, as President of the country for a period of a further two years. In early January 1993 200 members of the advisory council were selected to constitute the future membership of the country's legislature.

The establishment of the advisory council and the re-election of President Rabbani provoked yet further heavy fighting in Kabul and other provinces in early 1993. Owing to the worsening violence, all Western diplomats had left the capital by the end of January. In early March, however, President Rabbani, Hekmatyar, Mojaddedi and leaders of other major *mujahidin* factions held negotiations in Islamabad, Pakistan, at the end of which a peace accord was signed. Under the terms of the accord, an interim Government was to be established, which would hold power for 18 months; President Rabbani was to remain as Head of State, and Hekmatyar (or his nominee) was to assume the premiership of the acting Council of Ministers; a cease-fire was to be imposed with immediate effect; legislative elections were to be held within six months; a 16-member defence commission was to be formed, which would be responsible for the establishment of a national army; and all weaponry was to be seized from the warring factions in an attempt to restore peace and order. The peace accord was officially approved and signed by the Governments of Pakistan, Saudi Arabia and Iran.

Confronted with the difficult task of satisfying the demands of all the *mujahidin* groups, Hekmatyar was not able to present a new Council of Ministers until late May 1993. Each *mujahidin* faction was allocated two ministerial posts, with further positions left vacant for other representatives. Representatives from Gen. Dostam's group of predominantly Uzbek militiamen—known collectively as the National Islamic Movement (NIM) (Jonbesh-i Melli-i Islami)—were offered two posts in July. One of Hekmatyar's most noteworthy decisions in the formation of the new Council of Ministers was to remove one of his most powerful rivals, Ahmad Shah Masoud, from the crucial post of Minister of Defence. The new Prime Minister promised to hold a general election by October. The temporary headquarters of the Government were situated in Charasiab, Hekmatyar's military base, about 25 km south of Kabul.

Despite the signing of the Islamabad peace accord in March 1993, the violence between the various *mujahidin* groups did not cease, and hundreds of people were killed and wounded. The interim Government was beset by internal dissension and proved relatively ineffectual. Hekmatyar refused to co-operate with Rabbani, and frequently demanded the President's resignation. In September, however, it was reported that a new draft Constitution (known as the Basic Law) had been drawn up and approved by a special commission, in preparation for the holding of a general election. The fighting intensified in late December, when Gen. Dostam transferred his allegiance to his hitherto arch-enemy, Hekmatyar, and the supporters of the two combined to confront the forces of Rabbani and Masoud. The violence spread throughout the provinces, resulting in large numbers of military and civilian casualties and the internal displacement of thousands of people. Various unsuccessful attempts were made in 1994 by neighbouring countries and by international organizations to achieve a negotiated settlement between the main warring factions. In late June the Supreme Court ruled that Rabbani could retain the presidency for a further six months, but failed to grant a similar extension to Hekmatyar's premiership. Although President Rabbani's extended term in office expired at the end of December, he did not resign.

In the latter half of 1994, a new, hitherto unknown, militant grouping emerged in Afghanistan, known as the Taliban (the plural form of 'Talib', meaning 'seeker of religious knowledge'). The movement, which at the outset comprised an estimated 25,000 fighters (the majority of whom were reported to be young Pashtun graduates of fundamentalist Islamist schools established by Afghan refugees in Pakistan), advocated the adoption of extremist practices, including the complete seclusion of women from society. Although initially claiming that they had no interest in actually assuming power in Afghanistan, the Taliban, who were led by Mullah Mohammad Omar, won a major victory in October, when they captured the city of Qandahar from the forces of Hekmatyar, which had hitherto dominated the southern provinces. In February 1995 the Taliban routed Hekmatyar's men from their headquarters in Charasiab, and within a month they controlled 10 provinces, mostly in southern and south-eastern Afghanistan. However, the Taliban retreated from their advance on Kabul when Rabbani's troops launched a massive counter-offensive. By mid-1995, with both the Taliban and Hekmatyar's men held in check, President Rabbani and his supporters were enjoying an unprecedented level of authority and confidence in Kabul and its environs. This was reflected in Rabbani's reneging on his earlier promise of standing down from the presidency in late March and in the growing number of countries that were considering reopening their embassies in the Afghan capital. In mid-1995 talks were held between Rabbani and the Taliban, but relations between the two sides remained extremely strained. In early September the Taliban achieved a notable gain when they captured the key north-western city of Herat and the surrounding province from government forces.

The resurgence of the Taliban apparently provoked an attack on the Pakistani embassy in Kabul by hundreds of pro-Government demonstrators protesting against Pakistan's alleged support for the student militia; the embassy was destroyed by fire, one employee was killed and a number injured (including the ambassador himself). In response, the Afghan ambassador to Pakistan and six other Afghan diplomats were expelled from Islamabad. In October the Taliban launched a massive ground and air assault on Kabul, but by early January 1996 had failed to breach the capital's defences. The constant bombardment of the besieged city, however, resulted in hundreds of civilian deaths.

Despite the holding of exploratory negotiations between the Rabbani Government and major opposition parties in the first quarter of 1996, the fighting in and around Kabul intensified. The President's attempts at conciliation finally proved successful in late May when, in a critical development (known as the Mahipar Agreement), he persuaded Hekmatyar to rejoin the Government. Hekmatyar's forces arrived in the capital during May to defend the city against the Taliban. In late June Hekmatyar resumed the post of Prime Minister and President Rabbani appointed a new Council of Ministers in early July, which was to hold power for a period of six to 12 months pending a general election. In addition, under the terms of the Mahipar Agreement, a Constitution to cover the interim period was drawn up and published.

The political situation was radically altered in late September 1996 when, as a culmination of two weeks of sweeping military advances (including the capture of the crucial eastern city of Jalalabad), the Taliban seized control of Kabul following fierce clashes with government troops, who fled northwards together with the deposed Government. One of the Taliban movement's first actions in the captured capital was the summary execution of former President Najibullah and his brother. On assuming power, the Taliban declared Afghanistan a 'complete' Islamic state and appointed an interim Council of Ministers, led by Mullah Mohammad Rabbani, to administer the country (of which it now controlled about two-thirds). Pakistan, which was widely suspected of actively aiding the Islamist militia, was the first country officially to recognize the new regime. (By mid-November, however, few other countries or international organizations had followed suit—neither the UN, India, Russia nor Iran had given official recognition to the Taliban administration.) The Taliban imposed a strict and intimidatory Islamic code: women were ordered into purdah and were not permitted to enter employment or be formally educated beyond the age of eight years; television, non-religious music, gambling and alcohol were all banned; amputations and public stonings were enforced as forms of punishment; and compulsory attendance at mosques by all men was introduced.

In October 1996 a powerful military and logistical alliance was unexpectedly formed by Gen. Dostam, the former Minister of Defence who controlled six northern provinces, Masoud, and the leader of the Shi'a Hizb-i Wahadat-i Islami, Gen. Abdol Karim Khalili. By late October the anti-Taliban forces, whose leaders were now collectively known as the Supreme Council for the Defence of Afghanistan (the headquarters of which were situated in Gen. Dostam's stronghold of Mazar-i-Sharif), had launched a concerted offensive against Kabul in the hope of ousting the Islamist militia. Despite repeated calls for a cease-fire from various foreign governments and the UN, the fighting between the Taliban and the allied opposition continued into January 1997. In mid-January, following the rapid collapse of UN-sponsored talks in Islamabad, the Taliban launched an unexpected offensive, advancing north and capturing Bagram airbase and the provincial capital of Charikar. By late January the Taliban had made significant military gains and had pushed the front line to about 100 km north of Kabul. There was a dramatic development in mid-May when, following the defection of the Uzbek Gen. Abdul Malik and his men to the Taliban, the latter were able to capture the strategically important northern town of Mazar-i-Sharif. Gen. Dostam was reported to have fled to Turkey, and his position as leader of the NIM was assumed by Gen. Malik. The Taliban now controlled about 80% of the country, including all of the major towns and cities. Their position was also strengthened by the decision of Saudi Arabia and the United Arab Emirates (UAE) to accord formal recognition to the Taliban Government. Taliban control of Mazar-i-Sharif, however, was extremely brief, and within only three days of entering the town the movement was in full retreat. It appeared that Gen. Malik's tenuous alliance with the Taliban had collapsed almost immediately and his troops, together with

Shi'a militia, forced the newcomers out after ferocious fighting. The Taliban were soundly routed, and by early June their forces had retreated almost 200 km south of Mazar-i-Sharif.

The regional aspect of the Afghan conflict was highlighted at the beginning of June 1997 by the Taliban decision to close down the Iranian embassy in Kabul; the Iranian Government was widely suspected of actively aiding the anti-Taliban northern alliance. The alliance was reported to have been expanded and strengthened in early June by the inclusion of the forces of Hekmatyar and of the Mahaz-i-Melli-i-Islami (National Islamic Front), led by Pir Sayed Ahmad Gailani. This new coalition, which superseded the Supreme Council for the Defence of Afghanistan, was known as the United National Islamic Front for the Salvation of Afghanistan, commonly known as the United Front and the Northern Alliance. The United Front was the military wing of the exiled Government, the 'Islamic State of Afghanistan'. Despite the arrival of thousands of reinforcements from training camps in Pakistan (many of whom, however, were inexperienced teenagers), the Taliban suffered a series of military defeats in northern Afghanistan, and by late July the United Front forces were within firing range of Kabul, having recaptured Charikar and the airbase at Bagram. In the same month the UN Security Council demanded a cease-fire and an end to all foreign intervention in Afghanistan. In mid-1997 it was widely believed that the Taliban were supported by Pakistan and Saudi Arabia; on the opposing side, to various degrees, were ranged Iran, India, the Central Asian states (which feared the encroachment of Taliban fundamentalism) and Russia.

In mid-August 1997 it was reported that the United Front had appointed a new Government, based in Mazar-i-Sharif, with Rabbani continuing as President, Abdorrahim Ghafurzai as Prime Minister, Masoud as Minister of Defence and Gen. Malik as Minister of Foreign Affairs. The former Prime Minister in the anti-Taliban administration, Gulbuddin Hekmatyar, refused to recognize the new Government. Within a few days of its appointment, however, seven members of the new Government, including Prime Minister Ghafurzai, were killed in an aeroplane crash. In late August the anti-Taliban opposition alliance appointed Abdolghaffur Rawanfarhadi as the new Prime Minister.

In September 1997 Gen. Dostam was reported to have returned to Mazar-i-Sharif from Turkey, and in the following month the member parties of the United Front re-elected him as commander of the forces of the alliance and appointed him as Vice-President of the anti-Taliban administration. However, there were reports of a bitter rivalry between Gen. Dostam and Gen. Malik and skirmishes between their respective forces. Dostam's battle for supremacy with his rival led him to make overtures to the Taliban, including offers of exchanges of prisoners-of-war. Gen. Dostam also accused Gen. Malik of having massacred about 3,000 Taliban prisoners earlier in the year. By late November Gen. Dostam had resumed the leadership of the NIM, ousting Gen. Malik. In late October the Taliban unilaterally decided to change the country's name to the Islamic Emirate of Afghanistan and altered the state flag, moves that were condemned by the opposition alliance and all of Afghanistan's neighbours except Pakistan. In late 1997 the World Food Programme (WFP) launched an emergency operation to help people facing starvation in the impoverished central region of Hazarajat (held by the Shi'a Hizb-i Wahadat-i Islami), which had been blockaded by the Taliban since August. In January 1998, however, the UN was forced to suspend its airlifts of emergency supplies when Taliban aircraft bombed the area. Meanwhile, in mid-December 1997 the UN Security Council issued a communiqué expressing its concern at the alleged massacres of civilians and prisoners-of-war being perpetrated by various factions in Afghanistan.

In late March 1998 the UN ceased operating aid programmes in the southern province of Qandahar (where the political headquarters of the Taliban were located) following attacks on staff and constant harassment by the Taliban. In the same month there were reports of factional fighting between rival members of the United Front in and around Mazar-i-Sharif, highlighting the fragile nature of the anti-Taliban alliance. In late April, following the launch of a major diplomatic initiative by the USA, the Taliban and the United Front held talks, sponsored by the UN and the OIC, in Islamabad, the first formal peace negotiations between the two opposing sides for more than a year. In early May, however, the talks broke down, and fighting resumed to the north of Kabul.

On 1 August 1998 the Taliban captured the northern city of Shiberghan, Gen. Dostam's new headquarters, after a number of his Uzbek commanders allegedly accepted bribes from the Taliban and switched allegiance. Gen. Dostam was reported to have fled to the Uzbek border and thence to Turkey. Following the recapture of Mazar-i-Sharif by the Taliban (who allegedly now included considerable numbers of extremist volunteers from various other Islamic countries, including Pakistan, Saudi Arabia, Algeria and Egypt) in early August, 10 Iranian diplomats and one Iranian journalist were reported to have been captured and killed by Taliban militia. The Taliban, however, initially denied any knowledge of the whereabouts of the Iranian nationals. In early September Afghanistan and Iran appeared to be on the verge of open warfare, as 70,000 Iranian troops were deployed on the mutual border, and it emerged that nine of the missing Iranian nationals had, in fact, been murdered by members of the Taliban as they stormed Mazar-i-Sharif. (It was later reported that 2,000–6,000 Shi'a Hazara civilians had been systematically massacred by the guerrillas after recapturing the city.) Both Iran and Afghanistan massed more troops on the border; by mid-September 500,000 Iranian troops had reportedly been placed on full military alert. In mid-October, however, the Taliban agreed to free all Iranian prisoners being held in Afghanistan and to punish those responsible for the killing of the nine Iranian diplomats (or military advisers, according to the Taliban). By the end of the year the situation appeared much calmer, with the Taliban having expressed regret for the deaths of the Iranian nationals and Iran having scaled down its border forces and announced that it had no intention of invading Afghanistan.

Meanwhile, on 20 August 1998 the USA launched simultaneous air-strikes against alleged terrorist bases in eastern Afghanistan and Sudan, reportedly operated by the Saudi-born militant leader of the al-Qa'ida (Base) organization, Osama bin Laden (who was supported by the Taliban), in retaliation for the bombing of two US embassies in East Africa earlier that month. Many aid agencies withdrew their remaining expatriate staff from Afghanistan, fearing terrorist acts of vengeance. In September the Taliban suffered a considerable set-back when Saudi Arabia (one of only three countries officially to recognize the regime) withdrew its support and recalled its envoy from Kabul. The decision by the Saudi Government substantially to downgrade its relations with the Taliban appeared to have been prompted by its opposition to the reported brutality of the guerrilla authorities and to their sheltering of bin Laden. In the following month the Taliban stated that, although they were not willing to extradite the Saudi-born dissident, in the event of a lawsuit being filed against him, they would be prepared to place him on trial in Afghanistan. The Taliban also insisted that bin Laden (who had reportedly been resident in Afghanistan for at least two years) was under close supervision, with his activities and media access suitably restricted. In late November evidence submitted by the US Government to the Afghan Supreme Court was deemed by the latter as inadequate grounds for bin Laden's arrest.

In mid-September 1998 the Taliban captured the capital of Bamian province, a Shi'a stronghold; this victory meant that any substantial anti-Taliban opposition was effectively restricted to Masoud's stronghold in north-eastern Afghanistan. Taliban advances in the north alarmed Russia and the Central Asian states, which feared the unsettling potential of a militant Islamist army along their southern borders. In December the UN Security Council threatened the Taliban with the imposition of sanctions and called on the regime to commence negotiations with the opposition. Pakistan, on the other hand, demonstrated its diplomatic isolation with regard to the Afghan situation, by defending the Taliban and urging the other members of the UN to recognize their Government.

In January 1999 it was reported that the United Front had established a multi-ethnic Supreme Military Council, under the command of Masoud, the aim of which was to give fresh impetus to the anti-Taliban movement and to co-ordinate manoeuvres against Taliban forces in northern Afghanistan. Despite a certain degree of optimism being raised by the holding of UN-monitored direct peace talks between representatives of the Taliban and the United Front in February, March and July, ultimately very little was achieved as a result of the negotiations. In March, however, the first UN personnel returned to Afghanistan since their evacuation in August 1998 (following the murder of three UN employees), marking the beginning of a phased return of the organization's international staff to Afghanistan.

In July 1999, following reports that bin Laden was being sheltered in eastern Afghanistan, the USA imposed financial and economic sanctions on the Taliban regime in a further attempt to persuade it to hand over the militant leader (who the US authorities suspected of planning more atrocities) to stand trial in the USA. In response, the Taliban claimed that the sanctions would have very little impact and again refused to extradite bin Laden.

The Taliban continued to campaign for international recognition, to no avail. At the 1999 session of the UN General Assembly (held in September–November) the UN again rejected the Taliban request to represent Afghanistan; the seat remained under the control of President Rabbani, the leader of the 'Islamic State of Afghanistan'. In October 1999 the UN Secretary-General's Special Envoy to Afghanistan, Lakhdar Brahimi, announced his withdrawal from his mission, owing to the lack of progress (and particularly to the alleged negative attitude of the Taliban). In February 2000 Francesc Vendrell was appointed Head of the UN Special Mission to Afghanistan and Personal Representative of the UN Secretary-General, with the rank of Assistant Secretary-General. Relations between the UN and Afghanistan, however, remained tense, culminating in the UN's temporary withdrawal of its expatriate staff from Qandahar at the end of March, following an assault on UN offices by the Taliban.

In mid-November 1999 the UN Security Council imposed an embargo on all Taliban-controlled overseas assets and a ban on the international flights of the national airline, Ariana Afghan Airlines, as a result of the Afghan regime's continuing refusal to relinquish the suspected terrorist leader, bin Laden, to stand trial in the USA or in a third (possibly Islamic) country. Following the imposition of the sanctions, there were reports of large-scale demonstrations throughout Afghanistan, and international aid organizations once again came under attack. The impact of the sanctions was expected to be alleviated, however, by the reopening of key trade routes along the Afghan–Iranian border in late November. The Taliban Government expressed hopes that the trade with Iran would compensate for the significant decrease in imports of wheat and flour from Pakistan caused by the recent imposition of stricter border controls by the new military regime in Pakistan. Although the price of basic foodstuffs in Kabul and other towns declined dramatically as a result of renewed trade with Iran, the general economic circumstances in Kabul worsened. In February 2000 the UN relaxed the sanctions to permit the Taliban to operate flights to Mecca, in Saudi Arabia. In October an agreement was signed to allow weekly flights from Sharjah, in the UAE, to Qandahar, in southern Afghanistan.

During 2000 the Taliban and the United Front suffered internal discord, with defections of senior officials occurring on both sides. Heavy fighting, concentrated in the north of Kabul, resumed in early March. In the same month the military commander, Ismail Khan, escaped from prison in Qandahar and fled to Iran. The OIC hosted peace negotiations between representatives of the Taliban and the United Front in March and May, during which the two parties decided to exchange prisoners-of-war. No agreement, however, was reached on a cease-fire. In early June there was renewed fighting in northern and central Afghanistan, and by the end of July the Taliban had acquired more territory in the north of the country. As the fighting intensified throughout August, the Taliban became more confident of victory in the north, reopening training camps that had previously been closed down owing to international pressure.

At the beginning of September 2000 the Taliban captured Taloqan, the capital of Takhar province in the north of Afghanistan and the headquarters of the United Front. This victory represented a serious military and political set-back for Masoud and the United Front. In December the Taliban and the United Front entered negotiations conducted by Francesc Vendrell. Despite renewed attempts by the Taliban to end their diplomatic isolation, the UN continued to refute the Taliban claim to the Afghan seat at the UN. In December the UN Security Council passed a resolution, which stated that unless the Taliban surrendered bin Laden and closed down militant training camps by 19 January 2001, the international community would impose an arms embargo on the Taliban, tighten an existing embargo on flights and the 'freeze' on Taliban assets abroad, restrict the sale of chemicals used to produce heroin from poppies and close Ariana Afghan Airlines offices abroad. The weapons embargo would not affect the anti-Taliban forces. The Taliban refused to concede to the demands and, immediately after the UN's decision, shut down the UN special mission to Afghanistan and cancelled planned peace negotiations. By early January 2001 24 of the original 64 UN foreign workers had returned to Kabul. The sanctions were imposed in mid-January. Consequently, Francesc Vendrell's attempts to persuade the Taliban and their opposition to participate in open-ended negotiations collapsed.

In February 2001 the Taliban ordered the demolition of all statues in Afghanistan depicting living creatures, including the world's tallest standing Buddhas in Bamian. Despite widespread international condemnation, the destruction of much of Afghanistan's pre-Islamic cultural heritage was carried out in March. However, Hindu and Sikh statues, acknowledged as fundamental to the respective religious practices, were preserved. The order contravened a 1999 decree, which ordered the preservation of all ancient relics, thereby prompting speculation that members of bin Laden's al-Qa'ida had taken control of the Taliban by ousting the more moderate leaders.

In mid-April 2001 the Chairman of the Taliban Interim Council of Ministers and Gen. Commander of the Armed Forces of the Taliban, Mullah Mohammad Rabbani, died, owing to illness. He was later replaced as Gen. Commander by his brother, Mullah Ahmed. In May all UN political staff left Afghanistan in accordance with a Taliban order, a consequence of the fresh sanctions imposed in January. In July the Taliban issued another set of controversial edicts: the use of the internet was outlawed; women were banned from visiting picnic areas; and items such as tape recorders, telephone sets, musical instruments and lipstick were proscribed as non-Islamic.

In early August 2001 eight foreign and 16 Afghan aid workers of a German-based, Christian non-governmental organization were arrested by the Taliban on charges of Christian proselytization. A trial under the rules of *Shari'a* (Islamic religious law) of the foreign aid workers began in September. Shortly afterwards the Taliban offer to release the detained humanitarian workers in return for the release of Sheikh Omar Abdul Rahman, an Egyptian militant Islamist sentenced to life imprisonment in the USA, was rejected. Meanwhile, the Taliban closed down two other Christian aid organizations and ordered the foreign staff to leave the country.

At the end of June 2001 the US ambassador to Pakistan issued a statement in which he warned the Taliban that they would be held accountable if bin Laden carried out an attack against US interests. In response, the Taliban Minister of Foreign Affairs stated that the regime was not responsible for safeguarding US security outside Afghanistan. In late July the UN Security Council adopted a resolution that reinforced the sanctions imposed in January. Some 15 UN officials were to be posted in and around Afghanistan to monitor the success of the existing arms embargo. The resolution was censured for focusing solely on the Taliban and for failing to curb the United Front's arms supply.

Meanwhile, following the coup in Pakistan in October 1999, there were indications that relations between the Taliban and the new Pakistani administration, headed by Gen. Pervez Musharraf, might not prove as amicable as they had been since 1996. In his first major address to the Pakistani nation shortly after assuming power, Gen. Musharraf pledged to work for a 'truly representative government' in Afghanistan, and in the following month the State Bank of Pakistan complied with the UN sanctions in ordering a 'freeze' on all Taliban financial assets in Pakistan. In late January 2000, however, a delegation of the Islamic Emirate of Afghanistan, led by the Chairman of the Taliban Interim Council of Ministers, accepted a formal invitation to enter negotiations with Pakistani officials. Pakistan continued to offer economic aid and support to the Taliban and condemned the UN sanctions against Afghanistan. Although Gen. Musharraf strongly denied giving military assistance to the Taliban, allegations relating to the involvement of Pakistan's special forces in the Taliban campaign grew, following the latter's successful offensive in August–September 2000.

On 9 September 2001 Masoud was seriously injured in an attack by suicide bombers; some six days later he died. His deputy, Gen. Muhammed Qassim Fahim, was appointed acting military leader of the United Front. Evidence that emerged from deserted al-Qa'ida camps following the fall of the Taliban in Kabul in mid-November indicated that the Arab suicide bombers were linked to bin Laden.

The situation in Afghanistan drastically changed as a result of the terrorist attacks on New York and Washington, DC, USA, on 11 September 2001. Although bin Laden denied his involvement in the attacks, some two days after the events the US Secretary of State publicly identified bin Laden and his al-Qa'ida organization as principally responsible. The Taliban initially claimed that neither bin Laden nor Afghanistan had the means to carry out the attacks, warning that they would retaliate if the USA attacked Afghanistan. On 16 September the UN imposed diplomatic sanctions and an arms embargo on the Taliban. Meanwhile, the USA began to form an anti-terrorism coalition, with the assistance of the United Kingdom.

Pakistan came under considerable pressure to reverse its policy of supporting the Taliban and agreed to co-operate with the US-led coalition. On 17 September 2001 a Pakistani delegation issued Taliban leaders with an ultimatum to surrender bin Laden or face retaliation from the USA. A few days later a *shura* of Afghan clerics, under the leadership of Mullah Mohammad Omar, issued an edict for bin Laden to leave Afghanistan voluntarily. The *shura* also demanded that the UN and OIC hold independent investigations, and threatened to instigate a *jihad* (holy war) if the USA attacked Afghanistan. US officials, calling for unconditional surrender, considered the edict insufficient. At the same time, US President George W. Bush warned that the Taliban would also be targeted if they refused to extradite bin Laden and the rest of al-Qa'ida. It remained highly improbable that the Taliban would surrender bin Laden. Al-Qa'ida had become increasingly involved in Taliban affairs: in late August bin Laden had reportedly been appointed Commander-in-Chief of the Taliban forces.

In the mean time, the USA deployed aircraft around Afghanistan, in preparation for attack. The Taliban responded to the developments with preparations for *jihad*. On 26 September 2001 thousands of protesters set fire to the abandoned US embassy in Kabul. The next day Taliban officials announced that an edict had been delivered to bin Laden ordering him to leave the country. The US Government dismissed the edict and restated demands for the Taliban to surrender bin Laden to the US authorities, rejecting a Taliban offer to enter negotiations regarding the extradition.

The United Front had suffered a serious set-back when Masoud was fatally wounded two days before the terrorist attacks on the USA. However, speculation that it would receive military assistance from the anti-terrorism coalition as a result of the likely military intervention in Afghanistan encouraged the anti-Taliban coalition, which reported military successes against the Taliban in late September 2001. In early October there were reports that the USA was militarily assisting anti-Taliban groups within Afghanistan. The Taliban continued forcibly to conscript men to bolster their army, which in early October numbered 40,000 fighters. There were reports that al-Qa'ida provided the Taliban with several thousand fighters. In the mean time, the trial of the foreign aid workers continued. On 6 October an offer by a Taliban official to release the detainees in exchange for the withdrawal of the US-led military threats was dismissed. In mid-November the aid workers were rescued by anti-Taliban fighters and flown to Pakistan.

On 12 September 2001 the UN and other aid organizations began to remove their foreign staff from Afghanistan, owing to fears that the USA would launch retaliatory attacks against al-Qa'ida and the Taliban. Shortly afterwards the Taliban seized the UN Kabul office and shut down the Afghan communications network. The number of displaced people increased considerably; although accurate estimates of new refugees were not known, some reports estimated that 1.5m. Afghans had abandoned their homes in the latter half of September. Pakistan restricted entry to those at the border considered to be most in need of assistance. Nevertheless, thousands of refugees succeeded in entering Pakistan illegally. At the end of September communications were restored with Afghan humanitarian workers. WFP resumed emergency food deliveries to Kabul and Herat and northern Afghanistan on a trial basis; local aid workers were expected to distribute the aid. At the same time the Red Cross transported medical supplies to Kabul. In early October the US President announced a humanitarian aid programme for Afghans, in order to undermine the Taliban and to show Muslim countries that the USA was planning war against terrorism and not Islam. However, the proposal to link humanitarian aid with a pending military operation concerned humanitarian organizations.

On the evening of 7 October 2001 US-led forces began the aerial bombardment of suspected al-Qa'ida camps and strategic Taliban positions in Afghanistan. In addition to military strikes, aircraft released food and medicine parcels to Afghan civilians near the southern border with Pakistan; leaflets were also dropped offering protection and a reward in return for information on the whereabouts of al-Qa'ida leaders. Mullah Mohammad Omar responded by appealing to all Muslims to help defend Afghanistan, and as a result several thousand pupils of *madrassas* (mosque schools) in Pakistan and a number of Arab countries arrived in Afghanistan during October. A pre-recorded videotape of bin Laden's response to the military strikes was broadcast by the Qatar-based satellite television company Al-Jazeera. In the recording bin Laden declared war on the 'infidels' and warned the USA that attacks against it would continue until it withdrew from the Middle East. Although he did not claim responsibility for the attacks, bin Laden's comments were widely seen to be an implicit admission of his organization's involvement. Bin Laden also encouraged Muslims in countries that had offered assistance to the anti-terrorism coalition to rebel against their governments, thus provoking the sentiment that the US-led military strikes were against Afghanistan and Islam, as opposed to terrorism.

The US-led military operation, named 'Operation Enduring Freedom', achieved rapid results. After 10 days President George W. Bush announced that the Taliban regime's air defences had been destroyed. The nature of the attack changed when US and British ground forces, with Russian assistance, began an assault on Afghanistan on 20 October 2001. Some three days later it was announced that all of the identified al-Qa'ida training camps had been destroyed by air-strikes. The US-led military operation, however, also incurred failures, which resulted in civilian deaths. Evidence of civilian casualties adversely affected support for the military action. Saudi Arabia, which had hitherto remained silent about the military strikes, voiced its discontent in mid-October. In addition, tension rose in Pakistan; thousands of pro-Taliban fighters attempted to cross the border into Afghanistan. The USA's strategy also concerned members of the United Front; the bombing had not transformed the military balance in Afghanistan and by the end of October the United Front forces were still outnumbered. Nevertheless, rival commanders in the United Front launched a joint assault against the Taliban to recapture Mazar-i-Sharif and Taloqan. US servicemen were also killed in the conflict.

Initially, the US-led coalition avoided targeting Kabul in order to prevent the fractious United Front from capturing the capital. There were fears that while no alternative transitional government existed, the defeat of the Taliban in Kabul and other major cities would leave a power vacuum, resulting in anarchy. Some members of the United Front also voiced their concerns over occupying Kabul without a mandate; however, others regarded this strategy as a US-Pakistani plot to prevent the anti-Taliban opposition from advancing on Kabul and began to plan an early assault. In the mean time, the USA, the United Kingdom, other UN Security Council members and countries neighbouring Afghanistan began discussions for a broad-based transitional government for Afghanistan. At a meeting of United Front leaders in mid-October 2001 it was decided that the alliance would postpone an attack on Kabul for at least one month. At the same time, a delegation headed by the moderate religious leader, Pir Sayed Ahmad Gailani, held negotiations with the former King, Zahir Shah, in Rome, Italy, during which Gailani agreed to create a council, to be led by the former King. However, a meeting of more than 1,000 exiled Afghan commanders and tribal elders, chaired by Gailani, in Pakistan in late October revealed deep divisions between rival opposition groups. Some warned against the inclusion of the United Front, which was mainly composed of Tajiks, Uzbeks and Hazaras, in a transitional government that was to represent a majority Pashtun population. Senior representatives of the United Front and the former King were absent from the assembly. The outcome of the meeting caused grave concern for Western governments and the UN; many believed that Pakistan had sanctioned the conference in an attempt to encourage a resolute stand against support given by the West to the United Front. Plans to establish an alternative transitional council were hampered further by the capture and assassination of the Pashtun leader Abdul Haq by the Taliban. Haq entered Afghanistan on 21 October to attempt to mobilize Pashtuns to rebel against the Taliban; he was killed five days later.

The UN Secretary-General appointed a special representative for Afghanistan, Lakhdar Brahimi, to assist the formation of a transitional government. His first task was to negotiate an agreement between Afghanistan's neighbours regarding the council's composition. The USA had already requested the UN to supply a peace-keeping force that could secure Kabul; the UN refused, stating that it could not become involved while the war continued. Meanwhile, the humanitarian situation worsened.

On 10 October 2001 the UN resumed food aid. At the same time, the number of Afghan refugees attempting to leave the country increased dramatically; in early November UNHCR estimated that 135,000 refugees had entered Pakistan since 11 September.

In early November 2001 attacks against the Taliban in northern Afghanistan escalated. On 9 November the United Front captured Mazar-i-Sharif and proceeded to seize almost all of northern Afghanistan at an astonishing pace. The USA, United Kingdom and Pakistan advised the United Front not to enter Kabul until a leadership council was formed; however, on the night of 12 November the Taliban fled the capital and the next day, facing very little resistance, the United Front took over Kabul. Although the United Front immediately requested assistance from the US-led coalition to create a transitional government, it was impossible to do so while the majority Pashtun ethnic group remained under-represented. The USA and Pakistan had hitherto failed to attract defectors from the Pashtun Taliban leadership to join the council; in addition, US-led forces had given little support to anti-Taliban Pashtun leaders attempting to capture southern Afghanistan. Commanders of the United Front were soon in disagreement over the running of provinces in northern Afghanistan. Anti-Taliban forces from all ethnic backgrounds quickly advanced on southern Afghanistan and by the end of November had captured the Taliban stronghold of Kunduz. Unlike the factions belonging to the United Front, these groups were not united under a political alliance.

On 27 November 2001 the UN hosted a conference of 28 Afghan leaders representing the United Front, the Rome Group led by Zahir Shah, the pro-Iranian Cyprus Process and the Pakistan-backed Peshawar process (composed of Pashtun exiles and headed by Gailani), as well as other leading figures, in Bonn, Germany. On 5 December the leaders signed the Agreement on Provisional Arrangements in Afghanistan Pending the Re-establishment of Permanent Government Institutions, also known as the Bonn Agreement, stipulating the establishment of a 30-member multi-ethnic Interim Authority to preside for six months from 22 December. A Pashtun tribal chief, Hamid Karzai, was named Chairman of the Interim Authority, which was to comprise 11 Pashtuns, eight Tajiks, five Hazaras, three Uzbeks and three members of smaller tribal and religious groups. The United Front received the most seats; three of the leading members, Younis Qanooni, Gen. Muhammed Fahim and Dr Abdullah Abdullah, were allocated the interior, defence and foreign affairs portfolios respectively. Two female doctors were also granted posts in the executive council. Some leaders who were excluded from the government were dissatisfied with the outcome, including the former President Burhanuddin.

The Taliban regime's sole official contact with the outside world ended in late November 2001, when Pakistan severed all diplomatic links with the Taliban and closed their last remaining embassy. On 7 December the remaining members of the Taliban finally surrendered Qandahar and disappeared, marking the end of the Taliban regime. In the mean time, US ground forces were strengthened in an effort to find bin Laden and his supporters. Following unconfirmed reports that bin Laden and Mullah Mohammad Omar were hiding in the Tora Bora caves with the rest of the Islamist forces, the US-led coalition and United Front intensified the air and ground assault on the cave complex. However, after much of the region had been destroyed, there was no sign of the two leaders and their close associates. Some unconfirmed reports suggested that bin Laden had fled to Pakistan. Meanwhile, the USA and its allies continued to search for remaining Taliban and al-Qa'ida forces in Afghanistan. On 9 December WFP began a massive aid distribution programme in Kabul. The reopening of the Friendship Bridge between Afghanistan and Uzbekistan on the same day provided humanitarian agencies with a much-needed route by which to transport supplies. However, the poor weather conditions hampered the international relief campaign and most rural areas remained inaccessible, owing to safety concerns. Meanwhile, following the defeat of the Taliban regime, tens of thousands of refugees began to return to Afghanistan.

On 22 December 2001 the Interim Authority was inaugurated; Karzai was sworn in as Chairman. The country reinstated the Constitution of 1964, which combined *Shari'a* with Western concepts of justice. One of Karzai's first decisions was to appoint Gen. Dostam, who had initially boycotted the Government in protest at his exclusion, as Vice-Chairman and Deputy Minister of Defence. At the end of December the UN Security Council authorized, as envisaged in the Bonn Agreement, the deployment of an International Security Assistance Force (ISAF) to help maintain security in Kabul over the next six months. Some 19 countries were authorized to form a 5,000-strong security force, led by the United Kingdom.

In January 2002 the international community agreed to donate US $4,500m. over two-and-a-half years towards the reconstruction of Afghanistan. Also in that month a 21-member Special Independent Commission for the Convening of the Emergency Loya Jirga (commonly known as the Loya Jirga Commission) was established to devise the selection process and conduct of the Emergency Loya Jirga. Deployment of ISAF began in mid-January and remained confined to Kabul, despite Karzai's requests for the number of ISAF troops to be increased and the international force's mandate to be expanded to include security operations for the entire country. In May a UN Security Council Resolution approved the extension of ISAF for six months beyond June. In June Turkey assumed command of the security force. ISAF participated in joint patrols with Afghan police and assisted in creating and training a new Afghan National Army (ANA). It was intended that the ANA would eventually be a force of some 60,000, supported by a border guard of 12,000 and an air force of 8,000. Meanwhile, however, regional military commanders continued to reorganize their own armies, preventing scarce resources from being sent to the ANA and making the task of creating a multi-ethnic national army even more difficult. In early 2002 reports were already emerging of fighting among ethnic groups. In mid-February the Minister of Civil Aviation and Tourism, Abdul Rahman, was assassinated by a rival faction within the Interim Authority. The murder of Rahman, a staunch supporter of Zahir Shah, was evidently an attempt to deter the former monarch from returning to Afghanistan. In early April the Interim Authority claimed to have prevented an attempt allegedly organized by Hekmatyar to assassinate Karzai. Government officials accused Hekmatyar of seeking to depose the Interim Authority and assume control. Despite security concerns, former King Zahir Shah returned to Afghanistan as a 'private citizen' on 18 April.

In mid-January 2002 Afghanistan's main route connecting Kabul with the north, the Salang Pass, was reopened for the first time in 10 years, following a clearance operation by Russian and French teams. At the same time UN sanctions imposed on Ariana Afghan Airlines were lifted. The Interim Authority issued a decree banning poppy cultivation and the processing, trafficking and abuse of opiates. In February, however, reports were emerging that the large-scale planting of poppies had already taken place during the collapse of law and order in late 2001. In early April 2002 the Interim Administration introduced a radical programme to eradicate the crop. In accordance with the scheme, farmers would receive compensation for destroying their opium crops; those who refused would have their land seized by the Government and risk prosecution. However, the offer of compensation did not compare well with the lucrative sale of opium, and farmers carried out violent demonstrations throughout the country against the initiative. Despite attempts by the Government and the UN to curb the drugs trade, the annual survey conducted by the UN Office on Drugs and Crime (UNODC), published in October, reported that, owing to the planting of poppies in late 2001, Afghanistan had resumed its place as the world's largest producer of opium.

The number of refugees returning in 2002 surpassed all expectations. In early April UNHCR reported that more than 50,000 Afghan refugees were returning from Pakistan every week. In the same month UNHCR and the Iranian Government embarked on a joint voluntary repatriation programme to facilitate the return of more than 400,000 Afghans from Iran. By early December that target had almost been reached. At the end of 2002 UNHCR announced that more than 1.5m. refugees had returned from Pakistan. An estimated 2.5m. refugees remained outside Afghanistan, including 1.1m. in Iran and 1.2m. in Pakistan. In September, however, concerns were raised that Afghanistan was incapable of meeting the nutritional requirements of its population. Officials estimated that only 20%–30% of the country's land was cultivated in 2002, largely owing to the fourth successive year of drought. The crisis was exacerbated by the lack of sufficient humanitarian assistance from the international donor community. The rapid return of refugees placed an even greater strain on the humanitarian programme. Some 80% of the funds provided by the international agencies had been allocated to humanitarian aid, thus leaving only 20% available for the country's reconstruction programme. In mid-September Japan, Saudi Arabia and the USA announced a joint aid programme worth US $180m. for the repair and improvement of roads throughout Afghanistan.

Internecine fighting escalated as tribal commanders attempted to consolidate territorial and political influence in preparation for the Loya Jirga. The human rights organization Human Rights Watch issued a report in March 2002 detailing a rise in incidents of violence, killing, rape and ethnic persecution in northern Afghanistan, particularly aimed at Pashtun villagers. Many of the commanders held responsible for the violence were supposed supporters of the Interim Authority. The USA and UN attempted to mediate between rival commanders as violent clashes between ethnic factions continued. In February the UN brokered an agreement between the leaders of the three feuding factions in northern and north-western Afghanistan, Gen. Dostam, Gen. Atta Mohammed and Mohammed Mohaqqeq, according to which a 600-strong security force was to be established in the region representing all three factions. However, factional fighting continued in the region and throughout Afghanistan.

Meanwhile, the US-led coalition continued its search for the leaders of al-Qa'ida and the Taliban. In early February 2002 the former Taliban Minister of Foreign Affairs, Mawlawi Wakil Ahmad Motawakkil, surrendered himself to US forces in Qandahar. The search was often thwarted by the activities of regional Afghan (non-Taliban) military commanders. In early January, for example, the Interim Authority confirmed that seven senior Taliban members, who had surrendered to a local Afghan commander, had been released without the approval of the Interim Administration or the US-led coalition forces. 'Operation Anaconda', conducted by US-led forces against alleged Taliban and al-Qa'ida forces in the Shah-i Kot valley of Paktia province in March, was planned as a three-day assault, but developed into a 17-day conflict resulting in the deaths of coalition soldiers. Many al-Qa'ida and Taliban members fled to Khost province. US forces depended heavily on information provided by military commanders regarding the whereabouts of militant Islamists. This tactic was often to the USA's detriment, as complex tribal allegiances and enmities regularly dictated the type of information given by tribal commanders. Indeed, it was largely believed that bin Laden had been allowed to escape from Tora Bora in December 2001 (see above) by Afghans who claimed to be US allies. The USA's policy of hiring and arming local soldiers in the hope of capturing Islamist militants at times compounded the unstable political situation. In March 2002 the funds provided by the US forces in return for the assistance of Afghan soldiers were reportedly used by various military commanders in their attempt to secure control of Khost province. In April the mission to find the remnants of al-Qa'ida and the Taliban became more dangerous and volatile. In mid-April British troops launched their first major military assault, joining US and Afghan soldiers in Paktia. US-led forces conducted several smaller operations in eastern Afghanistan in May–June, with the support of Afghan ground troops, with some success. The USA's military strategy came under severe criticism after a wedding party in Uruzgan province was inadvertently bombed in early July. It appeared that US forces, not for the first time, had mistaken the traditional celebratory firing of weapons at an Afghan wedding for Taliban activity.

The election of 1,051 delegates to attend the Emergency Loya Jirga by district representatives took place in May–June 2002 under the monitoring of the UN and Loya Jirga Commission. International aid agencies, universities and other organizations chosen by the Commission appointed an additional 600 members to ensure that the assembly was balanced in terms of gender, geography, ethnicity and political beliefs. The Emergency Loya Jirga, which was due to commence on 10 June, was delayed, however, largely owing to tension over the former King Zahir Shah's candidature for the presidency. Zahir Shah eventually withdrew his candidature, reportedly under pressure from the USA, and announced his support for Karzai. Former President Burhanuddin Rabbani also renounced his candidature and declared his support for Karzai. The Emergency Loya Jirga convened on 11 June. Karzai won the presidential election, with 1,295 of the approximately 1,575 votes cast. Masooda Jalal, a doctor and the first woman ever to participate in an Afghan presidential election, came second with 171 votes; Mahfouz Nedai secured 109 votes. Some 83 voters abstained. The UN declared the elections flawed, with incidents of malpractice and intimidation of candidates, but fair. The Loya Jirga was also expected to choose the structure of the Transitional Authority and its principal staff; however, the decision-making took place largely outside the assembly tent. Debate in the assembly was reportedly obstructed by poor chairmanship and the lack of a clear agenda. Nevertheless, on 19 June the Loya Jirga approved the Transitional Authority cabinet, retaining most of the incumbent members of the Interim Authority. However, it failed to establish a Meli Shura (National Assembly). Instead, it was decided that a National Assembly Commission would be convened at a future date to discuss this matter. Karzai announced the creation of a number of other commissions to address the issues of defence, human rights, internal security reform and a new constitution.

In early July 2002 the Vice-President and Minister of Reconstruction, Haji Abdul Qadir, was assassinated, raising new concerns over the Transitional Authority's stability. Many observers held the remnants of the Taliban or al-Qa'ida responsible for the attack. In early September Karzai escaped an assassination attempt in Qandahar; hours later a bomb explosion in Kabul killed 30 people and injured at least 160 others. Afghan officials and Western diplomats believed that Hekmatyar had joined forces with remaining members of the Taliban and al-Qa'ida in south and east Afghanistan and had perpetrated the attacks in an attempt to depose the Transitional Authority. Hekmatyar had allegedly also held negotiations with other discontented regional leaders in an effort to form a wider alliance against the Afghan Government and US military presence in Afghanistan. Following the bomb attack some 800 additional ISAF troops were deployed across Kabul to carry out random searches of vehicles and to construct security checkpoints; police officers arrested more than 100 people in connection with the attack.

Reported incidents of factional fighting increased significantly in mid-2002. In July Karzai announced the establishment of a UN-supported security commission, which would begin the disarming of rebel troops and precipitate the creation of a national army. Despite commanding little control outside Kabul, Karzai warned military commanders that their powers would be removed unless they denounced factional fighting and joined the Government. In November the President dismissed more than 20 senior regional officials—including Gen. Abdul Hamid, the military commander of Mazar-i-Sharif—in an attempt to consolidate the Transitional Authority's jurisdiction outside Kabul.

In the mean time, rival military commanders Gen. Dostam and Gen. Atta Mohammed eventually negotiated a somewhat fragile cease-fire in October 2002 and agreed to support the security commission's disarmament programme. By mid-January 2003 thousands of weapons had been collected, but regional commanders remained as powerful as before and internecine fighting continued in Khost and Paktia provinces. At a conference focusing on Afghanistan's reconstruction, held in Germany in early December 2002, Karzai officially announced a plan to create a 70,000-strong multi-ethnic army. In January 2003 Karzai established four committees to accelerate the disarmament process and to recruit a national army. In October a three-year programme of disarmament, demobilization and reintegration, drawn up by the Transitional Administration and the USA, was launched. Shortly before, a law proscribing the participation of military commanders and armed factions in political life was approved by the authorities. In December Gen. Dostam and Gen. Mohammed surrendered army tanks and weapons to the ANA under a deal brokered by the Minister of Interior Affairs and British forces. Meanwhile, Karzai continued attempts to extend his control outside Kabul. In May 12 Afghan provincial governors signed an agreement to transfer customs revenues to the Transitional Administration after Karzai threatened to resign if the governors refused to accede to this demand.

In early September 2002 the Transitional Authority announced a currency reform programme designed to end the problem of hyperinflation and to stop regional commanders from printing their own banknotes to fund military operations. During a two-month period, commencing 7 October, old afghani notes were exchanged for new afghani notes at a rate of 1,000 old afghanis to one new afghani. In late November Afghan authorities prevented an attempt to assassinate Marshal (formerly Gen.) Fahim. At the same time, the UN Security Council approved the extension of the mandate of ISAF for one year beyond 20 December; Germany and the Netherlands agreed to assume joint command of the force from Turkey.

In March 2003 a number of new political parties were established and united under a single 'umbrella' movement: the National Front for Democracy in Afghanistan. The parties were not officially recognized by the Government, however, as the formation of political parties remained illegal. In August supporters of former King Zahir Shah launched Jonbesh-i Wahadat-i Melli (the Afghan National Unity Movement); Sultan Mahmoud Ghazi was elected Chairman of the new political party. Later that month the activities of a new political organization, Hizb-i Muttahid-i Melli (the United National Party), established by supporters of the former communist PDPA, were proscribed by the Supreme Court after being deemed 'anti-Islamic'. On 9 September the Government approved legislation allowing the creation of political parties. In August, meanwhile, the North Atlantic Treaty Organization (NATO) assumed formal control of ISAF. In mid-October the UN Security Council passed a resolution authorizing the expansion of the mandate of ISAF.

Meanwhile, in April 2003 the Afghan Constitutional Drafting Commission, which had been meeting since November 2002, completed its draft of a new constitution. A 35-member Constitutional Commission was established to review the draft and submit the proposed charter to a constitutional loya jirga for discussion and ratification. The charter, envisaging a strong presidential system of government and a bicameral legislature, was finally made public in early November. The draft provoked a wide range of reactions, including concerns about inadequate protection of women's rights and religious freedoms. On 14 December the Constitutional Loya Jirga convened. Some 502 delegates representing all 32 provinces of Afghanistan, as well as the country's ethnic groups, minorities and refugees, were divided into 10 committees to debate the draft constitution. Around three weeks of intense negotiations, which were marred by ethnic divisions and arguments, followed. There were fears that an agreement would not be reached when more than 40% of the delegates boycotted the voting process on 1 January 2004; however, following 'closed-door' negotiations led by Brahimi and the US ambassador to Afghanistan, a compromise was reached two days later.

On 4 January 2004 Afghanistan's new Constitution was approved by consensus rather than by actual vote, after the Chairman of the Loya Jirga called for endorsement of the document by asking the delegates to rise and stand. In certain respects the amended charter differed little from the earlier draft: it still provided for the introduction of a strongly presidential political system following the holding of presidential elections scheduled for June, despite a campaign by former *mujahidin* parties for the installation of a parliamentary state. The revised Constitution, however, added a second vice-presidential post and gave the National Assembly powers of veto over major presidential appointments and policies. The document made no specific reference to the role of *Shari'a*. The status of languages had proved one of the main issues that had delayed the finalization of the agreement; eventually, Pashto and Dari were identified as the national languages, with provision made for a third national language in areas where the language of the ethnic group forming the majority population differed. The charter also contained new human rights provisions and articulated the equal rights of men and women before the law. One of the most significant achievements was the ensuring of greater political representation for women: it was agreed that approximately 25% of seats in the Wolasi Jirga (House of Representatives) would be reserved for women; the President would appoint additional women to the Meshrano Jirga (House of Elders). Following the ratification of the Constitution, however, Human Rights Watch expressed concern that military commanders, factional leaders and ministers had been involved in political intimidation and electoral fraud before and during the holding of the Constitutional Loya Jirga. It was fairly evident that local factions continued to dominate Afghanistan's political processes and doubts were raised about whether the country could hold free and fair presidential elections in June and parliamentary elections by the end of the year. Furthermore, the failure to address adequately the role of *Shari'a*, and its relation to human rights safeguards, generated concerns that conservative elements in the judiciary would be able to implement interpretations of Islam that might violate human rights values. In July it was announced that the presidential election would be held on 9 October 2004. However, legislative elections, which were originally due to have been held at the same time, were to be deferred until 2005, owing to the ongoing unrest in the country.

Meanwhile, in March 2003 US-led forces launched 'Operation Valiant Strike', a major offensive to combat the regrouping of Taliban and al-Qa'ida fighters in southern Afghanistan. In early April, in response to an attack on US and Afghan forces by suspected Taliban members, US-led troops launched an assault on alleged remnants of the Taliban and al-Qa'ida in the Tor Ghar mountains of Afghanistan, close to the border with Pakistan. In early May the US Secretary of Defense, Donald Rumsfeld, announced that major combat operations had ended in Afghanistan and that US forces had begun to concentrate on the stabilization and reconstruction of the country. Despite this statement, the security situation remained fragile. In late June US-led forces launched a major assault on suspected Taliban and al-Qa'ida fighters along Afghanistan's border with Pakistan, in response to an increase in attacks on members of the Afghan Transitional Administration and ISAF. The Taliban, reportedly bolstered by new volunteers from Pakistan and by funds from drugs-trafficking, continued their campaign of violence. Humanitarian organizations were also affected by the increase in violent incidents. In November a French refugee worker was shot dead in Ghazni by suspected Taliban members. UNHCR consequently announced that it would temporarily withdraw foreign staff from large parts of southern and eastern Afghanistan. In the weeks preceding the Constitutional Loya Jirga, the Taliban increased the number of their attacks against foreign aid workers and contractors and US and Afghan soldiers. In early December US forces launched 'Operation Avalanche' in southern and eastern Afghanistan against Taliban and al-Qa'ida members. The operation was condemned, however, after 15 Afghan children and two adults were killed in two separate miscalculated aerial attacks. In early January 2004 ISAF assumed command of a Provincial Reconstruction Team (PRT) in Kunduz, as the pilot project for further expansion of the international security force. By the end of May 2005 ISAF controlled a total of nine PRTs, five in the north and four in the west of Afghanistan, allowing the US-led coalition to concentrate more on the volatile southern and eastern parts of the country.

Throughout 2004 violence and instability continued to affect significant areas of the country. In February five Afghan aid workers died following an ambush east of Kabul. In March the Minister of Civil Aviation and Tourism and son of Ismail Khan, Mirwais Sadiq, was killed in a reported grenade attack in Herat. Khan held the regional government commander, Gen. Zahir Nayebzada, responsible for his son's death, and violent clashes ensued between rival forces in the province. Nayebzada eventually fled, and Khan regained control of the city. President Karzai subsequently deployed forces of the ANA to Herat in an attempt to restore order. Meanwhile, US troops continued to engage in operations against the Taliban. By the end of May 90 US soldiers had reportedly been killed in Afghanistan since the commencement of military action in the country. In the following month the murder of 11 Chinese construction workers during an attack on a camp in the northern province of Kunduz, generally perceived to be one of the safer areas of the country, raised concerns regarding security for the forthcoming national elections. In the same month the killing of five Dutch workers from the international aid organization Médecins Sans Frontières (MSF), during an ambush of their vehicle in the province of Badghis, prompted MSF to withdraw completely from Afghanistan. MSF criticized the US-led coalition for endangering aid workers by failing to distinguish properly between humanitarian and military operations. Meanwhile, the Governor of Ghor, Ibrahim Malikzada, was ousted from his position following a violent power struggle between local militia commanders in the province. In an attempt to increase security in the country, and to ensure its expansion outside Kabul, NATO pledged to increase the size of ISAF from 6,500 to 10,000. The Government expressed its concern that the additional forces would be deployed only in the north of the country, stressing that they were most urgently needed in the southern and eastern provinces.

In September 2004, in an apparent attempt to assert his jurisdiction outside Kabul in advance of the impending presidential election, President Karzai dismissed Ismail Khan, the powerful Governor of Herat province, and offered him the cabinet post of Minister of Mines and Industries. Khan's dismissal provoked rioting in the province as his supporters confronted US troops, reportedly resulting in the deaths of seven people and injuries to a further 60, including 15 US soldiers. Khan subsequently rejected the ministerial portfolio, and Mohammed Khairkhwa was appointed to succeed him as Governor of Herat. Shortly afterwards President Karzai survived an assassination attempt when a rocket narrowly missed the US military helicopter in which he was travelling on an official visit to the south-east of the country. The Taliban claimed responsibility for the attack. In the same month the UN Security Council adopted a resolution extending the mandate of ISAF for one year.

On 9 October 2004 Afghanistan held its first direct presidential election. Despite some sporadic violence on the day of the election, no widespread disturbances were reported. Shortly after polling had begun, all 15 opposition candidates launched a boycott of the vote and demanded that it be abandoned, owing to alleged widespread electoral fraud. However, international observers announced in the following month that they had concluded, following an inquiry, that alleged irregularities during the poll were not considered significant enough to have altered the final result. Interim President Hamid Karzai was subsequently declared the winner, receiving 55.4% of the votes, sufficient to ensure that a second round of voting would not be necessary. Former Minister of Education Younis Qanooni came second, with 16.3% of the votes, followed by Mohammad Mohaqqeq, with 11.7%, and Gen. Abdul Rashid Dostam, with 10.0%. A reported 83.7% of the electorate participated in the poll. Concerns were, however, raised by the regional nature of Karzai's victory, which seemed largely to have been secured by voters in the Pashtun-majority provinces, indicating that he had not succeeded in appealing to all ethnic groups. Meanwhile, the kidnapping of three foreign UN workers by armed militants in Kabul in late October raised fears that insurgents were adopting new tactics in their efforts to undermine democracy in the country. The kidnappers, who were reportedly members of a militant group called the Jaish-e-Muslimeen (Army of Islam), threatened to kill the hostages unless their demands for the release of certain prisoners and the withdrawal of foreign troops from Afghanistan were met. However, the hostages were released unharmed in the following month after a series of raids by US soldiers and Afghan security forces. It was later reported that Afghan security personnel had killed one of the kidnappers during the raid and tortured another suspected kidnapper while in custody until he died.

In December 2004, following his inauguration, President Karzai announced the composition of his Cabinet. While Minister of Foreign Affairs Dr Abdullah Abdullah and Minister of Interior Affairs Ali Ahmad Jalali retained their portfolios, Marshal Fahim was replaced as Minister of Defence by Gen. Abdul Rahim Wardak. Hedayat Amin Arsala was allocated the commerce portfolio and Ismail Khan was appointed Minister of Energy and Water. However, several powerful regional commanders were not included in the new Cabinet, ostensibly owing to the fact that they did not satisfy a requirement that all cabinet ministers be educated to university level. Karzai was criticized for his failure to allocate more portfolios in the Pashtun-dominated Cabinet to other ethnic groups. In an attempt to address Afghanistan's continuing problems with the widespread cultivation of opium, a Ministry of Counter Narcotics was created, headed by Habibullah Qaderi. According to the UN, in 2004 the total area under poppy cultivation had increased by 64%, compared with the previous year, despite a government ban on the cultivation and trafficking of the drug. Meanwhile, defeated presidential candidate Younis Qanooni stated his intention to form a political party, New Afghanistan, to contest the forthcoming legislative elections, which, it was announced in March 2005, would be held in September of that year.

In May 2005 anti-US demonstrations occurred in several cities in Afghanistan, prompted by reports in the US-based publication *Newsweek* that interrogators at the US detention centre in Guantánamo Bay, Cuba, had allegedly desecrated copies of the Islamic holy text, the Koran. The demonstrations became violent in some places when police fired on protesters. At least 16 people were subsequently reported to have died. *Newsweek* later retracted the allegations. The consequent strain placed upon US-Afghan relations was intensified several days later when *The New York Times* published a report into the alleged abuse of Afghan detainees by US troops at a detention centre in Bagram. Shortly afterwards, President Karzai met with his US counterpart, George W. Bush, in Washington. Although the two leaders signed a memorandum of understanding with regard to a continued strategic partnership, Bush ruled out any possibility of Afghanistan assuming control of the US troops that remained in the country. In October reports that US soldiers, in contravention of Islamic religious tradition, had burned the bodies of two Taliban fighters whom they had killed, and then taunted Muslim villagers about the incident, contributed to further tensions in the bilateral relationship.

On 18 September 2005 an estimated 5,800 candidates, including several former Taliban officials, contested elections to the 249-member Wolasi Jirga and 34 provincial legislatures. A total of 68 seats in the Wolasi Jirga were reserved for women. The polls constituted Afghanistan's first democratic legislative elections since 1969. The nation-wide turn-out was an estimated 53% of the electorate, with the figure decreasing to only 36% in Kabul, a significant decline compared with the level of participation at the 2004 presidential election. The widespread disruption that al-Qa'ida and the Taliban had threatened to orchestrate on polling day did not materialize. A delegation from the European Union (EU) initially described the elections as having been 'free, fair and transparent', but concerns were later expressed as to possible instances of fraud and intimidation of voters. The results, which were announced in November, showed that many of those who had been elected were powerful factional figures, not aligned with any particular party, leading to fears that the country's legislature would be less a unified mechanism through which the central Government could assert its authority, and more a conduit for the re-emergence of provincial 'warlordism'. The newly elected National Assembly convened for the first time in December. Younis Qanooni, who was widely perceived to be the most prominent opposition figure in the legislature, was subsequently elected Speaker of the Wolasi Jirga, and Sibghatullah Mojaddedi Speaker of the Meshrano Jirga.

In the mean time, in late September 2005 Minister of Interior Affairs Ali Ahmad Jalali announced his resignation from the Cabinet, citing personal reasons. It was rumoured, however, that his departure was in part a result of disagreements concerning President Karzai's appointment of factional leaders to provincial posts. Zarar Ahmad Moqbel was subsequently appointed to replace him, on an acting basis. In March 2006 Karzai announced an extensive reorganization of the Cabinet, including the replacement of Dr Abdullah Abdullah as Minister of Foreign Affairs by Dr Rangin Dadfar Spanta, and the allocation of the interior affairs portfolio to Zarar Ahmad Moqbel on a permanent basis. The Cabinet was presented for approval to the Meli Shura in the following month. Of the 25 ministers nominated, 20 were approved by majority vote, while five were rejected. In August the remaining five positions were filled; new appointments included Mohammad Amin Farhang as Minister of Commerce and Industries and Hosna Banu Ghazanfar as Minister of Women's Affairs.

Provincial instability and violence, often co-ordinated by a resurgent Taliban, continued throughout 2005. More than 1,400 people were believed to have died over the course of the year during fighting with Taliban insurgents, while a number of US and British soldiers were also killed. Violence escalated towards the end of the year, with a number of suicide bombings, hitherto a rarity in Afghanistan, taking place. The attacks were believed to have been instigated by al-Qa'ida and the Taliban and carried out by foreign militants.

In 2006 the security situation deteriorated, with frequent suicide bombings and clashes between Taliban forces and coalition troops leading to a rising death toll of combatants and civilians. Much of the conflict was centred on the southern and eastern provinces of the country, including Helmand and Qandahar, where regular attacks and raids were carried out by both sides. On 29 May, when a road accident caused by a US army truck killed five or more Afghans, serious rioting erupted in Kabul, resulting in at least 14 deaths. In July the Minister of Defence, Gen. Abdul Rahim Wardak, declared that even a 70,000-strong Afghan army, a goal that was estimated to be three years from attainment, would be unable to provide adequate security and stability for the country, and speculated that a minimum of 150,000 national troops were actually required. This forecast was in stark contrast to the size of the existing Afghan army, which comprised approximately 30,000 soldiers. At the end of July NATO announced the expansion of the mandate of its 18,000 troops into the southern provinces, assuming control from US-led coalition forces in the area. The violence continued, with Taliban militants targeting, among others, government officials: on 10 September Abdul Hakim Taniwal, the Governor of Paktia province, was killed in a suicide bombing, and on 25 September the Director for Women's Affairs of Qandahar province, Safia Ama Jan, was assassinated. In the following month NATO forces, which had now increased to number approximately 30,000, assumed military command of the eastern provinces; with this transfer ISAF became responsible for international military operations throughout Afghanistan. At the end of October NATO air raids in Qandahar province were reported to have killed at least 25 civilians, prompting concern regarding the mounting number of civilian deaths in the conflict and a public apology from NATO's Supreme Commander. At the end of 2006 a number of reports were published estimating that up to 3,700 fatalities (around one-quarter of which were civilians) had occurred in Afghanistan that year as a result of the ongoing conflict, a significant and alarming increase compared with the previous year.

Official reports of record levels of opium production in Afghanistan in 2006, coupled with an increase in the amount of land under opium poppy cultivation, bolstered the notion that the resurgence of the Taliban and the growing importance of the opium industry were inextricably linked. Opium production levels showed no sign of falling in the following year: according to estimates published by UNODC, the land area under poppy cultivation increased by 17% in 2007, compared with the previous year, while actual opium production rose by 34%. Accordingly, Afghanistan, with its 93% share of the global market, consolidated its position as the world's leading supplier of opiates in 2007.

In February 2007 the British Ministry of Defence announced that the number of troops deployed in the south of Afghanistan was to be increased to 5,800. In March a senior Taliban commander confirmed that the insurgents were gathering strength for an imminent offensive. However, the Taliban suffered setbacks in the following months, with the deaths of several senior figures, including Mullah Dadullah, who was believed to have been the Taliban's most senior military commander and at the forefront of the planned offensive. None the less, attacks on government officials continued: Abdol Sabur Farid, a member of the Meshrano Jirga and former Prime Minister, was killed in May, and President Karzai himself survived an attempt on his life in June. Suicide bombings were an increasingly commonplace feature of insurgency activity in 2007; in June a bomb attack in Kabul resulted in some 35 fatalities, and at least 41 people were killed in a suicide bombing in Baghlan in November. Repeated calls made by President Karzai and human rights organizations for an increase in public vigilance failed to stem the alarming rate of civilian deaths, which was a cause for serious concern among Afghans and the international community, and garnered widespread media coverage. Both sides in the conflict were variously held responsible for the rising toll of casualties: in April a Human Rights Watch report condemned the insurgents' tactics, highlighting the large number of resultant civilian fatalities in 2006, while in June 2007 the International Committee of the Red Cross (ICRC) denounced the coalition forces' strategies, which had led to the deaths of numerous civilians in the preceding months. The British charity organization Oxfam estimated that around 600 civilians died in 2007 as a result of military operations conducted by both coalition and insurgency forces. During the year there were also several instances of hostage-taking, most notably the kidnapping of 23 South Korean Christian missionaries—who claimed to be involved in development projects rather than in work of a religious nature—by the Taliban in July. Two of the missionaries were subsequently killed by their kidnappers. Negotiations led to the release of two others; the remaining 19 were released at the end of August following an agreement between the South Korean Government and the Taliban, amid unconfirmed reports of a ransom payment. Meanwhile, in May the Meshrano Jirga had adopted legislation aimed at opening lines of communication with the Taliban, and in early September President Karzai expressed his willingness to enter into negotiations with the insurgents. Initially the Taliban appeared ready to accept this offer; however, in late September the Taliban stipulated the withdrawal of foreign troops from Afghanistan as a precondition for the holding of bilateral talks, thereby stalling the nascent process indefinitely. In early March 2008 a senior official in the Norwegian Ministry of Foreign Affairs, Kai Eide, was appointed as Special Envoy of the UN Secretary-General to Afghanistan.

In 2007 Afghan government troops were reported to have carried out independent operations for the first time, and in December it was estimated that the ANA would reach its target (set in 2001) of totalling 70,000 soldiers by early 2008. At the same time, however, the Afghan Ministry of Defence stated that idealistically the ANA should be expanded to 200,000 men in order to handle both external threats and the deteriorating security situation within Afghanistan itself. In February 2007 President Karzai revised a controversial bill granting amnesty to alleged war criminals of the preceding 30 years; in March the amended bill, which permitted prosecutions instigated by individuals whilst providing amnesty from state prosecution, was endorsed by the Wolasi Jirga and subsequently came into force. In mid-2007 the Minister of Foreign Affairs, Dr Rangin Dadfar Spanta, and the Minister of Refugees and Repatriation, Mohammad Akbar Akbar, were removed from office by a parliamentary vote of no confidence as a result of their alleged acquiescence over the forced repatriation of Afghan refugees from Iran; following the intervention of Karzai and the Supreme Court, however, Spanta retained his cabinet position. Meanwhile, in March a new political grouping entitled Jabhe-ye-Motahed-e-Milli (United National Front—UNF) was established, comprising senior government officials, members of Parliament, and former members of the United Front and of communist parties. With former President Burhanuddin Rabbani as its Chairman and prominent figures such as Gen. Dostam, Marshal Fahim, Younis Qanooni and Vice-President Ahmad Zia Masoud within its ranks, the UNF was expected to have a significant impact on Afghan politics. Many of the Front's political objectives were reportedly in agreement with those of Karzai, but a number diverged considerably. Among these latter aims was the UNF's advocacy of the abolition of the presidential system of government in favour of a parliamentary system.

The former King, Zahir Shah, died in Kabul on 23 July, prompting three days of official mourning.

On 22 December 2002 the Governments of Afghanistan, China, Iran, Pakistan, Tajikistan, Turkmenistan and Uzbekistan signed the Kabul Declaration on Good-Neighbourly Relations, in which they pledged never again to interfere in each other's affairs. On paper, the agreement signalled a new era of regional co-operation, yet, in reality, the situation was somewhat different. Afghan officials claimed that Iranian Revolutionary Guards were continuing to provide financial and military assistance to Ismail Khan; Russia was reportedly supporting Marshal Fahim and his army; and certain Saudis had allegedly resumed sending financial assistance to the remnants of the Taliban in Pakistan. In addition, the Uzbek President had provided Uzbek Gen. Dostam with his own bodyguards. Publicly, the Pakistani President supported Karzai and the USA's campaign against al-Qa'ida; at the same time, however, Pakistan's Inter-Services Intelligence (ISI) was reportedly giving sanctuary to senior Taliban members and other anti-Government military commanders, such as Hekmatyar.

In mid-February 2003 the Pakistani and Afghan military intelligence services held talks in Rome in an attempt to resolve deep-rooted differences. The Afghan delegation repeated its claims that the ISI was harbouring Islamist militants. The ISI, in turn, expressed its discontent at the Transitional Administration for granting India, Iran and Russia unrestricted movement around Afghanistan. The opening of Indian consulates in Jalalabad and Qandahar, close to the Afghan–Pakistani border, particularly riled the ISI. Some two months later, during an official visit to Pakistan, President Karzai urged the Pakistani Government to assist in curbing the cross-border attacks by militant Islamists. Relations were strained when Pakistan delivered a formal protest to Afghanistan in June over the dumping of the bodies of some 21 Taliban fighters on its territory; the Afghan authorities were forced to recover the bodies after Pakistani border guards discovered that the dead were, in fact, not Pakistani, but Afghan citizens. One month later, in a seemingly well-planned operation, the Pakistani embassy in Afghanistan was stormed and raided by hundreds of Afghans in protest against alleged incursions by Pakistani border troops into Afghan territory. The crowds were dispersed by Afghan police; Karzai apologized for the incident to the Pakistani President and promised to pay compensation. The embassy was reopened almost two weeks later. In January 2004 the Pakistani Prime Minister, Zafarullah Khan Jamali, paid his first ever official visit to Afghanistan; the two countries agreed to work together to combat cross-border infiltration. In 2005–06, however, despite a number of meetings between Afghan and Pakistani officials, relations were strained, with President Karzai and his Pakistani counterpart engaging in public recriminations over cross-border activities and the fight against the Taliban. In December 2006 Pakistan's proposal to lay landmines and construct fences along the Afghan–Pakistani border to prevent the cross-border movement of militants provoked a negative reaction from Karzai, who claimed that such a strategy would be divisive. Relations between the two countries appeared to improve with the holding of a joint 'peace jirga' in Kabul in August 2007. The four-day meeting, which was attended by some 650 tribal leaders from both countries, along with Karzai,

President Musharraf and other senior government officials, was convened with the aim of addressing shared issues such as security and terrorism. In August 2005 Indian Prime Minister Manmohan Singh visited Afghanistan, the first time an Indian Prime Minister had visited the country since 1975. During his visit the two countries signed several agreements relating to a wide range of issues and stressed the need for greater bilateral co-operation. In November 2005 Afghanistan was approved as the eighth member of the South Asian Association for Regional Co-operation (SAARC) at the 13th summit meeting of the organization, held in Dhaka, Bangladesh; it was formally admitted into SAARC at the 14th summit meeting, which took place in New Delhi, India, in April 2007.

Government

During 11–19 June 2002 an Emergency Loya Jirga, comprising an estimated 1,650 delegates, appointed a head of state and the principal staff of a broad-based, gender-sensitive Transitional Authority. A new Constitution was adopted by a Constitutional Loya Jirga in January 2004. The charter provided for a presidential system of government and a bicameral legislature. Direct presidential elections were held in October 2004, and the elected President was formally inaugurated in December. In September 2005 elections took place to the 249-member Wolasi Jirga (House of Representatives), the lower house of the Meli Shura (National Assembly), and 34 provincial councils. Following these elections, the upper house of the Meli Shura, the Meshrano Jirga (House of Elders), which comprised 102 members (three times the number of provinces in Afghanistan), was constituted; one-third of its members were elected by the provincial councils, one-third by district councils, and the remaining members were appointed by the President. The Meli Shura held its inaugural session in December 2005, thus concluding the Bonn Process, which had achieved its aim of establishing a democratically governed Islamic Republic of Afghanistan.

Defence

Following the defeat of the Taliban in December 2001, an International Security Assistance Force (ISAF) was deployed in Kabul and at Bagram airbase to help maintain security in the area. In August 2003 the North Atlantic Treaty Organization (NATO) assumed command of the force, which in late 2005 consisted of approximately 12,400 members from 35 countries. (This figure included about 2,000 troops deployed temporarily as Election Support Forces for the legislative elections that took place on 18 September 2005.) ISAF was also responsible for the training of the first battalion of the Afghan National Guard, which was operational in April 2003. In December of that year NATO began to expand its presence in the country by assuming command of a number of Provincial Reconstruction Teams (PRTs) in the north and west of Afghanistan. In 2005 planning had begun for an expansion of ISAF into the south of the country, and by October 2006 ISAF, numbering some 30,000 troops, had assumed control of international military operations throughout Afghanistan.

US and French forces began training the first set of recruits for a new multi-ethnic Afghan National Army (ANA) in May 2003. In December President Karzai announced that the ANA would eventually comprise 70,000 soldiers and ordered all private armies to disarm and merge into the ANA within one year. Four committees were established in January 2003 to accelerate the disarmament and army-building process. By mid-2006 the disarmament of the 60,000 militia fighters who had been identified and targeted for demobilization was believed to have been completed. By the end of 2007 the ANA was reported to be nearing its initial target of totalling 70,000 troops. It was envisaged that the army would be supported by a border guard of 12,000. There was to be a 70,000-strong paramilitary force, including police officers trained by German instructors.

Economic Affairs

In 2006, according to estimates by the World Bank, Afghanistan's gross national income (GNI), measured at average 2004–06 prices, was US $8,092.3m. In 2005/06, according to official estimates, Afghanistan's gross domestic product (GDP), excluding the illegal cultivation of poppies and production of drugs, was $6,851m. This implied a per head GDP of $303. During 1995–2006, it was estimated, the population increased at an average annual rate of 2.2%. According to the Asian Development Bank (ADB), GDP increased by 4.6% in 2003/04, by 12.6% in 2004/05 and by 10.3% in 2005/06. The IMF projected that GDP would rise by an estimated 12.0% in 2006/07.

Agriculture (including hunting, forestry and fishing), according to the ADB, contributed 39.5% of GDP in 2005/06. According to official figures, 69.6% of the economically active population were employed in the agricultural sector in 2002/03. Livestock plays an important role in the traditional Afghan economy and is normally a major source of income for the country's numerous nomadic groups. However, the total livestock population has been seriously depleted, owing to the many years of conflict and prolonged drought conditions. In 2002/03 the sector benefited from greater rainfall and the increased availability and better quality of seeds and fertilizers. There was further growth in 2003/04, aided by increased rainfall, an expansion of the area under crop cultivation and the return of significant numbers of refugees to their lands; cereal production expanded by 50%, compared with the previous year, to 5.4m. metric tons, the level Afghanistan required to be self-sufficient. Wheat production was estimated at 4m. tons in 2004, but this figure decreased to 3m. tons in 2005. Expansion was not as significant as had been expected, owing to the ongoing drought in some regions of the country. As a consequence of this drought, cereal production decreased in 2004/05. The country thus continued to be dependent on food assistance. In 2005/06 greater rainfall contributed to a recovery in the output of the agricultural sector; cereal production was reported to have increased significantly compared with the poor harvest of the previous year. According to ADB estimates, the GDP of the agricultural sector contracted by 2.1% in 2004/05, compared with the previous year, but increased by 2.8% in 2005/06.

According to the ADB, the industrial sector (including mining, manufacturing, construction and power) contributed 25.3% of GDP in 2005/06, and employed an estimated 6.2% of the economically active population in 2002/03, according to official figures. The construction sub-sector performed particularly well, owing to the extensive post-war reconstruction activity in the country. According to ADB estimates, sectoral GDP increased by 35.8% in 2004/05 and by 19.3% in 2005/06.

Mining and quarrying, according to IMF estimates, contributed 0.1% of GDP in 2004/05, and employed about 1.5% of the settled labour force in 1979. Natural gas was the major mineral export (accounting for about 23.6% of total export earnings, according to the IMF, in 1988/89). Salt, hard coal, copper, lapis lazuli, emeralds, barytes and talc are also mined. In addition, Afghanistan has small reserves of petroleum and iron ore. In 1998 the Taliban had claimed that monthly revenue from the allegedly renascent mining sector in Afghanistan totalled US $3.5m. (including revenue from the recently revived steel-smelting plant in Baghlan province). The rehabilitation of the mining industry was ongoing from 2003/04.

Manufacturing, according to IMF estimates, contributed 15.8% of GDP in 2004/05, and employed about 10.9% of the settled labour force in 1979. Afghanistan's major manufacturing industries included food products, cotton textiles, chemical fertilizers, cement, leather and plastic goods. In 1999 only one of the four existing cement plants in Afghanistan and about 10% of the textile mills remained in operation (prior to the Soviet invasion in 1979 there were about 220 state-owned factories operating in Afghanistan). The traditional handicraft sector has better survived the devastating effects of war, however, and carpets, leather, embroidery and fur products continue to be produced.

Energy is derived principally from petroleum (which is imported from Iran and republics of the former USSR, notably Turkmenistan) and coal. It has been estimated that Afghanistan has some 73m. metric tons of coal reserves. In 2003 the ADB undertook a feasibility study into the possibility of constructing a pipeline to transport natural gas from the Dauletabad gas fields in Turkmenistan to markets in Afghanistan, Pakistan and, potentially, India. The project had initially been proposed in 1990, but was postponed owing to political and security concerns until the establishment of the Interim Authority in 2001. A protocol concerning the pipeline was signed by the Governments of Afghanistan, Pakistan and Turkmenistan in December 2003. Although little further progress was made in the following year, prospects improved in early 2005 when the Indian Government authorized discussion of the planned pipeline as a means of providing gas for the Indian market. The ADB conducted another feasibility study in mid-2005, concluding that construction of the pipeline could potentially play an important role in ensuring security and stability in the region. The Afghan President, Hamid Karzai, continued to stress to donors that development of the pipeline was a priority for the country. In May 2006 the Indian Government endorsed India's participation in the project, and in September Indian officials participated in a meeting of what was to be known as the Turkmenistan-Afghanistan-Pakistan-India (TAPI) pipeline project. In November of that year the four project partners demanded that work on the project be accelerated.

Services, according to the ADB, contributed 35.3% of GDP in 2005/06, and employed an estimated 24.2% of the economically active population in 2002/03, according to official figures. The GDP of the service sector increased by 19.6% in 2004/05 and by 10.4% in 2005/06, according to ADB estimates. Sectoral growth was mainly driven by the expansion of the transport and telecommunications sub-sectors.

In 2006/07 there was a deficit of an estimated US $97.0m. on the current account of the balance of payments. In the same year a trade deficit of $3,509.2m. was recorded. In that year total exports (excluding opium-related exports) reached an estimated $1,923.8m. Total imports, meanwhile, increased to an estimated $5,095.5m. in 2006/07. Exports were projected to reach $2,074.8m. in 2007/08; imports were forecast to increase to $5,584.0m. In 2004/05 the principal exports were carpets and handicrafts, dried fruit and animal skins; the principal imports were machinery and equipment, food, and fabrics, clothing and footwear. In that year the principal market for exports was Pakistan (which purchased an estimated 84.6% of the total) and the principal source of imports was the People's Republic of China (providing an estimated 17.7%). Another major trading partner was India. These official statistics do not, however, include illegal trade and smuggling. If the illegal revenue from the export of opium were included, a large trade surplus would be recorded. In 2000 a UN Development Programme/World Bank study estimated that out of total exports of $1,200m., about $1,000m. was unofficially exported. In March 2003 Afghanistan signed a new preferential trade agreement with India. Two months earlier India and Iran had agreed to improve the road network linking Afghanistan with the Chabahar port in Iran. Afghanistan began to open trade routes with Central Asia in late 2002; in August 2003 a memorandum of understanding was signed with Uzbekistan. Trade relations with Pakistan, the USA and the European Union have also improved in recent years.

In the financial year ending 20 March 2007 there was a projected budgetary deficit of 15,802m. afghanis, which was expected to be covered by financial assistance. In 2002/03 Afghanistan received US $26.4m. in bilateral grants and $157.1m. in multilateral official development assistance (this did not include grants of $51.24m.). In 2005/06 donor grants and loans totalled an estimated 16,732m. afghanis. According to the ADB, consumer prices in Kabul rose by an estimated average of 13.3% in 2003/04, compared with the previous year, by 5.9% in 2004/05 and by 7.2% in 2005/06.

Afghanistan is a member of the UN Economic and Social Commission for Asia and the Pacific (ESCAP, see p. 35), the Colombo Plan (see p. 411), which seeks to promote economic and social development in Asia and the Pacific, the Asian Development Bank (ADB, see p. 182) and the Economic Co-operation Organization (ECO, see p. 238). In November 2005 it was approved as a full member of the South Asian Association for Regional Co-operation (SAARC, see p. 384) and formally admitted as the eighth member of the regional organization in April 2007. In April 2003 Afghanistan applied for membership to the World Trade Organization (WTO, see p. 396); it formally initiated its accession process in November 2005.

It is difficult to provide an accurate economic profile of Afghanistan, after many years of conflict, intermittent droughts and earthquakes and constant population movements. However, more reliable statistics have become available in recent years as government and financial institutions have been re-established. In 2002 problems such as severe food and fuel shortages, the lack of infrastructure and the difficulties posed by the return of thousands of refugees to their war-ravaged land began to be addressed. In early 2002 the Interim Authority devised a National Development Framework for the reconstruction programme, which focused on these challenges. It placed emphasis on allowing the private sector to lead Afghanistan's recovery and on streamlining the public administration. In January international donors pledged US $4,500m. worth of aid over five years towards the reconstruction of Afghanistan, of which some $1,800m. had been disbursed by March 2003. The bulk of these funds, however, was dedicated to humanitarian assistance, and only a small proportion was invested in the country's reconstruction programmes. Nevertheless, by the end of 2003 a number of infrastructure projects, funded by international financial institutions and individual countries, were under way or had reached completion. From 2003 the economy showed strong signs of recovery, largely owing to the end of major conflict and of prolonged drought, international financial assistance and government economic policies. A new currency was introduced in late 2002 and a sound monetary policy has since been in place; consequently, the exchange rate has been largely stable and domestic and international confidence in the new currency has increased. Efforts to develop a modern banking sector commenced in 2003; the central bank was granted autonomy and in September the Government approved a law allowing foreign banks to open branches in Afghanistan. The reorganization and modernization of the central bank was ongoing in 2004–06; by the end of 2004 seven new commercial banks had been granted licences to operate in the country, while three state-owned banks had gone into liquidation. Reconstruction of the education system was also under way; women were given equal employment rights, as well as access to education. In late 2005 the Government approved legislation intended to encourage both domestic and foreign private investment in Afghanistan by protecting the rights of investors. It was hoped that the new law would expedite private-sector development in the country. In March 2004 international donors meeting in Berlin, Germany, pledged $4,400m. in aid for Afghanistan for that year, to be followed by $8,200m. in aid over the following three years. In June 2004 a 'core budget' was adopted, consolidating operational and most development expenditure for the first time. Total public expenditure of 79,476m. afghanis was projected for 2006/07, of which 35,276m. afghanis was allocated for development projects. The economy was expected to continue to grow in 2006/07, driven primarily by foreign aid and investment. It was announced in late 2007 that a Chinese consortium had won the bid to develop Aynak mine, one of the world's largest copper deposits situated 22 km south-east of Kabul, at an estimated cost of around $3,000m. The project, which was expected to employ some 10,000 people, represented the largest single foreign investment in the country to date. There were other signs of rapid growth in the economy, such as the expanding mobile cellular telephone sector; agencies reported 150,000 new mobile telephone subscribers per month in 2007. Several serious risks to the economy remained, however. First, while the formal economy was recovering, so too was the criminal economy. Despite the introduction of a ban in January 2002 on poppy cultivation and the processing, trafficking and abuse of opiates, the large-scale planting of poppies during the collapse of law and order in late 2001 had allowed Afghanistan to resume its place as the world's largest supplier of opium, a position that it consolidated over the following years. In 2004, according to the UN Office on Drugs and Crime (UNODC), the area under poppy cultivation increased by 64%, compared with the previous year, and opium production was taking place in all 32 provinces (UNODC did not take into account the formation of two new provinces in early 2004, bringing the total number of provinces in Afghanistan to 34). In 2005, although the area under poppy cultivation decreased by 21%, compared with the previous year, drug production levels were relatively unaffected, showing a mere 2.4% decline. Opium production accounted for the equivalent of 47% of non-drug GDP in 2004/05. The opium trade, and the associated violence and corruption, posed a serious threat to the Afghan economy. It was hoped that the adoption of a National Drug Control Strategy in May 2003, which was intended to reduce opium production by 70% by 2008, and the creation of a Ministry of Counter Narcotics in December 2004, would achieve some success. However, in September 2006 UNODC warned of record levels of opium production for that year, along with an estimated increase of 59% in the area under poppy cultivation, compared with 2005. Efforts to curb production have continued to have little success. Although a British-led eradication programme costing some £70m. a year over three years was put in place in 2006, concentrating mainly on compensating farmers for growing less profitable crops, it has achieved only negligible results. The lack of security and limited rule of law has also hampered Afghanistan's successful reconstruction, especially in the provinces. During 2006–07 the situation deteriorated rapidly, particularly in the south and east of the country, with a Taliban insurgency, largely emanating from Pakistan, becoming increasingly dangerous. Furthermore, there were concerns that international financial assistance might decrease prematurely. These misgivings were heightened in early 2006, when it was reported that the US Agency for International Development (USAID) intended to reduce its funding for Afghanistan for that year to approximately $600m., compared with an allocation of around $1,000m. for 2005, unless the US Congress approved supplementary funding. However, in January–February 2006 international donors pledged an estimated $10,500m. of aid for the country within the framework of a new five-year development plan, the Afghanistan Compact. In conjunction with this, the Afghan Government introduced the Interim Afghanistan National Development Strategy (I-ANDS), which encompassed plans and goals for economic, political and social development. In July 2006 the 'Paris Club' of official creditors approved a cancellation of $1,600m. of Afghanistan's debt and rescheduled a further $800m.

Education

Before the Taliban rose to power, primary education began at seven years of age and lasted for six years. Secondary education, beginning at 13 years of age, lasted for a further six years. As a proportion of the school-age population, the total enrolment at primary and secondary schools was equivalent to 36% (males 49%; females 22%) in 1995.

Higher education was disrupted by the departure of many teaching staff from Afghanistan during more than 20 years of civil war. In 1991 there were six institutions of higher education (including Kabul University, which was founded in 1932) in Afghanistan; a total of 17,000 students were enrolled in these institutions in that year.

Following their seizure of power in September 1996, the Taliban banned education for girls over the age of eight, closed all the women's institutes of higher education and planned to draw up a new Islamic curriculum for boys' schools. In early 1998, however, there were still two co-educational universities functioning in Afghanistan (in areas not under Taliban control). According to Taliban figures, in September 1999 1,586,026 pupils were being educated by 59,792 teachers in 3,836 *madrassas* (mosque schools).

After the Taliban regime was defeated in late 2001, the Afghan Interim Administration (later the Afghan Transitional Authority), with the help of foreign governments and UN and humanitarian organizations, began to rehabilitate the education system. In March 2003 4.2m. boys and girls commenced a new academic year at some 7,000 schools around the country. The number of girls attending school increased by some 37%, compared with the previous year, to approximately 1.2m. The boy-girl ratio in education in 2003/04 had returned to pre-Taliban levels. However, the attendance of girls at schools in parts of southern and eastern Afghanistan remained very low. In March 2004 about 5.5m. children reportedly sought enrolment; primary enrolment in 2004/05 was equivalent to an estimated 86.5% of children in the relevant age-group. In 2004 UNICEF aimed to provide 4m. primary school children with access to high-quality education, especially girls and those living in remote areas. The organization also planned to rehabilitate 200 primary schools throughout Afghanistan, to provide basic training to at least 40,000 primary school teachers and to ensure that every primary school in Afghanistan had a clean water point. In addition, the Afghan Ministry of Education, assisted by UNICEF, was leading an initiative to establish community-based education, initially in six provinces, in order to provide basic educational opportunities for those with no access to formal schools. In March 2005 a nation-wide campaign promoting the value of education for girls was launched, in an attempt to encourage more girls to enrol in school; according to UNICEF, more than 1m. girls of primary-school age were still not attending classes. By April of that year 1,108 community-based schools had been created, attended by approximately 55,000 children. According to statistics issued by the Afghan Ministry of Education, in 2005 there were some 5.2m. children enrolled in primary and secondary levels of education. In 2004/05 secondary enrolment was equivalent to an estimated 16.2% of pupils in the relevant age-group. A report published by Human Rights Watch in July 2006, however, indicated that a climate of insecurity, poverty, negative attitudes towards education, and the active (and often violent) targeting of the education system and its staff and attendees, had effected a serious deterioration in the condition of, and access to, schooling in the country.

Kabul University opened for men and women in March 2002. Some 24,000 students enrolled at the higher education level. Foreign universities as well as governments and non-governmental organizations donated books and teaching materials. Universities in at least five other provinces were being rehabilitated.

In January 2003 UNESCO and the Afghan Transitional Administration launched a major project to boost literacy rates throughout Afghanistan.

Public Holidays

The Afghan year 1387 runs from 21 March 2008 to 20 March 2009, and the year 1388 runs from 21 March 2009 to 20 March 2010.

2008: 19 January* (Ashura, Martyrdom of Imam Husayn), 1 February* (Arafat Day), 15 February (Liberation Day, commemoration of *mujahidin* struggle against Soviet occupation and withdrawal of Soviet troops in 1989), 20 March* (Roze-Maulud, Birth of Prophet Muhammad), 21 March (Nauroz: New Year's Day, Iranian calendar), 28 April (Loss of the Muslim Nation), 1 May (Workers' Day), 19 August (Independence Day), 2 September* (first day of Ramadan), 1 October* (Id al-Fitr, end of Ramadan), 9 December* (Id al-Adha, Feast of the Sacrifice).

2009: 7 January*† (Ashura, Martyrdom of Imam Husayn), 1 February* (Arafat Day), 15 February (Liberation Day, commemoration of *mujahidin* struggle against Soviet occupation and withdrawal of Soviet troops in 1989), 9 March* (Roze-Maulud, Birth of Prophet Muhammad), 21 March (Nauroz: New Year's Day, Iranian calendar), 28 April (Loss of the Muslim Nation), 1 May (Workers' Day), 19 August (Independence Day), 22 August* (first day of Ramadan), 20 September* (Id al-Fitr, end of Ramadan), 27 November* (Id al-Adha, Feast of the Sacrifice), 27 December*† (Ashura, Martyrdom of Imam Husayn).

* These holidays are dependent on the Islamic lunar calendar and may vary by one or two days from the dates given.

† This festival occurs twice (in the Afghan years 1387 and 1388) within the same Gregorian year.

Weights and Measures

The metric system has been officially adopted but traditional weights are still used. One 'seer' equals 16 lb (7.3 kg).

AFGHANISTAN

Statistical Survey

Sources (unless otherwise stated): Central Statistics Authority, Block 4, Microrayon, Kabul; tel. (93) 24883; Central Statistics Office, Ansari Wat, Kabul; e-mail info@cso.gov.af; internet www.cso.gov.af.

Area and Population

AREA, POPULATION AND DENSITY

Area (sq km)	652,225*
Population (census results) 23 June 1979†	
Males	6,712,377
Females	6,338,981
Total	13,051,358
Population (official estimates)	
2002‡	21,800,000
2006§	22,575,900
Density (per sq km) at 2006	34.6

* 251,773 sq miles.

† Figures exclude nomadic population, estimated to total 2,500,000. The census data also exclude an adjustment for underenumeration, estimated to have been 5% for the urban population and 10% for the rural population.

‡ This figure includes an estimate for nomadic population (1.5m. in 2002), but takes no account of emigration by refugees. At the end of 2006 UNHCR estimated that the total Afghan refugee population numbered 2.0m., of whom 1.0m. were located in Pakistan and some 900,000 in Iran.

§ Males 11,545,800, females 11,030,100; estimate for settled population only.

PROVINCES
(2006, excluding nomad population, estimates)

	Area (sq km)	Population ('000)	Density (per sq km)	Capital
Kabul	4,462	3,138	703.3	Kabul
Kapisa	1,842	383	207.9	Mahmud-e-Iraqi
Parvan (Parwan)§	n.a.	573	n.a.	Charikar
Wardak*	8,938	517	57.8	Maidanshahr
Loghar (Logar)*	3,880	340	87.6	Pul-i-Alam
Ghazni	22,915	1,063	46.4	Ghazni
Paktika	19,482	377	19.4	Sharan
Paktia (Paktya)	6,432	478	74.3	Gardez
Khost†	4,152	498	119.9	Khost
Nangarhar	7,727	1,289	166.8	Jalalabad
Kunar (Kunarha)	4,942	390	78.9	Asadabad
Laghman	3,843	386	100.4	Mehter Lam
Nuristan (Nooristan)†	9,225	128	13.9	Nuristan
Badakhshan	44,059	823	18.7	Faizabad
Takhar	12,333	845	68.5	Taloqan
Baghlan*	21,118	779	36.9	Baghlan
Kunduz	8,040	851	105.8	Kunduz
Samangan	11,262	335	29.7	Aybak
Balkh	17,249	1,096	63.5	Mazar-i-Sharif
Jawzjan (Juzjan)	11,798	462	39.2	Shiberghan
Sar-e Pol (Sar-e-Pul)‡	15,999	483	30.2	Sar-e Pol
Faryab	20,293	859	42.3	Maymana
Badghis	20,591	430	20.9	Qaleh-ye-Now
Herat	54,778	1,578	28.8	Herat
Farah	48,471	438	9.0	Farah
—continued				
Nimroz	41,005	141	3.4	Zaranj
Helmand	58,584	799	13.6	Lashgar Gah
Qandahar (Kandahar)	54,022	1,012	18.7	Qandahar
Zabul	17,343	263	15.2	Qalat
Uruzgan (Urizan)§	n.a.	304	n.a.	Terin Kowt
Ghor	36,479	599	16.4	Chaghcharan
Bamian (Bamyan)	14,175	387	27.3	Bamian
Panjshir§	n.a.	133	n.a.	Bazarat
Daikundi§	n.a.	400	n.a.	Neli
Total	652,225	22,575,900	34.6	

* By 1996 the capital of Loghar province had changed to Pul-i-Alam from Baraki Barak and the capital of Wardak province had moved to Maidanshahr from Kowt-i-Ashrow; it was reported that the capital of Baghlan province had moved to Pul-e-Khomri: this was yet to be confirmed.

† Nuristan province (formerly part of Kunar and Laghman provinces) and Khost province (formerly part of Paktia province) had been created by 1991 and 1995, respectively.

‡ Sar-e Pol province (formerly part of Balkh, Jawzjan and Samangan provinces) had been created by 1990.

§ Panjshir province (formerly part of Parvan province) and Daikundi province (formerly part of Uruzgan province) were created in 2004.

PRINCIPAL TOWNS
(estimated settled population at 2006)

Kabul (capital)	2,536,300	Pul-e-Khomri	180,800
Qandahar	450,300	Jalalabad	168,600
Herat	349,000	Baghlan	149,300
Mazar-i-Sharif	300,600	Ghazni	141,000
Kunduz	264,100	Maymana	67,800

BIRTHS AND DEATHS
(annual averages, UN estimates)

	1990–95	1995–2000	2000–05
Birth rate (per 1,000)	51.7	51.5	49.3
Death rate (per 1,000)	20.5	20.3	19.6

Source: UN, *World Population Prospects: The 2006 Revision*.

Expectation of life (years at birth, WHO estimates): 41.9 (males 41.7; females 42.3) in 2005 (Source: WHO, *World Health Statistics*).

ECONOMICALLY ACTIVE POPULATION*
(ISIC major divisions, '000 persons aged 15–59 years, year ending 20 March, estimates)

	2000/01	2001/02	2002/03
Agriculture, hunting, forestry and fishing	4,986.1	5,082.6	5,181.4
Mining, quarrying, manufacturing and utilities	348.6	355.3	362.2
Construction	94.9	96.7	98.6
Wholesale and retail trade	490.4	499.9	509.6
Transport, storage and communications	163.1	166.3	169.5
Other services	1,083.6	1,104.5	1,126.0
Total	7,166.6	7,305.4	7,447.3

* Figures refer to settled population only.

AFGHANISTAN

Health and Welfare

KEY INDICATORS

Total fertility rate (children per woman, 2005)	7.3
Under-5 mortality rate (per 1,000 live births, 2005)	257
HIV/AIDS (% of persons aged 15–49, 2005)	<0.01
Physicians (per 1,000 head, 2001)	0.19
Hospital beds (per 1,000 head, 1990)	0.39
Health expenditure (2004): US $ per head (PPP)	18.9
Health expenditure (2004): % of GDP	4.4
Health expenditure (2004): public (% of total)	16.9
Access to water (% of persons, 2004)	39
Access to sanitation (% of persons, 2004)	34

For sources and definitions, see explanatory note on p. vi.

Agriculture

PRINCIPAL CROPS
('000 metric tons)

	2003	2004	2005
Wheat	3,480	2,293*	4,265*
Rice (paddy)	260	465	470*
Barley	240	220*	337*
Maize	210	234*	315*
Millet	17	20*	20*
Potatoes*	240	241	242
Sesame seed	23†	23†	22*
Cottonseed	37†	40*	41*
Watermelons*	95	92	92
Cantaloupes and other melons*	28	28	28
Grapes*	350	349	346
Sugar cane*	38	36	35
Plums*	35	35	35
Apricots*	38	38	38

* FAO estimate(s).
† Unofficial figure.

2006 ('000 metric tons, FAO estimates): Wheat 320; Rice 540; Barley 220; Maize 240; Millet 20.

Aggregate production ('000 metric tons, may include official, semi-official or estimated data): Total cereals 4,207 in 2003, 3,232 in 2004, 5,407 in 2005, 4,220 in 2006; Total roots and tubers 240 in 2003, 241 in 2004, 242 in 2005, 242 in 2006; Total pulses 42 in 2003, 42 in 2004, 42 in 2005, 42 in 2006; Total vegetables (incl. melons) 663 in 2003, 660 in 2004, 660 in 2005, 660 in 2006; Total fruits (excl. melons) 705 in 2003, 706 in 2004, 704 in 2005, 704 in 2006.

Source: FAO.

LIVESTOCK
('000 head, year ending 30 September)

	2002	2003	2004
Horses*	104	104	104
Asses, mules or hinnies*	950	950	950
Cattle	3,500*	3,700†	3,700*
Camels	200*	175	180*
Sheep	11,000*	8,800	8,800*
Goats	7,500*	7,300	7,300*
Chickens*	8,400	8,400	8,400

* FAO estimate(s).
† Unofficial figure.

2005: Figures assumed to be unchanged from 2004 (FAO estimates).
Source: FAO.

LIVESTOCK PRODUCTS
('000 metric tons, FAO estimates)

	2003	2004	2005
Cattle meat	144	157	165
Sheep meat	72	72	72
Goat meat	33	33	33
Chicken meat	16	16	16
Other meat	12	12	12
Cows' milk	2,035	2,035	2,035
Sheep's milk	132	132	132
Goats' milk	110	110	110
Hen eggs	18	19	20
Wool: greasy	11	11	11

Source: FAO.

Forestry

ROUNDWOOD REMOVALS
('000 cubic metres, excl. bark, FAO estimates)

	2003	2004	2005
Sawlogs, veneer logs and logs for sleepers*	856	856	856
Other industrial wood†	904	904	904
Fuel wood	1,388	1,427	1,467
Total	3,148	3,187	3,227

* Assumed to be unchanged from 1976.
† Assumed to be unchanged from 1999.

2006: Production assumed to be unchanged from 2005 (FAO estimates).
Source: FAO.

SAWNWOOD PRODUCTION
('000 cubic metres, incl. railway sleepers, FAO estimates)

	1974	1975	1976
Coniferous (softwood)	360	310	380
Broadleaved (hardwood)	50	20	20
Total	410	330	400

1977–2006: Annual production as in 1976 (FAO estimates).
Source: FAO.

Fishing

(metric tons, live weight, FAO estimates)

	2003	2004	2005
Total catch (freshwater fishes)	900	1,000	1,000

Source: FAO.

Mining

('000 metric tons, unless otherwise indicated, estimates)

	2001	2002	2003
Hard coal	190	185	185
Natural gas (million cu metres)*	3,000	3,000	3,000
Copper ore†	5	5	5
Salt (unrefined)	13	13	13
Gypsum (crude)	3	3	3

* Figures refer to gross output. Estimated marketed production was 2,500 million cubic metres per year in 2001–03.
† Figures refer to metal content.

Source: US Geological Survey.

AFGHANISTAN

Industry

SELECTED PRODUCTS
(year ending 20 March, '000 metric tons, unless otherwise indicated)

	1986/87	1987/88	1988/89
Margarine	3.5	3.3	1.8
Vegetable oil	4	n.a.	n.a.
Wheat flour*	187	203	166
Wine ('000 hectolitres)*	289	304	194
Soft drinks ('000 hectolitres)	8,500	10,300	4,700
Woven cotton fabrics (million sq metres)	58.1	52.6	32.1
Woven woollen fabrics (million sq metres)	0.4	0.3	0.3
Footwear—excl. rubber ('000 pairs)*	613	701	607
Rubber footwear ('000 pairs)*	2,200	3,200	2,200
Nitrogenous fertilizers†	56	57	55
Cement	103	104	70
Electric energy (million kWh)*‡	1,171	1,257	1,109

* Production in calendar years 1986, 1987 and 1988.
† Production in year ending 30 June.
‡ Provisional.

Wheat flour ('000 metric tons): 1,832 in 1994; 2,029 in 1995; 2,145 in 1996.

Nitrogenous fertilizers (provisional, year ending 30 June, '000 metric tons): 49 in 1994/95; 50 in 1995/96; 50 in 1996/97; 5 in 1997/98; 5 in 1998/99; 5 in 1999/2000.

Cement (year ending 20 March, '000 metric tons): 26.8 in 2002/03; 24.0 in 2003/04; 15.2 in 2004/05.

Electric energy (year ending 20 March, million kWh): 557 in 2002/03; 827 in 2003/04; 783 in 2004/05.

Sources: UN, *Industrial Commodity Statistics Yearbook* and *Statistical Yearbook for Asia and the Pacific*, FAO, US Geological Survey and IMF.

Finance

CURRENCY AND EXCHANGE RATES

Monetary Units
100 puls (puli) = 2 krans = 1 afghani (Af).

Sterling, Dollar and Euro Equivalents (29 September 2006)
£1 sterling = 93.697 afghanis;
US $1 = 50.100 afghanis;
€1 = 63.43 afghanis;
1,000 afghanis = £10.67 = $19.96 = €15.77.

Exchange Rate: The foregoing information refers to the official exchange rate. The official rate was maintained at US $1 = 1,000 afghanis between 1 May 1995 and 30 April 1996. From 1 May 1996 a rate of US $1 = 3,000 afghanis was in operation. However, this rate was applicable to only a limited range of transactions. There was also a market-determined rate, which was US $1 = 34,000 afghanis in March 2002. A new afghani, equivalent to 1,000 of the old currency, was introduced in October 2002.

OPERATING BUDGET
(million afghanis, year ending 20 March)

Revenue*	2004/05†	2005/06†	2006/07‡
Tax revenue	9,546	14,035	22,462
Taxes on income, profits and capital gains	995	2,621	4,178
Taxes on international trade and transactions	7,247	9,446	12,750
Other taxes	1,304	1,968	5,534
Non-tax revenue	3,254	6,617	4,553
Total	12,800	20,652	27,015

Expenditure§	2004/05†	2005/06†	2006/07‡
Wages and salaries	18,902	20,430	27,276
Purchase of goods and services	4,182	6,679	9,352
Transfers and subsidies	764	495	3,816
Pensions	889	1,540	2,065
Capital expenditure	1,979	3,054	1,220
Interest	—	150	471
Total	26,716	32,348	44,200

* Excluding donor assistance grants and loans (million afghanis): 14,984 in 2004/05 (estimate); 16,732 in 2004/05 (estimate); 18,595 in 2006/07 (projected), and development assistance grants and loans: 8,250 in 2004/05 (estimate); 19,251 in 2005/06 (estimate); 18,064 in 2006/07 (projected).
† Estimates.
‡ Projected.
§ Excluding development spending (million afghanis): 12,834 in 2004/05 (estimate); 21,089 in 2005/06 (estimate); 35,276 in 2006/07 (projected).

Source: IMF, *Islamic Republic of Afghanistan: Second Review Under the Three-Year Arrangement Under the Poverty Reduction and Growth Facility - Staff Report; Press Release on the Executive Board Discussion; and Statement by the Executive Director for the Islamic Republic of Afghanistan* (July 2007).

FOREIGN EXCHANGE RESERVES
(million afghanis at 20 March)

	2005/06*	2006/07*	2007/08†
Gold‡	19,230	19,230	23,006
Other	63,765	76,412	91,927
Total	82,995	95,643	114,933

* Estimates.
† Projections.
‡ Excluding gold held in palace vaults.

Source: IMF, *Islamic Republic of Afghanistan: Second Review Under the Three-Year Arrangement Under the Poverty Reduction and Growth Facility - Staff Report; Press Release on the Executive Board Discussion; and Statement by the Executive Director for the Islamic Republic of Afghanistan* (July 2007).

MONEY SUPPLY
(million afghanis at 20 March)

	2005/06*	2006/07*	2007/08†
Reserve money	46,300	57,569	65,808
Currency in circulation	44,629	50,177	59,090
Bank deposits with central bank	1,670	7,392	6,718

* Estimates.
† Projections.

Source: IMF, *Islamic Republic of Afghanistan: Second Review Under the Three-Year Arrangement Under the Poverty Reduction and Growth Facility - Staff Report; Press Release on the Executive Board Discussion; and Statement by the Executive Director for the Islamic Republic of Afghanistan* (July 2007).

COST OF LIVING
(Consumer Price Index for Kabul; base: 2002 = 100)

	2004	2005	2006
Food	109.3	113.7	119.0
Non-food	115.6	126.1	139.4
All items	111.8	118.4	126.9

Source: Asian Development Bank, *Key Indicators of Developing Asian and Pacific Countries*.

AFGHANISTAN

Statistical Survey

NATIONAL ACCOUNTS
(US $ million at current prices, year ending 20 March)

Expenditure on the Gross Domestic Product

	2003/04	2004/05	2005/06
Public consumption expenditure	449	561	665
Private consumption expenditure	6,024	6,992	7,883
Gross fixed capital formation	626	1,001	1,459
Total domestic expenditures	7,099	8,554	10,007
Exports of goods and services	1,999	1,805	1,727
Less Imports of goods and services	4,331	4,627	4,883
Gross domestic product at market prices	4,769	5,733	6,851

Gross Domestic Product by Economic Activity

	2003/04	2004/05	2005/06
Agriculture, hunting, forestry and fishing	2,149	2,332	2,617
Mining and quarrying } Manufacturing } Electricity, gas and water }	622	873	1,065
Construction	250	435	610
Wholesale and retail trade, restaurants and hotels*	428	511	574
Transport, storage and communications	543	511	635
Public administration	245	299	442
Other services, incl. finance	436	645	686
Sub-total	4,673	5,606	6,629
Indirect taxes, less subsidies	96	127	223
Gross domestic product at market prices	4,769	5,733	6,851

*Residual item including data discrepancies.

Source: Asian Development Bank, *Key Indicators of Developing Asian and Pacific Countries*.

BALANCE OF PAYMENTS
(US $ million, year ending 20 March)

	2005/06*	2006/07†	2007/08‡
Exports of goods§	1,794.8	1,923.8	2,074.8
Imports of goods	-4,317.0	-5,095.5	-5,584.0
Trade balance	-2,522.2	-3,171.7	-3,509.2
Services and other income (net)	-538.3	-505.9	-438.4
Balance on goods, services and income	-3,060.5	-3,677.6	-3,947.6
Current transfers (net)	3,103.6	3,580.5	3,703.0
Current balance	43.1	-97.0	-244.6
Capital and financial account (net)	360.8	391.2	443.2
Net errors and omissions	-42.9	46.4	-64.0
Overall balance	360.9	340.5	134.6

* Estimates.
† Preliminary estimate.
‡ Projected.
§ Excludes opium exports and flows associated with US Army and International Security Assistance Force activities.

Source: IMF, *Islamic Republic of Afghanistan: Second Review Under the Three-Year Arrangement Under the Poverty Reduction and Growth Facility - Staff Report; Press Release on the Executive Board Discussion; and Statement by the Executive Director for the Islamic Republic of Afghanistan* (July 2007).

OFFICIAL DEVELOPMENT ASSISTANCE
(US $ million)

	1998	1999	2000
Bilateral	88.5	104.2	88.2
Multilateral	65.7	38.3	52.7
Total	154.2	142.5	140.9
Grants	154.3	140.9	140.9
Loans	-0.1	1.6	—
Per caput assistance (US $)	7.4	6.7	6.5

Source: UN, *Statistical Yearbook for Asia and the Pacific*.

2002/03 (US $ million, excl. grants used for clearing debt arrears): Bilateral grants 26.4; Multilateral grants 157.1 (Source: IMF, *Islamic State of Afghanistan: 2003 Article IV Consultation—Staff Report; Public Information Notice on the Executive Board Discussion; and Statement by the Executive Director for the Islamic State of Afghanistan*).

External Trade

PRINCIPAL COMMODITIES
(US $ million, year ending 20 March)

Imports c.i.f.*	2002/03	2003/04	2004/05
Machinery and equipment	856	478	528
Chemical materials	173	220	3
Food	222	309	404
Fabrics, clothing and footwear	344	340	330
Household items and medicine	501	189	241
Total (incl. others)	2,452	2,101	2,177

Exports f.o.b.*	2002/03	2003/04	2004/05
Fresh fruits	9	8	13
Dried fruit	57	59	81
Animal skins	9	29	22
Wool	4	7	8
Carpets and handicrafts	14	21	156
Total (incl. others)	100	144	305

* Official recorded only; excluding re-exports.

Source: IMF, *Islamic Republic of Afghanistan: Selected Issues and Statistical Appendix* (March 2006).

PRINCIPAL TRADING PARTNERS
(US $ million, year ending 20 March)

Imports*	2002/03	2003/04	2004/05
China, People's Republic	20	382	385
Germany	49	84	182
India	37	122	83
Japan	999	299	353
Kazakhstan	22	7	13
Kenya	57	55	22
Korea, Republic of	113	22	79
Pakistan	207	181	326
Turkmenistan	50	14	26
Total (incl. others)	2,452	2,101	2,177

Exports†	2002/03	2003/04	2004/05
Belgium	3	—	—
Finland	9	1	—
Germany	6	2	1
India	27	11	20
Pakistan	26	99	258
Russia	3	8	4
United Arab Emirates	5	—	—
United Kingdom	—	3	1
USA	4	—	—
Total (incl. others)	100	144	305

* Figures refer to official recorded imports only and include re-exports.
† Excluding re-exports.

Source: IMF, *Islamic Republic of Afghanistan: Selected Issues and Statistical Appendix* (March 2006).

AFGHANISTAN

Transport

ROAD TRAFFIC
(year ending 20 March, motor vehicles in use)

	2002/03	2003/04	2004/05*
Passenger cars	71,222	176,723	197,449
Lorries	51,527	76,236	83,347
Buses	29,098	40,042	40,590
Motorcycles	13,189	33,098	62,417
Rickshaws	419	3,044	6,355
Taxicabs	33,057	52,392	49,414
Foreign vehicles	9,900	10,458	12,237

*Provisional.

Source: IMF, *Islamic Republic of Afghanistan: Selected Issues and Statistical Appendix* (March 2006).

CIVIL AVIATION
('000)

	2002/03	2003/04	2004/05*
Kilometres flown	2,986	9,714	12,898
Passengers carried	161	296	333
Passenger-km	325,000	552,000	681,000
Freight ton-km	6,214	23,496	20,624

*Provisional figures.

Source: IMF, *Islamic Republic of Afghanistan: Selected Issues and Statistical Appendix* (March 2006).

Tourism

	1996	1997	1998
Tourist arrivals ('000)	4	4	4
Tourism receipts (US $ million)	1	1	1

Source: World Tourism Organization, *Yearbook of Tourism Statistics*.

Communications Media

	2004	2005	2006
Telephones ('000 main lines in use)	50.0	100.0	165.0
Mobile cellular telephones ('000 subscribers)	600.0	1,200.0	2,520.4
Personal computers ('000 in use)	25.0	30.0	n.a.
Internet users ('000)	25.0	300.0	535.0
Broadband subscribers	200.0	200.0	500.0

Radio receivers ('000 in use): 2,400 in 1995; 2,550 in 1996; 2,750 in 1997.

Television receivers ('000 in use): 290 in 1998; 300 in 1999.

Sources: mainly UNESCO, *Statistical Yearbook* and UN, *Statistical Yearbook*.

Daily newspapers: *Number*: 15 in 1995, 12 in 1996; *Average circulation* ('000 copies): 200 in 1995 (estimate), 113 in 1996.

Education

(2002)

	Institutions	Teachers	Pupils
Pre-primary	147	3,286	9,367
Primary	4,876	58,312	3,083,434
Secondary*	1,994	34,271	621,801
Higher	n.a.	1,449	22,717

*Figures refer to general secondary education only, excluding vocational and teacher training.

Sources: Ministries of Education, of Higher Education and of Social and Labour Affairs, Kabul, and UNICEF.

Teachers (2003/04, unless otherwise indicated): Pre-primary 3,510; Primary 51,802 (2004/05); Secondary vocational 674 (2004/05); Tertiary 1,781 (Source: UNESCO Institute for Statistics).

Adult literacy rate (UNESCO estimates): 28.0% (males 43.1%; females 12.6%) in 2000 (Source: UNESCO Institute for Statistics).

Directory

The Constitution

On 5 December 2001 28 Afghan leaders signed the Agreement on Provisional Arrangements in Afghanistan Pending the Re-establishment of Permanent Government Institutions (also known as the Bonn Agreement), stipulating a timetable for the creation of a permanent constitution and the holding of free national elections. In accordance with the agreement, Afghanistan temporarily reverted to the Constitution of 1964. On 11–19 June 2002 an Emergency Loya Jirga (Grand National Council), comprising approximately 1,650 delegates, convened. The Loya Jirga appointed a broad-based, gender-sensitive Transitional Authority and a Head of State. The Transitional Authority, with the assistance of the UN, established a Constitutional Drafting Commission in November to draw up a new constitution. A new charter providing for a presidential system of government and a bicameral legislature following eventual elections by universal suffrage was approved by a Constitutional Loya Jirga in early January 2004. A democratic presidential election, based on the principles of the new Constitution, took place on 9 October, following which the President appointed a new Government. Legislative elections were held on 18 September 2005, to determine the composition of the Meli Shura (National Assembly). The first meeting of the Meli Shura in December signified the end of the transitional period of government that had been initiated with the holding of the Emergency Loya Jirga in 2002.

The Government

HEAD OF STATE

President: HAMID KARZAI (inaugurated as Chairman of Interim Authority 22 December 2001; elected as President of Transitional Authority by Loya Jirga 13 June 2002 and as President of the Islamic Republic of Afghanistan by direct popular vote 9 October 2004).

Vice-Presidents: AHMAD ZIA MASOUD, KARIM KHALILI.

CABINET
(April 2008)

Senior Minister in the Cabinet: HEDAYAT AMIN ARSALA.
Minister of Commerce: Dr MOHAMMAD AMIN FARHANG.
Minister of Defence: Gen. ABDUL RAHIM WARDAK.
Minister of Foreign Affairs: Dr RANGIN DADFAR SPANTA.
Minister of Finance: Prof. Dr ANWAR-UL-HAQ AHADI.
Minister of Interior Affairs: ZARAR AHMAD MOQBEL.
Minister of Economy: Dr MOHAMMAD JALIL SHAMS.
Minister of Communications and Information Technology: AMIRZAI SANGIN.
Minister of Border and Tribal Affairs: ABDUL KARIM BARAHAWI.
Minister of Refugees and Repatriation: SHER MOHAMMAD ETEBARI.
Minister of Mines and Industries: IBRAHIM ADIL.
Minister of Water and Energy: MOHAMMED ISMAIL KHAN.
Minister of Public Health: Dr MOHAMMAD AMIN FATEMI.
Minister of Agriculture: OBAIDOLLAH RAMIN.
Minister of Justice: MOHAMMAD SARWAR DANESH.
Minister of Culture and Youth Affairs: ABDUL KARIM KHORAM.
Minister of Hajj and Islamic Affairs: NEMATULLAH SHAHRANI.
Minister of Urban Development: MOHAMMAD YOUSEF PASHTUN.
Minister of Public Welfare: SUHRAB ALI SAFARI.

AFGHANISTAN

Minister of Work, Social Affairs, the Martyred and the Disabled: Noor Mohammad Karkin.
Minister of Higher Education: Dr Mohammad Azam Dadfar.
Minister of Transport and Aviation: Hamidullah Qaderi.
Minister of Education: Dr Mohammed Hanif Atmar.
Minister of Rural Rehabilitation and Development: Ehsan Zia.
Minister of Women's Affairs: Hosna Banu Ghazanfar.
Minister of Counter Narcotics: Gen. Khodaidad (acting).
Minister of State for Parliamentary Affairs: Dr Farooq Wardak.
National Security Adviser: Dr Zalmai Rassoul.

MINISTRIES

Office of the President: Gul Khana Palace, Presidential Palace, Kabul; e-mail president@afghanistangov.org; internet www.president.gov.af.

Ministry of Agriculture: Jamal Mena, Kart-i-Sakhi, Kabul; tel. (20) 2500315; e-mail info@agriculture.gov.af; internet www.agriculture.gov.af.

Ministry of Border and Tribal Affairs: Shah Mahmud Ghazi Wat, Kabul; tel. (20) 2101365.

Ministry of Commerce: Darulaman Wat, Kabul; tel. (20) 2290090; fax (20) 2500356; e-mail info@commerce.gov.af; internet www.commerce.gov.af.

Ministry of Communications and Information Technology: Mohammad Jan Khan Wat, Kabul; tel. (20) 2101107; fax (20) 2101708; e-mail khalid.saleem@moc.gov.af; internet www.moc.gov.af.

Ministry of Counter Narcotics: Kabul-Jalalabad Rd, Banaiey, Macroyan, Kabul; tel. (79) 9871886; e-mail info@mcn.gov.af; internet www.mcn.gov.af.

Ministry of Culture and Youth Affairs: Mohammad Jan Khan Wat, Kabul; tel. and fax (20) 2101301; fax (20) 2290088; e-mail aziza_ahmadyar@hotmail.com.

Ministry of Defence: Shash Darak, Kabul; tel. (20) 2100451; fax (20) 2104172.

Ministry of Economy: Kabul.

Ministry of Education: Mohammad Jan Khan Wat, Kabul; tel. (79) 9332015; e-mail awassay.arian@moe.gov.af; internet www.moe.gov.af.

Ministry of Finance: Pashtunistan Wat, Kabul; tel. (20) 2004199; fax (20) 2103439; e-mail info@mof.gov.af; internet www.mof.gov.af.

Ministry of Foreign Affairs: Malak Azghar Rd, Kabul; tel. (70) 104024; fax (20) 2100360; e-mail contact@mfa.gov.af; internet mfa.gov.af.

Ministry of Hajj and Islamic Affairs: nr District 10, Shir Pur, Shar-i-Nau, Kabul; tel. (20) 2201338.

Ministry of Higher Education: Karte Char, Kabul; tel. (20) 2500324; e-mail afmohe@hotmail.com; internet www.mohe.gov.af.

Ministry of Interior Affairs: Shar-i-Nau, Kabul; tel. (20) 32441.

Ministry of Justice: Pashtunistan Wat, Kabul; tel. (20) 2101325; e-mail info@moj.gov.af; internet www.moj.gov.af.

Ministry of Mines and Industries: Pashtunistan Wat, Kabul; tel. (20) 2100309; e-mail info@mom.gov.af; internet www.mom.gov.af.

Ministry of Public Health: Wazir Akbar Khan, Sub-district 9, Kabul; tel. (20) 2301377; e-mail info@moph.gov.af; internet www.moph.gov.af.

Ministry of Public Welfare: Microrayon 1, Kabul; tel. (20) 2301363; fax (20) 2301362.

Ministry of Refugees and Repatriation: Jungaluk, off Darlaman Rd, Kabul; e-mail afgmorr@afgmorr.com.

Ministry of Rural Rehabilitation and Development: Shah Mahmud Ghazi Wat, Kabul; tel. (70) 222118; e-mail info@mrrd.gov.af; internet www.mrrd.gov.af.

Ministry of Transport and Aviation: Ansari Wat, Kabul; tel. (20) 2101032; internet www.caa-af.org.

Ministry of Urban Development: Microrayon 3, Kabul.

Ministry of Water and Energy: Kabul.

Ministry of Women's Affairs: beside Cinema Zainab, Shar-i-Nau, Kabul; tel. and fax (20) 2201378; e-mail info@mowa.gov.af; internet www.mowa.gov.af.

Ministry of Work, Social Affairs, the Martyred and the Disabled: Old Microrayon, Kabul; tel. (20) 2300369.

President and Legislature

PRESIDENT

Presidential Election, 9 October 2004

Candidates	Votes	% of votes
Hamid Karzai	4,443,029	55.37
Younis Qanooni	1,306,503	16.28
Haji Mohammad Mohaqqeq	935,325	11.66
Abdul Rashid Dostam	804,861	10.03
Abdul Latif Pedram	110,160	1.37
Masooda Jalal	91,415	1.14
Sayed Ishaq Gailani	80,081	1.00
Others	253,162	3.15
Total	**8,024,536**	**100.00**

MELI SHURA
(National Assembly)

Meshrano Jirga
(House of Elders)

The Meshrano Jirga, the upper house of the Meli Shura, comprises 102 members (three times the number of provinces in Afghanistan). One-third are elected by provincial councils (for a four-year term), one-third by district councils (for a three-year term) and the remaining members are nominated by the President (for a five-year term). The Constitution requires that one-half of the members nominated by the President must be women.

Speaker: Prof. Sibghatullah Mojaddedi.

Wolasi Jirga
(House of Representatives)

The Wolasi Jirga, the lower house of the Meli Shura, comprises 249 directly elected members, all of whom serve a five-year term. Sixty-eight seats are reserved for women. The most recent election was held on 18 September 2005.

Speaker: Younis Qanooni.

Election Commission

Independent Electoral Commission of Afghanistan (IEC): IEC Compound, Jalalabad Rd, Paktia Kot, POB 979, Kabul; tel. (79) 9421095; e-mail info@iec.org.af; internet iec.org.af; established by 2004 Constitution; appointed by the President; functions performed by Joint Electoral Management Body (JEMB) during transitional period of govt; following elections to the Wolasi Jirga and Provincial Councils in 2005, the JEMB was dissolved and the IEC assumed regulation and supervision of all election activities from 2006; Pres. Dr Azizullah Lodin; Chief Electoral Officer Dr Daoud Ali Najafi.

Political Organizations

In September 2003 a new law allowing the formation of political parties was passed. By July 2007 more than 80 parties were registered with the Ministry of Justice, including the following:

Afghan Mellat (Afghan Social Democratic Party): National Bank Club, 3rd Floor, Nader Pashtoon Jadah, Kabul; tel. (70) 224793; e-mail afghanmellat@afghanmellat.org; internet www.afghanmellat.org; Pres. Prof. Dr Anwar-ul-Haq Ahady.

Da Afghanistan Da Solay Ghorzang Gond (Afghanistan Peace Movement): Kolola Poshta (adjacent to Dost Hotel), Kabul; tel. (79) 9311523; Leader Shahnawaz Tanai.

Harakat-i Islami i Afghanistan (Islamic Movement of Afghanistan): Street 4, Qala-i Fathullah, Shar-e-Nau, Kabul; tel. (79) 9343998; Leader Sayyed Mohammad Ali Jawed.

Hizb-i Adalat-i Islami Afghanistan (Islamic Justice Party of Afghanistan): nr Aryub Cinema, Bagh-e-Bala, District 4, Kabul; tel. (79) 9312641; f. 2004; Leader Mohammad Kabir Marzban.

Hizb-i Afghanistan-i Nawin (New Afghanistan Party): 1st Rd Khair Khana Phase One, Parwan Hotel Rd, District 11, Kabul; tel. (79) 9342942; f. 2005; Leader Younis Qanooni.

Hizb-i Afghanistan-i-Wahid (United Afghanistan Party): 53–54, Block 11, Qasiba-e-Khana Sazi, Kabul; tel. (70) 7803738; e-mail xl_branch_afg@yahoo.com; f. 1999; Leader Mohammad Wasel Rahimy.

Hizb-i Hambastagi Afghanistan (Solidarity Party of Afghanistan): Spare Parts St, Parwan 3, Kabul; tel. (70) 231590; Leader Abdul Khaleq Ne'mat.

Hizb-i Hambastagi-yi Melli-yi Jawanan-i Afghanistan (National Solidarity Youth Party of Afghanistan): Qandahar; f. 2004; Leader MOHAMMAD JAMIL KARZAI.

Hizb-i Harakat-i-Islami Mardum-i Afghanistan (Islamic Movement Party of the People of Afghanistan): Rd 2–3, Qala-i-Fatullah, Kabul; tel. (79) 9183484; f. 2004; Leader Al-Hajj SYED HUSSAIN ANWARI.

Hizb-i Harakat-i-Melli Wahdat-i-Afghanistan (National Movement for the Unity of Afghanistan): Jamia Mosque, 6th Floor, Karte 4, District 3, Kabul; tel. (70) 204847; f. 2004; Chair. MOHAMMAD NADIR ATASH.

Hizb-i Islami Afghanistan (Islamic Party of Afghanistan): Area A, Khushal Mena, Kabul; tel. (79) 9421474; Pashtun/Turkmen/Tajik; Leader MOHAMMED KHALED FAROOQI; c. 50,000 supporters; based in Iran in 1998–99.

Hizb-i Isteqlal-i Afghanistan (Independence Party of Afghanistan): Khair Khana, nr Al-Farooq Healthcare Clinic, Kabul; f. 2004; Leader Dr GHULAM FAROOQ NAJRABI.

Hizb-i Jumhuri-i Khwahan-i Afghanistan (Republican Party of Afghanistan): Zainaba St, 6th Rd, Qala-i-Fathullal, Kabul; tel. (70) 275107; f. 2003; supporter of presidential system of government; Leader SEBGHATULLAH SANGAR; c. 35,000 mems.

Hizb-i Kar wa Tawse'ah Afghanistan (Labour and Progress of Afghanistan Party): Karte 4, Rd 2, Kabul; f. 1999 in Pakistan; previously known as the National Reconciliation Party; Leader ZULFIQAR OMID.

Hizb-i Melli Afghanistan (National Party of Afghanistan): Apt 4, Block 12, Microrayon 1, Kabul; tel. (70) 298392; Leader ABDUL RASHID ARYAN.

Hizb-i-Melli Wahdat-i-Aqwam-i-Islami-i-Afghanistan (Party of National Unity of Muslim Tribes of Afghanistan): Bahadur Ulya, Khugiana, Nangarhar; Leader MOHAMMAD SHAH KHOGIANI.

Hizb-i Muttahid-i Melli (United National Party): Kabul; f. 2003 by members of the fmr communist People's Democratic Party of Afghanistan; proscribed until 2004; Leader Gen. NOORUL HAQ OLOMI.

Hizb-i Nizat-i Azady Wa Demokrasi-ye Afghanistan (Movement for Democracy and Freedom in Afghanistan): Karte 4, adjacent to Suraya Lycee, Kabul; tel. (70) 281953; f. 2004; Leader ABDUL RAQIB JAVED KOHISTANI.

Hizb-i Rastakhaiz-i Mardum-i Afghanistan (Renaissance Party of the People of Afghanistan): Apt 4, 1st Floor, Block 15, Tahya Maskan, Kabul; tel. (79) 9372310; f. 2003; Chair. SAYED ZAHER QAID OMULBELADI.

Hizb-i Rifah-i Mardum-i Afghanistan (Party of Welfare of the People of Afghanistan): Khwaja Musafir Bazaar, Paghman, Kabul; tel. (79) 9215852; f. 2004; Leader MIAGUL WASIQ.

Hizb-i Sahadat-i Mardum-i-Afghanistan (Welfare Popular Party of Afghanistan): Apt 1, Block 13, Air Force Blocks, Kabul; tel. (70) 204847; Leader MOHAMMAD ZUBAIR PAYROZ.

Hizb-i-Wahdat-i Islami Afghanistan (Islamic Unity Party of Afghanistan): Mokhabirat, Karte 4, Kabul; tel. (70) 2501413; Leader MOHAMMAD KARIM KHALILI.

Hizb-i Wahdat-i Islami Mardum-i Afghanistan (People's Islamic Unity Party of Afghanistan): House 3, Mohammadia St, Tapa-i-Salaam, Karte Sakhi, Kabul; tel. (70) 278276; represents Hazaras; advocate of equal rights, freedom and social justice; Leader Haji MOHAMMAD MOHAQQEQ.

Hizb-i Wahdat Melli Afghanistan (National Unity Party of Afghanistan): Qaisar Market, 2nd Floor, adjacent to Gul-i-Surkh Hotel, Old Kolola Poshta Sq., Kabul; tel. (79) 9210998; Leader ABDUL RASHID JALILI.

Jamiat-i Islami (Islamic Society): Karte Parwan, Phase 2, Badaam Bagh; tel. (70) 278950; Turkmen/Uzbek/Tajik; Leaders Prof. BURHANUDDIN RABBANI, Marshal MUHAMMAD FAHIM; Sec.-Gen. ENAYATOLLAH SHADAB; c. 60,000 supporters.

Jebha-i-Nejat-i-Melli (National Liberation Front): Pashtun; Leader Prof. HAZRAT SIBGHATULLAH MOJADDEDI; Sec.-Gen. ZABIHOLLAH MOJADDEDI; c. 15,000 supporters.

Junbesh-i Melli-i Islami (National Islamic Movement): f. 1992; formed mostly from troops of fmr Northern Command of the Afghan army; predominantly Uzbek/Tajik/Turkmen/Ismaili and Hazara Shi'a; Leader SAYED NOORULLAH; 65,000–150,000 supporters.

Kangra-i Melli Afghanistan (National Congress of Afghanistan): Kabul; e-mail mcnafghan@hotmail.com; internet mouv.national .afghan.free.fr; f. 2004; Leader ABDUL LATIF PEDRAM.

Mahaz-i-Melli-i-Islami (National Islamic Front): Malalai Wat, Interior Ministry Rd, Kabul; tel. (70) 231345; Pashtun; Leader SAYED AHMAD GAILANI; Dep. Leader HAMED GAILANI; c. 15,000 supporters.

Nizat-i Hambastagi Melli (National Solidarity Movement): St 6, Taimani, Kabul; tel. (79) 9486558; Chair. Pir SAYED ISHAQ GAILANI.

Nizat-i Melli-i Afghanistan (National Movement of Afghanistan): Taimani, St 1, Kabul; tel. (70) 277938; f. 2002; Leader AHMAD WALI MASOUD.

Tanzim-i Dawat-i Islami (Organization for Invitation to Islam): Ansari Sq., Rd 1, District 4, Kabul; tel. (70) 277007; Pashtun; fmrly Ittihad-i Islami; name changed as above 2005; Leader Prof. ABDUL RASUL SAYEF.

Zazman-i Inqilabi Zahmatkishanan-i Afghanistan (SAZA) (Revolutionary Organization of the Toilers of Afghanistan): Kabul; Tajik; Leader MAHBOOBULLAH KUSHANI.

The following are unregistered political parties:

Hizb-i Islami Khalis (Islamic Party Khalis): Pashtun; promotes establishment of an Islamic state in accordance with Qu'ran, Sunnah and Shariah doctrines; Leader Maulvi MOHAMMAD YUNUS KHALIS; c. 40,000 supporters.

Jabhe-ye-Motahed-e-Milli (United National Front—UNF): f. 2007; informal political grouping incl. fmr mems of United Front; advocates parliamentary system of govt rather than presidential system; mems incl. Younis Qanooni, Ahmad Zia Masoud, Gen. Abdul Rashid Dostam and Marshal Muhammad Qassim Fahim; Chair. Prof. BURHANUDDIN RABBANI.

Taliban: emerged in 1994; Islamist fundamentalist; mainly Sunni Pashtuns; in power 1996–2001; also active in the Federally Administered Tribal Areas of Pakistan; Leader Mullah MOHAMMAD OMAR; c. 12,000 supporters.

Diplomatic Representation

EMBASSIES IN AFGHANISTAN

Australia: c/o Serena Hotel, Froshgah St, Kabul; tel. (79) 9654840; Ambassador MARTIN QUINN.

Belgium: House 1–3, St 1, Taimani Wat, Qala-i-Fathullah, Kabul; tel. (70) 294149; e-mail kabul@diplobel.org; internet www.diplomatie.be/kabul; Ambassador PIETER LEENKNEGT.

Bulgaria: St 15, Shirpur St, Wazir Akbar Khan, Kabul; tel. (20) 2103257; fax (20) 2101089; e-mail bgembkabul@yahoo.com; Ambassador KRASIMIR TULECHKI.

Canada: House 256, St 15, Wazir Akbar Khan, POB 2052, Kabul; tel. (79) 9742800; fax (79) 9742805; e-mail kabul@international.gc.ca; internet www.international.gc.ca/afghanistan; Ambassador ARIF LALANI.

China, People's Republic: Sardar Shah Mahmoud Ghazi Wat, Kabul; tel. (20) 2102545; fax (20) 2102728; e-mail chinaemb_af@mfa.gov.cn; Ambassador YANG HOULAN.

Denmark: House 35–36, Road 13, Lane 1, Wazir Akbar Khan, Kabul; tel. and fax (20) 2300968; e-mail kblamb@um.dk; internet www.ambkabul.um.dk; Head of Mission JENS HAARLOV.

Egypt: Road 15, Wazir Akbar Khan, Kabul; tel. (20) 2021901; fax (20) 2104064; e-mail egypt_kabul@mfa.gov.eg; Ambassador MOHAMMAD SHARIF HASSAN RAYHAN.

Finland: House 39, Street 10, Lane 1, Wazir Akbar Khan, Kabul; tel. (20) 2103051; fax (60) 581504; e-mail sanomat.kab@formin.fi; internet www.finland.org.af; Ambassador TIMO OULA.

France: Cherpour Ave, Shar-i-Nau, POB 62, Kabul; tel. (70) 284032; e-mail chancellerie.kaboul-amba@diplomatie.gouv.fr; internet www.ambafrance-af.org; Ambassador RÉGIS KOETSCHET.

Germany: Wazir Akbar Khan, Mena 6, POB 83, Kabul; tel. (20) 2101512; fax (30) 50007518; e-mail zreg@kabu.auswaertiges-amt.de; internet www.kabul.diplo.de; Ambassador Dr HANS-ULRICH SEIDT.

Hungary: c/o Embassy of the Federal Republic of Germany, Zanbaq Sq., Wazir Akbar Khan, Mena 6, POB 83, Kabul; tel. (79) 7035375; e-mail huembkbl@gmail.com; Chargé d'affaires a.i. SANDOR MATYUS.

India: Malalai Wat, Shar-i-Nau, Kabul; tel. (873) 763095560; fax (873) 763095561; e-mail embassy@indembassy-kabul.com; Ambassador RAKESH SOOD.

Indonesia: Interior Ministry St, Shar-i-Nau, POB 532, Kabul; tel. and fax (20) 2201066; e-mail kabul.kbri@deplu.go.id; internet www.kbri-kabul.go.id; Chargé d'affaires Brig.-Gen. ERMAN HIDAYAT.

Iran: Charahi Shir Pur, Kabul; tel. (20) 2101393; Ambassador FADA-HOSSEIN MALEKI.

Italy: Great Masoud Rd, Kabul; tel. and fax (20) 2103144; e-mail ambasciata.kabul@esteri.it; internet www.ambkabul.esteri.it; Ambassador ETTORE FRANCESCO SEQUI.

Japan: House 83, St 15, Wazir Akbar Khan, Kabul; tel. (873) 762853777; fax (873) 761218272; e-mail ejafg1@web-sat.com; Ambassador JUNICHI KASUGE.

Kazakhstan: House 1, St 10, Wazir Akbar Khan, Kabul; tel. (70) 284296; e-mail sher60@mail.ru; Ambassador AGYBAY SMAGULOV.

AFGHANISTAN
Directory

Korea, Republic: Wazir Akbar Khan, St 10, House 34, Kabul; tel. (932) 02102481; fax (873) 762728481; e-mail kabul@mofat.go.kr; Ambassador SUNG-ZU KANG.

Libya: Charahi Zanbaq, Wazir Akbar Khan, Kabul; tel. (20) 2101084; fax (20) 290160; Chargé d'affaires MOHAMMAD AMER ALZAIDY.

Lithuania: House 2, St 1, Wazir Akbar Khan, Kabul; tel. (79) 9740521; e-mail biruteatiene@yahoo.com; Head of Mission and Chargé d'affaires BIRUTĖ ABRAITIENĖ.

Netherlands: House 2 and 3, St 4, Ansari and Ghiassudin Wat, Shar-i-Nau, Kabul; tel. (70) 286847; e-mail kab@minbuza.nl; internet www.mfa.nl/kab-en; Ambassador HANS BLANKENBERG.

Norway: St 15, Lane 4, Wazir Akbar Khan, Kabul; tel. (20) 2300899; e-mail emb.kabul@mfa.no; internet www.norway.org.af; Ambassador JAN ERIK LEIKVANG.

Pakistan: 10 Nijat Watt Rd, Wazir Akbar Khan, Kabul; tel. (20) 2300911; fax (20) 2300912; e-mail embassy@pakembassykbl.com; Ambassador TARIQ AZIZ-UD-DIN KHAN.

Russia: House 63, Lane 5, St 15, Wazir Akbar Khan, Kabul; tel. (20) 2300500; e-mail rusembafg@neda.af; Ambassador ZAMIR N. KABULOV.

Saudi Arabia: Shash Darak (behind Eyes Office), Kabul; tel. (20) 2102064; e-mail ksa_kemb@hotmail.com; Ambassador GHURAM BIN SAID BIN MALHAN.

Spain: House 274, 4R, St 15, Wazir Akbar Khan, Kabul; tel. (79) 9816349; e-mail embespaf@mail.mae.es; Ambassador JOSÉ TURPÍN.

Tajikistan: House 41, St 10, Wazir Akbar Khan, Kabul; tel. (20) 2101080; fax (20) 2300392; e-mail kabultj@tojikistan.com; Ambassador FARKHOD MAHKAMOV.

Turkey: House 134, Shah Mahmoud Ghazi Khan St, Kabul; tel. (20) 2101581; fax (20) 2101579; e-mail etokdemir@mfa.gov.tr; Ambassador İSMAIL ETHEM TOKDEMIR.

Turkmenistan: House 280, St 13, Lane 3, Wazir Akbar Khan, Kabul; tel. (20) 2300541; e-mail kabulemb@neda.af; Ambassador AMAN MOHAMMADY.

United Arab Emirates: Charahi Zambak, Wazir Akbar Khan, Kabul; tel. (20) 2101578; Ambassador ALI MUHAMMAD AL-SHAMSI.

United Kingdom: St 15, Roundabout Wazir Akbar Khan, POB 334, Kabul; tel. (70) 102000; fax (70) 102250; e-mail britishembassy.kabul@fco.gov.uk; internet www.britishembassy.gov.uk/afghanistan; Ambassador Sir SHERARD LOUIS COWPER-COLES.

USA: Great Masoud Rd, Kabul; tel. (20) 2300436; fax (20) 2301364; e-mail usambassadorkabul@state.gov; internet kabul.usembassy.gov; Ambassador WILLIAM BRAUCHER WOOD.

Uzbekistan: House 14, St 13, Wazir Akbar Khan, Kabul; tel. (20) 2300124; Ambassador PARVEZ MIRIYEVICH ALIYEV.

Judicial System

In December 2001, following more than 20 years of civil conflict, there no longer existed a functioning national judicial system in Afghanistan. In accordance with the Bonn Agreement signed in that month, Afghanistan temporarily reverted to the Constitution of 1964, which combined *Shari'a* with Western concepts of justice. A new Constitution was introduced in early 2004, which made no specific reference to the role of *Shari'a* but stated that Afghan laws should not contravene the main tenets of Islam. The Constitution made provision for the creation of a Supreme Court (Stera Mahkama) as the highest judicial organ in Afghanistan. Until the inauguration of the Court, which took place shortly after the Meli Shura (National Assembly) was officially opened on 19 December 2005, an interim Supreme Court, established in January 2005, functioned in the country.

The Supreme Court comprises nine members, including the Chief Justice, who are appointed by the President, subject to the approval of the Wolasi Jirga (House of Representatives).

Chief Justice: ABDUL SALAM AZIMI.

Attorney-General: ABDUL JABAR SABIT.

Religion

The official religion of Afghanistan is Islam. Muslims comprise 99% of the population, approximately 84% of them of the Sunni sect and the remainder of the Shi'ite sect. There are small minority groups of Hindus, Sikhs and Jews.

ISLAM

The High Council of Ulema and Clergy of Afghanistan: Kabul; f. 1980; 7,000 mems; Chair. Mawlawi ABDOL GHAFUR SENANI.

The Press

Many newspapers and periodicals stopped appearing on a regular basis or, in a large number of cases, ceased publication during the civil war. Following the defeat of the Taliban in late 2001, a number of newspapers and periodicals resumed publication or were established for the first time. In February 2002 the Media Law was amended, removing most restrictions on independent media. Newspapers and periodicals were required to obtain a licence under the legislation. By early 2005 more than 250 publications had been registered with the then Ministry of Information and Culture.

PRINCIPAL DAILIES

Anis (Friendship): Ministry of Communications and Information Technology, Mohammad Jan Khan Wat, Kabul; f. 1927; evening; Dari, Uzbek and Pashto; state-owned; news and literary articles; Editor-in-Chief Prof. GHOLAM SAKHI MONIR; circ. 5,000.

Arman-e Melli (Hope of the Nation): 4 Muslim St, Shar-i-Nau, Kabul; f. 2002 by the Afghan Interim Authority; now independent; Dari and Pashto; Editor-in-Chief MIR HAYDAR MOTAHAR; circ. 4,200.

Cheragh (Light): 112 Shar-i-Nau, Kabul; e-mail cheragh_daily@hotmail.com; Dari, Pashto and English; independent; Editor-in-Chief KATHERINE WEDA; circ. 17,000.

Erada (Intention): Parwan Mina, Cinema Baharistan, House 95, Hajji Mir Ahmad St, Kabul; tel. (70) 224787; e-mail eradadaily@hotmail.com; f. 2000 as weekly in Pakistan; relaunched as daily in Afghanistan 2002; independent; Dari and Pashto; Editor-in-Chief Haji SYED DAUD.

Eslah (Reform): Azadi Printing Press, 4th Floor, Microrayon Part II, Kabul; e-mail islahdaily@yahoo.com; f. 1921; Dari and Pashto; state-owned; Editor-in-Chief SHAMSOLHAQ ARIANFAR.

Hewad (Homeland): Azadi Press Centre, Microrayon, Kabul; tel. (20) 22279; f. 1949; Pashto and Dari; state-owned; Editor-in-Chief SHAH MAHMUD ZIARMAL; circ. 5,000.

Ittefaq-e Islam: Herat; f. 1920; Dari; Editor-in-Chief NAQIB AROIN; circ. 2,000.

Jahan-i-Naw (New World): Mazar-i-Sharif; Editor QAYOUM BAABAK.

Kabul Times: Azady Press Centre, Microrayon, POB 1560, Kabul; tel. (20) 61847; e-mail thekabultimes@yahoo.com; f. 1962 as Kabul Times, renamed Kabul New Times in 1980; ceased publication in 2001; revived in 2002 under new management; English; state-owned; Editor-in-Chief ABDUL HAQ WALEH.

Rah-e Nejat: Kabul; e-mail info@rahenejat.com; internet www.rahenejatdaily.com; fmrly weekly, daily from 2005; Dari and Pashto; independent; Editor-in-Chief SAYED MOHAMMAD ALEMI.

Sahar (Dawn): Mazar-i-Sharif; f. 2005; circ. 2,000.

Shari'at: Kabul.

PERIODICALS

Aamu: Aria Press, Kabul; quarterly; research; circ. 1,000.

Amanat: House 3, Moslem St, Shar-i-Nau, POB 1158, Kabul; tel. (70) 280988; weekly; organ of Hindukosh News Agency; Editor-in-Chief SYED SHABIR ABIR.

Ambastagi: Aria Press, Kabul; weekly; circ. 1,000.

Anees: Kabul; weekly; govt-supported; Editor AHMAD ZIA SYAMAK.

Awa-e Naw: Herat; fortnightly; independent; circ. 2,000.

Ayina-e Zan (Women's Mirror): House 186, St 12, Wazir Akbar Khan, Kabul; tel. (70) 0281864; e-mail womensmirror@hotmail.com; f. 2002; weekly; women's; Dari, Pashto and English; Chief Editor SHUKRIA BAREKZAI; circ. 3,000.

Cinema: Kabul; f. 2003; monthly; entertainment and culture; Editor-in-Chief SIDDIQ BARMAK.

Eqtedar-e Melli: POB 4024, Kartai Char, University Rd, Kabul; tel. (70) 283554; e-mail eqtedaremelli@yahoo.com; weekly; Dari and Pashto.

Farda (Tomorrow): POB 1758, Kabul; tel. (20) 2100199; fax (20) 2100699; e-mail farda-news@yahoo.com; weekly; Publr ABDUL GHAFUR AITEQAD; circ. 4,000.

Kabul Weekly: Afghan Visual Communication Institute, Malik Ashgar Crossroads, POB 1831, Kabul; tel. (20) 2101589; e-mail kabulweekly@lycos.com; internet www.ainaworld.org; f. 1993; banned in 1997, revived in 2002; Dari, Pashto and English; weekly; independent; political, social and cultural issues; Editor-in-Chief FAHIM DASHTY; Sec. ABDUL AKBAR; circ. 8,000.

Killid (The Key): The Killid Group Main Office, Kolola Pushta, Kabul; tel. (20) 2200573; fax (20) 2200574; e-mail killidweekly@thekillidgroup.com; internet www.thekillidgroup.com/c/divisions/killidweekly.htm; weekly; current affairs; Editor SEDIQULLAH BADR; circ. 25,000.

AFGHANISTAN

Malalai: Afghan Visual Communication Institute, Malik Ashgar Crossroads, Kabul; internet www.ainaworld.org; f. 2002; monthly; women's; Dari, Pashto and English; publ. of Aïna humanitarian org.; Chief Editor JAMILA MUJAHID; circ. 3,000.

Mojahed: POB 226, Kabul; e-mail mujahidweekly@yahoo.com; weekly; Dari and Pashto; Editor WAQIF HAKIMI.

Mursal: The Killid Group Main Office, Kolola Pushta, Kabul; tel. (20) 2200573; fax (20) 2200574; e-mail mursal@thekillidgroup.com; internet www.thekillidgroup.com/c/divisions/mursal.htm; f. 2003; weekly; Pashto and Dari; circ. 15,000.

Les Nouvelles de Kaboul (Kabul News): Afghan Visual Communication Institute, Malik Ashgar Crossroads, Kabul; tel. (70) 286215; e-mail dimitri.beck@ainaworld.org; internet www.ainaworld.org; f. 2002; quarterly; English and French; publ. of Aïna humanitarian org.; Chief Editor DIMITRI BECK; Propr and Dir SHAFIQA HABIBI.

Parvaz (Flight): Afghan Visual Communication Institute, Malik Ashgar Crossroads, Kabul; e-mail roshanak@ainaworld.org; internet www.ainaworld.org; f. 2002; Dari and Pashto; every two months; children's; Editor MIRHASAMADEEN BRUMAND; circ. 25,000.

Payam-e-Mujahid (Holy Warrior's Message): POB 5051, Kabul; e-mail payamemojahed@hotmail.com; internet www.payamemojahed.com; f. 1996; weekly; Dari and Pashto; sponsored by the Northern Alliance; Editor HAFIZ MANSOOR.

Roz (The Day): Kabul; f. 2002; monthly; women's; Dari, Pashto, French and English; Editor-in-Chief LAILOMA AHMADI.

Rozgaran: POB 2018, Clola Pushta, Kabul; tel. (70) 207933; e-mail rozgaran@yahoo.com; internet www.geocities.com/rozgaran2; f. 2004; Dari and Pashto.

Takhassos (Experts): Jadai Baghi Azadi, Herat; tel. (70) 280258; monthly; Dari; published by Council of Professionals; Editor MOHAMMAD RAFIQ SHAHIR.

Tolo-e Afghan: Qandahar; several times a week; Pashto; Editor-in-Chief ABDUL QODUS BAES.

Zanbil-e-Gham: Afghan Visual Communication Institute, Malik Ashgar Crossroads, Kabul; f. 1997; monthly; satirical; Editor OSMAN AKRAM; circ. 2,000.

NEWS AGENCIES

Afghan Islamic Press: POB 520, GPO, Peshawar, North-West Frontier Province, Pakistan; tel. (91) 5701100 (Peshawar); fax (91) 5842544 (Peshawar); e-mail info@afghanislamicpress.com; internet www.afghanislamicpress.com.

Ariana Press Agency: Kabul; f. 1987 in Dushanbe, Tajikistan; independent; publishes three newsletters.

Bakhtar News Agency (BNA): Ministry of Communications and Information Technology, Mohammad Jan Khan Wat, Kabul; tel. and fax (20) 2101304; e-mail meenawee13@yahoo.com; internet www.bakhtarnews.com.af; f. 1939; govt news agency; correspondents in 32 provinces; Dir-Gen. SULTAN AHMAD BAHEEN.

Hindukosh News Agency (HNA): House 3, Moslem St, Shar-i-Nau, POB 1158, Kabul; f. 2002; independent; offices in Herat, Qandahar and Mazar-i-Sharif; Dir SYED NAJIBULLAH HASHIMI.

Pajhwok Afghan News: Interior Ministry Rd, Shahr-e-Kabul, Kabul; tel. (20) 2201814; fax (20) 2201813; e-mail feedback@pajhwok.com; internet www.pajhwok.com; f. 2004; independent; regional bureaux in Mazar-i-Sharif, Qandahar, Herat and Jalalabad; news service provided in English, Pashto and Dari; Dir and Editor-in-Chief DANISH KAROKHEL.

PRESS ASSOCIATION

Afghanistan Independent Journalists' Association (AIJA): Maiwand Press Club, Alam Ganj, Kabul; fax (20) 70285515; f. 2003; Chair. ABDULHAMID HAAMI.

Afghanistan Women in Media Network: Afghan Media and Cultural Centre, Malik Ashgar Crossroads, Kabul; e-mail najibamaram@hotmail.com; f. 2002; association of female media staff; Pres. JAMILA MUJAHID; Vice-Pres. NAJIBA MARAM.

Publishers

Some of the following publishers were forced to close down during the Taliban regime. Since the Taliban's fall from power in December 2001, publishers have been slowly reopening, with the help of the UN and other international aid agencies and foreign publishing houses.

Afghan Book: POB 206, Kabul; f. 1969; books on various subjects, translations of foreign works on Afghanistan, books in English on Afghanistan and Dari language textbooks for foreigners; Man. Dir JAMILA AHANG.

Afghanistan Today Publishers: c/o The Kabul Times, Ansari Wat, POB 983, Kabul; tel. (20) 61847; publicity materials; answers enquiries about Afghanistan.

Ariana Press: Poli Jarkhi, Kabul; under the supervision of the Ministry of Culture and Youth Affairs; Dir ABDUL KADER.

Azady (Freedom) Press: Ministry of Culture and Youth Affairs, Mohammad Jan Khan Wat, Kabul; tel. (20) 2100113; under supervision of the Ministry of Culture and Youth Affairs; Dir JAHAN YAR.

Balhaqi Book Publishing and Importing Institute: POB 2025, Kabul; tel. (20) 26818; f. 1971 by co-operation of the Government Printing House, Bakhtar News Agency and leading newspapers; publishers and importers of books; Pres. MUHAMMAD ANWAR NUMYALAI.

Beihagi Publishers: Azady Press Centre, Microrayon, Kabul; tel. (20) 63623; books on Afghan culture; also prints information related to the Govt and its plans; Dir SADIQ AYAR.

Book Publishing Institute: Herat; f. 1970 by co-operation of Government Printing House and citizens of Herat; books on literature, history and religion.

Book Publishing Institute: Qandahar; f. 1970; supervised by Government Printing House; mainly books in Pashto language.

Educational Publications: Ministry of Education, Mohammad Jan Khan Wat, Kabul; tel. and fax (20) 200000; textbooks for primary and secondary schools in the Pashto and Dari languages; also three monthly magazines in Pashto and in Dari.

Historical Society of Afghanistan: Kabul; tel. (20) 30370; f. 1931; mainly historical and cultural works and two quarterly magazines: *Afghanistan* (English and French), *Aryana* (Dari and Pashto); Pres. AHMAD ALI MOTAMEDI.

Institute of Geography: Kabul University, Kabul; geographical and related works.

International Center for Pashto Studies: Kabul; f. 1975 by the Afghan Govt with the assistance of UNESCO; research work on the Pashto language and literature and on the history and culture of the Pashtun people; Pres. and Assoc. Chief Researcher J. K. HEKMATY; publs *Pashto* (quarterly).

Kabul University Press: Kabul; tel. (20) 42433; f. 1950; textbooks; two quarterly scientific journals in Dari and in English, etc.

Research Center for Linguistics and Literary Studies: Afghanistan Academy of Sciences, Akbar Khan Mena, Kabul; tel. (20) 26912; f. 1978; research on Afghan languages (incl. Pashto, Dari, Balochi and Uzbek) and Afghan folklore; publs *Kabul* (Pashto), *Zeray* (Pashto weekly) and *Khurasan* (Dari); Pres. Prof. MOHAMMED R. ELHAM.

GOVERNMENT PUBLISHING HOUSE

Government Printing House: Kabul; tel. (93) 26851; f. 1870; under supervision of the Ministry of Communications and Information Technology; Dir SAID AHMAD RAHAA.

PUBLISHERS' ASSOCIATION

Afghan Libraries' and Publishers' Association: Chari Ansari, between Ansari Crossroads and Popo Lano Restaurant, Kabul.

Broadcasting and Communications

TELECOMMUNICATIONS

Afghanistan Telecom Regulatory Authority (ATRA): Ministry of Communications and Information Technology, MOC Headquarters Tower, 10th Floor, Mohammad Jan Khan Wat, Kabul; tel. (20) 2101179; e-mail z.hamidy@atra.gov.af; internet atra.gov.af; succeeded Telecom Regulatory Board.

Afghan Telecom (AfghanTel): Post Parcel Bldg, 4th Floor, Mohammad Jan Khan Wat, Kabul; tel. (75) 2033333; fax (75) 2033344; e-mail info@afghantelecom.af; internet www.afghantelecom.af; f. 2004; state-owned; provides wireless and digital fixed-line services; 80% of shares offered for sale in March 2008; Dir AMIRZAI SANGIN.

Afghan Wireless Communication Company (AWCC): Agricultural Bank, 3rd Floor, Maiwand Wat, Kabul; tel. and fax (70) 803803; e-mail info@afghanwireless.com; internet www.afghan-wireless.com; f. 1999; jt venture between the Ministry of Communications and Information Technology and Telephone Systems International, Inc of the USA; reconstruction of Afghanistan's national and international telecommunications network; by June 2002 mobile and fixed-line telecommunications services covered Herat, Jalalabad, Kabul, Mazar-i-Sharif and Qandahar; the first centre providing internet services was opened in Kabul in July of that year; 1.3m. subscribers (July 2007); Chair. EHSAN BAYAT.

AFGHANISTAN

Etisalat Afghanistan (UAE): POB 800, Kabul; e-mail info@etisalat.af; internet www.etisalat.af; commenced operations in Afghanistan in 2007; GSM operator.

Telecom Development Co Afghanistan Ltd (Roshan): House 13, Main St, Wazir Akbar Khan, Kabul; tel. (79) 9977755; fax (79) 9978800; e-mail roshanca@roshan.af; internet www.roshan.af; f. 2002 by an international consortium comprising the Aga Khan Fund for Economic Development (AKFED), French cos Monaco Telecom International (MTI) and Alcatel, and US co MCT Corpn; 51% owned by AKFED, 36.75% by MTI and 12.25% by MCT Corpn; provides mobile telecommunications services; CEO KARIM KHOJA.

BROADCASTING

The media were severely restricted by the militant Taliban regime (1996–2001): television was banned and Radio Afghanistan was renamed Radio Voice of Shari'a. The overthrow of the Taliban in November–December 2001 led to the liberation of the media. On 13 November Radio Afghanistan was revived in Kabul; music was broadcast for the first time in five years. A few days later Kabul TV was resurrected, and a woman was employed as its newsreader. By early 2005 there were 42 radio stations and eight private television stations broadcasting in Afghanistan.

Radio

Radio-Television Afghanistan: St 10, Lane 2, Wazir Akbar Khan, POB 544, Kabul; tel. (20) 2101086; e-mail rtakabul@hotmail.com; revived in 2001; programmes in Dari, Pashto, Turkmen and Uzbek; Dir-Gen. MOHAMMAD ESHAQ; Head of Radio GHULAM HASSAN HAZRATI.

Balkh Radio and TV: Mazar-i-Sharif; Pashto and Dari; Chair. ABDORRAB JAHED.

Radio Herat: Herat.

Radio Kabul: Ansari Wat, Kabul; tel. (20) 2101087; Dir GHULAM HASSAN HAZRATI.

Voice of Freedom: Kabul; f. 2002; broadcasts one hour a day in Dari and Pashto; German-funded.

Independent

Arman FM: POB 1045, Central Post Office, Kabul; tel. (79) 9321010; e-mail info@arman.fm; internet www.arman.fm; f. 2003; Afghanistan's first privately owned independent FM radio station; broadcasts in Kabul, Mazar, Herat, Qandahar and Jalalabad; broadcasts popular music and culture 24 hours a day; Dir SAAD MOHSENI.

Radio Azad Afghan: Qandahar; f. 2004; broadcasts five hours daily; Dir ISMAIL TIMUR.

Radio Bamian: Bamian; f. 2003.

Radio Killid: The Killid Group Main Office, Kolola Pushta, Kabul; tel. (20) 2200573; fax (20) 2200574; internet www.thekillidgroup.com/c/divisions/radio.htm; f. 2003 by Development and Humanitarian Services for Afghanistan; broadcasts 24 hours daily; stations in Kabul and Herat; Man. NAJIBA AYUBI.

Radio Sahar: Herat; f. 2003; Dari; women's; broadcasts 12 hours daily; Dir HULAN KHATIBI; Station Man. HUMAIRA HABIB.

Radio Sharq: Jalalabad; f. 2003; broadcasts 12 hours daily.

Radio Tiraj Mir: Pol-e-Khomri; f. 2003; broadcasts 16 hours daily.

Voice of Afghan Women: Kabul; f. 2003; relaunched in 2005 following closure owing to lack of funds; dedicated to interests of women; Dir JAMILA MUJAHID.

Television

Radio-Television Afghanistan: see Radio.

Balkh Radio and TV: see Radio.

Herat TV: Herat; state-owned.

Kabul TV: Kabul; revived in 2001; broadcasts four hours daily; Dir HUMAYUN RAWI.

TV Badakhshan: Faizabad; f. 1987 as Faizabad TV, name changed in 2000; Pashto and Dari.

Independent

Afghan TV: Kabul; f. 2004; broadcasts 24 hours daily; Man. AHMED SHAH AFGHANZAI.

Aina (Mirror): Shebarghan; f. 2003; broadcasts to Jawzjan, Sar-e Pol and Balkh provinces and to the bordering areas of Turkmenistan and Uzbekistan; Dir SYED ANWAR SADAT.

Aryana TV: Kabul; broadcasts to 16 provinces in Afghanistan; f. 2005; Dir AHSANULLAH BAYAT.

Tolo TV: POB 225, Central Post Office, Kabul; tel. (79) 9321010; e-mail info@tolo.tv; internet www.tolo.tv; f. 2004; commercial station; broadcasts news, current affairs, entertainment, lifestyle and culture programmes; Dir SAAD MOHSENI.

Finance
(cap. = capital; brs = branches)

BANKING

The banking sector was under reconstruction from 2002, following the collapse of the Taliban regime in late 2001. In September 2003 the President approved a law allowing foreign banks to open branches in Afghanistan. By the end of 2004 11 foreign banks had begun operations in the country.

Central Bank

Da Afghanistan Bank (Central Bank of Afghanistan): Ibne Sina Wat, Kabul; tel. (20) 2100301; fax (20) 290047; e-mail info@centralbank.gov.af; internet www.centralbank.gov.af; f. 1939; main functions: banknote issue, modernize the banking system, re-establish banking relations with international banks, create a financial market system, foreign exchange regulation, govt and private depository; granted complete independence in September 2003; Gov. NUROLLAH DELAWARI; 76 brs.

Other Banks

Afghanistan International Bank: House 1608, behind Amani High School, Wazir Akbar Khan, POB 2074, Kabul; tel. (79) 9089898; fax (79) 9798989; e-mail info@aib.af; internet www.aib.af; f. 2004; established and managed by the ING Institutional and Government Advisory Group (Netherlands) on behalf of a consortium of Afghan and US investors; 75% owned by Afghan nationals, 25% owned by Asian Development Bank; cap. US $10m. (March 2004); CEO CORNELIS E. VERHEEZEN (acting).

Azizi Bank: Malik Asghar Sq., POB 221, Kabul; tel. (20) 2104470; fax (20) 21044701; e-mail info@azizibank.com; internet www.azizibank.af; f. 2006; Pres. and CEO DEEPAK SHRIVASTAVA.

Banke Millie Afghan (Afghan National Bank): Jade Ibne Sina, POB 522, Kabul; tel. (20) 21003311; fax (20) 2101801; e-mail info@bma.com.af; internet www.bma.com.af; f. 1933 as private bank, nationalized in 1976; Chair. and CEO MOHAMMAD NAIM DINDAR; Pres. Prof. Dr ABDUL QAYOUM ARIF; 20 brs in Afghanistan, 6 brs overseas.

BRAC Afghanistan Bank: Charai Torabaz Khan Zarghona Midan, Shar-i-Nau, Kabul; tel. (75) 2016827; e-mail info@bracafbank.com; internet www.bracafbank.com; f. 2006; business with retail sector and small and medium-sized enterprises; managed by a Bangladeshi team; CEO M. EHSANUL HAQUE.

Development Bank of Afghanistan: Shah Mahmod Ghazi Rd, opposite Chinese Embassy, Kabul; tel. (77) 6677222; e-mail info@bankdba.com; internet www.bankdba.com; f. 2006; Chair. of Supervisory Bd SERGEY M. TSOY; CEO MAKHMUD L. LSROILOVE.

Export Promotion Bank of Afghanistan: Park-e-Timor Shahi, Kabul; tel. (20) 2100284; fax (20) 2103947; e-mail epbafghan@yahoo.com; f. 1976; provides financing for exports and export-orientated investments; state-owned; operations suspended under Taliban rule in 1996–2001; CEO ABDUL HAMID MOHEBBI; 3 brs.

First MicroFinance Bank (FMFB): 2nd Floor, Park Plaza, Torabaz Khan Rd, Shar-i-Nau, Kabul; tel. (79) 9322765; e-mail info@fmfb.com.af; internet www.akdn.org/microfinance/Afghanistan/index.html#microfinance; f. 2004; 51% owned by Aga Khan Agency for Microfinance, 32% by Kreditanstalt fur Wiederaufbau, 17% by International Finance Corpn; provides sustainable financial services to the poor in order to contribute to poverty alleviation and economic development; CEO MUSLIM UL-HAQ.

Kabul Bank: 10–42 Turabaz Khan, Shar-i-Nau, Kabul; tel. (20) 2222666; fax (216) 84400171; e-mail info@kabulbank.af; internet www.kabulbank.af; f. 2004; Chair. SHERKHAN FARNOOD; CEO ASSANKHAN AKBAR; 4 brs.

Pashtany Bank: Mohammad Jan Khan Watt, Kabul; tel. (20) 2100306; fax (20) 2102905; e-mail info@pashtanybank.com; internet www.pashtanybank.com; f. 1955 to provide short-term credits, forwarding facilities, opening letters of credit, purchase and sale of foreign exchange; nationalized in 1975; Chair. ABDUL TAWAB; CEO HAYAT ULLAH DAYANI; 14 brs in Afghanistan, 3 brs in Pakistan.

INSURANCE

Afghan National Insurance Co: Second Ave, Kartai Parwan, nr fmr British Embassy, POB 329, Kabul; tel. and fax (20) 2200189; e-mail insurancenationalafghanco@yahoo.com; f. 1964; mem. of Asian Reinsurance Corpn; marine, aviation, fire, motor and accident insurance; Pres. Eng. AHMAD SHAH ALIZAI; Claims Man. S. OMAR.

AFGHANISTAN · Directory

Trade and Industry

GOVERNMENT AGENCIES

Afghanistan Investment Support Agency (AISA): opposite Ministry of Foreign Affairs, Kabul; tel. (20) 2103404; fax (20) 2103402; e-mail info@aisa.org.af; internet www.aisa.org.af; f. 2003; promotes and regulates domestic and foreign investment in the private sector; Pres. and CEO OMAR ZAKHILWAL.

Export Promotion Centre of Afghanistan (EPCA): off Karte Char 2nd St, Kabul; tel. (79) 9030800; e-mail gulistani@epca.org.af; internet www.epca.org.af; f. 2006; provides guidance for traders, collects and disseminates trade information; CEO SULEMAN FATIMIE.

CHAMBERS OF COMMERCE AND INDUSTRY

Afghan Chamber of Commerce and Industry: Mohammad Jan Khan Wat, Kabul; tel. (20) 26796; fax (20) 2290089; e-mail acci2002@hotmail.com; internet www.acci.org.af; Head Mola GHULAM MUHAMMAD ALIAQI.

Afghanistan International Chamber of Commerce: House 92, St 2, Shash Darak, Kabul; e-mail admin@aicc-online.org.af; internet www.aicc-online.org.af; f. 2004; Chair. AZARKHASH HAFIZI; CEO HAMIDULLAH FAROOQI.

Federation of Afghan Chambers of Commerce and Industry: Darulaman Wat, Kabul; f. 1923; includes chambers of commerce and industry in Ghazni, Qandahar, Kabul, Herat, Mazar-i-Sharif, Fariab, Jawzjan, Kunduz, Jalalabad and Andkhoy.

INDUSTRIAL AND TRADE ASSOCIATIONS

Afghan Carpet Exporters' Guild: Darulaman Wat, POB 3159, Kabul; tel. (70) 224575; f. 1967; non-profit, independent organization of carpet manufacturers and exporters; Pres. ZIAUDDIN ZIA; c. 1,000 mems.

Afghan Cart Company: Zerghona Maidan, Kabul; tel. (20) 2201309; fax (20) 290238; e-mail do_ik@yahoo.com; f. 1988; imports electrical goods, machinery, metal, cars, etc.; exports raisins, medical herbs, wood, animal hides, etc.; Pres. KABIR IMAQ.

Afghan Fruit Processing Co: Industrial Estate, Puli Charkhi, POB 261, Kabul; tel. (20) 65186; f. 1960; exports raisins, other dried fruits and nuts.

Afghan Raisin and Other Dried Fruits Institute: Sharara Wat, POB 3034, Kabul; tel. (20) 30463; exporters of dried fruits and nuts; Pres. NAJMUDDIN MUSLEH.

Afghanistan Karakul Institute: Puli Charkhi, POB 506, Kabul; tel. (20) 61852; f. 1967; exporters of furs; Pres. G. M. BAHEER.

Afghanistan Plants Enterprise: Puli Charkhi, POB 122, Kabul; tel. (20) 31962; exports plant-based medicines, plants and spices.

Animal Products Trading and Industrial Association: Ayub Khan Mina, South of Habibia High School, 2nd St, Darulaman Wat, Kabul; tel. and fax (75) 2023490; e-mail mohsin_ataie@yahoo.com; f. 1979; promotes and exports animal products, incl. wool and animal skins; Chief Officer M. MOHSIN ATAIE.

Handicraft Promotion and Export Centre: Sharara Wat, POB 3089, Kabul; tel. (20) 32935; Dir MOMENA RANJBAR.

Parapamizad Co Ltd: Jadai Nader Pashtoon, Sidiq Omar Market, POB 1911, Kabul; tel. (20) 22116; export/import co; Propr PADSHAH SARBAZ.

TRADE UNIONS

Afghanistan Lawyers' Union: Shar-i-Nau, Shaheed Charahi, Kabul; tel. (75) 2004342; e-mail lawyers_union@yahoo.com; Chair. Prof. QAZI.

Afghanistan National Union of Journalists: f. 2006; formed through merger of Afghanistan Gen. Union of Journalists, Free Journalist Union of Afghanistan and Nat. Union of Afghan Journalists; Pres. SAYYID HUSSAIN FAZIL SANCHARAKI.

All Afghanistan Federation of Trade Unions: Karte Nau, First St, Kabul; tel. (79) 9340196; e-mail zquraishi_kab_aaftu@hotmail.com; Chair. Z. QURAISHI.

National Union of Afghanistan Employees (NUAE): POB 756, Kabul; tel. (20) 23040; f. 1978 as Central Council of Afghanistan Trade Unions, to establish and develop the trade union movement, including the formation of councils and organizational cttees in the provinces; name changed in 1990; composed of seven vocational unions; 300,000 mems; Pres. of Cen. Council MOHAMMAD QASIM EHSAS; Vice-Pres. ASAD KHAN NACEIRY.

Transport

RAILWAYS

There is no railway system currently operating in Afghanistan. Plans to build a rail line linking Pakistan, Afghanistan and Turkmenistan were under discussion in the mid-2000s. In February 2007 construction began on a 202-km railway line, funded by the Iranian Government, from Torbat Heidarieh, Iran, to Herat, with completion of the project anticipated by March 2008. In July 2007 the Government of Turkmenistan commenced reconstruction of the retired Kushka—Torgondi railway line linking Afghanistan to the rail networks of Iran and Russia at an estimated cost of US $550,000.

ROADS

In 2001 there were an estimated 23,500 km of roads, of which more than 18,000 km were unpaved. All-weather highways link Kabul with Qandahar and Herat in the south and west, Jalalabad in the east and Mazar-i-Sharif and the Amu-Dar'ya (Oxus) river in the north. A massive reconstruction programme of the road system in Afghanistan began in early 2002. The Salang Highway was rehabilitated, thus reconnecting Kabul with the north. In November the first of five bridges across the River Pyanj on the Tajik–Afghan border was reopened for use. By late 2004 the reconstruction of the important 482-km highway linking Kabul and Qandahar had been completed. Meanwhile, reconstruction of the 566-km highway linking Qandahar and Herat began in mid-2004 and was initially expected to be completed by the end of 2006. In January 2007, however, there were reports by USAID that, owing to concerns over security on one section of the highway, the projected completion date of the reconstruction work had been postponed until 2008. In late 2005 work began on a bridge across the Amu-Dar'ya river, linking Sher Khan Bandar in Kunduz province with Tajikistan.

In early 2005 Afghanistan, Iran and Uzbekistan signed an agreement concerning construction of a trans-Afghan transportation corridor, a 2,400-km road that would link the Uzbek city of Termez and the Iranian port of Bandar Abbas with Mazar-i-Sharif and Herat.

Afghan Container Transport Company Ltd (ACTCO): House 43, St 2, Shar-i-Nau, POB 3165, Kabul; tel. and fax (20) 2201392; e-mail kabul@afghancontainers.com; internet www.afghancontainers.com; f. 1974; Vice-Pres. ALI DAD BEIGH ZAD.

Afghan Transit Company: Ghousy Market, Mohammad Jan Khan Wat, POB 530, Kabul; tel. (20) 2101733; fax (20) 2101734; e-mail aftrans14@hotmail.com; Chair M. AZAM KARGAR.

AFSOTR: Kabul; tel. (20) 2102358; e-mail afsotr@svt.ru; founded as Afghan Soviet Transportation Company; resumed operations in 1998; transport co; 90 vehicles.

Land Transport Company: Khoshal Mena, Kabul; tel. (20) 20345; f. 1943; commercial transport within Afghanistan.

Milli Bus Enterprise: Ministry of Transport and Aviation, Ansari Wat, Kabul; tel. (20) 2101032; state-owned and -administered; 900 buses; Pres. Eng. AZIZ NAGHABAN.

Salang-Europe International Transport and Transit: Kabul; f. 1991 as joint Afghan/Soviet co; 500 vehicles.

INLAND WATERWAYS

There are 1,200 km of navigable inland waterways, including the Amu-Dar'ya (Oxus) river, which is capable of handling vessels of up to about 500 dwt. River ports on the Amu-Dar'ya are linked by road to Kabul.

CIVIL AVIATION

In 2005 there were 22 airports in Afghanistan, including international airports at Kabul, Qandahar, Bagram and Kunduz. Plans were under way to relocate and upgrade the airport at Kabul and to upgrade the airports at Herat, Mazar-i-Sharif and Jalalabad to international standards.

Ariana Afghan Airlines: POB 76, Kabul; tel. (20) 2100351; fax (873) 762523846; e-mail info@flyariana.com; internet www.flyariana.com; f. 1955; merged with Bakhtar Afghan Airlines Co Ltd in 1985; 75% state-owned; flights to India, Pakistan, Germany, the Middle East and Russia; Pres. ZABIULLAH ESMATI.

KamAir: POB 62, Kabul; tel. and fax (20) 2200108; e-mail info@flykamair.com; internet www.flykamair.com; f. 2003; privately owned; domestic and regional flights; Pres. ZAMARIA KAMGAR.

Tourism

Afghanistan's potential tourism attractions include: Bamian, with its thousands of painted caves; Bandi Amir, with its suspended lakes; the Blue Mosque of Mazar; Herat, with its Grand Mosque and minarets; the towns of Qandahar and Girishk; Balkh (ancient Bactria), 'Mother of Cities', in the north; Bagram, Hadda and Surkh Kotal (of interest to archaeologists); and the high mountains of the Hindu Kush. Furthermore, ruins of a Buddhist city (known locally as Kaffir Got—'Fortress of the Infidels') dating from the second century were discovered in July 2002 in a remote valley in southern Afghanistan. The restoration of cultural heritage, sponsored by UNESCO, began in 2002. In 1998 an estimated 4,000 tourists visited Afghanistan and receipts from tourism amounted to around US $1m.

Afghan Tourist Organization (ATO): Ansari Wat, Shar-i-Nau, Kabul; tel. (20) 30323; f. 1958; Pres. Dr HESSAMUDDIN HAMRAH.

ALBANIA

Introductory Survey

Location, Climate, Language, Religion, Flag, Capital

The Republic of Albania lies in south-eastern Europe. It is bordered by Montenegro to the north, by Kosovo (a Serbian province, which made a unilateral declaration of independence on 17 February 2008) to the north-east, by the former Yugoslav republic of Macedonia (FYRM) to the east, by Greece to the south and by the Adriatic and Ionian Seas (parts of the Mediterranean Sea) to the west. The climate is Mediterranean throughout most of the country. The sea plays a moderating role, although frequent cyclones in the winter months make the weather unstable. The average temperature is 14°C (57°F) in the north-east and 18°C (64°F) in the south-west. The language is Albanian, the principal dialects being Gheg (north of the Shkumbin river) and Tosk, which is spoken in the south and has been the official dialect since 1952. Islam is the predominant faith, but there are small groups of Christians (mainly Roman Catholic in the north and Eastern Orthodox in the south). The national flag (proportions 5 by 7) is red, with a two-headed black eagle in the centre. The capital is Tirana (Tiranë).

Recent History

On 28 November 1912, after more than 400 years of Turkish rule, Albania declared its independence under a provisional Government. Although the country was occupied by Italy in 1914, its independence was re-established in 1920. Albania was declared a republic in 1925 and Ahmet Beg Zogu was elected President; proclaimed King Zog I in 1928, he reigned until he was forced into exile by the Italian occupation of Albania in April 1939. Albania was united with Italy for four years, before being occupied by German forces in 1943; the Germans withdrew one year later.

The communist-led National Liberation Front (NLF), established in 1941, was the most successful wartime resistance group and took power on 29 November 1944. Elections in December 1945 were contested by only communist candidates. The new regime was headed by Enver Hoxha, the leader of the Albanian Communist Party (ACP). King Zog was declared deposed, and the People's Republic of Albania was proclaimed on 11 January 1946. The ACP was renamed the Party of Labour of Albania (PLA) in 1948, the NLF having been succeeded by the Democratic Front of Albania (DFA) in 1945.

The communist regime developed close relations with Yugoslavia until the latter's expulsion from the Cominform (a Soviet-sponsored body co-ordinating the activities of European communist parties) in 1948. Albania, fearing Yugoslav expansionism, became a close ally of the USSR and joined the Moscow-based Council for Mutual Economic Assistance (CMEA) in 1949. Hoxha resigned as Head of Government in 1954, but retained effective national leadership as First Secretary of the PLA. Albania joined the Warsaw Treaty Organization (Warsaw Pact) in 1955, but relations with the USSR deteriorated when Soviet leaders attempted a rapprochement with Yugoslavia. The Albanian leadership declared its support for the People's Republic of China in the Sino–Soviet ideological dispute, prompting the USSR to suspend relations with Albania in 1961. Albania established increasingly close relations with China, ended participation in the CMEA in 1962 and withdrew from the Warsaw Pact in 1968. However, following the improvement of relations between China and the USA after 1972, and the death of Mao Zedong, the Chinese leader, in 1976, Sino-Albanian relations progressively deteriorated. In 1978 Albania declared its support for Viet Nam in its dispute with China, prompting the Chinese Government to suspend all economic and military co-operation with Albania.

A new Constitution was adopted in December 1976, and the country was renamed the People's Socialist Republic of Albania. In December 1981 Mehmet Shehu, the Chairman of the Council of Ministers (Prime Minister) since 1954, died as a result of a shooting incident. Although officially reported to have committed suicide, there were suggestions of a leadership struggle with Hoxha, and subsequent allegations that he had been executed. Following the death of Shehu, a new Government, headed by Adil Çarçani, hitherto the First Deputy Chairman, was established. In November 1982 Ramiz Alia replaced Haxhi Lleshi as the Head of State, as President of the Presidium of the Kuvendi Popullor (People's Assembly). A number of former state and PLA officials were reportedly executed in September 1983.

Enver Hoxha died in April 1985, and was succeeded as First Secretary of the PLA by Alia. In March 1986 Hoxha's widow, Nexhmije, was elected to the chairmanship of the General Council of the DFA. Alia was re-elected as First Secretary of the PLA and as President of the Presidium of the Kuvendi Popullor in November 1986 and February 1987, respectively. In the latter month Çarçani was reappointed Chairman of the Council of Ministers.

In November 1989 an amnesty for certain prisoners (including some political prisoners) was declared. From December a number of anti-Government demonstrations were reportedly staged, particularly in the northern town of Shkodër. In January 1990 Alia announced proposals for limited political and economic reform, including the introduction of a system of multi-candidate elections (although the leading role of the PLA was to be maintained). The judicial system was reorganized, the number of capital offences considerably reduced, the practice of religion (which had been prohibited in 1967) was again to be tolerated, and Albanians were to be granted the right to foreign travel. Following renewed unrest in July, in which anti-Government demonstrators in Tirana were violently dispersed by the security forces, more than 5,000 Albanians took refuge in foreign embassies, and were subsequently granted permission to leave the country. Meanwhile, the membership of both the Council of Ministers and the Political Bureau of the PLA had been reorganized. In late 1990 Alia announced proposals for more radical political reforms. In December it was announced that the establishment of independent political parties was to be permitted, prior to elections to the Kuvendi Popullor, scheduled for February 1991. In mid-December 1990, however, anti-Government demonstrators clashed with the security forces in several cities. Nexhmije Hoxha resigned from the chairmanship of the General Council of the DFA, and was replaced by Çarçani (who was, in turn, replaced in mid-1991).

On 20 February 1991, following widespread anti-Government demonstrations, Alia declared presidential rule. An eight-member Presidential Council was established, and a provisional Council of Ministers was appointed. Çarçani was replaced as Chairman of the Council of Ministers by Fatos Nano, a liberal economist, who had been appointed Deputy Chairman in late January. In late February the unrest finally ended. Following opposition pressure, the elections were postponed until the end of March. In mid-March a general amnesty for all political prisoners was declared. The first round of the multi-party legislative elections took place on 31 March, with second and third ballots on 7 and 14 April, respectively. The PLA and affiliated organizations won 169 of the 250 seats, while the Democratic Party of Albania (DPA) secured 75 seats and the Democratic Union of the Greek Minority (OMONIA) obtained five seats. The victory of the PLA, amid allegations of electoral malpractice, prompted dismay in some urban areas, where support for the DPA had been strong. Widespread protests ensued, and in Shkodër security forces opened fire on demonstrators, killing four.

In April 1991 an interim Constitution replaced that of 1976, pending the drafting of a new constitution. The country was renamed the Republic of Albania, and the post of executive President, to be elected by two-thirds of the votes cast in the Kuvendi Popullor, was created. Alia was subsequently elected to the new post, defeating the only other candidate, Namik Dokle, also of the PLA; all the opposition deputies abstained from voting. In May 1991 Nano was reappointed Chairman of the Council of Ministers, and the Government was again reorganized. In accordance with the provisions of the interim Constitution, Alia resigned from the leadership of the PLA. In June the continuing general strike forced the resignation of Nano's administration. A Government of National Stability was subsequently formed, with Ylli Bufi as Chairman of the Council of Ministers. The coalition included representatives of the PLA, the DPA, the Republican Party of Albania (RPA), the Social Democratic Party of Albania (SDPA) and the Agrarian Party of Albania

(APA). Gramoz Pashko, a prominent member of the DPA, was appointed Deputy Chairman of the Council of Ministers and Minister of the Economy. At a party congress later in June, the PLA was renamed the Socialist Party of Albania (SPA). In December the Chairman of the DPA, Sali Berisha, announced the withdrawal of the seven representatives of the party from the coalition Government. These withdrawals, which followed the dismissal of three RPA ministers, forced the resignation of Bufi's Government. Pending elections, Alia appointed an interim Government of non-party 'technocrats', under a new Prime Minister, Vilson Ahmeti.

A new electoral law, approved by the legislature in early February 1992, reduced the number of deputies in the Kuvendi Popullor from 250 to 140. Under provisions that defined legitimate political parties, organizations that represented ethnic minorities, such as OMONIA, were prohibited from contesting the forthcoming general election, prompting widespread protests from the Greek minority. At the general election, conducted in two rounds on 22 and 29 March, the DPA secured 92 of the 140 seats, the SPA 38, the SDPA seven, the Union for Human Rights Party (UHRP—supported by the minority Greek and Macedonian communities) two and the RPA one seat. According to official figures, 90% of the electorate participated. Following the defeat of the SPA, Alia resigned as President on 3 April. A few days later the new Kuvendi Popullor elected Berisha to the presidency. Berisha subsequently appointed a coalition Government dominated by the DPA, with Aleksander Meksi, of that party, as Prime Minister. The SDPA and RPA were each allocated one ministerial portfolio. In July the DPA secured 43% of the total votes cast at multi-party local elections, compared with the 41% obtained by the SPA. In September divisions within the DPA resulted in the defection of a number of prominent party members, who formed a new political grouping, the Democratic Alliance Party (DAP).

During 1992 a number of former communist officials were detained, including Nexhmije Hoxha, who was arrested on charges of corruption. In February 1993 Ahmeti was placed under house arrest, also following charges of corruption; further allegations concerning abuse of power resulted in the arrest of another former Prime Minister, Nano (by this time Chairman of the SPA), in July. Nexhmije Hoxha was imprisoned for nine years in January, having been convicted of embezzling state funds. (She was released in January 1997.) In August 1993 Alia was arrested on charges of abuse of power. Later that month Ahmeti was sentenced to two years' imprisonment. The trial of Nano commenced in April 1994, despite an international campaign on his behalf, organized by the SPA, and a European Parliament resolution appealing for his release. Nano was convicted of misappropriation of state funds during his premiership in 1991, and was sentenced to 12 years' imprisonment. In July 1994 Alia was sentenced to nine years' imprisonment, but was released in 1995.

In October 1994 a draft Constitution was finally presented to Berisha, and was submitted for endorsement at a national referendum, after it failed to obtain the requisite two-thirds' majority approval in the Kuvendi Popullor. As a result of Berisha's support for the draft Constitution (which was to vest additional powers in the President), the referendum was widely perceived as a vote of confidence in his leadership. At the referendum, which took place on 6 November, with the participation of 84.4% of the electorate, the draft Constitution was rejected by 53.9% of the voters, precipitating demands for a general election. In December Berisha effected an extensive reorganization of the Council of Ministers. The RPA, which held only one seat in the Kuvendi Popullor, withdrew from the governing coalition. The SDPA split into two factions; of these, only a new grouping, the Union of Social Democrats, remained in the coalition. In March 1995 the Chairman of the DPA, Eduard Selami, who opposed attempts to organize a further referendum on the draft Constitution, and who had accused Berisha of abuse of power, was removed from his post. Public discontent at a lack of improvement in economic conditions was demonstrated by a continued flow of illegal immigrants to Italy, which, in May, deployed troops along its coast in an attempt to stem the influx.

In September 1995 the Kuvendi Popullor adopted legislation prohibiting those in power under the former communist regime from holding public office until 2002 (thereby banning a large number of prospective candidates, including incumbent SPA deputies, from contesting legislative elections in 1996). In November 1995 a parliamentary commission initiated an inquiry, following the discovery of a mass grave near the border town of Shkodër. Families of the deceased urged the prosecution service to initiate charges against former members of the communist regime, including Alia, who had allegedly been responsible for the killing by border guards of nationals attempting to flee the country in 1990–92; Alia was detained in February 1996. Meanwhile, in December 1995 the Kuvendi Popullor approved legislation requiring senior civil servants to be investigated for their activities under the communist regime. In December 14 prominent former members of the communist regime were arrested on charges of involvement in the execution, internment and deportation of citizens. (In May 1996 three of the former officials received death sentences, which were later commuted to terms of imprisonment, while the remaining defendants received custodial sentences.)

The first round of the legislative elections took place on 26 May 1996. Following alleged electoral irregularities, the principal opposition parties, including the SPA, the SDPA and the DAP, withdrew from the poll and announced their rejection of the election results. A subsequent demonstration by the SPA was violently dispersed by the security forces. The second round of the elections took place on 2 June; as a result of opposition demands for a boycott, only 59% of the electorate participated in the poll (compared with 89% in the first round). According to official results, the DPA secured 101 of the 115 directly elected seats (25 seats were to be allocated on the basis of proportional representation). However, international observers, who included representatives of the Organization for Security and Co-operation in Europe (OSCE, see p. 354), formerly the Conference on Security and Co-operation in Europe (CSCE), reported that widespread malpractice and intimidation of voters had been perpetrated, and urged the Government to conduct fresh elections, while SPA deputies staged a hunger strike in protest at the results. Berisha rejected the allegations, but agreed to conduct further elections in 17 constituencies. The principal opposition parties continued their electoral boycott, demanding that fresh elections be held, under international supervision, in all constituencies. Consequently, the DPA won all the seats contested in the partial elections, held on 16 June, and secured a total of 122 of the 140 elective seats. The SPA won 10 of the remaining seats, while the UHRP and the RPA each secured three and the National Front two. (The SPA, however, refused to recognize the new legislature and boycotted its inaugural session.) In early July Meksi, who had been reappointed to the office of Prime Minister, formed a new Council of Ministers. In August the Government established a permanent Central Elections Commission (CEC), prior to proposed local government elections. Despite continued division within the SPA, Nano (who remained in prison) was re-elected as Chairman at a party congress in late August. In local government elections, which took place in two rounds in October, the DPA secured the highest number of votes in 58 of the 65 municipalities and in 267 of the 305 communes. Although the OSCE had withdrawn its observers, monitors from the Council of Europe (see p. 225) declared that, despite some irregularities, the elections had been conducted fairly.

In January 1997 the collapse of several popular 'pyramid' financial investment schemes, resulting in huge losses of individual savings, prompted violent anti-Government demonstrations, particularly in Tirana and the southern town of Vlorë. It was widely believed that members of the Government were associated with the pyramid schemes, which had allegedly financed widespread illegal activities; legislation was subsequently adopted prohibiting the schemes. The Government increased efforts to suppress the protests; large numbers of demonstrators were arrested and prominent opposition members were publicly assaulted by the security forces. In late January the Kuvendi Popullor granted Berisha emergency powers to restore order. Several people were reported to have been killed in ensuing violent clashes between security forces and protesters. None the less, on 3 March Berisha, whose mandate was due to expire in April, was re-elected unopposed by parliamentary deputies for a second five-year term (the SPA continued to boycott the Kuvendi Popullor).

Following an escalation in hostilities between insurgents (who seized armaments from military depots) and government troops in the south of the country, Berisha declared a state of emergency in early March 1997. However, insurgent groups gained control of the southern towns of Vlorë, Sarandë and Gjirokastër, and it was reported that large numbers of government forces had deserted or defected to join the rebels. Following negotiations with representatives of nine opposition parties, Berisha signed an agreement providing for the installation of an interim coalition government, pending elections in June, and offered an amnesty to rebels who surrendered to the authorities. A former SPA mayor of Gjirokastër, Bashkim Fino, was appointed to the office of Prime Minister. Berisha subsequently approved the formation of a Government of National Reconciliation, which included representatives of eight opposition parties. None the less, the insurgency continued, reaching the northern town of Tropojë and Tirana (where rebels seized the airport). All those detained in Tirana central prison, including Nano and Alia, were released; Berisha subsequently granted Nano an official pardon. Extreme hardship and concern that the fighting would escalate into widespread civil conflict prompted thousands of Albanians to flee to Italy, although later in March Italian naval authorities were ordered to intercept boats transporting Albanian refugees, in an effort to halt the exodus. By late March government forces had regained control of Tirana, although insurgent groups controlled the south of the country, while the north was largely held by paramilitary units loyal to Berisha. The Government requested military assistance in the restoration of civil order, and Fino appealed to the European Union (EU, see p. 244) for the establishment of a multinational force to supervise aid operations in Albania. At the end of March the UN Security Council endorsed an OSCE proposal that member states be authorized to contribute troops to the force. The 5,915-member Multinational Protection Force for Albania was established in April, with an official mission (Operation Alba) to facilitate the distribution of humanitarian assistance. The Force (which had a mandate to remain in the country for three months) was subsequently deployed in regions under government control in northern and central Albania.

In early April 1997 the SPA ended its boycott of the legislature. Later in April the National Council of the DPA endorsed Berisha's leadership of the party and removed a number of dissident members who had demanded his resignation. The son of King Zog I and claimant to the throne, Leka Zogu, returned to Albania in April, with the support of the monarchist Movement of Legality Party; the principal political parties had already agreed to conduct a referendum on the restoration of the monarchy. In May the Kuvendi Popullor adopted legislation regulating the operation of pyramid investment schemes. Later that month the Kuvendi Popullor approved a proposal submitted by the DPA on the introduction of a new electoral system, in accordance with which the number of legislative deputies was to be increased from 140 to 155, of whom 40 were to be elected on the basis of proportional representation. Further elections were scheduled for 29 June. The SPA and its allied parties agreed to participate in the elections, after Berisha complied with the stipulation that the CEC be appointed by the interim Government (rather than by himself).

Election campaigning was marred by violence, including several bomb explosions in Tirana. Leaders of the DPA and the SPA signed an agreement in Rome, Italy, pledging to abide by the results of the elections. On 29 June 1997 the first round of voting in the legislative elections took place; a referendum on the restoration of the monarchy was conducted on the same day. Despite the presence of the Multinational Protection Force (the mandate of which had been extended to mid-August), three people were reportedly killed in violent incidents on polling day. A further ballot took place in 32 constituencies on 6 July. OSCE observers subsequently declared the electoral process to have been conducted satisfactorily. Later in July the CEC announced that the SPA had secured 101 seats in the Kuvendi Popullor, while the DPA had won 29 seats; the SPA and its allied parties (the SDPA, the DAP, the APA and the UHRP) thereby secured the requisite two-thirds' majority for the approval of constitutional amendments that they had proposed earlier in the month. At the referendum held on 29 June, 66.7% of the electorate voted in favour of retaining a republic; this result was upheld by the Constitutional Court in late August. Meanwhile, on 24 July, following Berisha's resignation as President, the Kuvendi Popullor elected the Secretary-General of the SPA, Rexhep Mejdani, to that position. Parliamentary deputies also voted to end the state of emergency. The SPA proposed Nano to the office of Prime Minister, and a new Council of Ministers was appointed, which comprised representatives of the SPA and its allied parties, and retained Fino as Deputy Prime Minister. At the end of July the new Government's programme for the restoration of civil order and economic reconstruction received a legislative vote of confidence. The Kuvendi Popullor also voted in favour of auditing existing pyramid schemes and investigating those that had been dissolved, in an attempt to reimburse lost savings. In August the Government dispatched troops to the south of the country, in an effort to restore order in major towns that were under the control of rebel forces. It was subsequently announced that Vlorë had been recaptured and a number of rebel forces arrested. By mid-August the Multinational Protection Force had left Albania.

In September 1997 the Kuvendi Popullor established a parliamentary commission, which was to draft a new constitution, in accordance with the amendments proposed by the SPA. Later that month an SPA deputy shot and wounded Azem Hajdari, a prominent DPA official and close associate of Berisha, in the parliamentary building. Although the SPA deputy was subsequently charged with attempted murder, the DPA initiated a boycott of the legislature. In October Berisha was re-elected Chairman of the DPA. In the same month Alia and three other former senior officials were acquitted of genocide by a Tirana court (upholding a ruling of the Supreme Court), on the grounds that the charge did not exist under the penal legislation of the former communist Government.

Intermittent violent unrest continued in early 1998. In February an armed revolt by civilians and disaffected members of the local security forces in Shkodër was suppressed by government troops. In March the DPA announced that it was to end its boycott of the Kuvendi Popullor, in order to express support within the legislature for ethnic Albanians in the Serbian province of Kosovo (see below). In early July a parliamentary commission into the unrest of 1997 recommended that several senior DPA officials, including Berisha, be charged in connection with the deployment of the armed forces to suppress the protests. Later in July 1998 Nano announced that the constitutional commission had presented a draft text for approval by the Kuvendi Popullor in October, prior to its eventual endorsement by a national referendum.

In early September 1998 Hajdari was assassinated in Tirana. Berisha accused Nano of involvement in the killing, and the DPA resumed its boycott of the legislature. The incident prompted violent protests by DPA supporters, who seized government offices and occupied the state television and radio buildings. Government security forces regained control of the capital, after clashes with protesters, in which about seven people were reported to have been killed. Although Berisha denied government claims that the uprising constituted a coup attempt, the Kuvendi Popullor voted to revoke Berisha's exemption (as a parliamentary deputy) from prosecution, thereby allowing him to be charged with attempting to overthrow the Government. An OSCE delegation, which mediated subsequent discussions between the political parties, condemned Berisha for inciting unrest, but also criticized Nano for the continued corruption within his administration. At the end of September the Minister of Public Order resigned, amid widespread criticism of the Government's failure to improve public security. Shortly afterwards Nano tendered his resignation, following a meeting of the SPA leadership, having failed to reach agreement with the government coalition on the composition of a new Council of Ministers. Mejdani subsequently requested that the Secretary-General of the SPA, Pandeli Majko, form a new government. In October a new coalition Council of Ministers, headed by Majko, was installed. Later that month the Kuvendi Popullor approved the draft Constitution (with opposition deputies boycotting the vote). The new Constitution was submitted for endorsement at a national referendum, monitored by OSCE observers, on 22 November. The Government announced that 50.1% of the registered electorate had participated in the referendum, of whom 93.1% had voted in favour of adopting the draft. However, Berisha claimed that only 17% of the votes cast by a total of 35% of the electorate had been in favour of the new Constitution, and urged his supporters to stage further protests against the preliminary results of the referendum. The Government deployed additional security forces in Tirana in an effort to maintain public order. On 28 November the new Constitution was officially adopted, but Berisha subsequently announced that the DPA would continue to refuse to recognize it. In July 1999 a DPA congress voted in favour of ending the boycott of the legislature.

At an SPA party congress in September 1999 Nano was re-elected as party Chairman, narrowly defeating Majko. In October Majko resigned as Prime Minister. Mejdani subsequently nominated Ilir Meta (hitherto Deputy Prime Minister) as Prime Minister. Berisha announced that the DPA would boycott a parliamentary motion to approve Meta's new Council of Ministers, and that his supporters would stage mass protests, following the return of Nano to the SPA leadership. In early November the new Government was formally approved in the Kuvendi Popullor, despite the opposition boycott.

Local government elections took place in two rounds in October 2000, following the preparation of a new voters' register, with assistance from the UN Development Programme (UNDP, see p. 58). Official results indicated that the SPA had obtained control of a total of 252 communes and municipalities, while the DPA had secured 118. However, DPA supporters subsequently staged a series of protests against the election results, which the party refused to recognize. In December, amid the continuing dispute over the local government elections, inter-party discussions over proposed amendments to electoral regulations commenced, prior to forthcoming elections to the Kuvendi Popullor. In February 2001 the DPA and the SPA reached agreement on the adoption of a new electoral code.

In April 2001 President Mejdani announced that the first round of the legislative elections would take place on 24 June, with a second round in early July. Five opposition parties, led by the DPA, subsequently formed an electoral alliance, known as the Union for Victory. The first round of the elections to the legislature (which was to revert to a total of 140 deputies) took place as scheduled. Despite a number of minor violent incidents, the poll was judged by international observers to have been conducted satisfactorily. A second round took place on 8 July in 45 constituencies where no candidate had secured more than 50% of the votes cast. Ballots were repeated in four constituencies later in July, and in a further four in August, after opposition complaints of irregularities were upheld by the Constitutional Court. The Government subsequently announced that, according to provisional results, the SPA had retained its parliamentary majority. According to the final results, which were announced by the CEC on 21 August, the SPA won 73 of the 140 seats in the Kuvendi Popullor, and the Union for Victory secured 46 seats.

Following Meta's re-appointment as Prime Minister, a reorganized Council of Ministers, nominated by President Mejdani, was approved in early September 2001. The new Government retained representatives of the SDPA, notably the party Chairman, Skender Gjinushi, who was nominated to the post of Deputy Prime Minister and Minister of Labour and Social Affairs; Majko became Minister of Defence. (Deputies belonging to the Union for Victory boycotted the new Kuvendi Popullor, which commenced sessions in early September, in continued protest at the outcome of the elections, which Berisha alleged had been characterized by widespread fraud.) A vote expressing confidence in the new Government, and its political and social programme (which was intended to permit the country to accede rapidly to membership of the EU), was adopted by 84 deputies in the Kuvendi Popullor.

In October 2001, under pressure from the OSCE, which maintained that the elections had been conducted satisfactorily, the Union for Victory agreed to end its boycott of the Kuvendi Popullor, subject to several preconditions. In December severe division emerged within the SPA, after Nano publicly accused the Government of engaging in corrupt practices. In that month the Minister of Finance and the Minister of the Public Economy and Privatization (both members of the SPA) resigned from the Government, after being implicated in the corruption allegations. Two further SPA members also resigned their ministerial portfolios. Later in December Berisha was re-elected to the leadership of the DPA. At the end of that month attempts by Meta to appoint new ministers to the four vacant posts in the Government proved unsuccessful, since his nominees were repeatedly rejected by supporters of Nano in the Kuvendi Popullor. On 29 January 2002 Meta tendered his resignation, after the two SPA factions failed to reach agreement on a government reorganization. Majko (a compromise candidate, who was supported by Meta), the SPA's candidate for Prime Minister, was appointed to the office on 7 February. Following protracted negotiations between the two SPA factions and allied parties, the Kuvendi Popullor approved a new Council of Ministers on 22 February. Portfolios were divided between supporters of Nano and Meta, with Kastriot Islami, a former Deputy Prime Minister who was favoured by Nano, becoming Minister of Finance.

Following the establishment of the new, transitional Council of Ministers, deputies from the Union for Victory decided to resume participation in the Kuvendi Popullor. As the end of Mejdani's term of office approached, it became apparent that Nano would be unable to secure majority support in the legislature, owing to strong opposition from Berisha. Following prolonged negotiations between the SPA and the DPA, Alfred Moisiu, a retired general who had served in the Berisha administration, was selected as the candidate of both parties. He was elected by 97 of the 140 legislative deputies on 24 June 2002, and was inaugurated on 24 July. On the following day Majko resigned as Prime Minister. Moisiu subsequently appointed Nano to the premiership, and a new administration, again including members of both SPA factions, was approved at the end of the month, with Majko returning to his post as Minister of Defence; Meta was allocated the office of Deputy Prime Minister and Minister of Foreign Affairs.

Despite the efforts towards reconciliation of the two SPA factions, prior to forthcoming local government elections, continuing differences culminated in Meta's resignation from his government office in mid-July 2003, citing authoritarian behaviour on the part of Nano. The Minister of State for Integration, an ally of Meta, also tendered his resignation. At the end of July Nano's nomination of a long-standing supporter, Marko Bello, as Minister of Foreign Affairs was rejected in the Kuvendi Popullor, owing to the opposition of Meta's faction.

A new electoral code was adopted in June 2003. Local government elections, conducted throughout Albania on 12 October, were marred by a low rate of participation by the electorate, of less than 50%, and reports by OSCE observers of irregularities. Although the SPA claimed to have secured control of 36 municipalities, the DPA immediately contested the results and accused the authorities of extensive malpractice. Later that month Nano removed the Minister of Public Order, Luan Rama, after he had reportedly assaulted the editor of a local television station that had been critical of the Government. Subsequent nominations by Nano to the posts of Minister of Foreign Affairs and Minister of Public Order were again rejected in the Kuvendi Popullor. Meta declared that his faction would continue to obstruct further appointments until Nano agreed to reorganize the Government, and the offices remained vacant. In early November the SPA leadership adopted amendments to its statute, whereby public criticism of party decisions would be prohibited and the Chairman would automatically obtain the premiership. Following Moisiu's insistence that appointments be made to the vacant ministerial posts, at the end of November Nano finally conceded the necessity of a government reorganization, and commenced negotiations to secure the support of smaller parties within the Kuvendi Popullor. On 14 December, at the SPA annual congress, Nano was re-elected as party Chairman. Later that month Nano signed agreements with the leaders of the SDPA, the DAP, the APA, the UHRP, and a breakaway faction of the SDPA, establishing the Coalition for Integration, which adopted the principal objective of supporting Albania's rapid accession to the EU and the North Atlantic Treaty Organization (NATO, see p. 340). With the additional votes of deputies belonging to the allied parties, a government reorganization by Nano, which included the appointment of a former parliamentary Speaker, Namik Dokle, as Deputy Prime Minister, and Islami as Minister of Foreign Affairs, was approved by the Kuvendi Popullor on 29 December. Meanwhile, further municipal elections were conducted in parts of the country in December, after a court of appeal upheld DPA allegations and declared the results in a number of districts to be invalid; however, OSCE monitors reported further irregularities at some ballots.

In February 2004 some 20,000 people took part in demonstrations supported by the DPA in Tirana, accusing the Government of having failed to improve living standards and demanding Nano's resignation. Concerns regarding the independence of the press were raised in May, following the filing of a lawsuit against the leader of the opposition Christian Democratic Party of Albania (CDPA), Nikolle Lesi, whose *Koha Jonë* newspaper had accused Nano and his wife of corruption. Lesi was convicted of slander and ordered to pay a fine; however, in February 2005 an appeals court overturned the sentence, citing procedural violations in the original judgment. Meanwhile, in May 2004 Zogu created a new monarchist political organization, the Movement for National Development. In June the approval by the Kuvendi Popullor of legislation on restitution and compensation of property (providing for the payment of recompense to citizens whose property had been transferred to state ownership, following the accession to power of the NLF in November 1944) was welcomed by the OSCE as positive progress towards economic and social stability, although there was difficulty in reaching consensus on some aspects of the new legislation, with President

Moisiu demanding changes to certain articles. In July the Kuvendi Popullor approved further legislation providing for the payment of compensation to former political prisoners.

In September 2004 the ruling coalition was severely weakened by Meta's resignation from the SPA, following continued disputes with Nano, and his establishment of a new political party, the Socialist Movement for Integration. The SPA subsequently lost its parliamentary majority following the defection of several deputies to the new group. In February 2005, following protracted negotiations between the SPA and the DPA, with OSCE mediation, the parties signed a bilateral agreement on a new division of electoral zones, in advance of legislative elections. The plan was approved by the Kuvendi Popullor in early March. The elections took place on 3 July, with the participation of some 56% of voters. A second round of voting was held in three constituencies on 21 August, following complaints of electoral irregularities. According to the final results, announced in early September, the DPA and its allies won 80 of the 140 seats in the Kuvendi Popullor, while the SPA and allied parties secured 60 seats. Nano duly conceded defeat and resigned as Chairman of the SPA, but continued to declare the results illegitimate. The OSCE, which monitored the elections, concluded in its final report that, although the ballot only partly met international standards, some improvement in the conduct of elections in the country had been demonstrated. The new Kuvendi Popullor, at its inaugural session on 2 September, elected Jozefina Topalli as parliamentary Speaker. On the same day President Moisiu nominated Berisha as Prime Minister. Berisha announced that his Government would focus on combating corruption and on integration into the EU and NATO, pledging to implement extensive reforms in order to secure Albania's membership of those organizations. On 10 September the Kuvendi Popullor approved the new DPA-led, coalition Government in which the RPA, the New Democratic Party, the APA and the UHRP each received one portfolio. While prominent representatives of the DPA obtained several principal posts in the Government, the Chairman of the RPA, Fatmir Mediu, became Minister of Defence. In early October the Mayor of Tirana, Edi Rama, was elected leader of the SPA.

In July 2006 Nard Ndoka, who had replaced Lesi as Chairman of the CDPA in June, announced that the party was to join the Government, after it was offered the deputy foreign affairs portfolio. (In November 2007 Lesi left the CDPA and formed the breakaway Albanian Christian Democratic Movement.) In early December 2006, following the failure of parliamentary parties to agree on the adoption of electoral reform legislation or a date for forthcoming local government elections, Moisiu decreed that the poll would take place on 20 January 2007. However, opposition parties continued to demand a postponement, claiming that the Government had reneged on an agreement to prevent electoral malpractice. Despite appeals by the OSCE and Council of Europe, in early January the Chairman of the CEC confirmed that electoral preparations would not be completed by the scheduled date, owing to the dispute between government and opposition parties. Later that month, following an agreement between political parties, which included provisions on voter identification, Moisiu rescheduled the local government elections for 18 February (narrowly meeting a deadline stipulated by the Constitution). In early February Zogu announced his withdrawal from party politics. Numerous incidents were reported during the election campaign, including skirmishes between government and opposition supporters and political clashes in Himarë, a predominantly ethnic Greek coastal region.

The CEC announced that a number of organizational irregularities had been reported during the poll on 18 February 2007; an OSCE observer mission and the EU concluded that both preparations for and the conduct of the elections had failed to meet international standards. According to official results, the 10-party ruling coalition secured about 51.1% of the votes cast, and the SPA-led opposition alliance (known as Together for the Future) 42.9% (with about 48% of the registered electorate participating). Individually, however, the SPA won the greatest proportion of votes, with 23.2%, while the DPA received 20.6%. SPA candidates secured control of several principal municipalities; notably, Rama was re-elected as Mayor of Tirana, defeating the DPA candidate (Sokol Olldashi, hitherto the Minister of the Interior). In mid-March Berisha announced his intention of expediting the reform process and proposed a number of government changes (which included the replacement of the Deputy Prime Minister), in an effort to extend the ruling coalition and increase its parliamentary majority prior to the election of a new President in June. The reorganized Government was approved in the Kuvendi Popullor on 19 March. In mid-April Majko resigned as Secretary-General of the SPA. Later that month the Minister of Foreign Affairs, Besnik Mustafaj, announced his resignation; he was replaced by Lulzim Basha (hitherto the Minister of Public Works, Transport and Telecommunications). In May Rama was re-elected as Chairman of the SPA.

In June 2007 the election by the Kuvendi Popullor of a new President, to succeed Moisiu on the expiry of his second term in office on 24 July, was postponed, owing to dissent between the parties. In early March the DPA had selected Bamir Topi as its presidential candidate. The SPA objected to the DPA's nomination of Topi without consultation, and representatives of the international community urged the selection of a consensus candidate. By mid-July three rounds of voting in the Kuvendi Popullor had failed to elect a candidate; the SPA-led coalition boycotted the ballots, in which Topi was unable to secure the support of the three-fifths of deputies required for election. The parties' inability to agree on a candidate prompted increasing concern, since, under the terms of the Constitution, failure to elect a President after five rounds would necessitate the dissolution of the Kuvendi Popullor and holding of early legislative elections. The prolonged impasse was finally resolved by a fourth round of voting on 20 July, when, in contravention of the continued boycott, five members of the SPA, together with two of the DAP, voted for Topi. Consequently, Topi was elected by 85 votes, narrowly obtaining the required three-fifths' majority. Topi was inaugurated on 24 July.

In November 2007 the Minister of Justice, Ilir Rusmajli, tendered his resignation, shortly after that of the head of the prison service, who had made allegations of corruption involving Rusmajli's brother. (Rusmajli was succeeded by Enkelejd Alibeaj, hitherto the director of the government anti-corruption department.) Later that month Topi dismissed the Prosecutor-General, Theodhori Sollaku, on the recommendation of a parliamentary investigative committee's report, which had criticized Sollaku's perceived failure to address organized crime and the early release of a number of prisoners. Ina Rama, an appeals court judge with no political and business affiliations, was approved to succeed him by the Kuvendi Popullor, becoming the first woman to hold the post. In December the Kuvendi Popullor voted in favour of removing the parliamentary immunity of Basha, who was accused of having demonstrated bias towards a US-Turkish joint venture when awarding a road-construction contract in his previous ministerial post. Meanwhile, there was increasing concern at the extent of corrupt practices within Albania, as it was reported that during the second half of the year some 40 public officials had been arrested on corruption charges, particularly involving procurement irregularities in the construction sector. The Government subsequently announced the adoption of a comprehensive anti-corruption strategy. In March 2008 the Minister of Defence tendered his resignation and three state officials were arrested, after at least 17 people were killed in an explosion at a munitions depot near Tirana.

The gradual relaxation of Albania's isolationist policies culminated in 1990 in a declaration of its intention to establish good relations with all countries, irrespective of their social system. In July of that year Albania and the USSR formally agreed to restore diplomatic relations. Diplomatic relations between Albania and the USA (suspended since 1946) were re-established in March 1991. Albania was granted observer status at the 1990 CSCE summit meeting, and became a full member of the organization in June 1991. In May 1992 Albania and the European Community (now EU) signed a 10-year agreement on trade and co-operation. In June Albania, together with 10 other countries (including six of the former Soviet republics), signed a pact to establish the Black Sea Economic Co-operation (now the Organization of the Black Sea Economic Co-operation, see p. 367), which created a regional structure for economic co-operation. In December Albania was granted membership of the Organization of the Islamic Conference (OIC, see p. 369), and in the same month applied to join NATO, thus becoming the first former Warsaw Pact country formally to seek membership of the Western alliance. Albania joined NATO's 'Partnership for Peace' programme of military co-operation in April 1994. In July 1995 Albania was admitted to the Council of Europe, having agreed to adopt a new Constitution and to take measures to fulfil the Council's requirements concerning human rights. Negotiations on the signature of a Stabilization and Association Agreement with the EU officially commenced at the end of January 2003. In

April 2005 the European Commissioner responsible for Enlargement, Olli Rehn, emphasized the importance of the proper conduct of legislative elections and the need for reforms relating to the rule of law, land ownership, respect for human rights, freedom of the media and customs. In November a European Commission report on Albania's efforts towards European integration recognized that the conduct of the general election had been satisfactory, and welcomed the progress made by the country, although it identified corruption as an area of continuing concern. Following a positive recommendation issued by the European Commission in March 2006, the Stabilization and Association Agreement was officially signed between the Albanian Government and the EU on 12 June. The Kuvendi Popullor ratified the Agreement on 27 July. However, local elections in early 2007 (see above) were judged by the EU to have failed to meet international standards. In October NATO's Parliamentary Assembly adopted a resolution supporting the accession applications of Albania (together with Croatia and the former Yugoslav republic of Macedonia—FYRM). At a NATO summit meeting, convened in Bucharest, Romania, on 2 April 2008, it was announced that official invitations to begin accession negotiations were to be extended to Albania and Croatia.

Albania's relations with neighbouring Greece and Serbia (formerly part of the State Union of Serbia and Montenegro, and prior to that, Yugoslavia) have been strained. In August 1987 Greece formally ended the technical state of war with Albania that had been in existence since 1945. However, the status of the Greek minority in Albania, officially numbering some 59,000 at the 1989 census, but estimated to number some 300,000 by the Greek authorities, remained a sensitive issue. Relations between Albania and Greece deteriorated in 1993, owing to Greece's deportation of some 20,000 Albanian immigrants and to the alleged mistreatment of the Greek minority in southern Albania. Tensions were exacerbated further in April 1994, following a border incident in which two Albanian guards were killed; diplomatic expulsions ensued on both sides, and the border situation remained tense, with reports of minor skirmishes. In May six prominent members of the ethnic Greek organization OMONIA were arrested. Greece subsequently vetoed the provision of EU funds to Albania and increased deportations of illegal Albanian immigrants. In September five of the OMONIA detainees were convicted on charges including espionage and the illegal possession of weapons, and received custodial sentences. Following the verdict, Greece and Albania both recalled their ambassadors. In addition, Greece submitted formal protests to the UN and the EU regarding Albania's perceived maltreatment of its ethnic Greek population and closed the Kakavija border crossing, which had hitherto been used by Albanian migrant workers. One of the OMONIA defendants was pardoned in December, after Greece withdrew its veto on EU aid to Albania in November. In February 1995 the four remaining prisoners were released, allowing a subsequent improvement in bilateral relations. In June the Albanian Government approved a new education bill, which recognized the right of ethnic minorities to their own language and culture. In March 1996 the Greek President, Konstantinos Stefanopoulos, visited Albania, and a co-operation agreement was signed, apparently resolving outstanding issues of concern between the two nations. In August 1997 the Greek Government agreed to grant temporary work permits to illegal Albanian immigrants in Greece, in exchange for assistance from Albania in combating cross-border crime. In April 1998 the two countries signed a military co-operation agreement. A new border crossing between Albania and Greece was opened in May 1999. In February 2001 Albania and Greece signed an agreement on increased bilateral economic and financial co-operation. Nevertheless, concerns regarding the protection of the rights of the Greek minority in Albania, as well as of the rights of Albanians living in Greece, continued to be expressed. In late 2006 the Albanian and Greek authorities announced a joint plan for increased surveillance measures to combat endemic cross-border trafficking.

Relations with Yugoslavia deteriorated sharply in early 1989, when many ethnic Albanian demonstrators were killed during renewed unrest in the Serbian province of Kosovo (where the population was principally composed of ethnic Albanians). Kosovo (which was officially renamed Kosovo and Metohija under the Serbian Constitution of September 1990, which significantly reduced the autonomy of the provincial authorities) remained a focus of political and ethnic tension. In early 1998 Albania condemned increased Serbian military activity against the ethnic Albanian majority in Kosovo. In April clashes were reported on the Albanian border with Kosovo between Serbian troops and suspected members of the paramilitary Kosovo Liberation Army (KLA). The Albanian administration initiated measures to prevent the illicit transportation of armaments from northern Albania to KLA forces in Kosovo. By mid-1998 some 10,000 ethnic Albanian refugees had fled to northern Albania, following continued Serbian military reprisals against the ethnic Albanian population in Kosovo.

In March 1999, following the failure of diplomatic efforts to compel the Yugoslav President, Slobodan Milošević, to accede to NATO demands, NATO forces commenced an intensive aerial bombardment of Yugoslavia. The Albanian Government expressed support for the NATO military action, and allowed Albania's air and sea facilities to be used for NATO operations. Further Albanian troops were deployed on the northern border with Serbia in preparation for a possible Serbian retaliatory offensive. NATO troops (which later numbered about 8,000, and became known as AFOR) were dispatched to Albania to support humanitarian aid operations. The Government appealed for international financial assistance for the Kosovan refugee population, and requested a more rapid accession to NATO. In early April Yugoslav forces bombarded Albanian border villages during heavy fighting with the KLA in Kosovo, increasing international concern that a broader regional conflict might develop. Later that month Serbian troops advanced into Albanian territory, but were repelled by the armed forces. Meanwhile, the KLA had succeeded in establishing a supply route for the transportation of armaments from bases in northern Albania to Kosovo. Following the deployment of a NATO-led peace-keeping Kosovo Force (KFOR) in the province, under the terms of a peace agreement agreed with Milošević in June, refugees began rapidly to return to Kosovo from Albania and the FYRM. In September NATO announced that AFOR, which had been gradually withdrawing from the country, was to be replaced by a 1,200-member contingent to be known as Communications Zone West (COMMZ-W), which was mandated to maintain civil order in Albania and to support the KFOR mission in Kosovo. (In June 2002 COMMZ-W was officially dissolved, when a NATO headquarters was established at Tirana.) Following the removal from power of Milošević in September 2000, Albania and Yugoslavia formally restored diplomatic relations in January 2001. Bilateral diplomatic relations were upgraded to ambassadorial level in September 2002.

In February 1993 Albania refused to accept an application by the FYRM for membership of the CSCE, and it was only in April that Albania officially recognized the existence of the republic as an independent state. Albania was concerned at the perceived oppression of the ethnic Albanian minority in the FYRM, which constituted about 21% of the population, and the majority of whom were Muslims. Following the civil unrest in Albania in early 1997 (see above), a number of incursions into FYRM territory by armed groups of Albanian rebels were reported; two members of the FYRM's security forces were killed in September. In October the Ministers of Defence of Albania and the FYRM signed an agreement providing for increased security at the joint border between the two countries.

The outbreak of conflict between government forces and ethnic Albanian rebels, known as the National Liberation Army (NLA), in the FYRM in February 2001 prompted large numbers of ethnic Albanian civilians to take refuge in Albania. Relations between Albania and the FYRM became strained, although the Albanian authorities maintained their opposition to the NLA's reported aim of creating a 'Greater Albania'. In August the FYRM Government and NLA leaders signed a peace agreement (which included constitutional amendments, adopted in November, according Albanian and other minority languages official status), but the region remained unstable. In September 2003 the Albanian Government issued a statement condemning further extremist ethnic Albanian operations in the FYRM, and in November the Ministries of Defence of Albania, Greece and the FYRM pledged to increase military co-operation to address the issues of illegal immigration and cross-border organized crime. The Prime Minister of the FYRM, Vlado Buckovski, made an official visit to Albania in January 2005.

Negotiations between Kosovan Albanian and Serbian delegations on the final status of Kosovo commenced in early 2006 (see the chapter on Serbia). In February 2007 Albanian political leaders welcomed proposals presented by the Special Envoy of the UN Secretary-General for the future-status process for Kosovo. In June US President George W. Bush, who was received with public enthusiasm during an official visit to Albania (the first by an incumbent US President), expressed US support for the independence of Kosovo. Despite the extension of the period of discussions, the two negotiating sides proved unable to reach a settlement, while (owing to the continued opposition of Russia) the UN Security Council failed to approve a resolution on the future of Kosovo. Consequently, a newly installed Kosovan Government adopted a unilateral declaration of independence on 17 February 2008 (which was rapidly approved by the USA and a number of EU member states). The declaration was welcomed with public celebrations in Tirana, and acclaimed by Berisha, who announced that Albania officially recognized Kosovo as an independent and sovereign state. On 19 February the Council of Ministers approved the establishment of diplomatic relations with Kosovo at ambassadorial level.

Government

Under the Constitution adopted in November 1998, legislative power is vested in the unicameral Kuvendi Popullor (People's Assembly). The Kuvendi Popullor, which is elected for a term of four years, comprises 140 deputies, 100 of whom are directly elected in single-member constituencies. Parties receiving 2.5% or more of the votes cast, and party coalitions obtaining 4.0% or more in the first round of voting, are allocated further deputies in proportion to the number of votes secured, on the basis of multi-name lists of parties or party coalitions. The President of the Republic is Head of State, and is elected by the Kuvendi Popullor for a term of five years. Executive authority is held by the Council of Ministers, which is led by the Prime Minister as Head of Government. The Prime Minister is appointed by the President and appoints a Council of Ministers, which is presented for approval to the Kuvendi Popullor. For the purposes of local government, Albania is divided into 12 counties (*qarqe*—also called prefectures), 36 districts (*rrethe*), 65 municipalities and 309 communes. The representative organs of the basic units of local government are councils, which are elected by direct election for a period of three years. The Council of Ministers appoints a Prefect as its representative in each of the 12 counties.

Defence

As assessed at November 2007, the total strength of the Albanian armed forces was about 11,020: the army accounted for about 6,200, the air force for 1,370 and the navy for 1,100. The 500-strong paramilitary forces comprised an internal security force, based in Tirana, and units in major towns, together with 500 border police. There were around 2,350 members of joint forces. A programme of military reorganization, with assistance from European Governments and the USA, was scheduled for completion by 2010. Military service is compulsory and lasts for 12 months. The budget for 2007 allocated some 17,900m. leks to defence.

Economic Affairs

In 2006, according to World Bank estimates, Albania's gross national income (GNI), measured at average 2004–06 prices, was US $9,273m., equivalent to $2,960 per head (or $5,840 on an international purchasing-power parity basis). During 1996–2006, it was estimated, the population increased by an annual average of 0.1%, while gross domestic product (GDP) per head increased, in real terms, by an average of 4.9% per year. Overall GDP increased, in real terms, at an average annual rate of 5.0% in 1996–2006; growth of 5.0% was recorded in 2006.

Agriculture (including hunting and forestry) contributed an estimated 20.7% of GDP in 2005. The sector (including fishing) employed some 58.0% of the labour force in 2006. Increased private enterprise was permitted from 1990, and agricultural land was subsequently redistributed to private ownership. The principal crops are wheat, maize, watermelons, potatoes, tomatoes and grapes. Agricultural GDP increased at an average annual rate of 0.8%, in real terms, in 1996–2005, according to the World Bank; growth in the sector was 3.6% in 2004 and 2.6% in 2005.

Industry (comprising mining, manufacturing and construction) accounted for an estimated 24.0% of GDP in 2005, and employed 13.5% of the labour force in 2006. Principal contributors to industrial output include mining, energy generation and food-processing. Construction has been the fastest-growing sector in recent years, contributing 14.3% of GDP in 2006. Industrial GDP increased at an average rate of 5.8% per year, in real terms, during 1996–2005; the GDP of the sector increased by 4.3% in 2004, but declined by 3.4% in 2005.

Albania is one of the world's largest producers of chromite (chromium ore), possessing Europe's only significant reserves (an estimated 37m. metric tons of recoverable ore, constituting about 5% of total world deposits). The mining sector was centred on chromite and copper, following the closure of nickel and iron ore operations, together with more than one-half of the country's coal mines, in 1990. By 2003 annual chromite production had declined to 220,000 metric tons (compared with 587,000 tons in 1991), further declining to an estimated 160,300 tons in 2004, although output increased slightly in 2005, to 170,000 tons. By 2000 output of copper was no longer significant. Albania has petroleum resources and its own refining facilities, and since 1991 there has been considerable foreign interest in the exploration of both onshore and offshore reserves. Proven reserves of petroleum were estimated at 165m. barrels in 2002; production of petroleum reached some 448,000 metric tons in 2005.

The manufacturing sector contributed an estimated 8.9% of GDP in 2005. The sector is based largely on the processing of building materials, agricultural products, minerals and chemicals. According to the World Bank, manufacturing GDP increased, in real terms, at an average annual rate of 3.4% during 1996–2004; the GDP of the sector increased by 6.5% in 2001 and by 0.3% in 2002.

Hydroelectric generation accounted for some 98.3% of total electricity production in 2004. In 2005 imports of mineral fuels accounted for 8.6% of the value of total merchandise imports. A project funded by a US consortium, AMBO (Albania–Macedonia–Bulgaria Oil Corporation), and approved by the Albanian Government in December 2003, envisaged a 920-km pipeline, capable of transporting 750,000 barrels of petroleum per day, to connect the Bulgarian Black Sea port of Burgas with Vlorë, in southern Albania, by way of the former Yugoslav republic of Macedonia (FYRM), and carry petroleum exports from Russia and the Caspian Sea region. A final agreement on the construction of the proposed pipeline was reached in January 2007, and work was expected to commence by late 2008. In August 2007 construction of a thermal power plant commenced in Vlorë. The facility was scheduled to become operational in 2009; total capacity of the unit was projected at just under 100 MW.

Services provided an estimated 55.3% of GDP in 2005, and employed 28.4% of the labour force in 2006. The GDP of the services sector increased, in real terms, by an average of 6.9% per year during 1996–2006; growth was 8.0% in 2005 and 3.5% in 2006.

In 2006 Albania recorded a visible trade deficit of US $2,122.7m., and there was a deficit of $670.9m. on the current account of the balance of payments. In 2005 the principal source of imports (accounting for some 29.3%) was Italy; other major suppliers were Greece, Turkey and Germany. Italy was also the principal market for exports (accounting for 72.4% of the total); in addition, Greece was an important purchaser. The principal exports in 2005 were miscellaneous manufactured articles (which accounted for 60.7% of the total), manufactured products and crude materials. The main imports in that year were manufactured products, machinery and transport equipment, miscellaneous manufactured articles, food and live animals, chemical products, and mineral fuels and lubricants.

Albania's overall budget deficit in 2006 was estimated at 29,000m. leks, equivalent to 3.2% of GDP. At the end of 2005 Albania's total external debt was US $1,839m., of which $1,375m. was long-term public debt. In that year the cost of servicing the debt was equivalent to 2.5% of the value of exports of goods and services. In 1996–2006 the average annual rate of inflation was 6.8%; consumer prices increased by an estimated 2.4% in 2005 and by 2.4% in 2006. The rate of unemployment was 13.8% in 2006. Some sources estimated that over 35% of the Albanian labour force was working abroad in 2005.

Having reversed its long-standing policy of economic self-sufficiency, in 1991 Albania became a member of the World Bank, the IMF and the newly established European Bank for Reconstruction and Development (EBRD, see p. 239). In 1992 Albania became a founder member of the Black Sea Economic Co-operation group, now known as the Organization of the Black Sea Economic Co-operation (see p. 367). Albania joined the Central European Free Trade Agreement (CEFTA, see p. 411) in July 2007.

In 1992, in response to a serious economic crisis, the Government introduced an extensive programme of reforms. High interest rates, reduced subsidies, banking reforms and trade liberalization succeeded in reducing the budget deficit and stabilizing the currency. Funding under the IMF's Poverty Reduction and Growth Facility (PRGF) contributed to the restoration of high rates of growth, but poverty remained severe,

ALBANIA

particularly in rural areas. The increasing stability of the early 2000s attracted a number of foreign banks to the country, and the increasing availability of mortgages has assisted the growth of the construction industry. A significant advancement in the privatization programme was achieved with the sale of the country's Savings Bank in 2004, by which time the private sector accounted for some 75% of GDP. In January 2006 the IMF approved a further disbursement of funds, worth some US $24.7m., under the PRGF arrangement, in order to strengthen the financial system and improve governance. In the same month the World Bank agreed to disburse funds of some $196m. for 2006–09 to help combat poverty and unemployment and stimulate economic growth. The Government signed a Stabilization and Association Agreement with the EU in June 2006, although an EU report on local elections held in February 2007 cited organizational shortcomings and expressed concerns that international democratic standards were not being met. In November the European Commission extended funds of €42.5m. to support the Government's reform efforts. In mid-2007 some 80% of the state-owned telecommunications company, Albtelecom, was divested to a consortium of two Turkish companies, Turk Telekom and Calik Enerji. In response to long-standing problems with the electricity supply, the World Bank, Italian energy companies and private consultancies produced plans to rehabilitate hydro-power plants, reduce transmission losses and build new power stations. In January 2008 it was announced that redevelopment work, which included the replacement of five turbines, on one of the four hydropower facilities operating at the Drin river, in northern Albania, had been completed. Meanwhile, in November 2007 the IMF urged the Government to hasten the partial privatization of the State Electricity Corporation, KESh; the Government later announced that it planned to complete the sale of its distribution section by mid-2008. Real GDP was estimated to have risen by 6.0% in 2007; in part, this growth was attributed to the increasing availability of credit and continuing inflows of remittances, which together helped to stimulate domestic demand. At the beginning of 2008 the Government announced a new strategy to combat widespread corruption.

Education

Education in Albania is free and compulsory for children between the ages of six and 14 years. Enrolment at pre-primary schools was equivalent to 48% of children aged between three and six years (males 46%; females 50%) in 2002. In that year enrolment at primary schools included 97% of children in the relevant age-group (males 98%; females 96%), while secondary education enrolment included 71% of children in the appropriate age-group (boys 74%; girls 68%). In 2003/04 a total of 36,244 students were enrolled at Albania's institutions of higher education. Spending on education accounted for some 10.6% of government expenditure in 2004 (equivalent to some 3.0% of GDP). In October 2006 the European Investment Bank announced that it was to provide funds of €12.5m. to support the reform of education infrastructure and management in Albania.

Public Holidays

2008: 1 January (New Year's Day), 11 January (Republic Day), 21–24 March (Roman Catholic Easter), 28 April (Eastern Orthodox Easter), 1 May (International Labour Day), 1 October* (Small Bayram, end of Ramadan), 28 November (Independence and Liberation Day), 8 December* (Great Bayram, Feast of the Sacrifice), 25 December (Christmas Day).

2009: 1 January (New Year's Day), 11 January (Republic Day), 10–13 April (Roman Catholic Easter), 20 April (Eastern Orthodox Easter), 1 May (International Labour Day), 20 September* (Small Bayram, end of Ramadan), 27 November* (Great Bayram, Feast of the Sacrifice), 28 November (Independence and Liberation Day), 25 December (Christmas Day).

*These holidays are dependent on the Islamic lunar calendar and may vary by one or two days from the dates given.

Weights and Measures

The metric system is in force.

Statistical Survey

Sources (unless otherwise indicated): Institute of Statistics (Instituti i Statistikës), POB 8194, Tirana; tel. (4) 222411; fax (4) 228300; e-mail root@instat.gov.al; internet www.instat.gov.al; Bank of Albania (Banka e Shqipërisë), Sheshi Skënderbej 1, Tirana; tel. (4) 222752; fax (4) 223558; e-mail public@bankofalbania.org; internet www.bankofalbania.org.

Area and Population

AREA, POPULATION AND DENSITY

Area (sq km)	
Land	27,398
Inland water	1,350
Total	28,748*
Population (census results)	
2 April 1989	3,182,417
1 April 2001	
Males	1,530,443
Females	1,538,832
Total	3,069,275
Population (official estimates of annual averages)	
2004	3,127,263
2005	3,142,000†
2006	3,142,200†
Density (per sq km) in 2006	109.3

* 11,100 sq miles.
† Rounded figure.

COUNTIES (PREFECTURES)
(census of 1 April 2001)

County	Area (sq km)	Population	Density (per sq km)	Capital
Berat	1,799	193,020	107.4	Berat
Dibër	2,586	189,854	73.4	Peshkopi
Durrës	766	245,179	320.1	Durrës
Elbasan	3,199	362,736	113.4	Elbasan
Fier	1,890	382,544	202.4	Fier
Gjirokastër	2,884	112,831	39.1	Gjirokastër
Korçë	3,711	265,182	71.5	Korçë
Kukës	2,374	111,393	46.9	Kukës
Lezhë	1,619	159,182	98.3	Lezhë
Shkodër	3,562	256,473	72.0	Shkodër
Tiranë	1,652	597,899	361.9	Tiranë
Vlorë	2,706	192,982	71.3	Vlorë
Total	**28,748**	**3,069,275**	**106.8**	

PRINCIPAL TOWNS
(population at 2001 census, preliminary results)

Tiranë (Tirana, the capital)	343,078	Korçë (Koritsa)	55,130
Durrës (Durazzo)	99,546	Berat	40,112
Elbasan	87,797	Lushnjë	32,580
Shkodër (Scutari)	82,455	Kavajë	24,817
Vlorë (Vlonë or Valona)	77,691	Pogradec	23,843
Fier	56,297	Gjirokastër	20,630

Mid-2005 (incl. suburbs, UN estimate): Tirana 388,000 (Source: UN, *World Urbanization Prospects: The 2005 Revision*).

ALBANIA   Statistical Survey

BIRTHS, MARRIAGES AND DEATHS

	Registered live births Number	Rate (per 1,000)	Registered marriages Number	Rate (per 1,000)	Registered deaths Number	Rate (per 1,000)
1998	60,139	19.7	27,871	9.1	18,250	6.0
1999	57,948	19.0	27,254	8.9	16,720	5.5
2000	51,242	16.7	25,820	8.4	16,421	5.4
2001	54,283	17.7	25,717	8.4	15,813	5.1
2002	45,515	14.7	26,202	8.5	16,248	5.3
2003	47,012	15.1	27,342	8.8	17,967	5.8
2004	43,022	13.8	20,949	6.7	17,749	5.7
2005	39,612	12.6	n.a.	n.a.	17,427	5.5

Source: partly UN, *Population and Vital Statistics Report*.

Expectation of life (years at birth, WHO estimates): 70.9 (males 68.8; females 73.2) in 2005 (Source: WHO, *World Health Statistics*).

ECONOMICALLY ACTIVE POPULATION
('000, official estimates)

	2004	2005	2006
Agriculture, hunting, forestry and fishing	545	545	542
Mining and quarrying	6	6	5
Manufacturing	56	56	58
Electricity, gas and water	13	12	10
Construction	52	52	53
Wholesale and retail trade	64	64	68
Hotels and restaurants	17	15	16
Transport, storage and communications	20	19	19
Education	48	47	48
Health and social work	27	24	25
Other activities	81	90	90
Total employed	931	932	935
Registered unemployed	157	153	150
Total labour force	1,088	1,085	1,085
Males	660	655	n.a.
Females	428	430	n.a.

Source: partly ILO.

Health and Welfare

KEY INDICATORS

Total fertility rate (children per woman, 2005)	2.2
Under-5 mortality rate (per 1,000 live births, 2005)	18
HIV/AIDS (% of persons aged 15–49, 2005)	<0.02
Physicians (per 1,000 head, 2002)	1.31
Hospital beds (per 1,000 head, 2005)	3
Health expenditure (2004): US $ per head (PPP)	338.7
Health expenditure (2004): % of GDP	6.7
Health expenditure (2004): public (% of total)	44.1
Access to water (% of total population, 2004)	96
Access to sanitation (% of total population, 2004)	91
Human Development Index (2005): ranking	68
Human Development Index (2005): value	0.801

For sources and definitions, see explanatory note on p. vi.

Agriculture

PRINCIPAL CROPS
('000 metric tons)

	2004	2005	2006
Wheat and spelt	253.4	260.0	230.9
Barley	3.7	4.1	6.0
Maize	216.2	219.9	245.4
Rye	2.4	3.0	2.6
Oats	23.1	24.2	22.6
Potatoes	159.8	169.3	150.0
Sugar beet*	27.9	21.2	21.2
Dry beans	22.4	23.6	24.3
Olives	58.7	30.2	40.2
Sunflower seed	2.2	2.0	2.2
Tomatoes	152.0	152.0	164.9
Green beans	7.6	7.8	0.4
Watermelons	204.3	204.0	169.1
Oranges	4.9	5.2	3.7
Apples	15.0	16.0	27.6
Pears	4.0	4.3	4.8
Sour (Morello) cherries	14.4	19.0*	19.0*
Sweet cherries	6.9	7.2	7.7
Peaches and nectarines	4.8	5.6	7.5
Plums	19.0	16.0	18.0
Grapes	97.1	115.1	127.8
Figs	17.8*	18.0*	16.7
Tobacco (leaves)	2.1	1.9	2.0

* FAO estimate(s).

Aggregate production ('000 metric tons, may include official, semi-official or estimated data): Total cereals 498.8 in 2004, 511.2 in 2005, 507.5 in 2006; Total roots and tubers 159.8 in 2004, 169.3 in 2005, 150.0 in 2006; Total vegetables (incl. melons) 677.7 in 2004, 686.0 in 2005, 675.0 in 2006; Total fruits (excl. melons) 194.5 in 2004, 218.5 in 2005, 247.1 in 2006.

Source: FAO.

LIVESTOCK
('000 head, year ending September)

	2004	2005	2006
Horses	58	53	53*
Asses, mules or hinnies*	127	127	127
Cattle	654	655	634
Pigs	143	147	152
Sheep	1,794	1,760	1,830
Goats	944	941	940
Chickens	4,517	4,671	4,572

* FAO estimate(s).

Source: FAO.

LIVESTOCK PRODUCTS
('000 metric tons)

	2004	2005	2006
Cattle meat	39.6*	40.8	41.4
Sheep meat	13.5	13.1	13.6
Goat meat	7.9*	7.0†	7.4
Pig meat	10.1*	11.3	11.3
Chicken meat	9.0	9.0	10.0
Cows' milk	917	930	956
Sheep's milk	75.0	75.0	75.0
Goats' milk	72.0	71.0	71.0
Hen eggs	290	270†	270†
Wool: greasy	3.3	3.4	3.2

* Unofficial figure.
† FAO estimate.

Source: FAO.

ALBANIA
Statistical Survey

Forestry

ROUNDWOOD REMOVALS
('000 cubic metres, excl. bark)

	2001	2002	2003
Sawlogs, veneer logs and logs for sleepers	64.7	67.5	62.1
Pulpwood	13.3	15.1	—
Other industrial wood	—	—	13.1
Fuel wood	186.6	222.2	221.0
Total	264.6	304.8	296.2

2004–06: Figures assumed to be unchanged from 2003 (FAO estimates).
Source: FAO.

SAWNWOOD PRODUCTION
('000 cubic metres, incl. railway sleepers)

	2001	2002	2003
Coniferous (softwood)*	47	47	47
Broadleaved (hardwood)	150†	50†	50*
Total	197	97	97*

* FAO estimate(s).
† Unofficial figure.
2004–06: Figures assumed to be unchanged from 2003 (FAO estimates).
Source: FAO.

Fishing

(metric tons, live weight)

	2003	2004	2005
Capture	2,802	3,564	3,802
Common carp	350*	415	550
Bleak	280*	330	457
Crucian carp	300*	350	381
Silver carp	100*	68	140
Salmonoids	50*	57	12
Common sole	38	73	40
European hake	384	473	267
Gilthead seabream	8	8	25
Bogue	84	76	68
Surmullets	141	158	113
Mullets	68	135	230
European pilchard (sardines)	70	32	104
Aquaculture	1,473*	1,569	1,473
Mediterranean mussel	860*	800	860
Rainbow trout	350*	350	350
Gilthead seabream	250*	400	250
Total catch	4,275*	5,133	5,275

* FAO estimate.
Note: Figures exclude Sardinia coral (metric tons): 1.6 in 2003; 0.5 in 2004; n.a. in 2005.
Source: FAO.

Mining

('000 metric tons, unless otherwise indicated)

	2003	2004	2005
Lignite (brown coal)	18	13	12*
Crude petroleum (gross production)	359	400	448
Natural gas (gross production, million cu metres)	12	12	11
Chromium ore (gross weight)*	220	160	170
Bauxite	5	—	—
Kaolin*	—	300	310
Dolomite*	1,500	1,613	1,000
Olivinite (metric tons)*	200	200	200

* Estimate(s).
Source: US Geological Survey.

Industry

SELECTED PRODUCTS
('000 metric tons, unless otherwise indicated)

	2002	2003	2004
Wheat flour	93	38	82
Wine ('000 hectolitres)	7	9	n.a.
Cigarettes (million)	50	15	n.a.
Veneer sheets ('000 cubic metres)*	37	37	37
Paper and paperboard*	2.8	2.8	2.8
Motor spirit (petrol)	21	6	35
Kerosene	8	5	7
Gas-diesel (distillate fuel) oil	84	95	73
Residual fuel oils	80	45	67
Electric energy (million kWh)†	3,179	4,904	5,493

* Source: FAO.
† Source: Institute of Statistics, Tirana.
Source (unless otherwise indicated): UN, *Industrial Commodity Statistics Yearbook*.

Beer ('000 hectolitres): 155 in 2002; 144 in 2003; 298 in 2004.

Petroleum bitumen (asphalt) ('000 metric tons): 28 in 2002; 42 in 2003; 61 in 2004.

Cement ('000 metric tons): 348 in 2002; 578 in 2003; 573 in 2004.

Ferro-chromium ('000 metric tons): 23 in 2002; 38 in 2003; 35 in 2004 (Source: US Geological Survey).

Petroleum coke ('000 metric tons): 40 in 2002; 58 in 2003; 59 in 2004 (Source: US Geological Survey).

Crude steel ('000 metric tons): 100 in 2002; 100 in 2003; 100 in 2004 (estimate) (Source: US Geological Survey).

Finance

CURRENCY AND EXCHANGE RATES

Monetary Units
100 qindarka (qintars) = 1 new lek.

Sterling, Dollar and Euro Equivalents (30 November 2007)
£1 sterling = 169.445 lekë;
US $1 = 82.000 lekë;
€1 = 121.040 lekë;
1,000 lekë = £5.90= $12.20 = €8.26.

Average Exchange Rate (lekë per US $)
2004   102.780
2005   99.870
2006   98.103

ALBANIA

STATE BUDGET
('000 million lekë)

Revenue*	2004	2005	2006†
Tax revenue	166.0	183.8	205.5
Tax revenue from Tax and			
Customs Directorate	127.3	139.7	161.5
Value-added tax	58.2	64.5	74.3
Profit tax	16.3	19.2	22.3
Excise taxes	15.8	18.5	23.0
Small business tax	4.1	3.8	2.6
Income tax	6.9	7.4	8.6
Customs duties	13.9	13.6	14.0
Other taxes	12.1	12.7	13.0
Property and local taxes	5.0	7.5	9.3
Social security contributions	33.3	36.2	39.3
Other revenue	16.0	14.2	16.0
Total	**182.0**	**198.0**	**221.5**

Expenditure‡	2004	2005	2006†
Current expenditure	183.8	194.0	204.9
Wages	49.0	53.7	56.7
Interest	28.4	26.0	25.0
Operational and maintenance	24.0	24.5	25.8
Subsidies	5.1	3.7	3.8
Social security	50.2	55.9	60.0
Local government expenditure	15.9	20.0	22.7
Social protection transfers	11.5	10.2	10.8
Other§	−0.3	0.0	0.0
Capital expenditure	38.6	38.4	50.4
Total	**222.4**	**232.3**	**255.3**

* Excluding grants received ('000 million lekë): 2.6 in 2004; 6.2 in 2005; 4.8 in 2006 (preliminary).
† Preliminary.
‡ Excluding lending minus repayments ('000 million lekë): 1.4 in 2004; 1.9 in 2005; and 0.0 in 2006 (preliminary).
§ Including statistical discrepancy.

Source: IMF, *Albania: Third Review Under the Three-Year Arrangement Under the Poverty Reduction and Growth Facility, Review Under Extended Arrangement, and Financing Assurances Review - Staff Report; Staff Statement; Press Release on the Executive Board Discussion; and Statement by the Executive Director for Albania* (July 2007).

INTERNATIONAL RESERVES
(US $ million at 31 December)

	2004	2005	2006
Gold*	30.25	35.49	43.91
IMF special drawing rights	100.79	12.50	9.00
Reserve position in IMF	5.21	4.80	5.05
Foreign exchange	1,251.60	1,386.79	1,754.75
Total	**1,387.85**	**1,439.58**	**1,812.71**

* Valued at market-related prices.
Source: IMF, *International Financial Statistics*.

MONEY SUPPLY
('000 million lekë at 31 December)

	2004	2005	2006
Currency outside banks	138.09	149.67	163.26
Demand deposits at deposit money banks	20.69	33.21	50.94
Total money	**158.79**	**182.88**	**214.20**

Source: IMF, *International Financial Statistics*.

COST OF LIVING
(Consumer Price Index; base: December 2001 = 100)

	2004	2005	2006
Food and non-alcoholic beverages	103.4	102.9	103.9
Alcoholic beverages and tobacco	104.8	107.3	113.3
Clothing and footwear	89.3	87.0	84.7
Rent, water, fuel and power	108.8	118.3	124.4
Household goods and maintenance	97.9	96.3	95.5
Medical care	110.2	115.7	119.7
Transport	104.2	108.1	111.8
Communication	120.7	111.4	110.6
Recreation and culture	101.8	102.3	103.2
Education	126.2	133.6	141.3
All items (incl. others)	**104.9**	**107.4**	**110.0**

NATIONAL ACCOUNTS
(million lekë at current prices, preliminary)

Expenditure on the Gross Domestic Product

	2003	2004	2005*
Final consumption expenditure	597,453	669,770	711,117
Households	520,954	586,242	621,417
Non-profit institutions serving households	914	1,044	1,192
General government	75,585	82,484	88,508
Gross fixed capital formation	280,921	279,378	296,925
Changes in inventories†	−12,635	−29,956	10,157
Total domestic expenditure	**865,739**	**919,192**	**1,018,199**
Exports of goods and services	141,290	165,097	185,970
Less Imports of goods and services	312,931	333,265	386,794
GDP in market prices	**694,098**	**751,024**	**817,374**

* Provisional.
† Including statistical discrepancies.

Gross Domestic Product by Economic Activity

	2003	2004	2005*
Agriculture, hunting and forestry	149,013	151,562	152,859
Mining and quarrying	4,084	5,522	6,066
Manufacturing	50,844	62,509	65,562
Construction	87,047	94,432	106,162
Wholesale and retail trade, hotels and restaurants	139,654	147,009	165,606
Transport	33,870	36,045	38,329
Post and communications	20,919	25,209	27,725
Other services	147,817	157,347	177,904
Sub-total	**633,247**	**679,636**	**740,213**
Less Financial intermediation services indirectly measured	20,849	18,729	23,508
Gross value added in basic prices	**612,398**	**660,907**	**716,705**
Taxes on products	86,714	94,951	104,158
Less Subsidies on products	5,015	4,834	3,489
GDP in market prices	**694,098**	**751,024**	**817,374**

* Provisional.

BALANCE OF PAYMENTS
(US $ million)

	2004	2005	2006
Exports of goods f.o.b.	603.3	656.3	792.9
Imports of goods f.o.b.	−2,194.9	−2,477.6	−2,915.6
Trade balance	**−1,591.6**	**−1,821.3**	**−2,122.7**
Exports of services	1,003.5	1,164.6	1,504.0
Imports of services	−1,054.8	−1,382.9	−1,584.8
Balance on goods and services	**−1,642.9**	**−2,039.6**	**−2,203.5**
Other income received	203.7	226.7	332.1
Other income paid	−28.3	−52.6	−69.1
Balance on goods, services and income	**−1,467.5**	**−1,865.5**	**−1,940.5**
Current transfers received	1,200.2	1,519.2	1,426.3

ALBANIA

—continued	2004	2005	2006
Current transfers paid	−90.6	−225.1	−156.7
Current balance	−357.9	−571.5	−670.9
Capital account (net)	132.4	122.9	179.8
Direct investment abroad	−13.6	−4.1	−10.6
Direct investment from abroad	341.3	262.5	325.3
Portfolio investment assets	−3.6	−5.7	34.2
Other investment assets	−113.8	6.6	−210.7
Other investment liabilities	186.1	133.2	385.2
Net errors and omissions	115.3	203.8	237.0
Overall balance	286.1	147.8	269.2

External Trade

PRINCIPAL COMMODITIES
(million lekë)

Imports c.i.f.	2003	2004	2005
Food and live animals	32,613	34,262	33,936
Beverages and tobacco	8,256	7,734	8,036
Mineral fuels and lubricants	19,421	18,079	22,571
Chemical products	16,593	18,640	22,135
Manufactured products	56,965	57,838	67,591
Machinery and transport equipment	48,870	55,710	61,641
Miscellaneous manufactured articles	36,485	36,780	37,283
Total (incl. others)	225,983	236,072	261,710

Exports f.o.b.	2003	2004	2005
Food and live animals	2,314	2,584	2,595
Crude materials	4,732	5,817	6,943
Manufactured products	6,892	8,799	10,211
Machinery and transport equipment	1,933	2,453	2,715
Miscellaneous manufactured articles	37,008	39,489	39,920
Total (incl. others)	54,487	62,121	65,766

PRINCIPAL TRADING PARTNERS
(million lekë)*

Imports c.i.f.	2003	2004	2005
Austria	3,646	2,648	4,546
Brazil	1,643	3,294	2,341
Bulgaria	4,963	4,731	7,330
Croatia	3,458	3,068	3,107
France	2,447	3,858	3,234
Germany	12,777	14,583	14,227
Greece	45,287	43,644	43,044
Italy	75,640	76,699	76,719
Macedonia, former Yugoslav republic	1,901	2,460	3,202
Russia	6,387	6,590	10,562
Slovenia	3,233	1,824	1,886
Spain	3,870	3,518	4,432
Turkey	14,830	16,764	19,615
United Kingdom	5,460	1,518	2,420
Ukraine	5,656	5,860	7,495
USA	2,248	3,569	3,690
Total (incl. others)	225,983	236,072	261,710

Exports f.o.b.	2003	2004	2005
Austria	675	209	149
Germany	1,857	1,928	2,188
Greece	6,980	7,448	6,884
Italy	40,811	45,350	47,640
Macedonia, former Yugoslav republic	372	787	1,029
Serbia and Montenegro	1,284	3,090	3,262
Turkey	451	1,178	1,131
Switzerland	161	59	40
USA	277	318	658
Total (incl. others)	54,487	62,121	65,766

* Imports by country of origin; exports by country of destination.

Transport

RAILWAYS
(traffic)

	2002	2003	2004
Passengers carried ('000)	2,279.7	2,068.5	1,758.0
Passenger-km (million)	123	105	89
Freight carried ('000 metric tons)	348.6	517.0	417.3
Freight ton-km (million)	21	31	32

ROAD TRAFFIC
(motor vehicles in use at 31 December)

	2002	2003	2004
Passenger cars	148,531	174,782	190,004
Buses and coaches	21,026	21,693	25,066
Lorries and vans	51,960	53,900	46,809
Road tractors	2,670	2,957	1,966
Motorcycles and mopeds	3,400	3,896	4,877
Trailers	6,367	6,673	5,930

SHIPPING

Merchant Fleet
(registered at 31 December)

	2004	2005	2006
Number of vessels	76	77	75
Displacement ('000 gross registered tons)	72.8	74.8	74.7

Source: Lloyd's Register-Fairplay, *World Fleet Statistics*.

International Sea-borne Freight Traffic
('000 metric tons)

	1998	1999	2000
Goods loaded	108	120	132
Goods unloaded	1,536	2,040	2,424

Source: UN, *Monthly Bulletin of Statistics*.

Goods loaded and unloaded ('000 metric tons): 2,995 in 2001; 3,092 in 2002; 3,425 in 2003; 3,628 in 2004.

CIVIL AVIATION
(traffic on scheduled services)

	2002	2003	2004
Passengers ('000):			
arrivals	238	276	321
departures	257	285	329
Freight (metric tons):			
loaded	504	450	405
unloaded	1,066	1,173	1,153

Tourism

FOREIGN TOURIST ARRIVALS BY COUNTRY OF ORIGIN*

	2003	2004	2005
Germany	15,169	18,420	23,391
Greece	34,266	40,541	47,776
Italy	49,984	51,703	62,520
Macedonia, former Yugoslav republic	79,012	99,837	141,160
Turkey	9,734	11,402	14,595
United Kingdom	25,239	31,186	33,163
USA	16,497	22,060	30,108
Serbia and Montenegro	272,058	299,488	302,669
Total (incl. others)	557,210	645,409	747,837

* Figures refer to arrivals at frontiers of visitors from abroad, and include same-day visitors.

Tourism receipts (US $ million, incl. passenger transport): 537 in 2003; 756 in 2004; 880 in 2005.

Source: World Tourism Organization.

Communications Media

	2003	2004	2005
Telephones ('000 main lines in use)	255.0	274.6	353.6
Mobile cellular telephones ('000 subscribers)	1,100.0	1,259.6	1,530.2
Broadband subscribers ('000)	—	—	0.3
Internet users ('000)	30	75	188

Personal computers ('000 in use): 36 in 2002.

Television receivers ('000 in use): 480 in 2000.

Radio receivers ('000 in use): 810 in 1997.

Facsimile machines ('000 in use): 18.3 in 1999.

Book production (1991): 381 titles (including 18 pamphlets).

Daily newspapers (2006): Titles 5; Average circulation ('000 copies) 116.

Sources: UN, *Statistical Yearbook*; UNESCO, *Statistical Yearbook*; International Telecommunication Union.

Education

(2003/04)

	Institutions	Teachers	Students
Pre-primary	1,678	3,543	75,755
Primary	1,721	26,208	491,541
Secondary:			
general	309	4,625	96,637
vocational	53	1,508	21,724
Higher education*	11	3,997	36,244

* Figures include those enrolled at distance-learning institutions.

Source: Ministry of Education, Tirana.

Adult literacy rate (UNESCO estimates): 98.7% (males 99.2%; females 98.3%) in 2001 (Source: UNESCO Institute for Statistics).

Directory

The Constitution

On 21 October 1998 the Kuvendi Popullor (People's Assembly) approved a new Constitution, which had been drafted by a parliamentary commission. The Constitution was endorsed at a national referendum on 22 November, and was officially adopted on 28 November.

GENERAL PROVISIONS

Albania is a parliamentary republic. The Republic of Albania is a unitary state, with a system of government based on the separation and balancing of legislative, executive and judicial powers. Sovereignty is exercised by the people through their elected representatives. The Republic recognizes and protects the national rights of people who live outside the country's borders. Political parties are created freely, and are required to conform with democratic principles. The Republic does not have an official religion, and guarantees equality of religious communities. The economic system is based on a market economy, and on freedom of economic activity, as well as on private and public property. The armed forces ensure the independence of the country, and protect its territorial integrity and constitutional order. Local government in the Republic of Albania is exercised according to the principle of decentralization of public power. The official language is Albanian. The fundamental political, economic and social rights and freedoms of Albanian citizens are guaranteed under the Constitution.

LEGISLATURE

The Kuvendi Popullor comprises 140 deputies, and is elected for a term of four years. Some 100 deputies are elected directly in single-member constituencies. Parties receiving 2.5% or more of the votes cast, and party coalitions obtaining 4.0% or more in the first round of voting, are allocated further deputies in proportion to the number of votes won, on the basis of multi-name lists of parties or party coalitions. The Council of Ministers, every deputy and 20,000 voters each have the right to propose legislation. The Kuvendi Popullor makes decisions by a majority of votes, when more than one-half of the deputies are present.

PRESIDENT

The President of the Republic is the Head of State and represents the unity of the people. A candidate for President is proposed to the Kuvendi Popullor by a group of no fewer than 20 deputies. The President is elected by secret ballot by a majority of three-fifths of the members of the Kuvendi Popullor for a term of five years. A President may be re-elected only once.

COUNCIL OF MINISTERS

The Council of Ministers comprises the Prime Minister, Deputy Prime Minister and ministers. The President of the Republic nominates as Prime Minister the candidate presented by the party or coalition of parties that has the majority of seats in the Kuvendi Popullor. The Prime Minister, within 10 days of his appointment, forms a Council of Ministers, which is presented for approval to the Kuvendi Popullor.

ALBANIA

LOCAL GOVERNMENT

The units of local government are communes, districts, municipalities, and counties. The representative organs of the basic units of local government are councils, which are elected by general direct elections for a period of three years. The executive organ of a municipality or commune is the Chairman. The Council of Ministers appoints a Prefect in every county as its representative.

JUDICIARY

Judicial power is exercised by the High Court, as well as by the Courts of Appeal and the Courts of First Instance. The Chairman and members of the High Court are appointed by the President of the Republic, with the approval of the Kuvendi Popullor, for a term of nine years. Other judges are appointed by the President upon the proposal of the High Council of Justice. The High Council of Justice, of which the President of the Republic is Chairman, additionally comprises the Chairman of the High Court, the Minister of Justice, three members elected by the Kuvendi Popullor for a term of five years, and nine judges who are elected by a national judicial conference. The Constitutional Court arbitrates on constitutional issues, and determines the conformity of proposed legislation with the Constitution. The Constitutional Court comprises nine members, who are appointed by the President, with the approval of the Kuvendi Popullor, for a term of nine years.

The Government

HEAD OF STATE

President of the Republic: BAMIR TOPI (elected by vote of the Kuvendi Popullor 15 July 2007; took office 24 July 2007).

COUNCIL OF MINISTERS
(March 2008)

A coalition of the Democratic Party of Albania (PDSh), the Republican Party of Albania (PRSh), the New Democratic Party (PDR), the Environmentalist Agrarian Party (PAA), the Union for Human Rights Party (PBDNj) and the Christian Democratic Party of Albania (PDK).

Prime Minister: Prof. SALI BERISHA (DPA).
Minister of Finance: RIDVAN BODE (DPA).
Minister of Foreign Affairs: LULËZIM BASHA (DPA).
Minister of Economy, Trade and Energy: GENC RULI (DPA).
Minister of the Interior: BUJAR NISHANI (DPA).
Minister of Health: NARD NDOKA (CDPA).
Minister of Public Works, Transport and Telecommunications: SOKOL OLLDASHI (DPA).
Minister of Agriculture, Food and Consumer Protection: JEMIN GJANA (DPA).
Minister of Justice: ENKELEJD ALIBEAJ (DPA).
Minister of European Integration: MAJLINDA BREGU (DPA).
Minister of Tourism, Culture, Youth and Sports: YLLI PANGO (DPA).
Minister of Defence: GAZMEND OKETA (DPA).
Minister of Education and Science: GENC POLLO (NDP).
Minister of Labour, Social Affairs and Equal Opportunities: KOSTA BARKA (UHRP).
Minister of the Environment, Forestry and Water Administration: LUFTER XHUVELI (EAP).

MINISTRIES

Office of the President: Bulevardi Dëshmorët e Kombit, Tirana; tel. (4) 228437; fax (4) 236925; e-mail info@president.al; internet www.president.al.
Office of the Council of Ministers: Bulevardi Dëshmorët e Kombit 1, Tirana; tel. (4) 250474; fax (4) 237501; e-mail info@km.gov.al; internet www.km.gov.al.
Ministry of Agriculture, Food and Consumer Protection: Sheshi Skënderbej 2, Tirana; tel. (4) 232796; fax (4) 227924; e-mail gjana@hotmail.com; internet www.mbu.gov.al.
Ministry of Defence: Bulevardi Dëshmorët e Kombit, Tirana; tel. (4) 226601; fax (4) 228325; e-mail kontakt@mod.gov.al; internet www.mod.gov.al.
Ministry of Economy, Trade and Energy: Bulevardi Dëshmorët e Kombit 2, Tirana; tel. (4) 227617; fax (4) 234052; e-mail kabineti@mete.gov.al; internet www.mete.gov.al.
Ministry of Education and Science: Rruga Durrësit 23, Tirana; tel. (4) 226307; fax (4) 232002; e-mail rspahia@mash.gov.al; internet www.mash.gov.al.

Ministry of the Environment, Forestry and Water Administration: Rruga Durrësit 27, Tirana; tel. (4) 270630; fax (4) 270627; e-mail info@moe.gov.al; internet www.moe.gov.al.
Ministry of European Integration: Bulevardi Dëshmorët e Kombit, Tirana; tel. and fax (4) 228645; e-mail tatjana.kongoli@mie.gov.al; internet www.mie.gov.al.
Ministry of Finance: Bulevardi Dëshmorët e Kombit 4, Tirana; tel. (4) 267654; fax (4) 226111; e-mail secretary.minister@minfin.gov.al; internet www.minfin.gov.al.
Ministry of Foreign Affairs: Bulevardi Gjergj Fishta 6, Tirana; tel. (4) 364090; fax (4) 362084; e-mail info@mfa.gov.al; internet www.mfa.gov.al.
Ministry of Health: Bulevardi Bajram Curri 1, Tirana; tel. (4) 362937; fax (4) 362554; internet www.moh.gov.al.
Ministry of the Interior: Sheshi Skënderbej 3, Tirana; tel. (4) 247155; e-mail mb@moi.gov.al; internet www.moi.gov.al.
Ministry of Justice: Bulevardi Dëshmorët e Kombit, Tirana; tel. (4) 224041; fax (4) 228359; e-mail ministidre@albaniaonline.net.
Ministry of Labour, Social Affairs and Equal Opportunities: Rruga e Kavajes, Tirana; tel. (4) 240413; fax (4) 227779; e-mail molsa@icc-al.org; internet www.mpcs.gov.al.
Ministry of Public Works, Transport and Telecommunications: Sheshi Skënderbej 5, Tirana; tel. and fax (4) 232389; e-mail ministri@mpptt.gov.al; internet www.mpptt.gov.al.
Ministry of Tourism, Culture, Youth and Sports: Rruga Abdi Toptani, Tirana; tel. (4) 222508; fax (4) 232488; e-mail informacion@mtkrs.gov.al; internet www.mtkrs.gov.al.

Legislature

Kuvendi Popullor
(People's Assembly)

Bulevardi Dëshmorët e Kombit 4, Tirana; tel. (4) 237418; fax (4) 227949; e-mail marlind@parlament.al; internet www.parlament.al.
Speaker: JOZEFINA TOPALLI.

General Election, 3 July 2005*†

Party	A†	B†	Total
Democratic Party of Albania	56	—	56
Socialist Party of Albania	42	—	42
Republican Party of Albania‡	—	11	11
Social Democratic Party of Albania	—	7	7
Socialist Movement for Integration	1	4	5
Environmentalist Agrarian Party	—	4	4
New Democratic Party‡	—	4	4
Democratic Alliance Party	—	3	3
Christian Democratic Party of Albania‡	—	2	2
Social Democracy Party	—	2	2
Union for Human Rights Party	—	2	2
Liberal Democratic Union Party‡	—	1	1
Independent	1	—	1
Total	**100**	**40**	**140**

* A second round of voting was held on 21 August in three constituencies.
† Of the 140 legislative seats, 100 (A) are elected in single-mandate constituency seats, while 40 (B) are elected from party lists, on the basis of proportional representation.
‡ Participated in the election separately, as a member of the Alliance for Freedom, Justice and Well-Being.

Election Commission

Komisioni Qendror i Zgjyedhjeve (KQZ) (Central Election Commission—CEC): Pallati i Kongreseve; tel. and fax (4) 235362; e-mail foreign.rel@cec.org.al; internet www.cec.org.al; f. 1996; seven members: two elected by the Kuvendi Popullor, two by the President and three by the High Council of Justice; Chair. ÇLIRIM GJATA.

Political Organizations

Albanian Communist Party (ACP) (Partia Komuniste e Shqipërisë—PKSh): Tirana; fax (4) 233164; f. 1991; granted legal recognition 1998; Chair. HYSNI MILLOSHI.

ALBANIA

Directory

Albanian Green Party (Partia Të Gjelbërit e Shqipërisë): Rruga Bajram Curri Pall. 31/1/4, Tirana; tel. and fax (4) 246955; e-mail albgreens@tegjelberit.org; internet www.tegjelberit.org; f. 2001; ecologist; observer mem. of European Greens; Chair. EDLIR PETANAJ.

Christian Democratic Party of Albania (CDPA) (Partia Demokristiane e Shqipërisë—PDK): Rruga Dëshmorët e 4 Shkurtit, Tirana; tel. (4) 2240574; fax (4) 2233024; f. 1991; contested 2005 legislative elections as mem. of Alliance for Freedom, Justice and Well-being; Leader NARD NDOKA.

Democratic Alliance Party (DAP) (Partia Aleanca Demokratike—PAD): Tirana; f. 1992 by fmr mems of the Democratic Party of Albania; Chair. NERITAN ÇEKA; Sec.-Gen. EDMOND DRAGOTI.

Democratic Party of Albania (DPA) (Partia Demokratike e Shqipërisë—PDSh): Rruga Punëtorët e Rilindjes, Tirana; tel. (4) 228091; fax (4) 223525; e-mail profsberisha@albaniaonline.net; internet www.dpalbania.org; f. 1990; centre-right, pro-democracy, pro-market; Chair. Prof. Dr SALI BERISHA; Sec.-Gen. RIDVAN BODE.

Environmentalist Agrarian Party (EAP) (Partia Agrare Ambjentaliste—PAA): Rruga Budi 6, Tirana; tel. and fax (4) 231904; e-mail lxhuveli@europe.com; f. 1991; Chair. LUFTER XHUVELI.

Liberal Democratic Union Party (LDUP) (Partia Bashkimi Liberal Demokrat—PBLD): contested 2005 legislative elections as mem. of Alliance for Freedom, Justice and Well-being; Chair. ARJAN STAROVA.

Macedonian Alliance for European Integration (Makedonskata alijansa za evropska integratsija): f. 2005; aims to encourage greater participation of the Macedonian minority in politics and to contribute to Albania's Euro-Atlantic integration; participated indirectly in 2005 legislative elections through the Union for Human Rights Party (q.v.).

Movement of Legality Party (MLP) (Partia Lëvizja e Legalitetit—PLL): Tirana; e-mail levizja_legalitetit@yahoo.com; f. 1992; monarchist; contested 2005 legislative elections as part of the Movement for National Development, but subsequently announced its withdrawal from the alliance; Chair. EKREM SPAHIA.

Movement for Solidarity: Tirana; f. Sept. 2007 by fmr leader of the SPA; Leader FATOS NANO.

New Democratic Party (NDP) (Partia Demokrate e Re—PDR): Rruga M. Shyri 47, Tirana; tel. and fax (4) 269107; e-mail pdr@interalb.net; f. 2001 by fmr mems of the DPA; contested 2005 legislative elections as mem. of Alliance for Freedom, Justice and Well-being; Leader GENC POLLO.

Republican Party of Albania (RPA) (Partia Republika e Shqipërisë—PRSh): Tirana; f. 1991; contested 2005 legislative elections as mem. of Alliance for Freedom, Justice and Well-being; Chair. FATMIR MEDIU.

Social Democracy Party (SDP) (Partia Demokracia Sociale—PDS): Tirana; f. 2003 by breakaway faction of the SDP; Chair. PASKAL MILO.

Social Democratic Party of Albania (SDPA) (Partia Social Demokratike e Shqipërisë—PSDSh): Rruga Asim Vokshi 26, Tirana; tel. (4) 226540; fax (4) 227417; f. 1991; Chair. SKËNDER GJINUSHI.

Socialist Movement for Integration (SMI) (Lëvizja Socialiste për Integrim—LSI): Rruga Smai Frasheri 20/10, Tirana; tel. (4) 270412; fax (4) 270413; e-mail secretariat@lsi.al; internet www.lsi.al; f. 2004 by fmr mems of the SPA; moderate socialist; Chair. ILIR META; c. 40,000 mems (April 2005).

Socialist Party of Albania (SPA) (Partia Socialiste e Shqipërisë—PSSh): Tirana; tel. (4) 227409; fax (4) 227417; internet www.ps.al; f. 1941 as Albanian Communist Party; renamed Party of Labour of Albania in 1948, adopted present name in 1991; now rejects Marxism-Leninism and claims commitment to democratic socialism and a market economy; Chair. EDI RAMA; Sec.-Gen. ANDIS HARASANI; 110,000 mems.

Union for Human Rights Party (UHRP) (Partia Bashkimi për të Drejtat e Njeriut—PBDNj): Tirana; f. 1992; represents the Greek and Macedonian minorities; Leader VANGJEL DULE.

Diplomatic Representation

EMBASSIES IN ALBANIA

Austria: Rruga Frederik Shiroka 3, Tirana; tel. (4) 274855; fax (4) 233140; e-mail tirana-ob@bmaa.gv.al; Ambassador KLAUS DERKOWITSCH.

Bulgaria: Rruga Skënderbej 12, Tirana; tel. (4) 233155; fax (4) 232272; e-mail bgemb@interalb.net; internet www.mfa.bg/tirana; Ambassador TEODOR SPASOV RUSINOV.

China, People's Republic: Rruga Skënderbej 57, Tirana; tel. (4) 232385; fax (4) 233159; e-mail chinaemb_al@mfa.gov.cn; Ambassador WANG JUNLING.

Croatia: Rruga A. Toptani, Torre Drin 4, Tirana; tel. (4) 256948; fax (4) 230578; e-mail croemb.tirana@mvpei.hr; Ambassador DARKO JAVORSKI.

Czech Republic: Rruga Skënderbej 10, Tirana; tel. (4) 234004; fax (4) 232159; e-mail tirana@embassy.mzv.cz; internet www.mzv.cz/tirana; Ambassador MARKÉTA FIALKOVÁ.

Denmark: Rruga Nikolla Tupe 1/4, POB 1743, Tirana; tel. (4) 280600; fax (4) 280630; e-mail tiaamb@um.dk; internet www.ambtirana.um.dk; Ambassador NIELS SEVERIN MUNK.

Egypt: Rruga Skënderbej 43, Tirana; tel. (4) 233022; fax (4) 232295; Ambassador REFAAT AL-ANSARI.

France: Rruga Skënderbej 14, Tirana; tel. (4) 234054; fax (4) 234442; e-mail ambafrance.tr@adanet.com.al; internet www.ambafrance-al.org; Ambassador MARYSE DAVIET.

Germany: Rruga Skënderbej 8, Tirana; tel. (4) 274505; fax (4) 233497; e-mail info@tira.diplo.de; internet www.tirana.diplo.de; Ambassador BERND BORCHARDT.

Greece: Rruga Frederik Shiroka 3, Tirana; tel. (4) 274670; fax (4) 234290; e-mail gremb.tir@mfa.gr; internet www.greekembassy.al; Ambassador KONSTANTIN KOKOSSIS.

Holy See: Rruga e Durrësit 13, POB 8355, Tirana; tel. (4) 233516; fax (4) 232001; e-mail nunapal@icc-al.org; Apostolic Nuncio Most Rev. GIOVANNI BULAITIS (Titular Archbishop of Narona).

Hungary: Rruga Skënderbej 16, Tirana; tel. (4) 232238; fax (4) 233211; e-mail mission.tia@kum.hu; internet www.mfa.gov.hu/emb/tirana; Ambassador SÁNDOR MOLNÁRI.

Iran: Rruga Mustafa Matohiti 20, Tirana; tel. (4) 255038; fax (4) 230409; Ambassador HABIBOLLAH BIAZAR.

Italy: Rruga Lek Dukagjini 2, Tirana; tel. (4) 234045; fax (4) 250921; e-mail segreteriaambasciata.tirana@esteri.it; internet www.ambtirana.esteri.it; Ambassador SABA D'ELIA.

Libya: Rruga Dëshmorët e 4 Shkurtit 48, Tirana; tel. (4) 228101; fax (4) 232098; e-mail amblibi@abissnet.com.al; Chargé d'affaires a.i. MOULOUD O. A. AL-HAMUDI.

Macedonia, former Yugoslav republic: Rruga Kavajes 116, Tirana; tel. (4) 230909; fax (4) 232514; e-mail makambas@albnet.net; Ambassador BLAGORODNA MINGOVA-KREPIEVA.

Netherlands: Rruga Asim Zeneli 10, Tirana; tel. (4) 240828; fax (4) 232723; e-mail tir@minbuza.nl; internet www.mfa.nl/tir; Ambassador SWEDER VAN VOORST TOT VOORST.

Norway: Sky Tower, Rruga Dëshmorët e 4 Shkurtit 5; tel. (4) 256923; fax (4) 221507; e-mail embtia@mfa.no; Ambassador CARL SCHIØTZ WIBYE (resident in Skopje, former Yugoslav republic of Macedonia).

Poland: Rruga e Durrësit 123, Tirana; tel. (4) 234190; fax (4) 233364; e-mail polemb@albaniaonline.net; internet www.tirana.polemb.net; Ambassador (vacant).

Romania: Rruga Themistokli, Gjermeni 2, Tirana; tel. (4) 256071; fax (4) 256072; e-mail roemb@adanet.co.al; Chargé d'affaires GHEORGHE MICU.

Russia: Rruga Asim Zeneli 5, Tirana; tel. (4) 256040; fax (4) 256046; e-mail rusemb@icc.al.eu.org; Ambassador ALEKSANDR L. PRISHCHEPOV.

Saudi Arabia: Bulevardi Dëshmorët e Kombit; tel. and fax (4) 248306; e-mail embsaudarab@albaniaonline.net; Ambassador ABDULLAH S. AL-HAMDAN.

Serbia: Rruga Donika Kastrioti 9/1, Tirana; tel. (4) 232091; fax (4) 232089; e-mail ambatira@icc-al.org; internet www.tirana.mfa.gov.yu; Chargé d'affaires a.i. (vacant).

Spain: Rruga Skënderbej 43, Tirana; tel. (4) 274960; fax (4) 225383; e-mail emb.tirana@mae.es; Ambassador MANUEL MONTOBBIO DE BALANZÓ.

Switzerland: Rruga e Elbasanit 81, Tirana; tel. (4) 234888; fax (4) 234889; e-mail tir.vertretung@eda.admin.ch; internet www.eda.admin.ch/tirana; Ambassador YVANA ENZLER.

Turkey: Rruga Konferenca e Kavajes 31, Tirana; tel. (4) 233399; fax (4) 232719; e-mail turkemb@interalb.al; Ambassador SUPHAN ERKULA.

United Kingdom: Rruga Skënderbej 12, Tirana; tel. (4) 234973; fax (4) 247697; e-mail information.tiran@fco.gov.uk; internet www.britishembassy.gov.uk/albania; Ambassador FRASER WILSON.

USA: Rruga Elbasanit 103, Tirana; tel. (4) 247285; fax (4) 232222; e-mail wm_tirana@pd.state.gov; internet tirana.usembassy.gov; Ambassador Dr JOHN L. WITHERS, II.

Judicial System

The judicial structure comprises the Supreme Court, the Courts of Appeal and the Courts of First Instance. The Chairman and members of the Supreme Court are appointed by the President of the Republic, with the approval of the legislature, for a term of nine years. Other judges are appointed by the President upon the proposal of the High Council of Justice. The High Council of Justice comprises the President of the Republic (who is its Chairman), the Chairman of the High Court, the Minister of Justice, three members elected by the legislature for a term of five years, and nine judges of all levels who are elected by a national judicial conference. The Constitutional Court arbitrates on constitutional issues, and determines, *inter alia*, the conformity of proposed legislation with the Constitution. It is empowered to prohibit the activities of political organizations on constitutional grounds, and also formulates legislation regarding the election of the President of the Republic. The Constitutional Court comprises nine members, who are appointed by the President, with the approval of the legislature, for a term of nine years.

Supreme Court (Gjykata e Larte): Rruga Dëshmorët e 4 Shkurtit, Tirana; tel. (4) 228357; fax (4) 228837; e-mail supremecourt@albaniaonline.net; internet www.gjykataelarte.gov.al; Chief Justice THIMJO KONDI.

Constitutional Court (Gjykata Kushtetuese): Bulevardi Dëshmorët e Kombit, Tirana; tel. (4) 228357; fax (4) 228357; e-mail kujtim.osmani@gjk.gov.al; internet www.gjk.gov.al; Pres. Dr VLADIMIR KRISTO.

Office of the Prosecutor-General (Zyra e Prokurorit te Pergjithshem): Rruga Qemal Stafa 1, Tirana; tel. (4) 234850; fax (4) 229085; internet www.pp.gov.al; Prosecutor-General INA RAMA.

Religion

In May 1990 a prohibition on religious activities, enforced since 1967, was revoked, religious services were permitted and, from 1991, mosques and churches began to be reopened. Under the Constitution of November 1998, Albania is a secular state, which respects freedom of religious belief. On the basis of declared affiliation in 1945, it is estimated that some 70% of the population are of Muslim background, of whom about 75% are associated with Sunni Islam; many of the remainder are associated with the Bektashi sect, a Sufi dervish order. Muslims are mainly concentrated in the middle and, to some extent, the south of the country. Some 20% of the population are of Eastern Orthodox Christian background (mainly in the south) and some 10% are associated with the Roman Catholic Church (mainly in the north).

ISLAM

Albanian Islamic Community (Bashkesia Islame e Shqipërisë): Rruga Puntoret e Rilindjes, Tirana; e-mail icalb@yahoo.com; f. 1991; Chair. and Grand Mufti of Albania SELIM MUÇA.

Bektashi Sect

Albania is the world centre of the Bektashi sect.

World Council of Elders of the Bektashis: Tirana; f. 1991; Chair. Haxhi Dedebaba RESHAT BARDHI.

CHRISTIANITY

The Eastern Orthodox Church

Orthodox Autocephalous Church of Albania (Kisha Orthodhokse Autoqefale e Shqipërisë): Rruga e Kavajes 151, Tirana; tel. (4) 234117; fax (4) 232109; e-mail orthchal@orthodoxalbania.org; internet www.orthodoxalbania.org; the Albanian Orthodox Church was proclaimed autocephalous at the Congress of Berat in 1922, its status was approved in 1929 and it was recognized by the Ecumenical Patriarchate of Constantinople (İstanbul), Turkey, in 1936; Archbishop of Tirana, Durrës and all Albania ANASTASIOS YANNOULATOS.

The Roman Catholic Church

Many Roman Catholic churches have been reopened since 1990, and in September 1991 diplomatic relations were restored with the Holy See. Albania comprises two archdioceses, three dioceses and one apostolic administration. At 31 December 2005 there were an estimated 509,242 adherents in the country, equivalent to 12.9% of the population.

Bishops' Conference: Rruga Don Bosko 1, POB 2950, Tirana; tel. and fax (4) 247159; e-mail cealbania@albnet.net; Pres. Most Rev. RROK K. MIRDITA (Archbishop of Tirana-Durrës).

Archbishop of Shkodër-Pult: Most Rev. ANGELO MASSAFRA, Sheshi Gijon Pali II, Shkodër; tel. (22) 42744; fax (22) 43673; e-mail curiashkoder@hotmail.com.

Archbishop of Tirana-Durrës: Most Rev. RROK K. MIRDITA, Bulevardi Zhan d'Ark, Tirana; tel. (4) 232082; fax (4) 230727; e-mail arq@icc.al.org.

The Press

PRINCIPAL DAILIES

Albania: Rruga Sami Frashëri 8, Tirana; tel. (4) 229243; fax (4) 223198; e-mail albania@albaniaonline.net; independent; politics, society, culture; pro-Democratic Party of Albania (DPA); English summary; Editor-in-Chief LUFTI DERVISHI.

Albanian Daily News: Rruga Hoxha Tahsin 109/1/18, Tirana; tel. (4) 376132; fax (4) 227639; e-mail adn@albnet.net; internet www.albaniannews.com; f. 1995; in English, subscription-based online edition updated daily, printed weekly newspaper; Editor ARBEN LESKAJ.

Biznesi (Business): Rruga Don Bosko, Vilat e Reja, POB 2423, Tirana; tel. (4) 251422; fax (4) 233526; e-mail kontakt@biznesi.com.al; internet www.biznesi.com.al; Editor-in-Chief ORJETA ZHUPA.

Dita (The Day): Rruga Ymer Kurti, Pallati 6/2/3, Tirana; tel. and fax (4) 271131; e-mail gazetadita@gazetadita.com; independent; politics, society, culture; Editor-in-Chief YLLI MOLLA.

Ekonomia (Economy): Rruga Gjergj Fishta, pranë isch ekspozitës Shqipëria Sot, Tirana; tel. and fax (4) 250766; e-mail gazekonomia@albaniaonline.com; published by the Albanian Agency of Economic Development.

Gazeta 55 (Newspaper 55): Rruga e Dibrës 213; tel. and fax (4) 230035; e-mail gazeta55@albaniaonline.net; internet www.gazeta55.net; f. 1997; independent; right-wing; English summary; Editor-in-Chief ILIR NIKOLLA.

Gazeta Shqiptare (The Albanian Newspaper): Ish-Drejtoria e Uzines se AutoTraktoreve, Tirana; tel. (4) 359104; fax (4) 359116; e-mail redaksia@gazetashqiptare.com; internet balkanweb.com/gazetav4; f. 1927; re-established 1993; independent; politics, economics, culture; local news section; Editor-in-Chief ARJAN CANI.

Koha Jonë (Our Time): Rruga Dervish Hima 1, Tirana; tel. (4) 247004; fax (4) 239584; e-mail redaskj@kohajone.com; internet www.kohajone.com; f. 1991; independent; Editor-in-Chief EDISON KURANI; circ. 400,000.

Korrieri (The Courier): Rruga Dervish Hima 1, Tirana; tel. (4) 253574; fax (4) 253575; e-mail posta@korrieri.com; internet www.korrieri.com; independent; Editor-in-Chief SOKOL SHAMETAJ.

Panorama (Panorama): Rruga Jordan Misja, prapa shkollës Harry Fultz, Pallati 1, Kati i II-të, Tirana; tel. (4) 273207; fax (4) 273206; e-mail info@panorama.com.al; internet www.panorama.com.al; independent; politics, economics, culture, sports, arts; Editor-in-Chief ROBERT RAKIPLLARI.

Republika: Rruga Sami Frashëri, Pallatet e Aviacionit, Tirana; tel. and fax (4) 225988; e-mail republika@albaniaonline.net; organ of the Republican Party of Albania; Editor-in-Chief YLLI RAKIPI.

Rilindja Demokratike (Democratic Revival): Rruga Punëtorët e Rilindjes, pranë selisë së PD, Tirana; tel. (4) 232355; fax (4) 230329; e-mail gazetard@albaniaonline.net; internet www.rilindjademokratike.com; f. 1991; organ of the DPA; Editor-in-Chief ASTRIT PATOZI; circ. 50,000.

Shekulli (Century): Rruga Don Bosko, Vilat e Reja, Tirana; tel. (4) 233572; fax (4) 233526; e-mail kryeredaktori@shekulli.com.al; internet www.shekulli.com.al; independent; national and international politics, economics, culture; English summary; Editor-in-Chief ROBERT RAKIPLLARI.

Sot (Today): Rruga Donika Kastrioti 9/1; tel. (4) 382019; fax (4) 382020; e-mail gazeta@sot.com.al; internet www.sot.com.al; Albanian and English; current affairs; Editor-in-Chief DRITAN YLLI.

Sporti Shqiptar (Albanian Sports): Rruga Don Bosko, Vilat e Reja, Tirana; tel. (4) 220237; fax (4) 251420; e-mail posta@sportishqiptar.com.al; internet www.sportishqiptar.com.al; f. 1935; national and international sports; Publisher KOÇO KOKËDHIMA; circ. 10,000.

Tema: Zayed Business Center, Rruga Sulejman Delvina, 3rd Floor, Tirana; tel. and fax (4) 251073; e-mail gazetatema@albmail.com; internet www.gazetatema.net; independent; liberal; Editor-in-Chief MERO BAZE.

Zëri i Popullit (The Voice of the People): Bulevardi Zhan D'Ark, Tirana; tel. (4) 222192; fax (4) 227813; e-mail zeri@zeripopullit.com; internet www.zeripopullit.com; f. 1942; daily, except Mon.; organ of the Socialist Party of Albania (SPA); English summary; Editor-in-Chief ERION BRACE; circ. 105,000.

PERIODICALS

AENews: Rruga Jul Variboba 14, Tirana; tel. (69) 2076943; e-mail erebaragjergj@hotmail.com; internet www.albanianeconomy.com; online only; fmrly Albanian Economy; in English; corporate, business, economic, market, political and general news concerning Albania; Editor-in-Chief GJERGJ EREBARA.

Albanian Journal of Natural and Technical Sciences (AJNTS): Akademia e Shkencave e Shqipërisë, Sheshi Fan S. Noli 7, Tirana;

ALBANIA

tel. (4) 259657; fax (4) 227476; e-mail sbushati@akad.edu.al; two a year; published by the Academy of Sciences of Albania Publishing House; in English; all fields of natural and technical sciences; Editor-in-Chief Prof. Dr SALVATORE BUSHATI.

Albanian Observer: Rruga Perlat Rexhepi Pall. 9, Shkurtit 1/4, Tirana; tel. and fax (4) 227419; e-mail albatimes@aol.com; monthly; in English; business and economics; Editor-in-Chief TEODOR MISHA.

ARS (Revista Letrare Shqiptare—Albanian Literary Review): e-mail ars@arsalbania.com; f. 2002; monthly; Albanian and English; literature and literary criticism; Editor-in-Chief IRHAN JUBICA.

Atdheu (Fatherland): Tirana; e-mail levizja_legalitetit@yahoo.com; internet gazeta-atdheu.tripod.com; organ of the Legality Movement; Editor-in-Chief ASTRIT KOLA.

Bujqesia Shqiptare (Albanian Agriculture): Ministria e Bujqësisë, Ushqimit dhe Mbrojtjes së Konsumatorit, Sheshi Skënderbej 2, Tirana; tel. (4) 232796; fax (4) 227924; e-mail gjana@hotmail.com; monthly; organ of the Ministry of Agriculture, Food and Consumer Protection; agriculture, cattle-breeding and gardening.

Demokracia (Democracy): Bulevardi B. Curri 32, Tirana; tel. and fax (4) 275260; weekly; organ of the Union for Human Rights Party; primarily concerned with rights of minority ethnic groups.

Drita (The Light): Rruga Konferenca e Pezës 4, Tirana; tel. (4) 230212; fax (4) 230203; f. 1960; weekly; publ. by Union of Writers and Artists of Albania (Lidhja e Shkrimtarëve dhe Artistë); Editor-in-Chief BRISEIDA MEMA; circ. 31,000.

Drita Islame (Light of Islam): Tirana; e-mail gazeta@dritaislame.com; every two weeks; organ of the Albanian Islamic Community.

Femra Moderne (Modern Woman): Sheshi Avni Rustemi 12, mbrapa Shkolles Pedagogjike, 2nd Floor; e-mail femramoderne@abissnet.com.al; every two weeks; women's interest.

Gazeta Ballkan: Rruga Durrësit 61, Tirana; tel. and fax (4) 229954; internet www.ballkan.com; Editor-in-Chief ZAMIR ALUSHI.

Gjuha Jonë (Our Language): Akademia e Shkencave e Shqipërisë, Sheshi Fan Noli 7, Tirana; tel. (4) 256777; fax (4) 227476; e-mail encikloped@yahoo.com; f. 1981; quarterly; published by the Institute of Linguistics and Literature, Academy of Sciences of Albania Publishing House; Albanian language matters for the non-specialist; Editor-in-Chief Prof. Dr EMIL LAFE.

Identity (Identitet): L. Qemal Stafa, Rruga Daut Boriçi 874, Shkodër; tel. and fax (22) 41229; e-mail irsh@albnet.net; f. 1999; organ of Intelektualet e Rinj Shprese (Young Intellectuals, Hope), the principal aim of which is the development of Albanian civil society; English summary; Editor-in-Chief BLENDI DIBRA.

Iliria: Instituti i Arkeologjisë, Sheshi Nënë Tereza, Tirana; tel. and fax (4) 240712; e-mail instark@albmail.com; f. 1971; twice a year; published by the Archaeological Institute, Academy of Sciences of Albania Publishing House; concerned with archaeology studies in the fields of prehistory, antiquity and the early Middle Ages; in English and French, or in Albanian with English or French summaries; Editor-in-Chief Prof. Dr MUZAFER KORKUTI.

Intervista (The Interview): Rruga e Dibres 133, Tirana; tel. (4) 233164; independent; weekly; interviews with, and information on, leading Albanian and international figures.

Jeta (Life): Bulevardi Gjergj Fishta, pranë isch exsposites Shqiperia Sot, Tirana; tel. (4) 270913; fax (4) 270914; e-mail revistajeta@albaniaonline.net; internet www.revistajeta.com; f. 2000; monthly; general interest; illustrated; Gen. Dir ESMERALDA TONI.

Klan: Rruga Dervish Hima 1, Tirana; tel. (4) 256111; fax (4) 234424; e-mail redaksia@revistaklan.com; internet www.revistaklan.com; f. 1997.

Kultura Popullore (Folk Culture Magazine): Instituti i Kultures Popullore, Rruga Kont Urani 3, Tirana; tel. (4) 222323; e-mail ikp.alb@icc.al.org; f. 1980; annually; published by the Institute of Folk Culture, Academy of Sciences of Albania Publishing House; folk culture, anthropology; English summary; Editor-in-Chief Prof. Dr AFËRDITA ONUZI.

Mbrojtja (The Defence): Bulevardi Dëshmorët e Kombit, Tirana; tel. and fax (4) 225726; e-mail tanct@al.pims.org; internet www.mod.gov.al/botime/html/revista/revista.htm; f. 1931; monthly; publ. by the Ministry of Defence; Editor-in-Chief Prof. Dr ELMAZ LECI; circ. 1,500.

Mesuesi (The Teacher): Rruga Durrësit, pranë Ministrise se Arsimit dhe Shkences, Tirana; tel. (4) 227206; weekly; organ of the Ministry of Education and Science.

Ngjallja (The Resurrection): Kisha Orthodhokse Autoqefale e Shqipërisë, Rruga e Kavajes 151, Tirana; monthly; organ of the Orthodox Autocephalous Church of Albania.

Official Gazette of the Republic of Albania (Fletore Zyrtare): Kuvendi Popullor, Tirana; tel. (4) 228668; fax (4) 227949; f. 1945; occasional government review.

Pasqyra (The Mirror): Bulevardi Zogu I, Pall. A. Kelmendi, Tirana; tel. (4) 222956; fax (4) 229169; e-mail marketingu@pasqyra.com;

f. 1991; to replace *Puna* (Labour); f. 1945; weekly; organ of the left-wing Confederation of Albanian Trade Unions; Editor-in-Chief XHAFER SHATRI.

Përpjekja (Endeavour): Tirana; e-mail flubonja@hotmail.com; internet perpjekja.net; quarterly; culture and society; Editor-in-Chief FATOS LUBONJA.

Revista Pedagogjike: Rruga Naim Frashëri 37, Tirana; tel. (4) 223860; fax (4) 223860; f. 1945; quarterly; organ of the Institute i Studimeve Pedagogjike (Institute of Pedagogical Studies); educational development, psychology, didactic; Editor BUJAR BASHA; circ. 4,000.

Shëndeti (Health): M. Duri 2, Tirana; tel. (4) 227803; fax (4) 227803; f. 1949; monthly; publ. by the National Directorate of Health Education; issues of health and welfare, personal health care; Editors-in-Chief KORNELIA GJATA, AGIM XHUMARI.

Sindikalisti (Trade Unionist): Tirana; f. 1991; newspaper; organ of the right-wing Union of Independent Trade Unions of Albania; Editor-in-Chief VANGJEL KOZMAI.

Spektër: Rruga Aleksander Moisiu 76, ish-Kinostudio, Tirana; tel. and fax (4) 375511; e-mail revista_spekter@yahoo.com; internet www.spekter.com.al; f. 1991; every two weeks; general interest, illustrated; Editor-in-Chief BORA KOKEDHIMA.

Studia Albanica: Rruga Naim Frashëri 7, Tirana; tel. (4) 227476; fax (4) 227476; published by Academy of Sciences of Albania Publishing House; twice a year; history.

Studime Filologjike (Philological Studies): Instituti i Gjuhesisë dhe i Letersisë, Rruga Naim Frashëri 7, Tirana; tel. and fax (4) 235134; e-mail jbulo@albmail.com; f. 1964; quarterly; published by the Institute of Linguistics and Literature, Academy of Sciences of Albania Publishing House; philology, linguistics; English and French summaries; Editor-in-Chief Prof. JORGO BULO.

Studime Historike (Historical Studies): Instituti i Historisë, Rruga Naim Frashëri 7, Tirana; tel. and fax (4) 225869; e-mail alalaj@albmail.com; quarterly; published by the Institute of History, Academy of Sciences of Albania Publishing House; history; English and French summaries; f. 1964; Editor-in-Chief Prof. Dr ANA LALAJ.

Studime per Artin (Art Studies): Centre for Art Studies, Rruga Don Bosko 60, Tirana; tel. (4) 259667; fax (4) 228274; e-mail betim@sizmo.albnet.net; annually; published by the Centre for Art Studies, Academy of Sciences of Albania Publishing House; art, music, theatre, film.

Tirana Times: Rruga Dëshmorët e 4 Shkurtit 7/1, Tirana; tel. (4) 274203; fax (4) 270337; e-mail editor@tiranatimes.com; internet www.tiranatimes.com; f. 2005; weekly (hard copy), daily (online); in English; news, analysis, politics, business, culture; Dir and Managing Editor JERINA ŽALOSHNJA.

Universi i Librit Shqiptar (Universe of the Albanian Book): Rruga Muhamet Gjollesha, POB 1420; tel. (4) 240116; quarterly review of books published in Albanian and of foreign-language books about Albania, Albanian affairs, etc.

Ushtria (Army): Bulevardi Dëshmorët e Kombit, Tirana; tel. (4) 226701; e-mail kontakt@mod.gov.al; internet www.mod.gov.al/botime/html/ushtria/ushtria.htm; f. 1945; weekly; publ. by the Ministry of Defence; Editor-in-Chief BARDHYL GOSTNISHTI; circ. 3,200.

NEWS AGENCIES

Albanian Independent News Agency (AINA) (Agjensia e Lajmeve të Pavarura Shqiptare): Rruga 4 Dëshmorët Vila 80, Tirana; tel. (4) 241727; fax (4) 230094; e-mail aina@abissnet.com.al; f. 1996; Albanian and English; Dir ZENEL ÇELIKU.

Albanian Telegraphic Agency (ATA) (Agjencia Telegrafike Shqiptare—ATSh): Bulevardi Zhan D'Ark 23, Tirana; tel. (4) 235584; fax (4) 234230; e-mail atsh@albnet.net; internet www.ata-al.net; f. 1929; state-owned; domestic and foreign news; brs in provincial towns and in Kosovo; Dir-Gen. FRROK CUPI.

Alna (Albanian News Agency—Agjensi Private e pavarur Lajmesh në Shqiperi): Rruga Ismail Qemali, Tirana; tel. (4) 257001; fax (4) 256002; f. 2001.

PRESS ASSOCIATIONS

Albanian Media Institute: Rruga Gjin Bue Shpata 8, Tirana; tel. and fax (4) 229800; e-mail info@institutemedia.org; internet www.institutemedia.org; f. 1995; independent; produces books and publications on the Albanian and international media, incl. the *Albanian Media Newsletter* (monthly); Dir REMZI LANI.

Asscn of Professional Journalists of Albania: Rruga Dervish Hima 1, Tirana; tel. (4) 251923; fax (4) 251926; e-mail ashkullaku@hotmail.com; affiliated to International Federation of Journalists (Brussels, Belgium); Pres. ARMAND SHKULLAKU.

League of Albanian Journalists: Bulevardi Dëshmorët e Kombit, Tirana; tel. and fax (4) 228563; e-mail albania@albaniaonline.net;

ALBANIA — *Directory*

affiliated to International Federation of Journalists (Brussels, Belgium); Pres. YLLI RAKIPI.

Publishers

Academy of Sciences of Albania Publishing House (SHKENCA—Botime të Akademisë së Shkencave të RSH): Sheshi Fan S. Noli 7, Tirana; tel. (4) 250369; fax (4) 227476; publs include *Kultura Popullore*, *Studia Albanica*, *Studime Filologjike*, *Studime per Artin* and *Studime Historike*; Contact TATJANA NAÇI.

Agjensia Qëndrore e Tregtimit të Librit Artistik dhe Shkencor (AQTLASH—Central Agency of the Artistic and Scientific Book Trade): Rruga e Kavajës 42, Tirana; tel. and fax (4) 227246; Dir HAMIT ALIAJ.

Dituria: Rruga Frederik Shiroka 31, POB 1441, Tirana; tel. and fax (4) 251344; e-mail dituria@icc-al.org; f. 1991; dictionaries, calendars, encyclopedias, social sciences, biographies, fiction and non-fiction; Gen. Dir PETRIT YMERI.

Drejtoria e Informacionit Agro-Ushqimor (Agriculture and Food Information Directory): Rruga S. Kosturi, Tirana; tel. (4) 226147; f. 1970; publishes various agricultural periodicals; Gen. Dir Prof. AGO NEZHA.

Dudaj: Rruga Brigada VIII, pallati i Teknoprojektit, shk. 1/2/6, Tirana; tel. and fax (4) 249944; e-mail arlinda.h.dudaj@botimedudaj.com; internet www.botimedudaj.com; fiction and non-fiction; Dir ARLINDA HOVI DUDAJ.

Fan Noli: Rruga Bulev Shekip. Ere, Tirana; tel. (4) 242739; f. 1991; Albanian and foreign literature; Dir AGIM BYCI.

Neraida: Rruga Myslym Shyri 54/4/1, Tirana; tel. (4) 243310; fax (4) 262312; e-mail neraida@albaniaonline.net; fiction and non-fiction; f. 1995; Dir JANI MALO.

Ombra: Bulevardi Gjergj Fishta, Kompleksi Tirana 2000 4/2, Tirana; tel. (4) 224173; fax (4) 224986; e-mail ombragvg@albmail.com; f. 1998; Pres. GËZIM TAFA.

Omsca: Rruga Frederik Shiroka, Tirana; tel. and fax (4) 360793; e-mail omsca@abissnet.com.al; fiction; Dir LUAN PENGILI.

Onufri: Rruga Sulejman Pasha, Tirana; tel. (4) 220017; fax (4) 270399; e-mail info@onufri.com; internet www.onufri.com; literary; Dir BUJAR HUDHRI.

Shtëpia Botuese e Librit Shkollor: Tirana; tel. (4) 222331; f. 1967; educational books; Dir SHPËTIM BOZDO.

Shtëpia Botuese Naim Frashëri: Tirana; tel. (4) 227906; f. 1947; fiction, poetry, drama, criticism, children's literature, translations; Dir GAQO BUSHAKA.

Skanderbeg Books: Rruga H. H. Dalliu, Pallat Binjakët, Tirana; tel. and fax (4) 230721; e-mail fluturacka@abissnet.com.al; internet www.albliterature.com; literary fiction and non-fiction in translation; Dir FLUTURA AÇKA.

Toena: Rruga Muhamet Gjollesha, POB 1420, Tirana; tel. (4) 240116; fax (4) 227232; e-mail toena@icc.al.eu.org; history, social sciences, humanities, fiction, linguistics; Dir FATMIR TOCI.

Uegen: Rruga Ismail Qemali 30/1/4; tel. (4) 271150; fax (4) 233596; e-mail uegen@albnet.net; f. 1992; fiction, history, psychology, philosophy, etc.; Dir XHEVAIR LLESHI.

PUBLISHERS' ASSOCIATION

Albanian Publishers' Asscn: Rruga Dervish Hima 32, Tirana; tel. (4) 240116; fax (4) 240117; e-mail toena@icc.al.org; f. 1992; Pres. PETRIT YMERI.

Broadcasting and Communications

TELECOMMUNICATIONS

Albanian Mobile Communications (AMC): Rruga Gjergi Legisi, Laprakë, Tirana; tel. (4) 275000; fax (4) 235157; e-mail contact_us@amc.al; internet www.amc.al; f. 1996; fmrly state-owned, bought by a Greek-Norwegian consortium in 2000; operates mobile-telephone network; Man. Dir STEFANOS OKTAPODAS.

Albtelecom: Rruga Myslym Shyri 42, Tirana; tel. (4) 232169; fax (4) 233323; e-mail infocenter@atnet.com.al; internet www.atnet.com.al; 80% stake owned by consortium of Turk Telekom and Calik Enerji (both of Turkey); Chief Exec. ILIRIAN KUKA.

Vodafone Albania: Zayed Business Centre, Rruga Sulejman Delvina, POB 268/1, Tirana; tel. (4) 283072; fax (4) 283333; e-mail info.al@vodafone.com; internet www.vodafone.al; f. 2001; mobile cellular telecommunications; Gen. Dir THOMAS PAPASPYROU.

BROADCASTING

In 1991 state broadcasting was removed from political control and made subordinate to the Parliamentary Commission for the Media. By the end of 2000 the National Council of Radio and Television had licensed two national television stations, 45 local television stations, one national radio station and 31 local radio stations.

Regulatory Authority

National Council of Radio and Television (NCRT) (Këshilli Kombëtar i Radios dhe Televizionit—KKRT): Rruga Abdi Toptani, Ish Hotel Drini, Tirana; tel. (4) 226133; e-mail m.doda@kkrt.gov.al; internet www.kkrt.gov.al; f. 1999; Chair. MESILA DODA.

Radio

Radio Televizioni Shqiptar: Rruga Ismail Qemali 11, Tirana; tel. and fax (4) 222481; e-mail dushiulp@yahoo.com; internet rtsh.sil.at; f. 1938 as Radio Tirana; two channels of domestic services (19 and five hours daily) and a third channel covering international broadcasting (two services in Albanian and seven in foreign languages); several local channels; 65% state-funded; 35% funded through commercial advertising and fees; Chair. KASTRIST CAUSBI; Dir-Gen. EDUARD MAZI; Dir of Radio MARTIN LEKA.

Radio Klan: Rruga Myslim Shyri 8/1, Tirana; tel. (4) 240304; e-mail klan@albnet.net.

Top Albania Radio: Qendra Ndërkombëtare e Kulturës, Bulevardi Dëshmorët e Kombit, Tirana; tel. (4) 247492; fax (4) 247299; e-mail topalbaniaradio@albaniaonline.net; internet www.topalbaniaradio.com; Dir ENKELEJD JOTI.

Television

Radio Televizioni Shqiptar: Rruga Ismail Qemali 11, Tirana; tel. (4) 256056; fax (4) 256058; e-mail dushiulp@yahoo.com; internet rtsh.sil.at; f. 1960; broadcasts range of television programmes; 65% state–funded; 35% funded through commercial advertising and fees; Chair. KASTRIST CAUSBI; Dir-Gen. EDUARD MAZI; Dir of Television VENA ISAK.

Albanian Satellite Television (ALSAT TV): Rruga Siri Kodra, Tirana; tel. and fax (4) 271738; e-mail info@alsat.tv; internet www.alsat.tv; news satellite broadcasting in Albanian; from mid-2003 programmes also broadcast by local TV stations in Albania, the former Yugoslav republic of Macedonia and Kosovo.

Shijak TV: Rruga Kavajes, Sheshi Ataturk, Tirana; tel. and fax (4) 247135; e-mail shijaktv01@albaniaonline.net; internet www.shijaktv.com; Pres. GËZIM ISMAILI.

Top Channel TV: Qendra Ndërkombëtare e Kulturës, Bulevardi Dëshmorët e Kombit, Tirana; tel. (4) 253177; fax (4) 253178; e-mail info@top-channel.tv; internet www.top-channel.tv; Dir ENKELEJD JOTI.

TV Arberia: Pallati i Kultures, Kati III, Tirana; tel. (4) 243932; fax (4) 8301466; e-mail informacioni@telearberia.tv; internet www.telearberia.tv; Dir ESTELA DASHI.

TV Klan: Rruga Aleksander Moisiu 97, Ish-Kinostudio, Tirana; tel. (4) 347805; fax (4) 347808; e-mail info@tvklan.com; internet www.tvklan.com; Dir-Gen. ALEKSANDER FRANGAJ.

Finance

(cap. = capital; dep. = deposits; res = reserves; m. = million; brs = branches; amounts in lekë, unless otherwise stated)

BANKING

The Savings Bank of Albania, which accounted for more than 50% of activity in the banking sector, was sold to Raiffeisen Bank (of Austria) at the beginning of 2004. By November 2005, when the privatization of the financial sector had been largely completed, there were 16 commercial banks operating in the country, 14 of which were foreign-owned.

Central Bank

Bank of Albania (Banka e Shqipërisë): Sheshi Skënderbej 1, Tirana; tel. (4) 222152; fax (4) 223558; internet www.bankofalbania.org; f. 1992; cap. 750.0m., res −740.0m., dep. 70,951.0m. (Dec. 2006); Gov. ARDIAN FULLANI; 5 brs.

Other Banks

American Bank of Albania (Banka Amerikanë e Shqipërisë): Rruga Ismail Qemali 27, POB 8319, Tirana; tel. (4) 276000; fax (4) 248762; e-mail americanbank@ambankalb.com; internet www.albambank.com; f. 1998; owned by Albanian-American Enterprise Fund USA; cap. US $36.2m., res $7.5m., dep. $830.2m. (2007); Chair. MICHAEL GRANOFF; Pres. and CEO LORENZO RONCARI.

ALBANIA

Banka Credins: Rruga Ismail Qemali 21, Tirana; tel. (4) 234096; fax (4) 222916; e-mail info@bankacredins.com; internet www.bankacredins.com; f. 2003; cap. 1,369.4m., res −156.7m., dep. 24,633.5m. (Dec. 2006); Pres. ALEKSANDER PILO; Chair. ILIRJAN BUSHATI.

Banka Popullore: Bulevardi Dëshmorët e Kombit, Twin Towers, Tower 1, 9th Floor, Tirana; tel. (4) 280300; fax (4) 280441; e-mail info@bpopullore.com; internet www.bpopullore.com; f. 2004; 75% owned by Société Générale; cap. 1,474.0m., res −48.9m., dep. 26,858.9m. (Dec. 2006); Chair. EDVIN LIBOHOVA.

Emporiki Bank-Albania: Tirana Tower, Rruga e Kavajes 59, Tirana; tel. (4) 258755; fax (4) 258752; e-mail headoffice@emporiki.com.al; f. 1999 as Intercommercial Bank; name changed as above 2004; owned by Emporiki Bank of Greece; cap. €10.3m., res €0.2m., dep. €83.3m. (Dec. 2006); Chair. LEONIDAS ZONNIOS; CEO GEORGE CARACOSTAS.

Italian-Albanian Bank (Banka Italo Shqiptare/Banco Italo Albanese): Rruga e Barrikadave, Tirana; tel. (4) 235693; fax (4) 235700; e-mail biatia@adanet.com.al; internet www.bia.com.al; f. 1993; 40% state-owned; cap. US $15.5m., res $1.0m., dep. $160.7m. (Dec. 2005); Chair. GIUSEPPE CUCCURESE.

National Commercial Bank of Albania (Banka Kombëtare Tregtare ShA): Bulevardi Zhan D'Ark, Tirana; tel. (4) 250955; fax (4) 250956; e-mail bkt@bkt.com.al; internet www.bkt.com.al; f. 1993 by merger; privatized in 2000; cap. US $33.0m., res $0.6m., dep. $807.1m. (Dec. 2006); Chair. HALUK USULOY; 32 brs.

ProCredit Bank (Albania) (Banka ProCredit): Rruga Sami Frasheri, POB 2395, Tirana; tel. (4) 271272; fax (4) 271276; e-mail info@procreditbank.com.al; internet www.procreditbank.com.al; f. 1996 as Foundation for Enterprise Finance and Development; name changed to Fedad Bank ShA in 1999, and as above in 2003; cap. 1,535.3m., res 219.5m., dep. 24,033.2m. (Dec. 2006); Chair. C. P. ZEITINGER; CEO FRIEDER WÖHRMANN; 9 brs.

Raiffeisen Bank: Rruga e Kavajes 12, Tirana; tel. (4) 224540; fax (4) 230013; e-mail info@raiffeisen.al; internet www.raiffeisen.al; f. 1991 as Savings Bank of Albania; acquired by Raiffeisen Zentralbank Österreich AG (Austria) in Jan. 2004; cap. 4,348.2m., res 782.4m., dep. 208,924.8m. (Dec. 2006); CEO and Chair. STEVEN GRUNERUD; 37 brs.

Tirana Bank: Rruga Dëshmorët 4 Shkurtit, POB 2400/1, Tirana; tel. (4) 277700; fax (4) 263022; e-mail managingdirector@tiranabank.net; internet www.tiranabank.al; f. 1996; cap. 2,360.5m., res 543.8m., dep. 46,085.6m. (Dec. 2006); Chair. MIHALIS KOLAKIDIS.

United Bank of Albania: Rruga Dëshmorët e Kombit 8, POB 128, Tirana; tel. (4) 227408; fax (4) 233030; e-mail uba@albaniaonline.net; f. 1994; 40% state-owned; cap. US $12.5m., res $0.6m., dep. $26.1m. (Dec. 2006); fmrly Arab-Albanian Islamic Bank, present name adopted 2003; Chair. Sheikh SOLAIMAN ELKHEREIJI; Gen. Man. Dr A. WAHEED ALAVI; 3 brs.

STOCK EXCHANGE

Tirana Stock Exchange (Bursa e Tiranes): Rruga Dora D'Istria, Kutia Postare 274/1, Tirana; tel. and fax (4) 265058; e-mail tseinfo@abcom-al.com; internet www.tse.com.al; f. 1996; Gen. Dir ANILA FURERAJ.

INSURANCE

Agjensia Shqiptare e Garancisë (ASHG): Rruga Ismail Qemali Pall 34/1/2, Tirana; tel. (4) 247048; fax (4) 247047; e-mail aga@aga-al.com.

Atlantik: Rruga Themistokli Gërmenji 3/1, Tirana; tel. (4) 230506; fax (4) 235071; e-mail info@atlantik.com.al; internet www.atlantik.com.al; Gen. Dir DRITAN ÇELAJ.

Health Insurance Institute (Instituti i Sigurimeve të Kujdesit Shëndetsor): Rruga Sami Frashëri 8; tel. (4) 232844; e-mail fhopdari@yahoo.com; internet www.isksh.com.al; Dir ELVANA HANA.

Insurance Institute of Albania (INSIG) (Instituti i Sigurimeve të Shqipërisë): Rruga e Dibrës 91, Tirana; tel. (4) 270667; fax (4) 223838; e-mail info@insig.com.al; internet www.insig.com.al; f. 1991; 61% owned by Albanian Govt; European Bank for Reconstruction and Development (United Kingdom) and the International Finance Corpn each acquired 19.5% stake in 2004; all types of insurance; Gen. Dir SAIMIR ZEMBLAKU; 12 brs.

INTERSIG: Rruga Ali Demi; tel. and fax (4) 344718; e-mail intersig@albaniaonline.net; Gen. Dir VANGJEL BIRBO.

Sigal: Bulevardi i Zogu I 1, Tirana; tel. (4) 250220; fax (4) 233308; e-mail info@sigal.com.al; internet www.sigal.com.al; f. 1999; property, engineering, motor, marine, aviation, liability, accidents, banking, agriculture, credit, surety; Gen. Dir AVNI PONARI; 12 brs, 260 agencies (2005).

SIGMA: Rruga Migësia, Sheshi Wilson, POB 1714, Tirana; tel. (4) 258254; fax (4) 258253; Gen. Dir QEMAL DISHA.

INSURERS' ASSOCIATION

Association of Albanian Insurers (Shoqata e Siguruesve të Shqipërisë): Rruga Punëtoret e Rilindjes, Kulla I–14 katëshe 141, Tirana; tel. and fax (4) 221403; e-mail info@insurers-al.org; internet www.insurers-al.org; f. 2003; Gen. Sec. VALBONA KADUKU; Chair. AVNI PONARI.

Trade and Industry
PRIVATIZATION AGENCY

National Agency for Privatization (NAP) (Agjencia Kombetare e Privatizimit): Bulevardi Dëshmorët e Kombit, Tirana; tel. (4) 257457; fax (4) 227933; govt agency under the control of the Council of Ministers; prepares and proposes the legal framework concerning privatization procedures and implementation; Gen. Dir KOZETA FINO.

SUPERVISORY ORGANIZATIONS

Albkontroll: Rruga Skënderbej 45, Durrës; tel. (52) 23377; fax (52) 22791; f. 1962; brs throughout Albania; independent control body for inspection of goods for import and export, means of transport, etc.; Gen. Man. DILAVER MEZINI; 15 brs.

State Supreme Audit Control (Kontrolli I Larte I Shtetit): Bulevardi Dëshmorët e Kombit 3, Tirana; tel. and fax (4) 232491; e-mail klsh@klsh.org.al; internet www.klsh.org.al; Pres. ROBERT CEKU.

DEVELOPMENT ORGANIZATIONS

Albanian Centre for Foreign Investment Promotion (ANIH): Bulevardi Gjergj Fishta, Pallatat Shallvare, Tirana; tel. (4) 252976; fax (4) 222341; Exec. Dir ESTELA DASHI.

Albanian Development Fund (Fondi Shqiptar i Zhvillimit): Rruga Sami Frashëri 10, Tirana; tel. (4) 235597; fax (4) 234885; e-mail adf@albaniandf.org; internet www.a-d-f.org; Exec. Dir BENET BECI.

Albanian Economy Development Agency (AEDA): Bulevardi Zhan D'Ark, Tirana; tel. (4) 230133; fax (4) 228439; e-mail xhepa@cpfi.tirana.al; f. 1993; govt agency to promote foreign investment in Albania and to provide practical support to foreign investors; publishes *Ekonomia*; Chair. SELAMI XHEPA.

CHAMBERS OF COMMERCE

Union of Chambers of Commerce and Industry of Albania (Bashkimi i Dhomave të Tregtisë dhe Industrisë të Shqipërisë): Rruga Kavajes 6, Tirana; tel. and fax (4) 222934; f. 1958; Chair. ILIR ZHILLA.

Durrës Chamber of Commerce and Industry: Durrës; tel. (52) 22199; e-mail info@ccidr.tirana.al; f. 1988; Chair. ANDREA XHAVARA.

Elbasan Chamber of Commerce and Industry: Elbasan; tel. (54) 55490; e-mail cciel@albmail.com; Chair. VELI KAZAZI.

Shkodër Chamber of Commerce and Industry: Shkodër; tel. (224) 2460; fax (224) 3656; e-mail ccish@abissnet.com.al; Chair. ANTON LEKA.

Tirana Chamber of Commerce and Industry (Dhoma E Tregtise Dhe Industrise Tirane): Rruga Kavajes 6, Tirana; tel. (4) 232448; fax (4) 229779; e-mail ccitr@abissnet.com.al; internet www.cci.gov.al; f. 1926; Chair. GJOKË ULDEDAJ.

Vlorë Chamber of Commerce and Industry: Vlorë; tel. (33) 25737; e-mail ccivlore@gmail.com; Chair. EDMOND LEKA.

There are also chambers of commerce in Berat, Diber, Fier, Gjirokastër, Korçë, Kukës and Lezhë.

UTILITIES
Electricity

State Electricity Corporation of Albania (KESh) (Korporata Elektroenergjetikë Shqiptarë): Biloky Vasil Shanto, Tirana; tel. (4) 228434; fax (4) 232046; e-mail email@kesh.com.al; internet www.kesh.com.al; state corpn for the generation, transmission, distribution and export of electrical energy; govt-controlled; scheduled for transfer to private ownership; Gen. Dir (vacant).

TRADE UNIONS

During 1991 independent trade unions were established. The most important of these was the Union of Independent Trade Unions of Albania. Other unions were established for workers in various sectors of the economy.

Confederation of Albanian Trade Unions (Konfederata e Sindikatave të Shqipërisë—KSSh): Bulevardi Zogu I, Pall. A. Kelmendi, Tirana; tel. (4) 229169; fax (4) 222956; e-mail kssh@icc-al.org; internet www.konfederatasindikale.org; f. 1991; includes 12 trade

ALBANIA

union federations representing workers in different sectors of the economy; Chair. KOL NIKOLLAJ; 105,000 mems (2007).

Union of Independent Trade Unions of Albania (Bashkimi i Sindikatave të Pavarura të Shqipërisë—BSPSh): Tirana; f. 1991; Chair. (vacant).

Agricultural Trade Union Federation (Federata Sindikale e Bujqesise): Tirana; f. 1991; Leaders ALFRED GJOMO, NAZMI QOKU.

Free and Independent Miners' Union (Sindikata e Lire dhe e Pavarur e Minatoreve): Tirana; f. 1991; Chair. GEZIM KALAJA.

Trade Union Federation of Employees and Pensioners of Albania: Bulevardi Dëshmorët e Kombit, Tirana; tel. (4) 229169; Chair. PETRAQ TAPIA.

Transport

RAILWAYS

In 2004 there were 428 km of railway track in Albania.

Albanian Railways (Hekurudha Shqiptare): Rruga Skënderbej, Durrës; tel. and fax (52) 22037; CEO SOKOL KAPIDANI.

ROADS

In 2002 the road network comprised an estimated 18,000 km of classified roads, including 3,220 km of main roads and 4,300 km of secondary roads; 39% of the total network was paved. In December 2002 a 23.5-km road linking Greece with southern Albania was opened. In 2003 the Albanian Government secured financing from the World Bank, the European Investment Bank and the European Bank for Reconstruction and Development for a number of road-maintenance projects. As part of the European Union's Transport Corridor Europe–Central Asia (TRACECA) programme, the construction of a west–east highway (Corridor VIII) from the port of Durrës to the Black Sea, via the former Yugoslav republic of Macedonia and Bulgaria, has been undertaken. Corridor X, another TRACECA project, runs north–south from Hani i Hotit, at the border with Montenegro, to Tri Urat on the Greek frontier. A highway linking Tirana and Vlorë was completed in 2006.

SHIPPING

At December 2005 Albania's merchant fleet had 77 vessels, with a total displacement of 74,800 grt. The chief ports are those in Durrës, Vlorë, Sarandë and Shëngjin. Ferry services have been established between Durrës and three Italian ports (Trieste, Bari and Ancona) and between Sarandë and the Greek island of Corfu. Services also connect Vlorë with the Italian ports of Bari and Brindisi. The World Bank, the European Union and the Organization of the Petroleum Exporting Countries Fund For International Development have financed projects to improve existing port facilities.

Adetare Shipping Agency: Rruga Taulantia, Durrës; tel. (52) 23883; fax (52) 23666; e-mail adeag@albmail.com; f. 1991.

Albanian State Shipping Enterprise: Durrës; tel. (52) 22233; fax (52) 229111.

Durrës Port Authority: Lagija 1, Rruga Tregtare, Durrës; tel. (52) 23115; fax (52) 23427; e-mail apd@apdurres.com.al; internet www.apdurres.com.al; state-owned; Gen. Dir EDUARD NDREU.

CIVIL AVIATION

There is a small international airport at Rinas, 25 km from Tirana. Reconstruction of the airport was undertaken in the late 1990s, and it was privatized in April 2005. A civil and military airport was constructed at Pish Poro, 29 km from Vlorë, under an agreement between Albania and Italy. The construction of a second international airport (Zayed International Airport) at the north-eastern town of Kukës, with funding from the Government of the United Arab Emirates, was completed in November 2005.

General Directorate of Civil Aviation: Rruga e Kavajes, Perballe Xhamise, POB 205, Tirana; tel. and fax (4) 223969; e-mail dpac2@albanet.net; CEO AGRON DIBRA.

Ada Air: Rruga Kemal Stafa 262, Tirana; tel. (4) 256111; fax (4) 226245; e-mail contact@adaair.com; internet www.adaair.com; f. 1991; operates passenger and cargo flights to Greece, Italy, Serbia, Montenegro and Switzerland; Pres. MARSEL SKENDO; Gen. Dir ILIR ZEKA.

Albanian Airlines: Rruga Deshmoret e 4 Shkurtit 2, Tirana; tel. (4) 235162; fax (4) 235138; e-mail ticketing@albanianair.com; internet www.albanianairlines.com.al; f. 1992; acquired in 1995 by Aviation World Mak (Kuwait), and assumed present name; scheduled services to Germany, Italy and Turkey; Pres. FIKRY ABDUL WAHHAB; Man. Dir ASHRAF HASHEM.

Tourism

In 2005 there were some 747,837 international tourist arrivals. In that year receipts from tourism totalled US $880m., compared with $537m. in 2003. The main tourist centres include Tirana, Durrës, Sarandë, Shkodër and Pogradec. The Roman amphitheatre at Durrës is one of the largest in Europe. The ancient towns of Apollonia and Butrint are important archaeological sites, and there are many other towns of historic interest. However, expansion of the tourist industry has been limited by the inadequacy of Albania's infrastructure and a lack of foreign investment in the development of new facilities.

Albturist: Bulevardi Dëshmorët e Kombit 8, Hotel Dhajti, Tirana; tel. and fax (4) 251849; e-mail albturist.t.a.@albnet.net; brs in main towns and all tourist centres; 28 hotels throughout the country; Dir-Gen. BESNIK PELLUMBI.

Committee for Development and Tourism: Bulevardi Dëshmorët e Kombit 8, Tirana; tel. (4) 258323; fax (4) 258322; e-mail arskenderi@albaniaonline.com; govt body.

ALGERIA

Introductory Survey

Location, Climate, Language, Religion, Flag, Capital

The Democratic and People's Republic of Algeria lies in north Africa, with the Mediterranean Sea to the north, Mali and Niger to the south, Tunisia and Libya to the east, and Morocco and Mauritania to the west. The climate on the Mediterranean coast is temperate, becoming more extreme in the Atlas mountains immediately to the south. Further south is part of the Sahara, a hot and arid desert. Temperatures in Algiers, on the coast, are generally between 9°C (48°F) and 29°C (84°F), while in the interior they may exceed 50°C (122°F). Arabic is the official language, but French is widely used. Tamazight, the principal language of Algeria's Berber community, was granted 'national' status in 2002. Islam is the state religion, and almost all Algerians are Muslims. The national flag (proportions 2 by 3) has two equal vertical stripes, of green and white, with a red crescent moon and a five-pointed red star superimposed in the centre. The capital is Algiers (el-Djezaïr).

Recent History

Algeria was conquered by French forces in the 1830s and annexed by France in 1842. The territory was colonized with French settlers, and many French citizens became permanent residents. Unlike most of France's overseas possessions, Algeria was not formally a colony but was 'attached' to metropolitan France. However, the indigenous Muslim majority were denied equal rights, and political and economic power within Algeria was largely held by the settler minority.

On 1 November 1954 the principal Algerian nationalist movement, the Front de libération nationale (FLN), began a war for national independence, in the course of which about 1m. Muslims were killed or wounded. The French Government agreed to a cease-fire in March 1962, and independence was declared on 3 July 1962. In August the Algerian provisional Government transferred its functions to the Political Bureau of the FLN, and in September a National Constituent Assembly was elected (from a single list of FLN candidates) and a Republic proclaimed. A new Government was formed, with Ahmed Ben Bella, founder of the FLN, as Prime Minister.

A draft Constitution, providing for a presidential regime with the FLN as the sole party, was adopted in August 1963, and approved by popular referendum in September. Ben Bella was elected President, although real power remained with the bureaucracy and the army. In June 1965 the Minister of Defence, Col Houari Boumedienne, deposed Ben Bella in a bloodless coup and took control of the country as President of a Council of the Revolution, composed chiefly of army officers.

In 1975 Boumedienne announced a series of measures to consolidate the regime and enhance his personal power, including the drafting of a National Charter and a new Constitution, and the holding of elections for a President and National People's Assembly. The National Charter, which enshrined both the creation of a socialist system and the maintenance of Islam as the state religion, and a new Constitution (incorporating the principles of the Charter) were approved at referendums held in June and November 1976, respectively, and in December Boumedienne was elected President unopposed. The new formal structure of power was completed in February 1977 by the election of FLN members to the National People's Assembly.

President Boumedienne died in December 1978, and the eight-member Council of the Revolution took over the Government. In January 1979 the FLN adopted a new party structure, electing a Central Committee that was envisaged as the highest policy-making body both of the party and of the nation as a whole. The Committee's choice of Col Ben Djedid Chadli, commander of Oran military district, as the sole presidential candidate (having been named as party Secretary-General) was endorsed by a referendum in February. Unlike Boumedienne, Chadli appointed a Prime Minister, Col Muhammad Abd al-Ghani, anticipating constitutional changes approved by the National People's Assembly in June, which included the obligatory appointment of a premier. In mid-1980 the FLN authorized Chadli to form a smaller Political Bureau, with more limited responsibilities, thereby increasing the power of the President.

At a presidential election held in January 1984 Chadli's candidature was endorsed by 95.4% of the electorate. Chadli subsequently appointed Abd al-Hamid Brahimi as Prime Minister. In 1985 Chadli initiated a public debate on Boumedienne's National Charter, resulting in the adoption of a new National Charter at a special FLN congress in December. The revised Charter, which emphasized a state ideology based on the twin principles of socialism and Islam while encouraging the development of private enterprise, was approved by a referendum in January 1986. In July 1987 the National People's Assembly adopted legislation to permit the formation of local organizations without prior government approval: a ban remained, however, on associations that were deemed to oppose the policies of the Charter or to threaten national security.

During the second half of the 1980s opposition to the Government was increasingly manifest. In 1985 22 Berber cultural and human rights activists were imprisoned after being convicted of belonging to illegal organizations. In 1987 several leading activists of an Islamist group were killed by security forces, and some 200 of the group's members were given prison sentences. From mid-1988 severe unemployment, high consumer prices and shortages of essential supplies provoked a series of strikes, and in October rioting erupted in Algiers, spreading to Oran and Annaba. Chadli imposed a six-day state of emergency, and in November constitutional amendments allowing non-FLN candidates to participate in elections and making the Prime Minister answerable to the National People's Assembly (rather than to the President) were approved in a referendum. In December Chadli was elected President for a third term of office, obtaining 81% of the votes cast.

In February 1989 a new Constitution, signifying the end of the one-party socialist state, was approved by referendum. The formation of political associations outside the FLN was henceforth permitted, while the armed forces were no longer allocated a role in the development of socialism. The executive, legislative and judicial functions of the state were separated and made subject to the supervision of a Constitutional Council. In July legislation permitting the formation of political parties entered force (although these were still required to be licensed by the Government): by mid-1991 a total of 47 political parties had been registered, including a radical Islamist group, the Front islamique du salut (FIS), the Mouvement pour la démocratie en Algérie (MDA), which had been founded by Ben Bella in 1984, the Parti d'avant-garde socialiste (renamed Ettahaddi in 1993), the Parti social-démocrate (PSD) and the Berber Rassemblement pour la culture et la démocratie (RCD). Other legislation adopted in July 1989 further reduced state control of the economy, allowed the expansion of investment by foreign companies and ended the state monopoly of the press (although the principal newspapers remained under FLN control). In September Chadli appointed Mouloud Hamrouche, hitherto a senior official in the presidential office, as Prime Minister.

At local elections held in June 1990 the principal Islamist party, the FIS, received some 55% of total votes cast, while the FLN obtained about 32%. In July, following disagreement within the FLN concerning the pace of economic and political reform, the Prime Minister and four other ministers resigned from the party's Political Bureau. In a reorganization of the Council of Ministers in that month the defence portfolio was separated from the presidency for the first time since 1965. In December 1990 the National People's Assembly adopted a law whereby, after 1997, Arabic would be Algeria's only official language and the use of French and Berber in schools and in official transactions would be punishable offences. As a result of the new legislation more than 100,000 people demonstrated in Algiers against political and religious intolerance.

In April 1991 Chadli declared that Algeria's first multi-party general election would take place in late June. The FIS argued that a presidential election should be held simultaneously with, or shortly after, the general election, and in May organized an indefinite general strike and demonstrations to demand Chadli's resignation and changes in the electoral laws. Violent confrontations in June between Islamist activists and the security forces prompted Chadli to declare a state of emergency and postpone the general election; he also announced that he had accepted the resignation of the Prime Minister and his Government. The former Minister of Foreign Affairs, Sid-Ahmad Ghozali, was appointed premier, and he subsequently nominated a Council of Ministers consisting mainly of political independents.

Meanwhile, the FLN and the FIS reached a compromise whereby the strike was abandoned and legislative and presidential elections were to be held before the end of 1991. In July, however, army units arrested some 700 Islamists and occupied the headquarters of the FIS. Among those arrested were the party's President, Abbassi Madani, who had threatened to launch a *jihad* ('holy war') if the state of emergency was not ended, and Vice-President, Ali Belhadj; both were charged with armed conspiracy against the state. The state of emergency was revoked in September.

In October 1991, following revisions to the electoral code, Chadli formally announced that the first round of the multiparty general election to the newly enlarged 430-seat legislature would take place on 26 December, with a second round (in those constituencies where no candidate had secured an overall majority) scheduled for 16 January 1992. In all, 231 seats were won outright at the first round: the FIS took 188 seats (with 47.5% of the votes cast), the Front des forces socialistes (FFS) 25, the FLN just 15 and independents three. The FLN alleged widespread intimidation and electoral malpractice on the part of the FIS. On 11 January Chadli resigned as President, announcing that he had (one week earlier) dissolved the National People's Assembly. The following day the High Security Council (comprising the Prime Minister, three generals and two senior ministers) cancelled the second round of legislative voting, at which the FIS had been expected to consolidate its first-round victory, and on 14 January a five-member High Council of State (HCS) was appointed to act as a collegiate presidency until, at the latest, the expiry of Chadli's term of office in December 1993. The HCS was to be chaired by Muhammad Boudiaf, a veteran of the war of independence, but its most influential figure was believed to be Maj.-Gen. Khaled Nezzar, the Minister of Defence. The other members of the HCS were Ali Haroun (the Minister of Human Rights), Sheikh Tejini Haddam (the Rector of the Grand Mosque in Paris, France) and Ali Kafi (President of the war veterans' association, the Organisation nationale des moudjahidine—ONM). The constitutional legality of the HCS was disputed by all the political parties, including the FLN, while the FIS deputies who had been elected in December 1991 formed a 'shadow' assembly.

In February 1992 the HCS declared a 12-month state of emergency and detention centres were opened in the Sahara. The FIS, which was officially dissolved by the Government in March, claimed that 150 people had been killed, and as many as 30,000 detained, since the military-sponsored takeover. In April Boudiaf, as Chairman of the HCS, announced the creation of a 60-member National Consultative Council (NCC), which was to meet each month in the building of the suspended Assembly, although it was to have no legislative powers. In June Boudiaf promised a constitutional review, the dissolution of the FLN and a presidential election. Moreover, despite continuing violence, he ordered the release from detention of 2,000 FIS militants.

On 29 June 1992 Boudiaf was assassinated while making a speech in Annaba. The HCS ordered an immediate inquiry into the assassination, for which the FIS denied all responsibility. Ali Kafi succeeded Boudiaf as Chairman of the HCS, and Redha Malek, the Chairman of the NCC, was appointed as a new member of the HCS. In early July Ghozali resigned in order to enable Kafi to appoint his own Prime Minister. He was replaced by Belaid Abd es-Salam, who had directed Algeria's post-independence petroleum and gas policy. Abd es-Salam appointed a new Council of Ministers later in the month.

In July 1992 Madani and Belhadj were sentenced to 12 years' imprisonment for conspiracy against the state. Violent protests erupted in Algiers and quickly spread to other cities. Despite appeals by Abd es-Salam for a multi-party dialogue in an attempt to end civil strife, the Government attracted widespread criticism for reinforcing its emergency powers to repress any person or organization whose activities were deemed to represent a threat to stability. As political manoeuvring and attempts at reconciliation continued against a background of escalating violence, in February 1993 the state of emergency was renewed for an indefinite period. Yet the violence continued unabated, with terrorist attacks increasingly targeting not only political officials but also prominent intellectual and civilian figures. In June the HCS announced that it would dissolve itself in December, asserting that a modern democracy and free market economy would be created within three years of that date.

In July 1993 a retired general, Liamine Zéroual, succeeded Maj.-Gen. Nezzar as Minister of Defence, although Nezzar retained his post within the HCS. In August Redha Malek, who similarly remained a member of the HCS, replaced Abd es-Salam as Prime Minister. Malek, who appointed a new Council of Ministers in September, stated that the resolute stance against terrorism would be maintained, and rejected the possibility of dialogue with its perpetrators. In October the HCS appointed an eight-member National Dialogue Commission (NDC), which was charged with the preparation of a political conference to organize the transition to an elected and democratic form of government. In December it was announced that the HCS would not be disbanded until a new presidential body had been elected at the NDC conference in January 1994. However, all the main political parties (with the exception of the moderate Islamist Hamas) boycotted the conference. Liamine Zéroual (who retained the defence portfolio in the Council of Ministers) was inaugurated as President on 31 January for a three-year term, on the apparent recommendation of senior members of the military.

Malek resigned as Prime Minister in April 1994 and was replaced by Mokdad Sifi, hitherto Minister of Equipment. In May the President inaugurated a National Transition Council (NTC), an interim legislature of 200 appointed members, the aim of which was to provide a forum for debate pending legislative elections. With the exception of Hamas, most of the 21 parties that agreed to participate in the NTC were virtually unknown, and the 22 seats that were allocated to other major parties remained vacant.

In March 1994 an attack by Islamist militants on the high-security Tazoult prison, near Batna, resulted in the release of more than 1,000 political prisoners. Certain towns were virtually controlled by Islamist activists, and the deaths of a number of foreign nationals led several countries to advise their citizens to leave Algeria. In response to the rise in violence, the security forces intensified their campaign against armed Islamist groups, resorting to air attacks, punitive raids, torture and psychological warfare, and killing thousands of militants.

In August 1994 members of the FLN, the Parti du renouveau algérien (PRA), the MDA, Nahdah and Hamas engaged in what was termed a national dialogue with the Government; the meetings were boycotted, however, by Ettahaddi, the FFS and the RCD. At further negotiations held in early September discussion focused on two letters sent to the President by Abbassi Madani, purportedly offering a 'truce'. Madani and Belhadj were released from prison in mid-September and placed under house arrest; however, the FIS did not participate in the next round of national dialogue later that month, declaring that negotiations could take place only after the granting of a general amnesty, the rehabilitation of the FIS and the repeal of the state of emergency. The most prominent and radical Islamist militant group, the Groupe islamique armé (GIA), threatened reprisals if the FIS entered into dialogue with the regime, and intensified its campaign of violence against secular society by targeting educational institutions. In addition to the upheaval caused by Islamist violence, the RCD urged a boycott of the start of the school year, and in September Berber activists in the Kabylia region organized a general strike in protest at the exclusion of the Berber language, Tamazight, from the syllabus and at the prospect of the FIS entering the national dialogue. In May 1995 the RCD welcomed the establishment of a government body to oversee the teaching of Tamazight in schools and universities (commencing in October) and to promote its use in the official media.

Zéroual announced in October 1994 that a presidential election would be held before the end of 1995. However, the FIS and other opponents of the Algerian regime condemned the proposed organization of an election in the context of the ongoing civil conflict. In November 1994 representatives of several major Algerian parties, including the FIS, the FLN, the FFS and the MDA, attended a two-day conference in Rome, Italy, organized by the Sant' Egidio Roman Catholic community to foster discussion about the crisis in Algeria. The ensuing Sant' Egidio pact, endorsed by all the participants at a meeting in Rome in January 1995, rejected the use of violence to achieve or maintain power, and urged the Algerian regime to repeal the state of emergency and thereby facilitate negotiations between all parties. However, the pact was dismissed as a 'non-event' by the Government. In

April Zéroual resumed discussions with the legalized opposition parties in preparation for the presidential election. Talks with the FLN and the FFS quickly collapsed, however, as both rejected the prospect of participating in an election from which the FIS was excluded. Subsequent dialogue between the Government and the FIS also proved unsuccessful.

Some 40 candidates announced their intention to contest the presidential election, the first round of which was scheduled for 16 November 1995, but only four were confirmed as having attained the required 75,000 signatures from at least 25 of 48 provinces in order to qualify. Despite an appeal by the FLN, the FFS and the FIS for voters to boycott the election, official figures showed that some 75% of the electorate participated in the poll, in which Zéroual secured an outright victory, with 61.0% of the valid votes cast. Zéroual was inaugurated for a five-year term on 27 November. Shortly afterwards the Government announced the closure of the last of seven detention centres opened since 1992, thereby releasing some 650 prisoners, many of whom were Islamist sympathizers. In December 1995 Ahmed Ouyahia, a career diplomat, replaced Sifi as Prime Minister. Ouyahia's Government, named in January 1996, included two members of Hamas and a dissident leader of the FIS.

In April 1996, in an attempt to foster national reconciliation, Zéroual held bilateral discussions with more than 50 influential individuals, including leaders of trade unions and opposition groups; the FIS was not invited to participate. In the following month Zéroual announced his intention to hold legislative elections in early 1997. In addition, he proposed that a referendum be held, prior to the elections, on amendments to the Constitution: these included measures to increase the powers of the President while limiting his tenure to a maximum of two consecutive mandates; the creation of a Council of the Nation as a second parliamentary chamber (one-third of whose members would be chosen by the President); the establishment of a State Council (to regulate the administrative judiciary) and a High State Court; and, significantly, a ban on political parties that were based on religion, language, gender or regional differences. Some 1,000 delegates, including representatives of the FLN, Nahdah and Hamas, attended a government-sponsored conference on national concord held in September 1996. The conference was boycotted by the FFS, the RCD, Ettahaddi and the MDA. Zéroual subsequently withdrew his offer to include members of opposition parties in an expanded Council of Ministers and NTC. The proposed constitutional amendments were promulgated in December, having been approved by some 86% of the voters at a referendum held in November.

In January 1997 the Secretary-General of the FLN-affiliated Union Générale des Travailleurs Algériens (UGTA), Abd al-Hak Benhamouda, was shot dead in Algiers. Although an Islamist group claimed responsibility for the assassination, there was speculation that it may have been perpetrated by opponents within the regime. In February Zéroual announced that elections to the National People's Assembly would take place in mid-1997. Shortly afterwards the NTC adopted restrictive legislation concerning political parties in accordance with the amended Constitution; new electoral legislation replacing the majority system with proportional representation was also adopted. Later in February Abdelkader Bensalah, the President of the NTC, formed a centrist grouping, the Rassemblement national démocratique (RND). The RND received support from a wide range of organizations, including trade unions, anti-Islamist groups and the influential war veterans' ONM, and was closely linked with Zéroual and the Government. Several other political parties emerged in the months that followed, while certain existing parties changed their names to comply with the new legislation. Notably, Hamas became the Mouvement de la société pour la paix (MSP).

Some 39 political parties contested the elections to the National People's Assembly, held on 5 June 1997, although the FIS and Ettahaddi urged a boycott of the polls. As the preliminary results of the elections began to emerge, opposition leaders complained of irregularities during the electoral process, and accused officials of manipulating the results in favour of the RND. International observers were critical of the conduct of the elections, and commented that the rate of voter participation (officially estimated at 65.5% of the electorate) seemed unrealistically high. According to the final official results, the RND won 156 of the Assembly's 380 seats, followed by the MSP (69) and the FLN (62); Nahdah took 34 seats, the FFS 20 and the RCD 19. President Zéroual asked Ahmed Ouyahia to form a new Government, and later in June Ouyahia announced a new Council of Ministers, comprising members of the RND, the FLN and the MSP.

Following the RND's success at regional and municipal elections held in October 1997, the party's political dominance was consolidated with the appointment of the Council of the Nation in December. Of the Council's 96 seats indirectly elected by regional and municipal authorities, 80 were won by the RND, 10 by the FLN, four by the FFS and two by the MSP; President Zéroual appointed the remaining 48 members. In the following month the authorities disbanded some 30 political groupings, including Ettahaddi and the PSD, for failing to satisfy the legal requirements concerning political associations.

There were violent protests in Kabylia in June 1998 following the assassination of Lounès Matoub, a popular Berber singer and an outspoken critic of both the Government and the fundamentalist Islamist movement. There were further protests in July when controversial legislation on the compulsory use of the Arabic language in public life (see above) came into effect. Berber activists in Kabylia fiercely opposed the 'arabization' policy, demanding the recognition of Tamazight as an official language.

In September 1998 President Zéroual announced that a presidential election would be held before March 1999, nearly two years ahead of schedule. There was considerable speculation that the announcement had been prompted primarily by a power struggle within the regime between the faction loyal to the President and figures close to Lt-Gen. Muhammad Lamari, the Chief of Staff of the Army. Zéroual declared in October 1998 that the presidential election would be postponed until April 1999 to allow political parties to prepare their campaigns. In December 1998 Ouyahia resigned; he was replaced as premier by Smail Hamdani, a widely respected senior politician and former diplomat.

A total of 47 candidates registered to contest the presidential election; however, the Constitutional Council declared only seven eligible to stand. Although the senior generals had decided not to nominate a member of the armed forces for the presidency, Abdelaziz Bouteflika was believed to have the support of the military establishment, as well as that of the four main political parties and the UGTA. On the eve of the election, which took place on 15 April 1999, Bouteflika's six rivals withdrew their candidacies after Zéroual refused to postpone the poll following allegations of massive electoral fraud in favour of Bouteflika. Voting papers were, nevertheless, distributed for all seven candidates, and no official boycott of the election was organized. The credibility of the poll was, however, seriously diminished, and Bouteflika announced that he would accept the presidency only if there were both a high rate of voter participation and a large majority in his favour. According to official results, Bouteflika won 73.8% of the votes cast (his closest rival, Ahmed Taleb Ibrahimi, a former Minister of Foreign Affairs who was now supported by the outlawed FIS, secured 12.5%). However, this figure, together with the estimated official turn-out of more than 60%, was immediately disputed by his opponents, who maintained that only 23.3% of the registered electorate had participated, and that Bouteflika had received only 28% of the votes cast, compared with 20% for Ibrahimi. At his inauguration, on 27 April, Bouteflika emphasized the need for national reconciliation to end the civil conflict in Algeria, but pledged to continue the military campaign against terrorists and reaffirmed that the FIS would not be legalized.

Following clandestine negotiations between the Government and representatives of the FIS, in June 1999 the Armée islamique du salut (AIS, the armed wing of the FIS) announced the permanent cessation of its armed struggle against the Government. President Bouteflika's plans for a national reconciliation initiative were incorporated in a Law on Civil Concord, promulgated in July, whereby there was to be an amnesty for members of armed Islamist groups who surrendered within a six-month deadline and who were not implicated in mass killings, rape or bomb attacks on public places. The legislation was approved by 98.6% of those who voted in a national referendum in September. Meanwhile, Bouteflika exhibited unprecedented candour, admitting in August that the civil conflict of the past seven years had resulted in the deaths of at least 100,000 people (hitherto the authorities had put the number of deaths at 30,000). Bouteflika finally named his Council of Ministers in December; led by Ahmed Benbitour, a former Minister of Finance, the new Government comprised members of the FLN, the MSP, Nahdah, the RCD, the Alliance nationale républicaine (ANR), the RND and the PRA, all of which had supported Bouteflika's presidential campaign.

In early January 2000, following discussions between representatives of the Government, the army and the AIS, an agreement was reached whereby the AIS pledged to disband in return for the restoration of full civil and political rights to its former members. It was estimated that some 1,500–3,000 rebels were to be granted a full pardon under the agreement, some of whom were to be temporarily enlisted in an auxiliary unit to assist the security forces in apprehending members of the GIA and of a breakaway group from the GIA, the Groupe salafiste pour la prédication et le combat (GSPC, or Da'wa wal Djihad). In mid-January, following the expiry of the amnesty period specified under the Law on Civil Concord, the armed forces launched a concerted assault on rebel strongholds in the north-east and south-west of the country, in an attempt to eliminate remaining anti-Government factions. It was officially stated at this time that 80% of members of armed groups had surrendered. Meanwhile, the Government estimated that around 600 people (many of them civilians) had been killed between July 1999 and January 2000, mostly in incidents connected to the GIA and the GSPC. In July 2000 an article in the daily *Le Jeune Indépendant*, citing unofficial sources, claimed that some 1,100 civilians and an estimated 2,000 terrorists had been killed in Algeria since the expiry of the general amnesty in January. However, following visits to Algeria in mid-2000, the human rights organizations Amnesty International and the Fédération internationale des ligues des droits de l'homme reported that there had been a significant decline in violence and a clear improvement in the country's human rights situation, although concern was expressed about the fate of an estimated 22,000 missing persons who had disappeared since 1992.

In August 2000 Benbitour resigned the premiership and was replaced by Ali Benflis, a former Minister of Justice who had directed Bouteflika's presidential campaign. The composition of the new Government remained largely unchanged. At indirect elections in December 2000 for one-half of the 96 elective members of the Council of the Nation, the RND retained its comfortable majority, although its total number of seats was reduced from 80 to 74. President Bouteflika effected an extensive reorganization of the Council of Ministers in May 2001.

A sharp escalation in violence at the end of 2000 added weight to the arguments of those who believed that the amnesty under the Law on Civil Concord had done little to quell unrest. Indeed, more than 1,300 deaths (among Islamist fighters, government forces and civilians) were reported as a result of continuing attacks involving armed Islamist groups between late 2000 and the holy month of Ramadan in 2001, including the killing of four Russian expatriate workers in the Annaba region in January. Meanwhile, there were persistent rumours of tensions between Bouteflika, the military high command and those parties opposed to any appeasement with militant fundamentalists.

Meanwhile, violent clashes broke out in April 2001 between protesters and security forces in several villages in Kabylia following the death of a secondary school student (who had been apprehended for allegedly committing an assault during a robbery) in police custody at Beni Douala near the regional capital, Tizi Ouzou. Thousands of local inhabitants joined demonstrations, demanding a full inquiry into the incident and the withdrawal of paramilitary gendarmes from Kabylia. Tensions were further fuelled by anger among Kabyles at the poor social and economic conditions in the region. Days after the student was killed the situation was further inflamed when three young Kabyles were assaulted by gendarmes near Béjaïa. The incidents coincided with demonstrations traditionally held to mark the anniversary of the so-called 'Berber Spring' protests of 1980, when Berber activism for cultural and linguistic rights had first taken form, and although the two major political parties in Kabylia—the FFS and the RCD—appealed for calm, violence rapidly escalated throughout the area; as many as 80 people had reportedly died by the end of the month. In a televised address, Bouteflika announced the creation of a national commission of inquiry, to be headed by Mohand Issad, a lawyer originating from Kabylia, to investigate recent events in the region. Bouteflika also indicated that he planned revisions to the Constitution that would address the status of Tamazight, and revealed his intention to adopt a proposal making instruction in the Berber language compulsory in Tamazight-speaking areas. Furthermore, he accused unnamed groups both inside and outside the country of inciting extremism. Bouteflika's speech was strongly criticized by the main political groupings in Kabylia, and the RCD withdrew from the coalition Government. Increasingly violent demonstrations by Berbers took place in Kabylia during May and June 2001. In mid-June Prime Minister Benflis appeared on television to appeal for calm, and all protests in Algiers were prohibited.

By the end of June 2001 unrest had spread beyond Kabylia to the Aurès region, as well as to Annaba and Biskra. Official reports stated that 56 people had been killed, and 1,300 injured, since the violence first erupted. Despite repeated calls in the independent press for his resignation, Bouteflika declared that he would not relinquish the presidency and again urged rioters not to participate in what he termed an external plot to undermine the security of the country. In July the Issad commission issued its preliminary report into the events in Kabylia, in which it attached the blame for the rioting to the gendarmerie, maintaining that gendarmes had adopted a 'shoot-to-kill' policy and had acted in an illegal manner. However, the report failed to name those responsible for ordering the gendarmes' actions, and the commission complained of attempts, apparently on the part of vested interests within the security forces, to obstruct its investigations.

In August 2001 security forces blocked roads in order to prevent a large number of Berbers from marching on the capital, where they intended to present a list of 15 demands at the presidential palace. This 'El-Kseur platform' (named after the Kabyle town in which it had been drawn up) notably requested: the granting of official status to Tamazight without the holding of a referendum; the removal of all paramilitary gendarmes from Kabylia; the annulment of legal proceedings against demonstrators; and the trial by civilian courts of all those who had ordered or perpetrated crimes and their dismissal from the security forces or the civil service.

In September 2001 President Bouteflika formally invited Berber community and tribal leaders, known as the *Aarouch*, to present their demands for social and political change, and designated Benflis to act as interlocutor between the authorities and the Berbers. Relations between the two sides were, however, complicated by divisions within the Berber movement, as some Berber leaders were unwilling to enter into any negotiations with the Government. Nevertheless, official reports claimed that a meeting took place in October between Benflis and moderate *Aarouch*, at which Benflis informed them that the President had decided to grant Tamazight the status of a national language in a forthcoming constitutional amendment. Ongoing dialogue between moderate Berber representatives and the Government resulted in the adoption, in January 2002, of a series of resolutions, including proposals for the establishment of a special ministerial council to implement the creation of decentralized government councils in Kabylia at *wilaya* (department) level. The demand that the gendarmerie be withdrawn from Kabylia was, however, dismissed by Bouteflika as 'inconceivable'. The more radical *Aarouch* voiced their disapproval of the resolutions, stating that the El-Kseur platform was non-negotiable, and again insisted that the gendarmerie be withdrawn from Kabylia.

Meanwhile, in December 2001 the final report of the Issad commission had been published, confirming the initial findings that the gendarmerie had been to blame for the repression in Kabylia, and also expressing deep pessimism about the immediate future of the region. Emphasizing the increasing authority of the military throughout the country since 1992, the report stated that the responsibilities of the civil and military authorities had become blurred and denounced the subtle slide from 'a state of emergency to a state of siege'. Issad also condemned the military's widespread abuse of its powers and the laws of the country.

In a televised address in March 2002 Bouteflika officially announced that Tamazight would be recognized as a national language without the issue being put to a referendum. Accordingly, on 7 April the National People's Assembly voted almost unanimously in favour of amending the Constitution to grant Tamazight the status of a national language. Nevertheless, Kabyle leaders urged a boycott of the forthcoming legislative elections, and unrest continued in the region, which was brought to a standstill by a series of strikes.

A total of 23 parties contested elections to the newly enlarged National People's Assembly held on 30 May 2002, although the polls were boycotted by the FFS and the RCD. According to official results, the FLN won 199 of the 389 available seats (compared with 64 in the outgoing, 380-member legislature), while the RND suffered a significant loss of support, with its parliamentary representation reduced from 155 seats to just 47. Sheikh Abdallah Djaballah's Mouvement de la réforme nationale (MRN) took 43 seats, the MSP 38 (compared with 69 in 1997) and the Parti des travailleurs 21. Independent candidates secured a total of 30 seats. The overall credibility of the election was, however, undermined by a low rate of voter participation: only 46.2% of the country's 18m. eligible voters cast their ballot. Voter abstention was particularly high in Kabylia, with participation rates in Béjaïa and Tizi Ouzou recorded at just 2.6% and 1.8%, respectively. The FFS and the RCD demanded an annulment of the results, claiming that real voter turn-out had reached no more than 15%–20%.

Following the elections Bouteflika reappointed Ali Benflis as Prime Minister, and in June 2002 Benflis named a new coalition Government, in which the majority of the key figures from the outgoing administration retained their posts. The most notable promotion was that of Muhammad Terbeche, hitherto Minister-delegate to the Minister of Finance, in charge of the Budget, who replaced Mourad Medelci as Minister of Finance. Former Prime Minister Ahmed Ouyahia was appointed as Minister of State, Personal Representative of the President of the Republic. The new Council of Ministers included five women, among them an outspoken campaigner for women's rights, Khalida Toumi-Messaoudi, who was appointed Minister for Communications and Culture, and Government Spokesperson.

In July 2002, on the 40th anniversary of independence from French rule, some 50 people were killed in a bomb attack in Larba, to the south of Algiers; this brought the total number of conflict-related deaths since the beginning of the year to more than 800. The attack came just days after the army Chief of Staff, Lt-Gen. Lamari, had declared that the Government had won its campaign against the Islamist guerrillas. Some 150 people were estimated to have died in ongoing violence during July; certain sources reported that GIA leader Rachid Abou Tourab had been killed, along with 15 other GIA militants, during a raid by security forces in the Tamezguida forest, south of the capital. (Tourab's predecessor, Antar Zouabri, had been killed by security forces in February.)

Prior to local elections in October 2002, the persistence of divisions within the Berber movement was highlighted when the RCD, supported by the Coordination des aârchs, daïras et communes (CADC—also known as the Coordination des comités de villages Kabyles), announced that it would again boycott the polls. This was in direct contrast to the FFS, which was to present candidates in 40 of the country's 48 *wilayat*, maintaining that these would provide ordinary Kabyles with the possibility of attaining some form of political representation. At the elections the FLN won 668 of the 1,541 communes and thus secured control of 43 *wilayat*, although there were violent clashes in Kabylia, where demonstrators attempted to prevent voting from taking place.

There was a further escalation of violence in January 2003 after some 60 people, including at least 43 soldiers, were killed in an ambush by GSPC fighters near Batna. Although Algerian officials maintained that fewer than 1,000 Islamist rebels remained in the country, there were continued reports of attacks on civilians and security forces by the GIA and the GSPC throughout the first months of the year.

At the FLN party congress, held in March 2003, evidence of a serious rift between Benflis and Bouteflika emerged when Benflis announced his opposition to a number of Bouteflika's economic policies and withdrew the party's support for the President. Furthermore, it was rumoured that Benflis intended to stand as a candidate in the presidential election scheduled for April 2004. Benflis, who was re-elected Secretary-General of the FLN for a further five-year term, was also granted considerably increased powers, including the right to appoint senior party officials and to call extraordinary party congresses. In May 2003 Bouteflika dismissed Benflis as Prime Minister, reportedly owing to 'far-reaching divergencies' between the two men. The former Prime Minister, Ahmed Ouyahia, was subsequently appointed to succeed Benflis. Ouyahia announced a new coalition Government shortly afterwards, in which, most notably, Terbeche was replaced as Minister of Finance by Abdellatif Benachenhou.

In early July 2003 the two leaders of the proscribed FIS, Abbassi Madani and Ali Belhadj, were released, after having completed their 12-year gaol sentences. However, upon their release both men were issued with court orders prohibiting them from: engaging in any political activity; holding meetings; establishing a political, cultural, charitable or religious association; voting or standing as candidates in any election.

The Government announced in late July 2003 that it had agreed to reintroduce the use of Tamazight into Algeria's educational system, thereby fulfilling one of the demands of the El-Kseur platform. Ouyahia had, in May, urged local Berber leaders in Kabylia to negotiate with the authorities to bring an end to the violence in the region, and in June several senior members of the CADC had been released. President Bouteflika remained eager to resolve the ongoing crisis in Kabylia, and in August the Government granted more than €23m. in 'overdue' development aid to the region. In early January 2004 lengthy negotiations took place between the *Aarouch* and the Government, following which the authorities pledged to acquiesce to five of the six points deemed by the *Aarouch* to be 'prerequisites' before any further talks relating to the El-Kseur platform could take place; these included the release of all remaining prisoners and the annulment of legal proceedings against demonstrators detained during the riots of April 2001. The sixth point, regarding the dissolution of municipal and regional councils elected in Kabylia in October 2002 (when there was a widespread voter boycott), was settled in late January 2004, when the Government agreed to remove any councillors who had been elected illegally in the contested polls. Days later the Algerian authorities released a further five Berber leaders who had been imprisoned for their role in the rioting, and Ouyahia stated that the meetings had provided a 'fundamental turning point' in the process between the two sides. However, the negotiations collapsed following the Government's assertion that the status of Tamazight should be decided in a national referendum, and further unrest ensued in Kabylia, while the FFS declared that it would not participate in the forthcoming presidential election. It was announced in January 2005 that, following a new round of talks, the Government and the *Aarouch* had reached an agreement regarding implementation of the El-Kseur platform. Two joint committees were established to implement and monitor the agreement.

Meanwhile, in September 2003 Bouteflika effected a reorganization of the Council of Ministers, in which he dismissed a number of FLN ministers who had indicated their support for Benflis's presidential campaign. During late 2003 relations between Bouteflika and Benflis continued to deteriorate and in early October the remaining FLN ministers, who had pledged their support for Benflis, withdrew from the coalition Government. The following day, at an extraordinary congress of the FLN (which took place despite attempts by a number of party members opposed to Benflis to have the meeting prohibited), 1,375 of the 1,500 members present approved Benflis's candidature, thus confirming him as the party's representative at the 2004 presidential election. Bouteflika immediately carried out a further reshuffle of the Council of Ministers, appointing new ministers to the seven posts vacated by the Benflis loyalists.

In December 2003 the administrative chamber of the Algiers Court suspended all activities of the FLN after the pro-Bouteflika faction of the party lodged a complaint maintaining that the party congress held in April had been held illegally and that the results of the congress were 'null and void'. The party's bank accounts were frozen and its headquarters and provincial offices were closed down. The decision was condemned by Benflis, and in early January 2004 numerous FLN members protested against the decision outside the National People's Assembly. On 12 January a group of 11 leading politicians, including Benflis and four other former heads of government, signed a statement demanding the formation of an interim government ahead of the presidential election (citing the lack of impartiality in the current Government) and an independent body to oversee the polls. Prime Minister Ouyahia (whose party, the RND, had already declared its support for President Bouteflika were he to stand for re-election) responded to the communiqué by affirming that he had no intention of stepping down and pledging that the Government would organize a free and fair presidential election in the early part of the year. He also dismissed claims that the Government was restricting other political parties' access to state television and radio coverage.

Meanwhile, indirect elections took place on 30 December 2003 to renew 46 members of the Council of the Nation. The RND won 17 seats, while the (pro-Benflis) FLN obtained 11 seats, the Corrective Movement of the FLN 10, the MSP four, and the MRN and independents secured two seats each. One-half of the presidential appointees to the Council were also replaced on 8 January 2004. However, these elections and appointments were incomplete, principally owing to the unrest in Kabylia. By-elections for five seats in the Council were held on 23 February 2006.

During 2003 violent incidents in Algeria declined markedly; in that year, according to official figures, fewer than 900 people were killed as a result of violence involving Islamists and the security forces, compared with some 1,400 in 2002 and almost 1,900 in 2001. The Government attributed the decline in the number of attacks to the increased efficiency of the security forces, who had successfully dismantled many of the terrorists' support networks, and to divisions within the Islamist groups. It was claimed that the GIA, whose leader, Tourab, was apparently captured in November 2003 (despite reports of his death in July 2002), had been reduced to just 30 members, while internal divisions had reportedly caused a split in the GSPC, with three separate factions of the group operating in the country.

In advance of the 2004 presidential election, Bouteflika declared that a committee would be established to ensure the fairness and transparency of the ballot, and invited representatives of international organizations to observe the electoral process. In February Bouteflika announced his intention to run for a second term as President. Although more than 40 candidates put forward applications to contest the poll, only six obtained the requisite 75,000 signatures from more than one-half of the country's 48 provinces. Bouteflika was joined in the presidential race by Benflis; Sheikh Abdallah Djaballah, leader of the Islamist MRN; Saïd Saâdi, President of the RCD; Louisa Hanoune, head of the Parti des travailleurs; and Ali Fawzi Rebaïne, Secretary-General of the small nationalist party Ahd 54. Prior to the election there were increased allegations of fraudulent behaviour on the part of Bouteflika, who was accused of monopolizing state media and of using state funds to set his re-election campaign in motion before the electoral race had officially begun. The President dismissed these claims by insisting that the media remained unbiased and emphasizing that the elections would be monitored by neutral observers.

Bouteflika was decisively re-elected for a second term of office on 8 April 2004. He received 85.0% of the valid votes cast, while his nearest rival, Benflis, took 6.4%. Djaballah secured 5.0%, Saâdi 1.9%, Hanoune 1.0% and Rebaïne 0.6%. The rate of turn-out by eligible voters was reported to be 58.1%, although this rate was estimated to be as low as 18% in Kabylia. Bouteflika's rivals immediately accused the President of electoral malpractice; however, international observers declared the election to have been representative of popular will and free from any vote-rigging. Both Benflis and Saâdi boycotted Bouteflika's inauguration ceremony on 19 April, at which he vowed to resolve the Berber crisis and to improve the rights of women by readdressing the controversial family code of 1984. He also emphasized his commitment to his campaign for 'true national reconciliation'. Ahmed Ouyahia resigned as Prime Minister, as required under the Constitution, but was immediately reinstated and given the task of forming a new government. On 26 April 2004 Ouyahia named his new Council of Ministers, which retained most of the senior ministers from the previous administration. The new Government consisted principally of FLN members and non-partisan supporters of Bouteflika, with a few representatives from the RND and the MSP. Meanwhile, Benflis resigned as Secretary-General of the FLN. At an FLN congress held between the end of January and early February 2005 the Minister of State for Foreign Affairs, Abdelaziz Belkhadem, was elected to the post of Secretary-General and President Bouteflika was elected honorary President of the party.

In August 2004 the Chief of Staff of the Army, Lt-Gen. Muhammad Lamari, resigned on the grounds of ill health, although there was considerable speculation that his departure from the military might also signal the final withdrawal of the army from the political sphere. Lamari had issued a statement in January, in which he pledged the army's neutrality in the forthcoming presidential election and declared that it would remain neutral so long as the stability of the nation did not come under threat. Some analysts argued that the decision not to intervene in political affairs was prompted both by the military's determination that Algeria should join NATO and by pressure from Western countries, in particular the USA. Lamari was replaced by the Commander of the Land Force, Gen. Salah Ahmed Gaid.

Meanwhile, violence between the GSPC and the Algerian military began to escalate, particularly in Kabylia. In March 2004 it was reported that fighting had occurred between the Chadian military and a faction of the GSPC led by the group's second-in-command, Amari Saifi, resulting in the deaths of more than 40 militants. Saifi was wanted in Algeria and abroad for various crimes, including the kidnapping in 2003 of a group of 32 European tourists (see below) and the killing of 43 Algerian soldiers. It was announced in October 2004 that Saifi had been taken into Algerian custody, having been intercepted by Libyan authorities on the Chadian–Libyan border. Meanwhile, in June 2004 Nabil Sahraoui, the GSPC's leader since October 2003, was reportedly killed by the Algerian military in Kabylia during a gun battle that also killed four of his senior aides, including his likely successor, Abdi Abdelaziz. The army subsequently announced that it had 'completely neutralized' the leadership of the GSPC and had seized many of its weapons and documents. Shortly after the announcement of Sahraoui's death, an explosion at the Hamma power station near Algiers injured 11 people. The Government declared the explosion to be accidental; however, the GSPC later claimed responsibility and warned that further attacks would ensue. In September 2004 Sahraoui was replaced as leader of the GSPC by Abdelmalek Droukdal (also known as Abu Musab Abd al-Wadud).

The relationship between the national press and the Algerian authorities worsened in 2004, particularly during the run-up to the presidential election. The majority of the principal daily newspapers were highly critical of Bouteflika's re-election campaign and his overwhelming victory. In June the editor of the independent Algerian daily Le Matin, Muhammad Benchicou, was gaoled for two years, having been convicted of violating foreign exchange laws. In July the Government refused to print Le Matin until all unpaid bills had been settled, and the newspaper went out of circulation. Restrictions were extended to the international media when, in June, the Government suspended the activities of the Qatar-based satellite television channel Al-Jazeera in Algeria following the broadcast of a programme in which critics of the Bouteflika administration denounced the President's national reconciliation policy and the actions of several Algerian generals. In May 2006 Bouteflika announced that he intended to pardon those journalists convicted of 'outrage to state officials, institutions and the constitutional body, defamation and insult'. However, it subsequently became clear that only journalists whose trials had been completed would be released from gaol; of the 20 journalists recently imprisoned, the majority still awaited definitive judgments. Benchicou was not eligible for pardon, having been convicted of financial irregularities. Nevertheless, he was released in the following month, on completion of his two-year sentence.

In August 2004 a bill to improve women's rights was drawn up by the commission in charge of revising the family code, which had been established in October 2003. The new legislation was approved by the Government and sent for review by the Council of Ministers, despite fierce opposition from Islamist groups who considered that it went against the teachings of the Koran. The reform would make it illegal for a man to divorce his wife without stating clear grounds, and would allow a woman to receive financial support from her husband once they were divorced. Moreover, women would no longer have to seek permission from a male relative in order to marry. The Algerian authorities faced criticism in early 2005, however, when Amnesty International published a report highlighting their failure to protect women against 'rape, beatings and widespread legal and economic discrimination'. Furthermore, in February Bouteflika was criticized for having weakened the reform by overruling the removal from the legislation of the requirement that women ask permission from a male guardian in order to marry, following considerable pressure from religious groups. The amendments to the family code were approved by the National People's Assembly in March.

In January 2005 the Ministry of the Interior and Local Authorities announced that the GIA had been virtually destroyed following a military campaign during the latter part of 2004, in which they had arrested the group's leader, Noureddine Boudiafi, and later killed his replacement, Chabaâne Younès. The Ministry also confirmed that, despite reports to the contrary, former GIA leader Tourab had been killed by members of his own group in July 2004. In April 2005 14 civilians were killed by suspected GIA militants in a roadside ambush in the Blida region; later that month the group's 'emir', Boulenouar Oukil, was arrested on suspicion of having planned the attack. In June Amari Saifi was sentenced in absentia to life imprisonment, having been found guilty of forming a terrorist group and of 'propagating terror'.

President Bouteflika effected a partial reorganization of the Council of Ministers in May 2005, in a bid to revive the Government's economic reform programme. Abdelaziz Belkhadem was replaced as Minister of State for Foreign Affairs, but remained in the cabinet as Minister of State and Special Representative of the President. Mourad Medelci replaced Benachenhou as Minister of

Finance, and a new defence post was created (although Bouteflika continued to hold the position of Minister of Defence). Some commentators interpreted the reshuffle, which gave key posts to ministers who endorsed the majority of the Prime Minister's policies, as an attempt to consolidate Ouyahia's position.

In August 2005 Bouteflika announced that a referendum to decide whether to grant a partial amnesty to Islamist rebels who had surrendered their weapons after the January 2000 deadline (see above) would take place in the following month. The FFS and the RCD called for a boycott of the referendum on the grounds that an amnesty would 'consecrate impunity' for the crimes committed by the security forces during Algeria's civil war. In the run-up to the vote there was an increase in violence on the part of armed Islamists in Algiers, where some 44 people were killed in attacks during September. A reported 79.8% of the electorate participated in the referendum on 29 September, with 97.4% of voters approving the partial amnesty. However, the result was marred by reports of violence in Kabylia, with turn-out in Tizi Ouzou registered at just 11.4%. Amnesty International criticized the Charter for Peace and National Reconciliation, stating that it would simply 'obliterate crimes of the past'. More than 55 people were reportedly killed by militant Islamists in the first half of October alone.

The Government revealed the exact details of the partial amnesty in February 2006: those Islamist rebels who had not been involved in mass killings, rape or bomb attacks on public places would have six months to surrender to the authorities, while more than 2,000 armed Islamists imprisoned during the civil conflict would be pardoned and released by mid-March; a small number of detainees would have their sentences reduced. The release of the first group of prisoners, who included Belhadj and Abdelhak Layada, second-in-command of the GIA, took place in early March. Nevertheless, the threat of Islamist terrorism continued, and attacks attributed to militants of the GSPC resulted in the deaths of a number of Algerian security officials in April. By the time that the six-month amnesty expired, in August, the Minister of State for the Interior and Local Authorities, Noureddine Yazid Zerhouni, stated that only some 250–300 militants had given up their weapons; it was estimated that up to 800 Islamist fighters remained at large, most of these being members of the GSPC. In October three people were killed in co-ordinated bomb explosions outside police stations in Réghaïa and Dergana. In December the GSPC claimed responsibility for a roadside bomb attack near Algiers on two vehicles carrying employees of a US- and Algerian-owned engineering company, in which one man was killed and nine others, including six foreigners, were injured.

Meanwhile, in May 2006 Ouyahia resigned as Prime Minister. President Bouteflika subsequently appointed Belkhadem, who retained the post of FLN Secretary-General, to succeed him. Ouyahia had been strongly criticized for a perceived reluctance to use increased revenues from hydrocarbons exports to effect social reform, and a disagreement between premier Ouyahia and Belkhadem over proposed constitutional reforms had precipitated rumours of a rift within the presidential alliance. Bouteflika later appointed Hachemi Djiar to the hitherto vacant position of Minister of Information; all other portfolios remained unchanged.

It was reported in January 2007 that the GSPC had restyled itself as 'al-Qa'ida in the Islamic Maghreb' (AQIM). The announcement followed reports in September 2006 that the GSPC had joined the international al-Qa'ida (Base) organization led by the Saudi-born Islamist Osama bin Laden. It appeared during 2007 that an intensification of Islamist violence was being undertaken simultaneously in neighbouring Morocco and Tunisia, and there were widespread fears that attacks across North Africa were being co-ordinated by militant groups with an al-Qa'ida connection. It became increasingly evident that the newly radicalized GSPC was unprepared to join many of Algeria's other militant groups in giving up their weapons and renouncing violence, under President Bouteflika's Charter on Peace and National Reconciliation. Days after the GSPC had announced its name change, 15 people were killed following clashes between Algerian security forces and Islamist militants in Batna. During February at least six people died when a series of explosions targeting police stations were launched in eastern Algeria. In March seven police officers were killed in a militant attack in Tizi Ouzou, while four pipeline construction workers (from Russia and Ukraine), together with three Algerians, died in a further attack in Aïn Defla, south-west of the capital; AQIM claimed responsibility for both incidents. The same group declared that it had carried out car bomb attacks targeted at sites in Algiers in early April, in which 33 people were killed and more than 200 wounded; one of the bombs exploded close to the Prime Minister's office and was widely believed to be the country's first attack by a suicide bomber. Later that month Algerian military officials announced that the second-in-command of AQIM, Samir Saioud (also known as Samir Moussaâb), had been shot dead during fighting to the east of the capital. In June Italian authorities announced that at least 10 suspected militant Islamists thought to have been involved in the planning of the Algiers car bombings had been detained in the northern city of Milan.

The Government announced in February 2007 that elections to the National People's Assembly would be held in May and that, in preparation for the polls, the country's electoral lists were to be revised. The FFS responded by announcing in March that it intended to boycott the elections, as had been the case in 2002, citing its lack of confidence in the Algerian parliamentary system as a means of bringing about real political change. The FLN retained its dominance of the legislature following the 17 May 2007 polls, winning 136 of the 389 seats and thus an overall majority. This was, however, a poorer result for the party than had been the case in the previous elections, when the FLN had 199 representatives in the National People's Assembly. The RND again held the second highest number of seats, with 62 (compared with 48 in 2002), while the MSP increased its representation, taking 51 seats (compared with 38 in 2002). The PT fared well at the polls, with a gain of five seats, from 21 to 26. A notable result was the relative success of the RCD, which had boycotted the previous elections: the party achieved a total of 19 seats in the legislature. In contrast, the MRN, which had been the principal opposition movement in the outgoing Assembly, won only three seats. Independent candidates secured 33 seats (against 29 in 2002). Although the rate of voter participation was reported to have been the lowest since Algeria's independence, at only 36%, Zerhouni asserted that similar rates were not unusual in some Western democracies and denied that the new legislature would lack credibility. In early June 2007 President Bouteflika appointed a new, 38-member Council of Ministers, with Abdelaziz Belkhadem retaining the premiership. Notable changes in the composition of the Government were the replacement of Muhammad Bedjaoui as Minister of Foreign Affairs by the Minister of Finance, Mourad Medelci, while Karim Djoudi was chosen to replace Medelci in his former post.

In early July 2007 a suicide bombing apparently intended to coincide with the opening in Algeria of the All-Africa Games—one of the continent's most important sporting events—resulted in the deaths of at least eight people. The driver of a truck detonated his explosives at a military barracks near the town of Bouira, south-east of Algiers, in the Kabylia region. AQIM claimed responsibility for the attack, prompting Minister of State Zerhouni to state defiantly that such violence would not prevent the Government from continuing its 'relentless fight against terrorism'. Two further suicide bombings apparently carried out by the al-Qa'ida offshoot in Batna and Algiers in early September claimed up to 60 lives. The latest bomb attacks, the first of which was intended to assassinate President Bouteflika, resulted in an anti-violence demonstration in the capital by thousands of Algerians. The security forces appeared to have had some success against militant Islamism in early October, when it was reported that they had killed the deputy leader of AQIM, Hareg Zoheir (or Sofiane Abu Fasila), in Tizi Ouzou; Zoheir was thought to have been responsible for many of Algeria's recent bombings. Nevertheless, the violence continued at an alarming rate: in early December two suicide car bombings in separate districts of Algiers resulted in a large number of fatalities. (Estimates for the number of those killed ranged between an official figure of 26 and reports from other sources, such as medics, who claimed that around 70 people had lost their lives.) The first bomb exploded outside the Constitutional Court, while the second targeted UN offices, killing 17 personnel. This reportedly brought to 15 the number of terrorist attacks perpetrated in the country since the start of 2007; an estimated 491 people were believed to have died as a result of political violence by the end of 2007. Many commentators noted that the leadership of AQIM, which was said to be experiencing considerable levels of dissent within its various factions, had chosen to adopt suicide bombing as its principal method of operation, in contrast with the tactics traditionally used by militant Islamist groups in Algeria, and that civilians were increasingly being targeted as well as the armed forces, police and other state officials. In early January 2008 a car bomb attack against a police station and an ambush on a military convoy, both in the Algiers region, resulted in the deaths of four police officers and five soldiers, respectively. The authorities responded to this renewed violence, for which AQIM again claimed responsibility, by arresting many suspected militants and implementing a further tightening of security measures.

At local elections held in late November 2007 (postponed from October owing to the month of Ramadan) the FLN obtained some 30.0% of seats, against 24.5% for the RND and 11.3% for the Front national algérien. Recent changes to electoral legislation had restricted the number of parties eligible to participate in the polls. As in the general election of May, candidates of the FIS were not permitted to field candidates. However, most of Algeria's political organizations considered the local elections to have been conducted fairly. In early 2008 opposition politicians, academics and journalists launched a petition against plans by supporters of President Bouteflika to amend the Constitution (which stipulates that a President may only renew his term of office once) in order to allow Bouteflika to seek a third presidential term.

During the late 1970s and early 1980s the protracted struggle in Western Sahara embittered Algeria's relations with France, which supported the claims of Morocco. Algeria also criticized French military intervention elsewhere in Africa, while further grievances were the trade imbalance in favour of the former colonial power, recurrent disputes over the price of Algerian exports of gas to France, and the French Government's determination to reduce the number of Algerians residing in France. The Algerian military takeover in January 1992 was welcomed by the French Government, and French economic and political support for the Algerian regime increased in early 1993, following the appointment of Edouard Balladur as Prime Minister of France. Alleged Islamist militants residing in France continued to be prosecuted, and in August 1994, following the killing of five French embassy employees in Algiers, 26 suspected Algerian extremists were interned in northern France; 20 of them were subsequently expelled to Burkina Faso. In September the French embassy in Algiers confirmed that entry visas would be issued to Algerians only in exceptional cases. By November the number of French nationals killed by Islamist militants in Algeria had reached 21 and the French Government urged its citizens to leave Algeria. An Air France aircraft was hijacked at Algiers airport in December by members of the GIA, resulting in the deaths of three passengers and, later, in the killing of the hijackers by French security forces when the aircraft landed in France. The GIA claimed responsibility for numerous bomb attacks across France between July and November 1995, in which seven people were killed and more than 160 injured. In August 1996 the success of a visit to Algeria by Hervé de Charette, the French Minister of Foreign Affairs, was marred by the assassination of the French Roman Catholic Bishop of Oran only hours after meeting de Charette. In December four people were killed as a result of a bomb explosion on a passenger train in Paris, prompting speculation that the GIA had resumed its campaign of violence in France. In early 1998 a French court sentenced 36 Islamist militants to terms of imprisonment of up to 10 years for providing logistical support for the bomb attacks in France in 1995. A further 138 people stood trial in France in September 1998, accused of criminal association with Algerian terrorists.

In June 1999 the French National Assembly voted unanimously to abandon the official claim that the eight-year struggle between Algerian nationalists and French troops, which began in November 1954, had been no more than 'an operation for keeping order' and thus admitted that France had indeed fought in the Algerian war of independence. An apparent improvement in relations between Algeria and France was further signalled by a meeting in September 1999 between Bouteflika and the French President, Jacques Chirac, in New York, USA (the first meeting between the leaders of the two countries since 1992). In mid-June Bouteflika made a full state visit to France—the first of its kind by an Algerian Head of State—during which he addressed the French National Assembly and held talks with both Chirac and the French Prime Minister, Lionel Jospin. Although the visit produced few tangible results, it was regarded as a success and an important step towards ending the diplomatic isolation imposed on Algeria following the military takeover in 1992.

Algeria's relations with France were placed under strain from late 2000 by a series of much-publicized revelations, mainly regarding occurrences during the war of independence. In November Gen. Jacques Massu, who had commanded French troops during the Battle of Algiers in 1957, asserted in an interview with the French daily Le Monde that France should admit and condemn the use of torture by its forces during the conflict. In February 2001 the French Ministers of the Interior and of Defence held talks with their Algerian counterparts in Algiers. The meetings were, however, overshadowed by the recent publication of allegations of Algerian army involvement in the torture and massacre of civilians since 1992 (see above). In his book *Services spéciaux Algérie 1955-57: Mon témoignage sur la torture*, published in May 2001, a retired French general, Paul Aussarresses, admitted that he had, with the full knowledge and support of the French Government, personally tortured and killed 24 Algerian prisoners during the war of independence. In January 2002 Aussarresses, who had been deprived of his military rank, was convicted of 'apologizing for war crimes' and fined €7,500. Meanwhile, in August 2001 eight 'harkis'—Algerian Muslims who had served in the French army prior to independence—filed a formal complaint against the French Government for crimes and complicity in crimes against humanity. As many as 130,000 harkis were estimated to have been murdered by FLN troops following France's withdrawal from Algeria in 1962. In September 2001 President Chirac unveiled a plaque in Paris to commemorate those who were killed, and acknowledged his country's failure to halt the reprisals against the harkis. In November 2003 it was announced that Pierre Messmer, the French Minister of the Armed Forces during the latter stages of the war of independence, would face charges of committing 'crimes against humanity' for his role in the decision not to allow the harkis to settle in France.

Relations between the two countries improved markedly during 2002, and in March 2003 Jacques Chirac became the first French President to make a full state visit to Algeria since 1962. Bouteflika and Chirac signed the 'Declaration of Algiers', whereby both countries pledged to rebuild bilateral relations by holding annual meetings of their heads of state as well as twice-yearly talks between the two countries' ministers responsible for foreign affairs. The agreement was intended to initiate an 'exceptional partnership' between the two countries. In June 2003 Air France resumed flights to Algeria, which had been suspended since the hijacking of one of its aircraft in December 1994 (see above). President Chirac's official visit was repaid in August 2004 when Bouteflika visited France to mark the 60th anniversary of the Algerian landings in Provence, which had opened up a new front against the Nazi German occupiers. In May 2005 Bouteflika again urged France to acknowledge that Algerians had been tortured and killed during French colonial rule and, specifically, to admit to the massacre of 45,000 Algerian protesters who were demanding independence at the end of the Second World War in May 1945. In April 2006 the French Minister of Foreign Affairs, Philippe Douste-Blazy, visited Algiers for talks aimed at reviving the proposed treaty of friendship between the two countries. However, President Bouteflika insisted that Algerian public opinion was not ready for such a step, and in May relations became further strained after Bouteflika announced that the treaty would remain on hold until France issued an apology to the Algerian people for 'crimes' committed under colonialism. In November the French Minister of the Interior and Land Management, Nicolas Sarkozy, met Bouteflika for talks in Algiers; however, by late 2006 discussions regarding the treaty of friendship appeared to have reached an impasse. Following his recent election to the French presidency, in July 2007 Sarkozy visited Algeria and Tunisia, apparently to demonstrate the intention of his administration to forge even closer ties with the countries of the Maghreb. President Sarkozy undertook a further visit to Algiers in December, at which his failure to offer an explicit apology on behalf of the French nation for the era of colonial rule again angered some Algerian officials. Nevertheless, the French President did acknowledge that France's colonization of Algeria had been 'profoundly unfair', and the two countries signed several important bilateral agreements in the fields of petroleum, gas and nuclear energy. Moreover, the French Government announced subsequently that it was to offer financial compensation to thousands of harkis (see above).

During the 1980s Algeria attempted to achieve a closer relationship with the other countries of the Maghreb region (Libya, Mauritania, Morocco and Tunisia). The Maghreb Fraternity and Co-operation Treaty, signed by Algeria and Tunisia in March 1983 and by Mauritania in December, established a basis for the creation of the long-discussed 'Great Arab Maghreb'. Although bilateral relations continued to be affected by the dispute over Western Sahara, in May 1988 Algeria and Morocco restored diplomatic relations (severed in 1976) at ambassadorial level. Meeting in Algiers in June, the five Heads of State of the Maghreb countries announced the formation of a Maghreb commission to examine areas of regional integration. In February 1989 the leaders signed a treaty establishing the Union du Maghreb arabe (UMA, see p. 414), with the aim of encouraging economic co-operation and eventually establishing a full customs union. The Algerian army's intervention in January 1992 to prevent victory by the FIS in the general election provoked relief in Tunisia and Morocco that the establishment of a neighbouring fundamentalist state had been pre-empted.

Morocco imposed entry visas on Algerian nationals in August 1994, following the murder of two Spanish tourists in Morocco, allegedly by Algerian Islamist extremists. Algeria reciprocated by closing the border between the two countries and imposing entry visas on Moroccan nationals. Tensions eased slightly in September when Algeria announced the appointment of a new ambassador to Morocco, and in early 1995 negotiations commenced on the development of bilateral co-operation. However, in December King Hassan II of Morocco expressed his disapproval at Algeria's alleged continuing support for the independence of Western Sahara, and demanded that UMA activities be suspended. A UMA summit meeting, scheduled for later that month, was subsequently postponed. Following his accession to the presidency in April 1999, Bouteflika initially attempted further to improve bilateral relations during a visit to the Moroccan capital to attend the funeral of King Hassan. However, the rapprochement was halted in August, on the day when the imminent reopening of the common border was announced, by the massacre by the GIA of 29 civilians in the border region of Béchar. Bouteflika's public allegation that Morocco was providing sanctuary for the perpetrators of the attack extended to accusations of drugs-trafficking and arms-dealing on the Algerian border. In September Bouteflika accused both Morocco and Tunisia of acting against the interests of the UMA by negotiating separate agreements with the European Union (EU, see p. 244).

In February 2000 Algeria and Morocco both expressed their desire to improve bilateral relations, and in April Bouteflika met with the new Moroccan ruler, King Muhammad VI, at the Africa-EU summit held in Cairo, Egypt. The two leaders agreed to establish joint committees in an attempt to reduce the number of violent incidents on their mutual border, and joint military security operations began in May. In March 2001 a meeting in Algiers of the UMA's council of ministers responsible for foreign affairs ended acrimoniously following disagreements between Moroccan and Algerian delegations. Relations were further strained after Algeria announced its opposition to UN proposals for a settlement to the Western Sahara issue, as Algeria believed that the plans unduly favoured Morocco and would inevitably lead to the formal integration of the disputed territory into Morocco. (For further details, see the chapter on Morocco.) A UMA summit meeting scheduled to be held in Algiers in December 2003 was postponed just days before it was due to take place following Morocco's announcement that King Muhammad's place at the summit was to be taken by its Minister of Foreign Affairs and Co-operation, and amid reports that representatives from Libya and Mauritania would also not attend. In July 2004 talks between the Moroccan Minister of the Interior, Al Mustapha Sahel, and the Algerian Minister of State for the Interior and Local Authorities, Noureddine Yazid Zerhouni, recommenced in Algeria. The discussions, which were centred on the future of Western Sahara, were also attended by senior representatives of both France and Spain. However, Morocco remained opposed to the UN proposals, stating that they jeopardized its sovereignty, and the ongoing differences between Morocco and Algeria led to the eventual breakdown of the talks. A UMA summit meeting due to take place in Tripoli, Libya, in May 2005 was postponed indefinitely after King Muhammad announced that he would not be attending the summit owing to the continuing dispute with Algeria over Western Sahara. In September, however, Sahel announced that the Moroccan Government was committed to improving relations with Algeria and to negotiating a political end to the conflict. Tensions between the two countries increased again in October, during the Spanish/Moroccan immigration crisis (see the chapter on Morocco), when the Moroccan authorities accused Algeria of exploiting the issue for propaganda purposes.

In December 1996 the EU and Algeria began negotiations on Algeria's participation in a Euro-Mediterranean free trade zone. In January 2001 the President of the European Commission, Romano Prodi, visited Algeria, where he signed the financing protocols for a number of joint projects. In December negotiations for the EU-Algeria Euro-Mediterranean Association Agreement were concluded, and both parties formally signed the agreement in April 2002. It was ratified by the European Parliament in October and, following ratification by the requisite EU member states, entered effect on 1 September 2005.

The Algerian Government was swift to condemn the suicide attacks on New York and Washington, DC, on 11 September 2001, for which the USA held al-Qa'ida responsible, and to offer assistance for the USA's proposed 'coalition against terror'. Later that month the Algerian authorities handed the US authorities a list containing the profiles of some 350 Islamist militants it believed had links to bin Laden and al-Qa'ida. In November President Bouteflika visited Washington, where he met with President George W. Bush and reiterated his support for the US-led campaign. Algeria continued to assist the USA with anti-terrorist operations, and in September 2002 Algerian security forces killed a senior al-Qa'ida operative, who was alleged to be liaising with the GSPC, in a raid near Batna. In December the US Administration announced that it had for the first time agreed to sell weaponry and other military equipment to Algeria as part of the USA's policy of intensifying security co-operation with Algeria. In December 2003 the US Secretary of State, Colin Powell, visited Algeria for talks with President Bouteflika at which he praised Algeria's co-operation in the 'war on terror' and the strength of US-Algerian relations.

In March 2003 four Algerians were sentenced to terms of imprisonment ranging from 10 to 12 years by a court in Frankfurt, Germany, after being convicted of conspiracy to commit murder, conspiracy to plant a bomb and of weapons violations. The four men had been arrested in December 2000 in Strasbourg, France, where, it was alleged, they had intended to detonate a series of bombs. Meanwhile, in January 2003 five Algerians were arrested in London, United Kingdom, and charged with being 'concerned in the development or production of a chemical weapon' and with having materials 'connected with the commission, preparation or instigation of an act of terrorism'. A number of Algerians were also detained following a series of police raids across the United Kingdom later that month, and in April two Algerians were sentenced to 11 years' imprisonment for 'entering a funding arrangement for the purposes of terrorism'. In July another Algerian was gaoled for four years after being convicted of raising funds for al-Qa'ida. In June 2006 Algeria and the United Kingdom signed a memorandum of understanding on the extradition of Algerian citizens suspected of involvement in terrorist activity. Two such alleged Islamist militants were deported to Algeria in that month and another five reportedly agreed to be extradited in January 2007.

During February and March 2003 32 European tourists, including 16 Germans and 10 Austrians, disappeared in the Algerian Sahara. The Algerian authorities refused to confirm allegations that the tourists had been kidnapped by a terrorist group with close links to the GSPC, although some reports maintained that they had been taken as hostages to be exchanged for Islamist militants imprisoned in Europe. In April a senior Algerian army official stated that all 32 were alive but that they were being held by members of the GSPC outside the town of Illizi, close to the Libyan border. In early May government sources confirmed that talks were ongoing with the captors, and later that month 17 of the hostages were forcibly freed when Algerian special forces stormed the Islamists' hideout, reportedly killing at least nine of the kidnappers. In July it was claimed that the remaining 15 hostages had been moved to Mali, although one of the German hostages subsequently died from heatstroke. In August a Malian presidential spokesman announced that all 14 hostages had been released from captivity and that a 'major and positive role' in their release had been played by Libya's Qaddafi International Foundation for Charitable Associations (since renamed the Qaddafi Development Foundation), which had apparently paid €5m. to the kidnappers. There were also unconfirmed reports that Germany had paid the hostage-takers between €4m. and €15m. to secure the release of the prisoners. Libyan diplomats, however, denied that any ransom had been paid. Meanwhile, the German Chancellor, Gerhard Schröder, stated that German security forces would join Malian and Algerian troops in their search for the hostage-takers.

In July 2005 Algeria's chargé d'affaires in Iraq, the most senior Algerian diplomat in the country, and a colleague were abducted in the capital, Baghdad, by militants of the group known as al-

ALGERIA

Qa'ida in Iraq; they were killed six days later. The Algerian authorities consequently withdrew all diplomatic staff from Iraq.

During the first visit by a Russian leader to Algeria since the Soviet era, undertaken by President Vladimir Putin in March 2006, the two countries signed an agreement whereby Russia would cancel the estimated US $4,700m. of Algerian debt (some 25% of Algeria's total external debt), in exchange for which Algeria was to purchase an estimated $7,500m. of Russian weaponry and other military equipment.

Government

Under the 1976 Constitution (with modifications adopted by the National People's Assembly in June 1979 and with further amendments approved by popular referendum in November 1988, February 1989 and November 1996), Algeria is a multi-party state, with parties subject to approval by the Ministry of the Interior and Local Authorities. The Head of State is the President of the Republic, who is elected by universal adult suffrage for a five-year term, renewable once. The President presides over a Council of Ministers and a High Security Council. The President must appoint a Prime Minister as Head of Government, who appoints a Council of Ministers. The bicameral legislature consists of the 389-member National People's Assembly and the 144-member Council of the Nation. The members of the National People's Assembly are elected by universal, direct, secret suffrage for a five-year term. Two-thirds of the members of the Council of the Nation are elected by indirect, secret suffrage from regional and municipal authorities; the remainder are appointed by the President of the Republic. The Council's term in office is six years; one-half of its members are replaced every three years. Both the Head of Government and the parliamentary chambers may initiate legislation, which must be deliberated upon by the National People's Assembly and the Council of the Nation, respectively, before promulgation. The country is divided into 48 departments (*wilayat*), which are, in turn, sub-divided into communes. Each *wilaya* and commune has an elected assembly.

Defence

As assessed at November 2007, the estimated strength of the armed forces was 147,000 (including some 80,000 conscripts), comprising an army of 127,000, a navy of about 6,000 and an air force of an estimated 14,000. The defence budget for 2007 was estimated at AD 250,000m. Military service is compulsory for 18 months. There are paramilitary forces of about 187,200, controlled by the Ministry of Defence and the Directorate of National Security, and an estimated 150,000 self-defence militia and communal guards.

Economic Affairs

In 2006, according to estimates by the World Bank, Algeria's gross national income (GNI), measured at average 2004–06 prices, was US $101,206m., equivalent to $3,030 per head (or $6,900 on an international purchasing-power parity basis). During 1996–2006, it was estimated, the population increased at an average annual rate of 1.5%, while gross domestic product (GDP) per head increased, in real terms, by an average of 2.4% per year. Overall GDP increased, in real terms, at an average annual rate of 3.9% in 1996–2006; it grew by 3.0% in 2006.

Agriculture (including forestry and fishing) contributed 8.2% of GDP in 2005, and employed an estimated 23.0% of the labour force in 2005, according to FAO. Domestic production of food crops is insufficient to meet the country's requirements. The principal crops are wheat, barley, potatoes and tomatoes. Dates are Algeria's principal non-hydrocarbon export; onions, citrus fruits, watermelons and grapes are also grown, and wine has been an important export since the French colonial era. During 1995–2005 agricultural GDP increased at an average annual rate of 5.1%. Agricultural GDP increased by 1.9% in 2005.

Industry (including mining, manufacturing, construction and power) contributed 61.9% of GDP in 2005, and engaged 24.0% of the employed population in 2003. During 1995–2005 industrial GDP increased at an average annual rate of 4.1%. Industrial GDP increased by 5.5% in 2005.

The mining sector provides almost all of Algeria's export earnings, although it engaged only 1.2% of the employed population in 2003. Petroleum and natural gas, which together contributed 48.3% of GDP in 2005, are overwhelmingly Algeria's principal exports, providing 98.1% of total export earnings in 2004. Algeria's proven reserves of petroleum were 12,300m. barrels at the end of 2006, sufficient to maintain output at that year's levels—which averaged 2.01m. barrels per day (b/d)—for almost 17 years. As a member of the Organization of the Petroleum Exporting Countries (OPEC, see p. 373), Algeria is subject to production quotas agreed by the Organization's Conference. Proven reserves of natural gas at the end of 2006 totalled 4,500,000m. cu m, sustainable at that year's production level (totalling 84,500m. cu m) for more than 52 years. Algeria currently transports natural gas through two pipelines—one to Spain and Portugal via Morocco, and the other to Italy via Tunisia. Plans to construct a second pipeline linking Algeria to Italy via the island of Sardinia were at an advanced stage in early 2008, with the pipeline scheduled to begin transporting gas in 2011. Construction of a further pipeline enabling gas to be exported to Spain and thereafter France began in 2007; the project was due to be completed by 2009. Substantial reserves of iron ore, phosphates, barite (barytes), lead, zinc, mercury, salt, marble and industrial minerals are also mined, and the exploitation of gold reserves commenced in 2001. The GDP of the hydrocarbons sector increased by 6.1% in 1999 and by an estimated 4.9% in 2000, while that of other mining activities declined by 3.0% in 1999 but expanded by some 6.5% in 2000.

Manufacturing engaged 9.2% of the employed population in 2003, and, according to the World Bank, provided 5.6% of GDP in 2005. Measured by gross value of output, the principal branches of manufacturing are: food products, beverages and tobacco; metals, metal products, machinery and transport and scientific equipment; non-metallic mineral products; chemical, petroleum, coal, rubber and plastic products; wood, paper and products; and textiles and clothing. During 1995–2005 the GDP of the manufacturing sector declined at an average annual rate of 1.0%. However, manufacturing GDP increased by 3.3% in 2005.

Energy is derived principally from natural gas (which contributed 97.0% of total electricity output in 2004). Algeria is a net exporter of fuels, with imports of energy products comprising only an estimated 0.9% of the value of merchandise imports in 2004.

Services engaged 54.9% of the employed labour force in 2003, and provided 29.9% of GDP in 2005. During 1995–2005 the combined GDP of the service sectors increased at an average annual rate of 3.5%. Services GDP increased by 5.7% in 2005.

In 2005 Algeria recorded a visible trade surplus of US $26,470m., while there was a surplus of $21,180m. on the current account of the balance of payments. France was the principal source of imports in 2004 (providing 22.5% of the total); other important suppliers were Italy, Germany, the USA and the People's Republic of China. The USA was the principal market for exports (23.6%) in that year; other major purchasers were Italy, France, Spain and the Netherlands. The principal exports in 2004 were, overwhelmingly, mineral fuels and lubricants. The principal imports in that year were machinery and transport equipment, food and live animals, and basic manufactures.

In 2005 Algeria recorded an overall budget surplus of AD 896,400m., equivalent to 11.9% of GDP. Algeria's total external debt at the end of 2005 amounted to US $16,879m., of which $15,476m. was long-term public debt. In 2001 the cost of debt-servicing was equivalent to 19.5% of the value of exports of goods and services. The annual rate of inflation averaged 2.9% in 2000–06. Consumer prices increased by an average of 1.9% in 2005 and by 1.8% in 2006. According to an official labour force survey conducted between July and October 2006, some 12.3% of the labour force were unemployed, compared with an estimated 15.3% between July and September 2005.

Algeria is a member of the Union of the Arab Maghreb (UMA, see p. 414), which aims to promote economic integration of member states, and also of OPEC. A Euro-Mediterranean Association Agreement between Algeria and the European Union, signed in April 2002, entered into effect on 1 September 2005. Negotiations concerning Algeria's accession to the World Trade Organization (WTO, see p. 396), which commenced in 1987, were believed to be at an advanced stage in early 2008.

Despite the persistent high levels of unemployment and poverty in the country, Algeria's economy showed continuing signs of improvement during 2006–07. The economy remains reliant on hydrocarbons (which accounted for 98.1% of exports in 2004) and since international petroleum prices reached a record level in 2006, the Algerian Government was able to pay off its entire debt to the 'Paris Club' of official creditors by November. Many analysts commented, however, that in order to maintain its high level of GDP growth, the country would need to introduce further privatization of state-controlled companies to attract foreign investment. In October 2007 the Government announced the dissolution of 120 state-owned companies, after efforts to modernize them were deemed to have failed. By early 2008 the privatization programme was proceeding far more slowly than was originally anticipated. Algeria's rate of unemployment appeared to have decreased considerably in the first part of the decade (from 29.8% of the population in 2000 to 12.3% in 2006), although many commentators argued that this decline had been exaggerated. The country remained a leading exporter of liquified natural gas, exporting 28,750m. cu m in 2004, chiefly to Europe. Oil production reached 2.0m. b/d at the end of 2006—substantially in excess of agreed OPEC quotas. In October 2006 an amendment to legislation promulgated in March 2005 regarding foreign and private investment in the hydrocarbons sector was adopted by the National People's Assembly. The amendment to the hydrocarbons law restored the permission of the state energy company SONATRACH to hold a 51% stake in all discoveries and development projects, thus maximizing state revenues at a time when international hydrocarbons prices had risen sharply. However, many analysts expressed concerns that the amendment would precipitate a reduction in the level of foreign investment in Algeria's energy sector. In September 2007 a consortium led by the Spanish company Repsol was relieved of its majority stake in the Gassi Touil natural gas project by SONATRACH. It was reported in December that the Government was seeking an international partner to develop iron ore deposits in the south-eastern region of Gara Djebilet. The project would facilitate the building of an 800-km railway in order to transport the ore, and a steel plant to process it; once completed, the mine reportedly had the potential to become the largest source of iron ore in the world, and to assist in both job creation and diversification away from the hydrocarbons sector.

Education

Education, in the national language (Arabic), is officially compulsory for nine years between six and 15 years of age. Primary education begins at the age of six and lasts for six years. Secondary education begins at 12 years of age and lasts for up to six years (comprising two cycles of three years each). In 2004/05 the total enrolment at primary schools included 96.6% of children in the relevant age-group. The comparable ratio for secondary enrolment in 2003/04 was an estimated 66.2%. In mid-2003 the Government agreed to permit the use of the Berber language, Tamazight, as a language of instruction in Algerian schools. In 2005 some AD 78,000m. (11.5% of capital expenditure) was allocated to education and professional training by the central Government. Priority is being given to teacher-training, to the development of technical and scientific teaching programmes, and to adult literacy and training schemes. In addition to the 27 main universities, there are 16 other *centres universitaires* and a number of technical colleges. In 2004/05 a total of 755,463 students were enrolled in tertiary education.

Public Holidays

2008: 1 January (New Year), 10 January*† (Muharram, Islamic New Year), 19 January* (Ashoura), 20 March* (Mouloud, Birth of Muhammad), 1 May (Labour Day), 19 June (Ben Bella's Overthrow), 5 July (Independence Day), 30 July* (Leilat al-Meiraj, Ascension of Muhammad), 2 September* (Ramadan begins), 1 October* (Id al-Fitr, end of Ramadan), 1 November (Anniversary of the Revolution), 9 December* (Id al-Adha, Feast of the Sacrifice), 29 December*† (Muharram, Islamic New Year).

2009: 1 January (New Year), 7 January*‡ (Ashoura), 9 March* (Mouloud, Birth of Muhammad), 1 May (Labour Day), 19 June (Ben Bella's Overthrow), 5 July (Independence Day), 19 July* (Leilat al-Meiraj, Ascension of Muhammad), 22 August* (Ramadan begins), 20 September* (Id al-Fitr, end of Ramadan), 1 November (Anniversary of the Revolution), 27 November* (Id al-Adha, Feast of the Sacrifice), 18 December* (Muharram, Islamic New Year), 27 December*‡ (Ashoura).

* These holidays are dependent on the Islamic lunar calendar and may differ by one or two days from the dates given.

† This festival occurs twice (marking the start of the Islamic years AH 1429 and 1430) within the same Gregorian year.

‡ This festival occurs twice (in the Islamic years AH 1430 and 1431) within the same Gregorian year.

Weights and Measures

The metric system is in force.

Statistical Survey

Source (unless otherwise stated): Office National des Statistiques, 8 rue des Moussebilines, BP 202, Ferhat Boussad, Algiers; tel. (21) 63-99-74; fax (21) 63-79-55; e-mail ons@ons.dz; internet www.ons.dz.

Area and Population

AREA, POPULATION AND DENSITY

Area (sq km)	2,381,741*
Population (census results)†	
20 April 1987	23,038,942
25 June 1998	
Males	14,698,589
Females	14,402,278
Total‡	29,100,867
Population (official estimates at 31 December)	
2005	33,200,000
2006	33,800,000
Density (per sq km) at 31 December 2006	14.2

* 919,595 sq miles.
† Excluding Algerian nationals residing abroad, numbering an estimated 828,000 at 1 January 1978.
‡ Excluding 171,476 Sahrawi refugees in camps.

POPULATION BY WILAYA (ADMINISTRATIVE DISTRICT)
(1998 census)

	Area (sq km)	Population	Density (per sq km)
Adrar	439,700	311,615	0.7
Aïn Defla	4,897	660,342	134.9
Aïn Témouchent	2,379	327,331	137.6
Algiers (el-Djezaïr)	273	2,562,428	9,386.2
Annaba	1,439	557,818	387.6
Batna	12,192	962,623	79.0
el-Bayadh	78,870	168,789	2.1
Béchar	162,200	225,546	1.4
Béjaïa	3,268	856,840	262.2
Biskra (Beskra)	20,986	575,858	27.4
Blida (el-Boulaïda)	1,696	784,283	462.4
Borj Bou Arreridj	4,115	555,402	135.0
Bouira	4,439	629,560	141.8
Boumerdès	1,591	647,389	406.9
Chlef (el-Cheliff)	4,795	858,695	179.1
Constantine (Qacentina)	2,187	810,914	370.8
Djelfa	66,415	797,706	12.0
Ghardaïa	86,105	300,516	3.5
Guelma	4,101	430,000	104.9
Illizi	285,000	34,108	0.1
Jijel	2,577	573,208	222.4
Khenchela	9,811	327,917	33.4
Laghouat	25,057	317,125	12.7
Mascara (Mouaskar)	5,941	676,192	113.8
Médéa (Lemdiyya)	8,866	802,078	90.5
Mila	9,375	674,480	71.9
Mostaganem	2,175	631,057	290.1
M'Sila	18,718	805,519	43.0

ALGERIA

Statistical Survey

—continued	Area (sq km)	Population	Density (per sq km)
Naâma	29,950	127,314	4.3
Oran (Ouahran)	2,121	1,213,839	572.3
Ouargla	211,980	445,619	2.1
el-Oued	54,573	504,401	9.2
Oum el-Bouaghi	6,768	519,170	76.7
Relizane (Ghilizane)	4,870	642,205	131.9
Saïda	6,764	279,526	41.3
Sétif	6,504	1,311,413	201.6
Sidi-bel-Abbès	9,096	525,632	57.8
Skikda	4,026	786,154	195.3
Souk Ahras	4,541	367,455	80.9
Tamanrasset (Tamanghest)	556,200	137,175	0.3
et-Tarf	3,339	352,588	105.6
Tébessa (Tbessa)	14,227	549,066	38.6
Tiaret (Tihert)	20,673	725,853	35.1
Tindouf	159,000	27,060	0.2
Tipaza	2,166	506,053	233.6
Tissemsilt	3,152	264,240	83.8
Tizi Ouzou	3,568	1,108,708	310.7
Tlemcen	9,061	842,053	92.9
Total	2,381,741	29,100,867	12.2

PRINCIPAL TOWNS
(population at 1998 census)

Algiers (el-Djezaïr, capital)	1,519,570	Tébessa (Tbessa)	153,246
Oran (Ouahran)	655,852	Blida (el-Boulaïda)	153,083
Constantine (Qacentina)	462,187	Skikda	152,335
Batna	242,514	Béjaïa	147,076
Annaba	215,083	Tiaret (Tihert)	145,332
Sétif (Stif)	211,859	Chlef (el-Cheliff)	133,874
Sidi-bel-Abbès	180,260	el-Buni	133,471
Biskra (Beskra)	170,956	Béchar	131,010
Djelfa	154,265		

Mid-2005 ('000, incl. suburbs, UN estimate): Algiers 3,200; Oran 765 (Source: UN, *World Urbanization Prospects: The 2005 Revision*).

BIRTHS, MARRIAGES AND DEATHS*

	Registered live births†		Registered marriages		Registered deaths†	
	Number	Rate (per 1,000)	Number	Rate (per 1,000)	Number	Rate (per 1,000)
1999	594,000	19.8	163,126	5.4	141,000	4.7
2000	589,000	19.4	177,548	5.8	140,000	4.6
2001	619,000	20.0	194,273	6.3	141,000	4.6
2002	617,000	19.7	218,620	7.0	138,000	4.4
2003	649,000	20.4	240,463	7.6	145,000	4.6
2004	669,000	20.7	267,633	8.3	141,000	4.4
2005	703,000	21.4	279,548	8.5	147,000	4.5
2006	739,000	22.1	295,295	8.8	144,000	4.3

* Figures refer to the Algerian population only, and include adjustment for underenumeration.
† Excluding live-born infants dying before registration of birth.

Expectation of life (years at birth, WHO estimates): 70.8 (males 69.6; females 71.9) in 2005 (Source: WHO, *World Health Statistics*).

ECONOMICALLY ACTIVE POPULATION
('000 persons aged 15 years and over at September 2003)

	Males	Females	Total
Agriculture, hunting, forestry and fishing	1,308.9	102.8	1,411.8
Mining and quarrying	78.7	4.2	82.9
Manufacturing	406.3	210.3	616.7
Electricity, gas and water	93.4	11.1	104.6
Construction	790.4	9.5	799.9
Trade; repair of motor vehicles, motorcycles and personal household goods	853.7	27.2	880.9
Hotels and restaurants	97.6	4.9	102.5
Transport, storage and communications	384.5	20.9	405.4
Financial intermediation	49.5	18.1	67.6
Real estate, renting and business activities	53.6	14.4	68.0
Public administration and defence; compulsory social security	958.6	112.6	1,071.2
Education	400.3	227.5	627.7
Health and social work	143.2	101.9	245.0
Other community, social and personal service activities	124.0	59.4	183.4
Households with employed persons	4.6	7.6	12.2
Extra-territorial organizations and bodies	2.4	0.5	2.9
Activities not adequately defined	1.2	0.2	1.4
Total employed	5,751.0	933.0	6,684.1
Unemployed	1,759.9	318.3	2,078.0
Total labour force	7,510.9	1,251.3	8,762.1

Source: ILO.

2004 (sample survey, '000 persons aged 15 years and over, July–September): Total employed 7,798.4 (males 6,439.2, females 1,359.3); Unemployed 1,671.5 (males 1,370.4, females 301.1); Total labour force 9,469.9 (males 7,809.6, females 1,660.4).

2005 (sample survey, '000 persons aged 15 years and over, July–September): Total employed 8,044.2 (males 6,870.3, females 1,173.9); Unemployed 1,448.3 (males 1,199.1, females 249.2); Total labour force 9,492.5 (males 8,069.4, females 1,423.1).

2006 (sample survey, '000 persons aged 15 years and over, July–October): Total employed 8,868.8 (males 7,371.9, females 1,496.9); Unemployed 1,240.8 (males 988.3, females 252.6); Total labour force 10,109.6 (males 8,360.2, females 1,749.5).

Health and Welfare

KEY INDICATORS

Total fertility rate (children per woman, 2005)	2.4
Under-5 mortality rate (per 1,000 live births, 2005)	39
HIV/AIDS (% of persons aged 15–49, 2005)	0.10
Physicians (per 1,000 head, 2002)	1.1
Hospital beds (per 1,000 head, 2004)	1.7
Health expenditure (2004): US $ per head (PPP)	166.9
Health expenditure (2004): % of GDP	3.6
Health expenditure (2004): public (% of total)	72.5
Access to water (% of persons, 2004)	85
Access to sanitation (% of persons, 2004)	92
Human Development Index (2005): ranking	104
Human Development Index (2005): value	0.733

For sources and definitions, see explanatory note on p. vi.

ALGERIA

Agriculture

PRINCIPAL CROPS
('000 metric tons)

	2004	2005	2006
Wheat	2,731	2,415	2,688
Barley	1,212	1,033	1,236
Oats	89	78	89
Potatoes	1,896	2,157	2,181
Broad beans, dry	32	27	24
Chick-peas	16	14	13
Almonds	38	45	54
Olives	469	316	365
Rapeseed*	29	29	29
Cabbages	42	34	39
Artichokes	50	37	26
Tomatoes	1,092	1,023	796
Cauliflowers	53	51	59
Pumpkins, squash and gourds	158	189	158
Cucumbers and gherkins	92	98	93
Aubergines (Eggplants)	47	43	54
Chillies and green peppers	265	249	276
Dry onions	658	686	704
Garlic	52	46	54
Green beans	41	33	36
Green peas	98	110	82
Carrots	198	164	165†
Oranges	417	435	474
Tangerines, mandarins, clementines and satsumas	144	143	156
Lemons and limes	46	47	47
Apples	165	200	283
Pears	133	158	189
Apricots	88	145	167
Peaches and nectarines	80	95	118
Plums	38	46	66
Grapes	284	334	398
Watermelons	721	858	785
Figs	65	70	92
Dates	443	516	491
Tobacco (leaves)	8	7	7†

* Unofficial figures.
† FAO estimate.

Aggregate production ('000 metric tons, may include official, semi-official or estimated data): Total cereals 4,033 in 2004, 3,527 in 2005, 4,016 in 2006; Total roots and tubers 1,896 in 2004, 2,157 in 2005, 2,181 in 2006; Total vegetables (incl. melons) 4,164 in 2004, 4,280 in 2005, 3,986 in 2006; Total fruits (excl. melons) 1,990 in 2004, 2,284 in 2005, 2,588 in 2006.

Source: FAO.

LIVESTOCK
('000 head, year ending September)

	2004	2005	2006
Sheep	18,293	18,909	19,616
Goats	3,451	3,590	3,755
Cattle	1,614	1,586	1,608
Horses	45	43	44
Asses and mules	201	201	195
Camels	273	269	287
Chickens (million)*	125	125	125

* FAO estimates.
Source: FAO.

LIVESTOCK PRODUCTS
('000 metric tons)

	2004	2005	2006
Cattle meat	125*	120†	122†
Goat meat†	13	13	14
Chicken meat†	254	259	253
Rabbit meat†	7	7	7
Sheep meat†	172	178	185
Cows' milk†	1,300	1,298	1,320
Sheep's milk†	199	203	210
Goats' milk	191	184*	195†
Hen eggs†	180	172	172
Honey	3	3	3†
Wool: greasy	23	24	25

* Unofficial estimate.
† FAO estimate(s).
Source: FAO.

Forestry

ROUNDWOOD REMOVALS
('000 cubic metres, excl. bark, FAO estimates)

	2004	2005	2006
Pulpwood	29	23	23
Other industrial wood	93	50	50
Fuel wood	7,545	7,669	7,669
Total	**7,667**	**7,742**	**7,742**

Sawnwood production ('000 cubic metres, incl. railway sleepers, FAO estimates): 13 per year in 1975–2006.

Source: FAO.

Fishing

('000 metric tons, live weight)

	2003	2004	2005
Capture	141.5	113.5	126.3
Bogue	7.0	5.8	6.6
Jack and horse mackerels	7.9	6.0	10.6
Sardinellas	26.4	22.5	22.9
European pilchard (sardine)	70.3	63.8	69.5
European anchovy	1.7	1.4	3.1
Crustaceans and molluscs	4.1	4.0	4.7
Aquaculture*	0.4	0.6	0.4
Total catch*	**141.9**	**114.1**	**126.6**

* FAO estimates.
Source: FAO.

ALGERIA

Mining

('000 metric tons, unless otherwise indicated)

	2003	2004	2005*
Crude petroleum ('000 barrels)	580,000	589,870	611,950
Natural gas (million cu m)†	137,634	144,281	151,775
Iron ore (gross weight)	1,378	1,554	1,579
Zinc concentrates (metric tons)‡	2,796	231	4,463
Mercury (kilograms)‡	175,600	73,451	276
Phosphate rock§	905	1,017	878
Barite (Barytes)	46	48	53
Salt (unrefined)	191	183	197
Gypsum (crude)	350	1,058	1,460

* Preliminary.
† Figures refer to gross volume. Production on a dry basis (in million cu m) was: 98,754 in 2003; 98,111 in 2004; 98,784 in 2005 (preliminary).
‡ Figures refer to the metal content of ores or concentrates.
§ Figures refer to gross weight. The estimated phosphoric acid content (in '000 metric tons, estimated) was 280 in 2003; 300 in 2004; 260 in 2005 (preliminary).

Source: US Geological Survey.

Industry

SELECTED PRODUCTS
('000 metric tons, unless otherwise indicated)

	2002	2003	2004
Olive oil (crude)	24	26	30
Refined sugar	83	150	n.a.
Beer ('000 hectolitres)	283	186	n.a.
Soft drinks ('000 hectolitres)	184	189	n.a.
Footwear—excl. rubber ('000 pairs)	929	718	n.a.
Phosphate fertilizers*	122	153	n.a.
Naphthas†	4,098	4,164	3,096
Motor spirit (petrol)	1,939	1,893	1,925
Jet fuel†	1,393	1,315	986
Gas-diesel (distillate fuel) oils	6,044	6,186	6,340
Residual fuel oils	5,833	6,093	5,560
Lubricating oils	125	140	162
Petroleum bitumen (asphalt)	307	305	262
Liquefied petroleum gas:			
from natural gas plants	9,356	9,148	8,650
from petroleum refineries	600	608	573
Cement	9,277	8,192	9,000
Pig-iron for steel-making‡‡	960	965	994
Crude steel (ingots)‡	1,091	1,051	1,014
Zinc—unwrought	26.1	25.1	25.0
Refrigerators for household use ('000)	153	150	n.a.
Television receivers ('000)	289	292	n.a.
Buses and coaches—assembled (number)	243	190	n.a.
Lorries—assembled (number)	2,561	2,059	n.a.
Electric energy (million kWh)	27,647	29,571	31,250

* Production in terms of phosphoric acid.
† Provisional or estimated figure(s).
‡ Data from the US Geological Survey.

Source: mainly UN, *Industrial Commodity Statistics Yearbook*.

Finance

CURRENCY AND EXCHANGE RATES

Monetary Units
100 centimes = 1 Algerian dinar (AD).

Sterling, Dollar and Euro Equivalents (31 December 2007)
£1 sterling = 133.887 dinars;
US $1 = 66.830 dinars;
€1 = 98.380 dinars;
1,000 Algerian dinars = £7.47 = $14.96 = €10.16.

Average Exchange Rate (dinars per US $)
2005   73.276
2006   72.647
2007   69.292

GOVERNMENT FINANCE
(central government operations, '000 million AD)

Summary of Balances

	2003	2004	2005
Revenue and grants	1,947.4	2,215.2	3,082.7
Less Expenditure	1,691.4	1,891.8	2,052.0
Budget balance	256.1	323.4	1,030.6
Special accounts balance	186.9	109.9	−129.0
Less Net lending by Treasury	32.6	11.8	5.2
Overall balance	410.4	421.5	896.4

Revenue and Grants

	2003	2004	2005
Hydrocarbon revenue	1,350.0	1,570.7	2,352.7
SONATRACH dividends	65.0	85.0	85.0
Other revenue	594.6	644.1	730.0
Tax revenue	524.9	580.4	640.5
Taxes on income and profits	127.9	148.0	168.1
Wage income taxes	63.3	77.4	85.6
Taxes on goods and services	233.9	274.0	308.8
Customs duties	143.8	138.8	143.9
Registration and stamps	19.3	19.6	19.6
Non-tax revenue	69.7	63.7	89.5
Grants	2.9	0.4	0.0
Total	1,947.4	2,215.2	3,082.7

Expenditure

Expenditure by economic type	2003	2004	2005
Current expenditure	1,120.9	1,245.5	1,241.4
Personnel expenditure	398.0	446.8	492.2
War veterans' pensions	62.7	69.2	79.8
Material and supplies	58.8	71.7	76.0
Public services	161.4	176.5	187.5
Hospitals	59.3	63.2	61.7
Current transfers	326.1	396.1	332.7
Food subsidies	0.3	1.0	0.9
Youth Employment Support Fund	2.3	7.8	4.0
Interest payments	114.0	85.2	73.2
Capital expenditure	570.4	646.3	810.6
Total	1,691.4	1,891.8	2,052.0

ALGERIA

Statistical Survey

Sectoral allocation of capital expenditure*

	2003	2004	2005
Agriculture and fishery	15.8	8.5	12.0
Irrigation and waterworks	67.8	89.1	113.0
Industry and energy	5.9	0.2	0.3
Economic infrastructure	71.8	79.9	181.4
Housing	74.9	66.0	56.0
Education and professional training	60.0	61.8	78.0
Social infrastructure	31.5	30.8	32.7
Administrative infrastructure	30.5	21.3	32.0
Urban development	43.1	27.9	34.0
Unallocated	39.8	49.1	136.9
Total	441.1	434.6	676.3

* Commitment basis.

Source: IMF, *Algeria: Statistical Appendix* (March 2007).

CENTRAL BANK RESERVES
(US $ million at 31 December)

	2004	2005	2006
Gold*	303	279	294
IMF special drawing rights	1	3	5
Reserve position in IMF	132	122	128
Foreign exchange	43,113	56,178	77,781
Total	43,549	56,582	78,208

* National valuation.

Source: IMF, *International Financial Statistics*.

MONEY SUPPLY
('000 million AD at 31 December)

	2004	2005	2006
Currency outside banks	874.35	920.96	1,081.35
Demand deposits at deposit money banks	971.33	1,095.20	1,633.41
Total money (incl. others)	1,850.70	2,032.30	2,724.96

Source: IMF, *International Financial Statistics*.

COST OF LIVING
(Consumer Price Index; base: 2000 = 100)

	2003	2004	2005
Foodstuffs	111.0	116.4	116.6
Clothing	109.3	111.9	113.5
Rent (incl. fuel and light)	104.8	107.1	121.6
All items (incl. others)	109.5	114.5	116.7

2006: Foodstuffs 119.3; All items 118.8.

Source: ILO.

NATIONAL ACCOUNTS
('000 million AD at current prices)
Expenditure on the Gross Domestic Product

	2003	2004	2005
Government final consumption expenditure	777.5	847.0	890.0
Private final consumption expenditure	2,125.0	2,358.0	2,527.0
Increase in stocks	341.1	561.6	663.2
Gross fixed capital formation	1,265.1	1,476.9	1,661.0
Total domestic expenditure	4,508.7	5,243.5	5,741.2
Exports of goods and services	2,014.6	2,455.3	3,586.9
Less Imports of goods and services	1,259.4	1,572.0	1,809.4
GDP in purchasers' values	5,263.9	6,126.7	7,519.0

Gross Domestic Product by Economic Activity

	2003	2004	2005
Agriculture, forestry and fishing	515.3	578.9	577.0
Hydrocarbons*	1,868.9	2,329.3	3,394.0
Industry (excl. hydrocarbons)	344.9	368.8	393.0
Construction and public works	445.2	503.9	559.0
Government services	553.2	607.0	646.0
Non-government services	1,133.3	1,294.0	1,451.0
Sub-total	4,860.8	5,681.9	7,020.0
Import taxes and duties	403.1	445.1	499.0
GDP in purchasers' values	5,263.9	6,126.9	7,519.0

* Extraction and processing of petroleum and natural gas, including related services and public works.

Source: mainly IMF, *Algeria: Statistical Appendix* (March 2007).

BALANCE OF PAYMENTS
(US $ million)

	2003	2004	2005
Exports of goods f.o.b.	24,460	32,220	46,330
Imports of goods f.o.b.	−13,350	−17,950	−19,860
Trade balance	11,110	14,270	26,470
Exports of services	1,570	1,850	2,510
Imports of services	−2,920	−3,860	−4,780
Balance on goods and services	9,760	12,260	24,200
Other income received	760	990	1,430
Other income paid	−3,460	−4,590	−6,510
Balance on goods, services and income	7,060	8,660	19,120
Transfers (net)	1,750	2,460	2,060
Current balance	8,810	11,120	21,180
Direct investment (net)	620	620	1,060
Official capital (net)	−1,380	−2,230	−3,050
Short-term capital and net errors and omissions	−610	−260	−2,240
Overall balance	7,440	9,250	16,950

Source: IMF, *Statistical Appendix* (March 2007).

External Trade

Note: Data exclude military goods. Exports include stores and bunkers for foreign ships and aircraft.

PRINCIPAL COMMODITIES
(distribution by SITC, US $ million)

Imports c.i.f.	2002	2003	2004
Food and live animals	2,765.5	2,632.1	3,558.6
Dairy products and birds' eggs	506.8	520.4	821.8
Milk and cream	448.3	455.7	747.6
Cereals and cereal preparations	1,334.4	1,135.5	1,390.7
Wheat and meslin (unmilled)	974.8	878.3	1,026.7
Durum wheat (unmilled)	651.8	586.1	707.8
Crude materials (inedible) except fuels	327.7	406.0	460.4
Chemicals and related products	1,491.7	1,644.4	2,192.7
Medicinal and pharmaceutical products	656.4	765.0	1,005.2
Medicaments (incl. veterinary)	600.5	693.0	913.9
Basic manufactures	2,244.2	2,455.3	3,132.1
Iron and steel	919.1	1,048.7	1,337.3
Tubes, pipes and fittings	478.5	398.3	517.3

ALGERIA

Statistical Survey

Imports c.i.f.—continued	2002	2003	2004
Machinery and transport equipment	4,462.8	5,172.9	7,492.9
Power-generating machinery and equipment	382.6	410.8	686.7
Machinery specialized for particular industries	709.3	778.1	1,005.5
General industrial machinery, equipment and parts	1,096.8	1,193.3	1,545.2
Electrical machinery, apparatus, etc.	601.1	735.9	980.0
Telecommunications, sound recording and reproducing equipment	339.2	600.7	877.3
Road vehicles and parts*	824.6	1,049.9	1,794.7
Passenger motor vehicles (excl. buses)	326.6	428.2	870.7
Miscellaneous manufactured articles	618.3	740.0	888.1
Total (incl. others)	12,364.2	13,532.5	18,307.7

* Excluding tyres, engines and electrical parts.

Exports f.o.b.	2002	2003	2004
Mineral fuels, lubricants, etc.	18,238.5	24,129.6	31,491.6
Petroleum, petroleum products, etc.	10,407.6	14,094.1	20,492.3
Crude petroleum oils, etc.	7,956.4	11,346.3	17,570.5
Refined petroleum products	2,310.5	2,557.0	2,671.7
Gas (natural and manufactured)	7,829.3	10,035.1	10,994.8
Liquefied propane and butane	1,767.9	2,393.7	2,805.8
Petroleum gases, etc., in the gaseous state	3,065.2	3,682.2	4,258.6
Total (incl. others)	18,831.2	24,611.5	32,082.6

Source: UN, *International Trade Statistics Yearbook*.

PRINCIPAL TRADING PARTNERS
(US $ million)*

Imports c.i.f.	2002	2003	2004
Argentina	166.1	237.6	593.6
Austria	111.4	126.5	166.9
Belgium	296.0	311.2	490.9
Brazil	109.8	179.9	426.9
Canada	345.2	304.3	286.2
China, People's Republic	351.8	518.3	916.0
France (incl. Monaco)	2,777.0	3,233.4	4,125.3
Germany	878.2	879.5	1,209.3
India	85.6	136.9	217.0
Italy	1,172.7	1,273.1	1,547.5
Japan	383.6	379.9	656.6
Korea, Republic	213.9	220.0	361.1
Mexico	104.4	151.2	97.9
Netherlands	221.8	217.6	237.7
Poland	87.4	84.6	109.8
Russia	275.5	315.0	329.2
Spain	641.3	742.4	886.1
Sweden	100.9	248.5	320.5
Switzerland-Liechtenstein	101.2	148.2	217.0
Turkey	403.9	437.7	583.9
Ukraine	197.2	250.3	438.6
United Kingdom	314.4	410.8	393.0
USA	1,197.6	708.6	1,088.1
Total (incl. others)	12,364.2	13,532.5	18,307.7

Exports f.o.b.	2002	2003	2004
Belgium	469.5	706.5	737.3
Brazil	910.4	1,122.7	1,785.9
Canada	927.6	1,393.6	1,879.7
Egypt	146.8	307.1	447.5
France (incl. Monaco)	2,554.1	3,107.9	3,656.8
Germany	426.2	275.6	239.1
Indonesia	139.4	218.8	171.9
Italy	3,911.0	4,717.6	5,166.1
Netherlands	1,683.9	1,693.5	2,383.4
Portugal	335.0	541.4	863.1
Spain	2,247.3	2,993.0	3,608.7
Turkey	967.0	1,063.9	1,356.5
United Kingdom	382.7	392.7	497.5
USA	2,591.6	4,899.6	7,578.0
Total (incl. others)	18,831.2	24,611.5	32,082.6

* Imports by country of production; exports by country of last consignment.

Source: UN, *International Trade Statistics Yearbook*.

Transport

RAILWAYS
(traffic)

	1999	2000	2001
Passengers carried ('000)	32,027	n.a.	n.a.
Freight carried ('000 metric tons)	7,842	n.a.	n.a.
Passenger-km (million)	1,069	1,142	981
Freight ton-km (million)	2,033	1,980	1,990

Source: mostly UN, *Statistical Yearbook*.

2001 ('000 passenger journeys): 28,800 (Source: Railway Gazette).

ROAD TRAFFIC
(motor vehicles in use at 31 December)

	2000	2001	2002
Passenger cars	1,692,148	1,708,373	1,739,286
Lorries	296,145	298,125	300,171
Vans	609,617	612,523	615,663
Buses and coaches	42,791	44,323	46,136
Motorcycles	9,198	9,245	9,258

SHIPPING

Merchant Fleet
(registered at 31 December)

	2004	2005	2006
Number of vessels	138	129	127
Total displacement ('000 grt)	862.3	809.0	764.1

Source: Lloyd's Register-Fairplay, *World Fleet Statistics*.

International Sea-borne Freight Traffic
('000 metric tons)

	1997	1998	1999
Goods loaded	74,300	75,500	77,900
Goods unloaded	15,200	16,000	16,600

Note: Figures are rounded to the nearest 100,000 metric tons.

CIVIL AVIATION
(traffic on scheduled services)

	2001	2002	2003
Kilometres flown (million)	25	27	27
Passengers carried ('000)	2,076	1,876	2,019
Passenger-km (million)	2,722	2,605	2,672
Total ton-km (million)	264	251	258

Source: UN, *Statistical Yearbook*.

Tourism

FOREIGN TOURIST ARRIVALS BY COUNTRY OF ORIGIN*

	2003	2004	2005
France	106,042	138,473	153,398
Germany	7,049	7,306	9,392
Italy	10,571	10,642	13,676
Libya	9,391	10,007	11,803
Mali	14,453	11,520	12,817
Morocco	4,186	5,424	9,984
Spain	8,600	11,030	14,007
Tunisia	86,025	103,593	128,765
United Kingdom	4,549	6,956	8,126
Total (incl. others)	304,914	368,562	441,206

* Excluding arrivals of Algerian nationals resident abroad: 861,373 in 2003; 865,157 in 2004; 1,001,884 in 2005.

Tourism receipts (US $ million, incl. passenger transport): 112 in 2003; 178 in 2004; 184 in 2005.

Source: World Tourism Organization.

Communications Media

	2004	2005	2006
Telephones ('000 main lines in use)	2,487	2,572	2,841
Mobile cellular telephones ('000 subscribers)	4,882.4	13,661.4	20,998.0
Personal computers ('000 in use)	290	350	n.a.
Internet users ('000)	1,500	1,920	2,460
Broadband subscribers ('000)	36	195	195

1997: Radio receivers ('000 in use): 7,100; Facsimile machines (number in use) 7,000.

1998: Daily newspapers 24 (average circulation 796,440 copies); Non-daily newspapers 82 (average circulation 908,751 copies); Periodicals 106.

1999: Book production (titles) 133 (excl. pamphlets).

2001: Television receivers ('000 in use): 3,500.

2004: Daily newspapers 17.

Sources: UNESCO, *Statistical Yearbook*; UN, *Statistical Yearbook*; International Telecommunication Union.

Education

(2004/05, unless otherwise indicated)

	Institutions	Teachers	Pupils
Pre-primary	n.a.	2,465	71,265
Primary	17,041	171,471	4,361,744
Secondary	5,267	168,434	3,755,821
Tertiary	n.a.	756	755,463

Sources: UNESCO, *Statistical Yearbook* and Institute for Statistics, and Ministère de l'Education nationale.

1998/99 (Pre-primary and primary): 15,729 institutions; 170,562 teachers; 4,843,313 pupils.

Adult literacy rate (UNESCO estimates): 69.9% (males 79.6%; females 60.1%) in 2002 (Source: UNESCO Institute for Statistics).

Directory

The Constitution

A new Constitution for the Democratic and People's Republic of Algeria, approved by popular referendum, was promulgated on 22 November 1976. The Constitution was amended by the National People's Assembly on 30 June 1979. Further amendments were approved by referendum on 3 November 1988, on 23 February 1989 and on 28 November 1996. On 8 April 2002 the Assembly approved an amendment that granted Tamazight, the principal language spoken by the Berber population of the country, the status of a national language. The main provisions of the Constitution, as amended, are summarized below:

The preamble recalls that Algeria owes its independence to a war of liberation which led to the creation of a modern sovereign state, guaranteeing social justice, equality and liberty for all. It emphasizes Algeria's Islamic, Arab and Amazigh (Berber) heritage, and stresses that, as an Arab Mediterranean and African country, it forms an integral part of the Great Arab Maghreb.

FUNDAMENTAL PRINCIPLES OF THE ORGANIZATION OF ALGERIAN SOCIETY

The Republic
Algeria is a popular, democratic state. Islam is the state religion, and Arabic and Tamazight are the official national languages.

The People
National sovereignty resides in the people and is exercised through its elected representatives. The institutions of the State consolidate national unity and protect the fundamental rights of its citizens. The exploitation of one individual by another is forbidden.

The State
The State is exclusively at the service of the people. Those holding positions of responsibility must live solely on their salaries and may not, directly or by the agency of others, engage in any remunerative activity.

Fundamental Freedoms and the Rights of Man and the Citizen
Fundamental rights and freedoms are guaranteed. All discrimination on grounds of sex, race or belief is forbidden. Law cannot operate retrospectively, and a person is presumed innocent until proved guilty. Victims of judicial error shall receive compensation from the State.

The State guarantees the inviolability of the home, of private life and of the person. The State also guarantees the secrecy of correspondence, the freedom of conscience and opinion, freedom of intellectual, artistic and scientific creation, and freedom of expression and assembly.

The State guarantees the right to form political associations (on condition that they are not based on differences in religion, language, race, gender or region), the right to join a trade union, the right to strike, the right to work, to protection, to security, to health, to leisure, to education, etc. It also guarantees the right to leave the national territory, within the limits set by law.

Duties of Citizens
Every citizen must respect the Constitution, and must protect public property and safeguard national independence. The law sanctions the duty of parents to educate and protect their children, as well as the duty of children to help and support their parents. Every citizen must contribute towards public expenditure through the payment of taxes.

The National Popular Army
The army safeguards national independence and sovereignty.

Principles of Foreign Policy
Algeria subscribes to the principles and objectives of the UN. It advocates international co-operation, the development of friendly relations between states, on the basis of equality and mutual interest, and non-interference in the internal affairs of states.

POWER AND ITS ORGANIZATION

The Executive
The President of the Republic is Head of State, Head of the Armed Forces and responsible for national defence. He must be of Algerian origin, a Muslim and more than 40 years old. He is elected by universal, secret, direct suffrage. His mandate is for five years, and is renewable once. The President embodies the unity of the nation. The President presides over meetings of the Council of Ministers. He decides and conducts foreign policy and appoints the Head of Government, who is responsible to the National People's Assembly. The Head of Government must appoint a Council of Ministers. He drafts, co-ordinates and implements his government's programme, which he must present to the Assembly for ratification. Should the Assembly reject the programme, the Head of Government and the Council of Ministers resign, and the President appoints a new Head of Government. Should the newly appointed Head of Government's programme be rejected by the Assembly, the President dissolves the Assembly, and a general election is held. Should the President be unable to perform his functions, owing to a long and serious illness, the President of the Council of the Nation assumes the office for a maximum period of 45 days (subject to the approval of a two-thirds' majority in the National People's Assembly and the Council of the Nation). If the President is still unable to perform his functions after 45 days, the Presidency is declared vacant by the Constitutional Council. Should the Presidency fall vacant, the President of the Council of the Nation temporarily assumes the office and organizes presidential elections within 60 days. He may not himself be a candidate in the election. The President presides over a High Security Council, which advises on all matters affecting national security.

The Legislature
The legislature consists of the Assemblée Populaire Nationale (National People's Assembly) and the Conseil de la Nation (Council of the Nation, which was established by constitutional amendments approved by national referendum in November 1996). The members of the lower chamber, the National People's Assembly, are elected by universal, direct, secret suffrage for a five-year term. Two-thirds of the members of the upper chamber, the Council of the Nation, are elected by indirect, secret suffrage from regional and municipal authorities; the remainder are appointed by the President of the Republic. The Council's term of office is six years; one-half of its members are replaced every three years. The deputies enjoy parliamentary immunity. The legislature sits for two ordinary sessions per year, each of not less than four months' duration. The commissions of the legislature are in permanent session. The two parliamentary chambers may be summoned to meet for an extraordinary session on the request of the President of the Republic, or of the Head of Government, or of two-thirds of the members of the National People's Assembly. Both the Head of Government and the parliamentary chambers may initiate legislation, which must be deliberated upon respectively by the National People's Assembly and the Council of the Nation before promulgation. Any text passed by the Assembly must be approved by three-quarters of the members of the Council in order to become legislation.

The Judiciary
Judges obey only the law. They defend society and fundamental freedoms. The right of the accused to a defence is guaranteed. The Supreme Court regulates the activities of courts and tribunals, and the State Council regulates the administrative judiciary. The Higher Court of the Magistrature is presided over by the President of the Republic; the Minister of Justice is Vice-President of the Court. All magistrates are answerable to the Higher Court for the manner in which they fulfil their functions. The High State Court is empowered to judge the President of the Republic in cases of high treason, and the Head of Government for crimes and offences.

The Constitutional Council
The Constitutional Council is responsible for ensuring that the Constitution is respected, and that referendums, the election of the President of the Republic and legislative elections are conducted in accordance with the law. The Constitutional Council comprises nine members, of whom three are appointed by the President of the Republic, two elected by the National People's Assembly, two elected by the Council of the Nation, one elected by the Supreme Court and one elected by the State Council. The Council's term of office is six years; the President of the Council is appointed for a six-year term and one-half of the remaining members are replaced every three years.

The High Islamic Council
The High Islamic Council is an advisory body on matters relating to Islam. The Council comprises 15 members and its President is appointed by the President of the Republic.

Constitutional Revision
The Constitution can be revised on the initiative of the President of the Republic (subject to approval by the National People's Assembly and by three-quarters of the members of the Council of the Nation), and must be approved by national referendum. Should the Constitutional Council decide that a draft constitutional amendment does not in any way affect the general principles governing Algerian society, it may permit the President of the Republic to promulgate the amendment directly (without submitting it to referendum) if it has been approved by three-quarters of the members of both parliamentary chambers. Three-quarters of the members of both parliamentary chambers, in a joint sitting, may propose a constitutional amendment to the President of the Republic, who may submit it to referendum. The basic principles of the Constitution may not be revised.

The Government

HEAD OF STATE

President and Minister of National Defence: ABDELAZIZ BOUTEFLIKA (inaugurated 27 April 1999; re-elected 8 April 2004).

COUNCIL OF MINISTERS
(March 2008)

Prime Minister: ABDELAZIZ BELKHADEM.
Minister of State and Minister of the Interior and Local Authorities: NOUREDDINE YAZID ZERHOUNI.
Minister of State: BOUDJERRA SOLTANI.
Minister of Foreign Affairs: MOURAD MEDELCI.
Minister of Justice and Attorney-General: TAYEB BELAIZ.
Minister of Finance: KARIM DJOUDI.
Minister of Commerce: EL-HACHEMI DJAÂBOUB.
Minister of Energy and Mining: Dr CHAKIB KHELIL.
Minister of Water Resources: ABDELMALEK SELLAL.
Minister of Industry and of Investment Promotion: ABDELHAMID TEMMAR.
Minister of Religious Affairs and Awqaf (Religious Endowments): Prof. BOUABDELLAH GHLAMALLAH.
Minister of War Veterans: MUHAMMAD CHERIF ABBAS.
Minister of Urban and Rural Planning and the Environment and of Tourism: Dr CHERIF RAHMANI.
Minister of Transport: MUHAMMAD MAGHLAOUI.
Minister of Youth and Sports: HACHEMI DJIAR.
Minister of Agriculture and Rural Development: Dr SAÏD BARKAT.
Minister of Public Works: Dr AMAR GHOUL.
Minister of Health, Population and Hospital Reform: AMAR TOU.
Minister of Culture: KHALIDA TOUMI-MESSAOUDI.
Minister of Information: ABDERRACHID BOUKERZAZA.
Minister of Small and Medium-sized Enterprises and Handicrafts: MUSTAPHA BENBADA.
Minister of National Education: Prof. BOUBEKEUR BENBOUZID.
Minister of Higher Education and Scientific Research: RACHID HARROUBIA.
Minister of Postal Services, Information Technology and Telecommunications: BOUDJEMAÂ HAÏCHOUR.
Minister of Training and Vocational Education: Dr EL-HADI KHALDI.
Minister of Housing and Urban Development: NOUREDDINE MOUSSA.
Minister of Labour, Employment and Social Security: TAYEB LOUH.
Minister of National Solidarity: DJAMEL OULD ABBÈS.
Minister of Relations with Parliament: MAHMOUD KHEDRI.

ALGERIA

Minister of Fisheries and Fishing Resources: Dr SMAIL MIMOUNE.

Minister-delegate to the Minister of Foreign Affairs, in charge of Maghreb and African Affairs: ABDELKADER MESSAHEL.

Minister-delegate to the Minister of the Interior and Local Authorities, responsible for Local Authorities: DAHO OULD KABLIA.

Minister-delegate to the Minister of Health, Population and Hospital Reform, in charge of Family and Women's Affairs: NOUARA SAÂDIA DJAFFAR.

Minister-delegate to the Minister of National Defence: Gen. (retd) ABDELMALEK GUENAIZIA.

Minister-delegate to the Minister of Agriculture and Rural Development, in charge of Rural Development: Dr RACHID BENAÏSSA.

Minister-delegate to the Minister of Higher Education and Scientific Research, in charge of Scientific Research: SOUAD BENDJABALLAH.

Minister-delegate to the Minister of Finance, responsible for Financial Reform: FATIHA MENTOURI.

MINISTRIES

Office of the President: Présidence de la République, el-Mouradia, Algiers; tel. (21) 69-15-15; fax (21) 69-15-95; internet www.el-mouradia.dz.

Office of the Prime Minister: rue Docteur Saâdane, Algiers; tel. (21) 73-23-40; fax (21) 71-79-27; internet www.cg.gov.dz.

Ministry of Agriculture and Rural Development: 4 route des Quatre Canons, Algiers; tel. (21) 71-17-12; fax (21) 61-57-39.

Ministry of Commerce: Cité Zerhouni Mokhtar les El Mohamadia, Algiers; tel. (21) 89-00-74; fax (21) 89-00-34; e-mail info@mincommerce.gov.dz; internet www.mincommerce.gov.dz.

Ministry of Culture: BP 100, Palais de la Culture 'Moufdi Zakaria', Plateau des Annassers, Kouba, Algiers; tel. (21) 29-12-28; fax (21) 29-20-89; e-mail info@mcc.gov.dz.

Ministry of Defence: Les Tagarins, el-Biar, Algiers; tel. (21) 71-15-15; fax (21) 64-67-26.

Ministry of Energy and Mining: BP 677, Tower A, Val d'Hydra, Alger-Gare, Algiers; tel. (21) 48-85-26; fax (21) 48-85-87; e-mail info@mem-algeria.org; internet www.mem-algeria.org.

Ministry of Finance: Immeuble Maurétania, place du Pérou, Algiers; tel. (21) 71-13-66; fax (21) 73-42-76; e-mail algeriafinance@multimania.com; internet www.finances-algeria.org.

Ministry of Fisheries and Fishing Resources: Route des Quatre Canons, Algiers; tel. (21) 43-31-74; fax (21) 43-31-68; e-mail sg@mpeche.gov.dz; internet www.mpeche.gov.dz.

Ministry of Foreign Affairs: place Mohamed Seddik Benyahia, el-Mouradia, Algiers; tel. (21) 69-23-33; fax (21) 69-21-61; internet www.mae.dz.

Ministry of Health, Population and Hospital Reform: 125 rue Abd ar-Rahmane Laâla, el-Madania, Algiers; tel. (21) 27-29-00; fax (21) 27-96-41; e-mail webmaster@sante.dz; internet www.sante.dz.

Ministry of Higher Education and Scientific Research: 11 chemin Doudou Mokhtar, Ben Aknoun, Algiers; tel. (21) 91-23-23; e-mail info@mesrs.dz; internet www.mesrs.dz.

Ministry of Housing and Urban Development: 135 rue Mourad Didouche, Algiers; tel. (21) 74-07-22; fax (21) 74-53-83; e-mail mhabitat@wissal.dz; internet www.mhu.gov.dz.

Ministry of Industry and Investment Promotion: Immeuble de la Colisée, 2 rue Ahmed Bey, el-Biar, Algiers; tel. (21) 23-91-43; fax (21) 23-94-88; internet www.mppi.dz.

Ministry of Information: 2 rue des frères Bouaddou, Algiers; tel. (21) 54-47-67; fax (21) 54-12-08.

Ministry of the Interior and Local Authorities: 18 rue Docteur Saâdane, Algiers; tel. (21) 73-23-40; fax (21) 73-43-67.

Ministry of Justice: 8 place Bir Hakem, el-Biar, Algiers; tel. (21) 92-41-83; fax (21) 92-17-01; e-mail contact@mjustice.dz; internet www.mjustice.dz.

Ministry of Labour, Employment and Social Security: 44 rue Muhammad Belouizdad, 16600 Algiers; tel. (21) 65-99-99; fax (21) 66-34-56; e-mail informa@mtss.gov.dz; internet www.mtss.gov.dz.

Ministry of National Education: 8 rue de Pékin, el-Mouradia, Algiers; tel. (21) 60-67-57; fax (21) 60-57-82; e-mail education@men.dz; internet www.meducation.edu.dz.

Ministry of Postal Services, Information Technology and Telecommunications: 4 blvd Krim Belkacem, Algiers 16027; tel. (21) 71-12-20; fax (21) 71-92-71; e-mail contact@mptic.dz; internet www.mptic.dz.

Ministry of Public Works: 6 rue Moustafa Khalef, Ben Aknoun, Algiers; tel. (21) 91-49-47; fax (21) 91-35-85; e-mail info@mtp-dz.com; internet www.mtp-dz.com.

Ministry of Religious Affairs and Awqaf (Religious Endowments): 4 rue de Timgad, Hydra, Algiers; tel. (21) 60-88-20; fax (21) 69-15-69; e-mail redaction@marwakf-dz.org; internet www.marwakf-dz.org.

Ministry of Small and Medium-sized Enterprises and Handicrafts: Immeuble le Colisée, 4 rue Ahmed Bey, el-Biar, Algiers; tel. (21) 23-05-63; fax (21) 23-00-81; e-mail info@pmeart-dz.org; internet www.pmeart-dz.org.

Ministry of Social Action and National Solidarity: BP 31, Route nationale no 1, Les Vergers, Bir Khadem, Algiers; tel. (21) 44-99-46; fax (21) 44-97-26; e-mail cellulemassn@massn.gov.dz; internet www.massn.gov.dz.

Ministry of Training and Vocational Education: Route de Dély-Ibrahim, Ben Aknoun, Algiers; tel. (21) 91-15-28; fax (21) 60-09-36; e-mail abada@mfep.gov.dz; internet www.mfep.gov.dz.

Ministry of Transport: 1 chemin ibn Badis el-Mouiz (ex Poirson), el-Biar, Algiers; tel. (21) 92-98-85; fax (21) 92-98-94; e-mail contact@ministere-transports.gov.dz; internet www.ministere-transports.gov.dz.

Ministry of Urban and Rural Planning, the Environment and Tourism: rue des Quatre Canons, Bab-el-Oued, Algiers; tel. (21) 43-28-77; fax (21) 43-28-55; e-mail deeai@ifrance.com.

Ministry of War Veterans: 2 ave du Lt. Med Benarfa, el-Biar, Algiers; tel. (21) 92-23-55; fax (21) 92-35-16; e-mail mmoujahid@m-moudjahidine.dz; internet www.m-moudjahidine.dz.

Ministry of Water Resources: 3 rue du Caire, Kouba, Algiers; tel. (21) 68-95-00; e-mail deah@mre.gov.dz; internet www.mre.gov.dz.

Ministry of Youth and Sports: 3 rue Muhammad Belouizdad, place du 1er mai, 16600 Algiers; tel. (21) 65-55-55; e-mail ministre@mjs.dz; internet www.mjs.dz.

President and Legislature

PRESIDENT

Presidential Election, 8 April 2004

Candidate	Votes	% of votes
Abdelaziz Bouteflika	8,651,723	84.99
Ali Benflis	653,951	6.42
Sheikh Abdallah Djaballah	511,526	5.02
Saïd Saâdi	197,111	1.94
Louisa Hanoune	101,630	1.00
Ali Fawzi Rebaïne	63,761	0.63
Total*	10,179,702	100.00

* Excluding 329,075 invalid votes.

LEGISLATURE

National People's Assembly

President: ABDELAZIZ ZIARI.

General Election, 17 May 2007

	Votes	% of votes	Seats
Front de libération nationale (FLN)	1,314,494	22.95	136
Rassemblement national démocratique (RND)	597,712	10.44	62
Mouvement de la société pour la paix (MSP)	556,401	9.71	51
Parti des travailleurs (PT)	291,395	5.09	26
Rassemblement pour la culture et la démocratie (RCD)	185,616	3.24	19
Front national algérien (FNA)	241,594	4.22	15
Mouvement national pour la nature et le développement (MNND)	115,075	2.01	7
Nahdah	193,908	3.39	5
Mouvement pour la jeunesse et la démocratie (MJD)	130,992	2.29	5
Alliance nationale républicaine (ANR)	125,862	2.20	4
Mouvement de l'entente nationale (MEN)	121,961	2.13	4
Parti du renouveau algérien (PRA)	103,356	1.80	4
Infitah	150,423	2.63	3

ALGERIA

—continued	Votes	% of votes	Seats
Mouvement de la réforme nationale (MRN)	146,528	2.56	3
Front national des indépendants pour la concorde (FNIC)	112,263	1.96	3
Ahd 54	129,865	2.27	2
Mouvement national de l'espérance (MNE)	98,604	1.72	2
Rassemblement patriotique républicain (RPR)	84,497	1.48	2
Rassemblement algérien (RA)	100,391	1.75	1
Front national démocratique (FND)	78,596	1.37	1
Mouvement démocratique et social (MDS)	50,879	0.89	1
Independents	564,169	9.85	33
Others	233,246	4.07	—
Total	**5,727,827***	**100.00**	**389**

* Excluding 965,064 invalid votes.

Council of the Nation

President: ABDELKADER BENSALAH.
Elections, 30 December 2000 and 30 December 2003*

	Seats*
Rassemblement national démocratique (RND)	52
Front de libération nationale (FLN)	32
Mouvement de la société pour la paix (MSP)	10
Mouvement de la réforme nationale (MRN)	2
Front des forces socialistes (FFS)	1
Appointed by the President†	40
Total	**137‡**

* Deputies of the 144-member Council of the Nation serve a six-year term; one-half of its members are replaced every three years. Elected representatives are selected by indirect, secret suffrage from regional and municipal authorities.
† Appointed on 4 January 2001 and 8 January 2004.
‡ The elections held on 30 December 2003 to renew 46 members of the Council of the Nation, and the presidential appointments made on 8 January 2004, were incomplete, principally owing to the unrest in Kabylia (see Recent History). By-elections for five seats were held on 23 February 2006.

Political Organizations

Until 1989 the FLN was the only legal party in Algeria. Amendments to the Constitution in February of that year permitted the formation of other political associations, with some restrictions. The right to establish political parties was guaranteed by constitutional amendments in November 1996; however, political associations based on differences in religion, language, race, gender or region were proscribed. Some 24 political parties contested the legislative elections of May 2007. The most important political organizations are listed below.

Ahd 54 (Oath 54): 53 rue Larbi Ben M'Hedi, Algiers; tel. (21) 73-61-37; fax (21) 73-16-79; e-mail info@ahd54.org; internet www.ahd54.org; f. 1991; small nationalist party; Sec.-Gen. ALI FAWZI REBAÏNE.

Alliance nationale républicaine (ANR): Algiers; f. 1995; anti-Islamist; Leader REDHA MALEK.

Front des forces socialistes (FFS): 56 ave Souidani Boudjemaâ, el-Mouradia, 16000 Algiers; tel. (21) 69-41-41; fax (21) 48-45-54; internet www.ffs-dz.com; f. 1963; revived 1989; seeks greater autonomy for Berber-dominated regions and official recognition of the Berber language; Leader HOCINE AÏT AHMED; Sec.-Gen. KARIM TABBOU.

Front islamique du salut (FIS): Algiers; fax (21) 69-72-66; e-mail info@fisweb.org; internet www.fisweb.org; f. 1989; aims to emphasize the importance of Islam in political and social life; formally dissolved by the Algiers Court of Appeal in March 1992; Leader ABBASSI MADANI.

Front de libération nationale (FLN): 7 rue du Stade, Hydra, Algiers; tel. (21) 69-42-81; fax (21) 69-47-07; e-mail pfln@wissal.dz; internet www.pfln.dz; f. 1954; sole legal party until 1989; socialist in outlook, the party is organized into a Secretariat, a National Council, an Executive Committee, Federations, Kasmas and cells; under the aegis of the FLN are various mass political orgs, incl. the Union Nationale de la Jeunesse Algérienne and the Union Nationale des Femmes Algériennes; Pres. ABDELAZIZ BOUTEFLIKA; Sec.-Gen. ABDELAZIZ BELKHADEM.

Front national algérien (FNA): 18 rue Chaib Ahmed, 16100 Algiers; tel. (21) 73-07-88; fax (21) 73-30-96; e-mail fnatouati@yahoo.fr; internet www.fna.dz; f. 1999; advocates eradication of poverty and supports the Govt's peace initiative; Pres. MOUSSA TOUATI.

Mouvement pour l'autonomie de la Kabylie (MAK): internet www.makabylie.info; f. 2001; advocates autonomy for the north-eastern region of Kabylia within a federal Algerian state; Leader FERHAT MEHENNI.

Mouvement pour la démocratie et la citoyenneté (MDC): Tizi-Ouzou; f. 1997 by dissident members of the FFS; Leader SAÏD KHELIL.

Mouvement démocratique et social (MDS): 67 blvd Krim Belkacem, 16200 Algiers; tel. (21) 63-86-05; fax (21) 63-89-12; e-mail mds_pol@yahoo.fr; internet www.mds-algerie.com; f. 1998 by fmr mems of Ettahaddi; left-wing party; 4,000 mems; Sec.-Gen. AHMED MELIANI (acting).

Mouvement pour la jeunesse et la démocratie (MJD): advocates sexual equality; Pres. CHALABIA MAHDJOUBIA.

Mouvement de la réforme nationale (MRN) (El-Islah): Algiers; f. 1998; radical Islamist party; Sec.-Gen. Sheikh ABDALLAH DJABALLAH.

Mouvement de la société pour la paix (MSP) (Harakat Mujtamaa as-Silm): 63 rue Ali Haddad, Algiers; e-mail hms@hmsalgeria.net; internet www.hmsalgeria.net; fmrly known as Hamas; adopted current name in 1997; moderate Islamist party, favouring the gradual introduction of an Islamic state; Pres. BOUDJERRA SOLTANI.

Nahdah: blvd des Martyrs, 16100 Algiers; tel. (21) 74-85-14; fundamentalist Islamist group; Sec.-Gen. HABIB ADAMI.

Parti national pour la solidarité et le développement (PNSD): BP 110, Staoueli, Algiers; tel. and fax (21) 39-40-42; e-mail cherif_taleb@yahoo.fr; f. 1989 as Parti social démocrate; Leader MOHAMED CHERIF TALEB.

Parti du renouveau algérien (PRA): 8 ave de Pékin, 16209 el-Mouradia, Algiers; tel. (21) 59-43-00; Sec.-Gen. KAMEL BENSALEM; Leader NOUREDDINE BOUKROUH.

Parti républicain progressif (PRP): 3 rue Salah Gharbine, 16100 Algiers; tel. and fax (21) 74-61-25; f. 1990 as a legal party; Sec.-Gen. SLIMANE CHERIF.

Parti des travailleurs (PT): 2 rue Belkheir Hassan Badi, 16010 El Harrach, 16000 Algiers; tel. (21) 52-62-45; fax (21) 52-89-90; internet www.ptalgerie.com; workers' party; Leader LOUISA HANOUNE.

Rassemblement pour la culture et la démocratie (RCD): 40 rue Muhammad Chabane, el-Biar, Algiers; tel. (21) 92-50-76; fax (21) 92-51-01; e-mail info@rcd-algerie.org; internet www.rcd-algerie.org; f. 1989; social democratic and secular party; advocates inclusion of Berber traditions into the Algerian identity; Pres. SAÏD SADI.

Rassemblement national démocratique (RND): BP 10, Cité des Asphodèles, Ben Aknoun, Algiers; tel. (21) 91-64-10; fax (21) 91-47-40; e-mail contact@rnd-dz.com; internet www.rnd-dz.com; f. 1997; centrist party; Sec.-Gen. AHMED OUYAHIA.

Wafa wa al-Adl (Wafa): Algiers; f. 1999; unauthorized; Leader AHMED TALEB IBRAHIMI.

The following groups are in armed conflict with the Government:

Groupe islamique armé (GIA): f. 1992; was the most prominent and radical Islamist militant group in the mid-1990s, but has reportedly split into several factions which do not all adhere to one leader; Leader BOULENOUAR OUKIL.

Al-Qa'ida in the Islamic Maghreb (AQIM): f. 1998 as the Groupe salafiste pour la prédication et le combat (GSPC), a breakaway faction from the Groupe islamique armé; adopted current name in Jan. 2007, when it aligned itself with the militant Islamist al-Qa'ida (Base) network led by Osama bin Laden; particularly active to the east of Algiers and in Kabylia; as the GSPC, traditionally responded to preaching by Ali Belhadj, the second most prominent member of the proscribed Front islamique du salut; Leader ABDELMALEK DROUKDAL (also known as ABU MUSAB ABD AL-WADUD).

Diplomatic Representation

EMBASSIES IN ALGERIA

Angola: 12 rue Mohamed Khoudi, el-Biar, Algiers; tel. (21) 92-53-37; fax (21) 92-04-18; Ambassador HERMÍNIO ESCÓRCIO.

Argentina: 5 chemin Mohamed Drareni, Djenane, El Malik, Hydra, Algiers; tel. (21) 54-86-65; fax (21) 54-86-47; e-mail eargel@mrecic.gov.ar; Ambassador BIBIANA LUCÍA JONES.

ALGERIA

Austria: 17 chemin Abd al-Kader Gadouche, 16035 Hydra, Algiers; tel. (21) 69-10-86; fax (21) 69-12-32; e-mail algier-ob@bmeia.gov.at; Ambassador SYLVIA MEIER-KAJBIC.

Belgium: BP 341, 16030 el-Biar, Algiers; tel. (21) 92-26-60; fax (21) 92-50-36; e-mail algiers@diplobel.be; internet www.diplomatie.be/algiersfr; Ambassador BAUDOUIN VANDERHULST.

Benin: BP 103, 16 Lot du Stade Birkhadem, Algiers; tel. (21) 56-52-71; Ambassador LEONARD ADJIN.

Brazil: BP 246, 55 chemin Cheikh Bachir El-Ibrahimi, el-Biar, Algiers; tel. (21) 92-44-37; fax (21) 92-41-25; e-mail brasilia@wissal.dz; internet www.ambresil.dz; Ambassador SÉRGIO FRANÇA DANESE.

Bulgaria: 13 blvd Col Bougara, Algiers; tel. (21) 23-00-14; fax (21) 23-05-33; Ambassador DIMITAR DIMITROV.

Burkina Faso: BP 212, 23 Lot el-Feth, chemin ibn Badis el-Mouiz (ex Poirson), el-Biar, Didouche Mourad, Algiers; tel. (21) 92-33-39; fax (21) 92-73-90; e-mail abfalger@yahoo.fr; Ambassador MAMADOU SERME.

Cameroon: 26 chemin Cheikh Bachir El-Ibrahimi, 16011 el-Biar, Algiers; tel. (21) 92-11-24; fax (21) 92-11-25; e-mail ambacam_alger@yahoo.fr; Chargé d'affaires JEAN MISSOUP.

Canada: BP 48, 18 rue Mustapha Khalef, Ben Aknoun, 16000 Algiers; tel. (21) 91-49-51; fax (21) 91-49-73; e-mail alger@international.gc.ca; internet www.international.gc.ca/world/embassies/algeria; Ambassador PATRICK PARISOT.

Chad: Villa no 18, Cité DNC, chemin Ahmed Kara, Hydra, Algiers; tel. (21) 69-26-62; fax (21) 69-26-63; Ambassador El-Hadj MAHAMOUD ADJI.

Chile: 8 rue F. les Crêtes, Hydra, Algiers; tel. (21) 48-31-63; fax (21) 60-71-85; e-mail embchile@gecos.net; Ambassador PABLO MUÑOZ ROMERO.

China, People's Republic: 34 blvd des Martyrs, Algiers; tel. (21) 69-27-24; fax (21) 69-30-56; e-mail chinaemb_dz@mfa.gov.cn; internet dz.chineseembassy.org; Ambassador ZHANG SHIXIAN.

Congo, Democratic Republic: 111 Parc Ben Omar Kouba, Algiers; tel. (21) 59-12-27; Ambassador IKAKI BOMELE MOLINGO.

Congo, Republic: 111 Parc Ben Omar Kouba, Algiers; tel. (21) 58-68-00; Ambassador PIERRE N'GAKA.

Côte d'Ivoire: BP 260, Immeuble 'Le Bosquet', Parc Paradou, Hydra, Algiers; tel. (21) 69-23-78; fax (21) 69-30-32; e-mail acialg@yahoo.fr; Ambassador AMONCASSI SYLVESTRE AKA.

Croatia: Algiers; Ambassador MIRKO BOLFEK.

Cuba: 22 rue Larbi Alik, Hydra, Algiers; tel. (21) 69-21-48; fax (21) 69-32-81; e-mail ambcuba@wissal.dz; Ambassador ROBERTO BLANCO DOMÍNGUEZ.

Czech Republic: BP 358, Villa Koudia, 3 chemin Ziryab, Alger-Gare, Algiers; tel. (21) 23-00-56; fax (21) 23-01-03; e-mail algiers@embassy.mzv.cz; internet www.mzv.cz/algiers; Ambassador MILAN ŠARAPATKA.

Denmark: BP 384, 12 ave Emile Marquis, Lot Djenane el-Malik, Hydra, 16035 Algiers; tel. (21) 54-82-28; fax (21) 69-29-09; e-mail algamb@um.dk; internet www.ambalgier.um.dk; Ambassador OLE WØHLERS OLSEN.

Egypt: BP 297, 8 chemin Abd al-Kader Gadouche, 16300 Hydra, Algiers; tel. (21) 69-16-73; fax (21) 69-29-52; Ambassador ABD AL-AZIZ SHAWKI SEIF AN-NASR.

Finland: 10 rue des Cèdres, el-Mouradia, Algiers; tel. (21) 69-29-25; fax (21) 69-16-37; e-mail finamb@wissal.dz; Ambassador KAIJA ILANDER.

France: chemin Abd al-Kader Gadouche, 16035 Hydra, Algiers; tel. (21) 69-24-88; fax (21) 69-13-69; e-mail contact@ambafrance-dz.org; internet www.ambafrance-dz.org; Ambassador BERNARD BAJOLET.

Gabon: BP 125, Rostomia, 21 rue Hadj Ahmed Mohamed, Hydra, Algiers; tel. (21) 69-24-00; fax (21) 60-25-46; Ambassador YVES ONGOLLO.

Germany: BP 664, 165 chemin Sfindja, Alger-Gare, 16000 Algiers; tel. (21) 74-19-56; fax (21) 74-05-21; e-mail zreg@algi.diplo.de; internet www.algier.diplo.de; Ambassador Dr JOHANNES WESTERHOFF.

Ghana: 62 rue des Frères Benali Abdellah, Hydra, Algiers; tel. (21) 60-64-44; fax (21) 69-28-56; Ambassador LAWRENCE R. A. SATUH.

Greece: 60 blvd Col Bougara, 16030 el-Biar, Algiers; tel. (21) 92-34-91; fax (21) 92-34-90; e-mail gremb.alg@mfa.gr; Ambassador IOANNIS NEONAKIS.

Guinea: 43 blvd Central Saïd Hamdine, Hydra, Algiers; tel. (21) 69-20-66; fax (21) 69-34-68; Ambassador MAMADY CONDÉ.

Guinea-Bissau: BP 32, 17 rue Ahmad Kara, Colonne Volrol, Hydra, Algiers; tel. (21) 60-01-51; fax (21) 60-97-25; Ambassador JOSÉ PEREIRA BATISTA.

Holy See: 1 rue Noureddine Mekiri, 16021 Bolognine, Algiers (Apostolic Nunciature); tel. (21) 95-45-20; fax (21) 95-40-95; e-mail nuntiusalger2@yahoo.fr; Apostolic Nuncio Most Rev. THOMAS YEH SHENG-NAN (Titular Archbishop of Leptis Magna).

Hungary: BP 68, 18 ave des Frères Oughlis, el-Mouradia, Algiers; tel. (21) 69-79-75; fax (21) 69-81-86; e-mail huembalgoffice@djazairconnect.com; Ambassador Dr BÉLA MARTON.

India: BP 108, 14 rue des Abassides, 16030 el-Biar, Algiers; tel. (21) 92-32-88; fax (21) 92-40-11; e-mail indembalg@hotmail.com; Ambassador Dr ASHOK KUMAR AMROHI.

Indonesia: BP 62, 17 chemin Abd al-Kader Gadouche, 16070 el-Mouradia, Algiers; tel. (21) 69-49-15; fax (21) 69-49-16; e-mail kbrial@wissal.dz; Ambassador YULI MUMPUNI WIDARSO.

Iraq: 4 rue Abri Arezki, Hydra, Algiers; tel. (21) 69-31-25; fax (21) 69-10-97; e-mail algemb@iraqmofamail.net; Ambassador Dr ZIAD KHALID ABDALLI.

Italy: 18 rue Muhammad Ouidir Amellal, 16030 el-Biar, Algiers; tel. (21) 92-23-30; fax (21) 92-59-86; e-mail segretaria.algeri@esteri.it; internet www.ambalgeri.esteri.it; Ambassador GIAMPAOLO CANTINI.

Japan: BP 80, 1 chemin el-Bakri (ex Macklay), Ben Aknoun, Algiers; tel. (21) 91-20-04; fax (21) 91-20-46; Ambassador SHIMIZU KUMIO.

Jordan: 47 rue Ammani Belkalem, Hydra, Algiers; tel. (21) 69-20-31; fax (21) 69-15-54; e-mail jordan@wissal.dz; Ambassador ABDULLAH EL-AYYAM.

Korea, Democratic People's Republic: Algiers; tel. (21) 62-39-27; Ambassador PAK HO IL.

Korea, Republic: BP 92, 17 chemin Abd al-Kader Gadouche, Hydra, Algiers; tel. (21) 69-36-20; fax (21) 69-16-03; Ambassador KIM DENG-JI.

Kuwait: chemin Abd al-Kader Gadouche, Hydra, Algiers; tel. (21) 59-31-57; Ambassador SAUD FAISAL SAUD AD-DAWEESH.

Lebanon: 9 rue Kaïd Ahmad, el-Biar, Algiers; tel. (21) 78-20-94; Ambassador BASSAM ALI TARABAH.

Libya: 15 chemin Cheikh Bachir El-Ibrahimi, Algiers; tel. (21) 92-15-02; fax (21) 92-46-87; Ambassador ABD AL-MOULA EL-GHADHBANE.

Madagascar: BP 65, 22 rue Abd al-Kader Aouis, 16090 Bologhine, Algiers; tel. (21) 95-03-74; fax (21) 95-17-76; e-mail ambamadalg@yahoo.fr; Ambassador VOLA DIEUDONNÉ RAZAFINDRALAMBO.

Mali: Villa 15, Cité DNC/ANP, chemin Ahmed Kara, Hydra, Algiers; tel. (21) 69-13-51; fax (21) 69-20-82; Ambassador MAHAMADOU MAGASSOUBA.

Mauritania: 107 Lot Baranès, Aire de France, Bouzaréah, Algiers; tel. (21) 79-21-39; fax (21) 78-42-74; Ambassador MOHAMED LEMINE OULD MOHAMED VAL DIT ISSELMOU BABAMINE.

Mexico: BP 329, 25 chemin El-Bakri, Ben Aknoun, 16306 Algiers; tel. (21) 91-46-00; fax (21) 91-46-01; e-mail embamexargelia@gmail.com; Ambassador EDUARDO ROLDÁN ACOSTA.

Morocco: Villa nos 21 et 22, Cité al-Fath, Sable Rouge, el-Biar, Algiers; tel. (21) 69-14-08; fax (21) 69-29-00; e-mail ambmaroc@wissal.dz; Ambassador ABDELLAH BELKEZIZ.

Netherlands: BP 72, 23 chemin Cheikh Bachir El-Ibrahimi, el-Biar, Algiers; tel. (21) 92-28-28; fax (21) 92-29-47; e-mail alg@minbuza.nl; internet www.mfa.nl/alg; Ambassador HENK REVIS.

Niger: 54 rue Vercors Rostamia, Bouzaréah, Algiers; tel. (21) 78-89-21; fax (21) 78-97-13; Ambassador MOUSSA SANGARE.

Nigeria: BP 629, 27 bis rue Blaise Pascal, Algiers; tel. (21) 69-18-49; fax (21) 69-11-75; Ambassador ALIYU MOHAMMED.

Oman: BP 201, 52 rue Djamel Eddine, el-Afghani, Bouzaréah, Algiers; tel. (21) 94-13-10; fax (21) 94-13-75; Ambassador ALI ABDULLAH AL-ALAWI.

Pakistan: Villa no 50, allée des Feuilles Vertes, Sidi Yahia, Hydra, Algiers; tel. (21) 54-96-61; fax (21) 54-96-60; e-mail ambpakistan@wissal.dz; Ambassador ZAFARULLAH SHAIKH.

Peru: 20 ave Franklin Roosevelt, 1er étage, 16006 Algiers; tel. (21) 68-15-95; fax (21) 68-16-96; e-mail amb.perou@eepad.dz; Ambassador JOSÉ RAFAEL EDUARDO BERAÚN ARANÍBAR.

Poland: BP 60, 37 ave Mustafa Ali Khodja, el-Biar, Algiers; tel. (21) 92-25-53; fax (21) 92-14-35; e-mail marekmal@wissal.dz; Ambassador LIDIA MILKA-WIECZORKIEWICZ.

Portugal: 4 rue Mohamed Khoudi, el-Biar, Algiers; tel. (21) 92-53-14; fax (21) 92-53-13; e-mail embportdz@yahoo.fr; Ambassador LUÍS DE ALMEIDA SAMPAIO.

Qatar: BP 348, 7 chemin Doudou Mokhtar, Algiers; tel. (21) 91-20-09; fax (21) 91-20-11; Ambassador ALI MUBARAK MUHAMMAD AN-NUEIMI.

Romania: 24 rue Abri Arezki, Hydra, Algiers; tel. (21) 60-08-71; fax (21) 69-36-42; Ambassador VICTOR MIRCEA.

Russia: 7 chemin du Prince d'Annam, el-Biar, Algiers; tel. (21) 92-31-39; fax (21) 92-28-82; e-mail ambrussie@yandex.ru; internet www.ambrussie.gov.dz; Ambassador ALEKSANDR EGOROV.

Saudi Arabia: 62 rue Med. Drafini, chemin de la Madeleine, Hydra, Algiers; tel. (21) 60-35-18; Ambassador Dr SAMI BIN ABDULLAH BIN OTHMAN AS-SALIH.

Senegal: BP 720, 350 Parc Ben Omar Kouba, Alger-Gare, Algiers; tel. (21) 54-90-90; fax (21) 54-90-94; e-mail senegal@wissal.dz; Ambassador PAPA OUSMANE SEYE.

Serbia: BP 366, 7 rue des Frères Ben-hafid, Hydra, Algiers; tel. (21) 69-12-18; fax (21) 69-34-72; e-mail yuga@djazair-connect.com; Ambassador VLADIMIR KOHUT.

South Africa: 30 rue Capitain Hocine Slimane, 16000 el-Biar, Algiers; tel. (21) 23-03-84; fax (21) 23-08-27; e-mail sae@medianet.dz; Ambassador MZUVUKILE MAQETHUKA.

Spain: BP 142, 46 bis, rue Muhammad Chabane, el-Biar, Algiers; tel. (21) 92-27-13; fax (21) 92-27-19; e-mail emb.argel@mae.es; Ambassador JUAN BAUTISTA LEÑA CASAS.

Sudan: Algiers; tel. (21) 56-66-23; fax (21) 69-30-19; Ambassador YOUCEF FADUL AHMED.

Sweden: BP 263, rue Olof Palme, Nouveau Paradou, Hydra, Algiers; tel. (21) 54-83-33; fax (21) 54-83-34; e-mail ambassaden.alger@foreign.ministry.se; Ambassador HELENA NILSSON-LANNEGREN.

Switzerland: BP 443, Paradou, 2 rue no 3, 16035 Hydra, Algiers; tel. (21) 60-04-22; fax (21) 60-98-54; e-mail vertretung@alg.rep.admin.ch; Ambassador JEAN-CLAUDE RICHARD.

Syria: Domaine Tamzali, 11 chemin Abd al-Kader Gadouche, Hydra, Algiers; tel. (21) 91-20-26; fax (21) 91-20-30; Ambassador NUMEIR WAHIB GHANEM.

Tunisia: 5 rue du Bois, Hydra, 16405 Algiers; tel. (21) 60-13-88; fax (21) 69-23-16; Ambassador MUHAMMAD EL-FADHAL KHALIL.

Turkey: Villa Dar el-Ouard, chemin de la Rochelle, blvd Col Bougara, Algiers; tel. (21) 23-00-04; fax (21) 23-01-12; e-mail cezayir.be@mfa.gov.tr; Ambassador AHMET BIGALI.

Ukraine: 19 rue des Frères Benhafid, Hydra, Algiers; tel. (21) 69-13-87; fax (21) 69-48-87; e-mail emb_dz@mfa.gov.ua; Ambassador SERHIY BOROVYK.

United Arab Emirates: BP 165, Alger-Gare, 14 rue Muhammad Drarini, Hydra, Algiers; tel. (21) 69-25-74; fax (21) 69-37-70; Ambassador AHMAD AL-HOSANI.

United Kingdom: 12 rue Slimane Amirate, Hydra, Algiers; tel. (21) 23-00-68; fax (21) 23-00-67; e-mail britishembassy.algiers@fco.gov.uk; internet www.britishembassy.gov.uk/algeria; Ambassador ANDREW HENDERSON.

USA: BP 549, 4 chemin Cheikh Bachir El-Ibrahimi, el-Biar, 16000 Algiers; tel. (21) 69-12-55; fax (21) 69-39-79; e-mail algiers_webmaster@state.gov; internet algiers.usembassy.gov; Ambassador ROBERT S. FORD.

Venezuela: BP 297, 3 impasse Ahmed Kara, Algiers; tel. (21) 69-38-46; fax (21) 69-35-55; Ambassador MICHEL MUJICA RICARDO.

Viet Nam: 30 rue de Chenoua, Hydra, Algiers; tel. (21) 69-27-52; fax (21) 69-37-78; e-mail sqvnaler@djazair-conn.ect.com; Ambassador VU VAN DU.

Yemen: 18 chemin Mahmoud Drarnine, Hydra, Algiers; tel. (21) 54-89-50; fax (21) 54-87-40; Ambassador AHMAD ABDULLAH ABD AL-ELAH.

Judicial System

The highest court of justice is the Supreme Court (Cour suprême) in Algiers, established in 1963, which is served by 150 judges. Justice is exercised through 183 courts (tribunaux) and 31 appeal courts (cours d'appel), grouped on a regional basis. New legislation, promulgated in March 1997, provided for the eventual establishment of 214 courts and 48 appeal courts. The Court of Accounts (Cour des comptes) was established in 1979. Algeria adopted a penal code in 1966, retaining the death penalty. In February 1993 three special courts were established to try suspects accused of terrorist offences; however, the courts were abolished in February 1995. Constitutional amendments introduced in November 1996 provided for the establishment of a High State Court (empowered to judge the President of the Republic in cases of high treason, and the Head of Government for crimes and offences), and a State Council to regulate the administrative judiciary. In addition, a Conflicts Tribunal has been established to adjudicate in disputes between the Supreme Court and the State Council.

Supreme Court
rue du 11 décembre 1960, Ben Aknoun, Algiers; tel. and fax (21) 92-44-89; e-mail secretairegeneral@coursupreme-dz.org.

President of Supreme Court: KADDOUR BERRADJA.

Attorney-General: TAYEB BELAIZ.

Religion

ISLAM
Islam is the official religion, and the vast majority of Algerians are Muslims.

High Islamic Council
16 rue du 11 décembre 1960, Ben-Aknoun, 16030 Algiers; tel. (21) 91-54-10; fax (21) 91-54-09; e-mail hci@hci.dz; internet www.hci.dz.

President of the High Islamic Council: Dr CHEIKH BOUAMRANE.

CHRISTIANITY
The majority of the European inhabitants, and a few Arabs, are Christians, mostly Roman Catholics.

The Roman Catholic Church
Algeria comprises one archdiocese and three dioceses (including one directly responsible to the Holy See). In December 2005 there were an estimated 3,200 adherents in the country. The Bishops' Conference of North Africa (Conférence des Evêques de la Région Nord de l'Afrique—CERNA) moved from Algiers to Tunis, Tunisia, in 2004.

Archbishop of Algiers: Most Rev. HENRI TEISSIER, 22 chemin d'Hydra, 16030 el-Biar, Algiers; tel. (21) 92-56-67; fax (21) 92-55-76; e-mail evechealger@yahoo.fr.

Protestant Church
Protestant Church of Algeria: 31 rue Reda Houhou, 16110 Alger-HBB, Algiers; tel. and fax (21) 71-62-38; e-mail protestants_alger@yahoo.fr; 38 parishes; 7,000 mems; Pres. MOUSTAFA KRIM.

The Press

DAILIES
El Acil: 1 rue Kamel ben Djelit, Constantine; tel. and fax (31) 92-46-13; e-mail elacil_info@yahoo.fr; internet www.elacildz.com; f. 1993; French; Dir GHALIB DJABBOUR.

Akher Sâa: Intersection Bougandoura Miloud et Sakhri Abdelhamid, Annaba; tel. (38) 86-02-41; fax (38) 86-47-19; e-mail saidbel@hotmail.com; internet www.akhersaa-dz.com; Arabic; Dir SAÏD BELHADJOUDJA.

L'Authentique: 4 rue Abane Ramdane, Algiers; tel. (17) 06-13-80; fax (21) 74-27-15; e-mail laredaction@lauthentiquedz.net; internet www.lauthentiquedz.net; French; Editorial Dir NADJIB STAMBOULI.

Ech-Cha'ab (The People): 1 ave Pasteur, Algiers; tel. (21) 60-70-40; fax (21) 60-67-93; e-mail webmaster@ech-chaab.com; internet www.ech-chaab.com; f. 1962; Arabic; journal of the Front de libération nationale; Dir AZZEDINE BOUKERDOUSSE; circ. 24,000.

Ech-Chorouk El-Youmi: Maison de la presse Abdelkader Safir, Kouba, Algiers; tel. (21) 28-47-54; fax (21) 28-48-52; e-mail infos@ech-chorouk.com; internet www.echoroukonline.com; f. 2000; Arabic; Dir ALI FOUDIL.

Le Courier d'Algérie: Maison de la presse Abdelkader Safir, Kouba, Algiers; tel. and fax (21) 46-25-12; fax (21) 46-25-13; e-mail redactioncourrier@hotmail.com; internet www.lecourrier-dalgerie.com; f. 2003; French; Dir AHMED TOUMIAT.

La Dépêche de Kabylie: Maison de la presse Tahar Djaout, place du 1er mai, 16016 Algiers; tel. (21) 66-37-93; fax (21) 66-37-87; e-mail info@depechedekabylie.com; internet www.depechedekabylie.com; f. 2001; Dir IDIR BENYOUNÈS.

Djazair News: Maison de la presse Tahar Djaout, place du 1er mai, 16016 Algiers; tel. (21) 66-38-80; fax (21) 66-38-79; e-mail info@djazairnews.info; internet www.djazairnews.info; f. 2003; Arabic; Man. Dir HMIDA AYACHI.

L'Expression: Maison de la presse Abdelkader Safir, Kouba, Algiers; tel. (21) 68-94-55; fax (21) 28-02-29; e-mail ladirection@lexpressiondz.com; internet www.lexpressiondz.com; f. 2000; French; Editor AHMED FATTANI; circ. 70,000.

Al-Fedjr: Maison de la presse Tahar Djaout, place du 1er mai, 16016 Algiers; tel. and fax (21) 65-76-60; e-mail fadjr@al-fadjr.com; internet www.al-fadjr.com; f. 2000; Arabic; Dir ABDA HADDA HAZEM.

Horizons: 20 rue de la Liberté, Algiers; tel. (21) 73-67-24; fax (21) 73-61-34; e-mail info@horizons-dz.com; internet www.horizons-dz.com; f. 1985; evening; French; Dir NAÂMA ABBAS; circ. 35,000.

Le Jeune Indépendant: Maison de la presse Tahar Djaout, 1 rue Bachir Attar, place du 1er mai, 16016 Algiers; tel. (21) 67-07-48; fax (21) 67-07-46; f. 1990; French; circ. 60,000.

Al-Joumhouria (The Republic): 6 rue Bensenouci Hamida, Oran; tel. (41) 39-04-97; fax (41) 39-10-39; e-mail djoumhouria@yahoo.fr; f. 1963; Arabic; Editor BENAMEUR BOUKHALFA; circ. 20,000.

ALGERIA *Directory*

El Khabar: Maison de la presse Tahar Djaout, 1 rue Bashir Attar, place du 1er mai, 16016 Algiers; tel. (21) 67-07-05; fax (21) 67-04-63; e-mail admin@elkhabar.com; internet www.elkhabar.com; f. 1990; Arabic; Dir-Gen. ALI DJERI; circ. 450,000.

Liberté: BP 178, 37 rue Larbi Ben M'Hidi, Alger-Gare, Algiers; tel. (21) 64-34-34; fax (21) 64-34-35; e-mail webmaster@liberte-algeria.com; internet www.liberte-algerie.com; f. 1992; French; independent; Dir ALI OUAFEK; Editors SALIM TAMANI, AMAR OUALI; circ. 20,000.

El-Massa: Maison de la presse Abdelkader Safir, Kouba, Algiers; tel. (21) 59-54-19; fax (21) 59-64-57; e-mail info@el-massa.com; internet www.el-massa.com; f. 1977; evening; Arabic; Dir ABDERRAHMANE TIGANE; circ. 45,000.

El-Moudjahid (The Fighter): 20 rue de la Liberté, Algiers; tel. (21) 73-70-81; fax (21) 73-90-43; e-mail elmoudja@elmoudjahid.com; internet www.elmoudjahid.com; f. 1965; govt journal in French and Arabic; Dir ABDELMADJID CHERBAL; circ. 392,000.

An-Nasr (The Victory): BP 388, Zone Industrielle, La Palma, Constantine; tel. (31) 66-81-84; fax (31) 66-81-97; e-mail an-nasr@an-nasr.dz; internet www.an-nasr.dz; f. 1963; Arabic; Dir ELARBI OUANOUGHI; circ. 340,000.

La Nouvelle République: Maison de la presse Tahar Djaout, 1 rue Bachir Attar, place du 1er mai, 16016 Algiers; tel. and fax (21) 67-10-44; fax (21) 67-10-75; e-mail contact@lanouvellerepublique.com; internet www.lanouvellerepublique.com; French; Dir ABDELWAHAB DJAKOUNE.

Ouest Tribune: 13 Cité Djamel, 31007 Oran; tel. (41) 45-31-30; fax (41) 45-34-62; e-mail redaction@ouestribune-dz.com; internet www.ouestribune-dz.com; French; Dir ABDELKADER BENSAHNOUN.

Le Quotidien d'Oran: BP 110, 63 ave de l'ANP, 1 rue Laid Ould Tayeb, Oran; tel. (41) 32-63-09; fax (41) 32-51-36; e-mail admin@lequotidien-oran.com; internet www.lequotidien-oran.com; French; Dir-Gen. MUHAMMAD ABDOU BENABBOU.

Sawt al-Ahrar: 6 ave Pasteur, Algiers; tel. (21) 73-47-70; fax (21) 73-47-65; e-mail sawtalahrar@hotmail.com; internet www.sawt-alahrar.net; Arabic; Dir MUHAMMAD NADIR BOULAGROUNE.

Le Soir d'Algérie: Maison de la presse Tahar Djaout, 1 rue Bachir Attar, place du 1er mai, 16016 Algiers; tel. (21) 67-06-58; fax (21) 67-06-56; e-mail info@lesoirdalgerie.com; internet www.lesoirdalgerie.com; f. 1990; evening; independent information journal in French; Dir FOUAD BOUGHANEM; Editor NACER BELHADJOUDJA; circ. 80,000.

La Tribune: Maison de la presse Tahar Djaout, 1 rue Bachir Attar, place du 1er mai, 16016 Algiers; tel. (21) 68-54-21; fax (21) 68-54-22; e-mail latribun@latribune-online.com; internet www.latribune-online.com; f. 1994; current affairs journal in French; Dir HASSAN BACHIR-CHERIF; Editorial Dir ABDELKRIM GHEZALI.

La Voix de l'Oranie: 3 rue Rouis Rayah, Haï Oussama, 31000 Oran; tel. (41) 32-22-18; fax (41) 35-18-01; e-mail contact@voix-oranie.com; internet www.voix-oranie.com; French; Dir RAFIK CHARRAK.

El Watan: Maison de la presse, 1 rue Bachir Attar, place du 1er mai, 16016 Algiers; tel. (21) 68-21-83; fax (21) 68-21-87; e-mail admin@elwatan.com; internet www.elwatan.com; f. 1990; French; Dir OMAR BELHOUCHET; circ. 140,000.

El-Youm: Maison de la presse Tahar Djaout, 1 rue Bachir Attar, place du 1er mai, 16016 Algiers; tel. (21) 66-70-82; fax (21) 67-57-05; e-mail pubelyoum@yahoo.fr; Arabic; Dirs MAHFOUD HADJI, AMINA HADJI; Editor KHALED LAKHDARI; circ. 54,000.

WEEKLIES

Algérie Actualité: 2 rue Jacques Cartier, 16000 Algiers; tel. (21) 63-54-20; f. 1965; French; Dir KAMEL BELKACEM; circ. 250,000.

Les Débats: 2 rue Blvd Muhammad V, Algiers; tel. (21) 63-73-05; fax (21) 36-42-13; e-mail contact@lesdebats.com; internet www.lesdebats.com; French; Dir ABDERRAHMANE MAHMOUDI.

Al-Mohakik Assiri (The Secret Enquirer): 2 ave Nafaâ Hafaf, Algiers; tel. (21) 71-05-58; e-mail almohakik@yahoo.fr; internet www.almohakik.com; f. 2006; Arabic; Dir HABET HANNACHI.

La Nation: 33 rue Larbi Ben M'hidi, Algiers; tel. (21) 43-21-76; f. 1992; French; Dir ATTIA OMAR; Editor SALIMA GHEZALI; circ. 35,000.

Révolution Africaine: Algiers; tel. (21) 59-77-91; fax (21) 59-77-92; current affairs journal in French; socialist; Dir FERRAH ABDELLALI; circ. 50,000.

OTHER PERIODICALS

Al-Acala: 4 rue Timgad, Hydra, Algiers; tel. (21) 60-85-55; fax (21) 60-09-36; f. 1970; publ. by the Ministry of Religious Affairs and Endowments; fortnightly; Arabic; Editor MUHAMMAD AL-MAHDI.

Algérie Médicale: Algiers; f. 1964; publ. of the Union médicale algérienne; 2 a year; French; circ. 3,000.

Alouan (Colours): 119 rue Didouche Mourad, Algiers; f. 1973; cultural review; monthly; Arabic.

L'Auto Marché: 139 blvd Krim Belkacem; tel. (21) 74-44-59; fax (21) 74-14-63; e-mail contact@lautomarche.com; internet www.lautomarche.com; f. 1998; fortnightly; French; motoring; Dir MOURAD CHEBOUB.

Bibliographie de l'Algérie: Bibliothèque Nationale d'Algérie, BP 127, Hamma el-Annasser, 16000 Algiers; tel. (21) 67-18-67; fax (21) 67-29-99; f. 1963; lists books, theses, pamphlets and periodicals publ. in Algeria; 2 a year; Arabic and French; Dir-Gen. MUHAMMAD AÏSSA OUMOUSSA.

Le Buteur: Maison de la presse Tahar Djaout, 1 rue Bachir Attar, place du 1er mai, 16016 Algiers; tel. (21) 73-25-76; fax (21) 73-99-71; e-mail contact@lebuteur.com; internet www.lebuteur.com; Mon., Thur. and Sat.; French; sports; Dir BOUSAÂD KAHEL.

Ach-Cha'ab ath-Thakafi (Cultural People): Algiers; f. 1972; cultural monthly; Arabic.

Ach-Chabab (Youth): Algiers; journal of the Union Nationale de la Jeunesse Algérienne; bi-monthly; Arabic and French.

Ad-Djeich (The Army): Office de l'Armée Nationale Populaire, Algiers; f. 1963; monthly; Arabic and French; Algerian army review; circ. 10,000.

IT Mag: Co-opérative immobilière Charifa, A Bab Ezzouar, Algiers; tel. (21) 65-68-69; fax (21) 66-29-92; e-mail info@itmag-dz.com; internet www.itmag-dz.com; f. 2002; fortnightly; French; telecommunications and IT in North Africa; Dir ABDERRAFIQ KHENIFSA.

Journal Officiel de la République Algérienne Démocratique et Populaire: BP 376, Alger-Gare, Les Vergers, Bir Mourad Raïs, Algiers; tel. (21) 54-35-06; fax (21) 54-35-12; internet www.joradp.dz; f. 1962; Arabic and French.

Nouvelles Economiques: 6 blvd Amilcar Cabral, Algiers; f. 1969; publ. of the Institut Algérien du Commerce Extérieur; monthly; French and Arabic.

Révolution et Travail: Maison du Peuple, 1 rue Abdelkader Benbarek, place du 1er mai, Algiers; tel. (21) 66-73-53; journal of the Union Générale des Travailleurs Algériens (central trade union) with Arabic and French edns; monthly; Editor-in-Chief RACHIB AÏT ALI.

Revue Algérienne du Travail: 28 rue Hassiba Bouali, Algiers; f. 1964; labour publ.; quarterly; French; Dir. A. DJAMAL.

Ath-Thakafa (Culture): 2 place Cheikh ben Badis, Algiers; tel. (21) 62-20-73; f. 1971; every 2 months; cultural review; Editor-in-Chief CHEBOUB OTHMANE; circ. 10,000.

NEWS AGENCIES

Agence Algérienne d'Information (AAI): Maison de la presse Tahar Djaout, 1 rue Bachir Attar, place du 1er mai, 16016 Algiers; tel. (21) 67-07-44; fax (21) 67-07-32; e-mail aai@aai-online.com; internet www.aai-online.com; f. 1999; Dir HOURIA AÏT KACI.

Algérie Presse Service (APS): BP 444, 58 ave des Frères Bouadou, Bir Mourad Raïs, 16300 Algiers; tel. (21) 56-44-44; fax (21) 54-16-08; e-mail aps@aps.dz; internet www.aps.dz; f. 1961; provides news reports in Arabic, English and French.

Publishers

BERTI Editions: Lot en-Nadjah no 24, 16320 Dely Ibrahim, Algiers; tel. (21) 37-16-87; fax (21) 36-83-08; e-mail info@berti-editions.com; internet www.berti-editions.com; f. 1995; publishes books on medicine, law, finance and IT; Dir MUHAMMAD GACI.

Casbah Editions: Lot Saïd Hamdine, Hydra, 16012 Algiers; tel. (21) 54-79-10; fax (21) 54-72-77; internet www.casbaheditions.net; f. 1995; literature, essays, memoirs, textbooks and children's literature; Dir-Gen. SMAÏN AMZIANE.

Chihab: 10 ave Brahim Gharafa, Bab el-Oued, 16009 Algiers; tel. (21) 97-54-53; fax (21) 97-51-91; e-mail chihab@chihab.com; internet www.chihab.com/edition; f. 1989; publishes educational textbooks.

Editions Bouchène: 4 rue de l'oasis, Algiers; tel. (21) 59-69-23; e-mail edbouchene@wanadoo.fr; internet www.bouchene.com; f. 1998; publishes books on the Maghreb region.

Editions Dahlab: 108 rue de Tripoli, Hussein Dey, Algiers; tel. (21) 49-67-39; fax (21) 64-31-75; e-mail editiondahlab@yahoo.fr; history, social sciences, economy; Dir ABDELLAH CHEGHNANE.

Editions du Tell: 3 rue des Frères Yacoub Torki, 09000 Blida; tel. (25) 31-10-35; fax (25) 31-10-36; e-mail contact@editions-du-tell.com; internet www.editions-du-tell.com; f. 2002; publishes books on literature, history, economy and social sciences.

Entreprise Nationale des Arts Graphiques (ENAG): BP 75, Zone industriel de Réghaia, Algiers; tel. (21) 84-86-11; fax (21) 84-80-08; e-mail edition@enag.dz; internet www.enag.dz; f. 1983; art, literature, social sciences, economy, science, religion, lifestyle and textbooks; Dir F. BOUKHALOUA.

ALGERIA

Maison d'Édition El Amel: Cité 600, Logement EPLF 53, 15000 Tizi Ouzou; tel. (26) 21-96-55; fax (26) 21-07-21; law and political science publishers.

Office des Publications Universitaires (OPU): 1 place Centrale de Ben Aknoun, 16306 Algiers; tel. (21) 91-23-14; fax (21) 91-21-81; e-mail dg@opu-dz.com; internet www.opu-dz.com; publishes university textbooks; Dir-Gen. NOUREDDINE LACHEB.

Sedia: 17 bis, chemin du Réservoir, Hydra, 16035 Algiers; tel. (21) 60-14-82; fax (21) 60-14-84; e-mail sedia@sedia-dz.com; internet www.sedia-dz.com; f. 2000; part of the Hachette Livre group (France); literature and educational textbooks; Pres. and Dir-Gen. RADIA ABED.

Broadcasting and Communications

TELECOMMUNICATIONS

New legislation approved by the National People's Assembly in August 2000 removed the state's monopoly over the telecommunications sector and redefined its role to that of a supervisory authority. Under the legislation an independent regulator for the sector was created, and both the fixed-line and mobile sectors were opened to foreign competition.

Algérie Télécom: Route Nationale 5, Cinq Maisons, Mohammadia, 16130 Algiers; tel. (21) 82-38-38; fax (21) 82-38-39; e-mail contact@algerietelecom.dz; internet www.algerietelecom.dz; f. 2001 to manage and develop telecommunications infrastructure; privatization pending; Pres. and Dir-Gen. MOULOUD DJAZIRI.

Autorité de Régulation de la Poste et des Télécommunications (ARPT): 1 rue Kaddour Rahim, Hussein Dey, 16008 Algiers; tel. (21) 47-02-05; fax (21) 47-01-97; e-mail info@arpt.dz; internet www.arpt.dz; f. 2001; Pres. MUHAMMAD BELFODIL; Dir-Gen. FODIL BENYELLES.

Djezzy GSM: Orascom Telecom Algérie, rue Mouloud Feraoun, Lot no 8A, el-Beida, Algiers; tel. (70) 85-00-00; fax (70) 85-70-85; e-mail djezzy.entreprises@otalgerie.com; internet www.otalgerie.com; f. 2002; operates mobile cellular telephone network; some 13m. subscribers (Dec. 2007); Group Chair. NAGUIB SAWIRIS; Dir-Gen. HASSAN KABBANI.

Entreprise Nationale des Télécommunications (ENTC): 4–6 blvd Muhammad V, 16100 Algiers; tel. and fax (21) 63-73-93; f. 1978; national telecommunications org.; jt venture with Sweden; Dir-Gen. SIBAWAGHI SAKER.

Mobilis: Site Sider, 7 rue Belkacem Amani, Paradou, Hydra, Algiers; tel. (21) 54-71-63; fax (21) 54-72-72; e-mail commercial@mobilis.dz; internet www.mobilis.dz; f. 2003; subsidiary of Algérie Télécom; Pres. and Dir-Gen. LOUNIS BELHARRAT.

BROADCASTING

Radio

Radiodiffusion Algérienne: 21 blvd des Martyrs, Algiers; tel. (21) 48-37-90; fax (21) 23-08-23; e-mail info@algerian-radio.dz; internet www.algerian-radio.dz; govt-controlled; operates 30 local radio stations; Dir-Gen. AZZEDINE MIHOUBI.

Arabic Network: transmitters at Adrar, Aïn Beïda, Algiers, Béchar, Béni Abbès, Djanet, El Goléa, Ghardaïa, Hassi Messaoud, In Aménas, In Salah, Laghouat, Les Trembles, Ouargla, Reggane, Tamanrasset, Timimoun, Tindouf.

French Network: transmitters at Algiers, Constantine, Oran and Tipaza.

Kabyle Network: transmitter at Algiers.

Television

The principal transmitters are at Algiers, Batna, Sidi-Bel-Abbès, Constantine, Souk-Ahras and Tlemcen. Television plays a major role in the national education programme.

Télévision Algérienne (ENTV): 21 blvd des Martyrs, Algiers; tel. (21) 60-23-00; fax (21) 60-19-22; e-mail alger-contact@entv.dz; internet www.entv.dz; f. 1986; Dir-Gen. HABIB CHAWKI HAMRAOUI.

Finance

(cap. = capital; res = reserves; dep. = deposits; brs = branches; m. = million; amounts in Algerian dinars)

BANKING

Central Bank

Banque d'Algérie: Immeuble Joly, 38 ave Franklin Roosevelt, 16000 Algiers; tel. (21) 23-00-23; fax (21) 23-03-71; e-mail ba@bank-of-algeria.dz; internet www.bank-of-algeria.dz; f. 1962 as Banque Centrale d'Algérie; present name adopted 1990; bank of issue; cap. 40m., res 74,367.5m. (March 2006); Gov. MUHAMMAD LAKSACI; Sec.-Gen. KAMEL LONGO; 50 brs.

Nationalized Banks

Banque Al-Baraka d'Algérie: Haï Bouteldja Houidef, Villa no 1, Ben Aknoun, Algiers; tel. (21) 91-64-50; fax (21) 91-64-57; e-mail info@albaraka-bank.com; internet www.albaraka-bank.com; f. 1991; Algeria's first Islamic financial institution; owned by the Jeddah-based Al-Baraka Investment and Development Co (50%) and the local Banque de l'Agriculture et du Développement Rural (50%); cap. 500m., res 1,314.3m., dep. 31,720.0m. (Dec. 2005); Chair. ADNANE AHMAD YOUCEF; Gen. Man. HAFID MUHAMMAD SEDDIK.

Banque Extérieure d'Algérie (BEA): 48 rue des Trois Frères Bouadou, Bir Mourad Raïs, Algiers; tel. (21) 44-90-25; fax (21) 56-17-40; e-mail dircom@bea.dz; internet www.bea.dz; f. 1967; chiefly concerned with energy and maritime transport sectors; total assets 681,681m. (Dec. 2002); Dir-Gen. M. MOKHAZNI; 80 domestic brs, 1 abroad.

Banque du Maghreb Arabe pour l'Investissement et le Commerce (BAMIC): 7 rue Dubois, Hydra, Algiers; tel. (21) 69-45-43; fax (21) 60-19-54; e-mail bamic@bamic-dz.com; internet www.bamic-dz.com; f. 1988; owned by Libyan Arab Foreign Bank (50%) and by Banque Extérieure d'Algérie, Banque Nationale d'Algérie, Banque de l'Agriculture et du Développement Rural and Crédit Populaire d'Algérie (12.5% each); cap. 50m., res 16.2m. (Dec. 2005); Pres. MUHAMMAD DJELLAB; Dir-Gen. IBRAHIM AL-BISHARY.

Crédit Populaire d'Algérie (CPA): BP 411, 2 blvd Col Amirouche, 16000 Algiers; tel. (21) 63-57-05; fax (21) 63-57-13; e-mail info@cpa-bank.com; internet www.cpa-bank.com; f. 1966; specializes in light industry, construction and tourism; cap. and res 28,002m., total assets 367,847m. (Dec. 2002); Chair. EL HACHEMI MEGHAOUI; Dir-Gen. MUHAMMAD DJELLAB; 128 brs.

Development Banks

Banque de l'Agriculture et du Développement Rural (BADR): BP 484, 17 blvd Col Amirouche, 16000 Algiers; tel. (21) 63-49-22; fax (21) 63-51-46; e-mail dcm@badr-bank.net; internet www.badr-bank.net; f. 1982; wholly state-owned; finance for the agricultural sector; cap. 33,000m., res 1,995m., dep. 470,386m. (Dec. 2004); Dir-Gen. BOUALEM DJEBBAR; 270 brs.

Banque Algérienne de Développement (BAD): 21 blvd Zighout Youcef, Algiers; tel. (21) 73-99-04; e-mail bad@ist.cerist.dz; f. 1963; a public establishment with fiscal sovereignty; aims to contribute to Algerian economic devt through long-term investment programmes; cap. and res 7,125.4m., total assets 132,842.3m. (Dec. 2003); Pres. SADEK ALILAT; 4 brs.

Banque de Développement Local (BDL): 5 rue Gaci Amar, Staouéli, 16000 Algiers; tel. (21) 39-28-58; fax (21) 39-37-57; e-mail clientele@bdl.dz; internet www.bdl.dz; f. 1985; regional devt bank; cap. 13,390m. (2004); Pres. MUHAMMAD ARCELANE BACHTARZI; Dir-Gen. ABDELMADJID BAGHDADLI; 15 brs.

Caisse Nationale d'Epargne et de Prévoyance (CNEP): 42 blvd Khélifa Boukhalfa, Algiers; tel. (21) 71-33-53; fax (21) 71-70-22; e-mail infos@cnepbanque.dz; internet www.cnepbanque.dz; f. 1964; savings and housing bank; cap. and res 22.6m., total assets 443,239.6m. (Dec. 2001); Pres. and Dir-Gen. DJAMAL BESSA.

Private Banks

Algeria Gulf Bank: BP 26, route de Chérage, Dély Ibrahim, Algiers; tel. (21) 91-00-31; fax (21) 91-02-37; e-mail agbank_dz@hotmail.com; f. 2004; owned by United Gulf Bank, Bahrain (60%), Tunis International Bank (30%) and Jordan Kuwait Bank (10%); Dir-Gen. AMINE BAGHDADI.

Arab Leasing Corpn: BP 74, chemin Ahmed Ouaked, Dély Brahim, Algiers; tel. (21) 91-77-72; fax (21) 91-76-72; e-mail aleasinggroup@yahoo.fr; internet www.arableasing-dz.com; f. 2001; owned by Arab Banking Corpn (34%), The Arab Investment Co (25%), CNEP (20%) and other small shareholders; cap. and res 758m., total assets 801.6m. (Dec. 2002); Dir-Gen. ABDERREZAK TRABELSI.

BNP Paribas El-Djazair: 8 rue de Cirta, 16405 Hydra, Algiers; tel. (21) 60-39-42; fax (21) 60-39-29; e-mail mohamednazim.bessaih@bnpparibas.com; internet www.algerie.bnpparibas.com; f. 2001; cap. and res 2,125.1m., total assets 22,090.3m. (Dec. 2004); Chair. FATHI MESTIRI; Man. Dir FRANÇOIS EDOUARD DRION.

Trust Bank Algeria: 70 chemin Larbi Allik, Hydra, Algiers; tel. (21) 54-97-55; fax (21) 54-97-50; internet www.trust-bank-algeria.com; f. 2002; Pres. and Dir-Gen. KAMAL ABU NAHAL GHAZI; 3 brs.

Banking Association

Association des banques et des établissements financiers (ABEF): 03 chemin Romain, Val d'Hydra, el-Biar, Algiers; tel. (21)

91-55-77; fax (21) 91-56-08; e-mail abenkhalfa@gmail.com; f. 1995; serves and promotes the interests of banks and financial institutions in Algeria; Del.-Gen. ABDERRAHMANE BENKHALFA.

STOCK EXCHANGE

The Algiers Stock Exchange began trading in July 1999.

Commission d'Organisation et de Surveillance des Opérations de Bourse (COSOB): 17 Campagne Chkiken, 16045 Hydra, Algiers; tel. (21) 59-10-15; fax (21) 59-10-19; e-mail contact@cosob.org; internet www.cosob.org; f. 1993; Chair. BELKACEM IRATNI; Gen. Sec. ABDELHAKIM BERRAH.

INSURANCE

The insurance sector is dominated by the state; however, in 1997 regulations were drafted to permit private companies to enter the Algerian insurance market.

L'Algérienne des Assurances (2a): 1 rue de Tripoli, Hussein-Dey, Algiers; tel. (21) 47-68-72; fax (21) 47-65-73; e-mail info@assurances-2a.com; internet www.assurances-2a.com; f. 2004; general; Dir-Gen. TAHAR BALA.

Caisse Nationale de Mutualité Agricole: 24 blvd Victor Hugo, Algiers; tel. (21) 74-33-28; fax (21) 73-34-79; e-mail cnma@cnma.dz; internet www.cnma.dz; f. 1972; Dir-Gen. DJAMEL MADANI; 62 brs.

Cie Algérienne d'Assurances (CAAT): 52 rue des Frères Bouaddou, Bir Mourad Raïs, Algiers; tel. (21) 44-90-75; fax (21) 92-90-03; e-mail info@caat.dz; internet www.caat.dz; f. 1985; general; majority state ownership; Pres. and Dir-Gen. ABDELKRIM DJAFRI.

Cie Algérienne d'Assurance et de Réassurance (CAAR): 48 rue Didouche Mourad, 16000 Algiers; tel. (21) 63-20-72; fax (21) 63-13-77; e-mail caaralg@caar.com.dz; internet www.caar.com.dz; f. 1963 as a public corpn; partial privatization pending; Pres. and Dir-Gen. BRAHIM DJAMEL KASSALI.

Cie Centrale de Réassurance (CCR): Lot no 1, Saïd Hamdine, Bir Mourad Raïs, 16005 Algiers; tel. (21) 54-70-33; fax (21) 54-75-06; f. 1973; general; Pres. and Dir-Gen. DJAMEL ED-DIN CHOUAÏB CHOUITER.

Société Nationale d'Assurances (SAA): 5 blvd Ernesto Ché Guévara, Algiers; tel. (21) 71-47-60; fax (21) 71-22-16; f. 1963; state-sponsored co; Pres. and Dir-Gen. AMARA LATROUS.

Trust Algeria Assurances-Réassurance: 70 chemin Larbi Allik, 16405 Hydra, Algiers; tel. (21) 54-89-00; fax (21) 54-71-36; e-mail trustalgeria@ifrance.com; f. 1987; 60% owned by Trust Insurance Co (Bahrain), 17.5% owned by CAAR; Pres. and Dir-Gen. KAMAL ABU NAHAL GHAZI.

Trade and Industry

GOVERNMENT AGENCIES AND DEVELOPMENT ORGANIZATIONS

Agence Nationale de l'Aménagement du Territoire (ANAT): 30 ave Muhammad Fellah, Kouba, Algiers; tel. (21) 68-78-16; fax (21) 68-85-03; e-mail anat@anat.dz; internet www.anat.dz; f. 1980; Dir-Gen. MUHAMMAD MEKKAOUI.

Agence Nationale de Développement de l'Investissement (ANDI): 27 rue Muhammad Merbouche, Hussein-Dey, Algiers; tel. (21) 77-32-62; fax (21) 77-32-57; e-mail information@andi.dz; internet www.andi.dz; Dir-Gen. ABDELMADJID BAGHDADLI.

Agence Algérienne de Promotion du Commerce Extérieur (ALGEX): BP 191, Hassan Badi, el-Harrach, Algiers; tel. (21) 52-20-82; fax (21) 52-11-26; e-mail algex@info.dz; internet www.algex.dz; f. 2004; Dir-Gen. MUHAMMAD BENNINI.

Institut National de la Productivité et du Développement Industriel (INPED): 35000 Boumerdès; tel. (24) 81-78-34; fax (24) 81-58-59; e-mail dg@inped.edu.dz; internet www.inped.edu.dz; f. 1967; Dir-Gen. NOUREDDINE TABLIT.

Office National de Recherche Géologique et Minière (ORGM): BP 102, Cité Ibn Khaldoun, 35000 Boumerdès; tel. (24) 81-75-99; fax (24) 81-83-79; e-mail orgm-dg@orgm.com.dz; internet www.orgm.com.dz; f. 1992; mining, cartography, geophysical exploration; Dir-Gen. ABDELKADER SEMIANI.

CHAMBERS OF COMMERCE

Chambre Algérienne de Commerce et d'Industrie (CACI): BP 100, Palais Consulaire, 6 blvd Amilcar Cabral, place des Martyres, 16003 Algiers; tel. (21) 96-77-77; fax (21) 96-70-70; e-mail dsisec.caci@elwassit.dz; internet www.caci.dz; f. 1980; Pres. BRAHIM BENDJABER; Dir-Gen. MUHAMMAD CHAMI.

Chambre Française de Commerce et d'Industrie en Algérie (CFCIA): Villa Clarac, 3 rue des Cèdres, 16070 el-Mouradia, Algiers; tel. (21) 48-08-00; fax (21) 60-95-09; e-mail jf.heugas@cfcia.org; internet www.cfcia.org; f. 1975; c. 24,500 mems; Pres. MICHEL DE CAFFARELLI; Dir-Gen. JEAN-FRANÇOIS HEUGAS.

INDUSTRIAL ASSOCIATIONS

Centre d'Etudes et de Services Technologiques de l'Industrie des Matériaux de Construction (CETIM): BP 93, Cité Ibn Khaldoun, 35000 Boumerdès; tel. (24) 81-99-78; fax (24) 81-72-97; e-mail contact@cetim-dz.com; internet www.cetim-dz.com; f. 1982; Pres. and Dir-Gen. ABDENNOUR ADJTOUTAH.

Institut National Algérien de la Propriété Industrielle (INAPI): 42 rue Larbi Ben M'hidi, 16000 Algiers; tel. (21) 73-23-58; fax (21) 73-55-81; e-mail info@inapi.org; internet www.inapi.org; f. 1973; Dir-Gen. NABILA KADRI.

Institut National des Industries Manufacturières (INIM): 35000 Boumerdès; tel. (21) 81-62-71; fax (21) 82-56-62; f. 1973; Dir-Gen. YOUSUF OUSLIMANI.

STATE TRADING ORGANIZATIONS

Since 1970 all international trading has been carried out by state organizations, of which the following are the most important:

Entreprise Nationale d'Approvisionnement en Outillage et Produits de Quincaillerie Générale (ENAOQ): 5 rue Amar Semaous, Hussein-Dey, Algiers; tel. (21) 23-31-83; fax (21) 47-83-33; tools and general hardware; Dir-Gen. SMATI BAHIDJ FARID.

Entreprise Nationale d'Approvisionnements en Produits Alimentaires (ENAPAL): 29 rue Larbi Ben M'hidi, Algiers; tel. (21) 76-10-11; f. 1983; monopoly of import, export and bulk trade in basic foodstuffs; brs in more than 40 towns; Chair. LAÏD SABRI; Man. Dir BRAHIM DOUAOURI.

Office Algérien Interprofessionel des Céréales (OAIC): 5 rue Ferhat-Boussaad, Algiers; tel. (21) 23-73-04; fax (21) 23-70-83; f. 1962; responsible for the regulation, distribution and control of the national market and the importation of cereals and vegetables; Gen. Man. MUHAMMAD KACEM.

Office National de la Commercialisation des Produits Viti-Vinicoles (ONCV): 112 Quai Sud, Algiers; tel. (21) 73-82-59; fax (21) 73-72-97; e-mail dg@oncv-groupe.com; internet www.oncv-groupe.com; f. 1968; monopoly of importing and exporting products of the wine industry; Man. Dir SAÏD MEBARKI.

Société des Emballages Fer Blanc et Fûts (EMB-FBF): BP 245, Kouba, Route de Baraki, Gué de Constantine, Algiers; tel. (21) 89-94-23; fax (21) 83-05-29; e-mail info@emb-fbf.com; internet www.emb-fbf.com; Dir-Gen. HAMID ZITOUN.

UTILITIES

Regulatory Authority

Commission de Régulation de l'Electricité et du Gaz: Immeuble du Ministère de l'Energie et des Mines, Tour B, Val d'Hydra, Algiers; tel. (21) 48-81-48; fax (21) 48-84-00; e-mail contact@creg.mem.gov.dz; internet www.creg.gov.dz; f. 2005; Pres. NADJIB OTMANE.

Electricity

Entreprise Nationale de Travaux d'Electrification (KAHRIF): Villa Malwall, Aïn d'Heb, Médéa; tel. (25) 58-51-67; fax (25) 61-31-14; e-mail bousri@kahrif.com; internet www.kahrif.com; f. 1982; study of electrical infrastructure; Pres. and Dir-Gen. SAÂD BOUSRI.

Société Algérienne de l'Electricité et du Gaz (Sonelgaz Spa): 2 blvd Col Krim Belkacem, Algiers; tel. (21) 72-31-00; fax (21) 71-26-90; e-mail n.boutarfa@sonelgaz.dz; internet www.sonelgaz.dz; f. 1969; production, distribution and transportation of electricity and transportation and distribution of natural gas; Chair. and CEO NOUREDDINE BOUTARFA.

Gas

Linde Gas Algérie SpA (GI): BP 247, 23 ave de l'ALN, Hussein-Dey, Kouba, Algiers; tel. (21) 49-85-99; fax (21) 49-71-94; internet www.gaz-industriels.com.dz; f. 1972 as Entreprise Nationale des Gaz Industriels; production, distribution and commercialization of industrial and medical gas; Pres. and Dir-Gen. LAHOCINE BOUCHERIT; Gen. Man. RICHARD PERRAYON.

Société Algérienne de l'Electricité et du Gaz: (see under Electricity).

Water

Algérienne des Eaux (ADE): BP 548, 3 rue du Caire, Kouba, 16016 Algiers; tel. (21) 28-28-07; fax (21) 28-10-06; f. 1985 as Agence Nationale de l'Eau Potable et Industrielle et de l'Assainissement; state-owned co; Dir-Gen. ABDELKRIM MECHIA.

ALGERIA

STATE HYDROCARBONS AGENCIES AND COMPANIES

Agence Nationale pour la Valorisation des Ressources en Hydrocarbures (Alnaft): Ministère de l'Energie et des Mines, Tour B, Val d'Hydra, Algiers; tel. (21) 48-85-42; fax (21) 48-83-92; e-mail contact.alnaft@mem.gov.dz; f. 2005; Dir SID ALI BETATA.

Autorité de Régulation des Hydrocarbures (ARH): Ministère de l'Energie et des Mines, Tour B, Val d'Hydra, Algiers; tel. (21) 48-81-67; fax (21) 48-83-15; e-mail arh@arh.mem.gov.dz; f. 2005; Dir NOUREDDINE CHEROUATI.

Société Nationale pour la Recherche, la Production, le Transport, la Transformation et la Commercialisation des Hydrocarbures (SONATRACH): Djenane el-Malik, Hydra, Algiers; tel. (21) 54-70-00; fax (21) 54-77-00; e-mail sonatrach@sonatrach.dz; internet www.sonatrach-dz.com; f. 1963; exploration, exploitation, transport and marketing of petroleum, natural gas and their products; Pres. and Dir-Gen. MUHAMMAD MEZIANE; Gen. Sec. ABDELMALEK ZITOUNI.

The following companies are wholly owned subsidiaries of SONATRACH:

Entreprise Nationale de Canalisation (ENAC): rue Benyoucef Khattab, 16130 Mohammadia, Algiers; tel. (21) 53-85-49; fax (21) 53-85-53; piping; Vice-Pres. HOCINE CHEKIRED.

Entreprise Nationale de Forage (ENAFOR): BP 211, Hassi Messaoud, W. Ouargla; tel. (29) 73-75-95; fax (29) 73-80-26; e-mail laouadi@enafor.dz; f. 1981; drilling.

Entreprise Nationale de Géophysique (ENAGEO): BP 140, 30500 Hassi Messaoud, Ouargla; tel. (29) 73-77-00; fax (29) 73-72-12; internet www.enageo.com; f. 1981; seismic acquisition, geophysics; Dir-Gen. RÉDA RAHAL.

Entreprise Nationale des Grands Travaux Pétroliers (ENGTP): BP 09, Zone industrielle, Reghaïa, Boumerdès; tel. (24) 84-86-26; fax (24) 84-80-34; e-mail info@engtp.com; internet www.engtp.com; f. 1980; major industrial projects; Dir-Gen. MUHAMMAD RACHID MESSAOUD.

Entreprise Nationale de la Pétrochimie (ENIP): BP 215, Zone industrielle, 21000 Skikda; tel. (38) 74-52-86; fax (38) 74-52-80; e-mail inr@enip-dz.com; internet www.enip-dz.com; f. 1984; design and construction for petroleum-processing industry; Dir-Gen. YAHIA ZAKARIA KHADIR.

Entreprise Nationale des Services aux Puits (ENSP): BP 83, 30500 Hassi Messaoud, Ouargla; tel. and fax (29) 73-73-33; fax (29) 73-82-01; e-mail services.requests@enspgroup.com; internet www.enspgroup.com; f. 1981; oil-well services; Dir-Gen. RABAH LAKEHAL.

Entreprise Nationale des Travaux aux Puits (ENTP): BP 206–207, Base du 20 août 1955, 30500 Hassi Messaoud, Ouargla; tel. (29) 73-88-50; fax (29) 73-84-06; e-mail acila@entp-dz.com; internet www.entp-dz.com; f. 1981; oil-well construction; Pres. and Dir-Gen. ALI ACILA.

Société Nationale de Commercialisation et de Distribution des Produits Pétroliers (NAFTAL, SpA): BP 73, route des Dûnes, Chéraga, Algiers; tel. (21) 38-13-13; fax (21) 38-19-19; e-mail webmaster@naftal.dz; internet www.naftal.dz; f. 1987; international marketing and distribution of petroleum products; CEO SAÏD AKRETCHE.

Société Nationale de Génie Civil et Bâtiments (GCB, SpA): BP 110, blvd de l'ALNBoumerdès-Ville; tel. (24) 81-89-99; fax (24) 81-38-80; e-mail gcb@wissal.dz; civil engineering.

Société Nationale de Raffinage de Pétrole (NAFTEC): BP 130, Sidi Arcine, Baraki, Algiers; tel. (21) 67-21-12; fax (21) 67-21-96; f. 1988; refining of oil and petrochemicals; Dir-Gen. AKLI REMINI.

TRADE UNIONS

Ittahad as-Sahafiyin al-Jaza'iriyin (Algerian Journalists' Union): Maison de la presse Tahar Djaout, 1 rue Bachir Attar, place du 1er mai, 16016 Algiers; e-mail snjalgerie2006@yahoo.fr; f. 2001; Sec.-Gen. KAMEL AMARNI (acting).

Union Générale des Entrepreneurs Algériens (UGEA): Villa 28, quartier Aïn Soltane, les Oliviers, Birkhadem, Algiers; tel. and fax (21) 54-10-82; Pres. ABDELMADJID DENNOUNI.

Union Générale des Travailleurs Algériens (UGTA): Maison du Peuple, place du 1er mai, Algiers; tel. (21) 65-07-36; e-mail sgeneral@ugta.dz; internet www.ugta.dz; f. 1956; there are 10 national 'professional sectors' affiliated to the UGTA; Sec.-Gen. ABDELMADJID SIDI SAÏD.

Union Nationale des Paysans Algériens (UNPA): f. 1973; 700,000 mems; Sec.-Gen. KAMEL ALIOUI.

Directory

Transport

RAILWAYS

Entreprise Métro d'Alger: 178B Hassiba Ben Bouali, Algiers; tel. (21) 66-17-47; fax (21) 66-17-57; construction of a 26.5-km metro railway line began in 1991; initial 12.5-km section (16 stations) scheduled to open in two stages, starting in mid-2008; Dir-Gen. MUHAMMAD ZENDAOUI.

Infrafer (Entreprise Publique Economique de Réalisation des Infrastructures Ferroviaires): BP 208, 15 rue Colonel Amirouche, 35300 Rouiba; tel. (21) 85-67-02; fax (21) 85-49-62; e-mail info@infrafer.com; internet www.infrafer.com; f. 1987; responsible for construction and maintenance of track; Man. Dir SAIDI HASSANE.

Société Nationale des Transports Ferroviaires (SNTF): 21–23 blvd Muhammad V, Algiers; tel. (21) 71-15-10; fax (21) 74-81-90; e-mail dg-sntf@sntf.dz; internet www.sntf.dz; f. 1976 to replace Société Nationale des Chemins de Fer Algériens; 5,090 km of track, of which 289 km are electrified; daily passenger services from Algiers to the principal provincial cities and services to Tunisia and Morocco; Dir-Gen. ABD AL-ADIM BENALLEGUE.

ROADS

In 2004 there were an estimated 108,302 km of roads and tracks; some 70.2% of the road network was paved. The French administration built a good road system (partly for military purposes), which, since independence, has been allowed to deteriorate in places. New roads have been built linking the Sahara oil fields with the coast, and the Trans-Sahara highway is a major project. Construction of the 1,216-km East–West motorway, linking et-Tarf with Tlemcen, is scheduled for completion by 2010.

Agence Nationale des Autoroutes (ANA): BP 72M Mohammadia, El Harrach, Algiers; tel. (21) 53-09-63; fax (21) 53-09-62; e-mail dgana@ana.org.dz; internet www.ana.org.dz; f. 2005 to manage the construction and maintenance of the motorway network.

Société Nationale des Transports Routiers (SNTR): 27 rue des Trois Frères Bouadou, Bir Mourad Raïs, Algiers; tel. (21) 54-06-00; fax (21) 54-05-35; e-mail dg-sntr@sntr-groupe.com; internet www.sntr-groupe.com; f. 1967; goods transport by road; maintainance of industrial vehicles; Pres. and Dir-Gen. ABDELLAH BENMAÂROUF.

Société Nationale des Transports des Voyageurs (SNTV): Algiers; tel. (21) 66-00-52; f. 1967; long-distance passenger transport by road; Man. Dir MUHAMMAD DIB.

SHIPPING

Algiers is the main port, with anchorage of between 23 m and 29 m in the Bay of Algiers, and anchorage for the largest vessels in Agha Bay. The port has a total quay length of 8,380 m. There are also important ports at Annaba, Arzew, Béjaïa, Djidjelli, Ghazaouet, Mostaganem, Oran, Skikda and Ténès. Petroleum and liquefied gas are exported through Arzew, Béjaïa and Skikda. Algerian crude petroleum is also exported through the Tunisian port of La Skhirra. In December 2006 Algeria's merchant fleet totalled 127 vessels, with an aggregate displacement of 764,099 grt.

Cie Algéro-Libyenne de Transports Maritimes (CALTRAM): 19 rue des Trois Frères Bouadou, Bir Mourad Raïs, Algiers; tel. (21) 54-17-00; fax (21) 54-21-04; e-mail caltram@wissal.dz; f. 1974; Man. Dir A. KERAMANE.

Cie Nationale de Navigation (CNAN Group): BP 280, 2 quai no 9, Nouvelle Gare Maritime, Algiers; tel. (21) 42-33-89; fax (21) 42-31-28; f. 2003 as part of restructuring of the Société Nationale de Transports Maritimes-Compagnie Nationale Algérienne de Navigation (SNTM—CNAN); state-owned co which owns and operates fleet of 12 freight ships; rep. offices in Marseille (France) and La Spezia (Italy), and rep. agencies in Antwerp (Belgium), Barcelona (Spain), Hamburg (Germany) and the principal ports in many other countries; Dir-Gen. ALI BOUMBAR.

Entreprise Nationale de Réparation Navale (ERENAV): quai no 12, Algiers; tel. (21) 42-37-83; fax (21) 42-30-39; f. 1987; ship repairs; Pres. and Dir-Gen. REGAINIA GHAZI.

Entreprise Nationale de Transport Maritime de Voyageurs—Algérie Ferries (ENTMV): BP 467, 5–6 rue Jawharlal Nehru, 16001 Algiers; tel. (21) 42-33-01; fax (21) 42-33-63; e-mail entmv@algerieferries.com; internet www.algerieferries.com; f. 1987 as part of restructuring of SNTM-CNAN; responsible for passenger transport; operates car ferry services between Algiers, Annaba, Skikda, Alicante (Spain), Marseille (France) and Oran; Dir-Gen. BOUDJEMA CHERIET.

Entreprise Portuaire d'Alger (EPAL): BP 259, 2 rue d'Angkor, Alger-Gare, Algiers; tel. (21) 42-36-14; fax (21) 71-54-52; e-mail epal@portalger.com.dz; internet www.portalger.com.dz; f. 1982; responsible for management and growth of port facilities and sea pilotage; Dir-Gen. ABDELHAK BOUROUAÏ.

Entreprise Portuaire d'Annaba (EPAN): BP 1232, Môle Cigogne, Quai nord, 23000 Annaba; tel. (38) 86-31-31; fax (38) 86-54-15; e-mail epan@annaba-port.com; internet www.annaba-port.com; Man. Dir DJILANI SALHI.

Entreprise Portuaire d'Arzew (EPA): BP 46, 7 rue Larbi Tebessi, 31200 Arzew; tel. (41) 47-69-22; fax (41) 47-54-23; Man. Dir CHAÏB OUMER.

Entreprise Portuaire de Béjaïa (EPB): BP 94, 13 ave des frères Amrani, 06000 Béjaïa; tel. (34) 21-18-07; fax (34) 20-14-88; e-mail portbj@portdebejaia.dz; internet www.portdebejaia.com.dz; Dir-Gen. RABAH MOUSSAOUI.

Entreprise Portuaire de Djen-Djen (EPJ): BP 87, 18000 Jijel; tel. (34) 44-65-64; fax (34) 44-52-60; e-mail epjdjendjen@wissal.dz; internet www.djendjen-port.com.dz; f. 1984; Pres. and CEO MUHAMMAD ATMANE.

Entreprise Portuaire de Ghazaouet (EPG): BP 217, 13400 Ghazaouet; tel. (43) 32-32-37; fax (43) 32-32-55; e-mail contact@portdeghazaouet.com; internet www.portdeghazaouet.com; f. 1982; Gen. Man. ABDELMALEK BRAHIM.

Entreprise Portuaire de Mostaganem (EPM): BP 131, quai du Maghreb, 27000 Mostaganem; tel. (45) 21-14-11; fax (45) 21-78-05; Dir-Gen. M. CHERIF.

Entreprise Portuaire d'Oran (EPO): 1 rue du 20 août, 31000 Oran; tel. (41) 33-24-41; fax (41) 33-24-98; e-mail webmaster@oran-port.com; Chair. and Dir-Gen. M. S. LOUHIBI.

Entreprise Portuaire de Skikda (EPS): BP 65, 46 ave Rezki Rahal, 21000 Skikda; tel. (38) 75-68-50; fax (38) 75-20-15; e-mail info@skikda-port.com; internet www.skikda-port.com; Man. Dir LAÏDI LEMRABET.

Entreprise Portuaire de Ténès (EPT): BP 18, 02200 Ténès; tel. (27) 76-72-76; fax (27) 76-61-77; e-mail asiporttenes@yahoo.fr; Man. Dir KHALDI EL-HAMRI.

HYPROC Shipping Co (HYPROC SC): BP 7200, Zone des Sièges 'ZHUN-USTO', es-Seddikia, 31025 Oran; tel. (41) 47-62-62; fax (41) 47-32-75; e-mail hyproc@hyproc.com; internet www.hyproc.com; f. 1982 as Société Nationale de Transports Maritimes des Hydrocarbures et des Produits Chimiques; name changed as above in 2003; wholly owned subsidiary of SONATRACH; Pres. and Dir-Gen. MUSTAPHA ZENASNI.

NAFTAL Division Aviation Marine: BP 70, Aéroport Houari Boumedienne, Dar-el-Beïda, Algiers; tel. (21) 50-95-50; fax (21) 50-67-09; e-mail avm@ist.cerist.dz; Dir MESNOUS NOUREDDINE.

Société Générale Maritime (GEMA): BP 368, 2 rue Jawharlal Nehru, 16100 Algiers; tel. (21) 74-73-00; fax (21) 74-76-70; e-mail gemadg@gema-groupe.com; internet www.gema-groupe.com; f. 1987 as part of restructuring of SNTM-CNAN; shipping, ship-handling and forwarding; Dir-Gen. ALI LARBI CHERIF.

CIVIL AVIATION

Algeria's principal international airport, Houari Boumedienne, is situated 20 km from Algiers. Other international airports are situated at Constantine, Annaba, Tlemcen and Oran. There are, in addition, 65 aerodromes, of which 20 are public, and a further 135 airstrips connected with the petroleum industry.

Air Algérie (Entreprise Nationale d'Exploitation des Services Aériens): BP 858, 1 place Maurice Audin, Immeuble el-Djazair, Algiers; tel. (21) 74-24-28; fax (21) 61-05-53; e-mail contacts@airalgerie.dz; internet www.airalgerie.dz; f. 1953 by merger; state-owned from 1972; internal services and extensive services to Europe, North and West Africa, and the Middle East; Chair. and Dir-Gen. MUHAMMAD TAYEB BENOUIS; Sec.-Gen. NOUREDDINE BEZAOUCHA.

Tassili Airlines: BP 301, blvd Mustapha Ben Boulaïd, 30500 Hassi Messaoud; tel. (29) 73-80-25; fax (29) 73-84-24; f. 1997; wholly owned by SONATRACH; domestic passenger services.

Tourism

Algeria's tourist attractions include the Mediterranean coast, the Atlas mountains and the Sahara desert. In 2005 a total of 1,443,090 tourists visited Algeria, compared with 1,233,719 in 2004. Receipts from tourism totalled US $184m. in 2005. It was announced in early 2007 that the Government was investing some $1,000m. in the tourism sector; the construction of 42 new resorts was scheduled to be completed by 2015.

Agence Nationale de Développement Touristique (ANDT): BP 151, Sidi Fredj Staoueli, Algiers; tourism promotion; Dir-Gen. RACHID CHELOUFI.

Office National du Tourisme (ONT): 2 rue Ismail Kerrar, 16307 Algiers; tel. (21) 71-30-60; fax (21) 71-30-59; e-mail webmaster@algeriatourism.com; internet www.algeriantourism.com; f. 1988; state institution; oversees tourism promotion policy; Dir-Gen. MAGHMOUL LAÏD.

ONAT (Entreprise Nationale Algérienne de Tourisme): 126 bis A, rue Didouche Mourad, 16000 Algiers; tel. (21) 74-29-85; fax (21) 74-32-14; e-mail direction-marketing@onat-dz.com; internet www.onat-dz.com; f. 1983; Pres. and Dir-Gen. BELKACEMI HAMMOUCHE.

Touring Club d'Algérie (TCA): 30 rue Hassène Benaâmane, Les Vergers, Bir Mourad Raïs, Algiers; tel. (21) 54-13-13; fax (21) 54-39-53; e-mail sg-touring@algeriatouring.dz; internet www.algeriatouring.dz; f. 1963; Pres. ABDERRAHMANE ABDEDAÏM.

Touring Voyages Algérie: Centre commercial 'el-Hammadia', Bouzaréah, Algiers; tel. (21) 94-13-13; fax (21) 94-26-95; e-mail contact@touringvoyagesalgerie.dz; internet www.touringvoyagesalgerie.dz; f. 1995 to manage the commercial activities of Touring Club d'Algérie; 89% owned by Touring Club d'Algérie; Pres. and Dir-Gen. TAHAR SAHRI.

ANDORRA

Introductory Survey

Location, Climate, Language, Religion, Flag, Capital

The Principality of Andorra lies in the eastern Pyrenees, bounded by France and Spain, and is situated roughly midway between Barcelona and Toulouse. The climate is alpine, with much snow in winter and a warm summer. The official language is Catalan, but French and Spanish are also widely spoken. Most of the inhabitants profess Christianity and more than 90% are Roman Catholics. The civil flag (proportions 2 by 3) has three equal vertical stripes, of blue, yellow and red. The state flag has, in addition, the state coat of arms (a quartered shield above the motto *Virtus unita fortior*) in the centre of the yellow stripe. The capital is Andorra la Vella.

Recent History

Owing to the lack of distinction between the authority of the Consell General (General Council) of Andorra and the Co-Princes (Copríinceps—the President of France and the Spanish Bishop of Urgell) who have ruled the country since 1278, the Andorrans encountered many difficulties in their attempts to gain international status for their country and control over its essential services.

Until 1970 the franchise was granted only to third-generation Andorran males who were more than 25 years of age. Thereafter, women, persons aged between 21 and 25, and second-generation Andorrans were allowed to vote in elections to the Consell General. In 1977 the franchise was extended to include all first-generation Andorrans of foreign parentage who were aged 28 and over. The electorate remained small, however, when compared with the size of the population, and Andorra's foreign residents increased their demands for political and nationality rights. In December 2006 foreign residents comprised 63.6% of the total population. Immigration is on a quota system, being restricted primarily to French and Spanish nationals intending to work in Andorra.

Prior to 1993, political parties were not directly represented in the Consell General, but there were loose groupings with liberal and conservative sympathies. The country's only political organization, the Partit Democràtic d'Andorra (Andorran Democratic Party—PDA), was technically illegal and in the 1981 elections to the Consell General the party urged its supporters to cast blank votes.

In 1980, during discussions on institutional reform, representatives of the Co-Princes and the Consell General agreed that an executive council should be formed and that a referendum should be held on changes to the electoral system. In early 1981 the Co-Princes formally requested the Consell General to prepare plans for reform, in accordance with these proposals. Following the December elections to the Consell General, in January 1982 the new legislature elected Oscar Ribas Reig as Head of Government (Cap de Govern). Ribas appointed an executive of six ministers, who expressed their determination to provide Andorra with a written constitution. The formation of the executive body, known as the Govern, constituted the separation of powers between an executive and a legislature.

Severe storm damage in November 1982, and the general effects of the world-wide economic recession, led to the introduction of income tax in August 1983, in an effort to alleviate Andorra's budgetary deficit and to provide the Government with extra revenue for development projects. Subsequent government proposals for an indirect tax on bank deposits, hotel rooms and property sales encountered strong opposition from financial and tourism concerns, and prompted the Government's resignation in April 1984. Josep Pintat Solans, a local business executive, was elected unopposed by the Consell General as Head of Government in May. In August, however, the Ministers of Finance and of Industry, Commerce and Agriculture resigned, following disagreements concerning the failure to implement economic reforms (including the introduction of income tax). At the December 1985 elections to the Consell General the electorate was increased by about 27%, as a result of the newly introduced lower minimum voting age of 18 years. The Consell re-elected Josep Pintat as Head of Government in January 1986, when he won the support of 27 of its 28 members.

In September 1986 President François Mitterrand of France and the Bishop of Urgell, Dr Joan Martí Alanis, met in Andorra to discuss the principality's status in relation to the European Community (EC, now European Union—EU, see p. 244), as well as the question of free exchange of goods between EC member countries and Andorra, following Spain's admission to the Community in January of that year.

In April 1987 the Consejo Sindical Interregional Pirineos-Mediterráneo, a collective of French and Spanish trade unions, in conjunction with the Andorran Asociación de Residentes Andorranos, began to claim rights, including those of freedom of expression and association and the right to strike, on behalf of 20,000 of its members who were employed as immigrant workers in Andorra. Further proposals for institutional reforms were approved by the Consell General in October. The transfer to the Andorran Government of responsibility for such matters as public order was proposed, while the authority of the Co-Princes in the administration of justice was recognized. The drafting of a constitution for Andorra was also envisaged. The implementation of the reforms was, however, dependent on the agreement of the Co-Princes. In December municipal elections were held, at which 80% of the electorate voted; however, the number of citizens eligible to vote represented only 13% of Andorra's total population. For the first time, the election campaign involved the convening of meetings and the use of the media, in addition to traditional canvassing. Although there were no political parties as such, four of the seven seats were won by candidates promoting a conservative stance.

In April 1988 Andorra enacted legislation recognizing the Universal Declaration of Human Rights, adopted by the UN General Assembly in 1948. In June 1988 the first Andorran trade union was established by two French union confederations and by the Spanish Unión General de Trabajadores. (There were about 26,000 salaried workers in Andorra at this time, 90% of whom were of French or Spanish origin.) In the following month, however, the Consell General rejected the formation of the union, as the Consell did not recognize workers' right of association and prohibited the existence of any union.

Elections to the Consell General took place in December 1989, following which the reformist Ribas was elected as Head of Government, with the support of 22 members of the Consell. In June the Consell voted unanimously to establish a special commission to draft a constitution. The proposed document was to promulgate popular sovereignty and to limit the role of the Co-Princes. In April 1991 representatives of the Co-Princes agreed to recognize popular sovereignty in Andorra and to permit the drafting of a constitution, which would be subject to approval by referendum. In September, however, Ribas was threatened with a vote of 'no confidence' by traditionalist members of the Consell, who were opposed to the proposed constitution, which would effectively legalize political parties and trade unions. There followed a period of political impasse, during which no official budget was authorized for the principality. In January 1992, following small, but unprecedented, public demonstrations in protest against the political deadlock, Ribas and the Consell General resigned. The result of a general election, which took place in April, was inconclusive, necessitating a second round of voting one week later, following which supporters of Ribas controlled a narrow majority of the 28 seats. Accordingly, Ribas was re-elected as Head of Government.

At a referendum held in March 1993, in which 75.7% of the electorate participated, 74.2% of those who voted approved the draft Constitution. The document was signed by the Co-Princes in April, and was promulgated on 4 May. Under its provisions, the Co-Princes remained as Heads of State, but with greatly reduced powers, while Andorran nationals were afforded full sovereignty and (together with foreigners who had lived in Andorra for at least 20 years) were authorized to form and to join political parties and trade unions. The Constitution provided for the establishment of an independent judiciary and permitted the principality to formulate its own foreign policy and to join international organizations. The Co-Princes were to retain a

ANDORRA

right of veto over treaties with France and Spain that affected Andorra's borders or security.

The first general election under the terms of the new Constitution took place on 12 December 1993. One of the constitutional provisions was the implementation of a new system of partial proportional representation—one-half of the Consell General's 28 members were directly elected from a single national constituency by a system of proportional representation, the remainder being elected by Andorra's seven parishes (two for each parish). Ribas's Agrupament Nacional Democràtic (National Democratic Grouping—AND), the successor to the PDA, won eight seats, while Nova Democràcia (New Democracy—ND) and the Unió Liberal (Liberal Union—UL) each won five seats. In January 1994 Ribas was re-elected Head of Government, supported by the AND and the ND, together with the two representatives of the Iniciatíva Democràtica Nacional (National Democratic Initiative—IDN). Ribas announced that a priority of his administration would be the restoration of economic growth by means of financial reforms and infrastructural development. Opposition to Ribas's proposed budget and tax legislation, however, led in November to the adoption of a motion of 'no confidence' in the Government. Ribas immediately submitted his resignation; Marc Forné Molné, the leader of the UL, was subsequently elected Head of Government and was inaugurated in late December.

Forné's Government lacked an overall majority in the Consell General; however, the support of councillors from regional political organizations enabled the Government to adopt more than 30 acts between December 1994 and July 1996, including controversial legislation regarding foreign nationals (see Economic Affairs). After being censured twice in one year by the Consell General, Forné was obliged to announce an early general election, which took place in February 1997. The UL won an overall majority, securing 18 seats; the AND took six seats, while the ND and the IDN won two seats each. In April Forné announced the formation of a new, expanded Government. The UL was subsequently renamed the Partit Liberal d'Andorra (Andorran Liberal Party—PLA). In 2000 the AND split into two parties—the Partit Socialdemocràta (Social Democratic Party—PS) and the Partit Democràta (Democratic Party—PD).

Elections to the Consell General took place on 4 March 2001, when 81.6% of the registered electorate participated; however, the number of citizens eligible to vote represented only 20.7% of Andorra's total population. The PLA won 15 of the 28 seats, six seats were secured by the PS, the PD took five seats and the two remaining seats went to independent candidates. Forné was re-elected Head of Government by the Consell General and, in April, appointed a new Government, similar to the outgoing administration.

In May 2003 Joan Enric Vives i Sicilia succeeded Joan Martí Alanis as the Bishop of Urgell and therefore as ex officio Episcopal Co-Prince of Andorra. In September 2004 the PLA selected the former Minister of Foreign Affairs, Albert Pintat Santolària, as its candidate for Head of Government following the decision of Forné not to seek a new term of office. The PS signed a co-operation agreement in December 2004 with two other opposition parties, Renovació Democràtica (Democratic Renewal—RD) and the Grup d'Unió Parroquial Independents (Group of United Parish Independents—GUPI), to contest the forthcoming elections. Elections to the Consell General took place, as scheduled, on 24 April 2005; 80.4% of the electorate participated. The PLA won 14 seats, the PS secured 11, a coalition of two smaller centrist parties, the Centre Demòcrata Andorrà (Andorran Democratic Centre—CDA, the successor to the PD) and Segle 21 (21st Century) took two seats and the RD won one seat. Albert Pintat was elected Head of Government in a vote by the Consell General on 27 May, his candidacy being supported by the PLA and one of the CDA/Segle 21 councillors. Since no party had won an absolute majority, negotiations between the PLA and the CDA/Segle 21 coalition on the formation of a government commenced. However, an agreement on the division of portfolios was not reached and CDA/Segle 21 agreed to support only part of the PLA's programme. On 8 June the new PLA administration took office. Juli Minoves Triquell remained Minister of Foreign Affairs, also assuming responsibility for culture and co-operation, while Ferran Mirapeix Lucas became Minister of Finance, and Joel Font Coma was appointed as Minister of the Economy and Agriculture. In August 2006 CDA/Segle 21 expressed a desire to join the Government, proposing an allocation of two ministerial positions; the possibility of a definitive union between the two parties was also raised. However, the prospect of a representative of Segle 21 joining the Government was opposed by some members of the PLA, and discussion of the proposal was reported to have terminated in March 2007.

In early May 2007 Albert Pintat announced a reorganization of ministerial portfolios: Minoves was replaced as Minister of Foreign Affairs by Meritxell Mateu Pi (hitherto Minister of Housing, Youth, Higher Education and Research), although he retained the culture portfolio and gained responsibility for higher education, while Antoni Riberaygua Sasplugas was appointed Minister of Justice and the Interior. Xavier Jordana Rossell became Minister of Urbanization and Territorial Planning. Later that month Nicolas Sarkozy succeeded Jacques Chirac as President of France and therefore as ex-officio French Co-Prince of Andorra. In December the Minister of Tourism and the Environment, Antoni Puigdellívol Riberaygua, resigned from the Government, prompting a further ministerial reorganization: the tourism and environment portfolio was divided and its responsibilities were assumed by Minoves and Jordana, respectively.

Following the referendum of March 1993, Andorra formally applied for membership of the Council of Europe (see p. 225), gaining entry in October 1994. In June 1993 the Andorran Government signed a treaty of co-operation with France and Spain, which explicitly recognized the sovereignty of Andorra. In the following month Andorra became the 184th member of the UN. In 2003 Forné announced plans for Andorra to join the EU within 15 years. In June 2004 the Charter of Fundamental Social Rights of Workers (commonly known as the Social Charter) of the EU was ratified by the Consell General; however, certain articles of the Charter, relating to employment rights, were omitted. A co-operation agreement with the EU was signed in November and came into effect on 1 July 2005, together with an agreement on the taxation of savings income (see Economic Affairs).

Government

Andorra is a co-principality, under the suzerainty of the President of France and the Spanish Bishop of Urgell. However, since May 1993, when the Constitution of the Principality of Andorra was promulgated, these positions have been almost purely honorary.

The Consell General (General Council) currently comprises 28 councillors (although the number can be between 28 and 42), who are elected by universal suffrage for a four-year period. Two councillors are directly elected by each of the seven parishes of Andorra, and the remainder are elected from a single national constituency by a system of proportional representation. At its opening session the Consell elects as its head the Speaker (Síndic General) and the Deputy Speaker (Subsíndic General), who cease to be members of the Consell on their election. The Consell General elects the Head of Government (Cap de Govern), who, in turn, appoints ministers to the executive body, the Govern.

Andorra is divided into seven parishes, each of which is administered by a Communal Council. Communal councillors are elected for a four-year term by direct universal suffrage. At its opening session each Communal Council elects two consuls, who preside over it.

Defence

Andorra has no defence budget.

Economic Affairs

In 2000 Andorra's national revenue totalled an estimated US $1,275m., equivalent to $19,368 per head. During 1995–2006 the population grew at an estimated average rate of 2.2% per year. Traditionally an agricultural country, Andorra's principal crop is tobacco; livestock-rearing, particularly sheep, is also of importance. However, the agricultural sector (including forestry and hunting) accounted for only 0.3% of total employment (excluding unclassified occupations) in 2006 and Andorra is dependent on imports of foodstuffs to satisfy domestic requirements.

Industry in Andorra includes the manufacture of cigars and cigarettes, together with the production of textiles, leather goods, wood products and processed foodstuffs. In addition to forested timber, natural resources include iron, lead, alum and stone. Including manufacturing, construction and the production and distribution of electricity, industry provided 21.1% of total employment (excluding unclassified occupations) in 2006.

The country's hydroelectric power plant supplied about 12% of domestic needs in 2006, and Andorra is dependent on imports of electricity and other fuels from France and Spain. In 2006 fuel imports accounted for 5.9% of total merchandise imports. In early 2003 the Spanish electricity group Endesa reached an agreement with the Andorran authorities to supply one-half of Andorra's electricity requirements until December 2008. In 2006 a project to extend the production capacity of the hydroelectric plant commenced as part of a government strategic energy plan for 2006–15. The generation of electricity from the combustion of urban waste also began in 2006 and was to contribute 3% of Andorra's electricity supply in 2007. Andorra's total electricity consumption in 2006 amounted to 583m. GWh.

The services sector accounted for 78.6% of total employment (excluding unclassified occupations) in 2006. Tourism and tourist-related commerce are the principal contributors to GDP. Andorra attracts visitors owing to its well-developed facilities for winter sports and also the availability of low-duty consumer items. A total of 2.2m. tourists and 8.6m. excursionists (mostly from Spain and France) visited Andorra in 2007; the hotel industry provided 13.5% of total employment (excluding unclassified occupations) in 2006. The absence of income tax and other forms of direct taxation, in addition to the laws on secrecy governing the country's banks, favoured the development of Andorra as a tax haven. The banking and insurance sectors make a significant contribution to the economy.

Andorra's external trade is dominated by the import of consumer goods destined for sale, with low rates of duty, to visitors. In 2006 imports were valued at €1,416.7m. and exports at €120.1m. Spain and France are Andorra's principal trading partners, respectively providing 56.8% and 21.3% of imports and taking 69.6% and 15.2% of exports in 2006. The European Union (EU, see p. 244) as a whole provided 90.9% of imports and received 96.3% of exports in 2006.

In 2006, according to official figures, the budget balanced at €340.5m., but liabilities on the revenue account of the budget amounted to some €47m., prompting concerns about the continuing budget deficit. In the absence of direct taxation, the Government derives its revenue from levies on imports and on financial institutions, indirect taxes on petrol and other items, stamp duty and the sale of postage stamps. Total general government debt was equivalent to an estimated 18% of GDP in 2007. There is no recorded unemployment in Andorra: the restricted size of the indigenous labour force necessitates high levels of immigration. Consumer prices increased by an annual average of 3.4% in 2001–2006. The annual rate of inflation was 3.1% in 2006.

In March 1990 Andorra approved a trade agreement with the European Community (EC, now EU) which was effective from July 1991, allowing for the establishment of a customs union with the EC and enabling Andorran companies to sell non-agricultural goods to the EU market without being subject to the external tariffs levied on third countries. Andorra benefits from duty free transit for goods imported via EU countries. Agreements with the EU on co-operation and on the taxation of savings income (see below) entered into force on 1 July 2005. In early 2008 negotiations, which had commenced in 1997, for membership of the World Trade Organization (WTO, see p. 396) were ongoing. Andorra is an observer at the WTO.

Andorra has a small, open, prosperous economy, which is narrowly focused on the services sector, principally tourism and tourism-related commerce and banking. Although economic growth in the 2000s was robust, tourist arrivals declined by 5.3% in 2005 and 2.8% in 2006. This was partly due to poor weather conditions for winter sports, but was also attributable to the development of inexpensive ski resorts in countries such as Bulgaria, Slovenia and Serbia. In response to such competition, and as one element of a development project styled Andorra 2020, Andorra was increasing investment in tourist infrastructure and placing a new emphasis on the affluent sector of the market, including the promotion of Andorra as a conference centre. Andorra's lack of diversification made it vulnerable to changes in economic conditions, particularly in Spain and France, which accounted for most tourist and visitor arrivals. The principality's favourable tax regime and banking secrecy have fostered the development of a large financial sector. Controversial legislation was adopted in 1996 to allow certain foreign nationals to become 'nominal residents' (individuals who, for the purposes of avoiding taxation, establish their financial base in Andorra), on condition that they pay an annual levy, in addition to a deposit. The practice of granting this status (without the levy) had been suspended in 1992; however, in the mid-1990s those already accorded nominal residency were estimated to contribute 90% of Andorra's bank deposits. In mid-2000, under its initiative to abolish 'harmful tax practices', the Organisation for Economic Co-operation and Development (OECD, see p. 347) identified a number of jurisdictions as tax havens lacking financial transparency, and urged these to amend their national financial legislation. Many of the countries and territories identified agreed to follow a timetable for reform, with the aim of eliminating such practices by the end of 2005. Others at least entered into dialogue with OECD. A few, including Andorra, did neither and were designated by OECD as 'unco-operative tax havens'. In November 2004 the EU signed an agreement with Andorra on the taxation of savings income. Under the agreement, which came into effect on 1 July 2005, savings income, in the form of interest payments made in Andorra to residents of the EU, was to be subject to a withholding tax of 15%, rising to 35% in 2011. Andorra also signed an undertaking to introduce the concept of tax fraud as a criminal offence, although it maintained its banking secrecy laws. The agreement with the EU included a joint declaration of intent under which Andorra would negotiate on a bilateral basis with the EU its removal from the OECD list of unco-operative tax havens. However, by March 2008 Andorra remained one of only three countries still listed as unco-operative tax havens by OECD. The introduction of the withholding tax resulted in a significant increase in activity in the insurance industry, where savings-linked life insurance policies were not subject to the tax. Andorra's economy was expected to continue to expand at a moderate rate, although increased capital expenditure was expected to have a negative impact on the general government balance.

Education

Education is compulsory for children of between six and 16 years of age, and is provided free of charge by Catalan-, French- and Spanish-language schools. (Children educated under the French or Spanish state systems are required to study some Catalan.) Six years of primary education are followed by four years of secondary schooling. University education is undertaken abroad, although there are two centres for vocational training in Andorra—the Andorran University School of Nursing and the National School of Computer Studies. In 2005/06 there were a total of 10,789 pupils attending Andorra's schools (of whom 2,614 pupils were enrolled at pre-primary schools, 4,332 at primary schools, 3,597 at secondary schools and 246 at institutions providing non-university higher education). Of these, 3,612 were under the Andorran education system (where Catalan is the teaching medium), 3,636 were attending French-speaking schools and 3,541 were being educated under the Spanish system (secular and congregational). In 2002/03 1,288 students were enrolled at universities, including 307 studying in Andorra, 218 in France and 746 in Spain. In late 2007 the Government announced the introduction of a new baccalaureate examination, which was intended to facilitate direct access for students in the Andorran education system to universities in other European countries; the new examination was expected to enter into effect by June 2008. The 2008 budget allocated €73.6m. (17.0% of total projected expenditure) to education.

Public Holidays

2008: 1 January (New Year's Day), 6 January (Epiphany), 6 February (Carnival), 14 March (Constitution Day), 21 March (Good Friday), 24 March (Easter Monday), 1 May (Labour Day), 12 May (Whit Monday), 15 August (Assumption), 8 September (National Day), 1 November (All Saints' Day), 8 December (Immaculate Conception), 21 December (St Thomas' Day), 25 December (Christmas), 26 December (St Stephen's Day).

2009: 1 January (New Year's Day), 6 January (Epiphany), 24 February (Carnival), 14 March (Constitution Day), 10 April (Good Friday), 13 April (Easter Monday), 1 May (Labour Day), 1 June (Whit Monday), 15 August (Assumption), 8 September (National Day), 1 November (All Saints' Day), 8 December (Immaculate Conception), 21 December (St Thomas' Day), 25 December (Christmas Day), 26 December (St Stephen's Day).

Each Parish also holds its own annual festival, which is taken as a public holiday, usually lasting for three days, in July, August or September.

Weights and Measures

The metric system is in force.

ANDORRA

Statistical Survey

Source (unless otherwise stated): Servei d'Estudis, Ministeri de Finances, Carrer Prat de la Creu 62–64, Andorra la Vella AD500; tel. 865714; fax 829218; e-mail servest@andorra.ad; internet www.estadistica.ad.

AREA AND POPULATION

Area: 467.8 sq km (180.6 sq miles).

Population: 46,166 at census of 12 July 1989; 81,222, comprising: Andorrans 29,535, Spanish 27,638, Portuguese 12,789, French 5,104 and others 6,156 at 31 December 2006.

Density (31 December 2006): 173.6 per sq km.

Parishes (population at 31 December 2006): Andorra la Vella (capital) 24,211; Escaldes-Engordany 16,391; Encamp 13,685; Sant Julià de Lòria 9,448; La Massana 8,953; Canillo 5,067; Ordino 3,467.

Births, Marriages and Deaths (2006): Registered live births 843; Registered marriages 296; Registered deaths 260.

Expectation of Life (years at birth, WHO estimates): 80.3 (males 77.0; females 83.5) in 2005. Source: WHO, *World Health Statistics*.

Employment (2006): Agriculture, forestry and hunting 145; Industry 8,826 (Construction 6,908, Manufacturing 1,758, Production and distribution of electricity 160); Services 32,913 (Repair and sale of motor vehicles 11,454, Hotels 5,670, Real estate 4,147, Administration 4,332, Finance and insurance 1,559, Transport and storage 1,295, Education 632, Other services 3,824); Unclassified occupations 1,496; *Total* 43,380.

HEALTH AND WELFARE
Key Indicators

Total Fertility Rate (children per woman, 2005): 1.2.

Under-5 Mortality Rate (per 1,000 live births, 2005): 6.

Physicians (per 1,000 head, 2003): 3.70.

Hospital Beds (per 1,000 head, 2005): 2.7.

Health Expenditure (2004): US $ per head (PPP): 3,546.0.

Health Expenditure (2004): % of GDP: 7.1.

Health Expenditure (2004): public (% of total): 69.2.

For sources and definitions, see explanatory note on p. vi.

AGRICULTURE

Principal Crop (metric tons, 2005/06): Tobacco 315.2.

Livestock (head, 2006): Cattle 1,434; Sheep 2,524; Horses 859; Goats 508.

FINANCE

Currency and Exchange Rates: 100 cent = 1 euro (€). *Sterling and Dollar Equivalents* (31 December 2007): £1 sterling = €1.3609; US $1 = €0.6793; €10 = £7.35 = US $14.72. *Average Exchange Rate* (euros per US dollar): 0.8041 in 2005; 0.7971 in 2006; 0.7306 in 2007. Note: French and Spanish currencies were formerly in use. From the introduction of the euro, with French and Spanish participation, on 1 January 1999, fixed exchange rates of €1 = 6.55957 francs and €1 = 166.386 pesetas were in operation. Euro notes and coins were introduced on 1 January 2002. The euro and local currencies circulated alongside each other until 17 February (francs) and 28 February (pesetas), after which the euro became the sole legal tender.

Budget (€ million, 2006): *Revenue:* Indirect taxes 257.8; Property income 14.6; Other taxes and income 21.0; Assets 0.1; Liabilities 47.0; Total 340.5. *Expenditure:* Current expenditure 182.0 (Personnel emoluments 76.8, Goods and services 47.0, Interest payments 7.9, Current transfers 50.3); Capital expenditure 158.0 (Fixed capital investment 111.1, Capital transfers 46.8; Assets 0.5; Liabilities 0.0; Total 340.5.

Cost of Living (Consumer Price Index at December; base: 2001 = 100): All items 111.1 in 2004; 114.6 in 2005; 118.2 in 2006.

EXTERNAL TRADE

Principal Commodities (€ million, 2006): *Imports:* Live animals and animal products 65.3; Sugars and sugar-based substances 35.1; Alcoholic drinks and vinegars 58.0; Tobacco and tobacco substitutes 18.2; Flammable minerals, oils, petroleum 83.9; Pharmaceutical products 26.1; Essential oils, perfume and toiletries 95.8; Plastics and articles thereof 16.3; Clothes and clothing accessories, knitted 37.2; Clothes and clothing accessories, not knitted 78.8; Shoes and boots 29.3; Cast products in iron or steel 31.2; Nuclear reactors, boilers and mechanical engines 83.6; Electric machines, tools and materials 164.8; Automobile vehicles, tractors, motorcycles 146.0; Optical instruments 26.2; Toys, games and sports articles 33.2; Total (incl. others) 1,416.7. *Exports:* Sugars and sugar-based substances 34.7; Essential oils, perfumes and toiletries 3.5; Press products 3.2; Clothes and clothing accessories, not knitted 2.2; Cast products in iron or steel 2.0; Nuclear reactors, boilers and mechanical engines 7.4; Electric machines, tools and materials 14.7; Automobile vehicles, tractors, motorcycles 18.2; Optical instruments 7.7; Art objects, collection or antiques 3.1; Total (incl. others) 120.1.

Principal Trading Partners (€ million, 2006): *Imports c.i.f.:* European Union 1,287.4 (Spain 804.4; France 301.8); Other Europe 18.2; Africa 1.5; USA and Canada 9.6; Central and South America 4.9; Asia and Oceania 95.2; Total 1,416.7. *Exports f.o.b.:* European Union 115.7 (Spain 83.6; France 18.2); Other Europe 2.0; Africa 1.9; USA and Canada 0.1; Central and South America 0.2; Asia and Oceania 0.2; Total 120.1.

TRANSPORT

Road Traffic (registered motor vehicles, 2006): Passenger cars 47,566; Buses and coaches 202; Trucks (lorries) and vans 5,064; Tractors 354; Motorcycles 7,164.

TOURISM

Tourist Arrivals (country of residence, 2006): Spain 6,237,954; France 4,190,719; Total (incl. others) 10,736,722 (Visitors staying at least one night 2,226,922, Excursionists 8,509,800).

COMMUNICATIONS MEDIA

Radio Receivers (1997): 16,000 in use.

Television Receivers (2000): 36,000 in use (Source: UNESCO).

Daily Newspapers (2005): 2 titles published.

Telephones (main lines in use, 2006): 36,507.

Facsimile Machines (number in use, 1998): 5,000 (Source: UN, *Statistical Yearbook*).

Mobile Cellular Telephones (subscribers, 2006): 37,039.

Internet Users (2000): 6,192.

Source: partly International Telecommunication Union and Servei de Telecomunicacions d'Andorra.

EDUCATION

Pre-primary Enrolment (2005/06): Andorran schools 991; French schools 898; Spanish schools* 725.

Primary Enrolment (2005/06): Andorran schools 1,601; French schools 1,277; Spanish schools* 1,454.

Secondary Enrolment (2005/06): Andorran schools 946; French schools 1,300; Spanish schools* 1,351.

Non-university Higher Education Enrolment (2005/06): Andorran institutions 74; French institutions 161; Spanish institutions 11.

University Enrolment (2002/03): Andorra 307; France 218; Spain 746; Total (incl. others) 1,288.

*Including congregational schools.

Directory

The Constitution

The Constitution of the Principality of Andorra came into force on 4 May 1993, having been approved by the Andorran people in a referendum on 14 March. The official name of the independent state is Principat d'Andorra. The Constitution asserts that Andorra is 'a Democratic and Social independent state abiding by the Rule of Law', defines the fundamental rights, freedoms and obligations of Andorran citizens and delineates the functions and competences of the organs of state.

In accordance with Andorran tradition, the Co-Princes (Copríncep), respectively the Bishop of Urgell and the President of the French Republic, are titular Heads of State.

The legislature is the Consell General (General Council), which comprises between 28 and 42 members. Two members of the Consell General are elected to represent each of Andorra's seven parishes (Parròquies), and one-half are elected from a single national constituency by a system of proportional representation; members are elected to the Consell General for four years (or until the dissolution of the Consell General). Elections are on the basis of direct universal adult suffrage. The ruling organ of the Consell General is the Sindicatura, headed by a Speaker (Síndic General).

The Govern (the executive organ of state) is directed by the Head of Government (Cap de Govern), who is elected by the Consell General (and formally appointed by the Co-Princes) and who must command the support of the majority of the legislature's members. The Head of Government nominates government ministers, who may not at the same time be members of the Consell General. The Head of Government is restricted to two consecutive full terms of office.

The Constitution defines the composition and powers of the judiciary, the highest organ of which is the Higher Court of Justice (Consell Superior de Justícia).

The Constitution defines the functions of the communal councils (Comuns), which are the organs of representation and administration of the parishes.

Revision of the Constitution shall require the approval of two-thirds of the members of the Consell General and ratification by a referendum. The Consell General is advised on constitutional matters by the Institució del Raonador del Ciutadà, an independent institution established in 1998, responsible for the application of the Constitution.

The Constitutional Court is the supreme interpreter of the Constitution. Its decisions are binding for public authorities and for individuals.

The Government

HEADS OF STATE

Episcopal Co-Prince: JOAN ENRIC VIVES I SICÍLIA (Bishop of Urgell).
French Co-Prince: NICOLAS SARKOZY (President of France).

GOVERN
(March 2008)

Head of Government (Cap de Govern): ALBERT PINTAT SANTOLÀRIA.
Minister of the Presidency and Finance: FERRAN MIRAPEIX LUCAS.
Minister of Territorial Planning, Urbanization and the Environment: XAVIER JORDANA ROSSELL.
Government Spokesperson and Minister of Economic Development, Tourism, Culture and Universities: JULI MINOVES TRIQUELL.
Minister of Justice and the Interior: ANTONI RIBERAYGUA SASPLUGAS.
Minister of Foreign Affairs: MERITXELL MATEU PI.
Minister of Health, Welfare, the Family and Housing: MONTSERRAT GIL TORNÉ.
Minister of the Economy and Agriculture: JOEL FONT COMA.
Minister of Education, Vocational Training, Youth and Sports: ROSER BASTIDA ARENY.
Secretary-General: ESTEVE VIDAL FERRER.
Head of the Office of the Head of Government: ANNA ZAMORA PUIGCERCÓS.
Head of Protocol: ROSER SUÑÉ PASCUET.

MINISTRIES

Office of the Head of Government: Govern d'Andorra, Carrer Prat de la Creu 62–64, Edif. Administratiu, Andorra la Vella AD500; tel. 875700; fax 822882; e-mail comunicacio.gov@andorra.ad; internet www.presidencia.ad.
Ministry of Culture and Higher Education: Carrer Prat de la Creu 62–64, Edif. Administratiu, Andorra la Vella AD500; tel. 875634; fax 875637.
Ministry of the Economy and Agriculture: Govern d'Andorra, Carrer Prat de la Creu 62–64, Edif. Administratiu, Andorra la Vella AD500; tel. 875706; fax 861519.
Ministry of Education, Vocational Training, Youth and Sports: Avinguda Rocafort, Edif. Molí 21–23, Sant Julià de Lòria AD600; tel. 743300; fax 743311; internet www.esports.ad (sport).
Ministry of Foreign Affairs: Carrer Prat de la Creu 62–64, Edif. Administratiu, Andorra la Vella AD500; tel. 875700; fax 869559; e-mail exteriors.gov@andorra.ad.
Ministry of Health, Welfare, the Family and Housing: Avinguda Príncep Benlloch 30, Edif. Clara Rabassa, Andorra la Vella AD500; tel. 860345; fax 829347; e-mail iolanda_latorre@govern.ad; internet www.salutibenestar.ad (health, welfare, the family); internet www.habitatgegovern.ad (housing).
Ministry of Justice and the Interior: Carretera de l'OBAC, Edif. Administratiu de l'OBAC, Escaldes-Engordany AD700; tel. 872080; fax 869250.
Ministry of the Presidency and Finance: Carrer Prat de la Creu 62–64, Edif. Administratiu, Andorra la Vella AD500; tel. 875700; fax 860962; e-mail finances.gov@andorra.ad; internet www.presidencia.ad; internet www.finances.ad.
Ministry of Tourism and the Environment: Carrer Prat de la Creu 62–64, Edif. Administratiu, Andorra la Vella AD500; tel. 875702; fax 860184; e-mail turisme@andorra.ad (tourism); e-mail mediambient@andorra.ad (environment); internet www.andorra.ad (tourism); internet www.mediambient.ad (environment).
Ministry of Urbanization and Territorial Planning: Carrer Prat de la Creu 62–64, Edif. Administratiu, Andorra la Vella AD500; tel. 875701; fax 861313; e-mail mot@andorra.ad; internet www.muot.ad.

Legislature

GENERAL COUNCIL
(Consell General)

General Council (Consell General): Casa de la Vall, Andorra la Vella AD500; tel. 877877; fax 869863; e-mail consell_general@parlament.ad; internet www.consell.ad.
Speaker (Síndic General): JOAN GABRIEL I ESTANY (PLA).
Deputy Speaker (Subsíndica General): BERNADETA GASPÀ BRINGUERET (PLA).

General Election, 24 April 2005

Party	Votes cast	Seats
Partit Liberal d'Andorra	5,100	14
Partit Socialdemòcrata	4,711	11
Centre Demòcrata Andorrà/Segle 21	1,360	2
Renovació Democràtica	772	1
Els Verds d'Andorra	433	0
Total	12,376	28

Election Commission

Junta Electoral: Carrer Prat de la Creu 62–64, Edif. Administratiu, Andorra la Vella AD500; tel. 875700; e-mail portal@govern.ad; internet www.eleccions.ad; govt agency; Pres. DAVID MOYNAT ROSSELL.

Political Organizations

The establishment of political parties was sanctioned under the Constitution that was promulgated in May 1993.

Centre Demòcrata Andorrà (CDA) (Andorran Democratic Centre): Carrer dels Feners 15, 1° C, Andorra la Vella AD500; tel. 805778;

ANDORRA

fax 805779; e-mail secretariat@enrictarrado.com; internet www.centredemocrataandorra.com; f. 2000 as Partit Democràta (PD); name changed as above in 2003; Pres. JOSEP MARIA COSAN.

Partit Liberal d'Andorra (PLA) (Andorran Liberal Party): Carrer Babot Camp 13, 2°, Andorra la Vella AD500; tel. 807715; fax 869728; e-mail pla@pla.ad; internet www.partitliberal.ad; f. 1992 as Unió Liberal; Leader MARC FORNÉ MOLNÉ; Pres. ALBERT PINTAT SANTO-LÀRIA.

Partit Socialdemocràta (PS) (Social Democratic Party): Carrer Verge del Pilar 5, 3°, Andorra la Vella AD500; tel. 805262; fax 821746; e-mail psd@andorra.ad; internet www.partitsocialdemocrata.com; name changed following merger of Nova Democràcia and Agrupment Nacional Democràta in 2000; formed alliance with the RD and GUPI in Dec. 2004 to contest 2005 elections; Pres. MARIONA GONZÁLEZ REOLIT; First Sec. FRANCESC CASALS PANTEBRE; Parliamentary Leader JAUME BARTUMEU CASSANY.

Renovació Democràtica (RD) (Democratic Renewal): Avinguda Carlemany 67, 5° 2, Escaldes-Engordany AD700; tel. 801770; fax 821775; e-mail infopartit@renovaciodemocratica.com; internet www.renovaciodemocratica.com; formed alliance with the PS and GUPI in Dec. 2004 to contest 2005 elections.

Els Verds d'Andorra (The Andorran Greens): Ciutat de Consuegra 10, 1°, Edif. Orio, Andorra la Vella AD500; tel. 363797; e-mail verds@verds.ad; internet www.verds.ad; f. 2004; Pres. ISABEL LOZANO MUÑOZ.

Other parties are Acció Comunal d'Ordino (Local Action for Ordino), Bloc d'Acció Política (Bloc of Political Action), Democràcia Andorrana (Andorran Democracy), Grup d'Opinió Liberal (Group of Liberal Opinion), Partit Unió Laurediana (Lauredian Union), Segle 21 (21st Century), Unió Democràtica Andorrana (Andorran Democratic Union), Unió Nacional de Progrés (National Union for Progress) and Unió del Poble (People's Union). There is also a grouping of independents, the Grup d'Unió Parroquial Independents (Group of United Parish Independents—GUPI).

Diplomatic Representation

EMBASSIES IN ANDORRA

France: Carrer les Canals 38–40, POB 155, Andorra la Vella AD500; tel. 736700; fax 736731; e-mail ambassade.de.france@andorra.ad; internet www.ambafrance-ad.org; Ambassador GILLES CHOURAQUI.

Portugal: Carrer Prat de la Creu 59–65, 4°, Andorra la Vella AD500; tel. 805308; fax 869555; e-mail mail@andorra.dgaccp.pt; internet www.embaixadadeportugal.ad; Ambassador NUNO ANTÓNIO RIBEIRO DE BESSA LOPES.

Spain: Carrer Prat de la Creu 34, Andorra la Vella AD500; tel. 800030; fax 868500; e-mail embaspad@correo.mae.es; Ambassador EUGENI BREGOLAT OBIOLS.

Judicial System

Judicial power is vested, in the first instance, in the Magistrates' Courts (Batllia) and in the Judges' Tribunal (Tribunal de Batlles), the criminal-law courts (Tribunal de Corts) and the Higher Court of Justice (Tribunal Superior de la Justícia). The judiciary is represented, directed and administered by the Higher Council of Justice (Consell Superior de la Justícia), whose five members are appointed for single terms of six years. Final jurisdiction, in constitutional matters, is vested in the Constitutional Court (Tribunal Constitucional), whose four members hold office for no more than two consecutive eight-year terms.

The 1993 Constitution guarantees the independence of the judiciary.

Higher Council of Justice (Consell Superior de la Justícia): Carrer Prat de la Creu 8, Andorra la Vella AD500; tel. 808390; fax 868778; e-mail con.sup.justicia@andorra.ad; internet www.justicia.ad.

President of the Higher Council of Justice: LLUÍS MONTANYA TARRÉS.

Religion

More than 90% of the population of Andorra are Roman Catholic. Andorra forms part of the Spanish diocese of Urgell.

The Press

7 DIES: Carrer Bonaventura Riberaygua 39, 5°, Andorra la Vella AD500; tel. 877477; fax 863800; f. 1994; weekly; free; local issues, advertising; Dir. Gen IGNASI DE PLANELL; Dir ROSA MARI SORRIBES; circ. 30,000.

Butlletí Oficial del Principat d'Andorra: Avda Santa Coloma 91, Andorra la Vella AD500; tel. 724400; fax 724300; e-mail administrador_bopa@govern.ad; internet www.bopa.ad; official govt gazette; weekly.

Diari d'Andorra: Carrer Bonaventura Riberaygua 39, Andorra la Vella AD500; tel. 877477; fax 863800; e-mail redaccio@diariandorra.ad; internet www.diariandorra.ad; f. 1991; daily; local issues; Pres. MARC VILA AMIGÓ; Dir IGNASI DE PLANELL; circ. 17,165.

El Periòdic d'Andorra: Parc de la Mola 10, Torre Caldea, Escaldes-Engordany AD700; tel. 736200; fax 736210; e-mail redaccio@andorra.elperiodico.com; internet www.elperiodico.com/andorra; daily; local issues; Propr Grupo Zeta, SA (Spain); Dir JOSEP ANTON ROSSELL PUJOL.

Broadcasting and Communications

TELECOMMUNICATIONS

Servei de Telecomunicacions d'Andorra (Andorran Telecommunications Service—STA): Carrer Mossen Lluis Pujol 8–14, Santa Coloma AD500; tel. 875105; fax 725003; internet www.sta.ad; provides national and international telecommunications services; Dir JAUME SALVAT FONT.

BROADCASTING

In 2007 there were five radio stations in Andorra. In that year one television station was active in Andorra, and it was possible to receive broadcasts from television stations in neighbouring countries. Digital television broadcasts began in October 2004 and analogue broadcasting was phased out entirely in late September 2007.

Radio

Ràdio i Televisió d'Andorra, SA—Ràdio Nacional Andorra (RTVA): Baixada del Molí 24, Andorra la Vella AD500; tel. 873777; fax 863242; e-mail rtva@rtva.ad; internet www.rtva.ad; f. 1990 as an Andorran-owned commercial public broadcasting service; two stations: Ràdio Andorra and Andorra Música; Dir GUALBERT OSORIO ACHURRA.

Andorra7Ràdio: e-mail laradio@andorra7radio.com; internet www.andorra7radio.com.

R7P Ràdio: Avinguda Príncep Benlloch 24, Encamp AD200; tel. 731410; fax 731517; e-mail info@cadenapirenaica.com; internet www.cadenapirenaica.com; commercial broadcasting service, aimed at people aged 25–45 years; owned by Cadena Pirenaica de Ràdio i Televisió.

Ràdio Valira: Avinguda Príncep Benlloch 24, Encamp AD200; tel. 732000; fax 834831; e-mail info@cadenapirenaica.com; internet www.cadenapirenaica.com; f. 1985; commercial broadcasting service, aimed at people aged 40–65 years; owned by Cadena Pirenaica de Ràdio i Televisió.

Television

Ràdio i Televisió d'Andorra, SA—Andorra Televisió (RTVA): Baixada del Molí 24, Andorra la Vella AD500; tel. 873777; fax 864232; e-mail rtva@rtva.ad; internet www.rtva.ad; f. 1995 as an Andorran-owned commercial public broadcasting service; Dir-Gen. GUALBERT OSORIO ACHURRA.

Finance

(cap. = capital; res = reserves; dep. = deposits; m. = million; brs = branches; amounts in euros)

REGULATORY AUTHORITY

Institut Nacional Andorrà de Finances (INAF): Av. Príncep Benlloch 30, 3r, Andorra la Vella AD500; tel. 808898; fax 865977; e-mail inaf.sc@inaf.ad; internet www.inaf.ad; f. 1989; Pres. MANEL TORRENTALLÉ CAIRÓ; Dir Gen CARLES SALVADÓ MIRAS.

BANKS

In 2007 five banking groups were operating in Andorra.

Andorra Banc Agrícol Reig, SA (Andbanc): Carrer Manuel Cerqueda i Escaler 6, Escaldes-Engordany AD700; tel. 739011; fax 868905; e-mail corporate@andbanc.com; internet www.andbanc.com; f. 2001 by merger of Banca Reig and Banc Agrícol i Comercial d'Andorra; cap. 68.1m., res 273.6m., dep. 1,942.5m. (Dec. 2006); Chair. MANEL CERQUERDA I DONADEU; Gen. Man. JAUME SABATER I ROVIRA; 13 brs.

Banc Internacional d'Andorra SA (BIBM): Avinguda Meritxell 96, Andorra la Vella AD500; tel. 884488; fax 884499; e-mail bibm@bibm.ad; internet www.bibm.ad; f. 1958 as Banc International; merged with Banca Mora in 1976; cap. 42.4m., res 140.7m., dep. 2,741.0m. (Dec. 2006); Chair. JORDI ARISTOT MORA; Chief Exec. JOAN QUERA FONT; 11 brs.

Banca Privada d'Andorra SA (BPA): Avinguda Carlemany 119, POB 25, Escaldes-Engordany AD700; tel. 873501; fax 873515; e-mail bpa@bpa.ad; internet www.bpa.ad; f. 1962 as Banca Cassany SA; name changed as above in 1994; cap. 33.0m., res 44.0m., dep. 1,143.5m. (Dec. 2006); Pres HIGINI CIERCO NOGUER, RAMON CIERCO NOGUER; Gen. Man. JOAN PAU MIQUEL PRATS; 5 brs.

BancSabadell d'Andorra: Avinguda del Fener 7, Andorra la Vella AD500; tel. 735600; fax 735601; e-mail bsa@bsa.ad; internet www.bsa.ad; cap. 30.1m., res 0.1m., dep. 489.1m. (Dec. 2006); Chair. ROBERT CASSANY I VILA; Gen. Man. MIQUEL ALABERN I COMAS.

Crèdit Andorrà: Avinguda Meritxell 80, Andorra la Vella AD500; tel. 888600; fax 888601; e-mail comunicacio@creditandorra.ad; internet www.creditandorra.ad; f. 1949; merged with CaixaBank SA in 2007; cap. 70.0m., res 422.0m., dep. 3,488.2m. (Dec. 2006); Chair. ANTONI PINTAT; CEO JOSEP PERALBA; 17 brs.

Banking Association

Associació de Bancs Andorrans (ABA): Carrer Ciutat de Consuegra 16, Edif. L'Illa, Escala A-2°, Andorra la Vella AD500; tel. 807110; fax 866847; e-mail aba@aba.ad; internet www.aba.ad; f. 1960; Dir ANTONI ARMENGOL.

INSURANCE

In May 2006 there were 16 Andorran insurance companies registered, while a further 18 foreign companies were also authorized to operate in Andorra.

Assegurances Generals Andorra, SA: Sant Salvador 7, Edif. Rosella, Andorra la Vella AD500; tel. 877677; fax 860093; e-mail aga@andorra.ad; internet www.assegurancesgenerals.com; Pres. AMADEU CALVÓ CASAL.

Companyia Andorrana d'Assegurances, SA: Avinguda Meritxell 88, Andorra la Vella AD 500; tel. 806806; fax 824605; e-mail sinistres.caa@andorra.ad.

Financera d'Assegurances, SA: Babot Camp 11, Andorra la Vella AD500; tel. 890300; fax 864717; e-mail info@e-financera.com; internet www.e-financera.com; non-life.

Previsió i Futur, SA: Avinguda Meritxell 9, Andorra la Vella AD500; tel. 800333; fax 860237; e-mail info@previsioifutur.com; internet www.previsioifutur.com; f. 2000; life.

Trade and Industry

CHAMBER OF COMMERCE

Cambra de Comerç, Indústria i Serveis d'Andorra: Carrer Prat de la Creu 8, Andorra la Vella AD500; tel. 809292; fax 89293; e-mail ccis@andorra.ad; internet www.ccis.ad; Pres. FRANCESC PALLÀS VILADOMAT.

UTILITIES

Electricity

The Forces Elèctriques d'Andorra (FEDA) distributes 69% of energy used in Andorra, while four smaller companies, supplied by FEDA, distribute the rest of the electricity used.

Forces Elèctriques d'Andorra (FEDA): Avinguda de la Barta s/n, Encamp AD200; tel. 739100; fax 739118; e-mail feda@feda.ad; internet www.feda.ad; f. 1988; state-owned; imports, generates and distributes electricity; Pres. FERRAN MIRAPEIX LUCAS (Minister of the Presidency and of Finance); Dir-Gen. ALBERT MOLES BETRIU.

TRADE UNIONS

Sindical de Treballadors d'Andorra: Andorra la Vella AD500.

Unió Sindical d'Andorra (USdA): Andorra la Vella AD500; e-mail usda@andorra.ad; Sec.-Gen. GABRIEL UBACH.

Transport

RAILWAYS

In 2001 construction began of an overhead train system, which was expected to alleviate traffic problems in Andorra la Vella. The 8-km line was to link Sant Julià de Lòria and Escaldes-Engordany to the capital. The link was scheduled for completion by 2008. Until then, the nearest stations are Ax-les-Thermes, L'Hospitalet and La Tour de Carol, in France (with trains from Toulouse and Perpignan), and Puigcerdà, in Spain, on the line from Barcelona. There is a connecting bus service from all four stations to Andorra. In early 2008 the extension of the Spanish railway network as far as Andorra was being considered by the Catalan Government.

ROADS

A good road connects the Spanish and French frontiers, passing through Andorra la Vella. The Envalira tunnel, between Andorra and France, was opened in September 2002. Work began on the Dos Valires tunnel to link Encamp and La Massana in late 2005. The tunnel, which was expected to cost €73m., was scheduled to open in 2010. Two companies, Cooperativa Interurbana Andorrana and Hispano Andorrana, operate bus services within Andorra.

CIVIL AVIATION

In 2008 negotiations were continuing regarding the redevelopment of the airport at La Seu d'Urgell, located in Spanish territory 10 km from the border with Andorra, to be financed jointly by the Andorran, Spanish and Catalan administrations. The Government was also studying the feasibility of constructing an airport or heliport in Andorra.

Tourism

Andorra has attractive mountain scenery, and winter sports facilities are available at five skiing centres. Tourists are also attracted by Andorra's duty-free shopping facilities. A total of 2.2m. tourists visited Andorra in 2007, as well as 8.6m. excursionists, mainly from Spain and France. In 2004 the valley of Madriu was declared a UNESCO World Heritage Site.

Sindicat d'Iniciatíva Oficina de Turisme: Carrer Dr Vilanova, Edif. Davi, Andorra la Vella AD500; tel. 820214; fax 825823; e-mail sindicatdiniciativa@andorra.ad; Dir ROSER JORDANA.

Ski Andorra: Avinguda Tarragona 58-70, Despatx 14, Andorra la Vella AD500; tel. 805200; fax 865910; e-mail skiandorra@skiandorra.ad; internet www.skiandorra.ad; association of ski stations; Dir MARTA ROTÉS.

Unió Hotelera d'Andorra (Hotel Association of Andorra): Antic Carrer Major 18, Andorra la Vella AD500; tel. 820602; fax 861539; e-mail uhotelera@uha.ad; internet www.uha.ad; f. 1961; Pres. XAVIER PALOU SOLSONA; Sec.-Gen. JOAN ANDREU CACHAFEIRO VIDAL; 200 mems.

Each parish has its own tourist office.

ANGOLA

Introductory Survey

Location, Climate, Language, Religion, Flag, Capital

The Republic of Angola lies on the west coast of Africa. The province of Cabinda is separated from the rest of the country by the estuary of the River Congo and territory of the Democratic Republic of the Congo (DRC—formerly Zaire), with the Republic of the Congo lying to its north. Angola is bordered by the DRC to the north, Zambia to the east and Namibia to the south. The climate is tropical, locally tempered by altitude. There are two distinct seasons (wet and dry) but little seasonal variation in temperature. It is very hot and rainy in the coastal lowlands but temperatures are lower inland. The official language is Portuguese, but African languages (the most widely spoken being Umbundo, Lunda, Kikongo, Chokwe and Kwanyama) are also in common use. Much of the population follows traditional African beliefs, although a majority profess to be Christians, mainly Roman Catholics. The flag (proportions 2 by 3) has two equal horizontal stripes, of red and black; superimposed in the centre, in gold, are a five-pointed star, half a cog-wheel and a machete. A new flag was proposed by the Constitutional Commission in August 2003. The capital is Luanda.

Recent History

Formerly a Portuguese colony, Angola became an overseas province in 1951. African nationalist groups began to form in the 1950s and 1960s, including the Movimento Popular de Libertação de Angola (MPLA) in 1956, the Frente Nacional de Libertação de Angola (FNLA) in 1962 and the União Nacional para a Independência Total de Angola (UNITA) in 1966. Severe repression followed an unsuccessful nationalist rebellion in 1961, but, after a new wave of fighting in 1966, nationalist guerrilla groups were able to establish military and political control in large parts of eastern Angola and to press westward. Following the April 1974 *coup d'état* in Portugal, Angola's right to independence was recognized.

In January 1975 a transitional Government was established, comprising representatives of the MPLA, the FNLA, UNITA and the Portuguese Government. However, following violent clashes between the MPLA and the FNLA, by the second half of 1975 control of Angola was effectively divided between the three major nationalist groups, each aided by foreign powers. The MPLA (which held the capital) was supported by the USSR and Cuba, the FNLA by Zaire and Western powers (including the USA), while UNITA was backed by South African forces. The FNLA and UNITA formed a united front to fight the MPLA.

The Portuguese Government proclaimed Angola independent from 11 November 1975, transferring sovereignty to 'the Angolan people' rather than to any of the liberation movements. The MPLA proclaimed the People's Republic of Angola in Luanda under the presidency of Dr Agostinho Neto. The FNLA and UNITA proclaimed the Democratic People's Republic of Angola, based in Nova Lisboa (renamed Huambo). By the end of February 1976, however, the MPLA, aided by Cuban technical and military expertise, had effectively gained control of the whole country.

Neto died in September 1979, and José Eduardo dos Santos, hitherto the Minister of Planning, was elected party leader and President by the Central Committee of the Movimento Popular de Libertação de Angola—Partido do Trabalho (MPLA—PT, as the MPLA had been renamed in December 1977). Elections to the National People's Assembly (Assembléia Popular Nacional), which replaced the Council of the Revolution (Conselho da Revolução), were first held in 1980. Fresh elections, due to be held in 1983, were postponed until 1986, owing to political and military problems.

The MPLA—PT Government's recovery programme was continually hindered by security problems. Although the FNLA reportedly surrendered to the Government in 1984, UNITA conducted sustained and disruptive guerrilla activities, mainly in southern and central Angola, throughout the 1980s. In addition, forces from South Africa, which was providing UNITA with considerable military aid, made numerous armed incursions over the Angolan border with Namibia, ostensibly in pursuit of guerrilla forces belonging to the South West Africa People's Organisation (SWAPO), which was supported by the Angolan Government. UNITA's position was strengthened in 1986, when US military aid began to arrive and the US Government continued to provide covert military aid to UNITA until 1990. However, UNITA was excluded from a series of major peace negotiations, between Angola, Cuba and South Africa (with the unofficial mediation of the USA), which commenced in May 1988. By July the participants had agreed to a document containing the principles for a peace settlement that provided for independence for Namibia, the discontinuation of South African military support for UNITA and the withdrawal of Cuban troops from Angola. Following the conclusion of the New York accords on Angola and Namibia in December, the UN Security Council established the UN Angola Verification Mission (UNAVEM) to verify the phased withdrawal of Cuban troops from Angola, which was completed in May 1991.

In July 1990 the Central Committee of the MPLA—PT announced that the Government would allow Angola to 'evolve towards a multi-party system'. In October the Central Committee proposed a general programme of reform, including the replacement of the party's official Marxist-Leninist ideology with a commitment to 'democratic socialism', the legalization of political parties, the transformation of the army from a party institution to a state institution, the introduction of a market economy, a revision of the Constitution and the holding of multi-party elections in 1994, following a population census.

In March 1991 the Assembléia Popular approved legislation permitting the formation of political parties. On 1 May the Government and UNITA concluded a peace agreement in Estoril, Portugal, which provided for a cease-fire from 15 May, to be monitored by a joint political and military commission, with representatives from the MPLA—PT, UNITA, the UN, Portugal, the USA and the USSR. A new national army of 50,000 men was to be established, comprising equal numbers of government and UNITA soldiers. Free and democratic elections were to be held by the end of 1992. On 31 May the Government and UNITA signed a formal agreement in Lisbon, Portugal, ratifying the Estoril agreement. The UN Security Council agreed to establish UNAVEM II, with a mandate to ensure implementation of the peace accord. In July a new amnesty law was approved, under the terms of which amnesty would be granted for all crimes against state security as well as for military and common law offences committed before 31 May 1991.

In September 1991 the UNITA leader, Dr Jonas Savimbi, returned to Luanda for the first time since the civil war began in 1975, and UNITA headquarters were transferred to the capital from Jamba in October. In the following month dos Santos announced that legislative and presidential elections were to take place in September 1992.

Representatives of the Government and 26 political parties met in Luanda in January 1992 to discuss the transition to multi-party democracy. It was agreed in February that the elections would be conducted on the basis of proportional representation, with the President elected for a five-year term, renewable for a maximum of three terms. The legislature would be a national assembly, elected for a four-year term. In April the Assembléia Popular adopted electoral legislation incorporating these decisions and providing for the creation of a National Assembly (Assembléia Nacional) comprising 223 members (90 to be elected in 18 provincial constituencies and the remainder from national lists).

In April 1992 the Supreme Court approved UNITA's registration as a political party. In May the MPLA—PT voted to enlarge the membership of the Central Committee to include prominent dissidents who had returned to the party and removed the suffix Partido do Trabalho from the organization's official name. In August the legislature approved a further revision of the Constitution, removing the remnants of the country's former Marxist ideology, and deleting the words 'People's' and 'Popular' from the Constitution and from the names of official institutions. The name of the country was changed from the People's Republic of Angola to the Republic of Angola.

Increased tension and outbreaks of violence in the period preceding the general election seriously threatened to disrupt the electoral process. In early September 1992 in Cabinda province, the enclave that provides most of Angola's petroleum revenue, secessionist groups, notably the Frente de Libertação do Enclave de Cabinda (FLEC), intensified attacks on government troops. On 27 September the government Forças Armadas Populares de Libertação de Angola (FAPLA) and the UNITA forces were formally disbanded, and the new national army, the Forças Armadas de Angola (FAA), was established. However, the process of training and incorporating FAPLA and UNITA troops into the new 50,000-strong national army had been hindered by delays in the demobilization programme and fewer than 10,000 soldiers were ready to be sworn in as members of the FAA.

Presidential and legislative elections were held, as scheduled, on 29 and 30 September 1992. When preliminary results indicated victory for the MPLA in the elections to the new Assembléia Nacional, Savimbi accused the Government of electoral fraud, withdrew his troops from the FAA, and demanded the suspension of the official announcement of the election results until an inquiry into the alleged irregularities had been conducted. A second round of the presidential election was required to be held between dos Santos and Savimbi, as neither candidate had secured 50% of the votes cast in the first round. Savimbi agreed to participate in this second round on the condition that it be conducted by the UN, while the Government insisted that the election should not take place until UNITA had satisfied the conditions of the Estoril peace agreement by transferring its troops to assembly points or to the FAA.

Following the announcement, on 17 October 1992, of the official results of the elections, which the UN had declared to have been free and fair, violence broke out between MPLA and UNITA supporters in the cities of Luanda and Huambo. By the end of October hostilities had spread throughout Angola, with the majority of UNITA's demobilized soldiers returning to arms. On 20 November, following negotiations with UN diplomats, Savimbi agreed to abide by the results of the September elections, although he maintained that the ballot had been fraudulent. Subsequently dos Santos announced that the Assembléia Nacional would be inaugurated on 26 November. On that day delegations from the Government and UNITA issued a joint communiqué, declaring full acceptance of the validity of the May 1991 Estoril peace agreement and the intention to implement immediately a nation-wide cease-fire. However, UNITA's 70 elected deputies failed to attend the inauguration of the Assembléia. On 27 November dos Santos announced the appointment of Marcolino José Carlos Moco, the Secretary-General of the MPLA, as Prime Minister. At the end of November, in violation of the recently signed accord, hostilities broke out in the north of the country. On 2 December a new Council of Ministers was announced, including minor ministerial positions for members of the FNLA. In addition, one full and four deputy ministerial posts were reserved for UNITA, which was allowed one week to join the Government. UNITA subsequently nominated a number of its officials to the reserved posts. According to a statement by Moco, however, the appointment of UNITA officials to the Government was entirely dependent upon the implementation of the Estoril peace agreement.

In 1993–94 the UN continued its efforts to negotiate a permanent peace accord between the Government and UNITA. Meanwhile, civil war, in which both sides claimed military gains and suffered heavy losses, continued. In May 1993 the US President, Bill Clinton, announced that the USA was to recognize the Angolan Government. In September, following reports of an intensification of UNITA activity, the UN imposed an arms and petroleum embargo against the rebels, the 'freezing' of UNITA's foreign assets, and the expulsion of its representatives from Western capitals. However, in November UNITA agreed to withdraw its forces to UN-monitored confinement areas. In response, the UN agreed to delay the imposition of further sanctions against UNITA.

In December 1993 an agreement was reportedly reached between UNITA and the Government on issues concerning the demobilization and confinement of UNITA troops, the surrender of UNITA weapons to the UN, and the integration of UNITA generals into the FAA, prompting the UN again to postpone additional sanctions against the rebels. Talks resumed in Lusaka, Zambia, in January 1994, and agreement was reached on the formation, under UN supervision, of a national police force of 26,700 members, of which UNITA was to provide 5,500. Further talks culminated in the signing, on 17 February, of a document on national reconciliation. Acceptance of the September 1992 election results by both sides was also reaffirmed. However, progress at the Lusaka peace talks slowed as discussions advanced to the issue of UNITA's participation in government. Negotiations on the distribution of ministerial posts appeared to have reached an impasse in March 1994, although in May agreement was reached on the second round of the presidential election between dos Santos and Savimbi. Talks continued in Lusaka in late June, culminating in the signing of an 18-point document on national reconciliation.

In July 1994 President Nelson Mandela of South Africa hosted discussions in Pretoria between the Presidents of Angola, Mozambique and Zaire. The discussions concentrated on allegations of Zairean support for UNITA and resulted in the re-establishment of a joint defence and security commission between Angola and Zaire, with the aim of curbing the supply of armaments to the rebels. In August UNITA acceded to government insistence that its officials be permitted to participate in government institutions only after the total demilitarization of the movement, and an 11-point procedural accord, enabling discussions on full reconciliation, was signed.

In September 1994, following successive extensions, the UN Security Council further extended the mandate of UNAVEM II until 31 October. Talks continued throughout October, concentrating on the issue of Savimbi's security and the replacement of the joint political and military commission with a new joint commission, which was to be chaired by the UN Secretary-General's special representative and was to comprise representatives of the Government and UNITA and observers from the USA, Russia and Portugal. A peace accord was finally initialled on 31 October and formally signed on 20 November. However, hostilities continued beyond 22 November, when a permanent cease-fire was to have come into force, notably in Huambo and in Bié province.

In January 1995 a meeting took place at Chipipa, in Huambo province, between the Chief of General Staff of the FAA and his UNITA counterpart, at which agreement was reached on an immediate cessation of hostilities nation-wide. Nevertheless, the fighting continued. In February the UN Security Council adopted a resolution creating UNAVEM III. However, the deployment of the new peace-keeping mission remained conditional on the cessation of hostilities and the disengagement of government and UNITA forces.

In May 1995 dos Santos and Savimbi met in Lusaka for direct talks, which concluded with the ratification of the Lusaka peace accord. Savimbi recognized the status of dos Santos as President of Angola and pledged his full co-operation in the reconstruction of the nation. The two leaders agreed to accelerate the consolidation of the cease-fire, to create conditions for the deployment of UNAVEM III, to expedite the integration of UNITA troops into the FAA, and to establish a government of unity based on the provisions of the Lusaka accord (subsequent to the demobilization of the UNITA forces). Dos Santos requested that Savimbi immediately nominate the UNITA appointees to the new government.

In June 1995 the MPLA proposed a revision of the Constitution to create two new posts of Vice-President, of which one was to be offered to Savimbi, conditional upon the prior disbanding of UNITA forces. The other vice-presidency was to be assumed by Fernando José França van-Dúnem, the President of the Assembléia Nacional. Later that month Savimbi, who had publicly expressed his intention to accept the vice-presidency, declared the war in Angola to be at an end and appealed to neighbouring nations to prevent the traffic of arms to the country. In July the Assembléia approved the creation of the two new vice-presidential positions, and the UN announced that the deployment of UNAVEM III personnel would be completed by the end of August.

The cantonment of UNITA forces began officially in November 1995. However, continued hostilities were reported that month, including confrontations in the diamond-producing areas of the north-east and in Cabinda. By early February 1996 only some 8,200 UNITA troops had been cantoned, prompting the UN Security Council to renew the mandate of UNAVEM III.

In March 1996 discussions between dos Santos and Savimbi, conducted in Libreville, Gabon, resulted in agreement on the establishment of a government of national unity, in accordance with the provisions of the Lusaka accord. Savimbi proposed the UNITA governmental nominees, while dos Santos formally invited Savimbi to assume the vice-presidency. (Later in March, however, Savimbi demanded the appointment of other opposition members to the government of national unity, most notably the President of the FNLA, Holden Roberto.) Agreement was also reached in Libreville on the formation of a unified national army, which, it was envisaged, would be concluded in June. In subsequent talks it was agreed that 18 UNITA generals would be appointed to command posts in the new, unified FAA. It was also established that 26,300 of UNITA's total force of some 62,000 would be integrated into the FAA. In May agreement was reached on a programme to integrate UNITA troops into the FAA. During that month Savimbi introduced further conditions for his acceptance of the vice-presidency and expressed his intention to retain control of diamond-producing areas in north-eastern Angola. In mid-May the Government and a Cabinda secessionist faction, FLEC—Forças Armadas Cabindesas (FLEC—FAC), signed an agreement outlining the principles of a cease-fire. However, following renewed fighting later that month between government troops and the secessionists, the leader of FLEC—FAC, N'zita Henriques Tiago, declared that a definitive cease-fire would only follow the withdrawal of the FAA from Cabinda. A separate cease-fire had been signed with FLEC—Renovada (FLEC—R) in September 1995.

In mid-1996 public protests at deteriorating economic conditions and the high level of corruption within the state apparatus placed increasing political pressure on dos Santos, who responded in June with the dismissal of the administration. Moco was succeeded as Prime Minister by van-Dúnem. In August, following its party congress, UNITA issued a communiqué declining the appointment of Savimbi to the position of national Vice-President.

In November 1996 the Assembléia Nacional adopted a constitutional revision extending its mandate, which was due to expire that month, for a period of between two and four years, pending the establishment of suitable conditions for the conduct of free and fair elections. In April 1997 an agreement was reached to accord Savimbi the special status of official 'leader of the opposition'. Following the arrival of the full contingent of UNITA deputies and government nominees in Luanda, on 11 April the new Government of National Unity and Reconciliation was inaugurated. As envisaged, UNITA assumed a number of ministerial and deputy ministerial portfolios.

In May 1997 the Angolan Government officially recognized the new Government of Laurent-Désiré Kabila in the Democratic Republic of the Congo (DRC, formerly Zaire). The Angolan Government had actively supported Kabila's rebels during the civil war in Zaire, while UNITA, which relied on Zaire as a conduit for exporting diamonds and importing arms, had reportedly sent some 2,000 troops to support President Mobutu. In the light of the defeat of UNITA's main ally, the Government subsequently launched a military offensive on UNITA strongholds in the north-eastern provinces of Lunda-Sul and Lunda-Norte.

On 30 June 1997 the UN Security Council unanimously approved the discontinuation of UNAVEM III and its replacement by a scaled-down observer mission, the UN Observer Mission in Angola (MONUA), with a seven-month mandate to oversee the implementation of the remaining provisions of the Lusaka accord. In late July the UN condemned UNITA's failure to adhere to the Lusaka accord and threatened to impose further sanctions on the movement, including travel restrictions, if it did not take irreversible steps towards fulfilling its obligations.

In July 1997 government delegations from Angola and the Republic of the Congo met in Cabinda to discuss the security situation along the border between the Angolan exclave and the Congo, following armed clashes between Angolan soldiers and FLEC separatists apparently operating from Congolese territory. The talks resulted in proposals to strengthen border security, including the establishment of a joint police force, comprising representatives from both countries and the office of the UN High Commissioner for Refugees (UNHCR). However, in October it became evident that FAA troops were actively supporting the former Marxist ruler of the Congo, Gen. Denis Sassou-Nguesso, in his attempts to overthrow the Government of President Pascal Lissouba. Angola's involvement had been prompted by attacks on Cabinda by FLEC and UNITA forces operating from bases in the Congo provided by Lissouba. In mid-October Sassou-Nguesso's Cobra militia, with Angolan assistance, succeeded in securing his return to power in the Congo.

On 31 October 1997, as a result of UNITA's continued failure to meet its obligations under the peace accord, the UN Security Council finally ordered the implementation of additional sanctions against the movement. In November UNITA expressed its intention to continue to pursue a peaceful settlement, and during the ensuing months ceded further territory to state administration, including the important Cuango valley diamond mines in Lunda-Norte province.

In January 1998 a new schedule was agreed for the implementation of the Lusaka protocol. In early March UNITA announced the disbandment of its remaining forces, following which it received official recognition as a legally constituted party. Later that month the Government implemented the special status agreed for Savimbi, and legislation was adopted allowing him to retain a 400-strong personal guard. However, allegations persisted of preparations by UNITA for a resumption of hostilities. By June fighting had spread to 14 of the country's 18 provinces, displacing some 150,000 people. In August UNITA accused the observer countries in the joint commission of bias in the Government's favour and declared that it would no longer negotiate with them. On 31 August the Government suspended UNITA's government and parliamentary representatives from office.

On 2 September 1998 a group of five UNITA moderates issued a manifesto declaring the suspension of Savimbi and the introduction of an interim UNITA leadership, pending a general congress of the party. Although the group, which styled itself UNITA—Renovada (UNITA—R), commanded very limited support among UNITA's leaders in Luanda, the Government welcomed the development, recognizing UNITA—R as the sole and legitimate representative of UNITA in negotiations concerning the implementation of the Lusaka peace process. The UN Security Council continued to seek a dialogue between dos Santos and Savimbi as the only solution to the conflict. In late September the Government revoked the suspension of UNITA's representatives in the Government and legislature and in October the Assembléia Nacional revoked Savimbi's special status. In that month UNITA—R failed to impose its candidate to lead the UNITA parliamentary group when Abel Chivukuvuku was overwhelmingly re-elected as its Chairman. Chivukuvuku, while no longer claiming allegiance to Savimbi, was opposed to UNITA—R and subsequently formed his own wing of UNITA.

In November 1998, following increasingly frequent outbreaks of fighting, the UN Security Council demanded that UNITA withdraw immediately from territories that it had reoccupied through military action and complete the demilitarization of its troops. The military situation deteriorated considerably in December, prompting the Government to approve the introduction of compulsory military service.

In January 1999, in an effort to address the prevailing military and economic crisis, dos Santos assumed the role of Prime Minister, and in the same month UNITA—R conducted its first congress in Luanda, at which Eugénio N'Golo 'Manuvakola' was elected leader of the faction. In February the UN Security Council voted unanimously to end MONUA's mandate and withdraw its operatives by 20 March, on the grounds that conditions had deteriorated to such an extent that UN personnel were no longer able to function. In October the UN and the Government formally agreed on the establishment of a 30-member 'follow-up' mission, the UN Office in Angola (UNOA), which was to focus on issues concerning humanitarian assistance and human rights.

During 1999 the UN increased its efforts to impose sanctions on UNITA, with the appointment of Canada's ambassador to the UN, Robert Fowler, as Chairman of the UN Sanctions Committee. A UN report published in June disclosed the contravention of UN sanctions by a number of African heads of state, who were apparently involved in the trading of arms for UNITA-mined diamonds. In October 1999 the South African diamond company De Beers, which controls the majority of the international trade in diamonds, announced that it had placed a world-wide embargo on the purchase of all diamonds from Angola, except those whose acquisition was already under contract. The Angolan Government also attempted to stem the flow of illegal diamonds by introducing a strict regime of stone certification. In March 2000 a number of African leaders, as well as individuals in Belgium and Bulgaria, were criticized in a UN report for allegedly violating sanctions that had been imposed on UNITA following the discovery of the trade in illegally mined diamonds. In response, the Angolan Government announced the establishment of a state-owned company, which was to be responsible for centralizing and regulating the country's diamond trade. All marketing was transferred to the newly created Angolan Selling Corporation. In December the UN Angola Sanctions Committee issued a further report on the smuggling of UNITA diamonds, which confirmed that sanctions had failed to prevent the movement's involvement in the diamond trade, and accused several countries of supporting the illegal trade.

At the end of June 2000 the Angolan Government and UNITA representatives were reported to have held secret talks on the possible means of achieving peace in Angola. The conference was attended by the Angolan Deputy Minister of Foreign Affairs, George Chicoti, by 'Manuvakola' from UNITA—R and by Chivukukuvu from UNITA. Furthermore, in August the Angolan Chief of Staff of the Armed Forces, Gen. João de Matos, announced that Savimbi would no longer be prosecuted for his failure to uphold the cease-fire imposed following the 1992 elections. However, he also stated that, although a position would be made available in the Assembléia Nacional for Savimbi, he would not be offered the vice-presidency.

In October 2000 UNITA put forward a 12-point peace plan, including proposals for the formation of a 'broad consensus government' and the depoliticization of the armed forces, the police and public administration. The plan was rejected by the Government. Nevertheless, UNITA reiterated its desire to negotiate with the Angolan Government, on condition that the current Portuguese, US and Russian observers be replaced by Angolan nationals, that the sanctions imposed on UNITA in 1993 be revoked, and that the second round of the 1992 presidential election be held. In December the Assembléia Nacional approved draft amnesty legislation, which had been proposed by the MPLA as a direct response to appeals for reconciliation in Angola.

In June 2001, following an alleged declaration by Savimbi that UNITA forces had been conclusively defeated by the FAA, the Minister of Industry, Joaquim Duarte da Costa David, announced that the civil war had effectively ended. However, sporadic fighting between both factions persisted throughout mid-2001.

In September 2001 the Roman Catholic Church and civil movements in Angola launched an appeal for peace, calling for a cease-fire and the resumption of dialogue between the Government, UNITA and opposition parties. This appeal was supported by a coalition of 35 opposition parties, the Partidos da Oposição Civil, which advocated the establishment of a transitional government, to rule until such time as elections were held. In November dos Santos declared the civil war to be almost ended, on the grounds that UNITA had only a small number of troops remaining at its disposal.

On 22 February 2002 Savimbi was killed during an ambush by FAA soldiers in Moxico province. He was replaced as UNITA President by António Dembo; however, in early March his death was also reported. On 13 March the Government halted military offensives against UNITA, and on 30 March, following talks between the Government and UNITA's Chief-of-Staff, Gen. Abreu 'Kamorteiro' Muengo, both parties signed a memorandum of understanding, aimed at ending the civil war. On 4 April a cease-fire agreement was ratified, in which UNITA accepted the Lusaka protocol and agreed to the cantonment of its soldiers. Some 5,000 UNITA soldiers were to be integrated into the FAA, and UNITA representatives were to take up positions in central, provincial and local government.

By the end of July 2002 some 85,000 UNITA soldiers and an estimated 300,000 family members had registered in quartering camps, amid severe food shortages, but only 30,000 light arms had been turned over to the Government. Nevertheless, in early August UNITA announced that its military wing had been disbanded, following the integration of its soldiers into the FAA. Also in August, the UN Security Council established the UN Mission in Angola (UNMA) to succeed UNOA until 15 February 2003. On 23 August 2002 the Government and UNITA set a 45-day deadline for the full implementation of the Lusaka protocol, which was to be monitored by a UN-led joint commission, comprising representatives of the Government, UNITA and observer countries (Portugal, Russia and the USA). In October the inauguration of a new national political commission for UNITA, including former members of UNITA—R, marked the official reunification of the party; Gen. Paulo Lukamba 'Gato' was confirmed as interim leader of the party, pending a full congress.

In September 2002 João Lourenço, the Secretary-General of the MPLA, admitted the possibility of limited autonomy for Cabinda, but ruled out independence. Meanwhile, fighting continued in Cabinda between FAA troops and FLEC—FAC rebels. An FAA offensive took FLEC—FAC headquarters in Kungo-Shonzo in October, and in December the FAA claimed that it had also seized FLEC—R's main base. During February 2003 FLEC—R and FLEC—FAC forces in Cabinda were actively dispersed by the FAA, and 7,000 captured civilians were freed. Action against the Cabinda rebels was strengthened by a security pact between Angola, the Republic of the Congo and the DRC, which had been signed in January.

The FAA maintained forces in Cabinda throughout 2003, and by the middle of that year it was believed that, with the exception of some pockets of resistance in the north, the province had been pacified. FLEC—FAC continued to state that it was prepared to negotiate a peace agreement based on a level of autonomy for Cabinda within Angola, and in August the Government declared that it was willing to reopen negotiations on that basis. In September 2004 the merger was announced of FLEC—FAC and FLEC—R. The new grouping, which adopted the name FLEC, was led by N'Zita Henriques Tiago, while António Bento Bembe, previously the President of FLEC—R, became Secretary-General of the movement. A political wing, styling itself FLEC—Conselho Superior Alargado (FLEC—CSA), with the stated aim of achieving independence through political means, was subsequently established under the leadership of Liberal Nuno.

Meanwhile, in October 2002 the UN Development Programme reported that Angola was threatened with an 'extremely serious humanitarian crisis' as a result of the civil war, which had caused severe damage to political and economic structures and displaced some 4.3m. people. On 11 November, to mark the celebration of Angola's first peacetime Independence Day, UNITA declared its intention to accelerate the approval of new policies designed to aid the economy. Later that month the joint commission responsible for supervising the implementation of the Lusaka protocol was dissolved and replaced by a joint UNITA-Government mechanism.

In early December 2002 Fernando (Nando) da Piedade Dias dos Santos, hitherto Minister of the Interior, was appointed as Prime Minister, a post that President dos Santos had himself held since January 1999. The Council of Ministers was subsequently reshuffled, with the inclusion of the four UNITA representatives. Shortly afterwards the UN Security Council voted to lift all remaining sanctions on UNITA, having previously removed travel restrictions on officials of the former rebel group. Meanwhile, a Constitutional Commission (which had been established by the Assembléia Nacional in 1998) was considering proposals for a new draft constitution. Agreement was reached on a major point of contention in January 2003, when the Commission decided that the President of the Republic would remain Head of Government, as favoured by MPLA deputies; UNITA had advocated the devolvement of executive power to the Prime Minister. In mid-February UNMA withdrew from Angola, as scheduled. The demobilization of former UNITA soldiers continued throughout 2003. The Government closed the 35 quartering camps in June, and by November around 80,000 soldiers, along with their families, had been demobilized.

In January 2004 the Constitutional Commission was presented with a draft constitution and in mid-2004 the Government, which had identified 14 'key tasks' it wished to accomplish before calling concurrent legislative and presidential elections—including constitutional reform and the compiling of an electoral register—stated that polls would not take place until late 2006. A government report recommended that a minimum period of one year be allowed in order to prepare for the elections; however, several opposition parties, including UNITA, insisted that elections could take place in 2005 without constitutional reform and withdrew from the Commission in May 2004 in protest at the perceived lack of progress towards elections. In November the Commission was dissolved, after a draft constitutional bill had been presented to the Assembléia Nacional. Also in November President dos Santos indicated that a presidential election could be delayed to take place one year after the holding of legislative elections.

During late 2004 and early 2005 President dos Santos effected a series of minor reorganizations of the Council of Ministers and appointed several new Provincial Governors. Most notably, in mid-December the Minister of Justice, Paulo Tjipilika, was dismissed and replaced by Manuel da Costa Aragão, hitherto his deputy. Also in late 2004 the Government launched an anti-corruption campaign which resulted in the dismissal of various government officials.

In July 2005 the Supreme Court ruled that President dos Santos was eligible to stand for re-election, and in August, following approval by the Supreme Court, dos Santos signed into law legislation pertaining to the elections, which were expected to be held in late 2006. The legislation provided for, *inter alia*, the creation of a Comissão Nacional Eleitoral (CNE—National Electoral Commission). The 11-member CNE, presided over by a senior judge, Caetano de Sousa, was sworn in later in August 2005. However, owing to the lack of progress with preparations for the registration of voters, in late 2005 there remained considerable uncertainty as to whether the necessary infrastructure would be in place to enable the elections to be held in 2006.

In January 2006 the UNITA President, Isaías Samakuva, nominated replacements for 16 of the UNITA members of the Assembléia Nacional; however, the incumbents refused to co-operate. Four of these, including Jorge Alicerces Valentim, were subsequently expelled from the party, but the deadlock continued. In August a peace agreement was signed with the splintered secessionist movement FLEC in the Cabinda region (an area with over one-half of the country's petroleum resources), recognizing Cabinda as part of Angola but granting it special status, with a greater degree of autonomy than other provinces. Human rights organizations alleged that this deal had been imposed by force, and members of the Fórum Cabindês para o Diálogo claimed that the representative with whom the agreement had been reached, António Bento Bembe (see above), was not a valid spokesman (as did members of his own party).

In September 2006 a national campaign of civic education was launched, as a precursor to voter registration for the impending legislative and presidential elections; the first phase of voter registration commenced in November. However, in December the Council of the Republic cross-party advisory committee concluded that a postponement was necessary in order for sufficient preparatory time, with legislative elections likely to take place in mid-2008 and a presidential ballot in 2009. In the same month an amnesty was announced by the legislature for crimes against state security and crimes associated with the conflict in Cabinda, and in January 2007 a unit of FLEC soldiers was demobilized, with some members integrated into the Angolan army and police. In November Bembe was appointed to the Government, assuming the position of Minister without Portfolio.

Meanwhile, at the end of 2006 Samakuva announced that a UNITA party congress was to take place in 2007, following allegations of inadequacy regarding his leadership over the problem of the substitute parliamentarians (and allegations of embezzlement by Valentim). At the congress, which was held in July, Samakuva was re-elected to the presidency of the party, after comfortably defeating the sole challenger Chivukuvuku. In September the Government announced that the voter registration process had been completed and that some 8m. Angolans would be eligible to vote in the forthcoming polls. In late December President dos Santos stated that legislative elections would be held on 5–6 September 2008.

Between late 2002 and late 2003 the Angolan Government and UNHCR established separate tripartite commissions with Zambia, the DRC, Namibia, Botswana, the Republic of the Congo and South Africa, with the aim of facilitating the repatriation of Angolan refugees from these countries. In early 2003 there were an estimated 470,000 Angolan refugees in the region, including 210,000 in Zambia, 192,000 in the DRC and 24,000 in Namibia. By late 2006 around 370,000 of these had been repatriated by UNHCR or had returned without assistance. However, significant problems remained for returning refugees, notably the presence of anti-personnel mines, a lack of infrastructure and social services in rural areas, and disputes over land rights. In late 2003 the Council of Ministers approved draft legislation on land possession, which was adopted by the Assembléia Nacional in August 2004.

Following the internal uprising in August 1998 against the Kabila regime in the DRC, the Angolan Government moved swiftly to provide Kabila with military support against the rebels. In October, as the conflict escalated in the east of the DRC, Angola, in alliance with Namibia and Zimbabwe, stated that it would continue supporting Kabila until the rebels were defeated. Following the assassination of Kabila in January 2001, the Angolan Government announced its intention to allow its troops stationed in the DRC to remain there until further notice; moreover, several thousand additional Angolan troops were moved into that country later in January. However, by the end of October 2002 Angola, Namibia and Zimbabwe had completed the withdrawal of their troops from the DRC. Between December 2003 and August 2004 the Angolan authorities were reported to have expelled an estimated 120,000 illegal diamond workers, mostly from the DRC, from northern Angola.

In 2000 a French judicial inquiry was instigated into alleged arms-trafficking to Angola by a French company, Brenco International, and a French businessman, Pierre Falcone. The company, along with a number of prominent French politicians, was alleged to have engaged in money-laundering and the unauthorized sales of arms worth some US $600m. to the dos Santos Government in 1993–94. Falcone was placed under provisional detention in France in December 2000, but was released after one year, the maximum term allowed for temporary detention. French investigations into the sale of weapons to Angola, as well as the settlement of the country's debt to Russia, continued during 2005. Meanwhile, Falcone's appointment, in June 2003, as a plenipotentiary minister at the Angolan permanent delegation to UNESCO, entitling him to diplomatic immunity, provoked considerable international controversy and condemnation from Angolan opposition parties and civil society organizations.

In July 1996 Angola was among the five lusophone African countries that, together with Portugal and Brazil, formed the Comunidade dos Países de Língua Portuguesa (see p. 423), a Portuguese-speaking commonwealth seeking to achieve collective benefits from co-operation in technical, cultural and social matters. In 2004 Angola joined the African Peer Review Mechanism, a group designed to monitor economic and political development. In May 2007 the Governments of Angola and Mozambique signed an agreement on employment and social security, pledging to increase efforts in the fight against poverty and to provide better working conditions for their people.

Government

In March 1991 and in the first half of 1992 the Government of the Movimento Popular de Libertação de Angola—Partido do Trabalho (MPLA—PT) introduced a series of far-reaching amendments to the 1975 Constitution, providing for the establishment of a multi-party democracy (hitherto, no other political parties, apart from the ruling MPLA—PT, had been permitted). According to the amendments, legislative power was to be vested in the National Assembly (Assembléia Nacional), with 223 members elected for four years on the basis of proportional representation. Executive power was to be held by the President, who was to be directly elected for a term of five years (renewable for a maximum of three terms). As Head of State and Commander-in-Chief of the armed forces, the President was to govern with the assistance of an appointed Council of Ministers. Proposals for a new constitution remained under consideration in 2007.

For the purposes of local government, the country is divided into 18 provinces, each administered by an appointed Governor.

Legislative elections, held in September 1992, resulted in victory for the MPLA. However, in the presidential election, which was held at the same time, the MPLA's candidate and incumbent President, José Eduardo dos Santos, narrowly failed to secure the 50% of the votes necessary to be elected President. Following a resumption of hostilities between the União Nacional para a Independência Total de Angola (UNITA) and government forces, the conduct of a second round of the presidential election was held in abeyance, with dos Santos remaining in the presidency. In accordance with the terms of the Lusaka peace accord of November 1994, in April 1997 a new Government of National Unity and Reconciliation was inaugurated in which UNITA held four portfolios. However, following a resumption of hostilities, in August 1998 UNITA's government representatives were suspended from office. In 2004 the Government proposed that legislative elections be held in late 2006, with presidential elections expected to take place at a later date. In December 2007 it was announced that legislative elections would take place on 5–6 September 2008.

Defence

In accordance with the peace agreement concluded by the Government and the União Nacional para a Independência Total de Angola (UNITA) in May 1991 (see Recent History), a new 50,000-strong national army, the Forças Armadas de Angola (FAA), was established, comprising equal numbers of government forces, the Forças Armadas Populares de Libertação de Angola, and UNITA soldiers. Following elections in 1992, UNITA withdrew its troops from the FAA, alleging electoral fraud on the part of the Movimento Popular de Libertação de Angola, and hostilities resumed. After the signing of the Lusaka peace accord in November 1994, preparations for the confinement and demobilization of troops, and the integration of the UNITA contingent into the FAA, resumed. In 1995 the Government and UNITA reached agreement on the enlargement of the FAA to comprise a total of 90,000 troops, and discussions began concerning the potential formation of a fourth, non-combatant branch of the FAA, which would engage in public works projects. In mid-1997 the Government estimated that a residual UNITA force numbered some 25,000–30,000 troops, while UNITA claimed to have retained a force of only 2,963 'police'. In March 1998 UNITA issued a declaration announcing the complete demobilization of its forces. However, evidence of the existence of a large UNITA force became apparent with the escalation of widespread hostilities in Angola from mid-1998. Following the ratification of a peace agreement between UNITA and the Government in April 2002, some 5,000 former UNITA soldiers were incorporated into the FAA in mid-2002, and by November 2003 around 80,000 former combatants had been demobilized and were to be reintegrated into civilian life. As assessed at November 2006, the FAA had an estimated total strength of 107,000: army 100,000, navy 1,000 and air force 6,000. In addition, there was a paramilitary force numbering an estimated 10,000. The defence budget for 2007 was 172,000m. kwanza. It was estimated that the Frente de Libertação do Enclave de Cabinda had a total strength of 5,500 and UNITA had a strength of 5,000.

Economic Affairs

In 2006, according to estimates by the World Bank, Angola's gross national income (GNI), measured at average 2004–06 prices, was US $32,411.3m., equivalent to $1,980 per head (or $2,360 per head on an international purchasing-power parity basis). During 1996–2006, it was estimated, Angola's population increased at an average annual rate of 2.7%, while gross domestic product (GDP) per head increased, in real terms, by an average of 5.9% per year. Overall GDP increased, in real terms, at an average annual rate of 8.7% in 1996–2006; growth in 2006 was 14.6%.

According to the IMF, agriculture contributed an estimated 8.9% of GDP in 2006. An estimated 70.5% of the total working population were employed in the agricultural sector in 2005, according to FAO figures. Coffee is the principal cash crop. The main subsistence crops are cassava, sweet potatoes, potatoes, maize, sugar cane and bananas. Severe food shortages following a period of drought in late 2000 worsened in 2001, owing to continued low levels of agricultural productivity. The widespread presence of unexploded anti-personnel mines continued to be an obstacle to the successful redevelopment of the agricultural sector. From 2005 the Government commenced a programme of investment in the formerly flourishing fisheries sector, which held much potential for redevelopment. During 1996–2005, according to the World Bank, agricultural GDP increased at an average annual rate of 10.9%, and by 17.0% in 2005.

Industry (including mining, manufacturing, construction and power) provided an estimated 69.7% of GDP in 2006, and employed an estimated 10.5% of the labour force in 1991. The economic recovery in the country, as well as increased petroleum production and earnings, and Chinese sponsorship, led to strong expansion in the construction sector from 2005, with investment in the redevelopment of infrastructure. According to the World Bank, industrial GDP increased, in real terms, at an average annual rate of 9.3% in 1996–2005; growth in industrial GDP was 23.4% in 2005.

Mining contributed an estimated 61.8% of GDP in 2006 Petroleum production (including liquefied petroleum gas) accounted for an estimated 58.5% of GDP in that year. Angola's principal mineral exports are petroleum and diamonds. In addition, there are reserves of iron ore, copper, lead, zinc, gold, manganese, phosphates, salt and uranium. At the end of 2006 Angola had proven petroleum reserves of 9,000m. barrels, sufficient to sustain production at current levels for some 20 years.

The manufacturing sector provided an estimated 4.3% of GDP in 2006. The principal branch of manufacturing is petroleum refining. Other manufacturing activities include food-processing, brewing, textiles and construction materials. According to the World Bank, the GDP of the manufacturing sector increased at an average annual rate of 11.1% in 1996–2005; growth in manufacturing GDP was 24.9% in 2005.

Energy is derived mainly from hydroelectric power, which, according to the World Bank, provided 66.5% of Angola's electricity production in 2004, while petroleum accounted for 33.5%. Angola's power potential exceeds its requirements; however, power supply is erratic and the country lacks a national grid.

Services accounted for an estimated 21.4% of GDP in 2006, and engaged an estimated 20.1% of the labour force in 1991. In real terms, the GDP of the services sector increased at an average annual rate of 4.0% in 1996–2005. Services GDP increased by 1% in 2005.

In 2006 Angola recorded an estimated visible trade surplus of US $23,085m., while there was a surplus of $10,690m. on the current account of the balance of payments. In 2006 the principal source of imports was the Republic of Korea (17.3%); other major suppliers were the USA (14.3%) and Portugal (14.1%), while the countries of the European Union (see p. 244) supplied 35.2% of total imports. In that year the principal market for exports was the USA (38.6%); the People's Republic of China was also a significant purchaser of Angola's exports. The principal export in 2006 was crude petroleum, accounting for an estimated 94.2% of total export earnings, while diamonds contributed 3.6%. In 2007 it was estimated that Angola was the largest supplier of crude petroleum to the People's Republic of China.

In 2006 there was an estimated budget surplus of 103m. kwanza. Angola's total external debt at the end of 2006 was US $7,596m., of which $6,672m. was long-term public debt. In that year the cost of debt-servicing was equivalent to 8.7% of GDP. Consumer prices increased by an average of 24.8% in 2005 and by 11.7% in 2006, according to IMF figures.

Angola is a member of both the Common Market for Eastern and Southern Africa (see p. 205) and the Southern African Development Community (see p. 386), which was formed with the aim of reducing the economic dependence of southern African states on South Africa. In January 2007 Angola joined the Organization of the Petroleum Exporting Countries (see p. 373).

From independence, exploitation of Angola's extensive mineral reserves, hydroelectric potential and abundant fertile land was severely impaired by internal conflict, as well as an acute shortage of skilled personnel. Following the ratification of a cease-fire agreement in April 2002, Angola's prospects depended greatly on a resolution of the civil strife, the reintegration of the displaced population and the rehabilitation of the country's devastated infrastructure. Despite civil conflict, the development of the petroleum sector continued apace from the late 1990s, although much petroleum revenue was used to finance the Government's military expenditure. In 2004, according to the BP Statistical Review of World Energy, total national output of crude petroleum was 976,000 barrels per day (b/d) and the state petroleum company, SONANGOL, predicted that production would reach some 2m. b/d by 2008. These estimates appeared to be on target with an increase in production to 1.2m. b/d in 2005, and to 1.4m. b/d in 2006. Increasingly, Angola has been the beneficiary of investment and technical support from the People's Republic of China, accounting for a large proportion of Chinese investment in the continent. However, some concern was raised over the validity of figures regarding such investment, with the Ministry of Finance stating in October 2007 that credit from the China International Fund (based in Hong Kong) in 2005 was valued at US $2,900m., rather than the figure of $9,800m. suggested by the World Bank. Meanwhile, opposition parties and international observers maintained that while the Government was correct to seek ties with China, the benefits of the investment had not filtered through to the Angolan people, and that despite impressive recent economic growth, some two-thirds of the population continued to subside on less than $1 per day. Consumer price inflation was estimated to have reached its lowest level in some decades in 2006 at 11.7%, although the IMF was critical of the primary method utilized to achieve this effect (by strengthening the national currency financially on foreign exchange markets) and questioned its long term sustainability. An IMF paper in October 2007 highlighted a lack of reliable data required adequately to forecast inflation. The report additionally cited uncertainty over non-oil sector growth, and the shortcomings of infrastructure and institutions in the market that were hampering monetary policy. Production of petroleum was forecast to increase steeply in 2007 and 2008, thus supporting strong growth in GDP, in export earnings and in the surplus on the current account, given the continuing rise in international petroleum prices. GDP growth of 18.6% in 2006 far exceeded that of many African nations, and an estimated increase of 35.3% in 2007 placed Angola as the continent's most rapidly expanding economy. This growth was expected to continue into 2008, and the budget for that year provided for an increase of approximately 30% in both revenue and expenditure compared with 2007.

Education

Education is officially compulsory for eight years, between seven and 15 years of age, and is provided free of charge by the

ANGOLA

Government. Primary education begins at seven years of age and lasts for four years. Secondary education, beginning at the age of 11, lasts for up to seven years, comprising a first cycle of four years and a second of three years. As a proportion of the school-age population, the total enrolment at primary and secondary schools was 45% in 1991. According to UNESCO estimates, enrolment at primary schools in 2000/01 included 37% of children in the relevant age-group (boys 39%; girls 35%), while secondary enrolment was equivalent to 18% of children in the relevant age-group (boys 19%; girls 16%). In 1997/98 the Agostinho Neto university, in Luanda, at that time the country's only university, had 8,337 students. In November 2002 the Government announced plans for the construction of seven provincial universities, five science and technology institutes, three medical schools and a nutrition research centre. There are also four private universities. Much education is now conducted in vernacular languages rather than Portuguese. In 2004 the Government recruited 29,000 new teachers, to be trained by the UN Children's Fund (UNICEF). The 2006 budget allocated an estimated 83,500m. kwanza to education.

Public Holidays

2008: 1 January (New Year's Day), 4 January (Martyrs' Day), 4 February (Anniversary of the outbreak of the armed struggle against Portuguese colonialism), 5 February (Carnival Day), 8 March (International Women's Day), 27 March (Victory Day)*, 4 April (Peace and National Reconciliation Day), 14 April (Good Friday and Youth Day)*, 1 May (Workers' Day), 25 May (Africa Day), 1 June (International Children's Day), 1 August (Armed Forces' Day)*, 17 September (National Hero's Day, birthday of Dr Agostinho Neto), 2 November (All Souls' Day), 11 November (Independence Day), 1 December (Pioneers' Day)*, 10 December (Foundation of the MPLA Day)*, 25 December (Christmas Day and Family Day).

2009: 1 January (New Year's Day), 4 January (Martyrs' Day), 4 February (Anniversary of the outbreak of the armed struggle against Portuguese colonialism), 24 February (Carnival Day), 8 March (International Women's Day), 21 March (Good Friday), 27 March (Victory Day)*, 4 April (Peace and National Reconciliation Day), 14 April (Youth Day)*, 1 May (Workers' Day), 25 May (Africa Day), 1 June (International Children's Day), 1 August (Armed Forces' Day)*, 17 September (National Hero's Day, birthday of Dr Agostinho Neto), 2 November (All Souls' Day), 11 November (Independence Day), 1 December (Pioneers' Day)*, 10 December (Foundation of the MPLA Day)*, 25 December (Christmas Day and Family Day).

* Although not officially recognized as public holidays, these days are popularly treated as such.

Weights and Measures

The metric system is in force.

Statistical Survey

Source (unless otherwise stated): Instituto Nacional de Estatística, Av. Ho Chi Minh, CP 1215, Luanda; tel. 222322776; e-mail ine@angonet.gn.apc.org.

Area and Population

AREA, POPULATION AND DENSITY

Area (sq km)	1,246,700*
Population (census results)	
30 December 1960	4,480,719
15 December 1970	
Males	2,943,974
Females	2,702,192
Total	5,646,166
Population (UN estimates at mid-year)	
2005	16,095,000
2006	16,557,000
2007	17,024,000
Density (per sq km) at mid-2007	13.7

* 481,354 sq miles.

Source: partly UN, *World Population Prospects: The 2006 Revision*.

DISTRIBUTION OF POPULATION BY PROVINCE
(provisional estimates, mid-1995)

	Area (sq km)	Population	Density (per sq km)
Luanda	2,418	2,002,000	828.0
Huambo	34,274	1,687,000	49.2
Bié	70,314	1,246,000	17.7
Malange	87,246	975,000	11.2
Huíla	75,002	948,000	12.6
Uíge	58,698	948,000	16.2
Benguela	31,788	702,000	22.1
Kwanza-Sul	55,660	688,000	12.4
Kwanza-Norte	24,110	412,000	17.1
Moxico	223,023	349,000	1.6
Lunda-Norte	102,783	311,000	3.0
Zaire	40,130	247,000	6.2
Cunene	88,342	245,000	2.8
Cabinda	7,270	185,000	25.4
Bengo	31,371	184,000	5.9
Lunda-Sul	56,985	160,000	2.8
Cuando Cubango	199,049	137,000	0.7
Namibe	58,137	135,000	2.3
Total	**1,246,600**	**11,561,000**	**9.3**

PRINCIPAL TOWNS
(population at 1970 census)

Luanda (capital)	480,613		Benguela	40,996
Huambo (Nova Lisboa)	61,885		Lubango (Sá da Bandeira)	31,674
Lobito	59,258		Malange	31,559

Source: Direcção dos Serviços de Estatística.

Mid-2005 ('000, incl. suburbs, UN estimate): Luanda 2,766 (Source: UN, *World Urbanization Prospects: The 2005 Revision*).

BIRTHS AND DEATHS
(annual averages, UN estimates)

	1990–95	1995–2000	2000–05
Birth rate (per 1,000)	52.5	49.0	48.6
Death rate (per 1,000)	23.8	22.6	22.1

Source: UN, *World Population Prospects: The 2006 Revision*.

Expectation of life (years at birth, WHO estimates): 40.0 (males 38.6; females 41.4) in 2005 (Source: WHO, *World Health Statistics*).

ECONOMICALLY ACTIVE POPULATION
('000 persons, 1991, estimates)

	Males	Females	Total
Agriculture, etc.	1,518	1,374	2,892
Industry	405	33	438
Services	644	192	836
Total labour force	**2,567**	**1,599**	**4,166**

Source: UN Economic Commission for Africa, *African Statistical Yearbook*.

1996 (official estimates, '000 persons): Total employed 475,214; Unemployed 19,000; Total labour force 494,214 (males 379,166; females 115,049) (Source: ILO).

Mid-2005 (estimates in '000): Agriculture, etc. 5,218; Total (incl. others) 7,403 (Source: FAO).

ANGOLA

Health and Welfare

KEY INDICATORS

Total fertility rate (children per woman, 2005)	6.6
Under-5 mortality rate (per 1,000 live births, 2005)	260
HIV/AIDS (% of persons aged 15–49, 2005)	3.7
Physicians (per 1,000 head, 2004)	0.08
Hospital beds (per 1,000 head, 1990)	1.29
Health expenditure (2004): US $ per head (PPP)	37.5
Health expenditure (2004): % of GDP	1.9
Health expenditure (2004): public (% of total)	79.4
Access to water (% of persons, 2004)	53
Access to sanitation (% of persons, 2004)	31
Human Development Index (2005): ranking	162
Human Development Index (2005): value	0.446

For sources and definitions, see explanatory note on p. vi.

Agriculture

PRINCIPAL CROPS
('000 metric tons)

	2004	2005	2006
Wheat*	4	5	5
Rice (paddy)	10	9	9*
Maize	531	720	566*
Millet	123†	138	138*
Potatoes	242	307	593*
Sweet potatoes	630	659	685*
Cassava (Manioc)	8,587	8,606	8,810*
Sugar cane*	360	n.a.	360
Dry beans	76	108	100*
Groundnuts (in shell)	50	66	57†
Sunflower seed*	11	11	11
Oil palm fruit*	280	291	291
Cottonseed*	58	58	58
Tomatoes*	1	13	13
Onions and shallots (green)*	13	n.a.	13
Bananas*	300	306	306
Citrus fruit*	78	78	78
Pineapples*	40	41	41
Coffee (green)†	2	2	2

* FAO estimate(s).
† Unofficial figure(s).

Aggregate production ('000 metric tons, may include official, semi-official or estimated data): Total cereals 668 in 2004, 871 in 2005, 717 in 2006; Total roots and tubers 9,458 in 2004, 9,573 in 2005, 10,088 in 2006; Total vegetables (incl. melons) 271 in 2004, 271 in 2005, 271 in 2006; Total fruits (excl. melons) 450 in 2004, 457 in 2005, 457 in 2006.

Source: FAO.

LIVESTOCK
('000 head, year ending September, FAO estimates)

	2003	2004	2006
Cattle	4,150	3,680	4,150
Pigs	780	780	780
Sheep	340	297	340
Goats	2,050	2,050	2,050
Chickens	6,800	6,800	6,800

* Data for 2005 were unavailable.
Source: FAO.

LIVESTOCK PRODUCTS
('000 metric tons, FAO estimates)

	2004	2005	2006
Cattle meat	75.5	n.a.	85.0
Goat meat	9.2	9.2	9.2
Pig meat	27.9	29.6	29.6
Chicken meat	8.7	8.8	8.8
Game meat	7.5	n.a.	7.5
Sheep meat	1.2	1.3	1.3
Cows' milk	195.0	n.a.	195.0
Hen eggs	4.3	n.a.	4.3
Honey	23.0	23.8	23.8

Source: FAO.

Forestry

ROUNDWOOD REMOVALS
('000 cubic metres, excluding bark, FAO estimates)

	2003	2004	2005
Sawlogs, veneer logs and logs for sleepers	46	46	46
Other industrial wood	1,050	1,050	1,050
Fuel wood	3,402	3,487	3,574
Total	4,498	4,583	4,670

2006: Production assumed to be unchanged from 2005 (FAO estimates).
Source: FAO.

SAWNWOOD PRODUCTION
('000 cubic metres, including railway sleepers, FAO estimates)

	1983	1984	1985
Total	6	2	5

1986–2006: Annual production as in 1985 (FAO estimates).
Source: FAO.

Fishing

('000 metric tons, live weight)

	2003	2004	2005*
Freshwater fishes	10.0	10.0*	10.0
West coast sole	n.a.	8.3	8.2
West African croakers	18.9	18.3	19.0
Dentex	18.2	17.9	17.8
Cunene horse mackerel	28.1	34.9	35.0
Sardinellas	45.0	58.6	55.0
Chub mackerel	9.7	6.6	7.0
Total catch (incl. others)	211.5	240.0*	240.0

* FAO estimate(s).
Source: FAO.

ANGOLA

Statistical Survey

Mining

('000 metric tons, unless otherwise indicated)

	2003	2004	2005
Crude petroleum ('000 42-gallon barrels):			
crude	321,200	383,250	456,250
refinery products*	14,000	14,000	14,000
Salt (unrefined)	30	30	30
Diamonds ('000 carats):†			
industrial	570	610	700
gem	5,130	5,490	6,300

* Estimates; includes asphalt and bitumen.
† Reported figures, based on estimates of 90% of production at gem grade and 10% of production at industrial grade.

Source: US Geological Survey.

2006: Crude petroleum ('000 42-gallon barrels) 515,000; Liquefied petroleum gas ('000 barrels) 6,427; Diamonds ('000 carats) 9,157 (Source: IMF, *Angola: Selected Issues and Statistical Appendix*—October 2007).

Industry

SELECTED PRODUCTS
('000 metric tons, unless otherwise indicated)

	2001	2002	2003
Frozen fish	57.8	43.9	36.2
Wheat flour	20.3	21.0	38.2
Bread	313.7	n.a.	264.0
Beer ('000 hectolitres)	82.0	80.0	192.0
Non-alcoholic beverages ('000 hectolitres)	82.0	56.0	88.8
Jet fuels	330.9	352.5	324.8
Motor spirit (petrol)	107.2	104.6	95.9
Kerosene	31.2	36.9	43.9
Distillate fuel oils	501.7	461.0	407.5
Residual fuel oils	552.8	590.7	639.3
Butane gas	31.5	34.3	30.0
Cement	465.5	312.7	500.6

Source: IMF, *Angola: Selected Issues and Statistical Appendix* (April 2005).

2004 ('000 metric tons): Jet fuels 302; Motor gasoline 96; Naphthas 85; Kerosene 41; Distillate fuel oils 669; Residual fuel oils 604; Cement 250 (Source: UN, *Industrial Commodity Statistics Yearbook*).

Finance

CURRENCY AND EXCHANGE RATES

Monetary Units
100 lwei = 1 kwanza.

Sterling, Dollar and Euro Equivalents (30 December 2007)
£1 sterling = 150.301 kwanza;
US $1 = 75.023 kwanza;
€1 = 110.441 kwanza;
1,000 kwanza = £6.65 = $13.33 = €9.05.

Average Exchange Rate (kwanza per US $)
2005 87.159
2006 80.368
2007 76.706

Note: In April 1994 the introduction of a new method of setting exchange rates resulted in an effective devaluation of the new kwanza, to US $1 = 68,297 new kwanza, and provided for an end to the system of multiple exchange rates. Further substantial devaluations followed, and in July 1995 a 'readjusted' kwanza, equivalent to 1,000 new kwanza, was introduced. The currency, however, continued to depreciate. Between July 1997 and June 1998 a fixed official rate of US $1 = 262,376 readjusted kwanza was in operation. In May 1999 the Central Bank announced its decision to abolish the existing dual currency exchange rate system. In December 1999 the readjusted kwanza was replaced by a new currency, the kwanza, equivalent to 1m. readjusted kwanza.

BUDGET
('000 million kwanza)

Revenue	2004*	2005*	2006†
Tax revenue	597.3	1,050.3	1,394.2
Petroleum	469.3	862.1	1,172.1
Income tax	42.4	62.2	84.6
Tax on goods and services	36.5	54.9	56.1
Taxes on foreign trade	33.2	47.0	54.8
Taxes on properties	0.7	1.0	1.2
Other taxes	15.2	23.1	25.4
Contributions to social welfare	—	21.0	19.1
Grants	7.5	6.4	9.4
Other revenue	4.9	8.2	18.5
Total	**609.7**	**1,085.8**	**1,441.3**

Expenditure	2004*	2005*	2006†
Current	518.6	725.0	798.2
Personnel‡	170.4	246.7	296.3
Goods and services	156.2	245.1	255.4
Interest payments	38.6	53.5	56.3
Transfers	153.4	179.7	190.3
Capital	73.3	134.7	540.2
Total	**591.9**	**859.7**	**1,338.5**

* Estimates.
† Projections.
‡ Including wages and salaries of defence and public order personnel.

Source: Ministry of Finance, Luanda.

INTERNATIONAL RESERVES
(US $ million at 31 December)

	2004	2005	2006
IMF special drawing rights	0.23	0.21	0.23
Foreign exchange	1,373.82	3,196.64	8,598.35
Total	**1,374.05**	**3,196.85**	**8,598.58**

Source: IMF, *International Financial Statistics*.

MONEY SUPPLY
(million kwanza at 31 December)

	2004	2005	2006
Currency outside banks	45,933.1	59,692.6	71,588.7
Demand deposits at banking institutions	49,970.9	92,991.6	123,634.8
Total (incl. others)	**96,058.5**	**152,909.9**	**195,488.0**

Source: IMF, *International Financial Statistics*.

COST OF LIVING
(Consumer Price Index for Luanda at December; base: 1994 average = 100)

	1999	2000	2001
Food	3,551.1	11,211.2	22,494.2
Clothing	5,189.4	21,449.2	45,733.9
Rent, fuel and light	28,392.7	157,756.4	434,224.6
All items (incl. others)	5,083.6	18,723.6	40,456.1

Source: IMF, *Angola: Selected Issues and Statistical Appendix* (September 2003).

All items (Consumer Price Index for Luanda at December; base: 2000 = 100): 1,501.2 in 2004; 1,872.8 in 2005; 2,091.5 in 2006 (Source: IMF, *International Financial Statistics*).

ANGOLA

NATIONAL ACCOUNTS
Expenditure on the Gross Domestic Product
(US $ million at current prices)

	2004	2005	2006
Government final consumption expenditure	8,817.0	14,397.8	18,501.8
Private final consumption expenditure	5,997.8	7,899.2	9,633.7
Gross fixed capital formation	1,802.1	2,472.9	6,186.3
Increase in stocks			
Total domestic expenditure	16,616.9	24,769.9	34,321.8
Exports of goods and services	13,779.8	23,804.6	35,070.8
Less Imports of goods and services	10,621.5	15,763.8	22,132.6
GDP in purchasers' values (market prices)	19,775.2	32,810.7	47,260.0
GDP at constant 2000 prices	12,378.8	14,930.4	17,155.1

Source: African Development Bank.

Gross Domestic Product by Economic Activity
(million kwanza at current prices)

	2004	2005	2006*
Agriculture, forestry and fishing	142,500	206,800	322,900
Mining	988,800	1,923,700	2,241,300
Petroleum and gas	903,000	1,800,100	2,120,700
Manufacturing	66,100	102,300	154,400
Electricity and water	600	900	1,200
Construction	62,100	90,900	131,700
Trade	263,100	353,900	566,100
Other services	128,000	180,800	210,400
Sub-total	1,651,200	2,858,500	3,628,000
Import duties	900	1,200	1,600
Statistical discrepancy	4,800	–190,100	100
GDP at market prices	1,656,900	2,669,600	3,629,700

*Estimates.

Source: IMF, *Angola: Selected Issues and Statistical Appendix* (October 2007).

BALANCE OF PAYMENTS
(US $ million)

	2004	2005	2006
Exports of goods f.o.b.	13,475.0	24,109.4	31,862.2
Imports of goods f.o.b.	–5,831.8	–8,353.2	–8,777.6
Trade balance	7,643.2	15,756.2	23,084.6
Exports of services	322.8	176.8	1,484.2
Imports of services	–4,802.7	–6,791.0	–7,511.2
Balance on goods and services	3,163.3	9,142.0	17,057.7
Other income received	33.0	25.8	145.0
Other income paid	–2,516.6	–4,056.6	–6,322.9
Balance on goods, services and income	679.6	5,111.1	10,879.8
Current transfers received	124.4	172.5	59.5
Current transfers paid	–117.9	–145.8	–249.5
Current balance	686.2	5,137.9	10,689.8
Direct investment abroad	–35.2	–219.4	–190.6
Direct investment from abroad	1,449.2	–1,303.8	–37.7
Portfolio investment assets	–2.7	–1,267.0	–1,439.5
Other investment assets	–1,951.5	–1,850.1	–1,633.1
Investment liabilities	–83.0	1,525.5	–2,300.3
Net errors and omissions	277.3	–377.9	289.8
Overall balance	340.3	1,645.2	5,378.4

Source: IMF, *International Financial Statistics*.

External Trade

SELECTED COMMODITIES

Imports (million kwanza)	1983	1984	1985
Animal products	1,315	1,226	1,084
Vegetable products	2,158	3,099	2,284
Fats and oils	946	1,006	1,196
Food and beverages	2,400	1,949	1,892
Industrial chemical products	1,859	1,419	1,702
Plastic materials	431	704	454
Textiles	1,612	1,816	1,451
Base metals	1,985	3,730	2,385
Electrical equipment	3,296	2,879	2,571
Transport equipment	2,762	2,240	3,123
Total (incl. others)	20,197	21,370	19,694

Exports (US $ million)	2004	2005	2006*
Crude petroleum	12,441	22,583	29,961
Refined petroleum products	148	242	295
Gas (per barrel)	30	30	260
Diamonds	790	1,092	1,140
Coffee	0.3	0.3	0.2
Total (incl. others)	13,474	24,109	31,817

*Estimates.

Total imports (US $ million): 2,079 in 1998; 3,109 in 1999; 3,040 in 2000; 3,179 in 2001; 3,760 in 2002; 5,480 in 2003; 5,832 in 2004; 8,353 in 2005; 10,776 in 2006 (estimate).

Sources: Banco Nacional de Angola; African Development Bank; IMF, *Angola: Selected Issues and Statistical Appendix* (October 2007).

PRINCIPAL TRADING PARTNERS
(US $ million)*

Imports c.i.f.	2004	2005	2006
Brazil	392	572	707
European Union	2,225	2,747	4,188
Portugal	920	1,093	1,677
Korea, Republic	1,996	1,669	2,063
South Africa	525	600	747
USA	654	1,021	1,705
Total (incl. others)	7,033	8,136	11,905

Exports f.o.b.	2004	2005	2006
China, People's Republic	4,121	5,982	9,937
European Union	1,107	2,966	2,484
Portugal	2	30	63
France	747	1,585	1,413
South Africa	261	296	366
USA	4,361	8,042	11,068
Total (incl. others)	11,541	20,194	28,664

*Data are compiled on the basis of reporting by Angola's trading partners.

Source: IMF, *Direction of Trade Statistics*.

Transport

GOODS TRANSPORT
(million metric tons)

	1999	2000	2001
Road	2,500.0	5,727.3	4,708.6
Railway	123.2	179.8	242.6
Water	2,009.0	5,981.0	3,045.6

Source: IRF, *World Road Statistics*.

ANGOLA

PASSENGER TRANSPORT
(million passenger-km)

	1999	2000	2001
Road	73,644.9	111,455.7	166,044.7
Railway	3,467.3	3,194.9	3,722.3

Source: IRF, *World Road Statistics*.

ROAD TRAFFIC
(motor vehicles in use at 31 December, estimates)

	1997	1998	1999
Passenger cars	103,400	107,100	117,200
Lorries and vans	107,600	110,500	118,300
Total	211,000	217,600	235,500

2000–2002: data assumed to be unchanged from 1999 (estimates).
Source: UN, *Statistical Yearbook*.

SHIPPING
Merchant Fleet
(registered at 31 December)

	2004	2005	2006
Number of vessels	125	128	129
Total displacement (grt)	47,937	53,869	56,391

Source: Lloyd's Register-Fairplay, *World Fleet Statistics*.

International Sea-borne Freight Traffic
(estimates, '000 metric tons)

	1989	1990	1991
Goods loaded	19,980	21,102	23,288
Goods unloaded	1,235	1,242	1,261

Source: UN Economic Commission for Africa, *African Statistical Yearbook*.

CIVIL AVIATION
(traffic on scheduled services)

	2001	2002	2003
Kilometres flown (million)	3	3	4
Passengers carried ('000)	101	101	99
Passenger-km (million)	413	417	417
Total ton-km (million)	87	87	92

Source: UN, *Statistical Yearbook*.

Tourism

FOREIGN TOURIST ARRIVALS

Country of origin	2005
Belgium	7,459
Brazil	11,053
France	17,658
Germany	3,399
Italy	5,250
Philippines	4,697
Portugal	29,527
Russia	2,788
South Africa	13,294
Spain	7,368
United Kingdom	11,157
USA	13,896
Total (incl. others)	209,956

Tourism receipts (US $ million, incl. passenger transport): 63 in 2003; 82 in 2004; 103 in 2005.
Source: World Tourism Organization.

Communications Media

	2004	2005	2006
Telephones ('000 main lines in use)	94.3	96.8	98.2
Mobile cellular telephones ('000 subscribers)	740.0	1,611.1	2,264.2
Personal computers ('000 in use)	27	n.a.	n.a.
Internet users ('000)	75	85	85

Source: International Telecommunication Union.

Radio receivers ('000 in use, 1999): 840 (Source: UN, *Statistical Yearbook*).

Daily newspapers (2004): 1 (average circulation 35,0000 copies) (Source: UNESCO Institute for Statistics).

Book production (1995): 22 titles (all books) (Source: UNESCO, *Statistical Yearbook*).

Education

(1997/98)

	Teachers	Pupils
Pre-primary	n.a.	214,867*
Primary	31,062†	1,342,116
Secondary:		
general	5,138‡	267,399
teacher training	280§	10,772*
vocational	286‡	12,116*
Higher	776	8,337

* Figure for school year 1991/92.
† Figure for school year 1990/91.
‡ Figure for school year 1989/90.
§ Figure for school year 1987/88.

Source: mainly UNESCO Institute for Statistics.

Adult literacy rate (UNESCO estimates): 67.4% (males 82.9%; females 54.2%) in 2001 (Source: UNESCO Institute for Statistics).

Directory

The Constitution

The MPLA regime adopted an independence Constitution for Angola in November 1975. It was amended in October 1976, September 1980, March 1991, April and August 1992, and November 1996. The main provisions of the 1975 Constitution, as amended, are summarized below:

BASIC PRINCIPLES

The Republic of Angola shall be a sovereign and independent state whose prime objective shall be to build a free and democratic society of peace, justice and social progress. It shall be a democratic state based on the rule of law, founded on national unity, the dignity of human beings, pluralism of expression and political organization, respecting and guaranteeing the basic rights and freedoms of persons, whether as individuals or as members of organized social groups. Sovereignty shall be vested in the people, which shall exercise political power through periodic universal suffrage.

The Republic of Angola shall be a unitary and indivisible state. Economic, social and cultural solidarity shall be promoted between all the Republic's regions for the common development of the entire nation and the elimination of regionalism and tribalism.

ANGOLA
Directory

Religion

The Republic shall be a secular state and there shall be complete separation of the State and religious institutions. All religions shall be respected.

The Economy

The economic system shall be based on the coexistence of diverse forms of property—public, private, mixed, co-operative and family—and all shall enjoy equal protection. The State shall protect foreign investment and foreign property, in accordance with the law. The fiscal system shall aim to satisfy the economic, social and administrative needs of the State and to ensure a fair distribution of income and wealth. Taxes may be created and abolished only by law, which shall determine applicability, rates, tax benefits and guarantees for taxpayers.

Education

The Republic shall vigorously combat illiteracy and obscurantism and shall promote the development of education and of a true national culture.

FUNDAMENTAL RIGHTS AND DUTIES

The State shall respect and protect the human person and human dignity. All citizens shall be equal before the law. They shall be subject to the same duties, without any distinction based on colour, race, ethnic group, sex, place of birth, religion, level of education, or economic or social status.

All citizens aged 18 years and over, other than those legally deprived of political and civil rights, shall have the right and duty to take an active part in public life, to vote and be elected to any state organ, and to discharge their mandates with full dedication to the cause of the Angolan nation. The law shall establish limitations in respect of non-political allegiance of soldiers on active service, judges and police forces, as well as the electoral incapacity of soldiers on active service and police forces.

Freedom of expression, of assembly, of demonstration, of association and of all other forms of expression shall be guaranteed. Groupings whose aims or activities are contrary to the constitutional order and penal laws, or that, even indirectly, pursue political objectives through organizations of a military, paramilitary or militarized nature shall be forbidden. Every citizen has the right to a defence if accused of a crime. Individual freedoms are guaranteed. Freedom of conscience and belief shall be inviolable. Work shall be the right and duty of all citizens. The State shall promote measures necessary to ensure the right of citizens to medical and health care, as well as assistance in childhood, motherhood, disability, old age, etc. It shall also promote access to education, culture and sports for all citizens.

STATE ORGANS

President of the Republic

The President of the Republic shall be the Head of State, Head of Government and Commander-in-Chief of the Angolan armed forces. The President of the Republic shall be elected directly by a secret universal ballot and shall have the following powers:

- to appoint and dismiss the Prime Minister, Ministers and other government officials determined by law
- to appoint the judges of the Supreme Court
- to preside over the Council of Ministers
- to declare war and make peace, following authorization by the Assembléia Nacional
- to sign, promulgate and publish the laws of the Assembléia Nacional, government decrees and statutory decrees
- to preside over the National Defence Council
- to decree a state of siege or state of emergency
- to announce the holding of general elections
- to issue pardons and commute sentences
- to perform all other duties provided for in the Constitution.

Assembléia Nacional

The Assembléia Nacional is the supreme state legislative body, to which the Government is responsible. The Assembléia shall be composed of 223 deputies, elected for a term of four years. The Assembléia shall convene in ordinary session twice yearly and in special session on the initiative of the President of the Assembléia, the Standing Commission of the Assembléia or of no less than one-third of its deputies. The Standing Commission shall be the organ of the Assembléia that represents and assumes its powers between sessions.

Government

The Government shall comprise the President of the Republic, the ministers and the secretaries of state, and other members whom the law shall indicate, and shall have the following functions:

- to organize and direct the implementation of state domestic and foreign policy, in accordance with the decision of the Assembléia Nacional and its Standing Commission
- to ensure national defence, the maintenance of internal order and security, and the protection of the rights of citizens
- to prepare the draft National Plan and General State Budget for approval by the Assembléia Nacional, and to organize, direct and control their execution.

The Council of Ministers shall be answerable to the Assembléia Nacional. In the exercise of its powers, the Council of Ministers shall issue decrees and resolutions.

Judiciary

The organization, composition and competence of the courts shall be established by law. Judges shall be independent in the discharge of their functions.

Local State Organs

The organs of state power at provincial level shall be the Provincial Assemblies and their executive bodies. The Provincial Assemblies shall work in close co-operation with social organizations and rely on the initiative and broad participation of citizens. The Provincial Assemblies shall elect commissions of deputies to perform permanent or specific tasks. The executive organs of Provincial Assemblies shall be the Provincial Governments, which shall be led by the Provincial Governors. The Provincial Governors shall be answerable to the President of the Republic, the Council of Ministers and the Provincial Assemblies.

National Defence

The State shall ensure national defence. The National Defence Council shall be presided over by the President of the Republic, and its composition shall be determined by law. The Angolan armed forces, as a state institution, shall be permanent, regular and non-partisan. Defence of the country shall be the right and the highest indeclinable duty of every citizen. Military service shall be compulsory. The forms in which it is fulfilled shall be defined by the law.

The Government

HEAD OF STATE

President: JOSÉ EDUARDO DOS SANTOS (assumed office 21 September 1979).

COUNCIL OF MINISTERS
(March 2008)

Prime Minister: FERNANDO (NANDO) DA PIEDADE DIAS DOS SANTOS.
Deputy Prime Minister: AGUINALDO JAIME.
Minister of National Defence: Gen. KUNDI PAIHAMA.
Minister of the Interior: Gen. ROBERTO LEAL RAMOS MONTEIRO (NGONGO).
Minister of Foreign Affairs: JOÃO BERNARDO DE MIRANDA.
Minister of Justice: MANUEL DA COSTA ARAGÃO.
Minister of Territorial Administration: VIRGÍLIO FERREIRA FONTES PEREIRA.
Minister of Planning: ANA AFONSO DIAS LOURENÇO.
Minister of Finance: JOSÉ PEDRO DE MORAIS.
Minister of Petroleum: DESIDÉRIO DA GRAÇA VERÍSSIMO DA COSTA.
Minister of Fisheries: SALOMÃO LUHETO XIRIMBIMBI.
Minister of Industry: JOAQUIM DUARTE DA COSTA DAVID.
Minister of Agriculture and Rural Development: AFONSO PEDRO CANGA.
Minister of Geology and Mines: MANUEL ANTÓNIO AFRICANO NETO.
Minister of Public Administration, Labour and Social Security: Dr ANTÓNIO DOMINGOS PITRA DA COSTA NETO.
Minister of Health: ANASTÁCIO ARTUR RUBEN SICATO.
Minister of Education: ANTÓNIO BURITY DA SILVA NETO.
Minister of Culture: BOAVENTURA CARDOSO.
Minister of Science and Technology: JOÃO BAPTISTA NGANDAJINA.
Minister of Transport: ANDRÉ LUÍS BRANDÃO.
Minister of Posts and Telecommunications: LICÍNIO TAVARES RIBEIRO.
Minister of Family and the Promotion of Women: CÂNDIDA CELESTE DA SILVA.
Minister of Former Combatants: PEDRO JOSÉ VAN-DÚNEM.
Minister of Youth and Sports: JOSÉ MARCOS BARRICA.
Minister of Public Works: FRANCISCO HIGINO CARNEIRO.

ANGOLA

Minister of Commerce: JOAQUIM EKUMA MUAFUMUA.
Minister of Hotels and Tourism: EDUARDO JONATÃO CHINGUNJI.
Minister of Social Assistance and Reintegration: JOÃO BAPTISTA KUSSUMUA.
Minister of Social Communication: MANUEL ANTÓNIO RABELAIS.
Minister of Energy and Water: JOSÉ MARIA BOTELHO DE VASCONCELOS.
Minister of Urban Affairs and the Environment: SITA JOSÉ DIAKUMPUNA.
Minister without Portfolio: ANTÓNIO BENTO BEMBE.

Ministers in the Office of the Presidency

Secretary of the Council of Ministers: JOAQUIM ANTÓNIO CARLOS DOS REIS.
Minister in the Presidency and Head of the Civil House: AMERICO MARIA DE MORAIS GARCIA.
Civil Affairs: JOSÉ DA COSTA DE SILVA LEITÃO.
Military Affairs: MANUEL HELDER DIAS.
General Secretariat: JOSÉ MATEUS DE ADELINO PEIXOTO.

MINISTRIES

Office of the President: Protocolo de Estado, Futungo de Belas, Luanda; tel. 222370150; fax 222370366.
Office of the Prime Minister: Luanda.
Office of the Deputy Prime Minister: Luanda; tel. 222371032; fax 222370842; e-mail ministro.adj1m@netangola.com.
Ministry of Agriculture and Rural Development: Av. Comandante Gika 2, CP 527, Luanda; tel. 222322694; fax 222320553; e-mail gabminander@netangola.com; internet www.angola-portal.ao/MINADER/.
Ministry of Commerce: Palácio de Vidro, Largo 4 de Fevereiro, CP 1242, Luanda; tel. 222310626; fax 222310335; e-mail gamaarte63@yahoo.com.br; internet www.angola-portal.ao/MINCO.
Ministry of Culture: Av. Comandante Gika, Luanda; tel. and fax 222323979; e-mail mincultura@mincultura.gv.ao; internet www.angola-portal.ao/MINCULT.
Ministry of Education: Av. Comandante Gika, CP 1281, Luanda; tel. 222320653; fax 222321592; internet www.angola-portal.ao/MED/.
Ministry of Energy and Water: Av. 4 de Fevereiro 105, CP 2229, Luanda; tel. 222393681; fax 222298687; internet www.angola-portal.ao/MINEA/.
Ministry of Family and the Promotion of Women: Palácio de Vidro, Largo 4 de Fevereiro, Luanda; tel. and fax 222311728; e-mail phildelgado@netangola.com; internet www.angola-portal.ao/MINFAMU.
Ministry of Finance: Av. 4 de Fevereiro 127, CP 592, Luanda; tel. and fax 222338548; e-mail cdi@minfin.gv.ao; internet www.angola-portal.ao/MINFIN/.
Ministry of Fisheries: Edif. Atlântico, Av. 4 de Fevereiro 30, CP 83, Luanda; tel. 222311420; fax 222310199; e-mail geral@angola-minpescas.com; internet www.angola-minpescas.com.
Ministry of Foreign Affairs: Rua Major Kanhangulo, Luanda; tel. 222397490; fax 222393246; e-mail webdesigner@mirex.ebonet.net; internet www.angola-portal.ao/MIREX/.
Ministry of Former Combatants: Av. Comandante Gika 2, CP 3828, Luanda; tel. 222323865; fax 222320876; internet www.angola-portal.ao/MACVG.
Ministry of Geology and Mines: Av. Comandante Gika, CP 1260, Luanda; tel. 222322766; fax 222321655; e-mail min.geominas@ebonet.net; internet www.angola-portal.ao/MGM.
Ministry of Health: Rua 17 de Setembro, CP 1201, Luanda; tel. and fax 222338052; internet www.angola-portal.ao/MINSA/.
Ministry of Hotels and Tourism: Palácio de Vidro, Largo 4 de Fevereiro, Luanda; tel. 222310899; fax 222310629; internet www.angola-portal.ao/MINHOTUR.
Ministry of Industry: Rua Cerqueira Lukoki 25, CP 594, Luanda; tel. 222390728; fax 222392400; e-mail gmi@ebonet.net; internet www.angola-portal.ao/MIND/.
Ministry of the Interior: Av. 4 de Fevereiro 204, CP 2723, Luanda; tel. 222391049; fax 222395133; internet www.angola-portal.ao/MININT.
Ministry of Justice: Rua 17 de Setembro, CP 2250, Luanda; tel. and fax 222339914; e-mail minijus20@hotmail.com; internet www.angola-portal.ao/MINJUS/.
Ministry of National Defence: Rua 17 de Setembro, Luanda; tel. 222337530; fax 222334276; e-mail minden1@ebonet.net; internet www.angola-portal.ao/MINDEN.
Ministry of Petroleum: Av. 4 de Fevereiro 105, CP 1279, Luanda; tel. and fax 222385847; internet www.angola-portal.ao/MINPET/.
Ministry of Planning: Largo do Palácio do Povo, Cidade Alta, Luanda; tel. 222390188; fax 222339586; e-mail lourenco@compuserve.com; internet www.angola-portal.ao/MINPLAN/.
Ministry of Posts and Telecommunications: Rua Major Kanhangulo, Luanda; tel. 222311004; fax 222330776; e-mail sg_mct@snet.co.ao; internet www.angola-portal.ao/MCT/.
Ministry of Public Administration, Labour and Social Security: Rua do 1° Congresso do MPLA 5, Luanda; tel. 222338940; fax 222399507; e-mail mapess@ebonet.net; internet www.mapess.gv.ao.
Ministry of Public Works: Rua Frederich Engels 92, Luanda; tel. 222336715; fax 222392539.
Ministry of Science and Technology: Ilha do Cabo, Luanda; tel. and fax 222309794; e-mail dgmk@ebonet.com; internet www.angola-portal.ao/MINCIT/.
Ministry of Social Assistance and Reintegration: Av. Hoji Ya Henda 117, CP 102, Luanda; tel. 222341460; fax 222342988; internet www.angola-portal.ao/MINARS.
Ministry of Social Communication: Av. Comandante Valódia, 1° e 2° andares, CP 2608, Luanda; tel. and fax 222443495; e-mail mcs@netangola.com; internet www.angola-portal.ao/MCS.
Ministry of Territorial Administration: Av. Comandante Gika 8, Luanda; tel. 222321729; fax 222323272; internet www.angola-portal.ao/MAT.
Ministry of Transport: Av. 4 de Fevereiro 42, CP 1250-C, Luanda; tel. 222311303; fax 222311582.
Ministry of Urban Affairs and the Environment: Luanda; tel. 222336717; internet www.angola-portal.ao/MINUA/.
Ministry of Youth and Sports: Av. Comandante Valódia 229, 4° andar, Luanda; tel. and fax 222321118; internet www.angola-portal.ao/MINJUD.

PROVINCIAL GOVERNORS
(December 2007)

All Provincial Governors are ex officio members of the Government.
Bengo: JORGE INOCENCIO DOMBOLO.
Benguela: DUMILDE DAS CHAGAS SIMÕES RANGEL.
Bié: JOSÉ AMARO TATI.
Cabinda: JOSÉ ANÍBAL LOPES ROCHA.
Cuando Cubango: JORGE BIWANGO.
Cunene: PEDRO MUTINDE.
Huambo: AGOSTINHO NJAKA.
Huila: FRANCISCO JOSÉ RAMOS DA CRUZ.
Kwanza-Norte: HENRIQUE ANDRÉ JÚNIOR.
Kwanza-Sul: SERAFIM MARIA DO PRADO.
Luanda: JOB CASTELO CAPAPINHA.
Lunda-Norte: MANUEL FRANCISCO GOMES MAIATO.
Lunda-Sul: FRANCISCO TSCHIWISSA.
Malange: CRISTOVÃO DA CUNHA.
Moxico: JOÃO ERNESTO DOS SANTOS.
Namibe: ÁLVARO MANUEL DE BOAVIDA NETO.
Uíge: ANTÓNIO BENTO KANGULO.
Zaire: PEDRO SEBASTIÃO.

President and Legislature

PRESIDENT*

Presidential Election, 29 and 30 September 1992

Candidate	Votes	% of votes
José Eduardo dos Santos (MPLA)	1,953,335	49.57
Dr Jonas Malheiro Savimbi (UNITA)	1,579,298	40.07
António Alberto Neto (PDA)	85,249	2.16
Holden Roberto (FNLA)	83,135	2.11
Honorato Lando (PDLA)	75,789	1.92
Luís dos Passos (PRD)	59,121	1.47
Bengui Pedro João (PSD)	38,243	0.97
Simão Cacete (FPD)	26,385	0.67
Daniel Júlio Chipenda (Independent)	20,646	0.52
Anália de Victória Pereira (PLD)	11,475	0.29
Rui de Victória Pereira (PRA)	9,208	0.23
Total	**3,940,884**	**100.00**

*Under the terms of the electoral law, a second round of the presidential election was required to take place in order to determine which of the two leading candidates from the first round would

ANGOLA

be elected. A resumption of hostilities between UNITA and government forces prevented a second round from taking place. The electoral process was to resume only when the provisions of the Estoril peace agreement, concluded in May 1991, had been fulfilled. However, provision in the Lusaka peace accord of November 1994 for the second round of the presidential election was not pursued.

LEGISLATURE

Assembléia Nacional: CP 1204, Luanda; tel. 222334021; fax 222331118; e-mail assembleianacional@parlamento.ebonet.net; internet www.parlamento.ao.

President: ROBERTO DE ALMEIDA.

General Election, 29 and 30 September 1992

Party	Votes	% of votes	Seats*
MPLA	2,124,126	53.74	129
UNITA	1,347,636	34.10	70
FNLA	94,742	2.40	5
PLD	94,269	2.39	3
PRS	89,875	2.27	6
PRD	35,293	0.89	1
AD Coalition	34,166	0.86	1
PSD	33,088	0.84	1
PAJOCA	13,924	0.35	1
FDA	12,038	0.30	1
PDP—ANA	10,620	0.27	1
PNDA	10,281	0.26	1
CNDA	10,237	0.26	—
PSDA	19,217	0.26	—
PAI	9,007	0.23	—
PDLA	8,025	0.20	—
PDA	8,014	0.20	—
PRA	6,719	0.17	—
Total	**3,952,277**	**100.00**	**220**

* According to the Constitution, the total number of seats in the Assembléia Nacional is 223. On the decision of the National Electoral Council, however, elections to fill three seats reserved for Angolans resident abroad were abandoned.

Election Commission

Comissão Nacional Eleitoral (CNE): Av. Amílcar Cabral, 30–31, Luanda; tel. 222393825; e-mail info@cne.gv.ao; internet www.cne.gv.ao; f. 2005; government agency; Pres. ANTÓNIO CAETANO DE SOUSA.

Political Organizations

In 2007 there were over 130 political parties.

Aliança Democrática de Angola: Leader SIMBA DA COSTA.

Angolan Democratic Coalition (AD Coalition): Pres. EVIDOR QUIELA (acting).

Convenção Nacional Democrata de Angola (CNDA): mem. of POC; Leader PAULINO PINTO JOÃO.

Frente para a Democracia (FpD): Sec.-Gen. LUIS FERNANDES DO NASCIMENTO.

Frente de Libertação do Enclave de Cabinda (FLEC): f. 1963; comprises several factions, claiming total forces of c. 5,000 guerrillas, seeking the secession of Cabinda province; in Sept. 2004 the Frente de Libertação do Enclave de Cabinda—Forças Armadas Cabindesas (FLEC—FAC) and the Frente de Libertação do Enclave de Cabinda—Renovada (FLEC—R) merged under the above name; Leader N'ZITA HENRIQUES TIAGO; Sec.-Gen. ANTÓNIO BENTO BEMBE.

Frente de Libertação do Enclave de Cabinda—Conselho Superior Alargado (FLEC—CSA): f. 2004; political wing of FLEC; supports Cabindan independence through negotiation; Leader LIBERAL NUNO.

Frente Nacional de Libertação de Angola (FNLA): Av. Hoji Va Henda (ex Av. do Brasil) 91/306, CP 151, Luanda; tel. and fax 222344638; e-mail fnla@fnla-angola.org; internet www.fnla-angola.org; f. 1962; Pres. LUCAS NGONDA; Interim Sec.-Gen. NYMI A-SIMBI.

Movimento de Defesa dos Interesses de Angola—Partido de Consciência Nacional (MDIA—PCN) (Movement for the Defence of Angolan Interests—National Conscience Party): f. 1991; Pres. FILIPE PINTO SUAMINA; Sec.-Gen. AFONSO MAYTUKA.

Movimento Popular de Libertação de Angola (MPLA) (People's Movement for the Liberation of Angola): Luanda; e-mail mpla@ebonet.net; internet www2.ebonet.net/MPLA; f. 1956; in 1961–74 conducted guerrilla operations against Portuguese rule; governing party since 1975; known as Movimento Popular de Libertação de Angola—Partido do Trabalho (MPLA—PT) (People's Movement for the Liberation of Angola—Workers' Party) 1977–92; in Dec. 1990 replaced Marxist-Leninist ideology with commitment to 'democratic socialism'; absorbed the Fórum Democrático Angolano (FDA) in 2002; Chair. JOSÉ EDUARDO DOS SANTOS; Sec.-Gen. JULIÃO MATEUS PAULO.

Nova Democracia—União Eleitoral: f. 2006; a splinter group from the POC comprising the Frente Unida para Liberdade Democratica (FULD), the Movimento para Democracia de Angola (MPDA), the Partido Angolano Republicano (PAR), the Partido Social Independente de Angola (PSIA), the Partido Socialista Liberal (PSL) and the União Nacional para Democracia (UND); Sec.-Gen. QUINTINO DE MOREIRA.

Partido de Aliança de Juventude, Operários e Camponêses de Angola (PAJOCA) (Angolan Youth, Workers' and Peasants' Alliance Party): Pres. ALEXANDRE SEBASTIÃO ANDRÉ.

Partido Angolano Independente (PAI): Leader ADRIANO PARREIRA.

Partido de Apoio Democrático e Progresso de Angola (PADEPA): Luanda; f. 1995; Chair. JOSÉ CARLOS LEITÃO.

Partido Democrático Angolano (PDA): Leader ANTÓNIO ALBERTO NETO.

Partido Democrático Liberal de Angola (PDLA): Leader HONORATO LANDO.

Partido Democrático para o Progresso—Aliança Nacional de Angola (PDP—ANA): Interim Leader and Pres. SEDIANGANI MBIMBI.

Partido Democrático para o Progresso Social (PDPS): f. by members of the PRS; Pres. PAULO LUSENQUENY.

Partido Liberal Democrático (PLD): Rua Manuel Fernando Caldeira, 3c andar, Esquerda Município de Ingombotas, CP 10199, Luanda; tel. 222396968; fax 222395966; e-mail pld@ebonet.net; Leader ANÁLIA DE VICTÓRIA PEREIRA.

Partido Nacional Democrata de Angola (PNDA): Sec.-Gen. PEDRO JOÃO ANTÓNIO.

Partido Reformador de Angola (PRA): Leader RUI DE VICTÓRIA PEREIRA.

Partido Renovador Democrático (PRD): Leader LUÍS DOS PASSOS.

Partido Renovador Social (PRS): Pres. EDUARDO KWANGANA; Sec.-Gen. JOÃO BAPTISTA NGANDAJINA.

Partido Social Democrata (PSD): Leader BENGUI PEDRO JOÃO.

Partido Social Democrata de Angola (PSDA): Leader ANDRÉ MILTON KILANDONOCO.

Partidos de Oposição Civil (POC): Luanda; f. 2005; coalition comprising 13 small parties; formed to contest presidential and legislative elections; six parties left the coalition in December 2006 to form the Nova Democracia—União Eleitoral; Exec. Sec. MANUEL FERNANDES; Pres. PAULINO PINTO JOÃO.

Tendência de Reflexão Democrática (TRD): Luanda; Leader PAULO TJIPILIKA.

União Democrática Nacional de Angola (UDNA): Largo Teixeira de Pascoais 14/15, Vila Alice, Luanda; f. 1980s as underground movement; recognized by Supreme Court in 1994; Pres. FRANCISCO J. PEDRO KIZADILAMBA.

União Nacional para a Independência Total de Angola (UNITA): internet www.kwacha.net; f. 1966 to secure independence from Portugal; to secure independence from Portugal; later received Portuguese support to oppose the MPLA; UNITA and the Frente Nacional de Libertação de Angola conducted guerrilla campaign against the MPLA Govt with aid from some Western countries, 1975–76; supported by South Africa until 1984 and in 1987–88, and by USA after 1986; obtained legal status in March 1998, but hostilities between govt and UNITA forces resumed later that year; signed cease-fire agreement with the MPLA Govt in April 2002; joined the Govt in Dec. 2002; support drawn mainly from Ovimbundu ethnic group; Pres. ISAÍAS SAMAKUVA.

Other parties include the **Partido Angolano para Unidade Democrática e Progresso (PAUPD)**.

The **Fórum Cabindês para o Diálogo (FCD)** was formed in 2004 to provide a united platform for Cabindan separatists and civil-society leaders with which to negotiate with the Government. Its leader was ANTÓNIO BENTO BEMBE.

ANGOLA

Diplomatic Representation

EMBASSIES IN ANGOLA

Algeria: Rua Edif. Siccal, Rainha Ginga, CP 1389, Luanda; tel. 222332881; fax 222334785; e-mail ambalg@netangola.com; Ambassador TOUFIK DAHMANI.

Belgium: Av. 4 de Fevereiro 93, 3° andar, CP 1203, Luanda; tel. 222336437; fax 222336438; e-mail luanda@diplobel.org; internet www.diplomatie.be/luanda; Ambassador HUBERT COOREMAN.

Brazil: Rua Houari Boumedienne 132, Miramar, CP 5428, Luanda; tel. 222441307; fax 222444913; e-mail emb.bras@ebonet.net; Ambassador MARCELO DA SILVA VASCONCELOS.

Bulgaria: Rua Fernão Mendes Pinto 35/37, Alvalade, CP 2260, Luanda; tel. 222324213; fax 222321010; e-mail bulgemb@ebonet.net; Ambassador ELENKO ANDREEV.

Cape Verde: Rua Oliveira Martins 3, Luanda; tel. 222321765; fax 222320832; Ambassador DOMINGOS MASCARENHAS.

China, People's Republic: Rua Houari Boumedienne 196, Miramar, CP 52, Luanda; tel. 222341683; fax 222344185; e-mail shiguan@netangola.com; Ambassador ZHANG BEISAN.

Congo, Democratic Republic: Rua Cesário Verde 24, Luanda; tel. 222361953; Ambassador BOLANGAMBE YONGO.

Congo, Republic: Av. 4 de Fevereiro 3, Luanda; tel. 222310293; Ambassador CHRISTIAN GILBERT BEMBET.

Côte d'Ivoire: Rua Eng Armindo de Andrade 75, Miramar, CP 432, Luanda; tel. 222440878; fax 222440907; e-mail aciao@ambaci-angola.org; internet www.ambaci-angola.org; Ambassador ANNE GNAHOURET TATRET.

Cuba: Rua Che Guevara 42, Ingombotas, Luanda; tel. 222336749; fax 222339165; e-mail embcuba.ang@ebonet.net; Ambassador PEDRO ROSS LEAL.

Czech Republic: Rua Companhia de Jesus 43–45, Miramar, Luanda; tel. 222430646; fax 222447676; e-mail luanda@embassy.mzv.cz; Ambassador VLADIMÍR VÁLKY.

Egypt: Rua Comandante Stona 247, Alvalade, CP 3704, Luanda; tel. 222321590; fax 222323285; e-mail embegipto@ebonet.net; Ambassador BELAL ABD EL-WAHED EL-MASRY.

Equatorial Guinea: Luanda; Ambassador Gen. EUSTAQUIO NZENG ESONO.

France: Rua Reverendo Pedro Agostinho Neto 31–33, CP 584, Luanda; tel. 222334841; fax 222391949; e-mail cad.luanda-amba@diplomatie.gouv.fr; internet www.ambafrance-ao.org; Ambassador FRANCIS BLONDET.

Gabon: Av. 4 de Fevereiro 95, Luanda; tel. 222372614; Ambassador RAPHAËL NKASSA-NZOGHO.

Germany: Av. 4 de Fevereiro 120, CP 1295, Luanda; tel. 222334516; fax 222399269; e-mail germanembassy.luanda@ebonet.net; internet www.luanda.diplo.de; Ambassador Dr INGO WINKELMANN.

Ghana: Rua Cirilo da Conceição E Silva 5, 1A, CP 1012, Luanda; tel. 222338239; fax 222338235; e-mail embassyghana@ebonet.net; Ambassador KWASI BAAH-BOAKYE.

Guinea: Luanda.

Holy See: Rua Luther King 123, CP 1030, Luanda; tel. 222330532; fax 222332378; e-mail nunc.nuncio@snet.co.ao; Apostolic Nuncio Most Rev. GIOVANNI ANGELO BECCIU (Titular Archbishop of Roselle).

India: Rua Marquês das Minas 18A, Macalusso, CP 6040, Luanda; tel. 222392281; fax 222371094; e-mail indembluanda@ebonet.net; Ambassador (vacant).

Israel: Edif. Siccal, 11° andar, Rua Rainha Ginga, Luanda; tel. 222395295; fax 222396366; e-mail info@luanda.mfa.gov.il; internet luanda.mfa.gov.il; Ambassador BAHIJ MANSOUR.

Italy: Rua Americo Boavida 49–51, Ingombotas, CP 6220, Luanda; tel. 222331245; fax 222333743; e-mail segreteria.luanda@esteri.it; internet www.ambluanda.esteri.it; Ambassador TORQUATO CARDILLI.

Japan: Rua Armindo de Andrade 183–185, Miramar, Luanda; tel. 222442007; fax 222449888; Chargé d'affaires a.i. HIROAKI SANO.

Mali: Rua Padre Manuel Pombo 81, Maianga, Luanda; e-mail ambamali@netangola.com; Ambassador FAROUK CAMARA.

Morocco: Edif. Siccal, 10° andar, Rua Rainha Ginga, Luanda; tel. 222393708; fax 222338847; e-mail aluanda@supernet.ao; Ambassador ABDELLAH AIT EL HAJ.

Mozambique: Rua Amílcar Cabral 102, R/C CP 12117, Luanda; tel. and fax 222330811; fax 222332883; e-mail embamoc.Ida@netangola.com; Ambassador ANTÓNIO MATOSE.

Namibia: Rua dos Coqueiros 37, CP 953, Luanda; tel. 222395483; fax 222339234; e-mail embnam@netangola.com; Ambassador LINEEKELA MBOTI.

Netherlands: Edif. Secil, 6°, Av. 4 de Fevereiro 42, CP 3624, Luanda; tel. 222310686; fax 222310966; e-mail lua@minbuza.nl; internet mfa.nl/lua-en; Ambassador JAN GIJS SCHOUTEN.

Nigeria: Rua Houari Boumedienne 120, Miramar, CP 479, Luanda; tel. and fax 222340089; Ambassador ADAMU UMAR.

Norway: Rua de Benguela 17, Bairro Patrice Lumumba, CP 3835, Luanda; tel. 222449936; fax 222449248; e-mail emb.luanda@mfa.no; internet www.noruega.ao; Ambassador ARILD R. ØYEN.

Poland: Rua Comandante N'zagi 21–23, Alvalade, CP 1340, Luanda; tel. 222323088; fax 222323086; e-mail embpol@netangola.com; internet www.luanda.polemb.net; Chargé d'affaires a.i. PIOTR MYŚLIWIEC.

Portugal: Av. de Portugal 50, CP 1346, Luanda; tel. 222333027; fax 222390392; e-mail secretariado.emb@netcabo.co.ao; Ambassador FRANCISCO RIBEIRO TELLES.

Romania: Rua Ramalho Ortigão 30, Alvalade, Luanda; tel. and fax 222321076; e-mail ambromania@ebonet.net; Chargé d'affaires a.i. IACOB PRADA.

Russia: Rua Houari Boumedienne 170, CP 3141, Luanda; tel. 222445028; fax 222445320; e-mail rusemb@netangola.com; Ambassador ANDREI KEMARSKY.

São Tomé and Príncipe: Rua Armindo de Andrade 173–175, Luanda; tel. 222345677; Ambassador ARMINDO BRITO FERNANDES.

Serbia: Rua Comandante N'zagi 25–27, Alvalade, CP 3278, Luanda; tel. 222321421; fax 222321724; e-mail yugoemb@snet.co.ao; Ambassador DOBRIVOJ KACANSKI.

South Africa: Edif. Maianga, 1° e 2° andar, Rua Kwamme Nkrumah 31, Largo da Maianga, CP 6212, Luanda; tel. 222330593; fax 222398730; e-mail saemb.ang@netangola.com; internet www.sambangola.info; Ambassador THEMBA M. N. KUBHEKA.

Spain: Av. 4 de Fevereiro 95, 1° andar, CP 3061, Luanda; tel. 222391166; fax 222332884; e-mail emb.luanda@mae.es; Ambassador FRANCISCO JAVIER VALLAURE DE ACHA.

Sweden: Rua Garcia Neto 9, CP 1130, Luanda; tel. 222440706; fax 222443460; e-mail Erik.Aberg@foreign.ministry.se; internet www.swedenabroad.com/luanda; Ambassador ERIK ABERG.

Ukraine: Rua Companhia de Jesus 35, Miramar, Luanda; tel. 222447492; fax 222448467; e-mail emb_ao@mfa.gov.ua; Chargé d'affaires VOLODYMYR M. KOKHNO.

United Kingdom: Rua Diogo Cão 4, CP 1244, Luanda; tel. 222334582; fax 222333331; e-mail ppa.luanda@fco.gov.uk; internet www.britishembassy.gov.uk/angola; Ambassador RALPH PUBLICOVER.

USA: Rua Houari Boumedienne 32, Miramar, CP 6468, Luanda; tel. 222641000; fax 222641232; e-mail econusembassyluanda@yahoo.com; internet luanda.usembassy.gov; Ambassador DAN MOZENA.

Viet Nam: Rua Alexandre Peres 4, Maianga, CP 1774, Luanda; tel. 222390684; fax 222390369; e-mail dsqvnangola@netangola.com; Ambassador NGUYEN DINH.

Zambia: Rua Rei Katyavala 106–108, CP 1496, Luanda; tel. 222331145; Ambassador MARINA NSINGO.

Zimbabwe: Edif. Secil, Av. 4 de Fevereiro 42, CP 428, Luanda; tel. and fax 222311528; e-mail embzimbabwe@ebonet.net; Ambassador JAMES MANZOU.

Judicial System

There is a Supreme Court and Court of Appeal in Luanda. There are also civil, criminal and military courts.

Supreme Court: Rua 17 de Setembro, Luanda; fax 222335411; Pres. Dr CRISTIANO ANDRÉ.

Office of the Attorney-General: Rua 17 de Setembro, Luanda; tel. 222333171; fax 222333172; Attorney-General AUGUSTO DA COSTA CARNEIRO.

Religion

In 1998 it was estimated that 47% of the population followed indigenous beliefs, with 53% professing to be Christians, mainly Roman Catholic. There is a small Muslim community, which comprises less than 1% of the population.

CHRISTIANITY

In early 2005 some 85 Christian denominations were registered in Angola.

Conselho de Igrejas Cristãs em Angola (CICA) (Council of Christian Churches in Angola): Rua 15 24, Bairro Cassenda, CP 1301/1659, Luanda; tel. 222354838; fax 222356144; e-mail info@cicaangola.org; internet www.cicaangola.org; f. 1977 as Conselho Angolano de Igrejas Evangélicas; 14 mem. churches; five assoc.

mems; one observer; Pres. Rev. ALVARO RODRIGUES; Gen. Sec. Rev. LUÍS NGUIMBI.

Protestant Churches

Evangelical Congregational Church in Angola (Igreja Evangélica Congregacional em Angola—IECA): CP 1552, Luanda; tel. 222355108; fax 222350868; e-mail iecageral@snet.co.ao; f. 1880; 750,000 mems; Gen. Sec. Rev. AUGUSTO CHIPESSE.

Evangelical Pentecostal Church of Angola (Missão Evangélica Pentecostal de Angola): CP 219, Porto Amboim; 13,600 mems; Sec. Rev. JOSÉ DOMINGOS CAETANO.

United Evangelical Church of Angola (Igreja Evangélica Unida de Angola): CP 122, Uíge; 11,000 mems; Gen. Sec. Rev. A. L. DOMINGOS.

Other active denominations include the African Apostolic Church, the Church of Apostolic Faith in Angola, the Church of Our Lord Jesus Christ in the World, the Evangelical Baptist Church, the Evangelical Church in Angola, the Evangelical Church of the Apostles of Jerusalem, the Evangelical Reformed Church of Angola, the Kimbanguist Church in Angola, the Maná Church and the United Methodist Church.

The Roman Catholic Church

Angola comprises three archdioceses and 13 dioceses. At 31 December 2005 there were 11,503,140 adherents in the country, equivalent to 52.7% of the population.

Bishops' Conference

Conferência Episcopal de Angola e São Tomé (CEAST), CP 3579, Luanda; tel. 222443686; fax 222445504; e-mail ceast@snet.co.ao. f. 1967; Pres. Most Rev. DAMIÃO ANTÓNIO FRANKLIN (Archbishop of Luanda).

Archbishop of Huambo: Most Rev. JOSÉ DE QUEIRÓS ALVES, Arcebispado, CP 10, Huambo; tel. 241220130; fax 241220133; e-mail bispado-huambo@huambo.angonet.org.

Archbishop of Luanda: Most Rev. DAMIÃO ANTÓNIO FRANKLIN, Arcebispado, Largo do Palácio 9, CP 87, 1230-C, Luanda; tel. 222331481; fax 222334433; e-mail spastoral@snet.co.ao.

Archbishop of Lubango: Most Rev. ZACARIAS KAMWENHO, Arcebispado, CP 231, Lubango; tel. and fax 261230140; e-mail arquidiocese.lubango@netangola.com.

The Press

A free press was reinstituted in 1991, after 15 years of government control. In 2004 there were seven privately owned newspapers in Angola.

DAILIES

Diário da República: CP 1306, Luanda; official govt bulletin.

O Jornal de Angola: Rua Rainha Ginga 18–24, CP 1312, Luanda; tel. 222335531; fax 222333342; e-mail jornaldeangola@nexus.ao; internet www.jornaldeangola.com; f. 1975; state-owned; Dir JOSÉ RIBEIRO; mornings and Sun.; circ. 41,000.

PERIODICALS

Actual: Rua Fernando Pessoa 103, Vila Alice, CP 6959, Luanda; tel. and fax 222332116; e-mail actuals@hotmail.com; f. 2003; weekly; Editor JOAQUIM ALVES.

Agora: Rua Commandante Valódia 59, 2° andar, CP 24, Luanda; tel. and fax 222344680; e-mail agora-as@ebonet.net; f. 1996; weekly; Dir AGUIAR DOS SANTOS.

Angolense: Rua Cónego Manuel das Neves 83B, Luanda; tel. 222341501; fax 222340549; e-mail angolense@netangola.com; f. 1998; weekly; Dir AMÉRICO GONÇALVES.

O Apostolado: Rua Comandante Bula 118, São Paulo, CP 3579, Luanda; tel. 222432641; fax 222440628; e-mail direccao@apostolado .info; internet www.apostolado.info; current and religious affairs; Dir MAURÍCIO AGOSTINHO CAMUTO.

A Capital: Luanda; f. 2003; weekly; Dir FRANCISCO TANDALA.

Comércio Actualidade: Rua da Missão 81, CP 6375, Luanda; tel. 222334060; fax 222392216; e-mail actualidade@ebonet.net; f. 1993; weekly; Editor VICTOR ALEIXO.

Eme: Luanda; tel. 222321130; f. 1996; fortnightly; MPLA publ.; Dir FERNANDO FATI.

Folha 8: Rua Conselheiro Júlio de Vilhena 24, 5° andar, CP 6527, Luanda; tel. 222391943; fax 222392289; e-mail folha8@ebonet.net; f. 1994; two a week; Dir WILLIAM TONET.

Independente: Rua Gracia da Horta 9, Luanda; tel. and fax 222343968; weekly; Dir PEDRO NARCISO.

Jornal dos Desportos: Rua Rainha Ginga 18–24, CP 1312, Luanda; tel. 222335531; fax 222335481; e-mail jornaldosdesportos@hotmail .com; internet www.jornaldosdesportos.com; f. 1994; bi-weekly; Dir LUIS FERNANDO; Editorial Dir POLICARPO DA ROSA; circ. 5,000.

Lavra & Oficina: CP 2767-C, Luanda; tel. 222322421; fax 222323205; e-mail uea@uea-angola.org; internet www.uea-angola .org; f. 1975; journal of the União dos Escritores Angolanos (Union of Angolan Writers); monthly; circ. 5,000.

A Palavra: Luanda; f. 2003; weekly.

Semanário Angolense: Rua António Feliciano de Castilho 103, Luanda; tel. 222264915; fax 222263506; e-mail info@ semanarioangolense.com; internet www.semanarioangolense.net; f. 2003; independent; current affairs; Dir FELIZBERTO GRAÇA CAMPOS; weekly.

Tempos Novos: Av. Combatentes 244, 2° andar, CP 16088, Luanda; tel. and fax 222349534; f. 1995.

NEWS AGENCIES

In early 2006 legislation was passed by the Assembléia Nacional ending the governmental monopoly over news agencies.

Agência Angola Press (ANGOP): Rua Rei Katyavala 120, CP 2181, Luanda; tel. 222447343; fax 222447342; e-mail angop@ netangola.com; internet www.angolapress-angop.ao; f. 1975; Dir-Gen. MANUEL DA CONCEIÇÃO.

Centro de Imprensa Anibal de Melo (CIAM): Rua Cerqueira Lukoki 124, CP 2805, Luanda; tel. 222393341; fax 222393445; govt press centre; Dir Dr OLYMPIO DE SOUSA E SILVA.

Publishers

Chá de Caxinde: Av. do 1° Congresso do MPLA 20–24, CP 5958, Luanda; tel. 222336020; fax 222332876; e-mail chacaxinde@ebonet .net; f. 1999; Dir JAQUES ARLINDO DOS SANTOS.

Editorial Kilombelombe: Luanda; Dir MATEUS VOLÓDIA.

Editorial Nzila: Rua Comandante Valódia 1, ao Largo do Kinaxixi, Luanda; tel. 222447137; e-mail edinzila@hotmail.com.

Plural Editores: Rua Lucrécia Paim 16A (ex-Marquês de Minas), Bairro do Maculusso, Luanda; e-mail plural@pluraleditores.co.ao; internet www.pluraleditores.co.ao; f. 2005; 49% owned by Porto Editora (Portugal); technical and educational.

Ponto Um Indústria Gráfica: Rua Sebastião Desta Vez 55, Luanda; tel. 222448315; fax 222449424.

União dos Escritores Angolanos (UEA): Luanda; tel. and fax 222323205; e-mail uea@uea-angola.org; internet www.uea-angola .org.

GOVERNMENT PUBLISHING HOUSE

Imprensa Nacional, UEE: CP 1306, Luanda; f. 1845; Gen. Man. ANA MARÍA SOUSA E SILVA.

Broadcasting and Communications

TELECOMMUNICATIONS

Angola Telecom (AT): Rua das Quipacas 186, CP 625, Luanda; tel. 222311889; fax 222311288; e-mail Sec_CA@angolatelecom.com; internet www.angolatelecom.com; state telecommunications co; Dir-Gen. JOÃO AVELINO AUGUSTO MANUEL.

Movicel Telecomunicações, Lda: Rua Mãe Isabel 1, Luanda; tel. 222692000; fax 222692090; internet www.movicel.co.ao; f. 2002; mobile cellular telephone operator; Chair. MANUEL AVELINO; Exec. Dir MICHAEL ROUBICEK.

Mundo StarTel: Rua Ndunduma 188, São Paulo, Município de Sambizanga, Luanda; tel. 222432417; e-mail mundostartel@ netangola.com; 44% owned by Telecom Namibia.

Nexus Telecomunicações e Serviços SARL: Rua dos Enganos 1, 1° andar, Luanda; tel. 228740041; fax 228740741; e-mail nexus@ nexus.ao; internet www.nexus.ao; began operations mid-2004; fixed-line operator.

Unitel SARL: Sede Miramar, Rua Marechal Bróz Tito 77–79, Ingombotas, Luanda; tel. 222199100; fax 222447783; e-mail unitel@unitel.co.ao; internet www.unitel.co.ao; f. 1998; 25% owned by Portugal Telecom; private mobile telephone operator; Dir-Gen. NICOLAU JORGE NETO.

Regulatory Authority

Instituto Angolano das Comunicações (INACOM): Av. de Portugal 92, 7° andar, CP 1459, Luanda; tel. 222338352; fax 222339256; e-mail inacom.dg@netangola.com; internet www .inacom.og.ao; f. 1999; monitoring and regulatory authority; Dir-Gen. JOÃO BEIRÃO.

BROADCASTING
Radio

A decree on the regulation of radio broadcasting was approved in 1997. Since that time private operators had reportedly experienced difficulty in gaining permission to broadcast; although four private stations were operating in Luanda in the mid-2000s.

Rádio Nacional de Angola: Rua Comandante Gika, CP 1329, Luanda; tel. 222320192; fax 222324647; e-mail rna.dg@netangola.com; internet www.rna.ao; state-controlled; operates Canal A, Radio 5, Radio FM Estério, Radio Luanda and Radio N'gola Yetu; broadcasts in Portuguese, English, French, Spanish and vernacular languages (Chokwe, Kikongo, Kimbundu, Kwanyama, Fiote, Ngangela, Luvale, Songu, Umbundu); Dir-Gen. ALBERTO DE SOUSA.

Luanda Antena Comercial (LAC): Rua Luther King 5, CP 3521, Luanda; tel. 222394989; fax 222396229; e-mail lac@ebonet.net; internet www.nexus.ao/lac; popular music.

Radio CEFOJOR: Rua Luther King 123/4, Luanda; tel. 222336140; e-mail cefojor@hotmail.com; f. 2003; commercial station, provides journalistic training; Dir-Gen. JOAQUIM PAULO DA CONCEIÇÃO.

Rádio Ecclésia—Emissora Católica de Angola: Rua Comandante Bula 118, São Paulo, CP 3579, Luanda; tel. 222443041; fax 222443093; e-mail recclesia@recclesia.org; internet www.recclesia.org; f. 1955; broadcasts mainly restricted to Luanda; coverage of politics and current affairs; Dir-Gen. JOSÉ PAULO.

Radio Escola: Luanda; educational.

Rádio Morena Comercial, Lda: Rua Comandante Kassanji, CP 537, Benguela; tel. 272232525; fax 272234242.

The Voice of America (internet www.ebonet.net/voa) also broadcasts from Luanda.

Television

In early 2006 legislation was passed by the Assembléia Nacional ending the Government's monopoly over television and simplifying the radio licensing process. A digital television system, TV Cabo Angola, began broadcasting in early 2006.

Televisão Pública de Angola (TPA): Rua Ho Chi Minh, CP 2604, Luanda; tel. 222320272; fax 222323027; e-mail carlos.cunha@netangola.com; internet www.tpa.ao; f. 1976; state-controlled; 2 channels; Man. Dir CARLOS CUNHA.

Finance

(cap. = capital; res = reserves; dep. = deposits; m. = million; brs = branches; amounts in kwanza (equivalent to 1m. readjusted kwanza), unless otherwise indicated)

BANKING

All banks were nationalized in 1975. In 1995 the Government authorized the formation of private banks. In 2006 there were 12 commercial banks in Angola.

Central Bank

Banco Nacional de Angola: Av. 4 de Fevereiro 151, CP 1243, Luanda; tel. 222399125; fax 222390579; e-mail bna.cri@ebonet.net; internet www.bna.ao; f. 1976; bank of issue; Gov. Dr AMADEU DE JESÚS CASTELHANO MAURÍCIO; 6 brs.

Commercial Banks

Banco Comercial Angolano (BCA): Av. Comandante Valódia 83A, CP 6900, Luanda; tel. 222349548; fax 222349516; e-mail bca@snet.co.ao; f. 1997; 50% owned by Absa; cap. 0.9m., res 347.4m., dep. 1,799.3m. (Dec. 2002); Pres. Dr BENVINDO RAFAEL PITRA; 4 brs (2005).

Banco de Fomento Angola—BFA: Rua Amílcar Cabral 58, Luanda; tel. 222638900; fax 222638925; internet www.bfa.ao; f. 1993 as Banco Fomento Exterior; name changed to above in 2001; 100% owned by Banco BPI, SA, Portugal; cap. 3,522.0m., res 2,613.0m., dep. 75,168.4m. (Dec. 2004); CEO EMIDIO PINHEIRO; 38 brs (2005).

Banco Internacional de Crédito (BIC): Rua Cerqueira Lukoki 78–80, Luanda; tel. 222391526; fax 222391407; e-mail bancobic@bancobic.ao; internet www.bancobic.ao; f. 2005; 25% owned by Américo Amorim, Portugal; Chair. FERNANDO MENDES TELES.

Banco de Poupança e Crédito (BPC): Largo Saydi Mingas, CP 1343, Luanda; tel. 222390841; fax 222372529; e-mail bpc@bpc.ao; internet www.bpc.ao; f. 1956 as Banco Comercial de Angola; 100% state-owned; undergoing privatization in 2006; cap. 1,304.0m., res 2,574.3m., dep. 64,072.4m. (Dec. 2004); Chair. PAIXÃO ANTÓNIO JÚNIOR; brs throughout Angola.

Banco Regional do Keve SARL: Edif. Robert Hudson, Rua Rainha Ginga 77, CP 1804, Luanda; tel. 222394100; fax 222395101; e-mail servicoscentrais@bankeve.com; internet www.bankeve.com; f. 2003; Pres. AMILCAR AZEVEDO DA SILVA.

Banco Sol: Rua Rei Katyavala 110–112, Maculusso, Zona 8, Ingombotas, CP 814, Luanda; tel. 222402215; fax 222440226; e-mail banco.sol@ebonet.net; internet www.bancosol.co.ao; f. 2000; cap. 96.9m., res 389.9m., dep. 5,474.0m. (Dec. 2004); Pres. SEBASTIÃO BASTOS LAVRADOR.

Development Bank

Banco de Comércio e Indústria SARL: Rua Rainha Ginga, Largo do Atlético 79–83, POB 1395, Luanda; tel. 222330209; fax 222334924; e-mail falfredo@bci.ebonet.net; f. 1991; 91% state-owned; privatization pending; provides loans to businesses in all sectors; cap. US $9.5m., res $34.4m., dep. $247.3m. (Dec. 2002); Chair. ADRIANO RAFAEL PASCOAL; 5 brs.

Banco de Desenvolvimento de Angola (BDA): Luanda; f. 2006; Pres. FRANCO PAIXÃO.

Investment Bank

Banco Africano de Investimentos SARL (BAI): Rua Major Kanhangulo 34, CP 6022, Luanda; tel. 222335749; fax 222335486; e-mail baisede@bancobai.co.ao; internet www.bancobai.co.ao; f. 1997; 17.5% interest owned by Sonangol; cap. 6.5m., dep. 91,253.3m. (Dec. 2005); Pres. Dr MÁRIO ABÍLIO PALHARES; 15 brs.

Foreign Banks

Banco Comercial Português—Atlântico SA: Rua Rainha Ginga 83, CP 5726, Luanda; tel. 222397922; fax 222397397; e-mail atlantico_luanda@netangola.com; Gen. Man. MARIA NAZARÉ FRANCISCO DANG.

Banco Espírito Santo Angola SARL (BESA): Rua do 1° Congresso do MPLA 29, Bairro Ingombotas, Luanda; tel. 222693600; fax 222693698; internet www.besa.ao; f. 2002; 99.96% owned by Banco Espírito Santo SA, Lisbon; cap. US $7.0m., res $6.1m., dep. $205.3m. (Dec. 2004); Gen. Mans Dr CARLOS SILVA, Dr HELDER BATAGLIA.

Banco Totta de Angola SARL: Av. 4 de Fevereiro 99, CP 1231, Luanda; tel. 222332729; fax 222333233; e-mail tottango@ebonet.net; 99.98% owned by Banco Santander Totta; cap. €15.5m. (Dec. 2003); Man. Dir Dr MÁRIO NELSON MAXIMINO; 7 brs.

NovoBanco: Rua N'Dunduma 253/257, Bairro Miramar, Município Sambizanga, Luanda; tel. 222430040; fax 222430074; e-mail secretariado@novobanco.ao; internet www.novobanco.net; f. 2004; Pres. GABRIELE HEBER; Dir STEFAN WOLFF.

BNP Paribas, Citigroup and Equator Bank Ltd maintain offices in Luanda.

STOCK EXCHANGE

Bolsa de Valores e Derivativos do Angola (BVDA): Mutamba, Luanda; f. 2006.

INSURANCE

AAA Seguros SA: Rua Lenine 58, Luanda; tel. 222691331; fax 222691342; e-mail saovicente@aaa.co.ao; f. 2000; life and non-life; Pres. Dr CARLOS MANUEL DE SÃO VICENTE.

ENSA Seguros de Angola (Empresa Nacional de Seguros e Resseguros de Angola, UEE): Av. 4 de Fevereiro 93, CP 5778, Luanda; tel. 222332990; fax 222332946; e-mail geral@ensa.co.ao; internet www.ensaseguros.com; f. 1978; state-owned; to be privatized; Chair. MANUEL JOAQUIM GONÇALVES; Pres. and Dir-Gen. ALEIXO AUGUSTO.

GA Angola Seguros (Global Alliance Insurance Angola): Av. 4 de Fevereiro 79, 1° andar, Luanda; tel. 222330368; fax 222398815; e-mail blara@globalalliance.co.ao; internet www.globalalliance.co.ao; f. 2005; owned by Global Alliance Group (United Kingdom); Gen. Man BRIAN LARA.

Nova Sociedade de Seguros de Angola S.A. (Nossa Seguros): Av. 4 de Fevereiro 111, Luanda; tel. 222399909; fax 222399153; e-mail info@nossaseguros.com; internet www.nossaseguros.com.

Trade and Industry

GOVERNMENT AGENCIES

Corpo de Segurança de Diamantes (CSD): Luanda; f. 2004; security agency monitoring diamond mining sector.

Gabinete de Obras Especiais: Luanda; Dir MANUEL FERREIRA CLEMENTE JÚNIOR.

Gabinete de Reconstrução Nacional: Luanda; f. 2004; monitors economic and social reconstruction programmes; Dir MANUEL HELDER VIEIRA DIAS JÚNIOR.

Gabinete de Redimensionamento Empresarial: Rua Cerqueira Lukoki 25, 9° andar, CP 594, Luanda; tel. 222390496; fax 222392987; privatization agency.

Instituto de Desenvolvimento Agrário: Rua Comandante Gika, CP 2109, Luanda; tel. and fax 222323651; e-mail ida.canga@netangola.com; promotes agricultural development; Dir Eng. AFONSO PEDRO CANGA.

Instituto de Desenvolvimento Industrial de Angola (IDIA): Rua Cerqueira Lukoki 25, 8° andar, CP 594, Luanda; tel. and fax 222338492; e-mail idiadg@netangola.com; f. 1995; promotes industrial development; Dir KIALA NGONE GABRIELE.

Instituto de Investimento Estrangeiro (IIE): Rua Cerqueira Lukoki 25, 9° andar, CP 594, Luanda; tel. 222392620; fax 222393381; foreign investment agency.

Instituto Nacional de Cereais (INCER): Av. 4 de Fevereiro 101, CP 1105, Luanda; tel. and fax 222331611; promotes cereal crops; Dir-Gen. ESTEVÃO MIGUEL DE CARVALHO.

CHAMBER OF COMMERCE

Câmara de Comércio e Indústria de Angola (CCIA) (Angolan Chamber of Commerce and Industry): Largo do Kinaxixi 14, 1° andar, CP 92, Luanda; tel. 222444506; fax 222444629; e-mail ccira@ebonet.net; internet www.ccia.ebonet.net; Pres. ANTÓNIO JOÃO DOS SANTOS.

INDUSTRIAL AND TRADE ASSOCIATIONS

Associação Comercial de Benguela: Rua Sacadura Cabral 104, CP 347, Benguela; tel. 272232441; fax 272233022; e-mail acbenguela@netangola.com; internet www.netangola.com/acb; f. 1907; Pres. AIRES PIRES ROQUE.

Associação Comercial e Industrial da Ilha de Luanda (ACIL): Largo do Kinaxixi 9, Luanda; tel. 222341866; fax 222349677; Pres. PEDRO GODHINO DOMINGOS.

Associação Comercial e Industrial de Luanda (ACOMIL): Largo do Kinaxixi 14–30, Luanda; tel. 222335728; Pres. JOÃO ADÃO ANTÓNIO TIGRE.

Associação Comercial de Luanda (ASCANGOLA): Edif. Palácio de Comércio, 1° andar, CP 1275, Luanda; tel. 222332453.

Associação Industrial de Angola (AIA): Rua Manuel Fernando Caldeira 6, CP 6127, Luanda; tel. 222443504; fax 222392241; e-mail secretariado@aiaangola.com; internet www.aiaangola.com; Pres. JOSÉ SEVERINO.

Associação de Mulheres Empresárias: Largo do Kinaxixi 14, 3° andar, Luanda; tel. 222346742; fax 222343088; f. 1990; asscn of business women; Sec.-Gen. HENRIQUETA DE CARVALHO.

Rede Angolana do Sector Micro-Empresarial (RASME): Luanda; asscn of small businesses; Exec.-Co-ordinator BAY KANGUDI.

STATE TRADING ORGANIZATIONS

Angolan Selling Corporation (ASCORP): Edif. Soleil B, Rua Tipografia Mama Tita, Ingombotas, CP 3978, Luanda; tel. 222396465; fax 222397615; e-mail ascorpadmin@ebonet.net; f. 1999; 51% state-owned diamond-trading co; Pres. NOE BALTAZAR.

Direcção dos Serviços de Comércio (DNCI) (Dept of Trade): Palácio de Vidro, 3° andar, Largo 4 de Fevereiro 7, CP 1337, Luanda; tel. and fax 222310658; e-mail minco.dnci.gc@netangola.com; internet www.dnci.net; f. 1970; brs throughout Angola; Dir GOMES CARDOSO.

Exportang, UEE (Empresa de Exportações de Angola): Rua dos Enganos 1A, CP 1000, Luanda; tel. 222332363; co-ordinates exports.

Importang, UEE (Empresa de Importações de Angola): Calçada do Município 10, CP 1003, Luanda; tel. 222337994; f. 1977; co-ordinates majority of imports; Dir-Gen. SIMÃO DIOGO DA CRUZ.

Maquimport, UEE: Rua Rainha Ginga 152, CP 2975, Luanda; tel. 222339044; f. 1981 to import office equipment.

Mecanang, UEE: Rua dos Enganos, 1°–7° andar, CP 1347, Luanda; tel. 222390644; f. 1981 to import agricultural and construction machinery, tools and spare parts.

Nova Angomédica, UEE: Rua do Sanatório, Bairro Palanca, CP 2698, Luanda; tel. 222261366; fax 222260010; f. 1981; production and distribution of pharmaceutical goods; Gen. Dir JAILTON BATISTA DOS SANTOS.

Sociedade de Comercialização de Diamantes de Angola SARL (SODIAM): Edif. Endiama/De Beers, Rua Rainha Ginga 87, CP 1072, Luanda; tel. 222370217; fax 222370423; e-mail sodiamadmin@ebonet.net; f. 2000; part of the ENDIAMA group; diamond trading org.; Man. Dir MANUEL ARNALDO DE SOUSA CALADO.

STATE INDUSTRIAL ENTERPRISES

Bricomil: Rua Massano Amorim 79, Chicala, Luanda; tel. 222343895; fax 222342533; f. 1986; 55% state-owned; privatization planned; civil construction; 650 employees.

Companhia do Açúcar de Angola: Rua Direita 77, Luanda; production of sugar.

Empresa Abastecimento Técnico Material, UEE (EMATEC): Largo Rainha Ginga 3, CP 2952, Luanda; tel. 222338891; technical and material suppliers to the Ministry of National Defence.

Empresa de Construção de Edificações, UEE (CONSTROI): Rua Amílcar Cabral 167, 1° andar, Luanda; tel. 222333930; construction.

Empresa de Obras Especiais (EMPROE): Rua Ngola Kiluange 183–185, Luanda; tel. 222382142; fax 222382143; building and civil engineering.

Empresa de Pesca de Angola, UEE (PESCANGOLA): Luanda; f. 1981; state fishing enterprise, responsible to the Ministry of Fisheries.

Empresa de Rebenefício e Exportação do Café de Angola, UEE (CAFANGOL): Rua Robert Shields 4–6, CP 342, Luanda; tel. 222337916; fax 222332840; e-mail cafangol@nexus.ao; f. 1983; nat. coffee-processing and trade org.; Dir-Gen. ALVARO FARIA.

Empresa de Tecidos de Angola, UEE (TEXTANG): Rua N'gola Kiluanji-Kazenga, CP 5404, Luanda; tel. 222381134; production of textiles.

Empresa dos Tabacos de Angola: CP 1238, Luanda; tel. 222336995; fax 222336921; manufacture of tobacco products; Gen. Man. K. BITTENCOURT.

Empresa Nacional de Cimento, UEE (ENCIME): CP 157, Lobito; tel. 272212325; cement production.

Empresa Nacional de Comercialização e Distribuição de Produtos Agrícolas (ENCODIPA): Luanda; central marketing agency for agricultural produce; numerous brs throughout Angola.

Empresa Nacional de Diamantes de Angola (ENDIAMA), UEE: Rua Major Kanhangulo 100, CP 1247, Luanda; tel. and fax 222332718; f. 1981; commenced operations 1986; diamond mining; a number of subsidiary companies undergoing privatization; Pres. Dr MANUEL ARNALDO DE SOUSA CALADO.

Empresa Nacional de Ferro de Angola (FERRANGOL): Rua João de Barros 26, CP 2692, Luanda; tel. 222373800; iron production; Chair. DIAMANTINO PEDRO DE AZEVEDO; Dir ARMANDO DE SOUSA.

Empresa Nacional de Manutenção, UEE (MANUTECNICA): Rua 7, Av. do Cazenga 10, CP 3508, Luanda; tel. 222383646; assembly of machines and specialized equipment for industry.

Geotécnica Unidad Económica Estatal: Rua Angola Kilmanse 389–393, Luanda; tel. 222381795; fax 222382730; f. 1978; for surveying and excavation; Man. P. M. M. ELVINO, Jr.

Siderurgia Nacional, UEE: Rua Farol Lagostas, Luanda; tel. 222383587; f. 1963; nationalized 1980; scheduled for privatization; steelworks and rolling mill plant.

Sonangalp, Lda: Rua Manuel Fernando Caldeira 25, Luanda; tel. 222334527; fax 222333529; internet www.sonangalp.co.ao; f. 1994; 51% owned by Sonangol, 49% owned by Petrogal Angola (Portugal); fuel distribution; Pres. ANTÓNIO SILVESTRE.

Sociedade Nacional de Combustíveis de Angola (SONANGOL): Rua 1° Congreso do MPLA 8–16, CP 1316, Luanda; tel. 222632162; fax 2223919782; e-mail drh@sonangol.co.ao; internet www.sonangol.co.ao; f. 1976 for exploration, production and refining of crude petroleum, and marketing and distribution of petroleum products; sole concessionary in Angola, supervises on- and offshore operations of foreign petroleum cos; 11 subsidiaries, including shipping cos; holds majority interest in jt ventures with Cabinda Gulf Oil Co (Cabgoc), Fina Petróleos de Angola and Texaco Petróleos de Angola; CEO MANUEL VICENTE; c. 7,000 employees.

UTILITIES

Electricity

Empresa Nacional de Construções Eléctricas, UEE (ENCEL): Rua Comandante Che Guevara 185–187, CP 5230, Luanda; tel. 222446712; fax 222446759; e-mail encel@encel.co.ao; internet www.encel.co.ao; f. 1982; supplier of electromechanical equipment; Dir Gen. DANIEL SIMAS.

Empresa Nacional de Electricidade, EP (ENE): Edif. Geominas 6°–7° andar, CP 772, Luanda; tel. 222321499; fax 222323433; e-mail enepdg@netangola.com; f. 1980; production and distribution of electricity; Pres. and Dir-Gen. Eng. EDUARDO GOMES NELUMBA.

Water

Empresa Provincial de Água de Luanda (EPAL): Rua Frederick Engels 3, CP 1387, Luanda; tel. 222335001; fax 222330380; e-mail epalsdg@sney.co.ao; state-owned; Dir DIÓGENES OLIVEIRA.

TRADE UNIONS

Sindicato dos Jornalistas Angolanos (SJA): Rua Francisco Távora 8, 1° andar, CP 2140, Luanda; tel. 222331969; fax 222332420; e-mail sja@netangola.com; f. 1992; Pres. AVELINO MIGUEL; Gen. Sec. LUISA ROGÉRIO; 1,253 mems in 2003.

Sindicato Nacional de Professores (Sinprof): Rua da Missão 71, 4° andar, Luanda; tel. 222371780; e-mail sinprof@angonet.org; teachers' union; Gen. Sec. MIGUEL JOÃO FILHO.

União Nacional das Associações de Camponeses Angolanos (UNACA): Luanda; peasants' asscn; Gen. Sec. PAULO UIME.

União Nacional de Trabalhadores Angolanos (UNTA) (National Union of Angolan Workers): Av. 4 de Fevereiro 210, CP 28, Luanda; tel. 222334670; fax 222393590; e-mail untadis@netangola.com; f. 1960; Pres. MANUEL AUGUSTO VIAGE; c. 160,000 mems.

Transport

The transport infrastructure was severely dislocated by the civil war that ended in 2002. Subsequently, major rebuilding and upgrading projects were undertaken.

RAILWAYS

There are three main railway lines in Angola, the Benguela railway, which runs from the coast to the Zambian border, the Luanda–Malanje line, and the Moçamedes line, which connects Namibe and Cuando-Cubango. In 2004 only 850 km out of a total of almost 3,000 km of track were operational. A plan introduced in late 2004 to rehabilitate and extend the rail network was expected to take 11 years and to cost US $4,000m. In mid-2005 a project for rebuilding and upgrading the railway system was approved by the Southern African Development Community (SADC). The Benguela line—a significant export route—was scheduled to reopen in mid-2007, following demining and reconstruction work by Chinese workers.

Direcção Nacional dos Caminhos de Ferro: Rua Major Kanhangulo, CP 1250, Luanda; tel. 222370091; f. 1975; nat. network operating four fmrly independent systems covering 2,952 track-km; Dir JULIO BANGO.

Amboim Railway: Porto Amboim; f. 1922; 123 track-km; Dir A. GUIA.

Benguela Railway (Caminho de Ferro de Benguela—Empresa Pública): Praça 11 Novembro 3, CP 32, Lobito, Benguela; tel. 272222645; fax 272225133; e-mail cfbeng@ebonet.net; f. 1903; line completed 1928; owned by Govt of Angola; line carrying passenger and freight traffic from the port of Lobito across Angola, via Huambo and Luena, to the border of the Democratic Republic of the Congo (DRC, fmrly Zaire); 1,301 track-km; guerrilla operations by UNITA suspended all international traffic from 1975, with only irregular services from Lobito to Huambo being operated; the rehabilitation of the railway was a priority of a 10-year programme, planned by the Southern African Development Co-ordination Conference (SADCC, now SADC), to develop the 'Lobito corridor'; from 2001 rehabilitation of the line was under government control; in 2004 a consortium from China (People's Republic) agreed to rehabilitate the line to the DRC; Dir-Gen. DANIEL QUIPAXE; 1,700 employees.

Caminho de Ferro de Moçamedes (CFM): CP 130, Lubango; tel. 261221752; fax 261224442; e-mail gab.dir.cfm@netangola.com; f. 1905; main line from Namibe to Menongue, via Lubango; br. lines to Chibia and iron ore mines at Cassinga; 838 track-km; Dir-Gen. Dr JÚLIO BANGO JOAQUIM.

Luanda Railway (Empresa de Caminho de Ferro de Luanda, UEE): CP 1250-C, Luanda; tel. 222370061; f. 1886; serves an iron-, cotton- and sisal-producing region between Luanda and Malange; 536 track-km; Man. A. ÁLVARO AGANTE.

ROADS

In 2001 Angola had 51,429 km of roads, of which 7,944 km were main roads and 5,278 km were secondary roads. About 10.4% of roads were paved. It was estimated that 80% of the country's road network was in disrepair. In 2005–06 contracts were awarded to various foreign companies to upgrade the road network, including the main north–south coastal road. The Government planned a US $190m. programme to rebuild some 1,200 km of the network by 2008.

Direcção Nacional dos Transportes Rodoviárias: Rua Rainha Ginga 74, 1° andar, Luanda; tel. 222339390.

Instituto Nacional de Estradas de Angola (INEA): Rua Amílcar Cabral 35, 3° andar, CP 5667, Luanda; tel. 222332828; fax 222335754.

SHIPPING

The main harbours are at Lobito, Luanda and Namibe. The first phase of a 10-year SADCC (now SADC) programme to develop the 'Lobito corridor', for which funds were pledged in January 1989, was to include the rehabilitation of the ports of Lobito and Benguela. In January 2007 the Japanese authorities pledged US $9m. for the rehabilitation of the quays of Namibe and Lobito ports. The port of Luanda was due to be upgraded by 2010. In December 2006 Angola's registered merchant fleet comprised 129 vessels, totalling 56,391 grt.

Direcção Nacional da Marinha Mercante e Portos: Rua Rainha Ginga 74, 4° andar, Luanda; tel. 222332032.

Agenang, UEE: Rua Engracia Fragoso 47–49, Luanda; tel. 222336380; fax 222334392; state shipping co; scheduled for privatization.

Cabotang—Cabotagem Nacional Angolana, UEE: Av. 4 de Fevereiro 83A, Luanda; tel. 222373133; operates off the coasts of Angola and Mozambique; Dir-Gen. JOÃO OCTAVIO VAN-DÚNEM.

Empresa Portuária do Lobito, UEE: Av. da Independência 16, Lobito, Benguela; tel. 272222718; fax 272222719; e-mail eplobito@eplobito.com; internet www.eplobito.com; long-distance sea transport; Gen. Man. JOSÉ CARLOS GOMES.

Empresa Portuária de Luanda: CP 1229, Porto de Luanda; tel. 222393284; Pres. SÍLVIO BARROS VINHAS.

Empresa Portuária de Moçâmedes—Namibe, UEE: Rua Pedro Benje 10A e c, CP 49, Namibe; tel. 264260643; long-distance sea transport; Dir HUMBERTO DE ATAIDE DIAS.

Orey Angola, Lda: Largo 4 de Fevereiro 3, 3° andar, CP 583, Luanda; tel. 222310290; fax 222310882; e-mail orey@oreylad.ebonet.net; internet www.orey.com/angola; international shipping, especially to Portugal; Dir Commdt A. CARMONA E COSTA.

Sécil Marítima SARL, UEE: Edif. Secil, Av. 4 de Fevereiro 42, 1° andar, CP 5910, Luanda; tel. 222311334; fax 222311784; e-mail secilmaritima@msn.com; operates ports at Lobito, Luanda and Namibe; Gen. Man. MARIA AMÉLIA RITA.

CIVIL AVIATION

Angola's airport system is well-developed, but suffered some damage in the later years of the civil war. The 4 de Fevereiro airport in Luanda is the only international airport. During the mid-2000s airports at Luanda, Lobito, Soyo, Namibe, Saurimo, Uíge, Huambo and Bié were undergoing rehabilitation.

Direcção Nacional da Aviação Civil: Rua Frederich Engels 92, 6° andar, CP 569, Luanda; tel. 222339412.

Empresa Nacional de Aeroportos e Navegação Aerea (ENANA): Av. Amílcar Cabral 110, CP 841, Luanda; tel. and fax 222351267; e-mail cai_enana@snet.co.ao; administers airports; Chair. JORGE DOS SANTOS CORREIA MELO.

TAAG—Linhas Aéreas de Angola: Rua da Missão 123, CP 79, Luanda; tel. 222332338; fax 222390396; e-mail gci_taag@ebonet.net; internet www.nexus.ao/taag; f. 1938; internal scheduled passenger and cargo services, and services from Luanda to destinations within Africa and to Europe and South America; Chair. JESÚS NELSON PEREIRA MARTINS.

Angola Air Charter: Aeroporto Internacional 4 de Fevereiro, CP 3010, Luanda; tel. 222321290; fax 222320105; e-mail aacharter@independente.net; f. 1992; subsidiary of TAAG; CEO A. DE MATOS.

Air Nacoia: Rua Comandante Che Guevara 67, 1° andar, Luanda; tel. and fax 222395477; f. 1993; Pres. SALVADOR SILVA.

SONAIR SARL: Aeroporto Internacional 4 de Fevereiro, Luanda; tel. 222633502; fax 222321572; e-mail support.sonair@sonangol.co.ao; internet www.sonairsarl.com; f. 1998; subsidiary of SONANGOL; operates direct flights between Luanda and Houston, Texas, USA; Pres. Dr ANTÓNIO DOS SANTOS DOMINGOS.

Transafrik International Ltd: Aeroporto Internacional 4 de Fevereiro, Luanda; tel. 222353714; fax 222354183; e-mail info@transafrik.com; internet www.transafrik.com; f. 1986; operates international contract cargo services; CEO BJÖRN NÄF; Chief Financial Officer STEPHAN BRANDT.

Tourism

Angola's tourism industry is undeveloped as a result of the years of civil war, although its potential for development is great. Tourist arrivals totalled 209,956 in 2005 and receipts from tourism in that year amounted to US $103m.

National Tourist Agency: Palácio de Vidro, Largo 4 de Fevereiro, CP 1240, Luanda; tel. 222372750.

ANTARCTICA

Source: partly Scientific Committee on Antarctic Research, Scott Polar Research Institute, Lensfield Rd, Cambridge, CB2 1ER, United Kingdom; tel. (1223) 336550; fax (1223) 336549; e-mail info@scar.org; internet www.scar.org.

The Continent of Antarctica is estimated to cover 13,661,000 sq km. There are no indigenous inhabitants, but a number of permanent research stations have been established. W. S. Bruce, of the Scottish National Antarctic Expedition (1902–04), established a meteorological station on Laurie Island, South Orkney Islands, in 1903. After the expedition, this was transferred to the Argentine authorities (the British Government having declined to operate the station), who have maintained the observatory since 1904 (see Orcadas, below). The next permanent stations were established in 1944 by the United Kingdom, and then subsequently by other countries.

Tourism, which consists almost exclusively of 'eco-cruises', is promoted by the International Association of Antarctica Tour Operators (IAATO). The number of tourists visiting Antarctica in 2006/07 totalled 37,552 (compared with 4,700 in 1990/91), including 29,576 landed passengers. The rate of increase in tourist numbers led to expressions of concern in the early 2000s regarding the environmental impact of the industry on the region. In March 2008 the Antarctic and Southern Ocean Coalition, a consortium of non-governmental organizations concerned with the environmental protection of the region, urged the International Maritime Organization, through its Maritime Environment Protection Committee, to agree stringent vessel standards, equipment and procedures for ships entering Antarctic waters, notably the exclusion of shipping using heavy fuel oil and a mandatory requirement that vessels be ice-strengthened. In response, the Organization invited member states to submit proposals aimed at limiting the environmental impact of shipping on the Antarctic region.

To coincide with the 50th anniversary of International Geophysical Year, March 2007–March 2008 was designated International Polar Year, a joint initiative of the World Meteorological Organization (WMO, see p. 155) and the International Council for Science. (This period also represented the 125th and 75th anniversaries of the previous two International Polar Years.) Scientific research conducted under the designated International Polar Year was to run in the two years to March 2009, and was to involve more than 200 projects and more than 60 participating nations.

Wintering Stations

(The following list includes wintering stations south of latitude 60° occupied during austral winter 2008)

	Latitude	Longitude
ARGENTINA		
Belgrano II, Bertrab Nunatak, Luitpold Coast	77° 52' S	34° 38' W
Esperanza, Hope Bay	63° 23' S	56° 59' W
Jubany, King George Island	62° 14' S	58° 40' W
Marambio, Seymour Island	64° 14' S	56° 39' W
Orcadas, Laurie Island	60° 44' S	44° 44' W
San Martín, Barry Island	68° 07' S	67° 06' W
AUSTRALIA		
Casey, Vincennes Bay, Budd Coast	66° 17' S	110° 31' E
Davis, Ingrid Christensen Coast	68° 35' S	77° 58' E
Mawson, Mac. Robertson Land	67° 36' S	62° 52' E
BRAZIL		
Comandante Ferraz, King George Island	62° 05' S	58° 23' W
CHILE		
O'Higgins, Cape Legoupil	63° 19' S	57° 54' W
Frei, King George Island	62° 12' S	58° 58' W
Escudero, King George Island	62° 12' S	58° 58' W
PEOPLE'S REPUBLIC OF CHINA		
Chang Cheng (Great Wall), King George Island	62° 13' S	58° 58' W
Zhongshan, Princess Elizabeth Land	69° 22' S	76° 23' E
FRANCE		
Dumont d'Urville, Terre Adélie	66° 40' S	140° 00' E
FRANCE-ITALY*		
Concordia, Dome C	75° 06' S	123° 24' E
GERMANY		
Neumayer, Ekstrømisen	70° 38' S	08° 16' W
INDIA		
Maitri, Schirmacheroasen	70° 46' S	11° 44' E
JAPAN		
Syowa, Ongul	69° 00' S	39° 35' E
REPUBLIC OF KOREA		
King Sejong, King George Island	62° 13' S	58° 47' W
NEW ZEALAND		
Scott Base, Ross Island	77° 51' S	166° 46' E
NORWAY		
Troll	72° 00' S	02° 32' E
POLAND		
Arctowski, King George Island	62° 10' S	58° 28' W
RUSSIA		
Bellingshausen, King George Island	62° 12' S	58° 58' W
Mirny, Queen Mary Land	66° 33' S	93° 00' E
Novolazarevskaya, Prinsesse Astrid Kyst	70° 46' S	11° 52' E
Progress 2, Princess Elizabeth Land	69° 23' S	76° 23' E
Vostok, East Antarctica	78° 28' S	106° 48' E
SOUTH AFRICA		
SANAE IV, Vesleskarvet	71° 40' S	02° 50' W
UKRAINE		
Vernadsky, Argentine Islands	65° 14' S	64° 15' W
UNITED KINGDOM		
Halley, Brunt Ice Shelf, Caird Coast	75° 35' S	26° 32' W
Rothera, Adelaide Island	67° 34' S	68° 07' W
USA		
McMurdo, Ross Island	77° 51' S	166° 40' E
Palmer, Anvers Island	64° 47' S	64° 03' W
Amundsen-Scott		South Pole†
URUGUAY		
Artigas, King George Island	62° 11' S	58° 54' W

*The Concordia research station is a joint venture between France and Italy.

†The precise co-ordinates of the location of this station are: 89° 59' 85" S, 139° 16' 37" E.

Territorial Claims

Territory	Claimant State
Antártida Argentina	Argentina
Australian Antarctic Territory	Australia
British Antarctic Territory	United Kingdom
Dronning Maud Land	Norway
Ross Dependency	New Zealand
Terre Adélie	France
Territorio Chileno Antártico	Chile

These claims are not recognized by the USA or Russia. No formal claims have been made in the sector of Antarctica between 90° W and 150° W.

See also Article 4 of the Antarctic Treaty, below.

Research

Scientific Committee on Antarctic Research (SCAR) of the International Council for Science (ICSU): Secretariat: Scott Polar Research Institute, Lensfield Rd, Cambridge, CB2 1ER, United Kingdom; tel. (1223) 336550; fax (1223) 336549; e-mail info@scar.org; internet www.scar.org; f. 1958 to initiate, promote and co-ordinate scientific research in the Antarctic, and to provide scientific advice to the Antarctic Treaty System; 34 Full Mems; 8 ICSU Scientific Unions Mems; 4 Assoc. Mems.

President: Prof. CHRIS RAPLEY (United Kingdom).

Vice-Presidents: Prof. MAHLON C. KENNICUTT, II (USA), Prof. ZHANHAI ZHANG (People's Republic of China), Dr ANTONIO MELONI (Italy), Prof. Dr SERGIO A. MARENSSI (Argentina).

Executive Director: Dr COLIN P. SUMMERHAYES (United Kingdom).

Executive Officer: Dr MIKE SPARROW.

The Antarctic Treaty

The Treaty (summarized below) was signed in Washington, DC, on 1 December 1959 by the 12 nations co-operating in the Antarctic during the International Geophysical Year, and entered into force on 23 June 1961. The Treaty made provision for a review of its terms, 30 years after ratification; however, no signatory to the Treaty has requested such a review. The permanent Antarctic Treaty Secretariat was formally established, with its headquarters in Buenos Aires, Argentina, in September 2004.

Article 1. Antarctica shall be used for peaceful purposes only.
Article 2. On freedom of scientific investigation and co-operation.
Article 3. On exchange of information and personnel.
Article 4. i. Nothing contained in the present Treaty shall be interpreted as:

(a) a renunciation by any Contracting Party of previously asserted rights of or claims to territorial sovereignty in Antarctica;

(b) a renunciation or diminution by any Contracting Party of any basis of claim to territorial sovereignty in Antarctica which it may have whether as a result of its activities or those of its nationals in Antarctica, or otherwise;

(c) prejudicing the position of any Contracting Party as regards its recognition or non-recognition of any other State's right of or claim or basis of claim to territorial sovereignty in Antarctica.

Article 4. ii. No acts or activities taking place while the present Treaty is in force shall constitute a basis for asserting, supporting or denying a claim to territorial sovereignty in Antarctica or create any rights of sovereignty in Antarctica. No new claim, or enlargement of an existing claim, to territorial sovereignty in Antarctica shall be asserted while the present Treaty is in force.

Article 5. Any nuclear explosions in Antarctica and the disposal there of radioactive waste material shall be prohibited.

Article 6. On geographical limits and rights on high seas.

Article 7. On designation of observers and notification of stations and expeditions.

Article 8. On jurisdiction over observers and scientists.

Article 9. On consultative meetings.

Articles 10–14. On upholding, interpreting, amending, notifying and depositing the Treaty.

ORIGINAL SIGNATORIES

Argentina	France	Russia*
Australia	Japan	South Africa
Belgium	New Zealand	United Kingdom
Chile	Norway	USA

* As the successor to the former USSR.

Note: each Original Signatory to the Antarctic Treaty holds the status of Consultative Party.

ACCEDING STATES

Austria, Brazil, Bulgaria, Canada, the People's Republic of China, Colombia, Cuba, the Czech Republic, Denmark, Ecuador, Estonia, Finland, Germany, Greece, Guatemala, Hungary, India, Italy, the Democratic People's Republic of Korea, the Republic of Korea, the Netherlands, Papua New Guinea, Peru, Poland, Romania, Slovakia, Spain, Sweden, Switzerland, Turkey, Ukraine, Uruguay, Venezuela.

Brazil, Bulgaria, the People's Republic of China, Ecuador, Finland, Germany, India, Italy, the Republic of Korea, the Netherlands, Peru, Poland, Spain, Sweden, Ukraine and Uruguay have achieved consultative status under the Treaty, by virtue of their scientific activity in Antarctica.

Antarctic Treaty Secretariat: Leandro N. Alem 884, 4°, C1001AAQ Buenos Aires; tel. (11) 5169-1500; fax (11) 5169-1513; e-mail secret@ats.aq; internet www.ats.aq; Exec. Sec. JOHANNES HUBER.

ANTARCTIC TREATY CONSULTATIVE MEETINGS

Meetings of representatives of the original signatory nations of the Antarctic Treaty and acceding nations accorded consultative status are held annually to discuss scientific, environmental and political matters. The 31st meeting was scheduled to take place in Kyiv, Ukraine, on 2–13 June 2008.

Among the numerous measures that have been agreed and implemented by the Consultative Parties are several designed to protect the Antarctic environment and wildlife. These include the designation of Specially Protected Areas and Sites of Special Scientific Interest, a Convention for the Conservation of Antarctic Seals, and a Convention on the Conservation of Antarctic Marine Living Resources.

The Protocol on Environmental Protection to the Antarctic Treaty was adopted by the original signatory nations in October 1991. By late 1997 the Protocol had been ratified by all 26 of the then Consultative Parties, and it entered into force in January 1998. Under Article 7, any activity relating to mineral resources, other than scientific research, is prohibited. Article 25, on modification or amendment, states that a conference shall be held as soon as practicable if, after the expiration of 50 years from the date of entry into force of tne Protocol, any of the Antarctic Treaty Consultative Parties so requests; it further specifies that, in respect of Article 7, any proposed modification to the prohibition on mining activity shall be considered only if a regulatory regime is in place. The first four annexes to the Protocol, providing for environmental impact assessment, conservation of fauna and flora, waste disposal, and monitoring of marine pollution, entered into force with the Protocol; and a fifth annex, on area protection and management, entered effect in May 2002. A sixth annex, on liability arising from environmental emergencies, was adopted in June 2005, and was to take effect upon ratification by all Consultative Parties to the Protocol. The Protocol effectively superseded the provisions of the 1964 Agreed Measures for the Conservation of Antarctic Flora and Fauna, including area protection in Antarctica. At the 22nd Consultative Meeting, held in Tromsø, Norway, in May 1998, the Committee for Environmental Protection (CEP) was established, under the provisions of the Protocol on Environmental Protection. The CEP meets at the location of the annual Antarctic Treaty Consultative Meeting.

Committee for Environmental Protection (CEP): e-mail cep@cep.aq; internet www.cep.aq; Chair. Dr NEIL GILBERT (2006–08).

RECENT DEVELOPMENTS

In October 2006 WMO reported that the hole in the ozone layer formed over Antarctica was the most serious on record: the US National Aeronautics and Space Administration (NASA) had recorded the area of the hole in late September as having reached 29.5m. sq km. This marginally exceeded the area of the hole recorded in 2000 (29.4m. sq km), hitherto the largest recorded. Furthermore, according to WMO, there had been the greatest recorded mass deficit in 2006—of 40.8m. metric tons, compared with 39.6m. tons in 2000—with the effect that the mass of ozone over Antarctica was lower than that ever previously recorded. WMO data for 2007 showed that the hole was somewhat weaker than that in 2006, 2005 and 2000, but stronger than that in 2004 and 2002. WMO stated that the relatively smaller size of the ozone hole was not a sign of recovery, but was instead related to mild temperatures in the Antarctic stratosphere during the 2007 austral winter.

Substantial calving from ice shelves along the Antarctic Peninsula has fuelled speculation that this may be attributable to climate warming. In early 1995 the Larsen A ice shelf lost 1,300 sq km, and in 1998 the Larsen B and Wilkins ice shelves together lost 3,000 sq km. These calvings represented a much greater rate of loss than had been predicted. The B15 iceberg, which was the largest in the world (measuring 11,000 sq km) when it calved from the Ross Ice Shelf in 2000, also split into smaller bergs in October 2003. Moreover, in March 2002 the Larsen B ice shelf, which had a surface area of 3,250 sq km and was 200 m thick, collapsed and fragmented into small icebergs. Scientists expressed alarm at the speed of the disintegration of Larsen B, which took place in a period of less than one month. Climate records from the Antarctic Peninsula show an increase in average temperatures of some 3°C during the period 1951–2000. Studies published by US scientists in September 2004 reported evidence of glaciers thinning at twice the rate recorded in the mid-1990s, prompting fears that the West Antarctic ice sheet (which contains sufficient ice to raise sea levels by more than 6 m) could become destabilized. It was also claimed that following the collapse of an ice shelf, nearby inland glaciers flow up to eight times more quickly into the ocean (this had been shown to have occurred after the disintegration of Larsen B), causing sea levels to rise more rapidly than had previously been thought. A comprehensive survey of the region published in April 2005 reported that 87% of glaciers in the Antarctic Peninsula were retreating, and that the rate of retreat had increased markedly since 2000. A similar survey conducted in the 1950s showed a majority of glaciers to be increasing in size. Research published in March 2006, led by the University of Colorado, USA, gave evidence of the significant decline of the total mass balance of the Antarctic ice sheet. Satellite data indicated that the volume of ice being lost was raising global sea levels by some 0.4 mm per year. As much as 152 cu km was being lost annually from the ice sheet, with the bulk of the loss being from the West Antarctic sheet; the East Antarctic ice sheet was considered to be more stable. Research published by an international team of scientists in January 2008 estimated that 132,000m. metric tons of ice had been lost from West Antarctica in 2006, compared with 83,000m. tons in 1996. Loss of ice from the Antarctic Peninsula was estimated at 60,000m. tons, compared with 25,000m. tons 10 years earlier. Loss was concentrated at narrow glacier outlets with accelerating ice flow, suggesting that the mass balance of the entire ice sheet had been altered by glacier flow. (Previous simulation had suggested that the ice mass would increase in response to future climate change during the 21st century, owing to increased snowfall.) While recorded loss to the East Antarctic ice sheet was near zero in 1996–2006, the thinning of maritime sectors suggested to the researchers that this may change in the near future.

ANTIGUA AND BARBUDA

Introductory Survey

Location, Climate, Language, Religion, Flag, Capital

The country comprises three islands: Antigua (280 sq km—108 sq miles), Barbuda (161 sq km—62 sq miles) and the uninhabited rocky islet of Redonda (1.6 sq km—0.6 sq mile). They lie along the outer edge of the Leeward Islands chain in the West Indies. Barbuda is the most northerly (40 km—25 miles north of Antigua), and Redonda is 40 km south-west of Antigua. The French island of Guadeloupe lies to the south of the country, the United Kingdom Overseas Territory of Montserrat to the south-west and Saint Christopher and Nevis to the west. The climate is tropical, although tempered by constant sea breezes and the trade winds, and the mean annual rainfall of 1,000 mm (40 ins) is slight for the region. The temperature averages 27°C (81°F), but can rise to 33°C (93°F) during the hot season between May and October. English is the official language, but an English patois is commonly used. The majority of the inhabitants profess Christianity, and are mainly adherents of the Anglican Communion. The national flag consists of an inverted triangle centred on a red field; the triangle is divided horizontally into three unequal bands, of black, blue and white, with the black stripe bearing a symbol of the rising sun in gold. The capital is St John's, on Antigua.

Recent History

The British colonized Antigua in the 17th century. The island of Barbuda, formerly a slave stud farm for the Codrington family, was annexed to the territory in 1860. Until December 1959 Antigua and other nearby British territories were administered, under a federal system, as the Leeward Islands. The first elections under universal adult suffrage were held in 1951. The colony participated in the West Indies Federation, which was formed in January 1958 but dissolved in May 1962.

Attempts to form a smaller East Caribbean Federation failed, and most of the eligible colonies subsequently became Associated States in an arrangement that gave them full internal self-government while the United Kingdom retained responsibility for defence and foreign affairs. Antigua attained associated status in February 1967. A House of Representatives replaced the Legislative Council, the Administrator became Governor and the Chief Minister was restyled Premier.

In the first general election under associated status, held in February 1971, the Progressive Labour Movement (PLM) ousted the Antigua Labour Party (ALP), which had held power since 1946, by winning 13 of the 17 seats in the House of Representatives. George Walter, leader of the PLM, replaced Vere C. Bird, Sr, as Premier. However, a general election in February 1976 was won by the ALP, with 11 seats, while the seat representing Barbuda was won by an independent. Vere Bird, the ALP's leader, again became Premier, while Lester Bird, one of his sons, became Deputy Premier.

In 1975 the Associated States agreed to seek independence separately. In the 1976 elections the PLM campaigned for early independence while the ALP opposed it. In September 1978, however, the ALP Government declared that the economic foundation for independence had been laid, and a premature general election was held in April 1980, when the ALP won 13 of the 17 seats. There was strong opposition in Barbuda to gaining independence as part of Antigua, and at local elections in March 1981 the Barbuda People's Movement (BPM), which continued to campaign for secession from Antigua, won all the seats on the Barbuda Council. However, the territory finally became independent, as Antigua and Barbuda, on 1 November 1981, remaining within the Commonwealth. The grievances of the Barbudans concerning control of land and devolution of power were unresolved, although the ALP Government had conceded a certain degree of internal autonomy to the Barbuda Council. The Governor, Sir Wilfred Jacobs, became Governor-General, while the Premier, Vere Bird, Sr, became the country's first Prime Minister.

Following disagreements within the opposition PLM, George Walter formed his own political party, the United People's Movement (UPM), in 1982. In April 1984, at the first general election since independence, divisions within the opposition allowed the ALP to win all of the 16 seats that it contested. The remaining seat, representing Barbuda, was retained by an unopposed independent.

In November 1986 controversy surrounding a rehabilitation scheme at the international airport on Antigua led to an official inquiry, which concluded that Vere Bird, Jr (a senior minister and the eldest son of the Prime Minister), had acted inappropriately by awarding part of the contract to a company with which he was personally involved. The affair divided the ALP, with eight ministers (including Lester Bird, the Deputy Prime Minister) demanding the resignation of Vere Bird, Jr, and Prime Minister Bird refusing to dismiss him. The rifts within the ALP and the Bird family continued into 1988, when new allegations of corruption implicated Lester Bird. At a general election in March 1989 the ALP remained the ruling party by retaining 15 of the 16 seats that it had held previously. The United National Democratic Party (UNDP, formed by the merger of the UPM with the National Democratic Party) won more than 30% of the total votes, but only one seat. The Barbuda seat was won by the BPM.

In April 1990 the Government of Antigua and Barbuda received a diplomatic note of protest from the Government of Colombia regarding the sale of weapons to the Medellín cartel of drugs-traffickers in Colombia. The weapons had originally been sold by Israel to Antigua and Barbuda, but, contrary to regulation, were then immediately shipped on to Colombia in April 1989. The communication from the Colombian Government implicated Vere Bird, Jr, and the Prime Minister eventually agreed to establish a judicial inquiry. In October 1990 the Chamber of Commerce recommended the resignation of the Government, and in November the Government dismissed Vere Bird, Jr, and banned him for life from holding office in the Government. The head of the defence force, Col Clyde Walker, was also dismissed.

Discontent within the ALP (including dissatisfaction with the leadership of Vere Bird, Sr) provoked a serious political crisis in early 1991. The Minister of Finance, John St Luce, resigned in February, after claiming that the Prime Minister ignored his proposals for a restructuring of government. A subsequent cabinet reshuffle (in which Lester Bird lost his deputy premiership) provoked the immediate resignation of three ministers. In September, however, Lester Bird and John St Luce accepted invitations from the Prime Minister to rejoin the Cabinet.

In early 1992 further reports of corruption involving Vere Bird, Sr, provoked public unrest and demands for his resignation. In April the Antigua Caribbean Liberation Movement, the PLM and the UNDP consolidated their opposition to the Government by merging to form the United Progressive Party (UPP). In August further controversy arose when proposed anti-corruption legislation (which had been recommended following the Colombian arms scandal in 1991) was withdrawn as a result of legal intervention by the Prime Minister.

At a general election in March 1994 the ALP remained the ruling party, although with a reduced majority, having secured 11 seats; the UPP won five and the BPM retained the Barbuda seat. Following the election, Lester Bird assumed the premiership.

In February 1995 an ALP activist, Leonard Aaron, was charged with threatening to murder Tim Hector, editor of an opposition newspaper, *The Outlet*. It was reported that Hector's house had been burgled on several occasions, when material containing allegedly incriminating information relating to members of the Government had been stolen. Aaron was subsequently released, following the intervention of the Prime Minister. In May the Prime Minister's brother, Ivor Bird, was arrested following an incident in which he collected luggage at V. C. Bird International Airport from a Barbadian citizen from Venezuela that contained 12 kg of cocaine. *The Outlet* claimed that such an exchange had occurred on at least three previous occasions. Ivor Bird's subsequent release from police custody, upon payment of a fine of EC $200,000, attracted considerable criticism. In an attempt to improve the country's worsening reputation as a centre for drugs-trafficking, the Government proposed legislation in 1996 that aimed to curb the illegal drugs trade. A report published by the US Government in early 1998 found Antigua and Barbuda to be 'of primary concern' with regard to drugs-trafficking and money-laundering.

In May 1996 Vere Bird, Jr, who had been declared unfit for public office following a judicial inquiry in 1990 (see above), was controversially appointed to the post of Special Adviser to the Prime Minister. In September Molwyn Joseph resigned as Minister of Finance over allegations of corruption. His resignation followed an opposition protest at which the UPP leader, Baldwin Spencer, and seven other party members, including Tim Hector, were arrested (charges brought against them were later dismissed). A further demonstration took place at the end of the month, when some 10,000 people demanded a full inquiry into the affair and an early general election. In early December 1997, however, Joseph was reinstated in the Cabinet, an appointment that was vehemently condemned by the opposition.

In March 1997 the opposition BPM defeated the ALP's ally, the New Barbuda Development Movement, in elections to the Barbuda Council, winning all five of the contested seats and thus gaining control of all the seats in the nine-member Council. In the same month the High Court upheld a constitutional motion presented by Baldwin Spencer seeking the right of expression for the opposition on state-owned radio and television (denied during the electoral campaign in March 1994). In May and June the UPP boycotted sittings of the House of Representatives (the first legislative boycotts in the country's history) during a parliamentary debate on a proposed US $300m. tourism development on Guiana Island, claiming that the initiative had not been adequately publicized and would be detrimental to the island's ecology. The project was subsequently endorsed by legislature, but continued to provoke controversy. In December 1997 Vere Bird, Jr, was slightly wounded in a shooting incident on the same day as the Government agreed terms for the compulsory resettlement of the island's sole occupants, Cyril 'Taffy' Bufton and his wife. Bufton was subsequently charged with attempted murder, but was acquitted in October 1998. The UPP denied government allegations of its involvement in the attack.

Meanwhile, in August 1997 *The Outlet* published further allegations regarding government-supported drugs-trafficking, including a claim that a Colombian drugs cartel had contributed US $1m. to the ALP's election campaign in 1994. In response, Prime Minister Lester Bird obtained a High Court injunction in early September prohibiting the newspaper from publishing further material relating to the allegations. In November the printing presses of *The Outlet* were destroyed by fire, two days after the newspaper's editor, Tim Hector, had publicly alleged that a large consignment of 'sophisticated' weaponry had entered Antigua. The Government denied allegations that it was responsible for the fire, and stated that a shipment of 'basic' arms had been imported for police use.

At a general election held on 9 March 1999, the ALP increased its representation in the 17-seat House of Representatives from 11 to 12, at the expense of the UPP, which secured four seats; the BPM retained its single seat. Lester Bird was reappointed Prime Minister, and a new Cabinet was duly appointed, which again controversially included Vere Bird, Jr. Independent observers declared the election to have been free, although they expressed reservations concerning its fairness, owing to the ALP's large-scale expenditure and use of the media during its electoral campaign.

Also in March 1999 the US Government published a report that claimed that recent Antiguan financial legislation had weakened regulations concerning money-laundering and increased the secrecy surrounding 'offshore' banks. It also advised US banks to scrutinize all financial dealings with Antigua and Barbuda, which was described as a potential 'haven for money-laundering activities'. In April the United Kingdom issued a similar financial advisory to its banks. In response, in July Antigua and Barbuda became the first Eastern Caribbean country to bring into force a treaty with the USA on extradition and mutual legal assistance and in September established an independent body, the International Financial Sector Regulatory Body, to regulate 'offshore' banking. Although in 2000 Antigua and Barbuda's financial system was criticized by the Organisation for Economic Co-operation and Development (OECD, see p. 347) and by the Financial Action Task Force (FATF, see p. 416), in 2001 the FATF recognized the state as a 'fully co-operative jurisdiction against money laundering'. Furthermore by July the country had satisfied the United Kingdom that its financial institutions no longer needed special attention and in the following month the US Treasury withdrew its financial advisory notice. In December the Government signed a tax information exchange agreement with the USA and concluded a similar agreement with Australia and New Zealand in January 2004. In 2003 the Government strongly criticized OECD and the FATF for protecting the financial regimes of powerful states at the expense of smaller nations and for usurping the 'role of international organizations such as the World Trade Organization (WTO, see p. 396) in global governance'.

In January 2000 the Government established a commission, chaired by Sir Fred Philips, a former Governor of Saint Christopher and Nevis, to review the Constitution. It was to examine the role of the Government, political parties and non-governmental organizations, and was to focus on the maintenance of democracy and accountability. The commission's recommendations, reported in February 2002, included the replacement of the Queen as head of state with a President chosen by the majority party in Parliament, and amalgamation of the Senate and House of Representatives into a unicameral legislature, as well as a bill of rights and integrity legislation.

In May 2001 Dr Errol Cort, the Attorney-General, George 'Bacchanal' Walker, the Leader of Government Business in the Senate, and Bernard Percival, the former Minister of Health and head of the state-run Medical Benefits Scheme (MBS), were dismissed from their posts after the publication of an audit into alleged fraud in the MBS. An independent Commission of Inquiry into the funding and practices of the MBS, concluded in July 2002, recommended that a special prosecutor be appointed to examine charges against 12 people, including two former health ministers, implicated in abusing the scheme. The Inquiry also recommended the conversion of the MBS into a health insurance scheme run by an independent body, and stressed that the Government should not interfere with the scheme's operation. In April of that year fraud allegations arising from the Inquiry prompted the resignation of the Minister of Trade, Industry and Business Development, Hilroy Humphreys.

Also in April 2002 a further public dispute emerged, which prompted the Prime Minister to initiate a libel suit against leading members of the UPP, including Baldwin Spencer, as well as against an independent newspaper and radio station and a 15-year old girl. In early June the Prime Minister abandoned an initial attempt to obtain a court injunction against further repetition of the allegations, paying costs of EC $26,000 to his opponents. The libel case was scheduled to open in February 2003, but Bird dropped the suit against the newspaper and radio journalists before proceedings began. The case against the 15-year-old girl continued; however, she in turn initiated civil proceedings against the Prime Minister, before dropping the case in October.

In June 2003 Senator Asot Michael, the Minister of State in the Office of the Prime Minister with responsibility for Finance, resigned following accusations that he wielded more power in the ALP administration than was suitable for a non-elected politician. Michael's departure prompted Bird to effect a cabinet reorganization, which included the appointment of Longford Jeremy as Minister of Home Affairs, Information, Local Government and Youth Empowerment. Earlier in the same month Jeremy, along with four other deputies, had resigned the ALP whip for a short period after criticizing Bird's leadership. In November a UPP request for a motion of 'no confidence' in two government ministers, Molwyn Joseph and Gaston Brown, was denied by the Speaker; the opposition party alleged that both men received substantial sums of money from Allen Stanford, a US businessman and Chairman of the Bank of Antigua, during the negotiation of a real-estate transaction between the Government and the bank. In 2007 the ALP appeared to be renewing its links with Stanford at a time when the party was engaged in public disputes over various structural and management issues within the party.

At a general election on 23 March 2004 the opposition UPP, led by Baldwin Spencer, secured 12 out of the 17 parliamentary seats, thereby removing from government the ALP, which had held power since 1976. The ALP, which had been weakened by personal allegations surrounding Lester Bird and by a damaging contraction in the crucial tourism sector, secured only four seats. An extremely high voter turn-out—91.2% of the electorate—was interpreted as a strong indication of public resentment towards the Bird regime. The election in the remaining constituency, that of Barbuda, resulted in a tie between the incumbent BPM and a newly formed party, the Barbuda People's Movement for Change (BPMC); since neither candidate favoured a recount of the ballots, the island's electorate voted again on 20 April. Trevor Walker, the candidate of the BPM, was duly elected by a narrow margin. In advance of the general election a completely new electoral register was, with the assistance of the Electoral Office of Jamaica, prepared for the first time since 1975. Elimination of deceased and non-resident names reduced the list by more than one-fifth, while voters were issued with identity cards including a photograph and fingerprint, decreasing the risk that illegitimate votes would be cast. Spencer was sworn in as Prime Minister on 24 March.

Shortly after its removal from government, Bird's regime was again embroiled in controversy when Spencer ordered an investigation into accusations that the outgoing Prime Minister had illegally removed documents from state offices; Bird insisted he had only removed personal items and described the ensuing police search of his house as a 'witch hunt'. Spencer, in 2005, promised to investigate other alleged offences by Bird and his officials: in November it was reported that the Government was to sue the former Prime Minister and two erstwhile ALP cabinet ministers, Robin Yearwood and Hugh Marshall, Sr, for allegedly profiting from the sale of state lands.

In November 2005 the Government dismissed the board of the Antigua Public Utilities Authority (APUA), which had been appointed by Spencer in July 2004, following reports of financial irregularities and conflicts of interest, particularly regarding the proposed sale of APUA's digital mobile cellular telephone network (Personal Communications Services—PCS) to an Irish-owned multinational company, Digicel. Spencer transferred responsibility for APUA to the Office of the Prime Minister as part of a cabinet reorganization in December 2006, which also included the reassignment of a number of ministerial portfolios and the re-designation of several other ministry departments. APUA filed a lawsuit against five ex-cabinet ministers, including Bird, in June 2007, seeking to recover an estimated US $34m. allegedly misappropriated from the company and used to finance several projects around the country.

In July 2007 Louise Lake-Tack was sworn in as Governor-General, becoming the first woman in the country's history to assume this important role.

In foreign relations Antigua and Barbuda has traditionally followed a policy of non-alignment. In May 2006 the country was admitted to the Non-aligned Movement (see p. 424), although it has strong links with the USA. In September 2003 Antigua and Barbuda became the 67th nation to agree to grant immunity from prosecutions before the International Criminal Court (ICC) to US nationals accused of war crimes. In July the US Administration had rescinded military aid to several Caribbean nations, including Antigua and Barbuda, following their failure to agree to US terms over the ICC. In September 2001 the Government established diplomatic relations with Libya, after that country announced a US $1m. aid package to Antigua. The Government of Libya announced in September 2007 that it was to provide financial assistance for the development of the transport infrastructure in Antigua and Barbuda. Antigua and Barbuda is also a member of the CARICOM (see p. 196). In November 2003 the People's Republic of China granted Antigua a US $12m. loan, a large part of which was to fund the construction of a new sports stadium for the 2007 International Cricket Council Cricket World Cup, and in November 2006 the Antiguan Government received $7.5m. under the Bolivarian Alternative for Latin America (Alternativa Bolivariana para América Latina y el Caribe—ALBA) initiative—introduced by the Government of Venezuela to facilitate infrastructure and development programmes across the Caribbean region. The funds were intended for the upgrade of the V. C. Bird International Airport.

In 2003 the Government challenged US restrictions on 'offshore' internet gambling through the structures of the WTO (see p. 396), and in April 2005 received a ruling that was interpreted as partly in its favour. According to the Government, at least 10 new gambling companies were scheduled to open in 2006, to augment the 14 already in operation. The dispute continued unabated throughout 2006, aggravated by the successful passage of an 'Unlawful Internet Gambling Enforcement Act' in the US Congress on 30 September. In March 2007 the WTO Dispute Settlement Body ruled that the US ban was illegal and in May the USA announced that it would withdraw from any commitments relating to gambling under the General Agreement on Trade in Services (GATS). In June the Government of Antigua and Barbuda filed formal trade sanctions against the USA, demanding US $3,400m. in compensation, however the USA contended that the terms it had originally negotiated under the Agreement did not explicitly refer to internet gambling, thus rendering it exempt from the payment of such compensation. WTO arbitrators ruled in December 2007 that Antigua be awarded $21m. per year in compensation from the USA.

At the annual meeting of the International Whaling Commission in June 2006, Antigua voted, along with other members of the Organisation of Eastern Caribbean States (OECS, see p. 425), in favour of an end to a 20-year commercial whaling moratorium. The Government's apparent pro-whaling stance provoked allegations that Japanese financial assistance had amounted to bribery (Japan was in favour of ending the ban), and that the vote had jeopardized relations with environmental groups and other foreign investors. At the May 2007 meeting of the Commission Antigua was among several OECS countries to confirm their concurrence with a request, issued by Saint Vincent and the Grenadines, for an increase to those islands' commercial whaling quotas. An appeal for the protection of the indigenous and coastal population's rights to preserve their traditional fishing practices—and for acknowledgement of earlier recommendations, by Saint Christopher and Nevis, that a policy of appropriate management of marine resources be adopted as opposed to a complete ban—was presented to the Commission. Opposition to the proposed establishment of a marine mammal sanctuary in the French West Indies was also reiterated, particularly as marine territorial boundaries between the French dependencies and several Eastern Caribbean nations remained in dispute.

The signing of a joint communiqué between Antigua and Qatar on 9 October 2006, and subsequently with Bahrain on 20 October, signalled the commencement of a hitherto unprecedented diplomatic foray into the Middle East by the Caribbean state; a similar agreement was signed on 12 December with Singapore.

In September 2007 the Government signed an agreement to repay its outstanding debts to the International Criminal Police Organization. Non-payment of statutory contributions since 2001 had meant that Antigua and Barbuda had lost a number of member privileges, but the agreement allows the country to participate fully in the decision-making process of the organization.

The number of violent crimes in the country has increased rapidly in recent years: reported murders rose from three in both 2004 and 2005 to 12 in 2006 and nine in the first five months of 2007. The trend was attributed to an increase in the number of criminal deportees from the USA being repatriated to the region, and in 2007 the Government undertook a series of discussions with the US Department of Homeland Security, aimed at increasing co-operation between the two countries on this matter.

Government

Antigua and Barbuda is a constitutional monarchy. Executive power is vested in the British sovereign, as Head of State, and exercised by the Governor-General, who represents the sovereign locally and is appointed on the advice of the Antiguan Prime Minister. Legislative power is vested in Parliament, comprising the sovereign, a 17-member Senate and a 17-member House of Representatives. Members of the House are elected from single-member constituencies for up to five years by universal adult suffrage. The Senate is composed of 11 members (of whom one must be an inhabitant of Barbuda) appointed on the advice of the Prime Minister, four appointed on the advice of the Leader of the Opposition, one appointed at the discretion of the Governor-General and one appointed on the advice of the Barbuda Council. Government is effectively by the Cabinet. The Governor-General appoints the Prime Minister and, on the latter's recommendation, selects the other ministers. The Prime Minister must be able to command the support of a majority of the House, to which the Cabinet is responsible. The Barbuda Council has nine seats, with partial elections held every two years.

Defence

There is a small defence force of 170 men (army 125, navy 45). The US Government leases two military bases on Antigua. Antigua and Barbuda participates in the US-sponsored Regional Security System. The defence budget in 2007 was estimated at EC $14.0m.; some $4.3m. of the defence budget in that year was to be allocated specifically to the Antigua and Barbuda Defense Force to provide for equipment and an additional 150 recruits.

Economic Affairs

In 2006, according to estimates by the World Bank, Antigua and Barbuda's gross national income (GNI), measured at average 2004–06 prices, was US $937m., equivalent to $11,210 per head (or $13,500 per head on an international purchasing-power parity basis). During 1996–2005, it was estimated, the population increased at an average rate of 1.6% per year, while gross domestic product (GDP) per head increased, in real terms, by an average of 2.8% per year. Overall GDP increased, in real terms, at an average annual rate of 4.5% in 1996–2006. According to the Eastern Caribbean Central Bank (ECCB), real GDP increased by 12.5% in 2006.

Agriculture (including forestry and fishing) engaged 23.1% of the active labour force in 2005, according to estimates by the FAO. The sector contributed 3.1% of GDP in 2006. According to the ECCB, agricultural GDP increased, in real terms, between 1998 and 2006 at an average rate of 2.3% per year. The agricultural sector increased, in real terms, by 2.9% in 2006. The principal crops are cucumbers, pumpkins, sweet potatoes, mangoes, coconuts, limes, melons and the speciality 'Antigua Black' pineapple. Lobster, shrimp and crab farms are in operation.

Industry (comprising mining, manufacturing, construction and utilities) employed 14.6% of the active labour force in 2001 and provided 25.5% of GDP in 2006. The principal industrial activity is construction, accounting for 8.6% of total employment in 2001. Industrial GDP increased, in real terms, at an average rate of 8.6% per year during 1998–2006. It rose by 28.2% in 2006, mainly owing to a 35.0% expansion in the construction sector.

Mining and quarrying employed only 0.3% of the active labour force in 2001 and contributed 2.0% of GDP in 2006. The real GDP of the mining sector increased at an average rate of 8.4% per year during 1998–2006, mainly owing to recorded growth of 45.0% in 2006.

The manufacturing sector consists of some light industries producing garments, paper, paint, furniture, food and beverage products, and the assembly of household appliances and electrical components for export. Manufacturing contributed 1.7% of GDP in 2006. Construction provided 19.2% of GDP in the same year. In real terms, the GDP of the manufacturing sector increased at an average rate of 3.2% per year during 1998–2006. Manufacturing GDP increased by 5.0% in 2006.

Most of the country's energy production is derived from imported fuel. Imports of mineral fuels, lubricants and related materials accounted for 16.3% of total imports in 2000. In September 2005 the Government became one of 13 Caribbean administrations to sign the PetroCaribe accord, under which Antigua and Barbuda would be allowed to purchase petroleum from Venezuela at reduced prices.

Services provided 71.0% of employment in 2001 and 71.4% of GDP in 2006. The combined GDP of the service sectors increased, in real terms, at an average rate of 3.7% per year during 1998–2006. It rose by 7.0% in 2006. The islands' economy is heavily dependent on the tourism industry, which is particularly vulnerable to external factors, such as the behaviour of the world economy and the movement of tropical storms. Visitor arrivals decreased hugely in 2002 following a severe contraction in the US market, before recovering to an estimated 808,148 in 2004; however, visitors fell to 751,379 in 2005, recovering slightly in 2006 to a preliminary 755,385. Similarly, tourism receipts also fell in 2002, but recovered thereafter, reaching EC $915.5m. in 2005. Receipts were a preliminary $937.4m. in 2006. The real GDP of the hotels and restaurants sector declined in 2005 and 2006, by 1.1% and 2.4%, respectively, and its contribution to GDP fell to 8.4% in the later year (from 12.4% in 2004). The downturn in the sector followed amendments to the Western Hemisphere Travel Initiative—ratified by the US Congress in October 2006—which required all US citizens travelling to and from the Caribbean to hold a valid passport, a development described by the Caribbean Tourism Organization as potentially severely damaging to the region's tourism industry. The measures were to be implemented as early as January 2007, although cruise-ship passengers were to be exempt from the ruling until 1 January 2009. Most stop-over tourists are from the United Kingdom (32.3% in 2006), although a significant number (26.7% in 2006) are from the USA.

An independent body, the International Financial Sector Regulatory Body, was established in 1999 to regulate the 'offshore' financial services sector, operations of which in Antigua and Barbuda had hitherto been the subject of adverse international scrutiny (see Recent History). In 2001 the Financial Action Task Force (FATF, see p. 416) recognized Antigua and Barbuda as a 'fully co-operative jurisdiction against money-laundering'. In 2005 there were 15 licensed 'offshore' banks registered in the country, 11 of which were 'shell' banks with no physical presence; in excess of 30 further banks have been closed since 1999 for non-compliance with regulatory criteria.

Antigua and Barbuda recorded a visible trade deficit in 2006 of EC $1,052.1m. and a deficit of $439.2m. on the current account of the balance of payments. The country's principal trading partners are the other members of the Caribbean Community and Common Market (CARICOM, see p. 196), the USA, the United Kingdom and Canada. In 2000 the USA provided 49.3% of total imports and was also an important market for exports (mainly re-exports).

In 2006 there was a preliminary budgetary deficit of EC $231.4m. By the end of 2003 total external debt amounted to US $520.9m. In that year debt-servicing costs accounted for some 8.9% of the value of exports of goods and services, a figure that was expected to decrease slightly in 2004, to 8.5%. Total external and domestic debt was reported in the 2006 budgetary address as EC $1,112m. at September of that year. The annual average rate of inflation was 2.3% in 1993–2001. Consumer prices rose by 2.8% in 2004 and 2.6% in 2005. New tax legislation introduced in 2006 by the United Progressive Party sought to keep inflation below 3% by waiving the islands' customs tax on an increasing range of consumer products. The rate of unemployment in 2001 was reported to be 8.1% of the labour force.

Antigua and Barbuda is a member of CARICOM, the Organisation of Eastern Caribbean States (OECS, see p. 425), the Organization of American States (see p. 360), and is a signatory of the Cotonou Agreement (the successor agreement to Lomé Conventions) with the European Union (EU, see p. 244). Antigua and Barbuda is also a member of the Eastern Caribbean Securities Exchange (based in Saint Christopher and Nevis), established in 2001. In July 2007 the country joined the single market component of CARICOM's Single Market and Economy, full implementation of which was expected by 2015.

Despite some efforts at diversification, for example, the development of 'offshore' financial services, the economy of Antigua and Barbuda is dominated by tourism. The World Travel and Tourism Council estimated that in 2005 the tourism industry provided 35% of total employment. A decline in the rate of the country's economic expansion in 2001 (to 1.5%) was principally attributable to the weak performance of the tourism sector; equally, the improved growth of 2003 and 2004, which was estimated at 5.2% and 5.5%, respectively, reflected the receipt of record tourism earnings. Tourism earnings were expected to gain considerable momentum in 2007 from the hosting of the International Cricket Council Cricket World Cup in the Caribbean. According to the ECCB, economic growth was 12.5% in 2006, compared with 5.3% in 2005; however, the IMF reported more moderate growth of 8.0% in 2006. As well as tourism, the high growth rates have been attributed to increased revenues in the construction sector, which benefited from the necessary infrastructure improvements for the hosting of the Cricket World Cup. The IMF forecasts a slowdown in growth, to 4.8%, in 2007. It was hoped that the relatively stable economic situation would allow the Government to address the issue of the country's very large external debt, responsibility for which the IMF apportioned to 'years of fiscal mismanagement'. The debt stock was an estimated US $1,030m. in 2006. In view of this, the Antigua and Barbuda Sales Tax was implemented on 29 January 2007. Its introduction coincided with the revocation of several other taxes, all of which were further expected to facilitate a shift towards regional economic union, reflecting similar measures introduced by Antigua's Caribbean neighbours in recent years. The anticipated liberalization of the telecommunications sector in 2008 was expected to boost government revenues. The Government was also to receive an annual US $21m. from the USA after the World Trade Organization ruled in its favour in the two countries' dispute over internet gambling licences.

Education

Education is compulsory for 11 years between five and 16 years of age. Primary education begins at the age of five and normally lasts for seven years. Secondary education, beginning at 12 years of age, lasts for five years, comprising a first cycle of three years and a second cycle of two years. In 2000/01 there were 55 primary and 14 secondary schools; the majority of schools are administered by the Government. In the same year some 10,427 primary school pupils and 5,794 secondary school pupils were enrolled. Teacher-training and technical training are available at the

ANTIGUA AND BARBUDA

Antigua State College in St John's. An extra-mural department of the University of the West Indies offers several foundation courses leading to higher study at branches elsewhere. In November 2002 the European Union (see p. 244) agreed to provide funding for tertiary education worth EC $2.6m. Current government expenditure on education in 2006 was projected at $62.7m., equivalent to 9.4% of total budgetary expenditure.

Public Holidays

2008: 1 January (New Year's Day), 21 March (Good Friday), 24 March (Easter Monday), 2 May (Labour Day), 12 May (Whit Monday), 7 June (Queen's Official Birthday), 2 July (CARICOM Day), 4–5 August (Carnival), 1 November (Independence Day), 9 December (National Heroes' Day), 25–26 December (Christmas).

2009: 1 January (New Year's Day), 10 April (Good Friday), 13 April (Easter Monday), 2 May (Labour Day), 1 June (Whit Monday), 6 June (Queen's Official Birthday), 2 July (CARICOM Day), 3–4 August (Carnival), 1 November (Independence Day), 9 December (National Heroes' Day), 25–26 December (Christmas).

Weights and Measures

The imperial system is in use, but a metrication programme is being introduced.

Statistical Survey

Source (unless otherwise stated): Ministry of Finance, Economic Development and Planning, Govt Office Complex, Parliament Dr., St John's; tel. 462-5015; fax 462-4860; e-mail budget@candw.ag.

AREA AND POPULATION

Area: 441.6 sq km (170.5 sq miles).

Population: 62,922 at census of 28 May 1991; 77,426 (males 37,002, females 40,424) at census of 28 May 2001. Mid-2005 (estimate): 82,786 (Source: UN, *Population and Vital Statistics Report*).

Density (mid-2005): 187.5 per sq km.

Principal Town: St John's (capital), population 24,451 at 2001 census. *Mid-2005* (UN estimate, incl. suburbs): St John's 32,000 (Source: UN, *World Urbanization Prospects: The 2005 Revision*).

Births, Marriages and Deaths (registrations, 2001): Live births 1,366 (birth rate 18.04 per 1,000); Marriages 1,784 (marriage rate 23.55 per 1,000); Deaths 457 (death rate 6.03 per 1,000).

Expectation of Life (years at birth, WHO estimates): 72.6 (males 69.9; females 75.4) in 2005. Source: WHO, *World Health Statistics*.

Employment (persons aged 15 years and over, census of May 2001): Agriculture, forestry, hunting and fishing 946; Mining and quarrying 106; Manufacturing 1,541; Electricity, gas and water 513; Construction 3,122; Wholesale and retail trade 4,846; Restaurants and hotels 5,081; Transport, storage and communications 2,808; Financial intermediation 1,049; Real estate, renting and business activities 1,460; Community, social and personal services (incl. education, health and social work) 6,113; Public administration and defence 4,376; Activities not adequately defined 4,272; Total employed 36,233 (males 18,188, females 18,046) (Source: National Statistics Office). *Mid-2005* (estimates in '000): Agriculture, etc. 9; Total labour force 39 (Source: FAO).

HEALTH AND WELFARE
Key Indicators

Total Fertility Rate (children per woman, 2005): 2.2.

Under-5 Mortality Rate (per 1,000 live births, 2005): 12.

Physicians (per 1,000 head, 1999): 0.17.

Hospital Beds (per 1,000 head, 2005): 2.4.

Health Expenditure (2004): US $ per head (PPP): 516.2.

Health Expenditure (2004): % of GDP: 4.8.

Health Expenditure (2004): public (% of total): 70.6.

Access to Water (% of persons, 2004): 96.

Access to Sanitation (% of persons, 2004): 91.

Human Development Index (2005): ranking: 57.

Human Development Index (2005): value: 0.815.

For sources and definitions, see explanatory note on p. vi.

AGRICULTURE, ETC.

Principal Crops ('000 metric tons, 2005, FAO estimates): Cantaloupes and other melons 0.7; Vegetables (incl. melons) 2.8; Guavas, mangoes and mangosteens 1.2; Fruits (excl. melons) 9.7.

Livestock ('000 head, year ending September 2005, FAO estimates): Asses 1.6; Cattle 14.3; Pigs 2.8; Sheep 19.0; Goats 36.0; Poultry 105.0.

Livestock Products ('000 metric tons, 2005, FAO estimates): Cattle meat 0.5; Cows' milk 5.4; Hen eggs 0.3.

Fishing (metric tons, live weight, 2005): Groupers and seabasses 455; Snappers and jobfishes 296; Grunts and sweetlips 410; Parrotfishes 202; Surgeonfishes 254; Triggerfishes and durgons 61; Caribbean spiny lobster 309; Stromboid conches 528; Total catch (incl. others) 2,999.

Source: FAO.

INDUSTRY

Production (1988 estimates unless otherwise indicated): Rum 4,000 hectolitres; Wines and vodka 2,000 hectolitres; Electric energy (2004) 109m. kWh. Source: UN, *Industrial Commodity Statistics Yearbook*.

FINANCE

Currency and Exchange Rates: 100 cents = 1 Eastern Caribbean dollar (EC $). *Sterling, US Dollar and Euro Equivalents* (30 November 2007): £1 sterling = EC $5.579; US $1 = EC $2.700; €1 = EC $3.985; EC $100 = £17.92 = US $37.04 = €25.09. *Exchange rate*: Fixed at US $1 = EC $2.700 since July 1976.

Budget (EC $ million, 2006, preliminary): *Revenue:* Tax revenue 571.4 (Taxes on income and profits 115.7, Taxes on property 11.3, Taxes on domestic goods and services 120.0, Taxes on international transactions 324.4); Other current revenue 35.1; Capital revenue 5.0; Total 611.5, excl. grants received (55.0). *Expenditure:* Current expenditure 642.8 (Personal emoluments 266.8, Goods and services 119.1, Interest payments 98.1, Transfers and subsidies 158.7); Capital expenditure and net lending 200.1; Total 842.9. Source: Eastern Caribbean Central Bank.

International Reserves (US $ million at 31 December 2006): IMF special drawing rights 0.01; Foreign exchange 142.61; Total 142.62. Source: IMF, *International Financial Statistics*.

Money Supply (EC $ million at 31 December 2006): Currency outside banks 143.71; Demand deposits at deposit money banks 602.83; Total money 746.55. Source: IMF, *International Financial Statistics*.

Cost of Living (Consumer Price Index; base: January 2001 = 100): 105.2 in 2003; 108.1 in 2004; 110.9 in 2005. Source: IMF, *Antigua and Barbuda: Statistical Appendix* (July 2006).

Expenditure on the Gross Domestic Product (EC $ million at current prices, 2006): Government final consumption expenditure 492.48; Private final consumption expenditure 817.22; Gross capital formation 2,019.01; *Total domestic expenditure* 3,328.71; Exports of goods and services 1,567.53; *Less* Imports of goods and services 2,179.56; *GDP at market prices* 2,716.68. Source: Eastern Caribbean Central Bank.

Gross Domestic Product by Economic Activity (EC $ million at current prices, 2006): Agriculture, hunting, forestry and fishing 75.30; Mining and quarrying 49.40; Manufacturing 42.41; Electricity and water 62.03; Construction 466.40; Trade 219.89; Restaurants and hotels 204.82; Transport and communications 450.40; Finance, insurance, real estate and business services 357.31; Government services 359.79; Other community, social and personal service activities 142.90; *Sub-total* 2,430.65; *Less* Financial intermediation services indirectly measured 156.44; *Gross value added in basic prices* 2,274.21; Taxes, less subsidies, on products 442.46; *GDP in market prices* 2,716.67. Source: Eastern Caribbean Central Bank.

Balance of Payments (EC $ million, 2006): Goods (net) –1,052.1; Services (net) 740.1; *Balance on goods and services* –312.0; Income (net) –144.3; *Balance on goods, services and income* –456.3; Current

ANTIGUA AND BARBUDA

transfers (net) 17.1; *Current balance* –439.2; Capital account (net) 60.0; Direct investment (net) 512.7; Portfolio investment (net) 26.3; Other investments (net) –118.5; *Overall balance* 41.3. Source: Eastern Caribbean Central Bank.

EXTERNAL TRADE

Total Trade (EC $ million): *Imports f.o.b.:* 887.0 in 2002; 932.2 in 2003; 997.5 in 2004 (preliminary figure). *Exports f.o.b.:* 47.0 in 2002; 50.2 in 2003; 53.9 in 2004 (preliminary figure). Source: Eastern Caribbean Central Bank.

Principal Commodities (US $ million, 2000): *Imports:* Food and live animals 58.3 (Meat and meat preparations 11.6; Vegetables and fruit 13.4); Beverages and tobacco 13.4 (Beverages 12.5); Crude materials (inedible) except fuels 9.9; Mineral fuels, lubricants, etc. 55.1 (Refined petroleum products 52.9); Chemicals and related products 22.5; Basic manufactures 45.8; Machinery and transport equipment 93.6 (Telecommunications and sound equipment 17.3; Road vehicles 18.7); Miscellaneous manufactured articles 37.9. Total (incl. others) 338.2. *Exports:* Food and live animals 0.5; Crude materials (inedible) except fuels 0.5; Chemicals and related products 1.4 (Pigments, paints, varnishes, etc. 1.0); Basic manufactures 2.5 (Textiles, yarn, fabrics, made-up articles, etc. 0.8; Iron and steel 0.8); Machinery and transport equipment 14.1 (General industrial machinery and equipment 0.6; Telecommunications and sound equipment 7.7; Road vehicles 1.2); Miscellaneous manufactured articles 2.1; Total (incl. others) 22.5. Source: UN, *International Trade Statistics Yearbook*.

Principal Trading Partners (US $ million, 2000): *Imports:* Barbados 5.5; Canada 12.5; Japan 10.5; Korea, Republic 2.4; Netherlands Antilles 40.4; Saint Vincent and the Grenadines 3.2; Trinidad and Tobago 21.6; United Kingdom 25.0; USA 166.6; Venezuela 11.3; Total (incl. others) 338.2. *Exports:* Barbados 1.1; Canada 0.4; Dominica 0.7; France 0.6; Jamaica 0.1; Montserrat 1.5; Netherlands Antilles 1.7; Saint Christopher and Nevis 1.6; Saint Lucia 0.8; Saint Vincent and the Grenadines 3.1; Trinidad and Tobago 0.4; United Kingdom 4.4; USA 4.3; Total (incl. others) 22.5. Source: UN, *International Trade Statistics Yearbook*.

TRANSPORT

Road Traffic (registered vehicles, 1998): Passenger motor cars and commercial vehicles 24,000. Source: UN, *Statistical Yearbook*.

Shipping (international freight traffic, '000 metric tons, 1990): Goods loaded 28; Goods unloaded 113 (Source: UN, *Monthly Bulletin of Statistics*). *Merchant Fleet* (registered at 31 December): 1,086 vessels (total displacement 7,947,165 grt) in 2006 (Source: Lloyd's Register-Fairplay, *World Fleet Statistics*).

Civil Aviation (traffic on scheduled services, 2003): Kilometres flown (million) 12; Passengers carried ('000) 1,428; Passenger-km (million) 325; Total ton-km (million) 32. Source: UN, *Statistical Yearbook*.

TOURISM

Visitor Arrivals: 808,158 (267,627 stop-over visitors, 17,778 yacht passengers, 522,753 cruise-ship passengers) in 2004; 751,379 (267,106 stop-over visitors, 17,422 yacht passengers, 466,851 cruise-ship passengers) in 2005; 755,385 (273,414 stop-over visitors, 21,122 yacht passengers, 460,849 cruise-ship passengers) in 2006 (preliminary).

Tourism Receipts (EC $ million): 910.8 in 2004; 915.5 in 2005; 937.4 in 2006 (preliminary).

Source: Eastern Caribbean Central Bank.

COMMUNICATIONS MEDIA

Radio Receivers (1997): 36,000 in use*.
Television Receivers (1999): 33,000 in use*.
Telephones (2006): 40,000 main lines in use†.
Facsimile Machines (year ending 31 March 1997): 850 in use‡.
Mobile Cellular Telephones (2006): 102,000 subscribers†.
Internet Users (2006): 32,000†.
Broadband (2006): 5,700 subscribers†.
Daily Newspapers (2004): 2.
Non-daily Newspapers (1996): 4*.

* Source: UNESCO, *Statistical Yearbook*.
† Source: International Telecommunication Union.
‡ Source: UN, *Statistical Yearbook*.

EDUCATION

Pre-primary (1983): 21 schools; 23 teachers; 677 pupils.
Primary (2000/01): 55 schools; 525 teachers; 10,427 students.
Secondary (2000/01): 14 schools; 361 teachers; 5,794 students.
Special (2000/01): 2 schools; 15 teachers; 61 students.
Tertiary (1986): 2 colleges; 631 students.
Adult Literacy Rate (estimate): 85.8% in 2005 (Source: UN Development Programme, *Human Development Report*).

Directory

The Constitution

The Constitution, which came into force at the independence of Antigua and Barbuda on 1 November 1981, states that Antigua and Barbuda is a 'unitary sovereign democratic state'. The main provisions of the Constitution are summarized below.

FUNDAMENTAL RIGHTS AND FREEDOMS

Regardless of race, place of origin, political opinion, colour, creed or sex, but subject to respect for the rights and freedoms of others and for the public interest, every person in Antigua and Barbuda is entitled to the rights of life, liberty, security of the person, the enjoyment of property and the protection of the law. Freedom of movement, of conscience, of expression (including freedom of the press), of peaceful assembly and association is guaranteed and the inviolability of family life, personal privacy, home and other property is maintained. Protection is afforded from discrimination on the grounds of race, sex, etc., and from slavery, forced labour, torture and inhuman treatment.

THE GOVERNOR-GENERAL

The British sovereign, as Monarch of Antigua and Barbuda, is the Head of State and is represented by a Governor-General of local citizenship.

PARLIAMENT

Parliament consists of the Monarch, a 17-member Senate and the House of Representatives, which is composed of 17 elected members. Senators are appointed by the Governor-General: 11 on the advice of the Prime Minister (one of whom must be an inhabitant of Barbuda), four on the advice of the Leader of the Opposition, one at his own discretion and one on the advice of the Barbuda Council. The Barbuda Council is the principal organ of local government in that island, whose membership and functions are determined by Parliament. The life of Parliament is five years.

Each constituency returns one Representative to the House who is directly elected in accordance with the Constitution.

The Attorney-General, if not otherwise a member of the House, is an ex offico member but does not have the right to vote.

Every citizen over the age of 18 is eligible to vote.

Parliament may alter any of the provisions of the Constitution.

THE EXECUTIVE

Executive authority is vested in the Monarch and exercisable by the Governor-General. The Governor-General appoints as Prime Minister that member of the House who, in the Governor-General's view, is best able to command the support of the majority of the members of the House, and other ministers on the advice of the Prime Minister. The Governor-General may remove the Prime Minister from office if a resolution of no confidence is passed by the House and the Prime Minister does not either resign or advise the Governor-General to dissolve Parliament within seven days.

The Cabinet consists of the Prime Minister and other ministers and the Attorney-General.

The Leader of the Opposition is appointed by the Governor-General as that member of the House who, in the Governor-General's view, is best able to command the support of a majority of members of the House who do not support the Government.

ANTIGUA AND BARBUDA

CITIZENSHIP

All persons born in Antigua and Barbuda before independence who, immediately prior to independence, were citizens of the United Kingdom and Colonies automatically become citizens of Antigua and Barbuda. All persons born outside the country with a parent or grandparent possessing citizenship of Antigua and Barbuda automatically acquire citizenship, as do those born in the country after independence. Provision is made for the acquisition of citizenship by those to whom it would not automatically be granted.

The Government

HEAD OF STATE

Monarch: HM Queen ELIZABETH II (succeeded to the throne 6 February 1952).
Governor-General: LOUISE LAKE-TACK (took office on 17 July 2007).

CABINET
(April 2008)

Prime Minister and Minister of Foreign Affairs: BALDWIN SPENCER.
Deputy Prime Minister and Minister of Works and Transportation: WILMOTH DANIEL.
Minister of Finance and Economy: Dr ERROL CORT.
Minister of Justice and Public Safety: Sen. COLIN DERRICK.
Attorney-General and Minister of Legal Affairs: JUSTIN L. SIMON.
Minister of Health: JOHN HERBERT MAGINLEY.
Minister of Tourism, Civil Aviation, Culture and the Environment: HAROLD E. E. LOVELL.
Minister of Education, Sports and Youth Affairs: BERTRAND JOSEPH.
Minister of Agriculture, Lands, Marine Resources and Agro Industries: JOANNE MASSIAH (acting).
Minister of Housing and Social Transformation: HILSON BAPTISTE.
Minister of Labour, Public Administration and Empowerment: Dr JACQUI QUINN-LEANDRO.
Minister of State without Portfolio: Sen. AZIZ FARES HADEED.
Minister of State in the Ministry of Agriculture, Lands, Marine Resources and Agro Industry, with Responsibility for Marine Affairs and Food Production: Sen. JOANNE MASSIAH.
Minister of State in the Ministry of Education, Sports and Youth Affairs, with Responsibility for Sports and Youth Affairs: WINSTON WILLIAMS.
Minister of State in the Ministry of Tourism, Civil Aviation, Culture and the Environment, with Responsibility for Culture and Independence Celebrations: ELESTON ADAMS.
Minister of State in the Office of the Prime Minister, with Responsibility for Barbuda Affairs: TREVOR MYKE WALKER.
Minister of State in the Office of the Prime Minister, with Responsibility for Information, Broadcasting and Telecommunications: Sen. Dr EDMOND MANSOOR.
Minister of State in the Ministry of Housing and Social Transformation: ELESTON ADAMS.

MINISTRIES

Office of the Prime Minister, incorporating the Ministry of Energy and the Antigua Public Utilities Authority: Queen Elizabeth Highway, St John's; tel. 462-4956; fax 462-3225; e-mail cora.richards@antigua.gov.ag; internet www.antigua.gov.ag.
Ministry of Agriculture, Lands, Marine Resources and Agro Industries: Queen Elizabeth Highway, St John's; tel. 462-1543; fax 462-6104.
Ministry of Barbuda Affairs: Govt Office Complex, Parliament Dr., St John's.
Ministry of Ecclesiastics: Govt Office Complex, Parliament Dr., St John's.
Ministry of Education, Sports and Youth Affairs: Govt Office Complex, Queen Elizabeth Highway, St John's; tel. 462-4959; fax 462-4970; e-mail doristeen.etinoff@ab.gov.ag.
Ministry of Finance and Economy: Govt Office Complex, Parliament Dr., St John's; tel. 462-5015; fax 462-4860; e-mail minfinance@antigua.gov.ag.
Ministry of Foreign Affairs: Queen Elizabeth Highway, St John's; tel. 462-1052; fax 462-2482; e-mail foreignaffairs@ab.gov.ag; internet www.foreignaffairs.gov.ag.
Ministry of Health: St John's St, St John's; tel. 462-1600; fax 462-5003; e-mail minhealth@antigua.gov.ag.
Ministry of Housing and Social Transformation: Dickenson Bay Street, St John's; tel. 562-5303; fax 562-3637.
Ministry of Human Development: Govt Office Complex, Queen Elizabeth Highway, St John's; tel. 462-4959; fax 462-4970.
Ministry of Information, Broadcasting and Telecommunications: St John's.
Ministry of International Transportation: St John's St, St John's; tel. 462-0894; fax 462-1529.
Ministry of Justice: Government Complex, Parliament Drive, POB 118, St John's; tel. 462-0017; fax 562-5415.
Ministry of Labour, Public Administration and Empowerment: Cnr of Nevis St and Friendly Alley, St John's; tel. 462-3331; fax 462-1595; e-mail minlabour@antigua.gov.ag.
Ministry of Legal Affairs, Land and Commercial Registries and Office of the Attorney-General: Government Complex, Queen Elizabeth Highway, St John's; tel. 462-0017; fax 462-2465; e-mail legalaffairs@ab.gov.ag.
Ministry of National Security: Govt Office Complex, Parliament Dr., St John's.
Ministry of Works, Transportation and the Environment: St John's.
Ministry of Tourism, Civil Aviation, Culture and the Environment: Government Office Complex, Bldg 1, Queen Elizabeth Highway, St John's; tel. 462-0480; fax 462-2483; e-mail mblackman@tourism.gov.ag.

Legislature

PARLIAMENT

Senate

President: HAZELYN FRANCIS.
There are 17 nominated members.

House of Representatives

Speaker: D. GISELLE ISAAC-ARRINDELL.
Ex Officio Member: The Attorney-General.
Clerk: SYLVIA WALKER.

General Election, 23 March 2004*

Party	Votes cast	%	Seats
United Progressive Party	21,892	55.2	12
Antigua Labour Party	16,544	41.7	4
Barbuda People's Movement	408	1.0	1
Barbuda People's Movement for Change	394	1.0	—
Independents and rejected ballots	391	0.9	—
Total	39,629	100.0	17

* The table reflects the final election results after a rerun ballot on 20 April 2004 in the constituency of Barbuda following a tie between the Barbuda People's Movement and the Barbuda People's Movement for Change.

Political Organizations

Antigua Freedom Party (AFP): St John's; f. 2003; Leader GEORGE (RICK) JAMES.
Antigua Labour Party (ALP): S46 North St, POB 948, St John's; tel. 462-2235; e-mail alp@antigualabourparty.net; internet www.antigualabourparty.net; f. 1968; Leader LESTER BRYANT BIRD; Chair. GASTON BROWNE.
Barbuda People's Movement (BPM): Codrington; campaigns for separate status for Barbuda; Parliamentary Leader THOMAS HILBOURNE FRANK; Chair. FABIAN JONES.
Barbuda People's Movement for Change (BPMC): Codrington; f. 2004; effectively replaced Organisation for National Reconstruction, which was f. 1983 and re-f. 1988 as Barbuda Independence Movement; advocates self-government for Barbuda; Pres. ARTHUR SHABAZZ-NIBBS.
Democratic People's Party (DPP): St John's; f. 2003; Leader SHERFIELD BOWEN.
First Christian Democratic Movement (FCDM): St John's; f. 2003; Leader EGBERT JOSEPH.

ANTIGUA AND BARBUDA   Directory

National Labour Party (NLP): St John's; f. 2003.
National Movement for Change (NMC): St John's; f. 2002; Leader ALISTAIR THOMAS.
New Barbuda Development Movement: Codrington; linked with the Antigua Labour Party.
Organisation for National Development: Upper St Mary's St, St John's; f. 2003 by breakaway faction of the United Progressive Party; Chair. GLENTIS GOODWIN; Sec.-Gen. VALERIE SAMUEL.
United Progressive Party (UPP): UPP Headquaters Bldg, Upper Nevis St, POB 2379, St John's; tel. 481-3888; fax 481-3877; e-mail upp@uppantigua.ag; internet www.uppantigua.ag; f. 1992 by merger of the Antigua Caribbean Liberation Movement (f. 1979), the Progressive Labour Movement (f. 1970) and the United National Democratic Party (f. 1986); Leader BALDWIN SPENCER; Chair. LEON (CHAKU) SYMISTER.

Diplomatic Representation

EMBASSIES AND HIGH COMMISSION IN ANTIGUA AND BARBUDA

China, People's Republic: Cedar Valley, POB 1446, St John's; tel. 462-1125; fax 462-6425; e-mail chinaemb_ag@mfa.gov.cn; internet ag.chineseembassy.org/eng; Ambassador CHEN LIGANG.
Cuba: Embassy of the Republic of Cuba, Longfords Main Rd, St John's; tel. 562-5864; Ambassador Dr MARCELINO FAJARDO DELGADO.
United Kingdom: British High Commission, Price Waterhouse Centre, 11 Old Parham Rd, POB 483, St John's; tel. 462-0008; fax 562-2124; e-mail britishc@candw.ag; Commissioner TERRY KNIGHT.
Venezuela: Jasmine Court, Friar's Hill Rd, POB 1201, St John's; tel. 462-1574; fax 462-1570; e-mail embaveneantigua@yahoo.es; Ambassador JOSÉ LAURENCIO SILVA MÉNDEZ.

Judicial System

Justice is administered by the Eastern Caribbean Supreme Court (ECSC), based in Saint Lucia, which consists of a High Court of Justice and a Court of Appeal. Two of the Court's 16 High Court Puisne Judges are resident in and responsible for Antigua and Barbuda, and preside over the Court of Summary Jurisdiction on the islands. One of two ECSC Masters, chiefly responsible for procedural and interlocutory matters, is also resident in Antigua. Magistrates' Courts in the territory administer lesser cases.

Acting Chief Justice: BRIAN GEORGE KEITH ALLEYNE (resident in Saint Lucia).
Puisne Judges: ERROL THOMAS, LOUISE BLENMAN.
Master: CHERYL MATHURIN.
Solicitor-General: LEBRECHT HESSE.

Religion

The majority of the inhabitants profess Christianity, and the largest denomination is the Church in the Province of the West Indies (Anglican Communion).

CHRISTIANITY

Antigua Christian Council: POB 863, St Mary's St, St John's; tel. 462-5792; fax 462-2383; e-mail djr@candw.ag; f. 1964; five mem. churches; Pres. Rt Rev. DONALD J. REECE (Roman Catholic Bishop of St John's-Basseterre); Treas. MARY-ROSE KNIGHT.

The Anglican Communion

Anglicans in Antigua and Barbuda are adherents of the Church in the Province of the West Indies. The diocese of the North Eastern Caribbean and Aruba comprises 12 islands: Antigua, Saint Christopher (St Kitts), Nevis, Anguilla, Barbuda, Montserrat, Dominica, Saba, St Martin/St Maarten, Aruba, St Bartholomew and St Eustatius; the total number of Anglicans is about 60,000. The See City is St John's, Antigua.

Bishop of the North Eastern Caribbean and Aruba: Rt Rev. LEROY ERROL BROOKS, Bishop's Lodge, POB 23, St John's; tel. 462-0151; fax 462-2090; e-mail dioceseneca@candw.ag.

The Roman Catholic Church

The diocese of St John's-Basseterre, suffragan to the archdiocese of Castries (Saint Lucia), includes Anguilla, Antigua and Barbuda, the British Virgin Islands, Montserrat and Saint Christopher and Nevis. At 31 December 2005 there were an estimated 15,604 adherents in the diocese. The Bishop participates in the Antilles Episcopal Conference (whose Secretariat is based in Port of Spain, Trinidad and Tobago).

Bishop of St John's-Basseterre: Rt Rev. DONALD JAMES REECE, Chancery Offices, POB 836, St John's; tel. 461-1135; fax 462-2383; e-mail djr@candw.ag.

Other Christian Churches

East Caribbean Baptist Mission: POB 2678, St John's; tel. 462-2894; fax 462-6029; e-mail admin@baptistantigua.org; internet www.baptistantigua.org; f. 1991; mem. congregation of the Baptist Circuit of Churches in the East Caribbean Baptist Mission; Presiding Elder Dr HENSWORTH W. C. JONAS.
Methodist Church: c/o POB 863, St John's; Supt Rev. ELOY CHRISTOPHER.
St John's Church of Christ: Golden Grove, Main Rd, St John's; tel. and fax 461-6732; e-mail stjcoc@candw.ag; Contact EVANGELIST CORNELIUS GEORGE.
St John's Evangelical Lutheran Church: Woods Centre, POB W77, St John's; tel. and fax 462-2896; e-mail sjlutheran@candw.ag; Principal E. JOHN FREDRICH; Pastors Rev. ANDREW JOHNSTON, Rev. JOSHUA STERNHAGEN, Rev. JASON RICHARDS, Rev. PAUL WORKENTINE.

There are also Pentecostal, Seventh-day Adventist, Moravian, Nazarene, Salvation Army and Wesleyan Holiness places of worship.

The Press

Antigua Sun: 15 Pavilion Dr., Coolidge, POB W263, St John's; tel. 480-5960; fax 480-5968; e-mail editor@antiguasun.com; internet www.antiguasun.com; f. 1997; daily, Mon. to Fri; weekend publication SUN Weekend publ. Saturday; publ. by Sun Printing and Publishing Ltd; Man. Editor TIM PAYNE; Dir of Operations PATRICK HENRY.
Business Expressions: POB 774, St John's; tel. 462-0743; fax 462-4575; e-mail chamcom@candw.ag; monthly; organ of the Antigua and Barbuda Chamber of Commerce and Industry Ltd.
Daily Observer: LIAT Rd, Coolidge, POB 1318, St John's; tel. 480-1750; fax 480-1757; e-mail editor@antiguaobserver.com; internet www.antiguaobserver.com; independent; Publr WINSTON A. DERRICK; Editor MICHAEL BRANN; circ. 4,000.
The Worker's Voice: Emancipation Hall, 46 North St, POB 3, St John's; tel. 462-0090; f. 1943; 2 a week; official organ of the Antigua Labour Party and the Antigua Trades and Labour Union; Editor NOEL THOMAS; circ. 6,000.

Publishers

Antigua Printing and Publishing Ltd: Factory Rd, POB 670, St John's; tel. 462-1265; fax 462-6200.
Caribbean Publishing Co Ltd: Ryan's Place, Suite 1B, High St, POB 1451, St John's; tel. 462-2215; fax 462-0962.
Treasure Island Publishing Ltd: POB W283, Woods Centre, St John's; tel. and fax 463-7414.
West Indies Publishing Ltd: 3 Jasmine Court, Friars Hill Road, POB W883, St John's; tel. 461-0565; fax 461-9750; e-mail wip@westindiespublishing.com; internet www.westindiespublishing.com.

Broadcasting and Communications

TELECOMMUNICATIONS

Most telephone services are provided by the Antigua Public Utilities Authority (see Trade and Industry) and the Antiguan division of Cable & Wireless PLC (United Kingdom).

Antigua Public Utilities Authority Personal Communications Services (APUA PCS): Cassada Gardens, POB 416, St John's; tel. 480-7000; fax 480-7476; internet www.apua.ag; f. 2000; digital mobile cellular telephone network; proposed sale of 67% to Irish-owned consortium Digicel agreed in Nov. 2005; Gen. Man. ALLAN WILLIAMS.
Cable & Wireless (Antigua and Barbuda) Ltd: 42–44 St Mary's St, POB 65, St John's; tel. 480-4000; fax 480-4200; internet www.cwantigua.com; owned by Cable & Wireless PLC (United Kingdom).
Digicel Antigua and Barbuda: Antigua Wireless Ventures Ltd, POB W32, St John's; tel. 480-2050; fax 480-2060; internet www.digicelantiguaandbarbuda.com; acquired Cingular Wireless' Caribbean operations and licences in 2005; owned by an Irish

consortium; Chair. DENIS O'BRIEN; Eastern Caribbean CEO KEVIN WHITE.

BROADCASTING

Radio

ABS Radio: POB 590, St John's; tel. 462-3602; e-mail alex@hotmail.com; internet www.cmatt.com/abs.htm; f. 1956; subsidiary of Antigua and Barbuda Broadcasting Service (see Television); Programme Man. KENNY NIBBS.

Abundant Life Radio: Codrington Village, Barbuda; tel. 562-4821; e-mail afternoonpraise@gmail.com; internet www.abundantliferadio.com; f. 2001; began broadcasting on Antigua in 2003; Christian station; daily, 24-hour broadcasts; Man. Dir EVANGELIST CLIFTON FRANCOIS.

Caribbean Radio Lighthouse: POB 1057, St John's; tel. 462-1454; fax 462-7420; e-mail info@radiolighthouse.org; internet www.radiolighthouse.org; f. 1975; regional station; religious broadcasts in Spanish and English; operated by Baptist Int. Mission Inc (USA); Gen. Man. CURTIS L. WAITE.

Caribbean Relay Co Ltd: POB 1203, St John's; tel. 462-0994; fax 462-0487; e-mail cm-crc@candw.ag; jtly operated by British Broadcasting Corpn and Deutsche Welle.

Crusader Radio: Codrington Village, Barbuda; tel. 562-1075; fax 562-4611; internet www.crusaderradio.com; f. 2003; official station of the United Progressive Party.

Observer Radio: internet www.antiguaobserver.com; f. 2001; independently owned station; Gen. Man. WINSTON A. DERRICK.

ZDK Liberty Radio International (Radio ZDK): Grenville Radio Ltd, Bryant Pasture, Bird Rd, Ottos, POB 1100, St John's; tel. 462-1100; fax 462-1116; e-mail mail@radiozdk.com; internet www.radiozdk.com; f. 1970; commercial; also operates SUN Radio; Programme Dir IVOR BIRD; CEO E. PHILIP.

Television

Antigua and Barbuda Broadcasting Service (ABS): Directorate of Broadcasting and Public Information, POB 590, St John's; tel. 462-0010; fax 462-4442; scheduled for privatization; Dir-Gen. HOLLIS HENRY; CEO DENIS LEANDRO.

ABS Television: POB 1280, St John's; tel. 462-0010; fax 462-1622; f. 1964; Programme Man. JAMES TANNY ROSE.

CTV Entertainment Systems: 25 Long St, St John's; tel. 462-0346; fax 462-4211; cable television co; transmits 33 channels of US television 24 hours per day to subscribers; Programme Dir K. BIRD.

Finance

(cap. = capital; res = reserves; dep. = deposits; m. = millions; brs = branches)

BANKING

The Eastern Caribbean Central Bank, based in Saint Christopher, is the central issuing and monetary authority for Antigua and Barbuda.

ABI Bank Ltd: ABI Financial Center, 156 Redcliffe St, POB 1679, St John's; tel. 480-2700; fax 480-2751; e-mail abib@abifinancial.com; internet www.abifinancial.com; f. 1990 as Antigua Barbuda Investment Bank Ltd; ABI Financial Group comprising ABI Bank Ltd, AOB (Antigua Overseas Bank) Ltd, ABIT (ABI Trust Antigua) Ltd, ABID (ABI Development Co) Ltd and ABII (ABI Insurance Co) Ltd; cap. EC $18.2m., res EC $10.2m., dep. EC $751.5m. (Sept. 2006); Chair. SYLVIA O'MARD; Man. Dir MCALLISTER ABBOTT; 3 brs.

Antigua and Barbuda Development Bank: 27 St Mary's St, POB 1279, St John's; tel. 462-0838; fax 462-0839; f. 1974; Man. S. ALEX OSBORNE.

Antigua Commercial Bank: St Mary's and Thames Sts, POB 95, Loans, St John's; tel. 481-4200; fax 481-4229; e-mail acb@candw.ag; f. 1955; auth. cap. EC $5m.; Man. GLADSTON JOSEPH; 2 brs.

Bank of Antigua: 1000 Airport Blvd, Pavilion Dr., POB 315, Coolidge; tel. 480-5300; fax 480-5433; e-mail wmcdavid@stanfordeagle.com; internet www.bankofantigua.com; f. 1981; total assets EC $433m. (Dec. 2005); Man. Dir KENNY J. BYRON; Chair. ALLEN STANFORD; 3 brs.

Caribbean Union Bank Ltd: Friars Hill Rd, POB W2010, St. John's; tel. 481-8271; fax 481-8290; e-mail customerservice@caribbeanunionbank.com; internet www.caribbeanunionbank.com; f. 2005; total assets US $2.0m. (Sept. 2005); Chair. BRIAN STUART-YOUNG; Man. Dir VERE I. HILL; 1 br.

FirstCaribbean International Bank (Barbados) Ltd: POB 225, St John's; internet www.firstcaribbeanbank.com; adopted present name in 2002 following merger of Caribbean operations of CIBC and Barclays Bank PLC; Barclays relinquished its stake in June 2006; Exec. Chair. MICHAEL MANSOOR; Dir PAUL ASHE.

Global Bank of Commerce Ltd (GBC): 4 Woods Centre, Friars Hill Road, POB W1803, St. John's; tel. 480-2240; fax 462-1831; e-mail customer.service@gbc.ag; internet www.globalbank.ag; f. 1983; international financial services operator; total assets US $74.4m.; shareholder equity US $8.1m.; Chair. and CEO BRIAN STUART-YOUNG; 1 br.

RBTT Bank Caribbean Ltd: 45 High St, POB 1324, St John's; tel. 481-7200; fax 481-7270; e-mail marlon.rawlins@ag.rbtt.com; internet www.rbtt.com; Br. Man. MARLON RAWLINS.

In 2005 there were 15 registered 'offshore' banks in Antigua and Barbuda.

Regulatory Body

Financial Services Regulatory Commission (FSRC): FCIB Bldg, Old Parham Rd, POB 2674, St John's; tel. 481-1170; fax 463-0422; e-mail anuifsa@candw.ag; internet www.fsrc.gov.ag; fmrly known as International Financial Sector Regulatory Authority, adopted current name in 2002; Chair. LEBRECHT HESSE; Administrator LEROY KING.

STOCK EXCHANGE

Eastern Caribbean Securities Exchange: tel. (869) 466-7192; fax (869) 465-3798; e-mail info@ecseonline.com; internet www.ecseonline.com; based in Basseterre, Saint Christopher and Nevis; f. 2001; regional securities market designed to facilitate the buying and selling of financial products for the eight member territories—Anguilla, Antigua and Barbuda, Dominica, Grenada, Montserrat, Saint Christopher and Nevis, Saint Lucia and Saint Vincent and the Grenadines; Chair. Sir K. DWIGHT VENNER; Gen. Man. TREVOR BLAKE.

INSURANCE

Several foreign companies have offices in Antigua. Local insurance companies include the following:

ABI Insurance Co Ltd (ABII): ABI Financial Center, 156 Redcliffe St, POB 2386, St John's; tel. 480-2700; fax 480-2750; e-mail abib@abifinancial.com; internet www.abifinancial.com; f. 2000; subsidiary of the ABI Financial Group.

Antigua Insurance Co Ltd: Long St, POB 511, St John's; tel. 480-9000; fax 480-9035; e-mail anicol@candw.ag; internet www.anicolinsurance.com.

General Insurance Co Ltd: Upper Redcliffe St, POB 340, St John's; tel. 462-2346; fax 462-4482.

Selkridge Insurance Agency Ltd: 7 Woods Centre, POB W306, St John's; tel. 462-2042; fax 462-2466; e-mail selkins@candw.ag; internet www.aboutantigua.com/selkridge; f. 1961; agents for American Life Insurance Company (ALICO—American International Group) and Caribbean Alliance Insurance; Man. CHARLENE SELKRIDGE.

State Insurance Corpn: Redcliffe St, POB 290, St John's; tel. 462-3945; fax 462-2649; e-mail stateins@candw.ag; f. 1977; Chair. Dr VINCENT RICHARDS; Gen. Man. LYNDELL BUTLER.

Trade and Industry

DEVELOPMENT ORGANIZATIONS

Barbuda Development Agency: St John's; economic devt projects for Barbuda.

Development Control Authority: Cecil Charles Building, Cross Street, POB 895, St John's; tel. 462-6427; fax 462-1919; Chair. CHANDLAH CODRINGTON.

Industrial Development Board: Newgate St, St John's; tel. 462-1038; fax 462-1033; f. 1984.

St John's Development Corpn: Thames St, POB 1473, St John's; tel. 462-3925; fax 462-3931; e-mail info@stjohnsdevelopment.com; internet www.stjohnsdevelopment.com; f. 1986; manages the Heritage Quay Duty Free Shopping Complex, Vendors' Mall, Public Market and Cultural and Exhibition Complex; Exec. Dir Sen. ANTHONY STUART.

CHAMBER OF COMMERCE

Antigua and Barbuda Chamber of Commerce and Industry Ltd: Cnr of North and Popeshead Sts, POB 774, St John's; tel. 462-0743; fax 462-4575; e-mail chamcom@candw.ag; f. 1944 as Antigua Chamber of Commerce Ltd; name changed as above in 1991, following the collapse of the Antigua and Barbuda Manufacturers' Asscn; Pres. EVERETT CHRISTIAN; Exec. Dir HOLLY PETERS.

INDUSTRIAL AND TRADE ASSOCIATIONS

Antigua Cotton Growers' Association: Central Cotton Station, Friars Hill Rd, St John's; tel. 462-3871; fax 462-4962; f. 1945.

Antigua Fisheries Limited: Market St, POB 781, St John's; tel. 462-0512; e-mail fisheries@candw.ag; partly funded by the Antigua and Barbuda Development Bank; executing agency for the Antigua Fisheries Development Project (2004); aims to help local fishermen; Dir MICHAEL JAMES.

EMPLOYERS' ORGANIZATION

Antigua and Barbuda Employers' Federation: Upper High St, POB 298, St John's; tel. and fax and fax 462-0449; e-mail aempfed@candw.ag; f. 1950; affiliated to the International Organization of Employers and the Caribbean Employers' Confederation; 126 mems; Chair. PATRICK RYAN; Exec. Sec. HENDERSON BASS.

UTILITIES

Antigua Public Utilities Authority (APUA): Cassada Gardens, POB 416, St John's; tel. 480-7505; fax 462-4131; e-mail support@apua.ag; internet www.apua.ag; f. 1973; generation, transmission and distribution of electricity; internal telecommunications; collection, treatment, storage and distribution of water; transferred to the authority of the Office of the Prime Minister 31 December 2006; Gen. Man. ESWORTH MARTIN.

Antigua Power Co Limited: Old Parham Rd, POB 10, St John's; tel. 460-9461; e-mail cmills@candw.ag; electricity provider.

TRADE UNIONS

Antigua and Barbuda Meteorological Officers Association: c/o V. C. Bird International Airport, Gabatco, POB 1051, St John's; tel. and fax 462-4606; Pres. CICELY CHARLES.

Antigua and Barbuda Nurses Association (ABNA): Nurses Headquarters, Factory Rd, St John's; tel. 462-0251; fax 462-5003; Pres. ELNORA WARNER; Sec. ELAINE EDWARDS.

Antigua and Barbuda Public Service Association (ABPSA): All Saints Rd, POB 1285, St John's; tel. 562-4571; fax 461-5821; e-mail abpsa@candw.ag; Pres. JAMES SPENCER; Gen. Sec. ELLOY DE FREITAS; 550 mems.

Antigua and Barbuda Trades Union Congress (ABTUC): c/o Antigua and Barbuda Workers' Union, Freedom Hall, Newgate St, POB 940, St John's; tel. 462-0442; fax 462-5220; e-mail awu@candw.ag; Pres. MAURICE CHRISTIAN; Gen. Sec. DAVID JONES.

Antigua and Barbuda Union of Teachers: c/o Ministry of Education, Govt Office Complex, Queen Elizabeth Highway, St John's; tel. and fax 462-3750; internet www.abut.edu.ag; f. 1926; Pres. VERNEST MACK; Sec. RALSTON NICKEO.

Antigua Trades and Labour Union (ATLU): 46 North St, POB 3, St John's; tel. 462-0090; fax 462-4056; e-mail atandlu@hotmail.com; f. 1939; affiliated to the Antigua Labour Party; Pres. WIGLEY GEORGE; Gen. Sec. STAFFORD JOSEPH; about 10,000 mems.

Antigua and Barbuda Workers' Union (ABWU): Freedom Hall, Newgate St, POB 940, St John's; tel. 462-2005; fax 462-5220; e-mail awu@candw.ag; f. 1967 following split with ATLU; not affiliated to any party; Pres. Sen. CHESTER HUGHES; Gen. Sec. Sen. DAVID MASSIAH; 10,000 mems.

Transport

ROADS

There are 384 km (239 miles) of main roads and 781 km (485 miles) of secondary dry-weather roads. Of the total 1,165 km (724 miles) of roads, only 33% are paved.

SHIPPING

The main harbour is the St John's Deep Water Harbour. It is used by cruise ships and a number of foreign shipping lines. There are regular cargo and passenger services internationally and regionally. At Falmouth, on the south side of Antigua, is a former Royal Navy dockyard in English Harbour. The harbour is now used by yachts and private pleasure craft.

Antigua and Barbuda Port Authority: Terminal Bldg, Deep Water Harbour, POB 1052, St John's; tel. 462-0050; fax 462-2510; e-mail abpa@port.gov.ag; internet www.port.gov.ag; f. 1968; responsible to Ministry of Works, Transportation and the Environment; Chair. LLEWELLYN SMITH; Port Man. LESLIE WILLIAMS.

Caribbean Forwarders Ltd: North and Popeshead St, POB 530, St John's; tel. 480-1100; fax 480-1120.

Tropical Shipping: Antigua Maritime Agencies Ltd, Milburn House, Old Parham Rd, POB W1310, St John's; tel. 562-2934; fax 562-2935; internet www.tropical.com; f. 1992; operates between Canada, USA and the Caribbean; Pres. RICK MURRELL.

Vernon Edwards Shipping Co: Thames St, POB 82, St John's; tel. 462-2034; fax 462-2035; e-mail vedwards@candw.ag; cargo service to and from San Juan, Puerto Rico.

The West Indies Oil Co Ltd: Friars Hill Rd, POB 230, St John's; tel. 462-0140; fax 462-0543; e-mail wiocfs@candw.ag; f. 1970; petroleum refiner and supplier of petroleum products in the Caribbean; facilities in Antigua and Barbuda and Dominica; operates storage site for fuel shipments under the Venezuelan PetroCaribe initiative for distribution locally and to other OECS countries; CEO JOE FERNANDEZ.

CIVIL AVIATION

Antigua's V. C. Bird (formerly Coolidge) International Airport, 9 km (5.6 miles) north-east of St John's, is modern and accommodates jet-engined aircraft. There is a small airstrip at Codrington on Barbuda. Antigua and Barbuda Airlines, a nominal company, controls international routes, but services to Europe and North America are operated by American Airlines (USA), Continental Airlines (USA), Lufthansa (Germany) and Air Canada. Antigua and Barbuda is a shareholder in, and the headquarters of, the regional airline LIAT, which acquired Caribbean Star Airlines (another regional airline also based in Antigua) in October 2007. Other regional services are operated by Caribbean Airlines (Trinidad and Tobago) and Air BVI (British Virgin Islands).

LIAT (1974) Ltd: POB 819, V. C. Bird Int. Airport, St John's; tel. 480-5713; fax 480-5717; e-mail blancharda@liatairline.com; internet www.liatairline.com; f. 1956 as Leeward Islands Air Transport Services, jtly owned by 11 regional Govts; privatized in 1995; shares are held by the govts of Antigua and Barbuda, Montserrat, Grenada, Barbados, Trinidad and Tobago, Jamaica, Guyana, Dominica, Saint Lucia, Saint Vincent and the Grenadines and Saint Christopher and Nevis (30.8%), Caribbean Airlines (29.2%), LIAT employees (13.3%) and private investors (26.7%); merger negotiations with Caribbean Star Airlines were finalized in March 2007; deal was abandoned in July in favour of a buyout arrangement in which LIAT would acquire all remaining shares in Caribbean Star; scheduled passenger and cargo services to 19 destinations in the Caribbean; charter flights are also undertaken; Chair. JEAN STEWART HOLDER; CEO MARK DARBY.

Carib Aviation Ltd: POB W1396, St John's; tel. 481-2400; fax 481-2405; e-mail caribav@candw.ag; internet www.carib-aviation.com; f. 1973; charter co; operates regional services.

Tourism

Tourism is the country's main industry. Antigua offers a reputed 365 beaches, an annual international sailing regatta and Carnival week, and the historic Nelson's Dockyard in English Harbour (a national park since 1985). Barbuda is less developed, but is noted for its beauty, wildlife and beaches of pink sand. In 2005 there were some 260,530 stop-over visitors and 466,851 cruise-ship passengers. In the previous year 36.6% of stop-over visitors came from the United Kingdom. Expenditure by all visitors was estimated at EC $833.6m. in 2005.

Antigua and Barbuda Department of Tourism: c/o Ministry of Tourism and Civil Aviation, Queen Elizabeth Highway, POB 363, St John's; tel. 462-0480; fax 462-2483; e-mail deptourism@antigua.gov.ag; internet www.antigua-barbuda.org; Dir-Gen. LORRAINE HEADLEY.

Antigua Hotels and Tourist Association (AHTA): Island House, Newgate St, POB 454, St John's; tel. 462-0374; fax 462-3702; e-mail ahta@candw.ag; internet www.antiguahotels.org; Chair. TED ISAAC; Exec. Dir NEIL FORRESTER.

ARGENTINA
Introductory Survey

Location, Climate, Language, Religion, Flag, Capital

The Argentine Republic occupies almost the whole of South America south of the Tropic of Capricorn and east of the Andes. It has a long Atlantic coastline stretching from Uruguay and the River Plate to Tierra del Fuego. To the west lie Chile and the Andes mountains, while to the north are Bolivia, Paraguay and Brazil. Argentina also claims the Falkland Islands (known in Argentina as the Islas Malvinas), South Georgia, the South Sandwich Islands and part of Antarctica. The climate varies from sub-tropical in the Chaco region of the north to sub-arctic in Patagonia, generally with moderate summer rainfall. Temperatures in Buenos Aires are usually between 5°C (41°F) and 29°C (84°F). The language is Spanish. The great majority of the population profess Christianity: about 92% are Roman Catholics and about 2% Protestants. The national flag (proportions 14 by 9) has three equal horizontal stripes, of light blue (celeste), above white, above light blue. The state flag (proportions 1 by 2) has the same design with, in addition, a gold 'Sun of May' in the centre of the white stripe. The capital is Buenos Aires.

Recent History

During the greater part of the 20th century, government in Argentina tended to alternate between military and civilian rule. In 1930 Hipólito Yrigoyen, a member of the reformist Unión Cívica Radical (UCR), who in 1916 had become Argentina's first President to be freely elected by popular vote, was overthrown by an army coup, and the country's first military regime was established. Civilian rule was restored in 1932, only to be supplanted by further military intervention in 1943. A leading figure in the new military regime, Col (later Lt-Gen.) Juan Domingo Perón Sosa, won a presidential election in 1946. He established the Peronista party in 1948 and pursued a policy of extreme nationalism and social improvement, aided by his second wife, Eva ('Evita') Duarte de Perón, whose popularity greatly enhanced his position and contributed to his re-election as President in 1951. In 1954, however, his promotion of secularization and the legalization of divorce brought him into conflict with the Roman Catholic Church. In September 1955 President Perón was deposed by a revolt of the armed forces. He went into exile, eventually settling in Spain, from where he continued to direct the Peronist movement.

Following the overthrow of Perón, Argentina entered another lengthy period of political instability. Political control continued to pass between civilian (mainly Radical) and military regimes during the late 1950s and the 1960s. Congressional and presidential elections were conducted in March 1973. The Frente Justicialista de Liberación, a Peronist coalition, secured control of the Congreso Nacional (National Congress), while the presidential election was won by the party's candidate, Dr Héctor Cámpora. However, Cámpora resigned in July, to enable Gen. Perón, who had returned to Argentina, to contest a fresh presidential election. In September Perón was returned to power, with more than 60% of the votes.

Gen. Perón died in July 1974 and was succeeded as President by his widow, María Estela ('Isabelita') Martínez de Perón, hitherto Vice-President. The Government's economic austerity programme and the soaring rate of inflation led to widespread strike action, dissension among industrial workers, and demands for the President's resignation. In March 1976 the armed forces, led by Gen. Jorge Videla, overthrew the President and installed a three-man junta: Gen. Videla was sworn in as head of state. The junta made substantial alterations to the Constitution, dissolved the Congreso Nacional, suspended all political and trade union activity and removed most government officials from their posts. Several hundred people were arrested, while 'Isabelita' Perón was detained and later went into exile.

The military regime launched a ferocious offensive against left-wing guerrillas and opposition forces. The imprisonment, torture and murder of suspected left-wing activists by the armed forces provoked domestic and international protests. Repression eased in 1978, after all armed opposition had been eliminated.

In March 1981 Gen. Roberto Viola, a former member of the junta, succeeded President Videla and made known his intention to extend dialogue with political parties as a prelude to an eventual return to democracy. Owing to ill health, he was replaced in December by Lt-Gen. Leopoldo Galtieri, the Commander-in-Chief of the Army, who attempted to cultivate popular support by continuing the process of political liberalization initiated by his predecessor.

In April 1982, in order to distract attention from an increasingly unstable domestic situation, and following unsuccessful negotiations with the United Kingdom in February over Argentina's long-standing sovereignty claim, President Galtieri ordered the invasion of the Falkland Islands (Islas Malvinas) (see chapter on the Falkland Islands). The United Kingdom recovered the islands after a short conflict, in the course of which about 750 Argentine lives were lost. Argentine forces surrendered in June 1982, but no formal cessation of hostilities was declared until October 1989. Humiliated by the defeat, Galtieri was forced to resign, and the members of the junta were replaced. The army, under the control of Lt-Gen. Cristino Nicolaides, installed a retired general, Reynaldo Bignone, as President in July 1982. The armed forces were held responsible for the disastrous economic situation, and the transfer of power to a civilian government was accelerated. Moreover, in 1983 a Military Commission of Inquiry into the Falklands conflict concluded in its report that the main responsibility for Argentina's defeat lay with members of the former junta. Galtieri was sentenced to imprisonment, while several other officers were put on trial for corruption, murder and insulting the honour of the armed forces. In the same year the regime approved the Ley de Pacificación Nacional, an amnesty law which granted retrospective immunity to the police, the armed forces and others for political crimes that had been committed over the previous 10 years.

General and presidential elections were held on 30 October 1983, in which the UCR defeated the Peronist Partido Justicialista (PJ), attracting the votes of many former Peronist supporters. Dr Raúl Alfonsín, the UCR candidate, took office as President on 10 December. He promptly announced a radical reform of the armed forces, which led to the immediate retirement of more than one-half of the military high command. In addition, he repealed the Ley de Pacificación Nacional and ordered the court martial of the first three military juntas to rule Argentina after the 1976 coup, for offences including abduction, torture and murder. Public opposition to the former military regime was reinforced by the discovery and exhumation of hundreds of bodies from unmarked graves throughout the country. (It was believed that 15,000–30,000 people 'disappeared' during the so-called 'dirty war' between the former military regime and its opponents in 1976–83.) President Alfonsín also announced the formation of the National Commission on the Disappearance of Persons to investigate the events of the 'dirty war'. The trial of the former leaders began in April 1985. Several hundred prosecution witnesses gave testimonies which revealed the systematic atrocities and the campaign of terror perpetrated by the former military leaders. In December four of the accused were acquitted, but sentences were imposed on five others, including sentences of life imprisonment for Gen. Videla and Adm. Eduardo Massera (they were released in late 1990). In May 1986 all three members of the junta that had held power during the Falklands conflict were found guilty of negligence and received prison sentences, including a term of 12 years for Galtieri.

In late 1986 the Government sought approval for the Punto Final ('Full Stop') Law, whereby civil and military courts were to begin new judicial proceedings against members of the armed forces accused of violations of human rights, within a 60-day period ending on 22 February 1987. The pre-emptive nature of the legislation provoked widespread popular opposition but was, nevertheless, approved by the Congreso Nacional in December 1986. However, in May 1987, following a series of minor rebellions at army garrisons throughout the country, the Government announced new legislation, known as the Obediencia Debida ('Due Obedience') law, whereby an amnesty was to be declared for all but senior ranks of the police and armed forces. Therefore, under the controversial new law, of the 350–370 officers hitherto due to be prosecuted for alleged violations of human rights, only 30–50 senior officers were now to be tried.

In the campaign for the May 1989 elections, Carlos Saúl Menem headed the Frente Justicialista de Unidad Popular (FREJUPO) electoral alliance, comprising his own PJ grouping, the Partido Demócrata Cristiano (PDC) and the Partido Intransigente (PI). On 14 May the Peronists were guaranteed a return to power, having secured, together with the two other members of the FREJUPO alliance, 49% of the votes cast in the presidential election and 310 of the 600 seats in the electoral college. The Peronists were also victorious in the election for 127 seats (one-half of the total) in the Cámara de Diputados (Chamber of Deputies). The failure of attempts by the retiring and incoming administrations to collaborate, and the reluctance of the Alfonsín administration to continue in office with the prospect of further economic deterioration, left the nation in a political vacuum. Although Menem was scheduled to take office as President in December, the worsening economic situation compelled Alfonsín to resign five months early, and Menem assumed the presidency on 8 July.

In early 1990 the Government introduced a radical economic readjustment plan, incorporating the expansion of existing plans for the transfer to private ownership of many state-owned companies and the restructuring of the nation's financial systems. In August Erman González appointed himself head of the Central Bank and assumed almost total control of the country's financial structure. Public disaffection with the Government's economic policy was widespread. Failure to contain the threat of hyperinflation led to a loss in purchasing power, and small-scale food riots, looting, industrial action and demonstrations became more frequent. In January 1991 the Minister of the Economy, Antonio Erman González, was forced to resign following a sudden spectacular decline in the value of the austral in relation to the US dollar. He was succeeded by Domingo Cavallo.

In October 1989 the Government issued decrees pardoning 210 officers and soldiers who had been involved in the 'dirty war', as well as the governing junta during the Falklands conflict (including Gen. Galtieri) and leaders of three recent military uprisings (including Lt-Col Rico and Col Seineldín). Widespread public concern at the apparent impunity of military personnel further increased after a second round of presidential pardons was announced in late 1990.

In gubernatorial and congressional elections, held throughout 1991, the Peronists performed well. The success of the Peronist campaign was widely attributed to the popularity of Domingo Cavallo. Economic measures implemented by him included the abolition of index-linked wage increases and, most dramatically, the implementation of the 'Convertibility Plan', which linked the austral to the US dollar, at a fixed rate of exchange. This initiative soon achieved considerable success in reducing inflation, and impressed international finance organizations sufficiently to secure the negotiation of substantial loan agreements. In October the President issued a comprehensive decree ordering the removal of almost all of the remaining bureaucratic apparatus of state regulation of the economy, and in November the Government announced plans to accelerate the transfer to private ownership of the remaining public-sector concerns. Continuing economic success in 1992 helped to secure agreements for the renegotiation of repayment of outstanding debts with the Government's leading creditor banks and with the 'Paris Club' of Western creditor governments. The October 1993 elections to renew 127 seats in the Cámara de Diputados were won convincingly by the ruling PJ party.

An unexpected development in November 1993 was the return to political prominence of former President Alfonsín. While UCR opposition to Menem's presidential ambitions had remained vociferous, several opposition leaders, notably Alfonsín, feared that the UCR would be excluded from negotiations on constitutional reform, which was to be voted on at a national referendum scheduled for late that year. Consequently, Alfonsín entered into a dialogue with the President, resulting in a declaration, in November, that a framework for constitutional reform had been negotiated, apparently in return for Menem's postponement of the referendum and acceptance of modified reform proposals. In December the UCR national convention endorsed the terms of the agreement, which included the possibility of re-election of the President for one consecutive term, a reduction in the presidential term (to four years), the abolition of the presidential electoral college, the delegation of some presidential powers to a Chief of Cabinet, an increase in the number of seats in the Senate (Senado) and a reduction in the length of the mandate of all senators, a reform of the procedure for judicial appointments, the removal of religious stipulations from the terms of eligibility for presidential candidates, and the abolition of the President's power to appoint the mayor of the federal capital. The need for constitutional reform was approved by the Congreso later in the month. Following the convening of a Constituent Assembly in May 1994, a new Constitution was promulgated in August.

Menem's campaign for re-election in 1995 concentrated on the economic success of his previous administration and, despite the increasingly precarious condition of the economy, was sufficiently successful to secure 50% of the votes at the presidential election of 14 May, thereby avoiding a second ballot. José Octavio Bordón, the candidate of the Frente del País Solidario (Frepaso—a centre-left alliance of socialist, communist, Christian Democrat and dissident Peronist groups) was second with 29% of the votes, ahead of the UCR candidate, Horacio Massaccesi, who received 17% of the votes. However, Frepaso won the largest share of the 130 contested seats in the Cámara de Diputados at legislative elections conducted concurrently, and significantly increased its representation in the Senado (as did the Peronists), largely at the expense of the UCR. Menem was inaugurated as President for a second four-year term on 8 July.

Meanwhile, the Government's ongoing programme of economic austerity continued to provoke violent opposition, particularly from the public sector, where redundancies and a 'freeze' on salaries had been imposed in many provinces. In March 1995 the Government presented an economic consolidation programme aimed at protecting the Argentine currency against devaluation and supporting the ailing banking sector, which had been adversely affected by the financial crisis in Mexico in late 1994 (the so-called 'tequila effect'). Subsequent austerity measures adopted by provincial governments, together with a dramatic increase in the rate of unemployment, provoked widespread social unrest in the city of Córdoba and in the province of Río Negro in 1995.

In 1996 public disaffection with the Government was reflected in the PJ's poor performance in the first direct elections for the Mayor of the Federal District of Buenos Aires, as well as in concurrent elections to the 60-member Constituent Assembly (which was charged with drafting a constitution for the newly autonomous Federal District of Buenos Aires). In July the Government was again undermined by the resignations of the Minister of Justice and the Minister of Defence, whose parliamentary immunity was to be removed to allow investigations in connection with the illegal sale of armaments to Ecuador and Croatia. More significant was the dismissal of Cavallo as Minister of the Economy following months of bitter dispute with the President and other cabinet members. Roque Fernández, hitherto President of the Central Bank, assumed the economy portfolio. Cavallo became increasingly vociferous in his attacks against the integrity of certain cabinet members, and, in October, as Menem launched a well-publicized campaign against corruption after the discovery of wide-scale malpractice within the customs service, he accused the Government of having links with organized crime.

Industrial and social unrest increased in 1996 and 1997, owing to widespread discontent with proposed labour reforms, as well as reductions in public expenditure and high levels of unemployment. General strikes, organized by the Confederación General de Trabajo (CGT), the Congreso de los Trabajadores Argentinos (CTA) and the Movimiento de Trabajadores Argentinos (MTA), received widespread support in August and September 1996. In October relations between the Government and the trade unions deteriorated following the submission to the Congreso of controversial labour-reform legislation. In December, owing to legislative delays, President Menem introduced part of the reforms by decree, although a court declared the decrees to be unconstitutional in the following month. In May 1997 violent protests erupted across the country as police clashed with thousands of anti-Government demonstrators who had occupied government buildings and blockaded roads and bridges. In July some 30,000 people demonstrated in the capital to protest at the high level of unemployment, then estimated at more than 17%. A general strike in August, organized by the MTA and the CTA, was only partially observed, however.

At the mid-term congressional elections in October 1997 the UCR and Frepaso (who formed an electoral pact, the Alianza por el Trabajo, la Justicia y la Educación—ATJE, in order to present joint lists in certain constituencies) together won 46% of the votes and 61 of the 127 seats contested. In contrast, the PJ won 36% of the vote and 51 seats. The PJ thus lost its overall majority in the

Cámara de Diputados (its total number of seats being reduced to 118), while the UCR and Frepaso together increased their representation to 110 seats. More significant was the PJ's poor performance in the critical constituency of the province of Buenos Aires, where it received only 41% of the votes, compared with the ATJE's 48%.

A presidential election was held on 24 October 1999. The ATJE candidate, Fernando de la Rúa, ended 10 years of Peronist rule, winning 49% of the votes cast. The PJ contender, Eduardo Alberto Duhalde, secured 38% of the ballot. (Menem had been barred by the Supreme Court from contesting the presidency, despite attempting to amend the Constitution in order to stand.) The ATJE also performed well in concurrent congressional elections, winning 63 of the 130 seats up for renewal, while the PJ secured 50 seats and Acción por la República, led by Domingo Cavallo, won nine. The ATJE's total number of seats in the Cámara increased to 127—only two short of an absolute majority—in contrast to the PJ, whose representation was reduced to 101 seats. De la Rúa took office as President on 10 December. Later that month the new Congreso Nacional approved an austerity budget that reduced public expenditure by US $1,400m., as well as a major tax-reform programme and a federal revenue-sharing scheme.

In April 2000 the Senado approved a controversial major revision of employment law. The legislation met with public criticism and led to mass demonstrations by public sector workers and, subsequently, to two 24-hour national strikes organized by the CGT. Later that year the Government came under intense pressure after it was alleged that some senators had received bribes from government officials to pass the employment legislation. In September the Senado voted to end the immunity that protected law-makers, judges and government ministers from criminal investigation in order to allow an inquiry into the corruption allegations. The political crisis intensified on 6 October when Carlos Alvarez resigned as Vice-President, one day after a cabinet reorganization, in which two ministers implicated in the bribery scandal were not removed. One of these, former labour minister Alberto Flamarique, who was appointed presidential Chief of Staff in the reshuffle, resigned later the same day. The other, Fernando de Santibáñez, head of the state intelligence service, resigned in late October. Earlier that month the President of the Senado, José Genoud, also resigned after he too was implicated in the bribery allegations.

The economic situation continued to deteriorate in 2000 and 2001. In November 2000 thousands of unemployed workers blocked roads throughout the country to demand jobs, welfare programmes and improvements in standards of living. In the same month the country was paralysed by a 36-hour national strike, organized in response to the Government's proposed introduction of an IMF-backed economic recovery package that included a five-year 'freeze' on federal and provincial spending. Additional measures included a reform of the pension system and an increase in the female retirement age. In December the Congreso approved the reforms and, later in the month, the IMF agreed a package, worth an estimated US $20,000m., to meet Argentina's external debt obligations for 2001.

The resignation of the Minister of the Economy, José Luis Machinea, precipitated another political crisis in March 2001. The announcement by his successor, Ricardo López Murphy, of major reductions in public expenditure, resulted in several cabinet resignations. As a consequence, in late March a second reshuffle occurred, in which Domingo Cavallo was reappointed Minister of the Economy. In June Cavallo announced a series of measures designed to ease the country's financial situation. The most controversial of these was the introduction of a complex trade-tariff system that created multiple exchange rates (based on the average of a euro and a US dollar); this was, in effect, a devaluation of the peso for external trade, although the dollar peg remained in operation for domestic transactions. As Argentina's debt crisis intensified and fears of a default increased, a further emergency package, the seventh in 19 months, was implemented in July. A policy of 'zero deficit' was announced, whereby neither the federal Government nor any province would be allowed to spend more than it collected in taxes. In order to achieve this, state salaries and pensions were to be reduced by 13%. Despite mass protests and a one-day national strike, the measures were granted congressional approval at the end of July. Nevertheless, the economic situation continued to deteriorate. There were protests against the austerity measures in August and following the introduction of one-year bonds, known as 'patacones', as payment to 160,000 public sector workers.

Meanwhile, the Government encountered difficulties in effecting economic policies: negotiations with the opposition Peronists, who controlled the majority of Argentina's provincial governments, towards a 'zero deficit', were repeatedly stalled in late 2001.

The poor state of the economy contributed to the ATJE's poor performance in the legislative elections of October 2001. The PJ won control of the Cámara de Diputados and increased its lower-house representation to 116 seats overall. In comparison, the ATJE obtained 88 seats. In the Senado, which for the first time was directly elected by popular vote, the PJ increased its majority, winning 40 seats, while the ATJE secured 25 seats. The elections were marred by a high percentage of spoiled ballots (21%—in some provinces the number of spoiled ballots was higher than that for the winning candidate) and a high rate of abstention, about 28%, in a country where voting is obligatory.

In December 2001, as the economic situation deteriorated and the possibility of a default on the country's debt increased considerably, owing to the IMF's refusal to disburse more funds to Argentina, the Government introduced restrictions on bank account withdrawals and appropriated private pension funds. These measures proved to be extremely unpopular and resulted in two days of rioting and demonstrations nation-wide, in which at least 27 people died. On 20 December Cavallo resigned as Minister of the Economy and, following further rioting on the same day, President de la Rúa submitted his resignation. The newly appointed head of the Senado, Ramón Puerta, became acting President of the Republic, but was succeeded two days later by the Peronist Adolfo Rodríguez Saá. He, in turn, resigned one week later after protests against his proposed economic reforms (including the introduction of a new currency and the suspension of debt repayments) resulted in further unrest. On 1 January 2002 the former Peronist presidential candidate and recently elected Senator for the Province of Buenos Aires, Eduardo Alberto Duhalde, was elected President by the Congreso Nacional. He was Argentina's fifth President in less than two weeks. (The President of the Cámara de Diputados, Eduardo Camaño, was acting President from 31 December 2001 to 2 January 2002 following the resignation of Puerta as President of the Senado.) On 3 January Argentina officially defaulted on its loan repayments, reportedly the largest ever debt default, and three days later the Senado gave authorization to the Government to set the exchange rate, thus officially ending the 10-year-old parity between the US dollar and the peso. In the following month the Government initiated the compulsory conversion to pesos of US dollar bank deposits in order to prevent capital flight. This process of 'pesofication' led to many lawsuits (*amparos*) being brought by depositors against financial institutions in an attempt to recover their losses. However, in October 2004 the Supreme Court ruled that the 'pesofication' was not unconstitutional, thereby effectively ruling against future *amparos*.

Nevertheless, in February 2002 the Supreme Court had ruled that the restrictions imposed on bank withdrawals (the *corralito*) were unconstitutional. Some accounts were freed from the restrictions but, in order to forestall the complete collapse of the financial system, the Government imposed a six-month ban on legal challenges to the remainder of the bank withdrawal regime. Numerous bank holidays were also decreed to prevent another run on the banks and a further devaluation of the currency. A constitutional crisis ensued as the Congreso initiated impeachment proceedings against the unpopular Supreme Court Justices (see below). Later that month the Government signed a new tax-sharing pact with the provincial Governors, linking the monthly amount distributed to the provinces to tax collections, as recommended by the IMF. However, in late April Jorge Remes Lenicov resigned as Minister of the Economy following the Senado's refusal to support an emergency plan to exchange 'frozen' bank deposits for government bonds, despite an uncompromising message from the IMF that no further help would be available unless drastic reforms were forthcoming. He was replaced by Roberto Lavagna (the sixth Argentine economy minister in 12 months).

The economy achieved mixed progress during 2002. While the number of deposits in Argentine banks increased, Argentina still defaulted on a US $805m. loan instalment to the World Bank in November, thus jeopardizing the country's last remaining source of external finance. The situation was aggravated by disagreements between the Minister of the Economy and the President of the Central Bank over the *corralito* restrictions. Public anger against the Government and at the state of the economy did not subside, and in June two people were killed and dozens more injured when protesters demanding jobs and food clashed with the police. The following day thousands of anti-Government protesters marched in front of the Congreso building, and teachers and public sector workers went on strike.

In the latter half of 2002 congressional efforts to impeach the Supreme Court Justices for incompetence were repeatedly frustrated. The Cámara de Diputados failed to achieve quorum to begin the impeachment debate on five occasions but, in October, and after calls from the IMF for political consensus between the judiciary and the legislature, the impeachment bid was voted down in the Cámara. Nevertheless, later that month one Supreme Court judge resigned. Contentious decisions taken by the Supreme Court included ruling against the *corralito*, pay and pensions reductions for public sector workers and public utility price increases.

President Duhalde's announcement, in July 2002, that the presidential election would take place six months earlier than planned, on 30 March 2003, was intended to reduce political pressures on the Government during its ongoing negotiations with the IMF. In November 2002, following negotiations between the Government, legislators and provincial Governors, agreement was reached to postpone the presidential election until 27 April 2003. Internal rivalries within the ruling PJ, most notably between Duhalde (who supported the candidacy of the Santa Cruz Governor, Néstor Carlos Kirchner) and former President Carlos Menem, resulted in a bitter argument regarding the election of a Peronist candidate. Eventually, in late January 2003, the PJ congress voted to allow all three Peronist aspirants (namely Menem, Kirchner and Adolfo Rodríguez Saá) to contest the presidential election, despite a court order (obtained by Menem) ordering that a primary election be held. Menem had been the subject of a number of scandals in 2001 and 2002. In June 2001 he was placed under house arrest on charges of arms-trafficking; however, the charges against him were dismissed in November. He also refuted allegations that, while President, he had accepted a payment of US $10m. to suppress evidence of Iranian involvement in a bomb attack on a Jewish social centre in Buenos Aires in 1994 that had killed 86 people. Menem declared that the money was compensation that he had been awarded for his imprisonment during the military dictatorship and accused the Duhalde Peronist faction of attempting to sabotage his bid for a third presidential term.

At the presidential election on 27 April 2003 Menem obtained the largest share of the popular vote, with 24% of the votes cast, followed by Kirchner (representing the Frente para la Victoria—FPV—faction of the PJ), with 22% of the ballot. Ricardo López Murphy of the centre-right Movimiento Federal para Recrear el Crecimiento alliance came third with 16% of the ballot. The third Peronist candidate, former President Adolfo Rodríguez Saá, representing the Frente Movimiento Popular/Partido Unión y Libertad alliance, was narrowly defeated by Elisa M. A. Carrió of the Alternativa por una República de Iguales (ARI—later renamed the Afirmación para una República Igualitaria), who won 14% of the votes cast. As no candidate had secured the majority of votes required by the Constitution, a run-off ballot between the two leading candidates was scheduled for 18 May. However, faced with the very likely possibility of a decisive protest vote against him, on 14 May Menem withdrew his candidacy from the election. Kirchner was thus elected by default. He was sworn in as President on 25 May.

Upon taking office, the new President faced the problem of strengthening his relatively weak popular mandate, in order to fulfil his electoral pledges to address Argentina's severe social and economic problems. In his inauguration speech, Kirchner pledged to put the needs of the Argentine people before the demands of the IMF. He immediately announced a series of popular measures, which included the replacement of several high-ranking military and police commanders, the opening of an investigation into allegedly corrupt practices by several Supreme Court Justices (which prompted the resignation of the President of the Supreme Court in June) and increases in pensions and minimum wages. He also announced a programme of investment in infrastructure, particularly housing, intended to lower the high unemployment rate. Kirchner's new Cabinet included five ministers with previous government experience; most notably, Roberto Lavagna, the Minister of the Economy in the previous administration, retained his post. Lavagna had been widely credited with averting hyperinflation and a possible collapse in the financial system in 2002.

President Kirchner's increasing popularity in 2003 successfully translated into significant gains for the PJ in the legislative elections that were held during the latter half of the year, which resulted in a working majority for the PJ and its allies in both the Cámara de Diputados and the Senado (of 127 and 41 seats, respectively). Gubernatorial elections, also held during the second half of the year, further consolidated Kirchner's position; by December the PJ controlled 16 of the country's 24 provinces (including the Federal District of Buenos Aires). Moreover, the corruption inquiry within the Supreme Court resulted in the removal of four Justices, including the Court's President, Julio Nazareno, all of whom were considered to be hostile to the new President. However, a fifth Justice and ally of Kirchner, Antonio Boggiano, was charged with misconduct in October 2004 (he was dismissed from the Supreme Court in late September 2005). This impeachment process prompted the Kirchner Government to consider a radical reform of the Supreme Court with a view to reducing its size and remit.

Notwithstanding President Kirchner's pledges to improve social provisions, from 2003 frequent demonstrations against high levels of crime and unemployment continued to cause disruption across the country. Loosely organized groups of protesters, known as *piqueteros*, became increasingly radical during this period, erecting roadblocks and occupying both private and public institutions to demand jobs, redistribution of money and an end to a perceived culture of impunity. In April 2004 the federal Government announced a three-year anti-crime initiative; however, the plan failed to quell popular protests throughout the year.

In October 2004 the judges investigating the 1994 bomb attack in Buenos Aires issued a final report acquitting all Argentine suspects, owing to lack of evidence. However, the report severely criticized failures and procedural irregularities by the Menem administration, the judiciary, the intelligence services and federal judge Juan José Galeano, who had led the original investigation. Criminal investigations were subsequently initiated against Galeano, Carlos Corach (Minister of the Interior under Menem) and Hugo Anzorreguy (the former head of the Argentine intelligence service). In February 2005 Galeano was suspended from his post for six months by the Supreme Council of Magistrates (by 16 votes to one). Furthermore, in the same month the special unit of the Attorney-General's office investigating the bomb attack accused Menem of obstructing inquiries into the possible role of Argentine nationals. In July President Kirchner formally accepted that successive Governments had failed adequately to investigate the bombing and, on occasion, had sought to withhold relevant information; it was widely understood that this announcement would enable victims of the atrocity to receive state compensation. In August Galeano was dismissed from his post after the Supreme Court upheld two of 13 misconduct charges against him. In December 2004 Menem returned to Argentina from self-imposed exile in Chile after charges of financial impropriety against him were dropped. On his return he announced his intention to stand for re-election to the presidency.

At mid-term elections to the Congreso, held in October 2005, President Kirchner's FPV faction of the PJ secured a resounding victory over the faction of the party led by former President Eduardo Duhalde, Peronismo Federal. Following the ballot, the FPV bloc controlled 118 of the 257 seats in the Cámara de Diputados, compared with 31 held by Duhalde's faction, while the PJ bloc as a whole had 33 of the 72 senatorial seats. The UCR controlled 36 seats in the lower house and 11 in the Senado. The two PJ factions were bitterly divided throughout the electoral campaign, a division most evident in the hostile campaigning of Duhalde's wife, Hilda Beatriz González, and Kirchner's wife, Cristina E. Fernández de Kirchner, who were both elected as Senators for the Buenos Aires metropolitan area. President Kirchner declared the legislative election results to be a clear endorsement by the electorate of his Government, and in the following month he effected a major cabinet reshuffle, in which the ministers for the economy, foreign affairs and defence were replaced by ministers believed to be more closely aligned with his policies for regional integration and negotiations with the IMF.

In early July 2007 it was announced that Cristina Fernández de Kirchner would stand as the FPV candidate instead of her husband in the presidential election that was scheduled to be held on 28 October. The launch of Senator Fernández's campaign later in July was overshadowed by a number of allegations of corruption affecting the Government, notably the resignation of the Minister of Economy and Production, Felisa Miceli, following judicial investigations into the discovery of a large quantity of cash in her office. (Miceli was replaced by Miguel Peirano.) In the following month airport customs officers discovered nearly US $800,000 in cash in the suitcase of Guido Antonini Wilson, a Venezuelan businessman who was travelling from Venezuela to Argentina on an aircraft chartered by the state-owned company Energía Argentina, SA (ENARSA). Opposition parties accused the Government of illegally importing the money in order to fund Fernández's election campaign and demanded the resignation of the Minister of Federal Planning, Public Investment and Services, Julio De Vido.

In spite of these set-backs, Fernández won a decisive victory in the presidential election held on 28 October 2007, securing 44.9% of the votes cast, according to preliminary results, thereby avoiding the need for a run-off ballot. No candidate succeeded in unifying the opposition: Elisa Carrió of the ARI, representing the Coalición Cívica, obtained 23.0% of the vote, while Roberto Lavagna (who had resigned as Minister of Economy and Production in November 2005), leading the Concertación para Una Nación Avanzada (UNA)—a coalition consisting primarily of members of the UCR and of anti-Kirchner Peronists—received 16.9% of votes cast; Alberto Rodríguez Saá (brother of Adolfo Rodríguez Saá), also representing an anti-Kirchner faction of the PJ, received 7.7% of the ballot. The participation rate was put at approximately 74.1%. Following the concurrent partial elections to the Congreso the FPV legislative bloc emerged with 120 seats in the Cámara de Diputados and 42 seats in the Senado, thereby gaining an overall majority in the upper chamber, while the UCR's representation was reduced to 24 and eight seats, respectively. President Fernández was sworn in on 10 December. Her Cabinet retained seven members of the outgoing administration; one notable absence was that of the recently appointed Peirano, who was replaced as Minister of Economy and Production by Martín Lousteau, hitherto head of the state-owned Banco de la Provincia de Buenos Aires. (Lousteau, however, resigned in April 2008 and was replaced by Carlos Rafael Fernández.)

Despite public expressions of regret (in 1995 and 2004) by the heads of the navy, the army and the air force for crimes committed by the armed forces during 1976–83, issues concerning the 'dirty war' remained politically sensitive in the early 21st century. In January 1998 Alfredo Astiz, a notorious former naval captain, was deprived of his rank and pension after he defended the elimination of political opponents during the dictatorship. In the following month the Swiss authorities revealed that they had discovered a number of Swiss bank accounts belonging to former Argentine military officials, including Astiz and Antonio Domingo Bussi, then Governor of Tucumán. It was rumoured that the accounts contained funds stolen from the military regime from Argentines who had been detained or 'disappeared'. In July 2001 Astiz was arrested at the request of an Italian court on the grounds of his involvement in the murder of three Italian citizens during the 'dirty war'. He was released the following month. Astiz also remained the subject of extradition requests by the French and Swedish Governments. (In 1990 Astiz had been convicted in France, *in absentia*, and sentenced to life imprisonment for murder and in 2007 Astiz was convicted of the same crime, again *in absentia*, in an Italian court.) In April 2000 a mass grave was discovered in Lomas de Zamora, containing the remains of about 90 victims of the 'dirty war'. In July 2001 Videla was arrested, pending an inquiry into his role in 'Plan Condor', an alleged scheme among right-wing dictators in Argentina, Chile, Uruguay and Bolivia to eradicate leftist political opponents living in exile during the 1970s. In September he was ordered to stand trial for the abduction of 72 foreigners who were taken as part of 'Plan Condor'. In July 2002 the former dictator Gen. Galtieri was arrested, along with at least 30 others, on charges relating to the kidnapping and murder of opponents during the 'dirty war'. Specifically, the charges concerned the torture and murder of 20 members of the left-wing Montoneros guerrilla group in 1980. In September 2002 he was imprisoned, along with 24 other former military officers, pending trial. (Galtieri remained under house arrest until his death in January 2003.) In March 2003 the Congreso approved legislation repealing the Punto Final and Obediencia Debida laws (adopted in 1986 and 1987, respectively); however, the new legislation was not retrospective and would not affect those who had already received an amnesty. In June Gen. Videla was arrested in connection with the abduction and illegal adoption of children whose parents had been 'disappeared' during the dictatorship and placed under house arrest. As many as 300 infants born in special holding centres during the 'dirty war' were believed to have been abducted by the military and police. In late 2003 further arrests were made in connection with the alleged kidnappings, including that of former President Reynaldo Bignone, former army chief Lt-Gen. Cristino Nicolaides, former navy chief Vice-Adm. Rubén Oscar Franco and Alfredo Astiz. In March 2004 two former police officials were convicted of facilitating the illegal adoption of one such infant in a case that was seen to set a precedent for further possible prosecutions. In October the Supreme Court ruled that the state should pay compensation to Susana Yofre de Vaca Nervaja, who fled Argentina after her husband and son were killed by military personnel during the 'dirty war', as exile of this nature was equivalent to illegal detention. This ruling was widely expected to set a precedent for claims for compensation to be brought by others, thought to number between 10,000 and 50,000, who also fled Argentina during the years of military rule.

In 1996 a criminal investigation was begun in Spain regarding the torture, disappearance and killing of several hundred Spanish citizens in Argentina during 1976–83. A parallel investigation was initiated into the abduction of 54 children of Spanish victims during this period. In October 1997 Adolfo Scilingo, a former Argentine military official, was arrested in Madrid after admitting to his involvement in the 'dirty war'. However, he later retracted his confession, claiming it was given under duress, and contested the jurisdiction of the Spanish courts in this affair. His appeal was rejected in November 2004 and in April 2005 Scilingo was convicted of crimes against humanity, including the torture and murder of 30 prisoners; he was sentenced to 640 years' imprisonment. The Argentine Government expressed its approval of the verdict. During 1997 a Spanish High Court judge issued international arrest warrants for several other Argentine officers, including Adm. Massera and Gen. Galtieri. Following further investigations, in November 1999 international arrest warrants on charges of genocide, terrorism and torture were issued for 98 of those accused. In December the Spanish magistrate Baltasar Garzón issued international arrest warrants for 49 people, including former military presidents Videla and Galtieri, effectively confining them to Argentine territory. However, in January 2000 a federal judge refused to extradite them.

In July 2003 President Kirchner revoked a decree, issued by President de la Rúa in 2001, which had prevented the extradition of Argentine citizens suspected of human rights violations. Courts in Spain, France, Germany and Sweden have all since sought the extradition of former Argentine military personnel for crimes—including murder—committed against their citizens. In the following month the Senado approved legislation that would allow the annulment of the Punto Final and Obediencia Debida laws, and ratified a UN Convention that ostensibly removed all constitutional limitations on human rights prosecutions. In August 2004 the Supreme Court ruled, in reference to the assassination in Buenos Aires in 1974 of Carlos Prats (the former head of the Chilean army) and his wife, that crimes against humanity have no statutory limitations. In June 2005 the Supreme Court voted, by seven votes to one, to annul the Punto Final and Obediencia Debida laws. In September 2006 Miguel Etchecolatz, a former senior police officer, was sentenced to life imprisonment after being convicted on charges of murder, torture and kidnapping during the 'dirty war'. However, the day before he was sentenced an important witness in the case, Jorge Julio López, went missing. Many people, including the Governor of the Province of Buenos Aires, Felipe Solá, expressed fears that López's disappearance was linked to his testimony, and was intended to deter others from giving evidence in future cases.

In August 1991 Argentina and Chile reached a settlement regarding claims to territory in the Antarctic region; however, the sovereignty of the territory remained under dispute, necessitating the signing of an additional protocol in late 1996. In December 1998 the Presidents of the two countries signed a new agreement on the border demarcation of the contested 'continental glaciers' territory in the Antarctic region (despite the 1991 treaty); the accord became effective in June 1999 following ratification by the Argentine and Chilean legislatures. In February 1999, during a meeting held in Ushuaia, southern Argentina, President Menem and the Chilean President, Eduardo Frei Ruiz-Tagle, signed a significant defence agreement and issued a joint declaration on both countries' commitment to the consolidation of their friendship. Relations between the two countries were strained in mid-2004, however, following President Kirchner's decision to reduce exports of gas to Chile by some 25% in order to meet a critical shortfall in stocks for domestic consumption. The Chilean Government claimed that this violated an agreement signed in 1995. Following the election of

Michelle Bachelet Jeria to the Chilean presidency in January 2006, a bilateral group was established to resolve more effectively any future disagreements over energy matters. Nevertheless, in July the Government of Chile reacted angrily to Argentina's decision to introduce a surcharge on motor fuel sold to vehicles with foreign licence plates. The Argentine Government claimed the move was an attempt to deter foreign car owners from taking advantage of lower petrol prices there. In spite of this, in December the two countries announced the formation of a joint military force, the 'Cruz del Sur', which would participate in UN peace-keeping operations.

Full diplomatic relations were restored with the United Kingdom in February 1990, following senior-level negotiations in Madrid, Spain. The improvement in relations between Argentina and the United Kingdom prompted the European Community (now European Union, EU, see p. 244) to sign a new five-year trade and co-operation agreement with Argentina in April. In November Argentina and the United Kingdom concluded an agreement for the joint administration of a comprehensive protection programme for the lucrative South Atlantic fishing region. Subsequent agreements to regulate fishing in the area were made in 1992 and 1993. The question of sovereignty over the disputed islands was not resolved. The results of preliminary seismic investigations (published in late 1993), which indicated rich petroleum deposits in the region, were expected further to complicate future negotiations. Although a comprehensive agreement on exploration was signed by both countries in September 1995, negotiations on fishing rights in the region remained tense. In 1996 the Argentine Government suggested, for the first time, that it might consider shared sovereignty of the Falkland Islands with the United Kingdom. The proposal was firmly rejected by the British Government and by the Falkland Islanders, who reiterated their commitment to persuading the UN Special Political and Decolonization Committee to adopt a clause allowing the Islanders the right to self-determination. Relations between Argentina and the United Kingdom improved in January 1997 when the two countries agreed to resume negotiations on a long-term fisheries accord. Moreover, in October 1998 President Menem made an official visit to the United Kingdom, during which he held talks with the British Prime Minister, Tony Blair, on issues including the arms embargo, defence, trade and investment. Notably, Menem paid tribute to the British servicemen who died during the 1982 conflict, while he also appealed for an 'imaginative' solution to the Falkland Islands sovereignty issue. Earlier in 1998 relations with the United Kingdom had been strained by the presentation of draft legislation to the Congreso on the imposition of sanctions on petroleum companies and fishing vessels operating in Falkland Island waters without Argentine authorization. In late 1998 the United Kingdom partially lifted its arms embargo against Argentina. In July 1999 an agreement was reached providing for an end to the ban on Argentine citizens visiting the Falkland Islands and for the restoration of air links between the islands and South America, with stop-overs in Argentina to be introduced from October. In September Argentine and British government officials reached an understanding on co-operation against illegal fishing in the South Atlantic, and naval forces from both countries held joint exercises in the region in November. In August 2001 Tony Blair became the first British Prime Minister to make an official visit to Argentina; however, the issue of the sovereignty of the Falkland Islands was not discussed. In May 2005 the inclusion of the Falkland Islands as an Overseas Territory of the United Kingdom in the draft EU constitution provoked vociferous complaints from the Kirchner Government.

Argentina was a founder member of the Southern Common Market, Mercosur (Mercado Común del Sur, see p. 391), which came into effect on 1 January 1995. Mercosur, comprising Argentina, Brazil, Paraguay and Uruguay, removed customs barriers on 80%–85% of mutually exchanged goods, and was intended to lead to the eventual introduction of a common external tariff. The effects of economic recession and the devaluation of the Brazilian currency in January 1999 provoked a series of trade disputes within Mercosur during that year, particularly between Argentina and Brazil, the two largest members. However, a document, known as the 'Buenos Aires Consensus', signed in 2003 by President Kirchner and his Brazilian counterpart, Luiz Inácio (Lula) da Silva, agreed to study the creation of common institutions for resolving trade disputes, in addition to the eventual establishment of a Mercosur legislature.

From 2005 relations between Argentina and Uruguay were strained owing to the latter's decision to allow the construction of two pulp mills on the Uruguayan side of the River Uruguay by Botnia of Finland and Ence of Spain. The Argentine Government opposed the project on environmental grounds, although a World Bank study released in April 2006 concluded that the mills posed no threat to the environment. Argentina, however, demanded an independent assessment (the mills were partly financed by the World Bank) and ecological groups from Argentina erected roadblocks across bridges spanning the river. Following the failure of bilateral negotiations in April, Argentina filed a complaint with the International Court of Justice (ICJ) in The Hague, Netherlands, claiming that the mills violated the Statute of the River Uruguay signed by both countries in 1975. An initial finding by the ICJ in July dismissed Argentina's demand that the construction be halted, ruling that it would not cause irreversible damage to the environment. In September, however, the ongoing dispute prompted Ence to cancel its plans for a mill at the location in question, although construction of the Botnia plant continued. Also in September, a three-member arbitration panel appointed by Mercosur ruled that Argentina had failed to adhere to the trade agreement's free trade clauses by not preventing the ongoing roadblocks, although it also ruled that it had not done so intentionally. A final ruling by the World Bank, concurring with Uruguayan claims that the project met all international environmental standards, was dismissed by Argentina in October, and prompted further roadblocks across the bridges. At the end of November Uruguay asked the ICJ to intervene in the dispute by compelling Argentina to end the blockade of the bridges; however, the ICJ rejected the request in January 2007. In April, as a result of mediation by King Juan Carlos of Spain, representatives from both countries signed an agreement declaring their willingness to reach a resolution to the dispute. The inauguration by President Tabaré Vázquez of Uruguay of the Botnia mill in September provoked large-scale demonstrations by Argentine protesters; later in the month it was reported that the two sides had reached an agreement whereby the mill would delay starting production until after the presidential election in Argentina. In mid-November Vázquez authorized the plant to begin operations, and subsequently ordered the temporary closure of the border between the two countries in anticipation of violent protests.

Government

For administrative purposes Argentina comprises 23 provinces together with the Federal District of Buenos Aires. The provinces are generally subdivided into departments and municipalities.

Legislative power is vested in the bicameral Congress (Congreso): the Chamber of Deputies (Cámara de Diputados) has 257 members, elected by universal adult suffrage for a term of four years (with approximately one-half of the seats renewable every two years); the Senate (Senado) has 72 members, with three members drawn from each of the 23 provinces and the Federal District of Buenos Aires. Senators are elected for a six-year term (with one-third of the seats renewable every two years). In 2001, however, the entire Senate was renewed. The President is directly elected for a four-year term, renewable once. Each province has its own elected Governor and legislature, concerned with all matters not delegated to the federal Government.

Defence

The total strength of the regular armed forces, as assessed at November 2007, was 76,000, comprising a 41,400-strong army, a 20,000-strong navy and an air force of 14,600 men. There were also paramilitary forces numbering 31,240 men. Conscription was ended on 1 April 1995. The budget for 2007 put defence expenditure at 6,460m. new pesos.

Economic Affairs

In 2006, according to estimates by the World Bank, Argentina's gross national income (GNI), measured at average 2004–06 prices, was US $201,410m., equivalent to $5,150 per head (or $15,390 on an international purchasing-power parity basis). During 1996–2006, it was estimated, Argentina's population increased at an average rate of 1.0% per year, while gross domestic product (GDP) per head increased, in real terms, by an average of 1.5% per year. Overall GDP increased, in real terms, at an average annual rate of 2.6% in 1996–2006. Real GDP increased by a preliminary 8.5% in 2006.

Agriculture (including forestry and fishing) contributed an estimated 8.4% of GDP in 2006 and employed 8.7% of the economically active population in 2005, according to FAO estimates. The principal cash crops are wheat, maize, sorghum and soybeans. Beef production is also important. During 1995–2006 agricultural GDP increased at an average annual rate of 2.3%. According to official estimates, the GDP of the sector increased by 11.1% in 2005, and by 2.6% in 2006.

Industry (including mining, manufacturing, construction and power) engaged 18.4% of the employed labour force in 2001 and provided an estimated 35.6% of GDP in 2006. During 1995–2006 industrial GDP increased, in real terms, at an estimated average annual rate of 3.1%. According to official estimates, sectoral GDP increased by 10.1% in 2006.

Mining contributed an estimated 6.0% of GDP in 2006, and employed 0.3% of the working population in 2001. Although Argentina used to possess substantial deposits of petroleum and natural gas, as well as steam coal and lignite, few hydrocarbon deposits have been discovered since the mid-1990s. The GDP of the mining sector increased, in real terms, at an average estimated rate of 1.0% per year during 1995–2006; the sector's GDP decreased by 3.0% in 2006.

Manufacturing contributed an estimated 22.3% of GDP in 2006, and employed 11.4% of the working population in 2001. During 1995–2006 manufacturing GDP increased, in real terms, at an estimated average annual rate of 2.5%. According to official estimates, manufacturing GDP increased by 8.9% in 2006.

Energy is derived principally from natural gas, responsible for the production of 54.8% of total primary energy consumption in 2004. However, in early 2004 a critical shortage in the gas supply prompted the Government of President Néstor Carlos Kirchner to reduce the voltage in the national grid, ration gas supplies to various corporations and reduce exports of gas. Hydroelectricity produced 30.4% of Argentina's total energy requirements in 2004, while the country's two nuclear power-stations produced 7.8%. In 2005 imports of mineral fuels comprised an estimated 5.1% of the country's total imports.

Services engaged 69.3% of the employed labour force in 2001 and accounted for an estimated 56.0% of GDP in 2006. The combined GDP of the service sectors increased, in real terms, at an estimated average rate of 2.7% per year during 1995–2006; sectoral GDP increased by 8.1% in 2006.

In 2006 Argentina recorded a visible trade surplus of US $13,976m., and there was a surplus of $8,053m. on the current account of the balance of payments. In 2006 the principal source of imports was Brazil (34.4%), followed by the USA (12.6%). Brazil was also the principal recipient of exports, accounting for 17.6% of total exports in that year, again followed by the USA (8.9%). Other major trading partners in 2006 were the People's Republic of China, Chile, Spain, the Netherlands and Germany. The principal exports in 2006 were, according to provisional figures, mineral fuels, lubricants and related materials. The principal imports were, according to provisional figures, nuclear reactors, boilers, machines and mechanical appliances, vehicles and electrical machinery.

In 2008 there was a projected central government budget surplus of 7,976.3m. new pesos. Argentina's total external debt was US $114,335m. at the end of 2005, of which $61,952m. was long-term public debt. In that year the total cost of debt-servicing was equivalent to 20.7% of revenue from exports of goods and services. The annual rate of inflation averaged 5.4% in 1995–2006; consumer prices increased by 10.9% in 2006. The national unemployment rate was 11.4% in 2006.

Argentina is a member of the Latin American Integration Association (ALADI, see p. 331) and of Mercosur (Mercado Común del Sur, see p. 391). In December 2004 Argentina was one of 12 countries that were signatories to the agreement, signed in Cusco, Peru, creating the South American Community of Nations (Comunidad Sudamericana de Naciones, which was renamed the Union of South American Nations—Unión de Naciones Suramericanas, UNASUR, in April 2007), intended to promote greater regional economic integration.

From 1998 international prices for certain commodities fell, causing the trade and budget deficits to widen. The devaluation of the Brazilian currency in January 1999 exacerbated the situation and the economy entered recession. Throughout 2000 and 2001 the economic situation worsened. Faced with declining tax revenues, the Government failed to secure any further international funding, and in January 2002 a major default on the country's sovereign debt (estimated at US $155,000m.) to the IMF and a 30% devaluation of the peso inevitably ensued. In November 2002 the Government of Eduardo Duhalde announced its intention to default on payment obligations to the World Bank and the Inter-American Development Bank (IDB), in the absence of a new agreement with the IMF. Both institutions ceased to disburse funds with immediate effect. A new $6,700m. stand-by agreement was eventually reached with the IMF in January 2003, but in September, one month after the stand-by agreement expired, Argentina failed to repay $2,900m. owed to the IMF. In spite of what was effectively the largest default in the Fund's history, the IMF extended a new, favourable three-year deal to the Argentine Government, and in March 2004 the IMF agreed to release a further $3,100m. in loans, after the Government agreed to continue negotiations with private sector creditors. None the less, the Government of President Néstor Kirchner remained reluctant to honour international obligations at the expense of Argentina's fragile social stability, and negotiations with the IMF were suspended in the middle of the year after the Government refused to accede to the Fund's demand that Argentina increase its fiscal surplus. Nevertheless, following the implementation of a debt-conversion programme, by the end of February 2005 76.6% of Argentina's privately held debt (estimated at some $82,000m.) had been converted into several new types of bond. The plan was central to the Government's economic policy and its success facilitated Argentina's re-admission to international financial markets. Economic growth of 9.2% and a preliminary 8.5% was recorded in 2005 and 2006, respectively. Much of this improvement was owing to low international interest rates, record agricultural production, in addition to high world prices for Argentina's agricultural exports, and the devalued currency's positive impact on export levels. In an effort to liberate economic policy from IMF regulation, the Government repaid outstanding loans of some $9,500m. to the Fund in 2007. Nevertheless, at the end of that year, Argentina remained heavily indebted to both the 'Paris Club' of creditor nations and private creditors, with outstanding loans estimated at $6,000m. and $20,000m., respectively. Furthermore, concerns remained that continued economic growth was unsustainable without increased foreign investment, which largely depended on a reduction in the debt burden. It was estimated that the rate of investment would need to increase at an annual rate of 24% if Argentina was to be able to maintain high rates of growth. The economy was forecast to have expanded by 7.6% in 2007. The continued use of price controls eroded profitability in the energy sector and the resultant power shortages led to a downturn in industrial output as firms were unable to operate at full capacity, deterring investment in both the energy and industrial sectors. Argentina was also forced to import electricity from neighbouring Paraguay. The private sector hoped that the Government of Cristina Fernández de Kirchner, which took office in late 2007, would remove tariffs on utilities in 2008, a move which was likely to lead to a substantial increase in the rate of inflation. In 2007 the administration revised methodology used to calculate consumer prices, consequently the rate of inflation quoted by official sources was far lower than that calculated by independent organizations.

Education

Education from pre-school to university level is available free of charge. Education is officially compulsory for all children at primary level, between the ages of six and 14 years. Secondary education lasts for between five and seven years, depending on the type of course: the normal certificate of education (bachillerato) course lasts for five years, whereas a course leading to a technical or agricultural bachillerato lasts for six years. Technical education is supervised by the Consejo Nacional de Educación Técnica. In 1999 enrolment at primary schools included an estimated 99.3% of pupils in the relevant age-group. In 2003 enrolment at secondary schools included 79.1% of pupils in the relevant age-group. Non-university higher education, usually leading to a teaching qualification, is for three or four years, while university courses last for four years or more. There were 36 state universities and 48 private universities in 2001. Central government expenditure on education and culture in 2008 was forecast at 10,189.8m. new pesos (6.3% of total expenditure).

Public Holidays

2008: 1 January (New Year's Day), 21 March (Good Friday), 24 March (Truth and Justice Memorial Day), 2 April (Veterans' Day and Tribute to the Fallen of the Falklands (Malvinas) War), 1 May (Labour Day), 25 May (Anniversary of the 1810 Revolution), 16 June (Death of Gen. Manuel Belgrano), 9 July (Inde-

ARGENTINA

pendence Day), 18 August (Death of Gen. José de San Martín), 12 October (Columbus Day), 8 December (Immaculate Conception), 25 December (Christmas).
2009: 1 January (New Year's Day), 24 March (Truth and Justice Memorial Day), 2 April (Veterans' Day and Tribute to the Fallen of the Falklands (Malvinas) War), 10 April (Good Friday), 1 May (Labour Day), 25 May (Anniversary of the 1810 Revolution), 15 June (Death of Gen. Manuel Belgrano), 9 July (Independence Day), 17 August (Death of Gen. José de San Martín), 12 October (Columbus Day), 8 December (Immaculate Conception), 25 December (Christmas).

Weights and Measures
The metric system is in force.

Statistical Survey

Sources (unless otherwise stated): Instituto Nacional de Estadística y Censos, Avda Julio A. Roca 609, C1067AAB Buenos Aires; tel. (11) 4349-9200; fax (11) 4349-9601; e-mail ces@indec.mecon.gov.ar; internet www.indec.mecon.ar; Banco Central de la República Argentina, Reconquista 266, 1003 Buenos Aires; tel. (11) 4348-3500; fax (11) 4348-3955; e-mail sistema@bcra.gov.ar; internet www.bcra.gov.ar.

Area and Population

AREA, POPULATION AND DENSITY

Area (sq km)	2,780,403*
Population (census results)†	
15 May 1991	32,615,528
17–18 November 2001	
Males	17,659,072
Females	18,601,058
Total	36,260,130
Population (official estimates at mid-year)	
2005	38,592,150
2006	38,970,611
2007	39,356,383
Density (per sq km) at mid-2007	14.2

* 1,073,519 sq miles. The figure excludes the Falkland Islands (Islas Malvinas) and Antarctic territory claimed by Argentina.
† Figures exclude adjustment for underenumeration, estimated to have been 0.9% at the 1991 census.

PROVINCES
(official estimates at mid-2007)

	Area (sq km)	Population	Density (per sq km)	Capital
Buenos Aires—Federal District	203	3,034,161	14,946.6	
Buenos Aires—Province	307,571	14,917,940	48.5	La Plata
Catamarca	102,602	380,612	3.7	San Fernando del Valle de Catamarca
Chaco	99,633	1,042,881	10.5	Resistencia
Chubut	224,686	455,607	2.0	Rawson
Córdoba	165,321	3,311,280	20.0	Córdoba
Corrientes	88,199	1,002,416	11.4	Corrientes
Entre Ríos	78,781	1,242,547	15.8	Paraná
Formosa	72,066	532,238	7.4	Formosa
Jujuy	53,219	670,766	12.6	San Salvador de Jujuy
La Pampa	143,440	329,576	2.3	Santa Rosa
La Rioja	89,680	334,235	3.7	La Rioja
Mendoza	148,827	1,711,416	11.5	Mendoza
Misiones	29,801	1,061,590	35.6	Posadas
Neuquén	94,078	538,952	5.7	Neuquén
Río Negro	203,013	594,189	2.9	Viedma
Salta	155,488	1,202,753	7.7	Salta
San Juan	89,651	685,883	7.7	San Juan
San Luis	76,748	428,025	5.6	San Luis
Santa Cruz	243,943	221,871	0.9	Río Gallegos
Santa Fe	133,007	3,220,818	24.2	Santa Fe
Santiago del Estero	136,351	856,739	6.3	Santiago del Estero
Tierra del Fuego	21,571	122,531	5.7	Ushuaia
Tucumán	22,524	1,457,357	64.7	San Miguel de Tucumán
Total	**2,780,403**	**39,356,383**	**14.2**	Buenos Aires

PRINCIPAL TOWNS
(population at 2001 census)*

Buenos Aires (capital)	2,776,138	Malvinas Argentinas†	290,691
Córdoba	1,267,521	Berazategui†	287,913
La Matanza†	1,255,288	Bahía Blanca†	284,776
Rosario	908,163	Resistencia	274,490
Lomas de Zamora†	591,345	Vicente López†	274,082
La Plata†	574,369	San Miguel†	253,086
General Pueyrredón†	564,056	Posadas	252,981
San Miguel de Tucumán	527,150	Esteban Echeverría†	243,974
Quilmes†	518,788	Paraná	235,967
Almirante Brown†	515,556	Pilar†	232,463
Merlo†	469,985	San Salvador de Jujuy	231,229
Salta	462,051	Santiago del Estero	230,614
Lanús†	453,082	José C. Paz†	230,208
General San Martín†	403,107	Guaymallén	223,365
Moreno†	380,503	Neuquén	201,868
Santa Fe	368,668	Formosa	198,074
Florencio Varela†	348,970	Godoy Cruz	182,563
Tres de Febrero†	336,467	Escobar†	178,155
Avellaneda†	328,980	Hurlingham†	172,245
Corrientes	314,546	Las Heras	169,248
Morón†	309,380	Ituzaingó	158,121
Tigre†	301,223	San Luis	153,322
San Isidro†	291,505	San Fernando†	151,131

* In each case the figure refers to the city proper. At the 2001 census the population of the Buenos Aires agglomeration was 13,827,203.
† Settlement within the Province of Buenos Aires.

Mid-2005 ('000, incl. suburbs, UN estimates): Buenos Aires 12,550; Córdoba 1,423; Rosario 1,186; Mendoza 876; San Miguel de Tucumán 781 (Source: UN, *World Urbanization Prospects: The 2005 Revision*).

BIRTHS, MARRIAGES AND DEATHS

	Registered live births		Marriages		Registered deaths	
	Number	Rate (per 1,000)	Number	Rate (per 1,000)	Number	Rate (per 1,000)
1998	683,301	18.9	n.a.	n.a.	280,180	7.8
1999	686,748	18.8	n.a.	n.a.	289,543	7.9
2000	701,878	19.0	141,027	3.8	277,148	7.5
2001	683,495	18.2	130,533	3.5	285,941	7.6
2002	694,684	18.3	122,343	3.3	291,190	7.7
2003	697,952	18.4	129,049	3.4	302,064	8.0
2004	736,261	19.3	n.a.	n.a.	294,051	7.7
2005*	712,220	18.5	n.a.	n.a.	293,529	7.6

* Preliminary.

Source: mainly UN, *Demographic Yearbook* and *Population and Vital Statistics Report*.

Expectation of life (years at birth, WHO estimates): 75.0 (males 71.5; females 78.4) in 2005 (Source: WHO, *World Health Statistics*).

ARGENTINA

ECONOMICALLY ACTIVE POPULATION
(persons aged 14 years and over, census of November 2001)

	Males	Females	Total
Agriculture, hunting and forestry	805,293	92,228	897,521
Fishing	11,843	1,632	13,475
Mining and quarrying	35,068	2,911	37,979
Manufacturing	966,056	279,488	1,245,544
Electricity, gas and water	76,428	13,737	90,165
Construction	621,598	16,968	638,566
Wholesale and retail trade; repair of motor vehicles, motorcycles and personal and household goods	1,287,017	624,364	1,911,381
Hotels and restaurants	168,929	132,755	301,684
Transport, storage and communication	629,188	88,385	717,573
Financial intermediation	111,717	74,796	186,513
Real estate, renting and business activities	456,005	255,746	711,751
Public administration and defence; compulsory social security	649,790	319,490	969,280
Education	200,538	730,387	930,925
Health and social work	197,282	394,824	592,106
Other community, social and personal services	266,782	186,202	452,984
Private households with employed persons	85,213	701,219	786,432
Extra-territorial organizations and bodies	1,084	917	2,001
Activities not adequately described	243,200	184,107	427,307
Total employed	6,813,031	4,100,156	10,913,187
Unemployed	2,212,776	2,138,820	4,351,596
Total labour force	9,025,807	6,238,976	15,264,783

2003 (labour force survey of 31 urban agglomerations at May, '000 persons aged 10 years and over): Total employed 8,570.8 (males 4,887.7, females 3,683.1); Unemployed 1,583.6; Total labour force 10,154.4 (males 5,836.7, females 4,317.7).

2006 (labour force survey of 28 urban agglomerations at January–March, '000 persons aged 10 years and over): Total employed 9,565; Unemployed 1,233; Total labour force 10,798.

Health and Welfare

KEY INDICATORS

Total fertility rate (children per woman, 2005)	2.3
Under-5 mortality rate (per 1,000 live births, 2005)	16
HIV (% of persons aged 15–49, 2005)	0.6
Physicians (per 1,000 head, 1998)	3.01
Hospital beds (per 1,000 head, 2000)	4.1
Health expenditure (2004): US $ per head (PPP)	1,274.3
Health expenditure (2004): % of GDP	9.6
Health expenditure (2004): public (% of total)	45.3
Access to water (% of persons, 2004)	96
Access to sanitation (% of persons, 2004)	91
Human Development Index (2005): ranking	38
Human Development Index (2005): value	0.869

For sources and definitions, see explanatory note on p. vi.

Agriculture

PRINCIPAL CROPS
('000 metric tons)

	2004	2005	2006
Wheat	15,960	12,574	14,000
Rice (paddy)	1,060	1,027	1,193
Barley	1,004	894	1,268
Maize	14,951	20,483	14,446
Rye	37	92	33
Oats	536	227	243
Sorghum	2,160	2,894	2,328
Potatoes	2,021	2,432*	2,432*
Sweet potatoes*	276	272	272
Cassava (Manioc)*	173	176	176

—continued	2004	2005	2006
Sugar cane*	17,826	18,799	18,799
Dry beans	151	169	323
Soybeans (Soya beans)	31,500	38,300	40,467
Groundnuts (in shell)	419	593	496
Olives*	97	97	97
Sunflower seed	3,100	3,652	3,798
Artichokes*	88	89	89
Tomatoes*	664	660	660
Pumpkins, squash and gourds*	284	278	278
Chillies and green peppers*	130	134	134
Dry onions	699	773	773*
Garlic	143	116	116
Carrots and turnips*	248	252	252
Watermelons*	126	126	126
Cantaloupes and other melons*	79	78	78
Bananas*	171	167	167
Oranges	770†	792*	792*
Tangerines, mandarins, clementines and satsumas*	641	660	660
Lemons and limes	1,300†	1,393*	1,393*
Grapefruit and pomelos	170†	191*	191*
Apples	1,262	1,272*	1,272*
Pears	510	510*	510*
Peaches and nectarines	272	256*	256*
Plums and sloes	127	132*	132*
Grapes†	2,651	2,830	2,881
Tea (made)	70	68	68*
Mate	252	265	265*
Tobacco (leaves)	118*	164	164*
Cotton (lint)	112†	160†	160*

* FAO estimate(s).
† Unofficial estimate(s).

Aggregate production ('000 metric tons, may include official, semi-official or estimated data): Total cereals 35,750 in 2004, 38,239 in 2005, 33,556 in 2006; Total roots and tubers 2,470 in 2004, 2,880 in 2005, 2,880 in 2006; Total vegetables (incl. melons) 3,193 in 2004, 3,239 in 2005, 3,239 in 2006; Total fruits (excl. melons) 7,969 in 2004, 8,303 in 2005, 8,351 in 2006.

Source: FAO.

LIVESTOCK
('000 head, year ending September)

	2003	2004	2005
Horses*	3,655	3,655	3,655
Asses, mules or hinnies	283*	283*	n.a.
Cattle	50,869†	50,768†	50,768*
Pigs*	1,500	1,490	1,490
Sheep*	12,450	12,450	12,450
Goats*	4,200	4,200	4,200
Chickens*	110,700	95,000	95,000
Ducks	2,355*	2,355*	n.a.
Geese*	140	140	140
Turkeys*	2,900	2,900	2,900

* FAO estimate(s).
† Unofficial figure.

2006: Available data are assumed to be unchanged from 2005 (FAO estimates).

Source: FAO.

LIVESTOCK PRODUCTS
('000 metric tons)

	2004	2005	2006
Cattle meat	3,024	2,980	2,980*
Sheep meat*	52	52	52
Pig meat*	179	188	188
Horse meat*	56	56	56
Chicken meat	866	1,010	1,156
Cows' milk	8,100†	8,100*	8,100*
Hen eggs*	300	300	300
Honey*	88	93	93
Wool: greasy*	60	60	60

* FAO estimate(s).
† Unofficial figure.

Source: FAO.

ARGENTINA

Forestry

ROUNDWOOD REMOVALS
('000 cubic metres, excl. bark)

	2003	2004	2005
Sawlogs, veneer logs and logs for sleepers	3,259	3,055	3,455
Pulpwood	6,317	5,987	5,970
Other industrial wood	130	291	421
Fuel wood	3,972	5,584	4,372
Total	13,678	14,917	14,218

2006: Production assumed to be unchanged from 2005 (FAO estimates).
Source: FAO.

SAWNWOOD PRODUCTION
('000 cubic metres, incl. railway sleepers)

	2003	2004	2005
Coniferous (softwood)	1,066	948	1,079
Broadleaved (hardwood)	322	614	660
Total	1,388	1,562	1,739

2006: Production assumed to be unchanged from 2005 (FAO estimates).
Source: FAO.

Fishing

('000 metric tons, live weight)

	2003	2004	2005
Capture*	917.1	947.2	947.5
Southern blue whiting	44.6	50.2	36.7
Argentine hake	334.1	416.7	362.0
Patagonian grenadier	97.8	116.9	115.3
Argentine red shrimp	52.9	27.1	7.5
Patagonian scallop	50.7	49.2	39.5
Argentine shortfin squid	140.9	76.5	146.1
Aquaculture	1.6	1.8	2.4
Total catch*	918.7	949.1	949.9

* FAO estimates.

Note: The data exclude aquatic plants (metric tons, capture only): 3 in 2000. Also excluded are aquatic mammals, recorded by number rather than by weight. The number of La Plata River dolphins caught was 893 in 2003; 900 in 2004; nil in 2005.
Source: FAO.

Mining

('000 metric tons, unless otherwise indicated)

	2003	2004	2005*
Crude petroleum ('000 cu metres)	42,754	40,150	38,323
Natural gas (million cu metres)	48,876	50,254	48,738
Lead ore†	12.1	9.6*	10.7
Zinc ore†	29.8*	27.2*	30.2
Lithium‡	2.8	4.2*	5.9
Silver ore (kilograms)†	133,917	172,387	263,766
Copper ore†	199.0	177.1*	187.3
Gold ore (kilograms)†*	29,749	28,466	27,904
Boron	512.2	821.0	632.8
Gypsum (crude)	489.8	836.3	1,073.3
Clay (common)	1,682.2	2,284.3	6,023.9
Salt	1,667.8	1,458.9	1,747.5
Sand:			
for construction*	11,978.8	16,862.9	21,017.2
Silica (glass) sand	300.7	845.3*	461.2
Limestone	8,147.9	10,525.5*	12,476.5
Stone (various crushed)*	4,463.5	5,254.1	9,615.8
Rhodochrosite (kg)	23,915	109,476*	118,200
Gemstones (kg)	43,288	49,599*	69,241

* Estimate(s).
† Figures refer to the metal content of ores and concentrates.
‡ Lithium oxide (Li$_2$O) content.

Industry

SELECTED PRODUCTS
('000 metric tons, unless otherwise indicated)

	2003	2004	2005
Wheat flour	3,792	3,852	3,877*
Beer (sales, '000 hectolitres)†	12,950	13,410	13,960
Wine (sales, '000 hectolitres)	12,338	11,113	10,972
Cigarettes (sales, million packets)	1,990	1,890	1,862
Paper (excl. newspaper)	1,209	1,323	1,393
Aluminium	272	272	271
Iron (primary)	4,140	4,147	4,467
Crude steel	5,033	5,125	5,382
Rubber tyres for motor vehicles ('000, excl. tractors)	9,578	10,464	11,824
Portland cement	5,217	6,254	7,595
Refined petroleum ('000 cu metres)	32,958	33,622	33,552
Urea	1,300	1,365	1,249
Ammonia	884	858	797
Washing machines ('000 units)†	367	521	697
Home refrigerators ('000 units)†	149	241	352
Motor vehicles ('000)	110	171	183
Electric energy (million kWh)	85,260	92,000	96,900

* Provisional figure.
† Estimates.

2006 ('000 metric tons, unless otherwise indicated): Wheat flour 3,933; Beer (sales, '000 hectolitres) 14,825 (estimate); Wine (sales, '000 hectolitres) 11,104; Cigarettes (sales, million packets) 1,993; Electric energy 104,100m. kWh (estimate).

ARGENTINA

Finance

CURRENCY AND EXCHANGE RATES

Monetary Units
100 centavos = 1 nuevo peso argentino (new Argentine peso).

Sterling, Dollar and Euro Equivalents (31 December 2007)
£1 sterling = 6.269 new pesos;
US $1 = 3.129 new pesos;
€1 = 4.606 new pesos;
100 new pesos = £15.95= $31.96 = €21.71.

Average Exchange Rate (new pesos per US $)
2005   2.904
2006   3.054
2007   3.096

Note: From April 1996 to December 2001 the official exchange rate was fixed at US $1 = 99.95 centavos. In January 2002 the Government abandoned this exchange rate and devalued the peso: initially there was a fixed official exchange rate of US $1 = 1.40 new pesos for trade and financial transactions, while a free market rate was applicable to other transactions. In February, however, a unified 'floating' exchange rate system, with the rate to be determined by market conditions, was introduced.

BUDGET
(million new pesos, forecasts)*

Revenue	2006	2007	2008
Current revenue	100,059.1	119,294.0	168,322.1
Tax revenue	77,970.5	87,198.2	118,751.8
Direct	21,282.5	17,156.0	21,942.2
Indirect	56,688.0	70,042.2	96,809.7
Social security contributions	16,979.2	26,046.8	40,237.4
Sale of public goods and services	564.9	763.2	909.3
Property income	1,400.0	2,029.2	3,380.1
Other non-tax revenue	2,253.2	2,748.4	3,501.2
Current transfers	891.2	508.2	1,542.3
Capital revenue	1,102.8	1,097.8	1,140.7
Total	101,161.9	120,391.9	169,462.8

Expenditure	2006	2007	2008
Current expenditure	81,253.0	99,994.2	142,432.5
General administration	5,678.6	5,795.3	6,834.6
Legislative	469.9	552.0	710.7
Judicial	1,446.4	1,940.7	2,435.8
Foreign relations	752.9	900.6	1,082.5
Interior	2,009.6	1,200.1	1,169.5
Fiscal	21.7	40.6	204.4
Defence and security	6,540.0	7,536.4	9,370.5
Defence	3,123.2	3,550.6	4,250.6
Internal security	2,607.4	3,045.1	3,899.1
Penal system	392.7	473.8	608.4
Intelligence services	416.7	466.9	612.4
Social services	55,132.9	66,118.8	91,860.3
Health	3,331.3	4,199.9	5,930.2
Social welfare	5,516.0	2,976.2	3,718.7
Social security	35,184.0	46,323.0	66,504.9
Education and culture	6,352.9	7,903.5	10,189.8
Labour	3,461.1	2,934.7	2,614.5
Economy	3,255.6	6,409.9	15,158.1
Energy, fuel and mining	1,185.3	3,061.4	7,578.2
Communications	194.6	264.9	374.6
Transport	791.1	1,609.1	4,030.7
Agriculture	521.9	714.0	1,953.7
Industry	273.9	297.2	620.9
Debt-servicing	10,645.9	14,133.7	19,209.1
Capital expenditure	12,469.4	13,227.2	19,053.9
Total	93,722.4	113,221.4	161,486.5

*Budget figures refer to the consolidated accounts of the central Government.

Source: Oficina Nacional de Presupuesto, Secretaría de Hacienda, Ministerio de Economía, Buenos Aires.

Statistical Survey

INTERNATIONAL RESERVES
(US $ million at 31 December)

	2004	2005	2006
Gold (national valuation)	769	908	1,123
IMF special drawing rights	877	4,437	482
Foreign exchange	18,007	22,742	30,421
Total	19,653	28,087	32,026

Source: IMF, *International Financial Statistics*.

MONEY SUPPLY
(million new pesos at 31 December)

	2004	2005	2006
Currency outside banks	33,872	43,764	53,812
Demand deposits at commercial banks	22,055	27,478	24,570
Total money	55,927	71,242	78,382

Source: IMF, *International Financial Statistics*.

COST OF LIVING
(Consumer Price Index for Buenos Aires metropolitan area; annual averages; base: 2000 = 100)

	2004	2005	2006
Food, beverages and tobacco	165.1	183.3	205.5
Electricity, gas and other fuel	113.8	118.6	115.9
Clothing and footwear	168.2	187.2	215.6
All items (incl. others)	147.5	161.7	179.4

Source: ILO.

NATIONAL ACCOUNTS
(million new pesos at current prices)

National Income and Product

	2004	2005	2006
Gross domestic product (GDP) at market prices	447,643	531,939	654,439
Net primary income from abroad	−26,087	−18,029	−15,843
Gross national income (GNI)	421,556	513,910	638,596
Net current transfers	1,758	1,781	1,903
Gross national disposable income	423,314	515,691	640,499

Expenditure on the Gross Domestic Product
(preliminary)

	2004	2005	2006
Government final consumption expenditure	49,826	63,359	81,248
Private final consumption expenditure	281,189	326,275	386,305
Increase in stocks*	−2,014	−3,102	−2,124
Gross fixed capital formation	85,800	114,132	152,838
Total domestic expenditure	414,801	500,664	618,267
Exports of goods and services	115,075	133,346	162,035
Less Imports of goods and services	82,233	102,072	125,863
Gross domestic product (GDP) in market prices	447,643	531,939	654,439
GDP at constant 1993 prices	279,141	304,764	330,565

*Including statistical discrepancy.

ARGENTINA

Gross Domestic Product by Economic Activity
(preliminary)

	2004	2005	2006
Agriculture and forestry	41,886	44,760	48,759
Fishing and hunting	1,262	1,571	2,001
Mining and quarrying	23,542	28,820	36,235
Manufacturing	99,793	114,091	134,709
Electricity, gas and water supply	6,969	8,520	9,712
Construction	17,264	24,059	34,897
Wholesale and retail trade	48,453	57,999	69,127
Hotels and restaurants	9,936	12,559	16,344
Transport, storage and communications	37,524	44,428	53,565
Financial intermediation	17,044	21,402	28,048
Real estate, renting and business activities	45,987	53,599	65,962
Public administration and defence*	21,338	26,621	33,629
Education, health and social work	27,100	34,350	46,943
Other community, social and personal service activities†	16,278	20,047	24,862
Sub-total	414,374	492,825	604,793
Value-added tax	32,087	38,276	49,044
Import duties	3,250	3,877	5,139
Less Imputed bank service charge	2,068	3,039	4,536
GDP in market prices	447,643	531,939	654,440

* Including extra-territorial organizations and bodies.
† Including private households with employed persons.

BALANCE OF PAYMENTS
(US $ million)

	2004	2005	2006
Exports of goods f.o.b.	34,576	40,352	46,569
Imports of goods f.o.b.	−21,311	−27,302	−32,593
Trade balance	13,265	13,050	13,976
Exports of services	5,189	6,252	7,360
Imports of services	−6,634	−7,613	−8,417
Balance on goods and services	11,819	11,689	12,919
Other income received	3,463	4,092	5,270
Other income paid	−12,705	−10,719	−10,679
Balance on goods, services and income	2,577	5,061	7,509
Current transfers received	1,115	1,231	1,371
Current transfers paid	−532	−666	−827
Current balance	3,160	5,626	8,053
Capital account (net)	47	89	101
Direct investment abroad	−442	−1,151	−2,008
Direct investment from abroad	4,584	5,008	4,807
Portfolio investment assets	−77	1,368	−1
Portfolio investment liabilities	−9,339	−2,039	6,257
Other investment assets	−2,387	1,935	−3,522
Financial derivatives liabilities	—	—	−243
Other investment liabilities	−2,635	−3,661	−1,664
Net errors and omissions	95	444	1,128
Overall balance	−6,993	7,620	12,910

Source: IMF, *International Financial Statistics*.

External Trade

PRINCIPAL COMMODITIES
(US $ million)

Imports c.i.f.	2004	2005	2006*
Mineral fuels, lubricants and related products	922	1,425	1,604
Paper and cardboard	525	640	703
Rubber and manufactures of rubber	475	576	697
Organic chemicals and related products	1,622	1,721	1,914
Pharmaceutical products	545	625	763
Plastic and manufactures of laminate	1,164	1,497	1,628
Metalliferous ore	568	716	832
Electrical machinery	2,594	3,622	4,507
Vehicles	3,083	4,247	5,345
Nuclear reactors, boilers, machines and mechanical appliances	3,767	4,885	5,943
Optical instruments and apparatus, etc.	484	630	779
Total (incl. others)	22,445	28,687	34,151

Exports f.o.b.	2004	2005	2006*
Meat and meat products	1,025	1,452	1,430
Milk and milk products	656	740	929
Skins and leathers	819	814	886
Fish	791	782	1,210
Fats and oils	3,163	3,291	3,877
Cereals	2,690	2,808	2,955
Oil seeds and oleaginous fruits	1,832	2,444	1,961
Mineral fuels, lubricants and related materials	5,847	6,587	7,109
Mineral by-products	674	1,011	1,376
Metalliferous ore	647	1,053	1,311
Plastic and manufactures of laminate	941	1,149	1,217
Vehicles	2,054	2,883	4,023
Nuclear reactors, boilers and mechanical appliances	779	977	1,136
Total (incl. others)	34,576	40,387	46,456

* Provisional figures.

PRINCIPAL TRADING PARTNERS
(US $ million)*

Imports c.i.f.	2004	2005	2006†
Brazil‡	7,567	10,187	11,749
Chile‡	404	549	599
China, People's Republic§	1,737	2,682	3,153
France (incl. Monaco)	586	584	909
Germany	1,093	1,303	1,545
Italy	623	748	908
Japan	612	789	933
Mexico	758	793	1,111
Paraguay	380	453	505
Spain	517	571	614
United Kingdom	312	319	386
USA	3,432	4,046	4,294
Uruguay‡	227	269	301
Total (incl. others)	22,445	28,662	34,126

Exports f.o.b.	2004	2005	2006†
Belgium	249	262	298
Bolivia	299	380	380
Brazil‡	5,605	6,335	8,132
Canada	177	303	437
Chile‡	3,835	4,500	4,403
China, People's Republic§	3,055	3,336	3,643
Colombia	274	361	551
France (incl. Monaco)	295	381	553
Germany	727	871	1,126
Italy	948	984	1,095
Japan	363	304	398
Mexico	1,036	1,159	1,519

ARGENTINA

Exports f.o.b.—continued	2004	2005	2006†
Netherlands	1,243	1,352	1,443
Paraguay	522	509	621
Peru	500	600	729
South Africa	600	491	917
Spain	1,355	1,567	1,824
United Kingdom	406	375	490
USA	3,818	4,572	4,116
Uruguay‡	664	845	1,172
Venezuela	438	513	806
Total (incl. others)	34,576	40,387	46,083

* Imports by country of origin; exports by country of destination.
† Provisional figures.
‡ Including free trade zones.
§ Including Hong Kong and Macao.

Transport

RAILWAYS (traffic)

	2003	2004	2005
Passengers carried ('000)	381,726	400,692	417,266
Freight carried ('000 tons)	20,535	21,699	23,441
Passenger-km (million)	6,979	7,526	8,327
Freight ton-km (million)	11,001	11,603	12,262

ROAD TRAFFIC ('000 motor vehicles in use)

	1998	1999	2000
Passenger cars	5,047.8	5,056.7	5,386.7
Commercial vehicles	1,094.0	1,029.0	1,004.0

Source: UN, *Statistical Yearbook*.

SHIPPING

Merchant Fleet (registered at 31 December)

	2004	2005	2006
Number of vessels	507	522	565
Total displacement ('000 grt)	436.7	684.0	837.8

Source: Lloyd's Register-Fairplay, *World Fleet Statistics*.

International Sea-borne Freight Traffic ('000 metric tons)

	1996	1997	1998
Goods loaded	52,068	58,512	69,372
Goods unloaded	16,728	19,116	19,536

Source: UN, *Monthly Bulletin of Statistics*.

Total maritime freight handled ('000 metric tons): 118,965 in 2000; 125,685 in 2001; 120,514 in 2002; 130,775 in 2003; 137,213 in 2004 (Source: Dirección Nacional de Puertos y Vías Navegables).

CIVIL AVIATION

	2002	2003	2004
Kilometres flown (million)	131	131	165
Passengers carried ('000)	8,994	9,937	11,293
Passenger-km (million)	10,188	12,624	14,618
Total freight carried ('000 metric tons)	136	166	183

Tourism

TOURIST ARRIVALS BY REGION ('000)

	2002	2003	2004
Europe	323.7	456.0	555.1
USA and Canada	152.6	224.5	259.4
South America	2,094.5	1,970.6	2,151.3
Bolivia	119.1	59.7	69.0
Brazil	345.0	350.3	361.7
Chile	749.0	767.8	831.9
Paraguay	518.3	429.8	459.0
Uruguay	363.0	363.1	429.7
Total (incl. others)*	2,820.0	2,995.3	3,352.6

* Excluding nationals residing abroad.

Tourism receipts (US $ million, incl. passenger transport): 1,716 in 2002; 2,306 in 2003; 2,990 in 2004.

Source: World Tourism Statistics.

Communications Media

	2004	2005	2006
Telephones ('000 main lines in use)	8,760.6	9,441.7	9,459.8
Mobile cellular telephones ('000 handsets in use)	13,512.4	22,156.4	31,510.4
Internet users ('000)	6,153.6	6,863.5	8,183.7
Broadband subscribers ('000)	542.9	926.7	1,567.7
Personal computers ('000 in use)	3,200	3,200*	n.a.

* Estimate.

Television receivers ('000 in use): 11,800 in 2001.
Radio receivers ('000 in use): 24,300 in 1997.
Facsimile machines (estimate, '000 in use): 87 in 1998.
Book production: 13,148 titles in 2001.
Daily newspapers: 184 in 2004 (average circulation 1,363,000).

Sources: mainly UNESCO Institute for Statistics and *Statistical Yearbook*, and International Telecommunication Union.

Education

(2004)

	Institutions	Teachers	Students
Pre-primary	16,083	76,945	1,292,072
Primary	n.a.	306,285	4,727,783
EGB 1 and 2 (ages 6 to 11)	22,179	n.a.	4,575,818
Other primary	n.a.	n.a.	151,965
Secondary	n.a.	129,569	3,399,172
EGB 3 (ages 12 to 14)	15,063	34,103	1,823,519
Polimodal (ages 15 to 17)	6,908	95,466	1,150,548
Higher	1,879	n.a.	1,805,491
University	37	n.a.	1,273,156
Non-university	1,837	13,657	512,002
Special*	5	n.a.	20,333

* Including army, navy, police, aeronautical and art institutes.

Note: Figures include 2001 data for province of Corrientes.

Source: partly Red Federal de Información Educativa, *Relevamiento 2004*.

Adult literacy rate (UNESCO estimates): 97.2% (males 97.2%; females 97.2%) in 2001 (Source: UNESCO Institute for Statistics).

Directory

The Constitution

The return to civilian rule in 1983 represented a return to the principles of the 1853 Constitution, with some changes in electoral details. In August 1994 a new Constitution was approved, which contained 19 new articles, 40 amendments to existing articles and the addition of a chapter on New Rights and Guarantees. The Constitution is summarized below:

DECLARATIONS, RIGHTS AND GUARANTEES

Each province has the right to exercise its own administration of justice, municipal system and primary education. The Roman Catholic religion, being the faith of the majority of the nation, shall enjoy state protection; freedom of religious belief is guaranteed to all other denominations. The prior ethnical existence of indigenous peoples and their rights, as well as the common ownership of lands they traditionally occupy, are recognized. All inhabitants of the country have the right to work and exercise any legal trade; to petition the authorities; to leave or enter the Argentine territory; to use or dispose of their properties; to associate for a peaceable or useful purpose; to teach and acquire education, and to express freely their opinion in the press without censorship. The State does not admit any prerogative of blood, birth, privilege or titles of nobility. Equality is the basis of all duties and public offices. No citizens may be detained, except for reasons and in the manner prescribed by the law; or sentenced other than by virtue of a law existing prior to the offence and by decision of the competent tribunal after the hearing and defence of the person concerned. Private residence, property and correspondence are inviolable. No one may enter the home of a citizen or carry out any search in it without his consent, unless by a warrant from the competent authority; no one may suffer expropriation, except in case of public necessity and provided that the appropriate compensation has been paid in accordance with the provisions of the laws. In no case may the penalty of confiscation of property be imposed.

LEGISLATIVE POWER

Legislative power is vested in the bicameral Congreso (Congress), comprising the Cámara de Diputados (Chamber of Deputies) and the Senado (Senate). The Chamber of Deputies has 257 directly elected members, chosen for four years and eligible for re-election; approximately one-half of the membership of the Chamber shall be renewed every two years. Until October 1995 the Senate had 48 members, chosen by provincial legislatures for a nine-year term, with one-third of the seats renewable every three years. Since October 1995 elections have provided for a third senator, elected by provincial legislatures. In 2001 the entire Senate was renewed; one-third of the Senate was to be renewed every two years from 2003.

The powers of Congress include regulating foreign trade; fixing import and export duties; levying taxes for a specified time whenever the defence, common safety or general welfare of the State so requires; contracting loans on the nation's credit; regulating the internal and external debt and the currency system of the country; fixing the budget and facilitating the prosperity and welfare of the nation. Congress must approve required and urgent decrees and delegated legislation. Congress also approves or rejects treaties, authorizes the Executive to declare war or make peace, and establishes the strength of the Armed Forces in peace and war.

EXECUTIVE POWER

Executive power is vested in the President, who is the supreme head of the nation and controls the general administration of the country. The President issues the instructions and rulings necessary for the execution of the laws of the country, and takes part in drawing up and promulgating those laws. The President appoints, with the approval of the Senate, the judges of the Supreme Court and all other competent tribunals, ambassadors, civil servants, members of the judiciary, senior officers of the Armed Forces and bishops. The President may also appoint and remove, without reference to another body, the cabinet ministers. The President is Commander-in-Chief of all the Armed Forces. The President and Vice-President are elected directly for a four-year term, renewable only once.

JUDICIAL POWER

Judicial power is exercised by the Supreme Court and all other competent tribunals. The Supreme Court is responsible for the internal administration of all tribunals.

PROVINCIAL GOVERNMENT

The 23 provinces and the Federal District of Buenos Aires retain all the power not delegated to the Federal Government. They are governed by their own institutions and elect their own governors, legislators and officials.

The Government

HEAD OF STATE

President of the Republic: Cristina E. Fernández de Kirchner (took office 10 December 2007).
Vice-President: Julio César Cleto Cobos.

CABINET
(April 2008)

Cabinet Chief: Dr Alberto Angel Fernández.
Minister of the Interior: Aníbal Florencio Randazzo.
Minister of Foreign Affairs, International Trade and Worship: Jorge Taiana.
Minister of Defence: Dr Nilda Garré.
Minister of Economy and Production: Carlos Rafael Fernández.
Minister of Education: Juan Carlos Tedesco.
Minister of Science, Technology and Productive Innovation: Lino Barañao.
Minister of Labour, Employment and Social Security: Carlos Tomada.
Minister of Federal Planning, Public Investment and Services: Julio Miguel De Vido.
Minister of Health: Graciela Ocaña.
Minister of Justice and Human Rights: Aníbal Domingo Fernández.
Minister of Social Development: Alicia Kirchner.

MINISTRIES

General Secretariat to the Presidency: Balcarce 50, C1064AAB Buenos Aires; tel. (11) 4344-3674; fax (11) 4344-2647; e-mail dgi@presidencia.gov.ar; internet www.secretariageneral.gov.ar.

Ministry of Defence: Azopardo 250, 10°, 11° y 13°, C1107ADB Buenos Aires; tel. (11) 4346-8800; e-mail mindef@mindef.gov.ar; internet www.mindef.gov.ar.

Ministry of Economy and Production: Hipólito Yrigoyen 250, C1086AAB Buenos Aires; tel. (11) 4349-5000; e-mail sagpya@mecon.gov.ar; internet www.mecon.gov.ar.

Ministry of Education: Pizzurno 935, C1020ACA Buenos Aires; tel. (11) 4129-1000; e-mail info@me.gov.ar; internet www.me.gov.ar.

Ministry of Federal Planning, Public Investment and Services: Hipólito Yrigoyen 250, 11°, Of. 1112, C1086AAB Buenos Aires; tel. (11) 4349-6540; internet www.minplan.gov.ar.

Ministry of Foreign Affairs, International Trade and Worship: Esmeralda 1212, C1007ABR Buenos Aires; tel. (11) 4819-7000; e-mail webmaster@mrecic.gov.ar; internet www.cancilleria.gov.ar.

Ministry of Health: 9 de Julio 1925, C1073ABA Buenos Aires; tel. (11) 4379-9038; fax (11) 4381-2182; e-mail prensa@msal.gov.ar; internet www.msal.gov.ar.

Ministry of the Interior: 25 de Mayo 101/145, C1002ABC Buenos Aires; tel. (11) 4339-0800; fax (11) 4331-6376; internet www.mininterior.gov.ar.

Ministry of Justice and Human Rights: Sarmiento 329, C1041AAG Buenos Aires; tel. (11) 4328-3015; e-mail prensa@jus.gov.ar; internet www.jus.gov.ar.

Ministry of Labour, Employment and Social Security: Leandro N. Alem 650, C1001AAO Buenos Aires; tel. (11) 4311-2913; fax (11) 4312-7860; e-mail consultas@trabajo.gov.ar; internet www.trabajo.gov.ar.

Ministry of Science, Technology and Productive Innovation: Avda Córdoba 831, C1054AAH Buenos Aires; tel. (11) 4313-1477; fax (11) 4312-8364; e-mail webmaster@correo.secyt.gov.ar; internet www.secyt.gov.ar.

ARGENTINA

Ministry of Social Development: 9 de Julio 1925, 14°, C1073ABA Buenos Aires; tel. (11) 4379-3648; e-mail desarrollosocial@desarrollosocial.gov.ar; internet www.desarrollosocial.gov.ar.

President and Legislature

PRESIDENT

Election, 28 October 2007, provisional results

Candidates	Votes	% of votes cast
Cristina E. Fernández de Kirchner (Frente para la Victoria)	8,204,624	44.92
Elisa M. A. Carrió (Coalición Cívica)	4,191,361	22.95
Roberto Lavagna (Concertación Una Nación Avanzada*)	3,083,577	16.88
Alberto J. Rodríguez Saá (Frente Justicia, Unión y Libertad)	1,408,736	7.71
Fernando 'Pino' Solanas (Partido Socialista Autentico)	292,933	1.60
Jorge Omar Sobisch (Movimiento de las Provincias Unidas†)	284,161	1.56
Ricardo López Murphy (RECREAR)	264,746	1.45
Others	534,912	2.93
Total‡	18,265,050	100.00

*Electoral alliance founded by the Movimiento de Integración y Desarrollo.
†Electoral alliance comprising the Unión Popular, the Movimiento de Acción Vecinal and the Movimiento por la Dignidad y la Independencia.
‡In addition, there were 934,739 blank and 252,805 spoiled ballots.

CONGRESO

Cámara de Diputados
(Chamber of Deputies)

President: EDUARDO ALFREDO FELLNER.

The Cámara has 257 members, who hold office for a four-year term, with approximately one-half of the seats renewable every two years. The last election was held on 28 October 2007.

Distribution of Seats by Legislative Bloc, January 2008

	Seats
Frente para la Victoria—Partido Justicialista	120
Unión Cívica Radical (UCR)	24
Coalición Cívica	18
Propuesta Republicana (PRO)	10
Bloque de la Concertación*	10
Partido Socialista	10
ARI Autónomo 8+†	9
Peronista Federal‡	9
Frente Cívico por Santiago	6
Frente Justicia, Unión y Libertad	6
Encuentro Popular y Social	4
Movimiento Popular Neuquino	3
Unión Celeste y Blanca	2
Frente Movimiento Popular	2
Partido Nuevo Contra la Corrupción, por la Honestidad y la Transparencia	2
Partido Renovador de Salta	2
Frente Cívico y Social de Catamarca	2
Frente de Todos	2
Independent	1
Other parties	15
Total	257

*Supporters of President Cristina E. Fernández de Kirchner within the UCR.
†Members of the Afirmación para una República Igualitaria opposed to the party's inclusion within the Coalición Cívica.
‡Supporters of former President Eduardo Duhalde.

Senado
(Senate)

President: JULIO CÉSAR CLETO COBOS.

The Senate has 72 directly elected members, three from each province. One-third of these seats are renewable every two years. The last election was held on 28 October 2007.

Distribution of Seats by Legislative Bloc, January 2008

	Seats
Partido Justicialista—Frente para la Victoria	42
Unión Cívica Radical (UCR)	8
Afirmación para una República Igualitaria	2
Coalición Cívica	2
Concertación Plural	2
Frente Cívico por Santiago	2
Frente Cívico y Social de Catamarca	2
Fuerza Republicana	2
Justicialista San Luís	2
Others	8
Total	72

Provincial Administrators
(April 2008)

Mayor of the Federal District of Buenos Aires: MAURICIO MACRI (CPC).

Governort of the Province of Buenos Aires: DANIEL OSVALDO SCIOLI (PJ).

Governor of the Province of Catamarca: Dr EDUARDO BRIZUELA DEL MORAL (UCR).

Governor of the Province of Chaco: JORGE MILTON CAPITANICH (PJ).

Governor of the Province of Chubut: Dr MARIO DAS NEVES (PJ).

Governor of the Province of Córdoba: JUAN SCHIARETTI (PJ).

Governor of the Province of Corrientes: Dr ARTURO ALEJANDRO COLOMBI (UCR).

Governor of the Province of Entre Ríos: SERGIO DANIEL URRIBARRI (PJ).

Governor of the Province of Formosa: Dr GILDO INSFRÁN (PJ).

Governor of the Province of Jujuy: WALTER BASILO BARRIONUEVO (PJ).

Governor of the Province of La Pampa: OSCAR MARIO JORGE (PJ).

Governor of the Province of La Rioja: LUIS BEDER HERRERA-TERESITA LUNA (PJ).

Governor of the Province of Mendoza: CELSO ALEJANDRO JAQUE (PJ).

Governor of the Province of Misiones: MAURICE FABIÁN CLOSS (FR).

Governor of the Province of Neuquén: JORGE SAPAG (MPN).

Governor of the Province of Río Negro: Dr MIGUEL ANGEL SAIZ (UCR).

Governor of the Province of Salta: JUAN MANUEL URTUBEY (PJ).

Governor of the Province of San Juan: Dr JOSÉ LUIS GIOJA (PJ).

Governor of the Province of San Luis: Dr ALBERTO RODRÍGUEZ SAÁ (PJ).

Governor of the Province of Santa Cruz: DANIEL ROMAN PERALTA (PJ).

Governor of the Province of Santa Fe: HERMES BINNER (PS).

Governor of the Province of Santiago del Estero: Dr GERARDO ZAMORA (UCR).

Governor of the Province of Tierra del Fuego: MARÍA FABIANA RÍOS (ARI).

Governor of the Province of Tucumán: JOSÉ JORGE ALPEROVICH (PJ).

Election Commission

Cámara Nacional Electoral (CNE): Avda 25 de Mayo 245, C1002ABE Buenos Aires; tel. (11) 4331-8421; internet www.pjn.gov.ar; f. 1971; Pres. Dr RODOLFO EMILIO MUNNÉ.

Political Organizations

Afirmación para una República Igualitaria (ARI): Avda Callao 143, Buenos Aires; e-mail arinacional@ari.org.ar; internet www.ari.org.ar; f. 2001 as Alternativa por una República de Iguales; progressive party; contested the 2007 elections as part of the Coalición Cívica alliance; Leader ELISA M. A. CARRIÓ; Sec.-Gen. ELSA QUIROZ.

ARGENTINA

Alianza Nuevo Espacio Entrerriano: Gualeguaychú, Entre Ríos; provincial party; forms the Concertación Entrerriana bloc in the Congreso.

Autodeterminación y Libertad: Buenos Aires; tel. (11) 4773-2768; e-mail ayl@ayl.org.ar; internet www.ayl.org.ar; extreme left-wing; Leader LUIS ZAMORA.

Coalición Cívica: Buenos Aires; internet www.coalicioncivica.org.ar; f. 2007; electoral alliance mainly comprising the Afirmación por una República Igualitaria; Pres. ELISA M. A. CARRIÓ.

Compromiso para el Cambio (CPC): Edif. Anexo de la Cámara de Diputados, Riobamba 25, C1025ABA Buenos Aires; tel. (11) 6310-7710; e-mail ccambio@hcdn.gov.ar; internet www.cpcambio.org.ar; forms part of the Propuesta Republicana bloc in the Congreso; Leader MAURICIO MACRI.

Frente Cívico y Social: San Fernando del Valle de Catamarca; provincial alliance of UCR, dissident Peronists and others.

Frente Renovador para la Concordia (FR): Posadas, Misiones; provincial alliance.

Movimiento de Acción Vecinal (Frente País Solidario): Buenos Aires; contested the 2007 elections as part of the Movimiento de las Provincias Unidas electoral alliance.

Movimiento por la Dignidad y la Independencia (Modin): Yrigoyen 820, 2°G, Buenos Aires; e-mail modin@funescoop.com.ar; internet www.modin.org.ar; f. 1991; nationalist; contested the 2007 elections as part of the Movimiento de las Provincias Unidas electoral alliance; Pres. Lt-Col (retd) ENRIQUE CARLOS VENTURINO.

Movimiento de Integración y Desarrollo (MID): Ayacucho 49, C1025AAA Buenos Aires; tel. (11) 4954-0817; e-mail midinterior@mid.org.ar; internet www.mid.org.ar; f. 1963; supported candidacy of Roberto Lavagna in 2007 presidential election; Leader CARLOS ZAFFORE; 145,000 mems.

Movimiento Popular Neuquino (MPN): Neuquén; internet www.mpn.org.ar; f. 1961; provincial party; Pres. (vacant); Sec.-Gen. RICARDO HECTOR ROCA HALIL.

Movimiento al Socialismo (MAS): Chile 1362, C1098ABB Buenos Aires; tel. (11) 4381-2718; fax (11) 4381-2976; e-mail masarg@arnet.com.ar; internet www.mas.org.ar; Leaders RUBÉN VISCONTI, LUIS ZAMORA.

Partido Autonomista Nacional: Buenos Aires; Leader JOSÉ ANTONIO ROMERO FERIS.

Partido Comunista de Argentina: Entre Ríos 1039, C1080ABE Buenos Aires; tel. and fax (11) 4304-0066; e-mail central@pca.org.ar; internet www.pca.org.ar; f. 1918; Leader PATRICIO ECHEGARAY.

Partido Demócrata Cristiano (PDC): Combate de los Pozos 1055, C1222AAK Buenos Aires; tel. (11) 4305-1229; fax (11) 4306-8242; e-mail democracia_cristiana@fibertel.com.ar; internet www.democraciacristiana.com.ar; f. 1954; Leader ROBERTO PABLO MEYER.

Partido Demócrata Progresista (PDP): Chile 1934, C1227AAD Buenos Aires; e-mail progresista@tutopia.com; internet www.demoprogresista.org.ar; Pres. JOSÉ EDUARDO DE CARA.

Partido Federal: Buenos Aires; tel. (11) 4338-3071; e-mail mborrelli@federal.org.ar; internet www.federal.org.ar; f. 1973; Pres. Dr MARTÍN BORELLI.

Partido Intransigente: Riobamba 482, C1025ABJ Buenos Aires; tel. (11) 4954-2283; e-mail nacional@pi.org.ar; internet www.pi.org.ar; f. 1957; left-wing; Pres. Dr GUSTAVO CARDESA; Sec. CARMELO S. PRUDENTE; 90,000 mems.

Partido Justicialista (PJ): Domingo Matheu 130, C1082ABD Buenos Aires; tel. (11) 4954-2450; fax (11) 4954-2421; e-mail contacto@pj.org.ar; internet www.pj.org.ar; Peronist party; f. 1945; Supervisor Dr RAMÓN RUIZ; 3m. mems.

Frente Justicia, Unión y Libertad (Frejuli): Presidential Candidate ALBERTO J. RODRÍGUEZ SAÁ.

Frente para la Victoria: supported presidential candidacy of Cristina Fernández de Kirchner in 2007; Leader NÉSTOR CARLOS KIRCHNER.

Partido Nuevo Triunfo (PNT): Buenos Aires; e-mail pnt@libreopinion.com; internet pnt.libreopinion.com; f. 1990 as Partido de los Trabajadores; illegal extremist right-wing group; application for legal recognition ongoing; Pres. ALEJANDRO CARLOS BIONDINI; Vice-Pres. JORGE CASÓLIBA.

Partido Obrero: Ayacucho 448, C1026AAB Buenos Aires; tel. (11) 4953-3824; fax (11) 4954-5829; e-mail secprensa@po.org.ar; internet www.po.org.ar; f. 1982; Trotskyist; Pres. NÉSTOR PITROLA; Vice-Pres. GABRIELA ARROYO; 61,000 mems.

Partido Popular Cristiano (PPC): Entre Ríos; internet www.partidopopularcris.com.ar; f. 1954; Leader JOSÉ ANTONIO ALLENDE.

Partido Recrear para el Crecimiento (RECREAR): Avda de Mayo 605, 9°, Buenos Aires; tel. (11) 4342-2400; internet www.recrearargentina.org; forms part of the Propuesta Republicana bloc in the Congreso; Pres. RICARDO LÓPEZ MURPHY; Vice-Pres. JOSÉ MARÍA LLADÓS; Sec. RICARDO URQUIZA.

Partido Renovador de Salta: Rivadavia 453, C1002AAC Buenos Aires; f. 1982; Leader RICARDO GÓMEZ DIEZ.

Partido Socialista: Entre Ríos 488, 2°, Buenos Aires; tel. (11) 4383-2395; e-mail pscen@ar.inter.net; internet www.partidosocialista.com.ar; f. 2003 following merger of the Partido Socialista Democrático and the Partido Socialista Popular; Pres. RUBÉN HÉCTOR GIUSTINIANI; Sec.-Gen. OSCAR ROBERTO GONZÁLEZ.

Partido Socialista Auténtico: Sarandí 56, C1081ACB Buenos Aires; tel. and fax (11) 4952-3103; e-mail consultas@psa.org.ar; internet www.psa.org.ar; Sec.-Gen. MARIO MAZZITELLI; Pres. FERNANDO 'PINO' SOLANAS.

Partido Unidad Federalista (PaUFe): Buenos Aires; e-mail info@unidadfederalista.org.ar; internet www.paufe.org.ar; Leader LUIS ABELARDO PATTI.

Peronismo de Pie: Buenos Aires; f. 2006; dissident Peronist; mainly comprised of supporters of fmr Pres. Menem and fmr Pres. Duhalde; Pres. RAMÓN PUERTA.

Polo Social: Echeverría 441, 1878 Quilmes, C1437DLI Buenos Aires; tel. and fax (11) 4253-0971; e-mail polosocial@cscom.com.ar; f. 1999; mem. of the Mesa Coordinadora para un Nuevo Proyecto Nacional; Christian; Pres. LUIS FARINELLO.

Producción y Trabajo: San Juan; f. 2004; Leader ROBERTO GUSTAVO BASUALDO.

Propuesta Republicana: Alsina 1325, Buenos Aires; internet www.pro.com.ar; f. 2005; Leader MAURICIO MACRI.

Unión del Centro Democrático (UCeDé): Dorrego 2498, Casilla 1870, C1425GAO Buenos Aires; tel. (11) 4381-3763; e-mail wgutierrez@ucedeavellaneda.com.ar; f. 1980 as a coalition of eight minor political organizations; Pres. JORGE PEREYRA DE OLAZÁBAL; Vice-Pres. OSVALDO FANDIÑO.

Unión Cívica Radical (UCR): Alsina 1786, C1088AAR Buenos Aires; tel. and fax (11) 4375-2000; e-mail info@ucr.org.ar; internet www.ucr.org.ar; f. 1890; moderate; Pres. GERARDO RUBÉN MORALES; Gen. Sec MARIO JARAZ; 2.9m. mems.

Unión Popular: contested the 2007 elections as part of the Movimiento de las Provincias Unidas electoral alliance; Pres. JORGE OMAR SOBISCH.

Following the 2007 legislative elections the following political parties and groupings were also represented in the Congreso: Concertación Plural, Demócrata de Mendoza, Encuentro Popular y Social, Frente Cívico por Santiago, Frente Cívico y Social de Catamarca, Frente Movimiento Popular, Frente Producción y Trabajo, Frente de Todos, Fuerza Republicana, Justicialista San Luis, Partido Liberal de Corrientes, Partido Nuevo Contra la Corrupción, por la Honestidad y la Transparencia, Partido Renovador de Salta and Unión Celeste y Blanca.

OTHER ORGANIZATIONS

Asociación Madres de Plaza de Mayo: Hipólito Yrigoyen 1584, C1089AAD Buenos Aires; tel. (11) 4383-0377; fax (11) 4954-0381; e-mail madres@satlink.com; internet www.madres.org; f. 1979; formed by mothers of those who 'disappeared' during the years of military rule, it has since become a broad-based grouping with revolutionary socialist aims; Founder and Leader HEBE MARÍA PASTOR DE BONAFINI.

Corriente Clasista y Combativa (CCC): e-mail info@cccargentina.org.ar; internet www.cccargentina.org.ar; radical grouping; Leader CARLOS 'PERRO' SANTILLÁN.

Movimiento Barrios de Pie: e-mail correos@barriosdepie.org.ar; internet www.barriosdepie.org.ar; f. 2001; moderate grouping; Leader JORGE CEBALLOS.

Movimiento Libres del Sur: Humberto I° 542, Buenos Aires; tel. (11) 4307-3724; e-mail contacto@libresdelsur.org.ar; internet libresdelsur.org.ar; f. 2006; alliance of pro-President Kirchner *piquetero* groups; Leader HUMBERTO TUMINI.

Numerous other *piquetero* groupings also exist.

Diplomatic Representation

EMBASSIES IN ARGENTINA

Albania: Juez Tedín 3036, 4°, C1425CWH Buenos Aires; tel. (11) 4809-3574; fax (11) 4815-2512; e-mail ambasada.bue@netsat.com.ar; Ambassador REZAR BREGU.

Algeria: Montevideo 1889, C1021AAE Buenos Aires; tel. (11) 4815-1271; fax (11) 4815-8837; e-mail argeliae@interserver.com.ar; Ambassador AHCÈNE BOUKHELFA.

ARGENTINA

Angola: La Pampa 3452–56, C1430BXD Buenos Aires; tel. (11) 4554-8383; fax (11) 4554-8998; Ambassador Fernando Dito.

Armenia: José Andrés Pacheco de Melo 1922, C1126AAD Buenos Aires; tel. (11) 4812-2803; fax (11) 4816-8710; e-mail armenia@teletel.com.ar; Ambassador Vladimir Karmirshalyan.

Australia: Villanueva 1400, C1426BMJ Buenos Aires; tel. (11) 4779-3500; fax (11) 4779-3581; e-mail info.ba.general@dfat.gov.au; internet www.argentina.embassy.gov.au; Ambassador Peter Hussin.

Austria: French 3671, C1425AXC Buenos Aires; tel. (11) 4807-9185; fax (11) 4805-4016; e-mail buenos-aires-ob@bmaa.gv.at; internet www.austria.org.ar; Ambassador Dr Gudrun Graf.

Belarus: Cazadores 2166, C1428AVH Buenos Aires; tel. (11) 4788-9394; fax (11) 4788-2322; e-mail argentina@belembassy.org; Chargé d'affaires a.i. Oleg Malaev.

Belgium: Defensa 113, 8°, C1065AAA Buenos Aires; tel. (11) 4331-0066; fax (11) 4311-0814; e-mail buenosaires@diplobel.org; internet www.diplobel.org/argentina; Ambassador Koenraad Rouvroy.

Bolivia: Corrientes 545, 2°, C1043AAF Buenos Aires; tel. (11) 4394-6042; fax (11) 5217-1070; internet www.embajadadebolivia.com.ar; Chargé d'affaires a.i. Sixto Julio Valdez Cueto.

Bosnia and Herzegovina: 14 de Julio 1656, C1430END Buenos Aires; tel. and fax (11) 4554-9257; e-mail embajadabh@embajadabh.org.ar; internet www.embajadabh.org.ar; Chargé d'affaires a.i. Mario Đuragić.

Brazil: Cerrito 1350, C1010ABB Buenos Aires; tel. (11) 4515-2400; fax (11) 4515-2401; e-mail info@embrasil.org.ar; internet www.brasil.org.ar; Ambassador Mauro Vieira.

Bulgaria: Mariscal A. J. de Sucre 1568, C1428DUT Buenos Aires; tel. (11) 4781-8644; fax (11) 4781-1214; e-mail info@embular.int.ar; internet www.embular.int.ar; Ambassador Stephan Apostolov.

Canada: Tagle 2828, C1425EEH Buenos Aires; Casilla 1598, Correo Central 1000, Buenos Aires; tel. (11) 4808-1000; fax (11) 4808-1111; e-mail bairs-webmail@dfait-maeci.gc.ca; internet www.buenosaires.gc.ca; Ambassador Timothy Joseph Martin.

Chile: Tagle 2762, C1425EEF Buenos Aires; tel. (11) 4808-8600; fax (11) 4804-5927; e-mail data@embajadadechile.com.ar; internet www.embajadadechile.com.ar/home.asp; Ambassador Luis Osvaldo Maira Aguirre.

China, People's Republic: Crisólogo Larralde 5349, C1431APM Buenos Aires; tel. (11) 4543-8862; fax (11) 4545-1141; e-mail embchinaargentina@hotmail.com; internet ar.chineseembassy.org/esp; Ambassador Gang Zeng.

Colombia: Carlos Pellegrini 1363, 3°, C1011AAA Buenos Aires; tel. (11) 4325-0258; fax (11) 4322-9370; e-mail rodrigoholguin@embajadacolombia.int.ar; internet www.embajadacolombia.int.ar; Ambassador Jaime Bermúdez Merizalde.

Congo, Democratic Republic: Callao 322, 2°, C1022AAQ Buenos Aires; tel. (11) 4552-3942; e-mail rdcbuenos@hotmail.com; Chargé d'affaires a.i. Yemba Lohaka.

Costa Rica: Avda Callao 1769, 7°B, C1024AAD Buenos Aires; tel. (11) 4815-0072; fax (11) 4814-1660; e-mail embarica@fibertel.com.ar; Ambassador Maritza Castro Salazar.

Croatia: Gorostiaga 2104, C1426CTN Buenos Aires; tel. (11) 4777-6409; fax (11) 4777-9159; e-mail embajadada@embajadadacroacia.org.ar; Ambassador Mira Martinec.

Cuba: Virrey del Pino 1810, Belgrano, C1426DXH Buenos Aires; tel. (11) 4782-9049; fax (11) 4786-7713; e-mail argoficemb@ecuargentina.minrex.gov.cu; internet www.embacuba.com.ar; Ambassador Aramis Fuente Hernández.

Czech Republic: Junín 1461, C1113AAM Buenos Aires; tel. (11) 4807-3107; fax (11) 4807-3109; e-mail buenosaires@embassy.mzv.cz; internet www.mfa.cz/buenosaires; Ambassador Blanka Kovánksová.

Denmark: Avda Leandro N. Alem 1074, 9°, 1001 Buenos Aires; tel. (11) 4312-6901; fax (11) 4312-7857; e-mail bueamb@um.dk; internet www.buenosaires.um.dk; Ambassador Henrik Bramsen Hahn.

Dominican Republic: Santa Fe 830, 7°, C1059ABP Buenos Aires; tel. (11) 4312-9378; fax (11) 4894-2078; e-mail consuldo@hotmail.com; Ambassador Rafael Calventi.

Ecuador: Quintana 585, 9° y 10°, C1129ABB Buenos Aires; tel. (11) 4804-0073; fax (11) 4804-0074; e-mail embecuador@embecuador.ar; Ambassador Francisco Ernesto Proaño Arandi.

Egypt: Virrey del Pino 3140, C1426EHF Buenos Aires; tel. (11) 4553-3311; fax (11) 4553-0067; e-mail embegypt@fibertel.com.ar; Ambassador Youssef Hassan Shawki.

El Salvador: Suipacha 1380, 2°, C1011ACD Buenos Aires; tel. (11) 43251-0849; fax (11) 4328-7428; e-mail elsalvador@fibertel.com.ar; internet wwww.embajadaelsalvador.com.ar; Ambassador Guillermo Rubio Funes.

Directory

Finland: Santa Fe 846, 5°, C1059ABP Buenos Aires; tel. (11) 4312-0600; fax (11) 4312-0670; e-mail sanomat.bue@formin.fi; internet www.finlandia.org.ar; Ambassador Ritva Anneli Jolkkonen.

France: Cerrito 1399, C1010ABA Buenos Aires; tel. (11) 4515-2930; fax (11) 4515-0120; e-mail ambafr@abaconet.com.ar; internet www.embafrancia-argentina.org; Ambassador Frédéric Gabriel Charles Baleine du Laurens.

Germany: Villanueva 1055, C1426BMC Buenos Aires; tel. (11) 4778-2500; fax (11) 4778-2550; e-mail administracion@embajada-alemana.org.ar; internet www.embajada-alemana.org.ar; Ambassador Dr Rolf Schumacher.

Greece: Arenales 1658, C1061AAT Buenos Aires; tel. (11) 4811-4811; fax (11) 4816-2600; e-mail secretariagr@fibertel.com.ar; Ambassador Michael B. Christides.

Guatemala: Avda Santa Fe 830, 5°, C1059ABP Buenos Aires; tel. (11) 4313-9160; fax (11) 4313-9181; e-mail embagua@peoples.com.ar; Ambassador Luis Fernando González Davison.

Haiti: Avda Figueroa Alcorta 3297, C1425CKL Buenos Aires; tel. (11) 4802-0211; fax (11) 4802-3984; e-mail embajadahaiti@fibertel.com.ar; Ambassador Jean Marie Michel Raymond Mathieu.

Holy See: Alvear 1605, C1014AAD Buenos Aires; tel. (11) 4813-9697; fax (11) 4815-4097; e-mail nunciaturaapostolica@speedy.com.ar; Apostolic Nuncio Most Rev. Adriano Bernardini (Titular Archbishop of Faleri).

Honduras: Avda Callao 1564, 2A, C1024AAO Buenos Aires; tel. (11) 4803-0077; fax (11) 4807-5710; e-mail embajadadehonduras@fibertel.com.ar; Ambassador Carmen Eleonora Ortez Williams.

Hungary: Plaza 1726, C1430DGF Buenos Aires; tel. (11) 4553-3536; e-mail hungria@escape.com.ar; Ambassador Mátyás Józsa.

India: Avda Eduardo Madero 942, C1106ACW Buenos Aires; tel. (11) 4393-4001; fax (11) 4393-4063; e-mail indemb@indembarg.org.ar; internet www.indembarg.org.ar; Ambassador Rengaraj Viswanathan.

Indonesia: Mariscal Ramón Castilla 2901, C1425DZE Buenos Aires; tel. (11) 4807-2211; fax (11) 4802-4448; e-mail emindo@tournet.com.ar; internet www.indonesianembassy.org.ar; Ambassador Sunten Zephyrimus Manurung.

Iran: Avda Figueroa Alcorta 3229, CP 396, C1425CKL Buenos Aires; tel. (11) 4802-1470; fax (11) 4805-4409; e-mail embajadairan@fibertel.com.ar; Chargé d'affaires a.i. Mohsen Baharvand.

Ireland: Avda del Libertador 1068, 6°, C1112ABN Buenos Aires; tel. (11) 5787-0801; fax (11) 5787-0802; e-mail info@irlanda.org.ar; internet www.irlanda.org.ar; Ambassador Philomena Murnaghan.

Israel: Avda de Mayo 701, 10°, C1084AAC Buenos Aires; tel. (11) 4338-2500; fax (11) 4338-2624; e-mail info@buenosaires.mfa.gov.il; internet buenosaires.mfa.gov.il; Ambassador Rafael Eldad.

Italy: Billinghurst 2577, C1425DTY Buenos Aires; tel. (11) 4011-2100; fax (11) 4804-4914; e-mail ambasciata.buenosaires@esteri.it; internet www.ambbuenosaires.esteri.it; Ambassador Stefano Ronca.

Japan: Bouchard 547, 17°, C1106ABG Buenos Aires; tel. (11) 4318-8200; fax (11) 4318-8210; e-mail taishikan@japan.org.ar; internet www.ar.emb-japan.go.jp; Ambassador Shinya Nagai.

Korea, Republic: Avda del Libertador 2395, C1425AAJ Buenos Aires; tel. (11) 4802-9665; fax (11) 4803-6993; e-mail embcorea@cscom.com.ar; internet www.embcorea.org.ar; Ambassador Eui-Seung Hwang.

Kuwait: Uruguay 739, C1015ABO Buenos Aires; tel. (11) 4374-7202; fax (11) 4374-8718; e-mail info@kuwait.com.ar; internet www.embajadadekuwait.com.ar; Ambassador Saud Abd al-Aziz ar-Roumi.

Lebanon: Avda del Libertador 2354, C1425AAW Buenos Aires; tel. (11) 4802-0466; fax (11) 4802-2909; e-mail embajada@ellibano.com.ar; internet www.ellibano.com.ar; Ambassador Hicham Salim Hamdan.

Libya: 3 de Febrero 1358/62, C1426BJN Buenos Aires; tel. (11) 4788-3760; fax (11) 4784-9895; e-mail oficinapopularlibia@hotmail.com; Ambassador Dr Ali Y. Giuma ben Giuma.

Lithuania: Mendoza 1018, C1428DJD, Buenos Aires; tel. (11) 4788-2153; fax (11) 4785-7915; e-mail embajada@lituania.org.ar; internet ar.mfa.lt; Chargé d'affaires a.i. Laura Tupe.

Malaysia: Nicolás Villanueva 1040–48, C1426BMD Buenos Aires; tel. (11) 4776-0504; fax (11) 4776-0604; e-mail mwbaires@fibertel.com.ar; Ambassador Rohana Ramli.

Mexico: Arcos 1650, C1426BGL Buenos Aires; tel. (11) 4789-8800; fax (11) 4789-8836; e-mail embamexarg@interlink.com.ar; internet www.embamex.int.ar; Ambassador María Cristina de la Garza Sandoval.

Morocco: Castex 3461, C1425CDG Buenos Aires; tel. (11) 4801-8154; fax (11) 4802-0136; e-mail sifamarruecos@fibertel.com.ar; Ambassador Larbi Reffouh.

ARGENTINA

Netherlands: Edif. Porteño II, Olga Cossenttini 831, 3°, C1107BVA Buenos Aires; tel. (11) 4338-0050; fax (11) 4338-0060; e-mail bue@minbuza.nl; internet www.embajadaholanda.int.ar; Ambassador HENDRIK JACOB WILLEM SOETERS.

New Zealand: Carlos Pellegrini 1427, 5°, C1011AAC Buenos Aires; tel. (11) 4328-0747; fax (11) 4328-0757; e-mail kiwiargentina@datamarkets.com.ar; internet www.nzembassy.com/buenosaires; Ambassador ANNA LOUISE DUNCAN.

Nicaragua: Avda Santa Fe 1845, 7°B, C1123AAA Buenos Aires; tel. and fax (11) 4811-0973; e-mail embanic@fibertel.com.ar; Ambassador ZORAYA FABIOLA MASIS.

Nigeria: Juez Estrada 2746, Palermo, C1425CPD Buenos Aires; tel. (11) 4808-9245; fax (11) 4807-6423; e-mail info@nigerianembassy.org; internet nigerianembassy-argentina.org; Chargé d'affaires a.i. INALEGWU VICTOR OGAH.

Norway: Carlos Pelegrini 1427, 2°, C1011AAC Buenos Aires; tel. (11) 4328-8717; fax (11) 4328-9048; e-mail emb.buenosaires@mfa.no; internet www.noruega.org.ar; Ambassador NILS HAUGSTVEIT.

Pakistan: Gorostiaga 2176, C1426CTN Buenos Aires; tel. (11) 4775-1294; fax (11) 4776-1186; e-mail parepbaires@sinectis.com.ar; Ambassador ISHTIAQ HUSSAIN ANDRABI.

Panama: Santa Fe 1461, 1°, C1060ABA Buenos Aires; tel. (11) 4811-1254; fax (11) 4814-0450; e-mail epar@fibertel.com.ar; internet www.embajadadepanama.com.ar; Ambassador OLGA IVANIA GOLCHER DE MANNING.

Paraguay: Las Heras 2545, C1425ASC Buenos Aires; tel. (11) 4802-3826; fax (11) 4804-0437; Chargé d'affaires a.i. MYRIAM CELIA TORRES DE SEGOVIA.

Peru: Avda del Libertador 1720, C1425AAQ Buenos Aires; tel. (11) 4802-2000; fax (11) 4802-5887; e-mail embperu@arnet.com.ar; Ambassador JUDITH DE LA MATA FERNÁNDEZ DE PUENTE.

Philippines: Mariscal Ramón Castilla 3075/3085, C1425DZG Buenos Aires; tel. (11) 4807-3334; fax (11) 4804-1595; e-mail pheba@fibertel.com.ar; internet www.buenosairespe.com.ar; Chargé d'affaires a.i. EDGARDO R. MANUEL.

Poland: Marqués de Aguado 2870, C1425CEB Buenos Aires; tel. (11) 4802-9681; fax (11) 4802-9683; e-mail polemb@datamarkets.com.ar; Ambassador ZDZISŁAW JAN RYN.

Portugal: Maipú 942, 17°, C1006ACN Buenos Aires; tel. (11) 4312-0187; fax (11) 4311-2586; e-mail mebpor@embajadaportugal.org.ar; Ambassador JOAQUIM JOSÉ LEMOS FERREIRA MARQUES.

Romania: Arroyo 962–970, C1007AAD Buenos Aires; tel. and fax (11) 4326-5888; e-mail embarombue@rumania.org.ar; internet www.rumania.org.ar; Ambassador ION VILCU.

Russia: Rodríguez Peña 1741, C1021ABK Buenos Aires; tel. (11) 4813-1552; fax (11) 4815-6293; e-mail embrusia@fibertel.com.ar; internet www.argentina.mid.ru; Ambassador YURI P. KORCHAGIN.

San Marino: Avda Presidente Manuel Quintana 175, 1°A, C1014ACB Buenos Aires; tel. (11) 4815-3787; fax (11) 4815-9070; e-mail embajada@consulatosanmarino.org.ar; Ambassador STEFANO PISA DI MONTEROSA.

Saudi Arabia: Marqués de Aguado 2881, C1425CEA Buenos Aires; tel. (11) 4802-3375; fax (11) 4806-1581; e-mail embasaudita@fibertel.com.ar; internet www.embajadasaudi.org; Ambassador ESAM ABID ATH-THAGAFI.

Serbia: Marcelo T. de Alvear 1705, C1060AAG Buenos Aires; tel. (11) 4812-9133; fax (11) 4812-1070; e-mail yuembaires@ciudad.com.ar; Chargé d'affaires a.i. MARTIN SIMOVIĆ.

Slovakia: Figueroa Alcorta 3240, C1425CKY Buenos Aires; tel. (11) 4801-3917; fax (11) 4801-4654; e-mail embsl@fibertel.com.ar; Ambassador VLADIMIR GRACZ.

Slovenia: Santa Fe 846, 6°, C1059ABP Buenos Aires; tel. (11) 4894-0621; fax (11) 4312-8410; e-mail vba@mzz-dkp.gov.si; Ambassador AVGUŠTIN VIVOD.

South Africa: Marcelo T. de Alvear 590, 8°, C1058AAF Buenos Aires; tel. (11) 4317-2900; fax (11) 4317-2951; e-mail embasa@ciudad.com.ar; internet www.sudafrica.org.ar; Ambassador PETER GOOSEN.

Spain: Mariscal Ramón Castilla 2720, C1425DZB Buenos Aires; tel. (11) 4802-6031; fax (11) 4802-0719; Ambassador RAFAEL ESTRELLA PEDROLA.

Sweden: Tacuari 147, 6°, C1071AAC Buenos Aires; tel. (11) 4329-0800; fax (11) 4342-1697; e-mail ambassaden.buenos-aires@foreign.ministery.ce; internet www.swedenabroad.com/buenosaires; Ambassador ARNE LENNART RODIN.

Switzerland: Avda Santa Fe 846, 10°, C1059ABP Buenos Aires; tel. (11) 4311-6491; fax (11) 4313-2998; e-mail vertretung@bue.rep.admin.ch; internet www.eda.admin.ch/buenosaires_emb/s/home.html; Chargé d'affaires a.i. ERIC ALAIN MAYORAZ.

Syria: Callao 956, C1023AAP Buenos Aires; tel. (11) 4813-2113; fax (11) 4814-3211; Ambassador RIYAD AS-SINEH.

Thailand: Vuelta de Obligado 1947, 12°, C1428ADC Buenos Aires; tel. (11) 4774-4415; fax (11) 4773-2447; e-mail thaiembargen@fibertel.com.ar; Ambassador ANUCHA OSATHANOND.

Tunisia: Ciudad de la Paz 3086, C1429ACD Buenos Aires; tel. (11) 4544-2618; fax (11) 4545-6369; e-mail atbuenosaires@infovia.com.ar; Ambassador FETHI MANAI.

Turkey: 11 de Septiembre 1382, C1426BKN Buenos Aires; tel. (11) 4788-3239; fax (11) 4784-9179; e-mail turquia@fibertel.com.ar; Ambassador HAYRI HAYRET YALAV.

Ukraine: Conde 1763, C1426AZI Buenos Aires; tel. (11) 4552-0657; fax (11) 4552-6771; e-mail embucra@embucra.com.ar; internet www.embucra.com.ar; Ambassador OLEKSANDR NYKONENKO.

United Kingdom: Dr Luis Agote 2412, C1425EOF Buenos Aires; tel. (11) 4808-2200; fax (11) 4808-2274; e-mail askinformation.baires@fco.gov.uk; internet www.britain.org.ar; Ambassador Dr JOHN HUGHES.

USA: Avda Colombia 4300, C1425GMN Buenos Aires; tel. (11) 5777-4533; fax (11) 5777-4212; internet buenosaires.usembassy.gov; Ambassador EARL ANTHONY WAYNE.

Uruguay: Las Heras 1907, C1127AAB Buenos Aires; tel. (11) 4803-6030; fax (11) 4807-3050; e-mail embarou@impsat1.com.ar; internet www.embajadadeluruguay.com.ar; Ambassador FRANCISCO BUSTILLO BONASSO.

Venezuela: Virrey Loreto 2035, C1426DXK Buenos Aires; tel. (11) 4788-4944; fax (11) 4784-4311; e-mail contacto@embavenarg.org; Ambassador Gen. (retd) ARÉVALO ENRIQUE MÉNDEZ ROMERO.

Viet Nam: 11 de Septiembre 1442, C1426BKP Buenos Aires; tel. (11) 4783-1802; fax (11) 4782-0078; e-mail sqvnartn@fibertel.com.ar; Ambassador VAN LUNG THAI.

Judicial System

SUPREME COURT

Corte Suprema

Talcahuano 550, 4°, C1013AAL Buenos Aires; tel. (11) 4370-4600; fax (11) 4340-2270; e-mail jurisprudencia@cjsn.gov.ar; internet www.csjn.gov.ar.

The nine members of the Supreme Court are appointed by the President, with the agreement of at least two-thirds of the Senate. Members are dismissed by impeachment. In December 2006 the Congreso approved legislation reducing the number of judges to five.

President: RICARDO LUIS LORENZETTI.

Vice-President: ELENA I. HIGHTON DE NOLASCO.

Justices: EUGENIO RAÚL ZAFFARONI, ENRIQUE SANTIAGO PETRACCHI, JUAN CARLOS MAQUEDA, CARLOS S. FAYT, CARMEN MARÍA ARGIBAY.

OTHER COURTS

Judges of the lower, national or further lower courts are appointed by the President, with the agreement of the Senate, and are dismissed by impeachment. From 1999, however, judges were to retire on reaching 75 years of age.

The Federal Court of Appeal in Buenos Aires has three courts: civil and commercial, criminal, and administrative. There are six other courts of appeal in Buenos Aires: civil, commercial, criminal, peace, labour, and penal-economic. There are also federal appeal courts in: La Plata, Bahía Blanca, Paraná, Rosario, Córdoba, Mendoza, Tucumán and Resistencia. In August 1994, following constitutional amendments, the Office of the Attorney-General was established as an independent entity and a Council of Magistrates was envisaged. In December 1997 the Senate adopted legislation to create the Council.

The provincial courts each have their own Supreme Court and a system of subsidiary courts. They deal with cases originating within and confined to the provinces.

Attorney-General: Dr ESTEBAN RIGHI.

Religion

CHRISTIANITY

Federación Argentina de Iglesias Evangélicas (Argentine Federation of Evangelical Churches): José María Moreno 873, C1424AAI Buenos Aires; tel. and fax (11) 4922-5356; e-mail presidencia@faie.org.ar; internet www.faie.org.ar; f. 1938; 29 mem. churches; Pres. NICOLÁS ROSENTHAL; Sec. Rev. ADOLFO PEDROZA.

The Roman Catholic Church

At 31 December 2005 there were an estimated 36,557,365 Roman Catholics in Argentina.

ARGENTINA

Directory

Argentina comprises 14 archdioceses, 50 dioceses (including one each for Uniate Catholics of the Ukrainian rite, of the Maronite rite and of the Armenian rite), three territorial prelatures and an apostolic exarchate for Catholics of the Melkite rite. The Bishop of San Gregorio de Narek en Buenos Aires is also the Apostolic Exarch of Latin America and Mexico for Catholics of the Armenian rite, and the Archbishop of Buenos Aires is also the Ordinary for Catholics of other Oriental rites.

Bishops' Conference: Suipacha 1034, C1008AAV Buenos Aires; tel. (11) 4328-0993; fax (11) 4328-9570; e-mail seccea@cea.org.ar; internet www.cea.org.ar; f. 1959; Pres. Cardinal JORGE MARIO BERGOGLIO (Archbishop of Buenos Aires).

Armenian Rite

Bishop of San Gregorio de Narek en Buenos Aires: VARTAN WALDIR BOGHOSSIAN, Charcas 3529, C1425BMU Buenos Aires; tel. (11) 4824-1613; fax (11) 4827-1975; e-mail exarmal@pcn.net.

Latin Rite

Archbishop of Bahía Blanca: GUILLERMO JOSÉ GARLATTI, Avda Colón 164, B8000FTO Bahía Blanca; tel. (291) 455-0707; fax (291) 452-2070; e-mail arzobis@arzobispadobahia.org.ar.

Archbishop of Buenos Aires: Cardinal JORGE MARIO BERGOGLIO, Rivadavia 415, C1002AAC Buenos Aires; tel. (11) 4343-0812; fax (11) 4334-8373; e-mail arzobispado@arzbaires.org.ar; internet www.arzbaires.org.ar.

Archbishop of Córdoba: CARLOS JOSÉ ÑÁÑEZ, Hipólito Irigoyen 98, X5000JHN Córdoba; tel. and fax (351) 422-1015; e-mail info@arzobispado.org.ar; internet www.arzobispadocba.org.ar.

Archbishop of Corrientes: ANDRÉS STANOVNIK, 9 de Julio 1543, W3400AZA Corrientes; tel. and fax (3783) 422436; e-mail info@corrientes.arzobispado.net; internet corrientes.arzobispado.net.

Archbishop of La Plata: HÉCTOR RUBÉN AGUER, Calle 14 Centro 1009, B1900DVQ La Plata; tel. (221) 425-1656; e-mail arzobispadodelaplata@speedy.com.ar; internet www.arzolap.org.ar.

Archbishop of Mendoza: JOSÉ MARÍA ARANCIBIA, Catamarca 98, M5500CKB Mendoza; tel. (261) 423-3862; fax (261) 429-5415; e-mail arzobispadomza@supernet.com.ar.

Archbishop of Mercedes-Luján: AGUSTÍN ROBERTO RADRIZZANI, Calle 22 745, B6600HDU Mercedes; tel. (2324) 432-412; fax (2324) 432-104; e-mail arzomerce@yahoo.com.ar; internet www.basilicadelujan.org.

Archbishop of Paraná: MARIO LUIS BAUTISTA MAULIÓN, Monte Caseros 77, E3100ACA Paraná; tel. (343) 431-1440; fax (343) 423-0372; e-mail arzparan@arzparan.org.ar.

Archbishop of Resistencia: FABRICIANO SIGAMPA, Bartolomé Mitre 363, Casilla 35, H3500BLG Resistencia; tel. and fax (3722) 441908; e-mail arzobrcia@arnet.com.ar.

Archbishop of Rosario: JOSÉ LUIS MOLLAGHAN, Córdoba 1677, S2000AWY Rosario; tel. (341) 425-1298; fax (341) 425-1207; e-mail arzobros@uolsinectis.com.ar; internet www.delrosario.org.ar.

Archbishop of Salta: MARIO ANTONIO CARGNELLO, España 596, A4400ANL Salta; tel. (387) 421-4306; fax (387) 421-3101; e-mail arzobispadosalta@arnet.com.ar; internet www.arquidiocesissalta.org.ar.

Archbishop of San Juan de Cuyo: ALFONSO ROGELIO DELGADO EVERS, Bartolomé Mitre 250 Oeste, J5402CXF San Juan; tel. (264) 422-2578; fax (264) 427-3530; e-mail arzobispadosanjuan@infovia.com.ar.

Archbishop of Santa Fe de la Vera Cruz: JOSÉ MARÍA ARANCEDO, Avda Brig.-Gen. E. López 2720, S3000DCJ Santa Fe; tel. (342) 459-1780; fax (342) 459-4491; e-mail curia@arquisantafe.org.ar; internet www.arquisantafe.org.ar.

Archbishop of Tucumán: LUIS HÉCTOR VILLALBA, Avda Sarmiento 895, T4000GTI San Miguel de Tucumán; tel. (381) 431-0617; e-mail arztuc@arnet.com.ar; internet www.arztucuman.org.ar.

Maronite Rite

Bishop of San Charbel en Buenos Aires: CHARBEL GEORGES MERHI, Eparquía Maronita, Paraguay 834, C1057AAL Buenos Aires; tel. (11) 4311-7299; fax (11) 4312-8348; e-mail mcharbel@hotmail.com.

Melkite Rite

Apostolic Exarch: ABDO ARBACH, Exarcado Apostólico Greco-Melquita, Corrientes 276, X5000ANF Córdoba; tel. (351) 4210625.

Ukrainian Rite

Bishop of Santa María del Patrocinio en Buenos Aires: Rt Rev. MIGUEL MYKYCEJ, Ramón L. Falcón 3950, Casilla 28, C1407GSN Buenos Aires; tel. (11) 4671-4192; fax (11) 4671-7265; e-mail pokrov@ciudad.com.ar.

The Anglican Communion

The Iglesia Anglicana del Cono Sur de América (Anglican Church of the Southern Cone of America) was formally inaugurated in Buenos Aires in April 1983. The Church comprises seven dioceses: Argentina, Northern Argentina, Chile, Paraguay, Peru, Bolivia and Uruguay. The Primate is the Bishop of Argentina.

Bishop of Argentina: Rt Rev. GREGORY J. VENABLES, 25 de Mayo 282, C1002ABF Buenos Aires; Casilla 4293, Correo Central 1000, Buenos Aires; tel. (11) 4342-4618; fax (11) 4331-0234; e-mail diocesisanglibue@fibertel.com.ar; internet www.anglicanaargentina.org.ar.

Bishop of Northern Argentina: (vacant), Casilla 187, A4400ANL Salta; tel. (387) 431-1718; fax (387) 431-2622; e-mail sinclair@salnet.com.ar; jurisdiction extends to Jujuy, Salta, Tucumán, Catamarca, Santiago del Estero, Formosa and Chaco.

Protestant Churches

Convención Evangélica Bautista Argentina (Baptist Evangelical Convention): Virrey Liniers 42, C1174ACB Buenos Aires; tel. and fax (11) 4864-2711; e-mail ceba@sion.com; internet www.ceba.sion.com; f. 1909; Pres. EDUARDO LORENZO.

Iglesia Evangélica Congregacionalista (Evangelical Congregational Church): Perón 525, E3100BBK Paraná; tel. (43) 21-6172; f. 1924; 100 congregations, 8,000 mems, 24,000 adherents; Supt Rev. REYNOLDO HORSTT.

Iglesia Evangélica Luterana Argentina (Evangelical Lutheran Church of Argentina): Ing. Silveyra 1639-41, B1607BQM Villa Adelina, Buenos Aires; tel. and fax (11) 4766-7948; f. 1905; 30,000 mems; Pres. WALDOMIRO MAILI.

Iglesia Evangélica Luterana Unida (United Evangelical Lutheran Church): Marcos Sastre 2891, C1417FYE Buenos Aires; tel. and fax (11) 4501-3925; fax 4504-7358; e-mail ielu@ielu.org; mems; Pres. Rev. ALAN ELDRID.

Iglesia Evangélica del Río de la Plata (Evangelical Church of the River Plate): Mariscal Sucre 2855, C1428DVY Buenos Aires; tel. (11) 4787-0436; fax (11) 4787-0335; e-mail secretario@ierp.org.ar; internet www.iglesiaevangelica.org; f. 1899; 25,200 mems; Pres. FEDERICO HUGO SCHÄFER; Gen. Sec. JUAN ABELARDO SCHVIUDT.

Iglesia Evangélica Metodista Argentina (Methodist Church of Argentina): Rivadavia 4044, 3°, C1205AAN Buenos Aires; tel. (11) 4982-3712; fax (11) 4981-0885; e-mail secretariaadministracion@iglesiametodista.org.ar; internet www.iglesiametodista.org.ar; f. 1836; Bishop NELLIE RITCHIE.

JUDAISM

There are about 230,000 Jews in Argentina, mostly in Buenos Aires.

Delegación de Asociaciones Israelitas Argentinas (DAIA) (Delegation of Argentine Jewish Associations): Pasteur 633, 7°, C1028AAM Buenos Aires; tel. and fax (11) 4378-3200; e-mail daia@daia.org.ar; internet www.daia.org.ar; f. 1935; Pres. ALDO DONZIS; Sec.-Gen. Dr EDGARDO WAISSBEIN.

The Press

PRINCIPAL DAILIES

Buenos Aires

Ambito Financiero: Paseo Colón 1196, C1063ACY Buenos Aires; tel. (11) 4349-1500; fax (11) 4349-1505; e-mail mensajeseditor@ambito.com.ar; internet www.ambitoweb.com.ar; f. 1976; morning (Mon.–Fri.); business; Dir JULIO A. RAMOS; circ. 115,000.

Buenos Aires Herald: Azopardo 455, C1107ADE Buenos Aires; tel. (11) 4342-8476; fax (11) 4331-3370; e-mail info@buenosairesherald.com; internet www.buenosairesherald.com; f. 1876; English; morning; independent; Editor-in-Chief ANDREW GRAHAM-YOOLL; circ. 20,000.

Boletín Oficial de la República Argentina: Suipacha 767, C1008AAO Buenos Aires; tel. and fax (11) 4322-3982; internet www.boletinoficial.gov.ar; f. 1893; morning (Mon.–Fri.); official records publication; Dir JORGE EDUARDO FEIJOÓ; circ. 15,000.

Clarín: Piedras 1743, C1140ABK Buenos Aires; tel. (11) 4309-7500; fax (11) 4309-7559; e-mail cartas@claringlobal.com.ar; internet www.clarin.com; f. 1945; morning; independent; Dir ERNESTINA L. HERRERA DE NOBLE; circ. 616,000 (daily), 1.0m. (Sunday).

Crónica: Juan de Garay 40, C1063ABN Buenos Aires; tel. (11) 4361-1001; fax (11) 4361-4237; internet www.cronica.com.ar; f. 1963; morning and evening; Dirs MARIO ALBERTO FERNÁNDEZ (morning),

ARGENTINA

Directory

RICARDO GANGEME (evening); circ. 330,000 (morning), 190,000 (evening), 450,000 (Sunday).

El Cronista: Honduras 5663, C1414BNE Buenos Aires; tel. (11) 4121-9300; fax (11) 4778-6727; e-mail cronista@sadei.org.ar; internet www.cronista.com; f. 1908; morning; Dir NÉSTOR SCIBONA; circ. 65,000.

Diario El Popular: Vicente López 2626, Olivarría, 7400 Buenos Aires; tel. and fax (22) 8442-0502; e-mail diario@elpopular.com.ar; internet www.diarioelpopular.com.ar; f. 1974; morning; Dir ALBERTO ALBERTENGO; circ. 145,000.

La Gaceta: Beguiristain 182, 1870 Avellaneda, Buenos Aires; tel. (381) 4842200; fax (381) 4842311; Dir RICARDO WEST OCAMPO; circ. 35,000.

La Nación: Bouchard 551, C1106ABG Buenos Aires; tel. (11) 4319-1600; fax (11) 4319-1969; e-mail cescribano@lanacion.com.ar; internet www.lanacion.com.ar; f. 1870; morning; independent; Pres. JULIO SAGUIER; circ. 184,000.

Página 12: Belgrano 671, C1092AAG Buenos Aires; tel. (11) 6772-4400; fax (11) 4334-2335; e-mail lectores@pagina12.com.ar; internet www.pagina12.com.ar; f. 1987; morning; independent; Dir ERNESTO TIFFEMBERG; Editor FERNANDO SOKOLOWICZ; circ. 280,000.

La Prensa: Azopardo 715, C1107ADK Buenos Aires; tel. (11) 4349-1000; fax (11) 4349-1025; e-mail laprensa@interlink.com; internet www.interlink.com.ar/laprensa; f. 1869; morning; independent; Dir FLORENCIO ALDREY IGLESIAS; circ. 100,000.

La Razón: Río Cuarto 1242, C1168AFF Buenos Aires; tel. and fax (11) 4309-6000; e-mail larazon@arnet.com.ar; internet www.larazon.com.ar; f. 1992; evening; Dir OSCAR MAGDALENA; circ. 62,000.

El Sol: Hipólito Yrigoyen 122, Quilmes, 1878 Buenos Aires; tel. and fax (11) 4257-6325; e-mail autalan@elsolquilmes.com.ar; internet www.elsolquilmes.com.ar; f. 1927; Editor and Dir LUIS ANGEL AUTALÁN; Pres. RODRIGO GHISANI; circ. 25,000.

Tiempo Argentino: Buenos Aires; tel. (11) 4428-1929; Editor Dr TOMÁS LEONA; circ. 75,000.

PRINCIPAL PROVINCIAL DAILIES

Catamarca

El Ancasti: Sarmiento 518, K4700EML Catamarca; tel. and fax (3833) 431385; e-mail lector@elancasti.net.ar; internet www.elancasti.com.ar; f. 1988; morning; Dir ROQUE EDUARDO MOLAS; circ. 8,000.

Chaco

Norte: Carlos Pellegrini 744, H3500CDP Resistencia; tel. (3722) 428204; fax (3722) 426047; f. 1968; Dir MIGUEL A. FERNÁNDEZ; circ. 14,000.

Chubut

Crónica: Namuncurá 122, U9000BVD Comodoro Rivadavia; tel. (297) 447-1200; fax (297) 447-1780; e-mail diariocronica@diariocronica.com.ar; internet www.diariocronica.com.ar; f. 1962; morning; Dir HERMINIA M. PRESAS; Chief Editor HÉCTOR RODRÍGUEZ; circ. 15,000.

Córdoba

Comercio y Justicia: Mariano Moreno 378, X5000MRH Córdoba; tel. and fax (351) 422-0040; e-mail redaccion@comercioyjusticia.info; f. 1939; morning; economic and legal news with periodic supplements on architecture and administration; Pres. EDUARDO POGROBINKI; Dir JAVIER ALBERTO DE PASCUALE; circ. 5,800.

La Voz del Interior: Monseñor P. Cabrera 6080, X5008HKJ Córdoba; tel. (351) 475-7000; fax (351) 475-7247; e-mail lavoz@lavozdelinterior.com.ar; internet www.lavozdelinterior.com.ar; f. 1904; morning; independent; Dir Dr CARLOS HUGO JORNET; Editor FRANCO PICCATO; circ. 68,000.

Corrientes

El Litoral: Hipólito Yrigoyen 990, W3400AST Corrientes; tel. and fax (3783) 422227; internet www.corrientes.com.ar/el-litoral; f. 1960; morning; Dir CARLOS A. ROMERO FERIS; circ. 25,000.

El Territorio: Quaranta 4307, 3300 Posadas; tel. and fax (3752) 452100; e-mail info@territoriodigital.com; internet www.territoriodigital.com.ar; f. 1925; Dir GONZALO PELTZER; circ. 22,000 (Mon.–Fri.), 28,000 (Sunday).

Entre Ríos

El Diario: Buenos Aires y Urquiza, E2823XBC Paraná; tel. (343) 423-1000; fax (343) 431-9104; e-mail info@eldiarioentrerios.com.ar; internet www.eldiario.com.ar; f. 1914; morning; Dir Dr LUIS F. ETCHEVEHERE; circ. 25,000.

El Heraldo: Quintana 42, E3200XAE Concordia; tel. (345) 421-5304; fax (345) 421-1397; e-mail administracionelheraldo@infovia.com.ar; internet www.elheraldo.com.ar; f. 1915; evening; Editor Dr CARLOS LIEBERMANN; circ. 10,000.

Mendoza

Los Andes: San Martín 1049, M5500AAK Mendoza; tel. (261) 449-1280; fax (261) 449-1217; e-mail havila@losandes.com.ar; internet www.losandes.com.ar; f. 1982; morning; Dir ELVIRA CALLE DE ANTEQUEDA; Gen. Man. MIGUEL A. BAUZA; circ. 60,000.

Provincia de Buenos Aires

El Atlántico: Bolívar 2975, B7600GDO Mar del Plata; tel. (223) 435462; f. 1938; morning; Dir OSCAR ALBERTO GASTIARENA; circ. 20,000.

La Capital: Champagnat 2551, B7604GXA Mar del Plata; tel. (223) 478-8490; fax (223) 478-1038; e-mail diario@lacapitalnet.com.ar; internet www.lacapitalnet.com.ar; f. 1905; Dir FLORENCIO ALDREY IGLESIAS; circ. 32,000.

El Día: Avda A. Diagonal 80 817–21, B1925XAC La Plata; tel. (221) 425-0101; fax (221) 423-2996; e-mail redaccion@eldia.com; internet www.eldia.com; f. 1884; morning; independent; Dir RAÚL E. KRAISELBURD; circ. 54,868.

Ecos Diarios: Calle 62, No 2486, B7630XAF Necochea; tel. and fax (2262) 430754; e-mail ecosdiar@satlink.com; internet www.ecosdiarios.com; f. 1921; morning; independent; Dir GUILLERMO IGNACIO; circ. 6,000.

La Nueva Provincia: Rodríguez 55, B8000HSA Bahía Blanca; tel. (291) 459-0000; fax (291) 459-0001; e-mail info@lanueva.com; internet www.lanueva.com.ar; f. 1898; morning; independent; Dir DIANA JULIO DE MASSOT; circ. 22,000 (Mon.–Fri.), 30,000 (Sunday).

El Nuevo Cronista: Mercedes 619, 5°, B8000XAV Buenos Aires; tel. (11) 2324-4001; internet www.nuevocronista.com.ar.

La Voz del Pueblo: San Martín 991, B7500IKJ Tres Arroyos; tel. (2983) 430680; fax (2938) 430682; e-mail redaccion@lavozdelpueblo.com.ar; f. 1902; morning; independent; Dir ALBERTO JORGE MACIEL; circ. 8,500.

Río Negro

Río Negro: 9 de Julio 733, 8332, Gen. Roca, R8332AAO Río Negro; tel. (2941) 439300; fax (2941) 430517; e-mail comentario@rionegro.com.ar; internet www.rionegro.com.ar; f. 1912; morning; Editor NÉLIDA RAJNERI DE GAMBA.

Salta

El Tribuno: Ex Combatientes de Malvinas 3890, A4449XBN Salta; tel. (387) 424-6200; fax (387) 424-6240; e-mail redaccion@eltribuno.com.ar; internet www.eltribuno.com.ar; f. 1949; morning; Dir ROBERTO EDUARDO ROMERO; circ. 25,000.

San Juan

Diario de Cuyo: Mendoza 380 Sur, J5402GUH San Juan; tel. (264) 429-0038; fax (264) 429-0063; e-mail direcciondc@diariodecuyo.com.ar; internet www.diariodecuyo.com.ar; f. 1947; morning; independent; Dir FRANCISCO B. MONTES; circ. 20,000.

San Luis

El Diario de La República: Lafinur 924, D5700DCW San Luis; tel. and fax (2623) 422037; e-mail administracion@grupopayne.com.ar; internet www.eldiariodelarepublica.com; f. 1966; Dir-Gen. FELICIANA RODRÍGUEZ SAA; circ. 12,000.

Santa Fe

La Capital: Sarmiento 763, S2000CMK Rosario; tel. (341) 420-1100; fax (341) 420-1114; e-mail elagos@lacapital.com.ar; f. 1867; morning; independent; Dir CARLOS MARÍA LAGOS; circ. 65,000.

El Litoral: 25 de Mayo 3536, S3002DPJ Santa Fe; tel. (342) 450-2500; fax (342) 450-2530; e-mail litoral@litoral.com.ar; internet www.litoral.com.ar; f. 1918; morning; independent; Dir GUSTAVO VÍTTORI; circ. 37,000.

Santiago del Estero

El Liberal: Libertad 263, G4200CZC Santiago del Estero; tel. (385) 422-4400; fax (385) 422-4538; e-mail redaccion@elliberal.com.ar; internet www.elliberal.com.ar; f. 1898; morning; Exec. Dir JOSÉ LUIS CASTIGLIONE; Editorial Dir Dr JULIO CÉSAR CASTIGLIONE; circ. 20,000.

Tucumán

La Gaceta: Mendoza 654, T4000DAN San Miguel de Tucumán; tel. (381) 431-1111; fax (381) 431-1597; e-mail redaccion@lagaceta.com

ARGENTINA

.ar; internet www.lagaceta.com.ar; f. 1912; morning; independent; Dir ALBERTO GARCÍA HAMILTON; circ. 70,000.

WEEKLY NEWSPAPER

El Informador Público: Uruguay 252, 3° F, C1015ABF Buenos Aires; tel. (11) 4476-3551; fax (11) 4342-2628; f. 1986.

PERIODICALS

Aeroespacio: Avda Dorrego 4019, C1425GBE Buenos Aires; tel. and fax (11) 4514-1561; internet www.aeroespacio.com.ar; f. 1940; every 2 months; aeronautics; Dir CARLOS GUSTAVO RINALDI; circ. 24,000.

Billiken: Azopardo 579, C1107ADG Buenos Aires; tel. (11) 4346-0107; fax (11) 4343-7040; e-mail vzumbo@atlantida.com.ar; f. 1919; weekly; children's magazine; Dir JUAN CARLOS PORRAS; circ. 240,000.

Casas y Jardines: Sarmiento 643, C1405APE Buenos Aires; tel. (11) 445-1793; f. 1932; every 2 months; houses and gardens; publ. by Editorial Contémpora SRL; Dir NORBERTO M. MUZIO.

Chacra y Campo Moderno: Editorial Atlántida, SA, Azopardo 579, C1307ADG Buenos Aires; tel. (11) 4331-4591; fax (11) 4331-3272; f. 1930; monthly; farm and country magazine; Dir CONSTANCIO C. VIGIL; circ. 35,000.

Claudia: Córdoba 1345, 12°, C1055AAD Buenos Aires; tel. (11) 442-3275; fax (11) 4814-3948; f. 1957; monthly; women's magazine; Dir ANA TORREJÓN; circ. 150,000.

El Economista: Córdoba 632, 2°, C1054AAS Buenos Aires; tel. (11) 4322-7360; fax (11) 4322-8157; internet www.eleconomista.com.ar; f. 1951; weekly; financial; Dir Dr D. RADONJIC; circ. 37,800.

Fotografía Universal: Buenos Aires; monthly; circ. 39,500.

Gente: Azopardo 579, 3°, C1307ADG Buenos Aires; tel. (11) 433-4591; f. 1965; weekly; general; Dir JORGE DE LUJÁN GUTIÉRREZ; circ. 133,000.

El Gráfico: Paseo Colón 505, 2°, C1063ACF Buenos Aires; tel. (11) 5235-5100; fax (11) 5235-5137; e-mail elgrafico@elgrafico.com.ar; internet www.elgrafico.com.ar; f. 1919; weekly; sport; Editor MARTIN MAZUR; circ. 127,000.

Guía Latinoamericana de Transportes: Florida 8287, esq. Portinari, B1669GOK Del Viso (Ptdo de Pilar), Provincia de Buenos Aires; tel. (11) 4320-7004; fax (11) 4307-1956; f. 1968; every 2 months; travel information and timetables; Editor Dr ARMANDO SCHLECKER HIRSCH; circ. 7,500.

Humor: Venezuela 842, C1095AAR Buenos Aires; tel. (11) 4334-5400; fax (11) 411-2700; f. 1978; every 2 weeks; satirical revue; Editor ANDRÉS CASCIOLI; circ. 180,000.

Legislación Argentina: Talcahuano 650, C1013AAN Buenos Aires; tel. (11) 4371-0528; e-mail jurispru@lvd.com.ar; f. 1958; weekly; law; Dir RICARDO ESTÉVEZ BOERO; circ. 15,000.

Mercado: Rivadavia 877, 2°, C1002AAG Buenos Aires; tel. (11) 4346-9400; fax (11) 4343-7880; e-mail gacetillas@mercado.com.ar; internet www.mercado.com.ar; f. 1969; monthly; business; Dir MIGUEL ANGEL DIEZ; circ. 28,000.

Mundo Israelita: Pueyrredón 538, 1° B, C1032ABS Buenos Aires; tel. (11) 4961-7999; fax (11) 4961-0763; f. 1923; weekly; Editor Dr JOSÉ KESTELMAN; circ. 15,000.

Nuestra Arquitectura: Sarmiento 643, 5°, C1405APE Buenos Aires; tel. (11) 445-1793; f. 1929; every 2 months; architecture; publ. by Editorial Contémpora SRL; Dir NORBERTO M. MUZIO.

Para Ti: Azopardo 579, C1107ADG Buenos Aires; tel. (11) 4331-4591; fax (11) 4331-3272; e-mail redaccionparati@atlantida.com.ar; internet www.parati.com.ar; f. 1922; weekly; women's interest; Dir ANÍBAL C. VIGIL; circ. 104,000.

Pensamiento Económico: Leandro N. Alem 36, C1003AAN Buenos Aires; tel. (11) 4331-8051; fax (11) 4331-8055; e-mail cac@cac.com.ar; internet www.cac.com.ar; f. 1925; quarterly; review of Cámara Argentina de Comercio; Dir Dr CARLOS L. P. ANTONUCCI.

La Prensa Médica Argentina: Junín 845, C1113AAA Buenos Aires; tel. (11) 4961-9793; fax (11) 4961-9494; e-mail presmedarg@hotmail.com; f. 1914; monthly; medical; Editor Dr P. A. LÓPEZ; circ. 8,000.

Prensa Obrera: Ayacucho 444, C1026AAB Buenos Aires; tel. (11) 4953-3824; fax (11) 4953-7164; f. 1982; weekly; publication of Partido Obrero; circ. 16,000.

La Semana: Sarmiento 1113, C1041AAW Buenos Aires; tel. (11) 435-2552; general; Editor DANIEL PLINER.

La Semana Médica: Arenales 3574, C1425BEV Buenos Aires; tel. (11) 4824-5673; f. 1894; monthly; Dir Dr EDUARDO F. MELE; circ. 7,000.

Siete Días Ilustrados: Leandro N. Alem 896, C1001AAQ Buenos Aires; tel. (11) 432-6010; f. 1967; weekly; general; Dir RICARDO CÁMARA; circ. 110,000.

Técnica e Industria: Buenos Aires; tel. (11) 446-3193; f. 1922; monthly; technology and industry; Dir E. R. FEDELE; circ. 5,000.

Visión: French 2820, 2°A, C1425AWH Buenos Aires; tel. (11) 4825-1258; fax (11) 4827-1004; f. 1950; fortnightly; Latin American affairs, politics; Editor LUIS VIDAL RUCABADO.

Vosotras: Leandro N. Alem 896, 3°, C1001AAQ Buenos Aires; tel. (11) 432-6010; f. 1935; women's weekly; Dir ABEL ZANOTTO; circ. 33,000; monthly supplements.

Labores: circ. 130,000.

Modas: circ. 70,000.

NEWS AGENCIES

Agencia TELAM, SA: Bolívar 531, C1066AAK Buenos Aires; tel. (11) 4339-0330; fax (11) 4339-0353; e-mail telam@telam.com.ar; internet www.telam.com.ar; Gen. Man. HAEDO L. LAZZARO.

Diarios y Noticias (DYN): Julio A. Roca 636, 8°, C1067ABO Buenos Aires; tel. (11) 4342-3040; fax (11) 4342-3043; e-mail info@dyn.com.ar; internet www.dyn.com.ar; f. 1982; Pres. CARLOS LARIA.

Noticias Argentinas, SA (NA): Suipacha 570, 3° B, C1008AAL Buenos Aires; tel. (11) 4394-7522; fax (11) 4394-7648; e-mail infogral@noticiasargentinas.com; internet www.noticiasargentinas.com; f. 1973; Dir LUIS FERNANDO TORRES.

Foreign Bureaux

Agence France-Presse (AFP): Corrientes 456, 4°, Of. 41–42, C1043AAR Buenos Aires; tel. (11) 4394-0872; fax (11) 4393-9912; e-mail afp-baires@tournet.com.ar; internet www.afp.com; Bureau Chief FRÉDERIC GARLAN.

Agencia EFE (Spain): Moreau de Justo 1720, 1°, C1107AFJ Buenos Aires; tel. (11) 4311-1211; fax (11) 4312-7518; e-mail delegado@efe.com.ar; Bureau Chief ELÍAS GARCÍA.

Agenzia Nazionale Stampa Associata (ANSA) (Italy): San Martín 320, 6°, C1004AAH Buenos Aires; tel. (11) 4394-7568; fax (11) 4394-5214; e-mail ansabaires@infovia.com.ar; Bureau Chief ANTONIO CAVALLARI.

Associated Press (AP) (USA): Leandro N. Alem 712, 4°, C1001AAP Buenos Aires; tel. (11) 4311-0081; fax (11) 4311-0083; e-mail bcormier@ap.org; Bureau Chief WILLIAM CORMIER.

Deutsche Presse-Agentur (dpa) (Germany): Buenos Aires; tel. (11) 4311-5311; e-mail msvgroth@ba.net; Bureau Chief Dr HENDRIK GROTH.

Inter Press Service (IPS) (Italy): Buenos Aires; tel. (11) 4394-0829; Bureau Chief RAMÓN M. GORRIARÁN; Correspondent GUSTAVO CAPDEVILLA.

ITAR—TASS (Information Telegraphic Agency of Russia—Telegraphic Agency of the Sovereign Countries) (Russia): Córdoba 652, 11°E, C1054AAS Buenos Aires; tel. (11) 4392-2044; Dir ISIDORO GILBERT.

Magyar Távirati Iroda (MTI) (Hungary): Marcelo T. de Alvear 624, 3° 16, 1058 Buenos Aires; tel. (11) 4312-9596; Correspondent ENDRE SIMÓ.

Prensa Latina (Cuba): Buenos Aires; tel. (11) 4394-0565; e-mail prela@teletel.com.ar; Correspondent VÍCTOR CARRIBA.

Reuters (United Kingdom): Eduardo Madero 940, 25°, 1106 Buenos Aires; tel. (11) 4318-0600; fax (11) 4318-0698; Dir CARLOS PÍA MANGIONE.

Xinhua (New China) News Agency (People's Republic of China): Tucumán 540, 14°D, C1049AAL Buenos Aires; tel. (11) 4313-9755; Bureau Chief JU QINGDONG.

The following are also represented: Central News Agency (Taiwan), Interpress (Poland), Jiji Press (Japan).

PRESS ASSOCIATION

Asociación de Entidades Periodísticas Argentinas (ADEPA): Chacabuco 314, 3°, C1069AAH Buenos Aires; tel. and fax (11) 4331-1500; e-mail adepa@adepa.org.ar; internet www.adepa.org.ar; f. 1962; Pres. LAURO F. LAINO.

Publishers

Aguilar, Altea, Taurus, Alfaguara, SA de Ediciones: Leandro N. Alem 720, C1001AAP Buenos Aires; tel. (11) 4119-5000; fax (11) 4119-5021; e-mail info@alfaguara.com.ar; internet www.alfaguara.com.ar; f. 1946; general, literature, children's books; Pres. ESTEBAN FERNÁNDEZ ROSADO; Gen. Man. DAVID DELGADO DE ROBLES.

Aique: Valentín Gómez 3530, C1191AAP Buenos Aires; tel. and fax (11) 4865-5152; e-mail editorial@aique.com.ar; internet www.aique.com.ar; f. 1976; division of Aique Grupo Editor, SA.

ARGENTINA

Amorrortu Editores, SA: Paraguay 1225, 7°, C1057AAS Buenos Aires; tel. (11) 4816-5812; fax (11) 4816-3321; e-mail info@amorrortueditores.com; internet www.amorrortueditores.com; f. 1967; academic, social sciences and humanities; Man. Dir HORACIO DE AMORRORTU.

Az Editora, SA: Paraguay 2351, C1121ABK Buenos Aires; tel. (11) 4961-4036; fax (11) 4961-0089; e-mail contacto@az.com.ar; internet www.az.com.ar; f. 1976; educational, children's, literature, social sciences, medicine, law; Pres. DANTE OMAR VILLALBA.

Biblioteca Nacional de Maestros: c/o Ministerio de Educación, Ciencia y Tecnología, Pizzurno 935, planta baja, C1020ACA Buenos Aires; tel. (11) 4129-1272; fax (11) 4129-1268; e-mail gperrone@me.gov.ar; internet www.bnm.me.gov.ar; f. 1884; Dir GRACIELA PERRONE.

Carlos Lohlé, SA: Tacuarí 1516, C1139AAH Buenos Aires; tel. (11) 4427-9969; f. 1953; philosophy, religion, belles-lettres; Dir FRANCISCO M. LOHLÉ.

Club de Lectores: Avda de Mayo 624, C1084AAO Buenos Aires; tel. (11) 4342-6251; f. 1938; non-fiction; Man. Dir MERCEDES FONTENLA.

Cosmopolita, SRL: Piedras 744, C1070AAP Buenos Aires; tel. (11) 4361-8925; fax (11) 4361-8049; e-mail editorialcosmopolita@fullzero.com.ar; internet www.ed-cosmopolita.com.ar; f. 1940; science and technology; Man. Dir RUTH F. DE RAPP.

Crecer Creando Editorial: Callao 1225, 14°B, C1023AAF Buenos Aires; tel. and fax (11) 4812-4586; e-mail info@crecercreando.com.ar; internet www.crecercreando.com.ar; educational.

De Los Cuatro Vientos Editorial: Balcarce 1053, Local 2, C1064AAU Buenos Aires; tel. and fax (11) 4300-0924; e-mail info@deloscuatrovientos.com.ar; internet www.deloscuatrovientos.com.ar; Dir and Editor PABLO ALBORNOZ.

Ediciones Atril: Hortiguera 1411, C1406CKI Buenos Aires; tel. (11) 4924-3003; e-mail atril@interlink.com.ar.

Ediciones La Aurora: José María Moreno 873, 1°, C1424AAI Buenos Aires; tel. and fax (11) 4922-5356; f. 1925; general, religion, spirituality, theology, philosophy, psychology, history, semiology, linguistics; Dir Dr HUGO O. ORTEGA.

Ediciones de la Flor SRL: Gorriti 3695, C1172ACE Buenos Aires; fax (11) 4963-5616; e-mail edic-flor@datamarkets.com.ar; internet www.edicionesdelaflor.com.ar; f. 1966; fiction, poetry, theatre, juvenile, humour and scholarly; Co-Dirs ANA MARÍA T. MILER, DANIEL DIVINSKY.

Ediciones Librerías Fausto: Corrientes 1316, C1043ABN Buenos Aires; tel. (11) 4476-4919; fax (11) 4476-3914; f. 1943; fiction and non-fiction; Man. RAFAEL ZORRILLA.

Ediciones Macchi, SA: Alsina 1535/37, C1088AAM Buenos Aires; tel. (11) 446-2506; fax (11) 446-0594; e-mail info@macchi.com; internet www.macchi.com; f. 1947; economic sciences; Pres. RAÚL LUIS MACCHI.

Ediciones Nueva Visión, SAIC: Tucumán 3748, C1189AAV Buenos Aires; tel. (11) 4864-5050; fax (11) 4863-5980; e-mail ednuevavision@ciudad.com.ar; f. 1954; psychology, education, social sciences, linguistics; Man. Dir HAYDÉE P. DE GIACONE.

Ediciones del Signo: Julián Alvarez 2844, 1°A, C1425DHT Buenos Aires; tel. (11) 4861-3181; fax (11) 3462-5031; e-mail info@edicionesdelsigno.com.ar; internet www.edicionesdelsigno.com.ar; f. 1995; philosophy, psychoanalysis, politics and scholarly.

Editorial Abril, SA: Moreno 1617, C1093ABE Buenos Aires; tel. (11) 4331-0112; f. 1961; fiction, non-fiction, children's books, textbooks; Dir ROBERTO M. ARES.

Editorial Acme, SA: Santa Magdalena 635, C1277ACG Buenos Aires; tel. (11) 4328-1508; f. 1949; general fiction, children's books, agriculture, textbooks; Man. Dir EMILIO I. GONZÁLEZ.

Editorial Albatros, SACI: Torres Las Plazas, J. Salguero 2745, 5°, C1425DEL Buenos Aires; tel. (11) 4807-2030; fax (11) 4807-2010; e-mail info@albatros.com.ar; internet www.albatros.com.ar; f. 1945; technical, non-fiction, social sciences, sport, children's books, medicine and agriculture; Pres. ANDREA INÉS CANEVARO.

Editorial Argenta Sarlep SA: Corrientes 1250, 3°, Of. F, C1043AAZ Buenos Aires; tel. and fax (11) 4382-9085; e-mail argenta@millic.com.ar; internet www.editorialargenta.com.ar; f. 1970; literature, poetry, theatre and reference.

Editorial Bonum: Corrientes 6687, C1427BPE Buenos Aires; tel. and fax (11) 4554-1414; e-mail ventas@editorialbonum.com.ar; internet www.editorialbonum.com.ar; f. 1960; religious, educational and self-help.

Editorial Don Bosco: Don Bosco 4069, C1206ABM Buenos Aires; tel. (11) 4883-0111; fax (11) 4883-0115; e-mail administracion@edb.com.ar; internet www.edb.com.ar; f. 1993; religious and educational; Gen. Man. GERARDO BENTANCOUR.

Editorial Catálogos SRL: Independencia 1860, C1225AAN Buenos Aires; tel. and fax (11) 4381-5708; e-mail catalogos@ciudad.com.ar; internet www.catalogossrl.com.ar; religion, literature, academic, general interest and self-help.

Editorial Claretiana: Lima 1360, C1138ACD Buenos Aires; tel. (11) 427-9250; fax (11) 427-4015; e-mail editorial@editorialclaretiana.com.ar; internet www.editorialclaretiana.com.ar; f. 1956; Catholicism; Man. Dir DOMINGO ANGEL GRILLIA.

Editorial Claridad, SA: Viamonte 1730, 1°, C1055ABH Buenos Aires; tel. (11) 4371-5546; fax (11) 4375-1659; e-mail editorial@heliasta.com.ar; internet www.heliasta.com.ar; f. 1922; literature, biographies, social science, politics, reference, dictionaries; Pres. Dra ANA MARÍA CABANELLAS.

Editorial Columba, SA: Sarmiento 1889, 5°, C1044AAA Buenos Aires; tel. (11) 445-4297; f. 1953; classics in translation, 20th century; Man. Dir CLAUDIO A. COLUMBA.

Editorial Contémpora, SRL: Sarmiento 643, 5°, C1041AAM Buenos Aires; tel. (11) 445-1793; architecture, town planning, interior decoration and gardening; Dir NORBERTO C. MUZIO.

Editorial Difusión, SA: Sarandí 1065–67, C1222ACK Buenos Aires; tel. (11) 4941-0088; f. 1937; literature, philosophy, religion, education, textbooks, children's books; Dir DOMINGO PALOMBELLA.

Editorial Errepar: Paraná 725, C1017AAO Buenos Aires; tel. (11) 4370-8025; fax (11) 4383-2202; e-mail clientes@errepar.com; internet www.errepar.com; legal texts.

Editorial Glem, SACIF: Caseros 2056, C1264AAN Buenos Aires; tel. (11) 426-6641; f. 1933; psychology, technology; Pres. JOSÉ ALFREDO TUCCI.

Editorial Grupo Cero: Mansilla 2686, planta baja 2, C1425BPD Buenos Aires; tel. (11) 4328-0614; internet www.editorialgrupocero.com; fiction, poetry and psychoanalysis.

Editorial Guadalupe: Mansilla 3865, C1425BQA Buenos Aires; tel. (11) 4826-8587; fax (11) 4823-6672; e-mail ventas@editorialguadalupe.com.ar; internet www.editorialguadalupe.com.ar; f. 1895; social sciences, religion, anthropology, children's books and pedagogy; Man. Dir LORENZO GOYENECHE.

Editorial Heliasta, SRL: Viamonte 1730, 1°, C1055ABH Buenos Aires; tel. (11) 4371-5546; fax (11) 4375-1659; e-mail editorial@heliasta.com.ar; internet www.heliasta.com.ar; f. 1944; literature, biography, dictionaries, legal; Pres. Dra ANA MARÍA CABANELLAS.

Editorial Hispano-Americana, SA (HASA): Alsina 731, C1087AAK Buenos Aires; tel. (11) 4331-5051; f. 1934; science and technology; Pres. Prof. HÉCTOR OSCAR ALGARRA.

Editorial Inter-Médica, SAICI: Junín 917, 1°, C1113AAC Buenos Aires; tel. (11) 4961-9234; fax (11) 4961-5572; e-mail info@inter-medica.com.ar; internet www.inter-medica.com.ar; f. 1959; medicine and veterinary; Pres. SONIA MODYEIEVSKY.

Editorial Inter-Vet, SA: Avda de los Constituyentes 3141, C1427BLK, Buenos Aires; tel. (11) 451-2382; f. 1987; veterinary; Pres. JORGE MODYEIEVSKY.

Editorial Juris: Moreno 1580, S2000DLF Rosario, Santa Fe; tel. (341) 426-7301; e-mail editorialjuris@arnet.com.ar; internet www.editorialjuris.com; f. 1952; legal texts.

Editorial Kier, SACIFI: Santa Fe 1260, C1059ABT Buenos Aires; tel. (11) 4811-0507; fax (11) 4811-3395; e-mail ediciones@kier.com.ar; internet www.kier.com.ar; f. 1907; Eastern doctrines and religions, astrology, parapsychology, tarot, I Ching, occultism, cabbala, freemasonry and natural medicine; Pres. HÉCTOR S. PIBERNUS; Dir CRISTINA GRIGNA; Mans SERGIO PIBERNUS, OSVALDO PIBERNUS.

Editorial Losada, SA: Moreno 3362/64, C1209ABL Buenos Aires; tel. (11) 4373-4006; fax (11) 4375-5001; e-mail losada@editoriallosada.com; internet www.editoriallosada.com; f. 1938; general; Pres. JOSÉ JUAN FERNÁNDEZ REGUERA.

Editorial Médica Panamericana, SA: Marcelo T. de Alvear 2145, C1122AAG Buenos Aires; tel. (11) 4821-5520; fax (11) 4825-5006; e-mail info@medicapanamericana.com.ar; internet www.medicapanamericana.com.ar; f. 1962; medicine and health sciences; Pres. HUGO BRIK.

Editorial Mercosur: Dean Funes 923/25, C1231ABI Buenos Aires; tel. (11) 4822-4615; e-mail info@editorialmercosur.com; internet www.editorialmercosur.com; self-help and general interest.

Editorial del Nuevo Extremo: Juncal 4651, C1425BAE Buenos Aires; tel. (11) 4773-3228; fax (11) 473-8445; e-mail editorial@delnuevoextremo.com; internet www.delnuevoextremo.com; general interest.

Editorial Plus Ultra, SA: Callao 575, C1022AAF Buenos Aires; tel. (11) 4374-2953; f. 1964; literature, history, textbooks, law, economics, politics, sociology, pedagogy, children's books; Man. Editors RAFAEL ROMÁN, LORENZO MARENGO.

Editorial Santillana: Buenos Aires; f. 1960; education; Pres. JESÚS DE POLANCO GUTIÉRREZ.

ARGENTINA   *Directory*

Editorial Sigmar, SACI: Belgrano 1580, 7°, C1093AAQ Buenos Aires; tel. (11) 4383-3045; fax (11) 4383-5633; e-mail editorial@sigmar.com.ar; f. 1941; children's books; Man. Dir ROBERTO CHWAT.

Editorial Sopena Argentina, SACI e I: Maza 2138, C1240ADT Buenos Aires; tel. and fax (11) 4912-2383; f. 1918; dictionaries, classics, chess, health, politics, history, children's books; Dir MARTA A. J. OLSEN.

Editorial Stella: Viamonte 1984, C1056ABD Buenos Aires; tel. (11) 4374-0346; fax (11) 4374-8719; e-mail admin@editorialstella.com.ar; internet www.editorialstella.com.ar; general non-fiction and text-books; owned by Asociación Educacionista Argentina.

Editorial Sudamericana, SA: Humberto 545, 1°, C1103ACK Buenos Aires; tel. (11) 4300-5400; fax (11) 4362-7364; e-mail info@edsudamericana.com.ar; internet www.edsudamericana.com.ar; f. 1939; general fiction and non-fiction; Gen. Man. OLAF HANTEL.

Editorial Troquel, SA: Pichincha 967, C1219ACI Buenos Aires; tel. (11) 4308-3638; e-mail info@troguel.com.ar; internet www.troquel.com.ar; f. 1954; general literature and textbooks; Pres. GUSTAVO A. RESSIA.

Editorial Zeus SRL: Rosario, Santa Fe; tel. (341) 449-5585; fax (341) 425-4259; e-mail editorialzeus@citynet.net.ar; internet www.editorial-zeus.com.ar; legal texts; Editor and Dir GUSTAVO L. CAVIGLIA.

Emecé Editores, SA: Alsina 2062, C1090AAF Buenos Aires; tel. (11) 4954-0105; fax (11) 4953-4200; f. 1939; fiction, non-fiction, biographies, history, art, essays; Pres. ALFREDO DEL CARRIL.

Espasa Calpe Argentina, SA: Independencia 1668, C1100ABQ Buenos Aires; tel. (11) 4382-4043; fax (11) 4383-3793; f. 1937; literature, science, dictionaries; publ. Colección Austral; Dir GUILLERMO SCHAVELZON.

EUDEBA (Editorial Universitaria de Buenos Aires): Rivadavia 1573, C1033AAF Buenos Aires; tel. (11) 4383-8025; fax (11) 4383-2202; e-mail eudeba@eudeba.com.ar; internet www.eudeba.com.ar; f. 1958; university text books and general interest publications; Pres. PATRICIO GARRAHAN.

Fabril Editora, SA: Buenos Aires; tel. (11) 4421-3601; f. 1958; non-fiction, science, arts, education and reference; Editorial Man. ANDRÉS ALFONSO BRAVO; Business Man. RÓMULO AYERZA.

Galerna: Lambaré 893, C1185ABA Buenos Aires; tel. (11) 4867-1661; fax (11) 4862-5031; e-mail contacto@galerna.net; internet www.galernalibros.com; fiction, theatre, poetry and scholarly; Man. HUGO LEVÍN.

Gram Editora: Cochabamba 1652, C1148ABF Buenos Aires; tel. (11) 4304-4833; fax (11) 4304-5692; e-mail grameditora@infovia.com.ar; internet www.grameditora.com.ar; catholic.

Gránica Editorial: Lavalle 1634, 3° G, C1048AAN Buenos Aires; tel. (11) 4374-1456; fax (11) 4373-0669; e-mail granica.ar@granicaeditor.com; internet www.granica.com; juvenile and fiction.

Kapelusz Editora, SA: San José 831, C1076AAQ Buenos Aires; tel. (11) 5236-5000; fax (11) 5236-5005; e-mail jvergara@kapelusz.com.ar; internet www.kapelusz.com.ar; f. 1905; textbooks, psychology, pedagogy, children's books; Vice-Pres. RAFAEL PASCUAL ROBLES.

LexisNexis Argentina: Carlos Pellegrini 887, 1°, Buenos Aires; tel. (11) 5236-8888; e-mail info@ed-depalma.com; internet www.lexisnexis.com.ar; f. 1999; upon acquisition of Depalma and Abeledo-Perrot; periodicals and books covering law, politics, sociology, philosophy, history and economics.

Plaza y Janés, SA: Buenos Aires; tel. (11) 4486-6769; popular fiction and non-fiction; Man. Dir JORGE PÉREZ.

PUBLISHERS' ASSOCIATION

Cámara Argentina de Publicaciones: Lavalle 437, 6°, Of. D, C1047AAI Buenos Aires; tel. (11) 5218-9707; e-mail info@publicaciones.org.ar; internet www.publicaciones.org.ar; f. 1970; Pres. AGUSTÍN DOS SANTOS; Man. LUIS FRANCISCO HOULIN.

Broadcasting and Communications

Secretaría de Comunicaciones: Sarmiento 151, 4°, C1041AAC Buenos Aires; tel. (11) 4318-9410; fax (11) 4318-9432; internet www.secom.gov.ar; co-ordinates 30 stations and the international service; Sec. CARLOS LISANDRO SALAS.

Subsecretaría de Planificación y Gestión Tecnológica: Sarmiento 151, 4°, C1041AAC Buenos Aires; tel. (11) 4347-9970; Under-Sec. Ing. ALEJANDRA CABALLERO.

Subsecretaría de Radiocomunicaciones: Sarmiento 151, 4°, C1041AAC Buenos Aires; tel. (11) 4311-5909.

Subsecretaría de Telecomunicaciones: Sarmiento 151, 4°, C1041AAC Buenos Aires; tel. (11) 4311-5909.

Comité Federal de Radiodifusión (COMFER): Suipacha 765, 9°, C1008AAO Buenos Aires; tel. (11) 4320-4900; fax (11) 4394-6866; e-mail mlagier@comfer.gov.ar; internet www.comfer.gov.ar; f. 1972; controls various technical aspects of broadcasting and transmission of programmes; Insp. JULIO DONATO BÁRBARO.

TELECOMMUNICATIONS

Regulatory Bodies

Cámara de Informática y Comunicaciones de la República Argentina (CICOMRA): Córdoba 744, 2°, C1054AAT Buenos Aires; tel. (11) 4325-8839; fax (11) 4325-9604; e-mail cicomra@cicomra.org.ar; internet www.cicomra.org.ar; f. 1985; Pres. NORBERTO CAPELLÁN.

Comisión Nacional de Comunicaciones (CNC): Perú 103, 9°, C1067AAC Buenos Aires; tel. (11) 4347-9242; fax (11) 4347-9244; internet www.cnc.gov.ar; f. 1996; Pres. Dr ROBERTO CATALÁN; Insp. FULVIO MARIO MADARO.

Major Operators

AT&T Argentina: Alicia Moreau de Justo 400, C1107AAH Buenos Aires; internet www.att.com; Pres. of Global Operations PAULINO DO REGO BARROS, Jr.

Cía Ericsson SACI: Güemes 676, 1°, Vicente López PCIA, B1638CJF Buenos Aires; tel. (11) 4319-5500; fax (11) 4315-0629; e-mail infocom@cea.ericsson.se; internet www.ericsson.com.ar; Dir-Gen. Ing. ROLANDO ZUBIRÁN.

CTI Móvil: Avda de Mayo 878, C1084AAQ Buenos Aires; internet www.cti.com.ar; f. 1994; bought by América Móvil, SA de CV (Mexico) in 2003; mobile cellular telephone services.

Movistar: Corrientes 655, C1043AAG Buenos Aires; tel. (11) 4130-4000; internet www.movistar.com.ar; 98% owned by Telefónicas Móviles, SA (Spain); operates mobile telephone network.

Telcosur, SA: Don Bosco 3672, 5°, C1206ABF Buenos Aires; tel. (11) 4865-9060; e-mail telcosur@tgs.com.ar; internet www.telcosur.com.ar; f. 1998; 99% owned by Transportador de Gas del Sur (TGS); Operations Man. EDUARDO VIGILANTE; Commercial Man. EDUARDO MARTÍN.

Telecom Argentina: Alicia Moreau de Justo 50, C1107AAB Buenos Aires; tel. (11) 4968-4000; fax (11) 4968-1420; e-mail inversores@intersrv.telecom.com.ar; internet www.telecom.com.ar; provision of telecommunication services in the north of Argentina; Pres. AMADEO R. VÁZQUEZ.

RADIO

There are three privately owned stations in Buenos Aires and 72 in the interior. There are also 37 state-controlled stations, four provincial, three municipal and three university stations. The principal ones are Radio Antártida, Radio Argentina, Radio Belgrano, Radio Ciudad de Buenos Aires, Radio Excelsior, Radio Mitre, Radio El Mundo, Radio Nacional, Radio del Plata, Radio Rivadavia and Radio Splendid, all in Buenos Aires.

Radio Nacional Argentina (RNA): Maipú 555, C1006ACE Buenos Aires; tel. (11) 4325-4590; fax (11) 4325-4313; e-mail direccion@radionacional.gov.ar; internet www.radionacional.gov.ar; five radio stations: Nacional; Nacional Folklórica; Nacional Clásica; Nacional Faro; and RAE (q.v.); Exec. Dir ADELINA OLGA MONCALVILLO.

Radiodifusión Argentina al Exterior (RAE): Maipú 555, C1006ACE Buenos Aires; tel. (11) 4325-6368; fax (11) 4325-9433; e-mail rae@radionacional.gov.ar; f. 1958; broadcasts in seven languages to all areas of the world; Dir MARCELA CAMPOS.

Asociación de Radiodifusoras Privadas Argentinas (ARPA): Juan D. Perón 1561, 8°, C1037ACC Buenos Aires; tel. (11) 4382-4412; internet www.arpa.org.ar; f. 1958; an asscn of all but three of the privately owned commercial stations; Pres. ALBERTO VEIGA; Exec. Dir HECTOR J. PARREIRA.

TELEVISION

There are 42 television channels, of which 29 are privately owned and 15 are owned by provincial and national authorities. The national television network is regulated by the Comité Federal de Radiodifusión (see above).

The following are some of the more important television stations in Argentina: Argentina Televisora Color LS82 Canal 7, LS83 (Canal 9 Libertad), LV80 Telenueva, LU81 Teledifusora Bahiense SA, LV81 Canal 12 Telecor SACI, Dicor Difusión Córdoba, LV80 TV Canal 10 Universidad Nacional Córdoba, and LU82 TV Mar del Plata SA.

The Argentine Government holds a 20% stake in the regional television channel Telesur (q.v.), which began operations in May 2005 and is based in Caracas, Venezuela.

Asociación de Teleradiodifusoras Argentinas (ATA): Córdoba 323, 6°, C1054AAP Buenos Aires; tel. (11) 4312-4208; fax (11) 4315-4681; e-mail info@ata.org.ar; internet www.ata.org.ar; f. 1959; asscn

ARGENTINA

of 21 private television channels; Pres. CARLOS FONTAN BALESTRA; Sec. JORGE RENDO.

América: Fitzroy 1650, Buenos Aires; internet www.america2.com.ar; Programme Man. LILIANA PARODI.

Canal 13: Lima 1261, C1138ACA Buenos Aires; tel. (11) 4305-0013; fax (11) 4307-0315; e-mail prensa@artear.com; internet www.canal13.com.ar; f. 1989; leased to a private concession in 1992; Programme Man. ADRIÁN SUAR.

LS82 TV Canal 7: Figueroa Alcorta 2977, C1425CKI Buenos Aires; tel. (11) 4802-6001; fax (11) 4802-9878; e-mail info@canal7argentina.com.ar; internet www.canal7argentina.com.ar; state-controlled channel; Controller RICARDO PALACIO; Dir of News ANA DE SKALON; Dir of Drama LEONARDO BECHINI.

Canal 9: Dorrego 1708, C1414CKZ Buenos Aires; tel. (11) 777-2321; fax (11) 777-9620; e-mail webmaster@canal9.com.ar; internet www.canal9.com.ar; f. 1960; private channel; Pres. CARLOS GAUSTEIN; Dir-Gen. ENRIQUE TABOADA.

Telefé (Canal 11): Pavón 2444, C1248AAT Buenos Aires; tel. (11) 4941-9549; fax (11) 4942-6773; e-mail prensa@telefe.com; internet www.telefe.com.ar; private channel; Programme Man. CLAUDIO VILLARRUEL.

Finance

(cap. = capital; res = reserves; dep. = deposits; m. = million; brs = branches; amounts in nuevos pesos argentinos—$, unless otherwise stated)

BANKING

Central Bank

Banco Central de la República Argentina: Reconquista 266, C1003ABF Buenos Aires; tel. (11) 4348-3500; fax (11) 4348-3955; e-mail sistema@bcra.gov.ar; internet www.bcra.gov.ar; f. 1935 as a central reserve bank; bank of issue; all capital is held by the state; cap. and res $21,245m., dep. $50,577m. (Dec. 2005); Pres. MARTIN REDRADO.

Government-owned Commercial Banks

Banco del Chubut: Rivadavia 615, Rawson, U9103ANG Chubut; tel. (2965) 496-3050; fax (2965) 496-3051; internet www.bancochubut.com.ar; dep. $170.0m., total assets $456.8m. (May 1995); Pres. ERNESTO CARLOS REY.

Banco de la Ciudad de Buenos Aires: Florida 302, C1005AAH Buenos Aires; tel. (11) 4329-8600; e-mail bcdad39@sminter.com.ar; internet www.bancociudad.com.ar; municipal bank; f. 1878; cap. $378.9m., res $455.1m., dep. $7,359.5m. (Dec. 2005); Chair. and Pres. EDUARDO HECKER; 51 brs.

Banco de Inversión y Comercio Exterior, SA (BICE): 25 de Mayo 528/32, C1002ABL Buenos Aires; tel. (11) 4317-6900; fax (11) 4311-5596; e-mail info@bice.com.ar; internet www.bice.com.ar; f. 1991; cap. and res $1,130.4m. (Dec. 2004); Pres. and Chair. ESTEBAN DÓMINA; Gen. Man. JORGE GIACOMOTTI.

Banco de la Nación Argentina: Bartolomé Mitre 326, C1036AAF Buenos Aires; tel. (11) 4347-6000; fax (11) 4347-6316; e-mail mbravo@bna.com.ar; internet www.bna.com.ar; f. 1891; national bank; dep. $39,232.8m. (Dec. 2004); Pres. GABRIELA CIGANOTTO; Gen. Man. JUAN CARLOS FÁBREGA; 645 brs.

Banco de la Pampa SEM: Carlos Pellegrini 255, L6300DRE Santa Rosa; tel. (2954) 433008; fax (2954) 433196; e-mail cexterior@blp.com.ar; internet www.blp.com.ar; f. 1958; cap. $9.5m., res $134.6m., dep. $1,106.5m. (June 2005); Chair. OSCAR MARIO JORGE; Gen. Man. CARLOS DESINANO; 51 brs.

Banco de la Provincia de Buenos Aires: Avda Ingeniero Luis Monteverde 726, 1900 La Plata, Buenos Aires; tel. (11) 4347-0238; fax (11) 4348-9496; e-mail gsaldana@bpba.com.ar; internet www.bapro.com.ar; f. 1822; provincial govt-owned bank; cap. $1,250.0m., res $1,573.4m., dep. $19,412.8m. (Dec. 2006); Pres. GUILLERMO FRANCOS; Gen. Man. EDUARDO ORDÓÑEZ; 385 brs.

Banco de la Provincia de Córdoba: San Jerónimo 166, X5000AGD Córdoba; tel. (351) 420-7200; fax (351) 420-7407; internet www.bancor.com.ar; f. 1873; provincial bank; cap. $180.0m., res $29.9m., dep. $2,369.1m. (Dec. 2004); Pres. LUIS ENRIQUE GRUNHAUT; 150 brs.

Banco de la Provincia del Neuquén: Argentina 41, Q8300AYA Neuquén; tel. (299) 449-6618; fax (299) 449-6622; internet www.bpn.com.ar; f. 1960; dep. $232.8m., total assets $388.6m. (March 1995); Pres. FÉLIX RACCO; Vice-Pres. CARLOS ALBERTO SANDOVAL; 22 brs.

Banco Social de Córdoba: 27 de Abril 185, 1°, X5000AEC Córdoba; tel. (351) 422-3367; dep. $187.3m., total assets $677.3m. (June 1995); Pres. Dr JAIME POMPAS.

Banco de Tierra del Fuego: Maipú 897, V9410BJQ Ushuaia; tel. (2901) 441600; fax (2901) 441601; e-mail entradas@bancotdf.com.ar; internet www.bancotdf.com.ar; national bank; cap. and res $21.8m., dep. $54.2m. (June 1992); Pres. VICENTE EDUARDO FERNÁNDEZ; Gen. Man. EDUARDO LOMBARDI; 4 brs.

Nuevo Banco de la Rioja, SA: Rivadavia 702, F5300ACU La Rioja; tel. (3822) 430575; fax (3822) 430618; e-mail nblrsa@nblr.com.ar; internet www.nblr.com.ar; f. 1994; provincial bank; cap. $44.5m., dep. $134.0m., total assets $180.7m. (Dec. 2003); Pres. ELIAS SAHAD; Gen. Man. CLAUDIA L. DE BRIGIDO; 2 brs.

Nuevo Banco de Santa Fe, SA: 25 de Mayo 2499, S3000FTS Santa Fe; tel. (342) 4504700; fax (342) 440150; e-mail contactobc@bancobsf.com.ar; internet www.bancobsf.com.ar; f. 1847 as Banco Provincial de Santa Fe, adopted current name in 1998; provincial bank; cap. $90.8m., res $176.5m., dep. $3,637.6m. (Dec. 2005); Chair. ENRIQUE ESKINAZI; Exec. Dir MARCELO BUIL; 105 brs.

Private Commercial Banks

Banco BI Creditanstalt, SA: Bouchard 547, 24° y 25°, C1106ABG Buenos Aires; tel. (11) 4319-8400; fax (11) 4319-8230; internet www.bicreditanstalt.com.ar; f. 1971 as Banco Interfinanzas; name changed as above in 1997; cap. $41,100m. and res $403,711m., dep. $609.6m. (Dec. 2005); Pres. Dr MIGUEL ANGEL ANGELINO; Gen. Man. RICARDO RIVERO HAEDO.

Banco CMF, SA: Macacha Güemes 555, Puerto Madero, C1106BKK Buenos Aires; tel. (11) 4318-6800; fax (11) 4318-6859; e-mail cmfb@cmfb.com.ar; f. 1978 as Corporación Metropolitana de Finanzas, SA; adopted current name in 1999; cap. $49.0m., res $108.7m., dep. $495.1m. (Dec. 2004); Pres. and Chair. JOSÉ P. BENEGAS LYNCH.

Banco COMAFI: Roque S. Peña 660, C1035AAO Buenos Aires; tel. (11) 4347-0400; fax (11) 4347-0404; e-mail contactenos@comafi.com.ar; internet www.comafi.com.ar; f. 1984; assumed control of 65% of Scotiabank Quilmes in April 2002; total assets US $410.1m. (June 2001); Pres. GUILLERMO CERVIÑO; Vice-Pres. EDUARDO MASCHWITZ.

Banco de Corrientes: 9 de Julio 1099, esq. San Juan, W3400AYQ Corrientes; tel. (3783) 479300; fax (3783) 479372; e-mail bcteservicios@bcoctes.com.ar; internet www.bancodecorrientes.com.ar; f. 1951 as Banco de la República de Corrientes; adopted current name in 1993, after transfer to private ownership; cap. and res $120.0m., dep. $484.0m. (Dec. 2004); Pres. PEDRO DOMINGO GOIDA; 33 brs.

Banco Europeo para América Latina (BEAL), SA: Juan D. Perón 338, C1038AAH Buenos Aires; tel. (11) 4331-6544; fax (11) 4331-2010; e-mail bealbsa@interprov.com; f. 1914; cap. and res $60m., dep. $121m. (Nov. 1996); Gen. Mans JEAN PIERRE SMEETS, KLAUS KRÜGER.

Banco Finansur, SA: Corrientes 400, C1043AAQ Buenos Aires; tel. (11) 4324-3400; fax (11) 4322-4687; e-mail bafin@bancofinansur.com.ar; internet www.bancofinansur.com.ar; f. 1973 as Finansur Compañía Financiera, SA; adopted current name in 1993; cap. and res $17.3m., dep. $55.9m., total assets $107.6m. (Dec. 2003) Pres. JORGE SÁNCHEZ CÓRDOVA; 5 brs.

Banco de Galicia y Buenos Aires SA: Juan D. Perón 407, Casilla 86, C1038AAI Buenos Aires; tel. (11) 6329-0000; fax (11) 6329-6100; e-mail bancogalicia@bancogalicia.com.ar; internet www.bancogalicia.com.ar; f. 1905; cap. $468.6m., res $1,834.9m., dep. $6,207.0m. (Dec. 2004); Chair. ANTONIO R. GARCÉS; 281 brs.

Banco Itaú, SA (Brazil): 25 de Mayo 476, 2°, C1002ABJ Buenos Aires; tel. (11) 4325-6698; fax (11) 4394-1057; internet www.itau.com.ar; fmrly Banco Itaú Argentina, SA, renamed as above following purchase of Banco del Buen Ayre, SA, in 1998; cap. and res $20.2m., dep. $1.2m. (June 1992); Pres. OLAVO EGYDIO SETUBAL; 78 brs.

Banco Macro Bansud, SA: Sarmiento 447, C1041AAI Buenos Aires; tel. (11) 5222-6500; fax (11) 5222-6624; e-mail international@macrobansud.com.ar; internet www.macrobansud.com; f. 1995 as Banco Bansud after merger of Banesto Banco Shaw, SA, and Banco del Sud, SA; adopted current name in 2002 following merger with Banco Macro (f. 1988); cap. $608.9m., res $250.0m., dep. $4,349.2m. (Dec. 2005); Pres. JORGE HORACIO BRITO; 149 brs.

Banco Mariva, SA: Sarmiento 500, C1041AAJ Buenos Aires; tel. (11) 4321-2200; fax (11) 4321-2222; e-mail info@mariva.com.ar; internet www.mariva.com.ar; f. 1980; cap. and res $88.1m., dep. $179.5m. (Dec. 2004); Pres. RICARDO MAY.

Banco Patagonia Sudameris Argentina, SA: Juan D. Perón 500, C1038AAJ Buenos Aires; tel. (11) 4132-6055; fax (11) 4132-6059; e-mail international@patagoniasudameris.com.ar; internet www.patagoniasudameris.com.ar; f. 1912 as Banco Sudameris; adopted current name in 2003 following merger with Banco Patagonia; cap. $89.0m., res $11.5m., dep. $977.2m. (Dec. 1998); Chair. JOSÉ MARÍA DAGNINO PASTORE.

Banco Regional de Cuyo, SA: San Martín 841, M5500AAI Mendoza; tel. (261) 449-8800; fax (261) 449-8801; internet www

ARGENTINA

Directory

.bancoregional.com.ar; f. 1961; Pres. and Gen. Man. José Federico López; 12 brs.

Banco Río de la Plata, SA: Bartolomé Mitre 480, C1036AAH Buenos Aires; tel. (11) 4341-1000; fax (11) 4342-8962; internet www.bancorio.com.ar; f. 1908; cap. $440.2m., res $808.1m., dep. $13,716.8m. (Dec. 2004); Pres. José Luis Enrique Cristofani; 266 brs.

Banco de San Juan: Ignacio de la Roza 85, J5402DCA San Juan; tel. (264) 429-1000; fax (264) 421-4126; internet www.bancosanjuan.com; f. 1943; 25% owned by provincial govt of San Juan; 75% privately owned; Pres. Enrique Eskenazi; Gen. Man. Raúl Riobó; 8 brs.

Banco Santiago del Estero: Belgrano 529 Sur, G4200AAF Santiago del Estero; tel. (385) 422-2300; e-mail info@bse.com.ar; internet www.bse.com.ar; dep. $69.9m., total assets $101.6m. (Jan. 1995); Pres. Américo Daher.

Banco de Valores, SA: Sarmiento 310, C1041AAH Buenos Aires; tel. (11) 4323-6900; fax (11) 4334-1731; e-mail info@banval.sba.com.ar; internet www.bancodevalores.com; f. 1978; cap. $10.0m., res $45.4m., dep. $623.3m. (Dec. 2005); Pres. Jorge A. Cozzani; 1 br.

Banex: San Martín 136, C1004AAD Buenos Aires; tel. (11) 4340-3000; fax (11) 4334-4402; e-mail infobcra@banex.com.ar; internet www.banex.com.ar; f. 1998 by merger of Exprinter Banco with Banco San Luis, SA; cap. $34.5m., res $71.6m., dep. $406.4m. (Dec. 2005); Pres. Julio Patricio Supervielle; Gen. Man. Gabriel Coqueugniot; 23 brs.

BBVA Banco Francés, SA: Reconquista 199, C1003ABC Buenos Aires; tel. (11) 4346-4000; fax (11) 4346-4320; internet www.bancofrances.com; f. 1886 as Banco Francés del Río de la Plata, SA; changed name to Banco Francés, SA, in 1998 following merger with Banco de Crédito Argentino; adopted current name in 2000; cap. $368.1m., res $2,543.3m., dep. $10,654.1m. (Dec. 2002); Chair. Gervásio Collar Zavaleta; CEO and Gen. Man. Antonio Martínez-Jorquera; 308 brs.

HSBC Bank Argentina, SA: Avda de Mayo 701, 27°, C1084AAC Buenos Aires; tel. (11) 4344-3333; fax (11) 4334-6679; internet www.hsbc.com.ar; f. 1978 as Banco Roberts, SA; name changed to HSBC Banco Roberts, SA, in 1998; adopted current name in 1999; cap. $1,109.9m., res $1,068.4m., dep. $5,040.9m. (June 2004); Pres. Antonio M. Losada; 68 brs.

Nuevo Banco de Entre Ríos SA: Monte Caseros 128, E3100ACD Paraná; tel. (343) 423-1200; fax (343) 421-1221; e-mail exterior.cambios@nuevobersa.com.ar; internet www.nuevobersa.com.ar; f. 1935; provincial bank; transferred to private ownership in 1995; cap. $20.4m., dep. $624.5m. (Dec. 2002); Pres. Ricardo Matías Taddeo; 73 brs.

Nuevo Banco Industrial de Azul, SA: Córdoba 675, C1054AAF Buenos Aires; tel. (11) 4311-4666; fax (11) 4315-8113; e-mail info@bancoazul.com; internet www.bancoazul.com; f. 1971; Pres. and Gen. Man. Alberto Meta; 2 brs.

Nuevo Banco Suquía, SA: 25 de Mayo 160, X5000ELD Córdoba; tel. (351) 420-0200; fax (351) 420-0443; internet www.bancosuquia.com.ar; f. 1961 as Banco del Suquía, SA; adopted current name in 1998; dep. $2,051.0m. (June 2000); Pres. José P. Porta; Gen. Man. Raúl Fernández; 100 brs.

Co-operative Bank

Banco Credicoop Cooperativo Ltdo: Reconquista 484, C1003ABJ Buenos Aires; tel. (11) 4320-5000; fax (11) 4324-5891; e-mail credicoop@bancocredicoop.coop; internet www.credicoop.com.ar; f. 1979; cap. $0.7m., res $546.5m., dep. $2,324.9m. (June 2003); Pres. Raúl Guelman; Gen. Man. Carlos Heller; 227 brs.

Bankers' Associations

Asociación de Bancos del Interior de la República Argentina (ABIRA): Corrientes 538, 4°, C1043AAS Buenos Aires; tel. (11) 4394-3439; fax (11) 4394-5682; f. 1956; Pres. Dr Jorge Federico Christensen; Dir Raúl Passano; 30 mems.

Asociación de Bancos Públicos y Privados de la República Argentina (ABAPPRA): Florida 470, 1°, C1005AAJ Buenos Aires; tel. (11) 4322-6321; fax (11) 4322-6721; e-mail info@abappra.com.ar; internet www.abappra.com; f. 1959; Pres. Enrique Olivera; Man. Luis B. Bucafusco; 31 mems.

Federación de Bancos Cooperativos de la República Argentina (FEBANCOOP): Maipú 374, 9°/10°, C1006ACB Buenos Aires; tel. (11) 4394-9949; f. 1973; Pres. Omar C. Trillo; Exec. Sec. Juan Carlos Romano; 32 mems.

STOCK EXCHANGES

Mercado de Valores de Buenos Aires, SA: 25 de Mayo 367, 8°–10°, C1002ABG Buenos Aires; tel. (11) 4313-6021; fax (11) 4313-4472; e-mail merval@merval.sba.com.ar; internet www.merval.sba.com.ar; f. 1929; Pres. Pablo Aldazabal.

There are also stock exchanges at Córdoba, Rosario, Mendoza and La Plata.

Supervisory Authority

Comisión Nacional de Valores (CNV): 25 de Mayo 175, C1002ABC Buenos Aires; tel. (11) 4342-4607; fax (11) 4331-0639; e-mail webadm@cnv.gov.ar; internet www.cnv.gob.ar; monitors capital markets; Pres. Eduardo Hecker.

INSURANCE

In March 2001 there were 222 insurance companies operating in Argentina, of which 121 were general insurance companies. The following is a list of those offering all classes or a specialized service.

Supervisory Authority

Superintendencia de Seguros de la Nación: Julio A. Roca 721, 5°, C1067ABC Buenos Aires; tel. (11) 4338-4000; fax (11) 4331-9821; e-mail consultasydenuncias@ssn.gov.ar; internet www.ssn.gov.ar; f. 1938; Supt Miguel Baelo.

Major Companies

Argos Cía de Seguros Argentina, SA: Esmeralda 288, 6°, C1035ABF Buenos Aires; tel. (11) 4323-1200; fax (11) 4326-5851; Pres. Luis Ksairi.

Aseguradora de Créditos y Garantías, SA (ACG): Corrientes 415, 4°, C1043AAE Buenos Aires; tel. (11) 4320-7200; fax (11) 4320-7277; e-mail infoacg@bristolgroup.com.ar; internet www.bristolgroup.com.ar; f. 1961; part of the Bristol Group; Pres. Horacio G. Scapparone.

Aseguradores de Cauciones, SA: Paraguay 580, C1057AAF Buenos Aires; tel. (11) 5235-3700; fax (11) 5235-3784; e-mail consultas@caucion.com.ar; internet www.caucion.com.ar; f. 1968; all classes; Pres. José de Vedia.

Chiltington Internacional, SA: Reconquista 559, 8°, C1003ABK Buenos Aires; tel. (11) 4312-8600; fax (11) 4312-8884; e-mail msmith@chiltington.com.ar; internet www.chiltington.co.uk; Dir Martin Smith.

Chubb Argentina de Seguros, SA: Ing. Butty 240, 16°, C1001AFB Buenos Aires; tel. (11) 4510-1500; fax (11) 4510-1545; e-mail argentinainfo@chubb.com; internet www.chubb.com/international/argentina; f. 2003; Pres. Alfredo Lauro Rovira.

Columbia, SA de Seguros: Juan D. Perón 690, C1038AAN Buenos Aires; tel. (11) 4326-1240; fax (11) 4326-1392; f. 1918; all classes; Pres. Juan Pedro E. Castelli; Gen. Man. José Luis Pini.

El Comercio, Cía de Seguros a Prima Fija, SA: Corrientes 415, 3° y 5°, C1043AAE Buenos Aires; tel. (11) 4394-1300; fax (11) 4393-1311; internet www.bristolgroup.com.ar; f. 1889; all classes; Pres. Horacio Scapparone; Vice-Pres. Antonio Altieri.

Cía Argentina de Seguros de Créditos a la Exportación, SA: Corrientes 345, 7°, C1043AAD Buenos Aires; tel. (11) 4313-4303; fax (11) 4313-2919; internet www.casce.com; f. 1967; covers credit and extraordinary and political risks for Argentine exports; Pres. Dr Luis Orcoyen; Gen. Man. Dr Mariano A. García Galisteo.

General & Cologne Re (Sur), Cía de Reaseguros, SA: Arenales 707, 3°, C1061AAA Buenos Aires; tel. (11) 4114-7000; fax (11) 4114-7001; internet www.genre.com; Gen. Man. Juan J. Comerio.

La Meridional, Cía Argentina de Seguros SA: Juan D. Perón 646, C1038AAN Buenos Aires; tel. (11) 4909-7000; fax (11) 4909-7274; internet www.lameridional.com.ar; f. 1949; life and general; Pres. Guillermo V. Lascano Quintana; Gen. Man. Peter Hammer.

Metropol Cía Argentina de Seguros, SA: Sarmiento 1182–1190, 3°, Buenos Aires; tel. (11) 4443-3830; Pres. Carlos Alberto Pino.

Prudential Seguros, SA: Leandro N. Alem 855, 5°, C1001AAD Buenos Aires; tel. (11) 4891-5000; internet www.prudentialseguros.com.ar; Pres. Martín Eduardo Gauto.

La República Cía Argentina de Seguros Generales, SA: San Martín 627, 4°, C1004AAM Buenos Aires; tel. (11) 4314-1000; fax (11) 4318-8778; e-mail ccastell@republica.com.ar; internet www.republica.com.ar; f. 1928; group life and general; Pres. José Tomás Guzman Dumas; Gen. Man. Eduardo Escriña.

Royal & SunAlliance, Argentina: Buenos Aires; tel. (11) 4339-0000; internet www.royalsun.com.ar; f. 1996; Pres. Kelvin Edwards.

La Unión Gremial, SA: Lavalle 538, C1047AAL Buenos Aires; tel. (11) 4394-3342; fax (341) 425-9802; f. 1908; general; Gen. Man. Eduardo Ignacio Llobet.

Victoria Seguros, SA: Florida 556, C1005AAL Buenos Aires; tel. (11) 4322-1100; fax (11) 4325-9016; internet www.victoria.com.ar; Pres. Sebastián Bagó.

ARGENTINA

Zurich-Iguazú Cía de Seguros, SA: San Martín 442, C1004AAJ Buenos Aires; tel. (11) 4329-0400; fax (11) 4322-4688; f. 1947; all classes; Pres. RAMÓN SANTAMARINA.

Reinsurance

Instituto Nacional de Reaseguros: Julio A. Roca 694, C1067ABO Buenos Aires; tel. (11) 4334-0084; fax (11) 4334-5588; f. 1947; reinsurance in all branches; Pres. and Man. REINALDO A. CASTRO.

Insurance Associations

Asociación Argentina de Cías de Seguros (AACS): 25 de Mayo 565, 2°, C1002ABK Buenos Aires; tel. (11) 4312-7790; fax (11) 4312-6300; e-mail secret@aacsra.org.ar; internet www.aacsra.org.ar; f. 1894; 32 mems; Pres. ROBERTO F. E. SOLLITTO.

Asociación de Entidades Aseguradoras Privadas de la República Argentina (EAPRA): Esmeralda 684, 4°, C1007ABL Buenos Aires; tel. (11) 4393-2268; fax (11) 4393-2283; f. 1875; asscn of 12 foreign insurance cos operating in Argentina; Pres. Dr PIERO ZUPPELLI; Sec. BERNARDO VON DER GOLTZ.

Trade and Industry

GOVERNMENT AGENCIES

Agencia de Desarrollo de Inversiones: Julio A. Roca 651, 5°, Sector 20, C1067ABB Buenos Aires; tel. (11) 4349-3442; fax (11) 4349-3453; e-mail adi@mecon.gov.ar; internet www.inversiones.gov.ar; promotion of investment in Argentina; supervised by the Secretaría de Industria, Comercio y de la Pequeña y Mediana Empresa.

Cámara de Exportadores de la República Argentina: Roque S. Peña 740, 1°, C1035AAP Buenos Aires; tel. (11) 4394-4351; fax (11) 4328-1003; e-mail contacto@cera.org.ar; internet www.cera.org.ar; f. 1943; export promotion; 700 mems; Pres. Dr ENRIQUE S. MANTILLA.

Consejo Federal de Inversiones: San Martín 871, C1004AAQ Buenos Aires; tel. (11) 4317-0700; e-mail info@cfired.org.ar; internet www.cfired.org.ar; federal board to co-ordinate domestic and foreign investment and provide technological aid for the provinces; f. 1959; Sec.-Gen. Ing. JUAN JOSÉ CIÁCERA.

Dirección de Forestación (DF): Paseo Colón 982, anexo jardín, C1063ACW Buenos Aires; tel. (11) 4349-2124; fax (11) 4349-2102; e-mail bfores@mecon.gov.ar; assumed the responsibilities of the national forestry commission (Instituto Forestal Nacional—IFONA) in 1991, following its dissolution; supervised by the Secretaría de Agricultura, Ganadería, Pesca y Alimentación; maintains the Centro de Documentación e Información Forestal; Library Man. NILDA E. FERNÁNDEZ.

Instituto de Desarrollo Económico y Social (IDES): Araoz 2838, C1425DGT Buenos Aires; tel. (11) 4804-4949; fax (11) 4804-5856; e-mail ides@ides.org.ar; internet www.ides.org.ar; f. 1960; investigation into social sciences and promotion of social and economic devt; 700 mems; Pres. LUIS BECCARIA; Sec. ROSALIA CORTES.

Oficina Nacional de Control Comercial Agropecuario (ONCCA): Paseo Colón 922, C1063ACW Buenos Aires; tel. (11) 4349-2034; fax (11) 4349-2005; e-mail infooncca@mecon.gov.ar; internet www.oncca.gov.ar; oversees the agricultural sector; supervised by the Secretaría de Agricultura, Ganadería, Pesca y Alimentación.

Organismo Nacional de Administración de Bienes (ONABE): J. M. Ramos Mejía 1302, 3°, Of. 300, C1104AJN Buenos Aires; tel. (11) 4318-3458; e-mail prensa@onabe.gov.ar; internet www.onabe.gov.ar; responsible for overseeing privatization of state property.

Secretaría de Agricultura, Ganadería, Pesca y Alimentación: Paseo Colón 922, 1°, Of. 146, C1063ACW Buenos Aires; tel. (11) 4349-2000; fax (11) 4349-2292; e-mail comunica@sagpya.minproduccion.gov.ar; internet www.sagpya.mecon.gov.ar; f. 1871; undertakes regulatory, promotional, advisory and administrative responsibilities on behalf of the meat, livestock, agriculture and fisheries industries; Sec. MIGUEL SANTIAGO CAMPOS.

DEVELOPMENT ORGANIZATIONS

Instituto para el Desarrollo Social Argentino (IDESA): Belgrano 456, 4°, C1092AAR Buenos Aires; tel. (11) 4345-0775; e-mail atorres@idesa.org; internet www.idesa.org; Pres. OSVALDO GIORDANO; Exec. Dir ALEJANDRA TORRES.

Instituto Argentino del Petróleo y Gas: Maipú 645, 3°, C1006ACG Buenos Aires; tel. (11) 4325-8008; fax (11) 4393-5494; e-mail informa@iapg.org.ar; internet www.iapg.org.ar; f. 1958; established to promote the devt of petroleum exploration and exploitation; Pres. ENRIQUE RODOLFO POURTEAU.

Directory

Sociedad Rural Argentina: Florida 460, C1005AAJ Buenos Aires; tel. (11) 4324-4700; fax (11) 4324-4774; e-mail prensa@sra.org.ar; internet www.ruralarg.org.ar; f. 1866; private org. to promote the devt of agriculture; Pres. Dr LUCIANO MIGUENS; 9,400 mems.

CHAMBERS OF COMMERCE

Cámara Argentina de Comercio: Leandro N. Alem 36, C1003AAN Buenos Aires; tel. (11) 5300-9000; fax (11) 5300-9058; e-mail gerencia@cac.com.ar; internet www.cac.com.ar; f. 1924; Pres. CARLOS RAÚL DE LA VEGA.

Cámara de Comercio, Industria y Producción de la República Argentina: Florida 1, 4°, C1005AAA Buenos Aires; tel. (11) 4331-0813; fax (11) 4331-9116; e-mail cacipra@fibertel.com.ar; internet www.cacipra.org.ar; f. 1913; Pres. Dr MARÍA ARSENIA TULA; 1,500 mems.

Cámara de Comercio Exterior de Rosario: Córdoba 1868, Rosario, S2000AXD Santa Fe; tel. and fax (341) 425-7147; e-mail consultas@commerce.com.ar; internet www.commerce.com.ar; f. 1958; deals with imports and exports; Pres. JUAN CARLOS RETAMERO; Vice-Pres. GUILLERMO BECCANI; 150 mems.

Similar chambers are located in most of the larger centres and there are many foreign chambers of commerce.

INDUSTRIAL AND TRADE ASSOCIATIONS

Asociación Argentina de Químicos y Coloristas: Bulnes 1425, C1176ACA Buenos Aires; tel. (11) 4963-0394; e-mail aaqct@aaqct.org.ar; f. 1954; textile industry; Pres. GUILLERMO CEVASCO.

Asociación de Importadores y Exportadores de la República Argentina: Belgrano 124, 1°, C1092AAO Buenos Aires; tel. (11) 4342-0010; fax (11) 4342-1312; e-mail aiera@aiera.org.ar; internet www.aiera.org.ar; f. 1966; Pres. HORACIO CONSOLO; Man. ADRIANO DE FINA.

Asociación de Industrias Argentinas de Carnes: San Martín 390, 10°, C1004AAH Buenos Aires; tel. (11) 4394-9734; e-mail aiacsmm@cotelco.com.ar; meat industry; refrigerated and canned beef and mutton; Pres. JORGE BORSELLA.

Bodegas de Argentina: Güemes 4464, C1425BLF Buenos Aires; tel. (11) 4774-2529; fax (11) 4774-4873; e-mail sperez1904@sinectis.com; internet www.bodegasdeargentina.org; f. 1904; wine industry; Pres. LUCIANO COTUMACCIO; Man. MARIO J. GIORDANO.

Cámara de Sociedades Anónimas: Libertad 1340, C1016ABB Buenos Aires; tel. and fax (11) 4000-7399; e-mail camsocanon@camsocanon.com; internet www.camsocanon.com; Pres. JUAN CARLOS LANNUTTI; Man. EDUARDO BACQUÉ.

Centro de Exportadores de Cereales: Bouchard 454, 7°, C1106ABF Buenos Aires; tel. (11) 4311-1697; fax (11) 4312-6924; f. 1943; grain exporters; Pres. RAÚL S. LOEH.

Confederaciones Rurales Argentinas: México 628, 2°, C1097AAN Buenos Aires; tel. (11) 4261-1501; Pres. ARTURO J. NAVARRO.

Coordinadora de Actividades Mercantiles Empresarias: Buenos Aires; Pres. OSVALDO CORNIDE.

Federación Agraria Argentina (FAA): Alfonsina Storni 745, S2000DYA, Rosario, Santa Fe; tel. (341) 512-2000; fax (341) 512-2001; e-mail faaba@faa.com.ar; internet www.faa.com.ar; f. 1912; oversees the interests of small and medium-sized grain producers; Pres. EDUARDO BUZZI.

Federación Lanera Argentina: 25 de Mayo 516, 4°, C1002ABL Buenos Aires; tel. (11) 4878-8800; fax (11) 4878-8804; e-mail info@flasite.com; internet www.flasite.com; f. 1929; wool industry; Pres. JULIO AISENSTEIN; Sec. GEORGES J. LEFEBVRE; 40 mems.

EMPLOYERS' ORGANIZATION

Unión Industrial Argentina (UIA): Leandro N. Alem 1067, 11°, C1001AAF Buenos Aires; tel. (11) 4313-4474; fax (11) 4313-2413; e-mail uia@uia.org.ar; internet www.uia.org.ar; f. 1887; re-established in 1974 with the fusion of the Confederación Industrial Argentina (CINA) and the Confederación General de la Industria; following the dissolution of the CINA in 1977, the UIA was formed in 1979; asscn of manufacturers, representing industrial corpns; Pres. ALBERTO ALVAREZ GAIANI; Sec. JUAN CARLOS SACCO.

UTILITIES

Regulatory Authorities

Energía Argentina, SA (ENARSA): Neuquén; f. 2004; state-owned; Dir EXEQUIEL ESPINOSA.

Ente Nacional Regulador de la Electricidad (ENRE): Avda Eduardo Madero 1020, 10°, C1106ACX Buenos Aires; tel. (11) 4314-5805; fax (11) 4314-5416; internet www.enre.gov.ar; Vice-Pres. RICARDO MARTÍNEZ LEONE.

ARGENTINA

Ente Nacional Regulador del Gas (ENARGAS): Suipacha 636, 10°, C1008AAN Buenos Aires; tel. (11) 4325-9292; fax (11) 4348-0550; internet www.enargas.gov.ar; Insp. Dr JUAN CARLOS PEZOA.

Electricity

CAPEX: Melo 630, Vicente López, C1163ADB Buenos Aires; tel. (11) 4796-6000; e-mail info@capex.com.ar; internet www.capex.com.ar; f. 1988; electricity generation; Chair. ENRIQUE GÖTZ; Vice-Chair. ALEJANDRO GÖTZ.

Central Costanera, SA (CECCO): España 3301, C1107ANA Buenos Aires; tel. (11) 4307-3040; fax (11) 4307-1706; generation, transmission, distribution and sale of thermal electric energy; Chair. JAIME BAUZÁ BAUZÁ.

Central Puerto, SA (CEPU): Tomás Edison 2701, C1104BAB Buenos Aires; tel. (11) 4317-5000; fax (11) 4317-5099; electricity generating co; CEO HORACIO TURRI.

Comisión Nacional de Energía Atómica (CNEA): Avda del Libertador 8250, C1429BNP Buenos Aires; tel. (11) 4704-1384; fax (11) 4704-1176; e-mail freijo@cnea.edu.ar; internet www.cnea.gov.ar; f. 1950; scheduled for transfer to private ownership; nuclear energy science and technology; Pres. JOSÉ PABLO ABRIATA.

Comisión Técnica Mixta de Salto Grande (CTMSG): Leandro N. Alem 449, C1003AAE Buenos Aires; e-mail ctmsgda@sion.com; internet www.saltogrande.org; operates Salto Grande hydroelectric station, which has an installed capacity of 650 MW; joint Argentine-Uruguayan project; Pres. JULIO CÉSAR FREYRE.

Dirección Provincial de Energía: Calle 55, 570, La Reja, 1900 Buenos Aires; tel. (11) 4415-000; fax (11) 4216-124; e-mail webmaster@dpe.mosp.gba.gov.ar; internet www.dpe.mosp.gba.gov.ar; f. 1957; as Dirección de Energía de la Provincia de Buenos Aires; name changed as above in 2000; electricity co for province of Buenos Aires.

Empresa Distribuidora y Comercializadora Norte, SA (EDENOR): Azopardo 1025, C1107ADQ Buenos Aires; tel. (11) 4348-2121; fax (11) 4334-0805; e-mail ofitel@edenor.com.ar; internet www.edenor.com.ar; distribution of electricity; Pres. FERNANDO PONASSO.

Empresa Distribuidora Sur, SA (EDESUR): San José 140, C1076AAD Buenos Aires; tel. (11) 4381-8981; fax (11) 4383-3699; internet www.edesur.com.ar; f. 1992; distribution of electricity; Gen. Man. JOSÉ MARÍA HIDALGO.

Entidad Binacional Yacyretá: Eduardo Madero 942, 21°–22°, C1106ACW Buenos Aires; tel. (11) 4510-7500; e-mail rrpp@eby.org.ar; internet www.eby.org.ar; operates the hydroelectric dam at Yacyretá on the Paraná river; owned jointly by Argentina and Paraguay; completed in 1998, it is one of the world's largest hydroelectric complexes, consisting of 20 generators with a total generating capacity of 2,700 MW; Exec. Dir OSCAR ALFREDO THOMAS.

Hidronor Ingeniería y Servicios, SA (HISSA): Hipólito Yrigoyen 1530, 6°, C1089AAD Buenos Aires; tel. and fax (11) 4382-6316; e-mail info@hidronor.com; internet www.hidronor.com.ar; fmrly HIDRONOR, SA, the largest producer of electricity in Argentina; responsible for developing the hydroelectric potential of the Limay and neighbouring rivers; Pres. CARLOS ALBERTO ROCCA; transferred to private ownership in 1992 and divided into the following companies.

Central Hidroeléctrica Alicurá, SA: Leandro N. Alem 712, 7°, C1001AAP Buenos Aires.

Central Hidroeléctrica Cerros Colorados, SA: Leandro N. Alem 690, 12°, C1001AAO Buenos Aires.

Central Hidroeléctrica El Chocón, SA: Suipacha 268, 9°, Of. A, C1008AAF Buenos Aires.

Hidroeléctrica Piedra del Aguila, SA: Tomás Edison 1251, C1104AYL Buenos Aires; tel. and fax (11) 4311-3296; Pres. Dr JÉRÔME FERRIER; Gen. Man. HORACIO TURRI.

Transener, SA: Paseo Colón 728, 6°, C1063ACU Buenos Aires; tel. (11) 4342-6925; fax (11) 4342-7147; e-mail info-trans@transx.com.ar; internet www.transener.com.ar; energy transmission co; Gen. Man. SILVIO RESNICH.

Petrobrás Energía, SA: Maipú 1, 22°, C1084ABA Buenos Aires; tel. (11) 4344-6000; fax (11) 4331-8369; internet www.petrobrasenergia.com; f. 1946 as Pérez Companc, SA; petroleum interests acquired by Petrobrás of Brazil in 2003; operates the hydroelectric dam at Pichi Picún Leufu; Chair. JORGE GREGORIO PÉREZ COMPANC.

Gas

Asociación de Distribuidores de Gas (ADIGAS): Diagonal Norte 740, 5° B, C1035AAP Buenos Aires; tel. (11) 4393-8294; e-mail consultas@adigas.com.ar; internet www.adigas.com.ar; f. 1993 to represent newly privatized gas companies; Gen. Man. CARLOS ALBERTO ALFARO.

Distribuidora de Gas del Centro, SA: Hipólito Yrigoyen 475, X5000JHE Córdoba; tel. (351) 468-8100; fax (351) 468-1568; e-mail clientescentro@ecogas.com.ar; internet www.ecogas.com.ar/appweb/leo/centro/centro.php; state-owned co; distributes natural gas in Córdoba, Catamarca and La Rioja.

Distribuidora de Gas Cuyana, SA: Hipólito Yrigoyen 475, X5000JHE Córdoba; tel. (351) 468-8100; fax (351) 468-1568; e-mail clientescuyo@ecogas.com.ar; internet www.ecogas.com.ar/appweb/leo/cuyo/cuyo.php; state-owned co; distributes natural gas in Mendoza, San Juan, San Luis.

Gas Natural Ban, SA: Isabel la Católica 939, C1268ACS Buenos Aires; tel. (11) 4303-1380; internet www.gasnaturalban.com.ar; f. 1992; distribution of natural gas; Gen. Man. ANTONI PERIS MINGOT.

Metrogás, SA: Gregorio Aráoz de Lamadrid 1360, C1267AAB Buenos Aires; tel. (11) 4309-1434; fax (11) 4309-1025; f. 1992; gas distribution; Chair. RICK LYNN WADDELL; Dir LUIS AGUSTO DOMENECH.

Transportadora de Gas del Norte, SA: Don Bosco 3672, 3°, C1206ABF Buenos Aires; tel. (11) 4959-2000; fax (11) 4959-2242; internet www.tgn.com.ar; f. 1992; distributes natural gas; Gen. Man. FREDDY CAMEO.

Transportadora de Gas del Sur, SA (TGS): Don Bosco 3672, 5°, C1206ABF Buenos Aires; tel. (11) 4865-9050; fax (11) 4865-9059; e-mail totgs@tgs.com.ar; internet www.tgs.com.ar; f. 1992; processing and transport of natural gas; Gen. Dir EDUARDO OJEA QUINTANA.

Water

Aguas Argentinas: Buenos Aires; internet www.aguasargentinas.com.ar; distribution of water in Buenos Aires; privatized in 1993; Dir-Gen. JEAN-LOUIS CHAUSSADE.

TRADE UNIONS

Central de los Trabajadores Argentinos (CTA): Independencia 766, C1099AAU Buenos Aires; tel. (11) 4307-3829; e-mail internacional@cta.org.ar; internet www.cta.org.ar; dissident trade union confederation; Gen. Sec. VÍCTOR DE GENNARO; Int. Sec. PEDRO WASIEJKO.

Confederación General del Trabajo (CGT) (General Confederation of Labour): Azopardo 802, C1107ADN Buenos Aires; tel. (11) 4343-1883; e-mail secgral@cgtra.org.ar; internet www.cgtra.org.ar; f. 1984; Peronist; represents approx. 90% of Argentina's 1,100 trade unions; Sec.-Gen. HUGO MOYANO.

Movimiento de Trabajadores Argentinos (MTA): Buenos Aires; dissident trade union confederation.

Transport

Comisión Nacional de Regulación del Transporte (CNRT): Maipú 88, Apdo 129, C1000WAB Buenos Aires; tel. (11) 4819-3000; e-mail msenet@mecon.gov.ar; internet www.cnrt.gov.ar; regulates domestic and international transport services.

Secretaría de Transporte de la Nación: Hipólito Yrigoyen 250, 12°, C1086AAB Buenos Aires; tel. (11) 4349-7254; fax (11) 4349-7201; e-mail transporte@minplan.gov.ar; internet www.transporte.gov.ar; oversees and co-ordinates the Secretarías de Transporte Automotor, de Transporte Ferroviario, de Transporte Aerocomercial y de Puertos y Vías Navegables.

RAILWAYS

Lines: General Belgrano (narrow-gauge), General Roca, General Bartolomé Mitre, General San Martín, Domingo Faustino Sarmiento (all wide-gauge), General Urquiza (medium-gauge) and Línea Metropolitana, which controls the railways of Buenos Aires and its suburbs. There are direct rail links with the Bolivian Railways network to Santa Cruz de la Sierra and La Paz; with Chile, through the Las Cuevas–Caracoles tunnel (across the Andes) and between Salta and Antofagasta; with Brazil, across the Paso de los Libres and Uruguayana bridge; with Paraguay (between Posadas and Encarnación by ferry-boat); and with Uruguay (between Concordia and Salto). In 2005 there were 32,170 km of tracks.

Plans for the privatization of the state-run Ferrocarriles Argentinos (FA) were initiated in 1991. In 1993 central government funding for the FA was suspended and responsibility for existing intercity passenger routes was devolved to respective provincial governments. However, owing to lack of resources, few provinces have successfully assumed the operation of services, and many trains have been suspended. At the same time, long-distance freight services were sold as six separate 30-year concessions (including lines and rolling stock) to private operators. In the mid-1990s the FA was replaced by Ente Nacional de Administración de Bienes Ferroviarios (ENABIEF), which assumed responsibility for railway infrastructure and the rolling stock not already sold off. The Buenos Aires commuter system was divided into eight concerns (one of which incorporates the underground railway system) and was offered for

ARGENTINA

sale to private operators as 10- or 20-year (subsidized) concessions. The railway network is currently regulated by the Comisión Nacional de Regulación del Transporte (CNRT—see above).

Ferrocarriles Metropolitanos, SA (FEMESA): Bartolomé Mitre 2815, C1201AAA Buenos Aires; tel. (11) 4865-4135; fax (11) 4861-8757; internet www.femesa.com.ar; f. 1991 to assume responsibility for services in the capital; 820 km of track; concessions to operate services have been awarded to the following companies:

Ferrovías: Ramos Mejía 1430, C1104AJO Buenos Aires; tel. (11) 4314-1444; fax (11) 3311-1181; internet www.ferrovias.com.ar; f. 1994; operates northern commuter line (Belgrano Norte) in Buenos Aires; Pres. Gabriel Romero.

Metropolitano: Gen. Hornos 11, 3°, Of. 316A, C1154ACA Buenos Aires; tel. (11) 4778-5800; fax (11) 4778-5878; e-mail eltren@metropolitano.com.ar; internet www.metropolitano.com.ar; f. 1995; operates three commuter lines; 304-km network.

Metrovías (MV): Bartolomé Mitre 3342, C1201AAL Buenos Aires; tel. (11) 4959-6800; fax (11) 4866-3037; e-mail info@metrovias.com.ar; internet www.metrovias.com.ar; f. 1994; operates subway (Subterráneos de Buenos Aires—Subte, q.v.), a light rail line (Premetro) and Urquiza commuter line; Pres. Aldo Roggio.

Trenes de Buenos Aires, SA (TBA): Avda Ramos Mejía 1358, C1104AJN Buenos Aires; tel. (11) 4317-4400; fax (11) 4317-4409; e-mail prensa@tbanet.com.ar; internet www.tbanet.com.ar; took over operations of the Mitre and Sarmiento commuter lines from state in 1995; 400 km of track; Pres. Marcelo Calderón; Vice-Pres. Jorge Alvarez.

Cámara de Industriales Ferroviarios: Alsina 1609, 1°, C1088AAO Buenos Aires; tel. (11) 4371-5571; e-mail cifra@24horas.com; private org. to promote the devt of Argentine railway industries; Pres. Ana María Guibaudi.

The following consortia were awarded 30-year concessions to operate rail services in the 1990s:

ALL Mesopotámica: Santa Fe 4636, 3°, C1425BHV Buenos Aires; tel. (11) 4778-2425; fax (11) 4778-2493; internet www.rrdc.com/op_argentina_all_meso.html; f. 1993 as Ferrocarril Mesopotámico, bought by Brazil's América Latina Logística, SA, in 1999; operates freight services on the Urquiza lines; Exec. Dir Roberto Monteiro; 2,240 km of track.

Ferrobaires: Gen. Hornos 11, 4°, C1154ACA Buenos Aires; tel. (11) 4305-5174; fax (11) 4305-5933; e-mail calidadservicio@ferrobaires.gba.gov.ar; internet www.ferrobaires.gba.gov.ar; f. 1993; owned by the govt of the Province of Buenos Aires; local services; Pres. G. Crespo.

Ferroexpreso Pampeano (FEPSA): Conesa 1073, C1426AQU Buenos Aires; tel. (11) 4014-7900; operates services on the Rosario–Bahía Blanca grain lines; 5,094 km of track.

Ferrosur Roca (FR): Bouchard 680, 8°, C1106ABJ Buenos Aires; tel. (11) 4319-3900; fax (11) 4319-3901; e-mail ferrosur@elsitio.net; internet www.ferrosur.com.ar; f. 1993; operator of freight services on the Roca lines; 3,000 km of track.

Nuevo Central Argentino, SA (NCA): Avda Eduardo Madero 1020, 16°, C1106ACX Buenos Aires; f. 1993; operates freight services on the Bartolomé Mitre lines; 5,011 km of track.

Buenos Aires also has an underground railway system:

Subterráneos de Buenos Aires (Subte): Bartolomé Mitre 3342, C1201AAL Buenos Aires; tel. (11) 4862-6844; fax (11) 4864-0633; f. 1913; completely state-owned in 1951–93, responsibility for operations was transferred in 1993 to a private consortium, Metrovías (q.v.), with a 20-year concession; fmrly controlled by the Municipalidad de la Ciudad de Buenos Aires; five underground lines totalling 39.5 km, 69 stations, and a 7.4 km light rail line (Premetro) with 16 stations; Pres. Alberto Verra.

ROADS

In 2002 there were 215,434 km of roads, of which 29.5% were paved. Four branches of the Pan-American highway run from Buenos Aires to the borders of Chile, Bolivia, Paraguay and Brazil. In 1996 9,932 km of main roads were under private management. Construction work on a 41-km bridge across the River Plate (linking Punta Lara in Argentina with Colonia del Sacramento in Uruguay) was scheduled to begin in the late 1990s; however, by mid-2007 the agreement with Uruguay to build the bridge still had not been ratified by the Congreso.

Dirección Nacional de Vialidad: Julio A. Roca 783, C1067ABC Buenos Aires; tel. (11) 4343-8520; internet www.vialidad.gov.ar; controlled by the Secretaría de Transportes; Gen. Man. Nelson Guillermo Periotti.

Asociación Argentina de Empresarios Transporte Automotor (AAETA): Bernardo de Irigoyen 330, 6°, C1072AAH Buenos Aires; e-mail aaeta@sei.com.ar; internet www.aaeta.org.ar; f. 1941; Pres. Dr Juan Zunino.

Federación Argentina de Entidades Empresarias de Autotransporte de Cargas (FADEEAC): Sánchez de Bustamante 54, C1173AAB Buenos Aires; tel. (11) 4860-7700; fax (11) 4383-7870; e-mail fadeeac@fadeeac.org.ar; internet www.fadeeac.org.ar; Pres. Luis A. Morales.

There are several international passenger and freight services, including:

Autobuses Sudamericanos, SA: Tres Arroyos 287, C1414EAC Buenos Aires; tel. (11) 4857-3065; fax (11) 4307-1956; f. 1928; international bus services; car and bus rentals; charter bus services; Pres. Armando Schlecker Hirsch; Gen. Man. Miguel Angel Ruggiero.

INLAND WATERWAYS

There is considerable traffic in coastal and river shipping, mainly carrying petroleum and its derivatives.

Dirección Nacional de Construcciones Portuarias y Vías Navegables: España 221, 4°, Buenos Aires; tel. (11) 4361-5964; responsible for the maintenance and improvement of waterways and dredging operations; Dir Ing. Enrique Casals de Alba.

SHIPPING

There are more than 100 ports, of which the most important are Buenos Aires, Quequén and Bahía Blanca. There are specialized terminals at Ensenada, Comodoro Rivadavia, San Lorenzo and Campana (petroleum); Bahía Blanca, Rosario, Santa Fe, Villa Concepción, Mar del Plata and Quequén (cereals); and San Nicolás and San Fernando (raw and construction materials). In 2006 Argentina's merchant fleet totalled 565 vessels, with a combined aggregate displacement of 837,800 grt.

Administración General de Puertos: Avda Ing. Huergo 431, 1°, C1107AOE Buenos Aires; tel. (11) 4343-2425; fax (11) 4331-0298; e-mail institucionales@puertobuenosaires.gov.ar; internet www.puertobuenosaires.gov.ar; f. 1956; state enterprise for direction, administration and exploitation of all national sea- and river-ports; scheduled for transfer to private ownership; Gen. Sec. Dr Carlos Ferrari.

Capitanía General del Puerto: Julio A. Roca 734, 2°, C1067ABP Buenos Aires; tel. (11) 434-9784; f. 1967; co-ordination of port operations; Port Capt. Capt. Pedro Taramasco.

Administración General de Puertos (Santa Fe): Duque 1 Cabacera, Santa Fe; tel. (42) 41732.

Consorcio de Gestión del Puerto de Bahía Blanca: Dr Mario M. Guido s/n, 8103 Provincia de Buenos Aires; tel. (91) 57-3213; Pres. José E. Conte; Sec.-Gen. Claudio Marcelo Conte.

Terminales Portuarias Argentinas: Buenos Aires; operates one of five recently privatized cargo and container terminals in the port of Buenos Aires.

Terminales Río de la Plata: Buenos Aires; operates one of five recently privatized cargo and container terminals in the port of Buenos Aires.

Other private shipping companies operating on coastal and overseas routes include:

Antártida Pesquera Industrial: Calle Dr M. Moreno 1270, 5°, C1091AAZ Buenos Aires; tel. (11) 4381-0167; fax (11) 4381-0519; Pres. J. M. S. Miranda; Man. Dir J. R. S. Miranda.

Astramar Cía Argentina de Navegación, SAC: Buenos Aires; tel. (11) 4311-3678; fax (11) 4311-7534; Pres. Enrique W. Reddig.

Bottacchi SA de Navegación: Buenos Aires; tel. (11) 4392-7411; fax (11) 411-1280; Pres. Angel L. M. Bottacchi.

Maruba S. en C. por Argentina: Maipú 535, 7°, C1006ACE Buenos Aires; tel. (11) 4322-7173; fax (11) 4322-3353; Chartering Man. R. J. Dickin.

CIVIL AVIATION

Argentina has 10 international airports (Aeroparque Jorge Newbery, Córdoba, Corrientes, El Plumerillo, Ezeiza, Jujuy, Resistencia, Río Gallegos, Salta and San Carlos de Bariloche). Ezeiza, 35 km from Buenos Aires, is one of the most important air terminals in Latin America. More than 30 airports were scheduled for transfer to private ownership.

Aerolíneas Argentinas: Bouchard 547, 9°, C1106ABG Buenos Aires; tel. (11) 4317-3000; fax (11) 4320-2116; internet www.aerolineas.com.ar; f. 1950; 97.9% stake acquired by the Spanish company AirComet Marsans in 2001; services to North and Central America, Europe, the Far East, New Zealand, South Africa and destinations throughout South America; the internal network covers the whole country; passengers, mail and freight are carried; Pres. Antonio Mata.

Austral Líneas Aéreas (ALA): Corrientes 485, 9°, C1043AAE Buenos Aires; tel. (11) 4317-3600; fax (11) 4317-3777; internet www.austral.com.ar; f. 1971; domestic flights linking 27 cities in Argentina; Pres. MANUEL CASERO.

Aerovip: Ricardo Rojas 401, 5°, C1001AEA Buenos Aires; tel. (11) 4312-6954; fax (11) 4312-7080; f. 1999; domestic scheduled and charter flights.

Líneas Aéreas del Estado (LADE): Perú 710, C1068AAF Buenos Aires; tel. (11) 4361-7071; fax (11) 4362-4899; e-mail director@lade.com.ar; f. 1940; Dir GUILLERMO JOSÉ TESTONI.

Líneas Aéreas Federales, SA (LAFSA): Buenos Aires; f. 2003; founded following the suspension of operations of Líneas Aéreas Privadas Argentinas and Dinar Líneas Aéreas; co-operation accord signed with Southern Winds Líneas Aéreas in Sept. 2003 (annulled by the Govt in Feb. 2005); signed a co-operation accord with Línea Aérea Nacional de Chile in March 2005, with a view to the creation of Línea Aérea Nacional de Argentina.

Southern Winds Líneas Aéreas: Quaglia 262, Local 13, Buenos Aires; internet www.fly-sw.com; f. 1996; co-operation accord signed with Líneas Aéreas Federales, SA in Sept. 2003 (annulled by the Govt in Feb. 2005); Pres. JUAN MAGGIO.

Transporte Aéreo Costa Atlántica (TACA): Bernardo de Yrigoyen 1370, 1°, Ofs 25–26, C1086AAX Buenos Aires; tel. (11) 4307-1956; fax (11) 4307-8899; f. 1956; domestic and international passenger and freight services between Argentina and Bolivia, Brazil and the USA; Pres. Dr ARMANDO SCHLECKER HIRSCH.

Transportes Aéreos Neuquén: Diagonal 25 de Mayo 180, Q8341XAN Neuquén; tel. (299) 442-3076; fax (299) 448-8926; e-mail tancentr@satlink.com.ar; domestic routes; Pres. JOSÉ CHALÉN; Gen. Man. PATROCINIO VALVERDE MORAIS.

Valls Líneas Aéreas: Río Grande, Tierra del Fuego; f. 1995; operates three routes between destinations in southern Argentina, Chile and the South Atlantic islands.

Tourism

Argentina's superb tourist attractions include the Andes mountains, the lake district centred on Bariloche (where there is a National Park), Patagonia, the Atlantic beaches and Mar del Plata, the Iguazú falls, the Pampas and Tierra del Fuego. Tourist arrivals in Argentina in 2004 totalled some 3.4m. In that year tourism receipts amounted to US $2,990m.

Instituto Nacional de Promoción Turística: Suipacha 1111, 20°, C1088AAW Buenos Aires; tel. (11) 4316-1600; fax (11) 4313-6834; e-mail inprotur@turismo.gov.ar; internet www.argentina.travel.

Asociación Argentina de Agencias de Viajes y Turismo (AAAVYT): Viamonte 640, 10°, B6015XAA Buenos Aires; tel. (11) 4325-4691; fax (11) 4322-9641; e-mail secretaria@aaavyt.org.ar; internet www.aaavyt.org.ar; f. 1951; Pres. TOMÁS RICARDO ROZA; Sec. VERÓNICA REINHOLD.

ARMENIA

Introductory Survey

Location, Climate, Language, Religion, Flag, Capital

The Republic of Armenia is situated in the western South Caucasus, on the north-eastern border of Turkey. Its other borders are with Iran to the south, Azerbaijan to the east, and Georgia to the north. Naxçıvan, an exclave of Azerbaijan, is situated to the south. The climate is typically continental: dry, with wide temperature variations. Winters are cold, the average January temperature in Yerevan being −3°C (26°F), but summers can be very warm, with August temperatures averaging 25°C (77°F), although high altitude moderates the heat in much of the country. Precipitation is low in the Yerevan area (annual average 322 mm), but much higher in the mountains. The official language is Armenian, the sole member of a distinct Indo-European language group. It is written in the Armenian script. Most of the population are adherents of Christianity, the largest denomination being the Armenian Apostolic Church. There are also Russian Orthodox, Protestant, Islamic and Yazidi communities. The national flag (approximate proportions 2 by 3) consists of three equal horizontal stripes, of red, blue and orange. The capital is Yerevan.

Recent History

Although Armenia was an important power in ancient times, and formed the first Christian state, around AD 300, for much of its history it was ruled by foreign states. In 1639 Armenia was partitioned, with the larger, western part being annexed by the Osmanlı (Ottoman) Empire and the eastern region becoming part of the Persian Empire. In 1828 eastern Armenia was ceded to the Russian Empire by the Treaty of Turkmanchai. At the beginning of the 20th century Armenians living in western, or Anatolian, Armenia, under Ottoman rule, were subject to increasing persecution by the Turks. As a result of brutal massacres and deportations (particularly in 1915), the Anatolian lands were largely emptied of their Armenian population, and it was estimated that during 1915–22 some 1.5m. Armenians perished. After the collapse of Russian imperial power in 1917, Russian Armenia joined the anti-Bolshevik Transcaucasian Federation, which included Georgia and Azerbaijan. This collapsed when threatened by Turkish forces, and on 28 May 1918 Armenia was proclaimed an independent state. Without Russian protection, however, the newly formed republic was forced to cede territory around Kars to the Turks. Armenia was recognized as an independent state by the Allied Powers and by Turkey in the Treaty of Sèvres, signed on 10 August 1920. However, the rejection of the Treaty by the new Turkish leader, Mustafa Kemal, left Armenia vulnerable to renewed Turkish threats. In September Turkish troops attacked Armenia, but they were prevented from establishing full control over the country by the invasion of Russian Bolshevik troops, and the founding, on 29 November, of a Soviet Republic of Armenia. In December 1922 the republic became a member, together with Georgia and Azerbaijan, of the Transcaucasian Soviet Federative Socialist Republic (TSFSR), which, in turn, became a constituent republic of the USSR. In 1936 the TSFSR was dissolved, and the Armenian Soviet Socialist Republic (SSR) was formed as a full union republic of the USSR.

The Soviet authorities implemented a policy of forced modernization and industrialization. A programme to collectivize agriculture was enforced in 1930 and many thousands of peasants who opposed it were deported. Thousands more Armenians were executed or imprisoned during the late 1930s. During the Second World War (1939–45), Armenia avoided occupation by German forces, despite their invasion of the USSR in 1941. Consequently, the republic provided an essential source of labour for the Soviet economy, and as many as 600,000 Armenians served in the Soviet armies (of whom an estimated 350,000 were killed). In the late 1940s an estimated 150,000 Armenians of the diaspora returned to the republic.

The Soviet leader Mikhail Gorbachev's policies of perestroika (restructuring) and glasnost (openness), introduced following his accession to power in 1985, had little initial impact in Armenia. The first manifestations of the new policies were campaigns against corruption in the higher echelons of the Communist Party of Armenia (CPA). The most significant of the historical and ethnic concerns discussed from late 1987 was the status of Nagornyi Karabakh (known as Artsakh in Armenian), an autonomous oblast (region) within neighbouring Azerbaijan, largely populated by Armenians, control of which had been ceded to Azerbaijan in 1921 (see the chapter on Azerbaijan). In February 1988 up to 1m. people took part in demonstrations in Yerevan, the Armenian capital, organized by a group of Yerevan intellectuals, known as the Karabakh Committee, to support demands from Armenian inhabitants of Nagornyi Karabakh for the incorporation of the territory into the Armenian SSR. In response to increased unrest within Armenia, many Azeris began to leave the republic. Reports of ill-treatment of Azeris in Armenia and Nagornyi Karabakh led to anti-Armenian riots in Sumqayıt, Azerbaijan, in late February, in which 26 Armenians died. This event provoked further Armenian anger, which was compounded by the ruling of the Presidium of the USSR's Supreme Soviet (legislature) that Nagornyi Karabakh should remain under Azerbaijani jurisdiction. The inability of the local authorities to control ongoing unrest led to the dismissal, in May, of the First Secretary (leader) of the CPA. In December, however, the issue of Nagornyi Karabakh was temporarily subordinated to the problem of overcoming the effects of a severe earthquake, which had struck northern Armenia. Some 25,000 people were reported to have been killed and many thousands more were made homeless. Following the earthquake, members of the (outlawed) Karabakh Committee were arrested, ostensibly for interfering in relief work. They were released in May 1989, after huge demonstrations took place, protesting against their continued internment. Meanwhile, in January, the Soviet Government had formed a Special Administration Committee (SAC) of the Council of Ministers to preside over Nagornyi Karabakh, although the enclave remained under formal Azerbaijani jurisdiction. In September Azerbaijan announced the closure of its borders with Armenia, and prohibited trade with the republic, seriously affecting the reconstruction programme required in Armenia after the 1988 earthquake. In November the SAC was disbanded, and Azerbaijan resumed control over Nagornyi Karabakh. This prompted the Armenian Supreme Soviet to declare the territory part of a 'unified Armenian Republic', although this pronouncement was declared to be unconstitutional by the USSR Supreme Soviet in January 1990.

The increasing disillusionment with the Soviet Government was apparently responsible for the low level of participation in the elections to the Armenian Supreme Soviet, which took place in May–July 1990. The Armenian Pan-National Movement (APNM), the successor to the Karabakh Committee, was the largest single party, with some 35% of the seats in the legislature. Supported by other non-communist groups, Levon Ter-Petrossian, a leader of the APNM, was elected to the chairmanship of the Supreme Soviet. Vazgen Manukian, also an APNM leader, was appointed Prime Minister. On 23 August the legislature adopted a declaration of sovereignty, including a demand for international recognition that the Turkish massacres of Armenians in 1915 constituted genocide. The Armenian SSR was renamed the Republic of Armenia.

The Armenian Government refused to enter into the negotiations between Soviet republics on a new treaty of union, which took place in late 1990 and early 1991, and boycotted the referendum on the renewal of the USSR, which was held in March 1991 in nine republics. Instead, the legislature decided to conduct a referendum on secession from the USSR, to be held in September. In late April there was an escalation of tension in Nagornyi Karabakh. The Armenian Government denied any direct involvement in the violence, a claim disputed by Azerbaijan. Meanwhile, Armenia suggested that the Soviet leadership was supporting Azerbaijan, following the latter's agreement to sign the new union treaty.

The attempted coup in the Soviet and Russian capital, Moscow, in August 1991 provided further support for those advocating Armenian independence. According to the official results of the referendum organized by the republican authorities on 21 September, 99.3% of those participating (some 94.4% of the electorate) supported Armenia's reconstitution as 'an independent, democratic state outside the Union'. On 23 September, instead of conforming to the Soviet law on secession (which had been adopted in April and provided for a transitional period of at least five years before full independence could be achieved), the Supreme Soviet declared Armenia to be, thenceforth, a fully independent state. Meanwhile, a congress of the CPA voted to dissolve the party.

The independence declaration was followed, on 16 October 1991, by an election to the post of President of the Republic. Six candidates participated in the poll, which was won by Ter-Petrossian (with some 87% of the votes cast). The Armenian leadership joined the Commonwealth of Independent States (CIS, see p. 215), signing the founding Almaty (Alma-Ata) Declaration on 21 December. In early 1992 Armenia was admitted to the Conference on Security and Co-operation in Europe (CSCE—now the Organization for Security and Co-operation in Europe—OSCE, see p. 354) and the UN.

In 1992 economic conditions deteriorated, and there were widespread shortages of foodstuffs and fuel. The situation was exacerbated by the continuing conflict in Nagornyi Karabakh (see below), and also by fighting in neighbouring Georgia (which impeded supplies to Armenia) and the closure of borders with Azerbaijan. Compounding the economic crisis was an influx of refugees from Nagornyi Karabakh and elsewhere in Azerbaijan. There were also increasing indications of public dissatisfaction with the Ter-Petrossian administration, and in mid-August 1992 and in February 1993 mass rallies were staged in Yerevan to demand the President's resignation. Earlier in February Ter-Petrossian had dismissed the Prime Minister, Khosrov Haroutunian, and a new Council of Ministers was subsequently announced, headed by Hrant Bagratian, who was widely regarded as an economic reformist. However, the economic crisis intensified, partly as a result of Turkey, Azerbaijan's ally, closing its borders with Armenia and imposing economic sanctions against the country in April 1993. In the latter half of 1994 thousands of people participated in frequent anti-Government protests, organized by an association of opposition groups, known as the Union of Civic Accord. The assassination in December of a former mayor of Yerevan prompted the Government to effect a number of measures that it described as aimed at eliminating terrorism, the most radical of which was the suspension of the leading opposition party, the Armenian Revolutionary Federation (ARF, or Dashnaktsutiun), which had formed the Government of independent Armenia in 1918–20).

Armenia's first post-Soviet legislative elections were held in July 1995. Some 13 parties and organizations contested the 190 seats of the new Azgayin Zhoghov (National Assembly). Nine parties, including the ARF, were barred from participation. The Republican bloc (an alliance of six groups, led by the APNM) won a majority of the seats in the assembly (119), and 45 independent candidates were elected. In late July Ter-Petrossian appointed a new Government, in which Bagratian remained as Prime Minister. A referendum on a new constitution was held simultaneously with the general election. Of the 56% of the electorate who participated in the plebiscite, some 68% voted in favour of the Constitution, which granted wide-ranging executive authority to the President and provided for a smaller, 131-member Azgayin Zhoghov with effect from the next general election.

A presidential election was held on 22 September 1996. Ter-Petrossian was the candidate of the Republican bloc, while five opposition parties united to support Manukian, now the Chairman of the National Democratic Union (NDU). Although preliminary results indicated that Ter-Petrossian had been re-elected, the opposition made allegations of widespread electoral malpractice, and thousands staged protest rallies in Yerevan. International observers reported serious irregularities in the electoral proceedings. On 25 September supporters of Manukian stormed the Azgayin Zhoghov, injuring, among others, the Chairman and his deputy. According to the final results, Ter-Petrossian received 51.8% of the votes cast, and Manukian secured 41.3%. Bagratian resigned as Prime Minister, reportedly in response to opposition to his programme of economic reforms, in November; he was replaced by Armen Sarkissian. The latter resigned in March 1997 on grounds of ill health, and was succeeded by Robert Kocharian, hitherto the 'President' of the self-styled 'Republic of Nagornyi Karabakh', in what was regarded as an attempt by Ter-Petrossian to reduce pressure from nationalist opposition parties.

Following the resignation of Ter-Petrossian on 3 February 1998, owing to controversy over his support of an OSCE plan concerning Nagornyi Karabakh (see below), a presidential election was held on 16 and 30 March. In the second round of voting, Kocharian, the acting President, secured victory over the former CPA leader, Karen Demirchian, obtaining 59.5% of the votes cast, and was inaugurated as President on 9 April. On the following day Kocharian appointed Armen Darbinian, the erstwhile Minister of Finance and the Economy, as Prime Minister. In early May Kocharian legalized the ARF, and appointed two members of the party, including its leader, Vahan Hovhanissian, to positions in the Government.

In the elections to the Azgayin Zhoghov, held on 30 May 1999, the Unity bloc, an alliance of the Republican Party of Armenia (RPA) and the People's Party of Armenia (PPA), won 55 of 131 elective seats; 32 independent candidates were elected. The CPA secured 11 seats and the ARF obtained nine. On 11 June 1999 Darbinian (who became Minister of the Economy) was replaced as Prime Minister by Vazgen Sarkissian, the unofficial leader of the RPA and hitherto Minister of Defence. Meanwhile, Demirchian, by this time head of the PPA, was elected as legislative Chairman.

On 27 October 1999 five gunmen entered the Azgayin Zhoghov and opened fire, killing eight people, including Prime Minister Sarkissian, Demirchian and his two deputies, and a cabinet minister. The gunmen, who claimed no political affiliation, announced that they were seeking revenge against the 'corrupt political élite'. On their surrender the assailants were charged with murder and terrorist offences. (Their trial commenced in February 2001.) In the aftermath of the attack, the Ministers of the Interior and of National Security tendered their resignations. At the beginning of November 1999 Armen Khachatrian of the PPA was elected legislative Chairman. Aram Sarkissian, the younger brother of the murdered premier, was subsequently appointed Prime Minister. In May 2000 Kocharian dismissed Aram Sarkissian, appointing as his successor Andranik Markarian, the leader of the RPA, prior to the implementation of a cabinet reshuffle.

The PPA left the Unity bloc in September 2001. In October the PPA, together with the recently formed Republic grouping and the National Unity Party, organized a rally to demand the impeachment of the President, whom they accused of precipitating a socio-economic crisis in the country, acting in contravention of the Constitution and condoning terrorism. In April 2002 thousands of people participated in protests against the closure of the independent television station, A1+, which opposition parties claimed to be politically motivated, and further demands were made for the President's resignation. In the same month legislation was adopted abolishing the death penalty, although the new law was not to apply retroactively to those found guilty of perpetrating terrorist (including the parliamentary killings of October 1999) or paedophile offences. In September 2002 the Council of Europe (see p. 225) threatened Armenia with expulsion from the organization, unless it agreed to the unconditional abolition of capital punishment by June 2003. In September of that year the Government finally ratified a complete ban on capital punishment.

In August 2002 legislation was approved increasing the number of deputies elected by majority vote through single-mandate constituencies from 37 to 56. The composition of the Central Electoral Commission was also reorganized, with three of its nine members henceforth to be presidential appointments. In December 2002 the Ministry of Internal Affairs and the Ministry of National Security were restructured as non-ministerial institutions, and renamed the Police of the Republic of Armenia and the National Security Service, although the respective former ministers remained part of the Government.

Nine candidates participated in the presidential election held on 19 February 2003. Kocharian narrowly failed to secure the 50% required to secure an outright victory, attracting 49.5% of the ballot. In the second round, held on 5 March, Kocharian was re-elected as President with 67.5% of the votes cast, defeating Stepan Demirchian (the son of the assassinated parliamentary Chairman), the candidate of the PPA. Monitors from both the OSCE and the Council of Europe recorded irregularities in electoral procedure, and thousands of people took part in protests against the results, which were, none the less, declared valid by the Constitutional Court in mid-April.

Legislative elections were held on 25 May 2003, in which the pro-presidential RPA won 32 seats, the Law-Governed Country Party of Armenia received 18 seats, the Justice bloc (led by Demirchian, and comprising the Armenian Democratic Party of the former premier Aram Sarkissian, the National Democratic

Party, the People's Party of Armenia and the Union of National Democrats) secured 15 seats and the ARF obtained 11. However, once again international observers and opposition parties reported incidences of electoral malpractice. A referendum on proposed constitutional amendments, held simultaneously with the elections, failed to attract the support of the requisite one-third of registered voters. On 11 June the RPA, the Law-Governed Country Party and the ARF formed a coalition Government, again led by Markarian. The Chairman of the Law-Governed Country Party, Artur Baghdasarian, was appointed Chairman of the Azgayin Zhoghov. Members of both the Justice bloc and the National Unity Party boycotted parliamentary sessions until September, in protest at the results of the election.

In November 2003 Armen Sarkissian, brother of the former premiers Vazgen and Aram Sarkissian, was sentenced to 15 years' imprisonment, after being found guilty of organizing the killing of Tigran Naghdalian, the Chairman of the Board of Armenian Public Television and Radio, in December 2002. Sarkissian denied the charge, which he claimed had been politically motivated. In December 2003 six men were sentenced to life imprisonment for their involvement in the attack on the Azgayin Zhoghov in October 1999 (one other defendant was imprisoned for 14 years).

The legislative boycott by the parties of the Justice bloc and the National Unity Party was resumed from February 2004, following the refusal of the Azgayin Zhoghov to debate constitutional amendments allowing for a referendum of confidence in the President (the boycott continued on a selective basis for much of the following two years). In April–June 2004 demonstrations organized by those parties boycotting the legislature began in Yerevan, in protest against the conduct of the presidential election of 2003 and to urge Kocharian's resignation; demonstrators were, at times, forcibly dispersed and arrested by the security forces. Two of the Law-Governed Country Party's three ministerial representatives left office in 2004.

The issue of proposed constitutional reform (in relation to which the Government had committed itself, in negotiations with the Council of Europe, to holding a constitutional referendum by mid-2005 at the latest) remained a contentious topic within both the legislature and the Government. An initial draft document was rejected by the Venice Commission of the Council of Europe in May 2005. Draft constitutional amendments were finally approved by the Azgayin Zhoghov in September, although the main opposition parties appealed for a boycott of the referendum, which was scheduled for November. The proposed amendments were, *inter alia*, to limit the powers of the President and enhance those of the judiciary, in order to comply with Council of Europe standards. In October the USA announced a US $6m. plan to facilitate the conduct of free and fair elections in the country, to be implemented from 2006, in preparation for legislative elections in 2007 and a presidential election in 2008. The constitutional referendum took place on 27 November 2005, with a rate of participation by the electorate of some 65.3%, according to official figures, although these were strongly disputed by the opposition; the results indicated that some 94.5% of valid votes were cast in favour of the proposed constitutional amendments. In late November and early December a coalition of opposition parties held demonstrations in protest at the perceived falsification of the results. In mid-December Markarian acknowledged that some electoral violations had taken place, and in January 2006 the Parliamentary Assembly of the Council of Europe (PACE) issued a statement condemning the exaggerated rate of participation and the falsification of results.

Meanwhile, in November 2005 a number of former members of Republic, including former mayor of Yerevan Albert Bazeian and a former Minister of Defence, Vagarshak Haroutiunian, established the National Revival Party. In the same month Samuel Babaian, a high-profile former 'Minister of Defence' of Nagornyi Karabakh, established a new, moderate political party, Alliance. In December a prominent businessman and member of the legislature, Gagik Tsarukian, founded the Prosperous Armenia party, which became active in charitable activities, drawing accusations of 'vote buying' in advance of the legislative elections due to be held in May 2007.

On 12 May 2006 Baghdasarian resigned as Chairman of the Azgayin Zhogov and withdrew the Law-Governed Country Party of Armenia from the governing coalition; he had begun to position himself in opposition to the Government through criticism of its management of the referendum and by declaring a more overtly pro-Western and pro-North Atlantic Treaty Organization (NATO, see p. 340) foreign policy stance. Some members of the party defected to other political blocs in response to Baghdasarian's actions, including the Minister of Urban Planning, who retained his governmental post. The United Labour Party agreed to co-operate with the remaining members of the coalition and was allocated the ministerial portfolio for culture and other senior official posts. Tigran Torossian of the RPA was elected to succeed Baghdasarian as Chairman of the Azgayin Zhogov. In July the influential Minister of Defence, Serge Sarkissian, joined the ruling RPA and was appointed to a senior position in the party. In December 2006 the authorities claimed to have thwarted a plot to stage a coup; Zhirair Sefilian, a former military commander during the war in Nagornyi Karabakh, was arrested (and subsequently deported) as one of the founders of the recently formed Union of Armenian Volunteers, which was alleged to be behind the plot.

On 25 March 2007 Prime Minister Markarian died unexpectedly, having suffered a heart attack; he was succeeded as premier, on 4 April, by Serge Sarkissian, who had also been appointed as acting President of the RPA. Sarkissian was succeeded as Minister of Defence later in the month by the hitherto Chief of General Staff of the Armed Forces, Col-Gen. Mikhail Haroutunian; all other members of the outgoing government remained in post; however, the forthcoming parliamentary elections meant that these appointments were effectively on an interim basis.

Legislative elections were held according to schedule on 12 May 2007. The RPA garnered 33.91% of the votes cast, securing 64 seats, while its allies, Prosperous Armenia and the ARF, were placed second and third, with 15.13% of the ballot (25 seats) and 13.16% (16 seats), respectively. Two opposition parties obtained the minimum 5% threshold of votes required to secure parliamentary representation: the Law-Governed Country Party of Armenia attracted 7.05% of the vote (nine seats), while the Heritage Party won 6.00% (seven seats). The OSCE and the International Election Observation Mission (IEOM), which was supported by the OSCE and several European institutions, adjudged the polls, overall, to have been conducted fairly. However, the IEOM observed that regulations to prevent instances of vote-buying had not been adequately implemented and that there remained considerable inequality in the conditions under which the various parties had campaigned; the IEOM also identified a considerable proportion (17%) of polling stations at which vote-counting was deemed to have been poor. Four opposition parties, among them the Republican Party, filed appeals with the Constitutional Court, protesting against these and other alleged electoral irregularities and demanding the holding of fresh elections. However, their appeals were rejected by the Court, which ruled that the polls had been fair and free.

Despite securing an outright majority, the RPA reached an agreement with Prosperous Armenia and the ARF to form a coalition administration, which collectively controlled 105 of the 131 seats in parliament. Sarkissian was returned to the position of Prime Minister by President Kocharian and the new Azgayin Zhogov was inaugurated in early June 2007. The new Government was announced two weeks later, and included six new personnel; 11 of the ministries were allocated to the RPA, and three each to Prosperous Armenia and the ARF. The RPA's decision to enter into a coalition was widely perceived to reflect an intention on the part of Sarkissian to broaden his base of political support in advance of a forthcoming presidential election. By the time the Central Election Commission announced, in early November, that the poll was to be held on 19 February 2008, former President Ter-Petrossian had firmly established himself as the principal challenger to the candidacy of Sarkissian (who was formally nominated by the RPA as the party candidate on the following day). While Sarkissian focused his electoral campaign on a range of proposed measures intended to eradicate poverty, Ter-Petrossian's principal pledge was to secure the participation of the Nagornyi Karabakh leadership (with whom the former President had met in October 2007—see below) in any future peace negotiations, a scenario to which the Azerbaijani Government remained opposed. A total of nine candidates, including Sarkissian and Ter-Petrossian, had submitted formal applications by the registration deadline in December.

The presidential poll was duly conducted on 19 February 2008; according to official results, Sarkissian secured 52.8% of votes cast and Ter-Petrossian 21.5% of votes. Ter-Petrossian (and other opposition candidates) immediately attributed the results to widespread falsification and demanded that the ballot be repeated, prompting his followers to stage mass protests in his support. Ter-Petrossian claimed that he had been placed under house arrest. On 1 March President Kocharian declared a 20-day state of emergency, after the continued protests by opposition supporters in the capital, Yerevan, were violently suppressed by special police units and interior ministry forces, who killed eight demonstrators. A number of associates of Ter-Petrossian were detained, and some 30 prominent opposition members were subsequently arrested on charges of precipitating the clashes with the police. On 8 March the Constitutional Court upheld the final official election results, rejecting an appeal by Ter-Petrossian. On 9 April Kocharian nominated Tigran Sarkissian, hitherto the Governor of the Central Bank of Armenia, as Prime Minister, pending the approval of his appointment by the legislature and the formation of a new administration. Later in the month a new administration was formed, in which 10 of the 17 ministerial appointments remained unchanged. The new appointees included Armen Gevorgian as Deputy Prime Minister and Minister of Territorial Administration, Edvard Nalbandian as Minister of Foreign Affairs and Seyran Ohanian as Minister of Defence. The reorganization also incorporated the creation of a new ministry, of Emergency Situations.

The proclamation of Armenia's independence in September 1991 led to an escalation of hostilities in the disputed oblast of Nagornyi Karabakh in Azerbaijan. In that month the territory declared itself an independent republic, and violence intensified following the dissolution of the USSR in December. In January 1992 the President of Azerbaijan, Ayaz Mutalibov, placed the region under direct presidential rule; in the same month Azerbaijani forces surrounded and attacked Xankandi (Khankandi, or Stepanakert, in Armenian), the capital of Nagornyi Karabakh, while the Armenians laid siege to Şuşha (Shushi), a town with a mainly Azeri population. In May the Nagornyi Karabakh 'self-defence forces' (which the Armenian Government continued to claim were operating without its military support) captured Şuşha, thereby gaining complete control of the enclave and ending the bombardment of Xankandi. With the capture of the strategically important Laçin valley, the ethnic Armenian militia succeeded in opening a 'corridor' within Azerbaijan linking Nagornyi Karabakh with Armenia.

In June 1992 Azerbaijani forces launched a sustained counter-offensive in Nagornyi Karabakh, recapturing villages both inside and around the enclave, and expelling several thousand inhabitants, thus exacerbating the already urgent refugee crisis. In August Azerbaijani forces resumed the bombardment of Xankandi. In response, the Nagornyi Karabakh legislature declared a state of martial law, and a state defence committee, in close alignment with the Ter-Petrossian administration of Armenia, replaced the territory's Government.

In early 1993 ethnic Armenian forces undertook a series of successful offensives in and around Nagornyi Karabakh. With the capture of the Kelbacar district in April 1993, a second, lengthier corridor, linking the territory with Armenia, was formed, and ethnic Armenians effectively secured control of all Azerbaijani territory between Kelbacar in the north and Laçin in the south. Many thousands of Azeris fled or were expelled from their homes in this region. The Armenian position was further strengthened by the growing political turmoil in Azerbaijan in mid-1993 (see the chapter on Azerbaijan), and by late June Armenian forces had secured full control of Nagornyi Karabakh. The Armenian seizure of Azerbaijani territory prompted widespread international condemnation, particularly by Turkey and Iran, the latter fearing a massive influx of refugees. UN Security Council Resolutions 822 and 853, which demanded the withdrawal of occupying and local Armenian forces from Azerbaijan, went unheeded; hostilities intensified further, and more than 20% of Azerbaijan's total territory was reported to have been captured by the Nagornyi Karabakh forces, who had extended their operations as far south as the Azerbaijan–Iran border; Azerbaijani forces recaptured some territory in a counter-offensive launched in December. In February 1994 it was reported that as many as 18,000 people had been killed since 1988, with a further 25,000 wounded. The number of displaced Azeris was believed to have exceeded 1m.

A series of fragile cease-fire agreements was reached in early 1994. In May, following protracted mediation by the CSCE and Russia, a new cease-fire agreement was signed by the Ministers of Defence of Armenia and Azerbaijan and representatives of Nagornyi Karabakh. The agreement was formalized in July. Ter-Petrossian held talks with the President of Azerbaijan, Heydar Aliyev, in Moscow, in September, but Aliyev stated that his willingness to negotiate a peace accord depended on the unconditional withdrawal of Armenian forces from Azerbaijani territory. Negotiations were held at regular intervals throughout 1995, under the aegis of the OSCE's 11-nation Minsk Group, although only limited progress towards a political settlement was made. Nevertheless, only sporadic violations of the cease-fire were reported, and in May the three sides carried out a large-scale exchange of prisoners of war. Direct discussions between Armenia and Azerbaijan, which were held in conjunction with the OSCE negotiations, were initiated in December.

Elections to the post of 'President' of Nagornyi Karabakh, held in November 1996, were condemned by Azerbaijan and criticized by the Minsk Group as a hindrance to the peace process. Robert Kocharian, the incumbent, was re-elected with some 86% of the votes cast. In December Ter-Petrossian and Aliyev attended an OSCE summit meeting in Lisbon, Portugal. Following the submission of demands by Azerbaijan, the OSCE Chairman issued a statement recommending three principles that would form the basis of a future political settlement in the enclave: the territorial integrity of Armenia and Azerbaijan; the legal status of Nagornyi Karabakh, which would be granted broad autonomy within Azerbaijan; and security guarantees for the population of Nagornyi Karabakh. Armenia, however, refused to accept the terms of the statement.

Relations between Armenia and Azerbaijan deteriorated in early 1997, with both accusing one another of stockpiling weapons. Fresh elections to the post of 'President' of Nagornyi Karabakh in September, which were scheduled following the appointment of Kocharian as Prime Minister of Armenia, were won by Arkadii Ghukassian, with some 90% of the votes cast, but were criticized by the international community. Ghukassian reportedly rejected the OSCE peace settlement on the grounds that the proposals presupposed Azerbaijan's sovereignty over the territory. A subsequent statement by President Ter-Petrossian that Nagornyi Karabakh could hope neither to gain full independence, nor to be united with Armenia, appeared to indicate a significant change in policy, but the President's moderate approach to the crisis, which provoked much government disapproval, led to his resignation in February 1998. His replacement, Kocharian, had been expected to adopt a more nationalistic stance, although in November the Armenian Government accepted new proposals put forward by the Minsk Group for a settlement of the conflict, which were based on the principle of a 'common state'. They were, however, rejected by Azerbaijan. In March 2000 Ghukassian sustained serious injuries following an attack by gunmen in Xankandi. The former 'Minister of Defence' of Nagornyi Karabakh, Samuel Babaian, was subsequently sentenced to 14 years' imprisonment in February 2001 for having orchestrated the attack (he was, however, released under an amnesty in September 2004). Ghukassian was re-elected in August 2002, with some 88.4% of the votes. Meanwhile, despite several meetings between the Armenian and Azerbaijani Presidents in 1999–2002, no substantive progress was made in reaching a final resolution of the Nagornyi Karabakh conflict. Direct negotiations did not take place in 2003, and there were initial concerns that the Azerbaijani President elected in October of that year, Ilham Aliyev (the son of the former President, Heydar Aliyev), might prove less open to discussion. However, negotiations resumed in 2004. In January 2005 PACE approved a resolution on Nagornyi Karabakh, expressing concern at large-scale ethnic expulsions and the creation of mono-ethnic areas resulting from the conflict, which were described as resembling 'the terrible concept of ethnic cleansing'; the resolution clearly branded as unacceptable the occupation of Azerbaijani territory by ethnic Armenian forces. There was also concern among the international community over significant increases in the defence expenditure of the two countries. Negotiations continued in 2005–07 but the two sides failed to reach agreement on general principles that could serve as a draft accord for resolving the conflict. In July 2006 the Minsk Group publicized for the first time the details of its fundamental criteria for an agreement between the two countries. On 10 December the territory held an internationally unrecognized referendum, which affirmed the population's desire for independence from Azerbaijan. Greater efforts towards conciliation appeared to have been made by both Armenia and Azerbaijan in the latter stages of 2007 and in early 2008 (see the chapter on Azerbaijan). Meanwhile, following the election in July 2007 of Bako Sahakian—a former head of Nagornyi Karabakh's security service—as 'President' of the disputed territory, former Armenian President Ter-Petrossian was reported to have visited Nagornyi Karabakh in October to congratulate Sahakian.

In April 1997 the Armenian legislature ratified a treaty that allowed Russia to maintain military bases in Armenia for a period of 25 years. The ties between Russia and Armenia were reinforced by a declaration of alliance and co-operation, and a number of bilateral agreements were concluded in September 2000. A further, 10-year economic co-operation agreement was signed in 2001, during a visit to Armenia by the Russian President, Vladimir Putin. Armenia's relations with Georgia were generally cordial in the post-Soviet period, and the new President of Georgia, Mikheil Saakashvili, visited Armenia in March 2004, reaffirming the stability of relations between the two countries.

Meanwhile, relations with Turkey (which controlled large areas of historic Armenia, including Mount Ararat, regarded as a national symbol by many Armenians) remained uneasy, particularly following the closure of its borders with Armenia in 1993. Moreover, Turkey refused to allow the demarcation of its border with Armenia, owing to the presence of Russian border guards in that country. In September 2001 the first meeting of a Turkish-Armenian Reconciliation Commission (TARC), composed of members from both countries, was held in Istanbul, Turkey; at a second meeting, held in New York, USA, it was agreed to ask the New York-based International Centre for Transitional Justice to establish whether the Turkish massacre of Armenians in 1915–22 had constituted 'genocide'. In February 2003 it was reported that the International Centre for Transitional Justice had concluded that the massacres of 1915–22 could be interpreted as genocide, according to international criteria. (The TARC was officially dissolved in April 2004.) In December 2004, following an appeal from President Kocharian, the European Parliament issued a statement that Turkey should recognize that genocide against Armenians had taken place in 1915, and open its borders; in September 2005 the European Parliament issued a further non-binding resolution, which indicated that Turkey's refusal to recognize the killings as genocide could adversely affect its efforts to secure membership of the European Union (EU, see p. 244). In 2006 the lower house of the French legislature, the Assemblée nationale, voted in support of proposals to outlaw the denial of genocide against the Armenians in 1915, although it appeared unlikely that these proposals would form the basis of approved legislation. Both Armenia's campaign to secure recognition of the killings as constituting genocide and its continuing conflict with Azerbaijan remained serious obstacles to the development of closer relations. The murder of a prominent ethnic-Armenian Turkish journalist in Turkey in January 2007 further heightened the sensitivity of relations between the two countries.

In October 2007 the US House of Representatives' Foreign Affairs Committee voted in favour of a non-binding resolution branding the Turkish massacre of Armenians as genocide, which provoked outrage from Turkey. However, at least partly owing to public criticism from US President George W. Bush, who warned that the damage caused to US-Turkish relations by such a resolution would be considerable, by early 2008 the resolution had yet to be referred to the full House for debate and appeared to have stalled. Meanwhile, in mid-2007 the USA donated a US $1.2m. field hospital to a special Armenian peace-keeping battalion, and in August of that year it provided the battalion with $3m. worth of military equipment to facilitate the execution of operations jointly conducted with US and NATO forces.

Armenia generally enjoyed cordial relations with Iran, with a permanent bridge between the two countries being opened in 1995. In September 2004 President Hojatoleslam Dr Sayed Muhammad Khatami of Iran made a long-postponed official visit to Armenia, signing seven bilateral agreements with President Kocharian, which, *inter alia*, were to promote enhanced co-operation in energy and transport.

In June 2000 PACE voted to admit both Armenia and Azerbaijan to the Council of Europe; they became full members in January 2001. In June 2004 Armenia, Azerbaijan and Georgia were included in the EU's new European Neighbourhood Policy and in November 2006 a five-year action plan for co-operation was adopted, focusing on eight areas of priority.

Government
Under the Constitution of 1995, the President of the Republic is Head of State and Supreme Commander-in-Chief of the armed forces, but also holds broad executive powers. The President is directly elected for a term of five years (and for no more than two consecutive terms of office). The President appoints the Prime Minister (upon the approval of the majority of members of the Azgayin Zhoghov—National Assembly) and, on the Prime Minister's recommendation, the members of the Government. Legislative power is vested in the 131-member Azgayin Zhoghov, which is elected by universal adult suffrage for a term of five years. For administrative purposes, Armenia is divided into 11 regions (*marzer*), including the capital, Yerevan. The regions are subdivided into communities (*hamaynker*). Yerevan is a *hamaynk*, with an elected mayor.

Defence
Following the dissolution of the USSR in December 1991, Armenia became a member of the Commonwealth of Independent States (CIS, see p. 215) and its Collective Security Treaty. In April 2003 the Collective Security Treaty Organization (CSTO) was inaugurated as the successor to the CIS collective security system, with the participation of Armenia, Belarus, Kazakhstan, Kyrgyzstan, Russia and Tajikistan. After 1991 Armenia began to establish its own armed forces, which numbered some 42,080, as assessed at November 2007, including an army of 38,945 and an air force of 3,135. There is also a paramilitary force of an estimated 4,748. Military service is compulsory and lasts for two years (a draft law adopted in December 2002 provided for a 42-month alternative, civilian service). As assessed at November 2007 there were approximately 3,170 Russian troops stationed on Armenian territory. In October 1994 Armenia joined NATO's 'Partnership for Peace' (see p. 342) programme of military co-operation. In December 2005 Armenia agreed an Individual Partnership Action Plan with NATO, which identified areas of the sector in need of reform, as part of efforts to strengthen relations with the Alliance. Defence expenditure in Armenia increased substantially during the mid-2000s, as was also the case in neighbouring Azerbaijan. The budget for 2007 allocated an estimated 97,900m. drams to defence.

Economic Affairs
In 2006, according to estimates by the World Bank, Armenia's gross national income (GNI), measured at average 2004–06 prices, was US $5,799m., equivalent to $1,930 per head (or $5,890 on an international purchasing-power parity basis). During 1996–2006, it was estimated, the population decreased at an average rate of 0.6% per year, while gross domestic product (GDP) per head increased, in real terms, by an annual average of 10.0%. During 1996–2006, Armenia's overall GDP increased, in real terms, by an average of 9.4% annually. Real GDP increased by 14.0% in 2005 and by 13.4% in 2006.

According to the Asian Development Bank (ADB), agriculture and forestry contributed 19.1% of GDP in 2006 and, according to the International Labour Organization (ILO), employed 46.2% of the working population. (However, FAO estimated the proportion of the working population employed in agriculture at just 10.4% in 2005.) The principal crops are potatoes and other vegetables, cereals and fruit, primarily grapes. Private farms accounted for some 98% of agricultural production by 1998. During 1996–2006, according to estimates by the World Bank, agricultural GDP increased, in real terms, at an average annual rate of 5.0%. The GDP of the sector increased by 11.2% in 2005 but declined by 2.0% in 2006, according to the World Bank.

According to the ADB, in 2005 industry (including mining, manufacturing, construction and power) contributed 44.9% of GDP. The sector (excluding utilities) employed 15.6% of the working population in 2005, according to the ILO. World Bank estimates indicated that during 1996–2006 real industrial GDP increased by an average of 11.3% annually. According to World Bank figures, the GDP of the sector increased by 19.7% in 2005 and by 14.0% in 2006.

The mining sector has not yet been extensively developed. Copper, molybdenum, gold, silver and iron are extracted on a small scale, and there are reserves of lead and zinc. There are also substantial, but largely unexploited, reserves of mineral salt, calcium oxide and carbon. Production of gold decreased significantly in the 1990s, but the Government hoped to encourage a recovery in the industry, following the conclusion of an agreement with a Canadian company to develop new extraction facilities, the first of which went into production in 1998. Gold production increased in the early 2000s, from 600 kg of gold ore in 2000 to an estimated 2,100 kg in 2004. In December 2003 the Government approved a three-year programme for the stimulation of diamond production in Armenia. According to official figures, mining accounted for 17.4% of total industrial production in 2005.

In 2006, according to the World Bank, the manufacturing sector provided 18.6% of GDP. According to official figures, in 2005 the principal branches of manufacturing, measured by volume of production, were vehicles and transport equipment, chemicals and rubber and plastics. According to the World Bank, during 1996–2006 the GDP of the manufacturing sector increased, in real terms, at an average annual rate of 5.5%. Real sectoral GDP increased by 7.4% in 2005 and by 2.0% in 2006.

Armenia is heavily dependent on imported energy, much of which is supplied by Russia (petroleum and derivatives) and Turkmenistan (natural gas). In May 2004 an agreement was concluded on the construction of a 141-km natural gas pipeline to connect the pipeline networks of Armenia and Iran, to provide Armenia with supplies of Iranian natural gas (although this, too, was likely to be sourced from Turkmenistan); construction work commenced in 2005 and was expected to be completed in 2007. In early 2006 Armenia, like several other countries of the former USSR, began to be charged increased prices for the gas supplied to it by Russia. Armenia is thought likely to have significant reserves of petroleum and natural gas, but these remain undeveloped. By July 1999 Armenia had a surplus of electricity, some of which was exported to Georgia; a new, high-voltage electricity line opened between the two countries in December 2000, and two high-voltage lines were subsequently opened to permit exports of electric energy to Iran. In 2005 Armenia, Georgia and Iran pursued plans to integrate their electricity networks and the construction of a third line was planned. In September 1999 Armenia signed an initial agreement with the European Union (EU, see p. 244), providing for the closure of the country's sole nuclear power station, at Medzamor, by 2004. However, the Government subsequently claimed that the station could be operated safely for a longer period of time, following extensive renovation, and it sought international resources for the development of adequate alternative energy facilities; in the mean time the EU and the USA funded enhanced safety measures to permit the continued use of the station. The construction of some 15 small hydroelectric power stations was initiated in 2004, and the construction of joint Armenian-Iranian hydroelectric plants on the River Araks was proposed in the mid-2000s. In 2005 nuclear power contributed 41.8% of the country's electricity output, thermoelectric power produced 28.8% and hydroelectric power provided 29.4% of the total. Imports of mineral fuels comprised 14.7% of the value of merchandise imports in 2005 and imported electricity contributed 6% of the total consumed.

The services sector contributed 36.0% of GDP in 2006, according to the ADB, and ILO figures indicated that the sector engaged 38.2% of the employed labour force in that year. According to the World Bank, during 1996–2006 the GDP of the sector increased by an average of 9.3% annually, in real terms. According to the World Bank, services GDP increased by 10.8% in 2005 and by 15.0% in 2006.

In 2006 Armenia recorded a visible trade deficit of US $895.9m., while the deficit on the current account of the balance of payments was $117.1m. In 2006 the principal source of imports, according to official statistics, was Russia, which provided 16.6% of the total; other main sources were Belgium (7.2%), the United Arab Emirates (6.6%), the USA (6.2%), and Iran (6.1%). In the same year Germany was the main market for exports, accounting for 15.0% of the total. Other important purchasers were the Netherlands (12.9%), Russia (12.3%), Belgium (11.0%) and Israel (8.9%). The principal exports in 2006 were pearls, precious and semi-precious stones (in particular, diamonds), precious metals, imitation jewellery and coins; base metals; prepared foodstuffs, beverages and tobacco; mineral products and textiles. The principal imports in that year were pearls, precious and semi-precious stones, precious metals, imitation jewellery and coins; mineral products; machinery and electrical equipment; vehicles, aircraft and transport equipment; prepared foodstuffs, beverages and tobacco; chemicals; and vegetable products.

In 2005 there was a budgetary deficit of 29,650m. drams (equivalent to 1.3% of GDP). At the end of that year Armenia's total external debt was US $1,861m., of which $923m. was long-term public debt. In that year the cost of debt-servicing was equivalent to 7.9% of the value of exports of goods and services. According to ILO, consumer prices increased at an average annual rate of 5.6% in 1995–2005. Consumer prices decreased by 0.6% in 2005 and by 2.9% in 2006, according to data issued by the IMF. The rate of unemployment was 8.2% in 2005.

Armenia is a member of the IMF, the World Bank and the European Bank for Reconstruction and Development (EBRD, see p. 239), and it is also a member of the Organization of the Black Sea Economic Co-operation (BSEC, see p. 367). In February 2003 Armenia became a member of the World Trade Organization (WTO, see p. 396). Armenia joined the ADB in September 2005.

The critical economic situation in Armenia in the early 1990s was exacerbated by the closure by Azerbaijan and by Turkey of their borders with the country, in response to the conflict in Nagornyi Karabakh, resulting in widespread shortages and a decline in industrial production. A programme of reforms, including price liberalization and privatization, was initiated. By 2001 there was a significant improvement in economic performance, and GDP increased by an annual rate of more than 10% thereafter. In 2004 Armenia became eligible for the new US Millennium Challenge Account aid programme, and in December 2005 the USA agreed to disburse some US $235.6m., over a period of five years, to benefit infrastructural projects aimed at reducing rural poverty. However, the Government was required to implement measures to strengthen democracy and improve human rights in order to ensure the release of the funds. Meanwhile, in May 2005 the Government had reached agreement with the IMF on a second three-year Poverty Reduction and Growth Facility (PRGF) arrangement. The IMF emphasized the need to improve tax-collection methods; to strengthen the regulation of the financial system; to undertake further reform of the public-utility sector; and to combat corruption. According to the IMF, the Armenian economy grew by 11.1% in 2007, led by improvements in the construction and service sectors (both of which benefited from increased inflows of Foreign Direct Investment). Rising domestic demand, buoyed by a strong increase in remittances from abroad, also stimulated growth. In a report published in December 2007, the Fund recommended that Armenia take measures to ensure effective targeting of inflation, including granting the Central Bank full independence. Consumer prices were estimated to have risen by 3.7% in 2007, and were forecast to increase by 4.9% in 2008. The 2008 state budget incorporated a 60% rise in pensions payments (albeit from an extremely low base); expenditure on the health service was also scheduled to increase. GDP was forecast to increase, in real terms, by 10.0% in 2008, according to the IMF. Armenia's economic prospects would be ameliorated should there be a formal resolution of the conflict over Nagornyi Karabakh and the resumption of transport links with Azerbaijan and Turkey.

Education

Education is free and compulsory at primary and secondary levels. Until the early 1990s the general education system conformed to that of the Soviet system, but extensive changes were subsequently introduced, with greater emphasis placed on Armenian history and culture. Primary education usually began at seven years of age and lasted for four years. Secondary education, beginning at 11 years of age, comprised a first cycle of four years and a second of two years. In 2001/02, however, Armenia introduced an 11-year system of schooling. In 2005 total enrolment at pre-school establishments was equivalent to 21.5% of the relevant age-group. In 2004/05 primary enrolment included 78.8% of children in the relevant age-group, while the comparable ratio for secondary enrolment was 84.3%. In 2005/06 some 98.6% of students in general education schools were taught in Armenian, and 1.2% were mainly taught in Russian. Most instruction in higher institutions is in Armenian, although Russian is widely taught as a second language. Current expenditure on education and science from the state budget was 70,540m. drams in 2006 (15.5% of overall budgetary expenditure).

Public Holidays

2008: 1–2 January (New Year), 6 January (Christmas), 28 January (Army Day), 8 March (Women's Day), 24 April (Armenian Genocide Commemoration Day), 25–27 April (Easter), 1 May (Labour Day), 9 May (Victory and Peace Day), 28 May (Declaration of the First Armenian Republic Day), 5 July (Constitution Day), 21 September (Independence Day), 31 December (New Year's Eve).

2009: 1–2 January (New Year), 6 January (Christmas), 28 January (Army Day), 8 March (Women's Day), 17–19 April (Easter), 24 April (Armenian Genocide Commemoration Day), 1 May (Labour Day), 9 May (Victory and Peace Day), 28 May (Declaration of the First Armenian Republic Day), 5 July (Constitution Day), 21 September (Independence Day), 31 December (New Year's Eve).

Weights and Measures

The metric system is in force.

ARMENIA

Statistical Survey

Principal source: National Statistical Service of the Republic of Armenia, 0010 Yerevan, Republic Sq., Government House 3; tel. (10) 52-42-13; fax (10) 52-19-21; e-mail info@armstat.am; internet www.armstat.am.

Area and Population

AREA, POPULATION AND DENSITY

Area (sq km)	29,743*
Population (census results)†	
12 January 1989	3,287,677
10 October 2001	
Males	1,407,220
Females	1,595,374
Total	3,002,594
Population (official estimates at 1 January)‡	
2005	3,215,800
2006	3,219,200
2007	3,222,900
Density (per sq km) at 1 January 2007	108.4

* 11,484 sq miles (including inland water, totalling 1,278 sq km).
† Figures refer to *de facto* populations, although the methodology for calculating the relationship between *de jure* and *de facto* populations was amended for the 2001 census, and later figures are, therefore, not strictly comparable with those for 1989; the *de jure* total population for 2001 was 3,213,011.
‡ Figures include persons temporarily absent (475,200 at 1 January 1999).

POPULATION BY ETHNIC GROUP*
(permanent inhabitants, 2001 census)

	Number	%
Armenian	3,145,354	97.89
Yazidi	40,620	1.26
Others	27,037	0.84
Total	3,213,011	100.00

* According to official declaration of nationality; figures refer to *de jure* population.

MARZER (PROVINCES)
(1 January 2007)

Marz (Province)	Area (sq km)	Estimated population	Density (per sq km)	Capital
Yerevan City	227	1,104,900	4,867.4	Yerevan
Aragatsotn	2,753	140,000	50.9	Ashtarak
Ararat	2,096	275,100	131.3	Artashat
Armavir	1,242	280,200	225.6	Armavir
Gegharkunik	5,348	239,600	44.8	Gavar
Kotayk	2,089	276,200	132.2	Hrazdan
Lori	3,789	282,700	74.6	Vanadzor
Shirak	2,681	281,300	104.9	Gyumri
Syunik	4,506	152,900	33.9	Kapan
Tavush	2,704	134,200	49.6	Ijevan
Vayots Dzor	2,308	55,800	24.2	Yeghegnadzor
Total	29,743	3,222,900	108.4	—

PRINCIPAL TOWNS
(estimated population at 1 January 2006)

Yerevan (capital)	1,103,800	Etchmiadzin	56,700
Gyumri*	148,300	Hrazdan (Razdan)	52,800
Vanadzor†	105,500	Kapan	45,600

* Known as Leninakan between 1924 and 1991.
† Known as Kirovakan between 1935 and 1992.

BIRTHS, MARRIAGES AND DEATHS*

	Registered live births		Registered marriages		Registered deaths	
	Number	Rate (per 1,000)	Number	Rate (per 1,000)	Number	Rate (per 1,000)
1999	36,502	9.6	12,459	3.3	24,087	6.3
2000	34,276	9.0	10,986	2.9	24,025	6.3
2001	32,065	10.0	12,302	3.8	24,003	7.5
2002	32,229	10.1	13,682	4.3	25,554	8.0
2003	35,793	11.2	15,463	4.8	26,014	8.1
2004	37,520	11.7	16,975	5.3	25,679	8.0
2005	37,499	11.7	16,624	5.2	26,379	8.2
2006	37,639	11.7	16,887	5.2	27,202	8.5

* Rates for 1999–2000 are calculated from unrevised population estimates.

Expectation of life (years at birth, WHO estimates): 68.6 (males 65.0; females 72.0) in 2005 (Source: WHO, *World Health Statistics*).

ECONOMICALLY ACTIVE POPULATION
(annual averages, '000 persons)

	2004	2005	2006
Agriculture, hunting and forestry	507.0	507.5	504.3
Fishing	0.1	0.1	0.2
Mining and quarrying	6.9	7.0	7.6
Manufacturing	111.5	114.3	110.5
Electricity, gas and water supply	21.2	18.9	22.8
Construction	33.3	34.6	29.7
Wholesale and retail trade; repair of motor vehicles, motorcycles and personal household goods	103.2	108.9	105.9
Hotels and restaurants	3.9	5.7	7.7
Transport, storage and communications	46.5	49.7	48.6
Financial intermediation	5.6	6.1	6.6
Real estate, renting and business activities	18.3	19.1	23.3
Public administration and defence; compulsory social security	29.1	28.2	34.9
Education	100.5	98.7	100.8
Health and social work	49.8	50.6	48.8
Other community, social and personal service activities	44.8	48.4	40.8
Total employed	1,081.7	1,097.8	1,092.4
Registered unemployed	114.8	98.0	88.9
Total labour force	1,196.5	1,195.8	1,181.3

Source: ILO.

Health and Welfare

KEY INDICATORS

Total fertility rate (children per woman, 2005)	1.3
Under-five mortality rate (per 1,000 live births, 2005)	29
HIV (% of persons aged 15–49, 2005)	0.1
Physicians (per 1,000 head, 2003)	3.59
Hospital beds (per 1,000 head, 2005)	4.5
Health expenditure (2004): US $ per head (PPP)	225.6
Health expenditure (2004): % of GDP	5.4
Health expenditure (2004): public (% of total)	26.2
Access to water (% of persons, 2004)	92
Access to sanitation (% of persons, 2004)	83
Human Development Index (2005): ranking	83
Human Development Index (2005): value	0.775

For sources and definitions, see explanatory note on p. vi.

ARMENIA

Agriculture

PRINCIPAL CROPS
('000 metric tons)

	2004	2005	2006*
Wheat	291.6	258.4	140.0
Barley	131.1	110.8	60.0
Maize	19.3	14.1	0.7
Potatoes	576.4	564.2	541.6
Cabbages and brassicas	93.8	107.2	108.0
Tomatoes	229.5	234.9	236.0
Cauliflowers and broccoli	6.2	5.6	6.0
Cucumbers and gherkins	60.3	64.4	65.0
Dry onions	42.8	48.8	50.0
Garlic	7.3	8.7	10.0
Carrots and turnips	14.4	17.1	20.0
Watermelons	112.9	117.8	120.0
Apples	56.0†	85.7*	87.0
Pears	21.3†	35.4*	37.0
Apricots	5.4†	29.5	30.0
Peaches and nectarines	11.4†	62.0	64.0
Plums and sloes	11.0†	60.0	62.0
Grapes	148.9	164.4	166.0

* FAO estimate(s).
† Unofficial figure.

Aggregate production ('000 metric tons, may include official, semi-official or estimated data): Total cereals 451.6 in 2004, 391.8 in 2005, 211.7 in 2006; Total roots and tubers 576.4 in 2004, 564.2 in 2005, 541.6 in 2006; Total pulses 5.2 in 2004; 4.3 in 2005, 22.7 in 2006; Total vegetables (incl. melons) 713.6 in 2004, 781.5 in 2005, 795.7 in 2006; Total fruits (excl. melons) 262.5 in 2004, 480.0 in 2005, 493.0 in 2006.

Source: FAO.

LIVESTOCK
('000 head, year ending September)

	2004	2005	2006
Horses	13	12	12
Asses, mules or hinnies	7	7	7
Cattle	566	573	592
Pigs	85	89	138
Sheep	580	557	549
Goats	48	47	43
Rabbits	22	18	21
Chickens*	4,740	4,590	4,675
Turkeys*	284	272	280

* FAO estimates.
Source: FAO.

LIVESTOCK PRODUCTS
('000 metric tons)

	2004	2005	2006*
Cattle meat	33	34	35
Sheep meat	7	8	8
Pig meat	9	9	10
Chicken meat	4	5	5
Cows' milk	536	557	570
Sheep's milk	16	16*	22
Hen eggs	31*	29	29
Wool: greasy	1	1	1

* FAO estimate(s).
Source: FAO.

Forestry

ROUNDWOOD REMOVALS
('000 cubic metres, excluding bark)

	2004	2005	2006
Sawlogs, veneer logs and logs for sleepers	6	4	5
Fuel wood	59	39	60
Total	65	43	65

Source: FAO.

Fishing

(metric tons, live weight)

	2003	2004	2005*
Capture	569	218	220
Common carp	143	26	25
Crucian carp	63	40	40
Freshwater fishes	81	49	50
Trouts	151	62	60
Whitefishes	121	35	35
Aquaculture	1,064	813	813
Common carp	256	216	216
Crucian carp	47	45	45
Silver carp	382	229	229
Trouts	359	320	320
Total catch	1,633	1,031	1,033

* FAO estimates.
Source: FAO.

Mining

	2003	2004	2005
Copper concentrates (metric tons)*	18,068	17,700†	16,256
Molybdenum concentrates (metric tons)*	2,763	2,950†	3,030
Silver ores (kg)*†	4,000	4,000	4,000
Gold ores (kg)*	1,800	2,100	1,400
Salt ('000 metric tons)	32	32	35

* Figures refer to the metal content of ores and concentrates.
† Estimated production.
Source: US Geological Survey.

Industry

SELECTED PRODUCTS
('000 metric tons, unless otherwise indicated)

	2004	2005	2006
Wheat flour	147	140	n.a.
Wine ('000 hectolitres)	62	68	38
Beer ('000 hectolitres)	88	108	126
Soft drinks ('000 hectolitres)	362	320	n.a.
Cigarettes (million)	2,720	3,020	2,825
Wool yarn—pure and mixed (metric tons)	58	57	n.a.
Cotton yarn—pure and mixed (metric tons)	54	n.a.	n.a.
Woven cotton fabrics ('000 sq metres)	236	143	240
Woven woollen fabrics ('000 sq metres)	n.a.	1	n.a.
Carpets ('000 sq metres)	29	27	27
Cement	501	605	625
Electric energy (million kWh)	6,030	6,317	5,941

Finance

CURRENCY AND EXCHANGE RATES

Monetary Units
100 louma = 1 dram.

Sterling, Dollar and Euro Equivalents (31 May 2007)
£1 sterling = 609.48 drams;
US $1 = 304.22 drams;
€1 = 447.84 drams;
1,000 drams = £1.64 = $3.29 = €2.23.

Average Exchange Rate (drams per US $)
2005   477.69
2006   416.04
2007   342.08

Note: The dram was introduced on 22 November 1993, replacing the Russian (formerly Soviet) rouble at a conversion rate of 1 dram = 200 roubles. The initial exchange rate was set at US $1 = 14.3 drams, but by the end of the year the rate was $1 = 75 drams. After the introduction of the dram, Russian currency continued to circulate in Armenia. The rouble had been withdrawn from circulation by March 1994.

STATE BUDGET
(million drams)

Revenue	2004	2005	2006
Tax revenue	250,119	304,257	359,715
Value-added tax	117,903	146,783	165,912
Excises	40,657	38,638	39,858
Enterprise profits tax	32,011	46,557	65,329
Income tax	20,413	26,616	35,469
Customs duties	12,483	16,490	18,323
Fixed payments	11,742	12,963	15,074
Other taxes	14,977	16,207	19,733
Government duty	16,925	17,275	18,986
Non-tax incomes	12,394	29,218	32,638
Capital revenue	9,094	12,366	15,996
Other revenue	13,718	9,825	12,286
Total	302,249	372,941	439,620

Expense by economic type*	2004	2005	2006
Current expenditure	262,813	310,050	349,776
Wages	24,241	33,242	40,191
Interest	9,835	9,933	9,025
Subsidies	18,074	16,484	19,874
Current transfers	50,146	76,624	89,532
Goods and services	160,517	173,767	191,154
Capital expenditure	60,619	71,928	89,228
Net crediting	n.a.	13,191	15,974
Total	323,432	395,169	454,978

*Excluding lending minus repayments (million drams): 10,539 in 2004; 13,109 in 2005; 17,636 in 2006 (preliminary).

Outlays by function of government	2004	2005	2006
General public services	36,573	43,421	49,068
Defence	52,316	64,414	78,294
Public order and safety	24,588	33,263	40,203
Education and science	47,446	58,805	70,540
Health care	24,691	30,413	35,963
Social insurance	34,988	44,062	53,040
Culture, communication, religion and sport	8,486	10,412	13,597
Housing and community amenities	11,967	15,441	16,935
Fuel and energy production	9,552	10,759	1,544
Agriculture, fishery, forestry and waters	16,430	9,900	10,864
Industry and nature protection	3,138	3,199	5,290
Transport and communication	18,474	20,689	30,514
Other expenditures (transfer payments, debt obligations, etc.)	45,322	50,392	49,127
Total	333,970	395,169	454,978

INTERNATIONAL RESERVES
(US $ million at 31 December)

	2004	2005	2006
IMF special drawing rights	11.96	10.18	13.96
Foreign exchange	535.80	659.30	1,057.96
Total	547.76	669.48	1,071.92

Source: IMF, *International Financial Statistics*.

MONEY SUPPLY
(million drams at 31 December)

	2004	2005	2006
Currency outside banks	98,569	144,311	211,469
Demand deposits at commercial banks	33,283	57,095	83,141
Total money (incl. others)	132,414	202,056	171,034

Source: IMF, *International Financial Statistics*.

COST OF LIVING
(Consumer Price Index; base: 2000 = 100)

	2003	2004	2005
Food (incl. non-alcoholic beverages)	114.4	125.8	126.8
Electricity, gas and other fuels	102.1	103.8	106.0
Clothing (incl. footwear)	102.8	101.8	99.7
Rent	100.7	116.6	132.8
All items (incl. others)	109.2	116.3	117.0

Source: ILO.

2006 (Consumer Price Index; base: 2000 = 100): All items 120.9 (Source: IMF, *International Financial Statistics*).

NATIONAL ACCOUNTS
('000 million drams at current prices)
Expenditure on the Gross Domestic Product

	2004	2005	2006
Government final consumption expenditure	197.3	241.5	306.9
Private final consumption expenditure	1,570.4	1,706.7	1,922.1
Increase in stocks	19.4	8.4	4.3
Gross fixed capital formation	455.3	657.7	870.4
Total domestic expenditure	2,242.4	2,614.3	3,103.7
Exports of goods and services	522.5	604.0	576.7
Less Imports of goods and services	803.8	896.0	916.9
Statistical discrepancy*	−53.1	−78.5	−98.5
GDP in market prices	1,907.9	2,244.0	2,665.0

* Referring to the difference between the sum of the expenditure components and official estimates of GDP, compiled from the production approach.

ARMENIA

Gross Domestic Product by Economic Activity

	2004	2005	2006
Agriculture and forestry	431.1	421.5	473.5
Construction	297.2	487.4	711.5
Other industry*	366.3	422.1	402.8
Wholesale and retail trade; repair of motor vehicles; motorcycles and personal and household goods; hotels and restaurants	222.3	245.1	280.5
Transport, storage and communications	113.8	124.6	156.0
Financial intermediation; real estate, renting and business activities; public administration and defence; other community, social and personal service activities	341.6	380.9	455.0
Sub-total	1,772.3	2,081.6	2,479.3
Less Imputed bank service charges	24.2	27.2	32.3
Gross value added in basic prices	1,748.1	2,054.3	2,447.0
Taxes, *less* subsidies on products	159.9	189.7	218.0
GDP in market prices	1,907.9	2,244.0	2,665.0

*Comprising mining and quarrying, manufacturing, electricity, gas and water.

Source: Asian Development Bank, *Key Indicators of Developing Asian and Pacific Countries*.

BALANCE OF PAYMENTS
(US $ million)

	2004	2005	2006
Exports of goods f.o.b.	738.3	1,004.9	1,025.5
Imports of goods f.o.b.	−1,196.3	−1,592.8	−1,921.3
Trade balance	−458.0	−587.9	−895.9
Exports of services	332.6	411.1	484.7
Imports of services	−431.5	−531.1	−615.1
Balance on goods and services	−556.9	−707.9	−1,026.3
Other income received	397.5	457.5	624.3
Other income paid	−290.0	−325.0	−409.1
Balance on goods, services and income	−449.5	−575.4	−811.1
Current transfers received	514.8	603.5	791.7
Current transfers paid	−85.0	−79.9	−97.7
Current balance	−19.6	−51.7	−117.1
Capital account (net)	41.3	73.3	86.4
Direct investment abroad	−2.3	−6.7	−3.1
Direct investment from abroad	247.9	239.4	453.2
Portfolio investment assets	−0.5	−2.7	−0.2
Portfolio investment liabilities	−2.4	1.1	9.4
Other investment assets	−315.8	−170.7	−175.7
Other investment liabilities	89.7	102.3	150.5
Net errors and omissions	−5.5	2.4	−16.1
Overall balance	32.8	186.6	387.3

Source: IMF, *International Financial Statistics*.

External Trade

PRINCIPAL COMMODITIES
(distribution by HS, US $ million)

Imports c.i.f.	2004	2005	2006
Vegetable products	109.0	98.3	112.1
Cereals	72.6	53.7	60.7
Prepared foodstuffs; beverages, spirits and vinegar; tobacco and manufactured substitutes	112.7	145.9	163.8
Mineral products	209.4	297.4	366.0
Mineral fuels, mineral oils and products of their distillation; bituminous substances; mineral waxes	207.3	264.4	350.9
Products of chemical or allied industries	85.2	118.4	150.4
Textiles and textile articles	47.1	46.0	59.3
Natural or cultured pearls, precious or semi-precious stones, precious metals and articles thereof; imitation jewellery; coins	291.5	347.6	312.5
Base metals and articles thereof	60.8	94.1	163.7
Machinery and mechanical appliances; electrical equipment; sound and television apparatus	135.5	232.5	304.4
Nuclear reactors, boilers, machinery and mechanical appliances; parts thereof	69.1	156.6	168.6
Electrical machinery, equipment and parts; sound and television apparatus, and parts and accessories	66.4	75.9	135.8
Vehicles, aircraft, vessels and associated transport equipment	92.5	151.8	196.6
Vehicles other than railway or tramway rolling-stock, and parts and accessories thereof	90.4	146.6	195.7
Total (incl. others)	1,350.7	1,801.7	2,191.6

Exports f.o.b.	2004	2005	2006
Prepared foodstuffs; beverages, spirits and vinegar; tobacco and manufactured substitutes	69.2	96.9	95.1
Beverages, spirits and vinegar	57.0	84.3	79.1
Mineral products	99.6	93.5	136.6
Ores, slag and ash	72.8	51.4	93.5
Textiles and textile articles	44.0	37.0	35.5
Non-knitted clothing and accessories	28.0	22.4	20.9
Natural or cultured pearls, precious or semi-precious stones, precious metals and articles thereof; imitation jewellery; coins	299.3	336.3	301.0
Base metals and articles thereof	137.6	322.0	280.9
Iron and steel	70.5	243.7	167.6
Copper and articles thereof	37.7	50.6	77.2
Aluminium and articles thereof	16.9	4.4	7.9
Machinery and mechanical appliances; electrical equipment; sound and television apparatus	21.9	28.0	20.8
Optical, photographic, measuring and medical instruments and apparatus; clocks and watches; musical instruments	7.1	4.9	22.7
Total (incl. others)	722.9	973.9	985.1

ARMENIA

PRINCIPAL TRADING PARTNERS
(countries of consignment, US $ '000)

Imports c.i.f.	2004	2005	2006
Belgium	109,008	162,551	157,129
Bulgaria	11,038	11,709	19,423
China, People's Republic	13,379	27,173	52,547
Cyprus	18,929	10,554	9,632
France	17,979	39,668	37,147
Georgia	48,544	50,813	75,624
Germany	73,910	114,558	85,007
Greece	32,074	37,952	80,622
Iran	76,270	108,060	132,690
Israel	100,138	102,504	87,264
Italy	38,271	45,517	76,488
Luxembourg	41,287	24,213	2,234
Panama	54,051	70,767	75,453
Russia	179,679	268,484	364,775
Switzerland	46,085	86,106	85,264
Turkey	39,807	61,218	88,503
Ukraine	50,887	69,122	109,159
United Arab Emirates	65,225	107,326	145,192
United Kingdom	106,776	91,176	79,326
USA	104,824	116,327	136,692
Total (incl. others)	1,350,698	1,801,736	2,191,613

Exports f.o.b.	2004	2005	2006
Belgium	107,929	124,598	108,846
Canada	8,232	11,482	11,133
China, People's Republic	21,750	9,245	464
Georgia	29,062	46,833	54,649
Germany	83,180	152,108	148,028
Iran	30,560	28,513	29,643
Israel	98,356	112,241	87,448
Italy	28,433	25,594	28,928
Netherlands	26,269	133,110	126,946
Russia	77,898	119,004	121,156
Switzerland	45,354	34,666	72,100
Ukraine	10,479	13,703	22,554
United Arab Emirates	8,924	10,383	5,597
United Kingdom	1,194	419	7,618
USA	70,646	62,219	65,056
Total (incl. others)	722,912	973,921	985,108

Transport

RAILWAYS
(traffic)

	2004	2005	2006
Passenger journeys ('000)*	800	700	700
Passenger-km (million)	30.0	26.6	27.7
Freight carried ('000 metric tons)	2,629.6	2,612.3	2,719.6
Freight ton-km (million)	678.2	654.1	668.0

* Rounded figures.

CIVIL AVIATION
(traffic)

	2004	2005	2006
Passengers carried ('000)*	1,100	1,200	1,200
Passengers-km (million)	984.0	959.5	822.2
Freight carried ('000 metric tons)	9.2	9.3	9.3
Cargo ton-kilometres ('000)	10.0	10.7	12.4

* Rounded figures.

Tourism

ARRIVALS BY NATIONALITY

	2003	2004	2005
Argentina	9,855	14,935	17,560
Brazil	4,609	5,412	6,465
Canada	11,895	13,588	15,795
CIS countries*	58,744	72,996	89,968
France	9,754	12,368	14,294
Germany	7,771	10,688	12,966
Iran	22,750	25,650	27,458
Japan	3,850	5,585	7,681
Lebanon	9,875	11,556	13,411
Syria	8,790	10,985	13,941
United Kingdom	4,893	5,988	8,124
USA	30,844	39,965	43,869
Total (incl. others)	206,094	262,959	318,563

* Comprising Azerbaijan, Belarus, Georgia, Kazakhstan, Kyrgyzstan, Moldova, Russia, Tajikistan, Turkmenistan, Ukraine and Uzbekistan.

Tourism receipts: (US $ million, incl. passenger transport): 90 in 2003; 103 in 2004; 161 in 2005.

Source: World Tourism Organization.

Communications Media

	2003	2004	2005
Telephones ('000 main lines in use)	563.7	582.5	594.4
Mobile cellular telephones ('000 subscribers)	114.4	203.3	318.0
Personal computers ('000 in use)	103	200	n.a.
Internet users ('000)	140	150	161
Broadband subscribers	—	1,000	2,000
Book production:*			
titles	1,025	970	991
copies ('000)	660	427	796
Newspapers:			
titles	120	170	177
total circulation ('000 copies)	325	600	553
Periodicals:			
titles	77	112	120
total circulation ('000 copies)	309	412	401

* Including brochures.

2000: Television receivers ('000 in use) 860.

2006: Internet users ('000) 172.8.

Source: partly International Telecommunication Union.

Education

(2004/05, public institutions, unless otherwise indicated)

	Institutions	Teachers	Students
Pre-primary	623*	7,585†	47,800*
General	1,427	41,700	471,300
Gymnasia and lyceums	35	313	10,500
Specialized secondary schools	83	2,671	27,800
State higher schools (incl. universities)	22	7,152	73,700

* December 2005.
† 1998/99.

Adult literacy rate (UNESCO estimates): 99.4% (males 99.7%; females 99.2%) in 2001 (Source: UNESCO Institute for Statistics).

Directory

The Constitution

The Constitution was approved by a national referendum held on 5 July 1995. Several constitutional amendments were approved by a referendum held on 27 November 2005. The following is a summary of the Constitution's main provisions:

GENERAL PROVISIONS OF CONSTITUTIONAL ORDER

The Republic of Armenia is an independent democratic state; its sovereignty is vested in the people, who execute their authority through free elections, referendums and local self-government institutions and officials, as defined by the Constitution. Referendums, as well as elections of the President of the Republic, the Azgayin Zhoghov (National Assembly) and local self-government bodies, are carried out on the basis of universal, equal, direct suffrage by secret ballot. Through the Constitution and legislation, the State ensures the protection of human rights and freedoms, in accordance with the principles and norms of international law. A multi-party political system is guaranteed. The right to property is recognized and protected. Armenia conducts its foreign policy based on the norms of international law, seeking to establish neighbourly and mutually beneficial relations with all countries. The official language is Armenian.

FUNDAMENTAL HUMAN AND CIVIL RIGHTS AND FREEDOMS

The acquisition and loss of citizenship are prescribed by law. Armenian citizens may hold dual citizenship. No one shall be subject to torture or cruel treatment. Every citizen has the right to freedom of movement and residence within the republic, as well as the right to leave the republic. Every citizen has the right to freedom of thought, speech, conscience and religion. The right to establish or join associations, trade unions, political organizations, etc., is guaranteed, as is the right to strike for protection of economic, social and labour interests.

Every citizen has the right to social insurance in the event of old age, disability, sickness, widowhood, unemployment, etc. Every citizen has the right to education. Education is provided free at elementary and secondary state educational institutions. Citizens belonging to national minorities have the right to preserve their traditions and to develop their language and culture. Everyone charged with a penal offence has the right to be presumed innocent until proved guilty. The advocacy of national, racial and religious hatred, and the propagation of violence and war, are prohibited.

THE PRESIDENT OF THE REPUBLIC

The President of the Republic ensures the observance of the Constitution and the effective operation of the legislative, executive and juridical authorities. The President is the guarantor of the independence, territorial integrity and security of the republic and is elected by citizens of the republic for a period of five years. Any person who has the right to participate in elections, has attained the age of 35 years, and has been a resident citizen of Armenia for the preceding 10 years is eligible for election to the office of President. No person may be elected to the office for more than two successive terms.

The President signs and promulgates laws adopted by the Azgayin Zhoghov, or returns draft legislation to the Azgayin Zhoghov for reconsideration; may dismiss the Azgayin Zhoghov and declare special elections to it, after consultation with the Prime Minister and the Chairman of the Azgayin Zhoghov; appoints and dismisses the Prime Minister, following approval by the Azgayin Zhoghov; appoints and dismisses the members of the Government, upon the recommendation of the Prime Minister; appoints civil service officials, in cases prescribed by law; establishes deliberation bodies; represents Armenia in international relations, co-ordinates foreign policy, concludes international treaties, signs international treaties ratified by the Azgayin Zhoghov, and ratifies agreements between governments; appoints and recalls diplomatic representatives of Armenia to foreign countries and international organizations, and receives the credentials of diplomatic representatives of foreign countries; recommends to the legislature the candidacy of the Procurator-General, the Chairman of the Central Bank and the Chairman of the Control Chamber; appoints four members of the Constitutional Court and the Chairman, if the Azgayin Zhoghov has failed to fill this position in the period prescribed; is the Supreme Commander-in-Chief of the Armed Forces; takes decisions on the use of the Armed Forces; grants titles of honour; grants amnesties to convicts; and is immune from prosecution.

THE AZGAYIN ZHOGHOV

Legislative power is executed by the Azgayin Zhoghov. The Azgayin Zhoghov comprises 131 deputies, elected for a five-year term. Any person who has attained the age of 25 years and has been a permanent resident and citizen of Armenia for the preceding five years is eligible to be elected a deputy.

The Azgayin Zhoghov deliberates and enacts laws; has the power to express a vote of 'no confidence' in the Government; confirms the state budget, as proposed by the Government; supervises the implementation of the state budget; elects its Chairman (Speaker) and two Deputy Chairmen; appoints the Chairman and Deputy Chairman of the Central Bank, upon the nomination of the President; and appoints five members and the Chairman of the Constitutional Court, upon the recommendation of the Chairman in the Azgayin Zhoghov.

At the suggestion of the President of the Republic, the Azgayin Zhoghov declares amnesties; ratifies or declares invalid international treaties; and declares war. Upon the recommendation of the Government, the Azgayin Zhoghov confirms the territorial and administrative divisions of the republic.

THE GOVERNMENT

Executive power is realized by the Government. The Prime Minister directs the current activities of the Government and co-ordinates the activities of the Ministers.

The Government presents the programme of its activities to the Azgayin Zhoghov for approval; presents the draft state budget to the Azgayin Zhoghov for confirmation, ensures implementation of the budget and presents a report on its implementation to the Azgayin Zhoghov; ensures the implementation of state policy; and takes measures to strengthen adherence to the laws, to ensure the rights and freedoms of citizens, and to protect public order and the property of citizens.

JUDICIAL POWER

The courts of general competence are the tribunal courts of first instance, the review courts, the Court of Cassation and the courts of appeal. There are also economic, military and other courts. The guarantor of the independence of judicial bodies is the President of the Republic. The Chairman of the Court of Cassation is the Head of the Council of Justice, and does not have the right to vote. The Council consists of up to nine judges, elected by secret ballot for a period of five years by the General Assembly of Judges; two legal scholars appointed by the President; and two legal scholars appointed by the Azgayin Zhoghov. The Constitutional Court is composed of nine members, of whom the Azgayin Zhoghov appoints five and the President of the Republic appoints four. The highest court of appeal is the Court of Cassation, the members of which are appointed by the President of the Republic, for life.

TERRITORIAL ADMINISTRATION AND LOCAL SELF-GOVERNMENT

The administrative territorial units of the Republic of Armenia are provinces (*marzer*) and communities (*hamaynker*). Marzer are comprised of rural and urban communities. Local self-government takes place in the communities. Bodies of local self-government, community elders and the community head (city mayor or head of village) are to be elected for a four-year term. The Government appoints and dismisses regional governors, who carry out the Government's regional policy and co-ordinate the performance of regional services by state executive bodies. The city of Yerevan holds the status of a community, with an elected mayor.

The Government

HEAD OF STATE

President: SERGE SARKISSIAN (elected 19 February 2008, inaugurated 9 April 2008).

GOVERNMENT
(April 2008)

Prime Minister: TIGRAN SARKISSIAN.
Deputy Prime Minister and Minister of Territorial Administration: ARMEN GEVORGIAN.
Minister of Foreign Affairs: EDVARD NALBANDIAN.
Minister of Defence: SEYRAN OHANIAN.
Minister of Finance: TIGRAN DAVTIAN.

ARMENIA

Minister of Justice: GEVORG DANIELIAN.
Minister of Energy and Natural Resources: ARMEN MOVSISSIAN.
Minister of Labour and Social Affairs: AGHVAN VARDANIAN.
Minister of Health Care: HARUTYUN KUSHKIAN.
Minister of Agriculture: DAVID LOKIAN.
Minister of Environmental Protection: ARAM HAROUTUNIAN.
Minister of the Economy: NERSES YERITSIAN.
Minister of Education and Science: LEVON MKRTCHIAN.
Minister of Culture: HASMIK POGHOSSIAN.
Minister of Sport and Youth Affairs: ARMEN GRIGORIAN.
Minister of Transport and Communications: GURGEN SARKISSIAN.
Minister of Urban Development: VARDAN VARDANYAN.
Minister of Emergency Situations: MHER SHAHGELDIAN.

MINISTRIES

Office of the President: 0077 Yerevan, Marshal Baghramian Ave 26; tel. and fax (10) 52-23-64; e-mail press@president.am; internet www.president.am.

Office of the Prime Minister: 0010 Yerevan, Republic Sq. 1, Govt House; tel. (10) 52-03-60; fax (10) 15-10-35; internet www.gov.am/enversion/premier_2/primer_home.htm.

Ministry of Agriculture: 0010 Yerevan, Republic Sq., Govt House 3; tel. and fax (10) 52-46-41; internet www.minagro.am.

Ministry of Culture: 0010 Yerevan, Republic Sq. 1, Govt House 3; tel. (10) 52-93-49; fax (10) 52-39-22; e-mail mincult@xter.net.

Ministry of Defence: 0088 Yerevan, Proshian Settlement, G. Shaush St 60; tel. (10) 28-39-22; fax (10) 28-26-30; e-mail press@mil.am; internet www.mil.am.

Ministry of ehe Economy: 0010 Yerevan, M. Mkrtchian St 5; tel. (10) 56-61-85; fax (10) 52-65-77; e-mail info@minted.am; internet www.minted.am.

Ministry of Education and Science: 0010 Yerevan, Main Ave, Govt House 3; tel. and fax (10) 52-73-43; e-mail info@edu.am; internet www.edu.am.

Ministry of Emergency Situations: Yerevan.

Ministry of Energy and Natural Resources: 0010 Yerevan, Republic Sq., Govt House 2; tel. (10) 52-19-64; fax (10) 52-63-65; e-mail minenergy@minenergy.am; internet www.minenergy.am.

Ministry of Environmental Protection: 0010 Yerevan, Republic Sq., Govt House 3; tel. (10) 52-10-99; fax (10) 58-54-69; e-mail info@mnp.am; internet www.mnp.am.

Ministry of Finance: 0010 Yerevan, Melik-Adamian St 1; tel. (10) 59-53-04; fax (10) 54-58-15; e-mail mfe@mfe.am; internet mfe.gov.am.

Ministry of Foreign Affairs: 0010 Yerevan, Republic Sq., Govt House 2; tel. (10) 54-40-41; fax (10) 54-39-25; e-mail info@armeniaforeignministry.com; internet www.armeniaforeignministry.com.

Ministry of Health Care: 0010 Yerevan, Tumanian St 8; tel. (10) 58-24-13; fax (10) 15-10-97; internet www.moh.am.

Ministry of Justice: 0010 Yerevan, Vazgen Sarkissian St 3; tel. and fax (10) 58-21-57; e-mail justice@justice.am; internet www.justice.am.

Ministry of Labour and Social Affairs: 0010 Yerevan, Republic Sq., Govt House 3; tel. (10) 52-68-31; e-mail varduhii@mss.am; internet www.mss.am.

Ministry of Sport and Youth Affairs: 0010 Yerevan.

Ministry of Territorial Administration: 0010 Yerevan, Republic Sq., Govt House 2; tel. (10) 51-13-02; fax (10) 51-13-31; e-mail mta@mta.gov.am; internet www.region.am.

Ministry of Transport and Communications: 0010 Yerevan, Nalbandian St 28; tel. (10) 52-38-62; fax (10) 54-59-79; e-mail traceca@arminco.am; internet www.mtc.am.

Ministry of Urban Development: 0010 Yerevan, Republic Sq., Govt House 3; tel. (10) 58-90-80; fax (10) 52-32-00.

President

Presidential Election, 19 February 2008

Candidates	Votes	% of votes
Serge Sarkissian	862,369	52.82
Levon Ter-Petrossian	351,222	21.51
Artur Baghdasarian	272,427	17.69
Vahan Hovhanissian	100,966	6.18
Vazgen Manukian	21,075	1.29
Others	24,607	1.51
Total	**1,632,666**	**100.00**

Legislature

**Azgayin Zhoghov
(National Assembly)**

0095 Yerevan, Marshal Baghramian St 19; tel. (10) 58-82-25; fax (10) 52-98-26; internet www.parliament.am.

Chairman: TIGRAN TOROSSIAN.

General Election, 12 May 2007

Parties	% of votes	Seats	Total seats*
Republican Party of Armenia	33.91	41	64
Prosperous Armenia	15.13	18	25
Armenian Revolutionary Federation—Dashnaktsutyun	13.16	16	16
Law-Governed Country Party of Armenia	7.05	8	9
Heritage Party	6.00	7	7
Alliance	2.44	—	1
United Labour Party	4.39	—	—
National Unity Party	3.69	—	—
New Times Party	3.48	—	—
People's Party	2.74	—	—
Independents	—	—	9
Others	8.01	—	—
Total	**100.00**	**90**	**131**

* Including 41 seats filled by voting in single-member districts.

Election Commission

Central Electoral Commission (CEC): 0009 Yerevan, G. Kochar St 21A; tel. and fax (10) 54-35-23; e-mail cec@ielections.am; internet www.elections.am; Chair. GAREGIN AZARIAN.

Political Organizations

At January 2006 there were 74 duly registered parties in existence.

Alliance (Dashink): Yerevan; e-mail info@dashink.am; internet www.dashink.am; f. 2005; Leader SAMUEL BABAIAN.

Armenian Christian Democratic Union (HDQM): 0010 Yerevan, Vardanants St 8A; tel. (10) 54-11-33; fax (10) 54-37-87; e-mail cduarm@yahoo.com; f. 1990; Chair. KHOSROV HAROUTUNIAN.

Armenian Democratic Party: 0009 Yerevan, Koriun St 14; tel. and fax (10) 52-52-73; e-mail democracy@armenia.am; internet dem_party.tripod.com; f. 1992 by elements of Communist Party of Armenia; contested the parliamentary election of 2003 as part of the Justice (Artarutiun) bloc; Chair. ARAM SARKISSIAN.

Armenian Liberal Democratic Party (Ramgavar Azatagan—HRAK): 0070 Yerevan, Yervand Kochar St 19/6; tel. and fax (10) 57-23-97; e-mail hrak@arminco.com; internet www.hrak.am; f. 1991; centre-right; Chair. HAROUTIUN ARAKELIAN.

Armenian Pan-National Movement (APNM) (Haiots Hamazgaien Sharjoum–HHSh): 0010 Yerevan, Khanjian St 27; tel. (10) 57-04-70; f. 1989; Pres. LEVON TER-PETROSSIAN; Chair. ALEKSANDR ARZUMANIAN.

Armenian Revolutionary Federation—Dashnaktsutyun (ARF) (Hai Heghapokhakan Dashnaktsutiun): 0010 Yerevan, Mher Mkrtchian St 30; tel. (10) 52-15-02; fax (10) 52-04-26; e-mail info@arf.am; internet www.arfd.am; f. 1890; formed the ruling party in independent Armenia, 1918–20; prohibited under Soviet rule, but continued its activities in other countries; permitted to operate legally in Armenia from 1991; suspended in December 1994; legally reinstated 1998; 40,000 mems; Chair. HRANT MARKARIAN.

Association for Armenia Party (MHH): Yerevan; f. 2006; Leader VAHRAM BAGHDASARIAN.

Heritage Party (Zharangutyun): 0033 Yerevan, Vazgen Sarkissian St 7; tel. (10) 58-08-77; fax (10) 54-38-97; e-mail info@heritage.am; internet www.heritage.am; f. 2002; national liberal party; Chair. RAFFI HOVHANISSIAN; Chair. of Bd VARDAN KHACHATRIAN.

Law-Governed Country Party of Armenia (Orinats Yerkir—OY): 0009 Yerevan, Abovian St 43; tel. (10) 56-99-69; e-mail info@oek.am; internet www.oek.am; f. 1998; centrist; also known as the Rule of Law Party and the Legal State Party; absorbed the People's Democratic Party of Armenia in Nov. 2003; Head ARTUR BAGHDASARIAN; 41,000 mems.

Mighty Fatherland (Hzor Hayrenik): 0010 Yerevan, Tigran Mets Ave 9; tel. (10) 52-92-15; fax (10) 52-25-45; e-mail hzor_hayrenik@xter.net; f. 1997; Chair. VARDAN VARDAPETIAN; 11,500 mems.

National Democratic Party (AZhK): Yerevan, Paronyan St 11/4; tel. and fax (10) 56-21-50; e-mail ajk_info@web.am; internet www.ajk.am; f. 2001 following the division of the National Democratic Union; contested the 2003 parliamentary elections as part of the Justice (Artarutiun) bloc, but withdrew from the bloc in Dec. 2005; Leader SHAVARSH KOCHARIAN.

National Revival Party (AV): Yerevan; f. 2005 by former mems of Republic (q.v.); Chair. of Bd ALBERT BAZEIAN.

National Unity Party (Azgayin Miabanutiun—MAK): c/o Azgayin Zhoghov, 0095 Yerevan, Marshal Baghramian St 19; tel. (10) 58-01-37; f. 1998; Chair. ARTASHES GEGHAMIAN.

New Times Party (Nor Zhamanakner): 0001 Yerevan, Tumanian St 8; tel. (10) 56-83-17; fax (10) 56-83-39; e-mail nor_jamanakner@yahoo.com; f. 2003; Chair. ARAM KARAPETIAN.

People's Party (Zhoghovrdakan Kusaktsutyun): Yerevan; Leader TIGRAN KARAPETYAN.

People's Party of Armenia (PPA) (Hayastani Zhoghovrdakan Kusaktsutyun—HzhK): Yerevan; e-mail hzhk@freenet.am; internet www.ppa.am; f. 1998; contested the general election of May 2003 as part of the Justice (Artarutiun) bloc; Leader STEPAN DEMIRCHIAN.

Prosperous Armenia (Bargavach Hayastan Kusaktsutyun—BHK): Yerevan, Myasnikian 1; tel. (10) 54-88-07; e-mail info@bhk.am; internet www.bhk.am; f. 2006; Leader GAGIK TSARUKIAN.

Republic (Hanrapetutyun): 0002 Yerevan, Mashtots Ave 37/30; tel. (10) 53-86-34; e-mail republic@arminco.com; internet www.hanrapetutyun.am; f. 2001 by members of the Yerkrapah Union of Volunteers and fmr members of the Republican Party of Armenia; Leader ARAM SARKISSIAN.

Republican Party of Armenia (Haiastani Hanrapetakan Kusaktsutiun—RPA) (HHK): 0010 Yerevan, Melik-Adamian St 2; tel. (10) 58-00-31; fax (10) 50-12-59; e-mail hhk@hhk.am; internet www.hhk.am; f. 1990; national conservative party; Chair. of Bd and Acting Pres. SERGE SARKISSIAN.

Union of National Democrats: Yerevan; f. 2001 following a split in the National Democratic Union; contested the general election of May 2003 as part of the Justice (Artarutiun) bloc; Leader ARSHAK SADOIAN.

United Communist Party of Armenia (Hayastani Miatsial Komunistakan Kusaktsutyun—HMKK): Yerevan; f. 2003 by the merger of seven pro-communist parties, including the Renewed Communist Party of Armenia, the Party of Intellectuals, the Communist Party of the Working People and the United Progressive Communist; First Sec. YURI MANUKIAN.

Diplomatic Representation

EMBASSIES IN ARMENIA

Belarus: 0028 Yerevan, N. Duman St 12–14; tel. (10) 27-56-11; fax (10) 26-03-84; e-mail armenia@belembassy.org; Ambassador MARINA DOLGOPOLOVA.

Brazil: 0010 Yerevan, S. Yerevantzu 57; tel. (10) 50-02-09; fax (10) 53-69-55.

Bulgaria: Yerevan, Nor Aresh, Sofia St 16; tel. (10) 45-82-33; fax (10) 45-46-02; e-mail bulembassy@arminco.com; internet www.mfa.bg/yerevan; Ambassador TODOR STAIKOV.

China, People's Republic: 0019 Yerevan, Marshal Baghramian St 12; tel. (10) 56-00-67; fax (10) 54-57-61; e-mail chiemb@arminco.com; internet am.chineseembassy.org; Ambassador HONG JIUYIN.

Egypt: Yerevan, Sepuhi St 6A; tel. (10) 22-01-17; fax (10) 22-64-25; e-mail egyemb@arminco.com; Ambassador WAHID GALAL.

France: 0015 Yerevan, Grigor Lusavorichi St 8; tel. (10) 56-11-03; fax (10) 56-98-31; e-mail cad.erevan@diplomatie.gouv.fr; internet www.ambafrance-am.org; Ambassador SERGE SMESSOW.

Georgia: 0010 Yerevan, Aram St 42; tel. (10) 56-43-57; fax (10) 56-41-83; e-mail geoemb@netsys.am; internet www.armenia.mfa.gov.ge; Ambassador REVAZ GACHECHILADZE.

Germany: 0025 Yerevan, Charents St 29; tel. (10) 52-32-79; fax (10) 52-47-81; e-mail info@eriw.diplo.de; internet www.eriwan.diplo.de; Ambassador ANDREA WIKTORIN.

Greece: 0002 Yerevan, Demirchian St 6; tel. (10) 53-00-51; fax (10) 53-00-49; e-mail embassy@greekembassy.am; internet www.greekembassy.am; Ambassador IOANNIS KORINTHIOS.

India: 0019 Yerevan, Dzorapi St 50/2; tel. (10) 53-91-73; fax (10) 53-39-84; e-mail hoc@embassyofindia.am; internet www.indianembassy.am; Ambassador REENA PANDEY.

Iran: Yerevan, Budaghian St 1; tel. (10) 28-04-57; fax (10) 23-00-52; e-mail info@iranembassy.am; internet www.iranembassy.am; Ambassador ALIREZA HAGHIGHIAN.

Italy: 0010 Yerevan, Italiayi St 5; tel. (10) 54-23-35; fax (10) 54-23-41; e-mail segreteria.jerevan@esteri.it; internet www.ambjerevan.esteri.it; Ambassador MASSIMO CASSINELLI.

Kazakhstan: 0019 Yerevan, Marshal Baghramian 2–oi per. 1; tel. (10) 21-13-33; fax (10) 27-14-74; e-mail kazembassy@web.am; Ambassador AIYMDOC YE. BOZZHIGITOV.

Lebanon: 0010 Yerevan, Vardanants St 7; tel. (10) 52-65-40; fax (10) 52-69-90; e-mail libarm@arminco.com; Ambassador TONY BADAWI.

Lithuania: Yerevan, Noy 86; tel. (10) 74-19-64; fax (10) 74-19-63; Chargé d'affaires a.i. KĘSTUTIS STANKEVIČIUS.

Poland: 0010 Yerevan, Hanrapetutiun St 44A; tel. (10) 54-24-93; fax (10) 54-24-98; e-mail armpolemb@ct.futuro.pl; internet www.erewan.polemb.net; Ambassador TOMASZ KNOTHE.

Romania: Yerevan, Barbusse St 15; tel. (10) 27-53-32; fax (10) 22-75-47; e-mail ambrom@netsys.am; Ambassador RODINA CRINA PRUNARIU.

Russia: 0015 Yerevan, Grigor Lusavorichi St 13A; tel. (10) 56-74-27; fax (10) 56-71-97; e-mail info@rusembassy.am; internet www.armenia.mid.ru; Ambassador NIKOLAI V. PAVLOV.

Syria: 0019 Yerevan, Marshal Baghramian Ave 14; tel. (10) 52-40-36; fax (10) 54-52-19; e-mail syrem_ar@intertel.am; Chargé d'affaires a.i. Dr MAMOUN HARIRI.

Turkmenistan: 0028 Yerevan, Kievian St 19; tel. (10) 22-10-29; fax (10) 22-21-32; e-mail serdar@arminco.com; Ambassador KHIDIR SAPARLIYEV.

Ukraine: 0037 Yerevan, Arabkir 29/5/1; tel. (10) 22-97-27; fax (10) 25-13-83; e-mail emb_am@mfa.gov.ua; internet www.mfa.gov.ua/armenia; Ambassador OLEKSANDR I. BOZHKO.

United Kingdom: 0019 Yerevan, Marshal Baghramian Ave 34; tel. (10) 26-43-01; fax (10) 26-43-18; e-mail enquiries.yerevan@fco.gov.uk; internet www.britishembassy.am; Ambassador ANTHONY CANTOR.

USA: 0082 Yerevan, American Ave 1; tel. (10) 46-47-00; fax (10) 46-47-42; e-mail usinfo@usa.am; internet yerevan.usembassy.gov; Chargé d'affaires a.i. JOSEPH PENNINGTON.

Judicial System

A new judicial and legal system came into force in January 1999. The Supreme Court was replaced as the highest court of appeal by the Court of Cassation, and Appellate Courts replaced People's Courts. Members of the Court of Cassation were appointed by the President, for life. Following a constitutional referendum, held in November 2005, the President was to cede the chairmanship of the Council of Justice to the Chairman of the Court of Cassation; the Azgayin Zhoghov (National Assembly) was to appoint the Prosecutor-General; and the Council of Justice was to nominate the chairmen of all courts (including the Court of Cassation) and to draw up a list of proposed judges for approval by the President.

Constitutional Court

0019 Yerevan, Marshal Baghramian St 10; tel. (10) 58-81-40; fax (10) 52-99-91; e-mail armlaw@concourt.am; internet www.concourt.am. f. 1996; Chair. GAGIK HAROUTUNIAN.

Chairman of the Court of Cassation: HOVHANNES MANUKIAN, Yerevan, Hkorhrdaranayin St 6; tel. (10) 58-71-30; fax (10) 56-31-73.

Prosecutor-General: AGHVAN HOVSEPPIAN, 0010 Yerevan, V. Sarkissian St 5; tel. (10) 51-15-54; e-mail info@genpro.am; internet www.genproc.am.

Religion

The major religion is Christianity. The Armenian Apostolic Church is the leading denomination and was widely identified with the movement for national independence. There are also Russian Orthodox and Islamic communities, although the latter lost adherents as a result of the departure of large numbers of Muslim Azeris from the republic. Most Kurds are also adherents of Islam, although some are Yazidis. In 2006 10 religious organizations were registered in Armenia. (The Jehovah's Witness community was estimated to number 12,000, but failed to qualify for registration as its statutes were deemed to be in contravention of the Constitution.)

ADVISORY COUNCIL

Religious Council: Yerevan, c/o Department for National Minorities and Religious Affairs; tel. (10) 58-16-63; f. 2002 as a consultative council to advise the Government on religious affairs; was to comprise representatives of the Government, the Office of the Prosecutor-General, the Armenian Apostolic Church, and the Catholic and Protestant Churches.

CHRISTIANITY

Armenian Apostolic Church: Vagharshapat, Monastery of St Etchmiadzin; tel. (10) 28-57-37; fax (10) 15-10-77; e-mail holysee@etchmiadzin.am; internet www.holyetchmiadzin.am; nine dioceses in Armenia, 29 dioceses and bishoprics in the rest of the world; 15 monasteries and three theological seminaries in Armenia; Supreme Patriarch KAREKIN II (Catholicos of All Armenians).

The Roman Catholic Church

Armenian Rite

Armenian Catholics in Eastern Europe are under the jurisdiction of an Ordinary). At 31 December 2005 there were an estimated 220,000 adherents within this jurisdiction.

Ordinary: Most Rev. NECHAN KARAKAHIAN (Titular Archbishop of Adana of the Armenian Rite), 3101 Gyumri, Atarbekian St 82; tel. (312) 22-115; fax (312) 34-959; e-mail armorda@gyurmi.am.

Latin Rite

The Apostolic Administrator of the Caucasus (responsible for Latin Rite Roman Catholics in Armenia and Georgia) is resident in Tbilisi, Georgia (q.v.).

JUDAISM

In the early 2000s the Jewish community numbered around 1,000, and was located principally in Yerevan.

Mordechay Navi Jewish Religious Community of Armenia: 0018 Yerevan, Nar-Dosi St 23; tel. (10) 57-16-77; fax (10) 55-41-32; e-mail burger_mc@rambler.ru; internet www.yehudim.am; Chief Rabbi of Armenia GERSH MEIR BURSHTEIN; Chair. of the Jewish Community in Armenia RIMMA VARJAPETYAN.

The Press

PRINCIPAL NEWSPAPERS

In 2004 170 newspaper titles were published in Armenia. In 2003 107 of 120 titles were published in Armenian. Those listed below are in Armenian except where otherwise stated.

Aravot (Morning): 0023 Yerevan, Arshakuniats Ave 2, 15th Floor; tel. (10) 56-89-68; fax (10) 52-87-52; e-mail news@aravot.am; internet www.aravot.am; f. 1994; daily; Editor A. ABRAMIAN; circ. 5,000.

Azg (The Nation): 0010 Yerevan, Hanrapetutiun St 47; tel. (10) 52-16-35; fax (10) 56-28-63; e-mail azg2@arminco.com; internet www.azg.am; f. 1990; daily; Editor HAGOP AVETIKIAN; circ. 3,000.

Delovoi Ekspress (Business Express): 0005 Yerevan, Tigran Metsi Ave 67 A; tel. and fax (10) 57-31-25; e-mail editor@express.am; internet www.express.am; f. 1992; weekly; economic; in Russian; Editor EDUARD NAGDALIAN.

Golos Armenii (The Voice of Armenia): 0023 Yerevan, Arshakuniats Ave 2, 7th Floor; tel. (10) 52-77-23; fax (10) 52-89-08; e-mail gonline@press.arminco.com; internet www.golos.am; f. 1934 as *Kommunist*; 3 a week; in Russian; Editor F. NAKHSHKARIAN.

Grakan Tert (Literary Paper): 0019 Yerevan, Marshal Baghramian St 3; tel. (10) 52-05-94; e-mail gr_tert@freenet.am; f. 1932; weekly; organ of the Union of Writers; Editor NORAYR ADALIAN.

Haikakan Zhamanak (Armenian Times): 0016 Yerevan, Israelian St 37; tel. (10) 58-11-75; e-mail nikol@arminco.com; internet www.hzh.am; f. 1999; daily; Editor-in-Chief NIKOL PASHINIAN; circ. 6,000.

Haiots Ashkhar (Armenian World): Yerevan, Tumanian St 38; tel. (10) 53-32-11; fax (10) 53-88-65; e-mail hayashkh@arminco.com; f. 1997; daily; Editor G. MKRTCHIAN; circ. 3,500.

Iravunk (Right): 0002 Yerevan, Yeznik Koghbatsu St 50A; tel. (10) 53-27-30; fax (10) 53-41-92; e-mail info@iravunk.com; internet www.iravunk.com; f. 1989; twice weekly; opposition newspaper; Editor HAIK BABUKHANIAN; circ. 17,000.

Marzakan Haiastan (Sport Armenia): 0023 Yerevan, Arshakuniats Ave 5; tel. and fax (10) 52-62-41; f. 1956; weekly; sports; Editor S. MOURADIAN; circ. 3,000.

Novoye Vremya (New Times): 0023 Yerevan, Arshakuniats Ave 2, 3rd Floor; tel. (10) 52-69-46; fax (10) 52-73-62; e-mail nvremya@arminco.com; internet www.nv.am; f. 1992; 3 a week; in Russian; Editor R. A. SATIAN; circ. 5,000.

Respublika Armenia (Hayastani Hanrapetutiun): 0023 Yerevan, Arshakuniats Ave 2, 9th Floor; tel. and fax (10) 54-57-00; e-mail ra@arminco.com; internet www.ra.am; f. 1990; state-owned; twice weekly; in Russian; Editor YELENA KURDIYAN; circ. 3,000.

Vozny (Hedgehog): 0023 Yerevan, Arshakuniats Ave 2, 12th Floor; tel. (10) 52-63-83; f. 1954; Editor A. SAHAKIAN.

Yeter: Yerevan, A. Manukian St 5; tel. (10) 55-34-13; fax (10) 55-17-13; e-mail editor@eter.am; internet www.eter.am; weekly; independent; television and radio programming information; Editor G. KAZARIAN.

PRINCIPAL PERIODICALS

In 2003 77 periodicals were published, of which 51 were in Armenian. In 2004 112 periodicals were published.

Armenia: Finance and Economy: 0023 Yerevan, Arshakuniats Ave 2A, 10th Floor; tel. (10) 54-48-97; e-mail armef@arminco.com; f. 1999; Editor-in-Chief MHER DAVOIAN.

Armenia Now: Yerevan; tel. (10) 53-24-22; e-mail info@armenianow.com; internet www.armenianow.com; weekly; Editor-in-Chief JOHN HUGHES.

Aroghchapoutiun (Health): 0036 Yerevan, Halabian St 46; tel. (10) 39-65-36; e-mail mharut@dmc.am; f. 1956; quarterly; theoretical, scientific-methodological, and practical journal of the Ministry of Health Care; Editor M. A. MURADIAN; circ. 2,000–5,000.

Avangard: 0023 Yerevan, Arshakuniats Ave 2A, 4th Floor; tel. (10) 54-89-18; e-mail avangard-1@rambler.ru; internet www.avangard.nt.am; f. 1923; Editor JULIETA MARTIROSSIAN.

Ayb-Fe: 0015 Yerevan, Grigor Lusavorichi St 15; tel. (10) 56-07-16; fax (10) 56-90-42; e-mail oratert@a1plus.am; internet www.a1plus.am; weekly; Editor PERCHUHI TATURIAN.

Chorord Ishkhanutiun/Chetvertaya Vlast (The Fourth Estate): Yerevan, Abovian St 12, Rm 105, Hotel Yerevan 105; tel. (10) 52-02-12; e-mail chiog@arminco.com; internet www.chi.am; monthly; in Armenian and Russian; Editor SHOGHER MATEVOSSIAN.

Garoun (Spring): 0015 Yerevan, Grigor Lusavorichi St 15; tel. (10) 56-29-56; e-mail garoun@garoun.am; internet www.garoun.am; f. 1967; monthly; independent; fiction, poetry and socio-political issues; Editor V. S. AYVAZIAN; circ. 1,500.

Gitutyun ev Tekhnika (Science and Technology): 0048 Yerevan, Komitasa Ave 49/3; tel. (10) 23-37-27; e-mail giteknik@rambler.ru; f. 1963; monthly; journal of the Research Institute of Scientific-Technical Information and of Technological and Economic Research; Dir S. AGAJANIAN; Editor H. R. KHACHATRIAN; circ. 1,000.

Hanrapetakan: Yerevan, Melik-Adamian St 2; tel. (10) 58-00-31; fax (10) 50-12-59; internet www.hhk.am; f. 2003; ideological, political and analytical journal of the Republican Party of Armenia; monthly.

168 zham (168 Hours): Yerevan, Pushkin St 3A; tel. (10) 58-48-31; fax (10) 52-29-58; e-mail info@168.am; internet www.168.am; f. 1994; weekly; opposition; news; Editor-in-Chief SATIK SEIRANIAN.

Khorhrdaran (Parliament): Yerevan; tel. (10) 58-83-12; e-mail khorhrdaran@parliament.am; internet khorhrdaran.parliament.am; f. 2003; weekly; Editor HAMLET KHUBLARIAN.

Literaturnaya Armeniya (Literary Armenia): 0019 Yerevan, Marshal Baghramian St 3; tel. (10) 56-36-57; f. 1958; monthly; journal of the Union of Writers; fiction; in Russian; Editor A. M. NALBANDIAN.

Nork: Yerevan; f. 1934; fmrly *Sovetakan Grakanutiun* (Soviet Literature); monthly; journal of the Union of Writers; fiction; Russian; Editor R. G. OVSEPIAN.

New Yerevan Times: 0010 Yerevan, Arami St 3, 2nd Floor; tel. (10) 54-57-93; e-mail times@netsys.am; weekly; in English; Editor MARINA MKHITARIAN.

Yerkir (Country): 0010 Yerevan, Hanrapetutiun St 30; tel. (10) 52-15-01; fax (10) 52-04-26; e-mail erkir@arminco.com; internet www.yerkir.am; f. 1991; weekly; organ of the ARF; also published in Lebanon; Editor-in-Chief SPARTAK SEYRANIAN; circ. 2,500.

ARMENIA   *Directory*

NEWS AGENCIES

Arka News Agency: 0010 Yerevan, Pavstos Byuzand St 1/3; tel. (10) 52-21-52; fax (10) 52-40-80; e-mail arka@arminco.com; internet www.arka.am; f. 1996; economic, financial and political news; Russian and English.

Armenpress (Armenian News Agency): 0009 Yerevan, Isaahakian St 28, 4th Floor; tel. (10) 52-67-02; fax (10) 52-57-98; e-mail contact@armenpress.am; internet www.armenpress.am; f. 1922 as state information agency, transformed into state joint-stock company in 1997; Armenian, English and Russian; Dir H. ZORIAN.

Arminfo: 0009 Yerevan, Isaahakian St 28, 2nd Floor; tel. (10) 52-20-34; fax (10) 54-31-72; e-mail news@arminfo.am; internet www.arminfo.am; f. 1991 as Snark; name changed as above in 2001; Dir EMMANUIL MKRTCHIAN; Editor ALEKSANDR AVANISOV.

De Facto: Yerevan, Arshakuniats Ave 2, 9th Floor; tel. (10) 54-57-99; fax (10) 54-56-99; e-mail defacto@defacto.am; internet www.defacto.am.

Mediamax Armenian News Agency: 0012 Yerevan, Marshal Baghramian St 31A; tel. (10) 54-54-31; fax (10) 54-54-37; e-mail news@mediamax.am; internet www.mediamax.am; Dir ARA TADEVOSIAN; Editor-in-Chief DAVID ALAVERDIAN.

Noyan Tapan (Noah's Ark): 0009 Yerevan, Isaahakian St 28, 3rd Floor; tel. (10) 56-59-65; fax (10) 52-42-79; e-mail contact@noyan-tapan.am; internet www.nt.am; f. 1991; Dir TIGRAN HAROUTUNIAN.

PRESS ASSOCIATION

Union of Journalists of Armenia: Yerevan, Pushkin St 3A; tel. (1) 56-12-76; fax (1) 56-14-47; e-mail www@internews.am; f. 1959; Dir ASTGHIK GEVORGIAN.

Publishers

Academy of Sciences Publishing House: 0019 Yerevan, Marshal Baghramian St 24G; Dir KH. H. BARSEGHIAN.

Arevik Publishing House: 0009 Yerevan, Terian St 91; tel. (10) 52-45-61; fax (10) 52-05-36; e-mail arevick@netsys.am; internet www.arevik.am; f. 1986; political, scientific, fiction for children, textbooks; Pres. DAVID HOVHANNES; Exec. Dir ASTGHIK STEPANIAN.

Hayastan (Armenia Publishing House): 0009 Yerevan, Isaahakian St 28; tel. (10) 52-85-20; e-mail nunjan@hragir.aua.am; f. 1921; political and fiction; Dir VAHAGN SARKISSIAN.

Haikanuil Hanragitaran Hratarakchutioun (Armenian Encyclopedia Publishing House): 0001 Yerevan, Tumanian St 17; tel. (10) 52-43-41; fax (10) 52-27-33; e-mail encyclop@sci.am; internet www.encyclopedia.am; f. 1967; encyclopedias and other reference books; Editor H. M. AIVAZIAN.

Louys Publishing Co: 0009 Yerevan, Isaahakian St 28; tel. (10) 52-53-13; fax (10) 56-55-07; e-mail louys@arminco.com; f. 1955; textbooks; Dir H. Z. HAROUTUNIAN.

Nairi: 0009 Yerevan, Terian St 91; tel. and fax (10) 56-58-54; e-mail nairi_hrat@rambler.ru; f. 1991; fiction, science, translations and reference; Pres. HRACHIA TAMRAZIAN.

Tigran Mets (Tigran the Great) Publishing House: 0023 Yerevan, Arshakuniats St 2; tel. (10) 52-70-56; e-mail tigranmets2002@yahoo.com; fiction, poetry, science and children's books; Dir VREJ MARKOSSIAN.

Yerevan State University Publishing House: 0025 Yerevan, A. Manukian St 1; tel. (10) 55-55-70; fax (10) 55-46-41; e-mail pr-int@ysu.am; internet www.ysu.am; f. 1919; textbooks and reference books, history, literary criticism, science and fiction; Dir PERCH STEPANIAN.

Zangak-97: 0010 Yerevan, Vardanants St 8; tel. (10) 54-05-17; fax (10) 54-06-07; e-mail info@zangak.am; internet www.zangak.am; f. 2000; scientific works, school teaching manuals, literature for children, translations of foreign authors; Pres. SOKRAT MKRTCHIAN.

PUBLISHERS' ASSOCIATION

National Union of Armenian Publishers: 0009 Yerevan, Isahaakian St 28/22; tel. (10) 56-31-57; fax (10) 56-55-07; e-mail pubunion@gmail.com; f. 1999; Pres. SOS MOVSISSIAN.

Broadcasting and Communications

TELECOMMUNICATIONS

Armenia Telephone Co (ArmenTel): Yerevan, Azatutiun Ave 24; tel. (10) 54-91-00; fax (10) 28-98-88; internet www.armentel.com; f. 1995; 10% state-owned, 90% owned by VimpelCom (Russia); fixed line and mobile communications operator.

VivaCell: 0015 Yerevan, Argishti St 4/1; tel. (10) 56-87-77; fax (10) 56-92-22; e-mail info@vivacell.am; internet www.vivacell.am; f. 2004; mobile telecommunications provider; operated by K Telecom CJSC; Man. Dir RALPH YERIKIAN.

BROADCASTING

National Commission on Television and Radio (NCTR) (HRAH): 0002 Yerevan, Sarian St 22; tel. (10) 53-95-09; fax (10) 53-90-34; e-mail nctr@tvradio.am; internet www.tvradio.am; Dir GRIGOR AMALIAN.

Radio

Armenian Public Radio: 0025 Yerevan, A. Manukian St 5; tel. (10) 55-33-43; fax (10) 55-46-00; e-mail president@mediaconcern.am; internet www.armradio.am; domestic broadcasts in Armenian, Russian and Kurdish; external broadcasts in Armenian, Russian, Kurdish, Azerbaijani, Arabic, English, French, German, Spanish and Farsi; Dir-Gen. ARMEN AMIRIAN.

Television

Armenian Public Television: 0047 Yerevan, Hovsepian St 26; tel. (10) 56-95-74; fax (10) 56-24-60; internet www.armtv.com; state jt-stock co; Chair. of Council ALEKSAN HAROUTUNIAN; Exec. Dir ARMEN ARZUMANIAN.

Armenia TV: 0054 Yerevan, Yeghvard Ave 1; tel. (10) 36-69-25; fax (10) 36-68-52; e-mail mail@armeniatv.am; internet www.armeniatv.am; f. 1999; largest private television company in Armenia; transmits programming terrestrially, by cable and by satellite; Dir BAGRAT SARKISSIAN.

H2 (Armenian Second TV Channel): 0088 Yerevan, Ajapniak, Nazarbekian Distr., G. 3, Bl. 3/1; tel. (10) 39-88-31; fax (10) 39-56-40; e-mail h2@tv.am; internet www.tv.am; f. 1998; present name adopted 2005; Dir SAMVEL MAYRAPETIAN.

Shant TV: 0028 Yerevan, Kievian St 16, 10th Floor; tel. (10) 27-76-68; fax (10) 26-76-90; e-mail info@shanttv.am; internet www.shant-tv.com; f. 1994; private, independent; Pres. ARTHUR A. YEZEKIAN.

Finance

(cap. = capital; res = reserves; dep. = deposits; m. = million; brs = branches; amounts in drams, unless otherwise stated)

BANKING

Central Bank

Central Bank of the Republic of Armenia: 0010 Yerevan, Vazgen Sarkissian St 6; tel. (10) 58-38-41; fax (10) 52-38-52; e-mail mcba@cba.am; internet www.cba.am; f. 1993; state owned; cap. 100.0m., res 22,355.5m., dep. 225,326.7m. (Dec. 2006); Gov. (vacant).

Commercial Banks

At the end of 2005 there were 21 commercial banks (with 269 branches) in operation in Armenia.

ACBA-Credit Agricole Bank CJSC: 0009 Yerevan, Byron St 1; tel. (10) 56-85-58; fax (10) 54-34-85; e-mail acba@acba.am; internet www.acba.am; f. 1996 as Agricultural Co-operative Bank of Armenia; name changed as above Sept. 2006; cap. 1,519.3m., res 4,231.1m., dep. 28,021.6m. (Dec. 2005); Gen. Man. STEPAN GISHIAN.

Ardshininvestbank (ASHIB) (Bank for Industry, Construction and Investment): 0015 Yerevan, Grigor Lusavorichi St 13; tel. (10) 52-85-13; fax (10) 56-74-86; e-mail office@ashib.am; internet www.ashib.am; f. 2003 with acquisition of banking business of Ardshinbank and partially acquired the assets of Armagrobank; 58.6% owned by Business Investments Centre Ltd (Armenia), 19.5% owned by Rasko Armenia; cap. 11,143.7m., res 362.4m., dep. 55,882.6m. (Dec. 2006); Chair. of Bd ARAM ANDREASSIAN; 54 brs.

Armenian Development Bank: 0015 Yerevan, Paronian St 21/1; tel. (10) 59-14-00; fax (10) 59-14-05; e-mail info@armdb.com; internet www.armdb.com; f. 1990; Chief Exec. KAREN SARKISSIAN.

Armenian Economy Development Bank (Armeconombank) (AEB): 0002 Yerevan, Amirian St 23/1; tel. (10) 56-33-32; fax (10) 53-89-04; e-mail bank@aeb.am; internet www.aeb.am; f. 1988; jt-stock co; corporate banking; cap. 2,333.3m., res 413.1m., dep. 29,367.8m. (Dec. 2006); 25% owned by the European Bank for Reconstruction and Development; Chair. of Bd of Dirs SARIBEK SUKIASSIAN; CEO DAVIT SUKIASSIAN; 44 brs.

Armenian Import-Export Bank (Armimpexbank): 0010 Yerevan, Vazgen Sarkissian St 2; tel. (10) 58-99-06; fax (10) 56-59-58; e-mail office@impexbank.am; internet www.impexbank.am; f. 1992;

93.1% owned by CIE (United Kingdom); cap. 2,000m., res 338.0m., dep. 7,919.0m. (Dec. 2006); Chair. of Bd Levon Barkhudarian; CEO Ara Alexanian; 5 brs.

Armbusinessbank (ABB): 0010 Yerevan, Vardanants St 13; tel. (10) 52-39-29; fax (10) 54-58-35; e-mail info@armbusinessbank.am; internet www.armbusinessbank.am; f. 1992; as Arminvestbank; name changed Aug. 2006; 35% owned by Ukrprombank (Ukraine), 35% owned by Alpha-Garant (Ukraine), cap. 2,400m. (Sept. 2006); Chair. of Bd Ara Kirakossian.

Artsakhbank: 0028 Yerevan, Kievian St 3; tel. (10) 27-77-19; fax (10) 27-77-49; e-mail artsakhbank@ktsurf.net; internet www.artsakhbank.am; f. 1996; cap. 2,244.3m., res 393m., dep. 18,883.1m. (Dec. 2006); Chair. of Bd of Dirs Hratch Kaprielian; Chair. of Bd Kamo Nersissian; 12 brs.

Converse Bank: 0010 Yerevan, Vazgen Sarkissian St 26/1; tel. (10) 51-12-11; fax (10) 51-12-12; e-mail corr@conversebank.am; internet www.conversebank.com; f. 1994; 48.72% owned by Hudsotrade (Cyprus); cap. 1,233.1m., profits and res 2,817.0m., dep. 24,848.4m. (Dec. 2006); Dir-Gen. Artak Hanesian; 16 brs.

HSBC Bank of Armenia: 0009 Yerevan, Teryan St 66; tel. (10) 51-50-00; fax (10) 51-50-01; e-mail hsbc.armenia@hsbc.com; internet www.hsbc.am; f. 1996; 70% owned by HSBC Europe BV (Netherlands); cap. 2,437.6m., res −96.2m., dep. 70,702.4m. (Dec. 2006); Chief Exec. Timothy Slater; 4 brs.

InecoBank: 0001 Yerevan, Tumanian St 17; tel. (10) 56-37-25; fax (10) 54-51-66; e-mail inecobank@inecobank.am; internet www.inecobank.am; f. 1996; cap. 1,385.3m., res 2,252.1m., dep. 14,187.6m. (Dec. 2006); Chair. Avetis Baloyan.

Mellat Bank: 0010 Yerevan, Amirian St 6, POB 24; tel. (10) 58-13-54; fax (10) 54-08-85; e-mail mellat@netsys.am; internet www.mellatbank.am; f. 1995; wholly owned by Bank Mellat (Iran); cap. 3,522.1m. (Dec. 2006); Chair. and Gen. Dir Morteza Beheshtirouy.

Prometey Bank: 0010 Yerevan, Hanrapetutiun St 44/2; tel. (10) 56-20-36; fax (10) 54-57-19; e-mail intoperations@prometeybank.am; internet www.prometeybank.am; f. 1990; present name adopted 2001; cap. 3,538.5m. (Dec. 2005); res 52.1m., dep. 8,243.7m. (Dec. 2006); Chair. of Bd Emil Soghomonian.

Savings Bank

VTB Bank (Armenia): 375010 Yerevan, Nalbandian St 46; tel. (10) 58-04-51; fax (10) 56-55-78; e-mail headoffice@vtb.am; internet www.vtb.am; f. 1923 under the name Armsavingsbank; present name adopted 2006; 70.0% owned by Bank VTB (Russia); cap. 7,526.2m., res 420.2m., dep. 22,589.1m. (July 2007); Chair. Valery V. Ovsyannikov; 89 brs.

Banking Union

Union of Banks of Armenia: 0009 Yerevan, Koriun St 19A; tel. and fax (10) 52-77-31; e-mail uba@uba.am; internet www.uba.am; f. 1995; oversees banking activity; Pres. Stephen Gishyan; Exec. Dir Seyran Sargsyan.

COMMODITY AND STOCK EXCHANGES

Armenian Stock Exchange (Armex): 0010 Yerevan, Mher Mkrtchian St 5B, 3rd & 4th Floors; tel. (10) 54-33-21; fax (10) 54-33-24; e-mail info@armex.am; internet www.armex.am; f. 2001; Exec. Dir Armen G. Melikyan.

Yerevan Adamand Commodity and Raw Materials Exchange: 0010 Yerevan, Agatangeghos St 6/1; tel. (10) 56-31-15; fax (10) 56-52-28; e-mail ycre@cornet.am; internet www.yercomex.am; f. 1990; Dir Grigor Vardikian.

INSURANCE

In 2005 there were 23 licensed insurance companies in Armenia.

AHA Royal Insurance: 0010 Yerevan, Hanrapetutiun St 62/98; tel. (10) 52-67-30; fax (10) 52-67-40; e-mail aharoyal@insurer.am; internet www.insurer.am; f. 2004; insurance and reinsurance; Gen. Dir Hracha I. Karapetian.

Arajin Apahovagrakan: 0025 Yerevan, Charents St 1, 4th Floor; tel. (10) 57-51-18; fax (10) 55-94-73; e-mail info@arajin.am; f. 1995; general non-life insurance; Exec. Dir Paylak Ghukassian.

Cascade Insurance and Reinsurance Co (CIRCO): 0033 Yerevan, Hrachya Kochari St 5; tel. (10) 27-87-76; fax (10) 27-82-21; e-mail info@cascadeinre.com; internet www.cascadeinre.com; f. 2004; 35% owned by the European Bank for Reconstruction and Development; Gen. Dir Garnik Tonoyan.

Grand Insurance Co: 0002 Yerevan, Tumanian St 38; tel. (10) 56-03-92; fax (10) 51-28-23; f. 1999; Man. Dir Artak S. Antonian.

IngoArmenia: 0002 Yerevan, Demirchian St 38; tel. (10) 54-31-34; fax (10) 54-31-35; e-mail efes@arminco.com; internet www.ingoarmenia.am; f. 1997; as Efes; Gen. Dir Levon Altunian.

London-Yerevan Insurance Co: 0015 Yerevan, Sarian St 26/3; tel. (10) 54-16-50; fax (10) 54-25-58; e-mail admin@london-yerevan.acom; internet www.london-yerevan.com; f. 1998; wholly owned by Londongate Group (United Kingdom); Man. Dir Sona Dalalian.

Sil Insurance Co: 0018 Yerevan, Tigran Mets Ave 39; tel. (10) 53-52-90; fax (10) 56-52-34; f. 2000; risk reinsurance; Exec. Dir Hayk Baghramian.

State Insurance Armenia (Gosstrakh-Armenia): 0001 Yerevan, Hanrepetutiun St 76/3; tel. and fax (10) 56-06-89; e-mail info@gosstrax-armenia.am; f. 2001; Russian-Armenian joint venture; insurance and reinsurance; Man. Dir Vahan H Avetissian.

Trade and Industry

GOVERNMENT AGENCY

Armenian Development Agency (ADA): 0025 Yerevan, Charents St 17; tel. and fax (10) 54-22-72; e-mail info@ada.am; internet www.ada.am; f. 1998; foreign investment and export development; Gen. Dir Dr Vahagn Movsissian.

CHAMBER OF COMMERCE

Chamber of Commerce and Industry of the Republic of Armenia: 0010 Yerevan, Khanjian St 11; tel. (10) 56-01-84; fax (10) 58-78-71; e-mail armcci@arminco.com; internet www.armcci.am; f. 1959; Chair. Martin Sargsyan.

EMPLOYERS' ORGANIZATIONS

Armenian Business Small and Medium Entrepreneurship Association: 0010 Yerevan, Republic Sq., House of Unions 43; tel. (10) 56-31-50; fax (10) 56-02-29; e-mail invest@arminco.com; f. 1991; incl. Institute of Business Development and Human Resources, FOBIX Business Consulting Centre, Electronic Business Agency and Bankruptcy Protection Foundation; Pres. Seyran Avaghian.

Armenian Union of Manufacturers and Businessmen (Employers) of Armenia—UMB(E)A: 0010 Yerevan, Agatanghegos St 5; tel. and fax (10) 56-29-21; e-mail umba@arminco.com; internet www.umba.am; f. 1996; Chair. Arsen Khazarian.

TRADE ASSOCIATIONS

Union of Merchants of Armenia: 0037 Yerevan, Azatutioun Ave 1/1; tel. (10) 25-28-54; fax (10) 25-91-76; e-mail merchants@netsys.am; f. 1993; reorganized 1999; Pres. Tsolvard Gevorgian.

UTILITIES

Public Services Regulatory Commission of Armenia (PSRC): 0002 Yerevan, Sarian St 22; tel. (10) 52-25-22; fax (10) 52-55-63; e-mail info@psrc.am; internet www.psrc.am; f. 1997; fmrly Energy Commission of Armenia; Chair. Robert Nazarian.

Electricity

Electricity Networks of Armenia (ArmElNet—ENA): 0047 Yerevan, Armenakyian St 127; tel. (10) 54-21-63; fax (10) 54-36-83; e-mail elnet@arminco.com; internet www.ena.am; f. 2002; owned by Inter RAO UES (Russia); national electricity distributor comprising the four former regional electricity networks; Gen. Dir Eugene Gladunchik.

High Voltage Electric Networks (HV Networks): 0114 Yerevan, Zoravar Andranikian St 1; tel. (10) 72-00-10; fax (10) 72-01-21; e-mail hvn@arminco.am; f. 2003; comprises nine regions; Dir Sahak Abrahamian.

International Energy Corpn CJSC: 0014 Yerevan, Adontsi St 10B; tel. (10) 24-50-99; fax (10) 24-51-99; e-mail mailmek@mek.am; internet www.mek.am; f. 2003; wholly owned by Inter RAO EES, a subsidiary of Unified Energy System of Russia; manages Hrazdan Thermal Power Plant, Sevan-Hrazdan Hydroelectric Power Plant cascade and Armenian Nuclear Power Plant; Gen. Dir Michael Mantrov.

Operator of Electrical Energy System CJSC: 0009 Yerevan, Abovian St 27; tel. (10) 59-29-60; fax (10) 52-47-25; e-mail arm_eso@freenet.am; f. 2003; assumed part of the function of former state monopoly Armenergo.

Gas

ArmRosGazProm—ARG: 0091 Yerevan, Tbilisian St 43; tel. (10) 29-48-10; fax (10) 29-47-28; e-mail inbox@armrusgasprom.am; internet www.armrusgasprom.am; f. 1997; Armenian-Russian joint-stock co; 45% state-owned, 45% owned by Gazprom (Russia); sole natural gas producer in Armenia; Exec. Dir Karen Karapetian.

Water

Yerevan Water Supply and Sewerage (YWSC): Yerevan, Abovian St 66A; tel. (10) 56-95-13; fax (10) 56-93-357; provides water and sewerage services to Yerevan municipality; managed by Générale des Eaux (France); Gen. Dir D. ALEXANIAN.

TRADE UNIONS

At 1 January 2006 some 743 trade-union organizations were registered with the Ministry of Justice.

Confederation of Trade Unions of Armenia: 0010 Yerevan, Vazgen Sarkissian St 26; tel. (10) 58-36-82; fax (10) 54-33-82; e-mail boris@xar.am; Chair. MARTIN HAROUTUNIAN.

Transport

RAILWAYS

In 2005 there were 731 km of railway track in Armenia. There are international lines to Iran and Georgia; the lines to Azerbaijan and Turkey remained closed in 2007. In November 2004 it was agreed that rail transport between Russia and Armenia would be restored in 2005, with the co-operation of Georgia; the restoration of the Kavkaz (Russia)–Poti (Georgia) ferry route, with its railway facility, in January 2005 was also expected greatly to enhance the speed of cargo transport across the region.

Armenia Railways: 0005 Yerevan, Tigran Mets Ave 50; tel. (10) 52-04-28; fax (10) 57-36-30; e-mail arway@mbox.amilink.net; f. 1998; managed by Russian Railways; Pres. ARARAT KHRIMIAN.

Yerevan Metro: 0033 Yerevan, Marshal Baghramian St 76; tel. (10) 27-45-43; fax (10) 27-24-60; e-mail papiev@netsys.am; f. 1981; 12.1km, with 10 stations (2005); Gen. Dir VAHAGN HAKOPIAN.

ROADS

In 2005 there were an estimated 10,296 km of roads in Armenia. As a result of the closure of Azerbaijan's and Turkey's borders with Armenia, the Kajaran highway linking Armenia with Iran emerged as Armenia's most important international road connection; in December 1995 a permanent road bridge over the Araks (Aras, Araxes) river was opened.

CIVIL AVIATION

Zvartnots International Airport, 15 km west of Yerevan, is the main national airport; there are also international airports in Gyumri (Shirak) and Yerebuni (also near Yerevan).

Civil Aviation Department: 0042 Yerevan, Zvartnots Airport; tel. (10) 28-57-68; fax (10) 28-53-54; e-mail gayane.davtyan@aviation.am; internet www.aviation.am; f. 1933; Dir ARTYOM MOVSESIAN.

Armavia: 0042 Yerevan, Zvartnots Airport; tel. (10) 54-08-10; fax (10) 54-08-10; e-mail info@u8.am; internet www.u8.am; f. 1996; operates flights to destinations in Europe and Asia; Gen. Dir NORAIR BELLUIAN; 480 employees.

Tourism

Following secession from the USSR, tourism severely declined, although by the late 1990s some European firms were beginning to introduce tours to the country. According to the World Tourism Organization, tourism receipts amounted to US $161m. in 2005, compared with just $45m. in 1997. Armenia received an estimated 318,563 tourist arrivals in 2005. The major tourist attractions were the capital, Yerevan; Artashat, an early trading centre on the 'Silk Road'; and medieval monasteries. There was, however, little accommodation available outside the capital.

Directorate of Trade, Tourism and Services: Ministry of Trade and Economic Development, 0010 Yerevan, Mher Mkrtchian St 5; tel. (10) 58-94-94; fax (10) 56-61-23; e-mail garnikn@yahoo.com; Dir ARTAK DAVTIAN.

Tourism Armenia: 0010 Yerevan, 1 Proshian St 9; tel. (10) 53-45-01; fax (10) 52-25-83; e-mail tic@arminco.com; internet www.tourismarmenia.org; f. 1998; tourist information centre; Chair. KAREN GRIGORIAN.

Armenian Tourism Development Agency (ATDA): 0010 Yerevan, Nalbandian St 3; tel. (10) 54-23-03; fax (10) 54-47-92; e-mail help@armeniainfo.am; internet www.armeniainfo.am; f. 2001; Dir NINA HOVNANIAN.

AUSTRALIA

Introductory Survey

Location, Climate, Language, Religion, Flag, Capital

The Commonwealth of Australia occupies the whole of the island continent of Australia, lying between the Indian and Pacific Oceans and its offshore islands, principally Tasmania to the south-east. Australia's nearest neighbours are Timor-Leste (formerly East Timor) and Papua New Guinea, to the north. In the summer (November–February) there are tropical monsoons in the northern part of the continent (except for the Queensland coast), but the winters (July–August) are dry. Both the north-west and north-east coasts are liable to experience tropical cyclones between December and April. In the southern half of the country, winter is the wet season; rainfall decreases rapidly inland. Very high temperatures, sometimes exceeding 50°C (122°F), are experienced during the summer months over the arid interior and for some distance to the south, as well as during the pre-monsoon months in the north. The official language is English; 170 indigenous languages are spoken by Aboriginal and Torres Strait Islander peoples, who comprise 2.3% of the population according to the census of August 2006. The majority of the population profess Christianity (of whom 25.8% were Roman Catholic and 18.7% Anglican at the 2006 census). The national flag (proportions 1 by 2) is blue, with a representation of the United Kingdom flag in the upper hoist, a large seven-pointed white star in the lower hoist and five smaller white stars, in the form of the Southern Cross constellation, in the fly. The capital, Canberra, lies in one of two enclaves of federal territory known as the Australian Capital Territory (ACT).

Recent History

Since the end of the Second World War in 1945, Australia has played an important role in Asian affairs, and has strengthened its political and economic links with Indonesia, Japan, the People's Republic of China and other countries in the region. Australia has co-operated closely with the USA (in the context of ANZUS, see p. 422), and has given much aid to Asian and Pacific countries.

At the election of December 1949 the ruling Australian Labor Party (ALP) was defeated by the Liberal Party, in coalition with the Country Party. In January 1966 Sir Robert Menzies resigned after 16 years as Prime Minister, and was succeeded by Harold Holt, who was returned to office at elections in December of that year. However, Holt died in December 1967. His successor, Senator John Gorton, took office in January 1968 but resigned, after losing a vote of confidence, in March 1971. William McMahon was Prime Minister from March 1971 until December 1972, when, after 23 years in office, the Liberal-Country Party coalition was defeated at a general election for the House of Representatives. The ALP, led by Gough Whitlam, won 67 of the 125 seats in the lower chamber. Following a conflict between the Whitlam Government and the Senate, both Houses of Parliament were dissolved in April 1974, and a general election was held in May. The ALP was returned to power, although with a reduced majority in the House of Representatives. However, the Government failed to gain a majority in the Senate, and in October 1975 the Opposition in the Senate obstructed legislative approval of budget proposals. The Government was not willing to consent to a general election over the issue, but in November the Governor-General, Sir John Kerr, intervened and took the unprecedented step of dismissing the Government. A caretaker Ministry was installed under Malcolm Fraser, the Liberal leader, who formed a coalition Government with the Country Party. This coalition gained large majorities in both Houses of Parliament at a general election in December 1975, but the majorities were progressively reduced at general elections in December 1977 and October 1980.

Fraser's coalition Government was defeated by the ALP at a general election in March 1983. Robert (Bob) Hawke, who had replaced William (Bill) Hayden as Labor leader in the previous month, became the new Prime Minister and immediately organized a meeting of representatives of government, employers and trade unions to reach agreement on a prices and incomes policy (the 'Accord') that would allow economic recovery. Hawke called a general election for December 1984, 15 months earlier than necessary, and the ALP was returned to power with a reduced majority in the House of Representatives. The opposition coalition between the Liberal Party and the National Party (formerly known as the Country Party) collapsed in April 1987, when 12 National Party MPs withdrew from the agreement and formed the New National Party (led by the right-wing Sir Johannes Bjelke-Petersen, the Premier of Queensland), while the remaining 14 National Party MPs continued to support their leader, Ian Sinclair, who wished to remain within the alliance. Parliament was dissolved in June, in preparation for an early general election in July. The election campaign was dominated by economic issues. The ALP was returned to office with an increased majority, securing 86 of the 148 seats in the House of Representatives. The Liberal and National Parties announced the renewal of the opposition alliance in August. Four months later, Bjelke-Petersen was forced to resign as Premier of Queensland, under pressure from National Party officials.

During 1988 the Hawke Government suffered several defeats at by-elections, seemingly as a result of a decline in living standards and an unpopular policy of wage restraint. The ALP narrowly retained power at state elections in Victoria, but was defeated in New South Wales, where it had held power for 12 years. In May 1989 the leader of the Liberal Party, John Howard, was replaced by Andrew Peacock, and Charles Blunt succeeded Ian Sinclair as leader of the National Party. In July a commission of inquiry into alleged corruption in Queensland published its report. The report documented several instances of official corruption and electoral malpractice by the Queensland Government, particularly during the administration of Bjelke-Petersen. Following the publication of the report, support for the National Party within Queensland declined once more, and in December the ALP defeated the National Party in the state election (the first time that it had defeated the National Party in Queensland since 1957). By the end of 1991 four former members of the Queensland Cabinet and the former chief of the state's police force had received custodial sentences. The trial of Bjelke-Petersen, initially on charges of perjury and corruption but subsequently of perjury alone, resulted in dismissal of the case, when the jury failed to reach a verdict.

In February 1990 Hawke announced that a general election for the House of Representatives and for 40 of the 76 seats in the Senate was to be held on 24 March. The Government's position in the period preceding the election had been strengthened by the ALP's victory in Queensland in December 1989, the removal of an unpopular Labor leadership in Western Australia and its replacement by the first female Premier, Dr Carmen Lawrence, and by the support that it secured from environmental groups as a result of its espousal of 'green' issues. Although the opposition parties won the majority of the first-preference votes in the election for the House of Representatives, the endorsement of the environmental groups delivered a block of second-preference votes to the ALP, which was consequently returned to power, albeit with a reduced majority, securing 78 of the 148 seats. Following its defeat, Peacock immediately resigned as leader of the Liberal Party and was replaced by Dr John Hewson, a former professor of economics. Blunt lost his seat in the election and was succeeded as leader of the National Party by Timothy Fischer.

In September 1990, at a meeting of senior ALP members, government proposals to initiate a controversial programme of privatization were endorsed, effectively ending almost 100 years of the ALP's stance against private ownership. In October plans for constitutional and structural reform were approved in principle by the leaders of the six state and two territory governments. The proposed reforms envisaged the creation of national standards in regulations and services. They also aimed to alleviate the financial dependence of the states and territories on the Federal Government. These suggested reforms, however, encountered strong opposition from sections of the public services, the trade unions and the business community. In July 1991 the leaders of the federal and state Governments finally agreed to reforms in the country's systems of marketing, transport, trade and taxation, with the aim of creating a single national economy from 1992.

In June 1991, following months of divisions within the ALP, Hawke narrowly defeated a challenge to his leadership from Paul Keating, the Deputy Prime Minister and Treasurer, who accused the Prime Minister of reneging on a promise to resign in his favour before the next general election. This cast doubt on Hawke's credibility, as he had assured Parliament and the public in 1990 that he would continue as leader for the whole of the parliamentary term. Following his defeat, Keating resigned. In December 1991 Hawke dismissed John Kerin, Keating's replacement as Treasurer, following a series of political and economic crises. Hawke called another leadership election, but, on this occasion, he was defeated by Keating, who accordingly became Prime Minister. A major reorganization of the Cabinet followed.

Following the ALP's defeat in state elections in Tasmania, the party encountered further embarrassment in April 1992, when a by-election in Melbourne to fill the parliamentary seat vacated by Bob Hawke was won by a local football club coach, standing as an independent candidate. Meanwhile, Brian Burke, the former Premier of Western Australia, was arrested, having resigned as Australia's ambassador to Ireland and the Holy See in April 1991 following preliminary investigations by a Royal Commission into the financial dealings of the Labor Government of Western Australia in the 1980s. It was alleged that, during his term of office, he had misappropriated more than $A17,000 from a parliamentary expense account. In October 1992 the conclusions of the inquiry into the ALP's alleged involvement in corrupt practices in Western Australia were released. The Royal Commission was highly critical of the improper transactions between successive governments of Western Australia and business entrepreneurs. Burke's conduct drew particular criticism. In July 1994 he received a prison sentence of two years upon conviction on four charges of fraud; he was released in February 1995, but was sentenced to three years' imprisonment in February 1997 for the theft of $A122,000 from ALP funds. Furthermore, in February 1995 Ray O'Connor, Premier of Western Australia between 1982 and 1983, received a prison sentence of 18 months, having been found guilty of the theft in 1984 of $A25,000, intended as a donation to the Liberal Party. He was released in August 1995.

In September 1992 John Bannon, the ALP Premier of South Australia, became the seventh state Premier since 1982 to leave office in disgrace. His resignation was due to a scandal relating to attempts to offset the heavy financial losses incurred by the State Bank of South Australia. At state elections in Queensland in mid-September, the ALP administration of Wayne Goss was returned to power. In the following month, however, the ruling ALP was defeated in state elections in Victoria. Furthermore, in November a new financial scandal emerged: the federal Treasurer was alleged to have suppressed information pertaining to the former ALP Government of Victoria, which, in a clandestine manner prior to the state elections, was believed to have exceeded its borrowing limits.

By late 1992, therefore, the ALP's prospects of being returned to office at the forthcoming general election appeared to have been seriously damaged. Proposals for radical tax and economic reforms that were advocated by the federal opposition leader, Dr John Hewson, attracted much attention. At state elections in Western Australia in February 1993, the incumbent Labor Government was defeated. Dr Carmen Lawrence was replaced as Premier by Richard Court of the Liberal-National coalition.

Nevertheless, at the general election, held on 13 March 1993, the ALP was unexpectedly returned to office for a fifth consecutive term, having secured 80 of the 147 seats in the House of Representatives. In early 1994 the Government was embarrassed by the resignations of two ministers in connection with separate financial scandals. In May Dr John Hewson was replaced as leader of the Liberal Party by Alexander Downer, a supporter of the monarchy. Downer was therefore expected to lead the campaign against Paul Keating's proposal that Australia become a republic (see below). In January 1995, however, Downer resigned. The party leadership was resumed by John Howard, also a monarchist.

At state elections in New South Wales in March 1995 the ALP defeated the ruling Liberal-National coalition. Robert (Bob) Carr was appointed Premier. At a federal by-election in Canberra, however, the ALP suffered a serious reverse when, for the first time in 15 years, the seat fell to the Liberal Party. In July, at state elections in Queensland, the ALP Government of Wayne Goss was narrowly returned to office, only to be ousted following a by-election defeat in February 1996. In June 1995, meanwhile, the Deputy Prime Minister, Brian Howe, who intended to retire at the next general election, announced his resignation from the Cabinet. He was replaced by the Minister for Finance, Kim Beazley.

At the general election held on 2 March 1996 the Liberal-National coalition achieved a decisive victory, securing a total of 94 of the 148 seats in the House of Representatives. The ALP won only 49 seats. In the Senate the minor parties and independent members retained the balance of power. John Howard of the Liberal Party became Prime Minister, and immediately promised to give priority to the issues of industrial relations, the transfer to partial private ownership of the state telecommunications company, Telstra, and to expanding relations with Asia. The leader of the National Party, Tim Fischer, was appointed Deputy Prime Minister and Minister for Trade. Paul Keating was replaced as leader of the ALP by Kim Beazley.

Meanwhile, fears for Australia's tradition of racial tolerance continued to grow. In October 1996 Pauline Hanson, a newly elected independent member of the House of Representatives, aroused much controversy when, in a speech envisaging 'civil war', she reiterated her demands for the ending of immigration from Asia and for the elimination of special funding for Aboriginal people. The Prime Minister attracted criticism for his failure to issue a direct denunciation of the views of Hanson, a former member of the Liberal Party. In March 1997 Hanson established the One Nation party, which rapidly attracted support. In subsequent months, however, large protests against her policies took place in Perth, Melbourne and Canberra. Meanwhile, after his initial unemphatic response, the Prime Minister condemned her views. In August, as fears for Australian revenue from Asian investment, trade and tourism grew, the Government issued a document on foreign policy, in which Hanson's views were strongly repudiated and in which Australia's commitment to racial equality was reiterated. In November former Prime Ministers Keating, Hawke and Whitlam published a statement denouncing Pauline Hanson.

In early 1998 the long-standing tension between the National Farmers' Federation and the powerful Maritime Union of Australia (MUA) developed into a bitter dispute over trade unionists' rights when farmers established their own non-unionized stevedoring operation in Melbourne to handle their exports, in protest at high dockside costs and alleged inefficiency. The confrontation escalated in April, when Patrick Stevedores, a major cargo-handling company based in Sydney, dismissed its entire unionized work-force of 1,400 dockers, with the intention of replacing them with secretly trained contract workers. As part of its campaign to break the MUA monopoly (the offensive being supported by the Government), Patrick Stevedores drafted in hundreds of security guards to its 14 terminals around Australia, in an operation to lock out the dockers. The Federal Court, however, subsequently ruled that Patrick Stevedores had acted illegally and ordered the company to reinstate the 1,400 trade unionists. Following the rejection of an appeal to the High Court by Patrick Stevedores and the return to work of the dockers in May, the Prime Minister nevertheless pledged to press ahead with waterfront reform. Although the majority of Australians appeared to support the reform of labour practices in the country's ports, the Government's handling of the dispute had attracted much criticism.

Meanwhile, in December 1997 the New One Nation Party was established by former supporters of Pauline Hanson, who had apparently become disillusioned with her autocratic style of leadership. In June 1998, at state elections in Queensland, One Nation won 23% of first-preference votes, thus unexpectedly securing 11 of the 89 seats in the legislature and arousing renewed concern among tourism and business leaders. In August it was announced that an early general election was to be held in October. As the campaign commenced, former Prime Ministers Whitlam, Fraser, Hawke and Keating signed an open letter urging citizens not to support racist candidates at the forthcoming election.

At the election, conducted on 3 October 1998, the Liberal-National coalition was narrowly returned to office, winning a total of 80 of the 148 seats in the House of Representatives. The ALP increased its representation to 67 seats. Contrary to expectations, the One Nation party failed to win any representation in the lower house, the controversial Pauline Hanson losing her Queensland seat. (The one seat secured by One Nation in the Senate was subsequently subjected to a legal challenge, owing to the candidate's apparent failure to meet citizenship requirements—see below.) In a referendum held on the same day, the electorate of the Northern Territory unexpectedly rejected a proposal for the territory's elevation to full statehood.

In February 1999 Pauline Hanson was re-elected leader of One Nation, despite a series of defections, including the departure from the party of several of the 11 One Nation members of the Queensland legislature. At state elections in New South Wales in March, at which the ALP was returned to power, One Nation won two seats in the 42-member upper chamber. In June a court ruled that the One Nation Senator was ineligible to occupy her seat in the federal upper house, owing to her failure to renounce her British citizenship prior to the general election. She was subsequently replaced by another member of One Nation. In January 2000 police officers in Queensland and New South Wales raided premises belonging to the party, seizing hundreds of documents relating to its membership and financial structure. In April the Queensland Electoral Commission ruled that the party had been fraudulently registered by the falsification of significant sections of its 200-name membership list, in order to qualify for public funding in Queensland. Consequently, the party was ordered to repay some $A0.5m. of state funds which it had received. As the sole signatory on the registration papers, Pauline Hanson found herself personally responsible for the repayment. Hanson repaid the funds after a successful appeal for public donations, and she re-registered the One Nation party in January 2001 to contest the forthcoming Queensland state elections (see below).

Following state elections in Victoria in September 1999, the Liberal-National Premier, Jeffrey Kennett, was replaced by Stephen Bracks of the ALP. The defeat of the Liberal-National coalition was regarded as a set-back to the Federal Government's programme of economic reform, the transfer of public utilities to the private sector having been particularly unpopular among the voters of Victoria.

A marked increase in illegal immigration during 1999 and 2000 prompted the introduction of new legislation empowering Australian police to board vessels in international waters. In 1999 almost 2,000 illegal immigrants were intercepted by the authorities and transferred to detention centres in Australia, while many others were believed to have died in the attempt to enter the country. The issue of alleged maltreatment of illegal immigrants captured in Australia was highlighted by a series of protests at a privately managed detention centre in Woomera, South Australia. Moreover, in November the Government ordered an inquiry into allegations that children at the centre had been subjected to systematic sexual abuse. Campaigners, who had repeatedly appealed for more humane treatment of illegal immigrants, claimed that the Government had suppressed evidence of abuse at Woomera and other detention centres.

Australia's handling of immigration problems provoked international condemnation in August 2001 when the Prime Minister refused to admit 433 refugees, stranded on an overcrowded Norwegian cargo ship off Christmas Island, onto the Australian mainland. The Government, faced with a high court challenge, swiftly enacted new legislation empowering the navy to prevent migrants coming ashore and excluding remote Australian island territories from the definition of official landfall. The situation was eventually resolved when New Zealand, Nauru and Papua New Guinea agreed to accommodate the asylum-seekers whilst their applications were processed. In the interim, however, traffic in illegal immigrants attempting to reach Australia's outlying territories—the majority via Indonesia—continued to increase. The Government proposed its so-called 'Pacific solution', whereby neighbouring South Pacific nations could agree to host asylum-seekers during their processing on a continuing basis in exchange for substantial aid. Nauru signed an agreement to take up to 1,200 refugees at any one time, whilst Papua New Guinea prevaricated on the possibility of accommodating a further 1,000 people. Concerns about Australia's immigration policy again focused on the Woomera detention centre in January 2002, when 259 detainees began a hunger strike in protest at poor living conditions and at the long delays in the processing of their applications. In February the Australian Government announced that a representative of the UN High Commissioner for Human Rights and other observers would be permitted to inspect the camp between May and August.

A state election in Western Australia in February 2001 resulted in defeat for the governing Liberal-National coalition and the replacement of Premier Richard Court by the state's Labor leader, Geoffrey Gallop. Ongoing anxieties regarding illegal immigration were reflected in the unexpected success of One Nation, which secured almost 10% of votes at the poll. At the state election in Queensland in the same month, the ALP Government, led by Peter Beattie, was decisively re-elected. One Nation garnered 9% of the total votes.

A federal election took place on 10 November 2001. The Liberal-National coalition won 82 of the 150 seats in the House of Representatives, thus narrowly securing a third consecutive term of office. Despite its successes at state and territorial elections in Western Australia and the Northern Territory earlier in the year, the ALP won 65 seats, thus taking two fewer than at the previous federal election. Many political commentators attributed the coalition's apparent recovery to Howard's controversial handling of immigration issues, which had led to a surge in his popularity. Kim Beazley resigned as leader of the ALP and was replaced by Simon Crean, formerly the Shadow Treasurer. One Nation won no seats in either the House of Representatives or the Senate. (In December Pauline Hanson resigned as leader of the party to concentrate on contesting charges of electoral fraud brought against her in July 2001.)

John Howard announced the composition of his third Ministry in late November 2001, appointing six new cabinet ministers. Changes included the incorporation of the Department of Reconciliation and Aboriginal and Torres Strait Islander Affairs into the new portfolio of Immigration and Multicultural and Indigenous Affairs. The Department of Industry, Science and Resources became that of Industry, Tourism and Resources, emphasizing the tourism sector's growing importance to the Australian economy. At a state election in South Australia in February 2002, the ruling Liberal-National coalition was defeated. Michael Rann of the ALP was appointed Premier.

In mid-February 2002 the leader of the ALP accused the Prime Minister of having lied during the previous year's election campaign to boost his coalition's chances of victory, after it emerged that government claims that refugees in a ship intercepted by the Australian navy had thrown their children into the sea were false. John Howard, nevertheless, withstood a censure motion introduced in the House of Representatives. In late November the ruling ALP, led by Stephen Bracks, won a state election in Victoria. The Labor Government in New South Wales was re-elected in March 2003 for an unprecedented third term; Bob Carr was reappointed Premier. Meanwhile, in February the Senate approved a motion of no confidence in Howard over the Government's decision to deploy troops to the Middle East in preparation for a possible US-led military campaign to remove the regime of Saddam Hussain in Iraq. Although it had no legal impact, the motion—the first to be carried against a government in 102 years—was considered symbolic. Public demonstrations against Australia's anticipated involvement in the war took place throughout the month. In mid-March the Minister for Foreign Affairs announced that, owing to the Government's commitment to the US-led military campaign against Iraq (which began two days later), all Iraqi diplomatic staff would be expelled from the country with effect from 23 March. Public support for Howard rose substantially from May, largely owing to the apparent swift end to the conflict in Iraq and the absence of Australian casualties. In July, however, a former UN weapons inspector, Richard Butler, claimed that the Government had misled the public about Iraq's programme to develop weapons of mass destruction and demanded the Prime Minister's resignation. Howard denied this accusation; nevertheless, the ALP initiated a parliamentary inquiry on the Government's decision to participate in the war in Iraq. A former senior intelligence analyst, who had resigned in protest over Australia's involvement in the conflict, informed the inquiry in August that the Government had exaggerated and fabricated intelligence used to justify the case for war. Howard denied the allegations at a press conference. Meanwhile, in July Australia committed 870 troops to assist in the rehabilitation of Iraq. In February 2005 the Government announced that it would send 450 additional Australian troops to Iraq, despite having made a pledge in the previous year that it would not commit any more troops.

Protesters against the Government's mandatory detention of all asylum-seekers stormed the Woomera detention centre in March 2002. Most of the approximately 50 asylum-seekers who managed to escape were recaptured. In April riots took place at detention centres in Curtin and Port Hedland, Western Australia. In May the Government offered financial incentives to almost 1,000 Afghan asylum-seekers in detention centres throughout Australia and Nauru of $A2,000 each (with a limit of $A10,000 per family) if they returned to Afghanistan. The Government gave the detainees 28 days (from the day their asylum review process ended) to decide whether to accept the offer, which also included counselling, air fares and vocational training. International aid agencies criticized the scheme, stating that Afghanistan was not stable enough for asylum-seekers to return. By mid-July only 76 Afghans had accepted the offer. Concerns about the alleged maltreatment of asylum-seekers were raised again after supporters helped 34 detainees to escape from Woomera detention centre in late June. At the same time more than 120 inmates began a hunger strike in protest at poor living conditions and at the long delays in the processing of their applications. In the mean time, Australia's controversial efforts to deter refugees appeared to have been effective: the number of 'boat people' seeking asylum in Australia had declined significantly. In early December the Minister for Immigration and Multicultural and Indigenous Affairs, Philip Ruddock, announced plans to expand a programme to allow women and children asylum-seekers to live in the community rather than in the detention camps. The authorities employed tighter security measures at detention centres following riots at Woomera, Baxter, Port Hedland and on Christmas Island in late December.

In mid-March 2003 Ruddock announced that Woomera detention centre would be closed down in mid-April, for reasons of cost. Families faced being separated after it was agreed that fathers and husbands would be moved to the Baxter detention centre near Port Augusta, while women and children would have to continue to live in the community in Woomera. The Government, however, stated that discussions to establish a residential housing programme for women and children at Port Augusta would continue. Several days later it was announced that the Christmas Island detention centre would also be closed. In mid-April the Federal Court issued a ruling that the Government had no right to detain asylum-seekers indefinitely prior to deportation, even if the asylum-seeker had been refused permission to enter another country. The case was related to a Palestinian asylum-seeker who had been detained at the Woomera detention centre for eight months, after being denied refugee status, because Israel had initially refused to allow his repatriation. The Court had previously twice ordered the release of the asylum-seeker while awaiting deportation (he was later deported in September 2002), and on each occasion the Government appealed. The Court's rejection of the latest appeal represented a set-back to the Government's policy of detaining asylum-seekers; nevertheless, anxious to avoid a precedent that could affect the detention of hundreds of other asylum-seekers, Ruddock announced that the Government would seek an appeal at the High Court. In mid-August 2003 the High Court upheld the ruling and rebuked the Government for wasting its time. Nearly two weeks later the Family Court ordered the Government to release from custody five children who had been detained as illegal immigrants since January 2002. In October 2003 an eight-year-old Iranian asylum-seeker launched a lawsuit against the Government, claiming that he had suffered severe mental health problems caused by his detention in the Woomera centre. In the same month a government report was issued stating that 90% of the 'boat people' who had arrived in Australia's migration zone between July 1999 and June 2002 had eventually gained asylum. This figure challenged the Government's claim that the majority of asylum-seekers were economic migrants and not genuine refugees. The Government's immigration policy came under heavy criticism again in November 2003 when, in response to the arrival of an Indonesian boat carrying 14 Turkish Kurdish asylum-seekers at Melville Island, the Government immediately separated the island and 4,000 other small islands from the Australian migration zone. It then ordered an Australian warship to tow the boat to the Indonesian island of Yamdena. The UN High Commissioner for Refugees stated that Australia's exclusion of the islands was 'meaningless', since its obligations as a signatory to the UN refugee convention applied to its entire territory. The Indonesian Government insisted that its agreement to the Kurds' expulsion had neither been requested nor given. In May 2004 Australia's Human Rights and Equal Opportunities Commission issued a report describing the country's immigration detention system as 'cruel, inhumane and degrading', and urged the Government to release all child detainees within a month. In July, in a relaxation of the immigration policy, it was announced that some 9,500 asylum-seekers who had been released from detention centres since 1999 on temporary protection visas (renewable every three years) would henceforth be entitled to apply for permanent settlement in Australia.

In early June 2003 John Howard ended months of speculation by announcing that he intended to seek a fourth term in office. In mid-June the leader of the ALP, Simon Crean, won a leadership challenge mounted against him by his predecessor, Kim Beazley. Crean, however, failed to reunite his party and improve his popularity within the ALP, and in late November he resigned as leader of the opposition party. In early December the republican Mark Latham won the ALP leadership election, narrowly defeating Beazley. Meanwhile, in mid-August Richard Butler was appointed Governor of Tasmania, replacing Sir Guy Green. In the same month Pauline Hanson was convicted of electoral fraud by a court in Brisbane and sentenced to a three-year prison term; her conviction, however, was overturned by an appeals court in November. In late September a major reorganization of the Cabinet was announced. Changes included the transfer of the controversial Minister for Immigration and Multicultural and Indigenous Affairs, Philip Ruddock, to the post of Attorney-General; Senator Amanda Vanstone was allocated the immigration portfolio. At a state election in Queensland in February 2004, the ruling ALP was re-elected for a third term; Peter Beattie was reappointed Premier. In mid-February riots broke out in the predominantly Aboriginal district of Redfern in Sydney in protest against the death of an Aboriginal youth in an apparent cycling accident. At least four people were arrested and more than 30 police officers were injured during Sydney's worst violence in several years; three separate inquiries into the death of the youth and into the riots were launched the following day. (In August the New South Wales state coroner described the youth's death as a 'freak accident', exonerating the police of any blame.)

In early March 2004 the parliamentary committee on intelligence on Iraq's weapons of mass destruction published its report, largely exonerating the Government from claims that it had manipulated the intelligence used to justify Australia's involvement in the military campaign in Iraq. On the recommendation of the committee, the Prime Minister ordered an independent inquiry into the performance of the intelligence agencies in the period leading up to the war. In July the report judged that there had been an overall serious failure of intelligence relating to Iraq's alleged weapons of mass destruction, but that the Australian agencies' assessment of the available material had been more measured than that of their counterparts in the United Kingdom and the USA.

In April 2004 Prime Minister Howard announced controversial government plans to abolish the elected Aboriginal and Torres Strait Islander Commission (ATSIC), claiming that it had failed to improve conditions for the indigenous community since commencing operations in 1990. In response, the first national party for Aboriginal people, Your Voice, was launched in May 2004. Legislation to dismantle ATSIC was approved by the House of Representatives in June, but the Senate ordered an inquiry into the proposal. In the mean time, ATSIC's budget was transferred to government departments in July, and in December a new government-appointed advisory body on Aboriginal affairs, the 14-member National Indigenous Council, held its first meeting. In March 2005, following a report by the Senate committee, legislation was passed abolishing ATSIC.

In June 2004 the Anglican Archbishop of Adelaide, the Most Rev. Ian George, resigned after an independent inquiry reported that his diocese had mishandled more than 200 claims of sexual abuse by the clergy over a 50-year period. In August Richard Butler stood down as Governor of Tasmania, following threats from the state opposition to withdraw its support for him, after four senior members of his staff tendered their resignations; he was replaced by William Cox, hitherto Chief Justice of Tasmania. Meanwhile, an issue that had caused controversy at the federal election of 2001 re-emerged, when Mike Scrafton, a former government adviser, revealed that he had told Prime Minister Howard, prior to the election, that government claims that refugees in a ship intercepted by the Australian navy had thrown their children overboard (see above) were unsubstantiated. The Senate established an inquiry into Scrafton's allegations at the end of August 2004.

The Liberal-National coalition increased its majority in the House of Representatives at the federal election on 9 October 2004, securing 86 of the 150 seats, and gained an outright majority in the Senate. Prime Minister John Howard was thus returned to office for a fourth consecutive term. The ALP won 60 seats in the lower chamber, five fewer than at the 2001 election, surprising many political analysts, who had predicted a much closer result. The coalition's victory was widely attributed to the

AUSTRALIA

continued strong performance of the economy under Howard's Government. In December 2004 Senator Lyn Allison replaced Senator Andrew Bartlett as leader of the Australian Democrats Party, following the party's poor performance in the elections to the Senate, at which it had lost four of the eight seats previously held. In the same month the Senate committee investigating Mike Scrafton's claims concluded that his evidence was credible and clearly implied that the Prime Minister had misled the public over the so-called 'children overboard' affair in the period leading up to the 2001 election. However, the two Liberal senators on the five-member committee rejected these findings.

In January 2005 Mark Latham, leader of the ALP, announced his resignation from both the party leadership and the legislature, for health reasons. Kim Beazley was elected to succeed him as ALP leader later in that month, thus resuming the position. In March Australia's asylum policy came to the fore once again, following a ruling by the High Court that the country was obliged to accept refugees fleeing persecution in their homeland. John Howard subsequently announced that Australia's asylum policy would be slightly relaxed, and that a small number of detainees, who had been refused refugee status but were unable to return to their homelands, would be released and granted visas. In May the Minister for Immigration, Amanda Vanstone, announced that 201 cases of possible wrongful detention of immigrants would be reviewed, following a number of high-profile asylum cases that had attracted criticism in recent months. In June the Deputy Prime Minister and Minister for Transport and Regional Services, John Anderson, announced his resignation from both the Cabinet and the leadership of the National Party, citing health reasons. In consequence, in the following month a minor cabinet reorganization took place; Mark Vaile succeeded Anderson as both Deputy Prime Minister and National Party leader. Meanwhile, at elections to the 25-seat Northern Territory legislature in June, the ALP increased its majority, winning 19 seats. In July Bob Carr, long-serving Premier of New South Wales, announced his resignation; he was succeeded in August by Morris Iemma.

In December 2005 racially motivated rioting, believed to have been co-ordinated by right-wing extremists, broke out in the Sydney beach resort of Cronulla. As the disturbances continued, the New South Wales legislature approved emergency legislation to prevent civil unrest. The re-emergence of the race issue raised serious questions regarding the nature of Australian society.

In January 2006 the Premier of Western Australia, Geoffrey Gallop, resigned unexpectedly, on the grounds of ill health. He was subsequently replaced by Alan Carpenter. In the same month Dr Ken Michael was sworn in as Governor of the state, succeeding Lt-Gen. John Murray Sanderson. Also in January Robert Hill resigned as federal Minister for Defence, prompting a minor cabinet reorganization, in which he was succeeded by Dr Brendan Nelson, hitherto Minister for Education, Science and Training. In April Prof. David de Kretser was sworn in as Governor of Victoria. At the end of July Prime Minister John Howard announced his intention to seek a fifth term of office at the next federal election, scheduled for the latter part of 2007. Federal cabinet members Mark Vaile and Warren Truss exchanged portfolios in September 2006: Mark Vaile remained Deputy Prime Minister but also assumed responsibility for the transport and regional services portfolio, while Warren Truss became Minister for Trade. In December Kevin Rudd, the foreign affairs spokesman of the ALP, mounted a successful leadership challenge against Kim Beazley to become the federal Leader of the Opposition. Prime Minister Howard effected a ministerial reorganization in January 2007: among the appointees were Malcolm Turnbull as Minister for the Environment and Water Resources and Kevin Andrews as Minister for Immigration and Citizenship.

In March 2006, meanwhile, the ALP was returned to power at state elections in both South Australia and Tasmania. In September Peter Beattie of the ALP gained a fourth consecutive term as Premier of Queensland at state elections. The ALP's dominance of state politics continued with its victory at elections in Victoria in November, thus ensuring a third term for Premier Stephen Bracks; Bracks, however, resigned in July 2007 and was replaced by John Brumby. The ALP also prevailed at elections in New South Wales in March 2007, returning Premier Morris Iemma to office. In Queensland Premier Peter Beattie was succeeded by Anna Bligh in September, following the former's resignation.

The findings of the so-called Cole Inquiry were published in November 2006. Led by retired judge Terence Cole, the inquiry had been established at the end of 2005 in order to investigate allegations of misconduct or unlawful actions by Australian companies in connection with the UN's oil-for-food programme in Iraq (whereby the Government of Saddam Hussain had been permitted to use revenue from oil exports to purchase food and medicines in an attempt to alleviate the hardship resulting from the imposition of international sanctions). The Cole Inquiry received extensive press coverage during 2006, in part because of claims that the Government had repeatedly ignored warnings about the improper actions of the Australian Wheat Board (now AWB); Prime Minister Howard and Ministers Mark Vaile and Alexander Downer were all summoned to testify. The inquiry found that, in contravention of UN regulations, between 1999 and 2003 irregular payments totalling $A300m. had been made by AWB to the Government of Iraq in order to secure lucrative contracts under the oil-for-food programme. The Cole report exonerated the Government, but recommended that 11 former AWB executives face charges of corruption. In December 2006 AWB's long-standing monopoly of Australian wheat exports was temporarily removed.

In 2007 national politics were dominated by the anticipation of a federal election, which, it was announced in October, would be held on 24 November. In the weeks preceding the election, the Government sought to address general dissatisfaction over its stance on issues such as climate change and Aboriginal affairs, but it was the ALP that ultimately garnered enough public support to secure a majority in the House of Representatives: the Liberal Party won only 55 of the 150 seats, while the ALP secured 83 seats and the former's coalition partner, the National Party, won 10. Elections for 40 of the 76 Senate seats also resulted in the Liberal-National coalition's loss of its majority, although the newly elected Senators were not scheduled to take office until mid-2008. Prime Minister Howard suffered a humiliating personal defeat in his own long-held constituency of Bennelong. He was succeeded as Federal Parliamentary Leader of the Liberal Party by the erstwhile Minister of Defence, Dr Brendan Nelson. Kevin Rudd was sworn in as Prime Minister in early December, along with a Cabinet that included Julia Gillard as Deputy Prime Minister, Stephen Smith as Minister for Foreign Affairs and Wayne Swan as Treasurer. Fulfilling his election pledge, Rudd's first undertaking as Prime Minister was to ratify the Kyoto Protocol, negotiated in Japan in 1997, thereby committing Australia to reducing its emissions of carbon dioxide and other 'greenhouse gases'. Among other proposals, he reiterated his intention to withdraw Australian troops from Iraq and to reverse the previous Government's position on a formal apology to Aboriginals (see below).

On 12 October 2002 88 Australians were killed in a bomb explosion in a night-club on the Indonesian island of Bali. The Islamist militant group Jemaah Islamiah (JI) was held principally responsible for the attack, which killed more than 200 people in total. The Australian Government proscribed the organization, which was suspected of having links with the al-Qa'ida (Base) network, and successfully led a campaign to have JI listed as a terrorist organization by the UN. In an attempt to prevent retaliatory attacks against Muslims in Australia, the Prime Minister publicly declared that Islam was not responsible for the attack. However, a mosque and an Islamic school in Sydney were attacked in mid-October, prompting the Premier of New South Wales, Bob Carr, to establish a community harmony reference group to ease tensions. In early November the Government was accused of harassing Muslims, following a series of high-profile armed raids on the homes of Indonesian-born Muslims suspected of having connections with JI. Although the authorities denied the accusations, the raids antagonized the Muslim community and adversely affected relations with Indonesia. In mid-November Jack Roche, a British-born Australian, was charged with devising bomb attacks on the Israeli embassy in Canberra and the Israeli consulate in Sydney. Roche, a Muslim convert, who had earlier admitted to having met Osama bin Laden, the Saudi-born leader of al-Qa'ida, and Riduan Isamuddin, the suspected operations chief of JI, denied the charges. Having changed his plea to guilty, in late May 2004 Roche was convicted of plotting to attack the embassy, and was sentenced to nine years' imprisonment. In late March 2003 the Attorney-General announced a ban, effective immediately, on the Iraqi Kurdish Sunni Islamist fundamentalist group Ansar al-Islam. It was announced in mid-April that the Government had banned six more militant Islamist groups. In May the

Government decided to create a new counter-terrorist unit from the country's volunteer military reserve force. One month later the Senate approved anti-terrorism legislation giving significant new powers to the Australian Security Intelligence Organization, including the power to detain suspects for up to seven days without charge. In early February 2004 Australia and Indonesia co-hosted an anti-terrorism conference held on Bali, during which it was announced that a regional counter-terrorism centre would be established in the Indonesian capital, Jakarta. A bomb exploded outside the Australian embassy in Jakarta in September, killing at least nine people, mostly Indonesians, and injuring more than 180 others. JI was suspected of being responsible for the attack. In October 2005 Bali was once again the focus of a terrorist attack, with four Australian citizens being among 20 people killed in three suicide bombings on the island.

In September 2005 Prime Minister John Howard announced a series of proposals intended to strengthen Australia's anti-terrorism laws, including plans to make the incitement of terrorist acts a criminal offence and to detain suspects for up to 14 days without charge. The legislation initially met with opposition from several state leaders, owing to human rights concerns, but, following a meeting with Howard, state premiers agreed to support the legislation on the condition that a 'sunset clause' was included, guaranteeing that the laws would be reviewed after five years and would expire after 10 years. In November it was reported that Australian police had averted a potential terrorist attack by Islamist extremists upon an unspecified target in the country, arresting a number of suspects in raids in Sydney and Melbourne. Shortly before the arrests were made, and having been warned of a potential threat, the Senate had approved amendments to existing anti-terrorism legislation, enabling police to intervene at any stage of terrorist planning, however early, and to charge suspects without evidence of a specific terrorist act. Following the arrests, the new counter-terrorism proposals that Howard had announced in September were introduced into Parliament.

In March 1986, meanwhile, Australia's constitutional links with the United Kingdom were reduced by the Australia Act, which abolished the British Parliament's residual legislative, executive and judicial controls over Australian state law. In February 1992, shortly after a visit by Queen Elizabeth II, Paul Keating caused a furore by accusing the United Kingdom of abandoning Australia to the Japanese threat during the Second World War. Following a visit to the United Kingdom in September 1993, Keating announced that Australia was to become a republic by the year 2001, subject to approval by referendum. Sir William Deane succeeded William Hayden as Governor-General in February 1996, the former's term of office being scheduled to expire at the end of the year 2000. Although John Howard personally favoured the retention of the monarchy, in 1996 the new Prime Minister announced plans for a constitutional convention, prior to the holding of a referendum on the issue if necessary. In an unexpected development in January 1997, the Deputy Prime Minister put forward proposals for the removal from the Constitution of all references to the monarch and for the transfer of the Queen's functions to Australia's Chief Justice.

In February 1998 the Constitutional Convention was held. Following nine days of debate, a majority of the 152 delegates endorsed proposals to adopt a republican system and to replace the British monarch as Head of State. Although the Convention was dominated by republicans, delegates were divided over the method of election of a future head of state. In December it was confirmed that a referendum on the republican issue would be held in late 1999. In August 1999 the Federal Parliament gave approval to the wording of the question to be posed to the electorate, which was to be asked if support was forthcoming for an 'act to alter the Constitution to establish the Commonwealth of Australia as a republic with the Queen and Governor-General being replaced by a President appointed by a two-thirds' majority of the members of the Commonwealth Parliament'. At the referendum, conducted on 6 November 1999, 55% of voters favoured the retention of the monarchy. Moreover, some 61% of voters expressed opposition to a proposal to include a preamble to the Constitution, recognizing Aborigines as 'the nation's first people'. Although the result was regarded as a victory for Howard, who had campaigned for the retention of the monarchy, many observers interpreted the result as a rejection of the particular republican system offered, opinion polls having indicated that more than two-thirds of Australians would support the introduction of a republican system of government if the President were to be directly elected.

In June 2001 the Anglican Archbishop of Brisbane, Peter Hollingworth, was sworn in as Governor-General, succeeding Sir William Deane. In February 2002, as the Queen commenced a visit to Australia to celebrate her Golden Jubilee, Hollingworth refused to yield to pressure to resign over claims that he had deliberately concealed alleged cases of child abuse by the clergy in Queensland. The Prime Minister rejected calls to dismiss the Governor-General. On 11 May 2003 Hollingworth temporarily relinquished his post, pending the investigation of rape allegations against him. Sir Guy Green, the Governor of Tasmania, was appointed acting Governor-General. Hollingworth strongly denied the charge against him, which dated back to the 1960s. The woman accusing him of rape committed suicide in April, and on 23 May the case was dismissed at the request of her family. Although the Prime Minister continued to show support for Hollingworth, the Governor-General had lost the confidence of opposition parties, church leaders, child welfare campaigners, several senior government ministers and the public, and resigned on 25 May. The former Governor of Western Australia, Maj.-Gen. Michael Jeffery, was sworn in as the country's new Governor-General on 11 August.

In December 2003 the High Court ruled that long-term British residents without Australian citizenship who commit a crime in Australia could be deported to the United Kingdom. The judgment overturned the special status held by British residents, according to which they did not have to take Australian citizenship, and declared that any non-citizen who had arrived in the country after 26 January 1949 would henceforth be considered a foreign alien for immigration purposes. The ruling marked a further weakening of the relations between Australia and the United Kingdom. In March 2006 the Queen visited Australia. During her stay she made a speech upon the theme of the maturing of Australia as a nation, which was perceived by many commentators to hint at the possibility that the country was prepared to begin the transition towards a republican system of government. Prime Minister John Howard also commented that he was unsure whether Australia would choose to retain the monarchy after the Queen's death.

In May 1987 Australia and the United Kingdom began a joint operation to ascertain the extent of plutonium contamination resulting from British nuclear weapons testing at Maralinga in South Australia between 1956 and 1963. Many Australians were highly critical of the United Kingdom's apparent disregard for the environmental consequences of the tests and of the British authorities' failure to make adequate arrangements to protect the local Aboriginal people, who were now campaigning for a thorough decontamination of their traditional lands. In June 1993 Australia announced its acceptance of $A45m. in compensation from the British Government for the cost of the decontamination. In December 1994 the displaced Aboriginal people and the Federal Government reached agreement on a compensation settlement of $A13.5m., to be spent on health, employment and infrastructural projects. In March 2000 it was announced that a joint decontamination programme effected by the British and Australian Governments had been completed. However, the Australian Government issued a report in May stating that, despite the removal of 300,000 cu m of plutonium-contaminated topsoil during the operation, some 120 sq km of the territory were still considered too contaminated for permanent habitation, permitting only limited access. In March 2003, furthermore, the former head of the Maralinga Rehabilitation Committee declared the decontamination operation to have been a failure.

The sensitive issue of Aboriginal land rights was addressed by the Government in August 1985, when it formulated proposals for legislation that would give Aboriginal people inalienable freehold title to national parks, vacant Crown land and former Aboriginal reserves, in spite of widespread opposition from state governments (which had previously been responsible for their own land policies), from mining companies and from the Aboriginal people themselves, who were angered by the Government's withdrawal of its earlier support for the Aboriginal right to veto mineral exploitation. In October Ayers Rock (Uluru), in the Northern Territory, was officially transferred to the Mutijulu Aboriginal community, on condition that continuing access to the rock (the main inland tourist attraction) be guaranteed. In 1986, however, the Government abandoned its pledge to impose such federal legislation on unwilling state governments, and this led to further protests from Aboriginal leaders. In June 1991 the Government imposed a permanent ban on mining at an historical Aboriginal site in the Northern Territory.

An important precedent was established in June 1992, when the High Court overruled the concept of *terra nullius* (unoccupied land) by recognizing the existence of land titles that predated European settlement in 1788 in cases where a close association with the land in question had been continued; however, land titles legally acquired since 1788 were to remain intact. As a result of the 'Mabo' decision of 1992 (named after the Aboriginal claimant, Eddie Mabo), in December 1993 Parliament approved the Native Title Act, historic legislation granting Aboriginal people the right to claim title to their traditional lands. Despite the Prime Minister's personal involvement in the issue, the legislation aroused much controversy, particularly in Western Australia (vast areas of the state being vacant Crown land), where rival legislation to replace native title rights with lesser rights to traditional land usage, such as access for ceremonial purposes only, had been enacted. In March 1995 the High Court declared the Native Title Act to be valid, rejecting as unconstitutional Western Australia's own legislation. The ruling was expected to have widespread implications for the mining industry.

In October 1996, following protracted delays in the development of a valuable zinc mine in Queensland owing to Aboriginal land claims, the Howard Government announced proposals to amend the Native Title Act to permit federal ministers to overrule Aboriginal concerns if a project of 'major economic benefit' to Australia were threatened. Other proposed amendments included the simplification of the process of negotiation between potential developers and Aboriginal claimants. In December the Larrakia people of the Northern Territory presented a claim under the Native Title Act, the first such claim to encompass a provincial capital, namely Darwin. Meanwhile, in October the federal High Court upheld an appeal by two Aboriginal communities in Queensland (including the Wik people of Cape York) against an earlier ruling that prevented them from submitting a claim to land leased by the state government to cattle and sheep farmers. The Court's decision, known as the Wik judgment, was expected to encourage similar challenges to 'pastoral' leases, which covered 40% of Australia. Vociferous protests from farmers, who were strongly opposed to the co-existence of native title and pastoral leases, followed.

In April 1997 the first native title deed to be granted on mainland Australia was awarded to the Dunghutti people of New South Wales. In the same month the Prime Minister announced the introduction of legislation to clarify the issue of land tenure; a 10-point plan was to be drawn up in consultation with state governments and with representatives of the Aboriginal community. In September the Government introduced the Wik Native Title Bill, which was subsequently passed by the House of Representatives. In November, however, the Senate questioned the constitutional validity of the proposed legislation, whereby pastoralists' rights and activities would prevail over, but not extinguish (as had been assumed), the Aboriginal people's rights to native title. In December the Government refused to accept the Senate's proposed amendments to the legislation, thus raising the possibility of an early general election dominated by Aboriginal issues. In April 1998 the Senate rejected the legislation for a second time. Finally, in July, following a protracted and acrimonious debate, the Senate narrowly approved the Native Title Amendment Bill, thereby restricting the Aboriginal people's rights to claim access to Crown land leased to farmers. The passage of the controversial legislation was immediately denounced by Aboriginal leaders, who threatened to enlist international support for their cause. In the same month, however, the federal court of Darwin granted communal (but not exclusive or commercial) native title to the waters and sea-bed around Croker Island in the Northern Territory to five Aboriginal groups. With about 140 similar claims over Australian waters pending, the historic ruling represented the first recognition of native title rights over the sea. However, the area's traditional owners launched an appeal against the decision, insisting on the commercial right to negotiate on fishing and pearling activities. In March 1999, in a conciliatory gesture that settled a land claim case outstanding since 1845, the Tasmanian Government relinquished the site of a mission station at Wybellena, where 200 Aboriginal people had been forcibly resettled; most had subsequently died of disease and maltreatment.

The land rights movement suffered a set-back in August 2002 when the High Court in Canberra rejected a claim by the Miriuwung-Gajerrong people to territory in Western Australia and the Northern Territory that contained the Argyle diamond mine owned by the Anglo-Australian mining company Rio Tinto. The decision to give precedence to mining and petroleum leases over Aboriginal land rights appeared to reverse earlier court rulings that supported the land rights movement. In September, however, Rio Tinto offered to close the Jabiluka uranium mine in the Northern Territory following opposition to the project from the indigenous Mirrar people (the owners of the land) and environmental groups. The Mirrar people welcomed the proposal; the Government of the Northern Territory approved a plan to fill in the mine in August 2003. In 2007 Rio Tinto's revelation of its potential earnings from the Jabiluka mine prompted the Mirrar to reiterate their opposition to the project, which appeared unlikely to proceed without their permission. Meanwhile, in September 2002 the state Government of Western Australia agreed to return about 13.7m. ha of land to the Martu people. In December the Australian High Court rejected the Aboriginal Yorta Yorta people's claim to territory along the River Murray on the border of Victoria and New South Wales. A federal court ruling in September 2006 granted the Noongar Aboriginal people native title over more than 6,000 sq km of land in Western Australia, around and including Perth. The Government of Western Australia announced that it would appeal against the ruling, although Jim McGinty, the Attorney-General for Western Australia, maintained that the state Government did not wish to 'overturn native title', rather to reach a 'clearer understanding'. In the following month the federal Attorney-General, Philip Ruddock, announced that the federal Government intended to contest the ruling in order to clarify questions arising from the decision, including the issue of public access to vacant Crown land. In April 2007 the federal and state Governments' appeal was lodged in the Federal Court.

In November 1987 an official commission of inquiry into the cause of the high death rate among Aboriginal prisoners recommended immediate government action, and in July 1988 it was announced that 108 cases remained to be investigated. In August 1988 a UN report accused Australia of violating international human rights in its treatment of the Aboriginal people. In November the Government announced an inquiry into its Aboriginal Affairs Department, following accusations by the opposition coalition of nepotism and misuse of funds. The commission of inquiry published its first official report in February 1989. Following the report's recommendations, the Government announced the creation of a $A10m. programme to combat the high death rate among Aboriginal prisoners. In October an unofficial study indicated that Aboriginal people, although accounting for only 1% of the total population of Australia, comprised more than 20% of persons in prison. In May 1991 the report of the Royal Commission into Aboriginal Deaths in Custody was published. The report outlined evidence of racial prejudice in the police force and included more than 300 recommendations for changes in policies relating to Aboriginal people, aimed at improving relations between the racial groups of Australia and granting Aboriginal people greater self-determination and access to land ownership. In June Parliament established a Council for Aboriginal Reconciliation. In March 1992, Aboriginal deaths in custody having continued, radical plans for judicial, economic and social reforms, aimed at improving the lives of Aboriginal people, were announced. The Government made an immediate allocation of $A150m.; a total of $A500m. was to be made available over the next 10 years. In February 1993 the human rights organization Amnesty International issued a highly critical report on the prison conditions of Aboriginal people. In March 1996 Amnesty International claimed that Australia had made little progress with regard to its treatment of Aboriginal prisoners. In March 2000 the UN Committee on Elimination of Racial Discrimination issued a report denouncing Australia's treatment of its indigenous people. The report was particularly critical of the mandatory prison sentences for minor property offences in force in the Northern Territory and Western Australia, which appeared to target juvenile Aborigines. In July a legal case was initiated against the Australian Government accusing it of breaching the human rights of Aboriginal people with these harsh mandatory sentencing laws. In August 2001 the Australian Bureau of Statistics published its biannual survey of indigenous health, based on 1997–99 figures. It found the average life expectancy of Aboriginal men and women to be, respectively, 20 and 19 years less than that of other Australians. The Government claimed that $A220m. was being spent on Aboriginal health services in that year, to be increased to $A260m. by 2004. In November 2004 the death of an Aboriginal man in police custody prompted rioting by some 300 people on Palm Island, off the coast of Queensland, one of the country's largest Aboriginal communities.

In July 1996 the Roman Catholic Church issued an apology for its role in the forcible removal from their parents of tens of thousands of Aboriginal children, in a controversial practice of placement in white foster homes, where many were abused. This policy of assimilation had continued until the late 1960s. In August 1996 the new Governor-General, Sir William Deane, urged all state parliaments to affirm their support for reconciliation with the Aboriginal people. In May 1997 the publication of the findings of a two-year inquiry into the removal of as many as 100,000 Aboriginal children from their families had profound political repercussions. The author of the report, a distinguished former judge and President of the Human Rights and Equal Opportunities Commission, urged the Government to issue a formal apology to the 'stolen generation'. At a conference on reconciliation at the end of the month, the Prime Minister made an unexpected personal apology. The Government, however, repudiated the commission's assertion that the policy of assimilation had been tantamount to genocide and rejected recommendations that compensation be paid to victims. In December the Government reaffirmed that it would not issue a formal apology to the 'stolen generation'. A $A63m. programme to help reunite divided Aboriginal families was nevertheless announced. In February 1998 the Anglican Church apologized unreservedly for its part in the removal of Aboriginal children from their families. In May 2000, when 250,000 citizens took part in a march across Sydney Harbour Bridge, the Prime Minister refused to involve himself fully in the campaign for reconciliation between white and Aboriginal Australia, and ruled out any notion of a treaty. Two separate UN reports, released in March and July, were highly critical of Australia's treatment of the Aboriginal population; their findings were strongly rejected by the Australian Government. In August, at the conclusion of a test case brought in the Northern Territory by two members of the 'stolen generation', who hoped to win compensation for the trauma occasioned by their removal from their families, the Federal Court ruled that the Government was not obliged to pay punitive damages to the two Aboriginal claimants, on the grounds of insufficient evidence. As many as 30,000 similar cases had been pending. In December some 300,000 people took part in demonstrations in Melbourne and Perth in support of reconciliation between the white and indigenous communities, and the Prime Minister was subject to renewed pressure to apologize for the treatment of Aboriginal people by white settlers. A Senate committee recommended issuing an apology to the 'stolen generation' and establishing a reparations tribunal to deal with compensation claims. However, the Government strongly rejected the recommendations. In August 2001, at a human rights conference in Sydney, various indigenous and legal groups finalized a new proposal for a reparations tribunal; again the Government rejected it, insisting that its own $A60m. programme of practical assistance was sufficient. In November 2001 Pope John Paul II apologized to Australia's Aboriginal community for what he called the 'shameful injustices' of the past, asking for forgiveness for the Roman Catholic Church's role in forcibly removing Aboriginal children from their families. In October 2006 the Premier of Tasmania, Paul Lennon, announced that funds from a $A5m. compensation scheme would be made available to Tasmanian Aboriginal victims of the 'stolen generation' or their descendants.

In June 2007 the Howard Government announced plans to ban alcohol and certain types of pornography in Aboriginal communities in the Northern Territory, along with other federal measures formulated in response to reports of widespread child abuse and the appalling health and social conditions prevailing in the area. The controversial proposals attracted extensive press coverage, partly because critics felt that, at best, they represented an over-simplification of complex issues and, at worst, were a manifestation of inherent racism. However, the House of Representatives approved the relevant legislation in August. In February 2008 the new Prime Minister, Kevin Rudd, issued a formal apology to the 'stolen generation' at a parliamentary session. Rudd had previously maintained, however, that no compensation would be granted to victims; instead, his Government was to give priority to the improvement of health and educational services in Aboriginal areas.

In foreign affairs, the Hawke and Keating Governments placed greater emphasis on links with South-East Asia. This policy was continued by John Howard, who took office in 1996, pledging to expand relations with Asia. In January 1989 Hawke proposed the creation of an Asia-Pacific Economic Co-operation forum (APEC, see p. 176) to facilitate the exchange of services, tourism and direct foreign investment in the region. The inaugural APEC conference took place in Canberra in November 1989.

Australian relations with Indonesia, which had been strained since the Indonesian annexation of the former Portuguese colony of East Timor in 1976, improved in August 1985, when Hawke made a statement recognizing Indonesian sovereignty over the territory, but subsequently deteriorated, following the publication in a Sydney newspaper, in April 1986, of an article containing allegations of corruption against the Indonesian President, Gen. Suharto. Relations between Australia and Indonesia improved in December 1989, when they signed an accord regarding joint exploration for petroleum and gas reserves in the Timor Gap, an area of sea forming a disputed boundary between the two countries. Portugal, however, withdrew its ambassador from Canberra in protest, and in February 1991 instituted proceedings against Australia at the International Court of Justice. In June 1995 the Court refused to invalidate the exploration treaty. In April 1992 Paul Keating's visit to Indonesia, the new Prime Minister's first official overseas trip, aroused controversy, owing to the repercussions of the massacre of unarmed civilians in Dili, East Timor, by Indonesian troops in November 1991. In July 1995, owing to strong opposition in Australia, Indonesia was obliged to withdraw the appointment as ambassador to Canberra of Lt-Gen. (retd) Herman Mantiri, a former Chief of the General Staff of the Armed Forces and an apparent supporter of the November 1991 Dili massacre. Nevertheless, in December 1995 Australia and Indonesia unexpectedly signed a joint security treaty. In March 1996 a new Indonesian ambassador took up his appointment in Canberra, and in September, following a visit to Jakarta by John Howard, Indonesia accepted Australia's ambassador-designate.

Meanwhile, the investigation into the deaths of six Australia-based journalists (including two Britons) in East Timor in 1975 had been reopened, and in June 1996 a government report concluded that they had been murdered by Indonesian soldiers. In October 1996, as Australia continued to fail to denounce the Suharto Government's violations of human rights, Australian senators from all parties urged the Government to withdraw its recognition of Indonesian sovereignty over East Timor. In March 1997 Australia and Indonesia signed a treaty defining their seabed and 'economic zone' boundaries. The political unrest in Indonesia in early 1998, culminating in President Suharto's replacement in May, caused deep concern in Australia. In August the International Commission of Jurists, the Geneva-based human rights organization, reported that five of the six journalists had been murdered in an East Timorese village in October 1975 in an attempt to conceal the invasion of the territory, while the sixth man was killed in Dili in December of that year. Furthermore, it was claimed that the Australian embassy in Jakarta had been aware of the forthcoming invasion of East Timor but had failed to give adequate warning to the journalists. In October 1998, as newly emerging evidence continued to suggest that the truth had been suppressed and as interest in the matter was renewed in the United Kingdom, the Indonesian Government declared that it would not open an inquiry into the deaths of the two British journalists, maintaining that they and their colleagues had been killed in cross-fire. Australia, however, announced that its judicial inquiry was to be reopened. Government documents declassified in late 2000 proved conclusively that Australian officials had prior knowledge of Indonesia's plans to invade East Timor.

In January 1999, in a significant shift in its policy, Australia announced that henceforth it would support eventual self-determination for East Timor. (Australia had been the only developed nation to recognize Indonesia's annexation of the territory.) In late January, furthermore, Australia welcomed the Indonesian Government's declaration of its willingness to consider the possibility of full independence, if proposals for autonomy were rejected by the East Timorese people. During 1999, however, Australia became increasingly concerned at the deteriorating security situation in East Timor. The announcement of the result of the referendum on the future of East Timor, held in late August, at which the territory's people voted overwhelmingly in favour of independence (see the chapter on Timor-Leste) led to a rapid escalation of the violence. As pro-Jakarta militias embarked upon a campaign of murder and arson against innocent civilians, most of whom were forced to flee their homes, thousands of refugees were airlifted to safety in northern

Australia. With a commitment of 4,500 troops in its largest operation since the Viet Nam War, Australia took a leading role in the deployment of a multinational peace-keeping force, the first contingent of which landed in East Timor on 20 September 1999. Several Asian countries, however, in particular Malaysia and Thailand, along with Indonesia itself (which earlier in the month had suspended its security pact with Australia), were critical of Australia's bias towards pro-independence groups and of the country's apparent aggressive approach to its role in the operation, which some observers considered would have been more appropriately led by the Association of South East Asian Nations (ASEAN). A deterioration in relations between the two countries led President Abdurrahman Wahid of Indonesia to postpone an official visit to Australia in mid-2000. A series of postponements or cancellations of ministerial meetings followed.

In November 2000 the Australian Government agreed to help create an East Timor defence force, contributing some US $26m. over five years and providing training for police officers and border guards. Abdurrahman Wahid made a long-postponed official visit to Australia in June 2001, the first Indonesian President to do so in 26 years. In turn, John Howard was the first foreign leader to meet the next President of Indonesia, Megawati Sukarnoputri, when he visited the country in August. He affirmed that Australia would encourage the international community's support for Indonesia. However, the increasing numbers of immigrants, the majority from the Middle East, attempting to enter Australia by boat via Indonesia during 2000–01 proved contentious. Indonesia disclaimed responsibility for the many boatloads of asylum-seekers on the grounds that they had entered Indonesia illegally. The situation prompted senior-level talks between Australian and Indonesian officials in September 2001 which, however, failed to resolve the problem. Discussions resumed in November, when the Indonesian Minister of Foreign Relations visited Canberra. At an international forum on the issue of people-smuggling in February 2002, delegates agreed to pursue a 12-month programme, which included imposing stricter law enforcement and better information and intelligence-sharing, to combat smuggling and illegal immigration. In late February officials from Australia, Indonesia and Timor-Leste (formerly East Timor) held the first ever trilateral talks on future co-operation issues in Denpasar, on the Indonesian island of Bali. In September three Indonesians were convicted of attempting to smuggle 'illegal immigrants' into Australia in October 2001; they were sentenced to five years' imprisonment. Relations between Australia and Indonesia were strained as a result of Australia's treatment of Indonesian-born Muslims suspected of having links with the banned Islamist militant organization, JI, in the aftermath of the bomb attack on Bali in October 2002 (see above). Relations were placed under further stress in May 2005, when an Australian citizen, Schapelle Corby, was sentenced to a lengthy prison term by an Indonesian court, having been convicted of smuggling drugs into Indonesia. In March 2006 a diplomatic dispute developed between the two countries following the Australian Government's decision to grant temporary visas to several Indonesian asylum-seekers from the province of Papua. In the following month Prime Minister Howard announced a review of Australian immigration law, and in August the House of Representatives approved the Migration Amendment (Designated Unauthorised Arrivals) Bill, whereby it would be compulsory for asylum-seekers arriving by boat to be processed at offshore centres, rather than on the mainland. A few days later, however, the bill was withdrawn by the Government amid reports of significant opposition among members of the Senate. In November the Australian Minister for Foreign Affairs, Alexander Downer, and his Indonesian counterpart, Hassan Wirajuda, signed a treaty informally known as the Lombok Agreement, providing for the strengthening of bilateral relations and increased co-operation in the field of security.

In mid-December 2002 Timor-Leste's Parliament ratified a treaty with Australia on production, profit-sharing and royalty and tax distribution from oil and gas reserves. In August 2003 the two countries signed a memorandum of understanding to collaborate in combating terrorism. Australia's relations with Timor-Leste, however, were made difficult by disagreements over the maritime boundaries in the Timor Sea. Preliminary sea boundary talks between the two countries took place in November. The Prime Minister of Timor-Leste accused Australia of deliberately stalling negotiations after the latter refused to set a schedule for their completion. Australia stated that all its resources were being applied to other boundary discussions and that the dialogue with Timor-Leste might take decades. Little progress was made at the first round of negotiations, which took place in Dili in April 2004, with Australia rejecting appeals to submit the dispute to international arbitration. However, in August the Australian Minister for Foreign Affairs and his Timorese counterpart announced that they hoped to agree on a settlement framework by the end of 2004, following a warning from the Australian company Woodside Petroleum that if the dispute was not resolved by the end of the year, its gas project in the Timor Sea would not proceed. Talks on the maritime boundaries resumed in September and continued in October, but reached an impasse at the end of that month, and in January 2005, in the absence of any agreement, Woodside confirmed that it was halting development of the gas project. In January 2006 the two countries finally signed an agreement to share the revenue from the Greater Sunrise oil and gas field equally between them. However, the accord was criticized for including a condition that a final decision regarding the disputed maritime boundaries be postponed for at least 50 years. In October 2006 the Australian Minister for Foreign Affairs, Alexander Downer, and the ambassador of Timor-Leste to Australia, Hernani Coelho Da Silva, signed a Memorandum of Understanding, in order to ensure co-operation between the two countries in security operations in the Joint Petroleum Development Area.

In May 2006 an ongoing dispute within the Timor-Leste army, following the dismissal in April of almost 600 mutinous soldiers, provoked looting and violence in Dili (see the chapter on Timor-Leste). Australia responded to a request for assistance from the Timorese Government by leading a multinational security force comprising approximately 2,500 troops, drawn from Australia (the contingent of which numbered some 1,800), New Zealand, Malaysia and Portugal. The instability continued, albeit to a lesser degree, with occasional outbursts of violence, and in August the United Nations Integrated Mission in Timor-Leste (UNMIT) was established to address the situation. Also in August, the Australian Government announced the expansion of its army and police force in order to deal with security issues in South-East Asia and the Pacific region.

A crisis in Australia's relations with Malaysia arose in late 1993, when Paul Keating described the Malaysian Prime Minister as a 'recalcitrant' for his failure to attend the APEC summit meeting in Seattle, USA, in November. Relations subsequently improved, however, manifest in such initiatives as the Malaysia-Australia Dialogue (MAD), established in 1995 to encourage the long-term bilateral relationship at government-to-government level in education, business, the media and other sectors. In January 1996 Keating paid the first official visit to Malaysia by an Australian Prime Minister since 1984 and the ministerial-level Joint Trade Committee (JTC) talks were inaugurated. These led to the signing of a new trade and investment agreement, which took effect in January 1998. During 1999 Australia was critical of the continued detention and the trials of Anwar Ibrahim, the former Deputy Prime Minister and Minister of Finance (see the chapter on Malaysia). In early October 2002 the Australian Minister for Foreign Affairs met Myanma government officials and Myanma opposition leader Aung Sang Suu Kyi for discussions, during the first visit to Myanmar by an Australian minister for nearly 20 years. The Howard Government's more aggressive stance towards South-East Asia in late 2002 led to a deterioration in relations with the region. In early December the Prime Minister stated that he would be prepared to conduct pre-emptive strikes on militant organizations in neighbouring countries suspected of planning terrorist attacks on Australia. Malaysia warned Australia that any incursion into its territory would be considered as an act of war. Australia's growing interventionist stance towards its neighbours, in particular Solomon Islands and Papua New Guinea (see below), in 2003 encouraged Asian leaders to view the country increasingly as a 'deputy' of the USA. In March Australia and the Philippines signed an agreement on increased bilateral co-operation to counter international terrorism. Australia's relations with Malaysia appeared to improve following the succession of Abdullah Ahmad Badawi to the premiership of that country in October. In June 2004, during a visit to Malaysia by the Australian Minister for Foreign Affairs, Alexander Downer, agreement was reached to hold formal annual talks between the two countries' foreign ministers and separate regular consultations between senior security officials. However, the Malaysian Government dismissed a plan announced by John Howard in September to establish specialist counter-terrorist centres in South-East Asia and Australia, complaining that it had not been consulted about the proposal. In November, at a summit meeting of ASEAN leaders in Vientiane, Laos, Prime Minister Howard, together with his ASEAN and New Zealand counterparts, announced that negotiations would commence on a free trade agreement between Australia, ASEAN and New Zealand in early 2005. However, in December 2004 Australia provoked further tension with neighbouring countries when it proposed the creation of a coastal security zone extending five times as far as its territorial waters. Under this counter-terrorist measure, which came into effect in March 2005, all ships entering the 1,000-nautical mile zone would be monitored, with Australian naval and customs ships given powers to intercept and board all vessels suspected of constituting a terrorist threat. In April Prime Minister Abdullah Badawi visited Australia, the first visit to the country by a Malaysian leader in more than 20 years, as bilateral relations continued to improve. In the same month the President of Indonesia paid an official visit to the country. Australia's increasing involvement in regional affairs was emphasized by its attendance at the inaugural East Asia Summit meeting, held in Kuala Lumpur, Malaysia, in December.

Australia's relations with the People's Republic of China, meanwhile, were strained by the issue of China's nuclear-testing programme, and deteriorated further in September 1996 when the Dalai Lama, the exiled spiritual leader of Tibet, was received in Sydney by the Prime Minister. In March 1997, however, the Australian Prime Minister embarked upon an official visit to China, where he had discussions with Premier Li Peng. In July 1999, during a visit to Beijing by the Australian Minister of Foreign Affairs, Australia endorsed China's bid for membership of the World Trade Organization (WTO). The two countries also signed a bilateral trade pact. In September, however, President Jiang Zemin's visit to Australia was disrupted by pro-Tibet and Taiwan activists. Political and economic relations with China improved in the early 2000s, partly owing to Australia's refraining from criticizing China's human rights record. During President Hu Jintao's visit to Australia in October 2003 Australia agreed to supply China with liquefied natural gas for a period of 25 years. In June 2005 Sino-Australian relations were threatened by claims made by Chen Yonglin, a senior diplomatic official who had defected from the Chinese consulate in Sydney, that China maintained a significant espionage network in Australia. His allegations were supported by at least two other Chinese defectors. Chen and his family were subsequently granted permanent residency by the Australian authorities. In June 2007 the Australian Prime Minister, John Howard, held a meeting with the Dalai Lama in Sydney, despite opposition from the Chinese Government. Australia's relations with Japan were strained in the late 1990s by a fishing dispute relating to the latter's failure to curb its catches of the endangered southern bluefin tuna, as agreed in a treaty of 1993, of which New Zealand was also a signatory. In August 1999, however, an international tribunal ruled in favour of Australia and New Zealand. In March 2007 Prime Minister Howard and his Japanese counterpart, Shinzo Abe, signed an agreement on security in order to further bilateral co-operation, particularly in the areas of counter-terrorism and disaster relief.

In May 2000 diplomatic relations between Australia and the Democratic People's Republic of Korea, which had been severed in 1975, were restored. Discussions between the two nations, initiated by the North Korean Government in April 1999, had been dominated by the International Atomic Energy Agency's concerns over nuclear facilities and long-range missile testing. The Australian Minister of Foreign Affairs paid an official two-day visit to Pyongyang in November 2000. He confirmed that six North Korean officials were expected to participate in a nuclear-safeguards training course in Australia. An Australian trade mission organized by Austrade, Australia's trade and investment promotion agency, visited North Korea in December; discussions were held with North Korean officials regarding problems in the country's energy sector. Australia and North Korea agreed to establish, within two years, embassies in their respective capitals when North Korea's Minister of Foreign Affairs paid Australia a reciprocal visit in June 2001. Furthermore, a Memorandum of Understanding was signed to facilitate co-operation between Australian and North Korean scientists in agricultural research, including the participation of North Korean scientists in research programmes and on-the-job training activities in Australian research institutes. Plans to open an embassy in North Korea were deferred in late 2002, however, owing to North Korea's efforts to reactivate its nuclear weapons programme. In October 2006 North Korea's announcement that it had conducted its first test of a nuclear weapon prompted Australia to ban North Korean ships from its ports.

The viability of the ANZUS military pact, which was signed in 1951, linking Australia, New Zealand and the USA, was disputed by the US Government following the New Zealand Government's declaration, in July 1984, that vessels which were believed to be powered by nuclear energy, or to be carrying nuclear weapons, would be barred from the country's ports. Hawke did not support the New Zealand initiative, and Australia continued to participate with the USA in joint military exercises from which New Zealand had been excluded. However, the Hawke Government declined directly to endorse the US action against New Zealand, and in 1986 stated that Australia regarded its 'obligations to New Zealand as constant and undiminishing'. In September 1990 Australia and New Zealand signed an agreement to establish a joint venture to construct as many as 12 naval frigates to patrol the South Pacific. In February 1994 the USA announced its decision to resume senior-level contacts with New Zealand. In July 1996 Australia and the USA upgraded their defence alliance. In 1999 Australia's trading relations with the USA were strained by the latter's imposition of tariffs on imports of Australian lamb. In October Australia urged that the dispute be settled by means of a WTO panel; in December 2000 the WTO upheld the complaint, ruling that the tariffs violated global trade rules. Meanwhile, in July 2000 the US Secretary of Defense made an official visit to Australia, following which he re-emphasized the importance of bilateral defence ties; and the Ministers for Foreign Affairs and Defence participated in the Australia-US Leadership Dialogue in Washington, DC. In September 2001 Prime Minister John Howard condemned the terrorist attacks suffered by the USA and promised Australia's full support for the offensive in Afghanistan. In 2002 John Howard expressed his support for the USA's 'war on terror' and in early 2003 deployed some 2,000 troops to the Middle East in preparation for the US-led military campaign to oust the regime of Saddam Hussain in Iraq, which commenced in March. During a visit to Australia by US President George W. Bush in October, the US leader thanked and commended Australia for its support for the war in Iraq and the 'war on terror' during an address in Parliament. Two senators from the Green Party were expelled from the chamber for heckling President Bush, while an estimated 5,000 anti-Bush protesters held a demonstration outside the Parliament building. Relations between Australia and the USA were further strengthened in 2004 with the conclusion of a free trade agreement, which entered into force in January 2005, and with John Howard's visit to the USA in May 2006. In April 2007 the signing of an immigration agreement between Australia and the USA, whereby some asylum-seekers attempting to enter one country would be transferred to the other, was intended to deter illegal immigrants; critics claimed, however, that the agreement would have the opposite effect.

Owing to Australian opposition to French test explosions of nuclear weapons at Mururoa Atoll (French Polynesia) in the South Pacific Ocean, a ban on uranium sales to France was introduced in 1983. However, in August 1986 the Government announced its decision to resume uranium exports. In December Australia ratified a treaty declaring the South Pacific area a nuclear-free zone. France's decision, in April 1992, to suspend its nuclear-testing programme was welcomed by Australia. In June 1995, however, the French President's announcement that the programme was to be resumed provoked outrage throughout the Pacific region. The Australian ambassador to France was recalled, and the French consulate in Perth was destroyed in an arson attack. Further widespread protests followed the first of the new series of tests in September. Australia's relations with the United Kingdom were strained by the British Government's refusal to join the condemnation of France's policy. The final test was conducted in January 1996. On an official visit to Paris in September, the Australian Minister for Foreign Affairs adopted a conciliatory stance (which drew much criticism from anti-nuclear groups). A ban on new contracts for the supply of uranium to France, imposed in September 1995, was removed in October 1996. Meanwhile, Australia remained committed to achieving the elimination of all nuclear testing. In August, following a veto of the draft text by India and Iran at the UN Conference on Disarmament in Geneva, Switzerland, Australia took the initiative in leading an international effort to secure the passage of the Comprehensive Test Ban Treaty. In an unusual procedure, the Treaty was referred to the UN General Assembly, which voted overwhelmingly in its favour in September.

AUSTRALIA

Relations with neighbouring Pacific island states were strained in mid-1997. In July Australia was embarrassed by the unauthorized publication of a secret official document in which certain regional politicians were described as corrupt and incompetent. At a meeting of the South Pacific Forum (now Pacific Islands Forum, see p. 380) in September, the member countries failed to reach agreement on a common policy regarding mandatory targets for the reduction of emissions of the so-called 'greenhouse gases'. The low-lying nation of Tuvalu was particularly critical of Australia's refusal to compromise, the Australian Prime Minister declaring that the Pacific islands' concerns over rising sea levels were exaggerated. In July 2001 Australia declined Tuvalu's request to take in more Tuvaluan nationals. The Australian Government, committed to its 'Pacific solution', nevertheless made a verbal request for shelter for some of its many asylum-seekers to Tuvalu in November.

Australia's relations with Papua New Guinea were strained in early 1997 as a result of the latter's decision to engage the services of a group of mercenaries in the Government's operations against secessionists on the island of Bougainville. Fearing for the stability of the South Pacific region, the Australian Prime Minister denounced the use of foreign forces as unacceptable. In January 1998 a permanent cease-fire agreement between the Papua New Guinea Government and the Bougainville secessionists, which was to take effect in April, was signed in New Zealand. Australia reaffirmed its commitment to the provision of a peace-monitoring force. Since 1998 both Canberra and Townsville, in Queensland, had provided a neutral platform for rounds of negotiations regarding Bougainville's secession, and in August 2001 the Minister for Foreign Affairs, Alexander Downer, signed the Bougainville Peace Agreement as a witness. In October the Government concluded a deal with Papua New Guinea for that country to accommodate 223 asylum-seekers in exchange for $A1m. In December 2003 the Australian Government announced its intention to send around 300 police officers and civil servants to Papua New Guinea as part of a five-year operation to assist in the fight against crime and corruption. In July 2004 the National Parliament of Papua New Guinea approved legislation allowing the deployment of the Australian police officers and officials; the first contingent of police officers arrived in Bougainville in September. However, in May 2005, following a ruling by the Papua New Guinea Supreme Court that the deployment violated the Constitution, the police officers were withdrawn from the country. Tensions mounted between Australia and Papua New Guinea in October 2006 over the former's extradition request for an Australian lawyer, Julian Moti, to face criminal charges. Moti had been arrested in Port Moresby, but had escaped from Papua New Guinea to Solomon Islands, where he had previously been appointed Attorney-General (see below).

Australia played a leading role in the events following a coup in Solomon Islands, which took place in June 2000. The Australian navy dispatched a warship to assist in the evacuation of Australian and other nationals from the islands, while a similar ship anchored off shore served as a venue for negotiations between the two warring ethnic militias. The Australian Minister for Foreign Affairs led an international delegation with the aim of facilitating discussions between the factions. In October a peace agreement was signed in Townsville, which ended the two-year conflict; it was qualified and complemented by the Marau Peace Agreement, signed in February 2001. The Australian Government subsequently led an International Peace Monitoring Team, in an attempt to ensure continued stability in the islands. In September Australia contributed $A1.6m. towards financing democratic elections, and technical support was provided by the Australian Electoral Commission. In July 2003 an Australian-led regional peace-keeping force was deployed in Solomon Islands to restore law and order, leading many to believe that Australia was establishing itself as the 'neighbourhood policeman' in Asia. The force was welcomed by the inhabitants of the islands, and at the end of the year the operation was judged to have been a success. However, following the dispute arising from the Moti affair in October 2006 (see above), Prime Minister Manasseh Sogavare of Solomon Islands warned Australia that repeated extradition requests might lead to the expulsion of Australian peace-keepers from the country. Relations deteriorated further when Australian peace-keepers forcibly entered Sogavare's office in search of evidence relating to the Moti affair. At the Pacific Islands Forum meeting soon afterwards, Sogavare moved to diminish Australia's role in the Regional Assistance Mission to Solomon Islands (RAMSI); the Forum decided instead to establish a task force to evaluate its operations. In September 2007 Australia's extradition request for Julian Moti was formally rejected by the Solomon Islands Government. However, following Sogavare's removal from office in December and his replacement by Derek Sikua, Julian Moti was dismissed as Attorney-General, and the extradition request was subsequently granted.

The Australian Government intervened in the severe financial crisis experienced by Nauru in 2004, agreeing, in May, to provide a senior Treasury officer and finance department officials to assist in reorganizing the island's finances and a police commissioner and officers to help maintain law and order. In March 2007 it was announced that 83 Tamil asylum-seekers, who had reportedly fled from Sri Lanka via Indonesia, would be sent to Nauru.

In November 2006 pro-democracy protests in the Tongan capital, Nuku'alofa, led to serious rioting and the destruction of numerous buildings; several people were killed in the violence (see the chapter on Tonga). In response to an appeal from the Tongan Government, Australian and New Zealand security forces, including 50 soldiers and 35 police officers from Australia, were deployed in Tonga to restore stability.

The Australian Government responded to the military coup in Fiji in December 2006 by suspending military co-operation with the country and by banning those associated with the leader of the coup, Cdre Frank Bainimarama, from travelling to and via Australia. Towards the end of December the Government's sanctions against Fiji were extended to incorporate a suspension of aid to several areas of the public and legal sectors; aid to other spheres, including health and education, was to remain unaffected.

Government

Australia comprises six states and three territories. Executive power is vested in the British monarch and exercised by the monarch's appointed representative, the Governor-General, who normally acts on the advice of the Federal Executive Council (the Ministry), led by the Prime Minister. The Governor-General appoints the Prime Minister and, on the latter's recommendation, other Ministers.

Legislative power is vested in the Federal Parliament. This consists of the monarch, represented by the Governor-General, and two chambers elected by universal adult suffrage (voting is compulsory). The Senate has 76 members (12 from each state and two each from the Northern Territory and the Australian Capital Territory), who are elected by a system of proportional representation for six years when representing a state, with half the seats renewable every three years, and for a term of three years when representing a territory. The House of Representatives has 150 members, elected for three years (subject to dissolution) from single-member constituencies. The Federal Executive Council is responsible to Parliament.

Each state has a Governor, representing the monarch, and its own legislative, executive and judicial system. The state governments are essentially autonomous, but certain powers are placed under the jurisdiction of the Federal Government. All states except Queensland have an upper house (the Legislative Council) and a lower house (the Legislative Assembly or House of Assembly). The chief ministers of the states are known as Premiers, as distinct from the Federal Prime Minister. The Northern Territory (self-governing since 1978) and the Australian Capital Territory (self-governing since 1988) have unicameral legislatures, and each has a government led by a Chief Minister. The Jervis Bay Territory is not self-governing.

Defence

Australia's defence policy is based on collective security, and it is a member of the British Commonwealth Strategic Reserve and of ANZUS, with New Zealand and the USA. Australia also participates in the Five-Power Defence Arrangements, with New Zealand, Malaysia, Singapore and the United Kingdom. Australia's armed forces, as assessed at November 2007, numbered 51,293 (army 25,259, navy 12,784, air force 13,250). Defence expenditure for 2007 was budgeted at an estimated $A21,900m. Service in the armed forces is voluntary. In October 2001 Australia committed 1,550 service personnel to the International Coalition against Terrorism. In support of peace-keeping efforts, some 1,575 Australian troops were stationed in Iraq in November 2007. In the same month about 140 Australian military personnel remained in Solomon Islands.

Economic Affairs

In 2006, according to estimates by the World Bank, Australia's gross national income (GNI), measured at average 2004–06 prices, was US $738,479m., equivalent to US $35,990 per head (or US $34,060 per head on an international purchasing-power parity basis). During 1996–2006, it was estimated, the population increased at an average annual rate of 1.1%, while gross domestic product (GDP) per head increased, in real terms, by an average of 2.2%. Overall GDP increased, in real terms, at an average annual rate of 3.4% in 1996–2006. Compared with the previous year, GDP increased by 2.4% in 2006.

Agriculture (including forestry, hunting and fishing) contributed 2.3% of GDP in 2006/07. The sector engaged 3.5% of the employed labour force (excluding undefined activities) in 2006. The principal crops are wheat, fruit, sugar and cotton. Wheat production reached 25.1m. tons in 2005, before declining by more than 60% in 2006, to just 9.8m. tons, owing to drought conditions. Australia is the world's leading producer of wool. Export earnings from wool and other animal hair decreased from $3,545m. in 2002/03 to $2,258m. in 2005/06, reflecting a substantial decline in international prices for the commodity. In the year to March 2007 the contribution of wool to the country's exports reached only 1.9%. The export of wine is of increasing importance, having risen from 10m. litres in 1986 to 670m. litres in 2004/05. Australia has become one of the world's largest exporters of wine, with some 38% of the country's production being exported in 2006. The volume of grapes crushed in 2006/07, however, decreased by about 33%, owing to the impact of drought. In the year to June 2007 the value of wine exports totalled $A291,000m. Meat production is also important. Beef is Australia's leading meat export, although this (including veal) accounted for only about 2.8% of total export revenue in the year to March 2007. Between 1996 and 2004 agricultural GDP increased at an average annual rate of 2.0%. From 2002 agricultural production was severely affected by drought conditions, and in that year the GDP of the sector decreased by 23.8%, compared with 2001, before expanding by 31.3% in 2003, and contracting by 6.1% in 2004. Although there was some rainfall in mid-2003, water restrictions continued to constrain both agricultural producers and town dwellers in 2004–06. By 2007 the country's worst drought for a century had resulted in a critical situation, which was exacerbated by bushfires and also frosts.

Industry (comprising mining, manufacturing, construction and utilities) employed 21.3% of the working population (excluding activities not defined) in 2006, and provided 29.0% of GDP in 2006/07. Industrial GDP increased at an average rate of 2.7% per year between 1996 and 2004. Industrial output increased by 5.9% in 2006/07, in comparison with the previous 12-month period.

The mining sector employed 1.0% of the working population (excluding activities not defined) in 2006, and contributed 8.0% of GDP in 2006/07. Australia is one of the world's leading exporters of coal. Earnings from coal and related products in 2005/06 reached $A24,354m., accounting for 16.0% of total export receipts in that year. The other principal minerals extracted are iron ore, gold, silver, magnesite, petroleum and natural gas. Bauxite, zinc, copper, titanium, nickel, tin, lead, zirconium and diamonds are also mined. Between 1989/90 and 1996/97 the GDP of the mining sector increased at an average annual rate of 2.9%. This expansion continued at a similar rate between 1998/99 and 2006/07.

Manufacturing contributed 11.2% of GDP in 2006/07. The sector employed 10.4% of the working population (excluding undefined activities) in 2006. The principal branches of manufacturing include food, beverages and tobacco, equipment and machinery, chemical products and metal products. The manufacturing sector's GDP grew at an average annual rate of 1.7% between 1996 and 2004. Compared with the previous year, in 2003 the manufacturing sector's GDP grew by 0.9%, before declining by 1.0% in 2004.

Energy is derived principally from petroleum, natural gas and coal. Production of petroleum, however, declined from 33,320m. litres in 2002/03 to 24,315m. litres in 2005/06, before increasing to 28,555m. litres in 2006/07. Imports of crude petroleum and bituminous oils accounted for more than 7.4% of total import costs in 2005/06. The production of black coal increased from 348.9m. tons in 2002/03 to 409m. tons in 2006/07.

The services sector provided 68.8% of GDP in 2006/07, and engaged 75.2% of the employed labour force (excluding activities not defined) in 2006. The tourism industry has become a major source of foreign-exchange earnings. The number of visitor arrivals increased from 5.2m. in 2004 to more than 5.6m. in 2007. Tourism revenue increased from $A17,317m. in 2003/04 to $A18,257m. in 2004/05. It was estimated that in 2005/06 the tourism sector contributed 3.9% of GDP and accounted for 4.6% of total employment. The GDP of the services sector increased at an average annual rate of 4.1% between 1996 and 2004, rising by 3.1% in 2004.

In 2006 Australia recorded a visible trade deficit of US $9,524m., and there was a deficit of US $40,633m. on the current account of the balance of payments. In the year ending 30 June 2007 the People's Republic of China remained the principal source of imports (having overtaken the USA in the previous year), supplying 15.0%, compared with the USA's 13.8%. These nations were followed by Japan (9.6%) and Singapore (5.6%). Japan was the principal market for exports in 2006/07 (purchasing 19.4%), followed by China (13.6%). Other major trading partners are the Republic of Korea, New Zealand, the United Kingdom, Germany and Taiwan. The principal exports in 2005/06 included coal, iron ore, crude petroleum and non-monetary gold. The principal imports were passenger motor vehicles, crude petroleum, computing equipment and medicaments.

In the 2007/08 financial year a budgetary surplus of about $A11,171m. was forecast. In mid-2006 Australia's net external debt was equivalent to 51.0% of annual GDP, standing at $A493,828m., of which $A488,651m. was incurred by the private sector. An estimated average of 4.4% of the labour force were unemployed in 2007. The annual rate of inflation averaged 2.6% in 1995–2006. Consumer prices rose by 3.0% in 2007.

Australia is a member of the UN Economic and Social Commission for Asia and the Pacific (ESCAP, see p. 35), the Asian Development Bank (ADB, see p. 182), the Pacific Islands Forum (see p. 380), the Pacific Community (see p. 377) and the Colombo Plan (see p. 411). In 1989 Australia played a major role in the creation of the Asia-Pacific Economic Co-operation group (APEC, see p. 176), which aimed to stimulate economic development in the region. Australia is also a member of the Organisation for Economic Co-operation and Development (OECD, see p. 347), of the Cairns Group (see p. 464) and of the International Grains Council (see p. 408).

After 11 years of Liberal-National administration, Labor leader Kevin Rudd was appointed Prime Minister following the federal election of November 2007. Industrial relations had been a crucial area of focus during the election campaign, with Labor undertaking to restore to employees some trade union rights to collective bargaining. There had been criticism of Labor plans to transfer workers from individual contracts to common law agreements, with some arguing that this might reduce the flexibility of the labour force. Prior to its departure from office, the Liberal-National administration had granted approval to the long-awaited Gorgon gas project, off the north-western coast, which was expected to be the country's largest ever resources programme. Various overseas companies planned to collaborate in the development of a liquefied natural gas (LNG) plant, which was expected to produce 10m. metric tons of LNG per year. Investment of approximately $A20,000m. and the creation of 6,000 jobs were envisaged. Prolonged drought continued to have a detrimental impact upon the agricultural sector. Expansion in the wine industry, which for several years had been experiencing a large surplus in supply, was curtailed from 2007 when the year's grape harvest declined by 25%, to 1.4m. tons, the lowest production level since 2000. Nevertheless, the strength of other sectors, such as retail trade, ensured that the economy continued to perform well in 2007. The ratio of unemployed persons to vacancies declined to just 2.7, having averaged 13.7 in the 1990s. Following an estimated increase in GDP of 4.1% in 2007, however, growth was forecast to slow to 3.3% in 2008 and further decelerate, to 2.8%, in 2009. Although growth in consumption was expected to sustain momentum, owing to high levels of employment and increases in wages, concomitant with tax reductions, in early 2008 the new Government acknowledged that its principal economic challenge was that of containing inflationary pressures. During 2007 the central bank had raised its interest rate on two occasions, and in February 2008 the rate was increased to 7.0%, its highest point since 1976; a further rise, to 7.25%, was implemented in March 2008.

Education

Education is the responsibility of each of the states and the Federal Government. It is compulsory for all children from the ages of six to 15 years (16 in South Australia and Tasmania) and is free of charge. In most states and territories primary education generally begins with a preparatory year commencing at five years of age, followed by six or seven years of schooling. Secondary education, beginning at the age of 12, usually lasts for five or six years. In 2005 enrolment at primary schools included 96.6% of pupils in the relevant age group, while enrolment at secondary schools included an estimated 86.4% of pupils in the relevant age group. In 2006 there were 1,936,118 children enrolled in primary schools (of whom 29.4% attended non-government schools, the majority being Catholic institutions) and 1,431,918 in secondary schools (with 38.4% at non-government schools). Special services have been developed to fulfil the requirements of children living in the remote 'outback' areas, notably Schools of the Air, using two-way receiver sets. A system of one-teacher schools and correspondence schools also helps to satisfy these needs. In 2004 there were 48 publicly funded institutions of higher education. In the same year students totalled 830,058. Most courses last from three to six years. Public expenditure on education in the financial year 2007/08 was projected at $A17,752m.

Public Holidays*

2008: 1 January (New Year's Day), 28 January (Australia Day), 21–24 March (Easter), 25 April (Anzac Day), 9 June (Queen's Official Birthday, except Western Australia), 25–26 December (Christmas Day, Boxing Day).

2009: 1 January (New Year's Day), 26 January (Australia Day), 10–13 April (Easter), 25 April (Anzac Day), 8 June (Queen's Official Birthday, except Western Australia), 25–26 December (Christmas Day, Boxing Day).

* National holidays only. Some states observe these holidays on different days. There are also numerous individual state holidays.

Weights and Measures

The metric system is in force.

Statistical Survey

Source (unless otherwise stated): Australian Bureau of Statistics, POB 10, Belconnen, ACT 2616; tel. (2) 6252-7983; fax (2) 6251-6009; internet www.abs.gov.au.

Area and Population

AREA, POPULATION AND DENSITY

Area (sq km)	7,692,024*
Population (census results)†	
7 August 2001	18,769,249
8 August 2006	
Males	9,799,252
Females	10,056,036
Total	19,855,288
Population (official estimate at mid-year)	
2007*	21,017,200
Density (per sq km) at mid-2007	2.7

* 2,969,907 sq miles; including Jervis Bay Territory.
† Population is *de jure*.
‡ Including Jervis Bay Territory, Christmas Island and the Cocos (Keeling) Islands.

STATES AND TERRITORIES
(estimated population at mid-year 2007)

	Area (sq km)	Population	Density (per sq km)
New South Wales (NSW)	800,642	6,889,100	8.6
Victoria	227,416	5,205,200	22.9
Queensland	1,730,648	4,182,100	2.4
South Australia	983,482	1,584,500	1.6
Western Australia	2,529,875	2,105,800	0.8
Tasmania	68,401	493,300	7.2
Northern Territory	1,349,129	215,000	0.2
Australian Capital Territory (ACT)	2,358	339,900	144.1
Other territories*	73	2,300	—
Total	7,692,024	21,017,200	2.7

* Area refers to Jervis Bay Territory only, but population also includes data for Christmas Island and the Cocos (Keeling) Islands.

PRINCIPAL TOWNS
(population at census of August 2006)*

Sydney (capital of NSW)	4,119,190	Sunshine Coast	276,267
Melbourne (capital of Victoria)	3,592,591	Wollongong	263,535
Brisbane (capital of Queensland)	1,763,131	Hobart (capital of Tasmania)	200,525
Perth (capital of W Australia)	1,445,078	Geelong	160,991
Adelaide (capital of S Australia)	1,105,839	Townsville	143,328
Gold Coast-Tweed	527,660	Cairns	122,731
Newcastle	493,465	Toowoomba	114,479
Canberra (national capital)	323,056	Darwin (capital of N Territory)	105,991

* Figures refer to metropolitan areas, each of which normally comprises a municipality and contiguous urban areas.

BIRTHS, MARRIAGES AND DEATHS*

	Registered live births		Registered marriages		Registered deaths	
	Number	Rate (per 1,000)	Number	Rate (per 1,000)	Number	Rate (per 1,000)
1999	248,870	13.1	114,316	6.0	128,102	7.1
2000	249,636	13.0	113,429	5.9	128,291	6.8
2001	246,394	12.7	103,130	5.3	128,544	6.6
2002	250,988	12.8	105,435	5.4	133,707	6.7
2003	251,161	12.6	106,394	5.3	132,292	6.5
2004	254,246	12.6	110,958	5.5	132,508	6.3
2005	259,791	12.7	109,323	5.4	130,714	6.1
2006	265,949	12.8	114,222	5.5	133,739	6.0

* Data are tabulated by year of registration rather than by year of occurrence.

Expectation of life (years at birth, WHO estimates): 81.4 (males 79.0; females 83.7) in 2005 (Source: WHO, *World Health Statistics*).

IMMIGRATION AND EMIGRATION
(year ending 30 June)*

	2004/05	2005/06	2006/07
Permanent immigrants	123,420	131,590	140,150
Permanent emigrants	62,610	67,850	72,100

* Figures are rounded to the nearest 10 persons and refer to persons intending to settle in Australia, or Australian residents intending to settle abroad.

AUSTRALIA

ECONOMICALLY ACTIVE POPULATION
(annual averages, '000 persons aged 15 years and over, excluding armed forces)

	2004	2005	2006
Agriculture, hunting and forestry	348.9	349.6	345.5
Fishing	14.0	13.2	10.1
Mining and quarrying	78.9	92.1	102.6
Manufacturing	1,088.5	1,069.7	1,058.1
Electricity, gas and water	74.1	81.9	85.7
Construction	802.5	856.7	908.7
Wholesale and retail trade; repair of motor vehicles, motorcycles and personal and household goods	1,891.4	1,953.2	1,951.3
Hotels and restaurants	485.7	499.6	477.5
Transport, storage and communications	617.1	640.3	646.4
Financial intermediation	347.2	372.1	381.7
Real estate, renting and business activities	1,135.3	1,199.3	1,247.9
Public administration and defence; compulsory social security	566.9	583.3	605.8
Education	692.6	694.3	714.4
Health and social work	981.3	1,012.8	1,070.4
Other community, social and personal service activities	488.4	514.0	518.2
Private households with employed persons	2.6	0.4	0.5
Extra-territorial organizations and bodies	0.9	1.0	1.1
Not classified by economic activity	20.0	23.8	27.9
Total employed	9,636.3	9,957.3	10,153.8
Unemployed	570.6	535.0	525.6
Total labour force	10,206.9	10,492.3	10,679.4
Males	5,646.8	5,773.2	5,865.3
Females	4,560.1	4,719.1	4,814.1

Source: ILO.

Health and Welfare

KEY INDICATORS

Total fertility rate (children per woman, 2005)	1.7
Under-5 mortality rate (per 1,000 live births, 2005)	6
HIV/AIDS (% of persons aged 15–49, 2005)	0.1
Physicians (per 1,000 head, 2001)	2.5
Hospital beds (per 1,000 head, 2003)	3.99
Health expenditure (2004): US $ per head (PPP)	3,123.3
Health expenditure (2004): % of GDP	9.6
Health expenditure (2004): public (% of total)	67.5
Human Development Index (2005): ranking	3
Human Development Index (2005): value	0.962

For sources and definitions, see explanatory note on p. vi.

Agriculture

PRINCIPAL CROPS
('000 metric tons)

	2004	2005	2006
Wheat	21,905.1	25,090.0	9,819.0
Rice (paddy)	553.1	338.9	126.0
Barley	7,739.8	9,869.0	3,722.0
Maize	395.0	419.7	380.0
Oats	1,282.5	1,416.0	633.0
Millet	43.5	25.0	35.0
Sorghum	2,009.0	2,010.6	996.0
Triticale (wheat-rye hybrid)	615.1	675.0	595.0
Potatoes	1,310.4	1,288.3	1,288.3*
Sugar cane	36,993.5	37,822.2	38,169.0
Dry beans	27.3	20.5	15.0*
Dry broad beans	167.5	329.0	104.0
Dry peas	289.4	478.0	360.0
Chick-peas	135.2	116.0	108.0
Lentils	52.3	210.0	38.0

—continued	2004	2005	2006
Lupins	936.6	952.0	174.0
Soybeans (Soya beans)	59.8	44.7	55.0
Sunflower seed	56.7	60.9	95.0
Rapeseed	1,542.3	1,441.0	440.0
Cottonseed	493.7	912.3	844.4
Lettuce	127.2	132.0	132.0*
Tomatoes	474.2	408.0	408.0*
Cauliflower and broccoli	129.8	123.9	123.9*
Pumpkins, squash and gourds	94.6	89.9	89.9*
Dry onions	233.4	256.0	256.0*
Green peas	29.5	27.0	27.0*
Carrots and turnips	302.6	316.0	316.0*
Watermelons	126.9	108.4	108.4*
Cantaloupes and other melons	93.9	83.0	83.0*
Bananas	257.2	265.6	265.6*
Oranges	395.2	498.1	571.0
Tangerines, mandarins, clementines and satsumas	101.0	87.9	102.0
Apples	254.9	326.6	276.4
Pears	138.5	151.4	142.4
Peaches and nectarines	99.5	130.2	110.0†
Grapes	2,015.0	2,026.5	1,981.2
Pineapples	110.4	104.0	104.0*
Cotton (lint)	349.1	645.1	597.1

* FAO estimate.
† Unofficial figure.

Aggregate production ('000 metric tons, may include official, semi-official or estimated data): Total cereals 34,563.6 in 2004, 39,869.6 in 2005, 16,331.5 in 2006; Total roots and tubers 1,316.3 in 2004, 1,294.1 in 2005, 1,294.1 in 2006; Total vegetables (incl. melons) 1,896.1 in 2004, 1,824.7 in 2005, 1,824.7 in 2006; Total fruits (excl. melons) 3,606.0 in 2004, 3,857.5 in 2005, 3,821.4 in 2006.

Source: FAO.

LIVESTOCK
('000 head at 30 June)

	2004	2005	2006
Horses	219.1	221.0	221.0*
Cattle	27,465	27,782	28,560
Pigs	2,547.8	2,537.9	2,470.0
Sheep	101,287.4	101,124.9	100,100.0
Goats	594.7	461.5	461.5*
Chickens	83,404	75,903	74,500*
Ducks*	600	620	620
Turkeys*	1,550	1,600	1,600

* FAO estimate(s).

Source: FAO.

LIVESTOCK PRODUCTS
('000 metric tons)

	2004	2005	2006
Cattle meat	2,033	2,162	2,077
Sheep meat	561	595	626
Goat meat*	16.5	16.8	16.8
Pig meat	406.0	388.4	388.9
Horse meat*	21.3	21.3	21.3
Chicken meat	694.0	760.0	772.6
Duck meat*	9.5	9.6	9.6
Turkey meat*	28.0	28.7	28.7
Cows' milk	10,125	10,092	10,250
Hen eggs†	157.6	166.3	164.0
Honey*	18.0	18.5	18.5
Wool: greasy	509.5	519.7	519.7*

* FAO estimates.
† Unofficial figures.

Note: Figures for meat and milk refer to the 12 months ending 30 June of the year stated.

Source: FAO.

AUSTRALIA

Forestry

ROUNDWOOD REMOVALS
('000 cubic metres, excl. bark)

	2004	2005	2006
Sawlogs, veneer logs and logs for sleepers	12,655	12,655	12,680
Pulpwood	13,197	13,197	13,731
Other industrial wood	480	480	493
Fuel wood*	5,601	5,601	5,075
Total	31,933	31,933	31,979

* FAO estimates.
Source: FAO.

SAWNWOOD PRODUCTION
('000 cubic metres, incl. railway sleepers)

	2004	2005	2006
Coniferous (softwood)	3,415	3,456	3,596
Broadleaved (hardwood)	1,253	1,231	1,188
Total	4,668	4,687	4,784

Source: FAO.

Fishing

('000 metric tons, live weight, year ending 30 June)

	2002/03	2003/04	2004/05
Capture	215.2	229.7	245.9
Blue grenadier	8.9	8.9	6.7
Clupeoids	25.3	36.6	60.8
Australian spiny lobster	11.5	13.7	12.3
Penaeus shrimps	12.6	11.8	10.7
Scallops	9.6	9.3	15.4
Aquaculture	44.2	49.1	47.1
Atlantic salmon	15.2	16.5	16.0
Total catch	259.4	278.8	293.0

Note: Figures exclude aquatic plants ('000 metric tons, capture only): 8.9 in 2002/03; 12.6 in 2003/04; 14.2 in 2004/05. Also excluded are crocodiles, recorded by number rather than by weight. The number of estuarine crocodiles caught was: 15,325 in 2002/03; 12,232 in 2003/04; 20,194 in 2004/05. The number of Australian crocodiles caught was: 184 in 2002/03 and 65 in 2004/05; no figures were available for 2003/04. Also excluded are whales, recorded by number rather than weight. The number of Baleen whales caught was: 1 in 2002/03; 1 in 2003/04; 5 in 2004/05. The number of toothed whales (incl. dolphins) caught was: 29 in 2002/03; 41 in 2003/04; 44 in 2004/05. Also excluded are pearl oyster shells (metric tons, estimates): 200 in 2002/03; 200 in 2003/04; 200 in 2004/05.

Source: FAO.

Mining

(year ending 30 June, '000 metric tons, unless otherwise indicated)

	2004/05	2005/06	2006/07*
Black coal	393,000	398,000	409,000
Brown coal†	71,000	68,000	72,000
Crude petroleum (million litres)	27,311	24,315	28,555
Natural gas (million cu metres)	37,267	38,016	39,304
Iron ore: gross weight†	251,918	263,815	287,653
Copper ore†‡	905	936	859
Nickel ore†‡	192	186	192
Bauxite: gross weight	57,648	60,874	62,684
Bauxite: alumina content	17,161	17,826	18,506
Lead ore†‡	682	762	642
Zinc ore†‡	1,352	1,380	1,382
Tin ore (metric tons)†‡	2,055	1,805	2,061
Manganese ore (metallurgical): gross weight†	3,563	4,088	5,071

—continued	2004/05	2005/06	2006/07*
Ilmenite†	1,993	2,185	2,403
Leucoxene	68	87	174
Rutile†	174	184	277
Zirconium concentrates†	432	442	565
Silver (metric tons)†‡	2,303	2,218	1,674
Uranium (metric tons)‡	10,964	9,974	9,594
Gold (metric tons)†‡	266	250	251
Limestone	17,211	n.a.	n.a.
Salt (unrefined)†§	12,254	11,467	11,209
Diamonds ('000 carats, unsorted)	32,471	25,354	24,632

* Provisional.
† Estimated production.
‡ Figures refer to the metal content of ores and concentrates.
§ Excludes production in Victoria.

Source: Australian Bureau of Agricultural and Resource Economics, *Australian Mineral Statistics* and *Australian Commodity Statistics*.

Industry

SELECTED PRODUCTS
(year ending 30 June, '000 metric tons, unless otherwise indicated)

	2004/05	2005/06	2006/07
Pig-iron	6,080	6,765	n.a.
Raw steel	7,556	7,866	8,010
Aluminium—unwrought*	1,890	1,912	1,957
Copper—unwrought*	479	461	435
Lead—unwrought*	234	234	191
Zinc—unwrought*	464	446	496
Tin—unwrought (metric tons)*	445	736	321
Motor spirit (petrol—million litres)	17,913	16,528	n.a.
Fuel oil (million litres)	1,092	1,048	n.a.
Diesel-automotive oil (million litres)	12,822	10,154	n.a.
Aviation turbine fuel (million litres)	5,325	5,216	n.a.

* Primary refined metal only.

Sources: mainly Australian Bureau of Agricultural and Resource Economics, *Australian Mineral Statistics*, *Australian Commodity Statistics* and *Energy in Australia*.

Finance

CURRENCY AND EXCHANGE RATES

Monetary Units
100 cents = 1 Australian dollar ($A).

Sterling, US Dollar and Euro Equivalents (31 December 2007)
£1 sterling = $A2.272;
US $1 = $A1.134
€1 = $A1.670;
$A100 = £44.05 = US $88.16 = €59.89.

Average Exchange Rate (Australian dollars per US $)
2005 1.3095
2006 1.3280
2007 1.1951

AUSTRALIA

Statistical Survey

COMMONWEALTH GOVERNMENT BUDGET
($A million, year ending 30 June)

Revenue	2005/06	2006/07	2007/08*
Tax revenue	206,832	221,505	231,069
Income taxes	176,198	189,378	198,530
Individuals	114,431	117,614	119,560
Taxes on fringe benefits	4,084	3,754	4,110
Superannuation taxation	6,705	7,879	8,300
Companies	48,987	58,538	64,580
Petroleum resource rent tax	1,991	1,594	1,980
Excise and customs	26,914	28,379	28,910
Excise duty revenue	21,927	22,734	22,950
Other taxes	3,720	3,748	3,629
Non-tax revenue	15,086	15,504	15,691
Total	221,918	237,008	246,761

Expenditure	2005/06	2006/07	2007/08*
Defence	16,194	16,854	19,880
Education	15,883	16,898	17,752
Health	37,549	39,948	42,964
Social security and welfare	86,219	92,075	96,450
Economic services	16,680	17,847	20,321
General public services	12,790	14,615	15,768
Public-debt interest	3,628	3,592	3,485
Total (incl. others)	206,096	219,362	235,590

* Provisional figures.

Source: Government of Australia.

OFFICIAL RESERVES
(US $ million at 31 December)

	2004	2005	2006
Gold (national valuation)	1,123	1,316	1,121
IMF special drawing rights	195	193	200
Reserve position in IMF	1,706	776	428
Foreign exchange	33,901	40,972	52,821
Total	36,925	43,257	54,570

Source: IMF, *International Financial Statistics*.

MONEY SUPPLY
($A million at 31 December)

	2004	2005	2006
Currency outside banks	32,803	34,901	37,792
Demand deposits at trading and savings banks	211,102	233,984	260,762
Total money (incl. others)	243,950	268,904	298,570

Source: IMF, *International Financial Statistics*.

COST OF LIVING
(Consumer Price Index*; base 2000 = 100)

	2004	2005	2006
Food	117.1	120.0	129.2
Clothing	102.4	100.7	98.9
Rent†	110.4	112.9	116.5
Electricity, gas and other fuels	119.7	124.2	129.4
All items (incl. others)	113.1	116.1	120.2

* Weighted average of eight capital cities.
† Including expenditure on maintenance and repairs of dwellings; excluding mortgage interest charges and including house purchase and utilities.

Source: ILO.

NATIONAL ACCOUNTS
($A million, current prices, year ending 30 June)

National Income and Product

	2004/05	2005/06	2006/07
Compensation of employees	431,118	464,511	500,899
Gross operating surplus	284,467	312,417	345,856
Gross mixed income	80,259	83,066	85,551
Total factor incomes	795,844	859,994	932,305
Taxes, less subsidies, on production and imports	101,798	107,460	113,641
Statistical discrepancy	—	—	419
GDP in market prices	897,642	967,454	1,046,365
Net primary incomes from abroad	−32,407	−38,887	−47,131
Gross national income	865,235	928,567	999,234
Current taxes on income, wealth, etc.	989	1,001	958
Other current transfers (net)	−1,435	−1,478	−1,402
Gross disposable income	864,789	928,090	998,790

Expenditure on the Gross Domestic Product

	2004/05	2005/06	2006/07
Government final consumption expenditure	162,499	173,139	190,970
Private final consumption expenditure	521,028	547,458	581,873
Gross fixed capital formation	231,739	260,762	281,577
Change in inventories	4,641	277	2,345
Total domestic expenditure	919,907	981,636	1,056,765
Exports of goods and services	166,519	194,440	214,434
Less Imports of goods and services	188,784	208,622	225,132
Statistical discrepancy	—	—	298
GDP in market prices	897,642	967,454	1,046,365
GDP at constant 2005/06 prices	939,692	967,454	998,274

Gross Domestic Product by Economic Activity

	2004/05	2005/06	2006/07
Agriculture, hunting, forestry and fishing	25,794	26,353	21,183
Mining and quarrying	44,738	64,363	74,213
Manufacturing	93,748	96,008	104,151
Electricity, gas and water	19,668	21,115	21,242
Construction	56,618	61,550	70,297
Wholesale and retail trade	91,388	94,555	99,567
Hotels and restaurants	18,909	19,559	20,427
Transport, storage and communications	58,224	59,552	66,311
Finance and insurance	61,050	66,773	72,987
Property and business activities	102,936	110,718	125,079
Ownership of dwellings	66,171	70,012	75,963
Public administration and defence	33,761	37,412	40,279
Education	40,504	43,446	46,472
Health and community services	53,417	58,015	62,359
Cultural and recreational services	12,082	12,921	13,414
Personal and other services	16,839	17,642	18,360
Gross value added at basic prices	795,844	859,994	932,305
Taxes, less subsidies, on products	101,798	107,460	113,641
Statistical discrepancy	—	—	419
GDP in market prices	897,642	967,454	1,046,365

AUSTRALIA

BALANCE OF PAYMENTS
(US $ million)

	2004	2005	2006
Exports of goods f.o.b.	87,161	107,011	124,915
Imports of goods f.o.b.	-105,230	-120,383	-134,439
Trade balance	-18,069	-13,372	-9,524
Exports of services	28,485	31,047	33,014
Imports of services	-27,943	-30,505	-32,265
Balance on goods and services	-17,526	-12,830	-8,775
Other income received	14,307	16,420	21,627
Other income paid	-35,293	-44,129	-53,130
Balance on goods, services and income	-38,512	-40,539	-40,278
Current transfers received	3,145	3,277	3,227
Current transfers paid	-3,414	-3,638	-3,583
Current balance	-38,781	-40,900	-40,633
Capital account (net)	817	963	1,076
Direct investment abroad	-10,906	34,817	-21,025
Direct investment from abroad	36,613	-35,121	24,734
Portfolio investment assets	-25,081	-21,412	-42,452
Portfolio investment liabilities	39,403	58,760	95,487
Financial derivatives assets	19,056	14,497	9,025
Financial derivatives liabilities	-18,450	-15,985	-8,595
Other investment assets	-5,991	-3,200	-16,985
Other investment liabilities	3,992	15,065	9,405
Net errors and omissions	493	-227	-314
Overall balance	1,166	7,256	9,722

Source: IMF, *International Financial Statistics*.

External Trade

PRINCIPAL COMMODITIES*
(distribution by SITC, $A million, year ending 30 June)

Imports f.o.b.	2003/04	2004/05	2005/06
Crude petroleum oils	6,322	9,687	12,464
Refined petroleum oils	3,318	4,832	8,322
Medicaments (incl. veterinary)	4,898	5,718	5,942
Paper and paperboard	2,029	2,071	2,043
Automatic data-processing machines and units thereof, magnetic, optical readers; data transcribers and processors	5,127	5,792	6,081
Parts and accessories of office machines	2,149	2,141	2,215
Miscellaneous telecommunications equipment and parts, and accessories of radio, television, etc.	4,360	5,031	5,838
Motor vehicles principally designed for transport of persons (excl. public transport, incl. racing cars)	11,216	11,597	11,998
Motor vehicles for the transport of goods	3,111	4,036	4,353
Parts and accessories of motor vehicles	2,108	2,285	2,261
Aircraft and associated equipment; spacecraft (incl. satellites and launch vehicles) and parts thereof	3,817	3,685	4,293
Non-monetary gold (excl. gold ores and concentrates)	2,562	2,466	4,804
Total (incl. others)	130,997	149,469	167,603

Exports f.o.b.	2003/04	2004/05	2005/06
Meat of bovine animals, fresh, chilled or frozen	3,926	4,879	4,541
Wheat (incl. spelt) and meslin, unmilled	3,399	3,396	3,213
Wool and other animal hair	2,490	2,490	2,258
Iron ore and concentrates	5,277	8,120	12,511
Aluminium ores and concentrates (incl. alumina)	3,722	4,434	5,294
Coal, not agglomerated	10,916	17,144	24,350
Petroleum and bituminous oils, crude	4,643	5,693	6,004
Refined petroleum oils	1,994	2,388	3,096
Natural gas	2,174	3,199	4,347
Aluminium	3,809	4,139	5,206
Passenger motor vehicles	2,927	2,780	3,193
Non-monetary gold (excl. gold ores and concentrates)	5,652	5,642	7,274
Total (incl. others)	109,049	126,823	151,792

* Excludes commodities subject to a confidentiality restriction. Such commodities are included in the total.

PRINCIPAL TRADING PARTNERS
($A million, year ending 30 June)

Imports f.o.b.	2004/05	2005/06	2006/07
Canada	1,905	1,993	2,077
China, People's Republic	19,812	23,206	27,140
France	4,437	5,348	3,910
Germany	8,646	8,680	9,274
Indonesia	3,311	4,557	4,646
Ireland	1,917	1,847	2,120
Italy	4,494	4,187	4,869
Japan	17,161	17,337	17,399
Korea, Republic	5,006	6,491	6,012
Malaysia	5,920	6,750	6,602
New Zealand	5,337	5,481	5,615
Papua New Guinea	1,737	2,315	2,215
Singapore	7,245	10,562	10,132
Sweden	1,963	2,395	2,287
Taiwan	3,612	3,810	4,409
Thailand	4,202	5,390	7,222
United Kingdom	5,935	5,972	7,407
USA	21,270	22,776	24,908
Viet Nam	3,096	4,161	4,502
Total (incl. others)	149,469	167,603	180,805

Exports f.o.b.	2004/05	2005/06	2006/07
Canada	1,880	1,683	1,768
China, People's Republic	13,003	17,889	22,805
France	1,012	1,170	1,364
Germany	1,315	1,416	1,444
Hong Kong	2,709	2,897	3,038
India	6,055	7,333	10,102
Indonesia	3,407	3,979	4,240
Italy	1,544	1,560	1,742
Japan	24,955	30,982	32,631
Korea, Republic	9,720	11,691	13,097
Malaysia	2,581	2,528	3,103
Netherlands	1,794	2,578	2,976
New Zealand	9,163	8,728	9,434
Saudi Arabia	1,808	2,179	2,025
Singapore	3,362	4,200	4,638
South Africa	1,652	2,210	2,316
Taiwan	4,886	5,865	6,189
Thailand	3,900	4,219	4,256
United Kingdom	4,821	7,787	6,146
USA	9,462	9,781	9,804
Total (incl. others)	126,823	151,792	168,102

AUSTRALIA   Statistical Survey

Transport

RAILWAYS
(traffic)*

	1997/98	1998/99	1999/2000
Passengers carried (million)	587.7	595.2	629.2
Freight carried (millon metric tons)	487.5	492.0	508.0
Freight ton-km ('000 million)	125.2	127.4	134.2

* Traffic on government railways only.

Passengers carried (million): 610 in 2003/04; 616 in 2004/05.

Freight carried (million metric tons): 557.3 in 2001/02; 589.1 in 2002/03.

Freight ton-km ('000 million): 150.7 in 2001/02; 161.8 in 2002/03.

ROAD TRAFFIC
('000 vehicles registered at 31 March)

	2005	2006	2007
Passenger vehicles	10,896	11,189	11,462
Light commercial vehicles	2,030	2,114	2,190
Trucks*	499	476	490
Buses	73	75	78
Motorcycles	422	463	512

* Including camper vans, previously classified as passenger vehicles.

SHIPPING
Merchant Fleet
(registered at 31 December)

	2004	2005	2006
Number of vessels	652	671	672
Total displacement ('000 grt)	1,971.9	1,794.9	1,852.8

Source: Lloyd's Register-Fairplay, *World Fleet Statistics*.

International Sea-borne Traffic
('000 metric tons, year ending 30 June)

	2000/01	2001/02	2002/03
Goods loaded	496,204	506,317	540,570
Goods unloaded	54,579	58,041	62,459

CIVIL AVIATION
(traffic)*

	2003	2004	2005
International services ('000):			
Passenger arrivals	8,263.1	9,707.6	10,502.6
Passenger departures	9,663.5	9,663.5	10,373.8
Domestic services:			
Passengers carried ('000)	33,114	37,853	40,736
Passenger-km (million)	30,565	40,099	43,339

* Includes estimates for regional airline data.

1999 (metric tons): International freight carried 680,458; International mail carried 25,316; Domestic freight and mail carried 192,326.

Tourism

VISITOR ARRIVALS BY COUNTRY OF ORIGIN
('000)*

	2004	2005	2006
Canada	98.2	102.5	109.7
China, People's Republic	251.3	285.0	308.5
Germany	140.6	146.4	148.3
Hong Kong	137.2	159.5	154.6
Japan	710.4	685.5	650.9
Korea, Republic	211.9	250.4	260.9
Malaysia	166.8	165.9	150.3
New Zealand	1,032.7	1,098.7	1,075.7
Singapore	251.2	265.3	253.3
Taiwan	98.8	110.9	93.6
United Kingdom	676.2	708.3	734.2
USA	433.3	446.2	456.0
Total (incl. others)	5,215.0	5,497.0	5,532.4

* Visitors intending to stay for less than one year.

Receipts from tourism (US $ million): 15,510 in 2003; 18,908 in 2004; 20,637 in 2005 (Source: World Tourism Organization).

Communications Media

	2004	2005	2006
Telephones ('000 main lines in use)	10,370	10,120	9,940
Mobile cellular telephones ('000 subscribers)	16,480	18,420	19,760
Personal computers ('000 in use)	13,720	13,720	n.a.
Internet users ('000)	13,000	14,190	15,300
Broadband subscribers ('000)	834	1,787	3,900

Television receivers ('000 in use): 14,168 in 2001.

Source: International Telecommunication Union.

Radio receivers ('000 in use): 25,500 in 1997 (Source: UNESCO, *Statistical Yearbook*).

Facsimile machines ('000 in use): 900 in 1997 (Source: UN, *Statistical Yearbook*).

Book production (1994): 10,835 titles (Source: UNESCO, *Statistical Yearbook*).

Newspapers (2004): 49 dailies (estimated combined circulation 3,114,000); 435 non-dailies (circulation 433,000) (Source: UNESCO, *Statistical Yearbook*).

Education

(August 2006 unless otherwise indicated)

	Institutions	Teaching staff*	Students
Government schools	6,902	158,194	2,248,229†
Non-government schools	2,710	81,445	1,119,807†
Higher educational institutions‡	48§	78,189	830,058

* Full-time teaching staff and full-time equivalent of part-time teaching staff.
† Primary and secondary students. In 2006 the total at both government and non-government schools comprised 1,936,118 primary and 1,431,918 secondary students.
‡ March 2004 (Source: Department of Education, Science and Training).
§ Public institutions only.

Directory

The Constitution

The Federal Constitution was adopted on 9 July 1900 and came into force on 1 January 1901. Its main provisions are summarized below:

PARLIAMENT

The legislative power of the Commonwealth of Australia is vested in a Federal Parliament, consisting of HM the Queen (represented by the Governor-General), a Senate and a House of Representatives. The Governor-General may appoint such times for holding the sessions of the Parliament as he or she thinks fit, and may also from time to time, by proclamation or otherwise, prorogue the Parliament, and may in like manner dissolve the House of Representatives. By convention, these powers are exercised on the advice of the Prime Minister. After any general election Parliament must be summoned to meet not later than 30 days after the day appointed for the return of the writs.

THE SENATE

The Senate is composed of 12 senators from each state, two senators representing the Australian Capital Territory and two representing the Northern Territory. The senators are directly chosen by the people of the state or territory, voting in each case as one electorate, and are elected by proportional representation. Senators representing a state have a six-year term and retire by rotation, one-half from each state on 30 June of each third year. The term of a senator representing a territory is limited to three years. In the case of a state, if a senator vacates his or her seat before the expiration of the term of service, the houses of parliament of the state for which the senator was chosen shall, in joint session, choose a person to hold the place until the expiration of the term or until the election of a successor. If the state parliament is not in session, the Governor of the state, acting on the advice of the state's executive council, may appoint a senator to hold office until parliament reassembles, or until a new senator is elected.

The Senate may proceed to the dispatch of business notwithstanding the failure of any state to provide for its representation in the Senate.

THE HOUSE OF REPRESENTATIVES

In accordance with the Australian Constitution, the total number of members of the House of Representatives must be as nearly as practicable double that of the Senate. The number in each state is in proportion to population, but under the Constitution must be at least five. The House of Representatives is composed of 150 members, including two members for the Australian Capital Territory and two members for the Northern Territory.

Members are elected by universal adult suffrage and voting is compulsory. Only Australian citizens are eligible to vote in Australian elections. British subjects, if they are not Australian citizens or already on the rolls, have to take out Australian citizenship before thay can enrol and before they can vote.

Members are chosen by the electors of their respective electorates by the preferential voting system.

The duration of the Parliament is limited to three years.

To be nominated for election to the House of Representatives, a candidate must be 18 years of age or over, an Australian citizen, and entitled to vote at the election or qualified to become an elector.

THE EXECUTIVE GOVERNMENT

The executive power of the Federal Government is vested in the Queen, and is exercisable by the Governor-General, advised by an Executive Council of Ministers of State, known as the Federal Executive Council. These ministers are, or must become within three months, members of the Federal Parliament.

The Australian Constitution is construed as subject to the principles of responsible government and the Governor-General acts on the advice of the ministers in relation to most matters.

THE JUDICIAL POWER

See Judicial System, below.

THE STATES

The Australian Constitution safeguards the Constitution of each state by providing that it shall continue as at the establishment of the Commonwealth, except as altered in accordance with its own provisions. The legislative power of the Federal Parliament is limited in the main to those matters that are listed in section 51 of the Constitution, while the states possess, as well as concurrent powers in those matters, residual legislative powers enabling them to legislate in any way for 'the peace, order and good Government' of their respective territories. When a state law is inconsistent with a law of the Commonwealth, the latter prevails, and the former is invalid to the extent of the inconsistency.

The states may not, without the consent of the Commonwealth, raise or maintain naval or military forces, or impose taxes on any property belonging to the Commonwealth of Australia, nor may the Commonwealth tax state property. The states may not coin money.

The Federal Parliament may not enact any law for establishing any religion or for prohibiting the exercise of any religion, and no religious test may be imposed as a qualification for any office under the Commonwealth.

The Commonwealth of Australia is charged with protecting every state against invasion, and, on the application of a state executive government, against domestic violence.

Provision is made under the Constitution for the admission of new states and for the establishment of new states within the Commonwealth of Australia.

ALTERATION OF THE CONSTITUTION

Proposed laws for the amendment of the Constitution must be passed by an absolute majority in both Houses of the Federal Parliament, and not less than two or more than six months after its passage through both Houses the proposed law must be submitted in each state to the qualified electors.

In the event of one House twice refusing to pass a proposed amendment that has already received an absolute majority in the other House, the Governor-General may, notwithstanding such refusal, submit the proposed amendment to the electors. By convention, the Governor-General acts on the advice of the Prime Minister. If in a majority of the states a majority of the electors voting approve the proposed law and if a majority of all the electors voting also approve, it shall be presented to the Governor-General for Royal Assent.

No alteration diminishing the proportionate representation of any state in either House of the Federal Parliament, or the minimum number of representatives of a state in the House of Representatives, or increasing, diminishing or altering the limits of the state, or in any way affecting the provisions of the Constitution in relation thereto, shall become law unless the majority of the electors voting in that state approve the proposed law.

STATES AND TERRITORIES

New South Wales

The state's executive power is vested in the Governor, appointed by the Crown, who is assisted by an Executive Council composed of cabinet ministers.

The state's legislative power is vested in a bicameral Parliament, composed of the Legislative Council and the Legislative Assembly. The Legislative Council consists of 42 members directly elected for the duration of two parliaments (i.e. eight years), 21 members retiring every four years. The Legislative Assembly consists of 93 members and sits for four years.

Victoria

The state's legislative power is vested in a bicameral Parliament: the Upper House, or Legislative Council, of 44 members, elected for two terms of the Legislative Assembly; and the Lower House, or Legislative Assembly, of 88 members, elected for a minimum of three and maximum of four years. One-half of the members of the Council retires every three–four years.

In the exercise of the executive power the Governor is assisted by a cabinet of responsible ministers. Not more than six members of the Council and not more than 17 members of the Assembly may occupy salaried office at any one time.

The state has 88 electoral districts, each returning one member, and 22 electoral provinces, each returning two Council members.

Queensland

The state's executive power is vested in the Governor, appointed by the Crown, who is assisted by an Executive Council composed of Ministers. The state's legislative power is vested in the Parliament comprising the Legislative Assembly (composed of 89 members who are elected at least every three years to represent 89 electoral districts) and the Governor, who assents to bills passed by the Assembly. The state's Constitution anticipates that Ministers are also members of the Legislative Assembly and provides that up to 18 members of the Assembly can be appointed Ministers.

South Australia

The state's Constitution vests the legislative power in a Parliament elected by the people and consisting of a Legislative Council and a House of Assembly. The Council is composed of 22 members, one-half

AUSTRALIA

of whom retire every three years. Their places are filled by new members elected under a system of proportional representation, with the whole state as a single electorate. The executive has no authority to dissolve this body, except in circumstances warranting a double dissolution.

The 47 members of the House of Assembly are elected for four years from 45 electoral districts.

The executive power is vested in a Governor, appointed by the Crown, and an Executive Council consisting of 10 responsible ministers.

Western Australia

The state's administration is vested in the Governor, a Legislative Council and a Legislative Assembly.

The Legislative Council consists of 34 members, two of the six electoral regions returning seven members on a proportional representation basis, and four regions returning five members. Election is for a term of four years.

The Legislative Assembly consists of 57 members, elected for four years, each representing one electorate.

Tasmania

The state's executive authority is vested in a Governor, appointed by the Crown, who acts upon the advice of his premier and ministers, who are elected members of either the Legislative Council or the House of Assembly. The Council consists of 15 members who sit for six years, retiring in rotation. The House of Assembly has 25 members elected for four years.

Northern Territory

On 1 July 1978 the Northern Territory was established as a body politic with executive authority for specified functions of government. Most functions of the Federal Government were transferred to the Territory Government in 1978 and 1979, major exceptions being Aboriginal affairs and uranium mining.

The Territory Parliament consists of a single house, the Legislative Assembly, with 25 members. The first Parliament stayed in office for three years. As from the election held in August 1980, members are elected for a term of four years.

The office of Administrator continues. The Northern Territory (Self-Government) Act provides for the appointment of an Administrator by the Governor-General charged with the duty of administering the Territory. In respect of matters transferred to the Territory Government, the Administrator acts with the advice of the Territory Executive Council; in respect of matters retained by the Commonwealth, the Administrator acts on Commonwealth advice.

Australian Capital Territory

On 29 November 1988 the Australian Capital Territory (ACT) was established as a body politic. The ACT Government has executive authority for specified functions, although a number of these were to be retained by the Federal Government for a brief period during which transfer arrangements were to be finalized.

The ACT Parliament consists of a single house, the Legislative Assembly, with 17 members. The first election was held in March 1989. Members are elected for a term of three years.

The Federal Government retains control of some of the land in the ACT for the purpose of maintaining the Seat of Government and the national capital plan.

Jervis Bay Territory

Following the attainment of self-government by the ACT (see above), the Jervis Bay Territory, which had formed part of the ACT since 1915, remained a separate Commonwealth Territory, administered by the then Department of the Arts, Sport, the Environment and Territories. The area is governed in accordance with the Jervis Bay Territory Administration Ordinance, issued by the Governor-General on 17 December 1990.

The Government

Head of State: HM Queen ELIZABETH II (succeeded to the throne 6 February 1952).

Governor-General: Maj.-Gen. MICHAEL JEFFERY (assumed office 11 August 2003); (to be replaced by QUENTIN BRYCE on 5 September 2008).

THE MINISTRY
(April 2008)

Cabinet Ministers

Prime Minister: KEVIN RUDD.

Deputy Prime Minister and Minister for Education, Employment and Workplace Relations, and Social Inclusion: JULIA GILLARD.

Minister for Foreign Affairs: STEPHEN SMITH.

Treasurer: WAYNE SWAN.

Minister for Trade: SIMON CREAN.

Minister for Defence: JOEL FITZGIBBON.

Special Minister of State and Cabinet Secretary: Senator JOHN FAULKNER.

Minister for Broadband, Communications and the Digital Economy, and Deputy Leader of the Government in the Senate: Senator STEPHEN CONROY.

Minister for Finance and Deregulation: LINDSAY TANNER.

Minister for Immigration and Citizenship, and Leader of the Government in the Senate: Senator CHRIS EVANS.

Minister for Health and Ageing: NICOLA ROXON.

Minister for Families, Housing, Community Services and Indigenous Affairs: JENNY MACKLIN.

Minister for the Environment, Heritage and the Arts: PETER GARRETT.

Minister for Infrastructure, Transport, Regional Development and Local Government, and Leader of the House: ANTHONY ALBANESE.

Minister for Innovation, Industry, Science and Research: Senator KIM CARR.

Minister for Climate Change and Water: Senator PENNY WONG.

Minister for Human Services: Senator JOE LUDWIG.

Minister for Agriculture, Fisheries and Forestry: TONY BURKE.

Minister for Resources and Energy, and Tourism: MARTIN FERGUSON.

Attorney-General: ROBERT MCCLELLAND.

Other Ministers

Minister for Home Affairs and Territories: BOB DEBUS.

Minister for Competition Policy and Consumer Affairs, and Assistant Treasurer: CHRIS BOWEN.

Minister for Housing and the Status of Women: TANYA PLIBERSEK.

Minister for Defence Science and Personnel: WARREN SNOWDON.

Minister for Small Business, Independent Contractors and the Service Economy, and Minister assisting the Minister for Finance on Deregulation: CRAIG EMERSON.

Minister for Veterans' Affairs: ALAN GRIFFIN.

Minister for Ageing: JUSTINE ELLIOT.

Minister for Superannuation and Corporate Law: Senator NICK SHERRY.

Minister for Youth and Sport: Senator KATE ELLIS.

Minister for Employment Participation: BRENDAN O'CONNOR.

DEPARTMENTS

Department of the Prime Minister and Cabinet: 1 National Circuit, Canberra, ACT 2600; tel. (2) 6271-5111; fax (2) 6271-5414; internet www.dpmc.gov.au.

Department of Agriculture, Fisheries and Forestry: Edmund Barton Bldg, Blackall St, Barton, GPOB 858, Canberra, ACT 2601; tel. (2) 6272-3933; internet www.daff.gov.au.

Attorney-General's Department: Central Office, Robert Garran Offices, National Circuit, Barton, ACT 2600; tel. (2) 6250-6666; fax (2) 6250-5900; internet www.ag.gov.au.

Department of Broadband, Communications and the Digital Economy: GPOB 2154, Canberra, ACT 2601; tel. (2) 6271-1000; fax (2) 6271-1901; e-mail dcita.mail@dbcde.gov.au; internet www.dbcde.gov.au.

Department of Climate Change: GPOB 854, Canberra, ACT 2601; tel. (2) 6274-1888; e-mail communications@environment.gov.au; internet www.greenhouse.gov.au.

Department of Defence: Russell Offices, Russell Drive, Campbell, Canberra, ACT 2600; tel. (2) 6265-9111; e-mail webmaster@cbr.defence.gov.au; internet www.defence.gov.au.

Department of Education, Employment and Workplace Relations: GPOB 9880, Canberra, ACT 2601; tel. (2) 6240-8111; fax (2) 6240-8571; e-mail wwweditor@dest.gov.au; internet www.dest.gov.au.

Department of the Environment, Water, Heritage and the Arts: GPOB 787, Canberra, ACT 2601; tel. (2) 6274-1111; fax (2) 6274-1666; internet www.environment.gov.au.

AUSTRALIA

Department of Families, Housing, Community Services and Indigenous Affairs: Library and Information Service, Box 7788, Canberra Mail Centre, ACT 2610; tel. (2) 6244-6385; fax (2) 6244-7919; e-mail facsia.internet@facsia.gov.au; internet www.facs.gov.au.

Department of Finance and Deregulation: John Gorton Bldg, King Edward Tce, Parkes, ACT 2600; tel. (2) 6215-2222; fax (2) 6273-3021; e-mail feedback@finance.gov.au; internet www.finance.gov.au.

Department of Foreign Affairs and Trade: R. G. Casey Bldg, John McEwen Cres., Barton, ACT 0221; tel. (2) 6261-1111; fax (2) 6261-3111; internet www.dfat.gov.au.

Department of Health and Ageing: GPOB 9848, Canberra, ACT 2601; tel. (2) 6289-1555; fax (2) 6281-6946; e-mail enquiries@health.gov.au; internet www.health.gov.au.

Department of Human Services: POB 3959, Manuka, ACT 2603; tel. (2) 6223-4000; fax (2) 6223-4499; e-mail enquiries@humanservices.gov.au; internet www.humanservices.gov.au.

Department of Immigration and Citizenship: POB 25, Chan St, Belconnen, ACT 2616; tel. (2) 6264-1111; fax (2) 6225-6970; internet www.immi.gov.au.

Department of Infrastructure, Transport, Regional Development and Local Government: GPOB 594, Canberra, ACT 2601; tel. (2) 6274-7111; fax (2) 6257-2505; e-mail publicaffairs@infrastructure.gov.au; internet www.infrastructure.gov.au.

Department of Innovation, Industry, Science and Research: GPOB 9839, Canberra, ACT 2601; tel. (2) 6213-6000; fax (2) 6213-7000; e-mail inquiries@industry.gov.au; internet www.industry.gov.au.

Department of Resources, Energy and Tourism: GPOB 9839, Canberra, ACT 2601; tel. (2) 6276-1000; internet www.industry.gov.au.

Department of the Treasury: Langton Crescent, Parkes, ACT 2600; tel. (2) 6263-2111; fax (2) 6273-2614; e-mail department@treasury.gov.au; internet www.treasury.gov.au.

Department of Veterans' Affairs: POB 21, Woden, ACT 2606; tel. (2) 6289-6736; fax (2) 6289-6257; e-mail feedback@dva.gov.au; internet www.dva.gov.au.

Legislature

FEDERAL PARLIAMENT

Senate

President: ALAN FERGUSON.
Election, 24 November 2007

Party	Seats*
Liberal-National Coalition	37
Australian Labor Party	32
Greens	5
Family First	1
Other	1
Total	**76**

* The election was for 36 of the 72 seats held by state senators and for all four senators representing the Northern Territory and the Australian Capital Territory (see The Constitution). The newly elected state Senators were scheduled to take office on 1 July 2008.

House of Representatives

Speaker: HARRY JENKINS.
Distribution of seats following election, 24 November 2007

Party	Seats
Australian Labor Party	83
Liberal Party of Australia	55
National Party of Australia	10
Independents	2
Total	**150**

State and Territory Governments
(April 2008)

NEW SOUTH WALES

Governor: MARIE BASHIR, Level 3, Chief Secretary's Bldg, 121 Macquarie St, Sydney, NSW 2000; tel. (2) 9242-4200; fax (2) 9242-4266; internet www.nsw.gov.au.

Premier: MORRIS IEMMA (Labor), Level 40, Governor Macquarie Tower, 1 Farrer Place, Sydney, NSW 2000; tel. (2) 9228-5239; fax (2) 9228-3935; e-mail thepremier@www.nsw.gov.au; internet www.premiers.nsw.gov.au.

VICTORIA

Governor: Prof. DAVID DE KRETSER, Government House, Melbourne, Vic 3004; tel. (3) 9655-4211; fax (3) 9650-9050; internet www.governor.vic.gov.au.

Premier: JOHN BRUMBY (Labor), 1 Treasury Place, Melbourne, Vic 3000; tel. (3) 9651-5000; fax (3) 9651-5054; e-mail premier@dpc.vic.gov.au; internet www.premier.vic.gov.au.

QUEENSLAND

Governor: QUENTIN BRYCE, Government House, GPOB 434, Brisbane, Qld 4001; tel. (7) 3858-5700; fax (7) 3858-5701; e-mail govhouse@govhouse.qld.gov.au; internet www.govhouse.qld.gov.au.

Premier: ANNA BLIGH (Labor), Executive Bldg, 100 George St, Brisbane, Qld 4002; tel. (7) 3224-4500; fax (7) 3221-3631; e-mail ThePremier@premiers.qld.gov.au; internet www.premiers.qld.gov.au.

SOUTH AUSTRALIA

Governor: KEVIN SCARCE, Government House, North Terrace, Adelaide, SA 5000; tel. (8) 8203-9800; fax (8) 8203-9899; e-mail governors.office@saugov.sa.gov.au; internet www.governor.sa.gov.au.

Premier: MICHAEL (MIKE) RANN (Labor), 15th Floor, State Administration Centre, 200 Victoria Square, Adelaide, SA 5000; tel. (8) 8463-3166; fax (8) 8463-3168; e-mail premier@saugov.sa.gov.au; internet www.premier.sa.gov.au.

WESTERN AUSTRALIA

Governor: Dr KEN MICHAEL, Government House, St George's Terrace, Perth, WA 6000; tel. (8) 9429-9199; fax (8) 9325-4476; e-mail enquiries@govhouse.wa.gov.au; internet www.govhouse.wa.gov.au.

Premier: ALAN CARPENTER (Labor), 24th Floor, 197 St George's Terrace, Perth, WA 6000; tel. (8) 9222-9888; fax (8) 9322-1213; e-mail wa-government@dpc.wa.gov.au; internet www.premier.wa.gov.au.

TASMANIA

Governor: PETER UNDERWOOD, Government House, Lower Domain Rd, Hobart, Tas 7000; tel. (3) 6234-2611; fax (3) 6234-2556; internet www.dpac.tas.gov.au/governor.

Premier: PAUL LENNON (Labor), GPOB 123B, Hobart, Tas 7001; tel. (3) 6233-3464; fax (3) 6234-1572; e-mail premier@dpac.tas.gov.au; internet www.premier.tas.gov.au.

NORTHERN TERRITORY

Administrator: TOM PAULING, GPOB 497, Darwin, NT 0801; tel. (8) 8999-7103; fax (8) 8999-5521; e-mail governmenthouse.darwin@nt.gov.au; internet www.nt.gov.au/administrator.

Chief Minister: PAUL HENDERSON (Labor), GPOB 3146, Darwin, NT 0801; tel. (8) 8901-4000; fax (8) 8901-4099; e-mail chiefminister.nt@nt.gov.au; internet www.nt.gov.au.

AUSTRALIAN CAPITAL TERRITORY

Chief Minister: JONATHAN STANHOPE (Labor), Legislative Assembly Bldg, Civic Square, London Circuit, Canberra, ACT 2601; tel. (2) 6205-0104; fax (2) 6205-0433; e-mail canberraconnect@act.gov.au; internet www.act.gov.au.

Election Commission

Australian Electoral Commission (AEC): POB 6172, Kingston, ACT 2604; tel. (2) 6271-4411; fax (2) 6271-4558; e-mail info@aec.gov.au; internet www.aec.gov.au; f. 1984; statutory body; administers federal elections and referendums; Chair. Hon. JAMES BURCHETT; Electoral Commr IAN CAMPBELL.

AUSTRALIA   *Directory*

Political Organizations

Australians for Constitutional Monarchy (ACM): GPOB 9841, Sydney, NSW 2001; tel. (2) 9251-2500; fax (2) 9261-5033; e-mail acmhq@norepublic.com.au; internet www.norepublic.com.au; f. 1992; also known as No Republic; Nat. Convener Prof. DAVID FLINT.

Australian Democrats Party: 711 South Rd, Black Forest, SA 5035; tel. (8) 8371-1441; e-mail inquiries@democrats.org.au; internet www.democrats.org.au; f. 1977; comprises the fmr Liberal Movement and the Australia Party; Fed. Parl. Leader Senator LYN ALLISON; Nat. Pres. JOHN MCLAREN.

Australian Greens: GPOB 1108, Canberra, ACT 2601; tel. (2) 6162-0036; fax (2) 6247-6455; e-mail greens@greens.org.au; internet www.greens.org.au; f. 1992; Parl. Leader Senator BOB BROWN; National Convener ALISON XAMON.

Australian Labor Party (ALP): POB 6222, Kingston, ACT 2604; tel. (2) 6120-0800; fax (2) 6120-0801; e-mail info@cbr.alp.org.au; internet www.alp.org.au; f. 1891; advocates social democracy; trade unions form part of its structure; Fed. Parl. Leader KEVIN RUDD; Nat. Pres. JOHN FAULKNER; Nat. Sec. TIM GARTRELL.

Australian Republican Movement (ARM): GPOB 611, Canberra, ACT 2601; tel. (2) 6257-3705; fax (2) 6257-3670; e-mail republic@republic.org.au; internet www.republic.org.au; f. 1991; Chair. TED O'BRIEN; Exec. Officer PAMELA HUNT.

Communist Party of Australia: 74 Buckingham St, Surry Hills, NSW 2010; tel. (2) 9699-8844; fax (2) 9699-9833; e-mail cpa@cpa.org.au; internet www.cpa.org.au; f. 1971; fmrly Socialist Party; advocates public ownership of the means of production, working-class political power; Pres. Dr HANNAH MIDDLETON; Gen. Sec. PETER SYMON.

Family First: POB 1042, Campbelltown, SA 5074; tel. (8) 8369-0079; fax (8) 8266-4069; e-mail admin@familyfirst.org.au; internet www.familyfirst.org.au; supports family values; Chair. PETER HARRIS; Fed. Parl. Leader Senator STEVE FIELDING.

Liberal Party of Australia: Federal Secretariat, cnr Blackall and Macquarie Sts, Barton, ACT 2600; tel. (2) 6273-2564; fax (2) 6273-1534; e-mail libadm@liberal.org.au; internet www.liberal.org.au; f. 1944; advocates private enterprise, social justice, individual liberty and initiative; committed to national development, prosperity and security; Fed. Dir BRIAN LOUGHNANE; Fed. Parl. Leader Dr BRENDAN NELSON; Fed. Pres. CHRIS MCDIVEN.

National Party of Australia: John McEwen House, 7 National Circuit, Barton, ACT 2600; tel. (2) 6273-3822; fax (2) 6273-1745; e-mail federal.nationals@nationals.org.au; internet www.nationals.org.au; f. 1916 as the Country Party of Australia; adopted present name in 1982; advocates balanced national development based on free enterprise, with special emphasis on the needs of people outside the major metropolitan areas; Fed. Pres. JOHN TANNER; Fed. Parl. Leader WARREN TRUSS; Fed. Dir BRAD HENDERSON.

One Nation: POB 1199, Beenleigh, Qld 4207; tel. (7) 3287-4440; fax (7) 3287-4448; e-mail onenation@optusnet.com.au; internet www.onenationqld.com.au; f. 1997; opposes globalization and high immigration, advocates public ownership of major services; Pres. JIM SAVAGE.

Your Voice: POB 1245, Collingwood, Vic 3066; tel. (3) 9490-1498; fax (3) 9497-2222; e-mail peterl@VACCA.org; internet www.yourvoice.org.au; f. 2004; represents the interests of Aboriginal people; Co-Founder RICHARD FRANKLAND.

Diplomatic Representation

EMBASSIES AND HIGH COMMISSIONS IN AUSTRALIA

Afghanistan: POB 155, Deakin West, ACT 2600; tel. (2) 6282-7311; fax (2) 6282-7322; e-mail ambassador@afghanembassy.net; internet www.afghanembassy.net; Ambassador AMANULLAH JAYHOON.

Algeria: 9 Terrigal Crescent, O'Malley, ACT 2606; tel. (2) 6286-7355; fax (2) 6286-7037; e-mail info@algeriaemb.org.au; internet www.algeriaemb.org.au; Ambassador KAMERZAMANE BELRAMOUL.

Argentina: John McEwen House, Level 2, 7 National Circuit Barton, ACT 2600; tel. (2) 6273-9111; fax (2) 6273-0500; e-mail info@argentina.org.au; internet www.argentina.org.au; Ambassador PEDRO VILLAGRA DELGADO.

Austria: POB 3375, Manuka, ACT 2603; tel. (2) 6295-1533; fax (2) 6239-6751; e-mail canberra-ob@bmeia.gv.at; internet www.austria.org.au; Ambassador Dr HANNES PORIAS.

Bangladesh: POB 5, Red Hill, ACT 2603; tel. (2) 6290-0511; fax (2) 6290-0544; e-mail info@bangladoot-canberra.org; internet www.bangladoot-canberra.org; High Commissioner MD RESTADUL ISLAM (acting).

Belgium: 19 Arkana St, Yarralumla, ACT 2600; tel. (2) 6273-2501; fax (2) 6273-3392; e-mail canberra@diplobel.org; internet www.diplomatie.be/canberra; Ambassador FRANK CARRUET.

Bosnia and Herzegovina: 5 Beale Crescent, Deakin, ACT 2600; tel. (2) 6232-4646; fax (2) 6232-5554; e-mail embaucbr@tpg.com.au; internet www.bosnia.webone.com.au; Ambassador AMIRA KAPETANOVIĆ.

Botswana: 52 Culgoa Circuit, O'Malley, ACT 2606; tel. (2) 6290-7500; fax (2) 6286-2566; High Commissioner MOLOSIWA SELEPENG.

Brazil: GPOB 1540, Canberra, ACT 2601; tel. (2) 6273-2372; fax (2) 6273-2375; e-mail brazilemb@brazil.org.au; internet www.brazil.org.au; Ambassador FERNANDO DE MELLO BARRETO.

Brunei: 10 Beale Crescent, Deakin, ACT 2600; tel. (2) 6285-4500; fax (2) 6285-4545; e-mail canberra.australia@mfa.gov.bn; High Commissioner MOHAMMAD SAHRIP BIN OTHMAN.

Bulgaria: 33 Culgoa Circuit, O'Malley, ACT 2606; tel. (2) 6286-9711; fax (2) 6286-9600; e-mail embassy@bulgaria.org.au; Ambassador Dr LUBOMIR TODOROV.

Cambodia: 5 Canterbury Crescent, Deakin, ACT 2600; tel. (2) 6273-1259; fax (2) 6273-1053; e-mail cambodianembassy@ozemail.com.au; internet www.embassyofcambodia.org.nz/au.htm; Ambassador MEAS KIM HENG.

Canada: Commonwealth Ave, Canberra, ACT 2600; tel. (2) 6270-4000; fax (2) 6273-3285; e-mail cnbra@international.gc.ca; internet www.canada.org.au; High Commissioner MICHAEL LEIR.

Chile: 10 Culgoa Circuit, O'Malley, ACT 2606; tel. (2) 6286-2098; fax (2) 6286-1289; e-mail echileau@embachile-australia.com; internet www.embachile-australia.com; Ambassador JOSÉ BALMACEDA SERIGÓS.

China, People's Republic: 15 Coronation Drive, Yarralumla, ACT 2600; tel. (2) 6273-4780; fax (2) 6273-4878; e-mail chinaemb_au@mfa.gov.cn; internet au.china-embassy.org/eng; Ambassador ZHANG JUNSAI.

Croatia: 14 Jindalee Crescent, O'Malley, ACT 2606; tel. (2) 6286-6988; fax (2) 6286-3544; e-mail croemb@bigpond.com; Chargé d'affaires a.i. LJUBINKO MATEŠIĆ.

Cyprus: 30 Beale Crescent, Deakin, ACT 2600; tel. (2) 6281-0832; fax (2) 6281-0860; e-mail press@cyprus.org.au; internet www.cyprus.org.au; High Commissioner PHILIPPOS K. KRITIOTIS.

Czech Republic: 8 Culgoa Circuit, O'Malley, ACT 2606; tel. (2) 6290-1386; fax (2) 6290-0006; e-mail canberra@embassy.mzv.cz; internet www.mzv.cz/canberra; Ambassador KAREL PAŽOUREK.

Denmark: 15 Hunter St, Yarralumla, ACT 2600; tel. (2) (2) 6270-5333; fax (2) 6270-5324; e-mail cbramb@um.dk; internet www.canberra.um.dk; Ambassador SUSANNE HOFFMANN SHINE.

Ecuador: 6 Pindari Crescent, O'Malley, ACT 2606; tel. (2) 6286-4021; fax (2) 6286-1231; e-mail embecu@bigpond.net.au; internet www.embassyecuadoraustralia.org.au; Ambassador LUIS ANTONIO RODAS-POSSO.

Egypt: 1 Darwin Ave, Yarralumla, ACT 2600; tel. (2) 6273-4437; fax (2) 6273-4279; Ambassador MOHAMED M. TAWFIK.

Eritrea: 16 Bulwarra Close, O'Malley, ACT 2606; tel. (2) 6290-1991; fax (2) 6286-8902; Ambassador Dr ANDEAB GHEBREMESKEL.

Fiji: POB 159, Deakin West, ACT 2600; tel. (2) 6260-5115; fax (2) 6260-5105; e-mail admin@aus-fhc.org; High Commissioner EVISAKE KEDRAYATE (acting).

Finland: 12 Darwin Ave, Yarralumla, ACT 2600; tel. (2) 6273-3800; fax (2) 6273-3603; e-mail sanomat.can@formin.fi; internet www.finland.org.au; Ambassador GLEN LINDHOLM.

France: 6 Perth Ave, Yarralumla, ACT 2600; tel. (2) 6216-0100; fax (2) 6216-0127; e-mail embassy@ambafrance-au.org; internet www.ambafrance-au.org; Ambassador FRANÇOIS DESCOUEYTE.

Germany: 119 Empire Circuit, Yarralumla, ACT 2600; tel. (2) 6270-1911; fax (2) 6270-1951; e-mail info1@germanembassy.org.au; internet www.germanembassy.org.au; Ambassador Dr MARTIN LUTZ.

Ghana: 13 Numeralla St, O'Malley, ACT 2606; tel. (2) 6290-2110; fax (2) 6290-2115; e-mail info@ghanahighcom.org.au; internet www.ghanahighcom.org.au; High Commissioner KOFI SEKYIAMAH.

Greece: 9 Turrana St, Yarralumla, ACT 2600; tel. (2) 6273-3011; fax (2) 6273-2620; e-mail greekemb@bigpond.net.au; Ambassador GEORGE ZOIS.

Holy See: POB 3633, Manuka, ACT 2603 (Apostolic Nunciature); tel. (2) 6295-3876; fax (2) 6295-3690; Apostolic Nuncio Most Rev. GIUSEPPE LAZZAROTTO (Titular Archbishop of Numana).

Hungary: 17 Beale Crescent, Deakin, ACT 2600; tel. (2) 6282-3226; fax (2) 6285-3012; e-mail cbr.missions@kum.hu; internet www.hunconsydney.com; Ambassador GÁBOR CSABA.

AUSTRALIA

Directory

India: 3–5 Moonah Place, Yarralumla, ACT 2600; tel. (2) 6273-3999; fax (2) 6273-1308; e-mail hco@hcindia-au.org; internet www.hcindia-au.org; High Commissioner Sujatha Singh.

Indonesia: 8 Darwin Ave, Yarralumla, ACT 2600; tel. (2) 6250-8600; fax (2) 6273-6017; internet www.kbri-canberra.org.au; Ambassador Mohammad Hamzah Thayeb.

Iran: POB 705, Mawson, ACT 2607; tel. (2) 6290-2427; fax (2) 6290-2431; e-mail ambassador@iranembassy.org.au; internet www.iranembassy.org.au; Ambassador Mahmoud Movahhedi.

Iraq: 48 Culgoa Circuit, O'Malley, ACT 2606; tel. (2) 6286-2744; fax (2) 6286-8744; e-mail iraqembcnb@hotmail.com; internet www.iraqembassyaustralia.org; Ambassador Ghanim T. ash-Shibli.

Ireland: 20 Arkana St, Yarralumla, ACT 2600; tel. (2) 6273-3022; fax (2) 6273-3741; e-mail canberraembassy@dfa.ie; Ambassador Máirtín O'Fainnín.

Israel: 6 Turrana St, Yarralumla, ACT 2600; tel. (2) 6215-4500; fax (2) 6215-4555; e-mail info@canberra.mfa.gov.il; internet canberra.mfa.gov.il; Ambassador Yuval Rotem.

Italy: 12 Grey St, Deakin, ACT 2600; tel. (2) 6273-3333; fax (2) 6273-4223; e-mail ambasciata.canberra@esteri.it; internet www.ambcanberra.esteri.it; Ambassador Starace Janfolla.

Japan: 112 Empire Circuit, Yarralumla, ACT 2600; tel. (2) 6273-3244; fax (2) 6273-1848; e-mail cultural@japan.org.au; internet www.au.emb-japan.go.jp; Ambassador Taka-aki Kojima.

Jordan: 20 Roebuck St, Red Hill, ACT 2603; tel. (2) 6295-9951; fax (2) 6239-7236; e-mail jordan@jordanembassy.org.au; internet www.jordanembassy.org.au; Ambassador Rajab Sukayri.

Kenya: POB 1990, Canberra, ACT 2601; tel. (2) 6247-4788; fax (2) 6257-6613; e-mail khc-canberra@kenya.asn.au; High Commissioner John L. Lanyasunya.

Korea, Democratic People's Republic: 57 Culgoa Circuit, O'Malley, ACT 2606; tel. (2) 6286-4770; fax (2) 6286-4795; e-mail dprkembassy@hotmail.com; Ambassador Pang Song Hae.

Korea, Republic: 113 Empire Circuit, Yarralumla, ACT 2600; tel. (2) 6270-4100; fax (2) 6273-4839; e-mail info@korea.org.au; internet www.korea.org.au; Ambassador Cho Chang-Beom.

Kuwait: 5 Callemonda Rise, O'Malley, ACT 2606; tel. (2) 6286-7777; fax (2) 6286-3733; e-mail Kuwaitcan_2002@yahoo.com; internet www.kuwaitemb-australia.com; Ambassador Jamal al-Ghunaim.

Laos: 1 Dalman Crescent, O'Malley, ACT 2606; tel. (2) 6286-4595; fax (2) 6290-1910; e-mail laoemb@bigpond.net.au; internet www.laosembassy.net; Ambassador Khenthong Nuanthosing.

Lebanon: 27 Endeavour St, Red Hill, ACT 2603; tel. (2) 6295-7378; fax (2) 6239-7024; e-mail lebanemb@tpg.com.au; internet www.lebanemb.org.au; Ambassador Jean Daniel.

Libya: 50 Culgoa Circuit, O'Malley, ACT 2606; tel. (2) 6290-7900; fax (2) 6286-4522; Chargé d'affaires a.i. Mohamed A. K. Dalla.

Macedonia, former Yugoslav republic: POB 1890, Canberra, ACT 2601; tel. (2) 6282-6220; fax (2) 6282-6229; e-mail info@macedonianemb.org.au; internet www.macedonianemb.org.au; Ambassador Viktor Gaber.

Malaysia: 7 Perth Ave, Yarralumla, ACT 2600; tel. (2) 6273-1543; fax (2) 6273-2496; e-mail malcanberra@netspeed.com.au; internet www.malaysia.org.au; High Commissioner Dato' Haji Salim Hashim.

Malta: 38 Culgoa Circuit, O'Malley, ACT 2606; tel. (2) 6290-1724; fax (2) 6290-2453; e-mail maltahighcommission.canberra@gov.mt; High Commissioner Francis Tabone.

Mauritius: 2 Beale Crescent, Deakin, ACT 2600; tel. (2) 6281-1203; fax (2) 6282-3235; e-mail mhccan@cyberone.com.au; High Commissioner Marie France Roussety.

Mexico: 14 Perth Ave, Yarralumla, ACT 2600; tel. (2) 6273-3963; fax (2) 6273-1190; e-mail embamex@mexico.org.au; internet www.mexico.org.au; Ambassador Martha Ortiz de Rosas.

Morocco: 17 Terrigal Crescent, O'Malley, ACT 2606; tel. (2) 6290-0755; fax (2) 6290-0744; e-mail sifmacan@bigpond.com; internet www.moroccoembassy.org.au; Ambassador Badre Eddine Allali.

Myanmar: 22 Arkana St, Yarralumla, ACT 2600; tel. (2) 6273-3811; fax (2) 6273-3181; e-mail mecanberra@bigpond.com; internet www.myanmarembassycanberra.com; Ambassador U Thet Win.

Nepal: Suite 2.02, 24 Marcus Clarke St, Canberra, ACT 2601; tel. (2) 6162-1554; fax (2) 6162-1557; e-mail info@necan.gov.np; internet www.necan.gov.np; Ambassador Yogendra Dhakal.

Netherlands: 120 Empire Circuit, Yarralumla, ACT 2600; tel. (2) 6220-9400; fax (2) 6273-3206; e-mail can@minbuza.nl; internet www.netherlands.org.au; Ambassador Niek van Zutphen.

New Zealand: Commonwealth Ave, Canberra, ACT 2600; tel. (2) 6270-4211; fax (2) 6273-3194; e-mail nzhccba@bigpond.net.au; internet www.nzembassy.com/australia; High Commissioner John Larkindale.

Nigeria: POB 241, Civic Square, ACT 2608; tel. (2) 6282-7411; fax (2) 6282-8471; e-mail chancery@nigeria-can.org.au; internet www.nigeria-can.org.au; High Commissioner Dr Icha Emmanuel Ituma.

Norway: 17 Hunter St, Yarralumla, ACT 2600; tel. (2) 6273-3444; fax (2) 6273-3669; e-mail emb.canberra@mfa.no; internet www.norway.org.au; Ambassador Lars A. Wensell.

Pakistan: POB 684, Mawson, ACT 2607; tel. (2) 6290-1676; fax (2) 6290-1073; e-mail parepcanberra@internode.on.net; internet www.pakistan.org.au; High Commissioner Jalil Abbas Jilani.

Papua New Guinea: POB E6317, Kingston, ACT 2604; tel. (2) 6273-3322; fax (2) 6273-3732; internet www.pngcanberra.org; High Commissioner Charles W. Lepani.

Peru: POB 106, Red Hill, ACT 2603; tel. (2) 6273-7351; fax (2) 6273-7354; e-mail embassy@embaperu.org.au; internet www.embaperu.org.au; Ambassador Claudio de la Puente.

Philippines: 1 Moonah Place, Yarralumla, Canberra, ACT 2600; tel. (2) 6273-2535; fax (2) 6273-3984; e-mail cbrpe@philembassy.org.au; internet www.philembassy.org.au; Ambassador Ernesto Hernandez de Leon.

Poland: 7 Turrana St, Yarralumla, ACT 2600; tel. (2) 6273-1208; fax (2) 6273-3184; e-mail embassy@poland.org.au; internet www.poland.org.au; Chargé d'affaires a.i. Grzegorz Sokol.

Portugal: 23 Culgoa Circuit, O'Malley, ACT 2606; tel. (2) 6290-1733; fax (2) 6290-1957; e-mail embport@internode.on.net; Ambassador Dr Antonio J. Mendes.

Romania: 4 Dalman Crescent, O'Malley, ACT 2606; tel. (2) 6286-2343; fax (2) 6286-2433; e-mail roembcbr@cyberone.com.au; internet canberra.mae.ro; Chargé d'affaires a. i. Florina Sava.

Russia: 78 Canberra Ave, Griffith, ACT 2603; tel. (2) 6295-9033; fax (2) 6295-1847; e-mail rusembassy.australia@rambler.ru; internet www.australia.mid.ru; Ambassador Alexander Blokhin.

Samoa: POB 3274, Manuka, ACT 2603; tel. (2) 6286-5505; fax (2) 6286-5678; e-mail samoahcaussi@netspeed.com.au; High Commissioner Leiataua Dr Kilifoti S. Eteuati.

Saudi Arabia: POB 9162, Deakin, ACT 2600; tel. (2) 6282-6999; fax (2) 6282-8911; e-mail amb.auemb@mofa.gov.sa; internet www.saudiembassy.org.au; Ambassador Hassan Talat Nazer.

Serbia: POB 728, Mawson, ACT 2607; tel. (2) 6290-2630; fax (2) 6290-2631; e-mail serbembau@optusnet.com.au; Ambassador Milivoje Glisic.

Singapore: 17 Forster Crescent, Yarralumla, ACT 2600; tel. (2) 6271-2000; fax (2) 6273-9823; e-mail singhc_cbr@sgmfa.gov.sg; internet www.mfa.gov.sg/canberra; High Commissioner Eddie Teo.

Slovakia: 47 Culgoa Circuit, O'Malley, ACT 2606; tel. (2) 6290-1516; fax (2) 6290-1755; internet www.slovakemb-aust.org; Ambassador Dr Peter Prochacka.

Slovenia: POB 284, Civic Square, Canberra, ACT 2608; tel. (2) 6243-4830; fax (2) 6243-4827; e-mail vca@gov.si; internet www.gov.si/mzz-dkp/veleposlanistva/eng/canberra; Chargé d'affaires a.i. Bojan Bertoncelj.

Solomon Islands: POB 256, Deakin West, ACT 2600; tel. (2) 6282-7030; fax (2) 6282-7040; e-mail info@solomon.emb.gov.au; High Commissioner Victor Ngele.

South Africa: cnr State Circle and Rhodes Place, Yarralumla, ACT 2600; tel. (2) 6272-7365; fax (2) 6273-3543; e-mail info@sahc.org.au; internet www.sahc.org.au; High Commissioner Anthony Mongalo.

Spain: POB 9076, Deakin, ACT 2600; tel. (2) 6273-3555; fax (2) 6273-3918; e-mail emb.canberra@mae.es; internet www.mae.es/Embajadas/Canberra/es/Home; Ambassador Antonio Cosano Pérez.

Sri Lanka: 35 Empire Circuit, Forrest, ACT 2603; tel. (2) 6239-7041; fax (2) 6239-6166; e-mail admin@slhcaust.org; internet www.slhcaust.org; High Commissioner Kusumpala Balapatabendi.

Sweden: 5 Turrana St, Yarralumla, ACT 2600; tel. (2) 6270-2700; fax (2) 6270-2755; e-mail sweden@iimetro.com.au; internet www.swedenabroad.com/canberra; Ambassador Karin Ehnbom-Palmquist.

Switzerland: 7 Melbourne Ave, Forrest, ACT 2603; tel. (2) 6162-8400; fax (2) 6273-3428; e-mail vertretung@can.rep.admin.ch; internet www.eda.admin.ch/australia; Ambassador Christian Mühlethaler.

Syria: 41 Culgoa Circuit, O'Malley, ACT 2606; tel. (2) 6218-5200; fax (2) 6218-5250; e-mail info@syrianembassy.org.au; internet www.syrianembassy.org.au; Ambassador Tammam Sulaiman.

Thailand: 111 Empire Circuit, Yarralumla, ACT 2600; tel. (2) 6273-1149; fax (2) 6273-1518; e-mail info@thaiembassy.org.au; internet www.thaiembassy.org.au; Ambassador Bandhit Sotipalalit.

Timor-Leste: 25 Blaxland Crescent, Griffith, ACT 2603; tel. (2) 6260-8800; fax (2) 6239-7682; e-mail TL_Emb.Canberra@bigpond.com; Ambassador Hernani Filomena Coelho Da Silva.

AUSTRALIA

Turkey: 6 Moonah Place, Yarralumla, ACT 2600; tel. (2) 6234-0000; fax (2) 6273-4402; e-mail turkembs@bigpond.net.au; internet www.turkishembassy.org.au; Ambassador N. MURAT ERSAVCI.

Uganda: 7 Dunoon St, O'Malley, ACT 2606; tel. (2) 6286-1234; fax (2) 6286-1243; High Commissioner Dr CHRISTOPHER JAMES LUKABYO.

Ukraine: Level 12, St George Centre, 60 Marcus Clarke St, Canberra, ACT 2601; tel. (2) 6230-5789; fax (2) 6230-7298; e-mail ukremb@bigpond.com; internet www.ukremb.info; Ambassador VALENTYN ADOMAYTIS.

United Arab Emirates: 12 Bulwarra Close, O'Malley, ACT 2606; tel. (2) 6286-8802; fax (2) 6286-8804; e-mail uaeembassy@bigpond.com; internet www.uaeembassy.org.au; Ambassador Dr SAEED MUHAMMAD ASH-SHAMSI.

United Kingdom: Commonwealth Ave, Canberra, ACT 2600; tel. (2) 6270-6666; fax (2) 6273-3236; e-mail bhc.canberra@britaus.net; internet bhc.britaus.net/default.asp; High Commissioner HELEN LIDDELL.

USA: Moonah Place, Yarralumla, ACT 2600; tel. (2) 6214-5600; fax (2) 6214-5970; e-mail info@usembassy-australia.state.gov; internet canberra.usembassy.gov; Ambassador ROBERT D. MCCALLUM, Jr.

Uruguay: POB 5058, Kingston, ACT 2604; tel. (2) 6273-9100; fax (2) 6273-9099; e-mail urucan@iimetro.com.au; Chargé d'affaires a.i. ANDRÉS PELAEZ.

Venezuela: 7 Culgoa Circuit, O'Malley, ACT 2606; tel. (2) 6290-2968; fax (2) 6290-2911; e-mail embaustralia@venezuela-emb-org.au; internet www.venezuela-emb.org.au; Chargé d'affaires a. i. NELSÓN DÁVILA LAMEDA.

Viet Nam: 6 Timbarra Crescent, O'Malley, ACT 2606; tel. (2) 6286-6059; fax (2) 6286-4534; e-mail vembassy@webone.com.au; internet www.vietnamembassy.org.au; Ambassador NGUYEN THANH TAN.

Zimbabwe: 11 Culgoa Circuit, O'Malley, ACT 2606; tel. (2) 6286-2700; fax (2) 6290-1680; e-mail zimbabwe1@iimetro.com.au; Ambassador STEPHEN CHIKETA.

Judicial System

The judicial power of the Commonwealth of Australia is vested in the High Court of Australia, in such other Federal Courts as the Federal Parliament creates, and in such other courts as it invests with Federal jurisdiction.

The High Court consists of a Chief Justice and six other Justices, each of whom is appointed by the Governor-General in Council, and has both original and appellate jurisdiction.

The High Court's original jurisdiction extends to all matters arising under any treaty, affecting representatives of other countries, in which the Commonwealth of Australia or its representative is a party, between states or between residents of different states or between a state and a resident of another state, and in which a writ of mandamus, or prohibition, or an injunction is sought against an officer of the Commonwealth of Australia. It also extends to matters arising under the Australian Constitution or involving its interpretation, and to many matters arising under Commonwealth laws.

The High Court's appellate jurisdiction has, since June 1984, been discretionary. Appeals from the Federal Court, the Family Court and the Supreme Courts of the states and of the territories may now be brought only if special leave is granted, in the event of a legal question that is of general public importance being involved, or of there being differences of opinion between intermediate appellate courts as to the state of the law.

Legislation enacted by the Federal Parliament in 1976 substantially changed the exercise of Federal and Territory judicial power, and, by creating the Federal Court of Australia in February 1977, enabled the High Court of Australia to give greater attention to its primary function as interpreter of the Australian Constitution. The Federal Court of Australia has assumed, in two divisions, the jurisdiction previously exercised by the Australian Industrial Court and the Federal Court of Bankruptcy and was additionally given jurisdiction in trade practices and in the developing field of administrative law. In 1987 the Federal Court of Australia acquired jurisdiction in federal taxation matters and certain intellectual property matters. In 1991 the Court's jurisdiction was expanded to include civil proceedings arising under Corporations Law. Jurisdiction has also been conferred on the Federal Court of Australia, subject to a number of exceptions, in matters in which a writ of mandamus, or prohibition, or an injunction is sought against an officer of the Commonwealth of Australia. The Court also hears appeals from the Court constituted by a single Judge, from the Supreme Courts of the territories, and in certain specific matters from State Courts, other than a Full Court of the Supreme Court of a state, exercising Federal jurisdiction.

In March 1986 all remaining categories of appeal from Australian courts to the Queen's Privy Council in the United Kingdom were abolished by the Australia Act.

FEDERAL COURTS

High Court of Australia

POB 6309, Kingston, Canberra, ACT 2604; tel. (2) 6270-6811; fax (2) 6270-6868; e-mail enquiries@hcourt.gov.au; internet www.hcourt.gov.au.

Chief Justice: ANTHONY MURRAY GLEESON.

Justices: WILLIAM MONTAGUE CHARLES GUMMOW, MICHAEL DONALD KIRBY, KENNETH MADISON HAYNE, JOHN DYSON HEYDON, SUSAN MAREE CRENNAN, SUSAN MARY KIEFEL.

Federal Court of Australia

Chief Justice: MICHAEL ERIC JOHN BLACK.

In 2007 there were 49 other judges.

Family Court of Australia

Chief Justice: DIANA BRYANT.

In 2007 there were 40 other judges.

NEW SOUTH WALES

Supreme Court

Chief Justice: JAMES JACOB SPIGELMAN.
President: KEITH MASON.
Chief Judge in Equity: PETER WOLSTENHOME YOUNG.
Chief Judge at Common Law: PETER DAVID MCCLELLAN.

VICTORIA

Supreme Court

Chief Justice: MARILYN WARREN.
President of the Court of Appeal: CHRIS MAXWELL.

QUEENSLAND

Supreme Court

Chief Justice: PAUL DE JERSEY.
President of the Court of Appeal: MARGARET MCMURDO.
Senior Judge Administrator, Trial Division: JOHN H. BYRNE.

Central District (Rockhampton)

Resident Judge: PETER RICHARD DUTNEY.

Northern District (Townsville)

Resident Judge: KEIRAN ANTHONY CULLINANE.

Far Northern District (Cairns)

Resident Judge: STANLEY GRAHAM JONES.

SOUTH AUSTRALIA

Supreme Court

Chief Justice: JOHN JEREMY DOYLE.

WESTERN AUSTRALIA

Supreme Court

Chief Justice: WAYNE MARTIN.

TASMANIA

Supreme Court

Chief Justice: PETER GEORGE UNDERWOOD.

AUSTRALIAN CAPITAL TERRITORY

Supreme Court

Chief Justice: TERENCE JOHN HIGGINS.

NORTHERN TERRITORY

Supreme Court

Chief Justice: BRIAN ROSS MARTIN.

Religion

CHRISTIANITY

According to the provisional results of the population census of August 2006, Christians numbered 12,685,834.

National Council of Churches in Australia: Locked Bag 199, Sydney, NSW 1230; tel. (2) 9299-2215; fax (2) 9262-4514; e-mail secretariat@ncca.org.au; internet www.ncca.org.au; f. 1946; est. as Australian Council of Churches; assumed present name in 1994; 17 mem. churches; Pres. Rt Rev. RICHARD APPLEBY; Gen. Sec. Rev. JOHN HENDERSON.

The Anglican Communion

The constitution of the Church of England in Australia, which rendered the church an autonomous member of the Anglican Communion, came into force in January 1962. The body was renamed the Anglican Church of Australia in August 1981. The Church comprises five provinces (together containing 22 dioceses) and the extra-provincial diocese of Tasmania. According to the 2006 population census there were 3,718,248 adherents.

National Office of the Anglican Church

General Synod Office, Box Q190, QVB PO, Sydney, NSW 1230; tel. (2) 9265-1525; fax (2) 9264-6552; e-mail gsoffice@anglican.org.au; internet www.anglican.org.au; Gen. Sec. Rev. Canon BRUCE McATEER.

Archbishop of Adelaide and Metropolitan of South Australia: Most Rev. JEFFREY DRIVER, 26 King William Rd, North Adelaide, SA 5006; tel. (8) 8305-9350; fax (8) 8305-9399; e-mail mmessner@adelaide.anglican.com.au; internet www.adelaide.anglican.com.au.

Archbishop of Brisbane and Metropolitan of Queensland, Primate of Australia: Most Rev. Dr PHILLIP JOHN ASPINALL, Bishopsbourne, GPOB 421, Brisbane, Qld 4001; tel. (7) 3835-2218; fax (7) 3832-5030; e-mail archbishop@anglicanbrisbane.org.au; internet www.anglicanbrisbane.org.au.

Archbishop of Melbourne and Metropolitan of Victoria: Most Rev. Dr PHILIP FREIER, Bishopscourt, 120 Clarendon St, East Melbourne, Vic 3002; tel. (3) 9653-4220; fax (3) 9650-2184; e-mail archbishop@melbourne.anglican.com.au; internet www.melbourne.anglican.com.au.

Archbishop of Perth and Metropolitan of Western Australia: Most Rev. ROGER ADRIAN HERFT, GPOB W2067, Perth, WA 6846; tel. (8) 9325-7455; fax (8) 9325-6741; e-mail abcsuite@perth.anglican.org; internet www.perthanglicans.com.au.

also has jurisdiction over Christmas Island and the Cocos (Keeling) Islands.

Archbishop of Sydney and Metropolitan of New South Wales: Most Rev. Dr PETER F. JENSEN, POB Q190, QVB PO, Sydney, NSW 1230; tel. (2) 9265-1555; fax (2) 9261-4485; e-mail archbishop@sydney.anglican.asn.au; internet www.sydney.anglican.asn.au.

The Roman Catholic Church

Australia comprises five metropolitan archdioceses, two archdioceses directly responsible to the Holy See and 24 dioceses, including one diocese each for Catholics of the Maronite and Melkite rites, and one military ordinariate. According to the population census of August 2006, there were 5,126,882 adherents in the country.

Australian Catholic Bishops' Conference

GPOB 368, Canberra, ACT 2601; tel. (2) 6201-9845; fax (2) 6247-6083; e-mail gensec@catholic.org.au; internet www.acbc.catholic.org.au.

f. 1979; Pres. Most Rev. PHILIP WILSON (Archbishop of Adelaide); Sec. Rev. BRIAN LUCAS.

Archbishop of Adelaide: Most Rev. PHILIP WILSON, GPOB 1364, Adelaide, SA 5001; tel. (8) 8210-8108; fax (8) 8223-2307; e-mail cco@adelaide.catholic.org.au; internet www.adelaide.catholic.org.au.

Archbishop of Brisbane: Most Rev. JOHN ALEXIUS BATHERSBY, POB 936, New Farm, Brisbane, Qld 4005; tel. (7) 3131-5500; fax (7) 3358-1357; e-mail archbishop@bne.catholic.net.au; internet www.bne.catholic.net.au.

Archbishop of Canberra and Goulburn: Most Rev. MARK BENEDICT COLERIDGE, GPOB 89, Canberra, ACT 2601; tel. (2) 6248-6411; fax (2) 6247-9636; e-mail archbish@cg.catholic.org.au; internet www.cangoul.catholic.org.au.

Archbishop of Hobart: Most Rev. ADRIAN DOYLE, GPOB 62, Hobart, Tas 7001; tel. (3) 6208-6222; fax (3) 6208-6292; e-mail archbishop.assistant@aohtas.org.au; internet www.hobart.catholic.org.au.

Archbishop of Melbourne: Most Rev. DENIS JAMES HART, GPOB 146, East Melbourne, Vic 3002; tel. (3) 9926-5677; fax (3) 9926-5617; e-mail archbishop@melbourne.catholic.org.au; internet www.melbourne.catholic.org.au.

Archbishop of Perth: Most Rev. BARRY J. HICKEY, Catholic Church Office, 25 Victoria Ave, Perth, WA 6000; tel. (8) 9223-1351; fax (8) 9221-1716; e-mail archsec@perthcatholic.org.au; internet www.perthcatholic.org.au.

Archbishop of Sydney: Cardinal GEORGE PELL, Polding Centre, 133 Liverpool St, Sydney, NSW 2000; tel. (2) 9390-5100; fax (2) 9261-8312; e-mail chancery@ado.syd.catholic.org.au; internet www.sydney.catholic.org.au.

Orthodox Churches

Greek Orthodox Archdiocese of Australia: 242 Cleveland St, Redfern, Sydney, NSW 2016; tel. (2) 9698-5066; fax (2) 9698-5368; e-mail webmaster@greekorthodox.org.au; internet www.greekorthodox.org.au; f. 1924; 700,000 mems; Primate His Eminence Archbishop STYLIANOS.

The Antiochian, Coptic, Romanian, Serbian and Syrian Orthodox Churches are also represented.

Other Christian Churches

Baptist Union of Australia: Private Bag 8, Glebe, NSW 2037; tel. (2) 8572-3240; fax (2) 8572-3241; e-mail bua@baptist.org.au; internet www.baptist.org.au; f. 1926; 64,159 mems; 883 churches; Nat. Pres. ROSS CLIFFORD; Nat. Sec. NAOMI McCONNELL.

Churches of Christ in Australia: POB 101, Essendon North, Vic 3041; tel. (3) 9379-0085; fax (3) 9379-0015; e-mail president.nc@churchesofchrist.org.au; internet cofcaustralia.org/cofc-cms; 36,000 mems; Pres. Rev. RICHARD MENTEITH; Exec. Officer Rev. NIGEL PEGRAM.

Lutheran Church of Australia: National Office, 197 Archer St, North Adelaide, SA 5006; tel. (8) 8267-7300; fax (8) 8267-7310; e-mail president@lca.org.au; internet www.lca.org.au; f. 1966; 75,000 mems; Pres. Rev. M. P. SEMMLER.

United Pentecostal Church of Australia: POB 60, Woden, ACT 2606; over 3,000 adherents in 2008; Gen. Superintendent JOHN DOWNS.

Uniting Church in Australia: POB A2266, Sydney South, NSW 1235; tel. (2) 8267-4202; fax (2) 8267-4222; e-mail enquiries@nat.uca.org.au; internet uca.org.au; f. 1977 with the union of Methodist, Presbyterian and Congregational Churches; 300,000 mems; Pres. Rev. GREGOR HENDERSON; Gen. Sec. Rev. TERENCE CORKIN.

ISLAM

At the census of August 2006, the Muslim community was estimated to number 340,390.

The Australian Federation of Islamic Councils: 932 Bourke St, Zetland, Sydney, NSW 2017; tel. (2) 9319-6733; fax (2) 9319-0159; e-mail admin@afic.com.au; internet www.afic.com.au; Pres. IKEBAL PATEL.

JUDAISM

The Jewish community numbered 88,826 at the census of August 2006.

Great Synagogue: 166 Castlereagh St, Sydney, NSW; tel. (2) 9267-2477; fax (2) 9264-8871; e-mail admin@greatsynagogue.org.au; internet www.greatsynagogue.org.au; f. 1878; Sr Rabbi JEREMY LAWRENCE.

OTHER FAITHS

According to the August 2006 census, Buddhists numbered 418,757 and Hindus 148,127.

The Press

The total circulation of Australia's daily newspapers is very high, but in the remoter parts of the country weekly papers are even more popular. Most of Australia's newspapers are published in sparsely populated rural areas where the demand for local news is strong. The only newspapers that may fairly claim a national circulation are the dailies *The Australian* and *Australian Financial Review*, and the weekly magazines *The Bulletin*, *Time Australia* and *Business Review Weekly*, the circulation of most newspapers being almost entirely confined to the state in which each is produced.

ACP Publishing Pty Ltd: 54–58 Park St, Sydney, NSW 2000; tel. (2) 9282-8000; fax (2) 9267-4361; internet www.acp.com.au; publishes 60 magazines, including *Australian Women's Weekly*, *The Bulletin with Newsweek*, *Cleo*, *Cosmopolitan*, *Woman's Day*, *Dolly*, *Ralph* and *Wheels*; CEO SCOTT LORSON.

APN News and Media Ltd: Level 4, 100 William St, Sydney, NSW 2011; tel. (2) 9333-4999; fax (2) 9333-4900; e-mail info@apn.com.au;

AUSTRALIA

internet www.apn.com.au; Chair. JAMES J. PARKINSON; Chief Exec. BRENDAN M. A. HOPKINS.

Fairfax Media: POB 506, Sydney, NSW 2001; tel. (2) 9282-2833; fax (2) 9282-3133; e-mail rvictor@mail.fairfax.com.au; internet www.fxj.com.au; f. 1987; fmrly known as John Fairfax Holdings Ltd; merged with Rural Press Ltd 2007; Chair. RONALD WALKER; Chief Exec. DAVID E. KIRK; publs include *The Sydney Morning Herald*, *The Australian Financial Review* and *Sun-Herald* (Sydney), *The Age* and *BRW Publications* (Melbourne), and *The Canberra Times*; also provides online and interactive services.

The Herald and Weekly Times Ltd: POB 14999, Melbourne MC, Vic 8001; tel. (3) 9292-2000; fax (3) 9292-2002; internet www.heraldsun.news.com.au; acquired by News Ltd in 1987; Chair. JANET CALVERT-JONES; Man. Dir JULIAN CLARKE; publs include *Herald Sun*, *Sunday Herald Sun*, *The Weekly Times*, *MX*.

News Ltd: 2 Holt St, Surry Hills, Sydney, NSW 2010; tel. (2) 9288-3000; fax (2) 9288-2300; e-mail newsroom@news.com.au; internet www.news.com.au; Australian subsidiary of US News Corporation; Chair. and CEO JOHN HARTIGAN; controls *The Australian* and *The Weekend Australian* (national), *Daily Telegraph*, *Sunday Telegraph* (Sydney), *The Herald Sun* and *Sunday Herald Sun* (Victoria), *Northern Territory News* (Darwin), *Sunday Times* (Perth), *Townsville Bulletin*, *Courier Mail*, *Sunday Mail* (Queensland), *The Mercury* (Tasmania), *The Advertiser*, *Sunday Mail* (South Australia).

West Australian Newspapers Holdings Ltd: Newspaper House, 50 Hasler Rd, Osborne Park, WA 6017; tel. (8) 9482-3111; fax (8) 9482-9080; e-mail westinfo@wanews.com.au; internet thewest.com.au; Chair. P. J. MANSELL; Man. Dir and CEO K. N. STEINKE.

NEWSPAPERS

Australian Capital Territory

The Canberra Times: POB 7155, Canberra Mail Centre, ACT 2610; tel. (2) 6280-2122; fax (2) 6280-2282; internet www.canberratimes.com; f. 1926; daily and Sun.; morning; Editor-in-Chief JACK WATERFORD; Editor MARK BAKER; circ. 36,027 (Mon.–Fri.), 67,371 (Sat.), 36,892 (Sun.).

New South Wales

Dailies

The Australian: News Ltd, 2 Holt St, POB 4245, Surry Hills, NSW 2010; tel. (2) 9288-3000; fax (2) 9288-2250; e-mail letters@theaustralian.com.au; internet www.theaustralian.com.au; f. 1964; edited in Sydney, simultaneous edns in Sydney, Melbourne, Perth, Townsville, Adelaide and Brisbane; Editor-in-Chief CHRIS MITCHELL; Editor PAUL WHITTAKER; circ. 129,000 (Mon.–Fri.); *The Weekend Australian* (Sat.) 293,252.

Australian Financial Review: 201 Sussex St, GPOB 506, Sydney, NSW 2000; tel. (2) 9282-2833; fax (2) 9282-3137; e-mail edletters@afr.com.au; internet afr.com; f. 1951; distributed nationally; Publr/Editor-in-Chief MICHAEL GILL; Editor GLENN BURGE; circ. 85,537 (Mon.–Fri.), 85,392 (Sat.).

The Daily Telegraph: News Ltd, 2 Holt St, Surry Hills, NSW 2010; tel. (2) 9288-3000; fax (2) 9288-2300; e-mail news@dailytelegraph.com.au; internet www.dailytelegraph.com.au; f. 1879; merged in 1990 with *Daily Mirror* (f. 1941); 24-hour tabloid; Editor DAVID PENBERTHY; circ. 381,996 (Mon.–Fri.), 391,832 (Sat.).

The Manly Daily: 26 Sydney Rd, Manly, NSW 2095; tel. (2) 9977-3333; fax (2) 9977-1203; e-mail editor@manlydaily.com.au; internet www.manlydaily.com.au; f. 1906; Tue.–Sat.; Editor KATHY LIPARI; circ. 91,348.

The Newcastle Herald: 28–30 Bolton St, Newcastle, NSW 2300; tel. (2) 4979-5000; fax (2) 4979-5588; internet www.theherald.com.au; f. 1858; morning; 6 a week; Editor-in-Chief ROD QUINN; Gen. Man. JULIE AINSWORTH; circ. 53,082.

The Sydney Morning Herald: 201 Sussex St, GPOB 506, Sydney, NSW 2000; tel. (2) 9282-2833; fax (2) 9282-3253; internet www.smh.com.au; f. 1831; morning; Editor ALAN OAKLEY; circ. 231,508 (Mon.–Fri.), 400,000 (Sat.).

Weeklies

Bankstown Canterbury Torch: 47 Allingham St, Condell Park, NSW 2200; tel. (2) 9795-0000; fax (2) 9795-0096; e-mail torch@torchpublishing.com.au; internet www.torchpublishing.com.au; f. 1920; Wed.; owned by Torch Publishing Co Pty Ltd; Editor MARK KIRKLAND; circ. 90,066.

Northern District Times: Suite 2, 3 Carlingford Rd, Epping, NSW 2150; tel. (2) 9024-8777; fax (2) 9024-8788; e-mail gannons@cng.newsltd.com.au; internet www.northerndistricttimes.com.au; f. 1921; Wed.; Editor COLIN KERR; circ. 56,942.

The Parramatta Advertiser: 142–154 Macquarie St, Parramatta, NSW 2150; tel. (2) 9689-5370; fax (2) 9689-5388; internet www.parramattaadvertiser.com.au; f. 1933; Wed.; Editor JOHN BILIC; circ. 83,333.

St George and Sutherland Shire Leader: 633 Princess Hwy, Rockdale, NSW 2216; tel. (2) 9588-8888; fax (2) 9588-8887; e-mail leaderenquiries@fairfax.com.au; internet www.theleader.com.au; f. 1960; Tue. and Thur.; Editor ALBERT MARTINEZ; circ. 150,592.

Sun-Herald: GPOB 506, Sydney, NSW 2001; tel. (2) 9282-1679; fax (2) 9282-2151; internet www.sunherald.com.au; f. 1953; Sun.; Editor PHILIP MCLEAN; circ. 580,000.

Sunday Telegraph: GPOB 4245, Sydney, NSW 2001; fax (2) 9288-2307; e-mail letters@sundaytelegraph.com.au; internet www.sundaytelegraph.news.com.au; f. 1938; Editor NEIL BREEN; circ. 720,000.

Northern Territory

Daily

Northern Territory News: Printers Place, POB 1300, Darwin, NT 0801; tel. (8) 8944-9900; fax (8) 8981-6045; e-mail admin@ntn.newsltd.com.au; internet www.ntnews.com.au; f. 1952; Mon.–Sat.; Editor JULIAN RICCI; Gen. Man. DON KENNEDY; circ. 24,470.

Weekly

Sunday Territorian: Printers Place, GPOB 1300, Darwin, NT 0801; tel. (8) 8944-9722; fax (8) 8981-6045; e-mail sundayterritorian@ntn.newsltd.com.au; Sun.; Editor TIM PIGOT; circ. 21,605.

Queensland

Daily

The Courier-Mail: 41 Campbell St, Bowen Hills, Brisbane, Qld 4006; tel. (7) 3252-6011; fax (7) 3666-6696; e-mail fagand@gnp.newsltd.com.au; internet www.thecouriermail.news.com.au; f. 1933; morning; Editor DAVID FAGAN; Man. Editor ANNA REYNOLDS; circ. 208,902 (Mon.–Fri.), 332,335 (Sat.).

Weekly

The Sunday Mail: 41 Campbell St, Bowen Hills, Brisbane, Qld 4006; tel. (7) 3666-8000; fax (7) 3666-6787; internet www.news.com.au/couriermail/sundaymail; f. 1953; Editor LIZ DEEGAN; circ. 621,419.

South Australia

Daily

The Advertiser: 31 Waymouth St, Adelaide, SA 5000; tel. (8) 8206-2000; fax (8) 8206-3669; e-mail tiser@adv.newsltd.com.au; internet www.news.com.au/adelaidenow; f. 1858; morning; Editor MELVIN MANSELL; circ. 203,440 (Mon.–Fri.), 274,045 (Sat.).

Weekly

Sunday Mail: Level 2, 31 Waymouth St, GPOB 339, Adelaide, SA 5000; tel. (8) 8206-2000; fax (8) 8206-3646; e-mail gardnerp@adv.newsltd.com.au; internet www.news.com.au/adelaidenow; f. 1912; Editor PHILLIP GARDNER; circ. 331,755.

Tasmania

Dailies

The Advocate: POB 63, Burnie, Tas 7320; tel. (3) 6440-7409; fax (3) 6440-7340; e-mail news@theadvocate.com.au; internet nwtasmania.yourguide.com.au; f. 1890; morning; Editor PETER DWYER; circ. 25,623.

Examiner: 71–75 Paterson St, POB 99, Launceston, Tas 7250; tel. (3) 6336-7111; fax (3) 6334-7328; e-mail admin@examiner.com.au; internet www.examiner.com.au; f. 1842; morning; Editor DEAN SOUTHWELL; Chief Exec. TOM O'MEARA; circ. 38,721.

Mercury: 93 Macquarie St, Hobart, Tas 7000; tel. (3) 6230-0622; fax (3) 6230-0711; e-mail mercury.news@dbl.newsltd.com.au; internet www.themercury.news.com.au; f. 1854; morning; Man. Dir TONY YIANNI; Editor GARRY BAILEY; circ. 48,630 (Mon.–Fri.), 63,550 (Sat.).

Weeklies

Sunday Examiner: 71–75 Paterson St, Launceston, Tas 7250; tel. (3) 6336-7111; fax (3) 6334-7328; e-mail mail@examiner.com.au; internet www.examiner.com.au; f. 1924; Editor DEAN SOUTHWELL; circ. 42,000.

Sunday Tasmanian: 91–93 Macquarie St, Hobart, Tas 7000; tel. (3) 6230-0622; fax (3) 6230-0711; internet metro.newsmedianet.com.au;

f. 1984; morning; Man. Dir Rex Gardner; Editor Garry Bailey; circ. 61,391.

Victoria
Dailies

The Age: 250 Spencer St (cnr Lonsdale St), Melbourne, Vic 3000; tel. (3) 9600-4211; fax (3) 9601-2598; e-mail inquiries@theage.com.au; internet www.theage.com.au; f. 1854; morning, incl. Sun.; Editor-in-Chief Andrew Jaspan; Man. Dir Don Churchill; circ. 201,000 (Mon.–Fri.), 301,000 (Sat.), 210,000 (Sun.).

Herald Sun: HWT Tower, 40 City Rd, Southbank, Vic 3006; tel. (3) 9292-2000; fax (3) 9292-2112; e-mail news@heraldsun.com.au; internet www.heraldsun.news.com.au; f. 1840; Editor-in-Chief Peter Blunden; circ. 554,000.

Weekly

Sunday Herald Sun: HWT Tower, 40 City Rd, Southbank, Vic 3006; tel. (3) 9292-2963; fax (3) 9292-2080; e-mail sundayhs@hwt.newsltd.com.au; internet www.sundayheraldsun.com.au; f. 1991; Editor Simon Pristel; circ. 618,000.

Western Australia
Daily

The West Australian: POB D162, Perth, WA 6001; tel. (8) 9482-3111; fax (8) 9482-9080; internet www.thewest.com.au; f. 1833; morning; Editor Paul Armstrong; circ. 214,000 (Mon.–Fri.), 386,000 (Sat.).

Weekly

Sunday Times: 34 Stirling St, Perth, WA 6000; tel. (8) 9326-8326; fax (8) 9326-8316; e-mail editorial@sundaytimes.newsltd.com.au; internet www.sundaytimes.news.com.au; f. 1897; Man. Dir David Maguire; Editor Brett McCarthy; circ. 346,014.

PRINCIPAL PERIODICALS
Weeklies and Fortnightlies

The Bulletin: GPOB 3957, Sydney, NSW 2000; tel. (2) 9282-8227; fax (2) 9267-4359; e-mail bulletin@acpmagazines.com.au; internet www.thebulletin.com.au; f. 1880; weekly; business and current affairs; Editor-in-Chief John Lehmann; Editor Andrew Forbes; circ. 60,625.

Business Review Weekly (BRW): Level 24, Tower 1, 201 Sussex St, Sydney, NSW 2000; tel. (2) 9282-2822; fax (2) 9282-1095; e-mail brwonline@brw.fairfax.com.au; internet www.brw.com.au; f. 1981; Man. Editor Peter Roberts; circ. 45,467.

Computerworld Australia: POB 295, St Leonards, NSW 1590; tel. (2) 9901-0709; e-mail sandra_rossi@idg.com.au; internet www.computerworld.com.au; weekly; information technology news; Editor Sandra Rossi.

The Countryman: GPOB D162, Perth, WA 6840; tel. (8) 9482-3327; fax (8) 9482-3314; e-mail countryman@wanews.com.au; internet countryman.thewest.com.au; f. 1885; Thur.; farming; Editor Cameron Morse; circ. 10,500.

The Medical Journal of Australia: Locked Bag 3030, Strawberry Hills, NSW 2012; tel. (2) 9562-6666; fax (2) 9562-6699; e-mail medjaust@ampco.com.au; internet www.mja.com.au; f. 1914; fortnightly; Editor Dr Martin van der Weyden; circ. 27,532.

New Idea: 35–51 Mitchell St, McMahons Point, NSW 2060; tel. (2) 9464-3200; fax (2) 9464-3203; e-mail newidea@pacpubs.com.au; internet www.newidea.com.au; weekly; women's; Editor-in-Chief Robyn Foyster; Publr Suzanne Monks; circ. 402,038.

News Weekly: 582 Queensberry St, North Melbourne, Vic 3051; tel. (3) 9326-5757; fax (3) 9328-2877; e-mail nw@newsweekly.com.au; internet www.newsweekly.com.au; f. 1943; publ. by National Civic Council; fortnightly; Sat.; political, social, educational and trade union affairs; Editor Peter Westmore; circ. 9,000.

NW: 54 Park St, Sydney, NSW 2000; tel. (2) 9282-2000; internet nw.ninemsn.com.au; weekly; entertainment news; Editor Amy Sinclair; circ. 195,889.

People: Level 18, 66–68 Goulburn St, Sydney, NSW 2000; tel. (2) 9288-9648; fax (2) 9283-7923; e-mail mvine@acpmagazines.com.au; weekly; men's interest; Editor Martin Vine; circ. 59,083.

Picture: GPOB 5201, Sydney, NSW 2001; tel. (2) 9288-9686; fax (2) 9267-4372; e-mail picture@acp.com.au; weekly; men's interest; Editor Ashley Gray; circ. 88,903.

Queensland Country Life: cnr Finucane Rd and Delaney St, Ormiston, Qld 4160; tel. (7) 3826-8200; fax (7) 3821-1236; e-mail editorialsec.qcl@ruralpress.com; internet www.queenslandcountrylife.com; f. 1935; Thur.; Editor Mark Phelps; Gen. Man. John Warlters; circ. 32,976.

Stock and Land: 10 Sydenham St, Moonee Ponds, Vic 3039; tel. (3) 9287-0900; fax (3) 9370-5622; e-mail stockandland@ruralpress.com; internet www.stockandland.com; f. 1914; weekly; agricultural and rural news; Editor Susan McNair; circ. 12,363.

Take 5: 54–58 Park St, Sydney, NSW 2000; tel. (2) 9282-8000; fax (2) 9267-4361; weekly; Editor Belinda Wallis; circ. 252,548.

That's Life!: 35–51 Mitchell St, McMahons Point, NSW 2060; tel. (2) 9464-3300; fax (2) 9464-3480; e-mail thatslife@pacificmags.com.au; f. 1994; weekly; features; Editor Linda Smith; circ. 346,326.

Time South Pacific: Level 5, 61 Lavendar St, Milsons Pt, NSW 2061; tel. (2) 9434-2222; fax (2) 9954-0468; e-mail time.letters@timeinc.com.au; internet www.time.com/time/pacific; weekly; current affairs; Editor Steve Waterson; circ. 83,566.

TV Week: 54 Park St, Sydney, NSW 2000; tel. (2) 9288-9611; fax (2) 9283-4849; internet www.tvweek.ninemsn.com.au; f. 1957; Wed.; colour national; Editor Emma Nolan; circ. 290,818.

The Weekly Times: POB 14999, Melbourne City MC, Vic 8001; tel. (3) 9292-2000; fax (3) 9292-2697; e-mail wtimes@theweeklytimes.com.au; internet www.theweeklytimes.com.au; f. 1869; farming, regional issues, country life; Wed.; Editor Ed Gannon; circ. 78,900.

Woman's Day: POB 5245, Sydney, NSW 2001; tel. (2) 9282-8000; fax (2) 9267-4360; e-mail womansday@acp.com.au; internet womansday.ninemsn.com.au; weekly; circulates throughout Australia and NZ; Editor Alana House; circ. 765,170.

Monthlies and Others

Architectural Product News: Architecture Media Pty Ltd, Level 3, 4 Princes St, Port Melbourne, Vic 3207; tel. (3) 9646-4760; fax (3) 9646-4918; e-mail apn@archmedia.com.au; internet www.architecturemedia.com; 6 a year; Editorial Dir Sue Harris; circ. 24,584.

Australian Geographic: POB 321, Terrey Hills, NSW 2084; tel. (2) 9473-6700; fax (2) 9473-6790; e-mail order@ausgeo.com.au; internet editorial.australiangeographic.com.au; f. 1986; every 3 months; Man. Dir Rory Scott; Editorial Dir Dee Nolan; circ. 142,015.

Australian Good Taste: 170–180 Bourke Rd, Alexandria, NSW 2015; tel. (2) 9353-6666; fax (2) 9353-6699; e-mail goodtaste@fpc.com.au; internet www.australiangoodtaste.com.au; monthly; food and lifestyle; Editor Rebecca Cox; circ. 177,536.

Australian Gourmet Traveller: 54 Park St, Sydney, NSW 2000; tel. (2) 9282-8000; fax (2) 9267-4361; internet gourmettraveller.com.au; monthly; food and travel; Editor Anthea Loucas; circ. 77,500.

Australian Home Beautiful: 35–51 Mitchell St, McMahons Point, NSW 2060; tel. (2) 9464-3218; fax (2) 9464-3263; e-mail homebeautiful@pacificmags.com.au; internet www.homebeautiful.com.au; f. 1925; monthly; Editor Wendy Moore; circ. 65,533.

Australian House and Garden: 54 Park St, Sydney, NSW 2000; tel. (2) 9282-8456; fax (2) 9267-4912; e-mail h&g@acp.com.au; f. 1948; monthly; design, decorating, renovating, gardens, food and travel; Editorial Dir Anny Friis; Editor Maya Kelett; circ. 113,029.

Australian Journal of Mining: Informa Australia Pty Ltd, Level 2, 120 Sussex St, Sydney, NSW 2000; e-mail Paula.Wallace@informa.com.au; internet www.theajmonline.com; f. 1986; bi-monthly; mining and exploration throughout Australia and South Pacific; Editor Paula Wallace; circ. 5,875.

Australian Journal of Pharmacy: Level 5, 8 Thomas St, Chatswood, NSW 2067; tel. (2) 8117-9500; fax (2) 8117-9510; e-mail david.weston@appco.com.au; internet www.ajp.com.au; f. 1886; monthly; journal of the associated pharmaceutical orgs; Publr and Man. Editor David Weston; circ. 16,553.

Australian Law Journal: 100 Harris St, Pyrmont, NSW 2009; tel. (2) 8587-7000; fax (2) 8587-7104; e-mail alj@thomson.com.au; f. 1927; monthly; Editor Justice P. W. Young; circ 4,500.

Australian Photography: POB 606, Sydney, NSW 2001; tel. (2) 9281-2333; fax (2) 9281-2750; e-mail robertkeeley@yaffa.com.au; monthly; Editor Robert Keeley; circ. 9,010.

The Australian Women's Weekly: 54–58 Park St, Sydney, NSW 2000; tel. (2) 9282-8000; fax (2) 9267-4459; e-mail womensweekly@acpmagazines.com.au; internet www.ninemsn.com.au/aww; f. 1933; monthly; Editorial Dir Deborah Thomas; circ. 679,979.

Belle: 54 Park St, Sydney, NSW 2000; tel. (2) 9282-8000; fax (2) 9267-8037; e-mail belle@acp.com.au; f. 1975; every 2 months; interior design and architecture; Editor-in-Chief Neale Whitaker; circ. 27,272.

Better Homes and Gardens: 35–51 Mitchell St, McMahon's Point, NSW 2060; e-mail bhgmagenquiries@pacificmags.com.au; internet yahoo7.com.au/bhg; f. 1978; 13 a year; Editor Julia Zaetta; circ. 295,642.

Cleo: 54 Park St, Sydney, NSW 2000; tel. (2) 9282-8617; fax (2) 9267-4368; internet cleo.ninemsn.com.au/cleo; f. 1972; women's monthly; Editor Nedahl Stelio; circ. 170,123.

AUSTRALIA

Cosmopolitan: 54 Park St, Sydney, NSW 2000; tel. (2) 9282-8039; fax (2) 9267-4457; e-mail cosmo@acp.com.au; internet www.cosmopolitan.com.au; f. 1973; monthly; women's lifestyle; Editor SARAH WILSON; circ. 220,112.

Delicious: 170–180 Bourke Rd, Alexandria, NSW 2015; tel. (2) 9353-6666; fax (2) 9353-6699; e-mail delicious@fpc.com.au; internet www.deliciousmagazine.com.au; 11 a year; food and lifestyle; Editor TRUDI JENKINS; circ. 117,287.

Dolly: 54–58 Park St, Sydney, NSW 2000; tel. (2) 9282-8437; fax (2) 9267-4911; internet www.ninemsn.com.au/dolly; f. 1970; monthly; for young women; Editor BRONWYN MCCAHON; circ. 170,357.

Family Circle: Pacific Magazines, 35–51 Mitchell St, McMahons Point, NSW 2060; tel. (2) 9464-3471; fax (2) 9464-3506; internet www.familycircle.com.au; 13 a year; Editor SARAH BRYDEN-BROWN; circ. 87,301.

FHM: EMAP Australia, Level 6, 187 Thomas St, Haymarket, Sydney, NSW 2000; tel. (2) 9581-9400; fax (2) 9581-9570; e-mail incoming@emap.com.au; internet www.fhm.com.au; monthly; men's interest; Editor-in-Chief JOHN BASTICK; circ. 115,105.

Financial Review Smart Investor: 201 Sussex St, GPOB 506, Sydney, NSW 2000; tel. (2) 9282-2822; fax (2) 9603-3137; e-mail smartinvestor@afr.com.au; internet www.afrsmartinvestor.com.au; monthly; Editor NICOLE PEDERSEN-MCKINNON.

Gardening Australia: POB 199, Alexandria, NSW 1435; tel. (2) 9353-6666; fax (2) 9317-4615; e-mail gardeningaustralia@fpcliving.com.au; internet www.gardeningaustralia.com.au; f. 1991; monthly; Exec. Editor BRODEE MYERS-COOKE; circ. 87,000.

Girlfriend: 35–51 Mitchell St, McMahons Point, NSW 2060; tel. (2) 9464-3300; fax (2) 9464-3483; e-mail girlfriend@pacificmags.com.au; internet www.girlfriend.com.au; monthly; for teenage girls; Editor SARAH OAKES; circ. 145,123.

Good Health and Medicine: 54 Park St, Sydney, NSW 2000; tel. (2) 9282-8000; fax (2) 9267-4361; internet health.ninemsn.com.au/goodmedicine/goodmedicine.aspx; monthly; fmrly Good Medicine; health and beauty; Editor CATHERINE MARSHALL; circ. 64,624.

Houses: Architecture Media Pty Ltd, Level 3, 4 Princes St, Port Melbourne, Vic 3207; tel. (3) 9646-4760; fax (3) 9646-4918; e-mail houses@archmedia.com.au; internet www.architecturemedia.com/houses; f. 1989; 6 a year; Publisher/Editorial Dir SUE HARRIS; Editor MARK SCRUBY; circ. 19,877.

K-Zone: 35–51 Mitchell St, McMahons Point, NSW 2060; tel. (2) 9464-3300; fax (2) 9464-3483; e-mail kzone@pacificmags.com.au; internet www.kzone.com.au; monthly; youth lifestyle; Editor MATT PAROZ; circ. 114,330.

Marie Claire: 35–51 Mitchell St, McMahons Point, Sydney, NSW 2060; tel. (2) 9464-3177; e-mail marieclaire@pacificmags.com.au; internet www.marieclaire.com.au; monthly; fashion and lifestyle; Editor JACKIE FRANK; circ. 111,843.

Motor: Locked Bag 12, Oakleigh, Vic 3166; tel. (3) 9567-4200; fax (3) 9563-4554; e-mail motor@acpaction.com.au; internet carpoint.ninemsn.com.au/motor; f. 1954; monthly; Editor JESSE TAYLOR; circ. 50,085.

New Woman: EMAP Australia, Level 6, 187 Thomas St, Haymarket, NSW 2000; tel. (2) 9581-9400; fax (2) 9581-9570; internet www.newwoman.com.au; monthly; Editor FRAN SHEEN; circ. 81,026.

The Open Road: Level 23, 388 George St, Sydney, NSW 2000; tel. (2) 8222-2185; fax (2) 8222-2176; e-mail open.road@mynrma.com.au; internet www.theopenroad.com.au; f. 1927; every 2 months; journal of National Roads and Motorists' Asscn (NRMA); Publr BERNADETTE BRENNAN; Editor-in-Chief NEEDRA D'SOUZA; circ. 1,555,917.

Ralph: 54–58 Park St, Sydney, NSW 2000; tel. (2) 9282-8000; fax (2) 9267-4361; internet ralph.ninemsn.com.au; monthly; men's lifestyle; Editor MICHAEL PICKERING; circ. 103,356.

Reader's Digest: 26–32 Waterloo St, Surry Hills, NSW 2010; tel. (2) 9690-6111; fax (2) 9690-6211; e-mail editors.au@readersdigest.com; internet www.readersdigest.au.com; monthly; Editor-in-Chief BRUCE HEILBUTH; circ. 360,301.

Street Machine: Locked Bag 756, Epping, NSW 2121; tel. (2) 9868-4832; fax (2) 9869-7390; e-mail streetmachine@acpaction.com.au; monthly; motoring magazine; Editor GEOFF SEDDON; circ. 65,113.

Super Food Ideas: 170–180 Bourke Rd, Alexandria, NSW 2015; tel. (2) 9353-6666; fax (2) 9353-6699; e-mail superfoodideas@fpc.com.au; internet www.superfoodideas.com.au; 11 a year; Editor JENNIFER CONNELL; circ. 340,289.

TV Hits: 35–51 Mitchell St, McMahons Point, NSW 2060; tel. (2) 9464-2625; fax (2) 9464-3508; e-mail tvhits@pacificmags.com.au; internet www.tvhits.com.au; f. 1988; monthly; youth entertainment; Editor MELISSA HABCHI; circ. 48,563.

TV Soap: Level 5, Horwitz House, 55 Chandos St, St Leonards, NSW 2065; tel. (2) 9901-6132; fax (2) 9901-6116; e-mail tvsoap@horwitz.com.au; f. 1983; monthly; Editor VESNA PETROPOULOS; circ. 103,000.

Vogue Australia: 180 Bourke Rd, Alexandria, NSW 2015; tel. (2) 9353-6666; fax (2) 9353-0935; e-mail vogue@vogue.com.au; internet www.vogue.com.au; f. 1959; monthly; fashion; Editor KIRSTIE CLEMENTS; circ. 65,000.

Wheels: GPOB 4088, Sydney, NSW 2001; tel. (2) 9263-9732; fax (2) 9263-9702; e-mail wheels@acp.com.au; internet wheels.carpoint.ninemsn.com.au; f. 1953; monthly; international motoring magazine; Editor GED BULMER; circ. 68,155.

Your Garden: 35–51 Mitchell St, McMahons Point, NSW 2060; tel. (2) 9464-2671; fax (2) 9464-3487; e-mail yg@pacificmags.com.au; internet www.yourgarden.com.au; every three months; Editor PAUL URQUHART; circ. 46,300.

NEWS AGENCY

AAP: 3 Rider Blvd, Rhodes Waterside, Rhodes, NSW 2138; tel. (2) 9322-8000; fax (2) 9322-8888; e-mail info@aap.com.au; internet www.aap.com.au; f. 1983; owned by major daily newspapers of Australia; Chair. MICHAEL GILL; CEO CLIVE MARSHALL.

PRESS ASSOCIATIONS

Australian Press Council: Suite 10.02, 117 York St, Sydney, NSW 2000; tel. (2) 9261-1930; fax (2) 9267-6826; e-mail info@presscouncil.org.au; internet www.presscouncil.org.au; Chair. Prof. KEN MCKINNON.

Community Newspapers of Australia Pty Ltd: POB 234, Auburn, NSW 1835; tel. (2) 8789-7300; fax (2) 8789-7387; e-mail robyn@printnet.com.au; internet www.cna.org.au; Fed. Pres. GENE SWINSTEAD; Exec. Sec. ROBYN BAKER.

Country Press Association of SA Incorporated: 198 Greenhill Rd, Eastwood, SA 5063; tel. (8) 8373-6533; fax (8) 8373-6544; e-mail countrypsa@bigpond.com; internet www.cpasa.asn.au; f. 1912; represents South Australian country newspapers; Pres. T. MCAULIFFE; Exec. Dir R. M. MCCOY.

Country Press Australia: 113 Rosslyn St, West Melbourne, Vic 3003; tel. (3) 9320-8900; fax (3) 9328-1916; internet www.countrypress.net.au; f. 1906; 420 mems.

Queensland Country Press Association: POB 229, Kelvin Grove DC, Qld 4059; tel. (7) 3356-0033; fax (7) 3356-0027; e-mail qld@printnet.com.au; Pres. M. HODGSON; Sec. N. D. MCLARY.

Tasmanian Press Association Pty Ltd: 71–75 Paterson St, Launceston, Tas 7250; tel. (3) 6336-7111; Sec. TOM O'MEARA.

Victorian Country Press Association Ltd: 113 Rosslyn St, West Melbourne, Vic 3003; tel. (3) 9320-8900; fax (3) 9328-1916; internet www.vcpa.com.au; f. 1910; Pres. G. KELLY; Exec. Dir J. E. RAY; 110 mems.

Publishers

Allen and Unwin Pty Ltd: 83 Alexander St, Crows Nest, NSW 2065; tel. (2) 8425-0100; fax (2) 9906-2218; e-mail frontdesk@allenandunwin.com; internet www.allenandunwin.com; fiction, trade, academic, children's; Exec. Chair. and Publishing Dir PATRICK A. GALLAGHER; Man. Dir PAUL DONOVAN.

Australasian Medical Publishing Co Pty Ltd: Level 2, 26–32 Pyrmont Bridge Road, Pyrmont, NSW 2009; tel. (2) 9562-6666; fax (2) 9562-6600; e-mail ampco@ampco.com.au; internet www.ampco.com.au; f. 1913; scientific, medical and educational; CEO Dr MARTIN VAN DER WEYDEN.

Black Inc: Level 5, 289 Flinders Lane, Melbourne, Vic 3000; tel. (3) 9654-2000; fax (3) 9654-2290; e-mail enquiries@blackincbooks.com; internet www.blackincbooks.com; f. 2000; literary fiction and non-fiction; an imprint of Schwartz Publishing; Man. Dir SOPHY WILLIAMS.

Cambridge University Press (Australia): 477 Williamstown Rd, PB 31, Port Melbourne, Vic 3207; tel. (3) 8671-1411; fax (3) 9676-9966; internet www.cambridge.org/aus; scholarly and educational; Chief Exec. STEPHEN BOURNE.

Cengage Learning Australia Pty Ltd: Level 7, 80 Dorcas St, South Melbourne, Vic 3205; tel. (3) 9685-4111; fax (3) 9685-4116; e-mail aust.customerservice@cengage.com; internet www.cengage.com.au; fmrly Thomson Learning Australia, name changed as above 2007; educational; Man. Dir JOHN MEHAN.

Commonwealth Scientific and Industrial Research Organisation (CSIRO Publishing): 150 Oxford St, POB 1139, Collingwood, Vic 3066; tel. (3) 9662-7500; fax (3) 9662-7595; e-mail publishing@csiro.au; internet www.publish.csiro.au; f. 1926; scientific and technical journals, books, magazines, videos, CD-ROMs; Gen. Man. P. W. REEKIE.

Elsevier Australia: 30–52 Smidmore St, Marrickville, NSW 2204; tel. (2) 9517-8999; fax (2) 9517-2249; e-mail customerserviceau@

AUSTRALIA

elsevier.com; internet www.elsevier.com.au; a division of Reed International Books Australia Pty Ltd; health sciences, science and medicine; Man. Dir FERGUS HALL.

Encyclopaedia Britannica Australia Ltd: Level 1, 90 Mount St, North Sydney, NSW 2060; tel. (2) 9923-5600; fax (2) 9929-3758; e-mail feedback@britannica.com.au; internet www.britannica.com.au; reference, education, art, science and commerce; Man. Dir JAMES BUCKLE.

Harcourt Education Australia: POB 460, Port Melbourne, Vic 3207; tel. (3) 9245-7111; fax (3) 9245-7333; e-mail customerservice@harcourteducation.com.au; internet www.harcourteducation.com.au; primary, secondary and tertiary educational; division of Reed International; Man. Dir DAVID O'BRIEN.

Harlequin Enterprises (Australia) Pty Ltd: Locked Bag 2, Chatswood, NSW 2067; tel. (2) 9415-9200; fax (2) 9415-9292; internet www.eHarlequin.com.au; Man. Dir MICHELLE LAFOREST.

Hyland House Publishing Pty Ltd: 387–389 Clarendon St, South Melbourne, Vic 3205; tel. (3) 9818-5700; fax (3) 9818-5044; e-mail hyland3@netspace.net.au; internet www.greenweb.com.au/hyland; f. 1977; Aboriginal and children's literature, gardening, pet care; Rep. MICHAEL SCHOO.

Lansdowne Publishing: POB 1669, Crows Nest, NSW 1585; tel. and fax (2) 9436-2974; e-mail info@lanspub.com.au; internet www.lanspub.com.au; cookery, new age, interior design, gardening, health, history, spirituality; Chief Exec. STEVEN MORRIS.

LexisNexis: Tower 2, 475 Victoria Ave, Chatswood, NSW 2067; tel. (2) 9422-2222; fax (2) 9422-2444; e-mail customer.relations@lexisnexis.com.au; internet www.lexisnexis.com.au; f. 1910; div. of Reed Elsevier; legal and commercial; Man. Dir MAX PIPER.

McGraw-Hill Australia Pty Ltd: Level 2, 82 Waterloo Rd, North Ryde, NSW 2113; tel. (2) 9900-1800; fax (2) 9900-1980; e-mail cservice_sydney@mcgraw-hill.com; internet www.mcgraw-hill.com.au; educational, professional and technical; Man. Dir MURRAY ST LEGER.

Melbourne University Publishing Ltd: 187 Grattan St, Carlton, Vic 3053; tel. (3) 9342-0300; fax (3) 9342-0399; e-mail mup-info@unimelb.edu.au; internet www.mup.com.au; f. 1922; scholarly non-fiction, Australian history and biography; CEO and Publr LOUISE ADLER.

Murdoch Books: GPOB 4115, Sydney, NSW 2001; tel. (2) 8220-2000; fax (2) 8220-2558; e-mail inquiry@murdochbooks.com.au; internet www.murdochbooks.com.au; cooking, gardening, DIY, craft, gift, general leisure and lifestyle, narrative, history, non-fiction, travel memoirs and business; CEO JULIET ROGERS; Publishing Dir KAY SCARLETT.

National Library of Australia: Parkes Place, Canberra, ACT 2600; tel. (2) 6262-1111; fax (2) 6273-2545; e-mail csb@nla.gov.au; internet www.nla.gov.au; f. 1960; trade and library-related publications; Dir of Publications PAUL HETHERINGTON.

Oxford University Press: 253 Normanby Rd, South Melbourne, Vic 3205; tel. (3) 9934-9123; fax (3) 9934-9100; internet au.oup.com; f. 1908; general non-fiction and educational; Man. Dir MAREK PALKA.

Pan Macmillan Australia Pty Ltd: Level 25, BT Tower, 1 Market St, Sydney NSW 2000; tel. (2) 9285-9100; fax (2) 9285-9190; e-mail pansyd@macmillan.com.au; internet www.panmacmillan.com.au; general, reference, children's, fiction, non-fiction; Chair. R. GIBB.

Pearson Education Australia Pty Ltd: Unit 4, Level 3, 14 Aquatic Drive, Frenchs Forest, NSW 2086; tel. (2) 9454-2200; fax (2) 9453-0089; e-mail customer.service@pearsoned.com.au; internet www.pearsoned.com.au; f. 1957; mainly educational, academic, computer, some general; Man. Dir DAVID BARNETT.

Penguin Group (Australia): POB 701, Hawthorn, Vic 3122; tel. (3) 9811-2400; fax (3) 9811-2620; internet www.penguin.com.au; f. 1946; general; Man. Dir GABRIELLE COYNE; Publishing Dir ROBERT SESSIONS.

Random House Australia Pty Ltd: Level 3, 100 Pacific Highway, North Sydney, NSW 2060; tel. (2) 9954-9966; fax (2) 9954-4562; e-mail random@randomhouse.com.au; internet www.randomhouse.com.au; fiction, non-fiction and children's; Man. Dir MARGARET SEALE.

Reader's Digest (Australia) Pty Ltd: GPOB 4353, Sydney, NSW 2000; tel. (2) 9018-6000; fax (2) 9018-7000; e-mail editors.au@readersdigest.com; internet www.readersdigest.com.au; general; Man. Dir PAUL HEATH.

Scholastic Australia Pty Ltd: 76–80 Railway Crescent, Lisarow, NSW 2250; tel. (2) 4328-3555; fax (2) 4323-3827; internet www.scholastic.com.au; f. 1968; educational and children's; Man. Dir DAVID PEAGRAM.

Schwartz Publishing (Victoria) Pty Ltd: Level 5, 289 Flinders Lane, Melbourne, Vic 3000; tel. (3) 9654-2000; fax (3) 9654-2290; non-fiction; Dir MORRY SCHWARTZ.

Simon and Schuster (Australia) Pty Ltd: Suite 2, Lower Ground Floor, 14–16 Suakin St, Pymble, NSW 2073; tel. (2) 9983-6600; fax (2) 9988-4293; e-mail cservice@simonandschuster.com.au; non-fiction incl. anthropology, cooking, gardening, house and home, craft, parenting, health, history, travel, biography, motivation and management; Man. Dir and Publr JON ATTENBOROUGH.

Thames and Hudson Australia Pty Ltd: 11 Central Boulevard, Portside Business Park, Fishermans Bend, Vic 3207; tel. (3) 9646-7788; fax (3) 9646-8790; e-mail enquiries@thaust.com.au; internet www.thamesandhudson.com; art, history, archaeology, architecture, photography, design, fashion, textiles, lifestyle; Man. Dir PETER SHAW.

Thomson Legal & Regulatory, Australia: Level 5, 100 Harris St, Pyrmont, NSW 2009; tel. (2) 8587-7000; fax (2) 8587-7100; e-mail LRA.Service@thomson.com; internet www.thomson.com.au; legal, professional, tax and accounting; CEO TONY KINNEAR.

Thorpe-Bowker: C3, 85 Turner St, POB 101, Port Melbourne, Vic 3207; tel. (3) 8645-0300; fax (3) 8645-0395; e-mail customer.service@thorpe.com.au; internet www.thorpe.com.au; bibliographic, library and book trade reference; Gen. Man. GARY PENGELLY.

UNSW Press Ltd: University of New South Wales, Sydney, NSW 2052; tel. (2) 9664-0900; fax (2) 9664-5420; e-mail frontdesk.press@unsw.edu.au; internet www.unswpress.com.au; f. 1962; scholarly, general and tertiary texts; Man. Dir Dr ROBIN DERRICOURT.

University of Queensland Press: POB 6042, St Lucia, Qld 4067; tel. (7) 3365-7244; fax (7) 3365-7579; e-mail uqp@uqp.uq.edu.au; internet www.uqp.uq.edu.au; f. 1948; scholarly and general cultural interest, incl. Black Australian writers, adult and children's fiction; Gen. Man. GREG BAIN.

University of Western Australia Press: 35 Stirling Highway, Crawley, WA 6009; tel. (8) 6488-3670; fax (8) 6488-1027; e-mail admin@uwapress.uwa.edu.au; internet www.uwapress.uwa.edu.au; f. 1935; literary fiction, natural history, history, literary studies, Australiana, general non-fiction; Dir Assoc. Prof. TERRI-ANN WHITE.

John Wiley & Sons Australia, Ltd: POB 1226, Milton, Qld 4064; tel. (7) 3859-9755; fax (7) 3859-9715; e-mail brisbane@johnwiley.com.au; internet www.johnwiley.com.au; f. 1954; educational, reference and trade; Man. Dir PETER DONOUGHUE.

PUBLISHERS' ASSOCIATION

Australian Publishers Association Ltd: 60/89 Jones St, Ultimo, NSW 2007; tel. (2) 9281-9788; fax (2) 9281-1073; e-mail apa@publishers.asn.au; internet www.publishers.asn.au; f. 1948; 160 mems; Pres. JULIET ROGERS; Chief Exec. MAREE MCCASKILL.

Broadcasting and Communications

TELECOMMUNICATIONS

In October 2006 162 licensed telecommunications carriers were in operation.

AAPT Ltd: AAPT Centre, 9 Lang St, Sydney, NSW 2000; tel. (2) 9377-7000; fax (2) 9377-7133; internet www.aapt.com.au; f. 1991; part of Telecom New Zealand Group; long-distance telecommunications carrier.

Hutchison Telecoms Australia: POB 388, St Leonards, NSW 1590; tel. (2) 9964-4646; fax (2) 9964-4668; e-mail media@hutchison.com.au; internet www.hutchison.com.au; third generation (3G) mobile multimedia services; Chair. CANNING FOK KIN-NING; CEO NIGEL DEWS.

Optus Ltd: POB 1, North Sydney, NSW 2059; tel. (2) 9342-7800; fax (2) 9342-7100; internet www.optus.com.au; f. 1992; division of Singapore Telecommunications Ltd; general and mobile telecommunications, data and internet services, pay-TV; Chair. Sir RALPH ROBINS; Chief Exec. PAUL O'SULLIVAN.

Telstra Corpn Ltd: Level 14, 231 Elizabeth St, Sydney, NSW 2000; tel. (2) 9287-4677; fax (2) 9287-5869; internet www.telstra.com.au; general and mobile telecommunication services; Chair. DONALD G. MCGAUCHIE; Chief Exec. SOLOMON TRUJILLO.

Vodafone Australia Ltd: Tower A, 799 Pacific Highway, Chatswood, NSW 2067; tel. (2) 9415-7000; fax (2) 9878-7788; internet www.vodafone.com.au; mobile telecommunication services; CEO RUSSELL HEWITT.

Regulatory Authority

Australian Communications and Media Authority (ACMA): POB 13112, Law Courts, Melbourne, Vic 8010; tel. (3) 9963-6968; fax (3) 9963-6899; e-mail candinfo@acma.gov.au; internet www.acma.gov.au; f. 2005; Commonwealth regulator for telecommunications,

AUSTRALIA

broadcasting, internet and radiocommunications; Chair. CHRIS CHAPMAN.

BROADCASTING

Many programmes are provided by the non-commercial statutory corporation, the Australian Broadcasting Corporation (ABC). Commercial radio and television services are provided by stations operated by companies under licences granted and renewed by the Australian Communications and Media Authority (ACMA). They rely for their income on the broadcasting of advertisements. In late 2006 there were about 277 commercial radio stations in operation, and 54 commercial television stations.

In 1997 there were an estimated 25.5m. radio receivers. The number of television receivers in use totalled 14,168,000 in 2001.

Australian Broadcasting Corporation (ABC): 700 Harris St, Ultimo, POB 9994, Sydney, NSW 2001; tel. (2) 8333-1500; fax (2) 8333-5344; internet www.abc.net.au; f. 1932; est. as Australian Broadcasting Commission; became corporation in 1983; one national television network operating on about 700 transmitters, one international television service broadcasting via satellite to Asia and the Pacific and six radio networks operating on more than 6,000 transmitters; Chair. MAURICE NEWMAN; Man. Dir MARK SCOTT.

Radio Australia: international service broadcast by short wave and satellite in English, Indonesian, Standard Chinese, Khmer, Tok Pisin and Vietnamese.

Radio

Commercial Radio Australia Ltd: Level 5, 88 Foveaux St, Surry Hills, NSW 2010; tel. (2) 9281-6577; fax (2) 9281-6599; e-mail mail@commercialradio.com.au; internet www.commercialradio.com.au; f. 1930; represents the interests of Australia's commercial radio broadcasters; CEO JOAN WARNER.

Major Commercial Broadcasting Station Licensees

Associated Communications Enterprises (ACE) Radio Broadcasters Pty Ltd: Level 8C, 18 Albert Rd, South Melbourne, Vic 3205; tel. (3) 9645-9877; fax (3) 9645-9886; internet www.acecorporate.com; operates six stations; Chair. ROWLY PATERSON; Man. Dir S. EVERETT.

Austereo Pty Ltd: Ground Level, 180 St Kilda Rd, St Kilda, Vic 3182; tel. (3) 9230-1051; fax (3) 9593-9007; e-mail peter.harvie@austereo.com.au; internet www.austereo.com.au; operates 15 stations; Chair. PETER HARVIE; CEO MICHAEL E. ANDERSON.

Australian Radio Network Pty Ltd: 3 Byfield St, North Ryde, NSW 2113; tel. (2) 8899-9999; fax (2) 8899-9811; e-mail webmaster@arn.com.au; internet www.arn.com.au; operates 12 stations; CEO BOB LONGWELL.

Capital Radio: POB 1206, Mitchell, ACT 2911; tel. (2) 6452-1521; fax (2) 6452-1006; operates seven stations; Man. Dir KEVIN BLYTON.

DMG Radio Australia: Level 5, 75 Hindmarsh St, Adelaide, SA 5000; tel. (8) 8419-5000; fax (8) 8419-5062; e-mail enquiries@dmgradio.com.au; internet www.dmgradio.com.au; operates 9 stations; CEO PAUL THOMPSON.

Grant Broadcasting Pty Ltd: POB 1599, Crows Nest, NSW 2065; tel. (2) 9437-8888; fax (2) 9437-8881; operates 22 stations; Gen. Man. JANET CAMERON.

Greater Cairns Radio Ltd: Virginia House, Abbott St, Cairns, Qld 4870; tel. (7) 4050-0800; fax (7) 4051-8060; e-mail cnssales@dmgradio.com.au; Gen. Man. J. ELLER.

Macquarie Regional RadioWorks Pty Ltd: POB 4290, Sydney, NSW 2001; tel. (2) 9269-0646; fax (2) 9287-2772; internet theradio.com.au; operates 87 stations; Exec. Chair. TIM HUGHES; CEO RHYS HOLLERAN.

Radio 2SM Gold 1269: 8 Jones Bay Rd, Pyrmont, NSW 2009; tel. (2) 9922-1269; e-mail info@2sm.com.au; internet www.2sm.com.au; f. 1931; CEO and Chair. C. M. MURPHY.

RadioWest Hot FM: POB 10067, Kalgoorlie, WA 6430; tel. (8) 9021-2666; fax (8) 9091-2209; e-mail radio6KG@gold.net.au; f. 1931.

Regional Broadcasters (Australia) Pty: McDowal St, Roma, Qld 4455; tel. (7) 4622-1800; fax (7) 4622-3697; Chair. G. McVEAN.

RG Capital Radio Pty Ltd: Level 2, Seabank Bldg, 12–14 Marine Parade, Southport, Qld 4215; tel. (7) 5591-5000; fax (7) 5591-2869; operates 34 stations; Man. Dir RHYS HOLLERAN.

Rural Press Ltd: Cnr Pine Mt Rd and Hill St, Raymonds Hill, Qld 4305; tel. (7) 3201-6000; fax (7) 3812-3060; internet www.rpl.com.au; f. 1911; operates five stations; Gen. Man. RICHARD BURNS.

SEA FM Pty Ltd: POB 5910, Gold Coast Mail Centre, Bundall, Qld 4217; tel. (7) 5591-5000; fax (7) 5591-6080; operates 28 stations; Man. Dir RHYS HOLLERAN.

Southern Cross Broadcasting (Australia) Ltd: see under Television.

Super Radio Network: POB 1269, Pyrmont, NSW 2009; owned by Broadcast Operations Pty Ltd; operates 33 stations; Chair. BILL CARALIS.

Tamworth Radio Development Company Pty Ltd: POB 497, Tamworth, NSW 2340; tel. (2) 6765-7055; fax (2) 6765-2762; operates five stations; Man. W. A. MORRISON.

Tasmanian Broadcasting Network (TBN): POB 665G, Launceston, Tas 7250; tel. (3) 6431-2555; fax (3) 6431-3188; operates three stations; Chair. K. FINDLAY.

Tasmanian Radio Network: 109 York St, Launceston, Tas 7250; tel. (3) 6331-4844; fax (3) 6334-5858; internet www.bestmusicmix.com.au; operates six radio stations and part of Macquarie Regional Radioworks; Man. MATT RUSSELL.

Wesgo Ltd: POB 234, Seven Hills, NSW 2147; tel. (2) 9831-7611; fax (2) 9831-2001; operates eight stations; CEO G. W. RICE.

Television

Free TV Australia: 44 Avenue Rd, Mosman, NSW 2088; tel. (2) 8968-7100; fax (2) 9969-3520; e-mail contact@freetv.com.au; internet www.freetv.com.au; f. 1960; fmrly Commercial Television Australia; represents all commercial free-to-air broadcasters in Australia; Chair. DAVID LECKIE; CEO JULIE FLYNN.

Commercial Television Station Licensees

Amalgamated Television Services Pty Ltd: Mobbs Lane, Epping, NSW 2121; tel. (2) 9877-7777; fax (2) 9877-7888; f. 1956; originating station for Seven Network TV programming; Exec. Chair. KERRY STOKES.

Australian Capital Television Pty Ltd (Southern Cross Ten): Private Bag 10, Dickson, ACT 2602; tel. (2) 6242-2400; fax (2) 6241-9511; e-mail reception@southerncrossnsw.com.au; f. 1962; Gen. Man. GREG DODGSON.

Channel 9 South Australia Pty Ltd: 202 Tynte St, North Adelaide 5006; tel. (8) 8267-0111; fax (8) 8267-3996; internet www.nws9.com.au; f. 1959; Gen. Man. MARK COLSON.

Channel Seven Adelaide Pty Ltd: 45–49 Park Terrace, Gilberton, SA 5081; tel. (8) 8342-7777; fax (8) 8342-7717; f. 1965; mem. of Seven Network; Man. Dir TONY DAVISON.

Channel Seven Brisbane Pty Ltd: GPOB 604, Brisbane, Qld 4001; tel. (7) 3369-7777; fax (7) 3368-2970; f. 1959; operates one station; mem. of Seven Network; Man. Dir L. M. RILEY.

Channel Seven Melbourne Pty Ltd: 119 Wells St, Southbank, Vic 3006; tel. (3) 9697-7777; fax (3) 9697-7888; e-mail daspinall@seven.com.au; f. 1956; operates one station; Chair. KERRY STOKES; Man. Dir DAVID ASPINALL.

Channel Seven Perth Pty Ltd: POB 77, Tuart Hill, WA 6939; tel. (8) 9344-0777; fax (8) 9344-0670; f. 1959; Chair. C. S. WHARTON.

General Television Corporation Pty Ltd: 22–46 Bendigo St, POB 100, Richmond, Vic 3121; tel. (3) 9429-0201; fax (3) 9429-3670; internet www.nine.msn.com.au; f. 1957; operates one station; Man. Dir GRAEME YARWOOD.

Golden West Network Pty Ltd: Roberts Cres., Bunbury, WA 6230; tel. (8) 9721-4466; fax (8) 9792-2932; e-mail gwn.bunbury@gwn.com.au; internet www.gwn.com.au; f. 1967; subsidiary of Prime Television Ltd; operates three stations (SSW10, VEW and WAW); Gen. Man. W. FENWICK.

Imparja Television Pty Ltd: POB 52, Alice Springs, NT 0871; tel. (8) 8950-1411; fax (8) 8953-0322; e-mail imparja@imparja.com.au; internet www.imparja.com.au; CEO ALISTAIR FEEHAN.

Mt Isa Television Pty Ltd: 110 Canooweal St, Mt Isa, Qld 4825; tel. (7) 4743-8888; fax (7) 4743-9803; f. 1971; operates one station; Station Man. LYALL GREY.

NBN Television Ltd: 11–17 Mosbri Crescent, Newcastle, NSW 2300; tel. (2) 4929-2933; fax (2) 4926-2936; internet www.nbntv.com.au; f. 1962; operates one station; Man. Dir DENIS LEDBURY.

Network Ten Ltd: GPOB 10, Sydney, NSW 2000; tel. (2) 9650-1010; fax (2) 9650-1111; internet www.ten.com.au; f. 1964; operates Australian TV network and commercial stations in Sydney, Melbourne, Brisbane, Perth and Adelaide; Exec. Chair. NICK FALLOON; CEO GRANT BLACKLEY.

Nine Network Australia Pty Ltd: POB 27, Willoughby, NSW 2068; tel. (2) 9906-9999; fax (2) 9958-2279; internet www.ninemsn.com.au; f. 1956; division of Publishing and Broadcasting Ltd; operates three stations: TCN Channel Nine Pty Ltd (Sydney), Queensland Television Ltd (Brisbane) and General Television Corporation Ltd (Melbourne); CEO EDDIE McGUIRE.

Northern Rivers Television Pty Ltd: Peterson Rd, Locked Bag 1000, Coffs Harbour, NSW 2450; tel. (2) 6652-2777; fax (2) 6652-3034; f. 1965; CEO GARRY DRAFFIN.

Prime Television Group: 363 Antill St, Watson, ACT 2602; tel. (2) 6242-3700; fax (2) 6242-3889; e-mail primetv@primetv.com.au;

AUSTRALIA

internet www.primetv.com.au; Chair. PAUL RAMSAY; Dep. Chair MICHAEL S. SIDDLE.

Prime Television (Northern) Pty Ltd: POB 2077, Elermore Vale, NSW 2287; tel. (2) 4952-0500; fax (2) 4952-0502; internet www.primetv.com.au; Gen. Man. BRAD JONES.

Prime Television (Southern) Pty Ltd: POB 465, Orange, NSW 2800; tel. (2) 6361-6888; fax (2) 6363-1889; Gen. Man. D. EDWARDS.

Prime Television (Victoria) Pty Ltd: Sunraysia Highway, Ballarat, Vic 3350; tel. (3) 5337-1777; fax (3) 5337-1700; e-mail primetv@primetv.com.au; Gen. Man. TONY HOGARTH.

Queensland Television Ltd: GPOB 72, Brisbane, Qld 4001; tel. (7) 3214-9999; fax (7) 3369-3512; f. 1959; operated by Nine Network Australia Pty Ltd; Gen. Man. CHRIS TAYLOR.

Seven Network Ltd: Level 13, 1 Pacific Highway, North Sydney, NSW 2060; tel. (2) 9967-7903; fax (2) 9967-7972; internet www.seven.com.au; owns Amalgamated Television Services Pty Ltd (Sydney), Brisbane TV Ltd (Brisbane), HSV Channel 7 Pty Ltd (Melbourne), South Australian Telecasters Ltd (Adelaide) and TVW Enterprises Ltd (Perth); Exec. Chair. KERRY STOKES.

Seven Queensland: 140–142 Horton Parade, Maroochydore, Qld 4558; tel. (7) 5430-1777; fax (7) 5430-1767; f. 1965; fmrly Sunshine Television Network Ltd.

Southern Cross Broadcasting (Australia) Ltd: GPOB 1837, Melbourne, Vic 3001; tel. (3) 9243-2100; fax (3) 9682-5158; tel. comment@scbnetwork.com.au; internet www.southerncrossbroadcasting.com.au; f. 1932; operates four TV and four radio stations; Man. Dir ANTHONY E. BELL; Chair. JOHN C. DAHLSEN.

Southern Cross Television (TNT9) Pty Ltd: Watchorn St, Launceston, Tas 7250; tel. (3) 6344-0202; fax (3) 6343-0340; f. 1962; operates one station; Gen. Man. BRUCE ABRAHAM.

Special Broadcasting Service (SBS): Locked Bag 028, Crows Nest, NSW 1585; tel. (2) 9430-2828; fax (2) 9430-3047; e-mail sbs.com.au; internet www.sbs.com.au; f. 1980; national multi-cultural broadcaster of TV and radio; Chair. CARLA ZAMPATTI; Man. Dir SHAUN BROWN.

Spencer Gulf Telecasters Ltd: POB 305, Port Pirie, SA 5540; tel. (8) 8632-2555; fax (8) 8633-0984; e-mail dweston@centralonline.com.au; internet www.centralonline.com.au; f. 1968; operates two stations; Chair. P. M. STURROCK; Chief Exec. D. WESTON.

Swan Television & Radio Broadcasters Pty Ltd: POB 99, Tuart Hill, WA 6939; tel. (8) 9449-9999; fax (8) 9449-9900; Gen. Man. P. BOWEN.

Telecasters Australia Ltd: Level 8, 1 Elizabeth Plaza, North Sydney, NSW 2060; tel. (2) 9922-1011; fax (2) 9922-1033; internet www.telecasters.com.au; operates commercial TV services of TEN Queensland, TEN Northern NSW, Seven Central and Seven Darwin.

Territory Television Pty Ltd: POB 1764, Darwin, NT 0801; tel. (8) 8981-8888; fax (8) 8981-6802; f. 1971; operates one station; Gen. Man. A. G. BRUYN.

WIN Television Griffith Pty Ltd: 161 Remembrance Driveway, Griffith, NSW 2680; tel. (2) 6962-4500; fax (2) 6962-0979; e-mail murphyg@winnsw.com.au; fmrly MTN Television; Man. Dir GREG MURPHY.

WIN Television Loxton SA Pty Ltd: Murray Bridge Rd, POB 471, Loxton, SA 5333; tel. (8) 8584-6891; fax (8) 8584-5062; f. 1976; operates one station; Exec. Chair. E. H. URLWIN; Gen. Man. W. L. MUDGE.

WIN Television Mildura Pty Ltd: 18 Deakin Ave, Mildura, Vic 3500; tel. (3) 5023-0204; fax (3) 5022-1179; f. 1965; Chair. JOHN RUSHTON; Man. NOEL W. HISCOCK.

WIN Television NSW Network: Television Ave, Mt St Thomas, Locked Bag 8800, South Coast Mail Centre, NSW 2521; tel. (2) 4223-4199; fax (2) 4227-3682; internet www.wintv.com.au; f. 1962; Man. Dir K. KINGSTON; CEO JOHN RUSHTON.

WIN Television Qld Pty Ltd: POB 568 Rockhampton, Qld 4700; tel. (7) 4930-4499; fax (7) 4930-4490; Station Man. R. HOCKEY.

WIN Television Tas Pty Ltd: 52 New Town Rd, Hobart, Tas 7008; tel. (3) 6228-8999; fax (3) 6228-8991; e-mail wintas@wintv.com.au; internet www.wintv.com.au; f. 1959; Gen. Man. GREG RAYMENT.

WIN Television Vic Pty Ltd: POB 464, Ballarat, Vic 3353; tel. (3) 5320-1366; fax (3) 5333-1598; internet www.winnet.com.au; f. 1961; operates five stations; Gen. Man. MICHAEL TAYLOR.

Satellite, Cable and Digital Television

Digital television became available in metropolitan areas in January 2001 and was available in all major regional areas by 2004.

Austar United Communications: Level 29, AAP Centre, 259 George St, Sydney, NSW 2000; tel. (2) 9251-6999; fax (2) 9251-6136; e-mail austar@austarunited.com.au; internet www.austarunited.com.au; began operations in 1995; 459,819 subscribers (June 2004); CEO JOHN C. PORTER.

Australia Network: GPOB 9994, Sydney, NSW 2001; tel. (2) 8333-5598; fax (2) 8333-5305; internet australianetwork.com; international satellite service; broadcasts to countries and territories in Asia and the Pacific; owned by Australian Broadcasting Corpn.

Foxtel: 5 Thomas Holt Dr., North Ryde, NSW 2113; tel. (2) 9813-6000; fax (2) 9813-7303; e-mail corporateaffairs@foxtel.com.au; internet www.foxtel.com.au; owned by the News Corpn, Telstra Corpn and PBL; 800,100 subscribers (Aug. 2002); Chair. BRUCE AKHURST; CEO KIM WILLIAMS.

Optus Television: Tower B, Level 15, 16 Zenith Centre, 821–841 Pacific Highway, Chatswood, NSW 2067; provides cable television services in Sydney, Melbourne and Brisbane; 210,000 subscribers (March 1999).

Finance

(cap. = capital; p.u. = paid up; res = reserves; dep. = deposits; m. = million; brs = branches; amounts in Australian dollars)

Radical reforms of the financial sector were introduced in 1998. The banking system was opened up to greater competition. The licensing and regulation of deposit-taking institutions was supervised by the new Australian Prudential Regulation Authority, while consumer protection was the responsibility of the Australian Corporations and Financial Services Commission.

Australian Prudential Regulation Authority (APRA): GPOB 9836, Sydney, NSW 2000; tel. (2) 9210-3000; fax (2) 9210-3411; e-mail aprainfo@apra.gov.au; internet www.apra.gov.au; f. 1998; responsible for regulation of banks, insurance cos, superannuation funds, credit unions, building societies and friendly societies; Chair. Dr JOHN LAKER.

BANKING
Central Bank

Reserve Bank of Australia: 65 Martin Place, Sydney, NSW 2000; tel. (2) 9551-8111; fax (2) 9551-8000; e-mail rbainfo@rba.gov.au; internet www.rba.gov.au; f. 1911; responsible for monetary policy, financial system stability, payment system development; cap. 40m., res 1,116m., dep. 43,204m., total assets 105,447m., notes on issue 38,065m. (June 2006); Gov. GLENN STEVENS.

Development Bank

Rabobank Australia Ltd: GPOB 4577, Sydney, NSW 2001; tel. (2) 8115-4000; e-mail sydney.enquiry@rabobank.com; internet www.rabobank.com.au; f. 1978 as Primary Industry Bank of Australia Ltd; name changed as above 2003; cap. 123.2m., res 2.5m.; Chair. JAMES GRAHAM; CEO BRUCE DICK; 219 brs.

Trading Banks

ABN AMRO Australia Pty Ltd: Level 29, ABN AMRO Tower, 88 Phillip St, Sydney, NSW 2000; tel. (2) 8259-5000; fax (2) 8259-5444; e-mail au.mailbox@au.abnamro.com; internet www.abnamro.com.au; f. 1971; cap. 70m., res 590,000 (Dec. 2000); CEO ANGUS JAMES.

Arab Bank Australia Ltd: GPOB N645, Grosvenor Place, Sydney, NSW 1220; tel. (2) 9377-8900; fax (2) 9221-5428; e-mail service@arabbank.com.au; internet www.arabbank.com.au; cap. 55.0m., dep. 740.9m. (Dec. 2005); Chair. SAMIR KAWAR; Man. Dir JAMES WAKIM.

Australia and New Zealand Banking Group Ltd: 100 Queen St, 6th Floor, GPOB 537E, Melbourne, Vic 3000; tel. (3) 9273-5555; fax (3) 9658-2484; e-mail investor.relations@anz.com; internet www.anz.com; f. 1835; present name adopted in 1970; cap. 9,142m., dep. 227,665m. (Sept. 2006); Chair. CHARLES B. GOODE; CEO MICHAEL SMITH; 748 domestic brs, 204 overseas brs.

Bank of America Australia Ltd: Level 63, MLC Centre, 19–29 Martin Place, Sydney, NSW 2000; tel. (2) 9931-4200; fax (2) 9221-1023; f. 1964; Man. Dir JOHN LILES.

Bank of Queensland Ltd: 229 Elizabeth St, POB 898, Brisbane, Qld 4001; tel. (7) 3212-3333; fax (7) 3212-3399; internet www.boq.com.au; f. 1874; cap. 531.2m., res 61.0m., dep. 10,056.7m. (Aug. 2006); Chair. NEIL ROBERTS; Man Dir. DAVID P. LIDDY; 162 brs.

Bank of Tokyo-Mitsubishi UFJ Ltd: Level 25, Gateway, 1 Macquarie Place, Sydney, NSW 2000; tel. (2) 9296-1111; fax (2) 9247-4266; f. 1985; Gen. Man. K. TSUSHIMA.

Bank of Western Australia Ltd (BankWest): Level 47, BankWest Tower, 108 St George's Terrace, POB E237, Perth, WA 6001; tel. (8) 9449-7000; fax (8) 9449-7050; internet www.bankwest.com.au; f. 1895 as Agricultural Bank of Western Australia, est. 1945 as Rural and Industries Bank of Western Australia; present name adopted in 1994; 100% owned by HBOS Australia; cap. 872.3m., res

300,000, dep. 16,436.9m. (Dec. 2002); Chair. IAN C. R. MACKENZIE; Man. Dir SIMON WALSH; 87 brs.

Bankers' Trust Financial Group: GPOB 2675, Sydney, NSW 2001; tel. (2) 8222-7154; fax (2) 9274-5780; internet www.btal.com.au; f. 1986; division of Westpac Banking Corpn; CEO ROB COOMBE.

Bendigo Bank Ltd: 2nd Floor, Fountain Court, Bendigo, Vic 3550; tel. (3) 5433-9339; fax (3) 5433-9690; internet www.bendigobank.com.au; f. 1995; cap. 626.8m., res 69.0m., dep. 13,251.6m. (June 2006); Chair. ROBERT N. JOHANSON; Man. Dir ROBERT G. HUNT; 352 brs.

Citibank Pty Ltd: GPOB 40, Sydney, NSW 2000; tel. (2) 8225-0000; fax (2) 9239-9110; internet www.citibank.com.au; f. 1954; cap. 457m., res 1m., dep. 5,619m. (Dec. 1998); CEO (Australasia) AHMED FAHOUR; Man. Dir LES MATHESON.

Commonwealth Bank of Australia: Level 7, 48 Martin Place, Sydney, NSW 1155; tel. (2) 9378-2000; fax (2) 9378-3317; internet www.commbank.com.au; f. 1912; merged with Colonial Ltd in 2000; cap. 14,444m., res 1,904m., dep. 231,267m. (June 2006); Chair. JOHN SCHUBERT; CEO and Man. Dir RALPH NORRIS; more than 1,200 brs world-wide.

HSBC Bank Australia Ltd: Level 32, HSBC Centre, 580 George St, Sydney, NSW 2000; tel. (2) 9006-5888; fax (2) 9006-5440; e-mail pr@hsbc.com.au; internet www.hsbc.com.au; f. 1985; fmrly Hongkong Bank of Australia; cap. 926.2m., dep. 5,386.7m., res 0.06m. (Dec. 2005); Chair GRAHAM BRADLEY; CEO STUART DAVIS; 25 brs.

ING DIRECT (Australia) Ltd: GPOB 4094, Sydney, NSW 2001; tel. (2) 9028-4000; fax (2) 9028-4708; internet www.ingdirect.com.au; f. 1994; fmrly known as ING Bank; name changed as above 2007; CEO ERIK DROK.

Investec Bank (Australia) Ltd: Level 31, Chifley Tower, 2 Chifley Square, Sydney, NSW 2000; tel. (2) 9323-2000; fax (2) 9323-2002; e-mail australia@investec.com.au; internet www.investec.com/australia; fmrly N. M Rothschild & Sons; acquired by Investec Bank in July 2006; Chair. DAVID GONSKY; CEO BRIAN SCHWARTZ; 3 brs.

JPMorgan Australia: Level 32, Grosvenor Place, 225 George St, Sydney, NSW 2000; tel. (2) 9250-4111; internet www.jpmorgan.com/pages/jpmorgan/au/home; formed through merger of Ord Minnett, Chase Manhattan Bank, JPMorgan and Bank One; CEO ROB PRIESTLEY.

Macquarie Bank Ltd: 1 Martin Place, Sydney, NSW 2000; tel. (2) 8232-3333; fax (2) 8232-3350; internet www.macquarie.com.au; f. 1969 as Hill Samuel Australia Ltd; present name adopted in 1985; cap. 1,916m., res 639m., dep. 82,997m. (March 2006); Chair. DAVID S. CLARKE; Man. Dir and CEO W. RICHARD SHEPPARD; 4 brs.

National Australia Bank Ltd (NAB): 500 Bourke St, Melbourne, Vic 3000; tel. (3) 8641-3500; fax (3) 8641-4912; internet www.national.com.au; f. 1858; cap. 12,279m., res 1,064m., dep. 336,262m. (Sept. 2006); Chair. MICHAEL CHANEY; Group CEO JOHN STEWART; 2,349 brs.

SG Australia Ltd: Level 21, 400 George St, Sydney, NSW 2000; tel. (2) 9210-8000; fax (2) 9235-3941; internet sgcib.com; f. 1981; fmrly Société Générale Australia Ltd; CEO MICHEL L. MACAGNO.

St George Bank Ltd: Locked Bag 1, St George House, 4–16 Montgomery St, Kogarah, NSW 2217; tel. (2) 9952-1311; fax (2) 9952-1000; internet www.stgeorge.com.au; f. 1937 as building society; cap. 4,420m., res 169m., dep. 54,524m. (Sept. 2006); Chair. JOHN THAME; CEO PAUL FEGAN; 409 brs.

Standard Chartered Bank Australia Ltd: Level 1, 345 George St, Sydney, NSW 2000; tel. (2) 9232-9333; fax (2) 9232-9334; internet www.standardchartered.com/au; f. 1986; Chair. RICHARD NETTLETON; CEO EUGENE ELLIS.

Toronto–Dominion Australia Ltd: Level 24, 9 Castlereagh St, Sydney, NSW 2000; tel. (2) 9619-8888; internet www.tdbank.ca; f. 1970; Man. Dir KEITH MCQUEEN.

Westpac Banking Corporation: 275 Kent St, Sydney, NSW 2000; tel. (2) 9293-9270; fax (2) 9226-4128; internet www.westpac.com.au; f. 1817; cap. 5,468m., res 186m., dep. 258,107m. (Sept. 2006); CEO Dr DAVID MORGAN; 813 domestic brs, 195 brs in New Zealand, 48 other brs.

STOCK EXCHANGE

Australian Securities Exchange (ASX): Level 7, 20 Bridge St, Sydney, NSW 2000; tel. (2) 9227-0000; fax (2) 9227-0885; e-mail info@asx.com.au; internet www.asx.com.au; Australian Stock Exchange f. 1987 by merger of the stock exchanges in Sydney, Adelaide, Brisbane, Hobart, Melbourne and Perth, to replace the fmr Australian Associated Stock Exchanges; demutualized and listed Oct. 1998; Australian Securities Exchange formed through merger of Australian Stock Exchange and Sydney Futures Exchange July 2006; ASX group operates under the brand Australian Securities Exchange; spans markets for corporate control, capital formation and price discovery; operator, supervisor, central counter-party clearer and payments system facilitator; Chair. MAURICE NEWMAN; Man. Dir and CEO ROBERT ELSTONE.

Supervisory Body

Australian Securities and Investments Commission (ASIC): GPOB 9827, Sydney, NSW 2001; tel. (2) 9911-2200; fax (2) 9911-2333; internet www.asic.gov.au; f. 1990; corporations and financial products regulator; Chair. JEFFREY LUCY.

PRINCIPAL INSURANCE COMPANIES

Allianz Australia Ltd: GPOB 4049, Sydney, NSW 2001; tel. (2) 9390-6222; fax (2) 9390-6425; internet www.allianz.com.au; f. 1914; workers' compensation; fire, general accident, motor and marine; Chair. J. S. CURTIS; Man. Dir T. TOWELL.

AMP Ltd: AMP Bldg, 33 Alfred St, Sydney, NSW 2000; tel. (2) 9257-5000; fax (2) 9257-7886; internet www.amp.com.au; f. 1849; fmrly Australian Mutual Provident Society; life insurance; Chair. PETER MASON; CEO and Man. Dir ANDREW MOHL.

Aviva Australia Holdings Ltd: GPOB 2567W, 509 St Kilda Rd, Melbourne 3001; tel. (3) 9829-8989; fax (3) 9820-1534; internet www.avivagroup.com.au; f. 2000 as CGNU following merger of CGU and Norwich Union, renamed as above in 2003; CEO ALLAN GRIFFITHS.

AXA Asia Pacific Holdings Ltd: 447 Collins St, Melbourne, Vic 3000; tel. (3) 9616-3911; fax (3) 9618-4661; e-mail investor.relations@axa.com.au; internet www.axaasiapacific.com.au; f. 1869; fmrly The National Mutual Life Association of Australasia Ltd; financial advice, funds management, superannuation, retirement and savings products, life and trauma insurance, income protection; Chair. R. H. ALLERT; Group CEO A. PENN.

Calliden Insurance Ltd: Level 5, 114 Albert Rd, South Melbourne, Vic 3205; tel. (3) 8682-5702; fax (3) 9285-5020; e-mail feedback@calliden.com.au; internet www.calliden.com.au/business/calliden_insurance.cfm; general insurance products.

Catholic Church Insurances Ltd: 324 St Kilda Rd, Melbourne, Vic 3004; tel. (3) 9934-3000; fax (3) 9934-3460; internet www.ccinsurances.com.au; f. 1911; Chair. Most Rev. KEVIN MANNING (Bishop of Parramatta); Gen. Man. PETER RUSH.

The Copenhagen Reinsurance Co Ltd: 60 Margaret St, Sydney, NSW 2000; tel. (2) 9247-7266; fax (2) 9235-3320; internet www.copre.com; reinsurance; Gen. Man. DAVID KENNEDY.

General Reinsurance Australia Ltd: Level 24, 123 Pitt St, Sydney, NSW 2000; tel. (2) 8236-6100; fax (2) 9222-1500; f. 1961; reinsurance, fire, accident, marine; Chair. F. A. MCDONALD; Man. Dir C. J. CROWDER.

GIO Australia Holdings Ltd: POB 1464, Sydney, NSW 2001; tel. (2) 9255-8090; fax (2) 9251-2079; e-mail emailus@gio.com.au; internet www.gio.com.au; f. 1926; CEO PETER CORRIGAN.

Guild Insurance Ltd: Guild House, 40 Burwood Rd, Hawthorn, Vic 3122; tel. (3) 9810-9820; fax (3) 9819-5670; internet www.guildifs.com.au/insurance; f. 1963; Chair. ROBERT G. WATTS.

Insurance Australia Group Ltd: Level 26, 388 George St, Sydney, NSW 2000; tel. (2) 9292-9222; fax (2) 9292-8072; internet www.iag.com.au; f. 1926; fmrly NRMA Insurance Ltd; name changed as above 2002; Chair. JAMES STRONG; CEO MICHAEL HAWKER.

Lumley General Insurance Ltd: Lumley House, 309 Kent St, Sydney, NSW 2000; tel. (2) 9248-1111; fax (2) 9248-1198; e-mail general@lumley.com.au; internet www.lumley.com.au; CEO D. M. MATCHAM.

QBE Insurance Group Ltd: 82 Pitt St, Sydney, NSW 2000; tel. (2) 9375-4444; fax (2) 9235-3166; e-mail corporate@qbe.com; internet www.qbe.com; f. 1886; general insurance; Chair. E. J. CLONEY; CEO F. M. O'HALLORAN.

RAC Insurance Pty Ltd: 228 Adelaide Terrace, Perth, WA 6000; tel. (8) 9421-4444; fax (8) 9421-4593; internet rac.com.au; f. 1947; Gen. Man. TONY CARTER.

RACQ Insurance: POB 4, Springwood, Qld 4127; tel. (7) 3361-2444; fax (7) 3841-2995; e-mail bheath@racqi.com.au; internet www.racqinsurance.com.au; f. 1971; CEO BRADLEY HEATH (acting).

Suncorp Ltd: Level 18, 36 Wickham Tce, Brisbane, Qld 4000; tel. (7) 3835-5355; fax (7) 3836-1190; e-mail direct@suncorp.co.au; internet www.suncorp.com.au; f. 1996; CEO JOHN F. MULCAHY.

Swiss Re Australia Ltd: 363 George St, Sydney, NSW 2000; tel. (2) 8295-9500; fax (2) 8295-9804; internet www.swissre.com.au; f. 1962; Head of Australia and New Zealand operations KEITH SCOTT.

Vero Insurance Ltd: 465 Victoria Ave, Chatswood, NSW 2067; tel. (2) 9978-9000; fax (2) 9978-9807; e-mail veroinformation@vero.com.au; internet www.vero.com.au; fmrly RSA Insurance Australia Ltd; name changed as above 2003; CEO MARK MILLINER.

Wesfarmers Federation Insurance Ltd: 184 Railway Parade, Bassendean, WA 6054; tel. (8) 9273-5333; fax (8) 9378-2172; internet www.wfi.com.au; Gen. Man. R. J. BUCKLEY.

Westpac Life Ltd: 275 Kent St, Sydney, NSW 2000; internet www.westpac.com.au; f. 1986; CEO DAVID WHITE.

Zurich Financial Services Australia Ltd: 5 Blue St, North Sydney, NSW 2060; tel. (2) 9391-1111; fax (2) 9922-4630; e-mail client.service@zurich.com.au; internet www.zurich.com.au; CEO DAVID SMITH; Chair. NANCY MILNE.

Insurance Associations

Australian and New Zealand Institute of Insurance and Finance: Level 8, 600 Bourke St, Melbourne, Vic 3000; tel. (3) 9613-7200; fax (3) 9642-4166; e-mail ceo@theinstitute.com.au; internet www.theinstitute.com.au; f. 1884; provider of education, training, and professional devt courses across the region; 12,000 mems; 8,500 students; Pres. and Chair. of the Bd JOHN RICHARDSON; CEO JOAN FITZPATRICK.

Insurance Council of Australia Ltd: Level 3, 56 Pitt St, Sydney, NSW 2000; tel. (2) 9253-5100; fax (2) 9253-5111; internet www.insurancecouncil.com.au; f. 1975; Exec. Dir KERRIE KELLY.

Investment and Financial Services Association (IFSA): Level 24, 44 Market St, Sydney, NSW 2000; tel. (2) 9299-3022; fax (2) 9299-3198; e-mail ifsa@ifsa.com.au; internet www.ifsa.com.au; f. 1997 following merger of Australian Investment Managers' Association, Investment Funds Association and Life, Investment and Superannuation Association of Australia Inc; non-profit organization; Chair. CRAIG DUNN.

Trade and Industry

GOVERNMENT AGENCY

Austrade: Level 23, 201 Kent St, Sydney, NSW 2000; tel. (2) 9390-2000; fax (2) 9390-2024; e-mail info@austrade.gov.au; internet www.austrade.gov.au; f. 1931; export promotion agency; Chair. ROSS ADLER; CEO PETER O'BYRNE.

CHAMBERS OF COMMERCE

Australian Chamber of Commerce and Industry (ACCI): POB E14, Kingston, ACT 2604; tel. (2) 6273-2311; fax (2) 6273-3286; e-mail acci@acci.asn.au; internet www.acci.asn.au; Pres. NEVILLE SAWYER; CEO PETER HENDY.

Chamber of Commerce and Industry of Western Australia (CCIWA): POB 6209, East Perth, WA 6892; tel. (8) 9365-7555; fax (8) 9365-7550; e-mail info@cciwa.com; internet www.cciwa.com; f. 1890; 5,200 mems; Chief Exec. JAMES PEARSON; Pres. Dr PENNY FLETT.

Commerce Queensland: Industry House, 375 Wickham Terrace, Brisbane, Qld 4000; tel. (7) 3842-2244; fax (7) 3832-3195; e-mail info@commerceqld.com.au; internet www.commerceqld.com.au; f. 1868; operates World Trade Centre, Brisbane; 5,500 mems; Pres. BEATRICE BOOTH.

South Australian Employers' Chamber of Commerce and Industry Inc: Enterprise House, 136 Greenhill Road, Unley, SA 5061; tel. (8) 8300-0000; fax (8) 8300-0001; e-mail enquiries@business-sa.com; internet www.business-sa.com; f. 1839; 4,700 mems; Pres. ROB CHAPMAN; CEO PETER VAUGHAN.

Sydney Chamber of Commerce: Level 12, 83 Clarence St, Sydney, NSW 2000; tel. (2) 9350-8100; fax (2) 9350-8199; e-mail enquiries@thechamber.com.au; internet www.thechamber.com.au; f. 1825; offers advice to and represents over 70,000 businesses; Pres. Prof. TREVOR CAIRNEY; Exec. Dir PATRICIA FORSYTHE.

Tasmanian Chamber of Commerce and Industry: GPOB 793, Hobart, Tas 7001; tel. (3) 6236-3600; fax (3) 6231-1278; e-mail admin@tcci.com.au; internet www.tcci.com.au; CEO DAMON THOMAS.

Victorian Employers' Chamber of Commerce and Industry: Industry House, 486 Albert St, Melbourne, Vic 3002; tel. (3) 8662-5333; fax (3) 8662-5462; e-mail vecci@vecci.org.au; internet www.vecci.org.au; f. 1885; CEO NEIL COULSON.

AGRICULTURAL, INDUSTRIAL AND TRADE ASSOCIATIONS

Australian Business Ltd: Locked Bag 938, North Sydney, NSW 2059; tel. (2) 9458-7500; fax (2) 9923-1166; e-mail member.services@australianbusiness.com.au; internet www.australianbusiness.com.au; f. 1885; fmrly Chamber of Manufactures of NSW; Man. Dir and CEO KEVIN MACDONALD.

Australian Manufacturers' Export Council: POB E14, Queen Victoria Terrace, ACT 2600; tel. (2) 6273-2311; fax (2) 6273-3196; f. 1955; Exec. Dir G. CHALKER.

Australian Wine and Brandy Corporation (AWBC): POB 2733, Kent Town Business Centre, Kent Town, SA 5071; tel. (8) 8228-2000; fax (8) 8228-2022; e-mail awbc@awbc.com.au; internet www.wineaustralia.com; f. 1981; Chair. JOHN MOORE; Chief Exec. SAM TOLLEY.

Australian Wool Services Ltd: Wool House, 369 Royal Parade, Parkville, Vic 3052; tel. (3) 9341-9111; fax (3) 9341-9273; internet www.woolmark.com; f. 2001 following the privatization of the Australian Wool Research and Promotion Organisation; owner of The Woolmark Company; Chair. BARRY WALKER; Man. Dir (vacant).

Business Council of Australia: GPOB 1472, Melbourne, Vic 3001; tel. (3) 8664-2664; fax (3) 8664-2666; e-mail info@bca.com.au; internet www.bca.com.au; public policy research and advocacy; governing council comprises chief execs of Australia's major cos; Pres. GREIG GAILEY; Chief Exec. KATIE LAHEY.

Cotton Australia: Level 2, 490 Crown St, Surry Hills, NSW 2010; tel. (2) 9360-8500; fax (2) 9360-8555; e-mail talktous@cottonaustralia.com.au; internet www.cottonaustralia.com.au; Chair. BERNIE GEORGE.

Meat and Livestock Australia: Level 1, 165 Walker St, North Sydney, NSW 2060; tel. (2) 9463-9333; fax (2) 9463-9393; e-mail media@mla.com.au; internet www.mla.com.au; producer-owned co; represents, promotes, protects and furthers interests of industry in both the marketing of meat and livestock and industry-based research and devt activities; Chair. ARTHUR (DON) HEATLEY; Man. Dir DAVID PALMER.

National Farmers' Federation: POB E10, Kingston, ACT 2604; tel. (2) 6273-3855; fax (2) 6273-2331; e-mail nff@nff.org.au; internet www.nff.org.au; Pres. PETER CORISH; CEO BEN FARGHER.

Natural Resource Management Ministerial Council (NRMMC): NRMMC Secretariat, GPOB 858, Canberra, ACT 2601; tel. (2) 6272-4145; fax (2) 6272-4772; e-mail nrmmc@mincos.gov.au; internet www.mincos.gov.au; f. 2002 to replace the Agricultural and Resource Management Council of Australia and New Zealand; to promote the conservation and sustainable use of Australia's natural resources; mems comprising the Commonwealth/state/territory and New Zealand ministers responsible for environment, water and natural resources.

Primary Industries Ministerial Council (PIMC): Dept of Agriculture, Fisheries and Forestry, GPOB 858, Canberra, ACT 2601; tel. (2) 6272-5216; fax (2) 6272-4772; e-mail pimc@mincos.gov.au; internet www.mincos.gov.au; f. 2002 to develop and promote sustainable, innovative and profitable agriculture, fisheries, food and forestry industries; mems comprising the state/territory and New Zealand ministers responsible for agriculture, fisheries, food and forestry.

Trade Advisory Council (TAC): c/o Dept of Foreign Affairs and Trade, R. G. Casey Bldg, John McEwen Cres., Barton, ACT 0221; tel. (2) 6261-3236; fax (2) 6261-1385; e-mail tac@dfat.gov.au; internet www.dfat.gov.au/trade/formal_consultative_mechanisms.html; advises the Minister for Trade on business and investment issues; Chair. GEOFF ALLEN.

Winemakers' Federation of Australia (WFA): National Wine Centre, Botanic Rd, POB 2414, Kent Town, SA 5071; tel. (8) 8222-9255; fax (8) 8222-9250; e-mail wfa@wfa.org.au; internet www.wfa.org.au; f. 1990; Chief Exec. STEPHEN STRACHAN.

WoolProducers Australia: POB E10, Kingston, Canberra, ACT 2604; tel. (2) 6273-2531; fax (2) 6273-1120; e-mail woolproducers@nff.org.au; internet www.woolproducers.com.au; f. 2001; fmrly Wool Council Australia; represents wool-growers in dealings with the Federal Govt and industry; Pres. DONALD HAMBLIN.

EMPLOYERS' ORGANIZATIONS

Australian Co-operative Foods Ltd: 433 Victoria St, Wetherill Park, NSW 2164; tel. (2) 4821-1391; f. 1900; Man. Dir A. R. TOOTH.

Australian Industry Group: 51 Walker St, North Sydney, NSW 2060; tel. (2) 9466-5566; fax (2) 9466-5599; e-mail helpdesk@aigroup.asn.au; internet www.aigroup.asn.au; f. 1998 through merger of MTIA and ACM; 11,500 mems; Nat. Pres. TREVOR CARROLL; CEO HEATHER RIDOUT.

Australian Meat Industry Council: POB 1208, Crows Nest, NSW 1585; tel. (2) 9086-2200; fax (2) 9086-2201; e-mail admin@amic.org.au; internet www.amic.org.au; f. 1928; represents meat retailers, processors and small goods mfrs; Chair. TERRY NOLAN; CEO KEVIN COTTRILL.

NSW Farmers' Association: GPOB 1068, Sydney, NSW 2001; tel. (2) 8251-1700; fax (2) 8251-1750; e-mail emailus@nswfarmers.org.au; internet www.nswfarmers.org.au; f. 1978; CEO SHAUGHN MORGAN; Pres. JOCK LAURIE.

UTILITIES

Australian Institute of Energy: POB 193, Surry Hills, Vic 3127; tel. 1800-629-945; fax (3) 9898-0249; e-mail aie@aie.org.au; internet www.aie.org.au; f. 1977; Pres. MURRAY MEATON.

AUSTRALIA

Australian Water Association: POB 388, Artarmon, NSW 1570; tel. (2) 9413-1288; fax (2) 9413-1047; e-mail info@awa.asn.au; internet www.awa.asn.au; f. 1962; c. 4,000 mems; CEO TONY MOLLENKOPF; Pres. DAVID BARNES.

Energy Supply Association of Australia: GPOB 1823, Melbourne, Vic 3001; tel. (3) 9670-0188; fax (3) 9670-1069; e-mail info@esaa.com.au; internet www.esaa.com.au; CEO BRAD PAGE.

Electricity Companies

Country Energy: POB 718, Queanbeyan, NSW 2620; tel. 13-23-56; fax (2) 6589-8695; internet www.countryenergy.com.au; f. 2001 following merger of Advance Energy, Great Southern Energy and NorthPower; state-owned; electricity and gas distributor; Chair. BARBARA WARD; Man. Dir CRAIG MURRAY.

Delta Electricity: Level 12, Darling Park, 201 Sussex St, Sydney, NSW 2000; tel. (2) 9285-2700; fax (2) 9285-2777; e-mail raymond.madden@de.com.au; internet www.de.com.au; f. 1996; Chief Exec. JIM HENNESS.

ENERGEX: GPOB 1461, Brisbane, Qld 4001; tel. (7) 3407-4000; fax (7) 3407-4609; e-mail enquiries@energex.com.au; internet www.energex.com.au; spans Queensland and New South Wales; Chair. JOHN DEMPSEY (acting).

EnergyAustralia: 145 Newcastle Rd, Wallsend, NSW 2287; tel. (2) 4951-9346; fax (2) 4951-9351; internet www.energy.com.au; supplies customers in NSW; Chair. JOHN CONDE; Man. Dir GEORGE MALTABAROW.

Ergon Energy: POB 308, Rockhampton, Qld 4700; tel. (7) 3228-8222; fax (7) 3228-8118; e-mail customerservice@ergon.com.au; internet www.ergon.com.au; national retailer of electricity; Chair. KEITH HILLESS; Chief Exec. TONY BELLAS.

Power and Water Corpn: Energy House, 18–20 Cavenagh St, Darwin, NT 0800; tel. 1800-245-092; fax (8) 8924-7730; e-mail customerservice@powerwater.com.au; internet www.powerwater.com.au; state-owned; supplier of electricity, water and sewerage services in NT; Man. Dir ANDREW MACRIDES; Chair. NEIL PHILIP.

Powercor Australia Ltd: Locked Bag 14-090, Melbourne, Vic 8001; fax (3) 9683-4499; e-mail info@powercor.com.au; internet www.powercor.com.au; Chair. PETER TULLOCH; CEO SHANE BREHENY.

Snowy Hydro Ltd: POB 332, Cooma, NSW 2630; tel. (2) 6452-1777; fax (2) 6452-3794; e-mail info@snowyhydro.com.au; internet www.snowyhydro.com.au; Chair. RICK HOLLIDAY-SMITH; Man. Dir TERRY V. CHARLTON.

United Energy Ltd: Locked Bag 13, Mount Waverley, Vic 3149; fax (3) 9222-8588; e-mail info@mail.ue.com.au; internet www.ue.com.au; f. 1994 following division of State Electricity Commission of Victoria; transferred to private sector; distributor of electricity and gas.

Western Power Corpn: GPOB L921, Perth, WA 6842; tel. (8) 9326-4911; fax (8) 9326-4595; e-mail info@westernpower.com.au; internet www.wpcorp.com.au; f. 1995; principal supplier of electricity in WA; Chair. PETER MANSELL; CEO DOUG ABERLE.

Gas Companies

AlintaGas: GPOB W2030, Perth, WA 6846; internet www.alintagas.com.au; f. 1995; Chair. JOHN AKEHURST; CEO PETER MAGARRY (acting).

Allgas Energy Pty Ltd: 150 Charlotte St, Brisbane, Qld 4000; tel. (7) 3404-1822; fax (7) 3404-1821; e-mail corporate@allgas.com.au; internet www.allgas.com.au; f. 1885; Chief Exec. TOM BLOXSOM.

Australian Gas Light Co: AGL Centre, cnr Pacific Highway and Walker St, North Sydney, NSW 2060; tel. (2) 9921-2999; fax (2) 9957-3671; e-mail aglmail@agl.com.au; internet www.agl.com.au; f. 1837; Chair. MARK JOHNSON; Man. Dir. and CEO PAUL ANTHONY.

Envestra: 10th Floor, 81 Flinders St, Adelaide, SA 5000; tel. (8) 8227-1500; fax (8) 8277-1511; e-mail des.petherick@envestra.com.au; internet www.envestra.com.au; f. 1997 by merger of South Australian Gas Co, Gas Corpn of Queensland and Centre Gas Pty Ltd; purchased Victorian Gas Network in 1999; Chair. JOHN GEOFFREY ALLPASS; Man. Dir IAN BRUCE LITTLE.

Epic Energy: Level 8, 60 Collins St, Melbourne, Vic 3000; tel. (3) 8626-8400; fax (3) 8626-8454; internet www.epicenergy.com.au; f. 1996; privately owned gas transmission co; Chair. BRUCE MCKAY; Man. Dir and CEO ALAN FREER.

Origin Energy: Level 45, Australia Sq., 264–78 George St, Sydney, NSW 2000; tel. (2) 8345-5000; fax (2) 9252-9244; internet www.originenergy.com.au; Chair. H. KEVIN MCCANN; Man. Dir GRANT KING.

TRUenergy: Locked Bag 14060, Melbourne, Vic 8001; fax (3) 9299-2777; internet www.truenergy.com.au; formed through merger of TXU, Yallourn Energy and Auspower; owned by CLP Power Asia.

Water Companies

Melbourne Water Corpn: POB 4342, Melbourne, Vic 3001; tel. (3) 9235-7100; fax (3) 9235-7200; internet www.melbournewater.com.au; state-owned; Chair. CHERYL BATAGOL; Man. Dir ROB SKINNER.

Power and Water Corpn: see Electricity, above.

South Australian Water Corpn: 77 Grenfell St, Adelaide, SA 5000; tel. (8) 8204-1000; fax (8) 8204-1048; e-mail customerservice@sawater.com.au; internet www.sawater.com.au; state-owned; Chair. PHILIP PLEDGE; Chief Exec. ANNE HOWE.

South East Water Ltd: POB 1382, Moorabbin, Vic 3189; tel. (3) 9552-3000; fax (3) 9552-3001; internet www.southeastwater.com.au; f. 1995; state-owned; Chair. ELEANOR UNDERWOOD; Man. Dir DENNIS CAVAGNA.

Sydney Water Corpn: POB 53, Sydney South 1235; internet www.sydneywater.com.au; state-owned; Man. Dir KERRY SCHOTT; Chair. GABRIELLE KIBBLE.

Water Corpn: 629 Newcastle St, Leederville, WA 6007; tel. (8) 9420-2420; fax (8) 9420-3200; internet www.watercorporation.com.au; state-owned; Chair. PATRICK O'CONNOR; CEO Dr JIM GILL.

Yarra Valley Water Ltd: Private Bag 1, Mitcham, Vic 3132; tel. (3) 9874-2122; fax (3) 9872-1353; internet www.yvw.com.au; f. 1995; state-owned; Chair. ALAN CORNELL; Man. Dir TONY KELLY.

TRADE UNIONS

Australian Council of Trade Unions (ACTU): Level 2, 393 Swanston St, Melbourne, Vic 3000; tel. (3) 9663-5266; fax (3) 9663-4051; e-mail mailbox@actu.asn.au; internet www.actu.asn.au; f. 1927; br. in each state, generally known as a Trades and Labour Council; 46 affiliated trade unions; Pres. SHARAN BURROW; Sec. GREGORY COMBET.

Principal Affiliated Unions

Ansett Pilots Association (APA): POB 415, Essendon, Vic 3040; tel. (3) 9325-4233; fax (3) 9375-7405; e-mail secretary@apa.asn.au; internet www.apa.asn.au; Pres. AL CLARK; Sec. CON PROUSSALIS.

Association of Professional Engineers, Scientists & Managers, Australia (APESMA): POB 1272L, Melbourne, Vic 3001; tel. (3) 9695-8800; fax (3) 9696-9312; e-mail info@apesma.asn.au; internet www.apesma.asn.au; Nat. Pres. DARIO TOMAT; Nat. Sec. ROBERTA ESBITT; 25,000 mems.

Australasian Meat Industry Employees' Union (AMIEU): Level 1, 39 Lytton Rd, East Brisbane, Qld 4169; tel. (7) 3217-3766; fax (7) 3217-4462; e-mail admin@amieuqld.asn.au; internet www.amieu.asn.au; Fed. Pres. KATH EVANS; Fed. Sec. GRAHAM BIRD; 20,484 mems.

Australian Airline Flight Engineers Association (AAEA): Essendon, Vic 3040; f. 1984; Fed. Pres. JEFF SEABURN; Fed. Sec. RON HARE.

Australian Education Union (AEU): Ground Floor, 120 Clarendon St, Southbank, Vic 3006; tel. (3) 9693-1800; fax (3) 9693-1805; e-mail aeu@aeufederal.org.au; internet www.aeufederal.org.au; f. 1984; Fed. Pres. PATRICIA BYRNE; Fed. Sec. SUSAN HOPEGOOD; 170,000 mems.

Australian Manufacturing Workers' Union (AMWU): POB 160, Granville, NSW 2142; tel. (2) 9897-9133; fax (2) 9897-9274; e-mail amwu2@amwu.asn.au; internet www.amwu.asn.au; Nat. Pres. JULIUS ROE; Nat. Sec. DAVE OLIVER; 170,000 mems.

Australian Services Union (ASU): Ground Floor, 116 Queensberry St, Carlton South, Vic 3053; tel. (3) 9342-1400; fax (3) 9342-1499; e-mail asunatm@asu.asn.au; internet www.asu.asn.au; f. 1885; amalgamated in present form in 1993; Nat. Sec. PAUL SLAPE; 125,000 mems.

Australian Workers' Union (AWU): 685 Spencer St, West Melbourne, Vic 3003; tel. (3) 8327-0888; fax (3) 8327-0899; e-mail awu@alphalink.net.au; internet www.awu.net.au; f. 1886; Nat. Pres. BILL LUDWIG; Nat. Sec. BILL SHORTEN; 135,000 mems.

Communications, Electrical, Electronic, Energy, Information, Postal, Plumbing and Allied Services Union of Australia (CEPU): Suite 701, Level 7, 1 Rosebery Ave, Rosebery, NSW 2018; tel. (2) 9663-3699; fax (2) 9663-5599; e-mail edno@nat.cepu.asn.au; internet www.cepu.asn.au; Nat Pres. BRIAN BAULK; Nat. Sec. PETER TIGHE; 180,000 mems.

Community and Public Sector Union (CPSU): Level 5, 191–199 Thomas St, Haymarket, NSW 2000; tel. (2) 9334-9200; fax (2) 8204-6902; e-mail members@cpsu.org.au; internet www.cpsu.org.au; Nat. Pres. MARK GEPP; Nat. Sec. STEPHEN JONES; 200,000 mems.

Construction, Forestry, Mining and Energy Union (CFMEU): Box Q235, QVB PO, Sydney, NSW 1230; tel. (2) 9267-3393; fax (2) 9267-2460; internet www.cfmeu.asn.au; f. 1992 by amalgamation; Nat. Pres. TONY MAHER; Nat. Sec. JOHN SUTTON; 120,000 mems.

Finance Sector Union of Australia (FSU): GPOB 9893, 341 Queen St, Melbourne, Vic 3001; tel. 1300-366378; fax 1300-307943; e-mail fsuinfo@fsunion.org.au; internet www.fsunion.org.au; f. 1991; Nat. Pres. Carol Gordon; Nat. Sec. Leon Carter; 50,000 mems.

Health Services Union of Australia (HSUA): Level 2, 106–108 Victoria St, Carlton, Vic 3053; tel. (3) 9341-3328; fax (3) 9341-3329; e-mail hsu@hsu.net.au; internet www.hsu.net.au; Nat. Pres. Michael Williamson; Nat. Sec. Craig Thomson; 90,000 mems.

Independent Education Union of Australia (IEU): POB 1301, South Melbourne, Vic 3205; tel. (3) 9254-1830; fax (3) 9254-1835; e-mail ieu@ieu.org.au; internet www.ieu.org.au; Fed. Sec. Chris Watt; Fed. Pres. Richard Shearman; 63,000 mems.

Liquor, Hospitality and Miscellaneous Union (LHMU): Locked Bag 9, Haymarket, NSW 1240; tel. (2) 8204-3000; fax (2) 9281-4480; internet www.lhmu.org.au; f. 1992; Nat. Pres. Brian Daley; Nat. Sec. Louise Tarrant; 126,916 mems.

Maritime Union of Australia (MUA): 2nd Floor, 365 Sussex St, Sydney, NSW 2000; tel. (2) 9267-9134; fax (2) 9261-3481; e-mail muano@mua.org.au; internet www.mua.org.au; f. 1993; Nat. Sec. Paddy Crumlin; 10,012 mems.

Media, Entertainment & Arts Alliance (MEAA): POB 723, Strawberry Hills, NSW 2012; tel. (2) 9333-0999; fax (2) 9333-0933; e-mail mail@alliance.org.au; internet www.alliance.org.au; Fed. Sec. Christopher Warren; 30,000 mems.

National Union of Workers (NUW): POB 343, North Melbourne, Vic 3051; tel. (3) 9287-1850; fax (3) 9287-1818; e-mail nuwnat@nuw.org.au; internet www.nuw.org.au; Gen. Sec. Charles Donnelly; Gen. Pres. Doug Stevens; 100,000 mems.

Rail, Tram and Bus Union (RTBU): 83–89 Renwick St, Redfern, NSW 2016; tel. (2) 9310-3966; fax (2) 9319-2096; e-mail rtbu@rtbu-nat.abn.au; internet www.rtbu-nat.asn.au; Nat. Pres. R. Hayden; Nat. Sec. Roger Jowett; 35,000 mems.

Shop, Distributive & Allied Employees Association (SDA): 6th Floor, 53 Queen St, Melbourne, Vic 3000; tel. (3) 8611-7000; fax (3) 8611-7099; e-mail general@sda.org.au; internet www.sda.org.au; f. 1908; Nat. Pres. Don Farrell; Nat. Sec. Joe de Bruyn; 214,029 mems.

Textile, Clothing and Footwear Union of Australia (TCFUA): Ground Floor, 28 Anglo Rd, Campsie, NSW 2194; tel. (2) 9789-4188; fax (2) 9789-6510; e-mail tcfua@tcfua.org.au; f. 1919; Pres. Barry Tubner; Nat. Sec. Tony Woolgar; 21,354 mems.

Transport Workers' Union of Australia (TWU): POB 47, Parramatta, NSW 2124; tel. (2) 9912-0788; fax (2) 9689-1844; e-mail twu@twu.com.au; internet www.twu.com.au; Fed. Pres. Hughie Williams; Fed. Sec. John Allan; 82,000 mems.

Transport

Australian Transport Council: POB 594, Canberra, ACT 2601; tel. (2) 6274-7462; fax (2) 6274-8090; e-mail atc@infrastructure.gov.au; internet www.atcouncil.gov.au; f. 1993; mems include Australian and New Zealand ministers responsible for transport; Sec. Mike Jamieson.

State Transit Authority of New South Wales: 219–241 Cleveland St, Strawberry Hills, NSW 2010; tel. (2) 9245-5777; e-mail info@sydneybuses.nsw.gov.au; internet www.sta.nsw.gov.au; operates government buses and ferries in Sydney and Newcastle metropolitan areas; Chair. David Herlihy; CEO John Stott.

TransAdelaide (South Australia): GPOB 2351, Adelaide, SA 5001; tel. (8) 8218-2200; fax (8) 8218-4399; e-mail info@transadelaide.sa.gov.au; internet www.transadelaide.com.au; f. 1994; fmrly State Transport Authority; operates metropolitan train, bus, tram and Busway services; Gen. Man. Bill Watson.

RAILWAYS

In June 2003 there were 41,461 km of railways in Australia (including tram and light rail track). In September of that year the construction of a 1,400-km railway between Alice Springs and Darwin was completed. The rail link was to be used principally for transporting freight.

Pacific National: Locked Bag 90, Parramatta, NSW 2124; tel. (2) 8484-8000; fax (2) 8484-8154; e-mail communication@pacificnational.com.au; internet www.pacificnational.com.au; freight; fmrly National Rail Corporation Ltd; CEO Don Telford.

QR (Queensland Rail): POB 1429, Brisbane, Qld 4001; tel. (7) 3235-2180; fax (7) 3235-1799; internet www.qr.com.au; f. 1863; passenger commuter and long-distance services, freight and logistic services, track access and rail-specific expert services; Chair. John B. Prescott; CEO Bob Scheuber.

RailCorp: POB K349, Haymarket, NSW 1238; tel. (2) 8202-2000; fax (2) 8202-2111; internet www.railcorp.info; f. 1980; responsible for passenger rail and associated coach services in NSW; Chair. Ross Bunyon; Chief Exec. Vince Graham.

Victorian Rail Track (VicTrack): Level 17, 595 Collins St, Melbourne, Vic 3000; tel. (3) 9619-8850; fax (3) 9619-8851; e-mail victrack@victrack.com.au; internet www.victrack.com.au; f. 1997; Chair. Elana Robin; Chief Exec. John Sutton.

Western Australian Government Railways (Westrail): POB 8125, Perth 6849, WA; tel. (8) 9326-2000; fax (8) 9326-2500; statutory authority competing in the freight, passenger and related transport markets in southern WA; operates 1,029 main line route-km of track; Commr Reece Waldock (acting).

ROADS

In June 2004 there were 810,641 km of roads open for general traffic. In 1996 this included 1,000 km of freeways, a further 103 km of toll roads, 45,889 km of highways, 77,045 km of arterial and major roads and 30,596 km of secondary tourist and other roads. Local roads in urban areas account for 93,677 km of the network and those in rural localities for 537,278 km.

Austroads Inc: POB K659, Haymarket, NSW 2000; tel. (2) 9264-7088; fax (2) 9264-1657; e-mail austroads@austroads.com.au; internet www.austroads.com.au; f. 1989; assn of road transport and traffic authorities.

SHIPPING

In December 2006 the Australian merchant fleet comprised 672 vessels, with a total displacement of 1,852,800 grt.

Adsteam Marine Ltd: Level 22, Tower 2, 101 Grafton St, Bondi Junction, NSW 2022; tel. (2) 9369-9200; fax (2) 9369-9288; e-mail info@adsteam.com.au; internet www.adsteam.com.au; f. 1875; fmrly Adelaide Steamship Co; Man. Dir and Chief Exec. John Moller.

ANL Ltd (Australian National Line): GPOB 2238T, Melbourne, Vic 3004; tel. (3) 9257-0555; fax (3) 9257-0619; f. 1998; shipping agents; coastal and overseas container shipping and coastal bulk shipping; container management services; overseas container services to Hong Kong, People's Republic of China, Taiwan, the Philippines, Korea, Singapore, Malaysia, Thailand, Indonesia and Japan; extensive transhipment services; Chair. Jacques Saade; Man. Dir John Lines.

BHP Transport Pty Ltd: 27th Level, 600 Bourke St, POB 86A, Melbourne, Vic 3001; tel. (3) 9609-3333; fax (3) 9609-2400; Chair. D. Argus; Man. Dir P. Andersen.

William Holyman and Sons Pty Ltd: No. 3 Berth, Bell Bay, Tas 7253; tel. (3) 6382-2383; fax (3) 6382-3391; coastal services; Chair. R. J. Hoy.

CIVIL AVIATION

Eastern Australia Airlines: POB 538, Mascot, Sydney, NSW 2020; tel. (2) 9691-2333; fax (2) 9693-2715; internet www.qantas.com.au; subsidiary of Qantas; domestic flights; Gen. Man. Ashley Kilroy.

Jetstar Airways Pty Ltd: Tullamarine, POB 1503, Melbourne, Vic 3043; tel. (3) 8341-4901; internet www.jetstar.com.au; f. 2004; owned by Qantas Airways Ltd; low-cost domestic passenger service; Chief Exec. Alan Joyce.

National Jet Systems: National Drive, Adelaide Airport, SA 5950; tel. (8) 8154-7000; fax (8) 8154-7019; internet www.nationaljet.com.au; f. 1989; domestic services; Man. Dir Daniela Marsilli; Group Gen. Man. Commdr Robert Birks.

Qantas Airways Ltd: Qantas Centre, 203 Coward St, Mascot, NSW 2020; tel. (2) 9691-3636; fax (2) 9691-3339; internet www.qantas.com; f. 1920 as Queensland and Northern Territory Aerial Services; Australian Govt became sole owner in 1947; merged with Australian Airlines in Sept. 1992; British Airways purchased 25% in March 1993; remaining 75% transferred to private sector in 1995; services throughout Australia and to 36 countries, including destinations in Europe, Africa, the USA, Canada, South America, Asia, the Pacific and New Zealand; Chair. Leigh Clifford; CEO Geoff Dixon.

Sunstate Airlines: Lobby 3, Level 3, 153 Campbell St, Bowen Hills, Qld 4006; tel. (7) 3308-9022; fax (7) 3308-9088; e-mail edalessio@qantas.com.au; f. 1982; wholly owned by Qantas; operates passenger services within Queensland and to Newcastle (NSW) and Lord Howe Island; Gen. Man. Elsa d'Alessio.

Virgin Blue: Centenary Place, Level 7, 100 Wickham St, Brisbane, Qld; tel. (7) 3295-3000; e-mail customercare@virginblue.com.au; internet www.virginblue.com.au; domestic services; CEO Brett Godfrey.

AUSTRALIA

Tourism

The main attractions are the cosmopolitan cities, the Great Barrier Reef, the Blue Mountains, water sports and also winter sports in the Australian Alps, notably the Snowy Mountains. The town of Alice Springs, the Aboriginal culture and the sandstone monolith of Ayers Rock (Uluru) are among the attractions of the desert interior. Much of Australia's wildlife is unique to the country. Australia received more than 5.6m. foreign visitors in 2007. New Zealand, the United Kingdom, Japan, the USA and the People's Republic of China are the principal sources of visitors. Receipts from tourism totalled $A18,257m. in 2004/05.

Tourism Australia: GPOB 2721, Sydney, NSW 2001; tel. (2) 9360-1111; fax (2) 9331-6469; internet www.tourism.australia.com; f. 2004; government authority responsible for marketing of international and domestic tourism; Chair. RICK ALLERT; Man. Dir GEOFF BUCKLEY.

AUSTRALIAN EXTERNAL TERRITORIES
CHRISTMAS ISLAND

Introduction

Christmas Island lies 360 km south of Java Head (Indonesia) in the Indian Ocean. The nearest point on the Australian coast is North West Cape, 1,408 km to the south-east. Christmas Island has no indigenous population. The population was 1,508 at the 2001 census (compared with 1,906 in 1996), comprising mainly ethnic Chinese (some 70%), but there were large minorities of Malays (about 10%) and Europeans (about 20%). A variety of languages are spoken (more than 60% of the population spoke a language other than English in 2001), but English is the official language. The predominant religious affiliation is Buddhist (30% in 2006). The principal settlement and only anchorage is Flying Fish Cove.

Following annexation by the United Kingdom in 1888, Christmas Island was incorporated for administrative purposes with the Straits Settlements (now Singapore and part of Malaysia) in 1900. Japanese forces occupied the island from March 1942 until the end of the Second World War, and in 1946 Christmas Island became a dependency of Singapore. Administration was transferred to the United Kingdom on 1 January 1958, pending final transfer to Australia, effected on 1 October 1958. The Australian Government appointed Official Representatives to the Territory until 1968, when new legislation provided for an Administrator, appointed by the Governor-General. Responsibility for administration lies with the Attorney-General. In 1980 an Advisory Council was established for the Administrator to consult. In 1984 the Christmas Island Services Corporation was created to perform those functions that are normally the responsibility of municipal government. This body was placed under the direction of the Christmas Island Assembly, the first elections to which took place in September 1985. Nine members were elected for one-year terms. In November 1987 the Assembly was dissolved, and the Administrator empowered to perform its functions. The Corporation was superseded by the Christmas Island Shire Council in 1992.

In May 1994 an unofficial referendum on the island's status was held concurrently with local government elections. At the poll, sponsored by the Union of Christmas Island Workers, the islanders rejected an option to secede from Australia, but more than 85% of voters favoured increased local government control. The referendum was prompted, in part, by the Australian Government's plans to abolish the island's duty-free status (which had become a considerable source of revenue).

Since 1981 all residents of the island have been eligible to acquire Australian citizenship. In 1984 the Australian Government extended social security, health and education benefits to the island, and enfranchised Australian citizens resident there. Full income-tax liability was introduced in the late 1980s.

During the late 1990s an increasing number of illegal immigrants travelling to Australia landed on Christmas Island. In January 2001 Australian government officials denied claims by Christmas Islanders that some 86 illegal immigrants who had arrived at the island from the Middle East via Indonesia were being detained in inhumane conditions. Local people claimed that the detainees were sleeping on concrete floors and were being denied adequate food and medical care.

International attention was focused on Christmas Island in August 2001 when the *MV Tampa*, a Norwegian container ship carrying 433 refugees whom it had rescued from a sinking Indonesian fishing boat, was refused permission to land on the island. As the humanitarian crisis escalated, the Australian Government's steadfast refusal to admit the mostly Afghan refugees prompted international condemnation and led to a serious diplomatic dispute between Australia and Norway. The office of the UN High Commissioner for Refugees (UNHCR) and the International Organization for Migration (IOM) expressed grave concern at the situation. Hundreds of Christmas Island residents attended a rally urging the Australian Government to reconsider its uncompromising stance. In September the refugees were transferred (via Papua New Guinea and New Zealand) to Nauru, where their applications for asylum were to be processed. In the same month the Senate in Canberra approved new legislation, which excised Christmas Island and other outlying territories from Australia's official migration zone. The new legislation also imposed stricter criteria for the processing of asylum-seekers and the removal of their right to recourse to the Australian court system. Meanwhile, increasing numbers of asylum-seekers continued to attempt to reach Christmas Island via Indonesia. Among the many controversial incidents that occurred in the waters of Christmas Island in September–December 2001 was that of 186 Iraqis who jumped into the sea when ordered to leave Australian waters in October. They were temporarily housed on Christmas Island before being transferred to Nauru. According to Australian Immigration Department figures, 146 asylum-seekers were turned away from Christmas Island and Ashmore Reef in December 2001. In January 2002 211 asylum-seekers remained on Christmas Island awaiting transferral. In March the Government announced plans to establish a permanent detention centre on the island, the construction of which was expected to cost more than $A150m. The Government was thus preparing to accommodate an anticipated total of 18,000 illegal immigrants who were expected to arrive at Christmas Island during 2002–06. However, plans to scale down the project were announced in February 2003. In July of that year a boat carrying 53 asylum-seekers from Viet Nam was intercepted in Australian waters (the first such vessel to be found in the region since 2001), and its passengers were transferred to Christmas Island. In mid-2005 a total of 32 asylum-seekers remained in the Territory. Some 42 Indonesian refugees from Papua province arrived at Christmas Island in January 2006. They were granted temporary visas in March, while awaiting transfer to the Australian city of Melbourne. The construction of the 800-bed detention centre began in February 2005; some 100 construction workers were engaged on the project, which was expected to be completed during 2007. Speculation among certain observers that the Australian Government intended to use the completed centre as a military base for US forces was dismissed by official sources. However, the islanders became increasingly suspicious of the Government's intentions, particularly when unofficial information began to circulate that the building specifications of the project were similar to those used in high-security military facilities, such as those used to detain terrorists. The Australian Immigration Department would confirm only that it would be a modern detention facility. By late 2007 the estimated cost had reportedly increased to $A396m.; the centre opened in early 2008. Meanwhile, in February 2007 more than 80 Sri Lankan refugees, en route from Indonesia, were intercepted by a ship of the Australian navy and detained on Christmas Island, prior to being transferred to Nauru.

In January 2005 the President of the island's Chamber of Commerce offered to provide refuge on Christmas Island for up to 1,500 victims of the recent tsunami in the Indian Ocean. It was suggested that, as Christmas Island had numerous unused buildings, including a defunct casino resort (see below), plentiful supplies of clean water and strong links with South-East Asia, it would be an ideal haven for the victims, and would also be beneficial to the local economy. The Australian Government, however, did not support the proposals.

The health implications of the United Kingdom's nuclear experiments on Christmas Island in the 1950s were brought to the fore in 2007. Some 700 former military service personnel from the United Kingdom, Fiji and New Zealand instigated legal action against the British Government in an attempt to gain compensation for the significant deterioration in health that had allegedly resulted from their presence at the nuclear tests carried out on Christmas Island during the period of the Territory's administration by the United Kingdom. A parliamentary inquiry into the possibility of a link opened in the United Kingdom in October 2007.

The economy has been based on the recovery of phosphates. During the year ending 30 June 1984 about 463,000 metric tons were exported to Australia, 332,000 tons to New Zealand and 341,000 tons to other countries. Reserves were estimated to be sufficient to enable production to be maintained until the mid-1990s. In November 1987 the Australian Government announced the closure of the phosphate mine, owing to industrial unrest, and mining activity ceased in December. In 1990, however, the Government allowed private operators to recommence phosphate extraction, subject to certain conditions such as the preservation of the rainforest. A total of 220,000 metric tons of phosphates were produced in 1995. In 2001 the mine employed some 180 workers and contributed an estimated 16% to the Territory's economy as a whole. The owner of the mine, Phosphate Resources Ltd (trading as Christmas Island Phosphates), was thus the island's largest employer. A total of 570,000 metric tons of phosphate dust were exported in 2001/02, and phosphate exports were worth $A43.8m. in 1997/98. A new 21-year lease, drawn up by the Government and Phosphate Resources Ltd, took effect in February 1998. The agreement incorporated environmental safeguards and provided for a conservation levy, based on the tonnage of phosphate shipped, which was to finance a programme of rainforest rehabilitation. In mid-2007 Phosphate Resources instigated a legal challenge against the federal Government's refusal to allow access to nine areas of vacant land on Christmas Island. The company argued that, if these new leases were not granted, it would be obliged to cease its mining operations, thus jeopardizing 200 jobs and the island's entire economy.

The services sector engaged 65% of the employed labour force, according to the census of 2001. In that year the rate of unemployment was 8% of the workforce. Efforts have been made to develop the island's considerable potential for tourism. In 1989, in an attempt to protect the natural environment and many rare species of flora and fauna (including the Abbott's Booby and the Christmas frigate bird), the National Park was extended to cover some 70% of the island. A hotel and casino complex, covering 47 ha of land, was opened in November 1993. In 1994 revenue from the development totalled $A500m. A 50-room extension to the complex was constructed in 1995. In early 1997, however, fears for the nascent industry were expressed, following the decision by Ansett Australia to discontinue its twice-weekly air service to the island from September of that year. Despite the subsequent commencement of a weekly flight from Perth, Australia, operated by National Jet Systems, the complex was closed down in April 1998 and some 350 employees were made redundant. In July the resort's casino licence was cancelled and a liquidator was appointed to realize the complex's assets. The closure of the resort had serious economic and social repercussions for the island. An audit of tourist accommodation, conducted in May 2000, counted approximately 140 beds on the island. Only 60 visitors arrived on the island from overseas in 2001, according to official Australian figures. In August 2004 South Korean investors, willing to spend $A30m. on reopening the casino complex, met the Australian Minister for Territories. However, despite the strong support of a majority of islanders, who believed that the resort would regenerate the tourist industry and provide much-needed revenue, the Australian Government stated its opposition to the proposal. The decision prompted some islanders to protest outside the Australian administration offices.

Between 1992 and 1999 the Australian Government invested an estimated $A110m. in the development of Christmas Island's infrastructure as part of the Christmas Island Rebuilding Programme. The main areas of expenditure under this programme were a new hospital, the upgrading of ports facilities, school extensions, the construction of housing, power, water supply and sewerage, and the repair and construction of roads. In 2000 further improvements to marine facilities and water supply were carried out, in addition to the construction of new housing to relocate islanders away from a major rockfall risk area. In mid-2001 the Australian Government pledged a total of more than $A50m. for further developments including improvements to the airport and the road network, as well as an alternative port. The proposed additional port was to be constructed on the east coast of the island, allowing for the handling of sea freight and the launching of emergency vessels at times when the existing port at Flying Fish Cove is closed owing to north-west swells. These closures, which most commonly occur between December and March, had resulted in inflated costs for shipping companies and inconvenience for Christmas Islanders. The Australian Government announced in April 2004 that it would provide $A2.5m. to fund a new mobile telephone network for the Territory. It was hoped that enhanced communications would facilitate new business prospects for the island. The cost of the island's imports from Australia increased from $A13m. in 1998/99 to $A17m. in 1999/2000 and declined to $A16m. in 2000/01, when the Territory's exports to that country earned $A7m. In 1998/99 imports from New Zealand cost $NZ9m. Christmas Island purchased no imports from New Zealand in 2000/01, but exports to that country in the same year were worth $NZ4m. The 2007/08 budget envisaged operating revenue of $A6.4m. and expenditure of $A7.4m. Capital expenditure was projected at almost $A2.2.m. The 2001 census recorded 8.1% of the total labour force as being unemployed, compared with an estimated 7.5% in 1996.

Proposals for the development of a communications satellite launching facility on the island were under consideration in 1998. Christmas Island was chosen as a suitable site because of its proximity to the equator, which enables launch vehicles to lift heavier loads at no extra cost, compared with locations further from the equator. An assessment of the environmental impact was subsequently undertaken, and the scheme received government approval in May 2000. Following an agreement between the Governments of Australia and Russia in May 2001, preparations for the establishment of a space control centre on Christmas Island commenced. Australia and Russia were to contribute towards the project, the total cost of which was expected to be US $425m. The Christmas Island site was to be developed by the Asia Pacific Space Centre, an Australian company. The space centre was expected to become the world's first wholly privately owned land-based launch facility, with an operational lifespan of 15–20 years. Asia Pacific planned to launch 10–12 satellites annually. It was envisaged that the project would create many employment opportunities on the island (an estimated 400 new jobs during construction and 550 during operation) and lead to substantial infrastructural improvements, including the upgrading of airport and road facilities and the construction of a port on the east coast. However, environmentalists continued to express various concerns, in particular the potential impact of rocket launches on nesting seabirds. The project was subsequently delayed, and in mid-2007 the Australian Government threatened to withdraw its financial commitment of $A100m.

Statistical Survey

AREA AND POPULATION

Area: 136.7 sq km (52.8 sq miles).

Population: 1,508 at census of 7 August 2001; 1,349 (males 764, females 585) at census of 8 August 2006.

Density (August 2006): 9.9 per sq km.

Country of Birth (2006 census): Australia 609; Malaysia 412; United Kingdom 41; Singapore 39; Indonesia 21; New Zealand 20.

Births and Deaths (1985): Registered live births 36 (birth rate 15.8 per 1,000); Registered deaths 2.

Economically Active Population (persons aged 15 years and over, excl. overseas visitors, 2001 census): Agriculture, forestry and fishing 3; Mining 127; Manufacturing 9; Electricity, gas and water 21; Construction 71; Wholesale and retail trade, restaurants and hotels 100; Transport, storage and communications 44; Financing, insurance, real estate and business services 42; Government administration and defence 75; Community, social and personal services 148; Activities not stated or not adequately defined 29; *Total employed* 669 (males 442, females 227); Unemployed 59 (males 35, females 24); *Total labour force* 727 (males 482, females 245).

MINING

Natural Phosphates ('000 metric tons, official estimates): 285 in 1994; 220 in 1995.

FINANCE

Currency and Exchange Rates: Australian currency is used.

Budget ($A, year ending 30 June 2008, forecasts): Operating revenue 6,441,151 (General purpose funding 3,730,626; Welfare 127,500; Community amenities 327,608; Recreation and culture 977,250; Transport 1,040,075); Operating expenditure 7,405,511 (Governance 487,145; Law and order and public safety 152,580; Health 155,507; Welfare 401,498; Housing 149,103; Community amenities 847,458; Recreation and culture 2,141,249; Transport 2,818,815); Capital expenditure 2,152,021 (Welfare 40,000; Community amenities 307,027; Recreation and culture 362,060; Transport 1,326,934).

EXTERNAL TRADE

Principal Trading Partners (phosphate exports, '000 metric tons, year ending 30 June 1984): Australia 463; New Zealand 332; Total (incl. others) 1,136.

2000/01 ($A million): *Imports:* Australia 16. *Exports:* Australia 7. Source: Australian Bureau of Statistics, *Year Book Australia*.

2000/01 ($NZ million): *Exports:* New Zealand 4. Source: Ministry of Foreign Affairs and Trade, New Zealand.

TRANSPORT

International Sea-borne Shipping (estimated freight traffic, '000 metric tons, 1990): Goods loaded 1,290; Goods unloaded 68. Source: UN, *Monthly Bulletin of Statistics*.

TOURISM

Visitor Arrivals and Departures by Air: 14,513 in 1996; 3,895 in 1997; 2,712 in 1998. Source: *Year Book Australia*.

COMMUNICATIONS MEDIA

Radio Receivers (1997): 1,000 in use.

Television Receivers (per 1,000 population, 2004): 1,385.

Personal Computers (home users, 2001 census): 506.

Internet Users (2001 census): 464.

EDUCATION

Pre-primary (2005): 45 pupils.

Primary (2005): 192 pupils.

Secondary (2005): 129 pupils.

Source: Education Department of Western Australia.

AUSTRALIAN EXTERNAL TERRITORIES

Directory

The Government

The Administrator, appointed by the Governor-General of Australia and responsible to the Attorney-General, is the senior government representative on the island.

Administrator: NEIL LUCAS (non-resident).
Attorney-General's Department: c/o Department for Infrastructure, Transport, Regional Development and Local Government, POB 868, Christmas Island 6798, Indian Ocean; tel. (8) 9164-7901; fax (8) 9164-8245.
Shire of Christmas Island: George Fam Centre, POB 863, Christmas Island 6798, Indian Ocean; tel. (8) 9164-8300; fax (8) 9164-8304; e-mail chew@shire.gov.cx; internet www.christmas.shire.gov.cx; Community Services Man. CHEW BOON BENG; Pres. GORDON THOMSON.

Judicial System

The judicial system comprises the Supreme Court, District Court, Magistrate's Court and Children's Court.

Supreme Court
C/o Govt Offices, Christmas Island 6798, Indian Ocean; tel. (8) 9164-7911; fax (8) 9164-8530.
Judges (non-resident): ROBERT SHENTON FRENCH, MALCOLM CAMERON LEE.
Managing Registrar: JEFFREY LOW, Govt Offices, Christmas Island 6798, Indian Ocean; tel. (8) 9164-7901; fax (8) 9164-8530; e-mail jeffrey.low@dotars.gov.cx.

Religion

According to the census of 2006, a total of 407 (some 30%) Christmas Island residents were Buddhists, 266 (20%) were Muslims and 238 (18%) were Christians, of whom 157 were Roman Catholics and 81 were Anglicans. Within the Christian churches, Christmas Island lies in the jurisdiction of both the Anglican and Roman Catholic Archbishops of Perth, in Western Australia.

The Press

The Islander: Shire of Christmas Island, George Fam Centre, POB 863, Christmas Island 6798, Indian Ocean; tel. (8) 9164-8300; fax (8) 9164-8304; e-mail chong@shire.gov.cx; newsletter; fortnightly; Editor M. G. CHONG.

Broadcasting and Communications

BROADCASTING

Radio
Christmas Island Community Radio Service: f. 1967; operated by the Administration since 1991; daily broadcasting service by Radio VLU-2 on 1422 KHz and 102 MHz FM, in English, Malay, Cantonese and Mandarin; Station Man. WILLIAM TAYLOR.
Christmas Island Radio VLU2–FM: POB 474, Christmas Island 6798, Indian Ocean; tel. (8) 9164-8316; fax (8) 9164-8315; daily broadcasts on 102.1FM and 105.3FM in English, Malay, Cantonese and Mandarin; Chair. and Station Man. TONY SMITH.

Television
Christmas Island Television: POB AAA, Christmas Island 6798, Indian Ocean.

Finance

BANKING

Commercial Bank
Westpac Banking Corpn (Australia): Flying Fish Cove, Christmas Island, Indian Ocean; tel. (8) 9164-8221; fax (8) 9164-8241.

Trade and Industry

In April 2001 there were 67 small businesses in operation.
Administration of Christmas Island: POB 868, Christmas Island 6798, Indian Ocean; tel. (8) 9164-7901; fax (8) 9164-8245; operates power, public housing, local courts; Dir of Finance JEFFERY TAN.
Christmas Island Chamber of Commerce: POB 510, Christmas Island 6798, Indian Ocean; tel. (8) 9164-8856; fax (8) 9164-8322; e-mail info@cicommerce.org.cx; Pres. JOHN RICHARDSON; Vice-Pres. PHILLIP OAKLEY.
Shire of Christmas Island: George Fam Centre, POB 863, Christmas Island 6798, Indian Ocean; tel. (8) 9164-8300; fax (8) 9164-8304; e-mail margaret@shire.gov.cx; internet www.shire.gov.cx; f. 1992; est. by Territories Law Reform Act to replace Christmas Island Services Corpn; provides local govt services; manages tourism and economic development; CEO MARGARET ROBINSON.
Union of Christmas Island Workers (UCIW): Poon Saan Rd, POB 84, Christmas Island 6798, Indian Ocean; tel. (8) 9164-8471; fax (8) 9164-8470; e-mail uciw@pulau.cx; fmrly represented phosphate workers; Pres. FOO KEE HENG; Gen. Sec. GORDON THOMSON.

Transport

There are good roads in the developed areas. National Jet Systems operate a twice-weekly flight from Perth, via the Cocos (Keeling) Islands, and a private Christmas Island-based charter company operates services to Jakarta, Indonesia. In 1998 arrivals and departures by air in Christmas Island totalled 2,712 (compared with 3,895 in the previous year). The Australian National Line (ANL) operates ships to the Australian mainland. Cargo vessels from Fremantle deliver supplies to the island every four to six weeks. The Joint Island Supply System, established in 1989, provides a shipping service for Christmas Island and the Cocos Islands. The only anchorage is at Flying Fish Cove.

Tourism

Tourism has the potential to be an important sector of the island's economy. Visitors are attracted by the unique flora and fauna, much of which is found in the national park, which covers 63% of the island and contains large tracts of rainforest, as well as the waterfalls, beaches, coves and excellent conditions for scuba-diving and game-fishing. In 2000 there were approximately 90 hotel rooms on the island. The industry however, had been severely affected by the closure of the island's casino (one of the most profitable in the world) in 1998. Attempts by local business people to reopen the casino and its resort in 2004 were unsuccessful.
Christmas Island Tourism Association/Christmas Island Visitor Information Centre: POB 63, Christmas Island 6798, Indian Ocean; tel. (8) 9164-8382; fax (8) 9164-8080; e-mail cita@christmas.net.au; internet www.christmas.net.au.
Christmas Island Travel: Christmas Island 6798, Indian Ocean; tel. (8) 9164-7168; fax (8) 9164-7169; e-mail xch@citravel.com.au; internet www.citravel.com.au; Dir TAN SIM KIAT.
Island Bound Holidays: tel. (8) 9381-3644; fax (8) 9381 2030; e-mail info@islandbound.com.au.
Parks Australia: POB 867, Christmas Island 6798, Indian Ocean; tel. (8) 9164-8055; fax (8) 9164-8755; internet www.deh.gov.au/pa.

COCOS (KEELING) ISLANDS

Introduction

The Cocos (Keeling) Islands are 27 in number and lie 2,768 km north-west of Perth, in the Indian Ocean. The islands, with a combined area of 14 sq km (5.4 sq miles), form two low-lying coral atolls, densely covered with coconut palms. The climate is equable, with temperatures varying from 21°C (69°F) to 32°C (88°F), and rainfall of 2,000 mm per year. In 1981 some 58% of the population were of the Cocos Malay community, and 26% were Europeans. The Cocos Malays are descendants of the people brought to the islands by Alexander Hare and of labourers who were subsequently introduced by the Clunies-Ross family (see below). English is the official language, but Cocos Malay and Malay are also widely spoken. Most of the inhabitants are Muslims (75% in 2006). Home Island, which had a population of 446 in mid-1992, is where the Cocos Malay community is based. The only other inhabited island is West Island, with a population of 147 in mid-1992 and where most of the European community lives, the administration is based and the airport is located. The West Island population is composed mainly of the mainland-based employees of various government departments and their families. The total population of the islands was 621 at the census of both 1998 and August 2001, decreasing to 572 at the census of August 2006.

The islands were uninhabited when discovered by Capt. William Keeling, of the British East India Company, in 1609, and the first settlement was not established until 1826, by Alexander Hare. The islands were declared a British possession in 1857 and came successively under the authority of the Governors of Ceylon (now Sri Lanka), from 1878, and the Straits Settlements (now Singapore and part of Malaysia), from 1886. Also in 1886 the British Crown granted all land on the islands above the high-water mark to John Clunies-Ross and his heirs and successors in perpetuity. In 1946, when the islands became a dependency of the Colony of Singapore, a resident administrator, responsible to the Governor of Singapore, was appointed. Administration of the islands was transferred to the Commonwealth of Australia on 23 November 1955. The agent of the Australian Government was known as the Official Representative until 1975, when an Administrator was appointed. The Attorney-General is responsible for the governance of the islands. The Territory is part of the Northern Territory Electoral District.

In June 1977 the Australian Government announced new policies concerning the islands, which resulted in its purchase from John Clunies-Ross of the whole of his interests in the islands, with the exception of his residence and associated buildings. The purchase for $A6.5m. took effect on 1 September 1978. An attempt by the Australian Government to acquire Clunies-Ross' remaining property was deemed by the Australian High Court in October 1984 to be unconstitutional.

In July 1979 the Cocos (Keeling) Islands Council was established, with a wide range of functions in the Home Island village area (which the Government transferred to the Council on trust for the benefit of the Cocos Malay community) and, from September 1984, in most of the rest of the Territory.

On 6 April 1984 a referendum to decide the future political status of the islands was held by the Australian Government, with UN observers present. A large majority voted in favour of integration with Australia. As a result, the islanders were to acquire the rights, privileges and obligations of all Australian citizens. In July 1992 the Cocos (Keeling) Islands Council was replaced by the Cocos (Keeling) Islands Shire Council, composed of seven members and modelled on the local government and state law of Western Australia. The first Shire Council was elected in 1993. The Clunies-Ross family was declared bankrupt in mid-1993, following unsuccessful investment in a shipping venture, and the Australian Government took possession of its property.

In September 2001, following an increase in the numbers of illegal immigrants reaching Australian waters (see the section on Christmas Island), legislation was enacted removing the Cocos Islands and other territories from Australia's official migration zone. In October of that year the Australian Government sent contingency supplies to the islands as a precaution, should it be necessary to accommodate more asylum-seekers. This development provoked concern among many Cocos residents that the former quarantine station used as a detention centre might become a permanent asylum-processing facility under the order of the Australian Government. In December 123 Sri Lankan and Vietnamese asylum-seekers were housed at the station, which was built to accommodate only 40. They were transferred to Christmas Island in February 2002. The Government admitted that the establishment of an asylum-processing facility on Cocos might become necessary.

Although local fishing is good, some livestock is kept, and domestic gardens provide vegetables, bananas and papayas (pawpaws), the islands are not self-sufficient, and other foodstuffs, fuels and consumer items are imported from mainland Australia. Coconuts, grown throughout the islands, are the sole cash crop: total output was an estimated 7,600 metric tons in 2006, with copra production being estimated at 1,000 tons. In 2001/02 the Administration and the Shire provided support for a study investigating the potential economic benefits of various coconut products, including the production of high-quality carbon from coconut kernels and the manufacture of furniture from coconut palm wood. A clam farm was established in 2000. A Cocos postal service (including a philatelic bureau) came into operation in September 1979, and revenue from the service is used for the benefit of the community. In early 2000 the islands' internet domain name suffix, '.cc', was sold to Clear Channel, a US radio group, thus providing additional revenue. In October 2003 a ship carrying 52,000 Australian sheep was diverted to the Cocos Islands, having been refused entry in Saudi Arabia, where inspectors claimed to have found high levels of disease among the animals. Many islanders expressed concern over the arrangement and the Territory's lack of facilities to deal with the situation.

The islands have a small tourist industry. During August, September and October 2003 there were a total of 76 non-resident arrivals, of whom 28 were travelling on business and 19 were visiting relatives. Some controversy arose in July 2004 when it was revealed that the Australian Government had drawn up plans to develop a resort on the Cocos Islands without undertaking any consultation with the islanders.

The cost of the islands' imports from Australia increased from $A5m. in 1999/2000 to $A11m. in 2000/01. Exports to Australia totalled $A2m. in 1996/97, but by 2002 the Cocos Islands no longer exported any goods or produce. The Grants Commission estimated that the Australian Government's net funding of the Territory amounted to some $A18m. in 1999. In 2000/01 the Cocos Administration expended approximately $A9m. An estimated 19% of the total labour force was unemployed in 2001, 60% of whom were under the age of 30. The Shire Council and the Co-operative Society were the principal employers.

The Territory is important as a habitat for various species of flora and fauna. In December 1995 a national park (the Pulu Keeling National Park) was designated on North Keeling Island, an isolated island on an atoll 24 km to the north of the main island group, which is renowned for its populations of seabirds. The area has one of the largest breeding colonies of red-footed boobies in the world and is also important for frigate birds, common noddies and white terns, as well as the endangered sub-species the Cocos buff-banded rail. Public access to the Park is strictly controlled.

Statistical Survey

AREA AND POPULATION

Area: 14.1 sq km (5.4 sq miles).

Population: 621 at census of 7 August 2001; 572 (males 274, females 298) at census of 8 August 2006.

Density (August 2006): 40.6 per sq km.

Country of Birth (2006 census): Australia 512; Malaysia 22; Singapore 11; Kenya 3; Netherlands 3.

Births and Deaths (1986): Registered live births 12 (birth rate 19.8 per 1,000); Registered deaths 2.

Economically Active Population (persons aged 15 years and over, excl. overseas visitors, 2001 census): Agriculture, forestry and fishing 3; Mining 3; Manufacturing 6; Electricity, gas and water 7; Construction 24; Wholesale and retail trade, restaurants and hotels 32; Transport, storage and communications 26; Financing, insurance, real estate and business services 32; Government administration and defence 32; Community, social and personal services 47; Activities not stated or not adequately defined 18; *Total employed* 230.

AGRICULTURE

Production (metric tons, 2006, FAO estimate): Coconuts 7,600. Source: FAO.

INDUSTRY

Production (metric tons, 2006, FAO estimates): Copra 1,000; Coconut (copra) oil 650; Source: FAO.

FINANCE

Currency and Exchange Rates: Australian currency is used.

EXTERNAL TRADE

Principal Commodities (metric tons, year ending 30 June 1985): *Exports*: Coconuts 202. *Imports*: Most requirements come from Australia. The trade deficit is offset by philatelic sales and Australian federal grants and subsidies. *2000/01* ($A '000, imports from Australia): 11,000.

Source: *Year Book Australia*.

COMMUNICATIONS MEDIA

Radio Receivers (1992): 300 in use.

Personal Computers (home users, 2001 census): 142.

Internet Users (2001 census): 171.

EDUCATION

Pre-primary (2005): 19 pupils.

Primary (2005): 89 pupils.

Secondary (2005): 25 pupils.

AUSTRALIAN EXTERNAL TERRITORIES

Teaching Staff (2004): 17 (10 primary, 7 secondary).
Source: Education Department of Western Australia.

Directory

The Government

The Administrator, appointed by the Governor-General of Australia and responsible to the Attorney-General, is the senior government representative in the islands.
Administrator: NEIL LUCAS (non-resident).
Administrative Offices: Administration Bldg, Morea Close, Cocos (Keeling) Islands 6799, Indian Ocean; tel. (8) 9162-6600; fax (8) 9162-6691; e-mail cocosadmin@afp.gov.au.
Cocos (Keeling) Islands Shire Council: POB 1094, Home Island, Cocos (Keeling) Islands 6799, Indian Ocean; tel. (8) 9162-6649; fax (8) 9162-6668; e-mail info@shire.cc; internet www.shire.cc; f. 1992 by Territories Law Reform Act; Pres. RONALD GRANT; CEO MICHAEL SIMMS.

Judicial System

Supreme Court, Cocos (Keeling) Islands: c/o Australian Federal Police, Administration Bldg, Morea Close, Cocos (Keeling) Islands 6799, Indian Ocean; tel. (8) 9162-6600; fax (8) 9162-6691; Judge ROBERT SHENTON FRENCH; Additional Judge MALCOLM CAMERON LEE.

Magistrates' Court, Cocos (Keeling) Islands

Managing Registrar: ROBYN JENKINS, Cocos (Keeling) Islands 6799, Indian Ocean; tel. (8) 9162-6615; fax (8) 9162-6697.

Religion

According to the census of 2006, of the 572 residents, 431 (some 75%) were Muslims and 73 (13%) Christians. The majority of Muslims live on Home Island, while most Christians are West Island residents. The Cocos Islands lie within both the Anglican and the Roman Catholic archdioceses of Perth (Western Australia).

Broadcasting and Communications

BROADCASTING
Radio

Radio 6CKI Voice of the Cocos (Keeling) Islands: POB 1084, Cocos (Keeling) Islands 6799, Indian Ocean; tel. and fax (8) 9162-6666; e-mail 6cki@cki.cc; non-commercial; daily broadcasting service in Cocos Malay and English; Chair. KELLY EDWARDS.

Television

A television service, broadcasting Indonesian, Malaysian and Australian satellite television programmes and videotapes of Australian television programmes, began operating on an intermittent basis in September 1992.

Industry

Cocos (Keeling) Islands Co-operative Society Ltd: POB 1058, Home Island, Cocos (Keeling) Islands 6799, Indian Ocean; tel. (8) 9162-6708; fax (8) 9162-6764; e-mail admin@CocosCoOp.com; internet www.cocoscoop.com; f. 1979; conducts the business enterprises of the Cocos Islanders; activities include boat construction and repairs, copra and coconut production, sail-making, stevedoring and airport operation; owns and operates a supermarket and tourist accommodation; Chair. MOHAMMED SAID BIN CHONGKIN; Gen. Man. RONALD TAYLOR.

Transport

National Jet Systems operate a twice-weekly service from Perth, via Christmas Island, for passengers, supplies and mail to and from the airport on West Island. Cargo vessels from Singapore and Perth deliver supplies, at intervals of four to six weeks. The islands have a total of 10 km of sealed and 12 km of unsealed roads.

Cocos Trader: Cocos (Keeling) Islands 6799, Indian Ocean; tel. (8) 9162-6612; fax (8) 9162-6568; e-mail manpower@kampong.cc; shipping agent.

Tourism

Tourism is relatively undeveloped on the Cocos Islands, but has the potential to grow, owing to the islands' pristine beaches and coral reefs, which provide excellent opportunities for scuba-diving and snorkelling, and their unique flora and fauna. During August, September and October 2003 there were a total of 76 visitor arrivals, of whom 28 were travelling on business and 19 were visiting relatives. In 2005 there was one 28-room hotel on West Island and several self-catering villas available to tourists.

Cocos Island Tourism Association: Admiralty House, POB 1030, Cocos (Keeling) Islands 6799, Indian Ocean; tel. (8) 9162-6790; fax (8) 9162-6696; e-mail info@cocos-tourism.cc; internet www.cocos-tourism.cc.

Parks Australia: POB 1043, Cocos (Keeling) Islands 6798, Indian Ocean; tel. (8) 9162-6678; fax (8) 9162-6680; internet www.deh.gov.au/pa.

NORFOLK ISLAND

Introductory Survey

Location, Climate, Language, Religion, Capital

Norfolk Island lies off the eastern coast of Australia, about 1,400 km east of Brisbane, to the south of New Caledonia and 640 km north of New Zealand. The Territory also comprises uninhabited Phillip Island and Nepean Island, 7 km and 1 km south of the main island respectively. Norfolk Island is hilly and fertile, with a coastline of cliffs and an area of 34.6 sq km (13.3 sq miles). It is about 8 km long and 4.8 km wide. The climate is mild and subtropical, and the average annual rainfall is 1,350 mm, most of which occurs between May and August. The resident population, which numbered 1,863 in August 2006, consists of 'islanders' (descendants of the mutineers from HMS *Bounty*, evacuated from Pitcairn Island, who numbered 683 in 1996) and 'mainlanders' (originally from Australia, New Zealand or the United Kingdom). English and Norfuk, which combines elements of a local Polynesian dialect (related to Pitcairnese) and 18th-century English, are the official languages. Most of the population (67% at the 2001 census) adhere to the Christian religion. The capital of the Territory is Kingston.

Recent History

The island was uninhabited when discovered in 1774 by a British expedition, led by Capt. James Cook. Norfolk Island was used as a penal settlement from 1788 to 1814 and again from 1825 to 1855, when it was abandoned. In 1856 it was resettled by 194 emigrants from Pitcairn Island, which had become overpopulated. Norfolk Island was administered as a separate colony until 1897, when it became a dependency of New South Wales. In 1913 control was transferred to the Australian Government. Norfolk Island has a continuing dispute with the Australian Government concerning the island's status as a territory of the Commonwealth of Australia. There have been successive assertions of Norfolk Island's right to self-determination, as a distinct colony.

Under the Commonwealth Norfolk Island Act 1979, Norfolk Island is progressing to responsible legislative and executive government, enabling the Territory to administer its own affairs to the greatest practicable extent. Wide powers are exercised by the nine-member Legislative Assembly and by the Executive Council, comprising the executive members of the Legislative Assembly who have ministerial-type responsibilities. The Act preserves the Australian Government's responsibility for Norfolk Island as a territory under its authority, with the Minister for Infrastructure, Transport, Regional Development and Local Government as the responsible minister. The Act indicated that consideration would be given within five years to an extension of the powers of the Legislative Assembly and the political and administrative institutions of Norfolk Island. In 1985 legislative and executive responsibility was assumed by the Norfolk Island Government for public works and services, civil defence, betting and gaming, territorial archives and matters relating to the exercise of executive authority. In 1988 further amendments empowered the Legislative Assembly to select a Norfolk Island government auditor (territorial accounts were previously audited by the Commonwealth Auditor-General). The office of Chief Minister was replaced by that of the President of the Legislative Assembly. David Ernest Buffett was reappointed to this post following the May 1992 general election. A lack of consensus among members of the Executive Council on several major issues prompted early legislative elections in April 1994. The newly-elected seventh Legislative Assembly was significant in having three female members. Following elections in April 1997, in which 22 candidates contested the nine seats, George Smith was appointed President (subsequently reverting to the title of Chief Minister) of the eighth Legislative Assembly. At legislative elections in February 2000 three new members were elected to the Assembly, and Ronald Nobbs was subsequently appointed Chief Minister. Geoffrey Gardner, hitherto Minister for Health, replaced Nobbs as Chief Minister following the elections of November 2001. The incoming Assembly included four new members.

In December 1991 the population of Norfolk Island overwhelmingly rejected a proposal, made by the Australian Government, to include the island in the Australian federal electorate. The outcome of the poll led the Australian Government, in June 1992, to announce that it had abandoned the plan. Similarly, in late 1996 a proposal by the Australian Government to combine Norfolk Island's population with that of the federal capital of Canberra for record-keeping purposes was strongly opposed by the islanders.

In late 1997 the Legislative Assembly debated the issue of increased self-determination for the island. Pro-independence supporters argued that the Territory could generate sufficient income by exploiting gas- and oilfields in the island's exclusive economic zone.

In August 1998 a referendum proposing that the Norfolk Island electoral system be integrated more closely with that of mainland Australia (initiated in Canberra by the Minister for Regional Development, Territories and Local Government) was rejected by 78% of the Territory's electorate. A similar referendum in May 1999 was opposed by 73% of voters.

Frustration with the Australian Government's perceived reluctance to facilitate the transfer of greater powers to the Territory (as outlined in the Norfolk Island Act of 1979, see above) led the island's Legislative Assembly in mid-1999 to vote by seven members to one in favour of full internal self-government. Negotiations regarding the administration of crown land on the island, which continued in 2000, were seen as indicative of the islanders' determination to pursue greater independence from Australia.

In April 2002 a hotel worker from Sydney, Australia, was murdered. This was the first murder to occur on Norfolk Island in more than 150 years. As part of its investigation, the police force took fingerprints of the entire adult population in August. In July 2003 the Australian authorities stated that they had contacted more than 400 Australian and New Zealand nationals, who were visiting Norfolk Island at the time of the murder, to request fingerprints. In March 2004 the reward for information about the murder was tripled, and in May a further inquest was launched. A New Zealander was found guilty of the murder in March 2007, and sentenced to 24 years' imprisonment in July.

At a referendum held in August 2002 almost two-thirds of those who participated voted not to allow the operation of mobile telephones on the island. Furthermore, in March 2004 the Territory approved legislation to grant a monopoly on satellite internet connections to the government-owned Norfolk Telecom. The legislation, which was expected to put the Territory's private internet service provider, Norfolk Island Data Services, out of business, was criticized by the Australian Government.

Legislation was approved in March 2003 to amend the requirements for voting in Norfolk Island elections. Under the new system Australian, New Zealand and British citizens were to be allowed to vote after a residency period of 12 months (reduced from 900 days). The amendments, which followed a series of occasionally acrimonious discussions with the Australian Government, provoked concern among islanders who feared that succumbing to Australian pressure to reform the Norfolk Island Act would result in the effective removal of authority over electoral matters from island control. Moreover, a report by an Australian parliamentary committee published in July 2003 was critical of Norfolk Island's Government and public services. Many residents believed that the report constituted a further attempt by Australia to undermine their autonomy. The Chief Minister refuted the committee's claims, stating that he would refuse any offers of financial assistance from Canberra or any attempts to introduce income tax in return for access to services from the mainland. A further report by the Australian Government published later in the year alleged that officials on the island used intimidation to achieve political and financial gain and recommended that Norfolk Island's elections, government and financial matters should be overseen by Canberra.

The inhabitants of Norfolk Island were profoundly shocked when the Deputy Chief Minister and long-serving politician, Ivens Buffett, was shot dead in his office in mid-July 2004. A local man was arrested at the scene of the crime, although no motive was immediately apparent for the killing. It was subsequently revealed that the suspect was the politician's son.

A total of 14 candidates contested the legislative election held on 20 October 2004. Geoffrey Gardner, the Chief Minister, regained his seat in the nine-member Legislative Assembly, as did Speaker David Buffett. Two long-serving members, however, were defeated in the poll.

In early 2005 the Legislative Assembly declared Norfuk, the local creole spoken by around one-half of the island's population and described as a hybrid of Tahitian and 18th-century English, as an official language alongside English. The legislature's action was prompted by reports of a decline in the use of the language among islanders. Norfuk was subsequently introduced into the school curriculum on Norfolk Island, its usage having previously been forbidden in schools. In August 2007 the UN placed Norfuk on its list of endangered languages.

In June 2005 the environmental organization Greenpeace released photographic evidence of marine destruction caused by bottom trawling in international waters near Norfolk Island. The organization's claims, which had been repeatedly refuted by the fishing companies involved, were dramatically substantiated by photographs and film of centuries-old, endangered coral trees being removed from trawler nets and dumped in the sea. The New Zealand Government subsequently indicated its support for a UN moratorium on bottom trawler fishing in international waters, including areas such as the West Norfolk Ridge, described as a globally important area of marine biodiversity.

In February 2006, as the island's economy continued to deteriorate, the Australian Government unexpectedly announced that it was to resume responsibility for matters such as immigration, customs and quarantine, claiming that the existing arrangements under the Norfolk Island Act of 1979 had become too complex and costly for a community of the island's size to sustain. Two main alternative options were to be considered: a form of modified self-government that would allow greater powers for involvement by the Australian Government; and a model of local government whereby Australia might assume responsibility for state-type functions. Other options under consideration included the possibility of an island territory government with the power to legislate on local responsibilities. The island's revenue-raising capacities were also to be reviewed, along with the provision of basic services such as health and education. In December 2006, however, following the conclusion of this comprehensive review, it was declared that no restructuring of the system of governance was necessary, an announcement that brought mixed reactions from the people of Norfolk Island. While many in the Territory wished to retain a degree of autonomy, concerns remained over the future sustainability of the island's economy (see Economic Affairs).

In November 2006 a group of Norfolk Islanders challenged the introduction of new electoral laws requiring voters to be citizens of Australia. The group claimed that this did not take into consideration the fact that a proportion of Norfolk Island's adult population did not have Australian citizenship. However, lawyers for the Australian Government dismissed the argument. The group's claim that Norfolk Islanders represented a distinct community, and thus should be considered separately from Australia, was also dismissed as unfounded.

Following the legislative election of 21 March 2007, Andre Nobbs replaced David Buffett as the island's Chief Minister. Neville Christian was replaced as Speaker of the Legislative Assembly by Lisle Snell, but remained as Minister for Finance. Christopher Magri was appointed to the new post of Minister for Commerce and Industry. In October 2007, following Grant Tambling's departure from the post, Owen Walsh was appointed Administrator in an acting capacity.

Economic Affairs

Despite Norfolk Island's natural fertility, agriculture is no longer the principal economic activity. Agriculture and quarrying accounted for only 5.3% of all paid employment in 2001. About 400 ha of land are arable. The main crops are Kentia palm seed, cereals, vegetables and fruit. Cattle and pigs are farmed for domestic consumption. Development of a fisheries industry is restricted by the lack of a harbour. Some flowers and plants are grown commercially. The administration is increasing the area devoted to Norfolk Island pine and hardwoods. Seed and seedlings of the Norfolk Island pine are exported. Potential oil- and gas-bearing sites in the island's waters may provide a possible future source of revenue.

The Government is the most important employer, and there were 151 public sector workers in June 2003. Tourism is the island's main industry, and in 2001 some 28.4% of the employed labour force were engaged in tourism and recreation. A re-export industry has been developed to serve the island's tourist industry. The number of tourist arrivals increased from 28,219 in 2005/06 to 34,318 in 2006/07. The resurfacing of the island's main runway in mid-2005

AUSTRALIAN EXTERNAL TERRITORIES

allowed the airport to accommodate larger aircraft and would, it was hoped, improve the potential for an increase in tourist arrivals. The cessation of operations by the airline linking Norfolk Island with Australia in June 2005 and the initial uncertainty surrounding the establishment of a replacement service, however, illustrated the island's reliance on overseas airlines for the success and continuation of its important tourist industry.

In 2005/06 the cost of the island's imports, purchased mainly from Australia and New Zealand, reached almost $A32.1m., compared with $A41.3m. in 2000/01. Imports from New Zealand totalled $NZ5.9m. and exports to that country earned only $NZ14,000 in 2005/06. In 1999 the Norfolk Island Legislative Assembly announced plans to seek assistance from the Australian Government to establish an offshore financial centre on the island. The authorities receive revenue from customs duties (some $A3.9m., equivalent to 34.3% of total revenue in 2000/01), mail order services and the sale of postage stamps. Departure taxes are another source of government revenue. In mid-2005 it was announced that Norfolk Island was to introduce a 1% goods-and-services tax to raise funds for road projects and health services. The tax, to be known as the Norfolk Sustainability Levy, was to be implemented for an initial six-month trial period from December 2005, which was subsequently extended until the end of 2006. In November 2006 it was announced that the Norfolk Sustainability Levy was to be increased to 9% with effect from 1 January 2007. Following a major review (see Recent History), in December 2006 it was confirmed that Norfolk Island was to remain exempt from federal income taxes. Although the Territory would thus retain its attraction as a tax haven for wealthy individuals, many islanders expressed disappointment at the decision, as they had hoped that this potential source of government revenue might provide support in meeting the high costs of education and health care.

The 2005/06 budget envisaged revenue of almost $A25.0m. and expenditure of nearly $A24.8m. At the end of 2006 it was calculated that a total of $A36m. was required to finance the island's infrastructure but that less than 50% of this sum was available. The island's Government pledged to improve accountability and to continue its programme of economic reforms. Meanwhile, an independent financial assessment had indicated that the Government of Norfolk Island might become insolvent within two years.

In 1985 and 1986 the Governments of Australia and Norfolk Island jointly established the 465-ha Norfolk Island National Park. This was to protect the remaining native forest, which is the habitat of several unique species of flora (including the largest fern in the world) and fauna (such as the Norfolk Island green parrot, the guavabird and the boobook owl). Conservation efforts include the development of Phillip Island as a nature reserve.

Education

Education is free and compulsory for all children between the ages of six and 15. Pupils attend the government school from infant to secondary level. A total of 187 pupils were enrolled at infant and primary levels and 118 at secondary levels in 2002/03. Some 330 pupils were enrolled at all levels in 2005, although pupil numbers are subject to constant fluctuation, owing to the presence of numerous short-term workers and their families in the Territory. Students wishing to follow higher education in Australia are eligible for bursaries and scholarships. The budgetary allocation for education was more than $A2.4m. in 2006/07.

Weights and Measures

The metric system is in force.

Statistical Survey

Source: The Administration of Norfolk Island, Administration Offices, Kingston, Norfolk Island 2899; tel. 22001; fax 23177; internet www.norfolk.gov.nf.

AREA AND POPULATION

Area: 34.6 sq km (13.3 sq miles).

Population: 2,601 (males 1,257, females 1,344), including 564 visitors, at census of 7 August 2001; 2,523 (males 1,218, females 1,305), comprising 1,863 'ordinarily resident' and 660 visitors, at census of 8 August 2006.

Density (2006 census): 72.9 per sq km.

Births, Marriages and Deaths (2005/06, unless otherwise indicated): Live births 22; Marriages 35 (2002/03); Deaths 13.

Employment (ordinarily resident population aged 15 years and over, 2006 census): Agriculture, forestry and fishing 53; Mining and quarrying 13; Manufacturing 30; Electricity, gas and water 37; Construction 104; Wholesale and retail trade 280; Transport and storage 41; Communication 40; Finance, property and business services 49; Public administration and defence 67; Health 59; Education, museum and library services 48; Other community services 28; Restaurants, hotels, accommodation and clubs 206; Other recreational and personal services 97; Activities not stated or not adequately described 31; Total 1,183 (males 604, females 579).

FINANCE

Currency and Exchange Rates: Australian currency is used.

Budget (year ending 30 June 2006): Revenue $A24,965,400; Expenditure $A24,761,100.

Cost of Living (Retail Price Index, average of quarterly figures; base: October–December 1990 = 100): All items 159.7 in 2004; 168.6 in 2005; 181.1 in 2006.

EXTERNAL TRADE

2005/06 (year ending 30 June): *Imports:* $A32,065,392, mainly from Australia and New Zealand.

Trade with Australia ($A million, 2000/01): *Imports* 19.

Trade with New Zealand ($NZ '000, 2005/06): *Imports* 5,946; *Exports* 14.

TOURISM

Visitors (year ending 30 June): 33,742 in 2004/05; 28,219 in 2005/06; 34,318 in 2006/07.

COMMUNICATIONS MEDIA

Radio Receivers (1996): 2,500 in use.

Television Receivers (1996): 1,200 in use.

Telephones (2002/03): 2,374 main lines in use.

Internet Users (2002/03): 494.

Non-daily Newspaper (2002): 1 (estimated circulation 1,400).

EDUCATION

Institution (2003): 1 state school incorporating infant, primary and secondary levels.

Teachers (2004/05): Primary 8; Secondary 12.

Students (1999/2000): Infants 79; Primary 116; Secondary 119.

Directory

The Constitution

The Norfolk Island Act 1979 constitutes the administration of the Territory as a body politic and provides for a responsible legislative and executive system, enabling it to administer its own affairs to the greatest practicable extent. The preamble of the Act states that it is the intention of the Australian Parliament to consider the further extension of powers.

The Act provides for an Administrator, appointed by the Australian Government, who shall administer the government of Norfolk Island as a territory under the authority of the Commonwealth of Australia. The Administrator is required to act on the advice of the Executive Council or the responsible Commonwealth Minister in those matters specified as within their competence. Every proposed law passed by the Legislative Assembly must be effected by the assent of the Administrator, who may grant or withhold that assent, reserve the proposed law for the Governor-General's pleasure or recommend amendments.

The Act provides for the Legislative Assembly and the Executive Council, comprising the executive members of the Assembly who have ministerial-type responsibilities. The nine members of the Legislative Assembly are elected for a term of not more than three years under a cumulative method of voting: each elector is entitled to as many votes (all of equal value) as there are vacancies, but may not give more than four votes to any one candidate. The nine candidates who receive the most votes are declared elected.

The Government

The Administrator, who is the senior representative of the Commonwealth Government, is appointed by the Governor-General of Australia and is responsible to the Minister for Infrastructure, Transport, Regional Development and Local Government. A form of responsible legislative and executive government was extended to the island in 1979, as outlined above.

Administrator: OWEN WALSH (acting).

EXECUTIVE COUNCIL
(April 2008)

Chief Minister: ANDRE N. NOBBS.
Minister for Commerce and Industry: CHRISTOPHER A. C. MAGRI.
Minister for Finance: NEVILLE C. CHRISTIAN.
Minister for Tourism and Health: GEOFFREY GARDNER.
Minister for Environment, Education and Social Welfare: VICKY JACK.

MINISTRIES

All Ministries are located at: Old Military Barracks, Quality Row, Kingston, Norfolk Island 2899; tel. 22003; fax 22624; e-mail executives@assembly.gov.nf; internet www.norfolk.gov.nf; f. 1979.

GOVERNMENT OFFICES

Office of the Administrator: POB 201, New Military Barracks, Norfolk Island 2899; tel. 22152; fax 22681.

Administration of Norfolk Island: Administration Offices, Kingston, Norfolk Island 2899; tel. 22001; fax 23177; e-mail records@admin.gov.nf; internet www.norfolkisland.gov.nf; all govt depts; CEO RHONDA WHEATLEY.

Legislature

LEGISLATIVE ASSEMBLY

Nine candidates are elected for not more than three years. The most recent general election was held on 21 March 2007.

Speaker: LISLE SNELL.
Deputy Speaker: TIMOTHY J. SHERIDAN.
Other Members: ANDRE N. NOBBS, GEOFFREY R. GARDNER, CHRISTOPHER A. C. MAGRI, BRENDON A. CHRISTIAN, VICKY JACK, NEVILLE CHRISTIAN, IAN R. M. ANDERSON.

Judicial System

Supreme Court of Norfolk Island

Kingston.
Appeals lie to the Federal Court of Australia.
Chief Magistrate: RON CAHILL.
Judges: MARK SAMUEL WEINBERG (Chief Justice), PETER MICHAEL JACOBSON, SUSAN MARY KIEFEL.

Religion

The majority of the population professes Christianity (66.6%, according to the census of 2001), with the principal denominations being the Church of England (34.9%), the Roman Catholic Church (11.7%) and the Uniting Church (11.2%).

The Press

Norfolk Island Government Gazette: Kingston, Norfolk Island 2899; tel. 22001; fax 23177; internet www.info.gov.nf; weekly.

Norfolk Islander: Greenways Press, POB 150, Norfolk Island 2899; tel. 22159; fax 22948; e-mail news@islander.nf; f. 1965; weekly; Co-Editors TOM LLOYD, TIM LLOYD; circ. 1,350.

Broadcasting and Communications

TELECOMMUNICATIONS

Norfolk Telecom: New Cascade Rd, Kingston; e-mail kim@telecom.gov.nf; internet www.telecom.gov.nf; Man. KIM DAVIES.

BROADCASTING

Radio

Norfolk Island Broadcasting Service: New Cascade Rd, POB 456, Norfolk Island 2899; tel. 22137; fax 23298; e-mail manager@radio.gov.nf; internet www.norfolk.gov.nf/VL2NI.htm; govt-owned; non-commercial; broadcasts seven days per week; relays television and radio programmes from Australia and New Zealand; Broadcast Man. GEORGE SMITH.

Radio Norfolk: New Cascade Rd, POB 456, Norfolk Island 2899; tel. 22137; fax 23298; e-mail norfolk@radio.gov.nf; internet www.norfolk.gov.nf/VL2NI.htm; f. 1950s; govt-owned; Man. GEORGE SMITH.

Television

Norfolk Island Broadcasting Service: see Radio**Norfolk Island Television Service:** f. 1987; govt-owned; relays programmes of Australian Broadcasting Corpn, Special Broadcasting Service Corpn and Central Seven TV by satellite.

TV Norfolk (TVN): locally operated service featuring programmes of local events and information for tourists.

Finance

BANKING

Commonwealth Bank of Australia (Australia): Taylors Rd, Norfolk Island 2899; tel. 22144; fax 22805.

Westpac Banking Corpn Savings Bank Ltd (Australia): Burnt Pine, Norfolk Island 2899; tel. 22120; fax 22808.

Trade

Norfolk Island Chamber of Commerce Inc: POB 370, Norfolk Island 2899; tel. 22317; fax 23221; e-mail photopress@ni.net.nf; f. 1966; affiliated to the Australian Chamber of Commerce and Industry; 60 mems; Pres. GARY ROBERTSON; Sec. MARK MCGUIRE.

Norfolk Island Gaming Authority: POB 882, Norfolk Island 2899; tel. 22002; fax 22205; e-mail secgameauth@norfolk.net.nf; internet www.gamingauthority.nlk.nf; Dir KEVIN LEYSHON.

Transport

ROADS

There are some 53 km of paved roads and 27 km of unpaved roads.

SHIPPING

Norfolk Island is served by the three shipping lines, Neptune Shipping, Pacific Direct Line and Roslyndale Shipping Company Pty Ltd. A small tanker from Nouméa (New Caledonia) delivers petroleum products to the island and another from Australia delivers liquid propane gas.

CIVIL AVIATION

Norfolk Island has one airport, with two runways (of 2,437 m and 1,524 m), capable of taking medium-sized jet-engined aircraft. In 2005 work began to resurface the main runway (at a cost of $A12m.) in order to accommodate larger aircraft. In early 2008 Norfolk Air was operating services to Brisbane, Sydney, Melbourne and Newcastle, while Air New Zealand provided a twice-weekly service from Auckland. In April 2008 it was announced that Our Airline (formerly Air Nauru) was to resume its service to Norfolk Island, in a joint operation with Norfolk Air.

Norfolk Air: POB 475, Norfolk Island 2899; internet www.norfolkair.com; operated by Norfolk Island govt; CEO EWAN WILSON.

Tourism

Visitor arrivals totalled 34,318 in 2006/07, the majority of whom came from Australia. In 2002/03 tourist accommodation totalled 1,551 beds.

Norfolk Island Tourism: Taylors Rd, Burnt Pine, POB 211, Norfolk Island 2899; tel. 22147; fax 23109; internet www.norfolkisland.com.au; Chair. MARION CHRISTIAN; Gen. Man. TERRY WATSON.

Other Australian Territories

Ashmore and Cartier Islands

The Ashmore Islands (known as West, Middle and East Islands) and Cartier Island are situated in the Timor Sea, about 850 km and 790 km west of Darwin respectively. The Ashmore Islands cover some 93 ha of land and Cartier Island covers 0.4 ha. The islands are small and uninhabited, consisting of sand and coral, surrounded by shoals and reefs. Grass is the main vegetation. Maximum elevation is about 2.5 m above sea-level. The islands abound in birdlife, sea-cucumbers (bêches-de-mer) and, seasonally, turtles.

The United Kingdom took formal possession of the Ashmore Islands in 1878, and Cartier Island was annexed in 1909. The islands were placed under the authority of the Commonwealth of Australia in 1931. They were annexed to, and deemed to form part of, the Northern Territory of Australia in 1938. On 1 July 1978 the Australian Government assumed direct responsibility for the administration of the islands; this rests with a parliamentary secretary appointed by the Attorney-General. Periodic visits are made to the islands by the Royal Australian Navy and aircraft of the Royal Australian Air Force, and the Civil Coastal Surveillance Service makes aerial surveys of the islands and neighbouring waters. The oilfields of Jabiru and Challis are located in waters adjacent to the Territory.

In August 1983 Ashmore Reef was declared a national nature reserve. An agreement between Australia and Indonesia permits Indonesian traditional fishermen to continue fishing in the territorial waters and to land on West Island to obtain supplies of fresh water. In 1985 the Australian Government extended the laws of the Northern Territory to apply in Ashmore and Cartier, and decided to contract a vessel to be stationed at Ashmore Reef during the Indonesian fishing season (March–November) to monitor the fishermen.

During 2000–01 increasing numbers of refugees and asylum-seekers attempted to land at Ashmore Reef, hoping to gain residency in Australia. The majority had travelled from the Middle East via Indonesia, where the illegal transport of people was widespread. Consequently, in late 2000 a vessel with the capacity to transport up to 150 people was chartered to ferry unauthorized arrivals to the Australian mainland. In September 2001 the Australian Government introduced an item of legislation to Parliament excising Ashmore Reef and other outlying territories from Australia's migration zone. However, in March 2004 a group of nine women and six men, believed to be seeking asylum in Australia, was discovered on Ashmore Reef. A government spokesperson reiterated the Territory's exclusion from Australia's migration zone, stating that this would preclude the group from seeking any form of residency in the country.

In April 2005 the Australian Government invited petroleum exploration companies to bid for a number of leases which it had made available in an area covering some 920 sq km near the islands. In mid-2006 two permits were granted for exploration to take place in the territory's Bonaparte Basin.

Australian Antarctic Territory

The Australian Antarctic Territory was established by Order in Council in February 1933 and proclaimed in August 1936, subsequent to the Australian Antarctic Territory Acceptance Act (1933). It consists of the portion of Antarctica (divided by the French territory of Terre Adélie) lying between 45°E and 136°E, and between 142°E and 160°E. The Australian Antarctic Division (AAD) of the Department of the Environment, Sport and Territories (subsequently renamed the Department of the Environment and Water Resources and currently the Department of the Environment, Water, Heritage and the Arts) was established in 1948 as a permanent agency, and to administer and provide support for the Australian National Antarctic Research Expeditions (ANARE), which maintains three permanent scientific stations (Mawson, Davis and Casey) in the Territory. The area of the Territory is estimated to be 5,896,500 sq km (2,276,650 sq miles), and there are no permanent inhabitants, although there is a permanent presence of scientific personnel. Environmentalists expressed alarm at proposals in the late 1990s to encourage tourism in the Territory, which, they claimed, could damage the area's sensitive ecology. In November 2001 an international team of scientists commenced Australia's largest ever scientific expedition, to gather data on the influence of the Southern Ocean on the world's climate and the global carbon cycle. In January 2002 Australia attempted to expel Japanese whaling ships from the 200-nautical-mile exclusive economic zone it claimed to be under the jurisdiction of the Australian Antarctic Territory. However, the Government was severely criticized in mid-2005 for its failure to protect whales in its Antarctic territorial waters. Its reluctance to intercept Japanese whaling vessels in its territorial waters for 'diplomatic reasons' was blamed for the slaughter of more than 400 whales since 2000, when a whale sanctuary had been established in these waters. The Government allocated $A102.3m. to its Antarctic Programme in 2002/03. The Territory is administered by the Antarctic Division of the Department of the Environment, Water, Heritage and the Arts. Australia is a signatory to the Antarctic Treaty (see p. 575). As part of the Australian Government's commitment to establish regular flights to the Territory, a trial runway was constructed in the 2005/06 Antarctic summer season at the Wilkins Aerodrome, located 75 km from Casey. A full runway was opened in December 2007, with regular flights between Hobart Airport, in Tasmania, and Antarctica to become operational during the 2007/08 Antarctic summer season.

Coral Sea Islands Territory

The Coral Sea Islands became a Territory of the Commonwealth of Australia under the Coral Sea Islands Act of 1969. The Territory lies east of Queensland, between the Great Barrier Reef and longitude 156° 06′E, and between latitude 12°S and 24°S, and comprises several islands and reefs. The islands are composed largely of sand and coral, and have no permanent fresh water supply, but some have a cover of grass and scrub. The area has been known as a notorious hazard to shipping since the 19th century, the danger of the reefs being compounded by shifting sand cays and occasional tropical cyclones. The Coral Sea Islands have been acquired by Australia by numerous acts of sovereignty since the early years of the 20th century.

Spread over a sea area of approximately 780,000 sq km (300,000 sq miles), all the islands and reefs in the Territory are very small, totalling only a few sq km of land area. They include Cato Island, Chilcott Islet in the Coringa Group, and the Willis Group. In 1997 the Coral Sea Islands Act was amended to include Elizabeth and Middleton Reefs. A meteorological station, operated by the Commonwealth Bureau of Meteorology and with a staff of four, has provided a service on one of the Willis Group since 1921. The other islands are uninhabited. There are eight automatic weather stations (on Cato Island, Flinders Reef, Frederick Reef, Holmes Reef, Lihou Reef, Creal Reef, Marion Reef and Gannet Cay) and several navigation aids distributed throughout the Territory.

The Act constituting the Territory did not establish an administration on the islands, but provides means of controlling the activities of those who visit them. The Lihou Reef and Coringa-Herald National Nature Reserves were established in 1982 to provide protection for the wide variety of terrestrial and marine wildlife, which include rare species of birds and sea turtles (one of which is the largest, and among the most endangered, of the world's species of sea turtle). The Australian Government has concluded agreements for the protection of endangered and migratory birds with Japan and the People's Republic of China. The Governor-General of Australia is empowered to make ordinances for the peace, order and good government of the Territory and, by ordinance, the laws of the Australian Capital Territory apply. The Supreme Court and Court of Petty Sessions of Norfolk Island have jurisdiction in the Territory. The Territory is administered by a parliamentary secretary appointed by the Attorney-General. The area is visited regularly by the Royal Australian Navy.

Heard Island and the McDonald Islands

These islands are situated about 4,000 km (2,500 miles) south-west of Perth, Western Australia. The Territory, consisting of Heard Island, Shag Island (8 km north of Heard) and the McDonald Islands, is almost entirely covered in ice and has a total area of 369 sq km (142 sq miles). Sovereignty was transferred from the United Kingdom to the Commonwealth of Australia on 26 December 1947, following the establishment of a scientific research station on Heard Island (which functioned until March 1955). The islands are administered by the Antarctic Division of the Australian Department of the Environment, Water, Heritage and the Arts. There are no permanent inhabitants. However, in 1991 evidence emerged of a Polynesian community on Heard Island some 700 years before the territory's discovery by European explorers. The island is of considerable scientific interest, as it is believed to be one of the few Antarctic habitats uncontaminated by introduced organisms. Heard Island is about 44 km long and 20 km wide and possesses an active volcano, named Big Ben. In January 1991 an international team of scientists travelled to Heard Island to conduct research involving the transmission of sound waves, beneath the surface of the ocean, in order to monitor any evidence of the 'greenhouse effect' (melting of polar ice and the rise in sea-level as a consequence of pollution). The pulses of sound, which travel at a speed largely influenced by temperature, were to be received at various places around the world, with international co-operation. Heard Island was chosen for the experiment because of its unique location, from which direct paths to the five principal oceans extend. The McDonald Islands, with an area of about 1 sq km (0.4 sq miles), lie some 42 km west of Heard Island. Only two successful landings by boat have been recorded since the discovery of the McDonald Islands in the late 19th century. In late 1997 Heard Island and the McDonald Islands were accorded World Heritage status by UNESCO in recognition of their outstanding universal significance as a natural landmark.

In 1999 concern was expressed that stocks of the Patagonian toothfish in the waters around the islands were becoming depleted as a result of over-exploitation, mainly by illegal operators. (The popularity of the fish in Japan and the USA, where it is known as Chilean sea bass, increased significantly during the early 2000s.) This problem was highlighted in August 2003 when a Uruguayan fishing vessel was seized, following a 20-day pursuit over 7,400 km by Australian, South African and British patrol boats. The trawler had been fishing illegally in waters near Heard and McDonald and had a full cargo of Patagonian toothfish worth some US $1.5m. Experts feared that, if poaching continued at current rates, the species would become extinct by 2007. In response to this situation, the Australian Government announced in December 2003 that it was to send an ice-breaking patrol vessel with deck-mounted machine guns to police the waters around Heard and McDonald Islands. It was hoped that this action might serve to deter illegal fishing activity in the area, much of which was believed to involve international criminal organizations. However, it was reported that many vessels continued fishing in protected waters, including operations on the Banzare Bank, which in February 2005 was closed to fishing by the Convention for the Conservation of Arctic Marine Living Resources Commission. (An anomaly of international law meant that vessels flying flags of non-member countries of the Commission could not be evicted by Australian forces.) In August the Australian customs department announced that it was to train commandos to patrol the protected waters around Heard and McDonald for vessels fishing illegally. In September 2006 conservation groups petitioned the USA, a major importer of Patagonian toothfish, urging the Government to impose sanctions on Spain for failing to comply with laws governing fishing activities in the region.

In 2001 the Australian Government's Antarctic Division conducted a five-month scientific expedition to Heard Island. It claimed that glacial cover had retreated by 12% since 1947 as a result of global warming. In October 2002 the Australian Government declared the establishment of the Heard Island and McDonald Islands Marine Reserve. Covering 6.5m. ha, the marine reserve was to be the largest in the world, strengthening existing conservation measures and imposing an official ban on all fishing and petroleum and mineral exploitation. Among the many species of plant, bird and mammal to be protected by the reserve were the southern elephant seal, the sub-Antarctic fur seal and two species of albatross. Limited scientific research and environmental monitoring were to be allowed in the Marine Reserve. The Marine Reserve draft management plan, announced in 2005, proposed measures further to restrict human activity on the islands, in an attempt to protect their unique flora and fauna from damage and from introduced organisms.

AUSTRIA

Introductory Survey

Location, Climate, Language, Religion, Flag, Capital

The Republic of Austria lies in central Europe, bordered by Switzerland and Liechtenstein to the west, by Germany and the Czech Republic to the north, by Hungary and Slovakia to the east, and by Italy and Slovenia to the south. The mean annual temperature lies between 7°C and 9°C (45°F and 48°F). The population is 99% German-speaking, with small Croat- and Slovene-speaking minorities. The majority of the inhabitants profess Christianity: about 70% are Roman Catholics and about 5% are Protestants. The national flag (proportions 2 by 3) consists of three equal horizontal stripes, of red, white and red. The state flag has, in addition, the coat of arms (a small shield, with horizontal stripes of red separated by a white stripe, superimposed on a black eagle, wearing a golden crown and holding a sickle and a hammer in its feet, with a broken chain between its legs) in the centre. The capital is Vienna (Wien).

Recent History

Austria was formerly the centre of the Austrian (later Austro-Hungarian) Empire, which comprised a large part of central Europe. The Empire, under the Habsburg dynasty, was dissolved in 1918, at the end of the First World War, and Austria proper became a republic. The first post-war Council of Ministers was a coalition led by Dr Karl Renner, who remained Chancellor until 1920, when a new Constitution introduced a federal form of government. Many of Austria's inhabitants favoured union with Germany, but this was forbidden by the post-war peace treaties. In March 1938, however, Austria was occupied by Nazi Germany's armed forces and incorporated into the German Reich, led by the Austrian-born Adolf Hitler.

After Hitler's defeat in Austria, a provisional Government, under Renner, was established in April 1945. In July, following Germany's surrender to the Allied forces, Austria was divided into four zones, occupied respectively by forces of the USA, the USSR, the United Kingdom and France. At the first post-war elections to the 165-seat Nationalrat (National Council), held in November 1945, the conservative Österreichische Volkspartei (ÖVP, Austrian People's Party) won 85 seats and the Sozialistische Partei Österreichs (SPÖ, Socialist Party of Austria) secured 76. The two parties formed a coalition Government. In December Renner became the first Federal President of the second Austrian Republic, holding office until his death in December 1950. However, it was not until May 1955 that the four powers signed a State Treaty with Austria, recognizing Austrian independence, effective from 27 July; occupation forces left in October.

More than 20 years of coalition government came to an end in April 1966 with the formation of a Council of Ministers by the ÖVP alone. Dr Josef Klaus, the Federal Chancellor since April 1964, remained in office. The SPÖ achieved a relative majority in the March 1970 general election and formed a minority Government, with Dr Bruno Kreisky (a former Minister of Foreign Affairs, who had been party leader since 1967) as Chancellor. In April 1971 the incumbent President, Franz Jonas of the SPÖ, was re-elected, defeating the ÖVP candidate, Dr Kurt Waldheim, a former Minister of Foreign Affairs (who subsequently served two five-year terms as UN Secretary-General, beginning in January 1972). The SPÖ won an absolute majority of seats in the Nationalrat at general elections in October 1971 (when the number of seats was increased from 165 to 183) and October 1975. President Jonas died in April 1974, and the subsequent presidential election, held in June, was won by Dr Rudolf Kirchschläger, who had been the Minister of Foreign Affairs since 1970. He was re-elected for a second six-year term in 1980.

In November 1978 a government proposal to commission Austria's first nuclear power plant was defeated in a national referendum. Despite expectations that Chancellor Kreisky would resign, he received the full support of the SPÖ. At the general election in May 1979 the SPÖ increased its majority in the Nationalrat. The general election of April 1983, however, marked the end of the 13-year era of one-party government: the SPÖ lost its absolute majority in the Nationalrat and Kreisky, unwilling to participate in a coalition, resigned as Chancellor. The reduction in the SPÖ's representation was partly attributed to the emergence in the previous year of two environmentalist parties, which together received more than 3% of the total votes cast, but failed to win any seats. Kreisky's successor, Dr Fred Sinowatz (the former Vice-Chancellor and Minister of Education), took office in May, leading a coalition of the SPÖ and the right-of-centre Freiheitliche Partei Österreichs (FPÖ, Freedom Party of Austria). The new Government continued the social welfare policy that had been pursued by its predecessor, in addition to maintaining Austria's foreign policy of 'active neutrality'.

At the presidential election held in May 1986 the SPÖ candidate was Dr Kurt Steyrer (the Minister of Health and Environment), while Waldheim stood independently, although with the support of the ÖVP. The campaign was dominated by allegations that Waldheim, a former officer in the army of Nazi Germany, had been implicated in atrocities committed by the Nazis in the Balkans during 1942–45; the ensuing controversy divided the country and brought international attention to the election, which was won by Waldheim. The defeat of the SPÖ presidential candidate led Chancellor Sinowatz and four of his ministers to resign. Dr Franz Vranitzky, hitherto the Minister of Finance, became the new Chancellor. In September the FPÖ elected a controversial new leader, Dr Jörg Haider, who represented the far-right wing of his party. This precipitated the end of the governing coalition, and the general election for the Nationalrat, scheduled for April 1987, was brought forward to November 1986. No party won an absolute majority: the SPÖ won 80 seats, the ÖVP 77, the FPÖ 18 and an alliance of three environmentalist parties eight. Following several weeks of negotiations, a 'grand coalition' of the SPÖ and the ÖVP, with Vranitzky as Chancellor, was formed in January 1987.

Waldheim's election to the presidency was controversial both domestically and internationally, and Austria's relations with Israel and the USA, in particular, were severely strained. In February 1988 a specially appointed international commission of historians concluded that Waldheim must have been aware of the atrocities that had been committed. Waldheim refused to resign, but in June 1991 he announced that he would not seek a second presidential term.

At the general election held in October 1990 the SPÖ retained its position as the largest single party, increasing its number of seats to 81, while the ÖVP obtained only 60 seats; the FPÖ increased its representation to 33 seats. The FPÖ's success was attributed, in large part, to its support for restrictions on immigration, especially from eastern Europe. The Grüne Alternative Liste (GAL, Green Alternative List), an informal electoral alliance comprising Die Grüne Alternative (The Green Alternative) and the Vereinte Grüne Österreichs (United Green Party of Austria), increased the representation of environmentalist parties to nine. In December, following several weeks of negotiations, the SPÖ and the ÖVP formed a new coalition Government, again led by Vranitzky.

A congress of the SPÖ held in June 1991 voted to revert to the party's original name, the Sozialdemokratische Partei Österreichs (SPÖ, Social Democratic Party of Austria). In the same month Haider was dismissed as Governor of Carinthia (Kärnten) after publicly praising Hitler's employment policies. In December the Nationalrat approved government legislation whereby Austria became the only country in Europe able to reject asylum requests from individuals without identity papers. Following the imprisonment, in January 1992, of a prominent right-wing activist for demanding the restoration of the Nazi party, and the subsequent fire-bombing of a refugee hostel by neo-Nazis in northern Austria, the Nationalrat voted unanimously in February to amend anti-Nazi legislation. The minimum prison sentence for Nazi agitation was reduced from five years to one year (in order to increase the number of successful prosecutions) and denial of the Nazi Holocaust was made a criminal offence.

At the presidential election held in April 1992 the two main candidates were Dr Rudolf Streicher (hitherto the Minister of Public Economy and Transport), for the SPÖ, and Dr Thomas Klestil (a former ambassador to the USA), representing the ÖVP.

In a run-off ballot, held in May, Klestil received almost 57% of the votes cast; he assumed the presidency in July.

In January 1993 the FPÖ organized a national petition seeking to require the Nationalrat to debate the introduction of legislation that would halt immigration into Austria and impose stricter controls on foreign residents in the country. Some 417,000 people signed the petition (the constitutional requirement to force parliamentary debate was 100,000). The initiative was strongly opposed by a broad coalition of politicians, church leaders and intellectuals. In February five FPÖ deputies in the Nationalrat left the party, partly in protest at the petition on immigration, and formed a new political organization, the Liberales Forum (LiF, Liberal Forum), under the leadership of Dr Heide Schmidt, hitherto the Vice-President of the FPÖ.

In June 1994 a national referendum was held on the terms of Austria's entry into the European Union (EU, see p. 244). Some 66.4% of those who voted supported Austria's accession to the EU. Following the referendum Austria announced plans to sign the Partnership for Peace programme (see p. 342) of the North Atlantic Treaty Organization (NATO). Austria was formally admitted to the EU on 1 January 1995. Observer status at Western European Union (see p. 426) was subsequently granted.

At the general election held in October 1994 the ruling coalition lost its two-thirds' majority in the Nationalrat. The SPÖ obtained 66 seats, the ÖVP 52, and the FPÖ (which had campaigned against Austria's accession to the EU) 42. Die Grünen (the Greens) and the LiF also made gains, winning 13 and 10 seats, respectively. The success of the FPÖ's populist campaign, which had concentrated on countering corruption and immigration and had advocated referendum-based rather than parliamentary-based governance, unsettled the Austrian political establishment after years of relative consensus. At the end of November, following protracted negotiations, the SPÖ and ÖVP finally agreed to form a new coalition Government, with Vranitzky remaining as Chancellor.

The new SPÖ-ÖVP coalition was beleaguered by disagreements, mainly concerning differences in approach to the urgent need to reduce the annual budgetary deficit, in compliance with Austria's commitment, as a member of the EU, to future Economic and Monetary Union (EMU). In early 1995 five ministers, including the Vice-Chancellor, Dr Erhard Busek, resigned. Busek was replaced as Chairman of the ÖVP by Dr Wolfgang Schüssel. In October a rift between the SPÖ and ÖVP regarding the means of curtailing the 1996 budgetary deficit precipitated the collapse of the coalition. Consequently, a new general election was held in December 1995. The SPÖ improved upon its disappointing performance at the previous election, winning 71 seats. The ÖVP secured 53 seats, the FPÖ (also known as Die Freiheitlichen) 40, the LiF 10 and the Greens nine. In March 1996, following lengthy negotiations, the SPÖ and ÖVP agreed an economic programme and formed a new coalition Government, again under Vranitzky. However, in January 1997 Vranitzky unexpectedly resigned from the chancellorship. Viktor Klima, hitherto the Minister of Finance, replaced Vranitzky as Chancellor and as Chairman of the SPÖ.

In March 1998, following months of debate, the Government announced that Austria would not apply to join NATO, and would thereby preserve its traditional neutrality (as favoured by the SPÖ, but opposed by the ÖVP). Nevertheless, in April 1999 Austria, in conjunction with the three other officially neutral EU member countries, signed an EU declaration stating that the ongoing bombing of Serbia by NATO forces was, although regrettable, 'both necessary and warranted'. During the 1990s, in its capacity as a participant of NATO's Partnership for Peace programme (which it had joined in 1995), Austria contributed to peace-keeping operations in Bosnia and Herzegovina, authorized by the UN Security Council and effectively carried out under NATO command. Austria also provided substantial humanitarian aid to the thousands of refugees who suffered as a consequence of the wars and ethnic conflicts in the Balkans. In the aftermath of the suicide attacks on the USA in September 2001, the Chancellor, Wolfgang Schüssel, stated, in November, that Austria might consider abandoning its policy of neutrality and joining NATO at some time in the future. In early 2003, however, in the period immediately preceding the US-led military action to oust the regime of Saddam Hussein in Iraq, Austria refused permission for US fighter aircraft to fly over Austrian territory unless the action received UN authorization (which was ultimately not forthcoming).

At the presidential election held in April 1998 Klestil was re-elected emphatically, winning 63.5% of the votes cast. The FPÖ made significant gains at regional elections in March 1999, becoming the dominant party in Carinthia; Haider was subsequently elected Governor of Carinthia (having previously been dismissed from that post in 1991—see above). The general election held in October 1999 resulted in unprecedented success for the FPÖ, which narrowly took second place ahead of the ÖVP. The SPÖ won 65 seats, while the FPÖ and ÖVP both secured 52 and the Greens 14. The FPÖ had campaigned on a programme that included a halt to immigration, the obstruction of the projected eastwards expansion of the EU, the radical deregulation of the business sector and the introduction of a uniform low rate of income tax and of hugely increased child allowances for Austrian citizens. Haider appeared to have inflamed popular fears that the planned admission to the EU of Austria's eastern neighbours would flood the domestic market with cheap labour, thereby causing the level of unemployment to rise. During the FPÖ campaign Haider allegedly revived nationalist terminology previously employed by the Nazi regime; nevertheless, he consistently denied embracing neo-Nazi ideology. The election result was most widely regarded as a protest against the 12-year-old 'grand coalition', which had acquired a reputation for unwieldy bureaucracy and for sanctioning politically motivated appointments to public companies.

Following the election, protracted negotiations took place with a view to forming a new administration. In January 2000, after a failed attempt to reconstruct the SPÖ-ÖVP coalition, the SPÖ announced that it would not attempt to form a minority government. At the beginning of February President Klestil reluctantly presided over the inauguration of an ÖVP-FPÖ coalition Government, with Schüssel as Chancellor. Haider elected not to participate directly in the new administration, which included an FPÖ Vice-Chancellor, Dr Susanne Riess-Passer, and five FPÖ ministers (including those responsible for finance, justice and defence). Although the new coalition had committed itself to respecting human rights and had adopted a relatively moderate political programme, the participation in government of the FPÖ provoked strong opposition both within Austria and abroad. Israel and the USA immediately recalled their ambassadors from Vienna, while Austria's fellow EU member states each suspended bilateral political co-operation, maintaining diplomatic relations at a 'technical' level, pending the removal of the FPÖ from the coalition. In late February Haider announced that he was to resign as leader of the FPÖ, while retaining his position as Governor of Carinthia; few people, however, doubted that he would remain the *de facto* leader of the party.

In February 2000 Klima resigned as Chairman of the SPÖ and was replaced by Dr Alfred Gusenbauer. In April Gusenbauer apologized on behalf of his party for decades of political opportunism and acknowledged that the SPÖ had erred in embracing and promoting former Nazis after the Second World War in its efforts to become Austria's most powerful political force. He later established a commission of independent historians to investigate the matter. The commission reported in January 2005 that the SPÖ had actively recruited former Nazis in order to help them reintegrate into society, as had the ÖVP. The report noted that, while the Nazi holocaust against the Jews had stripped Austria of many professionals (thereby necessitating, to some extent, the parties' efforts at recruitment), the SPÖ ought to have made greater attempts at bringing back exiles following the war and differentiated between those who were 'merely Nazi party members' and those who had perpetrated crimes. Gusenbauer's initiative was expected to put pressure on the coalition Government to launch similar projects, but officials from both constituent parties claimed they had already dealt with the issue and had no plans to follow suit. However, in June 2000 Ernest Windholz, the newly elected head of the FPÖ in Lower Austria (Niederösterreich), provoked controversy by using a Nazi-era slogan to honour long-serving party members. The incident was thought to have harmed Austria's chances of having the diplomatic sanctions (see above) lifted. Prospects improved, however, at the end of June when Chancellor Schüssel agreed to the nomination by the President of the European Court of Human Rights of a three-person EU delegation to examine the Austrian Government's commitment to common European values (with particular regard to the rights of minority groups, immigrants and refugees and to the political philosophy of the FPÖ). The delegation visited Austria in late July, and issued its report in September, recommending that the sanctions be lifted on the grounds that they were counter-productive and tended to generate increased nationalist sentiment. Although the EU report did criticize the xenophobic tendencies of the FPÖ, it confirmed that Austria's treatment of minorities was superior to that of many other member states and that incidences of violence against foreigners were less frequent in Austria than in other EU countries. The report also criticized the FPÖ for trivializing Nazism and threatening press freedom by using libel suits to silence criticism. Concurrently, economic analysts reported that upholding the sanctions against Austria could adversely affect the single European currency, the euro. As a result, the EU lifted its sanctions in September, but warned that it would continue to monitor closely the influence of the FPÖ, and Haider, upon government policies.

By the end of 2000 the FPÖ's influence and popularity (which had, perversely, benefited from the temporary imposition of EU sanctions) was in decline. The party fared badly in regional elections in Styria (Steiermark) and Burgenland. In November the Minister of Science and Transport, Michael Schmid, resigned from the Government, citing the FPÖ's poor electoral performance. He was the third FPÖ minister to resign since the formation of the Government in February, prompting accusations that the party was unfit to govern. Schmid subsequently resigned from the FPÖ after refusing to pay one-half of his government pension into a party fund. Poor electoral results, instability and repeated indiscretions linking the party with Nazism were, however, overshadowed by the emergence of a major political scandal. In October a number of senior members of the FPÖ (including the Minister of Justice, Dr Dieter Böhmdorfer) were accused of using illicitly obtained police files to discredit opponents, including the former Minister of Finance, Dr Caspar Einem. Böhmdorfer rejected calls to resign, and in October survived a vote of confidence, the third such vote in his short ministerial career. By November the number of FPÖ members under investigation had risen to 67 and 11 police officers were suspended in connection with the scandal.

In late September 2001, purportedly as part of a plan to combat international terrorism following the devastating suicide attacks in the USA, Haider asserted that refugees from continents other than Europe seeking asylum within the EU should no longer be granted residence in Europe while their requests were being processed. The FPÖ also suggested the introduction of 'biometric' identification methods, a fortnightly 'control' of all asylum seekers and the immediate expulsion of any foreigners suspected of being involved in criminal activities. Furthermore, the FPÖ proposed the introduction of a so-called *Integrationsvertrag* ('integration contract') for immigrant workers and their families, including those who were already living in the country. Under this contract, immigrants would be obliged to attend courses and pass tests in German language and on citizenship; those who did not comply within four years would have their social security benefits gradually reduced, and, in extreme cases, would face expulsion from the country. The proposals provoked fierce criticism both within Austria and throughout the EU. Despite initial reservations, in early October the ÖVP endorsed the FPÖ's recommendations regarding asylum seekers and immigrants (with the exception of the proposal to deny those seeking asylum the right of temporary residence). Despite strong opposition from the SPÖ and the Greens, the proposed measures, including the introduction of the integration contract, were approved by the legislature and came into force on 1 January 2003.

The ÖVP-FPÖ coalition was characterized by periods of drive and reform intermittently supplanted by bouts of internecine strife. An internal power struggle within the FPÖ led to the resignation in September 2002 of a number of moderate FPÖ ministers, including the Vice-Chancellor, Riess-Passer. Hitherto, Schüssel had succeeded in persuading these ministers to eschew the more extremist elements of their party's credo, while himself adopting some of the FPÖ's more reasonable policies. Haider, believing that his party's influence was thus being undermined, had reverted to populist tactics in an effort to restore the FPÖ's perceived credentials as an 'anti-establishment' party. In February he had lost the support of many Austrians and had been severely criticized for making an unofficial visit to the Iraqi President, Saddam Hussain, in Baghdad. Haider's renewed bouts of invective against foreigners, the EU and even against Schüssel himself did nothing to improve his political standing or that of the FPÖ. With this increasing instability within the junior coalition party, Schüssel had little option but to dissolve the legislature on 20 September pending an early general election. On the same day Mathias Reichhold was elected as the new Chairman of the FPÖ, following Haider's refusal to stand for the post. When Reichhold resigned from the leadership of the FPÖ later that year owing to ill health, he was replaced by a staunch ally of Haider, Herbert Haupt.

At the general election held on 24 November 2002 the ÖVP received 42.3% of the votes cast, securing 79 seats (the party's largest single share of the votes in more than 30 years), mainly at the expense of the FPÖ, which obtained only 10.0% of the votes cast (18 seats), compared with 26.9% in 1999. Although the ÖVP was the party with the largest representation in the legislature, it did not have a sufficient number of seats to form a majority government. The Greens, many of whom were still mistrustful of Schüssel after his earlier co-operation with Haider, had already ruled out any coalition agreement with the ÖVP; many members of the SPÖ, too, were unwilling to form a coalition with the ÖVP in which their party would be the junior partner. At the end of February 2003, despite some apparent reluctance, Schüssel invited the FPÖ to form another coalition administration with the ÖVP; a new Council of Ministers was sworn in on 28 February. The new Government included only three ministers from the FPÖ, compared with five in the previous administration.

The FPÖ suffered heavy losses in regional elections held in September 2003, with the Greens, for the first time, receiving more votes than the right-wing party. The following month Haupt resigned as Vice-Chancellor (he was replaced by Hubert Gorbach of the FPÖ, who was the incumbent Minister of Transport, Innovation and Technology), while retaining his position as Minister of Social Security, Generations and Consumer Protection. Haupt was reported to have been under pressure to resign from Haider and was widely believed to have lost the support of his party over what it perceived as his poor media performance. Haupt was to remain as the nominal leader of the FPÖ pending party elections in 2004, but under the supervision of the party's new Managing Chairwoman, Haider's sister, Ursula Haubner. Many observers viewed the latter's appointment as evidence that Haider had again assumed control of the FPÖ. In March 2004 local elections were held in Carinthia; forecasts of an SPÖ victory were confounded when the FPÖ won 42.4% of the votes cast, compared with 38.4% for the SPÖ and only 11.6% for the ÖVP. Haider, therefore, retained the governorship of his home province. Notably, the FPÖ secured Haider's re-election with the help of the SPÖ, which in return gained influence in the state Government. In previous years the FPÖ had relied on the ÖVP for such support. Moreover, in supporting Haider, the SPÖ had broken a self-imposed prohibition on working with the FPÖ which had stood since 1986, when Haider was first appointed to the party leadership.

In October 2003 the Nationalrat approved amendments to Austria's asylum legislation that were intended to accelerate the asylum process; the office of the UN High Commissioner for Refugees, however, described the controversial amendments as 'among the most restrictive pieces of legislation' within the EU, whilst other critics claimed that the revised legislation was in breach of the Geneva Convention and the Austrian Constitution. The changes included measures such as deporting some asylum seekers while their appeals were under review, demanding full statements from asylum seekers within 72 hours of their arrival in Austria, and medically certifying cases involving traumatized people. According to government figures, in 2002 Austria received more asylum seekers per head of the population than any other EU member country, amounting to a total of some 39,000 cases, of which the Government claimed around 85% were economic migrants.

A presidential election was held on 25 April 2004, at which Dr Heinz Fischer of the SPÖ defeated Dr Benita Ferrero-Waldner of the ÖVP with 52.4% of the votes cast. It was widely held that the result of the election reflected growing public dissatisfaction with the governing coalition. On 5 July, just three days before the end of his term of office, President Klestil suffered a heart attack; he died the following day. Chancellor Schüssel temporarily assumed charge of Klestil's duties until 8 July, when Fischer was sworn in as the new President.

In June 2004 Böhmdorfer resigned as Minister of Justice and was replaced by Karin Miklautsch (also of the FPÖ). At a special conference held by the FPÖ in Linz in July Haubner was elected unopposed as the party's new Chairwoman. Other allies of Haider were appointed to key positions within the party. In October Ursula Plassnik of the ÖVP was appointed as Minister of Foreign Affairs, to replace Ferrero-Waldner, who had left to assume the post of European Commissioner for External Relations and European Neighbourhood Policy. In December Liese Prokop was appointed Minister of the Interior; her predecessor,

Dr Ernst Strasser, had resigned earlier that month to move into the private sector.

As a result of the continuing decline in support for the FPÖ, Haider split from the party in early April 2005 to form Bündnis Zukunft Österreich (BZÖ, Alliance for the Future of Austria). All of the FPÖ government ministers and several FPÖ members of parliament defected to the BZÖ, which replaced the FPÖ in the ruling coalition with the ÖVP, the ministers retaining their posts in the Government. Haider was elected as leader of the BZÖ at its founding conference in Salzburg. Later that month Heinz-Christian Strache was elected to the chairmanship of the FPÖ, replacing Haubner, who had joined the BZÖ. In mid-April Siegfried Kampl, a BZÖ member from Carinthia who was due to assume the Bundesrat's rotating presidency in July, provoked considerable controversy and widespread calls for his resignation when he denounced deserters from Austria's Nazi-era armed forces and deplored what he called the 'brutal persecution' of Austrian Nazis following the Second World War. Amid the ensuing furore, he initially announced that he would relinquish his parliamentary seat, but in late May he retracted this decision and stated his intention to take up the presidency of the Bundesrat as planned. (He did, however, resign from the BZÖ.) In June a constitutional amendment was adopted, with the support of all parties, allowing for the presidency of the chamber to be filled by any member from a province and not automatically by the delegate at the top of the province's list. Carinthia subsequently withdrew Kampl's nomination and designated Peter Mitterer as President of the Bundesrat for the last six months of 2005.

The SPÖ performed well at local elections held in three provinces in October 2005. In Styria the party defeated the ÖVP, which had previously held the governorship of the province for some 60 years without interruption. The results were also disappointing for the FPÖ and the BZÖ, which both failed to win any seats in the provincial assembly. The SPÖ increased its dominance in Burgenland, where it secured an absolute majority, and in Vienna, where only one-fifth of the votes were cast in favour of one of the government parties, the BZÖ taking only 1.2%. As a result of the provincial elections, the ruling ÖVP-BZÖ coalition lost its majority in the Bundesrat. In May 2006 Haider resigned as leader of the BZÖ; Peter Westenthaler, a former parliamentary leader of the FPÖ, was elected as his replacement in June.

In February 2006 David Irving, a British historian, was sentenced to three years' imprisonment by a court in Vienna after pleading guilty to the charge of Holocaust denial (which carries a maximum penalty of 10 years' imprisonment). He had been arrested in Styria in November 2005 in connection with comments he had made in Austria in 1989, in which he denied the existence of gas chambers at the Nazi concentration camp at Auschwitz. Austrian prosecutors subsequently sought to lengthen Irving's sentence, while the historian appealed for it to be reduced. On 20 December 2006 the Higher Provincial Court in Vienna ruled in favour of Irving and ordered his release on probation for the remainder of his sentence. On the following day Irving was deported to the United Kingdom and banned from returning to Austria.

Political activity in 2006 was dominated by the financial scandal surrounding the near collapse of the Bank für Arbeit und Wirtschaft AG PSK (BAWAG PSK), which was owned by the Austrian trades union federation, the Österreichischer Gewerkschaftsbund (ÖGB—Austrian Trade Union Federation), and had links to the SPÖ. Despite Gusenbauer's attempts to distance the party from the scandal, the emerging details of alleged embezzlement, corruption and excessive payments to directors resulted in a decline in support for the SPÖ. The party had previously been leading the opinion polls, largely owing to public dissatisfaction with Schüssel's programme of economic and social reforms. BAWAG was revealed to have accumulated huge debts in suspect investments and it was disclosed that officials had used the ÖGB strike fund in its attempts to conceal the losses. The federal Government intervened to prevent the collapse of the bank, which was later sold to a US-based company in December. The affair prompted the resignations of numerous bank and union officials and criminal charges were brought against several former BAWAG executives.

At the general election held on 1 October 2006, however, the SPÖ won 35.3% of the votes cast, securing 68 seats in the legislature (one fewer than in 2002), while the ÖVP won 34.3% (66 seats, compared with 79 in 2002). The Greens won 11.1% of the votes cast and the FPÖ 11.0% (21 seats apiece). The BZÖ narrowly exceeded the 4% minimum required to be allocated seats in the legislature, winning 4.1% of the votes cast (seven seats). The result of the election confounded many observers, who had predicted a victory for the ÖVP. The SPÖ were, however, unable to form a majority government and the two parties began talks over the formation of a 'grand coalition'. The ÖVP suspended negotiations with the SPÖ in early November, after the SPÖ allied itself at the first meeting of the new Nationalrat with the Greens and the FPÖ to initiate a parliamentary inquiry into a controversial purchase agreement entered into by the Government in 2002 for 18 fighter aircraft. The procurement of the Eurofighter aircraft represented the largest ever military purchase for Austria, a militarily neutral country, and had been opposed by the SPÖ from the outset. Indeed, opposition to the contract had been a central tenet of the SPÖ's election campaign. The SPÖ also instigated a parliamentary inquiry into banking sector reforms undertaken by the previous Government. Despite initial ÖVP insistence that negotiations could not continue until the inquiries were completed, the two parties recommenced negotiations in late November 2006. In December the Minister of the Interior, Liese Prokop, died; Chancellor Schüssel assumed the role on an acting basis, pending the formation of a new government.

Following protracted negotiations, on 8 January 2007 the SPÖ and ÖVP formed a 'grand coalition', giving the Government control of 134 of the 183 seats in the Nationalrat. The new Council of Ministers, comprising seven ministers each from the SPÖ and ÖVP, was sworn in on 11 January. Gusenbauer, as expected, became Chancellor and Wilhelm Molterer of the ÖVP was appointed as Vice-Chancellor and Minister of Finance. Schüssel announced his resignation as ÖVP Chairman in the light of the party's poor electoral performance, and Molterer, hitherto the leader of the ÖVP parliamentary group, assumed the leadership of the party. Gusenbauer was subsequently accused of reneging on election promises in order to reach an agreement with the ÖVP; notably, a commitment to abolish university admission fees was abandoned and a reduction in income tax was postponed. He was also criticized for conceding control of the key ministries of finance, foreign affairs and economy to the ÖVP. The new coalition's programme comprised austerity measures aimed at eradicating the budget deficit by 2010, with savings to be achieved largely by administrative reform, but also included increases in spending on education and social issues and a rise in personal contributions to the health system. Molterer was officially elected as ÖVP Chairman at the party congress in Salzburg in April 2007, while Schüssel assumed the role of leader of the ÖVP parliamentary group.

Relations between the coalition partners, which had been generally characterized by friction, were further strained in June 2007 by an announcement from the SPÖ Minister for Defence, Norbert Darabos, that he had signed a new contract with the manufacturers of the Eurofighter jets, reducing the number of aircraft involved from 18 to 15. The ÖVP expressed anger that Darabos had acted unilaterally and without consultation. The Greens and the FPÖ were also highly critical of the announcement, which had preceded the publication of the findings of the parliamentary investigation into the purchase. The parliamentary committee closed its inquiry in early July, concluding that although evidence of wrongdoing in the circumstances surrounding the awarding of the contract potentially justified a complete withdrawal, the probability of exposure to lengthy judicial proceedings initiated by the manufacturers of the aircraft, owing to a lack of conclusive proof of bribery, made such a course inadvisable. The inquiry focused on an unexplained payment from a lobbyist in 2002 to a company managed by the wife of an official from the Federal Ministry of Defence who shared responsibility for the decision to award the original contract. A motion of 'no confidence' in Darabos, tabled by the opposition parties, was not supported by the ÖVP and was thus easily defeated by the government majority in the Nationalrat.

In June 2007 the Nationalrat approved a proposal to extend the maximum parliamentary term from four to five years with effect from the next legislative election, which was scheduled to take place in 2010. Postal voting in national elections was to become available to everyone from that date. Members of the lower chamber also approved the reduction of the age of eligibility to vote in federal, provincial and European elections from 18 to 16 years; Austria thus became the first EU member state to grant voting rights to 16-year-olds at national level. The legislation was due to enter into effect at elections to the European Parliament, which were scheduled for June 2009.

The arrest in September 2007 of three Austrian citizens of Arab descent (one of whom was subsequently released on the grounds of insufficient evidence) on suspicion of broadcasting threats of violence via the internet provoked concern that militant Islamist organizations were active within Austria. The messages, broadcast in March 2007 by the internet platform Global Islamic Media Front, which was allegedly linked to the Islamist al-Qa'ida (Base) organization, threatened Austria and Germany with terrorist attacks if they did not withdraw their troops from Afghanistan. The trial of the two remaining suspects, a husband and wife who remained unnamed, began in March 2008. A further arrest linked to the internet broadcasts was made in Canada in September 2007, as part of a joint investigation with Austria. The detainee, Saïd Namouh, who was of Moroccan descent, was charged with conspiracy with one of the Austrian suspects to explode a car bomb in an undisclosed location. His trial was scheduled to begin in June 2008.

Austria's strict asylum legislation came under further scrutiny in mid-2007, following an appeal by two people of Kosovan origin against a court ruling requiring them to leave Austria. The case provoked opposition from the Greens and a number of SPÖ politicians, including the governor of the province in which the two asylum seekers had resided. However, in mid-December the Constitutional Court (Verfassungsgerichtshof) ruled that the two had no right to stay in Austria and ordered their deportation. The Minister for the Interior, Günther Platter, of the ÖVP, subsequently rejected calls to allow the family to remain in Austria on humanitarian grounds. Meanwhile, in early December the Nationalrat approved further reforms to asylum legislation, which the Government claimed would accelerate and enhance the asylum process. The measures included the removal of the right of unsuccessful asylum seekers to appeal to the Constitutional Court and the establishment of a special 'asylum court' (Asylgerichtshof) to hear such cases; this was due to enter into effect by mid-2008.

Relations between the two governing parties became increasingly acrimonious in March 2008, following the SPÖ's decision to support an opposition motion in the Nationalrat to establish a parliamentary commission of inquiry into abuses of office in the Federal Ministry of the Interior under the control of the ÖVP. The inquiry was prompted by two accusations by a former federal police chief, Herwig Haidinger: that errors in a child kidnapping case in 1998, which had led to the victim, Natascha Kampusch, being incarcerated for eight years until her escape from her captor in August 2006, had been suppressed in 2006 by the now deceased Minister for the Interior, Prokop, in order to avoid a political scandal shortly before the general election in October; and that in the same year the Ministry of the Interior had instructed Haidinger to pass findings from investigations into the BAWAG scandal (see above) to the ÖVP, prior to reporting them to the cross-party parliamentary commission of inquiry, in an attempt to find information to discredit the SPÖ during the forthcoming election campaign. Public levels of dissatisfaction with the Government remained high in early 2008, owing to the perception that continued clashes between the coalition partners were hindering policy implementation.

During the late 1990s a number of lawsuits were filed by US interests against several Austrian banks, which were accused of having profited during the Second World War from handling stolen Jewish assets. In November 1999 Bank Austria AG agreed to pay US $33m. as compensation to Holocaust survivors and, furthermore, to establish a humanitarian fund to assist survivors resident in Austria. Similar lawsuits were also filed against the Government, and in February 2000 Chancellor Schüssel appointed a former President of Bank Austria AG, Maria Schaumayer, as the co-ordinator in charge of Nazi-era compensation claims. In July the legislature approved the establishment of a €438m. fund, which was to be financed by unspecified contributions from the Government and from Austrian businesses that had profited from slave labour, to compensate an estimated 150,000 concentration camp inmates, who had been forced into slave labour by the Nazis. However, doubts subsequently arose as to whether Austrian businesses would agree to pay for their share of the compensation fund. Another potential problem facing the settlement of the slave labourers' claims was that 'class-action' lawyers were threatening not to drop their claims unless the agreement contained a firm commitment to a similarly extensive solution for the restitution of Jewish property. In January 2001, however, Austria signed an agreement with the USA to pay $500m. to compensate Jews for property lost when the Nazis took power, in return for the dismissal of survivors' lawsuits.

The Heads of Government of Austria, Hungary and Slovakia met on several occasions during the late 1990s in order to pursue co-operation on security and economic issues. In September 1999, however, Austria threatened to hinder Slovakia's entry into the EU, in protest at the alleged inadequacy of that country's nuclear safety standards. There were protests in the latter half of 2000 against the proposed activation of a Soviet-designed nuclear power installation at Temelín in the Czech Republic, 48 km from the border with Austria; both Austria and Germany claimed that the power plant was dangerously flawed. Despite a blockade of the Austro-Czech border staged by Austrian environmentalist protesters and despite pressure from the Austrian Government, which suspended imports of Czech electricity, the nuclear power plant commenced production in early October, after receiving authorization from the Czech nuclear safety office. Border protests were resumed, and, following negotiations between the Austrian and Czech authorities, an agreement was signed by the two countries in December under which the plant was not to operate at commercial capacity until a full evaluation of its safety and environmental impact had been completed by a joint Austro-Czech safety body under the supervision of the European Commission. In August 2001 the Czech authorities maintained that a report issued by the European Commission demonstrated the safety of the plant, and immediately commenced its reconnection with the national power network; this move met with strong criticism from the Austrian Government, which, together with the German authorities, continued to express concern over the safety of the plant. Later that year Chancellor Schüssel threatened to veto the Czech Republic's accession to the EU unless the matter were satisfactorily resolved. Further safety issues were subsequently agreed, however, and in April 2003 the Temelín installation commenced production at full capacity for an 18-month trial period, prior to entering into commercial operations by the end of 2004. In late 2003 the Austrian Government vehemently criticized alleged proposals by the Czech authorities to build two new reactor units at the Temelín power plant (with construction reportedly to commence in 2009). Relations between Austria and the Czech Republic were further marred by the latter's refusal to abolish the so-called Beneš Decrees—legislation enacted at the end of the Second World War, providing for the expulsion of about 2.5m. ethnic Sudeten Germans from the Czech Republic without recourse to compensation. Austria repeatedly threatened to block the Czech Republic's anticipated accession to the EU in 2004 unless the Decrees were annulled; the EU authorities, however, did not regard their abolition as a prerequisite for entry, and Austria did not carry out its threats. Following the Czech Republic's accession to the EU in May 2004, relations between the two countries improved. The Czech Prime Minister, Stanislav Gross, visited Vienna in September 2004 and Chancellor Schüssel visited Prague in January 2005. In January 2008 the Czech Prime Minister, Mirek Topolánek, visited Austria for talks with Chancellor Gusenbauer, principally regarding increased co-operation in policing and asylum policy and the ongoing dispute over the Temelín power plant. Following the talks, Gusenbauer stated that progress had been made on the issue of the Temelín installation and that Topolánek had denied the existence of plans to extend the plant. For his part, Topolánek reaffirmed the Czech Republic's desire to improve safety standards in its nuclear facilities.

In May 2005 the Austrian Parliament ratified the EU's Treaty establishing a Constitution for Europe. In early October a demand by Austria that a 'privileged partnership' with the EU be offered to Turkey rather than full membership threatened to delay the official launch of accession talks with that country. Austria was finally persuaded to withdraw this demand, and negotiations commenced. Observers suggested that Austria's concession on Turkey was linked to the decision to proceed with previously suspended talks with Croatia, whose bid for membership of the EU the Austrian Government supported. In April 2008 the Austrian Parliament ratified the Treaty of Lisbon, which had been signed by EU heads of state and of government in December 2007 and which replaced the rejected constitutional treaty.

The implementation in December 2007 of the Schengen agreement on border controls by nine Central and Eastern European countries, included four countries that share a border with Austria. In order to assuage public fears of mass migration, the Government promised to mount a guard on its borders, a move that provoked an angry reaction in the Czech Republic and

Hungary. Relations with Hungary were already strained following an attempt by the Austrian oil and gas company OMV to take over its Hungarian counterpart, MOL.

Controversy arose in November 2007 after the Nationalrat approved the deployment of up to 160 Austrian troops to Chad as part of the EU Force (EUFOR) peace-keeping mission in the east of that country, despite vociferous opposition to the proposal from the Greens, the FPÖ and the BZÖ. A limited deployment of Austrian troops took place in late January 2008. However, in early February an assault on the Chadian capital, N'Djamena, by forces opposed to President Idriss Deby forced the postponement of further troop arrivals. Despite the increased violence in Chad and calls by the opposition for Austria to withdraw from the mission, the Minister for Defence, Darabos, insisted that the deployment would recommence once EU approval had been granted.

Government

Austria is a federal republic, divided into nine provinces, each with its own provincial assembly and government. Legislative power is held by the bicameral Parliament (Parlament). The first chamber, the Nationalrat (National Council), has 183 members, elected by universal, direct adult suffrage for four years (subject to dissolution) on the basis of proportional representation. In 2007 the Nationalrat approved legislation extending the maximum parliamentary term from four to five years. The reform was due to enter into effect after the next legislative election, which was due in 2010. The second chamber, the Bundesrat (Federal Council), has 62 members, elected for varying terms by the provincial assemblies. The Federal Assembly (Bundesversammlung—a joint meeting of the Nationalrat and the Bundesrat) is convened for certain matters of special importance, for example to witness the swearing-in of the Federal President. The Federal President, elected by popular vote for six years, is the Head of State, and normally acts on the advice of the Council of Ministers, which is led by the Federal Chancellor, and which is responsible to the Nationalrat.

Defence

After the ratification of the State Treaty in 1955, Austria declared its permanent neutrality. To protect its independence, the armed forces were instituted. In 1995 Austria joined the 'Partnership for Peace' programme of the North Atlantic Treaty Organization (NATO), but reaffirmed its neutrality in March 1998, having evaluated and discounted the possibility of becoming a full member of NATO. Military service is compulsory and normally consists of six months' initial training, followed by a maximum of 30 days' reservist training over eight years (officers, non-commissioned officers and specialists undergo 90–120 days' of additional training); alternatively, military service may entail eight months' training, with no further reservist training. As assessed at November 2007, the total armed forces numbered some 39,600 (including an estimated 20,600 conscripts). The air force (numbering 6,700, of whom 3,400 were conscripts) is an integral part of the army. Total reserves in November 2007 numbered 66,000, compared with 100,700 in August 1999 and 200,000 in June 1992. The defence budget for 2008 amounted to an estimated €2,300m. In November 2004 the European Union (EU, see p. 244) ministers responsible for defence agreed to create 13 'battlegroups' (each numbering about 1,500 men), which could be deployed at short notice to crisis areas around the world. The EU battlegroups, two of which were to be ready for deployment at any one time, following a rotational schedule, reached full operational capacity from 1 January 2007. Austria was committed to contributing troops to a battlegroup with the Netherlands, Germany and Finland, which would be on standby for deployment to crisis areas in 2011. It was also committed to participate in another battlegroup with Germany and the Czech Republic, which was to be ready for deployment in 2012.

Economic Affairs

In 2006, according to estimates by the World Bank, Austria's gross national income (GNI), measured at average 2004–06 prices, was US $326,191m., equivalent to $39,590 per head (or $35,130 per head on an international purchasing-power parity basis). During 1996–2006 the population grew at an estimated average rate of only 0.3% per year, while gross domestic product (GDP) per head increased, in real terms, at an average annual rate of 1.9%. Overall GDP grew, in real terms, at an average annual rate of 2.3% in 1996–2006; growth was 3.1% in 2006.

The contribution of agriculture (including hunting, forestry and fishing) to GDP was 1.7% in 2006. In that year, according to the International Labour Organization (ILO), 5.5% of the employed labour force were engaged in the agricultural sector. Austrian farms produce more than 90% of the country's food requirements, and surplus dairy products are exported. The principal crops are sugar beet, maize, wheat and barley. The GDP of the agricultural sector increased, in real terms, at an average annual rate of 0.7% in 1996–2005; it rose by 7.7% in 2004, but declined by 8.6% in 2005.

Industry (including mining and quarrying, manufacturing, construction and power) contributed 30.7% of GDP in 2006; according to ILO, the sector engaged 28.2% of the employed labour force in that year. Industrial GDP increased, in real terms, at an average annual rate of 3.0% in 1996–2005; it increased by 3.2% in 2005.

In 2006 mining and quarrying contributed 0.5% of GDP; according to ILO, the sector employed 0.2% of the employed labour force in that year. The most important indigenous mineral resource is iron ore (2.0m. metric tons were mined in 2006). Austria also has deposits of petroleum, magnesite and tungsten. The GDP of the mining sector increased, in real terms, by 7.3% in 2004, it declined by 0.6% in 2005, but increased by 9.5% in 2006.

Manufacturing contributed 19.9% of GDP in 2006; according to ILO, the sector engaged 18.9% of the employed labour force in that year. Measured by the gross value of output, the principal branches of manufacturing in 2004 were metals and metal products (accounting for 16.6% of the total), non-electrical machinery (12.5%), electrical machinery and telecommunications equipment (10.1%), food products (9.4%), wood and paper products (8.6%), road vehicles and parts (6.9%) and chemicals and chemical products (6.2%). The GDP of the manufacturing sector increased, in real terms, at an average annual rate of 3.4% during 1996–2004; it grew by 4.7% in 2004.

Hydroelectric power resources provide the major domestic source of energy, accounting for 59.1% of total electricity production in 2004, followed by gas (17.8%), coal (14.8%) and petroleum (3.0%). Austria is heavily dependent on imports of energy, mainly from eastern Europe. Fuel imports accounted for 12.6% of the total cost of imports in 2005.

The services sector contributed 67.7% of GDP in 2006; according to ILO, the sector engaged 66.3% of the employed labour force in that year. Tourism has traditionally been a leading source of revenue, providing receipts of US $19,310m. in 2005 (including passenger transport). The GDP of the services sector increased, in real terms, at an average annual rate of 2.0% in 1996–2005; it grew by 1.6% in 2005.

In 2006, according to the IMF, Austria recorded a visible trade surplus of US $641m., and there was a surplus of $10,259m. on the current account of the balance of payments. According to official figures, in 2006 the principal source of imports was Germany (41.5%); other major suppliers were Italy (6.9%), the People's Republic of China (3.6%), Switzerland (including Liechtenstein, 3.5%), France (3.5%) and the USA (3.3%). Germany was also the principal market for exports (30.3%); other significant purchasers were Italy (8.9%), the USA (5.9%) and Switzerland (including Liechtenstein, 4.7%). The principal exports in 2006 were machinery and transport equipment (accounting for 42.1% of total export revenue) and basic manufactures (23.3%). The principal imports were also machinery and transport equipment, accounting for 36.1% of total import costs, basic manufactures (17.0%) and miscellaneous manufactured articles (13.8%).

The federal budget for 2006 produced a preliminary deficit of €5,800m., equivalent to 2.2% of GDP. The central Government's debt was equivalent to 62.2% of GDP in 2006. The average annual rate of inflation was 1.7% in 1996–2006. Consumer prices increased by 1.5% in 2006. In 2006 4.7% of the labour force were unemployed.

Austria joined the EU in January 1995 and participated in the introduction of the European single currency, the euro, on 1 January 1999. The country is also a member of the Organisation for Economic Co-operation and Development (OECD, see p. 347).

Austria is a small, wealthy country with an open economy, which is largely dependent on the export of manufactured products. Austria has enjoyed significant benefits from joining the EU in 1995, generally maintaining stronger growth than the average achieved in the euro area. Following stagnation in the economy in 2001–03, export-led GDP growth was strong in 2004–07. The economic resurgence was widely attributed to the successful implementation of much-needed structural reforms under the centre-right Government of Dr Wolfgang Schüssel (2000–06). The measures adopted included the reform of the pension system, the privatization of the postal service and

Telekom Austria, and tax reductions. The reduction in Austria's corporate tax rate from 34% to 25% in 2005, which was designed to prevent Austrian businesses from relocating to eastern Europe, attracted significant foreign investment and contributed to rapid growth on the Vienna Stock Exchange. Austria's geographical location and historical links with countries in Central and Eastern Europe helped it to take advantage of the eastward enlargement of the EU from 2004. Austria developed new markets in these rapidly growing economies and is the largest investor in many of the new EU member states, with investment encompassing not just manufacturing but also financial services and energy. Austria's strong economic performance in 2004–07 was also due to an increase in competitiveness, as a result of significant growth in productivity in conjunction with moderate wage rises, which was in part attributable to the country's social partnership system, whereby the Government, employers and employees co-operate over wages and economic policy. As an open economy, Austria remained vulnerable to fluctuations in the economic conditions of its principal trading partners, notably Germany, and thus benefited from the recovery in the German economy in the mid-2000s. A new 'grand coalition', which was formed in January 2007, was broadly committed to continuing the reforms initiated by the previous Government. Its programme included addressing inadequacies in the education system and further reforms of the labour market to help older, younger and less skilled workers to find employment. Additionally, legislation was adopted in 2007, following skilled labour shortages, particularly in the manufacturing and construction sectors, whereby work permits were to be extended to skilled workers from the new EU member states in 2008, although restrictions on unskilled labour were to remain in place until 2011. The new coalition was also committed to continuing to reduce the budget deficit, aiming to balance the budget by 2010, and to promoting innovation by planning to raise expenditure on research and development to above the equivalent of 3% of GDP. Tourism, which accounts for around 9% of GDP each year, was expected to perform strongly in 2008, as Austria and Switzerland were co-hosting the European Football Championships in June; around 1.4m. foreign visitors were expected to visit Austria during the tournament. In order to promote future economic development, Austria needed to improve infrastructural links with its Central and Eastern European neighbours. Growth was expected to slow slightly in 2008, as a result of worsening global economic conditions.

Education

The central controlling body is the Federal Ministry of Education, Arts and Culture. Provincial boards (Landesschulräte) supervise school education in each of the nine federal provinces. Budgetary expenditure on education in 2008 was forecast at €6,604m. (equivalent to 9.5% of total spending).

Education is free and compulsory between the ages of six and 15 years. In 2005/06 enrolment at pre-primary level included 88% of those in the relevant age-group and enrolment at primary level included an estimated 97% of children in the relevant age-group (males 96%; females 98%). In 2002/03 enrolment at secondary level included 89% of children in the relevant age-group. Children undergo four years' primary education at a Volksschule, after which they choose between two principal forms of secondary education. This may be a Hauptschule, which, after four years, may be followed by one of a variety of schools offering technical, vocational and other specialized training, some of which provide a qualification for university. Alternatively, secondary education may be obtained in an Allgemeinbildende höhere Schule, which provides an eight-year general education covering a wide range of subjects, culminating in the Reifeprüfung or Matura. This gives access to all Austrian universities. In June 2007 the Federal Minister for Education, Arts and Culture announced a proposal for a system of comprehensive education (Gesamtschulen) for children aged between 10 and 14 years; the new system was due to be introduced on a trial basis in six provinces in September 2008.

Opportunities for further education exist at 22 universities as well as 154 tertiary vocational institutions. There are also six schools of art and music, all of which have university status. University tuition fees were introduced in 2002. Institutes of adult education (Volkshochschulen) are found in all provinces, as are other centres operated by public authorities, church organizations and the Austrian Trade Union Federation. In addition, all Austrian citizens over the age of 24, and with professional experience, may attend certain university courses in connection with their professional career or trade. In 2005/06 enrolment at tertiary level was equivalent to 49% of those in the relevant age-group (males 44%; females 53%).

Public Holidays

2008: 1 January (New Year's Day), 6 January (Epiphany), 24 March (Easter Monday), 1 May (Labour Day and Ascension Day), 12 May (Whit Monday), 22 May (Corpus Christi), 15 August (Assumption), 26 October (National Holiday), 1 November (All Saints' Day), 8 December (Immaculate Conception), 25 December (Christmas Day), 26 December (St Stephen's Day).

2009: 1 January (New Year's Day), 6 January (Epiphany), 13 April (Easter Monday), 1 May (Labour Day), 21 May (Ascension Day), 1 June (Whit Monday), 11 June (Corpus Christi), 15 August (Assumption), 26 October (National Holiday), 1 November (All Saints' Day), 8 December (Immaculate Conception), 25 December (Christmas Day), 26 December (St Stephen's Day).

Weights and Measures

The metric system is in force.

Statistical Survey

Sources (unless otherwise stated): Statistik Austria, Hintere Zollamtsstr. 2B, 1033 Vienna; tel. (1) 711-28-76-55; fax (1) 711-28-77-28; e-mail info@statistik.gv.at; internet www.statistik.at; Austrian National Bank, Postfach 61, Otto-Wagner-Pl. 3, 1090 Vienna; tel. (1) 404-20-0; fax (1) 404-20-66-96; e-mail oenb.info@oenb.co.at; internet www.oenb.at.

Area and Population

AREA, POPULATION AND DENSITY

Area (sq km)	83,871*
Population (census results)†	
15 May 1991	7,795,786
15 May 2001	
Males	3,889,189
Females	4,143,737
Total	8,032,926
Population (official estimates of annual averages)	
2004	8,174,733
2005	8,233,306
2006	8,281,948
Density (per sq km) at 2006	98.7

* 32,383 sq miles.
† Figures include all foreign workers.

AUSTRIA

PROVINCES
(official estimates at mid-2006)

	Area (sq km)*	Population	Density (per sq km)	Capital (with population)†
Burgenland	3,965.5	279,803	70.6	Eisenstadt (11,334)
Kärnten (Carinthia)	9,536.0	560,492	58.7	Klagenfurt (90,141)
Niederösterreich (Lower Austria)	19,177.8	1,585,503	82.7	Sankt Pölten (49,121)
Oberösterreich (Upper Austria)	11,981.9	1,404,203	117.2	Linz (183,504)
Salzburg	7,154.2	528,809	73.9	Salzburg (142,662)
Steiermark (Styria)	16,391.9	1,202,911	73.4	Graz (226,244)
Tirol (Tyrol)	12,647.7	698,514	55.2	Innsbruck (113,392)
Vorarlberg	2,601.5	364,154	140.0	Bregenz (121,123)
Wien (Vienna)	414.7	1,657,559	3,997.0	—
Total	**83,871.1**	**8,281,948**	**98.7**	—

* According to the reorganization of Länder boundaries of 1 January 2005.
† At census of 15 May 2001.

PRINCIPAL TOWNS
(population at 1 January 2007)

Wien (Vienna, the capital)	1,664,146	Klagenfurt		92,397
Graz	247,698	Wels		58,623
Linz	188,894	Villach		58,480
Salzburg	149,016	Sankt Pölten		51,360
Innsbruck	117,693	Dornbirn		44,243

BIRTHS, MARRIAGES AND DEATHS*

	Registered live births Number	Rate (per 1,000)	Registered marriages Number	Rate (per 1,000)	Registered deaths Number	Rate (per 1,000)
1999	78,138	9.7	39,485	4.9	78,200	9.7
2000	78,268	9.7	39,228	4.8	76,780	9.5
2001	75,458	9.3	34,213	4.2	74,767	9.2
2002	78,399	9.7	36,570	4.5	76,131	9.5
2003	76,944	9.5	37,195	4.6	77,209	9.5
2004	78,968	9.7	38,528	4.7	74,292	9.1
2005	78,190	9.5	39,153	4.8	75,189	9.1
2006	77,914	n.a.	36,923	n.a.	74,295	n.a.

* Rates prior to 2001 are based on unrevised population estimates.

Expectation of life (years at birth, WHO estimates): 79.6 (males 76.7; females 82.2) in 2005 (Source: WHO, *World Health Statistics*).

IMMIGRATION AND EMIGRATION

Immigrants from:	2004	2005	2006
Europe	83,641	85,294	73,252
Bosnia and Herzegovina	5,074	4,763	3,398
Croatia	2,903	2,747	2,351
Germany	14,888	17,268	18,467
Hungary	3,159	3,692	3,889
Poland	7,111	7,245	6,145
Romania	5,357	5,332	4,794
Russia	6,075	3,929	2,436
Serbia and Montenegro	10,999	11,737	7,487
Slovakia	3,480	3,759	3,678
Turkey	8,078	7,920	5,047
Africa	5,487	4,850	3,466
Americas	3,770	4,068	3,788
Asia	10,897	10,740	9,543
China, People's Republic	1,887	1,620	1,135
Oceania	379	395	397
Stateless, undeclared or unknown	23,225	12,475	10,526
Total	**127,399**	**117,822**	**100,972**

Emigrants to:	2004	2005	2006
Europe	38,294	39,936	47,517
Bosnia and Herzegovina	2,374	2,255	2,297
Croatia	2,097	2,133	2,136
Germany	5,644	6,770	9,244
Hungary	1,875	2,276	2,537
Poland	1,983	2,574	3,001
Romania	3,244	3,480	3,723
Serbia and Montenegro	4,004	4,246	5,317
Slovakia	329	429	2,338
Turkey	2,609	2,941	3,350
Africa	2,178	2,471	3,006
Americas	2,152	2,756	4,071
USA	1,120	1,612	2,510
Asia	4,854	5,353	5,555
Oceania	314	314	386
Stateless, undeclared or unknown	31,663	17,820	12,960
Total	**76,817**	**68,650**	**73,495**

Note: Totals for immigration include Austrian nationals returning from permanent residence abroad: 18,452 in 2004; 16,367 in 2005; 15,588 in 2006.

ECONOMICALLY ACTIVE POPULATION
('000 persons aged 15 years and over)

	2004	2005	2006
Agriculture, hunting and forestry	187.3	210.3	216.7
Fishing	1.2	0.1	0.2
Mining and quarrying	8.6	8.6	9.8
Manufacturing	695.5	699.9	741.5
Electricity, gas and water supply	28.1	31.2	31.3
Construction	304.0	313.6	323.7
Wholesale and retail trade; repair of motor vehicles, motorcycles and personal and household goods	592.8	593.5	610.8
Hotels and restaurants	227.0	244.2	242.6
Transport, storage and communications	238.3	241.3	241.8
Financial intermediation	140.2	143.5	133.1
Real estate, renting and business activities	327.2	334.0	350.7
Public administration and defence; compulsory social security	254.1	238.6	253.0
Education	210.1	221.9	222.2
Health and social work	325.8	349.6	347.8
Other community, social and personal service activities	187.2	175.4	186.9
Private households with employed persons	8.5	9.6	10.0
Extra-territorial organizations and bodies	8.1	8.2	6.1
Total employed	**3,744.0**	**3,824.4**	**3,928.3**
Unemployed	194.6	207.7	195.6
Total labour force	**3,938.7**	**4,032.2**	**4,123.9**
Males	2,159.5	2,203.2	2,244.6
Females	1,779.1	1,829.0	1,879.2

Source: ILO.

Health and Welfare

KEY INDICATORS

Total fertility rate (children per woman, 2005)	1.4
Under-5 mortality rate (per 1,000 live births, 2005)	5
HIV/AIDS (% of persons aged 15–49, 2005)	0.3
Physicians (per 1,000 head, 2003)	3.38
Hospital beds (per 1,000 head, 2005)	7.7
Health expenditure (2004): US $ per head (PPP)	3,417.7
Health expenditure (2004): % of GDP	10.3
Health expenditure (2003): public (% of total)	75.6
Human Development Index (2005): ranking	15
Human Development Index (2005): value	0.948

For sources and definitions, see explanatory note on p. vi.

AUSTRIA

Agriculture

PRINCIPAL CROPS
('000 metric tons)

	2004	2005	2006
Wheat	1,718.8	1,453.1	1,396.3
Barley	1,006.7	879.6	914.1
Maize	1,653.8	1,724.8	1,471.7
Rye	213.5	163.7	93.8
Oats	138.8	128.4	131.2
Triticale (wheat-rye hybrid)	235.7	198.5	110.1
Potatoes	693.1	763.2	654.6
Sugar beet	2,901.9	3,083.8	2,493.1
Peas (dry)	122.1	90.3	89.9
Sunflower seed	77.9	80.8	84.6
Rapeseed	120.8	104.3	137.3
Cabbages	100.1	88.8	96.1
Lettuce	54.0	56.6	59.1
Onions (dry)	117.7	103.0	99.7
Carrots	81.3	79.4	77.2
Apples	484.1	452.6	509.1
Pears	124.4	118.3	117.2
Plums	69.6	61.6	80.3
Grapes	364.6	301.9	300.8

Aggregate production ('000 metric tons, may include official, semi-official or estimated data): Total cereals 5,319.8 in 2004, 4,903.1 in 2005, 4,460.0 in 2006; Total roots and tubers 693.1 in 2004, 763.2 in 2005, 654.6 in 2006; Total vegetables (incl. melons) 551.0 in 2004, 511.6 in 2005, 528.7 in 2006; Total fruits (excl. melons) 1,139.2 in 2004, 1,025.5 in 2005, 1,110.4 in 2006.

Source: FAO.

LIVESTOCK
('000 head at December)

	2004	2005	2006
Horses	80.1	85.0*	85.0*
Cattle	2,052.0	2,051.0	2,002.1
Pigs	3,154.3	3,209.3	3,160.4
Sheep	325.5	327.2	325.7
Goats	54.6	55.5	55.1
Chickens	12,354	n.a.	14,313
Ducks	83	n.a.	50*
Geese	40	22	21
Turkeys	550	700*	700*

* FAO estimate.

LIVESTOCK PRODUCTS
('000 metric tons)

	2004	2005	2006
Cattle meat	206.1	204.5	216.5
Sheep meat	6.6	6.6	7.2
Pig meat	514.7	510.1	514.0
Chicken meat	88.8	89.2	88.0*
Cows' milk	3,137.3	3,113.7	3,146.7
Sheep's milk	8.6	8.8	8.8
Goats' milk	12.3	13.4	13.4*
Hen eggs	87.0	89.3	90.0
Honey	6.9	6.2	6.0

* FAO estimate.
Source: FAO.

Forestry

ROUNDWOOD REMOVALS
('000 cubic metres, excl. bark)

	2004	2005	2006
Sawlogs, veneer logs and logs for sleepers	10,021	9,892	11,487
Pitprops (mine timber), pulpwood, and other industrial wood	2,922	2,894	2,943
Fuel wood	3,540	3,685	4,705
Total	16,483	16,471	19,135

Source: FAO.

SAWNWOOD PRODUCTION
('000 cubic metres, incl. railway sleepers)

	2004	2005	2006
Coniferous (softwood)	10,917	10,884	10,265
Broadleaved (hardwood)	216	190	242
Total	11,133	11,074	10,507

Source: FAO.

Fishing

(metric tons, live weight)

	2003	2004	2005
Capture	372	400	370
Freshwater fishes	372	400	370
Aquaculture	2,233	2,267	2,420
Common carp	337	306	321
Rainbow trout	1,594	1,640	1,729
Brook trout	217	230	246
Total catch	2,605	2,667	2,790

Source: FAO.

Mining

('000 metric tons, unless otherwise indicated)

	2004	2005	2006*
Brown coal (incl. lignite)	235	6	5
Crude petroleum ('000 barrels)	6,728	6,413	6,500
Iron ore: gross weight	1,882	2,048	2,000
Magnesite (crude)	715	694	700
Tungsten, concentrate (metric tons)†	1,400*	1,280	1,300
Gypsum and anhydrite (crude)	1,039	1,113	1,000
Kaolin (crude)	105	56	60
Basalt	5,197	3,166	3,200
Dolomite	5,907	6,291	6,200
Limestone and marble	24,158	25,576	25,000
Quartz and quartzite	294	249	250
Natural gas (million cu metres)	2,011	1,654	1,700

* Estimated production.
† Figures refer to metal content.
Source: US Geological Survey.

Industry

SELECTED PRODUCTS
('000 metric tons, unless otherwise indicated)

	2001	2002	2003
Wheat flour	278	287	282
Raw sugar	460*	456*	386
Wine ('000 hectolitres)	229	260	324
Beer ('000 hectolitres)	8,528	8,745	8,980
Woven cotton fabrics—pure and mixed (million sq metres)	62	56	95
Mechanical wood pulp	752	746	834
Chemical and semi-chemical wood pulp	1,544	1,557	1,594
Newsprint	766	730	784
Other printing and writing paper	4,162	4,506	4,684
Other paper and paperboard	1,786	1,801	1,831
Motor spirit (petrol)	1,922	1,927	1,811
Jet fuel	513	484	446
Distillate fuel oils	3,959	3,984	3,849
Residual fuel oils	1,047	1,012	1,062
Cement†	3,802	3,918	3,886
Crude steel†	5,887	6,208	6,261
Refined copper—unwrought: secondary†	69	65	65
Passenger motor cars (number)	131,098	132,768	118,650
Motorcycles, etc. (number)	40,088	52,911	n.a.
Electric energy (million kWh)	62,344	62,488	60,100

* Unofficial figure.
† Data from the US Geological Survey.

Sources: FAO; UN, *Industrial Commodity Statistics Yearbook*; International Road Federation, *World Road Statistics*.

2004 ('000 metric tons, unless otherwise indicated): Motor spirit (petrol) 1,738; Jet fuel 455; Distillate fuel oils 3,529; Residual fuel oils 1,032; Cement 3,976; Crude steel 6,530 (estimate); Refined copper—unwrought: secondary 74.2; Electric energy (million kWh) 64,125 (Sources: UN, *Industrial Commodity Statistics Yearbook*; US Geological Survey).

2005 ('000 metric tons): Cement 4,736; Crude steel 7,031; Refined copper—unwrought: secondary 72.3 (Source: US Geological Survey).

2006 ('000 metric tons, estimates): Cement 4,700; Crude steel 7,129; Refined copper—unwrought: secondary 72.6 (Source: US Geological Survey).

Finance

CURRENCY AND EXCHANGE RATES

Monetary Units
100 cent = 1 euro (€).

Sterling and Dollar Equivalents (31 December 2007)
£1 sterling = 1.3609 euros;
US $1 = 0.6793 euros;
€10 = £7.35 = $14.72.

Average Exchange Rate (euros per US $)
2005   0.8041
2006   0.7971
2007   0.7306

Note: The national currency was formerly the Schilling. From the introduction of the euro, with Austrian participation, on 1 January 1999, a fixed exchange rate of €1 = 13.7603 Schilling was in operation. Euro notes and coins were introduced on 1 January 2002. The euro and local currency circulated alongside each other until 28 February, after which the euro became the sole legal tender.

FEDERAL BUDGET
(€ million)

Revenue	2002	2003*	2004†
Total taxes and levies (net)	36,666	35,468	38,616
Gross tax revenue	54,951	53,498	57,618
Tax on wages and salaries	16,219	16,944	17,300
Tax on assessed income	3,126	2,677	3,000
Withholding tax	1,663	1,410	1,730
Corporate income tax	4,559	4,332	4,300
Turnover tax	17,639	16,472	19,000
Tobacco tax	1,297	1,329	1,350
Mineral oils tax	3,109	3,310	3,450
Car engine related insurance tax	1,185	1,217	1,250
Other taxes and levies	6,155	5,806	6,238
Transfers to provinces, municipalities, etc.	−16,176	−16,077	−16,602
Transfers to European Union	−2,108	−1,952	−2,400
Transfers from tax revenues	1,507	1,497	1,688
Social insurance contributions	7,331	7,473	7,952
Other revenue	13,924	13,454	10,980
Total	**59,428**	**57,892**	**59,237**

Expenditure‡	2002	2003*	2004†
Education	5,657	5,745	5,720
Research and development	2,566	2,581	3,514
Art and culture	689	660	489
Health	792	871	841
Social welfare	18,206	18,882	18,598
Housing construction	1,807	1,805	1,810
Transport	6,726	6,579	7,118
Agriculture and forestry	1,798	1,835	1,830
Industry and trade	874	761	1,199
Public-sector services	346	357	404
Private-sector services	179	232	219
Defence	1,624	1,721	1,702
Security and law enforcement	2,253	2,344	2,310
Other sovereign administration services	18,298	17,016	16,911
Total	**61,818**	**61,390**	**62,667**

* Provisional.
† Forecast.
‡ Excluding debt-servicing and currency swaps (including interest and charges, but excluding redemption payments) (€ million): 8,547 in 2002; 8,344 in 2003 (provisional); 8,329 in 2004 (forecast).

Note: Totals may not be equal to the sum of component parts, owing to rounding.

2004 (€ '000 million): Total revenue 60.3; Total expenditure 65.0.

2005 (€ '000 million): Total revenue 61.4; Total expenditure 66.0.

2006 (€ '000 million, preliminary): Total revenue 60.4; Total expenditure 66.2.

Source: Federal Ministry of Finance, Vienna.

NATIONAL BANK RESERVES
(US $ million at 31 December)

	2004	2005	2006
Gold*	4,330	4,989	5,901
IMF special drawing rights	160	147	190
Reserve position in IMF	935	394	247
Foreign exchange	6,763	6,298	6,573
Total	**12,188**	**11,828**	**12,911**

* Eurosystem valuation.

Source: IMF, *International Financial Statistics*.

AUSTRIA

MONEY SUPPLY
(€ '000 million at 31 December)

	2004	2005	2006
Currency issued*	14.11	15.90	17.65
Demand deposits at banking institutions	68.89	76.33	80.97

* Currency put into circulation by the Oesterreichische Nationalbank was (€ '000 million): 11.23 in 2004; 7.20 in 2005; 1.97 in 2006.

Source: IMF, *International Financial Statistics*.

COST OF LIVING
(Consumer Price Index; base: 2000 = 100)

	2004	2005	2006
Food and non-alcoholic beverages	109.0	110.4	112.5
Alcoholic beverages, tobacco	114.3	122.0	122.4
Housing, water, energy	109.2	114.9	119.8
Communication	94.9	86.9	81.7
Household goods/furnishings and operations	105.8	106.3	104.0
Clothing and footwear	104.0	104.0	103.7
Recreation and culture	105.8	106.3	107.2
Health	107.1	113.7	114.6
Education	141.1	144.1	154.9
Restaurants and hotels	111.2	113.7	116.2
Transport	107.4	110.8	113.8
Other goods and services	111.9	115.1	116.8
All items	108.1	110.6	112.2

NATIONAL ACCOUNTS

National Income and Product
(€ '000 million at current prices)

	2004	2005	2006
Compensation of employees	115.8	120.0	125.1
Gross operating surplus and mixed income	93.8	98.2	105.5
Taxes on production and imports, less subsidies	26.6	27.2	27.3
Gross domestic product (GDP) in market prices	236.2	245.3	257.9
Primary incomes (net)	−2.2	−2.5	−3.3
Gross national income (GNI)	234.0	242.8	254.6
Less Consumption of fixed capital	33.8	35.1	36.5
Net national income	200.2	207.8	218.1
Current transfers (net)	−2.4	−2.0	−2.2
Net national disposable income	197.8	205.7	215.9

Expenditure on the Gross Domestic Product
(€ '000 million at current prices)

	2004	2005	2006
Final consumption expenditure	175.6	182.3	189.3
Gross capital formation	50.4	50.7	53.8
Total domestic expenditure	226.0	233.0	243.1
Exports of goods and services	120.5	131.1	144.7
Less Imports of goods and services	110.3	119.1	130.1
Statistical discrepancy	−0.1	0.3	0.1
GDP in market prices	236.1	245.3	257.9

Gross Domestic Product by Economic Activity
(€ '000 million at current prices)

	2004	2005	2006
Agriculture, hunting, forestry and fishing	3.9	3.5	3.9
Mining and quarrying	1.0	1.0	1.2
Manufacturing	40.9	42.7	46.2
Electricity, gas and water	5.0	5.2	6.0
Construction	16.1	16.6	17.9
Wholesale and retail trade	27.6	28.2	29.2
Restaurants and hotels	9.7	10.1	10.6
Transport, storage and communications	15.0	14.9	15.1
Finance and insurance	11.4	11.4	12.7
Real estate and business services*	37.5	40.3	41.6
Public administration and defence	12.3	12.8	13.3
Other services	31.6	33.4	34.8
Sub-total	212.0	220.1	232.5
Taxes, less subsidies, on products	24.1	25.3	25.4
GDP in purchasers' values	236.1	245.3	257.9

* Including imputed rents of owner-occupied dwellings.

BALANCE OF PAYMENTS
(US $ million)

	2004	2005	2006
Exports of goods f.o.b.	112,070	117,233	134,302
Imports of goods f.o.b.	−109,020	−113,806	−133,661
Trade balance	3,050	3,427	641
Exports of services	49,153	53,921	45,202
Imports of services	−46,737	−49,107	−32,398
Balance on goods and services	5,466	8,241	13,445
Other income received	19,891	24,151	27,506
Other income paid	−21,216	−25,488	−29,336
Balance on goods, services and income	4,141	6,904	11,614
Current transfers received	5,314	6,257	4,368
Current transfers paid	−8,073	−8,908	−5,724
Current balance	1,382	4,252	10,259
Capital account (net)	−341	−237	−930
Direct investment abroad	−8,664	−10,078	−4,017
Direct investment from abroad	3,892	9,057	157
Portfolio investment assets	−32,677	−44,060	−30,753
Portfolio investment liabilities	31,695	30,396	43,316
Financial derivatives assets	144	283	—
Financial derivatives liabilities	−813	−129	−1,368
Other investment assets	−21,178	−29,966	−66,032
Other investment liabilities	24,983	42,870	49,647
Net errors and omissions	−272	−3,138	−1,142
Overall balance	−1,849	−750	−862

Source: IMF, *International Financial Statistics*.

AUSTRIA

External Trade

Note: Austria's customs territory excludes Mittelberg im Kleinen Walsertal (in Vorarlberg) and Jungholz (in Tyrol). The figures also exclude trade in silver specie and monetary gold.

SELECTED COMMODITIES
(distribution by SITC, € million)

Imports c.i.f.	2004	2005	2006
Food and live animals	4,673	5,058	5,426
Fruit and vegetables	1,210	1,349	1,373
Beverages and tobacco	568	560	566
Crude materials (inedible) except fuels	3,324	3,876	4,534
Cork and wood	844	900	1,153
Mineral fuels, lubricants, etc.	8,083	11,778	11,727
Crude petroleum and bituminous oils	4,552	6,114	7,377
Gas, natural and manufactured	1,197	1,748	2,442
Chemicals and related products	9,392	10,566	11,857
Medicinal and pharmaceutical products	2,991	3,366	3,905
Basic manufactures	14,451	14,969	17,678
Metal manufactures	3,522	3,714	4,253
Machinery and transport equipment	37,076	35,544	37,602
General industrial machinery and equipment	4,688	4,834	5,378
Road vehicles	11,059	11,054	11,537
Miscellaneous manufactured articles	13,081	13,584	14,367
Total (incl. others)	91,094	96,499	104,201

Exports f.o.b.	2004	2005	2006
Food and live animals	3,553	3,988	4,427
Dairy products and birds' eggs	731	741	798
Beverages and tobacco	1,596	1,763	1,972
Crude materials (inedible) except fuels	2,876	2,883	3,239
Cork and wood	1,479	1,458	1,578
Mineral fuels, lubricants, etc.	2,901	4,360	2,401
Crude petroleum and bituminous oils	616	976	970
Electricity	2,069	3,084	792
Chemicals and related products	8,177	9,308	10,972
Medicinal and pharmaceutical products	2,870	3,606	4,234
Basic manufactures	19,228	21,142	24,217
Metal manufactures	3,486	4,201	5,188
Machinery and transport equipment	40,329	39,441	43,656
General industrial machinery and equipment	5,093	5,565	6,399
Electrical machinery, apparatus and appliances, etc.	6,931	6,940	7,514
Road vehicles	10,843	11,168	12,582
Miscellaneous manufactured articles	10,654	11,293	12,297
Total (incl. others)	89,848	94,705	103,742

PRINCIPAL TRADING PARTNERS
(€ million)*

Imports c.i.f.	2004	2005	2006
Belgium-Luxembourg	1,764	1,739	1,993
China, People's Republic	2,296	2,981	3,777
Czech Republic	2,886	3,189	3,354
Finland	705	1,072	794
France	3,644	3,897	3,598
Germany	39,130	40,733	43,264
Hungary	2,603	2,464	2,587
Italy	6,234	6,389	7,183
Japan	1,999	1,885	1,931
Netherlands	2,557	2,706	3,049
Poland	1,112	1,489	1,617
Russia	1,403	2,262	2,399
Slovakia	1,814	1,696	1,788
Spain	1,390	1,388	1,549
Sweden	1,214	1,177	1,251
Switzerland-Liechtenstein	2,847	3,344	3,633
United Kingdom	1,754	1,852	2,049
USA	2,958	3,175	3,462
Total (incl. others)	91,094	96,499	104,201

Exports f.o.b.	2004	2005	2006
Belgium-Luxembourg	1,570	1,776	1,833
China, People's Republic	1,119	1,221	1,232
Croatia	1,219	1,224	1,320
Czech Republic	2,752	2,925	3,384
France	3,778	4,017	3,942
Germany	28,951	30,108	31,475
Hungary	3,338	3,223	3,508
Italy	7,706	8,187	9,235
Japan	1,051	1,025	1,100
Netherlands	1,660	1,700	1,862
Poland	1,630	1,891	2,393
Russia	1,390	1,701	2,254
Slovakia	1,377	1,640	1,768
Slovenia	1,986	1,711	1,873
Spain	2,214	2,615	2,896
Sweden	933	997	1,083
Switzerland-Liechtenstein	4,435	4,647	4,854
United Kingdom	3,765	3,845	3,922
USA	5,307	5,350	6,118
Total (incl. others)	89,848	94,705	103,742

* Imports by country of production; exports by country of consumption.

Transport

RAILWAYS
(traffic, Federal Railways only)

	2004	2005	2006
Number of passengers carried ('000)	187,900	191,600	195,900
Freight gross ton-km (millions)	71,371	69,489	73,441
Freight tons carried ('000)	85,427	86,820	91,577

ROAD TRAFFIC
(motor vehicles in use at 31 December)

	2004	2005	2006
Passenger cars	4,109,129	4,156,743	4,204,969
Buses and coaches	9,408	9,301	9,297
Goods vehicles	332,976	338,888	345,480
Motorcycles	315,638	326,286	338,721
Mopeds and motor scooters	296,522	301,425	306,592

AUSTRIA

SHIPPING

Merchant Fleet
(registered at 31 December)

	2004	2005	2006
Number of vessels	8	8	8
Total displacement ('000 grt)	34.1	34.1	34.1

Source: Lloyd's Register-Fairplay, *World Fleet Statistics*.

International Freight Traffic on the Danube
('000 metric tons, excl. transit traffic)

	2003	2004	2005
Goods loaded	1,567.3	1,635.2	1,653.0
Goods unloaded	5,225.1	6,071.6	6,069.5

CIVIL AVIATION
(Austrian Airlines, '000)

	2000	2001	2002
Kilometres flown	70,411	66,316	129,649
Passenger ton-km	914,870	846,385	1,434,582
Cargo ton-km	284,533	252,406	396,021
Mail ton-km	11,635	12,539	28,099

2003 (traffic, millions): Kilometres flown 130; Passengers carried 6.9; Passenger-km 14,558; Total ton-km 1,983 (Source: UN *Statistical Yearbook*).

Tourism

FOREIGN TOURIST ARRIVALS
(by country of origin, '000)*

	2003	2004	2005
Belgium	391.5	401.0	425.1
France	436.1	469.1	452.0
Germany	10,468.0	10,255.0	10,366.8
Italy	1,089.6	1,100.6	1,101.8
Netherlands	1,418.4	1,425.6	1,483.9
Switzerland-Liechtenstein	888.4	895.6	894.7
United Kingdom	662.7	721.9	757.0
USA	484.7	545.9	548.4
Total (incl. others)	19,077.6	19,372.8	19,952.4

* Arrivals at accommodation establishments.

Tourism receipts (US $ million, incl. passenger transport): 16,342 in 2003; 18,385 in 2004; 19,310 in 2005.

Source: World Tourism Organization.

Communications Media

	2004	2005	2006
Radio licences issued	3,051,142	3,238,424	3,211,797
Television licences issued	3,008,976	3,075,249	3,130,654
Telephones ('000 main lines in use)*	3,821	3,739	3,564
Mobile cellular telephones ('000 subscribers)*	7,992	8,650	9,255
Personal computers ('000 in use)*	4,729	4,996	n.a.
Internet users ('000)*	3,900	4,000	4,200
Broadband subscribers ('000)*	870	1,174	1,428
Daily newspapers	17	17	17
Weekly newspapers	229	226	263
Other periodicals	2,776	n.a.	2,735

* Source: International Telecommunication Union.

Facsimile machines ('000 in use): 210.0 in 1993; 240.0 in 1994; 284.7 in 1995 (Source: UN, *Statistical Yearbook*).

Education

(2005/06)

	Institutions	Staff	Students
Pre-primary*	7,063	37,620†	274,904
General primary and secondary	5,205	92,146	858,105
Compulsory vocational	160	4,505	128,287
Secondary technical and vocational	1,181	21,107	212,436
Teacher training:			
second level	51	1,341	13,079
third level	35	2,803	13,073
Universities‡	22	11,236	203,453
Tertiary vocational‡	169	3,454	25,727

* Including crèches.
† Including non-teaching staff.
‡ Excluding private institutions.

Directory

The Constitution

The Austrian Constitution of 1920, as amended in 1929, was restored on 1 May 1945. Its main provisions, with subsequent amendments, are summarized below:

Austria is a democratic republic, having a Federal President (Bundespräsident), elected directly by the people, and a bicameral legislature, the Parliament (Parlament), consisting of the National Council (Nationalrat) and the Federal Council (Bundesrat). The republic is organized on the federal system, comprising the nine federal provinces (Bundesländer) of Burgenland, Carinthia (Kärnten), Lower Austria (Niederösterreich), Upper Austria (Oberösterreich), Salzburg, Styria (Steiermark), Tyrol (Tirol), Vorarlberg and Vienna (Wien). Following reforms to the Constitution approved by the Nationalrat in June 2007, the age at which men and women are eligible to vote in all national and provincial elections was lowered from 18 to 16 years. (The reform was to take effect at elections to the European Parliament, scheduled for 2009.)

The Nationalrat consists of 183 members, elected by universal direct suffrage, according to a system of proportional representation. It functions for a maximum period of four years. In June 2007 the Nationalrat approved a reform extending the maximum duration of the parliamentary mandate to five years. (The reform was to take effect after the next general election, scheduled for 2010.)

The 62-member Bundesrat represents the Bundesländer. Lower Austria provides 12 members, Vienna and Upper Austria each 11, Styria nine, Tyrol five, Carinthia and Salzburg each four, and Burgenland and Vorarlberg each three. The seats are divided between the parties according to the number of seats that they control in each Provincial Assembly (Landtag) and are held during the life of the provincial government (Landesregierung) that they represent. Each Land, in turn, provides the President of the Bundesrat for a period of six months.

The Federal Assembly (Bundesversammlung—a joint meeting of the Nationalrat and the Bundesrat) is convened for certain matters of special importance, for example to witness the swearing-in of the Federal President. It can also be convened to declare war or to demand a referendum on the deposition of the President, if demanded by the Nationalrat.

The Federal President, elected by popular vote, is the Head of State and holds office for a term of six years. The President is eligible for re-election only once in succession. Although invested with special emergency powers, the President normally acts on the authority of the Federal Government, which is responsible to the Nationalrat for governmental policy.

The Federal Government consists of the Federal Chancellor, the Vice-Chancellor and the other ministers and state secretaries, who may vary in number. The Chancellor is chosen by the President, usually from the party with the strongest representation in the newly elected Nationalrat, and the other ministers are then selected by the President on the advice of the Chancellor.

If the Nationalrat adopts an explicit motion expressing 'no confidence' in the Federal Government or individual members thereof, the Federal Government or the federal minister concerned is removed from office.

All new legislative proposals must be read and submitted to a vote in both chambers of the Parliament. A new draft law is presented first to the Nationalrat, where it usually has three readings, and secondly to the Bundesrat, where it can be delayed or vetoed.

The Constitution also provides for appeals by the Government to the electorate on specific points by means of a referendum. If a petition supported by at least 100,000 electors, or by one-sixth of the electors in each of three separate provinces, is presented to the Government, the Government must submit it to the Nationalrat.

The Landtag exercises the same functions in each province as the Nationalrat does in the State. The members of the Landtag elect the Landesregierung, consisting of a provincial governor (Landeshauptmann) and his or her councillors (Landesräte). They are responsible to the Landtag.

The spheres of legal and administrative competence of both national and provincial governments are clearly defined. The Constitution distinguishes four groups:

1. Law-making and administration are the responsibility of the State: e.g. foreign affairs, justice and finance.
2. Law-making is the responsibility of the State, administration is the responsibility of the provinces: e.g. elections, population matters and road traffic.
3. The State formulates the rudiments of the law, the provinces enact the law and administer it: e.g. charity, rights of agricultural workers, land reform.
4. Law-making and administration are the responsibility of the provinces in all matters not expressly assigned to the State: e.g. municipal affairs.

The Government

HEAD OF STATE

Federal President: Dr HEINZ FISCHER (sworn in 8 July 2004).

COUNCIL OF MINISTERS
(March 2008)

A 'grand coalition' of the Sozialdemokratische Partei Österreichs (Social Democratic Party of Austria—SPÖ) and the Österreichische Volkspartei (Austrian People's Party—ÖVP).

Federal Chancellor: Dr ALFRED GUSENBAUER (SPÖ).
Vice-Chancellor and Federal Minister for Finance: WILHELM MOLTERER (ÖVP).
Federal Minister for European and International Affairs: Dr URSULA PLASSNIK (ÖVP).
Federal Minister for Transport, Innovation and Technology: WERNER FAYMANN (SPÖ).
Federal Minister for Education, Arts and Culture: Dr CLAUDIA SCHMIED (SPÖ).
Federal Minister for Health, the Family and Youth: Dr ANDREA KDOLSKY (ÖVP).
Federal Minister for the Interior: GÜNTHER PLATTER (ÖVP).
Federal Minister for Justice: Dr MARIA BERGER (SPÖ).
Federal Minister for Agriculture, Forestry, Environment and Water Management: JOSEF PRÖLL (ÖVP).
Federal Minister for Defence: NORBERT DARABOS (SPÖ).
Federal Minister for Social Security and Consumer Protection: Dr ERWIN BUCHINGER (SPÖ).
Federal Minister for Economics and Labour: Dr MARTIN BARTENSTEIN (ÖVP).
Federal Minister for Science and Research: Dr JOHANNES HAHN (ÖVP).
Federal Minister for Women, the Media and the Civil Service: DORIS BURES (SPÖ).
Secretaries of State in the Federal Chancellery: HEIDRUN SILHAVY (SPÖ), Dr REINHOLD LOPATKA (ÖVP).
Secretary of State in the Federal Ministry of European and International Affairs: Dr HANS WINKLER (Independent).
Secretary of State in the Federal Ministry of Finance: Dr CHRISTOPH MATZNETTER (SPÖ).
Secretary of State in the Federal Ministry of Transport, Innovation and Technology: CHRISTA KRANZL (SPÖ).
Secretary of State in the Federal Ministry of Economics and Labour: CHRISTINE MAREK (ÖVP).

Note: Government chief whips, the leaders of the parliamentary parties and the respective directors of the parliamentary groups (Klubdirektoren) are also members of the Council of Ministers.

MINISTRIES

Office of the Federal President: Hofburg, Leopoldinischer Trakt, 1014 Vienna; tel. (1) 534-22; fax (1) 535-65-12; e-mail buergerservice@hofburg.at; internet www.hofburg.at.

Office of the Federal Chancellor: Ballhauspl. 2, 1014 Vienna; tel. (1) 531-15-0; fax (1) 535-03-38-0; e-mail post@bka.gv.at; internet www.bka.gv.at.

Federal Ministry of Agriculture, Forestry, Environment and Water Management: Stubenring 1, 1012 Vienna; tel. (1) 711-00-0; fax (1) 711-00-21-40; e-mail infomaster@lebensministerium.at; internet www.lebensministerium.at.

Federal Ministry of Defence: Rossauer Lände 1, 1090 Vienna; tel. (1) 520-00; fax (1) 520-02-61-22; e-mail presse@bmlv.gv.at; internet www.bmlv.gv.at.

Federal Ministry of Economics and Labour: Stubenring 1, 1011 Vienna; tel. (1) 711-00-0; fax (1) 710-85-73; e-mail service@bmwa.gv.at; internet www.bmwa.gv.at.

Federal Ministry of Education, Arts and Culture: Minoritenpl. 5, 1014 Vienna; tel. (1) 531-20-00; fax (1) 531-20-30-99; e-mail ingrid.wurzinger@bmukk.gv.at; internet www.bmukk.gv.at.

Federal Ministry of European and International Affairs: Minoritenpl. 8, 1014 Vienna; tel. (5) 011-50-0; fax (5) 011-59-0; e-mail post@bmeia.gv.at; internet www.bmeia.gv.at.

Federal Ministry of Finance: Hintere Zollamtstr. 2B, 1030 Vienna; tel. (1) 514-33-0; fax (1) 512-78-69; e-mail buergerservice@bmf.gv.at; internet www.bmf.gv.at.

Federal Ministry of Health, the Family and Youth: Radetzkystr. 2, 1030 Vienna; tel. (1) 711-00-0; fax (1) 711-00-14-30-0; e-mail buergerservice@bmgfj.gv.at; internet www.bmgfj.gv.at.

Federal Ministry of the Interior: Herrengasse 7, 1014 Vienna; tel. (1) 531-26-0; fax (1) 531-26-10-86-13; e-mail infomaster@bmi.gv.at; internet www.bmi.gv.at.

Federal Ministry of Justice: Museumstr. 7, 1016 Vienna; tel. (1) 521-52-0; fax (1) 521-52-27-30; internet www.bmj.gv.at.

Federal Ministry of Science and Research: Minoritenpl. 5, 1014 Vienna; tel. (1) 531-20-0; fax (1) 531-20-90-99; e-mail petra.schaur@bmwf.gv.at; internet www.bmwf.gv.at.

Federal Ministry of Social Security and Consumer Protection: Stubenring 1, 1010 Vienna; tel. (1) 711-00-0; fax (1) 711-00-14-26-6; e-mail briefkasten@bmsk.gv.at; internet www.bmsk.gv.at.

Federal Ministry of Transport, Innovation and Technology: Radetzkystr. 2, Postfach 3000, 1030 Vienna; tel. (1) 711-62-65-0; fax (1) 711-62-65-74-98; e-mail info@bmvit.gv.at; internet www.bmvit.gv.at.

Federal Ministry of Women, the Media and the Civil Service: Bundeskanzleramt Österreich, Sektion II-Frauenangelegenheiten und Gleichstellung, Minoritenpl. 3, 1014 Vienna; tel. (1) 531-15-0; fax (1) 531-15-21-33; internet www.frauen.bka.gv.at.

President and Legislature

PRESIDENT

Presidential Election, 25 April 2004

Candidates	Votes	% of votes
Dr Heinz Fischer (SPÖ)	2,166,690	52.4
Dr Benita Ferrero-Waldner (ÖVP)	1,969,326	47.6
Total	4,136,016	100.0

PARLIAMENT

Nationalrat
(National Council)

President of the Nationalrat: BARBARA PRAMMER.

AUSTRIA

General Election, 1 October 2006

Party	Votes	% of votes	Seats
Sozialdemokratische Partei Österreichs (SPÖ)	1,663,986	35.34	68
Österreichische Volkspartei (ÖVP)	1,616,493	34.33	66
Die Grünen	520,130	11.05	21
Freiheitliche Partei Österreichs (FPÖ)	519,598	11.04	21
Bündnis Zukunft Österreich (BZÖ)	193,539	4.11	7
Liste Dr Martin—für Demokratie, Kontrolle, Gerechtigkeit	131,688	2.80	—
Kommunistische Partei Österreichs (KPÖ)	47,578	1.01	—
Others	15,269	0.32	—
Total	4,708,281	100.00	183

Bundesrat
(Federal Council)
(March 2008)

President of the Bundesrat: HELMUT KRITZINGER (January–June 2008).

Provinces	SPÖ	ÖVP	Die Grünen	Other	Total seats
Burgenland	2	1	—	—	3
Carinthia (Kärnten)	2	—	—	2	4
Lower Austria (Niederösterreich)	3	7	1	1	12
Upper Austria (Oberösterreich)	5	5	1	—	11
Salzburg	2	2	—	—	4
Styria (Steiermark)	5	4	—	—	9
Tyrol (Tirol)	1	3	1	—	5
Vorarlberg	1	2	—	—	3
Vienna (Wien)	7	2	1	1	11
Total	28	26	4	4	62

Governments of the Federal Provinces

BURGENLAND

Governor: HANS NIESSL (SPÖ).
President of the Landtag: WALTER PRIOR (SPÖ).
Election, 9 October 2005

Party	Seats
SPÖ	19
ÖVP	13
FPÖ	2
Die Grünen	2
Total	36

CARINTHIA (KÄRNTEN)

Governor: Dr JÖRG HAIDER (BZÖ).
President of the Landtag: JOSEF LOBNIG (BZÖ).
Election, 4 March 2004

Party	Seats
FPÖ*	16
SPÖ	14
ÖVP	4
Die Grünen	2
Total	36

* In 2005 15 representatives of the FPÖ left that party to join the Alliance for the Future of Austria (Bündnis Zukunft Österreich—BZÖ).

LOWER AUSTRIA (NIEDERÖSTERREICH)

Governor: Dr ERWIN PRÖLL (ÖVP).
President of the Landtag: HANS PENZ (ÖVP).
Election, 9 March 2008

Party	Seats
ÖVP	31
SPÖ	15
FPÖ	6
Die Grünen	4
Total	56

UPPER AUSTRIA (OBERÖSTERREICH)

Governor: Dr JOSEF PÜHRINGER (ÖVP).
President of the Landtag: ANGELA ORTHNER (ÖVP).
Election, 28 September 2003

Party	Seats
ÖVP	25
SPÖ	22
Die Grünen	5
FPÖ	4
Total	56

SALZBURG

Governor: GABI BURGSTALLER (SPÖ).
President of the Landtag: JOHANN HOLZTRATTNER (SPÖ).
Election, 17 March 2004

Party	Seats
SPÖ	17
ÖVP	14
FPÖ	3
Die Grünen	2
Total	36

STYRIA (STEIERMARK)

Governor: FRANZ VOVES (SPÖ).
President of the Landtag: SIEGFRIED SCHRITTWIESER (SPÖ).
Election, 2 October 2005

Party	Seats
SPÖ	25
ÖVP	24
KPÖ	4
Die Grünen	3
Total	56

TYROL (TIROL)

Governor: HERWIG VAN STAA (ÖVP).
President of the Landtag: Prof. HELMUT MADER (ÖVP).
Election, 28 September 2003

Party	Seats
ÖVP	20
SPÖ	9
Die Grünen	5
FPÖ	2
Total	36

VORARLBERG

Governor: Dr HERBERT SAUSGRUBER (ÖVP).
President of the Landtag: GEBHARD HALDER (ÖVP).

AUSTRIA

Election, 19 September 2004

Party	Seats
ÖVP	21
SPÖ	6
FPÖ	5
Die Grünen	4
Total	**36**

VIENNA (WIEN)

Bürgermeister (Mayor) and Governor: Dr MICHAEL HÄUPL (SPÖ).

President of the Landtag: JOHANN HATZL (SPÖ).

Election, 23 October 2005

Party	Seats
SPÖ	55
ÖVP	18
Die Grünen	14
FPÖ	13
Total	**100**

Election Commission

Bundeswahlbehörde (Federal Election Board): Bundesministerium für Inneres, Abteilung III/6, Postfach 100, 1014 Vienna; tel. (1) 53126-2464; e-mail wahl@bmi.gv.at; internet www.bmi.gv.at/cms/BMI_wahlen/bundeswahlbehoe/start.aspx; comprises 17 *Beisitzer* (assessors); 15 of the assessors are nominated by the political orgs represented in the Nationalrat; the remaining two are members of the judiciary; Chair. GÜNTHER PLATTER (Minister for the Interior).

Political Organizations

Bündnis Zukunft Österreich (BZÖ) (Alliance for the Future of Austria): Dorotheergasse 7/19–20, 1010 Vienna; tel. (1) 513-28-28; fax (1) 513-28-38-9; e-mail office@bzoe.at; internet www.bzoe.at; f. 2005 by split from Freiheitliche Partei Österreichs (FPÖ); proponent of social market-economy, controlled immigration and protection of Austria's cultural identity; Leader and Parliamentary Spokesman PETER WESTENTHALER; Gen.-Sec. GERALD GROSZ.

Freiheitliche Partei Österreichs (FPÖ/Die Freiheitlichen) (Freedom Party): Friedrich–Schmidt Pl. 4, 1080 Vienna; tel. (1) 512-35-35-0; fax (1) 513-35-35-9; e-mail bgst@fpoe.at; internet www.fpoe.at; f. 1955; partially succeeded the Verband der Unabhängigen (League of Independents, f. 1949); popularly known as Die Freiheitlichen; populist right-wing party advocating the participation of workers in management, stricter immigration controls and deregulation in the business sector; opposes Austria's membership of the EU; breakaway party, Bündnis Zukunft Österreich (BZÖ), formed in 2005; Chair. HEINZ-CHRISTIAN STRACHE.

Die Grünen (Greens): Rooseveltpl. 4–5, 1090 Vienna; tel. (1) 236-39-98-0; fax (1) 526-91-10; e-mail bundesbuero@gruene.at; internet www.gruene.at; f. 1986; campaigns for environmental protection, peace and social justice; Chair. and Leader of Parliamentary Group Prof. Dr ALEXANDER VAN DER BELLEN.

Kommunistische Partei Österreichs (KPÖ) (Communist Party of Austria): Drechslergasse 42, 1140 Vienna; tel. (1) 503-65-80-0; fax (1) 503-65-80-49-9; e-mail bundesvorstand@kpoe.at; internet www.kpoe.at; f. 1918; strongest in the industrial centres and trade unions; advocates a policy of strict neutrality; mem. party of European Left; Chairs MELINA KLAUS, Dr MIRKO MESSNER.

Liberales Forum (LiF) (Liberal Forum): Parlament, Dr Karl-Renner-Ring 3, 1017 Vienna; tel. (1) 503-06-67; fax (1) 503-06-67-20; e-mail office@lif.at; internet www.liberale.at; f. 1993 by fmr mems of Freiheitliche Partei Österreichs; Leader ALEXANDER ZACH.

Österreichische Volkspartei (ÖVP) (Austrian People's Party): Lichtenfelsgasse 7, 1010 Vienna; tel. (1) 401-26-0; fax (1) 401-26-10-9; e-mail email@oevp.at; internet www.oevp.at; f. 1945; Christian Democratic party; advocates an ecologically orientated social market-economy; Chair. WILHELM MOLTERER; Sec.-Gen. HANNES MISSETHON.

Sozialdemokratische Partei Österreichs (SPÖ) (Social Democratic Party of Austria): Löwelstr. 18, 1014 Vienna; tel. (1) 534-27-0; fax (1) 535-96-83; e-mail spoe@spoe.at; internet www.spoe.at; f. as the Social Democratic Party in 1889, subsequently renamed the Socialist Party, reverted to its original name in 1991; advocates democratic socialism and Austria's permanent neutrality; 500,000 mems; Chair. Dr ALFRED GUSENBAUER; Secs JOSEF KALINA, REINHARD WINTERAUER.

Diplomatic Representation

EMBASSIES IN AUSTRIA

Afghanistan: Lackierergasse 9/9, 1090 Vienna; tel. (1) 524-78-06; fax (1) 406-02-19; e-mail afg.emb.vie@chello.at; internet www.embassyofafghanistan.com; Chargé d'affaires a.i. WAHID MONAWAR.

Albania: Prinz-Eugen-Str. 18/1/5, 1040 Vienna; tel. (1) 328-86-56; fax (1) 328-86-58; e-mail albemb.vie@chello.at; Ambassador VALTER IBRAHIMI.

Algeria: Rudolfinergasse 18, 1190 Vienna; tel. (1) 369-88-53; fax (1) 369-88-56; e-mail office@algerische-botschaft.at; internet www.algerische-botschaft.at; Ambassador TAOUS FEROUKHI.

Andorra: Kärntner Ring 2A/13, 1010 Vienna; tel. (1) 961-09-09; fax (1) 961-09-09-50; e-mail office@ambaixada-andorra.at; Ambassador JOAN PUJAL LABORDA.

Angola: Seilerstätte 15/10–11, 1010 Vienna; tel. (1) 718-74-88; fax (1) 718-74-86; e-mail embangola.viena@embangola.at; internet www.embangola.at; Ambassador Dr FIDELINO LOY DE JESUS FIGUEIREDO.

Argentina: Goldschmiedgasse 2/1, 1010 Vienna; tel. (1) 533-84-63; fax (1) 533-87-97; e-mail embargviena@embargviena.at; Ambassador EUGENIO MARIA CURIA.

Armenia: Hadikgasse 28, 1140 Vienna; tel. (1) 522-74-79; fax (1) 522-74-81; e-mail armenia@armembassy.at; Ambassador Dr ASHOT HOVAKIMIAN.

Australia: Mattiellistr. 2, 1040 Vienna; tel. (1) 506-74-0; fax (1) 504-11-78; e-mail austemb@aon.at; internet www.australian-embassy.at; Ambassador PETER JAMES SHANNON.

Azerbaijan: Hügelgasse 2, 1130 Vienna; tel. (1) 403-13-22; fax (1) 403-13-23; e-mail vienna@mission.mfa.gov.az; Ambassador FUAD ISMAYILOV.

Belarus: Hüttelbergstr. 6, 1140 Vienna; tel. (1) 419-96-30-11; fax (1) 416-96-30-30; e-mail mail@byembassy.at; internet www.byembassy.at; Ambassador ALYAKSANDR SYCHOV.

Belgium: Wohllebengasse 6, 1040 Vienna; tel. (1) 502-07-0; fax (1) 502-07-22; e-mail vienna@diplobel.org; internet www.diplomatie.be/vienna; Ambassador CRISTINA FUNES-NOPPEN.

Belize: Franz Josefs Kai 13/5/16, Postfach 982, 1011 Vienna; tel. (1) 533-76-63; fax (1) 533-81-14; e-mail belizeembassy@utanet.at; Ambassador ALEXANDER PILETSKY.

Bolivia: Waaggasse 10/4, 1040 Vienna; tel. (1) 587-46-75; fax (1) 586-68-80; e-mail embolaustria@of-viena.at; Ambassador Dr HORACIO BAZOBERRY OTERO.

Bosnia and Herzegovina: Tivoligasse 54, 1120 Vienna; tel. (1) 811-85-55; fax (1) 811-85-69; e-mail bihembassyvienna@diplomats.com; Ambassador TOMISLAV LIMOV.

Brazil: Pestalozzigasse 4/2, 1010 Vienna; tel. (1) 512-06-31; fax (1) 513-83-74; e-mail mail@brasilemb.at; Ambassador JULIO CEZAR ZELNER GONÇALVES.

Bulgaria: Schwindgasse 8, 1040 Vienna; tel. (1) 505-31-13; fax (1) 505-14-23; e-mail amboffice@aon.at; Ambassador RADI NAIDENOV.

Burkina Faso: Prinz-Eugen-Str. 18/3A, 1040 Vienna; tel. (1) 503-82-64; fax (1) 503-82-64-20; e-mail s.r@abfvienne.at; internet www.abfvienne.at; Ambassador NOELLIE MARIE BÉATRICE DAMIBA.

Canada: Laurenzerberg 2/III, 1010 Vienna; tel. (1) 531-38-30-00; fax (1) 531-38-33-21; e-mail vienn@international.gc.ca; internet www.kanada.at; Ambassador MARIE GERVAIS-VIDRICAIRE.

Cape Verde: Schwindgasse 20, 1040 Vienna; tel. (1) 503-87-27; fax (1) 503-87-29; e-mail embcviena@nnweb.at; Chargé d'affaires a.i. HERCULES DO NASCIMENTO CRUZ.

Chile: Lugeck 1/3/10, 1010 Vienna; tel. (1) 512-92-08; fax (1) 512-92-08-33; e-mail echileat1@chello.at; Ambassador MILENKO ESTEBAN SKOKNIC TAPIA.

China, People's Republic: Metternichgasse 4, 1030 Vienna; tel. (1) 714-31-49; fax (1) 713-68-16; e-mail chinaemb_at@mfa.gov.cn; internet www.chinaembassy.at; Ambassador WU KEN.

Colombia: Stadiongasse 6–8/15, 1010 Vienna; tel. (1) 406-44-46; fax (1) 408-83-03; e-mail embcolviena@aon.at; internet www.embcol.or.at; Ambassador ROSSO JOSÉ SERRANO CADENA.

Costa Rica: Wagramerstr. 23/1/1 Top 2–3, 1220 Vienna; tel. (1) 263-38-24; fax (1) 263-38-24-5; e-mail embajadaaustria_costa.rica@chello.at; Ambassador ANA TERESA DENGO BENAVIDES.

Côte d'Ivoire: Stadiongasse 4/5, 1010 Vienna; tel. (1) 406-50-51; fax (1) 409-77-15; Ambassador YOUSSOUFOU BAMBA.

Croatia: Heuberggasse 10, 1170 Vienna; tel. (1) 485-95-24; fax (1) 480-29-42; e-mail vlprhbec@reinprecht.at; internet at.mfa.hr; Ambassador Prof. Dr ZORAN JAŠIĆ.

Cuba: Kaiserstr. 84, 1070 Vienna; tel. (1) 877-81-98; fax (1) 877-81-98-30; e-mail secembajador@ecuaustria.at; internet emba.cubaminrex.cu/austria; Ambassador NORMA MIGUELINA GOICOCHEA ESTENOZ.

Cyprus: Parkring 20, 1010 Vienna; tel. (1) 513-06-30; fax (1) 513-06-32; e-mail embassy2@cyprus.vienna.at; Ambassador KORNELIOS S. KORNELIOU.

Czech Republic: Penzingerstr. 11–13, 1140 Vienna; tel. (1) 899-58-0; fax (1) 894-12-00; e-mail vienna@embassy.mzv.cz; internet www.mzv.cz/vienna; Ambassador Dr JAN KOUKAL.

Denmark: Führichgasse 6, 1010 Vienna; tel. (1) 512-79-04-0; fax (1) 513-81-20; e-mail vieamb@um.dk; internet www.ambwien.um.dk; Ambassador HUGO OSTERGAARD-ANDERSEN.

Ecuador: Goldschmiedgasse 10/2/24, 1010 Vienna; tel. (1) 535-32-08; fax (1) 535-08-97; e-mail mecaustria@chello.at; Ambassador BYRON MOREJON ALMEIDA.

Egypt: Hohe Warte 50–54, 1190 Vienna; tel. (1) 370-81-04; fax (1) 370-81-04-27; e-mail egyptembassyvienna@egyptembassyvienna.at; internet www.egyptembassyvienna.at; Ambassador EHAB MUHAMMAD MOSTAFA FAWZI.

El Salvador: Prinz-Eugen-Str. 72/2/1, 1040 Vienna; tel. (1) 505-38-74; fax (1) 505-38-76; e-mail sgutierrez@rree.gob.sv; Ambassador VANESSA EUGENIA INTERIANO TOBAR.

Estonia: Wohllebengasse 9/13, 1040 Vienna; tel. (1) 503-77-61; fax (1) 503-77-61-20; e-mail saatkond@estwien.at; Ambassador KATRIN SAARSALU-LAYACHI.

Ethiopia: Wagramerstr. 14/1/2, 1223 Vienna; tel. (1) 710-21-68; fax (1) 710-21-71; e-mail office@ethiopianembassy.at; internet www.ethiopianembassy.at; Ambassador KONGIT WOLDEMARIAM SINEGIORGIS.

Finland: Gonzagagasse 16, 1010 Vienna; tel. (1) 531-59-0; fax (1) 535-57-03; e-mail sanomat.wie@formin.fi; internet www.finnland.at; Ambassador KIRSTI HELENA KAUPPI.

France: Technikerstr. 2, 1040 Vienna; tel. (1) 502-75-0; fax (1) 502-75-16-8; e-mail presse@ambafrvienne.at; internet www.ambafrance-at.org; Ambassador PIERRE VIAUX.

Georgia: Doblhoffgasse 5/5, 1010 Vienna; tel. (1) 403-98-48; fax (1) 403-98-48-20; e-mail vienna.emb@mfa.govge; internet www.austria.mfa.gov.ge; Ambassador VICTOR DOLIDZE.

Germany: Metternichgasse 3, 1030 Vienna; tel. (1) 711-54-0; fax (1) 713-83-66; e-mail info@wien.diplo.de; internet www.wien.diplo.de; Ambassador Dr GERHARD WESTDICKENBERG.

Greece: Argentinierstr. 14, 1040 Vienna; tel. (1) 506-15-0; fax (1) 505-62-17; e-mail gremb@griechischebotschaft.at; internet www.griechische-botschaft.at; Ambassador PANAGOTIS ZOGRAFOS.

Guatemala: Landstr. Hauptstr. 21/Top 9, 1030 Vienna; tel. (1) 714-35-70; fax (1) 714-35-70-15; e-mail embajada@embaguate.co.at; Ambassador LUIS ALBERTO PADILLA MENÉNDEZ.

Holy See: Theresianumgasse 31, 1040 Vienna; tel. (1) 505-13-27; fax (1) 505-61-40; e-mail nuntius@nuntiatur.at; internet www.nuntiatur.at; Apostolic Nuncio Most Rev. EDMOND FARHAT (Titular Archbishop of Byblos).

Hungary: Bankgasse 4–6, 1010 Vienna; tel. (1) 537-80-30-0; fax (1) 535-99-40; e-mail kom@huembvie.at; Ambassador Dr ISTVÁN HORVÁTH.

Iceland: Naglergasse 2/8, 1010 Vienna; tel. (1) 533-27-71; fax (1) 533-27-74; e-mail emb.vienna@mfa.is; internet www.iceland.org/at; Ambassador SVEINN BJÖRNSSON.

India: Kärntner Ring 2, 1015 Vienna; tel. (1) 505-86-66; fax (1) 505-92-19; e-mail indemb@eoivien.vienna.at; internet www.indianembassy.at; Ambassador SAURABH KUMAR.

Indonesia: Gustav-Tschermak-Gasse 5–7, 1180 Vienna; tel. (1) 479-23-0; fax (1) 479-05-57; e-mail unitkom@kbriwina.at; internet www.kbriwina.at; Ambassador TRIYONO WIBOWO.

Iran: Strohgasse 14C, 1030 Vienna; tel. (1) 712-26-50; fax (1) 713-57-33; e-mail public@iranembassy-wien.at; Chargé d'affaires a.i. ALI MESHKIN MEHR.

Iraq: Johannesgasse 26, Postfach 599, 1010 Vienna; tel. (1) 713-81-95; fax (1) 713-67-20; e-mail office@iraqembassy.at; Ambassador TARIQ AQRAWI.

Ireland: Rotenturmstr. 16–18, 5th Floor, 1010 Vienna; tel. (1) 715-42-46; fax (1) 713-60-04; e-mail vienna@dfa.ie; Ambassador FRANK COGAN.

Israel: Anton-Frank-Gasse 20, 1180 Vienna; tel. (1) 476-46-0; fax (1) 476-46-55-5; e-mail info-sec@vienna.mfa.gov.il; internet vienna.mfa.gov.il; Ambassador DAN ASHBEL.

Italy: Rennweg 27, 1030 Vienna; tel. (1) 712-51-21; fax (1) 713-97-19; e-mail ambasciata.vienna@esteri.it; internet www.ambvienna.esteri.it; Ambassador Dr MASSIMO SPINETTI.

Japan: Hessgasse 6, 1010 Vienna; tel. (1) 531-92-0; fax (1) 532-05-90; e-mail info@embjp.at; internet www.at.emb-japan.go.jp; Ambassador AKIO TANAKA.

Jordan: Rennweg 17/4, 1030 Vienna; tel. (1) 405-10-25; fax (1) 405-10-31; e-mail info@jordanembassy.at; internet www.jordanembassy.at; Ambassador MAKRAM QUEISI.

Kazakhstan: Felix-Mottl-Str. 23, 1190 Vienna; tel. (1) 367-66-57-11; fax (1) 367-91-75-33; e-mail embassy@kazakhstan.at; internet www.kazakhstan.at; Ambassador KAIRAT ABDRAKHMANOV.

Kenya: Neulinggasse 29/8, 1030 Vienna; tel. (1) 712-39-19; fax (1) 712-39-22; e-mail kenyarep-vienna@aon.at; Ambassador JULIUS KIPLAGAT KANDIE.

Korea, Democratic People's Republic: Beckmanngasse 10–12, 1140 Vienna; tel. (1) 894-23-13; fax (1) 894-31-74; e-mail d.v.r.korea.botschaft@chello.at; Ambassador KIM GWANG SOP.

Korea, Republic: Gregor-Mendel-Str. 25, 1180 Vienna; tel. (1) 478-19-91; fax (1) 478-10-13; e-mail mail@koreaemb.at; internet www.mofat.go.kr/austria; Ambassador KIM SUNG-HWAN.

Kuwait: Universitätsstr. 5/2, 1010 Vienna; tel. (1) 405-56-46; fax (1) 405-56-46-13; e-mail kuwaitem@eunet.at; Ambassador FAWZI ABD AL-AZIZ AL-JASEM.

Kyrgyzstan: Invalidenstr. 3/8, 1030 Vienna; tel. (1) 535-03-79; fax (1) 535-03-79-13; e-mail kyrbot@nnweb.at; Ambassador RINA N. PRIZHIVOIT.

Latvia: Stefan-Esders-Pl. 4, 1190 Vienna; tel. (1) 403-31-12; fax (1) 403-31-12-27; e-mail embassy.austria@mfa.gov.lv; Ambassador AVIARS GROZA.

Lebanon: Oppolzergasse 6/3, 1010 Vienna; tel. (1) 533-88-21; fax (1) 533-49-84; e-mail embassy.lebanon@inode.at; Chargé d'affaires a.i. ISHAYA AL-KHOURY.

Libya: Blaasstr. 33, 1190 Vienna; tel. (1) 367-76-39; fax (1) 367-76-01; e-mail office@libyanembassyvienna.at; Sec. of the People's Bureau AHMED M. A. MENESI.

Liechtenstein: Löwelstr. 8/7, 1010 Vienna; tel. (1) 535-92-11; fax (1) 535-92-11-4; e-mail info@vie.rep.llv.li; internet www.liechtenstein.li/fl-aussenstelle-wien; Ambassador Princess MARIA-PIA KOTHBAUER of Liechtenstein.

Lithuania: Löwengasse 47/4, 1030 Vienna; tel. (1) 718-54-67; fax (1) 718-54-69; e-mail amb.at@urm.lt; internet at.mfa.lt; Ambassador GIEDRIUS PUODŽIŪNAS.

Luxembourg: Sternwartestr. 81, 1180 Vienna; tel. (1) 478-21-42; fax (1) 478-21-44; e-mail vienne.amb@mae.etat.lu; Ambassador ARLETTE CONZEMIUS.

Macedonia, former Yugoslav republic: Maderstr. 1/10, 1040 Vienna; tel. (1) 524-87-56; fax (1) 524-87-53; e-mail macembassy@24on.cc; Ambassador Dr VESNA BOROZAN.

Malaysia: Floridsdorfer Hauptstr. 1–7, Florida Tower, 24th Floor, 1210 Vienna; tel. (1) 505-10-42-0; fax (1) 505-79-42; e-mail mwvienna@utanet.at; Ambassador MOHD ARSHAD MANZOOR HUSSAIN.

Malta: Opernring 5/1, 1010 Vienna; tel. (1) 586-50-10; fax (1) 586-50-10-9; e-mail maltaembassy.vienna@gov.mt; Ambassador CHRISTOPHER GRIMA.

Mexico: Operngasse 21/10, 1040 Vienna; tel. (1) 310-73-83; fax (1) 310-73-87; e-mail embamex@embamex.or.at; Ambassador ALEJANDRO DÍAZ Y PÉREZ DUARTE.

Moldova: Löwengasse 47/10, 1030 Vienna; tel. (1) 961-10-30; fax (1) 961-10-30-34; e-mail viena@mfa.md; Ambassador VICTOR POSTOLACHI.

Mongolia: Fasangartengasse 45–47, 1130 Vienna; tel. (1) 535-30-13; fax (1) 535-30-06; e-mail office@embassymon.at; internet www.embassymon.at; Ambassador LUVSANDAGVA ENKHTAIVAN.

Montenegro: Niebelungengasse 13, 1010 Vienna; tel. (1) 715-31-02; fax (1) 715-31-02-20; e-mail diplomat-mn@me-austria.eu; Ambassador VESKO GARČEVIĆ.

Morocco: Opernring 3–5, 1010 Vienna; tel. (1) 586-66-50; fax (1) 586-76-67; e-mail emb-pmissionvienna@morocco.at; Ambassador Dr OMAR ZNIBER.

Namibia: Ungargasse 33/5, 1030 Vienna; tel. (1) 402-93-71; fax (1) 402-93-70; e-mail nam.emb.vienna@speed.at; internet www.embnamibia.at; Ambassador SELMA ASHIPALA-MUSAVYI.

Netherlands: Opernring 5, 7th Floor, 1010 Vienna; tel. (1) 589-39; fax (1) 589-39-26-5; e-mail wen-public@minbuza.nl; internet www.mfa.nl/wen; Ambassador JUSTUS JONATHAN DE VISSER.

Nicaragua: Ebendorferstr. 10/3/12, 1010 Vienna; tel. (1) 403-18-38; fax (1) 403-27-52; e-mail embanic-viena@aon.at; Ambassador PIERO DARIO COEN MONTEALEGRE (resident in Rome, Italy).

Nigeria: Nordbahnstr. 36/2/5, 1020 Vienna; tel. (1) 712-66-85; fax (1) 714-14-02; e-mail he@nigeriaembassyvienna.com; internet www.nigeriaembassyvienna.com; Chargé d'affaires a.i. KENJIKA LINUS EKEDEDE.

Norway: Reisnerstr. 55–57, 1030 Vienna; tel. (1) 715-66-92; fax (1) 712-65-52; e-mail emb.vienna@mfa.no; internet www.norwegen.or.at; Ambassador BENGT OLAV JOHANSEN.

Oman: Währingerstr. 2–4/24–25, 1090 Vienna; tel. (1) 310-86-43; fax (1) 310-72-68; e-mail embassy.oman@chello.at; Ambassador BADR MUHAMMAD ZAHIR AL-HINAI.

Pakistan: Hofzeile 13, 1190 Vienna; tel. (1) 368-73-81; fax (1) 368-73-76; e-mail parepvienna@gmail.com; Ambassador SHAHBAZ SHAHBAZ.

Panama: Elisabethstr. 4–5/4/10, 1010 Vienna; tel. (1) 587-23-47; fax (1) 586-30-80; e-mail mail@empanvienna.co.at; Ambassador ISABEL DAMIÁN KAREKIDES.

Paraguay: Prinz-Eugen-Str. 18/1/2/7, 1040 Vienna; tel. (1) 505-46-74; fax (1) 941-98-98; e-mail embaparviena@chello.at; Chargé d'affaires a.i. NILDA FATIMA ACOSTA GARCETE.

Peru: Gottfried-Keller-Gasse 2/1–2, 1030 Vienna; tel. (1) 713-43-77; fax (1) 712-77-04; e-mail embajada@embaperuaustria.at; internet www.embaperuaustria.at; Ambassador CARLOS ALBERTO HIGUEROS RAMOS.

Philippines: Laurenzerberg 2, 1010 Vienna; tel. (1) 533-24-01; fax (1) 533-24-01-24; e-mail office@philippine-embassy.at; internet www.philippine-embassy.at; Ambassador LINGLINGAY LACANLALE.

Poland: Hietzinger Hauptstr. 42C, 1130 Vienna; tel. (1) 870-15-00-0; fax (1) 870-15-22-2; e-mail sekretariat@botschaftrp.at; internet www.wien.polemb.net; Chargé d'affaires a.i. JAROSŁAW DZIEDZIC.

Portugal: Opernring 3/1, 1010 Vienna; tel. (1) 586-75-36-0; fax (1) 586-75-36-99; e-mail portugal@portembassy.at; internet www.portembassy.at; Ambassador Dr JOAQUIM RAFAEL CAIMOTO DUARTE.

Romania: Prinz-Eugen-Str. 60, 1040 Vienna; tel. (1) 505-32-27; fax (1) 504-14-62; e-mail ambromviena@ambrom.at; internet viena.mae.ro; Chargé d'affaires a.i. ADRIANA LORETA STĂNESCU.

Russia: Reisnerstr. 45–47, 1030 Vienna; tel. (1) 712-12-29; fax (1) 712-33-88; e-mail rusemb@chello.at; internet www.austria.mid.ru; Ambassador STANISLAV V. OSADCHIY.

San Marino: Dr-Karl-Lueger-Pl. 5, 1010 Vienna; tel. (1) 586-21-80; fax (1) 586-22-35; e-mail pfk@pfk.at; Ambassador GIOVANNI CONTI (resident in San Marino).

Saudi Arabia: Formanekgasse 38, 1190 Vienna; tel. (1) 367-25-31; fax (1) 367-25-40; e-mail emb.saudiarabia.vienna@aon.at; Chargé d'affaires a.i. ABD AR-RAHMAN AS-SUHAIBANI.

Serbia: Rennweg 3, 1030 Vienna; tel. (1) 713-25-95; fax (1) 713-25-97; e-mail ambasada@amb.srbije.net; internet www.vienna.mfa.gov.yu; Ambassador DRAGAN VELIKIĆ.

Slovakia: Armbrustergasse 24, 1190 Vienna; tel. (1) 318-90-55-20-0; fax (1) 318-90-55-20-8; e-mail slovakembassy@vienna.mfa.sk; internet www.vienna.mfa.sk; Ambassador Dr PETER LIZAK.

Slovenia: Nibelungengasse 13/3, 1010 Vienna; tel. (1) 586-13-09; fax (1) 586-12-65; e-mail vdu@gov.si; Ambassador Prof. Dr ERNEST PETRIČ.

South Africa: Sandgasse 33, 1190 Vienna; tel. (1) 320-64-93; fax (1) 320-64-93-51; e-mail vienna.ambassador@foreign.gov.za; internet www.saembvie.at; Ambassador LESLIE MABANGAMBI GUMBI.

Spain: Argentinierstr. 34, 1040 Vienna; tel. (1) 505-57-88; fax (1) 505-57-88-25; e-mail embespat@mail.mae.es; internet www.mae.es/embajadas/viena/es; Ambassador JUAN MANUEL DE BARANDICA Y LUXÁN.

Sri Lanka: Rainergasse 1/2/5, 1040 Vienna; tel. (1) 503-79-88; fax (1) 503-79-93; e-mail embassy.srilanka@etelnet.at; internet www.embassy.srilanka.at; Ambassador ARUNI YASHODHA WIJEWARDANE.

Sudan: Reisnerstr. 29/5, 1030 Vienna; tel. (1) 710-23-43; fax (1) 710-23-46; e-mail sudanivienna@prioritytelecom.biz; Ambassador SAYED GALAL ED-DIN ES-SAYED AL-AMIN.

Sweden: Obere Donaustr. 49–51, Postfach 18, 1025 Vienna; tel. (1) 217-53-0; fax (1) 217-53-370; e-mail ambassaden.wien@foreign.ministry.se; internet www.swedenabroad.com/wien; Ambassador HANS LUNDBORG.

Switzerland: Prinz-Eugen-Str. 7, 1030 Vienna; tel. (1) 795-05-0; fax (1) 795-05-21; e-mail vie.vertretung@eda.admin.ch; internet www.eda.admin.ch/wien; Ambassador Dr OSCAR KNAPP.

Syria: Daffingerstr. 4, 1030 Vienna; tel. (1) 533-46-33; fax (1) 533-46-32; e-mail vienna_embassy@syrianembassy.jet2web.at; Ambassador MUHAMMAD BADI KHATTAB.

Tajikistan: Universitätsstr. 8/1A, 1090 Vienna; tel. and fax (1) 409-82-66; fax (1) 409-82-66-14; e-mail tajikembassy@chello.at; internet www.tajikembassy.org; Ambassador NURIDDIN T. SHAMSOV.

Thailand: Cottagegasse 48, 1180 Vienna; tel. (1) 478-33-35; fax (1) 478-29-07; e-mail thai.vn@embthai.telecom.at; Ambassador ADISAK PANUPONG.

Tunisia: Sieveringerstr. 187, 1190 Vienna; tel. (1) 581-52-81; fax (1) 581-55-92; e-mail at.vienne@aol.at; Ambassador Prof. MUHAMMAD DAOUAS.

Turkey: Prinz-Eugen-Str. 40, 1040 Vienna; tel. (1) 505-73-38-0; fax (1) 505-36-60; e-mail tuerkische-botschaft@chello.at; internet www.tuerkischebotschaftwien.at; Ambassador SELIM YENEL.

Turkmenistan: Argentinierstr. 22/11/EG, 1040 Vienna; tel. (1) 503-64-70; fax (1) 503-64-73; e-mail turkmenistan.botschaft@chello.at; Ambassador ESEN AYDOGDIYEV.

Ukraine: Naaffgasse 23, 1180 Vienna; tel. (1) 479-71-72; fax (1) 479-71-72-47; e-mail info@ukremb.at; internet www.ukremb.at; Ambassador VOLODYMYR YU. YELCHENKO.

United Arab Emirates: Peter-Jordan-Str. 66, 1190 Vienna; tel. (1) 368-14-55; fax (1) 368-44-85; e-mail emirats@aon.at; Ambassador AHMAD RASHID AD-DOSARI.

United Kingdom: Jaurèsgasse 12, 1030 Vienna; tel. (1) 716-13-0; fax (1) 716-13-29-99; e-mail info@britishembassy.at; internet www.britishembassy.at; Ambassador SIMON JOHN MEREDITH SMITH.

USA: Boltzmanngasse 16, 1090 Vienna; tel. (1) 313-39; fax (1) 310-06-82; e-mail embassy@usembassy.at; internet www.usembassy.at; Ambassador CHARLES A. GARGANO.

Uruguay: Palais Esterhazy, Wallnerstr. 4/3/17, 1010 Vienna; tel. (1) 535-66-36; fax (1) 535-66-18; e-mail uruvien@embuy.at; Ambassador JORGE PÉREZ OTERMIN.

Uzbekistan: Poetzleinsdorferstr. 49, 1180 Vienna; tel. (1) 315-39-94; fax (1) 315-39-93; e-mail botschaft@usbekistan.at; internet www.usbekistan.at; Chargé d'affaires a.i. KADYRJAN YUSUPOV.

Venezuela: Prinz-Eugen-Str. 72/1.OG/Steige 1/Top1.1, 1040 Vienna; tel. (1) 712-26-38; fax (1) 715-32-19; e-mail embajada@austria.gob.ve; internet www.austria.gob.ve; Chargé d'affaires a.i. VERÓNICA CALCINARI VAN DER VELDE.

Viet Nam: Félix-Mottl-Str. 20, 1190 Vienna; tel. (1) 368-07-55; fax (1) 368-07-54; e-mail embassy.vietnam@aon.at; Ambassador BA THAN NGUYEN.

Yemen: Reisnerstr. 18–20, 1st Floor, Top 3–4, 1030 Vienna; tel. (1) 503-29-30; fax (1) 505-31-59; e-mail yemenembassy.vienna@aon.at; Ambassador Dr AHMAD ALWAN MULHI AL-ALWANI.

Zimbabwe: Strozzigasse 10/15, 1080 Vienna; tel. (1) 407-92-36; fax (1) 407-92-38; e-mail z.vien@chello.at; internet www.zimbabweembassyvienna.at; Ambassador GRACE TSITSI MUTANDIRO.

Judicial System

The Austrian legal system is based on the principle of a division between legislative, administrative and judicial power. There are three supreme courts (Verfassungsgerichtshof, Verwaltungsgerichtshof and Oberster Gerichtshof). The judicial courts are organized into 141 local courts (Bezirksgerichte), 20 provincial and district courts (Landesgerichte), and four higher provincial courts (Oberlandesgerichte) in Vienna, Graz, Innsbruck and Linz.

SUPREME ADMINISTRATIVE COURTS

Verfassungsgerichtshof (Constitutional Court): Judenpl. 11, 1010 Vienna; tel. (1) 531-22-0; fax (1) 531-22-49-9; e-mail vfgh@vfgh.gv.at; internet www.vfgh.gv.at; f. 1919; deals with matters affecting the Constitution, examines the legality of legislation and administration; Pres. Prof. Dr KARL KORINEK; Vice-Pres. Dr BRIGITTE BIERLEIN.

Justices: Dr KURT HELLER, Dr KARL SPIELBÜCHLER, Dr HERBERT HALLER, Dr LISBETH LASS, Dr WILLIBALD LIEHR, Dr HANS GEORG RUPPE, Dr PETER OBERNDORFER, Dr RUDOLF MÜLLER, Dr GERHART HOLZINGER, Dr ELEONORE BERCHTOLD-OSTERMANN, Dr CLAUDIA KAHR, Dr CHRISTOPH GRABENWARTER.

Verwaltungsgerichtshof (Administrative Court): Judenpl. 11, 1010 Vienna; tel. (1) 531-11-0; fax (1) 531-11-508; internet www.vwgh.gv.at; deals with matters affecting the legality of administration; Pres. Prof. Dr CLEMENS JABLONER; Vice-Pres. Prof. Dr RUDOLF THIENEL.

Presidents of the Senate: Dr PETER BERNARD, Dr FRANZ HÖSZ, Dr GUNTHER GRUBER, Dr ILONA GIENDL, Dr RUDOLF MÜLLER, Dr PETER NOVAK, Dr GERHART MIZNER, Dr RUDOLF HARGASSNER, Dr LEOPOLD BUMBERGER, Dr KARL HÖFINGER, HERBERT HEINZL.

SUPREME JUDICIAL COURT

Oberster Gerichtshof: Schmerlingpl. 11, 1016 Vienna; tel. (1) 521-52-0; fax (1) 521-52-37-10; e-mail ogh.praesidium@justiz.gv.at; internet www.ogh.gv.at; Pres. Prof. Dr IRMGARD GRISS; Vice-Pres.

AUSTRIA

Dr BIRGIT LANGER (criminal matters), Dr RONALD ROHRER (civil matters).

Presidents of the Senate: Dr PETER SCHIEMER, Dr GERNOT FLOSSMANN, Dr PETER SCHINKO, Dr KARL MAYRHOFER, Dr JOSEF GERSTENECKER, Dr ILSA HUBER, Dr GÜNTER HOLZWEBER, Dr HELGE SCHMUCKER, Dr HERBERT PIMMER, Dr PETER BAUMANN, Dr ALFONS ZECHNER, Dr FRANZ ZEHETNER, Dr ECKART RATZ.

Religion

At the 2001 census, professed membership in major religions was as follows: Roman Catholic Church 74.0% of the population; Lutheran and Presbyterian churches (Evangelical Church, Augsburger and Helvetic confessions) 4.7%; Islam 4.2%; Judaism 0.1%; Eastern Orthodox (Russian, Greek, Serbian, Romanian and Bulgarian) 2.2%; other Christian churches 0.9%; other non-Christian religious groups 0.2%. Atheists accounted for 12% of respondents, while 2% did not indicate a religious affiliation. The vast majority of groups termed 'sects' by the Government are small organizations with fewer than 100 members. Among the larger groups are the Church of Scientology, with between 5,000 and 6,000 members, and the Unification Church, with approximately 700 adherents.

CHRISTIANITY

Ökumenischer Rat der Kirchen in Österreich (Ecumenical Council of Churches in Austria): Severin-Schreiber-Gasse 3, 1180 Vienna; tel. (1) 479-15-23-30-0; fax (1) 479-15-23-33-0; e-mail oerkoe@kirchen.at; internet www.kirchen.at; f. 1958; 14 mem. Churches, 10 observers; Pres. Bishop HERWIG STURM (Protestant Church of the Augsburg Confession); Vice-Pres. Mgr GOTTFRIED AUER (Roman Catholic Church), NICOLAE DURA (Romanian Orthodox Church); Secretary Mag. ERIKA TUPPY (Protestant Church of the Helvetic Confession).

The Roman Catholic Church

Austria comprises two archdioceses, seven dioceses and the territorial abbacy of Wettingen-Mehrerau (directly responsible to the Holy See). The Archbishop of Vienna is also the Ordinary for Catholics of the Byzantine rite in Austria (totalling an estimated 8,000). At 31 December 2005 there were an estimated 5,664,233 adherents (69.5% of the population).

Bishops' Conference

Österreichische Bischofskonferenz, Rotenturmstr. 2, 1010 Vienna; tel. (1) 516-11-32-80; fax (1) 516-11-34-36; e-mail sekretariat@bischofskonferenz.at; internet www.bischofskonferenz.at.
f. 1849; Pres. Cardinal Dr CHRISTOPH SCHÖNBORN (Archbishop of Vienna); Gen. Sec. Mgr Dr ÄGIDIUS ZSIFKOVICS.

Archbishop of Salzburg: Most Rev. Dr ALOIS KOTHGASSER, Kapitelpl. 2, 5020 Salzburg; tel. (662) 80-47-1100; fax (662) 80-47-1109; e-mail ordinariat.salzburg@ordinariat.kirchen.net; internet www.kirchen.net.

Archbishop of Vienna: Cardinal Dr CHRISTOPH SCHÖNBORN, Wollzeile 2, 1010 Vienna; tel. (1) 515-52-0; fax (1) 515-52-37-28; internet www.stephanscom.at.

The Anglican Communion

Within the Church of England, Austria forms part of the diocese of Gibraltar in Europe. The Bishop is resident in London, United Kingdom.

Archdeacon of the Eastern Archdeaconry: Ven. PATRICK CURRAN, Christ Church, Jaurèsgasse 17–19, 1030 Vienna; tel. and fax (1) 714-89-00; e-mail office@christchurchvienna.org; internet www.christchurchvienna.org.

Protestant Churches

Bund der Baptistengemeinden in Österreich (Fed. of Baptist Communities): Krummgasse 7/4, 1030 Vienna; tel. (1) 713-68-28; fax (1) 713-68-28-11; e-mail bund@baptisten.at; internet www.baptisten.at; Gen. Sec. WALTER KLIMT.

Evangelische Kirche Augsburgischen Bekenntnisses in Österreich (Protestant Church of the Augsburgian Confession): Severin-Schreiber-Gasse 3, 1180 Vienna; tel. (1) 479-15-23; fax (1) 479-15-23-110; e-mail bischof@evang.at; internet www.evang.at; 314,774 mems (2007); Bishop Dr MICHAEL BÜNKER.

Evangelische Kirche HB (Helvetischen Bekenntnisses) (Protestant Church of the Helvetic Confession): Dorotheergasse 16, 1010 Vienna; tel. (1) 513-65-64; fax (1) 512-44-90; e-mail kirche-hb@evang.at; 19,463 mems (2007); Landessuperintendent Hofrat Pfarrer THOMAS HENNEFELD.

Evangelisch-methodistische Kirche (United Methodist Church): Sechshauserstr. 56, 1150 Vienna; tel. (1) 604-53-47;

Directory

e-mail superintendent@emk.at; internet www.emk.at; Superintendent LOTHAR PÖLL.

Orthodox Churches

The Armenian Apostolic Church and the Bulgarian, Coptic, Greek, Romanian, Russian, Serbian and Syrian Orthodox Churches are active in Austria.

Other Christian Churches

Altkatholische Kirche Österreichs (Old Catholic Church in Austria): Schottenring 17, 1010 Vienna; tel. (1) 317-83-94; fax (1) 317-83-94-9; e-mail bischof.okoro@altkatholiken.at; internet www.altkatholiken.at; c. 18,000 mems; Bishop Dr JOHN OKORO.

ISLAM

In 2001 there were 338,988 Muslims in Austria.

Islamische Glaubensgemeinschaft in Österreich (Islamic Community of Austria—IGGIÖ): Bernardgasse 5, 1070 Vienna; tel. (1) 526-31-22; fax (1) 526-31-22-4; e-mail info@derislam.at; internet www.derislam.at; Pres. ANAS SCHAKFEH.

JUDAISM

There are five Jewish communities in Austria, the largest of which is in Vienna. At the end of 2004 there were 6,890 Jews in Vienna, and a combined total of 400 in Graz, Innsbruck, Linz and Salzburg.

Israelitische Kultusgemeinde Graz (Jewish Community in Graz): David-Herzog-Pl. 1, 8020 Graz; tel. (316) 712-46-8; fax (316) 720-43-3; e-mail office@ikg-graz.at; internet www.ikg-graz.at; Pres. GÉRARD SONNENSCHEIN.

Israelitische Kultusgemeinde Salzburg (Jewish Community in Salzburg): Lasserstr. 8, 5020 Salzburg; tel. (662) 872-22-8; e-mail office@ikg-salzburg.at; internet www.ikg-salzburg.at.

Israelitische Kultusgemeinde für Tirol und Vorarlberg (Jewish Community in Tyrol and Vorarlberg): Sillgasse 15, 6020 Innsbruck; tel. (512) 586-89-2; e-mail office@ikg-innsbruck.at; internet www.ikg-innsbruck.at; Pres. Dr ESTHER FRITSCH.

Israelitische Kultusgemeinde Wien (Jewish Community in Vienna): Seitenstettengasse 4, 1010 Vienna; tel. (1) 531-04-0; fax (1) 531-04-10-8; e-mail office@ikg-wien.at; internet www.ikg-wien.at; Pres. Dr ARIEL MUZICANT.

The Press

Austria's first newspaper was published in 1605. *Wiener Zeitung*, founded in 1703, is one of the world's oldest daily newspapers still in circulation. Restrictions on press freedom are permissible only within the framework of Article 10 (2) of the European Convention on Human Rights.

The Austrian Press Council (Presserat), founded in 1961, supervises the activities of the press. Vienna is the focus of newspaper and periodical publishing, although there is also a strong press in some provinces. The three highest circulation dailies are *Kronen-Zeitung*, *Kleine Zeitung* (Graz) and *Kurier*.

In 2006 there were 17 daily newspapers and 263 weekly newspapers in Austria; 2,735 other periodicals were active in that year.

PRINCIPAL DAILIES

Bregenz

NEUE Vorarlberger Tageszeitung: Gutenbergstr. 1, 6858 Schwarzach; tel. (5572) 501-850; fax (5572) 501-860; e-mail neue-redaktion@neue.vol.at; internet www.neue.vol.at; f. 1972; morning; independent; Editor ROBERT THOMA; circ. 6,914.

Vorarlberger Nachrichten: Gutenbergstr. 1, 6858 Schwarzach; tel. (5572) 501-993; fax (5572) 501-227; e-mail redaktion@vn.vol.at; internet www.vn.vol.at; morning; Editor EUGEN A. RUSS; circ. 64,684.

Graz

Kleine Zeitung: Schönaugasse 64, 8011 Graz; tel. (316) 87-50; fax (316) 87-54-03-4; e-mail redaktion@kleinezeitung.at; internet www.kleine.co.at; f. 1904; independent; Chief Editor HUBERT PATTERER; circ. 178,334.

Innsbruck

NEUE Zeitung für Tirol: Matthias-Schmid-Str. 10, 6020 Innsbruck; tel. (512) 72-82-0; e-mail kontakt@dieneue.at; internet www.dieneue.at; Mon.-Sat., fmrly Tues.-Sun; Editors-in-Chief PATRICIO HETFLEISCH, FLORIAN MADL; circ. 32,739.

Tiroler Tageszeitung: Ing.-Etzel-Str. 30, 6020 Innsbruck; tel. (512) 05-04-03; fax (512) 05-04-54-3; e-mail redaktion@tt.com;

AUSTRIA

internet www.tt.com; morning; independent; Chief Editor FRANK STAUD; circ. 88,901.

Klagenfurt

Kärntner Tageszeitung: Viktringer Ring 28, 9020 Klagenfurt; tel. (463) 58-66-0; fax (463) 58-66-28-0; e-mail redaktion@ktz.at; internet www.ktz.at; f. 1946; morning except Monday; Socialist; Chief Editor Dr HELLWIG VALENTIN; circ. 32,000.

Kleine Zeitung: Funderstr. 1A, 9020 Klagenfurt; tel. (463) 58-00-0; fax (463) 58-00-31-3; e-mail redaktion@kleinezeitung.at; internet www.kleine.co.at; independent; Editor REINHOLD DOTTOLO; circ. 90,571.

Linz

Neues Volksblatt: Hafenstr. 1–3, 4010 Linz; tel. (732) 76-06-0; fax (732) 77-92-42; e-mail volksblatt@volksblatt.at; internet www.volksblatt.at; f. 1869; organ of Austrian People's Party; Chief Editor Dr FRANZ ROHRHOFER.

Oberösterreichische Nachrichten: Promenade 23, 4010 Linz; tel. (732) 78-05-0; fax (732) 78-05-329; e-mail redaktion@nachrichten.at; internet www.nachrichten.at; f. 1865; morning; independent; Chief Editor GERALD MANDLBAUER; circ. 104,604.

Salzburg

Salzburger Nachrichten: Karolingerstr. 40, 5021 Salzburg; tel. (662) 83-73-30-1; fax (662) 83-73-39-9; e-mail redakt@salzburg.com; internet www.salzburg.com; f. 1945; morning; independent; Editor-in-Chief MANFRED PERTERER; circ. 69,339.

Salzburger Volkszeitung: Bergstr. 12, 5020 Salzburg; tel. (662) 87-94-91; fax (662) 87-94-91-13; e-mail redaktion@svz.at; internet www.svz.at; organ of Austrian People's Party; Editor KONNIE AISTLEITNER; circ. weekdays 12,030.

Wien
(Vienna)

Kronen-Zeitung: Muthgasse 2, 1190 Vienna; tel. (1) 360-10; fax (1) 369-83-85; e-mail chefredaktion@kronenzeitung.at; internet www.krone.at; f. 1900; independent; Editor HANS DICHAND; circ. weekdays 847,320, Sunday 1,362,521.

Kurier: Lindengasse 48–52, 1072 Vienna; tel. (1) 521-00-0; fax (1) 521-00-22-63; e-mail leser@kurier.at; internet www.kurier.at; f. 1954; independent; Chief Editor Dr CHRISTOPH KOTANKO; circ. weekdays 169,481, Sunday 325,521.

Die Presse: Hainburgerstr. 33A, 1030 Vienna; tel. (1) 514-14; fax (1) 514-14-368; e-mail chefredaktion@diepresse.com; internet www.diepresse.com; f. 1848; morning; independent; Chief Editor MICHAEL FLEISCHHACKER; circ. Mon.–Sat. 79,676.

Der Standard: Herrengasse 19–21, 1014 Vienna; tel. (1) 531-70; fax (1) 531-70-13-1; e-mail chefredaktion@derstandard.at; internet www.derstandard.at; f. 1988; independent; Editors-in-Chief OSCAR BRONNER, Dr GERFRIED SPERL; circ. 74,314.

Wiener Zeitung: Wiedner Gürtel 10, 1040 Vienna; tel. (1) 206-99-0; fax (1) 206-99-592; e-mail redaktion@wienerzeitung.at; internet www.wienerzeitung.at; f. 1703; morning; official govt paper; Chief Editor Dr ANDREAS UNTERBERGER; circ. 20,020.

PRINCIPAL WEEKLIES

Die Furche: Lobkowitzpl. 1, 1010 Vienna; tel. (1) 512-52-61; fax (1) 512-82-15; e-mail furche@furche.at; internet www.furche.at; f. 1945; Chief Editor RUDOLF MITLÖHNER; circ. 17,956.

IW-Internationale Wirtschaft: Nikolsdorfer Gasse 7–11, 1051 Vienna; tel. (1) 546-64-346; fax (1) 546-64-342; economics; Editor NIKOLAUS GERSTMAYER; circ. 13,430.

Kärntner Nachrichten: Stauderpl. 5, 9020 Klagenfurt; tel. (463) 511515; fax (463) 511515-51; e-mail office@abc-werbeagentur.at; f. 1954; Editors ARMIN KORDESCH, HELMUT PRASCH; circ. 17,500.

KirchenZeitung Diözese Linz: Kapuzinerstr. 84, 4020 Linz; tel. (732) 7610-3944; fax (732) 7610-3939; e-mail office@kirchenzeitung.at; internet www.kirchenzeitung.at; publ. by Archdiocese of Linz; Chief Editor MATTHÄUS FELLINGER; circ. 42,442.

Die Neue Wirtschaft: Nikolsdorfer Gasse 7–11, 1051 Vienna; tel. (1) 546-64-24-7; fax (1) 546-64-34-7; economics; circ. 25,650.

Neue Wochenschau: J. N. Bergerstr. 2, 7210 Mattersburg; tel. and fax (2622) 67-47-3; e-mail redaktion@wochenschau.at; internet www.wochenschau.at; f. 1908; Editor HELMUT WALTER; circ. 128,500.

NFZ (Neue Freie Zeitung): Postfach 81, 1013 Vienna; Esslinggasse 14–16, 1010 Vienna; tel. (1) 512-35-35-311; fax (1) 512-35-35-412; e-mail redaktion.nfz@fpoe.at; organ of Freedom Party; Chief Editor MICHAEL A. RICHTER; circ. 70,000.

Niederösterreichische Nachrichten: Gutenbergstr. 12, 3100 St Pölten; tel. (2742) 802-0; fax (2742) 802-14-80; e-mail chefredaktion@noen.at; internet www.noen.at; Chief Editor HARALD KNABL; circ. 131,989.

Oberösterreichische Rundschau: Hafenstr. 1–3, 4010 Linz; tel. (732) 76-16-0; fax (732) 76-16-302; e-mail office@rundschau.co.at; internet www.rundschau.co.at; Chief Editor Dr JOSEF ERTL; circ. 104,459.

Österreichische Bauernzeitung: Bruckerstr. 6, 1040 Vienna; tel. (1) 533-14-48; fax (1) 533-14-48-33; e-mail christine.demuth@bauernzeitung.at; internet www.bauernzeitung.at; publ. by Österreichischer Bauernbund; Dir FRITZ KALTENEGGER.

Präsent: Exlgasse 20, 6020 Innsbruck; tel. (512) 22-33; fax (512) 22-33-50-1; f. 1892; independent Catholic; Chief Editor PAUL MVIGG.

Rupertusblatt: Kaigasse 8, 5020 Salzburg; tel. (662) 87-22-23-0; fax (662) 87-22-23-13; e-mail rupertusblatt@kommunikation.kirchen.net; internet www.kirchen.at/rupertusblatt; publ. by Archdiocese of Salzburg; Chief Editor KARL ROITHINGER; circ. 14,147.

Samstag: Faradaygasse 6, 1030 Vienna; tel. (1) 795-94-13-5; e-mail samstag@heroldwien.at; f. 1951; weekly; independent; Chief Editor GERLINDE KOLANDA; circ. 41,000.

Der Sonntag: Stephanspl. 4/VI/DG, Postfach 152, 1014 Vienna; tel. (1) 512-60-63-39-71; fax (1) 512-60-63-39-70; e-mail redaktion@dersonntag.at; internet www.dersonntag.at; f. 1848 as the Wiener Kirchenzeitung; present name adopted 2004; publ. by the Archdiocese of Vienna; Chief Editor ELVIRA GROISS; circ. 20,576.

Volksstimme: Lichtensteinstr. 123/20, 1090 Vienna; tel. (1) 503-68-28; fax (1) 503-66-38; e-mail redaktion@volksstimme.at; internet www.volksstimme.at; f. 1994; Chief Editor WALTER BAIER.

POPULAR PERIODICALS

Agrar Post: Schulstr. 64, 2103 Langenzersdorf; tel. (2244) 46-47; f. 1924; monthly; agriculture.

Alles Auto: Beckgasse 24, 1130 Vienna; tel. (1) 877-97-11; fax (1) 877-97-114; e-mail redaktion@allesauto.at; internet www.allesauto.at; 10 a year; motoring; Chief Editor ENRICO FALCHETTO; circ. 47,783.

Austria-Ski: Olympiastr. 10, 6020 Innsbruck; tel. (512) 335-01-0; fax (512) 361-99-8; 6 a year; official journal of Austrian Skiing Asscn; Editor JOSEF SCHMID.

Auto Touring: ÖAMTC Verlag GmbH, Tauchnergasse 5, 3400 Klosterneuburg; tel. (2243) 404-0; fax (2243) 404-27-21; e-mail autotouring.redaktion@oeamtc.at; internet www.autotouring.at; monthly; official journal of the Austrian Automobile Organization; Chief Editor PETER PISECKER; circ. 1,315,000.

Format: Taborstr. 1–3, 1020 Vienna; tel. (1) 217-55-0; internet www.format.at; f. 1998; weekly; business; independent; Dir HELMUT HANUSCH; circ. 61,706.

Frauenblatt: Faradaygasse 6, 1032 Vienna; tel. (1) 795-94-13-5; e-mail samstag@heroldwien.at; women's weekly; Editor KURT MARKARITZER; circ. 22,300.

Die Ganze Woche: Heiligenstädter Str. 121, 1190 Vienna; tel. (1) 291-60-272; fax (1) 291-60-73; e-mail redaktion@dgw.at; internet www.dgw.at; f. 1985; circ. 341,220.

Gewinn: Stiftgasse 31, 1071 Vienna; tel. (1) 521-24-0; e-mail gewinn@gewinn.com; internet www.gewinn.com; monthly; business, economics, personal finances; Chief Editors Prof. Dr GEORG WEILAND, Dr MICHAEL FEMBEK; circ. 58,755.

Maxima: IZ NÖ Süd, Str. 3, Objekt 16, 2355 Wiener Neudorf; tel. (2236) 600-67-30; fax (2236) 600-67-70; e-mail redaktion@maxima.co.at; internet www.maxima.at; f. 1996; 10 a year; women's magazine; Chief Editor BRIGITTE FUCHS; circ. 72,703.

NEWS: Taborrstr. 1–3, 1020 Vienna; tel. (1) 213-12-0; fax (1) 213-12-666-1; e-mail redaktion@news.at; internet www.news.at; f. 1992; weekly; illustrated; Chief Editors JOSEF VOTZI, ANDREAS WEBER, CHRISTIAN NEUHOLD; circ. 240,297.

ORF nachlese: Würzburggasse 30, 1136 Vienna; tel. (1) 470-64-23; fax (1) 470-64-23-23; e-mail nachlese@orf.at; monthly; programme guide to television and radio broadcasts; Chief Editor CHRISTINE SCHNÖDL; circ. 74,479.

Profil: Taborstr. 1-3, 1020 Vienna; tel. (1) 534-70-0; fax (1) 535-32-50; e-mail redaktion@profil.at; internet www.profil.at; f. 1970; weekly; political, general; independent; Chief Editor CHRISTIAN RAINER; circ. 77,685.

RZ (Wochenschau): Lilienbrumgasse 7–9, 1020 Vienna; tel. (1) 993-99-0; fax (1) 993-99-10-11; e-mail info@rizit.at; internet www.rizit.at; f. 1936; weekly illustrated; Chief Editor PAUL WEISS.

Seitenblicke: Heinrich-Collin Str. 1/Top 1, 1140 Vienna; tel. (1) 90-220-0; fax (1) 220-990; e-mail redaktion@seitenblicke.at; internet www.seitenblicke.at; fortnightly; lifestyle, celebrity news; Chief Editor ANDREAS WOLLINGER; circ. 60,059.

Sportzeitung: Linke Wienzeile 40, 1060 Vienna; tel. (1) 585-57-57-0; fax (1) 585-57-57-411; e-mail sportzeitung@lwmedia.at; internet www.sportzeitung.at; f. 1949; weekly sports illustrated; Chief Editors Horst Hötsch, Gerhard Weber; circ. 10,915.

TOPIC: Königsklostergasse 7–15, 1060 Vienna; tel. (1) 535-57-83; e-mail topic@topmedia.at; internet www.mytopic.at; 11 a year; politics, economics and culture for young people; publ. by Austrian Youth Red Cross and Austrian Youth Book Club; Dir Dr Eva Lingens; circ. 106,258.

Trend: Taborstr. 1–3, 1020 Vienna; tel. (1) 213-12-0; fax (1) 213-12-66-00; e-mail redaktion@trend.at; internet www.trend.at; monthly; economics; Dir Helmut Hanusch; circ. 62,326.

TV-Media: Taborstr. 1–3, 1020 Vienna; tel. (1) 213-120; internet www.tv-media.at; weekly; illustrated; f. 1995; Chief Editor Atha Athanasiadis; circ. 252,582.

Vídeňské svobodné listy: Margaretenpl. 7/2/4, 1050 Vienna; tel. and fax (1) 587-83-08; fortnightly for Czech and Slovak communities in Austria; Editor Hana Herdova.

Welt der Frau: Lustenauerstr. 21, 4020 Linz; tel. (732) 77-00-01-11; fax (732) 77-00-01-24; e-mail info@welt-der-frau.at; internet www.welt-der-frau.at; women's monthly; Chief Editor Dr Christine Haiden; circ. 52,576.

Wiener: Lifestyle Zeitschriften Verlag GmbH, Davidgasse 79, 1100 Vienna; tel. (1) 601-17-249; fax (1) 601-17-350; e-mail wiener@lifestylezv.at; monthly; Chief Editor Peter Mosser; circ. 85,000.

SPECIALIST PERIODICALS

Eurocity: Leberstr. 122, 1110 Vienna; tel. (1) 740-95-53-5; fax (1) 740-95-53-8; e-mail redaktion@eurocity.at; internet www.eurocity.at; f. 1928; every 2 months; Chief Editor Georg Karp.

FSG Direkt: Altmannsdorferstr. 154–156, 1230 Vienna; tel. (1) 662-32-96; fax (1) 662-32-96-63-85; e-mail karin.stieber@oegbverlag.at; socialist industrial journal; formerly *Welt der Arbeit* ; Chief Editor Walter Kratzer; circ 47,500.

Itm Praktiker: ZB-Verlag, Marochallpl. 23/1/21, 1125 Vienna; tel. (1) 804-04-74; fax (1) 804-44-39; technical hobbies; Chief Editor Gerhard K. Buchberger; circ. 18,800.

Juristische Blätter (mit Beilage 'Wirtschaftsrechtliche Blätter'): Springer Verlag, Sachsenpl. 4, 1201 Vienna; tel. (1) 330-24-15-0; fax (1) 330-24-26; internet www.springer.at/jbl; f. 1872; monthly; nine editors.

Die Landwirtschaft: Wiener Str. 64, 3100 St Pölten; tel. (2742) 259-93-00; e-mail presse@lk-noe.at; internet www.lk-noe.at; f. 1923; monthly; agriculture and forestry; owned and publ. by Österreichischer Agrarverlag; Editor Gerd Rittenauer.

Liberale Zeichen: Dürergasse 6/10, 1060 Vienna; tel. (1) 503-06-67; fax (1) 503-06-67-20; e-mail office@lif.at; internet www.lif.at; 4 a year; organ of Liberal Forum.

Literatur und Kritik: Otto-Müller-Verlag, Ernest-Thun-Str. 11, 5020 Salzburg; tel. (662) 88-19-74; fax (662) 87-23-87; e-mail luk@omvs.at; internet www.omvs.at; f. 1966; 5 a year; Austrian and European literature and criticism; Editor Karl-Markus Gauss.

MEDIZIN Populär: Nibelungengasse 13, 1010 Vienna; tel. (1) 512-44-86-36; fax (1) 512-44-86-34; e-mail k.kirschbichler@aerzteverlagshaus.at; internet www.medizinpopulaer.at; monthly; health and fitness; Chief Editor Karin Kirschbichler; circ. 33,807.

Monatshefte für Chemie: Sachsenpl. 4–6, 1201 Vienna; tel. (1) 330-24-15-0; fax (1) 330-24-26; e-mail journals@springer.at; internet www.springer.at/mochem; f. 1880; monthly; chemistry; Chief Editor Heinz Falk.

Oeffentliche Sicherheit: Postfach 100, Herrengasse 7, 1014 Vienna; tel. (1) 531-26-2307; fax (1) 531-26-2504; e-mail sicherheit@mail.bmi.gv.at; internet www.bmi.gv.at/sicherheit; 6 a year; published by the Ministry of the Interior; Chief Editor Werner Sabitzer; circ. 15,000.

Österreichische Ärztezeitung: Nibelungengasse 13, 1010 Vienna; tel. (1) 512-44-86; fax (1) 512-44-86-24; e-mail b.ostermann@aerzteverlagshaus.at; internet www.aerztezeitung-oesterreich.at; f. 1945; 20 a year; organ of the Austrian Medical Board; Chief Editors Reinhard Hampel, Dr Agnes M. Mühlgassner.

Österreichische Ingenieur- und Architekten-Zeitschrift (ÖIAZ): Eschenbachgasse 9, 1010 Vienna; tel. (1) 587-35-36-0; fax (1) 253-303-379-27; e-mail office@oiav.at; internet www.oiav.at; f. 1849; 6 a year; Editor Peter Reichel; circ. 2,200.

Österreichische Monatshefte: Lichtenfelsgasse 7, 1010 Vienna; tel. (1) 401-26-53-2; f. 1945; monthly; organ of Austrian People's Party; Editor Gerhard Wilflinger.

Österreichische Musikzeitschrift: Hegelgasse 13, 1010 Vienna; tel. (1) 512-68-69; fax (1) 512-68-69-9; e-mail order@musikzeit.at; internet internet www.musikzeit.at; f. 1946; monthly; Editor Dr M. Diederichs-Lafite; circ. 5,000.

Reichsbund-Aktuell mit SPORT: Laudongasse 16, 1080 Vienna; tel. and fax (1) 405-54-06; e-mail info@amateurfussball.at; internet www.amateurfussball.at; f. 1917; monthly; Catholic; organ of Reichsbund, Bewegung für christliche Gesellschaftspolitik und Sport; Editor Walter Raming; circ. 12,000.

Wiener Klinische Wochenschrift: Sachsenpl. 4–6, 1201 Vienna; tel. (1) 330-24-15; fax (1) 330-24-26; e-mail journals@springer.at; internet www.springer.at/wkw; f. 1888; medical bi-weekly; Editors Wilfred Druml, Ulrich Jaeger.

Die Zukunft: Löwelstr. 18, 1014 Vienna; tel. (1) 534-27-280; fax (1) 534-27-282; monthly; organ of Social Democratic Party of Austria; Editor Albrecht K. Konecny; circ. 15,000.

NEWS AGENCY

APA (Austria Presse Agentur): Laimgrubengasse 10, 1060 Vienna; tel. (1) 360-60-0; fax (1) 360-60-30-99; e-mail chefredaktion@apa.at; internet www.apa.at; f. 1946; co-operative agency of the Austrian Newspapers and Broadcasting Co (private co); 37 mems; Man. Dir Dr Wolfgang Vyslozil; Chief Editor Michael Lang.

PRESS ASSOCIATIONS

Österreichischer Zeitschriften- und Fachmedien-Verband (Asscn of Periodical Publrs): Renngasse 12/6, 1010 Vienna; tel. and fax (1) 319-70-01; e-mail oezv@oezv.or.at; internet www.oezv.or.at; f. 1946; 155 mems; Pres. Dr Rudolf Bohmann; Man. Dir Dr Wolfgang Brandstetter.

Verband Österreichischer Zeitungen (Newspaper Asscn of Austria): Wipplingerstr. 15, 4th Floor, TOP 19, Postfach 144, 1013 Vienna; tel. (1) 533-79-79-0; fax (1) 533-79-79-422; e-mail gs@voez.at; internet www.voez.at; f. 1946; mems include 17 daily newspapers and 57 other newspapers and periodicals; Pres. Dr Horst Pirker; Dir Dr Walter Schaffelhofer.

Publishers

Akademische Druck- und Verlagsanstalt (ADEVA): Postfach 598, Auersperggasse 12, 8010 Graz; tel. (316) 36-44; fax (316) 36-44-24; e-mail info@adeva.com; internet www.adeva.com; f. 1949; scholarly reprints and new works, facsimile editions of Codices, fine art facsimile editions, music books and facsimile editions; Man. Dr Hubert Christian Konrad.

Betz, Annette, Verlag GmbH: Alser Str. 24, 1090 Vienna; tel. (1) 404-44-0; fax (1) 404-44-5; internet www.annettebetz.com; f. 1962; Man. Dir Dr Fritz Panzer.

Böhlau Verlag GmbH & Co KG: Wiesingerstr. 1, 1010 Vienna; tel. (1) 330-24-27-0; fax (1) 330-24-32; e-mail boehlau@boehlau.at; internet www.boehlau.at; f. 1947; history, law, philology, the arts, sociology; Dir Dr Peter Rauch.

Christian Brandstätter Verlag GmbH & Co KG: Wickenburggasse 26, 1080 Vienna; tel. (1) 512-15-43-0; fax (1) 512-15-43-23-1; e-mail info@cbv.at; internet www.cbv.at; f. 1982; the arts, lifestyle; Chair. Dr Christian Brandstätter.

Wilhelm Braumüller Universitäts Verlagsbuchhandlung GmbH: Servitengasse 5, 1090 Vienna; tel. (1) 319-11-59; fax (1) 310-28-05; e-mail office@braumueller.at; internet www.braumueller.at; f. 1783; politics, law, ethnology, literature and theatre, linguistics, history, journalism, sociology, philosophy, psychology, communications; university publrs; Dirs Brigitte Pfeifer, Konstanze Weber.

Czernin Verlags GmbH: Kupkagasse 4, 1080 Vienna; tel. (1) 403-35-63; fax (1) 403-35-63-15; e-mail office@czernin-verlag.com; internet www.czernin-verlag.com; f. 1999; philosophy, politics, literature, the arts; Dir Klaus Gadermaier.

Facultas Verlags- und Buchhandels AG: Berggasse 4, 1090 Vienna; tel. (1) 310-53-56; fax (1) 319-70-50; e-mail facultas@facultas.at; internet www.facultas.at; f. 2001 by merger of WUV Universitätsverlags GmbH and Servicebetriebe GmbH an der Wirtschaftsuniversität Wien; acquired Urban & Schwarzenberg GmbH in 2005; science, medicine, law, social sciences; Dir Thomas Stauffer.

Freytag-Berndt u. Artaria KG: Brunnerstr. 69, 1230 Vienna; tel. (1) 869-90-90-0; fax (1) 869-90-90-61; e-mail office@freytagberndt.at; internet www.freytagberndt.at; f. 1879; cartography, geography; atlases, maps, guides, geographical data; Dir Dr Christian Halbwachs; Publ. and Sales Man. Wolfgang Kubesch.

Kunstverlag Wolfrum: Augustinerstr. 10, 1010 Vienna; tel. (1) 512-53-98-0; fax (1) 512-53-98-57; e-mail wolfrum@wolfrum.at; internet www.wolfrum.at; f. 1919; art; Dir Hubert Wolfrum.

Leykam Buchverlagsgesellschaft mbH Nfg & Co KG: Ankerstr. 4, 8057 Graz; tel. (316) 281-08-55-30; fax (316) 281-08-55-39; e-mail verlag@leykam.com; internet www.leykamverlag.at; f. 1585; art,

AUSTRIA

literature, academic, law; Dirs Dr WOLFGANG HÖLZL, KLAUS BRUNNER.

LexisNexis Verlag ARD ORAC GmbH & Co KG: Marxergasse 25, 1030 Vienna; tel. (1) 534-52-0; fax (1) 534-52-14-0; e-mail verlag@lexisnexis.at; internet www.lexisnexis.at; f. 1946; legal books, periodicals and online databases; CEO PETER J. DAVIES; Dir Dr GERIT KANDUTSCH.

Linde Verlag Wien GmbH: Scheydgasse 24, 1211 Vienna; tel. (1) 246-30-0; fax (1) 246-30-23; e-mail office@lindeverlag.at; internet www.lindeverlag.at; f. 1925; business, economics, law; Dirs ANDREAS JENTZSCH, Dr ELEONORE BREITEGGER, Dr OSKAR MENNEL.

Manz'sche Verlags- und Universitätsbuchhandlung GmbH: Johannesgasse 23, 1010 Vienna; tel. (1) 531-61-0; fax (1) 531-61-18-1; e-mail verlag@manz.at; internet www.manz.at; f. 1849; law, tax and economic sciences; textbooks and school-books; Man. Dir SUSANNE STEIN-DICHTL; Publr Dr WOLFGANG PICHLER.

Wilhelm Maudrich KG: Spitalgasse 21A, 1096 Vienna; tel. (1) 402-47-12; fax (1) 408-50-80; e-mail medbook@maudrich.com; internet www.maudrich.com; f. 1909; medical.

Molden Verlag GmbH & Co KG: Palais Ferstel/Top 3038, Freyung 2, 1010 Vienna; tel. (1) 533-26-39; fax (1) 533-26-39-9; e-mail office@molden.at; internet www.molden.at; politics, literature, art; Dir MARION MAUTHE.

Musikverlag Doblinger: Dorotheergasse 10, 1010 Vienna; tel. (1) 515-03-0; fax (1) 515-03-51; e-mail music@doblinger.at; internet www.doblinger.at; f. 1876; music; Dir HELMUTH PANY.

Niederösterreichisches Pressehaus Druck- und Verlagsgesellschaft mbH (Residenz Verlag): Gutenbergstr. 12, 3100 St Pölten; tel. (2742) 802-14-15; fax (2742) 802-14-31; e-mail info@residenzverlag.at; internet www.residenzverlag.at; f. 1956; Dir HERWIG BITSCHE.

Otto Müller Verlag: Ernest-Thun-Str. 11, 5020 Salzburg; tel. (662) 88-19-74; fax (662) 87-23-87; e-mail info@omvs.at; internet www.omvs.at; f. 1937; general; Man. ARNO KLEIBEL.

Österreichischer Bundesverlag Schulbuch GmbH & Co KG: Frankgasse 4, 1090 Vienna; tel. (1) 401-36; fax (1) 401-36-185; e-mail office@oebv.at; internet www.oebv.at; educational books, dictionaries; Dir Dr RAINER STAHL.

Pinguin Verlag Pawlowski GmbH: Lindenbühelweg 2, 6021 Innsbruck; tel. (512) 28-11-83; fax (512) 29-32-43; f. 1945; illustrated books; Dir OLAF PAWLOWSKI.

Anton Schroll & Co: Spengergasse 37, 1051 Vienna; tel. (1) 544-56-41; fax (1) 544-56-41-66; f. 1884; also in Munich; art; Man. F. GEYER.

Springer-Verlag GmbH: Sachsenpl. 4–6, 1201 Vienna; tel. (1) 330-24-15-55-2; fax (1) 330-24-26-65; e-mail springer@springer.at; internet www.springer.at; f. 1924; medicine, science, technology, law, sociology, economics, architecture, art, periodicals; Man. Dir RUDOLF SIEGLE.

Leopold Stocker Verlag GmbH: Hofgasse 5, 8011 Graz; tel. (316) 82-16-36; fax (316) 83-56-12; e-mail stocker-verlag@stocker-verlag.com; internet www.stocker-verlag.com; f. 1917; history, nature, hunting, fiction, agriculture, textbooks; Dir WOLFGANG DVORAK-STOCKER.

Carl Ueberreuter Verlag: Alserstr. 24, 1090 Vienna; tel. (1) 404-44-0; fax (1) 404-44-5; e-mail office@vcu.ueberreuter.com; internet www.ueberreuter.at; non-fiction, children's; Man. Dir Dr FRITZ PANZER.

Universal Edition AG: Karlspl. 6, 1010 Vienna; tel. (1) 337-23-0; fax (1) 337-23-40-0; e-mail office@universaledition.com; internet www.universaledition.com; f. 1901; music; Dirs JOHANN JURANEK, ASTRID KOBLANCK, STEFAN RAGG.

VERITAS Verlags- und Buchhandlungsgesellschaft mbH & Co OHG: Hafenstr. 1–3, 4010 Linz; tel. (732) 77-64-51-22-50; fax (732) 77-64-51-22-39; e-mail kundenberatung@veritas.at; internet www.veritas.at; f. 1945; training materials, educational books; Dir MANFRED CHRISTL.

Verlag Brüder Hollinek und Co GmbH: Luisenstr. 20, 3002 Purkersdorf; tel. and fax (2231) 673-65; fax (2231) 673-65-24; e-mail office@hollinek.at; internet www.hollinek.at; f. 1872; science, law and administration, printing, reference works, dictionaries; Dir RICHARD HOLLINEK.

Verlag Jugend & Volk GmbH: Universitätsstr. 11, Postfach 54, 1016 Vienna; tel. (1) 407-27-07-0; fax (1) 407-27-07-22; e-mail verlag@jugendvolk.at; internet www.jugendvolk.at; f. 1921; trade, technical and educational books; Dir KARL KAZ.

Verlag Kremayr & Scheriau KG: Währinger Str. 76/8, 1090 Vienna; tel. (1) 713-87-70-0; fax (1) 713-87-70-20; e-mail office@kremayr-scheriau.at; internet www.kremayr-scheriau.at; f. 1951; non-fiction, history, lifestyle; Dir MARTIN SCHERIAU.

Verlag Oldenbourg: Neulinggasse 26, 1030 Vienna; tel. (1) 712-62-58-0; fax (1) 712-62-58-19; e-mail oldenbourg@veritas.at; f. 1959; subsidiary of VERITAS; Dir MANFRED CHRISTL.

Verlag Österreich GmbH: Kandlgasse 21, 1070 Vienna; tel. (1) 610-77-0; fax (1) 610-77-41-9; e-mail office@verlagoesterreich.at; internet www.verlagoesterreich.at; f. 1804; fmrly state-owned; acquired by JUSLINE Beteiligungs GmbH in 2000; law, CD-ROMs; Dir Prof. Dr NORBERT GUGERBAUER.

Verlag Styria Pichler GmbH & Co KG: Lobkowitzpl. 1, 1010 Vienna; tel. (1) 203-28-28-0; fax (1) 203-28-28-68-75; e-mail office@verlagsgruppestyria.at; internet www.verlagsgruppestyria.at; f. 2003 by merger of Styria Verlag and Pichler Verlag; biographies, theology, religion, philosophy; imprints: Styria Verlag, Pichler Verlag, Verlag Carinthia and Edition Oberösterreich; Man. Dir GERDA SCHAFFELHOFER.

Verlagsanstalt Tyrolia GmbH: Postfach 220, Exlgasse 20, 6020 Innsbruck; tel. (512) 223-32-02; fax (512) 223-32-06; e-mail buchverlag@tyrolia.at; internet www.tyrolia.at; f. 1888; geography, history, science, children's, religion, fiction; Chair. Dr GOTTFRIED KOMPATSCHER.

Paul Zsolnay Verlag GmbH: Prinz-Eugen-Str. 30, 1041 Vienna; tel. (1) 505-76-61-0; fax (1) 505-76-61-10; e-mail info@zsolnay.at; internet www.zsolnay.at; f. 1923; fiction, non-fiction; incl. Deuticke Verlag; Dirs MICHAEL KRÜGER, STEPHAN D. JOSS.

PUBLISHERS' ASSOCIATION

Hauptverband des Österreichischen Buchhandels (Assen of Austrian Publrs and Booksellers): Grünangergasse 4, 1010 Vienna; tel. (1) 512-15-35; fax (1) 512-84-82; e-mail sekretariat@hvb.at; internet www.buecher.at; f. 1859; Pres. Dr INGE KRALUPPER; 530 mems.

Broadcasting and Communications

REGULATORY BODY

Rundfunk und Telekom Regulierungs GmbH (RTR): Mariahilferstr. 77–79, 1060 Vienna; tel. (1) 580-58-0; fax (1) 580-58-91-91; e-mail rtr@rtr.at; internet www.rtr.at; f. 1997 as Telekom-Control GmbH; regulatory body for the broadcasting and telecommunications sector; Dirs Dr GEORG SERENTSCHY (Telecommunications), Dr ALFRED GRINSCHGL (Broadcasting).

TELECOMMUNICATIONS

Telekom Austria AG: Lassallestr. 9, 1020 Vienna; tel. and fax (1) 590-59-1-0; fax (800) 10-01-09; e-mail kundenservice@telekom.at; internet www.telekom.at; f. 1998; Dir-Gen. BORIS NEMSIC.

mobilkom austria AG: Obere Donaustr. 29, 1020 Vienna; tel. (1) 331-61-0; fax (800) 664-60-1; internet www.mobilkom.at; mobile cellular telecommunications; owned by Telekom Austria AG; Chair. RUDOLF FISCHER; CEO BORIS NEMSIC.

ONE GmbH: Brunnerstr. 52, 1210 Vienna; tel. (1) 277-28-0; internet www.one.at; f. 1998; frmly Connect Austria Gesellschaft für Telekommunikation GmbH; mobile cellular telecommunications; 50.10% owned by E.ON AG (Germany), 17.45% each by Telenor (Norway) and Orange SA (France) and 15.00% by TDC A/S (Denmark); CEO JØRGEN BANG-JENSEN.

tele.ring Telekom Service GmbH: Rennweg 97–99, Postfach 1012, 1030 Vienna; tel. (1) 795-85-60-30; fax (1) 795-85-65-86; e-mail info@telering.co.at; internet www.telering.at; wholly owned by T-Mobile Austria GmbH; Chair. ROBERT CHVÁTAL.

T-Mobile Austria GmbH: Rennweg 97–99, 1030 Vienna; tel. (1) 795-85-0; fax (1) 795-85-65-26; e-mail presse@t-mobile.at; internet www.t-mobile.at; f. 1996 as max.mobil; present name adopted 2002; subsidiary of T-Mobile International AG & Co KG (Germany); CEO ROBERT CHVÁTAL.

BROADCASTING

Radio

The state-owned Österreichischer Rundfunk (ORF) provides three national and nine regional radio channels, as well as an overseas service. The provision of radio services was liberalized in 1998, when a number of commercial radio stations were launched.

Österreichischer Rundfunk (ORF) (Austrian Broadcasting Company): Würzburggasse 30, 1136 Vienna; tel. (1) 870-70-30; fax (1) 878-70-33-0; e-mail kundendienst@orf.at; internet www.orf.at; f. 1924; state-owned; operates three national radio stations: Ö1, Hitradio Ö3 and FM4; nine regional radio stations (Ö2): Radio Burgenland, Radio Kärnten, Radio Niederösterreich, Radio Oberösterreich, Radio Salzburg, Radio Steiermark, Radio Tirol, Radio Vorarlberg, Radio Wien; two international radio stations: Radio Österreich 1 International and Radio 1476; two television channels: ORF1 and ORF2; operates satellite television channel, 3 Sat, in conjunction with ARD (Germany), SRG (Switzerland) and ZDF (Germany); also distributes content via teletext and internet; Dir-Gen. Dr ALEXANDER WRABETZ;

AUSTRIA
Directory

Dirs Dr WILLY MITSCHE (Radio), Prof. WOLFGANG LORENZ (Television), THOMAS PRANTNER (Online and New Media).

Private and Commercial Radio Operators

There are no national private or commercial radio operators. The following are the largest local radio operators.

Antenne Kärnten Regionalradio GmbH & Co KG: Suppanstr. 69, 9020 Klagenfurt; tel. (463) 458-88-45; fax (463) 458-88-90-5; internet www.antennekaernten.at; one FM station, Antenne Kärnten; broadcasts in Carinthia; Mans GOTTFRIED BICHLER, RUDOLF KUZMICKI, Dr KLAUS SCHWEIGHOFER.

Antenne Oberösterreich GmbH: Eisenhowerstr. 11, 4600 Wels; tel. and fax (7242) 351-29-9; e-mail info@antennewels.at; internet www.antennewels.at; one FM station, Antenne Wels 98.3; broadcasts in Oberösterreich; Man. Dr CHRISTOPH LEON.

Antenne Österreich GmbH (Niederlassung Salzburg): Friedensstr. 14A, 5020 Salzburg; tel. (662) 40-80-0; fax (662) 40-80-76; e-mail info@antennesalzburg.at; internet www.antennesalzburg.at; one FM station, Antenne Salzburg; broadcasts in Salzburg and Lienz; Mans JOHANNA PAPP, SYLVIA BUCHHAMMER.

Antenne Österreich GmbH (Niederlassung Tirol): Maria-Theresien-Str. 8, 6020 Innsbruck; tel. (512) 574-12-72-3; fax (512) 574-12-75-0; e-mail info@antennetirol.at; internet www.antennetirol.at; two FM stations, Antenne Tirol (Innsbruck) and Antenne Tirol (Unterland); broadcasts in Tyrol; Mans JOHANNA PAPP, SYLVIA BUCHHAMMER.

Antenne Österreich GmbH (Niederlassung Wien): Makartgasse 3, 1010 Vienna; tel. (1) 217-00-0; fax (1) 217-00-20-9; e-mail office@antennewien.at; internet www.antennewien.at; one FM station, Antenne Wien; broadcasts in Vienna; Mans JOHANNA PAPP, SYLVIA BUCHHAMMER.

Antenne Steiermark Regionalradio GmbH & Co KG: Am Sendergrund 15, 8143 Dobl; tel. (3136) 505-0; fax (3136) 505-11-1; e-mail info@antenne.net; internet www.antenne.net; one FM station, Antenne Steiermark; broadcasts in Styria; Mans GOTTFRIED BICHLER, Dr KLAUS SCHWEIGHOFER, RUDOLF KUZMICKI.

There are a further 64 private organizations licensed to broadcast.

Television

The state-owned Österreichischer Rundfunk (ORF) retained a monopoly over television broadcasting in Austria until 2001. It operates two terrestrial television channels and a satellite station in conjunction with German and Swiss companies. Digital television services, comprising three television channels, ORF1, ORF2 and a commercial service, ATV, were launched in October 2006. Digital broadcasts were initially available to 70% of the population. It was expected that analogue broadcasting would be discontinued in 2009.

Österreichischer Rundfunk: see Radio.

Private and Commercial Television Operators

ATV Privat-TV Services AG: Aspernbrückengasse 2, 1020 Vienna; tel. (1) 213-64-0; fax (1) 213-64-99-9; internet atvplus.at; f. 2003; private, commercial channel (ATVplus); CEO FRANZ PRENNER.

Premiere Fernsehen GmbH: Kreitnergasse 5, 1163 Vienna; tel. (1) 491-90-0; internet www.premiere.at; f. 2003; satellite operator offering films, sport and adult programming; wholly owned by Premiere AG (Germany).

Other channels available nationally through cable and satellite include Blue Movie 1, Blue Movie 2, Eurotic-TV, Fashion-TV, Gotv, INXTC TV, K-TV, Kabel Woche, Pro7 Austria, Raceon TV, Sat.1 Österreich, TV 6, TW1 and X-Plus TV.

Finance

(cap. = capital; res = reserves; dep. = deposits; m. = million; brs = branches; amounts in euros)

BANKS

Banks in Austria, apart from the National Bank, belong to one of five categories. The first category comprises banks that are organized as corporations (i.e. joint-stock and private banks), and special-purpose credit institutions; the second category comprises savings banks; and the third category comprises co-operative banks. Co-operative banks include rural credit co-operatives (Raiffeisenbanken) and industrial credit co-operatives (Volksbanken). The remaining two categories comprise the mortgage banks of the various Austrian Länder, and the building societies. The majority of Austrian banks (with the exception of the building societies) operate on the basis of universal banking, although certain categories have specialized. Banking operations are governed by the Banking Act of 1993 (Bankwesengesetz—BWG).

In 2006 there were 871 banks and credit organizations in Austria.

Central Bank

Oesterreichische Nationalbank (Austrian National Bank): Postfach 61, Otto-Wagner-Pl. 3, 1090 Vienna; tel. (1) 404-20; fax (1) 404-23-99; e-mail oenb.info@oenb.co.at; internet www.oenb.at; f. 1922; 70.3% state-owned; cap. 12m., res 4,114m., dep. 26,146m. (Dec. 2006); Pres. HERBERT SCHIMETSCHEK; Gov. Dr KLAUS LIEBSCHER; 3 brs.

Commercial Banks

Adria Bank AG: Gonzagagasse 16, 1010 Vienna; tel. (1) 514-09; fax (1) 514-09-43; e-mail headoffice@adriabank.at; internet www.adriabank.at; f. 1980; cap. 9,447m., res 19,149m., dep. 183,984m. (Dec. 2006); Chair. JURIJ DETICEK.

Alpenbank AG: Kaiserjägerstr. 9, 6020 Innsbruck; tel. (512) 599-77; fax (512) 562-01-5; e-mail private-banking@alpenbank.com; internet www.alpenbank.at; f. 1983 as Save Rössler Bank AG; name changed as above in 1991; cap. 10m., res 2m., dep. 90m. (Dec. 2006); Gen. Mans MARTIN STERZINGER, Dr HEIDI VEROCAI-DÖNZ.

Anglo Irish Bank (Austria) AG: Postfach 306, Rathausstr. 20, 1011 Vienna; tel. (1) 406-61-61-0; fax (1) 405-81-42; f. 1890 as Bankhaus Rosenfeld; present name adopted 1995; wholly owned by Anglo Irish Bank Corpn PLC (Ireland); cap. 7m., res 62m., dep. 501m. (Sept. 2006); Chair. and CEO MICHAEL MCGEE.

Bank Austria Creditanstalt AG: Vordere Zollamtstr. 13, 1010 Vienna; tel. (0) 50505-44610; fax (0) 50505-56149; e-mail info@ba-ca.com; internet www.ba-ca.com; f. 1991 as Bank Austria AG by merger of Österreichische Länderbank and Zentralsparkasse und Kommerzialbank; merged with Creditanstalt AG in 2002; present name adopted 2002; 96.3% owned by UniCredito Italiano, SpA; dep. 135,620m. (Dec. 2006); Group Chair. ALESSANDRO PROFUMO; Chair., Bd of Man. Dirs and CEO ERICH HAMPEL; 409 brs.

Bank Gutmann AG: Schwarzenbergpl. 16, 1010 Vienna; tel. (1) 502-20-0; fax (1) 502-202-249; e-mail mail@gutmann.at; internet www.gutmann.at; f. 1970 as Bank Gebrüd AG; present name adopted 1995; 83% owned by Gutmann Holding AG, 17% owned by partners; cap. 12m., res 20m., dep. 432m. (Dec. 2005); Chair. and Gen. Man. Dr RUDOLF F. STAHL.

Bank Vontobel Österreich AG: Rathauspl. 4, 5024 Salzburg; tel. (662) 810-40; fax (662) 810-47; e-mail vontobel@salzburg.co.at; f. 1885 as Bankhaus Berger & Co AG; name changed to Vontobel Bank AG 1998; present name adopted 2000; 99.95% owned by Vontobel Holding AG (Switzerland); cap. 10m., res 25m., dep. 176m. (Dec. 2006); Chair., Exec. Bd HENDRIK DANIELS.

Bank Winter & Co AG: Singerstr. 10, 1010 Vienna; tel. (1) 515-04-0; fax (1) 515-04-20-0; e-mail contact@bankwinter.com; internet www.bankwinter.com; f. 1892; re-established 1959; present name adopted 1986; dep. 1,842m., total assets 2,049m. (June 2006); Chair. and CEO THOMAS MOSKOVICS.

Bankhaus Carl Spängler und Co AG: Postfach 41, 5024 Salzburg; Schwarzstr. 1, 5020 Salzburg; tel. (662) 86-86-0; fax (662) 86-86-15-8; e-mail bankhaus@spaengler.at; internet www.spaengler.at; f. 1828; cap. 15m., res 32m., dep. 785m. (Dec. 2006); Gen. Man. HEINRICH SPÄNGLER; 10 brs.

Bankhaus Krentschker und Co AG: Am Eisernen Tor 3, 8010 Graz; tel. (316) 80-30-0; fax (316) 80-308-79; e-mail mail@krentschker.at; internet www.krentschker.at; f. 1924; 92.58% owned by Die Steiermärkische Bank und Sparkassen AG, 7.34% owned by Kärntner Sparkasse AG, 0.08% owned by private shareholders; cap. 14m., res 36m., dep. 921m. (Dec. 2006); Chair. Dr GEORG WOLF-SCHÖNACH; 3 brs.

Bankhaus Schelhammer und Schattera AG: Postfach 618, 1011 Vienna; Goldschmiedgasse 3, 1010 Vienna; tel. (1) 534-34; fax (1) 534-34-64; e-mail bank.office@schelhammer.at; internet www.schelhammer.at; f. 1832; cap. 40m., res 22m., dep. 516m. (Dec. 2006); Chair. HELMUT JONAS; 1 br.

BAWAG PSK Bank für Arbeit und Wirtschaft und Österreichische Postsparkasse Aktiengesellschaft (BAWAG PSK): Seitzergasse 2–4, 1010 Vienna; tel. (1) 534-53-0; fax (1) 534-53-2840; e-mail bawag@bawag.com; internet www.bawag.com; f. 1922 as Bank für Arbeit und Wirtschaft AG; merged with Österreichische Postsparkasse (PSK), the state-owned postal bank, in Aug. 2005; acquired by Cerberus Capital Management (USA) in 2006; cap. 250m., res 1,423m., dep. 44,318m. (Dec. 2006); Chair. EWALD NOWOTNY; 155 brs.

Capital Bank-Grawe Gruppe AG: Burgring 16, 8010 Graz; tel. (316) 807-20; fax (316) 807-23-90; e-mail office@capitalbank.at; internet www.capitalbank.at; f. 1922 as Gewerbe- und Handelsbank; present name adopted 2001; wholly owned by Grazer Wechselseitige Versicherung AG; cap. 10m., res 69m., dep. 411m. (Dec. 2006); CEO CHRISTIAN JAUK.

DenizBank AG: Kärntner Ring 12, 1010 Vienna; tel. (1) 503-93-96-0; fax (1) 503-93-96-133; e-mail service@denizbank.at; internet www.denizbank.at; f. 1996 as ESBANK AG; present name adopted 2003;

AUSTRIA

owned by DenizBank AS (Turkey); cap. 12m., res 41m., dep. 1,002m. (Dec. 2006); Chair., Supervisory Bd HAKAN ATES; Gen. Man. Dr ISMAIL ERGENER.

Investkredit Bank AG: Renngasse 10, 1010 Vienna; tel. (1) 531-35-0; fax (1) 531-35-98-3; e-mail invest@investkredit.at; internet www.investkredit.at; owned by Österreichische Volksbanken AG; cap. 46m., res 657m., dep. 10,362m. (Dec. 2006); Pres. FRANZ PINKL; Chair. Dr WILFRIED STADLER.

Kathrein und Co Privatgeschäftsbank AG: Postfach 174, Wipplingerstr. 25, 1013 Vienna; tel. (1) 534-51-0; fax (1) 534-51-221; e-mail privatgeschaeftsbank.ag@kathrein.at; internet www.kathrein.at; f. 1924; owned by Raiffeisen Zentralbank Österreich AG; cap. 20m., res 7m., dep. 308m. (Dec. 2005); Chair. Dr CHRISTOPH KRAUS; Dir Dr CLAUDIO CANTELE.

Meinl Bank AG: Postfach 99, Bauernmarkt 2, 1010 Vienna; tel. (1) 531-88-0; fax (1) 531-88-44-0; e-mail servicecenter@meinlbank.com; internet www.meinlbank.com; f. 1923; cap. 9m., res 38m., dep. 3,085m. (Dec. 2006); Chair., Supervisory Bd Dr WALTER JAKOBLJEVICH; Chair., Management Bd JULIUS MEINL; 2 brs.

Österreichische Verkehrskreditbank AG: Auerspergstr. 17, 1080 Vienna; tel. (1) 93-11-09-0; fax (1) 93-11-09-18; e-mail vst-sekretariat@verkehrskreditbank.at; internet www.verkehrskreditbank.at; f. 1969; owned by BAWAG PSK Bank für Arbeit und Wirtschaft PSK; cap. 4m., res 10m., dep. 635m. (Dec. 2006); Pres. STEPHAN KOREN; CEO MANFRED SOOS; Chair. ALEXANDER WIDDER.

Schoellerbank AG: Palais Rothschild, Renngasse 3, 1010 Vienna; tel. (1) 534-71-0; fax (1) 534-71-655; e-mail info@schoellerbank.at; internet www.schoellerbank.at; f. 1998 by merger of Schoellerbank AG (f. 1833) and Salzburger Kredit-und Wechsel-Bank AG (f. 1922); owned by Bank Austria Creditanstalt AG; cap. 20m., res 70m., dep. 1,200m. (Dec. 2006); Chair. JÜRGEN DANZMAYR.

VakifBank International AG: Kärntner Ring 17, 1010 Vienna; tel. (1) 512-35-20; fax (1) 512-35-20-22; e-mail office@vakifbank.at; internet www.vakifbank.at; f. 1999 as Vakifbank International (Wien) AG; present name adopted 2002; 90% owned by Türkiye Vakifar Bankası TAO, 10% owned by Pension Fund of Türkiye Vakifar Bankası TAO; cap. 16m., res 24m., dep. 326m. (Dec. 2006); Pres. BILAL KARAMAN; Gen. Man. NUMAN BEK.

VTB Bank (Austria) AG: Postfach 560, Parkring 6, 1011 Vienna; tel. (1) 515-35; fax (1) 515-35-29-7; e-mail general@vtb-bank.at; internet www.vtb-bank.at; f. 1974 as Donau-Bank AG; present name adopted 2006; owned by Bank for Foreign Trade (Russia); cap. 73m., res 251m., dep. 1,142m. (Dec. 2006); Chair. and CEO Dr RICHARD VORNBERG.

Zveza Bank RZZOJ (Bank und Revisionsverband rGmbH): Postfach 465, Paulitschgasse 5–7, 9010 Klagenfurt; tel. (463) 512-36-50; fax (463) 512-36-51-9; e-mail office@zvezabank.co.at; internet www.zvezabank.at; f. 1921 as Zveza Koroških zadrug/Verband Kärntner Genossenschaften; in 1949 name changed to Zveza slovenskih zadrug v Celovcu/Verband slowenischer Genossenschaften in Klagenfurt; present name adopted 1996; 55 mems, of which seven are credit co-operatives; cap. 7m., res 7m., dep. 247m. (Dec. 2006); Chair. Dr LUDWIG DRUML; Gen. Mans RUDOLF URBAN, JOSEF LANG.

Regional Banks

Allgemeine Sparkasse Oberösterreich Bank AG (Sparkasse Oberösterreich): Postfach 92, Promenade 11–13, 4041 Linz; tel. (0) 50100-40000; fax (0) 50100-940000; e-mail intl.division@sparkasse-ooe.at; internet www.sparkasse-ooe.at; f. 1849 as Allgemeine Sparkasse in Linz; present name adopted 1991; cap. 57m., res 341m., dep. 7,737m. (Dec. 2006); CEO Dr MARKUS LIMBERGER; 135 brs.

Bank für Tirol und Vorarlberg AG (BTV): Stadtforum, 6020 Innsbruck; tel. (512) 53-33-0; fax (512) 533-31-206; e-mail btv@btv.at; internet www.btv.at; f. 1904; cap. 50m., res 340m., dep. 6,427m. (Dec. 2006); Chair. PETER GAUGG; 40 brs.

BKS Bank AG: St. Veiter Ring 43, 9020 Klagenfurt; tel. (463) 58-58; fax (463) 58-58-94-3; e-mail bks@bks.at; internet www.bks.at; f. 1922; fmrly Bank für Kärnten und Steiermark AG, present name adopted 2005; cap. 50m., res 327m., dep. 4,420m. (Dec. 2006); Mans HEIMO PENKER, Dr HERTA STOCKBAUER; 6 brs.

Hypo Alpe-Adria-Bank AG: Postfach 517, Alpen-Adria-Pl. 1, 9020 Klagenfurt; tel. (0) 502-02-0; fax (0) 502-02-30-00; e-mail austria@hypo-alpe-adria.com; internet www.hypo-alpe-adria.com; f. 1896 as Kärntner Landes- und Hypothekenbank AG; present name adopted 1999; wholly owned by Hypo Alpe-Adria-Bank International AG; cap. 30m., res 158m., dep. 5,606m. (Dec. 2006); Chair., Exec. Bd KURT MAKULA; 2 brs.

Hypo Alpe-Adria-Bank International AG: Alpen Adria Pl. 1, 9020 Klagenfurt; tel. (0) 50202-0; fax (0) 50202-3000; e-mail international@hypo-alpe-adria.com; internet www.hypo-alpe-adria.com; f. 2004 from split of Hypo Alpe-Adria-Bank AG; operates in Bosnia and Herzegovina, Croatia, Italy, Liechtenstein, Montenegro, Serbia, and Slovenia; 52% owned by BayernLB (Germany), 26.5% owned by Grazer Wechselseitige Versicherungs AG; cap. 37m., res 589m., dep. 27,578m. (Dec. 2006); Chair., Supervisory Bd WERNER SCHMIDT; Chair., Management Bd Dr TILO BERLIN.

HYPO Investmentbank AG: Kremsergasse 20, 3100 St Pölten; tel. (2742) 49-20; fax (2742) 49-20-14-44; e-mail office@noehypo.at; internet www.noehypo.at; f. 1889; fmrly Niederösterreichische Landesbank-Hypothekenbank AG, present name adopted 2007; cap. 38m., res 150m., dep. 6,042m. (Dec. 2006); Pres. and Chair. HERBERT FICHTA; Gen. Man. HERBERT HÖCK; 26 brs.

Hypo Tirol Bank AG: Postfach 524, Hypo Passage 2, 6020 Innsbruck; tel. (512) 50-70-0; fax (512) 59-11-21-50; e-mail office@hypotirol.at; internet www.hypotirol.at; f. 1901 as Landes-Hypothekenbank Tirol AG; present name adopted 2000; owned by federal province of Tyrol; cap. 18m., res 361m., dep. 10,911m. (Dec. 2006); Pres. Dr JOHANN GRUBER; 20 brs.

Oberbank AG: Hauptpl. 10–11, 4020 Linz; tel. (732) 78-02-0; fax (732) 78-66-33; e-mail office@oberbank.at; internet www.oberbank.at; f. 1869 as Bank für Oberösterreich und Salzburg; present name adopted 1998; cap. 75m., res 756m., dep. 11,385m. (Dec. 2006); Pres. and CEO Dr FRANZ GASSELSBERGER; 110 brs and sub-brs.

Oberösterreichische Landesbank AG (Hypo Oberösterreich): Landstr. 38, 4020 Linz; tel. (70) 76-39-0; fax (70) 76-39-20-5; e-mail vorstand@hypo-ooe.at; internet www.hypo.at; f. 1891 as Oberösterreichische Landes-Hypothekenanstalt; present name adopted 1988; cap. 15m., res 180m., dep. 5,456m. (Dec. 2005); Pres. Dr WOLFGANG STAMPFL; Chair. and Gen. Man. Dr ANDREAS MITTERLEHNER; 18 brs.

Salzburger Landes-Hypothekenbank AG: Postfach 136, Residenzpl. 7, 5010 Salzburg; tel. (662) 804-60; fax (662) 804-64-64-6; e-mail office@hyposalzburg.at; internet www.hyposalzburg.at; f. 1909 as bank of the Government of Salzburg; present name adopted 1992; 50.02% owned by Hypo Holding GmbH, 25% owned by Oberösterreichische Landesbank AG, 14.97% owned by Raiffeisenlandesbank Oberösterreich AG, 10% owned by Salzburger Landesholding; cap. 15m., res 91m., dep. 4,160m. (Dec. 2006); Gen. Man. Dr REINHARD SALHOFER; 24 brs.

Steiermärkische Bank und Sparkassen AG (Steiermärkische Sparkasse): Postfach 844, Am Sparkassenpl. 4, 8010 Graz; tel. (0) 50100-36000; fax (0) 50100-936000; e-mail international@steiermaerkische.com; internet www.steiermaerkische.com; f. 1825 as Steiermärkischer Sparkasse Graz; present name adopted 1992 following merger; 74.1% owned by Steiermärkische Versicherungssparkasse, 25% owned by Erste Bank der oesterreichischen Sparkassen AG, 1.0% owned by employees; cap. 55m., res 531m., dep. 10,401m. (Dec. 2006); CEO Dr GERHARD FABISCH; Man. Dir Dr FRANZ KERBER; 172 brs.

Tiroler Sparkasse Bankaktiengesellschaft Innsbruck (Tiroler Sparkasse): Sparkassenpl. 1, 6020 Innsbruck; tel. (512) 59-10-0; fax (512) 59-10-50-0; internet www.tispa.at; f. 1822 as Sparkasse der Stadt Innsbruck; present name adopted 1990, following merger in 1975; 97.6% owned by AVS Beteiligungs GmbH, 1.8% owned by Erste Bank der oesterreichischen Sparkassen AG; cap. 66m., res 112m., dep. 3,610m. (Dec. 2006); Pres. ANDREAS TREICHL; 49 brs.

Volkskreditbank AG (VKB Bank): Postfach 116, Rudigierstr. 5–7, Pfarrpl. 12 und Domgasse 12, 4010 Linz; tel. (732) 76-37-0; fax (732) 76-37-29-0; e-mail international@vkb-bank.at; internet www.vkb-bank.at; f. 1872; wholly owned by Volkskredit Verwaltungsgenossenschaft; cap. 30m., res 190m., dep. 1,871m. (Dec. 2006); Chair., Supervisory Bd Dr RUDOLF TRAUNER; Dir-Gen. Dr ALBERT WAGNER; 45 brs.

Vorarlberger Landes- und Hypothekenbank AG: Hypo-Passage 1, 6900 Bregenz; tel. (5574) 414-0; fax (5574) 414-10-50; e-mail info@hypovbg.at; internet www.hypovbg.at; f. 1899 as Hypothekenbank des Landes Vorarlberg; name changed to Vorarlberger Landes- und Hypothekenbank 1990; status changed as above 1996; dep. 9,071m., total assets 10,047m. (Dec. 2006); Chair. Dr KURT RUPP; Man. Dirs Dr JODOK SIMMA, Dr JOHANNES HEFEL, Dr MICHAEL GRAHAMMER; 25 brs.

Specialized Banks

European American Investment Bank AG (Euram Bank): Palais Esterházy, Wallnerstr. 4, 1010 Vienna; tel. (1) 512-38-80; fax (1) 512-388-08-88; e-mail office@eurambank.com; internet www.eurambank.com; f. 1999; cap. 7m., res 5m., dep. 253m. (June 2005); CEO VIKTOR POPOVIC.

Kommunalkredit Austria AG: Türkenstr. 9, 1092 Vienna; tel. (1) 316-31-0; fax (1) 316-31-105; e-mail kommunal@kommunalkredit.at; internet www.kommunalkredit.at; f. 1958; 50.78% owned by Österreichische Volksbanken AG, 49% owned by Dexia Crédit Local SA (France), 0.22% owned by Austrian Asscn of Municipalities; dep.

AUSTRIA

23,325m., total assets 26,861m. (Dec. 2006); Chair., Supervisory Bd Franz Pinkl; CEO and Chair., Executive Bd Dr Reinhard Platzer.

Oesterreichische Kontrollbank AG: Postfach 70, Am Hof 4 & Strauchgasse 1–3, 1011 Vienna; tel. (1) 531-27-0; fax (1) 531-27-5237; e-mail public.relations@oekb.at; internet www.oekb.at; f. 1946; administration of guarantees, export financing, stock exchange clearing, organization and administration of domestic bond issues, central depository for securities and settlement of off-floor transactions, money market operations; cap. 130m., res 219m., dep. 24,848m. (Dec. 2006); Mans Dr Johannes Attems, Dr Rudolf Scholten.

Privatinvest Bank AG: Postfach 16, Griesgasse 11, 5010 Salzburg; tel. (662) 80-48-0; fax (662) 80-48-33-3; e-mail piag@piag.at; internet www.privatinvestbank.com; 74% owned by Reuschel & Co Finanz Service GmbH, 26% owned by Salzburger Sparkasse Bank AG; f. 1885 as Bankhaus Daghofer & Co AG; present name adopted 1990; cap. 6m., res 5m., dep. and bonds 210m. (Dec. 2007); CEO Hermann J. Manfred Reif Althammer; 1 br.

Savings Banks

Dornbirner Sparkasse Bank AG: Postfach 199, Bahnhofstr. 2, 6850 Dornbirn; tel. (50100) 740-00; fax (50100) 741-80; e-mail service@dornbirn.sparkasse.at; internet www.sparkasse.at/dornbirn; f. 1867; owned by Dornbirner Anteilsverwaltungssparkasse; cap. 10m., res 163m., dep. 1,741m. (Dec. 2006); Chair. Wolfgang Rümmele; Gen. Man. Dr Hubert Singer; 15 brs.

Erste Bank der Oesterreichischen Sparkassen AG (Erste Bank) (First Austrian Savings Bank): Postfach 162, Graben 21, 1010 Vienna; tel. (1) 501-00-0; fax (1) 501-00-9; e-mail service.center@erstebank.at; internet www.sparkasse.at/erstebank; f. 1819; present name adopted 1997; dep. 151,551m., total assets 181,703m. (Dec. 2006); Chair. Andreas Treichl; 984 brs in Austria.

Kärntner Sparkasse AG: Neuer Pl. 14, 9020 Klagenfurt; tel. (463) 588-80; fax (463) 588-82-91; e-mail info@kaerntnersparkasse.co.at; internet www.kaerntnersparkasse.at; f. 1835; 75% owned by private foundation Die Kärntner Sparkasse AG, 25% owned by Erste Bank der oesterreichischen Sparkassen AG; dep. 3,218m., total assets 3,680m. (Dec. 2006); Pres. Dr Hans Kostwein; Chair. and Gen. Man. Alois Hochegger; 52 brs.

Salzburger Sparkasse Bank AG: Postfach 180, Alter Markt 3, 5021 Salzburg; tel. (662) 80-40-0; fax (662) 80-40-81; internet www.sparkasse.at/salzburg; f. 1855 as Salzburger Sparkasse; present name adopted 1991; absorbed ALPHA-Beteiligungs GmbH in 1997; 98.69% owned by Erste Bank der oesterreichischen Sparkassen AG; cap. 34m., res 145m., dep. 3,657m. (Dec. 2006); Gen. Man. Johann Lassacher; 79 brs.

Co-operative Banks

Österreichische Volksbanken-AG (VBAG): Kollngasse 19, 1090 Vienna; tel. (1) 504-00-40; fax (1) 504-004-36-83; e-mail info@volksbank.com; internet www.volksbank.com; f. 1922 as Österreichische Zentralgenossenschaftskasse rGmbH; present name adopted 1974; cap. and res 2,846m., dep. and bonds 52,559m., total assets 67,429m. (Dec. 2006); Chair. and CEO Franz Pinkl; 79 brs.

Raiffeisen Centrobank AG: Postfach 272, Tegetthoffstr. 1, 1015 Vienna; tel. (1) 515-20-0; fax (1) 513-43-96; e-mail office@rcb.at; internet www.rcb.at; f. 1973 as Centro International Handelsbank; present name adopted 2001; 99.99% owned by Raiffeisen Zentralbank Österreich AG, 0.01% owned by Raiffeisen-Invest-Gesellschaft mbH; cap. 48m., res 27m., dep. 1,138m. (Dec. 2006); Chair. Dr Eva Marchart.

Raiffeisen Zentralbank Österreich AG (RZB-Austria): Am Stadtpark 9, 1030 Vienna; tel. (1) 717-07-0; fax (1) 717-07-17-15; internet www.rzb.at; f. 1927; dep. 100,179m., total assets 115,629m. (Dec. 2006); central institute of the Austrian Raiffeisen banking group; Chair., Supervisory Bd Dr Christian Konrad; Chair., Bd of Management Dr Walter Rothensteiner.

Raiffeisen-Landesbank Steiermark AG: Kaiserfeldgasse 5–7, 8010 Graz; tel. (316) 80-36-0; fax (316) 80-36-24-37; e-mail info@rlb-stmk.raiffeisen.at; internet www.rlbstmk.at; f. 1927; cap. 135m., res 498m., dep. and bonds 5,972m. (Dec. 2006); Chair., Bd of Management Markus Mair.

Raiffeisen-Landesbank Tirol AG (RLB Tirol AG): Adamgasse 1–7, 6020 Innsbruck; tel. (512) 530-50; fax (512) 530-52-229; e-mail andrea.zankl@rlb-tirol.at; internet www.rlb-tirol.at; f. 1894; cap. 80m., res 217m., dep. 4,342m. (Dec. 2006); Chair. Dr Hannes Schmid; 21 brs.

Raiffeisenlandesbank Kärnten-Rechenzentrum und Revisionsverband rGmbH: Raiffeisenpl. 1, 9020 Klagenfurt; tel. (463) 99300-22-70; fax (463) 993-00-36; internet www.raiffeisen.at/ktn; f. 1900 as Spar- und Darlehensverband Kärnten; present name adopted 1996; cap. 5m., res 111m., dep. 2,385m. (Dec. 2006); Chair. Dr Klaus Pekarek; Man. Dir Peter Gauper.

Directory

Raiffeisenlandesbank Niederösterreich-Wien AG: Friedrich-Wilhelm-Raiffeisen-Pl. 1, Raiffeisenhaus, 1020 Vienna; tel. (1) 517-00-17-00; e-mail info@raiffeisenbank.at; internet www.raiffeisenbank.at; f. 1898; dep. 13,782m., total assets 16,473m. (Dec. 2006); Chair., Supervisory Board Dr Christian Konrad; Chair., Management Board and CEO Erwin Hameseder.

Raiffeisenlandesbank Oberösterreich AG: Postfach 455, Europapl. 1A, 4021 Linz; tel. (732) 65-96-0; fax (732) 65-96-27-39; e-mail cb@rlbooe.at; internet www.rlbooe.at; f. 1900; cap. 241m., res 858m., dep. 18,651m. (Dec. 2006); Chair. Dr Ludwig Scharinger.

Raiffeisenlandesbank Vorarlberg Waren-und Revisions Verband rGmbH: Rheinstr. 11, 6900 Bregenz; tel. (5574) 40-50-0; fax (5574) 405-331; e-mail info@raiba.at; internet www.raiba.at; f. 1895; cap. 27m., res 120m., dep. 3,422m. (Dec. 2006); Gen. Mans Dr Karl Waltle, Dr Johannes Ortner, Wilfried Hopfner; 3 brs.

Raiffeisenverband Salzburg rGmbH: Postfach 6, Schwarzstr. 13–15, 5024 Salzburg; tel. (662) 88-86-0; fax (662) 88-86-597; e-mail friedrich.buchmueller@rvs.at; internet www.salzburg.raiffeisen.at; f. 1905 as Salzburgische Genossenschafts-Zentralkasse; present name adopted 1949; cap. 44m., res 224m., dep. 4,322m. (Dec. 2006); Chair. Günther Reibersdorfer.

Welser Volksbank rGmbH: Postfach 234, Pfarrgasse 5, 4601 Wels; tel. (7242) 495; fax (7242) 495-97; e-mail office@welser.volksbank.at; internet www.welser.volksbank.at; f. 1912 as Welser Handels- und Gewerbekasse rGmbH; present name adopted 1971; cap. 2m., res 21m., dep. 257m. (Dec. 2005); Chair. Dr Josef Steinböck; Gen. Man. Andreas Pirklbauer; 12 brs.

Bankers' Organization

Verband Österreichischer Banken und Bankiers (Asscn of Austrian Banks and Bankers): Postfach 132, Börsegasse 11, 1013 Vienna; tel. (1) 535-17-71-0; fax (1) 535-17-71-38; e-mail bv@bankenverband.at; internet www.voebb.at; f. 1945; Pres. Dr Stephan Koren; Gen. Sec. Maria Geyer; 64 mems and 17 extraordinary mems.

STOCK EXCHANGE

Wiener Börse (Vienna Stock Exchange): Wallnerstr. 8, 1010 Vienna; tel. (1) 531-65-0; fax (1) 532-97-40; e-mail board@wienerborse.at; internet www.wienerborse.at; f. 1771; two sections: Stock Exchange, Commodity Exchange; absorbed equity and futures exchanges in 1997; CEO Dr Heinrich Schaller, Dr Michael Buhl.

INSURANCE COMPANIES

In 2006 there were 60 insurance companies in Austria, with total assets of €82,871m.

Allgemeine Rechtsschutz Versicherungs-AG (ARAG): Favoritenstr. 36, 1041 Vienna; tel. (1) 531-02-0; fax (1) 531-02-1923; e-mail info@arag.at; internet www.arag.at; Man. Dr Herbert Kittinger.

Allianz Elementar Lebensversicherung-AG: Hietzinger Kai 101–105, 1130 Vienna; tel. (1) 878-07-0; fax (1) 878-07-27-03; e-mail office@allianz.at; internet www.allianz.at; life insurance; Chair., Supervisory Bd Dr Gerhard Rupprecht; Chair., Management Bd Dr Wolfram Littich.

Allianz Elementar Versicherungs-AG: Hietzinger Kai 101–105, 1130 Vienna; tel. (1) 878-07-0; fax (1) 878-07-53-90; e-mail office@allianz.at; internet www.allianz.co.at; f. 1860; all classes except life insurance; Chair., Supervisory Bd Dr Reiner Hagemann; Chair., Management Bd Dr Wolfram Littich.

AXA Nordstern Colonia Versicherungs-AG: Uraniastr. 2, 1010 Vienna; tel. (1) 711-50-0; fax (1) 711-50-212; e-mail kundendienst@axa-versicherung.at; internet www.axa-versicherung.at; Gen. Man. David Furtwängler.

Donau Allgemeine Versicherungs-AG: Schottenring 15, 1010 Vienna; tel. (1) 313-11; fax (1) 310-77-51; e-mail donau@donauversicherung.at; internet www.donauversicherung.at; f. 1867; all classes; Gen. Man. Hans Rauwauf.

Generali Versicherung AG: Landskrongasse 1–3, 1011 Vienna; tel. (1) 534-01; fax (1) 534-01-12-26; e-mail headoffice@generali.at; internet www.generali.co.at; f. 1882; as Erste Österreichische Allgemeine Unfall-Versicherungs-Gesellschaft; Gen. Man. Dr Hans Peer.

Grazer Wechselseitige Versicherung: Herrengasse 18–20, 8011 Graz; tel. (316) 80-37-0; fax (316) 80-37-41-4; f. 1828; all classes; Gen. Man. Dr Othmar Ederer.

Interunfall Versicherungs-AG: Tegetthoffstr. 7, 1011 Vienna; tel. (1) 514-03-0; fax (1) 514-03-4590; e-mail z-v@interunfall.at; internet www.interunfall.at; all classes (incl. reinsurance); Man. Dr Hans Peer.

Raiffeisen-Versicherung AG: Untere Donaustr. 25, 1021 Vienna; tel. (1) 211-19-0; fax (1) 211-19-11-34; e-mail kommunikation@

raiffeisen-versicherung.at; internet www.raiffeisen-versicherung.at; Dir Dr PETER EICHLER.

Salzburger Landes-Versicherung AG: Auersperstr. 9, 5021 Salzburg; tel. (662) 899-98-0; fax (662) 889-98-109; e-mail sekretariat@slv.co.at; internet www.slv.co.at; Gen. Man. Dr JOSEF GLASER.

Sparkassen Versicherung AG: Wipplingerstr. 36–38, 1011 Vienna; tel. (1) 313-81-0; fax (1) 313-81-300; e-mail sag@s-versicherung.co.at; internet www.s-versicherung.co.at; Gen. Man. Dr MICHAEL HARRER.

UNIQA Versicherungen AG: Untere Donaustr. 21, 1029 Vienna; tel. (1) 211-75-0; fax (1) 214-33-36; e-mail kommunikation@uniqa.at; internet www.uniqagroup.com; f. 1999; Chair. Dr KONSTANTIN KLIEN.

Wiener Städtische Allgemeine Versicherung AG: Schottenring 30, Ringturm, 1010 Vienna; tel. (1) 531-39-0; fax (1) 535-34-37; e-mail mail-us@wr.staedtische.co.at; internet www.staedtische.co.at; f. 1824; all classes; CEO Dr SIEGFRIED SELLITSCH.

Wüstenrot Versicherungs-AG: Alpenstr. 61, 5033 Salzburg; tel. (662) 6386-0; fax (662) 6386-623; e-mail versicherung@wuestenrot.at; internet www.wuestenrot.at; Gen. Man. HELMUT GEIER.

Zürich Versicherungs AG: Schwarzenbergpl. 15, 1015 Vienna; tel. (1) 501-25-0; fax (1) 505-04-85; internet www.zurich.at; f. 1876; all classes; CEO CHRISTIAN BAUER.

Insurance Organization

Verband der Versicherungsunternehmen Österreichs (Asscn of Austrian Insurance Cos): Schwarzenbergpl. 7, 1030 Vienna; tel. (1) 711-56-0; fax (1) 711-56-27-0; e-mail versver@ibm.net; internet www.vvo.at; f. 1945; Pres. Dr ALEXANDER HOYOS; Gen. Sec. HERBERT RETTER; 86 mems.

Trade and Industry

GOVERNMENT AGENCIES

Austrian Business Agency (ABA): Opernring 3, 1010 Vienna; fax (1) 586-86-59; e-mail office@aba.gv.at; internet www.aba.gv.at; Man. Dir RENÉ SIEGL.

Österreichische Industrieholding AG (ÖIAG): Dresdner Str. 87, 1201 Vienna; tel. (1) 711-14-0; fax (1) 711-14-24-5; e-mail oiag@oiag.at; internet www.oiag.at; f. 1970; Chair., Supervisory Bd Dr PETER MITTERBAUER; Man. Dir Dr PETER MICHAELIS.

CHAMBERS OF COMMERCE

All Austrian enterprises must by law be members of the Economic Chambers. The Federal Economic Chamber promotes international contacts and represents the economic interests of trade and industry on a federal level. Its Foreign Trade Organization includes about 90 offices abroad.

Wirtschaftskammer Österreich (Austrian Federal Economic Chamber): Wiedner Hauptstr. 63, 1045 Vienna; tel. (0) 590-90-0; fax (0) 590-90-02-50; e-mail wkoe@wko.at; internet www.wko.at; f. 1946; seven divisions: Crafts and Trades, Industry, Commerce, Bank and Insurance, Transport and Communications, Tourism and Leisure, Industry, Information and Consulting; these divisions are subdivided into branch asscns; Regional Economic Chambers with divisions and branch asscns in each of the nine Austrian provinces; Pres. Dr CHRISTOPH LEITL; Sec.-Gen. ANNA-MARIA HOCHHAUSER; c. 330,000 mems.

INDUSTRIAL AND TRADE ASSOCIATIONS

Wirtschaftskammer Österreich—Bundessparte Industrie: Wiedner Hauptstr. 63, 1045 Vienna; tel. (0) 590900-3420; fax (0) 590900-273; e-mail bsi@wko.at; internet www.wko.at; f. 1896; as Zentralverband der Industrie Österreichs (Central Fed. of Austrian Industry), merged into present org. 1947; Chair. Dr WERNER TESSMAR-PFOHL; Dir WOLFGANG DAMIANISCH; comprises the following industrial feds:

Fachverband der Audiovisions-und Filmindustrie Österreichs (Film): Postfach 327, Wiedner Hauptstr. 63, 1045 Vienna; tel. (0) 590900-3010; fax (0) 590900-276; e-mail krenmayr@fafo.at; internet www.fafo.at; Chair. DANIEL KRAUSZ; Man. Dir Dr WERNER MÜLLER; 2,500 mems.

Fachverband der Bekleidungsindustrie (Clothing): Wiedner Hauptstr. 63, 1045 Vienna; tel. (0) 590900-4903; fax (0) 590900-4908; e-mail pitnik@fashion-industry.at; internet www.fashion-industry.at; Chair. WOLFGANG SIMA; Dir FRANZ J. PITNIK; 195 mems.

Fachverband der Bergwerke und Eisenerzeugenden Industrie (Mining and Steel Production): Wiedner Haupstr. 3, 1045 Vienna; tel. (1) 512-46-01; fax (1) 512-46-01-20; e-mail fvil@wkoesk.wk.or.at; internet www.wko.at/bergbau-stahl; Dir HERBERT BARDACH; Sec. Ing. HERMANN PRINZ; 39 mems.

Fachverband der Chemischen Industrie (Chemicals): Postfach 325, Wiedner Hauptstr. 63, 1045 Vienna; tel. (1) 501-05-280; fax (1) 502-06-28-0; e-mail office@fcio.wko.at; internet www.fcio.at; Pres. Dr WOLFGANG FRANK; Gen. Dir Dr WOLFGANG EICKHOFF; 530 mems.

Fachverband der Elektro- und Elektronikindustrie—FEEI (Electrical): Mariahilfer Str. 37–39, 1060 Vienna; tel. (1) 588-39-0; fax (1) 586-69-71; e-mail info@feei.at; internet www.feei.at; Pres. ALBERT HOCHLEITNER; Man. Dir LOTHAR ROITNER; 350 mems.

Fachverband der Fahrzeugindustrie (Vehicles): Wiedner Hauptstr. 63, 1045 Vienna; tel. (0) 590900-4800; fax (0) 590900-289; e-mail kfz@wko.at; internet www.fahrzeugindustrie.at; Pres. BRUNO KRAINZ; Gen. Sec. WALTER LINSZBAUER; 200 mems.

Fachverband der Gas- und Wärmeversorgungsunternehmungen (Gas and Heating): Schubertring 14, 1010 Vienna; tel. (1) 513-15-88-0; fax (1) 513-15-88-25; e-mail office@gaswaerme.at; internet www.gaswaerme.at; Gen. Dir Dr KARL SKYBA.

Fachverband der Giessereiindustrie (Foundries): Postfach 339, Wiedner Hauptstr. 63, 1045 Vienna; tel. (0) 590900-3463; fax (0) 590900-279; e-mail giesserei@wko.at; Chair. PETER MAIWALD; Dir ADOLF KERBL; 60 mems.

Fachverband der Glasindustrie (Glass): Wiedner Hauptstr. 63, 1045 Vienna; tel. (0) 590-900-3448; fax (0) 590-900-281; e-mail office@fvglas.at; internet www.fvglas.at; Chair. RUDOLF SCHRAML; Dir ALEXANDER KRISSMANEK; 66 mems.

Fachverband der Holzindustrie (Wood): Postfach 123, Schwarzenbergpl. 4, 1037 Vienna; tel. (1) 712-26-01-0; fax (1) 713-03-09; e-mail office@holzindustrie.at; internet www.holzindustrie.at; f. 1947 as Fachverband der Sägeindustrie Österreichs; present name adopted 2000; Chair. Dr ERICH WIESNER; Dir Dr CLAUDIUS KOLLMANN; 1,800 mems.

Fachverband der Ledererzeugenden Industrie (Leather Production): Postfach 312, Wiedner Hauptstr. 63, 1045 Vienna 4; tel. (0) 590900-3453; fax (0) 590900-278; e-mail fvleder@wko.at; internet www.leather-industry.at; f. 1945; Chair. ULRICH SCHMIDT; Dir PETER KOVACS; 8 mems.

Fachverband der Lederverarbeitenden Industrie (Leather Processing): Postfach 313, Wiedner Hauptstr. 63, 1045 Vienna; tel. (0) 590900-3453; fax (0) 590900-278; e-mail fvleder@wko.at; internet www.shoes-leather.at; f. 1945; Chair. JOSEPH LORENZ; Dir PETER KOVACS; 45 mems.

Fachverband der Maschinen- und Stahlbauindustrie (Machinery and Steel Construction): Wiedner Hauptstr. 63, 1045 Vienna; tel. (1) 502-25; fax (1) 505-10-20; e-mail machinen@fms.at; internet www.fms.at; Pres. Dr CLEMENS MALINA-ALTZINGER; Dir JOHANN ZODER; 850 mems.

Fachverband der Metallwarenindustrie Österreichs (Metal Goods): Postfach 335, Wiedner Hauptstr. 63, 1045 Vienna; tel. (1) 501-05; fax (1) 505-09-28; internet www.fmwi.at; f. 1908; Chair. Ing. WOLFGANG WELSER; Gen. Man. Dr WOLFGANG LOCKER; 800 mems.

Fachverband der NE-Metallindustrie Österreichs (Austrian Non-Ferrous Metals Federation): Postfach 338, Wiedner Hauptstr. 63, 1045 Vienna; tel. (0) 590900-3309; fax (0) 590900-3378; e-mail nemetall@wko.at; f. 1946; Chair. GERHARD ESCHNER; Dir HERBERT BADRACH; 69 mems.

Fachverband der Mineralölindustrie (Petroleum): Wiedner Hauptstr. 63, 1045 Vienna; tel. (0) 590900-4892; fax (0) 590900-4895; e-mail office@oil-gas.at; internet www.oil-gas.at; f. 1947; Gen. Dirs Dr WOLFGANG RUDDENSDORFER, Dr CRISTOPH CAPEK; 21 mems.

Fachverband der Nahrungs- und Genussmittelindustrie (Provisions): Zaunergasse 1–3, 1030 Vienna; tel. (1) 712-21-21; fax (1) 712-21-21-35; e-mail fiaa@dielebensmittel.at; internet dielebensmittel.at; Chair. JOHANN MARIHART; Dir Dr MICHAEL BLASS; 480 mems.

Fachverband der Papier und Pappe verarbeitenden Industrie (Paper and Board Processing): Brucknerstr. 8, 1041 Vienna; tel. (1) 505-53-82-0; fax (1) 505-90-18; e-mail ppv@ppv.at; internet www.ppv.at; Chair. GUSTAV GLÖCKLER; 134 mems.

Fachverband der Papierindustrie (Paper): Gumpendorferstr. 6, 1061 Vienna; tel. (1) 588-86-0; fax (1) 588-86-33-3; e-mail austropapier@austropapier.at; internet www.austropapier.at; Chair. THOMAS M. SALZER; Dir Dr WERNER AURACHER; 30 mems.

Fachverband der Stein- und keramischen Industrie (Stone and Ceramics): Postfach 329, Wiedner Hauptstr. 63, 1045 Vienna; tel. (0) 590900-3531; fax (1) 505-62-40; e-mail steine@wko.at; internet www.baustoffindustrie.at; f. 1947; Chair. Dr CARL HENNRICH; Pres. Dr ERHARD SCHASCHL; 400 mems.

AUSTRIA   *Directory*

Fachverband der Textilindustrie Österreichs (Textiles): Rudolfspl. 12, Postfach 197, 1013 Vienna; tel. (1) 533-37-26-0; fax (1) 533-37-26-40; e-mail fvtextil@fvtextil.wk.or.at; internet www.textilindustrie.at; Pres. Dr PETER PFNEISL; Dir Dr WOLFGANG ZEYRINGER; 265 mems.

Geschäftsstelle Bau (Building): Schaumburgergasse 20/8, 1010 Vienna; tel. (1) 718-37-37; e-mail office@bau.or.at; internet www.bau.or.at; formerly Fachverband der Bauindustrie; Dir MANFRED KATZENSCHLAGER; 150 mems.

UTILITIES
Electricity

Burgenländische Elektrizitätswirtschafts-AG (BEWAG): Kasernenstr. 9, 7000 Eisenstadt; tel. (2682) 900-01-10-0; fax (2682) 900-01-90-0; e-mail info@bewag.at; internet www.bewag.at; f. 1958; owned by province of Burgenland (51%) and Burgenland Holding AG (49%); Chair. JOSEF KALTENBACHER.

Energie AG Oberösterreich: Böhmerwaldstr. 3, Postfach 298, 4021 Linz; tel. (70) 9000-0; fax (800) 8180-01; e-mail service@energieag.at; internet www.energieag.at; fmrly Oberösterreichische Kraftwerke AG; subsidiaries active in Germany, the Czech Republic, Hungary and Slovakia; Chair. Dr LEOPOLD WINDTNER.

Energie Steiermark AG: Leonhardstr. 59, 8010; tel. (316) 9000; fax (316) 387290; e-mail office@e-steiermark.com; internet www.estag.com; 75% (minus one share) owned by province of Steiermark; fmrly Steirische Wasserkraft- und Elektrizitäts-AG; Chair. Dr KARL-FRANZ MAIER.

Energie-Versorgung-Niederösterreich AG (EVN): EVN Pl., 2344 Maria Enzersdorf; tel. (2236) 200-0; e-mail info@evn.at; internet www.evn.at; Chair. Dr BURKHARD HOFER.

Kärntner Elektrizitäts-AG (KELAG): Arnulfpl. 2, Postfach 176, 9010 Klagenfurt; tel. (463) 525-0; fax (463) 525-1596; e-mail office@kelag.at; internet www.kelag.at; Chair. Dr HERMANN EGGER, HANS-JOACHIM JUNG.

Österreichische Elektrizitätswirtschafts-AG (Verbund): Am Hof 6A, 1010 Vienna; tel. (1) 531-13-0; fax (1) 531-13-41-91; e-mail info@verbund.at; internet www.verbund.at; federal electricity authority; operates national grid, sells electricity wholesale to the nine regional operators; Chair., Supervisory Bd Dr GILBERT FRIZBERG; Chair., Management Bd Dr MICHAEL PISTAUER.

Salzburg AG für Energie, Verkehr und Telekommunikation: Bayerhamerstr. 16, 5020 Salzburg; tel. (662) 88-84-0; fax (662) 88-84-17-0; e-mail offic@salzburg-ag.at; internet www.salzburg-ag.at; f. 2000 by merger of SAFE and Salzburger Stadtwerke; 42.56% owned by province of Salzburg, 31.31% by city of Salzburg and 26.13% by Energie Oberösterreich Service- und Beteiligungsverwaltungs-GmbH; Chair. Dr OTHMAR RAUS.

Tiroler Wasserkraftwerke AG (TIWAG): Eduard-Wallnöfer-Pl. 2, 6020 Innsbruck; tel. (0) 50607-0; fax (0) 50607-21714; e-mail office@tiwag.at; internet www.tiwag.at; Chair. FERDINAND EBERLE.

Vorarlberger Kraftwerke AG (VKW): Weidachstr. 6, 6900 Bregenz; tel. (5574) 601-0; fax (5574) 601-1710; e-mail unternehmen@vkw.at; internet www.vkw.at; Chair. Dr LUDWIG SUMMER.

Wien Energie GmbH: Schottenring 30, 1011 Vienna; tel. (1) 53123-0; fax (1) 800-500-801; e-mail info@wienenergie.at; internet www.wienenergie.at; Chair. MICHAEL OBENTRAUT.

Gas

BEGAS (Burgenländische Erdgasversorgungs AG): Kasernenstr. 10, 7000 Eisenstadt; tel. (2682) 709-0; fax (2682) 709-174; internet www.begas.at; Chair. RUDOLF SIMANDL, REINHARD SCHWEIFER.

Oberösterreichische Ferngas-AG: Neubauzeile 99, 4030 Linz; tel. (732) 38-83; fax (732) 37-72-19; Chair. MAX DOBRUCKT.

Steirische Ferngas-AG: Gaslaternenweg 4, 8041 Graz; tel. (316) 476-0; fax (316) 476-28-000; e-mail info@steirische.ferngas.at; internet www.steirische.ferngas.at; Chair. DOMINIQUE BAYEN, PETER KÖBERL, MAX PÖLZL.

Water

Water is supplied to 90% of the population by municipalities, either directly or through private companies in which they retain a majority stake. The remaining 10% of the population access water from private wells or small facilities organized as co-operative societies.

Österreichischer Wasser- und Abfallwirtschaftsverband (ÖWAV) (Austrian Water and Waste Management Asscn): Marc-Aurel-Str. 5, 1010 Vienna; tel. (1) 535-57-20-0; fax (1) 535-40-64; e-mail buero@oewav.at; internet www.oewav.at.

TRADE UNIONS

Österreichischer Gewerkschaftsbund (ÖGB) (Austrian Trade Union Fed.): Laurenzerberg 2, 1010 Vienna; tel. (1) 534-44; fax (1) 534-44-20-4; e-mail oegb@oegb.or.at; internet www.oegb.or.at; non-party union org. with voluntary membership; f. 1945; org. affiliated with ITUC and the European Trade Union Confederation (ETUC); Pres. RUDOLF HUNDSTORFER; Vice-Pres. ROSWITHA BACHNER, Dr NORBERT SCHNEDL.

Nine affiliated unions with a total membership of 1.3m. (2006):

Gewerkschaft Bau-Holz (Building Workers and Woodworkers): Ebendorferstr. 7, 1010 Vienna; tel. (1) 401-47; fax (1) 401-47-314; e-mail bau-holz@gbh.oegb.or.at; internet www.bau-holz.at; Chair. JOHANN HOLPER; 150,000 mems (2006).

Gewerkschaft der Chemiearbeiter (Chemical Workers): Stumpergasse 60, 1060 Vienna; tel. (1) 597-15-01; fax (1) 597-21-01-23; e-mail evelyn.gotschy@gdc.oegb.or.at; internet www.chemiearbeiter.at; Chair. ALFRED ARTMÄUER.

Gewerkschaft der Gemeindebediensteten (Municipal Employees): Maria-Theresien-Str. 11, 1090 Vienna; tel. (1) 313-16-0; fax (1) 313-16-83-81; e-mail gdg@gdg.at; internet www.gdg.at; Chair. CHRISTIAN MEIDLINGER; 153,459 mems (2006).

Gewerkschaft Kunst, Medien, Sport, freie Berufe (Musicians, Actors, Artists, Journalists, etc.): Maria-Theresien-Str. 11, 1090 Vienna; tel. (1) 313-16; fax (1) 313-16-77-00; e-mail sekretariat@kmsfb.oegb.or.at; internet www.kmsfb.at; f. 1945; Chair. Prof. HEINZ FIEDLER; Sec.-Gen. SABINE HEROLD; 11,603 mems (2003).

Gewerkschaft Metall-Textil-Nahrung (GMTN) (Metal Workers, Miners and Power Supply Workers—Textile, Leather and Garment Industry Workers—Agricultural, Food, Beverage and Tobacco Workers): Plösslgasse 15, 1041 Vienna; tel. (1) 501-46-0; fax (1) 534-44-10-32-70; e-mail gmtn@gmtn.at; internet www.gmtn.at; f. by merger of Gewerkschaft Metall-Bergbau-Energie and Gewerkschaft Textil, Bekleidung, Leder; joined by Gewerkschaft Agrar-Nahrung-Genuss in 2006; Chair. ERICH FOGLAR; 230,000 mems (2006).

Gewerkschaft Öffentlicher Dienst (Public Employees): Teinfaltstr. 7, 1010 Vienna; tel. (1) 534-54-0; fax (1) 534-54-207; e-mail goed@goed.at; internet www.goed.at; f. 1945; Chair. FRITZ NEUGEBAUER; 230,000 mems (2006).

Gewerkschaft der Post- und Fernmeldebediensteten (Postal and Telegraph Workers): Postfach 343, Biberstr. 5, 1010 Vienna; tel. (1) 512-55-11-0; fax (1) 512-55-11-52; e-mail gpf.post@gpf.oegb.or.at; internet www.gpf.at; Chair. GERHARD FRITZ; 64,533 mems (2004).

Gewerkschaft der Privatangestellten Druck, Journalismus und Papier (Commercial, Clerical and Technical Employees, Printing, Journalism and Paper Trade Workers): Alfred-Dallinger-Pl. 1, 1034 Vienna; tel. (1) 503-01; fax (1) 503-01-300; e-mail service@gpa-djp.at; internet www.gpa-djp.at; f. 2006 by merger of Gewerkschaft der Privatangestellten (f. 1945) and Gewerkschaft Druck, Journalismus und Papier (f. 1842); Chair. Dr DWORA STEIN.

Gewerkschaft vida: Margaretenstr. 166, 1051 Vienna; tel. (1) 546-41-0; e-mail info@vida.at; internet www.vida.at; f. 2006 by merger of Gewerkschaft der Eisenbahner, Gewerkschaft Handel, Transport, Verkehr and Gewerkschaft Hotel, Gastgewerbe, Persönlicher Dienst; Chair. RUDOLF KASKE; Sec.-Gen. NORBERT BACHER-LAGLER; 170,000 mems (2007).

Transport
RAILWAYS

ÖBB-Konzern (Austrian Federal Railways) operates more than 90% of all the railway routes in Austria. In 2006 ÖBB operated 5,702 km of track, of which 3,523 km were electrified.

ÖBB-Konzern (Austrian Federal Railways): Wienerbergstr. 11, 1100 Vienna; tel. (1) 930-00-0; fax (1) 930-00-25010; e-mail holding@oebb.at; internet www.oebb.at; f. 2004 following reorg. of Östereichische Bundesbahnen (ÖBB) in 2003; Chair. MARTIN HUBER; consists of ÖBB Holding AG (management) and the following orgs:

ÖBB-Dienstleistungs GmbH: Clemens-Holzmeister-Str. 6, 1100 Vienna; tel. (1) 930-00-13-06-1; fax (1) 930-00-25-01-2; e-mail dlg@oebb.at; information systems and personnel management; Man. FRANZ NIGL.

ÖBB-Infrastruktur Bau AG: Vivenotgasse 10, 1120 Vienna; tel. (1) 930-00-0; e-mail info@bau.oebb.at; internet www.oebb.at/bau; responsible for planning, construction and financing of rail infrastructure projects; provides power and telecommunications for the network; subsidiary: ÖBB-Immobilienmanagement GmbH (buildings management); Mans GILBERT TRATTNER, GEORG-MICHAEL VAVROVSKY.

ÖBB-Infrastruktur Betrieb AG: Elisabethstr. 9, 1010 Vienna; e-mail infra.kommunikation@oebb.at; rail network infrastructure; Chair. ALFRED ZIMMERMANN.

ÖBB-Personenverkehr AG: Wagramer Str. 17–19, 1220 Vienna; tel. (1) 930-00-0; e-mail service@pv.oebb.at; passenger transport; jointly responsible, with Rail Cargo Austria AG (q.v.),

AUSTRIA

for ÖBB-Traktion GmbH (locomotives) and ÖBB-Technische Services GmbH (technical services); subsidiary: ÖBB-Postbus GmbH; Mans Gabriele Lutter, Josef Halbmayr, Dr Stefan Wehinger.

Rail Cargo Austria AG: Erdberger Lände 40–48, 1030 Vienna; tel. (1) 577-50; fax (1) 577-50-71-9; e-mail kommunikation@railcargo.at; internet www.railcargo.at; freight and logistics; jointly responsible, with ÖBB-Personenverkehr AG (q.v.), for ÖBB-Traktion GmbH (locomotives) and ÖBB-Technische Services GmbH (technical services); subsidiary: Speditions Holding GmbH; Dirs Ferdinand Schmidt, Friedrich Macher, Dr Günther Riessland.

Other railway companies include: Achenseebahn AG, AG der Wiener Lokalbahnen, Graz-Köflacher Eisenbahn- und Bergbau GmbH, Lokalbahn, Montafonerbahn AG, Raab-Oedenburg-Ebenfurter Eisenbahn, Salzburger Stadtwerke AG-Verkehrsbetriebe, Steiermarkische Lokalbahnen, Stern & Hafferl Verkehrs GmbH, Zillertaler Verkehrsbetriebe AG.

ROADS

In 2003 Austria had some 133,928 km of classified roads, of which 2,050 km were motorways and 10,193 km were main roads.

INLAND WATERWAYS

The Danube (Donau) is Austria's only navigable river. It enters Austria from Germany at Passau and flows into Slovakia near Hainburg. The length of the Austrian section of the river is 350 km. Danube barges carry up to 1,800 metric tons, but loading depends on the water level, which varies considerably throughout the year. Cargoes are chiefly petroleum and derivatives, coal, coke, iron ore, iron, steel, timber and grain. The Rhine-Main-Danube Canal opened in 1992. A passenger service is maintained on the Upper Danube and between Vienna and the Black Sea. Passenger services are also provided on Bodensee (Lake Constance) and Wolfgangsee by Austrian Federal Railways, and on all the larger Austrian lakes.

CIVIL AVIATION

Civil aviation is regulated by the Federal Ministry of Transport, Innovation and Technology, as well as Austro Control GmbH (Austrian air traffic control), Österreichischer Aeroclub (the Austrian Aeroclub), Landeshauptleute (provincial governors) and Bezirksverwaltungsbehörden (district administrative authorities). The main international airport is located at Schwechat, near Vienna. There are also international flights from Graz, Innsbruck, Klagenfurt, Linz and Salzburg, and internal flights between these cities.

Principal Airlines

Austrian Airlines Group (Österreichische Luftverkehrs AG): Fontanastr. 1, 1107 Vienna; tel. (1) 517-66; fax (1) 688-55-05; e-mail public.relations@austrian.com; internet www.austrian.com; f. 1957; 42.75% state-owned; serves 130 cities in 66 countries worldwide; mem. of Star Alliance; Chair. Peter Michaelis; CEO Alfred Ötsch.

Austrian Arrows: Postfach 98, Fürstenweg 176, 6026 Innsbruck; tel. (512) 22-22-0; fax (512) 28-66-46; e-mail pressestelle@tyrolean.at; internet www.tyrolean.at; f. 1978 as Aircraft Innsbruck; renamed Tiroler Luftfahrt GmbH 1980; present name adopted 2003; brand name of Tyrolean Airlines; operates scheduled services and charter flights within Austria and to other European countries; Man. Dir Manfred Helldoppler.

Lauda Air Luftfahrt GmbH: Office Park 2, Postfach 56, 1300 Vienna-Schwechat; tel. (1) 7000-0; fax (1) 7000-790-15; e-mail info@laudaair.com; internet www.laudaair.com; f. 1979; became a scheduled carrier 1987; wholly owned by Austrian Airlines Group; operates scheduled passenger services and charter flights to Europe, Australia, the Far East and the USA; Chair. Thomas Suritsch.

Tourism

Tourism plays an important part in the Austrian economy. In 2006 Austria received 20.3m. foreign visitors at accommodation establishments. Receipts from the tourism sector, excluding passenger transport, totalled €13,267m. in 2006. The country's mountain scenery attracts visitors in both summer and winter, while Vienna and Salzburg, hosts to a number of internationally renowned arts festivals, are important cultural centres. In June 2008 Austria was due jointly to host (with Switzerland) the European Football Championships.

Österreich Werbung (Austrian National Tourist Office): Margaretenstr. 1, 1040 Vienna; tel. (1) 588-66-0; fax (1) 588-66-40; e-mail holiday@austria.info; internet www.austriatourism.com; f. 1955; Pres. Dr Martin Bartenstein (Federal Minister for Economics and Labour); CEO Dr Petra Stolba.

AZERBAIJAN

Introductory Survey

Location, Climate, Language, Religion, Flag, Capital

The Azerbaijan Republic is situated in the eastern South Caucasus, on the western coast of the Caspian Sea. To the south it borders Iran, to the west Armenia, to the north-west Georgia, and to the north the Republic of Dagestan, in Russia. The Naxçıvan Autonomous Republic is part of Azerbaijan, although it is separated from the rest of Azerbaijan by Armenian territory. Azerbaijan also includes the territory of the former Nagorno-Karabakh Autonomous Oblast (Nagornyi Karabakh), which is largely populated by Armenians. The Kura plain has a dry, temperate climate with an average July temperature of 27°C (80°F) and an average January temperature of 1°C (34°F). Average annual rainfall on the lowlands is 200 mm–300 mm, but the Lankaran plain normally receives between 1,000 mm and 1,750 mm. The official language is Azerbaijani, one of the South Turkic group of languages. Religious adherence corresponds largely to ethnic origins: almost all ethnic Azerbaijanis (Azeris) are Muslims, some 70% being Shi'ite and 30% Sunni. There are also Christian communities, mainly representatives of the Russian Orthodox and Armenian Apostolic denominations. The national flag (proportions 1 by 2) consists of three equal horizontal stripes, of pale blue, red and green, with a white crescent moon framing a white eight-pointed star on the central red stripe. The capital is Baku (Bakı).

Recent History

An independent state in ancient times, Azerbaijan was dominated for much of its subsequent history by foreign powers. Under the Treaty of Turkmanchai of 1828, Azerbaijan was divided between Persia (now Iran) and Russia. During the latter half of the 19th century petroleum was discovered in Azerbaijan, and by 1900 the region had become one of the world's leading petroleum producers. Immigrant Slavs began to dominate Baku and other urban areas.

After the October Revolution of 1917 in Russia, there was a short period of pro-Bolshevik rule in Baku before a nationalist Government took power and established an independent state on 28 May 1918, with Ganca (formerly Elisavetpol, but renamed Kirovabad in 1935–89) as the capital. Independent Azerbaijan was occupied by troops of both the Allied and Central Powers; after their withdrawal, it was invaded by the Red Army in April 1920, and on 28 April a Soviet Republic of Azerbaijan was established. In December 1922 the republic became a member of the Transcaucasian Soviet Federative Socialist Republic (TSFSR), a constituent republic of the newly formed USSR. The TSFSR was disbanded in 1936, and Azerbaijan became a full union republic, the Azerbaijan SSR.

Following the Soviet seizure of power in 1920, many nationalist and religious leaders and activists were persecuted or killed. In 1930–31 forced collectivization of agriculture led to peasant uprisings, which were suppressed by Soviet troops. The purges of 1937–38, under the Soviet leader, Stalin (Iosif V. Dzhugashvili), involved the execution or imprisonment of many prominent members of the Communist Party of Azerbaijan (CPA). In 1945 the Soviet Government attempted to unite the Azeri population of northern Iran with the Azerbaijan SSR, by providing military support for a local 'puppet' government in Iran; Soviet troops were forced to withdraw from Iran in the following year by US-British opposition.

In 1982 Heydar Aliyev, First Secretary of the CPA since 1969, was promoted to First Deputy Chairman of the USSR Council of Ministers, based in the Russian and Soviet capital, Moscow, while retaining his republican office; he remained influential at all-Union level until his dismissal from the Politburo in October 1987, amid popular dissatisfaction at widespread corruption within Azerbaijan. Although Azerbaijan had an annual trade surplus with the rest of the USSR, its income per head was the lowest of any of the Union Republics, except for those in Central Asia. Public grievances over the privileges enjoyed by the party leadership were expressed at demonstrations in November 1988, when protesters occupied the main square in Baku for 10 days.

The initial impetus for the demonstrations was the debate on the status of Nagornyi Karabakh (a nominally autonomous oblast, or region, within Azerbaijan, known as Artsakh in Armenian) and Naxçıvan (an exclave of Azerbaijan, with the status of Autonomous Republic, separated from metropolitan Azerbaijan by Armenia). Both territories were claimed by Armenia, on historical grounds, and Nagornyi Karabakh had a majority of Armenians among its population. Despite the apparent surrender of Azerbaijan's claims to Naxçıvan in 1920, Azerbaijani jurisdiction over the territory was guaranteed by the Soviet-Turkish Treaty of March 1921. (The 45%–50% of the republic's population that had been ethnically Armenian in 1919 had declined to less than 5% by 1989.) Nagornyi Karabakh had been a disputed territory during the period of Armenian and Azerbaijani independence (1918–20), but in June 1921 the Bolshevik Bureau for Caucasian Affairs (Kavburo) voted to unite Nagornyi Karabakh with Armenia. However, shortly afterwards, following intervention by Stalin, the decision was reversed. In 1923 the territory was declared an autonomous oblast within Azerbaijan.

Conflict over the territory re-emerged in February 1988, when the Nagornyi Karabakh regional soviet (council) requested the Armenian and Azerbaijani Supreme Soviets to agree to the transfer of the territory to Armenia. The Soviet and Azerbaijani authorities rejected the request, provoking huge demonstrations by Armenians in both Nagornyi Karabakh and Yerevan, the capital of Armenia. Azeris began leaving Armenia, and reports that refugees had been attacked led to three days of anti-Armenian violence in the Azerbaijani town of Sumqayıt. According to official figures, 32 people died, 26 of whom were Armenians. Disturbances continued, leading to a large-scale migration of refugees from both Armenia and Azerbaijan. In January 1989, in an attempt to end the tension, the Soviet Government suspended the activities of the Nagornyi Karabakh authorities and established a Special Administration Committee (SAC), responsible to the USSR Council of Ministers. The dispatch of some 5,000 Soviet troops did little to reduce tensions within Nagornyi Karabakh, where ethnic Armenians went on strike from May until September.

In 1989 the nationalist Popular Front Party of Azerbaijan (PFPA) was established. The PFPA organized a national strike in September and demanded discussion on the issues of sovereignty, Nagornyi Karabakh, the release of political prisoners and official recognition of the party. After one week, the Azerbaijan Supreme Soviet (Supreme Majlis) agreed to concessions to the PFPA, including official recognition, and on 23 September adopted a 'Constitutional Law on the Sovereignty of the Azerbaijan SSR'. Azerbaijan closed its borders and prohibited all trade with Armenia. In November the Soviet Government transferred control of Nagornyi Karabakh from the SAC to an Organizing Committee, dominated by Azeris. The Armenian Supreme Soviet denounced this decision and declared Nagornyi Karabakh to be part of a 'unified Armenian republic', prompting further outbreaks of violence in Nagornyi Karabakh and along the Armenian–Azerbaijani border, while growing unrest within Azerbaijan was exacerbated by the influx of refugees from Armenia.

In January 1990 radical members of the PFPA led assaults on CPA and government buildings in Baku. Border posts were attacked on the Soviet–Iranian border, and nationalist activists seized CPA buildings in Naxçıvan. Renewed violence against Armenians, with some 60 people killed in rioting in Baku, led to a hasty evacuation of the remaining non-Azeris from the city. On 19 January a state of emergency was declared in Azerbaijan, and Soviet troops were ordered into Baku, where the PFPA was in control. According to official reports, 131 people were killed, and some 700 wounded, during the Soviet intervention. The inability of the CPA to ensure stability led to the dismissal of Abdul Vezirov as First Secretary of the party; he was replaced by Ayaz Mutalibov.

Continuing unrest caused the scheduled elections to the republic's Supreme Soviet to be postponed until September–October 1990, and the continuing state of emergency severely disrupted campaigning by the opposition. When the new Supreme Soviet convened in February 1991, some 80% of its deputies were members of the CPA. The small group of opposition deputies united as the Democratic Bloc of Azerbaijan.

Unlike the other Caucasian republics (Armenia and Georgia), Azerbaijan declared a willingness to sign a new Union Treaty and participated in the all-Union referendum on the preservation of the USSR, which took place in March 1991. Official results of the referendum demonstrated qualified support for the preservation of the USSR, with 75.1% of the electorate participating, of whom 93.3% voted for a 'renewed federation'. In Naxçıvan, however, only 20% of voters supported the proposal.

In August 1991, following the attempted seizure of power in Moscow by the conservative communist 'State Committee for the State of Emergency', Mutalibov issued a statement that appeared to demonstrate support for the coup. Large demonstrations took place, demanding his resignation; the declaration of Azerbaijan's independence; the repeal of the state of emergency; and the postponement of the presidential election, scheduled for 8 September. The opposition was supported by Heydar Aliyev, now Chairman of the Supreme Soviet of Naxçıvan. Mutalibov responded by ending the state of emergency and resigning as First Secretary of the CPA; on 30 August the Azerbaijani Supreme Soviet voted to 'restore the independent status of Azerbaijan'. The election to the presidency proceeded, although it was boycotted by the opposition, with the result that Mutalibov was the only candidate. According to official results, he won 84% of the total votes cast. At a congress of the CPA, held later in September, it was agreed to dissolve the party.

Independence was formally declared on 18 October 1991. On 21 December Azerbaijan joined the Commonwealth of Independent States (CIS, see p. 215), signing the Almaty (Alma-Ata) Declaration. Following the dissolution of the USSR, hostilities intensified in Nagornyi Karabakh. In March 1992 Mutalibov resigned as President, owing to military reverses. He was replaced, on an interim basis, by Yagub Mamedov, the Chairman of the Milli Majlis, or National Assembly (which had replaced the Supreme Soviet following its suspension in late 1991), pending a presidential election in June. However, further military reverses, including the occupation of Azerbaijani territory between Nagornyi Karabakh and Armenia by ethnic Armenian forces, and the consequent expulsion from these areas of Azeris, prompted the Majlis to reinstate Mutalibov as President in May. His immediate declaration of a state of emergency and the cancellation of the forthcoming presidential election outraged the PFPA, which organized a large protest rally in Baku. The demonstrators occupied both the Majlis building and the presidential palace, and succeeded in deposing Mutalibov, who took refuge in Russia. In June the leader of the PFPA, Abulfaz Elchibey, was elected President of Azerbaijan in a popular vote, defeating four other candidates by a substantial margin.

The military defeats and continuing economic decline severely undermined the Government and led to divisions within the PFPA in early 1993. In June a rebel army, led by Col Surat Husseinov (the former Azerbaijani military commander in Nagornyi Karabakh), seized the city of Ganca and advanced towards Baku, with the apparent intention of deposing Elchibey. In an attempt to bolster his leadership, Elchibey summoned Heydar Aliyev to the capital, and in mid-June Aliyev was elected Chairman of the Milli Majlis. Following Elchibey's subsequent flight from the capital, Aliyev announced that he had assumed the powers of the presidency. In late June virtually all presidential powers were transferred, on an acting basis, to Aliyev by the Milli Majlis (which had voted to impeach Elchibey), and Husseinov was appointed Prime Minister, with control over the security services. A referendum of confidence in Elchibey (who had taken refuge in Naxçıvan and still laid claim to the presidency) was held in late August 1993; of the 92% of the electorate that participated, 97.5% voted against him. The Milli Majlis endorsed the result and announced a direct presidential election, which took place on 3 October. Aliyev was duly elected President, with 98.8% of the votes cast. The PFPA boycotted the election.

The domestic political situation remained tense during 1994. Opponents of President Aliyev and his New Azerbaijan Party (NAP) were subject to increasing harassment, and their media activities were severely restricted. The signature, in May, of a cease-fire agreement in Nagornyi Karabakh (see below) led to further unrest, and large anti-Government demonstrations were organized by the PFPA in Baku in May and September. In September the Deputy Chairman of the Milli Majlis and Aliyev's security chief were assassinated; three members of the OPON special militia attached to the Ministry of Internal Affairs were subsequently arrested. In early October 100 OPON troops, led by Rovshan Javadov, stormed the office of the Procurator-General, taking him and his officials hostage and securing the release of the three OPON members in custody. Aliyev described the incident as an attempted coup and declared a state of emergency in Baku and Ganca.

In the immediate aftermath of these events, other forces mutinied in Baku and elsewhere in Azerbaijan. In Ganca, rebel forces occupied government and strategic buildings, although troops loyal to Aliyev quickly re-established control. Husseinov was dismissed as Prime Minister, and replaced, on an acting basis, by Fuad Quliyev. However, Aliyev stated that he would head the Government for the immediate future, and initiated a series of dismissals of senior members of the Government and the armed forces. In mid-October 1994 the Milli Majlis voted unanimously to remove Husseinov's parliamentary immunity from prosecution (he was, however, believed to have fled to Russia).

Further political turmoil arose in March 1995, following a decree by the Government to disband OPON. In response, OPON forces seized government and police buildings in Baku and in north-western regions, and many casualties were reported, as government forces clashed with the OPON units. The rebellion was crushed when government troops stormed the OPON headquarters near Baku; Javadov and many of his men were killed, and some 160 rebels were arrested. Aliyev accused Elchibey and Husseinov of collusion in the attempted coup. Subsequently, the PFPA was also accused of involvement, and the party was banned. In April Aliyev extended the state of emergency in Baku until June, although that in Ganca was lifted. In May Quliyev was confirmed as Prime Minister.

Elections to the new, 125-member Milli Majlis took place on 12 November 1995. Of Azerbaijan's 31 officially registered parties, only eight were permitted to participate; of these, only two were opposition parties—the PFPA (recently relegalized) and the Azerbaijan National Independence Party (ANIP). Almost 600 nominally independent candidates were barred from participation. The elections were held under a mixed system of voting: 25 seats were to be filled by proportional representation on the basis of party lists and the remaining 100 by majority voting in single-member constituencies. These included the constituencies within Nagornyi Karabakh and the other territories occupied by ethnic Armenian forces (refugees from those regions voted in areas under Azerbaijani control). The results demonstrated widespread support for Aliyev's NAP, which won 19 of the 25 party-list seats (with the PFPA and the ANIP receiving three seats each). The NAP and independent candidates supporting Aliyev won most of the single-constituency seats. Of the remaining 28 seats in the Majlis, 27 were filled at subsequent 'run-off' elections, and one seat remained vacant. Some international observers declared that the elections had not been free and fair and that serious electoral violations had taken place. Concurrently with the election of the Milli Majlis, Azerbaijan's new Constitution was approved by 91.9% of the electorate in a national referendum. The Constitution provided for a secular state, headed by the President, who was accorded wide-ranging executive powers.

In early 1996 supporters of Husseinov and Elchibey received lengthy custodial sentences for their involvement in the alleged coup attempts of 1994 and 1995. In February 1996 two former government members were sentenced to death on charges of treason and several others were sentenced to death on conspiracy charges in the following months. Mutalibov, whom Aliyev had accused of conspiring with Javadov, was arrested in Russia in April, although the Russian authorities refused to extradite him, on the grounds of insufficient evidence. Repressive measures against the opposition continued. In July Fuad Quliyev resigned as Prime Minister, officially on grounds of ill health, after he was accused by Aliyev of hindering the process of reform; Artur Rasizade, hitherto first Deputy Prime Minister, was appointed in his stead, initially in an acting capacity. In September the Chairman of the Milli Majlis, Rasul Quliyev, resigned. Murtuz Aleskerov, a staunch supporter of Aliyev, was elected in his place. In January 1997 the authorities released details of an abortive coup in October 1996, which had reportedly been organized by, among others, Mutalibov and Husseinov. Charges were subsequently brought against some 40 alleged conspirators, and in early 1997 many people received prison sentences for their part in the attempted coups of October 1994 and March 1995. Husseinov was extradited from Russia in March 1997 and was sentenced to life imprisonment in February 1999. He received a presidential pardon in March 2004.

AZERBAIJAN

In January 1998 the Azerbaijani authorities accused Rasul Quliyev (who was now resident in the USA) of organizing a conspiracy to depose President Aliyev. In April Quliyev, who denied the accusations, was charged *in absentia* with alleged abuses of power while Chairman of the Milli Majlis. (Further charges were brought against him in October 2000.) A law regarding presidential elections was approved in June, which required candidates to collect 50,000 signatures to stand; the initially announced minimum level of voter participation of 50% was reduced to 25% in July. The opposition protested that the law favoured Aliyev's re-election, and launched a series of demonstrations to demand the cancellation of the election scheduled to be held in October. In September police and demonstrators clashed violently in Baku.

The presidential election was held, as planned, on 11 October 1998. According to official results, Aliyev was re-elected with 77.6% of the votes cast. Five other candidates contested the election, which was criticized by the Organization for Security and Co-operation in Europe (OSCE, see p. 354) and the Council of Europe (see p. 225) for failing to meet democratic standards. Unrest continued, owing to the opposition's dissatisfaction with the validity of the results. In late October the majority of government ministers, including the Prime Minister, were reconfirmed in their positions by President Aliyev. In December the Milli Majlis approved a revised Constitution for Naxçıvan, which defined the exclave as an 'autonomous state' within Azerbaijan. The amended Constitution had earlier been endorsed by the Naxçıvan legislature, the Ali Majlis (Supreme Assembly).

In April–June 1999 parliamentarians of the Democratic Congress, which comprised a total of 17 deputies, including those of the PFPA and the Civic Solidarity Party (CSP), boycotted the Milli Majlis, owing to conflict over draft legislation on municipal elections. Azerbaijan's first municipal elections since independence were held in December, thereby fulfilling a prerequisite for membership of the Council of Europe. However, widespread electoral violations were observed and repeat elections were subsequently held in those constituencies where the results had been deemed invalid.

In April 2000 a demonstration, attended by up to 20,000 people, was organized by the Democratic Congress, which demanded the introduction of measures to ensure that the legislative elections due to be held in November would be free and fair. Many arrests were made, and the security forces were accused of using excessive force. The death, in August, of Elchibey prompted the division of the PFPA into traditionalist and reformist factions; the Central Electoral Commission (CEC) recognized only the reformist wing, led by Ali Kerimli. In September the CEC refused to register eight opposition parties. Although the CEC's decision was revoked, following strong criticism from the US Administration, a number of political parties decided to boycott the legislative elections, which they condemned as undemocratic. The Democratic Congress was forced to restructure in October, when five parties, including the reformist branch of the PFPA, withdrew.

The legislative elections, held, as scheduled, on 5 November 2000, were condemned by the OSCE for the falsification of results and intimidatory practices, and country-wide protests followed. Of the 25 seats filled by proportional representation, 17 were obtained by the NAP and four by the PFPA, while the CPA and the CSP each secured two seats. Of the 99 seats contested in single-mandate constituencies, 62 were obtained by the NAP and 26 by independent candidates. The election results were invalidated in 11 constituencies; repeat elections were held on 7 January 2001. Divisions within the NAP became increasingly evident during 2001, with the emergence of a faction known as the '91st' group, the members of which were largely excluded from the party's political council, following a party congress held in November. Aliyev was re-elected as Chairman of the NAP and his son İlham (the Vice-Chairman of the State Oil Company of the Azerbaijan Republic—SOCAR) was elected to the newly created post of First Deputy Chairman.

On 24 August 2002 a referendum was held to seek approval for 39 proposed amendments to the Constitution, among the most notable of which were proposals for executive power to be transferred to the (presidentially appointed) Prime Minister, rather than the elected Chairman of the Milli Majlis, in the event of the President's inability to govern; and for the outcome of the presidential election to be determined by a straightforward majority of the votes cast, rather than the existing prerequisite of two-thirds. According to official figures, 96% of votes (cast by 84% of the electorate) were in favour of the constitutional amendments, although demonstrations followed, after reports by both opposition parties and observers from the OSCE and the USA of fraud and procedural violations. Protest rallies and demonstrations to demand the President's resignation continued into the first half of 2003.

In April 2003 President Aliyev collapsed while delivering a televised speech, and in subsequent months he reportedly travelled to Turkey and the USA for medical treatment. On 4 August an emergency session of the Milli Majlis approved İlham Aliyev's appointment as Prime Minister. Two days later Rasizade assumed the premiership, on an acting basis, to allow İlham Aliyev to campaign for the presidential election, scheduled to take place in October. In early October it was announced that Heydar Aliyev was formally to withdraw his candidacy, in favour of his son. Meanwhile, opposition demonstrations in September had resulted in violent clashes with the security forces.

The opposition failed to consolidate support in favour of one principal candidate, and İlham Aliyev secured 79.5% of the votes cast in the presidential election, held on 15 October 2003. The second-placed candidate, the Chairman of the Equality Party (Müsavat), İsa Qambar, obtained 12.1% of the votes cast, according to official results. However, both international observers and opposition parties reported widespread electoral malpractice. The opposition subsequently refused to recognize the validity of the election results and opposition protests, led by the Equality Party, were violently repressed by the authorities; there were reports of a number of deaths. İlham Aliyev was inaugurated as President at the end of October. The nomination of Rasizade as premier was approved by the Milli Majlis on 4 November, and the majority of ministers in the previous administration were subsequently reappointed. Heydar Aliyev's death was announced in mid-December. In the months following his election, İlham Aliyev implemented measures that were regarded as seeking to consolidate his position, including the announcement of new appointments to several senior government posts. In April 2004 Aliyev appointed a career diplomat, Elmar Mammedyarov, as Minister of Foreign Affairs, and in July dismissed Namik Abbasov as Minister of National Security, a position he had held for some 10 years. By January 2005 some 50 people had received custodial sentences for their involvement in the protests that followed İlham Aliyev's election as President.

Municipal elections were held on 17 December 2004, in which the NAP won 64.7% of seats and independent candidates received 31.1%. The elections failed to meet democratic norms, according to the OSCE. Three of the four largest opposition parties boycotted the elections in protest at pressure exerted by the authorities prior to the ballot, and the ANIP was the only major opposition party to participate; Etibar Mamedov resigned as party Chairman shortly after the elections.

Prior to the legislative elections scheduled for late 2005, a number of opposition parties established united blocs and many independent candidates formed alliances. However, the only groups to submit a sufficient number of candidates to be entitled to campaign by way of the broadcast media were the ruling NAP, the Azerbaijan Liberal Party, the Freedom bloc (Azadlıq—comprising the Equality Party, the PFPA and the Azerbaijan Democratic Party—ADP) and the New Policy bloc; the latter comprised the ANIP, the Azerbaijan Social Democratic Party, the For Azerbaijan public forum, the Intelligentsia Movement and various public figures and non-governmental organizations (NGOs). As a result of the constitutional changes approved in 2002, the legislative elections were the first in which candidates were campaigning for single-mandate seats, rather than on the basis of the mixed system of voting previously in place. Another development was the emergence of several youth groups, which modelled themselves on those that had helped to bring about political change in Serbia, Georgia and Ukraine; of these, New Thinking was the most prominent. The authorities, which initially responded by mobilizing young supporters of their own, in August 2005 detained the leader of New Thinking on conspiracy charges. None the less, several opposition leaders, detained on charges of inciting violence following the 2003 presidential election, were released from gaol, under amnesty, in March 2005, and public demonstrations in Baku, prohibited since October 2003, were once again authorized. Other measures were implemented in an attempt to improve the electoral environment, including: the accurate and transparent compilation of voter lists; the establishment of a public television channel; and the cessation of a ban on the sale of opposition newspapers on Baku's underground railway. In late October

2005 a ban on the monitoring of elections by NGOs that received more than one-third of their funding from abroad was lifted.

In mid-October 2005 Rasul Quliyev, the exiled leader of the ADP, was detained in Simferopol, Ukraine, after his aircraft was prevented from landing in Baku, where he had been intending to return in order to participate in the elections. Allegations emerged that a former Minister of Finance, Fikret Yusifov, had facilitated the transfer of large amounts of money from Quliyev to the prominent, reformist, Minister of Economic Development, Farhad Aliyev, in order to finance a coup attempt. In late October Farhad Aliyev and the Minister of Public Health, Ali Insanov, were dismissed from their government posts and arrested. Farhad Aliyev's brother, Rafiq Aliyev, the Chairman of the petroleum production and distribution company Azpetrol, was also reported to have been detained. Subsequently, there were reports that several other senior officials and prominent businessmen had been arrested. Heydar Babayev, the erstwhile head of the State Securities Commission and a long-term rival of Farhad Aliyev, succeeded him as Minister of Economic Development.

The legislative elections were held on 6 November 2005. Observers from the OSCE and the Council of Europe stated that, despite some improvement in electoral conduct, the polls failed to meet democratic standards. From 9 November opposition parties held large-scale demonstrations to protest against the conduct of the elections. However, in late November a fourth demonstration, organized by the Freedom bloc, was violently dispersed by the security forces, and further rallies were prohibited. Following the elections, Ilham Aliyev dismissed several regional governors for having failed to prevent electoral irregularities in a number of constituencies. On 1 December the Constitutional Court endorsed the results of the elections in 115 of the country's 125 constituencies, but annulled the results in the remainder (including two constituencies where opposition candidates, including Ali Kerimli of the PFPA, had achieved election). The NAP won 56 seats, non-party candidates obtained 43 seats and the Freedom bloc received six seats; a number of other parties also obtained representation. Repeat elections were held to those constituencies in which the initial results had been annulled on 13 May 2006; following these elections, the NAP held a total of 61 seats, and there were 46 independent deputies.

The newly elected Milli Majlis convened for the first time on 2 December 2005, and Oktai Asadov of the NAP replaced Aleskerov as legislative Chairman. Following the elections President Aliyev effected some long-anticipated personnel changes. These included the appointment in early December of Natiq Aliyev, hitherto the President of SOCAR, as Minister of Industry and Energy; the appointment in February 2006 of Col-Gen. Kamaladdin Heydarov, reputedly a powerful 'oligarch' (politically influential business executive) and rival of Farhad Aliyev, as Minister of Emergency Situations; and the dismissal in April of the Minister of Finance, Avaz Alekperov, who had held that office for nearly seven years. In addition, Abbas Abbasov, who had served as First Deputy Prime Minister for some 14 years, tendered his resignation in May. It was observed that many of the new appointees to power were derived from the energy industry. A new ministerial portfolio of Defence Industries was created, further accentuating the emphasis on the defence sector as a whole, the funding of which was increasing substantially during the mid-2000s.

Following the elections, the opposition again fragmented, largely owing to a lack of consensus over whether the small number of opposition candidates to have received seats should participate in the work of a Milli Majlis that opposition parties considered to be illegitimate. In November 2005 the ADP and the reformist wing of the PFPA announced their intention to boycott both the new legislature and the repeat elections scheduled to take place in 10 constituencies in May 2006. However, in February 2006 the Equality Party confirmed that it intended to participate in the work of the Milli Majlis and announced its withdrawal from the Freedom bloc; the party had won four of the six legislative seats hitherto controlled by the bloc. Meanwhile, in January the ANIP divided into two rival factions, one supporting the party's Chairman, Ali Aliyev, and the other supporting the founder of the party, honorary party leader and former Chairman, Etibar Mamedov, after Aliyev proposed withdrawing the ANIP from the New Policy bloc, and instead aligning it with the Freedom bloc.

Serious irregularities were again observed to have taken place during municipal elections held on 6 October 2006. Meanwhile, the repression of independent media intensified during 2006, the *Azadıq* (Freedom) newspaper and various associated organizations (the PFPA, Turan news agency and *Bizim Yol*—Our Way newspaper, the editor of which was abducted and severely beaten in May) were evicted from their shared address in November; one journalist was sentenced to gaol and, in December, another was attacked and stabbed. The broadcasting licence of the ANS television and radio station was revoked in November, while a subsequent round of tendering for broadcasting rights was postponed after ANS was the only candidate to have submitted an application. International organizations and officials appealed strongly to the Government for the protection of press freedom. In January 2007 the European Court of Human Rights ruled in favour of Sardar Jalaloğlu of the ADP, who stated that his treatment by the authorities following the presidential election of 2003 constituted torture. Also in January 2007 Jalaloğlu was instrumental in the decision of the ADP to alter its stance in relation to the Government to one of constructive opposition, thereby allowing for dialogue with the NAP. Several public rallies, organized by the Equality Party and the Freedom bloc, were staged during that month, in protest against the steep price increases imposed on fuel and utilities from the beginning of 2007 in line with IMF recommendations.

In November 2007 eight men suspected of having links to the transnational militant Islamist al-Qa'ida (Base) organization, led by the Saudi-born dissident Osama bin Laden, were apprehended by the authorities during a special security operation conducted in Sumqayıt. The arrests followed the detention in the previous month of a group of alleged militant Islamists whom the Government referred to as members of the austere Wahhabi sect, the distribution of literature promoting the beliefs of which had been banned in 2005.

Further repression of independent media was evident in 2007. In April Eynulla Fatullayev, Editor of the newspaper *Gündalik Azarbaycan* (Azerbaijan Daily) and the weekly publication *Realnyi Azarbaycan* (Real Azerbaijan), was sentenced to 30 months' imprisonment, having been convicted on charges of defaming the military in comments published on the internet that were attributed to Fatullayev, but which he strenuously denied having written. In July fresh charges of terrorism and inciting racial and ethnic hatred were brought against Fatullayev and in October he was convicted on these charges, together with a further charge of tax evasion, all of which, opponents of the Government suggested, had been fabricated merely to silence a dissenting voice; Fatullayev was sentenced to eight-and-a-half years' imprisonment. In December a journalist was sentenced to a three-month prison term for insulting a police officer.

In early 2008 revisions to the 1992 Law on Political Parties were reported to be in the process of being drafted; amendments to the legislation were expected to include new rules governing the financing of political organizations. Discussions were also ongoing into possible reform of the electoral code, although discussions, attended by representatives of the Council of Europe's Venice Commission, the Azerbaijani Government and representatives of Azerbaijani political organizations, were boycotted by the leading opposition parties—namely, the Equality Party and the Freedom bloc. Proposed amendments to the electoral code, however, were reported to focus on procedural technicalities, rather than promising substantive democratic reform in advance of the presidential election scheduled for 15 October.

Upon the USSR's disintegration in late 1991, the leadership of Nagornyi Karabakh declared the enclave to be an independent republic. Azerbaijan refused to accept the territory's attempts to secede, and in January 1992 Nagornyi Karabakh was placed under direct presidential rule. International efforts to negotiate a peace settlement foundered, owing to Azerbaijan's insistence that the conflict was a domestic problem. Military successes by the ethnic Armenian forces of Nagornyi Karabakh in early 1992 culminated in the creation, in May, of a 'corridor' through Azerbaijani territory around Laçin, linking Nagornyi Karabakh with Armenia. Despite a successful Azerbaijani counter-offensive in late 1992, ethnic Armenian forces were able to open a second corridor in early 1993, eventually obtaining control of the regions of Azerbaijan between Nagornyi Karabakh and Armenia. By August some 20% of Azerbaijan's territory had been seized by ethnic Armenian units, and large numbers of refugees fled the occupied territories. Although it did not directly accuse Armenia of aggression, the UN Security Council adopted a series of resolutions demanding an immediate cease-fire and the withdrawal of all occupying units from Azerbaijan. There were also strong protests by Turkey and Iran. In December Azerbaijani forces launched a new counter-offensive in Nagornyi Karabakh, recapturing some areas that had been lost to Armenian control, although suffering heavy casualties. Meanwhile, international efforts to halt the conflict continued, led by the 11-nation Minsk Group of the Conference on Security and Co-operation in Europe (CSCE—later OSCE). In early 1994 it was estimated that, since the conflict began in 1988, some 18,000 people had been killed and a further 25,000 had been wounded. The number of Azeri refugees was believed to have exceeded 1m.

In May 1994 Azerbaijan signed the so-called Bishkek Protocol, which had been adopted several days previously at a meeting of the CIS Inter-Parliamentary Assembly, with the approval of representatives of both Armenia and the self-styled 'Republic of Nagornyi Karabakh'. On 8 May the Nagornyi Karabakh leadership ordered its forces to cease hostilities, in accordance with the Protocol. Although isolated violations were subsequently reported, the cease-fire remained in force. In the latter half of the year efforts were made to co-ordinate the separate peace proposals of the CSCE Minsk Group and Russia. However, Azerbaijan refused either to negotiate a peace settlement or to discuss the future status of Nagornyi Karabakh until Armenian forces were withdrawn entirely from occupied Azerbaijani territory and Azeri refugees had returned to their homes. In May 1995 the exchange of prisoners of war and other hostages commenced. In April–June a new, 33-seat legislature was elected in Nagornyi Karabakh (replacing the 81-member Supreme Soviet). Robert Kocharian, hitherto Chairman of the State Defence Committee, was appointed to the new executive presidency. An election to the (internationally unrecognized) office of 'President' of Nagornyi Karabakh was held in November 1996, when Kocharian was elected with more than 85% of the votes cast. In December President Heydar Aliyev and his Armenian counterpart, Levon Ter-Petrossian, attended a summit meeting of the OSCE, in Lisbon, Portugal. Following demands by Azerbaijan, a statement was released by the OSCE Chairman, recommending three principles that would form the basis of a political settlement to the conflict: the territorial integrity of Armenia and Azerbaijan; legal status for Nagornyi Karabakh, which would be granted self-determination within Azerbaijan; and security guarantees for the population of Nagornyi Karabakh. However, Armenia refused to accept the terms of the statement.

The appointment of Kocharian as Prime Minister of Armenia in March 1997, and the consequent proposed presidential election in Nagornyi Karabakh, scheduled for September, were severely criticized by Aliyev. The election of Arkadii Ghukassian as 'President' of Nagornyi Karabakh in September threatened to hamper further progress on reaching a settlement, owing to his outright dismissal of the OSCE proposals; it was reported later in that month, however, that both Azerbaijan and Armenia had accepted a revised plan drawn up by the Minsk Group. In addition, in an apparently significant change in policy, Ter-Petrossian publicly admitted that Nagornyi Karabakh could expect neither to gain full independence, nor to be united with Armenia. Ter-Petrossian's cautious and moderate approach to the Nagornyi Karabakh crisis provoked much disapproval in Armenia and led to his resignation in February 1998; he was replaced by Kocharian. In November the Armenian Government announced that, despite some reservations, it officially accepted the latest proposals put forward by the Minsk Group, which were based on the principle of a 'common state' (comprising Azerbaijan and Nagornyi Karabakh). The Azerbaijani Government, however, rejected the proposals, claiming that they threatened the territorial integrity of Azerbaijan.

An escalation in hostilities in mid-1999 prompted mutual accusations by Azerbaijan and Armenia that the other was attempting to abrogate the 1994 cease-fire agreement. Presidents Kocharian and Aliyev met on several occasions in the latter half of 1999, but no substantive progress was made. Following an assassination attempt against Ghukassian in March 2000, the former 'Minister of Defence' of Nagornyi Karabakh, Samuel Babaian, was charged with organizing the attack, as part of a purported coup. (He was sentenced to 14 years' imprisonment in February 2001, but was released in September 2004.) Legislative elections were held in Nagornyi Karabakh on 18 June 2000. On 11 August 2002 Ghukassian was re-elected as 'President' of the territory, receiving 88.4% of the votes cast. Meanwhile, direct negotiations between the Armenian and Azerbaijani Presidents continued in 1999–2002, but little progress was made towards reaching a final solution to the dispute. No further talks took place in 2003, although negotiations resumed in 2004, under the administration of the new Azerbaijani President, İlham Aliyev.

In January 2005 the OSCE agreed to a request by Azerbaijan that it monitor settlements in the region, in which Azerbaijan claimed some 23,000 ethnic Armenians had been settled by the Armenian authorities, and report on its findings. On 25 January the Parliamentary Assembly of the Council of Europe adopted a resolution describing the occupation of Azerbaijani territory by ethnic Armenian forces as a 'grave violation' and stating that the conflict had led to 'ethnic expulsion and the creation of mono-ethnic areas that resemble the terrible concept of ethnic cleansing'. The resolution also urged Azerbaijani leaders to establish contacts with the leaders of the secessionist region (which they had hitherto refused to do) and refrain from the use of force. The resolution suggested, furthermore, that should the Minsk Group fail to resolve the situation, then a submission to the International Court of Justice should be considered. Legislative elections were held in Nagornyi Karabakh in June 2006, which were not recognized by Azerbaijan or the international community; the majority of votes were cast in favour of pro-Government parties. A referendum was held on 10 December, in which some 84% of eligible voters participated; a constitution defining the territory as an independent and sovereign state was approved by some 98.6% of the votes cast. Elections to the 'Presidency' of Nagornyi Karabakh were held on 19 July 2007, at which Bako Sahakian, a former head of the territory's security service, secured victory, attracting 85.4% of the votes cast. Negotiations to resolve the Nagornyi Karabakh conflict continued between the Armenian and Azerbaijani authorities throughout this time. In December 2007 the Armenian Prime Minister and Minister of Foreign Affairs both declared that the signing of a framework agreement with Azerbaijan could be achieved before the staging of presidential elections in Armenia, scheduled to take place on 18 February 2008, although this did not, in the event, ensue. Earlier in December 2007 Azerbaijan's Minister of Foreign Affairs, Mammedyarov, had attributed the failure to achieve a 'breakthrough' in negotiations to Armenia's alleged intractability; however, he also acknowledged that 'gradual progress' had been made during 2007. Speaking at a press conference a few days later, Mammedyarov stated that autonomy might be granted for Nagornyi Karabakh within Azerbaijan's territory, but stressed that Azerbaijan would not under any circumstance allow its territorial integrity to be compromised.

Although it signed the Almaty Declaration in December 1991, in October 1992 the Milli Majlis voted not to participate in the CIS. However, with the overthrow of the PFPA Government and the accession to power of Heydar Aliyev, the country's position regarding the CIS was reversed, and in September 1993 Azerbaijan was formally admitted to full membership of the body. None the less, Azerbaijan did not renew its membership of the CIS Collective Security Treaty in 1999, because of the continued occupation of Nagornyi Karabakh by ethnic Armenian troops, and in protest against Russia's continuing supply of armaments to Armenia. However, a visit to Azerbaijan by Russian President Vladimir Putin in January 2001, and the signature of a number of co-operation agreements, appeared to signal a new stage in relations between the two countries. President Heydar Aliyev undertook a reciprocal visit to Russia in January 2002, when a 10-year economic co-operation plan between the two countries was agreed. Furthermore, in September a bilateral agreement was signed on the delimitation of the Caspian Sea, according to which the seabed would be divided into national sectors, and the surface be used in common. A similar agreement had already been reached with Kazakhstan, and a trilateral agreement was signed in mid-May 2003. Although in November Azerbaijan expressed concern at new Russian-Armenian plans for defence co-operation, in February 2004 the newly elected President of Azerbaijan, İlham Aliyev, undertook an official visit to Russia, during which the so-called Moscow Declaration was signed, reaffirming bilateral agreements signed in 1997 and 2001; a further visit followed in early 2005. However, in December 2006 the Russian state-controlled natural gas monopoly Gazprom steeply increased the price of natural gas exports to Azerbaijan (contrary to the terms of an existing contract). Azerbaijan, therefore, ceased importing gas from Russia, rather than pay the increased costs, and also temporarily reduced its own petroleum exports to Russia, ostensibly to provide an alternative source of fuel to its own power stations. Relations were further undermined by the strong rapprochement between Russia and Armenia in 2006, and by Russia's decision to impose strict restrictions on migrant workers from April 2007, which was expected to affect many expatriate Azerbaijanis, whose remittances made a significant contribution to the national economy.

The strengthening of relations with Turkey, which had been cultivated by successive leaderships following independence in 1991, continued under the presidencies of both Heydar and İlham Aliyev. Throughout the conflict over Nagornyi Karabakh, Azerbaijan was supported by Turkey, which provided humanitarian and other aid and reinforced Armenia's international isolation by closing its borders with Armenia and prohibiting trade with that country. An intergovernmental agreement in support of the construction of a pipeline to connect the Azerbaijani petroleum fields near Baku with the Turkish port of Ceyhan, via Tbilisi, Georgia, was signed in October 1998 (see Economic Affairs). The BTC pipeline, as it was known, was inaugurated in May 2005 and became fully operational in the following year. From 2005 plans to complete a rail transport connection between Turkey, Georgia and Azerbaijan (Kars–Akhalkalaki–Tbilisi–Baku) were revived, despite criticism from the USA, which objected to the project's exclusion of Armenia. A ceremony to inaugurate construction of the railway was held in November 2007 and was attended by the Turkish, Georgian and Azerbaijani Presidents; the first tracks of the rail link were expected to be laid by April 2008. Also in November, the new Turkish President, Abdullah Gül, who had taken office in August, made an official visit to Azerbaijan, where he met with President Aliyev to discuss bilateral relations, economic ties and the Nagornyi Karabakh conflict.

In November 2006 a summit of leaders of Turkic-speaking nations (including Azerbaijan, Kazakhstan, Kyrgyzstan, Turkey and Turkmenistan, but not Uzbekistan) was held in Turkey, with strong support for the enhancement of economic and transport connections within the region. It was hoped that the strategic new energy supply routes through Azerbaijan could be extended to Central Asia, via the Caspian Sea (as well as by way of an eventual rail route). Azerbaijan also participated in the revival of the GUAM organization of states (Azerbaijan, Georgia, Moldova and Ukraine) in May 2006, which was renamed the Organization for Democracy and Economic Development—GUAM, to emphasise the Western orientation of its policy.

The large Azeri minority in neighbouring Iran (numbering an estimated 20m.) was regarded as a potential source of tension. Nevertheless, official relations between Iran and Azerbaijan remained amicable, and bilateral trade increased significantly in the 1990s. However, tensions arose over the status of the Caspian Sea, together with Azerbaijan's increasing involvement with international petroleum companies. In July 2001 an Iranian military patrol boat ordered Azerbaijani survey vessels leased by the company BP (of the United Kingdom) to leave a disputed area of the Sea. As a result, BP suspended its petroleum exploration operations in the southern Caspian, pending a resolution of the dispute. In May 2002 President Heydar Aliyev paid an official visit to Iran, signing a number of accords on bilateral co-operation, which were expected significantly to stimulate trade. A further agreement on economic co-operation was signed in October, which included plans for the construction of a pipeline to carry natural gas from Iran to Naxçıvan, and for improved transit links and customs procedures between the two countries. In November 2003, in Tehran, Iran, representatives of Azerbaijan, Iran, Kazakhstan, Russia and Turkmenistan signed a UN-sponsored framework Convention for the Protection of the Marine Environment of the Caspian Sea, which sought to alleviate environmental damage in the Caspian Sea region. In August 2004 President Sayed Muhammad Khatami of Iran visited Azerbaijan, signing 10 bilateral accords and making a commitment to further energy co-operation with Naxçıvan. President İlham Aliyev made a reciprocal visit to Iran in January 2005, where he signed further agreements and obtained permission for the establishment of an Azerbaijani consulate in the Iranian city of Tabriz, which had previously been denied by the Iranian authorities. In December Presidents Aliyev and Khatami attended a ceremony in Naxçıvan to inaugurate a new natural gas pipeline, and a memorandum of understanding on further co-operation in the energy sector was signed. International observers judged the improvement in relations between the two countries to be based on strategic diplomacy and the consolidation of allegiances by Iran, in response to increasingly belligerent statements against Iran made by senior members of the US Administration, particularly in response to the development of Iran's nuclear industry and its support for militant Islamist groups internationally. During a two-day visit to Baku in August 2007, Iranian President Mahmoud Ahmadinejad, who had assumed office in August 2005, held talks with President Aliyev, following which the Azerbaijani head of state spoke of a 'mutual understanding on all issues'. Five co-operation agreements, including one pertaining to energy matters, were signed during Ahmadinejad's first official visit to Azerbaijan.

US-Azerbaijani relations improved significantly in the mid-1990s, and in July 1997 President Heydar Aliyev visited the USA. A bilateral agreement on military co-operation was signed, and four contracts between SOCAR and US petroleum companies to develop offshore oilfields in the Caspian Sea were also concluded. New contracts for the development of the petroleum industry, worth US $10m., were signed during a visit to Washington, DC, USA, by Aliyev in April 1999, and a financial agreement on the construction of the BTC pipeline was signed in Washington in April 2000. In late 2001 the USA agreed to halt the provision of financial assistance to separatists in Nagornyi Karabakh and commit funds to Azerbaijan, through the temporary suspension of Amendment 907 to the Freedom Support Act of 1992 (establishing a foreign assistance programme to the countries of the former USSR), which prevented the donation of aid to Azerbaijan while that country's closure of the Armenian border remained in place. The waiver was renewed annually. In January 2004 a co-operation agreement was signed between Azerbaijan and the USA, which aimed to prevent the proliferation of weapons of mass destruction, and according to which the USA was to grant funds of $10m. to Azerbaijan for the strengthening of border security. In late 2005 Azerbaijan confirmed that two new, US-funded radar stations were under construction close to the Iranian and Russian borders, respectively. In October Azerbaijan and the USA co-hosted the second annual Black Sea and Caspian Sea Maritime Non-proliferation Conference, held in Baku. The USA was also active in funding security programmes, of particular benefit to the coastguard and naval troops (under its Caspian Guard Initiative), in order to strengthen protection for offshore oilfields and to help combat terrorism and smuggling. In April 2006 President İlham Aliyev made his first official visit to the USA. A proposal made by Russian President Vladimir Putin in June 2007 that elements of the planned US missile defence programme be located in Azerbaijan, instead of in the Czech Republic and Poland, as provided for by US plans that were strongly opposed by Russia, appeared unlikely to come to fruition.

In March 1992 Azerbaijan was admitted to the UN, and it subsequently became a member of the CSCE. In April 1996, together with Armenia and Georgia, Azerbaijan signed a co-operation agreement with the European Union—EU (see p. 244). Azerbaijan joined the North Atlantic Treaty Organization's (NATO) 'Partnership for Peace' (see p. 342) programme in May 1994, and was awarded observer status at the Alliance in June 1999. In January 2001 the country was inaugurated as a full member of the Council of Europe (as was Armenia). In June 2004 the EU included Azerbaijan in its new European Neighbourhood Policy, with the other two countries of the south Caucasus. In October 2006 Azerbaijan signed an action plan pertaining to its relations with the EU under this policy.

Government

Under the Constitution of November 1995, the President of the Azerbaijan Republic is Head of State and Commander-in-Chief of the armed forces. The President, who is directly elected for a five-year term of office, holds supreme executive authority in conjunction with the Cabinet of Ministers, which is appointed by the President and is headed by the Prime Minister. Supreme legislative power is vested in the 125-member Milli Majlis (National Assembly), which is directly elected for a five-year term. Azerbaijan is divided into 74 administrative districts (rayons) and the Naxçıvan Autonomous Republic, which forms an exclave to the west of metropolitan Azerbaijan, separated from the rest of the country by Armenian territory. By early 2008 central Government control did not extend to the former autonomous oblast (region) of Nagornyi Karabakh and seven rayons located between Nagornyi Karabakh and Armenia.

Defence

After obtaining independence in 1991, Azerbaijan began the formation of national armed forces. As assessed at November 2007, these numbered 66,740: an army of 56,840, a navy of 2,000 and an air force of 7,900. The Ministry of Internal Affairs controls a militia of some 10,000 and a border guard of an estimated 5,000. Military service lasts for 17 months (but may be extended for ground forces). As a member of the Commonwealth of Indepen-

AZERBAIJAN

dent States (CIS, see p. 215), Azerbaijan's naval forces operate under CIS (Russian) control. In May 1994 Azerbaijan became the 15th country to join NATO's 'Partnership for Peace' (see p. 342) programme of military co-operation. As in Armenia, military expenditure increased substantially during the mid-2000s. The 2007 budget allocated an estimated US $936m. to defence.

Economic Affairs

In 2006, according to World Bank estimates, Azerbaijan's gross national income (GNI), measured at average 2004–06 prices, was US $15,712m., equivalent to $1,850 per head (or $5,960 per head on an international purchasing-power parity basis). During 1996–2006, it was estimated, the population increased at an average rate of 0.9% per year, while gross domestic product (GDP) per head increased, in real terms, at an average annual rate of 12.4%. Overall GDP increased, in real terms, at an average annual rate of 13.4% in 1996–2006. Real GDP increased by 26.4% in 2005 and by 34.5% in 2006.

Agriculture (including fishing) contributed 7.6% of GDP in 2006, when some 39.1% of the working population were employed in the sector. The principal crops are grain, potatoes, tomatoes, barley, watermelons, sugar beet and apples. By mid-1999 some 80% of state-owned agriculture had passed into private ownership, and by the end of 2001 all collective farms had been privatized. During 1996–2006, according to World Bank estimates, agricultural GDP increased, in real terms, at an average annual rate of 5.9%. Agricultural GDP increased by 6.0% in 2006.

Industry (including mining, manufacturing, construction and power) contributed 69.6% of GDP in 2006. In that year, according to official sources, 12.7% of the working population were employed in the sector. According to the World Bank, during 1996–2006 industrial GDP increased, in real terms, by an annual average of 16.3%. Real sectoral GDP increased by 31.5% in 2006. Growth was driven principally by the mining sector.

Mining accounted for 55.2% of GDP in 2006, when the sector employed just 1.1% of the working population. Azerbaijan is richly endowed with mineral resources, the most important of which is petroleum. The country's known reserves of petroleum were estimated to total 1,000m. metric tons at the end of 2006, mainly located in offshore fields in the Caspian Sea, and production in 2005 was estimated at 32.5m. tons. In September 1994 the Azerbaijani Government and a consortium of international petroleum companies, the Azerbaijan International Operating Company (AIOC), concluded an agreement to develop the offshore oilfields. By 2000 SOCAR had signed more than 20 production-sharing agreements with international partners, largely for the exploration of new fields. Production of 'early' oil began in October 1997 and accounted for a 50% increase in overall petroleum extraction over the following two years. The petroleum was transported to the Russian Black Sea port of Novorossiisk, although technical problems with the pipeline and the conflict in Chechnya caused regular closures; a new section of the pipeline, avoiding Chechnya, was completed in March 2000. A further pipeline, transporting petroleum from Baku to the Georgian port of Supsa, opened in April 1999. In October 2000 the Government of Azerbaijan signed an agreement with SOCAR and a consortium of petroleum companies on the construction of a pipeline from Baku, via Tbilisi (Georgia), to Ceyhan in Turkey. Construction work on what became known as the BTC pipeline commenced in April 2003 and the Azerbaijani section was inaugurated in May 2005, with deliveries of petroleum through the pipeline commencing in mid-2006. Azerbaijan also has substantial reserves of natural gas, most of which are located offshore; however, owing to a lack of suitable infrastructure, Azerbaijan has been a net importer of gas. However, in 1999 a gas field was discovered at Şah Deniz in the Caspian Sea, with reserves estimated at 1,000,000m. cu m, and a gas pipeline was constructed to transport natural gas to Erzurum (Turkey), via Tbilisi, running parallel with the BTC pipeline. This new South Caucasus Pipeline commenced operations in late 2006, with an initial anticipated capacity of 6,000m. cu m per year. Other minerals extracted include gold, silver, iron ore, copper concentrates, alunite (alum-stone), iron pyrites, barytes, cobalt and molybdenum.

Manufacturing accounted for some 5.7% of GDP in 2006, when it employed 4.9% of the population. The GDP of the sector rose, in real terms, at an annual average rate of 3.3% in 1996–2005, according to the World Bank. Sectoral growth was 4.8% in 2005.

In 2004 only 28.4% of Azerbaijan's supply of primary energy was provided by petroleum and petroleum products, compared with 72.0% in 2000. However, natural gas accounted for 58.9% of production in 2004, compared with 19.8% in 2000. The remainder was provided by hydroelectric stations. In 2004 Azerbaijan participated in an agreement with Iran and Russia on the synchronization and parallel operation of their national power grids from March 2006, following the necessary construction work. From 2006 the Russian gas supplier Gazprom significantly increased the prices charged to several of the states of the former USSR, prompting Azerbaijan to reduce drastically its imports of Russian gas later in that year and to suspend SOCAR's petroleum exports via the Baku–Novorossiisk pipeline in early 2007, in order to fuel domestic thermal power stations. In November 2006 a memorandum on energy co-operation was signed between Azerbaijan and the EU. Mineral fuels accounted for 14.8% of merchandise imports in 2006.

In 2006 the services sector provided an estimated 22.9% of GDP and accounted for 48.3% of employment. During 1996–2006 the GDP of the services sector increased, in real terms, at an average annual rate of 9.4%. Growth of 11.2% was recorded in 2006, according to the World Bank.

In 2006 Azerbaijan recorded a visible trade surplus of US $7,745.3m., and there was a surplus of $3,707.6m. on the current account of the balance of payments. In that year the principal source of imports was Russia (22.4%). Other major sources of imports were the United Kingdom, Germany, Turkey and Turkmenistan. The main market for exports in 2006 was Italy (44.7%). Other important purchasers were Israel, Turkey, France, Russia, and Iran. The principal exports in 2006 were mineral products (accounting for 84.6% of the total). The principal imports were machinery and electrical equipment (29.4%), as well as vehicles and transportation equipment, mineral products, base metals and prepared foodstuffs.

Azerbaijan's budgetary surplus for 2006 was some 91.5m. manats (equivalent to some 0.5% of GDP). At the end of 2005 the country's total external debt was US $1,881m., of which $1,334m. was long-term public debt. The cost of debt-servicing in that year was equivalent to 2.6% of the value of exports of goods and services. According to the ADB, consumer price inflation increased by an average of 4.1% per year during 1995–2006. According to the International Labour Organization (ILO), the average annual rate of inflation was 9.5% in 2005 and 8.2% in 2006. Just 1.3% of the total labour force were registered as unemployed in 2006, although the actual rate of unemployment was thought to be considerably higher.

Azerbaijan is a member of the IMF and the World Bank. It has also joined the Islamic Development Bank (see p. 329), the European Bank for Reconstruction and Development (EBRD, see p. 239), the Economic Co-operation Organization (ECO, see p. 238), the Organization of the Black Sea Economic Co-operation (see p. 367) and the Asian Development Bank (ADB, see p. 182).

The dissolution of the USSR in 1991, the conflict in Nagornyi Karabakh and the disruption of trade routes through Armenia, Georgia and Chechnya (in Russia) caused significant economic problems in Azerbaijan. However, owing to its substantial mineral wealth, Azerbaijan's prospects for eventual economic prosperity were favourable. Agreements were concluded with international consortiums from the mid-1990s, and the development of export routes for the country's petroleum and natural gas reserves was expected greatly to improve the economic situation. In 1999 the State Oil Fund of Azerbaijan (SOFAZ) was established for the management of petroleum- and gas-related revenue. In 2004 Azerbaijan implemented a long-term strategy on the management of petroleum revenues, which was intended to stimulate growth and reduce poverty and underemployment in the non-petroleum sector, and passed legislation on structural reform of the banking sector. However, the privatization of the country's two largest banks remained to be completed in early 2007. Extremely rapid economic growth was recorded in 2005–06, owing to increased petroleum production (particularly from the offshore Azeri, Çıraǧ and deep water Güneşli oilfields, known collectively as ACG), natural gas production and the operational launch of the BTC pipeline, as well as increased international prices for petroleum, which led to a surplus on the current account of the balance of payments. State revenue increased significantly, in particular owing to the expiry of the preferential tax arrangements hitherto enjoyed by foreign petroleum companies involved in the development of the ACG oilfields. However, further structural reforms remained necessary to stimulate the non-petroleum sector and lead to increased investment in the long term. In early 2008 the Minister of Finance, Samir Sharifov, announced that GDP growth of 24.7% had been achieved in 2007, with growth in the non-oil sector at 11.0%. Growth was again driven by increased hydrocarbon revenues buoyed by elevated petroleum prices. According to SOCAR, oil exports in January–September 2007 amounted to 22.2m. metric tons, representing a 42.4% increase compared with the same period in 2006. In September 2007 year-on-year inflation of 16.5% was recorded, and inflation was expected to remain a cause for concern in the medium term.

Education

In the early 1990s the education system was reorganized, as part of overall economic and political reforms. Education is officially compulsory between the ages of six and 17 years. Primary education begins at six years of age and lasts for four years. Secondary education, beginning at the age of 10, comprises a first cycle of five years and a second cycle of two years. According to UNESCO estimates, there were 75,950 children enrolled at pre-primary institutions in 2004/05. In the same year total enrolment at the primary level included 84.5% of the school-age population, while the comparable ratio at the secondary level was 77.6%. Almost all secondary schools use Azerbaijani as the medium of instruction, although some 6% use Russian. There are 27 state-supported institutions of higher education and 15 private universities; courses of study for full-time students last between four and five years. Higher education institutes include Baku State University, which specializes in the sciences, and the State Petroleum Academy, which trains engineers for the petroleum industry. In 2006/07 some 129,141 students were enrolled in institutes of higher education. The state budget for 2006 allocated 479.0m. manats to education, representing 12.6% of total state expenditure in that year.

Public Holidays

2008: 1 January (New Year), 8 March (International Women's Day), 22 March (Novruz Bayramy, Spring Holiday), 9 May (Victory Day), 28 May (Republic Day), 15 June (Gayidish—Day of Liberation of the Azerbaijani People), 26 June (Day of the Foundation of the Army), 1 October* (Ramazan Bayramy, end of Ramadan), 18 October (Day of Statehood), 12 November (Constitution Day), 17 November (Day of National Revival), 8 December* (Kurban Bayramy, Feast of the Sacrifice), 31 December (Day of Azerbaijani Solidarity World-wide).

2009: 1 January (New Year), 8 March (International Women's Day), 20–21 March (Novruz Bayramy, Spring Holiday), 9 May (Victory Day), 28 May (Republic Day), 15 June (Gayidish—Day of Liberation of the Azerbaijani People), 26 June (Day of the Foundation of the Army), 20 September* (Ramazan Bayramy, end of Ramadan), 18 October (Day of Statehood), 12 November (Constitution Day), 17 November (Day of National Revival), 27 November* (Kurban Bayramy, Feast of the Sacrifice), 31 December (Day of Azerbaijani Solidarity World-wide).

* These holidays are dependent on the Islamic lunar calendar and may vary by one or two days from the dates given.

Weights and Measures

The metric system is in force.

Statistical Survey

Source (unless otherwise stated): State Statistical Committee of the Azerbaijan Republic, 1136 Baku, İnşaatçılar pr.; tel. (12) 438-64-98; fax (12) 438-24-42; e-mail sc@azstat.org; internet www.azstat.org.

Area and Population

AREA, POPULATION AND DENSITY

Area (sq km)	86,600*
Population (census results)†	
12 January 1989	7,021,178
27 January 1999	
Males	3,883,155
Females	4,070,283
Total	7,953,438
Population (official estimates at 1 January)	
2005	8,347,300
2006	8,436,400
2007	8,532,700
Density (per sq km) at 1 January 2007	98.5

* 33,400 sq miles.
† Figures refer to *de jure* population. The *de facto* total at the 1989 census was 7,037,867.

ETHNIC GROUPS
(permanent inhabitants, 1999 census)

	Number ('000)	%
Azeri	7,205.5	90.6
Lazs (Lezghi)	178.0	2.2
Russian	141.7	1.8
Armenian	120.7	1.5
Talish	76.8	1.0
Others	230.7	2.9
Total	**7,953.4**	**100.0**

AUTONOMOUS REPUBLIC
(estimated population at 1 January 2007)

	Area (sq km)	Population	Population density (per sq km)
Naxçıvan	5,500	379,500	69.0

PRINCIPAL TOWNS
(estimated population at 1 January 2007)

Bakı (Baku, the capital)	1,893,300	Naxçıvan	70,400
Ganca *	307,500	Yevlakh	54,700
Sumqayıt	268,800	Xankandi (Stepanakert)	53,000
Mingaçevir	95,500	Lankaran	48,500
Ali-Bayramlı	69,600	Ağdam	39,500

* Known as Kirovabad between 1935 and 1989.

BIRTHS, MARRIAGES AND DEATHS

	Registered live births		Registered marriages		Registered deaths	
	Number	Rate (per 1,000)	Number	Rate (per 1,000)	Number	Rate (per 1,000)
1999	117,539	14.9	37,382	4.8	46,295	5.9
2000	116,994	14.8	39,611	5.0	46,701	5.9
2001	110,356	13.8	41,861	5.2	45,284	5.7
2002	110,715	13.8	41,661	5.2	46,522	5.8
2003	113,467	14.0	56,091	6.9	49,001	6.0
2004	131,609	16.1	62,177	7.6	49,568	6.1
2005	141,901	17.2	71,643	8.7	51,962	6.3
2006	148,946	17.8	79,443	9.5	52,248	6.2

Expectation of life (years at birth, WHO estimates): 65.4 (males 63.7; females 67.2) in 2005 (Source: WHO, *World Health Statistics*).

AZERBAIJAN

ECONOMICALLY ACTIVE POPULATION
(ISIC major divisions, annual average, '000 persons)

	2004	2005	2006
Agriculture, hunting and forestry	1,502.7	1,510.0	1,548.0
Fishing	3.3	3.8	4.3
Mining and quarrying	41.9	42.2	45.0
Manufacturing	181.2	188.7	195.0
Electricity, gas and water supply	39.8	39.7	40.2
Construction	190.6	194.4	222.8
Wholesale and retail trade; repair of motor vehicles, motorcycles and household goods	630.7	638.8	650.4
Hotels and restaurants	12.4	14.2	22.0
Transport, storage and communications	190.5	191.5	201.8
Financial intermediation	13.1	13.2	13.4
Real estate, renting and business activities	100.0	100.6	106.7
Public administration and defence; compulsory social security	269.7	270.5	271.2
Education	330.8	335.3	339.4
Health and social work	174.6	177.2	180.5
Other community, social and personal service activities	127.3	129.5	131.7
Extra-territorial organizations and bodies	0.5	0.6	0.6
Total employed	3,809.1	3,850.2	3,973.0*
Unemployed	55.9	56.3	53.9
Total labour force	3,865.0	3,906.5	4,026.9

* Of which number males accounted for 2,054.1, and females 1,918.9.

Health and Welfare

KEY INDICATORS

Total fertility rate (children per woman, 2005)	1.8
Under-five mortality rate (per 1,000 live births, 2005)	89
HIV (% of persons aged 15–49, 2005)	0.10
Physicians (per 1,000 head, 2003)	3.55
Hospital beds (per 1,000 head, 2005)	8.2
Health expenditure (2004): US $ per head (PPP)	138.3
Health expenditure (2004): % of GDP	3.6
Health expenditure (2004): public (% of total)	25.0
Access to water (% of persons, 2004)	77
Access to sanitation (% of persons, 2004)	54
Human Development Index (2005): ranking	98
Human Development Index (2005): value	0.746

For sources and definitions, see explanatory note on p. vi.

Agriculture

PRINCIPAL CROPS
('000 metric tons)

	2004	2005	2006
Wheat	1,573.0	1,527.0	1,460.3
Rice (paddy)	10.2	8.3	5.1
Barley	349.9	368.9	399.7
Maize	152.9	151.4	145.9
Potatoes	930.4	1,083.1	999.3
Sugar beet	56.8	36.6	167.2
Hazelnuts	5.5	28.0	24.6
Cottonseed	83.4	120.7	80.0
Cabbages and other brassicas	92.4	96.9	100.2
Tomatoes	425.0	437.7	442.0
Cucumbers and gherkins	151.1	159.8	171.3
Dry onions	163.4	177.4	184.2
Garlic	19.9	21.1	23.9

—continued	2004	2005	2006
Watermelons*	355.3	363.8	362.1
Oranges	19.2	19.3	19.5
Apples	137.3	163.1	178.4
Pears	27.2	41.5	31.9
Apricots	6.8	16.2	18.7
Peaches and nectarines	6.7	16.0	16.8
Plums	14.7	21.5	18.9
Grapes	54.9	79.7	94.1
Tobacco (leaves)	6.5	7.1	4.8
Cotton (lint)	52.1	75.9	50.0

* Including melons, pumpkins and squash.

Aggregate production ('000 metric tons, may include official, semi-official or estimated data): Total cereals 2,086.6 in 2004, 2,056.2 in 2005, 2,011.6 in 2006; Total nuts 13.9 in 2004, 45.5 in 2005, 40.6 in 2006; Total pulses 26.9 in 2004, 29.3 in 2005, 28.9 in 2006; Total roots and tubers 930.4 in 2004, 1,083.1 in 2005, 999.3 in 2006; Total vegetables (incl. melons) 1,400.1 in 2004, 1,456.9 in 2005, 1,584.2 in 2006; Total fruits (excl. melons) 478.2 in 2004, 704.3 in 2005, 753.4 in 2006.

Source: FAO.

LIVESTOCK
('000 head, year ending September)

	2004	2005	2006
Horses	71	69	70
Asses, mules or hinnies	45	46	46
Cattle	2,007	2,077	2,148
Buffaloes	309	303	299
Pigs	23	23	21
Sheep	6,887	7,105	7,304
Goats	601	593	578
Chickens	16,928*	17,553*	18,276†
Turkeys	617*	700*	760

* Unofficial figure.
† FAO estimate.

Source: FAO.

LIVESTOCK PRODUCTS
('000 metric tons)

	2004	2005	2006
Cattle meat	69.1	71.5	75.6
Sheep meat	40.7	41.9	43.6
Pig meat	1.6	1.6	1.6
Chicken meat	32.3	34.7	35.0
Cows' milk	1,188.6	1,226.1	1,272.7
Hen eggs	46.4	49.0	45.7
Wool: greasy	12.3	13.1	13.6

Source: FAO.

Forestry

ROUNDWOOD REMOVALS
('000 cubic metres, excl. bark)*

	1998	1999	2000
Sawlogs, veneer logs and logs for sleepers	3,200	3,200	3,500
Pulpwood	3,200	3,200	3,500
Other industrial wood	—	—	100
Fuel wood	6,200	6,200	6,400
Total	12,600	12,600	13,500

* Unofficial figure(s).

2001–06: Production as in 2000 (FAO estimates).

Source: FAO.

AZERBAIJAN

Fishing

(metric tons, live weight)

	2003	2004	2005*
Capture	6,694	9,281	9,001
Azov sea sprat	6,145	8,899	8,630
Aquaculture	243	15	15
Total catch	6,937	9,296	9,016

* FAO estimates.

Source: FAO.

Mining

	2004	2005	2006
Crude petroleum ('000 metric tons)	15,548	22,214	32,268
Natural gas (million cu metres)	4,948	5,732	6,763

Source: Asian Development Bank, *Key Indicators of Developing Asian and Pacific Countries*.

Industry

SELECTED PRODUCTS
('000 metric tons, unless otherwise indicated)

	2000	2001	2002
Wheat flour	234	370	251
Wine ('000 hectolitres)	77	76	73
Beer ('000 hectolitres)	71	116	125
Mineral water ('000 hectolitres)	21	30	56
Soft drinks ('000 hectolitres)	478	442	564
Cigarettes	2,362	6,808	6,296
Cotton yarn—pure and mixed (metric tons)	700	2,000	1,300
Woven cotton fabrics ('000 metres)	1,000	3,000	3,000
Footwear, excluding rubber ('000 pairs)	122	220	339
Cement	251	523	848
Sulphuric acid	52	10	19
Caustic soda (Sodium hydroxide)	30	27	25
Bricks (million)	10	12	24
Electric energy (million kWh)	18,699	18,969	19,543
Jet fuels	580	543	507
Motor spirit (petrol)	357	598	610
Kerosene	175	81	143
Gas-diesel (distillate fuel) oil	1,957	1,562	1,593
Lubricants	229	34	21
Residual fuel oil (Mazout)	4,072	2,648	2,569

Source: mostly UN, *Industrial Commodity Statistics Yearbook*.

2004 ('000 metric tons, unless otherwise indicated): Cement 1,427.5; Motor spirit (petrol) 852.4; Kerosene 646.8; Gas-diesel (distillate fuel) oil 1,789.1; Residual fuel oil (Mazout) 2,520.8; Finished cotton fabrics ('000 sq m) 4,038; Electric energy ('000 million kWh) 21.7.

2005 ('000 metric tons, unless otherwise indicated): Cement 1,537.9; Motor spirit (petrol) 906.2; Kerosene 747.1; Gas-diesel (distillate fuel) oil 2,101.13; Residual fuel oil (Mazout) 3,060.7; Finished cotton fabrics ('000 sq m) 3,099.0; Electric energy ('000 million kWh) 22.9.

2006 ('000 metric tons, unless otherwise indicated): Cement 1,604.5; Motor spirit (petrol) 1,042.3; Kerosene 737.2; Gas-diesel (distillate fuel) oil 2,095.1; Residual fuel oil (Mazout) 2,825.4; Finished cotton fabrics ('000 sq m) 3,083.0; Electric energy ('000 million kWh) 24.0.

Finance

CURRENCY AND EXCHANGE RATES

Monetary Units
100 gopik = 1 new Azerbaijani manat.

Sterling, Dollar and Euro Equivalents (31 December 2007)
£1 sterling = 1.693 new manats;
US $1 = 0.845 new manats;
€1 = 1.244 new manats;
10 new manats = £5.91 = $11.83 = €8.04.

Average Exchange Rate (Azerbaijani manats per US $)
2005   0.9454
2006   0.8934
2007   0.8581

Note: The Azerbaijani manat was introduced in August 1992, initially to circulate alongside the Russian (formerly Soviet) rouble, with an exchange rate of 1 manat = 10 roubles. In December 1993 Azerbaijan left the rouble zone, and the manat became the country's sole currency. The manat was redenominated from 1 January 2006, with 1 new unit of currency (new manat) equivalent to 5,000 of the old currency. Figures in this survey are given in terms of the new manat, where possible.

STATE BUDGET
('000 million manats)

Revenue	2004	2005	2006
Tax revenue	1,232.2	1,767.0	3,153.8
Value-added tax	452.7	599.9	737.8
Excises	72.4	141.0	187.4
Taxes on profits	223.4	355.4	994.5
Tax on rents	97.8	53.5	100.2
Taxes on income	221.6	317.4	378.5
Taxes on international trade and transactions	101.5	205.2	241.2
Taxes on land	14.1	15.3	18.5
Other	48.7	79.2	495.7
Non-tax revenue	277.3	288.2	727.2
Total	1,509.5	2,055.2	3,881.2

Expenditure	2004	2005	2006
Finance of national economy	290.9	444.7	1,246.9
Finance of social and cultural activities	642.3	843.3	1,049.5
Education	294.1	372.5	479.0
Culture, mass media and sport	38.2	50.6	67.1
Health	73.5	115.3	161.9
Social security and welfare funds	236.5	305.0	341.5
Law-enforcement bodies	155.9	206.4	278.5
Expenses of state administration bodies	89.3	123.9	142.9
Other purposes	323.8	522.4	1,071.9
Total	1,502.1	2,140.7	3,789.7

INTERNATIONAL RESERVES
(US $ million at 31 December)

	2004	2005	2006
IMF special drawing rights	14.53	13.91	15.43
Reserve position in IMF	0.02	0.01	0.02
Foreign exchange	1,060.53	1,163.82	2,484.93
Total	1,075.08	1,177.74	2,500.38

Source: IMF, *International Financial Statistics*.

MONEY SUPPLY
(million new manats at 31 December)

	2004	2005	2006
Currency outside banks	477.79	547.44	1,311.35
Demand deposits at commercial banks	175.10	202.80	527.84
Total money (incl. others)	652.90	750.24	1,839.57

Source: IMF, *International Financial Statistics*.

AZERBAIJAN

COST OF LIVING
(Consumer Price Index; base: 2000 = 100)

	2004	2005	2006
Food (incl. tobacco)	120.9	134.1	150.2
Fuel	109.6	243.4	212.3
Clothing	110.0	108.5	122.9
All items (incl. others)	113.9	124.7	134.9

Source: ILO.

NATIONAL ACCOUNTS
(million new manats at current prices)

Expenditure on the Gross Domestic Product

	2004	2005	2006
Government final consumption expenditure	1,100.4	1,305.1	1,427.5
Private final consumption expenditure	4,760.9	5,274.6	6,315.9
Increase in stocks	23.9	28.3	29.7
Gross fixed capital formation	4,922.8	5,172.9	5,567.8
Total domestic expenditure	10,808.0	11,780.9	13,340.9
Exports of goods and services	4,161.8	7,881.8	12,467.0
Less Imports of goods and services	6,203.0	6,624.5	7,265.7
Statistical discrepancy	−236.6	−515.7	−806.4
GDP in purchasers' values	8,530.2	12,522.5	17,735.8

Source: IMF, *International Financial Statistics*.

Gross Domestic Product by Economic Activity

	2004	2005	2006
Agriculture and fishing	937.3	1,145.5	1,252.5
Mining	2,476.5	5,283.9	9,157.8
Manufacturing	706.6	812.4	943.2
Electricity, gas and water	85.5	93.8	102.3
Construction	1,062.1	1,171.6	1,334.7
Trade	655.6	832.0	1,038.7
Transport and communications	812.4	932.1	1,323.1
Finance	116.0	173.3	191.8
Public administration	332.6	377.6	415.5
Other	729.9	753.6	826.2
GDP at factor cost	7,914.5	11,576.0	16,585.7
Indirect taxes *less* subsidies	615.7	946.5	1,150.1
GDP in purchasers' values	8,530.2	12,522.5	17,735.8

Source: Asian Development Bank, *Key Indicators of Developing Asian and Pacific Countries*.

BALANCE OF PAYMENTS
(US $ million)

	2004	2005	2006
Exports of goods f.o.b.	3,743.0	7,649.0	13,014.6
Imports of goods f.o.b.	−3,581.7	−4,349.9	−5,269.3
Trade balance	161.3	3,299.1	7,745.3
Exports of services	492.0	683.0	939.9
Imports of services	−2,730.4	−2,653.0	−2,863.2
Balance on goods and services	−2,077.1	1,329.1	5,821.9
Other income received	65.3	201.8	280.0
Other income paid	−765.9	−1,847.4	−2,960.6
Balance on goods, services and income	−2,777.7	−316.6	3,141.3
Current transfers received	262.6	626.2	748.2
Current transfers paid	−74.1	−142.3	−182.0
Current balance	−2,589.2	167.3	3,707.6
Capital account (net)	−4.1	40.9	−3.8
Direct investment abroad	−1,204.8	−1,220.8	−705.5
Direct investment from abroad	3,556.1	1,679.9	−584.0
Portfolio investment assets	−18.1	−47.8	−34.4
Portfolio investment liabilities	—	78.3	22.3
Other investment assets	−360.4	−1,365.3	−1,416.7
Other investment liabilities	987.4	953.7	612.9
Net errors and omissions	−49.9	−125.7	−255.9
Overall balance	317.0	160.5	1,342.6

Source: IMF, *International Financial Statistics*.

External Trade

PRINCIPAL COMMODITIES
(US $ million)

Imports c.i.f.	2004	2005	2006
Vegetable products	232.0	171.9	201.7
Prepared foodstuffs, beverages, spirits and vinegar; tobacco and manufactured substitutes	113.8	194.5	273.2
Mineral products	507.1	641.0	779.8
Products of chemical or allied industries	132.9	183.8	249.2
Base metals and articles thereof	611.2	489.3	615.6
Machinery and mechanical appliances; electrical equipment; sound and television apparatus	1,084.6	1,402.9	1,547.3
Vehicles, aircraft, vessels and associated transportation equipment	242.0	420.9	877.8
Miscellaneous manufactured articles	151.5	163.6	86.7*
Total (incl. others)	3,515.9	4,211.2	5,267.6

Exports f.o.b.	2004	2005	2006
Vegetable products	n.a.	193.6	156.3
Mineral products	2,973.8	3,338.6	5,392.7
Products of the chemical industry	n.a.	131.8	193.0
Vehicles, aircraft, vessels and associated transportation equipment	144.0	272.3	84.8*
Total (incl. others)	3,615.5	4,347.2	6,372.2

*Excluding railway or tramway rolling stock, ships and air-transport facilities.

PRINCIPAL TRADING PARTNERS
(US $ million)

Imports c.i.f.	2004	2005	2006
China, People's Repub.	145.5	173.8	222.5
France	120.1	121.8	55.8
Georgia	14.5	45.5	49.2
Germany	198.5	256.3	403.8
India	47.0	55.9	57.4
Iran	45.3	76.3	85.9
Italy	106.7	94.6	124.6
Japan	127.1	70.6	188.2
Kazakhstan	236.7	95.3	127.3
Netherlands	152.7	160.4	90.9
Russia	569.4	717.2	1,181.6
Singapore	8.9	384.9	6.2
Sweden	66.6	72.4	84.4
Turkey	225.0	313.0	385.0
Turkmenistan	114.4	242.9	369.0
Ukraine	170.4	226.3	317.5
United Kingdom	421.8	385.0	453.8
USA	131.9	151.3	197.9
Uzbekistan	79.7	99.8	27.5
Total (incl. others)	3,515.9	4,211.2	5,267.6

AZERBAIJAN

Exports f.o.b.	2004	2005	2006
Bulgaria	49.3	100.9	6.3
China, People's Repub.	31.7	99.2	6.4
Croatia	109.2	176.9	3.6
France	66.9	406.7	347.5
Georgia	188.9	208.4	285.3
Germany	37.6	34.8	9.0
Greece	20.2	95.7	182.0
Iran	153.5	166.5	295.9
Israel	323.7	195.1	684.8
Italy	1,614.9	1,315.7	2,845.4
Romania	82.3	119.1	80.1
Russia	209.8	285.4	344.3
Singapore	2.8	123.1	34.0
Spain	5.6	76.0	52.8
Tajikistan	46.5	78.9	130.9
Turkmenistan	143.4	273.6	9.5
Turkey	182.6	276.0	388.1
USA	26.0	43.2	91.9
Total (incl. others)	3,615.5	4,347.2	6,372.2

Transport

RAILWAYS

	2004	2005	2006
Passengers carried ('000)	5,241	5,492	5,816
Passenger-km (million)	789	878	959
Freight carried (million metric tons)	20.7	26.2	29.7
Freight ton-km (million)	7,536	9,628	10,910

ROAD TRAFFIC
(vehicles in use at 31 December)

	2004	2005	2006
Passenger cars	438,964	479,447	548,979
Buses	20,991	26,735	27,474
Lorries and vans	80,918	90,852	97,395
Motorcycles and mopeds	4,993	3,562	3,408

SHIPPING
Merchant Fleet
(registered at 31 December)

	2004	2005	2006
Number of vessels	292	295	300
Total displacement ('000 grt)	663.8	672.8	692.9

Source: Lloyd's Register-Fairplay, *World Fleet Statistics*.

International Sea-borne Freight Traffic
('000 metric tons)

	1997	1998	1999
Goods loaded	7,128	7,812	7,176

Source: UN, *Monthly Bulletin of Statistics*.

Sea-borne imports ('000 metric tons): 5,118 in 2000; 7,029 in 2001; 7,853.4 in 2002.

Sea-borne exports ('000 metric tons): 703 in 2000; 996.3 in 2001; 1,057.3 in 2002.

Statistical Survey

CIVIL AVIATION
(traffic on scheduled services)

	2004	2005	2006
Passengers carried ('000)	1,094	1,211	1,336
Passenger-km (million)	1,450	1,588	1,686
Total ton-km (million)	315	310	290

Tourism

FOREIGN TOURIST ARRIVALS

Country of residence	2005	2006
CIS countries*	809,172	776,670
Iran	210,616	167,815
Turkey	17,841	1,7360
Total (incl. others)	1,261,686	1,258,578

* Comprising Armenia, Belarus, Georgia, Kazakhstan, Kyrgyzstan, Moldova, Russia, Tajikistan, Turkmenistan, Ukraine and Uzbekistan.

Tourism receipts (incl. passenger transport, US $ million): 70 in 2003; 79 in 2004; 100 in 2005 (Source: World Tourism Organization).

Communications Media

	2004	2005	2006
Telephones ('000 main lines in use)	1,013.4	1,094.2	1,188.7
Mobile cellular telephones ('000 subscribers)	1,456.5	2,242.0	3,323.5
Personal computers ('000 in use)	149	195	n.a.
Internet users ('000)	408	679	829
Broadband subscribers	900	2,200	2,200

1999: Daily newspapers (number) 15; Daily newspapers (circulation) 80,000; Non-daily newspapers (number) 329; Non-daily newspapers (circulation) 122,000.

2000: Television receivers ('000 in use) 2,000; Book production (titles, incl. pamphlets) 400.

2005: Facsimile machines (number of units) 5,237; Newspapers and magazines sent by post 17.3m.

Sources: UN, *Statistical Yearbook*, UNESCO, *Statistical Yearbook*, and International Telecommunication Union.

Education

(2006/07, unless otherwise indicated)

	Institutions	Teachers	Students
Pre-primary*	1,758	10,947	109,925
General (primary and secondary)	4,538	177,738	1,537,273
Specialized secondary education institutions	60	7,049	56,872
Higher	42	14,358	129,141

* Figures for state institutions only, 2004/05.

Adult literacy rate (UNESCO estimates): 98.8% (males 99.5%; females 98.2%) in 1999 (Source: UNESCO Institute for Statistics).

Directory

The Constitution

A new Constitution was endorsed by 91.9% of the registered electorate in a national referendum, held on 12 November 1995. The following is a summary of the Constitution's main provisions, including amendments to the status of Naxçıvan approved by the Milli Majlis (National Assembly) in December 1998.

GENERAL PROVISIONS

The Azerbaijan Republic is a democratic, secular and unitary state. State power is vested in the people, who implement their sovereign right through referendums and their directly elected representatives. No individual or organization has the right to usurp the power of the people. State power is exercised on the principle of the division of powers between the legislature, the executive and the judiciary. The supreme aim of the state is to ensure human and civil rights and freedoms. The territory of the Azerbaijan Republic is inviolable and indivisible. Azerbaijan conducts its foreign policy on the basis of universally accepted international law. The state is committed to a market economic system and to freedom of entrepreneurial activity. Three types of ownership—state, private and municipal—are recognized; natural resources belong to the Azerbaijan Republic. The state promotes the development of art, culture, education, medical care and science, and defends historical, material and spiritual values. All religions are equal by law; the spread of religions that contradict the principles of humanity is prohibited. The state language is Azerbaijani, although the republic guarantees the free use of other languages. The capital is Baku (Bakı).

MAJOR RIGHTS, FREEDOMS AND RESPONSIBILITIES

Every citizen has inviolable, undeniable and inalienable rights and freedoms. Every person is equal before the law and the courts, regardless of sex, race, nationality, religion, origin, property and other status, and political or other convictions. Every person has the right to life. Any person charged with a penal offence is considered innocent until proven guilty. Every person has the right to freedom of thought, speech, conscience and religion. Everyone has the right to protect their national and ethnic affiliation. No one is to be subject to torture or the degradation of human dignity. The mass media are free, and censorship is prohibited. Every person has the right to freedom of movement and residence within the republic, and the right to leave the republic. The right to assemble publicly is guaranteed, and every person has the right to establish a political party, trade union or other organization; the activity of unions that seek to overthrow state power is prohibited. Citizens of the Azerbaijan Republic have the right to participate in the political life of society and the state, and the right to elect and to be elected to government bodies, and to participate in referendums. Every person has the right to health protection and medical aid, and the right to social security in old age, sickness, disability, unemployment, etc. The state guarantees the right to free secondary education.

THE LEGISLATURE

The supreme legislative body is the 125-member Milli Majlis. Deputies are elected by universal, equal, free, direct suffrage, and by secret ballot, for a five-year term. Any citizen who has reached the age of 25 years is eligible for election, with the exception of those possessing dual citizenship, those performing state service, and those otherwise engaged in paid work, unless employed in the creative, scientific and education sectors. The instigation of criminal proceedings against a deputy, and his or her detention or arrest, are only permitted on the decision of the Milli Majlis, on the basis of a recommendation by the Prosecutor-General. The Milli Majlis passes legislation, constitutional laws and resolutions; ratifies or denunciates treaties, agreements and conventions; ratifies the state budget; gives consent to declare war, on the recommendation of the President of the Republic; confirms administrative and territorial divisions; and declares amnesties. Upon the nomination of the President, the Milli Majlis is authorized to approve the appointment of the Prime Minister and the Prosecutor-General; appoint and dismiss members of the Constitutional Court and Supreme Court; and appoint and dismiss the Chairperson of the National Bank. It also has the power to express a vote of 'no confidence' in the Government; to call a referendum; to initiate impeachment proceedings against the President, on the recommendation of the Constitutional Court; and to introduce draft legislation and other issues for parliamentary discussion.

EXECUTIVE POWER

The President, who is directly elected for a term of five years, is Head of State and Commander-in-Chief of the Armed Forces. Executive power is held by the President, who acts as guarantor of the independence and territorial integrity of the republic. Any university graduate aged 35 years or over, who has the right to vote, has been a resident of the republic for the preceding 10 years, has never been tried for a major crime, and who is exclusively a citizen of the Azerbaijan Republic, is eligible for election to the office of President. The President appoints and dismisses the Cabinet of Ministers, headed by the Prime Minister, which is the highest executive body.

The President calls legislative elections; concludes international treaties and agreements, and submits them to the Milli Majlis for ratification; signs laws or returns draft legislation to the Milli Majlis for reconsideration; proposes candidates for the Constitutional Court, the Supreme Court and the Economic Court, and nominates the Prosecutor-General and the Chairman of the National Bank; appoints and recalls diplomatic representatives of Azerbaijan to foreign countries and international organizations, and receives the credentials of diplomatic representatives; may declare a state of emergency or martial law; and grants titles of honour.

The President enjoys immunity from prosecution during his or her period in office. In the event that the President commits a grave crime, he may be removed from office on the recommendation of the Supreme Court and the Constitutional Court, and with the approval of the Milli Majlis.

THE JUDICIARY

Judicial power is implemented only by the courts. Judges are independent and are subordinate only to the Constitution and the law; they are immune from prosecution. Trials are held in public, except in specialized circumstances.

The Constitutional Court is composed of nine members, appointed by the Milli Majlis on the recommendation of the President. It determines, among other things, whether presidential decrees, resolutions of the Milli Majlis and of the Cabinet of Ministers, laws of the Naxçıvan Autonomous Republic, and international treaties correspond to the Constitution; and decides on the prohibition of the activities of political parties. The Supreme Court is the highest judicial body in administrative, civil and criminal cases; the Economic Court is the highest legal body in considering economic disputes.

THE NAXÇIVAN AUTONOMOUS REPUBLIC

The Naxçıvan Autonomous Republic forms an autonomous state that is an inalienable part of the Azerbaijan Republic. It has its own Constitution, which must not contravene the Constitution and laws of Azerbaijan. Legislative power in Naxçıvan is vested in the 45-member Ali Majlis (Supreme Assembly), which serves a five-year term, and executive power is vested in the Cabinet of Ministers. The Ali Majlis elects a Chairman from among its members, as the highest official in the Naxçıvan Autonomous Republic. The Ali Majlis is responsible for the budget, the approval of economic and social programmes; and the approval of the Cabinet of Ministers. The Ali Majlis may dismiss its Chairman and express 'no confidence' in the Cabinet of Ministers. Justice is administered by the courts of the Naxçıvan Autonomous Republic.

LOCAL SELF-GOVERNMENT

Local government in rural areas and towns, villages and settlements is exercised by elected municipalities.

RIGHTS AND LAW

The Constitution has supreme legal force. Amendments and additions may only be introduced following a referendum.

The Government

HEAD OF STATE

President: İLHAM HEYDAR OĞLU ALIYEV (inaugurated 31 October 2003).

CABINET OF MINISTERS
(March 2008)

Prime Minister: ARTUR TAHIR OĞLU RASIZADE.
First Deputy Prime Minister: YAGUB ABDULLA OĞLU AYYUBOV.
Deputy Prime Ministers: ELCHIN ILYAS OĞLU EFENDIYEV, ABID QOCA OĞLU SHARIFOV, ALI SAMIL OĞLU HASANOV.
Minister of Public Health: OGTAY SHIRALIYEV.
Minister of Foreign Affairs: ELMAR MAHARRAM OĞLU MAMMEDYAROV.
Minister of Agriculture and Produce: ISMET ABBASOV.

Minister of Internal Affairs: Col RAMIL IDRIS OĞLU USUBOV.
Minister of Culture and Tourism: ABULFAZ MURSAL OĞLU KARAYEV.
Minister of Education: MISIR CUMAYIL OĞLU MARDANOV.
Minister of Communications and Information Technology: ALI MAMMAD OĞLU ABBASOV.
Minister of Finance: SAMIR RAUF OĞLU SHARIFOV.
Minister of Justice: FIKRET FARRUKH OĞLU MAMMADOV.
Minister of Labour and Social Protection: FIZULI ALEKPEROV.
Minister of National Security: Lt-Gen. ELDAR AKHMED OĞLU MAKHMUDOV.
Minister of Defence: Col-Gen. SAFAR AKHUNDBALA OĞLU ABIYEV.
Minister of Defence Industries: YAVAR CAMALOV.
Minister of Emergency Situations: Col-Gen. KAMALADDIN HEYDAROV.
Minister of Industry and Energy: NATIQ ALIYEV.
Minister of Taxation: FAZIL MAMEDOV.
Minister of Youth and Sport: AZAD RAHIMOV.
Minister of Economic Development: HEYDAR AYDIN OĞLU BABAYEV.
Minister of Ecology and Natural Resources: HUSSEIN SEYID OĞLU BAGHIROV.
Minister of Transport: ZIYA ARZUMAN OĞLU MAMMEDOV.

MINISTRIES

Office of the President: 1066 Baku, İstiklal küç. 19; tel. (12) 492-17-26; fax (12) 492-35-43; e-mail office@apparat.gov.az; internet www.president.az.
Office of the Prime Minister: 1066 Baku, Lermontov küç. 68; tel. (12) 492-66-23; fax (12) 492-91-79; e-mail nk@cabmin.gov.az; internet www.cabmin.gov.az.
Ministry of Agriculture and Produce: 1016 Baku, Azadlıq meydani 1; tel. (12) 493-53-55.
Ministry of Communications and Information Technology: 1000 Baku, Azarbaycan pr. 33; tel. (12) 493-00-04; fax (12) 498-79-12; e-mail mincom@mincom.gov.az; internet www.mincom.gov.az.
Ministry of Culture and Tourism: 1000 Baku, Azadlıq meydani 1, House of Government, 3rd Floor; tel. (12) 493-43-98; fax (12) 493-56-05; e-mail mugam@culture.gov.az.
Ministry of Defence: 1139 Baku, Azarbaycan pr.; tel. (12) 439-41-89; fax (12) 492-92-50.
Ministry of Defence Industries: Baku.
Ministry of Ecology and Natural Resources: 1073 Baku, Bahram Agayev küç. 100A; tel. (12) 492-59-07; fax (12) 439-84-32; internet eco.gov.az.
Ministry of Economic Development: 1001 Baku, Niyazi küç. 23; tel. (12) 490-24-30; fax (12) 490-24-08; e-mail office@economy.gov.az; internet economy.gov.az.
Ministry of Education: 1008 Baku, Xatai pr. 49; tel. (12) 496-06-47; fax (12) 496-34-83; e-mail office@min.edu.az; internet edu.gov.az.
Ministry of Emergency Situations: Baku.
Ministry of Finance: 1022 Baku, Samed Vurghun küç. 83; tel. (12) 493-30-12; fax (12) 498-79-69; e-mail office@maliyye.gov.az; internet maliyye.gov.az.
Ministry of Foreign Affairs: 1009 Baku, S. Qurbanov küç. 4; tel. (12) 492-96-92; fax (12) 498-84-80; e-mail secretariat@mfa.gov.az; internet www.mfa.gov.az.
Ministry of Industry and Energy: 1012 Baku, Hasanbek Zardabi küç. 88; tel. (12) 447-05-84; fax (12) 431-90-05.
Ministry of Internal Affairs: 1005 Baku, Gusi Hajiyev küç. 7; tel. (12) 492-57-54; fax (12) 498-22-85; internet mia.gov.az.
Ministry of Justice: 1000 Baku, İnşaatçılar pr. 1; tel. (12) 430-01-16; fax (12) 430-09-81; e-mail contact@justice.gov.az; internet www.justice.gov.az.
Ministry of Labour and Social Protection: 1009 Baku, S. Asgarov küç. 85; tel. (12) 596-50-23; fax (12) 596-50-22; e-mail mlspp@mlspp.gov.az; internet www.mlspp.gov.az.
Ministry of National Security: 1602 Baku, Parlament pr. 2; tel. (12) 493-76-22; fax (12) 495-04-91; e-mail cpr@mns.gov.az; internet mns.gov.az.
Ministry of Public Health: 1014 Baku, Kicik Deniz küç. 4; tel. (12) 493-29-77; fax (12) 493-07-11; e-mail moh@alexd.baku.az.az; internet sehiyye.gov.az.
Ministry of Taxation: 1073 Baku, Landau küç. 16; tel. (12) 497-06-11; fax (12) 498-54-07; e-mail info@taxes.gov.az; internet www.taxes.gov.az.
Ministry of Transport: 1010 Baku, Uzeyir Hajibeyov küç. 72/4; tel. (12) 430-99-41; e-mail office@mintrans.az; internet mot.gov.az.
Ministry of Youth and Sport: 1072 Baku, Olimpiya küç. 4; tel. (12) 465-64-42; fax (12) 465-64-38; e-mail mys@mys.gov.az; internet mys.gov.az.

President

Presidential Election, 15 October 2003

Candidates	Votes	% of votes
İlham Aliyev (New Azerbaijan Party)	2,438,787	79.53
İsa Qambar (Equality Party)	372,385	12.14
Lala Şövket Hacıyeva (Independent)	100,558	3.28
Etibar Mamedov (Azerbaijan National Independence Party)	82,401	2.69
Others	72,270	2.36
Total	**3,066,401**	**100.00**

Legislature

Milli Majlis
(National Assembly)
1152 Baku, Parlament pr. 1; tel. (12) 439-97-50; fax (12) 493-49-43; e-mail azmm@meclis.gov.az; internet www.meclis.gov.az.
Chairman: OKTAI ASADOV.
General Election, 6 November 2005*

Parties and blocs	Seats
New Azerbaijan Party	61
Independents	46
Freedom bloc†	6
Civic Solidarity Party	3
Fatherland Party	2
Others	7
Total	**125**

* Including the results of repeat elections, held in 10 districts on 13 May 2006, in which the original results had been annulled, following confirmation of irregularities.
† Electoral bloc comprising the Azerbaijan Democratic Party, the Azerbaijan Popular Front Party and the Equality Party.

Election Commission

Central Electoral Commission: 1000 Baku, Rasul Rza küç. 3; tel. (12) 493-60-08; fax (12) 493-43-40; e-mail office@cec.gov.az; internet www.cec.gov.az; f. 1998; Chair. MAZAHIR PANAHOV.

Political Organizations

Azerbaijan Communist Party (CPA) (Azarbaycan Kommunist Partiyası—AKP): 1000 Baku, A. Agayev küç. 1; tel. (12) 494-89-37; disbanded Sept. 1991, re-established Nov. 1993; Chair. RAMIZ AHMADOV.
Azerbaijan Democratic Party (Azarbaycan Demokrat Partiyası): 1000 Baku, Sabayel Rayon, Acad. A. Alizade küç. 13; tel. (12) 496-07-22; fax (12) 496-18-61; e-mail adp2005@mail.ru; f. 1994; formed part of the Freedom bloc at legislative elections in 2005; Chair. RASUL BAYRAM OĞLU QULIYEV.
Azerbaijan Democratic Reforms Party (Azarbaycan Demokratik İslahatlar Siyasi Partiyası): 1010 Baku, Neftchilar pr. 65/5; tel. (12) 437-15-76; fax (12) 492-61-10; e-mail demreforms@party.az; internet www.demreforms.org; f. 2005; Chair. ASIM MOLLAZADE.
Azerbaijan Hope Party (Azarbaycan Ümid Partiyasi): 1000 Baku, Qanub küç. 19/29; tel. (12) 496-65-48; f. 2001; Chair. IQBAL AGAZADE.
Azerbaijan Islamic Party (Azarbaycan İslam Partiyası—AİP): 1000 Baku; tel. (12) 491-86-45; fax (12) 491-83-88; e-mail AIP@azer.net; f. 1992; officially proscribed since 1995; forms part of the Union of Pro-Azerbaijanist Forces; Chair. MOVSUM SAMADOV.
Azerbaijan National Democratic Party (Azarbaycan Milli Demokrat Partiyası): 1000 Baku; tel. (12) 494-89-37; f. 1993; nationalist; fmrly associated with the prohibited Grey Wolves (Boz Gurd) militia; Leader İSKANDAR MEJID OĞLU HAMIDOV.

AZERBAIJAN

Azerbaijan National Independence Party (ANIP) (Azarbaycan Milli İstiqlal Partiyası—AMIP): 1000 Baku, Nasimi rayon, Mirqasımov küç. 4; tel. (12) 441-53-09; e-mail nipa@azeri.com; f. 1992; centre-right, supports liberalization of the economy and strengthening of democratic institutions; opposed to administration of İlham Aliyev; formed part of the New Policy bloc in 2005; the party split into two rival factions in Jan. 2006: one (radical) headed by ALİ ALIYEV, which joined the reconfigured Freedom bloc in 2006; and the other in support of ETIBAR MAMEDOV, headed by AYAZ RUSTAMOV, which was formally registered with the authorities.

Azerbaijan Popular Party (Azarbaycan Xalq Partiyası): Baku; f. 1998; Chair. PANAH HUSSEINOV.

Azerbaijan Social Democratic Party (Azarbaycan Sosial Demokrat Partiyası—ASDP): 1014 Baku, 28 May küç. 3/11; tel. (12) 493-33-78; fax (12) 498-79-03; e-mail asdp@bakililar.az; f. 1989; formed part of the New Policy (Yeni Siyaset) bloc for the legislative elections of 2005; Co-Chair. ARAZ ALIZADEH, AYAZ MUTALIBOV; 5,672 mems (2002).

Civic Unity Party (Vatandaş Birliyi Partiyası): Baku, M. Sanani küç. 30; tel. (12) 495-39-47; f. 2000; Chair. SABIR HAJIYEV.

Classical Popular Front of Azerbaijan (CPFA): Baku; f. 2006; traditionalist faction of the Popular Front of Azerbaijan (q.v.); Chair. MIRMAHMUD MIRALI OĞLU FATAYEV.

Equality Party (Müsavat) (Müsavat Partiyası): 1025 Baku, Darnagül qasabası 30/97; tel. (12) 448-23-82; fax (12) 448-23-84; e-mail info@musavat.org; internet www.musavat.org; f. 1992 as revival of party founded in 1911 and in exile from 1920; withdrew from the Freedom bloc (formed in advance of legislative elections in 2005) in Feb. 2006; Chair. İSA QAMBAR; Gen. Sec. VURGUN EYYUB.

Fatherland Party (Ana Vatan Partiyası—AVP): 1000 Baku, Aziz Aliyev küç. 3; tel. (12) 493-82-92; f. 1992; supports administration of İlham Aliyev; represents interests of Naxçıvan Autonomous Republic in Azerbaijan; Leader FAZAIL AGAMALIYEV.

Great Creation Party (Böyük Quruluş Partiyası): Baku; e-mail info@bqp-az.info; internet www.bqp-az.info; f. 2003; nationalist; Leader FAZIL QAZANFAROĞLU.

Justice Party (Adalat) (Adalat Partiyası): 1000 Baku, Nasimi rayon, Ceyhun Hacıbayli küç. 2; tel. (12) 440-85-23; e-mail adalat@azinternet.com; f. 2001; mem. of the Democratic Azerbaijan alliance; Leader İLYAS İSMAYILOV; 21,000 mems.

New Azerbaijan Party (NAP) (Yeni Azarbaycan Partiyası—YAP): 1000 Baku, Bül-Bül pr. 13; tel. (12) 493-42-76; fax (12) 498-03-22; e-mail yap@bakinter.net; internet www.yap.org.az; f. 1992; Chair. İLHAM ALIYEV.

Popular Front Party of Azerbaijan (PFPA) (Azarbaycan Xalq Cabhasi Partiyası—AXCP): 1152 Baku, Milli Majlis, Mehti Hussein küç. 2; tel. (12) 498-07-94; e-mail axcp@axcp.org; f. 1989; formed part of the Freedom bloc formed prior to 2005 legislative elections; Chair. ALİ KERIMLI.

United Azerbaijan Popular Front Party (Bütöv Azarbaycan Xalq Cabhasi Partiyası) (BAXCP): 1000 Baku, 12-ci Aşırım küç. 70A; tel. (12) 492-96-23; fax (12) 461-29-42; e-mail qudrat@hasanquliyev.com; f. 2003 by fmr mems of reformist wing of Azerbaijan Popular Front Party; Leader QÜDRAT HASANQULIYEV.

Diplomatic Representation

EMBASSIES IN AZERBAIJAN

Belgium: 1073 Baku, Suleyman Dadaşov 19; tel. (12) 437-37-70; Ambassador FRANK GEERKENS.

Bulgaria: 1069 Baku-34, Oktai Kerimov küç. 34; tel. (12) 441-43-81; fax (12) 440-81-82; e-mail balkan@bg.embassy.in-baku.com; internet www.mfa.bg/baku; Ambassador IVAN K. PALCHEVA.

China, People's Republic: 1000 Baku, Khagani küç. 67; tel. (12) 493-65-87; fax (12) 498-00-10; e-mail chinaemb@azeurotel.com; Ambassador ZHANG HAIZHOU.

Egypt: 1000 Baku, Hasan Aliyev küç. 7; tel. (12) 498-79-06; fax (12) 498-79-54; e-mail emb.egypt@azeuro.net; Ambassador YOUSSEF AHMED IBRAHEM ASH-SHARKAWY.

France: 1000 Baku, Rasul Rza küç. 7, POB 36; tel. (12) 490-81-00; fax (12) 490-81-01; e-mail ambafranbakou@azerin.com; internet www.ambafrance.az; Chargé d'affaires a.i. JEAN-YVES BERTHAULT.

Georgia: 1073 Baku, Yasamal rayon, section 523, S. Dadashev küç. 29; tel. (12) 497-45-60; fax (12) 497-45-61; e-mail embgeo@azeurotel.com; internet www.az.mfa.gov.ge; Ambassador NIKOLOZ NATBILADZE.

Germany: 1005 Baku, Nizami küç. 340, ISR Plaza; tel. (12) 465-41-00; fax (12) 498-54-19; e-mail zreg@bakudiplo.org; internet www.baku.diplo.de; Ambassador Dr PEER STANCHINA.

Greece: 1004 Baku, Icheri Şeher, Kichik Gala küç. 86/88; tel. (12) 492-46-80; fax (12) 492-48-35; e-mail greekemb@azeurotel.com; Ambassador DIMIDIS TEMISTOKLES.

India: 1069 Baku, Sabayel rayon, Oktay Karimov küç. 31/39; tel. (12) 447-41-86; fax (12) 447-25-72; e-mail eibaku@adanet.az; Ambassador B. R. MUTHU KUMAR.

Iran: 1000 Baku, B. Sadarov küç. 4; tel. (12) 492-64-53; fax (12) 498-07-33; e-mail iranemb@azerin.com; Ambassador NASIR HAMIDI ZARE.

Iraq: 1000 Baku, Khagani küç. 9; tel. (12) 498-14-47; fax (12) 498-14-37; e-mail iraqyia@azeri.com; Ambassador ARSHAD OMAR ISMAYIL.

Israel: 1065 Baku, Izmir küç. 1033, Hyatt Tower III, 7th Floor; tel. (12) 490-78-81; fax (12) 490-78-92; e-mail info@baku.mfa.gov.il; internet baku.mfa.gov.il; Ambassador ARTHUR LENK.

Italy: 1004 Baku, Icheri Şeher, Kichik Gala küç. 44; tel. (12) 497-51-33; fax (12) 497-52-02; e-mail ambasciata.baku@esteri.it; internet www.ambbaku.esteri.it; Ambassador GIAN-LUIGI MASCIA.

Japan: 1065 Baku, Izmir küç. 1033, Hyatt Tower III, 6th Floor; tel. (12) 490-78-18; fax (12) 490-78-20; e-mail japan@emb.baku.az; Ambassador TADAKHIRU ABE.

Kazakhstan: 1000 Baku, Inglab küç. 90; tel. (12) 465-62-48; fax (12) 465-62-49; e-mail embassyk@azdata.net; Ambassador (vacant).

Korea, Republic: 1000 Baku; internet aze.mofat.go.kr.

Latvia: 1065 Baku, J. Jabbarli küç. 44; tel. (12) 436-67-78; fax (12) 436-67-79; e-mail embassy.azerbaijan@mfa.gov.lv; Ambassador MIHAILS POPKOVS.

Libya: 1000 Baku, H. Javid pr. 520, apt 20; tel. (12) 493-23-65; fax (12) 498-12-47; e-mail libyabak@azerin.com; Chargé d'affaires a.i. MUHAMMAD AL-GILEDI JABIR.

Lithuania: 1000 Baku, Istiglaliyat küç. 15; tel. (12) 498-71-91; fax (12) 493-03-48; e-mail amb.az@urm.lt; Ambassador KĘSTUTIS KUDZMANAS.

Moldova: 1073 Baku, H. Javid pr. 520, Block 12; tel. (12) 510-15-38; fax (12) 403-52-91; e-mail baku@mfa.md; Ambassador ION ROBU.

Norway: 1000 Baku, Nizami küç. 340, ISR Plaza, 11th floor; tel. (12) 497-43-25; fax (12) 497-37-98; e-mail emb.baku@mfa.no; internet www.norway.az; Ambassador JON RAMBERG.

Pakistan: 1000 Baku, Atatürk pr. 30; tel. (12) 436-08-39; fax (12) 436-08-41; e-mail parepbaku@artel.net.az; Ambassador ABDUL HAMID.

Poland: 1000 Baku, Icheri Şeher, Kichik Gala küç. 2; tel. (12) 492-01-14; fax (12) 492-02-14; e-mail embpol@azeurotel.com; internet www.baku.polemb.net; Ambassador KRYSZTOF KRAJEWSKI.

Qatar: 1000 Baku, pr. Aliyev; tel. (12) 496-78-00; fax (12) 496-78-01.

Romania: 1000 Baku, Hasan Aliyev küç. 125A; tel. (12) 465-63-78; fax (12) 456-60-76; e-mail rom_amb_baku@azdata.net; Ambassador NICOLAE URECHE.

Russia: 1022 Baku, Bakixanov küç. 17; tel. (12) 498-60-16; fax (12) 498-14-16; e-mail embrus@azdata.net; internet www.embrus-az.com; Ambassador VASILII N. ISTRATOV.

Saudi Arabia: 1073 Baku, S. Dadashov küç. 44/2; tel. (12) 497-23-05; fax (12) 497-23-02; e-mail najdiahbaku@azereurotel.com; Ambassador ALI HASAN JAFAR.

Switzerland: 1000 Baku, Rasul Rza küç. 11/28–30; tel. (12) 598-53-14; fax (12) 498-15-43; e-mail baku.vertretung@eda.admin.ch; internet www.eda.admin.ch/baku; Ambassador ALAIN GUIDETTI.

Turkey: 1000 Baku, Khagani küç. 27; tel. (12) 444-73-20; fax (12) 444-73-55; e-mail bakube@artel.net.az; Ambassador HUSEYIN AVNI KARSLI.

Turkmenistan: Baku; tel. (12) 440-99-00; fax (12) 61-39-69.

Ukraine: 1069 Baku, Y. Vezirov küç. 49; tel. (12) 449-40-95; fax (12) 449-40-96; e-mail emb_az@mfa.gov.ua; internet www.mfa.gov.ua/azerbaijan; Ambassador STEPAN V. VOLKOVETSKIY.

United Kingdom: 1010 Baku, Khagani küç. 45; tel. (12) 497-51-88; fax (12) 492-27-39; e-mail generalenquiries.baku@fco.gov.uk; internet www.britishembassy.az; Ambassador Dr CAROLYN BROWNE.

USA: 1007 Baku, Azadlıq pr. 83; tel. (12) 498-03-36; fax (12) 465-66-71; internet azerbaijan.usembassy.gov; Ambassador ANNE E. DERSE.

Uzbekistan: 1021 Baku, Patamdart, 1-chi Şosesi, 9-chi tor 437; tel. (12) 497-25-49; fax (12) 497-25-48; e-mail embuzb@azeronline.com; Ambassador ISMATILLA R. ERGASHEV.

Judicial System

The judicial system in Azerbaijan is implemented by the following courts: regional (municipal) courts; the Court on Grave Crimes; the Military Court on Grave Crimes; local economical courts; the Economic Court on Disputes arising from International Agreements; the Supreme Court of Naxçıvan Autonomous Republic; the Court of Appeal; the Economic Court; the Supreme Court.

Supreme Court
(Azarbaycan Respublikasi Ali Mahkamasi)

1601 Baku, Z. Xalilov küç. 540; tel. (12) 493-18-37; fax (12) 493-11-68; e-mail sudaba_hasanova@supremecourt.gov.az; internet www.supremecourt.gov.az.

The highest judicial body in civil, criminal, administrative and other cases, referring to the activity of the general courts; judges are nominated by the President of the Republic and confirmed in office by the Milli Majlis.

President: SÜDABA CAMŞID QIZI HASANOVA.

Office of the Prosecutor-General (Baş Prokurorluğu): 1001 Baku, Nigar Rafibayli küç. 7; tel. (12) 492-30-32; fax (12) 493-03-35; e-mail info@genprosecutor.gov.az; internet www.genprosecutor.gov.az; Prosecutor-General ZAKIR BEKIR OĞLU QARALOV.

Constitutional Court
(Azarbaycan Republikasi Konstitusiya Mahkamasi)

1005 Baku, Genjler meydani 1; tel. (12) 492-88-41; fax (12) 492-97-66; e-mail inter.dept@constitutional-court-az.org; internet www.constitutional-court-az.org.

f. 1998; comprises a Chairman and eight judges, who are nominated by the President and confirmed in office by the Milli Majlis for a term of office of 15 years. Only the President, the Milli Majlis, the Cabinet of Ministers, the Procurator-General, the Supreme Court and the legislature of the Naxçıvan Autonomous Republic are permitted to submit cases to the Constitutional Court.

Chairman: FARHAD SAHIB OĞLU ABDULLAYEV.

Religion

ISLAM

The majority (some 70%) of Azerbaijanis are Shi'ite Muslims; most of the remainder are Sunni (Hanafi school). In 1944 the Soviet authorities established a Spiritual Board of Muslims of the Caucasus, with spiritual jurisdiction over the Muslims of Armenia, Georgia and Azerbaijan. The Chairman of the Board, which is based in Baku, is normally a Shi'ite, while the Deputy Chairman is usually a Sunni. The severe restrictions on religious activity during the Soviet period were liberalized following Azerbaijani independence in 1991.

Spiritual Board of Muslims of the Caucasus: 1000 Baku; Chair. Sheikh ul-Islam Haci ALLASHUKUR PASHEZADE.

CHRISTIANITY

The Roman Catholic Church

The Church is represented in Azerbaijan by a Mission, established in October 2000. There were an estimated 320 adherents at 31 December 2005.

Superior: Rev. JÁN ČAPLA, 1069 Baku, Teimur Aliyev küç. 69B/1; tel. (12) 462-22-55; fax (12) 436-09-43; e-mail parish@catholic.baku.az.

The Russian Orthodox Church (Moscow Patriarchate)

Bishop of Baku and the Caspian Region: ALEKSANDR, 1010 Baku, Ş. Azizbekova küç. 205; tel. (12) 440-43-52; fax (12) 440-04-43; e-mail baku@eparchia.ru.

The Press

PRINCIPAL NEWSPAPERS

In Azerbaijani, except where otherwise stated.

525-ci Qazet/525-ya Gazeta: 1033 Baku, Ş. Mustafayev küç. 27/121; tel. (12) 466-67-98; fax (12) 466-25-20; e-mail 525@azdata.net; internet www.525ci.com; f. 1992; 5 a week; in Azerbaijani, English and Russian; Editor-in-Chief RASHAD MAJID.

Ayna/Zerkalo (Mirror): 1138 Baku, Sharifzadeh küç. 1; tel. and fax (12) 497-71-23; e-mail gazeta@zerkalo.az; internet www.ayna.az; internet www.zerkalo.az; f. 1990; daily; independent; Azerbaijani and Russian edns; Editor-in-Chief ELCIN SIXLINSKI; circ. 4,500 (daily).

Azadliq (Freedom): 1000 Baku, Khagani küç. 33; tel. (12) 498-90-81; fax (12) 498-78-18; e-mail mail@azadliq.com; internet www.azadliq.az; f. 1989; weekly; independent; organ of the Azerbaijan Popular Front; in Azerbaijani and Russian; Editor-in-Chief GANIMAT ZAKHIDOV.

Azarbaycan/Azerbaijan: 1073 Baku, Matbuat pr. 529/4; tel. (12) 438-20-87; fax (12) 439-43-23; internet www.azerbaijan.news.az; f. 1991; 5 a week; publ. by the Milli Majlis; in Azerbaijani and Russian; Editor-in-Chief BAKHTIYAR SADIGOV.

Azernews: 1002 Baku, S. Askerova küç. 85; tel. (12) 494-93-73; fax (12) 495-85-37; e-mail azernews@azeurotel.com; internet www.azernews.net; f. 1997; weekly; in Azerbaijani, Russian and English; in association with AssA-Irada news agency; Editor-in-Chief FAZIL ABBASOV; circ. 5,000–6,000.

Bakı Xabar (Baku News): 1000 Baku, Kicik Qala küç. 128; internet www.baku-xeber.com; f. 2003; newspaper of the Azerbaijan Democratic Party; 6 a week; Editor-in-Chief AYDIN QULIYEV; circ. 5,000 (2007).

Bakinskii Rabochii (The Baku Worker): 1146 Baku, Matbuat pr. 529; tel. (12) 438-00-29; e-mail bakrab@azerin.com; internet www.br.az; f. 1906; 5 a week; govt newspaper; in Russian; Editor I. VEKILOVA.

Baku Sun: 1073 Baku, İnşaatçılar pr. 2/42; tel. and fax (12) 497-55-31; e-mail editor@bakusun.baku.az; internet www.bakusun.az; f. 1998; weekly; in English; free of charge; Editor VALENTINA HUBER.

Bizim Asr: 1141 Baku, A. Alekperov küç. 83/23; tel. (12) 497-88-99; fax (12) 497-88-98; e-mail bizim_asr@media-az.com; internet bizimasr.media-az.com; f. 1999.

Bizim Yol (Our Way): Baku; tel. (12) 418-91-79; e-mail info@bizimyol.org; internet www.bizimyol.org; f. 2003; independent; weekly; associated with the Popular Front Party of Azerbaijan; Editor-in-Chief BAHADDIN HAZIYEV.

Day: Baku; e-mail editor@day.az; internet www.day.az; online only, in Russian and English.

Echo (Ekho): 1138 Baku, Sharifzadeh küç. 1; tel. (12) 497-51-74; fax (12) 447-41-50; e-mail gazeta@echo-az.com; internet www.echo-az.com; daily; in Russian; Editor-in-Chief RAUF TALISHINSKYI; circ. 10,000.

Ekspress (The Express): 1000 Baku, Khagani küç. 20B/43; tel. (12) 498-08-63; e-mail express@azeronline.com; internet www.express.com.az; Editor QAZANFAR BAYRAMOV.

İstiqlal (Independence): 1014 Baku, 28 May küç. 3–11; tel. (12) 493-33-78; fax (12) 498-75-55; e-mail istiklal@ngonet.baku.az; 4 a month; organ of the Azerbaijan Social Democratic Party; Editor ZARDUSHT ALIZADEH; circ. 5,000.

Respublika (Republic): 1146 Baku, Matbuat pr. 529; tel. (12) 438-01-14; fax (12) 438-01-31; e-mail resp@azdata.net; internet www.respublica.news.az; f. 1996; daily; govt newspaper; Editor-in-Chief T. AHMADOV; circ. 5,500.

Sharg (The East): 1000 Baku, Matbuat pr. 529; tel. (12) 447-37-80; fax (12) 439-00-79; e-mail sharq@azerin.com; internet www.sherg.az.

Xalq Qazeti (Popular Gazette): 1000 Baku, Bül-Bül pr. 18; tel. (12) 493-02-80; fax (12) 498-85-29; e-mail webmaster@xalqqazeti.com; internet www.xalqqazeti.com; f. 1919; fmrly *Kommunist*; 6 a week; organ of the Office of the President; Editor HASAN HASANOV.

Yezhednevnye Novosti (The Daily News): 1000 Baku, Terlan Aliyarbekov küç. 43; tel. and fax (12) 492-12-24; e-mail alpha@azeri.com; internet www.alpha.azeri.com; in Russian; Editor EMIL ASADOV; circ. 14,000.

Yeni Azerbaijan (A New Azerbaijan): 1000 Baku; tel. (12) 439-82-27; fax (12) 497-53-04; internet www.yeniazerbaycan.com; f. 1993; weekly; organ of the New Azerbaijan Party; Editor ALGYSH MUSAYEV; circ. 2,493.

Yeni Müsavat (A New Equality): 1000 Baku; tel. (12) 498-00-61; e-mail ymusavat@azeronline.com; independent; pro-opposition; Editor-in-Chief AZAR AYHAN (acting).

OTHER PRINCIPAL PERIODICALS

Caspian Business News (CBN): 1000 Baku, Safaroğlu küç. 219 B; tel. (12) 493-31-89; fax (12) 497-24-78; e-mail media@cbnmail.com; f. 2000; weekly; in English.

Dialog (Dialogue): 1000 Baku; f. 1989; fortnightly; in Azerbaijani and Russian; Editor R. A. ALEKPEROV.

Iki Sahil: 1025 Baku, A. Akhundov 22; tel. (12) 490-49-89; internet www.ikisahil.com; f. 1965; weekly; organ of the New Baku Oil-Refining Plant; Editor-in-Chief V. RAHIMZADEH; circ. 2,815.

Kirpi (Hedgehog): 1046 Baku, Matbuat pr. 529; tel. (12) 432-18-18; f. 1952; fortnightly; satirical; Editor A. M. AIVAZOV.

Literaturnyi Azerbaijan (Literary Azerbaijan): 1001 Baku, Khagani küç. 25; tel. (12) 493-51-00; e-mail sima@azeri.com; f. 1931; monthly; journal of the Union of Writers of Azerbaijan; fiction; in Russian; Editor-in-Chief M. F. VEKILOV.

Ulus (The Nation): 1000 Baku; tel. (12) 492-27-43; 2 a week; Editor TOFIK DADASHEV.

Vyshka—Oil (Oil derrick): 1073 Baku, Matbuat pr. 529; tel. and fax (12) 439-96-97; e-mail medina@vyshka.com; internet vyshka.com; f. 1928; weekly; independent; in Russian; Editor M. E. GASANOVA.

NEWS AGENCIES

Azadinform Information Agency: 1000 Baku, F. Amirov küç. 1; tel. (12) 498-48-59; fax (12) 498-47-60; e-mail azadinform@azerin

.com; internet azadinform.az; f. 1998; independent information agency; Chief Editor ASEF HAJIYEV.

AzartAc—Azarbaycan Dövlat Teleqraf Agentlıyı (Azerbaijan State Telegraph Agency—AzerTAg): 1000 Baku, Bül-Bül pr. 18; tel. (12) 493-59-29; fax (12) 493-62-65; e-mail azertac@azdata.net; internet www.azertag.net; f. 1920; provides information in Azerbaijani, Russian and English; Dir-Gen. ASLAN ASLANOV.

Azeri Press Agency (APA): 1001 Baku, İstiqlal küç. 31; tel. (12) 596-33-57; fax (12) 596-31-94; e-mail apa@azeurotel.com; internet www.apa.az; f. 2004; in Azerbaijani, Russian and English; Dir-Gen. VUSALA MAHIRGIZI.

Bilik Dünyasi Information Agency: 1000 Baku, D. Aliyev küç. 241/22; tel. (12) 493-55-61; fax (12) 498-18-41; e-mail bd@azdata.net.

Media-Press: 1141 Baku, A. Alekperov küç. 83/23; tel. (12) 497-07-05; fax (12) 497-88-98; e-mail news@mediapress.media-az.com; internet mediapress.media-az.com; f. 1999; owned by Media Holding; independent; Gen. Dir VUGAR GARADAGLY.

Trend Information-Analytical Agency: 1601 Baku, Fizuli küç 69; tel. (12) 497-31-72; fax (12) 497-30-89; e-mail infotrend@azdata.net; internet www.trend-az.com; f. 1995; in Azerbaijani, Russian and English; Dir-Gen. INGILAB AKHMEDOV.

Turan İnformasıya Agentlıyı: 1000 Baku, Khagani küç. 20/56; tel. (12) 598-42-26; fax (12) 598-38-17; e-mail turan@azeurotel.az; internet www.turaninfo.com; f. 1990; independent news agency; in Azerbaijani, Russian and English; Dir MEHMAN ALIYEV.

PRESS ASSOCIATIONS

Azerbaijan Journalists' Confederation (AJK): 1000 Baku, Khagani küç. 33; tel. (50) 335-27-95; fax (12) 498-78-18; e-mail hasret@akjib.org; f. 2002; 15 member organizations; Gen. Sec. AZER H. HASRET.

Azerbaijan Press Council (Azerbaycan Metbuat Surasi)): 1010 Baku, Nizami küç. 121/11; tel. and fax (12) 498-27-48; e-mail info@presscouncil.az; internet www.presscouncil.az; f. 2003; mediates disputes between the media and the authorities; acts as a self-regulatory body for the print media; Chair. AFLATUN AMASHOV.

Publishers

Azarbaycan Ensiklopediyasi (Azerbaijan Encyclopedia): 1004 Baku, Boyuk Gala küç. 41; tel. (12) 492-87-11; fax (12) 492-77-83; e-mail azenciklop@ctc.net.az; f. 1965; encyclopedias and dictionaries; Gen. Dir I. O. VELIYEV.

Azarneshr State Publishing House: 1005 Baku, Gusi Hajiyev küç. 4; tel. (12) 492-50-15; f. 1924; Dir A. MUSTAFAZADE; Editor-in-Chief A. KUSEINZADE.

Elm Azerbaijani Academy of Sciences Publishing House: 1000 Baku; scientific books and journals.

Gyanjlik (Youth): 1005 Baku, Gusi Hajiyev küç. 4; books for children and young people; Dir E. T. ALIYEV.

Ishyg (Light): 1601 Baku, Gogol küç. 6; illustrated publs; Dir G. N. ISMAILOV.

Madani-maarif Ishi (Education and Culture): 1073 Baku, Matbuat pr. 529; tel. (12) 432-79-17; Editor-in-Chief ALOVSAT ATAMALY OĞLU BASHIROV.

Medeniyyat (Culture) Publishing House: 1146 Baku, Matbuat pr. 146; tel. (12) 432-98-38; Dir SHAKMAR AKPER OĞLU AKPERZADE.

Sada: 1004 Baku, Boyuk Gala küç. 28; tel. (12) 492-75-64; fax (12) 492-98-43; reference.

Shur: 1000 Baku; tel. (12) 492-93-72; f. 1992; Dir GASHAM ISA OĞLU ISABEYLI.

Broadcasting and Communications

TELECOMMUNICATIONS

Azercell Telecom: 1139 Baku, Tbilisi pr. 61A; tel. (12) 496-70-07; fax (12) 430-05-68; internet www.azercell.com; f. 1996; jt-venture co between the Ministry of Communications and Information Technology and Fintur Holdings B.V. (Netherlands); Gen. Dir ESRA TAN.

Azerfon: 1102 Baku, Alatava küç. 2; tel. (12) 444-07-30; fax (12) 444-07-31; internet www.narmobile.az; f. 2005; provides mobile cellular communications under the Narmobile brand name.

AzTelecom Production Asscn: 1122 Baku, Tbilisi pr. 3166; tel. (12) 430-26-30; fax (12) 493-17-87; e-mail aztelekom@aztelekom.net; internet www.aztelekom.net; national monopoly fixed-line telecommunications operator; f. 1992; owned by the Ministry of Communications and Information Technology; privatization pending; Dir MUHAMMAD MAMEDOV.

Bakcell: 1000 Baku, U. Hajibeyov küç. 24; tel. (12) 498-94-44; fax (12) 498-92-55; e-mail bakcell@bakcell.com; internet www.bakcell.com; f. 1994; mobile telecommunications service provider; wholly owned by GTIB (Israel); Gen. Man. HAIM MAIMON.

RADIO AND TELEVISION

National Television and Radio Council (Milli Televiziya va Radio Şurası): 1000 Baku, Nizami küç. 105; tel. (12) 98-36-59; fax (12) 98-76-68; e-mail office@ntrc.gov.az; internet www.ntrc.gov.az; f. 2003; regulatory body, comprising nine members, six of whom are presidential appointees; Chair. NUSHIRAVAN MAGERRAMLI.

Azerbaijan Television and Radio Broadcasting Co: 1011 Baku, Mehti Hussein küç. 1; tel. (12) 492-72-53; fax (12) 439-54-52; internet www.aztv.az; f. 1956; closed jt-stock co

Azerbaijan National Television (AzTV): 1011 Baku, Mehti Hussein küç. 1; tel. (12) 492-38-07; fax (12) 497-20-20; e-mail alishanov@aztv.az; internet www.aztv.az; f. 1956; programmes in Azerbaijani, English and Russian; one channel; Chair. ARIF ALISHANOV.

Azerbaijan National Radio: 1011 Baku, Mehti Hussein küç. 1; tel. (12) 492-87-68; fax (12) 439-72-48; internet www.aztv.az; f. 1926; broadcasts in Azerbaijani, Arabic, English and Turkish; two channels and one international broadcasting studio; Head MOVLUD SULEIMAN.

Public Television and Radio Broadcasting Co (İctimai Televizya va Radiyo Yayımları Şirkati—ITV): Baku; tel. (12) 431-17-37; fax (12) 430-24-26; e-mail info@itv.az; internet www.itv.az; f. 2005; created from the second channel of the state broadcasting co (AzTV2); broadcasts in Azerbaijani and Armenian; Gen. Dir ISMAYIL OMAROV.

ANS Independent Broadcasting and Media Co (Azerbaijan News Service): 1073 Baku, Matbuat pr. 28/11; tel. (12) 497-72-67; fax (12) 498-94-98; e-mail ans@ans.az; internet www.ans.az; f. 1999; independent; broadcasts ANS-TV (f. 1990) and NAS-CHM Radio (f. 1994); Pres. VAHID MUSTAFAYEV.

Lider TV and Radio: 1141 Baku, A. Alekperov küç. 83/23; tel. (12) 497-88-99; fax (12) 497-87-77; e-mail mail@media-az.com; internet www.lidertv.com; f. 2000.

Regional Television Network of Azerbaijan (RTNA): Sumqayıt, Qarabağ Cinema, c/o Dunya TV; f. 2005; includes seven regional channels: Alternativ TV in Ganca; Mingaçevir TV, Xayal TV in Quba; Dunya TV in Sumqayıt; Lankaran TV and Simurq TV in Tovuz; Aygun TV in Zaqatala.

Finance

(cap. = capital; res = reserves; dep. = deposits; m. = million; brs = branches; amounts in manats, unless otherwise stated)

BANKING
Central Bank

National Bank of Azerbaijan: 1014 Baku, R. Behbutov küç. 32; tel. (12) 493-11-22; fax (12) 493-55-41; e-mail mail@nba.az; internet www.nba.az; f. 1992; central bank and supervisory authority; cap. 50,000m., res 244,509m., dep. 2,546,561m. (Dec. 2005); Chair. ELMAN RUSTAMOV.

State-owned Banks

International Bank of Azerbaijan: 1005 Baku, Nizami küç. 67; tel. (12) 493-00-91; fax (12) 493-40-91; e-mail ibar@ibar.az; internet www.ibar.az; f. 1992 to succeed br. of USSR Vneshekonombank; 50.2% owned by the Ministry of Finance; carries out all banking services; cap. 59.3m., res 18.9m., dep. 1,518.5m. (Dec. 2006); Chair. of Bd JAHANGIR F. HAJIYEV; 36 brs.

Kapital Bank: 1014 Baku, Fizuli küç. 71; tel. (12) 493-66-30; fax (12) 493-79-05; e-mail office@kapitalbank.az; internet www.kapitalbank.az; f. 2000 by merger; present name adopted 2005; cap. 12.0m., res 3.5m., dep. 104.4m. (Dec. 2006); Chair. RAUF RZAYEV; 87 brs.

Other Banks

At 1 August 2005 there were 43 banks operating in Azerbaijan, including two state-owned banks and 17 banks supported by foreign capital.

Amrahbank: 1000 Baku, Y. Safarov küç. 111; tel. (12) 497-88-60; fax (12) 497-88-63; e-mail info@amrahbank.com; internet www.amrahbank.com; f. 1993; cap. 6.8m., dep. 20.5m., total assets 29.4m. (Dec. 2006); Pres. YUNUS ILDIRIMZADEH; Chair. MAHMUD AGAMALIYEV.

AtaBank: 1010 Baku, Shamsi Badalbeyli küç. 102; tel. (12) 497-87-00; fax (12) 498-74-47; e-mail atabank@atabank.com; internet www.atabank.com; f. 1994; cap. 35,000m., res 0.0, dep. 119,362.2m. (Dec. 2005); Chair. of Sup. Bd AZAD JAVADOV; Chair. of Exec. Bd MOBIL SHARIFOV.

AZERBAIJAN

Azalbank: 1000 Baku, Nizami küç. 86; tel. (12) 498-60-56; fax (12) 498-97-01; e-mail azalbank@azalbank.az; internet www.azalbank.az; f. 1994; cap. 5m., dep. 10.4m., total assets 15.0m. (Dec. 2006); Chair. of Bd MAMADOV TEYMUR MAMED; 8 brs.

Azarbaycan Sanaye Banki (Azerbaijan Industry Bank): 1005 Baku, Azarbaycan pr. 3; tel. (12) 493-50-67; fax (12) 493-84-50; e-mail contact@asb.az; internet www.asb.az; f. 1996; fmrly Capital Investment Bank; present name adopted Nov. 2006; cap. 7.8m., res 1.4m., dep. 14.9m. (Dec. 2006); Pres. ABDULBARI GUZAL; Chair. of Bd of Dirs AHMET YEMAN.

Azerdemiryolbank: 1008 Baku, Qarabağ küç. 31; tel. (12) 440-24-29; fax (12) 496-09-77; e-mail damir@azerdemiryolbank.az; internet www.azerdemiryolbank.com; f. 1992; cap. 7.2m., res 3.8m., dep. 42.9m. (Dec. 2006); Chair. of Bd ROMAN AMIRJANOV; 10 brs.

Azer-Turk Bank: 1005 Baku, Islam Seferli küç. 5; tel. (12) 497-43-16; fax (12) 498-37-02; e-mail atb@azerturkbank.biz; internet www.azerturkbank.biz; f. 1995; 46% owned by Türkiye Cumhuriyeti Ziraat Bankasi AS (Turkey); 46% owned by Agrarkredit; cap. 23,462.9m., dep. 69,958.5m. (Dec. 2005); Chair. MEMMED MUSAYEV; Gen. Man. MEHMET SAMI ACAROZMEN.

Azerigazbank: 1073 Baku, Landau küç. 16; tel. (12) 497-50-17; fax (12) 498-96-15; e-mail azerigazbank@azerigazbank.com; internet www.azerigazbank.com; f. 1992; jt-stock investment bank; cap. 29,000m., res 0.0, dep. 223,286m. (Dec. 2005); Chair. AZER F. MOVSUMOV; 5 brs.

Bank of Baku: 1069 Baku, Atatürk pr. 40/42; tel. (12) 447-00-55; fax (12) 498-82-78; e-mail root@bankofbaku.com; internet www.bankofbaku.com; f. 1994; merged with Ilkbank in Feb. 2005; 40% owned by NAB DIS Ticarat (Turkey); 28.9% owned by Azpetrol Holding; cap. 6.8m., res 1.7m., dep. 57.1m. (Dec. 2006); Chair. of Bd SHAHRAM M. OROMI.

Bank Respublika: 1000 Baku, Khagani küç. 71; tel. (12) 598-08-00; fax (12) 598-08-80; e-mail info@bankrespublica.az; internet www.bankrespublica.az; f. 1992; cap. 7.2m., res 2.3m., dep. 98.5m. (Dec. 2006); Chair. of Exec. Bd KHADIJA HASANOVA.

Bank Standard: 1005 Baku, H. Hadjiyev küç. 4; tel. (12) 497-10-71; fax (12) 498-07-78; e-mail bank@bankstandard.com; internet www.bankstandard.com; f. 1995; present name adopted 2004; cap. 15.0m., res 8.5m., dep. 179.8m. (Dec. 2006); Chief Exec. SALIM KRIMAN.

DEBUT Bank: 1025 Baku, Babek pr. 16; tel. (12) 496-45-51; fax (12) 496-45-60; e-mail info@debutbank.az; internet www.debutbank.az; f. 1994; cap. 25,000m., res 2,881.1m., dep. 22,441m. (Dec. 2005); Pres. ANAR GARIBOV.

Günay Bank: 1095 Baku, Rasul Rza küç. 4/6; tel. (12) 498-04-55; fax (12) 498-14-39; e-mail gunaybank@azerin.com; internet www.gunaybank.com; f. 1992; cap. 28,580m., res 2,844m., dep. 64,432m. (Dec. 2005); Pres. AHAD SHIRINOV; Gen. Man. SHAKIR ABDULLAYEV; 1 br.

Rabitabank: 1001 Baku, B. Sardarov küç. 1; tel. (12) 492-57-61; fax (12) 497-11-01; e-mail rb@rabitabank.com; internet www.rabitabank.com; f. 1993; jt-stock commercial bank; operates mainly in telecommunications sector; cap. 23,135m., res 6,613m., dep. 124,986m. (Dec. 2005); Chair. of Council ZAKIR NURIYEV; 9 brs.

Unibank Commercial Bank: 1022 Baku, Raşid Behbudov küç. 57; tel. (12) 498-22-44; fax (12) 498-09-53; e-mail bank@unibank.az; internet www.unibank.az; f. 2002 by merger; cap. 6.6m., res 0.6m., dep. 90.0m. (Dec. 2006); Chair. and Chief Exec. FAIG HUSEYNOV; 8 brs.

United Credit Bank: 1025 Baku, N. Rafiyev küç. 49; tel. (12) 490-06-41; fax (12) 490-05-22; e-mail ucb@ucb.az; internet www.ucb.az; f. 1996; 81.39% owned by United Business Co Ltd; Chair. of Bd AZAD ISKENDEROV.

Association

Azerbaijan Association of Banks: 1001 Baku, B. Sardarov küç. 1; tel. (12) 497-58-29; fax (12) 497-15-15; e-mail bank_assoc@azeurotel.com; f. 1990; co-ordinates banking activity; Pres. ZAKIR NURIYEV; 47 mems.

STOCK EXCHANGE

Baku Stock Exchange (Bakı Fond Birjasi): 1000 Baku, Bül-Bül pr. 19; tel. (12) 498-85-22; fax (12) 493-77-93; e-mail info@bse.az; internet www.bse.az; f. 2000; Pres. ANAR AKHUNDOV.

INSURANCE

At January 2005 there were 30 insurance companies operating in Azerbaijan.

Ataşgah Insurance Co: Baku, Sabir küç. 3; tel. (12) 497-81-82; fax (12) 492-97-65; e-mail ateshgah@ateshgah.com; internet www.ateshgah.com; f. 1996; 30% owned by State Oil Co of Azerbaijan, 30% owned by Atlantic Reinsurance Co, 19% owned by Lukoil Azerbaijan; Man. ROBERT BRUNDRETT.

AZAL-sığorta: 1000 Baku, Khagani küç. 1/4; tel. (12) 598-39-50; fax (12) 598-38-02; e-mail azalsigorta@azalsigorta.com; internet www.azalsigorta.com; f. 1995; Man. Dir NIYAZI IMANOV.

Azergarant: 1001 Baku, H. Aslanov küç. 115/18; tel. (12) 493-81-65; fax (12) 493-81-02; e-mail azergarant@azdata.net; f. 1993; Pres. Dr ALEKPER MAMEDOV; Gen. Dir FAIG HUSSEINOV.

Azersığorta: 1014 Baku, Füzuli 69; tel. (12) 495-95-64; fax (12) 495-94-69; e-mail azersigorta@azeuro.net; Dir MEMMED MEMMEDOV.

Beynalxalq Sığorta Şirkati (International Insurance Co): 1065 Baku, J. Jabbarli küç. 40c, IIC Bldg; tel. (12) 596-22-02; fax (12) 596-22-12; e-mail iic@iic.az; internet www.iic.az; f. 2002; universal insurance co; wholly owned subsidiary of the International Bank of Azerbaijan; Dir FEYRUZ NOVRUZOV.

Günay Anadolu Sığorta: 1005 Baku, Terlan Aliyarbekov küç. 3; tel. (12) 498-13-56; fax (12) 498-13-60; e-mail office@gunaysigorta.in-baku.com; internet insurancegunayanadolu.com; f. 1992; Gen. Man. ALOVSET GOJAYEV.

MBask Insurance Co: 1095 Baku, Azi Aslanov küç. 90/9; tel. (12) 498-91-90; fax (12) 498-10-62; e-mail office@mbask.com; f. 1992; 30% owned by the European Bank for Reconstruction and Development (United Kingdom); 7 brs; Chair. of Bd of Dirs JAMIL MALIKOV.

MOST Insurance Co: 1073 Baku, H. Javid pr. 15/21; tel. (12) 497-37-60; fax (12) 433-08-58; Dir KAMAL MIRSAHIB OĞLU IBRAHIMOV.

Trade and Industry

GOVERNMENT AGENCY

Azerbaijan Export and Investment Promotion Foundation: 1000 Baku, U. Hajibeyov küç. 40, Government House; tel. (12) 598-01-47; fax (12) 598-01-52; e-mail office@azerinvest.com; internet www.azerinvest.com; f. 2003 under the Ministry of Economic Development.

CHAMBER OF COMMERCE

Chamber of Commerce and Industry: 1001 Baku, İstiklal küç 31/33; tel. (12) 492-89-12; fax (12) 497-19-97; e-mail expo@chamber.baku.az; Pres. SULEYMAN BAYRAM OĞLU TATLIYEV.

INDUSTRIAL AND TRADE ASSOCIATIONS

National Confederation of Entrepreneurs' (Employers') Organizations of Azerbaijan (Azarbaycan Respublikasi Sahibkarlar—İşagötüranlar—Taşkilatları Milli Konfederasiyasi—ASK): 1002 Baku, S. Askerova küç. 85; tel. (12) 494-90-16; fax (12) 494-99-76; e-mail aazerenterprise@artel.net.az; internet www.ask.org.az; f. 1999; Pres. ALEKPER MAMEDOV.

UTILITIES

Electricity

Azerenerji: 1005 Baku, A. Alizade küç. 10; tel. (12) 493-73-58; fax (12) 498-55-23; state-owned jt-stock co; power generation and transmission company; Pres. ETIBAR S. PIRVERDIYEV.

AliBayramlıelektrikşebeke (Ali Bayramlı Electricity Network): 1800 Ali Bayramlı; f. 2001; comprises the Azerbaijani electricity network's southern zone; managed by Bakı Yüksakgarginlikli Elektroavadanliq (BYGEA—Baku High Voltage Electrical Equipment Co).

Bakı Electrikşebeke (Baku Electricity Network): 1008 Baku, Kazumzada 20; tel. (12) 440-44-04; fax (12) 440-22-26; e-mail info@bakuelektrikshebeke.az; internet www.bakuelektrikshebeke.az; f. 2001.

Bayva-Enerji: 2000 Ganca, Ruzigar Gasimov küç. 10; tel. and fax (22) 56-97-40; e-mail bayva-qerbenerji@mail.ru; f. 2002 as Ganjalektrikşebeke; comprising the Azerbaijani electricity distribution network's western zone; managed by Bakı Yüksakgarginlikli Elektroavadanliq (BYGEA—Baku High Voltage Electrical Equipment); Gen. Dir RAMIZ AGAMALIYEV.

Naxçıvan Electrikşebeke (Naxçıvan Electricity Network): 7000 Naxçıvan; f. 2001; state-owned open jt-stock co; approximately 60% of electricity imported from Iran.

Gas

AzeriGaz: 1025 Baku, Yusif Safarov küç. 23; tel. (12) 490-42-52; fax (12) 490-42-55; e-mail azer_bayramov@azerigaz.com; f. 1992; transport, distribution, sale, compression and storage of natural gas; Chair. ALIKHAN MELIKHOV; 13,000 employees.

TRADE UNIONS

Confederation of Azerbaijan Trade Unions (AHIK): 1000 Baku, Genjler meydani 3; tel. and fax (12) 492-72-68; e-mail ahik@azerin.com; 1.3m. mems; Chair. SATTAR MEHBALIYEV.

Trade Union of Oil and Gas Industry Workers: 1033 Baku, Aga Neymatulla küç. 39; tel. (12) 467-69-53; fax (12) 447-15-85; e-mail oilunion@online.az; f. 1906; 161 local orgs in the petroleum and gas sectors; 67,900 mems (2003); Chair. JAHANGIR ALIYEV.

Transport

RAILWAYS

In 2005 there were 2,122 km of railway track, of which 1,270 km were electrified. The majority of total freight traffic is carried by the railways. Railways connect Baku with Tbilisi (Georgia) and Makhachkala (Dagestan, Russia). The rail link between metropolitan Azerbaijan and the Naxçıvan Autonomous Republic, and that to Yerevan (Armenia) are currently disrupted, owing to Azerbaijan's economic blockade of Armenia. An international line links Naxçıvan with Tabriz (Iran). There is an underground railway in Baku.

Azerbaijani Railways (ADDY): 1010 Baku, Dilara Aliyeva küç. 230; tel. (12) 498-44-67; fax (12) 498-85-47; e-mail info@addy.gov.az; internet addy.gov.az; f. 1992.

Baku Metro (Bakı Metropoliteni): 1073 Baku, H. Javid pr. 33A; tel. (12) 490-00-00; fax (12) 497-53-96; e-mail akhmedov_tagi@metro.gov.az; internet www.metro.gov.az; f. 1967; 20 stations on two lines (30 km); Gen. Man. TAGI M. AKHMEDOV.

ROADS

In 2004 the total length of roads in Azerbaijan was 25,021 km, of which 6,928 km were main roads; 92.6% of the road network was paved.

SHIPPING

Shipping services on the Caspian Sea link Baku with: Astrakhan, Russia; Türkmenbaşi (formerly Krasnovodsk), Turkmenistan; and the Iranian ports of Bandar Anzali and Bandar Nowshar. At 31 December 2006 the Azerbaijani merchant fleet comprised 300 vessels, with a combined displacement of 692,900 grt.

Baku Sea Port: 1010 Baku, U. Hajibeyov küç. 72; tel. (12) 493-67-74; fax (12) 493-36-72; e-mail port@sea.baku.az.

Shipowning Company

Caspian Shipping Company (Caspar): 1005 Baku, M. Rasulzade küç. 5; tel. (12) 493-20-58; fax (12) 493-53-39; internet www.caspar.baku.az; transports crude petroleum and petroleum products; operates cargo and passenger ferries; fleet of 69 vessels; Pres. A. A. BASHIROV.

CIVIL AVIATION

There are five airports in Azerbaijan, of which Heydar Aliyev Airport at Baku is the largest. Naxçıvan has its own airport.

Civil Aviation Administration: 1000 Baku, Azadlıq pr. 11; tel. (12) 493-44-34; fax (12) 498-52-37; e-mail azal_coordpt@azerin.com; Chief Inspector İLHAM G. AMIROV.

Azerbaijan Airlines (AZAL) (Azerbaijan Hava Yollari): 1000 Baku, Azadlıq pr. 11; tel. (12) 493-44-34; fax (12) 498-52-37; e-mail azal@azal.baku.az; f. 1992; formerly Azalavia; state airline operating scheduled and charter passenger and cargo services to Africa, the CIS, Europe, South-East Asia and the Middle East; Gen. Dir JAHANGIR ASKEROV.

IMAIR Airlines: 1000 Baku, Hazi Aslanov küç. 115; tel. (12) 493-41-71; fax (12) 493-27-77; e-mail root@imair.com; internet www.imair.com; f. 1995; independent airline operating international regular passenger and charter passenger and cargo services, mainly within the CIS region; Pres. FIZOULI ALEKPEROV.

Turan Air: 1010 Baku, 28 May küç. 68/64; tel. (12) 498-94-31; fax (12) 498-94-34; e-mail root@turan-air.com; internet www.turan-air.com; f. 1994; operates scheduled and charter passenger and cargo services, mainly within the former USSR; Gen. Dir VAGIF ISKENDEROV.

Tourism

Tourism is not widely developed. However, there are resorts on the Caspian Sea, including the Ganjlik international tourist centre, on the Apsheron Peninsula, near Baku, which has four hotels as well as camping facilities. There were 1,261,686 tourist arrivals in 2005, when receipts from tourism totalled US $100m. The number of tourist arrivals decreased to 1,258,578 in 2006.

Dept of Tourism of the Ministry of Culture and Tourism: 1004 Baku, Neftchilar pr. 65; tel. (12) 492-87-13; fax (12) 492-98-41; e-mail tourism@myst.co-az.net; Head TEYMUR MEHDIYEV.

THE BAHAMAS

Introductory Survey

Location, Climate, Language, Religion, Flag, Capital

The Commonwealth of the Bahamas consists of about 700 islands and more than 2,000 cays and rocks, extending from east of the Florida coast of the USA to just north of Cuba and Haiti, in the West Indies. The main islands are New Providence, Grand Bahama, Andros, Eleuthera and Great Abaco. Almost 70% of the population reside on the island of New Providence. The remaining members of the group are known as the 'Family Islands'. A total of 29 of the islands are inhabited. The climate is mild and sub-tropical, with average temperatures of about 30°C (86°F) in summer and 20°C (68°F) in winter. The average annual rainfall is about 1,000 mm (39 ins). The official language is English. Most of the inhabitants profess Christianity, the largest denominations being the Anglican, Baptist, Roman Catholic and Methodist Churches. The national flag (proportions 1 by 2) comprises three equal horizontal stripes, of blue, gold and blue, with a black triangle at the hoist, extending across one-half of the width. The capital is Nassau, on the island of New Providence.

Recent History

A former British colonial territory, the Bahamas attained internal self-government in January 1964, although the parliamentary system dates back to 1729. The first elections under universal adult suffrage were held in January 1967 for an enlarged House of Assembly. The Progressive Liberal Party (PLP), supported mainly by Bahamians of African origin and led by Lynden (later Sir Lynden) Pindling, won 18 of the 38 seats, as did the ruling United Bahamian Party (UBP), dominated by those of European origin. With the support of another member, the PLP formed a Government and Pindling became Premier (he was restyled Prime Minister in September 1968). At the next elections, in April 1968, the PLP won 29 seats and the UBP only seven.

In May 1969 the Bahamas Government was given increased responsibility for internal security, external affairs and defence. In the elections of September 1972, which were dominated by the issue of independence, the PLP maintained its majority. Following a constitutional conference in December 1972, the Bahamas became an independent nation, within the Commonwealth, on 10 July 1973. Pindling remained Prime Minister. The PLP increased its majority in the elections of July 1977 and was again returned to power in the June 1982 elections, with 32 of the 43 seats in the enlarged House of Assembly. The remaining 11 seats were won by the Free National Movement (FNM), which had reunited for the elections after splitting into several factions over the previous five years.

Trading in illicit drugs, mainly for the US market, has become a major problem for the country, since many of the small islands and cays are used by drugs-traffickers in their smuggling activities. In 1983 allegations of widespread corruption, and the abuse of Bahamian bank secrecy laws by drugs-traffickers and US tax evaders, led Pindling to appoint a Royal Commission to investigate thoroughly the drugs trade in the Bahamas. The Commission's hearings revealed the extent to which money deriving from this trade had permeated Bahamian social and economic affairs. Evidence presented to the Commission led to the resignation, in October 1984, of two cabinet ministers, and by November 1985 a total of 51 suspects had been indicted, including the assistant police commissioner. The Commission also revealed that Pindling had received several million dollars in gifts and loans from business executives, although it found no evidence of a link to the drugs trade. Despite this, the PLP was returned to power for a fifth consecutive term in June 1987.

In February 1988 new claims of official corruption were made at the trial in Florida, USA, of a leading Colombian drugs-trafficker. Pindling and the Deputy Prime Minister were alleged to have accepted bribes, but this was vehemently denied. In March 1990 the Minister of Agriculture, Trade and Industry, Ervin Knowles, resigned, following allegations of nepotism and the misuse of public funds. He was replaced by Perry Christie.

Campaigning for the August 1992 general election was disrupted by industrial unrest in the country's telephone and electricity companies, and by the continuing problems of the state airline, Bahamasair. Despite predictions of a PLP victory, the FNM won the election, securing 33 seats, while Pindling's party won the remaining 16. Hubert Ingraham, the FNM leader, replaced Pindling as Prime Minister, and announced a programme of measures aimed at increasing the accountability of government ministers, combating corruption and revitalizing the economy.

A marked increase in violent crime in parts of New Providence led the Government to announce the creation, in March 1995, of a special police unit to address the problem. Meanwhile, the trade in illegal drugs remained widespread in the country, and in late 1995 several local business leaders, as well as close relatives of a member of Parliament, were arrested in connection with a large seizure of cocaine. In October of that year the Prime Minister introduced further legislation that aimed to prevent the abuse of Bahamian banks by drugs-traffickers, and thus improve the reputation of the country's financial sector, particularly in the USA.

At a general election held in March 1997 the FNM won 34 of the 40 seats in a reduced House of Assembly, and the PLP six. The FNM's overwhelming victory in the election was attributed both to the Prime Minister's success in reversing the economic decline and the involvement of the PLP in various financial scandals. Most notably, Pindling was implicated in February in the findings of a public inquiry (instituted in 1993) to investigate alleged corruption and misappropriation of funds in the three principal state corporations. Following the election, Pindling resigned as leader of the PLP and was replaced by Christie.

Violent crime continued to be of major concern to Bahamians. In April 1998 the Government signed a convention drawn up by the Organization of American States (OAS, see p. 360) to ban illegal guns, amid a disturbing increase in gun-related crime. In September 1998, following the murders of several tourists, the Prime Minister increased security in tourist areas, and announced plans to limit the right of appeal against death sentences (the sentences of 17 prisoners had been commuted in January). The hanging in October of two convicted murderers caused controversy, despite growing public demand for execution as a deterrent against crime. The Government had rejected a last-minute plea for clemency from the European Union, on the grounds that both men had appeals pending at the Inter-American Court of Human Rights (IACHR, see p. 361). In August 1999 the Bahamian authorities were strongly criticized by human rights groups after they announced their intention to execute another two convicted murderers who had also submitted petitions to the IACHR. In March 2006 the Privy Council in the United Kingdom banned the mandatory death penalty for murder. Despite attempts to reduce levels of crime, the murder rate continued to be high. By mid-June 2007 a total of 39 murders had been reported, compared with some 24 in the same period of the previous year. There was also an increase in the number of rapes committed against tourists in 2005.

At the general election held on 2 May 2002 the PLP unexpectedly secured an overwhelming victory over the FNM, winning 29 of the 40 seats (with 50.8% of the vote) in the House of Assembly. The FNM retained seven seats (with 41.1% of the ballot). Independent candidates won the remaining four seats. The tourism minister and FNM leader-designate, Tommy Turnquest, failed to retain his seat, as did several other ministers. Notable appointments to Perry Christie's Cabinet included those of Allyson Maynard-Gibson to the newly created post of Minister of Financial Services and Investments and James Smith, the former Governor of the Central Bank, as Minister of State in the Ministry of Finance. The new Government pledged to establish a national health insurance system, as well as to undertake constitutional reform.

In November 2005 Dame Ivy Dumont, the Bahamas' first female Governor-General, resigned after four years in office.

Arthur Hanna was sworn in as her successor on 1 February 2006. Later in the same month Christie reorganized the Cabinet. The only new appointment was that of Bernard Nottage, a former deputy leader of the PLP who had left the party in 2000 to form the Coalition for Democratic Reform before returning in 2005, as Minister of Health and National Insurance.

On 19 September 2006 Chief Justice Sir Burton Hall disbanded the Bahamas' sole coroner's court, recommending that the system revert to its pre-1993 operations whereby all magistrates were empowered to function as coroners during inquests. This would, theoretically, accelerate the rate of hearings and clear the backlog of pending cases. The decision was apparently prompted by widespread public complaint that the inquest into the death of the 20-year old son of reality television star Anna Nicole Smith had been scheduled very promptly, in comparison with the delays normally encountered. The inquest was adjourned due to concerns about potential juror bias and the threat from Tropical Storm Noel and finally opened in November 2007. Similarly, allegations of preferential treatment abounded against the Government in relation to Smith's application for permanent residency, which was processed with unprecedented expediency and provoked demands for the resignation of the Minister of Immigration, Shane Gibson. The controversy continued into 2007, with Gibson tendering his resignation in February amid escalating public and political pressure—further exacerbated by allegations of an intimate involvement with Smith—although the minister maintained that he was innocent of any wrongdoing throughout. International media interest in the scandal had intensified following Smith's unexpected death earlier that month, adding to an increasingly curious political fracas in the months preceding the general election of 2 May.

November 2006 witnessed significant disruption within the Bahamas' judicial system when a supreme court ruling concluded that the Cabinet had acted illegally in failing to appoint a commission to review judicial salaries and, consequently, had compromised the independence of the judiciary. It was anticipated that the country's magistrates' courts would close pending the outcome of an appeal against the ruling. Despite the furore over judicial pay, on 18 December a contingent of Law Lords from the Privy Council sat in the Court of Appeal in Nassau, the first instance of the country's final appellate court operating outside London. The Bahamas retained the Privy Council as its ultimate court of appeal, in contrast to several other Caribbean countries that had instituted the Caribbean Court of Justice following its inauguration in April 2005.

In December 2006 a National Health Insurance Act was approved by the House of Assembly. The new legislation allowed private-sector participation in the national health-care system in an effort to improve the quality of public health care. Doctors, employers and trade unions opposed the reform on the grounds that the scheme, which was to cost an estimated US $235m. per year, was not financially viable. Although fears of a concomitant income tax were vehemently denied by the Government, in the same month the Minister of Finance conceded that the implementation of a value-added tax might be necessary to finance the programme.

The PLP was defeated at the general election of 2 May 2007, retaining 18 seats in the 41-seat House of Assembly, while the FNM won 23 seats. Voter turn-out was high, with some 91.3% of eligible voters participating in the poll. The former opposition party formed a new Government, with party leader Hubert Ingraham sworn in as Prime Minister on 4 May. Ingraham also assumed the portfolio for finance and Tommy Turnquest, who had regained his seat in the House of Assembly, became Minister of National Security and Immigration. Ingraham declared that his immediate areas of concern were security issues at Lynden Pindling International Airport, illegal immigration and land policy matters.

The Bahamas' traditionally close relationship with the USA was strained during the 1990s by the increasingly uncompromising attitude of the US authorities towards bank secrecy laws and drugs-smuggling in the islands. Following an improvement in bilateral relations in the late 1990s, prompted by a series of joint operations, there was a fall in the rate of suspected drugs-transhipment detection in the Bahamas. This decrease was reportedly in part attributable to the withdrawal of some US detection and monitoring aircraft following the terrorist attacks on the USA in September 2001. In late 2002 the relationship worsened after the then US ambassador to the Bahamas, J. Richard Blankenship, asserted that the judicial system did not penalize drugs-traffickers severely enough and urged a thorough reform of the Royal Bahamian Defence Force. A report published in March 2004 by the US Department of State suggested that 12% of cocaine imports to the USA were transhipped through the Jamaica-Cuba-Bahamas corridor. Relations with the USA, however, improved in July after the Bahamian Government amended the country's extradition laws to give the state increased rights of appeal against the release of a suspect by the courts. (Of some 50 recent US extradition requests, 35 had been rejected by Bahamian courts.) These rights were exercised in September 2006 when alleged leading drugs-trafficker Samuel Knowles was extradited to Miami, Florida, and a Czech-born financier with Grenadian, Venezuelan and Irish nationality was extradited to the USA on corruption charges. The latter's attorney was a PLP member of Parliament, and former legal partner of the Prime Minister. In October 2005 the US Government agreed to extend its funding of the Bahamas' anti-drugs programmes.

Meanwhile, relations with the Bahamas' other neighbours, Haiti and Cuba, were strained by the influx of large numbers of illegal immigrants from both countries. In 1995–2003 more than 35,000 Haitian illegal migrants and refugees were deported from the Bahamas, with a peak figure of 7,589 in 2001. In November 2003 the human rights organization Amnesty International released a report that criticized prison conditions in the Bahamas and accused the country of mistreating asylum-seekers from Cuba and Haiti; the Christie Government countered that the report was 'unbalanced'. A report published in late 2005 found the Haitian population in the Bahamas to total between 30,000 and 60,000. More than 1,000 'undocumented' Haitians were apprehended by the Bahamas Defence Force in 2006. The Bahamas hosted the twice-yearly forum for the discussion of regional countries' efforts to address illegal migration and the burgeoning narcotics trade on 8 June 2007. The Narcotics Joint Task Force, comprising government representatives from the Bahamas, Turks and Caicos Islands and the USA, identified increased cocaine traffic from Hispaniola as an immediate threat to both Caribbean territories and resolved to work towards a more comprehensive integration of their respective law enforcement agencies' efforts to combat the illegal transhipment of migrants and drugs in the region.

Diplomatic relations with countries outside the Caribbean region were bolstered in October 2006 when the Bahamian Minister of Foreign Affairs, Frederick Mitchell, visited his Turkish counterpart in Ankara, Turkey, promoting greater tourism possibilities between the two countries and confirming the Bahamas' support for Turkey's candidacy as a non-permanent member of the UN Security Council.

In 2000 the Bahamas was listed by the Financial Action Task Force (FATF, see p. 416) as a 'non-co-operative' jurisdiction, and by the Organisation for Economic Co-operation and Development (OECD, see p. 347) as a tax haven. The Bahamas also received the lowest grade of bank supervision in a report by the Financial Stability Forum, a group of international regulators, and remained classified as a 'Country of Primary Concern' in the US International Narcotics Control Strategy Report, partly because of its banking secrecy laws and the size of its 'offshore' financial sector. The Government responded by establishing, in October 2000, a Financial Intelligence Unit and by adopting legislation intended to encourage transparency in the sector. As a result, in August 2001 the FATF removed the Bahamas from its 'blacklist'. In January 2002 an agreement to share information on tax matters with the USA was signed, while in March OECD accepted the Bahamas' commitment to improve the transparency of its financial sector. In June 2005 the FATF announced that it would continue to monitor the Bahamas' financial sector in the near future.

The Government in 2005 rejected the opportunity to join the Caribbean Single Market and Economy (CSME), which was launched on 1 January 2006 under the auspices of the Caribbean Community and Common Market (CARICOM, see p. 196). The Government argued that the CSME, which enshrined monetary union and the free movement of people among its signatory states, would place too great an economic and social burden on the Bahamas, one of the wealthier countries in the region.

Government

Legislative power is vested in the bicameral Parliament. The Senate has 16 members, of whom nine are appointed by the Governor-General on the advice of the Prime Minister, four by the Leader of the Opposition and three after consultation with the Prime Minister. The House of Assembly has 40 members, elected for five years (subject to dissolution) by universal adult suffrage. Executive power is vested in the British monarch, represented by a Governor-General, who is appointed on the Prime Minister's recommendation and who acts, in almost all matters, on the advice of the Cabinet. The Governor-General appoints the Prime Minister and, on the latter's recommendation, selects the other ministers. The Cabinet is responsible to the House of Assembly.

Defence

The Royal Bahamian Defence Force, a paramilitary coastguard, is the only security force in the Bahamas, and numbered 860 (including 70 women), as assessed at November 2007. Defence expenditure in 2007 was budgeted at an estimated B $45m.

Economic Affairs

In 2002, according to estimates by the World Bank, the Bahamas' gross national income (GNI), measured at average 2000–02 prices, was US $4,899m., equivalent to US $15,800 per head (or US $16,350 per head on an international purchasing-power parity basis). During 1996–2006 it was estimated that the population increased at an average annual rate of 1.4%. In 1996–2002 gross domestic product (GDP) per head increased, in real terms, by an annual average of 1.1%. Overall GDP increased, in real terms, at an average rate of 2.6% per year in 1996–2002; according to the Eastern Caribbean Central Bank, real GDP increased by 2.6% in 2005.

Agriculture, hunting, forestry and fishing, which together accounted for only 2.3% of GDP in 2004 and engaged an estimated 3.6% of the employed labour force in 2006, were developed by the Government in the 1990s in an attempt to reduce dependence on imports. In 2003, however, agricultural production accounted for only 1.0% of total land area. An increase in some areas of agricultural output has, none the less, resulted in the export of certain crops, particularly of cucumbers, tomatoes, pineapples, papayas, avocados, mangoes, limes and other citrus fruits. The development of commercial fishing has concentrated on conchs and crustaceans. In 2004 exports of Caribbean spiny lobster (crawfish) provided 21.5% of domestic export earnings, and accounted for 98.5% of the fishing total. There is also some exploitation of pine forests in the northern Bahamas.

Industry (comprising mining, manufacturing, construction and utilities) employed an estimated 16.1% of the working population in 2004 (construction accounted for 10.5%) and provided 16.9% of GDP in 2004.

Mining and quarrying contributed only 1.1% of GDP in 2004. The sector (including utilities) provided an estimated 1.5% of employment in 2006. The islands' principal mineral resource is salt. Minerals provided 13.0% of total export earnings in 2005. In late 2002 the Government granted a licence to an international oil company to explore for petroleum in Bahamian waters.

The manufacturing sector contributed some 4.9% of GDP in 2004 and employed 4.4% of the working population in 2006. The sector declined following the closure, in 1985, of the country's petroleum refinery (plans to build a new refinery in Grand Bahama proposed in 2006 had not advanced significantly by the end of that year). The principal branches of manufacturing were beverages, chemicals and printing and publishing. Exports of rum accounted for 7.8% of export earnings in 2004. The construction sector experienced much activity in the latter part of the 20th century and early 21st century, owing to the construction of hotels, tourist complexes and harbour developments. Plans for the establishment of a US $20m. manufacturing facility on Grand Bahama were announced in October 2006; the plant was expected to become operational in 2007.

Most of the energy requirements of the Bahamas are fulfilled by the petroleum that Venezuela and, particularly, Mexico provide under the San José Agreement (originally negotiated in 1980), which commits both the petroleum producers to selling subsidized supplies, on favourable terms, to the developing countries of the region. Imports of mineral products accounted for 20.8% of the total value of imports in 2005. In 2005 the Bahamas signed the PetroCaribe agreement with Venezuela, under which the Bahamas would be allowed to purchase petroleum from that country at reduced prices.

Service industries constitute the principal sectors of the economy, providing some 80.8% of GDP in 2004 and about 78.2% of total employment in 2006. In 1999 an international container transhipment facility was completed at Freeport, Grand Bahama; it was to act as an intercontinental hub port serving North America, the Caribbean and South America. Petroleum transhipment on Grand Bahama remains an important activity. At the end of 2006 a total of 1,402 vessels were registered under the Bahamian flag. With a combined displacement of 40.8m. grt, the fleet was the third largest in the world. Banking is the second most important economic activity in the Bahamas and there is a large 'offshore' financial sector. In May 2000 a stock exchange, where it was planned to develop trading in global depository receipts for overseas companies, became operational; by late 2007 it was trading the shares of 19 local companies. Tourism is the predominant sector of the economy, directly accounting for 15% of GDP in 1998 and employing some 30% of the working population. In 2004 the sector expanded by 5.5%. In 2005 estimated travel receipts covered 96.0% of the cost of goods imported. In 2006 some 85.8% of stop-over visitors were from the USA, although attempts are being made to attract visitors from other countries and improve air access to resorts. Visitor arrivals increased from 4.41m. in 2002 to 4.73m. in 2006. Receipts from tourism also increased from B $1,760m. in 2002 to $2,056m. in 2006. The Bahamas receives more cruise-ship arrivals annually than any other Caribbean destination. Amendments to the Western Hemisphere Travel Initiative—ratified by US Congress on 4 October 2006—requiring all US citizens travelling to and from the Caribbean to hold a valid passport, were described by the Caribbean Tourism Organization as potentially severely damaging to the region's tourism industry, rendering efforts to broaden the principal tourist catchment area beyond the USA all the more urgent. The measures were to be implemented as early as January 2007, although cruise-ship passengers were to be exempt from the ruling until 1 January 2009. It was hoped that the Cricket World Cup, to which several Caribbean nations played host in March and April 2007, would generate significant tourism revenues and renew interest in the region.

In 2006 the Bahamas recorded a visible trade deficit of B $1,931.9m., and there was a deficit of $1,564.7m. on the current account of the balance of payments. The USA is the principal trading partner of the Bahamas, providing 83.9% non-petroleum imports and taking 70.0% of non-petroleum exports in 2005. The principal imports in 2005 were mineral products (20.8%), machinery and mechanical appliances (14.2%), beverages, spirits and tobaccos (8.4% of total imports), and vehicles and transport equipment (7.9%). In that year the principal exports were plastics and plastic products (27.6% of total exports), live animals and animal products (18.2%), and products of chemical or allied industries (15.0%).

In 2005/06 there was a budgetary deficit of B $51.5m., equivalent to some 4.9% of GDP. In 2006/07 there was a budgetary deficit of B $92.9m. At 31 December 2005 the external debt of the central Government was some $286.5m. The debt-service ratio in that year was equivalent to 3.3% of the value of goods and services. The cost of servicing foreign currency debt in 2004 was $64.8m., equivalent to 6.3% of current revenue. The annual rate of inflation averaged 1.7% in 1995–2006; consumer prices increased by 1.8% in 2006. The rate of unemployment stood at some 9.7% of the labour force in 2006.

The Bahamas is a member of the Caribbean Community and Common Market (CARICOM, see p. 196), the Organization of American States (OAS, see p. 360), the Association of Caribbean States (see p. 411), and is a signatory of the Cotonou Agreement (see p. 301) with the European Union (see p. 244). The Government applied for membership of the World Trade Organization (see p. 396) in 2004, but negotiations had not advanced significantly towards accession by the end of 2006 when a public consultation remained pending.

Economic expansion through foreign investment was restricted in the 1990s by fears of widespread corruption and instability (caused by the activities of illegal drugs-trafficking networks in the islands); however, investor confidence was reported to have increased in the 21st century and in 2005 the Bahamas was rated as one of the western hemisphere's leading international financial centres by a banking industry magazine. In 2000 the Bahamas had been listed by the Financial Action Task Force (FATF, see p. 416) as a 'non-co-operative jurisdiction' and by the Organisation for Economic Co-operation and Development (OECD, see p. 347) as a tax haven. Following the introduction of regulatory legislation in late 2000, in 2001 the FATF removed the country from its 'blacklist', and OECD followed suit in March 2002. Legal challenges were made against various aspects of the new financial legislation, (although by late 2006 no major challenge had succeeded) and, as a consequence, the Progressive Liberal Party (PLP) Government, which had been elected in May 2002, pledged to review the regime. None the less, by the end of 2006 the Government had not relaxed controls significantly and a number of criminal investigations and troubling incidents in 2002–06 underlined the need for continuing regulatory vigilance. Moreover, in 2005 a US Department of State report on global money-laundering and drugs-trafficking listed the Bahamas as a 'major money laundering country'. The divestment of the state electricity company and of the loss-making Bahamasair Holdings was expected during the PLP administration, although plans had not advanced beyond the preliminary stage by the end of 2007 and, indeed, those regarding the airline had been postponed indefinitely. The liberalization of the telecommunications sector, including the partial privatization of the Bahamas Telcommunications Corporation, was also pending. A reduction in revenue from the tourism sector led the Government in late 2003 to announce its intention to reform the fiscal regime: in particular, the country's dependence on customs and excise taxes and stamp duties, incompatible with future regional and international trade agreements, was to be reduced; the loss was expected to be offset by the introduction of value-added tax. Meanwhile, the tourism sector continued to expand, despite reports that the industry had suffered from negative publicity surrounding the high crime rate on the islands and in other Caribbean destinations. In late 2005 the Government granted permission for the construction of a B $3,500m. tourist resort on Grand Bahama; the project was expected to create over 4,000 permanent new jobs. Further developments agreed by the Government in 2006 included a US $700m. resort on the island of Eleuthra and a $1,300m. luxury golf and tourism facility on New Providence island, scheduled for completion in 2008. It was estimated that the projects would provide some 1,600 construction jobs and 1,100 permanent roles on conclusion. In late 2006 the Government reached an agreement with Vancouver Airport Services whereby the Canadian company would manage and operate the Bahamas' Lynden Pindling International Airport (formerly Nassau International Airport) until 2016 and oversee a $225m. expansion of facilities. Tourism numbers continue to benefit from the improved infrastructure. The economic outlook for 2007–08 remained positive. GDP increased by 4.0% in 2006, owing largely to increased activity in the construction sector related to tourism and residential infrastructure projects. Economic growth of 3.8% and 3.6% was forecast for 2007 and 2008, respectively.

Education

Education is compulsory between the ages of five and 16 years, and is provided free of charge in government schools. There are several private and denominational schools. Primary education begins at five years of age and lasts for six years. Secondary education, beginning at the age of 11, also lasts for six years and is divided into two equal cycles. In 2004/05 88.7% of children in the relevant age-group were enrolled at primary level. In the same year 81.2% of children in the relevant age-group were enrolled at secondary level. The University of the West Indies has an extra-mural department in Nassau, offering degree courses in hotel management and tourism. The Bahamas Hotel Training College was established in 1992. The Bahamas Law School, part of the University of the West Indies, opened in 1998. Technical, teacher-training and professional qualifications can be obtained at the two campuses of the College of the Bahamas.

Government expenditure on education in 2006/07 was budgeted at B $258.6m. (or 18.1% of total spending from the General Budget). In late 2005 the Inter-American Development Bank approved a $18m. loan to the Bahamas for a national education and training programme.

Public Holidays

2008: 1 January (New Year's Day), 21 March (Good Friday), 24 March (Easter Monday), 12 May (Whit Monday), 6 June (Labour Day), 10 July (Independence Day), 4 August (Emancipation Day), 12 October (Discovery Day/Columbus Day/National Heroes Day), 25–26 December (Christmas).
2009: 1 January (New Year's Day), 10 April (Good Friday), 13 April (Easter Monday), 1 June (Whit Monday), 5 June (Labour Day), 10 July (Independence Day), 3 August (Emancipation Day), 12 October (Discovery Day/Columbus Day/National Heroes Day), 25–26 December (Christmas).

Weights and Measures

The imperial system is used.

Statistical Survey

Source (unless otherwise stated): The Central Bank of the Bahamas, Frederick St, POB N-4868, Nassau; tel. 322-2193; fax 322-4321; e-mail cbob@centralbankbahamas.com; internet www.centralbankbahamas.com.

AREA AND POPULATION

Area: 13,939 sq km (5,382 sq miles).

Population: 255,095 at census of 2 May 1990; 303,611 (males 147,715, females 155,896) at census of 1 May 2000; 327,100 at mid-2006. *By Island* (2000): New Providence 210,832; Grand Bahama 46,994; Andros 7,686; Eleuthera 7,999. Source: partly World Bank, *World Development Indicators*.

Density (mid-2006): 23.5 per sq km.

Principal Town (population in '000, incl. suburbs, UN estimate): Nassau (capital) 233 in mid-2005. Source: UN, *World Urbanization Prospects: The 2005 Revision*.

Births, Marriages and Deaths (2003, unless otherwise indicated): Registered live births 5,054 (birth rate 16.0 per 1,000); Registered deaths 1,649 (death rate 5.2 per 1,000); Registered marriages (2000) 1,787 (marriage rate 5.8 per 1,000). Sources: UN, *Demographic Yearbook*, *Population and Vital Statistics Report*, and Caribbean Development Bank, *Social and Economic Indicators*.

Expectation of Life (years at birth, WHO estimates): 72.8 (males 69.9; females 75.6) in 2005. Source: WHO, *World Health Statistics*.

Economically Active Population (persons aged 15 years and over, excl. armed forces, May 2006): Agriculture, hunting, forestry and fishing 6,050; Mining, quarrying, electricity, gas and water 2,435; Manufacturing 7,435; Construction 20,620; Wholesale and retail 24,735; Hotels and restaurants 26,850; Transport, storage and communication 11,245; Finance, insurance, real estate and other business services 18,815; Community, social and personal services 49,400; Activities not adequately defined 475; *Total employed* 168,060 (males 86,565, females 81,495); Unemployed 13,830 (males 6,375, females 7,455); *Total labour force* 181,890 (males 92,940, females 88,950). Source: ILO.

HEALTH AND WELFARE

Key Indicators

Total Fertility Rate (children per woman, 2005): 2.2.
Under-5 Mortality Rate (per 1,000 live births, 2005): 15.
HIV/AIDS (estimated % of persons aged 15–49, 2005): 3.3.
Physicians (per 1,000 head, 1998): 1.05.
Hospital Beds (per 1,000 head, 2004): 3.4.
Health Expenditure (2004): US $ per head (PPP): 1,348.6.
Health Expenditure (2004): % of GDP: 6.8.
Health Expenditure (2004): public (% of total): 50.1.
Access to Water (% of persons, 2004): 97.
Access to Sanitation (% of persons, 2004): 100.
Human Development Index (2005): ranking: 49.
Human Development Index (2005): value: 0.845.

For sources and definitions, see explanatory note on p. vi.

AGRICULTURE, ETC.

Principal Crops ('000 metric tons, 2005, FAO estimates): Sweet potatoes 0.8; Sugar cane 55.5; Bananas 2.1; Lemons and limes 10.7; Grapefruit and pomelos 16.9; Vegetables (incl. melons) 23.0; Fruits (excl. melons) 33.5.

Livestock ('000 head, year ending September 2005, FAO estimates): Cattle 0.8; Pigs 5.0; Sheep 6.5; Goats 14.5; Poultry 3,000.

Livestock Products ('000 metric tons, 2005, FAO estimates): Chicken meat 8.6; Cows' milk 0.7; Hen eggs 0.9.

THE BAHAMAS

Forestry ('000 cubic metres, 2006, FAO estimates): *Roundwood Removals (excl. bark):* Sawlogs and veneer logs 17 (output assumed to be unchanged since 1992); *Sawnwood Production (incl. railway sleepers):* Coniferous (softwood) 1.4 (output assumed to be unchanged since 1970).

Fishing (metric tons, live weight, 2005, estimates): Capture 11,347 (Nassau grouper 263; Snappers 648; Caribbean spiny lobster 9,317; Stromboid conchs 578); Aquaculture 10; *Total catch* 11,357.

Source: FAO.

MINING

Production ('000 metric tons, 2005): Unrefined salt 1,270; Aragonite 2. Source: US Geological Survey.

INDUSTRY

Production (million kWh, 2005): Electric energy 2,015.32.

FINANCE

Currency and Exchange Rates: 100 cents = 1 Bahamian dollar (B $). *Sterling, US Dollar and Euro Equivalents* (31 December 2007): £1 sterling = B $2.003; US $1 = B $1.000; €1 = B $1.472; B $100 = £49.92 = US $100.00 = €67.93. *Exchange Rate:* Since February 1970 the official exchange rate, applicable to most transactions, has been US $1 = B $1, i.e. the Bahamian dollar has been at par with the US dollar. There is also an investment currency rate, applicable to certain capital transactions between residents and non-residents and to direct investments outside the Bahamas. Since 1987 this exchange rate has been fixed at US $1 = B $1.225.

General Budget (B $ million, 2006/07, budget): *Revenue:* Taxation 1,196.0 (Taxes on international trade and transactions 725.7; Taxes on property 70.7; Taxes on companies 78.7); Other current revenue 136.0; Capital revenue 6.5; Grants 0.5; Total 1,339.0. *Expenditure:* Current expenditure 1,269.6 (Wages and salaries 553.7, Goods and services 275.4, Interest payments 141.4, Subsidies and transfers 299.2); Capital expenditure and net lending 162.4; Total 1,431.9.

International Reserves (B $ million at 31 December 2006): Reserve position in IMF 9.4; Foreign exchange 451.9; Total 461.3. Source: IMF, *International Financial Statistics*.

Money Supply (B $ million at 31 December 2006): Currency outside banks 202; Demand deposits at deposit money banks 1,018; Total money (incl. others) 1,239. Source: IMF, *International Financial Statistics*.

Cost of Living (Consumer Price Index; base: 2000 = 100): 107.9 in 2004; 109.6 in 2005; 112.2 in 2006. Source: IMF, *International Financial Statistics*.

Gross Domestic Product (B $ million at current prices): 5,502.6 in 2003; 5,661.0 in 2004; 5,869.5 in 2005 (preliminary).

Expenditure on the Gross Domestic Product (B $ million at current prices, 2005, preliminary): Government final consumption expenditure 875.9; Private final consumption expenditure 3,980.9; Change in stocks 174.0; Gross fixed capital formation 1,752.0; *Total domestic expenditure* 6,782.8; Exports of goods and services 2,882.7; *Less* Imports of goods and services 3,624.4; Statistical discrepancy −171.6; *GDP in purchasers' values* 5,869.5.

Gross Domestic Product by Economic Activity (B $ million at current prices, 2004, provisional): Agriculture, hunting, forestry and fishing 120.6; Mining and quarrying 58.6; Manufacturing 262.0; Electricity and water 188.7; Construction 395.1; Wholesale and retail trade 668.3; Restaurants and hotels 624.5; Transport, storage and communications 507.6; Finance, insurance, real estate and business services 1,786.3; Government services 358.8; Education 269.6; Health 184.1; Other community, social and personal services 375.2; *Sub-total* 5,799.4; *Less* Financial intermediation services indirectly measured and other indirect taxes 829.4; *Gross value added in basic prices* 4,970.0; Taxes on products 568.0; *Less* Subsidies on products 45.3; Statistical discrepancy 168.2; *GDP in purchasers' values* 5,661.0.

Balance of Payments (B $ million, 2006, preliminary): Exports of goods f.o.b. 692.2; Imports of goods f.o.b. −2,624.1; *Trade balance* −1,931.9; Services (net) 533.3; *Balance on goods and services* −1,398.7; Other income (net) −218.0; *Balance on goods, services and income* −1,616.7; Current transfers (net) 52.1; *Current balance* −1,564.7; Capital account (net) −63.5; Financial account (net) 1,203.4; Net errors and omissions 345.6; *Overall balance* −79.1.

EXTERNAL TRADE

Principal Commodities (B $ million, 2005, distribution according to Harmonised System): *Imports c.i.f.:* Live animals and animal products 111.3; Beverages, spirits, tobacco, etc. 215.0; Mineral products 534.8; Products of chemical or allied industries 179.2; Plastics and articles thereof, etc. 101.3; Base metals and articles of base metals 173.4; Machinery, mechanical appliances, etc. 365.3; Vehicles, transport equipment, etc. 202.1; Miscellaneous manufactured articles 114.3; Total (incl. others) 2,567.2. *Exports (incl. re-exports) f.o.b.:* Live animals and animal products 78.2; Mineral products 55.5; Products of chemical or allied industries 64.4; Plastics and articles thereof, etc. 118.2; Machinery, mechanical appliances, etc. 32.0; Total (incl. others) 450.8.

Principal Trading Partners (B $ million, 2005): *Imports c.i.f.:* USA 2,155.1; Curaçao 184.4; Puerto Rico 49.9; Japan 30.3; Total (incl. others) 2,567.2. *Exports f.o.b.:* USA 295.2; France 35.5; Canada 19.1; United Kingdom 19.9; Total (incl. others) 450.8.

TRANSPORT

Road Traffic (vehicles in use, '000, 2001): Passenger cars 80; Commercial vehicles 25. Source: Auto and Truck International (Illinois), *World Automotive Market Report*.

Shipping: *Merchant Fleet* (vessels registered at 31 December 2006): Number 1,402; Displacement ('000 grt) 40,831 (Source: Lloyd's Register-Fairplay, *World Fleet Statistics*). *International Sea-borne Freight Traffic* (estimates, '000 metric tons, 1990): Goods loaded 5,920; Goods unloaded 5,705 (Source: UN, *Monthly Bulletin of Statistics*).

Civil Aviation (2003): Kilometres flown (million) 6; Passengers carried ('000) 1,601; Passenger-km (million) 388; Total ton-km of freight (million) 48. Source: UN, *Statistical Yearbook*.

TOURISM

Visitor Arrivals ('000): 5,004 (1,450 by air, 3,554 by sea) in 2004; 4,780 (1,515 by air, 3,265 by sea) in 2005; 4,731 (1,492 by air, 3,239 by sea) in 2006.

Tourism Receipts (B $ million, incl. passenger transport): 1,759 in 2003; 1,884 in 2004; 2,069 in 2005; 2,056 in 2006.

COMMUNICATIONS MEDIA

Radio Receivers (1997): 215,000 in use.

Television Receivers (1999): 73,000 in use.

Telephones (2005): 139,900 main lines in use.

Facsimile Machines (1996): 500 in use.

Mobile Cellular Telephones (2005): 186,000 subscribers.

Internet Users (2006): 103,000.

Broadband (2006): 13,400 subscribers.

Daily Newspapers (1996, unless otherwise indicated): 3 titles (total circulation 28,000 copies); 4 titles in 2004.

Sources: UN, *Statistical Yearbook*; UNESCO, *Statistical Yearbook*; International Telecommunication Union.

EDUCATION

Pre-primary (2002/03, unless otherwise indicated): 20 schools (1996/97); 338 teachers; 3,771 pupils.

Primary (2003/04, unless otherwise indicated): 113 schools (1996/97); 1,734 teachers; 34,040 pupils.

Secondary (2003/04, unless otherwise indicated): 37 junior/senior high schools (1990); 1,700 teachers; 28,070 students.

Tertiary (1987): 249 teachers; 5,305 students. In 2002 there were 3,463 students registered at the College of the Bahamas.

Sources: UNESCO, *Statistical Yearbook*; UN, Economic Commission for Latin America and the Caribbean, *Statistical Yearbook*; Caribbean Development Bank, *Social and Economic Indicators 2001*.

Adult Literacy Rate (UNESCO estimates): 95.8% (males 95.0%; females 95.0%) in 2003. Source: UN Development Programme, *Human Development Report*.

Directory

The Constitution

A representative House of Assembly was first established in 1729, although universal adult suffrage was not introduced until 1962. A new Constitution for the Commonwealth of the Bahamas came into force at independence, on 10 July 1973. The main provisions of the Constitution are summarized below.

Parliament consists of a Governor-General (representing the British monarch, who is Head of State), a nominated Senate and an elected House of Assembly. The Governor-General appoints the Prime Minister and, on the latter's recommendation, the remainder of the Cabinet. Apart from the Prime Minister, the Cabinet has no fewer than eight other ministers, of whom one is the Attorney-General. The Governor-General also appoints a Leader of the Opposition.

The Senate (upper house) consists of 16 members, of whom nine are appointed by the Governor-General on the advice of the Prime Minister, four on the advice of the Leader of the Opposition and three on the Prime Minister's advice after consultation with the Leader of the Opposition. The House of Assembly (lower house) has 40 members. A Constituencies Commission reviews numbers and boundaries at intervals of not more than five years and can recommend alterations for approval of the House. The life of Parliament is limited to a maximum of five years.

The Constitution provides for a Supreme Court and a Court of Appeal.

The Government

HEAD OF STATE

Monarch: HM Queen ELIZABETH II (succeeded to the throne 6 February 1952).
Governor-General: ARTHUR HANNA (took office 1 February 2006).

THE CABINET
(March 2008)

Prime Minister and Minister of Finance: HUBERT INGRAHAM.
Deputy Prime Minister and Minister of Foreign Affairs: THEODORE BRENT SYMONETTE.
Minister of National Security and Immigration: ORVILLE (TOMMY) TURNQUEST.
Minister of Tourism and Aviation: NEKO GRANT.
Minister of Agriculture and Marine Resources: LAWRENCE (LARRY) CARTWRIGHT.
Minister of Lands and Local Government: SIDNEY COLLIE.
Minister of Education, Youth, Sports and Culture: CARL BETHEL.
Minister of Health and Social Development: Dr HUBERT MINNIS.
Minister of Works and Transport: Dr EARL DEVEAUX.
Attorney-General and Minister of Legal Affairs: Sen. CLAIRE HEPBURN.
Minister of Maritime Affairs and Labour: Sen. DION FOULKES.
Minister of Housing and National Insurance: KENNETH RUSSELL.
Minister of State in the Ministry of Legal Affairs: THOMAS DESMOND BANNISTER.
Minister of State in the Ministry of Finance: ZHIVARGO LAING.
Minister of State in the Ministry of Tourism and Aviation: BRANVILLE MCCARTNEY.
Minister of State with responsibility for Immigration: Sen. ELMA CAMPBELL.
Minister of State with responsibility for Culture: CHARLES MAYNARD.
Minister of State with responsibility for Public Utilities: PHENTON NEYMOUR.
Minister of State with responsibility for Social Development: LORETTA BUTLER TURNER.
Minister of State with responsibility for Youth and Sports: BYRAN WOODSIDE.

MINISTRIES

Attorney-General's Office and Ministry of Legal Affairs: 7th Floor, Post Office Bldg, East Hill St, POB N-3007, Nassau; tel. 502-0400; fax 322-2255.
Office of the Prime Minister: Sir Cecil V. Wallace-Whitfield Centre, West Bay St, POB CB-10980, Nassau; tel. 327-5826; fax 327-5806; e-mail info@opm.gov.bs.
Office of the Deputy Prime Minister: East Hill St, POB N-3746, Nassau; tel. 322-7624; fax 328-8212; e-mail psmns@hotmail.com.
Ministry of Agriculture and Marine Resources: Levy Bldg, East Bay St, POB N-3028, Nassau; tel. 325-7502; fax 322-1767.
Ministry of Education, Youth, Sports and Culture: Thompson Blvd, POB N-3913, Nassau; tel. 502-2700; fax 322-8491; e-mail info@moe.gov.bs; internet moe.gov.bs.
Ministry of Finance: Cecil V. Wallace-Whitfield Centre, West Bay St, POB N-3017, Nassau; tel. 327-1530; fax 327-1618; e-mail mofgeneral@bahamas.gov.bs; internet www.bahamas.gov.bs/finance.
Ministry of Financial Services and Investments: Goodman's Bay Corporate Centre, POB N-7770, Nassau; tel. 356-5956; fax 356-5990; e-mail info@investbahamas.org; internet www.investbahamas.org.
Ministry of Foreign Affairs: East Hill St, POB N-3746, Nassau; tel. 322-7624; fax 328-8212; e-mail mfabahamas@batelnet.bs; internet www.mfabahamas.org.
Ministry of Health and Social Development: Meeting St, POB N-3730, Nassau; tel. 502-4700; fax 325-5421; internet www.bahamas.gov.bs/health.
Ministry of Housing and National Insurance: Claughton House, Frederick St, POB N-4849, Nassau; tel. 322-6027; fax 322-6064.
Ministry of Lands and Local Government: Manx Corporate Centre, West Bay St, POB N-3040, Nassau; tel. 328-2700; fax 328-1324.
Ministry of Maritime Affairs and Labour: Post Office Bldg, 2nd Floor, East Hill St, POB N-3008, Nassau; tel. 323-7814; fax 325-1920.
Ministry of National Security and Immigration: East Hill St, POB N-3746, Nassau; tel. 322-7624; fax 328-8212.
Ministry of Tourism and Aviation: Bolam House, George St, POB N-3701, Nassau; tel. 322-7500; fax 302-2098.
Ministry of Works and Transport: John F. Kennedy Dr., POB N-8156, Nassau; tel. 322-4830; fax 326-6629; e-mail admin@mowt.bs; internet www.bahamas.gov.bs/publicworks.

Legislature

PARLIAMENT

Senate

President: LYNN HOLOWESKO.
There are 16 nominated members.

House of Assembly

Speaker: ALVIN SMITH.
The House has 41 members.
General Election, 2 May 2007

Party	Seats
Free National Movement (FNM)	23
Progressive Liberal Party (PLP)	18
Total	**41**

Election Commission

Parliamentary Registration Department: c/o Ministry of National Security, Farrington Road, POB N-1653, Nassau; tel. 325-2888; fax 322-1637; e-mail errolbethel@hotmail.com; internet www.bahamas.gov.bs/parliamentary; Chair. ERROL BETHEL.

Political Organizations

Bahamas Democratic Movement (BDM): 71 Marathon Rd, POB SS 5685, Nassau; tel. 341-3991; fax 393-9777; e-mail info@bdmparty.com; internet www.bdmparty.com; f. 2000; Leader CASSIUS V. STUART; Chair. TOLONUS SANDS.

THE BAHAMAS
Directory

Bahamas Freedom Alliance (BFA): Nassau; formed Coalition Plus Labour alliance with the Coalition for Democratic Reform and the PLM to contest 2002 legislative elections; Leader D. HALSTON MOULTRIE.

Free National Movement (FNM): 144 Mackey St, POB N-10713, Nassau; tel. 393-7853; fax 393-7914; e-mail info@freenationalmovement.org; internet www.freenationalmovement.org; f. 1972; Leader HUBERT ALEXANDER INGRAHAM; Deputy Leader BRENT T. SYMONETTE.

People's Labour Movement (PLM): Nassau; formed Coalition Plus Labour alliance with BFA and the Coalition for Democratic Reform to contest 2002 legislative elections; Leader OBIE FERGUSON.

Progressive Liberal Party (PLP): Sir Lynden Pindling Centre, PLP House, Farrington Rd, POB N-547, Nassau; tel. 325-5492; fax 328-0808; internet www.myplp.com; f. 1953; centrist party; Leader PERRY G. CHRISTIE; Chair. RAYNARD S. RIGBY.

Diplomatic Representation

EMBASSIES IN THE BAHAMAS

China, People's Republic: 3 Orchard Terrace, Village Rd, POB SS-6389, Nassau; tel. 393-1415; fax 393-0733; e-mail chinaemb_bs@mfa.gov.cn; internet bs.china-embassy.org; Ambassador HU DINGXIAN.

Cuba: Cash Fountain Bldg, Armstrong and Shirley Sts, POB EE-15679, Nassau; tel. 356-3473; fax 356-3472; e-mail cubanembassy@coralwave.com; Ambassador FÉLIX WILSON HERNÁNDEZ.

Haiti: Sears House, Shirley St and Sears Rd, POB N-3036, Nassau; tel. 326-0325; fax 322-7712; Ambassador LOUIS HAROLD JOSEPH.

USA: Mosmar Bldg, Queen St, POB N-8197, Nassau; tel. 322-1181; fax 328-7838; e-mail embnas@state.gov; internet nassau.usembassy.gov; Ambassador NED L. SIEGEL.

Judicial System

The Judicial Committee of the Privy Council (based in the United Kingdom), the Bahamas Court of Appeal, the Supreme Court and the Magistrates' Courts are the main courts of the Bahamian judicial system.

All courts have both a criminal and civil jurisdiction. The Magistrates' Courts are presided over by professionally qualified Stipendiary and Circuit Magistrates in New Providence and Grand Bahama, and by Island Administrators sitting as Magistrates in the Family Islands.

Whereas all magistrates are empowered to try offences that may be tried summarily, a Stipendiary and Circuit Magistrate may, with the consent of the accused, also try certain less serious indictable offences. In September 2006 the Bahamas' sole coroner's court was disbanded and magistrates endowed with the power to hear inquests. The jurisdiction of magistrates is, however, limited by law.

The Supreme Court consists of the Chief Justice, two Senior Justices and six Justices. The Supreme Court also sits in Freeport, with two Justices.

Appeals in almost all matters lie from the Supreme Court to the Court of Appeal, with further appeal in certain instances to the Judicial Committee of the Privy Council.

Supreme Court of the Bahamas

Bank Lane, POB N-167, Nassau; tel. 322-3315; fax 323-6463; internet www.bahamassupremecourt.gov.bs; Chief Justice Sir BURTON HALL.

Registrar of the Supreme Court: ESTELLE G. GRAY EVANS, The Registry, Ansbacher House, East and Shirley Sts, POB N-167 Nassau; tel. 322-4348; fax 325-6895; e-mail registrar@courts.gov.bs.

Court of Appeal: Claughton House, 3rd Floor, POB N-3209, Nassau; tel. 328-5400; fax 323-4659; e-mail info@courtofappeal.org.bs; internet wwww.courtofappeal.org.bs; Pres. Dame JOAN SAWYER.

Magistrates' Courts: POB N-421, Nassau; tel. 325-4573; fax 323-1446; 15 magistrates and a circuit magistrate.

Office of the Attorney-General: Post Office Bldg, 3rd Floor, East Hill St, POB N-3007, Nassau; tel. 322-1141; fax 322-2255; Dir of Legal Affairs DEBORAH FRASER; Dir of Public Prosecutions BERNARD TURNER.

Registrar-General: (vacant), Rodney Bain Bldg, 50 Shirley St, POB N-532, Nassau; tel. 322-3316; fax 322-5553; e-mail registrargeneral@bahamas.gov.bs; internet www.bahamas.gov.bs/rgd.

Religion

Most of the population profess Christianity, but there are also small communities of Jews and Muslims.

CHRISTIANITY

In 2007 about 35% of the population were Baptists, 15% were Anglican and about 14% were Roman Catholic. Other important denominations included the Pentecostal Church, the Church of Christ and the Methodists.

Bahamas Christian Council: POB N-3103, Nassau; tel. 326-7114; f. 1948; 27 mem. churches; Pres. Rev. RICARDO GRANT.

The Roman Catholic Church

The Bahamas comprises the single archdiocese of Nassau. At 31 December 2005 there were an estimated 48,967 adherents in the Bahamas. The Archbishop participates in the Antilles Episcopal Conference (whose Secretariat is based in Port of Spain, Trinidad and Tobago). The Turks and Caicos Islands are also under the jurisdiction of the Archbishop of Nassau.

Archbishop of Nassau: Most Rev. PATRICK PINDER, The Hermitage, West St, POB N-8187, Nassau; tel. 322-8919; fax 322-2599; e-mail rcchancery@batelnet.bs.

The Anglican Communion

Anglicans in the Bahamas are adherents of the Church in the Province of the West Indies. The diocese also includes the Turks and Caicos Islands.

Archbishop of the West Indies, and Bishop of Nassau and the Bahamas: Most Rev. DREXEL WELLINGTON GOMEZ, Bishop's Lodge, Sands Rd, POB N-656, Nassau; tel. 322-3015; fax 322-7943; internet www.christchurchbahamas.org.

Other Christian Churches

Bahamas Conference of the Methodist Church: POB SS-5103, Nassau; tel. 393-3726; fax 393-8135; e-mail bcmc@bahamasmethodist.org; internet bahamasmethodist.org; 34 mem. churches; Pres. KENRIS L. CAREY.

Bahamas Conference of Seventh-day Adventists: Tonique Williams-Darling Hwy, POB N-356, Nassau; tel. 341-4021; fax 341-4088; e-mail info@bahamasconference.org; internet www.bahamasconference.org; Pres. Dr LEONARD JOHNSON.

Greek Orthodox Church: Church of the Annunciation, West St, POB N-823, Nassau; tel. 322-4382; e-mail frtedbita@annunciation.bs.goarch.org; internet www.annunciation.bs.goarch.org; f. 1928; part of the Archdiocese of North and South America, based in New York (USA); Priest Rev. TEODOR BITA.

Other denominations include African Methodist Episcopal, the Assemblies of Brethren, Christian Science, the Jehovah's Witnesses, the Salvation Army, Pentecostal, Presbyterian, Baptist, Lutheran and Assembly of God churches.

OTHER RELIGIONS

Bahá'í Faith

Bahá'í National Spiritual Assembly: POB N-7105, Nassau; tel. 326-0607; e-mail nsabaha@mail.com; internet www.bs.bahai.org.

Islam

There is a small community of Muslims in the Bahamas.

Islamic Centre: Carmichael Rd, POB N-10711, Nassau; tel. 341-6612; fax 364-6233; e-mail jamaa.ahlussunnah@gmail.com; internet www.geocities.com/nassaumasjid.

Islamic Centre Jamaat Ul-Islam: 13 Davies St, Oakes Field, POB N-10711, Nassau; tel. 325-0413.

Judaism

Most of the Bahamian Jewish community are based on Grand Bahama.

Bahamas Jewish Congregation Synagogue: Luis de Torres Synagogue, East Sunrise Hwy, POB F-1761, Freeport; tel. 373-2008; fax 373-2130; e-mail hurst100@yahoo.com; Pres. GEOFF HURST.

The Press

NEWSPAPERS

The Abaconian: Marsh Harbour, POB AB-20551, Abaco; tel. 367-2677; fax 367-3677; e-mail information@abaconian.com; internet abaconian.com; f. 1993.

The Bahama Journal: Media House, East St North, POB N-8610, Nassau; tel. 325-3082; fax 325-3996; internet www.jonesbahamas.com; daily; circ. 5,000.

The Freeport News: Cedar St, POB F-40007, Freeport; tel. 352-8321; fax 351-3449; e-mail oswaldtbrown@hotmail.com; internet freeport.nassauguardian.net; f. 1961; owned by *The Nassau Guardian*; daily; Gen. Man. DORLAN COLLIE; Editor ROBYN ADDERLEY; circ. 5,000.

The Nassau Guardian: 4 Carter St, Oakes Field, POB N-3011, Nassau; tel. 302-2300; fax 328-8943; e-mail editor@nasguard.com; internet www.thenassauguardian.com; f. 1844; daily; Gen. Man. CHARLES CARTER; Man. Editor ALISON BETHEL; circ. 15,000.

The Punch: POB N-4081, Nassau; tel. 322-7112; fax 323-5268; e-mail thepunch@coralwave.com; 2 a week; Editor IVAN JOHNSON; circ. 25,000.

The Tribune: Shirley St, POB N-3207, Nassau; tel. 322-1986; fax 328-2398; e-mail steve@100jamz.com; f. 1903; daily; Man. Editor JOHN MARQUIS; Contact STEPHEN HAUGHEY; circ. 15,000.

PERIODICALS

The Bahamas Financial Digest: Miramar House, 2nd Floor, Bay and Christie Sts, POB N-4824, Nassau; tel. 322-5030; fax 326-2849; e-mail bfd@bahamas.net.bs; f. 1973; 4 a year; business and investment; Publr and Editor MICHAEL A. SYMONETTE; circ. 15,890.

Bahamas Tourist News: Bayparl Bldg, Parliament St, POB N-4855, Nassau; tel. 322-4528; fax 322-4527; e-mail starpub@batelnet.bs; f. 1962; monthly; Editor BOBBY BOWER; circ. 371,000 (annually).

Nassau City Magazine: Miramar House, Bay and Christie Sts, POB N-4824, Nassau; tel. 356-2981; fax 326-2849.

Official Gazette: c/o Cabinet Office, POB N-7147, Nassau; tel. 322-2805; weekly; publ. by the Cabinet Office.

What's On Magazine: Woodes Rogers Wharf, POB CB-11713, Nassau; tel. 323-2323; fax 322-3428; e-mail info@whatsonbahamas.com; internet www.whatsonbahamas.com; monthly; Publr NEIL ABERLE.

Publishers

Bahamas Free Press Ltd: POB CB-13309, Nassau; tel. 323-8961.

Benchmark Publishing Co Ltd: Farrington Rd, POB CB-12957, Nassau; tel. 323-3398; fax 326-2020; e-mail benchmark@batelnet.bs.

Etienne Dupuch Jr Publications Ltd: Oakes Field, POB N-7513, Nassau; tel. 323-5665; fax 323-5728; e-mail info@dupuch.com; f. 1959; publishes *Bahamas Handbook*, *Trailblazer* maps, *What To Do* magazines, *Welcome Bahamas*, *Tadpole* (educational colouring book) series and *Dining and Entertainment Guide*; Dirs ETIENNE DUPUCH, JR, S. P. DUPUCH.

Guanima Press: East Bay St, POB CB-13151, Nassau; tel. 393-3221.

Media Enterprises Ltd: 31 Shirley Park Ave, POB N-9240, Nassau; tel. 325-8210; fax 325-8065; e-mail info@bahamasmedia.com; internet www.bahamasmedia.com; f. 1986; educational and other non-fiction books; Pres. and Gen. Man. LARRY A. SMITH; Publishing Dir NEIL E. SEALEY.

Printing Tours and Publishing: Miramar House, Bay and Christie Sts, POB N-4846, Nassau; tel. 356-2981; fax 356-7118.

Star Publishers Ltd: Bayparl Bldg, Parliament St, POB N-4855, Nassau; tel. 322-3724; fax 322-4527; e-mail starpub@bahamas.net.bs; CEO BOB BOWER.

Broadcasting and Communications

TELECOMMUNICATIONS

The telecommunications sector was in the process of being opened to private participation in 2008.

Bahamas Telecommunications Co (BTC): John F. Kennedy Dr., POB N-3048, Nassau; tel. 302-7008; fax 326-8423; internet www.btcbahamas.com; f. 1966, fmrly known as BaTelCo; state-owned; intended sale of 49% stake to private investors failed in 2003; a subsequent deal to privatize an identical share was negotiated with Bluewater Ventures but remained pending in early 2008; Chair. GREGORY BETHEL; Pres. and CEO LEON WILLIAMS.

Cable Bahamas Ltd: Robinson Rd at Marathon, POB CB-13050, Nassau; tel. 356-8940; fax 356-8997; e-mail info@cablebahamas.com; internet www.cablebahamas.com; f. 1995; provides cable television and internet services; Chair. and CEO BRENDAN PADDICK; Dir and Pres. ANTHONY BUTLER.

BROADCASTING

Radio

Broadcasting Corporation of the Bahamas: 3rd Terrace, Centreville, POB N-1347, Nassau; tel. 322-4623; fax 322-6598; internet www.znsbahamas.com; f. 1936; govt-owned; operates the ZNS radio and television network; Chair. CALSEY JOHNSON; Gen. Man. ANTHONY FOSTER.

Radio ZNS Bahamas: internet www.znsbahamas.com; f. 1936; broadcasts 24 hours per day on four stations: the main Radio Bahamas ZNS1, Radio New Providence ZNS2, which are both based in Nassau, Radio Power 104.5 FM, and the Northern Service (ZNS3—Freeport); f. 1973; Station Man. ANTHONY FORSTER; Programme Man. TANYA PINDER.

Cool 96 FM: Yellow Pine Street, POB F-40773, Freeport, Grand Bahama; tel. 351-2665; fax 352-8709; e-mail kflores@cool96fm.com; internet cool96fm.com; opened office in Nassau in Jan. 2005; Pres. and Gen. Man. ANDREA GOTTLIEB.

Love 97 FM: Bahamas Media House, East St North, POB N-3909, Nassau; tel. 356-2555; fax 356-7256; e-mail twilliams@jonescommunications.com; internet www.love97fm.com; operated by Jones Communications Ltd.

More 94 FM: Carmichael Rd, POB CR-54245, Nassau; tel. 361-2447; fax 361-2448; e-mail media@more94fm.com; internet www.more94fm.com.

One Hundred JAMZ: Shirley and Deveaux St, POB N-3207, Nassau; tel. 328-4771; fax 356-5343; e-mail michelle@100jamz.com; internet www.100jamz.com; operated by *The Tribune* newspaper; Gen. Man. STEPHEN HAUGHEY; Programme Dir ERIC WARD.

Television

Broadcasting Corporation of the Bahamas: see Radio.

Bahamas Television: f. 1977; broadcasts for Nassau, New Providence and the Central Bahamas; transmitting power of 50,000 watts; full colour; Programme Man. CARL BETHEL.

US television programmes and some satellite programmes can be received. Most islands have a cable television service.

Finance

The Bahamas developed into one of the world's foremost financial centres (there are no corporation, income, capital gains or with-holding taxes or estate duty), and finance has become a significant feature of the economy. At 31 December 2005 there were 250 'offshore' banks in operation in the islands.

BANKING
(cap. = capital; res = reserves; dep. = deposits; m. = million; brs = branches)

Central Bank

The Central Bank of the Bahamas: Frederick St, POB N-4868, Nassau; tel. 322-2193; fax 322-4321; e-mail cbob@centralbankbahamas.com; internet www.centralbankbahamas.com; f. 1974; bank of issue; cap. B $3.0m., res B $101.4m., dep. B $340.8m. (Dec. 2005); Gov. and Chair. WENDY M. CRAIGG.

Development Bank

The Bahamas Development Bank: Cable Beach, West Bay St, POB N-3034, Nassau; tel. 327-5780; fax 327-5047; internet bahamasdevelopmentbank.com; f. 1978 to fund approved projects and channel funds into appropriate investments; total assets B $58.3m. (Dec. 2004); Chair. K. NEVILLE ADDERLEY; Man. Dir GEORGE E. RODGERS; 3 brs.

Principal Banks

Bank of the Bahamas Ltd (Bank of the Bahamas International): Claughton House, Shirley and Charlotte Sts, POB N-7118, Nassau; tel. 326-2560; fax 325-2762; internet info.bob@bankbahamas.com; internet www.bankbahamasonline.com; f. 1970 as Bank of Montreal (Bahamas and Caribbean); name changed as above in 2002; 50% owned by Govt, 50% owned by c. 4,000 Bahamian shareholders; cap. B $12.0m., res B $8.7m., dep. B $398.3m. (June 2005); Chair. A. L. JARRETT; Man. Dir PAUL MCWEENEY; 10 brs.

Banque Privée Edmond de Rothschild Ltd: 51 Frederick St, POB N-1136, Nassau; tel. 328-8121; fax 328-8115; internet www.lcf-rothschild.bs; f. 1997; owned by Banque Privée Edmond de Rothschild SA, Geneva; cap. 15.0m. Swiss francs, res 12.0m. Swiss francs, dep. 26.9m. Swiss francs (Dec. 2005); Chair. ROBERT MISRAHI; Dir CLAUDE MESSULAM; Country Contact DOMINIQUE ADRIEN.

THE BAHAMAS

BNP Paribas (Bahamas) Ltd: Scotiabank Building, 3rd Floor, Rawson Square, POB N-4915, Nassau; tel. 326-5935; fax 326-5871; internet www.bnpparibas.com; Man. Dir ANDRÉ LAMOTHE.

BSI Overseas (Bahamas) Ltd (Italy): Bayside Executive Park, West Bay St, POB N-7130, Nassau; tel. 702-1200; fax 702-1250; internet www.bs.bsibank.com; f. 1969 as Banca della Svizzera Italiana (Overseas) Ltd; wholly owned subsidiary of BSI SA Lugano; name changed as above 1990; cap. US $10.0m., res US $25.8m., dep. US $2,476.7m. (Dec. 2006); Chair. RETO KESSLER; Man. Dir NICOLA GUSCETTI.

Canadian Imperial Bank of Commerce (CIBC) (Canada): Goodman's Bay Corporate Centre, West Bay St, POB 3933, Nassau; tel. 356-1800; fax 322-3692; e-mail privatebanking@cibc.com; internet www.cibc.com; Area Man. TERRY HILTS; 9 brs.

Citibank NA (USA): Citibank Bldg, 4th Floor, Thompson Blvd, Oakes Field, POB N-8158, Nassau; tel. 322-6800; fax 302-8625; internet www.citibank.com; Gen. Man. ALISON JOHNSTON; 2 brs.

Commonwealth Bank Ltd: East Bay St, POB SS 6263, Nassau; tel. 322-1154; fax 393-7663; e-mail cbinquiry@combankltd.com; internet www.combankltd.com; f. 1960; total assets B $17m. (Dec. 2002); Pres., CEO and Dir WILLIAM BATEMAN SANDS, Jr; Chair. T. BASWELL DONALDSON; 9 brs.

Crédit Suisse (Bahamas) Ltd (Switzerland): Bahamas Financial Centre, 4th Floor, Shirley and Charlotte Sts, POB N-4928, Nassau; tel. 356-8100; fax 326-6589; f. 1968; subsidiary of Crédit Suisse Zurich; portfolio and asset management, 'offshore' company management, trustee services, foreign exchange; cap. US $12.0m., res US $20.0m., dep. US $579.2m. (Dec. 2004); CEO and Man. Dir EUGEN SCHAEFLI; Chair. JOACHIM STRÄHLE.

Eni International Bank Ltd: British American Insurance House, 1st Floor, Marlborough St, POB SS-6377, Nassau; tel. 322-1928; fax 323-8600; e-mail eib-info@enibank.eni.it; f. 1971 as Tradinvest Bank and Trust Company of Nassau Ltd; changed name as above in 1985; cap. US $50.0m., dep. US $310.6m., total assets US $377.5m. (Dec. 2005); Pres., Chair. and Man. Dir PAOLO CARMOSINO.

FirstCaribbean International Bank Ltd: Bahamas International Banking Centre, Shirley St, POB N-8350, Nassau; tel. 302-6000; fax 302-6091; internet www.firstcaribbeanbank.com; f. 2002 following merger of Caribbean operations of Barclays Bank PLC and CIBC; Barclays Bank relinquished its stake to CIBC in June 2006; Exec. Chair. MICHAEL MANSOOR; CEO CHARLES PINK.

Guaranty Trust Bank Ltd: Lyford Manor Ltd, Lyford Cay, POB N-4918, Nassau; tel. 362-7200; fax 362-7210; e-mail info@guarantybahamas.com; internet www.guarantybahamas.com; f. 1962; cap. US $18.0m., res US $0.1m., dep. US $75.0m. (Jan. 2006); Chair. Sir WILLIAM C. ALLEN; Man. Dir JAMES P. COYLE.

HSBC Private Banking (Bahamas) Ltd (Switzerland): Centre of Commerce, 3rd Floor, Suite 306, 1 Bay St, POB N-4917, Nassau; tel. 502-2555; fax 502-2566; e-mail hfccfint@bahamas.net.bs; f. 1971 as Handelsfina Int.; name changed as above in 2002; cap. US $5.0m., res US $15.5m., dep. US $581.3m. (Dec. 1999); Chair. MARC DE GUILLEBON; CEO JEAN-JACQUES SALOMON.

National Bank of Canada (International) Ltd: Goodman's Bay Corporate Centre, Ground Floor, POB N-3015, Nassau; tel. 502-8100; fax 502-8166; e-mail info@nbclintl.com; f. 1978; 100% owned by Natcan Holdings International Ltd; cap. US $20.0m., dep. US $175.6m., total assets US $498.9m. (Oct. 2006); Pres. and Man. Dir JACQUES LATENDRESSE; Chair. ERIC LA FLAMME.

Overseas Union Bank and Trust (Bahamas) Ltd (Switzerland): Kings Court, 250 Bay St, POB N-8184, Nassau; tel. 322-2476; fax 323-8771; f. 1980; cap. US $5.0m., res US $6.2m., dep. US $97.9m. (Dec. 1997); Chair. Dr CARLO SGANZINI; Gen. Man. URS FREI.

Pictet Bank and Trust Ltd (Switzerland): Bldg No. 1, Bayside Executive Park, West Bay St and Blake Rd, POB N-4837, Nassau; tel. 302-2222; fax 327-6610; e-mail pbtbah@bahamas.net.bs; internet www.pictet.com; f. 1978; cap. US $1.0m., res US $10.0m., dep. US $126.2m. (Dec. 1995); Chair. CHRISTIAN MALLET; Pres. and Man. YVES LOURDIN.

Private Investment Bank Ltd: Devonshire House, Queen St, POB N-3918, Nassau; tel. 302-5950; fax 302-5970; f. 1984 as Bank Worms and Co International Ltd; renamed in 1990, 1996 and 1998; in 2000 merged with Geneva Private Bank and Trust (Bahamas) Ltd; wholly owned by Banque de Patrimoines Privés Genève BPG SA (Switzerland); cap. US $3.0m., res US $12.0m., dep. US $139.7m. (Dec. 2005); Chair. and Dir MARTIN A. MURBACH.

Royal Bank of Canada (Canada): Royal Bank House, 4th Floor, East Hill Street, POB N-7549, Nassau; tel. 356-8500; fax 328-7145; e-mail banks@rbc.com; internet www.rbc.com; f. 1869; Chair. DAVID P. O'BRIEN; Vice-Pres. MICHAEL F. PHELAN; 25 brs.

Scotiabank (Bahamas) Ltd (Canada): Scotiabank Bldg, Rawson Sq., POB N-7518, Nassau; tel. 356-1400; fax 326-0991; e-mail scotiabank.bs@scotiabank.com; internet www.bahamas.scotiabank.com; Man. Dir MINNA ISRAEL; Chair. RORY MACDONALD; 18 brs.

SG Hambros Bank and Trust (Bahamas) Ltd (United Kingdom): SG Hambros Bldg, West Bay St, POB N-7788, Nassau; tel. 302-5000; fax 326-6709; e-mail bahamas@sghambros.com; internet www.sghambros.com; f. 1936; above name adopted in 1998; cap. B $2.0m., res B $8.3m., dep. B $688.7m. (Dec. 2005); Chair. WARWICK NEWBURY; Man. Dir DOMINIQUE LEFEVRE.

UBS (Bahamas) Ltd (Switzerland): UBS House, East Bay St, POB N-7757, Nassau; tel. 394-9300; fax 394-9333; internet www.ubs.com/bahamas; f. 1968 as Swiss Bank Corpn (Overseas) Ltd, name changed as above 1998; wholly owned by UBS AG (Switzerland); cap. US $4.0m., dep. US $420.2m. (Dec. 1997); Chair. MARTIN LIECHTI; CEO ERIC TSCHIRREN.

Principal Bahamian Trust Companies

Ansbacher (Bahamas) Ltd: Ansbacher House, Bank Lane, POB N-7768, Nassau; tel. 322-1161; fax 326-5020; e-mail info@ansbacher.bs; internet www.ansbacher.com; incorporated 1957 as Bahamas International Trust Co Ltd; name changed 1994; cap. B $1.0m., res B $9.7m., dep. B $190.3m. (Sept. 1998); Man. Dir MICHAEL MAYHEW-ARNOLD.

Bank of Nova Scotia Trust Co. (Bahamas) Ltd: Scotia House, 404 East Bay St, POB N-3016, Nassau; tel. 393-8777; fax 393-5344; e-mail bahamas@scotiatrust.com; internet www.scotiabank.com; wholly owned by the Bank of Nova Scotia; Gen. Man. RAVI JESUBATHAM.

Oceanic Bank and Trust: TK House, Bayside Executive Park, West Bay St and Blake Rd, POB AP-59213, Nassau; tel. 502-8822; fax 502-8840; e-mail diane@oceanic.bs; internet www.oceanic.bs; f. 1969; COO DIANE C. BOWE-PINDLING.

Winterbotham Trust Co Ltd: Winterbotham Pl., Marlborough and Queen Sts, POB N-3026, Nassau; tel. 356-5454; fax 356-9432; e-mail adavidson@winterbotham.com; internet www.winterbotham.com; total assets US $11.8m. (Dec. 2006); Pres. and Man. Dir GEOFFREY HOOPER; CEO ALAN MCLEOD DAVIDSON; 2 brs.

Bankers' Organizations

Association of International Banks and Trust Companies in the Bahamas: Goodman's Bay Corporate Centre, West Bay St, POB N-7880, Nassau; tel. 356-3898; fax 328-4663; e-mail info@aibt-bahamas.com; internet www.aibt-bahamas.com; f. 1976; Chair. JAN F. C. MEZULANIK.

Bahamas Financial Services Board (BFSB): Goodman's Bay Corporate Centre, 1st Floor, West Bay St, POB N-1764, Nassau; tel. 326-7001; fax 326-7007; e-mail info@bsfb-bahamas.com; internet www.bfsb-bahamas.com; f. 1998; jt govt/private initiative responsible for overseas marketing of financial services; CEO and Exec. Dir WENDY C. WARREN; Chair. MICHAEL ALLEN.

Bahamas Institute of Financial Services (BIFS): Verandah House, Market St and Trinity Pl., POB N-3202, Nassau; tel. 325-4921; fax 325-5674; e-mail info@bifs-bahamas.com; internet www.bifs-bahamas.com; f. 1974 as Bahamas Institute of Bankers; name changed as above March 2003; Pres. NATHANIEL BENEBY, Jr; Chair. WILLIAM DELANCEY.

STOCK EXCHANGE

Bahamas International Securities Exchange (BISX): 8 Village Gdns, Village Rd and Village Gdns, POB EE-15672, Nassau; tel. 394-2503; fax 323-2504; e-mail info@bisxbahamas.com; internet www.bisxbahamas.com; f. 2000; 19 local companies listed at Dec. 2007; Chair. IAN FAIR; CEO KEITH DAVIES.

INSURANCE

The leading British and a number of US, Canadian and Caribbean companies have agents in Nassau and Freeport. Local insurance companies include the following:

Allied Bahamas Insurance Co Ltd: 93 Collins Ave, POB N-1216, Nassau; tel. 326-5439; fax 356-5472; general, aviation and marine.

Bahamas First General Insurance Co Ltd: 32 Collins Avenue, POB SS-6238, Nassau; tel. 302-3900; fax 302-3901; e-mail info@bahamasfirst.com; internet www.bahamasfirst.com; Pres. and CEO PATRICK G. W. WARD.

British American Financial: Independence Dr., POB N-4815, Nassau; tel. 461-1000; fax 361-2524; e-mail info@babfinancial.com; internet www.babinsurance.com; f. 1920 as British American Insurance Co; name changed as above in 2007 when comprehensive range of financial services added; wholly owned by local consortium, BAB Holdings Ltd, since Feb. 2007; Pres. and CEO CHESTER COOPER.

ColinaImperial Insurance Ltd: 308 Bay St, POB N-4728, Nassau; tel. 396-2100; fax 393-1710; e-mail info@colinaimperial.com; internet www.colinaimperial.com; Colina Insurance Co merged with Global Life Assurance Bahamas in July 2002; operates under above name; Pres. MONTGOMERY BRAITHWAITE.

Commonwealth General Insurance Co Ltd: POB N-4200, Nassau; tel. 322-8210; fax 322-5277; Man. Dir ALBERT ARCHER.

Family Guardian Insurance Co Ltd (FamGuard): East Bay St, POB SS-6232, Nassau; tel. 396-4000; fax 393-1100; internet www.famguardbahamas.com; Pres. and CEO PATRICIA A. HERMANNS; Chair. NORBERT BOISSIERE; f. 1965.

Security and General Insurance Co Ltd: POB N-3540, Nassau; tel. 326-7100; fax 325-0948; Gen. Man. MARK SHIRRA.

Summit Insurance Co Ltd: POB SS-19028, Nassau; tel. 394-2351; fax 394-2353; e-mail info@summitbah.com; internet www.summitbah.com; Chair. CEDRIC A. SAUNDERS; CEO and Dir TIMOTHY N. INGRAHAM.

Association

Bahamas General Insurance Association: Royal Palm Mall, Unit 8, Mackey St, POB N-860, Nassau; tel. 394-6625; fax 394-6626; e-mail bgia@batelnet.bs; Co-ordinator ROBIN B. HARDY.

Trade and Industry

DEVELOPMENT ORGANIZATIONS

Bahamas Agricultural and Industrial Corpn (BAIC): Levy Bldg, East Bay St, POB N-4940, Nassau; tel. 322-3740; fax 322-2133; e-mail baic@bahamas.net.bs; internet bahamasb2b.com/baic; f. 1981; an amalgamation of Bahamas Development Corpn and Bahamas Agricultural Corpn for the promotion of greater co-operation between tourism and other sectors of the economy through the development of small and medium-sized enterprises; Gen. Man. JEFFREY STUART.

Bahamas Financial Services Board (BFSB): see Finance—Bankers' Organizations.

Bahamas Investment Authority: Cecil V. Wallace-Whitfield Centre, POB CB-10980, Nassau; tel. 327-5970; fax 327-5907; e-mail info@opm.gov.bs; internet www.investbahamas.org; Dir BASIL ALBURY.

Nassau Paradise Island Promotion Board: Hotel Center, S. G. Hambros Bldg, West Bay St, Nassau; tel. 322-8381; fax 326-5346; e-mail rknowles@bahamashotels.org; internet www.nassauparadiseisland.com; f. 1970; Chair. GEORGE R. MYERS; Sec. MICHAEL C. RECKLEY; 30 mems.

CHAMBERS OF COMMERCE

Bahamas Chamber of Commerce: Shirley St and Collins Ave, POB N-665, Nassau; tel. 322-2145; fax 322-4649; e-mail info@thebahamaschamber.com; internet www.thebahamaschamber.com; f. 1935 to promote, foster and protect trade, industry and commerce; Pres. DIONISIO D'AGUILAR; Exec. Dir PHILIP SIMON; over 700 mems.

Grand Bahama Chamber of Commerce: POB F-40808, Freeport, Grand Bahama; tel. 352-8329; e-mail themanager@thegrandbahamachamberofcommerce.com; internet www.thegrandbahamachamberofcommerce.com; Pres. CHRISTOPHER LOWE; 227 mems.

EMPLOYERS' ASSOCIATIONS

Bahamian Contractors' Association: POB N-9286, Nassau; tel. 322-2145; fax 322-4649; e-mail info@bahamiancontractors.org; internet www.bahamiancontractors.org; Chair. TERRENCE KNOWLES; Sec. ROBIN OGILVIE.

Bahamas Association of Land Surveyors: POB N-10147, Nassau; tel. 322-4569; Pres. DONALD THOMPSON; Vice-Pres. GODFREY HUMES; 30 mems.

Bahamas Boatmen's Association: POB ES-5212, Nassau; f. 1974; Pres. and Sec. FREDERICK GOMEZ.

Bahamas Employers' Confederation: POB N-166, Nassau; tel. 328-5719; fax 322-4649; e-mail becon@bahamasemployers.org; internet www.bahamasemployers.org; f. 1966; Pres. BRIAN NUTT.

Bahamas Hotel Employers' Association: SG Hambros Bldg, West Bay, POB N-7799, Nassau; tel. 322-2262; fax 502-4221; e-mail bhea4mcr@hotmail.com; f. 1958; Pres. J. BARRIE FARRINGTON; Exec. Vice-Pres. MICHAEL C. RECKLEY; 16 mems.

Bahamas Institute of Chartered Accountants: Star Plaza, Mackey St, POB N-7037, Nassau; tel. 326-6619; fax 326-6618; internet www.bica.bs; f. 1971; Pres. DANIEL FERGUSON.

Bahamas Institute of Professional Engineers (BIPE): POB N-306, Nassau; tel. 322-3356; fax 323-8503; Pres. PAUL HANNA.

Bahamas Motor Dealers' Association (BMDA): POB N-3919, Nassau; tel. 328-7671; fax 328-1922; Pres. HARRY ROBERTS.

Bahamas Real Estate Association: Chamber of Commerce, Collins Ave, POB N-8860, Nassau; tel. 322-2145; fax 322-4649; e-mail info@bahamasrealestateassociation.com; internet www.bahamasrealestateassociation.com; Pres. W. LARRY ROBERTS; Sec. JAMES NEWBOLD.

Bahamas Society of Engineers: POB CB-11678, Nassau; tel. 394-5544; fax 394-6885; e-mail rgreene@batelnet.bs; internet www.bahamasengineers.org; f. 1998; Pres. CYPRIAN GIBSON; Sec. JAMIE MUSGROVE.

UTILITIES

Electricity

Bahamas Electricity Corpn (BEC): Big Pond and Tucker Rds, POB N-7509, Nassau; tel. 302-1000; fax 323-6852; e-mail customercare@bahamaselectricity.com; internet www.bahamaselectricity.com; f. 1956; state-owned; transfer to private ownership pending in mid-2007; provides 70% of the islands' power-generating capacity; Chair. FREDERIK GOTTLIEB; Gen. Man. KEVIN BASDEN.

Grand Bahama Power Co.: POB F-40888, Freeport; tel. 352-6611; fax 352-8449; e-mail rodgerjohnson@gb-power.com; internet www.gb-power.com; f. 1962 as Freeport Power Co Ltd; privately owned; Pres. and CEO TIMOTHY BORKOWSKI.

Gas

Tropigas: Gladstone Rd, POB SS-5833, Nassau; tel. 361-2695; fax 341-4875.

Water

Bahamas Water and Sewerage Corpn (WSC): 87 Thompson Blvd, POB N-3905, Nassau; tel. 302-5500; fax 328-3896; e-mail wscomplaints@wsc.com.bs; internet www.wsc.com.bs; f. 1976; operates under the auspices of the Ministry of Works and Transport; Chair. MICHAEL BARNETT; Gen. Man. GODFREY SHERMAN (acting).

TRADE UNIONS

All Bahamian unions are members of one of the following:

Commonwealth of the Bahamas Trade Union Congress: House of Labour, corner Wulff Rd and West Minnie St, POB N-3399, Nassau; tel. 394-6301; fax 394-7401; e-mail tuc@bahamas.net.bs; Pres. OBIE FERGUSON, Jr; Gen. Sec. TYRONE MORRIS; 12,500 mems.

National Congress of Trade Unions: Horseshoe Dr., POB GT-2887, Nassau; tel. 356-7457; fax 356-7459; e-mail mail@nctu-bahamas.org; Pres. JOHN PINDER (acting); Gen. Sec. ROBERT FARQUHARSON; 20,000 mems.

The main unions are as follows:

Bahamas Airport, Airline and Allied Workers' Union: Workers' House, Harold Rd, POB N-3364, Nassau; tel. 323-5030; fax 326-8763; e-mail aaawu@batelnet.com; f. 1958; Pres. NELERENE HARDING; Gen. Sec. GLADSTONE ADDERLEY; 550 mems.

Bahamas Brewery, Distillers Union: POB N-838, Nassau; tel. 362-1412; fax 362-1415; f. 1968; Pres. JOSEPH MOSS; Gen. Sec. RAFAEL HOLMES; 140 mems.

Bahamas Cement, Marine, Maintenance and Building Construction Allied Workers' Union: Wulff Rd, POB N-3399, Nassau; tel. 394-6302; fax 394-7401; Pres. ALFRED SMITH (acting); Gen. Sec. BERTRAM TURNQUEST.

Bahamas Communications and Public Officers' Union: Farrington Rd, POB N-3190, Nassau; tel. 322-1537; fax 323-8719; e-mail union@bcpou.com; internet www.bcpou.com; f. 1973; Pres. ROBERT A. FARQUHARSON; Gen. Sec. DENISE WILSON; 2,100 mems.

Bahamas Doctors' Union: Nassau; Pres. FRANCIS WILLIAMS; Gen. Sec. GEORGE SHERMAN.

Bahamas Electrical Workers' Union: 52 Poinciana Dr., POB GT-2535, Nassau; tel. 322-4289; fax 322-4711; e-mail bewupresident2002@batelnet.com; Pres. DENNIS WILLIAMS; Gen. Sec. STEPHANO GREENE.

Bahamas Gaming and Allied Workers' Union: Taxi Union Bldg, Old Airport Rd, Freeport; tel. 375-9804; fax 352-8837; e-mail bgawu@hotmail.com; Pres. DENNIS BRITTON; Gen. Sec. TIFFANY MARTIN.

Bahamas Hotel, Catering and Allied Workers' Union: Harold Rd, POB GT-2514, Nassau; tel. 325-0807; fax 325-6546; e-mail bhcawu@batelnet.com; f. 1958; Pres. ROY COLEBROOKE; Gen. Sec. LEO DOUGLAS; 6,500 mems.

Bahamas Maritime Port and Allied Workers' Union: Prince George Docks, POB FF-6501, Nassau; tel. 322-2049; fax 322-5545; Pres. FREDERICK N. RODGERS; Gen. Sec. MUNSINE DAVIS.

Bahamas Musicians' and Entertainers' Union: Horseshoe Dr., POB N-880, Nassau; tel. 322-3734; fax 323-3537; f. 1958; Pres. PERCIVAL SWEETING; Gen. Sec. PORTIA NOTTAGE; 410 mems.

Bahamas Nurses' Union: Centreville, Eighth Terrace, POB N-11530, Nassau; tel. and fax 325-3008; e-mail bnu_17199@hotmail.com; Pres. CLEOLA HAMILTON; Gen. Sec. ANEKA JOHNSON.

THE BAHAMAS

Bahamas Public Services Union: Wulff Rd, POB N-4692, Nassau; tel. 325-0038; fax 323-5287; f. 1959; Pres. JOHN PINDER; Sec.-Gen. SYNIDA DORSET; 4,247 mems.

Bahamas Taxi-Cab Union: Nassau St, POB N-1077, Nassau; tel. 323-5818; fax 323-6919; e-mail btcu@coralwave.com; Pres. LEON GRIFFIN; Gen. Sec. ROSCOE WEECH.

Bahamas Union of Teachers: Teachers' National Secretariat, 104 Bethel Ave, Stapledon Gardens, POB N-3482, Nassau; tel. 323-4491; fax 323-7086; e-mail froberts@bahamasunionofteachers.com; internet www.bahamasunionofteachers.com; f. 1945; Pres. IDA POITIER TURNQUEST; Sec.-Gen. BELINDA WILSON; over 3,500 mems.

Bahamas Utility Services and Allied Workers' Union: POB CB-13370, Nassau; tel. 323-3944; fax 322-5080; Pres. HUEDLEY MOSS; Gen. Sec. PAMELA RUSSELL.

Eastside Stevedores' Union: Wulff Rd, POB GT-2813, Nassau; tel. 322-4069; fax 323-7566; f. 1972; Pres. DAVID BETHEL; Gen. Sec. HAROLDINE STUBBS, Jr.

United Brotherhood of Longshoremen's Union: Wulff Rd, POB N-7317, Nassau; tel. 362-2570; f. 1959; Pres. JOSEPH MCKINNEY; Gen. Sec. DEGLANVILLE PANZA; 157 mems.

Transport

ROADS

There are about 966 km (600 miles) of roads in New Providence and 1,368 km (850 miles) in the Family Islands, mainly on Grand Bahama, Cat Island, Eleuthera, Exuma and Long Island. In 1999 57.4% of roads were paved.

SHIPPING

The principal seaport is at Nassau (New Providence), which can accommodate the very largest cruise ships. Passenger arrivals exceed 2m. annually. The other main ports are at Freeport (Grand Bahama), where a container terminal opened in 1997, and Matthew Town (Inagua). There are also modern berthing facilities for cruise ships at Potters Cay (New Providence), Governor's Harbour (Eleuthera), Morgan's Bluff (North Andros) and George Town (Exuma).

The Bahamas converted to free-flag status in 1976. The fleet's aggregate displacement was 40.8m. grt in December 2006 (the third largest national fleet in the world).

There is a weekly cargo and passenger service to all the Family Islands.

Bahamas Maritime Authority: POB N-4679, Nassau; tel. 394-3024; fax 394-3014; e-mail nassau@bahamasmaritime.com; internet www.bahamasmaritime.com; f. 1995; promotes ship registration and co-ordinates maritime administration.

Freeport Harbour Co Ltd: POB F-42465, Freeport; tel. 350-8000; fax 350-8044; internet www.freeportcontainerport.com; owned by Hutchison Port Holdings (HPH), Hong Kong; Gen. Man. MICHAEL J. POWER.

Grand Bahama Port Authority (GBPA): Pioneer's Way and East Mall, POB F-42666, Freeport; tel. 352-6611; fax 352-6184; internet www.gbpa.com; f. 1955; receivers were appointed to operate co in Nov. 2006 pending outcome of contested ownership trial which remained unresolved in February 2008; Chair HANNES BABAK; CEO Sir ALBERT MILLER.

Nassau Port Authority: Prince George Wharf, POB N-8175, Nassau; tel. 322-8832; fax 322-5545; e-mail portaja@batelnet.bs; regulates principal port of the Bahamas; Port Dir ANTHONY J. ALLENS.

Principal Shipping Companies

Bahamas Ferries: Potters Cay West, Nassau; tel. 323-2166; fax 393-7451; e-mail info@bahamasferries.com; internet www.bahamasferries.com; f. 1999; services Spanish Wells, Harbour Island, Current Island and Governors Harbour in Eleuthera, Morgan's Bluff and Fresh Creek in Andros, Sandy Point in Abaco and George Town in Exuma; Gen. Man. ALAN BAX.

Cavalier Shipping: Arawak Cay, POB N-8170, New Providence; tel. 328-3103; fax 323-8866.

Dockendale Shipping Co Ltd: Dockendale House, West Bay St, POB N-10455, Nassau; tel. 325-0448; fax 328-1542; e-mail dockship@dockendale.com; f. 1973; ship management; Man. Dir L. J. FERNANDES; Tech. Dir P. R. C. DATT.

Eleuthera Express Shipping Co: POB N-4201, Nassau.

Freeport Ship Services: 24 Logwood Rd, POB F-40423, Freeport; tel. 351-4343; fax 351-4332; e-mail info@freeportshipservices.com; internet www.freeportshipservices.com; f. 2003; privately owned co; affiliated to United Shipping Co Ltd; agents, customs brokers, logistics providers, chandlers; Pres. JEREMY CAFFERATA; Gen. Man. TROY CARTWRIGHT.

Grand Master Shipping Co: POB N-4208, Nassau.

Grenville Ventures Ltd: 43 Elizabeth Ave, POB CB-13022, Nassau.

HJH Trading Co Ltd: POB N-4402, Nassau; tel. 392-3939; fax 392-1828.

Pioneer Shipping Ltd: Union Wharf, POB N-3044, Nassau; tel. 325-7889; fax 325-2214.

Teekay Shipping Corporation: TK House, Bayside Executive Park, West Bay St & Blake Rd, POB AP-59212, Nassau; tel. 502-8820; fax 502-8840; internet www.teekay.com; petroleum transporting; Chair. C. SEAN DAY; Pres. and CEO BJORN MOLLER.

Tropical Shipping Co Ltd: Container Terminals Ltd, John Alfred Dock, Bay St, POB N-8183, Nassau; tel. 322-1012; fax 323-7566; internet www.tropical.com.

United Shipping Co (Nassau) Ltd: Centreville House, 5th Floor, Terrace 2, West Centreville, POB N-4005, Nassau; tel. 322-1340; fax 323-8779; e-mail operations@unitedshipping.com; internet www.unitedshipping.com; sister co of Freeport Ship Services; Chair. TERRY MUNDAY; Pres. BERLIN KEY.

CIVIL AVIATION

Lynden Pindling International Airport (formerly Nassau International Airport) (15 km—9 miles—outside the capital), Freeport International Airport (5 km—3 miles—outside the city, on Grand Bahama) and Marsh Harbour International Airport (on Abaco Island) are the main terminals for international and internal services. There are also important airports at West End (Grand Bahama) and Rock Sound (Eleuthera) and some 50 smaller airports and landing strips throughout the islands. A B $30m. airport improvement programme was completed in 2004 and an estimated US $250–300m. development of the Lynden Pindling International Airport was scheduled to commence in the second quarter of 2008 with the first new terminal expected to open in 2010. Construction of a further international airport terminal on the island of Mayaguana (563 km—350 miles—south-east of Nassau) commenced in May 2007.

Bahamasair Holdings Ltd: Windsor Field, POB N-4881, Nassau; tel. 377-8451; fax 377-7409; e-mail astuart@bahamasair.com; internet www.bahamasair.com; f. 1973; state-owned, proposed privatization plans shelved in late 2006 but revived in May 2007; scheduled services between Nassau, Freeport, Cuba, Jamaica, Dominican Republic, Turks and Caicos Islands, destinations within the USA and 20 locations within the Family Islands; Chair. BASIL SANDS; Man. Dir HENRY WOODS.

Western Air Limited: San Andros International Airport, POB AP 532900, Nassau; tel. 329-4000; fax 329-4013; e-mail info@westernairbahamas.com; internet www.westernairbahamas.com; f. 2001; private wholly Bahamian-owned company; scheduled services between Nassau, Freeport, San Andros and Bimini and on-demand charter flights throughout Bahamas, the Caribbean and Central and South America; Pres. and CEO REX ROLLE.

Tourism

The mild climate and beautiful beaches attract many tourists. In 2006 tourist arrivals totalled some 4,731,000, including 3,239,000 visitors by sea. The majority of stop-over arrivals (85.8% in 2005) were from the USA. Receipts from the tourism industry stood at B $2,056m. in 2006.

Bahamas Hotel Association: SG Hambros Bldg, Goodman's Bay, POB N-7799, Nassau; tel. 322-8381; fax 502-4220; e-mail bha@bahamashotels.org; internet www.bhahotels.com; Pres. RUSSELL MILLER; Exec. Vice-Pres. FRANK COMITO.

Hotel Corporation of the Bahamas: Marlborough St & Navy Lion Rd, POB N-9520, Nassau; tel. 356-4571; fax 356-4846; Chair. MICHAEL SCOTT; Chief Exec. DEPP BHATNAGER (acting).

Nassau Tourism and Development Board: POB N-4740, Nassau; tel. 326-0992; fax 323-2998; e-mail linkages@batelnet.bs; f. 1995; Chair. CHARLES KLONARIS.

BAHRAIN

Introductory Survey

Location, Climate, Language, Religion, Flag, Capital

The Kingdom of Bahrain consists of a group of some 36 islands, situated midway along the Persian (Arabian) Gulf, approximately 24 km (15 miles) from the east coast of Saudi Arabia (to which it is linked by a causeway), and 28 km from the west coast of Qatar. The construction of a causeway linking eastern Bahrain to Qatar (the Friendship Bridge) is planned. There are six principal islands in the archipelago, the largest of these being Bahrain itself, which is about 50 km long, and between 13 km and 25 km wide. To the north-east of Bahrain island, and linked to it by a causeway and road, lies Muharraq island, which is approximately 6 km long. Another causeway links Bahrain island with Sitra island. The climate is temperate from December to the end of March, with temperatures ranging from 19°C to 25°C, but becomes very hot and humid during the summer months. In August and September temperatures can rise to 40°C. The official language is Arabic, but English is also widely spoken. More than 80% of Bahraini citizens are Muslims, divided into two sects: Shi'ites (almost 60%) and Sunnis (more than 40%). Non-Bahrainis comprised an estimated 38.2% of the total population in December 2006. The national flag (proportions 3 by 5) is red, with a vertical white stripe at the hoist, the two colours being separated by a serrated line forming five white triangles. The capital is Manama, on Bahrain island.

Recent History

Bahrain, a traditional Arab monarchy, became a British Protected State in the 19th century. Under this arrangement, government was shared between the ruling Sheikh and his British adviser. Following a series of territorial disputes in the 19th century, Persia (renamed Iran in 1935) made renewed claims to Bahrain in 1928. This disagreement remained unresolved until May 1970, when Iran accepted the findings of a UN-commissioned report showing that the inhabitants of Bahrain overwhelmingly favoured complete independence, rather than union with Iran.

Sheikh Sulman bin Hamad al-Khalifa, who became ruler of Bahrain in 1942, was succeeded upon his death in November 1961 by his eldest son, Sheikh Isa bin Sulman al-Khalifa. Extensive administrative and political reforms were implemented in January 1970, when a supreme executive authority, the 12-member Council of State, was established, representing the first formal derogation of the ruler's powers. Sheikh Khalifa bin Sulman al-Khalifa, the ruler's eldest brother, was appointed President of the Council.

Meanwhile, in January 1968 the United Kingdom had announced its intention to withdraw British military forces from the area by 1971. In March 1968 Bahrain joined the nearby territories of Qatar and the Trucial States (now the United Arab Emirates—UAE), which were also under British protection, in the Federation of Arab Emirates. It was intended that the Federation should become fully independent, but the interests of Bahrain and Qatar proved to be incompatible with those of the smaller sheikhdoms, and both seceded from the Federation. Bahrain thus became a separate independent state on 15 August 1971, when a new treaty of friendship was signed with the United Kingdom. Sheikh Isa took the title of Amir, while the Council of State became the Cabinet, with Sheikh Khalifa as Prime Minister. A Constituent Assembly, convened in December 1972, formulated a new Constitution providing for a National Assembly to be comprised of 14 cabinet ministers and 30 elected members. The Constitution came into force on 6 December 1973, and elections to the new Assembly were conducted the following day. In the absence of political parties, candidates sought election as independents. In August 1975 the Prime Minister submitted his resignation, complaining that the National Assembly was obstructing the Government's initiatives for new legislation, particularly regarding national security. However, Sheikh Khalifa was reappointed and, at his request, the Assembly was dissolved by Amiri decree. New elections were to be held following minor changes to the Constitution and to the electoral law, but there were few subsequent signs that the National Assembly would be reconvened. With no elected legislative body, the ruling family continued to exercise near-absolute power. On 16 January 1993 a 30-member Majlis ash-Shoura (Consultative Council)—appointed by the ruling authorities and comprising a large number of business executives and some members of the old National Assembly—held its inaugural meeting. The Council was to act in a purely advisory capacity, with no legislative powers.

In March 1981 Bahrain was one of the six founder members of the Co-operation Council for the Arab States of the Gulf (or Gulf Co-operation Council—GCC, see p. 219), which was established in order to co-ordinate defence strategy and to promote freer trade and co-operative economic protection among Gulf states.

For many years there have been indications of tension between Shi'ite Muslims, who form a slender majority in Bahrain (and many of whom are of Iranian descent), and the dominant Sunni Muslims, to which sect the ruling family belongs. During the 1980s two plots to overthrow the Government, one of which was alleged to have Iranian support, were uncovered, as was a plan to sabotage Bahrain's petroleum installations, in which Iran was also alleged to be implicated. In December 1993 the human rights organization Amnesty International published a report criticizing the Bahraini Government's treatment of Shi'ite Muslims, some of whom had been forcibly exiled. In March 1994 the Amir issued a decree pardoning 64 Bahrainis who had been in exile since the 1980s and permitting them to return to Bahrain. In December 1994, however, Sheikh Ali Salman Ahmad Salman, a Muslim cleric, was arrested following his criticism of the Government and his public appeal for reform, particularly the restoration of the National Assembly. Widespread rioting ensued throughout Bahrain, especially in Shi'ite districts, and large-scale demonstrations were held in Manama in support of Sheikh Salman's demands and to petition for his release. Civil unrest continued despite the Amir's pledge to extend the powers of the Consultative Council; 12 people died and some 2,500 demonstrators were arrested in clashes with the security forces during December and January 1995. Sheikh Salman was deported and sought asylum in the United Kingdom (a request that was finally granted in July 1998). The unprecedented scale of the protests was widely attributed to a marked deterioration in socio-economic conditions in Bahrain, and in particular to a high level of unemployment.

There were further anti-Government demonstrations in Shi'ite districts in March and April 1995, following a police search of the property of an influential Shi'ite cleric, Sheikh Abd al-Amir al-Jamri, who was subsequently placed under house arrest and later imprisoned. In May and July several people received custodial sentences for damaging public installations, and one Bahraini was sentenced to death for the murder of a police officer in March. In June, in an apparent attempt to appease Shi'ite opposition leaders, the Prime Minister announced the first major government reorganization for 20 years; the new Cabinet included five Shi'ite ministers, although many strategic portfolios remained unchanged.

In August 1995 the Government initiated talks with Shi'ite opposition leaders in an effort to foster reconciliation, while the Amir issued a decree pardoning 150 people detained since the unrest. However, a report issued by Amnesty International in September indicated that as many as 1,500 demonstrators remained in detention in Bahrain, and that two prisoners had died in police custody following torture. Talks between the Government and opposition leaders collapsed in mid-September, although more than 40 political prisoners, among them Sheikh al-Jamri, were released later in the month. In October al-Jamri and six other opposition figures began a hunger strike in protest at the Government's refusal to concede to their demands, which included the release of all political prisoners and the restoration of the National Assembly. Following a large demonstration to mark the end of the hunger strike, the Government announced in November that it would take 'necessary action' to prevent future 'illegal' gatherings. In December the Amir declared an amnesty for nearly 150 prisoners, most of whom had been arrested during the recent disturbances. There were large-scale demonstrations in December and January 1996, in protest at the heavy deployment of security forces in Shi'ite districts and at the closure of two mosques. Opposition activists also suggested that Saudi Arabian and Indian security officers had been dispatched to reinforce the Bahrain police. In mid-January eight opposition leaders, including Sheikh al-Jamri, were arrested on charges of inciting unrest. In February Ahmad ash-Shamlan, a noted lawyer and writer, became the first prominent Sunni to be detained in connection with the disturbances, following his distribution of a statement accusing the Government of authoritarianism. A number of bomb explosions in February and March culminated in an arson attack on a restaurant in Sitra, in which seven Bangladeshi workers died. Also in March jurisdiction with regard to a number of criminal offences was transferred from ordinary courts to the High Court of Appeal, acting in the capacity of State Security Court. This move effectively accelerated the pace of court proceedings, while removing the right of appeal and limiting the role of the defence. In late March Isa Ahmad Hassan Qambar was executed by firing squad, having been condemned to death for killing a police officer during the unrest of March 1995 (see above). The execution—the first to take place in Bahrain since 1977—provoked mass protests by Bahrainis, while international human rights organizations challenged the validity of Qambar's confession and trial.

Civil tensions were exacerbated by the Government's announcement, in April 1996, of the creation of a Higher Council of Islamic Affairs (to be appointed by the Prime Minister and headed by the Minister of Justice and Islamic Affairs) to supervise all religious activity (including that of the Shi'ite community) in Bahrain. In June, however, the Amir sought to appease the demands of opposition reformers by announcing the future expansion of the Consultative Council from 30 to 40 members: a new 40-member Council was duly appointed by the Amir in September. Meanwhile, in July the State Security Court imposed death sentences on three of the eight Bahrainis convicted of the arson attack in Sitra, while four men were sentenced to life imprisonment. Although the death sentences provoked widespread domestic protests and international criticism, resulting in an appeal being permitted against the ruling, in October the Court of Cassation ruled that it had no jurisdiction to overturn the verdict. Towards the end of the year government plans to close a number of Shi'ite mosques resulted in further riots.

As unrest continued into early 1997, there were rumours of division within the ruling family concerning the use of force in response to the crisis. In January a National Guard was created, to provide support for the Bahrain Defence Force and the security forces of the Ministry of the Interior. The Amir's son, Hamad, was appointed to command the new force, prompting speculation that its primary duty would be to protect the ruling family. In March a week of anti-Government protests marked the first anniversary of the execution of Isa Ahmad Hassan Qambar. It was reported that since the outbreak of civil unrest at the end of 1994 some 28 people had been killed and 220 imprisoned in connection with the protests. In July and August 1997 two human rights groups produced reports criticizing the Bahrain police for allegedly making arbitrary arrests, using torture and arresting children as young as seven years of age. The Government rejected these reports, but did appear to respond to the allegations when, in November, the trial *in absentia* of eight prominent exiled activists (including Sheikh Ali Salman) on charges including the attempted overthrow of the regime resulted in the imposition of prison sentences of between five and 15 years. Although the activists claimed not to have been summoned to stand trial, their sentences were considered lenient in view of the severity of their alleged offences. Furthermore, during 1997 publishing restrictions were relaxed, and in December the Amir announced plans to allow greater media coverage of the activities of the Consultative Council. In February 1998 opposition groups welcomed the appointment of Khalid bin Muhammad al-Khalifa as the new head of the State Security Investigation Directorate (in place of a long-serving British national) and urged the continuing 'Bahrainization' of the security apparatus as a precondition for the initiation of dialogue between the regime and the opposition.

Sheikh Isa died on 6 March 1999. He was succeeded as Amir by his son, Crown Prince Sheikh Hamad bin Isa al-Khalifa, hitherto Commander-in-Chief of the Bahrain Defence Force and the National Guard; Sheikh Hamad's eldest son, Sheikh Salman bin Hamad al-Khalifa, became Crown Prince and also assumed his father's military command. Initially, opposition groups welcomed Sheikh Hamad's accession, which raised expectations of political change. In his first months in office Sheikh Hamad permitted Shi'ites to join the armed forces, allowed an investigation by Amnesty International into alleged brutality by the Sunni security forces and released more than 300 Shi'ite prisoners being held on security-related charges. However, the opposition claimed that 1,200–1,500 political prisoners remained in detention, and Sheikh Hamad was regarded as having failed to initiate prompt negotiations to end political unrest. In May he announced a limited cabinet reorganization. In July Sheikh al-Jamri, who was brought to trial in February, having been detained since 1996 under the terms of the 1974 Decree Law on State Security Measures (which allowed the imprisonment of suspects without trial for a period of up to three years), was sentenced to 10 years' imprisonment for espionage and inciting anti-Government unrest; a substantial fine was also imposed. Following intense international pressure Sheikh Hamad granted al-Jamri an official pardon the following day, although he remained effectively under house arrest. In August 1999 Bahrain's longest serving political prisoner, As-Sayed Jafar al-Alawi, was released from detention, having served 18 years of a 25-year prison sentence imposed in 1981 for plotting against the Government. In November–December 1999 the Amir ordered the release of some 345 detainees. In October, meanwhile, Sheikh Hamad issued a decree ordering the Consultative Council to establish a human rights committee. None the less, Amnesty International asserted in November 2000 that, while the human rights situation in Bahrain had improved (among the advances cited by the organization was the ratification, in March 1998, of the UN Convention against Torture and Other Cruel, Inhuman or Degrading Treatment or Punishment), the mechanisms that had facilitated past human rights violations remained in place.

In May 2000 the Prime Minister stated that municipal elections, on the basis of universal suffrage, would be held in early 2001 and that parliamentary elections would take place in 2004. In September 2000 four women, as well as a number of non-Muslims, were appointed for the first time to the Consultative Council. The Amir announced in November that a 46-member Supreme National Committee (SNC) had been formed to prepare a National Action Charter (NAC), which would outline the further evolution of Bahrain's political system. Among the SNC's recommendations, submitted in December, were that there should be a transition from an emirate to a constitutional monarchy, comprising a directly elected bicameral parliament (with women permitted both to vote and to seek election), a consultative chamber that would be appointed by the Government from all sections of society and an independent judiciary. Critics of the Bahrain regime dismissed the proposed transition to a monarchy as a pretext for the continuation of autocratic rule.

The new Charter was submitted for approval in a national referendum held on 14–15 February 2001 (at which Bahraini women were permitted to vote for the first time), and was duly endorsed by 98.4% of participating voters. Two committees were formed by Sheikh Hamad later that month. The tasks of the first committee, the Committee for the Activation of the National Charter, headed by the Crown Prince, were to implement the NAC and to define the respective roles of the legislature and the monarchy. The second committee, chaired by the Minister of Justice and Islamic Affairs, was required to oversee amendments to the Constitution. The Decree Law on State Security Measures and the State Security Court were both abolished. Prior to the referendum all political prisoners, including Sheikh al-Jamri, were reportedly released by the Amir. Moreover, following the removal of travel restrictions for members of the opposition, by March 2001 at least 100 political exiles had returned to Bahrain, among them Sheikh Ali Salman. Also in March 2001, prior to a visit by representatives of Amnesty International, the Government granted a licence to the independent Bahrain Human Rights Society (BHRS). Five new ministers were appointed to the Cabinet in a government reorganization effected in April.

On 14 February 2002 Sheikh Hamad announced the establishment of a constitutional monarchy in Bahrain, proclaiming himself King. The new monarch approved the amendments to the Constitution outlined in the NAC and dissolved the Consultative Council. Municipal elections were held on 9 May (with run-off voting one week later); however, female candidates—for the first time permitted to stand for public office—failed to win any seats on the five new regional councils.

Meanwhile, it was announced that Bahrain's first legislative elections for 27 years would take place, earlier than had previously been indicated, on 24 October 2002. In preparation for the elections, the Government approved a draft electoral law in June of that year. The new legislation was criticized by opposition groups on the grounds that it barred all trade unions and overtly political organizations from participating in the ballot; in September, however, King Hamad removed restrictions on campaigning by political groups. Opposition activists expressed strong concern, furthermore, that the unelected Consultative Council would have the same rights as the elected Majlis an-Nuab (Council of Representatives) in the bicameral parliament, and stated that they would boycott the polls. Meanwhile, in July the King ordered the establishment of an independent financial auditing court, with far-reaching powers to monitor state spending. The creation of a Constitutional Court was also approved by the Government: this became operational in April 2005.

At the elections to the Council of Representatives held on 24 October 2002, 21 of the 40 seats were won by independents and 'moderate' Sunni candidates, with the remaining 19 seats taken by more radical Islamists. The rate of participation by voters was recorded as 53.2% of the registered electorate. Reformists expressed their view that the newly elected legislature would not reflect the structure of Bahraini society, since a large proportion of the Shi'ite majority had boycotted the elections and female candidates had failed to win any seats (there had been eight women among a total of 174 candidates). Opposition groups, both leftist and Islamist, also complained that international human rights groups had not been permitted to monitor the elections. Moreover, there was considerable criticism of the policy of political naturalization adopted by the Amir (whereby Sunnis from the Eastern Province of Saudi Arabia were granted full voting rights), which was interpreted as a deliberate attempt to reduce the size of the Shi'ite majority. On 17 November the new Consultative Council, headed by Dr Faisal Radhi al-Mousawi, hitherto Minister of Health, was sworn in by the King; the number of women appointed to the Council remained unchanged at four. Earlier in November King Hamad named an expanded Cabinet, in which Dr Khalil bin Ibrahim Hassan succeeded al-Mousawi as Minister of Health. Other notable changes included the appointment of two Shi'ites, Dr Majid bin Hassan al-Alawi and Sheikh Jawad bin Salem al-Oraid, as Minister of Labour and Social Affairs and Minister of Justice, respectively. Meanwhile, legislation permitting the establishment of independent trade unions was ratified in November. (In January 2004 the General Federation of Bahrain Workers' Unions, which represents some 40 trade unions, was founded; by early 2007 the number of trade unions operating within Bahrain was reported to be in excess of 50.) In late 2002 the King declared 1 May, international Labour Day, as an official holiday.

In January 2004 17 parliamentary deputies applied for permission to question three cabinet ministers, including the Minister of Finance and National Economy, Abdullah bin Hassan Saif, about alleged irregularities in the administration of two pension funds—the first such request since the establishment of the Council of Representatives in 2002. The Speaker, Khalifa adh-Dhahrani, claimed that the move was unjustified and urged the deputies to withdraw their request. King Hamad, however, expressed his support for a parliamentary investigation into the alleged mismanagement. In September 2004 the Bahraini authorities closed down the Bahrain Centre for Human Rights (BCHR), an independent grouping authorized by the Government, and arrested its director, Abd al-Hadi al-Khawaja, for criticizing Bahrain's economic policies and human rights record and for demanding the removal of the Prime Minister. (The BCHR lost a court appeal against its closure in March 2006.) Later in September King Hamad warned his regime's critics not to abuse the country's 'openness and freedoms'; however, in November he ordered the release of al-Khawaja and 13 other people who had publicly demonstrated their support for the activist.

In April 2004 Dr Nada Haffadh replaced Dr Khalil Hassan as Minister of Health, thereby becoming the first woman to attain cabinet rank in Bahrain. In May King Hamad dismissed the long-serving Minister of the Interior, Sheikh Muhammad bin Khalifa al-Khalifa, following clashes between Bahraini police and mainly Shi'ite protesters who were demonstrating against US military operations in two Shi'ite holy cities in Iraq. Maj.-Gen. Sheikh Rashid bin Abdullah bin Ahmad al-Khalifa was named as his successor. A further reorganization of the Government was effected in January 2005: Dr Fatima al-Blushi became Bahrain's second female minister when she secured the social affairs portfolio (now separate from the labour portfolio), and Sheikh Ahmad bin Muhammad al-Khalifa was given the post of Minister of Finance and National Economy (replacing Saif, who had been questioned in parliament in 2004 in connection with the pension fund controversy).

In September 2005 King Hamad implemented further changes to the composition of the Cabinet. Sheikh Khalid bin Ahmad al-Khalifa, the former Bahraini ambassador to the United Kingdom, was appointed as Minister of Foreign Affairs, replacing Sheikh Muhammad bin Mubarak al-Khalifa, who remained one of three Deputy Prime Ministers and assumed additional responsibility for ministerial committees. Another notable change was the dissolution of the Ministry of Oil, the functions of which were transferred to a newly established National Oil and Gas Authority; the erstwhile Minister of State for Cabinet Affairs, Dr Abd al-Hussain bin Ali Mirza, was appointed Chairman of the new authority, while the Minister of Oil, Sheikh Isa bin Ali al-Khalifa, became Adviser to the Prime Minister on Oil and Industry Affairs.

In preparation for legislative elections scheduled for October 2006, in late 2005 the King's reform strategy was tested by the progress of the draft political societies law that would oblige political groupings to agree to certain conditions, such as a pledge to work within the existing Constitution and the refusal of funding from foreign benefactors, in order to receive a licence (in effect granting a group political party status) from the Ministry of Justice. Al-Wefaq National Islamic Society (or the Islamic National Accord Association), the largest Shi'ite group, which boycotted the 2002 parliamentary elections, agreed to register under the proposed regulations. The group, however, was reported to have split into two factions over the issue; as anticipated, the smaller of the two groups—now called al-Haq (Right)—did not compete in the 2006 elections, for which a concrete date of 25 November had since been designated.

In September 2006 Sheikha Haya bint Rashid al-Khalifa, a well-respected lawyer and former Bahraini ambassador to France, became the first Arab and Muslim woman to accede to the role of President of the UN General Assembly during its 61st session, held at the organization's headquarters in New York, USA. Meanwhile, in June of that year Mona Jassem al-Kawari became the first-ever female judge in Bahrain, and indeed in any of the Gulf Arab states, when she was appointed, by royal decree, as a judge in the Higher Civil Court.

During the months preceding the legislative polls, allegations of unscrupulous campaign tactics, coupled with the Government's veto on international election monitors, provoked tensions between the opposing Sunni and Shi'ite political assemblies and increased fears of an undemocratic ballot. In an effort to minimize such fears, and to preserve the political neutrality of the military sector, the Ministry of the Interior prohibited military staff from participating in election campaigns and appointed the BHRS as an independent election monitor. However, a report compiled by Dr Salah al-Bandar, Chancellor of Strategic Planning in the Ministry of Cabinet Affairs, and released in September 2006, accused several government officials of deliberately exacerbating sectarianism and of contriving unfairly to influence the elections. The escalating scandal in the wake of these revelations became known as 'Bandargate'; Dr Bandar, a Sudanese-born British citizen, was deported to the United Kingdom and Bahrain's Higher Criminal Court issued an edict prohibiting any press coverage or comment relating to the affair. The ensuing censorship of over 20 discussion and news websites, which remained unavailable to Bahrainis in early 2008, precipitated considerable unease among international human rights observers. The Government's policy of incremental naturalization also provoked controversy and protests in September 2006, amid allegations of politically motivated citizenship awards; such claims were strenuously denied by the Minister of the Interior. It was feared by opposition groups that changes to electoral boundaries since 2002 and exploitation of new naturalization legislation were altering the population balance, to Shi'ite disadvantage, and would threaten the integrity of the polls; the announcement that 5,000 non-Bahraini citizens of other GCC states would be permitted voting rights was interpreted as an effort to increase the number of Sunni voters. A large demonstration staged one day prior to the elections demanded an investigation into an alleged plot to marginalize the Shi'ite majority population and called for the resignation of Prime Minister Sheikh Khalifa bin Salman al-Khalifa.

The initial round of elections to the Council of Representatives on 25 November 2006 represented the second direct elections since the amendments to the Constitution, promulgated on 14 February 2002, and attracted strong voter turn-out, estimated at 73% of the 295,686 eligible Bahrainis. A run-off ballot was subsequently held on 2 December 2006 to determine the distribution of the remaining 11 contested seats. In the second round the Shi'ite opposition Al-Wefaq National Islamic Society, led by Sheikh Ali Salman, secured a further seat, and the mandate of an additional aligned independent brought its total presence in the Council to 18; however, Sunni candidates—comprising 12 Sunni Islamists and 10 independent Sunnis—achieved a majority, winning 22 seats. (Only one seat was attained by a liberal candidate.) Of 18 women among the 209 participating in the elections, only one attained a position on the Council: Latifa al-Qouood became the first female parliamentarian in the Gulf states when her constituency seat remained unopposed. Overall participation of registered voters in both polls was reported as 71%. The election results were contentious, however, as opposition organizations made applications to the Court of Cassation challenging several appointments on the grounds of illegal campaign practices perpetrated by Sunni Islamist groups. The principal three seats under debate were critical in determining the Sunni Islamists' retention of a ruling majority and consequently provoked much further political wrangling. The election of hardline politicians from both Sunni and Shi'ite organizations to the Council of Representatives prompted speculation of a more volatile parliament and fears that religious tensions might be exacerbated. Meanwhile, municipal elections were held simultaneously with the legislative polls.

On 5 December 2006 King Hamad announced the appointment of the new Consultative Council; its composition contrasted markedly with that of the newly elected Council of Representatives, and with the previous Consultative Council, since it included 10 female members and just two religious personalities (compared with 30 elected to the lower house); the selection was widely regarded as a counterbalancing measure to achieve a more representative parliament. Sheikh Khalifa presented his new 24-member Cabinet on 11 December, notably appointing a Shi'ite, Jawad bin Salem al-Arrayed, as one of three Deputy Prime Ministers for the first time in the kingdom's history. The Cabinet instituted one new portfolio pertaining to Oil and Gas Affairs, which was awarded to the head of the National Oil and Gas Authority, Dr Abd al-Hussain bin Ali Mirza, and also introduced the post of Minister of State for Defence Affairs, to which Dr Sheikh Muhammad bin Abdullah al-Khalifa was appointed. Members of Al-Wefaq boycotted parliament's inauguration on 15 December, protesting that the composition of the new Cabinet effectively marginalized the Shi'ite majority and alleging royal interference in the distribution of posts within the chamber. In the absence of Shi'ite participation from the first two working sessions of the new parliament, Sunnis were appointed to the speakership and deputy speakerships: Khalifa ad-Dhahranib was elected Speaker and Ghanem Albuainain and Salah Ali secured the latter positions. The boycott ended in early January 2007 with the presentation of the 2007–10 economic development plan.

In May 2007 the US-based Human Rights Watch submitted a letter to King Hamad, urging the holding of a full and independent investigation into allegations of torture suffered by two men detained in police custody, who were among those arrested following clashes between anti-riot police and opposition activists earlier that month. Further riots occurred in June, when the authorities used tear gas and rubber bullets to disperse a group of approximately 200 people who had gathered in the predominantly Shi'ite village of al-Malkiyah, to the west of Manama, to attend an authorized rally staged in protest at the erection of a wall that prevented local villagers from accessing the seafront and thus from embarking on fishing expeditions—the village's principal source of income. The demonstrators alleged that the wall had been built in order that a cousin of King Hamad might claim the land as his own. It was one of several riots to take place in al-Malkiyah during 2007, with similar events taking place in numerous other villages across Bahrain, and human rights groups claiming that hundreds of demonstrators had been injured in the clashes. The unrest appeared to indicate an intensification of sectarian tensions between the kingdom's Sunni and Shi'ite populations.

In July 2007 the UN Secretary-General, Ban Ki-Moon, bestowed Prime Minister Sheikh Khalifa with an award for the 'remarkable strides in reducing poverty' achieved by the Bahraini Government's urban development policies, provoking censure from human rights groups, which contested that the Prime Minister's poor human rights record should have precluded the presenting of any such commendation. Meanwhile, in June the so-called Truth and Reconciliation Committee (TRC) was officially established by a consortium of opposition and civic groups in order to secure justice for the alleged victims of human rights violations during unrest in the 1970s, 1980s and mid-1990s. The unofficial body was not supported by the Government, however, which insisted that the edicts of the NAC (introduced in 2001—see above), specifically the pardon granting immunity from prosecution to all those who might have committed human rights violations, should continue to be honoured. The founders of the TRC, however, contested that the pardon, which had also granted freedom to all political prisoners, was illegal under the terms of the Constitution.

There was further unrest in mid-December 2007, when Shi'a demonstrators gathered in the streets of the capital to commemorate those killed in the riots of December 1994 (see above) and to protest against human rights violations. Police again resorted to the use of tear gas and rubber bullets to disperse the crowds, injuring dozens of people, while one man was reported to have been killed. The authorities maintained that the man's death was due to natural causes, but the incident sparked further anger among the protesters, who claimed that the man had died as a result of inhaling tear gas, and clashes between the demonstrators and police intensified in subsequent days. Numerous people were arrested for various alleged offences, including theft of police weaponry, throwing incendiary devices at police officers and the attempted arson of police vehicles, and security forces were reported to have raided premises belonging to members of Shi'a opposition groups, arresting at least seven people. A number of those detained claimed to have been tortured while in police custody, claims adamantly refuted by the police but which, none the less, prompted the independent BHRS to apply to the authorities in late December for permission to visit the inmates; this permission was granted in mid-January 2008. While the BHRS welcomed the concession, it expressed its regret at the fact that it had taken so long to obtain, with the organization's Assistant Secretary-General noting that the time that had elapsed in the intervening period was sufficient for any physical signs of torture to have disappeared. An official at the Ministry of the Interior, meanwhile, stated that medical tests carried out on the relevant prisoners 'proved' that no form of torture had been committed.

Also in January 2008 various bills were drafted to amend legislation that might allow or even encourage human rights violations, including the 1964 Prison Law. According to draft legislation, the new Prison Law would afford greater rights to inmates, including the introduction of measures to ensure the right to worship freely under incarceration and to eradicate mistreatment at the hands of prison authorities. The proposed legislative amendments followed the parliamentary approval in December 2007 of a new anti-human trafficking law, after a US State Department report suggested that the Bahraini Government did not comply with international standards in this regard. As well as increasing the severity of punishments in the event of successful convictions, the new law also established a Human Trafficking Victims Assessment Commission, which was to provide medical and psychological aftercare for victims of people-smuggling.

In a development that was widely seen as an attempt to strengthen royal control over the military, King Hamad announced by royal decree, in January 2008, the disbandment of the Ministry of Defence and the appointment of Crown Prince Sheikh Salman bin Hamad al-Khalifa as Deputy Commander-in-Chief of the Bahrain Defence Force. The outgoing Minister of Defence, Maj.-Gen. Sheikh Khalifa bin Ahmad al-Khalifa, was appointed to the position of Commander-in-Chief of the Army, and the administration of matters pertaining to the military was henceforth to be managed by the Minister of State for Defence Affairs. The transfer of military authority from a government ministry to the direct control of the King, in his capacity as Commander-in-Chief of the Bahrain Defence Force, rendered the military, according to the terms of the Constitution, immune to scrutiny by the legislature. At a time when the condition of King Hamad's health was reported to be a source of some concern, the changes were also regarded as a means of preparing for the eventual handover of power to the Crown Prince. In mid-January Sheikh Salman identified disunity within the Government and a lack of co-ordinated endeavour as the principal reasons for the slow pace of economic reform. His comments, made in a letter written to the King, attracted widespread media coverage in Bahrain, and were generally interpreted as public criticism of Prime Minister Sheikh Khalifa and as further evidence of the increasing power and influence enjoyed by the future heir to the throne.

Although relations between Bahrain and Iran were upgraded to ambassadorial level in late 1990, the situation between the two countries began to deteriorate in the mid-1990s. While there was sufficient evidence to suggest largely domestic motivation for the recent increase in popular disaffection, the Bahraini authorities continued to imply that the disturbances were fomented by Iranian-backed militant Shi'ite fundamentalists seeking to destabilize the country. These allegations were frequently dismissed by Iran. In June 1996 the Bahraini Government announced that it had uncovered details of a plot, initiated in 1993 with support from fundamentalist Shi'ite groups in Iran, to oust the Government and ruling family in Bahrain and replace them with a pro-Iranian administration. It was claimed that a previously unknown Shi'ite group, Hezbollah Bahrain, had been established and financed by Iran's Revolutionary Guard. Young Bahraini Shi'ites were alleged to have received military training in Iran and at guerrilla bases in Lebanon, in preparation for a terrorist offensive in Bahrain, which had culminated in the unrest of the previous 18 months. Within days of the Government's announcement more than 50 Bahrainis had been arrested in connection with the alleged plot, many of whom admitted membership of Hezbollah Bahrain. The Iranian authorities denied any involvement in the planned insurrection, but bilateral relations were severely undermined by the unprecedented directness of the Bahrain Government's accusations; the two countries' respective ambassadors were withdrawn, and diplomatic relations were downgraded. During June 1996 more than 30 Bahrainis received prison sentences of between one and 13 years—for offences connected to the disturbances—from the State Security Court (and were therefore denied the right of appeal). In March 1997 59 Bahraini Shi'ites accused of belonging to Hezbollah Bahrain were brought to trial; similar charges had been made against a further 22 Shi'ites who, according to the Bahrain Government, were to be tried *in absentia*. The State Security Court sentenced 37 of the defendants to terms of imprisonment ranging from three to 15 years, and acquitted the others.

There was a period of *détente* in relations between most countries of the GCC and Iran following the election of Muhammad Khatami to the Iranian presidency in May 1997, and in December 1999 relations at ambassadorial level were formally restored between Bahrain and Iran. In March 2000 the Ministers of Foreign Affairs of the two countries met in Manama to discuss regional security as well as political and economic co-operation; a bilateral economic commission held its first meeting in that month. In early 2001 it was announced that Shi'ite Muslims of Iranian descent and whose families had lived in Bahrain for several generations were to be granted full Bahraini citizenship. However, relations deteriorated in 2005, following the publication in the Bahrain daily *Al-Ayam* of a cartoon that Iranians considered insulting to their Supreme Leader, Ayatollah Ali Khamenei. Moreover, Bahrain took umbrage at the display of pictures of Iranian religious leaders during the country's own Ashoura festival. By mid-2006 Bahrain and Iran (whose President, Mahmoud Ahmadinejad, had assumed office in August 2005) had taken steps to repair ties, with reciprocal visits of the two countries' ministers responsible for foreign affairs. In May Bahrain's Minister of Foreign Affairs, Sheikh Khalid bin Ahmad al-Khalifa, was reported to have ruled out the use of any military action against Iran over its nuclear programme (see the chapter on Iran), while urging the Iranian authorities to abide by international treaties.

In July 2007 an editorial was published in a conservative Iranian newspaper, in which its author revived claims that Bahrain was rightfully an Iranian province. The comments provoked angry scenes in Manama, with about 100 protesters descending upon the Iranian embassy to decry the claim. Distancing itself from the comments, the Iranian Government dispatched the Minister of Foreign Affairs, Manouchehr Mottaki, to meet with his counterpart in Manama and convey a public message of 'peace and friendship' to the Bahraini Government, while an official at the Iranian embassy stated that the editor's views should in no way be taken as an official Iranian position. Sheikh Khalid asserted that the editorial had not compromised bilateral relations, which, he insisted, remained strong. Another dispute followed in November, when the Crown Prince was quoted in two British newspapers—*The Daily Telegraph* and *The Times*—as having accused Iran of developing nuclear weaponry. Sheikh Khalid was subsequently reported to have stated that the Crown Prince's comments had been 'distorted'. Iranian President Ahmadinejad made an official visit to Manama later that month, where he held discussions with King Hamad. During his visit a memorandum of understanding pertaining to oil and gas was signed between the two countries (see Economic Affairs, below). In January 2008 the Iranian First Vice-President, Parviz Davoudi, extended an official invitation to Prime Minister Sheikh Khalifa to visit the Iranian capital, Tehran, expressing his hope that the visit would consolidate both diplomatic and economic relations between Iran and Bahrain.

In common with other Gulf states, Bahrain consistently expressed support for Iraq at the time of the Iran–Iraq War (1980–88). However, following the Iraqi invasion of Kuwait in August 1990, Bahrain firmly supported the implementation of UN economic sanctions against Iraq and permitted the stationing of US troops and combat aircraft in Bahrain. (Military co-operation with the USA had been close for many years.) In June 1991, following the liberation of Kuwait in February, it was confirmed that Bahrain would remain a regional support base for the USA, and later in the year the two countries signed a defence co-operation agreement. In January 1994 Bahrain signed further accords of military co-operation with the USA and the United Kingdom. Relations with Iraq remained strained, and in October hopes of improved relations receded when Iraqi forces were again deployed in the Iraq–Kuwait border area. In response, Bahrain deployed combat aircraft and naval units to join GCC and US forces in the defence of Kuwait. However, in February 1998 Bahrain strongly advocated a diplomatic solution to the ongoing dispute between Iraq and the UN weapons inspectors (see the chapter on Iraq), and refused to allow US military aircraft to launch attacks on Iraq from Bahraini bases. In June, as part of a wider US effort to reduce its military presence in the region, US military aircraft were withdrawn from Bahrain. A further US-led military campaign against Iraq in December was supported by the Bahraini authorities (the operation was centred in Manama, where the US Fifth Fleet is based), although Bahrain refrained from any public endorsement of the air-strikes.

Bahrain joined the other GCC states in condemning the suicide attacks on New York and Washington, DC, on 11 September 2001, and pledged to co-operate with the USA's attempts to forge an international 'coalition against terror', notably by freezing the financial assets of individuals or organizations allegedly linked to the militant Islamist al-Qa'ida (Base) network of Osama bin Laden, held by the USA to be principally responsible for the attacks. Nevertheless, in the aftermath of the suicide attacks, small demonstrations and 'bomb scare' telephone calls to US companies based in Bahrain indicated renewed antipathy towards the USA in some quarters. As in the other Gulf states, the overriding sentiment in Bahrain was that US-led military action, which began in Afghanistan in October, should not be directed against any Muslim target in the Middle East. As the momentum grew towards a US-led military campaign to oust the regime of Saddam Hussain in Iraq, anti-war riots became increasingly frequent in Bahrain, and in February 2003 police opened fire on a 2,000-strong violent demonstration outside the US embassy in Manama. Although King Hamad expressed hope that a diplomatic solution to the crisis might be found, Bahrain announced that it would contribute a frigate and an unspecified number of troops to the defence of Kuwait from possible Iraqi retaliation should the US-led campaign proceed. In March the Bahraini Government lent its support to an appeal by the UAE for Saddam Hussain to go into exile in order to save his country from the consequences of the US pursuit of 'regime change', and offered him asylum in Bahrain.

Following the commencement, later in March 2003, of US-led military action in Iraq, in April Bahrain ordered the expulsion of an Iraqi diplomat who was alleged to be linked to an explosion outside the Fifth Fleet base. Sporadic violent incidents and threats, believed to be related to the continued presence of the US military in Bahrain, continued throughout 2003–04. The bombing of the al-Askari Mosque (or Golden Mosque) in Samarra, one of the holiest Shi'ite shrines in Iraq, by insurgents in February 2006 prompted the largest demonstration in Bahrain for many years. In early 2006 the ongoing contention between the USA (among other countries) and Iran over the latter's nuclear programme was regarded in some quarters as a potential threat to Bahrain's security, and there was speculation that the issue could foster further domestic resentment towards the Bahraini Government's hosting of the US base: in the event of conflict, the US Fifth Fleet base in Bahrain was considered likely to be a priority target for Iranian military action. In an effort to combat terrorism, King Hamad presented a 'Protecting Society from Terrorist Acts' bill to parliament in July; despite protestations of human rights contravention by the UN and Amnesty International (among others), the legislation was ratified in August. (The UN Special Rapporteur on the promotion and protection of human rights while countering terrorism, Martin Scheinin, expressed particular concern over the threat posed to freedom of speech by the law's 'overly broad' definition of 'terrorist' activity.) In October 2007 three Bahraini nationals became the first people to go on trial under the remit of the controversial new legislation after they were charged with belonging to a terrorist cell plotting attacks on US interests in Manama, and of supporting insurgents loyal to the deposed Taliban regime in Afghanistan (q.v.). The defendants were among a group of six people detained by the Bahraini authorities in August, the other three of whom had subsequently been released without charge; a fourth Bahraini man and a Qatari citizen, who at early 2008 continued to evade capture, also went on trial, *in absentia*. In January 2008 all five were convicted and sentenced to six months' imprisonment; yet, despite the verdict, the leniency of the sentences was a source of intense irritation to the US Administration.

In April 1986 Qatari military forces raided the island of Fasht ad-Dibal, which had been artificially constructed on a coral reef (submerged at high tide), situated midway between Bahrain and Qatar; both countries claimed sovereignty over the island. Following GCC mediation, in May the two Governments agreed to destroy the island. Other areas of dispute between the two states were Zubarah (which was part of Bahraini territory until the early 20th century), in mainland Qatar, and the Hawar islands, which were believed to contain potentially valuable reserves of petroleum and natural gas. In July 1991 Qatar instituted proceedings at the International Court of Justice (ICJ) in The Hague, Netherlands, regarding the issue of the Hawar islands (in 1939 a British judgment had awarded sovereignty of the islands to Bahrain), Fasht ad-Dibal and Qit'at Jaradah (over which the British Government had recognized Bahrain's 'sovereign rights' in 1947), together with the delimitation of the maritime border between Qatar and Bahrain. The question of sovereignty was further confused in April 1992, when the Government of Qatar issued a decree redefining its maritime borders to include territorial waters claimed by Bahrain, and tensions were exacerbated by Qatar's persistent rejection of Bahrain's insistence that the two countries should seek joint recourse to the ICJ. Moreover, Bahrain had reportedly attempted to widen the issue to include its claim to the Zubarah region. Qatar applied unilaterally to the Court, and in February 1995 the ICJ ruled that it was competent to adjudicate in the dispute. Relations between Bahrain and Qatar deteriorated following the Bahrain Government's decision, in September, to construct a tourist resort on the Hawar islands, and remained tense subsequently, with the Bahraini Government advocating a regional solution to the dispute in preference to ICJ jurisdiction.

In December 1996 Bahrain boycotted the GCC annual summit convened in Doha, Qatar, at which it was decided to establish a quadripartite committee (comprising those GCC members not involved in the dispute) to facilitate a solution. The committee reportedly made some progress, and following senior-level ministerial meetings between Bahrain and Qatar in London, United Kingdom, and in Manama in early 1997, it was announced that diplomatic relations at ambassadorial level were to be established between the two countries. Qatar, however, was alone in nominating its diplomatic representative shortly afterwards. Regional efforts failed to find a solution to the territorial dispute, and the announcement of Bahraini construction plans on the Hawar islands (which, in addition to the opening of an hotel in mid-1997, included a housing complex and a causeway linking the islands to Bahrain) did little to further bilateral relations. Bahrain emphasized that it would disregard any ruling on the issue by the ICJ. At the end of 1999 the Amir of Qatar made his first official visit to Manama, during which it was agreed that a joint committee, headed by the Crown Princes of Bahrain and Qatar, would be established to encourage bilateral co-operation. Qatar also agreed to withdraw its petition from the ICJ in the event of the joint committee's reaching a solution to the territorial disputes. Senior-level contacts were furthered in January 2000, upon the first visit of the new Amir of Bahrain, Sheikh Hamad, to Qatar, and the two countries agreed to hasten the opening of embassies in Manama and Doha. In February, following the first meeting of the Bahrain-Qatar Supreme Joint Committee, it was announced that the possibility of constructing a causeway (the Friendship Bridge) to link the two states was to be investigated; Qatar officially named its ambassador to Bahrain on the same day. In May, however, Bahrain unilaterally suspended the Supreme Joint Committee pending the ruling of the ICJ. Hearings by the Court began later that month and were completed by the end of June. A verdict was issued in March 2001, whereby Bahrain was found to have sovereignty over the Hawar islands and Qit'at Jaradah, while Qatar held sovereignty over Zubarah, Janan island and the low-tide elevation of Fasht ad-Dibal; the Court drew a single maritime boundary between the two states. Both Bahrain and Qatar accepted the ICJ ruling. Later in March, following a high-profile visit by Sheikh Hamad to Doha, the two sides announced that meetings of the Supreme Joint Committee would resume. From early 2002 international oil companies were invited to submit bids to drill for oil and gas off the Hawar islands, which Sheikh Hamad also intended to transform into a major tourist resort. Approval for the construction of the causeway linking Bahrain to Qatar was finally given in May 2004, and a public commission to oversee the project, which was expected to cost in excess of US $2,000m., was appointed in February 2005. After protracted discussions, it was announced in September 2007 that construction of the causeway was scheduled to commence in May 2008 and would, it was hoped, be completed by 2011; however, the contract had yet to be awarded by March 2008.

Following an unusually short period of negotiations, in September 2004 Bahrain signed a free trade agreement (FTA) with the USA. In response, the Saudi Government, which claimed that the accord contravened the GCC's external tariff agreement (a view disputed by Bahrain), in January 2005 threatened to impose customs duties on foreign goods imported duty-free through GCC countries, a move that would affect US goods imported to Bahrain under the bilateral agreement. In December 2004 Crown Prince Abdullah of Saudi Arabia had failed to attend the GCC annual summit in Manama, a decision that for some commentators symbolized growing Saudi disapproval of the burgeoning relationship between Bahrain and the USA, and, in particular, indicated the seriousness of the dispute over the FTA. In what was interpreted as a punitive measure, which ran contrary to Bahrain's expectations, Saudi Arabia reduced petroleum transfers by withdrawing the extra output resulting from the doubling of capacity at the jointly owned Abu Saafa oilfield. Nevertheless, in May 2005 GCC ministers responsible for finance reportedly decided to allow bilateral commercial accords between individual member states and the USA, and the FTA was duly implemented following US congressional approval in December (although it did not become effective until August 2006). As part of the negotiations, in September 2005 Bahrain became the first GCC member to lift its ban on Israeli imports; however, Sheikh Muhammad bin Mubarak al-Khalifa, the Deputy Prime Minister and Minister of Foreign Affairs at the time, strongly denied that this represented the first step towards the establishment of diplomatic relations between Bahrain and Israel. In January 2007 the citizenship of a Kenya-born Bahraini athlete was revoked after the Bahrain Athletics Association (in conjunction with government officials) arbitrated that, by competing in the Israeli Tiberias Marathon, he had 'violated the laws of Bahrain', and emphasized that his participation in the event had not been officially endorsed.

The complete blockade by the Israeli Government in mid-January 2008 of the Gaza Strip, which was controlled by the Islamic Resistance Movement (Hamas—see the chapters on Israel and the Palestinian Autonomous Areas), provoked vociferous condemnation from various leading elements of Bahraini society. The Bahraini Supreme Council for Islamic Affairs publicly denounced the blockade—which the Palestinian authorities claimed had left approximately 1.5m. Palestinians without access to power, food and medical supplies—branding it 'a threat to regional and international peace and stability'. Meanwhile, George W. Bush became the first active US President to embark upon an official visit to Bahrain when he travelled to the Gulf state in January 2008 during a wider regional tour, intended to garner support for his proposals to broker peace between Israelis and Palestinians before the end of his presidential term in January 2009. King Hamad welcomed President Bush's visit as a reflection of the burgeoning relationship enjoyed by the two allies, and called for further bilateral military co-operation, while President Bush was unreserved in his praise of King Hamad and the Bahraini Government's endeavours to effect significant political change in the Gulf state. However, most commentators agreed that much remained to be done before Bahrain's leadership could claim truly to have achieved lasting democratic reform.

Government

A National Action Charter, drafted in late 2000 by a Supreme National Committee and approved in a national referendum held in February 2001, recommended the transition from an emirate to a constitutional monarchy. The Amir proclaimed himself King in February 2002, when the amended Constitution was promulgated. Subsequently, a bicameral legislature, comprising a directly elected legislative body and an appointed consultative chamber, was instituted. Elections to a 40-member Majlis an-Nuab (Council of Representatives) took place in October 2002, and a new Majlis ash-Shoura (Consultative Council), comprising 40 appointed members, was sworn in by the King in November of that year. However, the principal political formation of the Shi'ite majority boycotted the elections of 2002. Further legislative polls held in November 2006 resulted in the formation of a predominantly Islamist parliament; a new Consultative Council was designated by royal decree in December.

Defence

Military service is voluntary. As assessed at November 2007, the active Bahrain Defence Force consisted of 8,200 men (6,000 army, 700 navy, 1,500 air force). There were also paramilitary forces of an estimated 11,260 men (9,000 police, an estimated 2,000 national guard, an estimated 260 coastguard). The defence budget for 2007 was estimated at BD 205m. (excluding procurement).

Economic Affairs

In 2004, according to estimates by the World Bank, Bahrain's gross national income (GNI), measured at average 2002–04 prices, was US $10,288m., equivalent to $14,370 per head (or $19,670 per head on an international purchasing-power parity basis). During 1996–2006, it was estimated, the population increased at an average annual rate of 2.1%, while gross domestic product (GDP) per head increased, in real terms, by an average of 3.0% per year in 1996–2005. Overall GDP increased, in real terms, at an average annual rate of 5.2% per year in 1996–2005; growth was 6.9% in 2005.

According to FAO, agriculture (including hunting, forestry and fishing) engaged 0.8% of the labour force in 2005. In the same year the sector contributed 0.3% of GDP. The principal crops are dates, tomatoes, onions and lettuces. Livestock production is also important. Agricultural GDP decreased by an annual average rate of 2.6% in 2001–05. The GDP of the sector decreased by an estimated 3.2% in 2005.

Industry (comprising mining, manufacturing, construction and utilities) engaged 54.5% of the employed labour force in 2001, and provided 39.1% of GDP in 2005. During 2001–05 industrial GDP increased by an average of 3.4% per year; the sector expanded by an estimated 6.7% in 2005.

Mining and quarrying engaged 0.2% of the employed labour force in 2001, and contributed 23.0% of GDP in 2005. The major mining activities are the exploitation of petroleum and natural gas; in 2005 oil production alone accounted for 25.2% of GDP. At the beginning of 2005 Bahrain's proven published reserves of crude petroleum were estimated at just 100m. barrels. Including output from the Abu Saafa oilfield (situated between Bahrain and Saudi Arabia), all revenue from which was, until the field was expanded in 2004, allocated to Bahrain, total crude oil production for 2005 was recorded at 68.1m. barrels. Excluding output from Abu Saafa, Bahrain produced an estimated 13.1m. barrels of crude oil in 2006. Bahrain's reserves of natural gas at the end of 2006 were put at 90,000m. cu m, sufficient to maintain production (at 2006 levels) for just over eight years. Mining GDP decreased by an annual average of 3.6% in 2001–05. The sector's GDP decreased by some 6.6% in 2005.

In 2001 manufacturing engaged 25.6% of the employed labour force, and the sector provided 11.8% of GDP in 2005. Important industries include the petroleum refinery at Sitra, aluminium (Bahrain is the region's largest producer) and aluminium-related enterprises, shipbuilding, iron and steel, and chemicals. Since the mid-1980s the Government has encouraged the development of light industry. During 2001–05 manufacturing GDP increased at an average annual rate of 6.2%; the sector's GDP increased by an estimated 18.8% in 2005.

Industrial expansion has resulted in energy demand that threatens to exceed the country's 1,830-MW total installed generating capacity, particularly as not all of the installed capacity is operational, owing to the advanced age of a number of stations. (Fuel imports amounted to 57.7% of total merchandise imports in 2006, according to provisional figures.) The largely state-owned Aluminium Bahrain (Alba) smelter plant was supplementing domestic power generation in an attempt to accommodate the energy deficit. An agreement was signed in 2004 with Tractebel of Belgium and Kuwait's Gulf Investment Corpn to run the Al-Ezzal independent power project from April 2006; the project was intended to increase the country's generating capacity to some 2,800 MW by mid-2007. Tendering for the initial phase of a US $1,100m. regional electricity 'inter-exchange' grid, connecting members of the Co-operation Council for the Arab States of the Gulf (or Gulf Co-operation Council—GCC, see p. 219), was completed in 2006; the network was ultimately to achieve regional self-sufficiency in electricity generation to 2058. The first stage, connecting Qatar, Bahrain, Saudi Arabia and Kuwait, was scheduled for completion in 2008, with full interconnection expected by 2010. Meanwhile, in November 2007 Bahrain and Iran signed a memorandum of understanding, which, *inter alia*, provided for the supply of 28m. cu m per day of natural gas from Iran to Bahrain, which was expected to commence within three years, dependent upon the successful conclusion of negotiations and the construction of a pipeline to transport the gas.

The services sector engaged 44.6% of the employed labour force in 2001, and contributed 60.5% of GDP in 2005. The financial services industry, notably the operation of 'offshore' banking units (OBUs), is a major source of Bahrain's prosperity. In late 2006 there were 49 registered OBUs. Bahrain has developed as a principal centre for Islamic banking and other financial services. In January 2002 Bahrain became the first country to publish a full set of regulations, including requirements in terms of capital adequacy, risk management, asset quality, liquidity management and corporate governance, for its Islamic banking sector. The first International Islamic Financial Market, with a liquidity management centre and Islamic ratings agency based in Bahrain, was inaugurated in August. In October the Government launched the Bahrain Financial Harbour project, whereby the Manama port area was to be redeveloped in order to provide a home for the 'offshore' financial sector and to protect Bahrain's status as the leading financial centre in the Gulf. Completion of the project was initially anticipated by 2007, but subsequently revised to mid-2009. In September 2006 the country's central bank and financial regulator, the Bahrain Monetary Agency, was disbanded and its successor, the Central Bank of Bahrain, established by enactment of a new Central Bank of Bahrain and Financial Institutions Law. Bahrain's prominence in the Islamic financial sector was further emphasized by the decision, in early 2007, to base a proposed Islamic Financial Mediator Council in the country, which was designed to arbitrate in potential disputes between Islamic financial institutions. During 2001–05 the services sector showed an average GDP increase of 10.5% per year. The GDP of the sector increased by about 11.4% in 2005.

In 2006 Bahrain recorded a visible trade surplus of a provisional BD 1,179.7m., and there was a surplus of some BD 721.3m. on the current account of the balance of payments. According to provisional figures, in 2006 the principal sources of non-petroleum imports were Japan (accounting for 11.9% of the total), Saudi Arabia (11.6%), Australia, the People's Republic of China and the USA. Saudi Arabia provided most of Bahrain's petroleum imports. Saudi Arabia was also the principal customer for Bahrain's non-petroleum exports (20.9% of the total) in 2006; other important markets were the USA (9.3%), India (6.8%), Singapore and the UAE. The principal exports are petroleum, petroleum products and aluminium. Sales of mineral products provided an estimated 80.9% of total export earnings in 2006, according to provisional figures. The principal import is crude petroleum (for domestic refining): mineral products accounted for about 57.7% of total imports in 2006. The main category of non-petroleum imports (some 9.2% in 2006) is machinery and mechanical appliances, electrical, sound and television equipment.

In 2005 there was an actual budgetary surplus of BD 257.3m. (equivalent to 5.1% of GDP), in marked contrast to the anticipated deficit of BD 208.6m.; a surplus of BD 281.1m. was recorded in 2006. According to ILO, the annual rate of inflation averaged 0.5% in 1997–2006; according to central bank figures, consumer prices increased by an annual average of 2.1% in 2006. Some 71.5% of the employed labour force were non-Bahrainis in 2006. The official rate of unemployment was 5.6% in late 2001, but unofficial sources estimated unemployment to be at around 20% in 2005, a situation that precipitated a series of protests. A number of government training initiatives and reform of the sponsorship system of employment were implemented in 2006 in an attempt to address this problem. The Ministry of Labour suggested in early 2007 that unemployment levels among Bahrainis in the kingdom had declined to less than 5%, although Bahraini human rights activists and some economists contended that the actual figure remained significantly higher.

Bahrain is a member of the GCC, whose six members established a unified regional customs tariff in January 2003 and agreed to create a single market and currency no later than January 2010. The economic convergence criteria for the proposed monetary union were agreed at a heads of state meeting in Abu Dhabi, the UAE, in December 2005, and in January 2008 the GCC launched its common market. The country is also a member of the Organization of Arab Petroleum Exporting Countries (OAPEC, see p. 366), the Arab Monetary Fund (see p. 175) and the Islamic Development Bank (see p. 329).

In recognition of the fact that Bahrain's reserves of petroleum and natural gas are nearing exhaustion, the Government has introduced measures both to diversify the country's industrial base and to attract wider foreign investment. During the past decade the Government has encouraged greater participation of the private sector in economic development, and has adopted a gradual approach to the privatization of state enterprises (excluding the petroleum sector). Following the foundation of the Telecommunications Regulatory Authority in 2002, in April 2003 the Government ended the monopoly of the state-owned Bahrain Telecommunications Co over the rapidly expanding mobile phone services market by granting, to MTC Vodafone Bahrain, a second GSM licence. In January 2004 further plans to liberalize the telecommunications sector by inviting applications for new licences were announced. Agreements for the award of two national fixed wireless services licences to MTC Vodafone Kuwait (rebranded in September 2007 as Zain Bahrain) and a local company, Mena Telecom, were finalized in early 2007. Meanwhile, investor confidence was enhanced by moves towards political liberalization. Despite the continued fear of regional instability linked to the US-led military involvement in Iraq from 2003, and ongoing speculation regarding Iran's nuclear programme, the IMF reported growth of 7.6% in 2006. The implementation of a free trade agreement with the USA in August 2006 has also provided a further boost to economic growth; however, the deal caused tension between Bahrain and Saudi Arabia, which led to the latter country opting to take its full share of petroleum from the jointly owned Abu Saafa oilfield, effectively costing Bahrain the revenue from some 50,000 barrels per day. The Government announced in late 2007 that it was to create a US $2,600m. holding company for its energy-related assets, which was to operate under the auspices of the National Oil and Gas Authority. It was hoped that the new entity would stimulate the oil and gas sector, the bureaucracy of which had been subject to considerable criticism in recent years. Meanwhile, job creation for Bahraini nationals remained a significant challenge. Several high-profile employment schemes were introduced by the Government in 2006, including the 18-month National Employment and Training Programme (NETP)—which sought to encourage employment of Bahraini nationals in private companies and provide training and rehabilitation to job-seekers. Initial reports suggested that thousands of Bahrainis had registered under the NETP, although doubts remained as to the sustainability and security of jobs in the kingdom. The Government renewed its commitment to diversification away from the hydrocarbons sector in 2007, focusing its efforts particularly on financial services, which account for about one-fifth of annual GDP. The rise to eminence of the banking sectors in Qatar, Saudi Arabia and the UAE has caused the Bahraini Government to increase its efforts to promote the kingdom's offshore and Islamic banking facilities, in the hope of reasserting its financial dominance over its regional competitors. The first phase of the new $1,500m. Bahrain Financial Harbour (BFH) development project—the Financial Centre—was inaugurated in May 2007. It was hoped that the BFH, which was eventually to combine office space with residential, retail and leisure facilities on 380,000 sq m of reclaimed waterfront land in northern Manama, would generate a significant number of new jobs, for Bahraini citizens and foreign workers alike.

Education

Although education is not compulsory, it is provided free of charge up to the secondary level. The education system is composed of three different stages: primary and intermediate schooling, which together form 'basic education', and secondary schooling. Primary education lasts from six to 11 years of age; it is divided into two cycles, each comprising three years. Intermediate education lasts for three years, between the ages of 12 and 14. Entry to secondary education, which comprises three years between the ages of 15 and 17, is conditional on obtaining the Intermediate School Certificate or its equivalent. Students choose to follow one of the following curriculums: general (science or literary), commercial, technical or vocational. Private and religious education are also available. The University of Bahrain, established by Amiri decree in 1986, comprises five colleges: the College of Engineering, the College of Arts, the College of Science, the College of Education and the College of Business Administration. About 25,000 students were enrolled at the University in 2006. The Arabian Gulf University (AGU), funded by seven Arab governments, also provides higher education. The AGU comprises two colleges: the College of Medicine and Medical Sciences and the College of Graduate Studies, which together enrolled some 659 students in 2001/02. Construction of the Royal College of Surgeons, within Ireland Medical University of Bahrain at Muharraq, was under way, and was expected to be completed by August 2008, at an estimated cost of US $78.9m. In addition, ambitious plans to establish a Higher Education City, at a projected cost of $1,000m., were finalized in December 2006; the development, which was scheduled to become operational by 2011, was to include a full branch of a leading US university, an international research centre and a specialist academy. According to UNESCO, in 2004/05 the total enrolment at primary schools included 97.1% of children in the relevant age-group, while the comparable ratio for secondary enrolment was 90.0%. Budget forecasts for 2006 allocated BD 149.3m. (13.7% of total recurrent government expenditure) to the Ministry of Education.

Public Holidays

2008: 1 January (New Year's Day), 10 January*† (Muharram, Islamic New Year), 19 January* (Ashoura), 20 March* (Mouloud, Birth of the Prophet), 1 May (Labour Day), 1 October* (Id al-Fitr, end of Ramadan), 8–10 December* (Id al-Adha, Feast of the Sacrifice), 16 December (National Day), 29 December*† (Muharram, Islamic New Year).

2009: 1 January (New Year's Day), 7 January*‡ (Ashoura), 9 March* (Mouloud, Birth of the Prophet), 1 May (Labour Day), 20 September* (Id al-Fitr, end of Ramadan), 26–28 November* (Id al-Adha, Feast of the Sacrifice), 16 December (National Day), 18 December* (Muharram, Islamic New Year), 27 December*‡ (Ashoura).

* These holidays are dependent on the Islamic lunar calendar and may vary by one or two days from the dates given.

† This festival occurs twice (marking the start of the Islamic years AH 1429 and 1430) within the same Gregorian year.

‡ This festival occurs twice (in the Islamic years AH 1430 and 1431) within the same Gregorian year.

Weights and Measures

The metric system is being introduced.

# Statistical Survey

Sources (unless otherwise stated): Central Informatics Organization (formerly Central Statistics Organization), POB 33305, Manama; tel. 17727722; e-mail ciohelpdesk@cio.gov.bh; internet www.cio.gov.bh; Central Bank of Bahrain, POB 27, Bldg 96, Block 317, Rd 1702, Manama; tel. 17547777; fax 17530399; e-mail info@cbb.gov.bh; internet www.cbb.gov.bh; Ministry of Finance and National Economy, POB 333, Diplomatic Area, Manama; tel. 17530800; fax 17532713; e-mail mofne@batelco.com.bh; internet www.mofne.gov.bh.

AREA AND POPULATION

Area: 720.1 sq km (278.0 sq miles).

Population: 508,037 at census of 16 November 1991; 650,604 (males 373,649, females 276,955), comprising 405,667 Bahrainis (males 204,623, females 201,044) and 244,937 non-Bahraini nationals (males 169,026, females 75,911), at census of 7 April 2001. *December 2006* (estimate) 742,561 (males 427,164, females 315,397), comprising 459,012 Bahrainis (males 231,493, females 227,519) and 283,549 non-Bahraini nationals (males 195,671, females 87,878).

Density (December 2006): 1,031.2 per sq km.

Regions (populations at 2001 census): Hidd 11,637; Muharraq 91,939; Manama 153,395; Jidd Hafs 52,450; Northern 43,691; Sitra 43,910; Central 49,969; Isa Town 36,833; Rifa'a 79,985; Western 26,149; Southern 3,875; Hamad Town 52,718; *Total* 650,604 (incl. 4,053 nationals residing abroad).

Principal Towns (populations at 2001 census): Manama (capital) 153,395; Muharraq 91,939; Rifa'a 79,985; Hamad Town 52,718; Jidd Hafs 52,450. *Mid-2005* (UN estimate, incl. suburbs): Manama 162,000. Source: UN, *World Urbanization Prospects: The 2005 Revision*.

Births, Marriages and Deaths (2003): Registered live births 14,560 (birth rate 21.1 per 1,000); Registered marriages 5,373 (marriage rate 7.8 per 1,000); Registered deaths 2,114 (death rate 3.1 per 1,000). *2004:* Registered live births 14,968; Registered marriages 4,667; Registered deaths 2,215. *2005:* Registered live births 15,198; Registered deaths 2,222 (Sources: UN, *Demographic Yearbook* and *Population and Vital Statistics Report*).

Expectation of Life (years at birth, WHO estimates): 74.3 (males 73.3; females 75.8) in 2005. Source: WHO, *World Health Statistics*.

Economically Active Population (persons aged 15 years and over, economic activity covered by social welfare system only, 2001): Agriculture, hunting, forestry and fishing 1,439; Mining and quarrying 283; Manufacturing 43,134; Electricity, gas and water 3,465; Construction 44,899; Trade, restaurants and hotels 34,683; Transport, storage and communications 10,322; Financing, insurance, real estate and business services 8,774; Community, social and personal services 21,339; Activities not adequately defined 656; *Total employed* 168,994 (males 147,683, females 21,311), comprising 56,165 Bahrainis (males 42,781, females 13,384) and 112,829 non-Bahraini nationals (males 104,902, females 7,927).

Total Labour Force (persons aged 15 years and over, census of 2001): Total Bahrainis employed 110,987 (males 84,920, females 26,067); Total non-Bahrainis employed 180,391 (males 146,604, females 33,787); *Total employed* 291,378. Total Bahraini labour force (incl. unemployed) 127,123 (males 94,354, females 32,769); Total non-Bahraini labour force (incl. unemployed) 181,220 (males 147,123, females 34,097); *Total labour force* 308,343. *2006:* Total employed 351,862 (Bahrainis 100,385, non-Bahrainis 251,477).

HEALTH AND WELFARE
Key Indicators

Total Fertility Rate (children per woman, 2005): 2.4.

Under-5 Mortality Rate (per 1,000 live births, 2005): 11.

HIV/AIDS (% of persons aged 15–49, 2003): 0.2.

Physicians (per 1,000 head, 2004): 1.09.

Hospital Beds (per 1,000 head, 2005): 2.81.

Health Expenditure (2004): US $ per head (PPP): 871.4.

Health Expenditure (2004): % of GDP: 4.0.

Health Expenditure (2004): public (% of total): 67.2.

Human Development Index (2005): ranking: 41.

Human Development Index (2005): value: 0.866.

For sources and definitions, see explanatory note on p. vi.

AGRICULTURE, ETC.

Principal Crops ('000 metric tons, 2005, FAO estimates): Lettuce 1.1; Tomatoes 2.1; Dry onions 1.4; Bananas 0.7; Lemons and limes 1.0; Dates 15.0. *Aggregate Production* (may include official, semi-official or estimated data): Total vegetables (incl. melons) 8.0; Total fruits (excl. melons) 20.0.

Livestock ('000 head, 2005, FAO estimates): Cattle 9.0; Sheep 40.0; Goats 26.0.

Livestock Products ('000 metric tons, 2005, FAO estimates): Cattle meat 0.9; Sheep meat 1.6; Goat meat 5.7; Poultry meat 5.3; Cows' milk 10.5.

Fishing (metric tons, live weight, 2005): Capture 11,854 (Groupers 358; Emperors—Scavengers 146; Spinefeet—Rabbitfishes 1,802; Carangids 63; Blue swimming crab 3,246; Green tiger prawn 1,107); Aquaculture 3; *Total catch* 11,857.

Source: FAO.

MINING

Production (2006, estimates): Crude petroleum 13,085,000 barrels; Natural gas 10,700 million cubic metres. Source: US Geological Survey.

INDUSTRY

Production ('000 barrels, 2006, unless otherwise indicated): Liquefied petroleum gas 400 (estimate); Butane 1,020 (estimate); Propane 1,070 (estimate); Naphtha 1,790 (estimate); Motor spirit (Gasoline) 7,200 (estimate); Kerosene and jet fuel 20,800 (estimate); Distillate fuel oil 19,000 (estimate); Residual fuel oil 28,500 (estimate); Electric energy 9,752.9 million kWh; Aluminium (unwrought) 872,388 metric tons (estimate).

Source: partly US Geological Survey.

FINANCE

Currency and Exchange Rates: 1,000 fils = 1 Bahraini dinar (BD). Sterling, Dollar and Euro Equivalents (31 December 2007): £1 sterling = 753.3 fils; US $1 = 376.0 fils; €1 = 553.5 fils; 10 Bahraini dinars = £13.28 = $26.60 = €18.07. *Exchange Rate:* Fixed at US $1 = 376.0 fils (BD 1 = $2.6596) since November 1980.

Summary of Government Finance (central government operations, cash basis, BD million, 2005): Revenue 1,730.6; *Less* Expense 1,176.2; *Net cash inflow from operating activities* 554.4; *Less* Purchases of non-financial assets 151.17; Sales of non-financial assets 0.6; *Cash surplus/deficit* 403.9. Source: IMF, *Government Finance Statistics Yearbook*.

Revenue (central government operations, cash basis, BD million, 2005): Taxes 266.6 (Taxes on income, profits and capital gains 64.2; Taxes on goods and services 27.5; Taxes on international trade and transactions 155.4); Social contributions 59.6; Grants 39.7; Other revenue 1,364.7; *Total* 1,730.6. Source: IMF, *Government Finance Statistics Yearbook*.

Expense by Economic Type (central government operations, cash basis, BD million, 2005): Use of goods and services 203.2; Interest 62.1; Subsidies 151.4; Grants 21.9; *Total* (incl. others) 1,176.2. Source: IMF, *Government Finance Statistics Yearbook*.

Outlays by Function of Government (central government operations, incl. purchases of non-financial assets, cash basis, BD million, 2005): General public services 584.8 (Public debt transactions 62.1); Defence 182.6; Public order and safety 114.6; Economic affairs 18.1; Housing and community amenities 60.5; Health 103.1; Recreation, culture and religion 8.2; Education 193.4 (Secondary education 32.0; Tertiary education 161.4); Social protection 62.0; *Total* 1,327.3. Source: IMF, *Government Finance Statistics Yearbook*.

International Reserves (US $ million at 31 December 2004): Gold (valued at $44 per troy oz) 6.6; IMF special drawing rights 0.9; Reserve position in IMF 110.0; Foreign exchange 1,829.6; *Total* 1,947.1. Source: IMF, *International Financial Statistics*.

Money Supply (BD million at 31 December 2006): Currency outside banks 227.7; Demand deposits at commercial banks 1,058.1; *Total money* 1,285.8. Source: IMF, *International Financial Statistics*.

Cost of Living (Consumer Price Index; base: 1994/95 = 100): 104.4 in 2004; 107.1 in 2005; 109.3 in 2006.

Expenditure on the Gross Domestic Product (BD million, 2005, provisional): Government final consumption expenditure 775.94; Private final consumption expenditure 2,189.66; Increase in stocks, including net errors and omissions 45.32; Gross fixed capital formation 893.28 *Total domestic expenditure* 3,904.20; Exports of goods and services 4,394.20; *Less* Imports of goods and services 3,267.20; *GDP in purchasers' values* 5,031.19.

BAHRAIN

Gross Domestic Product by Economic Activity (BD million at current prices, 2005): Agriculture, hunting, forestry and fishing 19.2; Mining and quarrying 1,282.6; Manufacturing 655.8; Electricity and water 51.6; Construction 188.4; Trade 504.2; Restaurants and hotels 106.0; Transport, storage and communications 312.5; Finance and insurance 1,237.9; Real estate and business services 393.2; Government services 628.3; Households with employed persons and private non-profit institutions 26.1; Other community, social and personal services 159.3; *Sub-total* 5,565.1; *Less* Imputed bank service charge 593.3; *GDP at factor cost* 4,971.8; Import duties 59.4; *GDP in purchasers' values* 5,031.2.

Balance of Payments (BD million, 2006, provisional): Exports of goods f.o.b. 4,347.6; Imports of goods f.o.b. –3,220.5; Repairs on goods 52.6; *Trade balance* 1,179.7; Services (net) 262.0; *Balance on goods and services* 1,441.7; Other income (net) –144.7; *Balance on goods, services and income* 1,297.0; Current transfers (net) –575.6; *Current balance* 721.3; Capital account (net) 28.2; Direct investment abroad –368.5; Direct investment from abroad 1,096.0; Portfolio investment (net) –3,218.2; Other investment (net) 2,047.2; Net errors and omissions 3.0; *Overall balance* 309.1.

EXTERNAL TRADE

Principal Commodities (BD million, 2006, provisional): *Imports c.i.f.:* Mineral products 1,940.0; Products of chemical or allied industries 204.5; Base metals and articles thereof 195.8; Machinery and mechanical appliances, electrical equipment, and sound and television apparatus 308.2; Transport equipment 255.7; Total (incl. others) 3,362.8. *Exports f.o.b.:* Mineral products 3,517.5; Base metals and articles thereof 559.9; Total (incl. others) 4,347.6.

Principal Trading Partners (BD million, 2006, provisional): *Imports c.i.f.:* Australia 125.4; Brazil 43.0; China, People's Repub. 123.9; France 38.4; Germany 96.8; India 51.2; Italy 51.1; Japan 181.0; Korea, Repub. 38.3; Netherlands 23.9; Saudi Arabia 176.9; Switzerland 19.7; United Arab Emirates 82.7; United Kingdom 71.2; USA 108.5; Total (incl. others) 1,519.8. *Exports f.o.b.:* Australia 16.7; China, People's Repub. 8.7; India 59.9; Italy 13.4; Japan 32.4; Korea, Repub. 32.2; Kuwait 26.2; Netherlands 32.1; Oman 7.9; Pakistan 13.8; Qatar 34.6; Saudi Arabia 184.5; Singapore 57.7; Taiwan 26.3; United Arab Emirates 53.1; USA 82.0; Total (incl. others) 881.0. Note: Figures exclude trade in petroleum.

TRANSPORT

Road Traffic (registered motor vehicles in use, 2005): Private passenger cars 241,813; Private buses and coaches 5,590; Private lorries and vans 39,221; Motor cycles and mopeds 3,601; *Total* (incl. others): 314,033.

Shipping (international sea-borne freight traffic, '000 metric tons, 1990): *Goods Loaded:* Dry cargo 1,145; Petroleum products 12,140. *Goods Unloaded:* Dry cargo 3,380; Petroleum products 132 (Source: UN, *Monthly Bulletin of Statistics*). Merchant Fleet (31 December 2006): Registered vessels 166; Total displacement 328,350 grt (Source: Lloyd's Register-Fairplay, *World Fleet Statistics*).

Civil Aviation (2003): Kilometres flown (million) 40; Passengers carried ('000) 1,850; Passenger-km (million) 4,494; Total ton-km (million) 769. Figures include an apportionment (equivalent to one-quarter) of the traffic of Gulf Air, a multinational airline with its headquarters in Bahrain. Source: UN, *Statistical Yearbook*.

TOURISM

Tourist Arrivals (at national borders, excluding Bahraini nationals residing abroad): 4,844,497 in 2003; 5,667,331 in 2004; 8,350,703 in 2005.

Arrivals by Nationality (2004): India 418,767; Kuwait 213,821; Philippines 134,369; Saudi Arabia 3,415,008; United Kingdom 191,003; USA 149,321; *Total* (incl. others) 5,667,331.

Tourist Receipts (US $ million, incl. passenger transport): 1,206 in 2003; 1,504 in 2004; 1,603 in 2005.

Source: World Tourism Organization.

COMMUNICATIONS MEDIA

Radio Receivers ('000 in use, 1997): 338.

Television Receivers ('000 in use, 2000): 275.

Telephones ('000 main lines in use, 2006): 193.3.

Facsimile Machines (2002): 4,514 in use.

Mobile Cellular Telephones ('000 subscribers, 2006): 898.9.

Personal Computers ('000 in use, 2004): 121.

Internet Users ('000, 2006): 157.3.

Broadband Subscribers ('000, 2006): 38.6.

Book Production (1998, titles, first editions only): 92.

Daily Newspapers (1996): 4 (circ. 67,000 copies).

Non-daily Newspapers (1993): 5 (circ. 17,000 copies).

Other Periodicals (1993): 26 (circ. 73,000 copies).

Source: mainly UNESCO, *Statistical Yearbook,* and International Telecommunication Union.

EDUCATION

Pre-primary: 90 schools (1996/97); 449 teachers (1995/96); 12,308 pupils (1996/97) (Source: UNESCO, *Statistical Yearbook*).

Primary (2005/06): 82,943 pupils (males 42,442, females 40,501).

Intermediate (2005/06): 39,741 pupils (males 20,270, females 19,471).

General Secondary (2005/06): 11,738 pupils (males 4,136, females 7,602).

Commercial Secondary (2005/06): 8,954 pupils (males 3,902, females 5,052).

Industrial Secondary (2005/06): 5,335 pupils.

Religious Institutes (2005/06): 1,197 pupils.

Source: Ministry of Education.

Adult Literacy Rate (UNESCO estimates): 86.5% (males 86.6%; females 83.6%) in 2001. Source: UNESCO Institute for Statistics.

Directory

The Constitution

The 108-article Constitution that came into force on 6 December 1973 stated that 'all citizens shall be equal before the law' and guaranteed freedom of speech, of the press, of conscience and of religious beliefs. Other provisions included compulsory free primary education and free medical care. The Constitution also provided for a National Assembly, composed of 14 members of the Cabinet and 30 members elected by popular vote, although this was dissolved in August 1975. A National Action Charter was approved in a nation-wide referendum held on 14–15 February 2001. (The Charter had been prepared by a Supreme National Committee, created by Amiri decree in late 2000 with the task of outlining the future evolution of Bahrain's political system.) Principal among the Committee's recommendations were that there should be a transition from an emirate to a constitutional monarchy (the Amir proclaimed himself King on 14 February 2002), with a bicameral parliament (comprising a directly elected legislature and an appointed consultative chamber) and an independent judiciary. Bahraini women were to be permitted for the first time to hold public office and to vote in elections. The amended Constitution, promulgated on 14 February 2002, guaranteed the provisions of the National Action Charter. The kingdom's first direct elections to the 40-member Majlis an-Nuab (Council of Representatives) took place on 24 October 2002, and the new Majlis ash-Shoura (Consultative Council), also comprising 40 members, was appointed by the King on 17 November. Members of both chambers are appointed for terms of four years. Subsequent elections to the Majlis an-Nuab were held on 25 November 2006, and a new Majlis ash-Shoura was designated by royal decree on 5 December. Members of the lower house are required to be Bahraini nationals of at least 30 years of age, while those of the appointed chamber—who must also be Bahraini citizens—are to be aged at least 35.

The Government

HEAD OF STATE

King and Commander-in-Chief of Bahrain Defence Force: HM Sheikh HAMAD BIN ISA AL-KHALIFA (acceded as Amir 6 March 1999; proclaimed King 14 February 2002).

BAHRAIN

CABINET
(March 2008)

Prime Minister: Sheikh KHALIFA BIN SALMAN AL-KHALIFA.
Deputy Prime Minister responsible for Ministerial Committees: Sheikh MUHAMMAD BIN MUBARAK AL-KHALIFA.
Deputy Prime Ministers: Sheikh ALI BIN KHALIFA AL-KHALIFA, JAWAD BIN SALEM AL-ARRAYED.
Minister of Foreign Affairs: Sheikh KHALID BIN AHMAD AL-KHALIFA.
Minister of the Interior: Maj.-Gen. Sheikh RASHID BIN ABDULLAH BIN AHMAD AL-KHALIFA.
Minister of Justice and of Islamic Affairs: Sheikh KHALID BIN ALI AL-KHALIFA.
Minister of the Prime Minister's Court: Sheikh KHALID BIN ABDULLAH AL-KHALIFA.
Minister of Municipalities and Agriculture Affairs: MANSOOR BIN RAJAB.
Minister of Works and Housing: FAHMI BIN ALI AL-JOUDER.
Minister of Finance and National Economy: Sheikh AHMAD BIN MUHAMMAD AL-KHALIFA.
Minister of Information: JIHAD BU KAMAL.
Minister of Industry and Commerce: Dr HASSAN BIN ABDULLAH FAKHRO.
Minister of Education: Dr MAJID BIN ALI AN-NO'AIMI.
Minister of Health: Dr FAISAL AL-HAMAR.
Minister of Electricity and Water: Sheikh ABDULLAH BIN SALMAN AL-KHALIFA.
Minister of Labour: Dr MAJID BIN HASSAN AL-ALAWI.
Minister for Oil and Gas Affairs: Dr ABD AL-HUSSAIN BIN ALI MIRZA.
Minister of Social Development: Dr FATIMA AL-BLUSHI.
Minister of State for Consultative Council and Council of Representatives Affairs: Brig.-Gen. ABD AL-AZIZ MUHAMMAD AL-FADHIL.
Minister of State for Cabinet Affairs and Head of the Central Informatics Organization: Sheikh AHMAD BIN ATIYATALLAH AL-KHALIFA.
Minister of State for Defence Affairs: Dr SHEIKH MUHAMMAD BIN ABDULLAH AL-KHALIFA.
Minister of State for Foreign Affairs: Dr NIZAR AL-BAHARNA.

NON-CABINET ADVISERS WITH THE RANK OF MINISTER

Adviser to the Prime Minister on Legislative Authority Affairs: Dr MUHAMMAD ALI AS-SITRI.
Adviser to the Prime Minister on Oil and Industry Affairs: Sheikh ISA BIN ALI AL-KHALIFA.
Adviser to the Prime Minister on Security Affairs: Sheikh ABD AL-AZIZ BIN ATIYATALLAH AL-KHALIFA.

MINISTRIES

Royal Court: POB 555, Riffa Palace, Manama; tel. 17666666; fax 17663070.
Prime Minister's Court: POB 1000, Government House, Government Rd, Manama; tel. 17253361; fax 17533033; internet www.pmc.gov.bh.
Ministry of Cabinet Affairs: POB 26613, Manama; tel. 17223366; fax 17225202.
Ministry of Education: POB 43, Manama; tel. 17680105; fax 17687866; e-mail dir.relations@moe.gov.bh; internet www.education.gov.bh.
Ministry of Electricity and Water: POB 2, Manama; tel. 17533133; fax 17533035; internet www.mew.gov.bh.
Ministry of Finance and National Economy: POB 333, Diplomatic Area, Manama; tel. 17530800; fax 17532713; e-mail mofne@batelco.com.bh; internet www.mofne.gov.bh.
Ministry of Foreign Affairs: POB 547, Government House, Government Rd, Manama; tel. 17227555; fax 17212603; internet www.mofa.gov.bh.
Ministry of Health: POB 12, Sheikh Sulman Rd, Manama; tel. 17255555; fax 17252569; e-mail webmaster@health.gov.bh; internet www.moh.gov.bh.
Ministry of Industry and Commerce: POB 10908, Manama; tel. 17568000; fax 17581408; e-mail industry@industry.gov.bh; internet www.industry.gov.bh.
Ministry of Information: POB 253, Manama; tel. 17871111; fax 17682777; e-mail pr@info.gov.bh; internet www.info.gov.bh.
Ministry of the Interior: POB 13, Police Fort Compound, Manama; tel. 17272111; fax 17262169; internet www.interior.gov.bh.
Ministry of Islamic Affairs: POB 560, Diplomatic Area, Manama; tel. 17812812; fax 17812801; e-mail IslamicAffairs@moia.gov.bh; internet www.moia.gov.bh.
Ministry of Justice: POB 450, Diplomatic Area, Manama; tel. 175313333; fax 17536343; internet www.moj.gov.bh.
Ministry of Labour: POB 32333, Isa Town; tel. 17687800; fax 17686954; internet www.mol.gov.bh.
Ministry of Municipalities and Agriculture Affairs: POB 26909, Manama; tel. 17293693; fax 17293694; e-mail helpdesk@mun.gov.bh; internet www.mun.gov.bh.
Ministry of Social Development: POB 32868, Isa Town; tel. 17873999; fax 17682248; e-mail info@social.gov.bh; internet www.social.gov.bh.
Ministry of Works and Housing: POB 5, Manama; tel. 17545805; fax 17545608; e-mail info@mwh.gov.bh; internet www.mwh.gov.bh.

Legislature

The National Assembly provided for in the 1973 Constitution was dissolved in August 1975 and succeeded by a bicameral parliament (see Constitution), comprising a directly elected legislature and an appointed consultative chamber, which was instituted in 2002. The second direct elections to the 40-member legislature, the Majlis an-Nuab (Council of Representatives), were held on 25 November 2006; 12 seats were taken by Sunni Islamist candidates and 10 by independent Sunnis, with the remaining 18 seats being secured by opposition Shi'ite Islamists, incorporating one aligned independent. The new 40-seat Majlis ash-Shoura (Consultative Council) was appointed by the King on 5 December.

Political Organizations

Political parties are still prohibited in Bahrain. However, several political and civic societies (many of which were previously in exile) are now active in the country, and a number of new groups have been established since 2001. Restrictions on campaigning by political groups were revoked prior to the first elections to the new Majlis an-Nuab (Council of Representatives), held in October 2002. At the time of the second elections to the Council in November 2006 it was reported that there were 16 political alliances or blocs functioning in Bahrain. Prominent organizations include al-Wefaq National Islamic Society and the Islamic Action Society (both Shi'a Islamist), al-Asala and al-Menbar (both Sunni Islamist), and the National Democratic Action (left-wing).

Diplomatic Representation

EMBASSIES IN BAHRAIN

Algeria: POB 26402, Villa 579, Rd 3622, Adliya, Manama; tel. 17713669; fax 17713662; e-mail abdemyh@hotmail.com; Ambassador AHMAD BOUZIANE.
Bangladesh: POB 26718, House 2280, Rd 2757, Area 327, Adliya, Manama; tel. 17714717; fax 17710031; e-mail bangla@batelco.com.bh; internet www.banglaembassy.com.bh; Ambassador M. A. K. MAHMOOD.
Brunei: POB 15700, House 892, Rd 3218, Block 332, Mahooz, Manama; tel. 17720222; fax 17741757; e-mail kbbhhom@batelco.com.bh; Chargé d'affaires Haji AHMAD Haji JUMAAT.
China, People's Republic: POB 3150, Bldg 158, Rd 4156, Juffair Ave, Block 341, Manama; tel. 17723800; fax 17727304; e-mail chinaemb_bh@mfa.gov.cn; Ambassador LI ZHIGUO.
Egypt: POB 818, Mahouz, Manama; tel. 17720005; fax 17721518; e-mail egyembbh@batelco.com.bh; internet www.geocities.com/egyptemb; Ambassador Dr AZMY HASSAN KHALIFA.
France: POB 11134, Rd 1901, Bldg 51A, Block 319, Diplomatic Area, Manama; tel. 17298600; fax 17298607; e-mail chancellerie.manama-AMBA@diplomatie.gouv.fr; internet www.ambafrance-bh.org; Ambassador MALIKA BERAK.
Germany: POB 10306, Al-Hasan Bldg, 1st Floor, Sheikh Hamad Causeway, Area 317, Manama; e-mail germemb@batelco.com.bh; internet www.manama.diplo.de; tel. 17530210; fax 17536282; Ambassador Dr HUBERT LANG.
India: POB 26106, Bldg 182, Rd 2608, Area 326, Adliya, Manama; tel. 17712785; fax 17715527; e-mail indemb@batelco.com.bh; internet www.indianembassy-bah.com; Ambassador Dr BALAKRISHNA SHETTY.

BAHRAIN

Iran: POB 26365, Building 1034, Rd 3221, Area 332, Mahooz, Manama; tel. 17722880; fax 17722101; Chargé d'affaires REZA HONARVAR NAZARI.

Iraq: Al-Mahawez, Bldg 396, Rd 3207, Manama; tel. 17741472; fax 17720756; e-mail bhremb@iraqmofamail.net; Ambassador GHASSAN MUHSEN HUSSAIN.

Italy: PO Box 397, Villa 1554, Rd 5647, Block 356, Manama; tel. 17252424; fax 17277060; e-mail ambasciata.manama@esteri.it; internet www.italian-embassy.org.ae/Ambasciata_Manama; Ambassador CALOGERO DI GESU.

Japan: POB 23720, 55 Salmaniya Ave, Salmaniya 327, Manama; tel. 17716565; fax 17715059; e-mail jpembbh@batelco.com.bh; internet www.bh.emb-japan.go.jp; Ambassador TAKESHI KONDO.

Jordan: POB 5242, Villa 43, Rd 1901, Area 319, Manama; tel. 17291109; fax 17291980; e-mail jordemb@batelco.com.bh; Ambassador HUSSAIN AL-MAJALI.

Kuwait: POB 786, Rd 1703, Diplomatic Area, Manama; tel. 17534040; fax 17530278; Ambassador Sheikh AZZAM MUBARAK AS-SABAH.

Lebanon: Villa 1556, Rd 5647, Area 356, Manama; tel. 17579001; fax 17232535; e-mail lebem@batelco.com.bh; Ambassador AZIZ KAZZI.

Libya: POB 26015, Manama; tel. 17722252; fax 17722911; Chargé d'affaires ABD AL-HAMID M. AL-WINDI.

Malaysia: Bldg 2771, Rd 2835, Block 428, as-Seef District, Manama; tel. 17564551; fax 17564552; e-mail malmnama@kln.gov.my; internet www.kln.gov.my/perwakilan/manama; Ambassador NAIMUN ASHAKLI BIN MUHAMMAD.

Morocco: POB 26229, Villa 415, Rd 3207, Block 332, Mahooz, Manama; tel. 17740566; fax 17740178; e-mail sifamana@batelco.com; Ambassador MUHAMMAD AIT OUALI.

Oman: POB 26414, Bldg 37, Rd 1901, Diplomatic Area, Manama; tel. 17293663; fax 17293540; e-mail oman@batelco.com.bh; Ambassador SALIM ALI OMAR BAYAQOOB.

Pakistan: POB 563, Bldg 261, Rd 2807, Block 381, Segeiya, Manama; tel. 17244113; fax 17255960; e-mail parepbah@batelco.com.bh; internet www.pakistanembassy.com.bh; Ambassador IKRAMULLAH MEHSUD.

Philippines: POB 26681, Villa 992, Rd 3119, Area 331, Manama; tel. 17250990; fax 17258583; e-mail manamape@batelco.com.bh; Ambassador EDUARDO PABLO M. MAGLAYA.

Qatar: POB 15105, Villa 814, Rd 3315, Area 333, Mahooz, Manama; tel. 17722922; fax 17740662; Ambassador Sheikh ABDULLAH BIN THAMIR ATH-THANI.

Russia: POB 26612, Manama; tel. 17725222; fax 17725921; e-mail rusemb@batelco.com.bh; internet www.bahrain.mid.ru; Ambassador YURII ANTONOV.

Saudi Arabia: POB 1085, Bldg 82, Rd 1702, Block 317, Diplomatic Area, Manama; tel. 17537722; fax 17533261; Ambassador Dr ABDULLAH BIN IBRAHIM EL-KUWAIZ.

Senegal: Villa 25, Rd 33, Block 333, Mahooz, Manama; tel. 17821060; fax 17721650; Ambassador MAFODE NDONG.

Sudan: Villa 423, Rd 3614, Block 336, Manama; tel. 17717959; fax 17710113; e-mail sudanimanama@hotmail.com; Ambassador BUSHRA ASH-SHAIKH.

Syria: POB 11585, Villa 867, Rd 3315, Block 333, Malhouze, Manama; tel. 17722484; fax 17740380; e-mail syremb@batelco.com.bh; Ambassador SULEIMAN ADEL SARRA.

Thailand: POB 26475, Bldg 132, Rd 66, Block 360, Zinj Area, Manama; tel. 17246242; fax 17272714; e-mail thaimnm@mfa.go.th; internet www.mfa.go.th/web/1444.php?depid=269; Ambassador SUPHAT CHITRANUKROH.

Tunisia: POB 26911, House 54, Rd 3601, Area 336, Manama; tel. 17714149; fax 17715702; e-mail atmanama@batelco.bh; Ambassador KHALED AZ-ZITOUNI.

Turkey: POB 10821, Sehl Centre, 5th Floor, Bldg 81, Rd 1702, Area 317, Manama; tel. 17533448; fax 17536557; e-mail tcbahrbe@batelco.com.bh; Ambassador KHALDOUN OTHMAN.

United Arab Emirates: POB 26505, Villa 221, Rd 4007, Area 340, Manama; tel. 17748333; fax 17717724; Ambassador ABD AL-AZIZ BIN HADEF ASH-SHAMSI.

United Kingdom: POB 114, 21 Government Ave, Area 306, Manama; tel. 17574100; fax 17574161; e-mail bahrainchancery.bahrain@fco.gov.uk; internet www.britishembassy.gov.uk/bahrain; Ambassador JAMIE BOWDEN.

USA: POB 26431, Bldg 979, Rd 3119, Block 331, Zinj, Manama; tel. 17242700; fax 17270547; e-mail manamaconsular@state.gov; internet bahrain.usembassy.gov; Ambassador JOSEPH ADAM ERELI.

Yemen: Bldg 80, Rd 2802, Block 328, Umm al-Hassam, Manama; tel. 17822110; fax 17822078; Ambassador Dr ALI MANSOUR BIN MUHAMMAD.

Judicial System

Since the termination of British legal jurisdiction in 1971, intensive work has been undertaken on the legislative requirements of Bahrain. The Criminal Law is at present contained in various Codes, Ordinances and Regulations. All nationalities are subject to the jurisdiction of the Bahraini courts, which guarantee equality before the law irrespective of nationality or creed. The 1974 Decree Law on State Security Measures and the State Security Court were both abolished in February 2001. A Constitutional Court, consisting of seven members appointed by the King, became operational in April 2005.

Directorate of Courts: POB 450, Government House, Government Rd, Manama; tel. 17522252; fax 17532542.

Religion

At the April 2001 census the population was 650,604, distributed as follows: Muslims 528,393; Christians 58,315; others 63,896.

ISLAM

Muslims are divided between the Sunni and Shi'ite sects. The ruling family is Sunni, although the majority of the Muslim population (estimated at almost 60%) are Shi'ite.

CHRISTIANITY

The Anglican Communion

Within the Episcopal Church in Jerusalem and the Middle East, Bahrain forms part of the diocese of Cyprus and the Gulf. There are two Anglican churches in Bahrain: St Christopher's Cathedral in Manama and the Community Church in Awali. The congregations are entirely expatriate. The Dean of St Christopher's Cathedral is the Archdeacon in the Gulf, while the Bishop in Cyprus and the Gulf is resident in Cyprus.

Archdeacon in the Gulf: Very Rev. ALAN HAYDAY, St Christopher's Cathedral, POB 36, Al-Mutanabi Ave, Manama; tel. 17253866; fax 17246436; e-mail decani@batelco.com.bh; internet www.stchcathedral.org.bh.

Roman Catholic Church

A small number of adherents, mainly expatriates, form part of the Apostolic Vicariate of Arabia. The Vicar Apostolic is resident in the United Arab Emirates.

The Press

DAILIES

Akhbar al-Khaleej (Gulf News): POB 5300, Manama; tel. 17620111; fax 17621566; e-mail editor@aaknews.com; internet www.aaknews.com; f. 1976; Arabic; Chair. and Editor-in-Chief ANWAR ABD AR-RAHMAN; circ. 42,000.

Al-Ayam (The Days): POB 3232, Manama; tel. 17727111; fax 17729009; e-mail alayam@batelco.com.bh; internet www.alayam.com; f. 1989; Arabic; publ. by Al-Ayam Establishment for Press and Publications; Editor-in-Chief ISA ASH-SHAIJI; circ. 37,000.

Bahrain Tribune: POB 3232, Manama; tel. 17827111; fax 17827222; e-mail tribune@batelco.com.bh; internet www.bahraintribune.com; f. 1997; English; Editor-in-Chief BIKRAM VOHRA; circ. 13,000.

Gulf Daily News: POB 5300, Manama; tel. 17620222; fax 17622141; e-mail gdn1@batelco.com.bh; internet www.gulf-daily-news.com; f. 1978; English; Chair. ANWAR ABD AR-RAHMAN; Editor-in-Chief GEORGE WILLIAMS; circ. 11,000.

Khaleej Times: POB 26707, City Centre Bldg, Suite 403, 4th Floor, Government Ave, Manama; tel. 17213911; fax 17211819; e-mail ktimesbn@batelco.com.bh; internet www.khaleejtimes.com; f. 1978; English; based in Dubai (United Arab Emirates); circ. 72,565.

Al-Meethaq: Manama; tel. 17877777; fax 17784118; internet www.almeethaq.net; f. 2004; Arabic; supports the Govt's reform programme; publ. by Al-Meethaq Media and Publishing House; Editor-in-Chief MUHAMMAD HASSAN AS-SATRI.

Al-Waqt (The Time): POB 37744, Rifa'a; tel. 488444; fax 488448; e-mail alwaqt@alwaqt.net; internet www.alwaqt.net; f. 2006; Arabic;

BAHRAIN

Directory

independent; publ. by Time Media House; Chair. and Editor-in-Chief IBRAHIM BASHMI.

Al-Wasat: Dar al-Wasat for Publishing and Distribution, POB 31110, Manama; tel. 17596999; fax 17596900; e-mail news@alwasatnews.com; internet www.alwasatnews.com; Editor-in-Chief MANSOOR AL-JAMRI.

WEEKLIES

Al-Adhwaa' (Lights): POB 250, Old Exhibition Rd, Manama; tel. 17290942; fax 17293166; f. 1965; Arabic; publ. by Arab Printing and Publishing House; Chair. RAID MAHMOUD AL-MARDI; Editor-in-Chief MUHAMMAD QASSIM SHIRAWI; circ. 7,000.

BAPCO News: Bahrain Refinery, Sitra; tel. 17755049; fax 17755047; e-mail kathleen_croes@bapco.net.bh; internet www.bapco.com.bh; bi-weekly; English and Arabic; publ. by the Bahrain Petroleum Co BSC; Editors KATHLEEN CROES, KHALID F. MEHMAS; circ. 4,000.

Gulf Economic Monitor: POB 224, Exhibition Ave, Manama; tel. 17293131; fax 17293400; e-mail info@tradearabia.net; internet www.tradearabia.com; English; publ. by Al-Hilal Publishing and Marketing Group; Man. Dir RONNIE MIDDLETON.

Huna al-Bahrain (Here is Bahrain): POB 26005, Isa Town; tel. 17870166; fax 17686600; e-mail bahrainmag@info.gov.bh; internet www.info.gov.bh; f. 1957; Arabic; publ. by the Ministry of Information; Editor ABD AL-QADER AQIL; circ. 3,000.

Al-Mawakif (Attitudes): POB 1083, Manama; tel. 17231231; fax 17271720; f. 1973; Arabic; general interest; Editor-in-Chief MANSOOR M. RADHI; circ. 6,000.

Oil and Gas News: POB 224, Bldg 149, Exhibition Ave, Manama; tel. 17293131; fax 17293400; e-mail editor@oilandgasnewsworldwide.com; internet www.oilandgasnewsworldwide.com; f. 1983; English; publ. by Al-Hilal Publishing and Marketing Group; Editor-in-Chief CLIVE JACQUES; circ. 5,000.

Sada al-Usbou (Weekly Echo): POB 549, Manama; tel. 17291234; fax 17290507; f. 1969; Arabic; Owner and Editor-in-Chief ALI ABDULLAH SAYYAR; circ. 40,000 (in various Gulf states).

OTHER PERIODICALS

Arab Agriculture: POB 10131, Bahrain Tower, 8th Floor, Manama; tel. 17213900; fax 17211765; e-mail fanar@batelco.com.bh; internet www.fanarpublishing.com; f. 1984; annually; English and Arabic; publ. by Fanar Publishing WLL; Editor-in-Chief ABD AL-WAHED ALWANI; circ. 12,650.

Arab World Agribusiness: POB 10131, Bahrain Tower, 8th Floor, Manama; tel. 17213900; fax 17211765; e-mail fanar@batelco.com.bh; internet www.fanarpublishing.com; f. 1985; nine per year; English and Arabic; publ. by Fanar Publishing WLL; Editor-in-Chief ABD AL-WAHED ALWANI; circ. 18,715.

Al-Bahrain ath-Thaqafia: POB 2199, Manama; tel. 17290210; fax 17292678; e-mail aqaqeel@batelco.com.bh; quarterly; Arabic; publ. by the Ministry of Information; Editor MAI BINT MUHAMMAD AL-KHALIFA.

Bahrain This Month: POB 20461, Manama; tel. 17813777; fax 17813700; e-mail redhouse@batelco.com.bh; internet www.bahrainthismonth.com; f. 1997; monthly; English; Publr and Man. Dir GEORGE F. MIDDLETON; circ. 10,000.

Gulf Construction: POB 224, Exhibition Ave, Manama; tel. 17293131; fax 17293400; e-mail editor@gulfconstructiononline.com; internet www.gulfconstructionworldwide.com; f. 1980; monthly; English; publ. by Al-Hilal Publishing and Marketing Group; Editor BINA PRABHU GOVEAS; circ. 26,539.

Gulf Industry: POB 224, Manama; tel. 17293131; fax 17293400; e-mail editor@gulfindustryworldwide.com; internet www.gulfindustryworldwide.com; English; journal of industry and transport; publ. by Al-Hilal Publishing and Marketing Group; Editor SALVADOR ALMEIDA.

Al-Hayat at-Tijariya (Commerce Review): POB 248, Manama; tel. 17229555; fax 17224985; e-mail bahcci@batelco.com.bh; monthly; English and Arabic; publ. by Bahrain Chamber of Commerce and Industry; Editor KHALIL YOUSUF; circ. 7,500.

Al-Hidayah (Guidance): POB 450, Manama; tel. 17727100; fax 17729819; f. 1978; monthly; Arabic; publ. by Ministry of Islamic Affairs; Editor-in-Chief ABD AR-RAHMAN BIN MUHAMMAD RASHID AL-KHALIFA; circ. 5,000.

Middle East Expatriate: POB 224, Manama; tel. 17293131; fax 17292400; e-mail editor@middleeastpatonline.com; internet www.alhilalgroup.com/publications/mee.htm; monthly; English; publ. by Al-Hilal Publishing and Marketing Group; Editor BABU KALYANPUR; circ. 16,816.

Al-Mohandis (The Engineer): POB 835, Manama; tel. and fax 17727100; fax 17729819; e-mail mohandis@batelco.com.bh; internet www.mohandis.org; f. 1972; quarterly; Arabic and English; publ. by Bahrain Society of Engineers; Editor ISA ALI JANAHI.

Al-Musafir al-Arabi (Arab Traveller): POB 10131, Bahrain Tower, 8th Floor, Manama; tel. 17213900; fax 17211765; e-mail fanar@batelco.com.bh; internet www.fanarpublishing.com; f. 1984; six per year; Arabic; publ. by Fanar Publishing WLL; Editor-in-Chief ABD AL-WAHED ALWANI; circ. 36,000.

Al-Quwwa (The Force): POB 245, Manama; tel. 17291331; fax 17659596; f. 1977; monthly; Arabic; publ. by Bahrain Defence Force; Editor-in-Chief Maj. AHMAD MAHMOUD AS-SUWAIDI.

Travel and Tourism News Middle East: POB 224, Exhibition Ave, Manama; tel. 17293131; fax 17293400; e-mail hilalpmg@tradearabia.net; internet www.ttnworldwide.com; f. 1983; monthly; English; travel trade; publ. by Al-Hilal Publishing and Marketing Group; Publishing Dir KIM THOMPSON; circ. 12,370.

NEWS AGENCIES

Bahrain News Agency (BNA): Ministry of Information, POB 572, Manama; tel. 17689044; fax 17683825; e-mail news@bahrain.gov.bh; internet www.bna.bh; f. 2001 to cover local and foreign news; replaced Gulf News Agency as national news agency.

Gulf News Agency (GNA): POB 5421, Manama; tel. 17689044; fax 17683825; e-mail brtcnews@batelco.com.bh; internet www.bna.bh; f. 1978; transmits news to the Gulf region in Arabic and English; broadcasts on the same frequency as the BNA, the national news agency; Chief Editor KHALID ABDULLAH AZ-ZAYANI.

PRESS ASSOCIATION

Bahrain Journalists' Association (BJA): 2057, Rd 4156, Block 0341, Juffair, Manama 332; tel. 17811770; e-mail bja@batelco.com.bh; internet www.bja-bh.org; f. 2000; Chair. ISA ASH-SHAIJI; Sec.-Gen. JAWAD ABD AL-WAHAB; 250 mems.

Publishers

Arab Communicators: POB 551, Almoayyed Bldg, 6th Floor, Government Ave, Manama; tel. 17534664; fax 17531837; f. 1981; publrs of annual Bahrain Business Directory; Dirs AHMAD A. FAKHRI, HAMAD A. ABUL.

Fanar Publishing WLL: POB 10131, Manama; tel. 17213900; fax 17211765; e-mail fanar@batelco.com.bh; internet www.fanarpublishing.com; f. 1990; Editor-in-Chief ABD AL-WAHID ALWANI.

Gulf Saatchi and Saatchi: POB 5518, Manama; tel. 17226262; fax 17228660; e-mail infogulf@gulfad.com.bh; f. 1974; advertising and marketing communications; Chair. and Man. Dir KHAMIS AL-MUQLA.

Al-Hilal Publishing and Marketing Group: POB 224, Exhibition Ave, Manama; tel. 17293131; fax 17293400; e-mail info@tradearabia.net; internet www.tradearabia.com; f. 1977; specialist magazines and newspapers of commercial interest; Chair. A. M. ABD AR-RAHMAN; Man. Dir RONNIE MIDDLETON.

Manama Publishing Co WLL: POB 1013, Manama; tel. 17714289; fax 17713860; e-mail mecon@batelco.com.bh.

Al-Masirah Journalism, Printing and Publishing House: POB 5981, Manama; tel. 17258882; fax 17276178; e-mail almasera@batelco.com.bh.

Tele-Gulf Directory Publications WLL: POB 2738, Manama; tel. 17490000; fax 17490001; e-mail telegulf@batelco.com.bh; internet www.bahrainyellowpages.com.bh; f. 1977; publrs of annual Gulf Directory and Arab Banking and Finance, as well as Bahrain Telephone Directory with Yellow Pages and Banks in Bahrain; CEO JOHN MCISAAC.

GOVERNMENT PUBLISHING HOUSE

Directorate of Press and Publications: POB 253, Manama; tel. 17717525; e-mail jamaldawood@hotmail.com; internet www.info.gov.bh/en/PublicationPress/DirectorateofPressandPublications; Dir JAMAL DAWOOD.

Broadcasting and Communications

TELECOMMUNICATIONS

Regulatory Authority

Telecommunications Regulatory Authority (TRA): POB 10353, Taib Tower, 7th Floor, Diplomatic Area, Manama; tel. 17520000; fax 17532125; e-mail contact@tra.org.bh; internet www.tra.org.bh; f. 2002; Chair. Dr MUHAMMAD J. K. AL-GHATAM; Gen. Dir ALAN HORNE.

Principal Operators

Bahrain Telecommunications Co BSC (BATELCO): POB 14, Manama; tel. 17881881; fax 17311120; e-mail batelco@btc.com.bh; internet www.batelco.com.bh; f. 1981; cap. BD 120m.; 100% owned by Govt of Bahrain, financial institutions and public of Bahrain; launched mobile cellular telecommunications service, Sim Sim, in 1999; Chair. Sheikh HAMAD BIN ABDULLAH BIN MUHAMMAD AL-KHALIFA; CEO PETER KALIAROPOULOS.

Mena Telecom: POB 3173, NBB Tower, Government Ave, Manama; tel. 17203040; e-mail enquiries@menatelecom.com; internet www.menatelecom.com; f. 2003; provides fixed-line telephone, satellite, broadband internet and fixed wireless internet services; Chair. ABD AL-HAKEEM AL-KHAYYAT.

Zain Bahrain: Manama; tel. 36107107; internet www.bh.zain.com; f. 2003 under the name MTC Vodafone Bahrain; present name adopted Sept. 2007; acquired Celtel International (Holland) in 2005; 60% owned by Mobile Telecommunications Co (Kuwait), 40% by Bahraini Govt.

BROADCASTING

Radio

Bahrain Radio and Television Corpn: POB 702, Manama; tel. 17686000; fax 17681544; e-mail ceobrtc@batelco.com.bh; internet www.bahraintv.com; f. 1955; state-owned; two 10-kW transmitters; programmes are in Arabic and English, and include news, drama and discussions; Dir of Broadcasting ABD AR-RAHMAN ABDULLAH.

Radio Bahrain: POB 702, Manama; tel. 17871585; fax 17780911; internet www.radiobahrain.fm; f. 1977; commercial radio station in English language; Head of Station SALAH KHALID.

Television

Bahrain Radio and Television Corpn: POB 1075, Manama; tel. 17686000; fax 17681544; e-mail ceobrtc@batelco.com.bh; internet www.bahraintv.com; commenced colour broadcasting in 1973; broadcasts on five channels, of which the main Arabic and the main English channel accept advertising; offers a 24-hour Arabic news and documentary channel; covers Bahrain, eastern Saudi Arabia, Qatar and the United Arab Emirates; an Amiri decree in early 1993 established the independence of the Corpn, which was to be controlled by a committee; Dir H. AL-UMRAN.

Finance

(cap. = capital; res = reserves; dep. = deposits; m. = million; br.(s) = branch(es); amounts in Bahraini dinars unless otherwise stated)

BANKING

Central Bank

Central Bank of Bahrain (CBB): POB 27, Bldg 96, Block 317, Rd 1702, Diplomatic Area, Manama; tel. 17547777; fax 17530399; e-mail info@cbb.gov.bh; internet www.cbb.gov.bh; f. 1973 as Bahrain Monetary Agency; in operation from Jan. 1975; name changed as above in Sept. 2006; controls issue of currency, regulates exchange control and credit policy, organization and control of banking and insurance systems, bank credit and stock exchange; cap. 200.0m., res 187.0m., dep. 439.1m. (Dec. 2005); Gov. RASHID MUHAMMAD AL-MARAJ.

Locally incorporated Commercial Banks

Ahli United Bank BSC (AUB): POB 2424, Bldg 2495, Rd 2832, as-Seef District 428, Manama; tel. 17585858; fax 17580549; e-mail info@ahliunited.com; internet www.ahliunited.com; f. 2001 by merger of Al-Ahli Commercial Bank and Commercial Bank of Bahrain; cap. US $1,020m., res $1,290m., dep. $17,770m. (Dec. 2007); Chair. FAHAD AR-RAJAAN; Group CEO and Man. Dir ADEL EL-LABBAN; 20 brs.

Awal Bank BSC: POB 1735, Manama; tel. 17203333; fax 17203355; e-mail info@awal-bank.com; internet www.awal-bank.com; f. 2004; cap. US $750m., res $44.5m., dep. $3,150.0m.; Chair. MAAN A. AS-SANEA; CEO and Dir GERARD DELAFORGE.

Bahrain Islamic Bank BSC: POB 5240, As-Salam Tower, Diplomatic Area, Manama; tel. 17546111; fax 17535808; e-mail bahisl@batelco.com.bh; internet www.bahisl.com.bh; f. 1979; cap. 23.0m., res 28.9m., dep. 199.2m. (Dec. 2004); Chair. KHALID ABDULLAH AL-BASSAM; CEO YOUSUF SALEH KHALAF; 8 brs.

Bahraini Saudi Bank BSC (BSB): POB 1159, As-Saddah Bldg, Government Ave, Manama; tel. 17578999; fax 17210989; e-mail info@bsb.com.bh; internet www.bsb.com.bh; f. 1983; licensed as a full commercial bank; cap. 50.0m., res 4.6m., dep. 130.9m. (Dec. 2006); Chair. Sheikh FAHAD M. AL-ATHEL; CEO KHALID S. S. SHAHEEN; 6 brs.

BBK: POB 579, 43 Government Ave, Area 305, Manama; tel. 17223388; fax 17229822; e-mail bbkp@batelco.com.bh; internet www.bbkonline.com; f. 1971 as Bank of Bahrain and Kuwait BSC; name changed as above in 2005; cap. 64.0m., res 80.2m., dep. 1,493.3m. (Dec. 2006); Chair. MURAD ALI MURAD; 20 brs.

Future Bank BSC: POB 785, Government Rd, Manama; tel. 17224368; fax 17224402; e-mail futurebk@batelco.com.bh; f. 2004; owned by Ahli United Bank BSC, Bank Melli Iran and Bank Saderat Iran; cap. US $50m. (2004); CEO STEPHEN AUSTEN; 3 brs.

National Bank of Bahrain BSC (NBB): POB 106, Government Ave, Manama; tel. 17228800; fax 17228998; e-mail nbb@nbbonline.com; internet www.nbbonline.com; f. 1957; 49% govt-owned; cap. 54.0m., res 168.1m., dep. 1,426.2m. (Dec. 2006); Chair. ABDULLAH ALI KANOO; Gen. Man. ABD AR-RAZAK A. HASSAN AL-QASSIM; 25 brs.

Shamil Bank of Bahrain BSC (SBB): POB 3005, Seef Tower, As-Seef District, Manama; tel. 17585000; fax 17585151; e-mail alshamil@shamilbank.net; internet www.shamilbank.net; f. 1982 as Massraf Faisal al-Islami of Bahrain EC, renamed Faisal Islamic Bank of Bahrain in 1987 and as above in 2000; 60% owned by Ithmaar Bank BSC; cap. US $230.0m., res $123.3m., dep. $412.9m. (Dec. 2006); Chair. MUHAMMAD ABDULLAH AL-ANQARI; CEO MUHAMMAD A. R. HUSSAIN; 3 domestic brs, 1 abroad.

The International Banking Corpn BSC (TIBC): POB 1230, Bahrain Commercial Complex, 3rd Floor, Government Ave, Manama; tel. 17570300; fax 17530817; e-mail info@tibc.com.bh; internet www.tibc.com.bh; f. 2003; cap. US $600m., res $67.9m., dep. $1,446.8m.; Chair. SULEIMAN HAMAD AL-GOSAIBI.

Specialized Financial Institutions

Bahrain Development Bank (BDB): POB 20501, Manama; tel. 17511111; fax 17534005; e-mail info@bdb-bh.com; internet www.bdb-bh.com; f. 1992; invests in manufacturing, agribusiness and services; cap. 10.0m., res 0.4m., dep. 11.0m. (Dec. 2006); Chair. Sheikh IBRAHIM BIN KHALIFA AL-KHALIFA; Gen. Man. NEDHAL S. AL-AUJAN.

The Housing Bank: POB 5370, Diplomatic Area, Manama; tel. 17534443; fax 17533437; f. 1979; provides housing loans for Bahraini citizens and finances construction of commercial properties; wholly owned by Housing Bank for Trade and Finance (Jordan); Chair. Sheikh KHALID BIN ABDULLAH BIN KHALID AL-KHALIFA; Gen. Man. ISA SULTAN ADH-DHAWADI; 1 br.

'Offshore' Banking Units

Bahrain has been encouraging the establishment of 'offshore' banking units (OBUs) since 1975. An OBU is not permitted to provide local banking services, but is allowed to accept deposits from governments and large financial organizations in the area and make medium-term loans for local and regional capital projects. In late 2006 there were 49 OBUs in operation in Bahrain.

ABC Islamic Bank EC: POB 2808, ABC Tower, Diplomatic Area, Manama; tel. 17543000; fax 17536379; e-mail webmaster@arabbanking.com; internet www.arabbanking.com; f. 1987 as ABC Investment and Services Co (EC), name changed as above in 1998 when converted into Islamic bank; 100% owned by Arab Banking Corpn BSC; cap. US $42.5m., res $4.3m., dep. $548.8m. (Dec. 2005); Chair. ABD AL-MAJID BREISH; Man. Dir NAVEED KHAN.

Allied Banking Corpn (Philippines): POB 20493, Bahrain Tower, 11th Floor, Government Ave, Manama; tel. 17224707; fax 17210506; e-mail info@alliedbank.com.ph; internet www.alliedbank.com.ph; f. 1980; Chair. PANFILO O. DOMINGO; Gen. Man. RAMON R. LANDINGIN.

Alubaf Arab International Bank BSC: POB 11529, Sheraton Tower 13F, Manama; tel. 17531212; fax 17540094; f. 1982; 95.1% owned by Libyan Arab Foreign Bank; cap. US $50.0m., res $0.6m., dep. $4.8m. (Dec. 2005); Chair. RASHID AZ-ZAYANI.

Arab Bank PLC (Jordan): POB 813, Manama; tel. 17549000; fax 17541116; e-mail arabbank@batelco.com.bh; f. 1930; Senior Vice-Pres. and Man. HANI FADAYEL.

Arab Banking Corpn BSC: POB 5698, ABC Tower, Diplomatic Area, Manama; tel. 17543000; fax 17533062; e-mail webmaster@arabbanking.com; internet www.arabbanking.com; f. 1980; cap. US $1,000m., res $1,112m., dep. $21,332m. (Dec. 2006); Chair. MUHAMMAD LAYAS; Pres. and CEO GHAZI ABD AL-JAWAD.

Arab Investment Co SAA (Saudi Arabia): POB 5559, Bldg 2309, Rd 2830, As-Seef District 428, Manama; tel. 17588888; fax 17588885; e-mail taic@taicobu.com; f. 1982; Dir-Gen. Dr SALEH AL-HUMAIDAN.

BNP Paribas (France): POB 5253, UGB Bldg, 10th Floor, Diplomatic Area, Manama; tel. 17531152; fax 17531237; e-mail jean-christophe.durand@mideastbnpparibas.com; internet www.bahrain.bnpparibas.com; f. 1975; Regional Man. JEAN-CHRISTOPHE DURAND.

Gulf International Bank BSC (GIB): POB 1017, Ad-Duwali Bldg, 3 Palace Ave, Area 317, Manama; tel. 17534000; fax 17522633; e-mail info@gibbah.com; internet www.gibonline.com; f. 1975; cap.

BAHRAIN

Directory

US $2,500m. (Dec. 2007), res $373.5m., dep. $19,950.0m. (Dec. 2006); Chair. Sheikh Ibrahim bin Khalifa al-Khalifa; CEO Dr Khaled al-Fayez.

Korea Exchange Bank (Repub. of Korea): POB 5767, Yateem Centre Bldg, 5th Floor, Manama; tel. 17229333; fax 17225327; e-mail kebbn002@batelco.com.bh; f. 1977; Gen. Man. Chang-Han Oh.

MCB Bank Ltd (MCB) (Pakistan): POB 10164, Diplomatic Area, Manama; tel. 17533306; fax 17533308; e-mail mcbobubh@batelco.com.bh; f. 1947 as Muslim Commercial Bank Ltd, name changed as above in 2005; Chief Man. Naeem Afzal Khan.

National Bank of Abu Dhabi (UAE): POB 5886, Manama 304; tel. 17214450; fax 17210086; e-mail Hassan.Bahzad@nbad.com; f. 1977; Chief Dealer Hassan Behzad.

National Bank of Kuwait SAK: POB 5290, Bahrain BMB Centre, Diplomatic Area, Manama; tel. 17532225; fax 17530658; e-mail nbkbah@batelco.com.bh; f. 1977; Gen. Man. Ali Y. Fardan.

Standard Chartered Bank (United Kingdom): POB 29, Manama; tel. 17223636; fax 17225001; f. 1976; CEO Martin Fish.

State Bank of India: POB 5466, Bahrain Tower, Government Ave, Manama; tel. 17224956; fax 17224692; e-mail sbigen@batelco.com.bh; f. 1977; CEO Ashwini Kumar Sharma.

Yapi ve Kredi Bankasi AS (Turkey): POB 10615, c/o Bahrain Development Bank, Diplomatic Area, Manama; tel. 17530313; fax 17530311; f. 1982; Dir Turan Ungor.

Investment Banks

Al-Baraka Islamic Bank BSC (EC): POB 1882, Diplomatic Area, Manama; tel. 17535300; fax 17533993; e-mail baraka@batelco.com.bh; internet www.barakaonline.com; f. 1984 as Al-Baraka Islamic Investment Bank BSC (EC), current name adopted in 1998; cap. US $50.0m., res $5.7m., dep. $52.8m. (Dec. 2006); Chair. Mahmood Jamil Hassoubah; Gen. Man. Salah Ahmad Zaindabedin; 2 domestic brs, 11 abroad.

Bahrain Middle East Bank BSC (BMB Investment Bank): POB 797, BMB Centre, Diplomatic Area, Manama; tel. 17532345; fax 17530526; e-mail requests@bmb.com.bh; internet www.bmb.com.bh; f. 1982; fmrly Bahrain Middle East Bank EC; cap. US $52.3m., res $−5.9m., dep. $47.6m. (Dec. 2006); Chair. Wilson Benjamin; CEO Albert I. Kittaneh; 1 br.

Capital Management House (CMH): Bahrain; f. April 2006; cap. US $47.7m.; Islamic investment co licensed with the powers of an investment bank; Chair. Khalid al-Bassam; CEO Saad ash-Shamlan.

Gulf Finance House BSC: POB 10006, As-Salam Tower, Diplomatic Area, Manama; tel. 17538538; fax 17540006; e-mail info@gfhouse.com; internet www.gfhouse.com; f. 1999 as Gulf Finance House EC, name changed as above in 2004; cap. US $149.8m., res $56.3m., dep. $659.0m. (Dec. 2005); Chair. Esam Y. Janahi; CEO Peter Panayiotou (acting).

Investcorp Bank BSC: POB 5340, Investcorp House, Diplomatic Area, Manama; tel. 17532000; fax 17530816; e-mail info@investcorp.com; internet www.investcorp.com; f. 1982 as Arabian Investment Banking Corpn (Investcorp) EC, current name adopted in 1990; cap. US $400.0m., res $437.7m., dep. $755.3m. (June 2006); Pres. and CEO Nemir A. Kirdar; Chair. Abd ar-Rahman Salim al-Ateeqi.

Ithmaar Bank BSC (Closed): POB 2820, Seef Tower, 14th Floor, As-Seef District, Manama; e-mail info@ithmaarbank.com; internet www.ithmaarbank.com; f. 1984 as Faisal Investment Bank of Bahrain EC, a wholly owned subsidiary of Shamil Bank of Bahrain BSC until 2003, when it was sold to Dar al-Maal al-Islami and assumed name as above; total assets US $830.2m. (June 2006); Chair. Khalid Abdullah-Janahi.

Nomura Investment Banking (Middle East) EC: POB 26893, BMB Centre, 7th Floor, Diplomatic Area, Manama; tel. 17530531; fax 17530365; f. 1982; cap. US $25.0m., res $35.3m., dep. $0.2m. (Dec. 2005); Chair. Takumi Shibata.

TAIB Bank BSC: POB 20485, TAIB Tower, 79 Rd 1702, Diplomatic Area, Manama 317; tel. 17549494; fax 17533590; e-mail taib@taib.com; internet www.taibdirect.com; f. 1979 as Trans-Arabian Investment Bank EC, renamed TAIB Bank EC in 1994, current name adopted in 2004; cap. US $107.0m., res $62.6m., dep. $229.1m. (Dec. 2006); Chair. Sheikh Abd al-Aziz R. ar-Rashid; Vice-Chair. and CEO Iqbal G. Mamdani.

United Gulf Bank BSC: POB 5964, UGB Tower, Diplomatic Area, Manama; tel. 17533233; fax 17533137; e-mail info@ugbbah.com; internet www.ugbbah.com; f. 1980; cap. US $200.5m., res $173.1m., dep. $1,605.7m. (Dec. 2006); Chair. Faisal Hamad M. al-Ayyar; CEO William Khouri.

Other investment banks operating in Bahrain include Al-Amin Bank, Amex (Middle East) EC, Arcapita Bank BSC, Capital Union EC, Daiwa Securities SMBC Europe Ltd (Middle East), Investors Bank EC, Al-Khaleej Islamic Investment Bank (BSC) EC and Merrill Lynch Int. Bank Ltd.

STOCK EXCHANGE

Bahrain Stock Exchange (BSE): POB 3203, Manama; tel. 17261260; fax 17256362; e-mail info@bahrainstock.com; internet www.bahrainstock.com; f. 1989; 51 listed cos at Dec. 2007; linked to Muscat Securities Market (Oman) in 1995, and to Amman Financial Market (Jordan) in 1996; Chair. Rashid Muhammad al-Maraj; Dir Fouad A. Rahman Rashid.

INSURANCE

Locally incorporated companies include:

Al-Ahlia Insurance Co BSC: POB 5282, Chamber of Commerce Bldg, 4th Floor, King Faisal Rd, Manama; tel. 17225860; fax 17224870; e-mail alahlia@alahlia.com; internet www.alahlia.com; f. 1976; Chair. Hussain Ali Sajwani; Gen. Man. Yahya Nooruddin.

Arab Insurance Group BSC (ARIG): POB 26992, Arig House, Diplomatic Area, Manama; tel. 17544444; fax 17531155; e-mail info@arig.com.bh; internet www.arig.com.bh; f. 1980; owned by Govts of Kuwait, Libya and the United Arab Emirates (49.5%), and other shareholders; reinsurance and insurance; Chair. Khalid Ali al-Bustani; CEO Yassir Albaharna.

Bahrain Kuwait Insurance Co BSC: POB 10166, Diplomatic Area, Manama; tel. 17542222; fax 17530799; e-mail info@bkic.com; internet www.bkic.com; f. 1975; CEO Ibrahim Sharif ar-Rayes; Gen. Man. Walid Ahmad Mahmood.

Bahrain National Holding Co BSC (BNH): POB 843, Manama; tel. 17587300; fax 17583099; e-mail admin@bnhgroup.com; internet www.bnhgroup.com; f. 1998 by merger of Bahrain Insurance Co and National Insurance Co; all classes incl. life insurance; Chair. Qassim Muhammad Fakhro; CEO Mahmoud as-Soufi.

Gulf Union Insurance and Reinsurance Co: POB 10949, Manama Centre, Ground Floor, Manama; tel. 17215622; fax 17215421; e-mail guirco@batelco.com.bh; Chair. Sheikh Ibrahim bin Hamad al-Khalifa.

Solidarity Insurance Co: POB 18668, Manama; tel. 17578777; fax 17578787; e-mail mail@solidarity.cc; internet www.solidarity.cc; f. 2004 by Qatar Islamic Bank; Chair. Khalid Abdullah-Janahi; CEO Samir Ebrahim al-Wazzan.

Takaful International Co: POB 3230, B680 R2811, As-Seef District 428, Manama; tel. 17565656; fax 17582688; internet takafulweb.com; f. 1989 as Bahrain Islamic Insurance Co; restructured and renamed as above in 1998; Chair. Adel Abdullah al-Mannai; Gen. Man. Younis A. Jamal.

Insurance Association

Bahrain Insurance Association (BIA): POB 2851, Manama; tel. 17532555; fax 17536006; e-mail biabah@batelco.com.bh; internet www.bia-bh.com; f. 1993; 28 mem. cos; Chair. Ashraf Bseisu; Man. Mahnaz Ashrafi.

Trade and Industry

GOVERNMENT AGENCIES

Economic Development Board (EDB): POB 11299, Manama; tel. 17589999; fax 17589900; e-mail bahrain@bahrainedb.com; internet www.bahrainedb.com; f. 2000; assumed duties of Bahrain Promotions and Marketing Board (f. 1993) and Supreme Council for Economic Development (f. 2000) in 2001; provides national focus for Bahraini marketing initiatives; attracts inward investment; encourages devt and expansion of Bahraini exports; Chair. Sheikh Salman bin Hamad al-Khalifa; CEO Sheikh Muhammad bin Issa al-Khalifa.

National Oil and Gas Authority (NOGA): POB 1435, Manama; tel. 17312644; fax 17293007; e-mail info@noga.gov.bh; internet www.noga.gov.bh; f. 2005, for the regulation and devt of oil and gas related industries in the kingdom; Chair. Dr Abd al-Hussain bin Ali Mirza.

CHAMBER OF COMMERCE

Bahrain Chamber of Commerce and Industry: POB 248, Bldg 122, Rd 1605, Block 216, Manama; tel. 17229555; fax 17224985; e-mail bcci@bahrainchamber.org.bh; internet www.bahrainchamber.org.bh; f. 1939; 12,023 mems (Jan. 2007); Chair. Dr Essam Abdullah Yousuf Fakhro; CEO Ahmad Najem Abdullah an-Najem.

STATE HYDROCARBONS COMPANIES

Bahrain National Gas Co BSC (BANAGAS): POB 29099, Rifa'a; tel. 17756222; fax 17756991; e-mail bng@banagas.com.bh; internet

BAHRAIN

Directory

www.banagas.com.bh; f. 1979; responsible for extraction, processing and sale of hydrocarbon liquids from associated gas derived from onshore Bahraini fields; ownership is 75% Govt of Bahrain, 12.5% Caltex and 12.5% Arab Petroleum Investments Corpn (APICORP); produces approx. 3,000 barrels per day (b/d) of propane, 2,700 b/d of butane and 4,500 b/d of naphtha; Chair. Sheikh HAMAD BIN IBRAHIM AL-KHALIFA; Gen. Man. Dr Sheikh MUHAMMAD BIN KHALIFA AL-KHALIFA.

Bahrain Petroleum Co BSC (BAPCO): POB 25555, Awali; tel. 17704040; fax 17704070; e-mail info@bapco.net; internet www.bapco.com.bh; f. 2000 by merger of Bahrain National Oil Co (f. 1976) and Bahrain Petroleum Co (f. 1980); fully integrated co responsible for exploration, drilling and production of oil and gas; supply of gas to power-generating plants and industries, refining crude oil, international marketing of crude oil and refined petroleum products, supply and sale of aviation fuel at Bahrain International Airport, and local distribution and marketing of petroleum products; Chair. Dr ABD AL-HUSSAIN BIN ALI MIRZA; CEO Eng. ABD AL-KARIM AS-SAYED.

Gulf Petrochemical Industries Co BSC (GPIC): POB 26730, Manama; tel. 17731777; fax 17731047; e-mail gpic@gpic.com; internet www.gpic.com; f. 1979 as a joint venture between the Govts of Bahrain, Kuwait and Saudi Arabia, each with one-third equity participation; a petrochemical complex at Sitra, inaugurated in 1981; produces 1,200 metric tons of both methanol and ammonia per day; Chair. Sheikh ISA BIN ALI AL-KHALIFA; Gen. Man. A. RAHMAN A. HUSSEIN JAWAHERI.

UTILITIES

Ministry of Electricity and Water: see Ministries, above; provides electricity and water throughout Bahrain; partial privatization of the ministry's assets had been achieved by 2007 and further divestment was pending; privatization of electricity production was approved in December 2003.

Electricity

Directorate of Electricity: POB 2, King Faisal Rd, Manama; tel. 17533133; responsible for domestic and industrial electricity generation and distribution throughout Bahrain.

Water

Directorate of Water Supply: POB 326, Manama; tel. 17727009; responsible for water supply to all areas except Awali.

TRADE UNIONS

In November 2002 legislation was ratified to permit the establishment of independent trade unions. There were reported to be more than 50 trade unions operating within Bahrain by early 2007.

General Federation of Bahrain Workers' Unions (GFBWU): Manama; f. 2004; Chair. ABD AL-GHAFFAR ABD AL-HUSSAIN.

Transport

RAILWAYS

There are no railways in Bahrain, although plans for a regional rail network, connecting Bahrain with member countries of the Co-operation Council for the Arab States of the Gulf (or Gulf Co-operation Council—GCC), were under discussion in early 2008.

ROADS

In 2003 Bahrain had 3,498 km of roads, including 440 km of highways, main or national roads, 487 km of secondary or regional roads and 2,571 km of other roads; about 79.1% of roads were paved. A modern network of dual carriageways is being developed, and a 25-km causeway link with Saudi Arabia was opened in 1986. A three-lane dual carriageway links the causeway to Manama. Other causeways link Bahrain with Muharraq island and with Sitra island. Construction of the third Manama–Muharraq causeway—the Sheikh Khalifa bin Salman Causeway—which links Hidd on Muharraq island with the port of Mina Salman, was completed in late 2004. Approval for the construction of a causeway linking eastern Bahrain with Qatar was given in that year. The project was to be supervised by a committee established in February 2005 by the Governments of both countries, and was expected to cost over US $2,000m. After protracted discussions and numerous delays, it was announced in September 2007 that construction of the causeway was scheduled to commence in May 2008 and to be completed by 2011; however, the contract had yet to be awarded by March 2008.

Directorate of Roads: POB 5, Manama; tel. 17545555; fax 17532565; responsible for traffic engineering and planning, traffic control and safety, bridges, road design, maintenance and construction supervision; Dir WALEED Y. AS-SAIE.

SHIPPING

Numerous shipping services link Bahrain and the Gulf with Europe, the USA, Pakistan, India, the Far East and Australia.

The deep-water harbour of Mina Salman was opened in 1962; it has 13 conventional berths, two container terminals (one of which has a 400-m quay—permitting two 180-m container ships to be handled simultaneously) and a roll-on roll-off berth. Two nearby slipways can accommodate vessels of up to 1,016 metric tons and 73 m in length, and services are available for ship repairs afloat. During 2004 868 vessels called at Mina Salman, and in that year the port handled 4,230,600 tons of cargo.

In 1999 work began on the construction of a new port and industrial zone at Hidd, on Muharraq island. The port, Mina Khalifa bin Salman, which was scheduled to become operational in late 2008 (at an estimated cost of BD 170m.), was to have an annual handling capacity of 234,000 TEUs and to include a general cargo berth and two container berths with roll-on roll-off facilities. The privatization of Mina Salman was achieved in December 2006 when it came under the management of APM Terminals Bahrain; the joint venture also expected to assume the management and operation of Mina Khalifa bin Salman from 2008.

Directorate of Customs and Ports: (Customs) POB 15, Manama; tel. 17725333; fax 17727556; e-mail customs@batelco.com.bh; internet www.bahraincustoms.gov.bh; (Ports) POB 453, Manama; tel. 17725555; fax 17725534; e-mail brnport@batelco.com.bh; internet www.bahrainports.gov.bh; responsible for customs, ports and free zone activities; Pres. of Customs and Ports DAIJ BIN SALMAN BIN DAIJ AL-KHALIFA; Dir-Gen. of Ports SALEH ABDULLAH AL-MUSALLAM; Dir-Gen. of Customs MUHAMMAD ALI TALEB; Dir-Gen. of Free Zones IBRAHIM HASSAN SALMAN.

Arab Shipbuilding and Repair Yard Co (ASRY): POB 50110, Hidd; tel. 17671111; fax 17670236; e-mail asryco@batelco.com.bh; internet www.asry.net; f. 1974 by OAPEC members; 500,000-ton dry dock opened 1977; two floating docks in operation since 1992; new twin slipway to be operational by mid-2008; repaired 139 ships in 2006; Chair. Sheikh DAJI BIN SALMAN BIN DAIJ AL-KHALIFA; CEO CHRIS POTTER (acting).

Principal Shipping Agents

Dilmun Shipping Co Ltd EC: POB 11664, Manama; tel. 17534530; fax 17531287; e-mail dilmunbh@batelco.com.bh; Chair. Capt. PHILIP G. CARR.

The Gulf Agency Co (Bahrain) WLL: POB 412, Bldg 224, Rd 20, Muharraq Area, Manama; tel. 17339777; fax 17320498; e-mail bahrain@gacworld.com; internet www.gacworld.com; f. 1957; Man. Dir PETER GRONBERG.

Al-Jazeera Shipping Co WLL: POB 302, Manama; tel. 17728837; fax 17728217; Dir ALI HASSAN MAHMOUD.

Nass Group: POB 669, Manama; tel. 17725522; fax 17728184; e-mail nassbah@batelco.com.bh; internet www.aanass.com.bh; f. 1963 as Abdullah Ahmad Nass; Chair. ABDULLAH AHMAD NASS; Man. Dir SAMIR ABDULLAH NASS.

Ash-Sharif Group: POB 1322, Manama; tel. 17530535; fax 17537637; e-mail general@bahragents.com; Dirs ALI ABD AR-RASOOL ASH-SHARIF, KHALID ABD AR-RASOOL ASH-SHARIF.

UCO Marine Contracting WLL: POB 1074, Manama; tel. 17730816; fax 17732131; e-mail ucomarin@batelco.com.bh; Man. Dirs BADER AHMAD KAIKSOW, HASSAN SABAH AL-BINALI, ALI AL-MUSALAM.

Yusuf bin Ahmad Kanoo WLL: POB 45, Al-Khalifa Ave, Manama; tel. 17220220; fax 17229122; e-mail kanoomgt@batelco.com.bh; internet www.ybakanoo.com; f. 1890; air and shipping cargo services, commercial and holiday services; Chair. and CEO ABDULLAH ALI KANOO.

CIVIL AVIATION

Bahrain International Airport (BIA) has a first-class runway, capable of taking the largest aircraft in use. In 2007 BIA handled some 7.3m. passengers. Extension work to the airport's main terminal building was undertaken during the 1990s, in order to increase the airport's cargo-handling facilities. A three-phase project to expand the existing passenger terminal and create additional aircraft parking and access, at a total cost of US $350m., was under way in 2008; it was hoped to increase the annual passenger capacity of BIA to 18m. by 2009, and further, to 22m., by 2020.

Department of Civil Aviation Affairs: POB 586, Bahrain International Airport, Muharraq; tel. 17321000; fax 17325757; e-mail prelation@caa.gov.bh; internet www.bahrainairport.com; Under-Sec. A. RAHMAN AL-GAOUD.

Gulf Air: POB 138, Manama; tel. 17339339; fax 17224494; e-mail gfpr@batelco.com.bh; internet www.gulfairco.com; f. 1950 as Gulf Aviation Co; name changed 1974; wholly owned by the Govt of

BAHRAIN

Bahrain; services to the Middle East, South-East Asia, the Far East, Australia, Africa and Europe; Chair. MAHMOUD HASHIM AL-KOOHEJI; Pres. and CEO BJÖRN NÄF.

Tourism

There are several archaeological sites of importance in Bahrain, which is the site of the ancient trading civilization of Dilmun. There is a wide selection of hotels and restaurants, and a new national museum opened in 1989. The Government is currently promoting Bahrain as a destination for sports and leisure activities. In 2005 Bahrain received 8.4m. foreign visitors (excluding Bahraini nationals residing abroad). Income from tourism totalled US $1,603m. in 2005.

Bahrain Tourism Co (BTC): POB 5831, Manama; tel. 17530530; fax 17530867; e-mail btc@alseyaha.com; internet www.alseyaha.com; f. 1974; Chair. QASSIM MUHAMMAD FAKHROO; CEO ABDULNABI DAYLAMI.

Tourism Affairs: Ministry of Information, POB 26613, Manama; tel. 17201203; fax 17229787; e-mail btour@bahraintourism.com; internet www.bahraintourism.com; Asst Under-Sec. for Tourism Dr KADHIM RAJAB.

BANGLADESH

Introductory Survey

Location, Climate, Language, Religion, Flag, Capital

The People's Republic of Bangladesh lies in southern Asia, surrounded by Indian territory except for a short south-eastern frontier with Myanmar (formerly Burma) and a southern coast fronting the Bay of Bengal. The country has a tropical monsoon climate and suffers from periodic cyclones. The average temperature is 19°C (67°F) from October to March, rising to 29°C (84°F) between May and September. The average annual rainfall in Dhaka is 188 cm (74 ins), of which about three-quarters occurs between June and September. About 95% of the population speak Bengali, the state language, while the remainder mostly use tribal dialects. More than 85% of the people are Muslims, Islam being the state religion, and there are small minorities of Hindus, Buddhists and Christians. The national flag (proportions 3 by 5) is dark green, with a red disc slightly off-centre towards the hoist. The capital is Dhaka (Dacca).

Recent History

Present-day Bangladesh was formerly East Pakistan, one of the five provinces into which Pakistan was divided at its initial creation, when Britain's former Indian Empire was partitioned in August 1947. East Pakistan and the four western provinces were separated by about 1,000 miles (1,600 km) of Indian territory. East Pakistan was created from the former Indian province of East Bengal and the Sylhet district of Assam. Although the East was more populous, government was based in West Pakistan. Dissatisfaction in East Pakistan at its dependence on a remote central government flared up in 1952, when Urdu was declared Pakistan's official language. Bengali, the main language of East Pakistan, was finally admitted as the joint official language in 1954, and in 1955 Pakistan was reorganized into two wings, east and west, with equal representation in the central legislative assembly. However, discontent continued in the eastern wing, particularly as the region was under-represented in the administration and armed forces, and received a disproportionately small share of Pakistan's development expenditure. The leading political party in East Pakistan was the Awami League (AL), led by Sheikh Mujibur (Mujib) Rahman, who demanded autonomy for the East. A general election in December 1970 gave the AL an overwhelming victory in the East, and thus a majority in Pakistan's National Assembly. Sheikh Mujib should therefore have been appointed Prime Minister, but Pakistan's President, Gen. Yahya Khan, would not accept this, and negotiations on a possible constitutional compromise broke down. The convening of the new National Assembly was postponed indefinitely in March 1971, leading to violent protests in East Pakistan. The AL decided that the province should unilaterally secede from Pakistan, and on 26 March Sheikh Mujib proclaimed the independence of the People's Republic of Bangladesh ('Bengal Nation').

Civil war immediately broke out. President Yahya Khan outlawed the AL and arrested its leaders. By April 1971 the Pakistan army dominated the eastern province. In August Sheikh Mujib was secretly put on trial in West Pakistan. Resistance continued, however, from the Liberation Army of East Bengal (the Mukhti Bahini), which launched a major offensive in November. As a result of the conflict, an estimated 9.5m. refugees crossed into India. On 4 December India declared war on Pakistan, with Indian forces intervening in support of the Mukhti Bahini. Pakistan surrendered on 16 December, and Bangladesh became independent. Pakistan was thus confined to its former western wing. In January 1972 Sheikh Mujib was freed by Pakistan's new President, Zulfiqar Ali Bhutto, and became Prime Minister of Bangladesh. Under a provisional Constitution, Bangladesh was declared to be a secular state and a parliamentary democracy. The new nation quickly achieved international recognition, causing Pakistan to withdraw from the Commonwealth in January 1972. Bangladesh joined the Commonwealth in April. The members who had been elected from the former East Pakistan for the Pakistan National Assembly and the Provincial Assembly in December 1970 formed the Bangladesh Constituent Assembly. A new Constitution was approved by this Assembly in November 1972 and came into effect in December. A general election for the country's first Jatiya Sangsad (Parliament) was held in March 1973. The AL received 73% of the total votes and won 292 of the 300 directly elective seats in the legislature. Bangladesh was finally recognized by Pakistan in February 1974. Internal stability, however, was threatened by opposition groups which resorted to terrorism and included extremists such as Islamist fundamentalists and Maoists. In December a state of emergency was declared and constitutional rights were suspended. In January 1975 parliamentary government was replaced by a presidential form of government. Sheikh Mujib became President, assuming absolute power, and created the Bangladesh Peasants' and Workers' Awami League. In February Bangladesh became a one-party state.

In August 1975 Sheikh Mujib and his family were assassinated in a right-wing coup, led by a group of Islamist army officers. Khandakar Mushtaq Ahmed, the former Minister of Commerce, was installed as President; martial law was declared, and political parties were banned. A counter-coup on 3 November brought to power Brig. Khalid Musharaf, the pro-Indian commander of the Dhaka garrison, who was appointed Chief of Army Staff; on 7 November a third coup overthrew Brig. Musharaf's brief regime, and power was assumed jointly by the three service chiefs, under a non-political President, Abusadet Mohammed Sayem, the Chief Justice of the Supreme Court. A neutral non-party Government was formed, in which the reinstated Chief of Army Staff, Major-Gen. Ziaur Rahman (Gen. Zia), took precedence over his colleagues. Political parties were legalized again in July 1976.

An early return to representative government was promised, but in November 1976 elections were postponed indefinitely and, in a major shift of power, Gen. Zia took over the role of Chief Martial Law Administrator from President Sayem, assuming the presidency also in April 1977. He amended the Constitution, making Islam, instead of secularism, its first basic principle. In a national referendum held in May 99% of voters affirmed their confidence in President Zia's policies, and in June 1978 the country's first direct presidential election resulted in a clear victory for Zia, who formed a Council of Ministers to replace his Council of Advisers. Parliamentary elections followed in February 1979: in an attempt to persuade opposition parties to participate in the elections, Zia met some of their demands by repealing 'all undemocratic provisions' of the 1974 constitutional amendment, releasing political prisoners and withdrawing press censorship. Consequently, 29 parties contested the elections, in which Zia's Bangladesh Nationalist Party (BNP) received 49% of the total votes and won 207 of the 300 contested seats in the Jatiya Sangsad. In April 1979 a new Prime Minister was appointed, and martial law was repealed. The state of emergency was revoked in November.

Political instability recurred, however, when Gen. Zia was assassinated on 30 May 1981 during an attempted military coup, allegedly led by Maj.-Gen. Mohammad Abdul Manzur, an army divisional commander who was himself later killed in unclear circumstances. The Vice-President, Justice Abdus Sattar, assumed the role of acting President, but was confronted by strikes and demonstrations in protest against the execution of several officers who had been involved in the coup, and by pressure from opposition parties to reschedule the date of the presidential election. As the only person acceptable to the different groups within the BNP, Sattar was none the less nominated as the party's presidential candidate, and secured an overwhelming victory at the November election. President Sattar announced his intention of continuing the policies of the late Gen. Zia. He found it increasingly difficult, however, to retain civilian control over the country, and in January 1982 formed a National Security Council, which included military personnel, led by the Chief of Army Staff, Lt-Gen. Hossain Mohammad Ershad. On 24 March Gen. Ershad seized power in a bloodless coup, claiming that political corruption and economic mismanagement had become intolerable. The country was placed under martial law, with Ershad as Chief Martial Law Administrator (redesignated Prime Minister in October), aided by a mainly military Council of Advisers. Ershad nominated a retired judge, Justice Abul Chowdhury, as President. Political activities were banned, and several former ministers were later tried and imprisoned on charges of corruption.

Although the Government's economic policies achieved some success and gained a measure of popular support for Ershad, there were increasing demands in 1983 for a return to democratic government. The two principal opposition groups that emerged were an eight-party alliance headed by the AL under Sheikh Hasina Wajed (daughter of the late Sheikh Mujib), and a seven-party group led by the BNP under former President Sattar (who died in 1985) and Begum Khaleda Zia (widow of Gen. Zia). In September 1983 the two groups formed an alliance, the Movement for the Restoration of Democracy (MRD), and jointly issued demands for an end to martial law, for the release of political prisoners and for the holding of parliamentary elections before any other polls. In November the resumption of political activity was permitted, and it was announced that a series of local elections between December 1983 and March 1984 were to precede a presidential election and parliamentary elections later in the year. A new political party, the Jana Dal (People's Party), was formed in November 1983 to support Ershad as a presidential candidate. Following demonstrations demanding civilian government, the ban on political activity was reimposed at the beginning of December, only two weeks after it had been rescinded, and leading political figures were detained. On 11 December Ershad declared himself President.

Strikes and political demonstrations occurred frequently during 1984. Local elections, planned for March, were postponed, as the opposition objected to their taking place prior to the presidential and parliamentary elections, on the grounds that Ershad was trying to strengthen his power base. The presidential and parliamentary elections, scheduled for May, were also postponed until December, in response to persistent opposition demands for the repeal of martial law and for the formation of an interim neutral government to oversee a fair election. In October an offer by Ershad to repeal martial law if the opposition would participate in the elections was met with an appeal for a campaign of civil disobedience, which led to the indefinite postponement of the elections.

In January 1985 it was announced that parliamentary elections would be held in April, to be preceded by a partial relaxation of martial law: the Constitution was to be fully restored after the elections. The announcement was followed by the formation of a new Council of Ministers, composed entirely of military officers and excluding all members of the Jana Dal, in response to demands by the opposition parties for a neutral government during the pre-election period. Once more, the opposition threatened to boycott the elections, as President Ershad would not relinquish power to an interim government, and in March the elections were abandoned and political activity was again banned. This was immediately followed by a referendum, held in support of the presidency, in which Ershad reportedly received 94% of the total votes. Local elections were held in May, without the participation of the opposition, following which Ershad claimed that 85% of the elected council chairmen were his supporters, although not necessarily members of his party. In September a new five-party political alliance, the National Front (comprising the Jana Dal, the United People's Party, the Gonotantrik Party, the Bangladesh Muslim League and a breakaway section of the BNP), was established to promote government policies.

In January 1986 the 10-month ban on political activity was ended. The five components of the National Front formally became a single pro-Government entity, named the Jatiya Dal (National Party). In March President Ershad announced that parliamentary elections were to be held (under martial law) at the end of April. He relaxed martial law, however, by removing all army commanders from important civil posts and by abolishing more than 150 military courts and the martial law offices. These concessions fulfilled some of the opposition's demands, and candidates from the AL alliance (including Sheikh Hasina Wajed herself), the Jamaat-e-Islami Bangladesh and other smaller opposition parties consequently participated in the parliamentary elections—which eventually proceeded in May. However, the BNP alliance, led by Begum Khaleda Zia, boycotted the polls, which were characterized by allegations of extensive fraud, violence and intimidation. The Jatiya Dal won 153 of the 300 directly elective seats in the Jatiya Sangsad. In addition, 30 seats reserved for women were filled by nominees of the Jatiya Dal. In July a mainly civilian Council of Ministers was sworn in.

Mizanur Rahman Chowdhury, former General Secretary of the Jatiya Dal, was appointed Prime Minister.

In order to be eligible to stand as a candidate in the forthcoming presidential election, Ershad retired as Chief of Army Staff in August 1986, while remaining Chief Martial Law Administrator and Commander-in-Chief of the Armed Forces. In early September Ershad officially joined the Jatiya Dal, whereupon he was elected as Chairman of the party and nominated as its presidential candidate. The presidential election, held in October, was boycotted by both the BNP and the AL, and resulted in an overwhelming victory for Ershad over his 11 opponents.

In November 1986 the Jatiya Sangsad approved indemnity legislation, effectively legitimizing the military regime's actions since March 1982. Ershad repealed martial law and restored the 1972 Constitution. The opposition alliances criticized the indemnity law, stating that they would continue to campaign for the dissolution of the Jatiya Sangsad and the overthrow of the Ershad Government. In December 1986, in an attempt to curb increasing dissent, President Ershad formed a new Council of Ministers, including four AL members of the legislature. The Minister of Justice, Justice A. K. M. Nurul Islam, was appointed Vice-President.

Opposition groups continued to organize anti-Government strikes and demonstrations during 1987, often with the support of trade unions and student groups. In July the Jatiya Sangsad approved a bill enabling army representatives to participate alongside elected representatives in the district councils. The adoption of this controversial legislation provoked widespread and often violent strikes and demonstrations, organized by the opposition groups, which perceived the measure as an attempt by the President to entrench military involvement in the governing of the country despite the ending of martial law in November 1986. Owing to the intensity of public opposition, President Ershad was forced to withdraw the legislation in August 1987 and return it to the Jatiya Sangsad for reconsideration. In November, in a renewed effort to oust President Ershad, opposition groups combined forces and organized further protests. Thousands of activists were detained, but demonstrations and strikes continued. In an attempt to forestall another general strike, President Ershad declared a nation-wide state of emergency on 27 November, suspending political activity and civil rights and banning all anti-Government protests. Disturbances persisted, despite the imposition of curfews on the main towns. In December, as about 6,000 activists remained in detention, opposition parties in the Jatiya Sangsad announced that their representatives intended to resign their seats. After 12 opposition members had withdrawn and the 73 AL members had agreed to do likewise, President Ershad dissolved the Jatiya Sangsad. In January 1988 the President announced that parliamentary elections would be held on 28 February, but leaders of the main opposition parties declared their intention to boycott the proposed poll while Ershad remained in office. Local elections, held throughout Bangladesh in February, were not boycotted by the opposition but were marred by serious outbreaks of violence. The parliamentary elections (postponed until 3 March) were also characterized by widespread violence, as well as by alleged fraud and malpractice. The opposition's appeal for a boycott of the polls was widely heeded, with the actual level of participation by the electorate appearing to have been considerably lower than the Government's estimate of 50%. As expected, the Jatiya Dal won a large majority of the seats.

A radical reshuffle of the Council of Ministers later in March 1988 included the appointment of a new Prime Minister, Moudud Ahmed, a long-time political ally of Ershad and hitherto the Minister of Industry and a Deputy Prime Minister, in place of Mizanur Rahman Chowdhury. In response to an abatement in the opposition's anti-Government campaign, Ershad repealed the state of emergency in April. Despite strong condemnation by the political opposition and sections of the public, a constitutional amendment establishing Islam as Bangladesh's state religion was approved by an overall majority in the Jatiya Sangsad in June. By early September, however, political events had been completely overshadowed by monsoon floods, which, having begun in August, proved to be the most severe in the area's recorded history. Bangladesh suffered further flooding in December 1988 and January 1989, following a devastating cyclone in late November. At the end of 1988 the Government established a national Disaster Prevention Council.

In July 1989 the Jatiya Sangsad approved legislation limiting the tenure of the presidency to two electoral terms of five years each and creating the post of a directly elected Vice-President (in the event of the vice-presidency being vacated, however, the President could make a new appointment with the prior approval of the Jatiya Sangsad). In August Ershad appointed Moudud Ahmed as Vice-President to replace Justice A. K. M. Nurul Islam, who was dismissed following charges of inefficiency. Kazi Zafar Ahmed, formerly the Minister of Information and a Deputy Prime Minister, was in turn promoted to the post of Prime Minister. Local elections held in March 1990 were officially boycotted by the opposition parties, although many members participated on an individual basis. In April Ershad announced that he would present himself as a candidate in the presidential election, which was scheduled for mid-1991.

Opposition groups, with the support of thousands of students, co-operated to intensify their anti-Government campaign in late 1990. On 27 November President Ershad proclaimed a nation-wide state of emergency for the second time in three years, suspending civil rights, imposing strict press censorship and enforcing an indefinite curfew throughout the country. On the following day, however, army units were summoned to impose order in the capital as thousands of protesters defied the curfew and attacked police. Under increasing pressure from the opposition groups, Ershad resigned on 4 December and declared that parliamentary elections would be held before the presidential election; the state of emergency was revoked, and the Jatiya Sangsad was dissolved. Following his nomination by the opposition, Justice Shahabuddin Ahmed, the Chief Justice of the Supreme Court, was appointed Vice-President. He assumed the responsibilities of acting President and was appointed to lead a neutral interim Government pending fresh parliamentary elections. Shahabuddin Ahmed undertook a comprehensive reorganization of personnel in financial institutions, local government and the civil service in an effort to remove Ershad's appointees from important posts. The opposition parties welcomed these developments and abandoned their protest campaigns. They also demanded that Ershad be tried for alleged corruption and abuse of power. Ershad was placed under house arrest, and was later sentenced to 20 years' imprisonment for illegal possession of firearms and other offences. (In June 1995 the former President was acquitted of illegally possessing firearms, and his sentence was halved. In the following month, however, Ershad was sentenced to a further three years' imprisonment for criminal misconduct.)

The BNP alliance won an overall majority at parliamentary elections held in February 1991. Following discussions with the Jamaat-e-Islami, as a result of which the BNP was ensured a small working majority in the Jatiya Sangsad, Begum Khaleda Zia assumed office as Prime Minister. In May the Government was faced with the immense problems created by a devastating cyclone, which caused the deaths of as many as 250,000 people and wreaked massive economic damage. In August the Jatiya Sangsad approved a constitutional amendment ending 16 years of presidential rule and restoring the Prime Minister as executive leader (under the previous system, both the Prime Minister and the Council of Ministers had been responsible to the President). The amendment, which was approved by national referendum in the following month, reduced the role of the President, who was now to be elected by the Jatiya Sangsad for a five-year term, to that of a titular Head of State. Accordingly, a new President was elected by the Jatiya Sangsad in October. The successful candidate was the BNP nominee, former Speaker of the Jatiya Sangsad Abdur Rahman Biswas. In September the BNP had secured an absolute majority in the Jatiya Sangsad as a result of the party's success in a number of by-elections. In November, despite strong protest from the opposition parties, the Government abolished the *upazilla* (sub-district) system of rural administration, introduced by Ershad in 1982. Henceforth, all public functions at *upazilla* level were to be performed through executive orders of the central Government, pending the introduction of a new system of rural administration. To this end, the Government established a special committee to review all aspects of local government.

From late 1993 and into 1994 mass anti-Government demonstrations were organized by the opposition, which initiated a boycott of parliamentary proceedings in February 1994. The number of strikes and violent protests staged by the opposition multiplied in the latter half of the year, and culminated in the resignation of all the opposition members from the Jatiya Sangsad in December. In spite of the political chaos, compounded by the holding of further general strikes by the opposition, the Prime Minister pledged to use her party's parliamentary majority to maintain constitutional government.

The opposition co-ordinated further nation-wide strikes in late 1995, which were, at times, marked by outbreaks of violence. In response to the intensification of the anti-Government campaign, and in an attempt to break the political impasse caused by the refusal of the opposition parties to take part in forthcoming by-elections, the Jatiya Sangsad was dissolved in November at the request of the Prime Minister, pending the holding of a general election in early 1996. Despite opposition demands for a neutral interim government to oversee the election, the President requested that Begum Khaleda Zia's administration continue in office in an acting capacity. All of the main opposition parties boycotted the general election, which was held in mid-February, and independent monitors estimated the turn-out at only about 10%–15% of the registered electorate. Of the 207 legislative seats declared by the end of February, the BNP had won 205 (a partial repoll had been ordered in most of the 93 remaining constituencies where violence had disrupted the electoral process). The opposition refused to recognize the legitimacy of the polls, and announced the launch of a 'non-co-operation' movement against the Government. Renewed street protests rendered the country virtually ungovernable, and Begum Khaleda Zia eventually agreed to the holding of fresh elections under neutral auspices. The Prime Minister and her Government duly resigned on 30 March, and the Jatiya Sangsad was dissolved. President Biswas appointed former Chief Justice Muhammad Habibur Rahman as acting Prime Minister, and requested that a fresh general election be held, under the auspices of an interim neutral government, within three months. At the general election, held on 12 June, the AL won 146 of the 300 elective seats in the Jatiya Sangsad, the BNP 116, the Jatiya Dal 32 and the Jamaat-e-Islami three. An understanding was rapidly reached between the AL and the Jatiya Dal, the latter's major interest being the release of Ershad, who had secured a legislative seat from within prison. (The former President was released on bail in January 1997.) Sheikh Hasina Wajed was sworn in as Prime Minister on 23 June 1996.

On 23 July 1996 the AL's presidential nominee, retired Chief Justice and former acting President Shahabuddin Ahmed, was elected unopposed as Bangladesh's Head of State. In early September the AL won eight of the 15 seats contested in by-elections; this result gave the AL, which was also allocated 27 of the 30 nominated women's parliamentary seats in July, an absolute majority in the Jatiya Sangsad.

On assuming power, Sheikh Hasina Wajed had vowed to bring to justice those responsible for the assassination of her father, Sheikh Mujibur Rahman, in 1975. In November 1996 the Jatiya Sangsad voted unanimously to repeal the indemnity law enacted in 1975 to protect the perpetrators of the military coup in that year; the BNP and the Jamaat-e-Islami, however, boycotted the vote. The trial of 19 people accused of direct involvement in Sheikh Mujib's assassination began in March 1997, with 14 of the defendants being tried *in absentia*.

Agitation persisted throughout 1997. In addition to the disruption caused by a series of strikes and demonstrations organized by the BNP in conjunction with Islamist and right-wing groups (which frequently led to violent clashes between demonstrators and police), the efficacy of the Jatiya Sangsad was undermined by several boycotts of parliamentary proceedings organized by BNP deputies. In mid-1998 the opposition organized public demonstrations in protest at problems of law and order and at power failures. The BNP's foremost demand was the holding of fresh elections, reiterating the AL's earlier campaign. The AL, however, strengthened its position through a series of by-election victories. Thus the departure of the Jatiya Dal from the coalition in March had little effect on the ruling party's hold on power. In June and August Begum Khaleda Zia was charged with corruption and abuse of power, allegedly perpetrated during her tenure as premier (the charges were later dismissed as politically motivated).

In September 1998 the controversial feminist writer Taslima Nasreen was reported to have secretly returned to Bangladesh after four years in self-imposed exile. (Nasreen, whose allegedly anti-Islamic public stance and statements had made her the target of a campaign of vilification by fundamentalist Islamist groups in Bangladesh, had—with the apparent complicity of government officials—fled the country in August 1994 and been granted refuge in Sweden, shortly after a warrant had been issued for her arrest on blasphemy-related charges.) On her return, a fresh warrant for the writer's arrest on charges of blasphemy was issued by a Dhaka court. Islamist extremists organized street protests, reiterating their demand for Nasreen's immediate arrest and execution. In November 1998 Nasreen voluntarily surrendered herself before the High Court in Dhaka, where she was granted bail. In January 1999 the author again left Bangladesh for Sweden, following renewed death threats from Islamist extremists. The sale of her third novel was authorized in Bangladesh in 2001; however, her fourth book was banned by the Bangladeshi authorities in August 2002. In October a court outside Dhaka sentenced Nasreen *in absentia* to one year's imprisonment on charges of blasphemy.

Meanwhile, unrest continued throughout the latter half of 1999 and into 2000. The opposition boycotted parliamentary proceedings from January 2000, and persisted in its demands for the holding of early elections. Street demonstrations resumed in February. The announcement in the same month of the introduction of the controversial Public Safety Act, which permitted detention without trial for up to 90 days, provoked a three-day nation-wide strike. The opposition parties suspended their boycott of the Jatiya Sangsad in June in order to avoid disqualification (which would take effect after an absence of 90 working days from the legislature without the Speaker's approval). However, following accusations that the Government was conspiring to amend the Constitution, opposition members promptly resumed their boycott, claiming that they were not permitted to address the legislature (an allegation denied by the Speaker).

In August 2000 the High Court in Dhaka reduced the sentence imposed by a lower court on Ershad to five years' imprisonment, and stipulated the payment of a substantial fine and the confiscation of property for the misappropriation of funds during his tenure of power between 1983 and 1990. In accordance with the Constitution, Ershad was deprived of his parliamentary seat. Following an appeal in November 2000, and shortly after Ershad had begun his term of imprisonment, the Supreme Court reduced the sentence to three years and seven months; the former President was released on bail in April 2001, owing to illness. In May 2002 Ershad was sentenced to six months' imprisonment for attempting to influence the proceedings in a corruption case. Meanwhile, in early September 2000 the opposition leader, Begum Khaleda Zia, was accused by the anti-corruption unit of financial irregularities.

In June 2001 Sheikh Hasina Wajed became the first Prime Minister in the history of Bangladesh to complete a five-year term of office. In mid-July the Government resigned, and the Jatiya Sangsad was dissolved in order to allow an interim neutral administration to prepare for a general election, to be held within three months. The interim administration was established shortly afterwards under the leadership of former Chief Justice Latifur Rehman. The election campaign was reportedly the most violent in the country's history, and Rehman ordered the deployment of more than 50,000 troops to curb the unrest.

The general election proceeded on 1 October 2001, although voting was postponed in several constituencies owing to violent incidents. The AL claimed that voting had been manipulated as it became clear that the opposition alliance, led by the BNP, had won an overwhelming majority of the 300 directly elective seats in the Jatiya Sangsad; however, international monitors declared the poll to be free and fair. Immediately after the election the BNP leader, Begum Khaleda Zia, asserted, in an apparent effort to allay national and international concerns regarding the presence of two fundamentalist Islamist parties in the four-party alliance, that Bangladesh would not become an Islamic state. Following elections on 9 October in 15 of those constituencies where voting had been delayed, the BNP-led alliance controlled a total of 214 of the directly elective seats, the AL 62 and the Jatiya Dal 14. Meanwhile, the AL, refusing to accept the election results, boycotted the ceremony at which newly elected members of the legislature were sworn in. On 10 October Begum Khaleda Zia was sworn in as Prime Minister, and a new Council of Ministers was appointed the following day. At the end of October newly elected members of Parliament representing the opposition AL took the oath of office, but refused to join the opening session of the Jatiya Sangsad, in continuing protest against what they considered a rigged election; the opposition party also condemned violence allegedly perpetrated by the BNP-led alliance against AL members and religious minority groups, stating that it would not attend the Jatiya Sangsad until the Government demonstrated a greater commitment to curb the alleged violence. Reports of attacks, particularly against the Hindu minority, increased markedly after the victory of the BNP-led coalition. Many Hindus either sought refuge in AL offices or fled the country to neighbouring India. The Government admitted that some of the assertions were true, while dismissing reports of widespread attacks as overstated, and announced that an investigation would be conducted into alleged violent acts against religious minorities and into reports that Hindus had left the country. In May 2002 the human rights organization Amnesty International issued a report stating that the Bangladeshi Government had failed to take effective measures to curb attacks allegedly perpetrated by supporters of the BNP-led coalition, before, during and after the October 2001 election, against the Hindu community, other minorities and women. The report also claimed that the police had failed to protect the minorities and that custodial torture by members of the police and armed forces had taken place during and after the general election. The Government rejected the charges; while admitting to some of the incidents, the BNP-led coalition held its political opponents responsible for the criminal acts and undertook no official investigation into the alleged attacks. In August 2002 the Chief of the Hindu Unity Council warned that unless demands for the restoration of a secular Constitution, as originally devised immediately after Bangladesh's independence, were met, Hindus would remain 'second-class citizens' in the country.

In November 2001 Prof. A. Q. M. Badruddoza Chowdhury, a former Minister of Foreign Affairs, was declared President after his sole nominated opponent, Mohammad Rowshan Ali, withdrew his candidacy. Prof. Chowdhury immediately resigned from the BNP, and was sworn into office two days later. The AL (which had refused to participate in the presidential election) boycotted the oath-taking ceremony. In December the Jatiya Sangsad repealed the Father of the Nation Family Security Act. The Security Act, which had been approved in June under the AL administration, guaranteed lifelong security for Sheikh Hasina Wajed and her sister, the daughters of Sheikh Mujib (the 'father of the nation' according to the AL), because several convicted assassins of the latter remained at large; however, the Act was strongly criticized by the BNP, which considered its own founder, Gen. Zia, to be the 'father of the nation'. In March 2002 the AL demonstrated against the repealing of the Father of the Nation's Portrait Display and Preservation Act, which made it mandatory for government officials to display portraits of Sheikh Mujib in their offices.

AL members of Parliament continued their boycott of the Jatiya Sangsad until June 2002. The party also refused to take part in civic elections in April and carried out a policy of agitation, organizing a series of strikes in protest against higher taxes, crime and rises in fuel prices. In response to the opposition's campaign, the Government filed two corruption charges against Sheikh Hasina Wajed and other AL members in December 2001, in relation to a weapons contract with Russia signed in 1999.

In mid-June 2002 the President yielded to pressure from the BNP to resign from office after he failed to visit Gen. Zia's grave on the anniversary of the latter's assassination. The resignation was considered unconstitutional by many observers. Some two days later Begum Khaleda Zia appointed her son, Tarique Rahman, to the post of Secretary-General of the BNP, prompting claims that the Prime Minister intended eventually to relinquish power to Rahman. In early September the BNP candidate, Iajuddin Ahmed, was declared President by the Election Commission after it was established that the nomination papers of the two other candidates were invalid.

In late September 2002 bomb explosions in the south-western town of Satkhira occurred, killing at least 10 people and seriously injuring 150. Islamist militant groups were suspected to have carried out the attack, although none claimed responsibility. In mid-October the Government launched a campaign to curb crime; some 40,000 members of the armed forces had been enlisted to assist the police. The AL claimed that the Government was using this campaign as a guise for the harassment of opposition members. By the end of the month almost 3,500 people had been arrested, including two former AL ministers. Concerns were raised over the unusually high number of people who had died in army custody. In early January 2003 the Government approved a law granting the armed forces legal immunity for any actions carried out during the three-month operation against crime. Meanwhile, in December 2002 bomb explosions at four cinemas in the town of Mymensingh occurred, killing at least 18 people and injuring some 300. The Prime Minister rejected suggestions that the Islamist militant al-

Qa'ida (Base) organization was involved in the attack. However, it was claimed that Bangladeshi Islamist militant groups had collaborated with South-East Asian Islamist groups connected with al-Qa'ida since 1999. In mid-February 2003 the Government proscribed the activities of the militant Islamist organization Shahadat-e-Al-Hikma. In January–March almost 50 people were killed and 6,000 injured in violent incidents during the holding of staggered local elections. In late August two senior members of the AL were shot dead in Khulna, provoking a general strike in Dhaka by demonstrators demanding an end to lawlessness. A report published by the Bureau of Human Rights Bangladesh in September stated that 2,974 people had been killed in separate violent occurrences throughout Bangladesh between January and September.

Unrest continued throughout the latter half of 2003. In November the United Nations Development Programme (UNDP) and the Bangladeshi Government jointly produced a preliminary report on the country's 100,000-strong police force. The report stated that the deep-rooted problems of corruption, inadequate pay, low morale and understaffing within the force were adversely affecting Bangladesh's social and economic conditions. In January 2004 a bomb explosion at the Muslim Hazrat Shah Jalal shrine in Sylhet killed five people. In May a grenade attack at the shrine resulted in the deaths of three people and injuries to at least a further 100, including the British High Commissioner to Bangladesh, Anwar Chowdhury. By the end of that month more than 100 people had been arrested in connection with the attack. Meanwhile, in early May Ahsanullah Master, an AL legislator, was shot dead in his constituency. While the AL accused the Government of having ordered the attack, the Government blamed factional fighting within the AL.

In May 2004 the Jatiya Sangsad approved a bill of constitutional amendments (comprising the 14th Amendment to the Constitution) that made provision for the existing 300-member legislature to be enlarged to 345 members—45 seats were to be reserved for women (the constitutional provision for women to hold 30 seats in the legislature had lapsed in 2001). The AL and most other opposition parties boycotted the vote, on the grounds that the seats for women would be awarded on a proportional representation basis, rather than by direct election. (The 14th Amendment was formally introduced in December 2004.) In June the AL announced the end of the parliamentary boycott that it had initiated one year previously, following the return of several AL legislators to the Jatiya Sangsad in the previous month as a tribute to the deceased Ahsanullah Master. In April 2005 22 people were sentenced to death by a Dhaka court, having been convicted of Master's murder; a further six defendants were sentenced to life imprisonment. Fifteen of those convicted were sentenced *in absentia*, and most were members of the ruling BNP and its coalition partners.

In August 2004 another grenade attack on an AL rally in Dhaka resulted in the deaths of 20 people, including the President of the AL women's wing, Ivy Rahman. AL leader Sheikh Hasina Wajed was slightly injured. Widespread rioting subsequently occurred in Dhaka and 13 other towns in Bangladesh, and the AL called a series of general strikes in protest. Later in that month a previously unknown group, Hikmatul Zihad, claimed responsibility for the attack. In January 2005 an explosion at an AL rally in Habiganj, in the north-east of the country, killed five party activists, including Shah Kibria, a former Minister of Finance. The AL subsequently alleged that the Government was responsible for the attack, an accusation that the latter denied. The security situation in Bangladesh provoked increasing international disquiet, owing largely to the Government's ongoing failure to bring to justice the perpetrators of many of the violent incidents that had taken place in the country. In the following month foreign donors meeting in Washington, DC, USA, cited the deterioration in law and order as a cause for serious concern.

In February 2005 the Government acknowledged, for the first time, that fundamentalist Islamist groups were operating in the country and officially banned two such organizations, Jamatul Mujahideen Bangladesh (JMB) and Jagrata Muslim Janata Bangladesh (JMJB), which were believed to have been responsible for several bomb attacks on the offices of aid agencies. In March 10 people were charged with involvement in the January grenade attack that had resulted in the death of Shah Kibria. It was reported that eight of those accused were district officials or members of the ruling BNP. The arrests lent credence to opposition accusations that the BNP, acting through its coalition partner, the Jamaat-e-Islami Bangladesh, was covertly encouraging the activities of Islamist militant groups in the country. On 17 August approximately 500 small bombs exploded virtually simultaneously at around 300 locations across Bangladesh, killing two people. The JMB claimed responsibility for the attacks, and the AL alleged that the BNP had, once again, been complicit. Several arrests were subsequently made in connection with the bombings. However, the leaders of both banned organizations, who were suspected of having planned the attacks, evaded capture. In October another Islamist militant group, Harakat-ul-Jihad-i-Islami (HJI), was banned by the Government. Media reports suggested that the HJI had 'merged' with other militant groups in the country, including the JMB and the JMJB, in order to conduct a concerted terrorist campaign intended to effect the transformation of Bangladesh into an Islamic state. In November two bomb attacks on courthouses in Gazipur and Chittagong resulted in the deaths of nine people. The JMB was suspected of having perpetrated these attacks, which were believed to be the country's first suicide bombings. A spate of attacks in the area followed. Approximately 800 alleged members of the JMB had been arrested by the end of 2005, as the Government attempted to bring the deteriorating security situation under control. In January 2006 a member of the JMB became the first Islamist militant to be convicted of explosives offences in Bangladesh; he was sentenced to a 15-year prison term. In February 21 people received death sentences for carrying out six bomb attacks in Jhenidah district in August 2005 (part of the large-scale bombing campaign mentioned above). In the same month Ataur Rahman, who was reported to be the leader of the JMB's military wing, and two others were sentenced to 40 years' imprisonment for their involvement in the November 2005 courthouse bomb attacks. An additional four defendants, including Siddiqul Islam and Abdur Rahman, who were alleged to be senior figures in the JMB, were sentenced *in absentia* for abetting the bombings. In March 2006 Islam and Abdur Rahman were captured, and in May both were sentenced to death, along with five others, on murder charges arising from the November 2005 bombings. In August 2006 Ataur Rahman and two others were sentenced to death for their role in bomb attacks that took place in August and October 2005.

Meanwhile, in January 2006 the opposition, led by the AL, called a general strike, claiming that the Government was attempting to manipulate the electoral list in advance of the general election which was due to be held in January 2007. It demanded the resignation of three officials from the Electoral Commission, who were believed to favour the Government. In the following month the AL announced that it would end the parliamentary boycott that it had instigated one year previously, while continuing to co-ordinate a campaign of civil disobedience against the Government. Political and civil unrest continued throughout 2006, a year characterized by regular strikes, demonstrations and clashes between government and opposition supporters. In May, amid growing discontent over electricity shortages, Minister for Power Iqbal Hassan Mahmood's role in government was downgraded to that of Minister of State for Agriculture. The power portfolio was transferred to Anwarul Kabir Talukder, who resigned after four months, however, citing his failure to improve the power supply situation. Also in May, protests by garment workers demanding increased wages and a reduction in working hours erupted into violence. Numerous factories were damaged, and clashes with police led to at least one fatality. In August at least six people were killed in demonstrations against plans for the development of an opencast coal mine in Phulbari, which was to be operated by a British company, Asia Energy Corporation. The controversial project, which would have necessitated the relocation of around 50,000 people, was subsequently cancelled by the Government. In October several members of the BNP defected to form a new party, the Liberal Democratic Party, with the former President Prof. A. Q. M. Badruddoza Chowdhury and Col (retd) Oli Ahmed as its leaders; the new organization cited the fight against corruption as one of its main objectives.

Tensions mounted with the approach of the 2007 election, as increasingly vociferous demands for electoral reform were made by the AL and its coalition, including the installation of a non-partisan caretaker government and election officials, and a revision of the electoral roll. Prime Minister Khaleda Zia and her Government duly stepped down at the end of their term in office in October 2006, but confusion about their successors remained and the transition was marked by widespread protests and sporadic violence. The original nominee for Chief Adviser (the head of the caretaker government which was to oversee the election process), K. M. Hasan, declined the post following the AL's assertion that it would not contest the election should he take office, in view of his alleged support for the BNP. Shortly afterwards President Iajuddin Ahmed announced that he himself would assume the additional role of Chief Adviser in an attempt to curb the unrest. A team of advisers was also appointed, including Fazlul Haq and Akbar Ali Khan, but President Ahmed took charge of the key defence, foreign affairs and home affairs portfolios. Demonstrations by the AL-led opposition continued, however, as did its demands for the resignation of allegedly biased election officials and for further electoral reform. In November transport blockades called by the opposition coalition caused widespread disruption; in response, it was announced that the Chief Election Commissioner, Justice M. A. Aziz, was to go on leave for three months. Later in November the January date for the general election, set by the Bangladesh Election Commission, was rejected by the AL-led coalition. In December it was reported that the former President and the Chairman of the Jatiya Dal, Lt-Gen. Ershad, who earlier in the year had been acquitted of several corruption charges dating back to the previous decade, had decided to join the opposition coalition. (Ershad was later sentenced to two years' imprisonment on other corruption charges, leading to a ban on his participation in the election. In January 2007, however, a Dhaka court ruled that the former President had already served adequate time in prison, leaving him free to contest the elections.) Meanwhile, President Ahmed's deployment of army troops to control opposition protests prompted four members of his team of advisers to resign in December 2006; four new advisers were promptly appointed and the President placed the troops on standby rather than on active service. On 20 December the team of advisers announced that, in order to address the AL-led coalition's concerns, a second election commissioner was to retire temporarily and confirmed that the voter list was to be updated. Despite these concessions, however, Sheikh Hasina Wajed continued to deem the scheduled date of 22 January 2007 for the forthcoming elections as unacceptable, as—in her opinion—it did not allow sufficient time for the updates to be carried out. On 3 January 2007 the AL coalition announced a boycott of the elections and called for another transport blockade, provoking reports that the army was to be redeployed. The interim Government stood firm, however, stressing that, according to constitutional stipulations, it was required to hold elections within 90 days of assuming power. Thousands of protesters took to the streets in Dhaka as the nation-wide transport blockade was implemented. On 11 January both the European Union (EU) and the United Nations (UN) suspended their election observer missions in Bangladesh. On the same day President Ahmed stepped down as Chief Adviser, postponed the elections and declared a state of emergency; nine of the 10 advisers also resigned. Dr Fakhruddin Ahmed was sworn in as the new Chief Adviser on 12 January, and 10 new advisers were subsequently appointed. Dr Ahmed took control of the home affairs portfolio, among others, while responsibility for the Ministry of Finance was assumed by Dr A. B. Mirza Azizul Islam. On 21 January Justice M. A. Aziz, who in November 2006 had begun a three-month leave of absence, permanently stepped down as Chief Election Commissioner, followed by five election commissioners; Aziz was replaced by Dr A. T. M. Shamsul Huda. Under emergency rules, a ban on political activity came into effect, along with curbs on certain media reports. The electoral roll that had been released prior to the postponed elections was subsequently invalidated by the High Court. In April 2007 Dr Ahmed projected that elections would be held by the end of 2008, following the implementation of a programme of reform. In the same month speculation arose regarding a rumoured deal between the interim Government and Khaleda Zia to ensure the latter's permanent departure from Bangladesh. It was later reported that Sheikh Hasina Wajed's return to Bangladesh from a trip abroad had been blocked following a government warning that, should she set foot in the country, she would face arrest in relation to fatalities arising from protests in the previous year. At the end of the month, however, the Government stated that Sheikh Hasina Wajed was free to return to Bangladesh, and denied that Khaleda Zia was to be forced into exile.

In the mean time, the interim Government had embarked on a large-scale campaign against corruption, apparently as part of a wider attempt to overhaul the political system and prepare the country for free and fair elections. A new Chairman, former Chief of Army Staff Lt-Gen. (retd) Hasan Mashhud Chowdhury, was appointed to head the reconstituted Anti-Corruption Commission. Numerous senior political figures from both the BNP and the AL were detained, and several (including a number of former government ministers) were subsequently charged and convicted of corruption or other crimes. According to one news source, as many as 200,000 people, including politicians, business executives and officials, had been arrested by mid-2007, with emergency rules limiting civil liberties still in effect. Most noteworthy, however, were the arrests of the two dominant figures in Bangladeshi politics: Sheikh Hasina Wajed was detained in July on charges of extortion, and her erstwhile rival Khaleda Zia was arrested in September on corruption charges; both were denied bail and remained incarcerated in early 2008. There were intimations of a rift within the BNP in Zia's absence, with the reported appointment in October 2007 of M. Saifur Rahman as acting Chairman and Maj. (retd) Hafizuddin Ahmed as acting Secretary-General by a section of the party standing committee (Zia had reportedly replaced Secretary-General Abdul Mannan Bhuiyan with Khandaker Delwar Hossain in September). Meanwhile, there was growing discontent in certain quarters over the perceived severity of the emergency measures and the curtailment of civil rights, including the reported maintenance of media restrictions. In August clashes between students and security forces at universities in Dhaka, Chittagong, Sylhet and three other cities prompted the imposition of temporary curfews. The Government announced a partial suspension of its ban on political activity in the following month, while upholding restrictions on outdoor rallies and functions. Iajuddin Ahmed's term as President, which duly expired in early September, was extended in light of the delayed legislative elections. In November the lengthy process of transferring power over the judiciary away from the executive arm of government appeared to be complete, with the announcement that judges and magistrates would henceforth be selected by the Supreme Court.

In mid-November 2007 Bangladesh's vulnerability to natural disasters was once again highlighted when a devastating cyclone caused widespread destruction and resulted in the deaths of more than 3,200 people. In December 2007–January 2008 five advisers resigned from the interim Government. Although personal reasons were officially cited for four of these resignations, some observers suggested that the advisers' departure had not been entirely voluntary. Five new advisers, including former Attorney-General A. F. Hassan Ariff, were subsequently sworn in.

In foreign affairs, Bangladesh has traditionally maintained a policy of non-alignment. Relations with Pakistan improved in 1976: ambassadors were exchanged, and trade, postal and telecommunication links were resumed. In September 1991 Pakistan finally agreed to initiate a process of phased repatriation and rehabilitation of some 250,000 Bihari Muslims (who supported Pakistan in Bangladesh's war of liberation in 1971) still remaining in refugee camps in Bangladesh. The first group of Bihari refugees returned to Pakistan from Bangladesh in January 1993, but the implementation of the repatriation process was slow. Relations with Pakistan deteriorated in September 2000 when, at the UN Millennium Summit in New York, USA, the Prime Minister, Sheikh Hasina Wajed, condemned Pakistan's military leadership, ostensibly as part of a general request for the UN to take action against undemocratic changes of government. A diplomatic row ensued over who was responsible for the events during Bangladesh's war of liberation, culminating in the withdrawal of the Pakistani Deputy High Commissioner to Bangladesh. In July 2002 Pakistani President Pervez Musharraf paid a visit to Bangladesh, during which he expressed regret for the atrocities committed by Pakistani troops during the 1971 war. In February 2006 Prime Minister Khaleda Zia visited Pakistan to hold talks with her Pakistani counterpart, Shaukat Aziz; the latter hailed the visit, during which the two sides signed four memorandums of understanding on trade, agriculture, tourism, and standardization and quality control, as a turning point in bilateral relations.

Relations with India have been strained over the questions of cross-border terrorism (especially around the area of the Chittagong Hill Tracts, where Buddhist tribal rebels, the Shanti Bahini, waged a lengthy guerrilla campaign against the Bangladeshi police and Bengali settlers—see below) and of the Farrakka barrage, which was constructed by India on the Ganga river in 1975, so depriving Bangladesh of water for irrigation and river transport during the dry season. In December 1996, however, Indo-Bangladeshi relations were given a major boost following the signing of an historic 30-year water-sharing agreement. In January 1997 Indian Prime Minister H. D. Deve Gowda paid an official visit to Bangladesh, the first Indian premier to do so for 20 years. In June 1999, during a visit to Dhaka by Indian Prime Minister Atal Bihari Vajpayee to celebrate the inauguration of the first direct passenger bus service between Bangladesh and India, Vajpayee promised Bangladesh greater access to Indian markets and announced that India would give its neighbour US $50m. in credits over three years to help develop its transport and industrial infrastructure. In August the Bangladeshi Government was criticized by the opposition for its approval of proposals to permit the transhipment of Indian goods through Bangladesh to the north-eastern states of India by Bangladeshi transport companies (see above). In October 2003 Bangladesh and India signed another water-sharing agreement.

In June 1992 the Indian Government, under the provisions of an accord signed with Bangladesh in 1974, formally leased the Tin Bigha Corridor (a small strip of land covering an area of only 1.5 ha) to Bangladesh for 999 years. India maintained sovereignty over the corridor, but the lease gave Bangladesh access to its enclaves of Dahagram and Angarpota. In September 1997 India granted Nepal a transit route through a 60-km corridor in the Indian territory joining Nepal and Bangladesh, thus facilitating trade between those two countries. Despite the 1992 border agreement between Bangladesh and India, the issue of territorial rights to pockets of land or enclaves along the irregular border remained a source of dispute, and occasional efforts to resolve this problem failed to prevent intermittent clashes between border guards. The worst fighting between the two countries since 1976 took place in April 2001 on the Bangladeshi border with the Indian state of Meghalaya. Some 16 members of the Indian Border Security Forces (BSF) and three members of the Bangladesh Rifles (border guard) were killed. The situation was brought under control, and the two sides entered border negotiations in June and July, as a result of which two joint working groups were established to review the undemarcated section of the border.

Relations with India deteriorated in November 2002 as a result of accusations by India's Deputy Prime Minister and Minister of Home Affairs, Lal Krishna Advani, that al-Qa'ida had increased its activities in Bangladesh since the BNP-led coalition's assumption of power in October 2001. Advani also claimed that Bangladesh was covertly assisting al-Qa'ida and Pakistan's Inter-Services Intelligence Agency, and was providing refuge for Indian separatist groups. The Bangladeshi Government strongly denied the allegations. In January 2003 the Indian Government announced plans to deport some 16m. Bangladeshis who it claimed were working and living in India illegally, because they were perceived to be a security threat. The Bangladeshi Government rejected the claim as groundless. In mid-February the Bangladeshi Minister of Foreign Affairs visited India to discuss the issue of illegal immigration; India expressed dismay at the outcome of the negotiations. Meanwhile, the number of people stranded between the countries' borders increased. In September 2004 senior Bangladeshi and Indian officials held talks in Dhaka concerning water-sharing and security issues. Some progress was made in resolving the issue of water-sharing between the two countries, and an agreement was reached to co-ordinate border patrols by security forces in both countries. However, Bangladesh continued to deny the existence of Indian separatist groups within its borders. In the following month members of the two countries' border patrols exchanged fire when a dispute occurred as several Bangladeshis attempted to cross illegally into India. The Indian Government again claimed that a significant number of Indian insurgent groups had established bases in Bangladesh, an allegation emphatically denied by the Bangladeshi Government. Relations continued to be strained into 2005, with clashes between the two countries' border patrols occurring again in March of that year. Talks were held later in that month in an attempt to resolve the ongoing problems, which had been exacerbated by India's continued construction of a fence along the border, in contravention of its obligations under a 1974 treaty. The Indian Government claimed that the fence was intended to prevent illegal immigrants and insurgents from crossing the border. Several further clashes occurred in the following months, as relations remained tense.

In March 2006 Prime Minister Khaleda Zia, during her first official visit to India since her term in office began in 2001, held talks with the Indian Prime Minister, Dr Manmohan Singh, the President, A. P. J. Abdul Kalam, and other senior officials. The two countries signed agreements on trade and anti-drugs trafficking measures, and stressed their commitment to working together on security issues. Security, however, remained a point of contention between Bangladesh and India throughout 2006. There were various reports in the Indian media that the explosives used in the Mumbai bomb attacks in July originated in Bangladesh (an allegation that was vehemently denied by the Bangladesh Government), and in late July it was reported that intelligence agencies in New Delhi were to produce evidence of terrorist training camps located in Bangladesh. In August the Indian BSF gave a list of more than 100 militants, including several Assamese (Asomese) rebel leaders, to the Bangladesh Rifles, requesting that they be handed over. The BSF had also appealed for separatist camps on Bangladeshi soil to be dismantled. The Bangladesh Rifles, however, reportedly denied the existence of separatist bases in Bangladesh. In January 2007, as violence in the Indian state of Assam (Asom) escalated, the BSF again accused Bangladesh of harbouring leaders of the United Liberation Front of Assam (ULFA). The Indian Minister of External Affairs, Pranab Mukherjee, visited Bangladesh in February, participating in talks with President Iajuddin Ahmed, Chief Adviser Fakhruddin Ahmed and other senior government officials and political figures. According to Mukherjee, the two countries agreed to increase co-operation in their respective fights against terrorism. Military officials from Bangladesh and India held talks in Dhaka in October to work towards a resolution of border issues, with the two sides agreeing to provide each other with information and assistance in order to combat militant and criminal activity in border areas.

In 1989 the Government attempted to suppress the Shanti Bahini insurgency in the Chittagong Hill Tracts by introducing concessions providing limited autonomy to the region in the form of three new semi-autonomous hill districts. Voting to elect councils for the districts took place relatively peacefully in June, despite attempts at disruption by the Shanti Bahini, who continued to demand total autonomy for the Chakma tribals. The powers vested in the councils were designed to give the tribals sufficient authority to regulate any further influx of Bengali settlers to the districts (the chief complaint of the tribals since Bengalis were settled in the Chittagong Hill Tracts, as plantation workers and clerks, by the British administration in the 19th century). Despite these concessions, violence continued unabated, and refugees continued to flee across the border into India (the number of refugees living in camps in Tripura reached about 56,000). In May 1992 Bangladesh and India negotiated an agreement intended to facilitate the refugees' return. However, the refugees, fearing persecution by the Bangladesh security forces, proved reluctant to repatriate. Following the conclusion of a successful round of negotiations in early 1994, the process of phased repatriation commenced, although by August only about 2,000 refugees had returned. In December 1997 the Bangladeshi Government signed a peace agreement with the political wing of the Shanti Bahini ending the insurgency in the Chittagong Hill Tracts. The treaty offered the rebels a general amnesty in return for the surrender of their weapons and gave the tribal people greater powers of self-governance through the establishment of three new elected district councils (to control the area's land management and policing) and a regional council (the chairman of which was to enjoy the rank of a state minister). The peace agreement, which was strongly criticized by the opposition for representing a 'sell-out' of the area to India and a threat to Bangladesh's sovereignty, was expected to accelerate the process of repatriating the remaining refugees from Tripura (who totalled about 31,000 at the end of December 1997). By the end of 2000 most of the Chakma refugees had been repatriated, the district and regional councils were in operation, and a land commission had been established. In June 2001 it was reported that rioting in the Chittagong area had caused a new flow of refugees to Tripura. Following the accession to power of the BNP-led alliance in October, there were reports of thousands of members of Buddhist, Christian and Hindu minorities fleeing to Tripura. In May 2003 the Chakma tribal people held nation-wide demonstrations protesting against discrimination by Bengalis and the apparent reneging on the 1997 peace agreement. In December 2003 and January 2004 protesters in the south-eastern Hill Tracts succeeded in cutting off the region from the rest of the country as they demanded the full implementation of the 1997 agreement. In December 2005 the Government and the UNDP announced investment of US $50m. in the south-eastern Hill Tracts, in order to assist with implementation of the 1997 agreement by strengthening the local economy.

Bangladesh security forces were put on alert in late 2000, as tension along the border with Myanmar increased following reports that Myanmar was laying land-mines and that Myanma troops had been deployed in the border area. In January 2001 border guards exchanged fire, amid rising tension over a controversial dam project on the Naaf river, which Bangladesh claimed would cause flooding in its territory; the shooting took place after work began in Myanmar on the construction of an embankment. The Myanma authorities agreed to suspend the project. Shortly afterwards Myanmar alleged that Bangladesh had violated the two countries' 1979 border agreement by cultivating shrimps in the area, an accusation denied by the Bangladeshi Government. Border negotiations took place subsequently, but collapsed after the Myanma authorities refused to sign the minutes. In early February 2001, however, Myanmar agreed permanently to halt construction of the dam. The official visit of the Myanma ruler, Gen. Than Shwe, to Bangladesh in December 2002 indicated an improvement in relations. Meanwhile, some 250,000 Rohingyas had fled Myanmar's Northern Rakhine state in 1991–92. Myanmar had in August 1997 suspended a programme of voluntary repatriations agreed by the Bangladeshi and Myanma authorities in 1992, under which about 230,000 refugees had returned to Myanmar, although smaller-scale repatriations had resumed in late 1998 following intervention by the office of the UN High Commissioner for Refugees (UNHCR). According to UNHCR data, 16,000 of the Rohingyas remaining in Bangladesh were considered by the Government of Myanmar to be ineligible for repatriation, since they had not been authorized for return prior to August 1997, and 5,000 were unwilling to return owing to protection concerns; however, the Bangladeshi Government continued to favour repatriation of the refugees. In January 2002 the World Food Programme launched an appeal for US $2.1m. in assistance for 21,500 Myanma Rohingya Muslim refugees who remained in two camps in south-eastern Bangladesh. In 2003 UNHCR announced that it intended gradually to phase out its support for those refugees who remained in the camps, and to implement a 'self-sufficiency' plan intended to enable the integration of the refugee population into the local Bangladeshi community. However, the Government rejected the plan in September 2004. In late 2006, according to UNHCR figures, an estimated 26,000 refugees remained in the camps, the rate of repatriation having slowed considerably.

In September 2001 Bangladesh's interim administration agreed, with the support of the AL and BNP, to offer the USA use of Bangladeshi airspace and ports in the event of military action against Afghanistan, where the Taliban leadership was believed to be harbouring Osama bin Laden and other members of al-Qa'ida—held principally responsible by the USA for that month's suicide attacks against New York and Washington, DC. However, the US-led military campaign to oust the regime of Saddam Hussain in Iraq from March 2003 provoked anti-US and anti-British demonstrations in Dhaka at the end of March and during April. In June 2004 US Secretary of Defense Donald Rumsfeld visited Bangladesh and held talks with Prime Minister Begum Khaleda Zia. There were protests against his visit, as it was believed that he intended to request that Bangladesh contribute troops to assist the US-led coalition in Iraq. The Bangladeshi Minister of Foreign Affairs stressed that Bangladesh would not send any troops to the country without a UN mandate.

Bangladesh is a member of the South Asian Association for Regional Co-operation (SAARC, see p. 384), formally constituted in 1985, with Bhutan, India, the Maldives, Nepal, Pakistan and Sri Lanka. Included in SAARC's charter are pledges of non-interference by members in each other's internal affairs and a joint effort to avoid 'contentious' issues whenever the association meets. The SAARC Preferential Trading Arrangement (SAPTA) was signed in April 1993 and came into effect in December 1995. At the 12th SAARC summit meeting held in Islamabad, Pakistan, in January 2004, members signed an agreement stipulating the establishment of a South Asian Free Trade Area (SAFTA) by 1 January 2006 (SAFTA, however, was not due to enter fully into force until 2016). An additional protocol on terrorism was also signed. Bangladesh hosted the 13th SAARC summit meeting in December 2005.

Government

The role of the President, who is elected by the Jatiya Sangsad (Parliament) for a five-year term, is essentially that of a titular Head of State. Executive power is held by the Prime Minister, who heads the Council of Ministers. The President appoints the Prime Minister and, on the latter's recommendation, other ministers. The Jatiya Sangsad comprises 345 members, 300 of whom are elected by universal suffrage: an additional 45 female members are appointed by the elective members on the basis of proportional representation. The Jatiya Sangsad serves a five-year term, subject to dissolution.

For purposes of local government, the country is divided into 64 administrative districts.

Defence

Military service is voluntary. The armed forces, as assessed at November 2007, numbered 150,000: an army of 120,000, a navy of 16,000 and an air force of 14,000. The paramilitary forces totalled 63,910, and included the Bangladesh Rifles (border guard) of 38,000. Budget expenditure on defence was estimated at 52,830m. taka for 2007/08 (equivalent to 9.8% of total budgetary spending).

Economic Affairs

In 2006, according to estimates by the World Bank, Bangladesh's gross national income (GNI), measured at average 2004–06 prices, was US $69,921m., equivalent to $480 per head (or $2,340 per head on an international purchasing-power parity basis). During 1996–2006, it was estimated, the population increased at an average annual rate of 2.0%, while gross domestic product (GDP) per head increased, in real terms, by an average of 3.5% per year. Overall GDP increased at an average annual rate of 5.7% in 1999–2006. GDP grew by 6.6% in 2005/06 and by an estimated 6.5% in 2006/07. GDP was projected to increase by about 6.0% in 2007/08.

Agriculture (including hunting, forestry and fishing) contributed an estimated 18.9% of total GDP in 2006/07. According to UN figures, in 2005 50.8% of the total labour force was engaged in that sector. The principal sources of revenue in the agricultural sector are jute, tea, shrimps and fish. Raw jute and jute goods accounted for 3.8% of total export earnings in 2006/07. Despite severe flooding in 2000, Bangladesh achieved self-sufficiency in basic foods for the first time in 2000/01, mainly owing to increased rice production. According to official figures, agricultural production grew by 4.1% in 2003/04, largely owing to the expansion of the area under high-yielding variety crops. However, sectoral GDP was considerably affected in 2004/05 by the consequences of serious flooding in July–September 2004, expanding by only an estimated 2.2% in that year. According to the 2006/07 Bangladesh Bank annual report, the GDP of the crop and horticulture sub-sector increased by 5.0% in 2005/06, compared with the previous year, and was projected to increase by 1.9% in 2006/07. Agricultural GDP expanded at an average annual rate of 3.8% in 1996–2006.

Industry (including mining, manufacturing, power and construction) employed 10.7% of the working population in 1999/2000. The industrial sector contributed an estimated 28.5% of total GDP in 2006/07. During 1996–2006 industrial GDP increased at an average annual rate of 7.2%. According to official figures, growth in the industrial sector was 9.7% in 2005/06 and an estimated 9.5% in 2006/07.

Bangladesh's proven reserves of natural gas totalled 440,000m. cu m at the end of 2006. According to the US Geological Survey, production of natural gas increased from 14,000m. cu m in 2004/05 to 15,000m cu m in 2005/06. It is envisaged that an exportable surplus of natural gas may eventually be produced. In November 2004 the US company Unocal signed an agreement with the state-owned Petrobangla corporation to develop the country's most extensive gas field, at Bibiyana. Bangladesh possesses substantial deposits of coal (estimated at more than 1,000m. metric tons, although difficulties of exploitation continue to make coal imports necessary) and petroleum.

Manufacturing contributed an estimated 17.9% of GDP in 2006/07. The sector employed 9.8% of the working population in 2003. The principal branches of the manufacturing sector include textiles, food products, garments and chemicals. During 1996–2006 manufacturing GDP increased at an average annual rate of 6.6%. According to official figures, the GDP of the manufacturing sector grew by 10.8% in 2005/06 and by an estimated 11.2% in 2006/07.

Energy is derived principally from natural gas (which contributed 87.5% of total electricity output in 2004). Imports of petroleum products comprised 10.7% of the cost of total imports in 2006/07.

The services sector accounted for an estimated 52.6% of total GDP in 2006/07. In 1999/2000 24.5% of the employed labour force was engaged in the sector. The GDP of the services sector increased at an average annual rate of 5.5% during 1996–2006. According to official figures, the sector's GDP expanded by 6.4% in 2005/06 and by an estimated 6.7% in 2006/07.

In 2006, according to the IMF, Bangladesh recorded a visible trade deficit of US $2,889.7m., while there was a surplus of $1,196.1m. on the current account of the balance of payments. In 2006 the principal source of imports was India (which contributed 12.4% of the total), while the USA was the principal market for exports (accounting for 25.4% of the total). Other major trading partners were the People's Republic of China, Singapore, Germany and the United Kingdom. The principal exports in 2006/07 were ready-made garments (accounting for an estimated 25.4% of total export revenue), knitwear and hosiery products, frozen shrimp and fish and raw jute and jute goods. The principal imports were textiles (an estimated 11.8% of the total), capital machinery, petroleum products, and iron and steel.

In 2006/07, according to Bangladesh Bank figures, the overall budgetary deficit (excluding grants) was projected to amount to the equivalent of 3.7% of GDP. According to figures from the Asian Development Bank (ADB), Bangladesh's total external debt was US $18,934.5m. at the end of 2005, of which $17,937.7m. was long-term public debt. In that year the cost of debt-servicing was equivalent to 5.3% of total revenue from exports of goods and services. The annual rate of inflation averaged 5.3% in 1996–2006. According to the International Labour Organization (ILO), consumer prices increased by an average of 7.0% in 2005 and 6.8% in 2006. About 4.3% of the total labour force was unemployed in 2003.

Bangladesh is a member of the UN Economic and Social Commission for Asia and the Pacific (ESCAP, see p. 35), of the Asian Development Bank (ADB, see p. 182), of the South Asian Association for Regional Co-operation (SAARC, see p. 384) and of the Colombo Plan (see p. 411). Bangladesh is also a member of the International Jute Organization, which is based in Dhaka.

The problems of developing Bangladesh include widespread poverty, malnutrition and underemployment, combined with an increasing population and a poor resource base—this last factor means that the country is particularly vulnerable to adverse climatic conditions and to fluctuations in international prices for its export commodities. Despite the frequency of natural disasters, food security has improved somewhat in recent years, as have efforts to enhance production methods (notably through subsidies and the increased use of high-yielding variety crops), storage and distribution facilities. The birth rate has decreased considerably, owing to a successful nation-wide birth-control campaign. In the 1990s high rates of growth were achieved in exports of non-traditional items, particularly ready-made garments and knitwear. Furthermore, recent discoveries of huge reserves of natural gas appear to offer opportunities both in terms of domestic fuel self-sufficiency and, in the longer term, export potential. Nevertheless, the increasing fiscal deficit, exacerbated by the heavy losses incurred by state-owned enterprises, continues to cause concern, as does Bangladesh's heavy dependence on foreign aid: total disbursed aid in 2005/06 amounted to US $1,280m. In 2001/02 real GDP growth slowed to the lowest rate in six years, owing to a deceleration in all sectors of the economy. However, in the following years the economy regained momentum: exports and imports rose, the textile industry showed signs of recovery and the wider trade deficit was more than offset by the increased level of remittances from Bangladeshis working abroad. In 2003 the Government agreed to follow a three-year IMF poverty-reduction programme in exchange for a loan of $500m. The Government also revealed a set of measures to curb corruption and improve tax collection. The World Trade Organization's Multi-fibre Arrangement (MFA) expired at the end of 2004; however, contrary to expectations, Bangladesh's garment industry (which had previously benefited from MFA quotas limiting garments exports to developed countries) continued to perform well. None the less, the diversification of Bangladesh's export base became a government priority and in 2004/05 several measures were introduced to facilitate this process. Priority was accorded to the development of alternative areas with potential for growth, such as computer software and information and communication technologies, and financial incentives were introduced to encourage the expansion of different product areas. From 2004 it was feared that the deteriorating domestic security situation would discourage foreign investment in Bangladesh, although it was hoped that government action against Islamist militants from 2005 would reassure investors. Ongoing general strikes, orchestrated by the political opposition, also proved economically damaging, as did periodic severe flooding. It was hoped that the formation of an independent Anti-Corruption Commission in November 2004 would improve the country's image abroad and lead to increased foreign investment in the long term. However, in November 2005 the World Bank announced that it intended to cancel funding for three development projects in the country, owing to its exposure of corruption in the bidding process for contracts for the projects. Meanwhile, in January 2005 the Governments of Bangladesh, India and Myanmar announced that they had agreed, in principle, to co-operate on a gas pipeline and exploration project. It was intended that a pipeline would be constructed between Myanmar and India, passing through Bangladesh, which could receive as much as $125m. annually in transit and other fees from the agreement. In mid-2006 plans for the pipeline foundered as India declared its unwillingness to accept Bangladesh's preconditions; it seemed increasingly likely that the pipeline would bypass Bangladesh altogether. Also in mid-2006, a coal-mining project in Phulbari, which was to be undertaken by the British company Asia Energy Corporation and which was to cost an estimated $1,000m., was cancelled by the Government after violent demonstrations were organized in protest against the anticipated damage to the environment and local livelihoods. In 2004/05, despite continuing growth in exports, the current account of the balance of payments moved into deficit, owing to an increase in imports necessitated by high global petroleum prices and the effects of flooding in that year on foodgrain production. Increased petroleum prices had a significant effect upon Bangladesh's economy. The current account did, however, record a surplus in 2005/06, mainly due to an increase in export earnings and in remittances from abroad, coupled with a relative deceleration in import growth rates. Driven by ongoing expansion in the industrial and service sectors and the recovery of the agricultural sector, the economy continued to grow, with GDP increasing by an estimated 6.6%, in real terms, in 2005/06. Widespread social unrest during 2006, however, forced the postponement of the general election in January 2007 and the installation of an emergency transitional government. The new interim administration rapidly introduced measures to increase transparency in the banking sector, which had the effect of discouraging capital transfers as companies became less willing to expose their operations to government scrutiny. Consequently, the rate of importation declined in 2007, which, in turn, exacerbated food shortages and accelerated inflation. Inflows of foreign direct investment (FDI) had risen from $385m. in 2003/04 to $800m. in 2004/05, owing largely to the Government's active encouragement of foreign investors; in 2005/06, however, inflows fell to $743m. The level of FDI recovered marginally in 2006/07, reaching $760m., although it was expected to decline once again in 2007/08 in tandem with domestic investment. The climatic volatility of the region once more impeded the country's progress in 2007; a substantial portion of Bangladesh's rice crop was destroyed by Cyclone Sidr, which struck in Bangladesh in November. The adverse weather conditions also damaged the country's already beleaguered infrastructure. Subsequent aid disbursements reached almost US $500m. in late 2007 and, in addition, the ADB provided a loan of $400m. for the purpose of reconstruction.

Education

The Government provides free schooling for children of both sexes for eight years. Primary education, which is compulsory, begins at six years of age and lasts for five years. Secondary education, beginning at the age of 11, lasts for up to seven years, comprising a first cycle of three years, a second cycle of two years and a third cycle of two further years. In 2003/04 an estimated 93.8% of children (92% of boys; 95% of girls) in the relevant age-group attended primary schools. In 2002/03 enrolment at secondary schools included 48.0% of children (45% of boys; 51% of girls) in the relevant age-group. Secondary schools and colleges in the private sector vastly outnumber government institutions. In 2004/05 there were 26 state universities, including one for agriculture, one for Islamic studies and one for engineering and technology. The Government launched an Open University Project in 1992 at an estimated cost of US $34.3m. The 2007/08 budget allocated 86,590m. taka to education and technology (equivalent to 16.1% of total budgetary expenditure).

Public Holidays

2008: 1 January (New Year's Day), 10 January*† (Muharram, Islamic New Year), 21 February (Shaheed Day and International Mother Language Day), 17 March (Birth of the Father of the Nation), 20 March* (Birth of the Prophet), 26 March (Indepen-

BANGLADESH

dence Day), 14 April (Bengali New Year), 1 May (May Day), 19 May* (Buddha Purnima), 7 July (First Monday in July), 30 July (Shab-i Bharat, Ascension of the Prophet), 15 August (National Mourning Day), 28 August* (Janmashtami), 1 October* (Id al-Fitr, end of Ramadan), 18–21 October* (Durga Puja), 9 December* (Id al-Adha, Feast of the Sacrifice), 16 December (Victory Day), 25 December (Christmas Day), 26 December (Boxing Day), 29 December*† (Muharram, Islamic New Year), 31 December (Bank Holiday).

2009: 1 January (New Year's Day), 21 February (Shaheed Day and International Mother Language Day), 17 March (Birth of the Father of the Nation), 20 March* (Birth of the Prophet), 26 March (Independence Day), 14 April (Bengali New Year), 1 May (May Day), 8 May* (Buddha Purnima), 6 July (First Monday in July), 19 July (Shab-i Bharat, Ascension of the Prophet), 14 August* (Janmashtami), 15 August (National Mourning Day), September/October* (Durga Puja), 20 September* (Id al-Fitr, end of Ramadan), 8 December* (Id al-Adha, Feast of the Sacrifice), 16 December (Victory Day), 18 December* (Muharram, Islamic New Year), 25 December (Christmas Day), 26 December (Boxing Day), 31 December (Bank Holiday).

* Dates of certain religious holidays are subject to the sighting of the moon, and there are also optional holidays for different religious groups.

† This festival occurs twice (marking the start of the Islamic years AH 1429 and AH 1430) within the same Gregorian year.

Weights and Measures

The imperial system of measures is in force, pending the introduction of the metric system. The following local units of weight are also used:

1 maund = 82.28 lb (37.29 kg).
1 seer = 2.057 lb (932 grams).
1 tola = 180 grains (11.66 grams).

Statistical Survey

Source (unless otherwise stated): Bangladesh Bureau of Statistics, Statistics Division, Ministry of Planning, E-27/A, Agargaon, Sher-e-bangla Nagar, Dhaka 1207; tel. (2) 9118045; fax (2) 9111064; e-mail ndbp@bangla.net; internet www.bbs.gov.bd.

Area and Population

AREA, POPULATION AND DENSITY

Area (sq km)	143,998*
Population (census results)†	
11 March 1991	111,455,185
22 January 2001	
Males	67,731,320
Females	62,791,278
Total	130,522,598
Population (official estimates at mid-year)‡	
2004	136,700,000
2005	138,600,000
2006	141,800,000§
Density (per sq km) at mid-2006	984.7

* 55,598 sq miles.
† Including adjustment for underenumeration, estimated to have been 3.08% in 1991 and 4.95% in 2001.
‡ Based on sample vital registration system (SVRS).
§ Projected estimate.

ADMINISTRATIVE DIVISIONS
(2001 census, preliminary figures)

Division	Area (sq km)	Population ('000)*	Density (per sq km)
Barisal	13,297	8,514	640.3
Chittagong	33,771	25,187	745.8
Dhaka	31,119	40,592	1,304.4
Khulna	22,274	15,185	681.7
Rajshahi	34,513	31,478	912.1
Sylhet	12,596	8,291	658.2
Total	**147,570**	**129,247**	**875.8**

* Including adjustments for net underenumeration.

PRINCIPAL TOWNS
(population at 1991 census)*

Dhaka (capital)	3,612,850	Comilla	135,313
Chittagong	1,392,860	Nawabganj	130,577
Khulna	663,340	Dinajpur	127,815
Rajshahi	294,056	Bogra	120,170
Narayanganj	276,549	Sylhet	114,300
Sitakunda	274,903	Brahmanbaria	109,032
Rangpur	191,398	Tangail	106,004
Mymensingh (Nasirabad)	188,713	Jamalpur	103,556
Barisal (Bakerganj)	170,232	Pabna	103,277
Tongi (Tungi)	168,702	Naogaon	101,266
Jessore	139,710	Sirajganj	99,669

* Figures in each case refer to the city proper. The population of the largest urban agglomerations at the 1991 census was: Dhaka 6,487,459 (including Narayanganj and Tongi); Chittagong 2,079,968 (including Sitakunda); Khulna 921,365; Rajshahi 507,435; Mymensingh 273,350; Sylhet 225,541; Comilla 225,259; Rangpur 208,294; Barisal 202,746; Jessore 169,349; Bogra 161,155.

2001 (urban agglomerations, preliminary census figures): Dhaka 9,912,908 (including Narayanganj 230,294 and Tongi 281,928); Chittagong 3,202,710 (including Patiya 47,625); Khulna 1,227,239; Rajshahi 646,716.

Mid-2005 ('000, incl. suburbs, UN estimate): Dhaka 12,430 (Source: UN, *World Urbanization Prospects: The 2005 Revision*).

BIRTHS, MARRIAGES AND DEATHS*
(crude rates per 1,000 persons)

	Live births	Marriages	Deaths
2000	19.0	9.0	4.9
2001	18.9	8.9	4.8
2002	20.1	9.5	5.1
2003	20.9	10.4	5.9
2004	20.8	12.4	5.8

* Estimates based on sample vital registration system (SVRS). According to UN estimates, the average annual rates per 1,000 for births and deaths were: Births 33.6 in 1990–95, 29.4 in 1995–2000, 27.8 in 2000–05; Deaths 11.1 in 1990–95, 9.2 in 1995–2000, 8.2 in 2000–05 (Source: UN, *World Population Prospects: The 2006 Revision*).

1997 (provisional): Registered live births 3,057,000 (birth rate 24.6 per 1,000); Registered deaths 958,000 (death rate 7.7 per 1,000) (Source: UN, *Population and Vital Statistics Report*).

Marriages: 1,181,000 in 1997 (Source: UN, *Demographic Yearbook*).

Expectation of life (years at birth, WHO estimates): 62.5 (males 62.2; females 63.0) in 2005 (Source: WHO, *World Health Statistics*).

BANGLADESH

ECONOMICALLY ACTIVE POPULATION*
(sample survey, '000 persons aged 15 years and over, year ending June 2000)

	Males	Females	Total
Agriculture, hunting, forestry and fishing	17,256	14,914	32,171
Mining and quarrying	107	188	295
Manufacturing	2,346	1,436	3,783
Electricity, gas and water	116	18	134
Construction	999	100	1,099
Trade, restaurants and hotels	5,769	506	6,275
Transport, storage and communications	2,432	77	2,509
Financing, insurance, real estate and business services	357	46	403
Community, social and personal services	1,243	1,726	2,969
Activities not adequately defined	1,744	384	2,126
Total employed	32,369	19,395	51,764
Unemployed	1,083	666	1,750
Total labour force	33,452	20,061	53,514

* Figures exclude members of the armed forces.

Note: Totals may not be equal to sum of components, owing to rounding.

Source: ILO.

Mid-2005 (official estimates in '000): Agriculture, etc. 37,874; Total labour force 74,574 (Source: FAO).

Health and Welfare

KEY INDICATORS

Total fertility rate (children per woman, 2005)	3.1
Under-five mortality rate (per 1,000 live births, 2005)	73
HIV/AIDS (% of persons aged 15–49, 2005)	<0.1
Physicians (per 1,000 head, 2004)	0.26
Hospital beds (per 1,000 head, 2001)	0.30
Health expenditure (2004): US $ per head (PPP)	64.3
Health expenditure (2004): % of GDP	3.1
Health expenditure (2004): public (% of total)	28.1
Access to water (% of persons, 2004)	74
Access to sanitation (% of persons, 2004)	39
Human Development Index (2005): ranking	140
Human Development Index (2005): value	0.547

For sources and definitions, see explanatory note on p. vi.

Agriculture

PRINCIPAL CROPS
('000 metric tons, year ending 30 June)

	2003/04	2004/05	2005/06
Wheat	1,253	976	772
Rice (paddy)	36,236	39,796	43,729*
Millet	26	25*	25†
Potatoes	3,907	4,855	4,161
Sweet potatoes	320	311	327†
Sugar cane	6,484	6,423	6,423†
Other sugar crops	317	342	342†
Beans (dry)	144	49†	50†
Lentils	122	118	120†
Other pulses	163	168	136†
Groundnuts (in shell)	34	39	34*
Areca nuts (betel)	55	57†	55†
Coconuts	133	88†	88†
Rapeseed	211	191	235*
Sesame seed*	49	50	50
Linseed*	50	50	50
Cottonseed†	27	26	26
Cabbages	129	142	142†
Lettuce	32	32	32†
Spinach	29	29	29†
Tomatoes	120	122	122†
Cauliflowers and broccoli	101	109	109†
Pumpkins, squash and gourds	226	228†	228†

—continued	2003/04	2004/05	2005/06
Dry onions	272	589	589†
Garlic	73	90	90†
Beans (green)	59	61	61†
Cantaloupes and other melons	89†	82	82
Guavas, mangoes and mangosteens	243	228†	228†
Pineapples	213	235	235†
Bananas	707	899	899†
Papayas	51	51†	51†
Tea (made)	58	58	58†
Tobacco (leaves)	39	39†	39†
Ginger	48	49	49†
Jute†	801	801	801

* Unofficial figure(s).
† FAO estimate(s).

Aggregate production ('000 metric tons, may include official, semi-official or estimated data): Total cereals 37,759 in 2004, 41,156 in 2005, 45,010 in 2006; Total roots and tubers 4,228 in 2004, 5,167 in 2005, 4,488 in 2006; Total vegetables (incl. melons) 2,097 in 2004, 2,451 in 2005, 2,451 in 2006; Total spices 235 in 2004, 283 in 2005, 283 in 2006; Total fruits (excl. melons) 1,690 in 2004, 1,889 in 2005, 1889 in 2006.

Source: FAO.

LIVESTOCK
('000 head, year ending September, FAO estimates)

	2001	2002	2003
Cattle	24,100	24,300	24,500
Buffaloes	850	850	850
Sheep	1,143	1,194	1,260
Goats	34,400	36,900	36,900
Chickens	140	140	142
Ducks	12	11	12

2004–06: Figures assumed to be unchanged from 2003 (FAO estimates).

Source: FAO.

LIVESTOCK PRODUCTS
('000 metric tons, FAO estimates)

	2003	2004	2005
Cattle meat	180.0	180.0	180.0
Buffalo meat	3.6	3.6	3.6
Sheep meat	3.0	3.0	3.0
Goat meat	137	137	137
Chicken meat	102.0	109.6	114.2
Duck meat	14.0	13.7	13.6
Cows' milk	797	800	800
Buffalo milk	22.8	22.8	22.8
Sheep's milk	25.1	25.1	25.1
Goats' milk	1,416	1,416	1,416
Hen eggs	135	135	135
Other poultry eggs	26	26	26

2006: Figures assumed to be unchanged from 2005 (FAO estimates).

Source: FAO.

Forestry

ROUNDWOOD REMOVALS
('000 cubic metres, excl. bark)

	2003	2004	2005
Sawlogs, veneer logs and logs for sleepers*	174	174	174
Pulpwood	18	18†	18†
Other industrial wood	90	90†	90†
Fuel wood†	27,728	27,694	27,662
Total	28,010	27,976	27,944

* Annual output assumed to be unchanged since 1996.
† FAO estimate(s).

2006: Figures assumed to be unchanged from 2005 (FAO estimates).

Source: FAO.

BANGLADESH

SAWNWOOD PRODUCTION
('000 cubic metres, incl. railway sleepers)

	2001	2002	2003
Total (all broadleaved)	79*	255	388

* FAO estimate.
2004–06: Production assumed to be unchanged from 2003 (FAO estimates).
Source: FAO.

Fishing

('000 metric tons, live weight)

	2003	2004	2005
Capture	1,141.2	1,187.3	1,333.9
Freshwater fishes	646.4	661.1	781.8
Hilsa shad	199.0	255.8	275.9
Marine fishes	263.8	233.8	231.9
Aquaculture	857.0	914.8	882.1
Roho labeo	164.8	166.3	164.2
Catla	137.0	140.6	138.5
Silver carp	180.0	156.7	159.7
Penaeus shrimps	56.5	58.0	63.1
Total catch	1,998.2	2,102.0	2,216.0

Source: FAO.

Mining

(million cubic metres, year ending 30 June)

	2003/04	2004/05	2005/06
Natural gas	13,000	14,000	15,000

Source: US Geological Survey.

Industry

SELECTED PRODUCTS
('000 metric tons, unless otherwise indicated; year ending 30 June)

	2002/03	2003/04	2004/05
Cement	n.a.	1,850.2	365.4
Refined sugar	177.4	119.1	108.7
Cigarettes (million)	20,384	22,499	23,860
Cotton yarn ('000 bales)*	388	470	573
Woven cotton fabrics ('000 metres)	18,030	26,296	32,585
Jute fabrics†	312.1	282.3	n.a.
Paper	30.3	28.9	24.3
Fertilizers	2,263.5	2,198.2	2,102.3
Electric energy (million kWh)	n.a.	n.a.	21,165

* 1 bale = 180 kg.
† Production of jute mills.
2005/06: Cement 2,195,632 metric tons; Electric energy 22,741m. kWh.
Source: mostly Bangladesh Bank.

Finance

CURRENCY AND EXCHANGE RATES

Monetary Units
100 poisha = 1 taka.

Sterling, Dollar and Euro Equivalents (31 December 2007)
£1 sterling = 137.385 taka;
US $1 = 68.576 taka;
€1 = 100.951 taka;
1,000 taka = £7.28 = $14.58 = €9.91.

Average Exchange Rate (taka per US $)
2005   64.328
2006   68.933
2007   68.875

BUDGET
(million taka, year ending 30 June)

Revenue*	2005/06†	2006/07†	2007/08‡
Taxation	361,750	392,470	458,380
Import duties	82,350	82,790	93,540
Income and profit taxes	69,600	89,240	10,838
Excise duties	1,630	1,850	2,000
Value-added tax	123,980	136,830	158,900
Other revenue	86,930	102,250	114,630
Total	448,680	494,720	573,010

Expenditure§	2005/06†	2006/07†	2007/08‡
General public services	47,620	50,400	84,590
Local government and rural development	11,300	14,340	13,070
Defence	44,110	52,820	52,830
Public order and safety	31,970	41,310	43,220
Education and technology	64,580	80,200	86,590
Health	20,650	26,820	28,640
Social security and welfare	19,250	24,200	30,850
Housing	5,660	5,450	6,270
Recreation, culture and religious affairs	4,290	5,050	5,540
Fuel and energy	230	270	290
Agriculture, forestry and fishing	27,720	35,970	46,760
Industrial and economic services	2,870	2,010	3,080
Transport and communications	25,000	23,720	28,930
Interest payments	75,450	91,540	107,850
Gross current expenditure	380,700	454,120	538,520

* Excluding grants, loans and food account transactions.
† Revised figures.
‡ Forecasts.
§ Non-development expenditure, excluding loans and advances, domestic and foreign debt, food account operations and structural adjustment.
Source: Ministry of Finance (Finance Division).

PUBLIC-SECTOR DEVELOPMENT EXPENDITURE
(departmental allocation, million taka, year ending 30 June)

	2006/07	2007/08*
Agriculture	17,180	22,230
Local government and rural development	59,080	61,530
Industrial and economic services	3,020	3,870
Fuel and energy	30,070	45,570
Transport and communications	35,800	41,060
Housing	360	1,050
Education and technology	28,760	37,090
Health	22,750	26,060
Social security and welfare	4,980	8,190
Public order and safety	2,620	4,620
Defence	1,160	1,870
Recreation, culture and religious affairs	2,520	3,790
Public services	10,530	12,710
Total development expenditure†	218,830	269,640

* Forecasts.
† Including transfers (million taka): 2,830 in 2006/07; 4,640 in 2007/08.
Source: Ministry of Finance (Economic Relations Division).

BANGLADESH

Statistical Survey

INTERNATIONAL RESERVES
(US $ million at 31 December)

	2004	2005	2006
Gold*	49.9	58.1	71.4
IMF special drawing rights	1.2	0.9	1.3
Reserve position in IMF	0.3	0.3	0.4
Foreign exchange	3,170.9	2,766.0	3,803.9
Total	3,222.3	2,825.3	3,877.0

* Valued at market-related prices.

Source: IMF, *International Financial Statistics*.

MONEY SUPPLY
(million taka at 31 December)

	2004	2005	2006
Currency outside banks	166,445	201,415	295,418
Demand deposits at deposit money banks*	151,439	173,896	200,237
Total money (incl. others)	317,884	375,311	495,655

* Comprises the scheduled banks plus the agricultural and industrial development banks.

Source: IMF, *International Financial Statistics*.

COST OF LIVING
(Consumer Price Index, year ending 30 June; base: 1995/96 = 100)

	2004/05	2005/06	2006/07
Food, beverages and tobacco	158.1	170.4	184.2
Rent, fuel and lighting	141.4	152.0	162.3
Household requisites	143.2	151.2	162.6
Clothing and footwear	142.2	148.4	156.8
Transport and communications	179.9	191.7	201.2
All items (incl. others)	153.2	164.2	176.0

Source: Bangladesh Bank.

NATIONAL ACCOUNTS
(million taka at current prices, year ending 30 June)

Expenditure on the Gross Domestic Product

	2004/05	2005/06	2006/07*
Government final consumption expenditure	205,303	230,324	259,481
Private final consumption expenditure	2,759,817	3,085,199	3,458,817
Gross capital formation	909,241	1,024,795	1,137,307
Statistical discrepancy	72,351	77,664	141,802
Total domestic expenditure	3,946,712	4,417,982	4,997,407
Exports of goods and services	614,681	788,788	1,027,002
Less Imports of goods and services	854,323	1,049,491	1,349,436
GDP in purchasers' values	3,707,070	4,157,279	4,674,973
GDP at constant 1995/96 prices	2,669,740	2,846,726	3,032,068

* Provisional figures.

Gross Domestic Product by Economic Activity

	2004/05	2005/06	2006/07*
Agriculture and forestry	561,674	622,233	678,296
Fishing	154,564	163,168	173,335
Mining and quarrying	40,411	46,431	53,005
Manufacturing	587,952	689,227	810,066
Electricity, gas and water	49,090	53,915	57,680
Construction	290,608	327,970	367,701
Wholesale and retail trade	502,782	569,842	656,826
Hotels and restaurants	25,117	28,532	32,749
Transport, storage and communications	382,890	432,056	484,287
Finance and insurance	59,343	66,839	73,873
Real estate, renting and business services	297,443	321,569	349,151
Public administration and defence	96,374	110,355	126,846
Education	87,882	99,345	114,251
Health and social work	81,043	90,220	100,175
Other community, social and personal services	338,763	382,832	435,372
Sub-total	3,555,936	4,004,534	4,513,613
Import duties	151,134	152,745	161,360
GDP in purchasers' values	3,707,070	4,157,279	4,674,973

* Provisional figures.

Source: Bangladesh Bank.

BALANCE OF PAYMENTS
(US $ million)

	2004	2005	2006
Exports of goods f.o.b.	8,150.7	9,302.5	11,553.7
Imports of goods f.o.b.	−11,157.1	−12,501.6	−14,443.4
Trade balance	−3,006.5	−3,199.1	−2,889.7
Exports of services	1,083.0	1,249.0	1,333.8
Imports of services	−1,931.4	−2,206.7	−2,340.5
Balance on goods and services	−3,854.9	−4,156.8	−3,896.3
Other income received	102.6	116.6	177.4
Other income paid	−473.9	−910.2	−1,018.1
Balance on goods, services and income	−4,226.2	−4,950.4	−4,737.0
Current transfers received	3,960.4	4,785.0	5,941.3
Current transfers paid	−12.9	−10.8	−8.2
Current balance	−278.7	−176.2	1,196.1
Capital account (net)	142.1	261.7	152.5
Direct investment abroad	−4.1	−1.9	—
Direct investment from abroad	448.9	813.3	697.2
Portfolio investment assets	—	−0.1	−2.6
Portfolio investment liabilities	4.3	19.5	30.8
Other investment assets	−495.1	−865.3	−1,352.8
Other investment liabilities	711.0	176.8	747.6
Net errors and omissions	−25.0	−643.9	−603.5
Overall balance	503.4	−416.1	865.3

Source: IMF, *International Financial Statistics*.

FOREIGN AID DISBURSEMENTS
(US $ million, year ending 30 June)

	2003/04	2004/05	2005/06
Bilateral donors	495	440	406
Canada	21	8	62
China, People's Republic	—	19	33
Denmark	20	5	14
France	7	—	—
Germany	26	24	15
Japan	79	45	31
Kuwait	7	5	9
Netherlands	41	5	13
Norway	6	4	11
Sweden	11	—	—
United Kingdom	94	85	157

BANGLADESH

—continued	2003/04	2004/05	2005/06
USA	12	8	4
Multilateral donors	538	1,049	1,162
Asian Development Bank	172	208	265
International Development Association	225	696	635
European Union	21	8	73
International Fund for Agricultural Development	15	9	14
UN Development Programme	36	—	111
UNICEF	30	26	18
Islamic Development Bank	17	70	25
Total aid disbursements	1,033	1,488	1,568

Source: IMF, *Bangladesh: Statistical Appendix* (July 2007).

External Trade

PRINCIPAL COMMODITIES
(US $ million, year ending 30 June)

Imports c.i.f.	2004/05	2005/06	2006/07
Food grains	574	418	581
Edible oil	440	473	583
Petroleum products	1,253	1,400	1,709
Chemicals	509	580	668
Plastics, rubber and articles thereof	477	523	643
Cotton	666	742	858
Yarn	393	501	582
Textiles	1,571	1,728	1,892
Iron and steel	680	980	985
Machinery	1,211	1,539	1,929
Total (incl. others)	13,147	14,746	16,013

Exports f.o.b.	2004/05	2005/06	2006/07
Raw jute	96	148	147
Jute goods (excl. carpets)	307	361	321
Leather and leather products	221	257	266
Frozen shrimp and fish	421	460	515
Ready-made garments	3,598	4,084	4,658
Knitwear and hosiery products	2,819	3,817	4,554
Total (incl. others)	8,655	10,526	12,178

Source: Bangladesh Bank.

PRINCIPAL TRADING PARTNERS
(US $ million)

Imports c.i.f.	2004	2005	2006
China, People's Republic	1,446	1,870	3,165
Hong Kong	518	567	739
India	1,745	1,951	2,145
Japan	614	571	660
Korea, Republic	419	446	515
Singapore	873	852	989
Thailand	324	316	484
United Kingdom	283	323	192
USA	268	327	361
Total (incl. others)	11,590	14,291	17,350

Exports f.o.b.	2004	2005	2006
Belgium	253	269	493
Canada	247	275	470
France	526	545	628
Germany	1,102	1,144	1,610
Italy	305	326	486
Netherlands	247	275	470
Spain	240	299	454
Sweden	148	131	168
United Kingdom	849	795	1,249
USA	1,698	2,003	3,179
Total (incl. others)	7,586	8,494	12,495

Source: Asian Development Bank, *Key Indicators of Developing Asian and Pacific Countries*.

Transport

RAILWAYS
(traffic, year ending 30 June)

	1995/96	1996/97	1997/98
Passenger-km (million)	3,333	3,754	3,855
Freight ton-km (million)	689	782	804

Source: UN, *Statistical Yearbook*.

2005: Passengers (million) 42.2; Passenger-km (million) 4,160; Freight (million metric tons) 3.2; Freight ton-km (million) 817 (Source: Bangladesh Railway).

ROAD TRAFFIC
(motor vehicles in use at 31 December)

	1997	1998	1999*
Passenger cars	54,784	57,068	60,846
Buses and coaches	29,310	30,361	32,371
Lorries and vans	40,084	42,425	45,234
Road tractors	2,769	2,813	2,999
Motorcycles and mopeds	125,259	145,259	147,205
Total	252,206	277,926	288,655

* Estimates.

Source: International Road Federation, *World Road Statistics*.

SHIPPING

Merchant Fleet
(registered at 31 December)

	2004	2005	2006
Number of vessels	328	331	328
Total displacement ('000 grt)	456.0	474.9	444.4

Source: Lloyd's Register-Fairplay, *World Fleet Statistics*.

International Sea-borne Freight Traffic
('000 metric tons, year ending 30 June)

	2001/02	2002/03	2003/04
Total goods loaded	900	1,000	8,000
Total goods unloaded	14,800	13,600	15,7000

Source: UN, *Monthly Bulletin of Statistics*.

CIVIL AVIATION
(traffic on scheduled services)

	2001	2002	2003
Kilometres flown (million)	26	26	27
Passengers carried ('000)	1,110	1,172	1,205
Passenger-km (million)	4,323	4,503	4,583
Total ton-km (million)	593	677	697

Source: UN, *Statistical Yearbook*.

Tourism

TOURIST ARRIVALS BY COUNTRY OF NATIONALITY

	2003	2004	2005
Canada	5,847	8,964	4,519
China, People's Republic	7,021	9,238	6,892
India	84,704	80,469	86,231
Japan	6,523	7,857	6,269
Korea, Republic	7,465	6,575	5,332
Malaysia	3,689	4,750	1,045
Nepal	3,904	3,144	3,378
Pakistan	9,238	11,997	5,671
United Kingdom	42,138	52,410	27,292
USA	24,458	27,895	13,422
Total (incl. others)	244,509	271,270	207,662

Tourism receipts (US $ million, incl. passenger transport): 59 in 2003; 76 in 2004; n.a. in 2005.

Source: World Tourism Organization.

Communications Media

	2004	2005	2006
Telephones ('000 main lines in use)	831.0	1,070.0	1,134.0
Mobile cellular telephones ('000 subscribers)	2,781.6	9,000.0	19,131.0
Personal computers ('000 in use)	1,650	1,650	n.a.
Internet users ('000)	300	300	450

Radio receivers ('000 in use): 6,150 in 1997.

Television receivers ('000 in use): 2,200 in 2001.

Facsimile machines (number in use, year ending 30 June 1998, provisional): 75,000.

Newspapers (provisional, 1998): *Daily:* 233 titles with average circulation of 6,658,000. *Non-daily incl. periodicals:* 509 titles with average circulation of 9,256,000.

Books published: 483 titles in 1998.

Sources: mainly UNESCO, *Statistical Yearbook*; UN, *Statistical Yearbook*; International Telecommunication Union.

Education

(2004/05)

	Institutions	Teachers	Students
Primary schools	80,397	344,789	16,225,658
Secondary schools	18,500	232,929	7,398,552
Universities (government)	26	6,852	115,929

Technical and vocational institutes (2004/05): 2,728 institutions, 18,185 teachers, 241,336 students.

Source: Ministry of Education.

Adult literacy rate (official estimates): 51.6% (males 57.2%; females 45.8%) in 2004.

Directory

The Constitution

The members who were returned from East Pakistan (now Bangladesh) for the Pakistan National Assembly and the Provincial Assembly in the December 1970 elections formed the Bangladesh Constituent Assembly. A new Constitution for the People's Republic of Bangladesh was approved by this Assembly on 4 November 1972 and came into effect on 16 December 1972. Following the military coup of 24 March 1982, the Constitution was suspended, and the country was placed under martial law. On 10 November 1986 martial law was repealed and the suspended Constitution was revived. The main provisions of the Constitution, including amendments, are listed below.

SUMMARY

Fundamental Principles of State Policy

The Constitution was initially based on the fundamental principles of nationalism, socialism, democracy and secularism, but in 1977 an amendment replaced secularism with Islam. The amendment states that the country shall be guided by 'the principles of absolute trust and faith in the Almighty Allah, nationalism, democracy and socialism'. A further amendment in 1988 established Islam as the state religion. The Constitution aims to establish a society free from exploitation in which the rule of law, fundamental human rights and freedoms, justice and equality are to be secured for all citizens. A socialist economic system is to be established to ensure the attainment of a just and egalitarian society through state and co-operative ownership as well as private ownership within limits prescribed by law. A universal, free and compulsory system of education shall be established. In foreign policy the State shall endeavour to consolidate, preserve, and strengthen fraternal relations among Muslim countries based on Islamic solidarity.

Fundamental Rights

All citizens are equal before the law and have a right to its protection. Arbitrary arrest or detention, discrimination based on race, age, sex, birth, caste or religion, and forced labour are prohibited. Subject to law, public order and morality, every citizen has freedom of movement, of assembly and of association. Freedom of conscience, of speech, of the press and of religious worship are guaranteed.

GOVERNMENT

The President

The President is the constitutional Head of State and is elected by Parliament (Jatiya Sangsad) for a term of five years. He is eligible for re-election. The supreme control of the armed forces is vested in the President. He appoints the Prime Minister and other Ministers as well as the Chief Justice and other judges.

The Executive

Executive authority shall rest in the Prime Minister and shall be exercised by him either directly or through officers subordinate to him in accordance with the Constitution.

There shall be a Council of Ministers to aid and advise the Prime Minister.

The Legislature

Parliament (Jatiya Sangsad) is a unicameral legislature. It comprises 345 members, including 45 women members elected by the other members on the basis of proportional representation. Members of Parliament, other than the 45 women members, are directly elected on the basis of universal adult franchise from single territorial constituencies. Persons aged 18 years and over are entitled to vote. The parliamentary term lasts for five years. War can be declared only with the assent of Parliament. In the case of actual or imminent invasion, the President may take whatever action he may consider appropriate.

THE JUDICIARY

The Judiciary comprises a Supreme Court with High Court and an Appellate Division. The Supreme Court consists of a Chief Justice and such other judges as may be appointed by the President. The High Court division has such original appellate and other jurisdiction and powers as are conferred on it by the Constitution and by other law. The Appellate Division has jurisdiction to determine appeals from decisions of the High Court division. Subordinate courts, in addition to the Supreme Court, have been established by law.

BANGLADESH   *Directory*

ELECTIONS

An Election Commission supervises elections, delimits constituencies and prepares electoral rolls. It consists of a Chief Election Commissioner and other Commissioners as may be appointed by the President. The Election Commission is independent in the exercise of its functions. Subject to the Constitution, Parliament may make provision as to elections where necessary.

The Government

HEAD OF STATE

President: Prof. IAJUDDIN AHMED (took office 6 September 2002).

LIST OF ADVISERS
(April 2008)

Prime Minister Khaleda Zia and the Council of Ministers stepped down in October 2006, having completed a five-year term in office; national elections were scheduled for January 2007. In early November 2006 a team of advisers was sworn in to act as an interim government, to manage key portfolios and to supervise the election process. President Iajuddin Ahmed assumed the role of Chief Adviser. In January 2007, following widespread protests and demands for electoral reform, President Ahmed resigned as Chief Adviser, postponed the elections and declared a state of emergency. Dr Fakhruddin Ahmed was subsequently appointed as his successor in the role of Chief Adviser.

Chief Adviser in charge of the Cabinet Division, of Establishment, of Home Affairs and of the Election Commission Secretariat: Dr FAKHRUDDIN AHMED.

Adviser in charge of Law, Justice and Parliament Affairs, and of Religious Affairs: A. F. HASSAN ARIFF.

Adviser in charge of Finance and of Planning: Dr A. B. MIRZA AZIZUL ISLAM.

Adviser in charge of Shipping and of Liberation War Affairs: Maj.-Gen. (retd) M. A. MATIN.

Adviser in charge of Health and Family Welfare, and of Food and Disaster Management: Dr A. M. M. SHAWKAT ALI.

Adviser in charge of Primary and Mass Education, and of Women and Children's Affairs: RASHEDA K. CHOWDHURY.

Adviser in charge of Commerce and of Education: Dr HOSSAIN ZILLUR RAHMAN.

Adviser in charge of Communications and of Housing and Public Works: Maj.-Gen. (retd) GHULAM QUADER.

Adviser in charge of Local Government, Rural Development and Co-operatives, of Textiles and Jute, and of Labour and Employment: MUHAMMAD ANWARUL IQBAL.

Adviser in charge of Foreign Affairs, and of Expatriates' Welfare and Overseas Employment: Dr IFTEKHAR AHMED CHOWDHURY.

Adviser in charge of Agriculture and of Water Resources: Dr CHOWDHURY SAJJADUL KARIM.

MINISTRIES

Chief Adviser's Office: Old Sangsad Bhaban, Tejgaon, Dhaka 1215; tel. (2) 8151159; fax (2) 8113244; e-mail info@pmo.gov.bd; internet www.cao.gov.bd.

Ministry of Agriculture: Bangladesh Secretariat, Bhaban 4, 2nd 9-Storey Bldg, Dhaka; tel. (2) 832137; internet www.moa.gov.bd.

Ministry of Chittagong Hill Tracts Affairs: Dhaka; tel. (2) 7161774; e-mail nazma@mochta.gov.bd; internet www.mochta.gov.bd.

Ministry of Civil Aviation and Tourism: Bangladesh Secretariat, Bhaban 6, 19th Floor, Dhaka 1000; tel. (2) 866485.

Ministry of Commerce: Bangladesh Secretariat, Bhaban 3, Dhaka 1000; tel. (2) 716009; e-mail mincom@intechworld.net; internet www.mincom.gov.bd.

Ministry of Communications: Bangladesh Secretariat, Bhaban 7, 1st 9-Storey Bldg, 8th Floor, Dhaka 1000; tel. (2) 868752; fax (2) 866636; internet www.moc.gov.bd.

Ministry of Cultural Affairs: Bangladesh Secretariat, Dhaka 1000; tel. (2) 9570667; fax (2) 7169008; e-mail sas-moca@mailcity.com; internet www.moca.gov.bd.

Ministry of Defence: Gonobhaban Complex, Sher-i-Bangla Nagar, Dhaka; tel. (2) 8116955; e-mail modgob@bttb.net.bd; internet www.mod.gov.bd.

Ministry of Education: Bangladesh Secretariat, Bhaban 6, 17th–18th Floors, Dhaka 1000; tel. (2) 7168711; fax (2) 7167577; e-mail info@moedu.gov.bd; internet www.moedu.gov.bd.

Ministry of Environment and Forests: Bangladesh Secretariat, Bhaban 6, 13th Floor, Chamber 1307, Dhaka; tel. (2) 7167240; fax (2) 7169210; e-mail jsdev@moef.gov.bd; internet www.moef.gov.bd.

Ministry of Establishment: Dhaka; e-mail estabsec@moestab.gov.bd; internet www.moestab.gov.bd.

Ministry of Finance: Bangladesh Secretariat, Bhaban 7, 1st 9-Storey Bldg, 3rd Floor, Dhaka 1000; tel. (2) 8690202; fax (2) 865581; internet www.mof.gov.bd.

Ministry of Fisheries and Livestock: Bangladesh Secretariat, Bhaban 6, 5th and 14th Floors, Dhaka 1000; tel. (2) 7164700; fax (2) 7161117; e-mail jslmofl@accesstel.net; internet www.mofl.gov.bd.

Ministry of Food and Disaster Management: Bangladesh Secretariat, Dhaka; tel. (2) 7165405; e-mail info@mofdm.gov.bd; internet www.mofdm.gov.bd.

Ministry of Foreign Affairs: Segunbagicha, Dhaka 1000; tel. (2) 9562862; fax (2) 9555283; e-mail info@mofabd.org; internet www.mofa.gov.bd.

Ministry of Health and Family Welfare: Bangladesh Secretariat, Main Bldg, 3rd Floor, Dhaka; tel. (2) 832079; internet www.mohfw.gov.bd.

Ministry of Home Affairs: Bangladesh Secretariat, School Bldg, 2nd and 3rd Floors, Dhaka; tel. (2) 7169076; fax (2) 7164788; e-mail info@mha.gov.bd; internet www.mha.gov.bd.

Ministry of Housing and Public Works: Bangladesh Secretariat, Bhaban 5, Dhaka 1000; tel. (2) 7163639; fax (2) 7167125; e-mail jsamohpw@bangla.net; internet www.mohpw.gov.bd.

Ministry of Industries: Shilpa Bhaban, 91 Motijheel C/A, Dhaka 1000; tel. (2) 9567024; fax (2) 860588; e-mail indsecy@bttb.net.bd; internet www.moind.gov.bd.

Ministry of Information: Bangladesh Secretariat, 2nd 9-Storey Bldg, 8th Floor, Dhaka; tel. (2) 7168555; fax (2) 7167236; e-mail moisecretary@yahoo.com; internet www.moi.gov.bd.

Ministry of Labour and Employment: Bangladesh Secretariat, Bldg 7, 5th Floor, Dhaka; tel. (2) 7169215; fax (2) 7168660; internet www.mole.gov.bd.

Ministry of Land: Bangladesh Secretariat, Bhaban 4, 2nd 9-Storey Bldg, 3rd Floor, Dhaka; tel. (2) 7164131.

Ministry of Local Government, Rural Development and Co-operatives: LGED Bhaban, 4th Floor, Agargaon, Dhaka 1207; tel. (2) 8119138; fax (2) 8113144; e-mail zmsajjad@lged.org.

Ministry of Planning: Block No. 7, Sher-e-Bangla Nagar, Dhaka; tel. (2) 815142; fax (2) 822210.

Ministry of Post and Telecommunications: Bangladesh Secretariat, Bhaban 7, 6th Floor, Dhaka 1000; tel. (2) 864800; fax (2) 865775.

Ministry of Power, Energy and Mineral Resources: Bangladesh Secretariat, Bhaban 6, 1st Floor, Dhaka 1000; tel. (2) 865918; fax (2) 861110; internet www.powerdivision.gov.bd.

Ministry of Religious Affairs: Bangladesh Secretariat, Dhaka; tel. (2) 7165800; fax (2) 7165040.

Ministry of Science and Information and Communication Technology: Bangladesh Secretariat, Bhaban 6, 9th Floor, Ramna, Dhaka 1000; tel. (2) 7163639; fax (2) 7169606; e-mail most@bangla.net; internet www.mosict.gov.bd.

Ministry of Shipping: Bangladesh Secretariat, Bhaban 6, 8th Floor, Dhaka 1000; tel. (2) 7165774; internet www.mos.gov.bd.

Ministry of Social Welfare: Bangladesh Secretariat, Bhaban 6, New Bldg, Dhaka 1000; tel. (2) 7160452; fax (2) 7168969; e-mail secsw@bttb.net.bd; internet www.msw.gov.bd.

Ministry of Textiles and Jute: Bangladesh Secretariat, Bhaban 6, 7th Floor, Dhaka 1000; tel. (2) 8612250; fax (2) 8618766; e-mail jutebd@bangla.net; internet www.motj.gov.bd.

Ministry of Water Resources: Bangladesh Secretariat, Dhaka 1000; tel. (2) 7168688; internet www.mowr.gov.bd.

Ministry of Women and Children's Affairs: Bangladesh Secretariat, Bhaban 6, 3rd Floor, Osman Goni Rd, Dhaka 1000; tel. (2) 7163943; fax (2) 7162892; internet www.mwca.gov.bd.

Ministry of Youth and Sports: 62/3, Purana Paltan, Dhaka 1000; tel. (2) 7167053; fax (2) 7162344; e-mail secmys@bttb.net.bd; internet www.moysports.gov.bd.

President and Legislature

PRESIDENT

On 5 September 2002 the Bangladesh Nationalist Party's presidential candidate, Prof. IAJUDDIN AHMED, was declared elected unopposed by the Election Commission as Bangladesh's new Head of State.

BANGLADESH

JATIYA SANGSAD
(Parliament)

Speaker: JAMIRUDDIN SIRCAR.

General Election, 1 and 9 October 2001

	Seats*
Bangladesh Jatiyatabadi Dal (Bangladesh Nationalist Party—BNP)	199†
Awami League (AL)	62
Jamaat-e-Islami Bangladesh	17
Jatiya Dal	14‡
Jatiya Dal (Manju)	1
Bangladesh Krishak Sramik Party	1
Independents	6
Total	**300**

* In addition to the 300 directly elected members, a further 45 seats are reserved for women members.
† Includes six seats won by the Jatiya Dal (Naziur-Firoz) and the Islami Jatiya Oikya Jote.
‡ Includes several seats won by the Islami Jatiya Oikya Front.

Election Commission

Bangladesh Election Commission: Block 5/6, Election Commission Secretariat, Sher-e-Bangla Nagar, Dhaka 1207; tel. (2) 8113601; fax (2) 8117834; e-mail ecs@bol-online.com; internet www.ecs.gov.bd; f. 1972; independent; commrs appointed by the President; Chief Election Commr Dr A. T. M. SHAMSUL HUDA.

Political Organizations

Bangladesh Awami League (AL): 23 Bangabandhu Ave, Dhaka; e-mail info@albd.org; internet www.albd.org; f. 1949; supports parliamentary democracy; advocates socialist economy, but with a private sector, and a secular state; pro-Indian; 28-member central executive committee, 15-member central advisory committee and a 13-member presidium; Pres. Sheikh HASINA WAJED; Gen.Sec. SYED ASHRAFUL ISLAM (acting); c. 1,025,000 mems.

Bangladesh Jatiya League: Dhaka; f. 1970 as Pakistan National League, renamed in 1972; supports parliamentary democracy; Leader ATAUR RAHMAN KHAN; c. 50,000 mems.

Bangladesh Jatiyatabadi Dal (Bangladesh Nationalist Party—BNP): Banani Office, House 23, Rd 13, Dhaka; tel. (2) 8819525; fax (2) 8813063; e-mail bnpbd@e-fsbd.net; internet www.bnpbd.com; f. 1978 by merger of groups supporting Ziaur Rahman, including Jatiyatabadi Gonotantrik Dal (Jagodal—Nationalist Democratic Party); right of centre; favours multi-party democracy and parliamentary system of govt; Chair. Begum KHALEDA ZIA.

Bangladesh Khelafat Andolon (Bangladesh Caliphate Movement): 314/2 Lalbagh Kellar Morr, Dhaka 1211; tel. (2) 8612465; fax (2) 9881436; e-mail khelafat@cimabd.com; Supreme Leader SHAH AHMADULLAH ASHRAF IBN HAFEZZEE; Sec.-Gen. Maulana MUHAMMAD ZAFRULLAH KHAN.

Bangladesh Krishak Sramik Party (Peasants' and Workers' Party): Sonargaon Bhavan, 99 South Kamalapur, Dhaka 1217; tel. (2) 834512; f. 1914; renamed 1953; supports parliamentary democracy, non-aligned foreign policy, welfare state, guarantee of fundamental rights for all religions and races, free market economy and non-proliferation of nuclear weapons; 15-mem. exec. council; Pres. A. S. M. SULAIMAN; Sec.-Gen. RASHEED KHAN MEMON; c. 125,000 mems.

Bangladesh Muslim League: Dhaka; Pres. GOWHAR ALI KHAN; Sec.-Gen. Alhaj MOHAMMAD ZAMIR ALI.

Communist Party of Bangladesh: 'Mukti Bhaban', 21/1, Purana Paltan, Dhaka 1000; tel. (2) 9558612; fax (2) 9552333; e-mail info@cpbdhaka.com; internet www.cpbdhaka.org; f. 1968 following split from Communist Party of Pakistan; Pres. MANZURUL AHASAN KHAN; Gen. Sec. MUJAHIDUL ISLAM SELIM; c. 22,000 mems.

Freedom Party: f. 1987; Islamic; Co-Chairs Lt-Col (retd) SAID FARUQ RAHMAN, Lt-Col (retd) KHANDAKAR ABDUR RASHID.

Gonoazadi League: 30 Banagran Lane, Dhaka.

Gonotantrik Jatiya Party: Leader SHAFIUL ALAM PRADHAN.

Islami Jatiya Oikya Front (Islamic National Unity Front): Dhaka; coalition of parties, including Jatiya Dal.

Islami Oikya Jote (Islamic Unity Front): Dhaka; mem. of the BNP-led alliance; Leader Mufti SHAHIDUL ISLAM; Sec.-Gen. Mufti FAZLUL HAQ AMINI.

Islamic Solidarity Movement: 84 East Tejturi Bazar, Tejgaon, Dhaka 1215; tel. (2) 8121017; fmrly known as Islamic Democratic League; renamed as above in 1984; Pres. ANOWEAR ULLAH; Sec.-Gen. Maulana MUHAMMAD AZIZ UL-HOQ MURAD.

Jamaat-e-Islami Bangladesh: 505 Elephant Rd, Bara Maghbazar, Dhaka 1217; tel. (2) 9331581; fax (2) 9556626; e-mail info@jamaat-e-islami.org; internet www.jamaat-e-islami.org; f. 1941; Islamist party striving to establish an Islamic state through the democratic process; mem. of the BNP-led alliance; Chair. MOTIUR RAHMAN NIZAMI; Sec.-Gen. ALI AHSAN MOHAMMAD MUJAHID.

Jatiya Dal (National Party): c/o Jatiya Sangsad, Dhaka; e-mail ershad@dhaka.agni.com; internet www.jatiyaparty.org; f. 1983 as Jana Dal; reorg. 1986, when the National Front (f. 1985), a five-party alliance of the Jana Dal, the United People's Party, the Gonotantrik Dal, the Bangladesh Muslim League and a breakaway section of the Bangladesh Nationalist Party, formally converted itself into a single pro-Ershad grouping; advocates nationalism, democracy, Islamic ideals and progress; Chair. Lt-Gen. HOSSAIN MOHAMMAD ERSHAD; Sec.-Gen. A. B. M. RUHUL AMIN HAWLADER; in April 1999 a group of dissidents, led by MIZANUR RAHMAN CHOWDHURY and ANWAR HUSSAIN MANJU, formed a rival faction; another rival faction, led by Kazi FIROZ RASHID, was also formed.

Jatiya Samajtantrik Dal (Inu): f. 2002; breakaway faction of JSD; Pres. HASANUL HAQUE INU; Gen. Sec. SYED JAFAR SAZZAD.

Jatiya Samajtantrik Dal (JSD—S) (National Socialist Party): 23 DIT Ave, Malibagh Choudhury Para, Dhaka; f. 1972; left-wing; Leader SHAJAHAN SIRAJ; c. 5,000 mems.

Jatiya Samajtantrik Dal (Rab): breakaway faction of JSD; Pres. A. S. M. ABDUR RAB.

Jatiyo Janata Party: Janata Bhaban, 47A Toyenbee Circular Rd, Dhaka 1000; tel. (2) 9667923; f. 1976; social democratic; Chair. NURUL ISLAM KHAN; Gen. Sec. MUJIBUR RAHMAN HERO; c. 35,000 mems.

Liberal Democratic Party: Dhaka; f. 2006; comprises several former members of BNP; reported to have split into two factions June 2007; Exec. Chair. Col (retd) OLI AHMAD; Pres. A. Q. M. BADRUDDOZA CHOWDHURY.

National Awami Party—Bhashani–Mustaq (NAP): Dhaka; f. 1957; Maoist; Leader MUSTAQ AHMED; Gen. Sec. ABDUS SUBHANI.

National Awami Party—Muzaffar (NAP—M): 21 Dhanmandi Hawkers' Market, 1st Floor, Dhaka; f. 1957; reorg. 1967; Pres. MUZAFFAR AHMED; Sec.-Gen. PANKAJ BHATTACHARYA; c. 500,000 mems.

Parbattya Chattagram Jana Sanghati Samity (Chittagong Hill Tracts United Peoples' Party): Central Office, Kalyanpur, Rangamati 4500, Chittagong Hill Tracts; tel. (351) 61248; e-mail pcjss.org@gmail.com; internet www.pcjss.org; f. 1972; political wing of the Shanti Bahini; represents interests of Buddhist tribals in Chittagong Hill Tracts; Leader JATINDRA BODDHIPRIYA ('SHANTU') LARMA.

Samyabadi Dal: Dhaka; Marxist-Leninist; Leader DILIP BARUA.

Zaker Party: f. 1989; supports sovereignty and the introduction of an Islamic state system; Leader SYED HASMATULLAH; Mem. of the Presidium MUSTAFA AMIR FAISAL.

Diplomatic Representation

EMBASSIES AND HIGH COMMISSIONS IN BANGLADESH

Afghanistan: House CWN(C) 2A, 24 Gulshan Ave, Gulshan Model Town, Dhaka 1212; tel. (2) 9895994; fax (2) 9884767; e-mail afghanembassydhaka@yahoo.com; Ambassador AHMAD KARIM NAWABI.

Australia: 184 Gulshan Ave, Gulshan 2, Dhaka 1212; tel. (2) 8813101; fax (2) 8811125; e-mail ahc.dhaka@dfat.gov.au; internet www.bangladesh.embassy.gov.au; High Commissioner DOUGLAS FOSKETT.

Bhutan: House 12, Rd 107, Gulshan 2, Dhaka 1212; tel. (2) 8826863; fax (2) 8823939; e-mail bhtemb@bdmail.net; Ambassador Dasho TSHERING DORJI.

Brunei: House 26, Rd 6, Baridhara, Dhaka; tel. (2) 8819552; fax (2) 8819551; e-mail bruhcomm@citechco.net; High Commissioner Dato' Haji ABDUL RAHMAN BIN ABDUL HAMID.

Canada: House 16A, Rd 48, Gulshan 2, Dhaka 1212; tel. (2) 9887091; fax (2) 8823043; e-mail dhaka@international.gc.ca; internet www.international.gc.ca/bangladesh; High Commissioner BARBARA RICHARDSON.

China, People's Republic: Plots 2 and 4, Rd 3, Block 1, Baridhara, Dhaka; tel. (2) 8824862; fax (2) 8823004; e-mail chinaemb@bdmail.net; internet bd.china-embassy.org; Ambassador ZHENG QINGDIAN.

Denmark: House (NW) H 1, Rd 51, Gulshan Model Town, POB 2056, Dhaka 1212; tel. (2) 8811799; fax (2) 8813638; e-mail dacamb@um.dk; internet www.ambdhaka.um.dk; Ambassador EINAR H. JENSEN.

Egypt: House NE (N) 9, Rd 90, Gulshan Model Town, Dhaka 1212; tel. (2) 8858737; fax (2) 8858747; e-mail egypt_embassy_dhaka@themail.com; Ambassador FAYEZ MUSTAFA NOSEIR.

France: House 18, Rd 108, Gulshan Model Town, POB 22, Dhaka 1212; tel. (2) 8813811; fax (2) 8813812; internet www.ambafrance-bd.org; Ambassador CHARLEY CAUSERET.

Germany: 178 Gulshan Ave, Gulshan 2, Dhaka 1212; tel. (2) 8853521; fax (2) 8853528; e-mail aadhaka@optimaxbd.net; internet www.dhaka.diplo.de; Ambassador FRANK MEYKE.

Holy See: United Nations Rd 2, Diplomatic Enclave, Baridhara Model Town, POB 6003, Dhaka 1212; tel. (2) 8822018; fax (2) 8823574; e-mail nuntius@dhaka.net; Apostolic Nuncio JOSEPH MARINO.

India: House 2, Rd 142, Gulshan-I, Dhaka; tel. (2) 9889339; fax (2) 8817487; e-mail hc@hcidhaka.org; internet www.hcidhaka.org; High Commissioner PINAK RANJAN CHAKRAVARTY.

Indonesia: Plot No. 14, Rd 53, Gulshan 2, Dhaka 1212; tel. (2) 9881640; fax (2) 8810993; e-mail indhaka@bangla.net; internet www.jakarta-dhaka.com; Ambassador WARMAS HASAN SAPUTRA.

Iran: House No. 7, Rd 6, Baridhara Model Town, Dhaka; tel. (2) 8825896; fax (2) 8828780; e-mail dacembiran@yahoo.com; Ambassador HASSAN FARAZANDEH.

Italy: Plots 2 and 3, Rd 74/79, Gulshan Model Town, POB 6062, Dhaka 1212; tel. (2) 8822781; fax (2) 8822578; e-mail ambdhaka@dominox.com; internet dominox.com/italydhaka; Ambassador ITALA MARIA MARTA OCCHI.

Japan: 5 and 7, Dutabash Rd, Baridhara, Dhaka 1212; tel. (2) 8810087; fax (2) 8826737; e-mail information@embjp.accesstel.net; internet www.bd.emb-japan.go.jp; Ambassador MASAYUKI INOUE.

Korea, Democratic People's Republic: House 6, Rd 7, Baridhara Model Town, Dhaka; tel. (2) 601250; Ambassador MUN SONG MO.

Korea, Republic: 4 Madani Ave, Diplomatic Enclave, Baridhara, Dhaka; tel. (2) 8812088; fax (2) 8823871; e-mail embdhaka@embdhaka.org; internet bgd.mofat.go.kr; Ambassador SUK BUM PARK.

Kuwait: Plot 39, Rd 23, Block J, Banani, Dhaka 13; tel. (2) 8822700; fax (2) 8823753; e-mail dhaka@mofa.gov.kw; Ambassador ABDULLATIF AL-MAWASH.

Libya: NE(D), 3A Gulshan Ave (N), Gulshan Model Town, Dhaka 1212; tel. (2) 600141; Chargé d'affaires LUTFI ALAMIN M. MUGHRABI.

Malaysia: House 19, Rd 6, Baridhara, Dhaka 1212; tel. (2) 8827759; fax (2) 8823115; e-mail mwdhaka@citech-bd.net; internet www.kln.gov.my/perwakilan/dhaka; High Commissioner ABDUL MALEK ABDUL AZIZ.

Morocco: House 44, United Nations Rd, POB 6112, Baridhara, Dhaka; tel. (2) 8823176; fax (2) 8810028; e-mail sifmadac@citechco.net; internet www.morocco-dhaka.com; Ambassador MOHAMED HOURORO.

Myanmar: NE(L) 3, Rd 84, Gulshan 2, Dhaka 1212; tel. (2) 600988; fax (2) 8823740; e-mail mofa.aung@mptmail.net.mm; Ambassador U NYAN LYNN.

Nepal: United Nations Rd, Rd 2, Diplomatic Enclave, Baridhara, Dhaka; tel. (2) 601790; fax (2) 8826401; e-mail rnedhaka@bdmail.net; Ambassador PRADEEP KHATIWADA.

Netherlands: House 49, Rd 90, Gulshan Model Town, POB 166, Dhaka 1212; tel. (2) 8822715; fax (2) 8823326; e-mail dha@minbuza.nl; internet www.netherlandsembassydhaka.org; Ambassador BERENDINA MARIA (BEA) TEN TUSSCHER.

Nigeria: House 9, Rd 1, Baridhara, Dhaka; tel. (2) 8817944; fax (2) 8817989; High Commissioner (vacant).

Norway: House 9, Rd 111, Gulshan, Dhaka 1212; tel. (2) 8816276; fax (2) 8823661; e-mail emb.dhaka@mfa.no; internet www.norway.org.bd/info/embassy.htm; Ambassador INGEBJØRG STØFRING.

Pakistan: House NE(C) 2, Rd 71, Gulshan Model Town, Dhaka 1212; tel. (2) 8825388; fax (2) 8850673; e-mail parepdka@citech-bd.com; High Commissioner ALAMGIR BABUR.

Philippines: House 6, Rd 101, Gulshan 2, Dhaka 1212; tel. (2) 9881590; fax (2) 8823686; e-mail philemb1@citechco.net; Ambassador ZENAIDA TACORDA-RABAGO.

Qatar: House 1, Rd 79/81, Gulshan 2, Dhaka 1212; tel. (2) 9887429; fax (2) 9896071; e-mail dhaka@mofa.gov.qa; Ambassador IBRAHIM MOHAMMAD A. AL-ABDULLA.

Russia: NE(J) 9, Rd 79, Gulshan 2, Dhaka 1212; tel. (2) 8828147; fax (2) 8823735; e-mail info@rusdhaka.org; internet www.bangladesh.mid.ru; Ambassador GENNADII P. TROTSENKO.

Saudi Arabia: House 12, Rd 92, Gulshan (North), Dhaka 1212; tel. (2) 889124; fax (2) 883616; Ambassador ABDULLAH MOHAMMAD AL-OBAID AL-NAMLA.

Sri Lanka: House 4A, Rd 113, Gulshan Model Town, Dhaka 1212; tel. (2) 9896353; fax (2) 8823971; High Commissioner V. KRISHNAMOORTHY.

Sweden: House 1, Rd 51, Gulshan 2, Dhaka 1212; tel. (2) 8833144; fax (2) 8823948; e-mail berth.abrahamsson@foreign.ministry.se; internet www.swedenabroad.com/dhaka; Ambassador BRITT FALKMAN HAGSTRÖM.

Switzerland: House 31B, Rd 18, Banani, Dhaka 1213; tel. (2) 8812874; fax (2) 8823872; Ambassador Dr DORA RAPOLD.

Thailand: 18 & 20, Madani Ave, Baridhara, Dhaka 1212; tel. (2) 8812795; fax (2) 8854280; e-mail thaidac@mfa.go.th; internet www.thaidac.com; Ambassador CHALERMPOL THANCHITT.

Turkey: House 14A, Rd 62, Gulshan 2, Dhaka 1212; tel. (2) 8823536; fax (2) 8823873; e-mail dakkabe@citech-bd.com; Ambassador FERIT ERGIN.

United Arab Emirates: POB 6014, Dhaka 1212; tel. (2) 9882244; fax (2) 8823225; e-mail info@uaeembassydhaka.com; Ambassador KHALFAN BATTAL AL MANSOURI.

United Kingdom: United Nations Rd, Baridhara, POB 6079, Dhaka 1212; tel. (2) 8822705; fax (2) 8826181; e-mail Dhaka.Chancery@fco.gov.uk; internet www.ukinbangladesh.org; High Commissioner ANWAR CHOWDHURY.

USA: Madani Ave, Baridhara, POB 323, Dhaka 1212; tel. (2) 8824700; fax (2) 8823744; e-mail ustc@bangla.net; internet dhaka.usembassy.gov; Ambassador JAMES F. MORIARTY.

Viet Nam: House 8, Rd 51, Gulshan 2, Dhaka 1212; tel. and fax (2) 8854051; e-mail vietnam@citech-bd.com; internet www.vietnamembassy-bangladesh.org; Ambassador NGUYEN VAN THAT.

Judicial System

A judiciary, comprising a Supreme Court with High Court and Appellate Divisions, is in operation (see under Constitution). On 1 November 2007 the Government announced the formal separation of the judiciary from the executive.

Supreme Court

Dhaka 2; tel. (2) 433585.

Chief Justice: MOHAMMAD RUHUL AMIN.

Attorney-General: FIDA M. KAMAL.

Deputy Attorney-General: A. M. FAROOQ.

Religion

The results of the 2001 census classified 89.7% of the population as Muslims (the majority of whom were of the Sunni sect), 9.2% as caste Hindus and scheduled castes, and the remainder as Buddhists, Christians, animists and others.

Freedom of religious worship is guaranteed under the Constitution but, under the 1977 amendment to the Constitution, Islam was declared to be one of the nation's guiding principles and, under the 1988 amendment, Islam was established as the state religion.

ISLAM

Islamic Foundation Bangladesh: Agargaon, Sher-e-Bangla Nagar, Dhaka 1207; tel. (2) 9115010; fax (2) 9144235; e-mail islamicfoundationbd@yahoo.com; internet www.islamicfoundation.org.bd; f. 1975; under supervision of Ministry of Religious Affairs; Dir-Gen. SHAMSUL ALAM.

BUDDHISM

World Fellowship of Buddhists Regional Centre: Dharmarajik Buddhist Monastery, Atish Dipanker Sarak, Basabo, Dhaka 1214; tel. (2) 7205665; fax (2) 7202503; e-mail mahathero@dhammarajika.com; internet www.dhammarajika.com; f. 1962; Pres. Ven. SUDDHANANDA MAHATHERO; Sec.-Gen. P. K. BARUYA.

CHRISTIANITY

Jatiyo Church Parishad (National Council of Churches): POB 220, Dhaka 1000; tel. (2) 9332869; fax (2) 8312996; e-mail nccb@bangla.net; f. 1949 as East Pakistan Christian Council; four mem. churches; Pres. Dr SAJAL DEWAN; Gen. Sec. SUBODH ADHIKARY.

Church of Bangladesh—United Church

After Bangladesh achieved independence, the Diocese of Dacca (Dhaka) of the Church of Pakistan (f. 1970 by the union of Anglicans, Methodists, Presbyterians and Lutherans) became the autonomous Church of Bangladesh. In 2001 the Church had an estimated 14,000 members. In 1990 a second diocese, the Diocese of Kushtia, was established.

BANGLADESH

Bishop of Dhaka: Rt Rev. MICHAEL S. BAROI, St Thomas's Church, 54 Johnson Rd, Dhaka 1100; tel. (2) 7116546; fax (2) 7118218; e-mail cbdacdio@bangla.net.

Bishop of Kushtia: Rt Rev. PAUL SHISHIR SARKAR, Church of Bangladesh, 94 N. S. Rd, Thanapara, Kushtia; tel. (71) 54618; fax (71) 54618.

The Roman Catholic Church

For ecclesiastical purposes, Bangladesh comprises one archdiocese and five dioceses. At 31 December 2005 there were an estimated 304,935 adherents in the country.

Catholic Bishops' Conference: Archbishop's House, 1 Kakrail Rd, Ramna, POB 3, Dhaka 1000; tel. (2) 9358247; fax (2) 9127339; e-mail archbp@bangla.net; f. 1978; Pres. Most Rev. PAULINUS COSTA (Archbishop of Dhaka).

Secretariat: CBCB Centre, 24C Asad Ave, Mohammadpur, Dhaka 1207; tel. and fax (2) 9127339; e-mail cbcbsg@bdonline.com; Sec.-Gen. Rt Rev. THEOTONIUS GOMES (Titular Bishop of Zucchabar).

Archbishop of Dhaka: Most Rev. PAULINUS COSTA, Archbishop's House, 1 Kakrail Rd, Ramna, POB 3, Dhaka 1000; tel. (2) 8314384; e-mail archbp@bangla.net.

Other Christian Churches

Bangladesh Baptist Sangha: 33 Senpara Parbatta, Mirpur 10, Dhaka 1216; tel. (2) 8012967; fax (2) 9005842; e-mail bbsangha@bdmail.net; f. 1922; 35,150 mems (2004); Pres. Dr S. M. CHOWDHURY; Gen. Sec. Rev. ROBERT SARKAR.

In early 2002 there were about 51 denominational churches active in the country, including the Bogra Christian Church, the Evangelical Christian Church, the Garo Baptist Union, the Reformed Church of Bangladesh and the Sylhet Presbyterian Synod. The Baptist Sangha was the largest Protestant Church.

The Press

PRINCIPAL DAILIES

Bengali

Banglar Bani: 81 Motijheel C/A, Dhaka 1000; tel. (2) 9551173; e-mail bani@bangla.net; f. 1972; Editor Sheikh FAZLUL KARIM SALIM; circ. 20,000.

Daily Azadi: 9 C.D.A. C/A, Momin Rd, Chittagong; tel. (31) 612380; e-mail azadi@globalctg.net; f. 1960; Editor M. A. MALEK; circ. 13,000.

Daily Jugantor: 12/7, North Kamalpur, Dhaka 1217; tel. (2) 7102701; fax (2) 7101917; e-mail jugantor@gononet.com; internet www.jugantor.com; Editor GOLAM SARWAR.

Daily Sangbad: 36 Purana Paltan, Dhaka 1000; tel. (9) 9558147; fax (2) 9562882; e-mail sangbad@gononet.com; internet www.thedailysangbad.com; Editor BAZLUR RAHMAN; circ. 77,109.

Dainik Arthaneeti: Bangladesh Media Services Ltd, Biman Bhaban, 5th Floor, 100 Motijheel C/A, Dhaka 1000; tel. (2) 9667789; fax (2) 9555707; e-mail dartho@citecho.net; Editor ZAHIDUZZAMAN FARUQUE.

Dainik Bhorer Kagoj: Rahat Tower, 14 Link Rd, Banglamotor, Dhaka; tel. (2) 9666545; fax (2) 8618801; e-mail bkagoj@yahoo.com; internet www.bhorerkagoj.net; Editor SHYAMAL DUTTA (acting); circ. 50,000.

Dainik Birol: Dhaka; tel. (2) 7121620; fax (2) 8013721; Chair. of Editorial Bd ABDULLAH AL-NASER.

Dainik Inqilab: 2/1 Ramkrishna Mission Rd, Dhaka 1203; tel. (2) 9563162; fax (2) 9552881; e-mail inqilab@bttb.net; internet www.dailyinqilab.com; Editor A. M. M. BAHAUDDIN; circ. 180,025.

Dainik Ittefaq: 1 Ramkrishna Mission Rd, Dhaka 1203; tel. (2) 7122660; e-mail info@ittefaq.com; internet www.ittefaq.com; f. 1953; Editor RAHAT KHAN; circ. 200,000.

Dainik Jahan: 3/B Shehra Rd, Mymensingh; tel. (91) 5677; f. 1980; Editor MUHAMMAD HABIBUR RAHMAN SHEIKH; circ. 4,000.

Dainik Janakantha (Daily People's Voice): Globe Janakantha Shilpa Paribar, Janakantha Bhaban, Dhaka 1000; tel. (2) 9347780; fax (2) 9351317; e-mail janakantha@bttb.net.bd; internet www.dailyjanakantha.com; f. 1993; Man. Editor TOAB KHAN; Exec. Editor BORHAN AHMED; circ. 100,000.

Dainik Janata: 24 Aminbagh, Shanti Nagar, Dhaka 1217; tel. (2) 400498; e-mail djanata@dhaka.net; internet www.dailyjanata.com; Editor Dr M. ASADUR RAHMAN.

Dainik Janmabhumi: 110/2 Islampur Rd, Khulna; tel. (41) 721280; fax (41) 724324; e-mail janmo@khulna.bangla.net; f. 1982; Editor WADUDUR RAHMAN PANNA (acting); circ. 30,000.

Dainik Karatoa: Chalkjadu Rd, Bogra 5800; tel. (51) 63660; fax (51) 73057; e-mail abas@bttb.net.bd; internet www.karatoa.com; f. 1976; Editor MOZAMMEL HAQUE LALU; circ. 44,000.

Dainik Khabar: 137 Shanti Nagar, Dhaka 1217; tel. (2) 406601; f. 1985; Editor PATRA GIAS KAMAL CHOWDHURY; circ. 18,000.

Dainik Millat: Dhaka; tel. (2) 9560026; Editor CHOWDHURY MOHAMMAD FAROOQ.

Dainik Patrika: 85 Elephant Rd, Maghbazar, Dhaka 1217; tel. (2) 415057; fax (2) 841575; e-mail patrika@citechco.net; Publr and Chief Editor MIA MUSA HOSSAIN; Editor M. FAISAL HASSAN HASSAN (acting).

Dainik Purbanchal: Purbanchal House, 38 Iqbal Nagar Mosque Lane, Khulna 9100; tel. (41) 722251; fax (41) 721013; e-mail liakat@purbanchal.com; internet www.purbanchal.com; f. 1974; Editor LIAKAT ALI; circ. 46,000.

Dainik Rupashi Bangla: Abdur Rashid Rd, Natun Chowdhury Para, Bagicha Gaon, Comilla 3500; tel. (81) 76689; f. 1972; a weekly until 1979; Editor Prof. HASINA WAHAB; Publr and Printer ASHIK AMITAV; circ. 10,000.

Dainik Sangram: 423 Elephant Rd, Baramaghbazar, Dhaka 1217; tel. (2) 9346448; fax (2) 9330579; e-mail dsangram@gmail.com; internet www.dailysangram.com; f. 1970; Chair. ALI AHSAN MUHAMMAD MUJAHID; Editor ABUL ASAD; circ. 50,000.

Dainik Sphulinga: Amin Villa, P-5 Housing Estate, Jessore 7401; tel. (421) 6433; f. 1971; Editor Mia ABDUS SATTAR; circ. 14,000.

Jaijaidin: Jaijaidin Mediaplex, Love Rd, Tejgaon Industrial Area, Dhaka 1000; tel. (2) 8832222; fax (2) 8832233; e-mail jajadi@aitlbd.net; internet www.jaijaidin.com; f. 1984; Editor SHAFIK REHMAN; circ. 100,000.

Janabarta: 5 Babu Khan Rd, Khulna; tel. (41) 21075; f. 1974; Editor SYED SOHRAB ALI; circ. 4,000.

Jugabheri: Sylhet; tel. (821) 715461; f. 1931; Editor FAHMEEDA RASHEED CHOWDHURY; circ. 6,000.

Manav Jamin (Human Land): 21 Kazi Nazrul Islam Ave, Dhaka 1000; tel. (2) 9669193; fax (2) 8618130; e-mail manabzamin@yahoo.com; internet www.manabzamin.ne; f. 1998; tabloid; Editor MATIUR RAHMAN CHOUDHURY.

Naya Bangla: 101 Momin Rd, Chittagong; tel. (31) 206247; f. 1978; Editor ABDULLAH AL-SAGIR; circ. 12,000.

Prothom Alo: C. A. Bhaban, 100 Kazi Nazrul Islam Ave, Kaiwan Bazar, Dhaka 1215; tel. (2) 8110081; fax (2) 9130496; e-mail info@prothom-alo.com; internet www.prothom-alo.com; f. 1998; publ. by MediaStar Ltd; Editor MATIUR RAHMAN.

Protidin: Ganeshtola, Dinajpur; tel. (531) 4555; f. 1980; Editor KHAIRUL ANAM; circ. 3,000.

Sangbad: 36 Purana Paltan, Dhaka 1000; tel. (2) 9558147; fax (2) 9562882; e-mail sangbad@bangla.net; f. 1952; Editor AHMADUL KABIR; circ. 71,050.

Shamokal: 136 Tejgaon Industrial Area, Dhaka 1208; tel. (2) 9889821; fax (2) 8855981; e-mail info@shamokalbd.com; internet www.shamokal.com; Editor GOLAM SARWAR.

Swadhinata: Chittagong; tel. (31) 209644; f. 1972; Editor ABDULLAH AL-HARUN; circ. 4,000.

English

Bangladesh Observer: Observer House, 33 Toyenbee Circular Rd, Motijheel C/A, Dhaka 1000; tel. (2) 9555105; fax (2) 9562243; e-mail observer@dhaka.net; internet www.bangladeshobserveronline.com; f. 1949; morning; Editor IQBAL SOBHAN CHOWDHURY; circ. 75,000.

The Bangladesh Today: 9 Motijheel C/A, Dhaka 1000; tel. (2) 9556254; fax (2) 9565257; e-mail editor@thebangladeshtoday.com; internet www.thebangladeshtoday.com; Editor Col (retd) MAHMUD-UR RAHMAN CHOUDHURY (acting).

Daily Evening News: Dhaka; tel. (2) 7121619; fax (2) 8013721; Chair. of Editorial Bd ABDULLAH AL-NASER.

Daily Rupali: 28/A/3 Toyenbee Circular Rd, Dhaka 1000; tel. (2) 235542; fax (2) 9565558; e-mail network@bangla.net; Editor MAFUZUR RAHMAN MITA.

Daily Star: 19 Karwan Bazar, Dhaka 1215; tel. (2) 8124944; fax (2) 8125155; e-mail editor@thedailystar.net; internet www.thedailystar.net; f. 1991; Publr and Editor MAHFUZ ANAM; circ. 30,000.

Daily Tribune: 38 Iqbal Nagar Mosque Lane, Khulna 9100; tel. (41) 721944; fax (41) 721013; e-mail ferdousi@purbanchal.com; f. 1978; morning; Editor FERDOUSI ALI; circ. 24,000.

Financial Express: Tropicana Tower, 4th Floor, 45 Topkhana Road, POB 2526, Dhaka 1000; tel. (2) 9568154; fax (2) 9567049; e-mail tfe@bangla.net; internet www.financialexpress-bd.com; f. 1994; Editor MOAZZEM HOSSAIN.

The Independent: Beximco Media Complex, 32 Kazi Nazrul Islam Ave, Karwan Bazar, Dhaka 1215; tel. (2) 9129938; fax (2) 9127722; e-mail ind@bol-online.com; internet www.theindependent-bd.com; f. 1995; Editor MAHBUBUL ALAM.

BANGLADESH

New Age: Holiday Bldg, 30 Tejgaon Industrial Area, Dhaka 1208; tel. (2) 8153034; fax (2) 8112247; e-mail newagebd@global-bd.net; internet www.newagebd.com; f. 2003; Editor NURUL KABIR.

New Nation: 1 Ramkrishna Mission Rd, Dhaka 1203; tel. (2) 7122654; fax (2) 7122650; e-mail n_editor@bangla.net; internet nation.ittefaq.com; f. 1981; Editor MOSTAFA KAMAL MAJUMDER; circ. 15,000.

The News Today: 2 Outer Circular Rd, Mogh Bazar, Dhaka; tel. (2) 9355567; fax (2) 9355569; e-mail today@gononet.com; internet www.newstoday-bd.com; Editor REAZUDDIN AHMED.

People's View: 102 Siraj-ud-Daulla Rd, Chittagong; tel. (31) 227403; f. 1969; Editor SABBIR ISLAM; circ. 3,000.

PERIODICALS

Bengali

Aachal: Dhaka; weekly; Editor FERDOUSI BEGUM.

Adhuna: 1/3 Block F, Lalmatia, Dhaka 1207; tel. (2) 812353; fax (2) 813095; e-mail adab@bdonline.com; f. 1974; quarterly; publ. by the Asscn of Devt Agencies in Bangladesh (ADAB); Exec. Editor MINAR MONSUR; circ. 10,000.

Ahmadi: 4 Bakshi Bazar Rd, Dhaka 1211; tel. (2) 7300808; fax (2) 7300925; e-mail amgb@bol-online.com; f. 1925; fortnightly; Editor-in-Chief M. A. S. MAHMOOD; Exec. Editor MOHAMMAD M. RAHMAN.

Alokpat: 166 Arambagh, Dhaka 1000; tel. (2) 413361; fax (2) 863060; fortnightly; Editor RABBANI JABBAR.

Amod: Chowdhury Para, Comilla 3500; tel. (81) 65193; e-mail info@weeklyamod.com; internet www.weeklyamod.com; f. 1955; weekly; Editor SHAMSUN NAHAR RABBI; circ. 6,000.

Begum: 66 Loyal St, Dhaka 1; tel. (2) 233789; f. 1947; women's illustrated weekly; Editor NURJAHAN BEGUM; circ. 25,000.

Chakra: 242A Nakhalpara, POB 2682, Dhaka 1215; tel. (2) 604568; social welfare weekly; Editor HUSNEARA AZIZ.

Chitra Desh: 24 Ramkrishna Mission Rd, Dhaka 1203; weekly; Editor HENA AKHTAR CHOWDHURY.

Chitrali: Observer House, 33 Toyenbee Circular Rd, Motijheel C/A, Dhaka 1000; tel. (2) 9550938; fax (2) 9562243; f. 1953; film weekly; Editor PRODIP KUMAR DEY; circ. 25,000.

Ekota: 15 Larmini St, Wari, Dhaka; tel. (2) 257854; f. 1970; weekly; Editor AFROZA NAHAR; circ. 25,000.

Fashal: 28J Toyenbee Circular Rd, Motijheel C/A, Dhaka 1000; tel. (2) 233099; f. 1965; agricultural weekly; Chief Editor ERSHAD MAZUMDAR; circ. 8,000.

Ispat: Majampur, Kushtia; tel. (71) 3676; f. 1976; weekly; Editor WALIUR BARI CHOUDHURY; circ. 3,000.

Jhorna: 4/13 Block A, Lalmatia, Dhaka; tel. (2) 415239; Editor MUHAMMAD JAMIR ALI.

Kalantar: 87 Khanjahan Ali Rd, Khulna; tel. (41) 61424; f. 1971; weekly; Editor NOOR MOHAMMAD; circ. 12,000.

Kankan: Nawab Bari Rd, Bogra; tel. (51) 6424; f. 1974; weekly; Editor SUFIA KHATUN; circ. 6,000.

Kirajagat: National Sports Council, 62/63 Purana Paltan, Dhaka 1000; f. 1977; fortnightly; Editor MAHMUD HOSSAIN KHAN DULAL; circ. 10,000.

Kishore Bangla: Observer House, Motijheel C/A, Dhaka 1000; juvenile weekly; f. 1976; Editor RAFIQUL HAQUE; circ. 5,000.

Moha Nagar: 4 Dilkusha C/A, Dhaka 1000; tel. (2) 255282; Editor SYED MOTIUR RAHMAN.

Moshal: 4 Dilkusha C/A, Dhaka 1000; tel. (2) 231092; Editor MUHAMMAD ABUL HASNAT; circ. 3,000.

Muktibani: Toyenbee Circular Rd, Motijheel C/A, Dhaka 1000; tel. (2) 253712; f. 1972; weekly; Editor NIZAM UDDIN AHMED; circ. 35,000.

Natun Bangla: 44/2 Free School St Bylane, Hatirpool, Dhaka 1205; tel. (2) 866121; fax (2) 863794; e-mail mujib@bangla.net; f. 1971; weekly; Editor MUJIBUR RAHMAN.

Natun Katha: 31E Topkhana Rd, Dhaka; weekly; Editor HAJERA SULTANA; circ. 4,000.

Nipun: 520 Peyarabag, Magbazar, Dhaka 11007; tel. (2) 312156; monthly; Editor SHAJAHAN CHOWDHURY.

Parikrama: 65 Shanti Nagar, Dhaka; tel. (2) 415640; Editor MOMTAZ SULTANA.

Prohar: 35 Siddeswari Rd, Dhaka 1217; tel. (2) 404206; Editor MUJIBUL HUQ.

Protirodh: Dept of Answar and V.D.P. Khilgoan, Ministry of Home Affairs, School Bldg, 2nd and 3rd Floors, Bangladesh Secretariat, Dhaka; tel. (2) 405971; f. 1977; fortnightly; Editor ZAHANGIR HABIB-ULLAH; circ. 20,000.

Purbani: 1 Ramkrishna Mission Rd, Dhaka 1203; tel. (2) 256503; f. 1951; film weekly; Editor KHONDKER SHAHADAT HOSSAIN; circ. 22,000.

Robbar: 1 Ramkrishna Mission Rd, Dhaka; tel. (2) 256071; e-mail robbar@nation-online.com; internet www.robbar.com; f. 1978; weekly; Editor SYED TOSHARRAF ALI; circ. 20,000.

Rokshena: 13B Avoy Das Lane, Tiktuli, Dhaka; tel. (2) 255117; Editor SYEDA AFSANA.

Sachitra Bangladesh: 112 Circuit House Rd, Dhaka 1000; tel. (2) 402129; f. 1979; fortnightly; Editor A. B. M. ABDUL MATIN; circ. 8,000.

Sachitra Sandhani: 68/2 Purana Paltan, Dhaka; tel. (2) 409680; f. 1978; weekly; Editor GAZI SHAHABUDDIN MAHMUD; circ. 13,000.

Sandip Bhabhan: 28/A/3 Toyenbee Circular Rd, Dhaka; tel. (2) 235542; fax (2) 9565558; e-mail network@bangla.net; weekly; Editor MAFUZUR RAHMAN MITA.

Shaptahik Ekhon: Dhaka; internet www.weeklyekhon.com; weekly; Editor ALTAUS SAMAD.

Shishu: Bangladesh Shishu Academy, Old High Court Compound, Dhaka 1000; tel. (2) 230317; f. 1977; children's monthly; Editor GOLAM KIBRIA; circ. 5,000.

Sonar Bangla: 423 Elephant Rd, Mogh Bazar, Dhaka 1217; tel. (2) 8319065; fax (2) 8315571; e-mail news@weeklysonarbanglabd.com; internet www.weeklysonarbangla.com; f. 1961; Editor MUHAMMED QAMARUZZAMAN; circ. 25,000.

Swadesh: 19 B.B. Ave, Dhaka; tel. (2) 256946; weekly; Editor ZAKIUDDIN AHMED; circ. 8,000.

Tarokalok: Tarokalok Complex, 25/3 Green Rd, Dhaka 1205; tel. (2) 506583; fax (2) 864330; weekly; Editor AREFIN BADAL.

Tilotwoma: 14 Bangla Bazar, Dhaka; Editor ABDUL MANNAN.

English

ADAB News: 1/3, Block F, Lalmatia, Dhaka 1207; tel. (2) 327424; f. 1974; 6 a year; publ. by the Asscn of Devt Agencies in Bangladesh (ADAB); Editor-in-Chief AZFAR HUSSAIN; circ. 10,000.

Bangladesh: 112 Circuit House Rd, Dhaka 1000; tel. (2) 402013; fortnightly; Editor A. B. M. ABDUL MATIN.

Bangladesh Gazette: Bangladesh Government Press, Tejgaon, Dhaka; f. 1947; name changed 1972; weekly; official notices; Editor M. HUDA.

Bangladesh Illustrated Weekly: Dhaka; tel. (2) 23358; Editor ATIQUZZAMAN KHAN; circ. 3,000.

Cinema: 81 Motijheel C/A, Dhaka 1000; Editor Sheikh FAZLUR RAHMAN MARUF; circ. 11,000.

Detective: Polwell Bhaban, Naya Paltan, Dhaka 2; tel. (2) 402757; f. 1960; weekly; also publ. in Bengali; Editor SYED AMJAD HOSSAIN; circ. 3,000.

Dhaka Courier: Cosmos Centre, 69/1 New Circular Rd, Malibagh, Dhaka 1217; tel. (2) 408420; fax (2) 831942; e-mail dhakacourier@dhakacourier.net; internet www.dhakacourier.net; weekly; Exec. Editor ROUSHAN ZAMAN; circ. 18,000.

Holiday: Holiday Bldg, 30 Tejgaon Industrial Area, Dhaka 1208; tel. (2) 9122950; fax (2) 9127927; e-mail holiday@bangla.net; internet www.weeklyholiday.net; f. 1965; weekly; independent; Editor SAYED KAMALUDDIN; circ. 18,000.

Motherland: Khanjahan Ali Rd, Khulna; tel. (41) 61685; f. 1974; weekly; Editor M. N. KHAN.

Tide: 56/57 Motijheel C/A, Dhaka; tel. (2) 259421; Editor ENAYET KARIM.

Voice from the North: Dinajpur Town, Dinajpur; tel. (531) 3256; f. 1981; weekly; Editor Prof. MUHAMMAD MOHSIN; circ. 5,000.

Weekly Blitz: 169 Shahid Syed Nazrul Islam Sarani, Bijoy Nagar, Dhaka 1000; tel. (19) 326232; e-mail ediblitz@yahoo.com; internet www.weeklyblitz.net; f. 2003; weekly (Wednesdays); Publr and Editor SALAH UDDIN SHOAIB CHOUDHURY; circ. 7,500.

NEWS AGENCIES

Bangladesh Sangbad Sangstha (BSS) (Bangladesh News Agency): 68/2 Purana Paltan, Dhaka 1000; tel. (2) 9555036; fax (2) 9568970; e-mail bssadmin@bssnews.org; internet www.bssnews.net; f. 1972; Man. Dir and Chief Editor GAZIUL HASAN KHAN.

Islamic News Society (INS): 24 R. K. Mission Rd, Motijheel C/A, Dhaka 1203; tel. (2) 7121619; fax (2) 8013721; Editor ABDULLAH AL-NASER.

United News of Bangladesh (UNB): Cosmos Centre, 69/1 New Circular Rd, Malibagh, Dhaka 1217; tel. (2) 9345543; fax (2) 9344556; e-mail unbnews@dhaka.net; internet www.unbnews.org; f. 1988; independent; Chair. AMANULLAH KHAN.

PRESS ASSOCIATIONS

Bangladesh Press Council: 2nd Floor, House 497, Rd 33, Mohakhali, Dhaka 1206; tel. (2) 9862426; e-mail info@presscouncilbd.com; internet www.presscouncilbd.com; f. 1974; established under an act of Parliament to preserve the freedom of the press and maintain and

BANGLADESH

develop standards of newspapers and news agencies; Chair. Justice ABU SAYEED AHAMMED.

Bangladesh Sangbadpatra Karmachari Federation (Newspaper Employees' Fed.): Dhaka; tel. (2) 235065; f. 1972; Pres. MATIUR RAHMAN TALUKDER; Sec.-Gen. MIR MOZAMMEL HOSSAIN.

Bangladesh Sangbadpatra Press Sramik Federation (Newspaper Press Workers' Federation): 1 Ramkrishna Mission Rd, Dhaka 1203; f. 1960; Pres. M. ABDUL KARIM; Sec.-Gen. BOZLUR RAHMAN MILON.

Dhaka Union of Journalists: National Press Club, Dhaka; f. 1947.

Newspaper Owners' Association of Bangladesh: c/o The Independent, Beximco Media Complex, 32 Kazi Nazrul Islam Ave, Karwan Bazar, Dhaka 1215; f. 2002; promotes interests of newspaper industry; Pres. MAHBUBUL ALAM.

Overseas Correspondents' Association of Bangladesh (OCAB): 18 Topkhana Rd, Dhaka 1000; e-mail naweed@bdonline .com; f. 1979; Pres. ZAHIDUZZMAN. FARUQUE; Gen. Sec. SHAMIM AHMED; 60 mems.

Press Institute of Bangladesh: 3 Circuit House Rd, Dhaka 1000; tel. (2) 9330081; fax (2) 8317458; e-mail pib@bdonline.com; internet www.pib.gov.bd; f. 1976; trains journalists, conducts research, operates a newspaper library and data bank; Dir-Gen. HAIDAR ALI (acting).

Publishers

Academic Publishers: 35 Syed Awlad Hossain Lane, Dhaka 1100; tel. (2) 507355; fax (2) 863060; f. 1982; social sciences and sociology; Jt Man. Dir HABIBUR RAHMAN.

Agamee Prakashani: 36 Bangla Bazar, Dhaka 1100; tel. (2) 7111332; fax (2) 7123945; e-mail agamee@bdonline.com; f. 1986; fiction and academic; Chief Exec. OSMAN GANI.

Ahmed Publishing House: 7 Zindabahar 1st Lane, Dhaka; tel. (2) 36492; f. 1942; literature, history, science, religion, children's, maps and charts; Man. Dir KAMALUDDIN AHMED; Man. MESBAHUDDIN AHMED.

Ankur Prakashani: 40/1 Purana Paltan, Dhaka 1000; tel. (2) 9564799; fax (2) 9553635; e-mail ankur@agnionline.net; internet www.ankur-prakashani.com; f. 1986; academic and general; Dir MESBAHUDDIN AHMED.

Ashrafia Library: 4 Hakim Habibur Rahman Rd, Chawk Bazar, Dhaka 1000; Islamic religious books, texts, and reference works of Islamic institutions.

Asiatic Society of Bangladesh: 5 Old Secretariat Rd, Ramna, Dhaka; tel. (2) 9560500; fax (2) 7168853; e-mail asb@bangla.net; internet www.asiaticsociety.org.bd/journals.htm; f. 1952; periodicals on science, Bangla and humanities.

Bangla Academy (National Academy of Arts and Letters of Bangladesh): Burdwan House, 3 Kazi Nazrul Islam Ave, Dhaka 1000; tel. (2) 8619577; fax (2) 8612352; e-mail bacademy@citechco .net; internet www.banglaacademy.org.bd; f. 1955; higher education textbooks in Bengali, books on language, literature and culture, language planning, popular science, drama, encyclopaedias, translations of world classics, dictionaries; Dir-Gen. Dr ABUL KALAM MANZUR MORSHED; Pres. A. NISUZZAMAN.

Bangladesh Books International Ltd: Ittefaq Bhaban, 1 Ramkrishna Mission Rd, POB 377, Dhaka; tel. (2) 256071; f. 1975; reference, academic, research, literary, children's in Bengali and English; Chair. MOINUL HOSSEIN; Man. Dir ABDUL HAFIZ.

Bangladesh Publishers: 45 Patuatully Rd, Dhaka 1100; tel. (2) 233135; f. 1952; textbooks for schools, colleges and universities, cultural books, journals, etc.; Dir MAYA RANI GHOSAL.

Gatidhara: 38/2-Ka Bangla Bazar, POB 2723, Dhaka 1100; tel. (2) 7117515; fax (2) 7123472; e-mail gatidara@bdonline.com; f. 1988; academic, general and fiction; Publr and Chief Exec. SIKDER ABUL BASHAR.

Gono Prakashani: House 14/E, Rd 6, Dhanmondhi R/A, Dhaka 1205; tel. (2) 8617208; fax (2) 8613567; e-mail gk@citechco.net; f. 1978; science and medicine; Man. Dir SHAFIQ KHAN; Editor BAZLUR RAHIM.

Muktadhara: 22 Payridas Rd, Banglabazar, Dhaka 1100; tel. (2) 7111374; e-mail muktadhara1971@yahoo.com; f. 1971; educational and literary; Bengali and English; Dir JAHAR LAL SAHA; Man. Dir C.R. SAHA.

Mullick Brothers: 160–161, Dhaka New Market, Dhaka; tel. (2) 8619125; fax (2) 8610562; educational; Man. Dir KAMRUL HASAN MULLICK.

Osmania Book Depot: 30/32 North Brook Hall Rd, Dhaka 1100.

Rahman Brothers: 5/1 Gopinath Datta, Kabiraj St, Babu Bazar, Dhaka; tel. (2) 282633; educational.

Directory

Royal Library: Ispahani Bldg, 31/32 P. K. Roy Rd, Bangla Bazar, Dhaka; tel. (2) 250863.

Shahitya Prakash: 42 Topkhana Road, Dhaka 1000; tel. (2) 281327; fax (2) 863797; f. 1970; Prin. Officer MOFIDUL HOQUE.

University Press Ltd: Red Crescent House, 61 Motijheel C/A, POB 2611, Dhaka 1000; tel. (2) 9565444; fax (2) 9565443; e-mail upl@bttb .net.bd; internet www.uplbooks.com; f. 1975; educational, academic and general; Man. Dir MOHIUDDIN AHMED.

GOVERNMENT PUBLISHING HOUSES

Bangladesh Bureau of Statistics: Parishankhan Bhaban, E-27/A, Agargaon, Sher-e-Bangla Nagar, Dhaka 1207; tel. (2) 9118045; fax (2) 9111064; e-mail ndbp@bangla.net; internet www.bbs.gov.bd; f. 1971; statistical year book and pocket book, censuses, surveys, agricultural year book, special reports, etc.; Dir-Gen. A. Y. M. EKRAMUL HOQUE; Sec. BADIUR RAHMAN.

Bangladesh Government Press: Tejgaon, Dhaka 1209; tel. (2) 606316; f. 1972.

Department of Films and Publications: 112 Circuit House Rd, Dhaka 1000; tel. (2) 8331034; fax (2) 8331030; e-mail dfp_bd@yahoo .com; internet www.dfpbd.com; Dir-Gen. MIR MOSHARRAF HOSSAIN.

Press Information Department: Bhaban 6, Bangladesh Secretariat, Dhaka 1000; tel. (2) 7163639; fax (2) 7165942; e-mail pid_1@ bangla.net; internet www.bdpressinform.org/activities.htm.

PUBLISHERS' ASSOCIATIONS

Bangladesh Publishers' and Booksellers' Association: 3 Liaquat Ave, 3rd Floor, Dhaka 1100; tel. (2) 7111666; e-mail info@ publisher-bookseller.org; internet www.publisher-bookseller.org; f. 1972; Pres. ABU TAHER; 2,500 mems.

National Book Centre of Bangladesh: 5C Bangabandhu Ave, Dhaka 1000; f. 1963; to promote the cause of 'more, better and cheaper books'; organizes book fairs, publs a monthly journal; Dir FAZLE RABBI.

Broadcasting and Communications

TELECOMMUNICATIONS

Bangladesh Telecommunication Regulatory Commission (BTRC): Setu Bhaban, 4th Floor, New Airport Rd, Banani, Dhaka 1212; tel. (2) 9893917; fax (2) 9890029; e-mail info@btrc.org.bd; internet www.btrc.gov.bd; f. 2002; regulates the telecommunications sector; Chair. Maj.-Gen. (retd) MANZURUL ALAM; Vice-Chair. A. M. M. REZA-E-RABBI.

Bangladesh Telegraph and Telephone Board: Central Office, Telejogajog Bhaban, 37/E Eskaton Garden, Dhaka 1000; tel. (2) 8322661; fax (2) 832577; internet www.bttb.net; Chair. ABDUL MALEQUE AKHAND; Dir (International) MUHAMMAD HASSANUZZAMAN.

Aktel: 1st Floor, Silver Tower, 52 South Gulshan C/A, Gulshan 1, Dhaka 1212; e-mail 123@aktel.com; internet www.aktel.com; f. 1996; jt venture between Telekom Malaysia Bhd and A. K. Khan & Co Ltd; provides mobile cellular telephone services; Man. Dir AHMAD BIN ISMAIL.

BanglaLink: FM Center (Tiger House), Level 1, House SW(H)04, Gulshan Ave, Gulshan Model Town, Dhaka 1212; tel. (2) 9885770; fax (2) 8827265; e-mail info@banglalinkgsm.com; internet www .banglalinkgsm.com; f. 1998; owned by Orascom Telecom; provides mobile cellular telephone services; Man. Dir and CEO RASHID KHAN.

GrameenPhone Ltd: Celebration Pt, Plots 3 & 5, Rd 113A, Gulshan 2, Dhaka 1212; tel. (2) 9882990; fax (2) 9882970; e-mail info@ grameenphone.com; internet www.grameenphone.com; f. 1996 by Grameen Bank to expand cellular telephone service in rural areas; CEO ANDERS JENSEN.

Pacific Bangladesh Telecom Ltd: Pacific Centre, 14 Mohakhali C/ A, Dhaka 1212; tel. (2) 8822186; fax (2) 8823575; e-mail customerservice@citycell.com; internet www.citycell.com; Man. Dir FAISAL MORSHED KHAN; CEO CHYE HOON PIN.

Teletalk Bangladesh Ltd: House 41, Rd 27, Block A, Banani, Dhaka 1213; tel. (2) 8851060; fax (2) 9882828; e-mail info@teletalk .com.bd; internet www.teletalk.com.bd; f. 2004; govt-owned; controls mobile cellular telephone operations of Bangladesh Telegraph and Telephone Board; Man. Dir MUHAMMAD AMINUL HASSAN.

Warid Telecom International: POB 3016, Dhaka; fax (2) 8951786; internet www.waridtel.com.bd; f. 2005; owned by Abu Dhabi Group of United Arab Emirates; operates mobile cellular telephone services; CEO MUNEER FAROOQUI.

BROADCASTING
Radio

Bangladesh Betar: NBA House, 121 Kazi Nazrul Islam Ave, Shahabag, Dhaka 1000; tel. (2) 8615294; e-mail dgbetar@bd.drik

.net; internet www.betar.org.bd; f. 1971; govt-controlled; regional stations at Dhaka, Chittagong, Khulna, Rajshahi, Rangpur, Sylhet, Rangamati and Thakurgaon broadcast a total of approximately 160 hours daily; transmitting centres at Lalmai and Rangamati; external service broadcasts 8 transmissions daily in Arabic, Bengali, English, Hindi, Nepalese and Urdu; Dir-Gen. MAHBUBUL ALAM.

Television

ATN Bangla: WASA Bhaban, 1st Floor, 98 Kazi Nazrul Islam Ave, Kawran Bazar, Dhaka 1215; tel. (2) 8111207; fax (2) 8111876; e-mail info@atnbangla.tv; internet www.atnbangla.tv; f. 1997; private satellite channel; broadcasts in Bengali; Chair. MAHFUZUR RAHMAN.

Bangladesh Television (BTV): Television House, Rampura, Dhaka 1219; tel. (2) 9330131; fax (2) 8621839; e-mail info@btv.com.bd; internet www.btv.com.bd; f. 1964; govt-controlled; daily broadcasts on one channel from Dhaka station for 10 hours; transmissions also from nation-wide network of 14 relay stations; Dir-Gen. NASIMUL GHANI; Gen. Man. NAWAZISH ALI KHAN.

Channel-i: Impress Telefilm Ltd, 62/A, Shiddeshwari Rd, Dhaka 1217; tel. (2) 9332444; fax (2) 9338285; e-mail info@channel-i-tv.com; internet www.channel-i-tv.com; f. 1999; Dir SHYKH SERAJ.

NTV Bangladesh: BSEC Bhaban, 6th Floor, 102 Kazi Nazrul Islam Ave, Karwan Bazar, Dhaka 1215; tel. (2) 9143381; fax (2) 9143386; e-mail info@ntvbd.com; internet www.ntvbd.com; f. 2003; private satellite channel; Chair. M. ENAYETUR RAHMAN.

Finance

(cap. = capital; res = reserves; dep. = deposits; m. = million; brs = branches; amounts in taka)

BANKING

Central Bank

Bangladesh Bank: Motijheel C/A, POB 325, Dhaka 1000; tel. (2) 7126101; fax (2) 9566212; e-mail banglabank@bangla.net; internet www.bangladesh-bank.org; f. 1971; cap. 30m., res 59,503.5m., dep. 201,800.9m. (June 2006); Gov. SALEHUDDIN AHMED; 9 brs.

Nationalized Commercial Banks

Agrani Bank: 9D Dilkusha C/A, POB 531, Dhaka 1000; tel. (2) 9566160; fax (2) 9563662; e-mail enquiry@agranibank.org; internet www.agranibank.org; f. 1972; 100% state-owned; cap. 2,484.2m., res 292.2m., dep. 128,920.7m. (Dec. 2006); Chair. SIDDIQUR RAHMAN CHOWDHURY; Man. Dir SYED ABU NASER BUKHTEAR AHMED; 866 brs.

Janata Bank: 110 Motijheel C/A, POB 468, Dhaka 1000; tel. (2) 9565041; fax (2) 9564644; e-mail id-obd@janatabank-bd.com; internet www.janatabank-bd.com; f. 1972; 100% state-owned; cap. 2,593.9m., res 1,726.5m., dep. 182,946.5m. (Dec. 2006); Chair. SUHEL AHMED CHOUDHURY; Man. Dir MUHAMMAD MUKTER HUSSAIN; 847 brs in Bangladesh, 4 brs in the UAE.

Rupali Bank Ltd: Rupali Bhaban, 34 Dilkusha C/A, POB 719, Dhaka 1000; tel. (2) 9554122; fax (2) 9564148; e-mail rblhocom@bdcom.com; internet www.rupali-bank.com; f. 1972; cap. 1,250m., res 855.8m., dep. 59,967.9m. (Dec. 2003); Chair. Dr MOHAMMAD TAREQUE; Man. Dir ABDUL HAMID MIAH; 508 brs in Bangladesh, 1 br. in Pakistan.

Sonali Bank: 35–44 Motijheel C/A, POB 3130, Dhaka 1000; tel. (2) 9550426; fax (2) 9561410; e-mail sbhoitd@bttb.net; internet www.sonalibank.com.bd; f. 1972; 100% state-owned; cap. 3,272.2m., res 3,034.0m., dep. 290,140.1m. (Dec. 2005); Chair. Prof. MAHBUB ULLAH; Man. Dir TAHMILAR RAHMAN; 1,186 brs incl. 2 overseas brs.

Private Commercial Banks

Al-Arafah Islami Bank Ltd: Rahman Mansion, 161 Motijheel C/A, Dhaka; tel. (2) 9568007; fax (2) 9569351; e-mail alarafah@bangla.net; internet www.al-arafah.com; f. 1995; 100% owned by 23 sponsors; cap. 720m., res 10m., dep. 852.0m. (Feb. 2004); Chair. MUHAMMAD ANOWER HOSSAIN; Man. Dir MUHAMMAD ABDUS SAMAD SHEIKH.

Arab Bangladesh Bank Ltd: Head Office, BCIC Bhaban, 30–31 Dilkusha C/A, POB 3522, Dhaka 1000; tel. (2) 9560312; fax (2) 9564122; e-mail abbank@abbank.org; internet www.abbank.org; f. 1981; 99.3% owned by Bangladesh nationals and 0.7% by Bangladesh Govt; cap. 571.7m., res 1,456.5m., dep. 43,374.4m. (Dec. 2006); Chair. FAISAL MORSHED KHAN; Pres. and Man. Dir KAISER A. CHOWDHURY; 66 brs, 1 br. in India.

The City Bank Ltd: Jiban Bima Tower, 10 Dilkusha C/A, POB 3381, Dhaka 1000; tel. (2) 9565925; fax (2) 9562347; e-mail mail@thecitybank.com; internet www.thecitybank.com; f. 1983; 50% owned by sponsors and 50% by public; cap. 720.0m., res 1,205.2m., dep. 30,647.8m. (Dec. 2005); Chair. AZIZ AL-KAISER; Man. Dir DILWAR H. CHOUDHURY; 82 brs.

Dhaka Bank Ltd: Biman Bhaban, 100 Motijheel C/A, Dhaka 1000; tel. (2) 9554514; fax (2) 9556584; e-mail dhakabank@bdonline.com; internet www.dhakabankltd.com; f. 1995; cap. 1,289.5m., res 871.0m., dep. 41,553.6m. (Dec. 2006); Chair. JASMINE SULTANA; Man. Dir SHAHED NOMAN; 20 brs.

Dutch-Bangla Bank Ltd: 3rd, 4th, 5th and 10th Floors, Sena Kalyan Bhaban, 195 Motijheel C/A, Dhaka 1000; tel. (2) 7176390; fax (2) 9561889; e-mail id@dutchbanglabank.com; internet www.dutchbanglabank.com; f. 1996; cap. 202.1m., res 724.7m., dep. 40,111.5m. (Dec. 2006); Chair. ABUL HASNAT MOHAMMAD RASHIDUL ISLAM; Man. Dir MOHAMMED YEASIN ALI; 39 brs.

Eastern Bank Ltd: Jiban Bima Bhaban, 2nd Floor, 10 Dilkusha C/A, POB 896, Dhaka 1000; tel. (2) 9556360; fax (2) 9562364; e-mail info@ebl-bd.com; internet www.ebl-bd.com; f. 1992; appropriated assets and liabilities of fmr Bank of Credit and Commerce International (Overseas) Ltd; 83% owned by public, 17% owned by govt and private commercial banks; cap. 828.0m., res 2,293.9m., dep. 30,139.7m. (Dec. 2006); Chair. AHMED QUAMRUL ISLAM CHOWDHURY; Man. Dir and CEO ALI REZA IFTEKHAR; 22 brs.

International Finance Investment and Commerce Bank Ltd (IFICB): BSB Bldg, 8th, 10th & 16th–19th Floors, 8 Rajuk Ave, POB 2229, Dhaka 1000; tel. (2) 9563020; fax (2) 9562015; e-mail info@ificbankbd.com; internet www.ificbankbd.com; f. 1983; 35.5% state-owned; cap. 406.4m., res 964.4m., dep. 28,620.9m. (Dec. 2006); Chair. Al-haj MOHAMMAD MOSADDAK ALI; Man. Dir MASHIUR RAHMAN; 65 brs in Bangladesh.

Islami Bank Bangladesh Ltd (IBBL): Head Office, Islami Bank Tower, 40 Dilkusha C/A, POB 233, Dhaka 1000; tel. (2) 9563040; fax (2) 9564532; e-mail info@islamibankbd.com; internet www.islamibankbd.com; f. 1983 on Islamic banking principles; cap. 3,456m., res 6,551.2m., dep. 132,419m. (Dec. 2006); Chair. Prof. ABU NASSER MUHAMMED ABDUZ ZAHER; Exec. Pres. and CEO FARIDUDDIN AHMED; 177 brs.

Mercantile Bank Ltd: 61 Dilkusha C/A, Dhaka 1000; tel. (2) 9559333; fax (2) 9561213; e-mail mbl@bol-online.com; internet www.mblbd.com; f. 1999; cap. 1,199.1m., res 751.6m., dep. 32,462.5m. (Dec. 2006); Chair. MOHAMMED ABDUL JALIL; Man. Dir and CEO SHAH MOHAMMAD NURAL ALAM; 25 brs.

National Bank Ltd: 18 Dilkusha C/A, POB 3424, Dhaka 1000; tel. (2) 9563081; fax (2) 9563953; e-mail nblho@citechco.net; internet www.nblbd.com; f. 1983; 50% owned by sponsors and 50% by general public; cap. 805.5m., res 2,059.3m., dep. 40,350.9m. (Dec. 2006); Chair. PARVEEN HAQUE SIKDER; Man. Dir M. AMINUZZAMAN; 91 brs.

National Credit and Commerce Bank Ltd: 7–8 Motijheel C/A, GPOB 2920, Dhaka 1000; tel. (2) 9561902; fax (2) 9566290; e-mail nccbl@bdmail.net; internet www.nccbank-bd.com; f. 1993; 50% owned by sponsors, 50% by general public; cap. 1,201.8m., res 925.2m., dep. 28,147.3m. (Dec. 2006); Chair. TOFAZZAL HOSSAIN; Man. Dir MUHAMMAD NURUL AMIN; 49 brs.

ONE Bank Ltd: HRC Bhaban, 46 Kawaran Bazar C/A, Dhaka; tel. (2) 8122046; fax (2) 9134794; e-mail obl@onebankbd.com; internet www.onebankbd.com; f. 1999; cap. 888.0m., res 627.2m., dep. 20,253.3m. (Dec. 2006); Chair. SAYEED HOSSAIN CHOWDHURY; Man. Dir FARMAN R. CHOWDHURY.

Oriental Bank Ltd: T. K. Bhaban, 14th–16th Floors, 13 Karwan Bazar, Dhaka 1215; tel. (2) 9143361; fax (2) 9562768; internet www.oriental-bank.com; f. 1987 on Islamic banking principles; fmrly Al-Baraka Bank Bangladesh Ltd; name changed as above 2003; 34.68% owned by Al-Baraka Group, Saudi Arabia, 5.78% by Islamic Development Bank, Jeddah, 45.91% by local sponsors, 5.75% by Bangladesh Govt, 7.8% by general public; Chair. Dr MASUM AHMED CHOWDHURY; Man. Dir C. M. KOYES SAMI; 33 brs.

Prime Bank Ltd: Adamjee Court, Annex Bldg No. 2, 119–120 Motijheel C/A, Dhaka 1000; tel. (2) 9567265; fax (2) 9567230; e-mail info@primebank.com; internet www.prime-bank.com; f. 1995; cap. 1,750.0m., res 1,404.1m., dep. 54,724.1m. (Dec. 2006); Chair. Capt. IMAM ANWAR HOSSAIN; Man. Dir M. SHAHJAHAN BHUIYAN; 50 brs.

Pubali Bank Ltd: Pubali Bank Bhaban, 26 Dilkusha C/A, POB 853, Dhaka 1000; tel. (2) 9551614; fax (2) 9564009; e-mail pubali@bdmail.net; internet www.pubalibangla.com; f. 1959 as Eastern Mercantile Bank Ltd; name changed to Pubali Bank in 1972; 98.5% privately owned, 1.5% state-owned; cap. 1,200.0m., res 2,395.8m., dep. 48,676.0m. (Dec. 2006); Chair. HAFIZ AHMED MAZUMDAR; Man. Dir HELAL AHMED CHOWDHURY; 350 brs.

Social Investment Bank: 15 Dilkusha C/A, Dhaka 1000; tel. (2) 9559014; fax (2) 9559013; e-mail sibl@bdonline.com; internet www.siblbd.com; f. 1995; cap. 585.0m., res 395.7m., dep. 17,940.5m. (Dec. 2006); Chair. Maj. (retd) Dr REZAUL HAQUE; Man. Dir K. M. ASHADUZ ZAMAN; 5 brs.

Southeast Bank Ltd: 1 Dilkusha C/A, 3rd Floor, Dhaka 1000; tel. (2) 9550081; fax (2) 9550093; e-mail seastbk@citechco.net; internet www.sebankbd.com; f. 1995; cap. 2,112.7m., res 2,344.8m., dep.

46,056.2m. (Dec. 2006); Chair. ALAMGIR KABIR; Pres. and Man. Dir NEAZ AHMED; 32 brs.

United Commercial Bank Ltd: Federation Bhaban, 4th–6th Floors, 60 Motijheel C/A, POB 2653, Dhaka 1000; tel. (2) 9568690; fax (2) 9560587; e-mail info@ucbl.com; internet www.ucbl.com; f. 1983; 50% owned by sponsors, 45% by general public and 5% by Govt; Chair. Hajee YUNUS AHMED; Man. Dir HAMIDUL HUQ; 80 brs.

Uttara Bank Ltd: 90 Motijheel C/A, POB 818, Dhaka 1000; tel. (2) 9551162; fax (2) 7168376; e-mail ublid@citecho.net; internet www.uttarabank-bd.com; f. 1965 as Eastern Banking Corpn Ltd; name changed to Uttara Bank in 1972 and to Uttara Bank Ltd in 1983; cap. 199.7m., res 1,881.8m., dep. 39,360.2m. (Dec. 2006); Chair. AZHARUL ISLAM; Man. Dir and CEO SHAMSUDDIN AHMED; 203 brs.

Development Finance Organizations

Bangladesh House Building Finance Corpn (BHBFC): HBFC Bldg, 22 Purana Paltan, POB 2167, Dhaka 1000; tel. (2) 9562767; fax (2) 9561324; e-mail bhbfc@bangla.net; internet bhbfc.gov.bd; f. 1952; provides low-interest credit for residential house-building; 100% state-owned; cap. 972.9m. (Dec. 2003); Chair. A. S. ABDUL QADIR MAHMUD; Man. Dir Dr JADAB CHANDRA SAHA; 9 zonal offices, 13 regional offices and 2 camp offices.

Bangladesh Krishi Bank (BKB): 83–85 Motijheel C/A, POB 357, Dhaka 1000; tel. (2) 9560021; fax (2) 9561211; e-mail bkb@citechco.net; internet www.krishibank.org.bd; f. 1961; as the Agricultural Development Bank of Pakistan, name changed as above in 1973; provides credit for agricultural and rural devt; also performs all kinds of banking; 100% state-owned; cap. 1,400m., res 820.4m., dep. 44,611m. (June 2002); Chair. K. M. S. A. KAISER; Man. Dir M. FAZLUL HOQUE; 938 brs.

Bangladesh Samabaya Bank Ltd (BSBL): 'Samabaya Sadan', 9D Motijheel C/A, POB 505, Dhaka 1000; tel. (2) 9564628; f. 1948; provides credit for agricultural co-operatives; Chair. Dr ABDUL MOYEEN KHAN; Gen. Man. MUHAMMAD ABDUL WAHED.

Bangladesh Shilpa Bank (BSB) (Industrial Development Bank): Shilpa Bank Bhaban, 8 Rajuk Ave, POB 975, Dhaka; tel. (2) 9556786; fax (2) 9562061; e-mail misd@shilpabank.gov.bd; internet www.shilpabank.gov.bd; f. 1972; fmrly Industrial Devt Bank; provides long- and short-term financing for industrial devt in the private and public sectors; also provides underwriting facilities and equity support; 51% state-owned; cap. 2,000.0m., res 957.5m., dep. 710.4m. (June 2005); Chair. Dr MUHAMMAD AMINUL ISLAM BHUIYAN; Man. Dir MUHAMMAD AMANULLAH; 15 brs.

Bangladesh Shilpa Rin Sangstha (BSRS) (Industrial Loan Agency): BIWTC Bhaban, 5th Floor, 141–143 Motijheel C/A, Dhaka 1000; tel. (2) 9553546; fax (2) 9567057; f. 1972; 100% state-owned; Chair. Dr M. FARASHUDDIN; Man. Dir HAFIZ UL ISLAM; 4 brs.

Bank of Small Industries and Commerce Bangladesh Ltd (BASIC Bank): Suite 601–602, Sena Kalyan Bhaban, 6th Floor, 195 Motijheel C/A, Dhaka 1000; tel. (2) 9564830; fax (2) 9564829; e-mail basicho@citechco.net; internet www.basicbanklimited.com; f. 1988; 100% state-owned; cap. 300m., res 713m., dep. 10,698m. (Dec. 2002); Chair. MOHAMMAD NURUL AMIN; Man. Dir A. H. EKBAL HOSSAIN; 19 brs.

Export-Import Bank of Bangladesh Ltd: Printers' Bldg, 5 Rajuk Ave, Motijheel C/A, Dhaka 1000; tel. (2) 9561604; fax (2) 7162379; e-mail itd@eximbankbd.com; internet www.eximbankbd.com; f. 1999; cap. 3,3467.4m., res 810.9m., dep. 35,032.0m. (Dec. 2006); Chair. NAZRUL ISLAM MAZUMDER; Man. Dir KAZI MASIHUR RAHMAN; 32 brs.

Grameen Bank: Grameen Bank Bhavan, Mirpur 1, Dhaka 1216; tel. (2) 9005257-68; fax (2) 803559; internet www.grameen.com; f. 1976; provides credit for the landless rural poor; 6.97% owned by Govt; Chair. REHMAN SOBHAN; Man. Dir Dr MUHAMMAD YUNUS; 2,431 brs.

Infrastructure Development Co Ltd (IDCOL): UTC Bldg, 16th Floor, 8 Panthapath, Kawran Bazar, Dhaka 1215; tel. (2) 9114385; fax (2) 8116663; e-mail contact@idcol.org; internet www.idcol.org/; f. 1999; state-owned; Chair. MUHAMMAD AMINUL ISLAM BHUIYAN; Exec. Dir and CEO MUHAMMAD SHAHEEDUL HAQUE.

Investment Corpn of Bangladesh (ICB): BSB Bldg, 12th–15th Floors, 8 DIT Ave, POB 2058, Dhaka 1000; tel. (2) 9563455; fax (2) 9563313; e-mail icb@agni.com; internet www.icb.gov.bd; f. 1976; provides investment banking services; 27% owned by Govt; cap. 500.0m., res 691.1m. (June 2004); Chair. FEROZ AHMED; Man. Dir MUHAMMAD ZIAUL HAQUE KHONDKER; 7 brs.

Rajshahi Krishi Unnayan Bank: Sadharan Bima Bhaban, Kazihata, Greater Rd, Rajshahi 6000; tel. (721) 775008; fax (721) 775947; e-mail ho@rakub.org.bd; internet www.rakub.org.bd; f. 1987; 100% state-owned; Chair. MUHAMMAD YAHIA MOLLA; Man. Dir JAGLUL KARIM; 357 brs.

Banking Association

Bangladesh Association of Banks: Iqbal Centre, 12th Floor, 42 Kamal Atatürk Ave, Banani C/A, Dhaka 1213; tel. and fax (2) 8851015; e-mail bab@citechco.net; Chair. SYED MANZUR ELAHI.

STOCK EXCHANGES

Chittagong Stock Exchange: CSE Bldg, 1080 Sheikh Mujib Rd, Agrabad, Chittagong; tel. (31) 714632; fax (31) 714101; e-mail cse@csebd.com; internet csebd.com; Chair. M. K. M. MOHIUDDIN; CEO A. B. SIDDIQUE.

Dhaka Stock Exchange Ltd: 9F Motijheel C/A, Dhaka 1000; tel. (2) 9564601; fax (2) 9564727; e-mail dse@bol-online.com; internet www.dsebd.org; f. 1954; 278 listed cos; Pres. ABDULLAH BOKHARI; CEO SALAHUDDIN AHMED KHAN.

Regulatory Authority

Bangladesh Securities and Exchange Commission: Jiban Bima Tower, 15th, 16th and 20th Floors, 10 Dilkusha C/A, Dhaka 1000; tel. (2) 9568101; fax (2) 9563721; e-mail secbd@bdmail.net; internet www.secbd.org; f. 1993; Chair. FARUQ AHMAD SIDDIQI; CEO Dr MIRZA AZIZUL ISLAM.

INSURANCE

Department of Insurance: 74 Motijheel C/A, Dhaka 1000; attached to Ministry of Commerce; supervises activities of domestic and foreign insurers; Chief Controller of Insurance Dr MAHFUZUL HAQUE.

Bangladesh Insurance Association: Rupali Bima Bhaban, 7th Floor, 7 Rajuk Ave, Dhaka 1000; tel. (2) 9557330; fax (2) 9562345; e-mail bia@bdcom.com; Chair. NASIR A. CHOWDHURY.

Bangladesh General Insurance Co Ltd: 42 Dilkusha C/A, Dhaka 1000; tel. (2) 9555073; fax (2) 9564212; e-mail bgic@citechco.net; Chair. and Man. Dir M. A. SAMAD.

Eastern Insurance Co Ltd: 44 Dilkusha C/A, Dhaka 1000; tel. (2) 9563033; fax (2) 9569735; e-mail eicl@dhaka.net; Chair. MOHAMMED MOHSIN; Man. Dir A. K. M. IFTEKHAR AHMAD.

Jiban Bima Corpn: 24 Motijheel C/A, POB 346, Dhaka 1000; tel. (2) 9552047; fax (2) 868112; state-owned; comprises 37 national life insurance cos; life insurance; Man. Dir A. K. M. MOSTAFIZUR RAHMAN.

Pioneer Insurance Co Ltd: 6th Floor, Jiban Bima Bhaban, 10 Dilkusha C/A, Dhaka 1000; tel. (2) 9557674; fax (2) 9557676; e-mail piclho@msnbd.net; internet www.pioneerinsurancebd.com; f. 1996; Man. Dir Q. A. F. M. SERAJUL ISLAM.

Pragati Insurance Ltd: Pragati Bhaban, 12th Floor, 20–21 Kawran Bazar, Dhaka 1215; tel. (2) 8117996; fax (2) 8122980; e-mail pilbima@bangla.net; Man. Dir A. K. M. RAFIQUL ISLAM.

Reliance Insurance Ltd: BSB Bldg, 8 Rajuk Ave, Dhaka 1000; tel. (2) 9560105; fax (2) 9562005; e-mail info@reliance-bd.com; f. 1988; Man. Dir AKHTAR AHMED.

Sadharan Bima Corpn: 33 Dilkusha C/A, Dhaka 1000; tel. (2) 9552070; fax (2) 9564197; e-mail head-office@sbc.org.bd; internet www.sbc.gov.bd; state-owned; general insurance; Chair. SIDDIQUR RAHMAN CHOUDHURY; Man. Dir ELIAS AHMED.

Trade and Industry

GOVERNMENT AGENCIES

Board of Investment: Jiban Bima Tower, 19th Floor, 10 Dilkusha C/A, Dhaka 1000; tel. (2) 9563570; fax (2) 9562312; e-mail ecboi@bdmail.net; internet www.boi.gov.bd; f. 1989; Exec. Chair. KAMALUDDIN AHMED.

Export Promotion Bureau: TCB Bhaban, 1st Floor, 1 Kawran Bazar, Dhaka 1215; tel. (2) 9144821; fax (2) 9119531; e-mail info@epb.gov.bd; internet www.epb.gov.bd; f. 1972; attached to Ministry of Commerce; regional offices in Chittagong, Khulna, Rajshahi, Narayanganj, Comilla and Sylhet; Dir-Gen. KHALILUR RAHMAN; Vice-Chair. MUHAMMAD SHAHAB ULLAH.

Petrobangla (Bangladesh Oil, Gas and Mineral Corpn): Petrocenter Bhaban, 3 Kawran Bazar C/A, POB 849, Dhaka 1215; tel. (2) 8114972; fax (2) 9120224; e-mail petchair@petrobangla.org; internet www.petrobangla.org.bd; f. 1972; explores and develops gas, petroleum and mineral resources, manages Bangladesh Petroleum Exploration Co Ltd and Sylhet Gas Fields Ltd; Chair. Dr Sheikh ABDUR RASHID.

Planning Commission: Planning Commission Secretariat, G.O. Hostel, Sher-e-Bangla Nagar, Dhaka 1207; e-mail mohammadalibd@hotmail.com; internet www.plancomm.gov.bd; f. 1972; govt agency responsible for all aspects of economic planning and development including the preparation of the five-year plans and annual development programmes (in conjunction with appropriate govt ministries), promotion of savings and investment, compilation of statistics and evaluation of development schemes and projects; Planning Division Sec. JAFAR AHMAD CHOWDHURY.

Privatization Commission: Jiban Bima Tower, 14th Floor, 10 Dilkusha C/A, Dhaka 1000; tel. (2) 9551986; fax (2) 9556433; e-mail pb@bdonline.com; internet www.bangladeshonline.com/pb; f. 1993; Chair. KAZI ZAFRULLAH; Sec. ABDUL MAZID.

Trading Corpn of Bangladesh: 2nd Floor, TCB Bhaban, 1 Kawran Bazar, Dhaka 1215; tel. (2) 8111521; fax (2) 8113582; e-mail tcb@bdonline.com; internet www.tcb.gov.bd; f. 1972; national trade org. of the Ministry of Commerce; imports, exports and markets goods through appointed dealers and agents; Chair. MOHAMMAD ZIAUL ISLAM; Dir MOHAMMAD MUKHLESUR RAHMAN.

DEVELOPMENT ORGANIZATIONS

Bangladesh Chemical Industries Corpn: BCIC Bhaban, 30–31 Dilkusha C/A, Dhaka; tel. (2) 955280; fax (2) 9564120; e-mail bciccomp@bangla.net; internet www.bcic.gov.bd; Chair. Maj.-Gen. (retd) IMAMUZ-ZAMAN.

Bangladesh Export Processing Zones Authority (BEPZA): BEPZA Complex, House 19/D, Rd 6, Dhaka 1000; tel. (2) 9670530; fax (2) 8650060; e-mail chairman@epzbangladesh.org.bd; internet www.epzbangladesh.org.bd; f. 1983 to plan, develop, operate and manage export processing zones (EPZs) in Bangladesh; Exec. Chair. Brig.-Gen. ASHRAF ABDULLAH YUSUF.

Bangladesh Fisheries Development Corpn: 24–25 Dilkusha C/A, Dhaka 1000; tel. (2) 9552689; fax (2) 9563990; e-mail bfdc@citechco.net; f. 1964; under Ministry of Fisheries and Livestock; development and commercial activities; Chair. Brig.-Gen. (retd) CHOWDHURY KHALEQUZZAMAN; Sec. A. K. M. SHAHIDUL ISLAM.

Bangladesh Forest Industries Development Corpn: 73 Motijheel C/A, Dhaka; tel. (2) 9552010; fax (2) 9563990; Chair. M. ATIKULLAH.

Bangladesh Jute Mills Corpn: Adamjee Court, 115–120 Motijheel C/A, Dhaka 1000; tel. (2) 9558182; fax (2) 9567508; e-mail info@bjmc.gov.bd; internet www.bjmc.gov.bd; f. 1972; operates 32 jute mills; bags, carpet backing cloth, yarn, twine, tape, felt, floor covering, etc.; Chair. ATHARUL ISLAM.

Bangladesh Small and Cottage Industries Corpn (BSCIC): 137/138 Motijheel C/A, Dhaka 1000; tel. (2) 9565612; fax (2) 9550704; e-mail cbscic@aitlbd.net; f. 1957; Chair. MUHAMMAD SIRAJUDDIN.

Bangladesh Steel and Engineering Corpn (BSEC): BSEC Bhaban, 102 Kazi Nazrul Islam Ave, Dhaka 1215; tel. (2) 9115144; fax (2) 8112846; e-mail bsec@bdcom.com; internet www.bsec.gov.bd; 16 industrial units; Chair. MOHAMMAD ABU JAFAR; Gen. Man. (Marketing) ASHRAFUL HAQ; 2,826 employees.

Bangladesh Sugar and Food Industries Corpn: Adamjee Court 115–120, Motijheel C/A, Dhaka; tel. (2) 9565869; fax (2) 9550481; e-mail chinikal@bttb.net.bd; f. 1972; Chair. MOMTAJUL ISLAM.

CHAMBERS OF COMMERCE

Federation of Bangladesh Chambers of Commerce and Industry (FBCCI): Federation Bhaban, 60 Motijheel C/A, Dhaka 1000; tel. (2) 9560598; fax (2) 9560588; e-mail fbcci@bol-online.com; internet www.fbcci-bd.org; f. 1973; comprises 221 trade asscns and 77 chambers of commerce and industry; Pres. MIR NASIR HOSSAIN; Sec.-Gen. Col (retd) M. M. JAHANGIR.

Barisal Chamber of Commerce and Industry: Chamber Bhabab, Nasir Pool, Shaw Rd, POB 30, Barisal; tel. (431) 61876; fax (51) 66257; Pres. EBADUL HAQUE CHAN.

Bogra Chamber of Commerce and Industry: Chamber Bhaban, 2nd Floor, Kabi Nazrul Islam Rd, Jhawtola, Bogra 5800; tel. (51) 64138; fax (51) 66257; e-mail bccibgr@bttb.net.bd; f. 1963; Pres. Alhaj MOHAMMAD FAZLUR RAHMAN PAIKER; Sr Vice-Pres. GOLAM RASUL KHAN RANA.

Chittagong Chamber of Commerce and Industry: Chamber House, 38 Agrabad C/A, POB 481, Agrabad, Chittagong; tel. (31) 713366; fax (31) 710183; e-mail ccci@globalctg.net; internet www.chittagongchamber.com; f. 1959; more than 5,000 mems; Pres. SAIFUZZAMAN CHOWDHURY; Sec. OSMAN GANI CHOWDHURY.

Comilla Chamber of Commerce and Industry: Rammala Rd, Ranir Bazar, Comilla; tel. (81) 68075; Pres. AFZAL KHAN.

Dhaka Chamber of Commerce and Industry: Dhaka Chamber Bldg, 1st Floor, 65–66 Motijheel C/A, POB 2641, Dhaka 1000; tel. (2) 9552562; fax (2) 9560830; e-mail dcci@bangla.net; internet www.dhakachamber.com; f. 1958; 5,000 mems; Pres. MATIUR RAHMAN; Sr Vice-Pres. AM MUBASH-SHAR.

Dinajpur Chamber of Commerce and Industry: Chamber Bhaban, Maldhapatty, Dinajpur 5200; tel. (531) 63189; Pres. KHAIRUL ANAM.

Faridpur Chamber of Commerce and Industry: Chamber House, Niltuly, Faridpur; tel. (631) 63530; fax (631) 61070; Pres. KHANDOKER MOHSIN ALI.

Foreign Investors' Chamber of Commerce and Industry: 'Prime View', 7 Gulshan Ave, Gulshan 1, Dhaka 1212; tel. (2) 9892913; fax (2) 9893058; e-mail ficci@bangla.net; internet www.ficci.org.bd; f. 1963 as Agrabad Chamber of Commerce and Industry, name changed as above in 1987; Pres. MASIH AL-KARIM; Sec. M. A. MATIN.

Khulna Chamber of Commerce and Industry: 5 KDA C/A, Khulna; tel. (41) 721695; fax (41) 417937; e-mail kcci@bttb.net.bd; f. 1934; Pres. S. M. NAZRUL ISLAM.

Kushtia Chamber of Commerce and Industry: 15, S Rd, Kushtia; tel. (71) 54068; e-mail kushcham@kushtia.com; Pres. MOHAMMAD MOZIBAR RAHMAN.

Metropolitan Chamber of Commerce and Industry: Chamber Bldg, 4th Floor, 122–124 Motijheel C/A, Dhaka 1000; tel. (2) 9565208; fax (2) 9565212; e-mail sg@citechco.net; internet www.mccibd.org; f. 1904; 310 mems; Pres. KUTUBUDDIN AHMED; Sec.-Gen. C. K. HYDER.

Noakhali Chamber of Commerce and Industry: Noakhali Pourshara Bhaban, 2nd Floor, Maiydee Court, Noakhali; tel. (321) 5229; Pres. MOHAMMAD NAZIBUR RAHMAN.

Rajshahi Chamber of Commerce and Industry: Chamber Bhaban, Station Rd, PO Ghoramara, Rajshahi 6100; tel. (721) 772115; fax (721) 772412; f. 1960; 800 mems; Pres. MOHAMMAD LUTFAR RAHMAN.

Sylhet Chamber of Commerce and Industry: Chamber Bldg, Jail Rd, POB 97, Sylhet 3100; tel. (821) 714403; fax (821) 715210; e-mail scci@btsnet.net; Pres. MOHD MOHIUDDIN.

INDUSTRIAL AND TRADE ASSOCIATIONS

Bangladesh Frozen Foods Exporters' Association: 50/1 Inner Circular Rd, 2nd Floor, Shantinagar, Dhaka; tel. (2) 418720; fax (2) 837531; e-mail bffea@drik.dgd.toolnet.org; Pres. MAKSUDUR RAHMAN.

Bangladesh Garment Manufacturers' and Exporters' Association: 7–9 Karwanbazar, BTMC Bhaban, Dhaka 1215; tel. (2) 8115597; fax (2) 8113951; e-mail info@bgmea.com; internet www.bgmea.com; Pres. ANNISUL HUQ; Vice-Pres. NURUL HAQ SIKDAR.

Bangladesh Jute Association: BJA Bldg, 77 Motijheel C/A, Dhaka; tel. (2) 9552916; fax (2) 9560137; e-mail beejay@bangla.net; internet www.juteministry.org/html/bja.html; Chair. FARHAND AHMED AKHAND; Sec. S. H. PRODHAN.

Bangladesh Jute Exporters' Association: Nahar Mansion, 2nd Floor, 150 Motijheel C/A, Dhaka 1000; tel. (2) 9561102.

Bangladesh Jute Goods Association: Nahar Mansion, 2nd Floor, 150 Motijheel C/A, Dhaka 1000; tel. (2) 253640; f. 1979; 17 mems; Chair. M. A. KASHEM; Sec. Haji MOHAMMAD ALI.

Bangladesh Jute Mills Association: Adamjee Court, 4th Floor, 115–120 Motijheel C/A, Dhaka 1000; tel. (2) 9560071; fax (2) 9566472; e-mail bjmajutegood@agnionline.com; Chair. KAMRAN T. RAHMAN.

Bangladesh Jute Spinners' Association: 55 Purana Paltan, 3rd Floor, Dhaka 1000; tel. (2) 9551317; fax (2) 9562772; internet www.bjsa.org; f. 1979; 44 mems; Chair. SHABBIR YOUSUF; Sec. SHAHIDUL KARIM.

Bangladesh Knitwear Manufacturers' and Exporters' Association (BKMEA): National Plaza, 4th Floor, 1/G Free School St, Sonagargaon Rd, Dhaka; tel. (2) 8620377; fax (2) 9673337; e-mail info@bangla.net; internet www.bkmea.com; f. 1996; Pres. FAZLUL HOQUE.

Bangladesh Tea Board: 171–172 Baizid Bostami Rd, Nasirabad, Chittagong; tel. (31) 682903; fax (31) 682863; e-mail btb@spnetctg.com; internet www.teaboard.gov.bd; f. 1951; regulates, controls and promotes the cultivation and marketing of tea, both in Bangladesh and abroad; Chair. Brig.-Gen. MOSHARRAF HOSSAIN.

Bangladesh Textile Mills Association: Moon Mansion, 6th Floor, Block M, 12 Dilkusha C/A, Dhaka 1000; tel. (2) 9552799; fax (2) 9563320; e-mail btma@citechco.net; internet www.btmadhk.com; Chair. M. A. AWAL.

Bangladeshiyo Cha Sangsad (Tea Association of Bangladesh): 'Progressive Tower', 4th Floor, 1837 Sheikh Mujib Rd (Badamtali), Agrabad, Chittagong 4100; tel. (31) 716407; f. 1952; Chair. M. SALMAN ISPAHANI; Sec. G. S. DHAR.

UTILITIES

Electricity

Bangladesh Atomic Energy Commission (BAEC): 4 Kazi Nazrul Islam Ave, POB 158, Dhaka 1000; tel. (2) 5021600; fax (2) 8613051; e-mail baec@agni.com; f. 1964 as Atomic Energy Centre of the fmr Pakistan Atomic Energy Comm. in East Pakistan; reorg. 1973; operates an atomic energy research establishment and a 3-MW research nuclear reactor (inaugurated in January 1987) at Savar, an atomic energy centre at Dhaka, etc.; Chair. M. A. QUAIYUM; Sec. RAFIQUL ALAM.

BANGLADESH

Directory

Bangladesh Energy Regulatory Commission: Anchor Tower, Level 7, 1/1B Sonargaon Rd, Dhaka 1205; tel. (2) 9669925; internet www.berc.org.bd; f. 2004; regulates activities of power sector; Sec. ABDUL BARI.

Bangladesh Power Development Board: WAPDA Bldg, Motijheel C/A, Dhaka; tel. (2) 9562154; fax (2) 9564765; e-mail chbpdb@bol-online.com; internet www.bpdb.gov.bd; f. 1972; under Ministry of Power, Energy and Mineral Resources; generation, transmission and distribution of electricity; installed capacity 4,710 MW (2002); Chair. A. N. M. RIZWAN.

Dhaka Electric Supply Authority: Bidyut Bhaban, 1 Nawab Abdul Gani Rd, Dhaka 1000; tel. (2) 9563520; fax (2) 9566699; f. 1991; under Ministry of Power, Energy and Mineral Resources; Chair. S. M. SHAMSUL ALAM.

Dhaka Electric Supply Co Ltd (DESCO): House 3, Rd 24, Block K, Banani Model Town, Dhaka 1213; tel. (2) 8859642; fax (2) 823140; internet www.desco.org.bd; f. 1997; Chair. Brig.-Gen. NAZRUL HASAN; Man. Dir Eng. SALEH AHMED.

Power Grid Company of Bangladesh Ltd (PGCB): Red Crescent Concord Tower, 6th Floor, 17 Mohakhali C/A, Dhaka 1212; tel. and fax (2) 9888589; e-mail info@pgcb.org.bd; internet www.pgcb.org.bd; f. 1996; responsible for power transmission throughout Bangladesh; Chair. A. N. M. RIZWAN; Sec. MOHAMMAD SALIM.

Rural Electrification Board: House 3, Rd 12, Nikanja-2, Khilkhet, Dhaka 1229; tel. (2) 8924035; fax (2) 8916400; e-mail seict@reb.gov.bd; internet www.reb.gov.bd; under Ministry of Power, Energy and Mineral Resources; Chair. HABIB ULLAH MAJUMDER.

Water

Chittagong Water Supply and Sewerage Authority: Dampara, Chittagong; tel. (31) 621606; fax (31) 610465; f. 1963; govt corpn; Chair. SULTAN MAHMUD CHOWDHURY.

Dhaka Water Supply and Sewerage Authority: 98 Kazi Nazrul Islam Ave, Kawran Bazar, Dhaka 1215; tel. (2) 8116792; fax (2) 8112109; e-mail secretary@dwasa.org.bd; internet www.dwasa.org.bd; f. 1963; govt corpn; Man. Dir RAIHANUL ABEDIN.

TRADE UNIONS

In 2001 only 4.3% of the non-agricultural labour force was unionized. There were about 4,200 registered unions, organized mainly on a sectoral or occupational basis. There were 23 national trade unions to represent workers at the national level.

Bangladesh Free Trade Union Congress (BFTUC): 6A 1–19 Mirpur, Dhaka 1216; tel. (2) 8017001; fax (2) 8015919; e-mail bftuc@agni.com; Gen. Sec. M. R. CHOWDHURY; 115,000 mems.

Bangladesh Jatio Sramik League (BJSL): POB 2730, Dhaka; tel. (2) 282063; fax (2) 863470; 62,000 mems.

Transport

RAILWAYS

In July 2000 Bangladesh Railway and the Indian Railway Board signed an agreement to resume rail services on the Benapole–Petrapole route. The service opened fully in January 2001. In December regular rail services between Bangabandhu and Kolkata (Calcutta—India) resumed, as did those between Dhaka and Kolkata in April 2008.

Bangladesh Railway: Rail Bhaban, 16 Abdul Ghani Rd, Dhaka 1000; tel. (2) 9561200; fax (2) 9563413; e-mail dg_rail@bangla.net; internet www.railway.gov.bd; f. 1862; supervised by the Ministry of Communications; divided into East and West Zones, with East Zone HQ at Chittagong (tel. (31) 843200; fax (31) 843215) and West Zone HQ at Rajshahi (tel. (721) 761576; fax (721) 761982); total length of 2,855 route km; 459 stations; Dir-Gen. BELAYET HOSSAIN; Gen. Man. (East Zone) HALIM F. M. ABDUL MEAH; Gen. Man. (West Zone) MUHAMMAD AKHTARUZ ZAMAN.

ROADS

In 1999 the total length of roads in use was 207,486 km (19,775 km of highways, 17,297 km of secondary roads and 170,413 km of other roads), of which 9.5% were paved. In 1992 the World Bank approved Bangladesh's US $700m. Jamuna Bridge Project. The construction of the 4.8-km bridge, which was, for the first time, to link the east and the west of the country with a railway and road network, was begun in early 1994. The bridge, which was renamed the Bangabandhu Jamuna Multipurpose Bridge, was officially opened in June 1998.

In June 1999 the first direct passenger bus service between Bangladesh (Dhaka) and India (Kolkata) was inaugurated.

Bangladesh Road Transport Corpn: Paribahan Bhaban, 21 Rajuk Ave, Dhaka; tel. (2) 9555786; fax (2) 9555788; e-mail info@brtc.gov.bd; internet www.brtc.gov.bd; f. 1961; state-owned; operates transport services, incl. truck division; transports govt food grain; Chair. HEDAYETULLAH AL MAMUN.

INLAND WATERWAYS

In Bangladesh there are some 8,433 km of navigable waterways, which transport 70% of total domestic and foreign cargo traffic and on which are located the main river ports of Dhaka, Narayanganj, Chandpur, Barisal and Khulna. A river steamer service connects these ports several times a week. Vessels of up to 175m overall length can be navigated on the Karnaphuli river.

Bangladesh Inland Water Transport Corpn: 5 Dilkusha C/A, Dhaka 1000; tel. (2) 9552561; internet www.mos.gov.bd/biwtc.htm; f. 1972; 608 vessels.

SHIPPING

The chief ports are Chittagong, where the construction of a second dry-dock is planned, and Mongla, where a modern seaport is being developed.

Atlas Shipping Lines Ltd: 142 Sir Iqbal Rd, 3rd Floor, Khulna; tel. and fax (4) 1732669; e-mail atlas@khulna.bangla.net; Man. Dir S. U. CHOWDHURY; Gen. Man. M. KAMAL HAYAT.

Bangladesh Shipping Corpn: BSC Bhaban, Saltgola Rd, POB 641, Chittagong 4100; tel. (31) 724479; fax (31) 710506; e-mail bsc-ctg@spnetctg.com; internet www.mos.gov.bd/bsc.htm; f. 1972; maritime shipping; 13 vessels; Chair. MOFAZZAL HOSSAIN CHOWDHURY MAYA; Man. Dir JAMIL OSMAN.

Bengal Shipping Line Ltd: Palm View, 100A Agrabad C/A, Chittagong 4100; tel. (31) 714800; fax (31) 710362; e-mail bsl@mkrgroup.com; Chair. MOHAMMED ABDUL AWWAL; Man. Dir MOHAMMED ABDUL MALEK.

Broadway Shipping Line: 39 Dilkusha C/A, Dhaka 1223; tel. (2) 404598; fax (2) 412254.

Chittagong Port Authority: POB 2013, Chittagong 4100; tel. (31) 812200; fax (31) 710593; e-mail info@cpa.gov.bd; internet www.cpa.gov.bd; f. 1887; provides bunkering, ship repair, towage and lighterage facilities as well as provisions and drinking water supplies; Chair. MUHAMMAD FARUQUE.

Continental Liner Agencies: Facy Bldg, 3rd Floor, 87 Agrabad C/A, Chittagong; tel. (31) 721572; fax (31) 710965; Man. SAIFUL AHMED; Dir (Technical and Operations) Capt. MAHFUZUL ISLAM.

Nishan Shipping Lines Ltd: Monzoor Bldg, 1st Floor, 67 Agrabad C/A, Chittagong; tel. (31) 710855; fax (31) 710044; Dir Capt. A. K. M. ALAMGIR.

CIVIL AVIATION

There is an international airport at Dhaka (Zia International Airport), situated at Kurmitola, with the capacity to handle 5m. passengers annually. There are also airports at all major towns. In 1997 the civil aviation industry was deregulated to permit domestic competition to Biman Bangladesh Airlines.

Biman Bangladesh Airlines: Head Office, Balaka, Kurmitola, Dhaka 1229; tel. (2) 8917400; fax (2) 8913005; e-mail dgmcmis@bdbiman.com; internet www.bimanair.com; f. 1972; fmrly state-owned; transferred to private ownership in 2007; domestic services to seven major towns; international services to 19 destinations in the Middle East, the Far East, Europe, and North America; CEO and Man. Dir Dr M. A. MOMEN.

GMG Airlines: ABC House, 9th Floor, 8 Kamal Atatürk Ave, Banani, Dhaka 1213; tel. (2) 8825845; fax (2) 8826115; e-mail gmgair@gmggroup.com; internet www.gmgairlines.com; f. 1997; private, domestic airline; Dir (Flight Operations) Capt. HABIBUR RAHMAN; Man. Dir HAFIZUR RAHMAN BHUIYAN.

Tourism

Tourist attractions include the cities of Dhaka and Chittagong, Cox's Bazar—which has the world's longest beach (120 km)—on the Bay of Bengal, and Teknaf, at the southernmost point of Bangladesh. Tourist arrivals decreased from 271,270 in 2004 to 207,662 in 2005. Earnings from tourism reached US $76m. in 2004. The majority of visitors are from India, Pakistan, the People's Republic of China, the United Kingdom and the USA.

Bangladesh Parjatan Corpn (National Tourism Organization): 233 Biruttam Ziaur Rahman Rd, Tejgaon, Dhaka 1215; tel. (2) 8117855; fax (2) 8126501; e-mail bpcho@bangla.net; internet www.bangladeshtourism.gov.bd; f. 1973; there are four tourist information centres in Dhaka, and one each in Bogra, Chittagong, Cox's Bazar, Dinajpur, Khulna, Kuakata, Rangamati, Rangpur, Rajshahi and Sylhet; Chair. Dr MAHFUZUL HAQUE.

BARBADOS

Introductory Survey

Location, Climate, Language, Religion, Flag, Capital

Barbados is the most easterly of the Caribbean islands, lying about 320 km (200 miles) north-east of Trinidad. The island has a total area of 430 sq km (166 sq miles). There is a rainy season from July to November and the climate is tropical, tempered by constant sea winds, during the rest of the year. The mean annual temperature is about 26°C (78°F). Average annual rainfall varies from 1,250 mm (49 ins) on the coast, to 1,875 mm (74 ins) in the interior. The official language is English. Almost all of the inhabitants profess Christianity, but there are small groups of Hindus, Muslims and Jews. The largest denomination is the Anglican church, but about 90 other Christian sects are represented. The national flag (proportions 2 by 3) has three equal vertical stripes, of blue, gold and blue; superimposed on the centre of the gold band is the head of a black trident. The capital is Bridgetown.

Recent History

Barbados was formerly a British colony. The Barbados Labour Party (BLP) won a general election in 1951, when universal adult suffrage was introduced, and held office until 1961. Although the parliamentary system dates from 1639, ministerial government was not established until 1954, when the BLP's leader, Sir Grantley Adams, became the island's first Premier. He was subsequently Prime Minister of the West Indies Federation from January 1958 until its dissolution in May 1962.

Barbados achieved full internal self-government in October 1961. The Democratic Labour Party (DLP), formed in 1955 by dissident members of the BLP, won an election in December. The DLP's leader, Errol Barrow, became Premier, succeeding Dr Hugh Cummins of the BLP. When Barbados achieved independence on 30 November 1966, Barrow became the island's first Prime Minister, following another electoral victory by his party earlier in the month.

The DLP retained power in 1971, but in the general election of September 1976 the BLP, led by J. M. G. M. (Tom) Adams (Sir Grantley's son), ended Barrow's 15-year rule. The BLP successfully campaigned against alleged government corruption, winning a large majority over the DLP. At a general election in June 1981 the BLP was returned to office with 17 of the 27 seats in the newly enlarged House of Assembly. The DLP won the remainder of the seats. Adams died in March 1985 and was succeeded as Prime Minister by his deputy, Bernard St John, a former leader of the BLP.

At a general election in May 1986 the DLP won a decisive victory, winning 24 seats in the House of Assembly. Bernard St John and all except one of his cabinet ministers lost their seats, and Errol Barrow returned as Prime Minister after 10 years in opposition. In June it was announced that Barrow was to review Barbados' participation in the US-supported Regional Security System, the defence force that had been established soon after the US invasion of Grenada in October 1983. Under Adams, Barbados was one of the countries whose troops had supported the invasion. In June 1987 Barrow died suddenly. He was succeeded by L. Erskine Sandiford (hitherto the Deputy Prime Minister), who pledged to continue Barrow's economic and social policies. In September 1987, however, the Minister of Finance, Dr Richard (Richie) Haynes, resigned, accusing Sandiford of failing to consult him over financial appointments. Sandiford assumed the finance portfolio, but acrimony over government policy continued to trouble the DLP. In February 1989 Haynes and three other members of Parliament resigned from the DLP and announced the formation of the National Democratic Party (NDP). Haynes was subsequently appointed as leader of the parliamentary opposition.

At a general election in January 1991 the DLP won 18 of the 28 seats in the enlarged House of Assembly, while the BLP secured the remaining 10. The creation of a Ministry of Justice and Public Safety by the new Government and the reintroduction of flogging for convicted criminals reflected widespread concern over increased levels of violent crime on the island. Moreover, as a result of serious economic problems, a series of austerity measures was proposed in September. However, the proposals resulted in public unrest, which continued in 1992, as large numbers of civil servants and agricultural workers were made redundant. In 1993 and 1994 the increasing unpopularity of Sandiford's premiership provoked continued demands for his resignation, culminating, in June 1994, in his narrow defeat in a parliamentary motion of confidence. At a general election on 6 September the BLP won a decisive victory and Owen Arthur was subsequently appointed as Prime Minister.

In May 1995 Arthur announced the formation of a 10-member commission to advise the Government on possible reforms of the country's Constitution and political institutions. In July 1996 the commission was asked to consider, in particular, the continuing role of the British monarch as Head of State in Barbados. The commission's report, published in December 1998, recommended, as expected, the replacement of the British monarch with a ceremonial President. It also proposed changes in the composition of the Senate and the substitution of a jointly administered regional court for the existing highest judicial body, the Privy Council in the United Kingdom; in February 2001 Caribbean leaders agreed to establish such a court (see below).

In November 1998, owing to a recent significant increase in the number of violent crimes involving guns, stricter penalties for unlawful possession of firearms were introduced. Amid fears that the escalation in violent crime might affect the country's tourism industry, it was announced in October 1999 that an antifirearms unit was to be established in the police force. In July 2001 the Inter-American Development Bank (see p. 308) approved a US $8.75m. loan to help Barbados modernize and strengthen its justice and penal system. In November 2002 the Government established a National Commission on Law and Order to help develop a plan of action to combat the rising crime rate. By 2006 the annual murder rate of 13 people per 100,000 was among the lowest in the Caribbean, but still double the level of the mid-1990s. In October 2007 Attorney-General Dale Marshall announced plans to reform the prison system following a riot in 2005 in which Glendairy prison was burnt down: the replacement facility incorporated the classified separation of prisoners and a parole system.

The BLP received 65% of the total votes cast at the general election held in January 1999, taking 26 of the 28 seats in the House of Assembly; the two remaining seats were won by the DLP (the NDP did not contest the election). The heavy defeat for the DLP was largely attributed to the Government's recent successes in reviving the Barbadian economy, particularly in reducing unemployment. The Prime Minister announced an expanded 14-member Cabinet, including the new post of Minister of Social Transformation, whose major concern was to be poverty alleviation.

In April 1999 Trafalgar Square, in the centre of Bridgetown, was renamed National Heroes Square, and the decision was made to replace the statue of the British Admiral Lord Horatio Nelson that stood there, with one of Errol Barrow, the country's first Prime Minister. These developments, which reinforced existing differences between Barbados' two main ethnic communities, were seen as evidence that the country was beginning its transformation into a republic, an aim set out by Arthur on the BLP's re-election. With the aim of resolving any growing divisions, the Government organized a day of national reconciliation in July, while a 13-member Committee for National Reconciliation was also established. In August 2000 Arthur announced that there would be a referendum on the replacement of the monarchy with a republic, a move that had the support of all political parties. A series of fierce political controversies in neighbouring Trinidad and Tobago over the constitutional powers of the President in 2000–02 led to an enhanced appreciation in Barbados of the need for careful consideration of the relationship between an elected Government and a ceremonial President. In early 2002 the Deputy Prime Minister and Minister of Foreign Affairs and Foreign Trade, Billie Miller, announced that new constitutional legislation would be drafted by the end of the year; however, the only change made was an amendment approved in September to override human rights judgments by the Privy

Council, making it easier to make use of the death penalty. In April 2005, following many delays, the Caribbean Court of Justice (CCJ—see above), which replaced the United Kingdom-based Privy Council, was inaugurated in Trinidad and Tobago; however, by the end of 2007 only Barbados and Guyana had instituted the Court as their supreme appellate body. The CCJ issued its first seminal ruling in November 2006, endorsing a decision of the Appeal Court of Barbados to reduce to life imprisonment the death penalties requested against two convicted murderers, and thus demonstrating the CCJ's disinclination to reinstate capital punishment (1984 saw the last execution in Barbados).

A general election was held on 21 May 2003. The BLP conducted a strong electoral campaign that, notwithstanding the recent contraction of the tourism sector, emphasized the party's solid economic record. Some voters were reportedly concerned over allegations of serious mismanagement in the tourism sector, waste disposal and other public-sector projects. None the less, Owen Arthur's BLP secured a third successive victory, attracting 55.8% of the votes cast, and securing 23 of the 30 seats in the enlarged House of Assembly. The DLP did, however increase its share of the popular vote to 44.1% (from 35.1% in 1999) and its parliamentary strength to seven, while the BLP retained four of its seats only by narrow margins. Clyde Mascoll, a former Central Bank economist, was appointed DLP and opposition leader. Arthur, meanwhile, appointed Mia Mottley, the Attorney-General and Minister of Home Affairs, as Deputy Prime Minister, making her a strong favourite to be his eventual successor.

Meanwhile, in June 2003 the Governor-General, appointed by the British monarch on the recommendation of Owen Arthur, announced that the Government intended to transform Barbados into a republic during the BLP's current five-year term in office. In February 2005 Arthur announced that a referendum on the issue would be held by the end of the year; however, owing to legislative obstacles, it was later disclosed that the referendum would be further delayed. It had been hoped that the 40th anniversary of Barbados' independence from British colonial rule, in November 2006, would induce the promised plebiscite, but a consultation remained unrealized in late 2007 as Mottley revoked a statement made in November in which she announced that the referendum would be held concurrently with the next general election, to be held in January 2008.

In November 2005 the former DLP leader and President of the party, David Thompson, was again elected to lead the party, replacing Clyde Mascoll. Thompson, who had resigned the DLP leadership in 2001 complaining of inadequate support for his policies, was in August also re-elected DLP President, in succession to the incumbent candidate, Freundel Stuart. In January 2006 Mascoll defected from the DLP to join the BLP, and was rapidly appointed to the Cabinet as Minister of State in the Ministry of Finance in February. Among several other ministerial changes effected by Arthur, the most significant was the transfer of Deputy Prime Minister Mottley to the new Ministry of Economic Affairs and Development. Dale Marshall, hitherto Minister of Industry and International Business, replaced Mottley as Attorney-General and Minister of Home Affairs.

The opposition DLP won an overwhelming majority in the general election held on 15 January 2008, securing 52.7% of the votes cast and 20 seats in the 30-seat House of Assembly. The BLP won the remaining 10 seats. Arthur had been seeking an unprecedented fourth consecutive term in office, but immediately conceded defeat to Thompson, the leader of the DLP, who was sworn in as Prime Minister on the following day, when a new Cabinet was also installed. Following his party's defeat, Arthur announced his retirement from politics; Mia Mottley was to replace him as BLP leader.

The Governments of Barbados and Trinidad and Tobago agreed in late 1999 to draft a boundary delimitation treaty and to establish a negotiating mechanism to resolve trade disputes. The issue of boundary delimitation, however, remained unresolved, and in late January 2004 the Prime Minister of Trinidad and Tobago indicated that he would refer the matter to the Caribbean Community and Common Market (CARICOM, see p. 196). Relations between the two countries worsened early in the following month after several Barbadian fishermen were arrested in Trinidad and Tobago's waters; in response, in early February Arthur called an emergency cabinet meeting, after which it was announced that sanctions would be imposed against Trinidad and Tobago manufacturers. Later that month Barbados referred the dispute for arbitration under the UN Convention on the Law of the Sea. In January 2005 the Barbados Government formed a committee to investigate whether a significant natural gas discovery off east Trinidad fell within Barbadian maritime territory. The Government of Trinidad and Tobago insisted the discovery was within its jurisdiction. Hearings on the boundary dispute commenced in October 2005 at the International Dispute Resolution Centre, and in April 2006 a tribunal ruling established a boundary between the two states. This gave Barbados a large area to the south-east of the island, which had been claimed by Trinidad and Tobago, and was thought to have potential for deep-water oil and gas exploration. The tribunal rejected the Barbadian claim to a large area to the north of Tobago, but instructed the two countries to negotiate a fishing agreement for this area 'in good faith'. Despite both sides reporting progress in talks to establish an agreement, none had been concluded by late 2007. The Permanent Court of Arbitration's ruling conferred security on these new demarcations of jurisdiction, enabling Barbados to begin auctioning oil exploration rights to leading hydrocarbon companies: as many as 60 companies had expressed an interest in the 24 blocks prior to the deadline for bids of December 2007.

In late 1996 Barbados signed an agreement with the USA to co-operate with a regional initiative to combat the illegal drugs trade. The Government signed a similar agreement with the Organization of American States (OAS) in January 2005. The US Department of the Treasury froze the assets of a Barbados-registered 'offshore' company, Kattus Corporation, in December 2006 after it was implicated in the operations of a Colombian drugs cartel. In June 2000 Barbados officially declared its acceptance of the compulsory jurisdiction of the Inter-American Court of Human Rights (see p. 361), an institution of the OAS. Meanwhile, Barbados joined CARICOM's Caribbean Single Market and Economy (CSME), which was established on 1 January 2006. The CSME was intended to enshrine the free movement of goods, services and labour throughout the CARICOM region, although only six of the organization's 15 members were signatories to the new project from its inauguration. Projections resulting from the annual CARICOM Heads of Government Conference, held in Barbados in July 2007, indicated that the CSME would be fully operational by 2015.

Government

Executive power is vested in the British monarch, represented by a Governor-General, who acts on the advice of the Cabinet. The Governor-General appoints the Prime Minister and, on the latter's recommendation, other members of the Cabinet. Legislative power is vested in the bicameral Parliament, comprising a Senate of 21 members, appointed by the Governor-General, and a House of Assembly with 30 members, elected by universal adult suffrage for five years (subject to dissolution) from single-member constituencies. The Cabinet is responsible to Parliament. The island is divided into 11 parishes, all of which are administered by the central Government.

Defence

The Barbados Defence Force was established in 1978. The total strength of the Barbados armed forces, as assessed at November 2007, was estimated at 610; the army consisted of 500 members and the navy (coastguard) 110. There was also a reserve force of 430. The defence budget for 2007 was estimated at Bds $55m.

Economic Affairs

In 2003, according to estimates by the World Bank, the island's gross national income (GNI), measured at average 2001–03 prices, was US $2,507m., equivalent to US $9,270 per head (or US $15,060 on an international purchasing-power parity basis). Between 1996 and 2006 the population increased at an average rate of 0.3% per year. Barbados' gross domestic product (GDP) per head, increased, in real terms, at an average rate of 1.5% per year during 1995–2003. Overall GDP increased, in real terms, at an average annual rate of 2.4% in 1995–2005, according to estimates by the Central Bank of Barbados. Real GDP increased by 3.9% in 2005.

Agriculture (including hunting, forestry and fishing) contributed 3.7% of GDP in 2005, when the sector engaged an estimated 3.4% of the employed labour force. Sugar was traditionally the main commodity export, earning US $23.0m. in 2004, when output was 34,358 metric tons (compared with $27m. and 58,000 tons in 2000). However, the industry was in decline, and in 2005 rum superseded sugar as the principal domestic export commodity, yielding US $25.4m. in that year. This was in spite of a recovery in sugar production in 2005, when output of 38,210 tons was recorded (an increase of 11.3% over the preceding year), generating US $22.2m. in domestic export earnings. Output fell back to an unofficial 35,000 tons in 2006. The other principal crops, primarily for local consumption, are sweet potatoes, carrots, yams and other vegetables and fruit. Fishing was also developed in the late 20th century. The GDP of the agricultural sector declined, in real terms, at an average rate of 0.1% per year during 1995–2005. According to central bank estimates, agricultural GDP decreased by 5.7% in 2004, but expanded by an estimated 9.6% in 2005.

In 2005 industry accounted for an estimated 18.0% of GDP, and 16.7% of the working population were employed in all industrial activities (manufacturing, construction, quarrying and utilities) in that year. In real terms, industrial GDP increased at an average rate of 8.4% annually in 1995–2005, according to estimates by the Central Bank. Real industrial GDP increased by an estimated 7.2% in 2005. Industrial growth was mainly attributed to expansion of the construction sector, which experienced significant growth of an estimated 13.4% in 2005, owing to initial preparations for Barbados' joint hosting of the Cricket World Cup in 2007.

Owing to fluctuations in international prices, the production of crude petroleum declined substantially from its peak in 1985, to 328,000 barrels in 1997. As a result of an onshore drilling programme begun in 1997, production increased markedly, reaching 708,500 barrels in 1999; however, production fell thereafter and stood at a provisional 348,718 barrels in 2005. Production of natural gas decreased from 46.9m. cu m in 1998 to an estimated 24m. cu m in 2005. Imports of mineral fuels accounted for 12.7% of total imports in 2004. Mining and construction contributed 7.4% of GDP and employed 9.9% of the working population in 2005.

In 2005 manufacturing contributed 7.1% of GDP and employed 5.2% of the working population. Excluding sugar factories and refineries, the principal branches of manufacturing were chemical, petroleum, rubber and plastic products, food products and beverages and tobacco. According to central bank estimates, manufacturing GDP decreased, in real terms, at an average rate of 2.5% per year during 1995–2005; it increased, however, by an estimated 2.2% in 2005.

Service industries are the main sector of the economy, accounting for 78.4% of GDP and 79.3% of employment in 2005. The combined GDP of the service sectors increased, in real terms, at an average rate of 5.1% per year during 1995–2005, according to the Central Bank. The sector expanded by an estimated 3.0% in 2005. Business and financial services contributed 20.0% of GDP in 2005. The Government has encouraged the growth of 'offshore' financial facilities, particularly through the negotiation of double taxation agreements with other countries. In November 2004 there were 4,635 international business companies, 413 exempt insurance companies and, in January 2008, 56 'offshore' banks were registered. Barbados has an active anti-money-laundering regime, which was further strengthened by new legislation in 1998. Despite this, in May 2000 the Organisation for Economic Co-operation and Development (OECD, see p. 347) placed Barbados on a list of tax havens that were likely to incur countermeasures if they failed to modify tax regimes in line with OECD requirements. However, Barbados was removed from the OECD list in January 2002. Tourism made a direct contribution of an estimated 9.4% to GDP in 2005, when it employed 9.7% of the working population. Receipts from the tourism industry totalled US $905m. in 2005. Partly because of the reduction in the number of US tourists following the terrorist attacks in the USA of September 2001 and partly owing to the US Government's 'war on terror' that commenced shortly afterwards, stopover tourist arrivals decreased from 545,027 in 2000 to 497,899 in 2002, while cruise-ship passenger arrivals also decreased over the same period by 0.9%, to 523,253. By 2004, however, the number of stop-over tourist arrivals had recovered to some 551,500 in that year—a record figure—with the number of cruise-ship passengers totalling an estimated 721,300. Conversely, in 2005 the sector contracted slightly (by 0.7%), with stopover tourist arrivals decreasing to 547,500, and cruise-ship passenger numbers falling to 563,600. The downturn was largely attributed to pronounced increases in international fuel prices and the consequent curtailment of cruise-ship routes. Stop-over arrivals increased slightly in 2006, to 562,600, although cruise-ship passenger numbers continued to decline, falling to 539,100 in that year. Amendments to the Western Hemisphere Travel Initiative—ratified by US Congress on 4 October 2006—requiring all US citizens travelling to and from the Caribbean to hold a valid passport, were described by the Caribbean Tourism Organization as potentially severely damaging to the region's tourism industry; Barbados was exploring promotion of its tourism facilities beyond the US market, particularly focusing on the United Kingdom and the rest of the Caribbean, in an effort to offset the feared fall in arrivals. The US measures were to be implemented as early as January 2007, although cruise-ship passengers were to be exempt from the ruling until 1 January 2009.

In 2005 Barbados recorded a visible trade deficit of US $1,085.6m., while there was a deficit of $386.7m. on the current account of the balance of payments. In 2005 the USA was both the principal source of imports (36.5%) and the largest single recipient of exports (14.6%). Trinidad and Tobago was the second most important trading partner in 2003, accounting for 19.8% of imports and 11.4% of exports. The principal exports in 2004 were chemicals (13.4% of total exports), raw cane sugar (11.8%) and rum (11.4%). The principal imports were machinery and transport equipment and food and live animals.

For the financial year ending 31 March 2006 there was an estimated total budgetary deficit of Bds $237.9m., equivalent to 3.9% of GDP. At December 2005 the total external debt of Barbados was some $1,523m.; the cost of foreign debt-servicing, at $236m., was equivalent to 6.7% of the value of goods and non-factor services exports in that year. The average annual rate of inflation was 2.4% in 1995–2005. Consumer prices rose by an average of 6.0% in 2005 and by 7.3% in 2006. By the end of December 2005 the unemployment rate was 9.1%.

Barbados is a member of the Caribbean Community and Common Market (CARICOM, see p. 196) and of CARICOM's Caribbean Single Market and Economy, which was launched on 1 January 2006 (see Recent History), of the Inter-American Development Bank (see p. 308), of the Latin American Economic System (see p. 413) and of the Association of Caribbean States (see p. 411).

Political stability and consensus have contributed to the economic strengths of Barbados. Tourism dominates the economy but 'offshore' banking and sugar and rum production are also important. The sugar industry, however, has come under increased pressure to reform in recent years, particularly as further liberalization of international trade has made the island's principal export less competitive. A 36% retraction, to be implemented incrementally over three years, of the preferential markets and subsidized prices for sugar exports provided by the European Union (EU, see p. 244) was initiated in July 2006. Dissemination of EU funds to ameliorate the economic impact of the cuts was delayed until mid-2007, when an agreement was signed immediately providing US $3m. to Barbados. In early 2006 the Government allotted $150m. for the construction of a sugar-cane plant designed to produce electricity, ethanol and refined and speciality sugars for the local economy, as well as speciality sugar for export markets. Plans were also announced to cultivate more sugar-cane for fuel use on the island's existing sugar plantations. A consequence of the falling sugar prices has been a changing landscape, as fields of sugar cane are replaced with fruit bushes and the planting of vegetables. Tourists holidayed in Barbados in record numbers in 2006, when growth of some 2.8% was recorded, although this was offset by another fall in lower-spending cruise-ship passengers. The increase in stop-over visitors was attributed to development of facilities and a concerted promotion of the country overseas. The tourism sector was expected to perform well in 2007, owing to Barbados' joint hosting of the Cricket World Cup. Indeed, the sector recorded an 18% increase in the first six months of the year, compared with the same period in 2006. Further economic benefits from the Cricket World Cup were evident in the construction sector, both in preparation for the event, and in terms of improved infrastructure. GDP growth was forecast at 4.1% in 2007, compared with 3.8% in 2006, although this figure was expected to decline to 3.3% in 2008. Despite relatively strong growth, in September 2006 the IMF cautioned that stringent fiscal policies were necessary to control escalating credit levels, lower outstanding debt and address other 'significant macroeconomic imbalances'. It was expected that the new Democratic Labour Party Government, which took office following a general election in January 2008, would not significantly alter the economic policies pursued by its predecessor.

Education

Education is compulsory for 12 years, between five and 16 years of age. Primary education begins at the age of five and lasts for seven years. Secondary education, beginning at 12 years of age, lasts for five years. In 2004/05 enrolment at primary schools included 97.2% of pupils in the relevant age-group, and the comparable enrolment ratio at secondary schools was 95.1%. Tuition at all government schools is free. In the same year enrolment at tertiary level was some 48% of the relevant age-group (males 38.5%; females 57.5%). In 1998 7,538 students were enrolled at universities or similar institutions. Degree courses in arts, law, education, natural sciences and social sciences are offered at the Cave Hill campus of the University of the West Indies, a regional university comprising three principal campuses. A two-year clinical-training programme for medical students is conducted by the School of Clinic Medicine and Research of the University, while an in-service training programme for teachers is provided by the School of Education. A further three tertiary level institutions operate under the ambit of the Ministry of Education in Barbados. Government expenditure on education for 2005/06 was $425.7m., constituting 21.5% of total current expenditure. A US $213m. programme for curriculum reform and the introduction of technology into education, Edutech 2000, was scheduled for completion by 2010.

Public Holidays

2008: 1 January (New Year's Day), 21 January (Errol Barrow Day), 21 March (Good Friday), 24 March (Easter Monday), 28 April (National Heroes' Day), 1 May (Labour Day), 12 May (Whit Monday), 1 August (Emancipation Day), 4 August (Kadooment Day), 30 November (Independence Day), 25–26 December (Christmas).

2009: 1 January (New Year's Day), 21 January (Errol Barrow Day), 10 April (Good Friday), 13 April (Easter Monday), 28 April (National Heroes' Day), 4 May (Labour Day), 1 June (Whit Monday), 3 August (Emancipation Day), 4 August (Kadooment Day), 30 November (Independence Day), 25–26 December (Christmas).

Weights and Measures

The metric system is used.

Statistical Survey

Sources (unless otherwise stated): Barbados Statistical Service, National Insurance Bldg, 3rd Floor, Fairchild St, Bridgetown; tel. 427-7841; fax 435-2198; e-mail barstats@caribsurf.com; internet www.barbados.gov.bb/bgis.htm; Central Bank of Barbados, Tom Adams Financial Centre, Spry St, POB 1016, Bridgetown; tel. 436-6870; fax 427-9559; e-mail cbb.libr@caribsurf.com; internet www.centralbank.org.bb.

AREA AND POPULATION

Area: 430 sq km (166 sq miles).

Population: 257,082 (provisional) at census of 2 May 1990; 250,010 (males 119,926, females 130,084) (provisional) at census of 5 May 2000; 273,987 at December 2006.

Density (December 2006): 637.2 per sq km.

Ethnic Groups (*de jure* population, excl. persons resident in institutions, 1990 census): Black 228,683; White 8,022; Mixed race 5,886; Total (incl. others) 247,288.

Principal Town: Bridgetown (capital), population 5,928 at 1990 census; *Mid-2005* (population in '000, incl. suburbs): Bridgetown 142 (Source: UN, *World Urbanization Prospects: The 2005 Revision*).

Births, Marriages and Deaths (2002, provisional): Live births 3,812 (birth rate 14.1 per 1,000); Marriages (2000) 3,518 (marriage rate 13.1 per 1,000); Deaths 2,285 (death rate 8.4 per 1,000). Source: partly UN, *Population and Vital Statistics Report*.

Expectation of Life (years at birth, WHO estimates): 74.8 (males 71.0; females 78.4) in 2005. Source: WHO, *World Health Statistics*.

Economically Active Population (labour force sample survey, '000 persons aged 15 years and over, excl. armed forces, 2005, provisional): Agriculture, forestry and fishing 4.5; Manufacturing 7.0; Electricity, gas and water 2.1; Construction and quarrying 13.2; Wholesale and retail trade 18.5; Tourism 12.9; Transport, storage and communications 5.7; Finance, insurance, real estate and business services 10.8; Community, social and personal services 57.9; Statistical discrepancy 0.8; *Total employed* 133.5 (males 69.5, females 64.0); Unemployed 13.3; *Total labour force* 146.8 (males 75.0, females 71.8). Note: Totals may not be equivalent to the sum of components, owing to rounding.

HEALTH AND WELFARE

Key Indicators

Total Fertility Rate (children per woman, 2005): 1.5.

Under-5 Mortality Rate (per 1,000 live births, 2005): 12.

HIV/AIDS (% of persons aged 15–49, 2005, estimate): 1.5.

Physicians (per 1,000 head, 1999): 1.21.

Hospital Beds (per 1,000 head, 2004): 7.3.

Health Expenditure (2004): US $ per head (PPP): 1,150.7.

Health Expenditure (2004): % of GDP: 7.1.

Health Expenditure (2004): public (% of total): 63.5.

Access to Sanitation (% of persons, 2002): 99.

Human Development Index (2005): ranking: 31.

Human Development Index (2005): value: 0.892.

For sources and definitions, see explanatory note on p. vi.

AGRICULTURE, ETC.

Principal Crops ('000 metric tons, 2006, FAO estimates): Sweet potatoes 2.0; Yams 1.2; Avocados 0.6; Pulses 0.8; Coconuts 2.0; Tomatoes 1.1; Cucumbers 1.8; Chillies and peppers 1.3; Dry onions 0.6; String beans 1.0; Carrots and turnips 1.0; Okra 1.6; Green corn 0.7; Other vegetables (excl. melons) 4.0; Bananas 0.7; Other fruit 2.3.

Livestock ('000 head, year ending September 2006, FAO estimates): Horses 1.2; Asses, mules and hinnies 4.2; Cattle 10.3; Pigs 19.0; Sheep 10.8; Goats 5.1; Poultry 3,400.

Livestock Products ('000 metric tons, 2006): Cattle meat 0.3; Pig meat 2.1; Chicken meat 13.6; Cows' milk 6.8; Hen eggs 2.0.

Forestry ('000 cubic metres, FAO estimates): Roundwood removals 5 (output assumed to be unchanged since 1993).

Fishing (metric tons, live weight, 2005): Total catch 1,869 (Yellowfin tuna 293; Flyingfishes 864; Common dolphinfish 323).

Source: FAO.

MINING

Production (2005, provisional): Natural gas 24m. cu m; Crude petroleum 348,718 barrels; Cement 340,696,000 metric tons.

INDUSTRY

Selected Products (2003, unless otherwise indicated): Raw sugar 38,210 metric tons (2005); Rum 11,000,000 litres; Beer 6,900,000 litres; Cigarettes 65m. (1995); Batteries 17,165 (official estimate, 1998); Electric energy 793m. kWh (2005). Sources: partly UN, *Industrial Commodity Statistics Yearbook*, and IMF, *Barbados: Statistical Appendix* (May 2004).

FINANCE

Currency and Exchange Rates: 100 cents = 1 Barbados dollar (Bds $). *Sterling, US Dollar and Euro Equivalents* (31 December 2007): £1 sterling = Bds $4.007; US $1 = Bds $2.000; €1 = Bds $2.944; Bds $100 = £24.96 = US $50.00 = €33.97. *Exchange Rate*: Fixed at US $1 = Bds $2.000 since 1986.

Budget (Bds $ million, year ending 31 March 2006): *Revenue:* Tax revenue 1,885.7 (Direct taxes 765.6; Indirect taxes 1,120.1); Non-tax revenue 133.0; Total 2,018.8. *Expenditure:* Current 1,955.7 (Wages and salaries 674.3, Other goods and services 240.9, Interest payments 289.7, Transfers and subsidies 750.8); Capital (incl. net lending 67.6) 300.9; Total 2,256.7.

International Reserves (US $ million at 31 December 2006): IMF special drawing rights 0.03; Reserve position in IMF 8.20; Foreign exchange 627.86; Total 636.09. Source: IMF, *International Financial Statistics*.

Money Supply (Bds $ million at 31 December 2006): Currency outside banks 465.8; Demand deposits at commercial banks 1,903.1;

BARBADOS   *Directory*

Total money (incl. others) 2,473.7. Source: IMF, *International Financial Statistics*.

Cost of Living (Index of Retail Prices; base: 2000 = 100): 105.9 in 2004; 112.3 in 2005; 120.5 in 2006. Source: IMF, *International Financial Statistics*.

Gross Domestic Product (Bds $ million at constant 1974 prices): 976.1 in 2002; 996.0 in 2003; 1,043.4 in 2004; 1,083.9 in 2005. Source: Caribbean Development Bank, *Social and Economic Indicators*.

Expenditure on the Gross Domestic Product (Bds $ million at current prices, 2005): Government final consumption expenditure 1,293.6; Private final consumption expenditure 4,077.1; Increase in stocks 728.4; Gross fixed capital formation 764.6; *Total domestic expenditure* 6,863.7; Exports of goods and services 2,940.8; *Less* Imports of goods and services 3,682.2; *GDP in purchasers' values* 6,122.3. Source: Caribbean Development Bank, *Social and Economic Indicators*.

Gross Domestic Product by Economic Activity (estimates, Bds $ million at current prices, 2005): Agriculture, hunting, forestry and fishing 185; Mining and quarrying 44; Manufacturing 357; Electricity, gas and water 171; Construction 329; Wholesale and retail trade 886; Hotels and restaurants 569; Transport, storage and communications 328; Finance, insurance, real estate and business services 1,004; Government services 820; Other community, social and personal services 322; *GDP at factor cost* 5,014; Indirect taxes, *less* subsidies 1,108; *GDP in purchasers' values* 6,122.

Balance of Payments (US $ million, 2005): Exports of goods f.o.b. 378.6; Imports of goods f.o.b. −1,464.2; *Trade balance* −1,085.6; Exports of services 1,457.4; Imports of services −679.7; *Balance on goods and services* −307.9; Other income received 85.0; Other income paid −257.0; *Balance on goods, services and income* −479.9; Current transfers received 160.4; Current transfers paid −67.2; *Current balance* −386.7; Direct investment abroad −9.2; Direct investment from abroad 62.0; Portfolio investment assets −76.4; Portfolio investment liabilities 98.3; Financial derivatives assets 1.6; Financial derivatives liabilities 5.0; Other investment assets −238.5; Other investment liabilities 548.5; Net errors and omissions 17.8; *Overall balance* 22.3. Source: IMF, *International Financial Statistics*.

EXTERNAL TRADE

Principal Commodities (US $ million, 2004): *Imports c.i.f.*: Food and live animals 169.2; Beverages and tobacco 34.2; Mineral fuels, lubricants, etc. 13.9 (Refined petroleum products 5.0); Chemicals 124.2 (Medicaments 34.2); Basic manufactures 187.1 (Metal manufactures excl. iron and steel 46.4); Machinery and transport equipment 373.9 (Telecommunication equipment 78.5; Road vehicles 87.6); Miscellaneous manufactured articles 139.2; Total (incl. others) 1,093.7. *Exports f.o.b.*: Food and live animals 44.9 (Raw cane sugar 23.0); Beverages and tobacco 26.8 (Rum 22.3); Mineral fuels, lubricants, etc. 15.3 (all crude petroleum); Chemicals 26.3 (Medicaments 8.8); Basic manufactures 31.8 (Portland cement 12.6); Machinery and transport equipment 27.9; Miscellaneous manufactured articles 14.9; Total (incl. others) 195.0. *2005* (Bds $ million): Total imports 3,208.9; Total exports 718.9.

Principal Trading Partners (US $ million, 2004): *Imports c.i.f.*: Brazil 21.0; Canada 52.4; China, People's Republic 32.7; France 16.7; Germany 20.1; Guyana 15.5; Italy 9.4; Japan 60.4; Korea, Republic 35.9; Mexico 17.6; Netherlands 16.1; New Zealand 16.3; Sweden 6.4; Trinidad and Tobago 83.5; United Kingdom 77.2; USA 477.1; Total (incl. others) 1,093.7. *Exports f.o.b.*: Antigua and Barbuda 5.4; Canada 5.2; Dominica 3.9; France 3.5; Grenada 7.1; Guyana 7.0; Jamaica 12.3; Saint Christopher and Nevis 5.6; Saint Lucia 13.0; Saint Vincent and the Grenadines 9.6; Suriname 3.4; Trinidad and Tobago 27.8; United Kingdom 29.8; USA 38.9; Total (incl. others) 195.0.

Source: UN, *International Trade Statistics Yearbook*.

TRANSPORT

Road Traffic (motor vehicles in use, 2002): Private cars 81,648; Buses and coaches 736; Lorries and vans 6,962; Motor cycles and mopeds 1,856; Road tractors 921. Source: International Road Federation, *World Road Statistics*.

Shipping (estimated freight traffic, '000 metric tons, 1990): Goods loaded 206; Goods unloaded 538 (Source: UN, *Monthly Bulletin of Statistics*). *Total Goods Handled* ('000 metric tons, 2003): 1,003 (Source: Barbados Port Authority). *Merchant Fleet* (vessels registered at 31 December 2006): Number of vessels 104; Total displacement 607,215 grt (Source: Lloyd's Register-Fairplay, *World Fleet Statistics*).

Civil Aviation (1994): Aircraft movements 36,100; Freight loaded 5,052.3 metric tons; Freight unloaded 8,548.3 metric tons.

TOURISM

Tourist Arrivals ('000 persons): *Stop-overs*: 551.5 in 2004; 547.5 in 2005; 562.6 in 2006. *Cruise-ship Passengers*: 721.3 in 2004; 563.6 in 2005; 539.1 in 2006. Source: partly Caribbean Development Bank, *Social and Economic Indicators*.

Tourist Arrivals by Country ('000 persons, 2005): Antigua and Barbuda 7.1; Canada 47.7; Germany 7.0; Grenada 7.9; Guyana 18.7; Jamaica 8.0; Saint Lucia 15.6; Saint Vincent and the Grenadines 13.9; Trinidad and Tobago 30.9; United Kingdom 201.4; USA 131.0; Total (incl. others) 547.5. Source: World Tourism Organization.

Tourism Receipts (US $ million, incl. passenger transport): 767 in 2003; 785 in 2004; 905 in 2005.

Source: World Tourism Organization.

COMMUNICATIONS MEDIA

Radio Receivers (1999): 175,000 in use.

Television Receivers (2000): 83,000 in use.

Telephones (2006): 134,900 main lines in use.

Facsimile Machines (year ending 31 March 1997): 1,800 in use.

Mobile Cellular Telephones (2006): 206,200 subscribers.

Personal Computers (2005): 40,000 in use.

Internet Users (2006): 160,000.

Broadband Subscribers (2006): 31,900.

Newspapers: *Daily* (1996): 2 (circulation 53,000). *Non-daily* (1990): 4 (estimated circulation 95,000).

Sources: partly UNESCO, *Statistical Yearbook*, UN, *Statistical Yearbook*, and International Telecommunication Union.

EDUCATION

Pre-primary (1995/96): 84 schools; 529 teachers; 4,689 pupils. *2004*: 5,901 pupils.

Primary (2002): 109 schools; 1,823 teachers; 29,502 pupils. *2004*: 22,327 pupils.

Secondary (2002): 32 schools; 1,389 teachers; 21,436 pupils. *2004*: 21,300 pupils.

Tertiary (2002): 4 schools; 339 teachers; 11,226 students.

Source: Ministry of Education, Youth Affairs and Sport.

Adult Literacy Rate (UNESCO estimates): 99.7% (males 99.7%; females 99.7%) in 2003. Source: UN Development Programme, *Human Development Report*.

Directory

The Constitution

The parliamentary system has been established since the 17th century, when the first Assembly sat, in 1639, and the Charter of Barbados was granted, in 1652. A new Constitution came into force on 30 November 1966, when Barbados became independent. Under its terms, protection is afforded to individuals from slavery and forced labour, from inhuman treatment, deprivation of property, arbitrary search and entry, and racial discrimination; freedom of conscience, of expression, assembly, and movement are guaranteed.

Executive power is nominally vested in the British monarch, as Head of State, represented in Barbados by a Governor-General, who appoints the Prime Minister and, on the advice of the Prime Minister, appoints other ministers and some senators.

The Cabinet consists of the Prime Minister, appointed by the Governor-General as being the person best able to command a majority in the House of Assembly, and not fewer than five other ministers. Provision is also made for a Privy Council, presided over by the Governor-General.

Parliament consists of the Governor-General and a bicameral legislature, comprising the Senate and the House of Assembly. The Senate has 21 members: 12 appointed by the Governor-General on the advice of the Prime Minister, two on the advice of the Leader of the Opposition and seven as representatives of such interests as the Governor-General considers appropriate. The House of Assembly has (since 2003) 30 members, elected by universal adult suffrage for a term of five years (subject to dissolution). The minimum voting age is 18 years.

The Constitution also provides for the establishment of Service Commissions for the Judicial and Legal Service, the Public Service, the Police Service and the Statutory Boards Service. These Commissions are exempt from legal investigation; they have executive powers relating to appointments, dismissals and disciplinary control of the services for which they are responsible.

The Government

HEAD OF STATE

Monarch: HM Queen Elizabeth II (succeeded to the throne 6 February 1952).
Governor-General: Sir Clifford Husbands (appointed 1 June 1996).

THE CABINET
(April 2008)

Prime Minister and Minister of Finance, Economic Affairs and Development, Labour, Civil Service and Energy: David Thompson.
Attorney-General and Minister of Home Affairs: Freundel Stuart.
Minister of Agriculture and Rural Development: Haynesley Benn.
Minister of Trade, Industry and Commerce: George Hutson.
Minister of Education and Human Resources Development: Ronald Jones.
Minister of Foreign Affairs, Foreign Trade and International Business: Christopher Sinckler.
Minister of Health, National Insurance and Social Security: Dr David Estwick.
Minister of Housing and Lands: Michael Lashley.
Minister of Community Development and Culture: Steven Blackett.
Minister of Family, Youth Affairs, Sports and Environment: Dr Esther Byer-Suckoo.
Minister of Social Care, Constituency Empowerment and Urban Development: Dr Dennis Lowe.
Minister of Tourism: Richard Sealy.
Minister of Transport, Works and International Transport: John Boyce.
Minister of State in the Prime Minister's Office with Responsibility for Management, Administration and Training: Maxine McClean.
Minister of State in the Prime Minister's Office with Responsibility for Finance and Energy: Darcy Boyce.
Minister of State in the Prime Minister's Office with Responsibility for Employment, Labour Relations and the Social Partnership: Arni Walters.
Minister of State in the Ministry of Foreign Affairs, Foreign Trade and International Business: Donville Inniss.
Minister of State in the Ministry of Social Care, Constituency Empowerment and Urban Development: Patrick Todd.

MINISTRIES

Office of the Prime Minister: Government Headquarters, Bay St, St Michael; tel. 436-6435; fax 436-9280; e-mail info@primeminister.gov.bb; internet www.primeminister.gov.bb.
Ministry of Agriculture and Rural Development: Graeme Hall, POB 505, Christ Church; tel. 428-4150; fax 420-8444; e-mail info@agriculture.gov.bb; internet www.agriculture.gov.bb.
Ministry of Community Development and Culture: Government Headquarters, Bay St, St Michael; tel. 435-5133.
Ministry of Education and Human Resources Development: Elsie Payne Complex, Constitution Rd, St Michael; tel. 430-2705; fax 436-2411; e-mail mined1@caribsurf.com; internet www.mes.gov.bb.
Ministry of Family, Youth Affairs, Sports and Environment: Constitution Rd, St Michael; tel. 430-2704; fax 436-8909.
Ministry of Finance, Economic Affairs and Development, Labour, Civil Service and Energy: Government Headquarters, Bay St, St Michael; tel. 426-3179; fax 436-9280.
Ministry of Foreign Affairs, Foreign Trade and International Business: 1 Culloden Rd, St Michael; tel. 431-2200; fax 429-6652; e-mail info@foreign.gov.bb; internet www.foreign.gov.bb.
Ministry of Health, National Insurance and Social Security: Jemmott's Lane, St Michael; tel. 426-4669; fax 426-5570.
Ministry of Home Affairs: General Post Office Bldg, Level 5, Cheapside, Bridgetown; tel. 228-8950; fax 437-3794; e-mail mha@caribsurf.com.
Ministry of Housing and Lands: National Housing Corpn Bldg, 'The Garden', Country Rd, St Michael; tel. 467-7801; fax 435-0174; S. P. Musson Bldg, 1st Floor, Hinks St, Bridgetown; tel. 467-5710; fax 437-8859.
Ministry of Social Care, Constituency Empowerment and Urban Development: 4th Floor, Warrens Office Complex, St Michael; tel. 310-1604; fax 424-2908; e-mail info@socialtransformation.gov.bb.
Ministry of Tourism: Sherbourne Conference Centre, Two Mile Hill, St Michael; tel. 430-7504; fax 436-4828; e-mail barmot@sunbeach.net; internet www.barmot.gov.bb.
Ministry of Trade, Industry and Commerce: Pelican Industrial Estate, Fontabelle, St Michael; tel. 426-4452; fax 431-0056.
Ministry of Transport, Works and International Transport: The Pine, St Michael; tel. 429-2863; fax 437-8133; e-mail mpttech@caribsurf.com.
Office of the Attorney-General: Sir Frank Walcott Bldg, Culloden Rd, St Michael; tel. 431-7700; fax 228-5433; e-mail attygen@caribsurf.com.bb.

Legislature

PARLIAMENT

Senate

President: Sir Fred Gollop.
There are 21 members.

House of Assembly

Speaker: Ishmael Roett.
General Election, 15 January 2008

Party	% of total	Seats
Democratic Labour Party (DLP)	52.66	20
Barbados Labour Party (BLP)	47.14	10
Total (incl. others)	100.00	30

Election Commission

Electoral and Boundaries Commission: National Insurance Bldg, Fairchild St, Bridgetown; tel. 426-5909; fax 228-8132; e-mail donvillej@hotmail.com; Chair. Donville Johnson.

Political Organizations

Barbados Labour Party (BLP): Grantley Adams House, 111 Roebuck St, Bridgetown; tel. 429-1990; fax 427-8792; e-mail will99@caribsurf.com; internet labourparty.wordpress.com; f. 1938 as Barbados Progressive League, name changed as above 1946; moderate social democrat; Leader and Chair. Mia Mottley; Gen. Sec. William Duguid.
Clement Payne Movement (CPM): Crumpton St, Bridgetown; tel. 435-2334; fax 437-8216; internet cpmbarbados2@yahoo.com; f. 1988 in honour of national hero; non-electoral founding assoc. of the PEP; links to the Pan-Caribbean Congress and promotes international Pan-Africanism; Pres. David A. Comissiong; Gen. Sec. Bobby Clarke.

> **People's Empowerment Party (PEP):** Crumpton St, Bridgetown; tel. 429-9902; fax 437-8216; e-mail pepbarbados@yahoo.com; f. 2006 by the Clement Payne Movt; left-of-centre; Leader David Comissiong.

BARBADOS

Democratic Labour Party (DLP): 'Kennington', George St, Belleville, St Michael; tel. 429-3104; fax 427-0548; internet www.dlpbarbados.org; f. 1955; Pres. and Leader DAVID J. H. THOMPSON.

Diplomatic Representation

EMBASSIES AND HIGH COMMISSIONS IN BARBADOS

Brazil: Sunjet House, 3rd Floor, Fairchild St, Bridgetown; tel. 427-1735; fax 427-1744; e-mail brembarb@sunbeach.net; internet www.brazilbb.org; Ambassador ORLANDO GALVÊAS OLIVEIRA.

Canada: Bishops Court Hill, Pine Rd, POB 404, Bridgetown; tel. 429-3550; fax 429-3780; e-mail bdgtn@international.gc.ca; internet geo.international.gc.ca/latin-america/barbados; High Commissioner DAVID MARSHALL.

China, People's Republic: 17 Golf View Terrace, Golf Club Rd, POB 428, Rockley, Christ Church; tel. 435-6890; fax 435-8300; e-mail chinaemb_bb@mfa.gov.cn; internet bb.chineseembassy.org; Ambassador LIU HUANXING.

Cuba: Palm View, Erdiston Dr., Pine Hill, St Michael; tel. 435-2769; fax 435-2534; e-mail embajadadecuba@sunbeach.net; Ambassador PEDRO ANDRÉS GARCÍA ROQUE.

United Kingdom: Lower Collymore Rock, POB 676, Bridgetown; tel. 430-7800; fax 430-7813; e-mail britishhcb@sunbeach.net; internet www.britishhighcommission.gov.uk/barbados; High Commissioner DUNCAN JOHN RUSHWORTH TAYLOR.

USA: Wildey Business Park, Wildey, POB 302, Bridgetown BB 14006; tel. 436-4950; fax 227-4073; internet bridgetown.usembassy.gov; Ambassador MARY OURISMAN.

Venezuela: Hastings, Main Rd, Christ Church; tel. 435-7619; fax 435-7830; e-mail embaven@sunbeach.net; internet www.geocities.com/embaven; Ambassador JUAN CARLOS VALDEZ.

Judicial System

Justice is administered by the Supreme Court of Judicature, which consists of a High Court and a Court of Appeal. Final appeal lies with the Caribbean Court of Justice (CCJ), which was inaugurated in Port of Spain, Trinidad and Tobago, on 16 April 2005; previously, final appeals were administered by the Judicial Committee of the Privy Council in the United Kingdom. There are Magistrates' Courts for lesser offences, with appeal to the Court of Appeal.

Supreme Court: Judiciary Office, Coleridge St, Bridgetown; tel. 426-3461; fax 246-2405.

Chief Justice: Sir DAVID SIMMONS.

Justices of Appeal: FREDERICK WATERMAN; PETER A. WILLIAMS; JOHN CONNELL; SHERMAN MOORE.

Judges of the High Court: ELNETH KENTISH; CHRISTOPHER BLACKMAN; WILLIAM CHANDLER; MARGARET REIFER; KAYE GOODRIDGE; RANDALL WORRELL; JACQUELINE CORNELIUS; SONIA RICHARDS.

Registrar of the Supreme Court: S. MAUREEN CRANE-SCOTT.

Office of the Attorney-General: Sir Frank Walcott Bldg, Culloden Rd, St Michael; tel. 431-7700; fax 228-5433; e-mail attygen@caribsurf.com; Dir of Public Prosecutions CHARLES LEACOCK; e-mail cbleacock@inaccs.com.bb.

Religion

More than 100 religious denominations and sects are represented in Barbados, but the vast majority of the population profess Christianity. About 40% of the total population are Anglican, while the Pentecostal (8%) and Methodist (7%) churches are next in importance. There are also small groups of Hindus, Muslims and Jews.

CHRISTIANITY

Barbados Christian Council

Caribbean Conference of Churches Bldg, George St and Collymore Rock, St Michael; tel. 426-6014

The Anglican Communion

Anglicans in Barbados are adherents of the Church in the Province of the West Indies, comprising eight dioceses. The Archbishop of the Province is the Bishop of Nassau and the Bahamas, resident in Nassau, the Bahamas. In Barbados there is a Provincial Office (St George's Church, St George) and an Anglican Theological College (Codrington College, St John).

Bishop of Barbados: Rt Rev. JOHN WALDER DUNLOP HOLDER, Anglican Diocese of Barbados, Mandeville House, Henry's Lane, Collymore Rock, St Michael; tel. 426-2761; fax 426-0871; e-mail mandeville@sunbeach.com; internet barbados.anglican.org.

The Roman Catholic Church

Barbados comprises a single diocese (formed in January 1990, when the diocese of Bridgetown-Kingstown was divided), which is suffragan to the archdiocese of Port of Spain (Trinidad and Tobago). At 31 December 2005 there were an estimated 10,443 adherents in the diocese. The Bishop participates in the Antilles Episcopal Conference (currently based in Port of Spain, Trinidad and Tobago).

Bishop of Bridgetown: (vacant), Bishop's House, Ladymeade Gardens, St Michael, POB 1223, Bridgetown; tel. 426-3510; fax 429-6198.

Other Churches

Baptist Churches of Barbados: National Baptist Convention, President Kennedy Dr., Bridgetown; tel. 429-2697.

Church of God (Caribbean Atlantic Assembly): St Michael's Plaza, St Michael's Row, POB 1021, Bridgetown; tel. 427-5770; Pres. Rev. VICTOR BABB.

Church of Jesus Christ of Latter-Day Saints (Mormons)—West Indies Mission: Bridgetown; tel. 435-8595; fax 435-8278.

Church of the Nazarene: District Office, Eagle Hall, St Michael; tel. 425-1067; fax 435-6486.

Methodist Church: Bethel Church Office, Bay St, Bridgetown; tel. and fax 426-2223; e-mail methodist@caribsurf.com.

Moravian Church: Calvary Office, Roebuck St, St Michael; tel. 426-2337; fax 228-4381; e-mail calvarymoravian@sunbeach.net; Supt Rev. ERROL CONNOR.

Seventh-day Adventists (East Caribbean Conference): Brydens Ave, Brittons Hill, POB 223, St Michael; tel. 429-7234; fax 429-7234; e-mail info@eastcarib.org; internet eastcarib.org; Pres. DAVID BECKLES.

Wesleyan Holiness Church: General Headquarters, Whitepark Rd, Bank Hall; tel. 429-4888; internet www.carringtonwesleyan.org; District Supt Rev. C. WILLIAMS.

Other denominations include the Abundant Life Assembly, the African Orthodox Church, the Apostolic Church, the Assemblies of Brethren, the Berean Bible Brethren, the Bethel Evangelical Church, Christ is the Answer Family Church, the Church of God the Prophecy, the Ethiopian Orthodox Church, the Full Gospel Assembly, Love Gospel Assembly, the New Testament Church of God, the Pentecostal Assemblies of the West Indies, the People's Cathedral, the Salvation Army, Presbyterian congregations, the African Methodist Episcopal Church, the Mt Olive United Holy Church of America and Jehovah's Witnesses.

ISLAM

In 2005 there were an estimated 2,700 Muslims in Barbados.

Islamic Teaching Centre: Harts Gap, Hastings, Bridgetown; tel. 427-0120.

JUDAISM

Jewish Community: Nidhe Israel and Shaara Tzedek Synagogue, Rockley New Rd, POB 651, Bridgetown; tel. 427-0703; fax 436-8807; Pres. RACHELLE ALTMAN; Sec. SHARON ORAN.

HINDUISM

At the census of 1980 there were 411 Hindus on the island.

Hindu Community: Hindu Temple, Roberts Complex, Government Hill, St Michael, BB 11066; tel. 434-4638.

The Press

Barbados Advocate: POB 230, St Michael; tel. 467-2000; fax 434-1000; e-mail news@barbadosadvocate.com; internet www.barbadosadvocate.com; f. 1895; daily; Editor (vacant); circ. 11,413.

The Broad Street Journal: Plantation Complex, St Lawrence Main Rd, Christ Church; tel. 420-6245; fax 420-5477; e-mail bsj@caribsurf.com; internet www.broadstreetnews.com; f. 1993; weekly; business; Editor PATRICK R. HOYOS.

The Nation: Nation House, Fontabelle, POB 1203, St Michael; tel. 430-5400; fax 427-6968; e-mail nationnews@sunbeach.net; internet www.nationnews.com; f. 1973; daily; also publishes *The Midweek Nation*, *The Weekend Nation*, *The Sun on Saturday*, *The Sunday Sun* (q.v.) and *The Visitor* (a free publ. for tourists); owned by One Caribbean Media Ltd; Publr VIVIAN-ANNE GITTENS; Exec. Editor ROXANNE GIBBS; circ. 23,144 (Mon.–Fri.), 33,084 (weekend).

BARBADOS
Directory

Sunday Advocate: POB 230, St Michael; tel. 467-2000; fax 434-1000; e-mail news@sunbeach.net; internet www.barbadosadvocate.com; f. 1895; Editor REUDON EVERSLEY; circ. 17,490.

The Sunday Sun: Nation House, Fontabelle, St Michael; tel. 430-5400; fax 427-6968; e-mail sundaysun@sunbeach.net; internet www.nationnews.com; f. 1977; owned by One Caribbean Media Ltd; Dir HAROLD HOYTE; circ. 48,824.

NEWS AGENCIES

Caribbean Media Corporation (CMC): Harbour Industrial Estate, Unit 1B, Bldg 6A, St Michael, BB 11145; tel. 467-1037; fax 429-4355; e-mail admin@cmccaribbean.com; internet www.cananews.net; f. 2000 by merger of Caribbean News Agency (CANA) and Caribbean Broadcasting Union; COO ERROL CLARKE.

Foreign Bureaux

Inter Press Service (IPS) (Italy): POB 697, Bridgetown; tel. 426-4474; e-mail ipsnoramcarib@ipsnews.net; Regional Editor KATHERINE STAPP.

Agence France-Presse (AFP), Agencia EFE (Spain) and Xinhua (New China) News Agency (People's Republic of China) are also represented.

Publishers

Advocate Publishers (2000) Inc: POB 230, Fontabelle, St Michael; tel. 467-2000; fax 434-2020; e-mail news@barbadosadvocate.com.

Business Tutors: 124 Chancery Lane, Christ Church; tel. 428-5664; fax 429-4854; e-mail pchad@caribsurf.com; business, management, computers.

Carib Research and Publications Inc: POB 556, Bridgetown; tel. 438-0580; f. 1986; regional interests; CEO Dr FARLEY BRAITHWAITE.

Miller Publishing Co: Edgehill, St Thomas; tel. 421-6700; fax 421-6707; e-mail info@barbadosbooks.com; internet www.barbadosbooks.com; f. 1983; publs general interest books, tourism and business guides; Jt Man. Dirs KEITH MILLER, SALLY MILLER.

Nation Publishing Co Ltd: Nation House, POB 1203, Fontabelle, St Michael; tel. 430-5400; fax 427-6968; internet www.onecaribbeanmedia.net; owned by One Caribbean Media Ltd; Publr VIVIAN-ANNE GITTENS.

National Cultural Foundation of Barbados: West Terrace, St James; tel. 424-0909; fax 424-0916; internet www.ncf.bb.

Broadcasting and Communications

TELECOMMUNICATIONS

Cable & Wireless (Barbados) Ltd: POB 32, Wildey, St Michael; tel. 292-6140; fax 427-5808; e-mail bdsinfo@caribsurf.com; internet www.candwbet.com.bb; f. 1984; fmrly Barbados External Telecommunications Ltd; became Cable & Wireless BET Ltd, which merged with Barbados Telephone Co Ltd (BARTEL), Cable & Wireless Caribbean Cellular and Cable & Wireless Information Systems in 2002; provides international telecommunications services; owned by Cable & Wireless PLC (United Kingdom); Chair. Sir ALLAN C. FIELDS; Pres. DONALD ST CLAIR AUSTIN; Gen. Man. VINCENT YEARWOOD.

Digicel Barbados Ltd: The Courtyard, Hastings, Christ Church; tel. 434-3444; fax 426-3444; e-mail customercarebarbados@digicelgroup.com; internet www.digicelbarbados.com; f. 2003; awarded licence to operate cellular telephone services in March 2003; approval granted in Jan. 2006 for the acquisition of Cingular Wireless' operation in Barbados; owned by an Irish consortium; Dir RALPH (BIZZY) WILLIAMS.

Sunbeach Communications: 'San Remo', Belmont Rd, St Michael; tel. 430-1569; fax 228-6330; e-mail customerservice@sunbeach.net; internet www.sunbeach.net; f. 1995; licence to operate cellular telephone services obtained in March 2003, due to launch operations in 2007; Vtel (Saint Lucia) acquired controlling 52.9% share in Dec. 2006; Man. Dir IAN K. C. WORRELL.

TeleBarbados Inc: CGI Tower, 6th Floor, Warrens, St Michael; tel. 620-1000; fax 620-1010; e-mail info@telebarbados.com; internet www.telebarbados.com; f. 2005; to provide a range of telecommunications services in Barbados from 2006; awarded licence to operate fixed-line service in 2005; Pres. BRIAN HARVEY.

BROADCASTING
Radio

Barbados Broadcasting Service Ltd: Astoria, St George, Bridgetown; tel. 437-9550; fax 437-9203; e-mail action@sunbeach.net; f. 1981; operates BBS FM and Faith FM (religious broadcasting).

Caribbean Broadcasting Corporation (CBC): The Pine, POB 900, Wildey, St Michael; tel. 467-5400; fax 429-4795; e-mail customer@cbcbarbados.bb; internet www.cbcbarbados.bb; f. 1963; operates three radio stations; Gen. Man. CLAUDE GRAHAM.

CBC Radio 900 AM: tel. 434-1900; f. 1963; spoken word and news.

Quality 100.7 FM: international and regional music, incl. folk, classical, etc.

The One 98.1 FM: tel. 429-5522; f. 1984; popular music.

Starcom Network Inc: River Rd, Bridgetown; tel. 430-7300; fax 426-5377; internet www.starcomnetwork.net; f. 1935 as Radio Distribution; owned by One Caribbean Media Ltd; operates four radio stations; Man. Dir VICTOR FERNANDES.

Gospel 790 AM: Bridgetown; tel. 467-7355; e-mail gospel@starcomnetwork.net; f. 2000; gospel music; Supervisor RONALD CLARKE.

Hott 95.3 FM: Bridgetown; tel. 434-4688; e-mail hott@starcomnetwork.net; internet www.hott953.com; f. 1997; popular music.

Love FM 104: Bridgetown; tel. 434-5683; e-mail love@starcomnetwork.net; f. 1988 as Yess Ten-Four FM; popular music; Supervisor GAYNELLE MARSHALL; Programme Dir DENNIS JOHNSON.

VOB 92.9 FM: Bridgetown; tel. 430-7372; e-mail dennisjohnson@starcomnetwork.net; internet www.vob929.com; f. 1981; current affairs, sport, music; Programme Dir DENNIS JOHNSON.

Television

CBC TV: The Pine, POB 900, Wildey, St Michael; tel. 467-5400; fax 429-4795; e-mail news@cbcbarbados.bb; internet www.cbcbarbados.bb; f. 1964; part of the Caribbean Broadcasting Corpn (q.v.); Channel Eight is the main national service, broadcasting 24 hours daily; a maximum of 115 digital subscription channels will be available through Multi-Choice Television; Programme Man. CECILY CLARKE-RICHMOND.

DIRECTV: Nation House, Roebuck St, Bridgetown, St Michael; tel. 434-7328; e-mail directv@starcomnetwork.net; internet www.starcomnetwork.net/services/directv.htm; digital satellite television service; owned by the Starcom Network.

Finance

In 2007 there were approximately 5,000 international business companies and 54 'offshore' banks registered in Barbados.

BANKING
(cap. = capital; auth. = authorized; res = reserves; dep. = deposits; brs = branches; m. = million; amounts in Barbados dollars unless otherwise indicated)

Central Bank

Central Bank of Barbados: Tom Adams Financial Centre, Spry St, POB 1016, Bridgetown; tel. 436-6870; fax 427-9559; e-mail cbb.libr@caribsurf.com; internet www.centralbank.org.bb; f. 1972; bank of issue; cap. 2.0m., res 10.0m., dep. 502.6m. (Dec. 2005); Gov. MARION V. WILLIAMS; Deputy Gov. CARLOS A. HOLDER.

Commercial Banks

Barbados National Bank Inc (BNB): Independence Sq, POB 1002, Bridgetown; tel. 431-5700; fax 426-2606; internet www.bnbbarbados.com; f. 1978 by merger; privatized in 2003; 65% of shares owned by Republic Bank Ltd (Trinidad and Tobago); cap. 48.0m., res 99.5m., dep. 1,729.9m. (Sept. 2006); Chair. RONALD F. D. HARFORD; Man. Dir and CEO ROBERT LE HUNTE; 6 brs.

FirstCaribbean International Bank Ltd: Warrens, POB 503, St Michael; tel. 367-2300; fax 424-8977; e-mail firstcaribbeanbank@firstcaribbeanbank.com; internet www.firstcaribbeanbank.com; f. 2002; previously known as CIBC West Indies Holdings, adopted present name following merger of CIBC West Indies and Caribbean operations of Barclays Bank PLC; Barclays relinquished its stake to CIBC in June 2006; cap. and res 736.6m., dep. 7,733.7m. (Oct. 2005); Chair. MICHAEL K. MANSOOR; CEO CHARLES PINK; 9 brs.

Mutual Bank of the Caribbean Inc: Trident House, Lower Broad St, Bridgetown; tel. 431-4500; fax 429-5734; 2 brs.

RBTT Bank Barbados Ltd: Lower Broad St, POB 1007C, Bridgetown; tel. 431-2500; fax 431-2530; internet www.rbtt.com; f. 1984 as

BARBADOS

Caribbean Commercial Bank Ltd; purchased by RBTT Financial Holdings, Trinidad and Tobago in 2004 when current name adopted; cap. 25.0m., res 6.0m., dep. 258.5m. (Dec. 2002); Chair. DAVIS HACKETT; Pres. and CEO JOHN BEALE; 4 brs.

Regional Development Bank

Caribbean Development Bank: Wildey, POB 408, St Michael; tel. 431-1600; fax 426-7269; e-mail info@caribank.org; internet www.caribank.org; f. 1970; cap. US $155.7m., res US $14.1m., total assets US $944.9m. (Dec. 2005); Pres. Dr COMPTON BOURNE.

Trust Companies

Bank of Nova Scotia Trust Co (Caribbean) Ltd: Bank of Nova Scotia Bldg, Broad St, POB 1003B, Bridgetown; tel. 431-3120; fax 426-0969.

Barbados International Bank and Trust Co: Bissex House, Bissex, St Joseph; tel. 422-4629; fax 422-7994; e-mail bdosintlbank&trustco@caribsurf.com; f. 1981; 'offshore' banking; Chair. DOUGLAS LEESE.

Bayshore Bank and Trust (Barbados) Corp: Lauriston House, Lower Collymore Rock, POB 1132, Bridgetown, St Michael; tel. 430-8650; fax 430-5335; e-mail info@bayshorecapital.com; internet www.bayshorebank.com; chartered bank with affiliates in the Cayman Islands and Toronto, Canada; Chair. and CEO JOHN PERRY BUJOUVES.

Clico Mortgage & Finance Corporation: C. L. Duprey Financial Centre, Walrond St, Bridgetown; tel. 431-4716; fax 426-6168; e-mail info@clicomortgage.com; internet www.clicomortgage.com; f. 1984 as the Caribbean Commercial Trust Co Ltd; name changed as above in 1998; subsidiary of the C. L. Financial Group, based in Trinidad and Tobago; Pres. and CEO ANDREW N. ST JOHN.

Concorde Bank Ltd: The Corporate Centre, Bush Hill, Bay St, POB 1161, St Michael; tel. 430-5320; fax 429-7996; e-mail concorde@concordebb.com; f. 1987; cap. US $2.0m., res US $2.0m., dep. US $7.5m. (June 2006); Pres. GERARD LUSSAN; Man. MARINA CORBIN.

Ernst & Young Trust Corporation: Bush Hill, Bay St, POB 261, St Michael; tel. 430-3900; fax 429-6446.

FirstCaribbean International Trust and Merchant Bank (Barbados) Ltd: Warren, St Michael; tel. 367-2324; fax 421-7178; internet www.firstcaribbeanbank.com; known as CIBC Trust and Merchant Bank until 2002.

Globe Finance Inc: Rendezvous Court, Suite 6, Rendezvous Main Rd, Christ Church BB15112; tel. 426-4755; fax 426-4772; e-mail info@globefinanceinc.com; internet www.globefinanceinc.com; f. 1998; offers loans and hire purchasing financial services; Gen. Man. RONALD DAVIS.

Royal Bank of Canada Financial Corporation: Bldg 2, 2nd Floor, Chelston Park, Collymore Rock, POB 48B, St Michael; tel. 431-6580; fax 429-3800; Man. N. L. (ROY) SMITH.

St Michael Trust Corpn: Braemar Court, Deighton Rd, St Michael; tel. 467-6677; fax 467-6678; e-mail info@stmichael.bb; f. 1987.

STOCK EXCHANGE

Barbados Stock Exchange (BSE): Carlisle House, 1st Floor, Hincks St, Bridgetown; tel. 436-9871; fax 429-8942; e-mail marlon.yarde@bse.com.bb; internet www.bse.com.bb; f. 1987 as the Securities Exchange of Barbados; in 1989 the Govts of Barbados, Trinidad and Tobago and Jamaica agreed to link exchanges; cross-trading began in April 1991; reincorporated in 2001; Gen. Man. MARLON YARDE.

INSURANCE

The leading British and a number of US and Canadian companies have agents in Barbados. In 2007 there were 235 exempt and qualified exempt insurance companies registered in the country. Local insurance companies include the following:

Insurance Corporation of Barbados Ltd (ICB): Roebuck St, Bridgetown; tel. 427-5590; fax 426-3393; e-mail icb@icb.com.bb; internet www.icb.com.bb; f. 1978; 51% owned by BF&M Ltd of Bermuda; cap. Bds $3m.; Chair. GLENN M. TITTERTON; Man. Dir WISMAR A. GREAVES; Gen. Man. DENIS A. BRADSHAW.

Sagicor: Sagicor Financial Centre, Lower Collymore Rock, St Michael; tel. 467-7500; fax 436-8829; e-mail info@sagicor.com; internet www.sagicor.com; f. 1840 as Barbados Mutual Life Assurance Society (BMLAS); changed name as above in 2002 after acquiring majority ownership of Life of Barbados (LOB) Ltd; listed on the London international stock exchange in May 2007; Chair. J. ARTHUR L. BETHELL; Pres. and CEO DODRIDGE D. MILLER.

United Insurance Co Ltd: United Insurance Centre, Lower Broad St, POB 1215, Bridgetown; tel. 430-1900; fax 436-7573; e-mail united@caribsurf.com; f. 1976; Man. Dir DAVE A. BLACKMAN.

Association

Insurance Association of the Caribbean Inc: IAC Bldg, Collymore Rock, St Michael; tel. 427-5608; fax 427-7277; e-mail info@iac-caribbean.com; internet www.iac-caribbean.com; regional asscn; Pres. KEITH CHOLMONDELEY; Country Dir DAVIS BROWNE.

Trade and Industry

GOVERNMENT AGENCY

Barbados Agricultural Management Co Ltd (BAMC): Warrens, POB 719C, St Michael; tel. 425-0010; fax 425-0007; internet agriculture.gov.bb; f. 1993; Chair. LINDSAY HOLDER; Gen. Man. CARL SIMPSON.

DEVELOPMENT ORGANIZATIONS

Barbados Agriculture Development and Marketing Corpn (BADMC): Fairy Valley, Christ Church; tel. 428-0250; fax 428-0152; e-mail andrew.skeete@badmc.org; internet agriculture.gov.bb/default.asp?V_DOC_ID=813; f. 1993 by merger; programme of diversification and land reforms; Chair. TYRONE POWER; CEO ANDREW SKEETE.

Barbados Investment and Development Corpn: Pelican House, Princess Alice Highway, Bridgetown; tel. 427-5350; fax 426-7802; e-mail bidc@bidc.org; internet www.bidc.com; f. 1992 by merger; facilitates the devt of the industrial sector, especially in the areas of manufacturing, information technology and financial services; offers free consultancy to investors; provides factory space for lease or rent; administers the Fiscal Incentives Legislation; CEO ANTHONY SOBERS.

Barbados Small Business Association: 1 Pelican Industrial Park, Bridgetown; tel. 228-0162; fax 228-0163; e-mail theoffice@sba.org.bb; internet www.sba.org.bb; f. 1974; non-profit org. representing interests of small businesses; Pres. SANDRA HUSBANDS; Exec. Dir LYNETTE HOLDER.

CHAMBER OF COMMERCE

Barbados Chamber of Commerce and Industry: Nemwil House, 1st Floor, Collymore Rock, St Michael; tel. 426-2056; fax 429-2907; e-mail bdscham@caribsurf.com; internet www.bdscham.com; f. 1825; 220 mem. firms; some 345 reps; Pres. DICK STOUTE; Exec. Dir RUALL HARRIS.

INDUSTRIAL AND TRADE ASSOCIATIONS

Barbados Agricultural Society: The Grotto, Beckles Rd, St Michael; tel. 436-6683; fax 435-0651; e-mail TyronePower@sunbeach.net; Pres. TYRONE POWER; Gen. Man. JAMES PAUL.

Barbados Association of Medical Practitioners (BAMP): BAMP Complex, Spring Garden, St Michael; tel. 429-7569; fax 435-2328; e-mail bamp@sunbeach.net; internet www.bamp.org.bb; Pres. Dr CARLOS CHASE.

Barbados Association of Professional Engineers: Christie Bldg, Garrison Hill, St Michael BB14038; tel. 429-6105; fax 434-6673; e-mail engineers@caribsurf.com; internet www.bape.org; f. 1964; Pres. ROGER BLACKMAN; Hon. Sec. KAREN WALKES; 213 mems.

Barbados Hotel and Tourism Association (BHTA): POB 711C, Bridgetown; tel. 426-5041; fax 429-2845; e-mail info@bhta.org; internet www.bhta.org; f. 1952 as the Barbados Hotel Asscn; adopted present name in 1994; non-profit trade asscn; Pres. ALVIN JEMMOTT.

Barbados Manufacturers' Association: Bldg 1, Pelican Industrial Park, St Michael; tel. 426-4474; fax 436-5182; e-mail bmex-products@caribsurf.com; internet www.bma.org.bb; f. 1964; Pres. JAMES HUSBANDS; Exec. Dir BOBBI McKAY; 108 mem. firms.

EMPLOYERS' ORGANIZATION

Barbados Employers' Confederation: Braemar Court, Deighton Rd, POB 33B, Brittons Hill, St Michael; tel. 620-4753; fax 620-2907; e-mail becon@barbadosemployers.com; internet barbadosemployers.com; f. 1956; Pres. Dr HENSLEY SOBERS; Exec. Dir HARRY HUSBANDS; 235 mems (incl. assoc. mems).

UTILITIES

Electricity

Barbados Light and Power Co (BL & P): POB 142, Garrison Hill, St Michael; tel. 430-4300; fax 429-6000; internet www.blpc.com.bb; f. 1911; electricity generator and distributor; operates three stations with a combined capacity of 209,500 kW; Chair. IAN CUMMING; Man. Dir PETER WILLIAMS.

Gas

Barbados National Oil Co Ltd (BNOCL): POB 175, Woodbourne, St Philip; tel. 420-1800; fax 420-1818; e-mail ronhewitt@bnocl.com; internet www.bnocl.com; f. 1982; exploration and extraction of petroleum and natural gas; state-owned; Gen. Man. RONALD HEWITT; Op. Man. GORDON WORME; 88 employees.

National Petroleum Corporation (NPC): Wildey, St Michael; tel. 430-4020; fax 426-4326; gas production and distribution; Gen. Man. KEN LINTON.

Water

Barbados Water Authority: The Pine, St Michael; tel. 426-4134; fax 426-4507; e-mail bwa@caribsurf.com; f. 1980; Gen. Man. DENIS YEARWOOD.

TRADE UNIONS

Principal unions include:

Barbados Secondary Teachers' Union: Ryeburn House, Eighth Ave, Belleville, St Michael; tel. and fax 429-7676; e-mail bstumail@caribsurf.com; f. 1949; Pres. MARY-ANN REDMAN; Gen. Sec. MICHAEL HINDS; 375 mems.

Barbados Union of Teachers: Merry Hill, Welches, POB 58, St Michael; tel. 436-6139; fax 426-9890; e-mail but@hotmail.com; internet www.butbarbados.org; f. 1974; Pres. KAREN BEST; Gen. Sec. HERBERT GITTENS; 1,800 mems.

Barbados Workers' Union (BWU): 'Solidarity' House, Harmony Hall, POB 172, St Michael; tel. 426-3492; fax 436-6496; e-mail bwu@caribsurf.com; internet www.bwu-bb.org; f. 1941; operates a Labour College; Pres.-Gen. HUGH ARTHUR; Gen. Sec. Sir LEROY TROTMAN; 25,000 mems.

National Union of Public Workers: Dalkeith Rd, POB 174, St. Michael; tel. 426-7774; fax 436-1795; e-mail nupwbarbados@sunbeach.net; f. 1944 as the Barbados Civil Service Asscn; present name adopted in 1971; Pres. WALTER MALONEY; Gen. Sec. DENNIS CLARKE; 6,000 mems.

Transport

ROADS

Ministry of Public Works and Transport: The Pine, St Michael; tel. 429-2863; fax 437-8133; internet www.publicworks.gov.bb; maintains a network of 1,600 km (994 miles) of paved roads; Permanent Sec. DAVID DAISLEY (acting).

SHIPPING

Bridgetown harbour has berths for eight ships and simultaneous bunkering facilities for five. In October 2003 the Government announced a 10-year plan to expand the harbour, at an estimated cost of US $101m. The plan was to include the construction of a new sugar terminal and a new cruise-ship pier. Construction commenced in 2004.

Barbados Port Inc: University Row, Princess Alice Hwy, Bridgetown; tel. 430-4700; fax 429-5348; e-mail postmaster@barbadosport.com; internet www.barbadosport.com; f. 1979 as the Barbados Port Authority and was incorporated in 2003; Chair. LARRY TATEM; Man. Dir and CEO EVERTON WALTERS.

The Shipping Association of Barbados: Trident House, 2nd Floor, Lower Broad St, Bridgetown; tel. 427-9860; fax 426-8392; e-mail manager@shasba.com.bb; f. 1981; Pres. GLYNE ST HILL; Vice-Pres. MARC SAMPSON.

Principal Shipping Companies

Barbados Shipping and Trading Co Ltd (B. S. & T.): The Auto Dome, 1st Floor, Warrens, St Michael; tel. 417-5110; fax 417-5116; e-mail info@bsandtco.com; internet www.bsandtco.com; f. 1920; acquired by energy and industrial asscn Neal & Massy (Trinidad and Tobago) in March 2008; Chair. ALLAN C. FIELDS; CEO G. ANTHONY KING.

Bernuth Agencies: T. Geddes Grant White Park Rd, Bridgetown; tel. 431-3343.

Carlisle Shipping Ltd: Musson Bldg, Ground Floor, Hincks St, Bridgetown; tel. 431-8700.

DaCosta Mannings Inc (DMI): DMI Corporate Office, The Autodome, Warrens, POB 103, St Michael; tel. 431-8700; fax 228-8590; internet www.dacostamannings.com; f. 1995 following merger of DaCosta Ltd and Manning, Wilkinson & Challenor Ltd; shipping and retail company; acquired the shipping lines of T. Geddes Grant Bros in 2002; Chair. F. F. C. DELMAS; Man. Dir T. A. MAHON.

T. Geddes Grant Bros: White Park Rd, Bridgetown; tel. 431-3300.

Hassell, Eric and Son Ltd: Carlisle House, Hincks St, Bridgetown; tel. 436-6102; fax 429-3416; e-mail info@erichassell.com; internet www.erichassell.com; shipping agent, stevedoring contractor and cargo fowarder; Gen. Man. GERRIT SCHEPER; Operations Man. NOEL WALCOTT.

Tropical Shipping: Goddards Complex, Fontabelle Rd, St Michael; tel. 426-9990; fax 426-7750; e-mail president@tropical.com; internet www.tropical.com; Pres. RICK MURRELL.

CIVIL AVIATION

The principal airport is Grantley Adams International Airport, at Seawell, 18 km (11 miles) from Bridgetown. A US $100m. contract to build a new arrivals terminal was awarded in late 2001. The first phase of the project was under construction in 2006. Barbados is served by a number of regional and international airlines, including Air Jamaica, LIAT (1974) Ltd (Antigua), Air Canada and British Airways. An inter-island service, operating flights between Saint Lucia and Barbados (three days a week), was launched by the US-based American Eagle carrier in September 2007.

Barbados Civil Aviation Department: Grantley Adams International Airport, Bridgetown; e-mail aisbarbados@sunbeach.net; internet www.barbadoscivilaviation.com; Ministry of Tourism department operating as internal regulator of air transport; Dir E. ANTHONY ARCHER.

Tourism

The natural attractions of the island consist chiefly of the warm climate and varied scenery. In addition, there are many facilities for outdoor sports of all kinds. Tourism receipts (including passenger transport) totalled US $905m. in 2005. In 2006 the number of stop-over tourist arrivals was 562,600, while the number of visiting cruise-ship passengers was 539,100. There were some 7,000 hotel rooms on the island in 2003.

Barbados Hotel and Tourism Association (BHTA): see Trade and Industry.

Barbados Tourism Authority: Harbour Rd, POB 242, Bridgetown; tel. 427-2623; fax 426-4080; e-mail btainfo@barbados.org; internet www.barbados.org; f. 1993 to replace Barbados Board of Tourism; offices in London, New York, Los Angeles, Miami, Munich, Paris and Caracas; Chair. PETER ODLE; Pres. and CEO STUART LAYNE.

BELARUS

Introductory Survey

Location, Climate, Language, Religion, Flag, Capital

The Republic of Belarus is a land-locked state in north-eastern Europe. It is bounded by Lithuania and Latvia to the north-west, by Ukraine to the south, by Russia to the east, and by Poland to the west. The climate is of a continental type, with an average January temperature, in Minsk, of −5°C (23°F) and an average for July of 19°C (67°F). Average annual precipitation is between 560 mm and 660 mm. The official languages of the republic are Belarusian and Russian. The major religion is Christianity—the Eastern Orthodox Church and Roman Catholic Church (of both the Latin and Byzantine rites) being the largest denominations. The national flag (proportions 1 by 2) consists of two unequal horizontal stripes, of red over light green, with a red-outlined white vertical stripe at the hoist, bearing in red a traditional embroidery pattern. The capital is Minsk (Miensk).

Recent History

Following periods of Lithuanian and Polish rule, Belarus became a part of the Russian Empire in the late 18th century. During the 19th century there was a growth of national consciousness in Belarus and, as a result of industrialization, significant migration from rural to urban areas. After the February Revolution of 1917 in Russia, Belarusian nationalists and socialists formed a rada (council), which sought a degree of autonomy from the Provisional Government in Petrograd (St Petersburg). In November, after the Bolsheviks had seized power in Petrograd, Red Army troops were dispatched to Minsk, and the rada was dissolved. However, the Bolsheviks were forced to withdraw by the invasion of the German army. The Treaty of Brest-Litovsk, signed in March 1918, assigned most of Belarus to Germany. On 25 March Belarusian nationalists convened to proclaim a Belarusian National Republic (BNR), but it achieved only limited autonomy. After the Germans had withdrawn, the Bolsheviks easily reoccupied Minsk, and the Belarusian Soviet Socialist Republic (SSR) was declared on 1 January 1919.

In February 1919 the Belarusian SSR was merged with neighbouring Lithuania in a Lithuanian-Belarusian Soviet Republic (known as 'Litbel'). In April, however, Polish armed forces entered Lithuania and Belarus, and both were declared part of Poland. In July 1920 the Bolsheviks recaptured Minsk, and in August the Belarusian SSR was re-established; Lithuania became an independent state. However, the Belarusian SSR comprised only the eastern regions of the lands populated by Belarusians. Western territories were granted to Poland by the Treaty of Rīga, signed on 18 March 1921. The Treaty assigned Belarus's easternmost regions to the Russian Federation, but they were returned to the Belarusian SSR in 1924 and 1926. Meanwhile, the Belarusian SSR, with Ukraine and Transcaucasia, had joined with Russia to establish the Union of Soviet Socialist Republics (USSR) in December 1922.

The Soviet leadership's New Economic Policy of 1921–28, which permitted some liberalization of the economy, brought a measure of prosperity, and there was significant cultural and linguistic development. This period ended in 1929 with the emergence of Stalin (Iosif V. Dzhugashvili) as the dominant figure in the USSR, and the beginning of a campaign to collectivize agriculture, which was strongly resisted by the peasantry. The purges of the early 1930s were initially targeted against Belarusian nationalists and intellectuals, but by 1936–38 they had widened to include all sectors of the population.

After the invasion of Poland by German and Soviet forces in September 1939, the Belarusian SSR was enlarged by the inclusion of the lands that it had lost to Poland and Lithuania in 1921. Between 1941 and 1944 the Belarusian SSR was occupied by Nazi German forces; an estimated 2.2m. people died, including most of the Republic's Jewish population. At the Yalta conference, in February 1945, the Allies agreed to recognize the 'Curzon line' as the western border of the Belarusian SSR, thus endorsing the unification of western and eastern Belarus. In response to Soviet demands the Belarusian SSR (along with the Ukrainian SSR) became a member of the UN in its own right.

The immediate post-war period was dominated by the need to rehabilitate the republic's infrastructure. The requirements of the reconstruction programme and the local labour shortage led to an increase in Russian immigration and during the 1960s and 1970s the process of russification continued. The relative prosperity of the Republic effectively permitted the ruling Communist Party of Belarus (CPB) to resist implementing the economic and political reforms that were proposed by the Soviet leader, Mikhail Gorbachev, from 1985. However, intellectuals and writers campaigned for the greater use of the Belarusian language in education, while campaigners also demanded more information about the consequences of the explosion of April 1986 at the Chornobyl (Chernobyl) nuclear power station in northern Ukraine, which had affected large areas of southern Belarus.

There was, however, little opportunity for overt political opposition. A Belarusian Popular Front (BPF) was established in October 1988, but the CPB severely restricted its activities. None the less, the BPF did have some success in the elections to the all-Union Congress of People's Deputies, which took place in March 1989. In January 1990 a law was approved, declaring Belarusian to be the state language of the Republic, with effect from 1 September. The BPF was not officially permitted to participate in the elections to the Belarusian Supreme Soviet (Supreme Council), which took place in March. Instead, its members joined other pro-reform groups in a coalition known as the Belarusian Democratic Bloc (BDB). The BDB secured about one-quarter of the 310 seats that were decided by popular election; most of the remainder were won by CPB members loyal to the republican leadership. The opposition won most seats in the large cities, notably Gomel (Homiel) and Minsk, where Zyanon Paznyak, the leader of the BPF, was elected. When the Belarusian Supreme Soviet convened in May, the BDB deputies immediately demanded the adoption of a declaration of sovereignty. The CPB initially opposed this, but on 27 July a Declaration of State Sovereignty of the Belarusian SSR was adopted unanimously by the Belarusian Supreme Soviet. The declaration asserted the Republic's right to maintain armed forces, to establish a national currency and to exercise full control over its domestic and foreign policies, and stated the Republic's right to compensation for the damage caused by the nuclear accident at Chornobyl. The Belarusian Government appealed to the all-Union Government for a minimum of 17,000m. roubles to address the consequences of the disaster, but was offered only 3,000m. roubles.

The Belarusian Government took part in the negotiation of a new Treaty of Union in late 1990 and early 1991. The all-Union referendum on the preservation of the USSR took place in the Belarusian SSR on 17 March 1991; of the 83% of the electorate who participated, 83% voted in favour of Gorbachev's proposals for a renewed federation.

On 10 April 1991 a general strike took place, and an estimated 100,000 people attended a demonstration in Minsk. The Government agreed to economic concessions, including wage increases, but the strikers' political demands, including the resignation of the Belarusian Government and the depoliticization of republican institutions, were rejected. It was estimated that some 200,000 workers took part in a second general strike on 23 April, in protest at the legislature's refusal to reconvene. The Belarusian Supreme Soviet was eventually convened in May, although the authority of the CPB was threatened by internal dissent. In June 33 deputies joined the opposition as a 'Communists for Democracy' faction, led by Alyaksandr Lukashenka, the director of a state farm.

The Belarusian leadership did not strongly oppose the attempted coup, led by conservative communist elements, in Moscow, the Russian and Soviet capital, in August 1991. The Presidium of the Supreme Soviet released a neutral statement on the last day of the coup, but the Central Committee of the CPB declared its unequivocal support. Following the failure of the coup, Mikalay Dzemyantsei, the Chairman of the Supreme Soviet (republican head of state), was forced to resign; he was replaced by Stanislau Shushkevich, a centrist, pending an election. In addition, the Supreme Soviet agreed to nationalize CPB property and to suspend the CPB, pending an investigation into its role in the coup. On 25 August the legislature voted to grant constitutional status to the July 1990 Declaration of State Sovereignty, and declared the political and economic independence of Belarus.

On 19 September 1991 the Belarusian Supreme Soviet voted to rename the Belarusian SSR the Republic of Belarus, and also elected Shushkevich as its Chairman. On 8 December Shushkevich, with the Russian and Ukrainian Presidents, signed the Minsk Agreement, establishing a Commonwealth of Independent States (CIS, see p. 215), which was to have its headquarters in Minsk. On 21 December the leaders of 11 former Soviet republics confirmed this decision by the Almaty (Alma-Ata) Declaration.

In March 1993 the CPB formed an informal coalition, the Popular Movement of Belarus, with 17 other parties and groups opposed to independence. Divisions between the various branches of government became more pronounced during that year, and a major source of controversy was the drafting of a new constitution. Shushkevich and the BPF strongly opposed the establishment of Belarus as a presidential republic; nevertheless, the new Constitution, which provided for a presidential system, was adopted in March 1994. A further point of dispute was whether Belarus should adopt closer relations with Russia and the CIS (as advocated by the Supreme Council). Shushkevich and the BPF opposed signing the Collective Security Treaty concluded by six other CIS states in May 1992, on the grounds that this would contravene the Declaration of State Sovereignty, which defined Belarus as a neutral state, and lead to renewed Russian domination. None the less, in April 1993 the Supreme Council voted to authorize the signature of the Treaty. Shushkevich delayed doing so, and in July the legislature approved a vote of no confidence in him; Shushkevich remained in office until his failure to win a vote of confidence, held in January 1994 (by which time he had signed the Treaty), resulted in his dismissal. He was replaced by Mechislau Gryb. Meanwhile, in February 1993 the suspension on the CPB was lifted, and the party was re-established.

Allegations of corruption against the premier, Vyacheslau Kebich, and leading members of the Council of Ministers, coupled with the worsening economic situation, culminated in a BPF-led general strike in Minsk in February 1994, which forced Gryb to announce an early presidential election. Six candidates contested the post, including Kebich, Shushkevich, Paznyak and Lukashenka, head of the Supreme Council's anti-corruption committee since the previous year. In the first round of voting, held in June, no candidate secured an overall majority, although Lukashenka, with 47% of the valid votes cast, led by a considerable margin. In the second round, contested by Lukashenka and Kebich and held on 10 July, Lukashenka received 85% of the votes cast, and he was inaugurated as the first President of Belarus on 20 July. Mikhail Chigir, an economic reformist, became Chairman of a new Council of Ministers (Prime Minister).

In early 1995 there were repeated confrontations between Lukashenka and the Supreme Council over constitutional issues. In late January the Council voted for a second time to adopt legislation that would permit the removal of the President by a two-thirds' quorum in the Council. In March Lukashenka announced that, simultaneously with the legislative elections scheduled to take place in May, a referendum would be held on four policy questions. In early April, following the Council's rejection of all but one of the proposed questions (on closer integration with Russia), Lukashenka threatened to dissolve the legislature. A number of opposition deputies (including Paznyak) were forcibly evicted from the legislative building, where they had declared a hunger strike in protest at the referendum. Shortly after this action, deputies voted in favour of the inclusion in the referendum of the remaining three questions: to give Russian equal status with Belarusian as an official language; to abandon the state insignia and flag of independent Belarus in favour of a modified version of those of the Belarusian SSR; and to amend the Constitution in order to empower the President to suspend the Supreme Council in the event of unconstitutional acts. Some 65% of the electorate participated in the referendum, held on 14 May, at which all four questions received strong popular support.

On the same day, Belarus's first post-Soviet legislative elections were held. However, owing to stringent electoral regulations, only 18 of the 260 seats in the Supreme Council were filled.

A further 101 deputies were elected at 'run-off' elections held on 28 May 1995, but the necessary two-thirds' quorum was only achieved after two further rounds of voting, held on 29 November and 10 December, brought the total membership of the Supreme Council to 198. The CPB emerged with the largest number of seats in the new legislature (42), followed by the Agrarian Party (AP, with 33) and the United Civic Party of Belarus (UCPB—nine). Independent candidates accounted for 95 seats. The BPF failed to win representation in the Council, as the 62 seats remaining vacant, largely owing to low electoral participation, were mostly in areas where the BPF commanded its strongest support. The Supreme Council held its inaugural session in early January 1996. Syamyon Sharetski, the leader of the AP, was appointed Chairman of the Council, replacing Gryb.

Despite strong opposition and protests against government proposals to sign a new union treaty with Russia, President Lukashenka and the Russian President, Boris Yeltsin, signed the Treaty on the Formation of a Community of Sovereign Republics in Moscow on 2 April 1996. Although it did not establish a single state, the Treaty included extensive provisions covering military, economic and political co-operation. Following the Treaty's endorsement, confrontation between Lukashenka and the opposition parties increased. A warrant was issued in April for the arrest of Paznyak, who was accused of organizing the anti-union demonstrations; he fled the country and later applied for political asylum in the USA.

Lukashenka scheduled another national referendum for 24 November 1996 (with polling stations to be open from 9 November for those unable to vote on the later date), which was to consider, *inter alia*, proposed amendments to the 1994 Constitution. Relations between Lukashenka and the Constitutional Court deteriorated in November 1996, when the Court ruled that the approval of amendments to the Constitution would not be legally binding. The revocation of this decision by presidential decree provoked fierce criticism. The referendum ballot papers contained seven questions, four of which were proposed by Lukashenka: that amendments be made to the Constitution to extend the President's term of office from 1999 until 2001, to enable the President to issue decrees that would carry legal force, and to grant him extensive powers of appointment both to the judiciary and to an envisaged bicameral legislature; that Belarusian Independence Day be moved from 27 July (the anniversary of the Declaration of State Sovereignty) to 3 July (the anniversary of the liberation from the Nazis); that there be an unrestricted right to purchase and sell land; and that the death penalty be abolished. The remaining three questions were submitted by the Supreme Council in an attempt to curtail the President's powers, and proposed that there be a significant reduction in the powers of the President (in effect, virtually abolishing the presidency); that the Supreme Council be allowed to elect heads of local administration (hitherto appointed by the President); and that state institutions be funded from the budget, instead of from a non-budgetary fund controlled by the President.

Despite the inclusion of questions concerning proposed constitutional changes, copies of the draft Constitution were not available to the public by the time voting began. The Chairman of the Central Electoral Commission, Viktar Hanchar, stated that he would not approve the results of the voting, owing to electoral violations, and was dismissed by Lukashenka. The crisis worsened in November 1996, when Chigir resigned as Chairman of the Council of Ministers, urging that the referendum be cancelled; he was replaced, initially in an acting capacity, by Syarhey Ling. Some 10,000 people attended an anti-Government rally in Minsk, protesting at the restrictions on freedom of expression. The Organization for Security and Co-operation in Europe (OSCE, see p. 354) refused to send observers to monitor the referendum, and the Council of Europe (see p. 225) declared that the presidential draft of the amended Constitution did not comply with European standards. Meanwhile, 75 deputies in the Supreme Council submitted a motion to the Constitutional Court to begin impeachment proceedings against the President; although the Court had already found 17 decrees issued by Lukashenka to be unconstitutional, it was forced to abandon the motion, as deputies retracted their support.

The referendum results revealed considerable support for the President, but their accuracy was disputed. According to official figures, some 84% of the electorate took part, 70.5% of whom voted for the President's constitutional amendments; only 7.9% voted for those of the Supreme Council. The amended Constitution was published on 27 November 1996 and came into immediate effect.

Following the referendum, the Supreme Council divided into two factions. More than 100 deputies declared their support for Lukashenka, and adopted legislation abolishing the Supreme Council and establishing a 110-member Palata Predstaviteley (House of Representatives), which was to be the lower chamber of the new bicameral Natsionalnoye Sobraniye (National Assembly). Some 50 other deputies denounced the referendum as invalid and declared themselves to be the legitimate legislature. The Palata Predstaviteley convened shortly afterwards and elected Anatol Malafeyeu as its Chairman. Deputies were granted a four-year mandate, while the term of office of those opposed to the new legislature was curtailed to two months. Deputies elected in the by-elections held simultaneously with the referendum were denied registration. Legislation governing the formation of the upper house of the new legislature, the 64-member Soviet Respubliki (Council of the Republic), was approved by Lukashenka in December 1996: eight members were appointed by the President and the remaining 56 were elected by regional councils. The Soviet Respubliki convened in mid-January 1997, and elected Pavel Shypuk as its Chairman. Meanwhile, in protest at the constitutional amendments introduced by the referendum, the Chairman of the Constitutional Court and several judges announced their resignations.

In January 1997 the Public Coalition Government-National Economic Council (PCG-NEC), a 'shadow' cabinet, was formed, chaired by Genadz Karpenka. Doubts about the legitimacy of the referendum were expressed by international organizations, including the Council of Europe, which suspended Belarus's 'guest status', and the Permanent Council of the Parliamentary Assembly of the OSCE, which recognized the right of a delegation from the former Supreme Council, rather than members of the Palata Predstaviteley, officially to represent Belarus at that organization.

The signing with Russia of the Treaty of Union, and initialling of the Charter of the Union on 2 April 1997, by Presidents Lukashenka and Yeltsin (see below) prompted an anti-Union demonstration in Minsk, which was suppressed by the police, resulting in many arrests. Nevertheless, support for the union treaty appeared to be widespread, and some 15,000 people participated in a pro-Union rally in Minsk in mid-May. The Charter of the Union was signed in Moscow on 23 May. The Treaty and Charter were ratified shortly afterwards by the respective legislatures, and came into effect in mid-June.

Negotiations mediated by the Council of Europe and the European Union (EU, see p. 244) to end the confrontation between the former Supreme Council and the new legislature began in June 1997, but collapsed in July, following disagreement over which constitution was to form the basis of the discussions. In November the opposition launched a petition movement, Charter 97, which demanded greater democracy and that a presidential election be held in 1999, as required by the 1994 Constitution. A number of senior BPF members were arrested in April 1998 during an unauthorized rally to protest against the Treaty of Union. A further 30 demonstrators were arrested later in the month at a rally led by former members of the disbanded Supreme Council, urging Lukashenka's resignation for mismanaging the economy and destroying national culture (most notably in response to the increasing marginalization of the Belarusian language). In June legislation was approved that rendered defamation of the President an offence punishable by up to five years' imprisonment.

In November 1998 Lukashenka decreed the formation of a special economic committee, to be known as the National Headquarters, which was to supersede the Council of Ministers in economic policy. A new law on local elections was approved by the Palata Predstaviteley in December, effectively banning those with a police record or fine from standing in the local elections that were to be held in April 1999, thereby excluding numerous opposition candidates. In the event, the opposition organized an electoral boycott, and the majority of the seats in the elections were each contested by a single candidate.

Meanwhile, in January 1999 the 'Central Electoral Commission' of the former Supreme Council scheduled a 'shadow' presidential 'election' for 16 May (according to the 1994 Constitution Lukashenka's legitimate term of office was to expire in July 1999). In March the Commission's Chairman, Hanchar, was arrested, but was released after a 10-day hunger strike. Chigir was registered as a candidate for the election in March, but was detained in April, prompting speculation that his arrest was politically motivated. (In May 2000 Chigir was convicted of abuse of office and received a three-year, suspended sentence.) Following the death of Karpenka in April 1999, Gryb was elected Chairman of the PCG-NEC in November. In the event, it proved impossible to organize fixed polling stations for the poll, which was not recognized by the Government or by the international community. The election results were declared invalid later in the month, owing to alleged irregularities, despite a reported participation rate of 53%. In July Sharetski fled to Lithuania to avoid arrest following his designation by the Supreme Council as 'acting President' of Belarus.

In January 1999 Lukashenka had decreed that political parties, trade unions and other organizations were required to re-register by 1 July; those failing to do so were to be dissolved. By September only 17 of the 28 existing official parties had been re-registered. In late September supporters of the exiled BPF leader Paznyak formed a breakaway faction, known as the Conservative Christian Party of the BPF. At the end of October Vintsuk Vyachorka was elected Chairman of the 'rump' BPF, which changed its name to Revival—BPF in December, in order to comply with legislation banning the use of certain words in the names of non-governmental organizations (NGOs). In early September OSCE-mediated negotiations commenced between the Government and the opposition, concerning the legislative elections to be held in 2000; however, further talks were subject to government-proposed postponements, and opposition frustration was such that, when talks resumed in March 2000, its participation was much reduced. Subsequently, a number of critics of the President disappeared in unexplained circumstances. In May a former Minister of the Interior and campaigner for Chigir, Yuriy Zakharenka, went missing. His disappearance was followed by those of: Tamara Vinnikava, a former head of the National Bank, who had been under house arrest; an independent publisher; and Hanchar. It was officially claimed that the four had gone into hiding to attract attention to their political cause. In October 15,000 people were estimated to have taken part in an anti-Government 'Freedom March' in Minsk.

In February 2000 Ling resigned as Chairman of the Council of Ministers, and was replaced by Uladzimir Yermoshin, hitherto the Governor of Minsk City. In that month opposition parties agreed to boycott the parliamentary elections due to take place in October, in protest at not having been consulted about the preparation of a new draft electoral code. This decision appeared to prompt increased repression of both the unofficial media and the opposition. The peaceful staging, in March, of a second Freedom March resulted in the prohibition of demonstrations in the centre of the capital. A further demonstration, to commemorate the creation of the BNR in 1918, which took place later that month, in contravention of the ban, was suppressed by the security forces and resulted in hundreds of arrests. Many of those detained were journalists and international observers, and Lukashenka subsequently issued an apology. In the following month the Minister of Internal Affairs, Yuriy Sivakow, resigned, ostensibly for health reasons.

A large-scale anti-election rally by opposition activists preceded the elections to the Natsionalnoye Sobraniye. In the first round of voting, which was conducted on 15 October 2000, 41 seats were filled and the results of voting were declared invalid in 13 constituencies. A second round of voting for the remaining 56 seats took place on 29 October. The OSCE denounced the elections as neither free nor fair. The official rate of participation, at 60.6%, was widely believed to have been exaggerated, and the international community refused to recognize the validity of the elections, in which nominally independent candidates were reported to have obtained the majority of seats.

In November 2000 Lukashenka made a number of changes to government and security-service personnel. Notably, Ural Latypaw, hitherto Deputy Prime Minister and Minister of Foreign Affairs, was appointed State Secretary of the Security Council; he was replaced by Mikhail Khvastow. In February 2001 a further, minor reshuffle of the Council of Ministers and of security officials took place.

In mid-March 2001 President Lukashenka signed a decree imposing severe restrictions on the use of foreign financial assistance by both individuals and national organizations, prompting fears by opposition activists that the decree would prevent the deployment of observers from the OSCE at the presidential election due to take place in September. Repeat elections were held on 18 March and 1 April to fill the vacant seats remaining in the Palata Predstaviteley. The opposition held a third 'Freedom March' in Minsk on 25 March, at which a small number of arrests were made. In early May the five main opposition candidates for the presidency announced their intention to nominate a single joint candidate.

In June 2001 two former investigators at the Office of the Prosecutor-General, who had been granted asylum in the USA, claimed that senior government officials had organized the assassinations of political opponents to Lukashenka's regime, and alleged them to be responsible for the deaths of the missing opposition figures Hanchar and Zakharenka, as well as Dmitrii Zavadski, a cameraman for a Russian television channel, who had been missing since July 2000. The allegations were supported by the Chairman of the Federation of Trade Unions of Belarus, Uladzimir Hancharyk, who in July 2001 revealed documents that apparently linked the Prosecutor-General and former State Secretary of the Security Council, Viktar Sheyman, and the former Minister of Internal Affairs, Yuriy Sivakow, with the disappearance and presumed murder of Hanchar and Zakharenka. In late July the opposition selected Hancharyk as its candidate for the presidency; his election campaign focused on continuing allegations of the government-sanctioned assassination of opposition figures. In late August two state security agents released to the media a recorded testimony, in which they supported claims that Hanchar, together with a business associate, had been kidnapped and killed in September 1999 by a special police unit attached to the Ministry of Internal Affairs. Meanwhile, media outlets came under increased pressure to withdraw their support for Hancharyk, as a number of police raids took place throughout the month.

The presidential election was held, as scheduled, on 9 September 2001, although a constitutional provision had permitted some voting to begin on 4 September. This provision was criticized by the opposition, which asserted that it made the election difficult to monitor. Lukashenka was re-elected with 75.7% of the valid votes cast. Hancharyk received 15.7% of the votes, and the only other candidate, the leader of the Liberal Democratic Party of Belarus (LDPB), Syarhey Gaydukevich, received just 2.5%. The election was described as flawed by the OSCE, and Hancharyk urged the public to protest against Lukashenka's victory; however, a popular uprising failed to take place, and observers noted that voters, particularly in the rural areas where Lukashenka drew much of his support, feared that the election of a new, reformist leader might lead to increased economic hardship.

Following Lukashenka's inauguration on 20 September 2001, the Prime Minister, Uladzimir Yermoshin, tendered the resignation of his Government. Lukashenka subsequently reshuffled the Council of Ministers, reducing the number of ministries. In the same month Latypaw was appointed to head the presidential administration; his former post as State Secretary of the Security Council was filled by Lt-Gen. Genadz Nyavyhlas. At the beginning of October Lukashenka nominated former Deputy Prime Minister Genadz Navitsky as premier, and the appointment was approved by the Palata Predstaviteley on 10 October. In late 2001 and early 2002 a number of state officials and managers of state enterprises were arrested, as part of an anti-corruption campaign initiated by the President. The opposition media claimed the arrests to be politically motivated, and linked them to criticism of Lukashenka's economic policies. Meanwhile, in December 2001 Hancharyk resigned the chairmanship of the Federation of Trade Unions.

Meanwhile, in March 2002 two former police officers were sentenced to life imprisonment, having been found guilty of kidnapping Zavadski. However, there were claims that the charges had been fabricated to divert attention from the involvement of more senior government officials in the abduction. In May the state officials arrested since late 2001 began to receive terms of imprisonment. In July 2002 Chigir was given a three-year, suspended prison sentence, following his conviction for tax evasion. In September the editor of an independent newspaper was sentenced to two years' corrective labour, after accusing the President of having profited from illicit arms sales. Further journalists were dismissed in January 2003. The Government also began dramatically to reduce the broadcast of Russian programmes, which were often critical of Lukashenka; to this end, all radio and television companies were required to re-register by June 2003.

Local elections were held in two rounds in March 2003, amid opposition allegations of electoral irregularities. Many constituencies registered only one candidate for the ballot, and a substantial number of opposition candidates were reported to have been denied registration. In July the President dismissed premier Genadz Navitsky and three officials accused of failing to implement instructions concerning the agricultural sector, including Deputy Prime Minister Alyaksandr Papkow and the Minister of Agriculture and Food, Mikhail Rusy. The First Deputy Prime Minister, Syarhey Sidorsky, was appointed acting Prime Minister. In the same month Navitsky was elected to succeed the retiring Chairman of the Council of the Republic. In December Sidorsky was confirmed as Prime Minister, and a further reorganization of the Council of Ministers took place.

State repression of independent organizations and the media continued in 2003–04, with the closure of several NGOs, efforts to prevent the publication and distribution of independent and satirical newspapers and measures restricting access to Russian media. In November 2003 an opposition alliance, known as the 'Five Plus' Popular Coalition, was formed by the Belarusian Party of Labour, the Belarusian Social Democratic Assembly, Revival—BPF, the Party of Communists of Belarus and the UCPB. In January 2004 the coalition signed a co-operation agreement with the Belarusian Green Party and a number of NGOs, in advance of parliamentary elections. Restrictions on political parties increased from February, and in August the Supreme Court abolished the Belarusian Party of Labour by decree, attracting widespread criticism. Meanwhile, a former Governor of Minsk City and a prominent opponent of the Government, Mikhail Marinich, was arrested in April, on charges of stealing computer equipment from an NGO and embezzlement, prompting a number of incidents of unrest, including a widely observed strike in June. (In December Marinich was sentenced to five years' imprisonment, although the sentence was subsequently halved.) At the time of the legislative elections, which took place on 17 October, the opposition comprised three broad groupings: Five Plus; the 'Free Belarus' European Coalition, which included the Belarusian Social Democratic Assembly, and favoured EU membership rather than federation with Russia; and a youth bloc, the Young Belarusians. No opposition candidates won seats in the elections, which were the subject of intense scrutiny by international electoral observers; 96 nominally independent candidates were elected, the CPB obtained eight mandates, the AP three, and the LDPB one. According to official results of a constitutional referendum, which was held concurrently with the elections, 77.3% of those participating voted to approve an amendment that effectively removed obstacles to Lukashenka seeking a third term in 2006. The official rate of participation was almost 90%.

Meanwhile, in January 2004 the Parliamentary Assembly of the Council of Europe (PACE) published a preliminary report on the disappearances of Zakharenka, Hanchar, Zavadski and an associate of Hanchar, Anatol Krasouski. The report concluded that senior government officials, including Sheyman (who remained Prosecutor-General) and Sivakow, may have been involved, and urged member states of the Council of Europe to exert political pressure on the Belarusian Government to prompt an independent investigation into the alleged murders. In August Sivakow was banned by EU member states from entering Greece (he had been appointed as Minister of Sports and Tourism in January 2003, and planned to visit the summer Olympic Games), in a further attempt to persuade the Government to authorize an investigation.

In March 2005 a demonstration of up to 1,500 people demanding the resignation of Lukashenka was violently dispersed by the police. A smaller opposition rally took place in late April. Also in April Assembly and the Belarusian Social Democratic Party (National Assembly—Hramada) merged to form the Assembly (Hramada)—Belarusian Social-Democratic Party; Alyaksandr Kazulin was elected as the party's Chairman in July. In May the opposition activist Syarhey Skryabets was detained and sentenced on what were widely alleged to be politically motivated charges. On 31 May the President decreed that NGOs and independent media organizations were no longer permitted to include the words 'Belarusian' or 'national' in their names, and that, if necessary, they would have to re-register under new, approved, designations. In early June opposition leaders Mikalay Statkevich and Pavel Seyyarynets were sentenced to three years of corrective labour (subsequently reduced to two years) for having organized in late 2004 a series of unauthorized demonstrations protesting against the constitutional referendum. In the same month Andrei Klimaw, who had organized the demonstration held in March 2005, was imprisoned for 18 months.

At the beginning of October 2005 a congress of opposition groups nominated civil-society activist Alyaksandr Milinkevich as its sole candidate to stand against Lukashenka in the presidential election due to take place in 2006. In early December

2005 the Soviet Respubliki approved legislative amendments to the criminal code, which included measures to penalize citizens for activities deemed to threaten personal or public security, and for discrediting Belarus internationally; the measures were widely interpreted as forming part of efforts to curb opposition activity in advance of the presidential election, which was subsequently scheduled for 19 March 2006. In late December 2005 Lukashenka undertook a reorganization of the Council of Ministers, including the appointment of Alyaksandr Kosinets as Deputy Prime Minister with responsibility for social and economic affairs.

Meanwhile, the suppression of the media and NGOs continued. In late January 2006 PACE urged member states to give financial (and, if necessary, logistical) support to enable independent broadcasts to reach Belarus from abroad. In a separate development, the European Commission awarded €2m. to a German-led consortium for the initiation of foreign broadcasts to the country prior to the presidential election. In the days preceding the presidential election many opposition politicians and supporters were reported to have been detained by the authorities. Early results of the election, which took place, as scheduled, on 19 March, indicated that Lukashenka had been returned to office by a significant majority, and on the same day some 20,000 opposition supporters gathered to protest at alleged electoral malpractice on the part of the authorities. Further protests took place in the week following the election, and numerous arrests were made. Meanwhile, the OSCE announced that the election had failed to meet democratic standards, while Milinkevich demanded that the poll be repeated. According to the final results, Lukashenka received 83.0% of the votes cast, followed by Milinkevich, with 6.1%. Two other candidates, Gaydukevich and Kazulin, won 3.5% and 2.2% of the votes, respectively. Kazulin, who, with Milinkevich, had helped lead the protests, was arrested on 25 March, prompting international protests. Both the USA and the EU imposed visa bans and financial sanctions on Belarusian officials whom they alleged had been involved in electoral malpractice, leading to accusations from the Belarusian authorities of attempting to destabilize the country. Lukashenka was inaugurated as President on 8 April, and Sidorsky was subsequently reappointed as Prime Minister. In mid-April PACE urged the Belarusian authorities to hold new, and fair, presidential elections in accordance with the demands of the opposition. Later that month Milinkevich was detained, and sentenced to 15 days' imprisonment, having been found guilty of participating in an unauthorized demonstration. In July Kazulin was convicted on charges of disorderly conduct, both prior to and following the elections, and was sentenced to a prison term of five-and-a-half years. In August a petition signed by almost 6,000 people calling for the invalidation of official election results was submitted to the Supreme Court; however, the Court refused to consider the petition, insisting that the matter fell outwith its jurisdiction.

Meanwhile, in May 2006 Lukashenka effected a government reorganization, in which Viktar Bura, hitherto Deputy Chairman of the Minsk City Executive Committee, received the post of Deputy Prime Minister; five new ministers were appointed. In October the Palata Predstaviteley voted to amend Belarus's electoral legislation, prior to local elections that were scheduled to take place in January 2007; local elections were henceforth to be conducted in just one round, while the existing voting system was to be replaced by a simple 'first-past-the-post' system (in which the candidate with the most votes would be declared the winner). Also in October 2006 Milinkevich was awarded the European Parliament's Sakharov Prize for freedom of thought. In January 2007 the human rights organization Amnesty International recognized Kazulin, who had recently ended a two-month hunger strike, as a prisoner of conscience, and launched a campaign in support of his release.

The local elections were held on 14 January 2007; according to the Central Electoral Commission, voter turnout was 79.2% of the electorate, although independent observers disputed this figure. Despite presenting some 300 candidates, the opposition performed poorly, securing only two seats on local councils in elections that prompted further allegations of gross misconduct. Opposition parties claimed that their offices had been raided and their leaders detained, in acts of repression by government officials. The EU denounced the elections, on the grounds that they had failed to comply with democratic standards.

In March 2007 an authorized opposition demonstration was staged in Minsk, on the anniversary of the creation of the BNR in 1918; opposition leaders declared that up to 10,000 supporters had attended the rally and that some 100 had been detained. A series of arrests of youth opposition leaders in August and September prompted the EU to suspend the second round of negotiations with Belarus on energy security, which had been due to be held in October. The most prominent of those arrested, Zmitser Dashkevich, received an 18-month term of imprisonment in November, on charges of engaging in activities for an unregistered political organization. Meanwhile, the Ministry of Justice continued to reject applications for official registration by new opposition parties, including the Movement for Freedom, which had been established by Milinkevich in May. In October an opposition rally of some 5,000 people was staged in Minsk to demand that the Government meet 12 terms that had been stipulated by the European Commission in November 2006 as being conditional to Belarus's access to greater aid and trade co-operation within the European Neighbourhood Policy. In November a new social organization, White Rus, chaired by Minister of Education Alyaksandr Radzkow, was established to consolidate support for Lukashenka in advance of the legislative elections scheduled for 2008, although the organization itself was not expected to participate in the polling. In January 2008 special police violently dispersed an unauthorized demonstration of about 3,000 people in Minsk, which had been organized in protest at a new presidential decree restricting small-business activities; a number of participants who were arrested received fines or brief terms of imprisonment. Lukashenka subsequently accused the opposition of attempting to destabilize the country. Dashkevich and another youth opposition leader were granted an early release in January 2008, following protests by the EU and USA. In February Andrey Klimau, an opponent of Lukashenka who had been sentenced to two years' imprisonment in August 2007 for inciting revolution in an internet article, was also released. Later in February, following a mass demonstration in Minsk and international appeals, Lukashenka permitted the temporary release of Kazulin to attend his wife's funeral; however, Belarus refused a demand by the US Administration that the remainder of his sentence be commuted.

Following the dissolution of the USSR in 1991, Belarus's closest relations continued to be with member states of the CIS, in particular with Russia. Belarus signed the CIS Collective Security Treaty in December 1993, and accords on closer economic co-operation with CIS states followed. In April 1994 Belarus and Russia concluded an agreement on eventual monetary union. In March 1996 Belarus, Kazakhstan, Kyrgyzstan and Russia signed the Quadripartite Treaty, which envisaged a common market and a customs union between the four countries, as well as joint transport, energy and communications systems (Tajikistan signed the Treaty in 1998). In September 2003 Belarus, Kazakhstan, Russia and Ukraine signed a new agreement on the establishment of a common economic space. (However, following the election of the reformist, Viktor Yushchenko, as President of Ukraine in December 2004, Ukraine's commitment to the scheme was increasingly called into question by the three other signatories.) Meanwhile, in April 2003 Armenia, Belarus, Kazakhstan, Kyrgyzstan, Russia and Tajikistan had formally inaugurated the successor to the Collective Security Treaty, a new regional defence structure known as the Collective Security Treaty Organization. Belarus was, together with Kazakhstan, Kyrgyzstan, Russia and Tajikistan, a founding member of the Eurasian Economic Community (EURASEC, see p. 412), the creation of which was agreed upon in 2000 and the formal establishment of which took place in the following year; Armenia, Moldova and Ukraine were subsequently granted observer status, and Uzbekistan acceded to full membership in 2006. In October 2007 EURASEC leaders approved the legal basis for the establishment of a new customs union that was initially to comprise Belarus, Kazakhstan and Russia, with Kyrgyzstan, Tajikistan and Uzbekistan expected to join by 2011.

In April 1996 Belarus and Russia concluded the far-reaching Treaty on the Formation of a Community of Sovereign Republics, providing for closer economic, political and military integration. On 2 April 1997 a further Treaty of Union was signed by Yeltsin and Lukashenka, and a Charter of the Union, detailing the process of integration, was also initialled. The stated aim of the Union was the 'voluntary unification of the member states'. The Union's Parliamentary Assembly (provision for which had been made in the 1996 Treaty, and which had convened in March) was to comprise 36 members from the legislature of each country. The Charter was signed in Moscow on 23 May. Ratification of the documents by the respective legislatures took place in June, and the first official session of the Parliamentary Assembly followed shortly afterwards.

In November 1998 the Parliamentary Assembly of the Russia-Belarus Union voted for the creation of a unified, bicameral parliament. The upper chamber was to include deputies delegated by the legislatures of the two countries, and the lower chamber, comprising 25 Belarusian and 75 Russian deputies, was to be elected by direct universal suffrage. (However, by early 2008 the proposed unified legislature remained in abeyance.) On 25 December 1998 Presidents Lukashenka and Yeltsin signed an outline union accord. A draft treaty on unification was submitted for national discussion in October 1999. Lukashenka's hopes for the formation of a single state, which were much contested by the Belarusian opposition, were not shared by Russia, and the draft treaty did not fully satisfy the wishes of the Belarusian President. None the less, the signature of the treaty, which created a more formal union structure, officially known as the Union of the Russian Federation and Belarus, took place in Moscow on 8 December. The treaty was ratified in January 2000 and came into force on 26 January, when Lukashenka was appointed Chairman of the High State Council of the Union. Although progress towards a full union appeared to be advancing, President Vladimir Putin of Russia (who succeeded Yeltsin, initially in an acting capacity, in January of that year) remained more pragmatic than Lukashenka, in particular in his attitude towards the formation of joint armed forces, a measure that the Belarusian President strongly favoured. On 30 November, during a CIS summit meeting in Minsk, an agreement on the introduction of a single currency was signed; the agreement, according to which the Russian rouble was to be adopted as the union currency from 1 January 2005 and a new currency was to be adopted three years later, was ratified by the Natsionalnoye Sobraniye in April 2001. In November the eventual merger of the air defence systems of Belarus and Russia was announced, and a draft constitution of the Russia-Belarus Union was made public.

During 2002, however, relations with Russia worsened, owing to disagreements over the nature of the planned union. In mid-March Belarus and Russia reached agreement on the harmonization of customs and tax laws and the removal of trade barriers, but in late June, at a meeting held in St Petersburg, Russia, Putin publicly criticized Lukashenka's union plans. Subsequently, in mid-August, at a summit meeting held in Moscow, Putin presented Lukashenka with a new unification plan, which effectively provided for the absorption of the seven administrative regions of Belarus (rather than Belarus as a country) into the Russian Federation; Lukashenka denounced the plan as unacceptable and as an insult to Belarus's sovereignty. Detailed negotiations on monetary union commenced in April 2003, and by June it had been agreed that the Russian central bank was to supply Belarus with bank notes from 1 January 2005. However, the two countries' failure to sign a final agreement on the proposed single currency by the end of 2003, largely owing to demands by Lukashenka for the prior adoption of a constitutional act on the formation of the union state (together with guarantees of Belarusian independence), delayed its planned introduction indefinitely. In October 2005 a draft constitutional act was drawn up, which was to be submitted for approval by referendums to be held in both countries; however, by early 2008 no date for a referendum had been announced by either Belarus or Russia.

Meanwhile, bilateral relations were strained in 2003-04 by inconclusive negotiations over the settlement of Belarusian fuel arrears, together with plans by the Russian state-controlled energy supplier Gazprom to increase gas prices, which led to the repeated suspension of gas supplies in early 2004. A gas deal was signed in June 2004, after which Gazprom immediately resumed supplies to Belarus; a further agreement was signed in December 2005. Bilateral relations were damaged, when, in December 2006, the price of gas supplied by Gazprom to Belarus was more than doubled and an oil export duty was introduced by Russia (see Economic Affairs). In early January 2007 Belarus imposed a retaliatory levy on Russian oil passing through its territory. Russia subsequently accused Belarus of abstracting almost 80,000 metric tons of Russian crude oil intended for various countries in central and eastern Europe, and ceased the transit of oil supplies through Belarus. The situation was resolved three days later, when Belarus agreed to lift the transit duty and Russia in turn reduced its duty on oil exports.

In June 1998 a diplomatic scandal resulted from the enforced eviction of 22 diplomatic families from their residences outside Minsk, purportedly for repairs. This violation of the Vienna Convention, guaranteeing the inviolability of diplomatic residences, led to the recall from Belarus of the ambassadors from EU countries, a number of other European states and the USA and Japan. Belarusian envoys were expelled from the EU in June, and in the following month Belarusian officials were barred from entering its member states. The ban was subsequently adopted by several other European countries and the USA. In December, however, Belarus agreed to provide compensation to those forced to relocate. Lukashenka gave assurances that, henceforth, he would comply with international agreements. All heads of diplomatic missions accredited to Belarus, with the exception of the US ambassador, returned to Minsk in January 1999. The EU ban on Belarusian officials entering its territory was repealed in February, and the US ambassador returned to Minsk in September. However, relations with the USA remained uneasy during 2000, and the US Administration urged the Belarusian opposition to boycott the legislative elections of October. The US ambassador refused to attend Lukashenka's inauguration ceremony following the 2001 presidential election. From late 2001, after the suicide attacks against the USA of 11 September (see the chapter on the USA), the USA expressed increasing concern over the alleged illegal sale of arms to states accused of supporting terrorist activity. Notably, Belarus had developed close economic and military relations with Iraq, and was reported to have helped to upgrade Iraq's air defence systems, although the Belarusian Government denied having acted in contravention of UN sanctions. In October 2004 the US Congress approved the Belarus Democracy Act of 2004, which authorized financial assistance to organizations campaigning for democracy within Belarus and also prohibited US government agencies from providing non-humanitarian aid to the Belarusian Government. In January 2005 the US Secretary of State, Condoleezza Rice, described Belarus as an 'outpost of tyranny', and in April identified the country as the 'last dictatorship in Europe', urging that the presidential election due to take place in 2006 be free and fair. Following the election in March 2006, relations with the USA deteriorated still further, owing to that country's imposition of visa bans and financial sanctions on prominent Belarusian officials (see above). In December the US House of Representatives approved an extension to the 'Belarus Democracy Act of 2004' to cover the period 2007–08. In the same month the Canadian Government imposed economic sanctions on Belarus, in order to apply pressure on the regime to improve the country's human rights situation and to work towards democratic reform. In November 2007 a committee of the UN General Assembly voted in favour of a resolution criticizing human rights violations in Belarus. The USA subsequently implemented additional financial sanctions, 'freezing' assets belonging to Belarus's largest petrochemical company, Belneftekhim, on the grounds that it was controlled by Lukashenka. In addition, the US Administration announced that it intended to impose similar measures against other Belarusian enterprises unless the authorities released political prisoners, prompting Belarus to threaten to expel the US Ambassador. In February 2008 Lukashenka authorized the establishment of a European Commission office in Minsk. In early March, following Belarus's continued refusal to release Kazulin (see above), the USA extended sanctions to include all Belarusian petrochemical companies in which the state's share was 50% or more. The Belarus Government responded by recalling its ambassador in the USA for consultations; the US Administration subsequently complied with Belarus's request that the US ambassador leave the country, but insisted that this was on a temporary basis.

In 2005 tensions between Poland and Belarus, which is home to a substantial ethnic Polish minority (constituting some 4% of the population at the 1999 census), increased. In July armed police raided the office of the Union of Poles of Belarus, in Grodno, and reinstated the organization's former leader, who had been replaced at a convention in March, apparently owing to fears that the Union of Poles might unite with the domestic opposition in an attempt to overthrow the Lukashenka regime. Meanwhile, journalists working for associated Polish publications were compelled to pay large fines after protesting at the takeover of a Polish-language newspaper by the authorities. The Polish Government responded by recalling its ambassador to Belarus, following a series of earlier diplomatic expulsions by both sides, and appealed to the EU for assistance in protecting the Polish minority in Belarus. The Polish ambassador returned to Belarus in October. Relations deteriorated further in March 2006 when Poland imposed a visa ban on those officials whom it deemed responsible for malpractice pertaining to the presidential elections. Further animosity was generated in January 2007 by Belarusian border guards' refusal to grant entry into the country to Krzysztof Putra, Deputy Marshal of the Polish Senat (Senate).

A diplomatic row erupted between Belarus and Latvia in late July 2006, following the broadcast on Belarusian television of video footage purporting to show Reimo Smits, a Latvian diplomat, engaged in homosexual activity. Smits, who was also accused of, and subsequently charged with, the distribution of pornographic materials, was discharged from office and returned to Latvia. The Latvian Government filed a formal complaint about Smits's treatment and, in early August, recalled its ambassador from Minsk; the Government also expelled the first secretary of the Belarusian embassy in the Latvian capital, Rīga, alleging that he had engaged in actions that were 'incompatible with the status of a diplomat'. In October criminal proceedings against Smits were abandoned; the Latvian ambassador later returned to Minsk. After protracted delays, Belarus and Latvia concluded in the latter stages of 2006 the demarcation of their shared border, a project that had commenced in 1998.

With the dissolution of the USSR in December 1991, Belarus effectively became a nuclear power, with approximately 80 intercontinental ballistic missiles stationed on its territory. However, the Government described Belarus as a neutral and non-nuclear state, and in May 1992 Belarus signed the Lisbon Protocol to the Treaty on the Non-Proliferation of Nuclear Weapons (see p. 109), under which it pledged to transfer all nuclear missiles to Russia by 1999. Substantial amounts of financial and technical aid were pledged by the USA to help Belarus dismantle its nuclear arsenal, and the last remaining nuclear warhead was transported to Russia in late 1996. In September 2000 Belarus became a permanent member of the Non-aligned Movement (see p. 424).

Government

Under the Constitution of March 1994, which was amended in November 1996, legislative power is vested in the bicameral Natsionalnoye Sobraniye (National Assembly). The lower chamber, the 110-member Palata Predstaviteley (House of Representatives), is elected by universal adult suffrage for a term of four years. The upper chamber, the Soviet Respubliki (Council of the Republic), comprises 64 members: 56 members elected by organs of local administration, and eight members appointed by the President. The President is the Head of State, and is elected by popular vote for five years. Executive authority is exercised by the Council of Ministers, which is led by the Chairman (Prime Minister) and is responsible to the Natsionalnoye Sobraniye. For administrative purposes, Belarus is divided into six regions (*oblasts*) and the capital city of Minsk; the regions are divided into districts (*rayons*).

Defence

As assessed at November 2007, the total strength of Belarus's armed forces was 72,940, comprising an army of 29,600, an air force and air defence forces of 18,170, as well as 25,170 in centrally controlled units and Ministry of Defence staff. There are also paramilitary forces, controlled by the Ministry of Internal Affairs, which number 110,000, including a border guard of 12,000. Military service is compulsory and lasts for between nine and 12 months. In October 1994 it was announced that two Russian non-nuclear military installations were to remain in Belarus. The budget for 2007 allocated 1,130,000m. readjusted roubles to defence. In January 1995 Belarus joined the North Atlantic Treaty Organization's (NATO) 'Partnership for Peace' (see p. 342) programme of military co-operation.

Economic Affairs

In 2006, according to estimates by the World Bank, Belarus's gross national income (GNI), measured at average 2004–06 prices, was US $32,800m., equivalent to $3,380 per head. In terms of purchasing-power parity, GNI in that year was equivalent to $8,810 per head. During 1996–2006 the population declined at an average annual rate of 0.4%, while gross domestic product (GDP) per head increased by an annual average of 8.1%, in real terms. During 1996–2006, overall GDP increased, in real terms, by an average of 7.6% annually. Real GDP increased by 10.1% in 2006.

Agriculture (including forestry) contributed 9.3% of GDP in 2006. In that year 13.5% of the employed labour force were engaged in the sector, according to IMF figures. The principal crops are potatoes, grain and sugar beet. Large areas of arable land (some 1.6m. ha) remain unused after being contaminated in 1986, following the accident at the Chornobyl nuclear power station in Ukraine. The Belarusian authorities have largely opposed private farming, and by 1999 collective and state farms still accounted for some 83% of agricultural land. However, private farms produced the majority of Belarus's potatoes, fruit and vegetables, as well as a significant proportion of total livestock-product output. In 1998, according to the IMF, 49.8% of total crop output was produced by the private sector. During 1996–2006, according to World Bank estimates, real agricultural GDP increased at an average annual rate of 2.2%. Agricultural output increased, in real terms, by 2.0% in 2006.

Industry (comprising mining, manufacturing, construction and power) provided 41.4% of GDP in 2006, when it engaged 35.1% of the employed labour force, according to IMF figures. According to the World Bank, industrial GDP increased, in real terms, at an average annual rate of 10.9% during 1996–2006. Real industrial GDP increased by 10.4% in 2006.

Belarus has relatively few mineral resources, although there are small deposits of petroleum and natural gas, and important peat reserves. Peat extraction, however, was severely affected by the disaster at Chornobyl, since contaminated peat could not be burned. Some 2.4m. metric tons of peat for fuel were mined in 2005, according to US Geological Survey. Belarus produced 50% of the former USSR's output of potash; annual output of around 4.4 metric tons was reported by 2004. Less than 0.5% the labour force were engaged in mining and quarrying in 2001.

According to the World Bank, the manufacturing sector contributed an estimated 37.7% of GDP in 2006, and employed 26.5% of the labour force in 1994. Machine-building, power generation and chemicals are the principal branches of the sector. During 1996–2006 manufacturing GDP increased, in real terms, at an average annual rate of 12.2%, according to World Bank estimates. Overall sectoral GDP increased by 19.8% in 2006.

In 2004 much of Belarus's supply of energy was provided by natural gas (87.3%), with petroleum and petroleum products accounting for almost all of the remainder. In 2005, according to IMF figures, the country imported 98.2% of its crude-oil consumption, 99.9% of its natural gas consumption and 28.1% of its electricity consumption. Energy products comprised 33.8% of the total value of imports in 2005. There are two large petroleum refineries, at Novopolotsk and Mozyr.

The services sector provided 49.3% of GDP in 2006 and, according to the IMF, accounted for 51.4% of total employment. The sector is led by transport and communications and trade and catering, which accounted, respectively, for 7.5% and 7.5% of GDP in 2006. According to World Bank estimates, during 1996–2006 the GDP of the services sector increased, in real terms, at an average annual rate of 7.6%. Sectoral GDP increased by 11.8% in 2006.

In 2005 Belarus recorded a visible trade deficit of US $2,398.4m., and there was a deficit of $1,511.6m. on the current account of the balance of payments. Trading partners within the Commonwealth of Independent States (CIS, see p. 215) accounted for 64.9% of Belarus's imports and 43.6% of its exports in 2006. In that year Belarus's principal trading partner was Russia (which accounted for 58.6% of total imports and 34.7% of exports). In 2004 the principal exports were machinery and transport equipment, mineral products, basic manufactures, chemicals and related products, miscellaneous manufactured articles and foodstuffs. The principal imports were petroleum and gas, basic manufactures, machinery and transport equipment, chemicals and related products, and foodstuffs.

In 2004 the republican and local government budgets (excluding receipts from privatization) registered a surplus of 12,800m. roubles (equivalent to 0.03% of GDP). Belarus's total external debt was US $4,734m. at the end of 2005, of which $783m. was long-term public debt. In that year the cost of debt-servicing was equivalent to 3.7% of the value of exports of goods and services. During 1996–2006 consumer prices increased at an average rate of 61.8% per year. The average annual rate of inflation was 10.3% in 2005 and 7.0% in 2006. In July 2006 some 66,500 people were registered as unemployed. However, the true rate of unemployment was believed to be far higher, as many people were unwilling to register, owing to the low level of official benefits.

Belarus joined the IMF and the World Bank in 1992. It also became a member of the European Bank for Reconstruction and Development (EBRD, see p. 239). Belarus is pursuing membership of the World Trade Organization (WTO, see p. 396), at which it holds observer status, although its failure to introduce market economic principles made the prospect of accession unlikely in the short term. The IMF closed its Belarus office in 2004.

Following the dissolution of the USSR, Belarus was slow to adopt economic reforms, and economic policy was influenced by the country's aim of eventual integration with Russia. External conditions were regarded as having facilitated the success of the Belarusian economy in 2004–05, as the increase in international petroleum prices stimulated exports of refined petroleum products. Poverty had declined significantly, as strong growth in real wages and pensions was recorded. However, wages were expanding more rapidly than productivity, while foreign and private-sector investment in Belarus was likely to remain limited while the so-called golden share regulation, which permitted any company in which the Government retained as little as one share to come under renewed state control, remained in place. In 2002 the Government agreed to authorize the partial denationalization of the domestic natural gas importer, Beltransgaz, enabling the Russian state-controlled natural gas producer Gazprom to acquire a stake in the company, in return for the partial settlement of Belarus's energy arrears. In January 2007 Belarus imposed a levy on Russian oil passing through Belarusian territory in response to the introduction of an export duty by Russia. Later in the month Belarus agreed to pay Gazprom $100 per 1,000 cu m of gas (more than two times the price paid under the previous contract). In exchange, Belarus stood to gain overdue fees for Gazprom's 50% stake in Beltransgaz. Further revenues were expected for the following five years, as Belarus increased gas transit tariffs for use of its section of the Yamal pipeline almost two-fold. Protective tariffs were implemented to shield industry and consumers from the full impact of the rise in energy prices. Overall, consumer prices rose by 8.1% in 2007, while economic growth was estimated at 7.8%. Fuel exports declined in early 2007, resulting in an increase in the trade deficit. The energy sector encountered further problems in November, when the USA imposed economic sanctions on the petrochemical company Belneftekhim (see Recent History). The Belarusian authorities hoped that a series of co-operation agreements signed with the Venezuelan Government in December, including an agreement providing for the joint exploration of two oil-fields in Venezuela by the Belarusian state-owned Belarusneft and the Venezuelan state-owned petroleum company Petróleos de Venezuela, SA, would generate economic benefits for Belarus. The IMF projected a 10.1% rise in consumer prices and GDP growth of 6.8% in 2008.

Education

In 1998 a programme of education reform was initiated, extending the period of compulsory education from nine to 10 years, from six to 16 years of age. In 2001 the total enrolment at pre-primary level was equivalent to 70.8% of children in the relevant age group. Primary education usually begins at six years of age and lasts for four years. In 2004 enrolment at primary level included 89.9% of pupils of the relevant age-group. Secondary education, beginning at the age of 10, lasts for a further eight years, comprising a first cycle of six years and a (non-compulsory) second cycle of two years. In 2004 secondary enrolment included 87.3% of pupils in the relevant age-group. In 2005/06 some 138,593 pupils were enrolled at vocational and technical schools, while a further 154,100 were enrolled at specialized institutions of secondary education. In 2001/02 some 27.7% of all pupils were taught in Belarusian, and 72.2% were taught in Russian (0.1% were taught in Polish). At early 2007 there were 43 state-owned and 12 private higher education institutions, including 29 universities, as well as seven academies, 13 institutes, four higher colleges and two theological seminaries. In 2005/06 some 383,000 students were enrolled in higher education (equivalent to 393 per 10,000 inhabitants). Research is co-ordinated by the National Academy of Sciences of Belarus. Budgetary expenditure on education by all levels of government was 3,020,000m. roubles (equivalent to 17.2% of total budgetary spending) in 2004.

Public Holidays

2008: 1 January (New Year's Day), 7 January (Orthodox Christmas), 8 March (International Women's Day), 15 March (Constitution Day), 23 March (Roman Catholic Easter), 27 April (Orthodox Easter), 1 May (Labour Day), 6 May (Radunitsa, Remembrance Day), 9 May (Victory Day and State Flag Day), 3 July (Independence Day), 25 December (Roman Catholic Christmas).

2009: 1 January (New Year's Day), 7 January (Orthodox Christmas), 8 March (International Women's Day), 15 March (Constitution Day), 12 April (Roman Catholic Easter), 19 April (Orthodox Easter), 1 May (Labour Day), 6 May (Radunitsa, Remembrance Day), 8 May (State Flag Day), 9 May (Victory Day), 3 July (Independence Day), 25 December (Roman Catholic Christmas).

Weights and Measures

The metric system is in force.

Statistical Survey

Source: mainly Ministry of Statistics and Analysis, 220070 Minsk, pr. Partizanski 12; tel. (17) 249-42-78; fax (17) 249-22-04; e-mail minstat@mail.belpak.by; internet www.belstat.gov.by.

Area and Population

AREA, POPULATION AND DENSITY

Area (sq km)	207,595*
Population (census results)†	
12 January 1989	10,151,806
16 February 1999	
Males	4,717,621
Females	5,327,616
Total	10,045,237
Population (official estimates at 31 December)	
2004	9,800,100
2005	9,750,500
2006	9,714,500
Density (per sq km) at 31 December 2006	46.8

* 80,153 sq miles.

† Figures refer to the *de jure* population. The *de facto* total was 10,199,709 in 1989.

POPULATION BY ETHNIC GROUP
(1999 census, % of total population)

Belarusian	81
Russian	11
Polish	4
Ukrainian	2
Others	2
Total	**100**

ADMINISTRATIVE DIVISIONS*
(31 December 2006; figures are rounded)

Oblasts (Regions)	
Brest (Bieraście)	1,439,500
Gomel (Homiel)	1,475,900
Grodno (Horadnia)	1,114,100
Minsk (Miensk)	1,466,800
Mogilev (Mahilou̇)	1,137,500
Vitebsk (Viciebsk)	1,283,200
Capital City	
Minsk (Miensk)	1,797,500
Total	**9,714,200**

* The Belarusian names are given in parentheses after the more widely used Russian names, where they differ.

BELARUS

PRINCIPAL TOWNS*
(estimated population at 1 January 2001)

Minsk (Miensk, capital)	1,699,100	Borisov (Barysau)	150,900
Gomel (Homiel)	480,000	Pinsk	131,100
Mogilev (Mahilou)	360,600	Orsha (Vorsha)	124,000
Vitebsk (Viciebsk)	341,500	Mozyr (Mazyr)	110,700
Grodno (Horadnia)	307,100	Novopolotsk	102,100
Brest (Bieraście)	291,400	Soligorsk	101,900
Bobruysk (Babrujsk)	221,400	Lida	100,000
Baranovichi (Baranavichy)	168,800		

* The Belarusian names are given in parentheses after the more widely used Russian names, where they differ.

Mid-2005 ('000, incl. suburbs, UN estimate): Minsk 1,778 (Source: UN, *World Urbanization Prospects: The 2005 Revision*).

BIRTHS, MARRIAGES AND DEATHS

	Registered live births Number	Rate (per 1,000)	Registered marriages Number	Rate (per 1,000)	Registered deaths Number	Rate (per 1,000)
1998	92,645	9.1	71,354	7.0	137,296	13.5
1999	92,975	9.3	72,994	7.3	142,027	14.2
2000	93,691	9.4	62,485	6.2	134,867	13.5
2001	91,720	9.2	68,697	6.9	140,299	14.1
2002	88,743	8.9	66,652	6.7	146,655	14.8
2003	88,512	9.0	69,905	7.1	143,200	14.5
2004	88,943	9.1	60,265	6.1	140,064	14.3
2005	90,508	9.3	n.a.	n.a.	141,857	14.5

Source: partly UN, *Demographic Yearbook*.

Expectation of life (years at birth, WHO estimates): 68.8 (males 63.1; females 74.7) in 2005 (Source: WHO, *World Health Statistics*).

EMPLOYMENT
(monthly averages, '000 persons)*

	2004	2005	2006
Agriculture	473	458	444
Forestry	32	33	32
Industry†	976	974	969
Construction	237	261	267
Transport and communications	268	268	265
Trade and related services‡	251	260	263
Communal services	177	184	187
Health and social services	304	308	310
Education, culture and science	561	560	566
Banks and insurance	57	59	60
Administration	84	86	86
Other activities	74	74	71
Total employed	3,494	3,525	3,520
Unemployed	83	68	52
Total labour force	3,577	3,593	3,572

* Excluding small non-state enterprises.
† Comprising manufacturing (except printing and publishing), mining and quarrying, electricity, gas, logging and fishing.
‡ Including material and technical supply and procurement.

Source: IMF, *Republic of Belarus: Statistical Appendix* (September 2007).

Health and Welfare

KEY INDICATORS

Total fertility rate (children per woman, 2005)	1.2
Under-5 mortality rate (per 1,000 live births, 2004)	9
HIV/AIDS (% of persons aged 15–49, 2005)	0.3
Physicians (per 1,000 head, 2005)	4.55
Hospital beds (per 1,000 head, 2004)	11.1
Health expenditure (2004): US $ per head (PPP)	426.5
Health expenditure (2004): % of GDP	6.2
Health expenditure (2004): public (% of total)	74.9
Access to water (% of persons, 2004)	100
Access to sanitation (% of persons, 2004)	84
Human Development Index (2005): ranking	64
Human Development Index (2005): value	0.804

For sources and definitions, see explanatory note on p. vi.

Agriculture

PRINCIPAL CROPS
('000 metric tons)

	2004	2005	2006
Wheat	1,120.9	1,174.8	1,075.4
Barley	2,031.7	1,863.8	1,831.3
Maize	38.8	144.2	152.6
Rye	1,397.1	1,154.9	1,072.1
Oats	765.2	609.6	554.9
Buckwheat	11.9	7.3	5.1
Triticale (wheat-rye hybrid)	1,216.0	1,121.5	978.3
Potatoes	9,902.2	8,185.0	8,329.4
Sugar beet	3,088.3	3,065.2	3,980.3
Dry beans	115.0	111.3	800.0
Dry peas	110.4	50.8	46.8
Walnuts*	13.3	14.0	14.0
Sunflower seed†	20.0	15.0	20.0
Rapeseed	142.9	149.9	115.0
Linseed	22.6	19.5	11.1
Cabbages and other brassicas	573.4	529.8	568.6
Tomatoes	229.7	245.9	241.5
Cucumbers and gherkins	265.9	286.9	315.0
Dry onions	156.5	158.5	167.3
Carrots and turnips	296.3	280.9	319.2
Apples	204.0	204.6	488.8
Pears	33.5	35.3	61.1
Plums	35.9	46.5	66.9
Sour (Morello) cherries	22.7	27.6	46.9
Sweet cherries*	11.0	12.0	12.0
Flax fibre	56.6	50.4	29.2

* FAO estimates.
† Unofficial figures.

Aggregate production ('000 metric tons, may include official, semi-official or estimated data): Total cereals 6,590.0 in 2004, 6,089.4 in 2005, 5,686.1 in 2006; Total roots and tubers 9,902.2 in 2004, 8,185.0 in 2005, 8,329.4 in 2006; Total pulses 425.8 in 2004; 331.2 in 2005, 235.2 in 2006; Total vegetables (incl. melons) 2,042.5 in 2004, 2,014.1 in 2005, 2,180.5 in 2006; Total fruits (excl. melons) 369.4 in 2004, 394.7 in 2005, 729.8 in 2006.

Source: FAO.

LIVESTOCK
('000 head at 1 January)

	2004	2005	2006
Horses	192	181	168
Cattle	3,924	3,963	3,980
Pigs	3,287	3,407	3,545
Sheep	63	59	53
Goats	63	66	68
Chickens	24,558	25,037	28,476

Source: FAO.

BELARUS

LIVESTOCK PRODUCTS
('000 metric tons)

	2004	2005	2006
Cattle meat	223.8	255.8	271.8
Sheep meat	1.8	1.2	1.0
Pig meat	298.9	321.0	345.9
Chicken meat	100.6	115.2	145.2
Cows' milk	5,124.1	5,650.1	5,869.9
Hen eggs	163.9*	172.4*	197.4†

* Unofficial figure.
† FAO estimate.
Source: FAO.

Forestry

ROUNDWOOD REMOVALS
('000 cubic metres, excl. bark)

	2003*	2004*	2005†
Sawlogs, veneer logs and logs for sleepers	2,304	3,676	3,771
Pulpwood	1,612	1,847	1,895
Other industrial wood	2,531	1,833	1,881
Fuel wood	1,097	1,266	1,170
Total	7,543	8,622	8,716

* Unofficial figures.
† FAO estimates.
2006: Figures assumed to be unchanged from 2005 (FAO estimates).
Source: FAO.

SAWNWOOD PRODUCTION
('000 cubic metres, incl. railway sleepers)

	2003*	2004*	2005†
Coniferous (softwood)	2,064	2,157	2,110
Broadleaved (hardwood)	239	570	557
Total	2,304	2,727	2,667

* Unofficial figures.
† FAO estimates.
2006: Figures assumed to be unchanged from 2005 (FAO estimates).
Source: FAO.

Fishing

(metric tons, live weight)

	2003	2004	2005*
Capture	6,925	890	900
Freshwater bream	393	164	160
Common carp	4,953	26	30
Crucian carp	497	188	190
Northern pike	336	125	130
Aquaculture	5,393	4,150	4,150
Common carp	3,386	3,207	3,207
Crucian carp	1,608	721	721
Total catch	12,318	5,040	5,050

* FAO estimates.
Source: FAO.

Mining

('000 metric tons, unless otherwise indicated)

	2003	2004	2005
Crude petroleum	1,820	1,804	1,785
Natural gas (million cu metres)	254	245	228
Peat: for fuel	1,802	2,108	2,408

Source: US Geological Survey.

Industry

SELECTED PRODUCTS
('000 metric tons, unless otherwise indicated)

	2002	2003	2004
Refined sugar	666	n.a.	n.a.
Wheat flour	644	637	677
Ethyl alcohol ('000 hectolitres)	902	867	761
Other distilled alcoholic beverages('000 hectolitres)	1,885	1,682	1,512
Beer ('000 hectolitres)	2,026	2,056	2,272
Mineral water ('000 hectolitres)	1,900	1,873	1,777
Soft drinks ('000 hectolitres)	2,348	2,479	2,528
Cigarettes (million)	10,524	10,442	12,627
Bed linen, articles ('000)	3,690	3,253	3,959
Blouses, women's and girls' ('000)	1,315	1,158	1,151
Skirts, slacks and shorts for women and girls ('000)	2,706	2,792	3,420
Shirts, men's and boys' ('000)	2,230	1,923	1,858
Blankets ('000)	365	329	236
Carpets ('000 sq metres)	4,902	n.a.	n.a.
Footwear (excluding rubber, '000 pairs)	12,691	n.a.	n.a.
Plywood ('000 cu metres)	168	166	192
Paper and paperboard*	216.0	279.3	257.0
Benzene (Benzol)	34.5	n.a.	n.a.
Ethylene (Ethene)	121.2	n.a.	n.a.
Propylene (Propene)	69.7	n.a.	n.a.
Xylenes (Xylol)	50.7	n.a.	n.a.
Sulphuric acid (100%)	524	n.a.	n.a.
Nitrogenous fertilizers (a)*†	644.4	635.9	665.0
Phosphate fertilizers (b)*†	74.0	86.2	114.3
Potash fertilizers (c)*†	3,811.9	4,276.3	4,712.1
Non-cellulosic continuous fibres	130.7	125.4	n.a.
Cellulosic continuous filaments	11.5	11.0	n.a.
Soap	4.0	6.0	6.0
Rubber tyres: for agricultural and other off-road vehicles ('000)	156	183	231
Rubber tyres: for road motor vehicles ('000)	2,126	n.a.	n.a.
Rubber footwear ('000 pairs)	5,438	n.a.	n.a.
Quicklime	601	658	727
Cement	2,171	2,472	2,731
Domestic refrigerators ('000)	856	886	953
Radio receivers ('000)	47	31	21
Lorries (number)	16,544	n.a.	n.a.
Motorcycles ('000)	15	33	12
Bicycles ('000)	875	773	775
Watches ('000)	3,948	2,606	1,740
Electric energy (million kWh)	26,455	26,627	31,211

* Source: FAO.
† Production in terms of (a) nitrogen (N); (b) phosphorous pentoxide (P_2O_5); or (c) potassium oxide (K_2O).

Source (unless otherwise indicated): UN, *Industrial Commodity Statistics Yearbook*.

2005 (figures are rounded): Sausages ('000 metric tons) 257; Carpets ('000 sq metres) 7,400; Footwear ('000 pairs) 10,100; Particle board ('000 cu metres) 390; Paper ('000 metric tons) 69; Tyres for automobiles and agricultural machinery 3,052,000; Cement ('000 metric tons) 3,131; Tractors 41,500 units; Refrigerators and freezers 995,000 units; Television receivers 1,308,000 units; Bicycles (excl. children's) 438,000; Electric energy (million kWh) 31,000.

2006 (figures are rounded): Sausages ('000 metric tons) 278; Carpets ('000 sq metres) 7,000; Footwear ('000 pairs) 10,900; Particle board ('000 cu metres) 411; Paper ('000 metric tons) 63; Tyres for automobiles and agricultural machinery 3,563,000; Cement ('000 metric tons) 3,495; Tractors 49,200 units; Refrigerators and freezers 1,050,000 units; Television receivers 1,308,000 units; Bicycles (excl. children's) 454,000; Electric energy (million kWh) 31,800.

BELARUS

Finance

CURRENCY AND EXCHANGE RATES

Monetary Units
100 kopeks = 1 readjusted Belarusian rouble (rubel).

Sterling, Dollar and Euro Equivalents (31 November 2007)
£1 sterling = 4,449.0 readjusted roubles;
US $1 = 2,153.0 readjusted roubles;
€1 = 3,178.0 readjusted roubles;
10,000 readjusted Belarusian roubles = £2.25 = $4.64 = €3.15.

Average Exchange Rate (readjusted Belarusian roubles per US $)
2004   2,160.26
2005   2,153.82
2006   2,144.56

Note: The Belarusian rouble was introduced in May 1992, initially as a coupon currency, to circulate alongside (and at par with) the Russian (formerly Soviet) rouble. The parity between Belarusian and Russian currencies was subsequently ended, and the Belarusian rouble was devalued. In August 1994 a new Belarusian rouble, equivalent to 10 old roubles, was introduced. On 1 January 1995 the Belarusian rouble became the sole national currency, while the circulation of Russian roubles ceased. On 1 January 2000 a readjusted Belarusian rouble, equivalent to 1,000 of the former units, was introduced.

STATE BUDGET
('000 million roubles)

Revenue*	2002	2003	2004
Republican and local budget revenue:			
Tax revenue	6,263.4	9,333.6	12,660.5
Direct taxes on income and profits	1,684.5	2,369.0	3,538.8
Personal income tax	773.1	1,024.4	1,403.8
Profit tax	643.3	934.4	1,624.6
Enterprise income tax	136.8	173.3	233.3
Taxes on wage fund	220.4	273.2	391.2
Taxes on goods and services	3,311.7	4,837.2	6,401.7
Value-added tax	2,165.1	2,894.8	3,814.6
Excises	592.0	837.8	1,121.6
Property tax	390.5	728.8	957.0
Other current revenue	453.4	631.3	990.4
Capital revenue	21.8	15.7	27.0
Revenue from sales of assets	21.5	13.9	24.1
Revenue of budgetary funds	1,924.9	2,862.8	3,738.7
Sub-total	8,663.5	12,843.4	17,416.7
Social protection fund:			
Total revenue (incl. from state budget)	3,055.0	3,977.8	5,452.8
Less Transfers from the state budget	69.8	56.7	36.1
Total revenue	11,648.7	16,764.6	22,833.4

Expenditure	2002	2003	2004
Republican and local budget expenditure:			
Government administration	251.6	381.5	565.7
Defence	259.9	376.9	472.2
Law, order and security	461.0	654.1	920.7
Agriculture	178.8	520.3	766.6
Housing and communal services	612.4	940.9	1,174.7
Emergency funds, Chernobyl	307.0	376.4	489.0
Education	1,738.1	2,343.1	3,020.0
Health, sports and physical education	1,270.1	1,809.8	1,410.3
Servicing of state debt	154.2	175.7	209.8
Capital investment	323.6	533.4	807.5
Expenditure of budgetary funds	1,805.2	2,619.7	3,579.5
Others	520.4	935.0	970.7
Unallocated	1,252.9	1,666.3	2,207.8
Sub-total	9,135.1	13,333.1	17,594.6
Less Transfers to the social protection fund	69.8	56.7	36.1
Social protection fund expenditure	3,061.4	3,987.8	5,262.1
Total expenditure	12,126.7	17,264.3	22,820.6

* Excluding receipts from privatization.

Source: IMF, *Republic of Belarus: Statistical Appendix* (June 2005).

General government totals ('000 million roubles): *Revenue:* 23,004 in 2004 (revised); 30,825 in 2005; 33,940 in 2006. *Expenditure* (cash basis): 22,984 in 2004 (revised); 31,257 in 2005; 35,070 in 2006. (Source: IMF, *Republic of Belarus: 2006 Article IV Consultation—Staff Report; Public Information Notice on the Executive Board Discussion; and Statement by the Executive Director for the Republic of Belarus*, August 2006).

INTERNATIONAL RESERVES
(US $ million at 31 December)

	2004	2005	2006
IMF special drawing rights	0.01	0.03	0.04
Reserve position in IMF	0.03	0.03	0.03
Foreign exchange	749.33	1,136.56	1,098.84
Total	749.37	1,136.62	1,098.91

Source: IMF, *International Financial Statistics*.

MONEY SUPPLY
(million roubles at 31 December)

	2004	2005	2006
Currency outside banks	1,339.44	2,016.41	2,818.35
Demand deposits at deposit money banks	1,771.36	2,928.49	4,203.46
Total money (incl. others)	3,111.36	4,945.79	7,023.21

Source: IMF, *International Financial Statistics*.

COST OF LIVING
(Consumer Price Index; base: 2000 = 100)

	2003	2004	2005
Food (incl. beverages)	267.6	320.1	358.2
Fuel and light	1,374.1	1,623.2	1,645.6
Clothing (incl. footwear)	201.2	214.1	218.8
Rent	1,348.8	2,236.4	3,201.6
All items (incl. others)	295.0	348.3	384.3

2006 (Consumer Price Index; base: 2000 = 100): All items 411.2; Food (incl. beverages) 380.1.

Source: ILO.

BELARUS

NATIONAL ACCOUNTS
('000 million roubles at current prices)

Expenditure on the Gross Domestic Product

	2004	2005	2006
Final consumption expenditure	37,159	47,351	57,285
Households	26,130	32,955	40,402
Non-profit institutions serving households	729	872	1,079
Government	10,300	13,524	15,804
Gross capital formation	15,243	18,519	24,081
Gross fixed capital formation	13,568	17,254	22,400
Changes in inventories	1,675	1,265	1,681
Total domestic expenditure	52,402	65,870	81,366
Net exports of goods and services	−3,181	463	−3,396
Statistical discrepancy	771	−1,266	1,261
GDP in market prices	49,992	65,067	79,231
GDP at constant 2000 prices*	11,987.2	13,118.9	14,423.0

*Source: IMF, *International Financial Statistics*.

Gross Domestic Product by Economic Activity

	2004	2005	2006
Agriculture and forestry	4,424	5,468	6,317
Industry*	14,007	18,509	21,865
Construction	3,234	4,500	6,271
Transport and communications	4,829	6,172	7,318
Trade and catering	4,859	6,129	8,131
Material supply and procurement	263	309	339
Housing and public utilities	2,154	2,498	3,102
Health care	1,785	2,311	2,712
Education, culture and science	2,929	4,231	4,931
Other	4,352	5,821	6,948
GDP at factor cost	42,836	55,948	67,934
Taxes, *less* subsidies on products	7,156	9,119	11,297
GDP in market prices	49,992	65,067	79,231

*Principally mining, manufacturing, electricity, gas and water.

Source: IMF, *Republic of Belarus: Statistical Appendix* (September 2007).

BALANCE OF PAYMENTS
(US $ million)

	2004	2005	2006
Exports of goods f.o.b.	13,942.2	16,108.8	19,838.1
Imports of goods f.o.b.	−16,126.1	−16,609.7	−22,236.5
Trade balance	−2,183.9	−500.9	−2,398.4
Exports of services	1,747.0	1,959.3	2,299.2
Imports of services	−1,058.4	−1,249.5	−1,486.9
Balance on goods and services	−1,495.3	208.9	−1,586.1
Other income received	157.6	283.4	244.6
Other income paid	−159.1	−227.7	−351.9
Balance on goods, services and income	−1,496.8	264.6	−1,693.4
Current transfers received	390.6	280.5	301.6
Current transfers paid	−88.0	−111.4	−119.8
Current balance	−1,194.2	433.7	−1,511.6
Capital account (net)	49.3	40.5	70.5
Direct investment abroad	−1.3	−2.5	−3.0
Direct investment from abroad	163.8	305.0	354.0
Portfolio investment assets	3.2	−2.9	5.6
Portfolio investment liabilities	59.6	−38.6	−24.7
Financial derivatives assets	n.a.	1.9	0.0
Financial derivatives liabilities	n.a.	−2.2	−13.0
Other investment assets	−151.4	−492.1	−136.8
Other investment liabilities	972.3	170.9	1,525.1
Net errors and omissions	274.2	111.7	−250.0
Overall balance	175.5	525.5	16.2

Source: IMF, *International Financial Statistics*.

External Trade

PRINCIPAL COMMODITIES
(distribution by SITC, US $ million)

Imports c.i.f.	2002	2003	2004
Food and live animals	898.5	1,016.7	1,325.9
Crude materials (inedible) except fuels	368.3	470.0	595.1
Mineral fuels, lubricants, etc.	2,334.5	3,038.3	4,524.7
Petroleum, petroleum products and related materials	1,609.6	2,153.2	3,436.0
Gas, natural and manufactured	566.3	719.2	973.3
Chemicals and related products	969.0	1,217.2	1,631.9
Basic manufactures	1,677.4	2,162.0	3,216.1
Textile yarn, fabrics, etc.	266.3	322.2	403.3
Iron and steel	548.7	777.0	1,238.7
Machinery and transport equipment	2,018.2	2,581.8	3,774.8
Machinery specialized for particular industries	249.7	377.6	584.6
General industrial machinery and equipment	332.6	474.0	697.1
Electric machinery, apparatus and appliances, etc.	375.9	503.2	756.2
Road vehicles	555.2	583.1	807.6
Miscellaneous manufactured articles	448.0	584.1	764.1
Total (incl. others)	9,092.3	11,558.0	16,345.4

Exports f.o.b.	2002	2003	2004
Food and live animals	544.7	741.9	1,045.3
Crude materials (inedible) except fuels	389.4	432.3	515.4
Mineral fuels, lubricants, etc.	1,624.4	2,194.1	3,697.8
Petroleum, petroleum products, etc.	1,605.0	2,150.5	3,596.7
Refined petroleum products	1,478.8	1,960.6	3,295.7
Chemicals and related products	982.7	1,181.7	1,499.5
Fertilizers, manufactured	540.5	643.4	863.4
Potassium chloride	463.1	535.8	752.0
Basic manufactures	1,514.6	1,911.1	2,497.6
Textile yarn, fabrics, etc.	381.2	448.6	513.7
Iron and steel	321.5	443.3	683.2
Other metal manufactures	249.5	330.2	445.4
Machinery and transport equipment	1,915.3	2,280.4	3,042.0
Machinery specialized for particular industries	349.5	402.3	532.4
Electrical machinery, apparatus and appliances, etc.	388.7	500.6	637.6
Road vehicles	762.8	870.0	1,211.6
Lorries and special purposes motor vehicles	349.5	388.7	555.2
Miscellaneous manufactured articles	896.8	1,039.7	1,231.0
Clothing and accessories (excl. footwear)	292.1	340.9	400.7
Total (incl. others)	8,020.9	9,945.6	13,751.7

Source: UN, *International Trade Statistics Yearbook*.

2005 (US $ million): Total imports 16,708; Total exports 15,979.
2006 (US $ million): Total imports 22,351; Total exports 19,734.

BELARUS

PRINCIPAL TRADING PARTNERS
(US $ million)

Imports c.i.f.	2002	2003	2004
Brazil	104.5	89.2	97.0
China, People's Republic	46.4	71.7	158.0
Czech Republic	54.2	74.4	111.0
France	94.8	116.3	165.0
Germany	693.0	820.6	1,081.0
Italy	215.1	283.9	300.4
Lithuania	109.3	154.2	175.5
Netherlands	84.0	93.3	118.6
Poland	221.7	348.4	474.9
Russia	5,922.3	7,601.9	11,142.5
Sweden	99.5	98.4	98.4
Ukraine	290.6	362.0	544.9
United Kingdom	67.7	79.3	128.3
USA	103.3	150.1	195.5
Total (incl. others)	9,092.3	11,558.0	16,345.4

Exports f.o.b.	2002	2003	2004
Brazil	89.4	113.4	146.4
China, People's Republic	217.4	162.2	301.5
Denmark	26.2	105.8	131.1
Germany	347.9	421.1	502.8
Hungary	70.8	105.5	136.6
Italy	130.0	135.2	142.9
Latvia	520.1	344.3	326.0
Lithuania	256.7	264.9	356.2
Netherlands	279.0	413.8	924.4
Poland	273.3	434.1	728.7
Russia	3,977.1	4,879.8	6,462.9
Sweden	27.2	65.4	136.9
Ukraine	271.6	343.5	539.8
United Kingdom	493.7	938.3	1,147.5
USA	91.3	102.5	162.8
Total (incl. others)	8,020.9	9,945.6	13,751.7

Source: UN, *International Trade Statistics Yearbook*.

2005 (US $ million): *Imports:* Trade with CIS countries 11,142.5 (Moldova 72.3; Russia 10,118.2; Ukraine 893.9); Total (incl. others) 16,708. *Exports:* Trade with CIS countries 7,060.3 (Kazakhstan 183.5; Moldova 102.2; Russia 5,715.8; Ukraine 907.8); Total (incl. others) 15,979.

2006 (US $ million): *Imports:* Trade with CIS countries 14,511,7 (Moldova 81.1; Russia 13,099.1; Ukraine 1,223.7); Total (incl. others) 22,351. *Exports:* Trade with CIS countries 8,608,8 (Kazakhstan 259.4; Moldova 95.7; Russia 6,845.3; Ukraine 1,234.0); Total (incl. others) 19,734.

Transport

RAILWAYS
(traffic)

	2004	2005	2006
Passenger-km (million)	13,893	10,351	9,968
Freight ton-km (million)	40,331	43,559	45,723

ROAD TRAFFIC
(motor vehicles in use at 31 December)

	2001	2002	2004
Passenger cars	1,467,605	1,548,472	1,707,888
Buses and coaches	8,038	7,672	7,781
Road tractors	17,795	14,036	n.a.
Motorcycles and mopeds	535,996	525,005	454,612

Source: IRF, *World Road Statistics*.

CIVIL AVIATION
(traffic on scheduled services)

	2004	2005	2006
Passenger-km (million)	674	684	754
Total ton-km (million)	49	59	92

Tourism

FOREIGN TOURIST ARRIVALS

Country of nationality	2003	2004	2005
Cyprus	2,602	1,179	940
Germany	7,067	8,542	7,402
Israel	755	2,515	3,120
Italy	4,225	4,533	5,090
Latvia	7,665	4,978	7,409
Lithuania	7,458	5,317	8,249
Netherlands	1,347	954	868
Poland	10,287	5,563	2,983
Russia	6,801	11,681	27,097
United Kingdom	3,282	5,222	8,208
USA	3,376	5,518	4,274
Total (incl. others)	64,190	67,297	90,588

Tourism receipts (US $ million, incl. passenger transport): 339 in 2003; 362 in 2004; 346 in 2005.

Source: World Tourism Organization.

Communications Media

	1998	1999	2000
Television receivers ('000 in use)	3,300	3,400	3,500
Telephones ('000 main lines in use)	2,489.9	2,638.5	2,751.9
Facsimile machines (number in use)	19,472	23,847	26,925
Mobile cellular telephones (subscribers)	12,155	23,457	49,353
Internet users ('000)	7.5	50.0	180.0
Book production (incl. pamphlets):			
titles	6,073	6,064	7,686
copies ('000)	60,022	63,305	61,627
Daily newspapers:			
number	20	12	10
average circulation ('000)	1,559	1,094	1,101
Non-daily newspapers:			
number	560	578	600
average circulation ('000)	8,973	10,094	10,339
Other periodicals:			
number	318	331	354
average circulation ('000)	1,687	1,498	1,381

Radio receivers ('000 in use): 3,020 in 1997.

Telephones ('000 main lines in use): 2,862.4 in 2001; 2,967.2 in 2002; 3,071.3 in 2003; 3,175.9 in 2004; 3,284.3 in 2005.

Mobile cellular telephones ('000 subscribers): 138.3 in 2001; 462.6 in 2002; 1,118.0 in 2003; 2,239.3 in 2004; 4,098.0 in 2005.

Internet users ('000): 430.0 in 2001; 891.2 in 2002; 1,607.3 in 2003; 2,461.1 in 2004; 3,394.4 in 2005; 5,477.5 in 2006.

Broadband subscribers: 100 in 2003; 800 in 2004; 1,600 in 2005; 11,400 in 2006.

Sources: partly International Telecommunication Union; UNESCO, *Statistical Yearbook*.

Education

(2001/02, unless otherwise indicated)

	Institutions	Teachers	Students
Pre-primary	4,423	52,524	390,812
Primary (Grades 1–4)	4,187*	138,744	1,240,900*
Secondary (Grades 5–11)			
Vocational and technical	248	14,772	138,593
Specialized secondary	204*	12,748	154,100*
Higher	55*	21,684	383,000*
Institutions offering post-graduate studies	377	9,000	570,000

*2005/06.

Source: partly Ministry of Education, Minsk.

Adult literacy rate (UNESCO estimates): 99.6% (males 99.8%; females 99.4%) in 1999 (Source: UNESCO Institute for Statistics).

Directory

The Constitution

A new Constitution came into effect on 30 March 1994. An amended version of the Constitution became effective on 27 November 1996, following a referendum held on 24 November. A constitutional referendum, held on 17 October 2004, removed the former two-term limit for presidential tenure. The following is a summary of the main provisions of the Constitution:

PRINCIPLES OF THE CONSTITUTIONAL SYSTEM

The Republic of Belarus is a unitary, democratic, social state based on the rule of law. State power is exercised on the principle of division of powers between the legislature, executive and judiciary, which are independent of one another. The Republic is bound by the principle of supremacy of law and ensures that its laws comply with universally acknowledged principles of international law. Property may be owned by the State or privately. The mineral wealth, waters and forests are the sole and exclusive property of the State. Land for agricultural use is the property of the State. All religions and creeds are equal before the law. The official languages are Belarusian and Russian. The Republic aims to make its territory a neutral, nuclear-free state. The capital is Minsk (Miensk).

THE INDIVIDUAL, SOCIETY AND THE STATE

All persons are equal before the law and entitled without discrimination to equal protection of their rights and legitimate interests. The State ensures the freedom, inviolability and dignity of the individual. No person may be subjected to torture or cruel, inhuman or humiliating treatment or punishment. Freedom of movement is guaranteed. The freedom of expression and public assembly, and the right to form public associations, including trade unions, are guaranteed. Citizens have the right to participate in the solution of state matters, both directly and through freely elected representatives. The State shall create the conditions necessary for full employment. The right to health care is guaranteed. Each person has the right to housing and to education. Everyone has the right to preserve his or her ethnic affiliation, to use his or her native language and to choose the language of communication.

THE ELECTORAL SYSTEM AND REFERENDUMS

Elections and referendums are conducted by means of universal, free, equal and secret ballot. Deputies are elected by direct ballot. National referendums may be called by the President of the Republic of Belarus, by the Natsionalnoye Sobraniye (National Assembly) or by no fewer than 450,000 citizens eligible to vote. Local referendums may be called by local representative bodies or on the recommendation of no less than 10% of the citizens who are eligible to vote and resident in the area concerned. Decisions adopted by referendum may be reversed or amended only by means of another referendum.

THE PRESIDENT

The President is Head of State, the guarantor of the Constitution, and of the rights and freedoms of its citizens. The President is elected for a term of five years by universal, free, equal, direct and secret ballot.

The President calls national referendums; calls elections to the Natsionalnoye Sobraniye and local representative bodies; dissolves the chambers of the Natsionalnoye Sobraniye, as determined by the Constitution; appoints six members to the Central Electoral Commission; appoints the Chairman of the Cabinet of Ministers (Prime Minister) with the consent of the Palata Predstavitaley (House of Representatives); appoints and dismisses Ministers and other members of the Government, and considers the resignation of the Government; appoints, with the consent of the Soviet Respubliki (Council of the Republic), the Chairmen of the Constitutional, Supreme and Economic Courts, the judges of the Supreme and Economic Courts, the Chairman of the Central Electoral Commission, the Prosecutor-General, the Chairman and members of the board of the National Bank, and dismisses the aforementioned, having notified the Soviet Respubliki; appoints six members of the Constitutional Court, and other judges; may chair meetings of the Government; conducts negotiations and signs international treaties, appoints and recalls diplomatic representatives; declares a state of emergency; has the right to abolish acts of the Government and to suspend decisions of local councils of deputies; forms and heads the Security Council of the Republic of Belarus; is the Commander-in-Chief of the Armed Forces; imposes, in the event of military threat or attack, martial law. In instances determined by the Constitution, the President may issue decrees which have the force of law. The President may be removed from office for acts of treason and other grave crimes, by a decision of the Natsionalnoye Sobraniye.

THE NATSIONALNOYE SOBRANIYE

The Natsionalnoye Sobraniye (National Assembly) is a representative and legislative body, comprising two chambers: the Palata Predstavitaley and the Soviet Respubliki. The term of the Natsionalnoye Sobraniye is four years. The Palata Predstavitaley comprises 110 deputies, who are elected by universal, equal, free, direct suffrage and by secret ballot. The Soviet Respubliki is a chamber of territorial representation with 64 members, consisting of eight deputies from every region and from the capital city, elected by deputies of local councils. Eight members of the chamber are appointed by the President. Any citizen who has reached the age of 21 years may become a deputy of the Palata Predstavitaley. Any citizen who has reached the age of 30 years, and who has been resident in the corresponding region for no less than five years, may become a member of the Soviet Respubliki. The chambers of the Natsionalnoye Sobraniye elect their Chairmen.

The Palata Predstavitaley considers draft laws and the interpretation of laws. The Palata Predstavitaley calls elections for the presidency; grants consent to the President concerning the appointment of the Chairman of the Cabinet of Ministers; accepts the resignation of the President; and together with the Soviet Respubliki, takes the decision to remove the President from office.

The Soviet Respubliki approves or rejects draft laws adopted by the Palata Predstavitaley; consents to appointments made by the President; elects six judges of the Constitutional Court and six members of the Central Electoral Commission; considers charges of treason against the President; takes the decision to remove the President from office; considers presidential decrees on the introduction of a state of emergency, martial law, and general or partial mobilization.

On the proposal of the President, the Palata Predstavitaley and the Soviet Respubliki may adopt a law, delegating to him legislative powers to issue decrees which have the power of a law. However, he may not issue decrees making alterations or addenda to the Constitution or to policy laws.

THE GOVERNMENT

Executive power is exercised by the Cabinet of Ministers. The Government is accountable to the President and responsible to the Natsionalnoye Sobraniye. The Chairman of the Cabinet of Ministers is appointed by the President with the consent of the Palata Predstavitaley. The Government formulates and implements domestic and foreign policy; submits the draft national budget to the President; and issues acts that have binding force.

THE JUDICIARY

Judicial authority is exercised by the courts. Justice is administered on the basis of adversarial proceedings and equality of the parties involved in the trial. Supervision of the constitutionality of enforceable enactments of the State is exercised by the Constitutional Court, which comprises 12 judges, of whom six are appointed by the President and six are elected by the Soviet Respubliki.

LOCAL GOVERNMENT

Citizens exercise local and self-government through local councils of deputies, executive and administrative bodies and other forms of direct participation in state and public affairs. Local councils of deputies are elected by citizens for a four-year term, and the heads of local executive and administrative bodies are appointed and dismissed by the President.

APPLICATION OF THE CONSTITUTION AND THE PROCEDURE FOR AMENDING THE CONSTITUTION

Amendments and supplements to the Constitution are considered by the chambers of the Natsionalnoye Sobraniye on the initiative of the President, or of no fewer than 150,000 citizens who are eligible to vote. The Constitution may be amended or supplemented via a referendum.

The Government

HEAD OF STATE

President: ALYAKSANDR R. LUKASHENKA (inaugurated 20 July 1994; re-elected 9 September 2001; re-elected 19 March 2006).

COUNCIL OF MINISTERS
(April 2008)

Chairman (Prime Minister): SYARHEY S. SIDORSKY.
First Deputy Prime Minister: ULADZIMIR I. SEMASHKA.

BELARUS
Directory

Deputy Prime Ministers: Ivan M. Bambiza, Alyaksandr M. Kasinets, Andrey U. Kabyakow, Viktar P. Bura.

Minister of Agriculture and Food: Semyon B. Shapira.

Minister of Architecture and Construction: Alyaksandr Selyaznyou.

Minister of Communications and Information Technologies: Mikalay Pantsyaley.

Minister of Culture: Uladzimir F. Matveichuk.

Minister of Defence: Col.-Gen. Leanid S. Maltsaw.

Minister of the Economy: Mikalay P. Zaychanka.

Minister of Education: Alyaksandr M. Radzkow.

Minister for Emergency Situations: Enver R. Baryyew.

Minister of Energy: Alyaksandr Azyarets.

Minister of Finance: Mikalay P. Korbut.

Minister of Foreign Affairs: Syarhey M. Martynow.

Minister of Forestry: Pyotr M. Syamashka.

Minister of Health: Vasil I. Zharko.

Minister of Housing and Municipal Services: Uladzimir M. Belakhvostow.

Minister of Industry: Anatoly M. Rusetsky.

Minister of Information: Uladzimir U. Rusakevich.

Minister of Internal Affairs: Uladzimir U. Naumau.

Minister of Justice: Viktar G. Golovanou.

Minister of Labour and Social Protection: Uladzimir Patupchyk.

Minister for Natural Resources and Environmental Protection: Lyavontsy I. Kharouzhyk.

Minister of Sports and Tourism: Alyaksandr U. Hrihoraw.

Minister of Statistics and Analysis: Uladzimir I. Zinovsky.

Minister of Taxes and Duties: Hanna K. Dzeyka.

Minister of Trade: Alyaksandr I. Ivankow.

Minister of Transport and Communications: Uladzimir G. Sosnovsky.

Note: The following positions are also members of the Council of Ministers: Head of the Presidential Administration; President of the National Academy of Sciences; Chairman of the Management of the National Bank; and Chairmen of the following organizations: the Committee of State Control; the State Military-Industrial Committee; the Committee of State Security; the State Committee of Aviation; the Belarusian Republic Union of Consumer Societies; the State Committee of Border Troops; the State Committee of Science and Technology; and the State Customs Committee.

MINISTRIES

Office of the President: 220016 Minsk, vul. K. Marksa 38, Dom Urada; tel. (17) 222-60-06; internet www.president.gov.by.

Office of the Council of Ministers: 220010 Minsk, vul. Savetskaya 11; tel. (17) 222-69-05; fax (17) 222-66-65; e-mail contact@government.by; internet www.government.by.

Ministry of Agriculture and Food: 220050 Minsk, vul. Kirava 15; tel. (17) 227-37-51; fax (17) 227-42-96; e-mail kanc@mshp.minsk.by; internet mshp.minsk.by.

Ministry of Architecture and Construction: 220048 Minsk, vul. Myasnikova 39; tel. (17) 227-26-42; fax (17) 220-74-24; tel. mas@-mas.by; internet www.mas.by.

Ministry of Communications and Information Technologies: 220050 Minsk, pr. Nezavisimosti 10; tel. (17) 227-38-61; fax (17) 227-21-57; e-mail mpt@mpt.gov.by; internet www.mpt.gov.by.

Ministry of Culture: 220004 Minsk, pr. Pobeditelei 11; tel. (17) 203-75-74; fax (17) 223-90-45; e-mail admin@kultura.by; internet kultura.by.

Ministry of Defence: 220034 Minsk, vul. Kamunistychnaya 1; tel. (17) 297-12-12; fax (17) 289-19-74; internet www.mod.mil.by.

Ministry of the Economy: 220050 Minsk, vul. Bersona 14; tel. (17) 222-60-48; fax (17) 200-37-77; e-mail gen@plan.minsk.by; internet www.economy.gov.by.

Ministry of Education: 220010 Minsk, vul. Savetskaya 9; tel. (17) 227-47-36; fax (17) 200-84-83; e-mail root@minedu.unibel.by; internet www.minedu.unibel.by.

Ministry for Emergency Situations: 220050 Minsk, vul. Revolutsionnaya 5; tel. (17) 203-94-28; fax (17) 203-77-81; e-mail mcs@infonet.by; internet www.rescue01.gov.by.

Ministry of Energy: 220050 Minsk, vul. K. Marksa 14; tel. (17) 229-83-59; fax (17) 229-86-39; e-mail minsecretary@min.energo.net.by; internet www.minenergo.gov.by.

Ministry of Finance: 220048 Minsk, vul. Savetskaya 7; tel. (17) 227-27-26; fax (17) 222-45-93; e-mail web_mf@open.by; internet ncpi.gov.by/minfin.

Ministry of Foreign Affairs: 220030 Minsk, vul. Lenina 19; tel. (17) 227-29-22; fax (17) 227-45-21; e-mail mail@mfabelar.gov.by; internet www.mfa.gov.by.

Ministry of Forestry: 220039 Minsk, vul. Chkalova 6; tel. (17) 224-47-05; fax (17) 224-41-83; e-mail info@komleshoz.org; internet www.mlh.by.

Ministry of Health: 220048 Minsk, vul. Myasnikova 39; tel. (17) 222-60-33; fax (17) 222-62-97; e-mail mzrb@belcmt.by; internet minzdrav.by.

Ministry of Housing and Municipal Services: 220050 Minsk, vul. Bersona 16; tel. (17) 220-15-45; fax (17) 220-87-08; internet www.mjkx.gov.by.

Ministry of Industry: 220033 Minsk, pr. Partizansky 2; tel. (17) 224-95-95; fax (17) 224-87-84; e-mail minprom1@minprom.gov.by; internet minprom.gov.by.

Ministry of Information: 220004 Minsk, pr. Pobeditelei 11; tel. (17) 203-92-31; fax (17) 203-34-35; e-mail info@mininform.gov.by; internet www.mininform.gov.by.

Ministry of Internal Affairs: 220050 Minsk, vul. Gorodskoy Val 4; tel. (17) 218-78-08; fax (17) 226-12-47; e-mail admin@mvd.gov.by; internet mvd.gov.by.

Ministry of Justice: 220048 Minsk, vul. Kalektarnaya 10; tel. (17) 206-37-28; fax (17) 200-97-55; e-mail kanc@minjust.by; internet www.minjust.by.

Ministry of Labour and Social Protection: 220004 Minsk, pr. Pobeditelei 23, kor. 2; tel. (17) 206-38-84; fax (17) 222-49-30; e-mail press@mintrud.gov.by; internet mintrud.gov.by.

Ministry for Natural Resources and Environmental Protection: 220048 Minsk, vul. Kalektarnaya 10; tel. (17) 220-66-91; fax (17) 220-55-83; e-mail minproos@mail.belpak.by; internet minpriroda.by.

Ministry of Sports and Tourism: 220050 Minsk, vul. Kirava 8, kor. 2; tel. (17) 227-72-37; fax (17) 227-30-31; e-mail intersport@mst.by; internet www.mst.by.

Ministry of Statistics and Analysis: 220070 Minsk, pr. Partizansky 12; tel. (17) 249-42-09; fax (17) 249-22-04; e-mail minstat@mail.belpak.by; internet www.belstat.gov.by.

Ministry of Taxes and Duties: 220010 Minsk, vul. Savetskaya 9; tel. (17) 222-49-92; fax (17) 222-66-87; e-mail GNK@mail.belpak.by; internet www.nalog.by.

Ministry of Trade: 220050 Minsk, vul. Kirava 8, kor. 1; tel. and fax (17) 227-24-80; e-mail mintorgrb@mail.belpak.by; internet www.mintorg.gov.by.

Ministry of Transport and Communications: 220029 Minsk, vul. Chicherina 21; tel. (17) 234-11-52; fax (17) 239-42-26; e-mail mail@mintrans.by; internet www.mintrans.by.

President and Legislature

PRESIDENT

Presidential Election, 19 March 2006

Candidates	Votes	%
Alyaksandr Lukashenka	5,501,249	83.0
Alyaksandr Milinkevich	405,486	6.1
Syarhey Gaydukevich	230,664	3.5
Alyaksandr Kazulin	147,402	2.2
Total*	6,630,653	100.0

* Including invalid votes and votes cast against all candidates.

NATSIONALNOYE SOBRANIYE
(National Assembly)

Soviet Respubliki (Council of the Republic)

220016 Minsk, vul. Krasnoarmeiskaya 4; tel. (17) 227-46-74; fax (17) 227-23-18; e-mail cr@sovrep.gov.by; internet www.sovrep.gov.by.

Chairman: Genadz V. Navitsky.

The Soviet Respubliki is the upper chamber of the legislature and comprises 64 deputies. Of the total, 56 deputies are elected by regional councils (eight each from the six oblasts and the city of Minsk) and eight deputies are appointed by the President of the Republic.

BELARUS

Palata Predstaviteley (House of Representatives)
220010 Minsk, vul. Savetskaya 11; tel. (17) 227-25-14; fax (17) 222-31-78; e-mail admin@gov.house.by; internet house.gov.by.
Chairman: VADIM A. POPOV.

General Election, 17 October 2004

Parties or groups	Seats
Independents	98
Communist Party of Belarus	8
Agrarian Party	3
Liberal Democratic Party of Belarus	1
Total	**110**

Election Commission

Central Commission of the Republic of Belarus for Elections and Referendums: 220010 Minsk, vul. Savetskaya 11, Dom Pravitelstva; tel. and fax (17) 227-19-03; e-mail centrizb@pmrb.gov.by; internet www.rec.gov.by; f. 1989; Chair. LYDIA M. YERMOSHINA.

Political Organizations

Following the Government's imposition of stringent measures for re-registration in January 1999, the number of political parties officially registered with the Ministry of Justice was reduced from 28 to 17. A number of unregistered parties operated, but were not permitted to participate in elections. In early 2008 there were 15 officially registered political parties operating in Belarus, of which the most important are listed below.

Agrarian Party (AP) (Agrarnaya Partya): 220073 Minsk, vul. Zakharava 31; tel. (17) 220-38-29; fax (17) 249-50-18; f. 1992; Leader MIKHAIL V. SHYMANSKI.

Assembly (Hramada)—Belarusian Social-Democratic Party (Belaruskaya Satsyal-demakratychnaya Partya 'Hramada'): 220095 Minsk, pr. Rakasoŭskaga 52/1; tel. and fax (17) 246-86-94; e-mail bsdggramada@tut.by; f. 2005; the Belarusian Social Democratic Party (National Hramada), f. 1991, and the Belarusian Social-Democratic Hramada (f. 1998) merged in April 2005, although a dissenting faction of the Belarusian Social-Democratic Hramada remained; Chair. ANATOL I. LYUKOVICH.

Belarusian Green Party (Belaruskaya Partya Zyaleny): 246023 Gomel, vul. Brestskaya 6; tel. (23) 47-08-08; fax (23) 247-96-96; e-mail bpz@tut.by; f. 1994 as Belarusian Greenpeace Party, present name adopted 1999; Leader ALEH A. NOVIKAU.

Belarusian Patriotic Party (Belaruskaya Patryatychnaya Partya): 220089 Minsk, vul. Papanina 7; tel. (17) 226-32-60; f. 1994; Leader MIKALAY D. ULAKHOVICH.

Communist Party of Belarus (CPB) (Kamunistychnaya Partya Belarusi): 220029 Minsk, vul. Chicherina 21; tel. (17) 293-48-88; fax (17) 232-31-23; f. 1996; Chair. TATSYANA H. HOLUBEVA.

Conservative Christian Party of the Belarusian National Front (CCP/BPF): 220005 Minsk, pr. Masherova 8; tel. (17) 285-34-70; e-mail bpfs@narod.ru; internet www.pbpf.org; f. 1999 as a breakaway faction of the BNF; Chair. ZYANON S. PAZNYAK.

Liberal Democratic Party of Belarus (Liberalna-Demakratychnaya Partya Belarusi): 220005 Minsk, vul. Platonava 22, 12th Floor; tel. and fax (17) 231-63-31; e-mail ldpb@infonet.by; internet www.ldpb.net; f. 1994; advocates continued independence of Belarus, increased co-operation with other European countries and eventual membership of the European Union, and expansion of the private sector; Leader SYARHEY V. HAYDUKEVICH; approx. 50,000 mems (2004).

Revival—Belarusian National Front (Belaruski Narodny Front 'Adradzhenniye'): 220005 Minsk, pr. Masherova 8; tel. and fax (17) 284-50-12; e-mail pbnf@pbnf.org; internet www.pbnf.org; f. 1993; fmrly the Belarusian Popular Front, name changed as above Dec. 1999; anti-communist movement campaigning for democracy, genuine independence for Belarus and national and cultural revival; Chair. LIAVON BARSHCHEUSKI.

Social-Democratic Party of Popular Accord (Satsial-Demakratychnaya Partya Narodnay Zhody): 220050 Minsk, vul. K. Marksa 10; tel. (29) 686-35-65; fax (23) 274-12-60; f. 1992; Leader SYARHEY U. ERMAK.

United Civic Party (UCP) (Abyadnanaya Hramadzyanskaya Partya): 220123 Minsk, vul. Khoruzhey 22; tel. and fax (17) 289-50-09; e-mail ucpb@ucpb.org; internet www.ucpb.org; f. 1995; liberal-conservative; Chair. ANATOL U. LIABEDZKA.

Diplomatic Representation

EMBASSIES IN BELARUS

Armenia: 220050 Minsk, vul. Kirava 17; tel. and fax (17) 227-51-53; e-mail armrep@cis.minsk.by; Ambassador OLEG YESAIAN.

Azerbaijan: 220029 Minsk, vul. Vostochnaya 133/167; tel. (17) 293-32-99; fax (17) 237-27-51; e-mail azoffice_minsk@avilink.net; Ambassador ALI NAGHIYEV.

Bulgaria: 220030 Minsk, pl. Svoboda 11; tel. (17) 328-65-58; fax (17) 328-65-59; e-mail embassy@bulgaria.by; internet www.mfa.bg/minsk; Ambassador PETKO GANCHEV.

China, People's Republic: 220071 Minsk, vul. Brestyanskaya 22; tel. (17) 284-97-28; fax (17) 210-58-41; e-mail chinaemb_by@mfa.gov.cn; internet by.china-embassy.org; Ambassador WU HONGBIN.

Cuba: 220005 Minsk, vul. Krasnozvezdnaya 13; tel. (17) 200-03-83; fax (17) 200-23-45; e-mail oficome@belsonet.net; Ambassador OMAR SENÓN MEDINA QUINTERO.

Czech Republic: 220030 Minsk, Muzykalny per. 1/2; tel. (17) 226-52-44; fax (17) 211-01-37; e-mail minsk@embassy.mzv.cz; internet www.mzv.cz/minsk; Chargé d'affaires VLADIMÍR RUML.

France: 220030 Minsk, pl. Svabody 11; tel. (17) 210-28-68; fax (17) 210-25-48; e-mail webmestreby@diplomatie.fr; internet www.ambafrance-by.org; Ambassador MIREILLE MUSSO.

Germany: 220034 Minsk, vul. Zakharava 26; tel. (17) 217-59-00; fax (17) 294-85-52; e-mail germanembassy@mail.belpak.by; internet www.minsk.diplo.de; Ambassador Dr GEBHARDT WEISS.

Holy See: 220050 Minsk, vul. Valadarskaga 6; tel. (17) 289-15-84; fax (17) 289-15-17; e-mail nuntius@catholic.by; internet nunciature.catholic.by; Apostolic Nuncio MARTIN VIDOVIĆ (Titular Archbishop of Nona).

India: 220090 Minsk, vul. Kaltsova 4, kor. 5; tel. (17) 262-93-99; fax (17) 262-97-99; e-mail amb@indemb.bn.by; internet www.indembminsk.org; Ambassador R. K. TYAGI.

Iran: 220049 Minsk, vul. Suvorova 2; tel. (17) 207-66-99; fax (17) 207-61-99; Ambassador ABDULHAMID FEKRI.

Israel: 220033 Minsk, pr. Partizansky 6A; tel. (17) 298-43-92; fax (17) 298-44-03; e-mail info@minsk.mfa.gov.il; Ambassador ZE'EV BEN ARIE.

Italy: 220004 Minsk, vul. Rakovskaya 16B; tel. (17) 220-29-69; fax (17) 306-20-37; e-mail ambasciata.minsk@esteri.it; internet www.ambminsk.esteri.it; Ambassador NORBERTO CAPPELLO.

Japan: 220004 Minsk, pr. Pobeditelei 23/1; tel. (17) 223-62-33; fax (17) 210-21-69; Chargé d'affaires a.i. NAOTAKE YAMASHITA.

Kazakhstan: 220029 Minsk, vul. Kuibysheva 12; tel. (17) 234-30-23; fax (17) 334-96-50; e-mail kazemb@nsys.by; internet www.kazembassy.by; Ambassador BULAT G. ISKAKOV.

Kyrgyzstan: 220002 Minsk, vul. Starovilenskaya 57; tel. (17) 234-91-17; fax (17) 234-16-02; e-mail manas@nsys.minsk.by; internet kgembassy.by; Ambassador LIDIYA A. IMANALIYEVA.

Latvia: 220013 Minsk, vul. Doroshevicha 6A; tel. (17) 211-30-33; fax (17) 284-74-94; e-mail embassy.belarus@mfa.gov.lv; internet www.am.gov.lv/belarus; Ambassador MAIRA MORA.

Libya: 220000 Minsk, vul. Belaruskaya 4; tel. (17) 201-39-88; fax (17) 206-39-97; Ambassador ABDALLAH AL-MAGRAVI.

Lithuania: 220088 Minsk, vul. Zakharava 68; tel. (17) 285-24-48; fax (17) 285-33-37; e-mail amb.by@urm.ly; internet by.urm.lt; Ambassador EDMINAS BAGDONAS.

Moldova: 220030 Minsk, vul. Belaruskaya 2; tel. (17) 289-14-41; fax (17) 289-11-47; e-mail emmdby@anitex.by; Ambassador ION FILIMON.

Poland: 220034 Minsk, vul. Rumyantsova 6; tel. (17) 288-21-14; fax (17) 236-49-92; e-mail ambasada@minsk.polemb.net; internet www.minsk.polemb.net; Ambassador HENRIK LITWIN.

Romania: 220035 Minsk, zav. Maskvina 4; tel. (17) 203-77-26; fax (17) 211-21-63; e-mail romania@nsys.by; Chargé d'affaires a.i. DUMITRU BADEA.

Russia: 220002 Minsk, vul. Staravilenskaya 48; tel. (17) 250-36-66; fax (17) 250-36-64; e-mail kira1130@yahoo.com; internet www.belarus.mid.ru; Ambassador ALEKSANDR A. SURIKOV.

Serbia: 220034 Minsk, vul. Rumyantseva 4; tel. (17) 284-29-84; fax (17) 233-92-26; e-mail embassy.minsk@mfa.gov.yu; internet www.ambasadasrbije.info; Ambassador SRECKO DJUKIĆ.

Slovakia: 220034 Minsk, vul. Platonova 1B; tel. (17) 285-29-99; fax (17) 283-68-48; e-mail slovemb@iptel.by; internet www.mzv.sk/minsk; Chargé d'affaires REHÁK LUBOMÍR.

Syria: 220049 Minsk, vul. Suvorova 2; tel. (17) 280-37-08; fax (17) 280-72-00; Ambassador FARUK TAKH.

Tajikistan: 220050 Minsk, vul. Kirava 17; tel. (17) 222-37-98; fax (17) 227-76-13; e-mail tajikemb-belarus@mail.ru; Ambassador AMIRKHON SAFAROV.

BELARUS

Turkey: 220050 Minsk, vul. Valadarskaya 6; tel. (17) 227-13-83; fax (17) 227-27-46; e-mail trembassy@forenet.by; Ambassador BIRNUR FERTEKLIGIL.
Turkmenistan: 220050 Minsk, vul. Kirava 17; tel. (17) 222-34-27; fax (17) 222-33-67; Ambassador ATA GUNDOGDIYEV.
Ukraine: 220002 Minsk, vul. Staravilenskaya 51; tel. (17) 283-19-90; fax (17) 283-19-80; e-mail emb_by@mfa.gov.ua; internet www.belarus.mfa.gov.ua/belarus; Ambassador IHOR D. LIKHOVYI.
United Kingdom: 220030 Minsk, vul. K. Marksa 37; tel. (17) 210-59-20; fax (17) 220-23-06; e-mail britinfo@nsys.by; internet www.britishembassy.gov.uk/belarus; Ambassador (vacant).
USA: 220002 Minsk, vul. Staravilenskaya 46; tel. (17) 210-12-83; fax (17) 234-78-53; e-mail webmaster@usembassy.minsk.by; internet www.usembassy.minsk.by; Ambassador KAREN B. STEWART.
Venezuela: 220000 Minsk; tel. (17) 226-07-88; fax (17) 220-20-19; e-mail embavenbel@gmail.com; Chargé d'affaires AMÉRICO DÍAZ NUÑEZ.

Judicial System

Supreme Court: 220030 Minsk, vul. Lenina 28; tel. (17) 226-12-06; fax (17) 227-12-25; e-mail scjustrb@pmrb.gov.by; f. 1923; Chair. VALENTIN SUKALO.
Supreme Economic Court: 220050 Minsk, vul. Valadarskaya 8; tel. (17) 227-16-41; fax (17) 220-20-85; e-mail bxc@court.by; internet www.court.by; Chair. VIKTAR S. KAMYANKOV.
Office of the Prosecutor-General: 220050 Minsk, vul. Internatsionalnaya 22; tel. and fax (17) 206-57-27; e-mail info@prokuratura.gov.by; internet www.prokuratura.gov.by; Prosecutor-General GRYGORY A. VASILEVICH.
Constitutional Court: 220016 Minsk, vul. K. Marksa 32; tel. and fax (17) 227-80-12; e-mail ksrb@user.unibel.by; internet ncpi.gov.by/ConstSud; f. 1994; 12 mem. judges; Chair. PYOTR MIKLASHEVICH.

Religion

CHRISTIANITY

The major grouping is the Eastern Orthodox Church, but there are also an estimated 1.3m. adherents of the Roman Catholic Church. Of these, some 25% are ethnic Poles and there is a significant number of Catholics of the Eastern Rites.

The Eastern Orthodox Church

In 1990 Belarus was designated an exarchate of the Russian Orthodox Church (Moscow Patriarchate), known as the Belarusian Orthodox Church.
Belarusian Orthodox Church (Moscow Patriarchate): 220004 Minsk, vul. Osvobozhdeniya 10; tel. and fax (17) 223-25-05; e-mail orthobel@gin.by; 1,319 parishes (2004); Metropolitan of Minsk and Slutsk, Patriarchal Exarch of All Belarus His Eminence FILARET (VAKHROMEYEV).

The Roman Catholic Church

Although five Roman Catholic dioceses, embracing 455 parishes, had officially existed since the Second World War, none of them had a bishop. In 1989 a major reorganization of the structure of the Roman Catholic Church in Belarus took place. The dioceses of Minsk and Mogilev (Mahilou) were merged, to create an archdiocese, and two new dioceses were formed, in Grodno (Horadnia) and Pinsk. At 31 December 2005 the Roman Catholic Church had an estimated 1,003,000 adherents in Belarus (about 9.7% of the population).
Bishops' Conference of Belarusian Catholics: 220030 Minsk, pl. Svobody 9; tel. (17) 226-61-27; fax (17) 226-90-92; internet www.catholic.by; Pres. Most Rev. ALEKSANDR KASZKIEWICZ Bishop of Grodno.
Archdiocese of Minsk and Mogilev: 220030 Minsk, ul. Revolutsionna 1A; tel. (17) 226-62-44; fax (17) 226-90-92; e-mail archdioces@catholic.by; internet catholic.by; Archbishop Mgr TADEVUSH KANDRUSIEVICH.

Protestant Churches

Union of Evangelical Christian Baptists in the Republic of Belarus: 220107 Minsk, POB 25; tel. and fax (17) 295-67-84; e-mail office@baptist.by; internet www.baptist.by; f. 1989; Pres. NIKOLAY SINKOVETS.

ISLAM

There are small communities of Azeri and Tatar adherents of Islam. In 1994 the supreme administration of Muslims in Belarus, which had been abolished in 1939, was reconstituted. In mid-1998 there were some 4,000 Muslims and four mosques.

The Press

According to official figures, in 2002 there were 740 newspapers, 351 magazines and other periodicals and four information agencies in Belarus; 12 titles were published in a language other than Belarusian or Russian (primarily English, Polish or Ukrainian). Most daily newspapers are government-owned.

PRINCIPAL DAILIES

In Russian, except where otherwise stated. The Russian-based newspapers *Argumenty i Fakty* and *Komosomolskaya Pravda* (in a special edition, *Komsomolskaya Pravda v Belorusii*) also maintain a high rate of circulation in the country.
BDG Delovaya Gazeta (BDG Business Newspaper): 220039 Minsk, vul. Chekalova 12; tel. (17) 216-25-85; e-mail info@bdg.by; internet www.bdg.by; f. 1992; 2 a week; business affairs; suspended for three months in May 2003; subsequently printed in Smolensk, Russia; independent; in 2005 name changed from Belorusskaya Delovaya Gazeta (BDG), following a presidential decree restricting the use of certain words; Editor-in-Chief SVYATLANA KALONKINA.
Belaruskaya Niva (Belarusian Cornfield): 220013 Minsk, vul. B. Hmyalnitskaga 10A; tel. (17) 287-16-20; fax (17) 232-39-62; e-mail info@belniva.by; internet belniva.by; f. 1921; 5 a week; organ of the Cabinet of Ministers; in Belarusian and Russian; Editor E. SEMASHKO; circ. 34,021 (Aug. 2004).
Narodnaya Hazeta (The People's Newspaper): 220013 Minsk, vul. B. Hmyalnitskaga 10A; tel. (17) 268-28-70; fax (17) 268-25-29; e-mail info@ng.press.net.by; f. 1990; 5–6 a week; in Belarusian and Russian; Editor-in-Chief M. SHIMANSKY; circ. 90,000 (2000).
Narodnaya Volya (People's Will): Minsk; f. 1995; daily; independent; 5 a week; in Belarusian and Russian; Editor-in-Chief SVYATLANA KALONKINA; circ. 27,000.
Respublika (Republic): 220013 Minsk, vul. B. Hmyalnitskaga 10A; tel. (17) 287-16-15; fax (17) 287-16-12; e-mail info@respublika.info; internet www.respublika.info; 5 a week; in Belarusian and Russian; Editor ANATOLI LEMIASHONOK; circ. 101,000 (2005).
Sovetskaya Belorussiya (Soviet Belarus): 220013 Minsk, vul. B. Hmyalnitskaga 10A; tel. and fax (17) 232-14-32; e-mail admin@sb.by; internet sb.by; 5 a week; Editor-in-Chief PAVEL YAKUBOVICH; circ. 400,000 (2004).
Vechernii Minsk (Evening Minsk): 220005 Minsk, pr. Nezavisimosti 44; tel. (17) 284-50-44; fax (17) 288-28-35; e-mail vm@nsys.by; internet newsvm.com; f. 1967; Editor SYARHEY SVERKUNOU; circ. 30,000 (2007).
Znamya Yunosti (Banner of Youth): 220013 Minsk, vul. B. Hmyalnitskaga 10A; tel. and fax (17) 268-26-84; f. 1938; 5 a week; organ of the Cabinet of Ministers; Editor-in-Chief ELENA PHILIPTCHIK; circ. 9,000 (2000).
Zvyazda (Star): 220013 Minsk, vul. B. Hmyalnitskaga 10A; tel. (17) 268-29-19; fax (17) 268-27-79; f. 1917 as Zvezda; 5 a week; organ of the Cabinet of Ministers; in Belarusian; Editor ULADZIMIR B. NARKEVICH; circ. 90,000 (1998).

PRINCIPAL PERIODICALS

In Belarusian, except where otherwise stated.
Alesya: 220013 Minsk, pr. Nezavisimosti 77; tel. and fax (17) 232-20-51; e-mail magalesya@mail.ru; f. 1924; monthly; Editor TAMARA BUNTO; circ. 10,500 (2003).
Belarus: 220005 Minsk, vul. Zakharava 19; tel. (17) 284-80-01; f. 1930; monthly; publ. by the State Publishing House; journal of the Union of Writers of Belarus and the Belarusian Society of Friendship and Cultural Links with Foreign Countries; fiction and political essays; in Belarusian, English and Russian; Editor-in-Chief A. A. SHABALIN.
Belaruskaya Krynitsa (Belarusian Spring): 220065 Minsk, vul. Avakyana 38/59; tel. and fax (17) 220-67-56; e-mail b.krinica@tut.by; internet www.ibkby.com; f. 1991; monthly; journal of the Belarusian Public Organization of Social Development and Co-operation; Editor-in-Chief Dr PETR SILKO; circ. 5,000 (2006).
Chyrvonaya Zmena (The Red Rising Generation): 220013 Minsk, vul. B. Hmyalnitskaga 10A; tel. and fax (17) 232-21-03; f. 1921; weekly; Editor A. KARLUKIEVICH; circ. 5,000 (2000).
Gramadzyanin: Minsk; tel. (17) 229-08-34; fax (17) 272-95-05; publ. by the United Civic Party of Belarus.
Holas Radzimy (Voice of the Motherland): 220005 Minsk, pr. Nezavisimosti 44; tel. (17) 288-12-80; fax (17) 288-17-82; e-mail golas_radzimy@tut.by; internet www.belarus21.by; f. 1955; weekly;

BELARUS

articles of interest to Belarusians in other countries; Editor-in-Chief NATALIA SALUK.

Krynitsa (Spring): Minsk; tel. (17) 236-60-71; e-mail www.krynitsa@open.by; f. 1988; monthly; publ. by the state media holding, Literatura i Mastatstva; literary and cultural; Editor ALA KAPANELKA; circ. 2,100 (2001).

Kultura (Culture): 220029 Minsk, vul. Chicherina 1; tel. and fax (17) 289-34-66; e-mail kultura@tut.by; f. 1991; weekly; colour illustrated; incorporates *Mastatstva* (Arts); Editor-in-Chief LUDMILA KRUSHINSKAYA; circ. 4,000 (2005).

Litaratura i Mastatstva (Literature and Arts): 220034 Minsk, vul. Zakharava 19; tel. (17) 284-66-73; f. 1932; weekly; Editor ANATOL KAZLOU; circ. 3,428 (2007).

Maladosts (Youth): 220034 Minsk, vul. Zakharava 19; tel. (17) 284-79-85; f. 1953; monthly; publ. by the state media holding, Literatura i Mastatstva; novels, short stories, essays, translations, etc., for young people; Editor-in-Chief R. BARAVIKOVA.

Narodnaya Asveta (People's Education): 220023 Minsk, vul. Makayenka 12; tel. (17) 267-64-69; fax (17) 267-62-68; e-mail n_asveta@tut.by; internet www.n-asveta.com; f. 1924; publ. by the Ministry of Education; Editor-in-Chief ALLA V. MASLAVA.

Nasha Niva (Our Cornfield): 220050 Minsk, POB 537; tel. (17) 707-73-29; fax (29) 284-73-29; e-mail nn@promedia.by; internet www.nn.by; f. 1991; first founded in 1906; independent; weekly; Editor-in-Chief ANDREY SKURKO; circ. 2,500 (2007).

Navinki (News): Minsk; tel. www.navinki.net; private; weekly; satirical; Editor-in-Chief PAVLYUK KANAVALCHYK; circ. 3,000.

Neman (The River Nieman): 220005 Minsk, pr. Nezavisimosti 39; tel. (17) 213-40-72; fax (17) 213-44-61; f. 1945; monthly; publ. by the state media holding, Literatura i Mastatstva; literary; fiction; in Russian; Editor-in-Chief A. ZHOUK.

Polymya (Flame): 220005 Minsk, vul. Zakharava 19; tel. (17) 284-80-12; f. 1922; monthly; publ. by the state media holding, Literatura i Mastatstva; literary; fiction; Editor-in-Chief S. I. ZAKONNIKOU.

Salidarnasts (Solidarity): Minsk; weekly; private; independent trade-union newspaper; Editor-in-Chief ALYAKSANDR STARYKEVICH.

Tovarisch (Comrade): 220005 Minsk, pr. Nezavisimosti 46A; tel. (17) 202-08-14; fax (17) 231-80-36; e-mail ck_pkb@anitex.by; internet pkb.promedia.minsk.by; f. 1994; weekly newspaper of the Party of Communists of Belarus; Editor-in-Chief SYARGEY V. VOZNYAK; circ. 6,000 (2001).

Vozhyk (Hedgehog): 220013 Minsk, pr. Nezavisimosti 77; tel. and fax (17) 232-12-40; f. 1941; fortnightly; satirical; Editor-in-Chief MIKHAIL POZDNYAKOV; circ. 12,000 (1998).

Vyaselka (Rainbow): 220004 Minsk, vul. Kalektarnaya 10; tel. (17) 220-91-90; fax (17) 220-92-61; f. 1957; bi-annual; popular, for 5–10-year-olds; Editor-in-Chief V. S. LIPSKY.

PRESS ASSOCIATIONS

Belarusian Association of Journalists (Belaruskaya Asatsyyatsyya Zhurnalistau): 220030 Minsk, pl. Svabody 17/304; tel. (17) 226-70-98; fax (17) 203-63-66; e-mail baj@baj.by; internet www.baj.ru; f. 1995; Chair. ZHANNA LITVINA.

Belarusian Union of Journalists: 220034 Minsk, vul. Rumyantsava 3; tel. and fax (17) 294-51-95; 3,000 mems; Chair. A. GEMESCHINOK.

NEWS AGENCIES

BelaPAN: tel. (17) 232-55-01; fax (17) 232-56-57; e-mail mail@belapan.com; internet www.belapan.com; in Belarusian, English and Russian; independent, commercial information company.

Belta—Belarusian Telegraph Agency: 220030 Minsk, vul. Kirava 26; tel. (17) 227-19-92; fax (17) 227-13-46; e-mail oper@belta.by; internet www.belta.by; f. 1918; Gen. Dir DMITRIY A. ZHUK.

Interfaks Zapad (Interfax-West): 222050 Minsk, vul. Bersana 3; tel. (17) 222-42-75; fax (17) 222-42-76; e-mail infportal@interfax.minsk.by; subsidiary of Interfaks (Russia); regional bureaux in Brest, Vitebsk, Gomel, Grodno and Mogilev.

Publishers

In 2000 there were 7,686 titles published in Belarus (62m. copies).

Belarus: 220600 Minsk, pr. Nezavisimosti 79; tel. (17) 223-87-42; fax (17) 223-87-31; f. 1921; social, political, technical, medical and musical literature, fiction, children's, reference books, art reproductions, etc.; Dir MIKHALAY KAVALEVSKY; Editor-in-Chief ELENA ZAKONNIKOVA.

Belaruskaya Entsiklopediya (Belarusian Encyclopedia): 220072 Minsk, vul. Akademicheskaya 15A; tel. and fax (17) 284-17-67; e-mail belen@mail.belpak.by; f. 1967; encyclopedias, dictionaries, directories and scientific books; Editor-in-Chief G. P. PASHKOV.

Belaruskaya Navuka (Belarusian Science): 220141 Minsk, Staroborisovsky trakt 40; tel. (17) 263-76-18; e-mail belnauka@infonet.by; f. 1924; scientific, technical, reference books, educational literature and fiction in Belarusian and Russian; Dir LUDMILA PIETROVA.

Belarusky Dom Druku (Belarusian Printing House): 220013 Minsk, pr. Nezavisimosti 79; tel. (17) 287-17-03; fax (17) 231-67-74; e-mail dom.pechati@bdp.minsk.by; f. 1917; social, political, children's and fiction in Belarusian, Russian and other European languages; Dir ROMAN OLEINIK.

Belblankavyd: 220035 Minsk, vul. Timirazeva 2; tel. (17) 226-71-22; reference books in Belarusian and Russian; Dir VALENTINA MILOVANOVA.

Mastatskaya Litaratura (Literary Fiction): 220600 Minsk, pr. Pobeditelei 11; tel. (17) 223-48-09; f. 1972; fiction in Belarusian and Russian; Dir GEORGE MARCHUK.

Narodnaya Asveta (People's Education): 220004 Minsk, pr. Pobeditelei 11; tel. and fax (17) 203-61-84; e-mail director@narasveta.by; f. 1951; scientific, educational, reference literature and fiction in Belarusian, Russian and other European languages; Dir LARISA MINKO.

Vysheyshaya Shkola (Higher School): 220048 Minsk, pr. Pobeditelei 11; tel. (17) 203-70-08; fax (17) 223-54-15; e-mail market@vshph.com; internet www.vshph.com; f. 1954; textbooks and science books for higher educational institutions; in Belarusian, Russian and other European languages; absorbed the Universitetskaye publishing house in 2002; Dir ANATOL A. ZHADAN; Editor-in-Chief TETYANA K. MAIBORODA.

Yunatstva (Youth): 220600 Minsk, pr. Pobeditelei 11; tel. (17) 223-24-30; fax (17) 223-31-16; f. 1981; fiction and children's books; Dir ALYAKSANDR KOMAROVSKY.

Broadcasting and Communications

TELECOMMUNICATIONS

BelCel: 22005 Minsk, vul. Zolotaya Gorka 5; tel. (17) 282-02-82; fax (17) 276-11-11; e-mail belcel@belcel.by; internet www.belcel.com.by; f. 1993; 50% owned by Cable and Wireless (United Kingdom); mobile telecommunications services; Gen. Dir ARTEM H. ORANDZH; 23,000 subscribers (2003).

Beltelecom: 220030 Minsk, vul. Engelsa 6; tel. (17) 217-10-05; fax (17) 227-44-22; e-mail info@main.beltelecom.by; internet www.beltelecom.by; f. 1995; national telecommunications operator; Dir-Gen. KANSTANTIN TSIKAR.

Best: 220030 Minsk, vul. Chervonoarmeiska 24; tel. (17) 295-99-99; e-mail info@best.by; internet www.best.by; f. 2004; 25% owned by Beltelecom; provides mobile cellular telecommunications services.

MTS Belarus: 222043 Minsk, pr. Nezavisimosti 95; tel. (17) 237-98-98; e-mail info@mts.by; internet www.company.mts.by; f. 2002; mobile cellular communications; 49% owned by Mobile TeleSystems (Russia); Dir-Gen. ANDREI B. RUMYANTSEV; 465,500 subscribers (2004).

Velcom: 220002 Minsk, vul. Masherova 19; tel. (17) 222-49-01; fax (17) 206-62-52; e-mail pressa@velcom.by; internet www.velcom.by; f. 1999; mobile cellular telecommunications; 950,000 subscribers (2004); Gen. Dir MIKHAIL A. BATRANETS.

BROADCASTING

National State Television and Radio Company of Belarus (Belteleradiocompany): 220807 Minsk, vul. A. Makayenka 9; tel. (17) 264-88-43; fax (17) 264-81-82; e-mail pr@tvr.by; internet www.tvr.by; f. 1925; parent co of Belarusian Radio (q.v.) and Belarusian Television (q.v.); Chair. ULADZIMIR MATVYAYCHUK.

Radio

Belarusian Radio: 220807 Minsk, vul. Chyrvonaya 4; tel. (17) 239-58-10; fax (17) 284-85-74; e-mail radio-minsk@tvr.by; internet www.tvr.by; stations include Culture Channel, First National Channel (news), Radio Stalitsa (Capital Radio) and Radio Belarus (foreign service in Belarussian, Russian, German and English); Dir ULADZIMIR V. DEYAKAW.

Television

Belarusian Television: 220807 Minsk, vul. A. Makayenka 9; tel. (17) 269-97-72; fax (17) 267-81-82; e-mail pr@tvr.by; internet www.tvr.by; f. 1956; Dir ULADZIMIR V. ISAT.

BELARUS   *Directory*

Belarus-TV: 220807 Minsk, vul. A. Makayenka 9; tel. (17) 264-95-92; fax (17) 264-81-82; e-mail eksp@tvr.by; f. 2005; international satellite channel; Gen. Producer VIKTAR U. MAYUCHY.

First National Channel: 220807 Minsk, vul. A. Makayenka 9; tel. (17) 233-45-01; fax (17) 264-81-82; main state news channel; also shows entertainment, sport, films etc.

LAD: 220807 Minsk, vul. A. Makayenka 9; tel. (17) 264-88-43; fax (17) 264-81-82; f. 2003; family channel; Gen. Producer ALYAKSANDR B. SEMYARNYOW.

ONT—Obshchenatsionalnoye Televideniye (Nation-wide TV): Minsk; tel. (17) 290-66-84; e-mail press@ont.by; internet www.ont .by; f. 2002; 51% state-owned; broadcasts nation-wide; Chair. GRIGORIY L. KISEL.

TVS—Televizionnaya Veshchatelnaya Set (TBN—Television Broadcasting Network): 220072 Minsk, pr. Nezavisimosti 15A; tel. (17) 284-10-86; fax (17) 284-10-86; e-mail tbn@promedia.by; internet www.data.minsk.by/tbn; f. 1995; comprises 16 private television cos in Belarus's largest cities and an advertising co.

Finance

(cap. = capital; dep. = deposits; res = reserves; m. = million; brs = branches; amounts in readjusted Belarusian roubles, unless otherwise indicated)

BANKING

At October 2006 there were 30 commercial banks registered in Belarus.

Central Bank

National Bank of the Republic of Belarus: 220008 Minsk, pr. Nezavisimosti 20; tel. (17) 219-23-03; fax (17) 227-48-79; e-mail email@nbrb.by; internet www.nbrb.by; f. 1990; cap. 60,000m., res 525,029.5m., dep. 2,600,201m. (Dec. 2005); Chair. PETR P. PRAKAPOVICH; 6 brs.

Commercial Banks

Absolutbank: 220023 Minsk, pr. Nezavisimosti 95, POB 9; tel. (17) 237-07-02; fax (17) 264-24-43; e-mail root@absolutbank.by; internet www.absolutbank.by; f. 1993; closed jt-stock co; 51.9% owned by Theocritos Enterprises Ltd (Cyprus); 30.8% owned by Estudes Trading Ltd (Cyprus); cap. 11,040.7m., res 4,193.0m., dep. 48,435.8m. (Dec. 2006); Chair. BORIS G. CHEREDNIK; 3 brs.

Bank Moskva-Minsk (Moscow-Minsk Bank): 220002 Minsk, vul. Kamunistychnaya 49; tel. (17) 288-63-01; fax (17) 288-63-02; e-mail mmb@mmbank.by; internet www.mmbank.by; f. 2000; wholly owned by Bank of Moscow (Russia); cap. US $23.1m., dep. $126.6m., total assets $153.8m. (Dec. 2006); Dir Dr ALEKSANDR RAKOVETS; 5 brs.

Belagroprombank: 220036 Minsk, pr. Zhukov 3; tel. (17) 218-57-77; fax (17) 218-57-14; e-mail info@belapb.by; internet www.belapb .by; f. 1991; 99.2% state-owned; cap. 1,578,600m., res 145,100m., dep. 1,020,000m. (Dec. 2006); Chair. SERGEI N. ROUMAS; 118 brs.

Belarusbank: 220050 Minsk, vul. Myasnikova 32; tel. (17) 200-18-31; fax (17) 226-47-50; e-mail info@belarusbank.minsk.by; internet www.belarus-bank.by; f. 1995 following merger with Sberbank (Savings Bank; f. 1922); cap. 1,130,923m., res −3,270m., dep. 10,478,582.0m. (Dec. 2006); Chair. NADEZHDA A. YERMAKOVA; 136 brs.

Belarusian Industrial Bank (Belarusskii industrialnyi bank): 220004 Minsk, vul. Melnikaite 8; tel. (17) 223-95-78; fax (17) 209-42-06; e-mail bib@bib.by; internet www.bib.by; f. 1991; cap. 7,042.4m., res 8,733.1m., dep. 50,678.7m. (Dec. 2006); Chair. of Bd ANDREY KIREYEV.

Belgazprombank: 220121 Minsk, vul. Pritytsky 60/2; tel. (17) 259-40-24; fax (17) 259-45-25; e-mail bank@bgpb.by; internet www .belgazprombank.by; f. 1990; present name adopted 1997; 33.91% owned by Gazprombank (Russia), 33.91% owned by OAO Gazprom (Russia), 23.50% owned by Beltransgaz, 8.63% owned by the Ministry of the Economy; jt-stock bank; cap. 34,124m., dep. 434,556m., total assets 506,682m. (Dec. 2006); Chair. of Bd VIKTAR D. BABARIKO; 7 brs.

Belinvestbank—Belarusian Bank for Development and Reconstruction: 220002 Minsk, pr. Masherova 29; tel. (17) 289-28-99; fax (17) 289-35-22; e-mail corr@belinvestbank.by; internet www.belinvestbank.by; f. 2001 by merger; 66.0% owned by the State Committee for property; 15.6% owned by National Bank of the Republic of Belarus; universal bank; cap. 172,201m., res 20,898m., dep. 1,303,296m. (Dec. 2005); cap. 319,170.7,m, total assets 3,314,198.1m. (Dec. 2007); Chair. of Bd ALYAKSANDR E. RUTKOVSKY; 18 brs.

Belpromstroibank (BPS-Bank): 220005 Minsk, Blvd Muliavin 6; tel. (17) 210-13-14; fax (17) 210-03-42; e-mail inbox@bpsb.by; internet www.bpsb.by; f. 1923; 90% privately owned; cap. 99,878.8m., res 192,943.3m., dep. 1,821,296.0m. (Jan. 2007); Dir-Gen. GALINA P. KUKHORENKO; 37 brs.

Belvnesheconombank: 220050 Minsk, vul. Myasnikova 32; tel. (17) 238-12-15; fax (17) 226-48-09; e-mail office@bveb.minsk.by; internet www.bveb.by; f. 1991; 53.2% owned by Vneshekonombank (Bank for Foreign Economic Affairs—Russia), 20.0% by National Cosmos Bank (Russia); cap. 226,947m., dep. 702,437m., total assets 823,807m. (Dec. 2006); Chair. of Bd GEORGIY YEGOROV; 26 brs.

ITI Bank (International Trade and Investment Bank): 220030 Minsk, vul. Savetskaya 12; tel. (17) 200-68-80; fax (17) 200-17-00; e-mail office@itibank.by; internet www.itibank.by; f. 1999; 42.7% owned by Daltotrade Ltd (Cyprus), 38.9% owned by National Bank of the Republic of Belarus; cap. 51,616.2m., dep. 255,090.2m. (Jan. 2008); Chair. GENNADY S. ALEINIKOV; 5 brs.

Minski Tranzitnyi Bank (Minsk Transit Bank): 220033 Minsk, pr. Partizansky 6A; tel. (17) 213-29-00; fax (17) 213-29-09; e-mail cor@mtb.minsk.by; internet www.mtb.by; f. 1994; cap. US $43.8m., res $1.1m., dep. $41.6m. (Jan. 2008); Chair. of Bd ANDREY K. ZHISHKEVICH; 5 brs.

Paritetbank: 220090 Minsk, vul. Gamarnik 9/4; tel. (17) 288-32-50; fax (17) 228-38-47; e-mail info@paritetbank.by; internet www .paritetbank.by; f. 1974; present name adopted 2004; 98.77% owned by the National Bank of Belarus; cap. 93,368m. (April 2007); res 1,386.9m., dep. 85,007.7m. (Dec. 2005); Chair. of Bd SERGEI PANKOVETS; 8 brs.

Priorbank: 220002 Minsk, vul. V. Khoruzhey 31A; tel. (17) 289-90-87; fax (17) 289-91-91; e-mail info@priorbank.by; internet www .priorbank.by; f. 1989, present name since 1992; 63.045% owned by Raffeisen International Bank-Holding AG (Austria), 13.5% owned by the European Bank for Reconstruction and Development (United Kingdom); cap. 102,801m., res 247m., dep. 1,319,646m. (Dec. 2005); Chair. of Bd SERGEY A. KOSTYUCHENKO; 18 brs.

Slavneftebank: 220007 Minsk, vul. Fabritsius 8; tel. (17) 222-07-09; fax (17) 222-07-52; e-mail corr@snbank.by; internet www.snbank.by; f. 1996; 50.02% owned by VTB Bank (Russia); cap. 43,519m., res dep. 354,410m., total assets 411,747m. (Dec. 2006); Chair. of Bd ULADZIMIR V. IVANOV; 6 brs.

Trastbank: 220035 Minsk, vul. Ignatenka 11; tel. and fax (17) 250-43-88; fax (17) 228-52-31; e-mail root@trustbank.by; internet www .trustbank.by; f. 1994; jt-stock co; 37.4% owned by Delikates (Belarus), 35% owned by Libyan Arab Foreign Bank (Libya); fmrly Infobank, present name adopted Feb. 2005; cap. 14,501m., res 22,341.9m., dep. 94,675.5m. (Dec. 2006); Chair. IOSIF F. KARITSKY.

BANKING ASSOCIATION

Association of Belarusian Banks: 220005 Minsk, vul. Smolyachkova 9; tel. (17) 227-78-90; fax (17) 227-58-41; e-mail mail@abbanks .by; Chair. FELIX CHERNYAVSKY.

COMMODITY AND STOCK EXCHANGES

Belarusian Currency and Stock Exchange (Belorusskaya Valyutno-Fondovaya Birzha): 220013 Minsk, vul. Surganova 48 A; tel. (17) 209-41-03; fax (17) 209-41-10; e-mail bcse@bcse.by; internet www.bcse.by; f. 1998; currency and securities exchange trading organization, depository, clearing and information activities; value of trade US $8,934.5m. (2004); Gen. Dir PAVEL TSEKHANOVICH.

Belarusian Universal Commodity Exchange (BUTB): 220099 Minsk, vul. Kazintsa 2; tel. (17) 224-48-25; e-mail info@butb.by; internet www.butb.by; f. 2004; jt-stock co; trades in timber, metal and agricultural produce; Pres. ARKADII S. SALIKOV.

INSURANCE

AlVeNa: 220006 Minsk, vul. Mayakovskaya 14; tel. (17) 210-28-36; fax (17) 221-59-27; e-mail root@alvena.by; internet www.alvena.by; f. 1991; Belarusian-German jt-stock co; Dir-Gen. VIKTOR SIMONOV.

Bagach: 220104 Minsk, vul. Lynkova 19, bldg 1; tel. (17) 250-84-78; fax (17) 250-84-77; e-mail insure@bagach.gtp.by.

Belgosstrakh (Belarusian Republican Unitary Insurance Co): 220036 Minsk, vul. K. Libknekht 70; tel. (17) 259-10-21; fax (17) 213-08-05; e-mail bgs@belsonet.net; internet www.belgosstrakh.by; state-owned; Dir-Gen. VIKTAR I. SHOUST; 145 brs.

Belingosstrakh: 220050 Minsk, pr. Myasnikov 40; tel. (17) 203-58-78; fax (17) 217-84-19; e-mail bigs1@mail.belpak.by; f. 1992; non-life, property, vehicle and cargo insurance; Dir-Gen. ALYAKSANDR KHOMYAKOV.

Brolly: 220030 Minsk, vul. Uljanovskaya 31, POB 73; tel. (17) 210-46-33; fax (17) 222-48-71; e-mail brolly@brolly.by; internet www .brolly.by; f. 1994; offers 30 types of insurance; Gen. Dir VIKTOR A. LAVRUSHENKO.

Kupala: 220004 Minsk, vul. Nemiga 40; tel. (17) 200-80-71; fax (17) 200-80-13; e-mail office@kupala.by; internet www.kupala.by; f. 1993;

BELARUS

affiliate of Wiener Städtische Allgemeine Versicherung AG (Austria); Dir-Gen. VIKTOR S. NOVIK.

TASK: 220005 Minsk, pr. Nezavisimosti 58/9; tel. (17) 225-11-24; fax (17) 296-68-35; e-mail info@task.by; internet www.task.by; f. 1991; partly state-owned; all forms of insurance; Gen. Dir I. I. VOLKOV.

INSURANCE ASSOCIATION

Belarusian Insurance Union (BIU) (Belaruskii Strakhovoi Soyuz): 220114 Minsk, pr. Nezavisimosti 169/905; tel. (29) 650-08-91; fax (17) 218-14-65; e-mail info@biu.by; internet www.biu.by; f. 1992; 56 mems; Pres. VIKTAR HOMYARCHUK.

Trade and Industry

GOVERNMENT AGENCIES

Belarusian Foreign Investment Promotion Agency: 220004 Minsk, pr. Pobeditelei 7; tel. (17) 203-40-36; fax (17) 203-07-78; e-mail ncm@icetrade.by; internet www.export.by; Dir BORIS SMOLKIN.

Belarusian Fund for the Financial Support of Entrepreneurs (BFFSE): 220048 Minsk, vul. Myasnikova 39; e-mail fund@belpak.minsk.by; f. 1996.

CHAMBER OF COMMERCE

Belarusian Chamber of Commerce and Industry (Belorusskaya Torgovo-promyshlennaya Palata): 220035 Minsk, pr. Pobeditelei 14; tel. (17) 226-91-27; fax (17) 226-98-60; e-mail mbox@cci.by; internet www.cci.by; f. 1952; brs in Brest, Gomel, Grodno, Mogilev and Vitebsk; Pres. ULADZIMIR N. BOBROV.

EMPLOYERS' ORGANIZATION

Business Union of Entrepreneurs and Employers (Biznes Soyuz Predprinimatelei i Nanimatelei): 220033 Minsk, vul. Fabrichnaya 22; tel. (17) 298-11-49; fax (17) 298-27-92; e-mail bspn-org@nsys.by; internet www2.bspn.nsys.by; f. 1990; Pres. GEORGY BADEY.

UTILITIES

Electricity

Belenergo/Belenerha (Belarusian Energy Co): 220030 Minsk, vul. K. Marksa 14; tel. (17) 218-23-59; fax (17) 218-26-39; e-mail belenergo@bel.energo.by; internet www.energo.by; f. 1995; restructuring pending; generation, transmission and distribution of electric power; includes six regional generation companies; Chair. SYARHEY BELY.

Gas

Beltopgaz: 220002 Minsk, vul. V. Khoruzhey 3; tel. (17) 288-23-93; fax (17) 284-37-86; e-mail admin@topgas.by; internet www.topgas.by; f. 1992; distributes natural gas to end-users.

Beltransgaz: 220040 Minsk, vul. Nekrasov 9; tel. (17) 280-01-01; fax (17) 285-63-36; e-mail mail@btg.by; internet www.btg.by; natural gas transportation and supply; underground gas storage; Dir VLADIMIR MAYAROU.

TRADE UNIONS

Automobile and Agricultural Machinery Workers' Union: 220126 Minsk, pr. Pobeditelei 21/1103; tel. (17) 203-82-04; fax (17) 203-84-27; e-mail acmbel7@mail.belpak.by; f. 1990; Leader VALERY KUZMICH.

Belarusian Congress of Democratic Trade Unions (BKDP): 220095 Minsk, vul. Yakubova 80/80, etazh 15/2; tel. (17) 214-89-05; fax (17) 249-31-79; e-mail bcdtu@mail.ru; internet www.bkdp.org; f. 1993; alliance of four independent trade unions; Pres. ALYAKSANDR YARASHUK; International Sec. OLEG PODOLINSKI; 9,500 mems (2007).

Belarusian Peasants' Union (Syalansky Sayuz): 220199 Minsk, vul. Brestskaya 64/327; tel. (17) 277-99-93; Chair. KASTUS YARMOLENKA.

Federation of Trade Unions of Belarus (FPB): 220126 Minsk, pr. Pobeditelei 21; tel. (17) 210-43-37; fax (17) 203-89-93; e-mail contact@fpb.by; internet www.fpb.by; f. 1990; Chair. LEANID P. KOZIK.

Transport

RAILWAYS

In 2000 the total length of railway lines in use was 5,512 km. Minsk is a major railway junction, situated on the east–west line between Moscow and Warsaw, and the north-west–south-east line linking Lithuania and Ukraine. There is an underground railway in Minsk, the Minsk Metro, which has two lines (total length 27.6 km in 2007), with 23 stations.

Belarusian State Railways (Belorusskaya Zheleznaya Doroga): 220745 Minsk, vul. Lenina 17; tel. (17) 225-44-00; fax (17) 227-56-48; internet www.rw.by; f. 1992; Pres. VLADIMIR ZHERELO.

Minsk Metro: 220030 Minsk, pr. Nezavisimosti 6; tel. (17) 219-50-09; fax (17) 200-51-22; e-mail metro@minsktrans.by; internet www.minsktrans.by; f. 1984; two lines (30 km) with 25 stations (2007); Dir NIKOLAI T. ANDREYEV.

ROADS

At 31 December 2004 the total length of roads in Belarus was 93,310 km (comprising 15,377 km of main roads and 66,094 km of secondary roads). Some 87% of the total network was hard-surfaced.

CIVIL AVIATION

Minsk has two airports.

State Committee for Aviation: 220065 Minsk, vul. Aerodromnaya 4; tel. (17) 222-53-93; fax (17) 222-77-28; e-mail gka@ivcavia.com; internet www.ivcavia.com; Chair. VADZIM MELNIK.

Belavia Belarusian Airlines: 220004 Minsk, vul. Nemiga 14; tel. (17) 220-24-24; fax (17) 220-23-83; e-mail info@belavia.by; internet www.belavia.by; f. 1993; state carrier since 1996; operates services in Europe and to the CIS and the Middle East; Dir-Gen. ANATOLY GUSAROV.

Gomelavia: 246011 Gomel, Gomel Airport; tel. (23) 253-53-58; fax (23) 253-02-00; e-mail gomelavia@gomelavia.com.com; internet www.gomelavia.com; f. 1944; state-owned; includes Gomel Airport and Gomelavia Airlines; Dir ANATOLY KIRSANOV.

Tourism

Tourism is not developed. According to the World Tourism Organization, there were 90,588 tourist arrivals in 2005, when receipts from tourism (including passenger transport) amounted to US $346m.

Belintourist: 220004 Minsk, pr. Pobeditelei 19; tel. (17) 226-98-40; fax (17) 203-11-43; e-mail out@belintourist.by; internet www.belintourist.by; f. 1992; national tour operator; Dir MARIA I. FILIPOVICH.

BELGIUM

Introductory Survey

Location, Climate, Language, Religion, Flag, Capital

The Kingdom of Belgium lies in north-western Europe, bounded to the north by the Netherlands, to the east by Luxembourg and Germany, to the south by France, and to the west by the North Sea. The climate is temperate. Temperatures in the capital, Brussels, are generally between 0°C (32°F) and 23°C (73°F). Flemish (closely related to Dutch), spoken in the north (Flanders), and French, spoken in the south (Wallonia), are the two main official languages. Brussels (which is situated in Flanders) has bilingual status. Nearly 60% of the population are Flemish-speaking, about 40% are French-speaking and less than 1% have German as their mother tongue. The majority of the inhabitants profess Christianity, and about three-quarters of the population are Roman Catholics. The national flag (proportions 13 by 15) consists of three equal vertical stripes, of black, yellow and red.

Recent History

Since the Second World War, Belgium has promoted international co-operation in Europe. It is a founder member of many important international organizations, including the North Atlantic Treaty Organization (NATO, see p. 340), the Council of Europe (see p. 225), the European Union (EU, see p. 244) and the Benelux Economic Union (see p. 411).

In the latter half of the 20th century linguistic divisions were exacerbated by the political and economic polarization of Flemish-speaking Flanders in the north and francophone Wallonia in the south. The faster-growing and relatively prosperous population of Flanders has traditionally supported the conservative Flemish Christelijke Volkspartij (CVP—Christian People's Party) and the nationalist Volksunie—Vlaamse Vrije Democraten (VU—People's Union—Flemish Free Democrats), while Wallonia has traditionally been a stronghold of socialist political sympathies. Most major parties have both French and Flemish sections, as a result of a trend away from centralized administration towards greater regional control. Moderate constitutional reforms, introduced in 1971, were followed by further concessions: in 1972 the German-speaking Community gained representation in the Council of Ministers for the first time, and in 1973 linguistic parity was assured in central government. Provisional legislation, adopted in 1974, established separate Regional Councils and Ministerial Committees. The administrative status of Brussels remained contentious: the majority of the city's inhabitants are francophone, but the Flemish parties were, until the late 1980s, unwilling to grant the capital equal status with the other two regional bodies (see below).

In June 1977 the Prime Minister, Leo Tindemans, formed a coalition composed of the CVP and the francophone Parti Social Chrétien (PSC—Christian Social Party), which were collectively known as the Christian Democrats, the Socialists, the Front Démocratique des Francophones (FDF—French-speaking Democratic Front) and the VU. The Council of Ministers, in what became known as the Egmont Pact, proposed the abolition of the virtually defunct nine-province administration, and devolution of power from the central Government to create a federal Belgium, comprising three political and economic regions (Flanders, Wallonia and Brussels), and two linguistic communities. However, these proposals were not implemented. Tindemans resigned in October 1978 and the Minister of Defence, Paul Vanden Boeynants, was appointed Prime Minister in a transitional Government. Legislative elections in December caused little change to the distribution of seats in the Chamber of Representatives. Four successive Prime Minister-designates failed to form a new government, the main obstacle being the future status of Brussels. The six-month crisis was finally resolved when a new coalition Government was formed in April 1979 under Dr Wilfried Martens, the President of the CVP.

During 1980 the linguistic conflict worsened, sometimes involving violent incidents. Legislation was formulated, under the terms of which Flanders and Wallonia were to be administered by regional assemblies, with control of cultural matters, public health, roads, urban projects and 10% of the national budget, while Brussels was to retain its three-member executive. Belgium suffered severe economic difficulties during the late 1970s and early 1980s, and internal disagreement over Martens' proposals for their resolution resulted in the formation of four successive coalition Governments between April 1979 and October 1980. Proposed austerity measures, including a 'freeze' on wages and reductions in public expenditure at a time of high unemployment, provoked demonstrations and lost Martens the support of the Socialist parties. Martens also encountered widespread criticism over plans to install NATO nuclear missiles in Belgium. In April 1981 a new Government was formed, comprising a coalition of the Christian Democrats and the Socialist parties and led by Mark Eyskens (of the CVP), hitherto Minister of Finance. However, lack of parliamentary support for his policies led to Eyskens' resignation in September. In December Martens formed a new centre-right Government, comprising the Christian Democrats and the two Liberal parties. In 1982 Parliament granted special powers for the implementation of economic austerity measures; these were effective until 1984, and similar powers were approved in March 1986. Opposition to reductions in public spending was vigorous, with public sector trade unions undertaking damaging strike action throughout the 1980s.

In May 1985 a riot at a football match between English and Italian clubs at the Heysel Stadium in Brussels, which resulted in 39 deaths, precipitated demands for the resignation of the Minister of the Interior, Charles-Ferdinand Nothomb, of the PSC, over accusations of inefficient policing. In July the resignation, in connection with the issue, of six Liberal government ministers (including the Deputy Prime Minister, Jean Gol) led to the collapse of the coalition. Martens offered the resignation of his Government, but this was 'suspended' by King Baudouin I pending a general election, which was called for October. Meanwhile, however, controversy regarding educational reform provoked a dispute between the two main linguistic groups and caused the final dissolution of Parliament in September. The general election returned the Christian Democrats-Liberal alliance to power, and in November Martens formed his sixth Council of Ministers.

The Government collapsed in October 1987, as a result of continuing division between the French- and Flemish-speaking parties of the coalition. At the ensuing general election in December, the CVP sustained significant losses in Flanders, while the French-speaking Parti Socialiste (PS—Socialist Party) gained seats in Wallonia, and the Socialists became the largest overall grouping in the Chamber of Representatives. No party, however, had a clear mandate for power, and negotiations for a new coalition lasted 146 days. During this time Martens assumed a caretaker role, while a series of mediators, appointed by the King, attempted to reach a compromise. In May 1988 Martens was sworn in at the head of his eighth administration, after agreement was finally reached by the French- and Flemish-speaking wings of both the Christian Democrats and Socialist parties and by the VU.

The five-party coalition agreement committed the new Government to a programme of further austerity measures, together with tax reforms and increased federalization. In August 1988 Parliament approved the first phase of the federalization plan, intended ultimately to lead to a constitutional amendment, whereby increased autonomy would be granted to the country's Communities and Regions in several areas of jurisdiction, including education and socio-economic policy. It was also agreed that Brussels would have its own Regional Council, with an executive responsible to it, giving the city equal status with Flanders and Wallonia. In January 1989 Parliament approved the second phase of the federalization programme, allocating the public funds necessary to give effect to the regional autonomy that had been approved in principle in August 1988. The federal Constitution formally came into effect in July 1989.

A brief constitutional crisis in 1990 provoked widespread demands for a review of the powers of the Monarch, as defined by the Constitution. In March proposals for the legalization of abortion (in strictly controlled circumstances) received parliamentary approval. However, King Baudouin had previously stated that his religious convictions would render him unable to give royal assent to any such legislation. A compromise solution was reached in April, whereby Article 82 of the Constitution, which makes provision for the Monarch's 'incapacity to rule', was invoked. Baudouin thus abdicated for 36 hours, during which time the new legislation was promulgated. A joint session of Parliament was then convened to declare the resumption of Baudouin's reign. However, the incident prompted considerable alarm within Belgium: it was widely perceived as setting a dangerous precedent for the reinterpretation of the Constitution.

The Government was weakened by the resignation of both VU ministers in September 1991 and by the resultant loss of its two-thirds' parliamentary majority, necessary for the implementation of the third stage of the federalization programme. Further linguistic conflict between the remaining coalition partners led to Martens' resignation as Prime Minister in October and the subsequent collapse of the Government. However, King Baudouin rejected the resignations of Martens and the Council of Ministers. The Government remained in office until the next general election, which took place in November. The results of the election reflected a significant decline in popular support for all five parties represented in the outgoing Government. The Socialist parties remained the largest overall grouping in the Chamber of Representatives, although they sustained the highest combined loss of seats (nine). In March 1992 four of the five parties that had composed the previous Government, the CVP, the PSC, the Socialistische Partij (SP) and the PS (which together controlled 120 seats in the 212-member Chamber of Representatives), agreed to form a new administration; a leading member of the CVP, Jean-Luc Dehaene, was appointed Prime Minister. The new Government committed itself to the completion of the constitutional reforms that had been initiated under Martens' premiership. For several months, however, the coalition partners repeatedly failed to reach agreement, both on proposals for the implementation of the third stage of the federalization programme and on amendments to the 1993 budget. A compromise on both issues was eventually reached at the end of September 1992.

In July 1992 the Chamber of Representatives voted overwhelmingly in favour of ratifying the Treaty on European Union, agreed by the heads of government of member states of the European Community (now EU) at Maastricht, in the Netherlands, in December 1991. The Senate approved ratification in November 1992.

In February 1993 Parliament voted to amend the Constitution to create a federal state of Belgium, comprising the largely autonomous regions of Flanders, Wallonia and Brussels. The three regions, and the country's three linguistic groups, were to be represented by the following directly elected administrations: a combined administration for Flanders and the Flemish Community; regional administrations for Wallonia and Brussels; and separate administrations for French- and German-speakers. The regional administrations were to assume sole responsibility for the environment, housing, transport and public works, while the language community administrations were to supervise education policy and culture. Legislation to implement the reforms was enacted in July.

In July 1993 King Baudouin died; he was succeeded by his brother, Prince Albert of Liège (as King Albert II), in August.

In January 1994 three PS government ministers (including a Deputy Prime Minister, Guy Coëme) resigned from their posts, following allegations of their involvement in a bribery scandal in connection with the award, in 1988, of a defence contract to an Italian helicopter company. The PS was subsequently implicated in a similar scandal involving a French aviation company. In April 1996 Coëme and seven others were found guilty of fraud and abuse of public office. The scandal also led to the suicide in March 1995 of a retired Chief of Staff of the Air Force, the resignation in the same month of Frank Vandenbroucke, a Deputy Prime Minister and the Minister of Foreign Affairs, and the resignation of Willy Claes, a former Deputy Prime Minister and Minister of Foreign Affairs, as Secretary-General of NATO, and his eventual conviction in December 1998 on charges of corruption, fraud and forgery; he received a three-year suspended prison sentence. A former Deputy Prime Minister and erstwhile President of the PS, Guy Spitaels, Coëme and a French business executive were also convicted of corruption and each received a two-year suspended prison sentence.

At a general election held in May 1995 the ruling centre-left coalition retained significant support, securing a total of 82 seats in the Chamber of Representatives (membership of which had been reduced to 150), despite the ongoing investigation into alleged illegal activities by officials of the two Socialist parties. The performance of the extreme right-wing Vlaams Blok (Flemish Bloc) was not as strong as had been anticipated (the party having performed well in the mid-1994 elections to the European Parliament): despite winning nearly 28% of the votes cast in Antwerp, Belgium's second largest city, it received only 12% of the votes overall in Flanders. Elections to the regional assemblies were held concurrently. The CVP-PSC-PS-SP coalition was re-formed shortly after the election and in mid-June a new Council of Ministers was appointed, under Dehaene. The Government introduced several strict economic austerity measures in late 1995; public sector trade unions organized strike action in response. In April 1996 the Government, employers and trade unions agreed measures that aimed to reduce the high level of unemployment. The agreement was, however, short-lived, owing to the subsequent withdrawal of one of the main trade unions. In the following month Parliament granted the Dehaene administration special emergency powers to implement economic austerity measures by decree.

The latter half of 1996 was dominated by extreme public concern over allegations of endemic official corruption, following the discovery, in August, of an international paedophile network based in Belgium, and subsequent widespread speculation (fuelled by the arrests in September of several police officers) that this had received protection from the police force and from the judicial and political establishment. During September King Albert promised a thorough investigation of the network and, in an unprecedented gesture, demanded a review of the judicial system. In October, however, allegations of a conspiracy to impede the progress of the investigation were prompted by the removal from the case of Jean-Marc Connerotte, a widely respected senior investigating judge. The prevailing mood of national crisis was heightened by the arrests, during September, of Alain Van der Biest of the PS (a former federal Minister of Pensions) and four others, on charges connected with the assassination in 1991 of a former Deputy Prime Minister, André Cools. It was alleged that PS colleagues had ordered the killing in order to prevent Cools from disclosing corruption within the party. In June 1998 a Tunisian court found two Tunisian citizens guilty of the murder; however, the background to the assassination remained unclear. Although the motive remained elusive, in December 2001 Van der Biest, in addition to eight members of his entourage, was charged with murder for his part in the killing. However, Van der Biest, still protesting his innocence, committed suicide in March 2002 before he could be tried. Six members of his entourage were convicted in January 2004 of organizing the assassination, and were sentenced to between five and 20 years' imprisonment.

Meanwhile, in April 1997 a parliamentary committee investigating allegations of official corruption and mismanagement issued a report that claimed that rivalry between the country's various police and judicial divisions often prevented their effective co-operation; it recommended the establishment of a single integrated national police force. However, the committee found little evidence that paedophile networks had received official protection. In February 1998 the Government announced that, in place of the recommended integrated national police force, efforts would be made to facilitate 'voluntary co-operation contracts' between the various law enforcement services.

In April 1998 Marc Dutroux, a convicted paedophile whose arrest in August 1996 on charges of child kidnapping and murder had prompted the ongoing scrutiny of Belgium's national institutions, briefly escaped from police custody. (In June 2000 Dutroux was sentenced to five years' imprisonment for his escape.) The incident incited renewed public anger and precipitated the resignations of several high-ranking figures, including the commander of the national gendarmerie and the Ministers of the Interior and Justice. A proposed vote of 'no confidence' in the Dehaene Government, also ensuing from Dutroux's escape, was defeated in the Chamber of Representatives. Dehaene immediately reaffirmed his commitment to restructuring the police and judiciary. However, in May 2002 the parents of one of Dutroux's alleged victims declared a lack of confidence in the competence of the authorities and withdrew from the criminal investigation. Their principal complaint was the alleged obstruction of attempts to broaden the inquiry to include an investigation into allegations of Dutroux's involvement in a putative paedophile network that extended into the political and judicial establishment. The police completed their inquiry in August and Dutroux's trial began in March 2004. In June Dutroux was found guilty of the kidnapping, imprisonment and rape of six young girls and of three murders; he was sentenced to life imprisonment with no possibility of parole.

Preparations for the general election scheduled to be held in mid-June 1999 were overshadowed by the public announcement in late May that animal feed contaminated with industrial oil containing dioxin (a carcinogenic chemical) had been supplied to farms throughout Belgium from a factory near Ghent. Following the announcement, many food products were withdrawn from sale, while production was suspended at farms across Belgium. There was widespread public anger that, although veterinary inspectors had identified a problem as early as mid-March, it was not until May that the Ministry of Agriculture had suspended sales from the affected suppliers, and had informed authorities in neighbouring countries. On 1 June the Minister of Agriculture and Small and Medium-sized Enterprises and the Minister of Consumer Affairs, Public Health and the Environment resigned. In early June the EU announced that it was to demand the removal from sale, and destruction, of poultry, pork and cattle products from affected farms. The Belgian Government subsequently introduced a total ban on the slaughter and transportation of all poultry, cattle and pigs until it could confirm which farms had received the affected feed. On 7 June Dehaene took the unprecedented step of halting his electoral campaign, and announced an official parliamentary inquiry into the contamination. On 10 June, in an apparent attempt to assuage demands for compensation from farmers affected by the ban, the Government announced that slaughtering and exports could resume at farms that had not received the contaminated feed, despite the lack of a definitive list of dioxin-free farms. This relaxation of the temporary ban on production contravened the advice of the European Commission. The Commission later announced that it was to initiate legal proceedings against the Belgian Government over its handling of the crisis, which had led to imports of European food products being banned by many non-European countries (including the USA); however, the proceedings were dropped in June 2001.

At the general election, which was held on 13 June 1999, the Christian Democrats suffered heavy losses, mainly at the hands of the Liberals and the ecologist parties. The Vlaams Blok also showed significant gains. The Vlaamse Liberalen en Demokraten—Partij van de Burger (VLD—Flemish Liberals and Democrats—Citizens' Party) emerged as the largest single party, with 23 seats in the 150-member Chamber of Representatives, while the ecologist parties, Anders Gaan Leven (Agalev) and the Ecologistes Confédérés pour l'Organisation des Luttes Originales (Ecolo), almost doubled their representation, to 20 seats, and the Vlaams Blok became the fifth largest party in the lower house, with 15 seats. The CVP secured 22 seats and the PSC won 10 seats, while the Socialist parties obtained a combined total of 33 seats. The VLD also performed well in the elections to the Senate. The electoral defeat of the outgoing coalition was largely attributed to public dissatisfaction with the authorities' response to the dioxin crisis, compounded by general disquiet over the earlier scandals. On 12 July a new six-party coalition Government, led by the President of the VLD, Guy Verhofstadt, and comprising the VLD, the francophone Parti Réformateur Libéral (PRL), the two Socialist parties and the two ecologist parties, was sworn in. The new administration was the first Belgian Government in 40 years not to include the Christian Democrats, the first to include the ecologist parties, and the first to be headed by a Liberal Prime Minister since 1884.

The general popularity of the new Government was slightly undermined by the results of the local elections that took place in October 2000. Although the government parties performed well, their achievements were overshadowed by those of the Vlaams Blok, which had campaigned against immigration and in favour of independence for Flanders. The Vlaams Blok made significant advances in Flanders, particularly in Antwerp. It also performed well in Ghent and Mechelen and, surprisingly, in Brussels, where its share of the vote doubled in several districts. The Vlaams Blok remained unrepresented in any municipal government, owing to the refusal of any other party to co-operate with the group, but there were fears nevertheless that its extremist positions were altering political debate in Belgium. In September 2002 the Court of Appeal ruled that two human rights groups could begin legal proceedings seeking the dissolution of the Vlaams Blok, on the grounds that its xenophobic and racist views were in contravention of equal rights legislation.

In January 2001 the federal Council of Ministers approved a directive for the decriminalization, subject to parliamentary approval, of marijuana. Legislation legalizing the possession and cultivation of marijuana for personal use by persons aged over 18 years was subsequently approved by Parliament in early 2003. In October 2001 the Senate approved legislation enabling the legalization of euthanasia. In May 2002 the Chamber of Representatives endorsed a law that permitted adult patients suffering extreme physical or psychological pain resulting from an accident or terminal illness to seek the right to die. Despite opposition from the Roman Catholic Church, the law was promulgated in September. Legislation providing for marriage between homosexual couples was approved by the Senate in November and by the Chamber of Representatives in January 2003; it awarded homosexual couples similar rights to heterosexual couples, with the notable exception of the right to adopt children. However, legislation allowing homosexual couples to adopt children was subsequently approved by the Chamber of Representatives in December 2005. The legislation was approved by the Senate in April 2006.

In mid-August 2002 an agreement secured by the Minister of Foreign Affairs, Louis Michel, for the supply of 5,500 automatic rifles to the Government of Nepal caused divisions within the coalition Government. While Michel maintained that the sale would help the Nepalese administration counter Maoist rebel attempts to establish a communist dictatorship in the country, opponents, led by Agalev, claimed that the deal contravened EU directives against the sale of weapons to countries engaged in civil war. On 31 August the Government won a parliamentary vote of confidence by 87 votes to 38, although Verhofstadt was obliged to accede to a number of minor concessions concerning the deal. The first consignment of weapons arrived in Nepal in January 2003. In July of that year the Nieuw-Vlaamse Alliantie (N-VA—New Flemish Alliance), a small nationalist party, filed a suit against Michel under controversial Belgian war crimes legislation (see below), accusing him of complicity with alleged atrocities committed by the Nepalese military against the Maoist rebels.

In November 2002 the allegedly racially motivated murder of a man of Moroccan origin provoked rioting in Antwerp; police arrested some 160 people of North African origin in the city. Among the detainees was Abu Jahjah, the leader of an Arab militant group, the Arab European League (AEL). Originally from Lebanon, Jahjah rejected the assimilation of Arabs into Belgian society, demanding separate schools and the creation of self-governing Arab areas. He was subsequently charged with conspiracy to foment disorder. A week before the rioting began, members of the AEL had been pursuing police with video recorders to compile evidence of alleged racist behaviour by the authorities. The Vlaams Blok demanded that the organization be banned. Also in November a Tunisian member of the Islamist al-Qa'ida (Base) organization, Nizar Trabelsi, confessed that he had planned a suicide attack on a US air force installation in eastern Belgium, which was believed to contain nuclear warheads. Trabelsi was sentenced in October 2003 to 10 years' imprisonment, following his conviction for attempting to destroy public property, possession of firearms and membership of a private militia. At the same time a further 17 Islamist militants were also convicted for offences related to terrorism, while five others were acquitted. In late December 2007 Belgian police arrested 14 men on suspicion of planning to help Trabelsi to escape from prison. However, on the following day all 14 were released without charge; Trabelsi, for his part, denied the existence of such a plot. None the less, the interim federal Government insisted that heightened security measures, which had been implemented following the arrests and the resultant discovery of explosive materials and firearms in locations throughout Belgium, would remain in place until early January 2008.

In January 2003 Verhofstadt announced that a general election would take place a month earlier than scheduled, on 18 May. Verhofstadt was obliged to reorganize the Council of Ministers in early May, following the withdrawal of Ecolo from the six-party coalition Government. The Deputy Prime Minister and Minister of Mobility and Transport, Isabelle Durant, and the State Secretary for Energy and Sustainable Development, Olivier Deleuze, resigned after Durant had been deprived of responsibility for the transport portfolio following her refusal to implement a recently negotiated compromise on night flights over Brussels. The dispute over flight routes reflected Belgium's language divide, as the proposed route change would affect the predominantly French-speaking population of the city, whereas the previous arrangement caused greater disturbance to the Flemish-speaking residents. (Durant and Deleuze represented the French-speaking Ecolo, whereas Verhofstadt's VLD was Flemish-speaking.) The transport portfolio was allocated to the PS Deputy Prime Minister and Minister of Employment, Laurette Onkelinx, while responsibility for energy and sustainable development was awarded to a PRL government official, Alain Zenner.

Belgium's international profile was raised in 2003 by its Government's public opposition to the USA's policy of a preemptive military attack against Iraq, owing to the alleged failure of Saddam Hussain's regime to disarm in compliance with a resolution by the UN. The Belgian position, which was shared by the French and German Governments, also created a crisis in NATO as the three countries used their veto to reject US-supported defensive aid to Turkey in preparation for a potential war with Iraq. While opposition from Germany and France was successfully circumvented, the Belgian Government, which was under considerable pressure from domestic anti-war public opinion prior to a general election, remained isolated. The issue was resolved by the inclusion of Belgian amendments to the agreement to provide military aid to Turkey, notably the addition of an explicit reference to the framework of the UN for the peaceful solution of the crisis.

At the general election on 18 May 2003, in which 91.6% of the electorate participated, the outgoing centre-left Liberal and Socialist coalition was returned to power. The ecologist parties suffered heavy losses, while the controversial Vlaams Blok achieved the best result in its 25-year history. The VLD won 25 seats in the Chamber of Representatives, as did the PS. The Mouvement Réformateur (MR) coalition obtained 24 seats, while the Flemish wing of the Socialist party (renamed the Sociaal Progressief Alternatief—SP.A—in 2001) in an alliance with the smaller Flemish regional party, Spirit, won 23. The Christian Democrats (restyled the Christen-Democratisch en Vlaams Partij—CD&V—in 2001) secured 21 seats. The CD&V Chairman, Stefaan De Clerck, subsequently resigned and was replaced by Yves Leterme. The Vlaams Blok became the sixth largest party in the house, increasing its representation to 18 seats. It gained 18% of the Flemish vote and one-third of the votes cast in Antwerp. The growing popularity of the party stimulated debate about the counter-productiveness of the 12-year agreement by the principal political parties to exclude the Vlaams Blok from mainstream politics. The ecologist parties Ecolo and Agalev (later renamed Groen!) which had together won 20 seats in the 1999 election, were reduced to four representatives. The poor performance of the ecologist parties was partly attributed to their prominent role in promoting unpopular legislation such as the early introduction of an EU-mandated ban on tobacco advertising, which led to the loss of Belgium's right to stage a Formula One motor racing event. (The new Government, which excluded the ecologist parties, rescinded the early introduction of the ban in August 2003 in order to regain the right to host the annual event.) The VLD and the SP.A-Spirit coalition also performed well in the concurrent election to the Senate, each winning seven of the 40 directly elective seats. The CD&V and the PS each secured six seats, while the MR and the Vlaams Blok obtained five apiece.

On 28 May 2003 King Albert asked Verhofstadt to form a new government. Following negotiations between the Liberal and Socialist parties, a new coalition Government, comprising the VLD, the MR, the PS, the SP.A and Spirit, took office on 12 July. The Minister of Defence, André Flahaut, and the Minister of Foreign Affairs, Michel, who were both outspoken critics of the conflict in Iraq, retained their portfolios, as did the Minister of Finance, Didier Reynders, although the administration included nine new appointees. Verhofstadt's Government pledged to reduce personal income tax, to increase expenditure on health and justice, and to create 200,000 new jobs by 2007.

It was widely believed that the established parties' continued refusal to enter into coalition with the Vlaams Blok was counterproductive and, despite the Government's adoption of more stringent policies with regard to asylum seekers, the popularity of the Vlaams Blok grew. In the European and regional elections concurrently held on 10 June 2004, the Vlaams Blok increased its representation in the European Parliament to three of Belgium's 24 seats and it became the second largest party in the 124-member Flemish Parliament (while the VLD was only the fourth largest), with 32 seats. Following the poor performance of the ruling coalition parties in the regional elections, Verhofstadt effected a government reorganization (including five new appointments) later that month; the new administration was formally sworn in in July.

On 9 November 2004 the Supreme Court of Appeal found the Vlaams Blok guilty of promoting racial discrimination and ruled that freedom of speech should be curtailed in the interests of national security and to protect the rights of other people. The judgment upheld an earlier ruling made in April in a case brought by the government anti-racism agency. The Vlaams Blok was fined and lost access both to state funding and to television exposure, thus effectively forcing it to disband. The organization had been prepared for the court's decision and consequently changed its statutes and renamed itself Vlaams Belang (Flemish Interest). In a bid to capitalize on its growing popularity, the organization announced plans to broaden its appeal; on 4 November members had voted to moderate the party's policy on immigration.

In early 2005 linguistic divisions intensified, when French-speakers living on the outskirts of Brussels demanded that they be allowed to elect French-speaking politicians, despite Flemish being the sole official language of their communities, or, failing that, that the bilingual region of Brussels be extended into parts of surrounding Flemish-speaking districts; the request was rejected. In May, following the failure of negotiations aimed at resolving the issue, Verhofstadt announced that a decision on the matter was to be postponed until at least 2007. On 13 May the Government won a parliamentary vote of confidence called by Verhofstadt by 97 votes to 50.

On 7 October 2005 government proposals to reform the pension and social security systems prompted the first general strike in 12 years. The reforms, designed to expand the work-force by increasing employment among younger and older workers and, most controversially, by raising the minimum retirement age, were severely criticized by employers' organizations and trade unions. The 24-hour strike, which was organized by the Fédération Générale du Travail de Belgique (FGTB), caused severe disruption to schools, public transport and government services. Later the same month the FGTB was joined by the two other unions in calling for further industrial action, leading to a nation-wide strike on 28 October. On the same day some 80,000 protesters participated in a demonstration in Brussels against the proposals. Following the Government's introduction of a number of minor amendments, employers' groups agreed to the reforms. However, the trade unions remained dissatisfied and organized further industrial action, including a 24-hour strike at the Volkswagen factory on the outskirts of Brussels on 25 November.

In November 2005 the trial began in Brussels of 13 suspected Islamist militants who were accused of membership of the Groupe islamique combattant marocain, which had been linked with a series of suicide bombings in Casablanca, Morocco, in May 2003 and bomb attacks on three trains in Madrid, Spain, in March 2004. The 13 defendants, all Moroccans or Belgians of Moroccan descent, were charged with providing logistical support to the perpetrators of the attacks. The trial was the first to be conducted under anti-terrorism legislation adopted in December 2003. In mid-February 2006 three of the defendants were found guilty of providing logistical support; two were sentenced to seven years' imprisonment and the third to six years' imprisonment, while eight others were convicted of lesser charges and two were acquitted.

In mid-April 2006 the President of the extreme right-wing Front National (National Front), Daniel Féret, was sentenced to 250 hours of community service aiding the integration of migrants and barred from standing for election for 10 years following his conviction on charges of inciting racial hatred. An appeal by Féret against the sentence was rejected in early October.

Concern over increases in racist and anti-immigrant sentiment, particularly in Flanders, continued to dominate the political discourse. Spurious indications by the police that the assailants of a white youth killed at a railway station in Brussels were of North African origin (although two Polish-born suspects were later arrested in relation to the incident) were believed to have encouraged a spate of racially motivated crime. The rise in intolerance was often ascribed by members of other political parties to the influence of the extreme right-wing Vlaams Belang, notably the murder and attempted murder in May 2006 of two women from ethnic minorities by a youth whose family were prominent members of the party. (The youth was convicted of murder in October 2007 and sentenced to life imprisonment.) Vlaams Belang, for its part, insisted that it did not advocate violence.

In municipal elections held on 8 October 2006 Vlaams Belang, which had campaigned against immigration and in favour of independence for Flanders, expanded its influence beyond its traditional base in Antwerp, winning more than 20% of the vote in the 308 municipal councils in Flanders. In Antwerp, however, although Vlaams Belang won 33.5% of the vote, the SP.A-Spirit alliance won the largest representation with 35.5%. The VLD and other members of the governing coalition performed poorly in the municipal elections, largely reflecting voter dissatisfaction with federal policies, notably attempts at economic reform.

At the general election of 10 June 2007 the CD&V made significant gains in Flanders, mainly at the expense of the VLD, while the MR replaced the PS as the leading party in Wallonia. An alliance of the CD&V and the N-VA emerged as the largest group in the Chamber of Representatives, winning 30 seats of the 150 seats (compared with 23 seats in 2003), while the MR won 23 seats. The PS won 20 seats (compared with 25 in 2003), and the VLD, which contested the election as Open VLD in alliance with two smaller Flemish liberal parties, Liberaal Appèl Plus and Vivant, just 18 seats (compared with 25 in 2003). A collapse in support for the SP.A-Spirit alliance, which won 14 seats (compared with 23 in 2003), allowed Vlaams Belang to become the fifth largest party in the Chamber of Representatives, despite a reduction in its own representation from 18 seats in 2003 to 17 seats. The Centre Démocrate Humaniste (CDH) won 10 seats (compared with eight in 2003). In response to the poor electoral performance of the main coalition parties, Verhofstadt announced the resignation of the Council of Ministers, although the Government was to remain in office until the successful conclusion of negotiations over a new coalition agreement. In elections to the Senate, which were held concurrently, the Flemish Christian Democrats and the francophone Liberals also performed well; the CD&V/N-VA alliance won nine seats and the MR eight seats. Open VLD and Vlaams Belang each won five seats, while the PS took four.

In mid-July 2007 the leader of the CD&V, Leterme, was appointed by King Albert to the role of *formateur* (charged with forming a new government), and duly initiated formal discussions regarding a coalition agreement between the Christian Democrats and the Liberals. However, divisions quickly emerged between the Flemish- and French-speaking parties over proposals to devolve further powers to the regional and Community administrations and over boundary changes that would result in the incorporation of 35 districts surrounding Brussels—which, along with the 19 districts of the Brussels-Capital region, comprise the electoral constituency of Bruxelles-Hal-Vilvorde—into Flanders. (Although situated in Flanders, some of those districts comprise a majority of French-speaking inhabitants, who were able to vote for candidates belonging to francophone parties at federal and European elections, and had access to bilingual judicial institutions.) By mid-August the talks appeared to have reached an impasse, and on 23 August, King Albert suspended the negotiations, citing the inability of the main parties to reach a compromise. At the end of the month King Albert requested the newly appointed President of the Chamber of Representatives, Herman Van Rompuy of the CD&V, to assess the willingness of the main political parties to recommence talks over a coalition agreement.

Following the completion of Van Rompuy's mission in late September 2007, King Albert again asked Leterme to lead attempts to form a government. Talks progressed into October, and several agreements were reached on social and economic policies, notably regarding immigration. Nevertheless, later that month linguistic conflict erupted once more over the issues of devolution and boundary changes. Since the francophone parties failed to agree to demands for greater autonomy for Flanders by a deadline in early November set by the Flemish speakers, the Flemish members in the Chamber of Representatives supported a motion in favour of the division of the Bruxelles-Hal-Vilvorde constituency. The francophone parties then withdrew from the talks. On 1 December Leterme resigned as *formateur*, having failed to broker an agreement. Two days later, in an attempt to end the impasse, King Albert asked Verhofstadt to preside over negotiations to form an interim administration, which would have the power to pass a budget. On 21 December an interim coalition Government, comprising the CD&V, the MR, the VLD, the PS and the CDH, was sworn in. Verhofstadt remained as Prime Minister, while Leterme was appointed Deputy Prime Minister and Minister for the Budget and Structural Reform. Reynders retained his previous role as Deputy Prime Minister and Minister of Finance, while assuming extra responsibility for structural reform. The two deputy premiers were each appointed to lead a working group, with Reynders examining socio-economic policy issues and Leterme addressing the prospects for devolution. At the end of February the interim administration reached agreement on a budget for 2008 and on the less controversial devolution measures, facilitating the formation of a new government by 23 March, upon which date the interim mandate was due to expire.

By mid-March 2008 the five parties of the interim coalition had agreed a programme for government and on 20 March Verhofstadt submitted his resignation as Prime Minister. As had been envisaged under the interim coalition agreement, Leterme was then sworn in as Prime Minister by King Albert II. Reynders retained the roles of Deputy Prime Minister and Minister of Finance, though relinquishing responsibility for structural reform to the Minister of Justice, Jo Vandeurzen of the CD&V. The President of the CDH, Joëlle Milquet, entered the Government as one of five deputy prime ministers, also assuming the role of Minister of Employment and Equality, while Annemie Turtelboom and Vincent Van Quickenborne, both of the VLD, were appointed as Minister for Immigration and Asylum Policy and Minister for Enterprise and Deregulation, respectively. The Minister-President of the French Community, Marie Arena of the PS, vacated that post following her appointment as Minister for Social Integration, Pensions and Large Towns; she was succeeded by Rudy Demotte (also of the PS), who assumed responsibility for the French Community in addition to his duties as Minister-President of Wallonia. The agreed government programme focused principally on economic issues, including increasing pension benefits and reducing taxation, while the prospects for devolution continued to be considered by a group of senior politicians. A deadline of July was established for agreement on constitutional reform.

A three-year study by a group of historians commissioned by the Senate, published in February 2007, concluded that the Belgian authorities had collaborated in the persecution and deportation of Jews during the Second World War. Following publication of the report, Verhofstadt, who was the first Belgian premier to acknowledge Belgian complicity in the deportation of tens of thousands of Jews and made the country's first official apology to the Jewish community in 2002, recommended the inclusion of the events in school textbooks. In March 2008 a government commission announced that the sum of €35m. would be paid to Belgian Jews in compensation for the loss of property and goods during the Second World War.

From late 1988 Belgium's hitherto cordial relations with its former colonies underwent considerable strain. Proposals that Prime Minister Martens made in November 1988 regarding the relief of public and commercial debts owed to Belgium by Zaire (formerly the Belgian Congo, renamed the Democratic Republic of the Congo—DRC—in 1997) provoked allegations in the Belgian press of corruption within the Zairean Government and of the misappropriation of development aid. President Mobutu Sese Seko of Zaire responded by ordering the withdrawal of all Zairean state-owned businesses from Belgium and by demanding that all Zairean nationals resident in Belgium remove their assets from, and leave, their host country. In July 1989 the situation was apparently resolved following meetings between Martens and Mobutu, at which a new debt-servicing agreement was signed. However, relations again deteriorated when, in May 1990, the Mobutu regime refused to accede to demands for an international inquiry into the alleged massacre of as many as 150 students by the Zairean security forces. Mobutu accused Belgium of interfering in his country's internal affairs, and ordered the expulsion from Zaire of some 700 Belgian technical workers, together with the closure of three of Belgium's four consular offices. Following the collapse of public order in Zaire in September 1991, the Belgian Government dispatched 1,000 troops to Zaire for the protection of the estimated 11,000 Belgian nationals resident there. By the end of 1991 all the troops had been withdrawn and about 8,000 Belgian nationals had been evacuated. Prospects for the normalization of relations improved following the establishment of a transitional Government in Zaire in July 1992 and the removal of Zairean sanctions against Belgium. Relations deteriorated again, however, in January 1993, when, in response to rioting by troops loyal to President Mobutu, Belgium dispatched 520 troops to evacuate the remaining 3,000 Belgian nationals in Zaire. In October 1994 the Belgian Government pledged to resume humanitarian aid to Zaire. In August 1997, following the deposition of Mobutu's regime in May by the forces of Laurent-Désiré Kabila, it was announced that normal relations between Belgium and the DRC (as Zaire was now renamed) would be gradually restored.

The election of a new Government in Belgium in June 1999 led to an improvement in relations between Belgium and the DRC. The new Belgian Minister of Foreign Affairs, Michel, was determined to develop a new strategy towards the central African countries with which Belgium had historical ties. Following the assassination of the DRC's President Laurent-Désiré Kabila in January 2001, the Belgian Government intensified its attempts to relaunch the peace initiative in the region. During a visit to Belgium by the new DRC President, Kabila's son, Joseph, the Belgian Prime Minister urged Kabila to commit to peace negotiations under the auspices of the UN. Michel also aimed to add an 'ethical' dimension to Belgian foreign policy. Initiatives that reflected this new approach included an apology made by Belgium in February 2002 for its role in the murder of the Belgian Congo's first Prime Minister, Patrice Lumumba, in 1961. Although a report had found no direct link between the killing and the Belgian Government, it did conclude that ministers at the time bore a 'moral responsibility' by failing to prevent it. In July 2002 the state-funded Royal Museum for Central Africa announced that it had commissioned a review of Belgium's colonial past. This followed allegations by a US author, Adam Hochschild, in his book published in translation in Belgium in 1999, that 10m. Congolese had been killed as a result of policies adopted during the colonial rule of King Leopold II (1885–1908). The investigators presented their findings in 2004 (which, although disputing the actual number of Congolese killed during King Leopold's rule, did not deny that many atrocities had indeed taken place). Following a peace accord formalized in April 2003 and the installation in June of Joseph Kabila as leader of an interim DRC Government, in October the Belgian Government announced its intention to double its aid to the DRC to €82m. in 2004. Kabila met Verhofstadt in February 2004 as part of a European tour to secure investment in the DRC's devastated economy. Prior to Kabila's visit the Belgian Government announced that it would send military instructors to train DRC troops in peace-keeping operations. In October, however, the Government of the DRC recalled its ambassador from Brussels, in protest at remarks made by the Belgian Minister of Foreign Affairs, Karel de Gucht, criticizing the DRC authorities for their alleged continuing corrupt practices and lack of democracy.

In October 1990 the Martens Government dispatched 600 troops to protect some 1,600 Belgian nationals resident in Rwanda (part of the former Belgian territory of Ruanda-Urundi), when exiled opponents of the incumbent regime invaded that country. The Belgian Government insisted that the deployment was a purely humanitarian action, and stated that it would not agree to a request from the Rwandan Government for military assistance, citing unacceptable violations of human rights by the authorities. In late October a cease-fire agreement came into effect, and in early November Belgian forces were withdrawn from Rwanda. Nevertheless, the conflict in Rwanda continued during 1991–94. Following the signing of a peace accord in August 1993, some 420 Belgian troops were redeployed as part of a UN peace-keeping force; this was, however, unable to prevent an outbreak of extreme violence, beginning in April 1994, which resulted in the deaths of many hundreds of thousands of people. Following the execution of 10 Belgian troops in April, the Belgian Government withdrew its peace-keeping contingent. It also dispatched some 800 paratroopers to Rwanda to co-ordinate the evacuation of the estimated 1,500 Belgian expatriates remaining in the country, as well as other foreign nationals. In October 1998 three Belgian army officers were demoted, having been found negligent in not preventing the 10 troop fatalities in April 1994. The Belgian Ministries of Foreign Affairs and Defence rejected allegations, published in November 2003, of racist, aggressive and undisciplined behaviour by Belgian UN troops at the start of Rwanda's 1994 genocide. Verhofstadt denounced the author of the book, Gen. Romeo Dallaire, the Commander-in-Chief of the UN Assistance Mission for Rwanda from 1993–94, as unprofessional and noted that Dallaire had refused to testify before the Belgian Senate's Parliamentary Commission of Inquiry Regarding the Events in Rwanda, which took place in 1997–98. In April 2007 the trial of Bernard Ntuyahaga, a former Rwandan army major accused of involvement in the execution of the 10 Belgian troops in 1994, commenced in Brussels. Ntuyahaga had been arrested in Belgium in 2004, having travelled to that country voluntarily after the Belgian authorities had made several unsuccessful attempts to secure his extradition from Rwanda. In June 2007 Ntuyahaga was convicted of the murder of the 10 troops and sentenced to 20 years' imprisonment.

In June 2001 a Belgian court convicted four Rwandan nationals of war crimes for their role in the ethnic violence in Rwanda in 1994. The case was the first to be successfully conducted under legislation introduced in 1993, which endowed Belgian courts with universal jurisdiction in human rights cases. (Three of the four subsequently filed an appeal against their convictions.) In February 2002, however, the International Court of Justice ruled that Belgium did not have the right to try suspects who were protected by diplomatic immunity. In May the final hearing began in a Belgian appeals court for a case brought against the Israeli Prime Minister, Ariel Sharon, for war crimes allegedly committed against Palestinian refugees in Lebanon in 1982, when he was the Israeli Minister of Defence. However, in June judges ruled that the case could not be brought to trial since, according to the Belgian criminal code, alleged crimes committed outside the country required subjects to be on Belgian territory to be investigated and tried. Another human rights case, against President Laurent Gbagbo of Côte d'Ivoire, was similarly dismissed. In February 2003, however, the Supreme Court reversed the earlier ruling regarding Sharon, but recognized his diplomatic immunity so that proceedings against him were inadmissible while he remained the Israeli premier. However, the court ruled that proceedings against members of the Israeli Defence Forces who had served as senior commanders during the conflict in Lebanon could begin. Israel responded by recalling its ambassador from Belgium.

The 1993 law also jeopardized relations with the USA. In May 2003 Gen. Tommy Franks, the retiring US commander in Iraq, was indicted under the legislation by a Belgian lawyer representing 19 Iraqis. Despite the fact that the case was ended the following week under new procedures introduced in April to prevent the legislation being used for politically motivated litigation, the US Government demanded the abolition of the legislation. The US Secretary of Defense, Donald Rumsfeld, warned that US officials would be unable to attend meetings of NATO and threatened to withdraw US funding for a new NATO headquarters in Belgium. In July 2003 cases were initiated (and dismissed) against several other prominent US politicians, including the President, George W. Bush, as well as against the British Prime Minister, Tony Blair, for their roles in the military action in Afghanistan and Iraq. Legislation was passed in August that repealed the 1993 law and established a procedure for nullifying pending cases; it limited the jurisdiction of the law to cases involving Belgian citizens and long-term residents, and granted automatic legal immunity to all officials attending meetings at NATO and the EU. The repeal of the legislation was opposed by human rights organizations; in February 2004 a human rights group lodged an appeal demanding the partial annulment of the new legislation to eliminate alleged discrimination against the victims of genocide, war crimes and crimes against humanity.

Government

Belgium is a constitutional and hereditary monarchy, consisting of a federation of the largely autonomous regions of Brussels, Flanders and Wallonia and of the Flemish-, French- and German-speaking language communities. The central legislature consists of a bicameral Parliament (the Chamber of Representatives and the Senate). The Chamber has 150 members, all directly elected for a term of four years by universal adult suffrage, on the basis of proportional representation. The Senate has 71 normal members, of whom 40 are directly elected at intervals of four years, also by universal suffrage on the basis of proportional representation, 21 are appointed by the legislative bodies of the three language communities (see below), and 10 are co-opted by the elected members. In addition, children of the King are entitled to honorary membership of the Senate from 18 years of age and acquire voting rights at the age of 21. Members of both Houses serve for up to four years. Executive power, nominally vested in the King, is exercised by the Council of Ministers. The King appoints the Prime Minister and, on the latter's advice, other Ministers. The Council of Ministers is responsible to the Chamber of Representatives. The three regions and three linguistic communities are represented by the following directly elected legislative administrations: a combined administration for Flanders and the Flemish Community, regional administrations for Wallonia and Brussels, and separate administrations for French- and German-speakers. The regional administrations have sole responsibility for the environment, housing, transport and public works, while the language community administrations supervise education policy and culture. Under a constitutional amendment approved by the Chamber of Representatives in June 2001, the regions were also granted greater autonomy over taxation and public expenditure, agriculture, and policies regarding foreign aid and trade.

Defence
Belgium is a member of the North Atlantic Treaty Organization (NATO, see p. 340). As assessed at November 2006, the total strength of the armed forces was 39,690 (including 1,808 in the Medical Service and 16,236 in Joint Service), comprising an army of 12,571, a navy of 1,605 and an air force of 7,470. Total reserves numbered 2,040. The defence budget for 2006 was estimated at €2,790m. Compulsory military service was abolished in 1995. In 1996 the Belgian and Dutch navies came under a joint operational command, based at Den Helder, the Netherlands. In November 2004 the European Union (EU, see p. 244) ministers responsible for defence agreed to create 13 'battle-groups' (each numbering about 1,500 men), which could be deployed at short notice to crisis areas around the world. The EU battlegroups, two of which were to be ready for deployment at any one time, following a rotational schedule, reached full operational capacity from 1 January 2007. Belgium was committed to contributing troops to one battlegroup with France and another with participation from France, Germany and Luxembourg.

Economic Affairs
In 2006, according to estimates by the World Bank, Belgium's gross national income (GNI), measured at average 2004–06 prices, was US $404,730m., equivalent to $38,600 per head (or $35,090 per head on an international purchasing-power parity basis). During 1996–2006, it was estimated, the population increased at an average annual rate of 0.3%, while gross domestic product (GDP) per head increased, in real terms, by an average of 1.9% per year. Overall GDP increased, in real terms, at an average annual rate of 2.3% during 1996–2006; it rose by 3.2% in 2006.

Agriculture (including hunting, forestry and fishing) contributed 1.0% of GDP in 2006 and engaged 2.0% of the employed labour force in that year. The principal agricultural products are sugar beet, cereals and potatoes. Pig meat, beef and dairy products are also important. Exports of food and live animals accounted for 9.5% of Belgium's total export revenue in 2006. The agricultural sector was adversely affected by the dioxin contamination scandal (see Recent History) in the late 1990s. Agricultural GDP increased, in real terms, at an average annual rate of 1.5% in 1996–2005; it decreased by 7.8% in 2005.

Industry (including mining and quarrying, manufacturing, power and construction) contributed 24.3% of GDP in 2006 and engaged 24.7% of the employed labour force that year. Real industrial GDP increased at an average rate of 1.6% per year in 1996–2005; it expanded by 2.9% in 2004 before declining by 0.1% in 2005.

Belgium has few mineral resources, and the country's last coal mine closed in 1992. Extractive activities accounted for only 0.1% of GDP in 2006 and engaged only 0.2% of the employed labour force in that year. Belgium is, however, an important producer of copper, zinc and aluminium, smelted from imported ores. The sector's GDP declined at an average rate of 2.2% per year during 1995–2004; it declined by 1.6% in 2003, but increased by 10.5% in 2004.

Manufacturing contributed 17.1% of GDP in 2005 and engaged 16.8% of the employed labour force in 2006. In 2004 the main branches of manufacturing, in terms of value added, were chemicals, chemical products and man-made fibres (accounting for 18.6% of the total), basic metals and fabricated metal products (15.4%) and food products, beverages and tobacco (13.5%). During 1995–2004 manufacturing GDP increased at an average annual rate of 1.7%; it declined by 0.8% in 2003, but rose by 2.3% in 2004.

Belgium's seven nuclear reactors accounted for 56.1% of total electricity generation in 2004. A further 25.5% was produced by natural gas power stations and 13.6% by coal-fired stations. The country's dependence on imported petroleum and natural gas has increased since 1988, following the announcement by the Government in that year of the indefinite suspension of its nuclear programme and of the construction of a gas-powered generator. In December 2002 a bill was approved by the Chamber of Representatives to phase out the use of nuclear power by 2025, with the first nuclear power station scheduled to be closed in 2015. Fuel imports comprised an estimated 16.9% of the value of Belgium's total imports in 2006. The electricity market in Flanders was opened up to competition from July 2003, and the remainder of the electricity sector was fully liberalized in January 2007. The natural gas market was fully liberalized by July 2007.

The services sector contributed 74.7% of GDP in 2006 and engaged 73.3% of the employed labour force in that year. Financial services and the insurance sector provide significant contributions to GDP. The presence in Belgium of the offices of many international organizations and businesses is a significant source of revenue. Tourism is an expanding industry in Belgium, and in 2005 an estimated 6.7m. foreign tourists visited the country. Tourism receipts totalled US $10,879m. in that year. The GDP of the services sector increased at an average annual rate of 2.3% in 1996–2005; it increased by 1.8% in 2005.

In 2006 Belgium recorded a visible trade surplus of US $3,872m., and there was a surplus of $7,858m. on the current account of the balance of payments. Belgium's principal source of imports in 2006 was the Netherlands (providing 22.6% of the total); other major suppliers were Germany (16.2%), France (13.1%) and the United Kingdom (7.6%). The principal markets for exports in that year were France (accounting for 17.3% of the total) and Germany (also accounting for 17.3%); other major purchasers were the Netherlands (12.8%) and the United Kingdom (7.9%). The principal exports in 2006 were road vehicles, petroleum and related products, general industrial machinery, equipment and parts and iron and steel. The principal imports in that year were petroleum and related products, road vehicles, and general industrial machinery, equipment and parts.

In 2006 there was a budgetary surplus of €280.2m., equivalent to 0.1% of GDP. The country's total public debt was equivalent to 94.3% of GDP in 2005. The annual rate of inflation averaged 1.9% in 1996–2006. Consumer prices increased by an average annual of 2.3% in 2006. In 2006 8.2% of the labour force were unemployed.

Belgium is a member of the European Union (EU, see p. 244) and participated in the introduction of the European single currency, the euro, on 1 January 1999. Belgium is also a member of the Benelux Economic Union (see p. 411) and the European System of Central Banks (ESCB), which was inaugurated in 1998 under the auspices of the European Central Bank (see p. 256).

Belgium is a small open economy, which is reliant on exports and benefits from high levels of foreign investment. The first Verhofstadt administration, which presided over a period of growth in the economy, achieved the first budget surplus for 50 years (of 0.2% of GDP) in 2001. In June 2001 the Government attempted to address the imbalances in the performances of the regional economies in Belgium, granting greater fiscal control to the regions, with the discretion to raise or lower local taxes. At 95.9% of GDP in 2004, public debt fell below 100% of GDP for the first time in 20 years, although this was still far above the 60% limit set by the EU Stability and Growth Pact. Progress in job creation was considered essential for the long-term prospects of the economy, as social security and pension payments remained a serious burden on public finances. The Belgian employment rate was one of the lowest among EU member states, at 61.1% in 2006, compared with the EU target of 70% by 2010. On a federal level, Verhofstadt announced a number of measures to increase employment, including simplifying the business environment and expediting the process of establishing new businesses. The Prime Minister also announced that priority would be given to reducing social security contributions for older and younger employees and, controversially, that the minimum age for early retirement would be raised from 58 to 60 years from 2008. The retirement age for women was to be gradually raised to 65 by 2009. A wage agreement was confirmed between employers and unions in December 2006, allowing for 5% wage increases in 2007–08, owing to high business profits, although wage moderation was viewed as essential in order to reverse the recent decline in Belgian competitiveness in relation to neighbouring countries. Following the devolution of further powers to the regions, the Walloon and Flemish Governments adopted plans to regenerate the regional economies through investment in infrastructure, encouraging research and development and improving business. The Belgian economy performed well in 2007, but was adversely affected by the failure to form a government following the general election in June 2007, which resulted in the country being run by a caretaker Government with limited powers. The planned budget surplus of 0.3% of GDP for 2007 failed to materialize, as certain planned fiscal measures were not implemented, and a deficit of 0.1% of GDP was recorded. The surplus had been intended to help provide for the future associated health and welfare costs of an ageing population. The lack of a legitimate government was also expected to have a detrimental effect on foreign investment. An interim administration was established in December and agreement was finally reached on the 2008 budget at the end of February of that year. A balanced budget was envisaged, while funds of €340m. were made available to improve the minimum wage and pensions, which were being eroded by inflation, which was at its highest level since 1991. The principal pressures on inflation were increases in petroleum and food prices, which were largely beyond the control of the Government. Real GDP expanded by an estimated 2.7% in 2007, with growth supported by a significant increase in employment, which had a positive effect on consumption. GDP growth was anticipated to slow in 2008–09, although consumption, investment and export growth were expected to remain strong.

Education

Legislation granting responsibility for the formulation of education policy to the administrations of the Flemish-, French- and German-speaking communities came into effect in 1993. Education may be provided by the Communities, by public authorities or by private interests. All educational establishments, whether official or 'free' (privately organized), receive most of their funding from the Communities. Roman Catholic schools constitute the greatest number of 'free' establishments.

Full-time education in Belgium is compulsory between the ages of six and 16 years. Thereafter, pupils must remain in part-time education for a further two-year period. About 90% of infants attend state-financed nursery schools. Elementary education begins at six years of age and consists of three courses of two years each. Secondary education, beginning at the age of 12, lasts for six years and is divided into three two-year cycles or, in a few cases, two three-year cycles. According to UNESCO, enrolment at primary schools in 2005 included 98% of children (males 97%; females 98%) in the relevant age-group, while the comparable ratio at secondary schools was an estimated 97% (males 96%; females 97%).

The requirement for university entrance is a pass in the 'examination of maturity', taken after the completion of secondary studies. Courses are divided into 2–3 years of general preparation followed by two to three years of specialization. The French Community controls four universities, while the Flemish Community controls three such institutions; in addition, there are 11 university centres or faculties (six French, five Flemish). In 2004/05 a total of 122,405 students were enrolled in university-level establishments. Non-university institutions of higher education provide arts education, technical training and teacher training; in that year a total of 184,395 students were enrolled in such institutions. In that year enrolment at tertiary level was equivalent to 62.5% of those in the relevant age-group (males 56.6%; females 68.7%). A national study fund provides grants where necessary and almost 20% of students receive scholarships.

Regional expenditure on education was €8,788.6m. in Flanders and €5,778.3m. in Brussels and Wallonia in 2007, and was budgeted at €81.0m. in the German-speaking Community for 2006.

Public Holidays

2008: 1 January (New Year's Day), 24 March (Easter Monday), 1 May (Labour Day and Ascension Day), 12 May (Whit Monday), 11 July (Flemish Community), 21 July (Independence Day), 15 August (Assumption), 27 September (French Community), 1 November (All Saints' Day), 11 November (Armistice Day), 15 November (German-speaking Community), 25 December (Christmas Day).

2009: 1 January (New Year's Day), 13 April (Easter Monday), 1 May (Labour Day), 21 May (Ascension Day), 1 June (Whit Monday), 11 July (Flemish Community), 21 July (Independence Day), 15 August (Assumption), 27 September (French Community), 1 November (All Saints' Day), 11 November (Armistice Day), 15 November (German-speaking Community), 25 December (Christmas Day).

Weights and Measures

The metric system is in force.

Statistical Survey

Source: Institut National de Statistique, 44 rue de Louvain, 1000 Brussels; tel. (2) 548-62-11; fax (2) 548-63-67; e-mail info@statbel.mineco.fgov.be; internet www.statbel.fgov.be; National Bank of Belgium, 14 blvd de Berlaimont, 1000 Brussels; tel. (2) 221-21-11; fax (2) 221-31-00; e-mail info@nbb.be; internet www.nbb.be.

Area and Population

AREA, POPULATION AND DENSITY

Area (sq km)	30,528*
Population (census results)†	
1 March 1981	9,848,647
1 March 1991	
Males	4,875,982
Females	5,102,699
Total	9,978,681
Population (official estimates at 1 January)†	
2005	10,445,852
2006	10,511,382
2007	10,584,534
Density (per sq km) at 1 January 2007	346.7

* 11,787 sq miles.
† Population is *de jure*.

PROVINCES
(1 January 2007)

	Area (sq km)	Population	Density (per sq km)	Capital (with population)
Flemish region	13,521	6,117,440	452.4	
Antwerp	2,867	1,700,570	593.1	Antwerp (466,203)*
Brabant (Flemish)	2,106	1,052,467	499.7	Leuven (91,942)
Flanders (East)	2,982	1,398,253	468.9	Ghent (235,143)
Flanders (West)	3,144	1,145,878	364.5	Brugge (116,982)
Limburg	2,422	820,272	338.7	Hasselt (70,584)
Walloon region	16,845	3,435,879	204.0	
Brabant (Walloon)	1,091	370,460	339.6	Wavre (32,576)
Hainaut	3,786	1,294,844	342.0	Mons (91,196)
Liège	3,862	1,047,414	271.2	Liège (188,907)
Luxembourg	4,440	261,178	58.8	Arlon (26,548)
Namur	3,666	461,983	126.0	Namur (107,653)
Brussels-Capital	162	1,031,215	6,365.5	Brussels (145,917)
Total	30,528	10,584,534	346.7	

* Including Deurne and other suburbs.

BELGIUM

PRINCIPAL TOWNS
(population of city proper at 1 January 2007)

Antwerpen (Anvers, Antwerp)	466,203*	Mons (Bergen)	91,196
Gent (Gand, Ghent)	235,143	Mechelen (Malines)	78,900
Charleroi	210,550	Aalst (Alost)	77,790
Liège (Luik)	188,907	La Louvière	77,509
Bruxelles (Brussel, Brussels—capital)	145,917	Kortrijk (Courtrai)	73,777
Brugge (Bruges)	116,982	Hasselt	70,584
Namur (Namen)	107,653	Sint-Niklaas (Saint-Nicolas)	70,016
Leuven (Louvain)	91,942	Oostende (Ostende, Ostend)	69,115

*Including Deurne and other suburbs.

BIRTHS, MARRIAGES AND DEATHS

	Registered live births		Registered marriages*		Registered deaths†	
	Number	Rate (per 1,000)	Number	Rate (per 1,000)	Number	Rate (per 1,000)
1999	113,469	11.1	44,171	4.3	104,904	10.2
2000	114,883	11.2	45,123	4.4	104,903	10.2
2001	114,014	11.1	42,110	4.1	103,447	10.1
2002	111,225	10.8	40,434	3.9	105,642	10.2
2003	112,149	10.8	41,777	4.0	107,039	10.3
2004	115,618	11.1	43,326	4.1	101,946	9.8
2005	118,002	11.3	43,182	4.1	103,278	9.9
2006	121,382	11.5	44,850	4.3	101,587	9.7

*Including marriages among Belgian armed forces stationed outside the country and alien armed forces in Belgium, unless performed by local foreign authority.
† Including Belgian armed forces stationed outside the country, but excluding alien armed forces stationed in Belgium.

Expectation of life (years at birth, WHO estimates): 78.6 (males 75.6; females 81.5) in 2005 (Source: WHO, *World Health Statistics*).

ECONOMICALLY ACTIVE POPULATION*
('000 persons aged 15 and over)

	2004	2005	2006
Agriculture, hunting and forestry	81.4	85.5	82.9
Fishing	0.6	0.0	0.4
Mining and quarrying	6.8	9.3	9.4
Manufacturing	718.5	727.3	715.2
Electricity, gas and water supply	32.3	32.3	35.1
Construction	272.6	277.0	292.9
Wholesale and retail trade	565.3	568.0	559.4
Hotels and restaurants	132.0	143.8	140.1
Transport, storage and communications	313.3	313.5	320.0
Financial intermediation	152.3	162.0	155.6
Real estate, renting and business activities	378.7	368.8	404.4
Public administration and defence	419.4	419.8	422.1
Education	371.3	389.5	375.6
Health and social work	508.6	516.8	528.9
Other community, social and personal service activities	159.5	170.0	172.0
Private households with employed persons	13.3	20.8	23.7
Extra-territorial organizations and bodies	13.3	31.3	24.8
Total employed	4,139.2	4,235.3	4,262.8
Unemployed	380.3	390.3	383.2
Total labour force	4,519.5	4,625.6	4,646.0
Males	2,545.7	2,582.8	2,582.0
Females	1,973.8	2,042.8	2,063.7

*Includes professional armed forces, but excludes compulsory military service.

Source: ILO.

Health and Welfare

KEY INDICATORS

Total fertility rate (children per woman, 2005)	1.7
Under-5 mortality rate (per 1,000 live births, 2005)	5
HIV/AIDS (% of persons aged 15–49, 2005)	0.3
Physicians (per 1,000 head, 2002)	4.49
Hospital beds (per 1,000 head, 2004)	6.8
Health expenditure (2004): US $ per head (PPP)	3,132.9
Health expenditure (2004): % of GDP	9.7
Health expenditure (2004): public (% of total)	71.1
Human Development Index (2005): ranking	17
Human Development Index (2005): value	0.946

For sources and definitions, see explanatory note on p. vi.

Agriculture

PRINCIPAL CROPS
('000 metric tons)

	2004	2005	2006*
Wheat	1,913	1,768	1,583
Barley	305	302	367
Maize	638	634	576
Oats	31	29	27
Triticale (wheat-rye hybrid)	38	49	46
Potatoes	3,230	2,781	2,593
Sugar beet	6,216	5,983	5,667
Rapeseed	23	24	34
Cabbages and other brassicas	107	110	124
Lettuce and chicory	86	76	75
Spinach	85	96	100
Tomatoes	246	230	240
Cauliflowers and broccoli	86	86	93
Leeks and other alliaceous vegetables	170	169	175
Beans (green)	109	107	110
Peas (green)	78	58	66
Carrots and turnips	301	254	280
Mushrooms and truffles*	41	40	43
Chicory roots	768	694	363
Apples	356	325	325
Pears	231	212	215
Strawberries	44	42	44

*FAO estimates.

Aggregate production ('000 metric tons, may include official, semi-official or estimated data): Total cereals 2,932 in 2004, 2,787 in 2005, 2,606 in 2006; Total roots and tubers 2,470 in 2004, 2,781 in 2005, 2,593 in 2006; Total vegetables (incl. melons) 2,555 in 2004, 2,419 in 2005, 2,161 in 2006; Total fruits (excl. melons) 6,409 in 2004, 5,896 in 2005, 5,955 in 2006.

Source: FAO.

LIVESTOCK
('000 head, year ending September)

	2004	2005	2006
Horses	32	28	35
Cattle	2,739	2,699	2,669
Pigs	6,355	6,318	6,295
Sheep	151	152	154
Goats	25	26	26
Chickens	36,506	35,569	32,867
Turkeys	253	215	178

Source: FAO.

BELGIUM   *Statistical Survey*

LIVESTOCK PRODUCTS
('000 metric tons)

	2004	2005	2006*
Cattle meat	281	271	265
Sheep meat	4	2	2
Pig meat	1,054	1,015	1,008
Horse meat	3	3	3
Chicken meat	468	470*	484
Turkey meat*	7	7	7
Cows' milk	3,060	3,025	3,012
Hen eggs	230	198	244

* FAO estimate(s).
Source: FAO.

Forestry

ROUNDWOOD REMOVALS
('000 cubic metres, excluding bark)

	2004	2005	2006
Sawlogs, veneer logs and logs for sleepers	2,700	2,690	2,800
Pulpwood	1,375	1,430	1,430
Other industrial wood	175	170	175
Fuel wood*	600	650	670
Total	4,850	4,940	5,075

* FAO estimates.
Source: FAO.

SAWNWOOD PRODUCTION
('000 cubic metres, including railway sleepers)

	2004	2005	2006
Coniferous (softwood)	1,035	1,075	1,300
Broadleaved (hardwood)	200	210	220
Total	1,235	1,285	1,520

Source: FAO.

Fishing

('000 metric tons, live weight)

	2003	2004	2005
Capture	26.8	26.8	24.6
European plaice	6.5	6.1	5.1
Lemon sole	1.0	1.3	1.2
Common sole	5.1	4.7	4.4
Atlantic cod	1.9	1.9	2.1
Angler (Monk)	1.3	1.5	1.3
Rays	1.8	2.0	2.0
Aquaculture*	1.0	1.2	1.2
Total catch*	27.8	28.0	25.8

* FAO estimates.
Source: FAO.

Mining

('000 metric tons, unless otherwise indicated, estimated production)

	2003	2004	2005
Barite (Barytes)	30	30	30
Dolomite	3,500	3,500	3,500
Kaolin	300	300	300
Limestone	30,000	30,000	30,000
Petit granite—Belgian bluestone ('000 cubic metres)	916,200	916,200	916,200

Source: US Geological Survey.

Industry

SELECTED PRODUCTS
('000 metric tons, unless otherwise indicated)

	2002	2003	2004
Wheat flour*	1,361	1,318	n.a.
Refined sugar	967	1,016	n.a.
Margarine	221	233	n.a.
Beer ('000 hectolitres)	15,063	15,924	n.a.
Cigars and cigarettes (million)	257	261	n.a.
Cotton yarn—pure and mixed (metric tons)	18,105	15,407	n.a.
Woven cotton fabrics—pure and mixed (metric tons)†	34,115	26,739	n.a.
Synthetic fibres (metric tons)	41,710	38,095	n.a.
Wool yarn—pure and mixed (metric tons)	12,775	10,688	n.a.
Woven fabric from wool, silk, etc. (metric tons)†	3,330	2,950	n.a.
Synthetic fabrics (metric tons)	15,171	14,677	n.a.
Mechanical wood pulp‡	164	158	170
Newsprint‡	103	173	345
Other paper and paperboard‡	534	511	493
Sulphuric acid (100%)	705	623	n.a.
Jet fuels	2,067	2,048	2,143
Motor spirit (petrol)	5,775	5,865	5,789
Kerosene	78	62	78
Distillate fuel oils	12,464	13,013	12,327
Residual fuel oil	7,603	8,689	8,380
Petroleum bitumen (asphalt) ('000 42-gallon barrels)§‖	5,000	5,000	5,000
Liquefied petroleum gas ('000 42-gallon barrels)‖	7,600	7,264	9,000§
Coke-oven coke‖	2,967	3,200§	3,200§
Cement‖	8,152	7,469	7,379
Pig-iron (metric tons)‖	8,053	8,000§	8,000
Crude steel‖	11,495	11,128	11,698
Refined copper—unwrought‖	423	425	383
Refined lead—unwrought‖	88	65	62
Zinc—unwrought‖	239	244	257
Tin—unwrought (metric tons)‖	8,900	7,700	8,900
Passenger motor cars ('000)¶	950	804	n.a.
Commercial motor vehicles ('000)¶	103	95	n.a.
Electric energy (million kWh)	82,069	84,630	85,643

* Source: UN, *Industrial Commodity Statistics Yearbook*.
† Including blankets and carpets.
‡ Source: FAO.
§ Estimate(s).
‖ Source: US Geological Survey.
¶ Assembled wholly or mainly from imported parts.

2005: Mechanical wood pulp ('000 metric tons) 163; Newsprint ('000 metric tons) 265; Other paper and paperboard ('000 metric tons) 513; Petroleum bitumen (asphalt) ('000 42-gallon barrels) 5,000; Liquefied petroleum gas ('000 42-gallon barrels) 9,000; Cement 7,400 ('000 metric tons); Pig-iron ('000 metric tons) 8,000; Crude steel ('000 metric tons) 10,422; Refined copper—unwrought ('000 metric tons) 383; Refined lead—unwrought ('000 metric tons) 63; Zinc—unwrought ('000 metric tons) 222; Tin—unwrought (metric tons) 7,800.

Finance

CURRENCY AND EXCHANGE RATES

Monetary Units
100 cent = 1 euro (€).

Sterling and Dollar Equivalents (31 December 2007)
£1 sterling = 1.3609 euros;
US $1 = 0.6793 euros;
€10 = £7.35 = $14.72.

Average Exchange Rate (euros per US $)
2005   0.8041
2006   0.7971
2007   0.7306

Note: The national currency was formerly the Belgian franc. From the introduction of the euro, with Belgian participation, on 1 January 1999, a fixed exchange rate of €1 = 40.3399 Belgian francs was in operation. Euro notes and coins were introduced on 1 January 2002. The euro and local currency circulated alongside each other until 28 February, after which the euro became the sole legal tender.

BELGIUM

Statistical Survey

GENERAL GOVERNMENT BUDGET
(€ million)

Revenue	2004	2005	2006
Fiscal and parafiscal receipts	128,526.3	133,892.7	139,184.8
Direct taxes	48,344.7	51,123.4	52,377.8
Individuals	38,481.5	40,047.2	39,960.3
Companies	9,592.3	10,851.5	12,217.5
Other	270.9	224.7	200.0
Indirect taxes	37,506.7	39,429.4	41,714.4
Actual social contributions	40,489.8	41,459.3	42,931.4
Taxes on capital	2,185.1	1,880.6	2,161.2
Non-fiscal and non-parafiscal receipts	13,775.8	15,089.6	14,990.6
Total	**142,302.1**	**148,982.3**	**154,175.4**

Expenditure	2004	2005	2006
Current expenditure excluding interest charges	122,176.6	127,908.7	132,862.8
Compensation of employees	34,691.4	36,198.4	37,567.8
Intermediate consumption and paid taxes	10,615.0	10,760.3	11,139.3
Subsidies to companies	3,538.8	4,981.9	5,655.9
Social benefits	66,670.3	68,873.2	71,169.5
Current transfers to the rest of the world	3,084.5	3,200.8	3,297.2
Other current transfers	3,576.6	3,894.1	4,033.1
Interest charges	13,895.5	13,037.6	12,849.6
Capital expenditure	6,584.5	8,066.5	8,182.8
Gross capital formation	4,667.3	5,303.9	5,377.0
Other capital expenditure	1,917.2	2,762.6	2,805.8
Total	**142,656.6**	**149,012.8**	**153,895.2**

INTERNATIONAL RESERVES
(US $ million at 31 December)

	2004	2005	2006
Gold (Eurosystem valuation)	3,630	3,755	4,653
IMF special drawing rights	350	314	545
Reserve position in IMF	2,296	1,112	620
Foreign exchange	7,715	6,815	7,619
Total	**13,991**	**11,996**	**13,435**

Source: IMF, *International Financial Statistics*.

MONEY SUPPLY
(€ million at 31 December)

	2004	2005	2006
Currency issued*	17,223	19,434	21,618
Demand deposits at commercial banks	78,158	90,396	92,388

*Currency put into circulation by the Banque Nationale de Belgique was €126m. in 2004, €–1,018m. in 2005 and €–623m. in 2006.

Source: IMF, *International Financial Statistics*.

COST OF LIVING
(Consumer Price Index; base: 2000 = 100)

	2004	2005	2006
Food	110.4	112.5	115.0
Electricity, gas and other fuels	103.5	112.9	123.0
Clothing	104.0	104.3	106.5
Rent	108.8	111.0	114.9
All items (incl. others)	**108.0**	**111.0**	**113.0**

Source: ILO.

NATIONAL ACCOUNTS
(€ million at current prices)

National Income and Product

	2003	2004	2005
Compensation of employees	142,597.1	146,568.8	151,570.0
Gross operating surplus and mixed income	99,995.5	108,009.8	111,452.6
Taxes on production and imports	36,754.2	39,280.2	41,391.4
Less Subsidies	4,689.0	4,350.3	5,873.1
GDP in market prices	**274,657.8**	**289,508.5**	**298,540.9**
Primary incomes received from abroad	35,029.2	38,588.9	46,303.7
Less Primary incomes paid abroad	31,240.8	35,884.4	43,755.4
Gross national income (GNI)	**278,446.2**	**292,213.0**	**301,089.2**

Expenditure on the Gross Domestic Product

	2004	2005	2006
Private final consumption expenditure	152,804	158,673	165,968
Government final consumption expenditure	66,177	68,496	70,891
Gross fixed capital formation	56,204	59,036	64,182
Increase in stocks	2,593	3,390	4,835
Total domestic expenditure	**277,778**	**289,595**	**305,876**
Exports of goods and services	241,581	257,697	275,432
Less Imports of goods and services	229,850	248,751	267,224
GDP in market prices	**289,509**	**298,541**	**314,084**
GDP at constant 2004 prices	**289,509**	**292,607**	**301,851**

Gross Domestic Product by Economic Activity

	2003	2004	2005
Agriculture, hunting, forestry and fishing	2,753.3	2,865.8	2,925.0
Mining and quarrying	315.6	299.5	310.1
Manufacturing	42,750.2	44,731.7	45,351.3
Electricity, gas and water supply	5,822.9	5,541.0	5,417.9
Construction	11,937.8	12,515.9	12,911.0
Wholesale and retail trade; repair of motor vehicles, motorcycles and personal and household goods	31,534.8	33,721.9	34,611.2
Hotels and restaurants	4,093.1	4,226.3	4,213.7
Transport, storage and communications	20,008.5	21,070.1	22,403.1
Financial intermediation	14,308.8	15,607.5	15,286.6
Real estate, renting and business activities	54,072.2	56,520.6	59,062.0
Public administration and defence; compulsory social security	18,226.4	18,643.3	19,343.6
Education	16,398.9	16,959.1	17,845.2
Health and social work	16,934.4	18,000.0	18,841.0
Other community, social and personal service activities	5,620.6	6,012.4	6,248.6
Private households with employed persons	909.0	868.0	782.0
Gross value added in basic prices	**245,686.5**	**257,583.0**	**265,552.3**
Taxes, less subsidies, on products	28,971.3	31,925.5	32,988.6
GDP at market prices	**274,657.8**	**289,508.5**	**298,540.9**

2006 (€ million at current prices): Agriculture, hunting, forestry and fishing 2,831; Construction 14,256; Other industry 53,586; Trade, transport and communications 62,708; Financial, real estate, renting and business activities 80,488; Public administration and education 38,487; Other service activities 26,944; *Sub-total* 279,300; Taxes, less subsidies, on products 34,784; *GDP at market prices* 314,084.

Source: Service Statistiques financières et économiques, Banque Nationale de Belgique.

BELGIUM

BALANCE OF PAYMENTS
(US $ million)

	2004	2005	2006
Exports of goods f.o.b.	245,426	263,063	283,817
Imports of goods f.o.b.	−235,718	−257,137	−279,945
Trade balance	9,708	5,926	3,872
Exports of services	52,708	55,949	59,953
Imports of services	−49,023	−51,202	−54,855
Balance on goods and services	13,392	10,673	8,970
Other income received	48,891	57,962	65,011
Other income paid	−43,269	−52,556	−58,941
Balance on goods, services and income	19,014	16,079	15,040
Current transfers received	7,949	9,258	8,147
Current transfers paid	−14,427	−15,689	−15,330
Current balance	12,537	9,648	7,858
Capital account (net)	−497	−836	−481
Direct investment abroad	−34,682	−29,550	−60,916
Direct investment from abroad	44,415	33,649	69,258
Portfolio investment assets	−35,558	−43,497	−17,730
Portfolio investment liabilities	5,070	−1,215	18,491
Financial derivatives assets	−8,648	−9,657	−3,637
Financial derivatives liabilities	3,063	4,199	4,870
Other investment assets	−64,685	−87,390	−98,593
Other investment liabilities	80,365	125,016	80,499
Net errors and omissions	−2,103	−2,544	536
Overall balance	−723	−2,176	156

Source: IMF, *International Financial Statistics*.

External Trade

PRINCIPAL COMMODITIES
(distribution by Harmonized System, € million)

Imports c.i.f.	2004	2005	2006
Food and live animals	17,352.6	17,750.8	18,512.2
Mineral fuels, lubricants, etc.	24,042.1	33,639.3	37,111.1
Petroleum, petroleum products, etc.	21,987.7	30,874.0	34,157.8
Chemicals and related products	26,691.0	28,594.2	30,444.2
Organic chemicals	10,170.8	10,318.0	13,470.1
Pharmaceutical products	6,694.4	8,272.9	6,156.8
Plastics and rubber and related products	11,100.5	11,918.9	12,846.0
Textile yarn, fabrics, etc.	6,966.9	7,220.3	7,382.0
Precious pearls, stones and metals and coinage	11,608.7	13,042.4	12,084.4
Base metals and related products	15,377.3	15,970.4	20,802.3
Iron and steel	6,300.1	6,386.6	8,321.1
Machinery and equipment	31,395.6	33,051.9	33,380.0
General industrial machinery, equipment and parts	20,102.4	21,055.3	21,142.4
Electrical machinery, apparatus, etc.	11,293.3	11,996.5	12,237.7
Transport equipment	25,436.0	24,843.3	26,472.3
Road vehicles (incl. air-cushion vehicles) and parts	23,648.1	23,110.1	25,365.1
Total (incl. others)	188,875.2	205,747.9	220,195.8

Exports f.o.b.	2004	2005	2006
Food and live animals	19,509.3	20,198.9	21,151.7
Prepared foodstuffs, tobacco and its substitutes	9,562.5	9,903.7	9,562.5
Mineral fuels, lubricants, etc.	14,731.4	18,917.5	21,275.7
Petroleum, petroleum products, etc.	13,645.0	17,590.8	19,799.7
Chemicals and related products	30,647.8	32,330.3	34,515.8
Organic chemicals	9,210.8	10,219.4	11,157.0
Pharmaceutical products	8,530.2	9,082.8	9,568.0
Plastics and rubber and related materials	17,270.1	19,572.0	20,842.2
Textile yarn, fabrics, etc.	8,355.4	8,392.6	8,517.0
Precious pearls, stones, metals and coinage	11,974.2	13,455.0	13,137.7*
Base metals and related products	18,361.1	20,431.3	25,478.5*
Iron and steel	10,330.0	11,695.0	14,005.9*
Machinery and equipment	27,396.4	28,596.2	28,828.0*
General industrial machinery, equipment and parts	17,510.0	18,489.4	18,790.1*
Electrical machinery, apparatus, etc.	9,886.2	10,106.5	10,038.1*
Transport equipment	29,046.7	29,346.4	30,138.5*
Road vehicles (incl. air-cushion vehicles) and parts	28,216.5	28,241.2	29,419.0*
Total (incl. others)	197,074.0	210,811.4	223,206.8

* Preliminary figure.

PRINCIPAL TRADING PARTNERS
(€ million)*

Imports c.i.f.	2004	2005	2006
China, People's Republic	3,409.7	5,543.3	5,988.8
France†	25,954.5	26,674.3	28,754.3
Germany	31,154.2	32,351.4	35,637.8
Ireland	3,217.3	3,618.9	3,373.3
Israel	1,822.2	2,186.4	1,843.9
Italy	6,330.6	6,913.0	7,231.1
Japan	5,690.5	5,213.7	5,389.9
Netherlands	37,380.5	44,415.0	49,757.6
Norway	2,108.4	4,051.4	3,914.9
Russia	2,912.1	3,722.9	2,597.2
Spain	4,146.4	4,386.2	4,847.8
Sweden	4,670.9	4,916.7	5,135.6
United Kingdom	14,973.3	16,111.3	16,645.7
USA	10,792.6	9,715.4	10,181.9
Total (incl. others)	188,875.2	205,747.9	220,195.8

Exports f.o.b.	2004	2005	2006
Austria	2,258.9	2,183.3	2,457.5
France†	33,996.9	37,322.4	38,719.2
Germany	34,204.9	35,383.6	38,686.0
India	4,224.5	5,126.1	4,521.9
Israel	2,819.2	2,955.0	2,501.9
Italy	10,844.8	11,154.7	11,477.8
Japan	1,713.1	1,759.8	1,554.5
Luxembourg	4,555.0	5,111.7	5,126.9
Netherlands	25,549.9	26,466.2	28,459.2
Poland	2,284.8	2,706.2	3,220.5
Spain	8,017.9	8,415.9	8,657.2
Sweden	2,949.9	3,262.0	3,644.9
Switzerland	2,414.8	2,778.0	3,223.8
Turkey	2,169.1	2,307.6	2,515.4
United Kingdom	17,125.0	17,057.2	17,576.1
USA	8,751.4	9,539.1	9,419.0
Total (incl. others)	197,074.0	210,811.4	223,206.8

* Imports by country of production; exports by country of last consignment.
† Including trade with Overseas Departments (French Guiana, Guadeloupe, Martinique and Réunion).

BELGIUM
Statistical Survey

Transport

RAILWAYS
(traffic)

	2003	2004	2005
Domestic:			
Passenger journeys (million)	154.9	165.0	172.9
Passenger-km (million)	6,929	7,328	7,771
International:			
Passenger journeys (million)	13.4	13.4	13.7
Passenger-km (million)	1,337	1,348	1,379
Freight carried ('000 metric tons)	55,732	58,454	58,400
Freight ton-km (million)	7,293	7,691	7,980

Source: SNCB Railways.

ROAD TRAFFIC
(motor vehicles in use)

	2003	2004	2005
Passenger cars	4,820,868	4,874,426	4,918,544
Buses and coaches	15,060	15,328	15,391
Lorries and vans	556,397	578,124	604,437
Road tractors	47,102	47,394	47,646
Motorcycles and mopeds	319,480	322,762	346,293

SHIPPING

Merchant Fleet
(registered at 31 December)

	2004	2005	2006
Number of vessels	232	238	231
Displacement ('000 grt)	3,973.3	4,058.4	4,312.7

Source: Lloyd's Register-Fairplay, *World Fleet Statistics*.

International Sea-borne Freight Traffic
('000 metric tons, estimates)

	2001	2002	2003
Goods loaded	422,700	439,900	419,400
Goods unloaded	436,900	447,100	427,000

Source: UN, *Monthly Bulletin of Statistics*.

CIVIL AVIATION
(traffic)

	2001	2002	2003
Kilometres flown (million)	186	115	103
Passengers carried ('000)	8,489	2,342	2,904
Passenger-km ('000)	15,320	2,606	3,958
Total ton-km ('000)	2,356	890	961

Source: UN, *Statistical Yearbook*.

Tourism

TOURIST ARRIVALS BY COUNTRY OF ORIGIN*

Country of residence	2003	2004	2005
China, People's Rep.	107,016	114,456	108,702
France	940,628	985,341	1,011,482
Germany	780,911	753,131	748,295
Italy	231,085	220,976	216,169
Japan	114,452	126,523	111,985
Netherlands	1,746,093	1,701,337	1,711,355
Spain	214,992	230,205	247,798
United Kingdom	1,195,123	1,130,224	1,078,492
USA	274,906	288,709	292,050
Total (incl. others)	6,689,998	6,709,740	6,747,123

* Non-residents staying in accommodation establishments.

Tourism receipts (US $ million, excl. passenger transport): 8,848 in 2003; 10,091 in 2004; 10,879 in 2005.

Source: World Tourism Organization.

Communications Media

	2004	2005	2006
Telephones ('000 main lines in use)	4,801.0	4,767.0	4,718.7
Mobile cellular telephones ('000 subscribers)	9,131.7	9,460.0	9,659.8
Internet users ('000)	4,200	4,800	n.a.
Broadband subscribers ('000)	1,617.2	2,010.6	n.a.

Personal computers ('000 in use): 3,627 in 2004.

Facsimile machines ('000 in use): 180 in 1995; 190 in 1996.

Radio receivers ('000 in use): 8,000 in 1995; 8,050 in 1996; 8,075 in 1997.

Television receivers ('000 in use): 5,400 in 1999; 5,500 in 2000; 5,600 in 2001.

Daily newspapers: 29 in 2004 (circulation 1,706,000).

Sources: International Telecommunication Union, UN, *Statistical Yearbook*; UNESCO, *Statistical Yearbook*.

Education

(2005/06, unless otherwise indicated)

	Institutions		Students	
	French*	Flemish	French*	Flemish
Pre-primary	1,861†	2,218‡	177,078	234,530
Primary	1,960†	2,337‡	317,902	415,726
Secondary	645	1,307	371,213	457,351
Non-university higher education	329	22	83,210	102,367
University level	9	7	65,400	59,172

* 2004/05.
† Figure includes 1,728 joint pre-primary and primary institutions.
‡ Figure includes 2,050 joint pre-primary and primary institutions.

Teachers: *French (2004/05):* Pre-primary and primary 30,645; Secondary 36,038; Special education (pre-primary, primary and secondary) 6,450; Non-university higher education 10,055; University level 1,822. *Flemish (2005/06):* Pre-primary and primary 68,768; Secondary 76,706; Non-university higher education 11,439; University level 11,049.

Sources: Entreprise des Technologies Nouvelles de l'Information et de la Communication, *Short statistical overview of full-time and social promotion education*; Vlaams Ministerie van Onderwijs en Vorming, *Vlaams onderwijs in beeld*.

Directory

The Constitution

The Belgian Constitution has been considerably modified by amendments since its creation in 1831. Belgium is a constitutional monarchy. The central legislature consists of a bicameral Parliament (the Chamber of Representatives—Chambre des Représentants/Kamer van Volksvertegenwoordigers and the Senate—Sénat/Senaat). In July 1993 the Constitution was amended to provide for a federation of the largely autonomous regions of Brussels, Flanders and Wallonia and of the Flemish, French and German-speaking Communities. Article 1 of the Constitution states that 'Belgium is a federal state which consists of communities and regions'. The three regions and three linguistic groups are represented by the following directly elected legislative bodies: a combined administration for Flanders and the Flemish Community, regional administrations for Wallonia and Brussels, and separate community administrations for French- and German-speakers. Each body is elected for a term of four years. The regional administrations have sole responsibility for the local economy, the environment, housing, transport and public works, while the language community administrations supervise education policy and culture. In addition, in June 2001 a constitutional amendment was passed by Parliament granting the regions greater responsibility for taxation and public expenditure, agriculture, and issues relating to foreign aid and trade.

ELECTORAL SYSTEM

Members of Parliament must be at least 21 years of age, and they are elected by secret ballot according to a system of proportional representation. Suffrage is universal for citizens of 18 years or over, and voting is compulsory.

The Chamber of Representatives consists of 150 members, who are elected for four years unless the Chamber is dissolved before that time has elapsed. The Senate comprises 71 normal members, of whom 40 are directly elected, usually at intervals of four years, 21 are appointed by the legislative bodies of the three language communities (10 each from the Flemish and French Communities and one from the German-speaking Community), and 10 are co-opted by the elected members. Children of the King are entitled to honorary membership of the Senate from 18 years of age and acquire voting rights at the age of 21.

THE CROWN

The King has the right to veto legislation, but, in practice, he does not exercise it. The King is nominally the supreme head of the executive, but, in fact, he exercises his control through the Council of Ministers, which is responsible for all acts of government to the Chamber of Representatives. According to the Constitution, the King appoints his own ministers, but in practice, since they are responsible to the Chamber of Representatives and need its confidence, they are generally the choice of the Representatives. Similarly, the royal initiative is in the control of the ministry.

LEGISLATION

Legislation is introduced either by the federal Government or the members in the two Houses, and as the party complexion of both Houses is generally almost the same, measures passed by the Chamber of Representatives are usually passed by the Senate. Each House elects its own President at the beginning of the session, who acts as an impartial Speaker, although he is a party nominee. The Houses elect their own committees, through which all legislation passes. They are so well organized that through them the Legislature has considerable power of control over the Council of Ministers. Nevertheless, according to the Constitution (Article 68), certain treaties must be communicated to the Chamber only as soon as the 'interest and safety of the State permit'. Further, the Government possesses an important power of dissolution which it uses; a most unusual feature is that it may be applied to either House separately or to both together (Article 71).

Revision of the Constitution is to be first settled by an ordinary majority vote of both Houses, specifying the article to be amended. The Houses are then automatically dissolved. The new Chambers thereupon determine the amendments to be made, with the provision that in each House the presence of two-thirds of the members is necessary for a quorum, and a two-thirds' majority of those voting is required.

The Government

HEAD OF STATE

King of the Belgians: HM King ALBERT II (succeeded to the throne 9 August 1993).

THE COUNCIL OF MINISTERS
(March 2008)

A coalition of the Christen Democraten en Vlaams (CD&V, in alliance with the Nieuw-Vlaamse Alliantie—N-VA), the Mouvement Réformateur (MR), the Vlaamse Liberalen en Democraten—Partij van de Burger (VLD), the Centre Démocrate Humaniste (CDH) and the Parti Socialiste (PS).

Prime Minister: YVES LETERME (CD&V).
Deputy Prime Minister and Minister of Finance: DIDIER REYNDERS (MR).
Deputy Prime Minister and Minister of Social Affairs and Public Health: LAURETTE ONKELINX (PS).
Deputy Prime Minister and Minister of the Interior: PATRICK DEWAEL (VLD).
Deputy Prime Minister and Minister of Justice and of Institutional Reform: JO VANDEURZEN (CD&V).
Deputy Prime Minister and Minister of Employment and Equality: JOËLLE MILQUET (CDH).
Minister of Foreign Affairs: KAREL DE GUCHT (VLD).
Minister for Small and Medium-sized Enterprises, the Self-employed, Agriculture and Science Policy: SABINE LARUELLE (MR).
Minister for Pensions, Social Integration and Large Towns: MARIE ARENA (PS).
Minister of Defence: PIETER DE CREM (CD&V).
Minister for Climate and Energy: PAUL MAGNETTE (PS).
Minister of Development Co-operation: CHARLES MICHEL (MR).
Minister of the Civil Service and Public Enterprise: INGE VERVOTTE (CD&V).
Minister for Enterprise and Deregulation: VINCENT VAN QUICKENBORNE (VLD).
Minister for Immigration and Asylum Policy: ANNEMIE TURTELBOOM (VLD).

FEDERAL PUBLIC SERVICES AND MINISTRIES

Federal Public Service Office of the Prime Minister: 16 rue de la Loi, 1000 Brussels; tel. (2) 501-02-11; fax (2) 512-69-53; internet www.premier.be.

Federal Public Service of the Budget and Administration: 138/2 rue Royale, 1000 Brussels; tel. (2) 212-37-11; fax (2) 217-39-37; e-mail helene.chaineux@budget.fed.be; internet www.budgetfederal.be.

Ministry of Defence: 8 rue Lambermont, 1000 Brussels; tel. (2) 550-28-11; fax (2) 550-29-19; e-mail cabinet@mod.mil.be; internet www.mil.be.

Federal Public Service of the Economy, Small and Medium-sized Enterprises, the Self-employed and Energy: 50 rue de Progrès, 1210 Brussels; tel. (2) 277-51-11; fax (2) 277-51-07; e-mail info.eco@mineco.fgov.be; internet www.mineco.fgov.be.

Federal Public Service of Employment, Work and Social Dialogue: 1 rue Ernest Blerot, 1070 Brussels; tel. (2) 233-43-93 (Flemish); tel. (2) 233-40-23 (French); fax (2) 233-42-57; e-mail information@emploi.belgique.be.; internet www.emploi.belgique.be.

Federal Public Service of Finance: 33 blvd du Roi Albert II, BP 70, 1030 Brussels; tel. (2) 233-81-11; fax (2) 233-80-03; e-mail info@minfin.be; internet www.minfin.fgov.be.

Federal Public Service of Foreign Affairs, Foreign Trade and Development Co-operation: 15 rue des Petits Carmes, 1000 Brussels; tel. (2) 501-81-11; fax (2) 501-81-70; e-mail info@diplobel.fed.be; internet www.diplomatie.be.

Federal Public Service of Health, Food Chain Security and the Environment: Eurostation II, 40 place Victor Horta, bte 10, 1060 Brussels; tel. (2) 524-90-90; fax (2) 524-96-01; e-mail fonctionnaire-information@health.fgov.be; internet www.health.fgov.be.

Federal Public Service of Information and Communication Technology: 1–3 rue Marie-Thérèse, 1000 Brussels; tel. (2) 212-96-00; fax (2) 212-96-99; e-mail info@fedict.belgique.be; internet www.belgium.be/fedict.

BELGIUM

Federal Public Service of the Interior: 1 rue de Louvain, 1000 Brussels; tel. (2) 500-20-48 (French); tel. (2) 500-20-50 (Flemish); fax (2) 500-20-39; e-mail info@ibz.fgov.be; internet www.ibz.be.

Federal Public Service of Justice: 115 blvd de Waterloo, 1000 Brussels; tel. (2) 542-69-78; fax (2) 542-70-39; e-mail info@just.fgov.be; internet www.just.fgov.be.

Federal Public Service of Mobility and Transport: 56 rue du Progrès, 1210 Brussels; tel. (2) 277-34-08; fax (2) 277-42-58; e-mail info@mobilit.fgov.be; internet www.mobilit.fgov.be.

Federal Public Service of Personnel and Organization: 51 rue de la Loi, 1040 Brussels; tel. (2) 790-58-00; fax (2) 790-58-99; e-mail info@p-o.be; internet www.p-o.be.

Federal Public Service of Social Security and Public Institutions of Social Security: Eurostation II, 40 place Victor Horta, BP 20, 1060 Brussels; tel. (2) 528-60-31; fax (2) 528-69-53; e-mail social.security@minsoc.fed.be; internet socialsecurity.fgov.be.

Legislature

CHAMBRE DES REPRÉSENTANTS/KAMER VAN VOLKSVERTEGENWOORDIGERS
(Chamber of Representatives)

President: HERMAN VAN ROMPUY (CD&V).

General Election, 10 June 2007

Party	Votes cast	% of votes	Seats
CD&V/N-VA	1,234,950	18.51	30
MR	835,073	12.52	23
PS	724,787	10.86	20
Open VLD*	789,445	11.83	18
Vlaams Belang	799,844	11.99	17
SP.A-Spirit	684,390	10.26	14
CDH	404,077	6.06	10
Ecolo	340,378	5.10	8
Lijst Dedecker	268,648	4.03	5
Groen!	265,828	3.98	4
FN	131,385	1.97	1
Total (incl. others)	6,671,360	100.00	150

*A coalition of the VLD and two minor parties: Liberal Appeal Plus (Liberaal Appèl Plus) and Vivant.

SÉNAT/SENAAT
(Senate)

President: ARMAND DE DECKER (MR).

General Election, 10 June 2007

Party	Votes cast	% of votes	Seats
CD&V/N-VA	1,287,389	19.42	9
MR	815,755	12.31	6
Open VLD*	821,980	12.40	5
Vlaams Belang	787,782	11.89	5
PS	678,812	10.24	4
SP.A-Spirit	665,342	10.04	4
CDH	390,852	5.90	2
Ecolo	385,466	5.82	2
Groen!	241,151	3.64	1
Lijst Dedecker	223,992	3.38	1
FN	150,461	2.27	1
Total (incl. others)	6,551,519	100.00	40

*A coalition of the VLD and two minor parties: Liberal Appeal Plus (Liberaal Appèl Plus) and Vivant.

In addition, the Senate has 21 members appointed by the legislative bodies of the three language communities and 10 members co-opted by the elected members. Children of the monarch are entitled to honorary membership of the Senate from 18 years of age and acquire voting rights at the age of 21.

Advisory Councils

Conseil Central de l'Economie/Centrale Raad voor het Bedrijfsleven: 17–21 ave de la Joyeuse entrée, 1040 Brussels; tel. (2) 233-88-11; fax (2) 233-89-12; e-mail anro@ccecrb.fgov.be; internet www.ccecrb.fgov.be; f. 1948; representative and consultative body; advises the authorities on economic issues; 50 mems; Pres. Baron ROBERT TOLLET.

Conseil d'Etat/Raad van State: 33 rue de la Science, 1040 Brussels; tel. (2) 234-96-11; e-mail info@raadvst-consetat.be; internet www.raadvst-consetat.be; f. 1946; advisory body on legislative and regulatory matters; supreme administrative court; hears complaints against the actions of the legislature; 44 mems; Pres. R. ANDERSEN.

Regional and Community Administrations

Belgium is a federal state, and considerable power has been devolved to the regional administrations of Brussels, Wallonia and Flanders, and to the French, German-speaking and Flemish Communities. The regional authorities have sole responsibility for the environment, housing, transport and public works and for certain aspects of social welfare, while the community administrations are primarily responsible for cultural affairs and education. In addition, in June 2001 Parliament granted the regions greater responsibility for taxation and public expenditure, agriculture and matters relating to foreign aid and trade. The administrations of Flanders and of the Flemish Community are homologous.

REGION OF FLANDERS AND THE FLEMISH COMMUNITY

Minister-President: KRIS PEETERS (CD&V).

President of the Parliament: MARLEEN VANDERPOORTEN (VLD).

Vlaams Parlement (Flemish Parliament): Leuvensweg 86, 1011 Brussels; tel. (2) 552-45-45; fax (2) 552-45-00; e-mail informatheek@vlaamsparlement.be; internet www.vlaamsparlement.be; f. 1980.

Vlaamse Regering (Flemish Government): Boudewijnlaan 30, 1000 Brussels; tel. (2) 553-29-11; fax (2) 553-29-05; e-mail voorlichtingsambtenaar@vlaanderen.be; internet www.vlaamseregering.be; 10 mems.

Election, 13 June 2004

Party	Seats
Vlaams Belang	30
CD&V	29
SP.A-Spirit	25
VLD	24
Groen!	6
N-VA	6
Union des Francophones	1
Independents	3
Total	124

REGION OF WALLONIA

Minister-President: RUDY DEMOTTE (PS).

President of the Parliament: JOSÉ HAPPART (PS).

Le Parlement Wallon (Walloon Parliament): 24 rue Saint-Nicolas, 5000 Namur; tel. (81) 23-10-36; fax (2) 23-12-20; e-mail presse@parlement-wallon.be; internet www.parlement-wallon.be; elects Government of Wallonia.

Gouvernement Wallon (Walloon Government): 1 place de la Wallonie, Bât 2, 5100 Namur; tel. (81) 33-31-60; fax (81) 33-31-66; e-mail vancau@gov.wallonie.be; internet gov.wallonie.be; 9 mems.

Election, 13 June 2004

Party	Seats
PS	34
MR	20
CDH	14
FN	4
Ecolo	3
Total	75

REGION OF BRUSSELS-CAPITAL

Minister-President: CHARLES PICQUÉ (PS).

President of the Parliament: ERIC TOMAS (PS).

Parlement de la Région de Bruxelles-Capitale/Brussels Hoofdstedelijk Parlement (Parliament of the Region of Brussels-Capital): 22 rue du Chêne, 1005 Brussels; tel. (2) 549-62-11; fax (2) 549-62-12; e-mail greffe@parlbru.irisnet.be; internet www.parlbru.irisnet.be.

BELGIUM

Gouvernement de la Région de Bruxelles-Capitale/Brusselse Hoofdstedelijke Regering (Government of Brussels-Capital): 7–9 rue Ducale, 1000 Brussels; tel. (2) 506-32-11; fax (2) 514-40-22; internet www.bruxelles.irisnet.be; 8 mems.

Election, 13 June 2004

Party	Seats
French-speaking group	
PS	27
MR	23
CDH	11
Ecolo	7
FN	3
Independent	1
Dutch-speaking group	
Vlaams Belang	6
VLD	4
SP.A-Spirit	3
CD&V	3
Groen!	1
Total (incl. both groups)	89

FRENCH COMMUNITY

Minister-President: RUDY DEMOTTE (PS).

President of the Parliament: JEAN-FRANÇOIS ISTASSE (PS).

Parlement de la Communauté française de Belgique (Parliament of the French Community): 6 rue de la Loi, 1000 Brussels; tel. (2) 506-38-11; fax (2) 506-38-08; e-mail cellule-internet@pcf.be; internet www.pcf.be; comprises the 75 mems of the Walloon Parliament and 19 French-speaking mems of the Council of the Region of Brussels-Capital; 94 mems.

Gouvernement de la Communauté française Wallonie-Bruxelles (Government of the French Community): 15–17 place Surlet de Chokier, 1000 Brussels; tel. (2) 227-32-11; fax (2) 227-33-53; internet www.gouvernement-francophone.be; 6 mems.

GERMAN-SPEAKING COMMUNITY

Minister-President: KARL-HEINZ LAMBERTZ (SP).

President of the Parliament: LUDWIG SIQUET (SP).

Parlament der Deutschsprachigen Gemeinschaft in Belgien (Parliament of the German-speaking Community): Kaperberg 8, 4700 Eupen; tel. (87) 59-07-20; fax (87) 59-07-30; e-mail stephan.thomas@dgparlament.be; internet www.dgparlament.be.

Regierung der Deutschsprachigen Gemeinschaft in Belgien (Government of the German-speaking Community): Klötzerbahn 32, 4700 Eupen; tel. (87) 59-64-00; fax (87) 74-02-58; e-mail regierung@dgov.be; internet www.dglive.be; 4 mems.

Election, 13 June 2004

Party	Seats
CSP	8
PFF	5
SP	5
PJU-PDB	3
Ecolo	2
Vivant	2
Total	25

Election Commission

Direction des Elections/Directie van de Verkiezingen: Parc Atrium, 11 rue des Colonies, 1000 Brussels; tel. (2) 518-21-21; fax (2) 518-21-86; e-mail elections@rrn.fgov.be; internet www.ibz.rrn.fgov.be; part of the General Directorate of Institutions and Population, a department of the Federal Public Service of the Interior; Dir ETIENNE VAN VERDEGEM.

Political Organizations

Centre Démocrate Humaniste (CDH) (Humanist Democrats): 41 rue des Deux-Eglises, 1000 Brussels; tel. (2) 238-01-11; fax (2) 238-01-29; e-mail info@lecdh.be; internet www.lecdh.be; f. 1945 as Parti Social Chrétien/Christelijke Volkspartij (PSC/CVP); the PSC separated from the CVP by 1972, name changed as above in 2002; Pres. JOËLLE MILQUET; Vice-Pres ANDRÉ ANTOINE, MELCHIOR WATHELET.

Christen-Democratisch en Vlaams (CD&V) (Christian Democratic and Flemish): Wetstraat 89, 1040 Brussels; tel. (2) 238-38-11; fax (2) 238-38-71; e-mail info@cdenv.be; internet www.cdenv.be; f. 1945 as Parti Social Chrétien/Christelijke Volkspartij (PSC/CVP); CVP separated from PSC by 1972, renamed as above in 2001; Chair. ETIENNE SCHOUPPE (acting).

Christlich Soziale Partei (CSP) (Christian Social Party—German-speaking): Kaperberg 6, 4700 Eupen; tel. (87) 55-59-86; fax (87) 55-59-82; e-mail csp-fraktion@rdg.be; internet www.csp-dg.be; Pres. MATHIEU GROSCH.

Ecologistes Confédérés pour l'Organisation des Luttes Originales (Ecolo) (Ecologist Party—French-speaking): 52 ave de Marlagne, 5000 Namur; tel. (81) 22-78-71; fax (81) 23-06-03; e-mail ecolo.sf@ecolo.be; internet www.ecolo.be; Fed. Secs JEAN-MICHEL JAVAUX, ISABELLE DURANT, CLAUDE BROUIR.

Front National (FN): 12 clos du Parnasse, 1050 Brussels; tel. (2) 503-06-91; e-mail info.frontnational@skynet.be; internet www.frontnational.be; f. 1985; extreme right-wing nationalist party; Pres. DANIEL FÉRET.

Groen! (Green!) (Ecologist Party—Flemish-speaking): Sergeant De Bruynestraat 78–82, 1070 Anderlecht; tel. (2) 219-19-19; fax (2) 223-10-90; e-mail info@groen.be; internet www.groen.be; f. 1982; fmrly Anders Gaan Leven (Agalev), name changed as above in 2003; Chair. MIEKE VOGELS; Sec. JOHAN MALCORPS (acting).

Lijst Dedecker: f. 2007; liberal conservative; advocates greater independence for Flanders; Leader JEAN-MARIE DEDECKER.

Mouvement Réformateur (MR) (Reformist Movement): 84–86 ave de la Toison d'Or, 1060 Brussels; tel. (2) 500-35-11; fax (2) 500-35-00; e-mail mr@mr.be; internet www.mr.be; f. 2002; Pres. DIDIER REYNDERS.

Association of the following parties:

Front Démocratique des Francophones (FDF) (French-speaking Democratic Front): 127 chaussée de Charleroi, 1060 Brussels; tel. (2) 538-83-20; fax (2) 539-36-50; e-mail fdf@fdf.be; internet www.fdf.be; f. 1964; aims to preserve the French character of Brussels; Pres. OLIVIER MAINGAIN.

Mouvement des Citoyens pour le Changement (MCC): 50 rue de la Vallée, 1000 Brussels; tel. (2) 642-29-99; fax (2) 642-29-90; e-mail info@lemcc.be; internet www.lemcc.be; Pres. GÉRARD DEPREZ.

Parti Réformateur Libéral (PRL) (Liberal Party—French-speaking wing): 41 rue de Naples, 1050 Brussels; tel. (2) 500-35-11; fax (2) 500-35-00.

Partei für Freiheit und Fortschritt (PFF) (German-speaking wing of PRL): Kaperberg 6, 4700 Eupen; tel. (8) 755-59-88; fax (8) 755-59-83; e-mail ferdel.schroeder@euregio.net; internet www.pff.be; Pres. FERDEL SCHRÖDER.

Nieuw-Vlaamse Alliantie (N-VA) (New-Flemish Alliance): Liefdadigheidsstraat 39, 1210 Brussels; tel. (2) 219-49-30; fax (2) 217-35-10; e-mail info@n-va.be; internet www.n-va.be; f. 1954 as Volksunie—Vlaamse Vrije Democraten; name changed as above in 2001; Flemish nationalist party advocating an independent Flemish state within a federal Europe; Chair. BART DE WEVER; Sec. BART DE NIJN; 11,000 mems.

Partei der Deutschsprachigen Belgier (PJU-PDB) (Party of German-speaking Belgians): Kaperberg 6, 4700 Eupen; tel. (87) 55-59-87; fax (87) 55-59-84; e-mail info@pju-pdb.be; internet www.pju-pdb.be; f. 1971; promotes equality for the German-speaking minority; Chair. GUIDO BREUER; Parliamentary Leader GERHARD PALM.

Parti Communiste (PC) (Communist Party): 21 ave de Stalingrad, 1000 Brussels; tel. (2) 512-77-77; fax (2) 511-34-96; e-mail parti.communiste@skynet.be; internet www.particommuniste.be; f. 1921 as Parti Communiste de Belgique—Kommunistische Partij van België; name changed 1990; Pres. PIERRE BEAUVOIS; 5,000 mems.

Parti Humaniste/Humanistische Partij (PH–HP) (Humanist Party): 75 rue de Pavie, 1000 Brussels; tel. (2) 427-71-43; fax (2) 426-03-78; e-mail ph_hp_belgium@yahoo.fr; internet www.partihumaniste.be; f. 1994; promotes social equality and human rights; Pres. GILLES SMEDTS.

Parti Socialiste (PS) (Socialist Party—French-speaking wing): Maison du PS, 13 blvd de l'Empereur, 1000 Brussels; tel. (2) 548-32-11; fax (2) 548-33-80; e-mail secretariat@ps.be; internet www.ps.be; f. 1885 as the Parti Ouvrier Belge; split from the Flemish wing 1978; Pres. ELIO DI RUPO; Sec.-Gen. JEAN-POL BARAS.

Sozialistische Partei (SP): Klötzerbahn 8, 4700 Eupen; tel. (87) 55-77-43; e-mail info@buergerbuero.be; internet www.sp-dg.be; section of the PS, representing the German-speaking region; Pres. EDMUND STOFFELS; Sec. BERNI SCHMIDZ.

Partij van de Arbeid van België/Parti du Travail de Belgique (PvdA/PTB) (Workers' Party of Belgium): 171 blvd M. Lemonnier, BP 2, 1000 Brussels; tel. (2) 504-01-39; fax (2) 504-01-41; e-mail wpb@

wpb.be; internet www.wpb.be; f. 1979; Marxist; publ. Solidaire/Solidair (weekly); Pres. PETER MERTENS.

Rassemblement Wallonie-France (RWF-RBF) (Wallonia-France Union): 38 Jevigné, 4990 Lierneux; tel. (7) 265-41-60; e-mail rwf@rwf.be; internet www.rwf.be; f. 1999 by amalgamation of the Rassemblement Wallon (f. 1968), the Alliance Démocratique Wallonne and the Mouvement Wallon pour le Retour à la France; promotes the union of Wallonia with France; Pres. PAUL-HENRY GENDEBIEN.

Sociaal Progressief Alternatief (SP.A) (Socialist Party—Flemish wing): Grasmarkt 105/37, 1000 Brussels; tel. (2) 552-02-00; fax (2) 552-02-55; e-mail info@s-p-a.be; internet www.s-p-a.be; f. 1885; fmrly Socialistische Partij, renamed as above in 2001; Chair. CAROLINE GENNEZ; Sec. ALAIN ANDRÉ.

Spirit (Sociaal, Progressief, Internationaal, Regionalistisch, Integraal-democratisch en Toekomstgericht): Woeringenstraat 21, 1000 Brussels; tel. (2) 513-20-63; fax (2) 512-85-75; e-mail info@spirit.be; internet www.spirit.be; f. 2001; Chair. BETTINA GEYSEN.

Vivant (Voor Individuele Vrijheid en Arbeid in een Nieuwe Toekomst): Zuidlaan 25-27, 1000 Brussels; tel. (2) 513-08-88; fax (2) 502-01-07; e-mail info@vivant.org; internet www.vivant.org; liberal; contested the 2007 legislative elections as Open VLD, in alliance with the VLD and Liberaal Appèl Plus; Chair. ROLAND DUCHÂTELET.

Vlaams Belang (Flemish Interest): Madouplein 8–9, 1210 Brussels; tel. (2) 219-60-09; fax (2) 219-50-47; e-mail info@vlaamsbelang.org; internet www.vlaamsbelang.org; f. 1979 as Vlaams Blok as a breakaway party from the Volksunie; party disbanded and relaunched as Vlaams Belang in 2004; advocates Flemish separatism and is anti-immigration; Chair. FRANK VANHECKE.

Vlaamse Liberalen en Demokraten (VLD) (Flemish Liberals and Democrats—Liberal Party—Flemish-speaking wing): Melsensstraat 34, 1000 Brussels; tel. (2) 549-00-20; fax (2) 512-60-25; e-mail contact@openvld.be; internet www.openvld.be; f. 1961 as Partij voor Vrijheid en Vooruitgang; name changed as above in 1992; contested the 2007 legislative elections as Open VLD, in alliance with two minor parties, Liberaal Appèl Plus (Liberal Appeal Plus) and Vivant; Pres. BART SOMERS; Sec.-Gen. SOFIE STAELRAEVE; 72,000 mems.

Diplomatic Representation

EMBASSIES IN BELGIUM

Afghanistan: 61 ave de Wolvendael, 1180 Uccle; tel. (2) 761-31-66; fax (2) 761-31-67; e-mail ambassade.afghanistan@skynet.be; Ambassador ZIA NEZAM.

Albania: 30 rue Tenbosch, 1000 Brussels; tel. (2) 644-33-29; fax (2) 640-31-77; e-mail amba.brux@skynet.be; Ambassador MIMOZA HALIMI.

Algeria: 207–209 ave Molière, 1050 Brussels; tel. (2) 343-50-78; fax (2) 343-51-68; e-mail info@algerian-embassy.be; internet www.algerian-embassy.be; Ambassador HALIM BENATTALLAH.

Andorra: 10 rue de la Montagne, 1000 Brussels; tel. (2) 513-28-06; fax (2) 513-07-41; e-mail ambassade@andorra.be; internet www.andorra.be; Ambassador IMMA TOR FAUS.

Angola: 182 rue Franz Merjay, 1050 Brussels; tel. (2) 346-18-72; fax (2) 344-08-94; e-mail angola.embassy.belgium@skynet.be; Ambassador TOKO DIAKENGA SERÃO.

Argentina: 225 ave Louise, 3e étage, 1050 Brussels; tel. (2) 647-78-12; fax (2) 647-93-19; e-mail info@embargentina.be; Ambassador GUILLERMO MARCOS JACOVELLA.

Armenia: 28 rue Montoyer, 1000 Brussels; tel. (2) 348-44-00; fax (2) 348-44-01; e-mail armembel@sknet.be; internet www.armembassy.be; Ambassador VIGUEN TCHITETCHIAN.

Australia: Centre Guimard, 6–8 rue Guimard, 1040 Brussels; tel. (2) 286-05-00; fax (2) 230-68-02; e-mail austemb.brussels@dfat.gov.au; internet www.belgium.embassy.gov.au; Ambassador ALAN WILLIAM THOMAS.

Austria: 5 place du Champ de Mars, BP 5, 1050 Brussels; tel. (2) 289-07-00; fax (2) 513-66-41; e-mail bruessel-ob@bmeia.gv.at; internet www.aussenministerium.at/bruessel; Ambassador FRANZ CEDE.

Azerbaijan: 464 ave Molière, 1050 Brussels; tel. (2) 345-26-60; fax (2) 345-91-58; e-mail office@azembassy.be; internet www.azembassy.be; Ambassador EMIN EYYUBOV.

Bangladesh: 29–31 rue Jacques Jordaens, 1000 Brussels; tel. (2) 640-55-00; fax (2) 646-59-98; e-mail bdootbrussels@skynet.be; internet www.bangladeshembassy.be; Ambassador A. H. M. MONIRUZZAMAN.

Barbados: 100 ave F. D. Roosevelt, 1050 Brussels; tel. (2) 732-17-37; fax (2) 732-32-66; e-mail brussels@foreign.gov.bb; Ambassador ERROL HUMPHREY.

Belarus: 192 ave Molière, 1050 Brussels; tel. (2) 340-02-70; fax (2) 340-02-87; e-mail embbel@skynet.be; internet www.belembassy.org/belgium; Ambassador VLADIMIR SENKO.

Belize: 136 blvd Brand Witlock, 1200 Brussels; tel. (2) 732-62-04; fax (2) 732-62-46; e-mail embelize@skynet.be; Ambassador ALEXIS ROSADO.

Benin: 5 ave de l'Observatoire, 1180 Brussels; tel. (2) 374-91-92; fax (2) 375-83-26; e-mail ambabenin_benelux@yahoo.fr; Chargé d'affaires a.i. DÉSIRÉ AUGUSTE ADJAHI.

Bolivia: 176 ave Louise, BP 6, 1050 Brussels; tel. (2) 627-00-10; fax (2) 647-47-82; e-mail embajada.bolivia@embolbrus.be; internet www.embolbrus.be; Ambassador CRISTIAN MANUEL INCHAUSTE SANDOVAL.

Bosnia and Herzegovina: 15–17 rue Belliard, 7e étage, 1040 Brussels; tel. (2) 502-01-88; fax (2) 644-32-54; e-mail info@bh-embassy-belgium.org; internet www.bh-embassy-belgium.org; Ambassador NIKOLA RADOVANOVIĆ.

Botswana: 169 ave de Tervueren, 1150 Brussels; tel. (2) 735-20-70; fax (2) 735-63-18; e-mail botswana@brutele.be; Ambassador CLAURINAH TSHENOLO MODISE.

Brazil: 350 ave Louise, 6e étage, BP 5, 1050 Brussels; tel. (2) 640-20-15; fax (2) 640-81-34; e-mail brasbruxelas@beon.be; Ambassador ALMIR FRANCO DE SÁ BARBUDA.

Brunei: 238 ave F. D. Roosevelt, 1050 Brussels; tel. (2) 675-08-78; fax (2) 672-93-58; e-mail kedutaan-brunei.brussels@skynet.be; Ambassador Pengiran Haji ALIHASHIM bin Pengiran Haji YUSUF.

Bulgaria: 58 ave Hamoir, 1180 Brussels; tel. (2) 374-59-63; fax (2) 375-84-94; e-mail embassy@bulgaria.be; internet www.bulgaria.be; Ambassador HRISTO GEORGIEV.

Burkina Faso: 16 place Guy d'Arezzo, 1180 Brussels; tel. (2) 345-99-12; fax (2) 345-06-12; e-mail ambassade.burkina@skynet.be; internet www.ambassadeduburkina.be; Ambassador KADRÉ DÉSIRÉ OUEDRAOGO.

Burundi: 46 square Marie-Louise, 1000 Brussels; tel. (2) 230-45-35; fax (2) 230-78-83; e-mail ambassade.burundi@skynet.be; internet www.amb-burundi.be; Ambassador LAURENT KAVAKURE.

Cambodia: 264 ave de Tervueren, 1150 Brussels; tel. (2) 772-03-72; fax (2) 772-03-76; e-mail amcambel@skynet.be; Ambassador SUN SAPHOEUN.

Cameroon: 131–133 ave Brugmann, 1190 Brussels; tel. (2) 345-18-70; fax (2) 344-57-35; Chargé d'affaires a.i. JACQUES ALFRED NDOUMBE EBOULÉ.

Canada: 2 ave de Tervueren, 1040 Brussels; tel. (2) 741-06-11; fax (2) 741-06-43; e-mail bru@international.gc.ca; internet www.ambassade-canada.be; Ambassador LAURETTE GLASGOW.

Cape Verde: 29 ave Jeanne, 1050 Brussels; tel. (2) 646-62-70; fax (2) 646-33-85; e-mail emb.caboverde@skynet.be; Ambassador FERNANDO JORGE WAHNON FERREIRA.

Central African Republic: 416 blvd Lambermont, 1030 Brussels; tel. (2) 242-28-80; fax (2) 215-13-11; e-mail ambassade.centrafrique@skynet.be; Ambassador ARMAND-GUY ZOUNGUERE-SOKAMBI.

Chad: 52 blvd Lambermont, 1030 Brussels; tel. (2) 215-19-71; fax (2) 216-35-26; e-mail ambassade.tchad@chello.be; Ambassador MAÏTINE DJOUMBE.

Chile: 106 rue des Aduatiques, 1040 Brussels; tel. (2) 743-36-60; fax (2) 736-49-94; e-mail embachile@embachile.be; internet www.embachile.be; Ambassador JUAN SALAZAR SPARKS.

China, People's Republic: 463 ave de Tervueren, 1160 Brussels; tel. (2) 771-14-95; fax (2) 779-28-95; e-mail chinaemb_be@mfa.gov.cn; internet wwww.chinaembassy-org.be; Ambassador ZHANG QIYUE.

Colombia: 96A ave F. D. Roosevelt, 1050 Brussels; tel. (2) 649-56-79; fax (2) 646-54-91; e-mail colombia@emcolbru.org; internet www.emcolbru.org; Ambassador CARLOS HOLMES TRUJILLO GARCÍA.

Comoros: 63 rue Berthelot, 1190 Brussels; tel. and fax (2) 779-58-38; e-mail ambacom.bxl@skynet.be; Ambassador SULTAN CHOUZOUR.

Congo, Democratic Republic: 30 rue Marie de Bourgogne, 1040 Brussels; tel. (2) 213-49-81; fax (2) 213-49-95; e-mail secretariat.cmd@amba-rdcongo.be; Ambassador JEAN-PIERRE MUTAMBA TSHAMPANGA.

Congo, Republic: 16–18 ave F. D. Roosevelt, 1050 Brussels; tel. (2) 648-38-56; fax (2) 648-42-13; e-mail ambassade.congobrazza@skynet.be; Ambassador JACQUES OBIA.

Costa Rica: 489 ave Louise, BP 13, 1050 Brussels; tel. (2) 640-55-41; fax (2) 648-31-92; e-mail info@costaricaembassy.be; internet www.costaricaembassy.be; Ambassador ROBERTO ECHANDI.

Côte d'Ivoire: 234 ave F. D. Roosevelt, 1050 Brussels; tel. (2) 672-23-57; fax (2) 672-04-91; e-mail mailbox@ambcibnl.be; internet www.ambacibnl.be; Ambassador MARIE GOSSET.

BELGIUM

Directory

Croatia: 425 ave Louise, 1050 Brussels; tel. (2) 639-20-36; fax (2) 512-03-38; e-mail croemb.bruxelles@mvp.hr; internet be.mfa.hr; Ambassador BORIS GRIGIĆ.

Cuba: 77 rue Roberts-Jones, 1180 Brussels; tel. (2) 343-00-20; fax (2) 344-96-91; e-mail mision@embacuba.be; internet www.embacuba.be; Ambassador ELIO EDUARDO RODRÍGUEZ PERDOMO.

Cyprus: 61 ave de Cortenbergh, 1000 Brussels; tel. (2) 650-06-10; fax (2) 650-06-20; e-mail ambassade.cyprus@skynet.be; Ambassador CONSTANTINOS ELIADES.

Czech Republic: Czech House, 60 rue du Trône, 1050 Brussels; tel. (2) 213-94-01; fax (2) 213-94-02; e-mail brussels@embassy.mzv.cz; internet www.mzv.cz/brussels; Ambassador VLADIMÍR MÜLLER.

Denmark: 73 rue d'Arlon, 1040 Brussels; tel. (2) 233-09-00; fax (2) 233-09-32; e-mail bruamb@um.dk; internet www.ambbruxelles.um.dk; Ambassador JØRGEN MOLDE.

Djibouti: 204 ave F. D. Roosevelt, 1050 Brussels; tel. (2) 347-69-67; fax (2) 347-69-63; e-mail amb_djib@yahoo.fr; Ambassador MOHAMMED MOUSSA CHEHEM.

Dominican Republic: 12 ave Bel Air, 1180 Brussels; tel. (2) 346-49-35; fax (2) 346-51-52; e-mail embajadombxl@brutele.be; Ambassador FEDERICO ALBERTO CUELLO CAMILO.

Eastern Caribbean States: 42 rue de Livourne, 1000 Brussels; tel. (2) 534-26-11; fax (2) 539-40-09; e-mail ecs.embassies@skynet.be; Chargé d'affaires a.i. ARNOLD THOMAS.

Ecuador: 363 ave Louise, 1050 Brussels; tel. (2) 644-30-50; fax (2) 644-28-13; e-mail amb.equateur@skynet.be; internet www.ecuador.be; Ambassador FERNANDO YÉPEZ LASSO.

Egypt: 19 ave de l'Uruguay, 1000 Brussels; tel. (2) 663-58-00; fax (2) 675-58-88; e-mail eg.sec.be@hotmail.com; Ambassador Dr MAHMOUD KAREM MAHMOUD.

El Salvador: 171 ave de Tervueren, 1150 Brussels; tel. (2) 733-04-85; fax (2) 735-02-11; e-mail embajadabruselas@rree.gob.sv; Ambassador HÉCTOR GONZÁLEZ URRUTIA.

Equatorial Guinea: 6 place Guy Arezzo, 1180 Brussels; tel. (2) 346-25-09; fax (2) 346-33-09; e-mail guineaaecuatorial.brux@skynet.be; Ambassador VITORINO NKA OBIANG MAYE.

Eritrea: 15–17 ave Wolvendael, 1180 Brussels; tel. (2) 374-44-34; fax (2) 372-07-30; e-mail eri_emba_brus@hotmail.com; Ambassador GIRMA ASMERON TESFAY.

Estonia: 1 ave Isidore Gérard, 1160 Brussels; tel. (2) 779-07-55; fax (2) 779-28-17; e-mail saatkond@estemb.be; internet www.estemb.be; Ambassador MALLE TALVET-MUSTONEN.

Ethiopia: 231 ave de Tervueren, 1150 Brussels; tel. (2) 771-32-94; fax (2) 771-49-14; e-mail etebru@brutele.be; Ambassador BERHANE GEBRE-CHRISTOS.

Fiji: 92–94 square Eugène Plasky, 5e étage, 1030 Brussels; tel. (2) 736-90-50; fax (2) 736-14-58; e-mail info@fijiembassy.be; internet www.fijiembassy.be; Ambassador SEREMAIA TUINAUSORI CAVUILATI.

Finland: 58 ave des Arts, 5e étage, 1000 Brussels; tel. (2) 287-12-12; fax (2) 287-12-00; e-mail sanomat.bry@formin.fi; internet www.finlande.be; Ambassador AAPO PÖLHÖ.

France: 65 rue Ducale, 1000 Brussels; tel. (2) 548-87-11; fax (2) 548-87-32; e-mail ambafr@ambafrance-be.org; internet www.ambafrance-be.org; Ambassador DOMINIQUE BOCHÉ.

Gabon: 112 ave Winston Churchill, 1180 Brussels; tel. (2) 340-62-10; fax (2) 346-46-69; e-mail ambagabbelg@yahoo.fr; Ambassador RENÉ MAKONGO.

Gambia: 126 ave F. D. Roosevelt, 1050 Brussels; tel. (2) 640-10-49; fax (2) 646-32-77; e-mail info@gambiaembassy.be; internet www.gambiaembassy.be; Chargé d'affaires a.i. AMIE NYAN-ALABOSON.

Georgia: 62 ave de Tervueren, 1040 Brussels; tel. (2) 761-11-90; fax (2) 761-11-99; e-mail info@georgia-embassy.be; internet www.belgium.mfa.gov.ge; Ambassador SALOME SAMADASHVILI.

Germany: 8–14 rue Jacques de Lalaing, 1040 Brussels; tel. (2) 787-18-00; fax (2) 787-28-00; e-mail info@bruessel.diplo.de; internet www.bruessel.diplo.de; Ambassador Prof. Dr REINHARD BETTZEUGE.

Ghana: blvd Général Wahis 7, 1030 Brussels; tel. (2) 705-82-20; fax (2) 705-66-53; e-mail ghanaemb@chello.be; internet www.ghanaembassy.be; Ambassador NANA BEMA KUMI.

Greece: 10 rue des petits Carmes, 1000 Brussels; tel. (2) 545-55-00; fax (2) 545-55-85; e-mail ambagre@skynet.be; Ambassador GEORGE PAPADOPOULOS.

Grenada: 123 rue de Laeken, 1e étage, 1000 Brussels; tel. (2) 223-73-03; fax (2) 223-73-07; e-mail embassyofgrenadabxl@skynet.be; Ambassador JOAN-MARIE COUTAIN.

Guatemala: 185 ave Winston Churchill, 1180 Brussels; tel. (2) 345-90-58; fax (2) 344-64-99; e-mail embaguate.belgica@skynet.be; Ambassador ANTONIO FERNANDO ARENALES FORNO.

Guinea: 108 blvd Auguste Reyers, 1030 Brussels; tel. (2) 771-01-26; fax (2) 762-60-36; e-mail ambasssadedeguinee.bel@skynet.be; Ambassador AHMED TIDIANE SAKHO.

Guinea-Bissau: 80 ave Brugmann, 1190 Brussels; tel. (2) 347-72-76; Ambassador HENRIQUE ADRIANO DA SILVA.

Guyana: 12 ave du Brésil, 1000 Brussels; tel. (2) 672-62-16; fax (2) 675-55-98; e-mail embassy_guyana@skynet.be; Ambassador PATRICK IGNASIUS GOMES.

Haiti: 139 chaussée de Charleroi, 1060 Brussels; tel. (2) 649-73-81; fax (2) 640-60-80; e-mail ambassade@amb-haiti.be; Ambassador RAYMOND LAFONTANT, Jr.

Holy See: 9 ave des Franciscains, 1150 Brussels; tel. (2) 762-20-05; fax (2) 762-20-32; e-mail nonciature.ue.chencellerie@pro.tiscali.be; internet www.vatican.va; Apostolic Nuncio Most Rev. KARL-JOSEF RAUBER.

Honduras: 3 ave des Gaulois, 5e étage, 1040 Brussels; tel. (2) 734-00-00; fax (2) 735-26-26; e-mail ambassade.honduras@chello.be; internet www.honduras.be; Ambassador RAMÓN CUSTODIO ESPINOZA.

Hungary: 44 ave du Vert Chasseur, 1180 Brussels; tel. (2) 348-18-00; fax (2) 347-60-28; e-mail titkarsag.bxl@kum.be; Ambassador FERENC ROBÁK.

Iceland: 11 rond point Robert Schuman, 1040 Brussels; tel. (2) 238-50-00; fax (2) 230-69-38; e-mail emb.brussels@mfa.is; internet www.iceland.org/be; Ambassador STEFÁN HAUKUR JÓHANNESSON.

India: 217 chaussée de Vleurgat, 1050 Brussels; tel. (2) 640-91-40; fax (2) 648-96-38; e-mail admin@indembassy.be; internet www.indembassy.be; Ambassador DIPAK CHATTERJEE.

Indonesia: 294 ave de Tervueren, 1150 Brussels; tel. (2) 771-20-14; fax (2) 772-82-10; e-mail kbribxl@brutele.be; internet www.indonesian-embassy.be; Ambassador NADJIB RIPHAT KESOEMA.

Iran: 15 ave F. D. Roosevelt, 1050 Brussels; tel. (2) 627-03-50; fax (2) 762-39-15; e-mail secretariat@iranebassy.be; internet www.iranembassy.be; Ambassador ALIASGHAR KHAJI.

Iraq: 115 ave F. D. Roosevelt, 1050 Brussels; tel. (2) 374-59-92; fax (2) 374-76-15; e-mail ambassade.irak@skynet.be; Ambassador MUHAMMAD JAWAN AD-DOREKY.

Ireland: 50 rue Wiertz, 1050 Brussels; tel. (2) 235-66-76; fax (2) 235-66-71; e-mail embassybrussels@dfa.ie; Ambassador BRIAN NASON.

Israel: 40 ave de l'Observatoire, 1180 Brussels; tel. (2) 373-55-00; fax (2) 373-56-17; e-mail info@brussels.mfa.gov.il; internet brussels.mfa.gov.il; Ambassador TAMAR SAMASH.

Italy: 28 rue Emile Claus, 1050 Brussels; tel. (2) 643-38-50; fax (2) 648-54-85; e-mail ambbruxelles@esteri.it; internet www.ambbruxelles.esteri.it; Ambassador SANDRO MARIA SIGGIA.

Jamaica: 77 ave Hansel Soulie, 1000 Brussels; tel. (2) 230-11-70; fax (2) 234-69-69; e-mail emb.jam.brussels@skynet.be; Ambassador MARCIA YVETTE GILBERT-ROBERTS.

Japan: 58 ave des Arts, 6e étage, BP 17/18, 1000 Brussels; tel. (2) 513-23-40; fax (2) 513-15-56; e-mail info.embjapan@skynet.be; internet www.be.emb-japan.go.jp; Ambassador AZUZA HAYASHI.

Jordan: 104 ave F. D. Roosevelt, 1050 Brussels; tel. (2) 640-77-55; fax (2) 640-27-96; e-mail jordan.embassy@skynet.be; internet www.jordanembassy.be; Ambassador AHMAD KHALAF MASAADEH.

Kazakhstan: 30 ave Van Bever, 1180 Brussels; tel. (2) 373-38-90; fax (2) 374-50-91; e-mail kazakhstanembassy.be; internet www.kazakhstanembassy.be; Ambassador KONSTANTIN V. ZHIGALOV.

Kenya: 208 ave Winston Churchill, 1180 Brussels; tel. (2) 340-10-40; fax (2) 340-10-50; e-mail info@kenyabrussels.com; internet www.kenyabrussels.com; Ambassador MARX G. N. KAHENDE.

Korea, Republic: 175 chaussée de la Hulpe, 1170 Brussels; tel. (2) 662-57-77; fax (2) 675-52-21; e-mail eukorea@mofat.go.kr; Ambassador CHONG WOO-SEONG.

Kuwait: 43 ave F. D. Roosevelt, 1050 Brussels; tel. (2) 647-79-50; fax (2) 646-12-98; e-mail embassy.kwt@euronet.be; Ambassador NABILA ABDULLA AL-MULLA.

Kyrgyzstan: 47 rue de l'Abbaye, 1050 Brussels; tel. (2) 640-18-68; fax (2) 640-01-31; e-mail kyrgyz.embassy@skynet.be; Ambassador CHINGIZ AITMATOV.

Laos: 19–21 ave de la Brabançonne, 1000 Brussels; tel. (2) 740-09-50; fax (2) 734-16-66; e-mail ambalaobx@yucom.be; Ambassador THONGPHACHANH SONNASINH.

Latvia: 158 ave Molière, 1050 Brussels; tel. (2) 344-16-82; fax (2) 344-74-78; e-mail embassy.belgium@mfa.gov.lv; internet www.mfa.gov.lv/belgium; Ambassador RAIMONDS JANSONS.

Lebanon: 2 rue Guillaume Stocq, 1050 Brussels; tel. (2) 645-77-65; fax (2) 645-77-69; e-mail ambassade.liban@brutele.be; Chargé d'affaires a.i. ADNAN MANSOUR.

Lesotho: 45 blvd Général Wahis, 1030 Brussels; tel. (2) 705-39-76; fax (2) 705-67-79; e-mail lesothobrussels@hotmail.com; Ambassador 'MAMORUTI TIHELI.

BELGIUM

Liberia: 50 ave du Château, 1081 Brussels; tel. (2) 411-01-12; fax (2) 411-09-12; e-mail liberia.embassy@scarlet.be; Ambassador YOUNGOR S. TELEWODA.

Libya: 28 ave Victoria, 1000 Brussels; tel. (2) 647-37-37; fax (2) 640-90-76; e-mail tripoli@diplobel.org; Chargé d'affaires a.i. YOUSUF SIFAW HAFIANI.

Liechtenstein: 1 place du Congrès, 1000 Brussels; tel. (2) 229-39-00; fax (2) 219-35-45; e-mail ambassade.liechtenstein@bbru.llv.li; Ambassador HSH Prince NIKOLAUS of Liechtenstein.

Lithuania: 48 rue Maurice Liétart, 1150 Brussels; tel. (2) 772-27-50; fax (2) 772-17-01; e-mail info@lt-embassy.be; internet be.mfa.lt; Ambassador NIJOLĖ ŽAMBAITĖ.

Luxembourg: 75 ave de Cortenbergh, 1000 Brussels; tel. (2) 737-57-00; fax (2) 737-57-10; e-mail bruxelles.amb@mae.etat.lu; Ambassador ALPHONSE BERNS.

Macedonia, former Yugoslav republic: 209A ave Louise, 1050 Brussels; tel. (2) 734-56-87; fax (2) 732-07-17; e-mail ambassade.mk@skynet.be; Chargé d'affaires a.i. JORDAN PANEV.

Madagascar: 276 ave de Tervueren, 1150 Brussels; tel. (2) 770-17-26; fax (2) 772-37-31; e-mail info@ambassademadagascar.be; internet www.ambassademadagascar.be; Ambassador JEANNOT RAKOTOMALALA.

Malawi: 46 ave Hermann Debroux, 1160 Brussels; tel. (2) 231-09-80; fax (2) 231-10-66; e-mail embassy.malawi@skynet.be; internet www.embassymalawi.be; Ambassador BRAVE NDISALE.

Malaysia: 414A ave de Tervueren, 1150 Brussels; tel. (2) 776-03-40; fax (2) 762-50-49; e-mail mwbrussel@euronet.be; Ambassador Dato MUHAMMAD KAMAL bin YAN YAHAYA.

Mali: 487 ave Molière, 1050 Brussels; tel. (2) 345-74-32; fax (2) 344-57-00; e-mail mali@skynet.be; Ambassador IBRAHIM BOCAR BA.

Malta: 25 rue Archimède, 5e étage, 1000 Brussels; tel. (2) 238-27-04; fax (2) 238-27-07; e-mail tarcisio.zammit@gov.mt; Ambassador TARCISIO ZAMMIT.

Mauritania: 6 ave de la Colombie, 1000 Brussels; tel. (2) 672-47-47; fax (2) 672-20-51; e-mail info@amb-mauritania.be; Ambassador MOULAYE OULD MUHAMMAD LAGHDAF.

Mauritius: 68 rue des Bollandistes, 1040 Brussels; tel. (2) 733-99-88; fax (2) 734-40-21; e-mail ambmaur@skynet.be; Ambassador SUTIAWAN GUNESSEE.

Mexico: 94 ave F. D. Roosevelt, 1050 Brussels; tel. (2) 629-07-77; fax (2) 644-08-19; e-mail embamex@embamex.eu; internet www.embamex.eu; Ambassador SANDRA FUENTES-BERAIN.

Moldova: 57 ave F. D. Roosevelt, 1050 Brussels; tel. (2) 732-96-59; fax (2) 732-96-60; e-mail bruxelles@mfa.md; Ambassador VICTOR GAICIUC.

Monaco: 17 place Guy d'Arezzo, BP 7, 1180 Brussels; tel. (2) 347-49-87; fax (2) 343-49-20; e-mail ambassade.monaco@skynet.be; Ambassador JOSÉ BADIA.

Mongolia: 18 ave Besme, 1190 Brussels; tel. (2) 344-69-74; fax (2) 344-32-15; e-mail brussels.mn.embassy@chello.be; Ambassador AVIRMEDIN BATTÖR.

Morocco: 29 blvd St-Michel, 1040 Brussels; tel. (2) 736-11-00; fax (2) 734-64-68; e-mail sifamabruxe@euronet.be; Ambassador MUSTAPHA SALAHDINE.

Mozambique: 97 blvd St-Michel, 1040 Brussels; tel. (2) 736-25-64; fax (2) 732-06-64; e-mail maria_manuelalucas@yahoo.com; internet www.mozambiqueembassy.be; Ambassador MARIA MANUELA DOS SANTOS LUCAS.

Myanmar: 9 blvd Général Wahis, 1030 Brussels; tel. (2) 701-93-80; fax (2) 705-50-48; Chargé d'affaires a.i. HAN THU.

Namibia: 454 ave de Tervueren, 1150 Brussels; tel. (2) 771-14-10; fax (2) 771-96-89; e-mail info@namibiaembassy.be; internet www.namibiaembassy.be; Ambassador HANNO BURKHARD RUMPF.

Nepal: 210 ave de Brugmann, 1050 Brussels; tel. (2) 346-26-58; fax (2) 344-13-61; e-mail embn@skynet.be; internet www.nepalembassy.be; Chargé d'affaires a.i. AMBIKA D. LUINTEL.

Netherlands: 48 ave Hermann Debroux, 1160 Brussels; tel. (2) 679-17-11; fax (2) 679-17-75; e-mail bru@minbuza.nl; internet www.nederlandseambassade.be; Ambassador RUDOLF BEKINK.

New Zealand: 1 square de Meeûs, 7e étage, 1000 Brussels; tel. (2) 512-10-40; fax (2) 513-48-56; e-mail nzemb.brussels@xs4all.be; internet www.nzembassy.com/belgium; Ambassador PETER KENNEDY.

Nicaragua: 55 ave de Wolvendael, 1180 Brussels; tel. (2) 375-65-00; fax (2) 375-71-88; e-mail sky77706@skynet.be; Chargé d'affaires a.i. SANTIAGO URBINA GUERRERO.

Niger: 78 ave F. D. Roosevelt, 1050 Brussels; tel. (2) 648-61-40; fax (2) 648-27-84; e-mail ambanigerbrux@skynet.be; Ambassador ABDOU ABBARY.

Nigeria: 288 ave de Tervueren, 1150 Brussels; tel. (2) 762-52-00; fax (2) 762-37-63; e-mail nigeriabrussels@belgacom.net; internet www.nigeriabrussels.be; Ambassador ADEKUNLE OLADOKUN ADEYANJU.

Norway: 17 rue Archimède, 2e étage, 1000 Brussels; tel. (2) 646-07-80; fax (2) 646-28-82; e-mail emb.brussels@mfa.no; internet www.norvege.be; Ambassador JOSTEIN HELGE BERNHARDSEN.

Oman: 40–42 ave Hermann Debroux, 4e étage, C2, 1160 Brussels; tel. (2) 679-70-15; fax (2) 534-79-64; e-mail omanembassy@europe.com; Ambassador Sheikh GHAZI BIN SAID AL-BAHR AR-RAWAS.

Pakistan: 57 ave Delleur, 1170 Brussels; tel. (2) 673-80-07; fax (2) 675-83-94; e-mail parepbrussels@skynet.be; internet www.embassyofpakistan.be; Ambassador SAEED KHALID.

Panama: 18 blvd Général Jacques, 1050 Brussels; tel. (2) 649-07-29; fax (2) 648-92-16; e-mail embajada.panama@skynet.be; Ambassador PABLO GARRIDO ARAÚZ.

Papua New Guinea: 430 ave de Tervueren, 1150 Brussels; tel. (2) 779-06-09; fax (2) 772-70-88; e-mail kundu.brussels@skynet.be; Ambassador ISAAC B. LUPARI.

Paraguay: 475 ave Louise, BP 21, 1050 Brussels; tel. (2) 649-90-55; fax (2) 647-42-48; e-mail embapar@skynet.be; Chargé d'affaires a.i. RAÚL JOSÉ VERA BOGADO.

Peru: 179 ave de Tervueren, 1150 Brussels; tel. (2) 733-33-19; fax (2) 733-48-19; e-mail comunicaciones@embassy-of-peru.be; internet www.embaperu.be; Ambassador JORGE VALDEZ.

Philippines: 297 ave Molière, 1050 Brussels; tel. (2) 340-33-77; fax (2) 345-64-25; e-mail brussels@philembassy.be; Ambassador CRISTINA G. ORTEGA.

Poland: 29 ave des Gaulois, 1040 Brussels; tel. (2) 739-01-51; fax (2) 736-18-81; internet www.bruksela.polemb.net; Ambassador SŁAWOMIR CZARLEWSKI.

Portugal: 55 ave de la Toison d'Or, 1060 Brussels; tel. (2) 533-07-00; fax (2) 539-07-73; e-mail ambassade.portugal@skynet.be; Ambassador MANUEL NUNO TAVARES DE SOUSA.

Qatar: 51 rue de la Vallée, 1000 Brussels; tel. (2) 223-11-55; fax (2) 223-11-66; internet www.qatarembassy.be; Ambassador Sheikh MESHAL BIN HAMAD ATH-THANI.

Romania: 105 rue Gabrielle, 1180 Brussels; tel. (2) 345-26-80; fax (2) 346-23-45; e-mail secretariat@roumanieamb.be; internet bruxelles.mae.ro; Ambassador Dr ION JINGA.

Russia: 66 ave de Fré, 1180 Brussels; tel. (2) 374-34-00; fax (2) 374-26-13; e-mail amrusbel@skynet.be; internet www.belgium.mid.ru; Ambassador VADIM B. LUKOV.

Rwanda: 1 ave des Fleurs, 1150 Brussels; tel. (2) 763-07-21; fax (2) 763-07-53; e-mail ambarwanda@gmail.com; internet www.ambarwanda.be; Ambassador JOSEPH BONESHA.

Samoa: 20 ave de l'Orée, BP 4, 1050 Brussels; tel. (2) 660-84-54; fax (2) 675-03-36; e-mail samoaembassy@skynet.be; Ambassador TUALA FALANI CHAN TUNG.

San Marino: 62 ave F. D. Roosevelt, 1050 Brussels; tel. (2) 644-22-24; fax (2) 644-20-57; e-mail ambrsm.bxl@scarlet.be; Ambassador GIAN NICOLA FILIPPI BALESTRA.

São Tomé and Príncipe: Square Montgomery, 175 ave de Tervueren, 1150 Brussels; tel. (2) 734-89-66; fax (2) 734-88-15; e-mail ambassade.sao.tome@skynet.be; Chargé d'affaires a.i. ARMINDO BRITO FERNANDES.

Saudi Arabia: 45 ave F. D. Roosevelt, 1050 Brussels; tel. (2) 649-20-44; fax (2) 647-24-92; e-mail beemb@mofa.gov.sa; Ambassador ABDULLAH BIN YAHYUA AL-MOUALLIMI.

Senegal: 196 ave F. D. Roosevelt, 1050 Brussels; tel. (2) 673-00-97; fax (2) 675-04-60; e-mail senegal.ambassade@coditel.net; Ambassador (vacant).

Serbia: 11 ave Emile de Mot, 1050 Brussels; tel. (2) 647-26-52; fax (2) 647-29-41; e-mail ambaserbie@skynet.be; Chargé d'affaires a.i. ALEKSANDAR TASIC.

Sierra Leone: 410 ave de Tervueren, 1150 Brussels; tel. (2) 771-00-53; fax (2) 771-82-30; e-mail sierraleoneembassy@brutele.be; Ambassador FODE M. DABOR.

Singapore: 198 ave F. D. Roosevelt, 1050 Brussels; tel. (2) 660-29-79; fax (2) 660-86-85; e-mail singemb_bru@sgmfa.gov.sg; internet www.mfa.gov.sg/brussels; Ambassador ANIL KUMAR NAYAR.

Slovakia: 195 ave Molière, 1050 Brussels; tel. (2) 346-40-45; fax (2) 346-63-85; e-mail emb.brussel@mzv.sk; Ambassador PETER SOPKO.

Slovenia: 130A ave Louise, 1050 Brussels; tel. (2) 643-49-50; fax (2) 644-20-79; e-mail vbr@gov.si; internet www.gov.si/mzz-dkp/vbr/eng/index.html; Ambassador BORUT TREKMAN.

Solomon Islands: 17 ave Edouard Lacomble, 1040 Brussels; tel. (2) 732-70-85; fax (2) 732-68-85; e-mail siembassy@compuserve.com; Ambassador JOSEPH MA'AHANUA.

BELGIUM

Directory

South Africa: 17–19 rue Montoyer, 1040 Brussels; tel. (2) 285-44-00; fax (2) 285-44-02; e-mail embassy@southafrica.be; internet www.southafrica.be; Ambassador Dr ANIL SOOKLAL.

Spain: 19 rue de la Science, 1040 Brussels; tel. (2) 230-03-40; fax (2) 230-93-80; e-mail ambespbe@mail.mae.es; internet www.mae.es/embajadas/bruselas; Ambassador CARLOS GÓMEZ-MÚGICA SANZ.

Sri Lanka: 27 rue Jules Lejeune, 1050 Brussels; tel. (2) 344-53-94; fax (2) 344-67-37; e-mail sri.lanka@skynet.be; Ambassador K. J. WEERASINGHE.

Sudan: 124 ave F. D. Roosevelt, 1050 Brussels; tel. (2) 647-94-94; fax (2) 648-34-99; e-mail sudanbx@yahoo.com; Ambassador NAJEIB EL-KHEIR ABDELWAHAB.

Suriname: 379 ave Louise, BP 20, 1050 Brussels; tel. (2) 640-11-72; fax (2) 646-39-62; e-mail sur.amb.bru@online.be; Ambassador GERHARD O. HIWAT.

Swaziland: 188 ave Winston Churchill, 1180 Brussels; tel. (2) 347-47-71; fax (2) 347-46-23; Ambassador SOLOMON M. N. DLAMINI.

Sweden: 3 rue de Luxembourg, 1000 Brussels; tel. (2) 289-57-60; fax (2) 289-57-90; e-mail ambassaden.bryssel@foreign.ministry.se; internet www.swedenabroad.com/bryssel; Ambassador MAGNUS ROBACH.

Switzerland: 26 rue de la Loi, BP 9, 1040 Brussels; tel. (2) 285-43-50; fax (2) 230-37-81; e-mail bru.vertretung@eda.admin.ch; internet www.eda.admin.ch/bruxelles; Ambassador JEAN-JACQUES DE DARDEL.

Syria: 3 ave F. D. Roosevelt, 1050 Brussels; tel. (2) 648-01-35; fax (2) 646-40-18; e-mail ambsyrie@skynet.be; internet www.syrianembassy.be; Ambassador Dr MUHAMMAD AYMAN SOUSAN.

Tajikistan: 363–365 ave Louise, BP 14, 1050 Brussels; tel. (2) 640-69-33; fax (2) 649-01-95; e-mail tajemb-belgium@skynet.be; internet www.taj-emb.be; Ambassador SAIMUMIN S. YATIMOV.

Tanzania: 72 ave F. D. Roosevelt, 1050 Brussels; tel. (2) 640-65-00; fax (2) 640-80-26; e-mail tanzania@skynet.be; Ambassador SIMON U. R. MLAY.

Thailand: 2 square du Val de la Cambre, 1050 Brussels; tel. (2) 640-68-10; fax (2) 648-30-66; e-mail thaibxl@thaiembassy.be; internet www.thaiembassy.be; Ambassador PISAN MANAWAPAT.

Timor-Leste: 12 ave de Cortenbergh, BP 198, 1040 Brussels; tel. (2) 280-00-96; fax (2) 280-02-77; Ambassador JOSÉ ANTÓNIO AMORIM DIAS.

Togo: 264 ave de Tervueren, 1150 Brussels; tel. (2) 770-55-63; fax (2) 771-50-75; e-mail ambassade.togo@skynet.be; Ambassador FÉLIX KODJO SAGBO.

Trinidad and Tobago: 14 ave de la Faisanderie, 1150 Brussels; tel. (2) 762-94-00; fax (2) 772-27-83; e-mail info@embtrinbago.be; Chargé d'affaires a.i. KEITH DE FREITAS.

Tunisia: 278 ave de Tervueren, 1150 Brussels; tel. (2) 771-73-95; fax (2) 771-94-33; e-mail amb.detunisie@brutele.be; Ambassador ABDESSALEM HETIRA.

Turkey: 4 rue Montoyer, 1000 Brussels; tel. (2) 513-40-95; fax (2) 514-07-48; e-mail info@turkey.be; internet www.turkey.be; Ambassador FUAT TANLAY.

Turkmenistan: 106 blvd Reyers, 1030 Brussels; tel. (2) 648-18-74; fax (2) 648-19-06; e-mail turkmenistan@skynet.be; Ambassador KAKADJAN MOMMADOV.

Uganda: 317 ave de Tervueren, 1150 Brussels; tel. (2) 762-58-25; fax (2) 763-04-38; e-mail ugembrus@brutele.be; Ambassador STEPHEN T. KAPIMPINA KATENTA-APUULI.

Ukraine: 30–32 ave Albert Lancaster, 1180 Brussels; tel. (2) 379-21-00; fax (2) 379-21-79; e-mail embassy@ukraine.be; internet www.ukraine.be; Ambassador YAROSLAV KOVAL.

United Arab Emirates: 73 ave F. D. Roosevelt, 1050 Brussels; tel. (2) 640-60-00; fax (2) 646-24-73; e-mail uae-embassy@skynet.be; internet www.uaeembassybrussels.be; Ambassador MUHAMMAD SALEM OBAID AS-SUWEIDI.

United Kingdom: 85 rue d'Arlon, 1040 Brussels; tel. (2) 287-62-11; fax (2) 287-63-60; e-mail info@britain.be; internet www.britishembassy.gov.uk/belgium; Ambassador RACHEL ARON.

USA: 27 blvd du Régent, 1000 Brussels; tel. (2) 508-21-11; fax (2) 511-21-60; internet brussels.usembassy.gov; Ambassador SAM FOX.

Uruguay: 22 ave F. D. Roosevelt, 1050 Brussels; tel. (2) 640-11-69; fax (2) 648-29-09; e-mail uruemb@skynet.be; Ambassador Dr LUIS ALFREDO SICA BERGARA.

Uzbekistan: 99 ave F. D. Roosevelt, 1050 Brussels; tel. (2) 672-88-44; fax (2) 672-39-46; Ambassador ISAN M. MUSTAFAEV.

Vanuatu: 380 ave de Tervueren, 1150 Brussels; tel. and fax (2) 771-74-94; e-mail info@embassyvanuatu.net; Ambassador ROY MICKEY JOY.

Venezuela: 10 ave F. D. Roosevelt, 1050 Brussels; tel. (2) 639-03-40; fax (2) 647-88-20; e-mail embajada@venezuela-eu.org; internet www.venezuela-eu.org; Ambassador Dr ALEJANDRO ANTONIO FLEMING CABRERA.

Viet Nam: 1 blvd Général Jacques, 1050 Brussels; tel. (2) 374-79-61; fax (2) 374-93-76; e-mail vnemb.brussels@skynet.be; Ambassador NGUYEN MANH DUNG.

Yemen: 114 ave F. D. Roosevelt, 1050 Brussels; tel. (2) 646-52-90; fax (2) 646-29-11; e-mail yemen@skynet.be; Ambassador ABD AL-WAHAB MUHAMMAD ASH-SHAWKANI.

Zambia: 469 ave Molière, 1050 Brussels; tel. (2) 343-56-49; fax (2) 347-43-33; e-mail zambians_brussels@brutele.be; Chargé d'affaires a.i. MIYAMBO SIPANGULE.

Zimbabwe: 11 square Joséphine Charlotte, 1200 Brussels; tel. (2) 762-58-08; fax (2) 762-96-05; e-mail zimbrussels@skynet.be; Ambassador GIFT PUNUNGWE.

Judicial System

The independence of the judiciary is based on the constitutional division of power between the legislative, executive and judicial bodies, each of which acts independently. Judges are appointed by the crown for life, and cannot be removed except by judicial sentence. The judiciary is organized on four levels, from the judicial canton to the district, regional and national courts. The lowest courts are those of the Justices of the Peace and the Police Tribunals. Each district has one of each type of district court, including the Tribunals of the First Instance, Tribunals of Commerce and Labour Tribunals, and there is a Court of Assizes in each province. There are civil and criminal Courts of Appeal and Labour Courts in five regional centres (Antwerp, Brussels, Ghent, Liège and Mons). In addition to its regional competencies, the Court of Appeal in Brussels has jurisdiction in certain national matters. With the Supreme Court of Justice, these are the highest courts in the country. The Military Court of Appeal is in Brussels.

SUPREME COURT OF JUSTICE

Palais de Justice, 1 pl. Poelaert, 1000 Brussels; tel. (2) 508-61-11; fax (2) 508-67-50; internet www.juridat.be.

First President: GHISLAIN LONDERS.

President: I. VEROUGSTRAETE.

Counsellors: D. BATSELÉ, R. BOES, C. PARMENTIER, C. STORCK, P. MATHIEU, C. MATRAY, P. GOSSERIES, S. VELU, E. WAUTERS, E. DIRIX, E. STASSIJNS, A. FETTWEIS, E. GOETHALS, P. MAFFEI, J. DE CODT, F. CLOSE, D. PLAS, E. FETTWEIS, B. DEJEMEPPE, E. FORRIER, L. HUYBRECHTS, J.-P. FRÈRE, L. VAN HOOGENBEMT, B. DECONINCK, J. BODSON, P. CORNELIS, A. SMETRYNS, K. MESTDAGH, M. REGOUT.

Attorney-General: JEAN-FRANÇOIS LECLERCQ.

First Advocate-General: M. DE SWAEF.

Advocates-General: X. DE RIEMAECKER, D. THIJS, A. HENKES, R. LOOP, M. TIMPERMAN, G. DUBRULLE, P. DUINSLAEGER, T. WERQUIN, D. VANDERMEERSCH, J-M. GENICOT, C. VANDEWAL, R. MORTIER.

CIVIL AND CRIMINAL COURTS OF APPEAL

Antwerp: Waalse Kaai, 2000 Antwerp; tel. (3) 247-97-11; fax (3) 247-97-81; Pres. CHRISTIAN DE VEL; Attorney-Gen. CHRISTINE DEKKERS.

Brussels: Palais de Justice, 1 pl. Poelaert, 1000 Brussels; tel. (2) 508-65-91; fax (2) 508-64-50; First Pres. GUY DELVOIE; Attorney-Gen. MARC DE LE COURT.

Ghent: Gerechtsgebouw, Koophandelspl. 23, 9000 Ghent; tel. (9) 267-41-11; First Pres. JEAN-PAUL DE GRAEF; Attorney-Gen. FRANK SCHINS.

Liège: Palais de Justice, 16 pl. Saint Lambert, 4000 Liège; tel. (4) 232-56-36; fax (4) 232-56-37; First Pres. MICHEL JOACHIM; Attorney-Gen. CÉDRIC VISART DE BOCARME.

Mons: 1 rue des Droits de l'Homme, 7000 Mons; tel. (65) 37-90-11; First Pres. JEAN-LOUIS FRANEAU; Attorney-Gen. CLAUDE MICHAUX.

LABOUR COURTS

Antwerp: Cockerillkaai 39, 2000 Antwerp; tel. (3) 247-97-11; fax (3) 247-99-41; First Pres. BEATRICE HOMANS.

Brussels: 3 pl. Poelaert, 1000 Brussels; tel. (2) 508-61-27; fax (2) 519-81-48; First Pres. BEATRIX CEULEMANS.

Ghent: Brabantdam 33B, 9000 Ghent; tel. (9) 266-02-55; fax (9) 266-02-90; First Pres. ROGER VAN GREMBERGEN.

Liège: 89 rue St Gilles, 4000 Liège; tel. (4) 232-85-50; fax (4) 223-04-13; First Pres. JOËL HUBIN.

Mons: 1 rue des Droits de l'Homme, 7000 Mons; tel. (65) 37-92-51; fax (65) 37-92-53; First Pres. CHARLES DELIGNE.

Religion

CHRISTIANITY

The Roman Catholic Church

Belgium comprises one archdiocese and seven dioceses. At 31 December 2005 adherents represented some 74.9% of the total population.

Bishops' Conference

Bisschoppenconferentie van België/Conférence Episcopale de Belgique, 1 rue Guimard, 1040 Brussels; tel. (2) 509-96-93; fax (2) 509-96-95; e-mail ce.belgica@catho.kerknet.be; internet www.kerknet.be. f. 1981; Pres. Cardinal GODFRIED DANNEELS (Archbishop of Mechelen-Brussels).

Archbishop of Mechelen-Brussels: Cardinal GODFRIED DANNEELS, Aartsbisdom, Wollemarkt 15, 2800 Mechelen; tel. (15) 21-65-01; fax (15) 20-94-85; e-mail aartsbisdom@kerknet.be; internet www.kerknet.be.

Protestant Churches

Church of England: Holy Trinity Pro-Cathedral, 29 rue Capitaine Crespel, 1050 Brussels; tel. (2) 511-71-83; fax (2) 511-10-28; e-mail admin@htbrussels.com; internet www.htbrussels.com; Rev. Dr ROBERT INNES (Chaplain and Chancellor of the Pro-Cathedral of the Holy Trinity, Brussels).

Eglise Protestante Unie de Belgique (EPUB): 5 rue du Champ de Mars, 1050 Brussels; tel. and fax (2) 510-61-66; e-mail belpro@epub.be; internet www.protestanet.be; f. 1979; Pres. Rev. Dr GUY LIAGRE; 50,000 mems; publ. Mosaïque (monthly).

Lutheran Church of Belgium: ave de Mersch 10, 6700 Arlon; tel. (6) 323-27-90; f. 1964; 809 mems; Pres. Rev. JEAN LOUIS CORNEZ.

Mission Evangélique Belge: 158 blvd Lambermont, 1030 Brussels; tel. (2) 241-30-15; fax (2) 245-79-65; e-mail information@b-e-m.org; internet www.bez-meb.be; f. 1919; Dirs WILFRIED GOOSSENS, ERIC ZANDER; c. 12,000 mems.

Union of Baptists in Belgium (UBB): 85A Liebaertstraat, 8400 Ostend; tel. and fax (5) 932-46-10; e-mail verhaeghe6@cs.com; f. 1922; as Union of Protestant Baptists in Belgium; Pres. SAMUEL VERHAEGHE; Sec. EMMANUEL MUKWEGE.

The Orthodox Church

There are about 70,000 Greek and Russian Orthodox believers in Belgium.

Archbishop of Belgium (Ecumenical Patriarchate of Constantinople): Metropolitan PANTELEIMON, 71 ave Charbo, 1030 Brussels; tel. (2) 736-52-78; fax (2) 735-32-64; e-mail eglise.orthodoxe@belgacom.net; internet www.eglise-orthodoxe.be.

Archbishop of Brussels and Belgium (Moscow Patriarchate): Archbishop SIMON, 29 rue des Chevaliers, 1050 Brussels; tel. and fax (2) 513-33-74; e-mail info@archiepiskopia.be; internet www.archiepiskopia.be.

ISLAM

In 2007 there were more than 500,000 Muslims in Belgium, constituting about 5% of the total population.

Exécutif des Musulmans de Belgique/Executieve van de Moslims van België (EMB): Rouppeplein 16, 1000 Brussels; tel. (2) 648-35-60; e-mail info@embnet.be; internet www.embnet.be; f. 1999; promotes dialogue between Muslim community and the Government; Pres. COŞKUN BEYAZGÜL; 16 mems.

JUDAISM

The Jewish population in Belgium was estimated at between 40,000 and 50,000 in 2007.

Consistoire Central Israélite de Belgique (Central Council of the Jewish Communities of Belgium): 2 rue Joseph Dupont, 1000 Brussels; tel. (2) 512-21-90; fax (2) 512-35-78; e-mail consis@online.be; internet www.jewishcom.be; f. 1808; Chair. Prof. JULIEN KLENER; Sec.-Gen. MICHEL LAUB.

The Press

Article 25 of the Belgian Constitution states: 'The Press is free; no form of censorship may ever be instituted; no cautionary deposit may be demanded from writers, publishers or printers. When the author is known and is resident in Belgium, the publisher, printer or distributor may not be prosecuted.'

There is a trend towards concentration of ownership by a number of organizations, which control chains of publications, mostly divided along linguistic lines. The largest of those organizations are as follows:

Corelio NV: Gossetlaan 30, 1702 Groot-Bijgaarden; tel. (2) 467-22-11; internet www.corelio.be; f. 1914 as NV De Standaard; fmrly De Vlaamse Uitgeversmaatschappij (VUM), present name adopted 2006; owns six newspapers, incl. *De Standaard, Het Nieuwsblad* and *Het Volk*; 10 magazines and three radio stations; Chair. THOMAS LEYSEN; CEO PIET VAN ROE.

Groupe Rossel: 100 rue Royale, 1000 Brussels; tel. (2) 225-55-99; fax (2) 225-59-02; e-mail micheline.demeurisse@viarossel.be; internet www.rossel.be; f. 1887; newspapers and magazines; French titles: *L'Echo, Le Soir* and *Sud Presse* newspapers; also publishes *Grenz Echo* and *De Tijd*; Pres. PATRICK HURBAIN; CEO BERNARD MARCHANT.

Roularta Media Group NV: Meiboomlaan 33, 8800 Roeselare; tel. (5) 126-61-11; fax (5) 126-68-66; e-mail info@roularta.be; internet www.roularta.be; f. 1954; magazines and regional newspapers; Chair. Baron HUGO VANDAMME.

Sanoma Magazines Belgium NV: Telecomlaan 5–7, 1831 Diegem; tel. (2) 776-22-11; fax (2) 776-23-99; e-mail info@sanoma-magazines.be; internet www.sanoma-magazines.be; periodicals; f. 2002; owned by SanomaWSOY Group (Finland); CEO AIMÉ VAN HECKE.

PRINCIPAL DAILIES

Antwerpen
(Antwerp)

Gazet van Antwerpen: Katwilgweg 2, 2050 Antwerp; tel. (3) 210-02-10; fax (3) 219-40-41; e-mail gvaredactie@concentra.be; internet www.gva.be; f. 1891; Christian Democrat; Editor LUC RADEMAKERS; circ. 109,472 (2006).

De Lloyd/Le Lloyd: Vleminckstraat 18, 2000 Antwerp; tel. (3) 234-05-50; fax (3) 226-44-64; e-mail info@lloyd.be; internet www.lloyd.be; f. 1858; Flemish and French edns, with supplements in English; shipping, commerce, industry, transport, logistics; Dir MIRANDA KEUTERS; Editor-in-Chief GUY MINTIENS; circ. 10,600.

De Nieuwe Gazet: Brusselsesteenweg 347, 1730 Asse; tel. (3) 212-13-48; fax (3) 212-13-46; f. 1897; liberal; Chief Editor LUC VAN DER KELEN.

Arlon

L'Avenir du Luxembourg: 235 ave Général Patton, 6700 Arlon; tel. (63) 23-10-20; fax (63) 23-10-51; e-mail infoal@actu24.be; internet www.actu24.be; f. 1894; 100% owned by Corelio NV; Catholic; Editor-in-Chief BERNARD MOTTET; circ. 117,175 (with *Vers l'Avenir, Le Courrier de l'Escaut, Le Jour, Le Courrier*).

Bruxelles/Brussel
(Brussels)

La Capitale: 120 rue Royale, 1000 Brussels; tel. (2) 225-56-41; fax (2) 225-59-13; e-mail redaction.generale@sudpresse.be; internet www.lacapitale.be; f. 1944 as La Lanterne; independent; present name adopted 2002; owned by Sud Presse; Dir DIDIER HAMANN; Editor-in-Chief DIDIER SWYSEN.

La Dernière Heure/Les Sports: 127 blvd Emile Jacqmain, 1000 Brussels; tel. (2) 211-28-49; fax (2) 211-28-70; e-mail dh.redaction@dh.be; internet www.dhnet.be; f. 1906; independent Liberal; Dir FRANÇOIS LE HODEY; Chief Editor MICHEL MARTEAU; circ. 86,163 (2006).

L'Echo: 86C ave du Port, BP 309, 1000 Brussels; tel. (2) 423-16-11; e-mail info@lecho.be; internet www.lecho.be; f. 1881; economic and financial; Dir FREDERIK DELAPLACE; circ. 18,028 (2006).

Het Laatste Nieuws: Brusselsesteenweg 347, 1730 Asse-Kobbegem; tel. (2) 454-22-11; fax (2) 454-28-22; e-mail redactie.hln@persgroep.be; internet www.hln.be; f. 1888; Flemish; independent; Editors-in-Chief FRANK DEPOORTER, PAUL DAENEN; circ. 286,420 (2006, incl. *De Nieuwe Gazet*).

La Libre Belgique: 79 rue des Francs, 1040 Brussels; tel. (2) 744-44-44; fax (2) 211-28-32; e-mail llb.redaction@saipm.com; internet www.lalibre.be; f. 1884; independent; Editor-in-Chief MICHEL KONEN; circ. 47,221 (with *La Libre Belgique—Gazette de Liège*, 2006).

De Morgen: Brogniezstraat 54, 1070 Brussels; tel. (2) 556-68-11; fax (2) 520-35-15; e-mail info@demorgen.be; internet www.demorgen.be; Editors-in-Chief KLAUS VAN ISACKER, PETER MIJLEMANS; circ. 50,837 (2006).

Het Nieuwsblad: Gossetlaan 28, 1702 Groot-Bijgaarden; tel. (2) 467-22-50; fax (2) 466-30-93; e-mail nieuws@nieuwsblad.be; internet www.nieuwsblad.be; f. 1923; Dir PETER VANDEMEERSCH; Editor-in-Chief MICHEL VANDERSMISSEN; circ. 204,752 (with *De Gentenaar*, 2006).

Le Soir: 120 rue Royale, 1000 Brussels; tel. (2) 225-54-32; fax (2) 225-59-10; e-mail journal@lesoir.be; internet www.lesoir.be; f. 1887; independent; Dir-Gen. DANIEL VAN WYLICK; Editor-in-Chief BÉATRICE DELVAUX; circ. 94,225 (2006).

BELGIUM

De Standaard: Gossetlaan 28, 1702 Groot Bijgaarden; tel. (2) 467-22-40; fax (2) 467-26-96; e-mail hoofdredactie@standaard.be; internet www.standaard.be; f. 1914; Dir PETER VANDERMEERSCH; Editor-in-Chief BART STURTEWAGEN; circ. 87,769 (2006).

De Tijd: 86C ave du Port, BP 309, 1000 Brussels; tel. (3) 423-18-40; e-mail persberichten@tijd.be; internet www.tijd.be; f. 1968; economic and financial; Editor-in-Chief FRANK DEMETS; circ. 36,341 (2006).

Charleroi

La Nouvelle Gazette (Charleroi, La Louvière, Philippeville, Namur, Nivelles); La Province (Mons): 2 quai de Flandre, 6000 Charleroi; tel. (71) 27-89-79; fax (71) 66-74-27; e-mail redaction.generale@sudpresse.be; internet www.lanouvellegazette.be; f. 1878; owned by Sud Presse; Dir DIDIER HAMANN; Editor-in-Chief DEMETRIO SCAGLIOLA.

Vers L'Avenir Entre-Sambre et Meuse: 1 blvd du Centenaire, 5600 Philippeville; tel. (71) 66-23-40; fax (71) 66-23-49; e-mail infonam@actu24.be; internet www.actu24.be; f. 1900; Editor-in-Chief BRUNO MALTER.

Eupen

Grenz-Echo: Marktpl. 8, 4700 Eupen; tel. (87) 59-13-22; fax (87) 55-34-57; e-mail redaktion@grenzecho.be; internet www.grenzecho.be; f. 1927; German; independent Catholic; Dir ALFRED KÜCHENBERG; Editor-in-Chief GERARD CERMER; circ. 9,850 (2006).

Gent
(Ghent)

De Gentenaar: Kouter 150, 9000 Ghent; tel. (9) 268-72-70; fax (9) 268-72-71; e-mail de.gentenaar@nieuwsblad.be; internet www.gentenaar.be; f. 1879; Editor-in-Chief GERT DE VOS.

Het Volk: Kouter 150, 9000 Ghent; tel. (9) 268-72-70; fax (9) 268-72-71; e-mail hetvolkhoofdredactie@vum.be; internet www.hetvolk.be; f. 1891; Editor-in-Chief MICHEL VANDERSMISSEN; circ. 70,903 (2006).

Hasselt

Het Belang van Limburg: Herckenrodesingel 10, 3500 Hasselt; tel. (11) 87-88-00; fax (11) 87-89-00; e-mail hbvlsecretariaat@concentra.be; internet www.hbvl.be; f. 1879; Dir LUC RADEMAKERS; Editor-in-Chief IVO VANDEKERCKHOVE; circ. 98,352 (2006).

Liège

La Libre Belgique—Gazette de Liège: 26 blvd d'Avroy, 4000 Liège; tel. (4) 290-04-80; fax (4) 290-04-81; e-mail llb.gazettedeliege@saipm.com; internet www.lalibre.be; f. 1840; Editor-in-Chief PAUL VAUTE.

La Meuse: 38 blvd de la Sauvenière, 4000 Liège; tel. (4) 220-08-40; fax (4) 220-08-59; e-mail redliege.lameuse@sudpresse.be; internet www.lameuse.be; f. 1856; owned by Sud Presse; Dir DIDIER HAMANN; Editor-in-Chief MICHEL ROYER.

Mons

La Province: 29 rue des Capucins, 7000 Mons; tel. (65) 39-49-70; fax (65) 33-84-77; e-mail redaction.generale@sudpresse.be; internet www.laprovince.be; f. 1907; owned by Sud Presse; Dir DIDIER HAMANN; Editor-in-Chief DAVID FLAMENT.

Namur

Le Quotidien de Namur: 134 rue de Coquelet, 5010 Namur; tel. (81) 20-82-11; fax (81) 20-83-72; internet www.lequotidiendenamur.be; f. as La Meuse Namur; present name adopted 2002; owned by Sud Presse; Dir DIDIER HAMANN; Editor-in-Chief CHRISTINE BOLINNE.

Vers l'Avenir Namur et Basse Sambre: 38 route de Hannut, 5000 Namur; tel. (81) 24-88-11; fax (81) 22-00-87; e-mail infonam@actu24.be; internet www.actu24.be; f. 1918; 100% by Médiabel; Editor-in-Chief JEAN-FRANÇOIS PACCO.

Tournai

Le Courrier de l'Escaut: 10 rue de Paris, 7500 Tournai; tel. (69) 88-96-20; fax (69) 88-96-60; e-mail infoce@actu24.be; internet www.actu24.be; f. 1829; 100% owned by Médiabel; Editor-in-Chief JEAN-PIERRE DE ROUCK.

Verviers

Le Jour: 87 ave de Spa, 4802 Heusy; tel. (87) 32-20-90; fax (87) 32-20-89; e-mail infolj@actu24.be; internet www.actu24.be; f. 1894; 100% owned by Médiabel; Editor-in-Chief CLAUDE GILLET.

WEEKLIES

Atlas Weekblad: Condédreef 89, 8500 Kortrijk; tel. (56) 26-10-10; fax (56) 21-35-93; e-mail atlas@atlasweekblad.be; internet www.atlasweekblad.be; classified advertising, regional news and sports.

Boer en Tuinder: Diestsevest 40, 3000 Leuven; tel. (16) 28-60-00; internet www.boerenbond.be; f. 1891; agriculture and horticulture; Chair. NOËL DEVISCH; circ. 23,047.

De Bond: Langestraat 170, 1150 Brussels; tel. (2) 779-00-00; fax (2) 779-16-16; e-mail com@publicarto.be; internet www.publicarto.be; f. 1921; general interest; circ. 287,046 (2006).

Brugsch Handelsblad: 20 Sint-Jorisstraat, 8000 Brugge; tel. (50) 44-21-55; fax (50) 44-21-66; e-mail redactie.bhblad@roularta.be; internet www.kw.be; f. 1906; local news; includes De Krant van West-Vlaanderen as a supplement; Dir EDDY BROUCKAERT; Editor-in-Chief HEDWIG DACQUIN; circ. 40,000.

Ciné Télé Revue: 101 ave Reine Marie-Henriette, 1190 Brussels; tel. (2) 345-99-68; fax (2) 343-12-72; e-mail redaction@cinetelerevue.be; internet www.cinetelerevue.be; f. 1944 as Theatra Ciné Revue; present name adopted 1984; TV listings, celebrity news, family issues; circ. 378,856 (2006).

Dag Allemaal: Brandekensweg 2, 2627 Schelle; tel. (3) 880-84-50; internet www.dagallemaal.be; Tues.; general, celebrity gossip; owned by Persgroep Publishing; Editor-in-Chief ILSE BEYERS; 355,632 (2006).

Dimanche: 20 pl. de Vannes, 7000 Mons; tel. (65) 35-28-85; fax (65) 34-63-70; e-mail info@dimanche.be; internet www.dimanche.be; f. 1946; Catholic; current affairs; 22 local editions; Editor-in-Chief CHARLES DELHEZ; circ. 162,573 (2006).

European Voice: International Press Centre, Résidence Palace, rue de la Loi 155, BP 6, 1040 Brussels; tel. (2) 540-90-90; fax (2) 540-90-71; e-mail info@europeanvoice.com; internet www.europeanvoice.com; f. 1995; Thurs.; publ. by The Economist Newspaper Ltd (United Kingdom); EU policy-making, politics and business; Editor DANA SPINANT; circ. 18,388.

Femmes d'Aujourd'hui: Telecomlaan 5–7, 1831 Diegem; tel. (2) 776-28-50; fax (2) 776-23-99; e-mail femmesaujourdhui@sanoma-magazines.be; internet www.femmesaujourdhui.be; f. 1933; French; women's interest; publ. by Sanoma Magazines Belgium SA; Editor-in-Chief ANOUK VAN GESTEL; circ. 101,171 (2006).

Flair: Uitbreidingstraat 82, 2600 Berchem; tel. (3) 290-13-92; e-mail flairsec@flair.be; internet www.flair.be; women's interest; publ. by Sanoma Magazines Belgium SA; Editor-in-Chief AN BROUCKMANS; circ. (2006) 124,729 (Flemish); 38,554 (French).

Humo: Telecomlaan 5–7, 1831 Diegem; tel. (2) 776-24-20; fax (2) 776-23-24; e-mail redactie@humo.be; internet www.humo.be; general weekly and TV and radio guide in Flemish; Editor-in-Chief JÖRGEN OOSTERWAAL; circ. 229,713 (2006).

Joepie: Brandekensweg 2, 2627 Schelle; tel. (3) 880-84-65; fax (3) 844-61-52; e-mail redactie@joepie.be; internet www.joepie.be; f. 1973; owned by Persgroep Publishing; teenagers' interest; Dir-Gen. KOEN CLEMENT; Chief Editor TINNE MARANT; circ. 58,223 (2006).

Kerk en Leven: Halewijnlaan 92, 2050 Antwerp; tel. (3) 210-08-44; fax (3) 210-08-36; e-mail redactie.kerkenleven@kerknet.be; internet www.kerknet.be; f. 1942; Catholic; five regional edns; Editor TOON OSAER; circ. 436,554 (2006).

Knack: Raketstraat 50, 1130 Brussels; tel. (2) 702-46-51; fax (2) 702-46-52; e-mail knack@knack.be; internet www.knack.be; f. 1971; news magazine; owned by Roularta Media Group; Dir RIK VAN CAUWELAERT; Editor-in-Chief KARL VAN DEN BROECK; circ. 124,939 (2006).

Kortrijks Handelsblad: Doorniksewijk 83B, 8500 Kortrijk; tel. (56) 27-00-34; fax (56) 27-00-12; e-mail luc.demiddele@roularta.be; regional news; owned by Roularta Media Group; includes De Krant van West-Vlaanderen as a supplement; Chief Editor LUC DEMIDDELE.

De Krant van West-Vlaanderen: Meiboomlaan 33, 8800 Roeselare; tel. (51) 26-66-44; fax (51) 26-65-87; e-mail redactie.kvwvl@roularta.be; internet www.kw.be; regional news and sport; owned by Roularta Media Group; 11 different edns; included as a supplement with titles *De Weekbode*, *Het Wekelijks Nieuws*, *De Zeewacht*, *Brugsch Handelsblad*, *Kortrijks Handelsblad* ; Dir EDDY BROUCKAERT; Editor-in-Chief JAN GHEYSEN; circ. 74,545 (2006).

Landbouwleven/Le Sillon Belge: 92 ave Léon Grosjean, 1140 Brussels; tel. (2) 730-33-00; fax (2) 730-33-24; e-mail info@landbouwleven.be; internet www.sillonbelge.be; f. 1952; agriculture; Editorial Man. ANDRÉ DE MOL; circ. 30,693 (2006).

Libelle: Uitbreidingstraat 82, 2600 Berchem; tel. (3) 290-14-42; fax (3) 290-14-44; e-mail libelle@libelle.be; internet www.libelle.be; f. 1945; Flemish; women's interest; publ. by Sanoma Magazines Belgium SA; Dir AIMÉ VAN HECKE; Editor-in-Chief DITTE VAN DE VELDE; circ. 217,881 (2006).

Le Soir Magazine: 120 rue Royale, 1000 Brussels; tel. (2) 225-55-55; fax (2) 225-59-11; e-mail redaction@lesoirmagazine.com; internet

BELGIUM

www.lesoir.be; f. 1928; independent illustrated; Dir-Gen. DANIEL VAN WYLICK; Editor-in-Chief MICHEL MARTEAU; circ. 53,772 (2006).

Spirou: 52 rue Jules Destrée, 6001 Marcinelle; tel. (71) 60-05-00; fax (71) 60-05-99; e-mail spirou@dupuis.com; internet www.spirou.com; children's interest; publ. by Editions Dupuis SA; Editor-in-Chief SERGE HONOREZ; circ. 20,534 (2006).

Sport/Foot Magazine and Sport/Voetbal Magazine: 50 rue de la Fusée, BP 5, 1130 Brussels; tel. (2) 702-45-71; fax (2) 702-45-72; e-mail sportmagazine@roularta.be; internet www.sport.be/sportmagazine; f. 1980; owned by Roularta Media Group; Flemish and French; football; Editors-in-Chief JACQUES SYS, JOHN BAETE; 57,686 (2006).

Story: Uitbreidingsstraat 82, 2600 Berchem; tel. (3) 290-15-13; fax (3) 290-15-14; e-mail story@sanoma-magazines.be; f. 1975; Wed.; Flemish; women's interest; Dir AIMÉ VAN HECK; Editor-in-Chief THOMAS SIFFER; circ. 155,444 (2006).

De Streekkrant/De Weekkrant: Meiboomlaan 33, 8800 Roeselare; tel. (51) 26-61-11; fax (51) 26-68-66; e-mail streekkrant@roularta.be; internet www.streekkrant.be; f. 1949; local news; distributed free-of-charge; Propr Roularta Media Group; Editor JEAN-PIERRE VAN GIMST; circ. 2,116,252 (2006).

Télémoustique: Telecomlaan 5–7, 1831 Diegem; tel. (2) 776-25-20; fax (2) 776-23-14; e-mail telemoustique@sanoma-magazines.be; internet www.telemoustique.be; f. 1924; radio and TV; Dir AIMÉ VAN HECK; Editor JEAN-LUC CAMBIER; circ. 108,863 (2006).

Télépro/Telepro: 50 rue de la Fusée, 1130 Brussels; tel. (87) 30-87-31; fax (87) 31-35-37; e-mail courrier@telepromagazine.be; internet www.telepro.be; f. 1954; TV listings; owned by Roularta Media Group; Editor-in-Chief NADINE LEJAER; circ. 145,292 (2006).

TeVe-Blad: Uitbreidingsstraat 82, 2600 Berchem; tel. (3) 290-14-81; fax (3) 290-14-82; e-mail teveblad@sanoma-magazines.be; internet www.teveblad.be; f. 1981; Tues.; TV listings; Editor-in-Chief JAN VAN DE VLOEDT; circ. 174,746 (2006).

Trends/Trends Tendances: Brussels Media Centre, rue de la Fusée, 50, BP 4, 1130 Brussels; tel. (2) 702-48-00; fax (2) 702-48-02; e-mail trends@trends.be; internet www.trends.be; Flemish and French; economic analysis and business news; owned by Roularta Media Group; Editor-in-Chief GUIDO MUELENAER; circ. 42,057 (2006).

Le Vif/L'Express: rue de la Fusée 50, BP 6, 1130 Brussels; tel. (2) 702-47-01; fax (2) 702-47-02; e-mail levif@levif.be; internet www.levif.be; f. 1971; current affairs; owned by Roularta Media Group; Dir-Gen. AMID FALJAOUI; Editor-in-Chief DOROTHÉE KLEIN; circ. 80,712 (2006).

De Weekbode: Meiboomlaan 33, 8800 Roeselare; tel. (51) 26-61-11; fax (51) 26-65-87; regional news; owned by Roularta Media Group; includes *De Krant van West-Vlaanderen* as a supplement; Editor-in-Chief JAN GHEYSEN.

Het Wekelijks Nieuws Kust: Meiboomlaan 33, 8800 Roeselare; tel. (51) 26-62-60; fax (51) 26-65-87; e-mail sandra.rosseel@roularta.be; internet www.kw.be; Furnes, Dixmude and Belgian West coast local news; owned by Roularta Media Group; includes *De Krant van West-Vlaanderen* as a supplement; Editor-in-Chief SANDRA ROSSEEL.

Het Wekelijks Nieuws West: Meiboomlaan 33, 8800 Roeselare; tel. (51) 26-65-55; fax (51) 26-55-87; e-mail matthias.vanderaspoilden@roularta.be; internet www.kw.be; local newspaper; Editor MATTHIAS VANDERASPOILDEN; circ. 56,000.

De Zeewacht: Meiboomlaan 33, 8800 Roeselare; tel. (51) 26-62-74; fax (51) 26-65-87; e-mail kris.carlier@roularta.be; internet www.kw.be; Ostend local news; owned by Roularta Media Group; includes *De Krant van West-Vlaanderen* as a supplement.

Zondag Nieuws: Brandekensweg 2, 2627 Schelle; tel. (2) 220-22-11; fax (2) 217-98-46; f. 1958; general interest; circ. 48,101.

Zondagsblad: Forelstraat 22, 9000 Ghent; tel. (9) 265-68-02; fax (9) 223-16-77; f. 1949; circ. 48,101.

SELECTED OTHER PERIODICALS

axelle: 111 rue de la Poste, 1030 Brussels; tel. (2) 227-13-19; fax (2) 223-04-42; e-mail axelle@viefeminine.be; internet www.axellemag.be; f. 1917; 11 a year; feminist; circ. 18,524 (2006).

Le Cri du Citoyen: BP 1607, 1000 Brussels 1; tel. and fax (2) 217-48-31; e-mail redaction@lecriducitoyen.com; internet www.chez.com/lecriducitoyen; social comment; 10 a year; Editor FRANCESCO PAOLO CATANIA.

Goed Gevoel: Brandekensweg 2, 2627 Schelle; tel. (3) 880-84-50; e-mail redactie@goedgevoel.be; internet www.goedgevoel.be; monthly; health, psychology; owned by Persgroep Publishing; Editor-in-Chief FEMKE ROBBERECHTS; circ. 57,934 (2006).

International Engineering News (IEN Europe): Potvlietlaan 5B, 2600 Antwerp; tel. (3) 285-33-77; fax (3) 285-33-35; e-mail p.bondi@tim-europe.com; internet www.ien.eu; f. 1975; 10 a year; English; Man. Dir ORHAN ERENBERK; Editor PIOTR GABER; circ. 50,990.

Jet Magazine: Herckenrodesingel 10, 3500 Hasselt; tel. (11) 87-85-12; fax (11) 87-84-84; e-mail ksnoeckx@concentra.be; internet www.jetmagazine.be; fortnightly; distributed free-of-charge; general; circ. (2006) 401,309 (Antwerp), 338,202 (Limburg).

Marie Claire Belgique: Telecomlaan 5–7, 1831 Diegem; tel. (2) 776-26-40; e-mail marieclaire@sanoma-magazines.be; f. 1960; monthly; women's interest; Editor-in-Chief FABIENNE WILLAERT; circ. 20,125 (2006).

Le Moniteur de l'Automobile: 56 ave Général Dumonceau, 1190 Brussels; tel. (2) 333-32-20; fax (2) 333-32-10; e-mail contact.mab@moniteurautomobile.be; internet www.moniteurautomobile.be; fortnightly; motoring; Editor-in-Chief XAVIER DAFFE; circ. 24,806 (2006).

Nest: 50 rue de la Fusée, BP 3, 1130 Brussels; tel. (2) 702-45-21; fax (2) 702-45-42; e-mail info@nest.be; internet www.nest.be; 8 a year; Flemish and French; lifestyle; owned by Roularta Media Group; Dir TESSA VERMEIREN; Editor-in-Chief PETER VANDEWEERDT; circ. 115,327 (2006).

Plus Magazine: 50 rue de la Fusée, BP 10, 1130 Brussels; tel. (2) 702-49-01; fax (2) 702-46-02; e-mail redactie@plusmagazine.be; internet www.plusmagazine.be; monthly; Flemish and French; fmrly Notre Temps/Onze Tijd; senior citizens' interest; owned by Roularta Media Group; Editor-in-Chief ANNE VANDERDONCKT; circ. 139,503 (2006).

Sélection du Reader's Digest: 20 blvd Paepsem, 1070 Brussels; tel. (2) 526-81-11; fax (2) 526-81-12; e-mail service@readersdigest.be; internet www.rdb.be; f. 1947; monthly; general; Editor-in-Chief OELE STEENKS; circ. 33,165 (2006).

Vrouw & Wereld: Langestraat 170, 1150 Brussels; tel. (2) 799-00-00; fax (2) 799-16-16; e-mail com@publicarto.be; internet www.publicarto.be; f. 1920; 11 a year; women's interest; circ. 108,269 (2006).

Vrouwen met vaart: Remylaan 4B, 3018 Wijgmaal-Leuven; tel. (2) 624-39-99; fax (2) 624-39-09; e-mail kvlv@kvlv.be; internet www.kvlv.be; f. 1911; 10 a year; women's interest; circ. 113,208 (2006).

NEWS AGENCIES

Agence Belga (Agence Télégraphique Belge de Presse SA)/Agentschap Belga (Belgisch Pers-telegraafagentschap NV): 8B rue F. Pelletier, 1030 Brussels; tel. (2) 743-23-11; fax (2) 735-17-44; e-mail redaction@belga.be; internet www.belga.be; f. 1920; largely owned by daily newspapers; Dir-Gen. EGBERT HANS; Editors-in-Chief JEAN-PIERRE BREULET, MARC HOLLANDERS.

Agence Europe SA: 36 rue de la Gare, 1040 Brussels; tel. (2) 737-94-94; fax (2) 736-37-00; e-mail press@agenceurope.com; internet www.agenceurope.eu; f. 1953; daily bulletin on EU activities; Editor-in-Chief OLIVIER JEHIN.

PRESS ASSOCIATIONS

Association belge des Editeurs de Journaux/Belgische Vereniging van de Dagbladuitgevers: 22 blvd Paepsem, bte 7, 1070 Brussels; tel. (2) 558-97-60; fax (2) 558-97-68; e-mail mieke.vandewinkel@dagbladpers.org; f. 1964; 17 mems; Pres BRUNO DE CARTIER; Gen. Secs ALEX FORDYN (Flemish), MARGARET BORIBON (French).

Association générale des Journalistes professionnels de Belgique/Algemene Vereniging van de Beroepsjournalisten in België (AGJPB/AVBB): Résidence Palace, Bloc C, 155 rue de la Loi, 1040 Brussels; tel. (2) 235-22-60; fax (2) 235-22-72; e-mail info@ajp.be; internet www.agjpb.be; f. 1978 by merger of the Association Générale de la Presse Belge and the Union Professionnelle de la Presse Belge; 4,899 mems; affiliated to International Federation of Journalists (IFJ); Nat. Secs MARTINE SIMONIS (AGJPB), POL DELTOUR (AVBB).

Association des Journalistes de la Presse Périodique/Vereniging van Journalisten van de Periodieke Pers: 54 rue Charles Martel, 1000 Brussels; tel. (2) 230-09-99; fax (2) 231-14-59; e-mail info@ajpp-vjpp.be; internet www.ajpp-vjpp.be; f. 1891; Pres. CLAUDE MUYLS.

Fédération Belge des Magazines/Federatie van de Belgische Magazines (FEBELMA): 22/8 blvd Paepsem, 1070 Brussels; tel. (2) 558-97-50; fax (2) 558-97-58; e-mail magazines@febelma.be; internet www.febelma.be; f. 1956 as Fédération Nationale des Hebdomadaires d'Information; present name adopted 1999; Pres. PATRICK DE BORCHGRAVE; Sec. Gen. ALAIN LAMBRECHTS.

Principal Publishers

Acco CV: Brusselsestraat 153, 3000 Leuven; tel. (1) 662-80-00; fax (1) 662-80-01; e-mail uitgeverij@acco.be; internet www.acco.be; f. 1960; general reference, scientific books, periodicals; Dir and Publr BART DE PRINS.

BELGIUM

Uitgeverij Altiora Averbode NV: Abdijstraat 1, Postbus 54, 3271 Averbode; tel. (1) 378-01-82; fax (1) 378-01-83; e-mail altiora@verbode.be; internet www.averbode.com; f. 1993; educational, religious; publishing dept of Uitgeverij Averbode; Publishing Man. P. HERMANS.

Brepols Publishers NV: Begijnhof 67, 2300 Turnhout; tel. (1) 444-80-20; fax (1) 442-89-19; e-mail info@brepols.net; internet www.brepols.net; f. 1796; academic; Dir PAUL DE JONGH.

Editions Casterman SA: 132 rue Royale, BP 2, 1000 Brussels; tel. (2) 209-83-00; fax (2) 209-83-01; internet www.casterman.com; f. 1780; fiction, encyclopaedias, education, history, comic books and children's books; Man. Dir LOUIS DELAS.

Davidsfonds vzw: Blijde-Inkomststraat 79–81, 3000 Leuven; tel. (1) 631-06-00; fax (1) 631-06-08; e-mail info@davidsfonds.be; internet www.davidsfonds.be; f. 1875; general, reference, textbooks; Dir KATRIEN DE VREESE.

Editions Dupuis SA: 52 rue Jules Destrée, 6001 Marcinelle; tel. (7) 160-50-00; fax (7) 160-05-99; e-mail dupuis@dupuis.com; internet www.dupuis.com; f. 1898; children's fiction, periodicals and comic books for children and adults, multimedia and audiovisual; Dir-Gen. OLIVIER PERRARD.

Etablissements Emile Bruylant SA: 67 rue de la Régence, 1000 Brussels; tel. (2) 512-98-42; fax (2) 511-94-77; e-mail info@bruylant.be; internet www.bruylant.be; f. 1838; law; Pres. and Dir-Gen. JEAN VANDEVELD.

Uitgeverij EPO: Lange Pastoorstraat 25-27, 2600 Berchem; tel. (3) 239-68-74; fax (3) 218-46-04; e-mail uitgeverij@epo.be; internet www.epo.be; history, literature, travel, politics and social sciences; Dir MARTINE UYTTERHOEVEN; Publr JOS HENNES.

Glénat Bénélux: 131 rue Saint-Lambert, 1200 Woluwe St Lambert; tel. (2) 761-26-40; fax (2) 761-26-45; internet www.glenat.com; f. 1985; comics, magazines; Publr JACQUES GLÉNAT; Dir DOMINIQUE LEBLAN.

Groupe De Boeck SA: 39 rue des Minimes, 1000 Brussels; tel. (2) 548-07-11; fax (2) 513-90-09; e-mail gbd@deboeck.com; internet www.deboeck.com; f. 1795; French imprints: De Boeck Education, De Boeck Université, Duculot, Estem, Larcier; Dutch imprints: Uitgeverij De Boeck, Uitgeverij Larcier; educational, scientific, academic, medical, legal; Chair. ALAIN KOUCK; Man. Dir GEORGES HOYOS.

Groupe Erasme: 2 place Baudouin 1er, 5004 Bouge; tel. (8) 121-37-00; fax (8) 121-23-72; e-mail info@grouperasme.be; internet www.groupeerasme.be; f. 1979; imprints: Artel, D2H Didier Hatier-Hachette Education, Didier-Hatier, Erasme; school books; Dir GAËTANE PONET.

Editions Hemma SA: 106 rue Chevron, 4987 Chevron; tel. (8) 643-01-10; fax (8) 643-36-40; e-mail hemma@hemma.be; internet www.hemma.be; f. 1956; juveniles, educational books and materials; Dir ALBERT HEMMERLIN.

Houtekiet NV: Vrijheidstraat 33, 2000 Antwerp; tel. (3) 238-12-96; fax (3) 238-80-41; e-mail info@houtekiet.com; internet www.houtekiet.com; f. 1983; Publr LEO DE HAES.

Intersentia NV: Groenstraat 30, 2640 Mortsel; tel. (3) 680-15-50; fax (3) 658-71-21; e-mail mail@intersentia.be; internet www.intersentia.be; Publrs KRIS MOEREMANS, HANS KLUWER, NANCY DE BRAEKELEER.

Die Keure NV: Kleine Pathoekeweg 3, 8000 Brugge; tel. (5) 047-12-72; fax (5) 034-37-68; e-mail info@diekeure.be; internet www.diekeure.be; f. 1948; textbooks, law, political and social sciences; Dirs B. VANDENBUSSCHE (secondary schools), NIC PAPPIJN (primary schools).

Uitgeverij De Klaproos: Hostenstraat 4, 8670 Koksijde; tel. (5) 851-85-30; fax (5) 851-29-42; e-mail info@klaproos.be; internet www.klaproos.be; f. 1992; historical works; Dir SIEGFRIED DEBAEKE.

Uitgeverij Lannoo NV: Kasteelstraat 97, 8700 Tielt; tel. (5) 142-42-11; fax (5) 140-11-52; e-mail lannoo@lannoo.be; internet www.lannoo.com; f. 1909; general, reference; Man. Dir MATTHIAS LANNOO.

Editions du Lombard SA: 7 ave Paul-Henri Spaak, 1060 Brussels; tel. (2) 526-68-11; fax (2) 520-44-05; e-mail info@lombard.be; internet www.lombard.be; f. 1946; graphic novels; Gen. Man. FRANÇOIS PERNOT.

Manteau: Mechelsesteenweg 203, 2018 Antwerp; tel. (3) 285-72-00; fax (3) 285-72-99; e-mail info@standaarduitgeverij.be; internet www.standaarduitgeverij.be; f. 1932; literature; imprint of Standaard Uitgeverij NV; Dir ERIC WILLEMS.

Mercatorfonds: 2 rue du Midi, 1000 Brussels; tel. (2) 548-25-35; fax (5) 502-16-28; e-mail kunstboeken@mercatorfonds.be; internet www.mercatorfonds.be; f. 1965; art, ethnography, literature, music, geography and history; Dir JAN MARTENS.

Peeters: Bondgenotenlaan 153, 3000 Leuven; tel. (1) 623-51-70; fax (1) 622-85-00; e-mail peeters@peeters-leuven.be; internet www.peeters-leuven.be; f. 1856; academic; Dir P. PEETERS.

Uitgeverij Pelckmans NV: Kapelsestraat 222, 2950 Kapellen; tel. (3) 660-27-00; fax (3) 660-27-01; e-mail uitgeverij@pelckmans.be; internet www.pelckmans.be; f. 1893 as De Nederlandsche Boekhandel; present name adopted 1988; school books, scientific, general; Dirs J. PELCKMANS, R. PELCKMANS.

Plantyn NV: Waterloo Office Park, 161 drève Richelle, Batiment L, 1410 Waterloo; tel. (2) 427-42-47; fax (2) 427-79-03; e-mail editions.plantyn@woltersplantyn.be; internet www.woltersplantyn.be; f. 1959; education; Dir PATRICK GEYSEN.

Roularta Books: Meiboomlaan 33, 8800 Roeselare; tel. (5) 126-69-67; fax (5) 126-66-80; e-mail jan.ingelbeen@roularta.be; internet www.roulartabooks.be; f. 1988; owned by Roularta Media Group; Publr JAN INGELBEEN.

Sanoma Magazines Belgium NV: Telecomlaan 5–7, 1831 Diegem; tel. (2) 776-22-11; fax (2) 776-23-99; e-mail info@sanoma-magazines.be; internet www.sanoma-magazines.be; periodicals; f. 2002; owned by SanomaWSOY Group (Finland); CEO AIMÉ VAN HECKE.

Snoecks NV: Begijnhoflaan 452, 9000 Ghent; tel. (9) 267-04-11; fax (9) 267-04-60; e-mail snoecks@snoecks.be; internet www.snoecks.be; f. 1782; art books, travel guides; acquired by Deckers Druk in 2006; Editor HALBE DE JONG.

Standaard Uitgeverij NV: Mechelsesteenweg 203, 2018 Antwerp; tel. (3) 285-72-00; fax (3) 285-72-99; e-mail info@standaarduitgeverij.be; internet www.standaarduitgeverij.be; f. 1924; general, fiction, non-fiction, comics, dictionaries and professional literature; Dirs ERIC WILLEMS, JOHAN DE KONING, JOHAN VAN HULLE.

Kluwer: Ragheno Business Park, Motstraat 30, 2800 Mechelen; tel. (15) 36-10-00; fax (15) 36-11-91; e-mail info@kluwer.be; internet www.kluwer.be; law, business, scientific; subsidiary of Wolters Kluwer NV (Netherlands); CEO HENRI VAN ENGHELEN.

Yoyo Books: Hagelberg 33, 2250 Olen; tel. (1) 428-23-40; fax (1) 428-23-49; e-mail jo.dupre@yoyo-books.com; internet www.yoyo-books.com; imprints: Yoyo, Allegrio; educational, cookery; Man. Dir JO DUPRÉ.

PUBLISHERS' ASSOCIATIONS

Association des Editeurs Belges (ADEB): 34 ave Huart Hamoir, 1030 Brussels; tel. (2) 241-65-80; fax (2) 216-71-31; e-mail adeb@adeb.be; internet www.adeb.be; f. 1922; asscn of French-language book publrs; Dir BERNARD GÉRARD.

Vlaamse Uitgevers Vereniging (VUV): Te Boelaerlei 37, 2140 Borgerhout; tel. (3) 287-66-92; fax (3) 281-22-40; e-mail annemie.verheeke@boek.be; internet www.vuv.be; asscn of Flemish-language book publrs; Dir JACQUES GERMONPREZ.

Broadcasting and Communications

TELECOMMUNICATIONS

In January 1998 the Belgian telecommunications sector was fully opened to private sector competition. More than 300 private companies have subsequently registered as service providers.

Regulatory Authority

Institut Belge des Services Postaux et des Télécommunications/Belgisch Instituut voor Postdiensten en Telecommunicatie (IBPT/BIPT): 14 ave de l'Astronomie, BP 21, 1210 Brussels; tel. (2) 226-88-88; fax (2) 226-88-77; e-mail viviane.uyttersprot@ibpt.be; internet www.ibpt.be; Chair. ERIC VAN HEESVELDE.

Major Service Providers

BASE: Neerveldstraat 105, 1200 Brussels; tel. (484) 00-62-00; fax (484) 00-62-01; e-mail help@base.be; internet www.base.be; mobile cellular telephone operator; subsidiary of Koninklijke KPN NV (Netherlands); CEO STAN MILLER.

Belgacom: 27B blvd du Roi Albert II, 1030 Brussels; tel. (2) 202-41-11; fax (2) 203-65-93; e-mail about@belgacom.be; internet www.belgacom.be; total service operator; Chair. THÉO DILISSEN; Pres. and CEO DIDIER BELLENS.

Belgacom Mobile SA (Proximus): 55 rue du Progrès, 1210 Brussels; tel. (2) 205-40-00; fax (2) 205-40-40; internet www.proximus.be; wholly-owned subsidiary of Belgacom; mobile cellular telephone operator; Chair. DIDIER BELLENS; CEO MICHEL GEORGIS.

BT Ltd (Belgium): Telecomlaan 9, 1831 Diegem; tel. (2) 700-22-11; fax (2) 700-32-11; internet www.bt.be; Man. MICHEL DE COSTER.

Cable & Wireless Belgium SA: Zaventemsesteenweg 162, 1831 Diegem; tel. (2) 627-34-00; fax (2) 627-34-01; e-mail info.be@cw.com; internet www.cw.com; Dir BRUNO DAVOINE.

Coditel SA: 26 rue des Deux Eglises, 1000 Brussels; tel. (2) 226-55-11; fax (2) 219-77-25; e-mail business-solutions@coditel.be; internet www.coditel.be; acquired by Altice (France) in 2001; main cable operator in the Brussels region; Dir-Gen. Pascal Dormal.

KPN Belgium: Koningin Astridlaan 166, 1780 Wemmel; tel. (2) 610-30-00; fax (2) 610-30-10; e-mail info@versatel.be; internet www.versatel.be; fixed-line and internet provider for business; fmrly Versatel Belgium NV; Man. Dir Raj Raithatha.

Mobistar: 70 blvd A. Reyers, 1030 Brussels; tel. (2) 745-71-11; fax (2) 745-70-00; internet www.mobistar.be; f. 1995; mobile cellular telephone and fixed-line operator; owned by Orange SA (France); CEO Benoit Scheen; 3.2m. customers (2007).

Scarlet SA: Medialaan 50, 1800 Vilvoorde; tel. (2) 275-27-27; internet www.scarlet.be; f. 1997; offers fixed-line telephone and broadband internet services; acquired by Belgacom in 2008.

Telenet NV: Liersesteenweg 4, 2800 Mechelen; tel. (15) 33-30-00; fax (15) 33-39-99; e-mail communicatie@telenet.be; internet www.telenet.be; f. 1996; total service operator; acquired UPC Belgium 2007; CEO Duco Sickinghe.

TELE2 Belgique SA: BP 3, 1140 Brussels 14; tel. (2) 608-06-00; fax (70) 22-55-05; internet www.tele2.be; fixed-line telephone and broadband internet services; acquired by Koninklijke KPN NV (Netherlands) in 2007; Man. Dir Grégoire Dallemagne.

Verizon Belgium Luxembourg NV: 37 rue de la Science, 1040 Brussels; tel. (2) 400-80-00; fax (2) 400-84-00; e-mail info-belgium-be@be.verizonbusiness.com; internet www.verizonbusiness.com/be; subsidiary of Verizon Communications (USA); total service operator for business.

Voo: 28 rue d'Alsace-Lorraine, 1050 Brussels; tel. (2) 500-99-11; internet www.voo.be; f. 2006 by merger of ALE-Télédis and Brutélé; digital television, fixed-line telephone and broadband internet service provider; provides services to Brussels and Wallonia.

PUBLIC BROADCASTING ORGANIZATIONS
Flemish Community

TV Brussel: Flageygebouw, Belvédèrestraat 27, Postbus 1, 1050 Elsene; tel. (2) 702-87-30; fax (2) 702-87-41; e-mail jan.de.troyer@tvbrussel.be; internet www.tvbrussel.be; f. 1993; broadcasts news and Flemish-language programmes in Brussels-Capital and Flanders regions; funded by the Flemish Community; Dir Jan de Troyer.

Vlaamse Radio- en Televisieomroep NV (VRT): Auguste Reyerslaan 52, 1043 Brussels; tel. (2) 741-31-11; fax (2) 734-93-51; e-mail info@vrt.be; internet www.vrt.be; f. 1998; shares held by Flemish Community; operates six radio stations (Radio 1, Radio 2, Klara, Donna, Radio Brussel and RVi) and three television stations (Eén, Canvas and Ketnet); Chair. Guy Peeters; Man. Dir Dirk Wauters.

French Community

Radio-Télévision Belge de la Communauté Française (RTBF): 52 blvd Auguste Reyers, 1044 Brussels; tel. (2) 737-21-11; fax (2) 737-25-56; internet www.rtbf.be; operates six radio stations (La Première, VivaCité, Musiq'3, Classic 21, Pure FM and RTBF International) and three television stations (La Une, La Deux and RTBF Sat); Dir Gen. Jean-Paul Philippot; Dir of Radio Francis Goffin; Dir of Television Yves Bigot.

Télé Bruxelles: 32 rue Gabrielle Petit, 1080 Brussels; tel. (2) 421-21-21; fax (2) 421-21-22; e-mail contact@telebruxelles.be; internet www.telebruxelles.net; f. 1985; broadcasts programmes in French to Brussels-Capital and Wallonia regions; funded mainly by the French Community; Pres. Fabrice Cumps; Dir-Gen. Marc de Haan.

German-speaking Community

Belgisches Rundfunk- und Fernsehzentrum der Deutschsprachigen Gemeinschaft (BRF): Kehrweg 11, 4700 Eupen; tel. (87) 59-11-11; fax (87) 59-11-99; e-mail info@brf.be; internet www.brf.be; operates three radio stations (BRF1, BRF2 and BRF-DLF) and one television station (BRF TV); Dir Hans Engels.

COMMERCIAL, CABLE AND PRIVATE BROADCASTING

PRIME: Liersesteenweg 4, 2800 Mechelen; tel. (2) 716-53-53; fax (2) 716-54-54; e-mail service@prime.be; internet www.prime.be; f. 1989; operated by Telenet NV; broadcasts in Flemish.

Regionale TV Media: Z.1 Research Park 120, 1731 Zellik; tel. (2) 467-58-77; fax (2) 467-56-54; e-mail contact@rtvm.be; internet www.rtvm.be; group of 11 regional news broadcasters within Flanders; commercial.

TVI SA: 1 ave Ariane, 1200 Brussels; tel. (2) 337-68-11; fax (2) 337-68-12; internet www.rtl.be; owned by RTL Group, Luxembourg; commercial station; broadcasts in French.

Vlaamse Media Maatschappij: Medialaan 1, 1800 Vilvoorde; tel. (2) 255-32-11; fax (2) 252-37-87; e-mail info@vtm.be; internet www.vtm.be; f. 1987; commercial; broadcasts in Flemish; Dir-Gen. Peter Quaghebeur.

Finance

(cap. = capital; res = reserves; dep. = deposits; m. = million; brs = branches; amounts in euros, unless otherwise indicated)

BANKING

Commission bancaire, financière et des assurances/Commissie voor het Bank-, Financie- en Assurantiewezen: 12–14 rue du Congrès, 1000 Brussels; tel. (2) 220-52-11; fax (2) 220-52-75; e-mail cpb@cbfa.be; internet www.cbfa.be; f. 2004 by merger; supervisory body for the financial sector; Chair. Jean-Paul Servais; Sec.-Gen. Albert Niesten.

Central Bank

Banque Nationale de Belgique: 14 blvd de Berlaimont, 1000 Brussels; tel. (2) 221-21-11; fax (2) 221-31-01; e-mail info@nbb.be; internet www.nbb.be; f. 1850; bank of issue; cap. 10.0m., res 1,049.4m., total assets 82,776.4m. (Dec. 2006); Gov. Guy Quaden; Vice-Gov. Luc Coene; Dirs Marcia de Wachter, Jan Smets, Jean Hilgers, Françoise Masai, Peter Praet, Norbert de Batselier; 7 brs.

Development Bank

Gewestelijke Investeringsmaatschappij voor Vlaanderen (GIMV): Karel Oomsstraat 37, 2018 Antwerp; tel. (3) 290-21-00; fax (3) 290-21-05; e-mail info@gimv.be; internet www.gimv.com; f. 1980; promotes creation, restructuring and expansion of private cos; net assets 446m. (2007); Chair. Herman Daems; CEO Dirk Boogmans.

Major Commercial Banks

ABN AMRO Bank NV: Kanselarijstraat 17A, 1000 Brussels; tel. (2) 546-04-60; fax (2) 546-04-04; e-mail info@abnamro.be; internet www.abnamro.be; f. 1824; Chair. of Man. Bd Mark Fisher; Chair. of Supervisory Bd A. C. Martínez; 7 brs.

Antwerpse Diamantbank NV/Banque Diamantaire Anversoise SA/Antwerp Diamond Bank NV: Pelikaanstraat 53, 2018 Antwerp; tel. (3) 204-72-04; fax (3) 233-90-95; e-mail info@adia.be; internet www.antwerpdiamondbank.com; f. 1934; owned by KBC Bank NV; cap. 34.4m., res 128.8m., dep. 1,430.5m. (Dec. 2004); Chair. Guido Segers; Man. Dir and Chair. of Exec. Cttee Paul C. Goris.

AXA Bank Belgium NV: Grotesteenweg 214, 2600 Antwerp; tel. (3) 286-22-11; fax (3) 286-24-07; e-mail contact@axa-bank.be; internet www.axa.be; f. 1881 as ANHYP Bank NV; present name adopted 2000; cap. 6.3m., res 413.7m., dep 13,518.1m. (Dec. 2006); Chair., Bd of Dirs Alfred Bouckaert; Chair., Exec. Cttee Patrick Vaneeckhout; 5 brs.

Banca Monte Paschi Belgio SA/NV: 24 rue Joseph II, 1000 Brussels; tel. (2) 220-72-11; fax (2) 218-83-91; e-mail info@montepaschi.be; internet www.montepaschi.be; f. 1947 as Banco di Roma (Belgique); name changed 1992; cap. 41.2m., res 18.6m., dep. 1,105.4m. (Dec. 2006); Gen. Dir and Pres. of Exec. Cttee Luigi Macchiola.

Bank J. Van Breda & Co NV: Ledeganckkaai 7, 2000 Antwerp; tel. (3) 217-53-33; fax (3) 271-10-94; e-mail info@bankvanbreda.be; internet www.bankvanbreda.be; f. 1930; cap. 17.5m., res 182.3m., dep. 2,282.2m. (Dec. 2006); Pres., Exec. Cttee and Gen. Man. Carlo Henriksen; 42 brs.

Bank Degroof SA/Banque Degroof SA: 44 rue de l'Industrie, 1040 Brussels; tel. (2) 287-91-11; fax (2) 230-67-00; e-mail info@degroof.be; internet www.degroof.be; f. 1871; present name adopted 1998; cap. 41.7m., res 208.4m., dep. 3,159.0m. (Sept. 2006); Chair. Alain Siaens; CEO Regnier Haegelsteen.

Bank Delen NV/Banque Delen SA: Jan van Rijswijcklaan 184, 2020 Antwerp; tel. (3) 244-55-66; fax (3) 216-04-91; e-mail info@delen.be; internet www.delen.be; f. 1928; cap. 41.4m., res 4.7m., dep. 839.7m. (Dec. 2005); Pres. Jacques Delen; Chair. Jan Suykens; 5 brs.

Byblos Bank Europe SA: 10B rue Montoyer, 1000 Brussels; tel. (2) 551-00-20; fax (2) 513-05-26; e-mail byblos.europe@byblosbankeur.com; internet www.byblosbank.com.lb; f. 1976 as Byblos Arab Finance Bank (Belgium) SA; present name adopted 1998; cap. 20.0m., res 12.8m., dep. 439.4m. (Dec. 2006); Chair. Bassam A. Nassar; Man. Dir and Pres. Najah L. Salem.

CBC Banque SA: 5 Grand-Place, 1000 Brussels; tel. (2) 547-12-11; fax (2) 547-11-10; e-mail info@cbc.be; internet www.cbc.be; f. 1958; name changed as above 1998; cap. 89.6m., res 354.6m., dep. 7,841.4m. (Dec. 2005); Chair., Bd of Dirs Jan Huyghebaert; Chair., Exec. Cttee Christian Deleu; 115 brs.

Citibank Belgium NV/SA: 263 blvd Général Jacques, 1050 Brussels; tel. (2) 626-51-11; fax (2) 626-55-84; internet www.citibank.be; f. 1919; present name adopted 1992; cap. 44.9m., res 11.0m., dep. 1,950.0m. (Dec. 2000); Chair. José de Peñaranda; Pres. Frits Seegers.

BELGIUM

Directory

Crédit Agricole SA/Landbouwkrediet NV: 251 blvd Sylvain Dupuis, 1070 Brussels; tel. (2) 558-71-11; fax (2) 558-76-23; e-mail info@credit-agricole.be; internet www.landbouwkrediet.be; f. 1937; cap. 61.6m., res 157.8m., dep. 6,373.2m. (Dec. 2006); Pres. and CEO LUC VERSELE.

Crédit Professionnel SA/Beroepskrediet NV: 6–9 ave des Arts, 1210 Brussels; tel. (2) 289-82-00; fax (2) 289-89-90; e-mail info@bkcp.be; internet www.bkcp.be; f. 1992 as Caisse Nationale de Crédit Professionnel SA; name changed as above 1997; cap. 112.4m., res 121.9m., dep. 2,188.2m. (Dec. 2006); Chair., Bd of Dirs ERIC CHARPENTIER; Chair., Exec. Bd WERNER ROGIERS.

Delta Lloyd Bank NV: 23 ave de l'Astronomie, 1210 Brussels; tel. (2) 229-76-00; fax (2) 229-76-99; e-mail info@dlbank.be; internet www.dlbank.be; f. 1966 as Bankunie NV; above name adopted 2001; cap. 22.8m., res 10.9m., dep. 762.5m. (Dec. 1999); Pres. PIET VERBRUGGE.

Deutsche Bank SA/NV: 13 ave Marnix, 1000 Brussels; tel. (2) 551-65-11; fax (2) 551-66-66; internet www.deutschebank.be; f. 1893 as Banque de Commerce SA (Handelsbank NV); renamed Crédit Lyonnais Belgium 1989, bought by Deutsche Bank 1999; Chair. RAINER NESKE; Chief Exec. YVES DELACOLLETTE; 25 brs.

Dexia Bank Belgium SA: Pachécolaan 44, 1000 Brussels; tel. (2) 222-11-11; fax (2) 222-11-22; internet www.dexia.be; f. 1860 as Crédit Communal de Belgique SA; present name adopted 2000; cap. 958.1m., res 4,724.7m., dep. 228,759.3m. (Dec. 2006); Chair., Exec. Cttee STEFAN DECRAENE; 1,283 brs.

Euroclear Bank SA: 1 blvd du Roi Albert II, 1210 Brussels; tel. (2) 326-12-11; fax (2) 326-40-45; e-mail info@euroclear.com; internet www.euroclear.com; f. 2000; 100% owned by Euroclear SA/NV; cap. 285.5m., res 578.9m. dep. 9,756.1m. (Dec. 2006); CEO YVES POULLET.

Europabank NV: Burgstraat 170, 9000 Ghent; tel. (9) 224-73-11; fax (9) 223-34-72; e-mail europabank@europabank.be; internet www.europabank.be; f. 1964; 99.9% owned by Landbouwkrediet NV; cap. 1.6m., res 62.2m., dep. 660.7m. (Dec. 2006); Chair. LUC VERSELE; Pres. LUK OSTE; 36 brs.

Fortis Bank NV/Fortis Banque SA: 3 Montagne du Parc, 1000 Brussels; tel. (2) 511-26-311; fax (2) 565-49-29; e-mail info@fortisbank.com; internet www.fortisbank.com; f. 1822; present name adopted 1999 following merger of Generale Bank/Générale de Banque and ASLK-CGER Bank/Banque with the Fortis Group; banking, insurance and investments; dep. 591,835.0m., total assets 674,691.0m. (Dec. 2006); Chair., Bd of Dirs JEAN-PAUL VOTRON; Chair., Man. Cttee HERMAN VERWILST; 1,109 brs.

Goffin Bank NV/Goffin Banque SA: Verlorenbroodstraat 120, 9820 Merelbeke; tel. (9) 261-02-00; fax (9) 261-02-01; e-mail info@goffin.be; internet www.goffin.be; f. 1955 as Kempische Hypotheek en Finacierings Maatschappij; present named adopted 2001; cap. 11.0m., res 0.6m., dep. 174.6m. (Dec. 2005); Pres. A. G. SAVELKOUL-LOMMAERT; Chair. M. PIENS.

ING Belgium SA/NV: 24 ave Marnix, 1000 Brussels; tel. (2) 547-21-11; fax (2) 547-38-44; e-mail info@ing.be; internet www.ing.be; f. 1975 as Bank Brussels Lambert; acquired in 1998 by ING Groep (Netherlands); name changed as above in April 2003; cap. 2,350m., res 5,118.3m., dep. 160,875.7m. (Dec. 2006); Chair., Bd of Dirs CEES MAAS; Pres. and CEO LUC VANDERWALLE; 808 brs.

KBC Bank NV: Havenlaan 2, 1080 Brussels 8; tel. (2) 429-11-11; fax (2) 429-81-31; e-mail kbc.telecenter@kbc.be; internet www.kbc.be; f. 1935 as Kredietbank NV; merged with Bank von Roeselare NV and CERA Investment Bank NV in 1998; cap. and res 10,603.0m., dep. 223,927.0m. (Dec. 2006); Chair. JAN HUYGHEBAERT; Pres. ANDRÉ BERGEN.

Keytrade Bank SA: 100 blvd de Souverain, 1170 Brussels; tel. (2) 679-90-00; fax (2) 679-90-01; e-mail info@keytradebank.com; internet www.keytradebank.com; f. 2002 by merger of RealBank SA and VMS Keytrade.com; owned by Credit Agricole SA/Landbouwkrediet NV; cap. 15.3m., res 3.3m., dep. 370.3m. (Dec. 2004); Pres., CEO and Gen. Man. THIERRY TERNIER.

Santander Benelux SA/NV: 85 ave des Nerviens, 1040 Brussels; tel. (2) 286-54-11; fax (2) 230-09-40; f. 1914 as Société Hollandaise de Banque; present name adopted 2004; owned by Banco Santander Centro Hispano SA (Spain); cap. 39.6m., res 0.8m., dep. 487.5m. (Dec. 2005); Man. Dir GUILLERMO SANZ MURAT.

Banking Association

Association Belge des Banques et des Sociétés de Bourse/Belgische Vereniging van Banken en Beursvenootschappen (ABB/BVB): 36 rue Ravenstein, BP 5, 1000 Brussels; tel. (2) 507-68-11; fax (2) 512-58-61; e-mail abb-bvb@abb-bvb.be; internet www.abb-bvb.be; f. 1936; part of Fédération Belge du Secteur Financier (FEBELFIN); Pres. JAN VANHEVEL; CEO MICHEL VERMAERKE; 137 mems.

STOCK EXCHANGE

Euronext Brussels SA/NV: Palais de la Bourse, 1000 Brussels; tel. (2) 509-12-11; fax (2) 509-12-12; e-mail info.be@euronext.com; internet www.euronext.com; formed in 2000 by merger of Amsterdam, Paris and Brussels exchanges, and joined in 2002 by the Lisbon stock exchange and the London futures exchange Liffe; merged with New York Stock Exchange in 2007 to form NYSE Euronext; Chair. and CEO BRUNO COLMANT.

INSURANCE

Principal Insurance Companies

Aviabel, Compagnie Belge d'Assurances Aviation, SA: 54 ave Louise, 1050 Brussels; tel. (2) 349-12-11; fax (2) 349-12-90; e-mail insurance@aviabel.be; internet www.aviabel.be; f. 1935; aviation, insurance, reinsurance; Chair. BART DE SMET; CEO PHILIPPE VANDE WAL.

AXA: 25 blvd du Souverain, 1170 Brussels; tel. (2) 678-61-11; fax (2) 678-93-40; e-mail elly.bens@axa.be; internet www.axa.be; f. 1853; member of the AXA group; all branches; Pres. ALFRED BOUCKAERT; Chair., Exec. Cttee and Man. Dir EUGÈNE TEYSEN.

DVV Verzekeringen NV/Les AP Assurances SA: 6 ave Livingston, 1000 Brussels; tel. (2) 286-61-11; fax (2) 286-15-15; e-mail info@dvvlap.be; internet www.dvv.be; f. 1929; all branches; owned by Dexia Group; Chair. GUY ROELANDT.

Ethias: 24 rue des Croisiers, 4000 Liège; tel. (4) 220-31-11; fax (4) 220-30-05; e-mail info@ethias.be; internet www.ethias.be; f. 1919; fmrly Société Mutuelle des Administrations Publiques (SMAP), name changed as above in 2003; institutions, civil service employees, public administration and enterprises; CEO GUY BURTON.

Nateus Verzekeringen: Frankrijklei 79, 2000 Antwerp; tel. (3) 247-35-11; fax (3) 247-35-90; e-mail info@nateus.be; internet www.nateus.be; f. 2003 by merger of Naviga, Mauretus, and Aachener & Münchener; present name adopted 2005; all branches; specializes in insurance for transport sector; Chair., Management Bd HANS VERSTRAETE.

Euler Hermes Credit Insurance Belgium SA: 15 rue Montoyer, 1000 Brussels; tel. (2) 289-31-11; fax (2) 289-32-99; e-mail info.belgium@eulerhermes.com; internet www.eulerhermes.com/belgium; f. 1929 as Compagnie Belge d'Assurance-Crédit; present name adopted 1998; credit insurance, reinsurance; mem. of Allianz Group (Germany); CEO JEAN-LUC LOUIS.

Fortis Insurance Belgium: 53 blvd Emile Jacqmain, 1000 Brussels; tel. (2) 220-81-11; fax (2) 220-81-50; e-mail info.insurance.be@fortis.com; internet www.insurance.be.fortis.com; f. 2006 by merger of Fortis AG and FBAssurances; owned by Fortis Group; CEO BART DE SMET.

Generali Belgium SA: 149 ave Louise, 1050 Brussels; tel. (2) 403-81-11; fax (2) 403-88-99; e-mail generali_belgium@generali.be; internet www.generali.be; f. 1901; all branches; Pres. FRANS HEUS; Dir-Gen. THIERRY DELVAUX.

KBC SA/NV: Waaistraat 6, 3000 Leuven; tel. (07) 815-21-53; fax (03) 283-29-50; e-mail kbc24plus@verz.kbc.be; internet www.kbc.be; f. 1998; Chair. JAN HUYGHEBAERT.

Mercator Verzekeringen: Desguinlei 100, 2018 Antwerp; tel. (3) 247-21-11; fax (3) 247-27-77; e-mail info@mercator.be; internet www.mercator.be; CEO JAN DE MEULDER.

Insurance Associations

Assuralia: 29 square de Meeûs, 1000 Brussels; tel. (2) 547-56-11; fax (2) 547-56-00; internet www.assuralia.be; f. 1921; affiliated to Fédération des Entreprises de Belgique; Pres. C. DESSEILLE; Man. Dir MICHEL BAECKER; 95 mems.

Fédération des Courtiers d'Assurances et Intermédiaires Financiers de Belgique (FEPRABEL): 40 ave Albert-Elisabeth, 1200 Brussels; tel. (2) 743-25-60; fax (2) 735-44-58; e-mail info@feprabel.be; internet www.feprabel.be; f. 1934; Pres. ANDRÉ LAMOTTE; 500 mems.

Trade and Industry

GOVERNMENT AGENCIES

Flanders Investment and Trade: Gaucheretstraat 90, 1030 Brussels; tel. (2) 504-87-11; fax (2) 504-88-99; e-mail info@fitagency.be; internet www.flanderstrade.be; f. 1991; promotes foreign investment in Flanders and Flemish business abroad; Man. Dir CLAIRE TILLEKAERTS.

Société de Développement de la Région de Bruxelles-Capitale (SDRB): 6 rue Gabrielle Petit, 1080 Brussels; tel. (2) 422-51-11; fax (2) 422-51-12; e-mail info@brda.be; internet www.brda.be;

BELGIUM

f. 1974; promotes economic development in the capital; Pres. L. WILLAME; Man. Dir J. MEGANCK.

Société Régionale d'Investissement de Wallonie: 13 ave Destenay, 4000 Liège; tel. (4) 221-98-11; fax (4) 221-99-99; e-mail sriw@sriw.be; internet www.sriw.be; f. 1979; promotes private enterprise in Wallonia; Pres. JEAN-CLAUDE DEHOVRE.

PRINCIPAL CHAMBERS OF COMMERCE

There are chambers of commerce and industry in all major towns and industrial areas.

Chambre de Commerce de Bruxelles (BECI): 500 ave Louise, 1050 Brussels; tel. (2) 648-50-02; fax (2) 640-93-28; e-mail info@beci.be; internet www.beci.be; f. 1875; Pres. YVAN HUYGHEBAERT; 3,000 mems.

Chambre de Commerce et d'Industrie de Liège et de Verviers: rue Renkin 35, 4800 Verviers; tel. (8) 729-36-36; fax (8) 726-87-80; e-mail info@ccilv.be; internet www.ccilv.be; f. 1866; Dir XAVIER CIECHANOWSKI; 2,000 mems.

Voka—Kamer van Koophandel Antwerpen-Waasland: Markgravestraat 12, 2000 Antwerp; tel. (3) 232-22-19; fax (3) 233-64-42; e-mail info@voka.be; internet www.kvkaw.voka.be; f. 1969; Pres. JOHN STOOP; 3,000 mems.

INDUSTRIAL AND TRADE ASSOCIATIONS

Fédération des Entreprises de Belgique (VBO-FEB) (Federation of Belgian Companies): 4 rue Ravenstein, 1000 Brussels; tel. (2) 515-08-11; fax (2) 515-09-99; e-mail info@vbo-feb.be; internet www.vbo-feb.be; f. 1895; federates all the main industrial and non-industrial asscns; Chair. JEAN-CLAUDE DAOUST; CEO RUDI THOMAES; 33 full mems.

Agoria—Fédération Multisectorielle de l'Industrie Technologique (Multisector Federation for the Technology Industry): 80 blvd Auguste Reyers, 1030 Brussels; tel. (2) 706-78-00; fax (2) 706-78-01; e-mail info@agoria.be; internet www.agoria.be; f. 1946; present name adopted 2000; more than 1,200 mem. cos; CEO PAUL SOETE.

Fédération des Carrières de Petit Granit—Pierre Bleue de Belgique ASBL (Limestone): 1 chemin de Carrières, 7063 Neufvilles; tel. (67) 34-68-05; fax (67) 33-08-49; internet www.federationpierrebleue.be; f. 1948; Pres. FRANÇOIS RENIER.

Association Belge des Banques/Belgische Vereniging van Banken (ABB): see Finance above.

Association des Fabricants de Pâtes, Papiers et Cartons de Belgique (COBELPA) (Paper): 306 ave Louise, BP 11, 1050 Brussels; tel. (2) 646-64-50; fax (2) 646-82-97; e-mail general@cobelpa.be; internet www.cobelpa.be; f. 1940; Gen. Man. FIRMIN FRANÇOIS.

Brasseurs Belges (Breweries): Maison des Brasseurs, 10 Grand' Place, 1000 Brussels; tel. (2) 511-49-87; fax (2) 511-32-59; e-mail belgian.brewers@beerparadise.be; internet www.beerparadise.be; f. 1971; Chair. THEO VERVLOET.

Confédération Nationale de la Construction (CNC) (Civil Engineering, Road and Building Contractors and Auxiliary Trades): 34–42 rue du Lombard, 1000 Brussels; tel. (2) 545-56-00; fax (2) 545-59-00; e-mail info@confederatiebouw.be; internet www.cnc.be; f. 1946; Pres. DIRK CORDEEL; Man. Dir ROBERT DE MÜELENAERE; 14,000 mems.

Confédération Professionnelle du Sucre et de ses Dérivés (Sugar): 182 ave de Tervueren, 1150 Brussels; tel. (2) 775-80-69; fax (2) 775-80-75; e-mail info@subel.be; f. 1938; mems: 10 groups, 66 cos; Pres. E. KESSELS; Dir-Gen. M. ROSIERS.

Creamoda (Clothing): Leliegaarde 22, 1731 Zellik; tel. (2) 238-10-11; fax (2) 238-10-10; e-mail info@creamoda.be; internet www.belgianfashion.be; f. 1946; Dir-Gen. ERIK MAGNUS.

Fédération Belge de la Brique (Bricks): 19 rue des Chartreux, BP 19, 1000 Brussels; tel. (2) 511-25-81; fax (2) 513-26-40; e-mail info@brique.be; internet www.brique.be; f. 1947; Pres. CAMILLE VANPEE; Dir JO VAN DEN BOSSCHE; 35 mems.

Fédération Belge des Dragueurs de Gravier et de Sable (BELBAG) (Quarries): Maasstraat 82, Postbus 2, 3640 Kinrooi; tel. (8) 956-08-08; fax (8) 956-08-09; e-mail info@belbag.be; internet www.belbag.be; f. 1967; Pres. LUC SEVERIJNS.

Fédération Belge de l'Industrie Textile, du Bois et de l'Ameublement (FEDUSTRIA) (Textiles, Wood and Furniture): 5 allée Hof-ter-Vleest, BP 1, 1070 Brussels; tel. (2) 528-58-11; fax (2) 528-58-29; e-mail info@fedustria.be; internet www.fedustria.be; f. 2006 by merger of Febelbois and Fébeltex; Pres. MICHÈLE SIOEN; Dir-Gen. FA QUIX.

Fédération Belge des Industries Chimiques et des Sciences de la Vie (Essencia) (Chemical Industries and Life Sciences): 80 blvd Auguste Reyers, 1030 Brussels; tel. (2) 238-97-11; fax (2) 231-13-01; e-mail info@essencia.be; internet www.essencia.be; Pres. CARL VAN CAMP; Man. Dir YVES VERSCHUEREN; 700 mem. cos.

Fédération Belge des Industries Graphiques (FEBELGRA) (Graphic Industries): 20 rue Belliard, BP 16, 1040 Brussels; tel. (2) 512-36-38; fax (2) 513-56-76; e-mail info@febelgra.be; internet www.febelgra.be; f. 1978; Pres. ROBY VAN DAELE; 750 mems.

Fédération Belgo-Luxembourgeoise de l'Industrie du Tabac (FEDETAB) (Tobacco): 7 ave Lloyd George, 1000 Brussels; tel. (2) 646-04-20; fax (2) 646-22-13; e-mail tobacco@fedetab.be; f. 1947; Pres. G. VANDERMARLIÈRE.

Fédération d'Employeurs pour le Commerce International, le Transport et les Branches d'Activité Connexes (Employers' Federation of International Trade, Transport and Related Activities); inc. Fédération Patronale des Ports Belges: Brouwersvliet 33, Postbus 7, 2000 Antwerp; tel. (3) 221-99-90; fax (3) 221-99-09; e-mail cepa@cepa.be; internet www.cepa.be/htm/we-fr/index.htm; f. 1937; Pres. MARINO VERMEERSCH; Dir RENÉ DE BROUWER.

Fédération de l'Industrie Alimentaire/Federatie Voedingsindustrie (FEVIA) (Food): 43 ave des Arts, BP 7, 1040 Brussels; tel. (2) 550-17-40; fax (2) 550-17-54; e-mail info@fevia.be; internet www.fevia.be; f. 1937; Dir-Gen. CHRIS MORIS.

Fédération de l'Industrie du Béton (FEBE) (Precast Concrete): 12 rue Volta, 1050 Brussels; tel. (2) 735-80-15; fax (2) 734-77-95; e-mail mail@febe.be; internet www.febe.be; f. 1936; Dir EDDY DANO; 80 mem. cos.

Fédération de l'Industrie Cimentière Belge (FEBELCEM) (Cement): 8 rue Volta, 1050 Brussels; tel. (2) 645-52-11; fax (2) 640-06-70; e-mail info@febelcem.be; internet www.febelcem.be; f. 1949; Pres. BERNARD KÜNG; Dir-Gen. JEAN-PIERRE JACOBS.

Fédération des Industries Extractives et Transformatrices de Roches non-Combustibles (FEDIEX) (Extraction and processing of non-fuel rocks): 61 rue du Trône, 1050 Brussels; tel. (2) 511-61-73; fax (2) 511-12-84; e-mail info@fediex.org; internet www.fediex.be; f. 1942 as Union des Producteurs Belges de Chaux, Calcaires, Dolomies et Produits Connexes; name changed (as above) 1990; co-operative society; Pres. J.-B. DE JONGH.

Fédération des Industries Transformatrices de Papier et Carton (FETRA) (Paper and Cardboard): 715 chaussée de Waterloo, BP 25, 1180 Brussels; tel. (2) 344-19-62; fax (2) 344-86-61; e-mail info@fetra.be; internet www.fetra.be; f. 1946; Pres. PAUL PISSENS; Sec.-Gen. LIEVE VANLIERDE.

Fédération de l'Industrie du Verre (Glass): 89 ave Louise, 1050 Brussels; tel. (2) 542-61-20; fax (2) 542-61-21; e-mail info@vgi-fiv.be; internet www.vgi-fiv.be; f. 1947; Pres. VINCENT GUILLÉ; Man. Dir ROLAND DERIDDER.

Fédération Patronale des Ports Belges: Brouwersvliet 33, Postbus 7, 2000 Antwerp; tel. (3) 221-99-87; fax (3) 221-99-09; e-mail rene.debrouwer@cepa.be; Pres. PAUL VALKENIERS; Dir RENÉ DE BROUWER.

Fédération Pétrolière Belge (Petroleum): 39 ave des Arts, BP 2, 1040 Brussels; tel. (2) 508-30-03; fax (2) 511-05-91; e-mail info@petrolfed.be; internet www.petrolfed.be; f. 1926; Pres. MIGUEL DEL MARMOL; Sec.-Gen. GAËTAN VAN DE WERVE.

Groupement des Sablières (Sand and Gravel): Quellinstraat 49, 2018 Antwerp; tel. (3) 223-66-11; fax (3) 223-66-47; e-mail cathy.blervacq@sibelco.be; f. 1937; Pres. ALAIN SPECKAERT.

Groupement de la Sidérurgie (Iron and Steel): 5 ave Ariane, 1200 Brussels; tel. (2) 509-14-11; fax (2) 509-14-00; e-mail gsv@steelbel.be; internet www.steelbel.be; f. 1953; Pres. ROBRECHT HIMPE.

Lubricants Association Belgium (LAB) (Mineral Oils): 80 blvd Auguste Reyers, 1000 Brussels; tel. (2) 238-97-85; fax (2) 230-03-89; e-mail lab@essenscia.be; internet www.lubsbelgium.be; f. 1921; fmrly Industrie des Huiles Minérales de Belgique; Pres. C. DEVROEY; Sec. N. POISSONNIER; 44 mems.

Synergrid (Gas and Electricity Grid Operators): 4 ave Palmerston, 1000 Brussels; tel. (2) 237-11-11; fax (2) 230-44-80; e-mail info@synergrid.be; internet www.synergrid.be; f. 1946; Pres. D. DOBBENI; Sec. Gen. FERDINAND DE LICHTERVELDE.

Union des Armateurs Belges (Shipowners): Brouwersvliet 33, Postbus 9, 2000 Antwerp; tel. (3) 232-72-32; fax (3) 231-39-97; e-mail info@brv.be; internet www.brv.be; Chair. NICOLAS SAVERYS; Man. Dir MARC NUYTEMANS.

Union des Carrières et Scieries de Marbres de Belgique (UCSMB) (Marble): Heideveld 8, 1654 Huizingen; tel. (2) 361-36-81; fax (2) 361-31-55; e-mail info@ucsmb.be; internet www.ucsmb.be.

Union Professionnelle des Producteurs Belges de Fibres-Ciment (Fibre-Cement): Aerschotstraat 114, 9100 Sint-Niklaas; tel. (3) 760-49-31; fax (3) 777-47-84; e-mail infod@svk.be; f. 1941; Pres. ANDRÉ HOSTE; Sec. THOM MEERSCHMAN.

BELGIUM

Union de la Tannerie et de la Mégisserie Belges (UNITAN) (Tanning and Tawing): c/o 140 rue des Tanneurs, 7730 Estaimbourg; tel. (69) 36-23-23; fax (69) 36-23-10; f. 1962; Pres. ALBERT CAPPELLE; Dir BRUNO COLLE.

UTILITIES
Regulatory Authorities

Commission de Régulation de l'Electricité et du Gaz/Commissie voor de Regulering van de Elektriciteit en het Gas (CREG): 26–38 rue de l'Industrie, 1040 Bruxelles; tel. (2) 289-76-11; fax (2) 289-76-09; e-mail info@creg.be; internet www.creg.be; regulatory body for both gas and electricity markets; Pres. FRANÇOIS POSSEMIERS.

Commission de Régulation pour l'Energie en Région de Bruxelles-Capitale (BRUGEL): 92 Gulledelle, 1200 Brussels; tel. (800) 971-98; internet www.brugel.be; regulatory body for electricity and gas markets in Brussels-Capital region; Pres. MARIE-PIERRE FAUCONNIER.

Commission Wallonne pour l'Energie (CWaPE): 103–106 ave Gouverneur Bovesse, 5100 Jambes; tel. (8) 133-08-10; fax (8) 133-08-11; internet www.cwape.be; f. 2002; Pres. FRANCIS GHIGNY.

Vlaams reguleringsinstantie voor de elektriciteits- en gasmarkt (VREG) (Flemish Electricity and Gas Market Regulatory Authority): Graaf de Ferrarisgebouw, Koning Albert II-laan 20–19, 1000 Brussels; tel. (2) 553-13-79; e-mail info@vreg.be; internet www.vreg.be; f. 2001; responsible for regulation of distribution of gas and electricity at low-voltage and production of electricity from renewable sources; Chair. LUC PEETERS; Man. Dir ANDRÉ PICTOEL.

Electricity

Electrabel: Regentlaan 8, 1000 Brussels; tel. (2) 518-61-11; fax (2) 518-64-00; internet www.electrabel.com; f. 1905 as Electriciteitsmaatschappij der Schelde; name changed to Ebes following merger in 1956; present name adopted 1990; generates and distributes electricity and natural gas; part of Groupe Suez; CEO JEAN-PIERRE HANSEN.

SPE NV (Luminus): Regentlaan 47, 1000 Brussels; tel. (2) 229-19-50; fax (2) 218-61-34; e-mail info@spe.be; internet www.spe.be; became a public company in 2000; 51% acquired in 2005 by Segebel, jointly owned by Gaz de France and Centrica (United Kingdom); builds, operates and maintains power plants; supplies electricity and gas under brand name Luminus; CEO LUC STERCKX.

Gas

Distrigas: 10 rue de l'Industrie, 1000 Brussels; tel. (2) 557-30-01; fax (2) 557-31-12; e-mail info@distri.be; internet www.distrigas.eu; supply and sale of natural gas; f. 2001; CEO ERWIN VAN BRUYSEL.

Fluxys NV/SA: Kunstlaan 31, 1040 Brussels; tel. (2) 282-72-11; fax (2) 230-02-39; e-mail berenice.crabs@fluxys.net; internet www.fluxys.net; owns and operates Belgian gas network; CEO SOPHIE DUTORDOIR.

SPE NV (Luminus): see Electricity.

Total Belgium: 52 rue de l'Industrie, 1040 Brussels; tel. (2) 288-99-33; fax (2) 288-32-60; e-mail gaznat.ventes@total.com; internet www.be.total.com; CEO CHRISTOPHE DE MARGERIE.

Water

Société Wallonne des Eaux: 41 rue de la Concorde, 4800 Verviers; tel. (8) 787-87; fax (8) 734-28-00; e-mail info@swde.be; internet www.swde.be; f. 1986; water production and distribution; Pres. RENÉ THISSEN; Dir-Gen. ERIC VAN SEVENANT.

Vlaamse Maatschappij voor Watervoorziening: Belliardstraat 73, 1040 Brussels; tel. (2) 238-94-11; fax (2) 230-97-98; e-mail info@vmw.be; internet www.vmw.be; Chair. LUC ASSELMAN; Dir-Gen. BERNARD BREDA.

TRADE UNIONS

Algemeen Christelijk Vakverbond/Confédération des Syndicats Chrétiens (ACV-CSC): Haachtsesteenweg 579, 1031 Brussels; tel. (2) 246-31-11; fax (2) 246-30-10; e-mail international@acv-csc.be; internet www.acv-online.be; Pres. LUC CORTEBEECK; 1.7m. mems.

Affiliated unions:

ACV Bouw en Industrie/CSC Bâtiment et Industrie (Building and Industrial Workers): 31 rue de Trèves, 1040 Brussels; tel. (2) 285-02-11; fax (2) 230-74-43; e-mail bouw_industrie@acv-csc.be; internet acv-bouw-industrie.acv-online.be; f. 1998 by merger of the Centrale Chrétienne des Diverses Industries and the Centrale Chrétienne des Travailleurs du Bois et du Bâtiment; Pres. LUC VAN DESSEL; Sec.-Gen. ISABELLE PARENT; 230,000 mems.

ACV Energie Chemie/CSC Energie-Chimie (Chemical and Energy Workers): 31–33 rue des Trèves, 1040 Brussels; tel. (2) 285-03-03; fax (2) 285-03-20; e-mail acv-energie-chemie@acv-csc.be; internet acv-energie-chemie.acv-online.be; f. 1912; Pres. ALFONS DE POTTER; Gen. Sec. ITALO RODOMONTI.

ACV Openbare Diensten/CSC Services Publics (Public Service Workers): 21 ave de l'Héliport, 1000 Brussels; tel. (2) 208-23-16; fax (2) 208-23-20; e-mail carine.mabbe@acv-csc.be; internet www.ccsp.be; f. 1921; Pres. LUC HAMELINCK.

ACV-CSC Textura (Textile and Clothing Workers): Koning Albertlaan 27, 9000 Ghent; tel. (9) 222-57-01; fax (9) 220-45-59; e-mail acv.csc.textura@acv-csc.be; internet acv-textura.acv-online.be; f. 1886; fmrly Centrale Chrétienne des Ouvriers de Textile et du Vêtement de Belgique; Pres. DIRK UYTTENHOVE; Gen. Secs JAN CALLAERT, REIN DE TREMERIE.

ACV—Transcom/CSC—Transcom (Railway, post, telecommunications, water, transport, shipping, civil aviation, radio, television and cultural workers): Galerie Agora, 105 rue Marché aux Herbes, BP 40, 1000 Brussels; tel. (2) 549-07-60; fax (2) 549-07-77; e-mail acv-transcom@acv-csc.be; internet www.acv-transcom.be; f. 1919; Pres. MARC VAN LAETHEM; Vice-Pres. PIERRE BERTIN.

ACV Voeding en Diensten/CSC Alimentation et Services (Food and Service Industries): Kartuizersstraat 70, 1000 Brussels; tel. (2) 500-28-11; fax (2) 500-28-99; e-mail ccvd-ccas@acv-csc.be; internet acv-voeding-diensten.acv-online.be; f. 1919; Chair. LOUIS DE PRINS; Gen. Sec. PHILIPPE YERNA.

Centrale Chrétienne des Métallurgistes de Belgique (ACV-Metaal/CSC-Métal) (Metal Workers): 127 rue de Heembeek, 1120 Brussels; tel. (2) 244-99-11; fax (2) 244-99-90; e-mail ccmb@acv-csc.be; internet www.csc-metal.be; Pres. M. DE WILDE.

Centrale Nationale des Employés (CNE) (Private Sector Workers): 46 rue Pépin, 5000 Namur; tel. (8) 125-90-90; fax (8) 122-50-47; internet www.cne-gnc.be; represents private sector workers in French-speaking regions; Sec.-Gen. RAYMOND COUMONT; 120,000 mems.

Christelijk Onderwijzersverbond (COV) (Schoolteachers): Koningsstraat 203, 1210 Brussels; tel. (2) 227-41-11; fax (2) 219-47-61; e-mail cov@acv-csc.be; internet www.cov.be; f. 1893; Pres. G. BOURDEAUD'HUI; Sec.-Gen. ROMAIN MAES.

Christelijke Onderwijs Centrale (COC) (Teachers): Trierstraat 33, 1040 Brussels; tel. (2) 285-04-40; fax (2) 230-28-83; e-mail coc.brussel@acv-csc.be; internet www.coc.be; f. 1993 as a result of a merger of the Flemish wings of three teachers' unions; Chair. ERIC DOLFEN; Gen. Sec. LOUIS RAYMAEKERS.

CSC Enseignement: 16 rue de la Victoire, 1060 Brussels; tel. (2) 542-09-00; fax (2) 542-09-08; e-mail csc-enseignement@acv-csc.be; internet www.csc-e-fond.be; Sec.-Gen. PROSPER BOULANGE; 38,000 mems.

Centrale Chrétienne du Personnel de l'Enseignement Technique (CCPET) (Teachers in Technical Education): 16 rue de la Victoire, 1060 Brussels; tel. (2) 542-09-00; fax (2) 542-09-08; e-mail ccpet-uceo@acv-csc.be.

Centrale Chrétienne des Professeurs de l'Enseignement Moyen et Normal Libre (Lay Teachers in Secondary and Teacher-Training Institutions): 16 rue de la Victoire, 1060 Brussels; tel. (2) 543-68-00; fax (2) 543-68-10; e-mail cemnl@acv-csc.be; internet www.cemnl.be; Pres. WILLEM MILLER.

Landelijke Bediendencentrale-Nationaal Verbond voor Kaderpersoneel (LBC-NVK) (Private Sector Workers): Sudermanstraat 5, 2000 Antwerp; tel. (3) 220-87-11; fax (3) 220-89-83; e-mail lbc-nvk@acv-csc.be; internet lbc-nvk.acv-online.be; f. 1912; represents private sector workers in Flemish-speaking regions; Sec.-Gen. FERRE WYCKMANS; 300,000 mems (2007).

Sporta-vsb (Sport): Kartuizersstraat 70, 1000 Brussels; tel. (2) 500-28-30; fax (2) 500-28-39; e-mail sporta@acv-csc.be; internet sporta.acv-online.be; Nat. Sec. DIRK DE VOS.

Fédération Générale du Travail de Belgique (FGTB)/Algemeen Belgisch Vakverbond (ABVV): 42 rue Haute, 1000 Brussels; tel. (2) 506-82-11; fax (2) 506-82-29; e-mail xavier.verboven@abvv.be; internet www.abvv.be; f. 1898; affiliated to ITUC; Pres. RUDY DE LEEUW; Gen. Sec. XAVIER VERBOVEN; an asscn of seven branch unions, three inter-regional orgs and 17 regional orgs with a total membership of 1,403,415m. in 2006.

Affiliated unions:

ABVV Metaal (Metal Workers): Jacob Jordaenstraat 17, 1000 Brussels; tel. (2) 627-74-11; fax (2) 627-74-90; e-mail info@abvvmetaal.org; internet www.abvvmetaal.org; f. 2006; represents metal workers in Flanders; together with FGTB Métallurgistes de Wallonie–Bruxelles, forms Centrale du Métal/Centrale van Metaal; Pres. HERWIG JORISSEN; Gen. Sec. ORTWIN MAGNUS; 180,459 mems (2006).

BELGIUM

Directory

Belgische Transportarbeidersbond/Union Belge des Ouvriers du Transport (Belgian Transport Workers' Union): Paardenmarkt 66, 2000 Antwerp; tel. (3) 224-34-11; fax (3) 224-34-49; e-mail btb@btb-abvv.be; internet www.ubot-fgtb.be; f. 1913; Pres. IVAN VICTOR; 39,476 mems (2006).

Centrale Alimentation-Horeca-Services/Centrale Voeding-Horeca-Diensten (Catering and Hotel Workers): 18 rue des Alexiens, 1000 Brussels; tel. (2) 512-97-00; fax (2) 512-53-68; e-mail horval@horval.be; internet www.horval.be; f. 1912; Pres. ALFONS DE MEY; Gen. Sec. ALAIN DETEMMERMAN; 105,353 mems (2006).

Centrale Générale des Services Publics/Algemene Centrale der Openbare Diensten (Public Sector Workers): Maison des Huit Heures, 9–11 place Fontainas, 1000 Brussels; tel. (2) 508-58-11; fax (2) 508-59-02; e-mail general@cgsp.be; internet www.acod.be; f. 1945; Pres. KAREL STESSENS; Gen. Sec. CHRIS RENIERS; 299,258 mems (2006).

FGTB Centrale Générale/ABVV Algemene Centrale (Central Union, building, timber, glass, paper, chemicals and petroleum industries): 26–28 rue Haute, 1000 Brussels; tel. (2) 549-05-49; fax (2) 514-16-91; e-mail info@accg.be; internet www.accg.be; Pres. ALAIN CLAUWERT; Sec.-Gen. JACQUES MICHIELS; 364,246 mems (2006).

FGTB Métallurgistes de Wallonie—Bruxelles: rue de Namur 47, 5000 Beez; tel. (8) 126-51-11; fax (8) 126-51-22; e-mail info@mwb-fgtb.be; internet www.mwb-fgtb.be; f. 2006; represents metal workers in Wallonia and Brussels-Capital regions; together with ABVV Metaal, forms Centrale du Métal/Centrale van Metaal; Pres. ANTONIO DI SANTO; Gen. Sec. NICO CUE.

FGTB—Textile, Vêtement et Diamant/ABVV—Textiel, Kleding en Diamant (Textile, Clothing and Diamond Workers): Barrierestraat 13, 8200 Brugge; tel. (50) 72-95-70; fax (50) 72-95-80; e-mail abvvtkd.fgtbtvd@glo.be; f. 1994; Pres. DONALD WITTEVRONGEL; 40,562 mems (2006).

Syndicat des Employés, Techniciens et Cadres de Belgique/Bond der Bedienden, Technici en Kaders van België (Employees, Technicians, Administrative Workers, Graphical and Paper Workers—SETCa / BBTK): 42 rue Haute, 1000 Brussels; tel. (2) 512-52-50; fax (2) 511-05-08; e-mail nationaal@setca-fgtb.be; internet www.bbtk.org; f. 1891; Pres. CHRISTIAN ROLAND; Vice-Pres. CARLOS POLENUS; 365,371 mems (2006).

Other unions:

Centrale Générale des Syndicats Libéraux de Belgique/Algemeen Centrale der Liberalen Vakverbonden van België (CGSLB/ACLVB) (General Federation of Liberal Trade Unions of Belgium): Koning Albertlaan 95, 9000 Ghent; tel. (9) 222-57-51; fax (9) 221-04-74; e-mail cgslb@cgslb.be; internet www.cgslb.be; f. 1891; present name adopted 1939; Nat. Pres. JAN VERCAMST; 220,000 mems.

Fédération Wallonne de l'Agriculture (FWA): 47 chaussée de Namur, 5030 Gembloux; tel. (81) 60-00-60; fax (81) 60-04-46; e-mail fwa@fwa.be; internet www.fwa.be; f. 2001; Pres. RENÉ LADOUCE; Sec.-Gen. J.-P. CHAMPAGNE.

Nationale Unie der Openbare Diensten (NUOD)/Union Nationale des Services Publics (UNSP): 36 blvd Bischoffsheim, 1000 Brussels; tel. (2) 219-88-02; fax (2) 223-38-36; e-mail unsinues@swing.be; f. 1983; Pres. LUC MICHEL; Sec.-Gen. PHILIPPE LAMBERT.

Transport

RAILWAYS

The Belgian railway network is one of the densest in the world. Train services are operated by the Société Nationale des Chemins de Fer Belges (SNCB), while the infrastructure is owned and managed by Infrabel. In 2008 there were 3,536 km of standard-gauge railways, of which some 2,950 km were electrified. A high-speed railway network for northern Europe, linking Belgium, France, Germany, the Netherlands and the United Kingdom, was fully operational by November 2007. The high-speed link between Brussels and Paris, France, was completed in 1998, the Brussels–Antwerp section was finished in 2000, and in 2002 the Leuven–Liège line opened for public use.

Société Nationale des Chemins de Fer Belges/Nationale Maatschappij der Belgische Spoorwegen (SNCB/NMBS): 85 rue de France, 1060 Brussels; tel. (2) 526-37-79; fax (2) 526-37-76; internet www.b-rail.be; f. 1926; 100% owned by SNCB Holding; 187.5m. passengers were carried in 2006; Pres. and Man. Dir MARC DESCHEEMAECKER.

Infrabel: 110 rue Bara, 1070 Brussels; tel. (2) 525-41-34; fax (2) 525-90-02; e-mail oss-me@infrabel.be; internet www.infrabel.be; f. 2005; responsible for rail infrastructure management; 83% owned by SNCB Holding, 17% owned by Federal Govt; CEO LUC LALLEMAND.

Thalys International: 20 place Stéphanie, 1050 Brussels; tel. (2) 548-06-00; e-mail corporate@thalys.com; internet www.thalys.com; f. 1995 as Westrail International; present name adopted 1999; operates rail passenger services between Brussels and Amsterdam (Netherlands), Cologne (Germany) and Paris (France); 62% owned by Société Nationale des Chemins de fer Français, 28% by SNCB and 10% by Deutsche Bahn (Germany); CEO JEAN-MICHEL DANCOISNE.

ROADS

In 2004 there were 1,747 km of motorways and some 12,531 km of other main or national roads. There were also 1,349 km of secondary or regional roads and an additional 134,940 km of minor roads.

Société Régionale Wallonne du Transport: 96 ave Gouverneur Bovesse, 5100 Namur; tel. (81) 32-27-11; fax (81) 32-27-10; e-mail jean-claude.phlypo@tec-wl.be; internet www.infotec.be; f. 1991; operates light railways, buses and trams; Dir-Gen. JEAN-CLAUDE PHLYPO.

Société des Transports Intercommunaux de Bruxelles: 15 ave de la Toison d'Or, 1050 Brussels; tel. (2) 515-20-00; fax (2) 515-32-84; e-mail flauscha@stib.irisnet.be; internet www.stib.be; operates a metro service, buses and trams; Dir-Gen. ALAIN FLAUSCH.

Vlaamse Vervoermaatschappij (De Lijn): Motstraat 20, 2800 Mechelen; tel. (15) 44-07-11; fax (15) 44-09-98; e-mail marketing.cd@delijn.be; internet www.delijn.be; f. 1991; operates bus and tram services under commercial name *De Lijn*; Dir-Gen. INGRID LIETEN.

INLAND WATERWAYS

There are over 1,520 km of inland waterways in Belgium, of which 660 km are navigable rivers and 860 km are canals.

In 1989 waterways administration was divided between the Flemish region (1,055 km), the Walloon region (450 km) and the Brussels region (15 km).

Flemish region:

De Scheepvaart NV: Havenstraat 44, 3500 Hasselt; tel. (11) 29-84-00; fax (11) 22-12-77; e-mail info@descheepvaart.be; internet www.descheepvaart.be; f. 2004; manages inland waterway system between Antwerp and Netherlands border; Chair. WILLY CLAES.

Waterwegen en Zeekanaal NV: Oostdijk 110, 2830 Willebroek; tel. (3) 860-62-11; fax (3) 860-62-00; e-mail info@wenz.be; internet www.wenz.be; f. 2006 to replace Departement Leefmilieu en Infrastructuur Administratie Waterwegen en Zeewezen; Man. Dir LEO CLINCKERS.

Walloon region:

Direction Générale des Voies Hydrauliques: Centre administratif du MET, 8 blvd du Nord, 5000 Namur; tel. (81) 77-29-94; fax (81) 77-37-80; e-mail jlaurent@met.wallonie.be; internet voies-hydrauliques.wallonie.be; Dir-Gen. JACQUES LAURENT.

Brussels region:

Haven van Brussel: 6 place des Armateurs, 1000 Brussels; tel. (2) 420-67-00; fax (2) 420-69-74; e-mail portdebruxelles@port.irisnet.be; internet www.havenvanbrussel.irisnet.be; f. 1993; Chair. LAURENCE BOVY; Gen. Mans CHARLES HUYGENS, ALFONS MOENS.

SHIPPING

The modernized port of Antwerp is the second biggest in Europe and handles about 80% of Belgian foreign trade by sea and inland waterways. It is also the largest railway port and has one of the largest petroleum refining complexes in Europe. Antwerp has 154 km of quayside and 17 dry docks. Other ports include Zeebrugge, Ostend, Ghent, Liège and Brussels.

Antwerp Port Authority: Havenhuis, Entrepotkaai 1, 2000 Antwerp; tel. (3) 205-20-11; fax (3) 205-20-28; e-mail info@haven.antwerpen.be; internet www.haven.antwerpen.be; owns and manages docks on Right Bank of the river Schelde, also manages docks on Left Bank; CEO EDDY BRUYNINCKX.

Principal Shipping Companies

Ahlers Logistic and Maritime Services: Noorderlaan 139, 2030 Antwerp; tel. (3) 543-72-11; fax (3) 543-74-77; e-mail info@ahlers.com; internet www.ahlers.com; shipping agency, ship and crew management, forwarding; Exec. Chair. CHRISTIAN LEYSEN.

De Keyser Thornton: Oude Leeuwenui 25–27, 2000 Antwerp; tel. (3) 205-31-00; fax (3) 205-31-32; e-mail info@multimodal.be; internet www.dekeyserthornton.com; f. 1853; shipping agency, forwarding and warehousing services; Man. Dir PHILIP VAN TILBURG.

Manuport Group: Vosseschijnstraat 59, Haven 182, 2030 Antwerp; tel. (3) 204-93-00; fax (3) 204-93-01; e-mail info@manuportgroup.com; internet www.manuportgroup.com; forwarding, customs clearance, liner and tramp agencies, chartering, Rhine and inland barging, multi-purpose bulk/bags fertilizer, minerals and agri-bulk terminal; Pres. and CEO WALTER SIJMONS.

BELGIUM   Directory

P&O Ferries: Leopold II Dam 13, 8380 Zeebrugge; tel. (50) 54-22-11; fax (50) 54-23-00; internet www.ponsf.com; 6 ships; ro-ro ferry services between Zeebrugge, Hull, Middlesbrough and Tilbury; CEO ROBERT WOODS.

Transeuropa Ferries NV: Slijkensesteenweg 5, 8400 Ostend; tel. (5) 934-02-60; fax (5) 934-02-61; e-mail info@transeuropaferries.com; internet www.transeuropaferries.com; f. 2001; five ships; shipping, stevedoring and line representation; operates between Ostend and Ramsgate (United Kingdom).

CIVIL AVIATION

The main international airport is at Brussels, with a direct train service between the air terminal and central Brussels. There are also international airports at Antwerp, Charleroi, Liège and Ostend.

Brussels Airlines: b.house, Airport Building 26, Ringbaan, 1831 Diegem; tel. (2) 754-19-06; fax (2) 723-84-09; internet www.brusselsairlines.be; f. 2007 by merger of SN Brussels Airlines and Virgin Express; owned by SN Airholding; scheduled services within Europe and to Africa, Asia, the Middle East and North America; Pres. and CEO PHILIPPE VANDER PUTTEN.

Tourism

Belgium has several towns of rich historic and cultural interest, such as Antwerp, Bruges, Brussels, Durbuy, Ghent, Liège, Namur and Tournai. The country's seaside towns attract many visitors. The forest-covered Ardennes region is renowned for hill-walking and gastronomy. In 2005 tourist arrivals totalled 6.7m.; receipts from tourism in that year totalled US $10,879m.

Brussels Tourism.com (BT.c): 8 rue du Rouge Gorge, 1170 Brussels; tel. and fax (2) 672-82-22; e-mail info@brusselstourism.com; internet www.brusselstourism.com; f. 1998; Editor MARC HAULOT.

Office de Promotion du Tourisme Wallonie et Bruxelles: 30 rue Saint-Bernard, 1060 Brussels; tel. (7) 022-10-21; fax (2) 513-69-50; e-mail info@opt.be; internet www.belgique-tourisme.net; f. 1981; promotion of tourism in French-speaking Belgium; Dir-Gen. VIVIANE JACOBS.

Toerisme Vlaanderen: Grasmarkt 61, 1000 Brussels; tel. (2) 504-03-90; fax (2) 513-04-75; e-mail info@toerismevlaanderen.be; internet www.visitflanders.com; f. 1985; official promotion and policy body for tourism in Flemish region of Belgium; Administrator Gen. RAYMONDA VERDYCK.

BELIZE

Introductory Survey

Location, Climate, Language, Religion, Flag, Capital

Belize lies on the Caribbean coast of Central America, with Mexico to the north-west and Guatemala to the south-west. The climate is sub-tropical, tempered by trade winds. The temperature averages 24°C (75°F) from November to January, and 27°C (81°F) from May to September. Annual rainfall ranges from 1,290 mm (51 ins) in the north to 4,450 mm (175 ins) in the south. The average annual rainfall in Belize City is 1,650 mm (65 ins). Belize is ethnically diverse, the population (according to the 2000 census) consisting of 49% Mestizos (Maya-Spanish), 25% Creoles (those of predominantly African descent), 11% Amerindian (mainly Maya), 6% Garifuna ('Black Caribs', descendants of those deported from the island of Saint Vincent in 1797) and communities of Asians, Portuguese, German Mennonites and others of European descent. English is the official language and an English Creole is widely understood. Spanish is the mother-tongue of some 15% of the population but is spoken by many others. There are also speakers of Garifuna (Carib), Maya and Ketchi, while the Mennonites speak a German dialect. Most of the population profess Christianity, with about 76% being Roman Catholics in 2005. The national flag (proportions usually 3 by 5) is dark blue, with narrow horizontal red stripes at the upper and lower edges; at the centre is a white disc containing the state coat of arms, bordered by an olive wreath. The capital is Belmopan.

Recent History

Belize, known as British Honduras until June 1973, was first colonized by British settlers (the 'Baymen') in the 17th century, but was not recognized as a British colony until 1862. In 1954 a new Constitution granted universal adult suffrage and provided for the creation of a legislative assembly. The territory's first general election, in April 1954, was won by the only party then organized, the People's United Party (PUP), led by George Price. The PUP won all subsequent elections until 1984. In 1961 Price was appointed First Minister under a new ministerial system of government. The colony was granted internal self-government in 1964, with the United Kingdom retaining responsibility for defence, external affairs and internal security. Following an election in 1965, Price became Premier and a bicameral legislature was introduced. In 1970 the capital of the territory was moved from Belize City to the newly built town of Belmopan.

Much of the recent history of Belize has been dominated by the territorial dispute with Guatemala, particularly in the years prior to Belize's independence (see below). This was achieved on 21 September 1981, within the Commonwealth, and with Price becoming Prime Minister. However, the failure of the 1981 draft treaty with Guatemala, and the clash of opposing wings within the ruling party, undermined the dominance of the PUP, and the party's 30 years of rule ended at the general election held in December 1984. The new United Democratic Party (UDP) Government, led by Manuel Esquivel, pledged to revive Belize's economy through increased foreign investment. However, the PUP regained power following the general election of September 1989 and Price was again appointed Prime Minister.

The PUP called a general election in June 1993, 15 months before it was constitutionally due, following recent successes at local and by-elections. However, at the election the party performed poorly, securing only 13 seats in the House of Representatives. An alliance of the UDP and the National Alliance for Belizean Rights (NABR) secured the remaining 16 seats (the total number of seats having been increased from 28 to 29) and Esquivel was appointed Prime Minister.

In June 1994 the sale of citizenship, of which many Hong Kong Chinese had taken advantage, was officially ended, following criticism that the system was open to abuse. In June 1995 the Minister of Human Resources, Community and Youth Development, Culture and Women's Affairs, Phillip S. W. Goldson, was relieved of responsibility for immigration and nationality affairs, following allegations implicating him in the sale of false residence and visitor permits to nationals of the People's Republic of China and Taiwan. Reportedly some 5,000 such permits had been issued over the previous 12-month period, and the recipients then smuggled into the USA.

At the general election of August 1998 the PUP, led by Said Musa, won an overwhelming victory, securing 26 of the 29 seats in the House of Representatives. The UDP obtained the remaining three seats. The result reflected popular discontent with the outgoing Government's structural adjustment policies, including the introduction of value-added tax (VAT), which the PUP had pledged to repeal. The PUP had also promised to create 15,000 new jobs, to build 10,000 new houses and to reduce public utility tariffs. Following the defeat of his party, Esquivel, who had lost his seat in the House of Representatives, resigned as leader of the UDP. He was succeeded by Dean Barrow. On 1 September Said Musa was sworn in as Prime Minister.

In July 1999 Musa issued a statement rejecting allegations that Michael Ashcroft, a businessman with dual British/Belizean nationality and Belize's ambassador to the UN, had used improper influence in Belizean affairs and was involved in money-laundering. In March 2000 Ashcroft resigned his UN post after receiving a life peerage in the British House of Lords. In late 2000 the remit of an inquiry commissioned by the British Government into Belize's financial system was expanded to investigate public investment companies operating from Belize, including Ashcroft's Carlisle Holdings. In December 2001 it was announced that the Government had refused the United Kingdom's offer of £10m. of debt relief in exchange for a reform of its financial regime and an end to tax relief given to Carlisle Holdings and another company.

On 5 April 2000 Belize became the eighth country to ratify the Rome Statute of the International Criminal Court, which was to be established following its ratification by 60 states. On 14 February 2001, following legislative approval the previous November, the leaders of 11 Caribbean countries, including Belize, signed an agreement to establish a Caribbean Court of Justice, based in Trinidad and Tobago. The Court was to replace the Privy Council in the United Kingdom as the final court of appeal, and would allow the execution of convicted criminals. In late October the Attorney-General defended before a panel of the Inter-American Commission on Human Rights a proposed amendment to the Constitution that would prevent prisoners sentenced to death from appealing to the Privy Council in the United Kingdom. This followed a petition to the Commission by a group of prisoners who claimed that the amendment was incompatible with the Government's obligations to an Organization of American States (OAS) treaty on human rights. The Attorney-General maintained that Belize had the right to legislate in its own domestic affairs. In July 2004 parliament approved legislation sanctioning Belize's membership of the Caribbean Court of Justice in its original jurisdiction. However, the Government failed to garner the three-quarters' majority required to amend the Constitution that would have allowed Belize to participate fully as part of the appellate jurisdiction. Thus, the Privy Council remained Belize's final court of appeal.

In February 2002 the policy of economic citizenship was formally abolished. However, a report produced in late July by the Ministry of Foreign Affairs substantiated claims that the immigration authorities had apparently continued the practice illegally until that month. In late November a Commission of Inquiry into the economic citizenship programme reported that while no person was granted Belizean citizenship under the programme following its annulment in February, over 1,000 applications were approved during the first seven months of 2002 and a number of irregularities had been detected.

In October 2002 a High Seas Fishing Act was approved by the Government. Under the Act, the activities of fishing boats operating under the Belizean flag would be monitored by satellite and licences were to be issued from July 2003. In 2001 the Government had been accused of allowing illegal fishing to be carried out by foreign vessels using the Belizean flag as a so-called 'flag of convenience'.

In its campaign for the March 2003 general election the PUP, which had repealed the unpopular VAT during its 1998–2003 administration, promised that, if re-elected, it would abolish sales tax on basic items and move towards the eradication of personal income tax. The party had also pledged to provide access to primary and secondary education for all children. In the election, which took place on 5 March, the PUP won 22 seats in the House of Representatives, while the UDP increased its legislative representation to seven seats (from three). Musa became the country's first Prime Minister to be sworn in for a second term in office.

In January 2004 Musa announced a wide-ranging reallocation of cabinet portfolios. In line with pre-election pledges, a number of measures were implemented in that year to improve security, including the inauguration of a Police Information Technology Unit, a Scenes of Crimes Technicians' Unit and a Legal Affairs Office. In addition, a project to construct hurricane shelters and a disaster preparedness system was completed in mid-2005, following the destruction wreaked by 'Hurricane Iris' in October 2001. Access to education was also improved by the construction of more than 100 new classrooms and an increase in the provision of scholarships to the University of Belize. Nevertheless, in 2004 the PUP struggled to maintain popular support as protracted financial crises in the Development Finance Corporation (DFC) and the Social Security Board (SSB) forced the Government to reduce spending on social projects (see below).

An audit into the SSB's financial operations in 2004 found that it had made a series of unsecured loans, principally to the housing and tourism sectors and to the DFC, incurring substantial financial losses. A Senate Select Committee on Social Security was established in September to investigate the SSB's alleged maladministration between 1999 and 2004. In July 2006 the Committee disclosed that they had found evidence of negligence and recklessness in the purchase and sale of mortgage loans. Following the Committee's recommendations, the Government subsequently dismissed the SSB's General Manager and board of directors. Following a senate investigation, in December 2004 it was announced that the DFC was to be dissolved. The Government affirmed that upon liquidation of the Corporation's assets, priority would be given to the DFC's debt commitments to the SSB. In May 2005 a three-member commission, appointed by Musa, launched an investigation into the Corporation's failure. On 1 August 2006 the commission, chaired by David Price, began a public hearing into the reported mismanagement at the DFC.

The Musa Government's 2005/06 budget, announced in January 2005, introduced tax increases and withheld the payment of the final instalment of an agreed public-sector pay rise. The proposals were met with widespread industrial action, particularly in the education sector, and thousands participated in anti-Government protests. In late January the National Trade Union Congress of Belize organized a two-day general strike that resulted in the closure of many schools and businesses and the temporary loss of water, electricity and telephone services. Following negotiations with the civil servants' trade unions, Musa agreed to defer implementation of the tax increases until March. The Government also proposed to complete salary increases over three years.

In 2005 controversy arose over the ownership of Belize Telecommunications Ltd (BTL). In April 2001 the Government had sold the company to Carlisle Holdings. Three years later, in April 2004, it bought back those shares and immediately sold them to US company Innovative Communications Company (ICC). However, in early February 2005 the Government resumed control of BTL after it claimed that ICC had not met a payment deadline. ICC maintained that the default was owing to government failure to meet certain conditions regarding licensing agreements and guaranteed rates of return. In March the Chief Justice launched an inquiry into the various ownerships of BTL between April 2001 and February 2005.

On 11 March 2005 ICC was granted a temporary injunction by a court in Miami, Florida, USA, that returned control of BTL to the US company and reinstated four ICC-appointed board members. However, the Supreme Court of Belize ruled that the injunction was not enforceable in Belize. Meanwhile, members of the Belize Communication Workers' Union (BCWU) demanded that majority ownership of BTL be transferred to the company's employees. In mid-April the anti-Government feeling led to a strike by BTL employees and several days of violent protests by union members and students, during which shops were looted and more than 100 people were arrested. The armed forces were deployed to restore order in the capital. Protesters disrupted telephone services to large areas of the country and on 22 April the entire telecommunications network was suspended for several days. On 17 June the House of Representatives approved the sale of BTL shares: 20% would be sold to employees, 12.5% to a subsidiary of Carlisle Holdings, which already controlled 25% of BTL, and 5% to other Belizeans. The BCWU subsequently filed a complaint in the Supreme Court, asserting that the sale of a further 12.5% interest to Carlisle Holdings breached the share-ownership limit of 25%. However, in late August the Court of Appeals overturned earlier supreme court rulings upholding government action in BTL, and ruled that control of the telecommunications company be returned to ICC and that all sales of BTL shares since 9 February be annulled.

Furthermore, on 4 October 2005 Belize Water Services Company Ltd was renationalized after the Government reached agreement with the Anglo-Dutch company CASCAL to repurchase some 83% of the company for the same amount it sold the shares in 2001. Musa was expected to appoint a new board of directors and new management. The newly acquired shares were put on sale to the general public, with preference given to Belizean citizens.

Two former members of the Cabinet rejoined the Government in early November 2005: Mark Espat was installed as the Minister of National Development, Investment and Culture, while Cordel Hyde was appointed Minister of Defence, Housing, Sports and Youth.

In February 2006 the Leader of the Opposition, Dean Barrow, declared his intention to relinquish the presidency of the UDP were his party to lose the forthcoming municipal elections—the last to be held before the general election due in 2008. However, at the elections on 1 March 2006 the UDP won a convincing victory, obtaining 64 of the 67 local council seats at stake in nine municipalities. It was anticipated that the result, which marked the PUP's first major election defeat in a decade, was likely to influence government policy decisions in 2006–07. In what was widely interpreted as an attempt to gain public favour, the 2006/07 budget repealed some of the tax increases introduced in 2005.

In a cabinet reorganization in April 2006 Eamon Courtenay, who had been dismissed as Minister of Foreign Trade in December 2004, returned to government, assuming responsibility for foreign affairs and foreign trade, a portfolio hitherto held by Godfrey Smith. Smith retained responsibility for the Ministry of Tourism, Information and National Emergency Management. Francis Fonseca, the Attorney-General and Minister of Education, was given additional responsibility for labour. Vildo Marin, formerly Minister of Health and Labour, was installed as Minister of Agriculture and Fisheries. Marin replaced Michael Espat, who was appointed Minister of Works, while the former Minister of Works, Transport and Communications and Tourism, José Coye, was assigned the health, local government and transport and communications portfolios. Musa remained responsible for finance and the public service, while Deputy Prime Minister John Briceño retained responsibility for natural resources and the environment.

Musa dismissed Cordel Hyde and Mark Espat from the Cabinet in May 2007 after they failed to vote against a motion presented by the opposition, which criticized the Government for approving a loan to a private hospital-operating company in 2004 without consulting the Cabinet or House of Representatives. In the subsequent cabinet reshuffle, Musa assumed responsibility for the national development portfolio and Rodwell Ferguson replaced Hyde as Minister of Defence, Youth and Sports. The Minister of Agriculture and Fisheries Vildo Marin was also assigned the role of Deputy Prime Minister and Florencio Marin became Minister of Natural Resources and the Environment.

A new political party, the People's National Party, was launched in February 2007 with a stated agenda of combating corruption in the country and led by an environmentalist, Wil Maheia. The party joined a coalition, the National Belizean Alliance, to contest the February 2008 general election.

The opposition UDP won a convincing victory in the general election held on 7 February 2008, securing 25 of the 31 legislative seats and 57.0% of valid votes cast. The PUP's representation was significantly reduced, to the six remaining seats, after obtaining 41.0% of the vote. Some 74.5% of eligible voters participated in the poll. The UDP had campaigned against what it perceived as corruption and mismanagement in the Musa administration and its leader, Dean Barrow, had pledged to take steps to lower the cost of living by reforming the tax system and reducing utility rates. Barrow was sworn in as Prime Minister on 8 February. In a concurrent referendum, 61.5% of voters supported proposals for an elected Senate; Barrow had previously, however, declared his opposition to such an amendment to Belize's system of government.

In the US Department of State's 2006 Trafficking in Persons Report, published on 5 June, Belize was placed on the Tier Three list for failing to meet minimum standards to address the problem of human-trafficking and for making insufficient effort to improve conditions. However, Belize was removed from the list four months later after having been judged to have made sufficient progress in tackling the issue. In October 2007 the US Government provided a grant of US $40,000 to aid in the implementation of a three-year programme aimed at the prevention of human-trafficking crimes and the prosecution of those involved in such activities.

The frontier with Guatemala was agreed by a convention in 1859, but this was declared invalid by Guatemala in 1940. Guatemalan claims to sovereignty of Belize date back to the middle of the 19th century and were written into Guatemala's Constitution in 1945. In November 1975 and July 1977 British troops and aircraft were sent to protect Belize from the threat of Guatemalan invasion, and a battalion of troops and a detachment of fighter aircraft remained in the territory. In November 1980 the UN General Assembly overwhelmingly approved a resolution urging that Belize be granted independence (similar resolutions having been adopted in 1978 and 1979), and the United Kingdom decided to proceed with a schedule for independence, after having excluded the possibility of any cessation of land to Guatemala. A tripartite conference in March 1981 appeared to produce a sound basis for a final settlement, with Guatemala accepting Belizean independence in exchange for access to the Caribbean Sea through Belize and the use of certain offshore cayes and their surrounding waters. Further tripartite talks in the same year collapsed, however, as a result of renewed claims by Guatemala to Belizean land. With Belizean independence imminent, Guatemala made an unsuccessful appeal to the UN Security Council to intervene, severing diplomatic relations with the United Kingdom and sealing its border with Belize on 7 September. Tripartite talks in January 1983 collapsed when Belize rejected Guatemala's proposal that Belize should cede the southern part of the country. This claim was subsequently suspended. Belize is a member of the Caribbean Community and Common Market (CARICOM, see p. 196), whose summit conferences have consistently expressed support for Belize's territorial integrity against claims by Guatemala.

At independence the United Kingdom had agreed to leave troops as protection and for training of the Belize Defence Force. Discussions with Guatemala resumed in February 1985. In July the new draft Guatemalan Constitution omitted the previous unconditional claim to Belize, while Esquivel had previously acknowledged Guatemala's right of access to the Caribbean Sea, but no settlement was forthcoming. In April 1987 renewed discussions were held between Guatemala, the United Kingdom and Belize (although Belize was still regarded by Guatemala as being only an observer at the meetings), and in May 1988 the formation of a permanent joint commission (which, in effect, entailed a recognition of the Belizean state by Guatemala) was announced.

In September 1991 Belize and Guatemala signed an accord under the terms of which Belize pledged to legislate to reduce its maritime boundaries and to allow Guatemala access to the Caribbean Sea and use of its port facilities. In return, President Jorge Serrano Elías of Guatemala officially announced his country's recognition of Belize as an independent state and established diplomatic relations. In January 1992 the Maritime Areas Bill was approved in the Belizean House of Representatives. The legislation, however, had caused serious divisions within the UDP, leading to the formation, in January 1992, of the NABR (see above), led by the former UDP Deputy Leader, Derek Aikman. In November the Guatemalan legislature voted to ratify Serrano's decision to recognize Belize. Serrano, however, indicated that the accord was not definitive and that Guatemala maintained its territorial claim over Belize. In April 1993 Belize and Guatemala signed a non-aggression pact, affirming their intent to refrain from the threat or use of force against each other, and preventing either country from being used as a base for aggression against the other.

In January 1994 responsibility for the defence of Belize was transferred to the Belize Defence Force; all British troops were withdrawn by October, with the exception of some 180 troops who remained to organize training for jungle warfare. In March Guatemala formally reaffirmed its territorial claim to Belize, prompting the Belizean Minister of Foreign Affairs to seek talks with the British Government regarding assistance with national defence. In September 1996 the Ministers of Foreign Affairs of Belize and Guatemala conducted preliminary talks in New York, USA, concerning a resumption of negotiations on the territorial dispute. Further such discussions were conducted in Miami, Florida, USA, in February 1997. In November 1998, at a meeting of ambassadors and officials of both countries, conducted in Miami, agreement was reached on the establishment of a joint commission to deal with immigration, cross-border traffic and respect for the rights of both countries' citizens.

In February 2000 Guatemalan forces captured three members of the Belizean border patrol, who later escaped; the men were assisted in their escape by the Belizean ambassador, who was expelled from Guatemala as a result. Bilateral talks resumed in May and in August a panel of negotiators was installed at the headquarters of the OAS. In November the two countries signed an agreement to initiate joint patrols of the unofficial common border and to hold quarterly meetings between operational commanders.

In June 2002 the Ministers of Foreign Affairs from both countries met under OAS auspices to discuss the border dispute issue. Following further, OAS-mediated, negotiations in August, in early September proposals were outlined for a solution to the dispute. These included the provision that Guatemala would recognize Belize's land boundary as laid out in the treaty of 1859 and the creation of a model settlement, complete with modern amenities, for peasants and landless farmers in the border area. Guatemalan farmers occupying land within the Belizean border were to have priority rights of residency on this settlement. There was also provision for the establishment of a free trade agreement between the two countries and a Development Trust Fund, to be managed by the Inter-American Development Bank, with the money being used to alleviate poverty in the border region. In addition, Guatemala would be granted a 200-sq mile Exclusive Economic Zone in the Gulf of Honduras, although Belize and Honduras would retain fishing rights and 50% of any mineral resources discovered in the sea-bed. A Commission comprising Belize, Guatemala and Honduras would oversee the establishment and management of an Ecological Marine Park in coastal areas and a separate Tripartite Regional Fisheries Management Commission would manage fishing in the Gulf of Honduras. However, in September 2003 the Guatemalan Government announced that it planned to reject the OAS-proposed agreement. Delegations from the two countries met for further OAS-mediated negotiations in May 2004. Under discussion was the establishment of a Joint Commission that would explore means of promoting mutual confidence, such as a free trade agreement, a mutual legal assistance treaty and the joint promotion of tourism. In May 2005 Musa raised the possibility of bringing the dispute before the International Court of Justice (ICJ). However, in September, at the OAS headquarters in Washington, DC, representatives of the two countries signed a new Agreement on a Framework of Negotiation and Confidence-Building Measures between Belize and Guatemala. The first meetings under the new accord were held in November in Belize, with future meetings scheduled to take place every 45 days thereafter. In March 2006 a representative from Honduras and an expert on the UN Convention on the Law of the Sea were included in negotiations on the disputed maritime area. The meeting then proceeded to discuss other matters under the confidence-building agenda, including the issue of people-trafficking. Following almost two years of negotiations, in late March 2007 representatives of Belize and Guatemala also signed a preliminary trade accord: the agreement would allow 150 products to be traded duty-free. However, due to a lack of progress in the talks regarding the border area, in November the Secretary-General of the OAS reiterated the Prime Minister's suggestion that the two countries take the dispute to the ICJ. Musa said that a referendum would be held on this issue after the next general election, due to take place on 7 February 2008.

In August 2005 the Government signed a reciprocal shipboarding agreement with the USA in an attempt to prevent the transportation of weapons of mass destruction.

Government

Belize is a constitutional monarchy, with the British sovereign as Head of State. Executive authority is vested in the sovereign and is exercised by the Governor-General, who is appointed on the advice of the Prime Minister, must be of Belizean nationality, and acts, in almost all matters, on the advice of the Cabinet. The Governor-General is also advised by an appointed Belize Advisory Council. Legislative power is vested in the bicameral National Assembly, comprising a Senate (12 members appointed by the Governor-General) and a House of Representatives (31 members elected by universal adult suffrage for five years, subject to dissolution). The Governor-General appoints the Prime Minister and, on the latter's recommendation, other ministers. The Cabinet is responsible to the House of Representatives.

Defence

The Belize Defence Force was formed in 1978 and was based on a combination of the existing Police Special Force and the Belize Volunteer Guard. Military service is voluntary. Provision has been made for the establishment of National Service if necessary to supplement normal recruitment. As assessed at November 2006, the regular armed forces totalled an estimated 1,050, with some 700 militia reserves. In 1994 all British forces were withdrawn from Belize and in 2006 some 30 troops remained to organize training for jungle warfare. The defence budget for 2006 was an estimated BZ $32m. On 28 November 2005 the Belize National Coast Guard Service was inaugurated to combat drugs-trafficking, illegal immigration and illegal fishing in Belize's territorial waters. The Coast Guard comprised 58 volunteer officers from the Belize Defence Force, the Belize Police Department, the Customs and Excise Department, the National Fire Service, the Department of Immigration and Nationality Services, the Port Authority and the Fisheries Department.

Economic Affairs

In 2006, according to estimates by the World Bank, Belize's gross national income (GNI), measured at average 2004–06 prices, was US $1,084m., equivalent to US $3,650 per head (or $6,650 per head on an international purchasing-power parity basis). During 1996–2006 Belize's population grew at an average annual rate of 3.0%, while gross domestic product (GDP) per head increased, in real terms, at an average rate of 2.8%. Overall GDP increased, in real terms, at an average rate of 5.9% per year in 1996–2006; growth was 4.0% in 2006.

Although 38% of the country is considered suitable for agriculture, only an estimated 6.6% of total area was used for agricultural purposes in 2003. Nevertheless, agriculture, hunting, forestry and fishing employed an estimated 22.3% of the working population in 2005 and contributed an estimated 13.3% of GDP, at current prices, in 2006. The principal cash crops are citrus fruits (citrus concentrates accounted for 19.8% of total domestic exports in 2006), sugar cane (sugar accounted for 18.4%) and bananas (an estimated 9.3%). Having recovered from hurricane damage in 2001, banana production increased by 70.1% in 2003, leading to an increase in banana export revenues of 57.6%. Production and export revenues subsequently stabilized in 2004–05. Agricultural policy promotes the cultivation of crops for domestic consumption and the diversification of crops for export. Maize, red kidney beans and rice are the principal domestic food crops, and the development of crops, such as soybeans (soya beans), papayas, organic rice and cocoa is being encouraged. The country is largely self-sufficient in fresh meat and eggs. Belize has considerable timber reserves, particularly of tropical hardwoods, and the forestry sector is being developed. In 2004 forestry and logging revenues increased by 8.1%; this followed a 5.2% decline in the sector in 2003, owing to damage by the pine bark beetle, and to the introduction of a licensing system intended to limit the exploitation of mahogany, in accordance with the UN's Convention on International Trade in Endangered Species of Wild Fauna and Flora (CITES). Largely owing to a massive expansion in farmed shrimp production, the fishing sector increased by 110.5% in 2003. More modest increases, of 4.8% and 8.3%, were recorded in 2004 and 2005, respectively. In 2006 marine products were Belize's fourth largest export earner, providing 15.6% of total domestic export revenue. The real GDP of the agricultural sector increased at an average annual rate of 7.2% in 1996–2006; real agricultural GDP declined by 5.5% in 2006.

Industry (including mining, manufacturing, construction, water and electricity) employed 15.5% of the working population in 2005 and contributed 20.0% of GDP in 2006. Mining and quarrying accounted for an estimated 0.4% of GDP in 2006 and for only 0.2% of employment in 2005. Industrial GDP increased at an average annual rate of 6.0% in 1996–2006; real industrial GDP increased by 25.6% in 2006.

Manufacturing accounted for 11.7% of GDP in 2006 and employed 7.3% of the working population in 2005. Dominant activities are the manufacture of clothing and the processing of agricultural products, particularly sugar cane (for sugar and rum). Manufacturing GDP increased at an average rate of 7.3% per year during 1996–2006; the sector recorded a sharp increase of 35.3% in 2006.

Imports of fuels and lubricants accounted for 16.5% of the total cost of imports in 2005. In the late 1990s the Mollejón hydroelectric station, on the Macal River, began operations. In 2001 construction began of a controversial second hydroelectric dam at Chalillo on the Macal River; upon completion, the dam would be operated by its Canadian contractor, Fortis Inc, before transfer to state ownership in 2031. The dam was expected to provide 7.3 MW of electricity annually and, according to the Government, would meet Belize's energy needs for 50 years. Environmentalist groups contended that the dam would destroy the habitat of some 40 species of rare animals and birds, including the endangered scarlet macaw. Following a protracted appeals process, in January 2004 the Privy Council in the United Kingdom upheld the Belizean Government's decision that construction of the dam should proceed. The dam began generating electricity in November 2005. In 2004 Hydro Maya Ltd signed a 15-year agreement to provide 2.8 MW of electricity annually to Belize Electricity Ltd (BEL). Construction of a hydroelectric dam on the Rio Grande River, to generate the required power, was scheduled for completion in 2007. In 2005 Belize signed the PetroCaribe agreement with Venezuela, under which it would be allowed to purchase petroleum from that country at reduced prices. In the same year Belize Cogeneration Energy Ltd began construction of a bagasse-fuelled co-generation facility, adjacent to the Tower Hill sugar factory. The biomass plant was expected to begin generating electricity in 2008, supplying 13.5 MW to BEL and 9 MW to Belize Sugar Industries. Belize Natural Energy discovered Belize's first commercially viable oilfield in 2005, with proven recoverable reserves of 10m. barrels.

The services sector employed 62.3% of the working population in 2005 and contributed 66.8% of GDP in 2006. Tourism development is concentrated on promoting 'eco-tourism', based on the attraction of Belize's natural environment, particularly its rainforests and the barrier reef, the second largest in the world. The number of cruise-ship passengers decreased by 18.0% in 2006, while the number of stop-over visitors rose by 4.5%; overall tourist arrivals totalled 903,238 in that year, a decline of 12.9% compared with 2005. The GDP of the services sector increased, in real terms, at an average annual rate of 6.3% in 1996–2006; real sectoral GDP increased by 2.8% in 2006. Belize's 'offshore' financial centre opened in 1996 and in 2005 there were more than 27,000 registered active 'offshore' companies.

In 2006 Belize recorded an estimated trade deficit of BZ $185.7m. and an estimated deficit of BZ $24.7m. on the current account of the balance of payments. In 2005 the principal source of imports was the USA (accounting for 39.1% of the total), followed by Mexico. The USA was also the principal export market, accounting for 52.3% of total exports in 2005, followed by the United Kingdom (22.0%). The principal exports in 2005 were orange concentrate (21.2%), marine products (excluding aquarium fish, 20.7%) and sugar (16.9%). The principal imports in that year were machinery and transport equipment (16.8%) and mineral fuels and lubricants (16.5%).

For the financial year 2006/07 there was a projected budgetary deficit of BZ $97.8m. At the end of December 2006 Belize's total external debt was estimated at $1,911m., of which $229.8m. was domestic public debt. The annual rate of inflation averaged 1.6% in 2000–05. Consumer prices increased by 3.6% in 2005. In April 2005 some 11.0% of the economically active population were unemployed. Many Belizeans, however, work abroad, and remittances to the country from such workers are an important source of income. Emigration, mainly to the USA, is offset by the number of immigrants and refugees from other Central American countries, particularly El Salvador.

Belize is a member of the Caribbean Community and Common Market (CARICOM, see p. 196), the Organization of American States (OAS, see p. 360) and the Inter-American Development Bank (IDB, see p. 308). Belize is also a member of the Central American Integration System (SICA, see p. 201). As a member of the Commonwealth, Belize enjoys guaranteed access to the European Union (EU) under the Cotonou Agreement (see p. 301), and tariff-free access to the USA under the Caribbean Basin Initiative. Belize joined CARICOM's Caribbean Single Market and Economy (CSME), which was established on 1 January 2006. The CSME was intended to enshrine the free movement of goods, services and labour throughout the CARICOM region, although only six of the organization's 15 members were signatories to the new project from its inauguration.

The Musa administration, which assumed office in 1998, undertook wide-ranging measures to restructure the tax system and increase public investment. However, extensive hurricane damage in 2000 and 2001 had a negative impact on the economy. In 2003 public and publicly guaranteed debt reached 102.3% of GDP and the current account deficit was equivalent to 18.2% of GDP. In 2004 the Government introduced a series of measures intended to improve the collection of taxes, particularly land tax and customs duties, and subsequently imposed additional increases in business taxes, notably affecting banks, real estate agencies and casinos. The Government in 2005 also withheld the final instalment of agreed increases in pensions and public-sector salaries, a move that met with popular protests (see Recent History). Amendments to the Income and Business Tax Act were expected to capture 40% of revenues from the oil industry in the 2007/08 financial year; this sector had enjoyed impressive growth following the discovery of a large deposit of high quality crude oil in 2005. In order to process the additional revenue from this sector effectively and improve transparency, the Government established the Petroleum Revenue Management Fund. In early 2007, the Government successfully restructured 98.1% of its outstanding public debt; some US $960m. was converted into high yield bonds, scheduled to reach maturity in 2029. Belize experienced a period of economic uncertainty in 2005–06; in addition to the problems regarding external financing, the economy had to contend with restructuring in the agricultural sector (following the cessation of EU preferential prices for sugar and bananas in 2006). However, the impact on these sectors was less severe than expected. In 2007 Belize was accorded a portion of the sugar quota hitherto assigned to Saint Christopher and Nevis (following the closure of the industry there), which would increase exports to the EU by around 20%. In addition, areas involved in the cultivation of banana and sugar crop were expected to benefit from EU-funded rehabilitation schemes. An IMF review, published in December 2007, predicted economic growth of some 4.1% in 2007 and projected that GDP would increase by a further 3.0% in 2008.

Education

Education is compulsory for all children for a period of 10 years between the ages of five and 14 years. Primary education, beginning at five years of age and lasting for eight years, is provided free of charge, principally through subsidized denominational schools under government control. In 2004 enrolment at primary institutions was equivalent to 95.2% of children in the relevant age-group (males 94.6%; females 95.9%). Secondary education, beginning at the age of 13, lasts for four years. Enrolment at secondary schools in 2004 was equivalent to 71.4% of students in the relevant age-group (males 69.8%; females 73.1%).

In 1998/99 there were 2,853 students enrolled in 12 other educational institutions, which included technical, vocational and teacher-training colleges. There is an extra-mural branch of the University of the West Indies in Belize. In 2000 the University of Belize was formed through the amalgamation of five higher education institutions, including the University College of Belize and Belize Technical College. Budgetary expenditure on education in the financial year 2004/05 was projected at BZ $152.6m., representing 26.7% of total spending by the central Government.

Public Holidays

2008: 2 January (for New Year's Day), 10 March (for Baron Bliss Day), 21–24 March (Easter), 1 May (Labour Day), 26 May (for Sovereign's Day), 10 September (National Day), 22 September (Independence Day), 13 October (for Day of the Americas), 19 November (Garifuna Settlement Day), 25–26 December (Christmas).

2009: 1 January (New Year's Day), 9 March (for Baron Bliss Day), 10–13 April (Easter), 1 May (Labour Day), 24 May (for Sovereign's Day), 10 September (National Day), 21 September (Independence Day), 12 October (for Day of the Americas), 19 November (Garifuna Settlement Day), 25–26 December (Christmas).

Weights and Measures

Imperial weights and measures are used, but petrol and paraffin are measured in terms of the US gallon (3.785 litres).

Statistical Survey

Sources (unless otherwise stated): Statistical Institute of Belize, 1902 Constitution Drive, Belmopan; tel. 822-2207; internet www.statisticsbelize.org.bz; Central Bank of Belize, Gabourel Lane, POB 852, Belize City; tel. 223-6194; fax 223-6226; e-mail cenbank@btl.net; internet www.centralbank.org.bz.

AREA AND POPULATION

Area: 22,965 sq km (8,867 sq miles).

Population: 189,774 at census of 12 May 1991; 240,204 (males 121,278, females 118,926) at census of 12 May 2000; 311,480 (males 154,665, females 156,815) at mid-2007 (official estimate).

Density (mid-2007): 13.6 per sq km.

Districts (official estimates at mid-2007): Belize 93,215; Cayo 73,325; Orange Walk 47,145; Corozal 36,365; Stann Creek 32,180; Toledo 29,250.

Principal Towns (official estimates at mid-2007): Belize City (former capital) 63,670; San Ignacio/Santa Elena 18,265; Orange Walk 15,990; Belmopan (capital) 16,435; Dangriga (fmrly Stann Creek) 11,600; Corozal 9,100; San Pedro 10,445; Benque Viejo 8,160; Punta Gorda 5,255.

Births, Marriages and Deaths (provisional figures, 2003): Registered live births 7,440 (birth rate 27.3 per 1,000); Registered marriages 1,713 (marriage rate 6.3 per 1,000); Registered deaths 1,277 (death rate 4.7 per 1,000). *2005* (provisional): Registered live births 8,396; Registered deaths 1,369 (Source: UN, *Population and Vital Statistics Report*).

Expectation of Life (years at birth, WHO estimates): 70.5 (males 67.4; females 74.2) in 2005. Source: WHO, *World Health Statistics*.

Economically Active Population (April 2005): Agriculture 18,671; Forestry 961; Fishing 2,330; Mining and quarrying 211; Manufacturing 7,210; Electricity, gas and water 934; Construction 6,884; Wholesale and retail trade and repairs 15,944, Tourism (incl. restaurants and hotels) 12,865; Transport, storage and communications 3,553; Financial intermediation 1,594; Real estate, renting and business activities 2,084; General government services 10,033; Community, social and personal services 15,084; Other 231; *Total employed* 98,589; Total unemployed 12,197; *Total labour force* 110,786.

HEALTH AND WELFARE
Key Indicators

Total Fertility Rate (children per woman, 2005): 3.0.
Under-5 Mortality Rate (per 1,000 live births, 2005): 17.
HIV/AIDS (% of persons aged 15–49, 2005): 2.5.
Physicians (per 1,000 head, 2000): 1.05.
Hospital Beds (per 1,000 head, 2004): 1.3.
Health Expenditure (2004): US $ per head (PPP): 338.6.
Health Expenditure (2004): % of GDP: 5.1.
Health Expenditure (2004): public (% of total): 53.8.
Access to Water (% of persons, 2004): 91.
Access to Sanitation (% of persons, 2004): 47.
Human Development Index (2005): ranking: 80.
Human Development Index (2005): value: 0.788.

For sources and definitions, see explanatory note on p. vi.

AGRICULTURE, ETC.

Principal Crops ('000 metric tons, 2006, FAO estimates): Rice (paddy) 13.0; Maize 32.0; Sorghum 9.3; Sugar cane 1,149.5; Dry beans 4.0; Fresh vegetables 8.8 (FAO estimate); Bananas 82.0; Plantains 34.2; Oranges 226.1; Grapefruit and pomelos 52.3; Papayas 18.6. *Aggregate Production* ('000 metric tons, may include official, semi-official or estimated data): Vegetables (incl. melons) 10.2; Fruits (excl. melons) 419.6.

BELIZE

Statistical Survey

Livestock ('000 head, year ending September 2006, FAO estimates): Horses 5; Mules 5; Cattle 58; Pigs 21; Sheep 6; Chickens 1,600.

Livestock Products ('000 metric tons, 2006, FAO estimates): Cattle meat 2.4; Chicken meat 13.6; Pig meat 0.6; Cows' milk 3.6; Hen eggs 2,851.

Forestry (1995): *Roundwood Removals* ('000 cubic metres, excl. bark): Sawlogs, veneer logs and logs for sleepers 62, Fuel wood 126, Total 188. *Sawnwood Production* ('000 cubic metres, incl. railway sleepers): Coniferous (softwood) 5, Broadleaved (hardwood) 30, Total 35. *1996–2006*: Annual production as in 1995 (FAO estimates).

Fishing ('000 metric tons, live weight, 2005): Capture 3.9 (Albacore 7.2; Caribbean spiny lobster 439; Stromboid conchs 2,136); Aquaculture 10.6 (White leg shrimp 10.4); Total catch 14.5.

Source: FAO.

INDUSTRY

Production (2005, unless otherwise indicated): Raw sugar 100,435 long tons; Molasses 37,074 long tons; Cigarettes 78 million; Beer 1,891,000 gallons; Batteries 6,000; Flour 26,959,000 lb; Fertilizers 26,874,000 short tons; Garments 611,900 items; Soft drinks 4,929,000 gallons; Citrus concentrates 2,973,000 gallons (2004); Single strength juices 2,102,000 gallons (2004). Source: IMF, *Belize: Selected Issues and Statistical Appendix* (October 2006).

FINANCE

Currency and Exchange Rates: 100 cents = 1 Belizean dollar (BZ $). *Sterling, US Dollar and Euro Equivalents* (31 December 2007): £1 sterling = BZ $4.007; US $1 = BZ $2.000; €1 = BZ $2.944; BZ $100 = £24.96 = US $50.00 = €33.97. *Exchange rate:* Fixed at US $1 = BZ $2.000 since May 1976.

Budget (BZ $ million, year ending 31 March 2008, draft budget): *Revenue*: Taxation 593.9 (Taxes on income, profits 170.3; Taxes on property 5.6; Taxes on goods and services 237.9; International trade and transactions 180.1); Other current revenue 57.0; Capital revenue 10.1; Total 661.0, excl. grants (17.5). *Expenditure*: Current expenditure 585.2 (Personal emoluments 235.3, Pensions 39.0, Goods and services 203.0, Debt service 107.9); Capital expenditure 118.0; Total 703.2.

International Reserves (US $ million at 31 December 2006): IMF special drawing rights 2.91; Reserve position in the IMF 6.38; Foreign exchange 104.44; Total 113.72. Source: IMF, *International Financial Statistics*.

Money Supply (BZ $ million at 31 December 2006): Currency outside banks 136.88; Demand deposits at commercial banks 421.23; Total money (incl. others) 559.06. Source: IMF, *International Financial Statistics*.

Cost of Living (Consumer Price Index; base: 2000 = 100): All items 106.1 in 2003; 109.4 in 2004; 113.3 in 2005. Source: IMF, *International Financial Statistics*.

Expenditure on the Gross Domestic Product (BZ $ million at current prices, 2006): Government final consumption expenditure 330.3; Private final consumption expenditure 1,581.7; Increase in stocks 8.5; Gross fixed capital formation 461.0; *Gross domestic expenditure* 2,381.6; Exports of goods and services 1,541.5; *Less* Imports of goods and services 1,501.2; Statistical discrepancy 5.3; *GDP at market prices* 2,427.3.

Gross Domestic Product by Economic Activity (BZ $ million at current prices, 2006): Agriculture and forestry 220.0; Fishing 73.8; Mining and quarrying 9.5; Manufacturing 258.1; Electricity and water 88.4; Construction 85.6; Wholesale and retail trade, repairs 352.3; Restaurants and hotels 107.1; Transport, storage and communications 253.0; Financial intermediation 188.1; Real estate, renting and business services 179.8; Community, social and personal services 159.5; General government services 238.3; *Sub-total* 2,213.5; Taxes, less subsidies, on products 324.3; *Less* Financial intermediation services indirectly measured 110.6; *GDP at market prices* 2,427.2.

Balance of Payments (US $ million, 2006): Exports of goods f.o.b. 426.2; Imports of goods f.o.b. −611.9; *Trade balance* −185.7; Exports of services 355.4; Imports of services −150.2; *Balance on goods and services* 19.5; Other income received 10.0; Other income paid −128.2; *Balance on goods, services and income* −98.6; Current transfers (net) 74.0; *Current balance* −24.7; Capital account (net) 9.1; Financial account (net) 38.6; Net errors and omissions 4.2; *Overall balance* 27.2 (Source: IMF, *International Financial Statistics*).

EXTERNAL TRADE

Principal Commodities (BZ $ million, 2006): *Imports c.i.f.*: Food and live animals 118.2; Mineral fuels and lubricants 213.3; Chemicals and related products 93.6; Manufactured goods 164.3; Miscellaneous manufactured articles 102.4; Machinery and transport equipment 219.1; Commercial free zone 217.7; Export processing zone 158.0; Total (incl. others) 1,320.8. *Exports f.o.b.*: Orange concentrate 86.2; Marine products (excl. aquarium fish) 86.0; Sugar 100.1; Bananas 50.6; Garments 36.6; Papaya 31.0; Grapefruit concentrate 22.8; Total (incl. others) 536.4.

Principal Trading Partners (BZ $ million, 2006): *Imports c.i.f.*: USA 510.8; Mexico 120.9; United Kingdom 18.2; Canada 14.3; Total (incl. others) 1,320.8. *Exports f.o.b.* (excl. re-exports): USA 224.4; United Kingdom 88.5; Mexico 17.3; Total (incl. others) 536.4.

TRANSPORT

Road Traffic (vehicles in use, 1998): Passenger cars 9,929; Buses and coaches 416; Lorries and vans 11,339; Motorcycles and mopeds 270 (Source: IRF, *World Road Statistics*). *2002* (vehicles in use): Passenger cars 32,600; Commercial vehicles 7,800 (Source: UN, *Statistical Yearbook*).

Shipping (sea-borne freight traffic, '000 metric tons, 1996): Goods loaded 255.4; Goods unloaded 277.1. *Merchant Fleet* (vessels registered at 31 December 2006): Number of vessels 525; Total displacement 1,437,986 grt (Source: Lloyd's Register-Fairplay, *World Fleet Statistics*).

Civil Aviation (2002): Passenger arrivals 174,038. Source: IMF, *Belize: Statistical Appendix* (April 2004).

TOURISM

Tourist Arrivals: 1,082,268 (cruise-ship passengers 851,436, stopover visitors 230,832) in 2004; 1,036,904 (cruise-ship passengers 800,331, stop-over visitors 236,573) in 2005; 903,238 (cruise-ship passengers 655,929, stop-over visitors 247,309) in 2006.

Tourism Receipts (US $ million): 172.7 in 2004; 174.7 in 2005; 199.4 in 2006.

Source: Belize Tourism Board.

COMMUNICATIONS MEDIA

Radio Receivers (1997): 133,000 in use*.

Television Receivers (2000): 44,000 in use†.

Telephones (2006): 33,900 main lines in use†.

Facsimile Machines (1996): 500 in use‡.

Mobile Cellular Telephones (2005): 118,300 subscribers†.

Personal Computers (2004): 35,000 in use†.

Internet Users (2005): 34,000†.

Broadband Subscribers (2006): 5,600.

Book Production (1996): 107 titles*.

Non-daily Newspapers (1996): 10 (circulation 80,000)*.

* Source: UNESCO, *Statistical Yearbook*.
† Source: International Telecommunication Union.
‡ Source: UN, *Statistical Yearbook*.

EDUCATION

Pre-primary (2005/06): 142 schools, 282 teachers, 4,861 students.

Primary (2005/06): 288 schools, 2,829 teachers, 64,516 students.

Secondary (2005/06): 50 schools, 1,170 teachers, 16,696 students.

Higher (1997/98): 12 institutions, 228 teachers, 2,853 students.

Source: fmr Ministry of Education, Youth and Sports.

Adult Literacy Rate (UNESCO estimates): 76.9% (males 77.1%; females 76.7%) in 2003. Source: UN Development Programme, *Human Development Report*.

Directory

The Constitution

The Constitution came into effect at the independence of Belize on 21 September 1981. Its main provisions are summarized below:

FUNDAMENTAL RIGHTS AND FREEDOMS

Regardless of race, place of origin, political opinions, colour, creed or sex, but subject to respect for the rights and freedoms of others and for the public interest, every person in Belize is entitled to the rights of life, liberty, security of the person, and the protection of the law. Freedom of movement, of conscience, of expression, of assembly and association and the right to work are guaranteed and the inviolability of family life, personal privacy, home and other property and of human dignity is upheld. Protection is afforded from discrimination on the grounds of race, sex, etc., and from slavery, forced labour and inhuman treatment.

CITIZENSHIP

All persons born in Belize before independence who, immediately prior to independence, were citizens of the United Kingdom and Colonies automatically become citizens of Belize. All persons born outside the country having a husband, parent or grandparent in possession of Belizean citizenship automatically acquire citizenship, as do those born in the country after independence. Provision is made which permits persons who do not automatically become citizens of Belize to be registered as such. (Belizean citizenship was also offered, under the Belize Loans Act 1986, in exchange for interest-free loans of US $25,000 with a 10-year maturity. The scheme was officially ended in June 1994, following sustained criticism of alleged corruption on the part of officials. A revised economic citizenship programme, offering citizenship in return for a minimum investment of US $75,000, received government approval in early 1995, but was ended in 2002.)

THE GOVERNOR-GENERAL

The British monarch, as Head of State, is represented in Belize by a Governor-General, a Belizean national.

Belize Advisory Council

The Council consists of not less than six people 'of integrity and high national standing', appointed by the Governor-General for up to 10 years upon the advice of the Prime Minister. The Leader of the Opposition must concur with the appointment of two members and be consulted about the remainder. The Council exists to advise the Governor-General, particularly in the exercise of the prerogative of mercy, and to convene as a tribunal to consider the removal from office of certain senior public servants and judges.

THE EXECUTIVE

Executive authority is vested in the British monarch and exercised by the Governor-General. The Governor-General appoints as Prime Minister that member of the House of Representatives who, in the Governor-General's view, is best able to command the support of the majority of the members of the House, and appoints a Deputy Prime Minister and other Ministers on the advice of the Prime Minister. The Governor-General may remove the Prime Minister from office if a resolution of 'no confidence' is passed by the House and the Prime Minister does not, within seven days, either resign or advise the Governor-General to dissolve the National Assembly. The Cabinet consists of the Prime Minister and other Ministers.

The Leader of the Opposition is appointed by the Governor-General as that member of the House who, in the Governor-General's view, is best able to command the support of a majority of the members of the House who do not support the Government.

THE LEGISLATURE

The Legislature consists of a National Assembly comprising two chambers: the Senate, with 12 nominated members; and the House of Representatives, with 31 elected members. The Assembly's normal term is five years. An amendment to the Constitution in January 2002 expanded the appointed Senate to 12 persons from eight. Senators are appointed by the Governor-General: six on the advice of the Prime Minister; three on the advice of the Leader of the Opposition or on the advice of persons selected by the Governor-General; and one each on the advice of the Belize Council of Churches together with the Evangelical Association of Churches, the Belize Chamber of Commerce and Industry and the Belize Better Business Bureau, and the National Trade Union Congress in agreement with the Civil Society Steering Committee. If any person who is not a Senator is elected to be President of the Senate, he or she shall be an *ex-officio* Senator in addition to the 12 nominees.

Each constituency returns one Representative to the House, who is directly elected in accordance with the Constitution.

If a person who is not a member of the House is elected to be Speaker of the House, he or she shall be an *ex-officio* member in addition to the 31 members directly elected. Every citizen older than 18 years is eligible to vote. The National Assembly may alter any of the provisions of the Constitution.

The Government

HEAD OF STATE

Sovereign: HM Queen ELIZABETH II (succeeded to the throne 6 February 1952).

Governor-General: Sir COLVILLE YOUNG (appointed 17 November 1993).

THE CABINET
(March 2008)

Prime Minister and Minister of Finance: DEAN BARROW.

Deputy Prime Minister and Minister of Natural Resources and the Environment: GASPAR VEGA.

Attorney-General and Minister of Foreign Affairs and Foreign Trade: WILFRED ELRINGTON.

Minister of Economic Development, Commerce, Industry and Consumer Protection: ERWIN CONTRERAS.

Minister of Education: PATRICK FABER.

Minister of National Security: CARLOS PERDOMO.

Minister of Housing and Urban Development: MICHAEL FINNEGAN.

Minister of Works: ANTHONY (BOOTS) MARTINEZ.

Minister of Tourism and Civil Aviation: MANUEL HEREDIA.

Minister of Health: PABLO MARIN.

Minister of Labour, Local Government and Rural Development: GABRIEL MARTINEZ.

Minister of the Public Service, Governance Improvement and Elections and Boundaries: JOHN SALDIVAR.

Minister of Agriculture and Fisheries: RENE MONTERO.

Minister of Public Utilities, Transport, Communications and National Emergency Management: MELVIN HULSE.

Minister of Human Development and Social Transformation: EDEN MARTINEZ.

Minister of Youth, Sports and Culture: MARCEL CARDONA.

MINISTRIES

Office of the Prime Minister and Ministry of Finance: New Administration Bldg, Belmopan; tel. 822-2345; fax 822-0898; e-mail cabinet@btl.net.

Ministry of Agriculture and Fisheries: 2nd Floor, West Block Bldg, Belmopan; tel. 822-2241; fax 822-2409; e-mail minaf@btl.net; internet www.agriculture.gov.bz.

Ministry of the Attorney-General: General Office, Belmopan; tel. 822-2504; fax 822-3390; internet www.belizelaw.org.

Ministry of Economic Development, Commerce, Industry and Consumer Protection: Belmopan.

Ministry of Education: West Block Bldg, Belmopan; tel. 822-2380; fax 822-3389; e-mail moeducation.moes@gmail.com; internet www.moes.gov.bz.

Ministry of Foreign Affairs and Foreign Trade: New Administration Bldg, POB 174, Belmopan; tel. 822-2167; fax 822-2854; e-mail belizemfa@btl.net; internet www.mfa.gov.bz.

Ministry of Health: East Block Bldg, Independence Plaza, Belmopan; tel. 822-2068; fax 822-2942; e-mail seniorsecretary@health.gov.bz; internet health.gov.bz/moh.

Ministry of Housing and Urban Development: Curl Thompson Bldg, Belmopan; tel. 822-2218; fax 822-2195.

Ministry of Human Development and Social Transformation: West Block, Independence Plaza, Belmopan; tel. 227-7451; fax 227-1276; e-mail hsdbze@hotmail.com.

Ministry of Labour, Local Government and Rural Development: Belmopan; tel. 822-2663; fax 822-1275; e-mail labcommgovbz@yahoo.com.

Ministry of National Security: Belmopan.

Ministry of Natural Resources and the Environment: Market Sq., Belmopan; tel. 822-2226; fax 822-2333; e-mail info@mnrei.gov.bz; internet www.mnrei.gov.bz.

Ministry of the Public Service, Governance Improvement and of Elections and Boundaries: Belmopan; tel. 822-3765; fax 822-2206; e-mail ceo@mps.gov.bz.

Ministry of Public Utilities, Transport, Communications and National Emergency Management: Belmopan; tel. 822-2692; fax 822-3317; e-mail belizetransport@yahoo.com.

Ministry of Tourism and Civil Aviation: c/o Civil Aviation Dept, Belize City; tel. 225-2014; fax 225-2533; e-mail dcabelize@btl.net.

Ministry of Works: New 2 Power Lane, Belmopan; tel. 822-2131; fax 822-2298; e-mail works@btl.net.

Ministry of Youth, Sports and Culture: c/o Belize Archives and Records Service, 26–28 Unity Blvd, Belmopan; tel. 822-2248; fax 822-3140.

Legislature

NATIONAL ASSEMBLY

The Senate

President: PHILIP ZUNIGA.

There are 12 nominated members in addition to the current *ex officio* President.

House of Representatives

Speaker: ELIZABETH ZABANEH.
Clerk: CONRAD LEWIS.

General Election, 7 February 2008

	Votes cast	% of total	Seats
United Democratic Party (UDP)	66,203	57.0	25
People's United Party (PUP)	47,624	41.0	6
Others	2,367	2.0	—
Total	116,194	100.0	31

Election Commissions

Elections and Boundaries Commission: Belize City; e-mail electbound@btl.net; internet www.belize-elections.org; f. 1978; appointed by Governor-Gen; Chair. KARL H. MENZIES.

Elections and Boundaries Department: Mahogany St Extension, POB 913, Belize City; tel. 222-4042; fax 222-4991; e-mail electbound@btl.net; internet www.belize-elections.org; f. 1989; dept of the Office of the Prime Minister; Chief Elections Officer RUTH MEIGHAN (acting).

Political Organizations

People's United Party (PUP): 3 Queen St, Belize City; tel. 223-2428; fax 223-3476; internet www.pupbelize.bz; f. 1950; based on organized labour; publs *The Belize Times*; Leader JOHN BRICEÑO; Chair. FRANCIS FONSECA; Sec.-Gen. HENRY USHER; Deputy Leaders GODFREY SMITH, VILDO MARIN.

United Democratic Party (UDP): South End Bel-China Bridge, POB 1898, Belize City; tel. 227-2576; fax 227-6441; e-mail unitedd@btl.net; internet www.udp.org.bz; f. 1974 by merger of People's Development Movement, Liberal Party and National Independence Party; conservative; Leader DEAN BARROW; Chair. DOUGLAS SINGH.

People's National Party (PNP): Belize City; e-mail info@pnpbelize.org; internet www.pnpbelize.org; f. 2007; Leader WIL MAHEIA.

Diplomatic Representation

EMBASSIES AND HIGH COMMISSION IN BELIZE

Brazil: 12 Floral Park Ave, POB 548, Belmopan; tel. 822-0460; fax 822-8461; e-mail embbrazil@btl.net; internet www.abe.mre.gov.br; Ambassador ROBERTO COUTINHO.

China (Taiwan): 20 North Park St, POB 1020, Belize City; tel. 227-8744; fax 223-3082; e-mail embroc@btl.net; internet come.to/ROCBelize; Ambassador TING JOSEPH SHIH.

Costa Rica: 10 Unity Blvd, POB 288, Belmopan; tel. 822-1582; fax 822-1583; e-mail fborbon@btl.net; Ambassador FERNANDO BORBÓN ARIAS.

Cuba: 6087 Manatee Dr., Buttonwood Bay, POB 1775, Belize City; tel. 223-5345; fax 223-1105; e-mail embacuba@btl.net; internet embacu.cubaminrex.cu/beliceing; Ambassador EUGENIO MARTÍNEZ ENRÍQUEZ.

El Salvador: 49 Nanche St, POB 215, Belmopan; tel. 823-3404; fax 823-3569; e-mail embasalva@btl.net; Ambassador Dr JOSE SERGIO MENA.

Guatemala: 8 'A' St, King's Park, POB 1771, Belize City; tel. 233-3150; fax 235-5140; e-mail embbelice1@minex.gob.gt; Ambassador MANUEL ARTURO TÉLLEZ MIRALDA.

Honduras: 22 Gabourel Lane, POB 285, Belize City; tel. 224-5889; fax 223-0562; e-mail embahonbe@sre.hn; Ambassador MANUEL SANDOVAL CABRERA.

Mexico: 3 North Ring Road, Embassy Sq., Belmopan; tel. 822-2480; fax 822-2487; e-mail embamexbze@btl.net; internet www.sre.gob.mx/belice; Ambassador JOSÉ ARTURO TREJO NAVA.

Nicaragua: 124 Barrack Rd, Belize City; tel. 223-2666; fax 223-0978; e-mail embanicbelize@btl.net; Ambassador NORA GORDON.

United Kingdom: Embassy Sq., POB 91, Belmopan; tel. 822-2146; fax 822-2761; e-mail brithicom@btl.net; internet www.britishhighbze.com; High Commissioner JOHN YAPP.

USA: Floral Park Road, Belmopan; tel. 822-4011; fax 822-4012; e-mail embbelize@state.gov; internet belize.usembassy.gov; Ambassador ROBERT J. DIETER.

Venezuela: 17 Orchid Garden St, POB 49, Belmopan; tel. 822-2384; fax 822-2022; e-mail embaven@bt1.net; Ambassador OMAR JOSÉ VALDIVIESO.

Judicial System

Summary Jurisdiction Courts (criminal jurisdiction) and District Courts (civil jurisdiction), presided over by magistrates, are established in each of the six judicial districts. Summary Jurisdiction Courts have a wide jurisdiction in summary offences and a limited jurisdiction in indictable matters. Appeals lie to the Supreme Court, which has jurisdiction corresponding to the English High Court of Justice and where a jury system is in operation. From the Supreme Court further appeals lie to a Court of Appeal, established in 1967, which holds an average of four sessions per year. Final appeals are made to the Judicial Committee of the Privy Council in the United Kingdom.

Court of Appeal: Belize City; tel. 227-2907; Pres. ELLIOTT MOTTLEY; Justices of Appeal MANUEL SOSA, BOYD CAREY, DENNIS MORRISON.

Supreme Court: Supreme Court Bldg, Belize City; tel. 227-7256; fax 227-0181; e-mail chiefjustice@btl.net; internet www.belizelaw.org/supreme_court/chief_justice.html; Registrar ALDO SALAZAR; Chief Justice Dr ABDULAI OSMAN CONTEH.

Magistrate's Court: Paslow Bldg, Belize City; tel. 227-7164; Chief Magistrate MARGARET GABB-MACKENZIE.

Religion

CHRISTIANITY

Most of the population are Christian, the largest denomination being the Roman Catholic Church (an estimated 76% of the population in 2005). The other main groups are the Pentecostal, Anglican, Seventh-day Adventist, Methodist and Mennonite churches.

Belize Council of Churches: 149 Allenby St, POB 508, Belize City; tel. 227-7077; f. 1957 as Church World Service Cttee; present name adopted 1984; nine mem. churches, four assoc. bodies; Pres. Rev. LeRoy FLOWERS.

The Roman Catholic Church

Belize comprises the single diocese of Belize City-Belmopan, suffragan to the archdiocese of Kingston in Jamaica. At 31 December 2006 it was estimated that there were 218,938 adherents in the diocese. The Bishop participates in the Antilles Episcopal Conference (whose secretariat is based in Port of Spain, Trinidad and Tobago).

Bishop of Belize City-Belmopan: DORICK McGOWAN WRIGHT, Bishop's House, 144 North Front St, POB 616, Belize City; tel. 223-2122; fax 223-1922; e-mail episkopos@btl.net.

The Anglican Communion

Anglicans in Belize belong to the Church in the Province of the West Indies, comprising eight dioceses. The Archbishop of the Province is

BELIZE
Directory

the Bishop of the North Eastern Caribbean and Aruba, resident in St John's, Antigua and Barbuda.

Bishop of Belize: Rt Rev. PHILIP S. WRIGHT, Rectory Lane, POB 535, Belize City; tel. 227-3029; fax 227-6898; e-mail bzediocese@btl.net; internet www.belize.anglican.org.

Protestant Churches

Methodist Church in the Caribbean and the Americas (Belize/Honduras District) (MCCA): 75 Albert St, POB 212, Belize City; tel. 227-7173; fax 227-5870; f. 1824; c. 1,827 mems; District Pres. Rev. DAVID GOFF.

Mennonite Congregations in Belize: POB 427, Belize City; tel. 823-0137; fax 823-0101; f. 1958; an estimated 3,575 mems live in eight Mennonite settlements, the largest of which is Altkolonier Mennonitengemeinde with 1,728 mems; Bishop AARON HARDER.

Other denominations active in the country include the Presbyterians, Baptists, Moravians, Jehovah's Witnesses, the Church of God, the Nazarene Church, the Assemblies of Brethren and the Salvation Army.

OTHER RELIGIONS

There are also small communities of Hindus (106, according to the census of 1980), Muslims (110 in 1980), Jews (92 in 1980) and Bahá'ís.

The Press

Amandala: Amandala Press, 3304 Partridge St, POB 15, Belize City; tel. 202-4476; fax 222-4702; e-mail editor@amandala.com.bz; internet www.amandala.com.bz; f. 1969; 2 a week; independent; Publr EVAN X. HYDE; Editor RUSSELL VELLOS; circ. 45,000.

Ambergris Today: San Pedro Town, Ambergris Caye; tel. 226-3462; e-mail ambertoday@btl.net; internet www.ambergristoday.com; weekly; independent; Editor DORIAN NUÑEZ.

The Belize Times: 3 Queen St, POB 506, Belize City; tel. 224-5757; fax 223-1940; e-mail belizetime@btl.net; internet www.belizetimes.bz; f. 1956; weekly; party political paper of PUP; Editor-in-Chief ANDREW STEINHAUER; circ. 6,000.

Belize Today: Belize Information Service, East Block, POB 60, Belmopan; tel. 822-2159; fax 822-3242; monthly; official; circ. 17,000.

Government Gazette: Print Belize Ltd, 1 Power Lane, Belmopan; tel. 822-0194; fax 822-3367; e-mail admin@printbze.bz; internet www.printbelize.bz; f. 1871; official; weekly; CEO LAWRENCE J. NICHOLAS.

The Guardian: Ebony St and Bel-China Bridge, POB 1898, Belize City; tel. 207-5346; fax 227-5343; e-mail info@guardian.bz; internet www.guardian.bz; weekly; party political paper of UDP; Editor JOHN AVERY; circ. 5,000.

The Reporter: 147 Allenby St, POB 707, Belize City; tel. 227-2503; fax 227-8278; e-mail editor@belizereporter.bz; internet www.reporter.bz; f. 1967; weekly; Editor ANN MARIE WILLIAMS; circ. 6,500.

The San Pedro Sun: POB 35, San Pedro Town, Ambergris Caye; tel. 226-2070; fax 226-2905; e-mail spsun@sanpedrosun.net; internet www.sanpedrosun.net; f. 1993; weekly; Editors RON SNIFFIN, TAMARA SNIFFIN.

Publishers

Angelus Press Ltd: 10 Queen St, POB 1757, Belize; tel. 223-5777; fax 227-8825; e-mail angel@btl.net; internet www.anguspress.com; Gen. Man. AMPARO M. NOBLE.

Cubola Productions: Montserrat Duran, 35 Elizabeth St, Benque, Viejo del Carmen; tel. 932-0853; fax 932-2240; e-mail cubolabz@btl.net; internet www.belizebusiness.com/cubola; Dir MONTSERRAT CASADEMUNT.

Print Belize Ltd: 1 Power Lane, Belmopan; tel. 822-2293; fax 882-3367; e-mail admin@printbze.bz; internet www.printbelize.com; f. 1871; responsible for printing, binding and engraving requirements of all govt depts and ministries; publications include annual govt estimates, govt magazines and the official *Government Gazette*; CEO LAWRENCE J. NICHOLAS.

Broadcasting and Communications

TELECOMMUNICATIONS

In September 2001 the Government announced that the telecommunications sector was to be liberalized.

Public Utilities Commission (PUC): regulatory body for the telecommunications sector; see Utilities—Regulatory Body.

Belize Telemedia Ltd: Esquivel Telecom Centre, St Thomas St, POB 603, Belize City; tel. 223-2868; fax 223-1800; e-mail prdept@btl.net; internet www.belizetelemedia.net; f. May 2007; fmrly Belize Telecommunications Ltd (subsidiary of Innovative Communication Corpn (ICC) until taken over by the Govt in Feb. 2005); Chair. of Board of Dirs KEITH ARNOLD; Chair. of Exec. Cttee DEAN BOYCE.

RADIO

Love FM: 7145 Slaughterhouse Rd, POB 1865, Belize City; tel. 203-2098; fax 203-0529; e-mail lovefm@btl.net; internet www.lovefm.com; f. 1992; purchased Friends FM in 1998; Man. Dir RENE VILLANUEVA.

Radio Krem Ltd: 3304 Partridge St, POB 15, Belize City; tel. 227-5929; fax 227-4079; e-mail kremwub@hotmail.com; internet www.krembz.com; commercial; purchased Radio Belize in 1998.

Other private radio stations broadcasting in Belize include: Estereo Amor, More FM, My Refuge Christian Radio, Radio 2000 and Voice of America.

TELEVISION

Centaur Cable Network (CTV): 31 Clarke St, Orange Walk Town, Orange Walk; tel. 670-2216; fax 322-2216; internet www.ctv3belizenews.com; f. 1989; commercial.

Channel 5 Belize: POB 679, Belize City; tel. 227-3146; fax 227-4936; e-mail gbtv@btl.com; internet www.channel5belize.com; f. 1991; Man. Dir STEWART KROHN.

Tropical Vision (Channel 7): 73 Albert St, Belize City; tel. 227-3988; fax 227-5602; e-mail tvseven@btl.net; internet 7newsbelize.com; commercial; Man. NESTOR VASQUEZ.

Finance

(cap. = capital; res = reserves; dep. = deposits; brs = branches; amounts in BZ $, unless otherwise indicated)

BANKING

Central Bank

Central Bank of Belize: Gabourel Lane, POB 852, Belize City; tel. 223-6194; fax 223-6226; e-mail cenbank@btl.net; internet www.centralbank.org.bz; f. 1982; cap. 10m., res 16.4m., dep. 188.2m. (2005); Gov. SYDNEY CAMPBELL; Deputy Gov. MARION PALACIO.

Development Bank

Development Finance Corporation: Bliss Parade, Belmopan; tel. 822-2360; fax 822-3096; e-mail info@dfcbelize.org; internet www.dfcbelize.org; f. 1972; ceased to finance loans following a govt review in Dec. 2004; issued cap. 10m.; Chair. GLENN GODFREY; CEO TROY GABB; 5 brs.

Other Banks

Alliance Bank of Belize Ltd: 106 Princess Margaret Dr., POB 1988, Belize City; tel. 223-6783; fax 223-6785; e-mail info@alliance.bz; internet www.alliancebank.bz; f. 2001; dep. 6,876m., total assets 113.7m.; 3 brs.

Atlantic Bank Ltd: Cnr Freetown Rd and Cleghorn St, POB 481, Belize City; tel. 223-4123; fax 223-3907; e-mail atlantic@atlabank.com; internet www.atlabank.com; f. 1971; dep. 161.0m., total assets 191.9m. (2001); Gen. Man. SANDRA BEDRAN; 8 brs.

Atlantic International Bank Ltd: Cnr Freetown Rd and Cleghorn St, POB 481, Belize City; tel. 223-3152; fax 223-3528; e-mail atlantic@btl.net; internet www.atlanticibl.com; affiliated to Atlantic Bank Ltd; Gen. Man. RICARDO PELAYO.

Belize Bank Ltd: 60 Market Sq., POB 364, Belize City; tel. 227-7132; fax 227-2712; e-mail bblbz@belizebank.com; internet www.belizebank.com; subsidiary of BB Holdings; cap. US $2.2m., res US $5.2m., dep. US $376.9m. (2006); Chair. PHILIP C. JOHNSON; Sr Vice-Pres. LOUIS ANTHONY SWASEY; 10 brs.

Caye International Bank Ltd (CIBL): POB 11, Coconut Dr., San Pedro, Ambergris Caye; tel. 226-2388; fax 226-2892; e-mail cibl@btl.net; internet www.cayebank.bz; Pres. and CEO PETER ZIPPER; Exec. Vice-Pres. JOY A. FLOWERS.

FirstCaribbean International Bank Ltd (Barbados): 21 Albert St, POB 363, Belize City; tel. 227-7211; fax 227-8572; e-mail care@firstcaribbeanbank.com; internet www.firstcaribbeanbank.com; f. 2002 by merger of CIBC West Indies Holdings and Barclays Bank PLC Caribbean operations; Barclays relinquished its stake to CIBC in June 2006; Exec. Chair. MICHAEL MANSOOR; Exec. Dir CHARLES PINK.

BELIZE *Directory*

Provident Bank and Trust of Belize: 35 Barrack Rd, POB 1867, Belize City; tel. 223-5698; fax 223-0368; e-mail services@providentbank.bz; internet www.providentbelize.com; f. 1998; cap. US $6.0m., res US $1.5m., dep. US $105.9m. (2004); Chair. JOY VERNON GODFREY; Pres. JOSÉ MARIN.

There is also a government savings bank. In late 2001 the Government amended the exchange-control regulations to allow foreign-currency exchange bureaux.

INSURANCE

The insurance sector is regulated by the Office of the Supervisor of Insurance, part of the Ministry of Finance.

Atlantic Insurance Company Ltd: Atlantic Bank Bldg, 3rd Floor, Cnr Cleghorn St and Freetown Rd, Belize City; tel. 223-2657; fax 223-2658; e-mail info@atlanticinsurancebz.com; internet www.atlanticinsurancebz.com; f. 1990; Chair. Dr GUILLERMO BUESO; Gen. Man. MARTHA GUERRA.

Belize Insurance Centre: 212 North Front St, Belize City; tel. 227-7310; fax 227-4803; e-mail info@belizeinsurance.com; internet www.belizeinsurance.com; insurance broker; Gen. Man. CYNTHIA AWE.

RFG Insurance Co Ltd: Gordon House, 4638 Coney Dr., POB 661, Belize City; tel. 223-5734; fax 223-6734; e-mail info@rfginsurancebelize.com; internet www.rfginsurancebelize.com; f. 2005 by merger of F&G Insurance and Regent Insurance; underwriters of all major classes of insurance; Chair. CHRISTOPHER ROE; Man. Dir GUY HOWISON.

RFG Life Insurance Company Ltd: 81 North Front St, POB 661, Belize City; tel. 227-3744; fax 227-2022; e-mail info@rfglife.com; internet www.rfglife.com; f. 2005 through merger of the Life and Medical portfolios of F&G Insurance Company into Regent Life; Chair. ANTHONY FLYNN; Man. Dir PETER ALLANSON.

Trade and Industry

STATUTORY BODIES

Banana Control Board: c/o Ministry of Agriculture and Fisheries, West Block Bldg, 2nd Floor, Belmopan; management of banana industry; in 1989 it was decided to make it responsible to growers, not an independent executive.

Belize Agricultural Health Authority: Cnr Forest Dr. and Hummingbird Hwy, POB 169, Belmopan; tel. 822-0818; fax 822-0271; e-mail baha@btl.net; internet www.baha.bz; Man. Dir NERIE SANZ.

Belize Marketing and Development Corporation: 117 North Front St, POB 633, Belize City; tel. 227-7402; fax 227-7656; f. 1948 as Belize Marketing Board to encourage the growing of staple food crops; renamed as above in 2003; promotes domestic produce; Gen. Man. CARLOS MORENO.

Citrus Growers Association: Mile 9, Stann Creek Valley Rd, POB 7, Dangriga, Stann Creek District; tel. 522-3585; fax 522-2686; e-mail info@belizecitrus.org; internet www.belizecitrus.org; f. 1967; CEO BRIDGET CULLERTON; Exec. Sec. JUDITH WILLIAMS.

Coastal Zone Management Authority (CZMAI): POB 1884, Belize City; tel. 223-0719; fax 223-5738; e-mail czmbze@btl.net; internet www.coastalzonebelize.org; Man. Dir VIRGINIA VASQUEZ (acting).

Pesticides Control Board (PCB): Central Farm, Cayo District; tel. 824-2640; fax 824-3486; e-mail pcbinfo@btl.net; internet www.pcbbelize.com.

DEVELOPMENT ORGANIZATION

Belize Trade and Investment Development Service (BELTRAIDE): 14 Orchid Garden St, Belmopan; tel. 822-3737; fax 822-0595; e-mail beltraide@belizeinvest.org.bz; internet www.belizeinvest.org.bz; f. 1986 as a joint govt and private-sector institution to encourage export and investment; Exec. Dir LOURDES SMITH.

CHAMBERS OF COMMERCE

American Chamber of Commerce of Belize: 5.5 miles Western Hwy, Cucumber Beach Marina, POB 75 Belize City; tel. and fax 222-4344; e-mail regent@btl.net; internet www.amchambelize.org; Pres. MARIA ELENA SYLVESTRE; Sec. EARL PÉREZ.

Belize British Chamber of Commerce (BBCC): Embassy Sq., Ring Rd, Cayo District, POB 91, Belmopan; tel. 822-2146; fax 822-2761; internet www.belizebritishchamber.com; Chair. IAN BEAUMONT; Sec. MIKE HERNÁNDEZ, Jr.

Belize Chamber of Commerce and Industry: 63 Regent St, POB 291, Belize City; tel. 227-3148; fax 227-4984; e-mail bcci@btl.net; internet www.belize.org; f. 1920; Pres. EMILE MENA; Sec. CELINE CLELAND GÓMEZ; 300 mems.

EMPLOYERS' ASSOCIATIONS

Banana Growers' Association: Big Creek, Independence Village, Stann Creek District; tel. 523-2000; fax 523-2112; e-mail banana@btl.net.

Belize Sugar Cane Farmers' Association (BSCFA): 34 San Antonio Rd, Orange Walk; tel. 322-2005; fax 322-3171; f. 1959 to assist cane farmers and negotiate with the Sugar Cane Board and manufacturers on their behalf; 16 district brs.

Belize Livestock Producers' Association: 47.5 miles Western Hwy, POB 183, Belmopan; tel. 822-3883; e-mail blpa@btl.net; Chair. FRED HUNTER, Sr.

UTILITIES

Regulatory Body

Public Utilities Commission (PUC): 63 Regent St, Belize City; tel. 227-1176; fax 227-1149; e-mail consumeraffairs@puc.bz; internet www.puc.bz; regulatory body, headed by seven commissioners; replaced the Offices of Electricity Supply and of Telecommunications following enaction of the Public Utilities Commission Act in 1999; Chair. ROBERTO YOUNG.

Electricity

Belize Electricity Co Ltd (BECOL): 115 Barrack Rd, POB 327, Belize City; tel. 227-0954; fax 223-0891; e-mail bel@btl.net; internet www.fortisinc.com; wholly owned subsidiary of Fortis Inc (Canada); operates Mollejón 25.2 MW hydroelectric plant and Chalillo 7.3 MW hydroelctric facility, which supply electricity to Belize Electricity Ltd (BEL—see below); Pres. and CEO H. STANLEY MARSHALL.

Belize Electricity Ltd (BEL): 2.5 miles Northern Hwy, POB 327, Belize City; tel. 227-0954; fax 223-0891; e-mail pr@bel.com.bz; internet www.bel.com.bz; fmrly Belize Electricity Board, changed name upon privatization in 1992; Govt held 51% of shares until 1999; 70% owned by Fortis Inc (Canada), 27% owned by Social Security Board; Pres. and CEO LYNN R. YOUNG; Vice-Pres. RENE BLANCO; Chair. ROBERT USHER; 242 employees.

Water

Belize Water Services Ltd: POB 150, Central American Blvd, Belize City; tel. 222-4757; fax 222-5113; e-mail bws_ceosec@btl.net; internet bws.com.bz; f. 1971 as Water and Sewerage Authority (WASA); changed name upon privatization in March 2001; renationalized in Oct. 2005 prior to partial reprivatization in early 2006; Chair. NORRIS HALL.

TRADE UNIONS

National Trade Union Congress of Belize (NTUCB): POB 2359, Belize City; tel. 822-0677; fax 822-0283; e-mail ntucb@btl.net; Pres. RENE GÓMEZ; Gen. Sec. DYLAN RENEAU.

Principal Unions

Belize Communications Workers' Union (BCWU): POB 1005, Belize City; tel. 223-4809; fax 224-4300; e-mail bcwu@btl.net; Pres. PAUL PERRIOTT; Gen. Sec. CHRISTINE PERRIOTT.

Belize Energy Workers' Union: c/o Belize Electricity Board, 2.5 miles Northern Hwy, POB 1066, Belize City; tel. 227-0954; Pres. COLVILLE YOUNG; Gen. Sec. FLOYD HERRERA.

Belize National Teachers' Union: Racecourse St, POB 382, Belize City; tel. 223-4811; fax 223-5233; e-mail bntu@btl.net; Pres. JOHN PINELO; Exec. Sec. GEORGE FRAZER; 1,000 mems.

Belize Workers' Union: Tate St, Orange Walk Town; tel. 822-2327; Pres. HORRIS PATTEN.

Christian Workers' Union: 107B Cemetery Rd, POB 533, Belize City; tel. 227-2150; fax 227-8470; e-mail cwu@btl.net; f. 1962; general; Pres. JAMES MCFOY; Gen. Sec. ANTONIO GONZÁLEZ; 1,000 mems.

Public Service Union of Belize: 2 Mayflower St, POB 458, Belmopan; tel. 822-0282; fax 822-0283; e-mail belizepsu@btl.net; f. 1922; public workers; Pres. DYLAN RENEAU; Gen. Sec. LIZANDRO QUIROZ; 1,600 mems.

Transport

Department of Transport: East Block Bldg, 2nd Floor, Belmopan; tel. 822-0992; fax 822-0994; e-mail transcom@btl.net; Commr PHILLIP BRACKETT.

RAILWAYS

There are no railways in Belize.

ROADS

There are 2,872 km of roads, of which some 2,210 km (1,600 km of gravel roads, 300 km of improved earth roads and 310 km of unimproved earth roads) are unpaved. In 2004 construction of a double-lane bridge over the Sibun river was completed, funded by a BZ $3.6m. European Union (EU) grant and some BZ $1m. from the Government. In October 2006 construction of another two-lane bridge, this time over Silver Creek, was completed. The bridge was intended to expedite the transport of produce and other products from the southern agricultural area to markets in Belize City along the Hummingbird Highway and also provide access for emergency aid to the southern communities of Belize during the hurricane period. A north–south highway, funded by the Government and international donors was expected to be completed by mid-2009.

SHIPPING

There is a deep-water port at Belize City and a second port at Commerce Bight, near Dangriga (formerly Stann Creek), to the south of Belize City. There is a port for the export of bananas at Big Creek and additional ports at Corozal and Punta Gorda. Nine major shipping lines operate vessels calling at Belize City, including the Carol Line (consisting of Harrison, Hapag-Lloyd, Nedlloyd and CGM). A proposal to develop a cruise-ship port at Port Loyola at a cost of BZ $963.5m. was submitted to parliament in October 2004. Work had commenced on the project by September 2007, however a dispute between the operating companies and government of that time severely compromised future development; no revised deadline for completion had yet been declared by April 2008.

Belize Ports Authority: Caesar Ridge Rd, POB 633, Belize City; tel. 227-2480; fax 227-2500; e-mail bzportauth@bpa.org.bz; internet bpa.org.bz; f. 1980; Commr of Ports Maj. (retd) LLOYD JONES.

Marine & Services: 95 Albert St, POB 611, Belize City; tel. 227-2112; fax 227-5404; e-mail shipping@marineservices.bz; internet www.marineservices.bz; f. 1975; shipping and cargo services, cruise line agent; Gen. Man. JOSÉ GALLEGO.

Port of Belize Ltd: Caesar Ridge Rd, POB 2674, Belize City; tel. 227-2439; fax 227-3571; e-mail portbz@btl.net; internet www.portofbelize.com; operates the main port facility; CEO RAINELDO GUERRERO; Deputy CEO FRANCINE WAIGHT.

CIVIL AVIATION

Phillip S. W. Goldson International Airport, 14 km (9 miles) from Belize City, can accommodate medium-sized jet-engined aircraft. The runway was extended in 2000. There are 37 airstrips for light aircraft on internal flights near the major towns and offshore islands.

Belize Airports Authority (BAA): POB 1564, Belize City; e-mail aviation@btl.net; tel. 225-2045; fax 225-2439; e-mail bzeaa@btl.net; CEO PABLO ESPAT.

Maya Island Air: Municipal Airport, POB 458, Belize City; tel. 223-1140; fax 223-0576; e-mail info@mayaisland.com; internet www.mayaairways.com; f. 1997 as merger between Maya Airways Ltd and Island Air; operated by Belize Air Group; internal services, centred on Belize City, and charter flights to neighbouring countries; CEO EUGENE ZABANEH; Gen. Man. FERNANDO TREJOS.

Tropic Air: San Pedro, POB 20, Ambergris Caye; tel. 226-2012; fax 226-2338; e-mail reservations@tropicair.com; internet www.tropicair.com; f. 1979; operates internal services and services to Guatemala; Chair. CELI MCCORKLE; Man. Dir JOHN GREIF, III.

Tourism

The main tourist attractions are the beaches and the barrier reef, diving, fishing and the Mayan archaeological sites. There are nine major wildlife reserves (including the world's only reserves for the jaguar and for the red-footed booby), and government policy is to develop 'eco-tourism', based on the attractions of an unspoilt environment and Belize's natural history. The country's wildlife also includes howler monkeys and 500 species of birds, and its barrier reef is the second largest in the world. In February 1996 the Mundo Maya Agreement was ratified, according to which Belize, El Salvador, Guatemala, Honduras and Mexico would co-operate in the management of Mayan archaeological remains. There were some 437 hotels in Belize in 2002. In 2006 there were 903,238 tourist arrivals, of which some 655,929 were cruise-ship passengers, and tourism receipts totalled US $199.4m.

Belize Tourism Board: Lower Flat, New Horizon Investment Bldg, 3.5 miles Northern Hwy, POB 325, Belize City; tel. 223-1913; fax 223-1943; e-mail info@travelbelize.org; internet www.travelbelize.org; f. 1964; fmrly Belize Tourist Bureau; eight mems; Chair. THERESE RATH; Dir TRACY TAEGAR-PANTON.

Belize Tourism Industry Association (BTIA): 10 North Park St, POB 62, Belize City; tel. 227-5717; fax 227-8710; e-mail info@btia.org; internet www.btia.org; f. 1985; promotes sustainable tourism; Exec. Dir ANDREW GODOY; Dir Marketing and Information EFREN PEREZ; 500 mems.

BENIN

Introductory Survey

Location, Climate, Language, Religion, Flag, Capital

The Republic of Benin is a narrow stretch of territory in West Africa. The country has an Atlantic coastline of about 100 km (60 miles), flanked by Nigeria to the east and Togo to the west; its northern borders are with Burkina Faso and Niger. Benin's climate is tropical, and is divided into three zones: the north has a rainy season between July and September, with a hot, dry season in October–April; the central region has periods of abundant rain in May–June and in October; and there is year-round precipitation in the south, the heaviest rains being in May–October. Average annual rainfall in Cotonou is 1,300 mm. French is the official language, but each of the indigenous ethnic groups has its own language. Bariba and Fulani are the major languages in the north, while Fon and Yoruba are widely spoken in the south. It is estimated that 35% of the people follow traditional beliefs and customs; about 35% are Christians, mainly Roman Catholics, and the majority of the remainder are Muslims. The national flag (proportions 2 by 3) has a vertical green stripe at the hoist, with equal horizontal stripes of yellow over red in the fly. The administrative capital is Porto-Novo, but most government offices and other state bodies are presently in the economic capital, Cotonou.

Recent History

Benin, called Dahomey until 1975, was formerly part of French West Africa. It became a self-governing republic within the French Community in December 1958, and an independent state on 1 August 1960. The early years of independence were characterized by chronic political instability and by periodic regional unrest, fuelled by long-standing rivalries between north and south.

Elections in December 1960 were won by the Parti dahoméen de l'unité, whose leader, Hubert Maga (a northerner), became the country's first President. In October 1963 Maga was deposed in a coup led by Col (later Gen.) Christophe Soglo, Chief of Staff of the Army. Soglo served as interim Head of State until January 1964, when Sourou-Migan Apithy, a southerner and former Vice-President, was elected President. Another southerner, Justin Ahomadegbé, became Prime Minister. In November 1965 Gen. Soglo forced Apithy and Ahomadegbé to resign. A provisional Government was formed, but a further military intervention, in December, resulted in Soglo again assuming power. In December 1967 industrial unrest precipitated another coup, led by Maj. (later Lt-Col) Maurice Kouandété. Lt-Col Alphonse Alley, hitherto Chief of Staff, became interim Head of State, and Kouandété Prime Minister.

A new Constitution, providing for a return to civilian rule, was approved by referendum in March 1968, and a presidential election followed in May. However, all former Heads of State were banned from contesting the presidency and only about 26% of the electorate voted; the abstention rate reportedly reached 99% in northern regions. The election was declared void, and in June the military regime nominated Dr Emile-Derlin Zinsou as President. In December 1969 Zinsou was deposed by Kouandété, then Commander-in-Chief of the Army, and a three-member military Directoire assumed power. In March 1970 a presidential election was abandoned when counting revealed roughly equal support for the three main candidates—Ahomadegbé, Apithy and Maga—to whom the Directoire ceded power in May: it was intended that each member of this Presidential Council would act as Head of State, in rotation, for a two-year period. Maga was the first to hold this office and was succeeded in May 1972 by Ahomadegbé.

In October 1972 the civilian leadership was deposed by Maj. (later Brig.-Gen.) Mathieu Kérékou, Deputy Chief of Staff of the armed forces and a northerner. In September 1973 a Conseil national révolutionnaire (CNR) was established. Strategic sectors and financial institutions were acquired by the State, under Kérékou's regime, which pursued Marxist-based policies. In late 1975 the Parti de la révolution populaire du Bénin (PRPB) was established as the sole party, and Dahomey was renamed the People's Republic of Benin.

In August 1977 the CNR adopted a *Loi fondamentale* decreeing new structures in government. Elections to a new 'supreme authority', the Assemblée nationale révolutionnaire (ANR), took place in November 1979, when a single list of 336 'People's Commissioners' was approved by 97.5% of voters. At the same time a Comité exécutif national (CEN) was established to replace the CNR. The PRPB designated Kérékou as the sole candidate for President of the Republic, and in February 1980 the ANR unanimously elected him to this office. A gradual moderation in Benin's domestic policies followed. At legislative elections in June 1984 the single list of People's Commissioners was approved by 98% of voters, and in July the ANR re-elected Kérékou, again the sole candidate, as President.

In January 1987 Kérékou resigned from the army to become a civilian Head of State. At elections to the ANR in June 1989 89.6% of voters endorsed the single list of PRPB-approved candidates. In August the ANR re-elected Kérékou (once again the sole candidate) as President. At the end of the year Kérékou instituted major political changes, abandoning Marxism-Leninism as the official state ideology.

In February 1990 delegates at a conference of the 'active forces of the nation' voted to adopt a 'national charter' that was to form the basis of a new constitution. An interim Haut conseil de la République (HCR) was appointed to assume the functions of the ANR. Among the members of the HCR were former Presidents Ahomadegbé, Maga and Zinsou. Presidential and legislative elections, to be held in the context of a multi-party political system, were scheduled for early 1991. A former official of the World Bank (who had briefly been Minister of Finance and Economic Affairs in the mid-1960s), Nicéphore Soglo, was designated interim Prime Minister. The conference also voted to change the country's name to the Republic of Benin. The HCR was inaugurated in March 1990 and Soglo appointed a transitional Government; of the previous administration, only Kérékou remained in office. In May civilian administrators replaced the provincial military prefects, prior to an extensive restructuring of the armed forces. Legislation permitting the registration of political parties was promulgated in August.

A national referendum on the draft Constitution was conducted on 2 December 1990. Voters were asked to choose between two proposed documents, one of which incorporated a clause stipulating upper and lower age-limits for presidential candidates, and would therefore prevent the candidatures of Ahomadegbé, Maga and Zinsou. It was reported that 95.8% of those who voted approved one or other of the versions, with 79.7% of voters favouring the age-restriction clause.

Following legislative elections on 17 February 1991, the largest grouping in the new 64-member Assemblée nationale was an alliance of three pro-Soglo parties, which secured 12 seats. Kérékou and Soglo were among 13 candidates at the first round of the presidential election on 10 March. Soglo, who won 36.2% of the total votes cast, received his greatest support in the south of the country, while Kérékou, who received 27.3% of the overall vote, was reported to have secured the support of more than 80% of voters in the north. Soglo and Kérékou proceeded to a second round of voting on 24 March, when Soglo was elected President, with 67.7% of the total votes cast. Soglo was inaugurated as President on 4 April.

In June 1991 a 34-member pro-Soglo parliamentary grouping, styled Le Renouveau, was formed in the Assemblée nationale. In October 1992 15 deputies withdrew from Le Renouveau, alleging that Soglo was consistently excluding the legislature from the decision-making process. In July Soglo, who had previously asserted his political neutrality, had made public his membership of a political party, La renaissance du Bénin (RB), formed by his wife, Rosine Soglo, in 1992; he was appointed leader of the RB in July 1994.

In November 1994 the Assemblée nationale voted to establish an independent electoral supervisory body, the Commission électorale nationale autonome (CENA), despite resistance from Soglo, who also opposed a planned increase in the number of deputies from 64 to 83. Some 31 political organizations participated in the legislative elections held on 28 March

1995. In mid-April the Constitutional Court annulled the results of voting for 13 seats on the grounds of irregularities. Following by-elections in May, the RB held 20 seats in the Assemblée nationale, and other supporters of Soglo 13. Opposition parties held 49 seats, the most prominent being the Parti du renouveau démocratique (PRD), with 19 seats, and the Front d'action pour le renouveau et le développement—Alafia (FARD—Alafia), with 10; the latter had attracted considerable support from Kérékou supporters in the north, although the former President had not actively campaigned in the election. In June 1995 Bruno Amoussou, the leader of the opposition Parti social-démocrate (PSD), was elected President of the Assemblée nationale. Later that month a new Government was formed.

In January 1996 Kérékou announced his candidature at the presidential elections to be held later that year. While Soglo's economic policies had earned his administration the respect of the international financial community, there was internal disquiet that growth had been achieved at the expense of social concerns.

The first round of the presidential election, on 3 March 1996, was contested by seven candidates. Some 22.8% of the votes cast were invalidated by the Constitutional Court prior to the announcement of the official results, whereby Soglo secured 35.7% of the valid votes and Kérékou 33.9%, followed by the leader of the PRD, Adrien Houngbédji (19.7%), and Amoussou (7.8%). The rate of participation by voters was 86.9%. Most of the defeated candidates quickly expressed their support for Kérékou, among them Houngbédji, who had, in 1975, been sentenced to death *in absentia* for his part in a plot to overthrow Kérékou's military regime. The second round of voting took place on 18 March. Several days later the Constitutional Court announced Kérékou's election, with 52.5% of the valid votes. Some 78.1% of those eligible had voted, and less than 3% of the votes had been disallowed.

Elections to the 83 seats in the Assemblée nationale, held on 30 March 1999, were contested by more than 2,900 candidates, representing 35 parties and alliances. International monitors reported that the elections had been conducted peacefully and democratically. The combined opposition parties won a slender majority in the legislature, with 42 seats. The RB won the largest number of seats, with 27, principally in the south and centre, while FARD—Alafia, the PSD and other parties loyal to the President performed strongly in the north and west. The rate of participation by voters was in excess of 70%. Houngbédji was elected Speaker of the new assembly. In June Kérékou effected a government reshuffle, increasing the number of parties represented in the Council of Ministers from seven to 10, in an apparent effort to consolidate his support in the Assemblée nationale. In early 2000 Soglo and Houngbédji formed a new alliance of 10 opposition parties, which condemned the perceived corruption of the Kérékou administration, particularly in relation to the privatization of SONACOP.

In the period preceding the presidential election, scheduled for March 2001, Soglo was widely regarded as the sole credible challenger to Kérékou. Early results of the first round of the election, which was held on 4 March and contested by 17 candidates, indicated that Kérékou had gained the largest share of the vote, but had failed to secure an absolute majority; a second round, to be contested by Kérékou and Soglo, the second-placed candidate, was scheduled for 18 March. As campaigning proceeded, the Constitutional Court conducted a review of the election results declared by the CENA. Revised provisional results of the first round gave Kérékou 45.4% of the votes cast, Soglo 27.1%, Houngbédji 12.6% and Amoussou 8.6%. Following the declaration of the revised results, which indicated a participation rate of around 80%, there were calls for a boycott of the second round of voting, owing to alleged irregularities in the conduct of the first round. Soglo appealed to the Constitutional Court to annul the disputed results, and to rerun the election. On 16 March Soglo, having had his appeal rejected, withdrew his candidature. The Government postponed the second round of the election, which was thus to be contested by Kérékou and Houngbédji, firstly until 19 March and subsequently until 22 March. However, on 19 March Houngbédji also declared his dissatisfaction with the conduct of the election and withdrew from the second round. Consequently, Amoussou, who had previously declared his support for Kérékou, was now to challenge him for the presidency. Nine opposition members of the CENA resigned in protest at the conduct of the election. Voter participation in the second round of voting, duly held on 22 March, was significantly lower than in the first round, at about 55%. Two days after polling the CENA announced that Kérékou had won 84.1% of the valid votes cast. Kérékou was declared President for a further term, despite allegations that the depleted CENA was not qualified to organize the election.

In May 2001 Kérékou announced the formation of a new Government. Amoussou was reappointed to a senior position in the Council of Ministers, as Minister of State, responsible for the Co-ordination of Government Action, Future Planning and Development. One of the stated priorities of the new administration was to combat corruption, and the Government announced the implementation of what it termed a strategic plan to that end.

In late 2001 and early 2002 up to 32,000 civil servants and workers, primarily in the health and education sectors, participated in a series of nation-wide strikes, in support of demands for higher salaries and the withdrawal of proposals to introduce promotion on grounds of merit within the public sector. (Sporadic industrial unrest, notably within the civil service, had occurred intermittently since the mid-1990s.) In early March 2002 the Government reached agreement with six of the seven trade unions that had organized the strikes; wage arrears were to be paid and an increase in civil servants' salaries granted, while the question of procedures for promotions was to be referred to the Assemblée nationale.

Following the legislative elections held on 30 March 2003, a secure pro-presidential majority in the Assemblée nationale was formed for the first time since the introduction of multi-party elections in Benin. Pro-Kérékou parties and alliances won 52 of the 83 elective seats, and in mid-April the PRD, which had secured 11 seats, announced that it would, henceforth, also support the Government. The Union pour le Bénin du futur (UBF) emerged as the largest single party, with 31 seats. The representation of the RB, the largest party in the outgoing assembly, was reduced from 27 to 15 seats. Nine other parties or alliances won representation in the elections. It was reported that as many as one-half of the deputies elected to the new legislature had not served in the outgoing assembly. Among the new deputies elected was the President's son, Modeste Kérékou. At the end of April Antoine Idji Kolawolé, hitherto Minister of Foreign Affairs and African Integration, was elected as President of the Assemblée nationale, defeating Rosine Soglo. The formation of a new Government was announced in mid-June 2003: Amoussou was appointed to the most senior ministerial post in the new Government, as Minister of State, responsible for Planning and Development.

A major political concern during late 2003 was the alleged involvement of senior police and judicial officials with international criminal gangs involved in the smuggling of stolen motor cars based in Benin. The activities of these gangs had, in mid-August, resulted in the closure of the Beninois–Nigerian border for six days (see below). In late October, following the publication of a report by a recently formed presidential special commission on alleged links between government officials and organized criminal groups, the Beninois authorities announced that several senior police and judicial officials had been dismissed. In June 2004, in an unrelated case of corruption, 37 civil servants from the judiciary and the Ministry of Finance and the Economy were sentenced to between 30 months' and five years' imprisonment for their involvement in the embezzlement of more than 8,000m. francs CFA from state funds between 1996 and 2000.

In February 2005 President Kérékou effected a major cabinet reshuffle. Amoussou was removed from the Government and was replaced as Minister of State, responsible for Planning and Development by Zul Kifl Salami. During the course of 2005 the forthcoming presidential election (due to be held in March 2006) was the principal focus of political debate in Benin. There was widespread speculation that Kérékou might attempt either to implement constitutional changes in order to seek a third consecutive term of office as elected President or to postpone the election; indeed, in late 2005 senior members of the Government stated that a lack of budgetary funds could prevent the election from being held as scheduled, and suggested that presidential polling be held concurrently with the legislative elections scheduled for 2007. In January 2006 civil servants staged two days of strike action in protest against any such postponement. Moreover, the appointment, in late January, of Col (retd) Martin Dohou Azonhiho as Minister of State, responsible for National Defence, resulted in further controversy; Azonhiho, who had held several senior positions in Kérékou's military and Marxist governments from the mid-1970s had, prior to his appointment, been a vocal proponent of the postponement of the elections, and had served a prison sentence for embezzlement, prior to his release on parole in 2001. However, in January 2006 Kérékou announced that funding for the elections would be forthcoming, and at the end of the month the Constitutional Court approved 26 of the 29 presidential candidacies presented to it. In mid-February Rogatien Biaou was dismissed as Minister of Foreign Affairs, following the announcement that he was to be investigated on charges of corruption related to the illegal sale of land around the Beninois embassy to the USA.

The first round of presidential polling was held, as scheduled, on 5 March 2006. The CENA announced the results of voting on 12 March, several days later than expected. Boni Yayi, who had recently resigned as President of the Banque Ouest-Africaine de Développement to contest the election, received the largest share of the votes cast (35.64%), followed by Houngbédji, with 24.22%. Amoussou was placed third, with 16.29%, while Léhadi Vinagnon Vitoun Soglo, one of two sons of Nicephoré and Rosine Soglo to contest the election, was fourth, with 8.44%. Around 75% of the electorate voted. Yayi and Houngbédji progressed to a run-off poll, scheduled for 19 March. Despite several candidates, and, notably, Kérékou, expressing concern at possible fraudulent practice, international monitors described the election as broadly free and fair. Following the confirmation of the results by the Constitutional Court, the Court agreed to a request by the CENA that the second round of voting be postponed until 22 March; the CENA stated that the delay in announcing the results of the first round necessitated additional preparation time before the run-off poll. However, on 18 March Kérékou overruled the decision of the Constitutional Court to delay voting and announced that the election would take place, as initially proposed, on the following day. Despite the confusion caused by the rescheduling, voting duly proceeded on 19 March. According to the results of the second round, announced several days later by the Constitutional Court, Yayi was overwhelmingly elected as President, obtaining 74.52% of the votes cast; he was inaugurated as Head of State on 6 April. On 9 April Yayi appointed a new, 22-member Council of Ministers, of which 13 members were not affiliated to any political party. The most senior position, to which Pascal Koulpaki was appointed, was that of Minister of Development, Economy and Finance.

In late June 2006 it was reported that the Assemblée nationale had voted to extend its mandate from four years to five, thus postponing legislative elections, which were due to be held in March 2007, until 2008. However, in September 2006 the Constitutional Court ruled that the decision was invalid and in early February 2007 President Yayi confirmed that legislative elections would take place the following month. In mid-March a convoy in which President Yayi was returning from an election campaign rally in the north was attacked by gunmen as it travelled towards Cotonou; four members of the presidential guard were injured although the President's car was not hit and Yayi was unharmed.

The legislative elections were held on 31 March 2007, following a delay of one week, owing to organizational difficulties. According to provisional results released by the Constitutional Court in mid-April, the Force cauri pour un Bénin emergent, a pro-Yayi coalition of some 20 parties, took 35 of the 83 seats, while the Alliance pour une dynamique démocratique, of which Soglo's RB was a member, secured 20 seats. The PRD won 10 seats and a further nine parties or alliances secured parliamentary representation. The rate of voter participation was recorded at 58.7%. In June President Yayi named his new Government; of the 17 new appointments the most notable included Soulé Mana Lawani, who was awarded the finance portfolio, and Moussa Okanla, who became Minister of Foreign Affairs, African Integration, Francophone Affairs and Beninois Abroad. Kolpaki was again appointed to the most senior position, namely that of Minister of State, in charge of Planning, Development and the Evaluation of Public Action. In November a reorganization was effected in which the Ministry of Primary Education, Literacy and National Languages was split into two departments. Roger Gbegnonvi became the new Minister of Literacy and the Promotion of National Languages, while Christine Ouinsavi retained the primary education portfolio and assumed responsibility for nursery education.

Benin has in recent years played an active role in efforts to coordinate regional peace-keeping and humanitarian assistance operations, contributing troops to peace-keeping operations undertaken by the Economic Community of West African States (see p. 232) in Guinea-Bissau from late 1998 until mid-1999, in Côte d'Ivoire from early 2003, and in Liberia from September 2003.

Benin maintains generally good relations with neighbouring countries and joined the Community of Sahel-Saharan States (see p. 411) in March 2002. None the less, in mid-2000 a long-term dispute between Benin and Niger, over the ownership of various small islands in the Niger river, erupted after Nigerien soldiers reportedly sabotaged the construction of a Beninois administrative building on Lété Island. Meetings between representatives of the two Governments and arbitration by the Organization of African Unity (now the African Union, see p. 164) failed to resolve the dispute, and in April 2002 the two countries officially ratified an agreement (signed in 2001) to refer the dispute to the International Court of Justice (ICJ) in The Hague, Netherlands, for arbitration. Benin and Niger filed confidential written arguments with the Court, and in November 2003 a five-member Chamber formed to consider the case held its first public sitting. Both countries subsequently submitted counter-arguments, and a third written pleading was submitted by both parties in December of that year. (In June the UN had awarded Benin and Niger US $350,000 each towards the cost of resolving their dispute.) In July 2005 the ICJ issued a final ruling to the effect that 16 of the 25 disputed islands, including Lété, belonged to Niger; the Governments of both countries announced their acceptance of the ruling.

Benin and Nigeria launched joint police patrols along their common border in August 2001. However, renewed concerns about cross-border crime resulted in the unilateral closure, by the Nigerian authorities, of the frontier in August 2003. Following a meeting between the Presidents of the two countries later in the month, the border was reopened, and the Beninois and Nigerian authorities announced a series of measures intended to enhance co-operation to combat cross-border crime, including restrictions of certain types of export trade from Benin to Nigeria. Nevertheless, security around the common border was believed to have been the main focus of further discussions between Kérékou and President Gen. Olusegun Obasanjo of Nigeria in April 2004. In January 2005 it was announced that joint border patrols were to resume.

From late April 2005 thousands of Togolese sought refuge in Benin, having fled the violence that followed a presidential election in that country (see Recent History of Togo). In December the office of the UN High Commissioner for Refugees estimated that some 26,632 Togolese refugees had fled to Benin. By the end of 2006 the number of Togolese refugees remaining in Benin was reported to have decreased to 9,444.

Government

The Constitution of the Republic of Benin, which was approved in a national referendum on 2 December 1990, provides for a civilian, multi-party political system. Executive power is vested in the President of the Republic, who is elected by direct universal adult suffrage with a five-year mandate, renewable only once. The legislature is the 83-member Assemblée nationale, which is similarly elected, for a period of four years, by universal suffrage. The President of the Republic appoints the Council of Ministers, subject to formal parliamentary approval.

For the purposes of local administration, Benin is divided into 12 departments, each administered by a civilian prefect. These departments are further divided into a total of 77 communes.

Defence

As assessed at November 2007, the Beninois Armed Forces numbered an estimated 4,750 in active service (land army 4,300, navy 100, air force 350). Paramilitary forces comprised a 2,500-strong gendarmerie. Military service is by selective conscription, and lasts for 18 months. The estimated defence budget for 2007 was 26,200m. francs CFA.

Economic Affairs

In 2006, according to estimates by the World Bank, Benin's gross national income (GNI), measured at average 2004–06 prices, was US $4,665m., equivalent to $540 per head (or $1,160 on an international purchasing-power parity basis). During 1996–2006, it was estimated, the population increased at an average annual rate of 3.1%, while gross domestic product (GDP) per head increased, in real terms, by an average of 1.3% per year. Overall GDP increased, in real terms, at an average annual rate of 4.4% in 1996–2006; growth in 2006 was 4.1%.

According to preliminary figures, agriculture (including forestry and fishing) contributed 35.6% of GDP in 2005. In that year an estimated 49.1% of the labour force were employed in the sector, according to FAO. The principal cash crops are cotton (exports of which accounted for an estimated 65.0% of total exports in 2001), oil palm and cashew nuts. Benin is normally self-sufficient in basic foods; the main subsistence crops are cassava, yams and maize. The World Bank estimated that agricultural GDP increased at an average annual rate of 5.0% in 1996–2005; growth in 2005 was 4.4%.

Industry (including mining, manufacturing, construction and power) contributed 14.7% of GDP in 2005, according to preliminary figures, and engaged 10.4% of the employed labour force at the time of the 1992 census. According to the World Bank, industrial GDP increased at an average annual rate of 4.0% in 1996–2005; growth in 2005 was 4.6%.

Mining contributed only 0.3% of GDP in 2005, according to preliminary figures, and engaged less than 0.1% of the employed labour force in 1992. Petroleum extraction at Sémé was terminated on the grounds of unprofitability in 1998, contributing to a 82.2% decline in mining GDP in the following year. However, a contract signed between Benin and the multinational Zetah Oil Company in October 1999 envisaged the exploitation of Sémé's remaining petroleum reserves, estimated at some 22m. barrels, and operations recommenced in 2000. Marble and limestone are also exploited commercially. There are also deposits of gold, phosphates, natural gas, iron ore, silica sand, peat and chromium. The GDP of the mining sector declined at an average annual rate of 28.6% in 1994–2001; growth in mining GDP was negligible in 2001.

The manufacturing sector, which, according to preliminary figures, contributed 8.7% of GDP in 2005, engaged 7.8% of the employed labour force in 1992. The sector is based largely on the processing of primary products (principally cotton-ginning and oil-palm processing). Construction materials and some simple consumer goods are also produced for the domestic market. According to the World Bank, manufacturing GDP increased at an average annual rate of 4.0% in 1996–2005; growth in 2005 was 4.5%.

Benin is at present highly dependent on imports of electricity from Ghana (which supplied some 85% of total available production in 1996). It is envisaged that a hydroelectric installation on the Mono river, constructed and operated jointly with Togo, will reduce Benin's dependence on imported electricity, and a second such installation is under construction downstream. In 2004 hydroelectric sources were responsible for 1.2% of Benin's electricity production, while the remaining 98.8% was derived from petroleum. In 2000 the construction of a further electricity line, to run from Lagos, Nigeria, to Togo, through Benin, was proposed by the Governments of the three countries. A pipeline to supply natural gas from Nigeria to Benin, Togo and Ghana was expected to come on stream in early 2008, six years later than initially planned. Imports of mineral fuels and lubricants accounted for 23.0% of the value of total imports in 2004.

According to preliminary figures, the services sector contributed 49.6% of GDP in 2005, and engaged 31.8% of the employed labour force in 1992. The port of Cotonou is of considerable importance as an entrepôt for regional trade. According to the World Bank, the GDP of the services sector increased at an average annual rate of 4.2% in 1996–2005; the output of the sector increased by 0.9% in 2005.

In 2007, according to the IMF, Benin recorded a visible trade deficit of 261,800m. francs CFA, while there was a deficit of 164,700m. francs CFA on the current account of the balance of payments. In 2002 the principal source of imports (24.0%) was France; other major sources were the People's Republic of China, Côte d'Ivoire, Ghana and the United Kingdom. The principal market for exports in that year was Nigeria (22.2%); other important purchasers were India, Ghana, Indonesia and China. The principal exports in 2004 were textiles and cotton products (amounting to 69.5% of total exports), edible and oil-bearing fruits and tobacco products. The main imports in that year were food products (24.6% of the total) and mineral fuels and lubricants (23.0%).

In 2006 Benin recorded an overall budgetary deficit of just 7m. francs CFA (equivalent to 0.3% of GDP). The country's total external debt at the end of 2004 was US $1,916m., of which $1,827m. was long-term public debt. In 2003 the cost of debt-servicing was equivalent to 7.6% of the value of exports of goods and services. The annual rate of inflation, which had been negligible prior to the 50% devaluation of the CFA franc in January 1994, increased to 38.5% in that year, but slowed to an average of 3.5% per year in 1995–2002. The overall average annual rate of inflation between 1992 and 2006 was 6.0%. Consumer prices increased by 5.4% in 2005 and by 3.7% in 2006. About one-quarter of the urban labour force was estimated to be unemployed in 1997.

Benin is a member of the Economic Community of West African States (ECOWAS, see p. 232), of the West African organs of the Franc Zone (see p. 307), of the African Petroleum Producers' Association (APPA, see p. 407), of the Conseil de l'Entente (see p. 412) and of the Niger Basin Authority (see p. 413).

Benin experienced considerable economic growth during the 1990s, in part as a result of the country's perceived political stability, although more modest growth was recorded in the first half of the 2000s. In July 2000, as part of their initiative for heavily indebted poor countries (HIPCs), the IMF and the World Bank cancelled some US $460m. of Benin's debt and announced a further three-year enhanced HIPC programme for 2000–03. Also in that month the IMF approved funding of some $35.7m., under its Poverty Reduction and Growth Facility (PRGF), in support of the Government's economic programme for 2000–03. (In July 2002 the IMF announced that the PRGF arrangement was to be extended until 2004, and additional debt relief, amounting to $5m., was also granted under the HIPC initiative.) Although the primary marketing of the important crop of seed cotton was transferred, in January 2001, from the parastatal Société Nationale pour la Promotion Agricole (SONAPRA) to the private sector, the privatization of SONAPRA itself, which began in mid-2003 and which was expected to result in an eventual increase in the productivity of the sector, proceeded sporadically, amid protests by workers and unions that the company was being sold for less than its true value, while other privatization programmes were also subject to repeated delays. None the less, by the mid-2000s the country's cotton sector was one of the most liberalized in western or central Africa. In July 2005 Benin was among 18 countries to be granted 100% debt relief on multilateral debt agreed by the Group of Eight leading industrialized nations (G-8), subject to the approval of the lenders, and in 2006 Benin received some $1,100m. under the initiative. This was expected to be allocated towards spending on, *inter alia*, health and education. The further opening up of the cotton, telecommunications and electricity sectors to private capital, and the restructuring of the Port of Cotonou, to include the participation of private sector management, were expected to be priority measures for the Beninois authorities during the late 2000s. In June 2007 the African Development Bank approved a loan worth $48.6m. to Benin, Ghana and Togo, which would enable those countries to link their respective power grids and improve the reliability of their power production, while also lowering costs. Benin is particularly susceptible to droughts, which negatively affect the production capabilities of its hydroelectric power stations, and the project was also intended to safeguard overall electricity production. Meanwhile, a recovery in cotton production resulted in forecasted GDP growth of 3.8% for 2006, while inflation reached 3.8% in that year, according to the IMF. Cotton production continued its recovery in 2007, although at a slower pace. In spite of that and severe power shortages, the IMF projected an increase in GDP growth, to 4.0%, in 2007 and inflation was forecast to decline to 3.0%.

Education

The Constitution of Benin obliges the state to make a quality compulsory primary education available to all children. All public primary and secondary schools in Benin finance themselves through school fees. Primary education begins at six years of age and lasts for six years. Secondary education, beginning at 12 years of age, lasts for up to seven years, comprising a first cycle of four years and a second of three years. According to UNESCO estimates, primary enrolment in 2003/04 included 83% of children in the appropriate age-group (males 93%; females 72%), while enrolment at secondary schools in 2000/01 included 17% of children in the appropriate age group (males 23%; females 11%). In the 1990s the Government sought to extend the provision of education. In 1993 girls in rural areas were exempted from school fees, and in 1999 the Government created a 500m. francs CFA fund to increase female enrolment. The Université Nationale du Bénin, at Cotonou, was founded in 1970 and had a student population of approximately 9,000 in 1999/2000. A second university, in Parakou, with a student capacity of approximately 3,000, opened in 2001. In 2001 public expenditure on education totalled 71,100m. francs CFA.

BENIN

Statistical Survey

Public Holidays

2008: 1 January (New Year's Day), 10 January* (Vodoun national holiday), 16 January (Martyrs' Day, anniversary of mercenary attack on Cotonou), 21 March (Good Friday), 24 March (Easter Monday), 1 April (Youth Day), 1 May (Workers' Day and Ascension Day), 12 May (Whit Monday), 1 August (Independence Day), 15 August (Assumption), 1 October* (Id al-Fitr, end of Ramadan), 26 October (Armed Forces Day), 1 November (All Saints' Day), 30 November (National Day), 9 December* (Id al-Adha, Feast of the Sacrifice), 25 December (Christmas Day), 31 December (Harvest Day).

2009: 1 January (New Year's Day), 10 January (Vodoun national holiday), 16 January (Martyrs' Day, anniversary of mercenary attack on Cotonou), 1 April (Youth Day), 10 April (Good Friday), 13 April (Easter Monday), 1 May (Workers' Day), 21 May (Ascension Day), 1 June (Whit Monday), 1 August (Independence Day), 15 August (Assumption), 20 September* (Id al-Fitr, end of Ramadan), 26 October (Armed Forces Day), 1 November (All Saints' Day), 27 November* (Id al-Adha, Feast of the Sacrifice), 30 November (National Day), 25 December (Christmas Day), 31 December (Harvest Day).

*These holidays are dependent on the Islamic lunar calendar and may vary by one or two days from the dates given.

Weights and Measures

The metric system is in force.

Statistical Survey

Source (unless otherwise stated): Institut National de la Statistique et de l'Analyse Economique, BP 323, Cotonou; tel. 21-30-82-43; fax 21-30-82-46; e-mail insae@insae-bj.org; internet www.insae-bj.org.

Area and Population

AREA, POPULATION AND DENSITY

Area (sq km)	112,622*
Population (census results)	
15–29 February 1992	4,915,555
11 February 2002	
Males	3,284,119
Females	3,485,795
Total	6,769,914
Population (UN estimates at mid-year)†	
2005	8,490,000
2006	8,760,000
2007	9,033,000
Density (per sq km) at mid-2007	80.2

* 43,484 sq miles.
† Source: UN, *World Population Prospects: The 2006 Revision*.

ETHNIC GROUPS

2002 (percentages): Fon 39.2 (incl. Fon 17.6; Goun 6.3; Aïzo 4.3; Mahi 3.5; Ouémè 2.5; Torri 2.4; Kotafon 1.4; Tofin 1.3); Adja 15.2 (incl. Adja 8.7; Sahouè 2.6; Xwla 1.4; Mina 1.2); Yoruba 12.3 (incl. Nagot 6.8; Yoruba 1.8; Idaasha 1.5; Holli-Djè 1.4); Bariba 9.2 (incl. Bariba 8.3); Peulh 6.9 (incl. Peulh Fulfuldé 5.5); Otamari 6.1 (incl. Berba 1.4; Ditamari 1.3; Waama 1.0); Yoa Lokpa 4.5 (incl. Yoa 1.8; Lokpa 1.2); Dendi 2.5 (incl. Dendi 2.4); Others 2.7.

ADMINISTRATIVE DIVISIONS
(2002 census)

Département	Area (sq km)	Population	Population density (per sq km)
Alibori	25,683	521,093	20.3
Atacora	20,459	549,417	26.9
Atlantique	3,233	801,683	247.9
Borgou	25,310	724,171	28.6
Collines	13,561	535,923	39.5
Couffo	2,404	524,586	218.2
Donga	10,691	350,062	32.7
Littoral	79	665,100	8,419.0
Mono	1,396	360,037	257.9
Ouémé	2,835	730,772	257.8
Plateau	1,865	407,116	218.3
Zou	5,106	599,954	117.5
Total	**112,622**	**6,769,914**	**60.1**

PRINCIPAL TOWNS
(Communes, 2002 census)

Cotonou	665,100	Seme-Kpodji	115,238
Abomey-Calavi	307,745	Bohicon	113,091
Porto-Novo (capital)	223,552	Tchaourou	106,852
Djougou	181,895	Savalou	104,749
Banikoara	152,028	Malanville	101,628
Parakou	149,819	Ketou	100,499
Aplahoue	116,988	Kalale	100,026

Mid-2003 (incl. suburbs, UN estimate): Cotonou 827,754 (Source: UN, *World Urbanization Prospects: The 2003 Revision*).

Mid-2005 (incl. suburbs, UN estimate): Porto Novo 242,000 (Source: UN, *World Urbanization Prospects: The 2005 Revision*).

BIRTHS AND DEATHS
(annual averages, UN estimates)

	1990–95	1995–2000	2000–05
Birth rate (per 1,000)	46.3	44.0	42.2
Death rate (per 1,000)	13.9	12.8	12.6

Source: UN, *World Population Prospects: The 2006 Revision*.

2002: Birth rate 41.2 per 1,000; Death rate 12.3 per 1,000.

Expectation of life (years at birth, WHO estimates): 52.8 (males 52.3; females 53.2) in 2005 (Source: WHO, *World Health Statistics*).

ECONOMICALLY ACTIVE POPULATION
(persons aged 10 years and over, 1992 census)

	Males	Females	Total
Agriculture, hunting, forestry and fishing	780,469	367,277	1,147,746
Mining and quarrying	609	52	661
Manufacturing	93,157	67,249	160,406
Electricity, gas and water	1,152	24	1,176
Construction	50,959	696	51,655
Trade, restaurants and hotels	36,672	395,829	432,501
Transport, storage and communications	52,228	609	52,837
Finance, insurance, real estate and business services	2,705	401	3,106
Community, social and personal services	126,122	38,422	164,544
Activities not adequately defined	25,579	12,917	38,496
Total employed	**1,169,652**	**883,476**	**2,053,128**
Unemployed	26,475	5,843	32,318
Total labour force	**1,196,127**	**889,319**	**2,085,446**

Source: ILO, *Yearbook of Labour Statistics*.

2002 (census results): Total employed 2,811,753 (males 1,421,474, females 1,390,279); Unemployed 19,123 (males 12,934, females 6,189); Total labour force 2,830,876 (males 1,434,408, females 1,396,468).

Mid-2005 (estimates in '000): Agriculture, etc. 1,919; Total labour force 3,910 (Source: FAO).

BENIN

Health and Welfare

KEY INDICATORS

Total fertility rate (children per woman, 2005)	5.6
Under-5 mortality rate (per 1,000 live births, 2005)	150
HIV/AIDS (% of persons aged 15–49, 2005)	1.8
Physicians (per 1,000 head, 2004)	0.04
Hospital beds (per 1,000 head, 2005)	0.50
Health expenditure (2004): US $ per head (PPP)	40.4
Health expenditure (2004): % of GDP	4.9
Health expenditure (2004): public (% of total)	51.2
Access to water (% of persons, 2004)	67
Access to sanitation (% of persons, 2004)	33
Human Development Index (2005): ranking	163
Human Development Index (2005): value	0.437

For sources and definitions, see explanatory note on p. vi.

Agriculture

PRINCIPAL CROPS
('000 metric tons)

	2004	2005	2006*
Rice (paddy)	64.7	78.3	71.0
Maize	842.6	864.7	671.9
Millet	36.8	37.7	32.8
Sorghum	163.8	169.2	156.6
Sweet potatoes	50.0	64.0	53.8
Cassava (Manioc)	2,955.0	2,861.4	2,524.2
Yams	2,257.3	2,083.8	2,239.8
Sugar cane	68.5	64.3	37.8
Dry beans	93.8	104.6	80.2
Cashew nuts (in shell)*	40	47	41
Groundnuts (in shell)	151.7	140.3	99.4
Coconuts	20†	20†	20
Oil palm fruit*	244	257	245
Cottonseed	235†	190†	124
Tomatoes	144.2	143.3	113.6
Chillies and green peppers	33.6	50.9	59.4
Okra	69.5	76.2	77.4
Pineapples	110.8	121.2	80.1
Cotton (lint)	150†	122†	78

* FAO estimates.
† Unofficial figure.

Aggregate production ('000 metric tons, may include official, semi-official or estimated data): Total cereals 1,109 in 2004, 1,152 in 2005, 934 in 2006; Total roots and tubers 5,265 in 2004, 5,012 in 2005, 4,820 in 2006; Total pulses 119 in 2004, 123 in 2005, 90 in 2006; Total vegetables (incl. melons) 351 in 2004, 380 in 2005, 370 in 2006; Total fruits (excl. melons) 254 in 2004, 264 in 2005, 229 in 2006.

Source: FAO.

LIVESTOCK
('000 head, year ending September)

	2003	2004	2005*
Cattle	1,689	1,745	1,800
Sheep	670*	700*	750
Goats	1,300*	1,350*	1,380
Pigs	297	309	322
Chickens	10,000*	13,000*	13,000

* FAO estimate(s).

2006: Figures assumed to be unchanged from 2005 (FAO estimates).
Source: FAO.

LIVESTOCK PRODUCTS
('000 metric tons, FAO estimates)

	2004	2005	2006
Cattle meat	21.1	21.8	22.0
Goat meat	4.6	4.7	4.8
Pig meat	3.9	4.1	4.2
Chicken meat	12.1	12.3	16.0
Game meat	6.0	6.0	6.0
Cows' milk	27.2	28.1	28.9
Goats' milk	7.1	7.2	7.4
Hen eggs	9.4	9.4	10.1

Source: FAO.

Forestry

ROUNDWOOD REMOVALS
('000 cubic metres, excl. bark, FAO estimates)

	2003	2004	2005
Sawlogs, veneer logs and logs for sleepers	35	35	35
Other industrial wood	297	297	297
Fuel wood	162	162	6,061
Total	494	494	6,393

2006: Figures assumed to be unchanged from 2005 (FAO estimates).
Source: FAO.

SAWNWOOD PRODUCTION
('000 cubic metres, incl. railway sleepers)

	2002	2003	2004*
Total (all broadleaved)	46	31	31

* FAO estimate.
2005–06: Production as in 2004 (FAO estimate).
Source: FAO.

Fishing

('000 metric tons, live weight)

	2003	2004	2005
Capture	41.6	40.0	38.0
Tilapias*	10.9	10.2	10.2
Black catfishes*	1.5	1.4	1.4
Torpedo-shaped catfishes*	1.5	1.4	1.4
Mullets	2.1	2.1	2.1
Sardinellas	1.8	1.6	1.2
Bonga shad	1.7	1.6	1.6
European anchovy	1.5	1.1	0.9
Bluefish	1.5	1.3	n.a.
Freshwater crustaceans*	4.6	4.3	4.3
Penaeus shrimps*	2.4	2.3	2.3
Aquaculture	0.0	0.0	0.4
Total catch (incl. others)*	41.7	40.0	38.4

* FAO estimates.
Note: Figures exclude catches by Beninois canoes operating from outside the country.
Source: FAO.

Mining

(estimates)

	2004	2005	2006
Clay ('000 metric tons)	21	21	21
Gold (kg)	20	20	20

Source: US Geological Survey.

Industry

SELECTED PRODUCTS
('000 metric tons, unless otherwise indicated)

	2000	2001	2002
Cement (hydraulic)*	250	250	250
Beer of barley†	35.0	35.0	35.0
Beer of sorghum†	32.8	35.0	41.8
Salted, dried or smoked fish†	2.0	2.0	2.0
Palm oil†	15	15	15
Palm kernel oil	9.7‡	9.7‡	9.7†
Electric energy (million kWh)	57	90	92

* Data from the US Geological Survey.
† Estimate(s).
‡ Unofficial figure.

Cement (hydraulic, '000 metric tons, estimates): 250 in 2004; 250 in 2005; 250 in 2006 (Source: US Geological Survey).

Salted, dried or smoked fish ('000 metric tons): 2.4 in 2003 (Source: FAO).

Electric energy (million kWh): 80 in 2003; 81 in 2004.

Sources: mainly UN, *Industrial Commodity Statistics Yearbook*; FAO.

Finance

CURRENCY AND EXCHANGE RATES

Monetary Units
100 centimes = 1 franc de la Communauté financière africaine (CFA).

Sterling, Dollar and Euro Equivalents (31 December 2007)
£1 sterling = 892.70 francs CFA;
US $1 = 445.59 francs CFA;
€1 = 655.96 francs CFA;
10,000 francs CFA = £11.20 = $22.44 = €15.24.

Average Exchange Rate (francs CFA per US $)
2005   527.47
2006   522.89
2007   479.27

Note: An exchange rate of 1 French franc = 50 francs CFA, established in 1948, remained in force until January 1994, when the CFA franc was devalued by 50%, with the exchange rate adjusted to 1 French franc = 100 francs CFA. This relationship to French currency remained in effect with the introduction of the euro on 1 January 1999. From that date, accordingly, a fixed exchange rate of €1 = 655.957 francs CFA has been in operation.

BUDGET
('000 million francs CFA)

Revenue*	2005	2006†	2007‡
Tax revenue	334.0	378.8	416.5
Taxes on international trade and transactions§	174.8	207.4	221.4
Direct and indirect taxes	159.2	171.4	195.1
Non-tax revenue	49.4	38.1	43.2
Total	383.4	416.9	459.7

Expenditure	2005	2006†	2007‡
Salaries	130.3	135.0	145.1
Pensions and scholarships	26.5	29.3	31.6
Other expenditure and current transfers	182.2	194.9	177.2
Investment	144.2	113.4	219.4
Budgetary contribution	76.3	48.6	106.2
Financed from abroad	67.9	64.8	113.2
Interest due	6.9	5.8	7.3
External debt	5.6	5.6	5.6
Net lending	–0.8	1.2	—
Total	489.3	479.6	580.6

* Excluding grants received ('000 million francs CFA): 47.9 in 2005; 55.7 in 2006 (estimate); 65.1 in 2007 (projection).
† Estimates.
‡ Projections.
§ Including value-added taxes on imports.

Source: IMF, *Benin: Second Review Under the Three-Year Arrangement Under the Poverty Reduction and Growth Facility and Request for Waiver of a Performance Criterion - Staff Report; Press Release on the Executive Board Discussion; and Statement by the Executive Director for Benin* (June 2007).

INTERNATIONAL RESERVES
(excluding gold, US $ million at 31 December)

	2004	2005	2006
IMF special drawing rights	—	0.2	0.1
Reserve position in IMF	3.4	3.1	3.3
Foreign exchange	636.5	653.5	908.9
Total	639.9	656.8	912.3

Source: IMF, *International Financial Statistics*.

MONEY SUPPLY
('000 million francs CFA at 31 December)

	2004	2005	2006
Currency outside banks	129.9	193.3	253.1
Demand deposits at deposit money banks	198.6	225.3	239.5
Checking deposits at post office	8.1	29.9	9.8
Total money (incl. others)	337.2	449.4	503.1

Source: IMF, *International Financial Statistics*.

COST OF LIVING
(Consumer Price Index; base: 2000 = 100)

	2004	2005	2006
Food, beverages and tobacco	104.7	114.4	113.8
Clothing	101.2	101.4	103.1
All items (incl. others)	109.0	114.9	119.2

Source: ILO.

BENIN

Statistical Survey

NATIONAL ACCOUNTS
('000 million francs CFA at current prices)

Expenditure on the Gross Domestic Product

	2004	2005*	2006†
Final consumption expenditure	1,881.6	2,028.5	2,200.2
Households, incl. non-profit institutions serving households	1,622.9	1,753.5	1,906.1
General government	258.7	274.9	294.1
Gross capital formation	442.4	437.0	505.7
Gross fixed capital formation	415.5	444.9	481.1
Changes in inventories / Acquisitions, less disposals, of valuables	27.0	−8.0	24.6
Total domestic expenditure	2,324.0	2,465.5	2,705.9
Exports of goods and services	428.7	494.7	471.6
Less Imports of goods and services	612.7	656.2	708.7
GDP in market prices	2,140.0	2,304.0	2,468.8

Gross Domestic Product by Economic Activity

	2004	2005*	2006†
Agriculture, livestock, forestry, hunting and fishing	690.3	751.4	824.8
Mining	5.0	5.3	5.8
Manufacturing	167.6	184.6	192.5
Water, gas and electricity	25.9	28.4	30.1
Construction and public works	86.8	92.9	100.4
Trade	354.3	382.4	396.3
Transport and communications	163.7	173.9	184.6
Banks and insurance	39.6	41.6	44.1
Non-market services	224.4	238.9	255.9
Other services	199.5	210.9	222.3
Sub-total	1,957.1	2,110.3	2,256.8
Less Financial intermediation services indirectly measured	36.1	37.9	40.2
Import taxes and duties	219.0	231.6	252.2
GDP in purchasers' values	2,140.0	2,304.0	2,468.8

* Preliminary figures.
† Projected figures.

BALANCE OF PAYMENTS
('000 million francs CFA)

	2005	2006*	2007†
Exports of goods f.o.b.	171.6	147.2	192.3
Imports of goods f.o.b.	−393.3	−399.4	−454.1
Trade balance	−221.7	−252.3	−261.8
Exports of services	129.6	121.1	128.0
Imports of services	−154.4	−143.4	−155.0
Balance on goods and services	−246.5	−274.6	−288.8
Income (net)	−20.3	−18.1	−22.5
Balance on goods, services and income	−266.8	−292.7	−311.3
Private unrequited transfers	63.6	72.4	76.7
Public unrequited transfers	47.5	61.6	70.0
Current balance	−155.7	−158.7	−164.7
Capital account (net)	39.7	607.8	60.6
Medium- and long-term public capital	47.0	−517.4	61.6
Medium- and long-term private capital	58.7	56.4	27.7
Deposit money banks	−20.4	26.5	—
Short-term capital	55.0	53.5	—
Net errors and omissions	46.0	47.7	—
Overall balance	70.4	115.8	−14.8

* Estimates.
† Projections.

Source: IMF, *Benin: Second Review Under the Three-Year Arrangement Under the Poverty Reduction and Growth Facility and Request for Waiver of a Performance Criterion - Staff Report; Press Release on the Executive Board Discussion; and Statement by the Executive Director for Benin* (June 2007).

External Trade

PRINCIPAL COMMODITIES
('000 million francs CFA)

Imports c.i.f.	2002	2003	2004
Food products	119.0	124.0	115.7
Textiles, cotton products, etc.	44.6	34.2	30.3
Capital goods	74.0	93.0	82.5
Mineral fuels, lubricants, etc.	87.5	104.9	108.3
Chemicals, chemical products, etc.	35.3	23.9	21.1
Pharmaceutical products	27.2	21.6	20.7
Total (incl. others)	502.4	515.1	471.0

Exports f.o.b.	2002	2003	2004
Textiles, cotton products, etc.	93.5	111.1	110.3
Edible fruit, oil-bearing fruit	15.5	15.4	12.4
Tobacco products, cigarettes, etc.	2.5	5.7	10.3
Wood, wood products, etc.	5.5	2.9	2.0
Lime, cement, etc.	1.1	3.0	6.3
Total (incl. others)	167.5	157.8	158.7

PRINCIPAL TRADING PARTNERS
(US $ million)

Imports c.i.f.	2000	2001	2002
Belgium	10.5	17.4	13.8
China, People's Repub.	29.6	48.0	46.7
Côte d'Ivoire	50.9	32.7	40.8
France (incl. Monaco)	146.9	138.7	174.3
Germany	15.9	17.2	21.0
Ghana	26.7	29.4	40.4
India	8.9	8.5	14.1
Italy	20.1	22.1	23.5
Japan	16.9	18.5	20.5
Korea, Repub.	3.0	6.3	6.8
Mauritania	7.6	2.7	2.8
Netherlands	32.2	23.2	29.1
Nigeria	10.2	29.3	27.8
Pakistan	5.5	2.0	0.8
Saudi Arabia	9.5	6.5	4.7
Senegal	12.5	11.7	21.7
South Africa	3.2	11.0	18.1
Spain	16.1	13.5	13.3
Thailand	15.0	19.1	20.4
United Kingdom	18.2	20.9	36.0
USA	18.1	26.0	21.1
Total (incl. others)	547.1	601.9	727.0

BENIN

Statistical Survey

Exports f.o.b.	2000	2001	2002
Bangladesh	7.2	2.0	3.0
Belgium	4.4	4.0	3.1
Brazil	16.8	10.4	0.9
China, People's Repub.	0.4	0.4	16.9
France (incl. Monaco)	3.2	4.7	11.9
Germany	4.0	3.2	3.2
Ghana	4.9	10.7	26.5
India	59.8	55.7	43.3
Indonesia	9.4	10.2	24.1
Italy	12.0	8.3	12.8
Morocco	7.1	4.4	9.0
Netherlands	0.8	1.1	6.5
Niger	7.4	4.5	5.6
Nigeria	2.8	9.7	67.6
Pakistan	1.5	1.3	12.8
Portugal	2.3	1.8	3.1
Saudi Arabia	2.0	2.3	0.7
Spain	5.6	4.8	4.7
Switzerland-Liechtenstein	2.6	1.5	3.6
Thailand	7.2	7.9	12.6
Turkey	8.9	3.7	3.7
United Kingdom	0.9	2.5	1.9
Viet Nam	0.8	3.3	1.2
Total (incl. others)	188.4	181.8	304.0

Source: UN, *International Trade Statistics Yearbook*.

Transport

RAILWAYS
(traffic)

	1998	1999	2000
Passengers carried ('000)	699.8	n.a.	n.a.
Passenger-km (million)	112.0	82.2	156.6
Freight ton-km (million)	218.7	269.0	153.2

Source: mainly IMF, *Benin: Statistical Appendix* (August 2002).

2001 (traffic, million): Passenger-km 101; Net ton-km 316 (Source: UN, *Statistical Yearbook*).

2002 (traffic, million): Net ton-km 482 (Source: UN, *Statistical Yearbook*).

ROAD TRAFFIC
(motor vehicles in use)

	1994	1995	1996
Passenger cars	26,507	30,346	37,772
Buses and coaches	353	405	504
Lorries and vans	5,301	6,069	7,554
Road tractors	2,192	2,404	2,620
Motorcycles and mopeds	220,800	235,400	250,000

Source: IRF, *World Road Statistics*.

Passenger cars ('000 in use): 135.7 in 2002; 135.7 in 2003 (Source: UN, *Statistical Yearbook*).

Commercial vehicles ('000 in use): 18.8 in 2002; 19.2 in 2003 (Source: UN, *Statistical Yearbook*).

SHIPPING

Merchant Fleet
(registered at 31 December)

	2003	2004	2005
Number of vessels	6	6	6
Total displacement ('000 grt)	1.0	1.0	1.0

Source: Lloyd's Register-Fairplay, *World Fleet Statistics*.

International Sea-borne Freight Traffic
(at Cotonou, including goods in transit, '000 metric tons)

	2001	2002	2003
Goods loaded	380.5	462.2	469.4
Goods in transit	6.5	5.6	8.6
Goods unloaded	2,929.3	3,007.7	3,808.9
Goods in transit	984.9	514.7	838.1

Source: IMF, *Benin: Statistical Appendix* (November 2004).

CIVIL AVIATION
(traffic on scheduled services, domestic and international)*

	1999	2000	2001
Kilometres flown (million)	3	3	1
Passengers carried ('000)	84	77	46
Passenger-km (million)	235	216	130
Total ton-km (million)	36	32	19

* Including an apportionment of the traffic of Air Afrique.

Source: UN, *Statistical Yearbook*.

Tourism

FOREIGN VISITORS BY COUNTRY OF ORIGIN*

	2003	2004	2005
Angola	8,592	9,613	10,540
Austria	4,000	3,000	2,500
Belgium	3,500	3,125	4,630
Burkina Faso	2,200	3,750	3,900
Burundi	2,100	2,157	2,749
Cameroon	9,814	10,599	11,500
Central African Republic	2,000	1,877	880
Chad	1,870	2,110	1,950
Congo, Republic	37,781	36,376	35,320
Côte d'Ivoire	12,000	10,705	10,900
France	11,000	14,210	16,147
Gabon	6,830	5,878	1,600
Germany	2,500	1,520	1,900
Ghana	7,311	7,511	6,600
Guinea	730	1,810	1,320
Madagascar	1,800	1,102	2,172
Malawi	2,100	2,330	700
Mali	1,300	1,210	900
Niger	6,810	5,900	5,300
Nigeria	19,800	20,200	20,500
Senegal	3,800	1,100	1,339
Togo	10,400	11,200	10,590
Tunisia	1,724	1,918	1,885
USA	350	211	21
Total (incl. others)	175,000	173,500	176,000

* Arrivals of non-resident tourists at national borders, by country of residence.

Receipts from tourism (US $ million, incl. passenger transport): 107.9 in 2003; 121.9 in 2004; n.a. in 2005.

Source: World Tourism Organization.

Communications Media

	2004	2005	2006
Telephones ('000 main lines in use)	72.8	76.3	77.3
Mobile cellular telephones ('000 subscribers)	386.7	750.0	1,055.7
Personal computers ('000 in use)	30	32	n.a.
Internet users ('000)	100	425	700
Broadband subscribers	100	200	100

Facsimile machines (number in use): 1,064 in 1996.
Source: International Telecommunication Union.

Television receivers: ('000 in use): 272 in 2000 (Source: UNESCO, *Statistical Yearbook*).

1999: Radio receivers ('000 in use): 2,661; Daily newspapers 13 (average circulation 32,500 copies); Non-daily newspapers 2 (average circulation 44,000 copies); Periodicals 106 (average circulation 110,000 copies) (Sources: UNESCO, *Statistical Yearbook* and Institute for Statistics).

Book production: 84 titles (42,000 copies) in 1994 (first editions only); 9 titles in 1998. Sources: UNESCO, *Statistical Yearbook*, UNESCO Institute for Statistics.

Education

(2004/05, except where otherwise indicated)

	Institutions	Teachers	Males	Females	Total
Pre-primary	283*	640	8.8	8.7	17.5
Primary	4,178†	28,148	744.0	574.1	1,318.1
Secondary	145‡	14,410§	281.2	154.3	435.4
Tertiary‖	n.a.	672	15.8	3.9	19.8

* 1995/96.
† 1999/2000.
‡ 1993/94.
§ 2003/04.
‖ 2000/01.

Source: UNESCO, *Statistical Yearbook* and Institute for Statistics.

Adult literacy rate (UNESCO estimates): 34.7% (males 46.9%; females 23.3%) in 2004 (Source: UN Development Programme, *Human Development Report*).

Directory

The Constitution

A new Constitution was approved in a national referendum on 2 December 1990. Its main provisions are summarized below:

PREAMBLE

The Beninois People reaffirm their opposition to any political regime founded on arbitrariness, dictatorship, injustice and corruption, reassert their attachment to the principles of democracy and human rights, as defined in the United Nations Charter, the Universal Declaration of Human Rights and the African Charter of the Rights of Man and Peoples, proclaim their attachment to the cause of African Unity and solemnly adopt this new Constitution as the supreme Law of the State.

I. THE STATE AND SOVEREIGNTY

Articles 1–6: The State of Benin is an independent, sovereign, secular, democratic Republic. The capital is Porto-Novo. The official language is French. The principle of the Republic is 'government of the People, by the People and for the People'. National sovereignty belongs to the People and is exercised through elected representatives and by referendums. Political parties operate freely, as determined by the Charter of Political Parties, and must respect the principles of national sovereignty, democracy, territorial integrity and the secular basis of the State. Suffrage is universal, equal and secret.

II. RIGHTS AND DUTIES OF THE INDIVIDUAL

Articles 7–40: The State is obliged to respect and protect the sacred and inviolable rights of the individual, and ensures equal access to health, education, culture, information, vocational training and employment. Primary education is compulsory. The State progressively assures the provision of free public education. Private schools are permitted. Torture and the use of cruel or degrading punishment are prohibited, and detention is subject to strict limitations. All persons have the right to property ownership, to freedom of conscience and expression. The State guarantees the freedoms of movement and association. All are equal before the law. The State recognizes the right to strike. Military service is compulsory.

III. THE EXECUTIVE

Articles 41–78: The President of the Republic is the Head of State. Candidates for the presidency must be of Beninois nationality by birth or have been naturalized for at least 10 years, and must be aged 40–70 years. The President is elected for a mandate of five years, renewable only once, by an absolute majority of votes cast. If no candidate receives an absolute majority, a second round is to be held between the two highest placed candidates. The Constitutional Court oversees the regularity of voting and announces the results. No President may serve more than two mandates.

The President of the Republic holds executive power. Following consultation with the Bureau of the Assemblée nationale, he names the members of the Government, who may not hold any parliamentary mandate. The President of the Republic chairs the Council of Ministers and has various defined powers of appointment.

The President of the Republic promulgates laws adopted by the Assemblée nationale, and may demand the resubmission of a law to the Assemblée nationale prior to its promulgation. In the event that the President of the Republic fails to promulgate a law, the Constitutional Court may, in certain circumstances, declare the law as binding.

After consultation with the President of the Assemblée nationale and the President of the Constitutional Court, the President of the Republic may call a referendum on matters pertaining to human rights, sub-regional or regional integration or the organization of public powers. The President of the Republic is the Supreme Chief of the Armed Forces.

The President of the Republic may delegate certain specified powers to ministers. The President of the Republic or any member of his Government may be called to account by the Assemblée nationale.

IV. THE LEGISLATURE

i. The Assemblée Nationale

Articles 79–93: Parliament exercises legislative power and controls the activities of the Government. Deputies of the Assemblée nationale, who must be civilians, are elected by direct universal suffrage for four years, and may be re-elected. The Assemblée nationale elects its President and a Bureau. Deputies enjoy various conditions of immunity from prosecution.

ii. Relations between the Assemblée Nationale and the Government

Articles 94–113: Members of the Government may attend sessions of the Assemblée nationale. Laws are approved by a simple majority, although organic laws require an absolute majority and approval by the Constitutional Court. The Assemblée nationale authorizes any declaration of war. States of siege and of emergency are declared in the Council of Ministers, although the Assemblée nationale must approve the extension of any such state beyond 15 days.

Deputies may, by a three-quarters' majority, decide to submit any question to referendum. If the Assemblée nationale has not approved a balanced budget by 31 December of any year, the measures foreseen by the finance law may be implemented by ordinance.

V. THE CONSTITUTIONAL COURT

Articles 114–124: The Constitutional Court is composed of seven members, of which four are named by the Bureau of the Assemblée nationale and three by the President of the Republic, each for a mandate of five years, renewable only once. The President of the Constitutional Court is elected by his peers for a period of five years and is a senior magistrate or lawyer. The decisions of the Constitutional Court are not subject to appeal.

VI. THE JUDICIARY

Articles 125–130: The judiciary is independent of the legislature and of the executive. It consists of the Supreme Court, and other courts and tribunals created in accordance with the Constitution. Judges may not be removed from office. The President of the Republic appoints magistrates and is the guarantor of the independence of the judiciary, assisted by the Higher Council of Magistrates, the composition, attributes, organization and function of which are fixed by an organic law.

i. The Supreme Court

Articles 131–134: The Supreme Court is the highest jurisdiction of the State in administrative and judicial matters, and with regard to the accounts of the State and to local elections. The decisions of the Court are not subject to appeal. The President of the Supreme Court is appointed for five years by the President of the Republic. The President of the Supreme Court may not be removed from office during his mandate, which is renewable only once.

ii. The High Court of Justice

Articles 135–138: The High Court of Justice comprises the members of the Constitutional Court (other than its President), six deputies of the Assemblée nationale and the President of the Supreme Court. The High Court of Justice elects a President from among its members and is competent to try the President of the Republic and members of the Government in cases of high treason, crimes committed during the exercise of their functions and plots against state security. In the event of an accusation of high treason or of contempt of the Assemblée nationale, and in certain other cases, the President of the Republic and members of the Government are to be suspended from their functions. In the case of being found guilty of such charges, they are dismissed from their responsibilities.

VII. THE ECONOMIC AND SOCIAL COUNCIL

Articles 139–141: The Economic and Social Council advises on proposed laws, ordinances or decrees that are submitted to it. Proposed laws of an economic or social nature must be submitted to the Council.

VIII. THE HIGH AUTHORITY FOR BROADCASTING AND COMMUNICATION

Articles 142–143: The High Authority for Broadcasting and Communication assures the freedom of the press and all other means of mass communication. It oversees the equitable access of political parties, associations and citizens to the official means of communication and information.

IX. INTERNATIONAL TREATIES AND ACCORDS

Articles 144–149: The President of the Republic negotiates and ratifies international treaties and accords. Peace treaties, those relating to international organization or territorial changes and to certain other matters must be ratified by law.

X. LOCAL AUTHORITIES

Articles 150–153: The local authorities of the Republic are created by law and are freely administered by elected councils. Their development is overseen by the State.

XI. ON REVISION

Articles 154–156: The initiative for the revision of the Constitution belongs jointly to the President of the Republic, after a decision has been taken in the Council of Ministers, and to the Assemblée nationale, given a majority vote of three-quarters of its members. A revision requires approval by referendum, unless it is supported by a majority of four-fifths of the members of the Assemblée nationale. The republican and secular basis of the State may not be the subject of any revision.

XII. TRANSITIONAL AND FINAL DISPOSITIONS

Articles 157–160: This new Constitution must be promulgated within eight days of its adoption by referendum. The President of the Republic must assume office and the Assemblée nationale convene by 1 April 1991. The Haut Conseil de la République and the transitional Government will continue to exercise their functions until the installation of the new institutions.

The Government

HEAD OF STATE

President: Dr BONI YAYI (inaugurated 6 April 2006).

COUNCIL OF MINISTERS
(March 2008)

President: Dr BONI YAYI.
Minister of State, in charge of Planning, Development and the Evaluation of Public Action: PASCAL IRÉNÉE KOUPAKI.
Minister of State, in charge of National Defence: ISSIFOU KOGUI N'DOURO.
Minister of the Interior and Public Security: Gen. FÉLIX HESSOU.
Minister of Decentralization, Local Communities and Territorial Development: ISSA DÉMOLE MOKO.
Minister of Foreign Affairs, African Integration, Francophone Affairs and Beninois Abroad: MOUSSA OKANLA.
Minister of the Economy and Finance: SOULÉ MANA LAWANI.
Minister of Agriculture, Stockbreeding and Fisheries: ROGER DOVONOU.
Minister of Trade, Industry and Small and Medium-sized Enterprises: GRÉGOIRE AKOFODJI.
Minister of Mining, Energy and Water: SACCA LAFIA.
Minister of Health: KESSILE TCHALA.
Minister of Nursery and Primary Education: CHRISTINE OUINSAVI.
Minister of Literacy and the Promotion of National Languages: ROGER GBEGNONVI.
Minister of Secondary Education and Professional Training: BERNADETTE SOHOUDJI AGBOSSOU.
Minister of Higher Education and Scientific Research: VICENTIA BOCCO.
Minister of Youth, Sports and Leisure: GANIOU SOGLO.
Minister of Labour and the Civil Service: EMMANUEL TIANDO.
Minister of Culture, Tourism and Crafts: SOUMANOU SEÏBOU TOLÉBA.
Minister of Family and Children: GNIMBERE DANSOU.
Minister of Administrative and Institutional Reform: BIO GOUNOU IDRISSOU SINA.
Minister of the Environment and the Protection of Nature: JULIETTE KOUDENOUKPO BIAOU.
Minister of Microfinance and Youth and Women's Employment: SAKINATOU ABDOU ALFA OROU.
Minister of Town Planning, Housing, Land Reform and the Fight against Coastal Erosion: FRANÇOIS GBENOUPKO NOUDÉGBESSI.
Keeper of the Seals, Minister of Justice, Legislation and Human Rights: GUSTAVE ANANI CASSA.
Minister in charge of Relations with the Institutions, Government Spokesperson: ALEXANDRE HOUNTODJI.
Minister-delegate at the Presidency, in charge of Communication and New Technologies: DÉSIRÉ ADADJA.
Minister-delegate at the Presidency, in charge of Transport and Public Works: ARMAND ZINZINDOHOUÉ.

MINISTRIES

Office of the President: BP 1288, Cotonou; tel. 21-30-00-90; fax 21-30-06-36; internet www.gouv.bj.
Ministry of Administrative and Institutional Reform: BP 302, Cotonou; tel. 21-30-12-47; fax 21-30-18-51.
Ministry of Agriculture, Stockbreeding and Fisheries: 03 BP 2900, Cotonou; tel. 21-30-04-10; fax 21-30-03-26; e-mail sgm@agriculture.gouv.bj; internet www.agriculture.gouv.bj.
Ministry of Culture, Tourism and Crafts: 01 BP 2037, Guincomey, Cotonou; tel. 21-30-70-10; fax 21-30-70-31; e-mail sg@tourisme.gouv.bj; internet www.tourisme.gouv.bj.
Ministry of Decentralization, Local Communities and Territorial Development: Cotonou.
Ministry of the Economy and Finance: BP 302, Cotonou; tel. 21-30-02-81; fax 21-31-18-51; e-mail sgm@finance.gouv.bj; internet www.finance.gouv.bj.
Ministry of the Environment and the Protection of Nature: 01 BP 3621, Cotonou; tel. 21-31-55-96; fax 21-31-50-81; e-mail sg@environnement.gouv.bj; internet www.mehubenin.net.
Ministry of Family and Children: 01 BP 2802, Cotonou; tel. 21-31-67-08; fax 21-31-64-62; e-mail sgm@famille.gouv.bj; internet www.famille.gouv.bj.
Ministry of Foreign Affairs, African Integration, Francophone Affairs and Beninois Abroad: Zone Résidentielle, route de l'Aéroport, 06 BP 318, Cotonou; tel. 21-30-09-06; fax 21-30-19-70; e-mail sgm@etranger.gouv.bj; internet www.etranger.gouv.bj.

BENIN   *Directory*

Ministry of Health: Immeuble ex-MCAT, 01 BP 882, Cotonou; tel. 21-33-21-63; fax 21-33-04-62; e-mail sgm@sante.gouv.bj; internet www.sante.gouv.bj.

Ministry of Higher Education and Scientific Research: 01 BP 348, Cotonou; tel. 21-30-06-81; fax 21-30-57-95; e-mail sgm@recherche.gouv.bj; internet www.recherche.gouv.bj.

Ministry of the Interior and Public Security: BP 925, Cotonou; tel. 21-30-11-06; fax 21-30-01-59; e-mail sgm@securite.gouv.bj; internet www.securite.gouv.bj.

Ministry of Justice, Legislation and Human Rights: BP 2493, Cotonou; tel. 21-30-08-90; fax 21-30-18-21; e-mail sgm@justice.gouv.bj; internet www.justice.gouv.bj.

Ministry of Labour and the Civil Service: BP 907, Cotonou; tel. 21-31-26-18; fax 21-31-06-29; e-mail sgm@travail.gouv.bj; internet www.travail.gouv.bj.

Ministry of Microfinance and Youth and Women's Employment: Cotonou.

Ministry of Mining, Energy and Water: 04 BP 1412, Cotonou; tel. 21-31-29-07; fax 21-31-35-46; e-mail sgm@energie.gouv.bj; internet www.energie.gouv.bj.

Ministry of National Defence: BP 2493, Cotonou; tel. 21-30-08-90; fax 21-30-18-21; e-mail sgm@defense.gouv.bj; internet www.defense.gouv.bj.

Ministry of Primary Education, Literacy and National Languages: 01 BP 10, Porto-Novo; tel. 20-21-33-27; fax 20-21-50-11; e-mail sgm@enseignement.gouv.bj; internet www.enseignement.gouv.bj.

Ministry of Secondary Education and Professional Training: 10 BP 250, Cotonou; tel. and fax 21-30-56-15; e-mail sgm@formation.gouv.bj; internet www.formation.gouv.bj.

Ministry of Trade, Industry and Small and Medium-sized Enterprises: BP 363, Cotonou; tel. 21-30-76-46; fax 21-30-30-24; e-mail sgm@commerce.gouv.bj; internet www.commerce.gouv.bj.

Ministry of Youth, Sports and Leisure: 03 BP 2103, Cotonou; tel. 21-30-36-14; fax 21-38-21-26; e-mail sgm@jeunesse.gouv.bj; internet www.jeunesse.gouv.bj.

President and Legislature

PRESIDENT

Presidential Election, First Ballot, 5 March 2006

Candidate	Votes	% of votes
Boni Yayi	1,074,308	35.64
Adrien Houngbédji	727,239	24.13
Bruno Ange-Marie Amoussou	489,122	16.23
Léhadi Vinagnon Vitoun Soglo	253,478	8.41
Antoine Kolawole Idji	97,595	3.24
Lazare Maurice Sehoueto	61,195	2.03
Séverin Adjovi	53,304	1.77
Antoine Dayori	37,436	1.24
Others	208,812	6.93
Total	**3,014,167***	**100.00**

*Including 11,678 invalid votes, equivalent to 0.39% of the total.

Second Ballot, 19 March 2006

Candidate	Votes	% of votes
Boni Yayi	1,979,305	74.52
Adrien Houngbédji	673,937	25.37
Total	**2,656,070***	**100.00**

*Including 2,828 invalid votes, equivalent to 0.11% of the total.

LEGISLATURE

Assemblée nationale

BP 371, Porto-Novo; tel. 20-21-22-19; fax 20-21-36-44; e-mail assemblee.benin@yahoo.fr; internet www.assembleebenin.org.

President: MATHURIN NAGO.

General Election, 31 March 2007, provisional results

Party	Seats
Force cauris pour un Bénin émergent (FCBE)	35
Alliance pour une dynamique démocratique (ADD)	20
Parti du renouveau démocratique (PRD)	10
Force clé (FC)	4
Union pour la relève (UPR)	3
Alliance du renouveau (AR)	2
Coalition pour un Bénin émergent (CBE)	2
Force espoir (FE)	2
Union nationale pour la démocratie et le progrès (UNDP)	2
Alliance des forces du progrès (AFP)	1
Restaurer l'espoir (RE)	1
Parti pour la démocratie et le progrès social (PDPS)	1
Total	**83**

Election Commission

Commission électorale nationale autonome (CENA): Porto-Novo; f. 1994; 25 mems, of whom 18 are appointed by the Assemblée nationale, two by the President of the Republic, one by civil society; there are additionally four members of the Commission's permanent administrative secretariat; Pres. EUGENE CAPO CHICHI.

Advisory Council

Conseil économique et social (CES): ave Jean-Paul II, 08 BP 679, Cotonou; tel. 21-30-03-91; fax 21-30-03-13; e-mail ces@intnet.bj; internet www.ces-benin.org; f. 1994; 30 mems, representing the executive, legislature and 'all sections of the nation'; reviews all legislation relating to economic and social affairs; competent to advise on proposed economic and social legislation, as well as to recommend economic and social reforms; Pres. RAPHIOU TOUKOUROU.

Political Organizations

The registration of political parties commenced in August 1990. In mid-2002 there were more than 160 registered parties. In early 2008 the most important political parties included the following:

Alliance pour une dynamique démocratique (ADD): Leader NICÉPHORE SOGLO.

    Mouvement africain pour la démocratie et le progrès (MADEP): BP 1509, Cotonou; tel. 21-31-31-22; f. 1997; Leader El Hadj SÉFOU L. FAGBOHOUN.

    Parti social-démocrate (PSD): Leader BRUNO AMOUSSOU.

    La renaissance du Bénin (RB): BP 2205, Cotonou; tel. 21-31-40-89; f. 1992; Hon. Pres. NICÉPHORE SOGLO; Chair. ROSINE VIEYRA SOGLO.

    Rassemblement démocratique pour le développement—Nassara (RDD—Nassara): Leader RAMATOU BABA MOUSSA.

    Union des forces démocratiques (UFD): Parakou; f. 1994; Leader GEORGE SACCA.

Alliance étoile: f. 2002; Leader SACCA LAFIA.

    Union pour la démocratie et la solidarité nationale (UDS): BP 1761, Cotonou; tel. 21-31-38-69; Pres. SACCA LAFIA.

    Les verts du Bénin—Parti écologiste du Bénin: 06 BP 1336, Cotonou; tel. and fax 21-35-19-47; e-mail greensbenin@yahoo.fr; internet www.greensbenin.org; f. 1995; Pres. TOUSSAINT HINVI; Sec. PIERRE AHOUANOZIN.

Alliance des forces du progrès (AFP): Assemblée nationale, BP 371, Porto-Novo; Leader VALENTIN ADITI HOUDE.

Alliance impulsion pour le progrès et la démocratie (Alliance IPD): 04 BP 0812, Cotonou; tel. 21-35-20-03; f. 1999; Leader THÉOPHILE NATA.

Alliance MDC-PS-CPP: Assemblée nationale, BP 371, Porto-Novo; Leader DAMIEN ZINSOU MODÉRAN ALAHASSA.

    Congrès du peuple pour le progrès (CPP): Quartier Houéyiho, villa 061, cité BCEAO, BP 1565, Cotonou; tel. 21-38-52-55; Leader SÉDÉGNON ADANDE-KINTI.

    Mouvement pour le développement par la culture (MDC): Quartier Zogbohoué, BP 10, Cotonou; Pres. CODJO ACHODÉ.

    Parti du salut (PS): 06 BP 11, Cotonou; tel. 21-36-02-56; f. 1994; Leader DAMIEN MODÉRAN ZINSOU ALAHASSA.

Alliance du renouveau (AR): Leader MARTIN DOHOU AZONHIHO.

Coalition pour un Bénin émergent (CBE): Leader VENANCE GNIGLA.

Force cauris pour un Bénin émergent (FCBE): tel. 95-86-11-00; e-mail fcbe@gmail.com; internet www.fcbe2007.org; Pres. EXPÉDIT HOUESSOU; Sec.-Gen. DAVID NAHOUAN.

Force clé: Carré 315, ScoaGbéto, 01 BP 1435, Cotonou; tel. 21-35-09-36; f. 2003 on basis of Mouvement pour une alternative du peuple; Leader LAZARE SÈHOUÉTO.

Force espoir (FE): Leader ANTOINE DAYORI.

Mouvement pour le développement et la solidarité (MDS): BP 73, Porto-Novo; Leader SACCA MOUSSÉDIKOU FIKARA.

La nouvelle alliance (LNA): Assemblée nationale, BP 371, Porto-Novo; Leader SOULÉ DANKORO.

Union pour le progrès et la démocratie (UPD—Gamèsu): Assemblée nationale, BP 371, Porto-Novo; f. 2002 by mems of fmr Parti social démocrate; Pres. JEAN-CLAUDE HOUNKPONOU.

Nouvelle Alliance: Cotonou; f. 2006; Leader CORENTIN KOHOUE.

Parti pour la démocratie et le progrès social (PDPS): Leader EDMOND AGOUA.

Parti du renouveau démocratique (PRD): Immeuble Babo Oganla, 01 BP 1157, Porto-Novo; tel. 21-30-07-57; f. 1990; Leader ADRIEN HOUNGBÉDJI.

Rassemblement pour la démocratie et le panafricanisme (RDP): 03 BP 1050, Cotonou; tel. 21-32-02-83; fax 21-32-35-71; e-mail cotrans@leland.bj; f. 1995; Pres. DOMINIQUE O. HOUNGNINOU; Treas. JANVIER SETANGNI.

Restaurer l'espoir (RE): Leader CANDIDE AZANNAÏ.

Union pour le Bénin du futur (UBF): 03 BP 1972, Cotonou; tel. 21-33-12-23; e-mail amoussou@avu.org; f. 2002 by supporters of then Pres. Kérékou; separate faction, UBF 'Aller plus loin', formed Oct. 2004 under leadership of JOSEPH GANDAHO, comprising more than 30 pro-presidential parties and asscns; further, smaller, faction, the 'Alliance UBF' formed April 2005, led by ALAIN ADIHOU; Co-ordinator BRUNO AMOUSSOU.

Front d'action pour le renouveau, la démocratie et le développement—Alafia (FARD—Alafia): 01 BP 3238, Cotonou; tel. 21-33-34-10; f. 1994; Sec.-Gen. DANIEL TAWÉMA.

Union nationale pour la démocratie et le progrès (UNDP): Chair. EMILE DERLIN ZINSOU.

Union pour la relève (UPR): Gbégamey; Leader ISSA SALIFOU.

Diplomatic Representation

EMBASSIES IN BENIN

China, People's Republic: 2 route de l'Aéroport, 01 BP 196, Cotonou; tel. 21-30-07-65; fax 21-30-08-41; e-mail prcbenin@serv.eit.bj; internet bj.chineseembassy.org; Ambassador LI BEIFEN.

Congo, Democratic Republic: Carré 221, Ayélawadjè, Cotonou; tel. 21-30-00-01.

Cuba: ave de la Marina, face Hôtel du Port, 01 BP 948, Cotonou; tel. 21-31-52-97; fax 21-31-65-91; e-mail ecubaben@leland.bj; Ambassador MARTA FERNÁNDEZ PERAZA.

Denmark: Lot P7, Les Cocotiers, 04 BP 1223, Cotonou; tel. 21-30-38-62; fax 21-30-38-60; e-mail cooamb@um.dk; internet www.ambcotonou.um.dk; Ambassador GERT MEINECKE.

Egypt: Lot G26, route de l'Aéroport, BP 1215, Cotonou; tel. 21-30-08-42; fax 21-30-14-25; Ambassador OSAMA TAWFEEK BADR.

France: ave Jean-Paul II, BP 966, Cotonou; tel. 21-30-02-25; fax 21-30-07-57; e-mail ambafrance.cotonou@diplomatie.gouv.fr; internet www.ambafrance-bj.org; Ambassador HERVÉ BESANCENOT.

Germany: 7 ave Jean-Paul II, BP 504, Cotonou; tel. 21-31-29-67; fax 21-31-29-62; e-mail info@cotonou.diplo.de; internet www.cotonou.diplo.de; Ambassador Dr ALBRECHT CONZE.

Ghana: route de l'Aéroport, Lot F, Les Cocotiers, BP 488, Cotonou; tel. 21-30-07-46; fax 21-30-03-45; e-mail ghaemb02@leland.bj; Ambassador M. ADU.

Holy See: blvd de France, Quartier Awhouanléko/Djoméhountin, Zone des Ambassades, 08 BP 400, Cotonou; tel. 21-30-03-08; fax 21-30-03-10; e-mail noncia@intnet.bj; Apostolic Nuncio MICHAEL AUGUST BLUME (Titular Bishop of Alexanum).

Korea, Democratic People's Republic: Cotonou; Ambassador KIM PYONG GI.

Libya: Carré 36, Cotonou; tel. 21-30-04-52; fax 21-30-03-01; Ambassador TOUFIK ASHOUR ADAM.

Netherlands: ave Pape Jean Paul II, Route de l'aeroport, derrière le Tri Postal, 08 BP 0783, Cotonou; tel. 21-30-04-39; fax 21-30-41-50; e-mail cot@minbuza.nl; internet www.mfa.nl/cot; Ambassador C. G. WEIJERS.

Niger: derrière l'Hôtel de la Plage, BP 352, Cotonou; tel. 21-31-56-65; Ambassador LOMPO SOULEYMANE.

Nigeria: ave de France, Marina, BP 2019, Cotonou; tel. 21-30-11-42; fax 21-30-18-79; Ambassador EZEKEIL O. OLADEJI.

South Africa: Marina Hotel, blvd de la Merina, 01 BP 1901, Cotonou; tel. 21-30-72-17; e-mail foreign@intnet.bj; Ambassador SIKOSE NTOMBAZANA MJI.

Russia: Zone résidentielle, ave de la Marina, face Hôtel du Port, BP 2013, Cotonou; tel. 21-31-28-34; fax 21-31-28-35; e-mail benamrus@leland.bj; internet www.benin.mid.ru; Ambassador VLADIMIR S. TIMOSHENKO.

USA: Carré 125, rue Caporal Anani Bernard, 01 BP 2012, Cotonou; tel. 21-30-06-50; fax 21-30-06-70; internet usembassy.state.gov/benin; Ambassador GAYLEATHA B. BROWN.

Judicial System

Constitutional Court: BP 2050, Cotonou; tel. 21-31-16-10; fax 21-31-37-12; e-mail cconstitutsg@yahoo.fr; internet www.gouv.bj/institutions/cour_constitutionnelle/presentation.php; f. 1990; inaug. 1993; seven mems; four appointed by the Assemblée nationale, three by the President of the Republic; exercises highest jurisdiction in constitutional affairs; determines the constitutionality of legislation, oversees and proclaims results of national elections and referendums, responsible for protection of individual and public rights and obligations, charged with regulating functions of organs of state and authorities; Pres. CONCEPTIA L.-DENIS-OUINSOU; Sec.-Gen. MARCELLINE-CLAIRE GBÈHA AFOUDA.

High Court of Justice: 01 BP 2958, Porto-Novo; tel. 20-21-26-81; fax 20-21-27-71; tel. hcjbenin@intnet.bj; internet www.gouv.bj/institutions/haute_cour/presentation.php; f. 1990; officially inaugurated in 2001; comprises the six members of the Constitutional Court (other than its President), six deputies of the Assemblée nationale and the First President of the Supreme Court; competent to try the President of the Republic and members of the Government in cases of high treason, crimes committed in, or at the time of, the exercise of their functions, and of plotting against state security; Pres. CLOTILDE MEDEGAN NOUGBODE.

Supreme Court: 01 BP 330, Cotonou; tel. and fax 21-31-31-05; e-mail contact@coursupreme.bj; internet www.coursupreme.gouv.bj; f. 1960; highest juridical authority in administrative and judicial affairs and in matters of public accounts; competent in disputes relating to local elections; advises the executive on jurisdiction and administrative affairs; comprises a President (appointed by the President of the Republic, after consultation with the President of the Assemblée nationale, senior magistrates and jurists), presidents of the component chambers, a public prosecutor, four assistant procurators-fiscal, counsellors and clerks; Pres. SALIOÙ ABDOUDOU; Attorney-Gen. NESTOR DAKO; Pres. of the Judicial Chamber EDWIGE BOUSSARI; Pres. of the Administrative Chamber GRÉGOIRE Y. ALAYÉ; Pres. of the Chamber of Accounts FIRMIN DJIMENOU; Chief Clerk FRANÇOISE QUENUM.

Religion

Religious and spiritual cults, which were discouraged under Kérékou's military regime, re-emerged as a prominent force in Beninois society during the 1990s. At the time of the 2002 census it was estimated that some 38% of the population were Christians (mainly Roman Catholics) around 24% were Muslims, and around 17% followed the traditional *vodoun* religion, with a further 6% being adherents of other traditional religions.

CHRISTIANITY

The Roman Catholic Church

Benin comprises two archdioceses and eight dioceses. At 31 December 2005 there were an estimated 2.1m. Roman Catholics (about 27.7% of the population), mainly in the south of the country.

Bishops' Conference

Conférence Episcopale du Bénin, Archevêché, 01 BP 491, Cotonou; tel. 21-30-66-48; fax 21-30-07-07; e-mail cepiscob@intnet.bj; Pres. Most Rev. ANTOINE GANYÉ (Bishop of Dassa-Zoumé).

Archbishop of Cotonou: Most Rev. MARCEL HONORAT LÉON AGBOTON, Archevêché, 01 BP 491, Cotonou; tel. 21-30-01-45; fax 21-30-07-07; e-mail archeveche.cotonou@ifrance.com.

Archbishop of Parakou: Most Rev. FIDÈLE AGBATCHI, Archevêché, BP 75, Parakou; tel. 23-61-02-54; fax 23-61-01-09; e-mail archeveche@borgou.net.

BENIN

Protestant Church
There are an estimated 257 Protestant mission centres in Benin.

Eglise Protestante Méthodiste en République du Bénin (EPMB): 54 ave Mgr Steinmetz, 01 BP 34, Cotonou; tel. and fax 21-31-11-42; e-mail epmbenin@intnet.bj; f. 1843; Pres. Rev. Dr SIMON K. DOSSOU; Sec. Rev. Dr CÉLESTIN GB. KIKI; 101,000 mems (1997).

VODOUN
The origins of the traditional *vodoun* religion can be traced to the 14th century. Its influence is particularly strong in Latin America and the Caribbean, owing to the shipment of slaves from the West African region to the Americas in the 18th and 19th centuries.

Communauté Nationale du Culte Vodoun (CNCV): Ouidah; Pres. ADAN YOSSI GUÉDÉHOUNGUÉ.

ISLAM
Union Islamique du Bénin (UIB): Cotonou; Pres. Imam El Hadj MOHAMED AMED SANNI.

BAHÁ'Í FAITH
National Spiritual Assembly: BP 1252, Cotonou.

The Press

In 2001 there were 18 daily newspapers and 37 periodicals published in Benin.

DAILIES

L'Araignée: siège du cyber DOPHIA, face Cité Houeyiho, 01 BP 1357, Cotonou; tel. 21-30-64-12; fax (44) 21-32-18-84; e-mail direction@laraignee.org; internet www.laraignee.org; f. 2001; online only; politics, public affairs, culture, society, sport; Dir of Publishing FÉLIX ANIWANOU HOUNSA; Editor-in-Chief WILLÉANDRE HOUNGBÉDJI.

L'Aurore: face Clinique Boni, 05 BP 464, Cotonou; tel. 21-33-70-43; Dir PATRICK ADJAMONSI; circ. 1,500.

L'Autre Quotidien: 01 BP 6659, Cotonou; tel. 21-31-01-99; fax 21-31-02-05; e-mail lautreredaction@yahoo.fr; internet www.lautrequotidien.com; Dir ROMAIN TOÏ; Editor-in-Chief LÉON BRATHIER.

Bénin-Presse Info: 01 BP 72, Cotonou; tel. 21-31-26-55; fax 21-31-13-26; e-mail abpben@bow.intnet.bj; internet www.gouv.bj/presse/abp/index.php; bulletin of Agence Bénin-Presse; Dir YAOVI R. HOUNKPONOU; Editor-in-Chief JOSEPH VODOUNON.

Les Echos du Jour: Carré 136, Sodjatimè, 08 BP 718, Cotonou; tel. 21-33-18-33; fax 21-33-17-06; e-mail echos@intnet.bj; independent; Dir MAURICE CHABI; Editor-in-Chief SÉBASTIEN DOSSA; circ. 3,000.

Fraternité: face Station Menontin, 05 BP 915, Cotonou; tel. 21-38-47-70; fax 21-38-47-71; e-mail fraternite@fraternite-info.com; internet www.fraternite-info.com; Dir-Gen. MALICK SEIBOU GOMINA; Editor-in-Chief BRICE U. HOUSSOU.

L'Informateur: Etoile Rouge, Bâtiment Radio Star, Carré 1072C, 01 BP 5421, Cotonou; tel. and fax 21-32-66-39; f. 2001; Dir CLÉMENT ADÉCHIAN; Editor-in-Chief BRICE GUÉDÉ.

Le Matin: Carré 54, Tokpa Hoho, 06 BP 2217, Cotonou; tel. 21-31-10-80; fax 21-33-42-62; e-mail lematinonline@moncourrier.com; f. 1994; independent; Dir MOÏSE DATO; Editorial Dir LUC-AIMÉ DANSOU.

Le Matinal: Carré 153–154, Atinkanmey, 06 BP 1989, Cotonou; tel. 90-94-83-32; e-mail infodumatinal@yahoo.fr; internet www.actubenin.com; f. 1997; daily; Dir-Gen. CHARLES TOKO; Editor-in-Chief NAPOLÉON MAFORIKAN; circ. 5,000.

La Nation: Cadjèhoun, 01 BP 1210, Cotonou; tel. 21-30-02-99; fax 21-30-34-63; e-mail onip@communication.gouv.bj; internet www.gouv.bj/presse/lanation/index.php; f. 1990; official newspaper; Dir AKUÉTÉ ASSEVI; Editor-in-Chief HUBERT O. AKPONIKPE; circ. 4,000.

La Nouvelle Tribune: Lot 1409, Houéyiho II, 09 BP 336, Cotonou; tel. 21-30-65-16; Editor-in-Chief ALAIN ASSOGBA.

L'Oeil du Peuple: Carré 743, rue PTT, Gbégamey, 01 BP 5538, Cotonou; tel. 21-30-22-07; e-mail loeildupeuple@yahoo.fr; Dir CELESTIN ABISSI; Editor-in-Chief PAUL AGBOYIDOU.

Le Point au Quotidien: 332 rue du Renouveau, 05 BP 934, Cotonou; tel. 90-91-69-45; fax 21-32-25-31; e-mail info@lepointauquotidien.com; independent; Dir and Editor-in-Chief FERNANDO HESSOU; circ. 2,000.

Le Républicain: Les Presses d'Afrique, Carré 630, Tanto, 05 BP 1230, Cotonou; tel. and fax 21-33-83-04; e-mail lerepublicain@lerepublicain.org; independent; Editor-in-Chief ISIDORE ZINSOU.

Le Soleil: Carré 850, Sikècodji, 02 BP 8187, Cotonou; tel. 21-32-69-96; Dir MAURILLE GNANSOUNOU; Editor-in-Chief MATINI MARCOS.

La Tribune de la Capitale: Lot 03-46, Parcelle E, Houinmè, Maison Onifadé, Catchi, 01 BP 1463, Porto-Novo; tel. 20-22-55-69; e-mail latribunedelacapitale@yahoo.fr; internet www.latribunedelacapitale.com; Dir of Publication SETH EVARISTE HODONOU; Editor-in-Chief VINCENT LEZINME.

PERIODICALS

Afrique Identité: ave du Canada, Lot 1069 T, 02 BP 1215, Cotonou; Dir ANGELO AHOUANMAGMA; Editorial Dir SERGE AUGUSTE LOKO.

Agri-Culture: 03 BP 0380, Cotonou; tel. and fax 21-36-05-46; e-mail agriculture@uva.org; f. 1999; monthly; Editor-in-Chief JOACHIM SAÏZONOU; circ. 1,000.

L'Autre Gazette: 02 BP 1537, Cotonou; tel. 21-32-59-97; e-mail collegi@beninweb.org; Editor-in-Chief WILFRIED AYIBATIN.

L'Avenir: Carré 911, 02 BP 8134, Cotonou; tel. 21-32-21-23; fortnightly; political analysis; Dir CLAUDE FIRMIN GANGBE.

Bénin Hebdo: 03 BP 2332, Cotonou; tel. 90-92-24-09; Dir SANGARÉ NOUHOUN; Editor-in-Chief DENIS CHAUMEREUIL.

Bénin Info: 06 BP 590, Cotonou; tel. 21-32-52-64; fortnightly; Dir ROMAIN TOI.

Bénin Santé: 06 BP 1905, Cotonou; tel. 21-33-26-38; fax 21-33-18-23; fortnightly.

Le Canard du Golfe: Carré 240, Midombo, Akpakpa, 06 BP 59, Cotonou; tel. 21-32-72-33; e-mail lecanardugolfe@yahoo.fr; satirical; weekly; Dir F. L. TINGBO; Editor-in-Chief EMMANUEL SOTIKON.

Le Continental: BP 4419, Cotonou; Editor-in-Chief ARNAULD HOUNDETE.

La Croix du Bénin: Centre Paul VI, 01 BP 105, Cotonou; tel. and fax 21-32-11-19; e-mail andrequenum@yahoo.com; internet www.lacroixdubenin.com; f. 1946; twice a week; Roman Catholic; Editor Rev. Dr ANDRÉ S. QUENUM.

La Dernière Barque—Creuset de la Jeunesse Chrétienne Céleste: 06 BP 446, Cotonou; tel. 21-33-04-07; fax 21-33-42-14.

Emotion Magazine: 06 BP 1404, Cotonou; tel. 95-40-17-07; fax 21-32-21-33; e-mail emomagazine@yahoo.fr; f. 1998; every two months; cultural and social affairs; Dir of Publication ERIC SESSINOU HUANNOU; Editor-in-Chief BERNARD HERMANN ZANNOU; circ. 3,000 (2006).

L'Enjeu: 04 BP 0454, Cotonou; tel. 21-35-19-93; Editor-in-Chief MATHURIN ASSOGBA.

La Flamme: 01 BP 2582, Cotonou; tel. 21-30-69-03; Editor-in-Chief PHILIPPE NOUDJENOUME.

La Gazette du Golfe: Immeuble La Gazette du Golfe, Carré 902E, Sikècodji, 03 BP 1624, Cotonou; tel. 21-32-68-44; fax 21-32-52-26; e-mail gazettedugolfe@serv.eit.bj; f. 1987; weekly; Dir ISMAËL Y. SOUMANOU; Editor MARCUS BONI TEIGA; circ. 18,000 (nat. edn), 5,000 (international edn).

Le Gongonneur: 04 BP 1432, Cotonou; tel. 90-90-60-95; fax 21-35-04-22; e-mail dahoun@yahoo.com; Dir MATHIAS C. SOSSOU; Editor-in-Chief PASCALINE APHIA HOUNKANRIN.

Le Héraut: 03 BP 3417, Cotonou; tel. 21-36-00-64; e-mail franck.kouyami@auf.org; internet leheraut.org; monthly; current affairs; analysis; produced by students at Université nationale du Bénin; Dir GEOFFREY GOUNOU N'GOYE; Editor-in-Chief GABRIEL DIDEH.

Initiatives: 01 BP 2093, Cotonou; tel. 21-31-22-61; fax 21-31-59-50; e-mail cepepe@firstnet1.com; 6 a year; journal of the Centre de Promotion et d'Encadrement des Petites et Moyennes Entreprises.

Journal Officiel de la République du Bénin: BP 59, Porto-Novo; tel. 20-21-39-77; f. 1890; present name adopted 1990; official govt bulletin; fortnightly; Dir AFIZE DÉSIRÉ ADAMO.

Labari: BP 816, Parakou; tel. and fax 23-61-69-10; f. 1997; weekly; Dir DRAMANE AMI-TOURE; circ. 3,000.

La Lumière de l'Islam: Carré 163, 01 BP 4022, Cotonou; tel. and fax 21-31-34-59; monthly; Dir MOHAMED BACHIROU SOUMANOU.

Madame Afrique: Siège Mefort Inter Diffusion, Carré 1066, quartier Cadjehoun, 05 BP 1914, Cotonou; tel. 97-68-22-90; e-mail madafric@yahoo.fr; f. 2000; monthly; women's interest; Dir of Publication BERNARD G. ZANKLAN.

Le Magazine de l'Entreprise: BP 850, Cotonou; tel. 21-30-80-79; fax 21-30-47-77; e-mail oliviergat@hotmail.com; f. 1999; monthly; business; Dir A. VICTOR FAKEYE.

Nouvel Essor: Cotonou; tel. 21-32-43-13; monthly; Editor-in-Chief JEAN-BAPTISTE HOUNKONNOU.

Opérateur Économique: ave du Général de Gaulle, 01 BP 31, Cotonou; tel. 21-31-20-81; fax 21-31-22-99; monthly; published by Chambre de Commerce et d'Industrie du Bénin; Dir WASSI MOUFTAOU.

Le Perroquet: Carré 478, Quartier Bar-Tito, 03 BP 880, Cotonou; tel. 21-32-18-54; e-mail leperroquet2003@yahoo.fr; f. 1995; two a month; independent; news and analysis; Dir DAMIEN HOUESSOU; Editor-in-Chief SEPTOME ATCHÉKPE; circ. 4,000 (2004).

Le Piment: Carré 1965, Zogbo, 07 BP 0665, Cotonou; tel. 21-30-26-01; fax 21-31-25-81; 2 a month; independent; Editor-in-Chief JOACHIM GBOYOU.

Le Radical: 03 BP 0408, Cotonou; Dir ALASSANE BAWA.

Le Recadaire: 02 BP 308, Cotonou; tel. 21-22-60-11; e-mail lerecadaire@yahoo.com; Dir GUTEMBERT HOUNKANRIN.

La Région: Carré 1030, 05 BP 708, Cotonou; Editor-in-Chief ROMAIN CODJO.

La Réplique: BP 1087, Porto-Novo; tel. and fax 20-21-45-77; Dir EMILE ADECHINA; Editor-in-Chief JERÔME AKLAMAVO.

La Sirène: Carré 357, Sènadé, 01 BP 122, Cotonou; tel. 21-33-40-17; Dir ETIENNE HOUSSOU.

Le Télégramme: 06 BP 1519, Cotonou; tel. 21-33-04-18; fortnightly; Editor-in-Chief RENÉ NANA.

Le Temps: Kouhounou, 04 BP 43, Cotonou; tel. 21-30-55-06; 2 a month; Dir YAYA YOLOU; Editor-in-Chief GUY CONDÉ.

Le Tribune de l'Economie: BP 31, Cotonou; tel. 21-31-20-81; fax 21-31-32-99; monthly; Editor-in-Chief MOUFTAOU WASSI.

Press Association

Union des Journalistes de la Presse Privée du Bénin (UJPB): blvd de la République, près Cadmes Plus, 03 BP 383, Cotonou; tel. 21-32-52-73; e-mail ujpb@h2com.com; internet www.h2com.com/ujpb; f. 1992; asscn of independent journalists; Pres. AGAPIT N. MAFORIKAN.

NEWS AGENCY

Agence Bénin-Presse (ABP): BP 72, Cotonou; tel. and fax 21-31-26-55; e-mail abpben@intnet.bj; f. 1961; national news agency; section of the Ministry of Communication and the Promotion of New Technologies; Dir YAOVI R. HOUNKPONOU.

Publishers

AFRIDIC: 01 BP 269, 01 Porto-Novo; tel. 20-22-32-28; e-mail afridic@caramail.com; f. 1996; poetry, essays, fiction; Dir ADJIBI JEAN-BAPTISTE.

Editions de l'ACACIA: 06 BP 1978, Cotonou; tel. 21-33-04-72; e-mail zoundin@yahoo.fr; f. 1989; fmrly Editions du Flamboyant; literary fiction, history, popular science; Dir OSCAR DE SOUZA.

Editions des Diasporas: 04 BP 792, Cotonou; e-mail camouro@yahoo.fr; poetry, essays; Editor CAMILLE AMOURO.

Editions Ruisseaux d'Afrique: 04 BP 1154, Cotonou; tel. and fax 90-94-79-25; fax 21-30-31-86; e-mail ruisseau@leland.bj; f. 1992; children's literature; Dir BÉATRICE GBADO.

Editions Souvenir: 01 BP 2589, Porto-Novo; tel. 97-88-49-04; e-mail editsouvenir@voila.fr; youth and adult literature; Dir JEAN-BAPTISTE KUNDA LI FUMU'NSAMU.

Graphitec: 04 BP 825, Cotonou; tel. and fax 21-30-46-04; e-mail lewado@yahoo.com.

Imprimerie Notre Dame: BP 109, Cotonou; tel. 21-32-12-07; fax 21-32-11-19; e-mail lacroixbenin@excite.fr; f. 1974; Roman Catholic publications; Dir BARTHÉLÉMY ASSOGBA CAKPO.

Société Tunde: 06 BP 1925, Cotonou; tel. 21-30-15-68; fax 21-30-42-86; e-mail tunde.sa@tunde-sa.com; internet www.tunde-sa.com; f. 1986; economics, management; Pres. BABATOUNDÉ RASAKI OLLOFINDJI; Dir-Gen. ALFRED LAMBERT SOMA.

Star Editions: 01 BP 367, Recette principale, Cotonou; tel. 90-94-66-28; fax 21-33-05-29; e-mail star_editions@yahoo.fr; business, economics, science, poetry; Editor JOACHIM ADJOVI.

GOVERNMENT PUBLISHING HOUSE

Office National d'Edition, de Presse et d'Imprimerie (ONEPI): 01 BP 1210, Cotonou; tel. 21-30-02-99; fax 21-30-34-63; f. 1975; Dir-Gen. INNOCENT ADJAHO.

Broadcasting and Communications

TELECOMMUNICATIONS

Bénin Télécoms: Ganhi, 01 BP 5959, Cotonou; tel. 21-31-20-45; fax 21-31-38-43; e-mail Mail@benintelecoms.bj; internet www.benintelecoms.bj; f. 2004 to assume responsibility for telecommunications activities of fmr Office des Postes et des Télécommunications (OPT), in advance of proposed transfer of 55% stake to private ownership; Dir-Gen. PATRICK BENON.

Bell Bénin Communications (BBCOM): 02 BP 1886, Gbégamey; tel. 21-30-52-84; fax 21-30-84-84; internet www.bellbenin.net; f. 2002; mobile cellular telephone operator; Chief Exec. ISSA SALIFOU.

Libercom: blvd Saint-Michel, face Hall des Arts et de la Culture, 01 BP 5959, Cotonou; tel. 21-31-68-01; fax 21-31-68-00; f. 2000; mobile cellular telephone operator in Cotonou and Porto-Novo; 23,000 subscribers (2001).

MTN Bénin: 01 BP 5293, Cotonou; tel. 21-31-66-41; internet www.mtn.bj; f. 2000 as BéninCell; renamed as Areeba in 2005; operating licence suspended in Aug. 2007 following further rebranding; mobile cellular telephone operator in Cotonou, Porto-Novo and Parakou under network name Areeba; owned by Mobile Telephone Network International (South Africa); CEO MOHAMAD BADER; 267,583 subscribers (2005).

Moov Bénin: Immeuble Kougblenou, 5è étage, ave Mgr Steinmetz, Cotonou; e-mail moov@moov.bj; internet www.moov.bj; f. 2000 as Telcel Bénin; operating licence suspended in Aug. 2007 following rebranding; mobile cellular telephone operator in Cotonou, Porto-Novo, Abomey, Lokossa, other regions of southern Benin and in Parakou; Dir-Gen. TALIBI HAÏDRA; 130,000 subscribers (Jan. 2004).

BROADCASTING

Since 1997 the Haute Autorité de l'Audiovisuel et de la Communication has issued licences to private radio and television stations.

Haute Autorité de l'Audiovisuel et de la Communication (HAAC): 01 BP 3567, Cotonou; tel. 21-31-17-45; fax 21-31-17-42; e-mail haac@planben.intnet.bj; internet www.gouv.bj/institutions/haac/presentation_top.php; f. 1992; Pres. ALI ZATO.

Radio

In early 2002 there were nine commercial radio stations, 17 non-commercial stations and five rural or local stations broadcasting in Benin.

Office de Radiodiffusion et de Télévision du Bénin (ORTB): 01 BP 366, Cotonou; tel. 21-30-46-19; fax 21-30-04-48; e-mail ortb@intnet.bj; state-owned; radio programmes broadcast from Cotonou and Parakou in French, English and 18 local languages; Dir-Gen. JULIEN PIERRE AKPAKI; Dir FIDÈLE EDOH AYIKOUE.

Atlantic FM: 01 BP 366, Cotonou; tel. 21-30-20-41; Dir JOSEPH OGOUNCHI.

Radiodiffusion nationale du Benin: BP 366, Cotonou; tel. 21-30-10-96; f. 1953; Dir MOUFALIOU LIADY.

Radio Régionale de Parakou: BP 128, Parakou; tel. 23-61-07-73; Dir SÉNI SOUROU.

Bénin-Culture: BP 21, Association pour l'Institutionnalisation de la Mémoire et de la Pensée Intellectuelle Africaine, 01 BP 21, Porto-Novo; tel. 20-22-69-34; Head of Station ARMAND COVI.

Golfe FM-Magic Radio: 03 BP 1624, Cotonou; tel. 21-32-42-08; fax 21-32-42-09; e-mail golfefm@serv.eit.bj; internet www.eit.bj/golfefm.htm; Dir ISMAËL SOUMANOU.

Radio Afrique Espoir: Carré 123, 03 BP 203, Porto-Novo; tel. 20-21-34-55; fax 20-21-32-63; e-mail afespoir@intnet.bj; Dir RAMANOU KOUFERIDJI.

Radio Carrefour: 03 BP 432, Cotonou; tel. 21-32-70-50; fax 22-51-16-55; e-mail chrisdavak@yahoo.fr; f. 1999; production and broadcast of radio and television programmes; Dir-Gen. CHRISTOPHE DAVAKAN.

Radio FM-Ahémé: BP 66, Bopa, Mono; tel. 95-05-58-18; f. 1997; informative, cultural and civic education broadcasts; Dir AMBROISE COKOU MOUSSOU.

Radio Immaculée Conception: BP 88, Allada; tel. 21-36-80-97; e-mail satric@immacolata.com; internet www.immacolata.com; operated by the Roman Catholic Church of Benin; broadcasts to Abomey, Allada, Bembéréke, Cotonou, Dassa-Zoume, Djougou and Parakou; Dir Fr ALFONSO BRUNO.

Radio Maranatha: 03 BP 4113, Cotonou; tel. and fax 21-32-58-82; e-mail maranatha.fm@serv.eit.bj; internet www.eit.to/RadioMaranatha.htm; operated by the Conseil des Eglises Protestantes Evangéliques du Bénin; Dir Rev. CLOVIS ALFRED KPADE.

Radio Planète: 02 BP 1528, Immeuble Master Soft, Cotonou; tel. 21-30-30-30; fax 21-30-24-51; e-mail janvier@planetefm.com; internet www.planetefm.com; Dir JANVIER YAHOUEDEHOU.

Radio Solidarité FM: BP 135, Djougou; tel. 23-80-11-29; fax 23-80-15-63; Dir DAOUDA TAKPARA.

La Voix de la Lama: 03 BP 3772, Cotonou; tel. 21-37-12-26; fax 21-37-13-67; e-mail voix_delalama@yahoo.fr; f. 1998; non-commercial FM station, broadcasting on 103.8 Mhz from Allada; Dir SÉRAPHINE DADY.

La Voix de l'Islam: 08 BP 134, Cotonou; tel. 21-31-11-34; fax 21-31-51-79; e-mail islamben@leland.bj; operated by the Communauté musulmane de Zongo; Dir El Hadj MAMAN YARO.

Radio Wêkê: 05 BP 436, Cotonou; tel. 20-21-38-40; fax 20-21-37-14; e-mail issabadarou@hotmail.com; Promoter ISSA BADAROU-SOULÉ.

Benin also receives broadcasts from Africa No. 1, the British Broadcasting Corporation World Service and Radio France International.

Television

ORTB: (see Radio); Dir of Television PIERETTE AMOUSSOU.

ATVS: BP 7101, Cotonou; tel. 21-31-43-19; owned by African Television System-Sobiex; Dir JACOB AKINOCHO.

LC2—La Chaîne 2 (LC2): 05 BP 427, Cotonou; tel. 21-33-47-49; fax 21-33-46-75; e-mail lc2@intnet.bj; internet www.lc2international.tv; commenced broadcasts 1997; Pres. and Dir-Gen. CHRISTIAN LAGNIDE; Dir-Gen. NADINE LAGNIDE.

Telco: 44 ave Delorme, 01 BP 1241, Cotonou; tel. 21-31-34-98; e-mail telco@serv.eit.bj; relays five international channels; Dir JOSEPH JÉBARA.

TV+ International/TV5: 01 BP 366, Cotonou; tel. 21-30-10-96; Dir CLAUDE KARAM.

Finance

(cap. = capital; res = reserves; dep. = deposits; m. = million; br(s). = branch(es); amounts in francs CFA)

BANKING

Central Bank

Banque centrale des états de l'Afrique de l'ouest (BCEAO): ave Jean-Paul II, BP 325, Cotonou; tel. 21-31-24-66; fax 21-31-24-65; e-mail akangni@bceao.int; internet www.bceao.int; HQ in Dakar, Senegal; f. 1962; bank of issue for the mem. states of the Union économique et monétaire ouest-africaine (UEMOA, comprising Benin, Burkina Faso, Côte d'Ivoire, Guinea-Bissau, Mali, Niger, Senegal and Togo); cap. and res 859,313m., total assets 5,671,675m. (Dec. 2002); Gov. DAMO JUSTIN BARO (acting); Dir in Benin IDRISS LYASSOU DAOUDA; br. at Parakou.

Commercial Banks

Bank of Africa—Bénin (BOAB): ave Jean-Paul II, 08 BP 0879, Cotonou; tel. 21-31-32-28; fax 21-31-31-17; e-mail boa.dg@sobiex.bj; internet www.bank-of-africa.net; f. 1990; 35.2% owned by African Financial Holding; cap. 7,000m., res 12,884m., dep. 246,348m. (Dec. 2005); Chair. FRANÇOIS O. TANKPINOU; Dir-Gen. CHEIKH TIDIANE N'DIAYE (acting); 11 brs.

Banque Atlantique du Bénin: 109 rue des Cheminots, carré 107, 08 BP 682, Cotonou; tel. 21-31-81-63; fax 21-31-76-58; e-mail babn_support@banqueatlantique.net; Pres. SERGE GUETTA.

Banque Internationale du Bénin (BIBE): carrefour des Trois Banques, ave Giran, 03 BP 2098, Jéricho, Cotonou; tel. 21-31-55-49; fax 21-31-23-65; e-mail bibedi@leland.bj; f. 1989; owned by Nigerian commercial interests; cap. 9,000m., dep. 48,577m. (Dec. 2002); Chair. Dr G. A. T. OBOH; Man. Dir JEAN-PAUL K. AIDDO; 4 brs.

Continental Bank—Bénin (La Continentale): ave Jean-Paul II, carrefour des Trois Banques, 01 BP 2020, Cotonou; tel. 21-31-24-24; fax 21-31-51-77; e-mail contibk@intnet.bj; internet www.cbankbenin.com; f. 1993 to assume activities of Crédit Lyonnais Bénin; 43.61% state-owned; full transfer to private-sector ownership proposed; res 1,974m., dep. 23,230m., total assets 50,594m. (2005); Pres. NICOLAS ADAGBE; Dir-Gen. BENOÎT ZANNOU; 4 brs.

Diamond Bank Bénin: 308 rue du Révérend Père Colineau, 01 BP 955, Cotonou; tel. 21-31-79-27; fax 21-31-79-33; e-mail bao@diamondbank.com; 80% owned by Diamond Bank (Nigeria); cap. and res 1,939m., total assets 20,645m. (Dec. 2003); Chair. PASCAL GABRIEL DOZIE; Dir-Gen. BENJAMIN OVIOSU; 2 brs.

Ecobank Bénin: rue du Gouverneur Bayol, 01 BP 1280, Cotonou; tel. 21-31-40-23; fax 21-31-33-85; e-mail ecobankbj@ecobank.com; internet www.ecobank.com; f. 1989; 79% owned by Ecobank Transnational Inc (operating under the auspices of the Economic Community of West African States); total assets 159,922m., dep. 124,738m. (Dec. 2006); Pres., Chair. and Dir GILBERT MEDJE; Man. Dir CHRISTOPHE JOCKTANE LAWSON; 10 brs.

Finadev: ave du Commandant Decoeur, 01 BP 6335, Cotonou; tel. 21-31-40-81; fax 21-31-79-22; e-mail finadev2002@yahoo.fr; internet www.finadev.org; f. 1998; 25% owned by Financial Bank Bénin, 25% owned by FMO (Netherlands), 25% owned by International Finance Corpn; cap. and res 1,016.0m., total assets 6,254.6m. (Dec. 2005); Pres. RÉMY BAYSSET; Dir-Gen. CHRISTINE WESTERCAMP; 4 brs.

Financial Bank Bénin (FBB): Immeuble Ganhi, rue du Commandant Decoeur, 01 BP 2700, Cotonou; tel. 21-31-31-00; fax 21-31-31-04; e-mail info@financial-bank-bj.com; f. 1996; 43.5% owned by Financial BC (Togo); cap. and res 2,672.5m., total assets 60,334.8m. (Dec. 2003); Pres. ABDOULAYE MALLAM IDI; Dir-Gen. JEAN-LUC LABONTE; 8 brs.

Société Générale de Banques au Bénin (SGBBE): ave Clozel, Quartier Ganhi, 01 BP 585, Cotonou; tel. 21-31-83-00; fax 21-31-82-95; e-mail hotline.sogebenin@socgen.com; internet www.sogebenin.com; f. 2002; 67% owned by Genefitec, a wholly owned subsidiary of Groupe Société Générale (France); cap. and res 2,044.0m., total assets 25,503.0m. (Dec. 2003); Pres. AXELLE DE SAINT-AFFRIQUE.

Savings Bank

Caisse Nationale d'Epargne: Cadjèhoun, route Inter-Etat Cotonou-Lomé, Cotonou; tel. 21-30-18-35; fax 21-31-38-43; internet www.cne.opt.bj; state-owned; cap. and res 948.0m., total assets 27,512.5m. (Dec. 2002); Pres. CHARLES PRODJINOTHO; Dir ZAKARI BOURAHIMA.

Credit Institutions

Crédit du Bénin: 08 BP 0936, Cotonou; tel. 21-31-30-02; fax 21-31-37-01; Man. Dir GILBERT HOUNKPAIN.

Crédit Promotion Bénin: 03 BP 1672, Cotonou; tel. 21-31-31-44; fax 21-31-31-66; wholly owned by private investors; cap. 150m., total assets 409m. (Dec. 1998); Pres. BERNARD ADIKPETO; Man. Dir DÉNIS OBA CHABI.

Equipbail Bénin: blvd Jean-Paul II, 08 BP 0690, Cotonou; tel. 21-31-11-45; fax 21-31-46-58; e-mail equip.be@bkofafrica.com; internet www.bkofafrica.net/equipbail.htm; f. 1995; 58.7% owned by Bank of Africa—Bénin; cap. and res 1,229.2m., total assets 5,966.3m. (Dec. 2006); Pres. PAUL DERREUMAUX.

Financial Institution

Caisse Autonome d'Amortissement du Bénin: BP 59, Cotonou; tel. 21-31-47-81; fax 21-31-53-56; e-mail caa@firstnet.bj; f. 1966; govt owned; manages state funds; Man. Dir ADAM DENDE AFFO.

STOCK EXCHANGE

Bourse Régionale des Valeurs Mobilières (BRVM): Antenne Nationale des Bourses du Bénin, Immeuble Chambre de Commerce et d'Industrie du Bénin, ave Charles de Gaulle, 01 BP 2985, Cotonou; tel. 21-31-21-26; fax 21-31-20-77; e-mail patioukpe@brvm.org; internet www.brvm.org; f. 1998; national branch of BRVM (regional stock exchange based in Abidjan, Côte d'Ivoire, serving the member states of UEMOA); Man. in Benin PAULINE ATIOUKPE.

INSURANCE

A&C Bénin: Carré 21, 01 BP 3758, ave Delorme, Cotonou; e-mail info@acbenin.com; internet www.acbenin.com; all branches; Dir-Gen. JUSTIN HERBERT AGBOTON.

ASA Bénin: 01 BP 5508, Cotonou; tel. and fax 21-30-00-40; fmrly Société Nationale d'Assurance; Pres. EGOULETI MONTETCHO.

Assurances et Réassurance du Golfe de Guinée (ARGG): 04 BP 0851, Cadjehoun, Cotonou; tel. 21-30-56-43; fax 21-30-55-55; e-mail argg@intnet.bj; non-life insurance and re-insurance; Man. Dir COLETTE POSSET TAGNON.

Gras Savoye Bénin: Immeuble Aboki Hounkpehedji, 1er étage, ave Mgr Steinmetz, face de l'Immeuble Kougblenou, 01 BP 294 RP Cotonou; tel. 21-31-69-22; fax 21-31-69-79; e-mail gsbenin@leland.bj; affiliated to Gras Savoye (France); Man. GUY BIHANNIC.

SOBAC: Carré 5, ave Delorme, 01 BP 544, Cotonou; tel. 21-31-67-35; fax 21-31-67-34; e-mail sobac@intnet.bj; affiliate of AGF (France).

Union Béninoise d'Assurance-Vie: Place du Souvenir, 08 BP 0322, Cotonou; tel. 21-30-02-12; fax 21-30-07-69; e-mail uba@ubavie.com; f. 1994; cap. 500m.; 53.5% owned by Groupe SUNU (France); Man. Dir VENANCE AMOUSSOUGA.

Trade and Industry

GOVERNMENT AGENCIES

Cellule des Opérations de Dénationalisation (COD): 02 BP 8140, Cotonou; tel. 21-31-59-18; fax 21-31-23-15; Co-ordinator VICTORIN DOSSOU-SOGNON.

Centre Béninois de la Recherche Scientifique et Technique (CBRST): 03 BP 1665, Cotonou; tel. 21-32-12-63; fax 21-32-36-71; e-mail cbrst@bow.intnet.bj; internet www.cbrst-benin.org; f. 1986; promotes scientific and technical research and training; 10 specialized research units; Dir-Gen. Prof. MANSOUROU MOUDACHIROU.

Centre Béninois du Commerce Extérieur (CBCE): pl. du Souvenir, BP 1254, Cotonou; tel. 21-30-13-20; fax 21-30-04-36;

BENIN

Directory

e-mail cbce@bow.intnet.bj; internet www.cbce.africa-web.org; f. 1988; provides information to export cos.

Centre de Promotion et de l'Artisanat: à côté du Hall des Arts et de la Culture, BP 2651, Cotonou; tel. and fax 21-30-34-91; e-mail cpa.info@netcourrier.com; f. 1987; Dir BOIGRA KOMBIÉNI.

Centre de Promotion et d'Encadrement des Petites et Moyennes Entreprises (CEPEPE): face à la Mairie de Xlacondji, 01 BP 2093, Cotonou; tel. 21-31-44-47; fax 21-31-59-50; e-mail cepepe@firstnet.bj; internet www.cepepe.firstnet.bj; f. 1989; promotes business and employment; offers credits and grants to small businesses; undertakes management training and recruitment; publishes bi-monthly journal, *Initiatives*; Dir-Gen. THÉOPHILE CAPO-CHICHI.

Institut National de Recherches Agricoles du Bénin (INRAB): 01 BP 884, Cotonou; tel. 21-30-02-64; fax 21-30-37-70; e-mail inrabdg4@intnet.bj; internet www.bj.refer.org/benin_ct/rec/inrab/inrab.htm; f. 1992; undertakes research into agricultural improvements; publicizes advances in agriculture; Dir DAVID Y. ARODOKOUN.

Office Béninois de Recherches Géologiques et Minières (OBRGM): Ministry of Mining, Energy and Water Resources, 04 BP 1412, Cotonou; tel. 21-31-03-09; fax 21-31-41-20; e-mail nestorved@yahoo.fr; internet www.energie.gouv.bj/obrgm/index.htm; f. 1996 as govt agency responsible for mining policy, exploitation and research; Dir-Gen. NESTOR VEDOGBETON.

Office National d'Appui à la Sécurité Alimentaire (ONASA): PK3, route de Porto-Novo, 06 BP 2544, Cotonou; tel. 21-33-15-02; fax 21-33-02-93; e-mail onasamdr@intnet.bj; internet www.isicad.org/infoprix; f. 1992; distribution of cereals; Pres. IMAROU SALÉ; Dir-Gen. MOUSSA ASSOUMA.

Office National du Bois (ONAB): 01 BP 1238, Recette Principale, Cotonou; tel. 21-33-10-30; fax 21-33-19-56; e-mail mifor@intnet.bj; f. 1983; reorganized and partially privatized in 2002; forest development and management, manufacture and marketing of wood products; transfer of industrial activities to private ownership pending; Dir-Gen. PIERRE HOUAYE; Sec.-Gen. FRANCINE CHRISTMANN.

DEVELOPMENT ORGANIZATIONS

Agence Française de Développement (AFD): blvd de France, 01 BP 38, Cotonou; tel. 21-31-35-80; fax 21-31-20-18; e-mail afdcotonou@groupe-afd.org; internet www.afd.fr; fmrly Caisse Française de Développement; Country Dir DIDIER ROBERT.

Association Française des Volontaires du Progrès (AFVP): BP 344, Recette Principale, Cotonou; tel. 21-30-06-21; fax 21-30-07-78; e-mail afvpbn@intnet.bj; internet www.afvp.org; f. 1964; Nat. Delegate RÉMI HALLEGOUËT.

Mission de Coopération et d'Action Culturelle (Mission Française d'Aide et de Coopération): BP 476, Cotonou; tel. 21-30-08-24; administers bilateral aid from France; Dir BERNARD HADJADJ.

SNV Bénin (Société Néerlandais de Développement): 01 BP 1048, Carré 107, Zone Résidentielle, Rue du PNUD, Cotonou; tel. 21-31-21-22; fax 21-31-35-59; e-mail snvben@intnet.bj.

CHAMBER OF COMMERCE

Chambre de Commerce et d'Industrie du Bénin (CCIB): ave du Général de Gaulle, 01 BP 31, Cotonou; tel. 21-31-20-81; fax 21-31-32-99; e-mail ccib@bow.intnet.bj; internet www.ccib.bj; f. 1908; present name adopted 1962; Pres. ATAOU SOUFIANO; brs at Parakou, Mono-Zou, Natitingou and Porto-Novo.

EMPLOYERS' ORGANIZATIONS

Conseil National des Chargeurs du Bénin: 06 BP 2528, Cotonou; tel. 21-31-59-47; fax 21-31-59-07; e-mail cncb@intnet.bj; f. 1983; represents interests of shippers; Dir-Gen. PIERRE GANSARÉ.

Conseil National du Patronat du Bénin (CNP-Bénin): 01 BP 1260, Cotonou; tel. 21-30-74-06; fax 21-30-83-22; e-mail cnpbenin@yahoo.fr; internet www.cnpbenin.org; f. 1984 as Organisation Nationale des Employeurs du Bénin; Pres. SÉBASTIEN AJAVON; Sec.-Gen. VICTOR FAKEYE.

Fondation de l'Entrepreneurship du Bénin (FEB): pl. du Québec, 08 BP 1155, Cotonou; tel. 21-31-35-37; fax 21-31-37-26; e-mail fonda@intnet.bj; internet www.placequebec.org; non profit-making org.; encourages the devt of the private sector and of small and medium-sized businesses; Dir PIERRE DOVONOU LOKOSSOU.

Syndicat des Commerçants Importateurs et Exportateurs du Bénin: Cotonou; Pres. M. BENCHIMOL.

Syndicat Interprofessionnel des Entreprises Industrielles du Bénin: Cotonou; Pres. M. DOUCET.

Syndicat National des Commerçants et Industriels Africains du Bénin (SYNACIB): BP 367, Cotonou; Pres. URBAIN DA SILVA.

UTILITIES

Communauté Electrique du Bénin (CEB): Vedoko, BP 537, Cotonou; tel. 21-30-06-75; f. 1968; jt venture between Benin and Togo to exploit energy resources in the two countries; Dir N'PO CYR KOUAGOU.

Société Béninoise d'Electricité et d'Eau (SBEE): 01 BP 2047, Cotonou; tel. 21-31-21-45; fax 21-31-50-28; f. 1973; state-owned; production and distribution of electricity and water; separation of electricity and water sectors pending, prior to proposed privatization of electricity operations; Dir-Gen. SOULE MAMA LAWANI.

Société Nationale des Eaux du Bénin (SONEB): 92 ave Pope Jean-Paul II, 216 RP Cotonou; tel. 21-31-53-13; fax 21-31-11-08; e-mail info@soneb.com; internet www.soneb.com; f. 2003 to assume water activities of Société Béninoise d'Electricité et d'Eau; operates under supervision of Ministry responsible for water resources; utilises about 60 systems of drinkable water adductions, feeding 69 municipalities; Pres. EMILE LOUIS PARAÏSO; Dir-Gen. ALASSANE BABA-MOUSSA.

TRADE UNIONS

Centrale des Organisations Syndicales Indépendantes (COSI): Cotonou; tel. 21-30-20-12; principally active in the health and education sectors; Sec.-Gen. JOSÉ DE SOUZA.

Centrale Syndicale des Travailleurs du Bénin (CSTB): 03 BP 0989, Cotonou; tel. 21-30-13-15; fax 21-33-26-01; actively opposes privatization and the influence of the international financial community; linked to the Parti Communiste du Bénin; Sec.-Gen. GASTON AZOUA.

Centrale des Syndicats Autonomes du Bénin (CSA—Bénin): 1 Blvd St Michel, Bourse du Travail, 04 BP 1115, Cotonou; tel. 21-30-31-82; fax 21-30-23-59; e-mail csabenin@intnet.bj; principally active in private-sector enterprises; Sec.-Gen. GUILLAUME ATTIGBÉ.

Centrale des Syndicats du Secteur Privé et Informel du Bénin (CSPIB): 03 BP 2961, Cotonou; tel. 21-33-53-53.

Centrale des Syndicats Unis du Bénin (CSUB): Cotonou; tel. 21-33-10-27.

Confédération Générale des Travailleurs du Bénin (CGTB): 06 BP 2449, Cotonou; tel. 21-31-73-11; fax 21-31-73-10; e-mail cgtbpdd@bow.intnet.bj; principally active in public administration; Sec.-Gen. PASCAL TODJINOU; 33,275 mems (2002).

Confédération des Organisations Syndicales Indépendantes du Bénin (COSI—Benin): Bourse du Travail, 03 BP 1218, Cotonou; tel. 21-30-39-65; fax 21-33-27-82; e-mail cosibenin@intnet.bj; Sec.-Gen. GOERGES KAKAÏ GLELE.

Union Nationale des Syndicats de Travailleurs du Bénin (UNSTB): 1 blvd Saint-Michel, BP 69, Recette Principale, Cotonou; tel. and fax 21-30-36-13; e-mail unstb@yahoo.fr; principally active in public administration; sole officially recognized trade union 1974–90; 40,000 members in 2005, of which 25,000 in the informal sector; Sec.-Gen. EMMANUEL ZOUNON.

Transport

In 1996 the World Bank approved a credit of US $40m., to be issued through the International Development Association, in support of a major programme of investment in Benin's transport network. The integrated programme aimed to enhance Benin's status as an entrepôt for regional trade, and also to boost domestic employment and, by improving the infrastructure and reducing transport costs, agricultural and manufacturing output.

RAILWAYS

Organisation Commune Bénin-Niger des Chemins de Fer et des Transports (OCBN): BP 16, Cotonou; tel. 21-31-28-57; fax 21-31-41-50; e-mail ocbn@intnet.bj; f. 1959; 50% owned by Govt of Benin, 50% by Govt of Niger; total of 579 track-km; main line runs for 438 km from Cotonou to Parakou in the interior; br. line runs westward via Ouidah to Segboroué (34 km); also line of 107 km from Cotonou via Porto-Novo to Pobé (near the Nigerian border); extension to the Republic of Niger proposed; Dir-Gen. FLAVIEN BALOGOUN.

ROADS

In 2004 there were some 19,000 km of roads, including 1,805 km of paved roads.

Agence Générale de Transit et de Consignation (AGETRAC): blvd Maritime, BP 1933, Cotonou; tel. 21-31-32-22; fax 21-31-29-69; e-mail agetrac@leland.bj; f. 1967; goods transportation and warehousing.

Compagnie de Transit et de Consignation du Bénin (CTCB Express): Cotonou; f. 1986; Pres. SOULÉMAN KOURA ZOUMAROU.

SHIPPING

The main port is at Cotonou. In 2003 the port handled some 4,278,300 metric tons of goods.

Port Autonome de Cotonou (PAC): BP 927, Cotonou; tel. 21-31-28-90; fax 21-31-28-91; e-mail pac@leland.bj; internet www.portdecotonou.com; f. 1965; state-owned port authority; Dir-Gen. JOSEPH TCHAFFA.

Association pour la Défense des Intérêts du Port de Cotonou (AIPC) (Communauté Portuaire du Bénin): Port Autonome de Cotonou; tel. 21-31-17-26; fax 21-31-28-91; f. 1993; promotes, develops and co-ordinates port activities at Cotonou; Pres. ISSA BADAROU-SOULÉ; Sec.-Gen. CAMILLE MÉDÉGAN.

Compagnie Béninoise de Navigation Maritime (COBENAM): pl. Ganhi, 01 BP 2032, Cotonou; tel. 21-31-27-96; fax 21-31-09-78; e-mail cobenam@elodia.intnet.bj; f. 1974 by Govts of Algeria and Dahomey (now Benin); 100% state-owned; Pres. ABDEL KADER ALLAL; Man. Dir ARMAND PRIVAT KANDISSOUNON.

Maersk Bénin: Maersk House, Zone OCBN Lot 531, Parcelle B, 01 BP 2826, Cotonou; tel. 21-31-43-30; fax 21-31-56-60; e-mail BNNMKT@maersk.com; internet www.maerskline.com/bj; subsidiary of Maersk Line (Denmark); Dir DAVID SKOV.

SDV Bénin: route du Collège de l'Union, Akpakpa, 01 BP 433, Cotonou; tel. 21-31-21-19; fax 21-31-59-26; e-mail sdvbenin@bow.intnet.bj; f. 1986; affiliated to SDV Group (France); Pres. J. F. MIGNONNEAU; Dir-Gen. R. PH. RANJARD.

Société Béninoise d'Entreprises Maritimes (SBEM): BP 1733, Cotonou; tel. 21-31-23-57; fax 21-31-59-26; warehousing, storage and transportation; Dir RÉGIS TISSER.

Société Béninoise des Manutentions Portuaires (SOBEMAP): blvd de la Marina, BP 35, Cotonou; tel. 21-31-41-45; fax 21-31-53-71; e-mail infos@sobemap.com; internet www.sobemap.com; f. 1969; state-owned; Dir-Gen. WASSI BANKOLÉ.

Société Béninoise Maritime (SOBEMAR): Carré 8, Cruintomé, 08 BP 0956, Cotonou; tel. 21-31-49-65; fax 21-31-67-72; e-mail sobemar@intnet.bj.

CIVIL AVIATION

There is an international airport at Cotonou-Cadjehoun and there are secondary airports at Parakou, Natitingou, Kandi and Abomey.

Trans Air Bénin (TAB): Cotonou; f. 2000; regional flights; Dir BRICE KIKI.

Tourism

Benin's rich cultural diversity and its national parks and game reserves are the principal tourist attractions. About 176,000 tourists visited Benin in 2005. Receipts from tourism were estimated at US $121.9m. in 2004.

Direction de la Promotion et des Professions Touristiques: BP 2037, Cotonou; tel. 21-32-68-24; fax 21-32-68-23; e-mail dth@benintourism.com; internet www.benintourism.com.

BHUTAN

Introductory Survey

Location, Climate, Language, Religion, Flag, Capital

The Kingdom of Bhutan lies in the Himalaya range of mountains, with Tibet (the Xizang Autonomous Region), part of the People's Republic of China, to the north and India to the south. Average monthly temperature ranges from 4.4°C (40°F) in January to 17°C (62°F) in July. Rainfall is heavy, ranging from 150 cm (60 ins) to 300 cm (120 ins) per year. The official language is Dzongkha, spoken mainly in western Bhutan. Written Dzongkha is based on the Tibetan script. The state religion is Mahayana Buddhism, primarily the Drukpa school of the Kagyupa sect, although Nepalese settlers, who comprise about one-quarter of the country's total population, practise Hinduism. The Nepali-speaking Hindus dominate southern Bhutan and are referred to as southern Bhutanese. The national flag (proportions 2 by 3) is divided diagonally from the lower hoist to the upper fly, so forming two triangles, one orange and the other maroon, with a white dragon superimposed in the centre. The capital is Thimphu.

Recent History

The first hereditary King of Bhutan was installed in December 1907. An Anglo-Bhutanese Treaty, signed in 1910, placed Bhutan's foreign relations under the supervision of the Government of British India. After India became independent, this treaty was replaced in August 1949 by the Indo-Bhutan Treaty of Friendship, whereby Bhutan agreed to seek the advice of the Government of India with regard to its foreign relations but remained free to decide whether or not to accept such advice. King Jigme Dorji Wangchuck, installed in 1952, established the National Assembly (tshogdu chenmo) in 1953 and a Royal Advisory Council (lodoi tsokde) in 1965. He formed the country's first Council of Ministers (lhengye zhungtshog) in 1968. Bhutan became a member of the UN in 1971 and of the Non-aligned Movement in 1973.

King Jigme Dorji Wangchuck died in 1972 and was succeeded by the Western-educated 16-year-old Crown Prince, Jigme Singye Wangchuck. The new King stated his wish to preserve the Indo-Bhutan Treaty and further to strengthen friendship with India. In 1979, however, during the Non-aligned Conference and later at the UN General Assembly, Bhutan voted in opposition to India, in favour of Chinese policy. In 1983 India and Bhutan signed a new trade agreement concerning overland trade with Bangladesh and Nepal. India raised no objection to Bhutan's decision to negotiate directly with the People's Republic of China over the Bhutan-China border, and discussions between Bhutan and China were begun in 1984 (see below).

When Chinese authority was established in Tibet (Xizang) in 1959, Bhutan granted asylum to more than 6,000 Tibetan refugees. As a result of the discovery that many refugees were allegedly engaged in spying and subversive activities, the Bhutanese Government decided in 1976 to disperse them in small groups, introducing a number of Bhutanese families into each settlement. In June 1979 the National Assembly approved a directive establishing the end of the year as a time limit for the refugees to decide whether to acquire Bhutanese citizenship or accept repatriation to Tibet. By September 1985 most of the Tibetans had chosen Bhutanese citizenship, and the remainder were to be accepted by India. A revised Citizenship Act, adopted by the National Assembly in 1985, confirmed residence in Bhutan in 1958 as a fundamental basis for automatic citizenship (as provided for by the 1958 Nationality Act), but this was to be interpreted flexibly. Provision was also made for citizenship by registration for Nepalese immigrants who had resided in the country for at least 20 years (15 years if employed by the Government) and who could meet linguistic and other tests of commitment to the Bhutanese community.

The violent ethnic Nepalese agitation in India for a 'Gurkha homeland' in the Darjiling-Kalimpong region during the late 1980s and the populist movement in Nepal in 1988–90 (see the chapters on India and Nepal, respectively) spread into Bhutan in 1990. Ethnic unrest became apparent in that year when a campaign of intimidation and violence, directed by militant Nepalese against the authority of the Government in Thimphu, was initiated. In September thousands of southern Bhutanese villagers, and Nepalese who entered Bhutan from across the Indian border, organized demonstrations in border towns in southern Bhutan to protest against domination by the indigenous Buddhist Drukpa. The 'anti-nationals' (ngolops), as they were called by the Bhutanese authorities, demanded a greater role in the country's political and economic life and were bitterly opposed to official attempts to strengthen the Bhutanese sense of national identity through an increased emphasis on Tibetan-derived, rather than Nepalese, culture and religion (including a formal dress code, Dzongkha as the sole official language, etc.). Bhutanese officials, by contrast, viewed the southerners as recent arrivals who abused the hospitality of their hosts through acts of violence and the destruction of development infrastructure.

Most southern villagers are relatively recent arrivals from Nepal, and many of them have made substantial contributions to the development of the southern hills. The provision of free education and health care by the Bhutanese Government for many years attracted Nepalese who had been struggling to survive in their own country and who came to settle illegally in Bhutan. This population movement was largely ignored by local administrative officials, many of whom accepted incentives to disregard the illegal nature of the influx. The Government's policy of encouraging a sense of national identity, together with rigorous new procedures (introduced in 1988) to check citizenship registration, revealed the presence of thousands of illegal residents in southern Bhutan—many of whom had lived there for a decade or more, married local inhabitants and raised families. During the ethnic unrest in September 1990 the majority of southern villagers were coerced into participating in the demonstrations by groups of armed and uniformed young men (including many of Nepalese origin who were born in Bhutan). Many of these dissidents, including a large number of students and former members of the Royal Bhutan Army and of the police force, had fled Bhutan in 1989 and early 1990. In 1988–90 a large number of them resided in the tea gardens and villages adjoining southern Bhutan. Following the demonstrations that took place in Bhutan in September–October 1990, other ethnic Nepalese left Bhutan. In January 1991 some 234 persons, claiming to be Bhutanese refugees, reportedly arrived in the Jhapa district of eastern Nepal. In September, at the request of the Nepalese Government, the office of the UN High Commissioner for Refugees (UNHCR, see p. 66) inaugurated a relief programme providing food and shelter for more than 300 people in the *ad hoc* camps. By December the number of people staying in the camps had risen to about 6,000. This number was substantially augmented by landless and unemployed Nepalese, who had been expelled from Assam (Asom) and other eastern states of India. The small and faction-ridden ethnic Nepalese Bhutan People's Party (BPP) purported to lead the agitation for 'democracy' but presented no clear set of objectives and attracted little support from within Bhutan itself.

Between 1988 and the end of 1999 King Jigme personally authorized the release of more than 1,700 militants captured by the authorities. The King asserted that, while he had an open mind regarding the question of the pace and extent of political reform (including a willingness to hold discussions with any discontented minority group), his Government could not tolerate pressures for change if based on intimidation and violence. Although several important leaders of the dissident movement remained in custody, the King stated that they would be released upon a return to normal conditions of law and order. Violence continued in the disturbed areas of Samtse, Chhukha, Tsirang, Sarpang and Gelephu (then called Gelephug) throughout the early 1990s, and companies of trained militia volunteers were posted to these areas to relieve the forces of the regular army.

A number of southern Bhutanese officials (including the Director-General of Power, Bhim Subba, and the Managing Director of the State Trading Corporation, R. B. Basnet) absconded in June 1991 (on the eve of the publication of departmental audits) and went directly to Nepal, where they reportedly sought political asylum on the grounds of repression and atrocities against southern Bhutanese. These accusations were refuted by the Government in Thimphu. The former Secretary-General of the BPP, D. K. Rai, was tried by the High Court in Thimphu in May 1992 and was sentenced to life imprisonment for terrorist acts; a further 35 defendants received lesser sentences. Teknath Rizal, who was alleged to be responsible for the ethnic unrest and who had been held in prison since November 1989, came to trial, and was sentenced to life imprisonment in November 1993, having been found guilty of offences against the Tsawa Sum ('the country, the King, and the people'). (Rizal, together with 40 other 'political prisoners', was pardoned by the King and released from prison in December 1999; he decided to remain in Thimphu.)

In late 1991 and throughout 1992 several thousand legally settled villagers left southern Bhutan for the newly established refugee camps in eastern Nepal. The Bhutanese Government alleged that the villagers were being enticed or threatened to leave their homes by militants based outside Bhutan, in order to augment the population of the camps and gain international attention; the dissidents, by contrast, claimed that the Bhutanese Government was forcing the villagers to leave. The formation of the Bhutan National Democratic Party (BNDP), including members drawn from supporters of the BPP and with R. B. Basnet as its President, was announced in Kathmandu, Nepal, in February 1992. Incidents of ethnic violence, almost all of which involved infiltration from across the border by ethnic Nepalese who had been trained and dispatched from the camps in Nepal, reportedly diminished substantially in the first half of 1993, as talks continued between Bhutanese and Nepalese officials regarding proposals to resolve the issues at stake. The Nepalese Government steadfastly refused to consider any solution that did not include the resettlement in Bhutan of all ethnic Nepalese 'refugees' living in the camps (by November 1993 the number of alleged ethnic Nepalese refugees from Bhutan totalled about 85,000). This proposal was rejected by the Bhutanese Government, which maintained that the majority of the camp population merely claimed to be from Bhutan, had absconded from Bhutan (and thus forfeited their citizenship, according to Bhutan's citizenship laws), or had departed voluntarily after selling their properties and surrendering their citizenship papers and rights. The apparent deadlock was broken, however, when a joint statement was signed by the two countries' Ministers of Home Affairs in July, which committed each side to establishing a 'high-level committee' to work towards a settlement and, in particular, to fulfilling the following mandate prior to undertaking any other related activity: to determine the different categories of people claiming to have come from Bhutan in the refugee camps in eastern Nepal (which now numbered eight); and to specify the positions of the two Governments on each of these categories, which would provide the basis for the resolution of the problem. The two countries held their first ministerial-level meeting regarding the issue in Kathmandu in October, at which it was agreed that four categories would be established among the people in the refugee camps: '(i) bona fide Bhutanese who have been evicted forcefully; (ii) Bhutanese who emigrated; (iii) non-Bhutanese; and (iv) Bhutanese who have committed criminal acts' (henceforth referred to as Categories I, II, III and IV, respectively). Further meetings were held in 1994. Following the election of a new Government in Nepal in November of that year, however, little progress was made at joint ministerial meetings held in the first half of 1995. Nepal's communist Government demanded that all persons in the camps be accepted by Bhutan; the Bhutanese authorities, on the other hand, were prepared to accept only the unconditional return of any bona fide Bhutanese citizens who had left the country involuntarily. Nevertheless, diplomatic exchanges continued in the latter half of the year, despite serious political instability in Nepal.

In April 1996 a seventh round of talks, at foreign minister level, resulted in demands by Nepal that exceeded the mandate drawn up by the joint ministerial committee in mid-1993. It was widely understood that the Nepalese Government had again reverted to a requisition that all persons in the camps be accepted by Bhutan, regardless of status. This demand remained unacceptable to the Bhutanese Government. In August a UNHCR delegation visited Bhutan at the invitation of the authorities, who provided detailed information pertaining to the camps. Talks at ministerial level were held in 1997, without any public communiqué. Following informal discussions during the summit meeting of the South Asian Association for Regional Co-operation (SAARC, see p. 384) in Colombo, Sri Lanka, in July 1998, the Chairman of the Council of Ministers, Lyonpo Jigmi Y. Thinley, held talks with the Nepalese Prime Minister, G. P. Koirala. Thinley and Koirala agreed that bilateral negotiations would continue through their respective Ministers of Foreign Affairs on the issue of persons claiming refugee status in Nepal (who now numbered about 100,000). At the eighth round of joint ministerial negotiations, which was held in Kathmandu in September 1999, the Bhutanese Minister of Foreign Affairs agreed that some of those previously classified as voluntary emigrants (under Category II) might be reclassified as Category I (according to the Bhutanese Government, the number of people in this category totalled only about 3,000, while the Nepalese Government claimed that all of the camp dwellers had been compelled to leave Bhutan).

At the 10th round of joint ministerial negotiations, held in December 2000, the Bhutanese and Nepalese Ministers of Foreign Affairs agreed that nationality would be verified on the basis of the head of the refugee family for those over 25 years of age, and that refugees under 25 years of age would be verified on an individual basis. This important advance in bilateral negotiations signified a major concession by Bhutan, which had hitherto insisted that verification be conducted on an individual basis. By the end of January 2001 a Joint Verification Team (JVT), consisting of five officials each from the Nepalese and Bhutanese Governments, had concluded the inspection of the refugee camps. Verification of the nationality of 98,897 people claiming refugee status (including 13,000 minors born in the camp) began at the end of March, commencing with the Khudanabari camp. At a meeting in November the Ministers of Foreign Affairs of Bhutan and Nepal were unable to harmonize the positions of their respective Governments with regard to the four categories for the people in the camps. In late 2001 the verification of the Khudanabari camp had been completed; however, with the subsequent disagreements over harmonization, the process reached a standstill.

In January 2003 Bhutan hosted the 12th ministerial joint committee (MJC), at which the two Governments finally harmonized their positions on each of the four categories. Details of the results of the verification process at Khudanabari were published in June: 74 families (293 people) were in Category I (forcefully evicted Bhutanese people); 2,182 families (8,595 people) were in Category II (Bhutanese who had emigrated); 817 families (2,948 people) were in Category III (non-Bhutanese people); and 85 families (347 people) were in Category IV (Bhutanese who had committed criminal acts). Despite a new Nepalese Government from late May criticizing the agreements and several political parties in Nepal calling for the Nepalese Government to repudiate the deal, arrangements were being made to conduct the repatriation to Bhutan of most of the families in Category I by the end of 2003. It was agreed at the 15th MJC that the JVT would return to Jhapa in November to review the remaining appeals from people in the Khudanabari camp and then begin verification of the Sanischare camp. The committee also decided that Bhutan would be fully responsible for any Category I persons, while Category II people could apply for either Bhutanese or Nepalese citizenship, in accordance with the respective laws. However, in December 2003 the Bhutanese members of the JVT, while explaining the remaining procedures to Sector A residents of the Khudanabari camp, were attacked by several thousand other camp members protesting against the terms and conditions of the agreement. The JVT members were subsequently withdrawn to Thimphu and talks between Bhutan and Nepal were suspended. In March 2004 Teknath Rizal, Chairman of the Human Rights Council of Bhutan, began a hunger strike in Nepal, with the intention of drawing international attention to the plight of the refugees. Rizal ended his strike in the following month after receiving assurances from the Nepalese Government that it would attempt to enlist the involvement of UNHCR and India in restarting the stalled repatriation process. In September Rizal led a Nepalese delegation to the headquarters of UNHCR in Geneva, Switzerland, in a further attempt to raise the international profile of the refugees. In the following month the US Assistant Secretary of State for Population, Refugees and Migration, Arthur Dewey, visited the area and held discussions on how to end the stalemate. In October 2006 the US Government offered to resettle as many as 60,000 of the refugees. This met with a mixed response: some argued that third-country resettlement would amount to an exoneration of Bhutan's actions, while others welcomed the proposal. In the following month Australia, Canada and New Zealand also offered asylum to the refugees, although proposed intake numbers were not supplied. Bhutan reacted negatively to the Nepalese assertion, made at the UN General Assembly, that the refugee problem was a Bhutanese rather than a bilateral issue. UNHCR, which had urged Bhutan to allow repatriation, and the Nepalese Government began a census of the estimated 106,000 refugees in the Jhapa and Morang districts of Nepal in mid-November. In the same month the much anticipated negotiations between the Bhutanese and Nepalese Governments were postponed indefinitely—once at the request of Bhutan and a second time owing to the unsettled political situation in Nepal. The refugee issue was at the top of the agenda at the 86th session of Bhutan's National Assembly, which began in December. The Bhutanese Prime Minister, Lyonpo Khandu Wangchuck, expressed concern about the alleged infiltration of the refugee camps by terrorists and radicals, suggesting that repatriation of the refugees would challenge security and stability in Bhutan; the Nepalese Government and Bhutanese refugee groups, however, denied the veracity of the claim.

In January 2007 the Bhutanese Movement Steering Committee, a prominent refugee organization, urged the Nepalese Government to terminate discussions with Bhutan and to resolve the matter with the help of India (a course of action that was perhaps unlikely considering the Indian Minister of External Affairs' reiteration the previous month of India's reluctance to become involved in the dispute). In May an attempt by a group of 15,000 refugees to cross the Mechi bridge on the Indo–Nepalese border was foiled by Indian troops, who reportedly killed two people and injured a further 60. The march was organized by the National Front for Democracy, a coalition of exiled Bhutanese political groups, to coincide with the second round of 'mock' elections in Bhutan (see below). Following a visit to the refugee camps in November, the US Assistant Secretary of State for Population, Refugees and Migration, Ellen Sauerbrey, stated that the refugees were facing 'severe intimidation' from political leaders opposed to the offers of resettlement abroad. Nevertheless, in February 2008 Nepal began issuing exit permits to those who had opted for resettlement, and in March the first group of refugees left the camps for the USA and New Zealand.

In 1991 'Rongthong' Kinley Dorji (also styled Kuenley or Kunley), a former Bhutanese businessman accused of unpaid loans and of acts against the State, had absconded to Nepal and joined the anti-Government movement. In 1992 he established and became President of the Druk National Congress, claiming human rights violations in Bhutan. Following the signing of an extradition treaty between India and Bhutan in December, Kinley was arrested by the Indian authorities during a visit to Delhi in April 1997; he remained in detention until June 1998, when he was released on bail while his case was being examined by the Indian courts. Meanwhile, the extradition treaty was read to the 75th Assembly in July 1997, when demands for Kinley Dorji's return to Bhutan for trial were unanimously supported (as they were also at the 76th Assembly in 1998 and the 77th Assembly in 1999).

Important institutional changes were introduced in mid-1998, whereby King Jigme relinquished his role as head of government (while remaining Head of State) in favour of a smaller elected Council of Ministers, which was to enjoy full executive power under the leadership of a Chairman (elected by ministers, on a rotational basis, for a one-year term in office) who would be head of government. An act to regulate the Council of Ministers was presented to the 77th session of the National Assembly in mid-1999 and was subjected to extensive discussion and amendment. The rules as finally endorsed explicitly specified that the King had full power to dissolve the Council of Ministers.

At the 11th SAARC summit, held in Kathmandu in January 2002, the incumbent Chairman of the Council of Ministers, Lyonpo Khandu Wangchuck, was referred to as 'Prime Minister' of Bhutan, a title that subsequently became accepted usage. In accordance with a decree issued by King Jigme in September 2001, a committee to draft a written constitution for Bhutan was inaugurated in November. The 39-member committee was chaired by the Chief Justice and included the Chairman and members of the Royal Advisory Council, five government representatives, the Speaker of the National Assembly, representatives from each of the 20 local districts and two lawyers from the High Court. It was agreed that, on completion, the draft would be subjected to extensive public comment and review before being presented to the Assembly for formal approval. In December 2002 the preliminary draft of the constitution was presented by the committee to King Jigme; the King subsequently referred the draft to the Prime Minister for further scrutiny, envisaging widespread public debate. In November 2004 King Jigme presented a fourth draft of the proposed constitution to the Council of Ministers for discussion; the 34-article draft was made available for public review in March 2005. A second draft of the document, with several simplified clauses, was released for public review later that year.

The creation of four new ministerial positions (as part of a general reorganization of ministries) was announced in June 2003, bringing the total number of ministers to 10. In October 2004 the Crown Prince, Dasho Jigme Khesar Namgyel, was formally installed as the chhoetse penlop (heir to the throne) at a ceremony held at the Trongsa Dzong Buddhist monastery. In December a ban on sales of tobacco throughout the kingdom came into effect, making Bhutan the first country in the world completely to prohibit the substance. In February 2005 a complete ban on smoking in public places was announced. In September of that year Minister of Agriculture Lyonpo Sangay Ngedup was appointed Prime Minister, succeeding Lyonpo Yeshey Zimba. In December King Jigme announced that he intended to abdicate in favour of his son in 2008, the year in which Bhutan intended to hold its first national elections under the provisions of its new constitution. Meanwhile, appointments to the country's first constitutional posts were announced at the end of the year, in advance of the document's formal adoption. Dasho Kuenzang Wangdi became the country's first Chief Election Commissioner, while an Anti-Corruption Commission was also created.

The fifth draft of the Constitution, which was published in August 2005, provided for, amongst other things: the establishment of a democratic constitutional monarchy in accordance with the principle of hereditary succession; the establishment of a parliament consisting of the monarch, a 25-member National Council (Upper House) and a 47-member National Assembly (Lower House), with members of the latter body to be elected by universal secret ballot from constituencies with approximately equivalent populations; and for two political parties to be represented in the National Assembly, the election campaigns of which would be funded by the State. Within the National Council, 20 members—one representing each of the 20 electoral districts—were to be directly elected by a national vote, with the remaining five 'eminent members' to be selected by royal appointment.

In September 2006 the incumbent Minister of Foreign Affairs, Lyonpo Khandu Wangchuck, succeeded Sangay Ngedup as Prime Minister of Bhutan. Later in the month Chief Election Commissioner Wangdi announced that all registered parties would be able to contest the first round of the 2008 general election, following which the two parties with the largest number of votes would compete for parliamentary seats in the second and third rounds. A draft list of about 400,000 potential voters had already been prepared, but by December only around 338,000 electoral registration forms had been received. In January 2007 it was announced that 'mock' elections would be held: the first round took place on 21 April, and was followed by a second stage on 28 May. A further indication of progress being made with the electoral process was the declaration of 47 constituencies for the National Assembly in early March. Meanwhile, on 9 December 2006 King Jigme issued a kasho (a royal decree) in which he formally transferred his responsibilities as Head of State to Crown Prince Jigme Khesar Namgyel. In his first public speech King Jigme Khesar promised to continue on the path towards the establishment of parliamentary democracy. Legislation adopted by the 86th session of the National Assembly included bills relating to judicial services, immigration, and labour and employment. The session also reviewed drafts of election-related pieces of legislation, which were expected to be adopted by the new government in 2008: an election bill, a national referendum bill and a public election fund bill.

In June 2007 the King instructed the Chief Election Commissioner to conduct elections for the National Council in December of that year, a primary round for the National Assembly in February 2008, and a general election for the Assembly in March 2008. The Election Commission declared itself open to receive party nominations from 1 July 2007. In that month the Prime Minister and Minister of Foreign Affairs, Lyonpo Khandu Wangchuck, tendered the resignation of himself and six other ministers prior to joining the political process. Lyonpo Kinzang Dorji, hitherto Minister of Works and Human Settlement, assumed the role of Prime Minister at the head of a greatly diminished Council of Ministers. The National Assembly was dissolved on 31 July, and, prompted by the depleted status of the

Council of Ministers, from August the Royal Advisory Council similarly stood dissolved, in advance of the proposed October termination, in preparation for the inauguration of the new governmental structure.

Candidates in the National Council elections campaigned without party affiliation and the Election Commission ruled that only university graduates from approved institutions were eligible to stand. The latter restriction meant that the requisite minimum of two candidates was not available in five electoral districts before the date of the election, 31 December 2007. Consequently, a second stage of voting was held in these districts on 29 January 2008. Overall, some 53% of registered voters participated in the ballot. The 20 successful candidates, four of whom were women, were to serve five-year terms. An additional five members of the National Council were to be appointed by the King.

By January 2008 only two parties had successfully registered with the Election Commission ahead of elections to the National Assembly—the Druk Phuensum Tshogpa (DPT), led by former Prime Minister and Minister of Home and Cultural Affairs Lyonpo Jigmi Yozer Thinley, and the People's Democratic Party (PDP), headed by former Minister of Agriculture Lyonpo Sangye Ngedup. A third party, the recently formed Bhutan National Party, had its application for registration cancelled, while the application of the Bhutan People's United Party (established by a breakaway faction of the Druk Phuensum Tshogpa) was rejected by the Election Commission in November 2007. Consequently, the Commission announced that elections to the new National Assembly would be completed in one day (rather than in two rounds as originally envisaged) and the election date was set as 24 March.

In a rather worrying development, a series of bomb blasts occurred in Bhutan in January and February 2008. On 20 January four bombs were detonated in different locations, including one in the capital Thimphu, and a further explosion occurred behind a government office in Samste district on 4 February. No one was seriously hurt in the incidents. Leaflets of the Bhutan Communist Party (Marxist-Leninist-Maoist) were recovered from the site of the February explosion and police subsequently raided two training camps in southern Bhutan and arrested eight members of the party, which officials believed was attempting to disrupt preparations for the general election.

The DPT won an overwhelming majority in the elections to the National Assembly, which were held as scheduled on 24 March 2008, securing 45 seats and 67.0% of valid votes cast, while the PDP, the only other party contesting the ballot, won the remaining two seats. Voter turn-out was high, with 79.4% of the electorate participating in the polling. Lyonpo Jigmi Yozer Thinley was subsequently nominated as Prime Minister by the DPT and his premiership was endorsed by the King on 9 April. The new Council of Ministers was installed two days later and included key appointments for a number of former ministers: Khandu Wangchuk, who had previously served two terms as Prime Minister, was appointed Minister of Economic Affairs, while the finance portfolio was assigned to Wangdi Norbu, who had formerly held the same post. Ugyen Tshering and Yeshey Zimba were appointed as Minister of Foreign Affairs and Minister of Works and Human Settlement respectively. On 21 April the members of the National Assembly elected the Speaker and the Deputy Speaker of the lower house, and the first official joint session of both houses of the new legislature was scheduled to be held in early May.

Meanwhile, in mid-1999 the increasing modernization of Bhutan was illustrated by the inauguration of (limited) television and internet services and the election of nine women to the 1999 session of the National Assembly (this number had increased to 11 and 16 by 2000 and 2001, respectively). Furthermore, the mid-2001 assembly session for the first time elected a woman to the Royal Advisory Council. In mid-2002 revised rules for geog (village block) and district development committees to create a legal basis for local autonomy in development issues (a fundamental issue under the Ninth Plan) were approved by the National Assembly at its 80th session. In accordance with the 1999 Municipal Act, residents of Thimphu elected members of the municipal council in late December 2001. At the 81st session of the Assembly in mid-2003 the Royal Civil Service Commission (RCSC) was formally established as an autonomous body; the heads of the three branches of government (the judiciary, the legislature and the executive branch) would propose the commission members and their functions and responsibilities, while appointment of the RCSC Chairman would be on the advice of the King. A National Judicial Commission was established in September; its principal role was to professionalize further the appointment and tenure of judges in the court system. From November mobile cellular telephone services were provided for a limited number of towns and the major highways. By early 2008 B-Mobile had increased its coverage to include all 20 districts, and a new competitor, the Tashi Group, was to enter the telecommunications market in the same year.

By mid-1998 the most pressing security issue facing the country was judged to be the perceived threat from the presence of Assamese (Asomese) tribal (Bodo) and Maoist (United Liberation Front of Assam—ULFA) militants, who had established military training bases in the jungle border regions of south-eastern Bhutan. Particular concern was expressed regarding the Indian military incursions into Bhutanese territory in an attempt to expel the militants. In mid-1999 the Minister of Home Affairs reported that talks with ULFA leaders (in November 1998 and May 1999) had elicited the response that members of the ULFA had been forced to enter Bhutanese territory in 1992, but that they were not ready to leave Bhutan for at least another 18 months. They asserted that they were determined to fight until independence for Assam was achieved, but offered to reduce their military presence in Bhutan. After detailed discussion, assembly members decided that all supplies of food and other essentials to the ULFA and National Democratic Front of Bodoland (NDFB) must be stopped, that any Bhutanese who assisted the militants should be punished according to the National Security Act and that discussions should continue with the ULFA to seek a peaceful withdrawal of these forces from Bhutan. At the 78th session of the National Assembly in July 2000, members adopted a resolution stating that the problem should be solved through peaceful means, but that if negotiations failed military force should be used to evict the insurgents from Bhutanese territory. Some groups of militants began to return to India. However, most ULFA and Bodo militants, who had hitherto refrained from carrying out violent activities in Bhutan, were angered by the decision. In December some 13 people were killed when members of the Bodo Liberation Tigers (a group allegedly supported by the Indian security forces) attacked a convoy of Bhutanese vehicles on the Bhutan–India border. The act was perceived as a warning to the Bhutanese Government not to shelter ULFA and NDFB militants.

In October 2000 and May 2001 negotiations were held with leaders of the NDFB, during which they responded to a demand for the removal of their camps by declaring their intention to leave Bhutan, but would not commit themselves to a deadline. Following discussions in June, representatives of the ULFA agreed to seven points, including the removal of four of the nine military camps in Bhutan by December 2001 and the reduction in strength of the cadres in the remaining camps; further meetings were planned in order to find a solution to the issue of the remaining five camps. Members of the National Assembly were informed of the Government's preparations in the event of armed conflict with the militants: security had been strengthened, funds had been reserved for fuel supplies and medical support services, and contingency plans had been made to ensure the continued operation of the communications and transport systems.

On 31 December 2001 the army visited the four designated ULFA training camps and confirmed that these had been abandoned. Initially, however, the whereabouts of the militants was unknown. There were concerns that they had repositioned their camps elsewhere in Bhutan. In mid-2002 the Minister of Home Affairs confirmed that the ULFA had closed down a military training centre and three camps. The ULFA, however, had opened a new camp on a mountain ridge above the main Samdrup Jongkhar–Trashigang highway, raising the total number of camps remaining in Bhutan to six. In the mean time, the NDFB had three main camps and four mobile camps between Lhamoizingkha and Daifam. The Minister of Home Affairs also reported that the Government had only recently become aware that the Indian militant Kamtapur Liberation Organization (KLO) had established camps in Bhangtar sub-district (dungkhag) and near Piping in Lhamoizingkha sub-district. The KLO armed militants were Rajbansi tribals of north Bengal, bordering Chhukha and Samtse districts, who were campaigning for separate statehood for the Kamtapuris.

In mid-2002 the Minister of Home Affairs stressed that the presence of armed militants in Bhutan remained a grave threat. It appeared that no further negotiations could be held with the NDFB. The issue was further complicated by the presence of

KLO militants. Following extensive discussions, the National Assembly endorsed three decisions proposed by the Council of Ministers: first, to hold negotiations with the Chairman and the military commander of the ULFA; second, the Government would not agree to participate in any more meetings on the reduction of ULFA camps, but was prepared only to discuss the closure of the militants' main training camp and headquarters; and finally, if ULFA leaders refused to relocate their headquarters, there would be no option but to evict them physically. King Jigme informed the Assembly that it was important to hold talks with the ULFA and NDFB separately. Although the KLO was a new, relatively unknown group, the King warned that if the authorities had to resort to military action, they would have to deal with all three organizations. Little progress was achieved that year and in mid-2003 the Minister of Home Affairs, addressing the 81st session of the National Assembly, reported that the ULFA had increased the total number of camps inside Bhutan to eight, with an estimated 1,560 militants. The NDFB had eight camps, with about 740 militants. The KLO from West Bengal had three camps in Bhutan, with an estimated 430 militants. The Council of Ministers approved a contingency budget of up to Nu 2,000m. in the event of military action. King Jigme informed the Assembly that India had given its assurance that the Indian army would not enter Bhutan without the permission of the Council of Ministers and the National Assembly. He again stressed that, if the ULFA agreed to remove their central headquarters, other camps would subsequently close, and that, if the negotiations failed, military action would be aimed at all three militant groups. The Bhutanese Government subsequently made further efforts to seek a peaceful resolution of the issue of militants by directly addressing the three armed groups. The Government conducted negotiations with an ULFA delegation in October; however, these were unsuccessful, as were talks with the NDFB in late November. The Ministry of Home Affairs thus concluded that there was little chance of resolving the problem through dialogue, and it appeared that the Government would have to implement the decision of the 81st session of the National Assembly. Meanwhile, the KLO continued to fail to respond to any initiatives taken by the Bhutanese Government.

A 48-hour notice to leave Bhutan, issued to the militants by the Government on 13 December 2003, went unheeded. Accordingly, on 15 December the Royal Bhutan Army launched simultaneous attacks on most of the training camps, concentrating on the elimination of the general headquarters of the ULFA. By the end of the month the Government reported that all 30 camps had been captured and destroyed (14 of the camps belonged to the ULFA, the NDFB operated 11 camps and the KLO had five camps). Large quantities of armaments and ammunition were seized during the operation. In February 2004 the Chief of Staff of the Indian Army stated that the offensive, which had resulted in the deaths of at least 420 insurgents, had been highly successful. In March it was reported that the Royal Bhutan Army had launched another offensive against the remaining militants. In September a bomb explosion in Gelephu killed two people (both of Indian nationality) and injured a further 27; the NDFB was believed to have been responsible for the attack. Meanwhile, 111 people in six courts in various locations in Bhutan were convicted of aiding and abetting the NDFB, the ULFA and the KLO and were sentenced to prison terms of various lengths. In November King Jigme paid an official visit to India, meeting with Prime Minister Manmohan Singh and various other Indian officials during his six-day stay.

In December 2006 Bhutan and India finally concluded a border demarcation process that had been instigated more than four decades earlier, with the signing of some 62 strip maps and plans for boundary markers and pillars. In 2007 Indo-Bhutanese relations entered a new phase: a revised India-Bhutan Friendship Treaty, which was signed in February and ratified in March, ensured greater autonomy for Bhutan in external and military affairs and increased economic co-operation between the two countries, including free trade. The Treaty also allowed Bhutan to import arms from and through India, and guaranteed equality of justice for citizens of each country when residing in the other.

Following the relaxation of many policies in the People's Republic of China from 1978, and anticipating improved relations between India and China, Bhutan moved cautiously to assert positions on regional and world affairs that took into account the views of India but were not necessarily identical to them. Discussions with China regarding the formal delineation and demarcation of Bhutan's northern border began in 1984, and substantive negotiations commenced in 1986. At the 12th round of talks, held in Beijing, China, in December 1998, the Ministers of Foreign Affairs of Bhutan and China signed an official interim agreement (the first agreement ever to be signed between the two countries) to maintain peace and tranquillity in the Bhutan-China border area and to observe the status quo of the border as it was prior to May 1959, pending a formal agreement on the border alignment. The disputed area, which was 1,128 sq km during the early rounds of bilateral talks, was subsequently reduced to 269 sq km in three areas in the north-west of Bhutan. Meanwhile, demarcation of Bhutan's southern border was agreed with India, except for small sectors in the middle zone (between Sarpang and Gelephu) and in the eastern zone of Arunachal Pradesh and the *de facto* China–India border. Following bilateral discussions in Thimphu in September 1999, the 14th round of 'satisfactory' border discussions took place in Beijing in November 2000, at which Bhutan extended the area of its claim beyond the boundary offered by the Chinese Government. The three sections under discussion were in the Doglam, Sinchulumba and Dramana areas. Negotiations over the disputed boundary continued, with some agreement on the issue being reached following an intensive meeting between technical expert groups in July 2005. However, road construction and maintenance work carried out by China in the disputed border area caused some tensions from 2004, with the Bhutanese Government expressing concern that the work encroached upon its territory. The 18th round of Sino-Bhutanese boundary discussions was held in Beijing in August 2006, but the issue remained unresolved in early 2008 following reports of further Chinese border incursions in late 2007.

Government

In 2007–08 Bhutan was undergoing a transition from a modified form of constitutional monarchy to a parliamentary democracy. The former system of government, in place until 2007, was unusual in that power was shared by the monarchy (assisted by the Royal Advisory Council—lodoi tsokde), the Council of Ministers (lhengye zhungtshog), the National Assembly (tshogdu chenmo) and the Head Abbot (Je Khenpo) of Bhutan's 3,000–4,000 Buddhist monks. A special committee was convened in late 2001 to prepare a draft written constitution. A completed first draft was formally presented to King Jigme Singye Wangchuck in December 2002. The formal registration of political parties began in mid-2007, and the National Assembly and Royal Advisory Council were both subsequently dissolved. In accordance with the provisions of the draft constitution, the installation of a new Council of Ministers and a bicameral legislature, composed of a National Council and National Assembly, was scheduled to take place in mid-2008, following the holding of Bhutan's first general election. The National Council was to comprise 20 members elected by universal suffrage, together with five royal nominees; none would be affiliated to any political party. The National Assembly was to consist of 47 directly elected representatives with party affiliations. The final version of the draft constitution was expected to be adopted by the new Parliament in June 2008.

There are 20 local districts (dzongkhags), each headed by a Dzongda (district officer, in charge of administration and law and order) and a Drangpon (magistrate, in charge of judicial matters, formerly known as a Thrimpon). Dzongdas are appointed by the Royal Civil Service Commission and are responsible to the Commission and the Ministry of Home Affairs. Drangpons are responsible to the High Court. The principal officers under the Dzongda are the Dzongda Wongma and the Dzongrab, responsible for locally administered development projects and fiscal matters, respectively. Seven of the districts are further subdivided into sub-districts (dungkhags), and the lowest administrative unit in all districts is the block (geog) of several villages. There are geog yargye tshogchungs (GYT—Geog Development Committees) in each of the geogs (of which there were 205 in March 2007). New rules governing GYTs and dzongkhag yargye tshogchungs (DYTs—District Development Committees) were adopted by the National Assembly at its session in mid-2002, and in October secret ballots were held in all of the geogs to re-elect gups (heads of geogs), who, under the new rules, were to chair the GYT meetings. Other GYT members number between eight and 31, depending on the size of the block, and include a mangmi (deputy gup) and tshogpas (village elders). Public meetings (zomdue) are held periodically, at the village level, to discuss local issues.

Defence

The strength of the Royal Bhutanese Army, which is under the direct command of the King, is officially said to number just over

6,000, and is based on voluntary recruitment. Army training facilities are provided by an Indian military training team. Although India is not directly responsible for the country's defence, the Indian Government has indicated that any act of aggression against Bhutan would be regarded as an act of aggression against India.

Economic Affairs

In 2006, according to estimates by the World Bank, Bhutan's gross national income (GNI), measured at average 2004–06 prices, was US $915m., equivalent to $1,410 per head. During 1996–2006, it was estimated, the population increased at an average annual rate of 2.4%, while gross domestic product (GDP) per head increased, in real terms, by an average of 4.4% per year. Overall GDP increased, in real terms, at an average annual rate of 7.0% in 1996–2006. Real GDP growth was estimated at 7.8% in 2006. According to projections by the Asian Development Bank (ADB), growth in GDP was forecast to increase by around 18% in 2007 before decelerating to about 10% in 2008.

Agriculture (including livestock and forestry) contributed an estimated 22.3% of GDP in 2006. About 43.6% of the economically active population were employed in the sector in 2005. The principal sources of revenue in the agricultural sector are apples, oranges and cardamom. Timber production is also important; about 60% of the total land area is covered by forest. Agricultural GDP increased, in real terms, at an average annual rate of 2.3% in 2000–06; it rose by 1.7% in 2006.

Industry (including mining, manufacturing, utilities and construction) employed about 17.1% of the labour force in 2005, and contributed an estimated 37.9% of GDP in 2006. Industrial GDP increased at an average annual rate of 8.7% in 2000–06; growth in the sector was estimated at 10.0% in 2006.

Mining and quarrying contributed an estimated 2.4% of GDP in 2006. Calcium carbide is the principal mineral export (contributing 9.2% of total export revenue in 2003). Mineral products (including fuels) accounted for 9.8% of total exports in 2006. Gypsum, coal, limestone, slate and dolomite are also mined. Mining GDP increased at an average rate of 15.0% per year in 2000–06.

Manufacturing employed around 1.0% of the labour force in 2005, and contributed 7.4% of GDP in 2006. The most important sector is cement production, and there is a calcium carbide plant and a ferro-alloy plant. Small-scale manufacturers produce, *inter alia*, textiles, soap, matches, candles and carpets. Manufacturing GDP increased at an average annual rate of 4.1% in 2000–06; the sector grew by 3.0% in 2006.

Energy is derived principally from hydroelectric power. The Chhukha hydroelectric power (HEP) project, with a generating capacity of about 336 MW, provides electricity for domestic consumption and also for export to India. The Kurichhu HEP, which was completed in 2003, exported 90% of its electricity to India in the same year. The Indian-financed Tala HEP project was completed in July 2006 and was expected to generate about NU 2,000m. in revenue in that year. Expenditure on the project (including the cost of repairing damage by floods in 2000) was partially funded by India and amounted to some Nu 42,000m. In 2006 exports of electricity provided 26.5% of total export revenue, while in the same year the cost of imports of mineral products (including fuels) was equivalent to 17.2% of total import costs.

The services sector employed about 26.0% of the labour force in 2005, and contributed an estimated 39.2% of GDP in 2006. The tourism sector has become increasingly significant. In early 2006 a new, more flexible, tourism pricing policy was being considered, which could increase the royalty paid to the Bhutanese Government by tourists from US $65 to up to $100 for each night they stayed in the country during peak season. In 2006 the total number of foreign visitors to Bhutan increased by around 27%, compared with the previous year, to 17,342 and receipts from tourism rose by almost 30% to reach an estimated $24m. According to a number of media sources, visitor arrivals totalled a record 21,094 in 2007, earning the country about $30m. in tourism revenues. The GDP of the services sector increased at an average annual rate of 9.3% in 2000–06; sectoral GDP rose by 11.2% in 2006.

In the financial year ending 30 June 2007 Bhutan recorded a visible trade surplus of Nu 555.1m., following a number of years of widening trade deficits. The series of deficits had largely been owing to an increase in the cost of imports. Of particular note was the purchase of two aircraft by the Druk Air Corporation Limited in 2004. In 2006/07 there was a surplus of Nu 5,057.8m. on the current account of the balance of payments. In 2006 the principal source of imports (at an estimated 68.7% of the total) was India, which was also the main market for exports (an estimated 77.2% of the total). The principal exports in 2006 were electricity, machinery and mechanical appliances and mineral products. The principal imports in that year were machinery and mechanical appliances, mineral products and processed foods and beverages (including alcohol).

The 2006/07 budget envisaged a deficit of Nu 1,646.7m.—revenue (including grants) Nu 16,669.5m., expenditure (including net lending) Nu 18,316.2m. Bhutan's total external debt amounted to US $593.3m. at the end of 2005, all of which was long-term public debt. In 2002 the cost of debt-servicing was equivalent to 4.6% of the value of exports of goods and services. The average annual rate of inflation was 4.8% in 1996–2006. According to official sources, consumer prices increased by an annual average of 5.3% in 2006. In the early 21st century the rising level of unemployment among young people was beginning to cause concern; in 2004 the youth unemployment rate had increased to 5.5%, compared with 2.6% in 1998.

Bhutan is a member of the UN Economic and Social Commission for Asia and the Pacific (ESCAP, see p. 35), the Asian Development Bank (ADB, see p. 182), the Colombo Plan (see p. 411) and the South Asian Association for Regional Co-operation (SAARC, see p. 384), all of which seek to improve regional co-operation, particularly in economic development.

Bhutan's economic development has been guided by a series of five-year plans. The Ninth Plan, effective from July 2002, consisted, unlike previous plans, of separate programmes and budget allocations for individual sectors and dzongkhags (local districts). The dzongkhag plans became geog-based (a geog being a block of villages) through the devolution of powers to members of the Geog Development Committees, under new rules approved by the National Assembly at its 80th session. The central Government, however, maintained financial control in order to ensure budgetary discipline. Expenditure during 2002–07 was expected to total Nu 70,000m. Domestic revenue, which was forecast to reach Nu 30,000m., and external resources amounting to an estimated Nu 35,000m. (of which Nu 20,000m. was requested as assistance from India) were expected to cover the proposed outlay. GDP was forecast to grow at an average annual rate of 6%–7% during the five years of the Ninth Plan. The labour market was projected to expand in 2007, with sources claiming that some 50,000 young people would be looking for employment in that year. Consequently, King Jigme advised the Government to incorporate a Trust Fund for Employment into budgetary expenditure and specified a provision of US $100m. It was hoped that this large initial investment would provide the project with adequate scope to address Bhutan's unemployment problem, whilst protecting the Government's limited currency resources. The production of low-cost electricity by the Chhukha HEP project helped to stimulate growth in the industrial sector in the 1990s. In mid-2001 new legislation was enacted to reform the electricity supply industry and to develop and regulate the country's HEP resources; a Bhutan Electricity Authority was established. In the mid-2000s it was hoped that Bhutan's recently completed Kurichhu and Tala schemes would earn sufficient revenue for Bhutan to achieve economic self-reliance. In 2008 the Druk Green Power Corporation (DGPC) was established to consolidate and oversee the operations of the Chhukha, Kurichhu and Basochhu Hydropower Corporations. Meanwhile, the provision of electricity had been extended to 15,778 village homes by early 2007, well exceeding the target of 12,000 homes initially put forward by the Ninth Plan (which in mid-2006 had been expanded by a further year to mid-2008). The length of roads navigable by motor vehicles had also increased, from 4,007 km to 4,545 km as of June 2007, although 14% of the population still lived at least four hours' walk from the nearest road. In early 2008 the ADB provided US $15m. to assist local micro-, small- and medium-sized businesses, while the European Union (EU) promised to provide a total of €14m. during 2008–13 towards the implementation of poverty-reduction measures. The Tenth Five-Year Plan was announced in February 2008, the main aim of which was a reduction in levels of poverty; the expansion of the tourism industry was also highlighted. The Government hoped to attract as many as 100,000 tourists per year to the country and to increase employment in the tourism sector by 5%.

Multilateral investment in Bhutan's financial sector was agreed by the Government for the first time in September 1998, when the ADB and the US Citibank purchased shares in the Bhutan National Bank. Two important measures were implemented in 1999: a formal personal income tax (to be levied only on wealthier Bhutanese) was introduced, and the country was opened up to foreign investment (foreign investors were to be permitted up to 51% ownership in a joint venture), although the stock exchange remained closed to external investors. In 2003 Bhutan became a member of the Bay of Bengal Initiative for Multi-Sectoral Technical and Economic Co-operation (BIM-STEC) and a signatory to the group's free trade area. In the following year the country signed the Framework Agreement on the South Asia Free Trade Area (SAFTA), which became operational on 1 January 2006 but was not due to enter fully into force until 2016. Under SAFTA, as a Least Developed Contracting State, Bhutan would aim to reduce its tariffs to 30% by the end of 2007, before lowering them to between 0% and 5% over a period of eight years. It was hoped that membership of these trade groupings would enable Bhutan to develop its export markets and transport infrastructure and to become more economically integrated into the region.

Education

Education is not compulsory. Pre-primary education usually lasts for one year. Primary education begins at six years of age and lasts for five years. Secondary education, beginning at the age of 12, lasts for a further five years, comprising three cycles. Virtually free education is available (nominal fees are demanded), but there are insufficient facilities to accommodate all school-age children. In order to accommodate additional children, community primary schools (established in 1989 as 'extended classrooms', but renamed as above in 1991) were set up as essentially one-teacher schools for basic primary classes, whence children were to be 'streamed' to other schools. Enrolment at primary schools (excluding community primary schools) increased from 9,039 (including only 456 girls) in 1970 to 25,879 (including 12,526 girls) in 2005. Between 1970 and 2005 enrolment at secondary schools increased from 714 (boys 690; girls 24) to 82,781 (boys 42,765; girls 40,013). In 2007 there were 28,953 pupils in community primary schools. All schools are co-educational. English is the language of instruction and Dzongkha is a compulsory subject. Bhutan has no mission schools. By 2007 some 30 private schools had been established (the majority in Thimphu); these schools are under the supervision of the Ministry of Education. Owing to a shortage of qualified staff (despite the existence of two teacher-training institutes with a combined enrolment of 1,014 students in 2002), many Indian teachers are employed. In 2007 the total number of enrolled pupils was 171,912, and the total number of teachers was 6,610. In that year there were 1,274 educational institutions under the supervision of the Ministry of Education, including 249 community primary schools, 83 primary schools, 87 lower secondary schools, 37 middle secondary schools, 22 higher secondary schools and 777 non-formal education centres. At July 2007 there was one degree college and 16 post-secondary institutions. Some Bhutanese students were receiving higher education abroad. The 2007/08 budget allocated an estimated Nu 3,385m. (14% of total projected expenditure) to education.

Public Holidays

2008 and 2009: The usual Buddhist holidays are observed, as well as three days for Thimphu Tsechu (September/October, in Thimphu district only), the Winter Solstice, the Birthday of the fifth King Jigme Khesar Namgyel Wangchuck (21–23 February), the Birthday of the late third King Jigme Dorji Wangchuck (2 May), Coronation Day of the fourth King Jigme Singye Wangchuck (2 June), the Anniversary of the death of the late third King (7 August), the Birthday of the fourth King Jigme Singye Wangchuck (11 November), the movable Hindu feast of Dussehra and the National Day of Bhutan (17 December).

Weights and Measures

The metric system is in operation.

Statistical Survey

Source (unless otherwise stated): Royal Government of Bhutan, Thimphu.

Area and Population

AREA, POPULATION AND DENSITY

Area (sq km)	38,364*
Population (census results)	
30–31 May 2005†	
Males	364,482
Females	307,943
Total	672,425
Population (official estimates at May)	
2006	679,807
2007	692,044
Density (per sq km at May 2007)	18.0

* 14,812 sq miles; figure corresponds to official adjustment recorded in Ninth Plan.
† Including adjustment for estimated 37,443 persons with no permanent residence; the enumerated total was 634,982. The number of Bhutanese nationals was 552,996.

DISTRICTS
(population by dzongkhag at 2005 census)

Bumthang	16,116
Chhukha	74,387
Dagana	18,222
Gasa	3,116
Haa	11,648
Lhuentse	15,395
Mongar	37,069
Paro	36,433
Pemagatshel	13,864
Punakha	17,715
Samdrup Jongkhar	39,961
Samtse	60,100
Sarpang	41,549
Thimphu	98,676
Trashigang	51,134
Trashiyangtse	17,740
Trongsa	13,419
Tsirang	18,667
Wangdue Phodrang	31,135
Zhemgang	18,636
Total dzongkhags	634,982
No permanent residence	37,443
Total	672,425

BHUTAN

PRINCIPAL TOWNS
(1997 estimates)

Thimphu (capital)	45,000	Gelephu	12,500
Phuentsholing	45,000	Samdrup Jongkhar	12,500

Source: Thomas Brinkhoff, *City Population* (internet www.citypopulation.de).

2007 (official estimate at 1 January): Thimphu 95,000.

BIRTHS AND DEATHS
(annual averages, UN estimates)

	1990–95	1995–2000	2000–05
Birth rate (per 1,000)	35.7	29.3	22.4
Death rate (per 1,000)	12.6	10.0	7.8

Source: UN, *World Population Prospects: The 2006 Revision*.

2005 census (year ending 31 May 2005): Live births 12,538 (birth rate 20 per 1,000); Deaths 4,498 (death rate 7 per 1,000).

Expectation of life (years at birth, WHO estimates): 63.8 (males 62.4; females 65.4) in 2005 (Source: WHO, *World Health Statistics*).

EMPLOYMENT
('000 persons)

	2003	2004	2005
Agriculture and forestry	167.2	132.8	108.6
Mining and quarrying	0.4	0.1	2.8
Manufacturing	4.5	12.6	4.9
Electricity, gas and water supply	1.0	1.0	4.1
Construction	2.9	6.9	30.9
Wholesale and retail trade; repairs of motor vehicles and personal and household goods	6.9	4.8	6.7
Hotels and restaurants	1.3	1.4	4.0
Transport, storage and communications	0.2	2.6	8.1
Financial intermediation	0.3	2.5	2.3
Public administration and defence; compulsory social security	19.5	10.0	17.5
Education	3.5	3.9	7.8
Health and social work	2.7	2.4	2.5
Other community, social and personal service activities	11.4	29.1	48.7
Total	**221.8**	**210.1**	**249.0**

Source: Royal Monetary Authority of Bhutan, *Annual Report*.

2005 census: Total employed 308,998; Unemployed 7,236; Total labour force 316,234.

Health and Welfare

KEY INDICATORS

Total fertility rate (children per woman, 2005)	4.1
Under-5 mortality rate (per 1,000 live births, 2005)	75
HIV/AIDS (% of persons aged 15–49, 2005)	<0.1
Physicians (per 1,000 head, 2004)	0.05
Hospital beds (per 1,000 head, 2001)	1.6
Health expenditure (2004): US $ per head (PPP)	93.2
Health expenditure (2004): % of GDP	4.6
Health expenditure (2004): public (% of total)	64.2
Access to water (% of persons, 2004)	62
Access to sanitation (% of persons, 2004)	70
Human Development Index (2005): ranking	133
Human Development Index (2005): value	0.579

For sources and definitions, see explanatory note on p. vi.

Agriculture

PRINCIPAL CROPS
('000 metric tons)

	2003	2004	2005
Rice (paddy)	46*	54	50
Maize	50	91	74
Potatoes	40.5	47.4	31.7
Sugar cane†	12.8	12.8	12.8
Oranges	36.3	34.6†	33.3†
Apples	5.7	5.9	6.0†
Nutmeg, mace and cardamom†	5.8	6.0	6.2

* Unofficial figure.
† FAO estimate(s).

2006 (FAO estimates): Rice (paddy) 50; Maize 75; Potatoes 35.

Aggregate production ('000 metric tons, may include official, semi-official or estimated data): Total cereals 107.8 in 2003, 157.6 in 2004, 137.9 in 2005; Total roots and tubers 62.3 in 2003, 69.5 in 2004, 53.5 in 2005; Total vegetables (incl. melons) 5.2 in 2003, 7.7 in 2004, 5.4 in 2005; Total fruits (excl. melons) 76.9 in 2003, 76.7 in 2004, 71.8 in 2005.

Source: FAO.

LIVESTOCK
('000 head, year ending September)

	2004*	2005	2006
Horses	28*	25	26*
Asses, mules or hinnies*	28	27	n.a.
Cattle	372*	381	385*
Buffaloes*	2	2	n.a.
Pigs	41*	28	35*
Sheep	20*	18	18*
Goats*	30	30	n.a.
Chickens*	230	230	n.a.

* FAO estimate(s).

Source: FAO.

LIVESTOCK PRODUCTS
('000 metric tons, FAO estimates)

	2003	2004	2005
Cattle meat	5.1	5.1	5.1
Pig meat	1.1	1.3	1.3
Cows' milk	41.1	41.1	41.1
Buffaloes' milk	0.3	0.3	0.3
Hen eggs	0.2	0.2	0.2

Source: FAO.

Forestry

ROUNDWOOD REMOVALS
('000 cubic metres, excl. bark, FAO estimates)

	2003	2004	2005
Sawlogs, veneer logs and logs for sleepers	63	63	63
Other industrial wood	70	70	70
Fuel wood	4,413	4,479	4,546
Total	**4,546**	**4,612**	**4,679**

2006: Figures assumed to be unchanged from 2005 (FAO estimates).

Source: FAO.

BHUTAN

SAWNWOOD PRODUCTION
('000 cubic metres, incl. railway sleepers, FAO estimates)

	1998	1999	2000
Coniferous (softwood)	12	15	21
Broadleaved (hardwood)	6	7	10
Total	18	22	31

2001–06: Annual production as in 2000 (FAO estimates).

Source: FAO.

Fishing

(metric tons, live weight, FAO estimates)

	1999	2000	2001
Capture (Freshwater fishes)	300	300	300
Aquaculture (Freshwater fishes)	30	30	30
Total catch	330	330	330

2002–05: Capture 300 (FAO estimates).

Source: FAO.

Mining

('000 metric tons, unless otherwise indicated, estimates)

	2004	2005	2006*
Dolomite	452	389	410
Limestone	561	536	550
Gypsum	131	151	160
Coal	30	85	82
Marble chips ('000 sq m)	3	4	n.a.
Slate ('000 sq m)	12	0	1
Quartzite	43	53	50
Talc	40	43	45

* Estimates.

Iron ore ('000 metric tons, estimate): 5 in 2006.

Source: US Geological Survey.

Industry

GROSS SALES AND OUTPUT OF SELECTED INDUSTRIES
(million ngultrum)

	2004	2005	2006
Penden Cement Authority	851.8	807.0	1,041.8
Bhutan Ferro Alloys	748.3	651.2	678.3
Bhutan Fruit Products	174.1	69.4	134.7
Army Welfare Project*	233.8	240.0	279.4
Bhutan Carbide and Chemicals	731.6	760.2	—
Bhutan Board Products	546.2	158.3	251.8
Eastern Bhutan Coal Company	26.0	180.0	203.0
Druk Satair Corporation Ltd	140.4	172.9	258.4

* Manufacturer of alcoholic beverages.

Source: Royal Monetary Authority of Bhutan.

Electric energy (million kWh, year ending 30 June): 1,972.2 in 1995/96; 1,838.4 in 1996/97; 1,800.0 in 1997/98 (Source: Department of Power, Royal Government of Bhutan).

Revenue from the Chhukha, Basochhu and Kurichhu Hydroelectric Projects (million ngultrum): 2,875.0 (Internal consumption 271.4; Exports 2,603.5) in 2003; 3,077.4 (Internal consumption 365.7; Exports 2,711.7) in 2004; 3,780.5 (Internal consumption 586.5, Exports 3,194.0) in 2005; 5,581.8 (Internal consumption 603.0; Exports 4,978.8) in 2006 (Source: Department of Power, Royal Government of Bhutan).

Finance

CURRENCY AND EXCHANGE RATES

Monetary Units
100 chetrum (Ch) = 1 ngultrum (Nu).

Sterling, Dollar and Euro Equivalents (31 December 2007)
£1 sterling = 78.954 ngultrum;
US $1 = 39.410 ngultrum;
€1 = 58.015 ngultrum;
1,000 ngultrum = £12.67 = $25.37 = €17.24.

Average Exchange Rate (ngultrum per US $)
2005   44.101
2006   45.307
2007   41.389

Note: The ngultrum is at par with the Indian rupee, which also circulates freely within Bhutan. The foregoing figures relate to the official rate of exchange, which is applicable to government-related transactions alone. Since April 1992 there has also been a market rate of exchange, which values foreign currencies approximately 20% higher than the official rate of exchange.

GOVERNMENT FINANCE
(general government transactions, cash basis, million ngultrum, year ending 30 June)

Summary of Balances

	2001/02	2002/03	2003/04
Revenue	8,792.0	7,015.3	10,371.5
Less Expense	4,827.1	5,373.2	5,409.2
Net cash inflow from operating activities	3,965.0	1,642.1	4,962.2
Less Purchase of non-financial assets	4,953.4	4,517.2	4,393.0
Sales of non-financial assets	34.7	25.0	73.5
Cash surplus/deficit	−953.7	−2,850.1	642.7

Revenue

	2001/02	2002/03	2003/04
Taxes	2,414.6	2,713.6	2,446.6
Taxes on income, profit and capital gains	1,305.0	1,272.7	1,419.4
Taxes on goods and services	915.0	1,219.5	750.1
Grants	3,748.5	2,269.1	5,367.4
Other revenue	2,628.9	2,032.7	2,557.5
Total	8,792.0	7,015.3	10,371.5

Expense/Outlays

	2001/02	2002/03	2003/04
Compensation of employees	1,897.1	1,947.0	2,086.8
Use of goods and services	2,161.2	2,093.2	2,386.6
Interest	115.8	168.9	220.3
Subsidies	65.1	143.9	114.3
Grants	—	24.0	61.7
Social benefits	228.7	203.9	279.6
Other expense	359.2	792.3	260.0
Total	4,827.1	5,373.2	5,409.2

BHUTAN

Statistical Survey

Outlays by function of government*	2001/02	2002/03	2003/04
General public services	2,320.3	3,202.8	3,571.6
Public order and safety	482.4	519.8	552.7
Economic affairs	3,876.6	3,291.9	2,925.4
Agriculture, forestry, fishing and hunting	883.2	1,115.3	989.1
Fuel and energy	1,835.1	1,015.6	789.5
Transport	979.5	946.8	1,042.7
Housing and community amenities	340.8	411.1	501.7
Health	1,142.8	848.7	831.8
Recreation, culture and religion	183.6	139.6	155.7
Education	1,434.0	1,476.5	1,303.3
Statistical discrepancy	—	—	−40.0
Total	9,780.4	9,890.5	9,802.3

* Including purchases of non-financial assets.

Source: IMF, *Government Finance Statistics Yearbook*.

2004/05 (million ngultrum, year ending 30 June): *Revenue:* Total revenue 6,128.0 (Tax 3,382.4, Non-tax 2,683.7, Other 61.9); Grants 4,373.1 (India 2,625.0, Other 1,748.1); Total revenue and grants 10,501.1. *Expenditure (incl. net lending):* Total 12,893.7 (Current 6,170.6, Capital 6,723.0) (Source: Royal Monetary Authority of Bhutan, *Annual Report*).

2005/06 (million ngultrum, year ending 30 June): *Revenue:* Total revenue 7,027.4 (Tax 4,124.7, Non-tax 2,778.2, Other 124.5); Grants 6,424.7 (India 3,417.2, Other 3,007.5); Total revenue and grants 13,452.2. *Expenditure (incl. net lending):* Total 13,770.9 (Current 7,098.5, Capital 6,672.4) (Source: Royal Monetary Authority of Bhutan, *Annual Report*).

2006/07 (million ngultrum, year ending 30 June, preliminary): *Revenue:* Total revenue 9,951.0 (Tax 4,073.7, Non-tax 5,545.2, Other 332.1); Grants 6,718.5 (India 3,791.2, Other 2,927.3); Total revenue and grants 16,669.5. *Expenditure (incl. net lending):* Total 18,316.2 (Current 8,185.7, Capital 10,130.5) (Source: Royal Monetary Authority of Bhutan, *Annual Report*).

FOREIGN EXCHANGE RESERVES
(at 30 June)

	2004	2005	2006
Indian rupee reserves (million Indian rupees)	4,362.8	4,737.3	3,768.5
Royal Monetary Authority	1,822.4	2,539.7	200.8
Bank of Bhutan	1,988.3	1,833.6	3,120.5
Bhutan National Bank	552.1	364.0	447.2
Convertible currency reserves (US $ million)	287.4	354.3	453.1
Royal Monetary Authority*	249.0	316.0	399.0
Bank of Bhutan	31.3	24.9	26.4
Bhutan National Bank	7.0	13.4	27.7

* Includes tranche position in the IMF.

Source: Royal Monetary Authority of Bhutan.

MONEY SUPPLY
(million ngultrum at 31 December)

	2004	2005	2006
Currency outside banks*	2,070.7	2,404.4	2,762.5
Demand deposits at the Bank of Bhutan	5,983.1	6,565.2	7,575.6
Total money (incl. others)†	23,045.4	26,772.2	29,8493.4

* Including an estimate for Indian rupees.
† Including non-monetary deposits with the Royal Monetary Authority by financial institutions.

Source: Royal Monetary Authority of Bhutan.

COST OF LIVING
(Consumer Price Index at 31 December, excluding rent; base: 30 September 2003 = 100)

	2004	2005	2006
Food	104.2	109.4	115.1
Non-food items	106.9	112.1	118.1
All items	106.0	111.2	117.1

Source: National Statistical Bureau of the Planning Commission, Royal Government of Bhutan.

NATIONAL ACCOUNTS
(million ngultrum at current prices)

Expenditure on the Gross Domestic Product

	1998	1999	2000
Government final consumption expenditure	3,308	4,271	4,422
Private final consumption expenditure	9,322	10,067	11,329
Increase in stocks	45	108	49
Gross fixed capital formation	6,200	8,127	9,447
Total domestic expenditure	18,875	22,573	25,247
Exports of goods and services	5,148	5,714	6,456
Less Imports of goods and services	7,686	9,164	10,004
GDP in purchasers' values	16,337	19,122	21,698

Source: IMF, *International Financial Statistics*.

Gross Domestic Product by Economic Activity

	2004	2005	2006
Agriculture, forestry and livestock	7,864	8,256	8,859
Mining and quarrying	440	550	960
Manufacturing	2,361	2,560	2,924
Electricity and water	3,085	3,661	5,127
Construction	5,741	6,219	6,020
Wholesale and retail trade	1,726	2,089	2,374
Restaurants and hotels	169	212	301
Transport, storage and communications	3,295	3,891	4,496
Finance, insurance, real estate	2,280	2,873	3,400
Community and social services	3,823	4,472	4,989
Personal service, business and recreational activities	144	172	213
Sub-total	30,928	34,955	39,663
Taxes, less subsidies, on products	1,393	1,628	1,781
GDP at current prices	32,320	36,581	41,444
GDP at constant 2000 factor cost	27,269	29,201	31,673

Source: Royal Monetary Authority of Bhutan, *Annual Report*.

BALANCE OF PAYMENTS
(million ngultrum, year ending 30 June, estimates)

	2004/05	2005/06	2006/07*
Merchandise exports f.o.b.	9,457.1	13,959.8	22,674.3
Merchandise imports c.i.f.	−20,556.0	−19,456.5	−22,119.2
Trade balance	−11,099.0	−5,496.7	555.1
Exports of services	1,894.9	2,313.8	2,661.2
Imports of services	−3,647.9	−2,886.8	−2,519.2
Balance on goods and services	−12,852.0	−6,069.7	697.1
Other income received	537.2	813.3	1,159.5
Other income paid	−1,244.9	−1,125.8	−1,036.0
Balance on goods, services and income	−13,559.7	−6,382.2	820.6
Current transfers received	5,492.8	7,313.7	6,737.7
Current transfers paid	−2,420.5	−2,627.2	−2,500.4
Current balance	−10,487.4	−1,695.7	5,057.8
Capital transfers	4,586.4	1,751.5	1,111.8
Direct investment from abroad	401.5	273.9	3,238.1
Foreign aid (net of loans)	2,939.4	3,474.7	881.0
Other loans	89.2	347.0	−37.8
Other investment	1,456.9	—	—
Net errors and omissions	95.5	1,057.7	−5,066.6
Overall balance	−918.6	5,209.1	5,184.4

* Provisional.

Source: Royal Monetary Authority of Bhutan, *Annual Report*.

BHUTAN

Statistical Survey

OFFICIAL DEVELOPMENT ASSISTANCE
(US $ million)

	2000	2001	2002
Bilateral donors	33.7	42.5	42.9
Multilateral donors	19.6	18.0	30.6
Total	53.3	60.5	73.5
Grants	42.5	47.1	52.0
Loans	10.8	13.4	21.5
Per caput assistance (US $)	25.9	28.3	33.4

Source: UN, *Statistical Yearbook for Asia and the Pacific*.

External Trade

PRINCIPAL COMMODITIES
(million ngultrum)

Imports	2004	2005	2006
Animal products	436.8	570.2	631.4
Fruit, vegetables and cereal crops (incl. tea, coffee and spices)	646.3	773.7	846.6
Vegetable fats and oils	312.9	323.4	1,597.2
Processed foods and beverages (incl. alcohol)	779.0	903.1	919.0
Mineral products (incl. fuels)	2,226.2	2,748.8	3,259.2
Chemical products (incl. medicines and pharmaceuticals)	743.6	732.2	793.8
Plastics and rubber products	606.8	609.9	735.0
Wood and products thereof	132.4	133.3	141.8
Woodpulp and products thereof	271.9	277.6	287.7
Textiles, clothing and footwear	802.3	781.7	689.7
Machinery, mechanical appliances, base metals and products thereof, and electronic equipment	10,597.3	5,245.4	7,367.2
Transport vehicles and equipment*	570.9	548.7	903.3
Total (incl. others)	18,639.5	17,035.1	18,998.6

* Trade with India only.

Exports	2004	2005	2006
Fruit, vegetables and cereal crops (incl. tea, coffee and spices)	585.2	601.4	560.8
Processed foods and beverages (incl. alcohol)	417.3	619.0	418.5
Mineral products (incl. fuels)	816.4	1,244.4	1,836.1
Chemical products (including medicines and pharmaceuticals)*	712.5	714.0	587.0
Plastics and rubber products	291.8	298.0	262.1
Woodpulp and products thereof	281.6	314.7	257.7
Textiles, clothing and footwear	537.6	787.4	485.4
Machinery, mechanical appliances, base metals and products thereof, and electronic equipment	1,827.8	3,144.4	4,163.2
Electricity*	2,711.7	3,439.9	4,982.0
Total (incl. others)	8,271.2	11,386.1	18,771.8

* Trade with India only; figures for 2003 refer to sales of electricity from Chhukha and Kurichhu hydroelectric projects only.
Source: Royal Monetary Authority of Bhutan, *Annual Report*.

PRINCIPAL TRADING PARTNERS
(million ngultrum)

Imports c.i.f.	2004	2005	2006
China, People's Rep.	205.3	182.2	281.7
Germany	4,248.4	200.4	200.3
India	10,193.9	12,795.1	13,053.9
Indonesia	65.3	240.0	1,331.3
Japan	598.2	648.2	395.9
Korea, Republic	501.8	247.5	459.4
Malaysia	80.3	174.9	351.8
Russia	1.8	162.1	874.8
Singapore	420.1	447.2	515.1
Thailand	349.6	275.5	257.8
Total (incl. others)	18,639.5	17,035.1	19,012.0

Exports f.o.b.	2004	2005	2006
Bangladesh	410.7	561.8	470.1
India	7,761.6	9,969.8	14,488.0
Total (incl. others)	8,271.1	11,386.2	18,771.9

Source: Royal Monetary Authority of Bhutan, *Annual Report*.

Transport

Road traffic: At April 2003 there were 25,046 registered, roadworthy vehicles—10,574 light four-wheeled vehicles, 8,373 two-wheeled vehicles (motorcycles and scooters), 2,062 heavy vehicles (trucks, buses, bulldozers, etc.), 1,517 taxis and 730 others (Source: National Statistical Bureau, Ministry of Planning, Royal Government of Bhutan).

CIVIL AVIATION
(traffic on scheduled services)

	2001	2002	2003
Kilometres flown (million)	1	2	2
Passengers carried ('000)	35	41	36
Passenger-km (million)	47	61	56
Total ton-km (million)	4	6	5

Source: UN, *Statistical Yearbook*.

Tourism

FOREIGN VISITORS BY COUNTRY OF ORIGIN*

	2004	2005	2006
Australia	315	458	774
Austria	223	319	484
Canada	257	292	375
France	434	532	708
Germany	671	1,042	1,074
Italy	462	529	648
Japan	1,087	1,554	1,815
Netherlands	163	329	389
Spain	198	185	281
Switzerland	173	363	427
United Kingdom	954	1,462	5,018
USA	3,243	4,681	5,018
Total (incl. others)	9,249	13,626	17,342

* Figures relate to tourists paying in convertible currency.

Tourism receipts (US $ million): 12.5 in 2004; 18.5 in 2005; 24 in 2006.
Source: Royal Monetary Authority of Bhutan, *Annual Report*.

BHUTAN

Communications Media

	2004	2005	2006
Telephones ('000 main lines in use)	30.3	32.7	31.5
Mobile cellular telephones ('000 subscribers)	19.1	37.8	82.1
Personal computers ('000 in use)	11	n.a.	n.a.
Internet users ('000)	20	25	25

Radio receivers ('000 in use): 37 in 1997.

Television receivers ('000 in use): 13.5 in 2000.

Facsimile machines ('000 in use): 1.5 in 1998.

Sources: International Telecommunication Union; UNESCO, *Statistical Yearbook*.

Education

(2007 unless otherwise indicated)

	Institutions	Teachers	Students
Community primary schools	249	896	28,953
Primary schools	99	904	25,760
Lower secondary schools	88	1,627	48,966
Middle secondary schools	37	1,093	29,829
Higher secondary schools	29	852	18,686
Private schools*	23	334	5,421
Institutes	19	457	4,467
Non-formal education (NFE) centres	777	762	14,436

* Data for 2006.

Source: Ministry of Education, Thimphu.

Adult literacy rate (UNESCO estimates): 42.2% (males 56.3%; females 28.2%) in 1995 (Source: UNESCO, *Statistical Yearbook*).

Directory

The Constitution

Prior to 2008 the Kingdom of Bhutan had no formal constitution. However, the state system was a modified form of constitutional monarchy. Written rules, which were changed periodically, governed procedures for the election of members of the Council of Ministers, the Royal Advisory Council and the Legislature, and defined the duties and powers of those bodies.

A special committee was convened in late 2001 to prepare a draft written constitution (Tsa-Thrim). A completed first draft was formally presented to King Jigme Singye Wangchuck in December 2002, who then passed the draft to the Prime Minister. Another draft was submitted to King Jigme in mid-2003 for further revisions. In November 2004 King Jigme submitted a 34-article fourth draft to the Council of Ministers; the document was made public for review and comment in March 2005.

The fourth draft of the Constitution provided for, amongst other things: the establishment of a democratic constitutional monarchy in accordance with the principle of hereditary succession, with an age limit of 65 years to be imposed for both the monarch and public officials; the establishment of a parliament consisting of the monarch, the National Council and the National Assembly, with members of the National Assembly to be elected by universal secret ballot from constituencies with approximately equivalent populations; and for two political parties to be represented in the National Assembly, the election campaigns of which would be funded by the State. An additional draft (called the 'second draft' but in fact the fifth) was published in August 2005; the wording of this version was considerably simplified for easier comprehension. A further, final, version of the draft constitution was expected to be adopted by the new Parliament in June 2008.

The first round of elections to the National Council (Upper House) were held on 31 December 2007 and a second round (for the remaining five districts) took place on 29 January 2008. Under the new legislative structure, the Council would comprise 25 members (20 elected members, and five 'eminent members' nominated by the King), and would function as a house of review on security and national issues; Council members are required to be independent of any political party affiliation. (Registration of political parties was permitted from 1 July 2007.) A general election to the 47-member National Assembly (Lower House) was held on 24 March 2008, ahead of the convening of the new bicameral legislature, which was scheduled to take place in early May.

The Government

HEAD OF STATE

Druk Gyalpo ('Dragon King'): HM JIGME KHESAR NAMGYEL WANGCHUCK (succeeded to the throne on 21 December 2006).

LHENGYE ZHUNGTSHOG
(Council of Ministers)
(April 2008)

Prime Minister and Chairman: Lyonchhen JIGMI YOSER THINLEY.

Minister of Agriculture: Lyonpo PEMA GYAMTSHO.
Minister of Economic Affairs: Lyonpo KHANDU WANGCHUK.
Minister of Education: Lyonpo THAKUR SINGH POWDYEL.
Minister of Finance: Lyonpo WANGDI NORBU.
Minister of Foreign Affairs: Lyonpo UGYEN TSHERING.
Minister of Health: Lyonpo ZANGLEY DUKPA.
Minister of Home and Cultural Affairs: Lyonpo MINJUR DORJI.
Minister of Information and Communications: Lyonpo NANDA-LAL RAI.
Minister of Labour and Human Resources: Lyonpo DORJI WANGDI.
Minister of Works and Human Settlements: Lyonpo YESHEY ZIMBA.
Cabinet Secretary, Spokesperson for the Government: Dasho SHERUB TENZIN.

MINISTRIES AND OTHER MAJOR GOVERNMENT BODIES

Ministry of Agriculture: POB 252, Thimphu; tel. (2) 323765; fax (2) 323153; e-mail s_thinley@moa.gov.bt; internet www.moa.gov.bt.

Ministry of Economic Affairs: Tashichhodzong, POB 141, Thimphu; tel. (2) 322211; fax (2) 323617; e-mail kdorjee@druknet.bt; internet www.mti.gov.bt; internet www.tourism.gov.bt (Department of Tourism).

Ministry of Education: POB 112, Thimphu; tel. (2) 325325; fax (2) 325183; e-mail p_thinley@hotmail.com; internet www.education.gov.bt.

Ministry of Finance: Tashichhodzong, POB 117, Thimphu; tel. (2) 322223; fax (2) 323154; e-mail yanki@mof.gov.bt.

Ministry of Foreign Affairs: Convention Centre, POB 103, Thimphu; tel. (2) 322781; internet www.mfa.gov.bt.

Ministry of Health: Kawangsa, POB 108, Thimphu; tel. (2) 322602; fax (2) 323113; e-mail dr.gado@health.gov.bt; internet www.health.gov.bt.

Ministry of Home and Cultural Affairs: Tashichhodzong, POB 133, Thimphu; tel. (2) 322301; fax (2) 324320; internet www.mohca.gov.bt; internet www.ctf.gov.bt (Cultural Trust Fund); internet www.library.gov.bt (National Library).

Ministry of Information and Communications: POB 278, Thimphu; tel. (2) 322144; fax (2) 324860; e-mail info@moic.gov.bt; internet www.moic.gov.bt; overall responsibility for various corpns (Bhutan Post, Bhutan Telecom, BBS, Kuensel, Druk Air); Dept of Information and Media; Bhutan Information, Communication and Media Authority (fmrly Bhutan Communications Authority); Dept of Civil Aviation; Road Safety and Transport Authority; Dept of Information Technology.

Ministry of Labour and Human Resources: Thongsel Lam, Lower Motithang, POB 1036, Thimphu; tel. (2) 333867; fax (2) 326731; e-mail doe@molhr.gov.bt; internet www.molhr.gov.bt.

Ministry of Works and Human Settlements: POB 791, Thimphu; tel. (2) 327998; fax (2) 323122; e-mail mowhs@mowhs.gov.bt; internet www.mowhs.gov.bt.

Anti-Corruption Commission: POB 1113, Thimphu; tel. (2) 334863; fax (2) 334865; e-mail anticorruption@druknet.bt; internet www.anti-corruption.org.bt; f. 2006; Chair. Aum NETEN ZANGMO; Commrs THINLAY WANGDI, KEZANG JAMTSHO.

National Environment Commission: POB 466, Thimphu; tel. (2) 323384; fax (2) 323385; e-mail rnrec@druknet.bt; internet www.nec.gov.bt; Hon. Dep. Minister Dasho NADO RINCHEN; Dir SONAM YANGLEY.

Royal Audit Authority: POB 191, Kawajangsa, Thimphu; tel. (2) 322111; fax (2) 323491; e-mail bhutanaudit@bhutanaudit.gov.bt; internet www.raa.gov.bt; f. 1985; Auditor-Gen. UGYEN TSHEWANG.

Royal Civil Service Commission: POB 163, Thimphu; tel. (2) 322491; fax (2) 323086; internet www.rcsc.gov.bt; f. June 1982 under Royal Charter; successor to Dept of Manpower; restructured four times, most recently in October 2003; Chair. Dasho TASHI PHUNTSOG; Sec. Dasho BAP KESANG.

Cabinet Secretariat: Tashichhodzong, Thimphu; tel. (2) 321437; fax (2) 321438; e-mail cabinet@druknet.bt.

Legislature

The National Assembly (tshogdu chenmo—which was established in 1953) was dissolved on 31 July 2007. The following month the Royal Advisory Council was similarly disbanded, in preparation for the inauguration of a new governmental structure: a bicameral legislature, comprising a 25-member National Council and a newly configured 47-member National Assembly, was expected to be convened for its first full session in June 2008.

NATIONAL COUNCIL (UPPER HOUSE)

Within the National Council, 20 members—one representing each of the 20 electoral districts—were directly elected by a national vote, with the remaining five 'eminent persons' selected by royal appointment. The first round of elections to the National Council was held on 31 December 2007 in 15 districts, and a second round, held on 29 January 2008 in the five remaining districts, completed the voting process.

Chairperson: NAMGAY PENJOR.

Vice-Chairperson: Dasho KARMA URA.

Elected Members: TSHEWANG JURMI (Bumthang), TSHEWANG LHAMO (Chhukha), SONAM DORJI (Dagana), SANGAY KHANDU (Gasa), TSHERING DORJI (Haa), RINZIN (Lhuentse), NAICHU (Mongar), UGYEN TSHERING (Paro), JIGME RINZIN (Pemagatshel), NAMGAY PENJOR (Punakha), JIGME WANGCHUK (Samdrup Jongkhar), Dr MANI KUMAR RAI (Samtse), KARMA DONNEN WANGDI (Sarpang), SANGAY ZAM (Thimphu), SONAM KUENGA (Trashigang), Dr JAGAR DORJI (Trongsa), JUSTIN GURUNG (Tsirang), KESANG NAMGYEL (Trashiyangtse), SONAM YANGCHEN (Wangdue Phodrang), PEMA LHAMO (Zhemgang).

Appointed Members: Dasho KARMA URA, Drangpon KUENLEY TSHERING, KARMA YEZER RAYDI, KARMA DAMCHO NIDUP, TASHI WANGMO.

NATIONAL ASSEMBLY (LOWER HOUSE)

Speaker: Dasho JIGME TSHULTIM.
Deputy Speaker: YANGKHU TSHERING.
General Election, 24 March 2008

Party	% of votes	Seats
Druk Phuensum Tshogpa (DPT)	67	45
People's Democratic Party (PDP)	33	2
Total	100	47

Election Commission

In mid-April 2006 there were reported to be a total of 400,626 eligible voters in Bhutan.

A draft Election Bill 2008 was published in March 2007, featuring the proposed delimitation of 47 electoral constituencies to embrace all 205 geogs (blocks of several villages) of Bhutan: five were allocated to Trashigang, four to Samtse, three to Monggar and Pemagatshel respectively and two each for the remaining 16 districts. The allocation of constituencies to the 20 electoral districts, ensuring representation of no less than two and no more than seven representatives to Parliament from each, was enacted in the same month. Delimitation of constituencies was subject to review by the Election Commission at 10-year intervals. Registration of political parties was permitted from 1 July 2007.

Election Commission of Bhutan: Thimphu; tel. (2) 334761; fax (2) 334763; e-mail kwangdi@druknet.bt; internet www.election-bhutan.org.bt; f. 2006; appointed by the King; Chief Election Commr Dasho KUNZANG WANGDI; Election Commrs Dasho CHOGYAL DAGO RIGDZIN, Aum DEKI PEMA.

Political Organizations

Although previously banned in accordance with long-standing legislation, all political parties registered with the Election Commission were to be permitted to contest the first round of the 2008 legislative elections. Formal registration commenced in July 2007, although by March 2008 only two parties—the People's Democratic Party (PDP) and the Druk Phuensum Tshogpa (DPT)—had successfully registered with the Election Commission.

There are a number of anti-Government organizations, composed principally of Nepali-speaking former residents of Bhutan, based in Kathmandu, Nepal and New Delhi, India.

Bhutan Communist Party (Marxist-Leninist-Maoist): Nepal; f. 2003; advocates complete revolution in Bhutan; Gen. Sec. VIKALPA.

Bhutan Gorkha Liberation Front: f. 2003; based in southern Bhutan; Chair. TARA MUKARUNG.

Bhutan Gurkha National Liberation Front (BGNLF): Nepal; f. 1994; Vice-Pres. D. R. KATEL; Gen. Sec. LALIT PRADHAN.

Bhutan National Democratic Party (BNDP): POB 3334, Kathmandu, Nepal; tel. (1) 525682; f. 1992; also has offices in Delhi and Varanasi, India, and in Thapa, Nepal; Pres. (vacant); Vice-Pres. D. N. S. DHAKAL; Gen. Sec. Dr HARI P. ADHIKARI.

Bhutan People's Party (BPP): POB 13, Anarmani-4, Bhadrapur Rd, Birtamode, Jhapa, Nepal; tel. and fax (23) 542561; e-mail bpparty@ntc.net.np; internet www.bhutanpeoplesparty.org; f. 1990 as a successor to the People's Forum on Democratic Rights (f. 1989); advocates unconditional release of all political prisoners, judicial reform, freedom of religious practices, linguistic freedom, freedom of press, speech and expression, and equal rights for all ethnic groups; Pres. BALA RAM POUDYAL; Gen. Sec. DURGA GIRI.

Druk National Congress (DNC): B-125, 1st Floor, Dayanand Colony, Lajpat Nagar IV, New Delhi 110 024; tel. (11) 65641453; fax (11) 26472636; e-mail dnc@bhutandnc.com; internet www.bhutandnc.com; f. 1994; advocates democracy and human rights in Bhutan; Pres. 'RONGTHONG' KUNLEY DORJI; Gen. Sec. RINZIN DORJI.

Druk Phuensum Tshogpa (DPT): Chang Lam, Thimphu; tel. (2) 336336; fax (2) 335845; e-mail dpt@druknet.bt; internet www.dpt.bt; f. 2007 in asscn with five ministers of the outgoing Govt; Pres. Lyonpo JIGMI YOZER THINLEY; Gen. Sec. THINLEY JAMTSHO.

Human Rights Organization of Bhutan (HUROB): Patan Dhoka, POB 172, Lalitpur, Kathmandu, Nepal; tel. (1) 525046; fax (1) 526038; f. 1991; documents alleged human rights violations in Bhutan and co-ordinates welfare activities in eight refugee camps in Nepal for ethnic Nepalese claiming to be from Bhutan; Chair. S. B. SUBBA; Gen. Sec. OM DHUNGEL.

People's Democratic Party (PDP): Drizang Lam, Lower Motithang, Thimphu; tel. (2) 335557; fax (2) 335757; e-mail info@pdp.bt; internet www.pdp.bt; f. 2007 in asscn with a minister of the outgoing Govt; Leader SANGYE NGEDUP; Sec.-Gen. Lyonpo LAM KESANG.

Diplomatic Representation

EMBASSIES IN BHUTAN

Bangladesh: POB 178, Upper Choubachu, Thimphu; tel. (2) 322539; fax (2) 322629; e-mail bdoot@druknet.bt; Ambassador A. K. M. ATIQUR RAHMAN.

India: India House, Jungshina, Thimphu; tel. (2) 322162; fax (2) 323195; e-mail hocbht@druknet.bt; Ambassador SUDHIR VYAS.

Judicial System

Bhutan has Civil and Criminal Codes, which are based on those laid down by the Shabdrung Ngawang Namgyal in the 17th century. An independent judicial authority was established in 1961, but law was mostly administered at the district level until 1968, when the High Court was set up. Existing laws were consolidated in 1982, although annual or biennial conferences of Drangpons (previously styled Thrimpons) are held to keep abreast of changing circumstances and to recommend (in the first instance, to the King) amendments to existing laws. Most legislation is sent by the Council of Ministers to the National Assembly for approval and enactment. A substantially revised Civil and Criminal Procedure Code was endorsed by the 79th

National Assembly session in July 2001. In accordance with the law, a National Judicial Commission was established in September 2003. The principal role of the judicial board was to professionalize further the appointment and tenure of judges in the court system; the Chief Justice was to preside over the Commission. A revised Penal Code was adopted by the National Assembly in mid-2004. The historic Judicial Services Act, which was enacted by the National Assembly in January 2007, provided for the complete administrative independence of the judiciary with regard to personnel (excepting judges of the Supreme Court and High Court) through the establishment of a Judicial Services Council. Following the scheduled promulgation of the new Constitution in mid–2008, the Supreme Court of Bhutan (which was to consist of the Chief Justice and four Drangpons) was to be the highest appellate authority in the country.

High Court
(Thrimkhang Gongma)

Thimphu; tel. (2) 322344; fax (2) 322921; internet www.judiciary.gov.bt.

Established in 1968 to review appeals from Lower Courts, although some cases are heard at the first instance. The Full Bench is presided over by the Chief Justice. There are normally seven other judges (Drangpons), who are appointed by the King on the recommendation of the Chief Justice and who serve until their superannuation. Three judges form a quorum. Assistance to defendants is available through jabmis (certificated pleaders), whose responsibilities were formalized by the Jabmi Act in mid-2003. The operation of the legal system and proposed amendments are considered by regular meetings of all the judges and Drangpons (usually annually, or at least once every two years). Following the mid-1998 grant of governance to an elected Council of Ministers, major changes to the structure, administration and personnel of the High Court were implemented from mid-2001.

Chief Justice: Lyonpo SONAM TOBGYE.

Judges (Drangpons) of the High Court: Dasho THINLEY YOEZER, Dasho PASANG TOBGAY, Dasho KARMA D. SHERPA, Dasho K. B. GHALLEY, Dasho JIGME ZANGPO, Dasho SHERUB GYELTSHEN, Dasho SITHER NAMGYEL, Dasho KUENLEY TSHERING, Dasho TSHERING WANGCHUCK.

District Courts (Dzongkhag Thrimkhang): Each district has a court, headed by the drangpon (magistrate), which tries most cases. Appeals are made to the High Court, and less serious civil disputes may be settled by a gup or mandal (village headman) through written undertakings (genja) by the parties concerned.

All citizens have the right to make informal appeal for redress of grievances directly to the King, through the office of the gyalpoi zimpon (court chamberlain).

Office of the Attorney-General: POB 1045, Thori Lam, Lower Motithang, Thimphu; tel. (2) 326889; fax (2) 324606; e-mail oag@oag.gov.bt; internet www.oag.gov.bt; f. 2006; fmrly Office of Legal Affairs; Attorney-Gen. (vacant).

Religion

The state religion is Mahayana Buddhism, but the southern Bhutanese are predominantly followers of Hinduism. Buddhism was introduced into Bhutan in the eighth century AD by the Indian saint Padmasambhava, known in Bhutan as Guru Rimpoche. In the 13th century Phajo Drugom Shigpo made the Drukpa school of Kagyupa Buddhism pre-eminent in Bhutan, and this sect is still supported by the dominant ethnic group, the Drukpas. The main monastic group, the Central Monastic Body (comprising about 1,600 monks in Thimphu and Punakha), led by an elected Head Abbot (Je Khenpo), is directly supported by the State and spends six months of the year at Tashichhodzong and at Punakha, respectively. A further 2,120 monks, who are members of the District Monastic Bodies, are sustained by the lay population. The Council for Ecclesiastical Affairs oversees all religious bodies. Monasteries (Gompas) and shrines (Lhakhangs) are numerous. Religious proselytizing, in any form, is illegal.

Council for Ecclesiastical Affairs (Dratshang Lhentshog): POB 254, Thimphu; tel. (2) 322754; fax (2) 323867; e-mail dratshang@druknet.bt; f. 1984, replacing the Central Board for Monastic Studies, to oversee the national memorial chorten and all Buddhist meditational centres and schools of Buddhist studies, as well as the Central and District Monastic Bodies; daily affairs of the Council are run by the Central Monastic Secretariat; Chair. His Holiness the 70th Je Khenpo Trulku JIGME CHOEDRA; Sec. Dasho SANGAY WANGCHUCK; Dep. Sec. NGAWANG PHUNTSHO.

The Press

The Bhutan Review: Patan Dhoka, POB 172, Lalitpur, Kathmandu, Nepal; tel. 525046; fax 523819; f. 1993; monthly organ of the Human Rights Organization of Bhutan (HUROB); opposed to existing government policies.

Kuensel Corporation: POB 204, Thimphu; tel. (2) 322483; fax (2) 322975; e-mail editor@kuensel.com.bt; internet www.kuenselonline.com; f. 1965 as a weekly govt bulletin; reorg. as a national weekly newspaper in 1986; became autonomous corporation in 1992 (previously under Dept of Information), incorporating former Royal Government Press; also published weekly from Kanglung from Dec. 2005; in English and Dzongkha; offered 49% of shares to public in 2006, while Government retained controlling 51%; Man. Dir and Editor-in-Chief KINLEY DORJI; Editors TIKA RAM SHARMA (Nepali), PHUNTSO WANGDI (English), CHOKI DHENDUP (Dzongkha); 12,875 (English), 4,280 (Dzongkha).

Bhutan Times: POB 1365, Norzim Lam, Thimphu; tel. (2) 328450; fax (2) 328451; e-mail editor@bhutantimes.bt; internet www.bhutantimes.bt; f. 2006; weekly newspaper; publ. by Bhutan Times Ltd; initially in English edn only; publ. *Bhutan NOW* magazine; CEO TENZIN RIGDEN; Editor GOPILAL ACHARYA.

Bhutan Observer: POB 1112, Norzin Lam, Thimphu; tel. (2) 334890; fax (2) 327981; e-mail editor@bhutanobserver.com.bt; internet www.bhutanobserver.bt; f. 2006; weekly newspaper; publ. in English and Dzongkha, by KMT Printing Press Pvt Ltd; Man. Dir MANI DORJI; Man. Editor K. B. LAMA; Dir TENZIN WANGDI.

Broadcasting and Communications

TELECOMMUNICATIONS

Bhutan Infocomm and Media Authority (BICMA): Kawajangia, POB 1072, Thimphu; tel. (2) 321506; fax (2) 326909; internet www.bicma.gov.bt; f. 2000 as Bhutan Telecommunications Authority under Bhutan Telecommunications Act; telecommunications and media regulatory body; regulatory remit extended to include Information and Communication Technology and media services in 2005; began operations as autonomous authority, independent of Ministry of Information and Communications, from 1 January 2007; Dir KINLEY T. WANGCHUK.

Bhutan Telecom Ltd: POB 134, Thimphu; tel. (2) 322678; fax (2) 324312; e-mail info@telecom.net.bt; internet www.telecom.net.bt; f. 2000; state-owned public corpn; regulation authority; agency for satellite telephones; Chair. LAM DORJI; Exec. Dir Dasho SANGEY TENZING; Man. Dir THINLEY DORJI.

B-Mobile: c/o Bhutan Telecom, Drophenlam, POB 134, Drophenlam, Thimphu; tel. (2) 320194; fax (2) 320193; e-mail mkto@telecom.net.bt; internet www.telecom.net.bt; f. 2002; offered mobile cellular telephone services from Nov. 2003; covered Thimphu and most of Paro by mid-2004; coverage extended to all 20 districts by early 2008; more than 167,000 subscribers (2008); subsidiary of Bhutan Telecom Ltd; Gen. Man. TANDI WANGCHUK.

DrukNet: Bhutan Telecom, 2/28 Drophenlam, POB 134, Thimphu; tel. (2) 326998; fax (2) 328160; e-mail info@druknet.bt; internet www.druknet.bt; f. 1999; internet service provider; Head GANGA SHARMA; Gen. Man. JICHEN THINLEY.

Tashi InfoComm Ltd (TashiCell): Thimphu; f. 2008; first privately-owned mobile cellular telephone company in Bhutan; initially covered six western districts; more than 13,000 subscribers (2008); Exec. Dir TASHI TSHERING.

BROADCASTING
Radio

In 1994 there were 52 radio stations for administrative communications. Of these, 34 were for internal communications (to which the public had access), and three were external stations serving Bhutan House at Kalimpong and the Bhutanese diplomatic missions in India and Bangladesh. Following the passage of an Information, Communications and Media Act in June 2006, the country's first two private radio stations, *Radio Valley* and *Kuzoo FM*, were granted FM operating licences.

Bhutan Broadcasting Services Corporation (BBSC): POB 101, Thimphu; tel. (2) 323071; fax (2) 323073; e-mail bbs@bbs.com.bt; internet www.bbs.com.bt; f. 1973 as Radio National Youth Association of Bhutan (NYAB); became autonomous corporation in 1992 (previously under Dept of Information); short-wave radio station broadcasting daily in Dzongkha, Sharchopkha, Nepali (Lhotsamkha) and English; a daily FM programme (for Thimphu only) began in 1987; simultaneous broadcasting on FM for western Bhutan and parts of central and southern Bhutan began in 2000; a one-hour daily television service for Thimphu was introduced in mid-1999 and later increased to five hours in the morning and five in the evening; the nationwide television service expanded onto satellite in February 2007, allowing BBSC to broadcast to almost 40 countries; Chair. Dasho TASHI PHUNTSHOG; Man. Dir Aum PEMA CHHODEN.

Centennial Radio 101 FM: Ground Floor, Karma Tshongkhang Bldg, Thimphu; internet centennialradio.net; f. 2008; news, current affairs, music and entertainment programmes; CEO DORJI WANGCHUK.

Kuzoo FM: POB 419, Thimphu; tel. (2) 335984; fax (2) 335263; e-mail fm@kuzoo.net; internet www.kuzoo.net; f. 2006; broadcasts 24 hours a day on FM in Dzongkha and English; news, information and entertainment programmes.

Radio Valley: Rabten Lam, Thimphu; tel. (2) 323390; e-mail the_soundweaver@hotmail.com; internet www.radiovalley.bt; f. 2007; broadcasts 12 hours a day on FM; music, entertainment and information programmes to be broadcast upon commencement of full operations; Founder KINLEY CHOZOM.

Television

In June 1999 the BBSC started operating a television service (in Dzongkha and English) in Thimphu; the service was gradually to be expanded throughout the country. Broadcasts are limited to a few hours a day and consist principally of national news and documentaries about Bhutan. By March 2002, according to official figures, each of the two cable television operators was providing 45 channels. In mid-2006 television broadcasts were for five hours each evening (three hours in Dzongkha, two hours in English). Satellite broadcasting was introduced in February 2007.

Finance

(cap. = capital; auth. = authorized; p.u. = paid up; res = reserves; dep. = deposits; m. = million; brs = branches; amounts in ngultrum)

BANKING
Central Bank

Royal Monetary Authority (RMA): POB 154, Thimphu; tel. (2) 323111; fax (2) 322847; e-mail rma@rma.org.bt; internet www.rma.org.bt; f. 1982; bank of issue; frames and implements official monetary policy, co-ordinates the activities of financial institutions and holds foreign-exchange deposits on behalf of the Govt; cap. 4.4m., res 1,443.0m., dep. 11,017.3m. (June 2006); Chair. Lyonpo KINZANG DORJI; Man. Dir DAW TENZIN.

Commercial Banks

Bank of Bhutan Ltd: Samdrup Lam, POB 75, Phuentsholing; tel. (5) 252225; fax (5) 252641; e-mail bobho_hrd@druknet.bt; internet www.bobltd.com.bt; f. 1968; 20% owned by the State Bank of India and 80% by the Govt of Bhutan; wholly managed by Govt of Bhutan from 1997; cap. 100.0m., res 1,160.3m., dep. 15,174.5m. (Dec. 2006); Dirs nominated by the Bhutan Govt: Chair. KARMA Y. RAYDI; Dirs KARMA PENJOR, PEMA NADIK; Dirs nominated by the State Bank of India RAKESH SHARMA, P. S. PRAKESH RAO; 26 brs and 3 extension counters.

Bhutan National Bank (BNB): POB 439, Thimphu; tel. (2) 328577; fax (2) 328839; e-mail bnbpling@druknet.bt; internet www.bhutannationalbank.com; f. 1996; Bhutan's second commercial bank; partially privatized in 1998; 27.2% owned by Govt and 20.1% by Asian Development Bank; cap. 119.0m., res 705.6m., dep. 8,622.9m. (2006); Chair. Lyonpo YESHEY ZIMBA; Man. Dir KIPCHU TSHERING; 7 brs.

Development Bank

Bhutan Development Finance Corporation (BDFC): POB 256, Thimphu; tel. (2) 322579; fax (2) 323428; e-mail bdfc@druknet.bt; internet www.bdfcl.com.bt; f. 1988; provides industrial loans and short- and medium-term agricultural loans; cap. p.u. 100m., loans 1,114m. (2003); Chair. Dasho WANGDI NORBU; Man. Dir KARMA RANGDOL.

STOCK EXCHANGE

Royal Securities Exchange of Bhutan Ltd (RSEB): POB 742, Thimphu; tel. (2) 323995; fax (2) 323849; e-mail rseb@druknet.bt; f. 1993; supervised by the Royal Monetary Authority; open to Bhutanese nationals only; 16 listed cos (2006); Chair. DAW TENZIN; CEO TASHI YEZER.

INSURANCE

Royal Insurance Corporation of Bhutan: POB 77, Phuentsholing; tel. (5) 252453; fax (5) 252640; e-mail ricbho@druknet.bt; internet www.ricb.com.bt; f. 1975; provides general and life insurance and credit investment services; Chair. Lyonpo YESHEY ZIMBA; Man. Dir NAMGAY LHENDUP; 10 brs and development centres.

Trade and Industry

GOVERNMENT AGENCIES

Druk Holding and Investments Ltd: POB 1127, Motithang, Thimpu; tel. and fax (2) 335794; e-mail info@dhi.bt; internet www.dhi.bt; f. 2007 to manage the existing and future investments of the Govt; managed an initial grouping of 14 companies in sectors including hydropower, banking, minerals and natural resources; Chair. Lyonpo OM PRADHAN; CEO KARMA YONTEN.

Food Corporation of Bhutan (FCB): POB 80, Phuentsholing; tel. (5) 252241; fax (5) 252289; e-mail drukfood@druknet.bt; f. 1974; activities include procurement and distribution of food grains and other essential commodities through appointed Fair Price Shop Agents; marketing of surplus agricultural and horticultural produce through FCB-regulated market outlets; logistics concerning World Food Programme food aid; maintenance of buffer stocks to offset any emergency food shortages; maintenance of SAARC Food Security Reserve Stock; importing consumer goods from major Indian enterprises; exporting oranges and apples; Man. Dir SHERUB GYALTSHEN; 19 outlets and 100 Fair Price Shops.

Gross National Happiness Commission: Convention Centre, POB 127, Thimphu; tel. (2) 323176; fax (2) 325402; e-mail ldorji@pc.gov.bt; internet www.gnhc.gov.bt; f. 1971 as Planning Commission; headed by the King until 1991; reconstituted 1999 as department under Ministry of Finance; re-established as separate 11-mem. commission from Jan. 2006; renamed as above in Jan. 2008; proposes socio-economic policy guide-lines, issues directives for the formulation of development plans, ensures efficient and judicious allocation of resources, directs socio-economic research, studies and surveys, and appraises the Govt on the progress of development plans and programmes; Chair. Lyonpo KINZANG DORJI; Sec. KARMA TSHITEEM.

Natural Resources Development Corporation: Thimphu; tel. (2) 323834; fax (2) 325585; fmrly Forestry Development Corporation; renamed as above in 2007; fixes price of sand and timber; oversees quarrying and mining of sand; Chair. KARMA DUKPA; Man. Dir SANGAY GYALTSHEN.

State Trading Corpn of Bhutan Ltd (STCB): POB 76, Phuentsholing; tel. (5) 252745; fax (5) 252619; e-mail stcbl@druknet.bt; internet www.stcb.com.bt; f. 1969; manages imports and exports of vehicles, IT and construction materials on behalf of the Govt; Chair. SANGAY WANGDI; Man. Dir SAMDRUP K. THINLEY; brs in Thimphu (POB 272; tel. (2) 324785; fax (2) 322953; e-mail stcbthim@druknet.bt) and Kolkata (Calcutta), India (e-mail stcbkol@vsnl.net).

CHAMBER OF COMMERCE

Bhutan Chamber of Commerce and Industry (BCCI): Doebum Lam, POB 147, Thimphu; tel. (2) 322742; fax (2) 323936; e-mail bsdbcci@druknet.bt; internet www.bcci.com.bt; f. 1980; reorg. 1988; promotion of trade and industry and privatization, information dissemination, private-sector human resource development; 14 exec. mems; 20-mem. district executive committee; Pres. Dasho UGEN DORJI; Vice-Pres. and CEO Dasho BAP KINGA.

UTILITIES
Electricity

Bhutan Electricity Authority (BEA): Thimphu; e-mail ceo@bea.gov.bt; internet www.bea.gov.bt; f. 1991; regulates the electricity supply industry; CEO (vacant); Exec. Eng. PEM DORJEE.

Department of Energy: c/o Ministry of Economic Affairs, Tashichhodzong, POB 141, Thimphu; tel. (2) 322279; fax (2) 328278.

Basochhu Hydropower Corporation: Basochhu; tel. (2) 471021; fax (2) 471020; e-mail bhpc@druknet.bt; co-ordinates construction of dam and hydroelectric power-generating facilities; operates and maintains two power stations with a total installed capacity of 64MW; became part of Druk Green Power Corpn in 2008; Sr Plant Eng. OM BHANDARI.

Bhutan Power Corporation: POB 580, Thimphu; tel. (2) 325095; fax (2) 322279; e-mail hr@bpc.com.bt; internet www.bpc.com.bt; f. 2002; responsible for ensuring electricity supply for the whole country at an affordable cost by 2020 and for providing uninterrupted transmission access for export of surplus power; operations in 19 districts; Chair. YESHEY WANGDI; Man. Dir BHARAT TAMANG.

Chhukha Hydropower Corporation: Phuentsholing; tel. (5) 252575; fax (5) 252582; f. 1991; state-owned; 70% of power generated by the project is exported to India; became part of Druk Green Power Corpn in 2008; Chair. Lyonpo YESHEY ZIMBA; Man. Dir YESHEY WANGDI.

Kurichhu Project Authority: Gyelpozhing (Monggar); tel. (4) 744113; fax (4) 744130; e-mail kpa@druknet.bt; operates and maintains a 60-MW hydroelectric power-generating facility at Gyelpozhing; became part of Druk Green Power Corpn in 2008; Chair. Lyonpo KHANDU WANGCHUCK; Man. Dir TSHEWANG RINZIN.

Tala Hydroelectric Project Authority: THPA Office Complex, Gedu; tel. (5) 282001; fax (5) 282010; e-mail mdthpa@druknet.bt; co-ordinates construction of dam and hydroelectric power-generating facilities; Man. Dir R. N. KHAZANCHI.

Water

Thimphu City Corporation (Water Supply Unit): POB 215, Thimphu; tel. (2) 324710; fax (2) 324315; e-mail tda@druknet.bt; f. 1982; under Ministry of Home and Cultural Affairs from mid-2003; responsible for water supply of Thimphu municipality; Head BHIMLAL DHUNGEL.

TRADE UNIONS

Under long-standing legislation, trade union activity is illegal in Bhutan. During the 86th session of the National Assembly, which was held in December 2006/January 2007, the Labour Act was passed, permitting (among other things) the formation of 'workers' associations'.

Transport

ROADS AND TRACKS

In June 2005 there were 4,392.5 km of roads in Bhutan, of which 2,461.3 km were black-topped and included 1,579 km designated national highways. Surfaced roads link the important border towns of Phuentsholing, Gelephu, Sarpang and Samdrup Jongkhar in southern Bhutan to towns in West Bengal and Assam (Asom) in India. There is a shortage of road transport. Yaks, ponies and mules are still the chief means of transport on the rough mountain tracks. By 1990 most of the previously government-operated transport facilities (mainly buses and minibuses) on major and subsidiary routes had been transferred to private operators on the basis of seven-year contracts. Several major road construction and improvement projects were under development in 2006, including a 76-km highway connecting Samtse and Phuentsholing. A Roads Sector Master Plan (2007–27) envisaged the construction of 2,587.4 km of feeder roads throughout Bhutan, a second East–West Highway (794 km) stretching from Sipsu to Jomotshankha, and 410 km of highways to improve inter-connectivity between districts. It was hoped that 75% of the country's rural population would live within half a day's walk of the nearest road by the end of the 10th Five-Year Plan in 2012.

Road Safety and Transport Authority: Thimphu; tel. (2) 321282; fax (2) 321281; e-mail director_rsta@druknet.bt; f. 1995; under Ministry of Information and Communications; regulates all motor vehicle activities and surface transport services; Dir NIMA WANGDI.

Transport Corpn of Bhutan: Phuentsholing; tel. (5) 252476; f. 1982; subsidiary of Royal Insurance Corpn of Bhutan; operates direct coach service between Phuentsholing and Kolkata via Siliguri.

Other operators are **Barma Travels** (f. 1990), **Dawa Transport** (Propr SHERUB WANGCHUCK), **Dhendup Travel Service** (Phuentsholing; tel (5) 252437), **Gyamtsho Transport**, **Gurung Transport Service**, **Namgay Transport**, **Nima Travels** (Phuentsholing; tel. (5) 252384), and **Rimpung Travels** (Phuentsholing; tel. (5) 252354).

Lorries for transporting goods are operated by the private sector.

CIVIL AVIATION

There is an international airport at Paro, and a runway strip at Trashigang. There are also some 30 helicopter landing pads, which are used, by arrangement with the Indian military and aviation authorities, solely by government officials. The Council of Ministers approved the operation of a domestic helicopter service to improve mobility and to promote tourism; by mid-2003 five domestic heliports had been surveyed and found acceptable. The national carrier, Druk Air Corporation Limited, began operating helicopter services in 2005.

Department of Civil Aviation: c/o Ministry of Information and Communications, Woochu, Paro; tel. (8) 271347; fax (8) 271909; e-mail aviation@druknet.bt; state-owned; f. 1986; Dir PHALA DORJI.

Druk Air Corpn Ltd (Royal Bhutan Airlines): Head Office, Nemizampa, PO Paro; tel. (8) 271856; fax (8) 271861; e-mail drukair@druknet.bt; internet www.drukair.com.bt; national airline; f. 1981; became fully operational in 1983; services from Paro to Delhi and Gaya (winter only) in India, Bangladesh, Nepal and Thailand; additional services planned to increase utilization of aircraft; charter services available; helicopter services introduced in 2005; Chair. Lyonpo JIGMI Y. THINLEY; Man. Dir SANGAY TENZING.

Tourism

Bhutan was opened to tourism in 1975. In 2007 the total number of foreign visitors was 21,094, compared with 17,365 in 2006. Receipts from tourism in 2007 totalled US $30m., compared with $24m. in 2006. Tourists travel in organized 'package', cultural or trekking tours, or individually, accompanied by trained guides; independent, unaccompanied travel is not permitted within the kingdom. Hotels have been constructed at Phuentsholing, Paro, Bumthang, Wangduephodrang and Thimphu, with lodges at Trongsa, Trashigang and Monggar. In addition, there are many small privately operated hotels and guest-houses. Plans for several foreign-managed commercial hotels, in the style of resorts, were under way in the mid-2000s. The Government exercises close control over the development of tourism. In 1987 the National Assembly resolved that all monasteries, mountains and other holy places should be inaccessible to tourists from 1988 (this resolution is flexibly interpreted, however—e.g. Japanese Buddhist tour groups are permitted to visit 'closed' monasteries). In 1991 the Government began transferring the tourism industry to the private sector and licences were issued to new private tourism operators. Rules were introduced in 1995 asserting more stringent controls over private operators through the Tourism Authority of Bhutan (TAB). In 1998 the Government's tourism policy was liberalized further. In 2001 the TAB was reorganized as the Department of Tourism, under the Ministry of Trade and Industry (renamed the Ministry of Economic Affairs in 2007). The Government has identified and encouraged the industry's potential to grow and to provide significant employment opportunities. A levy of $10 per visitor contributed to a Tourist Development Fund, which by the end of 2002 amounted to more than Nu 10m. The Association of Bhutan Travel Operators (ABTO) was established in 1998 to act as a forum for co-ordinating tourism issues among the travel agencies. ABTO also surveyed new trekking routes in Haa, following the opening of the district to tourists from mid-2001. By the end of 2007 there were 349 registered tour operators in the country, but only 200 of these were actually functioning during that year.

Department of Tourism: POB 126, Thimphu; tel. (2) 323251; fax (2) 323695; e-mail dot@tourism.gov.bt; internet www.tourism.gov.bt; f. 2001 to replace Tourism Authority of Bhutan; under regulatory authority of Ministry of Economic Affairs; exercises overall authority over tourism policy, pricing, hotel, restaurant and travel agency licensing, visa approvals, etc.; Dir-Gen. LHATU WANGCHUCK.

Tourism Council of Bhutan: Thimpu; f. 2008; autonomous intergovernmental agency; manages and develops the tourism industry; aims to promote Bhutan as an 'exclusive tourist destination'; Chair. KINZANG DORJI; Dir-Gen. KESANG WANGDI.

Association of Bhutan Travel Operators (ABTO): POB 938, Thimphu; tel. (2) 322862; fax (2) 325286; e-mail abto@druknet.bt; internet www.abto.org.bt; f. 1998 to provide forum for members' views and to unite, supervise and co-ordinate activities of members; Chair. Dasho UGEN TSECHUP DORJI; 238 mem. tour operators (March 2008).

BOLIVIA

Introductory Survey

Location, Climate, Language, Religion, Flag, Capital

The Republic of Bolivia is a land-locked state in South America, bordered by Chile and Peru to the west, by Brazil to the north and east, and by Paraguay and Argentina to the south. The climate varies, according to altitude, from humid tropical conditions in the northern and eastern lowlands, which are less than 500 m (1,640 ft) above sea-level, to the cool and cold zones at altitudes of more than 3,500 m (about 11,500 ft) in the Andes mountains. The official languages are Spanish, Quechua and Aymará. Almost all of the inhabitants profess Christianity, and the great majority are adherents of the Roman Catholic Church. The national civil flag (proportions 2 by 3) has three equal horizontal stripes, of red, yellow and green. The state flag has, in addition, the national coat of arms in the centre of the yellow stripe. The legal capital is Sucre. The administrative capital and seat of government is La Paz.

Recent History

The Incas of Bolivia were conquered by Spain in 1538 and, although there were many revolts against Spanish rule, independence was not achieved until 1825. Bolivian history has been characterized by recurrent internal strife, resulting in a lengthy succession of presidents, and frequent territorial disputes with its neighbours, including the 1879–83 War of the Pacific between Bolivia, Peru and Chile, which resulted in the loss of Bolivia's coastline, and the Chaco Wars of 1928–30 and 1932–35 against Paraguay.

At a presidential election in May 1951 the largest share of the vote was won by Dr Víctor Paz Estenssoro, the candidate of the Movimiento Nacionalista Revolucionario (MNR), who had been living in Argentina since 1946. He was denied permission to return to Bolivia and contested the election *in absentia*. However, he failed to gain an absolute majority, and the incumbent President transferred power to a junta of army officers. This regime was itself overthrown in April 1952, when a popular uprising, supported by the MNR and a section of the armed forces, enabled Dr Paz Estenssoro to return from exile and assume the presidency. His Government, a coalition of the MNR and the Labour Party, committed itself to profound social revolution. The coalition nationalized the tin mines and introduced universal suffrage (the franchise had previously been limited to literate adults) and land reform. Dr Hernán Siles Zuazo, a leading figure in the 1952 revolution, was elected President for the 1956–60 term, and Dr Paz Estenssoro was again elected President in 1960. However, the powerful trade unions came into conflict with the Government, and in November 1964, following widespread strikes and disorder, President Paz Estenssoro was overthrown by the Vice-President, Gen. René Barrientos Ortuño, who was supported by the army. After serving with Gen. Alfredo Ovando Candía as Co-President under a military junta, Gen. Barrientos resigned in January 1966 to campaign for the presidency; he was elected in July.

President Barrientos encountered strong opposition from left-wing groups, including mineworkers' unions. There was also a guerrilla uprising in south-eastern Bolivia, led by Dr Ernesto ('Che') Guevara, the Argentine-born revolutionary who had played a leading role in the Castro regime in Cuba. However, the insurgency was suppressed by government troops, with the help of US advisers, and guerrilla warfare ended in October 1967, when Guevara was captured and killed. (In July 1997 Guevara's remains, together with those of three of his comrades, were finally located and returned to Cuba.) In April 1969 President Barrientos was killed in an air crash and Dr Luis Adolfo Siles Salinas, the Vice-President, succeeded to the presidency. In September, however, President Siles Salinas was deposed by the armed forces, who reinstated Gen. Ovando. He was forced to resign in October 1970, when, after a power struggle between right-wing and left-wing army officers, Gen. Juan José Torres González, who had support from leftists, emerged as President, pledging support for agrarian reform and worker participation in management. A 'People's Assembly', formed by Marxist politicians, radical students and leaders of trade unions, was allowed to meet and demanded the introduction of extreme socialist measures, causing disquiet in right-wing circles. President Torres was deposed in August 1971 by Col (later Gen.) Hugo Banzer Suárez, who drew support from the right-wing Falange Socialista Boliviana and a section of the MNR, as well as from the army. In June 1973 President Banzer announced an imminent return to constitutional government, but elections were later postponed to June 1974. The MNR withdrew its support and entered into active opposition.

Following an attempted military coup in June 1974, all portfolios within the Cabinet were assigned to military personnel. After another failed coup attempt in November, President Banzer declared that elections had been postponed indefinitely and that his military regime would retain power until at least 1980. All political and union activity was banned. Political and industrial unrest in 1976, however, led President Banzer to announce that elections would be held in July 1978. Allegations of fraud rendered the elections void, but Gen. Juan Pereda Asbún, the armed forces candidate in the elections, staged a successful military coup. In November 1978 his right-wing Government was overthrown in another coup, led by Gen. David Padilla Arancibia, Commander-in-Chief of the Army, with the support of national left-wing elements.

Presidential and congressional elections were held in July 1979. The presidential poll resulted in almost equal support for two ex-Presidents, Dr Siles Zuazo and Dr Paz Estenssoro, who were now leading rival factions of the MNR. The Congreso (Congress), which was convened in August to resolve the issue, failed to award a majority to either candidate. An interim Government was formed under Walter Guevara Arce, President of the upper house of the Congreso, but this administration was overthrown on 1 November by a right-wing army officer, Col Alberto Natusch Busch. He withdrew 15 days later after failing to gain the support of the Congreso, which elected Dra Lidia Gueiler Tejada, President of the Cámara de Diputados (Chamber of Deputies, the lower congressional house), as interim Head of State pending presidential and congressional elections scheduled for June 1980.

The result of the 1980 presidential election was inconclusive, and in July, before the Congreso could meet to decide between the two main contenders (again Siles Zuazo and Paz Estenssoro), a military junta led by an army commander, Gen. Luis García Meza, staged a coup—the 189th in Bolivia's 154 years of independence. In August 1981 a military uprising forced Gen. García to resign. In September the junta transferred power to another army commander, Gen. Celso Torrelio Villa, who declared his intention to return the country to democracy within three years. Labour unrest, provoked by Bolivia's severe economic crisis, was appeased by restitution of trade-union and political rights, and a mainly civilian Cabinet was appointed in April 1982. Elections were scheduled for April 1983. The political liberalization disturbed the armed forces, who attempted to create a climate of violence, and President Torrelio resigned in July 1982, amid rumours of an impending coup. The junta installed the less moderate Gen. Guido Vildoso Calderón, the Army Chief of Staff, as President. Unable to resolve the worsening economic crisis or to control a general strike, in September the military regime announced that power would be handed over in October to the Congreso that had originally been elected in 1980. Dr Siles Zuazo, who had obtained most votes in both 1979 and 1980, was duly elected President by the Congreso, and was sworn in for a four-year term in October 1982.

President Siles Zuazo appointed a coalition Cabinet consisting of members of his own party, the Movimiento Nacionalista Revolucionario de Izquierda (MNRI), the Movimiento de la Izquierda Revolucionaria (MIR) and the Partido Comunista de Bolivia (PCB). Economic aid from the USA and Europe was resumed, but the Government found itself unable to fulfil the expectations that had been created by the return to democratic rule. The entire Cabinet resigned in August 1983, and the President appointed a Cabinet in which the number of portfolios that were held by the right-wing of the MNRI, the Partido Demócrata Cristiano (PDC) and independents was increased. The MIR joined forces with the MNR and with business interests in rejecting the Government's policy of complying with IMF conditions for assistance, which involved harsh economic measures. The Government lost its majority in the Congreso and was confronted by strikes and mass labour demonstrations. In November the opposition-dominated Senado Nacional (Senate) approved an increase of 100% in the minimum wage, in defiance of the Government's austerity measures. Following a 48-hour general strike, the whole Cabinet resigned once again in December, in anticipation of an opposition motion of censure. In January 1984 President Siles Zuazo appointed a new coalition Cabinet, including 13 members of the previous Government.

In June 1984 the country was again thrown into turmoil by the temporary abduction of President Siles Zuazo. Two former cabinet ministers and some 100 right-wing army officers were arrested in connection with the kidnapping, which was believed to have been supported by leading figures in the illicit drugs trade.

At elections in July 1985, amid reports of electoral malpractice and poor organization, the right-wing Acción Democrática Nacionalista (ADN), whose presidential candidate was Gen. Hugo Banzer Suárez (the former dictator), received 29% of the votes cast, and the MNR obtained 26%, while the MIR was the leading left-wing party. At a further round of voting in the Congreso in August, an alliance between the MNR and the leading left-wing groups, including the MIR, enabled Dr Víctor Paz Estenssoro of the MNR to secure the presidency (which he had previously held in 1952–56 and 1960–64). The armed forces pledged their support for the new Government.

On taking office in August 1985, the new Government immediately introduced a very strict economic programme, designed to reduce inflation, which was estimated to have reached 14,173% in the year to August. The trade union confederation, the Central Obrera Boliviana (COB), rejected the programme and called an indefinite general strike in September. The Government responded by declaring the strike illegal and by ordering a 90-day state of siege throughout Bolivia. Leading trade unionists were detained or banished, and thousands of strikers were arrested. The strike was called off in October, when union leaders agreed to hold talks with the Government.

Throughout 1986 demonstrations and strikes were held by the COB in protest at the Government's austerity measures. Following a general strike in August, the Government imposed another 90-day state of siege. Social discontent persisted in 1987 and extensive unrest continued in 1988 (following a further increase in the price of petrol in February of that year), which culminated in April with a national hunger strike, called by the COB, to protest against the continuing austerity measures. These problems led to the resignation of the Cabinet in August, although all except four ministers were reappointed.

Presidential and congressional elections took place in May 1989. As no candidate had gained the requisite absolute majority, responsibility for the choice of President passed to the newly elected Congreso, which was to convene in August. Shortly before the second stage of the election, Gen. Hugo Banzer Suárez of the ADN withdrew his candidacy in order to support his former adversary, Jaime Paz Zamora of the MIR. The 46 ADN and 41 MIR seats in the Congreso were sufficient to assure a majority vote for Paz Zamora, who assumed the presidency. A coalition Government of 'national unity', the Acuerdo Patriótico, was then formed. At the same time, a joint political council (with undefined powers), headed by Banzer, was established.

From 1988 the Government increased its attempts to reduce the illegal production of coca. As a result, during 1989 clashes between the drugs-control troops, Unidad Móvil de Patrullaje Rural (UMOPAR), and drugs-traffickers intensified, particularly in the coca-processing region of northern Beni. By the middle of the year, however, it became clear that the Government had failed to attain the targets of its coca-eradication programme (begun in 1986 after the US Government had agreed to provide more than US $100m. in aid), having encountered staunch opposition from the powerful coca-growers' organizations. Paz Zamora was critical of the militaristic approach of the USA to coca eradication and emphasized the need for economic and social support. In May 1990, however, he accepted $35m. in military aid from the USA. In late 1990 reaction to US involvement in Bolivia became increasingly violent.

In December 1989 a serious institutional conflict arose when the Government allowed a former Minister of the Interior, Migration and Justice, Col Luis Arce Gómez, to be taken to Miami, Florida (USA), to be tried on drugs-trafficking charges, despite the absence of a formal extradition treaty between Bolivia and the USA. Arce Gómez had been on trial in Bolivia since 1986, accused of violating human rights. His extradition, therefore, constituted a contravention of Bolivian law, which states that a Bolivian cannot be extradited while undergoing trial in Bolivia. Following an acrimonious conflict between the Government and the judiciary, the Congreso temporarily suspended eight of the 12 supreme court judges in late 1990. In retaliation, the court threatened to annul the 1989 elections. The conflict was resolved in early 1991 with the signing by the country's five main political parties of a pact affirming the independence of the Supreme Court. In January 1991 a federal jury in Miami found Arce Gómez guilty on two charges of drugs-trafficking, and he was sentenced to 30 years' imprisonment.

In March 1991 the reputation of the Government was seriously undermined when three of its senior officials were forced to resign amid allegations of corruption. Moreover, the appointment in February of Col Faustino Rico Toro as the new head of Bolivia's anti-drugs-trafficking force, La Fuerza Especial de Lucha Contra el Narcotráfico (FELCN), had provoked widespread outrage. In addition to his alleged connections with illegal drugs-traffickers, Rico was accused of having committed human rights abuses during his tenure as Chief of Army Intelligence under the regime of Gen. Luis García Meza (1980–81). After considerable pressure from the USA (including the suspension of all military and economic aid), Rico resigned from his new position in early March. Later that month, following accusations by the USA linking them with illegal drugs-traffickers, the Minister of the Interior, Migration and Justice and the Chief of Police resigned from their posts, although both maintained their innocence. In July the Government announced a decree granting a period of amnesty, lasting 120 days, for drugs-traffickers to surrender voluntarily. A condition of the amnesty was that those giving themselves up confess their crimes and contribute effectively to the apprehension of other such criminals. In return, they were offered minimum prison sentences and the guarantee that they would not risk extradition to the USA. As many as seven of the country's most powerful drugs-traffickers were reported to have taken advantage of the amnesty.

Government plans to privatize state-owned enterprises, including the state mining corporation, COMIBOL, resulted in a series of strikes, organized by the COB, in late 1991 and early 1992, which eventually prompted the Government to suspend its programme of joint ventures between COMIBOL and private companies. Continued social unrest led to violent confrontation between protesters and troops throughout the country in early 1993, and the military occupation of La Paz in March of that year.

In April 1993 the Supreme Court found the former military dictator Gen. Luis García Meza guilty on 49 charges of murder, human rights abuses, corruption and fraud, and sentenced him, *in absentia*, to 30 years' imprisonment. Similar sentences were imposed on 14 of his collaborators. García Meza was arrested in Brazil in March 1994 and, following his extradition to Bolivia in October of that year, began his prison sentence in March 1995.

Presidential and congressional elections were held in June 1993. Sánchez de Lozada was the MNR's presidential candidate, while Banzer Suárez was supported by both the ADN and the MIR, as Paz Zamora was ineligible for re-election. Again, no candidate secured the requisite absolute majority, so a congressional vote was scheduled to take place in August to decide between the two main presidential contenders, Sánchez de Lozada and Banzer. However, Banzer withdrew from the contest, thereby leaving Sánchez de Lozada's candidacy unopposed. He was sworn in as President on 6 August. At legislative elections, conducted simultaneously, the MNR secured 69 of the 157 seats in the bicameral Congreso, while the ruling Acuerdo Patriótico coalition won only 43. The MNR subsequently concluded a pact with the Unión Cívica Solidaridad (UCS) and the Movimiento Bolivia Libre (MBL), thus securing a congressional majority.

Despite the new Government's stated intention to combat corruption in Bolivia's political and public life, evidence of fraudulent practice continued to feature widely in the country's affairs in 1994. In March former President Jaime Paz Zamora announced his retirement from political life following the presentation of a report by the FELCN to the Congreso alleging his co-operation with drugs-traffickers. (In January 1995 Paz Zamora announced his return to political life, however, while denying the allegations against him in the FELCN report.) In June the President of the Supreme Court and its third judge were found guilty of bribery by the Senado and were dismissed and banned from holding public office for 10 years.

In early 1995 government plans to privatize much of the education system and to restrict teachers' rights to union membership provoked industrial action by teachers nation-wide. In response to a call by the COB for an indefinite strike, and in an attempt to quell several weeks of civil unrest, the Government declared a state of siege for 90 days. Military units were deployed throughout the country, and 370 union leaders were arrested and banished to remote areas. However, protests continued nation-wide and the state of siege was extended by a further 90 days in July, owing to continued civil unrest, which had become particularly intense in the Chapare valley of Cochabamba, where, despite the introduction of a voluntary coca-eradication programme, UMOPAR forces had begun to occupy villages and to destroy coca plantations. Violent clashes between peasant farmers and UMOPAR personnel between July and September resulted in the arrest of almost 1,000 coca growers. Human rights organizations expressed alarm at the force with which UMOPAR was conducting its operations and at the number of peasants killed and injured in the campaign. In October the state of siege was revoked, and negotiations between the Government and the coca growers were undertaken, although the talks soon broke down.

Meanwhile, allegations implicating senior public officials in corruption and, particularly, the illegal drugs trade continued to emerge in 1995 and 1996. Four senior members of the FELCN were dismissed in September, following an investigation into their links with drugs-traffickers. A further 100 FELCN members were detained in November on drugs-related charges. Moreover, a serious political scandal erupted in October, following allegations that Guillermo Bedregal, the President of the Senado Nacional and a deputy leader of the MNR, had co-operated with leading drugs-traffickers. In early 1996 allegations concerning the abuse of the personal expenses system resulted in the resignation of 10 MNR members of the Congreso and the suspension of 12 others on criminal charges.

Continued opposition to the Government's capitalization programme led to further industrial unrest and a general strike in early 1996. In April more than 100,000 transport workers undertook a series of strikes and demonstrations in protest at the sale of the Eastern Railway to a Chilean company. Riots in La Paz resulted in damage to Chilean-owned railway property, which prompted threats from the Chilean Government to withdraw its investment from Bolivia. During violent clashes with the police several protesters were injured and one was killed. The dispute ended later in the month, when the COB signed an agreement with the Government which provided for modest public-sector wage increases, but did not include concessions in the Government's plans to continue implementation of its capitalization policies.

The proposed introduction of an agrarian reform law led to a series of protests in September and October 1996 by indigenous and peasant groups who feared that their land rights would be undermined by measures contained in the proposed legislation. In October the leaders of several peasant farmers' groups began a hunger strike, while the COB called an indefinite general strike. Shortly afterwards Sánchez de Lozada agreed to hold discussions with representatives of some of the indigenous and peasant groups (although not with the COB) and subsequently secured their support for the law by making a number of significant concessions.

Dissatisfaction with the continued privatization of major industrial companies in Bolivia, particularly in the mining sector, resulted in further unrest in late 1996. In December a group of miners occupied a pit at Amayapampa in northern Potosí to protest at the actions of the mine's Canadian operators, who, they alleged, had failed to pay local taxes and had caused damage to the environment. When troops arrived at the site to remove the miners 10 protesters were killed and 50 others injured in ensuing violent clashes. The incident provoked outrage throughout the country and was the subject of an investigation by the Organization of American States' Inter-American Human Rights Commission in 1997.

Presidential elections were held on 1 June 1997. The MNR's candidate was Juan Carlos Durán (Sánchez de Lozada was ineligible for re-election), the MIR presented Paz Zamora, while Banzer Suárez, in a fourth attempt to gain the presidency by democratic means, was the nominee of the ADN. In the event, Banzer secured 22% of the total votes, Durán won 18% and Paz Zamora received 17%. At legislative elections held concurrently the ADN failed to secure a majority of seats; however, it subsequently formed a pact with the MIR, the UCS and Condepa to form a congressional majority and, as a result, on 5 August Banzer was elected President for a newly extended term of five years. The inclusion of the MIR in the coalition prompted concern among some observers, as it was feared that previous allegations of corruption and of involvement in the illegal drugs trade against the party and, in particular, against Paz Zamora (see above) would jeopardize the country's ability to attract international aid and investment.

In February 1998 coca producers in the Cochabamba region announced their rejection of the Government's new anti-coca policy (the so-called 'Dignity Plan', which aimed to eradicate all illegal coca plantations by 2002), claiming that an agreement, signed in October 1997, to provide alternative development programmes had not been honoured. Moreover, many observers believed that similar policies had been ineffective, as, despite the provision of US finance worth US $500m. since 1990 to eradicate the crop, there had been no net reduction in coca production in Bolivia. Violent clashes ensued when army and police personnel converged on the region in April to implement the eradication programme, and in the following month the Government temporarily suspended the measures. More than 1,000 coca growers undertook an 800-km protest march from Chapare to La Paz in August to demand that the Government review its coca-eradication programme. The farmers denounced new measures, including the confiscation of land used for coca cultivation, the incarceration of new coca growers and the reduction, by more than 50%, of compensation rates paid to farmers who voluntarily ceased to grow coca. The Government rejected the protesters' demands, reiterating its intention to eradicate more than 9,000 ha of the crop by the end of the year. Demonstrations and roadblocks by coca growers in La Paz and Cochabamba during September were disrupted by security forces, leading to violent confrontation in many cases. The relocation of the headquarters of the armed forces from La Paz to Cochabamba in 1999 was widely interpreted as a further measure against coca growing. The Government, however, denied that a process of militarization of the Cochabamba region was being implemented. The Bolivian Government stated that funding for the programme had been received from the USA and the European Union (EU), but that a further US $300m. was required to develop alternative resources to replace revenue lost from the illegal sale of coca. By 1999 the amount of eradicated coca crops was estimated at 14,000 ha.

In mid-1999 a number of reforms of the judicial system were announced, including the appointment of a people's ombudsman, a constitutional tribunal and an independent judicial council. It was hoped that these measures, when implemented, would help to reduce levels of corruption, particularly with regard to the accountability of the police force. Bolivia's new penal code, which came into effect at the end of May 1999, was notable in that it formally incorporated into the country's legal system the customary law of indigenous Indian peoples.

In December 1999 a sharp increase in water charges in Cochabamba prompted violent demonstrations, which spread to other areas. Further violent protests and a general strike in April 2000 led to the imposition of a state of emergency by the Government and shortly afterwards resulted in the withdrawal of the policy. The Government was put under further pressure in September when striking teachers demanding higher salaries were joined by peasants protesting against the Government's plan to tax water used for crop irrigation. Violence ensued between the protesters and riot police, resulting in at least 10 fatalities. A settlement was achieved in October. Later in the month the Government acceded to coca growers' demands for a halt to the construction of new military bases in the Chapare region; however, the process of coca eradication intensified. In December President Banzer announced that most of the coca in the Chapare region had been eradicated (although it was subsequently revealed that some 6,000 ha remained).

In May 2001, following further protests against the Government's privatization and coca-eradication policies, a tentative agreement was reached in which seven commissions would be established, comprising representatives of government and civic opposition groups, to review government policy in areas such as agrarian reform, coca eradication and water privatization. Nevertheless, popular protests continued throughout the country.

In early August 2001 President Banzer resigned, owing to ill health. The Vice-President, Jorge Quiroga Ramírez, assumed the presidency on 6 August and immediately replaced 12 of the 16 members of the Government; almost one-half of the new Cabinet was not affiliated to any political party. The new Government's main stated aims were to stabilize the economy, implement anti-corruption measures and continue the dialogue with aggrieved peasants and indigenous groups. In that month the Government reached an agreement with the main peasant farmers' union to implement a US $70m. rural development programme.

Presidential and legislative elections were held on 30 June 2002. The main contenders in the presidential contest were former President Sánchez de Lozada, again representing the MNR, Manfred Reyes Villa of the centre-right Nueva Fuerza Republicana (NFR) and Juan Evo Morales Aima, a coca-grower leader, representing the left-wing Movimiento al Socialismo—Instrumento Político por la Soberanía de los Pueblos (MAS). In the event, Sánchez de Lozada won the largest share of the ballot (23%). Morales, who opposed the Government's free-market economic policy and its coca-eradication programme, performed unexpectedly well, coming second with 21% of the votes cast. As no candidate had achieved an absolute majority, however, responsibility for choosing the new President again passed to the Congreso. On 4 August it voted to appoint Sánchez de Lozada to the presidency once more. The MNR also won the largest number of seats (47) in the concurrently held legislative elections, followed by the MAS with 35 seats, the MIR with 31 seats and the NFR with 27 seats.

Following his inauguration on 6 August 2002, Sánchez de Lozada formed a coalition Government comprising representatives of the MNR, the MIR, the UCS, the MBL and the ADN, although the new Cabinet was dominated by MNR and MIR members. The new President's stated priorities were to continue the coca-eradication policy of his predecessor and to bring about economic recovery, by implementing a public-works programme. Sánchez de Lozada also pledged to review the country's privatization programme. However, the ruling coalition was a fragile one; the MNR could not rely on the support of the other alliance parties in the Congreso. This, coupled with the strong performance of the opposition parties in the elections led the new administration to encounter sustained resistance to its proposed agenda.

In light of renewed pressure from the US Administration to intensify eradication efforts, in September 2002 the Government held talks with coca-growers' representatives, led by Morales. The USA had threatened to suspend preferential access to certain US markets, agreed under the Andean Trade Promotion and Drug Eradication Act (ATPDEA), if Bolivia failed to meet the agreed eradication target of 9,000 ha of coca crops. The talks ended inconclusively. In October the USA published a report in which it was claimed that there were an estimated 24,400 ha of coca plantations in Bolivia in 2002, twice the agreed level, and that, contrary to government claims, new plantation rates exceeded eradication levels.

In response to the US study, the Government announced its intention to commission an independent survey of illegal coca plantations, as well as a review of legal cultivation levels (which stood at 12,000 ha in 2002). Peasant organizations insisted that eradication be suspended while the study was under way. In January 2003 coca growers staged roadblocks and demonstrations in protest at the Government's refusal to meet their demands. At the same time there were protests at legislation, approved in December 2002, which linked pensions to the consumer price index, rather than to the US dollar. Following two weeks of clashes with the police, in which 10 people were killed, President Sánchez de Lozada and Evo Morales agreed to restart negotiations on coca eradication, as well as on trade issues and the privatization programme.

In February 2003 the Sánchez de Lozada administration's budget proposals increased popular dissatisfaction still further. Faced with a fiscal deficit of more than 8.6% of gross domestic product, and under IMF pressure to secure new sources of revenue, the Government proposed increasing income tax rates. The new measure—known as an *impuestazo*, or 'tax shock'— drew widespread condemnation from representatives of middle- and lower-income groups, and prompted civil unrest. On 12 February, following the Government's dismissal of their 40% wage-increase demand, approximately 7,000 armed police officers joined civilian protests in central La Paz. During the ensuing confrontation with elements of the military 32 people were killed and the President was forced to withdraw to safety. The riots prompted the resignation, on 19 February, of the entire Cabinet. A new Government was appointed the following day. Seven ministers were reappointed to their previous posts and, in a measure intended to restore public confidence and reduce spending, President Sánchez de Lozada announced that the number of ministries would be reduced from 18 to 13.

In March 2003, following extensive negotiations with opposition groups, the Government announced revised budget proposals, including the withdrawal of the proposed *impuestazo*. In spite of its effective abandonment of the IMF-approved budget measures, in early April the Government reached a stand-by agreement with the Fund, worth US $118m., the first tranche of which was disbursed in early July. Furthermore, in August the opposition NFR announced that it was to join the ruling coalition. A subsequent cabinet reshuffle in the same month allocated significant portfolios to representatives of that party.

From 2001 proposals to construct a natural-gas pipeline from the southern department of Tarija to the Pacific had been met with public hostility. Opposition groups protested at the export of natural resources to Mexico and the USA. In March 2003 opposition to the project increased following the announcement by the international consortium overseeing the project that it favoured the Chilean port of Patillos as the location for the pipeline's export terminal. Patillos was on that part of the Pacific coastline Bolivia had lost to Chile in the late 19th century. Opposition groups accused the Government of putting foreign interests above domestic ones and also claimed that President Sánchez de Lozada had failed to fulfil economic pledges. Opposition continued to grow and in September there were strikes and roadblocks organized in protest.

In the following month, increasing civil unrest in El Alto, an industrial suburb of La Paz, culminated in military intervention, resulting in the deaths of some 36 people on 12 October 2003. The following day protests in La Paz fuelled by the events in El Alto resulted in further violent clashes with the army, and a further 13 deaths. The violent suppression of the protests prompted the resignation of the Vice-President, Carlos Mesa Gisbert, and the Minister of Economic Development, Jorge Torres, and the COB declared an indefinite general strike. On 15 October, in an attempt to restore order, the Government announced that it would hold a referendum on gas exports and would revise existing energy legislation. It also pledged to establish a constituent assembly to examine possible constitutional changes. Nevertheless, the civil unrest continued unabated and the death toll rose to an estimated 74. On 17 October Sánchez de Lozada resigned as President and travelled to the USA. Congress approved erstwhile Vice-President Mesa to succeed him. Mesa was sworn in as President on 18 October.

Upon taking office, President Mesa appointed a Cabinet largely composed of independent technocrats, and notably restored the indigenous affairs portfolio abolished in February 2003. The new President pledged to re-examine the contentious gas-export plan (suspended since 13 October) and reiterated the previous administration's pledges to hold a referendum on the pipeline through Chile, to establish a constituent assembly, and to revise energy legislation. Opposition groups agreed to a 90-day truce while the new Government began to implement these new policies. In December the new President announced plans to reduce the coca-eradication programme, in order to strengthen efforts to eliminate cocaine production. Peasant and coca growers' leaders expressed cautious approval of this new policy, although the US Government announced its opposition. In September 2004 President Mesa announced a new anti-drugs strategy that would receive some US $969m. in funding over the following four years. Instead of forcible eradication, the focus of this strategy would be to encourage the cultivation of alternative crops. Accordingly, in November the Government signed an agreement with Evo Morales (in his capacity as leader of the coca growers) to suspend the programme of forcible eradication in the Chapare region. On 14 October the Congreso voted to prosecute former President Lozada and all members of his Government over the decision to deploy troops to quell the civil unrest prompted by the gas-export proposals in October 2003 in El Alto, which resulted in considerable loss of life. It was thought likely that Lozada would eventually be tried *in absentia*. Efforts to secure his extradition from the USA to stand trial in Bolivia were increased by the Government of President Morales during 2007.

In accordance with President Mesa's pledges on taking office, in July 2004 a referendum was held on energy policy. The electorate was asked the following questions: if it agreed with the abrogation of the hydrocarbons law that had been reintroduced by President Sánchez de Lozada; if state intervention in the oil and gas industry should be increased; if the state oil company, Yacimientos Petrolíferos Fiscales Bolivianos (YPFB), should reclaim shares in privatized energy companies; if Bolivia's gas reserves should be used as a negotiating tool to regain access to the Pacific Ocean; and if reform of the energy sector under broadly left-wing principles should be allowed to proceed. All five of the Government's proposals were accepted, but, despite this clear mandate for change, the resulting draft legislation caused great controversy over the following months and, consequently, during this time several revisions were made to the Government's legislative proposals. Specifically, there was disagreement as to whether extant contracts with energy-sector companies should be voided and rewritten to provide for greater state control and revenue. Although various congressional, popular and indigenous groups strongly supported such moves, several foreign companies (notably, BP and Repsol) and foreign government delegations acting in their interests (notably, those of the USA, Brazil, Spain and the United Kingdom) voiced their opposition to any proposals they considered illegal under international law.

Also in late 2004, a broad-based coalition that included politicians, employers and trade unions from Santa Cruz and the oil- and gas-producing department of Tarija made increasingly vociferous demands for a referendum on greater regional autonomy or even full secession. This grouping was also opposed to an increased role of central government in the energy sector, fearing that this would deter foreign investment and increase corruption, inefficiency and political centralization. In furtherance of the aim for autonomy, a widely supported general strike was held in Santa Cruz and Tarija in November. The civil unrest continued in the following month, after the Government's announcement of significant increases in fuel prices was met with public protests across the country, particularly in Santa Cruz and El Alto. The COB called for President Mesa's resignation and announced that it was to organize an indefinite nationwide general strike from 11 January 2005. Throughout early 2005 the country suffered severe disruption from roadblocks and other acts of civil disobedience by protesters demanding, *inter alia*, a decrease in the price of fuel and a dramatic increase in government revenues from the hydrocarbon sector. In the face of such public opposition, on 19 January President Mesa announced that the fuel increases would be reduced from 23% to 15%. However, this was not enough to appease the protesters in Santa Cruz; on 28 January a mass rally was held in the department, at which the Comité Cívico pro Santa Cruz declared Santa Cruz to be autonomous and announced that it was to establish a provincial interim government. On the same day President Mesa announced that provincial gubernatorial elections would be held on 12 June (departmental prefects were hitherto appointed by the President). However, this measure first required approval by referendum in order to be constitutional, and a constituent assembly was duly appointed. In early February, in an attempt to restore confidence in his Government (and following the resignation of two cabinet members from Santa Cruz), Mesa effected a wide-ranging reallocation of cabinet portfolios; notably, three ministers from Santa Cruz were included in the new Government. However, faced with continued protests, on 8 March he submitted his resignation to the Congreso, declaring that he would only continue in office if a consensus could be reached to end the disruption; the Congreso rejected Mesa's resignation after an agreement was signed by the major congressional groups. On 16 March Evo Morales called for a temporary cessation of the roadblocks following the approval by the upper house of legislation that provided for a state royalty of 18% on hydrocarbons at the point of extraction and a further tax of 32%; Morales had initially favoured a royalty of 50%. Final approval of the legislation was given by the lower house on 5 May. Nevertheless, throughout April and May blockades, demonstrations and marches caused great disruption and shortages of goods and services nation-wide. Finally considering his position untenable, on 6 June President Mesa submitted his resignation to the Congreso, which was accepted following an emergency session convened in Sucre on 9 June. Owing to fears of exacerbating the civil conflict, the speakers of the Senado Nacional and the Cámara de Diputados, Hormando Vaca Díez and Mario Cossío Córtez, respectively, both waived their constitutional right to assume the presidency, which was instead assumed in a temporary capacity by a less partisan figure, Eduardo Rodríguez Veltzé, hitherto President of the Supreme Court.

Legislative and presidential elections were held on 4 December 2005. Evo Morales, candidate of the MAS, was elected to the presidency with 53.7% of valid votes cast, while former Vice-President Jorge Quiroga Ramírez of the conservative Poder Democrático y Social (PODEMOS) received 28.6% of the ballot. The MAS also secured the most votes in the concurrent legislative elections, winning 72 of 130 seats in the Cámara de Diputados and 12 of the 27 seats in the Senado Nacional, while PODEMOS secured 43 seats in the lower house and 13 in the upper house. Despite Morales' close alignment with the left-wing regimes of Venezuela and Cuba and his opposition to US counter-narcotics policy, the US Administration expressed its desire to work closely with the new Government.

Upon taking office on 22 January 2006, President Morales reiterated his electoral pledge to 'refound' the Bolivian state, by drafting a new constitution. To this end, in March a Government-sponsored enabling law was approved by the Congreso. The legislation, which received congressional approval only following several amendments, would allow for the election of a constituent assembly and a concurrently held referendum on regional autonomy. The referendums were held on 2 July. The MAS garnered 54.4% of the valid votes cast, which translated into 137 seats in the 255-seat Constituent Assembly, considerably short of the two-thirds' majority President Morales needed to be sure of gaining approval for his proposed reforms. PODEMOS secured only 15.0% of the ballot, or 60 seats, leaving it reliant on the support of other opposition parties to block government proposals. In the vote on regional autonomy, four of the country's nine departments were in favour of further devolution—Beni, Pando, Santa Cruz and Tarija. The Constituent Assembly convened on 6 August and was to draft a proposed constitution by August 2007, which would then be put to another referendum for approval. However, in early September 2006 opposition members withdrew from the Assembly after MAS representatives approved a resolution that decisions would need approval only by a simple majority, rather than the two-thirds' majority originally agreed. The impasse was ended in mid-November, after 10 independent members of the Assembly aligned themselves with the pro-Government bloc: it was agreed that the final proposed text of the constitution would require the approval of two-thirds of the members, but that individual clauses only needed a majority decision. Following further opposition, however, in January 2007 it was agreed that any individual clauses not accepted by a two-thirds' majority would also be put to a referendum, as well as the constitution as a whole.

In November 2006 the President attempted to weaken the power of the regional prefects (six of whom were from opposition parties) by proposing legislation that would allow the Congreso to censure and dismiss departmental heads. The Government claimed the move would allow it better to distribute revenues from oil-producing regions to poorer areas. In response, the governor of Cochabamba, Manfredo Reyes Villa, announced that a further referendum on autonomy should be held in the region. A majority of the electorate in Cochabamba had voted against autonomy in July; however, if another vote returned a different result, it would put the pro-autonomy departments into a majority. Government supporters in Cochabamba held a massive rally against the proposal in January 2007, demanding Reyes Villa's resignation. The protests and subsequent counter-protests descended into violence, with over 100 people injured and two killed. Reyes Villa was forced to flee the department, taking refuge in Santa Cruz, although he refused to resign. In an attempt to quell the unrest, the Government proposed a constitutional amendment allowing for the recall of any high-ranking official. Opposition parties indicated their support for the amendment, although not the proposal that those who had been elected with more than 50% of the votes would be exempt from the ruling (Morales had won almost 54% of the valid ballot).

On 1 May 2006 President Morales issued a decree establishing the state's ownership of the hydrocarbons sector and increasing taxes for foreign companies operating in the sector from 50% to 82%. Foreign companies had 180 days to sign new contracts with the state hydrocarbons company YPFB or else cease operations in Bolivia. Although the announcement was widely viewed as 'nationalization' of the hydrocarbons sector, foreign concerns would be allowed to remain in the country as minority shareholders. In the following month Morales issued another decree giving the state the power to seize land it deemed unproductive, in order to redistribute it to landless farmers. It was estimated that some 20–30m. ha of land could be affected. In the face of much protest from land-owners, particularly in eastern Bolivia, the President pledged that productive farms would be left alone, as would any land gained legally. In early November the Congreso approved a draft version of the reform, prompting protests from land-owning organizations. Then, at the end of the month, the Government succeeded in gaining senate approval for the law (and for numerous new contracts with foreign oil companies) by summoning alternate opposition senators to attend the legislative session. The new contracts with the foreign oil concerns were scheduled to come into force on 1 February 2007, although they were subsequently delayed: the lower house eventually approved the contracts in mid-April.

In December 2006 President Morales risked controversy, and the ire of the judiciary, when he appointed four supreme court judges by presidential decree after the Congreso had failed to reach consensus on the appointments. The President of the Supreme Court, Héctor Sandóval Parada, accused Morales of ignoring the Constitution's separation of powers. Morales maintained that the appointees would hold their posts in an acting capacity until their confirmation by the legislature. Disquiet at the arrangement continued into 2007 and culminated in a 24-hour strike by judges, magistrates and lawyers in June of that year. Moreover, a debate on the subject between government and opposition politicians in the Chamber of Deputies in August descended into physical fighting.

The Constituent Assembly finally came into operation in February 2007. Morales' proposals for the new constitution included new rights of determination for the indigenous majority, with their own political systems and legally recognized leaders, greater state control of the economy, the election of supreme court judges by popular vote (rather than their appointment by the Congreso) and the allowance of two consecutive five-year terms for Presidents. By July, however, disagreements over a proposal to transfer the seat of government back from La Paz to Sucre (where it had been located until 1899) led to disruption. A demonstration in La Paz, one of the largest in the country's history, was held in protest at the proposal. In August MAS delegates on the Assembly voted to exclude the issue from the agenda, prompting several weeks of unrest in Sucre. The Assembly was suspended for one month to allow both sides to seek a compromise. Some observers believed that the issue of relocating the capital from the poor Western Highlands to the relatively prosperous eastern region was being used by critics of Morales to sabotage his attempts to establish a more inclusive constitution, in which the country's wealth was more evenly distributed. Following the failure of both sides to agree on the issue, the delegates from PODEMOS continued to hold discussions in Sucre, insisting that talks take place in that city, thereby effectively boycotting the Assembly which had reconvened in mid-October. Unrest continued during November. Opposition governors from six of the country's nine departments approved a resolution calling for civil disobedience in response to Morales' plans to use profits from the hydrocarbons tax to fund a new pension scheme for Bolivians, diverting income that was previously sent to regional prefects. Meanwhile, some 10,000 supporters of Morales marched from El Alto to the opposition-controlled Senate in La Paz condemning the delegates in Sucre for stalling progress on the new constitution and thereby delaying projects such as the proposed pension plan. The constitution was approved on 9 December by the required two-thirds of members present, although not by two-thirds of the membership, owing to a boycott by opposition delegates. Claims of procedural irregularities led the opposition to denounce the vote as illegal. On 28 February 2008 President Morales approved legislation setting 4 May as the date for an initial national referendum on the draft constitution. However, resistance from the PODEMOS-led opposition—particularly regional prefects of the affluent 'media luna' region (Bolivia's gas-rich eastern lowlands, comprising four of the nine regional departments) who claimed the Government-sponsored charter favoured the country's indigenous population, and announced concurrent referenda upon proposals for greater regional autonomy—provoked considerable political turmoil. The National Electoral Court, Bolivia's supreme electoral authority, subsequently ruled that all referenda were to be postponed indefinitely owing, *inter alia*, to the logistical obstacles to public consultations at such short notice. Neither Morales' administration nor the conservative opposition demonstrated any signs of compromise in the ensuing weeks, despite appeals from international mediators, and no new date for voting on the controversial draft constitution had been announced by the end of April.

One of Morales' campaign pledges was to legalize the cultivation of coca. On taking office, the new President appointed a former coca grower, Felipe Cáceres García, to lead the country's anti-narcotics effort. In May 2006, following negotiations with representatives from the main coca-growing regions, the Government announced that voluntary eradication was to resume. However, growers in the Caranavi region were allowed to cultivate about 1,600 sq m of coca per household, a compromise already extended to the Chapare and Yungas regions. In July the President offered to ensure eradication of 5,000 ha of coca in return for the USA extending the terms of the ATPDEA, which was due to expire at the end of the year, a pledge supported by the main coca-growing organizations in the following month. In December Morales announced that the amount of land legally permitted for coca cultivation would be increased from 12,000 ha to 20,000 ha by 2010. The decision was criticized in a US report published in March 2007 which also berated Morales for advocating the industrialization of coca production. In the same month the Constituent Assembly approved a measure urging the UN to decriminalize coca and to refrain from 'using the name of the sacred leaf in their products'. The motion resulted from complaints that the US-based multi-national drinks company Coca-Cola used the name 'coca' to promote its products while exports of Bolivian products containing coca were banned. The Bolivian Government reacted angrily to a statement by the US ambassador in the La Paz in which he claimed that coca production and drugs-trafficking had increased under Morales' administration. Morales countered that right-wing opposition groups were receiving funding from the USA as part of its annual aid programme in Bolivia.

The issue of the participation of the Aymara, Quechua and Guaraní indigenous peoples in Bolivia's public life reached a critical phase in the early 21st century, following limited progress in the 1990s. Government decrees issued in 1990 acknowledging as Indian territory more than 1.6m. ha of tropical rainforest in northern Bolivia constituted an unprecedented act of recognition of Indian land rights. In September 2002 the Sánchez de Lozada administration announced a Land Reform Programme, under which some 1.2m. ha were to be bought by the Government and redistributed to some 11,000 landless families, at a cost of approximately US $2,500m. The Ministry for Peasants', Indigenous Peoples' and Ethnic Affairs, created in 2000, was abolished in February 2003 as part of the Government's cost-cutting programme, although it was re-established after President Mesa assumed power in October. (In January 2006 President-elect Morales announced his intention to form a cabinet including ministers of indigenous descent and to abolish the Ministry again, as its very existence, he claimed, constituted a form of discrimination.) Moreover, despite government claims that some 500,000 ha of land was available for redistribution, landless peasants continued to occupy farms illegally throughout 2004. In August land owned by the multinational hydrocarbons company BP was occupied until the Government agreed to accelerate the process of land redistribution. In early December there was an unprecedented level of indigenous political participation in municipal elections. In sharp contrast to the elections of 1999, in which candidates from just 18 parties stood, over 400 'citizen organizations' (mostly formed by local activist and indigenous groupings) fielded candidates. A large majority of constituencies were won by candidates from these new political groupings. The election in December 2005 of Bolivia's first President of indigenous descent, Evo Morales, was seen as a key development in indigenous peoples' political participation. In early June 2006, following the issuing of a decree on land reform (see above), President Morales handed over title deeds to 3.1m. ha of land in the east of the country to indigenous leaders. The gesture was largely symbolic, but it was expected that the land reform would grant indigenous and landless farmers almost 200,000 sq km of land by 2011.

Bolivia's relations with Peru and Chile have been dominated by the long-standing issue of possible Bolivian access to the Pacific Ocean. An agreement with Peru, completed in 1993, granted Bolivia free access from its border town of Desaguadero to the Pacific port of Ilo, Peru, until 2091. In August 2004, following talks to further economic integration, the Presidents of Bolivia and Peru signed a declaration of intent to create a special zone in Ilo for the exportation of Bolivian gas (see Economic Affairs).

Bolivia's desire to regain sovereign access to the Pacific continued to impair relations with Chile. In March 1997 (and again in May) failure to reach agreement on this matter led to the

BOLIVIA

Introductory Survey

suspension of talks which aimed to improve trade arrangements between the two countries. Relations deteriorated further in late 1997 when the Bolivian Government filed an official protest note to Chile regarding its failure to remove land-mines along the common border (planted during the 1970s). Although in mid-1999 Bolivia briefly renounced its demand of Chile for Pacific access in mid-1998, Chilean unwillingness to resume negotiations led to a return to diplomatic hostilities later that year. The Bolivian claim on Chile's Pacific coastline became a matter of greater regional concern in 2004 following the outspoken expressions of support from President Lt-Col (retd) Hugo Rafael Chávez Frías of Venezuela in November of the previous year; in January the Mesa Government announced it was withdrawing from trade agreement talks with Chile. Diplomatic interventions by Argentina and Brazil followed in an attempt to normalize relations between the countries concerned. The Chilean Government's decision in October to privatize the port of Arica elicited vehement objections from the Mesa administration, which feared this would adversely affect Bolivia's external trade, owing to significant increases in port tariffs (supposedly in contravention of the 1904 treaty that guaranteed duty-free passage of Bolivian goods through Arica). Soon after taking office in 2006, President Morales signalled his Government's intention to reopen negotiations with Chile over the issue, possibly in return for exporting Bolivian gas to Chile. Relations between the two countries improved significantly in May 2007 when the Commander-in-Chief of the Navy in Chile made the first ever official visit to La Paz, leading some observers to speculate that the possibility of a permanent access agreement for Bolivia might be closer than had previously been considered. Bolivia's Minister of Defence, Walker San Miguel, however, cautioned that, despite the encouraging developments, the two countries were not yet ready to re-establish diplomatic relations (which had been severed in 1978).

In 1992 Bolivia signed an agreement with Brazil for the construction of a 3,150-km pipeline to carry natural gas from Bolivia to southern Brazil. The outlines of the project, which was expected to cost US $1,800m. and was to be the largest of its kind in South America, were finalized, following considerable delay, in mid-1996. The pipeline (the first 1,970 km of which were completed in early 1999) transported an initial 3.7m. cu m of natural gas per day to Brazil, increasing to 30m. cu m by 2004.

Bolivia and Iran established closer bilateral relations in September 2007 following the signing of an industrial co-operation agreement and the investment by Iran of US $1,000m. in technology and trade and industry projects in Bolivia. The presidents of the two countries also signed a framework agreement expressing support for nuclear research for peaceful energy purposes. The US Government expressed concern at Iran's apparently increasing influence in the region.

Government

Legislative power is held by the bicameral Congreso Nacional (Congress), comprising a Senado Nacional (Senate), with 27 members and a Cámara de Diputados (Chamber of Deputies), comprising 130 members. Both houses are elected for a four-year term by universal adult suffrage. Executive power is vested in the President and the Cabinet, which is appointed by the President. The President is directly elected for five years. If no candidate gains an absolute majority of votes, the President is chosen by the Congreso. The country is divided, for administrative purposes, into nine departments, each of which is governed by a prefect.

Defence

Military service, for one year, is selective. As assessed at November 2006, the armed forces numbered 46,100 men, of whom the army had 34,800 (including 25,000 conscripts), the air force 6,500 and the navy 4,800. In 2006 the defence budget totalled 1,240m. bolivianos.

Economic Affairs

In 2006, according to World Bank estimates, Bolivia's gross national income (GNI), measured at average 2004–06 prices, totalled US $10,293m., equivalent to about $1,100 per head (or $2,890 per head on an international purchasing-power parity basis). During 1996–2006, it was estimated, the population increased at an average annual rate of 2.0%, while gross domestic product (GDP) per head increased, in real terms, by an average of 1.2% per year. Bolivia's overall GDP increased, in real terms, at an average annual rate of 3.3% in 1996–2006; GDP increased by an estimated 4.6% in 2006.

Agriculture (including forestry and fishing) contributed an estimated 13.5% of GDP in 2006. In 2000 some 4.9% of the working population was employed in agriculture. Wood and its products accounted for 2.1% of export earnings in 2006. The principal cash crops are edible oils (particularly of soybeans), nuts and sugar. Beef and hides are also important exports. According to the World Bank, in the period 1996–2006 agricultural GDP increased at an average annual rate of 2.7%; it rose by 3.4% in 2006.

Industry (including mining, manufacturing, construction and power) provided an estimated 32.9% of GDP in 2006. In 2000 some 28.2% of the working population was employed in industry. In 1996–2006 industrial GDP increased at an average annual rate of 3.1%; the rate increased by 3.2% in 2006.

Mining (including petroleum exploration) contributed a provisional 13.6% of GDP in 2006 and employed about 1.7% of the working population in 2000. Investment in petroleum exploration totalled an estimated US $1m. in 2002, compared with $374m. in 1998. In 2002 nine foreign companies were involved in petroleum exploration in the country. Zinc, tin, silver, gold, lead and antimony are the major mineral exports, while tungsten and copper continue to be mined. Exports of zinc and tin earned an estimated $548.4m. and $27.9m., respectively, in 2006. In 1996–2006 the GDP of the mining sector increased at an estimated average annual rate of 4.5%; mining GDP increased by an estimated 4.4% in 2006.

In 2006 manufacturing accounted for a provisional 14.2% of GDP and in 2000 some 15.3% of the working population was employed in the sector. According to official estimates, the GDP of this sector increased during 1996–2006 at an average annual rate of 3.2%; it rose by 8.1% in 2006.

Energy is derived principally from natural gas and hydroelectricity. In 2005 electricity generation totalled 5,040m. kWh, according to provisional figures issued by the US Energy Information Administration. Hydroelectricity accounted for 49% of Bolivia's total installed generating capacity in that year (2.5 GW), with thermal power-stations accounting for most of the remaining 51%. In the first half of 2005 production of crude petroleum averaged a reported 50,040 barrels per day, an increase of some 9% on production in the comparable period of 2004. In 2005 imports of mineral products comprised an estimated 10.7% of total merchandise imports. Earnings from exports of mineral products (including gas and petroleum) accounted for an estimated 58.8% of total export earnings in the same year. During the late 1990s several major new natural gas deposits were discovered, which increased the country's total known reserves considerably. At December 2006 proven reserves of natural gas put at 740,000m. cu m. In October TotalFinaElf announced the discovery of a new gasfield in the department of Chuquisaca, which geological surveys suggested would significantly increase Bolivia's natural gas reserves.

The services sector accounted for some 53.6% of GDP in 2006 and engaged 67.0% of the employed population in 2000. During 1996–2006 the GDP of this sector increased at an average annual rate of 3.2%; services GDP increased by 4.1% in 2006.

In 2006 Bolivia recorded a visible trade surplus of US $1,231.9m., and there was a surplus of $1,319.1m. on the current account of the balance of payments. In 2006 the main sources of imports were Brazil (20.4%), Argentina, the USA and Chile. Brazil (37.0%), the USA, Argentina and Colombia were the major recipients of Bolivian exports in 2006. The principal imports in that year included machinery, chemicals and chemical products and base metals and their manufactures. The principal legal exports were mineral fuels, lubricants, etc. and jewellery. However, it was estimated that a large proportion of Bolivia's export earnings came from the illegal trade in coca and its derivatives (mainly cocaine).

In 2006 Bolivia's overall budget deficit amounted to a preliminary 2,330.2m. bolivianos (equivalent to some 3.1% of GDP). The deficit for 2007 was envisaged to be 1,010.2m. bolivianos. Bolivia's total external debt at the end of 2005 was US $6,390m., of which $4,564m. was long-term public debt. The cost of debt-servicing in that year was equivalent to 14.8% of the total value of exports of goods and services. In 1996–2006 the average annual rate of inflation was 3.9%. Consumer prices increased by an average of 5.0% in 2006. In 2002 some 5.5% of the labour force was unemployed.

In May 1991 Bolivia was one of five Andean Pact countries to sign the Caracas Declaration providing the foundation for a common market. In October 1992 Bolivia officially joined the Andean free trade area, removing tariff barriers to imports from

Colombia, Ecuador and Venezuela. Bolivia also agreed to sign a free trade accord with Mexico in September 1994. In January 1997 a free trade agreement with Mercosur (see p. 391), equivalent to associate membership of the organization, came into effect. In mid-1999 an agreement on the rationalization of their respective customs systems (thus moving closer to the formation of a regional free trade area) was reached between Mercosur and the Andean Community (see p. 170); the two-year accord came into effect in August. Bolivia is a member of the Andean Community, and in 1989 the Andean Social Development Fund was established. The country is also a member of the Organization of American States (OAS, see p. 360), and of the Latin American Integration Association (ALADI, see p. 331). Bolivia became the 97th contracting party to GATT (which was superseded by the World Trade Organization, WTO, see p. 396, in 1995) in 1989. In December 2004 Bolivia was one of the founder signatories to the agreement signed in Cusco, Peru, creating the South American Community of Nations (Comunidad Sudamericana de Naciones), intended to promote greater regional economic integration and further the unification of Mercosur and the Andean Community. It had been anticipated that the new entity, to be styled after the EU, would become operational by 2007; however, by April 2008 implementation of the necessary legal frameworks, to achieve the integrated structure envisaged, remained incomplete. A treaty for the community—referred to as the Union of South American Nations (Unasur) since its reinvention at the first South American Energy Summit of 16 April 2007—was expected to be initialled in June 2008, with full functionality of economic union tentatively scheduled for 2019.

The country's severe debt burden was a major factor inhibiting economic growth in the early 21st century. Successive governments committed themselves to the maintenance of IMF-sponsored fiscal economic policies, although overall growth rates remained modest in relation to the rate of population increase. In December 2005 the IMF, under the heavily indebted poor countries (HIPC) initiative, approved the cancellation, from early January 2006, of all debt incurred prior to 2005, which amounted to some US $231m. New President Morales' 'nationalization' of the hydrocarbons sector in 2006 (see Recent History) increased state revenues, although worries remained that such decrees would deter foreign investment: the development of Bolivia's fossil fuels export sector had been seen as crucial to economic growth in the early 21st century and, to this end, a series of concessions for oil and natural gas projects were awarded in the late 1990s and early 2000s. At the beginning of 2007 Bolivia's economy was performing well: high international energy prices had increased export revenues and strengthened the current account, while an increased stock of international reserves meant Bolivia no longer required immediate IMF aid. In that year the state extended its policy of nationalization to key sectors of the mining industry, culminating in the acquisition of the Vinto iron smelter from the Swiss-based company Glencore International AG in February. The Government hoped to augment its economic strategy in the energy and minerals sectors via the relaunch of the Corporación Minera de Bolivia (COMIBOL). In late 2007 Morales signalled his intent to bring up to 35% of the economy under state control during his presidency. However, the political instability that ensued as a result of proposed constitutional reforms (see Recent History) threatened to undermine Bolivia's recent economic progress. Nonetheless, the IMF forecast that robust growth would be sustained, and a rate of 5.3% was projected for 2008, compared to 3.9% in 2007. The rise in export revenues from the hydrocarbons and minerals sector was expected to accelerate inflation; the IMF forecast that consumer prices would increase by 13.5% in 2008, compared to 8.5% in 2007. US policy towards Bolivia has consistently been aimed at the eradication of the coca leaf and, thus, the latter's own drugs policy has largely dictated the complexion of US–Bolivian relations. It was announced in February 2006 that US funding for counter-narcotics operations, budgeted at $91m. in 2005, was to be reduced to $80m. in 2006 and to $67m. in 2007.

Education
Primary education, beginning at six years of age and lasting for eight years, is officially compulsory and is available free of charge. Secondary education, which is not compulsory, begins at 14 years of age and lasts for up to four years. In 2004 enrolment at primary schools included 95.2% of pupils in the relevant age-group. In that year enrolment at secondary schools included 73.6% of students in the relevant age-group. There are eight state universities and two private universities. The Government of Evo Morales, which took office in 2006, launched an education programme, 'Yo sí puedo', to alleviate levels of illiteracy. Expenditure on education by the central Government in 2001 was 2,796.9m. bolivianos, representing 19.9% of total spending.

Public Holidays
2008: 1 January (New Year), 10 February (Oruro only), 21 March (Good Friday), 15 April (Tarija only), 1 May (Labour Day), 22 May (Corpus Christi), 25 May (Sucre only), 16 July (La Paz only), 6 August (Independence), 14 September (Cochabamba only), 24 September (Santa Cruz and Pando only), 1 October (Pando only), 1 November (All Saints' Day and Potosí), 10 November (Oruro only), 18 November (Beni only), 25 December (Christmas).

2009: 1 January (New Year), 10 February (Oruro only), 10 April (Good Friday), 15 April (Tarija only), 1 May (Labour Day), 25 May (Sucre only), 11 June (Corpus Christi), 16 July (La Paz only), 6 August (Independence), 14 September (Cochabamba only), 24 September (Santa Cruz and Pando only), 1 October (Pando only), 1 November (All Saints' Day and Potosí), 10 November (Oruro only), 18 November (Beni only), 25 December (Christmas).

Weights and Measures
The metric system is officially in force, but various old Spanish measures are also used.

BOLIVIA

Statistical Survey

Statistical Survey

Sources (unless otherwise indicated): Instituto Nacional de Estadística, José Carrasco 1391, Casilla 6129, La Paz; tel. (2) 222-2333; fax (2) 222-693; internet www.ine.gov.bo; Banco Central de Bolivia, Ayacucho esq. Mercado, Casilla 3118, La Paz; tel. (2) 240-9090; fax (2) 240-6614; e-mail bancocentraldebolivia@bcb.gov.bo; internet www.bcb.gov.bo.

Area and Population

AREA, POPULATION AND DENSITY

Area (sq km)	
Land	1,084,391
Inland water	14,190
Total	1,098,581*
Population (census results)†	
3 June 1992	6,420,792
5 September 2001	
Males	4,123,850
Females	4,150,475
Total	8,274,325
Population (official projections)	
2005	9,427,219
2006	9,627,269
2007	9,827,522
Density (per sq km) at 2007	8.9

* 424,164 sq miles.
† Figures exclude adjustment for underenumeration. This was estimated at 6.92% in 1992.

DEPARTMENTS
(official projections, 2007)

	Area (sq km)*	Population	Density (per sq km)	Capital ('000)
Beni	213,564	422,434	2.0	Trinidad (92,885)
Chuquisaca	51,524	621,383	12.1	Sucre (279,275)
Cochabamba	55,631	1,747,906	31.4	Cochabamba (595,254)
La Paz	133,985	2,715,016	20.3	La Paz (839,718)
Oruro	53,588	440,657	8.2	Oruro (232,241)
Pando	63,827	72,427	1.1	Cobija (36,162)
Potosí	118,218	776,568	6.6	Potosí (163,483)
Santa Cruz	370,621	2,546,881	6.9	Santa Cruz de la Sierra (1,482,255)
Tarija	37,623	484,249	12.9	Tarija (194,288)
Total	1,098,581	9,827,522	8.9	

* As at 2001 census.

PRINCIPAL TOWNS
(official projections, 2007)

Santa Cruz de la Sierra	1,451,597	Potosí	150,647
El Alto	858,186	Sacaba	134,518
La Paz (administrative capital)	835,186	Yacuiba	95,594
Cochabamba	595,226	Quillacollo	92,747
Sucre (legal capital)	256,225	Montero	91,952
Oruro	216,702	Trinidad	87,977
Tarija	176,787	Riberalta	80,422

BIRTHS AND DEATHS
(annual averages, UN estimates)

	1990–95	1995–2000	2000–05
Birth rate (per 1,000)	35.8	32.6	30.2
Death rate (per 1,000)	10.0	8.9	8.2

Source: UN, *World Population Prospects: The 2006 Revision*.

Expectation of life (years at birth, WHO estimates): 65.0 (males 63.3; females 66.8) in 2005 (Source: WHO, *World Health Statistics*).

ECONOMICALLY ACTIVE POPULATION
(labour force surveys, '000 persons aged 10 years and over, at November, urban areas only)

	1999	2000
Agriculture, hunting, forestry and fishing	77.4	102.7
Mining and quarrying	17.2	35.3
Manufacturing	370.5	320.1
Electricity, gas and water supply	5.5	15.9
Construction	176.5	218.9
Wholesale and retail trade; repair of motor vehicles, motorcycles and personal and household goods	542.5	536.1
Hotels and restaurants	126.8	124.4
Transport, storage and communications	173.0	144.3
Financial intermediation	17.5	20.0
Real estate, renting and business activities	71.7	95.8
Public administration and defence; compulsory social security	78.7	72.7
Education	135.6	132.8
Health and social work	63.2	48.8
Other community, social and personal service activities	76.6	98.8
Private households with employed persons	83.0	126.8
Extra-territorial organizations and bodies	1.2	2.8
Total employed	2,017.0	2,096.0
Unemployed	156.7	167.5
Total labour force	2,173.7	2,263.5
Males	1,204.6	1,248.1
Females	969.1	1,015.4

Source: ILO.

Mid-2005 (estimates in '000): Agriculture, etc. 1,650; Total labour force 3,850 (Source: FAO).

Health and Welfare

KEY INDICATORS

Total fertility rate (children per woman, 2005)	3.7
Under-5 mortality rate (per 1,000 live births, 2005)	65
HIV/AIDS (% of persons aged 15–49, 2005)	0.1
Physicians (per 1,000 head, 2001)	1.22
Hospital beds (per 1,000 head, 2004)	1.0
Health expenditure (2004): US $ per head (PPP)	185.9
Health expenditure (2004): % of GDP	6.8
Health expenditure (2004): public (% of total)	60.7
Access to water (% of persons, 2004)	85
Access to sanitation (% of persons, 2004)	46
Human Development Index (2005): ranking	117
Human Development Index (2005): value	0.695

For sources and definitions, see explanatory note on p. vi.

Agriculture

PRINCIPAL CROPS
('000 metric tons)

	2004	2005	2006
Wheat	116.0	131.2	148.9
Rice (paddy)	331.3	445.7	425.1
Barley	72.6	74.0	74.0
Maize	578.4	734.4	864.1
Sorghum	165.3	203.7	293.4
Potatoes	748.1	761.9	754.9
Cassava (Manioc)	362.9	370.5	373.6
Sugar cane	460.7	403.0	510.0*
Brazil nuts*	38.2	n.a.	38.2
Chestnuts*	38.8	41.0	41.0

BOLIVIA

Statistical Survey

—continued	2004	2005	2006
Soybeans (Soya beans)	1,611.8	1,690.2	1,350.0
Sunflower seeds	76.5	80.9	140.0†
Cottonseed*	53.0	56.2	56.2
Tomatoes	118.9	127.6	129.6
Pumpkins, squash and gourds*	118.9	123.3	123.3
Onions (dry)	31.7	32.3	33.3
Peas (green)	24.4	25.1	25.5
Broad beans, horse beans (dry)*	12.7	12.4	12.4
Carrots and turnips	28.2	28.7	29.5
Green corn	31.2	32.2	32.7
Watermelons*	22.6	23.9	23.9
Bananas	177.0	180.9	187.5
Plantains	432.8	443.4	450.1
Oranges	86.1	87.7	89.7
Tangerines, mandarins clementines and satsumas	34.5	35.4	36.5
Lemons and limes*	65.1	65.9	65.9
Grapefruit and pomelos*	30.2	30.6	30.6
Peaches and nectarines*	37.9	38.5	38.5
Grapes	28.9	29.8	31.0
Pineapples*	68.0	74.2	74.2
Papayas*	23.7	24.2	24.2
Coffee (green)	25.3	25.9	27.5
Cotton (lint)*	25.6	n.a.	25.6

* FAO estimate(s).
† Unofficial figure.

Aggregate production ('000 metric tons, may include official, semi-official or estimated data): Total cereals 1,296 in 2004, 1,622 in 2005, 1,839 in 2006; Total roots and tubers 1,215 in 2004, 1,236 in 2005, 1,233 in 2006; Total vegetables (incl. melons) 481 in 2004, 500 in 2005, 506 in 2006; Total fruits (excl. melons) 1,022 in 2004, 1,049 in 2005, 1,067 in 2006.

Source: FAO.

LIVESTOCK
('000 head, year ending September)

	2004	2005	2006
Horses	437	447	456
Asses, mules or hinnies*	717	717	717
Cattle	7,118	7,314	7,517
Pigs	2,282	2,390	2,488
Sheep	8,623	8,816	8,987
Goats	1,861	1,896	1,926
Chickens	67,401	73,140	80,598
Ducks*	295	295	295
Turkeys*	155	155	155

* FAO estimates.
Source: FAO.

LIVESTOCK PRODUCTS
('000 metric tons)

	2004	2005	2006
Cattle meat	172.0	172.0*	172.0*
Sheep meat	18.0	18.0*	18.0*
Goat meat*	5.8	5.8	5.8
Pig meat*	100.8	101.2	101.1
Chicken meat	155.5	167.8	167.8
Cows' milk*	233.7	233.7	233.7
Sheep's milk*	29.2	29.2	29.2
Goats' milk*	11.7	11.7	11.7
Hen eggs	n.a.	n.a.	5,615.0
Wool: greasy*	8.6	8.6	8.6

* FAO estimate(s).
Source: FAO.

Forestry

ROUNDWOOD REMOVALS
('000 cubic metres, excl. bark)

	2003	2004	2005
Sawlogs, veneer logs and logs for sleepers	650	730	810
Fuel wood	2,206	2,228	2,251
Total	2,856	2,958	3,061

2006: Figures assumed to be unchanged from 2005 (FAO estimates).
Source: FAO.

SAWNWOOD PRODUCTION
('000 cubic metres, incl. railway sleepers)

	2003	2004	2005
Total (all broadleaved)	347	402	408

2006: Figures assumed to be unchanged from 2005 (FAO estimates).
Source: FAO.

Fishing

(metric tons, live weight)

	2003	2004	2005
Capture	6,599	6,746	6,660
Freshwater fishes	5,615	5,548	5,510
Rainbow trout	124	310	300
Silversides (sand smelts)	860	888	850
Aquaculture	375	450	430
Rainbow trout	274	310	300
Total catch	6,974	7,196	7,090

Note: Figures exclude crocodiles and alligators, recorded by number rather than by weight. The number of spectacled caimans caught was: 43,528 in 2003; 36,299 in 2004; 51,330 in 2005.

Source: FAO.

Mining

(metric tons, unless otherwise indicated; figures for metallic minerals refer to the metal content of ores)

	2003	2004*	2005*
Crude petroleum ('000 barrels)	12,223	14,192	15,417
Natural gas (million cu feet, gross production)	360,272	447,483	518,137
Copper	344	576	714
Tin	16,386	18,114	18,694
Lead	9,353	10,252	11,093
Zinc	145,490	147,430	157,019
Tungsten (Wolfram)	556	508	658
Antimony	2,432	3,036	5,225
Silver	466	413	420
Gold (kg)	9,361	6,165	8,906

* Preliminary.

BOLIVIA

Industry

SELECTED PRODUCTS
('000 42-gallon barrels, unless otherwise indicated)

	2003	2004	2005
Cement ('000 metric tons)	1,138	1,276	1,440*
Liquefied petroleum gas	695	791*	864*
Distillate fuel oil	3,488	4,419*	4,450*
Kerosene	166	150*	151*
Motor spirit (petrol)*	3,450	3,867	3,726
Electric energy (million kWh)	4,340	4,542	4,778

* Provisional figure(s).

2001 (provisional): Flour ('000 metric tons): 788; Carbonated drinks ('000 hectolitres): 1,996; Beer ('000 hectolitres) 1,586; Cigarettes (packets) 75,373; Alcohol ('000 litres) 29,099.

Cement ('000 metric tons): 1,138 in 2003; 1,276 in 2004 (preliminary); 1,440 in 2005 (preliminary).

2005 (preliminary) Electric energy (million kWh): 4,778.

Source: partly US Geological Survey.

Finance

CURRENCY AND EXCHANGE RATES

Monetary Units
100 centavos = 1 boliviano (B).

Sterling, Dollar and Euro Equivalents (31 November 2007)
£1 sterling = 15.870 bolivianos;
US $1 = 7.680 bolivianos;
€1 = 11.336 bolivianos;
100 bolivianos = £6.30 = $13.02 = €8.82.

Average Exchange Rate (bolivianos per US $)
2004   7.9363
2005   8.0661
2006   8.0116

GENERAL BUDGET
(national treasury budget, million bolivianos, preliminary)

Revenue	2005	2006	2007
Current revenue	12,116.5	14,588.5	14,894.4
Tax revenue	8,013.5	12,771.1	12,679.5
Internal	7,363.5	11,988.2	11,691.1
Customs	471.2	546.1	746.8
Duties on hydrocarbons	1,072.0	730.5	1,152.6
Other current revenue	1,727.4	613.2	384.2
Repayment of loans	30.1	20.3	23.3
Current transfers	60.2	158.5	252.8
Grants	1,213.3	295.0	402.0
Capital transfers and sale of assets	13.8	—	—
Total	12,130.4	14,588.5	14,894.4

Expenditure	2005	2006	2007
Current expenditure	14,226.0	16,827.9	15,617.6
Personal services	6,215.5	6,788.8	8,310.7
Goods and services	835.4	755.7	727.4
Interest on debt	2,348.5	2,330.4	2,243.3
External	1,084.8	1,165.6	1,059.8
Internal	1,263.7	1,164.8	1,183.5
Current transfers	4,826.6	6,953.1	4,336.2
Payments	3,343.4	3,307.2	3,472.6
Capital expenditure	234.6	290.5	287.0
Total	14,460.5	17,118.5	15,904.6

INTERNATIONAL RESERVES
(US $ million at 31 December)

	2004	2005	2006
Gold (national valuation)	399.4	470.6	577.6
IMF special drawing rights	41.2	38.2	40.2
Reserve position in IMF	13.8	12.7	13.4
Foreign exchange	817.3	1,276.7	2,562.5
Total	1,271.7	1,798.2	3,193.7

Source: IMF, *International Financial Statistics*.

MONEY SUPPLY
(million bolivianos at 31 December)

	2004	2005	2006
Currency outside banks	3,865	5,594	8,012
Demand deposits at commercial banks	1,369	1,787	2,682
Total money (incl. others)	6,645	10,354	15,493

Source: IMF, *International Financial Statistics*.

COST OF LIVING
(Consumer Price Index for urban areas; base: 2000 = 100)

	2003	2004	2005
Food and beverages	103.2	109.3	115.7
Fuel and light	114.2	118.8	123.0
Clothing and footwear	109.0	111.4	114.7
Rent	109.0	111.0	112.3
All items (incl. others)	105.9	110.6	116.6

Source: ILO.

2006 (Consumer Price Index for urban areas; base: 2000 = 100): All items 121.6 (Source: IMF, *International Financial Statistics*).

NATIONAL ACCOUNTS
(million bolivianos at current prices, preliminary)

Expenditure on the Gross Domestic Product

	2004	2005	2006
Government final consumption expenditure	11,320	12,304	13,170
Private final consumption expenditure	47,281	50,763	56,635
Increase in stocks	−463	956	−718
Gross fixed capital formation	8,137	9,529	11,505
Total domestic expenditure	66,275	73,552	80,592
Exports of goods and services	21,680	27,381	37,997
Less Imports of goods and services	18,330	24,779	29,159
GDP at market prices	69,626	76,154	89,428
GDP at constant 1990 prices	24,928	25,936	27,137

BOLIVIA

Gross Domestic Product by Economic Activity

	2004	2005	2006
Agriculture, hunting, forestry and fishing	9,275.9	8,872.2	9,776.9
Mining and quarrying	6,582.4	7,550.1	9,899.3
Manufacturing	8,708.5	8,868.0	10,306.6
Electricity, gas and water	1,923.1	1,993.4	2,115.5
Construction	1,473.4	1,513.4	1,586.1
Trade	4,859.8	5,010.4	5,669.0
Hotels and restaurants	2,090.4	2,115.0	2,285.4
Transport, storage and communications	8,255.1	8,431.0	9,112.4
Finance, insurance, real estate and business services	6,840.3	7,149.8	7,831.1
Government services	8,643.1	9,275.0	10,063.4
Other community, social and personal services	3,626.4	3,730.9	4,012.7
Sub-total	62,278.4	64,509.2	72,658.4
Value-added tax / Import duties	9,294.0	13,849.6	19,429.6
Less Imputed bank charge	1,946.3	2,205.2	2,659.5
GDP in purchasers' values	69,626.1	76,153.8	89,428.3

BALANCE OF PAYMENTS
(US $ million)

	2004	2005	2006
Exports of goods f.o.b.	2,146.0	2,791.1	3,863.0
Imports of goods f.o.b.	−1,724.7	−2,182.6	−2,631.1
Trade balance	421.3	608.5	1,231.9
Exports of services	416.4	488.8	434.1
Imports of services	−606.7	−682.5	−805.5
Balance on goods and services	231.1	414.8	860.5
Other income received	76.0	121.2	214.5
Other income paid	−460.6	−497.6	−578.2
Balance on goods, services and income	−153.6	38.4	496.8
Current transfers received	542.6	648.7	895.1
Current transfers paid	−51.5	−64.7	−72.9
Current balance	337.5	622.4	1,319.1
Capital account (net)	—	8.7	1,813.2
Direct investment abroad	−2.8	−3.0	−3.0
Direct investment from abroad	65.4	−238.6	240.1
Portfolio investment assets	−35.4	−153.4	40.1
Other investment assets	94.3	123.8	−270.2
Other investment liabilities	239.0	451.8	−1,629.1
Net errors and omissions	−625.4	−374.5	−71.4
Overall balance	72.6	437.2	1,438.8

Source: IMF, *International Financial Statistics*.

External Trade

PRINCIPAL COMMODITIES
(distribution by SITC, US $ million)

Imports c.i.f.	2004	2005	2006
Vegetable products	112.9	122.4	130.5
Prepared foodstuffs (incl. beverages and tobacco)	89.8	95.0	114.1
Mineral fuels, lubricants, etc.	140.1	251.1	285.3
Chemicals and related products	282.5	341.9	372.1
Plastic and articles thereof	145.9	194.2	224.2
Wood and wood products	88.9	97.3	109.9
Textiles and textile products	92.0	88.1	95.5
Base metals and their manufactures	199.0	258.0	328.8
Machinery and mechanical appliances (incl. electrical equipment and parts thereof)	381.8	471.3	620.4
Transport equipment	194.3	236.9	326.3
Total (incl. others)	1,887.8	2,343.3	2,824.3

Exports f.o.b.	2004	2005	2006
Vegetable products	143.7	185.2	176.6
Prepared foodstuffs (incl. beverages and tobacco)	321.2	259.1	273.7
Animal and vegetable oils, fats and waxes	147.6	131.9	157.6
Mineral fuels, lubricants, etc.	1,142.0	1,689.1	2,854.8
Wood and wood products	58.3	69.5	90.3
Textiles and textile products	71.0	70.2	70.7
Jewellery, goldsmiths' and silversmiths' wares, etc.	163.2	215.0	286.1
Base metals and their manufactures	122.0	112.9	135.5
Total* (incl. others)	2,313.7	2,874.2	4,296.5

* Including re-exports (US $ million): 68.1 in 2004; 55.9 in 2005; 141.1 in 2006.

PRINCIPAL TRADING PARTNERS
(US $ million)

Imports c.i.f.	2004	2005	2006
Argentina	295.3	391.2	447.3
Brazil	486.7	513.8	576.3
Chile	111.4	162.4	234.6
China, People's Republic	107.9	136.0	192.1
Colombia	61.3	57.3	63.9
France	21.7	31.2	31.8
Germany	36.9	44.9	65.4
Italy	19.0	23.0	24.6
Japan	105.3	142.9	222.5
Korea, Republic	14.0	18.1	22.3
Mexico	36.3	50.9	49.2
Paraguay	19.2	22.8	23.7
Peru	127.3	152.3	189.4
Spain	27.4	36.0	39.8
USA	260.3	324.2	341.8
Total (incl. others)	1,887.8	2,343.3	2,824.3

Exports	2004	2005	2006
Argentina	122.6	260.2	370.4
Belgium	32.6	22.3	60.6
Brazil	710.9	1,001.5	1,561.9
Chile	47.6	37.1	60.1
Colombia	119.0	180.5	155.0
Germany	9.9	14.8	15.4
Italy	15.3	15.2	24.4
Japan	68.4	134.3	378.0
Mexico	20.9	19.9	20.7
Peru	134.6	123.7	231.9
Switzerland	52.4	107.4	210.4
United Kingdom	52.8	59.0	79.2
USA	330.8	384.5	360.0
Venezuela	242.6	159.2	199.9
Total* (incl. others)	2,254.4	2,810.4	4,223.3

* Including re-exports (US $ million): 68.1 in 2004; 55.9 in 2005; 141.1 in 2006.

Transport

RAILWAYS
(traffic)

	2002	2003	2004
Passenger-kilometres (million)	280	283	286
Net ton-kilometres (million)	873	901	1,058

Source: UN, *Statistical Yearbook*.

BOLIVIA

ROAD TRAFFIC
(motor vehicles in use at 31 December)

	2002	2003	2004
Passenger cars	26,229	127,222	138,729
Buses	27,226	43,588	49,133
Lorries and vans	30,539	225,028	251,801
Motorcycles	1,125	15,467	19,426

Source: IRF, *World Road Statistics*.

SHIPPING
Merchant Fleet
(registered at 31 December)

	2004	2005	2006
Number of vessels	85	68	68
Total displacement ('000 grt)	580.3	153.1	107.5

Source: Lloyd's Register-Fairplay, *World Fleet Statistics*.

CIVIL AVIATION
(traffic on scheduled services)

	2003	2004	2005
Kilometres flown (million)	22	22	22
Passenger-km (million)	1,744	1,779	1,903
Freight ton-km (million)	25	24	25

Source: UN Commission for Latin America and the Caribbean, *Statistical Yearbook*.

Tourism

ARRIVALS AT HOTELS
(regional capitals only)

Country of origin	2003	2004	2005
Argentina	31,242	36,320	41,610
Brazil	23,810	29,745	32,400
Canada	7,429	8,120	8,297
Chile	17,152	14,948	19,234
France	24,356	24,416	25,167
Germany	19,056	19,804	20,308
Israel	12,003	12,149	9,405
Italy	7,631	8,480	8,101
Japan	6,379	7,469	7,226
Netherlands	10,444	9,764	8,625
Peru	62,164	68,739	77,380
Spain	10,964	12,140	11,974
Switzerland	8,613	8,531	8,519
United Kingdom	20,434	20,616	20,801
USA	36,801	38,066	37,758
Total (incl. others)	367,036	390,888	413,267

Tourism receipts (US $ million, incl. passenger transport): 244 in 2003; 283 in 2004; 346 in 2005.

Source: World Tourism Organization.

Communications Media

	2004	2005	2006
Telephones ('000 main lines in use)	625.4	646.3	666.6
Mobile cellular telephones ('000 subscribers)	1,800.8	2,421.4	2,698.2
Personal computers ('000 in use)*	190	210	n.a.
Internet users ('000)	400	480	580
Broadband subscribers ('000)	8.7	13.0	n.a.

*Estimates.

Source: International Telecommunication Union.

Television receivers ('000): 990 in use in 2000 (Source: International Telecommunication Union).

Radio receivers ('000): 5,250 in use in 1997 (Source: UNESCO, *Statistical Yearbook*).

Daily newspapers: 18 in 1996 (average circulation 420,000 copies) (Source: UNESCO, *Statistical Yearbook*)

Education

(2003/04, unless otherwise indicated, estimates)

	Institutions	Teachers	Males	Females	Total
Pre-primary	2,294*	5,761	97.5	95.2	192.7
Primary	12,639†	64,426	790.0	755.8	1,545.8
Secondary:					
general	n.a.	42,756	541.2	491.1	1,032.3
technical/vocational‡	n.a.	2,148	17.3	32.3	49.6
Higher	n.a.	17,759	n.a.	n.a.	346.1

Students ('000)

*1988.
†1987.
‡2002/03 figure.

Source: UNESCO Institute for Statistics.

Adult literacy rate (UNESCO estimates): 86.7% (males 93.1%; females 80.7%) in 2001 (Source: UNESCO Institute for Statistics).

Directory

The Constitution

Bolivia became an independent republic in 1825 and received its first Constitution in November 1826. Since that date a number of new Constitutions have been promulgated. Following the *coup d'état* of November 1964, the Constitution of 1947 was revived. Under its provisions, executive power is vested in the President, who chairs the Cabinet. According to the revised Constitution, the President is elected by direct suffrage for a five-year term (extended from four years in 1997) and is not eligible for immediate re-election. In the event of the President's death or failure to assume office, the Vice-President or, failing the Vice-President, the President of the Senate becomes interim Head of State.

The President has power to appoint members of the Cabinet and diplomatic representatives from a panel proposed by the Senate. The President is responsible for the conduct of foreign affairs and is also empowered to issue decrees and to initiate legislation by special messages to Congress.

The Congreso Nacional (Congress) consists of a 27-member Senado Nacional (Senate) and a 130-member Cámara de Diputados (Chamber of Deputies). The Congreso meets annually and its ordinary sessions last only 90 working days, which may be extended to 120. Each of the nine departments (La Paz, Chuquisaca, Oruro, Beni, Santa Cruz, Potosí, Tarija, Cochabamba and Pando), into which the country is divided for administrative purposes, elects three senators. Members of both houses are elected for five years.

BOLIVIA

The supreme administrative, political and military authority in each department is vested in a prefect appointed by the President. The sub-divisions of each department, known as provinces, are administered by sub-prefects. The provinces are further divided into cantons. There are 94 provinces and some 1,000 cantons. The capital of each department has its autonomous municipal council and controls its own revenue and expenditure.

Public order, education and roads are under national control.

A decree issued in July 1952 conferred the franchise on all persons who had reached the age of 21 years, whether literate or illiterate. Previously the franchise had been restricted to literate persons. (The voting age for married persons was lowered to 18 years at the 1989 elections.)

A revised draft constitution was expected to be put to the electorate in a referendum during 2008.

The Government

HEAD OF STATE

President: Juan Evo Morales Aima (took office 22 January 2006).
Vice-President: Alvaro Marcelo García Linera.

THE CABINET
(March 2008)

Minister of Foreign Affairs and Worship: David Choquehuanca Céspedes.
Minister of the Interior: Alfredo Octavio Rada Vélez.
Minister of National Defence: Walker San Miguel Rodríguez.
Minister of Finance: Luis Alberto Arce Catacora.
Minister of Sustainable Development and Planning: Graciela Toro Ibáñez.
Minister of the Presidency: Juan Ramón de la Quintana.
Minister of Health and Sport: Walter Selum.
Minister of Labour: Walter Delgadillo Terceros.
Minister of Education and Culture: Magdalena Cajías de la Vega.
Minister of Rural, Agricultural and Environmental Development: Susana Rivero Guzmán.
Minister of Production and Small Businesses: Ángel Gonzalo Hurtado.
Minister of Hydrocarbons and Energy: Carlos Villega Quiroga.
Minister of Mines and Metallurgy: Luis Alberto Echazú.
Minister of Public Works and Services: Oscar Coca Antezana.
Minister without Portfolio responsible for Justice: Celima Torrico Rojas.
Minister without Portfolio responsible for Water: Walter Valda Rivera.

MINISTRIES

Ministry of Education and Culture: Casilla 6500, La Paz; tel. and fax (2) 220-3576; internet www.minedu.gov.bo.
Ministry of Finance: CP 3744, La Paz; tel. (2) 220-3434; e-mail webmaster@hacienda.gov.bo; internet www.hacienda.gov.bo.
Ministry of Foreign Affairs and Worship: Calle Ingavi, esq. Junín, La Paz; tel. (2) 237-1150; fax (2) 237-1155; e-mail mreuno@rree.gov.bo; internet www.rree.gov.bo.
Ministry of Health and Sport: Plaza del Estudiante, La Paz; tel. (2) 237-1373; fax (2) 239-1590; e-mail info@sns.gov.bo; internet www.sns.gov.bo.
Ministry of Hydrocarbons and Energy: Edif. Palacio de Comunicaciones, Avda Mariscal Santa Cruz, La Paz; e-mail minehidro@hidrocarburos.gov.bo; internet www.hidrocarburos.gov.bo.
Ministry of the Interior: Avda Arce 2409, esq. Belisario Salinas, La Paz; tel. (2) 237-0460; fax (2) 237-1334; e-mail mail@mingobierno.gov.bo; internet www.mingobierno.gov.bo.
Ministry of Labour: Calle Yanacocha, esq. Mercado, La Paz; tel. (2) 236-4164; fax (2) 237-1387; e-mail mintrabajo@unete.com; internet www.mintrabajo.gob.bo.
Ministry of Mines and Metallurgy: Edif. Palacio de Comunicaciones, 14°, Avda Mariscal Santa Cruz, La Paz; tel. (2) 231-0846; fax (2) 237-1241; e-mail boliviamin@acelerate.com; internet www.mineria.gov.bo.
Ministry of National Defence: Plaza Avaroa, esq. Pedro Salazar y 20 de Octubre 2502, La Paz; tel. (2) 232-0225; fax (2) 243-3153; e-mail correomaster@mindef.gov.bo; internet www.mindef.gov.bo.
Ministry of the Presidency: Palacio de Gobierno, Plaza Murillo, La Paz; tel. (2) 237-1082; fax (2) 237-1388.
Ministry of Production and Small Businesses: Edif. Palacio de Comunicaciones, Avda Mariscal Santa Cruz, La Paz; tel. (2) 237-5000; fax (2) 236-0534; e-mail despacho@desarrollo.gov.bo; internet www.desarrollo.gov.bo.
Ministry of Public Works and Services: La Paz; tel. (2) 241-9090; e-mail contacto@vivienda.gov.bo; internet www.vivienda.gov.bo.
Ministry of Rural, Agricultural and Environmental Development: Avda Camacho 1471, La Paz; e-mail despacho@maca.gov.bo; internet www.maca.gov.bo.
Ministry of Sustainable Development and Planning: Arce 2147, 4°, Casilla 12814, La Paz; tel. (2) 231-0860; fax (2) 231-7320; e-mail sdnp@coord.rds.org.bo; internet www.rds.org.bo.

President and Legislature

PRESIDENT

Election, 18 December 2005

Candidate	Valid votes	% of valid votes cast
Juan Evo Morales Aima (MAS)	1,544,374	53.74
Jorge Quiroga Ramírez (PODEMOS)	821,745	28.59
Samuel Doria Medina (FUN)	224,090	7.80
Michiaki Nagatani Morishita (MNR)	185,859	6.47
Felipe Quispe Huanca (MIP)	61,948	2.16
Total (incl. others)*	2,873,801	100.00

*In addition, there were 124,046 blank votes and 104,570 spoiled votes.

CONGRESO NACIONAL

President of the Senado Nacional: Santos Ramírez.
President of the Cámara de Diputados: Edmundo Novillo.

General Election, 18 December 2005

	Seats	
Party	Cámara de Diputados	Senado Nacional
Movimiento al Socialismo—Instrumento Político por la Soberanía de los Pueblos (MAS)	72	12
Poder Democrático y Social (PODEMOS)	43	13
Frente de Unidad Nacional (FUN)	8	1
Movimiento Nacionalista Revolucionario (MNR)	7	1
Total	130	27

Election Commission

Corte Nacional Electoral (CNE): Avda Sánchez Lima, esq. Pedro Salazar, Sopocachi, CP 8748, La Paz; tel. (2) 242-4221; fax (2) 241-6710; e-mail cne@cne.org.bo; internet www.cne.org.bo; Pres. José Luis Exeni Rodríguez.

Political Organizations

Acción Democrática Nacionalista (ADN): Calle Uruguay 454, La Paz; tel. (2) 242-3067; fax (2) 242-3412; e-mail mvberteros@aol.com; internet www.bolivian.com/adn; f. 1979; right-wing; Leader Mauro Bertero Gutiérrez; Nat. Exec. Sec. Jorge Landívar.

Alianza de Renovación Boliviana (ARBOL): La Paz; f. 1993; conservative; Leader Casiano Acalle Choque.

Comité Cívico pro Santa Cruz (CCSC): Avda Cañada Strongest 70, CP 1801, Santa Cruz; tel. (3) 334-2777; fax (3) 334-1812; e-mail info@comiteprosantacruz.org; internet www.comiteprosantacruz.org; f. 1950; right-wing autonomist grouping; Pres. Germán Antelo; Vice-Pres. Nino Gandarilla.

Comité Cívico de Tarija (CCT): Tarija; right-wing autonomist grouping; Pres. Roberto Ruiz.

Federación de Juntas Vecinales (FEJUVE): El Alto; left-wing grouping campaigning for civil rights and the nationalization of industries and utilities; Pres. ABEL MAMANI MARCA; Sec.-Gen. JORGE CHURA.

Frente Revolucionario de Izquierda (FRI): La Paz; left-wing; f. 1954; Leader OSCAR ZAMORA MEDINACELLI.

Frente de Unidad Nacional (FUN): Cochabamba; f. 2003; left-wing; Leader SAMUEL DORIA MEDINA.

Izquierda Unida: La Paz; internet www.bolivian.com/iu; Leader ALEJO VÉLIZ LAZO.

Katarismo Nacional Democrático (KND): La Paz; internet www.bolivian.com/knd/index.html; f. 1993; Pres. FERNANDO UNTOJA CHOQUE.

Movimiento Bolivia Libre (MBL): Edif. Camiri, Of. 601, Calle Comercio 972, esq. Yanacocha, Casilla 10382, La Paz; tel. (2) 234-0257; fax (2) 239-2242; internet www.bolivian.com/mbl; f. 1985; left-wing; breakaway faction of MIR; Leader FRANK BARRIOS; 60,000 mems.

Movimiento Indígena Pachakuti (MIP): indigenous movement; f. 2002; Leader FELIPE QUISPE HUANCA.

Movimiento de la Izquierda Revolucionaria (MIR): Avda América 119, 2°, La Paz; e-mail mir@ceibo.entelnet.bo; internet www.cibergallo.com; f. 1971; split into several factions in 1985; left-wing; 150,000 mems; Leader JAIME PAZ ZAMORA; Sec.-Gen. OSCAR EID FRANCO.

Movimiento sin Miedo: La Paz; internet www.bolivian.com/msm/index.html; f. 1999; left-wing; Leader JUAN DEL GRANADO.

Movimiento Nacionalista Revolucionario (MNR): Calle Estados Unidos y Panamá, Pasaje Puerto Príncipe 1487, Miraflores, La Paz; tel. (2) 212-8475; fax (2) 212-8479; e-mail giubedre@yahoo.es; internet www.mnr.org.bo; f. 1941; centre-right; Leader MIRTHA QUEVEDO ACALINOVIC; Sec.-Gen. FRANKLIN ANAYA VÁZQUEZ; 165,000 mems.

Movimiento Revolucionario Túpac Katarí de Liberación (MRTKL): Avda Baptista 939, Casilla 9133, La Paz; tel. (2) 235-4784; f. 1978; peasant party; Leader VÍCTOR HUGO CÁRDENAS CONDE; Sec.-Gen. NORBERTO PÉREZ HIDALGO; 80,000 mems.

Movimiento al Socialismo—Instrumento Político por la Soberanía de los Pueblos (MAS): Calle Capitán Ravelo 2334, entre Belisario Salinas y Rosendo Gutiérrez, 3°, Sopocachi, La Paz; e-mail webmaster@masbolivia.org; internet www.masbolivia.org; f. 1987; left-wing; Leader JUAN EVO MORALES AIMA.

Nueva Fuerza Republicana (NFR): Cochabamba; internet www.bolivian.com/nfr; f. 1996; centre-right; Leader MANFRED REYES VILLA.

Partido Comunista de Bolivia (PCB): La Paz; f. 1950; Leader MARCOS DOMIC; First Sec. SIMÓN REYES RIVERA.

Partido Demócrata Cristiano (PDC): Casilla 4345, La Paz; f. 1954; Pres. JORGE AGREDA VALDERRAMA; Sec. ANTONIO CANELAS-GALATOIRE; 50,000 mems.

Partido Obrero Revolucionario (POR): Correo Central, La Paz; f. 1935; Trotskyist; Leader GUILLERMO LORA.

Partido Revolucionario de la Izquierda Nacionalista (PRIN): Calle Colón 693, La Paz; f. 1964; left-wing; Leader JUAN LECHIN OQUENDO.

Partido Socialista (PS): La Paz; f. 1987; Leader JERES JUSTINIANO.

Partido de Vanguardia Obrera: Plaza Venezuela 1452, La Paz; Leader FILEMÓN ESCOBAR.

Plan Progreso: La Paz; f. 2004 by fmr mems of the MIR; Leader JOSÉ LUIS PAREDES.

Poder Democrático y Social (PODEMOS): La Paz; Leader JORGE QUIROGA RAMÍREZ.

Unión Cívica Solidaridad (UCS): Calle Mercado 1064, 6°, La Paz; tel. (2) 236-0297; fax (2) 237-2200; internet www.bolivian.com/ucs/index.html; f. 1989; populist; Leader JOHNNY FERNÁNDEZ; 102,000 mems.

Diplomatic Representation

EMBASSIES IN BOLIVIA

Argentina: Calle Aspiazú 497, esq. Sánchez Lima, Casilla 64, La Paz; tel. (2) 241-7737; fax (2) 242-2727; e-mail ebolv@mrecic.gov.ar; Ambassador HORACIO ANTONIO MACEDO.

Brazil: Edif. Multicentro, Torre B, Avda Arce s/n, esq. Rosendo Gutiérrez, Sopocachi, La Paz; tel. (2) 244-0202; fax (2) 244-0043; e-mail webmaster@brasil.org.bo; internet www.brasil.org.bo; Ambassador FREDERICO CEZAR DE ARAUJO.

China, People's Republic: Calle 1, Los Pinos 8532, Casilla 10005, La Paz; tel. (2) 279-3851; fax (2) 279-7121; e-mail emb-china@kolla.net; Ambassador ZHAO WUYI.

Colombia: Calle 9, 7835 Calacoto, La Paz; tel. (2) 278-4491; fax (2) 278-6510; e-mail elapaz@minrelext.gov.co; Ambassador JESÚS EDGAR PAPAMIJA DIAGO.

Costa Rica: Edif. San Miguel Arcángel 1420, 1°, Of. 102, Avda Montenegro en Calacoto, La Paz; tel. and fax (2) 279-8930; e-mail embcrbo@entelnet.bo; Ambassador MARÍA DE LOS ANGELES GUTIÉRREZ VARGAS.

Cuba: Bajo Irpavi Avda Gobles 20, entre 13 y 14, La Paz; tel. (2) 272-1157; fax (2) 272-3419; e-mail embacuba@acelerate.com; Ambassador LUIS FELIPE VÁSQUEZ VÁSQUEZ.

Denmark: Edif. Fortaleza, Avda Arce 2799, esq. Cordero, 9°, Casilla 9860, La Paz; tel. (2) 243-2070; fax (2) 243-3150; e-mail lpbamb@um.dk; internet www.amblapaz.um.dk; Ambassador CHARLOTTE SLENTE.

Ecuador: Edif. Hermman, 14°, Plaza Venezuela 1440, Casilla 406, La Paz; tel. (2) 278-4422; fax (2) 277-1043; e-mail eecuabolivia@mmrree.gov.ec; Ambassador LEONARDO CARRIÓN EGUIGURREN.

Egypt: Avda Ballivián 599, Casilla 2956, La Paz; tel. (2) 278-6511; fax (2) 278-4325; e-mail embajadaegipto@acelerate.com; Ambassador NAGWA MOHAMED AFIFI.

France: Avda Hernando Silés 5390, esq. Calle 8, Obrajes, Casilla 717, La Paz; tel. (2) 214-9900; fax (2) 214-9904; e-mail information@ambafrance-bo.org; internet www.ambafrance-bo.org; Ambassador ALAIN FOUQUET.

Germany: Avda Arce 2395, esq. Belisario Salinas, Casilla 5265, La Paz; tel. (2) 244-0066; fax (2) 244-1441; e-mail info@la-paz.diplo.de; internet www.la-paz.diplo.de; Ambassador ERICH RIEDLER.

Holy See: Avda Arce 2990, Casilla 136, La Paz; tel. (2) 243-1007; fax (2) 243-2120; e-mail nunapobol@acelerate.com; Apostolic Nuncio Most Rev. IVO SCAPOLO (Titular Archbishop of Tagaste).

Italy: Calle 5 (Jordán Cuellar) 458, Obrajes, La Paz; tel. (2) 278-8506; fax (2) 278-8178; e-mail segreteria.lapaz@esteri.it; internet www.italian-embassy.org.ae/ambasciata_lapaz; Ambassador SILVIO MIGNANO.

Japan: Calle Rosendo Gutiérrez 497, esq. Sánchez Lima, Casilla 2725, La Paz; tel. (2) 241-9110; fax (2) 241-1919; e-mail coopjapon@acelerate.com; internet www.bo.emb-japan.go.jp; Ambassador MITSUNORI SHIRAKAWA.

Mexico: Sánchez Bustamante 509, Casilla 430, La Paz; tel. (2) 277-2133; fax (2) 277-6085; e-mail embamex@acelerate.com; internet www.sre.gob.mx/bolivia; Ambassador ROBERTA LAJOUS VARGAS.

Netherlands: Edif. Hilda, 7°, Avda 6 de Agosto 2455, La Paz; tel. (2) 244-4040; fax (2) 244-3804; e-mail nllap@caoba.entelnet.bo; internet www.mfa.nl/lap-es; Ambassador MARTIN DE LA BEY.

Panama: Calle 10, 7853 Calacoto, Casilla 678, La Paz; tel. (2) 278-7334; fax (2) 279-7290; e-mail empanbol@ceibo.entelnet.bo; Ambassador AUGUSTO LUIS VILLARREAL AMARANTO.

Paraguay: Edif. Illimani II, 1°, Avda 6 de Agosto y Pedro Salazar, Casilla 882, La Paz; tel. (2) 243-3176; fax (2) 243-2201; e-mail embapar@acelerate.com; Ambassador NIMIA OVIEDO DE TORALES.

Peru: Calle F. Guachalla 300, Casilla 668, Sopocachi, La Paz; tel. (2) 244-1250; fax (2) 244-1240; e-mail embbol@caoba.entelnet.bo; Ambassador JUAN FERNANDO JAVIER ROJAS SAMANEZ.

Russia: Calacoto, Avda Walter Guevara Arce 8129, La Paz; tel. (2) 278-6419; fax (2) 278-6531; e-mail embrusia@ceibo.entelnet.bo; Ambassador VLADIMIR L. KULIKOV.

Spain: Avda 6 de Agosto 2827, Casilla 282, La Paz; tel. (2) 243-3518; fax (2) 211-3267; e-mail embespbo@correo.mae.es; Ambassador JUAN FRANCISCO MONTALBÁN CARRASCO.

Switzerland: Calle 13, esq. Avda 14 de Setiembre, Obrajes, Casilla 9356, La Paz; tel. (2) 275-1001; fax (2) 214-0885; e-mail vertretung@paz.rep.admin.ch; Chargé d'affaires a.i. JACQUES GREMAUD.

United Kingdom: Avda Arce 2732, Casilla 694, La Paz; tel. (2) 243-3424; fax (2) 243-1073; e-mail ppa@megalink.com; internet www.britishembassy.gov.uk/bolivia; Ambassador NIGEL BAKER.

USA: Avda Arce 2780, Casilla 425, La Paz; tel. (2) 243-0251; fax (2) 243-3900; internet lapaz.usembassy.gov; Ambassador PHILIP S. GOLDBERG.

Uruguay: Edif. Monroy Velez, 7°, Calle 21, 8350 Calacoto, La Paz, La Paz; tel. (2) 279-1482; fax (2) 212-9413; e-mail urulivia@acelerate.com; Ambassador ZORRILLA DE SAN MARTÍN LLAMAS.

Venezuela: Edif. Illimani, 4°, Avda Arce, esq. Campos, Casilla 441, La Paz; tel. (2) 243-1365; fax (2) 243-2348; e-mail embvzla@caoba.telnet.bo; Ambassador JULIO AGOSTO MONTES PRADO.

Judicial System

SUPREME COURT

Corte Suprema
Calle Pilinco 352, CP 211, Sucre; tel. (4) 645-1883; fax (4) 646-2696; e-mail cortesuprema@poderjudicial.gov.bo; internet suprema.poderjudicial.gov.bo.

Judicial power is vested in the Supreme Court. There are 12 members, appointed by Congress for a term of 10 years. The court is divided into four chambers of three justices each. Two chambers deal with civil cases, the third deals with criminal cases and the fourth deals with administrative, social and mining cases. The President of the Supreme Court presides over joint sessions of the courts and attends the joint sessions for cassation cases.

President of the Supreme Court: HÉCTOR SANDÓVAL PARADA.

DISTRICT COURTS

There is a District Court sitting in each Department, and additional provincial and local courts to try minor cases.

ATTORNEY-GENERAL

In addition to the Attorney-General at Sucre (appointed by the President on the proposal of the Senate), there is a District Attorney in each Department as well as circuit judges.

Attorney-General: PEDRO GARECA.

Religion

The majority of the population are Roman Catholics; there were an estimated 8.7m. adherents at 31 December 20056, equivalent to 83.6% of the population. Religious freedom is guaranteed. There are a number of Bahá'ís and a small Jewish community, as well as various Protestant denominations, in Bolivia.

CHRISTIANITY

The Roman Catholic Church

Bolivia comprises four archdioceses, six dioceses, two Territorial Prelatures and five Apostolic Vicariates.

Bishops' Conference

Conferencia Episcopal Boliviana, Calle Potosí 814, Casilla 2309, La Paz; tel. (2) 240-6855; fax (2) 240-6941; e-mail asc@scbbs-bo.com. f. 1972; Pres. Cardinal JULIO TERRAZAS SANDOVAL (Archbishop of Santa Cruz de la Sierra).

Archbishop of Cochabamba: Most Rev. TITO SOLARÍ, Avda Heroínas 152, esq. Zenteno Anaya, Casilla 129, Cochabamba; tel. (4) 425-6562; fax (4) 425-0522; e-mail arz_cbba@supernet.com.bo; internet www.iglesiacbba.org.

Archbishop of La Paz: Most Rev. EDMUNDO LUIS FLAVIO ABASTOFLOR MONTERO, Calle Ballivián 1277, Casilla 259, La Paz; tel. (2) 220-3690; fax (2) 220-3840; e-mail arzonslp@ceibo.entelnet.bo; internet www.arzobispadolapaz.org.

Archbishop of Santa Cruz de la Sierra: Cardinal JULIO TERRAZAS SANDOVAL, Calle Ingavi 49, Casilla 25, Santa Cruz; tel. (3) 332-4416; fax (3) 333-0181; e-mail asc@scbbs-bo.com.

Archbishop of Sucre: Most Rev. JESÚS GERVASIO PÉREZ RODRÍGUEZ, Calle Bolívar 702, Casilla 205, Sucre; tel. (4) 645-1587; fax (4) 646-0336; e-mail arzsucre@mara.scr.entelnet.bo.

The Anglican Communion

Within the Iglesia Anglicana del Cono Sur de América (Anglican Church of the Southern Cone of America), Bolivia forms part of the diocese of Peru. The Bishop is resident in Lima, Peru.

Protestant Churches

Baptist Union of Bolivia: Casilla 2199, La Paz; tel. (2) 222-9538; Pres. Rev. AUGUSTO CHUIJO.

Convención Bautista Boliviana (Baptist Convention of Bolivia): Casilla 3147, Santa Cruz; tel. and fax (3) 334-0717; f. 1947; Pres. EIRA SORUCO DE FLORES.

Iglesia Evangélica Metodista en Bolivia (Evangelical Methodist Church in Bolivia): Casillas 356 y 8347, La Paz; tel. (2) 249-1628; fax (2) 249-1624; autonomous since 1969; 10,000 mems; Bishop Rev. CARLOS INTIPAMPA.

BAHÁ'Í FAITH

National Spiritual Assembly of the Bahá'ís of Bolivia: Casilla 1613, La Paz; tel. (2) 278-5058; fax (2) 278-2387; e-mail noticias@bahai.org.bo; internet bahai.org.bo; mems resident in 5,161 localities; Gen. Sec. BADÍ HERNÁNDEZ.

The Press

DAILY NEWSPAPERS

Cochabamba

Opinión: General Acha 252, Casilla 287, Cochabamba; tel. (4) 425-4400; fax (4) 441-5121; e-mail opinion@opinion.com.bo; internet www.opinion.com.bo; f. 1985; Dir EDWIN TAPIA FRONTANILLA; Gen. Man. GRACIELA MÉNDEZ DE ESCOBAR.

Los Tiempos: Edif. Los Tiempos, Plaza Quintanilla-Norte, Casilla 525, Cochabamba; tel. (4) 425-4562; fax (4) 425-4577; e-mail contactos@lostiempos.com; internet www.lostiempos.com; f. 1943; morning; independent; Dir FERNANDO CANELAS; Man. Editor ALCIDES FLORES MONCADA; circ. 19,000.

La Paz

El Diario: Calle Loayza 118, Casilla 5, La Paz; tel. (2) 233-2233; fax (2) 236-3846; e-mail redinfo@diario.net; internet www.eldiario.net; f. 1904; morning; conservative; Dir ANTONIO CARRASCO GUZMÁN; Man. Editor RODRIGO TICONA ESPINOZA; circ. 55,000.

Jornada: Edif. Almirante Grau 672, Zona San Pedro, Casilla 1628, La Paz; tel. (2) 248-8163; fax (2) 248-7487; e-mail cartas@jornadanet.com; internet www.jornadanet.com; f. 1964; evening; independent; Dir DAVID RÍOS ARANDA; circ. 11,500.

La Razón: Colinas de Santa Rita, Auquisamaña, Casilla 13100, La Paz; tel. (2) 277-1415; fax (2) 277-0908; e-mail jcrocha@la-razon.com; internet www.la-razon.com; f. 1990; Dir JUAN CARLOS ROCHA CHAVARRÍA; Man. Editor GROVER YAPURA A.; circ. 35,000.

Oruro

La Patria: Avda Camacho 1892, Casilla 48, Oruro; tel. (2) 525-0761; fax (2) 525-0781; e-mail lapatria@coteor.net.bo; internet www.lapatriaenlinea.com; f. 1919; morning; independent; Dirs MARCELO MIRRALLES BOVÁ, ENRIQUE MIRALLES BONNECARRERE; Editor HUMBERTO APAZA OROZCO; circ. 6,000.

Potosí

El Potosí: Calle Cochabamba 35 (Junto a Unidad Sanitaria), Potosí; tel. and fax (2) 622-7835; e-mail elpotosi@entelnet.bo; internet www.elpotosi.net; f. 2001; Pres. GONZALO CANELAS TARDÍO; Man. Editor JUAN JOSÉ TORO MONTOYA.

Santa Cruz

El Deber: Avda El Trompillo 1144, Casilla 2144, Santa Cruz; tel. (3) 353-8000; fax (3) 353-9053; e-mail web@eldeber.com.bo; internet www.eldeber.com.bo; f. 1955; morning; independent; Dir Dr PEDRO RIVERO MERCADO; Man. Editor TUFFÍ ARÉ VÁZQUEZ; circ. 35,000.

La Estrella del Oriente: Calle Republiquetas 353, Santa Cruz; tel. (3) 332-9011; fax (3) 332-9012; e-mail info@laestrelladeloriente.net; internet www.laestrelladeloriente.net; f. 1864; Pres. CARLOS SUBIRANA S.; Dir CENTA RECK.

El Mundo: Parque Industrial MZ-7, Casilla 1984, Santa Cruz; tel. (3) 346-4646; fax (3) 346-5057; e-mail redaccion@mail.elmundo.com.bo; internet www.elmundo.com.bo; f. 1979; morning; owned by Santa Cruz Industrialists' Asscn; Pres. WALTER PAREJAS MORENO; Dir JUAN JAVIER ZEBALLOS GUTIÉRREZ; circ. 15,000.

El Nuevo Día: Avda Cristo Redentor 3355, Casilla 5344, Santa Cruz; tel. (3) 343-4040; fax (3) 342-5324; e-mail nuevodia@el-nuevodia.com; internet www.el-nuevodia.com; f. 1987; Pres. ALFREDO LEIGUE URENDA; Man. Editor RÓGER CUÉLLAR.

Sucre

Correo del Sur: Calle Kilómetro 7, No 202, Casilla 242, Sucre; tel. (4) 646-1531; fax (4) 646-0152; e-mail info@correodelsur.net; internet correodelsur.net; f. 1987; Pres. GONZALO CANELAS TARDÍO; Man. Editor RHAYKA FLORES.

PERIODICALS

Actualidad Boliviana Confidencial (ABC): Fernando Guachalla 969, Casilla 648, La Paz; f. 1966; weekly; Dir HUGO GONZÁLEZ RIOJA; circ. 6,000.

Aquí: Casilla 10937, La Paz; tel. (2) 234-3524; fax (2) 235-2455; f. 1979; weekly; circ. 10,000.

Bolivia Libre: Edif. Esperanza, 5°, Avda Mariscal Santa Cruz 2150, Casilla 6500, La Paz; fortnightly; govt organ.

Carta Cruceña de Integración: Casilla 3531, Santa Cruz de la Sierra; weekly; Dirs HERNÁN LLANOVARCED A., JOHNNY LAZARTE J.

BOLIVIA
Directory

Comentarios Económicos de Actualidad (CEA): Casilla 312097, La Paz; tel. (2) 242-4766; fax (2) 242-4772; e-mail veceba@caoba.entelnet.bo; f. 1983; fortnightly; articles and economic analyses; Editor GUIDO CÉSPEDES.

Información Política y Económica (IPE): Calle Comercio, Casilla 2484, La Paz; weekly; Dir GONZALO LÓPEZ MUÑOZ.

Informe R: La Paz; weekly; Editor SARA MONROY.

Notas: Edif. Mariscal de Ayacucho, 5°, Of. 501, Calle Loayza 233, Casilla 5782, La Paz; tel. (2) 233-5577; fax (2) 233-7607; e-mail arminda@agenciadenoticiasfides.net; internet www.agencia denoticiasfides.net; f. 1963; weekly; political and economic analyses; Editor JOSÉ GRAMUNT DE MORAGAS.

El Noticiero: Sucre; weekly; Dir DAVID CABEZAS; circ. 1,500.

Prensa Libre: Sucre; tel. (4) 646-2447; fax (4) 646-2768; e-mail prelibre@mara.scr.entelnet.bo; f. 1989; weekly; Dir JULIO PEMINTEL A.

Servicio de Información Confidencial (SIC): Elías Sagárnaga 274, Casilla 5035, La Paz; weekly; publ. by Asociación Nacional de Prensa; Dir JOSÉ CARRANZA.

Siglo XXI: La Paz; weekly.

Unión: Sucre; weekly; Dir JAIME MERILES.

Visión Boliviana: Calle Loayza 420, Casilla 2870, La Paz; 6 a year.

PRESS ASSOCIATIONS

Asociación Nacional de la Prensa: Avda 6 de Agosto 2170, Casilla 477, La Paz; tel. (2) 236-9916; Pres. Dr CARLOS SERRATE REICH.

Asociación de Periodistas de La Paz: Avda 6 de Agosto 2170, Casilla 477, La Paz; tel. (2) 236-9916; fax (2) 232-3701; f. 1929; Pres. MARIO MALDONADO VISCARRA; Vice-Pres. MARÍA EUGENIA VERASTEGUI A.

NEWS AGENCY

Agencia de Noticias Fides (ANF): Edif. Mariscal de Ayacucho, 5°, Of. 501, Calle Loayza, Casilla 5782, La Paz; tel. (2) 236-5152; fax (2) 236-5153; internet www.noticiasfides.com; f. 1963; owned by the Roman Catholic Church; Dir JOSÉ GRAMUNT DE MORAGAS; Man. Editor WALTER PATIÑO.

Publishers

Ediciones Runa: Calle España 459, Cochabamba; tel. (4) 523-389; e-mail edicionesruna@yahoo.com; internet www.geocities.com/edicionesruna; f. 1968; juvenile, educational and scholarly.

Editora Khana Cruz SRL: Avda Camacho 1372, Casilla 5920, La Paz; tel. (2) 237-0263; Dir GLADIS ANDRADE.

Editora Lux: Edif. Esperanza, Avda Mariscal Santa Cruz, Casilla 1566, La Paz; tel. (2) 232-9102; fax (2) 234-3968; f. 1952; Dir FELICISIMO TARILONTE PÉREZ.

Editorial los Amigos del Libro: Avda Ayacucho 0–156, Casilla 450, Cochabamba; tel. (4) 450-4150; fax (4) 411-5128; e-mail amigol@amigol.bo.net; e-mail gutten@amigol.bo.net; internet www.librosbolivia.com; f. 1945; general; Man. Dir WERNER GUTTENTAG; Gen. Man. INGRID GUTTENTAG.

Editorial Bruño: Loayza 167, Casilla 4809, La Paz; tel. (2) 233-1254; fax (2) 233-5043; e-mail brunol@caoba.entelnet.bo; f. 1964; Dir IGNACIO LOMAS.

Editorial Don Bosco: Avda 16 de Julio 1899, Casilla 4458, La Paz; tel. (2) 237-1449; fax (2) 236-2822; f. 1896; social sciences and literature; Dir GRAMAGLIA MAGLIANO.

Editorial Icthus: La Paz; tel. (2) 235-4007; f. 1967; general and textbooks; Man. Dir DANIEL AQUIZE.

Editorial Popular: Plaza Pérez Velasco 787, Casilla 4171, La Paz; tel. (2) 235-0701; f. 1935; textbooks, postcards, tourist guides, etc.; Man. Dir GERMÁN VILLAMOR.

Editorial Puerta del Sol: Edif. Litoral Sub Suelo, Avda Mariscal Santa Cruz, La Paz; tel. (2) 236-0746; f. 1965; Man. Dir OSCAR CRESPO.

Empresa Editora Proinsa: Avda Saavedra 2055, Casilla 7181, La Paz; tel. (2) 222-7781; fax (2) 222-6671; f. 1974; school books; Dirs FLOREN SANABRIA G., CARLOS SANABRIA C.

Gisbert y Cía, SA: Calle Comercio 1270, Casilla 195, La Paz; tel. (2) 220-2626; fax (2) 220-2911; e-mail libgis@entelnet.bo; f. 1907; textbooks, history, law and general; Pres. JAVIER GISBERT; Promotions Man. MARÍA DEL CARMEN SCHULCZEWSKI; Admin. Man. ANTONIO SCHULCZEWSKI.

Ivar American: Calle Potosí 1375, Casilla 6016, La Paz; tel. (2) 236-1519; Man. Dir HÉCTOR IBÁÑEZ.

Librería Editorial Juventud: Plaza Murillo 519, Casilla 1489, La Paz; tel. (2) 240-6248; f. 1946; textbooks and general; Dir GUSTAVO URQUIZO MENDOZA.

Librería El Ateneo SRL: Calle Ballivián 1275, Casilla 7917, La Paz; tel. (2) 236-9925; fax (2) 239-1513; Dirs JUAN CHIRVECHES D., MIRIAN C. DE CHIRVECHES.

Librería Dismo Ltda: Calle Comercio 806, Casilla 988, La Paz; tel. (2) 240-6411; fax (2) 231-6545; e-mail dismo@caoba.entelnet.bo; Dir TERESA GONZÁLEZ DE ALVAREZ.

Librería La Paz: Edif. Artemis, Calle Campos y Villegas, Casilla 539, La Paz; tel. (2) 243-4927; fax (2) 243-5004; e-mail liblapaz@ceibo.entelnet.bo; f. 1900; Dirs EDUARDO BURGOS R., CARLOS BURGOS M.

Librería La Universal SRL: Calle Ingavi 780, Casilla 2869, La Paz; tel. (2) 228-6634; f. 1958; Man. Dir ROLANDO CONDORI SALINAS.

Librería San Pablo: Calle Colón 627, Casilla 3152, La Paz; tel. (2) 232-6084; f. 1967; Man. Dir MARÍA DE JESÚS VALERIANO.

Santillana de Ediciones SA: Avda Arce 2333, La Paz; tel. (2) 441-122; fax (2) 442-208; e-mail info@santillanabo.com; internet www.santillanabo.com; Gen. Man. ANDRÉS CARDÓ.

PUBLISHERS' ASSOCIATION

Cámara Boliviana del Libro: Calle Capitán Ravelo 2116, Casilla 682, La Paz; tel. and fax (2) 211-3264; e-mail cabolib@entelnet.bo; internet www.cabolib.org.bo; f. 1947; Pres. ERNESTO MARTÍNEZ ACCHINI; Vice Pres. CAROLA OSSIO B.; Gen. Man. ANA PATRICIA NAVARRO.

Broadcasting and Communications

TELECOMMUNICATIONS

Cámara Nacional de Medios de Comunicación: Casilla 2431, La Paz.

Empresa Nacional de Telecomunicaciones (ENTEL): Calle Federico Zuazo 1771, Casilla 4450, La Paz; tel. (2) 231-3030; fax (2) 239-1789; tel. contacto@entelsa.entelnet.bo; internet www.entel.bo; f. 1965; privatized under the Govt's capitalization programme in 1995; 50% owned by Euro Telecom International NV (Netherlands); Pres. FRANCO BERTONE.

Superintendencia de Telecomunicaciones: Calle 13, No 8260, Calacoto, La Paz; tel. (2) 277-2266; fax (2) 277-2299; e-mail supertel@ceibo.entelnet.bo; internet www.sittel.gov.bo; f. 1995; govt-controlled broadcasting authority; Supt Ing. CLIFFORD PARAVICINI.

BROADCASTING

Regulatory Authority

Asociación Boliviana de Radiodifusoras (ASBORA): Edif. Jazmín, 10°, Avda 20 de Octubre 2019, Casilla 5324, La Paz; tel. (2) 236-5154; fax (2) 236-3069; broadcasting authority; Pres. RAÚL NOVILLO ALARCÓN.

Radio

The majority of radio stations are commercial. Broadcasts are in Spanish, Aymará and Quechua.

Educación Radiofónica de Bolivia (ERBOL): Calle Ballivian 1323, 4°, Casilla 5946, La Paz; tel. (2) 235-4142; fax (2) 239-1985; asscn of 28 educational radio stations in Bolivia; Gen. Sec. RONALD GREBE LÓPEZ.

Radio Fides: La Paz; e-mail sistemas@radiofides.com; internet www.radiofides.com; f. 1939; network of 28 radio stations; Roman Catholic; Pres. EDUARDO PÉREZ IRIBARNE.

Red Patria Nueva: Avda Camacho 1485, 6°, La Paz; tel. (2) 220-0473; e-mail illimani@comunica.gov.bo; f. 1932 as Compañía Radio Boliviana; govt-owned network; broadcasts across the country, often as Radio Illimani.

Television

ATB Red Nacional (Canal 9): Avda Argentina 2057, Casilla 9285, La Paz; tel. and fax (2) 222-9922; internet www.atb.com.bo; f. 1985; privately owned television network.

Bolivisión (Canal 4): Santa Cruz; internet www.bolivisiontv.com; f. 1997; privately owned television network; Exec. Pres. Ing. ERNESTO ASBÚN GAZAUI; Gen. Man. Lic. JEANNETTE ARRÁZOLA RIVERO.

Red Uno: Calle Romecín Campos 592, Sopocachi, La Paz; tel. (2) 242-1111; e-mail webmaster@reduno.com.bo; internet www.reduno.com.bo; f. 1985; commercial television station; offices in La Paz, Santa Cruz and Cochabamba; Dir Man. MARIO ROJAS.

Televisión Boliviana (TVB—Canal 7): Edif. La Urbana, 6° y 7°, Avda Camacho 1486, Casilla 900, La Paz; tel. (2) 237-6356; fax (2) 235-9753; f. 1969; govt network operating stations in La Paz, Oruro,

BOLIVIA   *Directory*

Cochabamba, Potosí, Chuquisaca, Pando, Beni, Tarija and Santa Cruz; Gen. Man. MIGUEL N. MONTERO VACA.

Televisión Universitaria (Canal 13): Edif. 'Hoy', 12°–13°, Avda 6 de Agosto 2170, Casilla 13383, La Paz; tel. (2) 235-9297; fax (2) 235-9298; internet www.umsanet.edu.bo; f. 1980; educational programmes; stations in Oruro, Cochabamba, Potosí, Sucre, Tarija, Beni and Santa Cruz; Dir Lic. ROBERTO CUEVAS RAMÍREZ.

Unitel (Canal 9): Km 5, Carretera antigua a Cochabamba, Santa Cruz; tel. (3) 352-7686; fax (3) 352-7688; e-mail webmaster@unitel.com.bo; internet www.unitel.tv; f. 1997; privately owned television network; Gen. Man. YAMILE IBAÑEZ CORREA.

Finance

(cap. = capital; res = reserves; dep. = deposits; m. = million; br(s) = branch(es); amounts are in bolivianos, unless otherwise stated)

BANKING

Supervisory Authority

Superintendencia de Bancos y Entidades Financieras: Plaza Isabel la Católica 2507, Casilla 447, La Paz; tel. (2) 243-1919; fax (2) 243-0028; e-mail sbef@sbef.gov.bo; internet www.sbef.gov.bo; f. 1928; Supt Lic. RÁUL MARCELO ZABALAGA ESTRADA.

Central Bank

Banco Central de Bolivia: Avda Ayacucho, esq. Mercado, Casilla 3118, La Paz; tel. (2) 237-4151; fax (2) 239-2398; e-mail sysweb@mail.bcb.gov.bo; internet www.bcb.gov.bo; f. 1911 as Banco de la Nación Boliviana; name changed as above in 1928; bank of issue; cap. 515.8m., res 8,064.4m., dep. 17,717.7m. (Dec. 2006); Pres. Lic. JUAN ANTONIO MORALES ANAYA; Gen. Man. Lic. JAIME VALENCIA.

Commercial Banks

Banco Bisa SA: Avda 16 de Julio 1628, Casilla 1290, La Paz; tel. (2) 231-7272; fax (2) 239-0033; e-mail bancobisa@grupobisa.com; internet www.bisa.com; f. 1963; cap. 479.7m., res 121.9m., dep. 4,192.6m. (Dec. 2006); Pres., CEO and Chair. Ing. JULIO LEÓN PRADO.

Banco de Crédito de Bolivia, SA: Calle Colón, esq. Mercado 1308, Casilla 907, La Paz; tel. (2) 233-0444; fax (2) 231-9163; e-mail mpaz@bancred.com.bo; internet www.bancodecredito.com.bo; f. 1993 as Banco Popular del Perú, SA; name changed as above 1994; owned by Banco de Crédito del Perú; cap. 315.5m., res 132.1m., dep. 4,447.8m. (Dec. 2006); Chair. DIONISIO ROMERO SEMINARIO; Gen. Man. GIANFRANCO FERRARI DE LAS CASAS; 7 brs.

Banco Económico SA-SCZ: Calle Ayacucho 166, Casilla 5603, Santa Cruz; tel. (3) 336-1177; fax (3) 336-1184; e-mail baneco@baneco.com.bo; internet www.baneco.com.bo; f. 1990; dep. US $244.9m., cap. US $24.4m., total assets US $269.3m. (Dec. 2006); Pres. IVO MATEO KULJIS FÜCHTNER; 14 brs.

Banco Ganadero SA-Santa Cruz: Calle 24 de Setiembre 110, Casilla 4492, Santa Cruz; tel. (3) 336-1616; fax (3) 333-2567; e-mail pcaceres@bancoganadero.co.bo; internet www.bancoganadero.com.bo; f. 1994; cap. 137.4m., res 1.4m., total assets 2,057.6m. (Dec. 2006); Pres. FERNANDO MONASTERIO NIEME; Gen. Man. RONALD GUTIÉRREZ LÓPEZ.

Banco Mercantil, SA: Calle Ayacucho 277, Casilla 423, La Paz; tel. (2) 240-9040; fax (2) 240-9158; e-mail aaguilar@bancomercantil.com.bo; internet www.bancomercantil.com.bo; f. 1905; cap. 394.2m., res 45.4m., dep. 3,884.9m. (Dec. 2005); Exec. Vice-Pres. JUAN CARLOS SALAUES ALMAREZ; Chair. EMILIO UNZUETA ZEGARRA; 37 brs.

Banco Nacional de Bolivia: Avda Camacho, esq. Colón 1312, Casilla 360, La Paz; tel. (2) 233-5353; fax (2) 231-0695; e-mail info@bnb.com.bo; internet www.bnb.com; f. 1871; cap. 261.0m., res 74.5m., dep. 4,845.5m. (Dec. 2005); Pres. GONZALO ARGANDOÑA; Gen. Man. PABLO BEDOYA; 9 brs.

Banco Santa Cruz, SA: Calle Junín 154, Casilla 865, Santa Cruz; tel. (3) 336-9911; fax (3) 335-0114; e-mail general@mail.bsc.com.bo; internet www.bsc.com.bo; f. 1965; 96% owned by Santander Central Hispano (Spain); Gen. Man. LISARDO PELÁEZ ACERO; 19 brs.

Banco Solidario, SA (BancoSol): Calle Nicolás Acosta, Casilla 13176, La Paz; tel. (2) 248-6563; fax (2) 248-6533; e-mail info@bancosol.com.bo; internet www.bancosol.com.bo; f. 1992; cap. 112.9m., res 13.8m., total assets 165.0m. (Dec. 2006); Pres. HERBERT MÜLLER COSTAS; Gen. Man. KURT KÖNIGSFEST.

Banco Unión, SA: Calle Libertad 156, Casilla 4057, Santa Cruz; tel. (3) 336-6869; fax (3) 334-0684; e-mail info@bancounion.com.bo; internet www.bancounion.com.bo; f. 1982; cap. 132.9m., res 5.3m., dep. 2,057.3m. (Dec. 2006); Pres. and Chair. JOSÉ ANTONIO CRIALES ESTRUGO; Gen. Man. RICARDO LINALE URIOSTE; 7 brs.

Banking Association

Asociación de Bancos Privados de Bolivia (ASOBAN): Edif. Cámara Nacional de Comercio, 15°, Avda Mariscal Santa Cruz, esq. Colombia 1392, Casilla 5822, La Paz; tel. (2) 237-6164; fax (2) 239-1093; e-mail info@asoban.bo; internet www.asoban.bo; f. 1957; Pres. EMILIO UNZUETA ZEGARRA; Vice-Pres PABLO BEDOYA, FRANCISCO MONASTERIOS; 18 mems.

STOCK EXCHANGE

Supervisory Authorities

Superintendencia de Pensiones, Valores y Seguros: Calle Reyes Ortiz, esq. Federico Zuazo, Edif. Torres Gundlach Este, 4°, Casilla 6118, La Paz; tel. (2) 233-1212; fax (2) 233-0001; e-mail spvs@spvs.gov.bo; internet www.spvs.gov.bo; Supt OSVALDO ANTONIO JAUREGUI CLAURE (acting).

Bolsa Boliviana de Valores SA: Edif. Zambrana, planta baja, Calle Montevideo 142, Casilla 12521, La Paz; tel. (2) 244-3232; fax (2) 244-2308; e-mail info@bolsa-valores-bolivia.com; internet www.bolsa-valores-bolivia.com; f. 1989; Gen. Man. Lic. ARMANDO ALVAREZ ARNAL.

INSURANCE

Supervisory Authority

Superintendencia de Pensiones, Valores y Seguros: see Stock Exchange—Supervisory Authorities.

Major Companies

Adriatica Seguros y Reaseguros, SA: Calle Libertad, esq. Cañoto 879, Casilla 1515, Santa Cruz; tel. (3) 336-6667; fax (3) 336-0600; e-mail adriaticasc@adriatica.com.bo; f. 1995; Pres. ANTONIO OLEA BAUDOIN.

Alianza, Cía de Seguros y Reaseguros, SA: Avda 20 de Octubre 2680, esq. Campos, Zona San Jorge, Casilla 1043, La Paz; tel. (2) 243-2121; fax (2) 243-2713; e-mail info@alianzaseguros.com; internet www.alianza.com.bo; f. 1991; Pres. JUAN MANUEL PEÑA ROCA.

Alianza Vida Seguros y Reaseguros, SA: Avda Viedma 19, Casilla 7181, Santa Cruz; tel. (3) 337-5656; fax (3) 337-5666; e-mail alejandroy@alianzaseguros.com; internet www.alianza.com.bo; f. 1999; Pres. RAÚL ADLER K.; Gen. Man. ALEJANDRO YBARRA CARRASCO.

Bisa Seguros y Reaseguros, SA: Edif. San Pablo, 13°, Avda 16 de Julio 1479, Casilla 3669, La Paz; tel. (2) 235-2123; fax (2) 239-2500; e-mail bisaseguros@grupobisa.com; internet www.bisaseguros.com; f. 1991; part of Grupo Bisa; Exec. Vice-Pres. ALEJANDRO MACLEAN CÉSPEDES.

La Boliviana Ciacruz de Seguros y Reaseguros, SA: Calle Colón, esq. Mercado 288, Casilla 628, La Paz; tel. (2) 220-3131; fax (2) 220-4087; e-mail rodrigo.bedoya@zurich.com; internet www.boliviana-ciacruz.com; f. 1946; owned by Zurich Bolivia group; all classes; Pres. GONZALO BEDOYA HERRERA; Gen. Man. RODRIGO BEDOYA DIEZ DE MEDINA.

Compañía de Seguros y Reaseguros Fortaleza, SA: Avda Virgen de Cotoca 2080, Casilla 1366, Santa Cruz; tel. and fax (3) 348-7273; e-mail nhinojosa@grupofortaleza.com.bo; internet www.grupofortaleza.com.bo; Pres. GUIDO HINOJOSA; Gen. Man. MARTHA O. LUCCA SUÁREZ.

Credinform International SA de Seguros: Edif. Credinform, Calle Potosí, esq. Ayacucho 1220, Casilla 1724, La Paz; tel. (2) 231-5566; fax (2) 220-3917; e-mail credinform@credinformsa.com; internet www.credinformsa.com; f. 1954; all classes; Pres. Dr ROBÍN BARRAGÁN PELÁEZ; Gen. Man. MIGUEL ANGEL BARRAGÁN IBARGÜEN.

International Health Insurance danmark Bolivia, SA: Edif. Tacuaral Equipetrol, Of. 203, Avda San Martín 1800, Santa Cruz; tel. (3) 341-2842; fax (3) 341-2832; e-mail bolivia@ihi.com; internet bolivia.ihi.com; travel and health insurance; Pres. PER BAY JØRGENSEN.

Nacional Vida Seguros de Personas, SA: Avda Monseñor Rivero 223, esq. Asunción, Santa Cruz; tel. (3) 371-6262; fax (3) 333-7969; e-mail nacionalvida@nacionalvida.com.bo; internet www.nacionalvida.com.bo; f. 1999; Pres. JUAN CARLOS ANTELO SALMÓN; Gen. Man. JOSÉ LUIS CAMACHO MISERENDINO.

Seguros y Reaseguros Generales 24 de Septiembre, SA: Avda Ejército Nacional 487, Santa Cruz; tel. and fax (3) 354-8484; e-mail seguros@caoba.entelnet.com.bo; f. 2001; Pres. Col ROBERTO FORONDA; Gen. Man. JOSEFINA SOLIZ DE FORONDA.

Seguros Illimani, SA: Edif. Mariscal de Ayacucho, 10°, Calle Loayza 233, Casilla 133, La Paz; tel. (2) 220-3040; fax (2) 239-1149; e-mail informaciones@segurosillimani.com; internet www.segurosillimani.com; f. 1979; all classes; Pres. FERNANDO ARCE GRANDCHANT.

BOLIVIA
Directory

La Vitalicia: Edif. Hoy, Avda 6 de Agosto 2860, Casilla 8424, La Paz; tel. (2) 212-5355; fax (2) 211-3480; e-mail aibanez@grupobisa.com; internet www.lavitaliciaseguros.com; f. 1988; part of Grupo Bisa; Pres. RUDY RIVERA DURÁN; Exec. Sec. EUGENIO LUCERO DEGLANE.

Insurance Association

Asociación Boliviana de Aseguradores: Edif. Castilla, 5°, Of. 510, Calle Loayza, esq. Mercado 250, Casilla 4804, La Paz; tel. (2) 220-1014; fax (2) 220-1088; e-mail aba@ababolivia.org; internet www.ababolivia.org; f. 1962; Pres. ALEJANDRO MACLEAN CÉSPEDES; Gen. Man. CARLOS BAUDOIN DÁVALOS.

Trade and Industry

GOVERNMENT AGENCIES

Centro de Promoción Bolivia (CEPROBOL): Calle Mercado 1328, 18°, La Paz; tel. (2) 233-6836; fax (2) 233-6996; e-mail ceprobol@ceprobol.gov.bo; internet www.ceprobol.gov.bo; promotes exports and foreign investment; Exec. Dir MARTÍN LÓPEZ.

Sistema de Regulación Sectorial (SIRESE): Edif. Capitán Ravelo, 8°, Calle Capitán Ravelo 2101, La Paz; tel. (2) 244-4545; fax (2) 244-4017; e-mail sg@sirese.gov.bo; internet www.sirese.gov.bo; f. 1994; regulatory body for the formerly state-owned companies and utilities; oversees the general co-ordination and growth of the regulatory system and the work of its Superintendencies of Electricity, Hydrocarbons, Telecommunications, Transport and Water; Supt-Gen. REYNALDO IRIGOYEN CASTRO.

DEVELOPMENT ORGANIZATIONS

Centro de Estudios para el Desarrollo Laboral y Agrario (CEDLA): Avda Jaimes Freyre 2940, esq. Muñoz Cornejo, Casilla 8630, La Paz; tel. (2) 241-3175; fax (2) 241-4625; e-mail cedla@cedla.org; internet www.cedla.org; f. 1985; agrarian and labour development; Exec. Dir CARLOS ARZE.

Consejo Nacional de Planificación (CONEPLAN): Edif. Banco Central de Bolivia, 26°, Calle Mercado, esq. Ayacucho, Casilla 3118, La Paz; tel. (2) 237-4151; fax (2) 235-3840; e-mail claves@mail.bcb.gov.bo; f. 1985.

Corporación de las Fuerzas Armadas para el Desarrollo Nacional (COFADENA): Avda 6 de Agosto 2649, Casilla 1015, La Paz; tel. (2) 237-7305; fax (2) 236-0900; e-mail gerencia_@acelerate.com; internet www.cofadena.org.bo; f. 1972; industrial, agricultural and mining holding co and devt org. owned by the Bolivian armed forces; Gen. Man. Col JOSÉ EDGAR BLACUTT BARRÓN.

Corporación Regional de Desarrollo de La Paz (CORDEPAZ): Avda Arce 2529, Edif. Santa Isabel, Casilla 6102, La Paz; tel. (2) 243-0313; fax (2) 243-2152; f. 1972; decentralized govt institution to foster the devt of the La Paz area; Pres. Lic. RICARDO PAZ BALLIVIÁN; Gen. Man. Ing. JUAN G. CARRASCO R.

Fondo Nacional de Desarrollo Regional (FNDR): La Paz; e-mail evalda@fndr.gov.bo; internet www.fndr.gov.bo; f. 1987; promotes local and regional devt, offering financing and support; assumed temporary responsibility for water supply in La Paz in Jan. 2007 following annulment of contracts with private water cos; Exec. Dir EDSON VALDA.

CHAMBERS OF COMMERCE

Cámara de Comercio e Industria de Pando: Casilla 227, Cobija; tel. (3) 842-3139; fax (3) 842-2291; e-mail cicpando@entelnet.bo; Pres. NEMESIO RAMÍREZ.

Cámara de Comercio e Industria de Potosí: Calle Matos 12, Casilla 159, Potosí; tel. and fax (2) 622-2641; e-mail camarap@cotapnet.com.bo; Pres. ISABEL SERRANO DE FERNÁNDEZ.

Cámara de Comercio de Oruro: Pasaje Guachalla s/n, Casilla 148, Oruro; tel. and fax (2) 525-0606; e-mail camacor@coteor.net.bo; f. 1895; Pres. ALVARO CORNEJO GAZCÓN; Gen. Man. LUIS CAMACHO VARGAS.

Cámara de Comercio y Servicios de Cochabamba: Calle Sucre E-0336, Casilla 493, Cochabamba; tel. (4) 425-7715; fax (4) 425-7717; e-mail gerencia@cadeco.org; internet www.cadeco.org; f. 1922; Pres. ORLANDO ORTIZ.

Cámara Departamental de Comercio de Beni: Casilla 96, Trinidad; tel. (3) 462-2365; fax (3) 462-1400; Pres. EDUARDO AVILA ALVERDI; Sec.-Gen. JOSÉ MAMERTO DURÁN.

Cámara Departamental de Industria y Comercio de Santa Cruz: Calle Suárez de Figueroa 127, esq. Saavedra, 3°, Casilla 180, Santa Cruz; tel. (3) 333-4555; fax (3) 334-2353; e-mail cainco@cainco.org.bo; internet www.cainco.org.bo; f. 1915; Pres. GABRIEL DABDOUB; Gen. Man. Lic. OSCAR ORTIZ ANTELO.

Cámara Departamental de Industria y Comercio de Tarija: Avda Bolívar 0413, esq. General Trigo, 1°, Casilla 74, Tarija; tel. and fax (6) 642-2737; e-mail caincotar@cosett.com.bo; Pres. JOSÉ MOLINA MITRU.

Cámara de Exportadores de La Paz (CAMEX): Avda Arce 2021 esq. Goitia, Casilla 789, La Paz; tel. (2) 244-4310; fax (2) 244-2842; e-mail camex@entelnet.bo; Pres. EDUARDO BRACAMONTE.

Cámara de Exportadores de Santa Cruz (CADEX): Avda Velarde 131, Santa Cruz; tel. (3) 336-2030; fax (3) 332-1509; e-mail cadex@cadex.org; internet www.cadex.org; f. 1986; Gen. Man. OSWALDO BARRIGA KARLBAUM.

Cámara de Industria y Comercio de Chuquisaca: Calle España 64, Casilla 33, Sucre; tel. (4) 645-1194; fax (4) 645-1850; f. 1923; Pres. MARCELO CUELLAR.

Cámara de Industria, Comercio y Servicios de Santa Cruz: Torre Cainco, Avda Las Américas, 7°, Casilla 180, Santa Cruz; tel. (3) 333-4555; fax (3) 334-2353; e-mail cainco@cainco.org.bo; internet www.cainco.org.bo; f. 1915.

Cámara Nacional de Comercio: Edif. Cámara Nacional de Comercio, Avda Mariscal Santa Cruz 1392, 1° y 2°, Casilla 7, La Paz; tel. (2) 237-8606; fax (2) 239-1004; e-mail cnc@boliviacomercio.org.bo; internet www.boliviacomercio.org.bo; f. 1890; 30 brs and special brs; Pres. GUILLERMO MORALES FERNÁNDEZ; Gen. Man. JOSÉ LUIS VALENCIA AQUINO.

Cámara Nacional de Exportadores (CANEB): Avda Arce 2017, esq. Goitia, Casilla 12145, La Paz; tel. (2) 234-1220; fax (2) 236-1491; e-mail caneb@entelnet.bo; f. 1970; Pres. LUIS NEMTALA YAMIN; Gen. Man. JORGE ADRIAZOLA REIMERS.

Cámara Nacional de Industrias de Bolivia: Edif. Cámara Nacional de Comercio, 14°, Avda Mariscal Santa Cruz 1392, Casilla 611, La Paz; tel. (2) 237-4477; fax (2) 236-2766; e-mail cni@entelnet.bo; internet www.bolivia-industry.com; f. 1937; eight depts throughout Bolivia; Pres. EDUARDO PEINADO T.; Gen. Man. GERARDO VELASCO T.

INDUSTRIAL AND TRADE ASSOCIATIONS

Asociación Nacional de Exportadores de Café (ANDEC): Calle Nicaragua 1638, Casilla 9770, La Paz; tel. (2) 224-4290; fax (2) 224-4561; e-mail andec@caoba.entelnet.bo; controls the export, quality and marketing of coffee producers; Exec. Pres. CARMEN DONOSO DE ARAMAYO.

Cámara Agropecuaria del Oriente: 3 anillo interno zona Oeste, Casilla 116, Santa Cruz; tel. (3) 352-2200; fax (3) 352-2621; e-mail caosrz@bibosi.scz.entelnet.bo; internet www.cao-bo.org; f. 1964; agriculture and livestock asscn for eastern Bolivia; Pres. RICARDO FRERKING ORTIZ; Gen. Man. WALTER NÚÑEZ RODRÍGUEZ.

Cámara Agropecuaria de La Paz: Avda 16 de Julio 1525, Casilla 12521, La Paz; tel. (2) 239-2911; fax (2) 235-2308; Pres. ALBERTO DE OLIVA MAYA; Gen. Man. JUAN CARLOS ZAMORANO.

Cámara Boliviana de Hidrocarburos: Radial 17 1/2 y Sexto Anillo, Santa Cruz; tel. (3) 353-8799; fax (3) 357-7868; e-mail cbh@cbh.org.bo; internet www.cbh.org.bo; f. 1986; Gen. Man. RAÚL KIEFFER G.

Cámara Departamental de Minería: Edif. Comboni Center, 5°, Calle Jordán 522, esq. San Martín, La Paz; tel. (2) 425-5263; e-mail camaramineria@hotmail.com; f. 1947; mining institute; Pres. FRANCISCO JAVIER BELLOTT; Sec.-Gen. FERNANDO MORALES.

Cámara Forestal de Bolivia: Prolongación Manuel Ignacio Salvatierra 1055, Casilla 346, Santa Cruz; tel. (3) 333-2699; fax (3) 333-1456; e-mail camaraforestal@cfb.org.bo; internet www.cfb.org.bo; f. 1969; represents the interests of the Bolivian timber industry; Pres. JUAN ABUAWAD CHAHUÁN; Gen. Man. Lic. ARTURO BOWLES OLHAGARAY.

Cámara Nacional de Industrias: Edif. Cámara Nacional de Comercio, 14°, Avda Mariscal Santa Cruz 1392, Casilla 611, La Paz; tel. (2) 237-4477; fax (2) 236-2766; e-mail cni@entelnel.bo; internet www.bolivia-industry.com; f. 1931; Pres. ROBERTO MUSTAFÁ; Man. GERARDO VELASCO T.

Comité Boliviano de Productores de Antimonio: Edif. El Condor, Batallón Colorados 1404, 14°, Casilla 14451, La Paz; tel. (2) 244-2140; fax (2) 244-1653; f. 1978; controls the marketing, pricing and promotion policies of the antimony industry; Pres. MARIO MARISCAL MORALES; Sec.-Gen. Dr ALCIDES RODRÍGUEZ J.

Comité Boliviano del Café (COBOLCA): Calle Nicaragua 1638, Casilla 9770, La Paz; tel. (2) 222-3883; fax (2) 224-4591; e-mail cobolca@ceibo.entelnet.bo; controls the export, quality, marketing and growing policies of the coffee industry; Gen. Man. MAURICIO VILLARROEL.

EMPLOYERS' ASSOCIATIONS

Asociación Nacional de Mineros Medianos: Calle Pedro Salazar 600, esq. Presbítero Medina, Casilla 6190, La Paz; tel. and fax (2) 241-

BOLIVIA
Directory

4123; e-mail anmm@caoba.entelnet.bo; f. 1939; asscn of 14 private medium-sized mining cos; Pres. Dr OSCAR BONIFAZ G.; Sec.-Gen. Dr HUGO URIONA.

Confederación de Empresarios Privados de Bolivia (CEPB): Calle Méndez Arcos 117, Plaza España, Zona Sopacachi, Casilla 4239, La Paz; tel. (2) 242-0999; fax (2) 242-1272; e-mail cepb@cepb.org.bo; internet www.cepb.org.bo; largest national employers' org.; Pres. ROBERTO MUSTAFÁ SCHNOR; Dir of Social and Institutional Affairs Lic. MAX GASTELÚ ZACONETA.

There are also employers' federations in Santa Cruz, Cochabamba, Oruro, Potosí, Beni and Tarija.

UTILITIES
Electricity

Superintendencia de Electricidad: Avda 16 de Julio 1571, La Paz; tel. (2) 231-2401; fax (2) 231-2393; e-mail webmaster@superele.gov.bo; internet www.superele.gov.bo; f. 1994; regulates the electricity sector; Supt ALEJANDRO NOWOTNY VERA; Gen. Sec. ROLANDO LÓPEZ.

Alternative Energy Systems Ltd (Talleres AES): Los Cafetales 2753, Cochabamba; tel. and fax (4) 445-3973; e-mail aesbol@freeyellow.com; internet aesbol.freeyellow.com; f. 1986; specialist manufacturers of alternative energy products including small water turbines, equipment for small hydro plants and pumping stations; Gen. Man. MIGUEL ALANDIA.

Compañía Boliviana de Energía Eléctrica, SA (COBEE): Avda Hernando Siles 5635, Casilla 353, La Paz; tel. (2) 278-2474; fax (2) 278-5920; e-mail cobee@cobee.com; internet www.cobee.com; f. 1925; largest private power producer and distributor, serving the areas of La Paz and Oruro; generated 27.2% of Bolivia's total electricity output in 2002; mainly hydroelectric; Pres. and Gen. Man. JULIO LEMAITRE SOLARES.

Compañía Eléctrica Central Bulo Bulo, SA (CECBB): Avda San Martín 1700, Equipetrol Norte, 6°, Santa Cruz; tel. (3) 346-0314; fax (3) 349-7800; e-mail carlosg@ipolbolivia.com.bo; f. 1999; generator co; 101.2 MW capacity in 2002; Gen. Man. RAMÓN BASCOPE PARADA.

Compañía Eléctrica Sucre, SA (CESSA): Calle Ayacucho 254, Sucre; tel. (4) 645-3126; fax (4) 646-0292; e-mail cessasucre@entelnet.bo; electricity distributor; Gen. Man. Ing. JOSÉ ANAVE LEÓN.

Cooperativa Rural de Electrificación Ltda (CRE): Avda Busch, esq. Honduras, Santa Cruz; tel. (3) 336-7777; fax (3) 336-9391; e-mail webmaster@cre.com.bo; internet www.cre.com.bo; electricity distributor; Gen. Man. CARMELO PAZ DURÁN; Sec.-Gen. JOSÉ ERNESTO ZAMBRANA.

Electropaz: Avda Illimani 1973, Miraflores, La Paz; tel. (2) 222-2200; fax (2) 222-3756; e-mail cpacheco@electropaz.com.bo; internet www.electropaz.com.bo; distributor serving La Paz area; Gen. Man. Ing. MAURICIO VALDEZ CÁRDENAS.

Empresa Corani, SA: Avda Oquendo 654, Edif. Las Torres Soler I, 9°, Cochabamba; tel. (4) 423-5700; fax (4) 425-9148; e-mail corani@corani.com; internet www.corani.com; generator co; 126 MW capacity in 2002; Pres. FREDERICK P. RENNER.

Empresa Eléctrica Valle Hermoso, SA (EVH): Calle Tarija 1425, esq. Adela Zamudio, Cala Cala, Cochabamba; tel. (4) 428-6600; fax (4) 428-6838; e-mail eballadares@evh.com.bo; internet www.evh.com.bo; generator co; 347.41 MW capacity in 2002; Pres. ENRIQUE HERRERA SORIA.

Empresa de Generación Guaracachi, SA (EGSA): Avda Brasil y Tercer Anillo Interno s/n, Santa Cruz; tel. (3) 346-0314; fax (3) 346-5888; e-mail central@egsa-bol.com; generator co; 347.41 MW capacity in 2002; Gen. Man. Ing. MAURICIO PERÓ DIEZ DE MEDINA.

Empresa de Luz y Fuerza Eléctrica Cochabamba, SA (ELFEC): Avda Heroínas 0686, Cochabamba; tel. (4) 425-9410; fax (4) 425-9427; e-mail sugerencias@elfec.com; internet www.elfec.com; electricty distributor; Gen. Man. Ing. JOSÉ D. TRONCOSO ESPARZA.

Empresa Nacional de Electricidad, SA (ENDE): Avda Ballivián 503, esq. México, 7°, Casilla Correo 565, Cochabamba; tel. (4) 452-0322; fax (4) 452-0318; f. 1962; former state electricity co; privatized under the Govt's capitalization programme in 1995 and divided into three arms concerned with generation, transmission and distribution, respectively; Gen. Man. Dr ENRIQUE GÓMEZ D'ANGELO.

Hidroeléctrica Boliviana, SA: Avda Fuerza Naval 22, La Paz; tel. (2) 277-0765; fax (2) 277-0933; e-mail hb@hidrobol.com; internet www.hidrobol.com; Gen. Man. Ing. ANGEL ZANNIER CLAROS.

Gas

Numerous distributors of natural gas exist throughout the country, many of which are owned by the petroleum distributor, Yacimientos Petrolíferos Fiscales Bolivianos (YPFB).

Yacimientos Petrolíferos Fiscales Bolivianos (YPFB): Calle Bueno 185, 6°, Casilla 401, La Paz; tel. (2) 235-6540; fax (2) 239-2596; e-mail webmaster@ypfb.gov.bo; internet www.ypfb.gov.bo; f. 1936; exploration, drilling, production, refining, transportation and distribution of petroleum; partially privatized in 1996; Pres. SANTOS RAMÍREZ; 4,900 employees.

Water

Superintendencia de Saneamiento Básico (SISAB): Edif. Cámara de Comercio, Avda Mariscal Santa Cruz 1392, Casilla 4245, La Paz; tel. (2) 231-0801; fax (2) 231-0554; e-mail contactos@sisab.gov.bo; f. 1999; regulates urban water supplies and grants service concessions and licences; Govt announced plans to replace SISAB with a decentralized regulatory authority in 2008/09; Supt ALVARO CAMACHO GARNICA.

Empresa Pública Social de Agua y Saneamiento (EPSAS): Villa Fátima, Avda de las Américas 705, Casilla 9359, La Paz; tel. (2) 221-0295; fax (2) 221-2454; internet www.fndr.gov.bo; f. 2007; state-owned water and sewerage provider in La Paz and El Alto; Gen. Man. VÍCTOR RICO.

CO-OPERATIVE

Instituto Nacional de Co-operativas (INALCO): Edif. Lotería Nacional, 4°, Avda Mariscal Santa Cruz y Cochabamba, La Paz; tel. (2) 237-4366; fax (2) 237-2104; e-mail inalcolp@ceibo.entelnet.bo; f. 1974; Pres. DAVID AYAVIRI.

TRADE UNIONS

Central Obrera Boliviana (COB): Edif. COB, Calle Pisagua 618, Casilla 6552, La Paz; tel. (2) 352-426; fax (2) 281-201; e-mail postmast@cob-bolivia.org; f. 1952; main union confederation; 800,000 mems; Exec. Sec. JAIME SOLARES QUINTANILLA; Pres. PEDRO CRUZ; Sec.-Gen. LUIS CHOQUETICLLA VÉLIZ.

Affiliated unions:

Central Obrera Departamental de La Paz: Estación Central 284, La Paz; tel. (2) 235-2898; Exec. Sec. GENARO TORRICO.

Confederación Sindical Unica de los Trabajadores Campesinos de Bolivia (CSUTCB): CP 11589, La Paz; tel. (2) 236-4975; f. 1979; peasant farmers' union; Sec.-Gen. FELIPE QUISPE HUANCA.

Federación de Empleados de Industria Fabril: Edif. Fabril, 5°, Plaza de San Francisco, La Paz; tel. (2) 240-6799; fax (2) 240-7044; Exec. Sec. ALEX GÁLVEZ.

Federación Sindical de Trabajadores Mineros de Bolivia (FSTMB): Plaza Venezuela 1470, Casilla 14565, La Paz; tel. (2) 235-9656; fax (2) 248-4948; f. 1944; mineworkers' union; Leader MIGUEL ZUBIETA; Gen. Sec. EDGAR RAMÍREZ SANTIESTÉBAN; 27,000 mems.

Federación Sindical de Trabajadores Petroleros de Bolivia: Calle México 1504, La Paz; tel. (2) 235-1748; Exec. Sec. NEFTALÍ MENDOZA DURÁN.

Central Obrera Regional (COR): El Alto; Exec. Sec. EDGAR PATANA.

Confederación General de Trabajadores Fabriles de Bolivia (CGTFB): Avda Armentia 452, Casilla 21590, La Paz; tel. (2) 237-1603; fax (2) 232-4302; e-mail dirabc@bo.net; f. 1951; manufacturing workers' union; Exec. Sec. ANGEL ASTURIZAGA; Gen. Sec. ROBERTO ENCINAS.

Transport
RAILWAYS

Empresa Nacional de Ferrocarriles (ENFE): Estación Central de Ferrocarriles, Plaza Zalles, Casilla 428, La Paz; tel. (2) 232-7401; fax (2) 239-2677; f. 1964; privatized in 1995; administers most of the railways in Bolivia; holding co for unauctioned former state assets; total networks: 3,608 km (1999); Andina network: 2,274 km; Oriental (Eastern) network: 1,424 km; Pres. J. L. LANDÍVAR.

Empresa Ferrocarril Andino, SA: Casilla 4350, La Paz; tel. and fax (2) 239-145; e-mail efasa@fca.com.bo; internet www.fca.com.bo; f. 1996; Pres. MIGUEL SEPÚLVEDA C.

Empresa Ferroviaria Oriental, SA (FCOSA): Avda Montes Final s/n, Casilla 108, Santa Cruz; tel. (3) 346-3900; fax (3) 346-3920; e-mail fcosa@fcosa.com; f. 1996; 50.0% owned by Genesee & Wyoming Inc (USA); Gen. Man. JAIME VALENCIA.

There are plans to construct a railway line with Brazilian assistance, to link Cochabamba and Santa Cruz. Plans were also mooted for the construction of a rail link between Santa Cruz and Mutún on the border with Brazil.

ROADS

In 2004 Bolivia had some 60,282 km of roads, of which an estimated 3,979 km (6.6%) were paved. Almost the entire road network is

BOLIVIA

concentrated in the Altiplano region and the Andes valleys. A 560-km highway runs from Santa Cruz to Cochabamba, serving a colonization scheme on virgin lands around Santa Cruz. The Pan-American Highway, linking Argentina and Peru, crosses Bolivia from south to north-west. In 1997 the Government announced the construction of 1,844 km of new roads in the hope of improving Bolivia's connections with neighbouring countries.

INLAND WATERWAYS

By agreement with Paraguay in 1938 (confirmed in 1939), Bolivia has an outlet on the River Paraguay. This arrangement, together with navigation rights on the Paraná, gives Bolivia access to the River Plate and the sea. The River Paraguay is navigable for vessels of 12-ft draught for 288 km beyond Asunción, in Paraguay, and for smaller boats another 960 km to Corumbá in Brazil. In late 1994 plans were finalized to widen and deepen the River Paraguay, providing a waterway from Bolivia to the Atlantic coast in Uruguay. However, work on the project was delayed, owing largely to environmental concerns.

In 1974 Bolivia was granted duty-free access to the Brazilian coastal ports of Belém and Santos and the inland ports of Corumbá and Port Velho. In 1976 Argentina granted Bolivia free-port facilities at Rosario on the River Paraná. In 1992 an agreement was signed with Peru, granting Bolivia access to (and the use, without customs formalities, of) the Pacific port of Ilo. Most of Bolivia's foreign trade is handled through the ports of Matarani (Peru), Antofagasta and Arica (Chile), Rosario and Buenos Aires (Argentina) and Santos (Brazil). An agreement between Bolivia and Chile to reform Bolivia's access arrangements to the port of Arica came into effect in January 1996.

Bolivia has over 14,000 km of navigable rivers, which connect most of Bolivia with the Amazon basin.

Bolivian River Navigation Co: f. 1958; services from Puerto Suárez to Buenos Aires (Argentina).

CIVIL AVIATION

Bolivia has 30 airports, including the two international airports at La Paz (El Alto) and Santa Cruz (Viru-Viru).

Dirección General de Aeronaútica Civil: Avda Mariscal Santa Cruz 1278, Casilla 9360; La Paz; tel. (2) 237-4142; e-mail dgacbol@ceibo-entelnet.bo; internet www.dgac.gov.bo; f. 1947; Dir-Gen. JAVIER GARCÍA SORUCO.

AeroSur: Calle Colón y Avda Irala 616, Casilla 3104, Santa Cruz; tel. (3) 336-4446; fax (3) 333-0666; e-mail aerosur@aerosur.com; internet www.aerosur.com; f. 1992 by merger of existing charter cos following deregulation; privately owned; Pres. OSCAR ALCOCER; Gen. Man. FERNANDO PRUDENCIO.

Lloyd Aéreo Boliviano, SAM (LAB): Casilla 132, Aeropuerto 'Jorge Wilstermann', Cochabamba; tel. (4) 425-1270; fax (4) 425-0766; e-mail presidencia@labairlines.com.bo; internet www.labairlines.com.bo; f. 1925; privatized under the Govt's capitalization programme in 1995; jtly owned by Bolivian Govt (48%), and private interests (52%); operates a network of scheduled services to 12 cities within Bolivia and to 21 international destinations in South America, Central America and the USA; Pres. Ing. ERNESTO ASBÚN; Gen. Man. JOSÉ RODRÍGUEZ.

Transportes Aéreos Bolivianos (TAB): Casilla 12237, La Paz; tel. (2) 237-8325; fax (2) 235-9660; f. 1977; regional scheduled and charter cargo services; Gen. Man. LUIS GUERECA PADILLA; Chair. PETER MARLIN GURD.

Transportes Aéreos Militares: Avda Montes 738, La Paz; tel. (2) 237-9286; internal passenger and cargo services; Dir-Gen. REMBERTO DURÁN.

Tourism

Bolivia's tourist attractions include Lake Titicaca, at 3,810 m (12,500 ft) above sea-level, pre-Incan ruins at Tiwanaku, Chacaltaya in the Andes mountains, which has the highest ski-run in the world, and the UNESCO World Cultural Heritage Sites of Potosí and Sucre. In 2005 some 413,267 foreign visitors arrived at hotels in Bolivian regional capitals. In 2004 receipts from tourism totalled US $265m. Tourists come mainly from South American countries, the USA and Europe.

Asociación Boliviana de Agencias de Viajes y Turismo (ABAVYT): Calle Colón 161, 3°, Casilla 8737, La Paz; tel. (2) 239-2033; fax (2) 212-6793; e-mail abavyt@caoba.entelnet.bo; internet www.abavyt.org; f. 1984; Pres. EUGENIO MONROY VÉLEZ.

BOSNIA AND HERZEGOVINA

Introductory Survey

Location, Climate, Language, Religion, Flag, Capital

Bosnia and Herzegovina is situated in south-eastern Europe. It is bounded by Croatia to the north, west and south-west, by Serbia to the east and by Montenegro to the south-east. There is a short south-western coastline on the Adriatic Sea around the town of Neum, which borders an exclave of Croatia, including Dubrovnik, to the south-east, while Croatia proper lies to the north-west. Bosnia and Herzegovina is a largely mountainous territory with a continental climate and steady rainfall throughout the year; in areas nearer the coast, however, the climate is more Mediterranean. The official languages are Bosnian, Croatian and Serbian. Bosnian and Croatian are written in the Latin script, while Serbian has traditionally been written in the Cyrillic script, but is sometimes also written in the Latin script. The Muslims (Bosniaks), the majority of whom belong to the Sunni sect, are the largest religious grouping in Bosnia and Herzegovina, comprising 43.7% of the population in 1991. Religious affiliation is roughly equated with ethnicity, the Serbs (31.4% of the population) belonging to the Serbian Orthodox Church and the Croats (17.3%) being members of the Roman Catholic Church. The national flag (proportions 1 by 2) consists of two unequal vertical sections of blue, separated by a yellow triangle, which is bordered on the left by a diagonal line of nine white, five-pointed stars. The capital is Sarajevo.

Recent History

The provinces of Bosnia and Herzegovina formed part of the Turkish Osmanlı (Ottoman) Empire for almost 400 years, but, following the Congress of Berlin of 1878, were administered by the Habsburg Empire of Austria-Hungary, which formally annexed the territories in 1908. The population of the provinces was composed of a mixture of Orthodox Christian Serbs, Roman Catholic Croats and Muslims (also referred to, particularly from the early 1990s, as Bosniaks). Serbian expansionist aims caused tension from the late 19th century, and in 1914, following the assassination of the heir to the Habsburg throne by a Bosnian Serb extremist in Sarajevo, Austria-Hungary declared war on Serbia, thereby precipitating the First World War. On 4 December 1918 the Kingdom of Serbs, Croats and Slovenes was proclaimed, under the Serbian monarchy. Bitter disputes ensued between Serbs and Croats (see the chapter on Croatia), however, and in 1929 King Aleksandar imposed a dictatorship, formally renaming the country Yugoslavia ('land of the Southern Slavs') in October.

Although officially banned in 1921, the Communist Party of Yugoslavia (CPY) operated clandestinely, and in 1937 Josip Broz (Tito) became its General Secretary. During the Second World War (1939–45) intense fighting took place between Croats and Serbs in Bosnia and Herzegovina, which was incorporated into a fascist Independent State of Croatia in 1941. From 1943, however, Tito's communist-led Partisan movement dominated most of Bosnia and Herzegovina, which, after the war, became one of the six constituent republics of the Yugoslav federation. In the 1960s Tito sought to counter increasing tension between the three principal ethnic groups of the republic, as well as maintaining a balance of power between the various ethnic groups of the Socialist Federal Republic of Yugoslavia (SFRY—as the country was renamed in 1963). Slav Muslims were granted a distinct ethnic status, as a nation of Yugoslavia, prior to the 1971 census. In that year a collective state presidency was established for Bosnia and Herzegovina, with a regular rotation of posts.

Communal affiliation proved to be a decisive factor in the elections held to the republican legislature, the Skupština Republike Bosne i Hercegovine (Assembly of the Republic of Bosnia and Herzegovina), in November and December 1990. The ruling League of Communists of Bosnia and Herzegovina was ousted, and three main nationalist parties emerged as the largest parties in the Skupština: the principally Muslim Party of Democratic Action (PDA), with 86 seats; the Serbian Democratic Party (SDP), with 72 seats; and the Croatian Democratic Union of Bosnia and Herzegovina (CDU—BH), an affiliate of the ruling party of Croatia, with 44 seats. The three nationalist parties also took all seven seats on the directly elected collective Presidency and formed a coalition administration for the republic. On 20 December they announced that the leader of the PDA, Alija Izetbegović (who had been imprisoned in 1983–88 on charges of, *inter alia*, promoting Muslim nationalism), was to be President of the Presidency, while members of the CDU—BH and the SDP were to be President of the Executive Council (Prime Minister) and President of the Skupština, respectively.

In 1991 the politics of Bosnia and Herzegovina were increasingly dominated by the Serb–Croat conflict. Following the declarations of independence by Slovenia and Croatia in June, Serb-dominated territories in Bosnia and Herzegovina declared their intent to remain within the Yugoslav federation. On 16 September a 'Serb Autonomous Region' (SAR) of Bosnian Krajina, based in the north-western city of Banja Luka, was proclaimed; this SAR was formed on the basis of a Serb 'Community of Municipalities of Bosnian Krajina', which had been formed in April, and which had announced its unification with the neighbouring 'SAR of Krajina' in Croatia in June. Armed incidents contributed to the rising tension throughout mid-1991, and the formation of further SARs was proclaimed, amid accusations that Serb nationalist elements sought to establish a 'Greater Serbia', with the support of the Yugoslav People's Army (JNA). In October the JNA assumed effective control of the southern multi-ethnic city of Mostar, north-west of the predominantly Bosnian Serb 'Old' Herzegovina.

In early October 1991 both the republican Presidency (with the dissenting votes of the Bosnian Serb members) and the PDA proposed to the Skupština that the republic declare its independence. Later that month the Serb deputies rejected the resolution as a move towards secession from the SFRY, and subsequently withdrew from the chamber. On 15 October, however, the remaining parliamentarians approved a resolution declaring the sovereignty of Bosnia and Herzegovina. The SARs rejected the declaration of sovereignty and declared that, henceforth, only the federal laws and Constitution would apply on their territory. On 24 October the Serb deputies of the republican legislature announced the formation of a Serb Narodna skupština (National Assembly). On 9–10 November a referendum, organized by the Bosnian Serb Narodna skupština, indicated overwhelming support for remaining in a common Serb state. On 9 January 1992 the formation of a 'Serb Republic (Republika Srpska) of Bosnia and Herzegovina', comprising Serb-held areas of the republic (about 65% of the total area), was proclaimed, headed by Dr Radovan Karadžić, the leader of the SDP. The republican Government immediately declared this secessionist Serb Republic, which was based in Banja Luka, to be illegal; in August it was renamed 'Republika Srpska'. Meanwhile, in a republic-wide referendum on 29 February–1 March, boycotted by the majority of Bosnian Serbs, 99.4% of the participating 63% of the electorate expressed support for the independence of Bosnia and Herzegovina. Izetbegović immediately declared the republic's independence and omitted the word 'socialist' from the new state's official title.

Following the declaration of independence, renewed Serb–Muslim tension led to clashes in Sarajevo, the republican capital, and elsewhere. On 18 March 1992, following mediation by the European Community (EC, now European Union—EU, see p. 244), the leaders of the Serb, Croat and Muslim communities signed an agreement providing for the division of Bosnia and Herzegovina into three autonomous units. In April fighting between the JNA and Muslim and Croat forces intensified, particularly following the recognition of Bosnia and Herzegovina's independence by the EC and the USA on 7 April; Serbian troops besieged Sarajevo and launched frequent mortar attacks on the city from the surrounding mountains and hills. Meanwhile, Bosnian Serb fighters and irregular troops from Serbia conducted a campaign of 'ethnic cleansing' in the areas they controlled, initially in the east and north-west of Bosnia, with the intent of creating an ethnically homogenous territory. Izetbegović requested foreign military intervention to support the republican Government, but the UN, while deploying a UN Protection Force (UNPROFOR) in Croatia, decided against the deployment of a peace-keeping force in the republic under the prevailing conditions. On 20 May the Government of Bosnia and Herzegovina declared the JNA to be an 'occupying force' and announced the formation of a republican army. Two days later Bosnia and Herzegovina was admitted to the UN, concurrently with Croatia and Slovenia. On 30 May the UN imposed economic sanctions against the recently established Federal Republic of Yugoslavia (FRY—comprising Serbia and Montenegro), in response to its involvement in the conflict in Bosnia and Herzegovina. In early June, in an apparent effort to placate the UN, Serbian leaders in Belgrade (the FRY capital) ordered the Bosnian Serbs to end the siege of Sarajevo and to surrender Sarajevo airport to UN control.

The proclamation, on 3 July 1992, by Croats in Western Herzegovina and central Bosnia, of an autonomous 'Croat Community of Herzeg-Bosna', covering about 30% of the territory of Bosnia and Herzegovina and headed by Mate Boban, was immediately declared to be illegal by Izetbegović's Government. Despite their political differences, Izetbegović and President Franjo Tuđman of Croatia signed a co-operation agreement in late July. Under this accord, the Governments of Bosnia and Herzegovina and of Croatia formed a Joint Defence Committee in September, and repeated demands that the UN end an armaments embargo (which had been imposed on the SFRY in September 1991, and which was subsequently determined to apply to all regions thereof, following the disintegration of the SFRY). However, hostilities erupted between Croats and Muslims in October, after several months of increasing tensions, and the towns of Mostar, Novi Travnik and Vitez were captured by Croat forces (the HVO). Mostar was subsequently proclaimed capital of Herzeg-Bosna, with the city effectively being split into Croat- and Muslim-controlled zones; the Serb population of the city, which had accounted for about 20% of the population prior to the conflict, had largely fled. In November the Croatian Government admitted for the first time that Croatian regular army units had been deployed in Bosnia and Herzegovina, and accordingly became a signatory to the latest cease-fire agreement in Bosnia and Herzegovina. In early December the UN Human Rights Commission declared that Bosnian Serbs were largely responsible for violations of human rights in Bosnia and Herzegovina. (Television broadcasts of concentration camps in Serb-held areas of the Bosnian Krajina, in which more than 1,500 Bosniaks were reported to have been killed, had provoked international outrage in August 1992.) Later in December the UN Security Council unanimously adopted a resolution condemning the atrocities, particularly the widespread rape of Bosniak women, and demanding access to all Serb detention camps.

In January 1993 the Co-Chairmen of the Geneva Peace Conference (a permanent forum for talks on the conflict), Lord (David) Owen (a former British Secretary of State for Foreign and Commonwealth Affairs) and Cyrus Vance (the UN mediator and a former US Secretary of State), visited Belgrade for talks with the President of Serbia, Slobodan Milošević. Their aim was to persuade him to convince the Bosnian Serbs to agree to a division of Bosnia and Herzegovina into 10 provinces (with three provinces allocated to each faction and Sarajevo as a province with special status). The peace plan was approved by Boban, and, in part, by Izetbegović, but was rejected by Karadžić, who insisted on the establishment of an autonomous Serb state within the territory of Bosnia and Herzegovina. In mid-January Milošević attended the peace talks in Geneva, Switzerland, for the first time. Karadžić, under pressure from Milošević and the President of the FRY, agreed to the constitutional proposals included in the plan and, subsequently, to the military arrangements. On 19–20 January the Bosnian Serb Narodna skupština, based at Pale, near Sarajevo, voted to accept the general principles of the Vance-Owen plan. On 22 February the UN Security Council adopted a resolution providing for the establishment of an international court to try alleged war criminals for acts committed since 1991 in the territories formerly included in the SFRY. On 31 March the UN Security Council adopted a resolution permitting the taking of 'all necessary measures' by UN member states or regional organizations to enforce a 'no-fly zone' imposed (by another Security Council resolution) on the airspace of Bosnia and Herzegovina in October 1992. During March 1993, at further peace talks, Izetbegović agreed to both the military arrangements and the proposed territorial divisions included in the Vance-Owen plan. In April, however, the Bosnian Serb assembly rejected the territorial arrangements, incurring international disapproval (including that of Serbia, which had endorsed the plan under pressure from UN and EC sanctions). In early Karadžić signed the Vance-Owen plan in Geneva, but two days later it was rejected by the Bosnian Serb assembly.

In May 1993 the USA, France, Russia, Spain and the United Kingdom signed a communiqué declaring that the arms embargo on the post-SFRY states would continue and that international armed forces would not intervene in the conflict; they proposed instead, with effect from 22 July, the creation of six designated 'safe areas' (Sarajevo, Bihać, Tuzla, Goražde, Srebrenica and Žepa), in which disarmed Bosniaks (who, unlike the Bosnian Serbs and Croats, lacked substantial external military support) would be settled, with the intention that they would be safe from Serb attack. In June a UN Security Council resolution permitted UNPROFOR to use force, including air power, in response to attacks against these 'safe areas'. In that month a joint Serb-Croat offensive began against the northern, predominantly Bosniak, town of Maglaj. In July intense fighting between Croats and Bosniaks for the control of Mostar commenced. Meanwhile, in late June new peace proposals were announced in Geneva by Owen and Thorvald Stoltenberg (who had replaced Vance as the UN mediator), under which Bosnia and Herzegovina would become a confederation of three ethnically determined states. Izetbegović refused to discuss the tripartite division of Bosnia and boycotted the remainder of the Geneva talks, although other members of the Presidency continued discussions.

On 30 July 1993 the three factions reached a constitutional agreement in Geneva on the reconstruction of Bosnia and Herzegovina into a confederation of three states, styled the 'Union of Republics of Bosnia and Herzegovina', under a central government with powers limited to foreign policy and trade. Under this agreement, Sarajevo would be placed under UN administration for a two-year transitional period. Despite this agreement and numerous negotiated cease-fires, fighting continued, and in early August the three Croat members of the Bosnian state Presidency (including the Prime Minister, who was consequently dismissed from that post) left the delegation to Geneva, in protest at Bosniak attacks on Croat populations, and instead joined the Croatian negotiators. On 28 August a 'Croat Republic of Herzeg-Bosna' was proclaimed in Grude, which proceeded to accept the Owen-Stoltenberg plan on condition that the Serbs and Bosniaks also accepted it. On the same day the Bosnian Serb assembly also voted in favour of the plan. On 31 August, however, a session of the Skupština Republike Bosne i Hercegovine rejected the Geneva plan, while agreeing to use it as a basis for further peace negotiations.

On 10 September 1993 Fikret Abdić, a Bosniak member of the state Presidency, announced the creation of an 'Autonomous Province of Western Bosnia' in the region around Bihać, in the extreme north-west, which, Abdić declared, was to form part of the 'Union of Republics of Bosnia and Herzegovina'. On 27 September Abdić was elected 'President' of the 'province' by a 'Constituent Assembly'. Abdić (who signed a peace agreement with representatives of the Bosnian Serbs), was subsequently dismissed from the state Presidency of Bosnia and Herzegovina. Izetbegović imposed martial law on the area and government forces attacked troops under Abdić's command.

In February 1994 the shelling of a Sarajevo market-place, killing at least 68 people and wounding 200 others, prompted the UN to threaten military intervention if Serb forces failed to cease their bombardment of the city. Following the issuing of an ultimatum by the North Atlantic Treaty Organization (NATO), the Bosnian Serbs withdrew most of their heavy weaponry from a 20-km 'exclusion zone' around the city, which, however, remained effectively blockaded. Moreover, the exclusion zone was frequently violated. In late February NATO forces shot down four Serb aircraft near Banja Luka, which had violated the UN prohibition of non-humanitarian flights over the country. The incident represented the first aggressive military action taken by NATO since its establishment. None the less, Bosnian Serb forces continued to shell Maglaj throughout March, while several of the 'safe areas' were also bombarded. Following a cease-fire agreed by the republican Government and the authorities of Herzeg-Bosna in late February 1994, Haris Silajdžić (Prime Minister of the republican Government since late October 1993) and Kresimir Zubak (who had replaced Boban as the leader of Herzeg-Bosna) signed an agreement on 18 March, in Washington, DC, USA, providing for the creation of a Federation on those territories controlled by Bosnian and Herzegovinian Croats and Bosniaks, with power to be shared equally between the two groups. A second 'preliminary' agreement was signed by Izetbegović and Tuđman, providing for the eventual creation of a loose confederation involving the Federation and

Croatia. In late March the accords were approved by the Herzeg-Bosna Assembly, and the new Constitution was ratified by the Skupština Republike Bosne i Hercegovine. In April, in response to the continued shelling of the 'safe area' of Goražde by Bosnian Serb forces, UN-sanctioned airstrikes were launched by NATO aircraft on Serb ground positions. However, Serb forces captured Goražde later that month, prompting strong criticism from the Russian Government, which hitherto had been perceived as sympathetic towards the Serbs, but which now indicated that it would not oppose the use of force against them. Bosnian Serb forces withdrew from Goražde in late April. On 26 April a new negotiating forum, the 'Contact Group', comprising representatives from France, Germany, Russia, the United Kingdom and the USA, was established.

In May 1994 the Ustavotvorna skupština Federacije Bosne i Hercegovine (Constituent Assembly of the Federation of Bosnia and Herzegovina) elected Zubak to the largely ceremonial post of President of the Federation at its inaugural meeting. Ejup Ganić, a Bosniak, was elected Vice-President of the Federation (he was concurrently a Vice-President of the collective Presidency of the Republic of Bosnia and Herzegovina) and Silajdžić was appointed Prime Minister of the Federation. A joint Government of the Federation and the Republic, led by Silajdžić, was appointed in late June.

Following peace negotiations in Geneva in early June 1994, a one-month republic-wide cease-fire was declared. By the end of the month, however, following reports of repeated violations, Bosnian government forces had captured Serb-held areas of central Bosnia. The Contact Group presented new peace proposals in early July, according to which the Federation would be granted 51% of the country's territory, thereby requiring the Bosnian Serbs to yield approximately one-third of the territory they controlled. Sensitive areas, including Sarajevo, Srebrenica, Goražde and Brčko, would be placed under UN and EU administration. On 17 July Izetbegović and Tuđman endorsed the Contact Group plan, which was also approved by the Skupština Republike Bosne i Hercegovine. However, the proposed territorial division was rejected by the Bosnian Serb Narodna skupština. Milošević subsequently criticized Bosnian Serb opposition to the plan, and in early August the FRY announced the closure of its borders with Bosnia and Herzegovina. On 5 August NATO airstrikes (the first since April) were launched against Bosnian Serb targets, in response to attacks against UN forces and the renewed shelling of Sarajevo. In late August 96% of participants of a referendum held in the Bosnian Serb-held areas reportedly voted to reject the Contact Group plan; this rejection was unanimously approved by the Bosnian Serb assembly on 1 September. Meanwhile, on 21 August the Bihać enclave, held by Abdić's forces, was captured by the government army of Bosnia and Herzegovina. In December the Contact Group issued proposals based on the July peace plan, which indicated the possibility of confederal links between a Bosnian Serb polity and the FRY. On 31 December the Bosnian Serb authorities and the republican Government signed a four-month cease-fire agreement, to take effect from the following day. Both sides expressed their readiness to resume peace negotiations based on the revised Contact Group plan. The cease-fire was generally observed during January 1995. However, intense fighting continued in the Bihać enclave between government forces and troops loyal to Abdić, who was supported by troops from the adjoining self-proclaimed 'Republic of Serbian Krajina' in Croatia. In February the USA refused to continue negotiations with Karadžić until the Bosnian Serb authorities accepted the Contact Group plan.

On 20 February 1995 representatives of the Bosnian Serbs and the Croatian Serbs signed a military pact, guaranteeing mutual assistance in the event of attack and providing for the establishment of a joint Supreme Defence Council. In early March, in response, a formal military alliance was announced between the armies of Croatia, the authorities of Herzeg-Bosna and the Government of the Republic of Bosnia and Herzegovina. On 8 April President Zubak of the Federation and Ejup Ganić, the Vice-President of both the Federation and of Bosnia and Herzegovina, signed an agreement in Bonn, Germany, on the implementation of principles for the entity, including the formation of unified police forces, local government and, eventually, armed forces. On 25 May, following a UN request in response to the continued bombardment of Sarajevo, NATO aircraft carried out strikes on Bosnian Serb ammunition depots. Serb forces responded by shelling five of the six 'safe areas' and, following further NATO airstrikes on 26 May, retaliated with a massive bombardment of Tuzla, which resulted in at least 70 deaths. Bosnian Serb troops subsequently disarmed and took hostage 222 UNPROFOR personnel in Goražde. In June defence ministers from NATO and other European states agreed on the creation of a 10,000-strong 'rapid reaction force' for Bosnia and Herzegovina, which was to operate under UN command from mid-July, with a mandate to provide 'enhanced protection' to UNPROFOR. However, although the UN denied that any deal had been reached with the Bosnian Serbs, the release of the remaining hostages coincided with the withdrawal of UNPROFOR from Bosnian Serb-controlled territory around Sarajevo.

On 11 July 1995 the eastern 'safe area' of Srebrenica was captured by Bosnian Serb fighters, after Dutch UNPROFOR troops based in the town were taken hostage, despite NATO airstrikes on Bosnian Serb tanks approaching the town. Following the capture of Srebrenica, an estimated 7,000–8,000 Muslim male civilians were massacred by Bosnian Serb forces, the largest atrocity to take place in Europe since the end of the Second World War.

Bihać was attacked on 20 July 1995, in a concerted effort by Bosnian Serbs, Croatian Serbs, and rebel Bosniaks led by Abdić. The situation in Bihać prompted the signature of a military co-operation agreement between Izetbegović and Tuđman on 22 July. Croatian and Herzeg-Bosna troops subsequently launched attacks on Serb positions around Bihać, thereby blocking Serb supply routes into the Krajina enclave.

Croatian government forces invaded the Croatian Serb-held Krajina on 4 August 1995, and rapidly recaptured the entire enclave, prompting a massive exodus of Serb civilians from the region into Serb-held areas of Bosnia and Herzegovina and into Serbia itself. On 6–7 August the siege of Bihać was ended by Bosnian government and Croatian troops. On 9 August a further peace initiative (devised by Richard Holbrooke, a US Assistant Secretary of State) was announced by the USA; the proposals, which were based on the Contact Group plan of 1994, none the less allowed the Bosnian Serb authorities to retain control of Srebrenica and Žepa (the latter of which they had captured in late July). On 28 August a mortar attack on a market in central Sarajevo, attributed to Bosnian Serb forces, resulted in at least 38 deaths. Two days later NATO responded by commencing a series of airstrikes (known as 'Operation Deliberate Force') on Serb positions throughout Bosnia and Herzegovina, which continued until 14 September and had the effect of markedly reducing the territory controlled by Bosnian Serb forces.

On 8 September 1995 major progress in the peace process was achieved when, at a meeting in Geneva, chaired by the Contact Group, the Ministers of Foreign Affairs of Bosnia and Herzegovina, Croatia and the FRY (the latter acting on behalf of the Bosnian Serbs) signed an agreement determining basic principles for a peace accord. These principles included the continuing existence of Bosnia and Herzegovina within its present borders, but the state was to comprise two administrative units, known as entities: the Federation of Bosnia and Herzegovina; and Republika Srpska, with each entity largely retaining its existing Constitution. In mid-September 'Operation Deliberate Force' was suspended, following the withdrawal of Bosnian Serb weaponry from the 'exclusion zone' around Sarajevo. Agreement on further basic principles for a peace accord was reached by the Ministers of Foreign Affairs of Bosnia and Herzegovina, Croatia and the FRY, meeting in New York, USA, on 26 September. Within the state parliament, Republika Srpska was to be apportioned one-third of the seats; the Federation was to control two-thirds of the seats (legislative decisions were only to be implemented, however, with the approval of at least one-third of the deputies of each entity). A collective presidency was also to be organized according to the one-third Serb to two-thirds Bosniak-Croat proportional division. A 60-day cease-fire came into effect on 12 October; the UN simultaneously announced its intention to reduce the number of peace-keeping troops in the area.

On 1 November 1995 peace negotiations between the three warring parties in the conflict began in Dayton, Ohio, USA. A comprehensive peace agreement was reached on 21 November, when Izetbegović, Tuđman and Milošević (the latter representing both the FRY and the Bosnian Serbs) initialled a General Framework Agreement for Peace in Bosnia and Herzegovina, dividing the country between the Federation of Bosnia and Herzegovina, with 51% of the territory, and Republika Srpska, with 49%, although the sovereignty of the state, which was henceforth to be known simply as Bosnia and Herzegovina, was to be maintained within its existing borders. Whereas the Government of Republika Srpska was to be highly centralized,

BOSNIA AND HERZEGOVINA

with a directly elected presidency and no level of local government other than that of municipality, power in the Federation was largely devolved to 10 cantonal administrations, as well as to municipalities. The Federation was to have a bicameral legislature, whereas that of Republika Srpska was to be unicameral. The Dayton accords included provisions for a state government with a democratically elected collective presidency and a parliament, and for a single monetary system, central bank and other economic institutions. It also stipulated the right of all refugees and displaced persons to return to their homes and either to have seized property returned to them or to receive fair compensation. Of the former 'safe areas' in eastern Bosnia, only Goražde was to remain under the control of the Federation; several south-eastern suburbs of Sarajevo were to form part of Republika Srpska, although most regions of the city were to be in the Federation. No agreement was reached, however, regarding the Posavina corridor, surrounded by Federation territory, connecting the northern sector of Republika Srpska with the southern sector, and control of the town of Brčko, and the river-port located at this point; the three sides agreed to place the issue under international arbitration. UNPROFOR troops were to be replaced by an international, NATO-commanded, 60,000-strong Implementation Force (IFOR), which was to be mandated to oversee the withdrawal of the warring parties from zones of separation and to monitor the agreed exchanges of territory. It was estimated that 200,000–250,000 people had been killed in the conflict in Bosnia and Herzegovina, and some 2.7m. (out of a total population of 4.4m. at the 1991 census) were believed to have been displaced.

Following the initialling of the Dayton peace accords, the UN suspended the remaining economic sanctions against the FRY and voted to remove gradually the arms embargo against the post-SFRY states. At a conference on the implementation of the Dayton peace accords, held in London, United Kingdom, in early December 1995, it was agreed that an Organization for Security and Co-operation in Europe (OSCE, see p. 354) mission would organize and monitor parliamentary elections in Bosnia and Herzegovina and that the Contact Group would be replaced by a Peace Implementation Council based in Brussels, Belgium. The Swedish former Prime Minister and EU envoy to the peace talks, Carl Bildt, was appointed High Representative of the International Community in Bosnia and Herzegovina, with responsibility for the implementation of the civilian aspects of the Dayton agreement. On 14 December the Dayton peace agreement was formally signed by Izetbegović, Tuđman and Milošević, and by President Bill Clinton of the USA and a number of European political leaders in Paris, France. The formal transfer of power from UNPROFOR to IFOR took place on 20 December.

On 30 January 1996 Hasan Muratović was elected by the state assembly as Prime Minister of Bosnia and Herzegovina, following the resignation from the premiership of Silajdžić; a new state Government was appointed on the same day, and a new Federation Government was appointed one day later. In mid-February, in response to unrest in Mostar (where tensions between Croats and Bosniaks remained intense), an emergency summit meeting took place in Rome, Italy, at which Izetbegović, Tuđman and Milošević reaffirmed their adherence to the Dayton agreement. A joint Croat-Bosniak security patrol, accompanied by officers from the UN International Police Task Force (IPTF) and Western European Union (WEU), subsequently began operating in Mostar.

By the end of April 1996 substantial progress had been made in the implementation of the military aspects of the Dayton agreement. However, the exchange of territory between the two entities did not proceed as envisaged in the peace agreement. From mid-January there was a mass exodus of ethnic Serbs from the Bosnian Serb-held suburbs of Sarajevo that were to be transferred to the control of the Federation. The Republika Srpska authorities in Pale were criticized for using intimidation to coerce the Serb inhabitants of these districts to resettle in towns in eastern regions of Republika Srpska from which Muslims had been driven during the war. By late March only about 10% of the pre-war Serb population in Sarajevo remained.

In May 1996 Bosniak and Croat leaders, meeting in Washington, DC, agreed on the merger of their armed forces and the return of refugees. The agreement on a unified Federation army was the principal precondition for the implementation of a US-sponsored training programme intended to give it equal military capabilities to that of Republika Srpska's armed forces. Given that Karadžić had been indicted by the International Criminal Tribunal for the former Yugoslavia (ICTY, see p. 18), based in The Hague, Netherlands, for war crimes, notably responsibility for the massacre at Srebrenica in July 1995, his continued position as President (and that of Gen. Ratko Mladić as head of the armed forces) was in breach of the Dayton agreement, which prohibited indicted war criminals from holding public office. In response to international pressure, Karadžić announced the delegation of some of his powers to his deputy, Dr Biljana Plavšić.

In mid-June 1996 ethnic Croats in Mostar announced a new Government of Herzeg-Bosna, in contravention of agreements that the autonomous state would be dissolved. At a summit meeting of the Presidents of Bosnia and Herzegovina, Croatia and Serbia, which was convened by the USA in Geneva in mid-August, Tuđman and Izetbegović agreed on the full establishment of Federation institutions by the end of the month.

In late June 1996 Western European countries issued an ultimatum to Karadžić to resign, on penalty of the reimposition of sanctions against Republika Srpska that had been suspended in April. In defiance of this, the SDP re-elected Karadžić as party leader. At the end of June Karadžić announced his temporary resignation and the appointment of Plavšić as the acting President of Republika Srpska. It was then confirmed that Karadžić would not contest the election to the presidency of Republika Srpska, and Plavšić was nominated as the SDP candidate. None the less, it was deemed unacceptable that Karadžić should remain as party leader, and the OSCE mission to Bosnia and Herzegovina declared that the SDP would be excluded from the elections if Karadžić retained any party office. In mid-July the ICTY issued arrest warrants for Karadžić and Mladić. Following intensive negotiations convened by Holbrooke with Milošević and Bosnian Serb leaders, on 19 July Karadžić resigned from the presidency and as head of the SDP.

During the electoral campaign there were increasing reports of harassment and violence in both the Federation and Republika Srpska. In late August 1996 the OSCE announced that municipal elections were to be postponed, in response to evidence that the Republika Srpska authorities were forcibly registering displaced Serbs in formerly Muslim-dominated localities. Elections were held on 14 September 1996 to the state Presidency and Predstavnički dom (House of Representatives—the lower chamber of the bicameral Parlamentarna skupština Bosne i Hercegovine—Parliamentary Assembly of Bosnia and Herzegovina). Elections also took place at entity level, to the Republika Srpska presidency and legislature, and to cantonal authorities within the Federation and to the Predstavnički dom Federacije (Federation House of Representatives—which formed the lower chamber of a bicameral Parlament Federacije—Federation Parliament). At the election to the state collective Presidency, Izetbegović won 80% of the Bosniak votes cast; Zubak (contesting the election as the candidate of the CDU—BH) 88% of the Croat votes; and Momčilo Krajišnik (of the SDP) 67% of the Serb votes. Having received the largest number of votes of the three winning presidential candidates, Izetbegović became Chairman of the Presidency. The PDA and the CDU—BH dominated both the Federation section of the Predstavnički dom and the Predstavnički dom Federacije; none the less, an alliance of social-democratic Bosniak and Croat parties, the Joint List of Bosnia and Herzegovina, and the Party for Bosnia and Herzegovina (led by Silajdžić) won a significant number of votes in the elections to both the state and Federation legislatures. The SDP secured a majority of votes in both the Serb section of the Predstavnički dom and in the Narodna skupština Republike Srpske. Plavšić was elected President of Republika Srpska, receiving 59% of the votes cast. Following the OSCE's endorsement of the election results, on 1 October 1996 the UN Security Council finally decided to remove sanctions against the FRY and Republika Srpska. A few days later Bosnia and Herzegovina and the FRY agreed to establish full diplomatic relations. The inauguration of the state Presidency took place on 5 October. The inaugural session of the bicameral Parlamentarna skupština (comprising the indirectly elected Dom Naroda—House of Peoples—and the Predstavnički dom) was postponed, owing to a boycott by the Serb deputies. In November 1996 Plavšić announced that she had dismissed Gen. Mladić as Commander of the Bosnian Serb armed forces.

Following a Peace Implementation Conference, held in London, it was announced, with effect from 20 December 1996, that IFOR would be replaced by a Stabilization Force (SFOR). In mid-December, after some delay, the Presidency appointed the two Co-Prime Ministers of the state Council of Ministers: Haris Silajdžić, and Boro Bosić of the SDP. Later in the month the dissolution of Herzeg-Bosna was announced and a Federation Prime Minister elected. The state Council of Ministers was appointed by the Co-Prime Ministers and approved by the inaugural session of the Parlamentarna škupština on 3 January 1997.

On 28 February 1997 Krajišnik signed, on behalf of Republika Srpska, an agreement with the FRY to foster mutual economic co-operation and to collaborate on regional security. The accord was ratified by the Narodna skupština Republike Srpske in March, despite Plavšić's opposition. In June Bildt was replaced as High Representative by Carlos Westendorp. In July Plavšić announced the dissolution of the Narodna skupština, scheduling parliamentary elections for September; this measure followed the assembly's opposition to the suspension of the entity's Minister of Internal Affairs by Plavšić. Although this action was supported by both the UN and the OSCE, it was strongly criticized by the entity's premier, Gojko Klicković, and a number of resolutions designed to undermine Plavšić were approved by the Narodna skupština. (Meanwhile, Plavšić was expelled from the SDP.) In August the Constitutional Court ruled that Plavšić's decision to dissolve the legislature had been illegal: the Narodna skupština proceeded to vote to disregard future decrees by her. The delayed municipal elections took place in both entities on 13–14 September, when the three main nationalist parties, the PDA, the CDU—BH and the SDP, received the majority of the votes cast. In late September a constitutional crisis in Republika Srpska was averted, following a meeting in Belgrade hosted by Milošević and attended by Plavšić and Krajišnik. A joint statement was issued detailing an agreement, whereby elections to the legislature would take place in November, and presidential elections for both Republika Srpska and the Serb member of the collective Presidency on 7 December.

Elections to the Narodna skupština Republike Srpske were held on 22–23 November 1997, under the supervision of the OSCE. Although the representation of the SDP was much reduced, to 24 seats, it remained the largest party in the legislature. A newly formed electoral alliance, the Coalition for a Single and Democratic Bosnia and Herzegovina, which included the PDA and the Party for Bosnia and Herzegovina, secured 16 seats, while the Serb National Alliance (SNA), recently established by Plavšić and the Serb Radical Party (SRP) each received 15 seats. At the inaugural session of the new assembly on 27 December, Plavšić nominated Mladen Ivanić, an economist with no political affiliation, as premier. However, in January 1998, following the failure of Ivanić's interparty talks, Milorad Dodik, the leader of the Party of Independent Social Democrats of Republika Srpska (PISD), and who was considered to be a moderate, secured sufficient parliamentary support to form a new government. At the end of January Dodik announced that government bodies were to be transferred from Pale to Banja Luka. In June 1998 the UN Security Council officially voted in favour of extending the mandate of SFOR to remain in the country indefinitely, with six-monthly reviews.

In April 1998 the OSCE dissolved the municipal assembly of Srebrenica in Republika Srpska, owing to its failure to assist in the resettlement of displaced Muslims there; a provisional executive council, headed by a senior OSCE official, was established to replace the assembly. In June Krajišnik criticized a motion by the Narodna skupština expressing 'no confidence' in its Speaker, Dragan Kalinić, and Deputy Speaker. Kalinić was subsequently elected as Chairman of the SDP, following the resignation of the incumbent.

In September 1998 elections took place to the state presidency and legislature, to the presidency and legislature of Republika Srpska, and to the Predstavnički dom Federacije. Izetbegović was re-elected as the Bosniak member of the collective Presidency. The Chairman of the Socialist Party of Republika Srpska (SPRS, a member of the SNA-led Accord Coalition), Živko Radišić, replaced Krajišnik, and the Chairman of the CDU—BH, Ante Jelavić, was elected as the Croat member of the Presidency. In the election to the presidency of Republika Srpska, the Chairman of the SRP, Dr Nikola Poplasen defeated Plavšić. The SDP retained 19 of the 83 seats in the Narodna skupština, while the Coalition for a Single and Democratic Bosnia and Herzegovina won 15 seats; the latter also secured 14 of the 42 seats in the Predstavnički dom and 68 of the 140 seats in the Predstavnički dom Federacije.

On 13 October 1998 the newly elected state Presidency of Bosnia and Herzegovina was inaugurated. Poplasen was inaugurated as President of Republika Srpska, pledging to maintain good relations with western Governments and to comply with the Dayton agreement. The major parties represented in the Narodna skupština Republike Srpske subsequently conducted negotiations on the appointment of a new Council of Ministers for the entity. The Accord Coalition, which held 32 seats, rejected Poplasen's nomination of Kalinić as Prime Minister, and supported the reappointment of Dodik to the post. In December the Parliament Federacije re-elected Ganić as President (to which post he had been elected in December 1997) and a new Federation Council of Ministers was established. In January 1999 Poplasen nominated Brane Miljus, a member of the PISD, as Prime Minister of Republika Srpska. The Accord Coalition objected to Miljus's candidacy, and Dodik announced his expulsion from the PISD. Later in January the Narodna skupština rejected Miljus's nomination to the office of Prime Minister.

In February 1999 Westendorp declared that supreme command of the armed forces of the two entities was to be transferred to the members of the collective state Presidency. However, the Republika Srpska Government announced that Poplasen would remain Commander of the entity's armed forces, pending a ruling by the state Constitutional Court. In early March Poplasen proposed a motion in the Narodna skupština Republike Srpske, in an attempt to instigate Dodik's dismissal. Westendorp announced Poplasen's removal from office, on the grounds that he had exceeded his authority. In the same month international arbitrators ruled that Serb control of Brčko would end, and that the town would henceforth be governed jointly by Republika Srpska and the Federation, under international supervision. The Narodna skupština rejected both the ruling on Brčko and Westendorp's decision to remove Poplasen from office. (It subsequently withdrew its opposition to Poplasen's dismissal, and Mirko Sarović, the incumbent Vice-President, provisionally assumed the presidential office.) In mid-April a new municipal Government of Serbs, Bosniaks and Croats was elected in Brčko. In March 2000 Brčko was established as a neutral district, and an Interim District Government, comprising representatives of the three ethnic groups, was established.

In June 1999 NATO announced that the strength of the SFOR contingent was to be reduced to about 16,500. In August Wolfgang Petritsch, hitherto the Austrian ambassador to the FRY, succeeded Westendorp as High Representative. Later in February the SPRS withdrew from the Accord Coalition of Republika Srpska, after Dodik dismissed the SPRS Deputy Prime Minister, Tihomir Gligorić. In March a senior Bosnian Croat commander, Gen. Tihomir Blaskić, was sentenced by the ICTY to 45 years' imprisonment (the most severe sentence issued by the Tribunal) for war crimes perpetrated against Muslims in 1992–93. (However, in July 2004 the ICTY reduced Blaskić's sentence to nine years on appeal, reversing most of the convictions against him on the grounds that he had not been responsible for atrocities perpetrated by forces under his command.) In early April 2000 Krajišnik was arrested in Pale by SFOR troops and extradited to the ICTY. (His trial finally commenced at the ICTY in February 2004; he pleaded not guilty to eight charges, including two relating to genocide.)

At municipal elections, held on 8 April 2000, the SDP won control of 49 of the 145 municipal councils (mainly in Republika Srpska), the CDU—BH secured 25 and the PDA 23; the multiethnic Social Democratic Party of Bosnia and Herzegovina (SDP BiH) made significant electoral gains in the Federation. In the same month the Predstavnički dom adopted legislation providing for the restructuring of the state Council of Ministers, which was to comprise a Chairman (appointed by the collective Presidency for an eight-month term) and five ministers. In late May the Federation Vice-President, Ejup Ganić, was expelled from the PDA, after failing to resign from his government office in compliance with the party's decision. In early June a new state Council of Ministers was appointed, after the Predstavnički dom confirmed the nomination of a non-party candidate, Spasoje Tusevljak, to the office of Chairman.

In September 2000 the Narodna skupština Republike Srpske adopted a motion, proposed by the SDP, expressing 'no confidence' in Dodik's administration. However, the Government submitted a legal challenge to the entity's Constitutional Court and announced that it would remain in office pending forthcoming legislative elections. In October Izetbegović retired from the collective state Presidency. A member of the CDU—BH, Martin Raguž, subsequently became Chairman of the Council of Ministers, replacing Tusevljak.

On 11 November 2000 elections to the Predstavnički dom, to the legislatures of both entities and to the presidency of Republika Srpska took place. The results of elections to the Predstavnički dom and the Predstavnički dom Federacije demonstrated a relative decline in support for the nationalist parties. In elections to the 42-member Predstavnički dom, the SDP BiH secured nine seats, the PDA eight seats, the SDP six seats and the CDU—BH five seats, while in the 140-member Predstavnički dom Federacije the PDA won 38 seats, the SDP BiH 37 seats, the CDU—BH 25 seats and the Party for Bosnia and Herzegovina 21 seats. The SDP secured 31 of the 83 seats in the Narodna skupština Republike Srpske, while the SPRS and the Party of Democratic Progress of Republika Srpska (PDP) each received 11 seats. Mirko Sarović, the SDP candidate, was elected to the presidency of Republika Srpska, with some 49.8% of votes cast, defeating Dodik. The SDP subsequently announced that it was to establish a parliamentary coalition with the PDP, the SPRS and the PDA, thereby securing a majority in the Narodna skupština.

In December 2000 Sarović designated Ivanić, who was now the leader of the PDP, as Prime Minister of Republika Srpska. In the following month Ivanić formed the entity's first multi-ethnic Council of Ministers. Meanwhile, the SDP BiH established parliamentary coalitions with a further nine non-nationalist parties (known as the Alliance for Change), which held 17 seats in the Predstavnički dom and 69 seats in the Predstavnički dom Federacije.

In January 2001 Plavšić surrendered to the ICTY, following her indictment in April 2000 on charges (that she denied) of involvement in the organization of a campaign of genocide and deportation against Bosniaks and Croats between July 1991 and December 1992. (She was provisionally released in August 2001, pending her trial.) In February 2001 three Bosnian Serbs were sentenced to terms of imprisonment by the ICTY for crimes against humanity perpetrated against Bosniak women in the eastern town of Foča in 1992 (the first case at the Tribunal concerning systematic rape and sexual enslavement). In the same month a former Herzeg-Bosna official received a custodial term of 25 years for authorizing crimes against humanity to be committed against Bosniaks in 1993–94.

In early February 2001 the Predstavnički dom rejected the nomination of Raguž to the office of Chairman of the Council of Ministers, owing to the opposition of the Alliance for Change deputies. The Presidency's subsequent designation to the post of a member of the SDP BiH, Božidar Matić, was endorsed, and on 22 February the Predstavnički dom approved a new state Council of Ministers. On 28 February the Predstavnički dom Federacije elected Karlo Filipović, of the SDP BiH, as President of the Federation. The new Federation Government notably included several members of the Alliance for Change. Meanwhile, in response to the rejection of Raguž's candidacy to the state premiership, a newly formed grouping of parties led by the CDU—BH, the self-styled 'Croat People's Assembly', declared self-government in three Croat-majority cantons. Petritsch subsequently dismissed Jelavić from the collective Presidency. Many Croat members of the armed forces and local officials also declared support for the Croat People's Assembly. On 28 March the Predstavnički dom voted in favour of appointing Jozo Križanović of the SDP BiH as the Croat member of the collective Presidency. Following negotiations with federal and international community officials, however, the Croat alliance agreed to end its boycott of state institutions in May.

In June 2001 Matić resigned as Chairman of the Council of Ministers, following the rejection by the Parlamentarna skupstina of proposed electoral legislation. On 7 July the state legislature accepted the nomination of Zlatko Lagumdžija, the leader of the SDP BiH and the hitherto Minister of Foreign Affairs, as the new Chairman of the Council of Ministers, and the legislation was approved in following month. Also in July the Narodna skupština Republike Srpske provisionally approved legislation providing for the entity's co-operation with the ICTY, notably requiring the Republika Srpska security forces to actively pursue and extradite war crime suspects. (The new legislation was adopted in October.) On 2 August the ICTY obtained its first conviction on charges of genocide, sentencing a former senior Serb army officer, Radislav Krstić, to 46 years' imprisonment for his responsibility for the massacre at Srebrenica in 1995. (In 2004 his sentence was reduced to 35 years on appeal.) In late September Gen. Sefer Halilović, a former Chief of Staff of the army of the Republic of Bosnia and Herzegovina, surrendered to the ICTY. Halilović was the most senior Bosniak official to be indicted by the Tribunal. (His trial commenced in January 2005, and he was acquitted of charges relating to the killing of Croat citizens by troops under his command in 1993 in November 2005.)

In October 2001 three former Herzeg-Bosna officials, who had been sentenced in 2000 for involvement in the killing of more than 100 Bosniaks in 1993, succeeded in having their convictions overturned on appeal, and the custodial terms of a further two detainees were reduced. In early November 2001 five Bosnian Serbs received terms of imprisonment at the ICTY for participating in the torture and killing of prisoners at Omarska detention camp in the Bosnian Krajina in 1992. Later that month Milošević (who had been extradited to the ICTY in June 2001 and had been charged with crimes against humanity relating to Croatia in 1991–92 and the Serbian province of Kosovo in 1999) was additionally indicted on the basis of responsibility for genocide in Bosnia and Herzegovina in 1992–95. (Milošević died in March 2006, while on trial at the ICTY.)

In March 2002 Dragan Mikerević of the PDP was appointed to the rotating chairmanship of the state Council of Ministers. Later in March the leading political parties, under pressure from Petritsch, reached agreement on the adoption of constitutional reforms (implemented the following month), which would ensure the representation of the three principal constituent peoples (Serb, Croat and Bosniak) at all levels of government throughout the country. Notably, a Vijeće Naroda (Council of Peoples—comprising eight Bosniaks, eight Croats, eight Serbs and four others, all of whom were to be elected by the Narodna skupština Republike Srpske) was established within the Republika Srpska legislature; among the principal duties of the Council was to be the selection of the entity's delegates to the state Dom Naroda. In May Petritsch issued a ruling providing for the adoption of judicial reforms, which would ensure the independent appointment of judges and prosecutors. On 27 May he announced the appointment of eight judges to a new Court of Bosnia and Herzegovina, which was to become the country's highest judicial organ. On the same day Sir Jeremy (Paddy) Ashdown, a British politician and former diplomat, replaced Petritsch as High Representative. Ashdown was additionally appointed to a new position, as EU Special Representative for Bosnia and Herzegovina. In June Ashdown dismissed the Federation Deputy Prime Minister and Minister of Finance, Nikola Grabovac, while the Republika Srpska Minister of Finance, Milenko Vracar, tendered his resignation, following pressure from Ashdown (who had criticized official malpractice in both entities).

In September 2002 an organ of the Republika Srpska Government issued a report disputing the veracity of the Srebrenica massacre and claiming that only some 2,000 members of the republican armed forces had been killed (mainly in military operations) in the region. The report was strongly condemned as a fabrication by the Bosniak community and by Ashdown. In October a Bosnian Serb former official, Milan Simić, was sentenced to five years' imprisonment on charges of having committed torture in 1992.

On 5 October 2002 elections were conducted to the state presidency, the presidency of Republika Srpska, the state and entity legislatures, and to the Federation cantonal assemblies. In the three ballots to the state Presidency, the Chairman of the PDA, Sulejman Tihić, was elected the Bosniak member, while Dragan Čović of the CDU—BH became the Croat member and Šarović of the SDP the Serb member. Dragan Cavić of the SDP secured the presidency of Republika Srpska. The SDP BiH-led alliance lost its majority in the Predstavnički dom following the polls, and the PDA became the largest single party, with 10 seats. The PDA also secured the highest number of seats (32) in the Predstavnički dom Federacije (which was reduced in size to 98 deputies), while the CDU—BH, contesting the elections in alliance with the Croatian Christian Democratic Union—Bosnia and Herzegovina, obtained 16 seats. The SDP BiH and the Party for Bosnia and Herzegovina each obtained 15 seats. In the elections to the Narodna skupština Republike Srpske, the SDP remained the largest party, with 26 seats, while the Alliance of Independent Social Democrats (AISD—as the PISD had become) obtained 19. At the end of October both the Minister of Defence and the army Chief of the General Staff of Republika Srpska resigned, after it emerged that an aviation company owned by the Republika Srpska authorities had exported military equipment to Iraq, in contravention of a UN armaments embargo (see the chapter on Iraq).

In November 2002 Mitar Vasiljević, the Bosnian Serb former leader of a paramilitary group, was sentenced to 20 years' imprisonment at the ICTY on two charges relating to atrocities perpetrated against Bosniaks in 1992–94. In December 2002 Cavić nominated Mikerević as Prime Minister of Republika Srpska. Also in December Ashdown introduced new legislation to strengthen the powers of the state Government: two new ministries, of security and justice, were to be established and the Prime Minister was henceforth to be appointed for a four-year term (replacing the system of rotation between the three ethnic representatives). The 14 Bosnian Serb delegates in the Predstavnički dom boycotted its first session in protest at these amendments. At the end of 2002 the mandate of the principally civilian security force, the UN Mission in Bosnia and Herzegovina (UNMIBH), officially expired, and the UN transferred responsibility for peace-keeping to an EU Police Mission, which was to supervise the reorganization and training of the country's security forces.

In January 2003 the Predstavnički dom approved the appointment of Adnan Terzić of the PDA, as Chairman of the state Government and a new Council of Ministers was formed. Although this Government was dominated by the three main nationalist parties (the PDA, the CDU—BH and the SDP), representatives of the PDP and the Party for Bosnia and Herzegovina were also included to ensure a legislative majority. Subsequently the Narodna skupština Republike Srpske approved Mikerević's nomination as entity Prime Minister and the formation of a new Government, which, in accordance with recently approved constitutional amendments, comprised eight Serb, five Bosniak and three Croat representatives. Later that month the Predstavnički dom Federacije elected a Croat, Niko Lozančić, to the presidency and, reflecting an amendment to the Federation's system of government, a Bosniak and a Serb to the office of joint Vice-President. The appointment of a new Federation Government, under Ahmet Hadžipašić, was approved in mid-February.

On 27 February 2003 the ICTY sentenced Plavšić to 11 years' imprisonment on the charge of crimes against humanity (seven other charges against her, including one of genocide, had been abandoned). On 2 April Sarović resigned as the Bosnian Serb member of the collective state Presidency, after being implicated in both the illicit exports to Iraq and alleged espionage activities by the Republika Srpska military. Ashdown announced the abolition of the Republika Srpska Supreme Military Council; command of the armed forces was transferred provisionally to the entity's President. Ashdown also removed all references of statehood from the Constitution of Republika Srpska. On 10 April the Predstavnički dom confirmed the nomination of Borislav Paravać, also of the SDP, to replace Sarović.

In July 2003 Željko Mejakić, the Bosnian Serb commander of the Omarska detention camp (who had originally been indicted in 1995), was transferred to the ICTY, having surrendered to the authorities in Serbia. At the end of July a former mayor of Prijedor, Dr Milomir Stakić, was sentenced to life imprisonment by the ICTY (the first time that the Tribunal had imposed this verdict) for his leading involvement in the campaign of 'ethnic cleansing' of non-Serbs from the region (involving the killing of 1,500 people and deportation of a further 20,000) in 1992–95. In October the international community pledged to finance the establishment of a new war crimes' court in Sarajevo, which would assume competence for a number of less important trials pending at the ICTY, enabling the Tribunal to complete operations in 2010, as scheduled.

In July 2003 a mass grave (the largest to be found), believed to contain the remains of some 700 Muslim males, who had been killed in Srebrenica in July 1995 was uncovered near the north-eastern town of Zvornik. In November a Banja Luka-based television station broadcast the results of an investigation by the Republika Srpska Government, conducted under pressure from Ashdown, into the Srebrenica massacre; the authorities conceded for the first time that Bosnian Serb forces had perpetrated the killings. During a state visit to Sarajevo in November Svetozar Marović, the President of Serbia and Montenegro (as the FRY had been renamed in February), issued a formal apology for the atrocities committed against Bosnian civilians during the 1992–95 conflict, and urged reconciliation.

In December 2003 a Bosnian Serb former army commander, Momir Nikolić, was sentenced at the ICTY to 27 years' imprisonment for his involvement in the Srebrenica massacre. Also in early December the first conviction relating exclusively to the siege of Sarajevo was imposed by the Tribunal on the commanding officer in 1992–94, Gen. Stanislav Galić, who was sentenced to 20 years' imprisonment.

In early January 2004, amid continuing pressure from the international community, SFOR, assisted for the first time by Republika Srpska military personnel, conducted a search operation in Pale, in an unsuccessful attempt to apprehend Karadžić.

Later that month Ashdown issued a decree providing for the reunification of Mostar (divided between six Croat- and Bosniak-controlled municipalities since 1993) into a single administration, thereby fulfilling one of the preconditions for signature of a Stabilization and Association Agreement (SAA) with the EU. In February 2004 Ashdown announced the dismissals of three security officials of Republika Srpska and the removal of Mirko Sarović from the presidium of the SDP, owing to suspicions of their complicity in attempts to prevent Karadžić's capture. The SDP refused to approve Sarović's dismissal and the party's leader, Dragan Kalinić, subsequently resigned in protest at Ashdown's decision. In mid-March the Predstavnički dom approved the nomination of Nikola Radovanović of the SDP as the first state Minister of Defence (following the rejection, at the instigation of Ashdown, of two extreme nationalist candidates). At the end of the month the state Constitutional Court ruled that the renaming since 1992 of some 13 municipalities in Republika Srpska with variants of the prefix 'Srpski' (Serbian) was unconstitutional; the Republika Srpska authorities subsequently agreed to rename these districts, but emphasized that they regarded this as a temporary measure. In mid-April Ashdown removed the Republika Srpska army Chief of Staff, who had failed to provide information required by a commission investigating the Srebrenica massacre. In June Ashdown dismissed 60 officials of Republika Srpska, including the Minister of the Interior, who were reportedly implicated in the continued failure of the authorities to locate and apprehend Karadžić. In September the ICTY sentenced Radislav Brđanin, the self-styled Deputy Prime Minister of Republika Srpska in 1992, to 32 years' imprisonment for involvement in crimes committed against Croats and Muslims in the Krajina region, although he was acquitted of the charge of genocide.

In municipal elections, held in October 2004, the PDA received the highest level of support in the Federation, while in Republika Srpska the SDP lost support to the AISD. In early October Ljubiša Beara, a former head of intelligence of the Bosnian Serb army charged with organizing the Srebrenica massacre, surrendered to security forces in Serbia and was extradited to the ICTY. In mid-October the commission established by the Republika Srpska authorities to investigate the Srebrenica massacre submitted a final report acknowledging that Bosnian Serb forces had, on that occasion, killed an estimated 7,800 Muslim males. In November the Republika Srpska Government (which continued to attract strong criticism from the international community for failing to apprehend any war crime suspects believed to be hiding on its territory) issued an official apology for the Srebrenica massacre.

On 22 November 2004 the UN Security Council approved a resolution authorizing the establishment of a new peace-keeping contingent under the command of the EU, and in December SFOR officially transferred authority to the new, 7,000-member EU Force (EUFOR), which incorporated many of the former members of the SFOR contingent. EUFOR was additionally mandated to assist Bosnia and Herzegovina in further progress towards European integration. In early December NATO rejected for the second time Bosnia and Herzegovina's application to join the 'Partnership for Peace' (PfP) programme, largely in response to the failure of the Republika Srpska authorities to co-operate with the ICTY. Ashdown responded by announcing the acceleration of military reforms: the entity Ministries of Defence were to be abolished by 2005, while a single police force under the state Minister of Security was to replace the three existing police and security agencies. In addition, Ashdown removed nine Republika Srpska security officials accused of complicity in the evasion from arrest of war crime suspects, and the USA imposed travel restrictions on the leadership of the PDP and the SDP. On 17 December Mikerević tendered his resignation as Prime Minister of Republika Srpska in protest at the dismissals. Ivanić announced his resignation from his post in the state Government as Minister of Foreign Affairs, although neither his resignation, nor those that had been threatened by other members of the state Government, were accepted. On 8 January 2005 Cavić nominated Pero Bukejlović of the SDP as Prime Minister of Republika Srpska.

In January 2005 the former deputy commander of a Serb detention camp, Savo Todorović, surrendered to the Republika Srpska authorities (the first war crimes suspect to do so). Todorović was extradited to the ICTY, which had indicted him on 18 charges relating to atrocities perpetrated against prisoners. In the same month two Bosnian Serbs were convicted by the ICTY for their involvement in the Srebrenica massacre: Col

Vidoje Blagojević received an 18-year sentence on a number of charges, including complicity in genocide, and Dragan Jokić was sentenced to a term of nine years.

In February 2005 the Narodna skupština Republike Srpske approved the SDP-dominated entity Government nominated by Bukejlović. Ivanić announced that the PDP was to remain in the state-level administration, and in March his threat of resignation and those of the other ministers were formally withdrawn. Later that month the Croat member of the state presidency, Dragan Ćović, was charged with corruption during his former tenure as Federation Minister of Finance; he was removed from office by Ashdown in March. (In May Ivo Miro Jović became the new Croat member of the state Presidency.)

The new War Crimes Chamber of the Court of Bosnia and Herzegovina commenced operations in March 2005, and by September the first war crimes indictee had been transferred to the Court from the ICTY, and proceedings for 86 cases were under way. Meanwhile, in May 62 of the 83 deputies in the Narodna skupština Republike Srpske voted against the establishment of a single state-level police structure. In June the Republika Srpska army Chief of General Staff was dismissed at the request of NATO and EUFOR commanders, following incidents during military induction ceremonies, in which new Republika Srpska army recruits had refused to pledge allegiance to Bosnia and Herzegovina. In July a special defence reform commission endorsed legislation (subject to approval by the state and entity legislatures) providing for the establishment of a joint multi-ethnic army with a unified command structure by 2007; the entity Ministries of Defence and system of military conscription were to be abolished. In August 2005 the Narodna skupština Republike Srpske approved the transfer of entity defence powers to the central government (with effect from the beginning of 2006). However, approval of the police reform (providing for the transfer of control of the service to state level) was obstructed by continued opposition from within the Government and legislature of Republika Srpska. In October the Narodna skupština Republike Srpske finally approved the proposals for police reform.

In 19 October 2005 the European Commissioner responsible for Enlargement, Olli Rehn, recommended that the Government of Bosnia and Herzegovina be invited to begin discussions on the signature of an SAA with the EU; these officially opened in November (with progress remaining conditional on implementation of the police and other reforms). Meanwhile, in October the former Chairman of the CDU—BH and a former member of the Presidency, Ante Jelavić, was sentenced to 10 years' imprisonment for the embezzlement of public funds in 1997, while serving as Minister of Defence in the Federation Government. (In August 2006 his conviction was overturned on a legal technicality and he evaded a further trial by fleeing to Croatia.) In November 2005 the three members of the state Presidency, attending a commemoration ceremony in Washington, DC to mark the 10th anniversary of the initialling of the Dayton accords, agreed, in principle, to initiate a process of constitutional reform, with the aim of strengthening the state institutions. The Federation and Republika Srpska Ministries of Defence and armed forces were officially dissolved on 1 January 2006, as authority over the military was transferred to the central state authorities.

In January 2006 US-supported inter-party discussions on constitutional reform were reconvened in Sarajevo. Issues of contention included reform of the parliamentary system and the proposed introduction of a single presidency. In that month the PDP opposed the adoption of the 2006 entity budget in the Narodna skupština Republike Srpske, and Ivanić announced the withdrawal of his party's support for the entity's Government in the legislature, prior to elections due to be held later that year. Nevertheless, Bukejlović refused to resign the premiership, claiming that the rejection of the budget reflected opposition to his campaign to eradicate corruption. On 26 January a parliamentary motion of 'no confidence', initiated by the AISD, was approved by 44 deputies in the 83-member chamber. Dodik (as leader of the AISD) subsequently indicated that the party commanded sufficient parliamentary support to secure approval for a new administration. On 31 January a German politician and former government minister, Dr Christian Schwarz-Schilling, succeeded Ashdown as High Representative; Schwarz-Schilling announced his intention of pursuing a less interventionist approach than his predecessor. On 4 February, in accordance with the Constitution, Čavić nominated Dodik as Prime Minister; Dodik subsequently formed a new administration, which was approved by the Narodna skupština on 28 February.

On 27 February 2006 a case submitted to the International Court of Justice (ICJ, see p. 20) at The Hague, Netherlands, in 1993 by Bosnia and Herzegovina against the FRY (represented by Serbia, as the successor state to the FRY and Serbia and Montenegro), claiming reparations for acts of genocide perpetrated against the Bosniak population in 1992–95, finally commenced.

In March 2006 the principal parties reached agreement on a number of draft constitutional reforms: these involved increasing the size of the state Council of Ministers by two portfolios, empowering the Prime Minister to appoint ministers, restructuring the Parlamentarna skupština Bosne i Hercegovine, and replacing the tripartite presidency with a single rotating president and two vice-presidents, to be elected by the legislature. The collective presidency subsequently adopted the reforms, which were to be submitted for approval by the Parlamentarna skupština prior to the forthcoming elections. On 26 April the Parlamentarna skupština narrowly failed to approve the constitutional reforms by the requisite majority of two-thirds of deputies, after four dissenting CDU—BH representatives formed a breakaway party, the Croatian Democratic Union 1990 of Bosnia and Herzegovina (CDU 1990).

In June 2006 Schwarz-Schilling announced plans for the closure of the Office of the High Representative at the end of June 2007, although the position of EU Special Representative (to which Schwarz-Schilling also had been appointed simultaneously) was to continue. The elections at national, entity and cantonal level, held on 1 October 2006, were pronounced by the OSCE to have been conducted satisfactorily. In the ballot for the Bosniak member of the tripartite presidency Haris Silajdžić of the Party of Bosnia and Herzegovina, was elected by 62.8% of votes cast, defeating the incumbent Bosniak representative, Tihić. Nebojša Radmanović, a member of the AISD, secured the post of Serb member of the presidency, with 53.3% of votes cast, while the SDP candidate took only 24.2% of votes. The successful Croat candidate, Željko Komšić, won 39.6% of votes cast; the incumbent Croat member of the presidency, Jović, who received 26.1% of votes, initially refused to concede defeat, on the grounds that Komšić, as a member of the multi-ethnic SDP BiH, was not a legitimate representative of the Croat people, but was subsequently obliged to relinquish his post. In the election to the 42-member Predstavnički dom, the PDA secured nine seats, while the Party for Bosnia and Herzegovina increased its representation to eight seats, the AISD obtained seven seats, and the SDP BiH five seats. The PDA also remained the leading party in the Predstavnički dom Federacije, with 28 seats; the Party for Bosnia and Herzegovina won 24 seats, and the SDP BiH 17 seats. The AISD achieved the largest representation in the Narodna skupština Republike Srpske, with 41 seats, two fewer than required for an absolute majority, while the SDP won only 17 seats. Milan Jelić of the AISD was elected to the Republika Srpska presidency with 48.8% of votes cast, replacing Čavić, who took 29.4% of votes.

In early October 2006 Krajišnik was convicted at the ICTY on five charges of crimes against humanity and sentenced to 27 years' imprisonment; however, he was acquitted of genocide and complicity in genocide. The three members of the collective presidency were inaugurated on 6 November 2006. The new Narodna skupština Republike Srpske was installed on 9 November, and Jelić, who pledged to eradicate corruption and crime in the entity, was inaugurated on the same day. In mid-November Jelić nominated Dodik as Prime Minister of Republika Srpska. Dodik renewed the ruling coalition of the AISD with the PDP and PDA, and a new Government, which included only five new ministers, was approved by the Narodna skupština on 30 November. Dodik subsequently reiterated opposition to the establishment of a single police structure at state level; implementation of the police reforms had become obstructed earlier that year after he demanded that they be reconsidered.

Following a summit meeting at the end of November 2006, NATO invited Bosnia and Herzegovina, together with Montenegro and Serbia, to join the PfP programme, on the grounds that substantive progress had been achieved in reforms. The ICTY Prosecutor, Carla Del Ponte, criticized NATO's decision and declared that the co-operation of Bosnia and Herzegovina, in particular of the Republika Srpska authorities, with the Tribunal continued to be unsatisfactory. (The three countries were officially admitted on 14 December.) In December the EU provisionally approved a staged reduction in EUFOR troops, from 6,000 to 2,500, stating that the improved security situation warranted such a withdrawal. (The EU confirmed this decision at the end of February 2007.)

Meanwhile, prolonged discussions regarding the establishment of the state Council of Ministers continued, with each of the three principal parties insisting on their own candidate for the office of Chairman. On 3 January 2007 agreement was finally reached on the appointment of Nikola Špirić of the AISD to the post. The Predstavnički dom approved a state Government proposed by Špirić on 9 February. At the end of January the Constitutional Court of Bosnia and Herzegovina abolished the coat-of-arms and flags of both Republika Srpska and the Federation, and the anthem of Republika Srpska, after both entity Governments failed to comply with a previous court ruling that the symbols should represent equally the three constituent ethnic groups. In February further inter-party discussions on police-sector reform ended in failure. On 26 February the ICJ ruled that the Serbian state was not directly responsible for genocide or complicity in genocide in Bosnia and Herzegovina in 1992–95. However, the Court declared that Serbia was in violation of its obligation under international law by having failed to prevent the 1995 massacre in Srebrenica and to co-operate fully with the ICTY. On 28 February 2007 the Peace Implementation Council of Bosnia and Herzegovina announced that the operations of the Office of the High Representative, which had been expected to end in June, were to be extended for a further year, although Schwarz-Schilling was to leave the post as scheduled. On 23 March Schwarz-Schilling annulled approval of a new Federation Government by the Predstavnički dom Federacije, on the grounds that his Office had not completed the process of checking ministerial candidates. A new five-party coalition Government, headed by Nedžad Branković of the PDA (hitherto the Minister of Transport and Communications), was finally approved in the Predstavnički dom Federacije on 30 March.

In late May 2007 a Serb war criminal, Radovan Stanković, who had been sentenced to 20 years' imprisonment by the Court of Bosnia and Herzegovina after being transferred from the ICTY, escaped from custody near Foča. In the same month a former Bosnian Serb army officer, Zdravko Tolimir, believed to be a close associate of Mladić and to be assisting his evasion of capture, was arrested on Republika Srpska territory, near the border with Serbia, and extradited to the ICTY. On 1 July a Slovakian diplomat, Miroslav Lajčák, officially succeeded Schwarz-Schilling as High Representative. In the same month the state and entity Governments signed an accord on public administration reform, which was required for the disbursement of EU funds and was also a precondition for the signature of an SAA. In August, after the main political leaders rejected a police-sector reform plan drafted by him, Lajčák insisted that agreement be reached on the issue by the end of September in order to allow the completion of negotiations on the SAA in 2007; he also criticized repeated demands by Dodik that a referendum be conducted in Republika Srpska on independence for the entity. A new police reform plan agreed between Silajdžić and Dodik shortly before the stipulated date was rejected by Lajčák as being insufficient to meet three main conditions stipulated by the EU (organization at state level, financing from a central budget and absence of political interference). In late October leaders of eight principal parties, meeting in Mostar, signed a declaration that the police should be restructured in accordance with the three EU principles, but failed to address the two main issues of dispute, that of the preservation of a Republika Srpska police force and the establishment of police districts that included territories from both entities.

In October 2007 Lajčák announced a number of measures for reforming parliamentary and government decision-making procedures, including new regulations to prevent representatives of one ethnic group from obstructing the adoption of legislation; Bosnian Serb politicians, including Dodik, threatened to boycott institutions if they were imposed. On 1 November Špirić resigned the state premiership in protest at Lajčák's decision, after the Peace Implementation Council expressed support for the reforms. At the end of November, following a protracted impasse, Bosnian Serb leaders ended resistance to the legislation proposed by Lajčák. Following an agreement by the political leaders to proceed with police-sector reforms in accordance with the EU criteria, the SAA was initialled on 4 December, with its signature remaining dependent on the implementation of the reforms. The EU decision was widely believed to reflect international concern that an expected declaration of independence from Serbia by the administration of Kosovo would increase secessionist aspirations in Republika Srpska.

On 9 December 2007 an election to the Republika Srpska presidency was conducted, following the death of Jelić as the result of a heart attack at the end of September; Rajko Kuzmanović of the AISD secured 41.3% of votes cast, defeating nine candidates, including Ognjen Tadić of the SDP (with 35.2%). At his presidential inauguration on 28 December, Kuzmanović stated his opposition to any further transfer of powers to central government from the entities. On the same day Špirić was reappointed to the state premiership. On 20 February 2008 the Predstavnički dom approved the unchanged Council of Ministers reappointed by Špirić. Following Kosovo's unilateral declaration of independence on 17 February, the Bosnian presidency announced that it would not extend recognition to Kosovo in the near future, owing to the opposition of the Serbian population. Protests against Kosovo's independence were staged in Banja Luka. On 21 February, prompted by demands from nationalist organizations, notably the SDP, the Narodna skupština Republike Srpske adopted a resolution declaring that the entity had the right to secede from Bosnia and Herzegovina if most UN and EU member nations recognized Kosovo's independence. A further police-reform plan, proposed by Lajčák, was approved by the Predstavnički dom on 10 April and by the Dom Naroda on 16 April; the compromise agreement abandoned the stipulation for the creation of a single police force, and provided for the establishment of seven state-level co-ordination bodies, with authority over the entity police forces. EU officials welcomed the measure as fulfilment of the final requirement for signature of the SAA.

Government

In accordance with the General Framework Agreement for Peace in Bosnia and Herzegovina, signed in December 1995, Bosnia and Herzegovina is a single state, which consists of two autonomous political entities: the Federation of Bosnia and Herzegovina and Republika Srpska. A civilian High Representative of the International Community in Bosnia and Herzegovina oversees government institutions and the implementation of the peace accords. The state Government of Bosnia and Herzegovina has a three-member collective presidency of one Bosniak, one Croat and one Serb. Members of the Presidency are directly elected for a term of four years, and are eligible to serve for only two consecutive terms. Chairmanship of the Presidency is rotated between the members every eight months. The bicameral Parlamentarna škupstina Bosne i Hercegovine (Parliamentary Assembly of Bosnia and Herzegovina) comprises the Dom Naroda (House of Peoples) and the Predstavnički dom (House of Representatives). The Predstavnički dom has 42 deputies, of whom 28 are directly elected from the Federation and 14 are directly elected from Republika Srpska for a four-year term. The Dom Naroda has 15 deputies, of whom 10 are selected by the Federation legislature and five by the Republika Srpska legislature for a four-year term. The Presidency appoints a Chairman of the state Council of Ministers (subject to the approval of the Predstavnički dom), who subsequently appoints the other ministers.

The Federation of Bosnia and Herzegovina and Republika Srpska each retain an executive presidency, government and legislature. The bicameral Parlament Federacije (Federation Parliament) has a 98-member Predstavnički dom Federacije (Federation House of Representatives), which is directly elected for a four-year term, and a 58-member Dom Naroda Federacije (Federation House of Peoples), comprising 17 Serb, 17 Bosniak, 17 Croat and seven other deputies, who are elected by the cantonal assemblies. The legislature of Republika Srpska comprises a 83-member Narodna skupština Republike Srpske (National Assembly of Republika Srpska), which is directly elected for a four-year term. This Assembly elects 28 delegates, of whom eight are Bosniaks, eight Croats, eight Serbs, and eight representatives of other ethnic groups, to a Vijeće naroda (Council of Peoples), which is responsible, *inter alia*, for electing the entity's representatives to the Dom Naroda. The Parlament Federacije elects a President and two joint Vice-Presidents, comprising one Bosniak, one Croat and one Serb, for a term of four years. The President and two Vice-Presidents of Republika Srpska are directly elected, for a four-year term. The Federation is divided into 10 cantons; each canton has an elected assembly and a President. The Federation comprises 84 and Republika Srpska 63 municipalities; in addition, the north-eastern town of Brčko was established as a neutral self-governing district in 2000, under the sovereignty of the state Government.

Defence

Under the terms of the Dayton agreement of 1995, the size of the armed forces of the two entities, the Federation and Republika Srpska, was restricted. In April 2003 the authorities announced a restructuring and reduction of the military, with the aim of establishing a unified defence command structure, a principal requirement for the country's accession to the North Atlantic Treaty Organization's (NATO) 'Partnership for Peace' (PfP, see p. 342) programme. A state-level Ministry of Defence was established in March 2004, and in November the first state armed forces unit, comprising troops from the country's three constitutive ethnic groups, was established. In December, after NATO rejected Bosnia and Herzegovina's application to join the PfP programme for a second time, the High Representative announced that the entity Ministries of Defence were to be abolished (thereby establishing a single state-level defence structure), and that the existing police and security agencies were to be merged to form a single police force. The Federation and Republika Srpska Ministries of Defence and armed forces were officially dissolved on 1 January 2006, thereby transferring authority over the military from the entity authorities to the central state government. A new police-reform plan, which, rather than stipulating the creation of a single police force, provided for the establishment of seven state-level co-ordination bodies, with authority over the entity police forces, was approved by both chambers of the state legislature in April 2008. Bosnia and Herzegovina was admitted to the PfP programme on 14 December 2006. As assessed at November 2007, the active armed forces of Bosnia and Herzegovina (which included an air force) numbered 9,047. Defence expenditure was budgeted at KM 220m. in 2006.

On 20 December 1995 power was formally transferred to an international, NATO-commanded, 60,000-strong 'Implementation Force' (IFOR), which was granted authority to oversee the implementation of the peace accord. In December 1996 IFOR was superseded by a Stabilization Force (SFOR), which initially comprised about 32,000 troops. At the end of 2002 the mandate of the UN Mission in Bosnia and Herzegovina (UNMIBH), established in 1995, was officially completed, and it was succeeded by a European Union Police Mission (EUPM), which had a mandate to supervise the reorganization and training of the country's security forces. At the beginning of February 2008 the EUPM comprised 168 police-officers, supported by 31 international civilian monitors. On 2 December 2004 SFOR officially transferred authority to a EU Force (EUFOR), which was authorized to maintain peace and to support the country's progress towards European integration. In February 2007 the EU confirmed plans for a staged reduction, from 6,000 to 2,500, of EUFOR troops, in view of the improvement in the country's security situation. At early 2008 EUFOR comprised 2,228 personnel from 29 countries (including six non-EU member states).

Economic Affairs

In 2006, according to World Bank estimates, Bosnia and Herzegovina's gross national income (GNI), measured at average 2004–06 prices, was US $11,649m., equivalent to $2,980 per head. During 1996–2006, it was estimated, the population of Bosnia and Herzegovina increased at an average annual rate of 1.4%, while gross domestic product (GDP) per head increased, in real terms, by an average of 7.8% per year. Overall GDP increased, in real terms, at an average annual rate of 9.2% in 1996–2006; real growth was 5.7% in 2006.

Agriculture (including forestry and fishing) contributed an estimated 10.1% of GDP in 2006, according to official figures, and employed 20.6% of the labour force. The major agricultural products are tobacco and fruit, and the livestock sector is also significant. Foodstuffs and live animals comprised 17.1% of total imports in 2006. According to World Bank estimates, the GDP of the agricultural sector declined, in real terms, by an annual average of 0.6% in 1996–2006. Sectoral growth was estimated at 3.7% in 2006.

Industry (mining, manufacturing, utilities and construction) contributed an estimated 23.9% of GDP in 2006. Some 30.7% of the labour force were employed in the industrial sector in 2006. According to World Bank estimates, industrial GDP increased, in real terms, by an annual average of 7.0% in 1996–2006. Industrial GDP increased by an estimated 7.7% in 2006.

The mining and quarrying sector contributed 2.2% of GDP in 2006. Bosnia and Herzegovina possesses extensive mineral resources, including iron ore, lignite, copper, lead, zinc and gold. Manufacturing contributed 11.5% of GDP in 2006. The manufacturing sector is based largely on the processing of iron ore, non-ferrous metals, coal, and wood and paper products. Manufacturing GDP increased, in real terms, by an annual average of 7.4% in 1996–2006. Manufacturing growth was estimated at 7.7% in 2006.

The civil conflict resulted in the destruction of much of the electric power system in Bosnia and Herzegovina. In 2004 some 52.1% of electricity production was derived from coal and 46.8% from hydroelectric power. Mineral fuels accounted for 16.5% of total imports in 2006.

The services sector contributed an estimated 66.0% of GDP in 2006, when it employed some 48.7% of the labour force. According to World Bank estimates, the GDP of the services sector increased, in real terms, by an annual average of 13.5% in 1996–2006. The GDP of the services sector was estimated to have increased by 5.2% in 2006.

In 2006 Bosnia and Herzegovina recorded a visible trade deficit of US $4,236.5m., and there was a deficit of $1,260.6m. on the current account of the balance of payments. In 2006 the principal source of imports was Croatia (which accounted for 16.7% of total imports); other important suppliers were Germany, Serbia and Montenegro and Italy. In that year the main market for exports was also Croatia (which accounted for 18.7% of the total); other significant purchasers were Italy, Serbia and Montenegro, Italy and Germany. The principal exports in 2006 were basic manufactures, machinery and transport equipment, and mineral fuels and lubricants. The main imports in that year were basic manufactures, machinery and transport equipment, and food and live animals.

Bosnia and Herzegovina's overall budget deficit for 2005 was KM 179.1m., according to projected figures, equivalent to 0.9% of GDP. The country's total external debt was estimated at US $5,564m. at the end of 2004 (of which $4,400m. was public debt), and the cost of debt-servicing was equivalent to about 4.8% of the value of exports of goods and services. Consumer prices, according to the IMF, declined by an average of 0.3% in 1998, and increased by 3.4% in 1999, by 5.0% in 2000, by 3.2% in 2001, and by 0.3% in 2002; the inflation rate was 0.5% in 2003, 0.3% in 2004, 3.6% in 2005 and 7.5% in 2006. The rate of unemployment was some 31.1% in 2006.

Bosnia and Herzegovina became a member of the IMF in December 1995 and was admitted to the World Bank in April 1996. In July 1999 the first summit meeting of the Stability Pact for South Eastern Europe took place in Bosnia and Herzegovina, with the aim of adopting a common strategy for regional stability. Bosnia and Herzegovina joined the Central European Free Trade Agreement (CEFTA) in September 2007.

The conflict in 1992–95 resulted in extensive damage to the economy. Following the signature of the Dayton peace agreement in December 1995, economic reconstruction commenced. The new national currency, the Convertible Mark, fixed at par with the German Deutsche Mark (and subsequently linked to the euro), was officially introduced in June 1998. In October agreement was reached with the 'Paris Club' of creditor governments on the reduction of external debt. Following large inflows of foreign assistance, the economy rapidly recovered under an IMF-supported reconstruction and development programme. During 2002 the High Representative imposed a series of economic regulations, with the ultimate aim of unifying principal sectors, such as telecommunications, banking, and tax and customs administration, throughout the country, as a prerequisite for eventual membership of the European Union (EU, see p. 244), and macroeconomic indicators continued to improve steadily. The most significant progress was demonstrated by the return of large numbers of refugees and internally displaced civilians, which was supported by foreign remittances. After the Republika Srpska and subsequently the state legislature agreed to essential police-sector reforms, negotiations on the signature of a Stabilization and Association Agreement (SAA) with the EU officially began in November 2005. As part of the process towards meeting EU standards, a series of economic measures, including improvement of the customs service, and of the regulation of public utilities and enterprises, was introduced. At the beginning of 2006 a single-rate value-added tax came into effect. The pace of privatization in the Federation remained slow during that year, but in Republika Srpska the sale of a majority share in a principal telecommunications company to the Serbian state-owned operator was finalized. There was a substantial rise in consumer prices in November 2007, notably for oil, while food prices also increased markedly. International officials attributed

BOSNIA AND HERZEGOVINA

the rises to higher international prices, although some analysts believed that an ongoing domestic political crisis was also a contributory factor (see Recent History). As price increases continued throughout early 2008, trade unions demanded that value-added tax on basic commodities be abolished or lowered. Meanwhile, on 4 December 2007, after political leaders had agreed to proceed with police reforms, the SAA was initialled with the Enlargement Commissioner, who indicated that the country had fulfilled many of its obligations for accession. The approval of a new police-reform plan by both chambers of the state legislature in April 2008 was expected to allow final signature of the Agreement to proceed.

Education

A nine-year system of elementary education, free and compulsory for all children between the ages of six and 15 years, was introduced throughout Bosnia and Herzegovina in 2003/04, replacing the 'eight-year school' cycle. Various types of secondary education available to all who qualify include: general secondary schools (gymnasiums), where children may follow a four-year course to prepare them for university entrance; vocational schools; and technical schools. The two entities (the Federation and Republika Srpska) have separate ministries of education, and authority over schooling in the Federation is further divided between the ten cantons, while the District of Brčko also has its own ministry. In 2003/04 some 374,915 pupils were enrolled in 1,871 primary schools, and 162,115 pupils attended 304 secondary schools. In 2005/06 some 60,860 students were enrolled in 72 higher education institutions in the Federation of Bosnia and Herzegovina, while 27,359 students were enrolled in 64 institutions in Republika Srpska. The higher education sector included seven universities (situated in Sarajevo, East Sarajevo, Banja Luka, Mostar—where there are two universities, Tuzla and Bihać). In August 2003 officials at state, entity and cantonal level signed an agreement to replace the country's three ethnically-based education systems with a single standardized system. However, the state Council of Ministers subsequently failed to endorse the new legislation. As a result, schooling remained ethnically divided, with entities and cantons continuing to control their own syllabuses.

Public Holidays

2008: 1–2 January (New Year), 6–7 January (Orthodox Christmas), 14–15 January (Orthodox New Year), 27 January (Orthodox St Sava's Day), 1 March (Independence Day), 21–24 March (Catholic Easter), 25–28 April (Orthodox Easter), 1 May (Labour Day), 15 August (Catholic Assumption), 1 October* (Small Bayram, end of Ramadan), 1 November (Catholic All Saints' Day), 25 November (National Statehood Day), 8 December* (Great Bayram, Feast of the Sacrifice), 25 December (Catholic Christmas).

2009: 1 January (New Year), 6–7 January (Orthodox Christmas), 14–15 January (Orthodox New Year), 27 January (Orthodox St Sava's Day), 1 March (Independence Day), 10–13 April (Catholic Easter), 17–20 April (Orthodox Easter), 1 May (Labour Day), 15 August (Catholic Assumption), 20 September* (Small Bayram, end of Ramadan), 1 November (Catholic All Saints' Day), 25 November (National Statehood Day), 27 November* (Great Bayram, Feast of the Sacrifice), 25 December (Catholic Christmas).

* These holidays are dependent on the Islamic lunar calendar and may vary by one or two days from the dates given.

Weights and Measures

The metric system is in force.

Statistical Survey

Source (unless otherwise stated): Agencija za statistiku Bosne i Hercegovine, 71000 Sarajevo, trg Bosne i Hercegovine 1; tel. and fax (33) 2206222; e-mail bhas@bih.net.ba; internet www.bhas.ba.

Area and Population

AREA, POPULATION AND DENSITY

Area (sq km)	
Land	51,197
Inland water	12
Total	51,209*
Population (census results)	
31 March 1981	4,124,008
31 March 1991	
Males	2,183,795
Females	2,193,238
Total	4,377,033
Population (official estimates)†	
2004	3,797,000
2005	3,808,000
2006	3,813,000
Density (per sq km) at 2006	74.5

* 19,772 sq miles.
† Approximate aggregates derived from separate annual population estimates of the Federation of Bosnia and Herzegovina Office of Statistics and the Republika Srpska Institute of Statistics.

POPULATION BY ETHNIC GROUP
(according to official declaration of nationality, 1991 census, provisional)

	Number	% of total population
Muslim	1,905,829	43.7
Serb	1,369,258	31.4
Croat	755,892	17.3
Yugoslav	239,845	5.5
Others	93,750	2.1
Total	**4,364,574**	**100.0**

CANTONS WITHIN THE FEDERATION
(at 31 December 2006, official estimates)

Canton	Population	Principal city (with population)
Bosna-Podrinje	33,717	Goražde (30,789)
Central Bosnia	256,191	Travnik (55,195)
Herzegovina-Neretva	227,630	Mostar (111,282)
Posavina	41,264	Orašje (20,721)
Sarajevo	418,891	Sarajevo (304,136)
Tuzla	496,280	Tuzla (131,414)
Una-Sana	287,624	Bihać (60,991)
West Herzegovina	82,082	Široki Brijeg (26,163)
Zenica-Doboj	401,590	Zenica (127,307)
'Canton 10'*	82,197	Livno (32,374)
Total	**2,327,466**	

* Formerly known as Herceg-Bosna Canton.

Source: Federation of Bosnia and Herzegovina Office of Statistics.

PRINCIPAL TOWNS
(population estimates at 31 December)

Sarajevo (capital)	304,136*		Cazin	61,926*
Banja Luka	224,647†		Gradišca	61,440†
Tuzla	131,414*		Bihać	60,991*
Zenica	127,307*		Travnik	55,195*
Mostar	111,282*		Živinice	54,248*
Bijeljina	109,211†		Zvornik-	51,688†
Prijedor	98,570†		Gračanica	51,364*
Doboj	80,464†		Lukavac	51,146*

* Estimate for 2006 (Source: Federation of Bosnia and Herzegovina Office of Statistics). The figure for Sarajevo excludes those areas of the city ('East Sarajevo') located in Republika Srpska.
† Estimate for 2004 (Source: Republika Srpska Institute of Statistics).

BOSNIA AND HERZEGOVINA

BIRTHS, MARRIAGES AND DEATHS

	Registered live births Number	Rate (per 1,000)	Registered marriages Number	Rate (per 1,000)	Registered deaths Number	Rate (per 1,000)
1998	45,007	12.3	22,398	6.1	28,679	7.9
1999	42,464	11.4	22,472	6.0	28,637	7.7
2000	39,563	10.5	21,897	5.8	30,482	8.1
2001	37,717	9.9	20,302	5.3	30,325	8.0
2002	35,587	9.3	20,122	5.3	30,155	7.9
2003	35,234	9.2	20,733	5.4	31,757	8.3
2004	35,151	9.1	22,252	5.8	32,616	8.5
2005	34,627	9.0	21,698	5.6	34,402	9.0

Note: Rates are based on official mid-year estimates of de facto population.

Expectation of life (years at birth, WHO estimates): 73.3 (males 69.9; females 76.8) in 2005 (Source: WHO, *World Health Statistics*).

EMPLOYMENT
(labour force survey at 31 March 2003)

	Males	Females	Total
Agriculture, hunting and forestry	14,503	3,447	17,950
Fishing	393	98	491
Mining and quarrying	18,203	2,051	20,254
Manufacturing	92,867	55,958	148,825
Electricity, gas and water supply	19,013	4,999	24,012
Construction	29,500	4,857	34,357
Wholesale and retail trade; repair of motor vehicles, motorcycles and personal and household goods	40,062	35,432	75,494
Hotels and restaurants	9,703	9,543	19,246
Transport, storage and communications	30,123	8,973	39,096
Financial intermediation	3,949	6,317	10,266
Real estate, renting and business activities	8,725	4,657	13,382
Public administration and defence; compulsory social security	26,565	20,351	46,916
Education	19,875	28,042	47,917
Health and social work	13,211	27,565	40,776
Other community, social and personal service activities	13,904	7,997	21,901
Activities not adequately defined	42,773	18,164	60,937
Total	**383,369**	**238,451**	**621,820**

Registered unemployed (annual averages): 434,087 in 2003; 455,836 in 2004; 489,869 in 2005.

2006 (labour force survey at April, '000 persons aged 15 years and over): Agriculture 167; Industry 249; Services 395; *Total employed* 811; Unemployed 366; *Total labour force* 1,177 (males 743, females 434).

Health and Welfare

KEY INDICATORS

Total fertility rate (children per woman, 2005)	1.3
Under-5 mortality rate (per 1,000 live births, 2005)	15
HIV/AIDS (% of persons aged 15–49, 2005)	<0.10
Physicians (per 1,000 head, 2003)	1.34
Hospital beds (per 1,000 head, 2005)	3
Health expenditure (2004): US $ per head (PPP)	603.0
Health expenditure (2004): % of GDP	8.3
Health expenditure (2004): public (% of total)	49.4
Access to water (% of persons, 2004)	97
Access to sanitation (% of persons, 2004)	95
Human Development Index (2005): ranking	66
Human Development Index (2005): value	0.803

For sources and definitions, see explanatory note on p. vi.

Agriculture

PRINCIPAL CROPS
('000 metric tons)

	2004	2005	2006
Wheat	319.0	248.3	232.5
Barley	62.5	51.9	62.4
Maize	990.4	1,004.1	993.9
Rye	9.9	7.5	10.7
Oats	57.0	37.9	41.5
Potatoes	447.1	458.6	410.4
Dry beans	14.2	13.5	14.5
Soybeans (Soya beans)	8.7	12.5	12.8
Cabbages	84.7	86.7	99.2
Tomatoes	39.7	30.7	40.7
Chillies and green peppers	48.2	36.1	43.0
Dry onions	34.5	34.3	41.5
Garlic	7.8	7.6	8.0
Carrots	19.3	21.0	18.9
Watermelons*	47.7	56.1	56.1
Grapes	21.7	23.3	21.5
Apples	53.3	52.2	58.1
Pears	19.8	22.5	23.0
Plums	167.8	96.0	123.2
Tobacco (leaves)	4.2	4.4	3.9

* FAO estimates.

Aggregate production ('000 metric tons, may include official, semi-official or estimated data): Total cereals 1,438.7 in 2004, 1,349.8 in 2005, 1,341.0 in 2006; Total roots and tubers 447.1 in 2004, 458.6 in 2005, 410.4 in 2006; Total vegetables (incl. melons) 809.0 in 2004, 798.5 in 2005, 836.7 in 2006; Total fruits (excl. melons) 286.8 in 2004, 227.4 in 2005, 261.1 in 2006.

Source: FAO.

LIVESTOCK
('000 head, year ending September)

	2004	2005	2006
Horses	28	27	26
Cattle	453	460	515
Pigs	595	653	712
Sheep	893	903	995
Chickens	9,476	10,340	13,331
Ducks	220*	250†	250†
Geese and guinea fowls	280*	300†	300†
Turkeys	220*	250	250†

* Unofficial figure.
† FAO estimate.

Source: FAO.

LIVESTOCK PRODUCTS
('000 metric tons)

	2004	2005	2006
Cattle meat	19.3	23.6	22.4
Sheep meat	1.5	1.7	1.9
Pig meat	8.2	8.9	9.8
Chicken meat	16.3	12.0	14.4
Cows' milk	582.6	629.4	662.4
Sheep's milk	16.4	18.2	20.0
Hen eggs	15.6	17.6	17.6

Source: FAO.

BOSNIA AND HERZEGOVINA

Forestry

ROUNDWOOD REMOVALS
('000 cubic metres, excluding bark)

	2003	2004	2005
Sawlogs, veneer logs and logs for sleepers	2,446	2,247	2,030
Pulpwood	144	196	155
Other industrial wood	293	240	259
Fuel wood	1,215	1,310	1,362
Total	4,098	3,993	3,806

2006: Figures assumed to be unchanged from 2005 (FAO estimates).
Source: FAO.

SAWNWOOD PRODUCTION
('000 cubic metres, including railway sleepers)

	2003	2004	2005*
Coniferous (softwood)	566.5	621.0	621.0
Broadleaved (hardwood)	321.4	698.0	698.0
Total	887.9	1,319.0	1,319.0

* FAO estimates.

2006: Figures assumed to be unchanged from 2005 (FAO estimates).
Source: FAO.

Fishing

(metric tons, live weight, FAO estimates)

	2003	2004	2005
Capture	2,000	2,000	2,000
Aquaculture	6,635	6,394	7,070
Common carp	1,900	2,363	2,450
Rainbow trout	3,800	3,430	3,720
Total catch	8,635	8,394	9,070

Source: FAO.

Mining

('000 metric tons, unless otherwise indicated)

	2003	2004	2005
Brown coal and lignite	9,006	8,896	9,000
Iron ore: metal content	63	140	150
Bauxite	573	917	900
Barite (Barytes) concentrate (metric tons)*	80	65	70
Salt	200	261	250
Gypsum (crude)	63	140	55

* Estimates.

Source: US Geological Survey.

Industry

SELECTED PRODUCTS
('000 metric tons, unless otherwise indicated)

	2001	2002	2003
Beer	480*	652*	1,316†
Cigarettes	690*	662*	5,062†
Crude steel‡	139	115	166
Aluminium (metal ingot)‡	95	102	113
Cement‡	703,843	912,611	890,179
Electric energy (million kWh)	10,327	10,785	11,250

* Excluding figures for the Federation.
† New series, not comparable with previous years' data.
‡ Source: US Geological Survey.

Source: UN, *Industrial Commodity Statistics Yearbook*.

2004 ('000 metric tons): Crude steel 117; Aluminium (metal ingot) 121; Cement 1,044,944. (Source: US Geological Survey).

2005 ('000 metric tons): Crude steel 283; Aluminium (metal ingot) 131; Cement 1,000,000. (Source: US Geological Survey).

Finance

CURRENCY AND EXCHANGE RATES

Monetary Units
  100 pfeninga = 1 konvertibilna marka (KM or convertible marka).

Sterling, Dollar and Euro Equivalents (31 December 2007)
  £1 sterling = KM 2.662;
  US $1 = KM 1.329;
  €1 = KM 1.956;
  KM 100 = £37.57 = $75.27 = €51.13.

Average Exchange Rate (KM per US $)
  2005 1.5727
  2006 1.5591
  2007 1.4290

Note: The new Bosnia and Herzegovina dinar (BHD) was introduced in August 1994, with an official value fixed at 100 BHD = 1 Deutsche Mark (DM). The DM, the Croatian kuna and the Yugoslav dinar also circulated within Bosnia and Herzegovina. On 22 June 1998 the BHD was replaced by the KM, equivalent to 100 of the former units. The KM was thus at par with the DM. From the introduction of the euro, on 1 January 1999, the German currency had a fixed exchange rate of €1 = DM 1.95583.

BUDGET
(KM million*)

Revenue†	2003	2004‡	2005§
Tax revenue	4,851.6	5,158.1	5,459.9
Indirect taxes	2,124.3	2,361.7	2,604.2
Trade taxes	624.1	533.6	503.6
Direct taxes	415.3	486.7	485.7
Social security contributions	1,687.9	1,776.1	1,866.3
Other revenue (incl. grants)	593.5	716.0	731.3
Total	5,445.1	5,874.0	6,191.2

BOSNIA AND HERZEGOVINA

Expenditure	2003	2004‡	2005§
Interest payments	108.0	53.5	91.5
Subsidies and transfers to non-public agents‖	2,385.3	2,477.5	2,478.1
Other current expenditure	2,809.5	3,231.9	3,435.8
Investment expenditure	987.6	838.2	788.3
Total	6,290.4	6,601.1	6,793.8

* Figures represent a consolidation of the budgetary accounts of: the central state Government; the federal and cantonal authorities in the Federation; and the central republican authorities (but not local and district administrations) in Republika Srpska.
† Excluding grants (KM million): 641.1 in 2003; 479.6 in 2004 (preliminary figure); 423.0 in 2005 (projected figure).
‡ Preliminary figures.
§ Projected figures.
‖ Excluding transfers by Federation Cantons.

Source: IMF, *Bosnia and Herzegovina: 2005 Article IV Consultation–Staff Report; Staff Supplement; Public Information Notice on the Executive Board Discussion; and Statement by the Executive Director for Bosnia and Herzegovina* (June 2005).

INTERNATIONAL RESERVES
(US $ million at 31 December)

	2004	2005	2006
IMF special drawing rights	1	—	—
Foreign exchange	2,407	2,531	3,371
Total	2,408	2,531	3,371

Source: IMF, *International Financial Statistics*.

MONEY SUPPLY
(KM million at 31 December)

	2004	2005	2006
Currency outside banks	−354	−159	1,978
Demand deposits at banks	1,762	2,303	2,989
Total money (incl. others)	1,763	2,534	5,553

Source: IMF, *International Financial Statistics*.

COST OF LIVING
(Retail Price Index; base: December of previous year = 100)

	2004	2005	2006*
All items (Federation)	99.7	103.0	106.9
All items (Republika Srpska)	101.9	105.2	108.4
All items (Bosnia and Herzegovina)	100.4	103.8	107.4

* Preliminary.

Source: Central Bank of Bosnia and Herzegovina, *Annual Report 2006*.

NATIONAL ACCOUNTS
(KM million at current prices)

Expenditure on the Gross Domestic Product
(estimates)

	2004	2005
Government final consumption expenditure	3,535.1	3,653.2
Private final consumption expenditure	15,139.1	16,682.3
Gross capital formation	4,520.2	4,902.4
Total domestic expenditure	23,194.4	25,237.9
Exports of goods and services	4,641.4	5,583.0
Less Imports of goods and services	11,155.6	12,643.2
GDP in purchasers' values	16,680.2	18,177.6

Note: GDP estimates may differ from respective figures for GDP by economic activity owing to differing methods of data compilation.

Gross Domestic Product by Economic Activity

	2004	2005	2006
Agriculture, hunting and forestry	1,397.6	1,468.9	1,605.3
Fishing	2.6	2.9	4.4
Mining and quarrying	283.7	332.3	357.0
Manufacturing	1,480.1	1,567.7	1,833.1
Electricity, gas and water	818.6	867.7	850.3
Construction	657.8	723.6	759.7
Wholesale and retail trade	1,923.2	2,135.1	2,532.5
Hotels and restaurants	471.3	486.5	565.1
Transport and communications	1,275.6	1,317.7	1,398.2
Financial intermediation	498.3	608.4	649.7
Real estate and business services	1,521.2	1,679.4	1,768.9
Public administration and defence	1,409.9	1,434.1	1,588.0
Education	641.8	680.0	821.9
Health and social welfare	631.6	663.2	723.2
Other personal services	334.5	377.4	436.4
Sub-total	13,347.8	14,344.6	15,893.7
Less Financial intermediation services indirectly measured	329.4	418.8	481.7
Gross value added in basic prices	13,018.4	13,925.8	15,412.0
Taxes, less subsidies, on products	2,767.6	3,002.0	3,693.9
GDP in market prices	15,786.0	16,927.9	19,105.9

BALANCE OF PAYMENTS
(US $ million)

	2004	2005	2006
Exports of goods f.o.b.	2,086.7	2,589.5	3,381.5
Imports of goods f.o.b.	−6,656.4	−7,544.5	−7,618.0
Trade balance	−4,569.7	−4,954.9	−4,236.5
Exports of services	863.5	950.3	1,118.8
Imports of services	−432.2	−459.2	−507.7
Balance on goods and services	−4,138.4	−4,463.8	−3,625.4
Other income received	643.6	648.7	690.1
Other income paid	−162.4	−195.7	−225.1
Balance on goods, services and income	−3,657.1	−4,010.8	−3,160.4
Current transfers received	2,073.2	2,094.6	2,125.6
Current transfers paid	−209.6	−199.3	−225.8
Current balance	−1,793.6	−2,115.6	−1,260.6
Capital account (net)	431.8	409.6	342.7
Financial account (net)	1,416.1	1,763.3	1,143.0
Net errors and omissions	398.5	431.1	337.8
Overall balance	452.8	488.4	562.8

Source: IMF, *International Financial Statistics*.

External Trade

SELECTED COMMODITIES
(KM million*)

Imports	2004	2005	2006
Food and live animals	1,958.6	1,981.7	1,945.0
Vegetable products	492.5	490.0	468.5
Prepared foodstuffs	1,090.9	1,094.5	1,149.2
Mineral fuels, lubricants, etc.	1,181.2	1,585.5	1,882.1
Chemicals and related products	877.0	1,037.5	1,062.6
Basic manufactures	2,759.6	3,259.9	3,501.3
Plastics and rubber	446.1	518.3	539.3
Wood and wood products	396.4	447.3	440.8
Textiles and textile articles	488.4	574.6	604.3
Articles of stone, plaster, cement and asbestos	312.9	319.2	290.4
Base metals and articles thereof	838.1	1,068.8	1,187.4
Machinery and transport equipment	2,149.6	2,892.2	2,618.0
Machinery and mechanical appliances	1,447.1	1,980.8	1,816.4
Transport equipment	702.5	911.4	801.6
Total (incl. others)	9,305.9	11,178.5	11,389.2

BOSNIA AND HERZEGOVINA

Exports	2004	2005	2006
Food and live animals	167.1	223.2	258.7
Prepared foodstuffs	96.4	120.2	143.0
Mineral fuels, lubricants, etc.	332.4	503.1	607.2
Basic manufactures	1,614.6	1,842.0	2,765.0
Wood and wood products	502.3	454.8	556.7
Textiles and textile articles	163.5	157.6	254.7
Base metals and articles thereof	701.9	947.0	1,389.1
Machinery and transport equipment	254.2	636.6	742.5
Electrical machinery and equipment	202.8	544.0	643.3
Transport equipment	51.4	92.6	99.2
Miscellaneous manufactured articles	201.3	231.4	400.5
Total (incl. others)	2,818.8	3,783.3	5,164.3

* Figures from the Customs Administration of the Federation, the Customs Administration of Republika Srpska and the Customs Service of Brčko District, not including adjustments.

Source: Central Bank of Bosnia and Herzegovina, *Annual Report 2006*.

PRINCIPAL TRADING PARTNERS
(KM '000)

Imports	2004	2005	2006
Austria	396,408	488,104	446,970
Croatia	1,633,847	1,886,484	1,907,044
France	176,498	251,630	208,581
Germany	1,021,218	1,605,765	1,398,466
Hungary	411,549	409,603	392,515
Italy	850,747	1,000,500	1,009,865
Serbia and Montenegro	946,962	1,135,162	1,108,219
Slovenia	712,071	779,943	833,548
Switzerland	158,430	182,857	268,813
Total (incl. others)	9,305,942	11,178,545	11,389,183

Exports	2004	2005	2006
Austria	136,048	163,432	313,807
Croatia	609,975	775,428	965,296
France	48,409	63,696	86,233
Germany	268,389	429,036	668,731
Hungary	22,698	142,643	165,097
Italy	492,555	496,275	713,413
Serbia and Montenegro	446,073	587,960	681,771
Slovenia	256,498	365,199	629,633
Switzerland	104,049	50,253	95,786
Total (incl. others)	2,818,780	3,783,280	5,164,339

Source: Central Bank of Bosnia and Herzegovina, *Annual Report 2006*.

Transport

RAILWAYS
(traffic)

	2001	2002	2003
Passengers ('000 journeys)	1,296	1,128	1,090
Freight carried ('000 metric tons)	5,400	6,600	6,799
Passenger-km (million)	48	48	55
Freight ton-km (million)	288	312	318

CIVIL AVIATION
(traffic on scheduled services)

	2001	2002	2003
Kilometres flown (million)	1	1	1
Passengers carried ('000)	65	66	73
Passenger-km (million)	44	43	47
Total ton-km (million)	6	5	6

Source: UN, *Statistical Yearbook*.

Tourism

FOREIGN TOURIST ARRIVALS BY COUNTRY OF ORIGIN
('000)*

Country of origin	2003	2004	2005
Austria	6	7	7
Croatia	28	30	32
Czech Republic	3	2	3
France	3	5	10
Germany	8	10	12
Italy	8	12	14
Poland	3	3	5
Serbia and Montenegro	40	49	51
Slovenia	18	20	26
Turkey	3	5	7
United Kingdom	5	5	6
USA	7	7	7
Total (incl. others)	166	190	217

* Figures refer to arrivals at frontiers by visitors from abroad, and include same-day visitors.

Tourism receipts (US $ million, incl. passenger transport): 404 in 2003; 543 in 2004; 604 in 2005.

Source: World Tourism Organization.

Communications Media

	2004	2005	2006
Telephones ('000 main lines in use)	951.5	968.9	989.0
Mobile cellular telephones ('000 subscribers)	1,407.4	1,594.4	1,887.8
Internet users ('000)	585.0	806.4	950.0
Broadband subscribers ('000)	6.6	13.7	40.0

Daily newspapers (government-controlled areas only): 2 (average circulation 520,000 copies) in 1995; 3 in 1996; 7 in 2004.

Non-daily newspapers (1992): 22 (average circulation 2,508,000 copies).

1997: Radio receivers ('000 in use) 940; Television receivers ('000 in use) 900.

Sources: UN, *Statistical Yearbook*; UNESCO, *Statistical Yearbook*; International Telecommunication Union.

Education

('2003/04* unless otherwise indicated)

	Institutions	Teachers	Males	Females	Total
Pre-primary†	195	983	n.a.	n.a.	12,794
Primary	1,871	21,661	192,679	182,236	374,915
Secondary	304	n.a.	81,337	80,778	162,115
Higher	105	n.a.	n.a.	n.a.	77,009

* Figures at end of academic year.
† Preliminary figures for Federation and Republika Srpska at beginning of 2005/06 academic year.

Sources: partly Federation of Bosnia and Herzegovina Office of Statistics and Republika Srpska Institute of Statistics.

Adult literacy rate (UNESCO estimates): 96.7% (males 99.0%; females 94.4%) in 2000 (Source: UNESCO Institute for Statistics).

Directory

The Constitution

The Constitution of Bosnia and Herzegovina was Annexe 4 to the General Framework Agreement for Peace in Bosnia and Herzegovina (known as the Dayton accords, after the town in Ohio, the USA, where negotiations took place in November 1995), signed in Paris, France, on 14 December 1995. Annexe 4 took effect as a constitutional act upon signature, superseding and amending the Constitution of the Republic of Bosnia and Herzegovina.

THE ENTITIES

Bosnia and Herzegovina comprises two 'entities': the Federation of Bosnia and Herzegovina and Republika Srpska, each of which has its own Government and institutions. (In March 2000, following completion of a demilitarization process, the north-eastern town of Brčko was established as a neutral district and placed under joint Serb, Croat and Bosniak authority.)

The Federation of Bosnia and Herzegovina

The Federation had been formed on 31 March 1994 on those territories controlled by the 'Croat Republic of Herceg-Bosna' and by the Government of the Republic of Bosnia and Herzegovina. The Federation Constitution provides for a balance of powers between Bosniak and Croat elements, with significant powers devolved to each of its ten constituent cantons. The Prime Minister of the Federation has a greater executive role than the Federation President; these two posts rotate between the two ethnic groups. There are also two Vice-Presidents. The Federation legislature is bicameral, comprising a 98-member Predstavnički dom Federacije (Federation House of Representatives), which is directly elected for a four-year term, and a Dom Naroda Federacije (Federation House of Peoples), comprising 17 Bosniak, 17 Croat, 10 Serb and seven other deputies, who are elected by the cantonal assemblies.

Republika Srpska

The 'Republika Srpska of Bosnia and Herzegovina' was proclaimed by the Bosnian Serb deputies of the Skupština Republike Bosne i Hercegovine (Assembly of the Republic of Bosnia and Herzegovina) on 27 March 1992, and subsequently comprised those territories within Bosnia and Herzegovina controlled by Serb forces. (The name was abbreviated to Republika Srpska in August 1992.) Its Constitution provides for an executive President (with two Vice-Presidents), a Government headed by a Prime Minister and the Narodna skupština Republike Srpske (National Assembly of Republika Srpska). Under constitutional amendments adopted in 2002 a 28-member Vijeće naroda (Council of Peoples), comprising eight Bosniak, eight Croat, eight Serb and four other delegates, was established within the entity legislature; its members are elected by the deputies of the Narodna skupština and are responsible, *inter alia*, for electing the entity's representatives to the upper chamber of the state legislature.

THE HIGH REPRESENTATIVE OF THE INTERNATIONAL COMMUNITY

The Office of a High Representative of the International Community, established by the Dayton Accords (and which office was subsequently extended to additionally comprise the role of Special Representative of the European Union—EU), is responsible for the civilian implementation of the terms of the peace settlement, holding the power to compel the entity governments to comply with the terms of the peace agreement and the state constitution and the authority to dismiss members of the entity Governments and organizations that fail to uphold the terms of the peace agreement.

STATE CONSTITUTION OF BOSNIA AND HERZEGOVINA

The Preamble declares the basic, democratic principles of the country and its conformity with the principles of international law. The Bosniaks, Croats and Serbs are declared to be the constituent peoples (along with others) of Bosnia and Herzegovina.

The continuity of Bosnia and Herzegovina with the former Republic of Bosnia and Herzegovina, within its existing international boundaries, is affirmed. Bosnia and Herzegovina is a democratic state, consisting of two Entities, the Federation of Bosnia and Herzegovina and Republika Srpska. The capital of the country, and of both Entities, is Sarajevo (although, in practice, most institutions and the Government of Republika Srpska are located in Banja Luka, while the government ministries of the Federation are shared between Sarajevo and Mostar). Citizenship is to exist both for Bosnia and Herzegovina and for the Entities.

The state institutions of Bosnia and Herzegovina are responsible for foreign policy (including trade and customs), overall financial policy, immigration and refugee issues, international and interentity law enforcement, common and international communications facilities, inter-entity transportation and air-traffic control. Any governmental functions or powers not reserved to the state institutions by this Constitution are reserved to the Entities, unless additional responsibilities are agreed between the Entities or as provided for in the General Framework Agreement. The Entities may establish special, parallel relations with neighbouring states, provided this is consistent with the sovereignty and territorial integrity of Bosnia and Herzegovina. The Constitution of Bosnia and Herzegovina has primacy over any inconsistent constitutional or legal provisions of the Entities.

Parlamentarna skupština Bosne i Hercegovine

Bosnia and Herzegovina has a bicameral legislature, the Parlamentarna skupština Bosne i Hercegovine (Parliamentary Assembly of Bosnia and Herzegovina). It consists of the Dom Naroda (House of Peoples) and the Predstavnički dom (House of Representatives). The Dom Naroda comprises 15 Members, five each from the Bosniaks, the Croats and the Serbs, who are elected for a term of four years. The Bosniak and Croat Delegates are selected by, respectively, the Bosniak and Croat Delegates to the Predstavnički dom Federacije, and the Serb Delegates by the Vijeće naroda (Council of Peoples) of the Narodna skupština Republike Srpske.

The Predstavnički dom consists of 42 Members, of whom two-thirds are directly elected from the territory of the Federation and one-third from the territory of Republika Srpska. Deputies are elected for a term of four years.

Each chamber of the Parlamentarna skupština rotates its chairmanship between three members.

The State Presidency

The office of the head of state consists of three Members: one Bosniak and one Croat, each directly elected from the Federation; and one Serb, directly elected from Republika Srpska. Members are elected for a term of four years and are restricted to two consecutive terms. Chairmanship of the Presidency is rotated between the Members every eight months. A Presidency decision, if declared to be destructive of a vital interest of an Entity, can be vetoed by a two-thirds' majority in the relevant body: the Narodna skupština Republike Srpske if the declaration was made by the Serb Member; or by the Bosniak or Croat Delegates in the Federation Dom Naroda if the declaration was made by, respectively, the Bosniak or Croat Members.

The Chairman of the Council of Ministers is nominated by the Presidency and confirmed in office by the Predstavnički dom. The Chairman of the Council of Ministers is required to be from a different constituent people than the Chairman of the Presidency. Other Ministers and Deputy Ministers are nominated by the Chairman of the Council of Ministers, and approved by the Predstavnički dom. No more than two-thirds of Ministers are to be from the territory of the Federation, and Deputy Ministers are to be from a different constituent people to their Minister.

Other Institutions and Provisions

The Constitutional Court has nine members, of which four are selected by the Predstavnički dom Federacije and two by the Narodna skupština Republike Srpske. The three remaining judges, at least initially, are to be selected by the President of the European Court of Human Rights. Judges usually serve until they are 70 years of age. The decisions of the Court are final and binding.

Anyone convicted or indicted by the International Criminal Tribunal for the former Yugoslavia is forbidden from standing for or holding public office. Amendments to the Constitution need a two-thirds majority of those present and voting in the Predstavnički dom.

The Government

HIGH REPRESENTATIVE OF THE INTERNATIONAL COMMUNITY IN BOSNIA AND HERZEGOVINA

Under the terms of the treaty and annexes of the General Framework Agreement for Peace in Bosnia and Herzegovina, signed in December 1995, the international community, as authorized by the UN Security Council, was to designate a civilian representative to oversee the implementation of the peace accords and the establishment of the institutions of the new order in Bosnia and Herzegovina.

High Representative of the International Community and Special Representative of the European Union to Bosnia and Herzegovina: MIROSLAV LAJČÁK, 71000 Sarajevo, Emerika Bluma 1; tel. (33) 283500; fax (33) 283501; internet www.ohr.int.

Principal Deputy High Representative: RAFFI GREGORIAN.

Senior Deputy High Representative: PETER BAS-BACKER.

BOSNIA AND HERZEGOVINA

STATE GOVERNMENT OF BOSNIA AND HERZEGOVINA

Presidency

The Dayton accords, which were signed into treaty in December 1995, provide for a three-member Presidency for the state, comprising one Bosniak (Muslim), one Croat and one Serb. The collective Presidency, which governs Bosnia and Herzegovina at state level, comprises a Chairman and a further two members, with the post of Chairman rotating every eight months between Bosniak, Croat and Serb representatives. The Presidency nominates a Chairman of the Council of Ministers (subject to the approval of the legislature), who appoints the other ministers.

Chairman of the Presidency: Prof. Dr HARIS SILAJDŽIĆ (Party for Bosnia and Herzegovina) (March–October 2008).

Member of the Presidency: ŽELJKO KOMŠIĆ (Social Democratic Party of Bosnia and Herzegovina).

Member of the Presidency: Prof. Dr NEBOJŠA RADMANOVIĆ (Alliance of Independent Social Democrats).

Council of Ministers
(March 2008)

A coalition of the Alliance of Independent Social Democrats (AISD), the Party for Bosnia and Herzegovina, the Croatian Democratic Union of Bosnia and Herzegovina (CDU—BH), the Croatian Democratic Union 1990 of Bosnia and Herzegovina (CDU 1990) and the Party of Democratic Action (PDA).

Chairman: NIKOLA ŠPIRIĆ (AISD).
Minister of Defence: SELMO CIKOTIĆ (PDA).
Minister of Justice: BARIŠA ČOLAK (CDU—BH).
Minister of Foreign Affairs: SVEN ALKALAJ (Party for Bosnia and Herzegovina).
Minister of Security: TARIK SADOVIĆ (PDA).
Minister of Civil Affairs: SREDOJE NOVIĆ (Independent).
Minister of Foreign Trade and Economic Relations: SLOBODAN PUHALAC (AISD).
Minister of Human Rights and Refugees: SAFET HALILOVIĆ (Party for Bosnia and Herzegovina).
Minister of Finance and the Treasury: DRAGAN VRANKIĆ (CDU—BH).
Minister of Communications and Transport: BOŽO LJUBIĆ (CDU 1990).

Ministries

Office of the State Presidency: 71000 Sarajevo, Musala 5; tel. (33) 664941; fax (33) 472491; internet www.predsjednistvobih.ba.

Office of the Chairman of the Council of Ministers: 71000 Sarajevo, trg Bosne i Hercegovine 1; tel. (33) 211581; fax (33) 205347; e-mail mmicevska@vijeceministara.gov.ba; internet www.vijeceministara.gov.ba.

Ministry of Civil Affairs: 71000 Sarajevo, Vojvode Putnika 3; tel. (33) 221073; fax (33) 221074; e-mail kabinet.zamjenika@mcp.gov.ba; internet www.mcp.gov.ba.

Ministry of Communications and Transport: 71000 Sarajevo, trg Bosne i Hercegovine 1; tel. (33) 284750; fax (33) 284751; e-mail info@mkt.gov.ba; internet www.mkt.gov.ba.

Ministry of Defence: 71000 Sarajevo, Bistrik 5; tel. (33) 286500; fax (33) 206094; e-mail mod@mod.gov.ba; internet www.mod.gov.ba.

Ministry of Finance and the Treasury: 71000 Sarajevo, trg Bosne i Hercegovine 1; tel. (33) 205345; fax (33) 471822; e-mail trezorbih@trezorbih.gov.ba; internet www.trezorbih.gov.ba.

Ministry of Foreign Affairs: 71000 Sarajevo, Musala 2; tel. (33) 281100; fax (33) 472188; e-mail info@mvp.gov.ba; internet www.mvp.gov.ba.

Ministry of Foreign Trade and Economic Relations: 71000 Sarajevo, Musala 9; tel. (33) 258840; fax (33) 265620; e-mail info@vet.gov.ba; internet www.mvt.gov.ba.

Ministry of Human Rights and Refugees: 71000 Sarajevo, trg Bosne i Hercegovine 1; tel. (33) 206673; fax (33) 206140; e-mail kabmin@mhrr.gov.ba; internet www.mhrr.gov.ba.

Ministry of Justice: 71000 Sarajevo, trg Bosne i Hercegovine 1; tel. (33) 223501; fax (33) 223504; e-mail kontakt@mpr.gov.ba; internet www.mpr.gov.ba.

Ministry of Security: 71000 Sarajevo, trg Bosne i Hercegovine 1; tel. (33) 213623; fax (33) 213628; e-mail bdautbasic@smartnet.ba; internet www.msb.gov.ba.

Presidency and Legislature

STATE PRESIDENCY

Election, 1 October 2006

	Votes	% of votes
Bosniak Candidates		
Haris Silajdžić (Party for Bosnia and Herzegovina)	350,520	62.80
Sulejman Tihić (Party of Democratic Action)	153,683	27.53
Mirnes Ajanović (Patriotic Bloc BOSS)	45,608	8.17
Others	8,381	1.50
Total	558,192	100.00
Croat Candidates		
Željko Komšić (Social Democratic Party of Bosnia and Herzegovina)	116,062	39.56
Ivo Miro Jović (Croatian Coalition)	76,681	26.14
Božo Ljubić (Croatian Democratic Union 1990 of Bosnia and Herzegovina)	53,325	18.18
Mladen Ivanković-Lijanović (People's Party Working for Betterment)	24,822	8.46
Zvonko Jurišić (Croatian Party of Rights)	20,350	6.94
Irena Javor-Korjenić (Independent)	2,143	0.73
Total	293,383	100.00
Serb Candidates		
Nebojša Radmanović (Alliance of Independent Social Democrats)	287,675	53.26
Mladen Bosić (Serbian Democratic Party)	130,824	24.22
Others	121,674	22.53
Total	540,173	100.00

PARLAMENTARNA SKUPŠTINA BOSNE I HERCEGOVINE
(Parliamentary Assembly of Bosnia and Herzegovina)

The Parlamentarna skupština Bosne i Hercegovine (Parliamentary Assembly of Bosnia and Herzegovina) comprises two chambers: a directly elected lower chamber, the Predstavnički dom (House of Representatives); and an indirectly elected upper chamber, the Dom Naroda (House of Peoples).

Predstavnički dom
(House of Representatives)

71000 Sarajevo, trg Bosne i Hercegovine 1; tel. (33) 284401; fax (33) 211028; e-mail branka.todorovic@parlament.ba; internet www.parlament.ba.

The Predstavnički dom has 42 deputies directly elected for a four-year term, of whom 28 are elected from the Federation and 14 from Republika Srpska.

Speaker: BERIZ BELKIĆ.

General Election, 1 October 2006

Party	FBiH*	RS† overall	Seats
	% of votes		
Party of Democratic Action	25.54	3.67	16.89	9
Party for Bosnia and Herzegovina	22.99	4.16	15.54	8
Alliance of Independent Social Democrats	0.85	46.93	19.08	7
Social Democratic Party of Bosnia and Herzegovina	15.40	2.12	10.15	5
Serbian Democratic Party	—	19.44	7.69	3
Croatian Coalition‡	7.99	0.20	4.91	3
Croats Together‖	6.10	0.11	3.73	2
Bosnian-Herzegovinian Patriotic Party—Sefer Halilović	4.41	0.16	2.72	1
Party of Democratic Progress of Republika Srpska	—	5.08	2.01	1
People's Party Working for Betterment	3.22	0.99	2.34	1
Democratic National Alliance	0.03	3.56	1.42	1
Democratic People's Community of Bosnia and Herzegovina	1.90	0.06	1.17	1
Others	11.56	13.52	12.33	—
Total	100.00	100.00	100.00§	42

* Federation of Bosnia and Herzegovina.
† Republika Srpska.

‡ A coalition of the Croatian Democratic Union of Bosnia and Herzegovina and the Croatian People's Union.
‖ A coalition of the Croatian Democratic Union 1990 of Bosnia and Herzegovina, the Croatian Christian Democratic Union—Bosnia and Herzegovina, the Croatian Democratic Christians, the Croatian Peasants' Party of Bosnia and Herzegovina and the Croatian Democratic Union of Bosnia and Herzegovina—HDU.
§ A total of 1,412,078 valid votes were cast, of which 853,372 were cast in the Federation of Bosnia and Herzegovina and 558,706 were cast in Republika Srpska.

Dom Naroda
(House of Peoples)

71000 Sarajevo, trg Bosne i Hercegovine 1; tel. (33) 284440; fax (33) 654357; e-mail aljosa.campara@parlament.ba; internet www.parlament.ba.

There are 15 deputies in the Dom Naroda (House of Peoples), of whom 10 are elected by the Dom Naroda Federacije (Federation House of Peoples) and five by the Vijeće Naroda (Council of Peoples) of the Narodna skupština Republike Srpske (National Assembly of Republika Srpska).

Speaker: ILIJA FILIPOVIĆ.

The Entities of Bosnia and Herzegovina

GOVERNMENT OF THE FEDERATION OF BOSNIA AND HERZEGOVINA

Following an agreement reached in Washington, DC, the USA, by representatives of the Republic of Bosnia and Herzegovina and the 'Croat Republic of Herzeg-Bosna' (declared on 28 August 1993), the Federation of Bosnia and Herzegovina was formed on 31 March 1994. The Federation was reorganized as one of the two constituent entities of Bosnia and Herzegovina in the peace agreements of 1995.

President: BORJANA KRIŠTO (Croatian Democratic Union of Bosnia and Herzegovina).
Vice-Presidents: SPOMENKA MIČIĆ (Party for Bosnia and Herzegovina), MIRSAD KEBO (Party of Democratic Action).

Government
(March 2008)

Prime Minister: Dr NEDŽAD BRANKOVIĆ.
Deputy Prime Minister and Minister of Finance: VJEKOSLAV BEVANDA.
Deputy Prime Minister and Minister of Culture and Sport: GAVRILO GRAHOVAC.
Minister of Internal Affairs: MUHIDIN ALIĆ.
Minister of Justice: FELIKS VIDOVIĆ.
Minister of Energy, Mining and Industry: VAHID HEĆO.
Minister of Transport and Communications: NAIL ŠEĆKANOVIĆ.
Minister of Labour and Social Policy: PERICA JELEČEVIĆ.
Minister of Displaced Persons and Refugees: EDIN MUŠIĆ.
Minister of Veterans and the Disabled of the War of Liberation: ZAHID CRNKIĆ.
Minister of Health: SAFET OMEROVIIĆ.
Minister of Education and Science: MELIHA ALIĆ.
Minister of Trade: DESNICA RADIVOJEVIĆ.
Minister of Urban Planning: SALKO OBHOĐAŠ.
Minister of Agriculture, Water Management and Forestry: DAMIR LJUBIĆ.
Minister of Development, Entrepreneurship and Crafts: VELIMIR KUNIĆ.
Minister of the Environment and Tourism: NEVENKO HERCEG.

Ministries

Office of the President: 71000 Sarajevo, Alipašina 41; tel. and fax (33) 472618; e-mail info@fbihvlada.gov.ba; internet www.fbihvlada.gov.ba.
Office of the Prime Minister: 71000 Sarajevo, Alipašina 41; tel. (33) 663649; fax (33) 444718; e-mail kabprem@fbihvlada.gov.ba.
Ministry of Agriculture, Water Management and Forestry: 71000 Sarajevo, Titova 15; tel. (33) 443338; fax (33) 663659; e-mail info@fmpvs.gov.ba; internet www.fmpvs.gov.ba.
Ministry of Culture and Sport: Sarajevo, Obala Maka Dizdara 2; tel. (33) 663693; fax (33) 664381; e-mail ggrahovac@fbihvlada.gov.ba.
Ministry of Development, Entrepreneurship and Crafts: 88000 Mostar, Stjepana Radića 33; tel. (36) 449120; fax (36) 449122; e-mail fmrpo@tel.net.ba.
Ministry of Displaced Persons and Refugees: 71000 Sarajevo, Alipašina 41; tel. (33) 663977; fax (33) 204552; e-mail fmsa_ras@fbihvlada.gov.ba.
Ministry of Education and Science: Mostar, Stjepana Radića 33; tel. (36) 355700; fax (33) 355742; e-mail fmonks@bih.net.ba.
Ministry of Energy, Mining and Industry: 88000 Mostar, Alekse Šantića bb; tel. (36) 513800; fax (36) 580015; e-mail fmeri-mo@bih.net.ba.
Ministry of the Environment and Tourism: 71000 Sarajevo, Alipašina 41; tel. (33) 562870; fax (33) 201602.
Ministry of Finance: 71000 Sarajevo, Mehmeda Spahe 5; tel. (33) 203147; fax (33) 203152; e-mail info@fmf.gov.ba; internet www.fmf.gov.ba.
Ministry of Health: 71000 Sarajevo, Titova 9; tel. and fax (33) 664245; e-mail moh@bih.net.ba.
Ministry of Internal Affairs: 71000 Sarajevo, Mehmeda Spahe 7; tel. (33) 280020; fax (33) 207606.
Ministry of Justice: 71000 Sarajevo, Valtera Perića 15; tel. and fax (33) 213155.
Ministry of Labour and Social Policy: 71000 Sarajevo, Vilsonovo šetalište 10; tel. (33) 661782; fax (33) 661783; e-mail fmsa@fbihvlada.gov.ba.
Ministry of Trade: 88000 Mostar, Ante Starčevića bb; tel. (36) 310148; fax (36) 318684; e-mail desnica.radivojevic@fmt.gov.ba; internet www.fmt.gov.ba.
Ministry of Transport and Communications: 88000 Mostar, Braće Fejića bb; tel. (36) 550025; fax (36) 550024; internet www.fmpik.gov.ba.
Ministry of Urban Planning: 71000 Sarajevo, Marsala Tita 9A; tel. and fax (33) 473124; e-mail fmpuio@fbihvlada.gov.ba.
Ministry of Veterans and the Disabled of the War of Liberation: 71000 Sarajevo, Alipašina 41; tel. (33) 212932; fax (33) 209333; e-mail kabinet@bih.net.ba; internet www.fmbi.gov.ba.

PARLAMENT FEDERACIJE

The bicameral Parlament Federacije (Federation Parliament) comprises two chambers: a directly elected lower chamber, the Predstavnički dom Federacije (Federation House of Representatives); and an indirectly elected upper chamber, the Dom Naroda Federacije (Federation House of Peoples).

Predstavnički dom Federacije
(Federation House of Representatives)

71000 Sarajevo; internet www.parlamentfbih.gov.ba.

The 98 deputies of the Predstavnički dom Federacije are directly elected for a four-year term.

Speaker: SAFET SOFTIĆ.

General Election, 1 October 2006

Party	Votes	% of votes	Seats
Party of Democratic Action	218,365	25.45	28
Party for Bosnia and Herzegovina	190,148	22.16	24
Social Democratic Party of Bosnia and Herzegovina	130,204	15.17	17
Croatian Coalition*	64,906	7.56	8
Croats Together†	54,210	6.32	7
Bosnian-Herzegovinian Patriotic Party—Sefer Halilović	35,223	4.10	4
Patriotic Bloc BOSS‡	27,200	3.17	3
People's Party Working for Betterment	27,132	3.16	3
Democratic People's Community of Bosnia and Herzegovina	16,014	1.87	2
Coalition for Equality§	21,152	2.46	1
Alliance of Independent Social Democrats	12,564	1.46	1
Others	60,987	7.11	—
Total	858,105	100.00	98

* A coalition of the Croatian Democratic Union of Bosnia and Herzegovina and the Croatian People's Union.
† A coalition of the Croatian Democratic Union 1990 of Bosnia and Herzegovina, the Croatian Christian Democratic Union—Bosnia and Herzegovina, the Croatian Democratic Christians, the Croatian Peasants' Party of Bosnia and Herzegovina and the Croatian Democratic Union of Bosnia and Herzegovina—HDU.
‡ A coalition of the Bosnian Party and the Social Democratic Union of Bosnia and Herzegovina.
§ A coalition of the Croatian Party of Rights and the New Croatian Initiative.

BOSNIA AND HERZEGOVINA

**Dom Naroda Federacije
(Federation House of Peoples)**
Sarajevo; tel. (33) 203246; fax (33) 205547; e-mail izmirhadziavdic@parlamentfbih.gov.ba; internet www.parlamentfbih.gov.ba.

The 51-member Dom Naroda Federacije comprises 17 Bosniak, 17 Croat, 10 Serb and seven other deputies, who are elected by the cantonal assemblies.

Speaker: STJEPAN KRESIĆ.

GOVERNMENT OF REPUBLIKA SRPSKA

The 'Serb Republic (Republika Srpska) of Bosnia and Herzegovina' was proclaimed on 27 March 1992. (In August 1992 the self-styled Republic changed its name to Republika Srpska.) According to the peace treaty of December 1995, Republika Srpska constituted one of the two territorial entities comprising Bosnia and Herzegovina, with 49% of the country's area. It retained its own executive presidency, government and parliament (henceforth known as the Narodna skupština Republika Srpska—the National Assembly of Republika Srpska). In January 1998 the Narodna skupština voted in favour of relocating Republika Srpska's administrative centre and *de facto* capital from Pale to Banja Luka. (According to the Republic's Constitution, the *de jure* capital is Sarajevo.)

President: RAJKO KUZMANOVIĆ (Alliance of Independent Social Democrats).

Vice-President: ADIL OSMANOVIĆ (Party of Democratic Action).

Vice-President: DAVOR ČORDAŠ (Croatian Democratic Union of Bosnia and Herzegovina).

Government
(April 2008)

Prime Minister: MILORAD DODIK.

Minister of Finance: ALEKSANDAR DZOMBIĆ.

Minister of Internal Affairs: STANISLAV CAĐO.

Minister of Justice: DZERARD SELMAN.

Minister of Administration and Local Government: ZORAN LIPOVAC.

Minister of the Economy, Energy and Development: (vacant).

Minister of Economic Affairs and Co-ordination: JASNA BRKIĆ.

Minister of Labour and the Protection of War Veterans: BOSKO TOMIĆ.

Minister of Trade and Tourism: PREDRAG GLUHAKOVIĆ.

Minister of Transport and Communications: NEDELJKO CUBRILOVIĆ.

Minister of Agriculture, Water Resources and Forestry: Dr RADIVOJE BRATIĆ.

Minister of Urban Planning, Housing and the Environment: FATIMA FETIBEGOVIĆ.

Minister of Education and Culture: ANTON KASIPOVIĆ.

Minister of Refugees and Displaced Persons: OMER BRANKOVIĆ.

Minister of Health and Social Welfare: RANKO SKRBIĆ.

Minister of Science and Technology: BAKIR AJANOVIĆ.

Minister of Family, Youth and Sport: Dr PROKO DRAGOSAVLJEVIĆ.

Ministries

Office of the President: 78000 Banja Luka, trg Srpskih Vladara 2; tel. (51) 211178; fax (51) 212018; e-mail info@predsjednikrs.net; internet www.predsjednikrs.net.

Office of the Prime Minister: 78000 Banja Luka, Vuka Karadžića 4; tel. (51) 331333; fax (51) 331366; e-mail kabinet@vladars.net; internet www.vladars.net.

Ministry of Administration and Local Government: 78000 Banja Luka, Vuka Karadžića 4; tel. (51) 331680; fax (51) 331681; e-mail muls@muls.vladars.net.

Ministry of Agriculture, Water Resources and Forestry: 78000 Banja Luka, Vuka Karadžića 4; tel. (51) 331634; fax (51) 331631; e-mail mps@mps.vladars.net.

Ministry of Economic Affairs and Co-ordination: 78000 Banja Luka, Vuka Karadžića 4; tel. (51) 331430; fax (51) 331436; e-mail meoi@meoi.vladars.net.

Ministry of the Economy, Energy and Development: 78000 Banja Luka, Vuka Karadžića 4; tel. (51) 331720; fax (51) 331721; e-mail mper@mper.vladars.net.

Ministry of Education and Culture: 78000 Banja Luka, Vuka Karadžića 4; tel. (51) 331424; fax (51) 331423; e-mail mp@mp.vladars.net.

Ministry of Family, Youth and Sport: 78000 Banja Luka, Vuka Karadžića 4; tel. (51) 331762; fax (51) 331761.

Ministry of Finance: 78000 Banja Luka, Vuka Karadžića 4; tel. (51) 331350; fax (51) 331351; e-mail mf@mf.vladars.net.

Ministry of Health and Social Welfare: 78000 Banja Luka, Vladike Platona bb; tel. (51) 348348; fax (51) 348346; e-mail mzsz@mzsz.vladars.net.

Ministry of Internal Affairs: 78000 Banja Luka, Desanke Maksimović 4; tel. (51) 334306; fax (51) 334304; e-mail mup@mup.vladars.net; internet www.mup.vladars.net.

Ministry of Justice: 78000 Banja Luka, Vuka Karadžića 4; tel. (51) 331582; fax (51) 331594; e-mail mpr@mpr.vladars.net.

Ministry of Labour and the Protection of War Veterans: 78000 Banja Luka, Vuka Karadžića 4; tel. (51) 331651; fax (51) 331652; e-mail mpb@mpb.vladars.net.

Ministry of Refugees and Displaced Persons: 78000 Banja Luka, Vuka Karadžića 4; tel. (51) 331470; fax (51) 331471; e-mail mirl@mirl.vladars.net.

Ministry of Science and Technology: 78000 Banja Luka, Vuka Karadžića 4; tel. (51) 331542; fax (51) 331548; e-mail mnk@mnk.vladars.net; internet www.mnk.vladars.net.

Ministry of Trade and Tourism: 78000 Banja Luka, Vuka Karadžića 4; tel. (51) 331523; fax (51) 331499; e-mail mtt@mtt.vladars.net; internet www.mtt.vladars.net.

Ministry of Transport and Communications: 78000 Banja Luka, Vuka Karadžića 4; tel. (51) 331611; fax (51) 331612; e-mail msv@msv.vladars.net.

Ministry of Urban Planning, Housing and the Environment: 78000 Banja Luka, Vladike Platona bb; tel. (51) 348600; fax (51) 316174; e-mail mgr@mgr.vladars.net.

PRESIDENT OF REPUBLIKA SRPSKA
Election, 9 December 2007

Candidate	Votes	% of votes
Rajko Kuzmanović (Alliance of Independent Social Democrats)	169,863	41.33
Ognjen Tadić (Serbian Democratic Party)	142,898	34.77
Mladen Ivanić (Party of Democratic Progress of Republika Srpska)	69,522	16.91
Slobodan Popović (Social Democratic Party of Bosnia and Herzegovina)	8,659	2.11
Mirko Blagojević (Serbian Radical Party—Dr Vojislav Šešelj—Bijeljina)	7,526	1.83
Nedžad Delić (Democratic Disabled People's Party of Bosnia and Herzegovina)	4,499	1.09
Others	8,056	1.96
Total	**411,023**	**100.00**

Narodna skupština Republike Srpske
(National Assembly of Republika Srpska)
51000 Banja Luka, Vuka Karadžića 2; tel. (51) 301099; fax (51) 301087; internet www.narodnaskupstinars.net.

Speaker: IGOR RADOJIČIĆ.

Election, 1 October 2006

Party	Votes	% of votes	Seats
Alliance of Independent Social Democrats	244,251	43.31	41
Serbian Democratic Party	103,035	18.27	17
Party of Democratic Progress of Republika Srpska	38,681	6.86	8
Democratic National Alliance	22,780	4.04	4
Party for Bosnia and Herzegovina	22,642	4.01	4
Socialist Party of Republika Srpska	20,031	3.55	3
Party of Democratic Action	19,137	3.39	3
Serbian Radical Party of Republika Srpska	16,454	2.92	2
Social Democratic Party of Bosnia and Herzegovina	14,079	2.50	1
Others	62,905	11.13	—
Total	**563,995**	**100.00**	**83**

Note: Following constitutional changes approved in 2002, the Narodna skupština Republike Srpske elects 28 delegates to a Vijeće naroda (Council of Peoples), who are responsible for, *inter alia*, nominating the entity's representatives to the state Dom naroda. These 28 members comprise eight Bosniaks, eight Croats, eight Serbs and four others. The current Chairman of the Vijeće naroda is DŽEVAD OSMANČEVIĆ

BOSNIA AND HERZEGOVINA

Election Commission

Centralna Izborna Komisija Bosne i Hercegovine (Central Election Commission of Bosnia and Herzegovina): 71000 Sarajevo, Mula Mustafe Bašeskije 6; tel. (33) 251300; fax (33) 251329; e-mail info@izbori.ba; internet www.izbori.ba; independent; Pres. STJEPAN MIKIĆ.

Political Organizations

Alliance of Independent Social Democrats (AISD) (Savez nezavisnih socijaldemokrata—SNSD): 78000 Banja Luka, Petra Kočića 5; tel. (51) 318492; fax (51) 318495; e-mail snsd@inecco.net; internet www.snsd.org; f. 1997 as Party of Independent Social Democrats; present name adopted 2001, following merger with Democratic Socialist Party; Chair. MILORAD DODIK; Sec.-Gen. IGOR RADOJIČIĆ.

Bosnian-Herzegovinan Patriotic Party—Sefer Halilović (Bosanskohercegovačka patriotska stranka—Sefer Halilović): 71000 Sarajevo, Husrefa Redžića 4; tel. (33) 216882; fax (33) 216881; e-mail bps@bih.net.ba; internet www.bps-sh.com.ba; f. 1996; Pres. SEFER HALILOVIĆ; Sec.-Gen. ŠEMSUDIN HADROVIĆ.

Bosnian Party (Bosanska Stranka—BOSS): 75000 Tuzla, Stari Grad 9; tel. and fax (35) 251035; e-mail boss.bh@inet.ba; socialist, supports policies of former Yugoslav leader Josep Broz (Tito); contested 2006 legislative elections as mem. of Patriotic Bloc BOSS, with the Social Democratic Union of Bosnia and Herzegovina; Chair. MIRNES AJANOVIĆ.

Civic Democratic Party of Bosnia and Herzegovina (Građanska Demokratska Stranka BiH): 71000 Sarajevo, Maršala Tita 9A; tel. (33) 213435; fax (33) 266630; Chair. IBRAHIM SPAHIĆ.

Croatian Christian Democratic Union—Bosnia and Herzegovina (Hrvatska Kršćanska Demokratska Unija—Bosne i Hercegovine): Mostar, Nikole Šubića Zrinskog 11; tel. and fax (80) 352051; e-mail hkdubih.hnz@tel.net.ba; contested 2006 legislative elections as mem. of the Croats Together coalition; Pres. MIJO IVANČIĆ-LONIĆ.

Croatian Democratic Christians (Hrvatski demokršćani): 88000 Mostar, Bogdana Mandića 10; tel. (36) 324613; contested 2006 legislative elections as mem. of the Croats Together coalition.

Croatian Democratic Union 1990 (CDU 1990) (Hrvatska Demokratska Zajednica 1990—HDZ 1990): 88000 Mostar, Nikole Šubića Zrinjskog 11/I; tel. (36) 449730; fax (36) 449737; e-mail hdz1990@tel.net.ba; internet www.hdz1990.org; f. 2006 by fmr mems of the Croatian Democratic Union of Bosnia and Herzegovina; contested 2006 legislative elections as mem. of the Croats Together coalition; Leader BOŽO LJUBIĆ.

Croatian Democratic Union of Bosnia and Herzegovina (CDU—BH) (Hrvatska Demokratska Zajednica Bosne i Hercegovine—HDZ BiH): 88000 Mostar, Kneza Domagoja bb; tel. (36) 310701; fax (36) 315024; e-mail hdzbih@hdzbih.org; internet www .hdzbih.org; f. 1990; affiliate of the CDU in Croatia; adopted new party statute July 2000; Croat nationalist party; contested legislative elections in 2006 as mem. of Croatian Coalition, in alliance with Croatian People's Union; Chair. DRAGAN ČOVIĆ; Gen.-Sec. VLATKO MEĐUGORAC.

Croatian Democratic Union of Bosnia and Herzegovina—HDU (Hrvatska demokratska unija BiH): 71000 Sarajevo, Tešanjska 9; tel. and fax (36) 321762; internet hdu-bih.tk; f. 2002 by fmr mems of Croatian Democratic Union of Bosnia and Herzegovina—HDZ; contested 2006 legislative elections as mem. of the Croats Together coalition; Chair. MIRO GRABOVAC-TITAN.

Croatian Party of Rights (Hrvatska stranka Prava): 88320 Ljubuški, Fra Petra Bakule 2; tel. and fax (36) 834917; Croat nationalist; contested 2006 legislative elections as mem. of Coalition for Equality, with the New Croatian Initiative; Pres. ZDRAVKO HRSTIĆ.

Croatian Peasants' Party of Bosnia and Herzegovina (Hrvatska Seljacka Stranka BiH): 71000 Sarajevo, Radićeva 4; tel. and fax (33) 551290; e-mail info@hssbih.co.ba; internet www.hssbih .co.ba; affiliated to Croatian Peasants' Party in Croatia; contested 2006 legislative elections as mem. of the Croats Together coalition; Chair. Prof. MARKO TADIĆ.

Croatian People's Union (Hrvatska narodna zajednica—HNZ): 71000 Sarajevo, Maršala Tita 9A; tel. and fax (33) 215146; contested legislative elections in 2006 as mem. of Croatian Coalition, in alliance with Croatian Democratic Union of Bosnia and Herzegovina.

Democratic Disabled People's Party of Bosnia and Herzegovina (Demokratska Stranka Invalida BiH): 75000 Tuzla, Zlatarska 4; tel. (35) 270091; Leader NEDŽAD DELIĆ.

Democratic Movement of Republika Srpska (Demokratski pokret Srpske—DEPOS): 78000 Banja Luka, Tina Ujevića 3; tel. (51) 308424; fax (51) 308463; Leader NEĐO ĐURIĆ.

Directory

Democratic National Alliance (Demokratski Narodni Savez): 78000 Banja Luka, Aleja Svetog Save 20; tel. (51) 219020; fax (51) 219033; internet www.dnsrs.org; f. 2000 by fmr mems of the Serb National Alliance; Chair. Dr MARKO PAVIĆ.

Democratic Party of Republika Srpska (Demokratska stranka Republike Srpske): 76300 Bijeljina, Kneza Miloša 26; tel. and fax (55) 201951; e-mail dsrs@bn.rstel.net; Pres. DRAGOMIR DUMIĆ.

Democratic People's Community of Bosnia and Herzegovina (Demokratska narodna zajednica BiH): 71000 Sarajevo, Hadži-Idrizova 8; tel. (33) 222297; e-mail dnzcazin@bih.net.ba; internet www .dnz-cazin.co.ba; Leader Dr HAFEZA SABLJAKOVIĆ.

Liberal Democratic Party (LDP) (Liberalno Demokratska Stranka): 71000 Sarajevo, Maršala Tita 9A; tel. and fax (33) 664540; e-mail centrala@liberali.ba; f. 2000 by merger of Liberal Party of Bosnia and Herzegovina and the Liberal Bosniak Organization; Chair. RASIM KADIĆ.

National Democratic Union (Narodna demokratska zajednica—NDZ): 77230 Velika Kladuša, Sulejmana Topića 7; tel. (37) 775340; fax (37) 770307; e-mail dnzbih@bih.net.ba; internet www.dnzbih.ba; f. 1996; Chair. RIFET DOLIĆ.

New Croatian Initiative (Nova Hrvatska Inicijativa): 71000 Sarajevo, Sime Milutinovića 2/II; tel. (33) 214602; fax (33) 214603; e-mail nhi@nhi.ba; internet www.nhi.ba; f. 1998 by fmr mems of the Croatian Democratic Union of Bosnia and Herzegovina; contested 2006 legislative elections as mem. of Coalition for Equality, with the Croatian Party of Rights; Chair. KREŠIMIR ZUBAK.

Party for Bosnia and Herzegovina (Stranka za Bosnu i Hercegovinu): 71000 Sarajevo, Maršala Tita 9A; tel. and fax (33) 214417; e-mail zabih@zabih.ba; internet www.zabih.ba; f. 1996; integrationist; member of the Coalition for a Single and Democratic Bosnia electoral alliance; Pres. HARIS SILAJDŽIĆ.

Party of Democratic Action (PDA) (Stranka Demokratske Akcije—SDA): 71000 Sarajevo, Mehmeda Spahe 14; tel. (33) 472192; fax (33) 650429; e-mail centrala@sda.ba; internet www .sda.ba; f. 1990; moderate Bosniak nationalist party that supports admission of Bosnia and Herzegovina to the European Union and formation of a Republic of Bosnia and Herzegovina as decentralized state composed of multi-ethnic regions, with Bosniaks, Croats and Serbs as members of a common Bosnian nation; Chair. SULEJMAN TIHIĆ; Sec.-Gen. MIRSAD CEMAN.

Party of Democratic Progress of Republika Srpska (PDP) (Partija Demokratskog Progresa Republike Srpske): 78000 Banja Luka, ul. Prvog Krajiškog Korpusa 130; tel. (51) 346210; fax (51) 300956; e-mail pdp@blic.net; f. 1999; moderate, supports equal rights for all ethnic groups, supports closer co-operation of Republika Srpska with the European Union; Chair. MLADEN IVANIĆ.

Pensioners' Party of Bosnia and Herzegovina (Stranka Penzionera BiH): 71000 Sarajevo, Azize Šaćirbegović 2; tel. and fax (33) 654837; Chair. HUSEIN VOJNIKOVIĆ.

Pensioners' Party of Republika Srpska (Penzionerska Stranka Republike Srpske): 78000 Banja Luka, Grčka 19; tel. (51) 301212; fax (51) 214789; Chair. STOJAN BOGOSAVAC.

People's Party Working for Betterment (Narodna stranka Radom za boljitak): 71000 Sarajevo, Kranjčevićeva 41; tel. (33) 550415; fax (33) 550416; internet www.zaboljitak.ba; f. 2001; Leader MLADEN IVANKOVIĆ-LIJANOVIĆ.

Radical Party of Republika Srpska (Radikalna Stranka Republike Srpske): 79101 Prijedor, Srpskih velikana bb; tel. and fax (52) 213428; e-mail goran-b@inecco.net; extreme Serb nationalist; Chair. GORAN ZMIJANJAC.

Serbian Democratic Party (SDP) (Srpska demokratska stranka—SDS BiH): 78000 Banja Luka, Kralja Petra I Karađorđevića; tel. (51) 212738; fax (51) 217640; f. 1990; allied to SDP of Serbia; Serb nationalist party; Chair. MLADEN BOSIĆ (acting).

Serbian Radical Party of Republika Srpska (Srpska Radikalna Stranka Republike Srpske—SRS): 78000 Banja Luka, Vidovdanska 53; tel. (51) 219428; e-mail srs-rs@teol.net; radical Serb nationalist, supports the notion of a 'Greater Serbia'; Chair. RADISLAV KANJERIĆ.

Serbian Radical Party of Republika Srpska—Dr Vojislav Šešelj—Bijeljina (Srpska Radikalna Stranka Republike Srpske—Dr Vojislav Šešelj—Bijeljina): 76300 Bijeljina, Karađorđeva 27; tel. (55) 203948; fax (55) 210539; extreme Serb nationalist party.

Social Democratic Party of Bosnia and Herzegovina (SDP BiH) (Socijaldemokratska Partija BiH): 71000 Sarajevo, Alipašina 41; tel. (33) 664044; fax (33) 644042; e-mail generalni.sekretar@ sdp-bih.org.ba; internet www.sdp-bih.org.ba; contested 2006 legislative elections as mem. of Patriotic Bloc BOSS, with the Bosnian Party; Chair. Dr ZLATKO LAGUMDŽIJA; Sec.-Gen. KARLO FILIPOVIĆ.

Social Democratic Union of Bosnia and Herzegovina (Socijaldemokratska Unija BiH): 71000 Sarajevo, Maršala Tita 9A; tel. (33) 201487; fax (33) 201557; e-mail sdubih@sdubih.org; internet www.sdubih.org; f. 2002 by fmr mems of Party for Bosnia and Herzegovina; Chair. SEJFUDIN TOKIĆ.

Socialist Party (Socijalistička Partija—SP): 78000 Banja Luka, Bana Lazarevića 7; tel. (51) 328750; fax (51) 328753; e-mail sprs@inecco.net; f. 1993 as br. of Socialist Party of Serbia; fmrly Socialist Party of Republika Srpska; Chair. ZIVKO RADIŠIĆ.

Diplomatic Representation

EMBASSIES IN BOSNIA AND HERZEGOVINA

Austria: 71000 Sarajevo, Džidžikovac 7; tel. (33) 279400; fax (33) 668339; e-mail sarajevo-ob@bmaa.gv.at; internet www.austrijska-ambasada.ba; Ambassador WERNER ALMHOFER.

Bulgaria: 71000 Sarajevo, Soukbunar 5; tel. (33) 668191; fax (33) 668182; e-mail possar@bih.net.ba; Ambassador (vacant).

Canada: 71000 Sarajevo, Grbavička 4/II; tel. (33) 222033; fax (33) 222044; e-mail sjevo@international.gc.ca; Ambassador DAVID HUTCHINGS.

China, People's Republic: 71000 Sarajevo, Braće Begića 17; tel. (33) 215102; fax (33) 215108; e-mail chinaemb_ba@mfa.gov.cn; Ambassador LIU WENXIN.

Croatia: 71000 Sarajevo, Mehmeda Spahe 20; tel. (33) 444330; fax (33) 472434; e-mail croemb.sarajevo@mvpei.hr; internet ba.mvp.hr; Ambassador Dr JOSIP VRBOŠIĆ.

Czech Republic: 71000 Sarajevo, Franjevačka 19; tel. (33) 447525; fax (33) 447526; e-mail sarajevo@embassy.mzv.cz; internet www.mzv.cz/wwwo/?zu=sarajevo; Ambassador JIŘÍ KUDĚLA.

Denmark: 71000 Sarajevo, Splitska 9; tel. (33) 665901; fax (33) 665902; e-mail sijamb@um.dk; internet www.danishembassy.ba; Ambassador NIELS-JORGEN NEHRING.

Egypt: 71000 Sarajevo, Nurudina Gackića 58; tel. (33) 666498; fax (33) 666499; e-mail eg.em.sa@bih.net.ba; Ambassador AHMED EL-SAYED KHATTAB.

France: 71000 Sarajevo, Kapetanović Ljubušaka 18; tel. (33) 668149; fax (33) 668103; e-mail ambsarayevo.presse@diplomatie.gouv.fr; internet www.ambafrance.ba; Ambassador MARYSE BERNIAU.

Germany: 71000 Sarajevo, ul. Buka bb; tel. (33) 275000; fax (33) 652978; e-mail info@sarajevo.diplo.de; internet www.sarajevo.diplo.de; Ambassador MICHAEL GEORG SCHMUNK.

Greece: 71000 Sarajevo, Obala Maka Dizdara I; tel. (33) 203516; fax (33) 203512; e-mail greekemb@bih.net.ba; Ambassador CONSTANTINA MAUROSKELIDOU.

Guinea-Bissau: 71000 Sarajevo, Radnička 2; tel. (33) 660948; fax (33) 655524; Ambassador DESIDERIUS OSTROGON DA COSTA.

Holy See: 71000 Sarajevo, Pehlivanuša 9; tel. (33) 551055; fax (33) 207863; e-mail nunbosnia@bih.net.ba; Apostolic Nuncio ALESSANDRO D'ERRICO (Titular Archbishop of Hyccarum).

Hungary: 71000 Sarajevo, Hasana Bibera 53; tel. (33) 205302; fax (33) 268930; e-mail hung.emb@bih.net.ba; internet www.mfa.gov.hu/emb/sarajevo; Ambassador IMRE VARGA.

Iran: 71000 Sarajevo, Obala Maka Dizdara 6; tel. (33) 650210; fax (33) 663910; e-mail iries1@bih.net.ba; Ambassador MOHAMMED REZA MORSHED ZADEH.

Italy: 71000 Sarajevo, Čekaluša 39; tel. (33) 218022; fax (33) 659368; e-mail ambsara@bih.net.ba; Ambassador ALESSANDRO FALLAVOLLITO.

Japan: 71000 Sarajevo, Bistrik 9; tel. (33) 209580; fax (33) 209583; Ambassador ITARU UMEZU.

Libya: 71000 Sarajevo, Tahtali sokak 17; tel. (33) 657534; fax (33) 663620; Ambassador IBRAHIM ALI TAGIURI.

Macedonia, former Yugoslav republic: 71000 Sarajevo, Splitska 57; tel. and fax (33) 206004; e-mail mak.amb@bih.net.ba; Ambassador MIHAILO TRPKOSKI.

Malaysia: 71000 Sarajevo, Radnicka 4A; tel. (33) 201578; fax (33) 667713; e-mail malsrjevo@bih.net.ba; Ambassador RAMLAN BIN IBRAHIM.

Malta: 71000 Sarajevo, Mula Mustafe Bašeskije 12; tel. and fax (33) 668632; e-mail lor.tac@tiscalinet.it; Ambassador Dr LORENZO TACCHELLA.

Montenegro: 71000 Sarajevo, Talirovića 4; tel. (33) 239925; fax (33) 239928; e-mail ambcg1@bih.net.ba; Ambassador RAMIZ BAŠIĆ.

Netherlands: 71000 Sarajevo, Grbavička 4; tel. (33) 562600; fax (33) 223413; e-mail sar@minbuza.nl; internet www.netherlandsembassy.ba; Ambassador KAREL E. VOSSKÜHLER.

Norway: 71000 Sarajevo, Ferhadija 20; tel. (33) 254000; fax (33) 666505; e-mail emb.sarajevo@mfa.no; internet www.norveska.ba; Ambassador JAN BRAATHU.

Pakistan: 71000 Sarajevo, Emerika Bluma 17; tel. (33) 211836; fax (33) 211837; Ambassador SHIREEN MOIZ.

Poland: 71000 Sarajevo, Dola 13; tel. (33) 201142; fax (33) 233796; e-mail amsar@bih.net.ba; internet www.sarajewo.polemb.net; Ambassador ANDRZEJ TYSZKIEWICZ.

Romania: 71000 Sarajevo, Tahtali sokak 13–15; tel. (33) 207447; fax (33) 668940; e-mail rumunska@bih.net.ba; Chargé d'affaires a.i. ADRIAN LÁRGEANU.

Russia: 71000 Sarajevo, Urjan Dedina 93–95; tel. (33) 668147; fax (33) 668148; e-mail rusembbih@lsinter.net; internet www.sarajevo.mid.ru; Ambassador KONSTANTIN V. SHUVALOV.

Saudi Arabia: 71000 Sarajevo, Koševo 44; tel. (33) 211861; fax (33) 212204; e-mail saudiembassy@epn.ba; Ambassador FAHAD BIN ABD AL-MUHSIN AL-ZEIDA.

Serbia: 71000 Sarajevo, Obala Maka Dizdara 3A; tel. (33) 260080; fax (33) 221469; e-mail srbamba@bih.net.ba; Ambassador GRUJICA SPASOVIĆ.

Slovakia: 71000 Sarajevo, Skopljanska 7; tel. (33) 716440; fax (33) 716410; e-mail emb.sarajevo@mzv.sk; internet www.sarajevo.mfa.sk; Ambassador MIROSLAV MOJŽITA.

Slovenia: 71000 Sarajevo, Bentbaša 7; tel. (33) 271260; fax (33) 271270; e-mail vsa@gov.si; internet sarajevo.veleposlanistvo.si; Ambassador NATAŠA VODUŠEK.

Spain: 71000 Sarajevo, Čekaluša 16; tel. (33) 278560; fax (33) 208758; Ambassador JOSÉ MARÍA CASTROVIEJO Y BOLÍBAR.

Sweden: 71000 Sarajevo, Ferhadija 20; tel. (33) 276030; fax (33) 276060; e-mail ambassaden.sarajevo@foreign.ministry.se; internet www.swedenabroad.se/sarajevo; Ambassador LARS ERIK WINGREN.

Switzerland: 71000 Sarajevo, Josipa Štadlera 15; tel. (33) 275850; fax (33) 570120; e-mail vertretung@sar.rep.admin.ch; internet www.eda.admin.ch/sarajevo; Ambassador ROLF LENZ.

Turkey: 71000 Sarajevo, Hamdije Kreševljakovića 5; tel. and fax (33) 472437; fax (33) 445260; e-mail turksa@bih.net.ba; Ambassador BÜLLENT TULUN.

United Kingdom: 71000 Sarajevo, Tina Ujevića 8; tel. (33) 444429; fax (33) 666131; e-mail britemb@bih.net.ba; internet www.britishembassy.gov.uk/bih; Ambassador MATTHEW JOHN RYCROFT.

USA: 71000 Sarajevo, Alipašina 43; tel. (33) 445700; fax (33) 659722; e-mail bhopa@state.gov; internet sarajevo.usembassy.gov; Ambassador CHARLES L. ENGLISH.

Judicial System

The Constitutional Court of Bosnia and Herzegovina has three international judges (selected by the President of the European Court of Human Rights) and six national judges (of whom four are elected by the Predstavnički dom Federacije and two by the Narodna skupština Republike Srpske). The Constitutional Court has competence regarding constitutional matters in both entities. The judicial system of each entity comprises a Constitutional Court, a Supreme Court and local district courts. The Court of Bosnia and Herzegovina, which was officially inaugurated on 27 January 2003, represents the country's highest judicial organ. The eight judges of the Court were appointed by the High Representative of the International Community.

Court of Bosnia and Herzegovina: 71000 Sarajevo, Kraljice Jelene 88; tel. (33) 707165; fax (33) 707224; e-mail pios@registrarbih.gov.ba; internet www.sudbih.gov.ba; inaugurated Jan. 2003; state-level court and highest judicial organ; comprises 37 judges (23 national and 14 international); 3 divisions (Criminal, Administrative and Appellate); War Crimes Chamber est. March 2005; Pres. KRESO MEDĐŽIDA.

Constitutional Court of Bosnia and Herzegovina: 71000 Sarajevo, Reisa Dzemaludina Causevića 6/III; tel. (33) 251210; fax (33) 561106; e-mail info@ccbh.ba; internet www.ccbh.ba; f. 1997; nine mems appointed until the age of 70; assumed role of fmr Human Rights Chamber in Dec. 2003; Pres. HATIDŽA HADŽIOSMANOVIĆ; Sec.-Gen. DUŠAN KALEMBER.

FEDERATION OF BOSNIA AND HERZEGOVINA

Constitutional Court of the Federation of Bosnia and Herzegovina: 71000 Sarajevo, Valtera Perića 15; tel. (33) 251650; fax (33) 251651.

Supreme Court of the Federation of Bosnia and Herzegovina: 71000 Sarajevo, Valtera Perića 15; tel. (33) 664751; fax (33) 553754; e-mail vrh.sud@bih.net.ba; internet www.vsfbih.ba; four chambers; Pres. AMIR JAGANJAĆ.

Office of the Federation Prosecutor: 71000 Sarajevo, Valtera Perića 11; tel. (33) 214990; Prosecutor ZDRAVKO KNEŽEVIĆ.

BOSNIA AND HERZEGOVINA Directory

REPUBLIKA SRPSKA

Constitutional Court of Republika Srpska: 78000 Banja Luka, Kralja Alfonsa 11; tel. and fax (51) 301218; e-mail contact@ustavnisud.org; internet www.ustavnisud.org; eight mems; Pres. RAJKO KUZMANOVIĆ; Sec. MIODRAG SIMOVIĆ.

Supreme Court of Republika Srpska: 78000 Banja Luka, Aleja Svetog Save bb; tel. (51) 211690; e-mail vrhovnisudrs@vrhovnisudrs.com; internet www.vrhovnisudrs.com; Pres. JOVO ROSIĆ.

Office of the Chief Prosecutor of Republika Srpska: 78000 Banja Luka, Kralja Petra I Karađorđevića 12; tel. (51) 218827; fax (51) 218834; e-mail rjt@inecco.net; internet www.tuzilastvo-rs.org; Prosecutor AMOR BUKIĆ.

Religion

Bosnia and Herzegovina has a diversity of religious allegiances, although as a result of the conflict of 1992–95, members of the various religious groupings have tended to live in separate regions of the country. The dominant single religion is Islam. The Reis-ul-ulema, the head of the Muslims in the territory comprising the former Yugoslavia, is resident in Sarajevo. Most of the adherents of Islam are ethnic Muslims or Bosniaks (Slavs who converted to Islam under the Ottoman Empire). Virtually all are adherents of the Sunni persuasion. Approximately one-half of the inhabitants are Christian, but these are divided between the Serbian Orthodox Church and the Roman Catholic Church. There is a small Jewish community.

ISLAM

Islamic Community of Bosnia and Herzegovina: 71000 Sarajevo, Isa-bega Ishakovica 2; tel. (33) 239404; fax (33) 441573; Reis-ul-ulema Dr MUSTAFA EFENDI CERIĆ.

CHRISTIANITY

The Serbian Orthodox Church

Metropolitan of Dabrobosna: NICOLAJ (MRDA), 71000 Sarajevo, Zelenih Beretki 3; tel. and fax (71) 210518; e-mail info@mitropolijadabrobosanska.org; internet www.mitropolijadabrobosanska.org.

The Roman Catholic Church

Bosnia and Herzegovina comprises one archdiocese and two dioceses. At 31 December 2005 adherents of the Roman Catholic Church numbered 462,586, representing about 15.5% of the total population.

Bishops' Conference

71000 Sarajevo, Kaptol 32; tel. and fax (33) 666867; e-mail bkbih@bih.net.ba; internet www.bkbih.org.

f. 1995; Pres. Cardinal VINKO PULJIĆ (Archbishop of Vrhbosna, Sarajevo).

Archbishop of Vrhbosna, Sarajevo: Cardinal VINKO PULJIĆ, 71000 Sarajevo, Kaptol 7; tel. (33) 218823; fax (33) 212937; e-mail kaptolka@bih.net.ba.

JUDAISM

Jewish Community of Bosnia and Herzegovina: 71000 Sarajevo, Hamdije Kreševljekoviće 59; tel. (33) 229666; fax (33) 229667; e-mail jakob_99@yahoo.com; internet www.benevolencija.eu.org; f. 1565; Pres. JAKOB FINCI.

The Press

PRINCIPAL DAILIES

Dnevni Avaz (Daily Herald): 71000 Sarajevo, Džemala Bijedića 185; tel. (33) 281393; fax (33) 281414; e-mail webmaster@avaz.ba; internet www.avaz.ba; f. 1995; Editor-in-Chief SAMIR MUSLIĆ; circ. 15,700 (2001).

Dnevni List (Daily News): 88000 Mostar, Ante Starčevića 56; tel. (36) 313370; e-mail national-holding@tel.net.ba; internet www.dnevni-list.ba.

Glas Srpske (Voice of Republika Srpska): 78000 Banja Luka; fmrly *Glas Srpski* (Serbian Voice); Editor-in-Chief TOMO MARIĆ; Deputy Editor-in-Chief NIKOLA GUZIJAN.

Jutarnje Novine (Morning News): Sarajevo; e-mail irfan_ljevakovic@jutarnje.ba; internet www.jutarnje.ba; fmrly *Vecernje Novine* (Evening News); Dir IRFAN LJEVAKOVIĆ; circ. 10,000 (2001).

Nezavisne novine (The Independent): 78000 Banja Luka, Krajiškikh brigada 8; tel. (51) 331800; fax (51) 331810; e-mail desk@nezavisne.com; internet www.nezavisne.com; f. 1995; Editor-in-Chief DRAGAN JERINIĆ; circ. 7,500 (2001).

Oslobođenje (Liberation): 71000 Sarajevo, Džemala Bijedića 185; tel. (33) 467723; fax (33) 4680504; internet www.oslobodjenje.com.ba; f. 1943; morning; Editor-in-Chief SENKA KURTOVIĆ; circ. 15,700 (2001).

WEEKLY NEWSPAPERS

Dani (Days): 71000 Sarajevo, Skenderpašina 4; tel. (33) 220462; fax (33) 651789; e-mail bhdani@bih.net.ba; internet www.bhdani.com; independent; political and cultural; Editor-in-Chief EMIR IMAMOVIĆ; circ. 25,500 (2001).

Hrvatska Riječ (Croat Voice): 71000 Sarajevo, Titova 9A/4; tel. and fax (33) 444621; e-mail h_rijec@bih.net.ba; internet www.hrvatska-rijec.com; Croat weekly; Editor-in-Chief ALENKO ZORNIJA.

Ljiljan: 71000 Sarajevo, Sime Milutinovica Sarajlije 12; tel. (33) 664895; fax (33) 664697; e-mail ljiljan@bih.net.ba; internet www.nippljiljan.com; official newspaper of the PDA; Editor-in-Chief DŽEMALUDIN LATIĆ; circ. 8,000 (2001).

Slobodna Bosna (Free Bosnia): 71000 Sarajevo, Čekaluša Čikma 6; tel. (33) 444041; fax (33) 444895; e-mail info@slobodna-bosna.ba; independent; national and international politics; Editor SENAD AVDIĆ; circ. 28,000 (2001).

Start: 71000 Sarajevo, La Benevolencije 6; tel. and fax (33) 260210; e-mail redakcija@startbih.info; internet www.startbih.info; independent; Editor NIK DENAMEDA.

PERIODICALS

Buka: 78000 Banja Luka; tel. and fax (51) 319130; internet www.6yka.com; internet magazine published by the Banja Luka Centre for Informational Decontamination of the Young (Centar za informativnu dekontaminaciju mladih iz Banjaluke); Editor-in-Chief ALEKSANDAR TRIFUNOVIĆ.

Naša Ognjišta—Hrvatski katolički mjesečnik (Our Hearth—Croat Catholic Monthly): 80240 Tomislavgrad, trg fra Mije Čuića 1; tel. (34) 352295; fax (34) 352808; e-mail nasa.ognjista@tel.net.ba; internet www.nasa-ognjista.com; monthly; Editor-in-Chief GABRIJEL MIOČ.

Reporter: 78000 Banja Luka, Grčka 20; tel. (51) 221220; fax (51) 221228; e-mail rep@inecco.net; f. 1996; independent; Editor PERICA VUČINIĆ.

Svjetlo Riječi (Light of the Word): 71000 Sarajevo, Zagrebačka 18; tel. (33) 726200; fax (33) 661364; e-mail svjetlo@svjetlorijeci.ba; internet www.svjetlorijeci.ba; f. 1983; Franciscan; monthly; Dir PETAR MATANOVIĆ; Editor-in-Chief ZDRAVKO KUJUNDŽIJA.

NEWS AGENCIES

Federation News Agency (FENA): 71000 Sarajevo, Cemalusa 1; tel. (33) 445247; e-mail direktor@fena.ba; internet www.fena.ba; f. 2000; Dir ZEHRUDIN ISAKOVIĆ; Editor-in-Chief ZORAN ILIĆ.

ONASA (Oslobođenje News Agency): 71000 Sarajevo, Zmaja od Bosna 4; tel. (33) 276580; fax (33) 276599; e-mail onasa@onasa.com.ba; internet www.onasa.com.ba; f. 1994; Gen. Man. ELVIRA BEGOIĆ.

SNRA—Srpska Novinska Agentsija (News Agency of Republika Srpska): 75320 Bijeljina, Sofke Nikolić 66; tel. (55) 201819; fax (55) 201810; e-mail redakcija@srna.co.yu; internet www.srna.co.yu; f. 1992; bureaux in Banja Luka and East Sarajevo (Republika Srpska); Man. Dir DRAGAN DAVIDOVIĆ.

Publishers

Novi Glas (New Voice): 78000 Banja Luka, Borisa Kidriča 1; tel. (51) 12766; fax (51) 12758; general literature; Dir MIODRAG ŽIVANOVIĆ.

JP NIO Službeni List BiH Sarajevo (Co for Newspaper Publication Organization, Official Gazette of Bosnia and Herzegovina, Sarajevo): 71000 Sarajevo, Magribija 3; tel. (33) 663470; e-mail slist@bih.net.ba; internet www.sllist.ba; publishes legislation and other official publications; Dir MEHMEDALIJA HUREMOVIĆ.

Svjetlost (Light): 71000 Sarajevo, Petra Preradovića 3; tel. (33) 212144; fax (33) 272352; internet www.svjetlost.ba; f. 1945; textbooks and literature, religion; Dir SAVO ZIROJEVIĆ.

TKD Šahinpašić: 71000 Sarajevo, Soukbunar 12; tel. (33) 220111; fax (33) 668856; e-mail info@btcsahinpasic.com; internet www.btcsahinpasic.com; f. 1989; publishers, importers, exporters and retailers of books; Dir-Gen. TAJIB ŠAHINPAŠIĆ.

Zoro (Sarajevo): 71000 Sarajevo, Šenoina 14; tel. and fax (33) 214454; e-mail zorosa@bih.net.ba; internet www.zoro.hr; f. 1994 in Zagreb (Croatia); Dir SAMIR FAZLIĆ.

PUBLISHERS' ASSOCIATION

Assen of Publishers and Booksellers of Bosnia and Herzegovina: 71000 Sarajevo, Maršala Tita 9A; tel. (33) 266621; fax (33) 266630; e-mail ibrosa@bih.net.ba; internet www.uik.ba; f. 2005; Pres. IBRAHIM SPAHIĆ.

Broadcasting and Communications

TELECOMMUNICATIONS

Three principal service providers of telecommunications operate in Bosnia and Herzegovina: BH Telecom, which operates chiefly in Sarajevo and in Bosniak-majority cantons of the Federation; HT Mostar in Croat-majority cantons of the Federation; and Telekom Srpske in Republika Srpska.

BH Telecom d.d. Sarajevo: 71000 Sarajevo, Obala Kulina Bana 8; tel. (33) 232651; fax (33) 212288; e-mail zinajda.kesan@bhtelecom.ba; internet www.bhtelecom.ba; jt-stock co; operates mobile cellular network under the brand name 'BH Mobile'; Chief Exec. HAMDO KATICA.

Hrvatske telekomunikacije Mostar (HT Mostar): 88000 Mostar, Kneza Branimira; tel. and fax (36) 395555; fax (36) 395269; e-mail info@ht.ba; internet www.ht.ba; f. 1995; CEO STIPE PRLIĆ.

Eronet: 88000 Mostar, Tvrtka Miloša bb; tel. (39) 663311; fax (39) 663391; e-mail info@eronet.ba; tel. www.eronet.ba; internet www.eronet.ba; f. 1996; 51% owned by Hrvatske Telekomunikacije Mostar, 49% owned by T-Hrvatski Telecom (Croatia); mobile cellular telecommunications; provides coverage in Western, Southern, Central and Northern regions of Bosnia and Herzegovina.

Telekom Srpske: 78000 Banja Luka, Kralja Petra I Karađorđevića 61A; tel. (51) 240100; fax (51) 211150; e-mail ts.office@telekom-rs.com; internet www.telekomsrpske.com; 65% share owned by Telekom Srbija (Serbia); Dir-Gen. PREDRAG ĆULIBRK.

M:Tel: 78000 Banja Luka, Mladena Stojanovića 4; e-mail s.markovic@telekomsrpske.com; internet www.mtel.ba; fmrly Mobi's; present name adopted 2007; mobile cellular communications; provides coverage in a majority of regions of Bosnia and Herzegovina; f. 1999; Dir MILENKO CVIJANOVIĆ; 506,500 subscribers (2003).

BROADCASTING

In 2002 there were 183 licensed broadcasters in Bosnia and Herzegovina (42 television stations and 141 radio stations), in addition to three nation-wide public broadcasters. In total, there were 78 public and 105 private broadcasting media outlets in the country, of which there were 16 public and 26 private television stations, and 62 public and 79 private radio stations.

Regulatory Authority

Communication Regulatory Agency (Regulatorna agencija za komunikacije—RAK): 71000 Sarajevo, Mehmeda Spahe 1; tel. (33) 250600; fax (33) 713080; e-mail info@rak.ba; internet www.rak.ba; f. 2001; Dir-Gen. KEMAL HUSEINOVIĆ.

Radio

Public Broadcasting Service of Bosnia and Herzegovina: 71000 Sarajevo, Bulevar Meše Selimovića 12; tel. (33) 464073; fax (33) 461556; e-mail mehmed.agovic@bhrt.ba; internet www.bhrt.ba; f. 1945; Dir-Gen. MEHMED AGOVIĆ; Dir of TV MILENKO VOČKIĆ; Dir of Radio SENADA ĆUMUROVIĆ.

Radio of the Federation of Bosnia and Herzegovina (Radio Federacije Bosne i Hercegovine): 71000 Sarajevo, Bulevar Mesa Selimovica 12; tel. (33) 455102; fax (33) 455103; e-mail esadc@rtvbih.ba; internet www.rtvbih.ba?Program/radio%20FbiH; Dir CEROVIĆ ESAD.

Radio-Televizija Republike Srpske (RTRS) (Radio and Television of Republika Srpska): 78000 Banja Luka, Kralja Petra I Karađorđevića 129; tel. (51) 300817; fax (51) 321812; e-mail rtrs@rtrs.tv; internet www.rtrs.tv; f. 1992; Gen. Man. DRAGAN DAVIDOVIĆ.

Bosnian Radio Network (Bosanska Radio Mreža—BORAM): 71000 Sarajevo, Cumurija 2; tel. (33) 202099; fax (33) 261231; e-mail web@bih.net.ba; internet www.web1.bih.net.ba; network of 20 local stations; nation-wide broadcasts from 2002.

Radio Slon: 75000 Tuzla, ul. S. Karamehmedović 39; tel. (35) 205530; fax (35) 250053; e-mail redakcija@radioslon.ba; internet www.radioslon.ba; f. 1995; Dir ŠABAN PIRIĆ.

Radio Stari Grad: 71000 Sarajevo, Urijan Dedina 7; tel. (33) 251435; fax (33) 251426; e-mail rsg@rsg.ba; internet www.rsg.ba; Gen. Dir ADNAN OSMANGIĆ.

Radio ZID: 71000 Sarajevo, Husrefa Redžića 8; commenced broadcasts March 1993; independent radio station; cultural and educative programmes; broadcasts to Sarajevo and to neighbouring areas in Federation of Bosnia and Herzegovina and in Republika Srpska; Chair. ZDRAVKO GREBO; Editor-in-Chief VLADO AZINOVIĆ.

Studio 99: Sarajevo; e-mail redakcija@ntv99.ba; internet www.ntv99.ba; f. 1995; independent radio and tv station; political and current affairs; Editor-in-Chief ADIL KULENOVIĆ; Editor of Programmes ERINA GAKIĆ.

Television

Public Broadcasting Service of Bosnia and Herzegovina: 71000 Sarajevo, Bulevar Meše Selimovića 12; tel. (33) 464073; fax (33) 461556; e-mail mehmed.agovic@bhrt.ba; internet www.bhrt.ba; f. 1945; Dir-Gen. MEHMED AGOVIĆ; Dir of TV MILENKO VOČKIĆ; Dir of Radio SENADA ĆUMUROVIĆ.

Federation of Bosnia and Herzegovina Television (Federalna Televizija BiH—FTV): 71000 Sarajevo, Bulevar Meše Selimovića 12; tel. (33) 462511; fax (33) 455148; e-mail tvdesk02@rtvfbih.ba.

Radio-Televizija Republike Srpske (RTRS) (Radio and Television of Republika Srpska): 78000 Banja Luka, Kralja Petra I Karađorđevića 129; tel. (51) 300817; fax (51) 321812; e-mail rtrs@rtrs.tv; internet www.rtrs.tv; f. 1992; Gen. Man. DRAGAN DAVIDOVIĆ.

Alternativna Televizija Informisanje: 78000 Banja Luka, Kralja Petra I Karađorđevića 2; tel. and fax (51) 320770; e-mail info@atvbl.com; internet www.atvbl.com; f. 1996; Dir NATAŠA TEŠANOVIĆ.

NTV Hayat: 71000 Sarajevo, Avdage Sahinagica 14; tel. (33) 271110; fax (33) 271111; e-mail ntvhayat@ntvhayat.com; internet www.ntvhayat.com; f. 1991; broadcasts 18 hours daily; Dir-Gen. ELVIR ŠVRAKIĆ.

Zetel: 72000 Zenica, Stara čaršija bb; tel. (32) 403900; fax (32) 284076; e-mail zetel@bih.net.ba; f. 1992; independent; transmits 13 hours per day to Zenica and surrounding area; cultural, political, educational and sports programmes; Dir ŽELJKO LINCNER.

Finance

(cap. = capital; res = reserves; dep. = deposits; m. = million; amounts in konvertibilna marka—KM, convertible marks; brs = branches)

BANKING

At the end of 2005 33 banks were operating in Bosnia and Herzegovina (of which three were state-owned, eight were domestic private banks and 22 were foreign-owned banks). In that year total assets of the banking system were equivalent to 75.3% of GDP.

Central Bank

Central Bank of Bosnia and Herzegovina: 71000 Sarajevo, Maršala Tita 25; tel. (33) 278100; fax (33) 278299; e-mail contact@cbbh.ba; internet www.cbbh.ba; replaced the National Bank of the Federation of Bosnia and Herzegovina, and the National Bank of Republika Srpska, which ceased monetary operations in Aug. 1997; cap. 25.0m., res 276.0m., dep. 3,028.4m. (Dec. 2006); Gov. KEMAL KOZARIĆ.

Selected Banks

Balkan Investment Bank a.d. Banja Luka: 78000 Banja Luka, Bana Milosavljevića 8; tel. (51) 245000; fax (51) 245188; e-mail contact@bib.ba; internet www.bib.ba; f. 2000; 49.99% owned by UAB Ukio banko investicine grupe (Lithuania); cap. 18.0m., res 0.1m., dep. 108.0m. (Dec. 2006); Chair. ARNAS ZALYS.

Bobar Banka a.d.: 76300 Bijeljina, Njegoseva 1; tel. (55) 211153; fax (55) 201863; e-mail office@bobarbanka.com; internet www.bobar.com; f. 1998; cap. 16.7m., res 0.1m., dep. 50.5m. (Dec. 2006); Gen. Man. DRAGAN RADUMILO.

HVB Central Profit Banka d.d.: 71000 Sarajevo, Zelenih Beretki 24; tel. (33) 533433; fax (33) 533688; e-mail info@hvb-cpb.ba; internet www.hvb-cpb.ba; f. 1919; present name adopted 2004; 80.0% owned by Bank Austria Creditanstalt AG (Austria); cap. 69.6m., res 16.5m., dep. 962.2m. (Dec. 2005); Gen. Man. ALEXANDER ZSOLNAI.

Hypo Alpe-Adria-Bank a.d. Banja Luka: 78000 Banja Luka, Aleja Svetog Save 13; tel. (51) 336500; fax (51) 336518; e-mail bank.bl.bih@hypo-alpe-adria.com; internet www.hypo-alpe-adria.ba; f. 2002; 99.6% owned by Hypo Alpe-Adria-Bank International AG (Austria); cap. 100.8m., res 7.9m., dep. 1,003.4m. (Dec. 2006); Chair. GÜNTER STRIEDINGER.

Hypo Alpe-Adria Bank d.d.: 88000 Mostar, Kneza Branimira 2B; tel. and fax (36) 444200; fax (36) 444235; e-mail bank.bih@hypo-alpe-adria.com; internet www.hypo-alpe-adria.ba; f. 1999; present name adopted 2001; subsidiary of Hypo Alpe-Adria-Bank International AG (Austria); cap. 140.0m., res 16.4m., dep. 1,498.1m. (Dec. 2006); Pres. GÜNTER STRIEDINGER.

BOSNIA AND HERZEGOVINA

NLB Razvojna Banka a.d.: 78000 Banja Luka, Milana Tepića 4; tel. (51) 242101; fax (51) 221623; e-mail info@lhbbank.com; internet www.razvojnabanka.com; f. 1998; present name adopted 2006; 50.6% stake purchased by NLB d.d. (Slovenia) in Sept. 2005; cap. 23.0m., res 2.3m., dep. 308.2m. (Dec. 2005); Gen. Dir Radovan Bajić; 56 brs.

NLB Tuzlanska Banka d.d. Tuzla: 75000 Tuzla, Maršala Tita 34; tel. (35) 259259; fax (35) 250596; e-mail info@nlbtuzlanskabanka.ba; internet www.nlbtuzlanskabanka.ba; f. 1990; present name adopted 2006; 93.2% owned by NLB d.d. (Slovenia); cap. 33.6m., res 15.1m., dep. 542.9m. (Dec. 2006); Chair. Matej Narat; 16 brs.

Nova Banka a.d. Bijeljina: 76300 Bijeljina, ul. Jovana Dučića br. 17; tel. (55) 230300; fax (55) 201410; e-mail office@novabanka.com; internet www.novabanka.com; f. 1992; present name adopted 1999; cap. 38.6m., res 6.1m., dep. 322.2m. (Dec. 2006); Pres. Mihajlo Vidić; Chair. Zivojin Krajisnik.

ProCredit Bank d.d.: 71000 Sarajevo, Emerika Bluma 8; tel. (33) 250950; fax (33) 250971; e-mail procreditbank@procreditbank.ba; internet www.procreditbank.ba; f. 1997; present name adopted 2003; cap. 15.7m., res 1.6m., dep. 176.8m. (Dec. 2006); Dir Peter Moelders.

Raiffeisen Bank d.d. Bosna i Hercegovina: 71000 Sarajevo, Danijela Ozme 3; tel. (33) 287100; fax (33) 213851; e-mail info.rbbh@rbb-sarajevo.raiffeisen.at; internet www.raiffeisenbank.ba; f. 1992; present name adopted 2000; cap. 89.3m., res 80.1m., dep. 2,220.5m. (Dec. 2005); Pres. Dr Hebert Stepić.

Turkish Ziraat Bank Bosnia d.d.: 71000 Sarajevo, Ferhadija 29 and Dženetića Čikma 2; tel. (33) 564100; fax (33) 564101; e-mail ziraat@bih.net.ba; internet www.ziraatbosnia.com; f. 1996; 68% owned by Türkiye Cumhuriyeti Ziraat Bankası (Turkey), 32% by Ziraat International (Germany); cap. 60.0m., res 2.2m., dep. 75.0m. (Dec. 2007); Chair. Mehmet Mumcuoglu; 9 brs.

UniCredit Zagrebačka Banka d.d.: 88000 Mostar, Kardinala Štepinca bb; tel. (36) 312112; fax (36) 312129; e-mail ana.rozic@unizaba.ba; internet www.unizaba.ba; f. 1992; present name adopted 2004; cap. 83.2m., res 0.1m., dep. 1,451.4m. (Dec. 2006); Chair. Franjo Luković.

Union Banka d.d. Sarajevo: 71000 Sarajevo, Dubrovačka 6; tel. (33) 561000; fax (33) 219201; e-mail unionban@bih.net.ba; internet www.unionbank.ba; f. 1955; 91.5% state-owned; cap. 34.1m., res 9.9m., dep. 109.6m. (Dec. 2006); Dir Esad Bekteševič.

Vakufska Banka d.d. Sarajevo: 71000 Sarajevo, Ferhadija 4; tel. (33) 200598; fax (33) 200597; e-mail vakufska@vakuba.ba; internet www.vakuba.ba; f. 1992; cap. 15.9m., dep. 86.2m. (Dec. 2006); Pres. Amir Rizvanović.

Volksbank BH d.d.: 71000 Sarajevo, Fra Anđela Zvizdovića 1; tel. (33) 295601; fax (33) 295603; e-mail info@volksbank.ba; internet www.volksbank.ba; cap. 47.0m., res 3.2m., dep. 276.0m. (Dec. 2006); Gen. Man. Reinhold Kolland.

Islamic Bank

Bosna Bank International d.d. Sarajevo: 71000 Sarajevo, trg Djece Sarajeva bb; tel. (33) 275131; fax (33) 203122; e-mail info@bbi.ba; internet www.bbi.ba; f. 2000; 45.5% owned by Islamic Development Bank (Saudi Arabia), 27.3% by Abu Dhabi Islamic Bank (United Arab Emirates), 27.3% by Dubai Islamic Bank (United Arab Emirates); cap. 50.1m., res 0.0m., dep. 84.9m. (Dec. 2006); Chair. Abdul Aziz al-Muhairi.

Banking Agencies

Banking Agency of the Federation of Bosnia and Herzegovina (Agencija za Bankarstvo Federacije Bosne i Hercegovine): 71000 Sarajevo, Koševo 3; tel. (33) 721400; fax (33) 668811; e-mail public@fba.ba; internet www.fba.ba; f. 1996; Chair. Eldar Arnautović; Dir Zlatko Bars.

Banking Agency of Republika Srpska (Agencija za Bankarstvo Republike Srpske): 78000 Banja Luka, Vase Pelagića 11a; tel. (51) 218111; fax (51) 216665; e-mail office@abrs.ba; internet www.abrs.ba; f. 1998; Chair. of Bd Novo Plakalović; Dir Dushanka Novaković.

STOCK EXCHANGE

Sarajevo Stock Exchange: 71000 Sarajevo, Zvizdovića 1; tel. (33) 251462; fax (33) 251478; e-mail uprava@sase.ba; internet www.sase.ba; f. 2002; Dir-Gen. Zlatan Dedić.

Trade and Industry

GOVERNMENT AGENCIES

Foreign Investment Promotion Agency of Bosnia and Herzegovina: 71000 Sarajevo, Branilaca Sarajeva 21; tel. (33) 278000; fax (33) 278081; e-mail fipa@fipa.gov.ba; internet www.fipa.gov.ba; f. 1999; Gen. Dir Haris Bašić.

Federation of Bosnia and Herzegovina

Privatization Agency of the Federation of Bosnia and Herzegovina: 71000 Sarajevo, Alipašina 41; tel. (33) 212884; fax (33) 212883; e-mail apfbih@bih.net.ba; internet www.apf.com.ba; Dir Adnad Mujagić.

Securities Commission of the Federation of Bosnia and Herzegovina (Komisija za vrijednosne papire Federacije Bosne i Hercegovine): 71000 Sarajevo, Čemaluša 9; tel. (33) 665897; fax (33) 211655; e-mail komvp@komvp.gov.ba; internet www.komvp.gov.ba; f. 1999; Pres. Hasan Ćelam.

Republika Srpska

Republika Srpksa Directorate for Privatization: 78000 Banja Luka, Mladena Stoganovića 4; tel. (51) 308311; fax (51) 311245; e-mail dip@inecco.net; internet www.rsprivatizacija.com; Dir Borislav Obradović.

Republika Srpska Securities Commission (Komisija za khartije od vrijednosti Republike Srpske): 78000 Banja Luka, Vuka Karadžića 6; tel. (51) 218361; fax (51) 218362; e-mail kontakt@khov-rs.org; internet www.khov-rs.org/Index.htm; Pres. Branka Bodroža.

DEVELOPMENT ORGANIZATIONS

Federation Development Planning Institution (Federacija BiH Federalni zavod za programiranje razvoja): 71000 Sarajevo, Alipašina 41; tel. (33) 667272; fax (33) 212625; e-mail info@fzzpr.gov.ba; internet www.fzzpr.gov.ba; Dir Prof. Nešet Muminagić.

CHAMBERS OF COMMERCE

Chamber of Commerce of Bosnia and Herzegovina (Privredna Komora BiH): 71000 Sarajevo, Branislava Đurđeva 10; tel. (33) 663631; fax (33) 663632; e-mail cis@komorabih.com; internet www.komorabih.com; Pres. Milan Lovrić.

Chamber of Commerce of the Federation of Bosnia and Herzegovina—Sarajevo (Privredna Komora FBiH—Sarajevo): 71000 Sarajevo, Branislava Đurđeva 10; tel. (33) 217782; fax (33) 217783; e-mail info@kfbih.com; internet www.kfbih.com; f. 1999; Pres. Jaso Lasić.

Chamber of Commerce of the Federation of Bosnia and Herzegovina—Mostar (Privredna Komora FBiH—Mostar): 88000 Mostar, Zagrebačka 10; tel. (36) 332963; fax (36) 332966; e-mail gkfbih@tel.net.ba; internet www.kfbih.com; Sec. Željana Bevanda.

Chamber of Commerce of Republika Srpska (Privredna komora RS): 78000 Banja Luka, Đure Daničića 1; tel. (51) 215744; fax (51) 215565; internet www.komorars.ba; Pres. Borko Đurić.

UTILITIES

Electricity

Elektroprivreda BiH: 71000 Sarajevo, Vilsonovo Šetalište 15; tel. and fax (33) 751000; fax (33) 751008; e-mail e.kreso@elektroprivreda.ba; internet www.elektroprivreda.ba; generation, transmission and distribution of electric energy; Dir-Gen. Enver Kreso.

Gas

BH-Gas: 71000 Sarajevo, Hamdije Cemerlića 2; tel. (33) 279000; fax (33) 661621; e-mail management@bh-gas.ba; internet www.bh-gas.ba; f. 1997; Man. Dir Almir Bećarević.

Water

Vodno Područje Slivova Rijeke Save: 71000 Sarajevo, ul. Grbavička 4/3; tel. (33) 209827; fax (33) 209903; e-mail info@voda.ba; internet www.voda.ba; Dir Mehmed Buturović.

TRADE UNIONS

Confederation of Independent Trade Unions of Bosnia and Herzegovina (Savez samostalnih sindikata Bosne i Hercegovine—SSSBiH): 71000 Sarajevo, Obala Kulina Bana 1; tel. (33) 202029; fax (33) 664872.

Confederation of Trade Unions of Republika Srpska (Savez sindikata Republike Srpske—SSRS): 78000 Banja Luka, Srpska 32; tel. (51) 310711; fax (51) 304241Chair. Čedo Bolaš.

Transport

RAILWAYS

Following the outbreak of hostilities in 1992, the state railway company was divided into three regional state-owned companies: the Bosnia and Herzegovina Railway (ŽBH); the Herceg-Bosnia Railway (ŽHB); and the Republika Srpska Railway (ŽRS). In 1998 ŽBH and ŽHB were merged to form Railways of the Federation of Bosnia and Herzegovina (ŽFBH). In late 2005 (by which time services had reached only about 25% of the pre-war level), the European Bank for Reconstruction and Development announced lending of some €70m., as part of a €169m. financial programme for the renovation and improvement of the country's rail network.

Željeznice Federacije Bosne i Hercegovine (ŽFBH) (Railways of the Federation of Bosnia and Herzegovina): 71000 Sarajevo, Musala 2; tel. (33) 616637; fax (33) 652396; e-mail zbh@bih.net.ba; Gen. Dir NARCIS DŽUMHUR.

Željeznice Republike Srpske (ŽRS) (Railways of Republika Srpska): 74000 Doboj, Svetog Save 71; tel. (53) 224050; fax (53) 222247; e-mail zrs.kp@doboj.net.

ROADS

Bosnia and Herzegovina's road network covers some 22,600 km, comprising 3,788 km of main roads, 4,842 km of regional roads and about 14,000 km of local roads.

Federation Road Directorate: 71000 Sarajevo, Terezisa 54; tel. (33) 250400; internet www.jpdcfbh.ba; Dir LJUBO PRAVDIĆ.

Republika Srpska Directorate for Roads: 78000 Banja Luka, Vase Pelagića 10; tel. (51) 309061; fax (51) 308316; Dir NEMANJA VASIĆ.

Centrotrans-Eurolines d.d. Sarajevo: 71000 Sarajevo, Mula Mustafa Bašeskije 5; tel. (33) 464045; fax (33) 464040; e-mail info@centrotrans.ba; internet www.centrotrans.ba; f. 1963; principal provider of inter-city passenger coach services domestically and between Bosnia and Herzegovina and the rest of Europe; Gen. Man. MUHAMED SACIRAGIĆ.

CIVIL AVIATION

The country has an international airport at Sarajevo, and three smaller civil airports, at Tuzla, Banja Luka and Mostar.

Department of Civil Aviation of Bosnia and Herzegovina: 71000 Sarajevo, Fehima Efendije Čurčića 6; tel. (33) 251350; fax (33) 251351; e-mail bhdca@bhdca.gov.ba; internet www.bhdca.gov.ba; f. 1997; Dir-Gen. DORĐE RATKOVICA.

Federation Civil Aviation Department (FEDCAD) (Federalna Direkcija za Civilnu Avijaciju): 88000 Mostar, Ante Starčevića bb; tel. (36) 449230; fax (36) 327811; e-mail info@fedcad.gov.ba; internet www.fmpik.gov.ba/sektori/civ_avio.html; Dir AMADEO MANDIĆ.

Republika Srpska Civil Aviation Department (RSCAD): 78250 Laktaši, Mahovljani bb, Međunarodni Aerodrom Banja Luka; tel. (51) 337500; fax (51) 337503; e-mail rscad@rscad.org; internet www.rscad.org; Dir DEJAN TODOROVIĆ.

B&H Airlines: 71000 Sarajevo, Kurta Schorka 36; tel. (33) 460783; fax (33) 466338; e-mail bkasumagic@airbosna.ba; internet www.airbosna.ba; f. 1994 as Air Bosna; ceased operations in 2003, relaunched as B&H Airlines in 2005; 51% state-owned; regular services to Croatia, Germany, Switzerland and Turkey.

Tourism

Despite the destruction or damage of many historic monuments, and the prevalence of landmines in many regions, Bosnia and Herzegovina has many sites of potential interest to tourists. These include mountain scenery, ski resorts and spas, rivers and waterfalls, the historic cities of Sarajevo, Mostar, Travnik, Trebinje and Jajce, and one resort on the Adriatic Sea, at Neum. A film festival has been held annually in Sarajevo since 1995. Tourist arrivals increased from 139,000 in 2001 to 217,000 in 2005, in which year receipts from tourism (including passenger transport) totalled US $604m.

Tourism Asscn of the Federation of Bosnia and Herzegovina: 71000 Sarajevo, Branilaca Sarajeva 21/4; tel. (33) 352900; fax (33) 252901; e-mail tour.off@bih.net.ba; internet www.bhtourism.ba.

Ministry of Trade and Tourism of Republika Srpska: see The Entities (Republika Srpska, The Government—Ministries).

BOTSWANA

Introductory Survey

Location, Climate, Language, Religion, Flag, Capital

The Republic of Botswana is a land-locked country in southern Africa, with South Africa to the south and east, Zimbabwe to the north-east and Namibia to the west and north. A short section of the northern frontier adjoins Zambia. The climate is generally sub-tropical, with hot summers. Annual rainfall averages about 457 mm (18 ins), varying from 635 mm (25 ins) in the north to 228 mm (9 ins) or less in the western Kalahari desert. The country is largely near-desert, and most of its inhabitants live along the eastern border, close to the main railway line. English is the official language, and Setswana the national language. Most of the population follow traditional animist beliefs, but several Christian churches are also represented. The national flag (proportions 2 by 3) consists of a central horizontal stripe of black, edged with white, between two blue stripes. The capital is Gaborone.

Recent History

Botswana was formerly Bechuanaland, which became a British protectorate, at the request of the local rulers, in 1885. It was administered as one of the High Commission Territories in southern Africa, the others being the colony of Basutoland (now Lesotho) and the protectorate of Swaziland. The British Act of Parliament that established the Union of South Africa in 1910 also allowed for the inclusion in South Africa of the three High Commission Territories, on condition that the local inhabitants were consulted. Until 1960 successive South African Governments asked for the transfer of the three territories, but the native chiefs always objected to such a scheme.

Bechuanaland became the independent Republic of Botswana, within the Commonwealth, on 30 September 1966, with Sir Seretse Khama, the leader of the Botswana Democratic Party (BDP) taking office as the country's first President. The BDP won elections to the National Assembly, with little opposition, in 1969, 1974 and 1979.

Upon Khama's death in July 1980, Dr Quett Masire (later Sir Ketumile Masire), hitherto Vice-President and Minister of Finance, was appointed to the presidency. Following elections to the National Assembly in September 1984, at which the BDP again achieved a decisive victory, Masire was re-elected President by the legislature.

In October 1989 the BDP received 65% of the votes cast at a general election to the National Assembly, winning 27 of the 30 elective seats (the remaining three seats were won by the principal opposition party, the Botswana National Front—BNF), and the new legislature re-elected Masire for a third term as President.

In March 1992 the Vice-President and Chairman of the BDP, Peter Mmusi, resigned as Vice-President and Minister of Local Government and Lands, while the party's Secretary-General, Daniel Kwelagobe, resigned as Minister of Agriculture, having been accused of corruption involving the illegal transfer of land. Festus Mogae, the Minister of Finance and Development Planning, was appointed as the new Vice-President. In June Mmusi and Kwelagobe were suspended from the Central Committee of the BDP; both were, however, re-elected to their former positions within the party in July 1993. In July 1995 the Minister of Presidential Affairs and Public Administration, Ponatshego Kedikilwe, was elected Chairman of the BDP—a post that had remained vacant since the death of Mmusi in October 1994.

At the general election held in October 1994 the BDP, which received 53.1% of the votes cast, won 26 of the 40 available seats, while the BNF, which obtained 37.7% of the votes, increased its representation to 13 seats. More than 70% of registered voters participated in the election. The National Assembly subsequently re-elected Masire to the presidency.

In August 1997 the National Assembly formally adopted a constitutional amendment restricting the presidential mandate to two terms of office and providing for the automatic succession to the presidency of the Vice-President, in the event of the death or resignation of the President. In September a national referendum endorsed further revisions, lowering the age of eligibility to vote from 21 to 18 years and providing for the establishment of an independent electoral commission. In November Masire announced his intention to retire from politics in March 1998. In accordance with the amended Constitution, Vice-President Mogae was inaugurated as President on 1 April 1998, pending elections to be held in 1999, and subsequently appointed a new Cabinet, in which the only new minister was Lt-Gen. Seretse Ian Khama, son of Botswana's first President (the late Sir Seretse Khama) and hitherto Commander of the Botswana Defence Force (BDF). Khama received the portfolio of presidential affairs and public administration, and was later designated as Mogae's Vice-President, subject to his election to the National Assembly. Kedikilwe was appointed Minister of Finance and Development Planning. Khama was elected to the National Assembly in July, and was sworn in as Vice-President in the same month.

Meanwhile, hostility between Kenneth Koma, the leader of the BNF, and his deputy, Michael Dingake, had led to a split in the party. In June 1998 the Botswana Congress Party (BCP) was formed, under the leadership of Dingake and the following month the BCP was declared the official opposition, after 11 of the BNF's 13 deputies joined the new party.

At the general election, held in mid-October 1999, the BDP received 57.2% of the votes and increased its representation in the National Assembly from 26 to 33 seats, while the number of seats held by the BNF (with 26.0% of the votes) fell significantly to only six seats. The BCP (having received 11.9%) obtained just one seat; 77.3% of the electorate participated in the polls. Mogae was re-elected to the presidency by the National Assembly on 20 October and formed a new Cabinet the following day.

The Government's attempts to relocate San (Bushmen) people from their homeland within the Central Kalahari Game Reserve to a new settlement outside the Reserve provoked international concern from 1996. It was claimed that officials had forced many San to move by disconnecting water supplies and threatening military intervention; 2,160 San had been resettled by mid-2001, according to reports. At the end of January 2002 the Government withdrew services to the remaining San living in the Reserve (estimated to number 500–700), in accordance with a decision announced in August 2001. A legal appeal brought to a halt the process of relocation but the return of hunting rights to the San was rejected on a technicality in April 2002. In August a delegation from the European Union (EU, see p. 244) accused the Government of providing false information about the number of San remaining in the Reserve, and of failing to fulfil their human rights requirements, including the supply of fresh water. In October the Government awarded some P2m. in compensation to more than 3,000 San who had been removed from the Reserve. In late 2002 Survival International, a lobby group for the rights of indigenous peoples, alleged that the Government had relocated the San in order to allow mining companies to explore for diamonds in the Reserve; the Government vehemently rejected these claims, maintaining that it was acting in the socio-economic interests of the San. Some 243 San commenced legal action against the Government in late 2003 in order to be permitted to live in the Reserve. In mid-2005 the Government removed a clause in the Constitution granting protection to San and other minorities, and some analysts argued that this was designed to undermine the court challenge. In December 2006 the High Court ruled that the removal of the San from the Reserve had been 'unlawful and unconstitutional' and confirmed their right to live on the Reserve, but also decreed that the Government was not obliged to provide services to them. Following the announcement of the decision some 100 San returned to the Reserve, although it was reported that the Government was attempting to limit the number of returnees.

Meanwhile, in November 2001 a number of changes to the structure and conditions of service of the judiciary were approved in a national referendum, although less than 5% of the electorate were reported to have participated in the vote. Ethnic tensions arose over a clause providing for an increase in the retirement age for judges. Pitso Ya Batswana, a Tswana nationalist group, claimed that this proposal was evidence of the over-representation in the judiciary and other professions of the Kalanga people, who constituted approximately 10% of the population, and that the referendum represented an attempt by the Kalanga community to advance its own interests. However, the Kalanga, together with numerous other ethnic groups, were not recognized in the Constitution as one of the eight tribes with the right to be represented in the House of Chiefs, Botswana's second legislative house. The Government had established a constitutional commission in July 2000 to investigate allegations of discrimination against minority groups, including the Kalanga, Wayeyi and San. On the basis of the recommendations of this commission, in December 2001 the Government presented a number of draft constitutional amendments. Under the proposals, the House of Chiefs would be renamed the Ntlo ya Dikgosi and its membership increased from 15 to 35, comprising 30 members elected by senior tribal authorities and five members appointed by the President. Elections to the Ntlo ya Dikgosi would be held every five years. In April 2002 the draft amendments were revised to allow the eight paramount chiefs to retain their ex officio status in the chamber. The proposed amendments were submitted to the legislature in late 2003. Approval of the increase in membership was announced in late December 2005.

In June 2002 the National Assembly approved legislation providing for an expansion in its directly elected membership from 40 to 57, with effect from the next general election (due in 2004), and a gradual increase in both the number of ministries, from 12 to 16, and in the number of assistant ministers, from four to eight.

In early 2003 dissidents from the BNF, led by Koma, who had been expelled from the party in 2002, formed a new party, the New Democratic Front. In July 2003, at the BDP congress, Vice-President Khama defeated Kedikilwe to become Chairman of the party. Later that month Lesego Motsumi replaced Joy Phumaphi as Minister of Health.

At the election to the newly enlarged legislature, held on 30 October 2004, the BDP secured 44 seats, although it obtained a smaller share of the vote (51.7%) than at the previous general election. The BNF received 26.1% of the votes cast and increased its representation to 12 seats, while the BCP (with 16.6%) retained its solitary parliamentary seat. The rate of voter participation was recorded at 74.6%. President Mogae was sworn in for a second and final term of office on 2 November; he was expected to step down from the presidency at the end of March 2008, to be succeeded by Vice-President Khama. Eleven new appointees were included in the reshuffled Cabinet, nine of whom were newly elected members of the National Assembly.

In January 2007 President Mogae effected a reorganization of the Cabinet. Most notably, Kwelagobe was appointed to the newly created post of Minister for Public Service in the Office of the President, responsible for the Public Service, the Ombudsman, the Independent Electoral Commission and the National AIDS Co-ordinating Agency, while Ponatsego Kedikilwe assumed the minerals, energy and water affairs portfolio, replacing Charles Tibone, who became Minister of Labour and Home Affairs. The appointment to the Cabinet of Kwelagobe and Kedikelwe was regarded as an attempt to address the divisions that had adversely affected the BDP during 2005–06. Maj.-Gen. Moeng Pheto, who assumed the newly established role of Minister of Youth, Sports and Culture, was regarded by many in the country as an unsuitable choice for the post and there were demands for his resignation and for the appointment of a minister better able to relate to the needs of Botswana's youth.

In July 2007 President Mogae announced that, as expected, he would relinquish the presidency in March 2008. In accordance with the Constitution, Vice-President Khama was to succeed Mogae.

Although, as one of the 'front-line' states, Botswana did not have diplomatic links with the apartheid regime in South Africa, it was (and remains) heavily dependent on its neighbour for trade and communications. Botswana is a member of the Southern African Development Community (SADC, see p. 386), which superseded the Southern African Development Co-ordination Conference (SADCC) in 1992. SADC, of which South Africa became a member in 1994, has its headquarters in Gaborone.

From independence, it was the Botswana Government's stated policy not to permit any guerrilla groups to operate from its territory. Relations with South Africa deteriorated in May 1984, when President Masire accused the South African Government of exerting pressure on Botswana to sign a non-aggression pact, aimed at preventing the alleged use of Botswana's territory by guerrilla forces of the (then outlawed) African National Congress of South Africa (ANC). In the second half of the 1980s South African forces launched a number of raids on alleged ANC bases in Botswana, causing several deaths. Owing to Botswana's vulnerable position, however, the Government did not commit itself to the imposition of economic sanctions against South Africa when this was recommended by SADCC in August 1986. In 1988–89 Botswana took action against the extension onto its territory of hostilities between South African government and anti-apartheid forces. Two South African commandos, who had allegedly opened fire on Botswana security forces while engaged in a raid, were sentenced to 10 years' imprisonment, nine South Africans were expelled for 'security reasons', and five ANC members were convicted on firearms charges. It was reported in August 1989 that the South African army had erected an electrified fence along a 24-km section of the South Africa–Botswana border, in order to halt the reputed threat of guerrilla infiltration into South Africa via Botswana.

With the dismantling of apartheid in the first half of the 1990s, Botswana's relations with South Africa improved markedly, and full diplomatic relations were established in June 1994. In April 1999 Botswana and South Africa signed a bilateral agreement on the administrative merger of their adjacent national parks. The Kgalagadi Transfrontier Park was formally opened in May 2000 by President Mogae and President Thabo Mbeki of South Africa. In November the inaugural meeting of the Botswana-South Africa joint permanent commission on defence and security was held in Gaborone.

In August 1998 Botswana participated in attempts made by SADC to resolve a political crisis in Lesotho, where opposition parties were demanding the annulment of elections held in May of that year. Following an increase in civil and military unrest and reports of an imminent coup attempt, on 22 September some 200 members of the BDF and 600 South African troops entered Lesotho, in response to requests from the Prime Minister, Pakalitha Mosisili. The SADC-sponsored military intervention encountered strong resistance from dissident members of the Lesotho armed forces and civilians, but after three days of heavy fighting and looting, in which more than 70 people died, relative calm was restored to the devastated capital, Maseru. In early 1999 the role of the BDF troops in Lesotho was the subject of debate in Botswana itself, and in May all the remaining SADC forces were withdrawn. A group of instructors from Botswana and South Africa remained in Lesotho, in an advisory and training capacity, until May 2000.

Botswana and Zimbabwe established full diplomatic relations in May 1983 and the first meeting of the Botswana-Zimbabwe joint commission for co-operation was held in October 1984. In the mid-1990s the Botswana Government expressed concern at the growing number of illegal immigrants in the country, the majority of whom were from Zimbabwe; of more than 40,000 illegal immigrants repatriated during 1995, more than 14,000 were Zimbabwean. Relations between the two countries were further strained in 2000, when Zimbabwe's construction of a railway line from Bulawayo (its second largest city) to Beitbridge (on the border with South Africa) severely reduced transit freight traffic on Botswana Railways. Following the controversial re-election of Robert Mugabe to the Zimbabwean presidency in March 2002, the Botswana Government became more critical of government policy in Zimbabwe, as the economic crisis in that country prompted an influx of immigrants into Botswana, with many entering illegally. In late 2003 the Botswana Government began erecting a 3m-high electrified fence along the border with Zimbabwe, ostensibly to prevent the spread of foot-and-mouth disease, although it was widely regarded as a measure to prevent the entry of further illegal immigrants, with those already in Botswana estimated to number more than 100,000 in early 2004; by the end of that year the number was estimated at more than 200,000. Some 2,500 people—mainly Zimbabweans—were being deported every month, and the Government sought to amend the Immigration Act of 2003 to impose higher fines and stricter sentences on those deemed to have entered the country illegally. During April–September 2006 the Botswana Government deported some 30,000 illegal Zimbabwean immigrants.

Following Namibian independence, in July 1990 it was announced that a commission for bilateral co-operation was to be established by Botswana and Namibia. In 1992, however, a border dispute developed between the two countries regarding their rival territorial claims over a small island (Sedudu-Kasikili) in the Chobe river. In early 1995 the two states agreed to present the issue of the demarcation of their joint border for arbitration at the International Court of Justice (ICJ), in The Hague, Netherlands, and in February 1996 the two countries signed an agreement committing themselves in advance to the

BOTSWANA

Court's eventual judgment. Meanwhile, Namibia appealed to Botswana to remove its troops—stated by the Botswana authorities to be anti-poaching patrols—and national flag from the island. In early 1997 it was reported that Namibia had been angered by Botswana's erection of a fence along Namibia's Caprivi Strip, which separates the two countries to the north; Botswana insisted, however, that the fence was simply a measure to control the spread of livestock diseases. In January 1998 an emergency meeting of the Botswana-Namibia joint commission on defence and security was held to discuss ownership of another island (Situngu) in the Chobe river, following allegations by Namibia that the BDF had occupied the island and was stealing crops planted by Namibian farmers resident there. In December 1999 the ICJ granted Botswana control over Sedudu-Kasikili. A joint technical commission was subsequently established to consider other demarcation disputes between Botswana and Namibia, and in March 2003 its report was accepted by the Presidents of both countries.

Meanwhile, in late 1998 relations between the two countries were further strained by the arrival in Botswana of more than 300 refugees (a number of whom were reportedly leading political dissidents) from the Caprivi Strip in Namibia. President Mogae rejected Namibian demands for the extradition of the refugees, whose number had increased to more than 2,000 by early 1999. In May, however, a formal agreement was signed by the two Governments, according to which prominent dissidents among the refugees would be allowed to leave Botswana for another country and an amnesty would be extended to other refugees returning to Namibia. In response to a request from the Namibian Government, in September 2001 the Gaborone Magistrates' Court ruled in favour of the extradition of a group of 13 suspected Caprivi separatists who were wanted to stand trial for alleged high treason; however, this decision was reversed by Botswana's High Court in December 2002. Meanwhile, in April 2002 officials from Botswana and Namibia concluded a tripartite agreement with the office of the UN High Commissioner for Refugees (UNHCR) on the voluntary repatriation of Namibian refugees in Botswana. Between August and October around 800 refugees were repatriated to Namibia (although UNHCR reported that none of them originated from the Caprivi Strip), leaving some 1,200 in Botswana, who remained reluctant to return. In December 2003 UNHCR and human rights groups criticized the deportation from Botswana to Namibia of a further eight Caprivians, seven of whom were subsequently charged with high treason over alleged separatist activities; the authorities in Botswana claimed that the eight had lost their refugee status by visiting Namibia after being granted asylum in Botswana.

Government

Legislative power is vested in Parliament, consisting of the President and the National Assembly. The National Assembly is elected for a term of five years and comprises 57 members directly elected by universal adult suffrage, together with four members who are elected by the National Assembly from a list of candidates submitted by the President; the President and the Attorney-General are also ex officio members of the Assembly. The President is restricted to two terms of office. He appoints and leads a Cabinet, which is responsible to the Assembly. The President has powers to delay implementation of legislation for six months, and certain matters also have to be referred to the House of Chiefs for approval, although this advisory body has no power of veto. In December 2005 the Assembly approved legislation according to which the House of Chiefs was renamed the Ntlo ya Dikgosi and its membership increased from 15 to 35, comprising 30 members elected by senior tribal authorities and five members appointed by the President; elections to the Ntlo ya Dikgosi would be held every five years. Local government is effected through nine district councils and four town councils.

Defence

Military service is voluntary. As assessed at November 2007, the total strength of the Botswana Defence Force (BDF) was some 9,000, comprising an army of 8,500 and an air force of 500. In addition, there was a paramilitary police force of 1,500. There were plans to enlarge the strength of the army to 10,000 men. Projected budgetary expenditure on defence in 2007 was P1,700m. In August 2005 the Government announced plans to recruit women into the BDF.

Introductory Survey

Economic Affairs

In 2006, according to estimates by the World Bank, Botswana's gross national income (GNI), measured at average 2004–06 prices, was US $10,380m., equivalent to $5,900 per head (or $12,250 on an international purchasing-power parity basis). During 1996–2006, it was estimated, the population increased by an average of 0.6% per year, while gross domestic product (GDP) per head also increased, in real terms, by an average of 6.1% per year. Overall GDP increased, in real terms, at an average annual rate of 6.7% in 1996–2006; growth in 2006 was 4.2%.

Agriculture (including hunting, forestry and fishing) contributed 1.9% of GDP in 2005/06 and engaged 30.9% of the total labour force in 2006. The principal agricultural activity is cattle-raising (principally beef production), which supports about one-half of the population and contributes more than 80% of agricultural GDP. As a member of the African, Caribbean and Pacific (ACP) group of states and a signatory to successive Lomé Conventions, Botswana has traditionally enjoyed preferential trade relations with the European Union (EU, see p. 244), including a quota to supply 18,916 metric tons of beef per year. Under the Cotonou Agreement, which was concluded in mid-2000, the quota was to be phased out by 2007, when Botswana and the other ACP states were to establish reciprocal trade arrangements with the EU in order to achieve compatibility with the rules of the World Trade Organization (see p. 396). In November 2007 it was announced that an interim agreement had been concluded that allowed Botswana to export beef duty free to the EU market and removed any limitations on export quotas. Negotiations were, nevertheless, to continue with the aim of finalizing an Economic Partnership Agreement between the EU and Southern African Development Community (SADC, see p. 386) members. The main subsistence crops are roots and tubers, pulses, vegetables and sorghum, although Botswana is not self-sufficient in basic foods. Agricultural GDP decreased by 1.4% per year during 1996–2006; it declined by 7.5% in 2005, but increased by 2.9% in 2006.

Industry (including mining, manufacturing, construction and power) engaged 14.7% of the employed labour force in 2006 and provided 50.9% of GDP in 2005/06. Industrial GDP increased at an average annual rate of 7.9% in 1996–2006; growth of 4.3% was recorded in 2006.

Mining contributed 40.5% of GDP in 2005/06, although the sector engaged only 2.6% of the employed labour force in 2006. In terms of value, Botswana is the world's largest producer of diamonds (which accounted for 73.5% of export earnings in 2006, according to provisional figures, and some two-thirds of foreign exchange in 2002); copper-nickel matte and soda ash are also exported. In addition, coal, gold, cobalt and salt are mined, and there are known reserves of plutonium, asbestos, chromite, fluorspar, iron, manganese, potash, silver, talc and uranium. In 1998 a new minerals code included measures to encourage non-diamond mining projects. According to provisional official figures, the GDP of the mining sector increased, in real terms, at an average annual rate of 9.0% in 1996/97–2005/06; mining GDP grew by 18.1% in 2005, but decreased by 4.4% in 2005/06.

Manufacturing engaged 6.6% of the employed labour force in 2006 and provided 3.5% of GDP in 2005/06. The GDP of the manufacturing sector increased at an average annual rate of 3.1% in 1996–2006; growth in 2006 was 5.0%.

Energy is derived principally from fuel wood and coal; the use of solar power is currently being promoted as an alternative source of energy. According to provisional figures, imports of fuels accounted for 17.2% of the value of total imports in 2006.

The services sector contributed 47.2% of GDP in 2005/06, and engaged 54.4% of the employed labour force in 2006. Within the sector, tourism is of considerable importance, being the third largest source of total foreign exchange. The GDP of the services sector increased at an average annual rate of 5.7% in 1996–2006; growth in 2006 was 4.2%.

In 2006, according to provisional figures, Botswana recorded a visible trade surplus of P11,422.6m., and there was a surplus of P11,926.0m. on the current account of the balance of payments. In 2006 countries of the Southern African Customs Union (SACU—see below) provided 86.5% of imports, while European countries (excluding the United Kingdom) provided 3.0%. The United Kingdom took 72.2% of exports in 2006; other important purchasers were the countries of SACU (6.7%). The principal exports in 2006 were diamonds and copper-nickel matte. The principal imports were fuels, machinery and electrical equipment, food, beverages and tobacco, chemicals and rubber products, vehicles and transport equipment and metals and metal products.

In the financial year to 31 March 2006 the central Government recorded a budgetary surplus of P4,328.6m. Botswana's external debt totalled US $524m. at the end of 2004, of which $488.63m. was long-term public debt. In 2005 the cost of debt-servicing was equivalent to 1.3% of the value of exports of goods and services. The average annual rate of inflation was 8.5% in 2000–06; consumer prices increased by 11.6% in 2006. Some 19.6% of the labour force were unemployed in 2001.

Botswana is a member of SADC and (with Lesotho, Namibia, South Africa and Swaziland) of SACU. In September 2000 SADC commenced the implementation phase of its Protocol on Trade, which provided for the establishment of a regional free-trade area; all trade tariffs between member countries were to be eliminated gradually over a 12-year period.

Since the 1970s Botswana's development from one of the poorest countries in the world to a stable middle-income country has been based predominantly on the successful exploitation of diamonds and other minerals. In 2004 Botswana was Africa's third largest mineral producer by value; however, the need to reduce the country's dependence on the mining industry has been recognized in recent years, and the Government's ninth National Development Plan (2003/04–2008/09) aimed to effect economic diversification by targeting growth in other sectors and embracing recent technological developments. The tourism sector, which contributes some 15% of GDP and engages about 10% of the employed labour force, was expected to benefit greatly from the hosting of the 2010 Association Football World Cup in neighbouring South Africa, and a number of major tourism projects were under way in 2007, including the development of Botswana's first golf resort and of the world's largest game park, which, once completed, would extend into Angola, Namibia, Zambia and Zimbabwe. Nevertheless, the Botswana Government continued to find ways of exploiting the country's natural mineral resources and in late 2007 it agreed to co-operate with Japan in order to attempt to locate new deposits of rare metals, in particular platinum. In exchange for using that country's satellite technology in the process, Botswana agreed to grant Japan access to any deposits that were uncovered. Other government priorities included the creation of new employment opportunities, attracting foreign investment and the maintenance of macroeconomic stability and financial discipline. Meanwhile, despite these positive developments, the HIV/AIDS pandemic represented a significant threat to continued economic growth, diminishing the work-force and depleting government resources through expenditure on projects to counter the disease. The 2006/07 budget allocated resources totalling P650m. to HIV/AIDS programmes; however, uptake of antiretroviral drugs remained poor and in 2005 only 54,378 patients were receiving such medication. With more than one-quarter of the population estimated to be infected with HIV, estimated average adult life expectancy had declined from around 60 years in the early 1990s to 41.5 years by 2005, and was expected to fall further in future years. The Government forecast GDP growth of 4.6% in 2007/08, compared with 4.0% in the previous year, although high rates of unemployment and poverty and the projected decline in mineral reserves were expected to provide serious challenges to the Government's ability to sustain positive economic development.

Education

Although education is not compulsory in Botswana, enrolment ratios are high. Primary education begins at seven years of age and lasts for up to seven years. Secondary education, beginning at the age of 13, lasts for a further five years, comprising a first cycle of three years and a second of two years. According to UNESCO estimates, enrolment at primary schools in 2003/04 included 82% of children in the relevant age-group (boys 81%; girls 83%), while the comparable ratio for secondary enrolment was 61% (boys 58%; girls 64%). School fees were abolished in 1987; however, in October 2005 legislation was approved to reintroduce fees for secondary education from January 2006. Botswana has the highest teacher-pupil ratio in Africa, but continues to rely heavily on expatriate secondary school teachers. Tertiary education is provided by the University of Botswana (which was attended by 15,725 students in 2005) and the affiliated College of Technical and Vocational Education. There are also some 49 other technical and vocational training centres, including the Institutes of Health Sciences, the Botswana College of Agriculture, the Roads Training College, the Colleges of Education (Primary and Secondary), and the Botswana Institute of Administration and Commerce. Expenditure on education by the central Government in 2007/08 was forecast at P6,009.9m. (representing 23.2% of total government spending).

Public Holidays

2008: 1–2 January (New Year), 21–24 March (Easter), 1 May (Ascension Day and Labour Day), 1 July (Sir Seretse Khama Day), 21–22 July (President's Day), 30 September (Botswana Day), 25–26 December (Christmas).
2009: 1–2 January (New Year), 10–13 April (Easter), 1 May (Labour Day), 21 May (Ascension Day), 1 July (Sir Seretse Khama Day), 20–21 July (President's Day), 30 September (Botswana Day), 25–26 December (Christmas).

Weights and Measures

The metric system is in use.

Statistical Survey

Source (unless otherwise stated): Central Statistics Office, Private Bag 0024, Gaborone; tel. 352200; fax 352201; e-mail csobots@gov.bw; internet www.cso.gov.bw.

Area and Population

AREA, POPULATION AND DENSITY

Area (sq km)	581,730*
Population (census results)	
21 August 1991	1,326,796
17 August 2001	
Males	813,488
Females	867,375
Total	1,680,863
Population (UN estimates at mid-year)†	
2005	1,836,000
2006	1,858,000
2007	1,882,000
Density (per sq km) at mid-2007	3.2

* 224,607 sq miles.
† Source: UN, *World Population Prospects: The 2006 Revision*.

ADMINISTRATIVE DISTRICTS
(population at census of August 2001)

Barolong	47,477		Kweneng	230,535
Central	501,381		Lobatse	29,689
Central Kalahari				
Game Reserve	689		Ngamiland	122,024
Chobe	18,258		Ngwaketse West	10,471
Delta	2,688		North-East	49,399
Francistown	83,023		Orapa	9,151
Gaborone	186,007		Selebi-Phikwe	49,849
Ghanzi	32,481		South-East	60,623
Jwaneng	15,179		Southern	113,704
Kgalagadi	42,049		Sowa	2,879
Kgatleng	73,507			

BOTSWANA

PRINCIPAL TOWNS
(population at August 2001 census)

Gaborone (capital)	186,007	Serowe		42,444
Francistown	83,023	Kanye		40,628
Molepolole	54,561	Mahalapye		39,719
Selebi-Phikwe	49,849	Mochudi		36,692
Maun	43,776	Lobatse		29,689

Mid-2005 (incl. suburbs, UN estimate): Gaborone 210,000 (Source: UN, *World Urbanization Prospects: The 2005 Revision*).

BIRTHS AND DEATHS
(annual averages, UN estimates)

	1990–95	1995–2000	2000–05
Birth rate (per 1,000)	32.4	29.1	26.0
Death rate (per 1,000)	7.2	12.1	16.3

Source: UN, *World Population Prospects: The 2006 Revision*.

2001 (12 months prior to August 2001 census): Births 53,735 (birth rate 41.1 per 1,000); Deaths 20,823 (death rate 12.4 per 1,000) (Source: UN, *Demographic Yearbook*).

Expectation of life (years at birth, WHO estimates): 41.5 (males 41.7; females 41.3) in 2005 (Source: WHO, *World Health Statistics*).

ECONOMICALLY ACTIVE POPULATION
(number of persons aged 7 years and over, 2006 labour force survey)

	Males	Females	Total
Agriculture, hunting, forestry and fishing	103,924	65,407	169,331
Mining and quarrying	12,396	1,716	14,112
Manufacturing	16,020	19,963	35,982
Electricity, gas and water supply	2,697	1,537	4,234
Construction	22,169	4,265	26,434
Wholesale and retail trade; repair of motor vehicles, motorcycles and personal and household goods	28,791	50,804	79,596
Hotels and restaurants	3,848	10,968	14,816
Transport, storage and communications	10,292	5,381	15,674
Financial intermediation	3,018	5,406	8,424
Real estate, renting and business services	15,338	9,778	25,116
Public administration and defence; compulsory social security	34,372	25,417	59,789
Education	15,190	27,987	43,177
Health and social work	5,503	8,612	14,114
Other community, social and personal service activities	5,277	5,283	10,560
Private households with employed persons	8,013	18,247	26,261
Extra-territorial organizations and bodies	456	439	895
Activities not adequately defined	—	78	78
Total employed	**287,303**	**261,290**	**548,594**

Health and Welfare

KEY INDICATORS

Total fertility rate (children per woman, 2005)	3.0
Under-5 mortality rate (per 1,000 live births, 2005)	120
HIV/AIDS (% of persons aged 15–49, 2005)	24.1
Physicians (per 1,000 head, 2004)	0.40
Hospital beds (per 1,000 head, 2003)	2.20
Health expenditure (2004): US $ per head (PPP)	504.3
Health expenditure (2004): % of GDP	6.4
Health expenditure (2004): public (% of total)	62.9
Access to water (% of persons, 2004)	95
Access to sanitation (% of persons, 2004)	42
Human Development Index (2005): ranking	124
Human Development Index (2005): value	0.654

For sources and definitions, see explanatory note on p. vi.

Agriculture

PRINCIPAL CROPS
('000 metric tons)

	2003	2004*	2005*
Maize	1.6	7.1	7.4
Sorghum	32.3	19.6	15.9
Sunflower seed*	7	8	9
Roots and tubers*	93	96	99
Pulses*	18.5	17.1	16.6
Vegetables*	16.4	16.3	16.2
Fruit*	10.6	10.3	10.1

* FAO estimates.

2006: Figures assumed to be unchanged from 2005 (FAO estimates).

Source: FAO.

LIVESTOCK
('000 head, year ending September, FAO estimates)

	2003	2004	2005
Cattle	3,100	3,100	3,100
Horses	33	33	33
Asses	332.5	332.5	332.5
Sheep	300	300	300
Goats	1,700	1,850	1,950
Pigs	8	8	8
Poultry	4,000	4,000	4,000

2006: Figures assumed to be unchanged from 2005 (FAO estimates).

LIVESTOCK PRODUCTS
('000 metric tons)

	2003	2004	2005*
Cattle meat	26.9	26.6*	25.1
Goat meat*	4.7	5.1	5.4
Chicken meat*	5.4	5.4	5.4
Other meat*	14.0	14.1	14.1
Cows' milk*	101.5	101.5	101.5
Goats' milk*	3.9	3.9	3.9
Hen eggs*	64.3	64.3	64.3

* FAO estimate(s).

2006: Figures assumed to be unchanged from 2005 (FAO estimates).

Source: FAO.

Forestry

ROUNDWOOD REMOVALS
('000 cubic metres, excl. bark, FAO estimates)

	2003	2004	2005
Industrial wood	105.0	105.0	105.0
Fuel wood	649.6	655.0	660.8
Total	754.6	760.0	765.8

2006: Figures assumed to be unchanged from 2005 (FAO estimates).

Source: FAO.

BOTSWANA

Statistical Survey

Fishing

(metric tons, live weight)

	2003	2004	2005
Tilapias	72	102	83
Other freshwater fishes	50	59	49
Total catch	122	161	132

Note: Figures exclude aquatic mammals, recorded by number rather than weight. According to FAO estimates, the number of Nile crocodiles caught was: 9 in 2003; nil in 2004; nil in 2005.

Source: FAO.

Mining

(metric tons, unless otherwise indicated)

	2003	2004	2005*
Hard coal	822,780	913,087	984,876
Copper ore†‡	24,292	21,195	26,704
Nickel ore‡	27,400	22,292	28,212
Cobalt†‡	294	223	326
Salt	229,432	208,319	243,945
Diamonds ('000 carats)	30,412	31,125	31,890
Soda ash (natural)	309,350	263,358	279,085
Sand and gravel ('000 cu metres)	1,485	2,330	2,110

* Preliminary.
† Figures refer to the metal content of matte; product smelted was granulated nickel-copper-cobalt matte.
‡ Figures refer to the nickel content of matte and include some product not reported as milled.

Source: US Geological Survey.

Industry

SELECTED PRODUCTS

	2001	2002	2003
Beer ('000 hectolitres)	1,692	1,396	1,198
Soft drinks ('000 hectolitres)	431	389	405
Electric energy (million kWh)	1,047	1,050	920

Electric energy (million kWh): 1,042 in 2004.

Source: UN, *Industrial Commodity Statistics Yearbook*.

Finance

CURRENCY AND EXCHANGE RATES

Monetary Units
100 thebe = 1 pula (P).

Sterling, Dollar and Euro Equivalents (31 May 2007)
£1 sterling = 12.304 pula;
US $1 = 6.223 pula;
€1 = 8.372 pula;
100 pula = £8.13 = $16.07 = €11.95.

Average Exchange Rate (pula per US $)
2004   4.693
2005   5.110
2006   5.837

BUDGET
(million pula, year ending 31 March)

Revenue*	2005/06	2006/07†	2007/08‡
Taxation	20,130.0	24,417.3	24,555.7
Mineral revenue	11,045.1	11,374.2	10,890.0
Customs and excise	3,929.9	7,361.9	7,398.3
Non-mineral income taxes	3,003.2	3,315.6	3,553.4
Other taxes	2,151.8	2,365.6	2,714.0
General sales tax/VAT	1,978.9	2,190.8	2,519.4
Other current revenue	2,023.6	1,886.1	2,299.8
Interest	97.3	36.2	58.7
Other property income	912.0	696.6	999.9
Fees, charges, etc.	957.6	1,092.5	1,191.2
Sales of fixed assets and land	56.8	60.7	50.1
Total	**22,153.6**	**26,303.4**	**26,855.5**

Expenditure§	2005/06	2006/07†	2007/08‡
General services (incl. defence)	5,268.0	6,244.6	7,517.7
Social services	8,127.0	10,735.1	12,058.0
Education	4,197.4	5,481.4	6,009.9
Health	2,056.4	2,686.7	3,378.4
Housing, urban and regional development	1,082.8	1,601.1	1,541.4
Food and social welfare programme	189.5	151.0	119.2
Other community and social services	600.9	815.0	1,009.0
Economic services	2,347.1	3,473.6	4,368.9
Agriculture, forestry and fishing	791.8	689.6	757.0
Mining	−134.7	147.7	193.7
Electricity and water supply	931.7	1,013.7	1,064.1
Roads	324.5	814.5	840.3
Others	433.8	808.3	1,513.9
Transfers	1,889.8	1,956.2	1,967.6
Deficit grants to local authorities	1,571.9	1,678.6	1,823.1
Interest on public debt	317.9	277.6	144.5
Total	**17,631.9**	**22,409.5**	**25,912.3**

* Excluding grants received (million pula): 113.0 in 2005/06; 493.5 in 2006/07; 323.6 in 2007/08.
† Estimates.
‡ Budget estimates.
§ Including net lending (million pula): −306.1 in 2005/06; −47.2 in 2006/07; −60.8 in 2007/08.

Source: Bank of Botswana, Gaborone, *Annual Report 2006*.

INTERNATIONAL RESERVES
(US $ million at 31 December)

	2004	2005	2006
IMF special drawing rights	53.46	50.85	55.53
Reserve position in IMF	31.84	10.59	9.40
Foreign exchange	5,576.13	6,247.62	7,927.47
Total	**5,661.43**	**6,309.06**	**7,992.40**

Source: IMF, *International Financial Statistics*.

MONEY SUPPLY
(million pula at 31 December)

	2004	2005	2006
Currency outside banks	632	625	753
Demand deposits at commercial banks	2,989	3,206	4,387
Total money (incl. others)	**4,225**	**3,998**	**5,157**

Source: IMF, *International Financial Statistics*.

BOTSWANA

COST OF LIVING
(Consumer Price Index; base: 2000 = 100)

	2003	2004	2005
Food (incl. beverages)	125.0	130.9	137.9
Clothing (incl. footwear)	112.4	114.8	116.9
Housing	138.0	153.9	163.9
Fuel	118.0	125.2	147.1
All items (incl. others)	125.8	134.4	146.1

2006: All items 163.0.
Source: ILO.

NATIONAL ACCOUNTS
(million pula at current prices, year ending 30 June, provisional figures)

National Income and Product

	1998/99	1999/2000	2000/01
Domestic primary incomes	17,098.6	19,867.7	22,944.3
Consumption of fixed capital	2,647.4	3,068.5	3,623.2
Gross domestic product (GDP) at factor cost	19,746.0	22,936.2	26,567.5
Taxes on production and imports	1,887.8	2,106.9	2,188.9
Less Subsidies	110.0	100.0	120.0
GDP in market prices	21,523.8	24,943.1	28,636.5

Expenditure on the Gross Domestic Product

	2003/04	2004/05	2005/06
Government final consumption expenditure	9,286.2	10,811.2	11,785.6
Private final consumption expenditure	12,243.7	13,846.2	15,022.7
Increase in stocks	9,183.8	7,990.8	4,559.1
Gross fixed capital formation	8,867.8	9,797.9	10,402.9
Total domestic expenditure	39,581.5	42,446.1	41,770.3
Exports of goods and services	17,875.6	24,279.3	32,125.5
Less Imports of goods and services	14,624.1	17,104.5	16,758.3
Statistical discrepancy	−260.0	—	—
GDP in purchasers' values	42,573.0	49,620.9	57,137.4
GDP at constant 1993/94 prices	20,941.2	22,865.7	22,672.1

Source: Bank of Botswana, Gaborone, *Annual Report 2006*.

Gross Domestic Product by Economic Activity

	2003/04	2004/05	2005/06
Agriculture, hunting, forestry and fishing	951.8	899.9	1,027.9
Mining and quarrying	15,078.9	19,222.4	22,178.0
Manufacturing	1,647.5	1,772.5	1,895.6
Water and electricity	1,058.9	1,216.2	1,398.0
Construction	2,103.4	2,241.7	2,426.9
Trade, restaurants and hotels	4,894.4	5,082.5	6,116.0
Transport, post and telecommunications	1,398.6	1,519.1	2,040.5
Finance, insurance and business services	4,517.4	5,169.7	5,919.3
Government services	7,231.8	8,104.1	9,509.6
Social and personal services	1,594.7	1,884.7	2,259.2
Sub-total	40,477.5	47,112.7	54,771.0
Less Imputed bank service charge	1,577.4	1,799.8	2,250.8
GDP at basic prices	38,900.1	45,312.9	52,520.2
Import duties	1,971.8	2,315.0	2,643.5
Taxes on products	1,918.9	2,240.4	2,254.8
Less Subsidies on products	217.8	247.4	281.1
GDP in purchasers' values	42,573.0	49,620.9	57,137.4

Source: Bank of Botswana, Gaborone, *Annual Report 2006*.

BALANCE OF PAYMENTS
(million pula)

	2004	2005*	2006†
Exports of goods f.o.b.	17,344.6	22,634.5	26,558.3
Imports of goods f.o.b.	−13,440.5	−14,440.1	−15,135.7
Trade balance	3,904.1	8,195.5	11,422.6
Exports of services	3,511.3	4,496.6	4,523.6
Imports of services	−3,715.3	−4,331.9	−3,911.5
Balance on goods and services	3,700.1	8,360.2	12,034.7
Other income received	1,065.5	2,330.1	2,604.5
Other income paid	−5,882.6	−6,478.3	−6,474.4
Balance on goods, services and income	−1,117.0	4,212.0	8,164.8
Current transfers received	3,486.7	4,578.9	4,949.2
Current transfers paid	−1,017.6	−1,112.8	−1,188.1
Current balance	1,352.0	7,678.5	11,926.0
Capital account (net)	149.2	160.8	125.7
Direct investment abroad	181.9	−285.5	−119.1
Direct investment from abroad	1,835.2	1,423.7	1,591.9
Portfolio investment assets	−2,055.3	−2,067.0	−3,448.1
Portfolio investment liabilities	−137.0	83.0	n.a.
Other investment assets	−985.1	−777.8	n.a.
Other investment liabilities	−396.0	1,328.1	484.4
Net errors and omissions	−216.8	−508.0	−102.7
Overall balance	−271.8	7,035.6	10,255.8

* Estimates.
† Provisional.
Source: Bank of Botswana, Gaborone, *Annual Report 2006*.

External Trade

PRINCIPAL COMMODITIES
(million pula, provisional figures)

Imports c.i.f.	2004	2005	2006
Food, beverages and tobacco	2,201.6	2,244.2	2,488.2
Fuels	1,783.5	2,209.0	3,083.4
Chemicals and rubber products	1,812.0	1,983.5	2,357.7
Wood and paper products	660.1	689.6	737.1
Textiles and footwear	753.4	792.1	899.1
Metals and metal products	1,257.7	1,239.5	1,456.1
Machinery and electrical equipment	2,660.9	2,713.7	2,996.2
Vehicles and transport equipment	2,167.1	2,080.3	1,737.8
Total (incl. others)	15,165.0	16,086.2	17,902.1

Exports f.o.b.	2004	2005	2006
Meat and meat products	240.5	376.4	477.0
Diamonds	12,434.5	16,863.9	19,431.8
Copper-nickel matte	1,578.3	2,314.9	3,618.9
Textiles	560.9	1,119.7	916.7
Vehicles and parts	568.8	572.8	183.6
Total (incl. others)	16,486.6	22,506.8	26,435.5

PRINCIPAL TRADING PARTNERS
(million pula, provisional figures)

Imports c.i.f.	2004	2005	2006
SACU*	12,681.4	13,604.0	15,481.0
Zimbabwe	239.2	248.2	279.1
United Kingdom	215.9	204.3	193.4
Other Europe	925.3	888.1	541.3
Korea, Repub.	21.5	29.5	32.4
USA	210.7	201.9	156.7
Total (incl. others)	15,165.0	16,086.2	17,902.1

BOTSWANA

Exports f.o.b.	2004	2005	2006
SACU*	1,572.5	2,052.4	1,784.0
Zimbabwe	614.5	937.0	1,486.1
Other Africa	67.0	139.7	215.8
United Kingdom	12,265.2	17,011.2	19,101.3
Other Europe	301.8	291.2	504.0
USA	264.4	498.0	489.0
Total (incl. others)	16,486.6	22,506.8	26,435.5

*Southern African Customs Union, of which Botswana is a member; also including Lesotho, Namibia, South Africa and Swaziland.

Transport

RAILWAYS
(traffic)

	2002	2003	2004
Number of passengers ('000)	528.1	572.0	406.2
Freight ('000 metric tons)	2,080.2	1,995.8	1,974.1

Source: Botswana Railways.

Passenger-km (million): 528.1 in 2002; 572.0 in 2003 (Source: International Road Federation, *World Road Statistics*).

Freight net ton-km (million): 920.2 in 2003; 636.7 in 2004 (Source: International Road Federation, *World Road Statistics*).

ROAD TRAFFIC
(registered vehicles)

	2003	2004	2005
Cars	65,479	74,465	83,039
Light duty vehicles	75,355	79,122	79,812
Trucks	9,394	9,942	10,349
Buses	7,407	8,749	9,490
Tractors	2,957	3,068	2,913
Others (incl. trailers, motorcycles and tankers)	13,236	13,919	14,461
Total	173,828	189,265	200,064

CIVIL AVIATION
(traffic on scheduled services, million)

	2001	2002	2003
Kilometres flown	3	3	3
Passenger-km	77	80	83
Total ton-km	7	8	8

Source: UN, *Statistical Yearbook*.

Passengers carried: 482,740 in 2003; 533,684 in 2004; 552,350 in 2005.

Freight carried (metric tons): 682.9 in 2003; 756.8 in 2004; 920.6 in 2005.

Tourism

FOREIGN TOURIST ARRIVALS

Country of origin	2002	2003	2004
Namibia	64,001	69,587	57,542
South Africa	527,505	514,708	626,207
United Kingdom	20,548	18,518	24,069
Zambia	25,637	83,588	72,492
Zimbabwe	454,847	550,994	576,328
Total (incl. others)	1,273,784	1,405,535	1,522,807

2005: Total foreign tourist arrivals 1,675,000.

Receipts from tourism (US $ million, excl. passenger transport): 457 in 2003; 549 in 2004; 562 in 2005.

Source: World Tourism Organization.

Communications Media

	2004	2005	2006
Telephones ('000 main lines in use)	136.5	132.0	136.9
Mobile cellular telephones ('000 subscribers)	563.8	823.1	979.8
Internet users ('000)	60	60.0	n.a.
Broadband subscribers ('000)	n.a.	1.6	n.a.

Personal computers ('000 in use): 80 in 2004.

Source: International Telecommunication Union.

Television receivers ('000 in use): 40 in 2000 (Source: UNESCO, *Statistical Yearbook*).

Radio receivers ('000 in use): 237 in 1997 (Source: UNESCO, *Statistical Yearbook*).

Facsimile machines: 3,529 in use in 1997/98 (Source: UNESCO, *Statistical Yearbook*).

Book production (first editions only): 158 titles in 1991, including 61 pamphlets (Source: UNESCO, *Statistical Yearbook*).

Daily newspapers: 2 in 2004 (average circulation 75,278) (Source: UNESCO, *Statistical Yearbook*).

Non-daily newspapers: 3 in 1996 (average circulation 51,000 copies); 9 in 2004 (Source: UNESCO, *Statistical Yearbook*).

Other periodicals: 14 titles in 1992 (average circulation 177,000 copies) (Source: UNESCO, *Statistical Yearbook*).

Education

(2004/05, unless otherwise indicated)

	Institutions	Teachers	Students
Primary	770*	13,057	330,888
Secondary	278*	12,093	165,377
General programmes	n.a.	10,842	154,494
Technical and vocational programmes	50*	1,251	10,883
Tertiary	2†	529	10,950

* 2003 figure.
† 2001 figure; number of colleges of education.

Source: Ministry of Education, Gaborone; UNESCO Institute for Statistics.

Agricultural college (2004): Teachers 120; Students 850 (Source: Botswana College of Agriculture).

University (2005): Teachers 791; Students 15,725 (Source: University of Botswana).

Adult literacy rate (UNESCO estimates): 81.2% (males 80.4%; females 81.8%) in 2003 (Source: UNESCO Institute for Statistics).

Directory

The Constitution

The Constitution of the Republic of Botswana took effect at independence on 30 September 1966; it was amended in August and September 1997. Its main provisions, with subsequent amendments, are summarized below:

EXECUTIVE

President

Executive power lies with the President of Botswana, who is also Commander-in-Chief of the armed forces. Election for the office of President is linked with the election of members of the National Assembly. The President is restricted to two terms of office. Presidential candidates must be over 30 years of age and receive at least 1,000 nominations. If there is more than one candidate for the Presidency, each candidate for office in the Assembly must declare support for a presidential candidate. The candidate for President who commands the votes of more than one-half of the elected members of the Assembly will be declared President. In the event of the death or resignation of the President, the Vice-President will automatically assume the Presidency. The President, who is an ex officio member of the National Assembly, holds office for the duration of Parliament. The President chooses four members of the National Assembly.

Cabinet

There is also a Vice-President, whose office is ministerial. The Vice-President is appointed by the President and deputizes in the absence of the President. The Cabinet consists of the President, the Vice-President and other Ministers, including Assistant Ministers, appointed by the President. The Cabinet is responsible to the National Assembly.

LEGISLATURE

Legislative power is vested in Parliament, consisting of the President and the National Assembly, acting after consultation in certain cases with the Ntlo ya Dikgosi. The President may withhold assent to a Bill passed by the National Assembly. If the same Bill is again presented after six months, the President is required to assent to it or to dissolve Parliament within 21 days.

Ntlo ya Dikgosi

Formerly known as the House of Chiefs, the Ntlo ya Dikgosi comprises the Chiefs of the eight principal tribes of Botswana as ex officio members, four members elected by sub-chiefs from their own number, and three members elected by the other 12 members of the Ntlo ya Dikgosi. Bills and motions relating to chieftaincy matters and alterations of the Constitution must be referred to the Ntlo ya Dikgosi, which may also deliberate and make representations on any matter. Following a review, in December 2005 it was announced that the membership of the Ntlo ya Dikgosi would be increased from 15 to 35.

National Assembly

The National Assembly consists of 40 members directly elected by universal adult suffrage, together with four members who are elected by the National Assembly from a list of candidates submitted by the President; the President, the Speaker and the Attorney-General are also ex officio members of the Assembly. The life of the Assembly is five years. In June 2002 the National Assembly voted to increase its membership from 40 directly elected members to 57, with effect from the following general election.

The Constitution contains a code of human rights, enforceable by the High Court.

The Government

HEAD OF STATE

President: Lt-Gen. SERETSE KHAMA IAN KHAMA (took office 1 April 2008).
Vice-President: Lt-Gen. MOMPATI S. MERAFHE.

CABINET
(April 2008)

President: Lt-Gen. SERETSE KHAMA IAN KHAMA.
Vice-President: Lt-Gen. MOMPATI S. MERAFHE.
Minister of Presidential Affairs and Public Administration: DANIEL KWELAGOBE.
Minister of Local Government: Dr MARGARET N. NASHA.
Minister of Trade and Industry: D. NEO MOROKA.
Minister of Finance and Development Planning: BALEDZI GAOLATHE.
Minister of Youth, Sports and Culture: GLADYS KOKORWE.
Minister of Minerals, Energy and Water Affairs: PONATSHEGO KEDIKILWE.
Minister of Communications, Science and Technology: PELONOMI VENSON-MOITOYI.
Minister of Defence, Justice and Security: DIKGAKGAMATSO SERETSE.
Minister of Agriculture: CHRISTIAN DE GRAAF.
Minister of Works and Transport: JOHNNIE SWARTZ.
Minister of Labour and Home Affairs: PETER SIELE.
Minister of Health: LESEGO MOTSUMI.
Minister of Foreign Affairs and International Co-operation: PHANDU SKELEMANI.
Minister of Environment, Wildlife and Tourism: ONKOKAME MOKAILA.
Minister of Education and Skills Development: JACOB NKATE.
Minister of Lands and Housing: NONOFO MOLEFHI.
Attorney-General: Dr ATHALIAH MOLOKOMME.

In addition, there were eight Assistant Ministers.

MINISTRIES

Office of the President: Private Bag 001, Gaborone; tel. 3950825; fax 3950858; e-mail op.registry@gov.bw; internet www.gov.bw/government/ministry_of_state_president.html#office_of_the_president.

Ministry for the Administration of Justice: Gaborone.

Ministry of Agriculture: Private Bag 003, Gaborone; tel. 3950602; fax 3975805; internet www.gov.bw/government/ministry_of_agriculture.html.

Ministry of Communications, Science and Technology: Private Bag 00414, Gaborone; tel. 3910384; fax 3907236; internet www.gov.bw/government/ministry_of_communications_science_and_technology.html.

Ministry of Education: Chief Education Officer, Block 6 Bldg, 2nd Floor, Government Enclave, Gaborone; Private Bag 005, Gaborone; tel. 3655400; fax 3655458; e-mail moe.webmaster@gov.bw; internet www.moe.gov.bw/moe/index.html.

Ministry of Environment, Wildlife and Tourism: Private Bag 0047, Standard House, 2nd Floor, Main Mall, Gaborone; tel. 3953024; fax 3908675.

Ministry of Finance and Development Planning: Private Bag 008, Gaborone; tel. 395-0201; fax 3905742; e-mail kmutasa@gov.bw; internet www.finance.gov.bw.

Ministry of Foreign Affairs and International Co-operation: Private Bag 00368, Gaborone; tel. 3600700; fax 3913366; e-mail csmaribe@gov.bw; internet www.gov.bw/government/ministry_of_foreign_affairs.html.

Ministry of Health: Private Bag 0038, Gaborone; tel. 3170585; e-mail moh-webmaster@gov.bw; internet www.moh.gov.bw.

Ministry of Labour and Home Affairs: Private Bag 002, Gaborone; tel. 3611100; fax 3913584; e-mail msetimela@gov.bw; internet www.gov.bw/government/ministry_of_labour_and_home_affairs.html.

Ministry of Lands and Housing: Private Bag 00434, Gaborone; tel. 3904223; fax 3911591.

Ministry of Local Government: Private Bag 006, Gaborone; tel. 354100; fax 352091; internet www.mlg.gov.bw.

Ministry of Minerals, Energy and Water Affairs: Khama Cres., Private Bag 0018, Gaborone; tel. 3656600; fax 3972738; internet www.gov.bw/government/ministry_of_minerals_energy_and_water_affairs.html.

Ministry of Trade and Industry: Private Bag 004, Gaborone; tel. 3601200; fax 3971539; internet www.mti.gov.bw.

Ministry of Works and Transport: Private Bag 007, Gaborone; tel. 3958500; fax 3913303; internet www.gov.bw/government/ministry_of_works_and_transport.html.

Ministry of Youth, Sports and Culture: Gaborone.

BOTSWANA   *Directory*

Legislature

NTLO YA DIKGOSI

The Ntlo ya Dikgosi has a total of 15 members. Following a review, in December 2005 it was announced that the membership would be increased from 15 to 35 members.

Chairperson: Chief MOSADI SEBOKO.

NATIONAL ASSEMBLY

Speaker: PATRICK BALOPI.
General Election, 30 October 2004

Party	Votes	% of votes	Seats
Botswana Democratic Party	213,308	51.7	44
Botswana National Front	107,451	26.1	12
Botswana Congress Party	68,556	16.6	1
Botswana Alliance Movement	11,716	2.8	—
Botswana People's Party	7,886	1.9	—
Others*	3,482	0.8	
Total	**412,399**	**100.0**	**57†**

* Including independents and candidates representing the New Democratic Front and MELS Movement of Botswana.
† The President and the Attorney-General are also ex officio members of the National Assembly.

Election Commission

Independent Electoral Commission (IEC): Government Enclave, Block 8, 7th Floor, Private Bag 00284, Gaborone; tel. 3612400; fax 3900581; e-mail iecwebmaster@gov.bw; internet www.iec.gov.bw; f. 1997; Chair. J. Z. MOSOJANE.

Political Organizations

Botswana Alliance Movement (BAM): Private Bag BO 210, Gaborone; tel. 3913476; fax 3914634; f. 1998 as an alliance of opposition parties—the Botswana Labour Party, United Socialist Party (PUSO), Botswana People's Party (BPP), Botswana Progressive Union, United Action Party and Independence Freedom Party—to contest the 1999 general election; the BPP withdrew in July 2000; Pres. EPHRAIM LEPETU SETSHWAELO; Chair. MOTSAMAI K. MPHO; Sec.-Gen. MATLHOMOLA MODISE.

Botswana Congress Party (BCP): Plot 364, Extension 4, Independence Ave, Gabarone; POB 2918, Gaborone; tel. and fax 3181805; internet www.bcp.org.bw; f. 1998 following split from the BNF; Pres. GILSON SALESHANDO; Nat. Chair. BATISANI MASWIBILI; Sec.-Gen. TAOLO LUCAS.

Botswana Democratic Party (BDP) (Domkrag): POB 28, Tsholetsa House, Gaborone; tel. 3952564; fax 3913911; internet www.bdp.org.bw; f. 1962 as the Bechuanaland Democratic Party; Pres. FESTUS G. MOGAE; Chair. Lt-Gen. SERETSE KHAMA IAN KHAMA; Sec.-Gen. DANIEL K. KWELAGOBE; Exec. Sec. Dr BATLANY COMMA SEREMA.

Botswana National Front (BNF): POB 1720, Gaborone; tel. 3951789; fax 3184970; e-mail botswananationalfront@yahoo.com; f. 1966; incl. fmr mems of the United Socialist Party (PUSO), which split from the BNF in 1994 later to re-affiliate in 2005; Pres. OTSWELETSE MOUPO; Chair. NEHEMIAH MODUBULE; Sec.-Gen. AKANYANG MAGAMA.

Botswana People's Party (BPP): POB 484, Francistown; f. 1960; Leader BERNARD BALIKANI.

Botswana Workers' Front (BWF): POB 597, Jwaneng; tel. 5880420; f. 1993 following split from the BNF; mems may retain dual membership of the BNF; Leader SHAWN NTHAILE.

MELS Movement of Botswana: POB 501818, Gaborone; tel. 3906005; fax 3933241; e-mail joinaandass@botsnet.bw; f. 1984; Marxist-Leninist; Leader THEMBA JOINA; Vice-Pres. EPHRAIM MAKGETHO.

New Democratic Front (NDF): Gaborone; f. 2003 following split from the BNF; affiliated to the BCP since mid-2006; Leader DICK BAYFORD.

Social Democratic Party (SDP): POB 201818, Gaborone; tel. 3956516; f. 1994 following split from the BNF; Leader RODGERS SEABUENG.

Diplomatic Representation

EMBASSIES AND HIGH COMMISSIONS IN BOTSWANA

Angola: 2715 Phala Cres., Private Bag BR 111, Gaborone; tel. 3900204; fax 3975089; e-mail angolaemb@info.bw; Ambassador JOSÉ AGOSTINHO NETO.

China, People's Republic: 3096 North Ring Rd, POB 1031, Gaborone; tel. 3953270; fax 3900147; e-mail chinaemb_bw@mfa.gov.cn; internet bw.china-embassy.org; Ambassador DING XIAOWEN.

Cuba: Plot 5198, Village, POB 40261, Gaborone; tel. 3951750; fax 3911485; Ambassador JORGE LUIS LÓPEZ TORMO.

France: 761 Robinson Rd, POB 1424, Gaborone; tel. 3973863; fax 3971733; e-mail frambbots@info.bw; Ambassador JEAN-PIERRE COURTOIS.

Germany: Professional House, 3rd Floor, Segoditshane Way, Broadhurst, POB 315, Gaborone; tel. 3953143; fax 3953038; e-mail info@gaborone.diplo.de; internet www.gaborone.diplo.de; Ambassador ULF HANEL.

India: Plot 5375, President's Dr., Private Bag 249, Gaborone; tel. 3972676; fax 3974636; e-mail administration@hci.org.bw; internet www.highcommissionofinida.org.bw; High Commissioner V. N. HADE.

Kenya: Plot 786, Independence Ave, Private Bag 297, Gaborone; tel. 3951408; fax 3951409; e-mail kenya@info.bw; internet www.kenyamission-botswana.com; High Commissioner CHARLES MBAKA.

Libya: Plot 8851 (Government Enclave), POB 180, Gaborone; tel. 3952481; fax 356928; Ambassador ASSED MOHAMED ALMUTAA.

Namibia: Plot 186, Morara Close, POB 987, Gaborone; tel. 3902181; fax 3902248; High Commissioner TSUKHOE GOWASES.

Nigeria: Plot 1086–92, Queens Rd, The Mall, POB 274, Gaborone; tel. 3913561; fax 3913738; High Commissioner MARIUS U. OFFOR.

Russia: Plot 4711, Tawana Close, POB 81, Gaborone; tel. 3953389; fax 3952930; e-mail embrus@info.bw; internet www.botswana.mid.ru; Ambassador IGOR S. LIAKIN-FROLOV.

South Africa: Plot 29, Queens Rd, Private Bag 00402, Gaborone; tel. 3904800; fax 3905501; e-mail sahcgabs@botsnet.bw; High Commissioner DIKGANG F. MOOPELOA.

Sweden: Development House, 4th Floor, The Mall, Private Bag 0017, Gaborone; tel. 3953912; fax 3953942; e-mail ambassaden.gaborone@foreign.ministry.se; internet www.swedenabroad.com/gaborone; Chargé d'affaires a.i. MARIE ANDERSSON DE FRUTOS.

United Kingdom: Plot 1079–1084, Main Mall, off Queens Rd, Private Bag 0023, Gaborone; tel. 3952841; fax 3956105; e-mail bhc@botsnet.bw; internet www.britishhighcommission.gov.uk/botswana; High Commissioner FRANCIS (FRANK) JAMES MARTIN.

USA: Embassy Enclave, off Khama Cres., POB 90, Gaborone; tel. 3953982; fax 3956947; e-mail ircgaborone@state.gov; internet botswana.usembassy.gov; Ambassador KATHERINE H. CANAVAN.

Zambia: POB 362, Gaborone; tel. 3951951; fax 3953952; High Commissioner CECIL HOLMES.

Zimbabwe: Plot 8850, POB 1232, Gaborone; tel. 3914495; fax 3905863; Ambassador THOMAS MANDIGORA.

Judicial System

There is a High Court at Lobatse and a branch at Francistown, and Magistrates' Courts in each district. Appeals lie to the Court of Appeal of Botswana. The Chief Justice and the President of the Court of Appeal are appointed by the President.

Chief Justice: JULIAN NGANUNU.

High Court

Private Bag 1, Lobatse; tel. 5330396; fax 5332317.

Judges of the High Court: ISAAC K. B. LESETEDI, MARUPING DIBOTELO, UNITY DOW, MOATLHODI MARUMO, STANLEY SAPIRE.

President of the Court of Appeal: PATRICK TEBBUTT.

Justices of Appeal: STANLEY MOORE, JULIAN NGANUNU, HEIN GROSSKOPF, NEVILLE ZIETSMAN, NICHOLAS JOHN MCNALLY, RODGER KORSAH, CHRIS PLEWMAN.

Registrar and Master: GODFREY NTHOMIWA.

Office of the Attorney-General

Private Bag 009, Gaborone; tel. 3954700; fax 3957089.

Attorney-General: Dr ATHALIAH MOLOKOMME.

Religion

The majority of the population hold animist beliefs; an estimated 30% are thought to be Christians. There are Islamic mosques in Gaborone and Lobatse. The Bahá'í Faith is also represented.

CHRISTIANITY

Botswana Council of Churches (Lekgotla la Dikereke mo Botswana): POB 355, Gaborone; tel. and fax 3951981; e-mail bots.christ.c@info.bw; f. 1966; Pres. Rev. ODIRILE E. MERE; Gen. Sec. DAVID J. MODIEGA; 24 mem. churches and orgs.

The Anglican Communion

Anglicans are adherents of the Church of the Province of Central Africa, covering Botswana, Malawi, Zambia and Zimbabwe. The Church comprises 15 dioceses, including one in Botswana. The current Archbishop of the Province is the Bishop of Upper Shire in Malawi. The Province was established in 1955, and the diocese of Botswana was formed in 1972. There were some 10,500 adherents at mid-2000.

Bishop of Botswana: Rt Rev. MUSONDA TREVOR S. MWAMBA, POB 769, Gaborone; tel. 3953779; fax 3913015; e-mail acenter@info.bw.

Protestant Churches

There were an estimated 178,000 adherents in the country at mid-2000.

African Methodist Episcopal Church: POB 141, Lobatse; tel. 5407520; e-mail mobeat@bpc.bw; Presiding Elder Rev. MOSES P. LEKHORI.

Evangelical Lutheran Church in Botswana (Kereke ya Luthere ya Efangele mo Botswana): POB 1976, Gaborone; tel. 3952227; fax 3913966; e-mail elcb@info.bw; f. 1979; Bishop Rev. PHILIP J. ROBINSON; 43 congregations; c. 25,000 mems (2004).

Evangelical Lutheran Church in Southern Africa (Botswana Diocese): POB 400, Gaborone; tel. 3953976; Bishop Rev. M. NTUPING.

Methodist Church of Southern Africa (Gaborone Circuit): POB 260, Gaborone; tel. 3167627; Circuit Supt Rev. ODIRILE E. MERE.

United Congregational Church of Southern Africa (Synod of Botswana): POB 1263, Gaborone; tel. 3952491; synod status since 1980; Chair. Rev. D. T. MAPITSE; Sec. Rev. M. P. P. DIBEELA; c. 24,000 mems.

Other denominations active in Botswana include the Church of God in Christ, the Dutch Reformed Church, the Mennonite Church, the United Methodist Church and the Seventh-day Adventists.

The Roman Catholic Church

Botswana comprises one diocese and an apostolic vicariate. The metropolitan see is Bloemfontein, South Africa. The church was established in Botswana in 1928, and had an estimated 63,926 adherents (some 6.4% of the total population) in the country at 31 December 2005. The Bishop participates in the Southern African Catholic Bishops' Conference, currently based in Pretoria, South Africa.

Bishop of Gaborone: Rt Rev. BONIFACE TSHOSA SETLALEKGOSI, POB 218, Bishop's House, Plot 162, Queens Rd, Gaborone; tel. 3912958; fax 3956970; e-mail gabs.diocese@botsnet.bw.

Vicar Apostolic of Francistown: Rt Rev. FRANKLYN NUBUASAH, POB 702, Francistown; tel. 2413601; fax 2417183.

The Press

DAILY NEWSPAPERS

Dikgang tsa Gompieno (Daily News): Mass Media Complex, Western Bypass, Private Bag 0060, Gaborone; tel. 3653065; fax 3901675; e-mail dailynews@gov.bw; internet www.mcst.gov.bw/dailynews; f. 1964; Mon.–Fri.; publ. by Dept of Information and Broadcasting; Setswana and English; Editor ME GOLEKANYE MOLAPISI; circ. 60,000.

Mmegi/The Reporter: Segogwane Way, Plot 8901, Broadhurst, Private Bag BR 50, Gaborone; tel. 3974784; fax 3905508; e-mail dikgang@mmegi.bw; internet www.mmegi.bw; f. 1984 as *Mmegi wa Dikgang*; daily; publ. by Dikgang Publishing Co; Setswana and English; Man. Editor TITUS MBUYA; circ. 20,000; also publishes the weekly *Mmegi Monitor* (f. 2000, Monday, circ. 16,000).

PERIODICALS

Botswana Advertiser/Northern Advertiser: 5634 Nakedi Rd, Broadhurst Industrial, POB 130, Gaborone; tel. 3914788; fax 3182957; e-mail martin@simplymarketing.co.bw; f. 1971; owned by Screen Print (Pty) Ltd; weekly; English; circ. 90,000 (Botswana Advertiser), 35,000 (Northern Advertiser); Gen. Man. MARTIN CHIBANDA.

The Botswana Gazette: 125 Sedimosa House, Millennium Park, Kgale View, POB 1605, Gaborone; tel. 3912833; fax 3972283; e-mail production@gazette.bw; internet www.gazette.bw; f. 1985; publ. by News Co Botswana; weekly; Man. Dir CLARA OLSEN; Editor AUBREY LUTE; circ. 17,000.

Botswana Guardian: Plot 14442, Kamushungo Rd, G-West Industrial Site, POB 1641, Gaborone; tel. 3908432; fax 3908457; internet www.botswanaguardian.co.bw; f. 1983; weekly; publ. by Pula Printing & Publishing (Pty) Ltd; English; Editor OUTSA MOKONE; circ. 21,505.

Botswana Journal of Technology: University of Botswana, Private Bag 0061, Gaborone; tel. 3554210; fax 3952309; e-mail ngowiab@mopipi.ub.bw; 2 a year; science and technology; Reviews Editor Prof. ALFRED B. NGOWI.

Business and Financial Times: Unit 9, Plot 64, Gaborone International Commerce Park, POB 402396, Gaborone; tel. 3939911; fax 3939910; e-mail bftimes@info.bw; Publr JAFFAR KATERYA MBUI; Editor JIMMY SWIRA.

The Clarion: POB 397, Gaborone; tel. 3930709; fax 3930708; Editor SELLO MOTSETA.

Fame Magazine: F5, Fairground Mall, POB 2214, Gaborone; tel. and fax 3907711; e-mail kudadi@yahoo.com.

Flair Magazine: Plot 22055, Mocha House, Unit Z, POB 21606, Gaborone; tel. 3911349; fax 3911359; monthly; Editor BOITSHEPO BALOZWI.

Francistown News and Reviews: POB 632, Francistown; tel. and fax 2412040; weekly; English.

Kutlwano: Private Bag BR 139, Gaborone; tel. 3653500; fax 3653630; e-mail kutlwano@gov.bw; monthly; publ. by Dept of Information Services; Setswana and English; Editor BOME MATSHABA; circ. 15,000.

The Midweek Sun: Plot 14442, Kamushungo Rd, G-West Industrial Site, POB 00153, Gaborone; tel. 3908408; fax 3908457; internet www.midweeksun.co.bw; f. 1989; weekly; English; Editor MIKE MOTHIBI; circ. 17,971.

Mokgosi Newspaper: Plot 134, Madirelo, Tlokweng, POB 46530, Gaborone; tel. 3936868; fax 3936869; e-mail mokgosi@mmegi.bw.

The Ngami Times: Mabudutsa Ward, Private Bag BO 30, Maun; tel. 6864807; fax 6860257; e-mail tnt@info.bw; internet www.ngamitimes.com; f. 1999; owned by The Ngami Times Botswana (Pty) Ltd; weekly; English; Editor NORMAN CHANDLER.

Sunday Standard: Postnet Kgale View, Private Bag 351, Suite 287, Gaborone; tel. 3188784; fax 3188795; internet www.sundaystandard.info; Editor OUTSA MOKONE.

Sunday Tribune: POB 41458, Gaborone; tel. and fax 3926431; weekly.

Tautona Times: Office of the President, Private Bag 001, Gaborone; tel. 3975154; fax 3902795; e-mail jramsay@gov.bw; f. 2003; weekly; electronic press circular publ. by the Office of the Pres; Press Sec. Dr JEFF RAMSAY.

The Voice: Plot 170, Unit 7, Commerce Park, POB 40415, Gaborone; tel. 3161585; fax 3932822; e-mail voicebw@yahoo.com; internet www.thevoicebw.com; f. 1992 as *The Francistowner*; weekly; Publr BEATA KASALE; Man. Editor DONALD MOORE; Editor EMANG BOKHUTLO; circ. 29,000.

Wena Magazine: POB 201533, Gaborone; tel. and fax 3907678; e-mail environews@it.bw; f. 1998; 6 a year; English and Setswana; environmental issues; Editor and Publr FLORA SEBONI-MMEREKI; circ. c. 8,000.

The Zebra's Voice: National Museum, 331 Independence Ave, Private Bag 00114, Gaborone; tel. 3974616; fax 3902797; e-mail bemotswakhumo@gov.bw; internet www.botswana-museum.gov.bw; f. 1980; quarterly; cultural affairs; Editor BERLINAH MOTSWAKHUMO; circ. 5,000.

NEWS AGENCIES

Department of Information Services, Botswana Press Agency (BOPA): Private Bag BR 139, Gaborone; tel. 3653525; fax 3653626; e-mail bopa@gov.bw; f. 1981; News Editor MABEL KEBOTSAMANG.

PRESS ORGANIZATIONS

Botswana Journalists' Association (BOJA): POB 60518, Gaborone; tel. 3974435; f. 1977; represents professional journalists; affiliated to the Int. Fed. of Journalists; Chair. SECHELE SECHELE; Sec.-Gen. RAMPHOLO MOLEFHE; 55 mems (1999).

Botswana Media Consultative Council (BMCC): POB 2679, Gaborone; tel. 71624382; e-mail botswanamedia@info.bw; internet

BOTSWANA

www.botswanamedia.bw; f. 1998; promotes the devt of a democratic media; Chair. Dr JEFF RAMSAY; Exec. Sec. ANTOINETTE O. CHIGODORA; 40 mem. orgs (1999).

Publishers

A. C. Braby (Botswana) (Pty) Ltd: Unit 3/A/2, Western Industrial Estate, 22100 Phase 4 Industrial, POB 1549, Gaborone; tel. 3971444; fax 3973462; e-mail customercare@brabys.co.za; internet www.brabys.com/bw/; business directories.

Botsalo Books: Gaborone International Commerce Park, Kgale, Plot 59/60, Unit 5, POB 1532, Gaborone; tel. 3912576; fax 3972608; e-mail botsalo@botsnet.bw; internet www.abcdafrica.com/botsalobooks.

The Botswana Society (BotSoc): Unispan Bldg, Lot 54, International Commerce Park, Kgale, POB 71, Gaborone; tel. 3919673; fax 3919745; e-mail baybooks@it.bw; internet www.botsoc.org.bw; f. 1968; archaeology, arts, history, law, sciences; Pres. FESTUS G. MOGAE.

Heinemann Educational Botswana (Pty) Ltd: Plot 20695, Unit 4, Magochanyana Rd, POB 10103, Village Post Office, Gaborone; tel. 3972305; fax 3971832; e-mail hein@info.bw; internet www.heinemann.co.za; Man. Dir LESEDI SEITEI.

Lentswe la Lesedi (Pty): POB 2365, Gaborone; tel. 314017; fax 314634; e-mail publisher@lightbooks.net; f. 1992

Lightbooks Publishers: Digitec House, 685 Botswana Rd, The Mall, POB 2365, Gaborone; tel. 3903994; fax 3914017; e-mail publisher@lightbooks.net; internet www.lightbooks.net; f. 1992; commercial publishing division of Lentswe la Lesedi (Pty); scholarly, research, women's issues, journals, reports; Publr CHARLES BEWLAY.

Longman Botswana (Pty) Ltd: Plot 14386, West Industrial Site, New Lobatse Rd, POB 1083, Gaborone; tel. 3922969; fax 3922682; e-mail carlson@longman.info.bw; f. 1981; subsidiary of Pearson Education, UK; educational; Man. Dir J. K. CHALASHIKA.

Macmillan Botswana Publishing Co (Pty) Ltd: Plot 50635, Block 10, Airport Rd, Gaborone; tel. 3911770; fax 3911987; e-mail leburu.sianga@macmillan.bw; CEO FELICITY LEBURU-SIANGA.

Medi Publishing: Phakalane Phase 1, Medie Close, Plot No. 21633, POB 47680, Gaborone; tel. 3121110; e-mail medi@it.bw; f. 1995; scholarly; Publishing Dir PORTIA TSHOAGONG.

Mmegi Publishing House (MPH): Plot 8901, Segogwane Way, Broadhurst, Private Bag BR 298, Gaborone; tel. 3952464; fax 3184977; e-mail ntebela@mmegi.bw; academic and general.

Morula Press: Business School of Botswana, Ext. 2, 222 Independence Ave, Selemelo, POB 402492, Gaborone; tel. 3906134; fax 3904809; f. 1994; business, law.

Printing and Publishing Co (Botswana) (Pty) Ltd (PPCB): Plot 5634 Nakedi Rd, Broadhurst Industrial, POB 130, Gaborone; tel. 3914788; fax 3182957; e-mail ppcb@info.bw; internet www.ppcb.co.bw; educational; Man. Dir Y. MUSSA; Gen. Man. GAVIN BLAMIRE.

GOVERNMENT PUBLISHING HOUSE

Department of Government Printing and Publishing Service: Private Bag 0081, Gaborone; tel. 353202; fax 312001; Dir O. ANDREW SESINYI.

Broadcasting and Communications

TELECOMMUNICATIONS

Botswana Telecommunications Authority (BTA): 206–207 Independence Ave, Private Bag 00495, Gaborone; tel. 3957755; fax 3957976; internet www.bta.org.bw; f. 1996; independent regulator for the telecommunications industry; Chair. Dr JOHN MOTHIBI; CEO THARI G. PHEKO.

Botswana Telecommunications Corpn (BTC): POB 700, Gaborone; tel. 3958000; fax 3952777; internet www.btc.bw; f. 1980; state-owned; privatization pending; fixed-line telecommunications provider; Chair. WILFRED MANDLEBE; CEO VINCENT T. SERETSE.

Mascom: Tsholetsa House, Plot 4705/6, Botswana Rd, Main Mall, Private Bag BO298, Bontleng, Gaborone; tel. 3903396; fax 3903445; internet www.mascom.bw; f. 1998; 60% owned by DECI; 40% owned by Econet Wireless; mobile cellular telecommunications provider; CEO JOSE GERALDES.

Orange Botswana: Camphill Bldg, Plot 43002/1, Private Bag BO64, Bontleng, Gaborone; tel. 3163370; fax 3163372; internet www.orange.co.bw; f. 1998 as Vista Cellular; present name adopted in 2003; 49% owned by Orange SA, France; 46% owned by Mosokelatsebeng Cellular; mobile cellular telecommunications provider; CEO (vacant).

BROADCASTING

The Department of Information and Broadcasting operates 21 radio stations across the country from bureaux in Gaborone, Kanye, Serowe and Francistown. The National Broadcasting Board was preparing to issue three further licences for private commercial radio stations in addition to those already held by Ya Rona FM and GABZ FM.

Department of Information and Broadcasting: Private Bag 0060, Gaborone; tel. 3658000; fax 564416; internet www.dib.gov.bw; f. 1978 following merger between Information Services and Radio Botswana; Dir O. ANDREW SESINYI.

Radio

Radio Botswana (RB1): Private Bag 0060, Gaborone; tel. 3952541; fax 3957138; e-mail rbeng@info.bw; state-owned; f. 1965; fmrly Radio Bechuanaland; culture, entertainment, news and current affairs programmes; broadcasts 18 hours daily in Setswana and English; Dir ANDREW SESINYI; Head of Programmes M. GABAKGORE.

Radio Botswana (RB2) (FM 103): Private Bag 0060, Gaborone; tel. 3653000; fax 3653346; e-mail mmphusu@gov.bw; f. 1992; contemporary entertainment; Head of Programmes MONICA MPHUSU.

GABZ FM 96.2: Private Bag 319, Gaborone; tel. 3170905; fax 3181443; e-mail feedback@gabzfm.co.bw; f. 1999; owned by Thari Investment; entertainment, news and politics; broadcasts in Setswana and English; Man. Dir KENNEDY OTSHELENG.

Yarona FM 106.6: POB 1607, Gaborone; tel. 3912305; fax 3901063; e-mail info@yaronafm.co.bw; internet www.yaronafm.co.bw; f. 1999; owned by Copacabana Investment; Station Man. DUMI LOPANG.

Television

Botswana Television (BTV): Private Bag 0060, Gaborone; tel. 3658000; fax 3900051; internet www.btv.gov.bw; f. 2000; broadcasts local and international programmes eight hours daily (Mon.–Fri.) and 10 hours (Sat.–Sun.); 60% local content; Gen. Man. BANYANA SEGWE.

GBC TV: Plot 53996, Mogochama St, opposite Coca Cola, POB 921, Gaborone; tel. 3957654; fax 3901875; e-mail gbctv@info.bw; f. 1988; operated by Gaborone Broadcasting Co (Pty) Ltd; 49% owned by Sabido (South Africa); Setswana and English; rebroadcasts foreign TV programmes; Man. Dir MIKE KLINCK.

TV Association of Botswana: Gaborone; relays SABC-TV and BOP-TV programmes from South Africa.

Finance

(cap. = capital; res = reserves; dep. = deposits; m. = million; brs = branches; amounts in pula)

BANKING

Central Bank

Bank of Botswana: POB 712, Private Bag 154, 17938 Khama Cres., Gaborone; tel. 3606000; fax 3913890; e-mail selwej@bob.bw; internet www.bankofbotswana.bw; f. 1975; bank of issue; cap. 25m., res 19,352.5m., dep. 14,012.8m. (Dec. 2005); Gov. LINAH MOHOHLO.

Commercial Banks

African Banking Corpn of Botswana Ltd (ABC): ABC House, Tholo Office Park, Plot 50669, Fairground Office Park, POB 00303, Gaborone; tel. 3905455; fax 3902131; e-mail abcbw@africanbankingcorp.com; internet www.africanbankingcorp.com; f. 1989 as ulc (Pty) Ltd; name changed to African Banking Corpn (Pty) Ltd in 2001; present name adopted in 2002; subsidiary of ABC Holdings Ltd; financial services and investment banking; operates in Botswana, Mozambique, Tanzania, Zambia and Zimbabwe; total assets 1,902.1m. (Dec. 2005); Chair. OLIVER M. CHIDAWU; Pres. JITTO KURIAN.

Bank of Baroda (Botswana) Ltd: Plot 50370, Ground Floor, Acumen Park, Fairgrounds, Gaborone; tel. 3188878; fax 3188879; e-mail botswana@barodabank.co.bw; internet www.bankofbaroda.com; f. 2001; subsidiary of the Bank of Baroda, India; Man. Dir R. S. SETIA; Chief Man. G. V. SESHADRI.

Barclays Bank of Botswana Ltd: Barclays House, 6th Floor, Plot 8842, Khama Cres., POB 478, Gaborone; tel. 3952041; fax 3913672; e-mail AFCAR.Psavery@barclaysmail.com; internet www.barclays.com; f. 1975 as local successor to Barclays Bank Int. Ltd; 74.9% owned by Barclays Bank PLC, UK; total assets 5,239.5m. (Dec. 2004); Chair. MBIGANYI CHARLES TIBONE; Man. Dir THULISIZWE JOHNSON; 48 brs.

First National Bank of Botswana Ltd: Finance House, 5th Floor, Plot 8843, Khama Cres., POB 1552, Gaborone; tel. 3642600; fax 3906130; e-mail achalwe@fnbbotswana.co.bw; internet www.fnbbotswana.co.bw; f. 1991; 69.5% owned by First Nat. Bank Holdings Botswana Ltd; total assets 7,213.1m. (June 2006); Chair. HENRY C. L. HERMANS; Man. Dir DANNY H. ZANDAMELA; 14 brs.

Kingdom Bank Africa Limited: Plot 133, Ext. 3, Independence Ave, Gaborone; POB 45078, Riverwalk, Gaborone; tel. 3906863; fax 3906874; f. 2003; Chair. NIGEL CHANKIRA; Man. Dir IRENE CHAMNEY; Exec. Dir TAPIWA SHAMU.

Stanbic Bank Botswana Ltd: Stanbic House, 1st Floor, Plot 50672, Fairground (off Machel Dr.), Private Bag 00168, Gaborone; tel. 3901600; fax 3900171; internet www.stanbic.co.bw; f. 1992; subsidiary of Standard Bank Investment Corpn Africa Holdings Ltd; cap. and res 170.5m., total assets 2,443.1m. (Dec. 2004); Chair. G. H. ABDOOLA (acting); Man. Dir D. W. KENNEDY; Exec. Dir T. FERREIRA; 6 brs.

Standard Chartered Bank Botswana Ltd: Standard House, 5th Floor, Queens Rd, The Mall, POB 496, Gaborone; tel. 3601500; fax 3972933; internet www.standardchartered.com/bw; f. 1975; 75% owned by Standard Chartered Holdings (Africa) BV, Amsterdam; total assets 4,729.7m. (Dec. 2005); Chair. P. L. STEENKAMP; Man. Dir NIGEL R. JONES; 14 brs; 4 agencies.

Other Banks

Botswana Savings Bank: Tshomarelo House, POB 1150, Gaborone; tel. 3952326; fax 3952608; e-mail marketing@bsb.bw; internet www.bsb.bw; f. 1992; cap. and res 48.4m., dep. 101.5m. (March 2000); Chair. F. MODISE; Man. Dir MICHAEL LESOLLE.

Letshego: POB 318, Gaborone; tel. 3180635; fax 3957949; e-mail letshego@info.bw; f. 1998; micro-finance; 43.8% owned by Micro Provident Ltd; 34.9% owned by the Int. Finance Corpn, Netherlands Devt Finance Co, Pan-African Investment Partners and Pan-Commonwealth African Partners; total assets 328.0m. (Oct. 2005); Chair. C. M. LEKAUKAU; Man. Dir J. A. CLAASSEN.

National Development Bank: Development House, Queens Rd, Main Mall, POB 225, Gaborone; tel. 3952801; fax 3974446; e-mail bmojalemotho@ndb.bw; internet www.ndb.bw; f. 1963; total assets 566.9m. (March 2005); Chair. LESEDI SEITEI (acting); CEO OAITSE M. RAMASEDI; 5 brs.

STOCK EXCHANGE

Botswana Stock Exchange: Finance House, 4th Floor, Unit 11, Millennium Office Park, Kgale Mews, Private Bag 00417, Gaborone; tel. 3180201; fax 3180175; e-mail enquiries@bse.co.bw; internet www.bse.co.bw; f. 1989; commenced formal functions of a stock exchange in 1995; Chair. LOUIS G. NCHINDO; CEO Dr T. T. K. MATOME; 25 cos and 32 securities firms listed in 2004.

INSURANCE

Botswana Eagle Insurance Co Ltd: Eagle House, Plot 54479, Fairgrounds, POB 1221, Gaborone; tel. 3188888; fax 3188911; e-mail john.main@botswanaeagle.co.za; f. 1976; subsidiary of Zurich Insurance Co South Africa Ltd, fmrly South African Eagle Insurance Co Ltd; Man. JOHN MAIN.

Botswana Insurance Holdings Ltd (BIHL): Block A, Fairgrounds Office Park, POB 336, Gaborone; tel. 3645100; fax 3905884; f. 1975; 54% owned by African Life Assurance Co Ltd (Aflife), South Africa; total assets 80.8m. (Dec. 2006); Chair. MCLEAN C. LETSHWITI.

Botswana Life Insurance Ltd: Botswana Life Insurance House, Nyerere Dr., Private Bag 00296, Gaborone; tel. 3645100; fax 3905884; e-mail Webmaster@blil.co.bw; internet www.botswanalifeinsurance.com; subsidiary of BIHL; life insurance; CEO REGINA VAKA.

Metropolitan Life of Botswana Ltd: Standard House, 1st Floor, Queens Rd, Main Mall, Private Bag 231, Gaborone; tel. 3624300; fax 3624423; e-mail jvdhoven@metropolitan.co.za; internet www.metropolitan.co.bw; f. 1996; 75% owned by Metropolitan South Africa, 25% owned by the Botswana Devt Corpn; Chair. JUSTIN VAN DEN HOVEN; Exec. Man. LEEBA FOUCHE.

Mutual and Federal Insurance Co of Botswana Ltd: Private Bag 00347, Gaborone; tel. 3903333; fax 3903400; e-mail jbekker@mf.co.za; f. 1994; subsidiary of Mutual and Federal, South Africa; Man. Dir JACK BEKKER.

Trade and Industry

GOVERNMENT AGENCIES

Botswana Housing Corpn (BHC): POB 412, Gaborone; tel. 3605100; fax 3952070; e-mail info@bhc.bw; internet www.bhc.bw; f. 1971; provides housing for central govt and local authority needs and assists with private sector housing schemes; Chair. MACLEAN C. LETSHWITI; CEO MOOTIEMANG R. MOTSWAISO.

Citizen Entrepreneurial Development Agency (CEDA): 205 Independence Ave, 1st Floor, Private Bag 00504, Gaborone; tel. 3170895; fax 3170896; internet www.ceda.co.bw; f. 2001; develops and promotes citizen-owned enterprises; provides business training and financial assistance; Chair. H. P. MAHLOANE; CEO Dr THAPELO C. MATSHEKA.

Department of Food Resources: POB 96, Gaborone; tel. 3954124; f. 1982; procurement, storage and distribution of food commodities under the Drought Relief Programme; Admin. Officer M. S. SEHLULANE.

Department of Town and Regional Planning: Private Bag 0042, Gaborone; tel. 3658596; fax 3913280; e-mail rchephethe@gov.bw; f. 1972; responsible for physical planning policy and implementation; Dir R. CHEPHETHE.

Public Enterprises Evaluation and Privatisation Agency (PEEPA): Twin Towers, East Wing, 2nd Floor, Fair Grounds Office Park, Private Bag 00510, Gaborone; tel. 3188807; fax 3188662; e-mail peepa@peepa.co.bw; internet www.peepa.co.bw; f. 2001; responsible for commercializing and privatizing public parastatals; CEO JOSHUA GALEFOROLWE.

DEVELOPMENT ORGANIZATIONS

Botswana Council of Non-Governmental Organisations (BOCONGO): Tebelelo Kgethang, Private Bag 00418, Gaborone; tel. 3911319; fax 3912935; e-mail bocongo@bocongo.org.bw; internet www.bocongo.org.bw; Exec. Dir BABOLOKI TLALE; 84 mem. orgs.

Botswana Development Corpn Ltd: Private Bag 160, Moedi, Plot 50380, Gaborone International Showgrounds (off Machel Dr.), Gaborone; tel. 3651300; fax 3904193; e-mail enquiries@bdc.bw; internet www.bdc.bw; f. 1970; Chair. S. S. G. TUMELO; Man. Dir KENNETH O. MATAMBO.

Botswana Enterprise Development Unit (BEDU): POB 0014, Plot 1269, Lobatse Rd, Gaborone; f. 1974; promotes industrialization and rural devt; Dir J. LINDFORS.

Botswana Export Development and Investment Authority (BEDIA): Plot 28, Matsitama Rd, The Main Mall, POB 3122, Gaborone; tel. 3181931; fax 3181941; e-mail bedia@bedia.bw; internet www.bedia.bw; f. 1998; promotes and facilitates local and foreign investment; Chair. MORAGO NGIDI; CEO (vacant).

Botswana International Financial Services Centre (BIFSC): Plot 50676, Block B, Fairground Office Park, Private Bag 160, Gaborone; tel. 3605000; fax 3913075; e-mail ifsc@ifsc.co.bw; internet www.ifsc.co.bw; f. 2003; govt-owned; Chair. H. C. L. HERMANS; CEO ALAN P. BOSHWAEN.

Department of Trade and Investment Promotion (TIPA), Ministry of Trade and Industry: Private Bag 00367, Gaborone; tel. 3951790; fax 3905375; promotes industrial and commercial investment, diversification and expansion; offers consultancy, liaison and information services; participates in overseas trade fairs and trade and investment missions; Dir D. TSHEKO.

Financial Services Co of Botswana (Pty) Ltd: POB 1129, Finance House, Khama Cres., Gaborone; tel. 3951363; fax 3957815; f. 1974; hire purchase, mortgages, industrial leasing and debt factoring; Chair. M. E. HOPKINS; Man. Dir R. A. PAWSON.

Integrated Field Services: Ministry of Trade and Industry, Private Bag 004, Gaborone; tel. 3953024; fax 3971539; promotes industrialization and rural devt; Dir B. T. TIBONE.

RETENG: the Multicultural Coalition of Botswana: POB 402786, Gaborone; tel. 71654345; fax 3937779; f. 2003; umbrella org. composed of human rights advocacy and conservation groups, and public-service and private-sector unions; Sec.-Gen. Prof. LYDIA NYATHI-RAMAHOBO.

CHAMBER OF COMMERCE

Botswana National Chamber of Commerce and Industry: POB 20344, Gaborone; tel. 3952677; Dir MODIRI J. MBAAKANYI.

INDUSTRIAL AND TRADE ASSOCIATIONS

Botswana Agricultural Marketing Board (BAMB): Plot 130, Unit 3–4, Gaborone International Finance Park, Private Bag 0053, Gaborone; tel. 3951341; fax 3952926; internet www.bamb.co.bw; Chair. L. R. MANTHE; CEO M. MPHATHI.

Botswana Meat Commission (BMC): Plot 621, 1 Khama Ave, Private Bag 4, Lobatse; tel. 5330619; fax 5332228; e-mail marketing@bmc.bw; internet www.bmc.bw; f. 1966; slaughter of livestock, export of hides and skins, carcasses, frozen and chilled boneless beef; operates tannery and beef products cannery; Exec. Chair. Dr MOTSHUDI V. RABOROKGWE; Gen. Man. JOHNSON BOJOSI.

EMPLOYERS' ORGANIZATIONS

Botswana Confederation of Commerce, Industry and Manpower (BOCCIM): BOCCIM House, POB 432, Gaborone; e-mail boccim@info.bw; internet www.boccim.co.bw; f. 1971; Pres. IQBAL EBRAHIM; Exec. Dir ELIAS DEWAH; 1,700 mems.

Botswana Teachers' Union (BTU): Plot 0019, BTU Rd Mogoditshane; BTU Centre, Private Bag 0019, Mogoditshane; tel. 3906774; fax 3909838; e-mail btu@it.bw; internet www.btu.co.bw; f. 1937 as the Bechuanaland Protectorate African Teachers' Asscn; present name adopted 1966; affiliated to Education Int.; merger discussions under way in mid-2006 with Botswana Primary Teachers Asscn (BOPRITA—Pres. SAM MALETE), Asscn of Botswana Tertiary Lecturers (ABOTEL—Pres. ALLEN KEITSENG) and BOSETU; Pres. JAPHTA RADIBE; Sec.-Gen. KEORAPETSE A. KGASA; 13,000 mems.

UTILITIES

Electricity

Botswana Power Corpn (BPC): Motlakase House, Macheng Way, POB 48, Gaborone; tel. 3603203; fax 3973563; e-mail selatot@bpc.bw; internet www.bpc.bw; f. 1971; parastatal; operates power station at Morupule (132 MW); Chair. E. RAKHUDU; Acting CEO JACOB N. RALERU.

Water

Department of Water Affairs: Khama Cres., Private Bag 0018, Gaborone; tel. 3656600; fax 3972738; e-mail dwa@global.bw; provides public water supplies for rural areas.

Water Utilities Corpn: Private Bag 00276, Gaborone; tel. 3604400; fax 3973852; e-mail metsi@wuc.bw; internet www.wuc.bw; f. 1970; 100% state-owned; supplies water to main urban centres; Chair. NOZIPHO MABE; Chief Exec. FRED MAUNGE.

CO-OPERATIVES

Department of Co-operative Development: POB 86, Gaborone; tel. 3950721; fax 3951657; e-mail vmosele@gov.bw; f. 1964; promotes marketing and supply, consumer, dairy, horticultural and fisheries co-operatives, thrift and loan societies, credit societies, a co-operative union and a co-operative bank; Commissioner VIOLET MOSELE.

TRADE UNIONS

Botswana Federation of Trade Unions (BFTU): POB 440, Gaborone; tel. and fax 3952534; f. 1977; affiliated to the Int. Trade Union Confed., the Org. of African Trade Union Unity and the Southern African Trade Union Co-ordination Council (SATUCC); Pres. RONALD DUST BAIPIDI; 25,000 mems (2001).

Affiliated Unions

Botswana Bank Employees' Union (BOBEU): Ext. 4, South Ring Rd, Dilalelo, POB 111, Gaborone; tel. 3905893; Gen. Sec. ALFRED SELEKE.

Botswana Construction Workers' Union: POB 1508, Gaborone; tel. 352534; fax 357790; affiliated to the Building and Wood Workers Int.; Gen. Sec. JOSHUA KESIILWE.

Botswana Diamond Sorters and Valuators' Staff Union (BDSVU): POB 1186, Gaborone; affiliated to the Int. Fed. of Chemical, Energy, Mine and Gen. Workers' Unions; Gen. Sec. EDWARD KELONEILWE.

Botswana Hotel, Wholesalers, Furniture, Agricultural and Commercial General Workers' Union (BHWFACGWU): POB 62, Gaborone; tel. 3911874; fax 3959360; f. 2006 by merger of Botswana Agricultural Marketing Board Workers' Union, Botswana Commercial and Gen. Workers' Union (f. 1988), Botswana Hotel Travel and Tourism Union, and Botswana Wholesale Furniture and Retail Workers' Union.

Botswana Mining Workers' Union (BMWU): POB 86, Orapa; tel. 2970331; fax 2970067; affiliated to the Int. Fed. of Chemical, Energy, Mine and General Workers' Unions; Chair. CHIMBIDZANI CHIMIDZA; Sec.-Gen. JACK TLHAGALE.

Botswana Postal Services Workers' Union (BOPSWU): POB 87, Gaborone; Chair. AARON LEFU.

Botswana Power Corpn Workers' Union (BPCWU): Private Bag 0053, Gaborone; affiliated to the Int. Fed. of Chemical, Energy, Mine and General Workers' Unions; Gen. Sec. MAVIS KOOGOTSITSE.

Botswana Railways Amalgamated Workers' Union (BRAWU): POB 181, Gaborone; affiliated to the Int. Transport Workers' Fed.; Chair. LETLAMPONA MOKGALAJWE.

Botswana Telecommunications Employees' Union (BOTEU): Gaborone; Pres. LESETSWE KOFA.

National Amalgamated Local and Central Government, Parastatal, Statutory Body and Manual Workers' Union (NALCPMWU): Ext. 15, Plot No. 4946/7, Jawara Rd, POB 374, Gaborone; tel. 352790; fax 357790; e-mail nalcg.pwu@info.bw; affiliated to the Public Services Int.; Chair. DAVID OTHUSITSE BINA TSALAILE; Gen. Sec. SIMON KGAOGANANG.

Other affiliated unions include: the Air Botswana Employees' Union; the Botswana Beverages and Allied Workers' Union; the Botswana Central Bank Staff Union; the Botswana Housing Corpn Staff Union; the Botswana Institute of Development Management Workers' Union; the Botswana Manufacturing and Packaging Workers' Union; the Botswana Meat Industry Union; the Botswana National Development Bank Staff Union; the Botswana Private Medical and Health Services Workers' Union; the Botswana Savings Bank Employees' Union; the Botswana Vaccine Institute Staff Union; and the Rural Industry Promotions Co Workers' Union.

Principal Non-affiliated Unions

Botswana Secondary Teachers' Trade Union (BOSETU): Unit 5, Commerce Park, Broadhurst, POB 404341, Gaborone; tel. 3937472; fax 3170845; f. 1986 as Botswana Fed. for Secondary School Teachers; present name adopted on achieving union status in 2006; Pres. ERIC DITAU.

Botswana Landboard and Local Authority Workers Union (BLLAWU): Private Bag 40, Francistown; tel. and fax 2413312; internet www.bulgsa.org.bw; affiliated to the Public Services Int.; fmrly the Botswana Unified Local Govt Service Asscn; renamed in 2007 on achieving union status; Pres. PELOTSHWEU A. D. S. BAENG; Sec.-Gen. MOTELEBANE SHEPPARD MOTELEBANE.

Transport

RAILWAYS

The 960-km railway line from Mafikeng, South Africa, to Bulawayo, Zimbabwe, passes through Botswana and has been operated by Botswana Railways (BR) since 1987. In 1997 there were 888 km of 1,067-mm-gauge track within Botswana, including three branches serving the Selebi-Phikwe mining complex (56 km), the Morupule colliery (16 km) and the Sua Pan soda-ash deposits (175 km). BR derives 85%–90% of its earnings from freight traffic, although passenger services do operate between Gaborone and Francistown, and Lobatse and Bulawayo. Through its links with Spoornet, which operates the South African railways system, and the National Railways of Zimbabwe, BR provides connections with Namibia and Swaziland to the south, and an uninterrupted rail link to Zambia, the Democratic Republic of the Congo, Angola, Mozambique, Tanzania and Malawi to the north. However, freight traffic on BR was severely reduced following Zimbabwe's construction, in 1999, of a rail link from Bulawayo to Beitbridge, on its border with South Africa.

Botswana Railways (BR): Private Bag 52, Mahalapye; tel. 4711375; fax 4711385; e-mail marketing@botrail.bw; internet www.botswanarailways.co.bw; f. 1986; Chair. IQBAL EBRAHIM; CEO ANDREW LUNGA.

ROADS

In 1999 there were 10,217 km of roads, including 3,360 km of main roads, and 2,210 km of secondary roads. Some 55% of the road network was paved, including a main road from Gaborone, via Francistown, to Kazungula, where the borders of Botswana, Namibia, Zambia and Zimbabwe meet. (In 2004 some 6,116 km of road were bitumenized.) The construction of a 340-km road between Nata and Maun was completed in the late 1990s. Construction of the 600-km Trans-Kalahari Highway, from Jwaneng to the port of Walvis Bay on the Namibian coast, commenced in 1990 and was completed in 1998. A car-ferry service operates from Kazungula across the Zambezi river into Zambia.

Department of Road Transport and Safety: Private Bag 0026, Gaborone; tel. 3905442; responsible for national road network; responsible to the Ministry of Works and Transport; Dir MOSES K. SEBOLAI.

CIVIL AVIATION

The main international airport is at Gaborone. Four other major airports are located at Kasane, Maun, Francistown and Ghanzi. In 2000 there were also 108 airfields throughout the country. Scheduled services of Air Botswana are supplemented by an active charter and business sector. In September 2005 the Government announced that the Department of Civil Aviation would be converted into a parastatal company, the Civil Aviation Authority.

Air Botswana: POB 92, Sir Seretse Khama Airport, Gaborone; tel. 3952812; fax 3974802; internet www.airbotswana.co.bw; f. 1972; 45% state-owned; transfer to private sector suspended in April 2004; domestic services and regional services to countries in eastern and southern Africa; Chair. G. N. THIPE; Gen. Man. LANCE BROGDEN; 150,000 passengers per year.

BOTSWANA

Tourism

There are five game reserves and three national parks, including Chobe, near Victoria Falls, on the Zambia–Zimbabwe border. Efforts to expand the tourism industry include plans for the construction of new hotels and the rehabilitation of existing hotel facilities. In 2004 foreign tourist arrivals were estimated at 1,522,807, compared with 1,405,535 in 2003. Receipts from tourism increased from an estimated US $319m. in 2002 to $549m. in 2004.

Department of Tourism: Private Bag 0047, Main Mall, Queens Rd, Standard House, 2nd Floor, Gaborone; tel. 3953024; fax 3908675; internet www.botswana-tourism.gov.bw; f. 1994; Dir KELEBAONE D.G. MASELESELE.

Department of Wildlife and National Parks: POB 131, Gaborone; tel. 3971405; fax 3912354; e-mail dwnp@gov.bw; Dir J. MATLHARE.

Hospitality and Tourism Association of Botswana (HATAB): Private Bag 00423, Gaborone; tel. 3957144; fax 3903201; e-mail hatab@hatab.bw; internet www.hatab.bw; f. 1982; fmrly Hotel and Tourism Asscn of Botswana; CEO MORONGOE NTLOEDIBE-DISELE.

BRAZIL

Introductory Survey

Location, Climate, Language, Religion, Flag, Capital

The Federative Republic of Brazil, the fifth largest country in the world, lies in central and north-eastern South America. To the north are Venezuela, Colombia, Guyana, Suriname and French Guiana, to the west Peru and Bolivia, and to the south Paraguay, Argentina and Uruguay. Brazil has a very long coastline on the Atlantic Ocean. Climatic conditions vary from hot and wet in the tropical rainforest of the Amazon basin to temperate in the savannah grasslands of the central and southern uplands, which have warm summers and mild winters. In Rio de Janeiro temperatures are generally between 17°C (63°F) and 29°C (85°F). The official language is Portuguese. Almost all of the inhabitants profess Christianity, and about 78% are adherents of the Roman Catholic Church. The national flag (proportions 7 by 10) is green, bearing, at the centre, a yellow diamond containing a blue celestial globe with 26 white five-pointed stars (one for each of Brazil's states), arranged in the pattern of the southern firmament, below an equatorial scroll with the motto 'Ordem e Progresso' ('Order and Progress'), and a single star above the scroll. The capital is Brasília.

Recent History

Formerly a Portuguese possession, Brazil became an independent monarchy in 1822, and a republic in 1889. A federal constitution for the United States of Brazil was adopted in 1891. Following social unrest in the 1920s, the economic crisis of 1930 resulted in a major revolt, led by Dr Getúlio Vargas, who was installed as President. He governed the country as a benevolent dictator until forced to resign by the armed forces in December 1945. During Vargas's populist rule, Brazil enjoyed internal stability and steady economic progress. He established a strongly authoritarian corporate state, similar to fascist regimes in Europe, but in 1942 Brazil entered the Second World War on the side of the Allies.

A succession of ineffectual presidential terms (including another by Vargas, who was re-elected in 1950) failed to establish stable government in the late 1940s and early 1950s. President Jânio Quadros, elected in 1960, resigned after only seven months in office, and in September 1961 the Vice-President, João Goulart, was sworn in as President. Military leaders suspected Goulart, the leader of the Partido Trabalhista Brasileiro (PTB), of communist sympathies, and they were reluctant to let him succeed to the presidency. As a compromise, the Constitution was amended to restrict the powers of the President and to provide for a Prime Minister. However, following the appointment of three successive premiers during a 16-month period of mounting political crisis, the system was rejected when a referendum, conducted in January 1963, approved a return to the presidential system of government.

Following a period of economic crisis, exacerbated by allegations of official corruption, the left-wing regime of President Goulart was overthrown in April 1964 by a bloodless right-wing military coup led by Gen. (later Marshal) Humberto Castelo Branco, the Army Chief of Staff, who was promptly elected President by the National Congress (Congresso Nacional). In October 1965 President Castelo Branco assumed dictatorial powers, and all political parties were banned. In December, however, two artificially created parties, the pro-Government Aliança Renovadora Nacional (ARENA) and the opposition Movimento Democrático Brasileiro (MDB), were granted official recognition. President Castelo Branco nominated as his successor the Minister of War, Marshal Artur da Costa e Silva, who was elected in October 1966 and took office in March 1967 as President of the redesignated Federative Republic of Brazil (a new Constitution was introduced simultaneously). The ailing President da Costa e Silva was forced to resign in September 1969 and was replaced by a triumvirate of military leaders.

The military regime granted the President wide-ranging powers to rule by decree. In October 1969 the ruling junta introduced a revised Constitution, vesting executive authority in an indirectly elected President. The Congresso Nacional, suspended since December 1968, was recalled and elected Gen. Emílio Garrastazú Médici as President. Médici was succeeded as President by Gen. Ernesto Geisel and Gen. João Baptista de Figueiredo, respectively. Despite the attempts of both Presidents to pursue a policy of *abertura*, or opening to democratization, opposition to military rule intensified throughout the 1970s and early 1980s. In November 1982 the government-sponsored Partido Democrático Social (PDS) suffered significant losses at elections to the Câmara dos Deputados (Chamber of Deputies), state governorships and municipal councils. However, the PDS secured a majority of seats in the Senado Federal (Federal Senate) and, owing to pre-election legislation, seemed set to enjoy a guaranteed majority in the electoral college, scheduled to choose a successor to Gen. Figueiredo in 1985.

However, in July 1984 Vice-President Antônio Chaves de Mendonça and the influential Marco de Oliveira Maciel, a former Governor of Pernambuco, formed an alliance of liberal PDS members with members of the Partido do Movimento Democrático Brasileiro (PMDB), which, in December, became an official political party, the Partido Frente Liberal (PFL). This offered the opposition a genuine opportunity to defeat the PDS in the electoral college and at the presidential election, conducted in January 1985, the PFL candidate, Tancredo Neves (Prime Minister in 1961–62) was elected as Brazil's first civilian President for 21 years. However, Neves died before he could be inaugurated and, as a result, the PFL vice-presidential candidate, José Sarney, took office as President in April. President Sarney affirmed his commitment to fulfilling the objectives of the late President-designate. In May the Congresso Nacional approved a constitutional amendment restoring direct elections by universal suffrage.

The introduction in February 1986 of an anti-inflation programme, the Cruzado Plan, proved, initially, to be successful. Support for the Government was demonstrated in November at elections to the Congresso Nacional, which was to operate as a Constitutional Assembly (Assembléia Constitucional). In June 1988 the Assembly approved a presidential mandate of five years. The first round of voting for the presidential election was provisionally set for 15 November 1989, thereby enabling Sarney to remain in office until March 1990. This *de facto* victory for the President precipitated a series of resignations by some of the leading members of the PMDB, who subsequently formed a new centre-left party, the Partido da Social Democracia Brasileira (PSDB). The Constitution was approved by the Congresso Nacional on 22 September 1988 and was promulgated in early October. Among its 245 articles were provisions transferring many hitherto presidential powers to the legislature. In addition, censorship was abolished, as was the National Security Law, whereby many political dissidents had been detained; the minimum voting age was lowered to 16 years; and the principle of habeas corpus was recognized. However, the Constitution offered no guarantees of land reform, and was thought by many to be nationalistic and protectionist.

Brazil's first presidential election by direct voting since 1960 took place on 15 November 1989. The main contenders were the conservative Fernando Collor de Mello, of the newly formed Partido de Reconstrução Nacional (PRN), Luiz Inácio Lula da Silva of the left-wing Partido dos Trabalhadores (PT) and Leonel Brizola of the centre-left Partido Democrático Trabalhista (PDT). A second round in December, contested by the two leading candidates, Collor de Mello and da Silva, was won by Collor de Mello, with 53% of the votes cast. Following his inauguration on 15 March 1990, the new President announced an ambitious programme of economic reform, entitled 'New Brazil' (known as the 'Collor Plan'), with the principal aim of reducing inflation, which had reached a monthly rate of more than 80%. A new currency, the cruzeiro (to replace, at par, the novo cruzado) was also introduced. A second economic plan, presented as an intensification of the Collor Plan, was implemented in February 1991. In March Collor de Mello announced a new Plan for National Reconstruction, which envisaged further deregulation and rationalization of many state-controlled areas, including the ports, and the communications and fuel sectors.

Collor de Mello's position became increasingly precarious towards the end of 1991, after allegations of mismanagement of federal funds were made against his wife and several associates in the President's home state of Alagoas. During informal multi-party negotiations in September 1991, the President attempted to achieve greater congressional consensus and to reinforce his own mandate. In the same month, Collor de Mello presented a comprehensive series of proposals for constitutional amendment before the Congresso. Nevertheless, allegations of high-level corruption persisted into 1992 and the President failed to dispel suspicions sufficiently to attract the wider political participation in government necessary to facilitate the passage of legislation through an increasingly ineffectual Congresso Nacional. In May the President became the focus of further allegations which appeared to implicate him in a number of corrupt practices orchestrated by Paulo César Farias, Collor de Mello's 1989 election campaign treasurer. As a result, the Congresso Nacional established a special commission of inquiry to investigate the affair and in early September, after the commission had delivered its report, and bolstered by massive popular support, a congressional committee authorized the initiation of impeachment proceedings against the President. On 29 September the Câmara dos Deputados voted to proceed with the impeachment of the President for abuses of authority and position, prompting the immediate resignation of the Cabinet. On 2 October Collor de Mello surrendered authority to Vice-President Itamar Franco for a six-month period, pending the final pronouncement regarding his future in office, to be decided by the Senado.

In December 1992 the Senado voted overwhelmingly to proceed with Collor de Mello's impeachment and to indict the President for 'crimes of responsibility'. Within minutes of the opening of the impeachment trial on 29 December, however, Collor de Mello announced his resignation from the presidency. Itamar Franco was immediately sworn in to serve the remainder of Collor de Mello's term. On the following day the Senado, which had agreed to continue with proceedings against Collor de Mello, announced that the former President's political rights (including immunity from prosecution) were to be removed. In January 1993 the Supreme Court announced that Collor de Mello was to stand trial as an ordinary citizen on charges of 'passive corruption and criminal association', and in December the Court endorsed the Senado's eight-year ban on his holding public office. In December 1994, however, the tribunal voted to acquit Collor de Mello of the charges, owing to insufficient evidence. In January 1998 the former President was cleared of charges of illegal enrichment.

In April 1993 the PDT announced its withdrawal from the ruling coalition, following Franco's decision to proceed with the privatization of the prestigious national steel company, the Companhia Siderúrgica Nacional (CSN). In August the Partido Socialista Brasileiro (PSB) also withdrew from the coalition, and in the following month the PMDB national council narrowly defeated a motion to end its association with the Government. The fragility of the Government was exacerbated by a new corruption scandal in October, in which numerous senior politicians were implicated in a fraudulent scheme in which political influence was allegedly exercised in order to secure state projects for individual construction companies, in exchange for bribes. In April 1994 the Congresso Nacional concluded a review of the Constitution, having adopted just six amendments, including a reduction in the length of the presidential term from five to four years.

Allegations of corruption and misconduct preceding the elections in October 1994 forced the replacement of the vice-presidential running mates of both Minister of the Economy Fernando Henrique Cardoso and of da Silva and the withdrawal from the contest of the PL's presidential candidate. Cardoso, whose candidacy was supported by the PFL, the PTB, the Partido Liberal (PL) and the business community, won the presidential contest in the first round, following a campaign that had focused largely on the success of his economic initiatives, which included the introduction of a new currency, the real.

Cardoso was inaugurated as President on 1 January 1995. The multi-party composition of his new Cabinet demonstrated the new President's need to maintain a broad base of congressional support in order to secure prompt endorsement for proposed constitutional reform of the taxation and social security systems. However, opposition to the ongoing programme of economic stabilization and to renewed efforts by the Government to introduce constitutional amendments, including those that would end state monopolies in the telecommunications and petroleum sectors, resulted, in May 1995, in a general strike. The President's decision to order military intervention in a number of crucial petroleum refineries was widely interpreted as evidence of the Government's intent to undermine the concerted action of the political opposition and the trade unions. However, a number of amendments, including to the petroleum and telecommunication sectors, were subsequently approved by the Senado.

By December 1995, however, Cardoso's integrity had been seriously compromised by the alleged involvement of a number of his political associates in irregular financial transactions, and by an influence-peddling scandal arising from the award to a US company of the contract for development of an Amazon Regional Surveillance System (Sivam). Meanwhile, investigation of the so-called 'pink folder' of politicians continued during 1996, as the banking sector was plunged into further crisis. In March it was revealed that the Government had withheld details of a US $5,000m. fraud perpetrated at the Banco Nacional a decade earlier. Moreover, it emerged that the Government had extended a recent credit facility of $5,800m. to the bank in order to facilitate its merger with UNIBANCO in 1995.

Cardoso's own popularity benefited from the success of the Government's attempts to control inflation. In June 1996 the Government announced details of the next phase of its massive divestment programme. Several companies in the power sector, 31 ports and the prestigious mining company Companhia Vale do Rio Doce (CVRD) were among those state concerns to be offered for sale. In July the Government announced that the state telecommunications company, Telebrás, together with large sections of the rail and power networks, would be privatized by the end of 1998. Further reductions in public spending were announced in August and October. In March 1997 legislation was approved ending the long-standing monopoly of Petróleo Brasileiro (Petrobras) over the petroleum industry. In November legislation to reform the civil service was also approved by the Congresso.

In mid-1997 a constitutional amendment to permit the President to stand for re-election in 1998 was approved by the Senado, and was swiftly ratified by Cardoso. In July an investigation by the Senado into a financial scandal arising from fraudulent bond issues had concluded that 20 prominent politicians and senior officials (including three state governors, the mayor of São Paulo, Celso Pitta, and his predecessor, Paulo Maluf) had been involved in a criminal operation. A total of 161 financial institutions, including Banco Bradesco, Brazil's largest private bank, were implicated in the scandal. In January 1998 Celso Pitta was found guilty of fraud; he finally stood down in 2000, after being impeached. In October 2004 Maluf was found guilty of sending R $5,000m. of public funds abroad. He also faced other charges of corruption, and was arrested in September 2005.

Despite his declared commitment to further economic austerity measures, in October 1998 Cardoso, again the PSDB's candidate, became the first President to be re-elected for a second consecutive term. At the concurrent legislative elections, the PSDB also performed well, securing 99 of the 513 seats in the lower chamber, while its electoral allies—the PFL, PMDB, Partido Progressista (PP) and PTB—won a total of 278 seats, bringing the coalition's total representation to 377.

In January 1999 Itamar Franco, the newly elected Governor of Minas Gerais, declared that the state was defaulting on its debt to the federal Government, indirectly precipitating the devaluation of the Brazilian currency. In the same month, however, both chambers of the Congresso Nacional endorsed long-proposed reforms to the country's munificent pension system, considerably enhancing the prospects of President Cardoso's programme of fiscal austerity. However, the Government suffered a set-back in March following the withdrawal of the PTB from the ruling coalition. The administration came under further pressure in May when the PFL announced its intention to present its own candidate at the next presidential election. In August demonstrations against the Government's economic and social policies culminated in the arrival in Brasília of as many as 100,000 marchers, comprising political opponents led by the PT, trade unionists and landless individuals.

In October 1999 a congressional commission of inquiry into allegations of organized crime exposed a nation-wide criminal network that allegedly encompassed politicians, government officials, judges, police officers, business executives and banking officials. Embarrassed by the scale of the revelations (which extended to reports of drugs-trafficking within the parliament building), President Cardoso announced the establishment of a new anti-corruption force to combat organized crime. In an effort to improve accountability and to strengthen congressional powers of investigation, the Senado approved a constitutional amendment to restrict presidential use of provisional measures, to which successive Governments had frequently resorted as a means to circumvent the cumbersome legislative process.

Investigations into government corruption and organized crime continued during 2001 and 2002. In October 2001 Jader Barbalho, the President of the Senado, resigned his post after it emerged that he had been involved in corrupt activities while Governor of the state of Pará in the 1980s. Meanwhile, in April the credibility of the ruling coalition was further undermined by the unauthorized release of telephone transcripts secretly recorded by police during investigations into the disappearance of some US $830m. from the Amazonian development agency, Superintendência do Desenvolvimento da Amazônia (SUDAM), with which Barbalho was personally connected. In the following month two senators and one cabinet minister resigned after allegations of corruption.

In the presidential election of 6 October 2002 Lula da Silva, once again the PT's candidate, secured 46% of the votes cast in the first round ballot. José Serra, the government-backed PMDB candidate, was second placed with 23% of the ballot, followed by PSB nominee Anthony Garotinho with 18% and Ciro Gomes, the candidate of the centre-left PPS, who secured 12% of the ballot. As no candidate had achieved the required 50%, a second ballot between the two leading candidates was held on 27 October. Aided by the support of Garotinho, Gomes and Sarney, da Silva secured 61% of the votes cast in this round (the largest ever proportion of the vote since the system's introduction in 1945), while Serra attracted 39%. In congressional elections, also held on 6 October, da Silva's party took 91 of the 513 seats in the Câmara dos Deputados and increased its representation in the Senado to 14 seats. The PFL secured 84 lower-house seats, followed by the PMDB with 74 seats and the PSDB with 71 seats. The PFL's representation in the Senado remained unchanged, at 19 seats; however, the number of PMDB senators decreased, from 27 seats to 19, as did the PSDB's upper-house representation, from 16 to 11 seats. President da Silva took office on 2 January 2003. Owing to the fractured nature of the new Congresso Nacional, the new President needed support from the centrist parties in order to form a Government, and duly entered a coalition agreement with the PFL and the PMDB. Da Silva's new Cabinet was dominated by members of the PT, although it also included representatives from the PPS, PDT, PSB and the PL.

Upon assuming the presidency, da Silva affirmed his intention to proceed with a promised 'zero hunger' poverty alleviation programme, to effect pension reform, and to modernize Brazil's tax system. In addition to the postponement of a large defence project, the new President announced immediate spending cuts in all areas of government, in order to fund the anti-hunger campaign. The public sector social security system, whereby civil servants could retire on much greater pensions than were paid to private sector workers, was widely seen as a symptom of the inequality within Brazilian society. The Government's proposed reform of the sector would make provision for the taxing of pensions and raise the retirement age. The proposals provoked discontent among government workers and the PT's traditional allies in the trade union movement, and in early July 2003 a one-day strike was held in protest, in which, it was claimed, over one-half of government employees participated. Nevertheless, in early August the Câmara dos Deputados approved the reforms, although the Government was forced to make several alterations to the legislation; it received senate approval in December. It was estimated that the reforms would reduce the social security deficit by R $50,000m. over 20 years.

President da Silva also promised major reform of the tax system. The proposed changes, announced in April 2003, were intended to rationalize the existing system, reduce levies on industry and export sectors, and improve collection. They included standardizing the rate of value-added tax (which varied between states), making permanent the temporary financial tax introduced by the Cardoso Government, and, in an attempt to ensure the support of regional Governors, replacing the federal property tax with a state levy. In September the Câmara dos Deputados approved the reforms. In mid-December the Senado followed suit, but not before the Government was again forced to make concessions to legislators and state Governors. In January 2004 the first of three stages of tax reform came into effect.

In January 2004 President da Silva effected his first major ministerial reshuffle. He significantly changed his social policy team and broadened the governing coalition to include two ministers from the centrist PMDB. In the following month evidence emerged that the former deputy of Cabinet Chief José Dirceu, Waldomiro Diniz, had offered government contracts in exchange for 2002 presidential campaign contributions from the head of an illegal gambling operation in the state of Rio de Janeiro. Diniz was dismissed from his post and a criminal investigation begun, as well as, eventually, a federal parliamentary investigation into the affair. The revelations prompted President da Silva to issue a decree outlawing bingo halls, although the ruling was overturned by the Senado in early May. The Government was also criticized for obstructing the federal inquiry. The final report of the parliamentary investigation into the scandal was published in June 2006 (see below): it recommended that Diniz, as well as former Minister of Finance Antônio Palocci (see below) and a close associate of the President, Paulo Okamoto, be indicted on corruption charges.

In June 2004 following a difficult passage through the Câmara dos Deputados, the Government's proposal to increase the minimum wage by R $20 per week was rejected by the Senado, which instead proposed an increase of R $35. (Da Silva had pledged to double the minimum wage by 2007, but claimed that the Government could not raise the extra revenue needed to pay minimum wage-linked pensions.) In July the Central Unica dos Trabalhadores (CUT) trade-union confederation organized marches across the country in protest at the Government's economic performance. Furthermore, from August the passing of legislation in the Câmara came to a standstill after deputies refused to vote on a number of presidential decrees (which took precedence over other legislation). The deputies were protesting at a controversial decree earlier in the month granting cabinet status to the Governor of the Central Bank, Henrique Meirelles. This gave him a level of legal immunity in relation to a senate investigation into alleged tax evasion. The congressional deadlock, which threatened the passage of crucial government legislation (see below), was only ended in November after the da Silva administration agreed to pledge R $600m. to projects sponsored by members of the Congresso Nacional. Most of the Government's ambitious judicial reforms were approved by the Senado later that month. The proposals included the creation of a supervisory council for the judiciary, and gave the Supreme Court power to set binding precedents for lower courts. In the following month a law allowing for joint public-private investment in infrastructure projects was approved by both legislative chambers in the same day. The approval of the legislation was an integral part of the Government's plan to increase foreign investment in the country.

In early November 2004 the Minister of Defence, José Viegas, resigned in protest at what was seen by many as an attempt by the military to justify the torture that took place during the period of military rule in Brazil. The Vice-President, José Alencar Gomes da Silva, assumed responsibility for the defence portfolio. In late 2004 divisions within the governing coalition emerged: in mid-December the Minister of National Integration, Ciro Gomes, resigned after his party, the PPS, announced its departure from the coalition, accusing the Government of being too 'conservative'. Then, one day later, members of the PMDB, which was the biggest party in the Senado and the second largest in the Câmara, also voted to leave the coalition Government, citing da Silva's failure to pursue an active social policy. The vote, however, which was instigated by right-wing members of the party, exposed fissures within the PMDB when its two cabinet members and several of its senators and deputies refused to abide by the decision (the vote was ruled invalid by the high court). In September further allegations of corruption within the government ranks emerged: it was announced that more than 500 deputies and government officials were being investigated as part of an inquiry into money-laundering at the Banco do Estado do Paraná (Banestado) during the 1990s. In December a congressional investigation recommended that 91 of these be indicted. Gustavo Franco, a former governor of the Central Bank, and Celso Pitta, the former mayor of São Paulo, were among those named.

In early June 2005 a videotape was shown on national television that appeared to show proof that bribes had been offered to employees of the state-run postal service, the Empresa Brasileira de Correios e Telégrafos, and the reinsurance company,

IRB-Brasil Resseguros, in return for contracts. A recipient of the bribes accused Roberto Jefferson, the President of the PTB, of organizing the cash incentive scheme; Jefferson denied the allegation, claiming it was politically motivated, and, in turn, accused the PT leadership of running a system of institutional bribery, known as the *mensalão*, in 2003 and 2004. This was a scheme whereby deputies from other parties allegedly received a monthly allowance for supporting government-sponsored legislation. Jefferson cited President da Silva's Cabinet Chief, José Dirceu, as the organizer of the *mensalão*. On 14 June 2005, appearing before a Câmara dos Deputados ethics committee, Jefferson repeated this accusation. Two days later Dirceu resigned, to be followed in the following month by Sílvio Pereira, Delúbio Soares and José Genoíno, respectively, Secretary-General, Treasurer and President of the PT. Pereira and Soares stepped down in early July after being implicated by Jefferson in the scandal, while Genoíno resigned several days later after an assistant to his brother (a regional PT treasurer) was arrested in possession of US $100,000 in cash. Genoíno was replaced on an interim basis by Tarso Genro, who resigned his post as Minister of Education. Dirceu was replaced as Cabinet Chief by Dilma Rousseff, a former PT activist who had previously held the mines and energy portfolio. In order to maintain the support of the PMDB, President da Silva was forced to effect further cabinet reshuffles in July, which increased the number of ministries held by that party, at the expense of the PT. However, the Minister of Social Security, Romero Jucá, of the PMDB, was replaced after he had been implicated in a separate corruption scandal concerning irregular loans.

Also in July 2005, Marcos Valério de Souza, an advertising executive, appeared before the congressional committee investigating the *mensalão* affair; it was alleged that the bribes paid to deputies were laundered through accounts held in his name. The committee subsequently recommended that Valério be arrested. In mid-July, in what was widely seen as an attempt to slow down the investigation, a judge ordered that the inquiry should be carried out by the Supreme Court, rather than the police.

In early August 2005 Valdemar Costa Neto, the President of the PL, a party allied to the Government, resigned owing to his alleged involvement in the *mensalão* scheme. Following his resignation Costa Neto claimed that the President had been aware of the irregular practices in his party. President da Silva's problems worsened on 22 August when his Minister of Finance, Antônio Palocci, was also accused of having accepted illegal payments from a waste management company while he was mayor of Ribeirão Preto. At the end of the month Roberto Jefferson further alleged that the PT also received payments from a state-owned electricity company. The President was dealt a further blow in early September when his Vice-President and Minister of Defence, José Alencar Gomes da Silva, announced he was leaving the PL, citing the party's involvement in the *mensalão* scandal (he subsequently joined the Partido Municipalista Renovador, a recently created party linked to the Igreja Universal do Reino de Deus).

A report published in early September 2005 by the two congressional investigation committees into the *mensalão* and post office corruption scandals recommended that 18 deputies, including José Dirceu, be impeached for their role in the affairs. All but one of the deputies belonged to the PT or allied parties. On 14 September the legislature voted to dismiss Roberto Jefferson from the Câmara dos Deputados. One week later Sergio Cavalcanti, the President of the Câmara dos Deputados (and a member of the PP), resigned following allegations that he too had accepted bribes. The case was, however, unconnected to the *mensalão* scandal. Later that month the Government's position appeared to improve when Aldo Rebelo, a member of the Partido Comunista do Brasil (PC do B) and a coalition ally, who had previously held a ministerial post, was elected to succeed Cavalcanti. A further indication that the da Silva administration had not suffered lasting damage was the election, in October, of Ricardo Berzoini to the PT presidency. Berzoini represented the *Campo Majoritário* faction of the PT, seen by many as responsible for bringing the party to power. The faction supported the Government's policies, but its leadership had been implicated in the corruption scandals. In the same month Eduardo Azeredo resigned as President of the opposition PSDB amid allegations that he had also accepted money from Marcos Valério de Souza to fund a gubernatorial election in 1998.

In November 2005 the congressional committee investigating the corruption scandals concluded its inquiry. It found that the PT had given money to deputies from pro-Government parties in return for legislative support. It also reported that public funds had been illegally transferred through the Banco do Brasil to the PT. It recommended that former PT Treasurer Soares be charged in relation to the bribes and related money-laundering. In early December José Dirceu was finally dismissed from the Câmara dos Deputados after deputies voted to impeach him. It was subsequently revealed that he was also to be questioned by the police in connection with the murder in 2002 of Celso Daniel, the mayor of Santo André in the state of São Paulo. Although a new bankruptcy law and legislation on joint public-private investment were approved in early 2005, the ongoing corruption scandals that dogged the Government throughout the year, together with the resulting congressional investigations, prevented the Government advancing its legislative programme.

After being implicated in a series of corruption scandals, Palocci finally resigned as Minister of Finance in late March 2006 when it was revealed that he had leaked the financial details of a man who had accused him of frequenting parties also attended by prostitutes. He was replaced by Guido Mantega, President of the Banco Nacional do Desenvolvimento Econômico e Social and a former minister. Mantega announced that he would continue existing economic policy, although he had previously been a critic of Palocci's monetary programme. At the end of the month it was announced that six members of the Cabinet would resign in order to contest senatorial, congressional and gubernatorial elections due in October. Notably, Waldir Pires replaced José Alencar Gomes da Silva as Minister of Defence (although Alencar remained Vice-President).

In May 2006 a sustained outbreak of violence in São Paulo paralysed the city and led to an estimated 138 deaths (44 of whom were police officers). The rioting had been prompted by an organized uprising in gaols in the region by gang members unhappy at being transferred to higher-security institutions. The Senado reacted to the violence by approving stricter legislation on gang membership and organized crime. Nevertheless, a similiar wave of co-ordinated violent crime broke out in Rio de Janeiro at the end of December. It was alleged that imprisoned gang leaders ordered other gang members to instigate lawlessness in protest at being moved to prisons in different parts of the country. Some 25 people were murdered during the riots, including eight passengers on a bus that was set ablaze. The Government deployed over 20,000 police officers in the city in an attempt to restore law and order. A further 21 people, all thought to be gang members, were killed in a further outbreak of violence in the city in April 2007. In response to the increase in lawlessness, in June the Government initiated a security plan, intended to combat youth crime in particular, and announced an expansion of the National Security Force, an élite federal body that provided additional troops to over-deployed state police forces.

Corruption scandals involving Brazilian politicians, and da Silva's Government in particular, continued to emerge in the months preceding the presidential election of October 2006. As well as the publication of the congressional investigation's final report into the bingo hall scandal (see above) in June, in the same month the Congresso agreed to establish a commission to investigate allegations that, in 2003, federal health officials accepted bribes in return for buying ambulances and other emergency equipment at inflated prices. As well as the police investigation requesting interviews with 170 members of the Congresso, in July the former PT health minister, Humberto Costa, was implicated in the affair. Then, in September, President da Silva's electoral campaign manager, Ricardo Berzoini, and a senior adviser, Freud Godoy, resigned after being accused of attempting to incriminate the PSDB's José Serra, a candidate in the São Paulo gubernatorial contest, in the ambulance-purchasing scandal.

In spite of the widespread corruption allegations levelled at his Government, da Silva continued to enjoy high levels of popularity among voters in the months preceding the 2006 presidential election. However, in the first round of voting, held on 1 October, da Silva failed to secure the necessary amount of votes to avoid a run-off ballot: the incumbent President garnered 48.6% of the valid votes cast, while Geraldo Alckmin, the former Governor of the state of São Paulo and the PSDB's candidate, won 41.6% of the ballot. The next highest placed nominee was Heloísa Helena of the Partido Socialismo e Liberdade, with just 6.9% of the votes. Helena was a former PT member who stood as an anti-corruption candidate. It was widely accepted that the numerous scandals had cost da Silva a first round victory, as well as the President's refusal to participate in a televised debate with other nominees in the week before the ballot. Nevertheless, in a second round ballot on 29 October da Silva comfortably secured a second term in office, attracting 58.3m. votes, some 60.8% of the valid ballot, compared with the 37.5m. votes (39.2% of the total) garnered by Alckmin. In the congressional elections, also held on 1 October, the PMDB (which did not put forward a presidential candidate) won the most seats, 89, in the 513-seat lower chamber, while the PT returned 83 deputies. The PSDB and the PFL both secured 65 seats, followed by the PP with 42 and the PFL (an ally of the PSDB) with 27. Some 27 seats were contested in the 81-seat Senado: following voting the PMDB held 20 upper-house seats, the PFL and the PSDB won 16 each, the PT secured 12 seats, and the PTB and the PDT won four senators each.

Lacking an absolute majority in the Congresso, the President immediately announced that he intended to govern 'by consensus' in his second term. To this end, in November 2006 he secured the congressional support of the PT and of most of the factions of the internally divided PMDB. However, the parties were ideologically at odds and it seemed unlikely that the consensus would endure. Indeed, in the same month, a dispute arose over the post of President of the Câmara: traditionally the position was filled by a representative of the party with the most seats, which was the PMDB, but the PT maintained that as its deputies had secured a greater number of votes, it should be allowed to nominate the new speaker. At the beginning of February 2007 Aldo Chinaglia, the candidate supported by the PT and the PMDB, secured the lower house presidency. Chinaglia defeated the incumbent speaker, Aldo Rebeldo of the PC do B, in a second round of voting following a bitterly fought contest.

President da Silva was inaugurated on 1 January 2007. The President declared that his main priority in his second term in office would be economic growth and continuing the poverty alleviation programmes of his first term, in particular the successful Bolsa Família programme, from which, by the end of 2006, some 11m. families were expected to have benefited. He also pledged to address the problem of violent crime, prompted by the violence in Rio de Janeiro at the end of 2006. Da Silva carried out a long-awaited reallocation of cabinet portfolios in March 2007: the PMDB increased its ministerial representation to five portfolios as the President attempted to appease all the factions of the party. The PMDB's greater prominence in the Cabinet was at the expense of smaller parties in the governing coalition, particularly the PSB and the Partido Republicano Brasileiro (as the Partido Municipalista Renovador had become in 2006). The PT's cabinet representation was also reduced, although PT appointees remained in the more important ministries.

Cases of corruption continued to affect the Government into da Silva's second term of office. In May 2007 a police investigation into embezzlement of federal funds implicated the Minister of Mines and Energy, Silas Rondeau, as well as two state governors. Rondeau resigned in response to the accusation, although he maintained his innocence, and was replaced in January 2008 by Edison Lobão. Later in May 2007 an article in the magazine *Veja* alleged that the President of the Senado, Renan Calheiros, a close ally of da Silva, had accepted bribes from the construction company Mendes Júnior. Subsequent newspaper reports accused Calheiros of producing false evidence in his efforts to deny the allegations. Following its investigation into the affair the Senado's ethical council recommended the impeachment of Calheiros, who had resisted repeated demands for his resignation; however, in a secret ballot held in September a substantial majority of senators voted not to indict the chamber's President. Calheiros did agree to a temporary leave of absence in early October while investigations into the allegations continued. After evidence emerged implicating him in further illegal practices, in late November the ethical council again recommended that he be deprived of his seat in the upper house; however, Calheiros resigned as President in early December, shortly before the Senado voted against his impeachment. (He was replaced by Garibaldi Alves, Filho.) The controversy surrounding Calheiros contributed to the Senado's rejection, later in December, of legislation to extend a tax on financial transactions, the Contribuição Provisória sobre Movimentação Financeira, for a further four-year period, represented the Government's first major defeat in the Congresso Nacional since da Silva gained power. Meanwhile, Walfrido dos Mares Guia, the Minister of Institutional Relations—responsible for relations between the executive and the legislature—also resigned in November after being accused by the public prosecution service of fraud in a 1998 gubernatorial election, and was succeeded by José Múcio Monteiro, Filho.

In July 2007 a passenger aircraft crashed into a building at Congonhas airport in São Paulo, resulting in the deaths of 200 people. Together with another fatal mid-air crash in September 2006, the disaster highlighted major weaknesses in the country's air traffic control system, which was controlled by the Ministry of Defence. Da Silva subsequently dismissed the Minister of Defence, Waldir Pires, and appointed Nelson Jobim as his successor.

In August 2007 the Supreme Court indicted 40 people on charges related to the *mensalão* affair, including Jefferson, Dirceu, Soares, Genoíno and Valério. In October the same court ruled that parliamentary seats and other elected offices belonged to the parties that were elected to fill them, rather than the individual office-holders. The ruling, which extended a decision of the Higher Electoral Court given in February applying only to the Câmara dos Deputados, was expected to lead to greater political stability by ending the common practice whereby politicians would change parties in exchange for favours.

From the mid-1990s the Landless Peasant Movement, the Movimento dos Trabalhadores Rurais Sem-Terra (MST), came to increasing prominence. During 1995 the MST organized a number of illegal occupations of disputed land in support of demands for an acceleration of the Government's programme of expropriation of uncultivated land for distribution to landless rural families. Rapidly deteriorating relations between the authorities and the MST were exacerbated in April 1996 by the violent intervention of the local military police in a demonstration in the State of Pará, which resulted in the deaths of 19 demonstrators. Widespread public outrage prompted the Government to announce new measures to accelerate the process of land reform in April 1997. In early 1998 the MST intensified its campaign for land reform and in March thousands of activists occupied government premises, a campaign that led to the suspension of São Paulo's land-expropriation proceedings. In May 2000, in one of the largest demonstrations in history by the movement, over 30,000 members of the MST occupied a number of public buildings, including the Ministry of Finance and the Ministry of Agrarian Reform, to demand land reform. The occupations prompted the Government to introduce legislation preventing further land invasions. In October it was announced that loans were to be made available for those already settled on their own land.

Following the election of Lula da Silva to the presidency in October 2002, the MST, traditional supporters of the PT, agreed to a temporary suspension of illegal land occupations. However, in March 2003 the MST declared its autonomy from the Government amid concerns that its policies were more conservative than expected, and resumed its policy of land invasions. In January 2007 the Government announced that it had reached 95% of its landless resettlement targets in 2003–06; however, this figure was disputed by landless organizations. Following a truce with the PT during President da Silva's re-election campaign in 2006, in April 2007 the MST again resumed its policy of land invasions.

The murder, in December 1988, of Francisco (Chico) Mendes, the leader of the rubber-tappers' union and a pioneering ecologist brought Brazil's environmental problems to international attention. Widespread concern was expressed that large-scale development projects, together with the 'slash-and-burn' farming techniques of cattle ranchers, peasant smallholders and loggers, and the release of large amounts of mercury into the environment by an estimated 60,000 gold prospectors (or *garimpeiros*) in the Amazon region, presented a serious threat to the survival of both the indigenous Indians and the rainforest. International criticism of the Government's poor response to the threat to the environment persisted into the 2000s. Of particular concern to many international observers was the plight of the Yanomami Indian tribe in Roraima. It was estimated that, since the arrival of the *garimpeiros* in the region, some 10%–15% of the Yanomami's total population had been exterminated as a result of pollution and disease, introduced to the area by the gold prospectors. Legislation to provide greater protection for Brazil's natural resources, through the establishment of criminal penalties for illegal activities, was introduced in February 1998. In August 2002 Cardoso's Government created the world's biggest national park in the Tumucumaque Mountains, with funding promised by the World Bank and the UN's Global Environmental Facility. In September 2003 President da Silva was criticized by environmentalists following the announcement of a four-year government infrastructure plan, which aimed to increase electricity output and improve transport links in the Amazon region.

It was claimed that the plan would accelerate rainforest destruction. In January 2004 the Government announced that, despite protests by farmers, it would continue its plans to create an Indian reservation of 1.75m. ha in Roraima. In March 2005 the human rights organization Amnesty International issued a report criticizing the failure of the Government to halt the ill treatment of Brazil's indigenous populations (a second report published in December also condemned the lack of progress in stopping extra-judicial police killings).

In 1990 a series of bilateral trade agreements was signed with Argentina, representing the first stage in a process which led to the establishment of a Southern Cone Common Market (Mercado Comum do Sul—Mercosul, see p. 391), also to include Paraguay and Uruguay. Mercosul came into effect on 1 January 1995, following the signing, by the Presidents of the four member nations, of the Ouro Prêto Protocol. Customs barriers on 80%–85% of mutually exchanged goods were removed immediately.

In May 2006 relations between Brazil and Bolivia threatened to become strained after President Evo Morales of Bolivia announced the effective nationalization of his country's hydrocarbons industry. The state-owned Petrobras was a significant investor in Bolivia's petroleum and gas sectors: although the Brazilian Government accepted the 82% tax increase on profits, it refused to accept any increases in the cost of gas imports, or any expropriation of Petrobras assets in Bolivia.

At the fifth Ministerial Conference of the World Trade Organization (WTO), held in Cancún, Mexico, in September 2003 Brazil led a group of countries opposed to the policy of subsidizing agricultural products as practised by the USA and the European Union. This group of developing nations (which came to be known as the 'G-20' group) demanded an end to subsidies in industrialized countries, in return for opening up their markets. In October 2003 President da Silva and his Argentine counterpart, Néstor Kirchner, signed the so-called 'Buenos Aires Consensus' on regional co-operation, which committed both countries to a common stance in negotiations towards the proposed Free Trade Area of the Americas (FTAA). However, in early 2008 negotiations remained at an impasse; in November 2005 the so-called Fourth Summit of the Americas, in Argentina, had ended without any further agreement. In January 2004 Brazil commenced a two-year term as a member of the UN's Security Council and began to campaign for a permanent seat on the Security Council. The da Silva administration expanded trade links with Asia, particularly the People's Republic of China. In June 2004 Brazil sent 1,200 troops to Haiti to cope with the deteriorating security situation there, and took command of the UN peace-keeping troops stationed in the country.

In May 1994 Brazil declared its full adherence to the 1967 Tlatelolco Treaty for the non-proliferation of nuclear weapons in Latin America and the Caribbean. The Treaty was promulgated by presidential decree in September 1994. Brazil signed the international Treaty on the Non-Proliferation of Nuclear Weapons (see p. 109) in June 1997. President Cardoso ratified this and also the Comprehensive Test Ban Treaty (see p. 109) in July 1998.

Government

Under the 1988 Constitution, the country is a federal republic comprising 26 States and a Federal District (Brasília). Legislative power is exercised by the bicameral Congresso Nacional (National Congress), comprising the Senado Federal (Federal Senate—members elected by the majority principle in rotation for eight years) and the Câmara dos Deputados (Chamber of Deputies—members elected by a system of proportional representation for four years). The number of deputies is based on the size of the population. Election is by universal adult suffrage. Executive power is exercised by the President, elected by direct ballot for four years. The President appoints and leads the Cabinet. Each State has a directly elected Governor and an elected legislature. For the purposes of local government, the States are divided into municipalities.

Defence

Military service, lasting 12 months, is compulsory for men between 18 and 45 years of age. As assessed at November 2007, the armed forces totalled 367,901: army 238,200 (including 89,000 conscripts), navy 62,261 (including at least 11,000 conscripts) and air force 67,440. Public security forces number about 385,600. Defence expenditure for 2007 was budgeted at R $39,000m. In November 2007 the Government announced an increase of approximately 50% in defence expenditure for 2008.

Economic Affairs

In 2006, according to estimates by the World Bank, Brazil's gross national income (GNI), measured at average 2004–06 prices, was US $892,806m., equivalent to US $4,730 per head (or $8,800 per head on an international purchasing-power parity basis). During 1996–2006, it was estimated, the population increased at an average annual rate of 1.0%, while gross domestic product (GDP) per head increased, in real terms, by an average of 1.4% per year. Overall GDP increased, in real terms, at an average annual rate of 2.5% in 1996–2006; real GDP grew by 3.7% in 2006.

Agriculture (including hunting, forestry and fishing) engaged 20.5% of the economically active population in 2005, according to official figures, and contributed 5.1% of GDP in 2006. The principal cash crops are soya beans, coffee, tobacco, sugar cane and cocoa beans. Subsistence crops include wheat, maize, rice, potatoes, beans, cassava and sorghum. Beef and poultry production are also important, as is fishing (particularly tuna, crab and shrimp). In March 2005 the Câmara dos Deputados (Chamber of Deputies) approved legislation, already passed by the Senado (Senate), permitting the use of genetically modified crops. During 1996–2006, according to the World Bank, agricultural GDP increased at an average annual rate of 3.9%. Agricultural GDP increased by 5.2% in 2006.

Industry (including mining, manufacturing, construction and power) employed 21.4% of the working population in 2005 and provided 30.9% of GDP in 2006. During 1996–2006, according to the World Bank, industrial GDP increased at an average annual rate of 2.0%. Industrial GDP increased by 2.7% in 2006.

Mining contributed 4.0% of GDP in 2004. Mining GDP grew by 10.4% in 2002. The major mineral exports are iron ore (haematite—in terms of iron content, Brazil is the largest producer in the world), manganese, tin and aluminium. Gold, phosphates, platinum, uranium, copper and coal are also mined. In 2006 Brazil supplied an estimated 93.5% of the world's total output of columbium and was among the largest producers of bauxite, graphite, iron ore, manganese, niobium, tantalum and tin. Brazil's proven reserves of petroleum were put at 12,200m. barrels at December 2006. The discovery of significant oil deposits off the coast of Rio de Janeiro in November 2007 was expected to increase total reserves to an estimated 20,000m. barrels.

Manufacturing contributed 23.0% of GDP in 2004. In 2005 the sector engaged 14.1% of the economically active population. There is considerable state involvement in a broad range of manufacturing activity. While traditionally dominant areas, including textiles and clothing, footwear and food- and beverage-processing, continue to contribute a large share to the sector, more recent developments in the sector have resulted in the emergence of machinery and transport equipment (including road vehicles and components, passenger jet aircraft and specialist machinery for the petroleum industry), construction materials (especially iron and steel), wood and sugar cane derivatives, and chemicals and petrochemicals as significant new manufacturing activities. According to the World Bank, manufacturing GDP increased at an average rate of 1.7% per year in 1996–2006; the sector's GDP grew by 1.6% in 2006.

In 2004, according to the World Bank, 82.8% of total electricity production was provided by hydroelectric power. Other energy sources, including petroleum, coal and nuclear power, accounted for the remaining 17.2%. Attempts to exploit further the country's vast hydroelectric potential were encouraged by the completion of ambitious dam projects at Itaipú, on the border with Paraguay (expected to produce as much as 35% of Brazil's total electricity requirements when fully operational), and at Tucuruí, on the Tocantins river. In 2005 the Senado voted in favour of the construction of a new hydroelectric power-station at Belo Monte in Pará, while more new plants were planned. In that year the privatization of Brazil's hydroelectricity sector began with the auctioning of seven hydroelectric plants. The Angra I nuclear power plant, inaugurated in 1985, has subsequently operated only intermittently, while financial constraints hindered the completion of the Angra II plant, which became operational in mid-2000, preventing further development of the country's nuclear programme. There were plans to build Angra III, and in June 2007 the Government approved resumption of construction of the plant, which had been halted owing to a lack of funding and environmental concerns. The first module of a uranium-enrichment plant came into operation in Rio de Janeiro in May 2006. In 2004 the Government made public its plan to construct a natural gas pipeline connecting the Urucu natural gas reserve in Amazonia to neighbouring cities. The pipeline was expected to carry 4.7m. cu m per day on becoming operational by mid-2008. Brazil is a major producer of ethanol from sugar cane, and in 2008 production of ethanol was forecast to increase to over 21,300m. litres, an increase of more than 20%, over the 2007 figure. Imports of mineral fuels and lubricants comprised 16.6% of the value of total merchandise imports in 2006.

The services sector contributed an estimated 64.0% of GDP in 2006 and engaged 57.9% of the employed labour force in 2005. According to the World Bank, the GDP of the services sector increased at an average rate of 3.4% per year in 1996–2006. The GDP of the services sector increased by 4.1% in 2006.

In 2006 Brazil recorded a trade surplus of US $46,155m. There was a surplus of $13,276m. on the current account of the balance of payments. In 2006 the principal source of imports (16.0%) was the USA, which was also the principal market for exports (18.0%). Other major trading partners were Germany, Argentina, the Netherlands, Mexico and the People's Republic of China. The principal exports in 2005 were iron ore and concentrates, soya beans and related products, and crude petroleum and fuels. The principal imports in 2006 were mineral fuels and lubricants, chemicals and pharmaceutical goods, and minerals.

The 2006 federal budget recorded expenditure of R $493,450m. and revenue of R $543,253m. Brazil's external debt was US $187,994m. at the end of 2005, of which US $94,497m. was long-term public debt. In that year the cost of debt-servicing was equivalent to 44.8% of the value of exports of goods and services. According to the IMF, the annual rate of inflation averaged 7.9% in 2000–06. Consumer prices increased by 4.2% in 2006. Official figures indicated an average unemployment rate of 9.3% of the labour force in 2005.

Brazil is a member of the Latin American Integration Association (ALADI, see p. 331), the Southern Cone Common Market (Mercado Comum do Sul—Mercosul, see p. 391), the Association of Tin Producing Countries (ATPC) and the Cairns Group (see p. 464). Brazil also joined the Comunidade dos Países de Língua Portuguesa (CPLP, see p. 423), founded in 1996. In December 2004 Brazil was one of 12 countries that were signatories to the agreement, signed in Cusco, Peru, creating the South American Community of Nations (Comunidad Sudamericana de Naciones, which was renamed the Union of South American Nations—Unión de Naciones Suramericanas, UNASUR, or, in Portuguese, União das Nações Sul-Americanas—UNASUL, in April 2007), intended to promote greater regional economic integration.

On beginning a second term in office in January 2007, President da Silva announced a new macroeconomic strategy: the Programa de Aceleração do Crescimento was expected to stimulate capital investment, develop credit markets and reduce government expenditure. It was hoped that these measures would encourage growth in the private sector. With a greater provision of credit available, the state would be able to finance planned infrastructure works. In early 2007 the Government also announced plans to introduce a series of indirect value-added taxes, to be administered at both a national and state level. It was hoped that these reforms would reduce the scope of individual states to set competitive tax rates on production. Tax revenues rose substantially in 2007, and the budget deficit was estimated to have decreased to the equivalent of 2.0% of GDP (compared with 3.3% in 2006). Overall growth was put at 4.4% for 2007; while consumer prices rose by just 3.6%. Interest rates remained relatively low in that year, which improved access to consumer credit and boosted domestic consumption. Investment also rose in 2007 and an associated increase in employment (particularly in the agricultural and industrial sectors) fuelled further growth. However, the rejection by the Senado of the Contribuição Provisória sobre Movimentação Financeira in December 2007, which would have extended a provisional tax on financial transactions for a further four-year period, was a serious set-back for the Government, depriving it of an estimated R $40,000m. in revenue for 2008. The IMF forecast more modest growth of 4.0% for 2008, as the effects of the US economic downturn reached Brazil. External demand for commodities was expected to fall in 2008, as were international prices for metal products—a major Brazilian export—and the trade surplus was likely to decline as a result. Brazil continued to develop its highly lucrative ethanol sector, and in March 2007 the Governments of Brazil and the USA signed agreements intended to increase production and exports. Furthermore, it was hoped that the discovery of a huge offshore oil deposit (lying approximately 155 miles south of Rio de Janeiro) in November would help to reduce the energy sector's reliance on imports.

Education

Education is free in official pre-primary and primary schools and is compulsory between the ages of seven and 14 years. Primary education begins at seven years of age and lasts for eight years. Secondary education, beginning at 15 years of age, lasts for three years and is also free in official schools. According to UNESCO, in 2003/04 enrolment at primary schools included 95.3% of children in the relevant age group, while in secondary schools enrolment included 77.8% of pupils in the relevant age-group. The federal Government is responsible for higher education, and in 2003 there were 163 universities, of which 79 were state-administered. Numerous private institutions exist at all levels of education. Expenditure on education by the central Government was forecast at R $14,157m. for 2003.

Public Holidays

2008: 1 January (New Year's Day—Universal Confraternization Day), 2–6 February (Carnival), 21 March (Good Friday), 21 April (Tiradentes Day—Discovery of Brazil), 1 May (Labour Day and Ascension Day), 22 May (Corpus Christi), 7 September (Independence Day), 12 October (Our Lady Aparecida, Patron Saint of Brazil), 2 November (All Souls' Day), 15 November (Proclamation of the Republic), 25 December (Christmas Day).

2009: 1 January (New Year's Day—Universal Confraternization Day), 21–25 February (Carnival), 10 April (Good Friday), 21 April (Tiradentes Day—Discovery of Brazil), 1 May (Labour Day), 21 May (Ascension Day), 11 June (Corpus Christi), 7 September (Independence Day), 12 October (Our Lady Aparecida, Patron Saint of Brazil), 2 November (All Souls' Day), 15 November (Proclamation of the Republic), 25 December (Christmas Day).

Other local holidays include 20 January (Foundation of Rio de Janeiro) and 25 January (Foundation of São Paulo).

Weights and Measures

The metric system is in force.

Statistical Survey

Sources (unless otherwise stated): Economic Research Department, Banco Central do Brasil, SBS, Quadra 03, Bloco B, 70074-900 Brasília, DF; tel. (61) 3414-1074; fax (61) 3414-2036; e-mail coace.depec.@bcb.gov.br; internet www.bcb.gov.br; Instituto Brasileiro de Geografia e Estatística (IBGE), Centro de Documentação e Disseminação de Informações (CDDI), Rua Gen. Canabarro 706, 2° andar, Maracanã, 20271-201 Rio de Janeiro, RJ; tel. (21) 2142-4781; fax (21) 2142-4933; e-mail ibge@ibge.bov.br; internet www.ibge.gov.br.

Area and Population

AREA, POPULATION AND DENSITY

Area (sq km)	8,514,877*
Population (census results)†	
1 August 1996	157,070,163
1 August 2000	
Males	83,576,015
Females	86,223,155
Total	169,799,170
Population (official projected estimates at mid-year)	
2005	184,184,264
2006	186,770,562
2007	189,335,118
Density (per sq km) at mid-2007	22.2

* 3,287,611 sq miles.
† Excluding Indian jungle population (numbering 45,429 in 1950).
2007 (official population count, including estimates, at 1 April): 183,900,000.

ADMINISTRATIVE DIVISIONS
(official projected estimates at mid-2007)

State	Area (sq km)	Population	Density (per sq km)	Capital
Acre (AC)	152,581	693,251	4.5	Rio Branco
Alagoas (AL)	27,768	3,085,100	111.1	Maceió
Amapá (AP)	142,815	636,665	4.5	Macapá
Amazonas (AM)	1,570,746	3,399,236	2.2	Manaus
Bahia (BA)	564,693	14,083,825	24.9	Salvador
Ceará (CE)	148,826	8,335,887	56.0	Fortaleza
Espírito Santo (ES)	46,078	3,519,734	76.4	Vitória
Goiás (GO)	340,087	5,840,657	17.2	Goiânia
Maranhão (MA)	331,983	6,265,065	18.6	São Luís
Mato Grosso (MT)	903,358	2,910,272	3.2	Cuiabá
Mato Grosso do Sul (MS)	357,125	2,331,212	6.5	Campo Grande
Minas Gerais (MG)	586,528	19,719,228	33.6	Belo Horizonte
Pará (PA)	1,247,690	7,249,167	5.8	Belém
Paraíba (PB)	56,440	3,650,315	64.7	João Pessoa
Paraná (PR)	199,315	10,511,844	52.7	Curitiba
Pernambuco (PE)	98,312	8,590,864	87.4	Recife
Piauí (PI)	251,529	3,065,448	12.2	Teresina
Rio de Janeiro (RJ)	43,696	15,738,533	360.2	Rio de Janeiro
Rio Grande do Norte (RN)	52,797	3,084,091	58.4	Natal
Rio Grande do Sul (RS)	281,749	11,080,359	39.3	Porto Alegre
Rondônia (RO)	237,576	1,590,007	6.7	Porto Velho
Roraima (RR)	224,299	415,271	1.9	Boa Vista
Santa Catarina (SC)	95,346	6,049,194	63.4	Florianópolis
São Paulo (SP)	248,209	41,663,522	167.9	São Paulo
Sergipe (SE)	21,910	2,033,408	92.8	Aracaju
Tocantins (TO)	277,621	1,358,929	4.9	Palmas
Distrito Federal (DF)	5,802	2,434,034	419.5	Brasília
Total	**8,514,877**	**189,335,118**	**22.2**	—

PRINCIPAL TOWNS
(official projected estimates at mid-2006)*

São Paulo	11,016,703	Jaboatão	651,355
Rio de Janeiro	6,136,652	São José dos Campos	610,965
Salvador	2,714,018	Contagem	603,376
Fortaleza	2,416,920	Uberlândia	600,368
Belo Horizonte	2,399,920	Sorocaba	578,068
Brasília (capital)	2,383,784	Ribeirão Preto	559,650
Curitiba	1,788,559	Cuiabá	542,861
Manaus	1,688,524	Feira de Santana	535,820
Recife	1,515,052	Juíz de Fora	509,125
Porto Alegre	1,440,939	Aracaju	505,286
Belém	1,428,368	Ananindeua	498,095
Guarulhos	1,283,253	Joinville	496,051
Goiânia	1,220,412	Londrina	495,696
Campinas	1,059,420	Belford Roxo	489,002
São Luís	998,385	Niterói	476,669
São Gonçalo	973,372	São João de Meriti	466,996
Maceió	922,458	Aparecida de Goiânia	453,104
Duque de Caxias	855,010	Campos dos Goytacazes	429,667
Nova Iguaçu	844,583	Santos	418,375
São Bernardo do Campo	803,906	São José do Rio Preto	415,508
Teresina	801,971	Mauá	413,943
Natal	789,896	Caxias do Sul	412,053
Campo Grande	765,247	Betim	407,003
Osasco	714,950	Florianópolis	406,564
Santo André	673,234	Vila Velha	405,374
João Pessoa	672,081		

* Figures refer to *municípios*, which may contain rural districts.

BIRTHS, MARRIAGES AND DEATHS
(official estimates based on annual registrations)

	Live births Number*	Rate (per 1,000)	Marriages Number	Deaths Number†	Rate (per 1,000)
1999	4,209,768	25.1	788,744	966,010	5.8
2000	4,107,757	24.1	732,721	945,492	5.6
2001	3,743,651	21.7	710,121	953,519	5.5
2002	3,853,869	22.1	715,166	987,966	5.7
2003‡	3,649,996	20.9	746,727	996,729	6.3
2004‡	3,314,521	20.6	806,968	1,022,369	6.3
2005‡	3,312,754	20.4	835,846	1,004,420	6.3
2006‡	3,156,327	n.a.	889,828	1,033,405	n.a.

* Including births registered but not occurring during that year: 1,552,155 in 1999; 1,496,335 in 2000; 1,234,297 in 2001; 1,272,814 in 2002; 827,534 in 2003; 500,817 in 2004; 438,001 in 2005; 357,199 in 2006.
† Including deaths registered but not occurring during that year: 22,486 in 1999; 20,792 in 2000; 25,174 in 2001; 29,491 in 2002; 29,012 in 2003; 27,530 in 2004; 27,315 in 2005; 13,194 in 2006.
‡ Rates are official estimates calculated in accordance with official estimated mid-year population projections, and are not strictly comparable with rates for previous years.

Expectation of life (years at birth, WHO estimates): 71.1 (males 67.7; females 74.6) in 2005 (Source: WHO, *World Health Statistics*).

BRAZIL

Statistical Survey

ECONOMICALLY ACTIVE POPULATION
('000 persons aged 10 years and over, labour force sample survey at September)*

	2003	2004	2005
Agriculture, hunting, forestry and fishing	16,409.4	17,733.8	17,813.8
Industry (excl. construction)	11,387.0	12,402.7	12,998.4
Manufacturing industries	10,749.1	11,723.6	12,322.3
Construction	5,157.6	5,354.4	5,635.8
Commerce and repair of motor vehicles and household goods	14,047.5	14,653.2	15,484.7
Hotels and restaurants	2,858.3	3,023.1	3,183.5
Transport, storage and communication	3,680.6	3,894.2	3,962.2
Public administration	3,942.2	4,203.9	4,262.4
Education, health and social services	7,087.3	7,409.3	7,651.7
Domestic services	6,081.9	6,472.5	6,658.6
Other community, social and personal services	2,947.0	3,498.3	3,297.4
Other activities	5,455.6	5,723.4	5,943.4
Activities not adequately defined	196.2	227.4	198.1
Total employed	79,250.6	84,596.3	87,090.0
Unemployed	8,537.0	8,263.8	8,942.0
Total labour force	87,787.7	92,860.1	96,032.0

* Data coverage excludes rural areas of Acre, Amapá, Amazonas, Pará, Rondônia and Roraima.

Health and Welfare

KEY INDICATORS

Total fertility rate (children per woman, 2005)	2.3
Under-5 mortality rate (per 1,000 live births, 2005)	33
HIV/AIDS (% of persons aged 15–49, 2005)	0.5
Physicians (per 1,000 head, 2000)	1.15
Hospital beds (per 1,000 head, 2002)	2.6
Health expenditure (2004): US $ per head (PPP)	1,519.7
Health expenditure (2004): % of GDP	8.8
Health expenditure (2004): public (% of total)	54.1
Access to water (% of persons, 2004)	90
Access to sanitation (% of persons, 2004)	75
Human Development Index (2005): ranking	70
Human Development Index (2005): value	0.800

For sources and definitions, see explanatory note on p. vi.

Agriculture

PRINCIPAL CROPS
('000 metric tons)

	2004	2005	2006
Wheat	5,818	4,659	2,482
Rice (paddy)	13,277	13,192	11,505
Barley	397	326	201
Maize	41,788	35,113	42,632
Oats	460	522	382
Sorghum	2,159	1,521	1,556
Buckwheat*	48	50	50
Potatoes	3,047	3,130	3,138
Sweet potatoes	539	514	515*
Cassava (Manioc)	23,927	25,872	26,713
Yams*	234	236	236
Sugar cane	415,206	422,957	455,291
Dry beans	2,967	3,022	3,437
Brazil nuts (in shell)*	29	30	30
Cashew nuts (in shell)	188	153	236
Soybeans (Soya beans)†	49,550	51,182	52,356
Groundnuts (in shell)	236	315	239
Coconuts	3,117	3,119	2,787
Oil palm fruit*	550	580	580
Castor oil seed	139	169	92
Sunflower seed†	200	94	120
Cottonseed	2,466†	1,785*	1,785*
Tomatoes	3,516	3,453	3,273

—continued	2004	2005	2006
Onions (dry)	1,158	1,138	1,175
Garlic	86	86	88
Watermelons	1,719	1,505	1,505*
Cantaloupes and other melons*	180	190	190
Bananas	6,584	6,803	7,088
Oranges	18,314	17,853	18,059
Tangerines, mandarins, clementines and satsumas	1,163	1,233	1,233*
Lemons and limes	986	1,031	1,031*
Grapefruit and pomelos*	68	68	68
Apples	980	851	861
Peaches and nectarines	236	235	235*
Grapes	1,291	1,233	1,220
Guavas, mangoes, mangosteens	1,358	1,348	1,348*
Avocados	171	169	169*
Pineapples	2,216	2,292	2,487
Persimmons	162	165	165*
Cashew-apple*	1,610	1,650	1,650
Papayas	1,612	1,574	1,574*
Coffee beans (green)‡	2,466	2,140	2,593
Cocoa beans	196	209	199
Mate	403	430	430*
Sisal and other agave fibres	199	207	248
Cotton (lint)†	1,196	n.a.	n.a.
Tobacco (leaves)	921	889	905
Natural rubber	99	104	104*

* FAO estimate(s).
† Unofficial figure(s).
‡ Official figures, reported in terms of dry cherries, have been converted into green coffee beans at 50%.

Aggregate production ('000 metric tons, may include official, semi-official or estimated data): Total cereals 59,017 in 2004, 55,669 in 2005, 59,017 in 2006; Total roots and tubers 30,602 in 2004, 29,752 in 2005, 30,602 in 2006; Total vegetables (incl. melons) 8,958 in 2004, 8,722 in 2005, 8,581 in 2006; Total fruits (excl. melons) 37,292 in 2004, 36,952 in 2005, 37,736 in 2006.

Source: FAO.

LIVESTOCK
('000 head, year ending September)

	2003	2004	2005
Cattle	195,552	204,513	207,157
Buffaloes	1,149	1,134	1,174
Horses	5,828	5,787	5,787
Asses, mules or hinnies	2,554	2,555	2,580
Pigs	32,305	33,085	34,064
Sheep	14,556	15,058	15,588
Goats	9,582	10,047	10,307
Chickens	921,323	944,298	999,041
Ducks*	3,550	3,550	n.a.
Turkeys*	14,800	16,200	16,200

* FAO estimates.

2006: Figures assumed to be unchanged from 2005 (FAO estimates).

Source: FAO.

LIVESTOCK PRODUCTS
('000 metric tons)

	2003	2004	2005
Cattle meat	7,230	7,774	7,774*
Sheep meat*	68	76	76
Goat meat*	41	41	41
Pig meat	3,059	3,110	3,140*
Horse meat*	21	22	n.a.
Chicken meat	7,760	8,668	8,507*
Cows' milk	22,944	24,202	25,333
Goats' milk*	135	135	135
Hen eggs, in shell	1,571	1,616	1,675
Other poultry eggs, in shell	61	66	75
Honey	30	33	34
Wool: greasy	11	11	11

* FAO estimate(s).

2006: Production assumed to be unchanged from 2005 (FAO estimates).

Source: FAO.

BRAZIL

Forestry

ROUNDWOOD REMOVALS
('000 cubic metres, excl. bark, FAO estimates)

	2003	2004	2005
Sawlogs, veneer logs and logs for sleepers	42,732	39,931	47,190
Pulpwood	71,007	60,473	63,425
Other industrial wood	6,799	6,354	7,509
Fuel wood	135,542	136,637	137,756
Total	256,081	243,395	255,880

2006: Figures assumed to be unchanged from 2005 (FAO estimates).
Source: FAO.

SAWNWOOD PRODUCTION
('000 cubic metres, incl. railway sleepers)

	2003	2004	2005
Coniferous (softwood)	8,660	8,990	8,935
Broadleaved (hardwood)	14,430	14,490	14,622
Total	23,090	23,480	23,557

2006: Figures assumed to be unchanged from 2005.
Source: FAO.

Fishing

('000 metric tons, live weight)

	2003	2004	2005
Capture	712.1	746.2	750.3
Characins	94.3	96.5	95.1
Freshwater siluroids	75.1	83.2	84.5
Weakfishes	46.9	40.4	42.5
Whitemouth croaker	39.8	37.0	30.6
Brazilian sardinella	25.3	53.4	42.7
Aquaculture	277.6*	269.7	257.8
Common carp	49.6	45.2	42.5
Tilapias	62.6	69.1	67.9
Whiteleg shrimp	90.2	75.9	63.1
Total catch	989.8*	1,015.9	1,008.1

* FAO estimate.

Note: Figures exclude aquatic mammals, recorded by number rather than by weight. The number of whales and dolphins caught was: 133 in 2002; 358 in 2003; 299 in 2004; 18 in 2005. Also excluded are crocodiles. The number of spectacled caimans caught was: 12,851 in 2003; 7,004 in 2004; 650 in 2005.
Source: FAO.

Mining

('000 metric tons, unless otherwise indicated)

	2003	2004	2005
Hard coal[1,2]	6,000	6,000	6,000
Crude petroleum ('000 barrels)	562,137	544,799	614,697
Natural gas (million cu m)	15,792	16,971	17,699
Iron ore:			
gross weight	230,707	261,675	280,862
metal content	153,190	173,752	185,369
Copper (metric tons)	173,378	208,020	199,043
Nickel ore (metric tons)[3]	44,928	51,886	74,198
Bauxite	17,363	20,914	21,000
Lead concentrates (metric tons)[3]	10,652	14,737	16,063
Zinc (metric tons)	262,998	265,987	267,374
Tin concentrates (metric tons)[3]	11,011	11,762	9,236
Manganese ore[1]	6,500	n.a.	n.a.
Chromium ore (metric tons)[4]	155,063	253,002	252,102
Tungsten concentrates (metric tons)[3]	30	262	458
Ilmenite (metric tons)	120,160	133,000	127,142
Rutile (metric tons)	2,303	2,117	2,069
Zirconium concentrates (metric tons)[5]	27,198	25,263	25,657
Silver (kilograms)[6]	31,440	35,497	38,134

—continued	2003	2004	2005
Gold (kilograms)[7]	40,416	47,596	38,292[1]
Bentonite (beneficiated)	199	227	221
Kaolin (beneficiated)	2,081	2,381	2,410
Magnesite (beneficiated)	306	366	387
Phosphate rock[8]	5,584	5,690	5,488
Potash salts[9]	416	403	405
Fluorspar (Fluorite) (metric tons)[10]	56,346	57,772	66,512
Barite (Barytes) (beneficiated) (metric tons)	57,452	59,612	44,041
Quartz (natural crystals) (metric tons)	7,420	18,116	17,860
Salt (unrefined):			
marine	5,144	5,206	5,738
rock	1,420	1,442	1,559
Gypsum and anhydrite (crude)	1,592	1,475	1,582
Graphite (natural) (metric tons)	70,739	76,332	75,515
Asbestos (fibre) (metric tons)	231,117	252,067	236,047
Mica (metric tons)[1]	4,000	4,000	4,000
Vermiculite (beneficiated) (metric tons)	26,055	25,103	24,191
Talc (crude)	369	418	401
Pyrophyllite (crude)	200[1]	200	200
Diamonds, gem and industrial ('000 carats)[1,11]	400	300	300

[1] Estimated production.
[2] Figures refer to marketable products.
[3] Figures refer to the metal content of ores and concentrates.
[4] Figures refer to the chromic oxide (Cr_2O_3) content.
[5] Including production of baddeleyite-caldasite.
[6] Figures refer to primary production only. The production of secondary silver (in kilograms) was: 50,000 in 2003; 45,000 in 2004–2005.
[7] Including official production by independent miners (*garimpeiros*): 14,350 kg in 2003; 19,088 kg in 2004; 8,351 kg in 2005.
[8] Figures refer to the gross weight of concentrates. The phosphoric acid (P_2O_5) content (in '000 metric tons) was: 2,005 in 2003; 2,181 in 2004; 2,044 in 2005.
[9] Figures refer to the potassium oxide (K_2O) content.
[10] Acid-grade and metallurgical-grade concentrates.
[11] Figures refer to officially reported diamond output plus official Brazilian estimates of diamond output by independent miners (*garimpeiros*).
Source: US Geological Survey.

Industry

SELECTED PRODUCTS
('000 metric tons, unless otherwise indicated)

	2001	2002	2003
Beer ('000 hl)	91,372	79,883	76,921
Soft drinks ('000 hl)	86,742	94,538	86,618
Wood pulp (sulphate and soda)	4,524	5,134	6,309
Newsprint	230	230	163
Caustic soda	961	1,052	722
Fertilizers*	7,597	8,071	9,353
Electric energy (million kWh)	328,509	345,671	364,339.
Pig-iron	27,391	29,694	32,039
Crude steel*	26,717	29,604	31,147
Cement*	38,026	38,026	34,010
Passenger cars (units)	296,000	326,000	344,000
Buses and Coaches (units)	23,163	22,826	26,990
Lorries (units)	77,431	68,558	78,938
Motorcycles (units)	741,000	851,000	948,000

* Source: Ministério de Desenvolvimento, Indústria e Comércio Exterior, Brasília.

Source: mostly UN, *Industrial Commodity Statistics Yearbook*.

2004 ('000 metric tons, unless otherwise indicated): Fertilizers 9,734; Paper 8,452; Crude steel 32,909; Aluminium 1,457; Cement 34,413; Cellulose 9,620; Motor vehicles ('000 units) 2,317.

2005 ('000 metric tons, unless otherwise indicated): Fertilizers 8,534; Paper 8,597; Crude steel 31,610; Aluminium 1,498; Cement 36,673; Cellulose 10,352; Motor vehicles ('000 units) 2,528.

2006 ('000 metric tons, unless otherwise indicated): Fertilizers 8,778; Paper 8,774; Crude steel 30,901; Aluminium 1,604; Cement 39,516; Cellulose 11,139; Motor vehicles ('000 units) 2,606.

Source: Ministério de Desenvolvimento, Indústria e Comércio Exterior, Brasília.

BRAZIL

Finance

CURRENCY AND EXCHANGE RATES

Monetary Units
100 centavos = 1 real (plural: reais).

Sterling, Dollar and Euro Equivalents (30 April 2007)
£1 sterling = 3.531 reais;
US $1 = 1.771;
€1 = 2.409 reais;
100 reais = £28.32 = $56.48 = €41.52.

Average Exchange Rates (reais per US $)
2005   2.4344
2006   2.1753
2007   1.9471

Note: In March 1986 the cruzeiro (CR $) was replaced by a new currency unit, the cruzado (CZ $), equivalent to 1,000 cruzeiros. In January 1989 the cruzado was, in turn, replaced by the new cruzado (NCZ $), equivalent to CZ $1,000 and initially at par with the US dollar (US $). In March 1990 the new cruzado was replaced by the cruzeiro (CR $), at an exchange rate of one new cruzado for one cruzeiro. In August 1993 the cruzeiro was replaced by the cruzeiro real, equivalent to CR $1,000. On 1 March 1994, in preparation for the introduction of a new currency, a transitional accounting unit, the Unidade Real de Valor (at par with the US $), came into operation, alongside the cruzeiro real. On 1 July 1994 the cruzeiro real was replaced by the real (R $), also at par with the US $ and thus equivalent to 2,750 cruzeiros reais.

BUDGET
(R $ million)*

Revenue	2004	2005	2006
Tax revenue	318,347	360,682	392,542
Income tax	101,386	124,520	137,375
Tax on profits of legal entities	19,957	26,428	28,188
Value-added tax on industrial products	22,695	26,428	28,188
Tax on financial operations and export duty	5,228	6,103	6,786
Import duty	9,201	9,080	10,036
Other taxes and duties	35,861	29,450	33,334
Social security contributions	77,918	87,615	92,340
Contributions to Social Integration Programme and Financial Reserve Fund for Public Employees	19,704	22,014	24,277
Provisional contribution on financial transactions	26,397	29,273	32,090
Social welfare contributions	93,765	108,433	123,521
Other income	7,503	19,261	27,190
Total	419,615	488,376	543,253

Expenditure	2004	2005	2006
Transfers to state and local governments†	67,559	83,938	92,779
Personnel	83,655	92,231	105,031
Social service and welfare transfers	125,751	146,010	165,586
Other expenditures	93,285	113,382	130,054
Total	370,250	435,561	493,450

* Figures refer to cash operations of the National Treasury, including the collection and transfer of earmarked revenues for social expenditure purposes. The data exclude the transactions of other funds and accounts controlled by the Federal Government.
† Constitutionally mandated participation funds.

CENTRAL BANK RESERVES
(US $ million at 31 December)

	2004	2005	2006
Gold*	195	225	277
IMF special drawing rights	4	29	8
Foreign exchange	52,736	53,545	85,553
Total	52,935	53,799	85,838

*Valued at market-related prices.

Source: IMF, *International Financial Statistics*.

MONEY SUPPLY
(R $ million at 31 December)

	2004	2005	2006
Currency outside banks	52,018	58,268	68,918
Demand deposits at deposit money banks	75,459	85,936	104,672
Total money (incl. others)	127,477	144,204	173,590

Source: IMF, *International Financial Statistics*.

COST OF LIVING
(Consumer Price Index; base: 2000 = 100)

	2004	2005	2006
Food	146.5	151.0	151.0
Clothing and footwear	135.2	147.3	156.1
Rent	148.6	158.3	165.7
All items (incl. others)	141.7	151.4	157.8

Source: ILO.

NATIONAL ACCOUNTS
(R $ million at current prices)

National Income and Product

	2001	2002	2003
Compensation of employees	444,067	486,457	554,149
Net operating surplus	490,327	564,323	668,926
Net mixed income	60,469	61,618	69,757
Gross domestic product (GDP) at factor cost	994,863	1,112,397	1,292,832
Taxes on production and imports	208,578	237,061	263,350
Less Subsidies	4,704	3,430	
GDP in market prices (purchasers' values)	1,198,736	1,346,028	1,556,182
Primary incomes received from abroad	8,185	10,434	10,902
Less Primary incomes paid abroad	53,689	62,706	66,384
Statistical discrepancy	220	328	332
Gross national income (GNI)	1,153,452	1,294,084	1,501,032
Current transfers from abroad	4,936	8,341	9,694
Less Current transfers paid abroad	1,069	1,074	941
Net national disposable income	1,157,318	1,301,351	1,509,785

Expenditure on the Gross Domestic Product

	2004	2005	2006
Final consumption expenditure	1,307,578	1,454,087	1,865,142
Households	975,245	1,075,343	1,402,136
Non-profit institutions serving households			
General government	332,332	378,745	463,006
Gross capital formation	376,573	398,598	389,428
Gross fixed capital formation	346,335	385,943	390,134
Changes in inventories	30,238	12,655	–706
Acquisitions, less disposals, of valuables			
Total domestic expenditure	1,684,151	1,852,685	2,254,570
Exports of goods and services	318,387	324,988	340,409
Less Imports of goods and services	235,917	240,075	272,159
GDP in purchasers' values (market prices)	1,766,621	1,937,598	2,322,818
GDP at constant 1990 prices	16,341	16,713	n.a.

Source: IMF, *International Financial Statistics*.

BRAZIL

Gross Domestic Product by Economic Activity

	2002	2003	2004
Agriculture, hunting, forestry and fishing	104,908	138,191	159,643
Mining and quarrying	40,724	54,888	65,895
Manufacturing	280,129	337,457	380,467
Electricity, gas and water	43,206	47,594	54,280
Construction	95,469	100,952	115,101
Trade, restaurants and hotels	92,190	107,502	123,490
Transport, storage and communications	63,483	78,338	81,813
Finance, insurance, real estate, business services and dwellings	227,819	240,005	253,029
Government services	195,934	220,461	254,678
Other community, social and personal services	130,615	144,876	166,384
Sub-total	1,274,477	1,470,263	1,654,780
Less Imputed bank service charges	75,332	74,660	73,278
Gross value added in basic prices	1,199,145	1,395,603	1,581,502
Taxes, less subsidies, on products	146,883	160,579	185,119
GDP in market prices	1,346,028	1,556,182	1,766,621

Source: UN Economic Commission for Latin America and the Caribbean, *Statistical Yearbook*.

2005 (R $ million): Agriculture, hunting, forestry and fishing 145,829; Industry (incl. mining, manufacturing, energy and construction) 690,601; Services 985,325; *Sub-total* 1,821,755; Imputed bank service charge –93,236; *Gross value added in basic prices* 1,728,519; Taxes, less subsidies, on products 209,080; *GDP in market prices* 1,937,598.

2006 (R $ million): Agriculture, hunting, forestry and fishing 102,891; Industry (incl. mining, manufacturing, energy and construction) 617,965; Services 1,278,771; *Gross value added in basic prices* 1,999,627; Taxes, less subsidies, on products 323,191; *GDP in market prices* 2,322,818.

BALANCE OF PAYMENTS
(US $ million)

	2004	2005	2006
Exports of goods f.o.b.	96,475	118,308	137,470
Imports of goods f.o.b.	–62,835	–73,551	–91,355
Trade balance	33,641	44,757	46,115
Exports of services	12,584	16,095	19,460
Imports of services	–17,261	–24,243	–29,116
Balance on goods and services	28,963	36,609	36,459
Other income received	3,199	3,194	6,438
Other income paid	–23,719	–29,162	–33,927
Balance on goods, services and income	8,443	10,642	8,970
Current transfers received	3,582	4,050	4,847
Current transfers paid	–314	–493	–541
Current balance	11,711	14,199	13,276
Capital account (net)	339	663	869
Direct investment abroad	–9,471	–2,517	–28,202
Direct investment from abroad	18,166	15,193	18,782
Portfolio investment assets	–755	–1,771	523
Portfolio investment liabilities	–3,996	6,655	9,051
Financial derivatives assets	467	508	482
Financial derivatives liabilities	–1,145	–548	–99
Other investment assets	–2,196	–3,792	–8,898
Other investment liabilities	–4,379	72	23,820
Net errors and omissions	–2,144	–1,096	968
Overall balance	6,599	27,566	30,571

Source: IMF, *International Financial Statistics*.

External Trade

PRINCIPAL COMMODITIES
(US $ million)

Imports f.o.b.	2004	2005	2006
Capital goods	12,145	15,387	91,351
Industrial machinery	3,279	4,251	5,310
Other fixed equipment	2,530	3,312	3,971
Office machines and equipment	2,685	3,381	4,305
Parts of capital goods for industry	1,519	1,745	2,010
Moveable transport equipment	610	969	1,404
Parts and accessories of industrial machinery	1,068	1,240	1,347
Consumer goods	6,864	8,484	11,997
Non-durable goods	3,674	4,556	5,918
Foodstuffs	1,059	1,374	1,728
Pharmaceuticals	1,454	1,684	2,171
Durable goods	3,190	3,928	6,079
Passenger vehicles	583	819	1,914
Jewellery	920	1,124	1,393
Mineral fuels and lubricants	10,315	11,925	15,197
Raw materials and intermediate goods	33,512	37,804	45,237
Chemicals and pharmaceutical goods	9,638	10,699	12,243
Intermediate goods and parts thereof	5,591	6,700	7,818
Minerals	5,073	6,372	9,205
Transport equipment and parts	4,912	5,912	6,290
Agricultural products (excl. foodstuffs)	2,213	2,360	3,189
Total (incl. others)	62,836	73,600	91,351

Exports f.o.b.	2004	2005	2006
Basic goods	28,529	34,732	40,285
Iron ore and concentrates	4,759	7,297	8,949
Crude petroleum and fuels	2,528	4,164	6,894
Soybeans and products thereof	8,666	8,210	8,082
Coffee	1,750	2,516	2,928
Beef and poultry	4,457	5,743	6,058
Semi-manufactured goods	13,433	15,963	19,523
Sugar	1,511	2,382	3,936
Iron and steel in primary forms	2,124	2,304	2,277
Pulp and waste paper	1,722	2,034	2,479
Manufactured goods	53,137	65,353	75,018
Passenger cars	3,352	4,395	4,597
Aeroplanes	3,269	3,168	3,241
Parts and accessories for motor vehicles and tractors	1,979	2,475	2,972
Flat-rolled products of iron or non-alloy steel	2,007	2,383	2,718
Devices, transmitters, receivers and components	1,379	2,733	2,901
Refined sugar	1,129	1,537	2,231
Total (incl. others)	96,678	118,529	137,807

BRAZIL

PRINCIPAL TRADING PARTNERS
(US $ million)*

Imports f.o.b.	2004	2005	2006
Argentina	5,570	6,241	8,053
Belgium-Luxembourg	640	760	997
Canada	866	1,019	1,194
Chile	1,399	1,746	2,866
China, People's Republic	3,710	5,355	7,990
France	2,289	2,700	2,838
Germany	5,072	6,144	6,503
Italy	2,049	2,276	2,571
Japan	2,869	3,405	3,840
Korea, Republic	1,730	2,327	3,106
Mexico	704	844	1,310
Netherlands	618	587	786
Paraguay	298	319	296
Spain	1,176	1,333	1,431
United Kingdom	1,355	1,376	1,417
USA	11,531	12,853	14,817
Uruguay	523	494	618
Total (incl. others)	62,836	73,600	91,351

Exports f.o.b.	2004	2005	2006
Argentina	7,391	9,930	11,740
Belgium-Luxembourg	1,932	2,197	3,015
Canada	1,202	1,947	2,281
Chile	2,556	3,624	3,914
China, People's Republic	5,442	6,835	8,402
France	2,194	2,507	2,669
Germany	4,047	5,032	5,691
Italy	2,909	3,229	3,836
Japan	2,774	3,483	3,895
Korea, Republic	1,430	1,897	1,963
Mexico	3,958	4,074	4,458
Netherlands	5,919	5,286	5,749
Paraguay	873	963	1,234
Spain	1,988	2,177	2,330
United Kingdom	2,122	2,597	2,829
USA	20,403	22,810	24,773
Uruguay	671	853	1,013
Total (incl. others)	96,678	118,529	137,807

* Imports by country of purchase; exports by country of last consignment.

Transport

RAILWAYS
(figures are rounded)

	2003	2004	2005
Passengers ('000)			
Long distance	1,553	1,557	1,451
Metropolitan	133,900	141,900	144,300
Passenger-km ('000, long distance only)	469,330	475,186	451,943
Freight ('000 metric tons)	345,111	377,776	388,592
Freight ton-km (million)	182,644	205,711	221,633

Source: Agência Nacional de Transportes Terrestres (ANTT), Ministério dos Transportes, Brasília.

ROAD TRAFFIC
(motor vehicles in use at 31 December)

	2003	2004
Passenger cars	23,757,230	24,936,541
Buses and coaches	468,295	493,973
Lorries and vans	5,511,133	5,800,529
Motorcycles and mopeds	6,195,949	7,039,675

Source: IRF, *World Road Statistics*.

SHIPPING
Merchant Fleet
(registered at 31 December)

	2004	2005	2006
Number of vessels	494	510	525
Total displacement ('000 grt)	2,628	2,343	2,281

Source: Lloyd's Register-Fairplay, *World Fleet Statistics*.

International Sea-borne Freight Traffic
('000 metric tons)

	2000	2001	2002
Goods loaded	288,202	315,135	342,675
Goods unloaded	191,072	191,072	186,330

Source: Ministério dos Transportes.

CIVIL AVIATION
(embarked passengers, mail and cargo)

	2003	2004	2005
Number of passengers ('000)	33,420	36,988	44,504
Passenger-km (million)*	44,045	47,462	50,689
Freight ton-km ('000)†	6,801,204	7,477,424	8,185,256

* Source: UN Economic Commission for Latin America and the Caribbean, *Statistical Yearbook*.
† Including mail.

Source: mostly Departamento de Aviação Civil (DAC), Comando da Aeronáutica, Ministério da Defesa, Brasília.

Tourism

FOREIGN TOURIST ARRIVALS

Country of origin	2004	2005	2006
Argentina	922,484	992,299	921,061
Bolivia	60,239	68,670	55,169
Canada	66,895	75,100	62,603
Chile	155,026	169,953	148,327
France	224,160	263,829	275,913
Germany	294,989	308,598	277,182
Italy	276,563	303,878	291,898
Japan	60,806	68,066	74,638
Mexico	65,707	73,118	70,862
Netherlands	102,480	109,708	86,122
Paraguay	204,758	249,030	198,958
Portugal	336,988	357,640	312,521
Spain	155,421	172,979	211,741
Switzerland	83,113	89,789	84,816
United Kingdom	150,336	169,514	169,627
USA	705,997	793,559	721,633
Uruguay	309,732	341,647	290,240
Total (incl. others)	4,793,703	5,358,170	5,018,991

Receipts from tourism (US $ million): 3,222 in 2004; 3,861 in 2005; 4,314 in 2006.

Source: Instituto Brasileiro de Turismo—EMBRATUR, Brasília.

Communications Media

	2004	2005	2006
Telephones in use ('000 main lines)	42,382.2	39,853.0	38,800.2
Mobile cellular telephones ('000 subscribers)	65,605.0	86,210.0	99,918.6
Personal computers ('000 in use)	19,350	n.a.	n.a.
Internet users ('000)	22,000	32,130	42,600
Broadband subscribers ('000)	3,157.5	4,385.1	5,921.9

Source: International Telecommunication Union (ITU).

Radio receivers ('000 in use): 71,000 in 1997 (Source: UNESCO, *Statistical Yearbook*).

Television receivers ('000 in use): 58,283 in 2000 (Source: International Telecommunication Union (ITU)).

Book production ('000 titles): 21,689 in 1998 (Source: UNESCO Institute for Statistics).

Daily newspapers: 532 (average circulation, '000 copies): 6,552 in 2004 (Source: UNESCO Institute for Statistics).

Non-daily newspapers: 2,472 in 2004 (Source: UNESCO Institute for Statistics).

Facsimile machines: 500,000 in 1997 (Source: UN, *Statistical Yearbook*).

Education

(2006, unless otherwise indicated)

	Institutions	Teachers	Students
Pre-primary	107,375	309,881	7,016,095
Literacy classes (Classe de Alfabetização)*	27,670	37,508	598,589
Primary	159,016	1,665,341	33,282,663
Secondary	24,131	519,935	8,906,820
Higher	1,859*	265,053	4,861,390

* 2003 figure(s).

Source: Ministério da Educação, Brasília.

Adult literacy rate (UNESCO estimates): 88.6% (males 88.4%; females 88.8%) in 2004 (Source: UNESCO Institute for Statistics).

Directory

The Constitution

A new Constitution was promulgated on 5 October 1988. The following is a summary of the main provisions:

The Federative Republic of Brazil, formed by the indissoluble union of the States, the Municipalities and the Federal District, is constituted as a democratic state. All power emanates from the people. The Federative Republic of Brazil seeks the economic, political, social and cultural integration of the peoples of Latin America.

All are equal before the law. The inviolability of the right to life, freedom, equality, security and property is guaranteed. No one shall be subjected to torture. Freedom of thought, conscience, religious belief and expression are guaranteed, as is privacy. The principles of habeas corpus and 'habeas data' (the latter giving citizens access to personal information held in government data banks) are granted. There is freedom of association, and the right to strike is guaranteed.

There is universal suffrage by direct secret ballot. Voting is compulsory for literate persons between 18 and 69 years of age, and optional for those who are illiterate, those over 70 years of age and those aged 16 and 17.

Brasília is the federal capital. The Union's competence includes maintaining relations with foreign states, and taking part in international organizations; declaring war and making peace; guaranteeing national defence; decreeing a state of siege; issuing currency; supervising credits, etc.; formulating and implementing plans for economic and social development; maintaining national services, including communications, energy, the judiciary and the police; legislating on civil, commercial, penal, procedural, electoral, agrarian, maritime, aeronautical, spatial and labour law, etc. The Union, States, Federal District and Municipalities must protect the Constitution, laws and democratic institutions, and preserve national heritage.

The States are responsible for electing their Governors by universal suffrage and direct secret ballot for a four-year term. The organization of the Municipalities, the Federal District and the Territories is regulated by law.

The Union may intervene in the States and in the Federal District only in certain circumstances, such as a threat to national security or public order, and then only after reference to the National Congress.

LEGISLATIVE POWER

Legislative power is exercised by the Congresso Nacional (National Congress), which is composed of the Câmara dos Deputados (Chamber of Deputies) and the Senado Federal (Federal Senate). Elections for deputies and senators take place simultaneously throughout the country; candidates for the Congresso must be Brazilian by birth and have full exercise of their political rights. They must be at least 21 years of age in the case of deputies and at least 35 years of age in the case of senators. The Congresso meets twice a year in ordinary sessions, and extraordinary sessions may be convened by the President of the Republic, the Presidents of the Câmara and the Senado, or at the request of the majority of the members of either house.

The Câmara is made up of representatives of the people, elected by a system of proportional representation in each State, Territory and the Federal District for a period of four years. The total number of deputies representing the States and the Federal District will be established in proportion to the population; each Territory will elect four deputies.

The Senado is composed of representatives of the States and the Federal District, elected according to the principle of majority. Each State and the Federal District will elect three senators with a mandate of eight years, with elections after four years for one-third of the members and after another four years for the remaining two-thirds. Each Senator is elected with two substitutes. The Senado approves, by secret ballot, the choice of Magistrates, when required by the Constitution; of the Attorney-General of the Republic, of the Ministers of the Accounts Tribunal, of the Territorial Governors, of the president and directors of the central bank and of the permanent heads of diplomatic missions.

The Congresso is responsible for deciding on all matters within the competence of the Union, especially fiscal and budgetary arrangements, national, regional and local plans and programmes, the strength of the armed forces and territorial limits. It is also responsible for making definitive resolutions on international treaties, and for authorizing the President to declare war.

The powers of the Câmara include authorizing the instigation of legal proceedings against the President and Vice-President of the Republic and Ministers of State. The Senado may indict and impose sentence on the President and Vice-President of the Republic and Ministers of State.

Constitutional amendments may be proposed by at least one-third of the members of either house, by the President or by more than one-half of the legislative assemblies of the units of the Federation. Amendments must be ratified by three-fifths of the members of each house. The Constitution may not be amended during times of national emergency, such as a state of siege.

EXECUTIVE POWER

Executive power is exercised by the President of the Republic, aided by the Ministers of State. Candidates for the Presidency and Vice-Presidency must be Brazilian-born, be in full exercise of their political rights and be over 35 years of age. The candidate who obtains an absolute majority of votes will be elected President. If no candidate attains an absolute majority, the two candidates who have received the most votes proceed to a second round of voting, at which the candidate obtaining the majority of valid votes will be elected President. The President holds office for a term of four years and (under an amendment adopted in 1997) is eligible for re-election.

The Ministers of State are chosen by the President and their duties include countersigning acts and decrees signed by the President, expediting instructions for the enactment of laws, decrees and regulations, and presentation to the President of an annual report of their activities.

The Council of the Republic is the higher consultative organ of the President of the Republic. It comprises the Vice-President of the Republic, the Presidents of the Câmara and Senado, the leaders of the majority and of the minority in each house, the Minister of Justice, two members appointed by the President of the Republic, two elected by the Senado and two elected by the Câmara, the latter six having a mandate of three years.

The National Defence Council advises the President on matters relating to national sovereignty and defence. It comprises the Vice-President of the Republic, the Presidents of the Câmara and Senado, the Minister of Justice, military Ministers and the Ministers of Foreign Affairs and of Planning.

JUDICIAL POWER

Judicial power in the Union is exercised by the Supreme Federal Tribunal; the Higher Tribunal of Justice; the Regional Federal Tribunals and federal judges; Labour Tribunals and judges; Electoral Tribunals and judges; Military Tribunals and judges; and the States' Tribunals and judges. Judges are appointed for life; they may not undertake any other employment. The Tribunals elect their own controlling organs and organize their own internal structure.

The Supreme Federal Tribunal, situated in the Union capital, has jurisdiction over the whole national territory and is composed of 11 ministers. The ministers are nominated by the President after approval by the Senado, from Brazilian-born citizens, between the ages of 35 and 65 years, of proved judicial knowledge and experience.

The Government

HEAD OF STATE

President: LUIZ INÁCIO LULA DA SILVA (PT) (took office 2 January 2003, re-elected 29 October 2006).
Vice-President: JOSÉ ALENCAR GOMES DA SILVA (PRB).

THE CABINET
(March 2008)

The Cabinet is composed of members of the Partido dos Trabalhadores (PT), the Partido Socialista Brasileiro (PSB), the Partido do Movimento Democrático Brasileiro (PMDB), the Partido Progressista (PP), the Partido Verde (PV), the Partido Republicano Brasileiro (PRB), the Partido Trabalhista Brasileiro (PTB) and Independents.

Minister of Foreign Affairs: CELSO LUIZ NUNES AMORIM (Ind.).
Minister of Justice: TARSO FERNANDO HERZ GENRO (PT).
Minister of Finance: GUIDO MANTEGA (PT).
Minister of Defence: NELSON AZEVEDO JOBIM (PT).
Minister of Agriculture, Fisheries and Food Supply: REINHOLD STEPHANES (PMDB).
Minister of Agrarian Development: GUILHERME CASSEL (PT).
Minister of Labour and Employment: CARLOS ROBERTO LUPI (PDT).
Minister of Transport: ALFREDO PEREIRA DO NASCIMENTO (PRB).
Minister of Cities: MÁRCIO FORTES DE ALMEIDA (PP).
Minister of Planning, Budget and Administration: PAULO BERNARDO SILVA (PT).
Minister of Mines and Energy: EDISON LOBÃO (PMDB).
Minister of Culture: GILBERTO PASSOS GIL MOREIRA (PV).
Minister of the Environment: MARIA OSMARINA MARINA DA SILVA VAZ DE LIMA (PT).
Minister of Development, Industry and Trade: MIGUEL JOÃO JORGE, Filho (Ind.).
Minister of Education: FERNANDO HADDAD (PT).
Minister of Health: JOSÉ GOMES TEMPORÃO (PMDB).
Minister of Institutional Relations: JOSÉ MÚCIO MONTEIRO, Filho (PTB).
Minister of National Integration: GEDDEL QUADROS VIEIRA LIMA (PMDB).
Minister of Social Security: LUIZ MARINHO (PT).
Minister of Social Development and the Fight against Hunger: PATRUS ANANIAS DE SOUSA (PT).
Minister of Communications: HÉLIO CALIXTO COSTA (PMDB).
Minister of Science and Technology: SÉRGIO MACHADO REZENDE (PSB).
Minister of Sport: ORLANDO SILVA DE JESUS, Júnior (PT).
Minister of Tourism: MARTA TERESA SUPLICY (PT).

Comptroller-General: JORGE HAGE, Sobrinho.
Cabinet Chief: DILMA VANA ROUSSEFF (Ind.).
There are also five Secretaries of State.

MINISTRIES

Office of the President: Palácio do Planalto, Praça dos Três Poderes, 70150-900 Brasília, DF; tel. (61) 3411-1225; e-mail protocolo@planalto.gov.br; internet www.presidencia.gov.br.

Office of the Civilian Cabinet: Palácio do Planalto, 4° andar, Praça dos Três Poderes, 70150-900 Brasília, DF; tel. (61) 2411-1221; e-mail casacivil@planalto.gov.br; internet www.presidencia.gov.br/casacivil.

Ministry of Agrarian Development: Esplanada dos Ministérios, Bloco A, Ala Norte, 70054-900 Brasília, DF; tel. (61) 3314-8003; fax (61) 3322-0492; e-mail miguel.rossetto@mda.gov.br; internet www.mda.gov.br.

Ministry of Agriculture, Fisheries and Food Supply: Esplanada dos Ministérios, Bloco D, 70043-900 Brasília, DF; tel. (61) 3218-2828; fax (61) 3225-9046; e-mail gm@agricultura.gov.br; internet www.agricultura.gov.br.

Ministry of Cities: Esplanada dos Ministérios, Bloco A, Anexo 2, 70050-901 Brasília, DF; tel. (61) 2108-1000; fax (61) 3223-5243; e-mail cidades@cidades.gov.br; internet www.cidades.gov.br.

Ministry of Communications: Esplanada dos Ministérios, Bloco R, 8° andar, 70044-900 Brasília, DF; tel. (61) 3311-6000; fax (61) 3311-6731; e-mail imprensa@mc.gov.br; internet www.mc.gov.br.

Ministry of Culture: Esplanada dos Ministérios, Bloco B, 4° andar, 70068-900 Brasília, DF; tel. (61) 3316-2171; fax (61) 3225-9162; e-mail gm@minc.gov.br; internet www.cultura.gov.br.

Ministry of Defence: Esplanada dos Ministérios, Bloco Q, 70049-900 Brasília, DF; tel. (61) 3312-4000; fax (61) 3225-4151; e-mail faleconosco@defesa.gov.br; internet www.defesa.gov.br.

Ministry of Development, Industry and Foreign Trade: Esplanada dos Ministérios, Bloco J, 70053-900 Brasília, DF; tel. (61) 3425-7000; fax (61) 3425-7230; e-mail asint@desenvolvimento.gov.br; internet www.desenvolvimento.gov.br.

Ministry of Education: Esplanada dos Ministérios, Bloco L, 70047-900 Brasília, DF; tel. (61) 2104-8731; fax (61) 2104-9172; e-mail henriquepaim@mec.gov.br; internet www.mec.gov.br.

Ministry of the Environment: Esplanada dos Ministérios, Bloco B, 5°–9° andares, 70068-900 Brasília, DF; tel. (61) 4009-1000; fax (61) 4009-1756; e-mail marina.silva@mma.gov.br; internet www.mma.gov.br.

Ministry of Finance: Esplanada dos Ministérios, Bloco P, 5° andar, 70048-900 Brasília, DF; tel. (61) 3412-2000; fax (61) 3226-9084; e-mail se.dff@fazenda.gov.br; internet www.fazenda.gov.br.

Ministry of Foreign Affairs: Palácio do Itamaraty, Esplanada dos Ministérios, Bloco H, 70170-900 Brasília, DF; tel. (61) 3411-6161; fax (61) 3225-1272; e-mail da@mre.gov.br; internet www.mre.gov.br.

Ministry of Health: Esplanada dos Ministérios, Bloco G, 70058-900 Brasília, DF; tel. (61) 3315-2425; fax (61) 3224-8747; internet www.saude.gov.br.

Ministry of Justice: Esplanada dos Ministérios, Bloco T, 70064-900 Brasília, DF; tel. (61) 3429-3000; fax 3224-0954; e-mail acs@mj.gov.br; internet www.mj.gov.br.

Ministry of Labour and Employment: Esplanada dos Ministérios, Bloco F, 5° andar, 70059-900 Brasília, DF; tel. (61) 3317-6000; fax (61) 3317-8257; e-mail ouvidoria@mte.gov.br; internet www.mte.gov.br.

Ministry of Mines and Energy: Esplanada dos Ministérios, Bloco U, 70065-900 Brasília, DF; tel. (61) 3319-5555; fax (61) 3225-5407; internet www.mme.gov.br.

Ministry of National Integration: Esplanada dos Ministérios, Bloco E, 70067-901 Brasília, DF; tel. (61) 3414-5972; fax 3321-9125; e-mail impresa@integracao.gov.br; internet www.integracao.gov.br.

Ministry of Planning, Budget and Administration: Esplanada dos Ministérios, Bloco K, 70040-906 Brasília, DF; tel. (61) 3429-4300; fax (61) 3321-7745; e-mail secretario.executivo@planejamento.gov.br; internet www.planejamento.gov.br.

Ministry of Science and Technology: Esplanada dos Ministérios, Bloco E, 4° andar, 70067-900 Brasília, DF; tel. (61) 3317-7500; fax (61) 3317-7764; e-mail lfernandes@mct.gov.br; internet www.mct.gov.br.

Ministry of Social Development and the Fight against Hunger: Esplanada dos Ministérios, Bloco C, 5° andar, 70046-900 Brasília, DF; tel. (61) 3313-1822; e-mail marcialopes@mds.gov.br; internet www.mds.gov.br.

Ministry of Social Security: Esplanada dos Ministérios, Bloco F, 70059-900 Brasília, DF; tel. (61) 3317-5151; fax (61) 3317-5407; internet www.mps.gov.br.

BRAZIL

Ministry of Sport: Esplanada dos Ministérios, Bloco A, 70054-906 Brasília, DF; tel. (61) 217-31800; fax (61) 3217-1707; e-mail ouvidoria@esporte.gov.br; internet www.esporte.gov.br.

Ministry of Tourism: Esplanada dos Ministérios, Bloco U, 70065-900 Brasília, DF; tel. (61) 3310-9491; e-mail ouvidoria@turismo.gov.br; internet www.turismo.gov.br.

Ministry of Transport: Esplanada dos Ministérios, Bloco R, 70044-900 Brasília, DF; tel. (61) 3311-7000; fax (61) 3311-7876; e-mail alfredo.nascimento@transportes.gov.br; internet www.transportes.gov.br.

Secretariat of Institutional Relations of the Presidency of the Republic: Palácio do Planalto, 4º andar, Praça dos Três Poderes, 70150-900 Brasília, DF; tel. (61) 3411-1042; fax (61) 3411-1470; e-mail sripr@planalto.gov.br; internet www.presidencia.gov.br/estrutura_presidencia/scpai.

President and Legislature

PRESIDENT

Election, First Round, 1 October 2006

Candidate	Valid votes cast	% of valid votes cast
Luiz Inácio Lula da Silva (PT)	46,662,365	48.61
Geraldo Alckmin (PSDB)	39,968,369	41.64
Heloísa Helena (P-SOL)	6,575,393	6.85
Cristovam Buarque (PDT)	2,538,844	2.64
Ana Maria Rangel (PRP)	126,404	0.13
José Maria Eymael (PSDC)	63,294	0.07
Luciano Bivar (PSL)	62,064	0.06
Total	**95,996,733**	**100.00**

In addition, there were 8,823,412 invalid votes.

Election, Second Round, 29 October 2006

Candidate	Valid votes cast	% of valid votes cast
Luiz Inácio Lula da Silva (PT)	58,295,042	60.83
Geraldo Alckmin (PSDB)	37,543,178	39.17
Total	**95,838,220**	**100.00**

In addition, there were 1,351,448 blank ballots and 4,808,553 spoiled ballots.

CONGRESSO NACIONAL

Câmara dos Deputados

Chamber of Deputies: Palácio do Congresso Nacional, Edif. Principal, Praça dos Três Poderes, 70160-900 Brasília, DF; tel. (61) 3216-0000; internet www.camara.gov.br.

President: ARLINDO CHINAGLIA (PT).

The Chamber has 513 members who hold office for a four-year term.

General Election, 1 October 2006

Party	Valid votes cast	% of valid votes cast	Seats
Partido do Movimento Democrático Brasileiro (PMDB)	13,580,517	14.57	89
Partido dos Trabalhadores (PT)	13,989,859	15.01	83
Partido da Social Democracia Brasileira (PSDB)	12,691,043	13.62	65
Partido da Frente Liberal (PFL)	10,182,308	10.93	65
Partido Progressista	6,662,309	7.15	42
Partido Socialista Brasileiro (PSB)	5,732,464	6.15	27
Partido Democrático Trabalhista (PDT)	4,854,017	5.21	24
Partido Liberal (PL)	4,074,618	4.37	23
Partido Trabalhista Brasileiro (PTB)	4,397,743	4.72	22
Partido Popular Socialista (PPS)	3,630,462	3.90	21
Partido Verde (PV)	3,368,561	3.61	13
Partido Comunista do Brasil (PC do B)	1,982,323	2.13	13
Partido Social Cristão (PSC)	1,747,863	1.88	9
Partido Trabalhista Cristão (PTC)	806,662	0.87	4
Partido Socialismo e Liberdade (P-SOL)	1,149,619	1.23	3
Partido da Mobilização Nacional (PMN)	875,686	0.94	3
Partido de Reedificação da Ordem Nacional (PRONA)	907,494	0.97	2
Partido Humanista da Solidariedade (PHS)	435,328	0.47	2
Partido Trabalhista do Brasil (PT do B)	311,833	0.33	1
Partido dos Aposentados da Nação (PAN)	264,682	0.28	1
Partido Republicano Brasileiro (PRB)	244,059	0.26	1
Total (incl. others)	**93,184,830**	**100.00**	**513**

There was a total of 11,593,921 blank or invalid votes. Voter turn-out was 83.27% of the total of 125,827,119 registered voters.

Senado Federal

Federal Senate: Palácio do Congresso Nacional, Praça dos Três Poderes, 70165-900 Brasília, DF; tel. (61) 3311-4141; fax (61) 3311-3190; e-mail webmaster.secs@senado.gov.br; internet www.senado.gov.br.

President: GARIBALDI ALVES, Filho (PMDB).

The 81 members of the Senate are elected by the 26 States and the Federal District (three Senators for each) according to the principle of majority. The Senate's term of office is eight years, with elections after four years for one-third of the members and after another four years for the remaining two-thirds.

In the elections of 1 October 2006 27 seats were contested. In that month the PMDB was represented by 20 senators, the PFL and the PSDB by 16 each, the PT by 12, the PTB and the PDT by four each, the PL by three, the PSB and the PRB by two each, and the P-SOL and the PC do B by one each.

Governors

STATES

Acre: BINHO MARQUES (PT).
Alagoas: TEOTÔNIO BRANDÃO VILELA, Filho (PSDB).
Amapá: ANTÔNIO WALDEZ GÓES (PDT).
Amazonas: CARLOS EDUARDO DE SOUZA BRAGA (PMDB).
Bahia: JACQUES WAGNER (PT).
Ceará: CID GOMES (PSB).
Espírito Santo: PAULO HARTUNG (PMDB).
Goiás: ALCIDES RODRIGUES, Filho (PP).
Maranhão: JACKSON LAGO (PDT).
Mato Grosso: BLAIRO BORGES MAGGI (PPS).
Mato Grosso do Sul: ANDRÉ PUCCINELLI (PMDB).
Minas Gerais: AÉCIO NEVES (PSDB).
Pará: ANA JÚLIA CAREPA (PT).
Paraíba: CÁSSIO RODRIGUES DA CUNHA LIMA (PSDB).
Paraná: ROBERTO REQUIÃO DE MELLO E SILVA (PMDB).
Pernambuco: EDUARDO HENRIQUE ACCIOLI CAMPOS (PSB).
Piauí: JOSÉ WELLINGTON BARROSO DE ARAÚJO DIAS (PT).
Rio de Janeiro: SÉRGIO CABRAL, Filho (PMDB).
Rio Grande do Norte: WILMA MARIA DE FARIA (PSB).
Rio Grande do Sul: YEDA CRUSIUS (PSDB).
Rondônia: IVO NARCISO CASSOL (PPS).
Roraima: JOSÉ DE ANCHIETA JÚNIOR (PSDB).
Santa Catarina: LUIZ HENRIQUE DA SILVEIRA (PMDB).
São Paulo: JOSÉ SERRA (PSDB).
Sergipe: MARCELO DÉDA (PT).
Tocantins: MARCELO MIRANDA (PMDB).

FEDERAL DISTRICT

Brasília: JOSÉ ROBERTO ARRUDA (PFL).

BRAZIL *Directory*

Election Commission

Tribunal Superior Eleitoral (TSE): Praça dos Tribunais Superiores, Bloco C, 70096-900 Brasília, DF; tel. (61) 3316-3000; fax (61) 3322-0603; e-mail webmaster@tse.gov.br; internet www.tse.gov.br; Pres. MARCO AURÉLIO MENDES DE FARIAS MELLO.

Political Organizations

In early 2008 a total of 27 political parties were registered with the Tribunal Superior Eleitoral.

Democratas (DEM): Senado Federal, Anexo 1, 26° andar, 70165-900 Brasília, DF; tel. (61) 3311-4305; fax (61) 3224-1912; e-mail democratas25@democratas.org.br; internet www.dem.org.br; f. 1985 as the Partido da Frente Liberal by moderate mems of the PDS and PMDB; re-founded in 2007 under present name; Pres. RODRIGO MAIA; Gen. Sec. JONAS PINHEIRO.

Partido Comunista do Brasil (PC do B): SCN, Quadra 01, Bloco C, Edifício Brasília Trade Center, Sala 2010, 70711-902 Brasília, DF; tel. (61) 3327 9736; fax (61) 3327 9736; e-mail secretariageral@pcdob.org.br; internet www.pcdob.org.br; f. 1922; Pres. RENATO REBELO; 185,000 mems.

Partido Democrático Trabalhista (PDT): Rua Marechal Câmara 160, 4° andar, 20050 Rio de Janeiro, RJ; tel. (21) 2232-1016; fax (21) 2262-8834; e-mail fio@pdt.org.br; internet www.pdt.org.br; f. 1980; fmrly the Partido Trabalhista Brasileiro, renamed 1980 when that name was awarded to a dissident group following controversial judicial proceedings; mem. of Socialist International; Pres. CARLOS LUPI; Gen. Sec. MANOEL DIAS.

Partido da Mobilização Nacional: Rua Martins Fontes, 197, 3° andar, Conj. 32, 01050-906 São Paulo, SP; e-mail pmn.sp@ig.com.br; internet www.pmn.org.br; f. 1984; Pres. OSCAR NORONHA, Filho; Sec.-Gen. TELMA RIBEIRO DOS SANTOS.

Partido do Movimento Democrático Brasileiro (PMDB): Câmara dos Deputados, Edif. Principal, 70160-900 Brasília, DF; tel. (61) 3318-5120; e-mail presidente@pmdb.org.br; internet www.pmdb.org.br; f. 1980 by moderate elements of fmr Movimento Democrático Brasileiro; merged with Partido Popular in 1982; Pres. MICHEL TEMER; Sec.-Gen. MAURO LOPES; factions include the Históricos and the Movimento da Unidade Progressiva (MUP).

Partido Popular Socialista (PPS): SCS, Quadra 7, Bloco A, Edif. Executive Tower, Sala 826/828, Pátio Brasil Shopping, Setor Comercial Sul, 70307-000 Brasília, DF; tel. (61) 3218-4123; fax (61) 3218-4112; e-mail pps23@pps.org.br; internet www.pps.org.br; f. 1922; Pres. ROBERTO FREIRE; Sec.-Gen. RUBENS BUENO.

Partido Progressista (PP): Senado Federal, Anexo 1, 17° andar, 70165-900 Brasília, DF; tel. (61) 3311-3041; fax (61) 3311-3984; internet www.pp.org.br; f. 1995 as Partido Progressista Brasileiro by merger of Partido Progressista Reformador, Partido Progressista and Partido Republicano Progressista; adopted present name 2003; right-wing; Pres. FRANCISCO DORNELLES; Sec.-Gen. BENEDITO DOMINGOS.

Partido da República (PR): SCN, Quadra 02, Bloco D, Torre A, Sala 601, Asa Norte, 70712-930 Brasília, DF; tel. and fax (61) 3202-9922; e-mail pr22@partidodarepublica.org.br; internet www.partidodarepublica.org.br; f. 2006 by merger of Partido Liberal and Partido de Reedificação da Ordem Nacional; Pres. SÉRGIO VICTOR TAMER.

Partido Republicano Brasileiro (PRB): SDS, Edif. Miguel Abadya, Bloco L 30, Sala 320, 70394-901 Brasília, DF; tel. and fax (61) 3223-9069; f. 2005 as Partido Municipalista Renovador; name changed as above in 2006; political wing of Igreja Universal do Reino de Deus; Pres. VITOR PAULO ARAÚJO DOS SANTOS.

Partido Social Cristão (PSC): Rua Pouso Alegre, 1388, Santa Teresa, 31015-030 Belo Horizonte, MG; tel. (31) 3467-1390; fax (31) 3467-6522; e-mail psc@psc.org.br; internet www.psc.org.br; f. 1970 as Partido Democrático Republicano; Pres. VITOR JORGE ADBALA NÓSSEIS; Sec.-Gen. ANTONIO OLIBONI.

Partido da Social Democracia Brasileira (PSDB): SGAS, Quadra 607, Edif. Metrópolis, Asa Sul, 70200-670 Brasília, DF; tel. (61) 3424-0500; fax (61) 3424-0515; e-mail tucano@psdb.org.br; internet www.psdb.org.br; f. 1988; centre-left; formed by dissident mems of parties incl. the PMDB, PFL, PDT, PSB and PTB; Pres. SÉRGIO GUERRA; Sec.-Gen. RODRIGO DE CASTRO.

Partido Social Liberal (PSL): SCS, Quadra 01, Bloco E, Edif. Ceará, Sala 1004, 70303-900 Brasília, DF; tel. and fax (61) 3322-1721; fax (61) 3032-6832; e-mail contato@pslnacional.org.br; internet www.pslnacional.org.br; f. 1994; Pres. LUCIANO CALDAS BIVAR; Sec.-Gen. RONALDO NÓBREGA MEDEIROS.

Partido Socialismo e Liberdade (P-SOL): SCS, Quadra 1, Bloco E, Edifício Ceará, Salas 1203–04, 70303-900 Brasília, DF; tel. and fax (61) 3963- 1750; e-mail secretaria@psol.org.br; internet www.psol.org.br; f. 2004 by fmr PT mems; Pres. HELOÍSA HELENA.

Partido Socialista Brasileiro (PSB): SCLN 304, Bloco A, Sobreloja 1, Entrada 63, 70736-510 Brasília, DF; tel. (61) 3327-6405; fax (61) 3327-5196; e-mail psb@psbnacional.org.br; internet www.psbnacional.org.br; f. 1947; Pres. EDUARDO CAMPOS; Sec.-Gen. RENATO CASAGRANDE.

Partido dos Trabalhadores (PT): Rua Silveira Martins 132, Centro, 01019-000 São Paulo, SP; tel. (11) 3243-1313; fax (11) 3243-1345; e-mail presidencia@pt.org.br; internet www.pt.org.br; f. 1980; first independent labour party; associated with the *autêntico* br. of the trade union movt; 350,000 mems; Pres. RICARDO JOSÉ RIBEIRO BERZOINI.

Partido Trabalhista Brasileiro (PTB): SAS Quadra 1, Bloco M, Edif. Libertas, Loja 101, 70070-935 Brasília, DF; tel. (61) 2101-1414; fax (61) 2101-1400; e-mail ptb@ptb.org.br; internet www.ptb.org.br; f. 1980; Pres. ROBERTO JEFFERSON MONTEIRO FRANCISCO; Sec.-Gen. ANTÔNIO CARLOS DE CAMPOS MACHADO.

Partido Trabalhista Cristão (PTC): Av. Nilo Peçanha 50, Sala 506, Centro, Rio de Janeiro 20220-460, RJ; tel. (21) 3974-3523; fax (21) 2220-1832; e-mail ptcnacional@uol.com.br; internet www.ptc.org.br; fmrly the Partido da Reconstrução Nacional; Christian party; Pres. DANIEL S. TOURINHO; Sec.-Gen. RIVAILTON PINTO VELOSO DA SILVA.

Partido Verde (PV): Edif. Miguel Badya Bloco L, sala 218, Brasília, DF; tel. (61) 3366-1569; e-mail nacional@pv.org.br; internet www.pv.org.br; Pres. JOSÉ LUIZ DE FRANÇA PENNA; Organizing Sec. CARLA PIRANDA.

Other political parties include the Partido da Causa Operária (PCO), the Partido Republicano Progressista (PRP), the Partido Social Democrata Cristão (PSDC; internet www.psdc.org.br), the Partido Trabalhista do Brasil (PT do B)and the Partido Humanista da Solidariedade (PHS; internet www.phs.org.br).

OTHER ORGANIZATIONS

Movimento dos Trabalhadores Rurais Sem Terra (MST): Alameda Barão de Limeira, 1232 Campos Elíseos, 01202-002 São Paulo, SP; tel. (11) 3361-3866; e-mail semterra@mst.org.br; internet www.mst.org.br; landless peasant movt; Pres. JOÃO PERO STÉDILE; Nat. Co-ordinator GILMAR MAURO.

Other rural movements include the Organização da Luto no Campo (OLC) and the Movimento de Liberação dos Sem Terra (MLST), a dissident faction of the MST.

Diplomatic Representation

EMBASSIES IN BRAZIL

Algeria: SHIS, QI 09, Conj. 13, Casa 01, Lago Sul, 70472-900 Brasília, DF; tel. (61) 3248-4039; fax (61) 3248-4691; e-mail sanag277@bsb.terra.com.br; Ambassador MOHAMMED ACHACHE.

Angola: SHIS, QL 06, Conj. 5, Casa 01, 71620-055 Brasília, DF; tel. (61) 3248-4489; fax (61) 3248-1567; e-mail emb.angola@tecnolink.com.br; internet www.angola.org.br; Ambassador LEOVIGILDO DA COSTA E SILVA.

Argentina: SHIS, QL 02, Conj. 01, Casa 19, Lago Sul, 70442-900 Brasília, DF; tel. (61) 3364-7600; fax (61) 3364-7666; e-mail ebras@mrecic.gov.br; internet www.brasil.embajada-argentina.gov.ar; Ambassador JUAN PABLO LOHLÉ.

Australia: SES, Av. Das Nações, Quadra 801, Conj. K, Lote 7, 70200-010 Brasília, DF; tel. (61) 3226-3111; fax (61) 3226-1112; e-mail embaustr@dfat.gov.au; internet www.brazil.embassy.gov.au; Ambassador NEIL ALLAN MULES.

Austria: SES, Av. das Nações, Quadra 811, Lote 40, 70426-900 Brasília, DF; tel. (61) 3443-3111; fax (61) 3443-5233; e-mail brasilia-ob@bmaa.gv.at; Ambassador WERNER BRANDSTETTER.

Belgium: SES, Av. das Nações, Quadra 809, Lote 32, 70422-900 Brasília, DF; tel. (61) 3443-1133; fax (61) 3443-1219; e-mail brasilia@diplobel.org; internet www.belgica.org.br; Ambassador JOHAN BALLEGEER.

Benin: SHIS, QI 9, Conj. 11, Casa 24, Lago Sul, 71625-110 Brasília, DF; tel. (61) 3248-2192; fax (61) 3248-5440; e-mail ambabeninbrasilia@yahoo.fr; Ambassador ISIDORE BENJAMIN AMÉDÉE MONSI.

Bolivia: SHIS, QI 19, Conj. 13, Casa 19, 71655-130 Brasília, DF; tel. (61) 3366-3432; fax (61) 3366-3136; e-mail embolivia-brasilia@embolivia.org.br; internet www.embolivia-brasil.org.br; Ambassador RENÉ MAURICIO DORFLER OCAMPO.

Bulgaria: SEN, Av. das Nações, Quadra 801, Lote 08, 70432-900 Brasília, DF; tel. (61) 3223-6193; fax (61) 3323-3285; e-mail bulgaria@linkexpress.com.br; Ambassador NIKOLAY TZATCHEV.

BRAZIL
Directory

Cameroon: SHIS, QI 09, Conj. 07, Casa 01, 71625-070 Brasília, DF; tel. (61) 3248-5403; fax (61) 3248-0443; e-mail embcameroun@embcameroun.org.br; internet www.embcameroun.org.br; Ambassador Martin Mbarga Nguele.

Canada: SES, Av. das Nações, Quadra 803, Lote 16, 70410-900 Brasília, DF; tel. (61) 3424-5400; fax (61) 3424-5490; e-mail brsla@international.gc.ca; internet www.dfait-maeci.gc.ca/brazil; Ambassador Paul Hunt.

Cape Verde: SHIS, QL 14, Conj. 03, Casa 08, Lago Sul, 71640-035 Brasília, DF; tel. (61) 3248-0543; fax (61) 3364-4059; e-mail embcvbrasil@embcv.org.br; internet www.embcv.org.br; Ambassador Daniel António Pereira.

Chile: SES, Av. das Nações, Quadra 803, Lote 11, 70407-900 Brasília, DF; tel. (61) 2103-5151; fax (61) 3322-0714; e-mail embchile@embchile.org.br; Ambassador Alvaro Humberto Abel Diaz Pérez.

China, People's Republic: SES, Av. das Nações, Quadra 813, Lote 51, 70443-900 Brasília, DF; tel. (61) 2198-8200; fax (61) 3346-3299; e-mail chinaemb_br@mfa.gov.cn; internet www.embchina.org.br; Ambassador Chen Duqing.

Colombia: SES, Av. das Nações, Quadra 803, Lote 10, 70444-900 Brasília, DF; tel. (61) 3226-8997; fax (61) 3224-4732; e-mail embjcol@embcol.org.br; internet www.embcol.org.br; Ambassador Tony Jozame Amar.

Congo, Democratic Republic: SHIS, QL 06, Conj. 04, Casa 15, Lago Sul, CP 71620-045 Brasília, DF; tel. (61) 3365-4822; fax (61) 3365-4823; e-mail ambaredeco@ig.com.br; Chargé d'affaires a.i. Baudouin Mayola ma Lulendo.

Costa Rica: SRTV/N 701, Conj. C, Ala A, Salas 308/310, Edif. Centro Empresarial Norte, 70710-200 Brasília, DF; tel. (61) 328-32219; fax (61) 3328-2243; e-mail embcostaricabr@solar.com.br; Ambassador Jorge Alfredo Robles Arias.

Côte d'Ivoire: SEN, Av. das Nações, Lote 09, 70473-900 Brasília, DF; tel. (61) 3321-7320; fax (61) 3321-1306; e-mail cotedivoire@cotedivoire.org.br; internet www.cotedivoire.org.br; Ambassador Daouda Diabate.

Croatia: SHIS, QI 09, Conj. 11, Casa 03, 71625-110 Brasília, DF; tel. (61) 3248-0610; fax (61) 3248-1708; e-mail embaixada.croacia@terra.com.br; Ambassador Rade Marélic.

Cuba: SHIS, QI 05, Conj. 18, Casa 01, 71615-180 Brasília, DF; tel. (61) 3248-4710; fax (61) 3248-6778; e-mail embacuba@uol.com.br; internet www.embaixadacuba.org.br; Ambassador Pedro Juan Núñez Mosquera.

Czech Republic: SES, Via L3 Sul, Quadra 805, Lote 21, CP 170, 70414-900 Brasília, DF; tel. (61) 3242-7785; fax (61) 3242-7833; e-mail brasilia@embassy.mzv.cz; internet www.mzv.cz/brasilia; Chargé d'affaires a.i. Jana Chaloupková.

Denmark: SES, Av. das Nações, Quadra 807, Lote 26, 70416-900 Brasília, DF; tel. (61) 3445-3443; fax (61) 3445-3509; e-mail bsbamb@um.dk; internet www.ambbrasilia.um.dk; Ambassador Christian Kønigsfeldt.

Dominican Republic: SHIS, QL 06, Conj. 07, Casa 02, 71626-075 Brasília, DF; tel. (61) 3248-1405; fax (61) 3364-3214; e-mail embdombrasil@serex.gov.do; Ambassador Manuel Morales Lama.

Ecuador: SHIS, QI 11, Conj. 09, Casa 24, 71625-290 Brasília, DF; tel. (61) 3248-5560; fax (61) 3248-1290; e-mail embeq@solar.com.br; internet www.embequador.org.br; Ambassador Eduardo Rodrigo Alfonso Mora-Anda.

Egypt: SEN, Av. das Nações, Lote 12, 70435-900 Brasília, DF; tel. (61) 3323-8800; fax (61) 3323-1039; e-mail embegito@opengate.com.br; internet www.opengate.com.br/embegito; Ambassador Muhammad Abd al-Fattah Abdallah.

El Salvador: SHIS, QL 10, Conj. 01, Casa 15, Lago Sul, 71630-100 Brasília, DF; tel. (61) 3364-4141; fax (61) 3364-2459; e-mail elsalvador@embelsalvador.brte.com.br; Ambassador César Edgardo Martínez Flores.

Equatorial Guinea: SHIS, QL 10, Conj. 09, Casa 01, 70630-095 Brasília, DF; tel. (61) 3364-4185; fax (61) 3364-1641; Ambassador Teodoro Biyogo Nsué Okomo.

Finland: SES, Av. das Nações, Quadra 807, Lote 27, 70417-900 Brasília, DF; tel. (61) 3443-7151; fax (61) 3443-3315; e-mail brasilia@finlandia.org.br; internet www.finlandia.org.br; Ambassador Ilpo Ilmari Manninen.

France: SES, Av. das Nações, Quadra 801, Lote 04, 70404-900 Brasília, DF; tel. (61) 3312-9100; fax (61) 3312-9108; e-mail france@ambafrance.org.br; internet www.ambafrance.org.br; Ambassador Antoine Pouillieute.

Gabon: SHIS, QL 08, Conj. 03, Casa 01, Lago Sul, 71620-235 Brasília, DF; tel. (61) 3248-3536; fax (61) 3248-2241; e-mail mgabao@terra.com.br; Ambassador Benjamin Legnongo-Ndumba.

Germany: SES, Av. das Nações, Quadra 807, Lote 25, 70415-900 Brasília, DF; tel. (61) 3442-7000; fax (61) 3443-7508; e-mail info.brasilia@alemanha.org.br; internet www.brasilia.diplo.de; Ambassador Friedrich Prot von Kunow.

Ghana: SHIS, QL 10, Conj. 08, Casa 02, 70466-900 Brasília, DF; tel. (61) 3248-6047; fax (61) 3248-7913; e-mail ghaembra@zaz.com.br; Ambassador Samuel Kofi Dadey.

Greece: SES, Av. das Nações, Quadra 805, Lote 22, 70480-900 Brasília, DF; tel. (61) 3443-6573; fax (61) 3443-6902; e-mail info@emb-grecia.org.br; internet www.emb-grecia.org.br; Ambassador Andonios Nicolaidis.

Guatemala: SHIS, QI 03, Conj. 10, Casa 01, Lago Sul, 71605-001 Brasília, DF; tel. (61) 3365-1908; fax (61) 3365-1906; e-mail embaguate-brasil@minex.gob.gt; Ambassador Carlos Jiménez Licona.

Guinea: SHIS QL 02, Conj. 07, Casa 09, Lago Sul, 71610-075 Brasília, DF; tel. (61) 3365-1301; fax (61) 3365-4921; e-mail ambaguibrasil@terra.com.br; Ambassador Fodé Touré.

Guyana: SHIS, QI 05, Conj. 19, Casa 24, 71615-190 Brasília, DF; tel. (61) 3248-0874; fax (61) 3248-0886; e-mail embguyana@embguyana.org.br; internet www.embguyana.org.br; Ambassador Marilyn Cheryl Miles.

Haiti: SHIS, QL 10, Conj. 06, Casa 16, Lago Sul, 71630-065 Brasília, DF; tel. (61) 3248-6860; fax (61) 3248-7472; e-mail embhaiti@terra.com.br; Ambassador (vacant).

Holy See: SES, Av. das Nações, Quadra 801, Lote 01, 70401-900 Brasília, DF; tel. (61) 3223-0794; fax (61) 3224-9365; e-mail nunapost@solar.com.br; Apostolic Nuncio Most Rev. Lorenzo Baldisseri (Titular Archbishop of Diocletiana).

Honduras: SHIS, QI 19, Conj. 07, Casa 34, Lago Sul, 71655-070 Brasília, DF; tel. (61) 3366-4082; fax (61) 3366-4618; e-mail embhonduras@ig.com.br; Ambassador Victor Manuel Lozano Urbina.

Hungary: SES, Av. das Nações, Quadra 805, Lote 19, 70413-900 Brasília, DF; tel. (61) 3443-0836; fax (61) 3443-3434; e-mail huembbrz@terra.com.br; internet www.hungria.org.br; Ambassador Dr Csaba Pólyi.

India: SHIS, QL 08, Conj. 08, Casa 01, 71620-285 Brasília, DF; tel. (61) 3248-4006; fax (61) 3248-7849; e-mail indemb@indianembassy.org.br; internet www.indianembassy.org.br; Ambassador Hardeep Singh Puri.

Indonesia: SES, Av. das Nações, Quadra 805, Lote 20, 70479-900 Brasília, DF; tel. (61) 3443-8800; fax (61) 3443-6732; e-mail kbribrasilia@persocom.com.br; internet www.indonesia-brasil.org.br; Ambassador Bali Moniaga.

Iran: SES, Av. das Nações, Quadra 809, Lote 31, 70421-900 Brasília, DF; tel. (61) 3242-5733; fax (61) 3224-9640; e-mail webiran@webiran.org.br; internet www.webiran.org.br; Ambassador (vacant).

Iraq: SES, Av. das Nações, Quadra 815, Lote 64, 70430-900 Brasília, DF; tel. (61) 3346-2822; fax (61) 3346-7034; e-mail embaixadairaque@terra.com.br; Chargé d'affaires a.i. Hussein Ali Abd al-Baqi Rammah.

Ireland: SHIS QL 12, Conj. 05, Casa 09, Lago Sul, Brasília, DF; tel. (61) 3248-8800; fax (61) 3248-8816; e-mail brasiliaembassy@dfa.ie; Ambassador Michael Hoey.

Israel: SES, Av. das Nações, Quadra 809, Lote 38, 70424-900 Brasília, DF; tel. (61) 2105-0500; fax (61) 2105-0555; e-mail info@brasilia.mfa.gov.il; internet brasilia.mfa.gov.il; Ambassador Tzipora Rimon.

Italy: SES, Av. das Nações, Quadra 807, Lote 30, 70420-900 Brasília, DF; tel. (61) 3442-9900; fax (61) 3443-1231; e-mail embitalia@embitalia.org.br; internet www.italian-embassy.org.ae/ambasciata_brasilia; Ambassador Michele Valensise.

Japan: SES, Av. das Nações, Quadra 811, Lote 39, 70425-900 Brasília, DF; tel. (61) 3442-4200; fax (61) 3242-0738; e-mail consularjapao@yawl.com.br; internet www.br.emb-japan.go.jp; Ambassador Ken Shimanouchi.

Jordan: SHIS, QI 09, Conj. 18, Casa 14, 70483-900 Brasília, DF; tel. (61) 3248-5414; fax (61) 3248-1698; e-mail emb.jordania@apis.com.br; Ambassador Ramez Zaki Odeh Goussous.

Kenya: SHIS, QL 10, Conj. 08, Casa 08, Lago Sul, 71630-085 Brasília, DF; tel. (61) 3364-0691; fax (61) 3364-0978; e-mail brazil@mfa.go.ke; Ambassador Pius Namachanja.

Korea, Democratic People's Republic: SHIS, QI 25, Conj. 10, Casa 11, Brasília, DF; tel. (61) 3367-1940; fax (61) 3367-3177; e-mail embcorea@hotmail.com; Ambassador Pak Hyok.

Korea, Republic: SEN, Av. das Nações, Lote 14, 70436-900 Brasília, DF; tel. (61) 3321-2500; fax (61) 3321-2508; e-mail emb-br@mofat.go.kr; internet bra-brasilia.mofat.go.kr; Ambassador Choi Jong-Hwa.

Kuwait: SHIS, QI 05, Chácara 30, Lago Sul, 71600-550 Brasília, DF; tel. (61) 3213-2333; fax (61) 3248-0969; e-mail kuwait@opendf.com.br; Ambassador WALEED AHMAD MUHAMMAD AHMAD AL-KANDARI.

Lebanon: SES, Av. das Nações, Quadra 805, Lote 17, 70411-900 Brasília, DF; tel. (61) 3443-5552; fax (61) 3443-8574; e-mail embaixada@libano.org.br; internet www.libano.org.br; Ambassador FOUAD EL-KHOURY GHANEM.

Libya: SHIS, QI 15, Chácara 26, Lago Sul 71600-750 Brasília, DF; tel. (61) 3248-6710; fax (61) 3248-0598; e-mail emblibia@terra.com.br; Ambassador SALEM OMAR ABDULLAH AZ-ZUBAIDI.

Malaysia: SHIS, QI 05, Chácara 62, 70477-900 Brasília, DF; tel. (61) 3248-5008; fax (61) 3248-6307; e-mail mwbrasilia@persocom.com.br; Ambassador Dato' ISMAIL BIN MUSTAPHA.

Mauritania: Hotel Meliá Comfort, apt. 1606, SHS, Quadra 6, Conj. A, Bloco D, Asa Sul, 70316-000 Brasília, DF; tel. (61) 3218-4700; Ambassador N'DIAYE KANE.

Mexico: SES, Av. das Nações, Quadra 805, Lote 18, 70412-900 Brasília, DF; tel. (61) 3244-1011; fax (61) 3244-1755; e-mail embamexbra@cabonet.com.br; internet www.mexico.org.br; Ambassador ANDRÉS VALENCIA BENAVIDES.

Morocco: SEN, Av. das Nações, Quadra 801, Lote 02, 70432-900 Brasília, DF; tel. (61) 3321-4487; fax (61) 3321-0745; e-mail sifamarbr@onix.com.br; Ambassador FARIDA JAIDI.

Mozambique: SHIS, QL 12, Conj. 07, Casa 09, 71630-275 Brasília, DF; tel. (61) 3248-4222; fax (61) 3248-3917; e-mail embamoc-bsb@uol.com; Ambassador MURADE ISAAC MIGUIGY MURARGY.

Myanmar: SHIS, QI 13, Conj. 08, Casa 09, Lago Sul, 71615-340 Brasília, DF; tel. (61) 3248-3747; fax (61) 3364-2747; e-mail mebrsl@brnet.com.br; Ambassador U HTEIN WIN.

Namibia: SHIS QI 09, Conj. 08, Casa 11, Lago Sul, 71625-080 Brasília, DF; tel. (61) 3248-6274; fax (61) 3248-7135; e-mail info@embassyofnamibia.org.br; internet www.embassyofnamibia.org.br; Ambassador HOPELONG UUSHONA IPINGE.

Netherlands: SES, Av. das Nações, Quadra 801, Lote 05, 70405-900 Brasília, DF; tel. (61) 3961-3200; fax (61) 3961-3234; e-mail bra@minbuza.nl; internet www.mfa.nl/brasil; Ambassador ONNO HATTINGA VAN'T SANT.

New Zealand: SHIS, QI 09, Conj. 16, Casa 01, 71625-160 Brasília, DF; tel. (61) 3248-9900; fax (61) 3248-9916; e-mail zelandia@nwi.com.br; Ambassador ALISON MANN.

Nicaragua: SHIS, QL 16, Conj. 04, Casa 15, 71640-245 Brasília, DF; tel. (61) 3248-1115; fax (61) 3248-1120; e-mail embanibra@terra.com.br; Ambassador SARA MARÍA TÓRREZ RUIZ.

Nigeria: SEN, Av. das Nações, Lote 05, 70459-900 Brasília, DF; tel. (61) 3226-1717; fax (61) 3226-5192; e-mail admin@nigerianembassy-brazil.org; internet www.nigerianembassy-brazil.org; Ambassador KAYODE GARRICK.

Norway: SES, Av. das Nações, Quadra 807, Lote 28, 70418-900 Brasília, DF; tel. (61) 3443-8720; fax (61) 3443-2942; e-mail emb.brasilia@mfa.no; internet www.noruega.org.br; Ambassador TURID B. RODRIGUES EUSÉBIO.

Pakistan: SHIS, QL 12, Conj. 02, Casa 19, 71630-225 Brasília, DF; tel. (61) 3364-1632; fax (61) 3248-0246; e-mail parepbra@bruturbo.com; Ambassador MUHAMMAD HAROON SHAUKAT.

Panama: SHIS, QI 03, Conj. 09, Casa 11, 71605-290 Brasília, DF; tel. (61) 3248-7309; fax (61) 3248-2834; e-mail empanamabr@embaixada.brte.com.br; Ambassador JUAN BOSCO BERNAL YANIS.

Paraguay: SES, Av. das Nações, Quadra 811, Lote 42, 70427-900 Brasília, DF; tel. (61) 3242-3732; fax (61) 3242-4605; e-mail embapar-sec1@yawl.com.br; Ambassador LUIS GONZÁLEZ ARIAS.

Peru: SES, Av. das Nações, Quadra 811, Lote 43, 70428-900 Brasília, DF; tel. (61) 3242-9933; fax (61) 3244-9344; e-mail embperu@embperu.org.br; internet www.embperu.org.br; Ambassador HUGO CLAUDIO DE ZELA MARTÍNEZ.

Philippines: SEN, Av. das Nações, Lote 01, 70431-900 Brasília, DF; tel. (61) 3223-5143; fax (61) 3226-7411; e-mail pg@persocom.com.br; Ambassador TERESITA V. G. BARSANA.

Poland: SES, Av. das Nações, Quadra 809, Lote 33, 70423-900 Brasília, DF; tel. (61) 3212-8000; fax (61) 3242-8543; e-mail embaixada@polonia.org.br; internet www.polonia.org.br; Ambassador JACEK JUNOSZA-KISIELEWSKI.

Portugal: SES Sul, Av. das Nações, Quadra 801, Lote 02, 70402-900 Brasília, DF; tel. (61) 3032-9600; fax (61) 3032-9642; e-mail embaixadaportugal@embaixadaportugal.org.br; internet www.embaixadadeportugal.org.br; Ambassador FRANCISCO MANUEL SEIXAS DA COSTA.

Qatar: SHIS, QL 20, Conj. 01, Casa 19, Lago Sul, 71650-115 Brasília, DF; tel. (61) 3366-1005; fax (61) 3366-1115; e-mail qatarbsb@embcatar.org.br; Ambassador JAMAL NASSER SULTAN AL-BADR.

Romania: SEN, Av. das Nações, Lote 06, 70456-900 Brasília, DF; tel. (61) 3226-0746; fax (61) 3226-6629; e-mail romenia@solar.com.br; Ambassador MIHAI ZAMFIR.

Russia: SES, Av. das Nações, Quadra 801, Lote A, 70476-900 Brasília, DF; tel. (61) 3223-3094; fax (61) 3226-7319; e-mail emb@embrus.brte.com.br; internet www.brazil.mid.ru; Ambassador VLADIMIR L. TYURDENEV.

Saudi Arabia: SHIS, QL 10, Conj. 09, Casa 20, 70471-900 Brasília, DF; tel. (61) 3248-3523; fax (61) 3284-1142; e-mail embsaud@terra.com.br; internet www.saudiembassy.org.br; Chargé d'affaires a.i. HODA OMAR SALEH AL-OYAIDI.

Senegal: SEN, Av. das Nações, Lote 18, 70800-400 Brasília, DF; tel. (61) 3223-6110; fax (61) 3322-7822; e-mail senebrasilia@senebrasilia.com.br; internet www.senebrasilia.org.br; Ambassador FODÉ SECK.

Serbia: SES, Av. das Nações, Quadra 803, Lote 15, 70409-900 Brasília, DF; tel. (61) 3223-7272; fax (61) 3223-8462; e-mail embaixadaservia@terra.com.br; Ambassador DUŠAN GAJIĆ.

Slovakia: Av. das Nações, Quadra 805, Lote 21, 70414-900 Brasília, DF; tel. (61) 3443-1263; fax (61) 3443-1267; e-mail eslovaca@brasil.mfa.sk; Ambassador MARIÁN MASARIK.

South Africa: SES, Av. das Nações, Quadra 801, Lote 06, 70406-900 Brasília, DF; tel. (61) 3312-9500; fax (61) 3322-8491; e-mail saemb@solar.com.br; internet www.africadosul.org.br; Ambassador LINDIWE DAPHNE ZULU.

Spain: SES, Av. das Nações, Quadra 811, Lote 44, 70429-900 Brasília, DF; tel. (61) 3244-2121; fax (61) 3242-1781; e-mail embespbr@correo.mae.es; Ambassador RICARDO PEIDRÓ CONDE.

Sri Lanka: SHIS, QI 09, Conj. 09, Casa 07, Lago Sul, 71625-090 Brasília, DF; tel. (61) 3248-2701; fax (61) 3364-5430; e-mail lankaemb@yawl.com.br; Ambassador SWANDA HENNEDIGE SHANTHA KOTTEGODA.

Sudan: SHIS, QI 11, Conj. 5, Casa 13, Lago Sul, 71635-050 Brasília, DF; tel. (61) 3248-4835; fax (61) 3248-4833; e-mail sdbrasilia@sudanbrasilia.org; internet www.sudanbrasilia.org; Ambassador RAHAMTALLA MOHAMED OSMAN.

Suriname: SHIS, QI 09, Conj. 08, Casa 24, 71625-080 Brasília, DF; tel. (61) 3248-6706; fax (61) 3248-3791; e-mail surinameemb@terra.com.br; Ambassador GEORGINE MAVIS DEMON-BELGRAEF.

Sweden: SES, Av. das Nações, Quadra 807, Lote 29, 70419-900 Brasília, DF; tel. (61) 3442-5200; fax (61) 3443-1187; e-mail ambassaden.brasilia@foreign.ministry.se; internet www.suecia.org.br; Ambassador ANNIKA MARKOVIC.

Switzerland: SES, Av. das Nações, Quadra 811, Lote 41, 70448-900 Brasília, DF; tel. (61) 3443-5500; fax (61) 3443-5711; e-mail vertretung@bra.rep.admin.ch; internet www.dfae.admin.ch/brasilia; Ambassador RUDOLF BAERFUSS.

Syria: SEN, Av. das Nações, Lote 11, 70434-900 Brasília, DF; tel. (61) 3226-0970; fax (61) 3223-2595; e-mail embsiria@uol.com.br; Ambassador (vacant).

Tanzania: SHIS, QI 09, Conj. 16, Casa 20, Lago Sul, 71615-190, Brasília, DF; tel. (61) 3364-2629; fax (61) 3248-3361; e-mail tanrepbrasilia@yahoo.com.br; Ambassador JORAM MUKAMA BISWARO.

Thailand: SEN, Av. das Nações, Lote 10, 70433-900 Brasília, DF; tel. (61) 3224-6943; fax (61) 3323-7502; e-mail thaiemb@linkexpress.com.br; Ambassador SIREE BUNNAG.

Trinidad and Tobago: SHIS, QL 02, Conj. 02, Casa 01, 71665-028 Brasília, DF; tel. (61) 3365-1132; fax (61) 3365-1733; e-mail trinbago@terra.com.br; Ambassador MONICA JUNE CLEMENT.

Tunisia: SHIS, QI 11, Conj. 01, Casa 23, 71625-210 Brasília, DF; tel. (61) 3248-7277; fax (61) 3248-7355; e-mail at.brasilia@terra.com.br; Ambassador SEIFEDDINE CHERIF.

Turkey: SES, Av. das Nações, Quadra 805, Lote 23, 70452-900 Brasília, DF; tel. (61) 3242-1850; fax (61) 3242-1448; e-mail turquia@conectanet.com.br; Ambassador AHMET GÜRKAN.

Ukraine: SHIS QI 05, Conj. 04, Casa 02, 71615-040 Brasília, DF; tel. (61) 3365-3889; fax (61) 3365-2127; e-mail brucremb@zaz.com.br; internet www.ucrania.org.br; Ambassador VOLODYMYR LAKOMOV.

United Arab Emirates: SHIS, QI 05, Chácara 54, 71600-580 Brasília, DF; tel. (61) 3248-0717; fax (61) 3248-7543; e-mail uae@uae.org.br; internet www.uae.org.br; Ambassador YOUSEF ALI AL-USAIMI.

United Kingdom: SES, Quadra 801, Conj. K, Lote 08, 70408-900 Brasília, DF; tel. (61) 3329-2300; fax (61) 3329-2369; e-mail contato@reinounido.org.br; internet www.reinounido.org.br; Ambassador Dr PETER COLLECOTT.

USA: SES, Av. das Nações, Quadra 801, Lote 03, 70403-900 Brasília, DF; tel. (61) 3321-7000; fax (61) 3325-9136; e-mail ircbsb@state.gov; internet brasilia.usembassy.gov; Ambassador CLIFFORD M. SOBEL.

Uruguay: SES, Av. das Nações, Quadra 803, Lote 14, 70450-900 Brasília, DF; tel. (61) 3322-1200; fax (61) 3322-6534; e-mail urubras@

BRAZIL   *Directory*

emburuguai.org.br; internet www.emburuguai.org.br; Ambassador Pedro Humberto Vaz Ramela.

Venezuela: SES, Av. das Nações, Quadra 803, Lote 13, 70451-900 Brasília, DF; tel. (61) 3322-1011; fax (61) 3226-5633; e-mail emb@embvenezuela.org.br; internet www.embvenezuela.org.br; Ambassador Julio José García Montoya.

Viet Nam: SHIS, QI 09, Conj. 10, Casa 01, Lago Sul, 71625-100 Brasília, DF; tel. (61) 3364-7856; fax (61) 3364-5836; e-mail embavina@yahoo.com; Ambassador Nguyen Thac Dinh.

Zambia: SHIS, QL 10, Conj. 6, Casa 10, Lago Sul, 71630-065 Brasília, DF; tel. and fax (61) 3248-3494; e-mail zambiaembassybr@yahoo.com; Ambassador Albert M. Muchanga.

Zimbabwe: SHIS, QI 03, Conj. 10, Casa 13, Brasília, DF; tel. (61) 3365-4801; fax (61) 3365-4803; e-mail zimbrasilia@uol.com.br; internet www.zimbabue-brasilia.org.br; Ambassador Thomas Sukutai Bvuma.

Judicial System

The judiciary powers of the State are held by the following: the Supreme Federal Court, the Higher Court of Justice, the five Regional Federal Courts and Federal Judges, the Higher Labour Court, the 24 Regional Labour Courts, the Conciliation and Judgment Councils and Labour Judges, the Higher Electoral Court, the 27 Regional Electoral Courts, the Electoral Judges and Electoral Councils, the Higher Military Court, the Military Courts and Military Judges, the Courts of the States and Judges of the States, the Court of the Federal District and of the Territories and Judges of the Federal District and of the Territories.

The Supreme Federal Court comprises 11 ministers, nominated by the President and approved by the Senate. Its most important role is to rule on the final interpretation of the Constitution. The Supreme Federal Court has the power to declare an act of Congress void if it is unconstitutional. It judges offences committed by persons such as the President, the Vice-President, members of the Congresso Nacional, Ministers of State, its own members, the Attorney-General, judges of other higher courts, and heads of permanent diplomatic missions. It also judges cases of litigation between the Union and the States, between the States, or between foreign nations and the Union or the States; disputes as to jurisdiction between higher Courts, or between the latter and any other court, in cases involving the extradition of criminals, and others related to the writs of habeas corpus and habeas data, and in other cases.

The Higher Court of Justice comprises 33 members, appointed by the President and approved by the Senado. Its jurisdiction includes the judgment of offences committed by State Governors. The Regional Federal Courts comprise at least seven judges, recruited when possible in the respective region and appointed by the President of the Republic. The Higher Labour Court comprises 17 members, appointed by the President and approved by the Senado. The judges of the Regional Labour Courts are also appointed by the President. The Regional Electoral Courts are composed of seven members. The Higher Military Court comprises 15 life members, appointed by the President and approved by the Senate; three from the navy, four from the army, three from the air force and five civilian members. The States are responsible for the administration of their own justice, according to the principles established by the Constitution.

SUPREME FEDERAL COURT

Supremo Tribunal Federal: Praça dos Três Poderes, 70175-900 Brasília, DF; tel. (61) 3217-3000; fax (61) 3316-5483; internet www.stf.gov.br.

President: Ellen Gracie Northfleet.

Vice-President: Gilmar Ferreira Mendes.

Justices: José Celso de Mello, Filho, Marco Aurelio Mendes de Farias Mello, Antonio Cezar Peluso, Carlos Ayres Britto, Joaquim Benedito Barbosa Gomes, Eros Roberto Grau, Enrique Ricardo Lewandowski, Cármen Lúcia Antunes Rocha, Carlos Alberto Menezes Direito.

Attorney-General: Antônio Fernando de Barros e Silva de Souza.

Director-General (Secretariat): Sérgio José Américo Pedreira.

Religion

According to the census of 2000, there were around 125m. Roman Catholics, 26m. Evangelical Christians, 1m. Jehovah's Witnesses, and 2m. Spiritualists. Other faiths include Islam (27,239), Buddhism (214,873) and Judaism (86,825). There are also followers of African and indigenous religions.

CHRISTIANITY

Conselho Nacional de Igrejas Cristãs do Brasil (CONIC) (National Council of Christian Churches in Brazil): Edif. Ceará, Sala 713, SCS, Quadra 01, Bloco E, 70303-900 Brasília, DF; tel. and fax (61) 3321-8341; e-mail conic.brasil@terra.com.br; internet www.conic.org.br; f. 1982; six mem. churches; Pres. Pastor Carlos Augusto Möller; Exec. Sec. Rev. Luiz Alberto Barbosa.

The Roman Catholic Church

Brazil comprises 41 archdioceses, 212 dioceses(including one each for Catholics of the Maronite, Melkite and Ukrainian Rites), 13 territorial prelatures and one personal apostolic administration. The Archbishop of São Sebastião do Rio de Janeiro is also the Ordinary for Catholics of other Oriental Rites in Brazil (estimated at 10,000 in 1994). The great majority of Brazil's population are adherents of the Roman Catholic Church. Adherents at 31 December 2005 represented an estimated 78.1% of the population.

Bishops' Conference: Conferência Nacional dos Bispos do Brasil, SE/Sul Quadra 801, Conj. B, CP 02067, 70259-970 Brasília, DF; tel. (61) 3313-8300; fax (61) 3313-8303; e-mail info@cnbb.org.br; internet www.cnbb.org.br; f. 1980; statutes approved 2002; Pres. Cardinal Geraldo Majella Agnelo (Archbishop of São Salvador da Bahia, BA); Sec.-Gen. Odilo Pedro Scherer.

Latin Rite

Archbishop of São Salvador da Bahia, BA, and Primate of Brazil: Cardinal Geraldo Majella Agnelo, Cúria Metropolitana, Rua Martin Afonso de Souza 270, 40100-050 Salvador, BA; tel. (71) 328-6699; fax (71) 328-0068; e-mail gma@atarde.com.br.

Archbishop of Aparecida, SP: Raymundo Damasceno Assis.

Archbishop of Aracaju, SE: José Palmeira Lessa.

Archbishop of Belém do Pará, PA: Orani João Tempesta.

Archbishop of Belo Horizonte, MG: Walmor Oliveira de Azevedo.

Archbishop of Botucatu, SP: Aloysio José Leal Penna.

Archbishop of Brasília, DF: João Braz de Aviz.

Archbishop of Campinas, SP: Bruno Gamberini.

Archbishop of Campo Grande, MS: Vitório Pavanello.

Archbishop of Cascavel, PR: Mauro Aparecido dos Santos.

Archbishop of Cuiabá, MT: Milton Antônio dos Santos.

Archbishop of Curitiba, PR: Moacyr José Vitti.

Archbishop of Diamantina, MG: João Bosco Oliver de Faria.

Archbishop of Feira de Santana, BA: Itamar Navildo Vian.

Archbishop of Florianópolis, SC: Murilo Sebastião Ramos Krieger.

Archbishop of Fortaleza, CE: José Antônio Aparecido Tosi Marques.

Archbishop of Goiânia, GO: Washington Cruz.

Archbishop of Juiz de Fora, MG: Eurico dos Santos Veloso.

Archbishop of Londrina, PR: Orlando Brandes.

Archbishop of Maceió, AL: Antônio Muniz Fernandes.

Archbishop of Manaus, AM: Luiz Soares Vieira.

Archbishop of Mariana, MG: Geraldo Lyrio Rocha.

Archbishop of Maringá, PR: Anuar Battisti.

Archbishop of Montes Claros, MG: José Alberto Moura.

Archbishop of Natal, RN: Matias Patrício de Macêdo.

Archbishop of Niterói, RJ: Alano Maria Pena.

Archbishop of Olinda e Recife, PE: José Cardoso Sobrinho.

Archbishop of Palmas, PR: Alberto Taveira Corrêa.

Archbishop of Paraíba, PB: Aldo de Cillo Pagotto.

Archbishop of Porto Alegre, RS: Dadeus Grings.

Archbishop of Porto Velho, RO: Moacyr Grechi.

Archbishop of Pouso Alegre, MG: Ricardo Pedro Chaves Pinto, Filho.

Archbishop of Ribeirão Preto, SP: Joviano de Lima.

Archbishop of São Luís do Maranhão, MA: José Belisário da Silva.

Archbishop of São Paulo, SP: Cardinal Odilo Pedro Scherer.

Archbishop of São Sebastião do Rio de Janeiro, RJ: Cardinal Eusébio Oscar Scheid.

Archbishop of Sorocaba, SP: Eduardo Benes de Sales Rodrigues.

Archbishop of Teresina, PI: Celso José Pinto da Silva.

Archbishop of Uberaba, MG: Aloísio Roque Oppermann.

Archbishop of Vitória, ES: Luiz Mancilha Vilela.

BRAZIL

Archbishop of Vitória da Conquista, BA: (vacant).

Maronite Rite

Bishop of Nossa Senhora do Líbano em São Paulo, SP: EDGAR MADI.

Melkite Rite

Bishop of Nossa Senhora do Paraíso em São Paulo, SP: FARES MAAKAROUN.

Ukrainian Rite

Bishop of São João Batista em Curitiba, PR: VALDOMIRO KOUBETCH.

The Anglican Communion

Anglicans form the Episcopal Anglican Church of Brazil (Igreja Episcopal Anglicana do Brasil), comprising eight dioceses.

Igreja Episcopal Anglicana do Brasil: Av. Ludolfo Boehl 256, Teresópolis, 91720-150 Porto Alegre, RS; tel. and fax (51) 3318-6200; e-mail sec.gral@ieab.org.br; internet www.ieab.org.br; f. 1890; 103,021 mems (1997); Primate Rt Rev. MAURÍCIO JOSÉ ARAÚJO DE ANDRADE; Sec.-Gen. Rev. FRANCISCO DE ASSIS DA SILVA.

Protestant Churches

Igreja Cristã Reformada do Brasil (Christian Reformed Church of Brazil): Rua Domingos Rodrigues, 306/Lapa, 05075-000 São Paulo, SP; tel. (11) 5260-7514; f. 1932; Pres. Rev. ANTÔNIO BONZOI; 500 mems.

Igreja Evangélica de Confissão Luterana no Brasil (IECLB): Rua Senhor dos Passos 202, 4° andar, 90020-180 Porto Alegre, RS; tel. (51) 3221-3433; fax (51) 3225-7244; e-mail secretariageral@ieclb.org.br; internet www.ieclb.org.br; f. 1949; 715,000 mems; Pres. Pastor Dr WALTER ALTMANN; Vice-Pres. Pastor HOMERO SEVERO PINTO.

Igreja Evangélica Congregacional do Brasil: Rua Dom Pedro 1616, 85960-000 Marechal Cândido Rondon, PR; tel. (45) 254-2448; e-mail web@iecb.org.br; internet www.iecb.org.br; f. 1942; 148,836 mems (2000); Pres. Rev. H. DORIVAL L. SEIDEL.

Igreja Evangélica Luterana do Brasil: Av. Cel. Lucas de Oliveira 894, Bairro Mont'Serrat, 90440-010 Porto Alegre, RS; tel. (51) 3332-2111; fax (51) 3332-8145; e-mail ielb@ielb.org.br; internet www.ielb.org.br; f. 1904; 230,215 mems; Pres. Rev. PAULO MOISÉS NERBAS; Sec. Rev. RONY RICARDO MARQUARDT.

Igreja Maná do Brasil: Travesa da Imprensa 26, Centro 12900-460 Bragança Paulista, SP; tel. (11) 4032-8104; e-mail adm_brasil@igrejamana.com; internet www.igrejamana.com.

Igreja Metodista do Brasil: Av. Piassanguaba 3031, Planalto Paulista, 04060-004 São Paulo, SP; tel. (11) 6813-8600; fax (11) 5594-3328; e-mail sede.nacional@metodista.org.br; internet www.metodista.org.br; 136,470 mems (2002); Exec. Sec. Bishop JOÃO ALVES DE OLIVEIRA.

Igreja Presbiteriana Unida do Brasil (IPU): Edif. Vitória Center, Av. Princesa Isabel 629, 1210/1, 29010-360 Vitória, ES; tel. and fax (27) 3222-8024; e-mail ipu@ipu.org.br; internet www.ipu.org.br; f. 1978; Moderator Rev. GERSON ANTÔNIO URBAN.

BAHÁ'Í FAITH

Comunidade Bahá'í do Brasil (Bahá'í Community of Brazil): SHIS, QL 08, Conj. 02, CP 7035, 71620-970 Brasília, DF; tel. (61) 3364-3594; fax (61) 3364-3470; e-mail info@bahai.org.br; internet www.bahai.org.br; f. 1965; Sec. CARLOS ALBERTO SILVA.

BUDDHISM

Sociedade Budista do Brasil (Buddhist Society—Rio Buddhist Vihara): Dom Joaquim Mamede 45, Lagoinha, Santa Tereza, 20241-390 Rio de Janeiro, RJ; tel. (21) 2526-1411; e-mail sbbrj@yahoo.com; internet www.geocities.com/sbbrj; f. 1972; Pres. JORGE ALOICE GOMES.

OTHER RELIGIONS

Sociedade Taoísta do Brasil (Daoist Society): Rua Cosme Velho 355, Cosme Velho, 22241-090 Rio de Janeiro, RJ; tel. (21) 2225-2887; e-mail info@taoismo.org.br; internet www.taoismo.org.br; f. 1991.

The Press

The most striking feature of the Brazilian press is the relatively small circulation of newspapers in comparison with the size of the population. The newspapers with the largest circulations are *O Dia* (250,000), *O Globo* (350,000), *Folha de São Paulo* (560,000), and *O Estado de São Paulo* (242,000). The low circulation is mainly owing to high costs resulting from distribution difficulties. In consequence there are no national newspapers. In 2000 a total of 465 daily newspaper titles, with an average circulation of 7,883,000, and 2,010 non-daily newspapers were published in Brazil.

DAILY NEWSPAPERS

Belém, PA

O Liberal: Rua Gaspar Viana 253, 66020 Belém, PA; e-mail redacao@orm.com.br; internet www.oliberal.com.br; f. 1946; Pres. LUCIDEA MAIORANA; circ. 20,000.

Belo Horizonte, MG

Diário da Tarde: Av. Getúlio Vargas 291, 30112-020 Belo Horizonte, MG; tel. (31) 3263-5229; internet www.estaminas.com.br/dt; f. 1931; evening; Editor FÁBIO PROENÇA DOYLE; total circ. 150,000.

Diário do Comércio: Av. Américo Vespúcio 1660, Nova Esperança, 31230-250 Belo Horizonte, MG; tel. (31) 3469-1011; fax (31) 3469-1080; e-mail redacaodc@diariodocomercio.com.br; internet www.diariodocomercio.com.br; f. 1932; Pres. LUIZ CARLOS MOTTA COSTA.

Estado de Minas: Av. Getúlio Vargas 291, 30112-020 Belo Horizonte, MG; tel. (31) 3263-5105; fax (31) 3263-5024; e-mail gerais.em@uai.com.br; internet www.uai.com.br/em; f. 1928; morning; independent; Pres. and Dir BRITALDO SILVEIRA SOARES; circ. 65,000.

Hoje em Dia: Rua Padre Rolim 652, Santa Efigênia, 30130-090 Belo Horizonte, MG; tel. (31) 3236-8120; fax (31) 3236-8046; e-mail comercial@hojeemdia.com.br; internet www.hojeemdia.com.br; Man. Dir REINALDO GILLI.

Blumenau, SC

Jornal de Santa Catarina: Rua São Paulo 1120, 89010-000 Blumenau, SC; tel. (47) 3340-1400; e-mail redacao@santa.com.br; internet www.santa.com.br; f. 1971; Dir (vacant); circ. 25,000.

Brasília, DF

Correio Brasiliense: SIG, Quadra 02, Lote 340, 70610-901 Brasília, DF; tel. (61) 3214-1100; fax (61) 3214-1157; e-mail geral@correioweb.com.br; internet www.correioweb.com.br; f. 1960; Pres. and Dir ÁLVARO TEIXEIRA DA COSTA; circ. 30,000.

Jornal de Brasília: SIG, Trecho 1, Lotes 585/645, 70610-400 Brasília, DF; tel. (61) 3343-8000; fax (61) 3226-6735; e-mail redacao@jornaldebrasilia.com.br; internet www.jornaldebrasilia.com.br; f. 1972; Dir-Gen. FERNANDO CÂMARA; circ. 25,000.

Campinas, SP

Correio Popular: Rua 7 de Setembro 189, Vila Industrial, 13035-350 Campinas, SP; tel. (19) 3736-3050; fax (19) 3234-8984; e-mail webmaster@rac.com.br; internet www.cpopular.com.br; f. 1927; Editorial Dir NELSON HOMEM DE MELLO; circ. 40,000.

Curitiba, PR

O Estado do Paraná: Parque Gráfico e Administração, Rua João Tschannerl 800, Cidade da Comunicação, Jardim Mercês, 80820-010 Curitiba, PR; tel. (41) 3331-5000; fax (41) 3335-2838; e-mail oestado@parana-online.com.br; internet www.parana-online.com.br; f. 1951; Pres. PAULO CRUZ PIMENTEL; Dir Supt YVONNE LUNARDELLI PIMENTEL; circ. 15,000.

Gazeta do Povo: Rua Pedro Ivo 459, Centro, 80010-020, Curitiba, PR; tel. (41) 3321-5000; fax (41) 3321-5300; e-mail atendimento@tudoparana.com; internet canais.ondarpc.com.br/gazetadopovo; f. 1919; Pres. FRANCISCO CUNHA PEREIRA, Filho; circ. 40,000.

Tribuna do Paraná: Parque Gráfico e Administração, Rua João Tschannerl 800, Cidade da Comunicação, Jardim Mercês, CP 869, 80820-010 Curitiba, PR; tel. (41) 3331-5000; fax (41) 3335-2838; e-mail tribuna@parana-online.com.br; internet www.parana-online.com.br; f. 1956; Dir YVONNE LUNARDELLI PIMENTEL; circ. 15,000.

Florianópolis, SC

O Estado: Rodovia SC-401, Km 3, 88030-900 Florianópolis, SC; tel. and fax (48) 3239-8888; internet www.oestado.com.br; f. 1915; Pres. JOSÉ MATUSALÉM DE CARVALHO COMELLI; Gen. Editor SANDRA ANNUSECK; circ. 20,000.

Fortaleza, CE

Jornal O Povo: Av. Aguanambi 282, 60055 Fortaleza, CE; tel. (85) 3255-6250; fax (85) 3231-5792; e-mail centraldeatendimento@opovo.com.br; internet www.opovo.com.br/opovo; f. 1928; evening; Pres. DEMÓCRITO ROCHA DUMMAR; Editor-in-Chief FÁTIMA SUDÁRIO; circ. 20,000.

BRAZIL

Tribuna do Ceará: Av. Desembargador Moreira 2900, 60170-002 Fortaleza, CE; tel. (85) 3247-3066; fax (85) 3272-2799; e-mail tc@secrl.com.br; f. 1957; Dir José A. Sancho; circ. 12,000.

Goiânia, GO

Diário da Manhã: Av. Anhanguera 2833, Setor Leste Universitário, 74610-010 Goiânia, GO; tel. (62) 3267-1000; internet www.dm.com.br; f. 1980; Editor Batista Custódio; circ. 16,000.

O Popular: Rua Thómas Edson, Quadra 07, Setor Serrinha, 74835-130 Goiânia, GO; tel. (62) 3250-1220; fax (62) 3250-1270; e-mail dca@opopular.com.br; internet www2.opopular.com.br; f. 1938; Pres. Jaime Câmara Júnior; circ. 65,000.

João Pessoa, PB

Correio da Paraíba: Av. Pedro II, Centro, João Pessoa, PB; tel. (83) 3216-5000; fax (83) 3216-5009; e-mail assinante@portalcorreio.com.br; internet www.correiodaparaiba.com.br; Exec. Dir Beatriz Ribeiro.

Londrina, PR

Folha de Londrina: Rua Piauí 241, 86010-420 Londrina, PR; tel. (43) 3374-2000; fax (43) 3321-1051; e-mail caf@folhadelondrina.com.br; internet www.bonde.com.br/folha; f. 1948; Pres. João Milanez; circ. 40,000.

Manaus, AM

A Crítica: Av. André Araújo, Km 3, 69060 Manaus, AM; tel. (92) 3643-1200; fax (92) 3643-1234; internet www.acritica.com.br; f. 1949; Dir Rita Araújo Calderaro; circ. 19,000.

Natal, RN

Diario de Natal: Av. Deodoro da Fonseca 245, Petrópolis, 59012-600, Natal, RN; tel. (84) 4009-0166; e-mail albimar@diariodenatal.com.br; internet www.diariodenatal.com.br; Pres. Gladstone Vieira Belo; Dir Albimar Furtado.

Niterói, RJ

O Fluminense: Rua da Conceição 188, Loja 118, Niterói Shopping, Niterói, RJ; tel. (21) 2620-6168; fax (21) 2620-8636; internet www.ofluminense.com.br; f. 1878; Man. Editor Marcelo Leite; circ. 80,000.

A Tribuna: Rua Barão do Amazonas 31, 2403-0111 Niterói, RJ; tel. (13) 2102-7000; fax (13) 3219-4466; e-mail icarai@urbi.com.br; f. 1936; daily; Dir-Supt Gustavo Santano Amóro; circ. 10,000.

Palmas, TO

O Girassol: Av. Teotônio Segurado 101 Sul, Conj. 01, Edif. Office Center, 77015-002 Palmas, TO; tel. and fax (63) 3225-5456; e-mail ogirassol@uol.com.br; internet www.ogirassol.com.br; Pres. Wilbergson Estrela Gomes; Exec. Editor Sonielson Luciano de Sousa.

Porto Alegre, RS

Zero Hora: Av. Ipiranga 1075, Azenha, 90169-900 Porto Alegre, RS; tel. (51) 3218-4900; fax (51) 3218-4700; internet www.zerohora.com.br; f. 1964; Pres. Nelson Sirotsky; circ. 165,000 Monday, 170,000 weekdays, 240,000 Sunday.

Recife, PE

Diário de Pernambuco: Rua do Veiga 600, Santo Amaro, 50040-110 Recife, PE; tel. (81) 2122-7666; fax (81) 2122-7603; e-mail diario@pernambuco.com; internet www.pernambuco.com/diario; f. 1825; morning; independent; Pres. Joezeil Barros; circ. 31,000.

Ribeirão Preto, SP

Jornal Tribuna da Ribeirão Preto: Rua São Sebastião 1380, Centro, 14015-040 Ribeirão Preto, SP; tel. and fax (16) 3632-2200; e-mail tribuna@tribunariberao.com.br; internet www.tribunariberao.com.br; Dir Francisco Jorge Rosa, Filho.

Rio de Janeiro, RJ

O Dia: Rua Riachuelo 359, 20235-900 Rio de Janeiro, RJ; fax (21) 2507-1228; internet odia.terra.com.br; f. 1951; morning; centrist labour; Pres. Gigi Carvalho; Editor-in-Chief Alexandre Freeland; circ. 250,000 weekdays, 500,000 Sundays.

O Globo: Rua Irineu Marinho 35, CP 1090, 20233-900 Rio de Janeiro, RJ; tel. (21) 2534-5000; fax (21) 2534-5510; internet oglobo.globo.com; f. 1925; morning; Editor-in-Chief Joyce Jane; circ. 350,000 weekdays, 600,000 Sundays.

Jornal do Brasil: Av. Paulo de Frontin 568, Fundos, Rio Comprido, 20261-243 Rio de Janeiro, RJ; tel. (21) 2323-1000; e-mail jb@jbonline.com.br; internet www.jb.com.br; f. 1891; morning; Catholic, liberal; Vice-Pres. Ricardo Carvalho; circ. 200,000 weekdays, 325,000 Sundays.

Jornal do Commercio: Rua do Livramento 189, 20221-191 Rio de Janeiro, RJ; tel. and fax (21) 2223-8500; e-mail jornaldocommercio@jcom.com.br; internet www.jornaldocommercio.com.br; f. 1827; morning; Pres. Mauricio Dinepi; circ. 31,000 weekdays.

Jornal dos Sports: Rua Pereira de Almeida 88, Praça de Bandeira, 20260-100 Rio de Janeiro, RJ; tel. (21) 2563-0363; e-mail falatorcedor@jsports.com.br; internet www.jsports.com.br; f. 1931; morning; sporting daily; Man. Dir Armando G. Coelho; circ. 39,000.

Salvador, BA

Correio da Bahia: Rua Professor Aristides Novis 123, Federação, 40210-630 Salvador, BA; tel. (71) 3203-1864; fax (71) 3203-1880; e-mail comercial@correiodabahia.com.br; internet www.correiodabahia.com.br; f. 1978; Editorial Dir Wilson Maron.

A Tarde: Av. Tancredo Neves 1092, Caminho das Árvores, 41822-900 Salvador, BA; tel. (71) 3340-8888; fax (71) 3231-1064; e-mail suporte@atarde.com.br; internet www.atarde.com.br; f. 1912; evening; Pres. Regina Simões de Mello Leitão; circ. 54,000.

Santarém, PA

O Impacto—O Jornal da Amazônia: Av. Presidente Vargas 3728, Caranaza, 68040-060 Santarém, PA; tel. (93) 3523-3330; fax (93) 3523-9131; e-mail oimpacto@oimpacto.com.br; internet www.oimpacto.com.br; Pres. Admilton Almeida.

Santo André, SP

Diário do Grande ABC: Rua Catequese 562, Bairro Jardim, 09090-900 Santo André, SP; tel. (11) 4435-8100; fax (11) 4434-8250; e-mail online@dgabc.com.br; internet www.dgabc.com.br; f. 1958; Editorial Dir Paula Fontenelle; circ. 78,500.

Santos, SP

A Tribuna: Rua João Pessoa 129, Santos, SP; tel. (13) 2102-7000; e-mail atribuna@atribuna.com.br; internet www.atribuna.com.br; f. 1984; Dir Roberto M. Santini; Editor-in-Chief Marcio Calves; circ. 40,000.

São Luís, MA

O Imparcial: Empresa Pacotilha Ltda, Rua Assis Chateaubriand s/n, Renascença 2, 65075-670 São Luís, MA; tel. (98) 3212-2000; e-mail redacao@pacotilha.com.br; internet www.oimparcial.com.br; f. 1926; Dir-Gen. Pedro Batista Freire.

São Paulo, SP

DCI (Diário Comércio, Indústria e Serviços): Rua Bacaetava 191, 1° andar, 04705-010 São Paulo, SP; tel. (11) 5094-5200; e-mail redacao@dci.com.br; internet www.dci.com.br; f. 1933; morning; Man. Dir António Carlos Rios Corral; circ. 50,000.

Diário do Comércio: Associação Comercial de São Paulo, Rua Boa Vista 51, 6° andar, Centro, 01014-911 São Paulo, SP; tel. (11) 3244-3322; fax (11) 3244-3046; e-mail dcomercio@acsp.com.br; internet www.dcomercio.com.br; Pres. Guilherme Afif Domingos.

Diário de São Paulo: Rua Major Quedinho 90, Centro, São Paulo, SP; tel. (11) 3658-8000; internet www.diariosp.com.br; f. 1884; fmrly Diário Popular; evening; owned by O Globo; Exec. Dir (vacant); circ. 90,000.

O Estado de São Paulo: Av. Celestino Bourroul 68, 1° andar, 02710-000 São Paulo, SP; tel. (11) 3959-8500; fax (11) 3266-2206; e-mail falecom@estado.com.br; internet www.estado.com.br; f. 1875; morning; independent; Dir Ruy Mesquita; circ. 242,000 weekdays, 460,000 Sundays.

Folha de São Paulo: Alameda Barão de Limeira 425, 6° andar, Campos Elíseos, 01202-900 São Paulo, SP; tel. (11) 3224-3678; fax (11) 3224-7550; e-mail folha@uol.com.br; internet www.folha.com.br; f. 1921; morning; Pres. Luís Frias; circ. 557,650 weekdays, 1,401,178 Sundays.

Gazeta Mercantil: Vila Olimpia, Rua Ramos Batista 444, 11° andar, CP 04552-020 São Paulo, SP; tel. (11) 2126-5000; e-mail relacionamento@gazetamercantil.com.br; internet www.gazeta.com.br; f. 1920; business paper; Pres. Luiz Ferreira Levy; circ. 80,000.

Jornal da Tarde: Av. Eng. Caetano Álvares 55, Limão, 02598-000 São Paulo, SP; tel. (11) 3959-8500; fax (11) 3856-2257; e-mail pergunta@jt.com.br; internet www.jt.com.br; f. 1966; evening; independent; Dir Fernão Lara Mesquita; circ. 120,000, 180,000 Mondays.

BRAZIL

Vitória, ES

A Gazeta: Rua Charic Murad 902, 29050 Vitória, ES; tel. (27) 3321-8333; fax (27) 3321-8720; e-mail aleite@redegazeta.com.br; internet gazetaonline.globo.com; f. 1928; Editorial Dir ANTÓNIO CARLOS LEITE; circ. 19,000.

PERIODICALS

Rio de Janeiro, RJ

Antenna-Eletrônica Popular: Av. Marechal Floriano 151, 20080-005 Rio de Janeiro, RJ; tel. (21) 2223-2442; fax (21) 2263-8840; e-mail antenna@anep.com.br; internet www.anep.com.br; f. 1926; monthly; telecommunications and electronics, radio, TV, hi-fi, amateur and CB radio; Dir MARIA BEATRIZ AFFONSO PENNA; circ. 15,000.

Conjuntura Econômica: Praia de Botafogo 190, Sala 923, 22253-900 Rio de Janeiro, RJ; tel. (21) 2559-6040; fax (21) 2559-6039; e-mail conjunturaeconomica@fgv.br; internet www.fgv.br/conjuntura.htm; f. 1947; monthly; economics and finance; published by Fundação Getúlio Vargas; Editor-in-Chief LUIZ GUILHERME SCHYMURA DE OLIVEIRA; circ. 25,000.

ECO21: Av. Copacabana 2, Gr. 301, 22010-122 Rio de Janeiro, RJ; tel. (21) 2275-1490; e-mail eco21@eco21.com.br; internet www.eco21.com.br; monthly; ecological issues; Dirs LÚCIA CHAYB, RENÉ CAPRILES.

São Paulo, SP

Caros Amigos: Rua Fidalga 162, Vila Madalena, São Paulo, SP; tel. (11) 3819-0130; fax (11) 3038-1415; e-mail atendimento.carosamigos@tmktbrasil.com.br; internet www.carosamigos.com.br; f. 1997; monthly; political; Editor SÉRGIO DE SOUZA; circ. 50,000.

Casa e Jardim: Av. Jaguaré 1485, 05342-900 São Paulo, SP; tel. (11) 3797-7000; e-mail casaejardim@edglobo.com.br; internet revistacasaejardim.globo.com; f. 1953; monthly; homes and gardens, illustrated; Gen. Dir JUAN OCERIN; circ. 120,000.

Claudia: Editora Abril, Av. das Nações Unidas 7221, Pinheiros 05425-902, São Paulo, SP; tel. (11) 3037-2000; fax (11) 5087-2100; e-mail claudia.abril@atleitor.com.br; internet claudia.abril.com.br; f. 1962; monthly; women's interest; Dir-Gen. JAIRO MENDES LEAL; circ. 460,000.

Criativa: Av. Jaguaré 1485, 05346-902 São Paulo, SP; tel. (11) 3767-7812; fax (11) 3767-7771; e-mail criativa@edglobo.com.br; internet www.criativa.globo.com; monthly; women's interest; Dir JUAN OCERIN; circ. 121,000.

Digesto Econômico: Associação Comercial de São Paulo, Rua Boa Vista 51, Centro, 01014-911 São Paulo, SP; tel. (11) 3244-3092; fax (11) 3244-3355; e-mail admdiario@acsp.com.br; internet www.acsp.com.br; every 2 months; Pres. ELVIO ALIPRANDI; Chief Editor JOÃO DE SCANTIMBURGO.

Elle: Editora Abril, Av. das Nações Unidas 7221, 16° andar, Pinheiro, 05425-902 São Paulo, SP; tel. (11) 3037-5451; fax (11) 3037-5197; e-mail elle.abril@atleitor.com.br; internet www.elle.com.br; f. 1988; monthly; women's interest; Editor LENITA ASSEF; circ. 100,000.

Exame: Editora Abril, Av. das Nações Unidas 7221, Pinheiros, 05425-902 São Paulo, SP; tel. (11) 3037-2000; fax (11) 3037-2027; e-mail redacao.exame@abril.com.br; internet www.exame.com.br; f. 1967; 2 a week; business; Editorial Dir CLÁUDIA VASSALLO; circ. 168,300.

Isto É: Rua William Speers 1000, 05067-900 São Paulo, SP; tel. (11) 3618-4566; fax (11) 3611-7211; e-mail atendimento@editora3.com.br; internet www.terra.com.br/istoe; politics and current affairs; Editorial Dir CARLOS JOSÉ MARQUES.

Máquinas e Metais: Alameda Olga 315, 01155-900, São Paulo, SP; tel. (11) 3824-5300; fax (11) 3666-9585; e-mail info@arandanet.com.br; internet www.arandanet.com.br; f. 1964; monthly; machine and metal industries; Editor JOSÉ ROBERTO GONÇALVES; circ. 15,000.

Marie Claire: Av. Jaguaré 1485, 05346-902 São Paulo, SP; tel. (11) 3767-7000; internet revistamarieclaire.globo.com; monthly; women's interest; Editorial Dir MÔNICA DE ALBUQUERQUE LINS SERINO; circ. 273,000.

Micromundo-Computerworld do Brasil: Rua Caçapava 79, 01408 São Paulo, SP; tel. (11) 3289-1767; monthly; computers; Gen. Dir ERIC HIPPEAU; circ. 38,000.

Placar: Editora Abril, Av. das Nações Unidas 7221, 14° andar, Pinheiro, 05425-902 São Paulo, SP; tel. (11) 3037-2000; fax (11) 5087-2100; e-mail placar.abril@atleitor.com.br; internet placar.abril.com.br; f. 1970; monthly; soccer; Dir MARCELO DURATE; circ. 127,000.

Quatro Rodas: Av. das Nações Unidas 7221, 14° andar, 05425-902 São Paulo, SP; fax (11) 3037-5039; internet quatrorodas.abril.com.br; f. 1960; monthly; motoring; Editor MARCIO ISHIKAWA; circ. 250,000.

Revista O Carreteiro: Rua Palacete das Aguias 395, Vila Alexandria, 04635-021 São Paulo, SP; tel. (11) 5031-8646; fax (11) 5031-8647; e-mail redacao@ocarreteiro.com.br; internet www.ocarreteiro.com.br; f. 1970; monthly; transport; Commercial Dir EDSON PEREIRA COELHO; circ. 100,000.

Saúde: Editora Abril, Av. das Nações Unidas 7221, 15° andar, Pinheiro, 05425-902 São Paulo, SP; tel. (11) 3037-4885; fax (11) 3037-4867; e-mail saude.abril@atleitor.com.br; internet saude.abril.com.br; monthly; health; Dir-Gen JAIRO MENDES LEAL; circ. 180,000.

Veja: Editora Abril, Av. das Nações Unidas 7221, Pinheiro, 05425-902 São Paulo, SP; tel. (11) 3347-2121; fax (11) 3037-5638; e-mail veja@abril.com.br; internet vejaonline.abril.com.br; f. 1968; news weekly; Dirs JOSÉ ROBERTO GUZZO, TALES ALVARENGA, EURIPEDES ALCÁNTARA; circ. 1,200,000.

NEWS AGENCIES

Agência o Estado de São Paulo: Av. Eng. Caetano Alvares 55, Bairro do Limão, 02588-900 São Paulo, SP; tel. (11) 3856-3500; fax (11) 3856-2940; internet www.estadao.com.br; Rep. SAMUEL DIRCEU F. BUENO.

Agência O Globo: Rua Irineu Marinho 35, 2° andar, Centro, 20233-900 Rio de Janeiro, RJ; tel. (21) 2534-5757; e-mail agenciaoglobo@oglobo.com.br; internet www.agenciaoglobo.com.br; f. 1974; Dir CARLOS LEMOS.

Agência JB (Agência Jornal do Brasil): Av. Paulo de Frontin 568, Fundos, Rio Comprido, 20261-243 Rio de Janeiro, RJ; tel. (21) 2101-4148; fax (21) 2101-4428; e-mail ajb@jb.com.br; internet www.agenciajb.com.br; f. 1966; Exec. Dir EDGAR LISBOA.

Folhapress: Alameda Barão de Limeira 401, 4° andar, 01290-900 São Paulo, SP; tel. (11) 3224-3123; fax (11) 3224-4778; e-mail folhapress@folhapress.com.br; internet www.folhapress.com.br; Gen. Man. RAIMUNDO CUNHA.

PRESS ASSOCIATIONS

Associação Brasileira de Imprensa (ABI): Rua Araújo Porto Alegre 71, Centro, 20030-010 Rio de Janeiro, RJ; tel. (21) 2282-1292; e-mail abi@abi.org.br; internet www.abi.org.br; f. 1908; 4,000 mems; Pres. MAURÍCIO AZÊDO.

Associação Nacional de Editores de Revistas (ANER): Rua Deputado Lacerda Franco 300, 15°, Conj. 155, 05418-000 São Paulo, SP; tel. (11) 3030-9390; fax (11) 3030-9393; e-mail info@aner.org.br; internet www.emrevista.com.br/emrevista/fixos/expediente.asp; Pres. JAIRO MENDES LEAL; Exec. Dir MARIA CÉLIA FURTADO.

Federação Nacional dos Jornalistas (FENAJ): HIGS 707, Bloco R, Casa 54, 70351-718 Brasília, DF; tel. (61) 3244-0650; fax (61) 3242-6616; e-mail fenaj@fenaj.org.br; internet www.fenaj.org.br; f. 1946; represents 31 regional unions; Pres. SÉRGIO MURILLO DE ANDRADE.

Publishers

Ao Livro Técnico Indústria e Comércio Ltda: Rua Sá Freire 36/40, São Cristóvão, 20930-430 Rio de Janeiro, RJ; tel. (21) 2580-6230; fax (21) 2580-9955; internet www.editoraaolivrotécnico.com.br; f. 1933; textbooks, children's and teenagers' fiction and non-fiction, art books, dictionaries; Man. Dir REYNALDO MAX PAUL BLUHM.

Atual Editora, Ltda: São Paulo, SP; tel. (11) 5071-2288; fax (11) 5071-3099; e-mail atendprof@atualeditora.com.br; internet www.atualeditora.com.br; f. 1973; school and children's books, literature; Dirs GELSON IEZZI, OSVALDO DOLCE.

Barsa Planeta Internacional: Rua Rego Freitas 192, Vila Buarque, CP 299, 01059-970 São Paulo, SP; tel. (11) 3225-1900; fax (11) 3225-1960; e-mail atendimento@barsaplaneta.com.br; internet www.barsa.com/; f. 1951; reference books.

Ebid-Editora Páginas Amarelas Ltda: Rua São José 90, 4° andar; tel. (21) 3824-8287; fax (21) 3824-8300; f. 1947; commercial directories.

Ediouro Publicações, SA: Rua Nova Jerusalém 345, CP 1880, Bonsucesso, 21042-235 Rio de Janeiro, RJ; tel. (21) 3882-8416; e-mail editoriallivros@ediouro.com.br; internet www.ediouro.com.br; f. 1939; general; Pres. JORGE CARNEIRO.

Editora Abril, SA: Av. das Nações Unidas 7221, Pinheiros, 05425-902 São Paulo, SP; tel. (11) 3037-2000; fax (11) 5087-2100; e-mail abril@abril.com.br; internet www.abril.com.br; f. 1950; magazines; Pres. ROBERTO CIVITA.

Editora Atica, SA: Rua Barão de Iguape 110, 01507-900 São Paulo, SP; tel. (11) 3346-3000; fax (11) 3277-4146; e-mail editora@atica.com.br; internet www.atica.com.br; f. 1965; textbooks, Brazilian and African literature; Pres. VICENTE PAZ FERNANDEZ.

Editora Atlas, SA: Rua Conselheiro Nébias 1384, 01203-904 São Paulo, SP; tel. (11) 3357-9144; fax (11) 3221-5859; e-mail diretoria@editora-atlas.com.br; internet www.editoraatlas.com.br; f. 1944; business administration, economics, accounting, law, education, social sciences; Pres. LUIZ HERRMANN, Jr.

BRAZIL   *Directory*

Editora do Brasil, SA: Rua Conselheiro Nébias 887, Campos Elíseos, CP 4986, 01203-001 São Paulo, SP; tel. (11) 3226-0211; fax (11) 3222-5583; e-mail editora@editoradobrasil.com.br; internet www.editoradobrasil.com.br; f. 1943; education; Pres. Dr CARLOS COSTA.

Editora Brasiliense, SA: Rua Airi 22, Tatuapé, 03310-010 São Paulo, SP; tel. and fax (11) 6198-1488; e-mail brasilienseedit@uol.com.br; internet www.editorabrasiliense.com.br; f. 1943; education, racism, gender studies, human rights, ecology, history, literature, social sciences; Man. YOLANDA C. DA SILVA PRADO; Vice-Pres. MARIA TERESA B. DE LIMA.

Editora Campus: Rua Sete de Setembro 111, 16° andar, 20050-002 Rio de Janeiro, RJ; tel. (21) 3970-9300; fax (21) 2507-1991; e-mail c.rothmuller@campus.com.br; internet www.campus.com.br; f. 1976; business, computing, non-fiction; imprint of Elsevier since 2002; Man. Dir CLAUDIO ROTHMULLER.

Editora Delta, SA: Av. Nilo Peçanha 50, 2817, 20020-100 Rio de Janeiro, RJ; tel. (21) 2262-5243; internet www.delta.com.br; f. 1930; reference books; Pres. ANDRÉ KOOGAN BREITMAN.

Editora Educacional Brasileira, SA: Rua XV de Novembro 178, Salas 101/04, CP 7498, 80000 Curitiba, PR; tel. (41) 2223-5012; f. 1963; biology, textbooks and reference books.

Editora Expressão e Cultura—Exped Ltda: Estrada dos Bandeirantes 1700, Bloco H, 22710-113 Rio de Janeiro, RJ; tel. (21) 2444-0649; fax (21) 2444-0651; e-mail exped@ggh.com.br; internet www.exped.com.br; f. 1966; textbooks, literature, reference; Gen. Man. RICARDO AUGUSTO PAMPLONA VAZ.

Editora FTD, SA: Rua Rui Barbosa 156, Bairro Bela Vista, 01326-010 São Paulo, SP; tel. (11) 3253-5011; fax (11) 3288-0132; internet www.ftd.com.br; f. 1902; textbooks; Pres. JOÃO TISSI.

Editora Globo, SA: Av. Jaguaré 1485/1487, 05346-902 São Paulo, SP; tel. (11) 3767-7400; fax (11) 3767-7870; e-mail globolivros@edglobo.com.br; internet globolivros.globo.com; f. 1957; fiction, engineering, agriculture, cookery, environmental studies; Gen. Man. JUAN OCERIN.

Editora e Gráfica Miguel Couto, SA: Rua da Passagem 78, Loja A, Botafogo, 22290-030 Rio de Janeiro, RJ; tel. (21) 2541-5145; f. 1969; engineering; Dir PAULO KOBLER PINTO LOPES SAMPAIO.

Editora Lê, SA: Rua Januária 437, Floresta, Belo Horizonte, MG; tel. (31) 3423-3200; e-mail editora@le.com.br; internet www.le.com.br; f. 1967; textbooks.

Editora Lemi, SA: Av. Nossa Senhora de Fátima 1945, CP 1890, 30000 Belo Horizonte, MG; tel. (31) 3201-8044; f. 1967; administration, accounting, law, ecology, economics, textbooks, children's books and reference books.

Editora Melhoramentos Ltda: Rua Tito 479, 05051-000 São Paulo, SP; tel. (11) 3874-0854; fax (11) 3874-0855; e-mail blerner@melhoramentos.com.br; internet www.melhoramentos.com.br; f. 1890; general non-fiction; children's books, dictionaries; Dir BRENO LERNER.

Editora Michalany Ltda: Rua Laura dos Anjos Ramos 420, Jardim Santa Cruz—Interlagos, 04455-350 São Paulo, SP; tel. (11) 5611-3414; fax (11) 5614-1592; e-mail editora@editoramichalany.com.br; internet www.editoramichalany.com.br; f. 1965; biographies, economics, textbooks, geography, history, religion, maps; Dir DOUGLAS MICHALANY.

Editora Moderna, Ltda: Rua Padre Adelino 758, Belenzinho, 03303-904, São Paulo, SP; tel. (11) 6090-1316; fax (11) 6090-1369; e-mail moderna@moderna.com.br; internet www.moderna.com.br; Pres. RICARDO ARISSA FELTRE.

Editora Nova Fronteira, SA: Rua Bambina 25, Botafogo, 22251-050 Rio de Janeiro, RJ; tel. (21) 2131-1111; fax (21) 2537-2659; e-mail sac@novafronteira.com.br; internet www.novafronteira.com.br; f. 1965; fiction, psychology, history, politics, science fiction, poetry, leisure, reference; Pres. CARLOS AUGUSTO LACERDA.

Editora Record, SA: Rua Argentina 171, São Cristóvão, CP 884, 20001-970 Rio de Janeiro, RJ; tel. (21) 2585-2000; fax (21) 2585-2085; e-mail record@record.com.br; internet www.record.com.br; f. 1941; general fiction and non-fiction, education, textbooks, fine arts; Pres. SÉRGIO MACHADO.

Editora Revista dos Tribunais Ltda: Rua do Bosque 820, 01136-000 São Paulo, SP; tel. (11) 3613-8400; fax (11) 3613-8474; e-mail gmarketing@rt.com.br; internet www.rt.com.br; f. 1912; law and jurisprudence books and periodicals; Dir CARLOS HENRIQUE DE CARVALHO, Filho.

Editora Rideel Ltda: Av. Casa Verde 455, Casa Verde, 02519-000 São Paulo, SP; tel. and fax (11) 6238-5100; e-mail sac@rideel.com.br; internet www.rideel.com.br; f. 1971; general; Dir ITALO AMADIO.

Editora Saraiva: Av. Marquês de São Vicente 1697, CP 2362, 01139-904 São Paulo, SP; tel. (11) 3933-3366; fax (11) 861-3308; e-mail diretoria.editora@editorasaraiva.com.br; internet www.editorasaraiva.com.br; f. 1914; education, textbooks, law, economics; Pres. JORGE EDUARDO SARAIVA.

Editora Scipione Ltda: Praça Carlos Gomes 46, 01501-040 São Paulo, SP; tel. (11) 3241-2255; e-mail scipione@scipione.com.br; internet www.scipione.com.br; f. 1983; owned by Editora Abril, SA; school-books, literature, reference; Dir LUIZ ESTEVES SALLUM.

Editora Vigília, Ltda: Belo Horizonte, MG; e-mail lerg@planetarium.com.br; tel. (31) 3337-2744; fax (31) 3337-2834; f. 1960; general.

Editora Vozes, Ltda: Rua Frei Luís 100, CP 90023, 25689-900 Petrópolis, RJ; tel. (24) 2233-9000; fax (24) 2231-4676; e-mail editorial@vozes.com.br; internet www.vozes.com.br; f. 1901; Catholic publrs; theology, philosophy, history, linguistics, science, psychology, fiction, education, etc.; Dir ANTÔNIO MOSER.

Instituto Brasileiro de Edições Pedagógicas, Ltda (Editoras IBEP Nacional): Av. Alexandre Mackenzie 619, Jaguaré, 05322-000 São Paulo, SP; tel. (11) 6099-7799; fax (11) 6694-5338; e-mail editoras@ibep-nacional.com.br; internet www.ibep-nacional.com.br; f. 1965; textbooks, foreign languages and reference books; Dirs JORGE YUNES, PAULO C. MARTI.

Lex Editora, SA: Rua da Consolação 77, 01301-000 São Paulo, SP; tel. (11) 2126-6000; fax (11) 2126-6001; e-mail wsoares@aduaneiras.com.br; internet www.lex.com.br; f. 1937; legislation and jurisprudence; Dir CARLOS SERGIO SERRA.

Livraria Francisco Alves Editora, SA: Rua Uruguaiana, 94, 13° andar, centro, 20050-091 Rio de Janeiro, RJ; tel. (21) 2221-3198; fax (21) 2242-3438; f. 1854; textbooks, fiction, non-fiction; Pres. CARLOS LEAL.

Livraria José Olympio Editora, SA: Rua da Glória 344, 4° andar, Glória, 20241-180 Rio de Janeiro, RJ; tel. (21) 2509-6939; fax (21) 2242-0802; f. 1931; juvenile, science, history, philosophy, psychology, sociology, fiction; Dir MANOEL ROBERTO DOMINGUES.

Pallas Editora: Rua Frederico de Albuquerque 56, Higienópolis, 21050-840 Rio de Janeiro, RJ; tel. and fax (21) 2270-0186; e-mail pallas@alternex.com.br; internet www.pallaseditora.com.br; f. 1980; Afro-Brazilian culture.

Thomson Pioneira: Condomínio E-Business Park, Rua Werner Siemens 111, Prédio 20, Espaço 03, Lapa de Baixo, 05069-900 São Paulo, SP; tel. (11) 3665-9900; fax (11) 3665-9901; internet www.thomsonlearning.com.br; f. 1960 as Editora Pioneira; acquired by Thomson Learning in 2000; architecture, computers, political and social sciences, business studies, languages, children's books; Dirs ROBERTO GUAZZELLI, LILIANA GUAZZELLI.

PUBLISHERS' ASSOCIATIONS

Associação Brasileira de Editores de Livros (Abrelivros): Rua Turiassu 143, conj. 101/102, 05005-001 São Paulo, SP; tel. and fax (11) 3826-9071; e-mail contato@abrelivros.org.br; internet www.abrelivros.org.br; f. 1991; 27 mems; Pres. JOÃO ARINOS RIBEIRO DOS SANTOS.

Associação Brasileira do Livro (ABL): Av. 13 de Maio 23, 16° andar, Sala 1619/1620, 20031-000 Rio de Janeiro, RJ; tel. and fax (21) 2240-9115; e-mail abralivro@uol.com.br; Pres. ADENILSON JARBAS CABRAL.

Câmara Brasileira do Livro: Cristiano Viana 91, 05411-000 São Paulo, SP; tel. and fax (11) 3069-1300; e-mail marketing@cbl.org.br; internet www.cbl.org.br; f. 1946; Pres. ROSELY BOSCHINI.

Sindicato Nacional dos Editores de Livros (SNEL): Rua da Ajuda 35, 18° andar, Centro, 20040-000 Rio de Janeiro, RJ; tel. (21) 2533-0399; fax (21) 2533-0422; e-mail snel@snel.org.br; internet www.snel.org.br; 200 mems; Pres. PAULO ROBERTO ROCCO.

There are also regional publishers' associations.

Broadcasting and Communications

TELECOMMUNICATIONS

Regulatory Authority

Agência Nacional de Telecomunicações (ANATEL): SAUS Quadra 06, Blocos C, E, F e H, 70070-940 Brasília, DF; tel. (61) 2312-2000; fax (61) 2312-2264; e-mail biblioteca@anatel.gov.br; internet www.anatel.gov.br; f. 1998; regional office in each state; Supt NILBERTO DINIZ MIRANDA.

Major Operators

Amazônia Celular: Rua Levindo Lopes 258, 4° andar, Savassi, 31040-170 Belo Horizonte, MG; internet www.amazoniacelular.com.br; mobile cellular provider in the Amazon region; 1.2m. customers.

AT&T Brazil: Torre Sul, 7°, Rua James Joule 65, São Paulo, SP; internet www.att.com.

BRAZIL   *Directory*

Brasil Telecom: SIA Sul, Área dos Servicos Públicos, Lote D, Bloco B, 71215-000 Brasília, DF; tel. (61) 3415-1128; fax (61) 3415-1133; internet www.brasiltelecom.com.br; fixed line services in 10 states; also operates mobile cellular network, Brasil Telecom Celular; Chair. MODESTO SOUZA BARROS CARVALHOSO; Pres. HENRIQUE SUTTON DE SOUSA NEVES.

Claro: Rua Mena Barreto 42, Botafogo, 22271-100 Rio de Janeiro, RJ; internet www.claro.com.br; f. 2003 by mergers; owned by Telmex (Teléfonos de México, SA); mobile cellular provider; 14.3m. customers.

CTBC (Companhia de Telecomunicações do Brasil Central): Av. Afonso Pena 3928, Bairro Brasil, 38400-668 Uberlândia, MG; internet www4.ctbctelecom.com.br; f. 1954; owned by Grupo Algar; mobile and fixed-line provider in central Brazil.

Empresa Brasileira de Telecomunicações, SA (Embratel): Av. Presidente Vargas 1012, CP 2586, 20179-900 Rio de Janeiro, RJ; tel. (21) 2519-8182; e-mail cmsocial@embratel.net.br; internet www.embratel.com.br; f. 1965; operates national and international telecommunications system; owned by Telmex (Teléfonos de Mexico, SA).

Sercomtel Celular, SA: Rua João Cândido 555, 86010-000 Londrina, PR; tel. 0800 400 4343; e-mail casc@sercomtel.com.br; internet www.sercomtelcelular.com.br; f. 1998; mobile cellular network provider; Pres. JOÃO BATISTA DE REZENDE.

Telefônica SP: Rua Martiniano de Carvalho 851, Bela Vista, 01321-000 São Paulo, SP; tel. (11) 3549-7200; fax (11) 3549-7202; e-mail webmaster@telesp.com.br; internet www.telesp.com.br; fmrly Telecomunicações de São Paulo (Telesp), privatized in 1998; subsidiary of Telefónica, SA (Spain); 41m. customers.

Telemar: Rua Lauro Müller 116, 22° andar, Botafogo, Rio de Janeiro, RJ; tel. (21) 2815-2921; fax (21) 2571-3050; internet www.telemar.com.br; f. 1998 as Tele Norte Leste; fixed line services in 16 states; Chair. CARLOS JEREISSATI; Pres. MANOEL DE SILVA.

Oi: internet www.oiempresa.com.br; f. 2002; subsidiary of Telemar; mobile cellular services in 16 states.

Telemig Celular: internet www.telemigcelular.com.br; mobile cellular provider in Minas Gerais; 2.6m. customers.

TIM (Telecom Italia Mobil): Av. das Américas 3434, 5° andar, Barra da Tijuca, 22640-102 Rio de Janeiro, RJ; internet www.tim.com.br; f. 1998 in Brazil; mobile cellular provider; 24.1m. customers (2006).

Vivo: Av. Chucri Zaidan 2460, 5°, 04583-110 São Paulo, SP; tel. (11) 5105-1001; internet www.vivo.com.br; owned by Telefónica Móviles, SA of Spain (50%) and Portugal Telecom; mobile telephones; Pres. ROBERTO OLIVEIRA DE LIMA; 24.6m. customers.

BROADCASTING

RADIOBRÁS (Empresa Brasileira de Radiodifusão): SCRN 502, Bloco B 80, Edif. Marilda Figueiredo, Sala 308, CP 070747, 70720-502 Brasília, DF; tel. (61) 3327-4348; fax (61) 3327-4378; e-mail faleconosco@radiobras.gov.br; internet www1.radiobras.gov.br; f. 1975; state-run radio and television network; Pres. EUGÊNIO BUCCI.

Radio

The main broadcasting stations in Rio de Janeiro are: Rádio Nacional, Rádio Globo, Rádio Eldorado, Rádio Jornal do Brasil, Rádio Tupi and Rádio Mundial. In São Paulo the main stations are Rádio Bandeirantes, Rádio Mulher, Rádio Eldorado, Rádio Gazeta and Rádio Excelsior; and in Brasília: Rádio Nacional, Rádio Alvorada, Rádio Planalto and Rádio Capital.

The state-run corporation RADIOBRÁS (q.v.) owns the following radio stations:

Rádio Nacional AM de Brasília: CP 259, 7017-750 Brasília, DF; f. 1958; Man. CRISTINA GUIMARÃES.

Rádio Nacional da Amazônia: CP 258, 70359-970 Brasília, DF; internet www.radiobras.gov.br; f. 1977; Man. SOFÍA HAMMOE.

Rádio Nacional FM de Brasília: CP 070747, 70720-502 Brasília, DF; f. 1977; broadcasts to the Distrito Federal and surrounding areas; Man. CARLOS SENNA.

Rádio Nacional do Rio de Janeiro: f. 2004.

Television

The main television networks are:

RBS TV: Rua do Acampamento 2250B, Passo do Príncipe, 96425-250 Bagé, RS; tel. (53) 240-5300; internet www.rbs.com.br; f. 1957; major regional network; operates Canal Rural and TVCOM; Group Pres. JAYME SIROTSKY.

TV Bandeirantes: Rádio e Televisão Bandeirantes Ltda, Rua Radiantes 13, Morumbi, 05699-900 São Paulo, SP; tel. (11) 3742-3011; fax (11) 3745-7622; e-mail cat@band.com.br; internet www.band.com.br; 65 TV stations and repeaters throughout Brazil; Pres. JOÃO CARLOS SAAD.

TV Brasil—Canal Integración: CP 08840, 70312-920 Brasília, DF; tel. (61) 3325-5203; fax (61) 3325-5454; e-mail contacto@tvbrasil.tv.br; internet www.tvbrasil.tv.br; f. 2005; owned by RADIOBRÁS; broadcasts internationally via satellite in Portuguese and Spanish; Gen. Co-ordinator ROBSON MOREIRA.

TV da Gente: internet www.tvdagente.com.br; f. 2005; part of Grupo Bandeirantes de Comunicação; Afro-Brazilian channel; Founder JOSÉ DE PAULA NETO.

TV Nacional (Canal 2): Brasília, DF; tel. (21) 3327-4523; public tv station; broadcasts to the Distrito Federal and surrounding areas; owned by RADIOBRÁS; Head ANDREÁ FASSINA.

TV Record—Rede Record de Televisão—Radio Record, SA: Rua de Várzea 240, Barra Funda, 01140-080 São Paulo, SP; tel. (11) 3660-4761; fax (11) 3660-4756; e-mail tvrecord@rederecord.com.br; internet www.tvrecord.com.br; Pres. JOÃO BATISTA R. SILVA; Exec. Vice-Pres. H. GONÇALVES.

TV Rede Globo: Rua Lopes Quintas 303, Jardim Botânico, 22460-010 Rio de Janeiro, RJ; tel. (21) 2540-2000; fax (21) 2294-2092; e-mail webm@redeglobo.com.br; internet www.redeglobo.com.br; f. 1965; 8 stations; national network; Dir ADILSON PONTES MALTA.

TV SBT—Sistema Brasileira de Televisão—Canal 4 de São Paulo, SA: Av. Das Comunicações 4, Vila Jaraguá, 06278-905 São Paulo, SP; tel. (11) 7087-3000; fax (11) 7087-3509; internet www.sbt.com.br; Vice-Pres. GUILHERME STOLIAR.

Broadcasting Associations

Associação Brasileira de Emissoras de Rádio e Televisão (ABERT): Centro Empresarial Varig, SCN Quadra 04, Bloco B, Sala 501, Centro Empresarial Varig Brasília, 70714-500 Brasília, DF; tel. (61) 2104-4600; e-mail abert@abert.org.br; internet www.abert.org.br; f. 1962; mems: 32 shortwave, 1,275 FM, 1,574 medium-wave and 80 tropical-wave radio stations and 258 television stations (1997); Pres. DANIEL PIMENTEL SLAVIERO; Exec. Dir FLÁVIO CAVALCANTI JÚNIOR.

There are regional associations for Bahia, Ceará, Goiás, Minas Gerais, Rio Grande do Sul, Santa Catarina, São Paulo, Amazonas, Distrito Federal, Mato Grosso and Mato Grosso do Sul (combined) and Sergipe.

Finance

(cap. = capital; dep. = deposits; res = reserves; m. = million; brs = branches; amounts in reais, unless otherwise stated)

BANKING

Conselho Monetário Nacional (CMN): Setor Bancário Sul, Quadra 03, Bloco B, Edif. Sede do Banco do Brasil, 21° andar, 70074-900 Brasília, DF; tel. (61) 3414-1945; fax (61) 3414-2528; e-mail cmn@bcb.gov.br; f. 1964 to formulate monetary policy and to supervise the banking system; Pres. GUIDO MANTEGA (Minister of Finance).

Central Bank

Banco Central do Brasil: Setor Bancário Sul, Quadra 03, Mezanino 01, Bloco B, 70074-900 Brasília, DF; tel. (61) 3414-1955; fax (61) 3223-1033; e-mail secre.surel@bcb.gov.br; internet www.bcb.gov.br; f. 1965 to execute the decisions of the Conselho Monetário Nacional; bank of issue; total assets 483,691.9m. (Dec. 2005); Gov. HENRIQUE DE CAMPOS MEIRELLES; 10 brs.

State Commercial Banks

Banco do Brasil, SA: Setor Bancário Sul, Quadra 01, Bloco C, Lote 32, Edif. Sede III, 70073-901 Brasília, DF; tel. (61) 3310-3406; fax (61) 3310-2561; e-mail ri@bb.com.br; internet www.bb.com.br; f. 1808; cap. 11,912.8m., res 8,845.3m., dep. 210,428.4m. (Dec. 2006); Pres. and Vice-Chair. ANTÔNIO FRANCISCO LIMA NETO; 15,133 brs.

Banco do Estado do Rio Grande do Sul, SA (Banrisul): Rua Caldas Junior 108, 7° andar, 90018-900 Porto Alegre, RS; tel. (51) 3215-2501; fax (51) 3215-1715; e-mail cambio_dg@banrisul.com.br; internet www.banrisul.com.br; f. 1928; cap. 900m., res 395.1m., dep. 12,266.9m. (Dec. 2006); Pres. ARIO ZIMMERMANN; 352 brs.

Banco do Estado de Santa Catarina, SA: Praça XV Novembro 329, 6° andar, Bairro Centro, 88010-901 Florianópolis, SC; tel. (48) 3239-9000; fax (48) 3239-9052; e-mail decam@besc.com.br; internet www.besc.com.br; f. 1962; acquired by Banco do Brasil, SA in 2007; cap. 1,319.1m., res −1,155.5m., dep. 2,354.3m. (Dec. 2006); Pres. EURIDES LUIZ MESCOLOTTO.

Banco do Nordeste do Brasil, SA: Av. Paranjana 5700, Passaré, 60740-000 Fortaleza, CE; tel. (85) 3299-3000; fax (85) 3299-3674; e-mail info@banconordeste.gov.br; internet www.banconordeste.gov.br; f. 1952; cap. 1,299.0m., res 203.3m., dep. 2,872.1m. (Dec. 2006); Pres. and CEO BYRON COSTA DE QUEIROZ; 186 brs.

BRAZIL   *Directory*

Other state commercial banks are the Banco do Estado do Pará and Banestes—the Banco do Estado do Espirito Santo.

Private Banks

Banco ABC Brasil, SA: Av. Juscelino Kubitschek 1400, 3°–5° andares, 04543-000 São Paulo, SP; tel. (11) 3170-2000; fax (11) 3170-2001; e-mail abcbrasil@abcbrasil.com.br; internet www.abcbrasil.com.br; f. 1989 as Banco ABC—Roma SA; 84% owned by Arab Banking Corpn BSC (Bahrain); cap. 248.4m., res 190.4m., dep. 1,655.3m. (Dec. 2006); Pres. and Gen. Man. TITO ENRIQUE DA SILVA NETO; 2 brs.

Banco ABN AMRO Real, SA: Av. Brigadeiro Luís Antônio 1824, 9° andar, 01317-002 Bela Vista, SP; tel. (11) 3174-9615; fax (11) 3174-7052; internet www.bancoreal.com.br; f. 1925 as Banco Real, SA; present name adopted 2000 following purchase by Banco ABN Amro, SA; owned by ABN AMRO Bank, NV (Netherlands); cap. 7,593.7m., res 2,092.0m., dep. 73,754.7m. (Dec. 2006); 847 brs.

Banco Alfa de Investimento SA: Alameda Santos 466, 4° andar, 01418-000 Paraíso, SP; tel. (11) 3175-5074; fax (11) 3171-2438; e-mail alfanet@alfa.com.br; internet www.bancoalfa.com.br; f. 1998; cap. 303.0m., res 452.5m., dep. 6,788.1m. (Dec. 2005); Pres. PAULO GUIHERME MONTEIRO LOBATO RIBEIRO; 9 brs.

Banco da Amazônia, SA: Av. Presidente Vargas 800, 66017-000 Belém, PA; tel. (91) 4008-3421; fax (91) 4008-3243; e-mail cambio@bancoamazionia.com.br; internet www.bancoamazonia.com.br; f. 1942; state-owned; cap. 1,205.2m., res 493.9m., dep. 1,181.8m. (Dec. 2006); Pres. ABIDIAS JOSÉ DE SOUZA, JÚNIOR; 92 brs.

Banco BBM, SA: Av. Tancredo Neves 1632, Caminho das Arvores, 41820-020 Salvador, BA; tel. (71) 4009-6000; fax (71) 4009-6001; internet www.bancobbm.com.br; f. 1858 as Banco de Bahia; present name adopted 1998; cap. 258.7m., res 402.3m., dep. 8,271.7m. (Dec. 2006); Pres. PEDRO HENRIQUE MARIANI BITTENCOURT; 7 brs.

Banco BEC, SA: Rua Pedro Pereira 481, 3° andar, 60035-000 Fortaleza, CE; tel. (85) 3255-1818; fax (85) 3255-1933; e-mail bec@bec.com.br; internet www.bec.com.br; f. 1964 as Banco do Estado do Ceará; present name adopted in 2006; owned by Banco Bradesco, SA; cap. 242.3m., res 114.0m., dep. 1,107.3m. (Dec. 2004); Pres. JOÃO BATISTA SANTOS; 4 brs.

Banco BMC, SA: Av. das Nações Unidas 12995, 24° andar, 04578-000 São Paulo, SP; tel. (11) 5503-7780; fax (11) 5503-7676; e-mail bancobmc@bmc.com.br; internet www.bmc.com.br; f. 1939 as Banco Mercantil de Crédito, SA; adopted current name in 1990; cap. 164.8m., res 72.9m., dep. 1,208.7m. (Dec. 2005); Chair. and CEO FRANCISCO JAIME NOGUEIRA PINHEIRO; 16 brs.

Banco BMG, SA: Av. Alvares Cabral 1707, Santo Agostinho, 30170-001 Belo Horizonte, MG; tel. (31) 3290-3700; fax (31) 3290-3168; e-mail bancobmg@bancobmg.com.br; internet www.bancobmg.com.br; f. 1930; cap. 510.0m., res 493.8m., dep. 2,573.3m. (Dec. 2006); Pres. FLÁVIO PENTAGNA GUIMARÃES; 10 brs.

Banco Bradesco, SA: Cidade de Deus, Vila Yara, 06029–900 Osasco, SP; tel. (11) 3681-4011; fax (11) 3684-4630; internet www.bradesco.com.br; f. 1943 as Banco Brasileiro de Descontos; present name adopted 1989; cap. 14,200.0m., res 10,436.4m., dep. 137,216.9m. (Dec. 2006); Pres. MÁRCIO ARTUR LAURELLI CYPRIANO; 3,021 brs.

Banco Brascan, SA: Av. Almirante Barroso 52, 30° andar, Centro, 20031-000 Rio de Janeiro, RJ; tel. (21) 3231-3000; fax (21) 3231-3231; internet www.bancobrascan.com.br; f. 1968; cap. 201.3m., res 103.2m., dep. 545.8m. (Dec. 2006); Pres. ANTÔNIO PAULO DE AZEVEDO SODRE.

Banco Dibens, SA: Rua Boa Vista 162, 6° andar, Centro, 01014-902 São Paulo, SP; tel. (11) 3243-7535; fax (11) 3243-7534; internet www.dibens.com.br; f. 1989; jtly owned by UNIBANCO and Grupo Verdi; cap. 179.2m., res 23.6m., dep. 1,420.3m. (Dec. 2005); Pres. MAURO SADDI; 23 brs.

Banco Fibra: Av. Brig. Faria Lima 3064, 11°–12° andares, Itaim Bibi, 01451-000 São Paulo, SP; tel. (11) 3847-6700; fax (11) 3847-6962; e-mail bancofibra@bancofibra.com.br; internet www.bancofibra.com.br; f. 1989; cap. 350.0m., res 90.6m., dep. 7,174.1m. (Dec. 2006); CEO JOÃO AYRES RABELLO, Filho.

Banco Industrial do Brasil: Av. Juscelino Kubitschek 1703, 2°–4° andares, Itaim Bibi, 04543-000 São Paulo, SP; tel. (11) 3049-9700; fax (11) 3049-9810; internet www.bancoindustrial.com.br; f. 1994; cap. 124.7m., res 52.3m., dep. 1223.6m. (Dec. 2005); Pres. CARLOS ALBERTO MANSUR.

Banco Industrial e Comercial, SA (Bicbanco): Av. Paulista 1048, Bela Vista, 01310-100 São Paulo, SP; tel. (11) 3179-9000; fax (11) 3179-9277; internet www.bicbanco.com.br; f. 1938; cap. 332.0m., res 195.3m., dep. 5,854.2m. (Dec. 2006); Pres. JOSÉ BEZERRA DE MENEZES; 30 brs.

Banco Indusval, SA (Banco Indusval Multistock): Rua Boa Vista, 7°–12° andares, Centro, 01014-000 São Paulo, SP; tel. (11) 3315-5677; fax (11) 3315-0166; e-mail banco@indusval.com.br; internet www.indusval.com.br; f. 1980; cap. 106.6m., res 43.1m., dep. 724.5m. (Dec. 2006); Pres. MANOEL FELIX CINTRA NETO.

Banco Itaú, SA: Praça Alfredo Egydio de Souza Aranha 100, Torre Itaúsa, 04344-902 São Paulo, SP; tel. (11) 5019-1549; fax (11) 5019-1133; e-mail investor.relations@itau.com.br; internet www.itau.com.br; f. 1944 as Banco Central de Crédito; present name adopted 1973; cap. 10,174.9m., res 1,262.0m., dep. 113,546.7m. (Dec. 2005); Pres. and CEO ROBERTO EGYDIO SETÚBAL; 3,044 brs.

Banco Itaú BBA, SA: Av. Brig. Faria Lima 3400, 4° andar, 04538-132 São Paulo, SP; tel. (11) 3708-8000; fax (11) 3708-8172; e-mail bancoitaubba@itaubba.com.br; internet www.itaubba.com.br; f. 1967 as Banco do Estado de Minas Gerais, SA; present name adopted 2004; acquired by Banco Itaú in 2002; cap. 2,77.2m., res 2,195.6m., dep. 37,105.1m. (Dec. 2005); Pres. and CEO CANDIDO BOTELHO BRACHER; 6 brs.

Banco Mercantil do Brasil, SA: Rua Rio de Janerio 654, 6° andar, Centro, 30160–912 Belo Horizonte, MG; tel. (31) 3239-6314; fax (31) 3239-6975; e-mail sac@mercantil.com.br; internet www.mercantil.com.br; f. 1943 as Banco Mercantil de Minas Gerais, SA; cap. 214.4m., res 269.3m., dep. 3,915.3m. (Dec. 2005); Pres. MILTON DE ARAÚJO; 201 brs.

Banco Paulista, SA: Rua Boa Vista, 2° andar, Centro, 01014-907 São Paulo, SP; tel. (11) 3117-6000; fax (11) 3117-6220; e-mail cambiobp@bancopaulista.com.br; internet www.bancopaulista.com.br; f. 1989; cap. 32.3m., res 13.8m., dep. 210.9m. (Dec. 2005); Pres. ALVARO AUGUSTO VIDIGAL.

Banco de Pernambuco SA (Bandepe): Edif. Bandepe, 5° andar, Cais do Apolo 222, Bairro do Recife, 50030-230 Recife, PE; tel. (11) 3425-6385; fax (11) 0812-2097; internet www.bandepe.com.br; f. 1938 as Banco do Estado de Pernambuco; present name adopted 2000; cap. 2,768.4m., res 150.3m., dep. 1,095.8m. (Dec. 2005); Pres. CELSO ANTUNES DA COSTA; 66 brs.

Banco Pine SA: Alameda Santos 1940, 12°–13° andares, Cerqueira Cesar, 01418-200 São Paulo, SP; tel. (11) 3372-5200; fax (11) 3372-5403; e-mail bancopine@uol.com.br; internet www.bancopine.com.br; f. 1997; cap. 248.5m., res 86.7m., dep. 2,494.8m. (Dec. 2006); Man. Dirs Dr NELSON NOGUEIRA PINHEIRO, NORBERTO NOGUEIRA PINHEIRO.

Banco Rural, SA: Av. Presidente Wilson 927, 20065-900 Rio de Janeiro, RJ; tel. (21) 3210-1310; fax (21) 3220-0198; internet www.rural.com.br; f. 1964 as Banco Rural de Minas Gerais; present name adopted 1980; cap. 177.7m., res 43.6m., dep. 961.5m. (Dec. 2005); Pres. KÁTIA RABELLO; 54 brs.

Banco Safra, SA: Av. Paulista 2100, 9° andar, 01310-930 São Paulo, SP; tel. (11) 3175-7575; fax (11) 3175-7211; internet www.safra.com.br; f. 1940; cap. 1,411.9m., res 2,390.8m., dep. 42.563.4m. (Dec. 2006); Pres. CARLOS ALBERTO VIEIRA; 77 brs.

Banco Société Générale Brasil, SA: Av. Paulista 2300, 9° andar, Cerqueira Cesar, 01310-300 São Paulo, SP; tel. (11) 3217-8000; fax (11) 3217-8090; internet www.sgbrasil.com.br; f. 1981 as Banco Sogeral; present name adopted 2001; cap. 319.8m., res –88.2m., dep. 503.4m. (Dec. 2005); Pres. FRANÇOIS DOSSA.

Banco Sudameris Brasil, SA: Av. Paulista 1000, 01310-912 São Paulo, SP; tel. (11) 3170-9899; fax (11) 3289-1239; internet www.sudameris.com.br; f. 1910; present name adopted 1979; cap. 1,423.0m., res 212.8m., dep. 10,021.7m. (Dec. 2005); Exec. Dir YVES L. J. LEJEUNE; 270 brs.

Banco UBS Pactual, SA: Torre Corcovado, 6°, Praia de Botafago 501, 22250-040 Rio de Janeiro, RJ; tel. (21) 2514-9600; fax (21) 2514-8600; e-mail webmaster@pactual.com.br; internet www.pactual.com.br; f. 1983; present name adopted 2006 following acquisition by UBS Ag (Switzerland); cap. 208.7m., res 416.5m., dep. 17,310.1m. (Dec. 2005); Pres. JOSE MARIA ARIAS MOSQUERA; 2 brs.

Banco Votorantim, SA: Av. Roque Petroni Jr 999, 16° andar, Vila Gertrudes, 04707-910 São Paulo, SP; tel. (11) 5185-1700; fax (11) 5185-1900; internet www.bancovotorantim.com.br; f. 1991; cap. 2,380.0m., res 1,654.9m., dep. 31,860.4m. (Dec. 2005); Pres. JOSÉ ERMÍRIO DE MORAES NETO.

Banif—Banco Internacional do Funchal (Brasil), SA: Rua Minas de Prata 30, 16°–17° andares, 04552-080 São Paulo, SP; tel. (11) 3165-2066; fax (11) 3073-0345; e-mail rosmar.vidigal@bancobanif.com.br; internet www.bancobanif.com.br; f. 1999 as Banco Banif Primus, SA; present name adopted 2005; owned by Banif Comercial SGPS, SA (Portugal); cap. 53.7m., res 2.3m., dep. 644.7m. (Dec. 2006); Pres. HORÁCIO DA SILVA ROQUE.

Unibanco (União de Bancos Brasileiros, SA): Av. Eusébio Matoso 891, 15° andar, 05423-901 São Paulo, SP; tel. (11) 3584-1980; fax (11) 3584-1585; e-mail investor.relations@unibanco.com.br; internet www.ir.unibanco.com; f. 1924; cap. 8,000.0m., res 1,920.9m., dep. 55,523.1m. (Dec. 2005); Chair. PEDRO MOREIRA SALLES; 809 brs.

BRAZIL
Directory

Development Banks

Banco de Desenvolvimento de Minas Gerais, SA (BDMG): Rua da Bahia 1600, 30160-907 Belo Horizonte, MG; tel. (31) 3219-8000; fax (31) 3226-3292; internet www.bdmg.mg.gov.br; f. 1962; owned by the state of Minas Gerais; long-term credit operations; cap. 717.9m., res 42.0m., total assets 1,623.5m. (Dec. 2006); Pres. ROMEU SCARIOLI.

Banco Nacional do Desenvolvimento Econômico e Social (BNDES): Av. República do Chile 100, Centro, 20031-917 Rio de Janeiro, RJ; tel. (21) 2277-7447; fax (21) 3088-7447; internet www.bndes.gov.br; f. 1952 to act as main instrument for financing of devt schemes sponsored by the Govt and to support programmes for the devt of the national economy; charged with supervision of privatization programme of the 1990s; cap. 12,500.1m., res 576.4m., dep. 8,617.0m. (June 2002); Chair. LUCIANO COUTINHO.

Investment Bank

Banco Fininvest, SA: Rua da Passagem 170, 7° andar, 20030-021 Rio de Janeiro, RJ; tel. (21) 3097-4725; fax (21) 3820-5323; internet www.fininvest.com.br; f. 1961 as Fininvest SA Crédito Financiamento e Investimento; present name adopted 1989; owned by UNIBANCO; cap. 87.7m., res 629.1m., dep. 1,805.4m. (Dec. 2005); Pres. ALVARO OSÓRIO LONGO MUSA DOS SANTOS.

State-owned Savings Bank

Caixa Econômica Federal: SBS, Quadra 04, Lotes 3–4, 16° andar, 70092-900 Brasília, DF; tel. (61) 3414-8543; fax (61) 3414-9740; e-mail genit@caixa.gov.br; internet www.caixa.gov.br; f. 1861; cap. 6,556.2m., res 2,626.3m., dep. 155,009.1m. (Dec. 2006); Pres. MARIA FERNANDA RAMOS COELHO; 2,026 brs.

Foreign Banks

American Express Bank (Brasil) Banco Múltiplo, SA (USA): Av. Bridadeiro Faria Lima 1355, 16° andar, 01452-022 São Paulo, SP; tel. (11) 3030-3000; fax (11) 3030-3030; e-mail biamex@biamex.com.br; internet www.biamex.com.br; f. 1988 as Mantrust SRL; present name adopted Dec. 2003; cap. 132.1m., res −35.3m., dep. 241.6m. (Dec. 2005); Pres. JOHN HARRIMAN.

Banco Sumitomo Mitsui Brasileiro, SA: Av. Paulista 37, 12° andar, Paraiso, 01311-902 São Paulo, SP; tel. (11) 3178-8000; fax (11) 3289-1668; f. 1958; present name adopted 2001; cap. 309.4m., res −5.0m., dep. 187.3m. (Dec. 2004); Pres. TAKEAKI MISUMI; 1 br.

Banco de Tokyo-Mitsubishi UFJ Brasil, SA: Av. Paulista 1274, Bela Vista, 01310-925 São Paulo, SP; tel. (11) 3268-0211; fax (11) 3268-0453; internet www.br.bk.mufg.jp; f. 1972 as Banco de Tokyo; cap. 186.9m., res 137.4m., dep. 318.4m. (Dec. 2004); Pres. AKIRA TAKEUCHI; 2 brs.

Deutsche Bank SA Banco Alemao: Rua Alexandre Dumas 2200, 04717-910 São Paulo, SP; tel. (11) 5189-5000; fax (11) 5189-5100; internet www.deutsche-bank.com.br; f. 1911; cap. 302.5m., res 273.3m., dep. 1,913.3m. (Dec. 2005); Pres. and CEO ALEXANDRE AOUDE.

HSBC Bank Brasil SA-Banco Multiplo: Edif. Palácio Avenida, 4° andar, Travessa Oliveira Belo 34, Centro, 80020-030 Curitiba, PR; tel. (41) 3321-6161; fax (41) 3340-2660; internet www.hsbc.com.br; f. 1997; cap. 2,146.8m., res 1,224.4m., dep. 36,222.5m. (Dec. 2005); Pres. YOUSSEF ASSAAD NASR; 939 brs.

Banking Associations

Associação Nacional dos Bancos de Investimentos—ANBID: Av. Brig. Faria Lima 2179, 2° andar, 01451-001 São Paulo, SP; tel. (11) 3471-4200; fax (11) 3471-4230; e-mail anbid@anbid.com.br; internet www.anbid.com.br; investment banks; Pres. ALFREDO EGYDIO SETÚBAL; Supt LUIZ KAUFMAN.

Federação Brasileira dos Bancos: Avda Brigadeiro Faria Lima 1485, 15° andar, Torre Norte, Pinheiros, 01452-921 São Paulo, SP; tel. (11) 3244-9800; fax (11) 3107-8486; internet www.febraban.org.br; f. 1966; Dir-Gen. WILSON ROBERTO LEVORATO.

Sindicato dos Bancos dos Estados do Rio de Janeiro e Espírito Santo: Av. Rio Branco 81, 19° andar, Rio de Janeiro, RJ; Pres. THEÓPHILO DE AZEREDO SANTOS; Vice-Pres. Dr NELSON MUFARREJ.

Sindicato dos Bancos dos Estados de São Paulo, Paraná, Mato Grosso e Mato Grosso do Sul: Rua Líbero Badaró 293, 13° andar, 01905 São Paulo, SP; f. 1924; Pres. PAULO DE QUEIROZ.

There are other banking associations in Maceió, Salvador, Fortaleza, Belo Horizonte, João Pessoa, Recife and Porto Alegre.

STOCK EXCHANGES

Comissão de Valores Mobiliários (CVM): Rua 7 de Setembro 111, Centro, 20050-901 Rio de Janeiro, RJ; tel. (21) 3233-8686; e-mail ouvidor@cvm.gov.br; internet www.cvm.gov.br; f. 1977 to supervise the operations of the stock exchanges and develop the Brazilian securities market; regional offices in Brasília and São Paulo; Chair. MARIA HELENA DOS SANTOS FERNANDES DE SANTANA.

Bolsa de Mercadorias e Futuros (BM&F) (Brazilian Mercantile and Futures Exchange): Praça Antônio Prado 48, 01010-901 São Paulo, SP; tel. (11) 3119-2000; fax (11) 3342-7565; e-mail bmf@bmf.com.br; internet www.bmf.com.br; f. 1985; trading centre and clearing house for assets, securities and derivatives; offices in Brasília, Rio de Janeiro, Campo Grande, Santos, New York (USA) and Shanghai (China); Pres. MANOEL FELIX CINTRA NETO; CEO EDEMIR PINTO.

Bolsa de Valores do Rio de Janeiro: Praça XV de Novembro 20, 20010-010 Rio de Janeiro, RJ; tel. (21) 2514-1069; fax (21) 2514-11107; e-mail info@bvrj.com.br; internet www.bvrj.com.br; f. 1845; focuses on the trading of fixed income govt bonds and foreign exchange; Chair. EDSON FIGUEIREDO MENEZES; Supt-Gen. SÉRGIO PÓVOA.

Bolsa de Valores de São Paulo (BOVESPA): Rua XV de Novembro 275, 01013-001 São Paulo, SP; tel. (11) 3233-2000; fax (11) 3233-3550; e-mail bovespa@bovespa.com.br; internet www.bovespa.com.br; f. 1890; offices in Rio de Janeiro and Porto Alegre; Pres. RAYMUNDO MAGLIANO, Filho; CEO GILBERTO MIFANO.

There are commodity exchanges at Paraná, Porto Alegre, Vitória, Recife, Santos and São Paulo.

INSURANCE

Supervisory Authorities

Superintendência de Seguros Privados (SUSEP): Rua Buenos Aires 256, 4° andar, 20061-000 Rio de Janeiro, RJ; tel. (21) 3086-9800; e-mail gabin@susep.gov.br; internet www.susep.gov.br; f. 1966; part of the Ministry of Finance; offices in Brasília, São Paulo and Porto Alegre; Pres. GUIDO MANTEGA (Minister of Finance); Supt ARMANDO VERGÍLIO DOS SANTOS JÚNIOR.

Conselho de Recursos do Sistema Nacional de Seguros Privados, de Previdência Abierta e de Capitalização (CRSNSP): Rua Buenos Aires 256, 20061-000 Rio de Janeiro, RJ; tel. (21) 3806-9815; f. 1966 as Conselho Nacional de Seguros Privados (CNSP); changed name in 1998; part of the Ministry of Finance; Pres. AGOSTINHO DO NASCIMENTO NETTO; Sec. THERESA CHRISTINA CUNHA MARTINS.

Federação Nacional dos Corretores de Seguros Privados, de Capitalização, de Previdência Privada e das Empresas Corretoras de Seguros (FENACOR): Rua Senador Dantas 74, 10° andar, 20031-205 Rio de Janeiro, RJ; tel. (21) 3077-4777; fax (21) 3077-4798; e-mail leoncio@fenacor.com.br; internet www.fenacor.com.br; Pres. ROBERTO SILVA BARBOSA.

Federação Nacional das Empresas de Seguros Privados e de Capitalização (FENASEG): Rua Senador Dantas 74, Centro, 20031-200 Rio de Janeiro, RJ; tel. (21) 2510-7777; e-mail fenaseg@fenaseg.org.br; internet www.fenaseg.org.br; f. 1951; Pres. JOÃO ELISIO FERRAZ DE CAMPOS.

IRB-Brasil Resseguros: Av. Marechal Câmara 171, Castelo, 20020-901 Rio de Janeiro, RJ; tel. (21) 2272-0200; fax (21) 2240-8775; e-mail info@irb-brasilre.com.br; internet www.irb-brasilre.com.br; f. 1939; state-owned reinsurance co; fmrly Instituto de Resseguros do Brasil; offices in Brasília, São Paulo, Porto Alegre, New York (USA) and London (United Kingdom); reinsurance; Pres. EDUARDO HITIRO NAKAO.

Principal Companies

The following is a list of the principal national insurance companies, selected on the basis of assets. The total assets of insurance companies operating in Brazil were US $21,465.7m. in December 2003.

AGF Vida e Previdência, SA: São Paulo, SP; separated from AGF Brasil Seguros and sold to Itaú in 2003; total assets US $218.2m. (Dec. 2003).

Bradesco Saúde, SA: Rua Barão de Itapagipe 225, Rio Comprido, 20261-901 Rio de Janeiro, RJ; tel. (21) 2503-1101; fax (21) 2293-9489; internet www.bradescosaude.com.br; health insurance; CEO and Dir MARCIO ARTUR LAURELLI CYPRIANO.

Bradesco Seguros e Previdência, SA: Rua Barão de Itapagipe 225, 20269-900 Rio de Janeiro, RJ; tel. (21) 2503-1101; fax (21) 2293-9489; internet www.bradescoseguros.com.br; f. 1934; general; total assets US $354.7m. (Dec. 2003); Pres. LUIZ CARLOS TRABUCO CAPPI.

Bradesco Vida e Previdência, SA: Cidade de Deus s/n, Vila Yara, São Paulo, SP; tel. (11) 3684-2122; fax (11) 3684-5068; internet www.bradescoprevidencia.com.br; f. 2001; life insurance; total assets US $8,530.2m. (Dec. 2003); Pres. MARCO ANTÔNIO ROSSI.

Brasilprev Seguros e Prevedência, SA: Rua Verbo Divino 1711, Chácara Santo Antônio, 04719-002 São Paulo, SP; tel. (11) 5185-4240; e-mail atendimento@brasilprev.com.br; internet www

BRAZIL
Directory

.brasilprev.com.br; f. 1993; all classes; 50% owned by Banco do Brasil; total assets US $1,933.5m. (Dec. 2003); Pres. FUAD NOMAN.

Caixa Seguros: SCN Quadra 01, Bloco A, Edif. 1, 15–17° andares, Asa Norte, 70711-900 Brasília, DF; tel. (61) 2192-2400; fax (61) 3328-8869; internet www.caixaseguros.com.br; f. 1967; fmrly Sasse, Cia Nacional de Seguros; changed name to Sasse Caixa Seguros in 1998 and as above in 2000; general; total assets US $2,509m. (Dec. 2005); Pres. THIERRY MARC CLAUDE CLAUDON.

Caixa Vida e Previdência, SA: SCN Quadra 1, Bloco A, Edif. 1, 15° andar, 70711-900 Brasília, DF; tel. (61) 2192-2400; fax (61) 3328-0600; internet www.caixaprevidencia.com.br; part of Caixa Seguros group; total assets US $451.6m. (Dec. 2003).

Cia de Seguros Aliança do Brasil, SA: Rua Manuel da Nóbrega 1280, 9° andar, 04001-004 São Paulo, SP; tel. (11) 4689-5638; internet www.aliancadobrasil.com.br; f. 1996; total assets US $324.4m. (Dec. 2003); Pres. KHALID MOHAMMED RAOUF.

HSBC Vida e Previdência (Brasil), SA: Rua Teniente Francisco Ferreira de Souza 805, Bloco 1, Ala 4, Vila Hauer, 81570-340 Curitaba, PR; tel. (41) 3217-4555; fax (41) 3321-8800; e-mail spariz@hsbc.com.vr; internet www.hsbc.com.br; f. 1938; all classes; total assets US $499.3m. (Dec. 2004); Supt Dir VILSON ANDRADE; Pension Funds Dir SIDNEY PARIZ.

Icatu Hartford Seguros, SA: Av. Presidente Wilson 231, 10° andar, 20030-021 Rio de Janeiro, RJ; tel. 0800-285-3000; e-mail online@icatu.com.br; internet www.icatu-hartford.com.br; total assets US $329.2m. (Dec. 2003).

Itaú Seguros, SA: Praça Alfredo Egydio de Souza Aranha 100, Bloco A, 04344-920 São Paulo, SP; tel. (11) 5019-3322; fax (11) 5019-3530; e-mail itauseguros@itauseguros.com.br; internet www.itauseguros.com.br; f. 1921; all classes; total assets US $325.4m. (Dec. 2003); Pres. LUIZ DE CAMPOS SALLES.

Itaú Vida e Previdência, SA: internet www.itau.com.br; part of the Itaú group; total assets US $1,808.4m. (Dec. 2003).

Liberty Paulista Seguros, SA: Rua Dr Geraldo Campos Moreira 110, 04571-020 São Paulo, SP; tel. (11) 5503-4000; fax (11) 5505-2122; internet www.libertypaulista.com.br; f. 1906; general; total assets US $156.7m. (Dec. 2003); Pres. LUIS MAURETTE.

Marítima Seguros, SA: Rua Col. Xavier de Toledo 114, 10° andar, São Paulo, SP; tel. (11) 3156-1000; fax (11) 3156-1712; internet www.maritima.com.br; f. 1943; Pres. FRANCISCO CAIUBY VIDIGAL; Dir-Gen. MILTON BELLIZIA, Filho.

Porto Seguro Cia de Seguros Gerais: Rua Guaianazes 1238, 12° andar, 01204-001 São Paulo, SP; tel. (11) 3366-5199; fax (11) 3366-5140; internet www.portoseguro.com.br; f. 1945; life, automotive and risk; total assets US $518.6m. (Dec. 2003); Pres. ROSA GARFINKEL.

Real Seguros, SA: Rua Samapiao Viana 44, 04004-902 Paraíso, SP; tel. (11) 3054-7000; internet www.realseguros.com.br; f. 1969; in 1999 became part of ABM AMRO group; general; total assets US $165.8m. (Dec. 2003).

Real Vida e Previdência, SA: Rua Sampaio Viana 44, 04004-902 Paraíso, SP; tel. (11) 3054-7000; internet www.bancoreal.com.br; f. 1969; became part of the ABM AMRO group in 1999; total assets US $495.1m. (Dec. 2003).

Santander Seguros, SA: internet www.santander.com.br; part of the Banco Santander; total assets US $467.3m. (Dec. 2003).

Sul América, Cia Nacional de Seguros: Rua da Quitanda 86, 20091-000 Rio de Janeiro, RJ; tel. (21) 2506-8585; fax (21) 2506-8807; internet www.sulamerica.com.br; f. 1895; life and risk; total assets US $221.9m. (Dec. 2003); Pres. RONY CASTRO DE OLIVEIRA LYRIO.

Sul América Seguros de Vida e Previdência, SA: Rua Pedro Avacine 73, Morumbi, 05679-160 São Paulo, SP; tel. (11) 3779-7000; fax (11) 3758-8972; internet www.sulamerica.com.br; total assets US $348.3m. (Dec. 2003).

Unibanco AIG Seguros e Previdência: Av. Eusébio Matoso 1375, 05423-180 São Paulo, SP; tel. (11) 3039-4082; fax (11) 3039-4074; internet www.unibancoaig.com.br; f. 2001 by merger of Unibanco Seguros and AIG Brasil; part of the Unibanco AIG group; life; Pres. JOSÉ CASTRO ARAÚJO RUDGE.

Trade and Industry

GOVERNMENT AGENCIES

Agência Nacional de Petróleo (ANP): Av. Rio Branco 65, 12° andar, 20090-004 Rio de Janeiro, RJ; tel. (21) 2112-8100; fax (21) 2112-8129; internet www.anp.gov.br; f. 1998; regulatory body of the petroleum industry; Dir-Gen. HAROLDO BORGES RODRIGUES LIMA.

Agência de Promoção de Exportações do Brasil (APEX Brasil): SBN Quadra 1, Bloco B, 10° andar, Edif. CNC, 70041-902 Brasília, DF; tel. (61) 3426-0202; fax (61) 3426-0263; e-mail apex@apexbrasil.com.br; internet www.apexbrasil.com.br; f. 2003; promotes Brazilian exports; CEO ALESSANDRO GOLOMBIEWSKI TEIXEIRA.

Câmara de Comércio Exterior (CAMEX): Ministério do Desenvolvimento, Indústria e Comércio Exterior, Bloco J, 70053-900 Brasília, DF; tel. (61) 2109-7483; e-mail camex@desenvolvimento.gov.br; internet www.desenvolvimento.gov.br; f. 2003; part of Ministry of Development, Industry and Trade; formulates and co-ordinates export policies; Exec. Sec. MÁRIO MUGNAINI JÚNIOR.

Companhia de Pesquisa de Recursos Minerais (CPRM): Serviço Geológico do Brasil, SGAN, Quadra 603, Conj. J, Parte A, 1° andar, 70830-030 Brasília, DF; tel. (61) 3426-5252; fax (61) 3225-3985; e-mail seus@rj.cprm.gov.br; internet www.cprm.gov.br; mining research, attached to the Ministry of Mines and Energy; regional offices in Manaus (Amazonas), Belém (Pará), Salvador (Bahia), Belo Horizonte (Minas Gerais), São Paulo (São Paulo) and Porto Alegre (Rio Grande do Sul); Pres. AGAMENON DANTAS.

Conselho Nacional de Desenvolvimento Científico e Tecnológico (CNPq): SEPN 507, 3° andar, Sala 300, 70740-901 Brasília, DF; tel. (61) 2108-9400; fax (61) 2108-9487; e-mail presidencia@cnpq.br; internet www.cnpq.br; f. 1951; scientific and technological development council; Pres. ERNEY FELÍCIO PLESSMANN DE CAMARGO.

Conselho Nacional de Desenvolvimento Rural Sustentável (CONDRAF): SCN, Quadra 01, Edif. Palácio do Desenvolvimento 8° andar, 70057-900 Brasília, DF; tel. (61) 2191-9880; e-mail condraf@mda.gov.br; internet www.condraf.org.br; f. 2000; to promote sustainable rural development; Pres. GUILHERME CASSEL (Minister of Agrarian Development).

Departamento Nacional da Produção Mineral (DNPM): SAN, Quadra 1, Bloco B, 3° andar, 70041-903 Brasília, DF; tel. (61) 3312-6666; fax (61) 3312-6918; e-mail dire@dnpm.gov.br; internet www.dnpm.gov.br; f. 1934; responsible for geological studies and control of exploration of mineral resources; part of Ministry of Mines and Energy; Dir-Gen. MIGUEL ANTONIO CEDRAZ NERY.

Empresa Brasileira de Pesquisa Agropecuária (EMBRAPA): Parque Estação Biológica (PqEB) s/n, 70770-901 Brasília, DF; tel. (61) 3448-4433; fax (61) 3347-1041; e-mail sac@embrapa.br; internet www.embrapa.br; f. 1973; attached to the Ministry of Agriculture, Fisheries and Food Supply; agricultural research; Pres. SILVIO CRESTANA.

Instituto Brasileiro de Geografia e Estatística (IBGE): Centro de Documentação e Disseminação de Informações (CDDI), Rua Gen. Canabarro 706, 2° andar, Maracanã, 20271-201 Rio de Janeiro, RJ; tel. (21) 2142-4781; fax (21) 2142-4933; e-mail ibge@ibge.gov.br; internet www.ibge.gov.br; f. 1936; produces and analyses statistical, geographical, cartographic, geodetic, demographic and socio-economic information; Pres. (IBGE) EDUARDO PEREIRA NUNES; Supt (CDDI) DAVID WU TAI.

Instituto Brasileiro do Meio Ambiente e Recursos Naturais Renováveis (IBAMA): SCEN Trecho 2, 70818-900 Brasília, DF; tel. (61) 3316-1205; fax (61) 3226-5094; e-mail webmaster@ibama.gov.br; internet www.ibama.gov.br; f. 1967; responsible for the annual formulation of national environmental plans; Pres. MARCUS LUIZ BARROSO BARROS.

Instituto Nacional de Colonização e Reforma Agraria (INCRA): Edif. Palácio do Desenvolvimento, 70057-900 Brasília, DF; tel. (61) 3411-7474; e-mail comunicacao.social@incra.gov.br; internet www.incra.gov.br; f. 1970; land reform agency; Pres. ROLF HACKBART.

Instituto Nacional de Metrologia, Normalização e Qualidade Industrial (INMETRO): Rua Santa Alexandrina 416, 5° andar, Rio Comprido, 20261-232 Rio de Janeiro, RJ; tel. and fax (21) 2563-2970; e-mail homepage@inmetro.gov.br; internet www.inmetro.gov.br; f. 1973; part of Ministry of Development, Industry and Trade.

Instituto Nacional da Propriedade Industrial (INPI): Praça Mauá 7, 18° andar, Centro, 20081-240 Rio de Janeiro, RJ; tel. (21) 2139-3000; fax (21) 2263-2539; e-mail inpipres@inpi.gov.br; internet www.inpi.gov.br; f. 1970; part of Ministry of Development, Industry and Trade; intellectual property, etc.; Pres. ROBERTO JAGUARIBE GOMES DE MATTOS.

Instituto de Pesquisa Econômica Aplicada (IPEA): Av. Presidente António Carlos 51, 13° andar, 20020-010 Rio de Janeiro, RJ; tel. (21) 3804-8000; fax (21) 2240-1920; e-mail faleconosco@ipea.gov.br; internet www.ipea.gov.br; also has an office in Brasília; f. 1970; economics and planning institute; Pres. LUIZ HENRIQUE PROENÇA SOARES.

REGIONAL DEVELOPMENT ORGANIZATIONS

Agência de Desenvolvimento da Amazônia (ADA): Av. Almirante Barroso 426, Marco, 66090-900 Belém, PA; tel. (91) 4008-5442; fax (91) 4008-5456; e-mail gabinete@ada.gov.br; internet www.ada.gov.br; f. 2001; to co-ordinate the development of resources in Amazonia; Dir-Gen. DJALMA BEZERRA MELLO.

BRAZIL

Directory

Companhia de Desenvolvimento dos Vales do São Francisco e do Parnaíba (CODEVASF): SGAN, Quadra 601, Conj. 1, Edif. Manoel Novaes, 70830-901 Brasília, DF; tel. (61) 3223-8819; fax (61) 3311-7814; internet www.codevasf.gov.br; f. 1974; promotes integrated development of resources of São Francisco and Parnaíba Valley; part of Ministry of National Integration; Pres. LUIZ CARLOS EVERTON DE FARIAS.

Superintendência de Desenvolvimento do Nordeste (SUDENE): Praça Ministro João Gonçalves de Souza s/n, Edif. Sudene, 50670-900 Recife, PE; tel. (81) 2102-2119; e-mail gabinete@sudene.gov.br; internet www.sudene.gov.br; f. 2007 to replace Agência de Desenvolvimento do Nordeste (f. 2001); Supt PAULO SÉRGIO DE NORONHA FONTANA.

Superintendência da Zona Franca de Manaus (SUFRAMA): Av. Ministro João Gonçalves de Souza s/n, Distrito Industrial, 69075-830 Manaus, AM; tel. (92) 3321-7000; fax (92) 3237-6549; e-mail cas@suframa.gov.br; internet www.suframa.gov.br; assists in the development of the Manaus Free Zone; Supt FLÁVIA SKROBOT BARBOSA GROSSO.

AGRICULTURAL, INDUSTRIAL AND TRADE ORGANIZATIONS

Associação Brasileira do Alumínio (ABAL) (Brazilian Aluminum Association): Rua Humberto I 220, 4° andar, Vila Mariana, 04018-030 São Paulo, SP; tel. (11) 5904-6450; fax (11) 5904-6459; e-mail aluminio@abal.org.br; internet www.abal.org.br; f. 1970; represents aluminium producing and processing cos; 66 mem. cos.

Associação Brasileira de Celulose e Papel—Bracelpa: Rua Afonso de Freitas 409, Bairro Paraíso, 04006-900 São Paulo, SP; tel. (11) 3885-1845; fax (11) 3885-3689; e-mail faleconosco@bracelpa.org.br; internet www.bracelpa.org.br; f. 1932; pulp and paper association; Pres. HORACIO LAFER PIVA.

Associação Brasileira das Indústrias de Óleos Vegetais (Abiove) (Brazilian Association of Vegetable Oil Industries): Av. Vereador José Diniz 3707, 7° andar, Conj. 73, 04603-004 São Paulo, SP; tel. (11) 5536-0733; fax (11) 5536-9816; internet www.abiove.com.br; f. 1981; 10 mem. cos; Pres. CARLO LOVATELLI.

Associação Brasileira dos Produtores de Algodão (ABRAPA): SAGN, Quadra 601, Modulo K, Edif. CNA, Asa Norte, 70830-010 Brasília, DF; tel. (61) 2109-1606; fax (61) 2109-1607; e-mail abrapa@abrapa.com.br; internet www.abrapa.com.br; f. 1999; cotton producers' association; Exec. Dir HÉLIO TOLLINI.

Associação de Comércio Exterior do Brasil (AEB) (Brazilian Foreign Trade Association): Av. General Justo 335, 4° andar, 20021-130 Rio de Janeiro, RJ; tel. (21) 2544-0048; fax (21) 2544-0577; e-mail aebbras@aeb.org.br; internet www.aeb.org.br; exporters' association; Vice-Pres. JOSÉ AUGUSTO DE CASTRO.

Associação Comercial do Rio de Janeiro (ACRJ): Rua da Calendária 9, 11°–12° andares, Centro, 20091-020 Rio de Janeiro, RJ; tel. and fax (21) 2291-1229; fax (21) 2514-1229; e-mail acrj@acrj.org.br; internet www.acrj.org.br; f. 1820; Pres. OLAVO EGYDIO MONTEIRO DE CARVALHO.

Associação Comercial de São Paulo (ACSP): Rua Boa Vista 51, Centro, 01014-911 São Paulo, SP; tel. (11) 3244-3322; fax (11) 3244-3355; e-mail infocem@acsp.com.br; internet www.acsp.com.br; f. 1894; Pres. ALENCAR BURTI.

Centro das Indústrias do Estado de São Paulo (CIESP): Av. Paulista 1313, 01311-923 São Paulo, SP; tel. (11) 3549-3232; e-mail atendimento@ciesp.com.br; internet www.ciesp.org.br; f. 1928; asscn of small and medium-sized businesses; Pres. CLÁUDIO VAZ.

Confederação da Agricultura e Pecuária do Brasil (CNA): SGAN, Quadra 601, Modulo K, 70830-903 Brasília, DF; tel. (61) 2109-1400; fax (61) 2109-1397; e-mail cna@cna.org.br; internet www.cna.org.br; f. 1964; national agricultural confederation; Exec. Vice-Pres. PIO GUERRA.

Confederação Nacional do Comércio (CNC): Av. General Justo 307, 20021-130 Rio de Janeiro, RJ; tel. (21) 3804-9200; e-mail cncrj@cnc.com.br; internet www.cnc.com.br; national confederation comprising 35 affiliated federations of commerce; Pres. ANTÔNIO JOSÉ DOMINGUES DE OLIVEIRA SANTOS.

Confederação Nacional da Indústria (CNI) (National Confederation of Industry): SBN, Quadra 01, Bloco C, Edif. Roberto Simonsen, 70040-903 Brasília, DF; tel. (61) 3317-9989; fax (61) 3317-9994; e-mail sac@cni.org.br; internet www.cni.org.br; f. 1938; national confederation of industry comprising 27 state industrial federations; membership of some 1,016 employers' unions; Pres. ARMANDO DE QUEIROZ MONTEIRO NETO; Dir JOSÉ AUGUSTO COELHO FERNANDES.

Conselho dos Exportadores de Café Verde do Brasil (CECAFE): Av. Nove de Julho 4865, Torre A, Conj. 61, Chácara Itaim, 01407-200 São Paulo, SP; tel. (11) 3079-3755; fax (11) 3167-4060; internet www.cecafe.com.br; f. 1999 through merger of Federação Brasileira dos Exportadores de Café and Associação Brasileira dos Exportadores de Café; council of green coffee exporters; Dir-Gen. GUILHERME BRAGA ABREU PIRES, Filho.

Federação Brasileira da Indústria Farmacêutica (Febrafarma): SAS, Quadra 1, Bloco N, Edif. Terra Brasilis, Salas 701 a 704, 70070-010 Brasília, DF; tel. and fax (61) 3323-8586; internet www.febrafarma.org.br; f. 2002; represents pharmaceutical industry; 15 mem. cos representing 267 manufacturers; Exec. Pres. CIRO MORTELLA.

Federação das Indústrias do Estado do Rio de Janeiro (FIRJAN): Centro Empresarial FIRJAN, Av. Graça Aranha 1, Rio de Janeiro, RJ; tel. (21) 2563-4389; e-mail centrodeatendimento@firjan.org.br; internet www.firjan.org.br; regional manufacturers' asscn; 103 affiliated sindicates representing almost 16,000 cos.

Federação das Indústrias do Estado de São Paulo (FIESP): Av. Paulista 1313, 01311-923 São Paulo, SP; tel. (11) 3549-4499; e-mail atendimento@fiesp.org.br; internet www.fiesp.org.br; regional manufacturers' asscn; Pres. PAULO SKAF.

Instituto Brasileiro do Mineração (IBRAM) (The Brazilian National Mining Association): SHIS, Quadra 12, Conj. 0, Casa 4, 71630-205 Brasília, DF; tel. (61) 3248-0155; fax (61) 3248-4940; e-mail ibram@ibram.org.br; internet ibram.org.br; f. 1976 to foster the development of the mining industry; Pres. and Dir PAULO CAMILLO VARGAS PENNA.

Instituto Brasileiro de Siderurgia (IBS): Av. Rio Branco 181, 28° andar, 20040-007 Rio de Janeiro, RJ; tel. (21) 2141-0001; fax (21) 2262-2234; e-mail ibs@ibs.org.br; internet www.ibs.org.br; f. 1963; steel cos org.; Exec. Pres. RINALDO CAMPOS SOARES.

Instituto Nacional de Tecnologia (INT): Av. Venezuela 82, 8° andar, 20081-312 Rio de Janeiro, RJ; tel. (21) 2123-1100; fax (21) 2123-1284; e-mail divulga@int.gov.br; internet www.int.gov.br; f. 1921; co-operates in national industrial development; Dir JOÃO LUIZ HANRIOT SELASCO.

Serviço de Apoio às Micro e Pequenas Empresas (Sebrae): SEPN, Quadra 515, Lote 03, Bloco C, Asa Norte, 70770-530 Brasília, DF; tel. (61) 3348-7100; fax (61) 3347-3581; internet www.sebrae.com.br; f. 1972; supports small- and medium-sized enterprises; Pres. PAULO TARCISO OKAMOTTO; Sec.-Gen. EJAIR SIQUEIRA ALVES.

União Democrática Ruralista (UDR): Av. Col. Marcondes 983, 6° andar, Sala 62, Centro, 19010-080 Presidente Prudente, SP; tel. (11) 3221-1082; fax (11) 3232-4622; e-mail udr.org@uol.com.br; internet www.udr.org.br; landowners' organization; Pres. LUIZ ANTÔNIO NABHAN GARCIA.

STATE HYDROCARBONS COMPANIES

Petróleo Brasileiro, SA (Petrobras): Av. República do Chile 65, Centro, 20031-912 Rio de Janeiro, RJ; tel. (21) 3224-1510; fax (21) 3224-6055; internet www.petrobras.com.br; f. 1953; production of petroleum and petroleum products; owns 16 oil refineries; net profit US $10,135.7m. (2005); Pres. JOSÉ SÉRGIO GABRIELLI DE AZEVEDO; Sec.-Gen. HÉLIO SHIGUENOBU FUJIKAWA; 53,933 employees; subsidiary cos are Petrobras Transporte, SA (Transpetro), Petrobras Comercializadora de Energia, Ltda, Petrobras Negócios Eletrônicos, SA, Petrobras International Finance Company (PIFCO) and Downstream Participações, SA, and cos listed below:

Petrobras Distribuidora, SA: Rua General Canabarro 500, Maracanã, 20271-900 Rio de Janeiro, RJ; tel. (21) 3876-4477; fax (21) 3876-4977; internet www.br.com.br; f. 1971; distribution of all petroleum by-products; Pres. MARIA DAS GRAÇAS SILVA FOSTER; 3,758 employees.

Petrobras Gás, SA (Gaspetro): Av. República do Chile 65, Centro, 20031-912 Rio de Janeiro, RJ; tel. (21) 3534-0439; fax (21) 3534-1080; e-mail sac@petrobras.com.br; internet www.gaspetro.com.br; f. 1998; Pres. JOSÉ MARIA CARVALHO DE RESENDE; Sec.-Gen. CARLOS AUGUSTO FRAZÃO DE AZEVEDO.

Petrobras Química, SA (Petroquisa): Av. República do Chile 65, 9° andar, Centro, 20031-912 Rio de Janeiro, RJ; tel. (21) 3224-1455; fax (21) 2262-1521; e-mail contato.petroquisa@petrobras.com.br; internet www.petroquisa.com.br; f. 1968; petrochemicals industry; controls 27 affiliated companies and four subsidiaries; Pres. JOSÉ LIMA DE ANDRADE NETO.

UTILITIES

Regulatory Agencies

Agência Nacional de Energia Elétrica (ANEEL): SGAN 603, Módulo J, 70830-030 Brasília, DF; e-mail aneel@aneel.gov.br; internet www.aneel.gov.br; f. 1939 as Conselho Nacional de Águas e Energia Elétrica, present name adopted 1996; Dir-Gen. JERSON KELMAN.

Comissão Nacional de Energia Nuclear (CNEN): Rua General Severiano 90, Botafogo, 22290-901 Rio de Janeiro, RJ; tel. (21) 2173-2000; fax (21) 2173-2003; e-mail corin@cnen.gov.br; internet www

BRAZIL

.cnen.gov.br; f. 1956; state organization responsible for management of nuclear power programme; Pres. ODAIR DIAS GONÇALVES.

Electricity

In December 2005 seven out of a total of 17 hydroelectric power-stations were successfully auctioned by ANEEL. Following a drought in 2002, the Government attempted to diversify the electricity-production sector, by encouraging the development of wind power and biofuels.

Centrais Elétricas Brasileiras, SA (Eletrobrás): Edif. Petrobras, Rua Dois, Setor de Autarquias Norte, 70040-903 Brasília, DF; tel. (61) 3223-5050; fax (61) 3225-5502; e-mail maryann@eletrobras.gov.br; internet www.eletrobras.gov.br; f. 1962; govt holding company responsible for planning, financing and managing Brazil's electrical energy programme; 52% govt-owned; scheduled for division into eight generating cos and privatization; Pres. ALOISIO MARCOS VASCONCELOS NOVAIS.

Centrais Elétricas do Norte do Brasil, SA (Eletronorte): SCN, Quadra 6, Conj. A, Blocos B/C, 70718-900 Brasília, DF; tel. (61) 3429-5151; fax (61) 3328-1463; e-mail ouvidoria@eln.gov.br; internet www.eln.gov.br; f. 1973; serves Amapá, Acre, Amazonas, Maranhão, Mato Gross, Pará, Rondônia, Roraima and Tocantins; Pres. CARLOS R. A. NASCIMENTO.

Boa Vista Energia, SA: Av. Capitão Ene Garcêz 691, Centro, 69310-160 Boa Vista, RR; tel. (95) 2621-1400; internet www.boavistaenergia.gov.br; f. 1997; subsidiary of Eletronorte; electricity distribution; Pres. CARLOS AUGUSTO ANDRADE SILVA.

Centrais Elétricas do Sul do Brasil, SA (Eletrosul): Rua Deputado Antônio Edu Vieira 999, Pantanal, 88040-901 Florianópolis, SC; tel. (48) 3231-7000; fax (48) 3234-4040; internet www.eletrosul.gov.br/home; Gerasul responsible for generating capacity; f. 1968; Pres. RONALDO DOS SANTOS CUSTÓDIO (acting).

Companhia de Geração Térmica de Energia Elétrica (CGTEE): Rua Sete de Setembro 539, 90010-190 Porto Alegre, RS; tel. (51) 3287-1500; fax (51) 3287-1566; internet www.cgtee.gov.br; f. 1997; became part of Eletrobrás in 2000; Dir-Pres. SERENO CHAISE.

Companhia Hidro Elétrica do São Francisco (Chesf): 333 Edif. André Falcão, Bloco A, Sala 313 Bongi, Rua Delmiro Golveia, 50761-901 Recife, PE; tel. (81) 229-2000; fax (81) 229-2390; e-mail chesf@chesf.com.br; internet www.chesf.gov.br; f. 1948; Exec. Dir DILTON DA CONTI OLIVEIRA.

Eletrobrás Termonuclear, SA (Eletronuclear): Rua da Candelária 65, Centro, 20091-906 Rio de Janeiro, RJ; tel. (21) 2588-7000; fax (21) 2588-7200; internet www.eletronuclear.gov.br; f. 1997 by fusion of the nuclear branch of Furnas with Nuclebrás Engenharia (NUCLEN); operates two nuclear facilities, Angra I and II; Angra III under construction and scheduled to come into operation in 2008; Pres. JOSÉ DRUMOND SARAIVA; Dir Pres. OTHON LUIZ PINHEIRO DA SILVA.

Furnas Centrais Elétricas, SA: Rua Real Grandeza 219, Bloco A, 16° andar, Botafogo, 22281-031 Rio de Janeiro, RJ; tel. (21) 2528-3970; fax (21) 2528-4480; e-mail presiden@furnas.com.br; internet www.furnas.gov.br; f. 1957; Pres. JOSÉ PEDRO RODRIQUES DE OLIVEIRA.

Manaus Energia, SA (ME): Manaus, AM; tel. (92) 3621-1110; internet www.manausenergia.com.br; f. 1895; became subsidiary of Eletronorte in 1997; electricity distributor; Pres. Dr WILLAMY MOREIRA FROTA.

Centrais Elétricas de Rondônia, SA (CERON): Rua José de Alencar 2613, Centro Porto Velho, RO; tel. (69) 216-4000; internet www.ceron.com.br; f. 1968; Dir-Pres. PAULO ROBERTO DOS SANTOS SILVEIRA.

Centrais Elétricas de Santa Catarina, SA (CELESC): Av. Itamarati 160, Bairro Itacorubi, 88034-900 Florianópolis, SC; tel. (48) 3231-5000; fax (48) 3231-6530; e-mail celesc@celesc.com.br; internet www.celesc.com.br; production and distribution of electricity throughout state of Santa Catarina; Dir and Pres. EDUARDO PINHO MOREIRA, Filho.

Companhia de Eletricidade do Acre (ELETROACRE): Rua Valério Magalhães 226, Bairro do Bosque, 69909-710 Rio Branco, AC; tel. (68) 3212-5700; fax (68) 3223-1142; internet www.eletroacre.com.br; f. 1965; Pres. EDILSON SOMÕES CADAXO SOBRINHO.

Companhia de Eletricidade do Estado da Bahia (COELBA): Av. Edgard Santos 300, Cabula IV, 41186-900 Salvador, BA; tel. (71) 370-5130; fax (71) 370-5132; internet www.coelba.com.br; f. 1960; Pres. MOISÉS AFONSO SALES, Filho.

Companhia de Eletricidade do Estado do Rio de Janeiro (CERJ): Rua Visconde do Rio Branco 429, Centro, 24020-003 Niterói, RJ; tel. (21) 2613-7120; fax (21) 2613-7196; e-mail cerj@cerj.com.br; internet www.cerj.com.br; f. 1907; privatized in 1996; Pres. ALEJANDRO DANÚS CHIRIGHIN.

Directory

Companhia Energética de Alagoas (CEAL): Av. Fernandes Lima 3496, Gruta de Lourdes, 57057-900 Maceió, AL; tel. (82) 3218-9300; internet www.ceal.com.br; f. 1961; Man. Dir JOAQUIM BRITO.

Companhia Energética do Amazonas (CEAM): Manaus, AM; internet www.ceam-am.com.br; f. 1964; owned by Eletrobrás; electricity generating and distribution co; Pres. Dr WILLAMY MOREIRA FROTA.

Companhia Energética de Brasília (CEB): SCRS, Quadro 503, Bloco B, Lotes 13/14, Brasília, DF; tel. 0800 610196; e-mail info@ceb.com.br; internet www.ceb.com.br; services in DF; also operates gas distribution co CEBGAS.

Companhia Energética do Ceará (COELCE): Av. Barão de Studart 2917, Dionísio Torres, 60120-002 Fortaleza, CE; tel. (85) 3247-1444; fax (85) 3216-4088; e-mail ouvidoria@coelce.com.br; internet www.coelce.com.br; f. 1971; Pres. and Dir CRISTIÁN EDUARDO FIERRO MONTES.

Companhia Energética do Maranhão (CEMAR): Av. Colares Moreira 477, Renascença II, São Luis, MA; internet www.cemar-ma.com.br; f. 1958 as Centrais Elétricas do Maranhão; changed name as above in 1984; owned by PPL Global, Inc, USA; Tech. Dir MARCELINO MACHADODA CUNHA NETO.

Companhia Energética de Minas Gerais (CEMIG): Av. Barbacena 1200, 30190-131 Belo Horizonte, MG; tel. (31) 3299-4900; fax (31) 3299-3700; e-mail atendimento@cemig.com.br; internet www.cemig.com.br; f. 1952; 51% state-owned, 33% owned by Southern Electric Brasil Partipações Ltda; Pres. DJALMA BASTOS DE MORAIS.

Companhia Energética de Pernambuco (CELPE): Av. João de Barros 111, Sala 301, 50050-902 Recife, PE; tel. (81) 3217-5168; e-mail celpe@celpe.com.br; internet www.celpe.com.br; state distributor of electricity; CEO JOÃO BOSCO DE ALMEIDA.

Companhia Energética do Piauí (CEPISA): Av. Maranhão 759, Sul, 64.001-010 Teresina, PI; tel. (86) 3221-8000; internet www.cepisa.com.br; f. 1962; 99% of shares bought by Eletrobrás in 1997; distributor of electricity in state of Piauí; Pres. GUILHERME FURST; Exec. Dir JOSÉ RICARDO PINHEIRO DE ABREU (acting).

Companhia Energética de São Paulo (CESP): Av. Nossa Senhora do Sabará 5312, Bairro Pedreira, 04447-011 São Paulo, SP; tel. (11) 5613-2100; fax (11) 3262-5545; e-mail inform@cesp.com.br; internet www.cesp.com.br; f. 1966; Pres. MAURO GUILHERME JARDIM ARCE.

Companhia Paranaense de Energia (COPEL): Rua Coronel Dulcídio 800, 80420-170 Curitiba, PR; tel. (41) 3331-4209; fax (41) 3331-4376; e-mail copel@copel.com; internet www.copel.com; f. 1954; state distributor of electricity and gas; Pres. JOÃO BONIFÁCIO CABRAL JÚNIOR; Exec. Dir RUBENS GHILARDI.

Companhia Paulista de Força e Luz (CPFL): Rodovia Campinas Mogi-Mirim Km 2.5, 10388-900 Campinas, SP; tel. (19) 3253-8704; fax (19) 3252-7644; internet www.cpfl.com.br; provides electricity through govt concessions; Pres. WILSON PINTO FERREIRA JÚNIOR.

Eletricidade de São Paulo, SA (ELETROPAULO): Av. Alfredo Egidio de Souza Aranha 100, 04791-900 São Paulo, SP; tel. (11) 5546-1467; fax (11) 3241-1387; e-mail administracao@eletropaulo.com.br; internet www.eletropaulo.com.br; f. 1899; acquired by AES in 2001; Pres. MARC ANDRÉ PERREIRA.

Espírito Santo Centrais Elétricas, SA (ESCELSA): Rua Sete de Setembro 362, Centro, CP 01-0452, 29015-000 Vitória, ES; tel. (27) 3321-9000; fax (27) 3322-0378; e-mail ri@energiasdobrasil.com.br; internet www.escelsa.com.br; f. 1968; CEO ANTÓNIO EDUARDO DA SILVA OLIVA.

Indústrias Nucleares do Brasil, SA (INB): Rua Mena Barreto 161, Botafogo, 22271-100 Rio de Janeiro, RJ; tel. (21) 2536-1600; fax (21) 2537-9391; e-mail inbrio@inb.gov.br; internet www.inb.gov.br; f. 1988; Pres. ALFREDO TRANJAN, Filho.

Itaipú Binacional: Av. Tancredo Neves 6731, 85866-900 Foz de Iguaçu, PR; tel. (45) 3520-5252; fax (45) 3520-3015; e-mail itaipu@itaipu.gov.br; internet www.itaipu.gov.br; f. 1974; jtly owned by Brazil and Paraguay; hydroelectric power-station on Brazilian-Paraguayan border; 1.3m. GWh of electricity produced in 2004; Dir-Gen. (Brazil) JORGE MIGUEL SAMEK.

LIGHT—Serviços de Eletricidade, SA: Av. Marechal Floriano 168, CP 0571, 20080-002 Rio de Janeiro, RJ; tel. (21) 2211-7171; fax (21) 2233-1249; e-mail light@lightrio.com.br; internet www.lightrio.com.br; f. 1905; electricity generation and distribution in Rio de Janeiro; fmrly state-owned, sold to a Brazilian-French-US consortium in 1996; controlled by EdF (France) from 2002; in 2006 79.4% holding sold to Brazilian group Rio Minas Energia Participaçoes, SA (RME) with EdF retaining 10% share; generating capacity of 850 MW; Pres. JOSÉ LUIZ ALQUÉRES.

Sistema Cataguazes-Leopoldina: Praça Rui Barbosa 80, 36770-000 Cataguases, MG; tel. (32) 3429-6000; fax (32) 3421-4240; internet www.cataguazes.com.br; f. 1905 as Companhia Força e Luz Cataguazes-Leopoldina, adopted current name in 2007; subsidiary of Energisa, SA; concerned with generation and distribution of electrical energy.

Gas

Companhia Distribuidora de Gás do Rio de Janeiro (CEG): Av. Pedro II 68, São Cristóvão, 20941-070 Rio de Janeiro, RJ; tel. (21) 2585-7575; fax (21) 2585-7070; internet www.ceg.com.br; f. 1969; gas distribution in the Rio de Janeiro region; privatized in July 1997.

Companhia de Gás de Alagoas, SA (ALGÁS): Rua Comendador Palmeria 129, Farol, 57051-150 Maceió, AL; tel. (82) 216-3600; fax (82) 216-3628; e-mail algas@algas.com.br; internet www.algas.com.br; 51% state-owned; Dir and Pres. Dr GERSON DA FONSECA.

Companhia de Gás de Bahia (BAHIAGÁS): Av. Tancredo Neves 450, Sala 1801, Edif. Suarez Trade, 41820-020 Salvador, BA; tel. (71) 340-9000; fax (71) 341-9001; e-mail bahiagas@bahiagas.com.br; internet www.bahiagas.com.br; f. 1991; 51% state-owned; Pres. Dr LUIZ FERNANDO MUELLER KOSER.

Companhia de Gás do Ceará (CEGÁS): Av. Santos Dumont 7700, 5°–6° andares, 20941-070 Fortaleza, CE; tel. (85) 3265-1144; fax (85) 3265-2026; e-mail cegas@secrel.com.br; internet www.cegas.com.br; 51% owned by the state of Amazonas; Pres. Dr JOSÉ REGO, Filho.

Companhia de Gás de Minas Gerais (GASMIG): Av. Álvares Cabral 1740, 7° andar, 30170-001 Belo Horizonte, MG; tel. (31) 3291-2001; e-mail gasmig@gasmig.com.br; internet www.gasmig.com.br; Pres. DJALMA BASTOS DE MORAIS.

Companhia de Gás de Pernambuco (COPERGÁS): Av. Eng. Domingo Ferreira 4060, 15° andar, 51021-040 Recife, PE; tel. (81) 3463-2000; e-mail copergas@copergas.com.br; internet www.copergas.com.br; 51% state-owned; Pres. Dr ALDO GUEDES.

Companhia de Gás do Rio Grande do Sul (SULGÁS): Rua 7 de Setembro 1069, Edif. Santa Cruz, 5° andar, 90010-190 Porto Alegre, RS; tel. and fax (51) 3220-2200; fax (51) 3220-2201; internet www.sulgas.rs.gov.br; f. 1993; 51% state-owned; 49% owned by Petrobras; Pres. EDVILSON BRUM.

Companhia de Gás de Santa Catarina (SCGÁS): Rua Antônia Luz 255, Centro Empresarial Hoepcke, 88010-410 Florianópolis, SC; tel. (48) 3229-1200; fax (48) 3229-1230; internet www.scgas.com.br; f. 1994; 51% state-owned; Pres. IVAN CÉSAR RANZOLIN.

Companhia de Gás de São Paulo (COMGÁS): Rua Olimpíadas 205, 10° andar, Vila Olímpia, 04551-000 São Paulo, SP; tel. (11) 4504-5000; e-mail comgas@comgas.com.br; internet www.comgas.com.br; f. 1978; distribution in São Paulo of gas; sold in April 1999 to consortium including British Gas PLC and Royal Dutch/Shell Group; Pres. LUIS DOMENECH.

Companhia Paraibana de Gás (PBGÁS): Av. Epitácio Pessoa 4840, Sala 210, 1° andar, Tambaú, 58030-001 João Pessoa, PB; tel. (83) 3247-2244; e-mail cicero@pbgas.com.br; internet www.pbgas.pb.gov.br; f. 1995; 51% state-owned; Pres. and Dir MANOEL DE DEUS ALVES.

Companhia Paranaense de Gás (COMPAGÁS): Rua Pasteur 463, Edif. Jatobá, 7° andar, Batel, 80250-080 Curitiba, PR; tel. (41) 3312-1900; fax (41) 3222-6633; e-mail compagas@mail.copel.br; internet www.compagas.com.br; f. 1998; 51.0% owned by Copel Participaçoes, SA, 24.5% by Gaspetro and 24.5% by Mitsui Gás e Energia do Brasil; Pres. Dr ANTÔNIO FERNANDO KREMPEL.

Companhia Potiguar de Gás (POTIGÁS): Av. Brancas Dunas 485, Lojas 1 e 2, Salas de 101 a 106, Candelária, 59064-720 Natal, RN; tel. (84) 3206-8500; e-mail ismael@potigas.com.br; internet www.potigas.com.br; 17% state-owned; Pres. NELSON HERMÓGENES DE MEDEIROS FREIRE.

Companhia Rondoniense de Gás, SA (RONGÁS): Av. Carlos Gomes 1223, Sala 403, Centro, 78903-000 Porto Velho, RO; tel. and fax (69) 229-0333; e-mail rongas@enter-net.com.br; internet www.rongas.com.br; f. 1998; 17% state-owned; Pres. GERSON ACURSI.

Empresa Sergipana de Gás, SA (EMSERGÁS): Rua Dom Bosco 1223 B, Suíça, 49050-220 Aracaju, SE; tel. (79) 3226-5213; e-mail emsergas@infonet.com.br; internet www.emsergas.com.br; Pres. Dr LUIZ MACHADO MENDONÇA.

Water

Águas e Esgotos do Piauí (AGESPISA): Av. Mal Castelo Branco 101, Cabral, 64000 Teresina, PI; tel. (86) 2239-300; internet www.agespisa.com.br; f. 1962; state-owned; water and waste management; Pres. MERLONG SOLANO.

Companhia de Agua e Esgosto de Ceará (CAGECE): Rua Lauro Vieira Chaves 1030, Fortaleza, CE; tel. (85) 3101-1735; fax (85) 3101-1742; internet www.cagece.com.br; state-owned; water and sewerage services; Gen. Man. JOSÉ DE RIBAMAR DA SILVA.

Companhia Algoas Industrial (CINAL): Rodovia Divaldo Suruagy, Km 12, 57160-000 Marechal Deodoro, AL; tel. (82) 3269-1100; fax (82) 3269-1199; internet www.cinal.com.br; f. 1982; management of steam and treated water; Dir Pres. FRANCISCO CARLOS RUGA.

Companhia Espírito Santense de Saneamento (CESAN): Av. Governador Bley, 186, Edif. BEMGE, 29010-150 Vitória ES; tel. (27) 3132-8200; fax (27) 3132-8271; e-mail comunica@cesan.com.br; internet www.cesan.com.br; f. 1968; state-owned; construction, maintenance and operation of water supply and sewerage systems; Pres. PAULO RUY VALIM CARNELLI.

Companhia Estadual de Aguas e Esgotos (CEDAE): Rua Sacadura Cabral 103, 9° andar, 20081-260 Rio de Janeiro, RJ; tel. (21) 2296-0025; fax (21) 2296-0416; internet www.cedae.rj.gov.br; f. 1975; state-owned; water supply and sewerage treatment; Pres. ALBERTO JOSÉ MENDES GOMES.

Companhia Pernambucana de Saneamento (COMPESA): Av. Cruz Cabugá 1387, Bairro Santo Amaro, 50040-905 Recife, PE; tel. (81) 421-1711; fax (81) 421-2712; state-owned; management and operation of regional water supply in the state of Pernambuco; Pres. GUSTAVO DE MATTO PONTUAL SAMPAIO.

Companhia Riograndense de Saneamento (CORSAN): Rua Caldas Júnior 120, 18° andar, 90010-260 Porto Alegre, RS; tel. (51) 3215-5691; e-mail ascom@corsan.com.br; internet www.corsan.com.br; f. 1965; state-owned; management and operation of regional water supply and sanitation programmes; Dir MÁRIO RACHE FREITAS.

Companhia de Saneamento Básico do Estado de São Paulo (SABESP): Rua Costa Carvalho 300, 05429-900 São Paulo, SP; tel. (11) 3388-8000; internet www.sabesp.com.br; f. 1973; state-owned; supplies basic sanitation services for the state of São Paulo, including water treatment and supply; Pres. GESNER JOSÉ DE OLIVEIRA, Filho.

TRADE UNIONS

Central Unica dos Trabalhadores (CUT): Rua Caetano Pinto 575, Brás, 03041-000 São Paulo, SP; tel. (11) 2108-9200; fax (11) 2108-9310; e-mail duvaier@cut.org.br; internet www.cut.org.br; f. 1983; central union confederation; left-wing; Pres. ARTHUR ENRIQUE DA SILVA SANTOS; Gen. Sec. SEVERE QUINTINO MARQUES.

Confederação Geral dos Trabalhadores (CGT): Rua Tomaz Gonzaga 50, 2° andar, Liberdade, 01506-020 São Paulo, SP; tel. (11) 3209-6577; e-mail cgt@cgt.org.br; internet www.cgt.org.br; f. 1986; fmrly Coordenação Nacional das Classes Trabalhadoras; represents 1,012 labour organizations linked to PMDB, containing 6.3m. workers; Pres. ANTÔNIO CARLOS DOS REIS MEDEIROS; Sec.-Gen. FRANCISCO CANÍNDE PEGADO DO NASCIMENTO.

Confederação Nacional dos Metalúrgicos (Metal Workers): Alameda dos Tupinás 248, Planalto Paulista, 04069-000 São Paulo, SP; tel. (11) 5584-8440; e-mail imprensa@cnmcut.org.br; internet www.cnmcut.org.br; f. 1985; Pres. CARLOS ALBERTO GRANA; Gen. Sec. VALTER SANCHES.

Confederação Nacional das Profissões Liberais (CNPL) (Liberal Professions): SAU/SUL, Quadra 06, Bloco K, Edif. Belvedere, 70070-915 Brasília, DF; tel. (61) 2103-1683; e-mail cnpldf@cnpl.org.br; internet www.cnpl.org.br; f. 1953; Pres. FRANSCISCO ANTONIO FEIJÓ; Sec.-Gen. LUIZ SERGIO DA ROSA LOPES.

Confederação Nacional dos Trabalhadores na Indústria (CNTI) (Industrial Workers): SEP/NORTE, Quadra 505, Conj. A, 70730-540 Brasília, DF; tel. (61) 3274-4150; fax (61) 3274-7001; e-mail cnti@cnti.org.br; internet www.cnti.org.br; f. 1946; Pres. JOSÉ CALIXTO RAMOS; Sec.-Gen. JOSÉ SEBASTIÃO DOS SANTOS.

Confederação Nacional dos Trabalhadores no Comércio (CNTC) (Commercial Workers): Av. W/5 Sul, SGAS Quadra 902, Bloco C, 70390-020 Brasília, DF; tel. (61) 3217-7100; fax (61) 3217-7122; e-mail secretaria@cntc.org.br; internet www.cntc.org.br; f. 1946; Pres. ANTÔNIO ALVES DE ALMEIDA.

Confederação Nacional dos Trabalhadores em Transportes Marítimos, Fluviais e Aéreos (CONTTMAF) (Maritime, River and Air Transport Workers): SDS, Edif. Venâncio V, Grupos 501503, 70393-900 Brasília, DF; tel. (61) 3225-0789; fax (61) 3322-6383; e-mail conttmaf@conttmaf.org.br; internet www.conttmaf.org.br; f. 1957; Pres. SEVERINO ALMEIDA, Filho.

Confederação Nacional dos Trabalhadores em Comunicações e Publicidade (CONTCOP) (Communications and Advertising Workers): SCS, Quadra 02, Edif. Serra Dourada, 7° andar, 70300-902 Brasília, DF; tel. (61) 3224-7926; fax (61) 3224-5686; e-mail contcop@contcop.org; internet contcop.org; f. 1964; 350,000 mems; Pres. ANTÔNIO MARIA THAUMATURGO CORTIZO.

Confederação Nacional dos Trabalhadores nas Empresas de Crédito (CONTEC) (Workers in Credit Institutions): SEP-SUL, Av. W/4, EQ 707/907 Conj. A/B, 70390-078 Brasília, DF; tel. (61) 3244-5833; fax (61) 3224-2743; e-mail contec@yawl.com.br; internet www.contec.org.br; f. 1958; Pres. LOURENÇO FERREIRA DO PRADO.

Confederação Nacional dos Trabalhadores em Estabelecimentos de Educação e Cultura (CNTEEC) (Workers in Education and Culture): SAS, Quadra 4, Bloco B, 70070-908 Brasília, DF; tel. (61) 3321-4140; fax (61) 3321-2704; internet www.cnteec.org.br; f. 1966; Pres. MIGUEL ABRÃO NETO.

BRAZIL	*Directory*

Confederação Nacional dos Trabalhadores na Agricultura (CONTAG) (Agricultural Workers): SMPW, Quadra 01, Conj. 02, Lote 02, Núcleo Bandeirante, 71735-102 Brasília, DF; tel. (61) 2102-2288; fax (61) 2102-2299; e-mail contag@contag.org.br; internet www.contag.org.br; f. 1964; represents 25 state federations and 3,630 syndicates, 15m. mems; Pres. Manoel José dos Santos; Sec.-Gen. David Wylkerson Rodrigues de Souza.

Força Sindical (FS): Rua Galvão Bueno 782, Liberdade, São Paulo, SP; tel. (11) 3277-5877; e-mail secgeral@fsindical.org.br; internet www.fsindical.org.br; f. 1991; 8.3m. mems (1999); Pres. Paulo Pereira da Silva.

Transport

Agência Nacional de Transportes Terrestres (ANTT): SBN, Quadra 2, Bloco C, 70040-020 Brasília, DF; tel. (61) 3410-1990; e-mail ouvidoria@antt.gov.br; internet www.antt.gov.br; f. 2002; govt agency; oversees road and rail infrastructure; Dir-Gen. José Alexandre Nogueira Resende.

RAILWAYS

In 2003 there were 29,605 km of railway lines. There are also railways owned by state governments and several privately owned railways. In 2001 railways accounted for 20.7% of all freight traffic, and in 2002 for 1.0% of passenger transport.

América Latina Logística do Brasil, SA (ALL): Rua Emilio Bertolini 100, Cajuru, Curitiba, PR; tel. (41) 2141-7555; e-mail caall@all-logistica.com; internet www.all-logistica.com; f. 1997; 6,586 km in 2003; Pres. Bernardo Hees.

Associação Nacional dos Transportadores Ferroviários (ANTF): Setor de Autarquias Sul, Quadra 05, Edif. OAB, Sala 509, 70070-050 Brasília, DF; tel. (61) 3226-5434; fax (61) 3221-0135; internet www.antf.org.br; promotes railway devt; 11 mem. cos; Pres. Julio Fontana Neto; Exec. Dir. Rodrigo Vilaça.

Companhia Brasileira de Trens Urbanos (CBTU): Estrada Velha da Tijuca 77, Usina, 20531-080 Rio de Janeiro, RJ; tel. (21) 2575-3399; fax (21) 2571-6149; internet www.cbtu.gov.br; f. 1984; fmrly responsible for surburban networks and metro systems throughout Brazil; 252 km in 1998; the transfer of each city network to its respective local government was under way; Pres. Luiz Otávio Mota Valadares.

Gerência de Trens Urbanos de João Pessoa (GTU/JP): Praça Napoleão Laureano 1, 58010-040 João Pessoa, PB; tel. (83) 3241-4240; fax (83) 3241-6388; 30 km.

Gerência de Trens Urbanos de Maceió (GTU/MAC): Rua Barão de Anadiva 121, 57020-630 Maceió, AL; tel. (82) 221-1839; fax (82) 223-4024; 32 km.

Gerência de Trens Urbanos de Natal: Praça Augusto Severo 302, 59012-380 Natal, RN; tel. (84) 221-3355; fax (84) 221-0181; 56 km.

Superintendência de Trens Urbanos de Belo Horizonte (STU/BH-Demetrô): Av. Afonso Pena 1500, 11° andar, 30130-005 Belo Horizonte, MG; tel. (31) 3250-4021; fax (31) 3250-4053; e-mail metrobh@gold.horizontes.com.br; f. 1986; 21.3 km open in 2002; Gen. Man. M. L. L. Siqueira.

Superintêndencia de Trens Urbanos de Recife (STU/REC): Rua José Natário 478, Areias, 50900-000 Recife, PE; tel. (81) 3455-4655; fax (81) 3455-4422; f. 1985; 53 km open in 2002; Supt Fernando Antônio C. Dueire.

Superintendência de Trens Urbanos de Salvador (STU/SAL): Praça Onze de Decembro s/n, Bairro Calçada, 40410-360 Salvador, BA; tel. (71) 313-9512; fax (71) 313-8760; 14 km.

Companhia Cearense de Transportes Metropolitanos, SA (Metrofor): Rua 24 de Maio 60, 60020-001 Fortaleza, CE; tel. (85) 3101-7100; fax (85) 3101-4744; e-mail metrofor@metrofor.ce.gov.br; internet www.metrofor.ce.gov.br; f. 1997; 46 km; Dir Rômulo dos Santos Fortes.

Companhia Ferroviária do Nordeste: Av. Francisco de Sá 4829, Bairro Carlito Pamplona, 60310-002 Fortaleza, CE; tel. (85) 4008-2525; e-mail kerley@cfn.com.br; internet www.cfn.com.br; 4,534 km in 2003; Dir Martiniano Dias.

Companhia do Metropolitano de São Paulo: Rua Augusta 1626, 01304-902 São Paulo, SP; tel. (11) 3371-7411; fax (11) 3283-5228; internet www.metro.sp.gov.br; f. 1974; 4-line metro system, 61.3 km open in 2007; Pres. José Jorge Fagali.

Companhia Paulista de Trens Metropolitanos (CPTM): Av. Paulista 402, 5° andar, 01310-000 São Paulo, SP; tel. (11) 3371-1530; fax (11) 3285-0323; e-mail ctpm@ctpm.sp.gov.br; internet www.ctpm.sp.gov.br; f. 1992 to incorporate suburban lines fmrly operated by the CBTU and FEPASA; 286 km; Dir and Pres. Mário Manuel Seabra Rodrigues Bandeira.

Empresa de Trens Urbanos de Porto Alegre, SA: Av. Ernesto Neugebauer 1985, 90250-140 Porto Alegre, RS; tel. (51) 2129-8000; e-mail secos@trensurb.com.br; internet www.trensurb.gov.br; f. 1985; 33.8 km open in 2004; Pres. Marco Arildo Prates da Cunha.

Estrada de Ferro do Amapá (EFA): Av. Santana 429, Porto de Santana, 68925-000 Santana, AP; tel. (96) 231-1719; fax (96) 281-1175; f. 1957; operated by Indústria e Comércio de Minérios, SA; 194 km open in 2003; Dir Supt José Luiz Ortiz Vergulino.

Estrada de Ferro Campos do Jordão: Rua Martin Cabral 87, CP 11, 12400-000 Pindamonhangaba, SP; tel. (12) 3644-7408; fax (12) 3643-2951; internet www.efcj.com.br; f. 1924; operated by the Tourism Secretariat of the State of São Paulo; Dir Arthur Ferreira dos Santos.

Estrada de Ferro Carajás: Av. dos Portugueses s/n, 65085-580 São Luís, MA; tel. (98) 3218-4000; fax (98) 3218-4530; f. 1985 for movement of minerals from the Serra do Carajás to the port at Ponta da Madeira; operated by the Companhia Vale do Rio Doce; 892 km open in 2002; Supt Juares Salibra.

Estrada de Ferro do Jari: Vila Mongouba s/n, Monte Dourado, 68230-000 Pará, PA; tel. (91) 3736-6526; fax (91) 3736-6490; transportation of timber and bauxite; 68 km open; Dir Armindo Luiz Baretta.

Estrada de Ferro Mineração Rio do Norte, SA: Praia do Flamengo 200, 5° e 6° andares, 22210-030 Rio de Janeiro, RJ; tel. (21) 2205-9112; fax (21) 2545-5717; 35 km open in 2003; Pres. Antônio João Torres.

Estrada de Ferro Paraná-Oeste, SA (FERROESTE): Av. Iguaçú 420, 7° andar, 80230-902 Curitiba, PR; tel. (41) 3321-3151; fax (41) 3233-2147; e-mail ferroest@pr.gov.br; internet www.pr.gov.br/ferroeste; f. 1988; serves the grain-producing regions in Paraná and Mato Grosso do Sul; privatized in 1996; 248 km in 2005; Pres. Martin Roeder.

Estrada de Ferro Vitória-Minas: Av. Carandaí 1115, 13° andar, Funcionários, 30130-915 Belo Horizonte, MG; tel. (31) 3279-4545; fax (31) 3279-4676; f. 1942; operated by Companhia Vale de Rio Doce; transport of iron ore, general cargo and passengers; 905 km open in 2003; Dir José Francisco Martins Viveiros.

Ferrovia Bandeirante, SA (Ferroban): Rua Dr Sales de Oliveira 1380, Vila Industrial, 13035-270 Campinas, SP; tel. (19) 3735-3100; fax (19) 3735-3196; e-mail ferroban@ferroban.com.br; internet www.ferroban.com.br; f. 1971 by merger of five railways operated by São Paulo State; transferred to private ownership in Nov. 1998; fmrly Ferrovia Paulista; 4,236 km open in 2003; Dir João Gouveia Ferrão Neto.

Ferrovia Centro Atlântica, SA: Rua Sapucaí 383, Floresta 30150-904, Belo Horizonte, MG; tel. (31) 3279-5520; fax (31) 3279-5709; e-mail thiers@centro-atlantica.com.br; internet www.fcasa.com.br; f. 1996; following the privatization of Rede Ferroviária Federal, SA; owned by Companhia Vale do Rio Doce (CVRD) since 2003; industrial freight; 8,000 km.

Ferrovia Norte-Sul: Av. Marechal Floriano 45, Centro, 20080-003 Rio de Janeiro, RJ; tel. (21) 2253-9659; fax (21) 2263-9119; e-mail valecascom@ferrovianortesul.com.br; internet www.ferrovianortesul.com.br; 2,066 km from Belém to Goiânia; Dir José Francisco das Neves.

Ferrovia Novoeste, SA: Rua do Rócio 351, 3° andar, 04552-905 São Paulo, SP; tel. (11) 3845-4966; fax (11) 3841-9252; e-mail silviam@uol.com.br; 1,622 km in 2003; Man. Dir Nélson de Sampaio Bastos.

Ferrovia Tereza Cristina, SA (FTC): Rua dos Ferroviários 100, Bairro Oficinas, 88702-230 Tubarão, SC; tel. (48) 3621-7700; fax (48) 3621-7747; e-mail ftc@ftc.com.br; internet www.ftc.com.br; 164 km in 2007; Man. Dir Benony Schmitz, Filho.

Ferrovias Norte do Brasil, SA (FERRONORTE): Rua do Rócio 351, 3° andar, Vila Olímpia, 04552-905 São Paulo, SP; tel. (11) 3845-4966; fax (11) 3841-9252; e-mail jhomero@novoeste.com.br; internet www.ferronorte.com.br; f. 1988; 403 km in 2003; affiliated with Ferrovia Novoeste and Ferroban; Man. Dir Nelson de Sampaio Bastos.

Metrô Rio: Av. Presidente Vargas 2000, Col. Centro, 20210-031 Rio de Janeiro, RJ; tel. (21) 3211-6300; e-mail sac@metrorio.com.br; internet www.metrorio.com.br; 2-line metro system, 42 km open in 1997; operated by Opportans Concessão Metroviária, SA; Pres. Alvaro J. M. Santos.

MRS Logística, SA: Praia de Botafogo 228, Sala 1201E, Ala B, Botafogo, 22359-900, Rio de Janeiro, RJ; tel. (21) 2559-4610; internet www.mrs.com.br; f. 1996; 1,974 km in 2003; CEO Julio Fontana Neto.

Transporte Urbano do Distrito Federal (DFTRANS): SES, Quadra 4, Lote 6, Brasília, DF; tel. (61) 3324-0376; internet www.dmtu.df.gov.br; the first section of the Brasília metro, linking the capital with the western suburb of Samambaia, was inaugurated in 1994; Dir Leonardo de Faria e Silva.

ROADS

In 2003 there were 1,751,862 km of roads in Brazil, of which 196,094 km were paved. Brasília has been a focal point for inter-regional development, and paved roads link the capital with every region of Brazil. The building of completely new roads has taken place predominantly in the north. Roads are the principal mode of transport, accounting for 61.1% of freight traffic in 2001, and 95% of passenger traffic, including long-distance bus services, in 2002. Major projects include the 5,000-km Transamazonian Highway, running from Recife and Cabedelo to the Peruvian border, the 4,138-km Cuiabá–Santarém highway, which will run in a north–south direction, and the 3,555-km Trans-Brasiliana project, which will link Marabá, on the Trans-Amazonian highway, with Aceguá, on the Uruguayan frontier. A 20-year plan to construct a highway linking São Paulo with the Argentine and Chilean capitals was endorsed in 1992 within the context of the development of the Southern Cone Common Market (Mercosul). In 2004 an agreement was reached to construct a highway linking the Brazilian state of Acre with the coast of Peru.

Departamento Nacional de Infra-Estrutura de Transportes (DNIT) (National Roads Development): SAN, Quadra 3, Lote A, Edif. Núcleo dos Transportes, 70040-902 Brasília, DF; tel. (61) 3315-4000; fax (61) 3315-4050; e-mail diretoria.geral@dner.gov.br; internet www.dner.gov.br; f. 1945 to plan and execute federal road policy and to supervise state and municipal roads in order to integrate them into the national network; Exec. Dir ROGÉRIO GONZALES ALVES.

INLAND WATERWAYS

River transport plays only a minor part in the movement of goods. There are three major river systems, the Amazon, Paraná and the São Francisco. The Amazon is navigable for 3,680 km, as far as Iquitos in Peru, and ocean-going ships can reach Manaus, 1,600 km upstream. Plans have been drawn up to improve the inland waterway system and one plan is to link the Amazon and Upper Paraná to provide a navigable waterway across the centre of the country.

Agência Nacional de Transportes Aquaviários (ANTAQ): SEPN, Quadra 514, Conj. 3, Edif. ANTAQ, 70760-545 Brasília, DF; tel. (61) 3447-1035; fax (61) 3447-1040; e-mail asc@antaq.gov.br; internet www.antaq.gov.br; Dir-Gen. FERNANDO ANTÔNIO BRITO FIALHO.

Administração da Hidrovia do Nordeste (AHINOR): Rua da Paz 561, 65020-450 São Luiz, MA; tel. and fax (98) 231-5122; e-mail ahinor@elo.com.br; Pres. JOSÉ OSCAR FRAZÃO FROTA.

Administração da Hidrovia do Paraguai (AHIPAR): Rua Treze de Junho 960, Corumbá, MS; tel. (67) 231-2841; fax (67) 231-2661; internet www.ahiper.gov.br; Supt PAULO CÉSAR C. GOMES DA SILVA.

Administração da Hidrovia do Paraná (AHRANA): Av. Brig. Faria Lima 1884, 6° andar, 01451-000 São Paulo, SP; tel. (11) 2106-1600; fax (11) 3815-5435; e-mail ahrana@ahrana.gov.br; internet www.ahrana.gov.br; Supt LUIZ EDUARDO GARCIA.

Administração da Hidrovia do São Francisco (AHSFRA): Praça do Porto 70, Distrito Industrial, 39270-000 Pirapora, MG; tel. (38) 3741-2555; fax (38) 3741-2510; e-mail superint@ahsfra.gov.br; internet www.ahsfra.gov.br; Supt SEBASTIÃO MARQUES DE OLIVEIRA.

Administração das Hidrovias da Amazônia Oriental (AHIMOR): Rua Joaquim Nabuco 8, Nazaré, 66055-300 Belém, PA; tel. (91) 3039-7700; fax (91) 3039-7721; e-mail ahimor@ahimor.gov.br; internet www.ahimor.gov.br; Supt MICHEL DIB TACHY.

Administração das Hidrovias do Sul (AHSUL): Praça Oswaldo Cruz 15, 3° andar, 90030-160 Porto Alegre, RS; tel. (51) 3228-3677; fax (51) 3226-9068; Supt JOSÉ LUIZ F. DE AZAMBUJA.

Administração das Hidrovias do Tocantins e Araguaia (AHITAR): Av. 85 971, Setor Sul, 74080-010 Goiânia, GO; tel. (62) 3225-1744; fax (62) 3229-2181; e-mail ahitar@terra.com.br; internet www.ahitar.com.br; Supt JOSENIR GONÇALVES NASCIMENTO.

Empresa de Navegação da Amazônia, SA (ENASA): Rodovia Arthur Bernardes 1000, Val-de-Cães, 66115-000 Belém, PA; tel. (91) 3257-6868; fax (91) 3257-4308; f. 1967; cargo and passenger services on the Amazon river and its principal tributaries, connecting the port of Belém with all major river ports; Pres. LORIWAL DE MAGALHÃES; 48 vessels.

SHIPPING

There are more than 40 deep-water ports in Brazil, all but one of which (Imbituba) are directly or indirectly administered by the Government. The majority of ports are operated by state-owned concerns (Cia Docas do Pará, Estado de Ceará, Estado do Rio Grande do Norte, Bahia, Paraíba, Espírito Santo, Rio de Janeiro and Estado de São Paulo), while a smaller number (including Suape, Cabedelo, São Sebastião, Paranaguá, Antonina, São Francisco do Sul, Porto Alegre, Itajaí, Pelotas and Rio Grande) are administered by state governments.

The ports of Santos, Rio de Janeiro and Rio Grande have specialized container terminals handling more than 1,200,000 TEUs (20-ft equivalent units of containerized cargo) per year. Santos is the major container port in Brazil, accounting for 800,000 TEUs annually. The ports of Paranaguá, Itajaí, São Francisco do Sul, Salvador, Vitória and Imbituba cater for containerized cargo to a lesser extent.

Total cargo handled by Brazilian ports in 2002 amounted to 529m. tons.

Brazil's merchant fleet comprised 525 vessels, with a combined aggregate displacement of 2.3m. grt, in December 2006.

Departamento de Marinha Mercante: Coordenação Geral de Transporte Maritimo, Av. Rio Branco 103, 6° e 8° andar, 20040-004 Rio de Janeiro, RJ; tel. (21) 2221-4014; fax (21) 2221-5929; Dir PAULO OCTÁVIO DE PAIVA ALMEIDA.

Port Authorities

Administração do Porto de Manaus (SNPH): Rua Marquês de Santa Cruz 25, Centro, 69005-050 Manaus, AM; tel. (92) 3621-4300; fax (92) 3621-4300; internet faleconosco@portodemanaus.com.br; internet www.portodemanaus.com.br; private; operates the port of Manaus.

Administração do Porto de São Francisco do Sul (APSFS): Av. Eng. Leite Ribeiro 782, CP 71, 89240-000 São Francisco do Sul, SC; tel. (47) 3471-1200; fax (47) 3471-1211; e-mail porto@apsfs.sc.gov.br; internet www.apsfs.sc.gov.br; Dir-Gen. ARNALDO S. THIAGO.

Administração dos Portos de Paranaguá e Antonina (APPA): Rua Antonio Pereira 161, 83221-030 Paranaguá, PR; tel. (41) 3420-1100; fax (41) 3423-4252; internet www.pr.gov.br/portos; Port Admin. OSIRIS STENGHEL GUIMARÃES.

Companhia Docas do Espírito Santo (CODESA): Av. Getúlio Vargas 556, Centro, 29020-030 Vitória, ES; tel. (27) 3132-7360; fax (27) 3132-7311; e-mail assecs@codesa.com.br; internet www.codesa.com.br; f. 1983; Dir HENRIQUE GERMANO ZIMMER.

Companhia das Docas do Estado de Bahia: Av. da França 1551, 40010-000 Salvador, BA; tel. (71) 3320-1100; fax (71) 3320-1375; e-mail codeba@codega.com.br; internet www.codeba.com.br; administers the ports of Salvador, Aratu and Ilhéus; Dir NEWTON FERREIRA DIAS.

Companhia Docas do Estado de Ceará (CDC): Praça Amigos da Marinha s/n, Mucuripe, 60182-640 Fortaleza, CE; tel. (85) 3266-8800; fax (85) 3266-88943-2433; internet www.docasdoceara.com.br; administers the port of Fortaleza.

Companhia Docas do Estado de São Paulo (CODESP): Av. Conselheiro Rodrigues Alves s/n, Macuco, 11015-900 Santos, SP; tel. (13) 3234-7000; fax (13) 3222-3068; e-mail codesp@carrier.com.br; internet www.portodesantos.com; administers the ports of Santos, Charqueadas, Estrela, Cáceres, Corumbá/Ladário, and the waterways of Paraná (AHRANA), Paraguai (AHIPAR) and the South (AHSUL); Pres. JOSÉ CARLOS MELLO REGO.

Companhia Docas de Imbituba (CDI): Porto de Imbituba, Av. Presidente Vargas 100, 88780-000 Imbituba, SC; tel. (48) 3255-0080; fax (48) 3255-0701; e-mail docas@cdiport.com.br; internet www.cdiport.com.br; private-sector concession to administer the port of Imbituba; Pres. NILTON GARCIA DE ARAUJO.

Companhia Docas do Pará (CDP): Av. Presidente Vargas 41, 2° andar, 66010-000 Belém, PA; tel. (91) 3182-9000; fax (91) 3216-2048; e-mail webmaster@cdp.com.br; internet www.cdp.com.br; f. 1967; administers the ports of Belém, Miramar, Santarém Obidos, Altamira, São Francisco, Marabá and Vila do Conde; Dir-Pres. ELDER JOSÉ PINHEIRO CHAVES.

Companhia Docas da Paraíba (DOCAS-PB): Porto de Cabedelo, Rua Presidente João Pessoa s/n, 58310-000 Cabedelo, PB; tel. (83) 3228-2805; fax (83) 3228-2619; e-mail porto-pb@zaitek.com.br; administers the port of Cabedelo.

Companhia Docas do Rio de Janeiro (CDRJ): Rua do Acre 21, 20081-000 Rio de Janeiro, RJ; tel. (21) 2219-8617; fax (21) 2253-0528; e-mail cdrj@portosrio.gov.br; internet www.portosrio.gov.br; administers the ports of Rio de Janeiro, Niterói, Itaguaí and Angra dos Reis; Pres. ANTÔNIO CARLOS SOARES LIMA.

Companhia Docas do Rio Grande do Norte (CODERN): Av. Hildebrando de Góis 220, Ribeira, 59010-700 Natal, RN; tel. (84) 4005-5311; e-mail administrativo@codern.com.br; internet www.codern.com.br; administers the ports of Areia Branca, Natal and Maceió; Dir RENATO FERNANDES DA SILVA.

Empresa Maranhense de Administração Portuária (EMAP): Porto do Itaquí s/n, 65085-370 São Luís, MA; tel. (98) 216-6000; fax (98) 216-6060; internet www.portodoitaqui.com.br; f. 2001 to administer ports of Itaquí as concession from the state of Maranhão; Pres. FERNANDO ANTONIO BRITO, Filho.

Sociedade de Portos e Hidrovias do Estado de Rondônia (SOPH): Terminal dos Milagres 400, Balsa, 78900-750 Porto Velho, RO; tel. (69) 229-2134; fax (69) 229-3943; operates the port of Porto Velho; Dir OBEDES OLIVEIRA DE QUEIROZ.

SUAPE—Complexo Industrial Portuário Governador Eraldo Gueiros: Rodovia PE-060, Km 10, Engenho Massangana, 55590-972 Município de Ipojuca, PE; tel. (81) 3527-5000; fax (81) 3527-5064; e-mail presidenciasuape.pe.gov.br; administers the port of Suape.

Superintendência do Porto de Itajaí: Rua Blumenau 5, Centro, 88305-101 Itajaí, SC; tel. (47) 3341-8023; fax (47) 3341-8075; e-mail atendimento@portoitajai.com.br; internet www.portoitajai.com.br; Supt WILSON FRANCISCO REBELO.

Superintendência do Porto de Rio Grande (SUPRG): Av. Honório Bicalho s/n, CP 198, 96201-020 Rio Grande do Sul, RS; tel. (53) 3231-1366; fax (53) 3231-1857; internet www.portoriogrande.com.br; f. 1996.

Superintendência do Porto de Tubarão: Porto de Tubarão, 29072-970 Vitória, ES; tel. (27) 3228-1053; fax (27) 3228-1682; operated by the Companhia Vale do Rio Doce mining co; Port Dir CANDIDO COTTA PACHECO.

Superintendência de Portos e Hidrovias do Estado do Rio Grande do Sul (SPH): Av. Mauá 1050, 4° andar, 90010-110 Porto Alegre, RS; tel. (51) 3288-9200; fax (51) 3288-9220; e-mail executiva@sph.rs.gov.br; internet www.sph.rs.gov.br; administers the ports of Porto Alegre, Pelotas and Cachoeira do Sul, the São Gonçalo canal and other waterways; Dir-Supt ROBERTO FALCÃO LAURINO.

State-owned Company

Companhia de Navegação do Estado de Rio de Janeiro: Praça 15 de Novembro 21, 20010-010 Rio de Janeiro, RJ; tel. (21) 2533-6661; fax (21) 2252-0524; Pres. MARCOS TEIXEIRA.

Private Companies

Aliança Navegação e Logística, Ltda: Rua Verbo Divino 1547, Bairro Chácara Santo Antônio, 04719-002 São Paulo, SP; tel. (11) 5185-5600; fax (11) 5185-5624; e-mail alianca@sao.alianca.com.br; internet www.alianca.com.br; f. 1950; cargo services to Argentina, Uruguay, Europe, Baltic, Atlantic and North Sea ports; Pres. ARSÊNIO CARLOS NÓBREGA.

Companhia de Navegação do Norte (CONAN): Av. Rio Branco 23, 25° andar, 20090-003 Rio de Janeiro, RJ; tel. (21) 2223-4155; fax (21) 2253-7128; f. 1965; services to Brazil, Argentina, Uruguay and inland waterways; Chair. J. R. RIBEIRO SALOMÃO.

Companhia de Navegação do São Francisco: Av. São Francisco 1517, 39270-000 Pirapora, MG; tel. (38) 3741-1444; fax (38) 3741-1164; Pres. JOSÉ HUMBERTO BARATA JABUR.

Companhia Interamericana de Navegação e Comercio—CINCO: Av. 14 de Março 1700, 79370-000 Ladário, MS; tel. (67) 226-1010; fax (67) 226-1718; e-mail luiz.assy@cinconav.com.br; internet www.cinconav.com.br; f. 1989; Paraguay and Parana Rivers water transportation; Dirs LUIZ ALBERTO DO AMARAL ASSY, MICHEL CHAIM.

Companhia Libra de Navegação: Rua São Bento 8, 8° andar, Centro, 20090-010 Rio de Janeiro, RJ; tel. (21) 2203-5000; fax (21) 2283-3001; internet www.libra.com.br.

Frota Oceânica e Amazonica, SA (FOASA): Av. Venezuela 110, CP 21-020, 20081-310 Rio de Janeiro, RJ; tel. (21) 2203-3838; fax (21) 2253-6363; e-mail foasa@pamar.com.br; f. 1947; Pres. JOSÉ CARLOS FRAGOSO PIRES; Vice-Pres. LUIZ J. C. ALHANATI.

Petrobras Transporte, SA (TRANSPETRO): Edif. Visconde de Itaboraí, Av. Presidente Vargas 328, 20091-060 Rio de Janeiro, RJ; internet www.transpetro.com.br; f. 1998; absorbed the Frota Nacional de Petroleiros (FRONAPE) in 1999; transport of petroleum and related products; 53 vessels; Pres. SERGIO MACHADO.

Vale do Rio Doce Navegação, SA (DOCENAVE): Av. Graça Aranha 26, 8°–9° andar, 20005-900 Rio de Janeiro, RJ; fax (21) 3814-4971; internet www.docenave.com.br; bulk carrier to Japan, Arabian Gulf, Europe, North America and Argentina; Pres. ALVARO DE OLIVEIRA, Filho.

Wilson Sons Agência Marítima: Rua Jardim Botânico 518, 3° andar, 22461-000 Rio de Janeiro, RJ; tel. (21) 2126-4222; fax (21) 2126-4190; e-mail box@wilsonsons.com.br; internet www.wilsonsons.com.br; f. 1837; shipping agency, port operations, towage, small shipyard.

CIVIL AVIATION

There are 2,014 airports and airstrips and 417 helipads. Of the 67 principal airports 22 are international, although most international traffic is handled by the two airports at Rio de Janeiro and two at São Paulo. There were 16,454 aircraft registered in Brazil in 2003.

Agencia Nacional de Aviação Civil: Aeroporto International de Brasília, Setor de Concessionárias, Lote 5, 71608-900 Brasília, DF; tel. (61) 3905-2673; internet www.anac.gov.br; f. 2005; Dir-Pres. (vacant).

Empresa Brasileira de Infra-Estrutura Aeroportuária (Infraero): SCS, Quadra 04, Bloco A, 58, Edif. Infraero, 6° andar, 70304-902 Brasília, DF; tel. (61) 3312-3222; fax (61) 3321-0512; e-mail webmaster@infraero.gov.br; internet www.infraero.gov.br; Pres. (vacant).

Principal Airlines

GOL Transportes Aéreos, SA: Rua Tamios 246, Jardim Aeropuerto, 04630-000 São Paulo, SP; tel. (11) 5033-4200; internet www.voegol.com.br; f. 2001; low-cost airline; Man. Dir CONSTANTINO OLIVEIRA JÚNIOR.

Líder Táxi Aéreo, SA: Av. Santa Rosa 123, 31270-750 Belo Horizonte, MG; tel. (31) 3490-4500; fax (31) 3490-4600; internet www.lideraviacao.com.br; helicopters and small jets; f. 1958; Pres. JOSÉ AFONSO ASSUMPÇÃO.

Oceanair Linhas Aéreas, Ltda: Av. Marechal Câmara 160, Sala 1532, Centro, 20020-080 Rio de Janeiro, RJ; tel. (21) 2544-2181; fax (21) 2215-7181; internet www.oceanair.com.br; f. 1998; domestic services; Pres. GERMAN EFROMOVICH.

Pantanal Linhas Aéreas, SA: Av. das Nações Unidas 10989, 8° andar, Conj. 81, 04578-000 São Paulo, SP; tel. (11) 3040-3900; fax (11) 3846-3424; e-mail pantanal@uninet.com.br; internet www.pantanal-airlines.com.br; f. 1993; regional services.

TAM Linhas Aéreas, SA (Transportes Aéreos Regionais—TAM): Av. Jurandir 856, Lote 4, 1° andar, Jardim Ceci, 04072-000 São Paulo, SP; tel. (11) 5582-8811; fax (11) 5578-5946; e-mail tamimprensa@tam.com.br; internet www.tam.com.br; f. 1976; scheduled passenger and cargo services from São Paulo to destinations throughout Brazil and in Argentina, Paraguay, France and the USA; Pres. DANIEL MANDELLI MARTIN.

VARIG, SA (Viação Aérea Rio-Grandense): Av. Almirante Silvio de Noronha 365, Bloco C, 4° andar, 20021-010 Rio de Janeiro, RJ; tel. (21) 3814-5869; fax (21) 3814-5703; internet www.varig.com.br; f. 1927; bought by Volo do Brasil in mid-2006; international services throughout North, Central and South America, Africa, Western Europe and Asia; domestic services to major Brazilian cities; cargo services; also operates the domestic regional subsidiary airlines Nordeste and Rio-Sul; Chair. DAVID ZYLBERSZTAJAN; CEO MARCELO BOTTINI.

VARIG LOG (VARIG Lógistica, SA): Rua Fidencio Ramos 223, 04551-010 São Paulo, SP; tel. (11) 3119-7003; e-mail atendimento.variglog@variglog.com; internet www.variglog.com; f. 2000; owned by Volo do Brasil; cargo airline.

VASP, SA (Viação Aérea São Paulo): Praça Comte-Lineu Gomes s/n, Aeroporto Congonhas, 04626-910 São Paulo, SP; tel. (11) 5532-3000; fax (11) 5542-0880; internet www.vasp.com.br; f. 1933; privatized in 1990; domestic services throughout Brazil; international services to Argentina, Belgium, the Caribbean, South Korea and the USA; Pres. WAGNER CANHEDO AZEVEDO.

Tourism

In 2006 some 5.0m. tourists visited Brazil. In that year receipts from tourism totalled US $4,314m. Rio de Janeiro, with its famous beaches, is the centre of the tourist trade. Like Salvador, Recife and other towns, it has excellent examples of Portuguese colonial and modern architecture. The modern capital, Brasília, incorporates a new concept of city planning and is the nation's show-piece. Other attractions are the Iguaçu Falls, the seventh largest (by volume) in the world, the tropical forests of the Amazon basin and the wildlife of the Pantanal.

Associação Brasileira da Indústria de Hotéis (ABIH): SCN, Quadra 01, Bloco F, Lojas 121 e 125, Térreo, 70711-905 Brasília, DF; tel. and fax (61) 3326-1177; e-mail abihnacional@abih.com.br; internet www.abih.com.br; f. 1936; hoteliers' asscn; Pres. ERALDO ALVES DA CRUZ.

Instituto Brasileiro de Turismo (EMBRATUR): SCN, Quadra 02, Bloco G, 3° andar, 70710-500 Brasília, DF; tel. (61) 3429-7777; fax (61) 3429-7710; e-mail presidencia@embratur.gov.br; internet www.braziltour.com; f. 1966; Pres. JEANINE PIRES.

BRUNEI

Introductory Survey

Location, Climate, Language, Religion, Flag, Capital

The Sultanate of Brunei (Negara Brunei Darussalam) lies in South-East Asia, on the north-west coast of the island of Borneo (most of which comprises the Indonesian territory of Kalimantan). It is surrounded and bisected on the landward side by Sarawak, one of the two eastern states of Malaysia. The country has a tropical climate, characterized by consistent temperature and humidity. Annual rainfall averages about 2,540 mm (100 ins) in coastal areas and about 3,300 mm (130 ins) in the interior. Temperatures are high: average daily temperatures range from 24°C (75°F) to 32°C (90°F). The principal language is Malay, although Chinese is also spoken and English is widely used. The Malay population (an estimated 66.7% of the total in 2006) are mainly Sunni Muslims. Most of the Chinese in Brunei (11.1% of the population) are Buddhists, and some are adherents of Confucianism and Daoism. Europeans and Eurasians are predominantly Christians, and the majority of indigenous tribespeople (Iban, Dayak and Kelabit—3.6% of the population) adhere to various animist beliefs. The flag (proportions 1 by 2) is yellow, with two diagonal stripes, of white and black, running from the upper hoist to the lower fly; superimposed in the centre is the state emblem (in red, with yellow Arabic inscriptions). The capital is Bandar Seri Begawan (formerly called Brunei Town).

Recent History

Brunei, a traditional Islamic monarchy, formerly included most of the coastal regions of North Borneo (now Sabah) and Sarawak, which later became states of Malaysia. During the 19th century the rulers of Brunei ceded large parts of their territory to the United Kingdom, reducing the sultanate to its present size. In 1888, when North Borneo became a British Protectorate, Brunei became a British Protected State. In accordance with an agreement made in 1906, a British Resident was appointed to the court of the ruling Sultan as an adviser on administration. Under this arrangement, a form of government that included an advisory body, the State Council, emerged.

Brunei was invaded by Japanese forces in December 1941, but reverted to its former status in 1945, when the Second World War ended. The British-appointed Governor of Sarawak was High Commissioner for Brunei from 1948 until the territory's first written Constitution was promulgated in September 1959, when a further agreement was made between the Sultan and the British Government. The United Kingdom continued to be responsible for Brunei's defence and external affairs until the Sultanate's declaration of independence in 1984.

In December 1962 a large-scale revolt broke out in Brunei and in parts of Sarawak and North Borneo. The rebellion was undertaken by the 'North Borneo Liberation Army', an organization linked with the Parti Rakyat Brunei (PRB—Brunei People's Party), led by Sheikh Ahmad Azahari, which was strongly opposed to the planned entry of Brunei into the Federation of Malaysia. The rebels proclaimed the 'revolutionary State of North Kalimantan', but the revolt was suppressed, after 10 days' fighting, with the aid of British forces from Singapore. A state of emergency was declared, the PRB was banned, and Azahari was given asylum in Malaya. In the event, the Sultan of Brunei, Sir Omar Ali Saifuddin III, decided in 1963 against joining the Federation. From 1962 he ruled by decree, and the state of emergency remained in force. In October 1967 Saifuddin, who had been Sultan since 1950, abdicated in favour of his son, Hassanal Bolkiah, who was then 21 years of age. Under an agreement signed in November 1971, Brunei was granted full internal self-government.

In December 1975 the UN General Assembly adopted a resolution advocating British withdrawal from Brunei, the return of political exiles and the holding of a general election. Negotiations in 1978, following assurances by Malaysia and Indonesia that they would respect Brunei's sovereignty, resulted in an agreement (signed in January 1979) that Brunei would become fully independent within five years. Independence was duly proclaimed on 1 January 1984, and the Sultan took office as Prime Minister and Minister of Finance and of Home Affairs, presiding over a Cabinet of six other ministers (including two of the Sultan's brothers and his father, the former Sultan).

The future of the Chinese population, which controlled much of Brunei's private commercial sector but had become stateless since independence, appeared threatened in 1985, when the Sultan indicated that Brunei would become an Islamic state in which the indigenous, mainly Malay, inhabitants, known as *bumiputras* ('sons of the soil'), would receive preferential treatment. Several Hong Kong and Taiwan Chinese, who were not permanent Brunei residents, were repatriated.

In May 1985 a new political party, the Parti Kebangsaan Demokratik Brunei (PKDB—Brunei National Democratic Party), was formed. The new party, which comprised business executives loyal to the Sultan, based its policies on Islam and a form of liberal nationalism. However, the Sultan forbade employees of the Government (about 40% of the country's working population) to join the party. Persons belonging to the Chinese community were also excluded from membership. Divisions within the new party led to the formation of a second group, the Parti Perpaduan Kebangsaan Brunei (PPKB—Brunei National Solidarity Party), in February 1986. This party, which also received the Sultan's official approval, placed greater emphasis on co-operation with the Government, and was open to both Muslim and non-Muslim ethnic groups.

During 1985 and 1986 the adoption of a more progressive style of government became apparent. The death of Sir Omar Ali Saifuddin, the Sultan's father, in September 1986 was expected to accelerate modernization. In October the Cabinet was enlarged to 11 members, and commoners and aristocrats were assigned portfolios that had previously been held by members of the royal family. In February 1988, however, the PKDB was dissolved by the authorities after it had demanded the resignation of the Sultan as Head of Government (although not as Head of State), an end to the 26-year state of emergency and the holding of democratic elections. The official reason for the dissolution of the party was its connections with a foreign organization, the Pacific Democratic Union. The leaders of the PKDB, Abdul Latif Hamid and Abdul Latif Chuchu, were arrested, under the provisions of the Internal Security Act, and detained until March 1990. Abdul Latif Hamid died in May of that year. In January 1990 the Government ordered the release of six political prisoners, who had been detained soon after the revolt in 1962.

In 1990 the Government encouraged the population to embrace *Melayu Islam Beraja* (MIB—Malay Islamic Monarchy) as the state ideology. This affirmation of traditional Bruneian values for Malay Muslims was widely believed to be a response to an increase in social problems, including the abuse of alcohol and mild narcotics. Muslims were encouraged to adhere more closely to the tenets of Islam, greater emphasis was laid on Islamic holiday celebrations, and the distribution of alcohol was discouraged.

In 1994 a constitutional committee, appointed by the Government and chaired by the Minister of Foreign Affairs, Prince Mohamad Bolkiah, submitted a recommendation that the Constitution be amended to provide for an elected legislature. In February 1995 the PPKB was given permission to convene a general assembly, at which Abdul Latif Chuchu, the former Secretary-General of the PKDB, was elected President. Latif Chuchu was, however, compelled to resign shortly afterwards, owing to a condition of his release from detention in 1990. In May 1998 the PKDB was permitted to hold a further annual general meeting, at which Hatta Zainal Abidin, the son of a former opposition leader, was elected party President.

In February 1997 the Sultan replaced his brother, Prince Jefri Bolkiah, as Minister of Finance. It was rumoured that the Sultan's assumption of the finance portfolio was due to alleged financial disagreements rather than Prince Jefri's frequently criticized lifestyle. In March the Sultan and Prince Jefri denied accusations of misconduct made by a former winner of a US beauty contest, Shannon Marketic. A US court granted the Sultan immunity from legal action in August, owing to his status as a foreign head of state; this immunity was extended to Prince

Jefri in March 1998. Similar allegations against Prince Jefri, submitted to a court in Hawaii, resulted in an undisclosed financial settlement, following the judge's rejection of Prince Jefri's claims to immunity. Marketic subsequently appealed against the granting of exemption from prosecution in her case. Further allegations concerning the extravagant lifestyle of Prince Jefri emerged in a court case in the United Kingdom in February, in which Jefri was being sued for £80m. by two former business associates, Watche (Bob) and Rafi Manoukian. The Manoukian brothers claimed that Prince Jefri had reneged on two property agreements; Prince Jefri was counter-suing them for £100m., alleging that they had exploited their relationship with him to amass considerable wealth. The case, which was unreported in Brunei, was also settled out of court for an undisclosed sum.

In March 1998, after 14 years in office, the Minister of Health, Dato' Dr Haji Johar bin Dato' Haji Noordin, was dismissed, reportedly owing to the inadequacy of his response to the haze over Brunei caused by forest fires in Indonesia and Malaysia. The resignations of the Attorney-General, Pengiran Haji Bahrin bin Pengiran Haji Abbas (who was granted leave from his position as Minister of Law), and of the Solicitor-General were accepted by the Sultan in June. An acting Attorney-General and Solicitor-General were appointed, while the Sultan assumed temporary responsibility for the law portfolio. On 10 August the Sultan's son, Prince Al-Muhtadee Billah Bolkiah, was installed as the heir to the throne.

Prince Jefri, who had left Brunei in April 1998, was removed as Chairman of the Brunei Investment Agency (BIA), the organization responsible for the country's overseas investments, at the end of July, following the collapse earlier in the month of his business conglomerate, the Amedeo Development Corporation. (The Amedeo Development Corporation was formally liquidated by the High Court of Brunei in July 1999, with reported debts of at least US $3,500m.) Prince Jefri was also removed from the boards of seven communications companies. He claimed that he was the victim of a conspiracy of conservative Islamists, led by his estranged brother, Prince Mohamad Bolkiah (the Minister of Foreign Affairs), and the Minister of Education, Pehin Dato' Haji Abdul Aziz bin Pehin Haji Umar. Prince Jefri's removal from positions of authority took place amid a more rigorous enforcement of the ban on alcohol and the confiscation from retailers of non-Islamic religious artefacts. Abdul Aziz, who replaced Prince Jefri as Chairman of the BIA, also headed an investigation (which was initiated in June) into the finances of the BIA. In September Abdul Aziz announced that large amounts of government funds had been misappropriated during Prince Jefri's tenure as Chairman. In January 2000, following a long period during which the Government made no significant comment about the misappropriation of BIA funds or about the role of the Sultan's younger brother in the affair, Prince Jefri returned to Brunei after many months of self-imposed exile. Private negotiations ensued between Prince Jefri and the parties involved in the investigation. These negotiations failed, however, and in February the Government and the BIA began civil proceedings against Prince Jefri, alleging his improper withdrawal and use of substantial BIA funds during the period in which he had served as Minister of Finance and Chairman of the BIA; 71 other people were named in the action, including Prince Jefri's eldest son, Prince Muda Abdul Hakeem. In May an out-of-court settlement was reached whereby the domestic and overseas assets that had been acquired by Prince Jefri with funds derived from the BIA were to be returned to the State. These assets were sold for £5.5m. at a public auction in August 2001.

In October 2000 Haji Awang Kassim, Prince Jefri's former confidential secretary, who was also former deputy managing director of the BIA and a prominent figure in Amedeo management, was arrested, following his extradition from the Philippines. Civil proceedings were also instigated against another six of Prince Jefri's former colleagues. In the mean time, the legal dispute over responsibility for Amedeo's huge losses continued. In October 2001 the Sultan, dissatisfied with the unsuccessful and expensive attempts by leading international accountancy and law companies, requested his newly created local company, Global Evergreen, to resolve the long-standing dispute with more than 300 creditors who were owed an estimated B $1,000m. Negotiations proceeded swiftly, and creditors were strongly recommended to accept a new, highly favourable offer whereby they would be repaid on a 'sliding scale' according to the magnitude of their claim. Larger claims would be dealt with on an individual basis. The settlement brought to an end much of the legal contention arising from the Government's closure of the company two years previously.

In May 2002 it was reported that 13 foreign Global Evergreen employees (of whom three were citizens of Australia, four of the United Kingdom, five of New Zealand and one of Malaysia), who had been investigating the whereabouts of the state funds that had disappeared as a result of the Amedeo scandal, had been refused permission to leave the country, ostensibly owing to visa irregularities. It was thought that, during the course of their investigation, they had angered both the chairman of the company and the Minister of Home Affairs, Pehin Dato' Haji Isa bin Pehin Haji Ibrahim. They were granted permission to leave Brunei shortly afterwards. In August the Sultan formally swore in Dato' Seri Paduka Dr Haji Ahmad bin Haji Jumat as the Minister of Development and Pehin Dato' Haji Abu Bakar bin Haji Apong as the Minister of Health. Meanwhile, following the introduction in October 2001 of a Local Newspapers (Amendment) Order establishing more stringent controls over Brunei's newspapers, the English-language *News Express* was forced to shut down its operations in September 2002; it had been unable to comply with new financial requirements.

In March 2004 it was reported that a businessman and two retired senior army and police intelligence officers had been imprisoned without trial under the Internal Security Act for allegedly 'leaking' government secrets. The police officer, Nordin bin Haji Mohamad Noor, was also accused of treason, having allegedly provided classified documents to a foreign country.

In September 2004 the 21-member Legislative Council, suspended since 1984, was reconvened in order to debate several proposed amendments to the country's Constitution. Later in that month it approved a series of constitutional amendments. These envisaged, amongst other changes, the direct election of 15 members of an expanded 45-member Legislative Council, although the remaining 30 members would be appointed by the Sultan. No schedule was established for the holding of the elections, nor was there any reference to an end to the national state of emergency that had been in place since 1962. Consequently, the extent to which the changes represented genuine progress towards democracy in Brunei was debatable.

In May 2005 the Sultan effected a major cabinet reorganization, in which four prominent ministers were dismissed. Pehin Dato' Haji Isa was replaced as Minister of Home Affairs and Special Adviser to the Prime Minister by Pehin Dato' Haji Adanan bin Mohammad Yusof; Pehin Dato' Haji Abdul Aziz was replaced by Pehin Dato' Haji Abdul Rahman Taib as Minister of Education; the communications portfolio was transferred from Pehin Dato' Haji Zakaria to Pehin Dato' Haji Abu Bakar; and Pehin Dato' Haji Mohammad Daud was chosen to replace Pehin Dato' Haji Hussein as Minister of Culture, Youth and Sports. The changes also included the creation of a new Ministry of Energy (the portfolio for which was allocated to Pehin Dato' Haji Yahya bin Bakar) and the appointment of Pehin Dato' Lim Jock Seng to the position of Minister of Foreign Affairs II, rendering him the first ethnic Chinese official to be included within the Bruneian cabinet. The Sultan also appointed 10 new Deputy Ministers, including two from the corporate sector.

In September 2005 the Sultan dissolved the existing Legislative Council and appointed 29 new members. The enlargement of the Council received widespread approval, but in early 2008 there was still no indication of a date for the holding of elections. Meanwhile, in August 2006 the total number of legal political organizations in Brunei was increased to three upon the establishment of the Parti Pembangunan Bangsa (PPB, or National Development Party—NDP). Founded by the former secretary-general of the PRB, Awang Muhammad Yasin Affendy bin Abdul Rahman, the PPB—the stated goal of which was to support the Government by promoting adherence to the values of MIB—had attracted a membership of approximately 700 people by April 2006, in which month the party's first congress was convened.

In March 2006 the Legislative Council held a six-day session principally for the purpose of approving the National Budget for 2006/07, following the completion of which the Council was adjourned. In May the Government announced that state laws governing the granting of citizenship to foreign nationals resident in Brunei were to be relaxed. Effective as of 15 May, any foreign male national married to a Bruneian woman for 15 years (if he had been born in Brunei) or for 20 years (if born outside Brunei) could apply for permanent citizenship. Furthermore, foreign nationals possessing professional skills of direct benefit to the country and those contributing to Brunei's economic growth and commanding assets and/or investments worth in excess of B $500,000 (approximately US $319,040) would also be eligible. However, all applicants would still be required to demonstrate both written and oral proficiency in Malay and be expected to possess a comprehensive understanding of Bruneian culture.

In various *titah* (royal addresses) during 2005 and 2006, the Sultan repeatedly stressed the need to revive the religious education system. A second Islamic university was to be established, and the Sultan insisted that emphasis be given to the teaching of Islamic religious knowledge in schools, the ultimate goal of the schooling system being to produce 'educated, skilled and pious Bruneians'.

Brunei has developed close relations with the members of the Association of South East Asian Nations (ASEAN, see p. 185), in particular Singapore, and became a full member of the organization immediately after independence. Brunei also joined the UN, the Commonwealth (see p. 206) and the Organization of the Islamic Conference (see p. 369) in 1984. In September 1992 Brunei was formally admitted to the Non-aligned Movement (see p. 424).

Relations with the United Kingdom, meanwhile, had become strained during 1983, following the Brunei Government's decision, in August, to transfer the management of its investment portfolio from the British Crown Agents to the newly created BIA. However, normal relations were restored in September, when the British Government agreed that a battalion of Gurkha troops, stationed in Brunei since 1971, should remain in the country after independence, at the Sultanate's expense, specifically to guard the oil and gas fields.

In July 1990, in response to the uncertainty over the future of US bases in the Philippines (see the chapter on the Philippines), Brunei joined Singapore in offering the USA the option of operating its forces from Brunei. A bilateral memorandum of understanding was subsequently signed, providing for up to three visits a year to Brunei by US warships. Under the terms of the memorandum, Brunei forces were to train with US personnel.

In late 1991 Brunei established diplomatic relations with the People's Republic of China at ambassadorial level. As a member of ASEAN, Brunei's relations with Viet Nam improved during 1991 (following Viet Nam's withdrawal from Cambodia in September 1989) and in February 1992 diplomatic relations between the two countries were formally established during a visit to Brunei by the Vietnamese Prime Minister. In October 1993 the Brunei Government announced the establishment of diplomatic relations at ambassadorial level with Myanmar.

Conflicting claims (from Brunei, Viet Nam, the People's Republic of China, the Philippines, Malaysia and Taiwan) to all, or some, of the uninhabited Spratly Islands, situated in the South China Sea, remained a source of tension in the region. Brunei is the only claimant not to have stationed troops on the islands, which are both strategically important and possess potentially large reserves of petroleum. During the 1990s attempts to resolve the dispute through a negotiated settlement resulted in little progress, and military activity in the area increased. Talks at the annual summit meeting of ASEAN ministers of foreign affairs held in Hanoi, Viet Nam, in July 2001 failed to make any further advances in ending the impasse. However, during the annual ASEAN summit meeting held in Phnom-Penh, Cambodia, in November 2002, the members of the grouping signed an agreement with China approving a 'code of conduct' for the islands, which was aimed at resolving the conflict.

In February 2000 Brunei hosted its first Asia-Pacific Economic Co-operation (APEC, see p. 176) Senior Officials' Meeting, attended by 3,000 delegates from 21 countries. In April an ASEAN Regional Forum (ARF) meeting to discuss security issues was held in Brunei. In November Brunei hosted the annual summit meeting of APEC leaders; attended by some 6,000 delegates, this was the largest international event ever held in the country.

In January 2001 the Sultan launched 'Visit Brunei Year' and 'Visit ASEAN Year 2002', in association with the regional Asian Tourism Forum. In August 2001 Brunei was the venue for the first International Islamic Exposition, attended by representatives from 25 other countries. In November Brunei hosted the seventh summit meeting of ASEAN leaders, which was also attended by representatives from the People's Republic of China, Japan and South Korea. At the end of the meeting Brunei pledged its support for a programme proposed by Philippine President Gloria Arroyo, which focused on encouraging close regional co-operation in countering international terrorism in the aftermath of the September suicide attacks on the USA. In late July and early August 2002 the 35th ASEAN Ministerial Meeting, the ninth ARF and the Post-Ministerial Meeting were held in Brunei; ASEAN leaders subsequently signed a Declaration on Counter-Terrorism with the USA. In September 2002 the 34th ASEAN Economic Ministers' Meeting was also convened in the country.

Relations with China continued to strengthen. In September 2004, during an official visit to the People's Republic, the Sultan and Chinese President Hu Jintao signed several memoranda of understanding (MOU), which were intended to increase co-operation in areas such as trade and investment, education and judicial affairs. During a reciprocal visit to Brunei by President Hu Jintao in April 2005, several more bilateral agreements were signed, under the terms of which the need for diplomatic and official visas for travel between the two countries was waived; other areas of focus included energy, public health, tourism, education and military training. One indirect consequence of this burgeoning relationship was the closure in March 2006 of the Taiwanese Economic and Cultural Representative Office in Bandar Seri Begawan; in November, however, it was announced that the Office was to reopen. During 2006 several Bruneian senior officials, including the Minister of Foreign Affairs and Trade and the Minister of Home Affairs, conducted visits to the Chinese capital of Beijing. In October Sultan Hassanal attended a meeting in the Chinese city of Nanning, convened to commemorate the 15th anniversary of the first ASEAN-China dialogue.

Diplomatic relations were established with numerous countries in 2005–06, including Venezuela in July 2005 and in 2006 with Samoa (in February), Iceland (in April), Estonia (in May), and Moldova and Angola (both in October). In June 2006 Brunei and Japan, which remained a major market for the former's exports, held inaugural negotiations aimed at securing a bilateral free trade agreement, and a second round of talks was conducted in October. In June 2007 the Sultan and the Japanese Prime Minister signed the resultant Brunei-Japan Economic Partnership Agreement (BJEPA) in Tokyo. Brunei's relations with other Islamic nations continued to develop, and in April 2006 the Sultan made his first state visits to Qatar and the United Arab Emirates. In February 2007 diplomatic relations were established with Afghanistan.

In 2005 Brunei became the 191st member state of the United Nations Educational, Scientific and Cultural Organization (UNESCO, see p. 137). Accession to the international body was expected to prove of considerable benefit to Brunei in various fields, including science and technology policy development, as well as education and communications networking. In 2007 Brunei was admitted to the International Labour Organization (ILO, see p. 124).

Government

The 1959 Constitution confers supreme executive authority on the Sultan. He is assisted and advised by four Constitutional Councils: the Religious Council, the Privy Council, the Council of Cabinet Ministers and the Council of Succession. Following the rebellion of 1962, certain provisions of the Constitution (including those pertaining to elections and to a fifth Council, the Legislative Council) were suspended, and the Sultan has since ruled by decree. However, in September 2004 the 21-member Legislative Council was convened for the first time since the country became independent in 1984 and approved several constitutional amendments, including one providing for the direct election of 15 members of an expanded 45-member Legislative Council. The remaining members were to be appointed by the Sultan. In September 2005 the Sultan appointed a new, enlarged Legislative Council comprising 29 members. No schedule was established for the holding of the elections.

Defence

As assessed at November 2007, the Royal Brunei Malay Regiment numbered 7,000: army 4,900; navy 1,000; air force 1,100. Military service is voluntary, but only Malays are eligible for service. Paramilitary forces comprised an estimated 2,250 personnel, including 1,750 Royal Brunei Police and a Gurkha Reserve Unit numbering about 400–500. A 110-strong unit of the British army was stationed in Brunei in 2007. There were also 500 troops from Singapore operating a training school in Brunei. Defence expenditure in 2007 was budgeted at an estimated B $519m.

Economic Affairs

In 1998, according to estimates by the World Bank, Brunei's gross national income (GNI), measured at average 1996–98 prices, was US $7,754m., equivalent to US $24,100 per head (or US $24,910 on an international purchasing-power parity basis). In 1996–2006, it was estimated, the population increased by an annual average of 2.3%, while gross domestic product (GDP) per head decreased, in real terms, by an average of 0.4% per year during 1996–2004. According to figures from the Asian Development Bank (ADB), Brunei's overall GDP increased at an estimated average annual rate of 2.0% during 1995–2006. Real GDP grew by 0.4% in 2005 and by an estimated 5.1% in 2006.

Agriculture (including forestry and fishing) employed less than an estimated 0.6% of the working population in 2005 and provided 0.7% of GDP in 2006. In 2000 an estimated 1.3% of the total land area was cultivated; the principal crops include rice, cassava, bananas and pineapples. In the 1990s Brunei imported about 80% of its total food requirements. According to figures from the ADB, during 1995–2006 the GDP of the agricultural sector increased, in real terms, at an estimated average annual rate of 5.3%. Agricultural GDP expanded by 1.4% in 2005 but declined by 10.1% in 2006.

Industry (comprising mining, manufacturing, construction and utilities) employed 21.4% of the working population according to the results of the 2001 census, and contributed an estimated 73.4% of GDP in 2006. According to figures from the ADB, total industrial GDP increased at an average annual rate of 1.4% in 1995–2006. Industrial GDP declined by 1.8% in 2005 before increasing by an estimated 4.1% in 2006.

Brunei's economy relies almost entirely on its petroleum and natural gas resources, although reforms designed to reduce this dependence were introduced in July 2005 (see below). Mining and quarrying employed only 2.7% of the working population according to the results of the 2001 census. In 2005 the oil and gas sector accounted for 75.2% of total GDP. Proven reserves of petroleum at the end of 2006 amounted to 1,100m. barrels, sufficient to sustain production at that year's levels (averaging 221,000 barrels per day) for approximately 13-and-a-half years. Output of natural gas in 2006 totalled 12,300m. cu m, from proven reserves at the end of that year of some 340,000m. cu m (sustainable for approximately 27 years). In 2005 exports of mineral fuels accounted for 94.2% of total exports. The GDP of the petroleum and gas sector increased by an annual average of 0.8% in 2000–05, declining by 1.0% in 2004 and by 2.6% in 2005.

The manufacturing sector employed 8.5% of the working population according to the results of the 2001 census and contributed 10.5% of GDP in 2006. Since the mid-1980s Brunei has attempted to expand its manufacturing base. In the mid-1990s the textile industry provided the largest non-oil-and-gas revenue; other industries included cement, mineral water, canned food, dairy products, silica sands products, footwear and leather products, the design and manufacture of printed circuits, publishing and printing. The expiry on 31 December 2004 of the Multi-Fibre Arrangement (MFA—the international quota system governing trade in textiles and garments), combined with increased competition from the People's Republic of China and India, was expected significantly to hinder the performance of Brunei's textiles industry in subsequent years. According to ADB figures, during 1995–2006 manufacturing GDP increased by an annual average of 1.8%. The GDP of this sector declined by 2.0% in 2005 but increased by 0.8% in 2006.

Services employed 77.2% of the working population according to the results of the 2001 census, and provided an estimated 25.9% of GDP in 2006. In that year the finance sector contributed 3.0% of GDP, and the sector comprising wholesale and retail trade contributed 2.6%. In 2000 the Islamic Development Bank of Brunei was established, in an effort to transform Brunei into an important financial centre. The tourism sector was also being actively promoted as an important part of Brunei's policy of diversification away from its reliance on petroleum and natural gas. In 2000 1.3m. people visited Brunei, and in 1998 receipts from tourism totalled US $37m. Following the terrorist attacks on the USA in September 2001, tourist arrivals in that year declined to 840,272. Arrivals totalled 815,054 in 2005. According to figures from the ADB, during 1995–2006 the combined GDP of the service sectors increased, in real terms, at an average rate of 3.1% per year. The GDP of the services sector increased by 4.1% in 2005 and by an estimated 7.4% in 2006.

In 2005 Brunei recorded a visible trade surplus of US $4,836m., predominantly attributable to the high volume of petroleum exports and as a result of high investment income from abroad. In the same year there was a surplus of US $5,339m. on the current account of the balance of payments. In 2006 the principal source of imports (providing 30.9%) was Singapore; other major suppliers were Malaysia, the United Kingdom, the People's Republic of China and Japan. The principal market for exports in that year was Japan, which accounted for 31.6% of total exports (mainly natural gas on a long-term contract); other significant purchasers were Indonesia, the Republic of Korea (also a purchaser of natural gas), Australia and the USA. In 2005 principal imports comprised machinery and transport equipment, basic manufactures, food and live animals and miscellaneous manufactured articles; principal exports were mineral fuels and lubricants.

For the fiscal year ending March 2007 there was a projected budgetary surplus of just B $6m., compared with B $3,355m. in the previous year, largely owing to an anticipated decline in oil and gas revenues. Brunei has no external public debt. Annual inflation averaged 0.4% in 1995–2003; consumer prices increased by 0.9% in 2004, by 1.2% in 2005 and by 0.1% in 2006. Foreign workers, principally from Malaysia and the Philippines, have helped to ease the labour shortage resulting from the small size of the population, and comprised about 41% of the labour force in 2000. However, the rate of unemployment was estimated at 4.0% in 2006, reflecting a shortage of non-manual jobs for the well-educated Bruneians.

Brunei is a member of the Association of South East Asian Nations (ASEAN, see p. 185). In October 1991 the member states formally announced the establishment of the ASEAN Free Trade Area (AFTA), which was to be implemented over 15 years (later reduced to 10), and, as a member of ASEAN, Brunei endorsed Malaysia's plan for an East Asia Economic Caucus. AFTA was formally established in 2002. Brunei was a founder member of the Asia-Pacific Economic Co-operation (APEC, see p. 176) forum, initiated in November 1989, and is also a member of the UN Economic and Social Commission for Asia and the Pacific (ESCAP, see p. 35), which aims to accelerate economic progress in the region. In 1994 the East ASEAN Growth Area (EAGA) was established, encompassing Mindanao, in the Philippines, Sarawak and Sabah, in Malaysia, Kalimantan and Sulawesi, in Indonesia, and Brunei. Brunei became a member of the Asian Development Bank (ADB, see p. 182) in April 2006.

A report released by the Brunei Darussalam Economic Council (BDEC) in February 2000 warned of the unsustainable nature of the country's economy. In an address delivered in the same month, the Sultan stressed the importance of the development of alternative sources of revenue, in an unprecedented acknowledgement of the country's fundamental economic problems. In July 2005 the Sultan announced a series of reforms designed to attract foreign investors and to reduce Brunei's dependence on the oil and gas sector. Although the strength of international petroleum prices from 2005 was advantageous to Brunei, with the economy reportedly growing by 8.9% in 2006, the Sultanate's excessive reliance on the oil and gas sector remained a major concern. In April 2006 it was announced that a special centre dedicated to effecting the transfer of information and communications technology skills to local Bruneians was to be established. In January 2008 the Government announced its long-term development strategy, the Wawasan (National Vision) Brunei 2035, which aimed to improve per caput incomes and to diversify economic activities. Eight strategic areas were identified: education, economics, security, institutional development, local business development, infrastructural development, social security and the environment. In particular, modifications in the education system were to be made in order better to address the requirements of the changing economy. Plans to increase the scope of the social security system were accorded priority, as were measures to improve business conditions for small and medium-sized enterprises. The country's immediate economic concerns were summarized in the Ninth National Development Plan, encompassing the period 2007–12, which envisaged an average annual rate of growth of 6%. Expenditure of B $9,500m. was allocated to the plan; social services, transport and communications, along with the information technology sector, were scheduled to benefit from substantial outlays.

Education

Education is free and is compulsory for 12 years from the age of five years. Islamic studies form an integral part of the school curriculum. Pupils who are Brunei citizens and reside more than 8 km (5 miles) from their schools are entitled to free accommodation in hostels, free transport or a subsistence allowance. Schools are classified according to the language of instruction, i.e. Malay,

BRUNEI

English or Chinese (Mandarin). In 2004/05 enrolment at pre-primary level was equivalent to 52% of children in the relevant age-group (males 52%; females 52%). Primary education lasts for six years from the age of six years. Secondary education, usually beginning at 12 years of age, lasts for seven years, comprising a first cycle of three years (lower secondary), a second of two years (upper secondary) and a third of two years (pre-tertiary). In 2004/05 enrolment at secondary level was equivalent to 94% of children in the relevant age group (males 91%; females 96%). In the same year there were 204 pre-primary and primary schools, 41 secondary schools, six vocational colleges, six Arabic schools, one teacher-training college and two institutes of higher education, including one university. The University of Brunei Darussalam was formally established in 1985, but many students continue to attend universities abroad, at government expense. In the budget for 2005/06 the Government allocated B $633.8m. in operating expenditure to the Ministry of Education. A second national university, the Universiti Islam Sultan Sharif Ali (UNISAA), was established in mid-2007.

Public Holidays

2008: 1 January (New Year's Day), 10 January*† (Hijrah, Islamic New Year), 7 February‡ (Chinese New Year), 23 February (National Day), 20 March* (Hari Mouloud, Birth of the Prophet), 31 May (Royal Brunei Armed Forces Day), 15 July (Sultan's Birthday), 30 July* (Israk Mikraj, Ascension of the Prophet Muhammad), 1 September* (Beginning of Ramadan), 30 September* (Memperingati Nuzul Al-Quran, Anniversary of the Revelation of the Koran), 1 October* (Hari Raya Aidilfitri, end of Ramadan), 8 December* (Hari Raya Aidiladha, Feast of the Sacrifice), 29 December*† (Hijrah, Islamic New Year).

2009: 1 January (New Year's Day), 26 January‡ (Chinese New Year), 23 February (National Day), 9 March* (Hari Mouloud, Birth of the Prophet), 31 May (Royal Brunei Armed Forces Day), 15 July (Sultan's Birthday), 20 July* (Israk Mikraj, Ascension of the Prophet Muhammad), 22 August* (Beginning of Ramadan), 17 September* (Memperingati Nuzul Al-Quran, Anniversary of the Revelation of the Koran), 21 September* (Hari Raya Aidilfitri, end of Ramadan), 28 November* (Hari Raya Aidiladha, Feast of the Sacrifice), 18 December* (Hijrah, Islamic New Year).

* These holidays are dependent on the Islamic lunar calendar and may vary by one or two days from the dates given.

† This festival occurs twice (marking the start of the Islamic years AH 1429 and 1430) within the same Gregorian year.

‡ The first day of the first moon of the lunar calendar.

Weights and Measures

The metric system has been introduced.

Statistical Survey

Sources (unless otherwise stated): Department of Economic Planning and Development, Prime Minister's Office, Block 2A, Jalan Ong Sum Ping, Bandar Seri Begawan BA 1311; tel. 2244433; fax 2230236; e-mail info@jpke.gov.bn; Brunei Economic Development Board, Block 2K, Bangunan Keraajan, Jalan Ong Sum Ping, Bandar Seri Begawan BA 1311; tel. 2230111; fax 2230063; e-mail info@bedb.com.bn; internet www.bedb.com.bn.

AREA AND POPULATION

Area: 5,765 sq km (2,226 sq miles); *By District:* Brunei/Muara 570 sq km (220 sq miles), Seria/Belait 2,725 sq km (1,052 sq miles), Tutong 1,165 sq km (450 sq miles), Temburong 1,305 sq km (504 sq miles).

Population (excluding transients afloat): 260,482 at census of 7 August 1991; 332,844 (males 168,925, females 163,919) at census of 21 August 2001; 383,000 (males 203,300, females 179,700) in 2006 (provisional estimate). *By District* (2006, provisional estimates): Brunei/Muara 264,700; Seria/Belait 63,900; Tutong 44,400; Temburong 10,000; Total 383,000.

Density (2006): 66.4 per sq km.

Ethnic Groups (2006 provisional estimates): Malay 255,500, Chinese 42,700, Others 84,800, Total 383,000.

Principal Towns: Bandar Seri Begawan (capital): population 27,285 at 2001 census; Kuala Belait: population 21,200 at 1991 census; Seria: population 21,100 at 1991 census; Tutong: population 13,000 at 1991 census. *Mid-2005* (incl. suburbs, UN estimate): Bandar Seri Begawan 64,000 (Source: UN, *World Urbanization Prospects: The 2005 Revision*).

Births, Marriages and Deaths (2005): Live births 6,933 (birth rate 18.7 per 1,000); Marriages 2,258; Deaths 1,072 (death rate 2.9 per 1,000).

Expectation of Life (years at birth, WHO estimates): 77.3 (males 75.9; females 78.5) in 2005. Source: WHO, *World Health Statistics*.

Economically Active Population (persons aged 15 years and over, 2001 census, provisional): Agriculture, hunting, forestry and fishing 1,994; Mining and quarrying 3,954; Manufacturing 12,455; Electricity, gas and water 2,639; Construction 12,301; Trade, restaurants and hotels 20,038; Transport, storage and communications 4,803; Financing, insurance, real estate and business services 8,190; Community, social and personal services 79,880; *Total employed* 146,254 (males 85,820, females 60,434); Unemployed 11,340 (males 6,734, females 4,606); *Total labour force* 157,594 (males 92,554, females 65,040). *2006* (provisional estimates): Total employed 173,100; Registered unemployed 7,300; Total labour force 180,400 (males 111,600, females 68,800).

HEALTH AND WELFARE

Key Indicators

Total Fertility Rate (children per woman, 2005): 2.4.

Under-5 Mortality Rate (per 1,000 live births, 2005): 9.

HIV/AIDS (% of persons aged 15–49, 2005): <0.1.

Physicians (per 1,000 head, 2000): 1.01.

Hospital Beds (per 1,000 head, 2003): 2.59.

Health Expenditure (2004): US $ per head (PPP): 620.9.

Health Expenditure (2004): % of GDP: 3.2.

Health Expenditure (2004): public (% of total): 79.7.

Human Development Index (2005): ranking: 30.

Human Development Index (2005): value: 0.894.

For sources and definitions, see explanatory note on p. vi.

AGRICULTURE, ETC.

Principal Crops ('000 metric tons, 2006): Rice (paddy) 1.0 (FAO estimate). *Aggregate Production* ('000 metric tons, may include official, semi-official or estimated data): Total vegetables (incl. melons) 10.5; Total fruits (excl. melons) 5.4.

Livestock ('000 head, 2006, FAO estimates): Cattle 1.3; Buffaloes 5.0; Sheep 3.0; Goats 3.0; Pigs 1.8; Chickens 13,000.

Livestock Products ('000 metric tons, 2006, FAO estimates): Cattle meat 2.8; Chicken meat 16.2; Hen eggs 6.0.

Forestry ('000 cubic metres, 2006, FAO estimates): *Roundwood Removals:* Sawlogs, veneer logs and logs for sleepers 101.1; Other industrial roundwood 11.0; Fuel wood 11.6; Total 123.7. *Sawnwood Production:* Total (all broad-leaved) 50.9.

Fishing (metric tons, live weight, 2005, estimates): Capture 2,400; Aquaculture 708 (Blue Shrimp 432); *Total catch* 3,108.

Source: FAO.

MINING

Production (2005, estimates): Crude petroleum ('000 barrels, incl. condensate) 70,000; Natural gas (million cu m, gross) 13,500. Source: US Geological Survey.

INDUSTRY

Production ('000 barrels, 2005, unless otherwise indicated): Motor spirit (petrol) 1,780 (estimate); Distillate fuel oils 1,220 (estimate); Residual fuel oil 540 (estimate); Cement ('000 metric tons) 266; Electric energy (million kWh) 2,913. Sources: mostly UN, *Industrial Commodity Statistics Yearbook*; and US Geological Survey.

FINANCE

Currency and Exchange Rates: 100 sen (cents) = 1 Brunei dollar (B $). *Sterling, US Dollar and Euro Equivalents* (31 December

BRUNEI

2007): £1 sterling = B $2.887; US $1 = B $1.441; €1 = B $2.122; B $100 = £34.63 = US $69.39 = €47.13. *Average Exchange Rate* (Brunei dollars per US $): 1.6644 in 2005; 1.5889 in 2006; 1.5071 in 2007. Note: The Brunei dollar is at par with the Singapore dollar.

Budget (B $ million, year ending 31 March 2007, projected figures): *Revenue:* Tax revenue 2,966 (Oil and gas sector 2,750); Non-tax revenue 2,240, (Oil and gas sector 1,966); Total 5,206. *Expenditure:* Current expenditure 3,600 (Personal emoluments 1,577, Other annual recurrent charges 1,354, Charged expenditure 669); Capital expenditure 1,600 (Special expenditure charges 700; Development expenditure 900); Total 5,200. Source: IMF, *Brunei Darussalam: Statistical Appendix* (December 2006).

International Reserves (US $ million, 2006): IMF special drawing rights 16.84; Reserve position in IMF 36.97; Foreign exchange 469.47; Total 523.28. Source: IMF, *International Financial Statistics*.

Money Supply (B $ million, 2006): Currency outside banks 641.4; Demand deposits at banks 3,324.2; Total money 3,965.6. Source: IMF, *International Financial Statistics*.

Cost of Living (Consumer Price Index, all items; base: 2000 = 100): 99.4 in 2004; 100.6 in 2005; 100.7 in 2006. Source: IMF, *International Financial Statistics*.

Gross Domestic Product (B $ million at constant 2000 prices): 11,419.4 in 2004; 11,463.7 in 2005; 11,903.1 in 2006 (forecast).

Gross Domestic Product by Economic Activity (B $ million in current prices, 2006): Agriculture, hunting, forestry and fishing 129; Mining and quarrying 10,913; Manufacturing 1,925; Electricity, gas and water 104; Construction 540; Wholesale and retail trade 486; Transport and communications 504; Finance 553; Public administration 2,009; Others 1,209; *GDP in purchasers' values* 18,370. Source: Asian Development Bank, *Key Indicators of Developing Asian and Pacific Countries*.

Balance of Payments (US $ million, 2005, estimates): Exports of goods 6,249; Imports of goods −1,413; *Trade balance* 4,836; Exports of services 617; Imports of services −1,111; *Balance on goods and services* 4,342; Other income received 1,563; Other income paid −190; *Balance on goods, services and income* 5,715; Current transfers received 0; Current transfers paid −376; *Current balance* 5,339; Capital balance −12; Direct investment (net) 167; Portfolio investment (net) 21; Other investment (net) −2,151; Net errors and omissions −3,375; *Overall balance* −11.

EXTERNAL TRADE

Principal Commodities (US $ million, 2005): *Imports c.i.f.:* Food and live animals 259; Chemicals 138; Basic manufactures 367; Machinery and transport equipment 478; Miscellaneous manufactured articles 161; Total (incl. others) 1,491. *Exports f.o.b.:* Mineral fuels 5,886; Miscellaneous manufactured articles 191; Machinery and transport equipment 125; Total (incl. others) 6,250.

Principal Trading Partners (US $ million, 2006): *Imports:* People's Republic of China 110; Germany 38; Hong Kong 32; Japan 107; Republic of Korea 79; Malaysia 380; Singapore 632; Thailand 91; United Kingdom 161; USA 53; Total (incl. others) 2,047. *Exports:* Australia 750; People's Republic of China 196; Indonesia 1,344; Japan 2,070; Republic of Korea 839; Singapore 200; Thailand 117; USA 523; Total (incl. others) 6,555. Source: Asian Development Bank, *Key Indicators of Developing Asian and Pacific Countries*.

TRANSPORT

Road Traffic (registered vehicles, 2001): Private cars 188,720; Goods vehicles 17,828; Motorcycles and scooters 7,162; Buses and taxis 2,267; Others 4,470. *2004:* Passenger cars 226,000; Commercial vehicles 22,000 (Source: UN, *Statistical Yearbook*).

Merchant Fleet (displacement, '000 grt at 31 December): 479.4 in 2004; 478.8 in 2005; 478.5 in 2006. Source: Lloyd's Register-Fairplay, *World Fleet Statistics*.

International Sea-borne Shipping (freight traffic, '000 freight tons, 2005): Goods loaded 87.9; Goods unloaded 1,675.9. Note: One freight ton equals 40 cubic feet (1.133 cubic metres) of cargo.

Civil Aviation (million, 2004): Kilometres flown 28; Passengers carried 1; Passenger-km 3,591; Total ton-km 473. Source: UN, *Statistical Yearbook*.

TOURISM

Foreign Visitor Arrivals by Nationality (arrivals at national borders, 2005): Indonesia 43,421; Malaysia 667,692; Philippines 46,853; Singapore 8,109; United Kingdom 10,129; Total (incl. others) 815,054. Source: World Tourism Organization.

Tourism Receipts (US $ million): 38 in 1996; 39 in 1997; 37 in 1998. Source: World Bank.

COMMUNICATIONS MEDIA

Radio Receivers (2000, estimate): 362,712 in use.

Television Receivers (2000, estimate): 216,223 in use.

Telephones (2006): 80,200 direct exchange lines in use. Source: International Telecommunication Union.

Facsimile Machines (1996, estimate): 2,000 in use. Source: UN, *Statistical Yearbook*.

Mobile Cellular Telephones ('000 subscribers, 2006): 254.0.

Personal Computers ('000 in use, 2004): 31. Source: International Telecommunication Union.

Internet Users ('000, 2006): 165.6. Source: International Telecommunication Union.

Broadband Subscribers ('000, 2006): 10.5. Source: International Telecommunication Union.

Book Production (1992): 25 titles; 56,000 copies. *1998:* 38 titles. Source: UNESCO, *Statistical Yearbook*.

Newspapers (2002): Daily 4; Non-daily 3 (English 2, with circulation of 22,000 copies; Malay 3, with circulation of 39,500 copies; Malay and English 1, with circulation of 10,000 copies).

Other Periodicals (1998): 15 (estimated combined circulation 132,000 copies per issue).

EDUCATION

Pre-primary and Primary (2006): 211 schools (including some schools also offering secondary education), 4,382 teachers and 58,885 pupils.

General Secondary (2006): 34 schools (excluding schools offering primary education also), 3,986 teachers and 42,997 pupils.

Nursing/Technical/Vocational (2006): 13 colleges, 540 teachers and 3,168 students.

Teacher Training (2006): 1 college, 45 teachers and 417 students.

Higher Education: 3 institutes (incl. 1 university) in 2006; 488 teachers and 4,242 students in 2005.

Adult Literacy Rate (UNESCO estimates): 92.7% (males 95.2%; females 90.2%) in 2004. Source: UNESCO Institute for Statistics.

Directory

The Constitution

Note: Certain sections of the Constitution relating to elections and the Legislative Council were in abeyance between 1962 and 2004.

A new Constitution was promulgated on 29 September 1959 (and amended significantly in 1971 and 1984). Under its provisions, sovereign authority is vested in the Sultan and Yang Di-Pertuan (Head of State), who is assisted and advised by five Councils: the Religious Council, the Privy Council, the Council of Cabinet Ministers, the Legislative Council and the Council of Succession. Power of appointment to the Councils is exercised by the Sultan.

The 1959 Constitution established the Chief Minister as the most senior official, with the British High Commissioner as adviser to the Government on all matters except those relating to Muslim and Malay customs.

In 1971 amendments were introduced reducing the power of the British Government, which retained responsibility for foreign affairs, while defence became the joint responsibility of both countries.

In 1984 further amendments were adopted as Brunei acceded to full independence and assumed responsibility for defence and foreign affairs.

BRUNEI

Directory

In 2004 further amendments were approved by the newly reconvened Legislative Council, allowing for an expanded Council of 45 members, including 15 directly elected members.

THE RELIGIOUS COUNCIL
In his capacity as head of the Islamic faith in Brunei, the Sultan and Yang Di-Pertuan is advised on all Islamic matters by the Religious Council, whose members are appointed by the Sultan and Yang Di-Pertuan.

THE PRIVY COUNCIL
This Council, presided over by the Sultan and Yang Di-Pertuan, is to advise the Sultan on matters concerning the Royal prerogative of mercy, the amendment of the Constitution and the conferment of ranks, titles and honours.

THE COUNCIL OF CABINET MINISTERS
Presided over by the Sultan and Yang Di-Pertuan, the Council of Cabinet Ministers considers all executive matters.

THE LEGISLATIVE COUNCIL
The role of the Legislative Council is to scrutinize legislation. However, following political unrest in 1962, provisions of the Constitution relating, *inter alia*, to the Legislative Council were amended, and the Legislative Council did not meet between 1984 and 2004. In the absence of the Legislative Council, legislation is enacted by royal proclamation.

In July 2004 the Sultan announced that the Legislative Council would be reinstated by the end of that year. It was duly reconvened in September. Its 21 members were appointed by a governmental committee. However, the state of emergency that had been declared in 1962 was to remain in force and the Sultan was to continue to rule by decree.

In September 2005 the Sultan dissolved the existing Legislative Council and appointed a new Council comprising 29 members.

THE COUNCIL OF SUCCESSION
Subject to the Constitution, this Council is to determine the succession to the throne, should the need arise.

ADMINISTRATIVE DISTRICTS
The State is divided into four administrative districts, in each of which is a District Officer responsible to the Prime Minister and Minister of Home Affairs.

The Government

HEAD OF STATE
Sultan and Yang Di-Pertuan: HM Sultan Haji HASSANAL BOLKIAH (succeeded 5 October 1967; crowned 1 August 1968).

COUNCIL OF CABINET MINISTERS
(April 2008)

Prime Minister, Minister of Defence and of Finance: HM Sultan Haji HASSANAL BOLKIAH.
Senior Minister at the Prime Minister's Office: HRH Prince Haji AL-MUHTADEE BILLAH BOLKIAH.
Minister of Foreign Affairs and Trade: HRH Prince Haji MOHAMED BOLKIAH.
Minister of Home Affairs and Special Adviser to the Prime Minister: Pehin Dato' Haji ADANAN BIN Pehin Dato' Haji MOHAMMAD YUSOF.
Minister of Education: Pehin Dato' Haji ABDUL RAHMAN TAIB.
Minister of Industry and Primary Resources: Dato' Seri Paduka Dr Haji AHMAD BIN Haji JUMAT.
Minister of Religious Affairs: Pehin Dato' Dr Haji MOHAMAD ZAIN BIN Haji SERUDIN.
Minister of Development: Pehin Dato' Paduka Haji ABDULLAH BIN Haji BAKAR.
Minister of Health: Pehin Dato' Paduka Haji SUYOI BIN Haji OSMAN.
Minister of Culture, Youth and Sports: Pehin Dato' Haji MOHAMMAD BIN Haji DAUD.
Minister of Communications: Pehin Dato' Haji ABU BAKAR BIN Haji APONG.
Minister of Energy: Pehin Dato' Paduka Haji YAHYA BIN Haji BAKAR.
Minister of Finance II: Pehin Dato' Paduka Haji ABDULLAH RAHMAN BIN Haji IBRAHIM.
Minister of Foreign Affairs and Trade II: Pehin Dato' Seri Paduka LIM JOCK SENG.

There are, in addition, 10 deputy ministers.

MINISTRIES
Office of the Prime Minister (Jabatan Perdana Menteri): Istana Nurul Iman, Bandar Seri Begawan BA 1000; tel. 2223626; fax 2228106; e-mail info@pmo.gov.bn; internet www.pmo.gov.bn.

Ministry of Communications (Kementerian Perhubungan): Jalan Menteri Besar, Bandar Seri Begawan BB 3910; tel. 2383838; fax 2380127; e-mail info@mincom.gov.bn; internet www.mincom.gov.bn.

Ministry of Culture, Youth and Sports (Kementerian Kebudayaan, Belia dan Sukan): Simpang 336-17, Jalan Kebangsaan, Bandar Seri Begawan BA 1210; tel. 2380667; fax 2380235; e-mail info@kkbs.gov.bn; internet www.kkbs.gov.bn.

Ministry of Defence (Kementerian Pertahanan): Bolkiah Garrison, Bandar Seri Begawan BB 3510; tel. 2386371; fax 2331615; e-mail info@mindef.gov.bn; internet www.mindef.gov.bn.

Ministry of Development (Kementerian Pembangunan): Old Airport, Jalan Berakas, Bandar Seri Begawan BB 3510; tel. 2241911; e-mail info@mod.gov.bn; internet www.mod.gov.bn.

Ministry of Education (Kementerian Pendidikan): Old Airport, Jalan Berakas, Bandar Seri Begawan BB 3510; tel. 2382233; fax 2380050; e-mail feedback@moe.edu.bn; internet www.moe.gov.bn.

Ministry of Energy: Office of the Prime Minister, Istana Nurul Iman, Bandar Seri Begawan BA 1000; tel. 2383001; fax 2384455.

Ministry of Finance (Kementerian Kewangan): Tingkat 5, Bangunan Kementerian Kewangan, Commonwealth Dr., Jalan Kebangsaan, Bandar Seri Begawan BB 3910; tel. 2241991; fax 2226132; e-mail info@finance.gov.bn; internet www.finance.gov.bn.

Ministry of Foreign Affairs and Trade (Kementerian Hal Ehwal Luar Negeri dan Perdagangan): Jalan Subok, Bandar Seri Begawan BD 2710; tel. 2261293; fax 2262904; e-mail info@mfa.gov.bn; internet www.mfa.gov.bn.

Ministry of Health (Kementerian Kesihatan): Jalan Menteri Besar, Bandar Seri Begawan BB 3910; tel. 2226640; fax 2240980; e-mail moh2@brunet.bn; internet www.moh.gov.bn.

Ministry of Home Affairs (Kementerian Hal Ehwal Dalam Negeri): Jalan Menteri Besar, Bandar Seri Begawan BB 3910; tel. 2223225; e-mail info@home-affairs.gov.bn; internet www.home-affairs.gov.bn.

Ministry of Industry and Primary Resources (Kementerian Perindustrian dan Sumber-sumber Utama): Jalan Menteri Besar, Bandar Seri Begawan BB 3910; tel. 2382822; fax 2382807; e-mail MIPRS2@brunet.bn; internet www.industry.gov.bn.

Ministry of Religious Affairs (Kementerian Hal Ehwal Ugama): Jalan Menteri Besar, Jalan Berakas, Bandar Seri Begawan BB 3910; tel. 2382525; fax 2382330; e-mail info@religious-affairs.gov.bn; internet www.religious-affairs.gov.bn.

Legislature

THE LEGISLATIVE COUNCIL
In September 2005 the Sultan dissolved the existing Legislative Council and appointed a new Council comprising 29 members.

Speaker: Haji MOHAMMED YASSIN.

Political Organizations

Parti Pembangunan Bangsa (PPB) (National Development Party): Bandar Seri Begawan BS 1710; tel. 2459500; f. 2005; Pres. MUHAMMAD YASIN AFFENDY BIN ABDUL RAHMAN; Sec.-Gen. Haji AMINORASHID Haji GHAZALI.

Parti Perpaduan Kebangsaan Brunei (PPKB) (Brunei National Solidarity Party—BNSP): Bandar Seri Begawan; f. 1986 after split in PKDB (see below); ceased political activity in 1988, but re-emerged in 1995; Pres. Dr Haji ABDUL BIN CHUCHU.

Former political organizations included: Parti Rakyat Brunei (PRB—Brunei People's Party), banned in 1962 and leaders all exiled; Barisan Kemerdeka'an Rakyat (BAKER—People's Independence Front), f. 1966 but no longer active; Parti Perpaduan Kebangsaan Rakyat Brunei (PERKARA—Brunei People's National United Party), f. 1968 but no longer active; and Parti Kebangsaan Demokratik Brunei (PKDB—Brunei National Democratic Party—BNDP), f. 1985 and dissolved by government order in 1988.

BRUNEI — Directory

Diplomatic Representation

EMBASSIES AND HIGH COMMISSIONS IN BRUNEI

Australia: Level 6, DAR Takaful IBB Utama, Jalan Pemancha, Bandar Seri Begawan BS 8711; tel. 2229435; fax 2221652; e-mail austhicom.brunei@dfat.gov.au; internet www.bruneidarussalam.embassy.gov.au; High Commissioner RUTH ADLER.

Bangladesh: 10 Simpang 83-20, Jalan Sungai Akar, Kampong Sungai Akar, Bandar Seri Begawan BC 3915; tel. 2342420; fax 2342421; e-mail bdoot@brunet.bn; High Commissioner MOHAMMAD HEDAYATUL ISLAM CHOWDHURY.

Cambodia: 8 Simpang 845, Kampong Tasek, Meradun, Jalan Tutong, Bandar Seri Begawan BF 1520; tel. 2654046; fax 2650646; e-mail cambodia@brunet.bn; Ambassador NAN SY.

Canada: 5th Floor, Jalan McArthur Bldg, 1 Jalan McArthur, Bandar Seri Begawan BS 8711; tel. 2220043; fax 2220040; e-mail bsbgn@international.gc.ca; internet www.dfait-maeci.gc.ca/Brunei; High Commissioner LÉOPOLD BATTEL.

China, People's Republic: 1, 3 & 5 Simpang 462, Kampong Sungai Hanching, Jalan Muara, Bandar Seri Begawan BC 2115; tel. 2334163; fax 2335710; e-mail chinaemb.bn@mfa.gov.cn; internet bn.china-embassy.org/eng; Ambassador TONG XIAOLING.

France: Kompleks Jalan Sultan, Units 301–306, 3rd Floor, 51–55 Jalan Sultan, Bandar Seri Begawan BS 8811; tel. 2220960; fax 2243373; e-mail france@brunet.bn; internet www.ambafrance-bn.org; Ambassador PATRICK BONNEVILLE.

Germany: Kompleks Bangunan Yayasan Sultan Haji Hassanal Bolkiah, Unit 2.01, Block A, 2nd Floor, Jalan Pretty, Bandar Seri Begawan BS 8711; tel. 2225547; fax 2225583; e-mail prgerman@brunet.bn; internet www.bandar-seri-begawan.diplo.de; Ambassador CONRAD KARL CAPPELL.

India: 'Baitussyifaa', Simpang 40–22, Jalan Sungai Akar, Bandar Seri Begawan BC 3915; tel. 2339947; fax 2339783; e-mail hicomind@brunet.bn; internet www.brunet.bn/gov/emb/india; High Commissioner R. V. WARJRI.

Indonesia: Simpang 528, Lot 4498, Kampong Sungai Hanching Baru, Jalan Muara, Bandar Seri Begawan BC 2115; tel. 2330180; fax 2330646; e-mail kbribsb@brunet.bn; Ambassador HERIJANTO SOEPRAPTO.

Iran: 400 Kampong Anggerek Desa, Berakas, Bandar Seri Begawan BB 3717; tel. 2330020; fax 2330021; Ambassador ABOLFAZL KHAZAEI TARSHIZI.

Japan: 1 & 3 Jalan Jawatan Dalam, Lot 37355, 33 Simpang 122, Kampong Kiulap, Bandar Seri Begawan BE 1518; tel. 2229265; fax 2229481; e-mail embassy@japan.com.bn; internet www.bn.emb-japan.go.jp; Ambassador NISAKA YOSHINOBU.

Korea, Republic: 17 Simpang 462, Kampong Hancing Baru, Jalan Muara, Bandar Seri Begawan BC 2115; tel. 2330248; fax 2330254; e-mail koreaemb@brunet.bn; Ambassador HWANG WONG-KUN.

Laos: Lot 19824, 11 Simpang 480, Jalan Kebangsaan Lama, off Jalan Muara, Bandar Seri Begawan BC 4115; tel. 2345666; fax 2345888; e-mail LAOSEMBA@brunet.bn; Ambassador BOUNTHONG VONGSALY.

Malaysia: 61 Simpang 336, Jalan Kebangsaan, Kampong Sungai Akar, Bandar Seri Begawan BC 1211; tel. 2345652; fax 2345654; e-mail mwbrunei@brunet.bn; High Commissioner Datuk ALI ABDULLAH.

Myanmar: 14 Lot 2185/46292, Simpang 212, Jalan Kampong Rimba, Gadong, Bandar Seri Begawan BE 3119; tel. 2450506; fax 2451008; e-mail myanmar@brunet.bn; Ambassador U TIN HTUN.

Oman: 35 Simpang 100, Kampong Pengkalan, Jalan Tungku Link, Gadong, Bandar Seri Begawan BE 3719; tel. 2446953; fax 2449646; e-mail omnembsb@brunet.bn; Ambassador AHMAD BIN MOHAMMED BIN ZAHER AL-HINAI.

Pakistan: 8 Simpang 31, Jalan Bunga Jasmin, Beribi, Gadong, Bandar Seri Begawan; tel. 2424600; fax 2424603; e-mail hcpak@brunet.bn; internet www.brunet.bn/gov/emb/pakistan; High Commissioner Maj.-Gen. (retd) SYED HAIDAR JAWED.

Philippines: 17 Simpang 126, Km 2, Jalan Tutong, Bandar Seri Begawan BA 2111; tel. 2241465; fax 2237707; e-mail bruneipe@brunet.bn; Ambassador VIRGINIA H. BENAVIDEZ.

Saudi Arabia: 1 Simpang 570, Kampong Salar, Jalan Muara, Bandar Seri Begawan BA 1429; tel. 2792821; fax 2792826; e-mail saudibru@brunet.bn; Ambassador ESAM BIN AHMED BIN JAMAL ABID AL-THAGAFI.

Singapore: 8 Simpang 74, Jalan Subok, Bandar Seri Begawan; tel. 2262741; fax 2262743; e-mail singhc_bwn@sgmfa.gov.sg; internet www.mfa.gov.sg/brunei; High Commissioner JOSEPH K. H. KOH.

Thailand: 2 Simpang 682, Jalan Tutong, Kampong Bunut, Bandar Seri Begawan BF 1320; tel. 2653108; fax 2653032; e-mail thaiemb@brunet.bn; Ambassador SORNSILP POLTEJA.

United Kingdom: POB 2197, Bandar Seri Begawan BS 8674; tel. 2222231; fax 2234315; e-mail brithc@brunet.bn; internet www.britishhighcommission.gov.uk/brunei; High Commissioner JOHN SAVILLE.

USA: Teck Guan Plaza, 3rd Floor, Jalan Sultan, Bandar Seri Begawan BS 8811; tel. 2220384; fax 2225293; e-mail amembassy_bsb@state.gov; internet bandar.usembassy.gov; Ambassador EMIL SKODON.

Viet Nam: 9 Simpang 148-3, Jalan Telanai, Bandar Seri Begawan BA 2312; tel. 2456483; fax 2456485; e-mail vnembassy@yahoo.com; Ambassador HA HONG HAI.

Judicial System

SUPREME COURT

The Supreme Court consists of the Court of Appeal and the High Court. Syariah (*Shari'a*) courts coexist with the Supreme Court and deal with Islamic laws.

Office of the Supreme Court

Km 11/2, Jalan Tutong, Bandar Seri Begawan BA 1910; tel. 2225853; fax 2241984; e-mail judiciarybn@hotmail.com; internet www.judicial.gov.bn/supr_court.htm.

Chief Registrar: Haji HAIROLARNI ABDULLAH MAJID.

The Court of Appeal

Composed of the President and two Commissioners appointed by the Sultan. The Court of Appeal considers criminal and civil appeals against the decisions of the High Court and the Intermediate Court. The Court of Appeal is the highest appellate court for criminal cases. In civil cases an appeal may be referred to the Judicial Committee of Her Majesty's Privy Council in London if all parties agree to do so before the hearing of the appeal in the Brunei Court of Appeal.

President: Sir NOEL PLUNKETT POWER.

The High Court

Composed of the Chief Justice and judges sworn in by the Sultan as Commissioners of the Supreme Court. In its appellate jurisdiction, the High Court considers appeals in criminal and civil matters against the decisions of the Subordinate Courts. The High Court has unlimited original jurisdiction in criminal and civil matters.

Chief Justice: Dato' Seri Paduka MOHAMMED SAIED.

OTHER COURTS

Intermediate Courts: have jurisdiction to try all offences other than those punishable by the death sentence and civil jurisdiction to try all actions and suits of a civil nature where the amount in dispute or value of the subject/matter does not exceed B $100,000.

The Subordinate Courts

Presided over by the Chief Magistrate and magistrates, with limited original jurisdiction in civil and criminal matters and civil jurisdiction to try all actions and suits of a civil nature where the amount in dispute does not exceed B $50,000 (for Chief Magistrate) and B $30,000 (for magistrates).

Chief Magistrate: ROSTAINA BINTI Pengiran Haji DURAMAN.

The Courts of Kathis

Deal solely with questions concerning Islamic religion, marriage and divorce. Appeals lie from these courts to the Sultan in the Religious Council.

Chief Kathi: Dato' Seri SETIA Haji SALIM BIN Haji BESAR.

Attorney-General: Dato' Paduka Haji KIFRAWI BIN Dato' Paduka Haji KIFLI, Attorney-General's Chambers, The Law Bldg, Km 1, Jalan Tutong, Bandar Seri Begawan BA 1910; tel. 2244872; fax 2223100; e-mail info@agc.gov.bn; internet www.agc.gov.bn.

Solicitor-General: Datin Paduka MAGDALENE CHONG.

Religion

The official religion of Brunei is Islam, and the Sultan is head of the Islamic community. The majority of the Malay population are Muslims of the Shafi'is school of the Sunni sect; at the 1991 census Muslims accounted for 67.2% of the total population. The Chinese population is either Buddhist (accounting for 12.8% of the total population at the 1991 census), Confucianist, Daoist or Christian. Large numbers of the indigenous ethnic groups practise traditional animist forms of religion. The remainder of the population are mostly Christians, generally Roman Catholics, Anglicans or members of the American Methodist Church of Southern Asia. At the 1991 census Christians accounted for 10.0% of the total population.

BRUNEI   *Directory*

ISLAM
Supreme Head of Islam: HM Sultan Haji HASSANAL BOLKIAH (Sultan and Yang Di-Pertuan).

CHRISTIANITY
The Anglican Communion
Within the Church of the Province of South East Asia, Brunei forms part of the diocese of Kuching (Malaysia).

The Roman Catholic Church
Brunei comprises a single apostolic prefecture. At December 2005 an estimated 6.2% of the population were adherents.
Prefect Apostolic: Rev. CORNELIUS SIM, Church of Our Lady of the Assumption, POB 527, Bandar Seri Begawan BS 8671; tel. 2222261; fax 2238938; e-mail frcsim@brunet.bn; internet www.bruneicola.com.

The Press
NEWSPAPERS
Borneo Bulletin: Locked Bag No. 2, MPC (Old Airport, Berakas), Bandar Seri Begawan BB 3510; tel. 2451468; fax 2451461; e-mail brupress@brunet.bn; internet www.brunet.bn/news/bb; f. 1953; daily; English; independent; owned by QAF Group; Editor CHARLES REX DE SILVA; circ. 25,000.

Brunei Darussalam Newsletter: Dept of Information, Prime Minister's Office, Istana Nurul Iman, Berakas, Bandar Seri Begawan BB 3510; tel. 2383400; fax 2382012; e-mail info@bruneinewsletter.info; internet www.bruneinewsletter.info; monthly; English; govt newspaper; distributed free; Chief Editor Haji MAHRUB Haji MURNI; Editor SASTRA SARINI BINTI Haji JULAINI; circ. 3,000.

The Brunei Times: Wisma Haji Mohd Taha, 3rd Floor, Jalan Gadong, Bandar Seri Begawan BC 4119; tel. 2428333; fax 2454752; e-mail theeditor@bruneitimes.com.bn; internet www.bruneitimes.com; f. 2006; daily; English; Editor-in-Chief Haji JOHARI ACHEE.

Daily News Digest: Dept of Information, Prime Minister's Office, Istana Nurul Iman, Bandar Seri Begawan BA 1000; English; govt newspaper.

Media Permata: Locked Bag No. 2, MPC (Old Airport, Berakas), Bandar Seri Begawan BB 3510; tel. 2451468; fax 2451461; e-mail mediapermata@brunet.bn; internet www.brunei-online.com/mp; f. 1995; daily (not Sun.); Malay; owned by QAF Group; Editor ABDUL LATIF; circ. 10,000.

Pelita Brunei: Dept of Information, Prime Minister's Office, Old Airport, Berakas BB 3510; tel. 2383941; fax 2381004; e-mail pelita@brunet.bn; internet www.brunet.bn/news/pelita; f. 1956; weekly (Wed.); Malay; govt newspaper; distributed free; Editor TIMBANG BIN BAKAR; circ. 27,500.

Salam: c/o Brunei Shell Petroleum Co Sdn Bhd, Seria KB 3534; tel. 3375951; fax 3374189; e-mail editorial@shell.com; internet www.bsp.com.bn/main/mediacentre/publications.asp; f. 1953; monthly; Malay and English; distributed free to employees and shareholders of the Brunei Shell Petroleum Co Sdn Bhd; Editor AZRINA TAIB; circ. 46,000.

Publishers

Borneo Printers & Trading Sdn Bhd: POB 2211, Bandar Seri Begawan BS 8674; tel. 2651387; fax 2654342; e-mail bptl@brunet.bn.

Brunei Press Sdn Bhd: Lots 8 & 11, Perindustrian Beribi II, Jalan Gadong, Bandar Seri Begawan BE 1118; tel. 2451468; fax 2451462; e-mail brupress@brunet.bn; internet www.bruneipress.com.bn; f. 1953; Gen. Man. REGGIE SEE.

Capital Trading & Printing Pte Ltd: POB 1089, Bandar Seri Begawan; tel. 2244541.

Leong Bros: 52 Jalan Bunga Kuning, POB 164, Seria; tel. 322381.

Offset Printing House: Lot Q37, 4 Simpang 5, Lambak Kanan Industrial Area, Berakas, Bandar Seri Begawan BB 1714; tel. 2390797; fax 2390798; e-mail offset@brunei.bn; f. 1980; Gen. Man. KENNY TEO.

The Star Press: Bandar Seri Begawan; f. 1963; Man. F. W. ZIMMERMAN.

GOVERNMENT PUBLISHING HOUSE
Government Printer: Government Printing Department, Office of the Prime Minister, Bandar Seri Begawan BB 3510; tel. 2382541; fax 2381141; e-mail jpkkuu@brunet.bn; internet www.printing.gov.bn; f. 1975; Dir MOHIDIN Haji DAUD.

Broadcasting and Communications
TELECOMMUNICATIONS
Authority for Info-Communications Technology Industry (AiTi): Block B14, Simpang 32–35, Kampong Anggrek Desa, Jalan Berakas, Bandar Seri Begawan BB 3713; tel. 2323232; fax 2382447; e-mail info@aiti.gov.bn; internet www.aiti.gov.bn; f. 2003; assumed responsibility for regulating and representing the telecommunications industry following the corporatization of the Dept of Telecommunications of Brunei in April 2006; also entrusted with the development of the information and communication technology industry; Chair. Dato' Paduka Haji MOHAMMAD YUSSOF Haji MOHAMMAD HASSAN.

DST Communications Sdn Bhd: 1st Floor, Block D, Yayasan Sultan Haji Hassanal Bolkiah Kompleks, Bandar Seri Begawan BS 8711; tel. 2232323; fax 2232922; internet www.dst-group.com/dstcom; mobile service provider; signed agreement with Alcatel in 2003 to improve provision of mobile services in Brunei; Man. Dir Pengiran Haji MOHAMED ZIN BIN Pengiran DAMIT.

Telekom Brunei Bhd (TelBru): Bangunan Ibu Pejabat Telekom Brunei, Old Airport, Jalan Berakas, Bandar Seri Begawan BB 3510; tel. 2321321; fax 2382444; internet www.telbru.com.bn; fmrly known as Jabatan Telekom Brunei (Dept of Telecommunications of Brunei); name changed as above upon corporatization in April 2006; telecommunications services provider; Chair. Dato' Paduka Haji OTHMAN BIN Haji YAAKUB; Man. Dir SONG KIN KOI.

BROADCASTING
Radio
Radio Televisyen Brunei (RTB): Prime Minister's Office, Jalan Elizabeth II, Bandar Seri Begawan BS 8610; tel. 2243111; fax 2241882; e-mail gts@rtb.gov.bn; internet www.rtb.gov.bn; f. 1957; five radio networks: four broadcasting in Malay, the other in English, Chinese (Mandarin) and Gurkhali; also broadcasts on the internet; Dir Haji OSMAN Haji MOHAMMAD (acting).

The British Forces Broadcasting Service (Military) broadcasts a 24-hour radio service to a limited area.

Television
Kristal Astro Sdn Bhd: Unit 1-345, 1st Floor, Gadong Properties Centre, Gadong, Bandar Seri Begawan BE 4119; tel. 2456828; fax 2420682; f. 2000; jt venture between Kristal Sdn Bhd and Malaysian Measat Broadcast Network Systems Sdn Bhd; provides more than 30 digital satellite subscription channels.

Kristal TV: DST Network Sdn Bhd, Unit 1-345, 1st Floor, Gadong Properties Centre, Gadong, Bandar Seri Begawan BE 4119; tel. 2456828; fax 2420682; f. 1999; 14 television channels.

Radio Televisyen Brunei (RTB): Prime Minister's Office, Jalan Elizabeth II, Bandar Seri Begawan BS 8610; tel. 2243111; fax 2241882; e-mail director@rtb.gov.bn; internet rtbinfo@rtb.gov.bn; f. 1975; three television channels, incl. one satellite channel; five radio channels; Dir Haji OSMAN Haji MOHAMMAD (acting).

Finance
(cap. = capital; res = reserves; dep. = deposits; brs = branches; amounts in Brunei dollars unless otherwise stated)

BANKING
The Department of Financial Services (Treasury), the Brunei Currency and Monetary Board and the Brunei Investment Agency (see Government Agencies, below), under the Ministry of Finance, perform most of the functions of a central bank. In 2004 there were 11 banks, including six foreign banks and two offshore banks.

Commercial Banks
Baiduri Bank Bhd: Block A, Units 1–4, Kiarong Complex, Lebuhraya Sultan Hassanal Bolkiah, Bandar Seri Begawan BE 1318; tel. 2268300; fax 2455599; e-mail bank@baiduri.com; internet www.baiduri.com; f. 1994; cap. 30m., res 32.0m., dep. 1,329.7m. (Dec. 2003); Chair. Pengiran ANAK ISTERI Pengiran ANAK HAJJAH ZARIAH; Gen. Man. PIERRE IMHOF; 10 brs.

Islamic Bank of Brunei Bhd: Lot 159, Bangunan IBB, Jalan Pemancha, POB 2725, Bandar Seri Begawan BS 8711; tel. 2235687; fax 2235722; e-mail ibb@brunet.bn; internet www.ibb.com.bn; f. 1981 as Island Development Bank; name changed from International Bank of Brunei Bhd to present name in Jan. 1993; practises

Islamic banking principles; plans for merger with Islamic Development Bank of Brunei Bhd announced in Feb. 2006; Chair. Haji ABDUL RAHMAN bin Haji ABDUL KARIM; Man. Dir Haji ZAINASALLEHEN BIN Haji MOHAMED TAHIR; 13 brs.

Islamic Development Bank of Brunei Bhd (IDBB): Ground–4th Floors, Kompleks Setia Kenangan, Kampong Kiulap, Jalan Gadong, Bandar Seri Begawan BE 1518; tel. 2233430; fax 2233540; e-mail dbbcom@brunet.bn; internet www.idbb-bank.com.bn; f. 1995 as Development Bank of Brunei Bhd; name changed to present in July 2000; practises Islamic banking principles; plans for merger with the Islamic Bank of Brunei Bhd announced in Feb. 2006; Chair. Pehin Dato' Haji AHMAD WALLY SKINNER; Man. Dir Pengiran Datin Paduka Hajah URAI Pengiran ALI; 4 brs.

Foreign Banks

Citibank NA (USA): Darussalam Complex, 12–15 Jalan Sultan, Bandar Seri Begawan BS 8811; tel. 2243983; fax 2237344; e-mail glen.rase@citicorp.com; Country Head GLEN RASE; 2 brs.

The Hongkong and Shanghai Banking Corpn Ltd (HSBC) (Hong Kong): Jalan Sultan, cnr Jalan Pemancha, Bandar Seri Begawan BS 8811; tel. 2252252; fax 2241316; e-mail hsbc@hsbc.com.bn; internet www.hsbc.com.bn; f. 1947; acquired assets of National Bank of Brunei in 1986; CEO TAREQ MUHMOOD; 10 brs.

Maybank (Malaysia): 1 Jalan McArthur, Bandar Seri Begawan BS 8711; tel. 2226462; fax 2226404; e-mail maybank@brunet.bn; f. 1960; Country Man. AZIZUL ABDUL RASHID; 3 brs.

RHB Bank Bhd (Malaysia): Unit G.02, Block D, Kompleks Bangunan Yayasan Sultan Haji Hassanal Bolkiah, Ground Floor, Jalan Pretty, Bandar Seri Begawan BS 8711; tel. 2231329; fax 2237487; e-mail rhbbsb@brunet.bn; internet www.rhbbank.com.my/cbob/brunei.shtm; fmrly Sime Bank Bhd; Country Man. APANDI BIN KLOMPOT; 1 br.

Standard Chartered Bank (United Kingdom): 1st Floor, 51–55 Jalan Sultan, POB 186, Bandar Seri Begawan BS 8811; tel. 2242386; fax 2220103; e-mail scb.brunei@bn.standardchartered.com; internet www.standardchartered.com/bn; f. 1958; CEO HANS THEILKUHL; 8 brs.

United Overseas Bank Ltd (Singapore): Units 10–11, Bangunan D'Amin Jaya, Lot 54989, Kampong Kiarong, Bandar Seri Begawan BE 1318; tel. 2225477; fax 2240792; f. 1973; Gen. Man. GEORGE LAI TED MIN; 2 brs.

Offshore Banks

The Brunei International Financial Centre (BIFC), under the Ministry of Finance, supervises the activities of the offshore banking sector in Brunei.

Royal Bank of Canada: 1 Jalan McArthur 4A, 4th Floor, Bandar Seri Begawan BS 8711; tel. 2224366; fax 2224368; internet www.rbcprivatebanking.com/brunei; Gen. Man. MATTHEW YONG.

Sun Hung Kai International Bank (Brunei) Ltd (Hong Kong): Bandar Seri Begawan; f. 2004; Dir P. H. MARK.

STOCK EXCHANGE

In May 2002 the International Brunei Exchange Ltd (IBX) was granted an exclusive licence to establish an international securities exchange in Brunei.

International Brunei Exchange Ltd (IBX): The Empire, Muara-Tutong Highway, Jerudong BG 3122; tel. 2611222; fax 2611020; e-mail info@ibx.com.bn; f. 2001; CEO B. C. YONG.

INSURANCE

General Companies

The Asia Insurance Co Ltd: Unit A1 & A2, 1st Floor, Block A, Bangunan Hau Man Yong, Simpang 88, Kampong Kiulap, Bandar Seri Begawan BE 1518; tel. 2236100; fax 2236102; e-mail asiains_d.wong@brunet.bn; f. 1929; Br. Man. DAVID WONG KOK MIN.

Aviva Insurance Bhd: Unit 311, 3rd Floor, Kompleks Mohd Yussof, Mile 1½, Jalan Tutong, Bandar Seri Begawan BA 1714; tel. 2223632; fax 2220965; e-mail aviva@brunet.bn; fmrly CGU Insurance Bhd; Man. LIANG VOON CHIANG.

AXA Insurance (B) Sdn Bhd: Units 604–606, 6th Floor, Jalan Sultan Complex, 51–55 Jalan Sultan, Bandar Seri Begawan BS 8811; tel. 2226138; fax 2243474; fmrly GRE Insurance (B) Sdn Bhd; Man. MOK HAI TONG.

BALGI Insurance (B) Sdn Bhd: Unit 7, Simpang 88, Bangunan Haji Ahmad bin Hassan and Anak-Anak, Kampong Kiulap, Bandar Seri Begawan BE 1518; tel. 2234020; fax 2233981; Man. Dir PATRICK SIM SONG JUAY.

Borneo Insurance Sdn Bhd: Unit 103, Bangunan Kambang Pasang, Km 2, Jalan Gadong, Bandar Seri Begawan BE 4119; tel. 2420550; fax 2428550; Man. LIM TECK LEE.

Cosmic Insurance Corpn Sdn Bhd: Block J, Unit 11, Abdul Razak Complex, 1st Floor, Jalan Gadong, Bandar Seri Begawan BE 3919; tel. 2427112; fax 2427114; Man. RONNIE WONG.

ING General Insurance International NV: Shop Lot 86, 2nd Floor, Jalan Bunga Raya, Kuala Belait KA 1131; tel. 3335338; fax 3335338; Man. SHERRY SOON PECK ENG.

Liberty Citystate Insurance Pte Ltd: 1st Floor, Unit 25, Block C, Bangunan Hau Man Yong Complex, Simpang 88, Kampong Kiulap, Bandar Seri Begawan BE 1518; tel. 2238282; fax 2236848; e-mail libertyintl@brunet.bn; Man. ROBERT LAI CHIN YIN.

Malaysia National Insurance Bhd: 9 Bangunan Haji Mohd Salleh Simpang 103, 1st Floor, Jalan Gadong, Bandar Seri Begawan BE 4119; tel. 2443393; fax 2427451; e-mail tsang.py@brunet.bn; Man. ANDREW AK NYAGORN.

MBA Insurance Sdn Bhd: First Floor, Units 15–17, Lot 9784, Bangunan Haji Hassan Abdullah, Kampong Menglait, Jalan Gadong, Bandar Seri Begawan BE 3978; tel. 2441535; fax 2441534; e-mail mbabrunei@brunet.bn; Man. CHEAH LYE CHONG.

Motor and General Insurance Sdn Bhd: 6 Bangunan Hasbullah II, Km 4, Jalan Gadong, Bandar Seri Begawan BE 3919; tel. 2440797; fax 2445342; Man. Dir Haji ABDUL AZIZ BIN ABDUL LATIF.

National Insurance Co Bhd: 3rd Floor, Scouts' Headquarters Bldg, Jalan Gadong, Bandar Seri Begawan BE 1118; tel. 2426888; fax 2429888; e-mail insurance@brunet.bn; internet www.national.com.bn; f. 1969; Gen. Man. NICHOLAS CHENG.

Royal and Sun Alliance Insurance (Global) Ltd: Unit 7, 1st Floor, Block B, Kiarong Complex, Lebuhraya Sultan Hassanal Bolkiah, Bandar Seri Begawan BE 1318; tel. 2423233; fax 2423325; Gen. Man. TOMMY LEONG TONG KAW.

South East Asia Insurance (B) Sdn Bhd: Unit 2, Block A, Abdul Razak Complex, 1st Floor, Jalan Gadong, Bandar Seri Begawan BE 3919; tel. 2443842; fax 2420860; Gen. Man. SHIM WEI HSIUNG.

Standard Insurance (B) Sdn Bhd: 2 Bangunan Hasbullah I, Ground Floor, Bandar Seri Begawan BE 3719; tel. 2450077; fax 2450076; e-mail feedback@standard-ins.com; internet www.standard-ins.com; Man. PAUL KONG.

Winterthur Insurance (Far East) Pte Ltd: c/o Borneo Co (B) Sdn Bhd, Lot 9771, Km 3½, Jalan Gadong, Bandar Seri Begawan BE 4119; tel. 2422561; fax 2424352; Gen. Man. ANNA CHONG.

Life Companies

American International Assurance Co Ltd: Unit 509, Wisma Jaya Building, 5th Floor, 85–94 Jalan Pemancha, Bandar Seri Begawan BS 8811; tel. 2239112; fax 2221667; e-mail Kenneth-WC.Ling@AIG.com; Man. SAJAN RAMAN.

The Asia Life Assurance Society Ltd: Unit 2, 1st Floor, Block D, Abdul Razak Complex, Jalan Gadong, Bandar Seri Begawan BE 4119; tel. 2423755; fax 2423754; e-mail asialife@simpur.net.bn; Br. Man. JOSEPH WONG SIONG LION.

The Great Eastern Life Assurance Co Ltd: Suite 1, Badi'ah Complex, 2nd Floor, Jalan Tutong, Bandar Seri Begawan BA 2111; tel. 2243792; fax 2225754; e-mail gelife@brunet.bn; Man. HELEN YEO.

Takaful (Composite Insurance) Companies

Insurans Islam TAIB Sdn Bhd: Bangunan Pusat Komersil dan Perdagangan Bumiputera, Ground Floor, Jalan Cator, Bandar Seri Begawan BS 8811; tel. 2237724; fax 2237729; e-mail insuranstaib@brunet.bn; internet www.insuranstaib.com.bn; f. 1993; provides Islamic insurance products and services; Gen. Man. OSMAN MOHAMAD JAIR.

Takaful Bank Pembangunan Islam Sdn Bhd (TBPISB): Unit 10, Komplex Seri Kiulap, Kampong Kiulap, Gadong, Bandar Seri Begawan BE 1518; tel. 2237220; fax 2237045; internet www.takafulbpisb.com; f. 2001; fmrly Takaful IDBB Sdn Bhd; name changed as above in 2003; Islamic life and non-life insurance products; Chair. Pehin Dato' Haji AHMAD WALLY SKINNER; Man. Dir Haji AISHATUL AKMAR SIDEK.

Takaful IBB Bhd: Unit 5, Block A, Kiarong Complex, Lebuhraya Sultan Hassanal Bolkiah, Bandar Seri Begawan BE 1318; tel. 2451804; fax 2451808; e-mail takaful@brunet.bn; f. 1993; Chair. Pehin Dato' Haji ABU BAKAR BIN Haji APONG DAUD.

Insurance Association

General Insurance Association of Negara Brunei Darussalam (GIAB): Unit C2-2, Block C, Shakirin Complex, Kampong Kiulap, Bandar Seri Begawan BE 1318; tel. 2237898; fax 2237858; e-mail giab@brunet.bn; internet www.giab.com.bn; f. 1986; 15 mems; Chair. DOROTHY NEWN.

Trade and Industry

GOVERNMENT AGENCIES

Brunei Currency and Monetary Board (BCMB): Tingkat 5, Bangunan Kementerian Kewangan, Commonwealth Dr., Jalan Kebangsaan, Bandar Seri Begawan BB 3910; tel. 2383999; fax 2382232; e-mail bcb@brunet.bn; internet www.finance.gov.bn/bcb/bcb_index.htm; f. 1967; maintains control of currency circulation; fmrly Brunei Currency Board; name changed as above Feb. 2004; Chair. HM Sultan Haji HASSANAL BOLKIAH (Minister of Finance); CEO MOHAMED ROSLI SABTU.

Brunei Darussalam Economic Council (BDEC): Bandar Seri Begawan; internet www.brudirect.com/BruneiInfo/info/BD_EconomicCouncil.htm; f. 1998; convened to examine the economic situation in Brunei and to recommend short- and long-term measures designed to revitalize the economy; Chair. HRH Prince MOHAMED BOLKIAH.

Brunei International Financial Centre (BIFC): Tingkat 14, Ministry of Finance, Commonwealth Dr., Jalan Kebangsaan, Bandar Seri Begawan BB 3910; tel. 2383747; fax 2383787; e-mail bifc@finance.gov.bn; internet www.bifc.finance.gov.bn; f. 2000; regulates international financial sector and encourages development of Brunei as investment destination; Dir MOHAMED ROSLI SABTU; CEO ROBERT MILLER.

Brunei Investment Agency: Tingkat 11, Bangunan Kementerian Kewangan, Commonwealth Dr., Jalan Kebangsaan, Bandar Seri Begawan BB 3910; e-mail dramin.abdullah@bia.com.bn; f. 1973; Man. Dir Haji MOHAMMAD AMIN LIEW ABDULLAH.

DEVELOPMENT ORGANIZATIONS

Brunei Economic Development Board (BEDB): Block 2K, Bangunan Kerajaan, Jalan Ong Sum Ping, Bandar Seri Begawan BA 1311; tel. 2230111; fax 2230063; e-mail info@bedb.com.bn; internet www.bedb.com.bn; f. 2001; promotes Brunei as an investment destination; facilitates and assists industrial development; Chair. Dato' TIMOTHY ONG; CEO Dato' Paduka VINCENT CHEONG.

Brunei Industrial Development Authority (BINA): Ministry of Industry and Primary Resources, Km 8, Jalan Gadong, Bandar Seri Begawan BE 1118; tel. 2444100; fax 2423300; e-mail bruneibina@brunet.bn; internet www.bina.gov.bn; f. 1996; Dir SHARIFUDDIN BIN Haji METALI (acting).

Brunei Islamic Trust Fund (Tabung Amanah Islam Brunei): Block A, Unit 2, Ground Floor, Kiarong Complex, Lebuhraya Sultan Hj Hassanal Bolkiah, Bandar Seri Begawan BE 1318; tel. 2452666; fax 2450877; f. 1991; promotes trade and industry; Chair. Haji YAHYA BIN Haji IBRAHIM.

Brunei Trade and Enterprise Development Council: Bandar Seri Begawan; facilitates the industrialization of Brunei; Chair. Dato' Seri Paduka Dr Haji AHMAD BIN Haji JUMAT.

Semaun Holdings Sdn Bhd: Unit 10, Block B, Warisan Mata-Mata Complex, Kg. Mata-Mata, Gadong, BE 1718; tel. 22456064; fax 2456060; e-mail semaun@brunet.bn; internet www.semaunholdings.com; promotes industrial and commercial development through direct investment in key industrial sectors; 100% govt-owned; the board of directors is composed of ministers and senior govt officials; Chair. Pehin Orang Kaya Amar Pahlawan Dato Seri Setia Dr AWG HAJI AHMAD; Dep. Man. Dir HAJAH ASMAH HAJI SAMAN Haji FAIZAL Haji MOHD YAAKUB.

CHAMBERS OF COMMERCE

Brunei Darussalam International Chamber of Commerce and Industry: Unit 401–403A, 4th Floor, Wisma Jaya, Jalan Pemancha, Bandar Seri Begawan BS 8811; tel. 2228382; fax 2228389; Chair. Haji AHMAD BIN Haji ISA; Sec. Haji SHAZALI BIN Dato' Haji SULAIMAN; 108 mems.

Brunei Malay Chamber of Commerce and Industry: Unit B1, 2nd Floor, Lot 44252, Kampong Kiulap, Bandar Seri Begawan BE 1518; tel. 2237113; fax 2237112; f. 1964; Pres. Dato' A. A. HAPIDZ; 160 mems.

Chinese Chamber of Commerce: Chinese Chamber of Commerce Bldg, 2nd–4th Floors, 72 Jalan Roberts, Bandar Seri Begawan BS 8811; tel. 2235494; fax 2235492; e-mail ccc@brunet.bn; Pres. ROBERT KOH HOE KIAT.

Indian Chamber of Commerce: Lot 20021, Taman Aman Complex, Jalan Gadong-Tutong, Kampong Beribi, Bandar Seri Begawan BE 3188; tel. and fax 2650793.

National Chamber of Commerce and Industry of Brunei Darussalam (NCCIBD): Unit 1, Block D, Beribi Industrial Complex 1, Jalan Gadong, Bandar Seri Begawan BE 1118; tel. 2444959; fax 2447397; e-mail abas@nccibd.com; Pres. Haji RAZALI BIN Haji JOHARI; Sec.-Gen. Haji ABDUL SAMAN AHMAD.

STATE HYDROCARBON COMPANIES

Brunei LNG Sdn Bhd: Lumut KC 2935, Seria; tel. 3236901; fax 3236892; e-mail GP-External-Affairs@BruneiLNG.com; internet www.blng.com.bn; f. 1969; natural gas liquefaction; owned jtly by the Brunei Govt (50%), Shell and Mitsubishi Corpn; operates LNG plant at Lumut, which has a capacity of 7.2m. metric tons per year; Man. Dir FRED SMEENK.

Brunei National Petroleum Co Sdn Bhd (PetroleumBrunei): Unit 2.02, 2nd Floor, Block D, Yayasan Sultan Haji Hassanal Bolkiah Complex, Jalan Pretty Bandar Seri Begawan BS 8711; tel. 2230720; fax 2230654; e-mail pb@pb.com.bn; internet www.pb.com.bn; f. 2001; wholly govt-owned; CEO ALIAS Haji MOHD YUSOF (acting).

Brunei Shell Marketing Co Bhd: Maya Puri Bldg, 36/37 Jalan Sultan, POB 385, Bandar Seri Begawan; tel. 2229304; fax 2240470; internet www.bsm.com.bn; f. 1978 (from the Shell Marketing Co of Brunei Ltd), when the Govt became equal partner with Shell; markets petroleum and chemical products throughout Brunei; Man. Dir MAT SUNY Haji MOHD HUSSEIN.

Brunei Shell Petroleum Co Sdn Bhd (BSP): Jalan Utara, Panagia, Seria KB 3534; tel. 3373999; fax 3372040; internet www.shell.com.bn; f. 1957; the largest industrial concern in the country; 50% state holding; Man. Dir MARK CARNE; Dep. Man. Dir Haji ZAINAL ABIDIN Haji MOHAMED ALI.

Jasra International Petroleum Sdn Bhd: RBA Plaza, 2nd Floor, Jalan Sultan, Bandar Seri Begawan; tel. 2228968; fax 2228929; petroleum exploration and production; Man. Dir ROBERT A. HARRISON.

TRADE UNIONS

Trade unions are legal in Brunei, but must be registered with the Government. In 2003 there were three officially registered trade unions, all in the petroleum sector, with a total membership constituting less than 5% of that sector's work-force. These included:

Brunei Oilfield Workers' Union: XDR/11, BSP Co Sdn Bhd, Seria KB 3534; f. 1964; 470 mems; Pres. SUHAINI Haji OTHMAN; Sec.-Gen. ABU TALIB BIN Haji MOHAMAD.

Transport

RAILWAYS

There are no public railways in Brunei. The Brunei Shell Petroleum Co Sdn Bhd maintains a 19.3-km section of light railway between Seria and Badas.

ROADS

In 2000 there were 3,358 km of roads in Brunei, of which 2,468 km were paved. The main highway connects Bandar Seri Begawan, Tutong and Kuala Belait. A 59-km coastal road links Muara and Tutong. The Eighth National Development Plan (2001–05) prioritized the development of Brunei's roads and, in particular, the construction of a network of main roads that would connect Brunei/Muara, Tutong, Kuala Belait and Temburong. In September 2002 construction of the 15-km Jalan Lumut Bypass was completed.

Land Transport Department: Jalan Beribi Gadong, Bandar Seri Begawan BE 1110; tel. 2451979; fax 2424775; e-mail latis@brunet.bn; internet www.land-transport.gov.bn; f. 1962; Dir Haji MOHAMMAD ALIMIN BIN Haji MOHAMMAD TANJONG.

SHIPPING

Most sea traffic is handled by a deep-water port at Muara, 28 km from the capital, which has a 611-m wharf and a draught of 8 m. The port has a container terminal, warehousing, freezer facilities and cement silos. In October 2000 a plan to deepen the port to enable its accommodation of larger vessels was announced. The original, smaller port at Bandar Seri Begawan itself is mainly used for local river-going vessels, for vessels to Malaysian ports in Sabah and Sarawak and for vessels under 30 m in length. There is a port at Kuala Belait, which takes shallow-draught vessels and serves mainly the Shell petroleum field and Seria. At Lumut there is a 4.5-km jetty for liquefied natural gas (LNG) carriers.

Four main rivers, with numerous tributaries, are an important means of communication in the interior, and boats or water taxis are the main form of transport for most residents of the water villages. Larger water taxis operate daily to the Temburong district.

Bee Seng Shipping Co: 7 Block D, Sufri Complex, Km 2, Jalan Tutong, POB 1777, Bandar Seri Begawan; tel. 2220033; fax 2221815; e-mail beeseng@brunet.bn.

Belait Shipping Co (B) Sdn Bhd: B1, 2nd Floor, 94 Jalan McKerron, Kuala Belait 6081; POB 632, Kuala Belait; tel. 3335418; fax 3330239; f. 1977; Man. Dir Haji FATIMAH BINTE Haji ABDUL AZIZ.

Brunei Gas Carriers Sdn Bhd (BGC): Bandar Seri Begawan 1518; internet www.syarikatbgc.com; f. 1998; LNG shipping co; owned jtly by the Prime Minister's Corpn (80%), Shell Gas BV (10%) and Diamond Gas Carriers BV (10%); one vessel operated by Shell Int. Trading and Shipping Co. Ltd; Man. Dir IBRAHIM Haji MOHD YASSIN (acting).

Brunei Shell Tankers Sdn Bhd: Seria KB 3534; tel. 3373999; f. 1986; owned jtly by the Prime Minister's Corpn (50%), Shell Petroleum Ltd (25%) and Diamond Gas Carriers BV (25%); seven vessels operated by Shell International Trading and Shipping Co Ltd; delivers LNG to overseas markets; Man. Dir MARCEL P. LUIJTEN.

Harper Wira Sdn Bhd: B2 Bangunan Haji Mohd Yussof, Jalan Gadong, Bandar Seri Begawan 3180; tel. and fax 2448529.

Inchcape Borneo: Bangunan Inchcape Borneo, Km 4, Jalan Gadong, Bandar Seri Begawan; tel. 2422396; fax 2424352; f. 1856; Gen. Man. LO FAN KEE.

New Island Shipping: POB 850, Bandar Seri Begawan 1908; tel. 2451800; fax 2451480; f. 1975; Chair. TAN KOK VOON; Man. JIMMY VOON.

Pansar Co Sdn Bhd: 1st Floor, 27 Kompleks Mubibbah 3, Jalan Gadong, Bandar Seri Begawan 3180; tel. 2445246; fax 2445247.

Seatrade Shipping Co: POB 476, Bandar Seri Begawan 1904; tel. 2421457; fax 2425824; e-mail seatradefang@brunet.bn.

Silver Line (B) Sdn Bhd: Muara Port; tel. 2445069; fax 2430276.

Wei Tat Shipping and Trading Co: Mile 41, Jalan Tutong, POB 103, Bandar Seri Begawan; tel. 265215.

CIVIL AVIATION

There is an international airport at Berakas, near Bandar Seri Begawan, which can handle up to 1.5m. passengers and 50,000 metric tons of cargo per year. The Brunei Shell Petroleum Co Sdn Bhd operates a private airfield at Anduki for helicopter services.

Department of Civil Aviation: Brunei International Airport, Bandar Seri Begawan BB 2513; tel. 2330142; fax 2331706; e-mail dea@brunet.bn; internet www.civil-aviation.gov.bn; Dir Haji KASIM BIN Haji LATIP.

Royal Brunei Airlines Ltd: RBA Plaza, Jalan Sultan, POB 737, Bandar Seri Begawan BS 8671; tel. 2212222; fax 2244737; e-mail feedback@rba.com.bn; internet www.bruneiair.com; f. 1974; operates services within the Far East and to the Middle East, Australia and Europe; Chair. Dato' Paduka Haji ABDUL HAMID BIN Haji MOHAMED YASSIN; CEO RAY SAYER.

Tourism

Tourist attractions in Brunei include the flora and fauna of the rain forest and the national parks, as well as mosques and water villages. The year 2001 was designated 'Visit Brunei Year'; in that year there were 840,272 foreign visitor arrivals, excluding excursionists. In 2005 the number of arrivals was estimated at 815,054. In 1998 international tourist receipts totalled US $37m.

Brunei Tourism: c/o Ministry of Industry and Primary Resources, Jalan Menteri Besar, Bandar Seri Begawan BB 3910; tel. 2382822; fax 2382824; e-mail info@tourismbrunei.com; internet www.bruneitourism.travel; Dir-Gen. Sheikh JAMALUDDIN Sheikh MOHAMED.

BULGARIA

Introductory Survey

Location, Climate, Language, Religion, Flag, Capital

The Republic of Bulgaria lies in the eastern Balkans, in south-eastern Europe. It is bounded by Romania to the north, by Turkey and Greece to the south, by Serbia to the west and by the former Yugoslav republic of Macedonia to the south-west. The country has an eastern coastline on the Black Sea. The climate is one of fairly sharp contrasts between winter and summer. Temperatures in Sofia are generally between −5°C (23°F) and 28°C (82°F). The official language is Bulgarian, a Southern Slavonic language, written in the Cyrillic alphabet. Minority languages include Turkish and Macedonian. The majority of the population are Christian, most of whom are members of the Bulgarian Orthodox Church, although there is a substantial minority of Muslims. The national flag (proportions 2 by 3) has three equal horizontal stripes, of white, green and red. The capital is Sofia.

Recent History

After almost 500 years of Ottoman rule, Bulgaria declared itself an independent kingdom in 1908. In both the First and Second World Wars Bulgaria allied itself with Germany, and in 1941 joined in the occupation of Yugoslavia. Soviet troops occupied Bulgaria in 1944. In September the Fatherland Front, a left-wing alliance formed in 1942, seized power, with help from the USSR, and installed a Government, led by Kimon Georgiev. In September 1946 the monarchy was abolished, following a popular referendum, and a republic was proclaimed. The first post-war election was held in October, when the Fatherland Front received 70.8% of the votes cast and won 364 seats—of which 277 were held by the Bulgarian Communist Party (BCP)—in the 465-member Narodno Sobraniye (National Assembly). In November Georgi Dimitrov, the First Secretary of the BCP, became Chairman of the Council of Ministers (Prime Minister) in a Government formed by members of the Fatherland Front. All opposition parties were abolished and a new Constitution was adopted in December 1947, when Bulgaria was designated a People's Republic. Dimitrov was replaced as Prime Minister by Vasil Kolarov in March 1949, but remained leader of the BCP until his death in July. His successor as party leader, Vulko Chervenkov, became Prime Minister in February 1950.

Todor Zhivkov succeeded Chervenkov as leader of the BCP in 1954, although Chervenkov remained Prime Minister until 1956, when he was replaced by Anton Yugov. Following an ideological struggle within the BCP, Zhivkov was Prime Minister from 1962 until 1971, when, after the adoption of a new Constitution, Zhivkov became the first President of the newly formed State Council. At a BCP Congress held in 1981 the party's leader was restyled General Secretary. In June, following elections to the Narodno Sobraniye, a new Government was formed; Grisha Filipov, a member of the BCP's Political Bureau, succeeded Stanko Todorov, who had been Prime Minister since 1971. In March 1986 Filipov was replaced by Georgi Atanasov, a former Vice-President of the State Council.

In local elections in March 1988, the nomination of candidates other than those endorsed by the BCP was permitted. Candidates presented by independent public organizations and workers' collectives obtained about one-quarter of the total votes cast. On 10 November 1989 Zhivkov was removed from his post of General Secretary of the BCP and from the Political Bureau. He was replaced as General Secretary by Petar Mladenov, Minister of Foreign Affairs since 1971, who also became President of the State Council. In mid-November 1989 the Narodno Sobraniye voted to abolish part of the penal code prohibiting 'anti-State propaganda' and to grant an amnesty to those convicted under its provisions. Zhivkov was subsequently denounced by the BCP, and an investigation into corruption during his tenure was initiated. In 1990 Zhivkov was arrested on charges of embezzlement of state funds. (In January 1994 Zhivkov was sentenced to seven years' imprisonment on these charges, but in February 1996 his appeal against the sentence was upheld.)

In early December 1989 Angel Dimitrov became leader of the Bulgarian Agrarian People's Union (BAPU, the sole legal political party apart from the BCP, with which it was originally allied); the BAPU was subsequently reconstituted as an independent opposition party. In mid-December the BCP proposed amendments to the Constitution and the adoption of a new electoral law to permit free elections to be held. In January 1990 the Narodno Sobraniye voted to remove from the Constitution the article guaranteeing the BCP's dominant role in society and approved legislation permitting citizens to form independent groups and to stage demonstrations. Discussions regarding political and economic reforms commenced in early January 1990 between the BCP, the BAPU and the Union of Democratic Forces (UDF), which comprised several dissident and independent groups. In early February the BCP adopted a new manifesto, pledging its commitment to the separation of party and state, and the introduction of a multi-party system, while retaining its Marxist orientation. The President of the State Council, Mladenov, proposed the formation of an interim coalition government, pending elections to the Narodno Sobraniye. The UDF and the BAPU, however, rejected Mladenov's invitation to participate in such a coalition. Accordingly, the new Council of Ministers, appointed on 8 February 1990, was composed solely of BCP members, chaired by Andrei Lukanov, who was regarded as an advocate of reform.

There was unrest in February 1990, when an estimated 200,000 supporters of the UDF gathered in Sofia to demand the end of BCP rule. Following discussions in March, with the participation of the BAPU and other political and public organizations, it was finally agreed that Mladenov was to be re-elected as President, pending elections to a Velikoto Narodno Sobraniye (Grand National Assembly), which would be empowered to approve a new constitution. It was also decided to dissolve the State Council. In April the Narodno Sobraniye adopted an electoral law, together with legislation that provided for political pluralism and guaranteed the right to form political parties. Meanwhile, the BCP was reconstituted as the Bulgarian Socialist Party (BSP).

Following an electoral campaign marred by acts of intimidation and violence, elections to a 400-member Velikoto Narodno Sobraniye were held in two rounds in June 1990. The BSP won 211 seats, but failed to obtain the two-thirds' majority of seats necessary to secure support for the approval of constitutional reforms. The UDF obtained 144 seats. The Movement for Rights and Freedoms (MRF), which had been established earlier in 1990 to represent the country's Muslim minority (principally ethnic Turks), secured 23 seats. The BAPU won 16 seats. The UDF rejected the BSP's invitation to join a coalition government. In July Mladenov announced his resignation as President, following a campaign of protests led by students. Zhelyu Zhelev, the Chairman of the UDF, was elected to replace him in early August. Zhelev was succeeded as Chairman of the UDF first by Petar Beron, hitherto the party's Secretary, and, from December, by Filip Dimitrov.

The severe deterioration in the economy in 1990 resulted in widespread shortages of food and fuel. Increasing division between conservative and reformist elements within the BSP became manifest in November, when 16 BSP delegates to the Velikoto Narodno Sobraniye announced their decision to form a separate group, as a result of which the party no longer held an absolute majority. Following a four-day general strike organized by Podkrepa, a trade union confederation formed in the previous year, Lukanov's Government resigned at the end of the month. Subsequent discussions resulted in the formation of a new 'government of national consensus' in mid-December, comprising members of the BSP, the UDF, the BAPU and four independents. Dimitar Popov, a lawyer with no party affiliation, had been elected in early December to chair the new Council of Ministers.

In mid-November 1990 the Velikoto Narodno Sobraniye voted to rename the country the Republic of Bulgaria and to remove from the national flag the state emblem, which included communist symbols. The Velikoto Narodno Sobraniye adopted a new Constitution in mid-July 1991; it subsequently voted to dissolve itself, although it continued sessions in an interim capacity, pending legislative elections. (The new Constitution provided for elections to be held, on an *ad hoc* basis, to a Velikoto Narodno Sobraniye, the sole body empowered to adopt a new constitution and sanction territorial changes or certain constitutional amendments, although the permanent legislative body was to be the Narodno Sobraniye.) The Constitution stipulated a five-year residency qualification for presidential candidates, effectively disqualifying the candidacy of Simeon Sakskoburggotski (Saxe-Coburg Gotha—'Simeon II'), the pretender to the Bulgarian throne, who had lived in exile since 1946. At the elections to the new, 240-seat Narodno Sobraniye, held on 13 October 1991, the UDF obtained the largest proportion of the votes cast (34.4%) and a total of 110 seats, narrowly defeating an alliance led by the BSP, which won 106 seats. The MRF became the third-strongest political force, securing 24 seats. The new Council of Ministers, composed principally of UDF members, was announced in early November. Dimitrov, the leader of the UDF, was elected Chairman of the new Government. A direct presidential election was held in January 1992 in two rounds, following which Zhelev was re-elected for a five-year term, receiving 53% of the votes cast in the 'run-off' poll.

In April 1992 the Government adopted legislation restoring ownership of land and property that had been transferred to the state during 1947–62; legislation approving the privatization of state-owned companies followed. In May Dimitrov implemented an extensive reorganization of the Council of Ministers.

Meanwhile, relations between President Zhelev and the UDF became increasingly strained. At the end of October 1992 MRF and BSP deputies in the Narodno Sobraniye defeated the Government in a motion of confidence proposed by Dimitrov; the Government subsequently resigned. In November Zhelev invited Dimitrov to form a new government. The MRF, however, declined to form a coalition with the UDF, and Dimitrov's nomination was thus defeated in the Narodno Sobraniye. President Zhelev rejected the candidacy of a BSP nominee and, following the failure of the UDF and the MRF to reach agreement for a coalition, in December the MRF nominated an academic, Prof. Lyuben Berov, hitherto an economic adviser to Zhelev, as Prime Minister. The UDF accused Berov of collaborating with the former communist regime and organized a large rally to protest against his candidacy. Although the majority of UDF deputies abstained, Berov was approved as Prime Minister on 30 December by 124 votes to 25. Berov's proposed Council of Ministers, principally composed of non-partisan 'technocrats', was also accepted by the Narodno Sobraniye.

In March 1993 internal divisions within the UDF became more apparent when a breakaway faction of the party formed a new, pro-Berov organization, the New Union for Democracy (NUD); in response, the UDF intensified its campaign of opposition. Demonstrations were staged by the UDF in Sofia and several other cities in June, accusing Zhelev of attempting to restore communism, and demanding immediate elections. In June the Vice-President, Blaga Dimitrova, resigned. The crisis subsided when three votes expressing 'no confidence' in Berov's Government, proposed by the UDF in the Narodno Sobraniye, proved unsuccessful.

By May 1994 the Berov Government had survived its seventh motion of 'no confidence', after the controversial introduction of value-added tax (VAT), increases in fuel prices and a dramatic decline in value of the national currency, the lev, prompted thousands of demonstrators to protest in Sofia. In September Berov's Government submitted its resignation, owing to criticism of the organization of the privatization programme that had commenced in June. Both the BSP and the UDF refused presidential mandates to form a new Government. In October Zhelev dissolved the Narodno Sobraniye and announced that a general election would take place in December.

At the general election, which was held on 18 December 1994, the BSP (in alliance with two small parties) obtained an outright majority in the Narodno Sobraniye, with 125 seats (43.5% of the total votes cast); the UDF won 69 seats. A new Government, headed by the Chairman of the BSP, Zhan Videnov, was appointed in January 1995.

In February 1995 the Narodno Sobraniye amended the 1992 property restitution law (see above), extending for a further three years the deadline by which certain properties had to be restored to their rightful owners. In March the Government drafted a programme for mass privatization. At municipal elections in October–November, the ruling coalition won 195 of a total of 255 mayoralties, although the UDF secured the mayoralties in the country's three main cities. In January 1996 a motion of 'no confidence' in the Videnov administration, proposed in protest at a severe shortage of grain, was defeated, although the situation prompted the resignations of the Deputy Prime Minister and two ministers. In June the UDF proposed a motion expressing 'no confidence' in the Government's management of the economy, which was, however, defeated by a large majority. In October 1996 former Prime Minister Andrei Lukanov was assassinated.

In the first round of the presidential election, held on 27 October 1996, Petar Stoyanov, a lawyer and senior member of the UDF, secured 44.1% of the votes cast; Ivan Marazov of the BSP, the candidate of a newly formed electoral alliance, Together for Bulgaria, received only 27.0% of the votes. In the second round of voting, which took place on 3 November, Stoyanov was elected to the presidency, with 59.7% of the votes cast. In December the UDF staged a series of demonstrations to demand early legislative elections and the resignation of the Government. On 21 December Videnov tendered his resignation as both Prime Minister and BSP leader. Georgi Parvanov, who was a supporter of Videnov, subsequently replaced him as Chairman of the BSP. At the end of December the Narodno Sobraniye voted by a large majority to accept the resignation of Videnov's Government. The UDF, however, intensified its campaign of demonstrations; in early January an attempt by protesters to seize the parliamentary building was suppressed by security forces.

On 19 January 1997 Stoyanov was inaugurated as President, and later in the month the BSP agreed to form a new government, pending legislative elections. In early February the BSP announced the appointment of a new Council of Ministers under Nikolai Dobrev (the Minister of the Interior in the previous administration). However, Dobrev agreed to relinquish the BSP's mandate to form a government, owing to concern that protests and strikes by supporters of the UDF might escalate into civil conflict. The consultative National Security Council adopted recommendations (which were approved by the legislature) that the President should appoint an interim council of ministers, dissolve the Narodno Sobraniye and schedule legislative elections. In March the interim Government, led by the mayor of Sofia, Stefan Sofiyanski, announced that Videnov was to be charged with criminal negligence as a result of government policies that had caused the severe shortage of grain in 1995–96; the Minister of Agriculture in the Videnov administration was also prosecuted.

At the elections to the Narodno Sobraniye, conducted on 19 April 1997, the UDF secured 137 seats, while the BSP (which again contested the elections in alliance with other parties, as the Democratic Left) obtained only 58 seats; three other groups obtained legislative representation. Later in April the UDF nominated the party Chairman, Ivan Kostov, as Prime Minister, and in May he was confirmed in that position by the Narodno Sobraniye.

Local government elections took place in October 1999: the UDF won 31.3% of the votes cast and the BSP secured 29.4%. In December Kostov reorganized the Council of Ministers. In May 2000 Kostov's administration survived its third vote of 'no confidence' in the Narodno Sobraniye, and in February 2001 the legislature rejected a further 'no confidence' motion, proposed in response to a perceived increase in crime. Meanwhile, in January, in advance of presidential and legislative elections, the BSP attempted to consolidate support by forming an alliance, known as the Coalition for Bulgaria, with smaller leftist and nationalist groups. In April the former monarch, Simeon Sakskoburggotski, who returned to Bulgaria at the beginning of the month, failed to be permitted legally to register his new National Movement as a party. None the less, in May the Movement was permitted to form an alliance with two smaller, registered parties, the Party of Bulgarian Women and the Oborishte Party for National Revival, as the National Movement Simeon II (NMSII), in order to participate in the legislative elections. Sakskoburggotski (who was not permitted to be the official leader of the Movement) asserted that he had no desire to restore the monarchy, and pledged to combat official corruption and reform the economy, in order to fulfil the criteria for membership of the European Union (EU, see p. 244).

In the general election, held on 17 June 2001, the NMSII received 42.7% of the votes cast, obtaining 120 seats, while the UDF secured only 18.2% of the votes (51 seats). The NMSII held just one seat fewer than the 121 required to secure an absolute majority in the Narodno Sobraniye; however, it had declared its intention to form a coalition government throughout its election campaign, and it approached the MRF (which held 21 legislative seats) and the UDF as potential partners. The MRF agreed to be represented in government, but the UDF refused to participate in a government that comprised members of the MRF; the BSP subsequently became an informal coalition partner. Saksko- burggotski was sworn in as Prime Minister on 24 July. The Council of Ministers, in which two ministerial portfolios were allocated to both the MRF and the BSP, was approved by the Narodno Sobraniye on the same day. Kostov subsequently resigned his leadership of the UDF.

In the first round of voting in the presidential election, held on 11 November 2001, at which the rate of participation by the electorate was just 39.2% (less than the 50% demanded by the Constitution), Parvanov, contesting the election for the Coalition for Bulgaria, won 36.4% of the votes cast, and the incumbent, Stoyanov, who stood as an independent candidate, secured 34.9% of the votes. Parvanov confirmed his victory in a second round of voting on 18 November, in which he obtained 54.1% of the votes cast; the rate of voter participation was some 54.6%. The result of the election, which was largely unanticipated, was widely interpreted as an expression of protest by a frustrated electorate. Parvanov was sworn in as President on 19 January 2002 and took office three days later.

In December 2001 the Government released a report, which accused the former Kostov administration of unscrupulous actions with regard to the privatization process, and announced the establishment of an investigative commission. In March five members of the Narodno Sobraniye left the NMSII, in protest at Sakskoburggotski's perceived failure to fulfil electoral pledges. In April the NMSII was finally legally registered as a political party, and Sakskoburggotski was elected as its Chairman.

In October 2002 the Narodno Sobraniye voted in favour of closing the third and fourth reactors of the Kozloduy nuclear power plant (in compliance with EU demands) following Bulgaria's accession to the Union, which was not anticipated before 2007. However, in November 2002 the Government signed an agreement with the EU, according to which it undertook to decommission the reactors by 2006. Later in November 2002 the Government defeated votes of 'no confidence' brought by the UDF and the Coalition for Bulgaria, both of which rejected the agreement.

Following efforts by the Supreme Administrative Court to suspend the sales of both the state tobacco company, Bulgartabac, and the Bulgarian Telecommunications Company in late 2002, in January 2003 the Narodno Sobraniye approved controversial legislation removing the Court's power to prevent the privatization of principal state enterprises, which were, instead, to be decided by the Government, with the approval of the legislature. Although Parvanov exercised his right of veto in February, later that month the Narodno Sobraniye voted to override the presidential veto. A petition was subsequently lodged with the Constitutional Court by Parvanov, the UDF and the BSP, and in April the Court ruled that the amendments to the privatization bill had been unconstitutional. Meanwhile, in February five legislative deputies had left the NMSII, alleging widespread corruption within the Government, thereby reducing the governing coalition's legislative majority to just 10 seats.

In July 2003 the Prime Minister reorganized the Council of Ministers. In July the Narodno Sobraniye approved draft electoral legislation that introduced a mixed system of voting, whereby one-half of the 240 legislative deputies were to be elected by majority vote in their constituencies, and the remainder by proportional representation from a national list of candidates. In late September the Narodno Sobraniye passed a number of amendments to the Constitution, as part of wider efforts to reform the judiciary and combat organized crime. The failure to address the strength of criminal structures had been widely regarded as a principal weakness of Sakskoburggotski's Government.

In municipal elections, conducted in October–November 2003, the BSP and the UDF secured the majority of seats. In mid-January 2004 Ekaterina Mihailova resigned her position as deputy leader of the UDF, in protest at the leadership of Nadezhda Mihailova. The latter was re-elected to the party leadership in February, prompting 26 UDF members, including the party's former Chairman, Kostov, to leave the party. Kostov subsequently founded a new party, Democrats for a Strong Bulgaria (DSB).

In February 2005 the Narodno Sobraniye voted by a narrow majority to dismiss its Chairman, Ognyan Gerdzhikov. Gerdzhikov had been accused of systematically violating the Narodno Sobraniye's rules of procedure, after he refused to allow parliament to discuss the failed sale of Bulgartabac to British-American Tobacco (of the United Kingdom and the USA). He was replaced by Borislav Velikov. The issue inspired a sixth vote of 'no confidence' in Sakskoburggotski's Government, which the ruling coalition narrowly survived, having received the support of a grouping that had left the NMSII earlier in the year, The New Time. In the same month, in an attempt to strengthen the ruling coalition before the legislative elections due to take place later that year, the Prime Minister reorganized the Council of Ministers. The parliamentary leader of The New Time, Miroslav Sevlievski, was appointed as Minister of Energy and Energy Resources, while Sevlievski's predecessor in that post, Milko Kovachev, was appointed as Deputy Prime Minister and Minister of the Economy.

At the elections to the Narodno Sobraniye, held on 25 June 2005, the BSP-led Coalition for Bulgaria secured 82 of the 240 seats in the legislature and 34.2% of the votes cast; the NMSII received 53 seats and 22.1% of the votes, and the MRF secured 34 seats and 14.2% of the votes. A newly formed coalition of extreme right-wing and nationalist parties, the Attack National Union (Attack—subsequently the Attack Party), secured 21 seats (8.8% of the votes). The rate of participation by the electorate was relatively low, at some 55.7%. In mid-July President Parvanov granted BSP leader Sergey Stanishev a mandate to form a government. However, in late July Stanishev's proposed Council of Ministers, comprising members of the Coalition for Bulgaria and the MRF, failed to secure sufficient support in the legislature, and the NMSII, as the second strongest faction in the Narodno Sobraniye, was subsequently awarded a new mandate to form a government. However, Sakskoburggotski abandoned efforts to form a new coalition administration and, as pressure increased for Bulgaria to make progress with the reforms needed to secure membership of the EU in 2007, on 16 August the Narodno Sobraniye approved a three-party coalition Government led by Stanishev. The new Council of Ministers comprised nine members of the BSP, five members of NMSII, three members of the MRF and one independent minister. Each of the three coalition partners nominated a Deputy Prime Minister. Meanwhile, in July Georgi Pirinski, a former Minister of Foreign Affairs and Deputy Chairman of the BSP, was elected as the new Chairman of the Narodno Sobraniye.

In October 2005 former President Stoyanov was appointed as leader of the UDF, replacing Nadezhda Mihailova, who had been widely blamed for divisions in the UDF that had led to the party receiving just 20 seats in the legislative elections (compared with 51 in 2001). The first round of presidential voting, held on 22 October 2006 and contested by seven candidates, proved inconclusive because the rate of electoral participation, at 44.3%, was below the 50% required by the Constitution for the polling to be valid. The first-placed candidate, the incumbent, Parvanov, who secured some 64.0% of the votes cast, progressed to a 'run-off' vote against Volen Siderov of Attack (who secured 21.5% of the votes cast), on 29 October. Attack alleged voting irregularities in the first round of the election and announced that it would decide whether to launch a formal challenge to the results after the second ballot. Although the rate of participation by the electorate was again low, at 42.5%, Parvanov won 75.9% of the votes in the second round of voting, thereby becoming the first post-communist president of Bulgaria to succeed in being elected to a second term of office. Parvanov was inaugurated on 22 January 2007.

At elections to the European Parliament in May 2007, both the UDF and DSB failed to secure representation, prompting the resignations of Stoyanov and Kostov from the leadership of their respective parties; the BSP and the Citizens for European Development of Bulgaria (GERB), a newly established centre-right opposition party headed by the Mayor of Sofia, Boyko Borisov, each secured five of the 18 available seats. The NMSII only obtained one seat, and in the following month reconstituted itself as the National Movement for Stability and Progress (NMSP). In early June Stanishev announced that he had accepted the resignations of the Minister of the Economy and Energy, Rumen Ocharov, following allegations against him of corruption by the National Investigative Service, and the Minister of Justice, Georgi Petkanov. New appointments to these offices were approved by the legislature on 18 July.

At municipal elections, which were conducted on 28 October and 4 November 2007, GERB won the mayoral polls in the country's principal towns. Berisov, who was re-elected Mayor of Sofia, subsequently demanded the resignation of the Government. In April 2008 the Minister of the Interior, Rumen Petkov, resigned from the Government, after allegations emerged of endemic corruption, involving connections between senior interior ministry officials and organized crime leaders. The BSP, the MRF and the NMSP reached agreement on a government reorganization, in which four ministers (including Petkov) were replaced. The hitherto ambassador to Germany, Meglena Plugchieva, was appointed to the new post of Deputy Prime Minister, with responsibility for EU funds; these changes were approved by the Narodno Sobraniye on 24 April.

Negotiations on Bulgaria's accession to the EU, which was conditional on the Government's fulfilment of certain criteria, began in March 2000, and Bulgaria hoped to be admitted as a full member in 2007. In March 2004 the European Parliament praised Bulgaria's reform efforts and endorsed the planned date of 2007 for Bulgaria's accession, and in June Bulgaria (along with Romania) officially concluded the negotiation process with the EU (although the EU reserved the right, for the first time, to postpone the accession date by up to one year if necessary). Bulgaria and Romania signed formal accession agreements with the EU on 25 April 2005. In October the European Commission emphasized that Bulgaria's accession to the EU depended on its ability to, *inter alia*, combat organized crime and reform the judicial system. In January 2006 the Supreme Judicial Council appointed Boris Velchev as Prosecutor-General, replacing Nikola Filtchev, who, together with the Sakskoburggotski Government, had attracted criticism for its tolerance of the continued prevalence of organized crime in Bulgaria. In early February 2007 the Narodno Sobraniye adopted a number of constitutional amendments designed to improve the performance of the judiciary, in accordance with European Commission recommendations on judicial reform. Bulgaria (along with Romania) formally acceded to the EU on 1 January of that year. However, this culmination of the new member states' respective preparatory reform efforts was tempered by extensive labour market restrictions imposed by existing EU members, only nine of which had guaranteed unlimited access to migrant workers from Bulgaria and Romania following the accession date. Additional constraints on membership rights, together with domestic power deficits following nuclear reactor closures at the end of 2006 in compliance with EU accession preconditions, provoked considerable animosity between Bulgaria and the original bloc members and instigated some reciprocal restrictions against economic migrants from those countries refusing or limiting access to Bulgarians. In early 2008, in view of the continuing domestic electricity shortages, the Government initiated an official campaign to gain support for the reopening of the third and fourth reactors at the Kozloduy nuclear installation (despite the opposition of the EU to such proposals).

Bulgaria's establishment of formal relations with the former Yugoslav republic of Macedonia (FYRM) in January 1992 prompted harsh criticism from the Greek Government, although relations with Greece appeared to improve thereafter. In November 1993 the FYRM expressed its desire to establish full diplomatic relations with Bulgaria, and in the following month Bulgaria announced that it was to open an embassy in the FYRM and relax border procedures between the two states. In February 1999 Prime Minister Kostov and the Prime Minister of the FYRM, Ljubčo Georgievski, signed a declaration pledging that neither country had a territorial claim on the other. In March the Ministers of Defence of Bulgaria and the FYRM signed a joint declaration providing for increased military co-operation, including joint exercises and the supply of military equipment to the FYRM, in connection with the aim of both countries to join the North Atlantic Treaty Organization (NATO, see p. 340). Changes to Bulgaria's visa regime, requiring visitors from both the FYRM and Serbia to hold a visa in addition to a valid passport, took effect from Bulgaria's accession to full EU membership, on 1 January 2007. Public opposition in Bulgaria to the aerial bombardment of Yugoslavia (Serbia and Montenegro) by NATO forces in March–June 1999, increased, after a misdirected NATO missile damaged a private residence on the outskirts of Sofia in April. Nevertheless, the Bulgarian Narodno Sobraniye approved a decision made by the Council of Ministers to allow NATO use of the country's airspace.

Relations between Bulgaria and Russia improved in 1992, following the signature of co-operation agreements, and the visit of the Russian President, Boris Yeltsin, to Sofia in August. In April 1998 the Bulgarian Government signed an agreement with the Russian national gas company, Gazprom, providing for the supply and transit of Russian gas. In December 2000 Russia expressed its disappointment at Bulgaria's decision to terminate, in accordance with conditions for accession to the EU, a 1978 bilateral agreement on visa-free travel, with effect from June 2001. However, in March 2003 Russian President Vladimir Putin visited Bulgaria, resulting in strongly enhanced economic relations, despite failing to persuade Bulgaria to withdraw its support for US-led military action in Iraq (see below). In early 2008 President Vladimir Putin of Russia made an official visit to Bulgaria; major energy accords signed between the two countries included a project for Russia to construct a second nuclear power installation in the northern town of Belene and an agreement (finalized in March 2007) on the establishment of a pipeline to transport Russian petroleum from the Bulgarian Black Sea port of Burgas to Alexandroupolis, on the Greek Aegean coast.

Relations with neighbouring Turkey were intermittently strained from the mid-1980s, when the Zhivkov regime began a campaign of forced assimilation of Bulgaria's ethnic Turkish minority (an estimated 9% of the total population). In May 1989 Bulgarian militia units violently suppressed demonstrations by an estimated 30,000 ethnic Turks in eastern Bulgaria and in June more than 80,000 ethnic Turks were expelled from Bulgaria, although the Bulgarian authorities claimed that the Turks had chosen to settle in Turkey, following a relaxation in passport regulations. By mid-August an estimated 310,000 Bulgarian Turks had crossed into Turkey, and in late August the Turkish Government closed the border. In the following month a substantial number of the Bulgarian Turks, disillusioned with conditions in Turkey, began to return to Bulgaria. The Turkish Government repeatedly proposed that discussions with the Bulgarian Government be held, under the auspices of the UN High Commissioner for Refugees, to establish the rights of the Bulgarian Turks and to formulate a clear immigration policy. Finally, Bulgaria agreed to negotiations and friendly relations between Bulgaria and Turkey were restored by late 1991.

Meanwhile, in December 1989 some 6,000 Pomaks (ethnic Bulgarian Muslims) held demonstrations to demand religious and cultural freedoms, as well as an official inquiry into alleged atrocities against Pomaks during Zhivkov's tenure of office. In January 1990 anti-Turkish demonstrations were held in the Kurdzhali district of southern Bulgaria, in protest at the Government's declared intention to restore civil and religious rights to the ethnic Turkish minority. Despite continuing demonstrations by Bulgarian nationalist protesters, in March the Narodno Sobraniye approved legislation that permitted ethnic Turks and Pomaks to use their original, non-Slavic names. This development was welcomed by the Turkish Government. Nevertheless, inter-ethnic disturbances continued, particularly in the Kurdzhali region, during 1990. In May 1992 Prime Minister Dimitrov visited Turkey, and the two countries signed a treaty of friendship and co-operation. In July 1995 a visit by President Süleyman Demirel of Turkey to Bulgaria indicated a significant improvement in Bulgarian-Turkish relations. In June 1998 the Narodno Sobraniye ratified an agreement demarcating the border between Bulgaria and Turkey (which had been signed during an official visit to Sofia by the Turkish Prime Minister, Mesut Yılmaz, in December 1997). In February 2001 Bulgaria and Turkey signed a joint protocol on combating terrorism and organized crime.

Bulgaria's relations with the USA strengthened during 2002, and in February 2003 the Narodno Sobraniye voted to allow US forces to make use of Bulgarian airspace, as well as the airbase at Sarafovo, on the Black Sea, for military operations during the impending US-led campaign to remove the regime of Saddam Hussain in Iraq (see the chapter on Iraq); Bulgaria had previously offered its support to the USA during its military campaign in Afghanistan from late 2001 (see the chapter on Afghanistan). The conflict in Iraq (which commenced in March 2003) was strongly opposed by a number of European countries, notably France, and in February the French President, Jacques Chirac, had condemned both Bulgaria and Romania as 'irresponsible' in offering the USA their support. Bulgaria dispatched some 470 troops to support the US-led military campaign in Iraq. In October 2005 the incoming Deputy Prime Minister and Minister of Foreign Affairs, Ivaylo Kalfin, announced that Bulgarian troops would be withdrawn after the Iraqi parliamentary elections, scheduled for 15 December, and the last Bulgarian troops left Iraq later that month. Since August 2003 19 Bulgarians (13 soldiers and six civilians) had been killed in Iraq. In February 2006 the Narodno Sobraniye approved the deployment of a 155-member mission to maintain security at a refugee camp in Ashraf, Iraq, for a one-year period; its mandate was extended until March 2008 and subsequently until March 2009. Meanwhile, negotiations to allow the sharing of Bulgarian military bases with US troops were well advanced; the Narodno Sobraniye had approved the measure in December 2003. Further agreements on the joint use of military facilities were to be signed in early 2008.

Diplomatic relations with Libya suffered a significant setback in December 2006, following a ruling by the Libyan Supreme Court that five Bulgarian nurses and an accompanying Palestinian doctor were to be sentenced to death; a Bulgarian doctor received a four-year jail term. The medical personnel had been indicted in 1999 on charges of having deliberately infected over 400 Libyan children (of which 50 subsequently died) with the HIV virus reportedly during trials to develop a cure for the disease. A death sentence had originally been handed down in 2005 in respect of the defendants, but was later repealed and a retrial ordered by the Libyan Supreme Court, amid international condemnation of the original proceedings. Allegations that the incarcerated Bulgarians had been subject to torture, the acquittal of nine Libyan health workers on similar charges, and growing evidence that the HIV virus had been present in some of the children for a prolonged period prior to the arrival of the Bulgarian workers in Libya further exacerbated Bulgarian outrage at the decision. The EU, the US Secretary of State, and the Bulgarian President and Prime Minister expressed their consternation at the decision, prompting a hostile response from the Libyan Ministry of Foreign Affairs. Death sentences were again imposed after the retrial in December 2006, and were upheld by the Libyan Supreme Court in July 2007. Later in July, however, following the negotiation of a compensation agreement, the Court commuted the sentences to life imprisonment and the five nurses were repatriated to Bulgaria shortly afterwards subsequently (receiving a pardon from President Parvanov). In August the Bulgarian Government announced the cancellation of some US $56.6m. in debt incurred by Libya in the 1980s.

In mid-1992 Bulgaria became a member of the Council of Europe (see p. 225), and in May 1994 Bulgaria was granted associate partnership status by Western European Union (WEU, see p. 426). In 1996 Bulgaria submitted an official application for membership of the EU, and acceded to full membership of the Union in January 2007. Meanwhile, in October 1996 Bulgaria joined the World Trade Organization (see p. 396). In November 2002, at a NATO summit meeting held in Prague, Czech Republic, seven countries, including Bulgaria, were formally invited to become full members in 2004. Bulgaria duly joined the Alliance on 29 March 2004.

Government

Legislative power is held by the unicameral Narodno Sobraniye (National Assembly), comprising 240 members, who are elected for four years by universal adult suffrage. The President of the Republic (Head of State) is directly elected for a period of five years, and is also Supreme Commander-in-Chief of the Armed Forces. The Council of Ministers, the highest organ of state administration, is elected by the Narodno Sobraniye. For local administration purposes, Bulgaria comprises 28 regions (divided into a total of 259 municipalities).

Defence

The total strength of the armed forces, as assessed at November 2007, was 40,747, comprising an army of 18,773, an air force of 9,344, a navy of 4,100, and 8,530 centrally controlled and Ministry of Defence staff. There were also paramilitary forces comprising an estimated 12,000 border guards, 18,000 railway and construction troops and 4,000 security police, and a total of 303,000 reserves. The budget for 2007 allocated some 1,190m. new leva to defence. Bulgaria joined the North Atlantic Treaty Organization's (NATO) 'Partnership for Peace' (see p. 342) programme of military co-operation in 1994 and became a full member of the Alliance on 29 March 2004. The modernization of the national defence force, and its operation on a professional basis, which were stipulated as preconditions of Bulgaria's accession to the EU, were agreed in November 2006. Compulsory military service was officially ended on 1 December 2007.

Economic Affairs

In 2006, according to estimates by the World Bank, Bulgaria's gross national income (GNI), measured at average 2004–06 prices, was US $30,733m., equivalent to $3,990 per head (or $10,140 per head on an international purchasing-power parity basis). During 1996–2006, it was estimated, the population decreased at an average rate of 0.8% per year, while gross domestic product (GDP) per head increased, in real terms, at an average annual rate of 4.7%. According to the World Bank, Bulgaria's overall GDP increased, in real terms, by an average of 3.9% annually during 1996–2006. Real GDP increased by 6.1% in 2006.

Agriculture contributed some 9.3% of GDP in 2005, according to preliminary figures, and the sector (including hunting, forestry and fishing) engaged 8.1% of the employed labour force in 2006. In 1990 private farming was legalized, and by the end of 1999 some 96% of farmland had been restituted, in its former physical boundaries, to former owners and their heirs. The principal crops are wheat, maize, barley, sunflower seeds, potatoes, tomatoes, melons and grapes. Bulgaria is a major exporter of wine, and there is a large exportable surplus of processed agricultural products. During 1996–2006, according to the World Bank, the average annual GDP of the agricultural sector increased, in real terms, by 2.3%. Real agricultural GDP decreased by 8.6% in 2005, and by 1.9% in 2006.

Industry provided some 30.4% of GDP in 2005, according to preliminary figures, and the sector (including mining, manufacturing, construction and utilities) engaged 34.5% of the employed labour force in 2006. According to the World Bank, industrial GDP increased, in real terms, at an average annual rate of 3.8% in 1996–2006. Real industrial GDP increased by 8.3% in 2006.

In 2005 mining accounted for some 1.6% of GDP, while in 2006 mining and quarrying engaged 1.2% of the employed labour force. Coal, iron ore, copper, manganese, lead and zinc are mined, and petroleum is extracted on the Black Sea coast.

The manufacturing sector accounted for 18.7% of GDP in 2005 and engaged 24.0% of the employed labour force in 2006. Based on the value of output, in 1999 the main branches of manufacturing were food products, beverages and tobacco products, machinery, refined petroleum products, basic metals, chemicals and chemical products, and clothing. In real terms, the GDP of the manufacturing sector increased at an average annual rate of 6.1% in 1997–2006. The GDP of the sector increased by 6.0% in 2006.

Bulgaria's production of primary energy in 2001 was equivalent to 54.0% of gross consumption. Coal and nuclear power, the latter of which is produced by the country's sole nuclear power station, at Kozloduy, are the main domestic sources of energy, despite the closure of four of the six reactors at the plant by 2006 (see below). A second nuclear power plant, at Belene, was scheduled to be completed by 2011, which would, it was hoped, partially offset the negative impact on domestic electricity production of the closure of the reactors at Kozloduy. In 2003 nuclear power provided 40.9% of electric energy, while coal accounted for 46.1% of electricity production. Mineral fuels comprised 17.4% of the value of merchandise imports in 2006.

The services sector contributed some 60.3% of GDP in 2005, according to preliminary figures, and engaged 57.4% of the employed labour force in 2006. Tourism revenue increased significantly in 2002–05. The World Bank estimated that the real GDP of the services sector increased by an annual average of 2.3% during 1996–2006. The real GDP of the sector increased by 6.1% in 2006.

In 2006 Bulgaria recorded a visible trade deficit of US $6,809.4m., and there was a deficit of $5,009.8m. on the current account of the balance of payments. In that year the principal sources of imports were Russia, which provided 17.3% of the total, and Germany, which provided 12.4%. Italy, Turkey and Greece were also major suppliers. The main market for exports in 2006 was Turkey (taking 11.4% of the total); Italy, Germany and Greece were also significant purchasers. The principal exports in 2006 were metals (including iron and steel), clothing and footwear, petroleum products, and machines and equipment. The principal imports in that year were crude petroleum and natural gas, machinery and equipment, textiles, and vehicles.

In 2005 Bulgaria recorded a budgetary surplus of an estimated 2,650m. new leva (equivalent to 6.2% of GDP). Bulgaria's total external debt at the end of 2005 was US $16,786m., of which $4,587m. was long-term public debt. In that year the cost of debt-servicing was equivalent to 31.2% of revenue from exports of goods and services. The annual rate of inflation averaged 32.2% in 1996–2006. Consumer prices increased by 1,158.3% in 1997, but by only 18.7% in 1998 and by 2.6% in 1999, and the rate of inflation remained relatively low thereafter. Consumer prices increased by 7.3% in 2006. According to Bulgaria's National Statistical Institute, 6.6% of the labour force were registered as unemployed in the third quarter of 2007.

BULGARIA

In 1990 Bulgaria became a founding member of the European Bank for Reconstruction and Development (EBRD, see p. 239). Bulgaria is a member of the Organization of the Black Sea Economic Co-operation (see p. 367). The country acceded to the European Union (EU, see p. 244) on 1 January 2007.

In May 1996 there was a dramatic reduction in the value of the lev, and in September the IMF suspended the disbursement of funds. In March 1997 agreement was reached with the IMF on the adoption of structural reforms. The Government established a currency control board in July, which fixed the exchange rate of the lev to that of the German Deutsche Mark (and subsequently the euro). In order to comply with conditions for EU membership, two of the Kozloduy nuclear power installation's reactors were closed at the end of 2002; although an agreement reached with the EU in November, on the closure of two additional reactors by 2006, was subsequently ruled to be illegal, the requirement was reinstated and the facilities were decommissioned in December of that year. Meanwhile, the privatization of the Bulgarian Telecommunications Company was completed in January 2005. In March 2007 Russia, Bulgaria and Greece signed a final agreement on the construction of a pipeline to transport Russian petroleum from the Bulgarian Black Sea port of Burgas to Alexandroupolis, on the Greek Aegean coast. Continuing its commitment to privatization, the Government formulated a new strategy for the divestment of Bulgaria Air, which culminated in the sale of the airline to the Balkan Hemus Group, a consortium of locally owned companies, in October 2006. As large inflows of foreign investment continued following EU accession at the beginning of 2007, other projects proceeded rapidly, including the construction of a new business district. Two large, foreign projects to transform the airport district were initiated. The IMF welcomed the rising budget surplus (which was stimulated further by the introduction of a new corporate tax rate of 10% in 2007) as a reflection of the Government's fiscal discipline. GDP growth in 2007 was estimated to exceed 6% for the fourth consecutive year. The burgeoning economy has led to the growth of a middle class and an increase in wages, although it was reported that the difference in salary growth between the public and private sectors continued to widen, while inflation (recorded at 9.3% in August 2007, on a year-on-year basis) remained high.

Education

Education is free and compulsory between the ages of seven and 16 years. Children between the ages of three and six years may attend kindergartens (in 2005/06 some 73.7% of pre-school age children attended). A 12-year system of schooling was introduced in 1998. Primary education (grades one to four), beginning at seven years of age, lasts for four years. Secondary education (grades five to 12), from 11 years of age, lasts for up to eight years, comprising two cycles of four years each. Secondary education is undertaken at general schools, which provide a general academic course, or vocational and technical schools, and art schools, which offer specialized training. In addition, basic schools cover both primary and lower secondary grades, while combined schools can cater for pupils from grades one to 12. In 2005/06 primary enrolment included 99.5% of children in the relevant age-group, while enrolment at lower secondary and upper secondary schools included 84.9% and 78.0%, respectively, of those in the relevant age-group. In 2005/06 enrolment in universities and higher colleges was equivalent to 26.4% of those in the relevant age-group. In 2004/05 there were a total of 43 higher educational institutions, with a total enrolment of 219,477 students, and an additional 10 colleges. Tuition fees for university students were introduced in mid-1999. The 2005 state budget allocated some 1,815m. new leva to education (representing 11.2% of total outlay by the central Government).

Public Holidays

2008: 1 January (New Year), 3 March (National Day), 21–24 March (Easter), 1 May (Labour Day), 6 May (St George's Day), 24 May (Education Day), 6 September (Unification Day), 22 September (Independence Day), 1 November (Commemoration of the Leaders of the Bulgarian National Revival), 24–26 December (Christmas).

2009: 1 January (New Year), 3 March (National Day), 10–13 April (Easter), 1 May (Labour Day), 6 May (St George's Day), 24 May (Education Day), 6 September (Unification Day), 22 September (Independence Day), 1 November (Commemoration of the Leaders of the Bulgarian National Revival), 24–26 December (Christmas).

Weights and Measures

The metric system is in force.

Statistical Survey

Sources (unless otherwise indicated): National Statistical Institute, 1038 Sofia, ul. P. Volov 2; tel. (2) 985-77-00; fax (2) 985-76-40; e-mail info@nsi.bg; internet www.nsi.bg; Bulgarian National Bank, 1000 Sofia, bul. A. Battenberg 1; tel. (2) 914-51-203; fax (2) 980-24-25; e-mail press_office@bnbank.org; internet www.bnb.bg; Center for Economic Development, 1408 Sofia, ul. J. K. Ivan Vazov 1/9; tel. (2) 953-42-04; e-mail stat@ced.bg; internet www.stat.bg.

Area and Population

AREA, POPULATION AND DENSITY

Area (sq km)*	110,994†
Population (census results)	
4 December 1992	8,487,317
1 March 2001	
Males	3,862,465
Females	4,066,436
Total	7,928,901
Population (official estimates at 31 December)	
2004	7,761,049
2005	7,718,750
2006	7,679,290
Density (per sq km) at 31 December 2006	69.2

* Including territorial waters of frontier rivers (261.4 sq km).
† 42,855 sq miles.

ETHNIC GROUPS
(2001 census)

	Number	%
Bulgarian	6,655,210	83.94
Turkish	746,664	9.42
Roma	370,908	4.68
Others*	156,119	1.97
Total	**7,928,901**	**100.00**

* Including 62,108 (0.78% of the total) who chose not to be defined by ethnic group, and 24,807 (0.31%) who did not respond to the question on ethnicity.

BULGARIA

ADMINISTRATIVE REGIONS
(official estimates at 31 December 2006)

	Area (sq km)	Population	Density (per sq km)
City Oblast			
Sofia City	1,038.8	1,237,891	1,191.7
Oblasts			
Blagoevgrad	6,468.8	330,034	51.0
Burgas	7,610.6	417,810	54.9
Dobrich	4,692.5	204,738	43.6
Gabrovo	2,069.5	134,490	65.0
Kardzhali	4,023.0	157,463	39.1
Khaskovo	4,032.0	264,312	65.6
Kyustendil	3,004.2	150,792	50.2
Lovech	4,131.0	157,407	38.1
Montana	3,587.6	164,057	45.7
Pazardzhik	4,382.2	296,281	67.6
Pernik	2,356.7	139,677	59.3
Pleven	4,187.1	301,634	72.0
Plovdiv	5,595.1	706,413	126.3
Razgrad	2,647.9	137,853	52.1
Ruse	2,625.9	255,315	97.2
Shumen	3,376.5	197,632	58.5
Silistra	2,878.1	132,699	46.1
Sliven	3,731.7	209,169	56.1
Smolyan	3,520.6	129,731	36.8
Sofia	7,389.4	258,397	35.0
Stara Zagora	4,905.6	358,342	73.0
Targovishche	2,756.0	134,264	48.7
Varna	3,822.8	456,915	119.5
Veliko Tarnovo	4,693.5	280,883	59.8
Vidin	3,112.3	114,769	36.9
Vratsa	4,189.1	205,797	49.1
Yambol	4,165.1	144,525	27.5
Total	110,993.6	7,679,290	69.2

Each oblast is named after its capital city.

PRINCIPAL TOWNS
(population at 2001 census)

Sofia (capital)	1,173,988	Sliven	136,148
Plovdiv	338,302	Pazardzhik	127,918
Varna	320,668	Pernik	104,626
Burgas (Bourgas)	209,479	Shumen	104,473
Ruse (Roussé)	178,435	Dobrich*	100,000
Stara Zagora	167,708	Khaskovo	99,181
Pleven	149,174	Veliko Tarnovo	90,504

*Known as Tolbukhin in 1949–90.

Mid-2005 ('000, incl. suburbs, UN estimate): Sofia 1,093 (Source: UN, *World Urbanization Prospects: The 2005 Revision*).

BIRTHS, MARRIAGES AND DEATHS

	Registered live births		Registered marriages*		Registered deaths	
	Number	Rate (per 1,000)	Number	Rate (per 1,000)	Number	Rate (per 1,000)
1997	64,125	7.7	34,772	4.2	121,861	14.7
1998	65,361	7.9	35,591	4.3	118,190	14.3
1999	72,291	8.8	35,540	4.3	111,786	13.6
2000	73,679	9.0	35,164	4.3	115,087	14.1
2001	68,180	8.6	31,974	4.0	112,368	14.2
2002	67,262	8.5	29,218	3.7	112,858	14.3
2003	67,359	8.6	30,645	3.9	111,927	14.3
2004	69,886	9.0	n.a.	4.0	110,110	14.2

*Including marriages of Bulgarian nationals outside the country, but excluding those of aliens in Bulgaria.

Source: partly UN, *Population and Vital Statistics* and *Monthly Bulletin of Statistics*.

2005: Birth rate 9.2 per 1,000; Marriage rate 4.3 per 1,000; Death rate 14.6 per 1,000.

2006: Birth rate 9.6 per 1,000; Marriage rate 4.3 per 1,000; Death rate 14.7 per 1,000.

Expectation of life (years at birth): 72.6 (males 69.1; females 76.3) in 2006.

Statistical Survey

ECONOMICALLY ACTIVE POPULATION
(labour force survey, '000 persons aged 15 years and over)

	2004	2005	2006
Agriculture, hunting, forestry and fishing	282.1	265.4	252.2
Mining and quarrying	38.9	36.9	38.2
Manufacturing	697.2	728.7	745.1
Electricity, gas and water supply	62.5	64.0	58.9
Construction	169.7	190.6	230.0
Wholesale and retail trade; repair of motor vehicles, motorcycles and personal and household goods	435.6	447.1	494.0
Hotels and restaurants	140.6	150.2	156.4
Transport and communications	211.6	213.9	220.3
Financial intermediation	34.4	37.8	39.1
Real estate, renting and business activities	132.2	141.6	147.1
Public administration and defence; compulsory social security	220.8	214.1	225.0
Education	210.4	207.2	214.9
Health and social work	157.0	159.6	163.8
Other community, social and personal service activities	127.2	120.8	125.1
Activities not adequately defined	1.7	2.1	—
Total employed	2,922.2	2,980.0	3,110.0
Unemployed	399.8	334.2	305.7
Total labour force	3,322.0	3,314.2	3,415.8

Source: ILO.

Health and Welfare

KEY INDICATORS

Total fertility rate (children per woman, 2005)	1.2
Under-5 mortality rate (per 1,000 live births, 2005)	15
HIV/AIDS (% of persons aged 15–49, 2005)	<0.10
Physicians (per 1,000 head, 2003)	3.6
Hospital beds (per 1,000 head, 2005)	6.4
Health expenditure (2004): US $ per head (PPP)	671.2
Health expenditure (2004): % of GDP	8.0
Health expenditure (2004): public (% of total)	57.6
Access to water (% of persons, 2004)	99
Access to sanitation (% of persons, 2004)	99
Human Development Index (2005): ranking	53
Human Development Index (2005): value	0.824

For sources and definitions, see explanatory note on p. vi.

Agriculture

PRINCIPAL CROPS
('000 metric tons)

	2004	2005	2006
Wheat	3,961.2	3,478.1	3,301.9
Rice (paddy)	28.1	20.2	20.0
Barley	1,180.8	657.9	546.3
Maize	2,123.0	1,585.7	1,587.8
Rye	17.0	13.6	12.7
Oats	101.5	50.1	30.5
Triticale (wheat-rye hybrid)	27.6	22.6	25.7
Potatoes	573.2	375.5	386.1
Sugar beet	26.4	24.7	26.8
Dry beans	9.3	10.1	4.9
Sunflower seed	1,078.8	934.9	1,196.6
Cabbages	116.9	69.3	72.7
Asparagus*	12.0	15.1	15.1
Tomatoes	237.6	126.5	213.0
Pumpkins, squash and gourds*	16.0	3.7	3.1
Cucumbers and gherkins	86.6	44.7	61.5
Aubergines (eggplants)	40.1	11.0	7.8
Chillies and green peppers	124.9	72.2	156.7
Dry onions	44.6	14.3	20.3
Green beans	14.5	4.1	3.2
Carrots	34.0	4.2	13.3

BULGARIA

Statistical Survey

—continued	2004	2005	2006
Mushrooms	1.3	1.4	1.9
Watermelons	100.2	75.0	135.9
Apples	39.4	26.1	26.1*
Apricots	18.5	10.6	10.6*
Sweet cherries	21.4	18.2	18.2*
Peaches and nectarines	22.5	14.8	14.8*
Plums	49.2	18.0	18.0*
Strawberries	11.5	6.6	8.8
Grapes	351.5	266.2	266.2*
Tobacco (leaves)	69.6	58.3	42.0

* FAO estimate(s).

Aggregate production ('000 metric tons, may include official, semi-official or estimated data): Total cereals 7,462.8 in 2004, 5,839.1 in 2005, 5,531.8 in 2006; Total roots and tubers 573.2 in 2004, 375.5 in 2005, 386.1 in 2006; Total vegetables (incl. melons) 990.0 in 2004, 522.1 in 2005, 788.8 in 2006; Total fruits (excl. melons) 525.2 in 2004, 369.1 in 2005, 371.3 in 2006.

Source: FAO.

LIVESTOCK
('000 head at 1 January each year)

	2004	2005	2006
Horses	126.3	n.a.	125.0*
Asses	143.7	n.a.	145.0*
Cattle	728.3	671.6	621.8
Pigs	1,032.3	931.4	943.0
Sheep	1,598.6	1,692.5	1,602.3
Goats	725.3	718.1	608.4
Poultry	21,552	19,495	19,488

* FAO estimate.

Source: FAO.

LIVESTOCK PRODUCTS
('000 metric tons)

	2004	2005	2006
Cattle meat	30.8	29.8	22.9
Sheep meat	14.3	17.7	18.1
Goat meat	6.2	6.7	5.6
Pig meat	78.3	74.5	77.0
Poultry meat	83.0	97.1	92.2*
Cows' milk	1,344.8	1,286.9	1,298.7
Buffaloes' milk	6.2	7.0	7.1
Sheeps' milk	117.7	105.1	107.5
Goats' milk	129.4	109.1	102.3
Hen eggs	97.4	97.0	99.2
Other poultry eggs	0.1	0.5	1.3
Honey	8.0	11.2	10.1
Wool: greasy	6.5	6.5	6.5*

* FAO estimate.

Source: FAO.

Forestry

ROUNDWOOD REMOVALS
('000 cubic metres, excl. bark)

	2003	2004	2005
Sawlogs, veneer logs and logs for sleepers	1,581	1,334	1,367
Pulpwood	971	1,649	1,723
Other industrial wood*	94	94	94
Fuel wood	2,187	2,909	2,678
Total	4,833	5,986	5,862

* FAO estimates.

2006: Production assumed to be unchanged from 2005 (FAO estimates).

Source: FAO.

SAWNWOOD PRODUCTION
('000 cubic metres, incl. sleepers)

	2002*	2003*	2004
Coniferous (softwood)	253	253	431
Broadleaved (hardwood)	79	79	138
Total	332	332	569

* FAO estimates.

2005–06: Figures assumed to be unchanged from 2004 (FAO estimates).

Source: FAO.

Fishing

('000 metric tons, live weight)

	2003	2004	2005
Capture	12.0	8.3	5.4
Common carp	0.8	1.0	0.7
European sprat	9.2	2.9	2.3
Sea snails	0.3	2.4	0.5
Aquaculture	4.5	2.5	3.1
Common carp	0.8	0.6	0.9
Other cyprinids	1.6	n.a.	n.a.
Rainbow trout	0.0	1.2	1.2
Total catch	16.5	10.7	8.6

Source: FAO.

Mining

('000 metric tons, unless otherwise indicated)

	2003	2004	2005
Anthracite	9	—	—
Other hard coal	44	170	96
Lignite	24,597	23,385	22,193
Other brown coal	3,044	3,071	2,620
Crude petroleum	27	30	27
Natural gas (million cu metres)	11	333	537
Iron ore: gross weight	466	83	—
Iron ore: metal content	127	27	—
Copper ore*†	116	107	112
Copper concentrate†	92	80	94
Lead—mine output†	31	25	32
Lead concentrate*†	24.6	19.0	22.0
Zinc—mine output†	31.0	19.0	22.0
Zinc concentrate*†	18.8	15.5	17.5
Silver—mine output (metric tons)†	50	60	60
Gold (kilograms)‡	2,142	2,431	3,868
Bentonite	146	225	181
Kaolin (raw)	1,137	1,291	1,381
Barite (Barytes)	637	237*	230
Salt (unrefined)	1,882	1,900	1,900
Gypsum and anhydrite (crude)	168	176	188

* Estimated production.
† Figures relate to the metal content of ores and concentrates.
‡ Figures relate to metal production.

Source: US Geological Survey.

BULGARIA

Statistical Survey

Industry

SELECTED PRODUCTS
('000 metric tons, unless otherwise indicated)

	2001	2002	2003
Wheat flour	637	548	551
Refined sugar	181	191	195
Wine ('000 hectolitres)	1,230	1,139	1,462
Beer ('000 hectolitres)	4,097	3,888	4,355
Cigarettes (million)	26,659	23,227	25,914
Cotton yarn (metric tons)[1]	20,700	18,500	16,100
Woven cotton fabrics[2,3]	68,700	45,300	n.a.
Wool yarn (metric tons)[1]	3,700	4,300	3,800
Woven woollen fabrics[3]	8,000	9,300	7,100
Footwear (excl. rubber, '000 pairs)	4,054	7,036	6,675
Chemical and semi-chemical wood pulp	95	95	95
Packing containers of paper and paperboard	86	103	80
Sulphuric acid (100%)	620	751	n.a.
Nitrogenous fertilizers[4]	337	193	199
Phosphate fertilizers[5]	102	120	n.a.
Clay building bricks (million)	144	173	192
Cement	2,061	2,141	2,398
Rolled iron (metric tons)	1,598	1,490	n.a.
Aluminium (base alloys, metric tons)	1,400	1,900	2,000
Refined copper—unwrought (metric tons)	41,900	40,700	n.a.
Refined lead—unwrought (metric tons)	168,500	151,600	n.a.
Zinc—unwrought (metric tons)	88,600	83,000	89,400
Crude steel (ingots)[6]	1,972	1,860	2,317
Pig iron, steel-making (incl. foundry)[6]	1,211	1,072	1,386
Lathes (number)	1,937	1,813	2,068
Fork-lift trucks (number)[7]	1,154	1,232	1,337
Refrigerators—household ('000)	145	202	244
Construction: dwellings completed (number)[8]	5,937	6,153	n.a.
Electric energy (million kWh)	43,969	42,679	42,600

[1] Pure and mixed yarn. Figures for wool include yarn of man-made staple.
[2] Pure and mixed fabrics, after undergoing finishing processes.
[3] Million square metres.
[4] Nitrogen (N) content.
[5] Phosphorous pentoxide (P_2O_5) content.
[6] Source: International Iron and Steel Institute (Brussels).
[7] Both electric and motor fork-lift trucks.
[8] Including restorations and conversions.

2004 ('000 metric tons, unless otherwise indicated): Wheat flour 562; Beer ('000 hectolitres) 3,997; Cigarettes (million) 24,462; Cement 2,043; Lathes (number) 2,324; Electrical energy (million kWh) 41,621.

Source: mostly UN, *Industrial Commodity Statistics Yearbook*.

Finance

CURRENCY AND EXCHANGE RATES

Monetary Units
100 stotinki (singular: stotinka) = 1 new lev (plural: leva).

Sterling, Dollar and Euro Equivalents (31 December 2007)
£1 sterling = 2.667 new leva;
US $1 = 1.331 new leva;
€1 = 1.960 new leva;
100 new leva = £37.50 = $75.12 = €51.03.

Average Exchange Rate (new leva per US$)
2005   1.5741
2006   1.5593
2007   1.4291

Note: On 5 July 1999 a new lev, equivalent to 1,000 old leva, was introduced. In January 1999 the value of the old lev had been linked to the German currency, the Deutsche Mark (DM), when an official exchange rate of 1 DM = 1,000 old leva was established. The new lev was thus at par with the DM. From the establishment of the euro, on 1 January 1999, the German currency had a fixed exchange rate of €1 = 1.95583 DM.

GOVERNMENT FINANCE
(general government operations, cash basis, million new leva)

Summary of Balances

	2003	2004	2005
Revenue	13,817	15,662	17,607
Less Expense	12,906	13,911	14,957
Net cash inflow from operating activities	911	1,751	2,650
Less Purchases of non-financial assets	1,162	1,284	1,718
Sales of non-financial assets	253	190	401
Cash surplus/deficit	1	657	1,334

Revenue

	2003	2004	2005
Taxes	7,634	8,903	10,293
Taxes on income, profits and capital gains	2,201	2,186	2,271
Taxes on goods and services	4,813	5,988	7,179
General taxes on goods and services	3,101	3,891	4,798
Excises	1,544	1,885	2,188
Social contributions	3,654	4,080	4,410
Grants	297	440	498
Other revenue	2,232	2,239	2,407
Total	13,817	15,662	17,607

Expense/Outlays

Expense by economic type	2003	2004	2005
Compensation of employees	2,313	2,575	2,690
Use of goods and services	3,509	3,830	4,135
Interest	723	697	686
Subsidies	940	868	876
Social benefits	5,128	5,542	6,098
Other expense	293	399	472
Total	12,906	13,911	14,957

Outlays by functions of government*	2003	2004	2005
General public services	1,569	1,622	1,549
Defence	826	875	922
Public order and safety	962	1,071	1,158
Economic affairs	1,668	1,890	2,122
Transport	692	775	838
Housing and community amenities	497	586	733
Health	1,698	1,769	2,009
Recreation, culture and religion	286	304	341
Education	1,505	1,652	1,815
Social protection	4,805	5,235	5,625
Total	13,816	15,005	16,274

* Including purchases of non-financial assets.

Source: IMF, *Government Finance Statistics Yearbook*.

2006 (million new leva): Total revenue and grants 18,203.8; Total expenditure and lending minus repayments 15,890.0 (Source: IMF, *International Financial Statistics*).

INTERNATIONAL RESERVES
(US $ million at 31 December)

	2004	2005	2006
Gold*	445.9	654.2	813.1
IMF special drawing rights	13.1	1.0	1.1
Reserve position in IMF	51.0	47.2	49.9
Foreign exchange	8,712.1	7,992.4	10,892.1
Total	9,222.1	8,694.8	11,756.2

* Valued at market-related prices.

Source: IMF, *International Financial Statistics*.

BULGARIA

MONEY SUPPLY
(million new leva at 31 December)

	2004	2005	2006
Currency outside banks	4,627.9	5,395.5	6,230.7
Demand deposits at deposit money banks	5,163.9	6,898.3	9,718.5
Total money (incl. others)	10,297.9	12,443.0	16,078.4

Source: IMF, *International Financial Statistics*.

COST OF LIVING
(Consumer Price Index; base: 2000 = 100)

	2004	2005	2006
Food	112.5	117.0	123.4
Fuel and light	142.8	154.1	162.0
Clothing	98.3	99.2	102.6
Rent	124.7	132.3	139.5
All items (incl. others)	123.4	129.6	139.0

Source: ILO.

NATIONAL ACCOUNTS
(million new leva at current prices)
Expenditure on the Gross Domestic Product

	2004	2005	2006
Government final consumption expenditure	7,151	7,709	8,537
Private final consumption expenditure	26,919	30,033	33,958
Gross fixed capital formation	7,969	10,347	12,878
Changes in inventories	1,006	1,624	2,792
Total domestic expenditure	43,045	49,713	58,165
Exports of goods and services	22,123	25,766	31,420
Less Imports of goods and services	26,603	32,692	40,741
Statistical discrepancy	257	11	245
GDP in market prices	38,823	42,797	49,091

Source: IMF, *International Financial Statistics*.

Gross Domestic Product by Economic Activity

	2003	2004	2005*
Agriculture and forestry	3,485	3,576	3,327
Fishing	14	14	14
Mining	440	530	566
Manufacturing	5,516	5,989	6,750
Electricity, gas and water	1,652	1,722	1,626
Construction	1,364	1,668	2,026
Trade	2,186	2,506	2,950
Transport	2,195	2,365	2,634
Communications	1,971	2,205	2,318
Financial services	1,147	1,382	1,682
Other services	10,258	11,213	12,130
Gross value added in basic prices	30,227	33,169	36,023
Less Financial intermediation services indirectly measured	−753	−1,043	−1,360
Taxes on products	4,841	5,856	6,913
Import duties	231	292	372
GDP in market prices	34,547	38,275	41,948

* Preliminary figures.

Source: IMF, *Bulgaria: Selected Issues and Statistical Appendix* (August 2006).

BALANCE OF PAYMENTS
(US $ million)

	2004	2005	2006
Exports of goods f.o.b.	9,931.2	11,754.1	15,064.1
Imports of goods f.o.b.	−13,619.1	−17,204.4	−21,873.5
Trade balance	−3,688.0	−5,450.3	−6,809.4
Exports of services	4,029.4	4,404.1	5,043.7
Imports of services	−3,238.4	−3,403.8	−4,111.9
Balance on goods and services	−2,896.9	−4,450.0	−5,877.6
Other income received	1,539.3	1,515.6	1,602.3
Other income paid	−1,235.9	−1,323.2	−1,555.2
Balances on goods, services and income	−2,593.5	−4,257.6	−5,830.4
Current transfers received	1,121.0	1,238.0	1,039.6
Current transfers paid	−198.6	−224.7	−219.0
Current balance	−1,671.1	−3,244.2	−5,009.8
Capital account (net)	204.0	256.3	227.9
Direct investment abroad	217.0	−307.6	−155.6
Direct investment from abroad	2,662.2	4,252.1	5,171.7
Portfolio investment assets	9.6	29.4	−273.4
Portfolio investment liabilities	57.9	374.0	609.1
Financial derivatives assets	−85.9	−112.5	−176.8
Financial derivatives liabilities	—	0.5	7.9
Other investment assets	−1,784.5	16.7	−2,356.1
Other investment liabilities	2,351.9	2,134.3	3,988.7
Net errors and omissions	370.8	−772.3	253.9
Overall balance	2,331.8	2,626.7	2,287.6

Source: IMF, *International Financial Statistics*.

External Trade

PRINCIPAL COMMODITIES
(€ million)

Imports c.i.f.	2004	2005	2006
Furniture and household appliances	394.6	469.8	602.0
Medicines and cosmetics	425.4	466.0	527.5
Automobiles	385.2	480.0	567.2
Ores	449.7	590.3	998.3
Iron and steel	458.6	585.1	802.1
Textiles	1,356.6	1,343.3	1,412.3
Plastics and rubber	552.8	696.3	844.3
Machines and equipment	1,052.5	1,395.7	1,626.8
Electrical machines	350.2	459.6	595.5
Vehicles	837.0	1,198.8	1,354.8
Spare parts and equipment	413.6	510.0	610.1
Crude petroleum and natural gas	1,482.6	2,283.4	3,189.3
Total (incl. others)	11,619.5	14,667.7	18,375.0

Exports f.o.b.	2004	2005	2006
Food	348.6	405.2	430.8
Clothing and footwear	1,549.4	1,540.0	1,611.0
Furniture and household appliances	279.5	314.7	361.9
Iron and steel	805.3	763.2	885.7
Other metals	746.6	942.7	1,703.7
Chemicals	254.6	280.4	301.7
Textiles	293.5	308.3	361.1
Raw materials for the food industry	277.9	408.6	413.4
Machines and equipment	357.0	415.1	490.1
Petroleum products	624.6	975.6	1,589.8
Other mineral fuels and electricity	184.0	246.3	269.9
Total (incl. others)	7,984.9	9,466.3	11,982.6

BULGARIA

Statistical Survey

PRINCIPAL TRADING PARTNERS
(€ million)

Imports c.i.f.	2004	2005	2006
Austria	274.8	316.8	386.9
Belgium	167.7	181.2	211.4
Brazil	189.9	252.2	365.5
China	377.1	567.4	761.7
Czech Republic	196.6	213.2	266.1
France	617.1	687.3	753.3
Germany	1,693.4	1,998.2	2,276.5
Greece	667.7	735.0	907.5
Hungary	141.0	171.4	232.2
Italy	1,141.6	1,318.4	1,602.6
Japan	151.4	176.9	247.6
Netherlands	193.0	210.6	233.0
Poland	173.1	238.9	360.3
Romania	342.3	547.4	691.9
Russia	1,469.8	2,294.2	3,173.1
Spain	244.0	271.9	321.2
Sweden	134.2	174.4	178.9
Switzerland	138.9	146.8	192.5
Turkey	700.1	888.3	1,101.9
Ukraine	471.2	560.0	570.8
United Kingdom	282.1	335.3	349.5
USA	254.1	362.8	369.7
Total (incl. others)	11,619.5	14,667.7	18,375.0

Exports f.o.b.	2004	2005	2006
Austria	175.8	177.8	226.9
Belgium	474.4	564.2	775.1
France	359.2	435.4	494.6
Germany	816.1	928.9	1,150.1
Greece	794.0	891.2	1,060.9
Italy	1,043.2	1,132.5	1,209.1
Macedonia, former Yugoslav republic	166.4	188.1	242.7
Netherlands	101.6	115.3	152.1
Poland	80.3	103.3	163.0
Romania	316.8	356.8	478.8
Russia	100.7	122.1	164.5
Spain	268.9	307.8	378.0
Switzerland	51.2	68.0	110.6
Turkey	797.9	990.7	1,369.6
United Kingdom	199.7	208.3	282.6
USA	356.7	286.4	324.7
Serbia and Montenegro	276.9	282.4	443.3
Total (incl. others)	7,984.9	9,466.4	11,982.6

Transport

RAILWAYS
(traffic)

	2001	2002	2003
Passengers carried ('000)	41,817	33,719	35,206
Passenger-kilometres (million)	2,990	2,598	2,517
Freight carried ('000 metric tons)	19,285	18,500	20,070
Freight net ton-kilometres (million)	4,904	4,628	5,274

ROAD TRAFFIC
(motor vehicles in use at 31 December)

	2000	2001	2002
Passenger cars	1,908,392	2,085,730	2,254,222
Buses and coaches	41,971	42,870	44,255
Lorries and vans	271,463	245,962	262,641
Motorcycles and mopeds	519,212	526,046	520,296

2004: Passenger cars 2,438,383; Buses 36,000; Lorries and vans 317,681; Motorcycles 137,955.

Source: International Road Federation, *World Road Statistics*.

INLAND WATERWAYS
(traffic)

	2000	2001	2002
Passengers carried ('000)	76	67	60
Passenger-kilometres (million)	1	—	—
Freight carried ('000 metric tons)	1,846	1,300	1,621
Freight ton-kilometres (million)	397	365	571

SHIPPING

Merchant Fleet
(registered at 31 December)

	2004	2005	2006
Number of vessels	113	123	134
Total displacement ('000 grt)	789.5	894.2	875.5

Source: Lloyd's Register-Fairplay, *World Fleet Statistics*.

Sea-borne Traffic
(international and coastal)

	2000	2001	2002
Freight ('000 metric tons)	18,619	16,737	15,557
Freight ton-kilometres (million)	74,391	67,551	60,814

CIVIL AVIATION
(traffic)

	2001	2002	2003
Passengers carried ('000)	234	63	311
Kilometres flown (million)	6	1	7
Passenger-kilometres (million)	362	57	457
Total ton-kilometres (million)	31	5	42

Source: UN, *Statistical Yearbook*.

Tourism

ARRIVALS OF FOREIGN VISITORS

Country of origin	2004	2005	2006
Czech Republic	102,045	116,111	111,429
Germany	565,337	545,265	481,118
Greece	707,453	615,219	550,571
Israel	79,172	97,773	81,080
Macedonia, former Yugoslav republic*	655,974	545,861	506,193
Poland	99,684	102,775	107,416
Romania*	91,539	144,312	323,106
Russia	120,523	144,841	182,374
Serbia and Montenegro*	655,974	513,482	590,367
Sweden	96,131	98,206	98,813
United Kingdom	259,092	353,023	392,977
Total (incl. others)	4,010,326	4,090,421	4,364,557

* Includes 'shuttle traders'.

Tourism receipts (US $ million, incl. passenger transport): 2,051 in 2003; 2,797 in 2004; 3,026 in 2005 (Source: World Tourism Organization).

Communications Media

	2004	2005	2006
Telephones ('000 main lines in use)	2,726.8	2,490.0	2,399.4
Mobile cellular telephones ('000 subscribers)	4,729.7	6,244.9	8,253.4
Internet users ('000)	1,234.0	1,591.7	1,870.0
Broadband subscribers ('000)	—	165.5	384.3
Book production:*			
titles	6,432	6,029	6,562
copies ('000)	4,286	3,917	4,138
Newspapers:			
titles	424	423	446
total circulation ('000 copies)	318,070	310,023	325,733
Magazines:†			
titles	712	746	778
total circulation ('000 copies)	12,902	13,665	22,159

* Including pamphlets.
† Including bulletins.

Facsimile machines (number in use): 15,000 in 1995 (estimate).

Television receivers (number in use): 3,692,000 in 2000.

Sources: partly UN, *Statistical Yearbook*, UNESCO, *Statistical Yearbook*, and International Telecommunication Union.

Education

(2006/07)

	Institutions	Teachers	Students
Kindergartens	2,470*	19,305	206,745
General and special schools:			
primary	252	17,054	267,584
basic	1,791	n.a.	n.a.
lower secondary	20	25,567	276,057
upper secondary	170	33,927†	357,286
combined schools	421	n.a.	n.a.
Vocational	506	n.a.	n.a.
Colleges	10	2,136	26,953‡
Universities and equivalent	43	21,300	231,739§

* Excluding dependent half-day kindergartens.
† Including teaching staff in interschools centres.
‡ Qualification degree 'specialist'.
§ Including 4,816 post-graduates studying for 'specialist' degrees.

Adult literacy rate (UNESCO estimates): 98.2% (males 98.7%; females 97.7%) in 2001 (Source: UNESCO Institute for Statistics).

Directory

The Constitution

The Constitution of the Republic of Bulgaria, summarized below, took effect upon its promulgation, on 13 July 1991.

FUNDAMENTAL PRINCIPLES

The Republic of Bulgaria is to have a parliamentary form of government, with all state power derived from the people. The rule of law and the life, dignity and freedom of the individual are guaranteed. The Constitution is the supreme law; the power of the State is shared between the legislature, the executive and the judiciary. The Constitution upholds principles such as political and religious freedom (although no party may be formed on separatist, ethnic or religious lines), free economic initiative and respect for international law.

THE NARODNO SOBRANIYE

The Narodno Sobraniye (National Assembly) is the legislature of Bulgaria. It consists of 240 members, elected for a four-year term. Only Bulgarian citizens aged over 21 years (who do not hold a state post or another citizenship and are not under judicial interdiction or in prison) are eligible for election to parliament. A member of the Narodno Sobraniye ceases to serve as a deputy while holding ministerial office. The Narodno Sobraniye is a permanently acting body, which is free to determine its own recesses and elects its own Chairman and Deputy Chairmen.

The Narodno Sobraniye may function when more than one-half of its members are present, and may pass legislation and other acts by a majority of more than one-half of the members present, except where a qualified majority is required by the Constitution. The most important functions of the legislature are: the enactment of laws; the approval of the state budget; the scheduling of presidential elections; the election and dismissal of the Chairman of the Council of Ministers (Prime Minister) and of other members of the Council of Ministers; the declaration of war or conclusion of peace; the foreign deployment of troops; and the ratification of any fundamental international instruments to which the Republic has agreed.

THE PRESIDENT OF THE REPUBLIC

The Head of State, the President of the Republic, is assisted by a Vice-President. The President and Vice-President are elected jointly, directly by the voters, for a period of five years. A candidate must be eligible for election to the Narodno Sobraniye, but also aged over 40 years and a resident of the country for the five years previous to the election. To be elected, a candidate must receive more than one-half of the valid votes cast, in an election in which more than one-half of the eligible electorate participate. If necessary, a second ballot must then be conducted, contested by the two candidates who received the most votes. The one who receives more votes becomes President. The President and Vice-President may hold the same office for only two terms. If the President resigns, is incapacitated, impeached or dies, the Vice-President carries out the presidential duties. If neither official can perform their duties, the Chairman of the Narodno Sobraniye assumes the prerogatives of the Presidency, until new elections take place.

The President's main responsibilities include the scheduling of elections and referendums, the conclusion of international treaties and the promulgation of laws. The President is responsible for appointing a Prime Minister-designate (priority must be given to the leaders of the two largest parties represented in the Narodno Sobraniye), who must then attempt to form a government.

The President has certain emergency powers, usually subject to the later approval of the Narodno Sobraniye. Many of the President's actions must be approved by the Chairman of the Council of Ministers. The President may return legislation to the Narodno Sobraniye for further consideration, but can be overruled.

THE COUNCIL OF MINISTERS

The principal organ of executive government is the Council of Ministers, which supervises the implementation of state policy and the state budget, the administration of the country and the Armed Forces, and the maintenance of law and order. The Council of Ministers is headed and co-ordinated by the Chairman (Prime Minister), who is responsible for the overall policy of government. The Council of Ministers, which also includes Deputy Chairmen and Ministers, must resign upon the death of the Chairman or if the Narodno Sobraniye votes in favour of a motion of 'no confidence' in the Council or in the Chairman.

JUDICIAL POWER

The judicial branch of government is independent. The Supreme Court of Cassation, which exercises supreme judicial responsibility for the precise and equal application of the law by all courts. The Supreme Administrative Court rules on all challenges to the legality of acts of any organ of government. The Supreme Judicial Council is responsible for appointments within the ranks of the justices, prosecutors and investigating magistrates, and recommends to the President of the Republic the appointment or dismissal of the Chairmen of the two Supreme Courts and of the Chief Prosecutor (they are each appointed for a single, seven-year term). These last three officials are, *ex officio*, members of the Supreme Judicial Council, together with 22 others, who must be practising lawyers of at least 15 years' professional experience. These members are elected for a term of five years, 11 of them by the Narodno Sobraniye and 11 by bodies of the judiciary. The Supreme Judicial Council is chaired by the Minister of Justice, who is not entitled to vote.

LOCAL SELF-GOVERNMENT

Bulgaria is divided into regions and municipalities. Municipalities are the basic administrative territorial unit at which local self-government is practised; their principal organ is the municipal council, which is elected directly by the population for a term of four years. The council elects a mayor. Regional government is entrusted to regional governors (appointed by the Council of Ministers) and administrations, and is responsible for regional policy and the implementation of state policy at a local level.

THE CONSTITUTIONAL COURT

The Constitutional Court consists of 12 justices, four of whom are elected by the Narodno Sobraniye, four appointed by the President of the Republic and four elected by the justices of the two Supreme Courts. Candidates must have the same eligibility as for membership of the Supreme Judicial Council. They serve a single term of nine years, but a part of the membership changes every three years. A chairman is elected by a secret ballot of the members.

The Constitutional Court provides binding interpretations of the Constitution. It rules on the constitutionality of: laws and decrees; competence suits between organs of government; international agreements; national and presidential elections; and impeachments. A ruling of the Court requires a majority of more than one-half of the votes of all the justices.

CONSTITUTIONAL AMENDMENTS AND THE ADOPTION OF A NEW CONSTITUTION

Except for those provisions reserved to the competence of a Velikoto Narodno Sobraniye (see below), the Narodno Sobraniye is empowered to amend the Constitution with a majority of three-quarters of all its Members, in three ballots on three different days. Amendments must be proposed by one-quarter of the parliamentary membership or by the President. In some cases, a majority of two-thirds of all the Members of the Narodno Sobraniye will suffice.

Velikoto Narodno Sobraniye

A Velikoto Narodno Sobraniye (Grand National Assembly) consists of 400 members, elected by the generally established procedure. It alone is empowered to adopt a new constitution, to sanction territorial changes to the Republic, to resolve on any changes in the form of state structure or form of government, and to enact amendments to certain parts of the existing Constitution (including those concerning the direct application of the Constitution, the domestic application of international agreements, the irrevocable nature of fundamental civil rights and of certain basic individual rights even in times of emergency or war).

Any bill requiring the convening of a Velikoto Narodno Sobraniye must be introduced by the President of the Republic or by one-third of the members of the Narodno Sobraniye. A decision to hold elections for a Velikoto Narodno Sobraniye must be supported by two-thirds of the members of the Narodno Sobraniye. Enactments of the Velikoto Narodno Sobraniye require a majority of two-thirds of the votes of all the members, in three ballots on three different days. A Velikoto Narodno Sobraniye may resolve only on the proposals for which it was elected, whereupon its prerogatives normally expire.

The Government

HEAD OF STATE AND VICE-PRESIDENT

President: GEORGI PARVANOV (took office 22 January 2002; re-elected 29 October 2006).
Vice-President: ANGEL MARIN.

COUNCIL OF MINISTERS
(April 2008)

A coalition of the Bulgarian Socialist Party (BSP), the National Movement for Stability and Progress (NMSP) and the Movement for Rights and Freedoms (MRF).
Prime Minister: SERGEY STANISHEV (BSP).
Deputy Prime Minister and Minister of Foreign Affairs: IVAILO KALFIN (BSP).
Deputy Prime Minister and Minister of Education and Science: DANIEL VALCHEV (NMSP).
Deputy Prime Minister and Minister of Disaster Prevention: EMEL ETEM (MRF).
Deputy Prime Minister, in charge of EU Funds: MEGLENA PLUGCHIEVA (BSP).
Minister of European Affairs: GERGANA GRANCHAROVA (NMSP).
Minister of the Economy and Energy: PETAR DIMITROV (BSP).
Minister of Finance: PLAMEN ORESHARSKI (Independent).
Minister of Defence: NIKOLAY TSONEV (NMSP).
Minister of the Interior: MIHAIL MIKOV (BSP).
Minister of Justice: MEGLENA TACHEVA (NMSP).
Minister of Labour and Social Policy: EMILIA MASLAROVA (BSP).
Minister of State Administration and Administrative Reform: NIKOLAY VASILEV (NMSP).
Minister of Transport: PETAR MUTAFCHIEV (BSP).
Minister of Regional Development and Public Works: ASSEN GAGAUZOV (BSP).
Minister of the Environment and Water: Dr DZHEVDET CHAKAROV (MRF).
Minister of Agriculture and Food Supply: VALERI TSVETANOV (MRF).
Minister of Health: EVGENIY ZHELEV (BSP).
Minister of Culture: STEFAN DANAILOV (BSP).

MINISTRIES

Office of the President: 1123 Sofia, bul. Dondukov 2; tel. (2) 923-93-33; e-mail press@president.bg; internet www.president.bg.

Council of Ministers: 1194 Sofia, bul. Dondukov 1; tel. (2) 940-29-99; fax (2) 980-20-56; e-mail iprd@government.bg; internet www.government.bg.

Ministry of Agriculture and Food Supply: 1040 Sofia, bul. Hristo Botev 55; tel. (2) 980-99-27; fax (2) 980-62-56; e-mail press@mzp.government.bg; internet www.mzgar.government.bg.

Ministry of Culture: 1040 Sofia, bul. A. Stamboliyski 17; tel. (2) 940-08-63; fax (2) 981-81-45; e-mail press@mc.government.bg; internet www.mc.government.bg.

Ministry of Defence: 1000 Sofia, ul. Dyakon Ignatiy 3; tel. (2) 922-09-22; fax (2) 987-32-28; e-mail presscntr@mod.bg; internet www.md.government.bg.

Ministry of Disaster Prevention: 1000 Sofia, pl. Sv. Nedelia 6; tel. (2) 940-14-01; fax (2) 940-15-99; internet www.mdpba.government.bg.

Ministry of the Economy and Energy: 1000 Sofia, ul. Slavyanska 8; tel. (2) 940-71-00; fax (2) 987-21-90; e-mail public@mi.government.bg; internet www.mi.government.bg.

Ministry of Education and Science: 1540 Sofia, bul. Dondukov 2; tel. (2) 921-77-44; fax (2) 988-26-93; e-mail press_mon@minedu.government.bg; internet www.minedu.government.bg.

Ministry of the Environment and Water: 1000 Sofia, ul. U. Gladston 67; tel. (2) 940-62-31; fax (2) 988-59-13; e-mail vivanova@moew.government.bg; internet www.moew.government.bg.

Ministry of European Affairs: 1040 Sofia, ul. Al. Zhendov 2; tel. (2) 971-32-12; fax (2) 971-29-06; e-mail mtsankova@mfa.government.bg; internet www.evroportal.bg.

Ministry of Finance: 1000 Sofia, ul. G. S. Rakovski 102; tel. (2) 985-920-22; fax (2) 985-920-24; internet www.minfin.government.bg.

Ministry of Foreign Affairs: 1040 Sofia, ul. Al. Zhendov 2; tel. (2) 971-14-08; fax (2) 870-30-41; e-mail iprd@mfa.government.bg; internet www.mfa.government.bg.

Ministry of Health: 1000 Sofia, pl. Sv. Nedelya 5; tel. (2) 930-011-01; fax (2) 981-26-39; e-mail press@mh.government.bg; internet www.mh.government.bg.

Ministry of the Interior: 1000 Sofia, ul. 6-ti Septemvri 29; tel. (2) 982-20-14; fax (2) 982-20-47; internet www.mvr.bg.

Ministry of Justice: 1040 Sofia, ul. Slavyanska 1; tel. (2) 988-48-23; fax (2) 981-91-57; e-mail pr@justice.government.bg; internet www.mjeli.government.bg.

Ministry of Labour and Social Policy: 1051 Sofia, ul. Triaditsa 2; tel. (2) 811-94-43; fax (2) 988-44-05; e-mail mlsp@mlsp.government.bg; internet www.mlsp.government.bg.

Ministry of Regional Development and Public Works: 1000 Sofia, ul. Kiril i Metodiy 17–19; tel. (2) 940-54-30; fax (2) 987-58-56; e-mail press@mrrb.government.bg; internet www.mrrb.government.bg.

Ministry of State Administration and Administrative Reform: 1000 Sofia, ul. Aksakov 1; tel. (2) 940-11-58; fax (2) 940-11-81; e-mail press@mdaar.government.bg; internet www.mdaar.government.bg.

Ministry of Transport: 1000 Sofia, ul. Dyakon Ignatiy 9; tel. (2) 940-95-00; fax (2) 987-18-05; e-mail press@mtc.government.bg; internet www.mtc.government.bg.

BULGARIA

President

Presidential Election, First Round, 22 October 2006

Candidate	Votes	% of votes
Georgi Parvanov (Bulgarian Socialist Party)	1,780,119	64.05
Volen Siderov (Attack Party)	597,175	21.49
Nedelcho Beronov (Independent)	271,078	9.75
Others	131,001	4.71
Total	**2,779,373**	**100.00**

Second Round, 29 October 2006

Candidate	Votes	% of votes
Georgi Parvanov (Bulgarian Socialist Party)	2,050,488	75.95
Volen Siderov (Attack Party)	649,387	24.05
Total	**2,699,875**	**100.00**

Legislature

Narodno Sobraniye (National Assembly)

1169 Sofia, pl. Narodno Sobraniye 2; tel. (2) 939-39; fax (2) 981-31-31; e-mail infocenter@parliament.bg; internet www.parliament.bg.

Chairman: Georgi Pirinski.

General Election, 25 June 2005

Party	% of votes	Seats
Coalition for Bulgaria*	34.17	82
National Movement Simeon II	22.08	53
Movement for Rights and Freedoms	14.17	34
Attack National Union	8.75	21
United Democratic Forces	8.33	20
Democrats for a Strong Bulgaria	7.08	17
Bulgarian People's Union	5.42	13
Total	**100.00**	**240**

*A coalition of eight parties, led by the Bulgarian Socialist Party.

Election Commission

Central Election Committee: 1169 Sofia, pl. A. Battenberg 1; tel. (2) 971-10-02; fax (2) 986-16-79; Chair. Lena Dzhelepova.

Political Organizations

Attack Party (Partiya Ataka): 1784 Sofia, bul. Tsargradsko shose 113; tel. and fax (2) 846-51-31; e-mail volenataka@abv.bg; internet www.atakabg.com; f. 2005 as Attack National Union by coalition of the National Movement for the Salvation of the Fatherland, the Bulgarian National Patriotic Party and the Union of Patriotic Forces and Militaries of the Defence Reserve; subsequently constituted as a political party; populist, anti-Western; Leader Volen Siderov.

Bulgarian Agrarian National Union—People's Union (Balgarski Zemedelski Naroden Sayuz—BZNS—NS): 1000 Sofia, pl. Slaveikov 4A; tel. and fax (2) 987-05-77; e-mail office@zns.bg; internet www.zns.bg; contested 2005 legislative elections as part of the United Democratic Forces coalition; Pres. Stefan Lichev.

Bulgarian Social Democrats (Balgarski Sotsialdemokrati): 1504 Sofia, ul. E. Yosif 37; tel. (2) 981-09-55; fax (2) 973-24-76; internet www.pbs-d.bg; fmrly Bulgarian Social Democratic Party (United); contested 2005 legislative elections as part of the Coalition for Bulgaria; Pres. Georgi Anastasov.

Bulgarian Socialist Party (BSP) (Balgarska Sotsialisticheska Partiya): 1000 Sofia, ul. Positano 20; tel. (2) 981-85-52; fax (2) 981-20-10; e-mail info@bsp.bg; internet www.bsp.bg; f. 1891 as the Bulgarian Social Democratic Party (BSDP); renamed as above in 1990; contested legislative elections in 2005 as part of the Coalition for Bulgaria; Chair. Sergey Stanishev.

Citizens for European Development of Bulgaria (Grazhdani za evropeysko razvitie na Balgariya—GERB): 1463 Sofia, pl. Balgaria 1, NDK Administration Bldg 17; tel. (2) 490-13-13; fax (2) 490-09-51; e-mail info@gerb-bg.com; internet www.gerb-bg.com; f. Dec. 2006; centre-right; Leader Boyko Borisov; Chair. Tsvetan Tsvetanov.

Communist Party of Bulgaria (Komunisticheska Partiya na Balgariya): 1404 Sofia, bul. P. J. Todorov 5B; tel. and fax (2) 959-16-73; e-mail spasov21@yahoo.com; f. 1996; breakaway party of fmr Bulgarian Communist Party (renamed Bulgarian Socialist Party 1990); Chair. Vladimir Spasov.

Democratic Party (Demokraticheskata Partiya): 1303 Sofia, bul. Botev 61; tel. (2) 930-80-30; fax (2) 930-80-31; re-formed 1990; contested the 2005 legislative elections as part of the United Democratic Forces coalition; Chair. Aleksandar Pramatarski.

Democrats for a Strong Bulgaria (DSB) (Demokrati za silna Balgariya): 1000 Sofia, bul. Vitosha 18; tel. (2) 400-99-21; fax (2) 980-53-34; e-mail mediacentre@dsb.bg; internet www.dsb.bg; f. 2004; right-wing; Chair. Ivan Kostov.

Green Party (Zelena Partiya v Balgariya): 1000 Sofia, ul. Lavele 30; tel. (2) 987-05-92; fax (2) 987-85-38; e-mail office@greenparty.bg; internet www.greenparty.bg; f. 1989; contested 2005 legislative elections as part of the Coalition for Bulgaria; Chair. Dimitar Bongalov.

IMRO—Bulgarian National Movement (VMRO—Balgarsko natsionalno dvizhenie—VMRO—BND): 1301 Sofia, ul. Pirotska 5; tel. (2) 980-25-82; fax (2) 980-25-83; e-mail vmro@vmro.org; internet www.vmro.org; fmrly Inner Macedonian Revolutionary Organization—Bulgarian National Movement; contested the legislative elections of 2005 as part of the Bulgarian People's Union alliance; Chair. Krassimir Karakachanov.

Movement for Rights and Freedoms (MRF) (Dvizhenie za Prava i Svobodi—DPS): 1301 Sofia, bul. Al. Stamboliyski 45A; tel. (2) 811-44-66; fax (2) 811-44-60; e-mail press@dps.bg; internet www.dps.bg; f. 1990 to represent interests of Muslim minority in Bulgaria; supports integration of Bulgaria into the European Union (EU) and North Atlantic Treaty Organization (NATO); Pres. Akhmed Dogan.

National Movement for Stability and Progress (NMSP) (Natsionalno dvizhenie za stabilnost i vazhod—NDSV): 1000 Sofia, ul. Vrabcha 23; tel. (2) 921-81-63; fax (2) 921-81-65; e-mail ndsv@ndsv.bg; internet www.ndsv.bg; f. 2001 by supporters of the former monarch; registered as a political party, National Movement Simeon II, in 2002; name changed June 2007; Chair. Simeon Sakskoburggotski.

The New Time (Novoto vreme): Sofia, bul. Vitocha 12; tel. (2) 980-23-76; fax (2) 981-45-17; e-mail party@novotovreme.bg; internet www.novotovreme.bg; f. 2003 by fmr mems of National Movement Simeon II; Leader Emil Koshlukov.

Union of Democratic Forces (UDF) (Sayuz na Demokratichnite Sili—SDS): 1000 Sofia, bul. Rakovski 134; tel. (2) 930-61-00; fax (2) 980-97-77; e-mail ahristova@sds.bg; internet www.sds.bg; f. 1989; supports the integration of Bulgaria into the EU; pro-market; contested 2005 legislative elections as part of the United Democratic Forces coalition; Chair. Plamen Yurukov.

Union of Free Democrats (Sayuz na svobodnite demokrati—SSD): 1000 Sofia, bul. Levski 91; tel. (2) 989-59-99; fax (2) 989-69-99; e-mail press@ssd.bg; internet www.ssd.bg; f. 2001 as a breakaway faction of the Union of Democratic Forces; supports greater integration of Bulgaria into the EU and NATO; contested the legislative elections of 2005 as part of the Bulgarian People's Union alliance; Leader Stefan Sofianski.

Diplomatic Representation

EMBASSIES IN BULGARIA

Afghanistan: 1618 Sofia, Ovcha Kupel, ul. Boryana 61/216A/15; tel. (2) 955-61-96; fax (2) 955-99-76; e-mail ariana@sofianet.net; Ambassador Karsimir Tulechki.

Albania: 1504 Sofia, ul. Krakra 10; tel. (2) 943-38-57; fax (2) 943-30-69; e-mail aembassy.sofia@mfa.gov.al; Ambassador Bujar Skendo.

Algeria: 1000 Sofia, ul. Slavyanska 16; tel. (2) 980-22-50; Ambassador Zine el-Abidine Hachichi.

Argentina: 1000 Sofia, ul. D. Tsankov 36, POB 635; tel. (2) 971-25-39; e-mail arebulg@mbox.contact.bg; Ambassador Gerónimo Cortés Funes.

Armenia: 1606 Sofia, ul. 20-ti April 11; tel. and fax (2) 952-60-46; e-mail armembsof@omega.bg; Ambassador Sergei Manaserian.

Austria: 1000 Sofia, ul. Shipka 4; tel. (2) 932-90-32; fax (2) 981-05-67; e-mail sofia-ob@bmaa.gov.at; Ambassador Dr Karl Diem.

Belarus: 1113 Sofia, ul. Kokiche 20; tel. (2) 965-28-43; e-mail embassyblr@omega.bg; internet www.belembassy.org/bulgaria; Ambassador Vyacheslav H. Kachanov.

BULGARIA

Belgium: 1164 Sofia, ul. V. Zavera 1; tel. (2) 988-72-90; fax (2) 963-36-38; e-mail sofia@diplobel.be; internet www.diplomatie.be/sofia; Ambassador PHILIPPE BEKE.

Brazil: 1113 Sofia, ul. F. Zh. Kyuri 19/1/6; tel. (2) 971-98-19; fax (2) 971-28-18; internet www.brazil-bg.info; Ambassador PAULO AMÉRICO VEIGA WOLOWSKI.

China, People's Republic: 1113 Sofia, ul. A. von Khambolt 7; tel. (2) 973-38-73; fax (2) 971-10-81; e-mail webmaster@chinaembassy.bg; internet bg.chineseembassy.org; Ambassador ZHANG WANXUE.

Colombia: Sofia, ul. Al. Zhendov 1; tel. (2) 971-31-03; fax (2) 972-76-60.

Croatia: 1504 Sofia, ul. Veliko Tarnovo 32; tel. (2) 943-32-25; fax (2) 946-13-55; e-mail croemb.sofia@mvp.hr; Ambassador DRAŽEN VUKOV COLIĆ.

Cuba: 1113 Sofia, ul. K. Sharkelov 1; tel. (2) 972-09-96; fax (2) 972-04-60; e-mail consulado@embacuba.bg.com; Ambassador GERARDO SUÁREZ ÁLVAREZ.

Cyprus: 1164 Sofia, ul. Dzheimz Baucher i Plachkovitsa 1A/1; tel. (2) 961-77-30; fax (2) 862-94-70; e-mail cyprusembasofia@netbg.com; Ambassador GIORGOS GIORGIS (resident in Athens, Greece).

Czech Republic: 1504 Sofia, ul. Ya. Sakazov 9; tel. (2) 946-11-11; fax (2) 946-18-00; e-mail sofia@embassy.mzv.cz; internet www.mzv.cz/sofia; Ambassador MARTIN KLEPETKO.

Denmark: 1000 Sofia, bul. Dondukov 54, POB 1393; tel. (2) 917-01-00; fax (2) 980-99-01; e-mail sofamb@um.dk; internet www.ambsofia.um.dk; Ambassador SVEND BOJE MADSEN.

Egypt: 1000 Sofia, ul. 6-ti Septemvri 5, POB 1025; tel. (2) 987-02-15; fax (2) 980-12-63; e-mail egembsof@spnet.net; Ambassador HEBA SALAH AD-DIN AL-MARASSY.

Finland: 1000 Sofia, Bacho Kiro 26; tel. (2) 810-21-10; fax (2) 810-21-11; e-mail sanomat.sof@formin.fi; internet www.finland.bg; Ambassador KAUKO JÄMSÉN.

France: 1504 Sofia, ul. Oborishte 27–29; tel. (2) 965-11-00; fax (2) 965-11-20; internet www.ambafrance-bg.org; Ambassador ETIENNE DE PONCINS.

Georgia: 1113 Sofia, ul. Krichim 65; tel. (2) 862-54-04; fax (2) 868-42-98; e-mail saelcho.sofia@mbox.contact.bg; internet www.bulgaria.mfa.gov.ge; Ambassador TEIMURAZ SHARASHENIDZE.

Germany: 1113 Sofia, ul. F. Zh. Kyuri 25, POB 869; tel. (2) 918-38-00; fax (2) 963-16-58; e-mail reg1@sofi.diplo.de; internet www.sofia.diplo.de; Ambassador MICHAEL GEIER.

Greece: 1504 Sofia, ul. San Stefano 33; tel. (2) 843-30-85; fax (2) 843-30-86; e-mail info@greekembassy-sofia.bg; internet info.greekembassy-sofia.org; Ambassador DANAE-MAGDALENE KOUMANA-KOU.

Holy See: 1000 Sofia, ul. 11-ti Avgust 6, POB 9; tel. (2) 981-21-97; fax (2) 981-61-95; e-mail nuntius@mbox.digsys.bg; Apostolic Nuncio GIUSEPPE LEANZA (Titular Archbishop of Lilibeo).

Hungary: 1000 Sofia, ul. 6-ti Septemvri 57; tel. (2) 963-11-35; fax (2) 963-21-10; e-mail embassy.sof@kum.hu; internet www.mfa.gov.hu/emb/sofia; Ambassador Dr JENŐ FALLER.

India: 1000 Sofia, bul. Patriarkh Evtimii 31; tel. (2) 986-76-72; fax (2) 980-12-89; e-mail ambsofia@inet.bg; internet www.indembsofia.org; Ambassador LAL DINGLIANA.

Indonesia: 1087 Sofia, bul. Simeonovsko shose 53/4; tel. (2) 962-52-40; fax (2) 962-58-42; e-mail kbrisofia@indonesia.bg; internet www.indonesia.bg; Ambassador R. BROTO UTOMO.

Iran: 1087 Sofia, ul. V. Levski 77; tel. (2) 987-61-73; fax (2) 980-22-60; Ambassador FEREIDUN HAKBIN.

Iraq: 1113 Sofia, ul. A. P. Chekhov 21-23; tel. (2) 973-33-48; fax (2) 971-11-97; e-mail sofemb@iraqmofamail.net; Ambassador HAIDER SHAIAA AL-BARAK.

Ireland: 1000 Sofia, Platinum Business Centre, ul. Bacho Kiro 26–28; tel. (2) 985-34-25; fax (2) 983-33-02; e-mail info@embassyofireland.bg; Ambassador GEOFFREY KEATING.

Israel: 1463 Sofia, pl. Bulgaria 1, NDK Administration Bldg; tel. (2) 951-50-44; fax (2) 952-11-01; e-mail info@sofia.mfa.gov.il; internet sofia.mfa.gov.il; Ambassador NOAH GAL-GENDLER.

Italy: 1000 Sofia, ul. Shipka 2; tel. (2) 921-73-00; fax (2) 980-37-17; e-mail ambasciata.sofia@esteri.it; internet www.ambsofia.esteri.it; Ambassador GIOVAN BATTISTA CAMPAGNOLA.

Japan: 1087 Sofia, ul. Lyulyakova gradina 14; tel. (2) 971-27-08; fax (2) 971-10-95; internet www.bg.emb-japan.go.jp; Ambassador TSUNEHARU TAKEDA.

Korea, Democratic People's Republic: 1087 Sofia, bul. A. Sakharov 4; tel. (2) 977-53-48; Ambassador JO SUNG JU.

Korea, Republic: 1414 Sofia, pl. Bulgaria 1, NDK Administration Bldg; tel. (2) 965-01-62; e-mail korean-embassy@mofat.go.kr; Ambassador CHEONG JAI-SIK.

Kuwait: 1700 Sofia, bul. Simeonovsko shose 15; tel. (2) 962-56-89; fax (2) 962-45-84; e-mail kuwaitembassy-bulgaria@spnet.net; Ambassador AHMAD ABDULLAH A. BUZUOBAR.

Lebanon: 1113 Sofia, ul. F. Zh. Kyuri 19; tel. (2) 971-31-69; fax (2) 973-32-56; Ambassador HIKMAT AWWAD.

Libya: 1784 Sofia, bul. A. Sakharov 1; tel. (2) 974-35-56; fax (2) 974-32-73; Ambassador TAHIR BENSHABAN.

Macedonia, former Yugoslav republic: 1113 Sofia, ul. F. Zh. Kyuri 17/2/1; tel. (2) 870-15-60; fax (2) 971-28-32; e-mail todmak@bgnet.bg; Ambassador ABDIRAMAN ALITI.

Moldova: 1142 Sofia, bul. G.S. Rakovski 152; tel. (2) 935-60-11; fax (2) 980-64-75; e-mail sofia@mfa.md; Ambassador VEACESLAV MADAN.

Mongolia: 1113 Sofia, ul. F. Zh. Kyuri 52; tel. (2) 865-90-12; fax (2) 963-07-45; e-mail mongemb@gmail.com; Ambassador BADAMDORJ BATKHISHIG.

Morocco: 1407 Sofia, bul. Tchervena Stena 1/1; tel. (2) 865-11-26; fax (2) 865-48-11; e-mail ambmarsofia@mbox.contact.bg; Ambassador GHAILANI DLIMI.

Netherlands: 1504 Sofia, ul. Oborishte 15, POB 91; tel. (2) 816-03-00; fax (2) 816-03-01; e-mail sof@minbuza.nl; internet www.netherlandsembassy.bg; Ambassador WILLEM VAN EE.

Peru: Sofia, ul. F. Zh. Kyuri 17/2/2; tel. (2) 971-37-08; fax (2) 973-33-46; e-mail peru@mail.bol.bg; Chargé d'affaires JULIO VEGA ERAUSQUÍN.

Poland: 1000 Sofia, ul. Chan Krum 46; tel. (2) 987-26-10; fax (2) 987-29-39; e-mail polamba@internet-bg.net; internet www.sofia.polemb.net; Ambassador ANDRZEJ PAPIERZ.

Portugal: 1504 Sofia, ul. Ivatz voyvoda 6; tel. (2) 943-36-67; fax (2) 943-30-89; e-mail embport@online.bg; Ambassador MÁRIO JESUS DOS SANTOS.

Romania: Sofia, bul. Mihai Eminescu 4; tel. (2) 971-28-58; fax (2) 973-34-12; e-mail ambsofro@vip.bg; internet sofia.mae.ro; Ambassador MIHAIL ROȘIANU.

Russia: 1087 Sofia, ul. D. Tsankov 28; tel. (2) 963-16-63; fax (2) 963-41-03; e-mail info@russia.bg; internet www.russia.bg; Ambassador ANATOLII V. POTAPOV.

Serbia: 1504 Sofia, ul. Veliko Tarnovo 3; tel. (2) 946-16-33; fax (2) 946-10-59; e-mail sofia@emb-serbia.com; internet www.emb-serbia.com; Ambassador (vacant).

Slovakia: 1504 Sofia, bul. Ya. Sakazov 9; tel. (2) 942-92-10; fax (2) 942-92-35; e-mail embassy@sofia.mfa.sk; internet www.mzv.sk/sofia; Ambassador MICHAL KOTTMAN.

Spain: 1087 Sofia, ul. Sheynovo 27; tel. (2) 943-30-32; fax (2) 946-12-01; e-mail embespbg@mail.mae.es; Ambassador FERNANDO ARIAS GONZALEZ.

Sweden: 1113 Sofia, ul. A. Nobel 4, POB 620; tel. (2) 930-19-60; fax (2) 973-37-95; e-mail ambassaden.sofia@foreign.ministry.se; internet www.swedenabroad.com/sofia; Ambassador BERTIL ROTH.

Switzerland: 1504 Sofia, ul. Shipka 33; tel. (2) 942-01-00; fax (2) 946-11-86; e-mail vertretung@sof.rep.admin.ch; Ambassador THOMAS FELLER.

Syria: 1087 Sofia, bul. Simeonovsko shose 13A; tel. (2) 962-45-80; fax (2) 962-53-89; Chargé d'affaires SADDIK SADDIKNI.

Turkey: 1087 Sofia, bul. V. Levski 80; tel. (2) 935-55-00; fax (2) 981-93-58; e-mail turkel@techno-link.com; Ambassador HAYDAR BERK.

Ukraine: 1618 Sofia, Ovcha Kupel, ul. Boryana 29; tel. (2) 955-94-78; fax 955-52-47; e-mail puvrb@mail.bol.bg; internet www.mfa.gov.ua/bulgaria; Ambassador VIKTOR M. KALNYK.

United Kingdom: 1000 Sofia, ul. Moskovska 9; tel. (2) 933-92-22; fax (2) 933-92-50; e-mail britembinf@mail.orbitel.bg; internet www.british-embassy.bg; Ambassador STEVE WILLIAMS.

USA: 1407 Sofia, ul. Kozyak 16; tel. (2) 937-51-00; fax (2) 937-53-20; e-mail sofia@usembassy.bg; internet bulgaria.usembassy.gov; Ambassador JOHN R. BEYRLE.

Venezuela: 1087 Sofia, ul. Tulovo 1; tel. (2) 943-30-61; fax (2) 943-30-10; e-mail embavenez@mbox.digsys.bg; Ambassador BOANERGES SALAZAR.

Viet Nam: 1113 Sofia, ul. Zhetvarka 1; tel. (2) 963-26-09; fax (2) 963-36-58; e-mail dsqvnsofia@eml.cc; Ambassador NGUYEN VAN DAC.

Judicial System

The 1991 Constitution provides for justice to be administered by the Supreme Court of Cassation, the Supreme Administrative Court, courts of appeal, courts of assizes, military courts and district courts. The main legal officials are the justices, or judges, of the higher courts, the prosecutors and investigating magistrates. The judicial system is independent, most appointments being made or recom-

BULGARIA

mended by the Supreme Judicial Council. The Constitutional Court is the final arbiter of constitutional issues.

Supreme Court of Cassation: 1000 Sofia, bul. Vitosha 2; tel. (2) 987-76-98; fax (2) 988-39-85; internet www.vks.bg; Chair. IVAN GRIGOROV.

Supreme Administrative Court: 1301 Sofia, bul. A. Stamboliyski 18; tel. (2) 988-49-02; fax (2) 981-87-51; e-mail vas_pressroom@sac.government.bg; internet www.sac.government.bg; Chair. KONSTANTIN PENCHEV.

Constitutional Court: 1594 Sofia, bul. Dondukov 1; tel. (2) 987-50-08; fax (2) 987-19-86; e-mail s.petrova@constcourt.government.bg; internet www.constcourt.bg; Chair. RUMEN YANKOV; Sec.-Gen. KIRIL A. MANOV.

Supreme Judicial Council (Vissh Sadeben Savet): 1000 Sofia, ul. Saborna 9; tel. (2) 981-79-74; fax (2) 980-76-32; e-mail vss_adm@inet.bg; internet www.vss.justice.bg.

Office of the Prosecutor-General: 1040 Sofia, bul. Vitosha 2; tel. and fax (2) 987-82-65; fax (2) 989-01-10; e-mail prb@prb.bg; internet www.prb.bg; Prosecutor-Gen. Dr BORIS VELCHEV.

Religion

Most of the population professes Christianity, the main denomination being the Bulgarian Orthodox Church. The 1991 Constitution guarantees freedom of religion, although Eastern Orthodox Christianity is declared to be the 'traditional religion in Bulgaria'. There is a significant Islamic minority, most of whom are ethnic Turks, although there are some ethnic Bulgarian Muslims, known as Pomaks. There is a small Jewish community.

CHRISTIANITY

Bulgarian Orthodox Church: 1090 Sofia, ul. Oborishte 4, Synod Palace; tel. (2) 987-56-11; fax (2) 989-76-00; f. 865; autocephalous Exarchate 1870 (recognized 1945); administered by the Bulgarian Patriarchy; 11 dioceses in Bulgaria and two dioceses abroad (Diocese of North and South America and Australia, and Diocese of West Europe), each under a Metropolitan; Chair. of the Bulgarian Patriarchy His Holiness Patriarch MAKSIM.

Armenian Apostolic Orthodox Church: Sofia 1080, ul. Nishka 31; tel. (2) 988-02-08; 20,000 adherents (1996); administered by Bishop DIRAYR MARDIKIYAN, resident in Bucharest, Romania; Chair. of the Diocesan Council in Bulgaria OWANES KIRAZIAN.

The Roman Catholic Church

The Latin (Western) Rite, which is organized in two dioceses, both directly responsible to the Holy See, had an estimated 67,000 adherents at 31 December 2005. The Byzantine-Slav (Eastern) Rite is organized in one apostolic exarchate, which had 10,107 adherents at that time.

Bishops' Conference: 1606 Sofia, ul. Lulin Planina 5; tel. (2) 953-04-06; fax (2) 952-61-86; e-mail proykov@gmail.com; Pres. Most Rev. CHRISTO NIKOLOV PROYKOV (Titular Bishop of Briula).

Western Rite

Bishop of Nicopolis: PETKO CHRISTOV, 7000 Ruse, ul. Bratya Simeonovi 26A; tel. (82) 83-52-45; fax (82) 82-28-81; e-mail dio_nicop@elits.rousse.bg.

Bishop of Sofia and Plovdiv: GEORGI JOVCHEV, 4000 Plovdiv, bul. Maria Luisa 3; tel. (32) 62-20-42; fax (32) 62-15-22; e-mail manolov@seznam.cz.

Eastern Rite

Apostolic Exarch of Sofia: CHRISTO NIKOLOV PROYKOV (Titular Bishop of Briula), 1606 Sofia, ul. Lulin Planina 5; tel. (2) 953-04-06; fax (2) 952-61-86; e-mail cproykov@technolink.bg.

ISLAM

Supreme Muslim Theological Council: 1000 Sofia, ul. Bratya Miladinovi 27; tel. (2) 987-73-20; fax (2) 939-00-23; an estimated 708 regional imams; Chair. RIDVAN KADIOV; Chief Mufti of the Muslims in Bulgaria FIKRI SALI.

JUDAISM

Central Jewish Theological Council: 1000 Sofia, ul. Ekzarkh Yosif 16; tel. (2) 983-12-73; fax (2) 983-50-85; e-mail sofia_synagogue@mail.orbitel.bg; internet www.sofiasynagogue.com; 5,000 adherents (1992); Head ROBERT DJERASSI.

The Press

PRINCIPAL DAILIES

24 Chasa (24 Hours): 1504 Sofia, bul. Tzarigradsko 47; tel. (2) 44-19-45; fax (2) 433-93-39; f. 1991; wholly owned by Westdeutsche Allgemeine Zeitung (Germany); Editor-in-Chief VALERI NAIDENOV; circ. 330,000.

Balgarska Armiya (Bulgarian Army): 1080 Sofia, ul. I. Vasov; tel. (2) 987-47-93; fax (2) 987-91-26; f. 1944 as *Narodna Armiya* (People's Army), name changed 1991; organ of the Ministry of Defence; Editor-in-Chief Col VLADI VLADKOV; circ. 30,000.

Chernomorsky Far (Black Sea Lighthouse): 8000 Burgas, ul. Milin Kamak 9; tel. (56) 84-22-48; fax (56) 84-01-78; f. 1958; independent regional newspaper; Editorial Dir GEORGI INGILISOV; circ. 37,000.

Dneven Trud (Daily Labour): 1000 Sofia, bul. Dondukov 52; tel. (2) 980-12-69; fax (2) 980-26-26; f. 1998; owned by Westdeutsche Allgemeine Zeitung (Germany); Editor TOSHO TOSHEV.

Dnevnik (Daily): 1000 Sofia, ul. I. Vazov 16; tel. (2) 937-63-00; fax (2) 937-62-35; internet www.dnevnik.bg; f. 2001; Editor-in-Chief GALYA PROKOPIEVA.

Duma (Word): 1000 Sofia, ul. Positano 20, POB 382; tel. (2) 980-12-91; fax (2) 980-52-91; e-mail bsp@mail.bol.bg; internet www.duma.bg; f. 1990 as organ of the Bulgarian Socialist Party; resumed publication in Oct. 2001; Editor-in-Chief VYACHESLAV TUNEV.

Maritza: 4000 Plovdiv, bul Kh. Botev 27A; tel. (32) 60-34-50; fax (32) 60-34-22; e-mail mpolit@maritsa.com; internet www.digsys.bg/bgnews/maritsa; f. 1991; Editor-in-Chief ANTON BAYEV; circ. 30,000.

Monitor: 1504 Sofia, bul. D. Tsankov 37; tel. (2) 960-22-07; fax (2) 960-22-13; e-mail info@zone168.com; internet www.monitor.bg; Editor-in-Chief PETYO BLSKOV.

Narodno Delo (People's Cause): 9000 Varna, bul. Kh. Botev 3; tel. (52) 23-10-71; fax (52) 23-90-67; f. 1944; six a week; regional independent; business, politics and sport; Editor-in-Chief DIMITAR KRASIMIROV; circ. 56,000.

Noshten Trud (Night Labour): 1000 Sofia, bul. Dondukov 52; tel. and fax (2) 987-70-63; f. 1992; five a week; Editor-in-Chief PLAMEN KAMENOV.

Nov Glas (New Voice): 5500 Lovech, ul. G. Dimitrov 24; tel. (68) 222-42; f. 1988; regional independent; Editor-in-Chief VENETSII GEORGIEV.

Novinar: 1505 Sofia, ul. Oborishte 44; tel. (2) 943-55-22; fax (2) 943-45-32; e-mail novinar@novinar.net; internet www.novinar.org; f. 1992; Editor-in-Chief Dr STOYKO TONEV; circ. 45,000 (1997).

Pari (Money): 1202 Sofia, ul. Industrialna 11; tel. (2) 917-87-02; fax (2) 917-87-03; e-mail office@pari.bg; internet www.pari.bg; f. 1991; 5 a week; financial and economic news online; Bulgarian and English; Editor-in-Chief STEFAN NEDELCHEV; circ. 10,000.

Podkrepa (Support): 1000 Sofia, ul. Ekzarkh Yosif 37; tel. (2) 983-12-27; fax (2) 946-73-74; f. 1991; organ of the Podkrepa (Support) Trade Union Confederation; Editor-in-Chief (vacant).

Sega: 1164 Sofia, bul. Dzh. Bauchar 23; tel. (2) 969-43-00; e-mail prepress@segbg.com; internet www.segabg.com; f. 1998; Editor-in-Chief DIMITRANA ALEKSANDROVA.

Shipka: Khaskovo; tel. (38) 12-52-52; fax (38) 3-76-28; f. 1988; independent regional newspaper; Editor-in-Chief DIMITAR DOBREV; circ. 25,000.

Sport: 1000 Sofia, Vassil Levski Stadium, Sektor V, POB 88; tel. (2) 88-03-43; fax (2) 88-36-28; f. 1927; Editor-in-Chief IVAN NANKOV; circ. 80,000.

Standart News Daily: 1504 Sofia, bul. Tzarigradsko 47; tel. (2) 960-43-43; fax (2) 960-43-12; e-mail root@standartnews.com; internet www.standartnews.com; f. 1992; Editor-in-Chief YULY MOSKOV; circ. 110,000.

Trud (Labour): 1000 Sofia, bul. Dondukov 52; tel. (2) 987-98-05; fax (2) 980-11-40; f. 1923; organ of the Confederation of Independent Trade Unions in Bulgaria; Editor-in-Chief TOSHO TOSHEV; circ. 200,000.

Zemedelsko Zname (Agrarian Banner): Sofia; tel. (2) 87-38-51; f. 1902; organ of the Aleksandar Stamboliyski Bulgarian Agrarian People's Union; Editor ILIYA DANOV.

Zemya (Earth): 1000 Sofia, ul. 11-ti Avgust 18; tel. (2) 88-50-33; fax (2) 83-52-77; f. 1951 as *Kooperativno Selo* (Co-operative Village); renamed 1990; fmrly an organ of the Ministry of Agriculture; Editor-in-Chief KOSTA ANDREEV; circ. 53,000.

PRINCIPAL PERIODICALS

166 Politzeiski Vesti (166 Police News): 1680 Sofia, ul. Solun 25–26, J. K. Belite Brezi; tel. (2) 82-30-30; fax (2) 82-30-28; f. 1945; fmrly *Naroden Strazh*; weekly; criminology and public security; Editor-in-Chief PETAR VITANOV; circ. 22,000.

BULGARIA
Directory

168 Chasa (168 Hours): 1504 Sofia, bul. Tzarigradsko 47; tel. (2) 433-92-88; fax (2) 433-93-15; f. 1990; weekly; business, politics, entertainment; owned by Westdeutsche Allgemeine Zeitung (Germany); Editor-in-Chief Vaselka Valileva; circ. 93,000.

Avto-Moto Svyat (Automobile World): 1000 Sofia, pl. Pozitano 3; tel. and fax (2) 897-23-10; fax (2) 873-75-27; e-mail yoka@abv.bg; f. 1957; monthly; illustrated publication on cars and motor sports; Editor-in-Chief Yordanka Karamfilova; circ. 3,600 (2007).

Az Buki (Alphabet): 1113 Sofia, bul. Tzarigradsko 125; tel. and fax (2) 870-52-98; e-mail azbuki@minedu.government.bg; f. 1991; weekly; for schools; sponsored by the Ministry of Education; Editor-in-Chief Zlatomir Zlatanov; circ. 4,000.

Bulgarski Fermer (Bulgarian Farmer): 1202 Sofia, ul. Industrialna 11; f. 1990; weekly; Editor-in-Chief Vassil Asparuhov; circ. 20,000.

Computer: 1504 Sofia, ul. Panayot Volov 11; tel. and fax (2) 943-41-28; e-mail office@newteck.bg; internet www.newteck.bg; f. 1991; monthly; information technology; Editor-in-Chief Petar Petrov; circ. 7,000.

Computer World: 1421 Sofia, bul. Hr. Smirnenski 1B/1111; tel. (2) 963-20-17; fax (2) 963-28-41; f. 1991; weekly; US-Bulgarian jt-venture; information technology; Editor-in-Chief Tatiana Hinova; circ. 7,000.

Durzhaven Vestnik (State Gazette): 1169 Sofia, bul. A. Battenberg 1; tel. (2) 986-10-76; e-mail dv@nt52.parliament.bg; f. 1879; two a week; official organ of the Narodno Sobraniye; two bulletins of parliamentary proceedings and the publication in which all legislation is promulgated; Editor-in-Chief Ivan Gajdarski; circ. 42,000.

Ekho (Echo): 1000 Sofia, ul. V. Levski 75; tel. (2) 87-54-41; f. 1957; weekly; organ of the Bulgarian Tourist Union; tourism publication; Editor-in-Chief Lubomir Gligorov; circ. 7,000.

Film: Sofia; e-mail film@online.bg; f. 1993; monthly; Editor Dima Dimova; circ. 11,000.

Ikonomichesky Zhivot (Economic Life): 1000 Sofia, bul. Dondukov 11; tel. (2) 987-95-06; fax (2) 987-65-60; e-mail ikonzhiv@dir.bg; f. 1966; weekly; independent; marketing and finance; Editor-in-Chief Vasil Aleksiev; circ. 10,000.

Kapital: 1000 Sofia, ul. I. Vazov 20; tel. (2) 981-58-16; fax (2) 987-69-07; internet www.capital.bg; f. 1993; weekly; Man. Editor Filip Harmandjiev; circ. 30,000 (1999).

Krile (Wings): 1784 Sofia, POB 11; tel. (2) 974-51-26; fax (2) 974-51-25; f. 1911; fmrly *Kam Nebeto*, renamed 1991; monthly; official organ; civil and military aviation; Pres. and Editor-in-Chief Rossen Kaludov Pantcheliev; circ. 20,000.

Kultura (Culture): 1040 Sofia, ul. A. Battenberg 4; tel. (2) 988-33-22; fax (2) 980-04-95; e-mail kultura@online.bg; internet www.online.bg/kultura; f. 1957; weekly; issue of the Culture Space Foundation; arts, publicity and cultural affairs; Editor-in-Chief Koprinka Chervenkova; circ. 5,000.

Kurier 5 (Courier 5): 1000 Sofia, bul. Tzarigradsko 47; tel. (2) 46-30-26; f. 1991; weekdays; advertising newspaper; Editor-in-Chief Stepan Eramian; circ. 30,000.

LIK: 1000 Sofia, bul. Tzarigradsko 49; weekly; publication of the Bulgarian Telegraph Agency; literature, art and culture; Editor-in-Chief Sirma Veleva; circ. 19,000.

Literaturen Forum (Literary Forum): 1000 Sofia, ul. Rakovski 136; tel. (2) 88-10-69; fax (2) 88-10-69; e-mail litforum@slovoto.org; internet www.slovo.bg/litforum; f. 1990; weekly; independent; Dir Marin Georgiev; circ. 5,300.

Makedonia (Macedonia): 1301 Sofia, ul. Pirotska 5; tel. (2) 80-05-32; fax (2) 87-46-64; e-mail mpress@virbus.bg; f. 1990; weekly; organ of the IMRO (Bulgarian National Movement)-Union of Macedonian Societies; Editor-in-Chief Dinko Draganov; circ. 22,000.

Napravi Sam (Do It Yourself): 1504 Sofia, ul. Panayot Volov 11; tel. and fax (2) 943-41-28; e-mail newteck@einet.bg; internet www.newteck.bg; f. 1981; monthly; Editor-in-Chief Georgi Balanski; circ. 8,000.

Nie Zhenite (We the Women): Sofia; f. 1990; weekly; organ of the Democratic Union of Women; Editor-in-Chief Evginia Kiranova.

Nov Den (New Day): 1000 Sofia, ul. Lege 5; tel. (2) 77-39-82; f. 1991; weekly; organ of the Union of Free Democrats; Editor-in-Chief Ivan Kalchev; circ. 25,000.

Novo Vreme (New Time): 1000 Sofia, ul. Positano 20; tel. (2) 981-62-58; fax (2) 980-52-91; e-mail novovreme@novovreme.com; internet www.novovreme.com; six a year; organ of the Bulgarian Socialist Party; Editor-in-Chief I. Borisov.

Paraleli: 1040 Sofia, bul. Tzarigradsko 49; tel. (2) 87-40-35; f. 1964; weekly; illustrated publication of the Bulgarian Telegraph Agency; Editor-in-Chief Krassimir Drumev; circ. 50,000.

Pardon: 1504 Sofia, bul. Tzarigradsko 47; tel. (2) 43-431; f. 1991; weekly; satirical publication; Editor-in-Chief Chavdar Shinov; circ. 8,560.

Pogled (Review): Sofia; tel. (2) 87-70-97; fax (2) 65-80-23; f. 1930; weekly; organ of the Union of Bulgarian Journalists; Editor-in-Chief Damyan Obrechkov; circ. 47,300.

Prava i Svobodi (Rights and Freedoms): 1000 Sofia, bul. A. Stamboliyski 45; f. 1990; weekly; organ of the Movement for Rights and Freedoms; politics, culture; Editor-in-Chief (vacant); circ. 7,500.

Pro i Anti: 1000 Sofia, POB 1078; tel. (2) 66-18-75; fax (2) 963-42-36; e-mail anti_bg@yahoo.co.uk; internet www.pro-anti.net; f. 1991; weekly; Editor-in-Chief Vasil Stanilov; circ. 7,000.

Starshel (Hornet): 1000 Sofia, ul. S. Karadja 26; tel. and fax (2) 988-08-16; e-mail starshel@bulmail.net; internet www.starshel.bg; f. 1946; weekly; satirical; Editor-in-Chief Miakhail Veshim; circ. 45,200.

Televiziya i Radio (Television and Radio): 1756 Sofia, bul. Tsarigradsko 111; tel. (2) 970-01-88; fax (2) 974-36-93; e-mail petmar@mail.techno-link.com; f. 1964; weekly; broadcast listings; Editor-in-Chief Lubomir Yankov; circ. 30,000 (1999).

Tsarkoven Vestnik (Church Newspaper): 1000 Sofia, ul. Oborishte 4; tel. (2) 87-56-11; f. 1900; weekly; organ of the Bulgarian Orthodox Church; Editor-in-Chief Dimitar Kirov; circ. 4,000.

Uchitelsko Delo (Teachers' Cause): Sofia; tel. and fax (2) 981-35-28; internet www.sbubg.info/udelo; f. 1905; weekly; organ of the Union of Bulgarian Teachers; Editor-in-Chief Margarita Cholakova; circ. 12,000.

Zdrave (Health): Sofia; tel. (2) 44-30-26; f. 1955; monthly; published by Bulgarian Red Cross; Editor-in-Chief Yakov Yanakiev; circ. 55,000.

Zhenata Dnes (Women Today): 1000 Sofia, bul. Narodno Sobraniye 12; tel. (2) 89-16-00; f. 1946; monthly; Editor-in-Chief Botio Angelov; circ. 50,000.

NEWS AGENCIES

Balgarska Telegrafna Agentsia (BTA) (Bulgarian Telegraph Agency): 1024 Sofia, bul. Tzarigradsko 49; tel. (2) 92-62-42; fax (2) 986-22-89; e-mail bta@bta.bg; internet www.bta.bg; f. 1898; official news agency; domestic, Balkan and international news in Bulgarian and English; also economic and sports news; publishes weekly surveys of science and technology, international affairs, literature and art; Gen. Dir Maksim Minchev.

Sofia-Press Agency: 1040 Sofia, ul. Slavyanska 29; tel. (2) 88-58-31; fax (2) 88-34-55; f. 1967; publishes socio-political and scientific literature, fiction, children's and tourist literature, publications on the arts, a newspaper, magazines and bulletins in foreign languages.

PRESS ASSOCIATION

Union of Bulgarian Journalists: 1000 Sofia, ul. Ekzarkh Yosif 37; tel. (2) 83-19-95; fax (2) 83-54-84; f. 1944; Pres. Chavdar Tonchev; 5,500 mems.

Publishers

Balgarski Khudozhnik (Bulgarian Artist) Publishing House: 1504 Sofia, ul. Shipka 6; tel. (2) 946-72-85; fax (2) 946-02-12; e-mail filchev@vip.bg; f. 1952; art books, children's books; Dir Bouyan Filchev.

Balgarski Pisatel (Bulgarian Writer) Publishing House: 1000 Sofia, ul. 6-ti Septemvri 35; tel. (2) 87-58-73; fax (2) 87-24-95; publishing house of the Union of Bulgarian Writers; Bulgarian fiction and poetry, criticism; Dir Gertcho Atanasov.

Christo G. Danov State Publishing House (Darzhavno Izdatelstvo 'Christo G. Danov'): 4005 Plovdiv, ul. S. Chalakov 1; tel. (32) 23-12-01; fax (32) 26-05-60; f. 1855; fiction, poetry, literary criticism; Dir Nacho Christoskov.

Prof. Marin Drinov Academic Publishing House (Bulgarian Academy of Sciences) (Izdatelstvo na Bulgarskata Akademiya na Naukite 'Prof. Marin Drinov'): 1113 Sofia, ul. G. Bonchev 6; tel. (2) 72-09-22; fax (2) 870-40-54; e-mail director@baspress.com; internet www.baspress.com; f. 1869; scientific works and periodicals of the Bulgarian Academy of Sciences; Dir Yatchko Ivanov.

Medizine i Fizkultura (Medicine and Physical Culture) Publishing House (Izdatelstvo 'Medizina i Fizkultura'): 1080 Sofia, pl. Slaveikov 11; tel. (2) 987-99-75; fax (2) 987-13-08; e-mail medpubl@abv.bg; internet www.medpubl.com; f. 1948; privately owned; medicine; Dir Emilia Nikolova.

Military Publishing House (Voenno Izdatelstvo): 1000 Sofia, ul. I. Vazov 12; tel. (2) 980-27-66; fax (2) 980-27-99; e-mail evtimov@vi-books.com; internet www.vi-books.com; Dir Ronmen Evtimov.

BULGARIA

Nauka i Izkustvo (Sciences and Arts) Publishing House: 1000 Sofia, pl. Slaveikov 11; tel. (2) 987-47-90; fax (2) 987-24-96; e-mail nauk_izk@sigma-bg.com; f. 1948; Man. Loreta Pushkarova.

Narodna Kultura (National Culture) Publishing House: 1000 Sofia, ul. A. Kanchev 1, POB 421; tel. (2) 987-80-63; e-mail nauk-izk@sigma-bg.com; f. 1944; general; Dir Petar Manolov.

Prosveta (Enlightenment) Publishing House: 1618 Sofia, ul. Zemedelska; tel. (2) 818-20-20; fax (2) 818-20-19; e-mail prosveta@intech.bg; internet www.prosveta.net; f. 1945; educational publishing house; Chair. Joana Tomova; Dir Yonko Yonchev.

Reporter Publishing House: 1184 Sofia, bul. Tsarigradsko 113; tel. (2) 975-23-82; fax (2) 975-23-84; e-mail reporter@techno-link.com; internet www.reporter-bg.com; f. 1990; private publishers of fiction and documentary literature; Man. Krum Blagov.

Sinodalno (Synodal) Publishing House: 1000 Sofia, ul. Oborishte 4; tel. (2) 87-56-11; religious publishing house; Dir Angel Velitehkov.

Technica Publishing House: 1000 Sofia, pl. Slaveikov 1; tel. (2) 987-12-83; fax (2) 987-49-06; e-mail upravitel@technica-bg.com; internet www.technica-bg.com; f. 1958; textbooks for professional, higher and university education, technical literature, dictionaries and handbooks; Exec. Man. Maria Damianova Paraskova.

Zemizdat Publishing House: 1504 Sofia, bul. Tsarigradsko 47; tel. (2) 44-18-29; f. 1949; specializes in works on agriculture, shooting, fishing, forestry, livestock-breeding, environmental studies and popular scientific literature and textbooks; Dir Petar Angelov.

PUBLISHERS' ASSOCIATION

Bulgarian Book Association: 1000 Sofia, pl. Slaveikov 11, POB 1046; tel. (2) 986-79-70; fax (2) 986-79-93; e-mail bba@otel.net; internet www.abk.bg; f. 1994; Exec. Dir Petko Dyulgerov; Chair. Yonko Yonchev.

Broadcasting and Communications

TELECOMMUNICATIONS

Communications Regulation Commission (CRC): 1000 Sofia, ul. Gurko 6; tel. (2) 981-29-49; fax (2) 971-27-29; e-mail info@crc.bg; internet www.crc.bg; f. 2002; Pres. Gergana Petrova Sarbova-Bozhilova.

Association of Bulgarian Broadcasters (ABBRO): 1504 Sofia, bul. Evlogi Georgiev 44; tel. (2) 946-16-20; fax (2) 944-29-79; e-mail office@abbro-bg.org; internet www.abbro-bg.org; f. 1997; independent non-profit organization; represents 60 private media companies, including 160 radio and television stations; Exec. Dir Antoaneta Arsova.

Bulgarian Telecommunications Co (Balgarska Telekomunikatsionna Kompaniya—BTC): 1606 Sofia, bul. Totleben 8; tel. (2) 949-46-24; fax (2) 952-10-98; e-mail pc@btc.bg; internet www.btc.bg; 65% owned by Viva Ventures (Austria), a subsidiary of Advent International (USA); Chair. Joanna James; 23,000 employees.

Cosmo Bulgaria Mobile EAD (Globul): 1715 Sofia, bul. Mladost 4; tel. (2) 942-80-00; fax (2) 942-80-10; e-mail customercare@globul.bg; internet www.globul.bg; f. 2001; subsidiary of Cosmote Group (Greence); Chief Exec. Athanasios Katsiroubas; 2.4m. subscribers (Sept. 2006).

Mobikom (Radiotelecommunication Company Mobikom): 1000 Sofia, POB 101; tel. (2) 974-40-27; fax (2) 960-56-13; internet www.mobikom.com; f. 1992; 49% owned by Cable and Wireless (USA), 39% owned by Bulgarian Telecommunications Co; Man. Dir John Munnery.

Mobiltel: 1309 Sofia, Ilinden, ul. Kukush 1/8; tel. (88) 850-00-31; fax (88) 850-00-32; e-mail pr@mobiltel.bg; internet www.mtel.bg; f. 1994; owned by Telekom Austria AG from 2006; provides mobile telecommunications services and internet; 5m. subscribers (Dec. 2007); CEO Josef Vinatzer.

BROADCASTING

National Radio and Television Council: 1504 Sofia, ul. San Stefano 29; Dir Ivan Borislavov.

Radio

Bulgarian National Radio (Balgarsko Natsionalno Radio): 1040 Sofia, bul. D. Tsankov 4; tel. (2) 963-43-30; fax (2) 963-44-64; internet www.bnr.bg; f. 1929; two Home Service programmes; local stations at Blagoevgrad, Plovdiv, Shumen, Stara Zagora and Varna. Foreign Service broadcasts in Bulgarian, Albanian, Arabic, English, French, German, Greek, Russian, Serbian, Spanish and Turkish; Dir-Gen. Polya Stancheva.

BG Radio: 1000 Sofia, POB 48; tel. (2) 951-62-24; fax (2) 952-38-45; e-mail bgradio@bgradio.net; internet www.bgradio.net; f. 2001; commercial music station; wholly owned by Metromedia International Telecommunications Inc (USA); Chief Exec. Nikolay Yanchovichin.

Television

bTV: 1463 Sofia, pl. Balgaria 1, NDK Administration Bldg; tel. (2) 917-68-00; fax (2) 952-14-83; internet www.btv.bg; f. 2000; daily transmission of commercial news, family entertainment and locally-produced programmes, on bTV channel; owned by Balkan News Corpn Plc, a subsidiary of News Corpn Ltd (Australia); Chief Exec. Marty Pompadur.

Bulgarian National Television (Bulgarska Natsionalna Televiziya): 1504 Sofia, ul. San Stefano 29; tel. (2) 944-63-29; fax (2) 946-12-10; internet www.bnt.bg; f. 1959; daily transmission of programmes on Channel 1 and Efir 2 and on the satellite channel—TV Bulgaria; Dir-Gen. Ulyana Prumova; 3,000 employees.

New Television (Novo Televiziya): 1000 Sofia, bul. N. Valtsarov 55; tel. (2) 933-18-40; fax (2) 933-18-20; e-mail pr@ntv.bg; internet www.ntv.bg; f. 1994; privately owned; news and entertainment.

Finance

(cap. = capital; dep. = deposits; res = reserves; m. = million; amounts in new leva unless otherwise stated)

BANKING

At early 2006 35 commercial banks were in operation in Bulgaria (of which six were branches of foreign banks).

Central Bank

Bulgarian National Bank (Bulgarska Narodna Banka): 1000 Sofia, bul. A. Battenberg 1; tel. (2) 914-51-203; fax (2) 980-24-25; e-mail press_office@bnbank.org; internet www.bnb.bg; f. 1879; bank of issue; cap. 20m., res 2,091.3m., dep. 3,593.7m. (Dec. 2006); Gov. Ivan Iskrov; 3 brs.

Commercial Banks

Central Co-operative Bank (Tsentralna Kooperativna Banka): 1086 Sofia, bul. G. S. Rakovski 103; tel. (2) 926-62-66; fax (2) 926-62-02; e-mail office@ccbank.bg; internet www.ccbank.bg; f. 1991; cap. 72.8m., res 31.9m., dep. 1,010.4m. (Dec. 2006); Chair. Nikola Damyanov; 45 brs.

Commercial Bank Allianz Bulgaria (Targovska Banka Aliantz Balgaria): 1202 Sofia, bul. Mariya Luiza 79; tel. (2) 921-54-07; fax (2) 981-93-07; e-mail admin@bank.allianz.bg; internet bank.allianz.bg; f. 1997 as Yambol Commercial Bank; 79.3% owned by Allianz Bulgaria Holding AD; cap. 47.8m., res 15.0m., dep. 792.2m. (Dec. 2006); Chair. of Supervisory Bd Maxim Sirakov; Chair. of Management Bd Dimitar Zhelev; 39 brs.

Corporate Commercial Bank (Korporativna Targovska Banka): 1000 Sofia, ul. Graf Ignatiev 10, POB 632; tel. (2) 980-93-62; fax (2) 980-89-48; e-mail corpbank@corpbank.bg; internet www.corpbank.bg; f. 1989 as BSFK Bulgarsovinvest; present name adopted 1994; cap. 50.0m., res 25.2m., dep. 929.2m. (Dec. 2006); Chair. of Supervisory Bd Tzvetan Vasilev; 10 brs.

DSK Bank (Banka DSK): 1036 Sofia, ul. Moskovska 19; tel. (2) 939-12-20; fax (2) 980-64-77; e-mail office@dskbank.bg; internet www.dskbank.bg; f. 1951 as State Savings Bank; present name adopted 1998; provides general retail banking services throughout the country; wholly owned by National Savings and Commercial Bank—OTP Bank (Hungary); cap. 94.0m., res 636.9m., dep. 5,226.1m. (Dec. 2006); Chair. and Chief Exec. Sandor Csanyi; 352 brs and offices.

DZI Bank: 1000 Sofia, bul. Dondukov 4–6; tel. (2) 930-71-36; fax (2) 980-26-23; e-mail info@dzibank.bg; internet www.dzibank.bg; f. 1994; cap. 50.0m., res 10.6m., dep. 901.3m. (Dec. 2005); Chair. Diana Mladenova; Chief Exec. Dir Krasimir Angarski.

EIBank—Economic and Investment Bank (SIBank—Stopanka i investitsionna banka): 1000 Sofia, ul. Slavyanska 2; tel. (2) 939-92-40; fax (2) 981-25-26; e-mail info@hq.eibank.bg; internet www.eibank.bg; f. 1994 as Bulgarian-Russian Investment Bank; present name adopted 2000; cap. 69.7m., res 61.7m., dep. 1,197.6m. (Dec. 2006); Chair. and Exec. Dir Vassil Simov; 16 brs.

First Investment Bank (Parva Investitsionna Banka): 1797 Sofia, bul. Dragan Tzankov 37; tel. (2) 817-11-00; fax (2) 970-95-97; e-mail fib@fibank.bg; internet www.fibank.bg; f. 1993; 20% owned by the European Bank for Reconstruction and Development; cap. 100.0m., res 39.6m., dep. 2,825.9m. (Dec. 2006); Chair. of Supervisory Bd Georgi Dimitrov Mutafchiev; 102 brs.

Investbank: 1404 Sofia, bul. Bulgaria 83A; tel. (2) 818-61-44; fax (2) 854-81-99; e-mail office@ibank.bg; internet www.ibank.bg; f. 1994; present name adopted 2002; cap. 32.3m., res 3.4m., dep. 484.8m. (Dec. 2006); Chair. of Supervisory Bd Petia Slavova; 60 brs.

Municipal Bank (Obshchinska Banka): 1000 Sofia, ul. Vrabcha 6; tel. (2) 930-01-85; fax (2) 930-01-83; e-mail contacts@municipalbank .bg; internet www.municipalbank.bg; f. 1996; cap. 25.0m., res 13.3m., dep. 546.2m. (Dec. 2006); Chair. of Supervisory Bd Dimitar Kolev; 63 brs.

Piraeus Bank Bulgaria AD: 1000 Sofia, ul. Vitosha 3; tel. (2) 980-56-54; fax (2) 981-85-79; e-mail haralampievb@piraeusbank.bg; internet www.piraeusbank.bg; f. 1994, as Commercial Bank Mollov; adopted the name Eurobank Plc in 1997; following bank's acquisition in 2005 by Piraeus Bank SA (Greece), in April 2006 name changed as above; cap. 50.8m., res 3.9m., dep. 445.0m. (Dec. 2005); Chair. Michael Colakides.

Postbank—Balgarska Poshchenska Banka: 1048 Sofia, bul. Tsar Osvoboditel 14; tel. (2) 951-68-40; fax (2) 963-40-35; e-mail main@postbank.bg; internet www.postbank.bg; f. 1991; privatized in 1999; cap. 109.9m., res 75.3m., dep. 1,260.4m. (Dec. 2005); Chair. and Chief Exec. Antonios C. Hassiotis; 112 brs and offices.

Raiffeisenbank (Bulgaria) EAD: 1504 Sofia, ul. Gogol 18–20; tel. (2) 919-85-101; fax (2) 943-45-28; internet www.rbb.bg; f. 1994; wholly owned by Raiffeisen International Beteiligungs (Austria); cap. 94.9m., res 40.6m., dep. 2,962.9m. (Dec. 2006); Chair. and Exec. Dir Momchil Andreev.

Societe Generale Expressbank AD Varna: 9000 Varna, bul. Vl. Varnenchik 92; tel. (52) 68-61-00; fax (52) 60-16-81; e-mail office@sgexpressbank.bg; internet www.sgexpressbank.bg; f. 1993; present name adopted 2005; 97.95% owned by Société Générale (France); cap. 28.5m., res 127.8m., dep. 993.8m. (Dec. 2006); Chief Exec. Philippe Lhotte; 20 brs.

UniCredit Bulbank AD: 1000 Sofia, Sveta Nedelya Sq. 7; tel. (2) 923-21-11; fax (2) 988-46-36; e-mail info@sof.bulbank.bg; internet www.bulbank.bg; f. 1964; fmrly Bulbank AD; name changed May 2007, after merger with Hebros Bank and HVB Bank Biochim AD; cap. 166.4m., res 117.3m., dep. 3,416.2m. (Dec. 2006); Chair. Andrea Moneta; 91 brs.

United Bulgarian Bank (Obedinena Balgarska Banka): 1040 Sofia, ul. Sv. Sofia 5; tel. (2) 811-28-00; fax (2) 988-08-22; e-mail info@ubb.bg; internet www.ubb.bg; f. 1993; universal commercial bank; 99.9% owned by National Bank of Greece SA; cap. 76.0m., res 15.2m., dep. 2,380.6m. (Dec. 2005); Chair. Ioannis Georgios Pehlivanidis; 134 brs.

STOCK EXCHANGE

Bulgarian Stock Exchange: 1303 Sofia, ul. Triushi 10; tel. (2) 937-09-34; fax (2) 937-09-46; e-mail bse@bse-sofia.bg; internet www .bse-sofia.bg; Chair. Viktor Papazov; Chief Exec. Bistra Ilkova.

INSURANCE

Bulstrad: 1000 Sofia, pl. Pozitano 5; tel. (2) 985-66-10; fax (2) 985-61-03; e-mail pubic@bulstrad.bg; internet www.bulstrad.bg; f. 1961; 31% owned by TBIH Group (Netherlands); all classes of insurance and reinsurance; Chair. of Bd and Chief Exec. Rumen Yanchev; 14 brs.

DZI Insurance: 1000 Sofia, Georgi Benkovski St 3; tel. (2) 981-57-99; fax (2) 987-45-33; e-mail general.ins@dzi.bg; internet www.dzi .bg; f. 1946; privatization approved in 2002; all areas of insurance; Chair. Dancho Danchev; 27 agencies, 101 brs.

Evroins: 1797 Sofia, bul. G. M. Dimitirov 16; tel. (2) 965-15-25; fax (2) 965-15-26; e-mail office@euroins.bg; internet www.euroins.bg; f. 1996; business and general insurance; Chair. Supervisory Bd Assen Hristov; 87 agencies and offices.

Municipal Insurance Co. (Obshchinska Zastrakhovatelna Kompaniya): 1504 Sofia, bul. Ya. Sakazov 48; tel. (2) 943-11-82; fax (2) 943-11-92; internet www.ozk.bg; f. 1996; Exec. Dir Kalin Glavchev.

Uniqa Life Insurance Co Bulgaria: 1000 Sofia, ul. Iskar 8; tel. (2) 935-95-95; fax (2) 935-95-96; internet www.uniqa.bg; subsidiary of Uniqa (Austria); frmly Vitosha-Zhivot (Vitosha Life) Insurance Co.

Trade and Industry

GOVERNMENT AGENCY

Privatization Agency (Agentsia za Privatizatsiya): 1000 Sofia, ul. Aksakov 29; tel. (2) 987-75-79; fax (2) 981-62-01; e-mail rstaneva@ priv.government.bg; internet www.priv.government.bg; f. 1992; Exec. Dir Todor Nikolov.

INTERNATIONAL FREE-TRADE ZONES

Burgas Free-Trade Zone: 8000 Burgas, ul. Trapezitsa 5, POB 154; tel. (56) 84-20-47; fax (56) 84-15-62; e-mail info@freezonebourgas .com; internet www.freezonebourgas.com; f. 1989; Exec. Dir Vassiliy Skripka.

Dragoman Free-Trade Zone: 2210 Dragoman, ul. G. Dimitrov 33; tel. and fax (2) 954-93-39.

Plovdiv Free-Trade Zone: 4003 Plovdiv, ul. V. Tarnovo 25,; tel. (32) 65-02-86; fax (32) 65-08-33; e-mail frzone@plovdiv.techno-link .com; internet www.freezone-plovdiv.com; f. 1990; Exec. Dir Aleksandar Nikolov.

Ruse (Rousse) Free-Trade Zone: 7000 Ruse, Tutrakan bul. 71, POB 107; tel. (82) 83-11-13; fax (82) 83-11-12; e-mail trade@ freezone-rousse.bg; internet www.freezone-rousse.bg; f. 1988; Exec. Man. Raytcho Raykov.

Svilengrad Free-Trade Zone: 6500 Svilengrad; tel. (359) 379-74-45; fax (359) 379-75-41; e-mail sbz@svilengrad.com; internet www .svilengrad.com/sbz; f. 1990; Exec. Dir Dimo Harakchiev.

Vidin Free-Trade Zone: 3700 Vidin; tel. (94) 60-20-40; fax (94) 60-20-46; internet www.vidin.net/ftz; f. 1988; Gen. Man. K. Marinov.

CHAMBER OF COMMERCE

Bulgarian Chamber of Commerce and Industry (BCCI): 1058 Sofia, ul. Parchevich 42; tel. (2) 987-26-31; fax (2) 987-32-09; e-mail bcci@bcci.bg; internet www.bcci.bg; f. 1895; promotes economic relations and business contacts between Bulgarian and foreign cos and orgs; organizes participation in international fairs and exhibitions; publishes economic publs in Bulgarian and foreign languages; organizes foreign trade advertising and publicity; provides legal and economic consultations, etc.; registers all Bulgarian cos trading internationally (more than 46,945 at the end of 2006); Pres. Bozhidar Bozhinov; 28 regional chambers.

EMPLOYERS' ASSOCIATIONS

Bulgarian Industrial Association—Union of Bulgarian Business (Balgarska Stopanska Kamara—Sayuz na balgarskiya biznes): 1000 Sofia, ul. Alabin 16–20; tel. (2) 932-09-11; fax (2) 987-26-04; e-mail office@bia-bg.com; internet www.bia-bg.com; f. 1980; assists Bulgarian economic enterprises with promotion and foreign contacts; economic analysis; legal and arbitration services; intellectual property protection; training and qualification; Chair. and Exec. Pres. Bozhidar Danev.

Employers Association of Bulgaria (EABG) (Sayuz na Rabotodatelite v Balgariya): 1202 Sofia, ul. Industrialna 11; tel. (2) 917-88-68; fax (2) 917-88-61; internet www.eabg.org; f. 2000; Chair. Vasil Vasilev.

Union for Private Economic Enterprise in Bulgaria (UPEE) (Sayuz za Stopansko Initsiativa—SSI): 1407 Sofia, ul. T. Notchev 30; tel. (2) 962-47-84; fax (2) 962-48-36; internet www.ssi-bg.org; f. 1989; voluntary asscn of private enterprises; Chair. of Bd Dr Borislav Borisov; 140 brs.

Vazrazhdane (Renaissance) Union of Bulgarian Private Entrepreneurs (UPBE) (Vazrazhdane sayuz na chastnite predpremachi): 1504 Sofia, bul. Dondukov 68; tel. (2) 926-24-17; fax (2) 926-74-12; e-mail vuzrazdane@union-vuzrazdane.com; internet www.union-vuzrazdane.com; f. 1989; Chair. Dobromir Gushcherov.

UTILITIES

Electricity

National Electricity Company (Natsionalna Elektricheska Kompania—NEK): 1040 Sofia, ul. Veslets 5; tel. (2) 986-18-19; fax (2) 980-12-43; e-mail nek@nek.bg; internet www.nek.bg; f. 1991; wholly state-owned; responsible for hydroelectric power generation; national transmission of electricity; centralized purchase and sale of electrical energy; supervision of national power system; Chair. of Bd Galina Tocheva; Exec. Dir Lubomir Velkov.

Gas

Bulgargaz: 1336 Sofia, bul. P. Vladigerov 66, POB 3; tel. (2) 939-64-22; fax (2) 925-04-01; e-mail hq@bulgargaz.com; internet www .bulgargaz.com; f. 1973; renamed 1990; state-owned; import, transmission, distribution, storage and transit of natural gas; Chair. Gati al-Jebouri; Chief Exec. Kiril Georgiev Gegov.

Overgaz: 1407 Sofia, ul. F. Kutev 5; tel. (2) 428-32-22; fax (2) 962-17-24; e-mail administration@overgas.bg; internet www.overgas.bg; f. 1992; 50% owned by Gazprom (Russia), 50% by Overgas Holding AD (Bulgaria); holds a majority share in 27 local gas distribution companies, including Sofiagas EAD and Varnagas AD; Exec. Dir Sasho Dontchev.

TRADE UNIONS

Confederation of Independent Trade Unions in Bulgaria (CITUB) (Konfederatsia na Nezavisitimite Sindikati v Bulgaria—KNSB): 1040 Sofia, bul. Makedonia 1; tel. (2) 917-04-79; fax (2) 988-59-69; internet knsb-bg.org; f. 1904; name changed from Bulgarian Professional Union and independence declared from all parties and state structures in 1990; in 1998 remained the main trade-union organization; approx. 75 mem. federations and four associate mems (principal mems listed below); Chair. ZHELYAZKO KHRISTOV; Sec. MILADIN STOYNOV; some 3m. mems.

Podkrepa (Support) Trade Union Confederation: 1000 Sofia, ul. A. Kanchev 2; tel. (2) 981-45-51; fax (2) 981-29-28; e-mail international_department@podkrepa.org; internet www.podkrepa.org; f. 1989; 36 regional and 30 branch union orgs; Chair. KONSTANTIN TRENCHEV; 155,000 mems (2007).

Principal CITUB Trade Unions

Federation of Independent Agricultural Trade Unions: 1606 Sofia, ul. D. Hadzhidimov 29; tel. (2) 952-15-40; Pres. LYUBEN KHARALAMPIEV; 44,600 mems.

Federation of Independent Trade Unions of Construction Workers: Sofia; tel. (2) 801-60-03; Chair. NIKOLAI RASHKOV; 220,000 mems.

Federation of the Independent Trade Unions of Employees of the State and Social Organizations: 1000 Sofia; tel. (2) 987-98-52; Chair. PETAR SUCHKOV; 144,900 mems.

Federation of Light-Industry Trade Unions: 1040 Sofia, bul. Makedonia 1; tel. (2) 988-15-70; fax (2) 988-15-20; Chair. YORDAN IVANOV.

Federation of Trade Unions in the Chemical Industry: 1040 Sofia, bul. Makedonia 1; tel. (2) 987-39-07; Pres. LYUBEN MAKOV.

Federation of Trade Union Organizations in the Forestry and Woodworking Industries: 1606 Sofia, ul. Vladayska 29; tel. (2) 952-31-21; fax (2) 951-73-97; Pres. PETAR ABRACHEV.

Independent Trade Union Federation for Trade Co-operatives, Services and Tourism: 1000 Sofia, ul. 6-ti Septemvri 4; tel. (2) 988-02-51; Chair. PETAR TSEKOV; 212,221 mems.

Trade Union of Bulgarian Teachers: 1000 Sofia, ul. Gen. Parensov 11; tel. (2) 987-78-18; fax (2) 988-17-94; e-mail seb@internet-bg.net; internet sbu.internet-bg.net; f. 1905; Pres. YANKA TANEVA; 186,153 mems.

Transport

RAILWAYS

Bulgarian State Railways EAD (Balgarski Darzhavni Zheleznitsi—BDZh/BDZ): 1080 Sofia, ul. I. Vazov 3; tel. (2) 981-11-10; fax (2) 981-71-51; e-mail bdz@bdz.bg; internet www.bdz.bg; f. 1888; operates passenger and freight railway services; wholly state-owned; Chair. of Bd of Dirs GEORGI PETARNEICHEV; Exec. Dir OLEG PETKOV; 17,832 employees (2006).

National Railway Infrastructure Company (Natsionalna Kompania 'Zhelezoputna Infrastruktura'): 1080 Sofia, ul. I. Vazov 3; e-mail intrel_1@rail.infra.bg; internet www.rail-infra.bg; f. 2002 to assume infrastructure responsibilities of Bulgarian State Railways into two entities; Chair. ANELIA KRUSHKOVA; Gen. Dir DIMITAR GAIDAROV.

Railway Transport Executive Agency (Zhelezoputna Administratsiya): 1080 Sofia, ul. I. Vazov 3; tel. (2) 940-94-27; fax (2) 987-67-69; e-mail aburov@mtc.government.bg; internet www.railbg.com; f. 2001; regulatory and control functions; Exec. Dir GEORGI NIKOLOV.

ROADS

There were 44,033 km of roads in Bulgaria in 2004, of which 2,961 km were principal roads. Two international motorways traverse the country and a motorway links Sofia to the coast.

SHIPPING AND INLAND WATERWAYS

The Danube (Dunav) River is the main waterway, with Ruse (Rousse) and Lom the two main ports. The largest Black Sea ports in Bulgaria are at Varna and Burgas.

Bulgarian Ports National Co (BPA) (Natsionalna Kompania 'Pristanishta'): 1000 Sofia, ul. Gen. Gurko 5; tel. (2) 940-97-73; fax (2) 987-94-80; e-mail bpa@port.bg; internet www.port.bg; f. 2000; Gen. Dir Capt. PEYCHO MANOLOV.

Bulgarian River Shipping Co (Parakhodstvo Balgarsko Rechno Plavane): 7000 Ruse, pl. Otets Paisiy 2; tel. (82) 82-20-81; fax (82) 82-21-30; e-mail main@brp.bg; internet www.brp.bg; f. 1935; shipment of cargo and passengers on the Danube; storage, handling and forwarding of cargo; scheduled for privatization; Chair. STEFAN ZAGOROV; Gen. Dir VRANGEL NIKIFOROV.

Bulgarski Morski Flot Co: 9000 Varna, ul. Panaguirishte 17; tel. (52) 22-63-16; fax (52) 22-53-94; carriage of goods and passengers on waterways; Dir-Gen. ATANAS YONKOV.

Burgas (Bourgas) Port Authority: 8000 Burgas, ul. A. Battenberg 1; tel. (56) 82-22-22; fax (56) 82-21-56; e-mail headoffice@port-burgas.com; internet www.port-burgas.com; Chair. NELY BENEVA; Exec. Dir ARGIR BOIADJIEV.

Navigation Maritime Bulgare: 9000 Varna, Primorski bul. 1; tel. (52) 63-31-00; fax (52) 63-30-33; e-mail office@navbul.com; internet www.navbul.com; f. 1892; scheduled for privatization; sea transport and ship repair; owns 78 tankers, bulk carriers and container, ferry, cargo and passenger vessels with a capacity of 1.35m. dwt; owns Varna shipyard; Dir-Gen. Capt. HRISTO DONEV; 5,000 employees.

Varna Port Authority: 9000 Varna, pl. Slaveykov 1; tel. (52) 60-21-91; fax (52) 63-29-53; e-mail headoffice@port-varna.bg; internet port-varna.bg; Exec. Dir DANAIL PAPAZOV.

CIVIL AVIATION

There are three international airports in Bulgaria, at Sofia, Varna and Burgas, and seven other airports for domestic services.

Civil Aviation Administration (Grazhdanska Vazdukhoplavatelna Administratsiya): 1000 Sofia, ul. Dyakon Ignatii 9; tel. (2) 937-10-47; fax (2) 980-53-37; e-mail caa@caa.bg; internet www.caa.bg; Dir-Gen. ZAHARI ALEKSIEV.

Air Sofia: 1000 Sofia, bul. Patriiarkh Evtimii 64; tel. (2) 981-09-25; fax (2) 980-29-07; e-mail airsofia@airsofia.com; internet www.airsofia.com; f. 1992; international charter flights; Pres. LILIAN TODOROV; Man. Dir GEORGI IVANOV.

Bulgaria Air: 1540 Sofia, bul. Brussels 1, Sofia Airport; tel. (2) 402-03-06; fax (2) 937-32-54; e-mail office@air.bg; internet www.air.bg; f. 2002 as successor to Balkan Bulgarian Airlines (Balkanair); 99.99% owned by Balkan Hemus Group; international passenger and cargo services; Chair. of Bd JORDAN KARAMALAKOV; Chief Exec. ZLATIN SARASTOV.

Tourism

Bulgaria's tourist attractions include the resorts on the Black Sea coast, mountain scenery and ski resorts and historic centres. In 2006 there were 4,364,557 foreign visitor arrivals. Receipts from tourism (including passenger transport) totalled US $3,026m. in 2005.

Bulgarian Tourist Chamber: 1000 Sofia, ul. Sv. Sofia 8; tel. (2) 987-40-59; fax (2) 986-51-33; e-mail btch@btch.org; internet www.btch.org; f. 1990; assists tourism enterprises, provides training, and co-ordinates non-governmental organizations; Chair. TSVETAN TONCHEV.

Balkantourist: 1000 Sofia, bul. Tsar Osvoboditel; tel. (2) 987-01-91; fax (2) 988-41-77; e-mail sofia.agency@balkantourist.bg; internet www.balkantourist.bg; f. 1948; privately owned; leading tour operator and travel agent; Exec. Dir NELLY SANDALSKA.

BURKINA FASO

Introductory Survey

Location, Climate, Language, Religion, Flag, Capital

Burkina Faso is a land-locked state in West Africa, bordered by Mali to the west and north, by Niger to the east, and by Benin, Togo, Ghana and Côte d'Ivoire to the south. The climate is hot and mainly dry, with an average temperature of 27°C (81°F) in the dry season (December–May). A rainy season occurs between June and October. Levels of rainfall are generally higher in the south than in the north; average annual rainfall in Ouagadougou is 718 mm (28 ins). The official language is French, and there are numerous indigenous languages (principally Mossi), with many dialects. The majority of the population follow animist beliefs; about 30% are Muslims and some 10% Christians, mainly Roman Catholics. The national flag (proportions 2 by 3) has two equal horizontal stripes, of red and green, with a five-pointed gold star in the centre. The capital is Ouagadougou.

Recent History

Burkina Faso became a self-governing republic (as Upper Volta) within the French Community in December 1958 and achieved independence on 5 August 1960, with Maurice Yaméogo as President. In January 1966 Yaméogo was deposed in a *coup d'état*, led by Lt-Col (later Gen.) Sangoulé Lamizana, the army Chief of Staff, who took office as President and Prime Minister. The new regime dissolved the legislature, suspended the Constitution and established a Conseil suprême des forces armées. A new Constitution, approved by referendum in June 1970, provided for a return to civilian rule after a four-year transitional period. The Union démocratique voltaïque (UDV) won 37 of the 57 seats in elections for an Assemblée nationale, held in December. In early 1971 Lamizana appointed the UDV leader, Gérard Ouédraogo, as Prime Minister at the head of a mixed civilian and military Council of Ministers.

In February 1974 Lamizana announced that the army had again assumed power. The Assemblée nationale was replaced in July by a Conseil national consultatif pour le renouveau, with 65 members nominated by the President. Political activity resumed in October 1977, and in the following month a referendum approved a draft Constitution providing for a return to civilian rule. The UDV won 28 of the 57 seats at elections to a new Assemblée nationale, held in April 1978, while the Union nationale pour la défense de la démocratie (UNDD), led by Hermann Yaméogo (the son of the former President), secured 13 seats. In May Lamizana was elected President, and in July the Assemblée elected Lamizana's nominee, Dr Joseph Conombo, as Prime Minister.

In November 1980 Lamizana was overthrown in a bloodless coup, led by Col Saye Zerbo, and a new Government, comprising both army officers and civilians, was formed. Opposition to the Zerbo regime soon emerged, and in November 1982 Zerbo was deposed by a group of non-commissioned army officers. Maj. Jean-Baptiste Ouédraogo emerged as leader of the new regime, and a predominantly civilian Government was formed. A power struggle within the Government became apparent with the arrest, in May 1983, of radical left-wing elements, including the recently appointed Prime Minister, Capt. Thomas Sankara. Sankara and his supporters were released following a rebellion by commandos under the leadership of Capt. Blaise Compaoré.

In August 1983 Sankara seized power in a violent coup. A Conseil national révolutionnaire (CNR) was established, and Jean-Baptiste Ouédraogo and other opponents of the new administration were placed under house arrest. Compaoré, as Minister of State at the Presidency, became the regime's second-in-command. Administrative, judicial and military reforms were announced, and citizens were urged to join Comités pour la défense de la révolution, which played an important role in consolidating Sankara's position. In August 1984 the country was renamed Burkina Faso ('Land of the Incorruptible Men').

In December 1985 a long-standing border dispute with Mali erupted into a six-day war that left some 50 people dead. The conflict centred on a reputedly mineral-rich area known as the Agacher strip. Following a cease-fire, arranged by the regional defence grouping, Accord de non-agression et d'assistance en matière de défense, and as a result of an interim decision on the dispute delivered by the International Court of Justice (ICJ) in January 1986, troops were withdrawn from the Agacher area; both countries accepted the ICJ's ruling, made in December, that the territory be divided equally between the two.

In October 1987 a self-styled Front populaire (FP), led by Compaoré, overthrew the CNR in a coup, in which Sankara was killed. A predominantly civilian Council of Ministers included seven members of the previous administration. Compaoré became Head of State. In April 1989 a new political grouping, the Organisation pour la démocratie populaire/Mouvement du travail (ODP/MT), was established, under the leadership of Clément Oumarou Ouédraogo. The dismissal of government members who had declined to join the new party was an indication that the ODP/MT was to assume a prominent role in Compaoré's regime.

In August 1989 an amnesty was proclaimed for all political prisoners. In the following month it was announced that the Commander-in-Chief of the Armed Forces and Minister of People's Defence and Security, Maj. Jean-Baptiste Boukary Lingani, and the Minister of Economic Promotion, Capt. Henri Zongo, had been executed, together with two others, following the discovery of a plot to overthrow Compaoré. It was widely believed that Lingani and Zongo had been opposed to aspects of economic reform, notably the principle of co-operation with the IMF and the World Bank (funding negotiations with which had begun in 1988). Compaoré subsequently assumed personal responsibility for defence.

The first congress of the FP, in March 1990, sanctioned the establishment of a commission to draft a new constitution that would define a process of 'democratization'. In April Clément Oumarou Ouédraogo was dismissed from the Council of Ministers and replaced as Secretary for Political Affairs of the FP and as Secretary-General of the ODP/MT by Roch Marc-Christian Kaboré, hitherto Minister of Transport and Communications. In September Kaboré was appointed as a Minister of State. The final draft of the Constitution, which was completed in late 1990, referred to Burkina Faso as a 'revolutionary, democratic, unitary and secular state'. Multi-party legislative and presidential elections, by universal suffrage, were to take place, while provision was made for the establishment of a second, appointed and consultative chamber of the legislature, the Chambre des représentants, to be composed of the 'active forces of the nation'. In March 1991 the ODP/MT adopted Compaoré as the party's presidential candidate and renounced its Marxist-Leninist ideology. In May a congress was convened to restructure the FP and to provide for the separation, upon the adoption of the draft constitution, of the functions of the FP and the organs of state. Delegates also approved the rehabilitation of Maurice Yaméogo, and an appeal was made to all political exiles to return to Burkina.

About 49% of the registered electorate voted in the constitutional referendum, which took place on 2 June 1991: of these, 93% were reported to have endorsed the new Constitution, which thereby took effect on 11 June. A transitional Government, in which the ODP/MT retained a dominant role, was subsequently appointed, its most senior member being Kaboré (as Minister of State, responsible for the Co-ordination of Government Action). In July Hermann Yaméogo (who had been a senior member of the FP in early 1990, but was subsequently expelled from the organization), now leader of the Alliance pour la démocratie et la fédération (ADF), and several other representatives of parties outside the FP were appointed to the Government. In August, however, Yaméogo (who had announced his intention to contest the presidency) was one of three government members who resigned in protest against proposed electoral procedures. Seven further opposition members resigned from the transitional administration in September. Grouped in a Coordination des forces démocratiques (CFD), the opposition organized rallies and demonstrations in support of the campaign for a national conference. Attempts to achieve a compromise failed, and in October five CFD candidates withdrew from the presidential contest.

The presidential election proceeded on 1 December 1991, when Compaoré (who had resigned from the army to contest the presidency as a civilian) was elected, unopposed, with the support of 90.4% of those who voted. The CFD claimed that an abstention rate of 74.7% reflected the success of its appeal for a boycott of the poll. Compaoré was inaugurated as President on 24 December and four opposition members were appointed to the Government in February 1992, including Hermann Yaméogo as Minister of State. Meanwhile, shortly after the election Clément Oumarou Ouédraogo was assassinated and further disturbances followed Ouédraogo's funeral. Apparently in response, the Government announced the indefinite postponement of the legislative elections, which had been scheduled for January.

Some 27 political parties contested the legislative elections, which were finally held on 24 May 1992. The ODP/MT won 78 of the 107 seats in the Assemblée des députés du peuple (ADP), and nine other parties secured representation. The rate of participation by voters was reported to have been around 35%. In June Compaoré appointed Youssouf Ouédraogo, hitherto President of the Economic and Social Council, as Prime Minister. Although his Council of Ministers included representatives of seven political parties, the ODP/MT was allocated most strategic posts.

In March 1994 Ouédraogo resigned, apparently prompted by the failure of the Government to negotiate a settlement for salary increases acceptable to workers' representatives, following the 50% devaluation of the CFA franc in January. Kaboré was appointed as the new premier. In February 1996 Kadré Désiré Ouédraogo, hitherto Deputy Governor of the Banque centrale des états de l'Afrique de l'ouest, replaced Kaboré as Prime Minister. At this time the ODP/MT and 10 other parties merged to form the Congrès pour la démocratie et le progrès (CDP), which was dominated by close allies of Compaoré, and the new premier subsequently joined the party.

Constitutional amendments and a new electoral code were approved by the ADP in January 1997. Notably, restrictions were removed on the renewal of the Head of State's mandate (hitherto renewable only once), the number of parliamentary seats was to be increased to 111 with effect from the forthcoming elections, and the ADP was renamed the Assemblée nationale. Elections to that body took place in May, contested by some 569 candidates from 13 parties. The CDP won a resounding victory, securing 101 seats.

In April 1998, following consultations with pro-Government and opposition parties, the Council of Ministers adopted legislation providing for the establishment of an independent electoral commission: the 27-member Commission électorale nationale indépendante (CENI) was to be composed of six representatives of the parliamentary majority and an equal number of opposition delegates, together with civic representatives.

Several prominent opposition figures, among them Hermann Yaméogo, whose party had become the Alliance pour la démocratie et la fédération—Rassemblement démocratique africain (ADF—RDA), and Joseph Ki-Zerbo, the leader of the principal opposition party in the legislature, the Parti pour la démocratie et le progrès (PDP), declined to participate in the presidential election held on 15 November 1998. Compaoré was challenged by two minor candidates. The provisional results confirmed a decisive victory for Compaoré, with 87.5% of the valid votes cast. Despite the appeal by a prominent opposition coalition, the Groupe du 14 février (G-14f), for a boycott, the rate of voter participation, at 56.1%, was considerably higher than in 1991. A new Government, again headed by Kadré Désiré Ouédraogo, was appointed in January 1999.

The political climate deteriorated rapidly after Norbert Zongo, the managing editor of the newspaper *L'Indépendant*, was found dead, together with three colleagues, in December 1998. Zongo, a frequent critic of the Compaoré regime, had been investigating allegations that David Ouédraogo, a driver employed by François Compaoré, younger brother and special adviser of the President, had been tortured and killed by members of the presidential guard. Opposition groups refused to participate in a commission of inquiry into Zongo's apparent murder established by presidential decree in January 1999, stating that a similar commission had failed to bring to justice those responsible for the assassination of Clément Oumarou Ouédraogo in 1991. In its final report, submitted in May 1999, the commission of inquiry stated that it had been unable to prove the identity of the culprits, but indicated the likelihood that the members of the presidential guard implicated in the death of David Ouédraogo were also responsible for the murders of the journalists. In mid-May three opposition leaders, including Halidou Ouédraogo, the Chairman of the Collectif d'organisations démocratiques de masse et de partis politiques, and Hermann Yaméogo, were arrested by the security forces, accused of denouncing the presidential guard and of having plotted a *coup d'état*. Two were released after a brief detention, but Yaméogo remained in custody for three days. Shortly afterwards Compaoré stated that the examining magistrate responsible for the Zongo case would be given his full support. He further announced a reorganization of the presidential guard, an amnesty for all those arrested in recent protests and compensation for the relatives of the victims of the murders that had provoked the political crisis.

In June 1999 Compaoré established a Collège des sages, composed of Burkinabè state elders, and religious and ethnic leaders. The 16-member Collège was to promote national reconciliation and to investigate unpunished political crimes since independence. In mid-June the Collège ordered the arrest of the three members of the presidential guard accused of the murder of David Ouédraogo. The Collège's report, published in August, recommended the formation of both a government of national unity and a 'commission of truth and justice' to oversee the transition to a truly plural political system and to investigate unresolved political murders, including that of Sankara. The Collège further recommended the creation of a commission to investigate possible political reforms. Opposition organizations rejected the proposed amnesty for those implicated during the investigations of the commission of truth and justice and criticized the need for the President to assent to any proposed reforms. Meanwhile, proposals to form a government of national unity were impeded by the demands of most opposition parties that legal action be expedited in the cases of David Ouédraogo and Norbert Zongo. Thus, the reshuffled Council of Ministers, announced in October, included just two, relatively uninfluential, representatives of the opposition. In November, the two advisory commissions, the formation of which had been recommended by the Collège des sages, were inaugurated. Despite official assurances that the commissions' findings would be binding, the G-14f refused to participate.

In January 2000 the ruling CDP organized a public demonstration in favour of the proposals made by the commission on political reform, including a restriction of the presidential mandate to no more than two successive terms. The Assemblée nationale subsequently voted to revise the electoral code and to accord greater powers to a restructured CENI. The opposition, however, criticized what they perceived to be the limited nature of the reforms and expressed their determination to boycott any elections until the Ouédraogo and Zongo cases had been fully resolved. The commission on national reconciliation published its report in February, urging the prosecution of those suspected of involvement in the embezzlement of public funds and in political killings. The commission also called for greater freedom of speech, of the press, and of assembly, the resolution of legal proceedings in the Ouédraogo and Zongo cases, the enactment of an amnesty law, and the construction of a monument to former President Sankara.

The Assemblée nationale approved revisions to the electoral code in April 2000; under the new regulations, which introduced a system of proportional representation, 90 deputies would be elected from regional lists, while 21 would be elected from a national list. The new legislation also reduced the presidential mandate from seven to five years, renewable only once. However, as the new limits were not to take effect until the next election, Compaoré would be permitted to contest the presidential elections due in 2005 and 2010. In addition, the Assemblée approved significant judicial reforms, which provided for the eventual abolition of the Supreme Court and the replacement of its four permanent chambers with four new state institutions: a Constitutional Council, a Council of State, a Court of Appeal and a National Audit Court.

In November 2000 Kadré Désiré Ouédraogo resigned as Prime Minister; he was succeeded by Paramanga Ernest Yonli, hitherto the Minister of the Civil Service and Institutional Development. Compaoré subsequently formed a 36-member Council of Ministers, including 12 members of the opposition. The new appointments resulted from an agreement reached by Yonli and representatives from seven political parties, including the CDP and the ADF—RDA, but not the principal opposition party, the PDP, which refused to participate. The agreement specified the parties' conditions for joining the Government, notably the prompt and thorough completion of pending legal cases. The leaders of the participating parties were to meet with the Prime Minister every three months to evaluate the implementation of the accord.

Meanwhile, the trial of the soldiers accused of murdering David Ouédraogo began in August 2000. The military tribunal sentenced two members of Compaoré's presidential guard, including Marcel Kafando, head of the guard at the time of Ouédraogo's death, to 20 years' imprisonment, with a third member sentenced to 10 years'. In February 2001 Kafando was charged with arson and the murder of Norbert Zongo and three others. In March, at a rally attended by some 30,000 people, President Compaoré apologized for 176 unpunished crimes allegedly committed by state representatives since independence in 1960. This act constituted the most significant element of a 'day of forgiveness' that had been proposed by the Collège des sages, but which was boycotted by, among others, relations of Sankara and Zongo. Dissatisfaction at the Government's failure to resolve the Zongo case continued, and in June 2001 several thousand people participated in a demonstration in Ouagadougou calling for those whom they believed to have ordered the killing of Zongo, including François Compaoré, to be brought to justice. However, in August, following the appointment of two of their members to the CENI, the constituent parties of the G-14f announced their intention to contest the forthcoming legislative elections. Michel Tapsoba, a human rights activist, was elected as Chairman of the CENI in the following month. In November it was announced that the judicial investigation into Kafando's alleged involvement in Zongo's death had been hampered by the poor health of the defendant. (In August 2006 an appeals court confirmed the dismissal of all charges against Kafando.)

In February 2002 the Assemblée nationale adopted a constitutional amendment, providing for the abolition of the Chambre des représentants, following the failure to appoint replacement representatives for those whose terms had expired in December 2001. The Government announced proposals for the eventual replacement of the Chambre by a Conférence générale de la nation, the membership and responsibilities of which were to be determined in due course.

On 5 May 2002 some 30 parties contested elections to the Assemblée nationale. The CDP remained the largest party, securing 57 of the 111 seats, with 49.5% of the votes cast, although its representation was much reduced. The ADF—RDA won 17 seats, with 12.6% of the votes cast, becoming the largest opposition party, followed by the PDP—PS (as the PDP had become, following its merger with the Parti socialiste burkinabè in mid-2001), with 10 seats. Kaboré was elected as President of the Assemblée nationale in June, prior to the reappointment of Yonli as Prime Minister. Despite the slim majority held by the CDP in the Assemblée nationale and the precedent set by the inclusion of ministers from opposition parties in the outgoing administration, the new 31-member Government did not contain any representatives of the opposition.

In October 2003 the Government announced that the authorities had prevented a planned *coup d'état*. By January 2004 some 15 members of the armed forces, including several members of the presidential guard, and two civilians, notably Norbert Tiendrébéogo, the Chairman of the Front des forces sociales, had been arrested on suspicion of involvement in the alleged plot. (International arrest warrants remained outstanding for a further two civilians.) It was announced that the detainees were to face charges of threatening the security of the State. The reputed leader of the group, Capt. Luther Ouali, was subsequently to convicted of treason and complicity with a foreign power and sentenced to 10 years' imprisonment. In mid-January President Compaoré effected a minor government reshuffle, in which the Minister of Defence, Gen. Kouamé Lougué, was dismissed and replaced by Yéro Boly, hitherto head of the presidential administration.

In April 2004 the Assemblée nationale approved an amendment to the electoral code, changing the electoral unit from the region, which number 15, to the province, of which there are 45. The vote was boycotted by most opposition parties, which claimed that they would be disadvantaged by the revised electoral code as they would be unable to field candidates in all 45 electoral units. The amendment represented a return to the system in place prior to the reforms adopted in 2000: these were regarded as having contributed to the opposition's success in increasing significantly its legislative representation in the 2002 elections.

In September 2004 Hermann Yaméogo and his cousin, Noël Yaméogo, were detained in connection with allegations that they had passed false intelligence reports regarding the alleged existence of mercenary training camps in Burkina to the Governments of Côte d'Ivoire and Mauritania. In October Noël Yaméogo was indicted on charges of treason and violating state security, while police confiscated the passport of Hermann Yaméogo, who, as a deputy, held immunity from prosecution. Both men denied the allegations made against them. Some 16 opposition parties held a rally in Ouagadougou in October to demand the immediate release of Noël Yaméogo, and later called for an international inquiry to be conducted into the alleged involvement of the Compaoré regime in several regional crises. Noël Yaméogo was freed pending trial in February 2005.

In March 2005 it was announced that the first round of the presidential election would take place on 13 November. Local elections, which had previously also been expected to be held in early November, were postponed until 12 February 2006. In the following months a number of candidates for the presidency emerged, including three candidates representing a 12-party opposition alliance, known as Alternance 2005, namely: Hermann Yaméogo now of the Union nationale pour la démocratie et le développement (UNDD); Philippe Ouédraogo of the Parti africain de l'indépendance; and Bénéwendé Stanislas Sankara of the Union pour la renaissance—Mouvement sankariste. Other candidates included Tiendrébéogo, for the FSS, and Prof. Ali Lankoandé (who had recently succeeded Ki-Zerbo as the party's President) for the PDP—PS. In June Compaoré announced his intention to seek a further term as the candidate of the CDP (28 smaller parties also declared their support for Compaoré); this announcement, although widely anticipated, was a cause of some controversy, and prompted several opposition parties, including those of Alternance 2005, to demand a ruling by the Constitutional Court as to whether the constitutional amendments approved in 2000 (which, notably, restricted Presidents to two terms of office) applied retroactively.

Compaoré implemented a minor reorganization of the Government in September 2005. Following a ruling by the Constitutional Court in October confirming that Compaoré was entitled to contest both the forthcoming election, and that scheduled to be held in 2010, Hermann Yaméogo announced that he was to withdraw from the contest (although his name remained on the ballot paper), and the UNDD called for a campaign of civil disobedience against what it termed a 'forceful step towards the installation of an absolute republican monarch'.

The presidential election was held, as scheduled, on 13 November 2005. According to official results, Compaoré obtained an overwhelming victory, securing 80.35% of the votes cast; the second-placed candidate was Bénéwendé Stanislas Sankara, with just 4.88%. Around 57% of the registered electorate participated in the election, and international election observers declared themselves largely satisfied with the conduct of the election, although some concern was expressed at relatively low levels of voter registration. Compaoré was inaugurated to a further term of office on 20 December. In January 2006 he reappointed Yonli as Prime Minister, heading a new Government that included several members of opposition parties, although many of the principal positions remained unchanged from the outgoing administration.

In May 2006 civil servants seeking increased pay observed a two-day strike, while several thousand people demonstrated in Ouagadougou against escalating fuel prices. An outbreak of violence between the army and the police in December, which resulted in five deaths, further underlined the fragile nature of the country's stability. (The politicization of the army was regarded as a dangerous contributory factor.) Summits of both Economic Community of West African States (ECOWAS, see p. 232) and the West African Economic and Monetary Union—UEMOA organizations, which were scheduled to take place in Ouagadougou, were postponed as a result of the unrest.

Legislative elections held on 6 May 2007 were contested by 47 parties. The CDP increased its majority in the Assemblée nationale, securing 73 of the 111 available seats (16 more than in the 2002 elections); the ADF—RDA took 14 and the remaining seats were shared by 11 parties. Voter turn-out was reported to be 56.4%. The following month Prime Minister Yonli tendered his resignation and that of his Government. President Compaoré subsequently named Tertius Zongo, hitherto the Burkinabè ambassador to the USA, as Yonli's successor and in mid-June a new Council of Ministers was sworn in. The new administration included Djibril Ypéné Bassolet as Minister of Foreign Affairs and Regional Co-operation, Zakaria Koté as Minister of Justice, Keeper of the Seals and Assane Sawadogo, who was awarded the security portfolio.

BURKINA FASO

Compaoré has, in recent years, gained wide recognition for his efforts as a regional mediator and as a proponent of inter-African conflict-resolution initiatives. In the early 1990s, however, relations with some members of ECOWAS suffered a reverse, owing to the Compaoré Government's support for Charles Taylor's rebel National Patriotic Front of Liberia (NPFL) and Burkina's refusal to participate in the military intervention by the ECOWAS cease-fire monitoring group (ECOMOG) in Liberia. However, in February 1997 the Burkinabè legislature approved legislation authorizing the participation of military personnel in ECOMOG, and members of the country's military subsequently remained in Liberia to assist in the training of new armed forces. In early 1999 President Ahmed Tejan Kabbah of Sierra Leone and the Nigerian Government alleged that Burkina Faso and Liberia were co-operating to provide support and supply arms to the rebel fighters of the Revolutionary United Front (RUF) in Sierra Leone. In early 2000 a report to the UN Security Council accused Burkina of having supplied weapons to the RUF in exchange for diamonds on several occasions. It was also alleged that Burkina had supplied weapons to Liberia and to Angolan rebel groups, despite international embargoes on the supply of weapons to those countries. The report was strenuously denied by the Burkinabè Government. Two missions from the UN Security Council visited Burkina Faso in mid-2000, at the invitation of the Burkinabè authorities, to investigate the claims regarding the breaching of arms embargoes against Angola and Sierra Leone. Although Compaoré, in May 2001, criticized a decision by the UN to impose travel restrictions on Liberian officials, relations with the Taylor Government subsequently deteriorated. In July 2002 the Burkinabè Government hosted a conference intended to promote a peaceful resolution of the political crisis in Liberia, at which Taylor's Government was not represented. Moreover, Compaoré stated that he regarded Taylor's resignation as President of Liberia in August 2003 as a positive development, which would encourage the stabilization of the region.

Burkina Faso has maintained close ties with Libya, and was a founder member of the Libyan-sponsored Community of Sahel-Saharan States (see p. 411) in 1997.

In early November 1999 a dispute over land rights between Burkinabè settlers in the south-west of Côte d'Ivoire and the indigenous minority Krou population led to the violent and systematic expulsion from the region of several hundred Burkinabè plantation workers. Several deaths were reported, and some 20,000 expatriates subsequently returned to Burkina. Following the *coup d'état* in Côte d'Ivoire in December, the military authorities assured the Government of Burkina that the expulsions would cease and that measures would be taken in order to allow workers to return. None the less, tensions between the two countries intensified as the former Prime Minister of Côte d'Ivoire, Alassane Ouattara, was excluded from participation in the Ivorian presidential election of October 2000 because of his Burkinabè origins. Following a coup attempt in Abidjan in early January 2001, which the Ivorian Government attributed to the influence of unnamed, neighbouring states, attacks on Burkinabè expatriates in Côte d'Ivoire reportedly increased; by late January it was reported that up to 10,000 Burkinabè were returning to Burkina each week. In early July a meeting between Compaoré and the Ivorian President, Laurent Gbagbo, in Sirte, Libya, was reported to have defused tensions somewhat between the two countries.

Following the outbreak of unrest in northern Côte d'Ivoire in mid-September 2002, Gbagbo again alleged that an unnamed, neighbouring country was implicated in the rebellion; these allegations were widely believed to refer to Burkina, although the Burkinabè Government denied any involvement in the uprising. However, in late November, following an attack on the residence of the Burkinabè President in Abidjan, the Ivorian Minister of Agriculture and Rural Development met Compaoré to express the Ivorian Government's regret for the attack. A statement by Compaoré in an interview with the French newspaper *Le Parisien*, in late January 2003, to the effect that the restoration of peace in Côte d'Ivoire would necessitate the resignation of Gbagbo as President of that country, led to a further deterioration in relations between the two countries. As a result of the upsurge in violence in Côte d'Ivoire, at least 350,000 Burkinabè citizens were reported to have fled Côte d'Ivoire for Burkina by mid-2003. The Burkinabè authorities closed the common border of the two countries in September 2002, reopening it in September 2003. Relations between the two countries subsequently became more cordial, and in late 2003 Compaoré hosted meetings with several prominent Ivorian leaders, including Gbagbo, Prime Minister Seydou Diarra and former rebel leader Guillaume Soro, emphasizing the need to develop bilateral co-operation. However, following the renewed outbreak of violence in Côte d'Ivoire in November, Compaoré again commented, this time in the French daily *Le Figaro*, that it would be impossible to resolve the Ivorian conflict under the present regime in that country.

During 2003–04 the Mauritanian President Col Maaouiya Ould Sid'Ahmed Taya and his administration repeatedly accused the Government of Burkina Faso of supporting a series of attempted *coups d'état* in Mauritania. The Burkinabè authorities denied claims that, in collaboration with Libya, they had provided refuge, funding, arms and training facilities to the rebels, particularly Saleh Ould Hnana and Capt. Abderahmane Ould Mini, who admitted attempting to overthrow President Taya's regime during the trial of 181 suspects which commenced in Mauritania in late 2004. Also among the accused, tried *in absentia*, was Sidi Mohamed Mustapha Ould Limam Chavi, a Mauritanian-born adviser to President Compaoré. In protest at the alleged conduct of the Burkinabè Government, President Taya did not attend the 10th Summit of La Francophonie, held in Ouagadougou in November 2004. Relations between Burkina Faso and Mauritania improved following the overthrow of Taya's regime in August 2005, with the new President, Col Ely Ould Mohamed Vall, attending President Compaoré's inauguration to a new term of office in December. In March 2006 Compaoré consolidated relations by paying a state visit to Nouakchott, the Mauritanian capital.

Government

Under the terms of the Constitution of June 1991, as subsequently revised, executive power is vested in the President and in the Government, and is counterbalanced by a legislative Assemblée nationale, and by an independent judiciary. Presidential and legislative elections are conducted by universal adult suffrage, in the context of a multi-party political system. The President is elected for a seven-year term, and delegates to the Assemblée nationale are elected for a five-year term. In April 2000 the Assemblée nationale adopted legislation, effective from the next elections, which reduced the presidential mandate from seven to five years, renewable only once, and introduced a system of proportional representation for elections to the Assemblée nationale, according to which 90 deputies would be elected from a regional list, while 21 would be elected from a national list. The President is empowered to appoint a Prime Minister; however, the Assemblée nationale has the right to veto any such appointment.

Burkina is divided into 45 provinces, each of which is administered by a civilian governor.

Defence

National service is voluntary, and lasts for two years on a part-time basis. As assessed at November 2007, the active armed forces numbered 10,800 (army 6,400, air force 200, gendarmerie 4,200). Other units include a 'security company' of 250 and a part-time people's militia of 45,000. The defence budget for 2007 was estimated at 44,600m. francs CFA.

Economic Affairs

In 2006, according to estimates by the World Bank, Burkina Faso's gross national income (GNI), measured at average 2004–06 prices, was US $6,311m., equivalent to $460 per head (or $1,330 on an international purchasing-power parity basis). During 1996–2006, it was estimated, the population increased at an average annual rate of 3.0%, while gross domestic product (GDP) per head increased, in real terms, by an average of 1.8% per year. Overall GDP increased, in real terms, at an average annual rate of 4.8% in 1996–2006; growth in 2006 was 5.6%.

Agriculture (including forestry and fishing) contributed 34.0% of GDP in 2005. According to FAO estimates about 92.1% of the labour force were employed in agriculture in 2005. The principal cash crop is cotton (exports of which accounted for an estimated 69.1% of the value of total exports in 2004). Smaller amounts of other crops, including karité nuts (sheanuts) and sesame seed, are also exported. The main subsistence crops are sorghum, millet and maize. Burkina is almost self-sufficient in basic foodstuffs in non-drought years. Livestock-rearing is of considerable significance, contributing 9.7% of GDP in 2002 and an estimated 12.1% of export revenue in 2004. According to the African Development Bank (ADB), during 1995–2006 agricultural GDP increased at an average annual rate of 5.8%. Agricultural GDP increased by 4.1% in 2006.

Industry (including mining, manufacturing, construction and power) contributed 19.6% of GDP in 2005, but engaged only 3.5% of the employed labour force in 2003. According to the ADB, during 1995–2006 industrial GDP increased at an average annual rate of 8.6%; industrial GDP increased by 6.9% in 2006.

Although Burkina has considerable mineral resources, extractive activities accounted for just 0.1% of GDP in 2005, and engaged only 0.5% of the employed labour force in 2003. However, the development of reserves of gold (exports of which contributed an estimated 3.0% of the value of total exports in 2004) has since brought about an increase in the sector's economic importance, while there is considerable potential, subject to the development of an adequate infrastructure, for the exploitation of manganese, zinc and limestone. In mid-2007 it was reported that the recently reopened gold mine at Taparko-Bouroum had yielded its first metal for 20 years. Production was expected to amount to some 1,700 kg in 2007, and was projected to increase to almost 4,000 kg by 2009. The country's other known mineral reserves include phosphates, silver, lead and nickel.

The manufacturing sector engaged only 2.0% of the employed labour force in 2003, and contributed 12.7% of GDP in 2005. The sector is dominated by the processing of primary products: major activities are cotton-ginning, the production of textiles, food-processing (including milling and sugar-refining), brewing and the processing of tobacco and of hides and skins. Motorcycles and bicycles are also assembled. According to the ADB, manufacturing GDP increased at an average annual rate of 7.4% in 1995–2006; growth of 6.3% was recorded in 2006.

Two hydroelectric stations supplied 19.5% of Burkina's electricity output in 2005; the remainder (80.5%) was derived from thermal power stations (using imported fuel). The country's hydropower capacity is being expanded, and in 2000 the interconnection of the south of Burkina Faso with the electricity network of Côte d'Ivoire was finalized; a link with Ghana's electricity grid is also planned. Imports of mineral fuels and related products accounted for an estimated 19.9% of the value of total merchandise imports in 2005.

The services sector contributed 46.3% of GDP in 2005, and engaged 7.8% of the employed labour force in 1996. According to the ADB, the GDP of the services sector increased at an average annual rate of 6.1% in 1995–2006; growth was 5.8% in 2006.

According to the IMF, in 2006 Burkina recorded a visible trade deficit of 302,000m. francs CFA, while there was a deficit of an estimated 339,000m. francs CFA on the current account of the balance of payments. In 2005 the principal sources of imports were France (which provided 18.7% of the total) and Côte d'Ivoire (18.0%). The principal market for exports in that year was Togo (taking 41.1% of exports). Other major purchasers were Ghana (16.6%) and Côte d'Ivoire (10.4%). The principal exports in that year were food products, manufactured articles, beverages and tobacco and products of the chemical and allied industries. In the same year the principal imports were machinery and transportation equipment, manufactured articles, and mineral fuels and related products.

In 2006 Burkina recorded an estimated overall budget deficit of 192,900m. francs CFA, equivalent to 6.1% of GDP. The budget deficit for 2007 was projected at 218,900 francs CFA. Burkina's total external debt was US $1,967m. at the end of 2004, of which $1,823m. was long-term public debt. In 2003 the cost of debt-servicing was equivalent to 10.3% of the value of exports of goods and services. The annual rate of inflation, which was negligible prior to the 50% devaluation of the CFA franc in January 1994, increased to 25.1% in 1994, but slowed thereafter, to 7.4% in 1995. In 1996–2006 the average annual rate of inflation was 2.4%. Consumer prices increased by 6.4% in 2005, and by 2.4% in 2006. Some 71,280 people were unemployed in 1996, according to the national census, equivalent to only 1.4% of the total labour force. According to official figures the unemployed population represented 2.8% in 2003 and the inactive population represented 15.0%, giving a combined rate of 17.4%.

Burkina is a member of numerous regional organizations, including the Economic Community of West African States (ECOWAS, see p. 232), the West African organs of the Franc Zone (see p. 307), the Conseil de l'Entente (see p. 412), the Liptako–Gourma Integrated Development Authority (see p. 413), and the Permanent Inter-State Committee on Drought Control in the Sahel (CILSS, see p. 414).

Burkina Faso has experienced strong growth since the devaluation of the CFA franc in 1994, as the competitiveness of its principal exports has been enhanced. However, it remains one of the poorest nations in the world and, largely owing to its very poor health and education indicators, was ranked 174th out of 177 countries on the UN Development Programme's 2006 human development index. In June 2003 the IMF approved a Poverty Reduction and Growth Facility (PRGF), equivalent to some US $34m., in support of the Government's economic programme for 2003–06, which aimed to contain inflation at less than 3% and achieve annual real GDP growth of 5.2% by 2005. In the event, heavy rainfall in 2003 facilitated a record cotton crop of some 500,000 metric tons, which, together with high international cotton prices, contributed to GDP growth of 8.0% for that year, according to the IMF, while growth of 4.6% was recorded in 2004. Strong cereal and cotton harvests in 2005 offset the negative impacts on the economy from lower international cotton prices and high international petroleum prices, and in that year Burkina Faso was among 18 countries to be granted 100% debt relief on multilateral debt agreed by the Group of Eight leading industrialized nations (G-8), subject to the approval of the lenders. In accordance with long-standing IMF recommendations, electricity tariffs were increased in 2006, and in mid-2007 the World Bank approved a loan worth $38.8m. to improve access to electricity and offer employment opportunities in the sector—only 18.5% of the country's population were reported to have access to electricity at that time. The IMF estimated GDP growth in 2007 of 4.2%, citing the main reason for the slowdown as reduced cotton production (some 30% less than the previous year) as a result of rains late in the harvest. Meanwhile, world cotton prices continued to decrease, and it was hoped that Burkina's continued reliance on cotton would be somewhat eased by the projected increase in gold production; however, further decreasing the dependency on a narrow resource base remained a priority if the strong economic growth of the previous decade was to be maintained.

Education

Education is provided free of charge, and is officially compulsory for six years between the ages of seven and 14. Primary education begins at seven years of age and lasts for six years. Secondary education, beginning at the age of 13, lasts for a further seven years, comprising a first cycle of four years and a second of three years. Enrolment levels are among the lowest in the region. According to UNESCO estimates, in 2003/04 primary enrolment included 40.5% of children in the relevant age-group, while secondary enrolment included only 9.5% of children in the appropriate age-group. There are three state-owned higher education institutions: a university in Ouagadougou, a polytechnic university at Bobo-Dioulasso and an institute of teacher training at Koudougou. There are also 11 private higher education institutions. The number of students enrolled at tertiary-level institutions in 2001/02 was 15,535. In 2000 spending on education represented 11.0% of total budgetary expenditure.

Public Holidays

2008: 1 January (New Year's Day), 8 March (International Women's Day), 20 March* (Mouloud, Birth of the Prophet), 24 March (Easter Monday), 1 May (Labour Day and Ascension Day), 5 August (Independence Day), 15 August (Assumption), 1 October* (Aid es Segheir, end of Ramadan), 1 November (All Saints' Day), 9 December* (Aid el Kebir—Tabaski, Feast of the Sacrifice), 11 December (Proclamation of the Republic), 25 December (Christmas).

2009: 1 January (New Year's Day), 8 March (International Women's Day), 9 March* (Mouloud, Birth of the Prophet), 2 April (Easter Monday), 1 May (Labour Day), 21 May (Ascension Day), 5 August (Independence Day), 15 August (Assumption), September* (Aid es Segheir, end of Ramadan), 1 November (All Saints' Day), 27 November* (Aid el Kebir—Tabaski, Feast of the Sacrifice), 11 December (Proclamation of the Republic), 25 December (Christmas).

*These holidays are dependent on the Islamic lunar calendar and may vary by one or two days from the dates given.

Weights and Measures

The metric system is in force.

BURKINA FASO

Statistical Survey

Source (except where otherwise stated): Institut National de la Statistique et de la Démographie, 555 blvd de la Révolution, 01 BP 374, Ouagadougou 01; tel. 50-32-49-76; fax 50-32-61-59; e-mail insd@cenatrin.bf; internet www.insd.bf.

Area and Population

AREA, POPULATION AND DENSITY

Area (sq km)	274,200*
Population (census results)	
10 December 1996	10,312,609
9–23 December 2006 (preliminary)	
Males	6,635,318
Females	7,094,940
Total	13,730,258
Density (per sq km) at 2006 census	50.1

* 105,870 sq miles.

ETHNIC GROUPS

1995 (percentages): Mossi 47.9; Peul 10.3; Bobo 6.9; Lobi 6.9; Mandé 6.7; Sénoufo 5.3; Gourounsi 5.0; Gourmantché 4.8; Tuareg 3.1; others 3.1 (Source: La Francophonie).

PROVINCES
(population at 2006 census, preliminary)

	Population	Capital	Population of capital
Balé	213,897	Boromo	30,305
Bam	277,092	Kongoussi	68,807
Banwa	267,934	Solenzo	118,424
Bazèga	238,202	Kombissiri	66,342
Bougouriba	102,507	Diébougou	41,348
Boulgou	542,286	Tenkodogo	124,053
Boulkiemdé	498,008	Koudougou	131,825
Comoé	400,534	Banfora	106,815
Ganzourgou	319,830	Zorgo	46,898
Gnagna	407,739	Bogandé	82,892
Gourma	304,169	Fada N'Gourma	123,594
Houet	902,662	Bobo-Dioulasso (rural)	61,919
Ioba	197,186	Dano	43,829
Kadiogo	1,523,980	Ouagadougou	1,181,702
Kénédougou	283,463	Orodara	30,332
Komandjari	80,047	Gayéri	48,814
Kompienga	75,662	Pama	36,503
Kossi	272,233	Nouna	70,010
Koulpélogo	259,395	Ouargaye	34,288
Kouritenga	330,342	Koupéla	57,632
Kourwéogo	136,017	Boussé	41,455
Léraba	124,422	Sindou	18,484
Lorom	142,990	Titao	66,379
Mouhoun	298,088	Dédougou	86,324
Nahouri	155,463	Pô	50,360
Namentenga	327,749	Boulsa	80,453
Nayala	162,869	Toma	29,003
Noumbiel	69,992	Batié	31,793
Oubritenga	237,290	Ziniaré	62,026
Oudalan	197,240	Gorom-Gorom	104,587
Passoré	322,873	Yako	79,408
Poni	254,371	Gaoua	52,090
Sanguié	297,230	Réo	59,779
Sanmatenga	598,232	Kaya	114,807
Séno	264,815	Dori	98,006
Sissili	212,628	Léo	50,378
Soum	348,341	Djibo	60,599
Sourou	219,826	Tougan	66,706
Tapoa	341,782	Diapaga	32,260
Tuy	224,159	Houndé	72,723
Yagha	159,485	Sebba	31,983
Yatenga	547,952	Ouahigouya	122,677
Ziro	175,607	Sapouy	54,618
Zondoma	168,955	Gourcy	80,689
Zoundwéogo	244,714	Manga	32,033
Total	**13,730,258**		

PRINCIPAL TOWNS
(population at 2006 census, preliminary)

Ouagadougou (capital)	1,181,702	Kaya	51,778
Bobo-Dioulasso	435,543	Tenkodogo	40,839
Koudougou	82,720	Fada N'gourma	40,815
Banfora	72,144	Dédougou	37,793
Ouahigouya	70,957	Houndé	34,669

Note: Figures refer to town proper, and totals may differ from provincial capitals as a result.

BIRTHS AND DEATHS
(annual averages, UN estimates)

	1990–95	1995–2000	2000–05
Birth rate (per 1,000)	49.0	47.7	45.9
Death rate (per 1,000)	17.1	16.4	15.7

Source: UN, *World Population Prospects: The 2006 Revision*.

Expectation of life (years at birth, WHO estimates): 48.8 (males 48.3; females 49.2) in 2005 (Source: WHO, *World Health Statistics*).

ECONOMICALLY ACTIVE POPULATION
(1996 census, persons aged 10 years and over)

	Males	Females	Total
Agriculture, hunting, forestry and fishing	2,284,744	2,229,124	4,513,868
Mining and quarrying	2,946	1,033	3,979
Manufacturing	46,404	25,161	71,565
Electricity, gas and water	2,279	534	2,813
Construction	20,678	398	21,076
Trade, restaurants and hotels	98,295	126,286	224,581
Transport, storage and communications	20,024	556	20,580
Finance, insurance, real estate and business services	10,466	2,665	13,131
Community, social and personal services	76,690	27,236	103,926
Activities not adequately defined	15,104	13,712	28,816
Total employed	2,577,630	2,426,705	5,004,335
Unemployed	51,523	19,757	71,280
Total labour force	2,629,153	2,446,462	5,075,615

Mid-2005 ('000, estimates): Agriculture, etc. 5,793; Total labour force 6,289 (Source: FAO).

Health and Welfare

KEY INDICATORS

Total fertility rate (children per woman, 2005)	6.5
Under-5 mortality rate (per 1,000 live births, 2005)	191
HIV/AIDS (% of persons aged 15–49, 2005)	2.0
Physicians (per 1,000 head, 2004)	0.05
Hospital beds (per 1,000 head, 1996)	1.42
Health expenditure (2004): US $ per head (PPP)	76.5
Health expenditure (2004): % of GDP	6.1
Health expenditure (2004): public (% of total)	54.8
Access to water (% of persons, 2004)	61
Access to sanitation (% of persons, 2004)	13
Human Development Index (2005): ranking	176
Human Development Index (2005): value	0.370

For sources and definitions, see explanatory note on p. vi.

BURKINA FASO   Statistical Survey

Agriculture

PRINCIPAL CROPS
('000 metric tons)

	2004	2005	2006*
Rice (paddy)	74.5	93.5	189.2
Maize	481.5	799.1	905.7
Millet	937.6	1,196.3	1,198.7
Sorghum	1,399.3	1,552.9	1,553.8
Sweet Potatoes	40.9	70.8	71.0
Yams	89.7	18.3	19.0
Sugar cane*	450	450	450
Cow peas (dry)	276.3	444.7	450.0
Bambara beans	27.8	40.0	40.0
Groundnuts (in shell)	245.3	220.5	221.0
Cottonseed	315†	370†	373
Okra*	26	26	26
Cotton (lint)†	210	250	290

* FAO estimate(s).
† Unofficial figure(s).

Aggregate production ('000 metric tons, may include official, semi-official or estimated data): Total cereals 2,902.0 in 2004, 3,649.5 in 2005, 3,858.2 in 2006; Total pulses 329.2 in 2004, 509.7 in 2005, 515.0 in 2006; Total roots and tubers 132.8 in 2004, 90.9 in 2005, 93.5 in 2006; Total vegetables (incl. melons) 228.1 in 2004, 225.9 in 2005, 232.0 in 2006; Total fruits (excl. melons) 76.6 in 2004, 76.3 in 2005, 78.1 in 2006.

LIVESTOCK
('000 head, year ending September)

	2003	2004*	2005*
Cattle	7,312	7,653	8,010
Sheep	6,703	6,854	7,009
Goats	10,306	10,367	10,709
Pigs	1,887	2,076	2,284
Chickens	24,384	25,052	25,739
Horses	36	37	39
Asses, mules or hinnies	915	970	1,028
Camels	15	15	15

* FAO estimates.

2006: Production assumed to be unchanged from 2005 (FAO estimates).
Source: FAO.

LIVESTOCK PRODUCTS
('000 metric tons, FAO estimates)

	2004	2005	2006
Cattle meat	101.0	105.5	105.5
Sheep meat	16.0	16.4	16.4
Goat meat	26.9	27.7	27.8
Pig meat	29.9	32.9	32.9
Chicken meat	30.1	31.0	30.9
Other meat	8.0	8.2	8.2
Cows' milk	168.4	190.8	190.8
Goats' milk	37.3	38.6	38.6
Hen eggs	43.8	45.0	42.7

Source: FAO.

Forestry

ROUNDWOOD REMOVALS
('000 cubic metres, excluding bark)

	2004	2005*	2006*
Sawlogs, veneer logs and logs for sleepers	73	73	73
Other industrial wood	1,098*	1,098	1,098
Fuel wood	8,040	10,533	11,060
Total	9,211	11,704	12,231

* FAO estimate(s).
Source: FAO.

SAWNWOOD PRODUCTION
('000 cubic metres)

	2004	2005	2006
Total (all broadleaved)	1.2	1.1	0.7

Source: FAO.

Fishing

(metric tons, live weight)

	2003	2004*	2005
Capture	9,000	9,000	9,000
Freshwater fishes	9,000	9,000	9,000
Aquaculture	5	5	6*
Total catch	9,005	9,005	9,006*

* FAO estimate(s).
Source: FAO.

Mining

(estimates)

(estimates)

	2004	2005	2006
Cement (metric tons)	30,000	30,000	30,000
Gold (kg)	1,125	1,397	1,571

Source: US Geological Survey.

Industry

SELECTED PRODUCTS
(metric tons, unless otherwise indicated)

	2000	2001	2002
Edible oils	17,888	19,452	19,626
Shea (karité) butter	186	101	21
Flour	12,289	13,686	10,005
Pasta	211	n.a.	n.a.
Sugar	43,412	46,662	47,743
Beer ('000 hl)	494	500	546
Soft drinks ('000 hl)	221	222	250
Cigarettes (million packets)	85	78	78
Printed fabric ('000 sq metres)	275	n.a.	n.a.
Soap	12,079	9,240	9,923
Matches (cartons)	9,358	4,956	3,009
Bicycles (units)	22,215	17,718	20,849
Mopeds (units)	16,531	19,333	19,702
Tyres ('000)	397	599	670
Inner tubes ('000)	2,655	3,217	2,751
Electric energy ('000 kWh)	390,322	364,902	361,000

Electric energy ('000 kWh): 444,554 in 2003; 473,249 in 2004; 516,225 in 2005.

Source: mainly IMF, *Burkina Faso: Selected Issues and Statistical Appendix* (September 2005).

Finance

CURRENCY AND EXCHANGE RATES

Monetary Units
100 centimes = 1 franc de la Communauté financière africaine (CFA).

Sterling, Dollar and Euro Equivalents (31 December 2007)
£1 sterling = 892.702 francs CFA;
US $1 = 445.593 francs CFA;
€1 = 655.957 francs CFA;
10,000 francs CFA = £11.20 = $22.44 = €15.24.

Average Exchange Rate (francs CFA per US $)
2005   527.47
2006   522.89
2007   479.27

Note: An exchange rate of 1 French franc = 50 francs CFA, established in 1948, remained in force until January 1994, when the CFA franc was devalued by 50%, with the exchange rate adjusted to 1 French franc = 100 francs CFA. This relationship to French currency remained in effect with the introduction of the euro on 1 January 1999. From that date, accordingly, a fixed exchange rate of €1 = 655.957 francs CFA has been in operation.

BUDGET
('000 million francs CFA)

Revenue*	2005†	2006†	2007‡
Tax revenue	336.8	362.3	413.5
Income and profits	79.7	85.7	99.6
Domestic goods and services	185.8	194.3	224.4
International trade	60.7	71.3	73.3
Non-tax revenue	28.4	30.1	36.9
Total	365.2	392.4	450.4

Expenditure§	2005†	2006†	2007‡
Current expenditure	332.4	386.4	419.5
Wages and salaries	141.4	159.9	182.7
Goods and services	75.3	82.2	93.4
Interest payments	18.2	17.3	8.2
Current transfers	97.6	126.9	135.2
Capital expenditure	322.7	361.9	424.9
Total	655.1	748.3	844.4

* Excluding grants received ('000 million francs CFA): 131.5 in 2005; 177.6 in 2006; 178.0 in 2007.
† Estimates.
‡ Projected.
§ Excluding net lending ('000 million francs CFA): –13.2 in 2005; –14.6 in 2006; –2.9 in 2007.

Source: IMF, *Burkina Faso: Sixth Review Under the Arrangement Under the Poverty Reduction and Growth Facility and Request for Waiver of Performance Criteria and Augmentation of Access, and Ex Post Assessment of Longer-Term Program Engagement - Staff Reports; Press Release on the Executive Board Discussion; and Statement by the Executive Director for Burkina Faso* (October 2006).

INTERNATIONAL RESERVES
(excluding gold, US $ million at 31 December)

	2004	2005	2006
IMF special drawing rights	0.2	0.2	—
Reserve position in IMF	11.3	10.5	11.1
Foreign exchange	657.6	427.7	543.7
Total	669.1	438.4	554.8

Source: IMF, *International Financial Statistics*.

MONEY SUPPLY
('000 million francs CFA at 31 December)

	2004	2005	2006
Currency outside banks	175.0	153.3	141.2
Demand deposits at deposit money banks*	193.9	194.9	220.6
Checking deposits at post office	4.5	2.7	3.5
Total money (incl. others)	378.2	351.8	366.6

* Excluding the deposits of public establishments of an administrative or social nature.

Source: IMF, *International Financial Statistics*.

COST OF LIVING
(Consumer Price Index; base: 2000 = 100)

	2004	2005	2006
Food, beverages and tobacco	104.9	120.2	120.0
Clothing	110.3	110.2	112.7
Housing, water, electricity and gas	111.0	111.3	116.4
All items (incl. others)	109.0	116.0	118.8

Source: ILO.

NATIONAL ACCOUNTS
('000 million francs CFA in current prices)

Expenditure on the Gross Domestic Product

	2003	2004	2005
Final consumption expenditure	2,308.9	2,601.2	2,808.0
Households, incl. non-profit institutions serving households	1,791.0	2,019.8	2,199.9
General government	517.9	581.4	608.1
Gross capital formation	515.6	479.9	565.1
Gross fixed capital formation	500.2	559.3	625.1
Changes in inventories	15.4	–79.4	–60.0
Total domestic expenditure	2,824.5	3,081.1	3,373.1
Exports of goods and services	212.9	286.5	294.1
Less Imports of goods and services	533.8	667.3	682.2
GDP in market prices	2,503.6	2,700.2	2,985.0

Gross Domestic Product by Economic Activity

	2003	2004	2005
Agriculture, livestock, forestry and fishing	799.4	803.2	940.5
Mining	1.5	1.6	1.8
Manufacturing	337.1	347.0	350.8
Electricity, gas and water	46.4	55.0	65.3
Construction and public works	92.5	111.5	125.9
Trade	309.8	364.8	388.2
Transport and communications	89.9	98.6	117.9
Other market services	260.0	297.2	324.8
Non-market services	398.4	426.0	452.8
Sub-total	2,335.0	2,504.9	2,768.0
Import taxes and duties	168.6	195.3	217.0
GDP in market prices	2,503.6	2,700.2	2,985.0

Source: Banque centrale des états de l'Afrique de l'ouest.

BURKINA FASO

BALANCE OF PAYMENTS
('000 million francs CFA, estimates)

	2004	2005	2006
Exports of goods f.o.b.	249	252	319
Imports of goods f.o.b.	–498	–556	–621
Trade balance	–249	–304	–302
Services (net)	–121	–138	–142
Balance on goods and services	–370	–442	–444
Income (net)	–16	–22	–21
Balance on goods, services and income	–386	–464	–465
Private unrequited transfers (net)	20	21	29
Official unrequited transfers (net)	80	95	96
Current balance	–286	–348	–339
Capital transfers (net)	106	115	818
Official capital (net)	94	112	–506
Private capital (net)*	21	17	78
Net errors and omissions	8	—	—
Overall balance	–57	–103	50

*Including portfolio investment and direct foreign investment.

Source: IMF, *Burkina Faso: Request for a Three-Year Arrangement Under the Poverty Reduction and Growth Facility - Staff Report; Press Release on the Executive Board Discussion; and Statement by the Executive Director for Burkina Faso* (October 2006).

External Trade

PRINCIPAL COMMODITIES
('000 million francs CFA)

Imports f.o.b.	2003	2004	2005
Food products	66.1	65.2	85.5
Mineral fuels, lubricants and related products	76.6	93.9	123.5
Chemical products	67.0	83.7	94.1
Manufactured articles	102.4	129.0	139.5
Machinery and transport materials	113.6	131.9	145.0
Total (incl. others)	446.8	534.6	619.2

Exports f.o.b.	2003	2004	2005
Food	12.4	16.4	12.7
Beverages and tobacco	8.9	6.1	4.1
Oils and fats (animal and vegetable)	4.0	2.9	2.0
Machinery and transport materials	6.5	6.5	3.4
Manufactured articles	7.7	3.8	7.8
Total (incl. others)	182.5	206.6	175.0

PRINCIPAL TRADING PARTNERS
('000 million francs CFA)*

Imports c.i.f.	2003	2004	2005
Belgium-Luxembourg	25.5	28.8	26.7
Benin	45.5	36.6	42.1
Chile	3.3	3.2	7.6
China, People's Repub.	12.0	21.2	16.7
Côte d'Ivoire	39.9	85.2	111.4
France	97.8	112.9	115.9
Germany	13.8	12.2	9.9
Ghana	17.3	14.4	36.3
India	10.6	9.1	17.3
Italy	6.4	7.8	10.5
Japan	9.2	9.3	9.2
Netherlands	6.2	6.7	6.2
Pakistan	0.0	0.1	7.1
Russia	9.8	6.2	2.3
Senegal	10.3	22.4	7.9
Spain	6.0	5.8	10.4
Thailand	2.5	5.2	8.0
Togo	81.9	71.6	70.8
USA	9.1	11.4	16.2
Total (incl. others)	446.8	534.6	619.2

Exports f.o.b.	2003	2004	2005
Belgium-Luxembourg	0.9	0.2	2.4
Benin	5.5	3.8	1.4
Côte d'Ivoire	3.6	18.1	18.3
France	8.5	14.7	17.2
Ghana	49.3	34.9	29.1
Mali	6.7	1.7	3.2
Niger	6.8	7.8	4.0
Switzerland	7.4	20.5	16.5
Togo	89.5	97.1	71.9
United Kingdom	0.0	2.5	1.1
Total (incl. others)	182.5	206.6	175.0

*Figures refer to recorded trade only.

Transport

RAILWAYS

	2002	2003	2004*
Freight traffic ('000 metric tons)	869.7	179.7	293.9
Passengers ('000 journeys)	320.6	87.5	116.6

*Estimates.

Source: IMF, *Burkina Faso: Selected Issues and Statistical Appendix* (September 2005).

2003: Passengers carried 87.5; Passenger-km (million) 9,980; Freight carried 179.7; Freight ton-km 128,795.

2005: Freight ton-km (million) 674,877.

ROAD TRAFFIC
('000 motor vehicles in use)

	1998	1999	2000
Passenger cars	25.3	26.3	26.5
Commercial vehicles	14.9	19.6	22.6

2001–03: Figures as in 2000.

Source: UN, *Statistical Yearbook*.

2005 ('000): Private cars 84.2; Lorries 20.1; Vans 20.1; Public transport 5.7; Tractors 8.2; Motorbikes and mopeds 100.0.

BURKINA FASO

CIVIL AVIATION
(traffic on scheduled services)*

	2001	2002	2003
Kilometres flown (million)	2	1	1
Passengers carried ('000)	100	53	54
Passenger-km (million)	158	29	29
Total ton-km (million)	22	3	3

* Including an apportionment of the traffic of Air Afrique.

Source: UN, *Statistical Yearbook*.

Tourism

FOREIGN VISITORS BY COUNTRY OF ORIGIN*

	2003	2004	2005
Belgium	4,984	6,482	6,438
Benin	6,443	8,765	9,186
Canada	3,000	4,548	6,048
Côte d'Ivoire	9,229	14,924	14,454
France	47,663	62,510	77,220
Germany	4,683	5,523	5,190
Ghana	3,831	5,456	4,914
Guinea	2,759	4,528	3,534
Italy	3,215	3,727	5,244
Mali	7,785	12,411	12,018
Mauritania	1,652	1,834	1,854
Netherlands	2,734	2,932	3,198
Niger	7,016	11,455	10,836
Nigeria	2,328	4,097	3,366
Senegal	5,950	9,882	9,792
Switzerland	4,025	5,192	3,828
Togo	5,394	6,961	7,974
United Kingdom	2,475	3,618	3,288
USA	6,030	6,872	7,290
Total (incl. others)	163,123	222,201	244,728

* Arrivals at hotels and similar establishments.

Receipts from tourism (US $ million, incl. passenger transport): 23 in 2000; 25 in 2001.

Source: World Tourism Organization.

Communications Media

	2004	2005	2006
Telephones ('000 main lines in use)	85.2	91.2	94.8
Mobile cellular telephones ('000 subscribers)	395.9	633.6	1,016.6
Personal computers ('000 in use)	29	31	n.a.
Internet users ('000)	53.2	64.6	80.0
Broadband subscribers ('000)	0.2	0.4	1.7

Source: International Telecommunication Union.

Television receivers ('000 in use): 140 in 2000 (Source: UNESCO, *Statistical Yearbook*).

Radio receivers ('000 in use): 370 in 1997 (Source: UNESCO, *Statistical Yearbook*).

Daily newspapers (national estimates): 4 (average circulation 14,200 copies) in 1997; 4 (average circulation 14,500 copies) in 1998; 5 in 2004 (Source: UNESCO Institute for Statistics).

Non-daily newspapers: 9 (average circulation 42,000 copies) in 1995 (Source: UNESCO, *Statistical Yearbook*).

Book production: 12 titles (14,000 copies) in 1996 (first editions only); 5 in 1997 (Sources: UNESCO, *Statistical Yearbook*, UNESCO Institute for Statistics).

Education

(2004/05, except where otherwise indicated, private and public institutions)

	Institutions	Teachers	Males	Females	Total
Pre-primary	147*	473†	7.3†	6.6†	13.9†
Primary	n.a.	26,938	715.3	555.5	1,270.8
Secondary	496†	8,471‡	175.1	120.3	295.4
Tertiary	n.a.	1,984	19.4	8.6	27.9

* 1997/98.
† 2001/02.
‡ 2003/04.

Source: mostly UNESCO Institute for Statistics.

Adult literacy rate (UNESCO estimates): 23.6% (males 31.4%; females 16.6%) in 2005 (Source: UNESCO Institute for Statistics).

Directory

The Constitution

The present Constitution was approved in a national referendum on 2 June 1991, and was formally adopted on 11 June. The following are the main provisions of the Constitution, as amended in January 1997, April 2000 and February 2002:

The Constitution of the 'revolutionary, democratic, unitary and secular' Fourth Republic of Burkina Faso guarantees the collective and individual political and social rights of Burkinabè citizens, and delineates the powers of the executive, legislature and judiciary.

Executive power is vested in the President, who is Head of State, and in the Government, which is appointed by the President upon the recommendation of the Prime Minister. With effect from the November 2005 election, the President is elected, by universal suffrage, for a five-year term, renewable only once (previously, a seven-year term had been served).

Legislative power is exercised by the multi-party Assemblée nationale. Deputies are elected, by universal suffrage, for a five-year term. The number of deputies and the mode of election is determined by law. The President appoints a Prime Minister and, at the suggestion of the Prime Minister, appoints the other ministers. The President may, having consulted the Prime Minister and the President of the Assemblée nationale, dissolve the Assemblée nationale. Both the Government and the Assemblée nationale may initiate legislation.

The judiciary is independent and, in accordance with constitutional amendments approved in April 2000 (see Judicial System), consists of a Court of Cassation, a Constitutional Council, a Council of State, a National Audit Court, a High Court of Justice, and other courts and tribunals instituted by law. Judges are accountable to a Higher Council, under the chairmanship of the Head of State, who is responsible for guaranteeing the independence of the judiciary.

The Constitution also makes provision for an Economic and Social Council, for a Higher Council of Information, and for a national ombudsman.

The Constitution denies legitimacy to any regime that might take power as the result of a *coup d'état*.

The Government

HEAD OF STATE

President: BLAISE COMPAORÉ (assumed power as Chairman of the Front populaire 15 October 1987; elected President 1 December 1991; re-elected 15 November 1998 and 13 November 2005).

COUNCIL OF MINISTERS
(March 2008)

President: BLAISE COMPAORÉ.
Prime Minister: TERTIUS ZONGO.
Minister of State, Minister of Health: BÉDOUMA ALAIN YODA.

BURKINA FASO

Minister of the Economy and Finance: Jean-Baptiste Marie Pascal Compaoré.
Minister of Agriculture, Water Resources and Fisheries: Laurent Sédgo.
Minister of Justice, Keeper of the Seals: Zakaria Koté.
Minister of Defence: Yéro Boly.
Minister of Foreign Affairs and Regional Co-operation: Col Djibril Ypéné Bassolet.
Minister of Transport: Gilbert G. Noël Ouédraogo.
Minister of the Civil Service and State Reform: Seydou Bouda.
Minister of Territorial Administration and Decentralization: Clément Pengdwendé Sawadogo.
Minister of Security: Assane Sawadogo.
Minister of Mines, Quarries and Energy: Abdoulaye Abdoulkader Cissé.
Minister of Trade, Business Promotion and Crafts: Mamadou Sanoh.
Minister of Culture, Tourism and Communication, Spokesperson for the Government: Philippe Sawadogo.
Minister of Infrastructure and Improving Access to Isolated Regions: Hippolyte Lingani.
Minister of Secondary and Higher Education and Scientific Research: Prof. Joseph Paré.
Minister of Basic Education and Literacy: Marie Odile Bonkoungou.
Minister of the Environment and Quality of Life: Salifou Sawadogo.
Minister of Labour and Social Security: Jérôme Bougouma.
Minister with Special Duties at the Presidency, responsible for Economic Analysis and Forecasting: Gueda Jacques Ouédraogo.
Minister of Youth and Employment: Justin Koutaba.
Minister of Social Action and National Solidarity: Pascaline Tamini.
Minister of Animal Resources: Sékou Bâ.
Minister for the Promotion of Human Rights: Salamata Sawadogo.
Minister of Posts and of Information and Communication Technology: Joachim Tankoano.
Minister for the Promotion of Women: Céline M. Yoda.
Minister of Housing and Town Planning: Vincent D. Dabilgou.
Minister of Sport and Leisure: Mori Ardjouma Jean-Pierre Palm.
Minister in charge of Relations with Parliament: Cécile Beloum.
Minister-delegate attached to the Minister of the Economy and Finance, responsible for the Budget: Lucien Marie Noël Bembamba.
Minister-delegate attached to the Minister of Foreign Affairs and Regional Co-operation, responsible for Regional Co-operation: Minata Samaté.
Minister-delegate attached to the Minister of Territorial Administration and Decentralization, responsible for Local Communities: Soungalo Ouattara.
Minister-delegate attached to the Minister of State, Minister of Agriculture, Water Resources and Fisheries, responsible for Agriculture: Issaka Maïga.
Minister-delegate attached to the Minister of Basic Education and Literacy, responsible for Literacy and Non-formal Education: Ousseini Tamboura.
Minister-delegate attached to the Minister of Secondary and Higher Education and Scientific Research, responsible for Technical and Professional Education: Maxime Somé.

MINISTRIES

Office of the President: 03 BP 7030, Ouagadougou 03; tel. 50-30-66-30; fax 50-31-49-26; e-mail info@presidence.bf; internet www.presidence.bf.

Office of the Prime Minister: 03 BP 7027, Ouagadougou 03; tel. 50-32-48-89; fax 50-31-47-61; e-mail webmaster@primature.gov.bf; internet www.primature.gov.bf.

Ministry of Agriculture, Water Resources and Fisheries: 03 BP 7005, Ouagadougou 03; tel. 50-32-41-14; fax 50-31-08-70; internet www.agriculture.gov.bf.

Ministry of Animal Resources: 03 BP 7026, Ouagadougou 03; tel. 50-32-61-07; fax 50-31-84-75; internet www.mra.gov.bf.

Ministry of Basic Education and Literacy: 03 BP 7032, Ouagadougou 03; tel. 50-30-66-00; fax 50-31-42-76; internet www.meba.gov.bf.

Ministry of the Civil Service and State Reform: Immeuble de la Modernisation, 922 ave Kwamé N'Krumah, 03 BP 7006, Ouagadougou 03; tel. 50-30-19-52; fax 50-30-19-55; internet www.fonction-publique.gov.bf.

Ministry of Culture, Tourism and Communication: 03 BP 7007, Ouagadougou 03; tel. 50-33-09-63; fax 50-33-09-64; e-mail mcat@cenatrin.bf; internet www.culture.gov.bf.

Ministry of Defence: 01 BP 496, Ouagadougou 01; tel. 50-30-72-14; fax 50-31-36-10; internet www.defense.gov.bf.

Ministry of the Economy and Finance: 03 BP 7050, Ouagadougou 03; tel. 50-32-42-11; fax 50-31-27-15; internet www.finances.gov.bf.

Ministry of the Environment and Quality of Life: 565 rue Agostino Neto, Koulouba, 03 BP 7044, Ouagadougou 03; tel. 50-32-40-74; fax 50-30-70-39; e-mail messp@liptinfor.bf; internet www.environnement.gov.bf.

Ministry of Foreign Affairs and Regional Co-operation: rue 988, blvd du Faso, 03 BP 7038, Ouagadougou 03; tel. 50-32-47-34; fax 50-30-87-92; e-mail webmaster.mae@mae.gov.bf; internet www.mae.gov.bf.

Ministry of Health: 03 BP 7035, Ouagadougou 03; tel. 50-32-61-88; internet www.sante.gov.bf.

Ministry of Housing and Town Planning: Ouagadougou.

Ministry of Infrastructure and Improving Access to Isolated Regions: 03 BP 7011, Ouagadougou 03; tel. 50-30-73-33; fax 50-31-84-08; internet www.mith.gov.bf.

Ministry of Justice: 01 BP 526, Ouagadougou 01; tel. 50-32-48-33; fax 50-31-71-37; e-mail webmestre@justice.bf; internet www.justice.gov.bf.

Ministry of Labour and Social Security: 01 BP 7016, Ouagadougou 01; tel. 50-30-09-60; fax 50-31-88-01; e-mail emploi@metss.gov.bf; internet www.emploi.gov.bf.

Ministry of Mines, Quarries and Energy: 01 BP 644, Ouagadougou 01; tel. 50-31-84-29; fax 50-31-84-30; internet www.mines.gov.bf.

Ministry of Posts and of Information and Communication Technology: 387 ave Georges Conseiga, 01 BP 5175, Ouagadougou 01; tel. 50-33-73-85; fax 50-33-73-87; internet www.mpt.bf.

Ministry for the Promotion of Human Rights: 11 BP 852 CMS, Ouagadougou 11; tel. 50-32-49-85; fax 50-31-64-20; e-mail secretariat@mpdh.gov.bf; internet www.mpdh.gov.bf.

Ministry for the Promotion of Women: 01 BP 303, Ouagadougou 01; tel. 50-30-01-04; fax 50-30-01-02; e-mail secretariat@mpf.gov.bf; internet www.mpf.gov.bf.

Ministry of Relations with Parliament: 01 BP 2079, Ouagadougou 01; tel. 50-32-40-70; fax 50-30-78-94; e-mail cab_mrp@yahoo.fr; internet www.mrp.gov.bf.

Ministry of Secondary and Higher Education and Scientific Research: 03 BP 7047, Ouagadougou 03; tel. 50-32-45-67; fax 50-32-61-16; e-mail laya.saw@messrs.gov.bf; internet www.messrs.gov.bf.

Ministry of Security: 01 BP 6466, Ouagadougou 01; tel. 50-31-68-91; fax 50-31-58-87.

Ministry of Social Action and National Solidarity: 01 BP 515, Ouagadougou 01; tel. 50-30-68-75; fax 50-31-67-37; internet www.action-sociale.gov.bf.

Ministry of Sport and Leisure: 03 BP 7035, Ouagadougou 03; tel. 50-32-47-86; fax 50-33-08-18; internet www.sports.gov.bf.

Ministry of Territorial Administration and Decentralization: 01 BP 526, Ouagadougou 01; tel. 50-32-48-33; fax 50-31-72-00; internet www.matd.gov.bf.

Ministry of Trade, Business Promotion and Crafts: 01 BP 514, Ouagadougou 01; tel. 50-32-48-28; fax 50-31-70-53; internet www.commerce.gov.bf.

Ministry of Transport: 03 BP 7011, Ouagadougou 03; tel. 50-30-73-33; fax 50-31-84-08.

Ministry of Youth and Employment: 03 BP 7035, Ouagadougou 03; tel. 50-32-47-96; fax 30-31-84-80; internet www.emploi.gov.bf.

President and Legislature

PRESIDENT
Presidential Election, 13 November 2005

Candidate	Votes	% of votes
Blaise Compaoré	1,660,148	80.35
Bénéwendé Stanislas Sankara	100,816	4.88
Kilachia Laurent Bado	53,743	2.60
Philippe Ouédraogo	47,146	2.28
Ram Ouédraogo	42,061	2.04
Ali Lankoandé	35,949	1.74
Norbert Michel Tiendrébéogo	33,353	1.61
Soumane Touré	23,266	1.13
Gilbert Bouda	21,658	1.05
Pargui Emile Paré	17,998	0.87
Others	30,132	1.46
Total	**2,066,270**	**100.00**

LEGISLATURE

Assemblée nationale
01 BP 6482, Ouagadougou 01; tel. 50-31-46-84; fax 50-31-45-90.
President: ROCH MARC CHRISTIAN KABORÉ.

General Election, 6 May 2007

Parties	% of total votes*	National list seats	Total seats†
CDP	58.85	9	73
ADF—RDA	10.70	2	14
UPR	4.30	1	5
UNIR—MS	3.89	1	4
CFD/B‡	2.34	1	3
PDS	3.28	1	2
PDP—PS	2.51	—	2
RDB	2.09	—	2
UPS	1.74	—	2
PAREN	1.29	—	1
RPC	1.15	—	1
UDPS	1.03	—	1
PAI	0.83	—	1
Total (incl. others)	**100.00**	**15**	**111**

* Including votes from regional and national party lists.
† Including seats filled by voting from regional lists, totalling 96.
‡ The Coalition des forces démocratiques du Burkina, an electoral alliance of six parties.

Election Commission

Commission électorale nationale indépendante (CENI): 01 BP 5152, Ouagadougou 01; tel. 50-30-00-52; fax 50-30-80-44; e-mail ceni@fasonet.bf; internet www.ceni.bf; f. 2001; 15 mems; Pres. MOUSSA MICHEL TAPSOBA.

Advisory Council

Conseil économique et social: 01 BP 6162, Ouagadougou 01; tel. 50-32-40-91; fax 50-31-06-54; e-mail ces@ces.gov.bf; internet www.ces.gov.bf; f. 1985; present name adopted in 1992; 90 mems; Pres. THOMAS SANON.

Political Organizations

A total of 47 political parties contested the legislative elections held in May 2007. In that year the most important political parties included the following:

Alliance pour la démocratie et la fédération—Rassemblement démocratique africain (ADF—RDA): 01 BP 1991, Ouagadougou 01; tel. 50-30-52-00; f. 1990 as Alliance pour la démocratie et la fédération; absorbed faction of Rassemblement démocratique africain in 1998; several factions broke away in 2000 and in mid-2003; Pres. GILBERT NOËL OUÉDRAOGO.

Alliance pour le progrès et la liberté (APL): Ouagadougou; tel. 50-31-16-01; Sec.-Gen. JOSÉPHINE TAMBOURA-SAMA.

Congrès pour la démocratie et le progrès (CDP): 1146 ave Dr Kwamé N'Krumah, 01 BP 1605, Ouagadougou 01; tel. 50-31-50-18; fax 50-31-43-93; e-mail contact@cdp-burkina.org; internet www.cdp-burkina.org; f. 1996 by merger, to succeed the Organisation pour la démocratie populaire/Mouvement du travail as the principal political org. supporting Pres. Compaoré; social democratic; Pres. ROCH MARC CHRISTIAN KABORÉ.

Convention nationale des démocrates progressistes (CNDP): Ouagadougou; tel. 50-36-39-73; f. 2000; Leader ALFRED KABORÉ.

Convention panafricaine sankariste (CPS): BP 44, Bokin; tel. 40-45-72-93; f. 1999 by merger of four parties, expanded in 2000 to include two other parties; promotes the policies of fmr Pres. Sankara; Pres. NONGMA ERNEST OUÉDRAOGO.

Convention pour la démocratie et la fédération (CDF): Ouagadougou; tel. 50-36-23-63; f. 1998; Pres. AMADOU DIEMDIODA DICKO.

Convergence pour la démocratie sociale (CDS): Ouagadougou; f. 2002; socialist, opposed to Govt of Pres. Compaoré; Chair. VALERIE DIEUDONNÉ SOMÉ; Exec. Sec.-Gen. SESSOUMA SANOU.

Front des forces sociales (FFS): BP 255, Ouagadougou; tel. 50-32-32-32; f. 1996; Sankarist; member of the Groupe du 14 février and opposition Collectif d'organisations démocratiques de masse et de partis politiques; Chair. NORBERT MICHEL TIENDRÉBÉOGO.

Front patriotique pour le changement (FPC): BP 8539, Ouagadougou; tel. 70-25-32-45; Pres. TAHIROU IBRAHIM ZON.

Mouvement du peuple pour le socialisme—Parti fédéral (MPS—PF): BP 3448, Ouagadougou; tel. 50-36-50-72; f. 2002 by split from PDP—PS; Leader Dr PARGUI EMILE PARÉ.

Mouvement pour la tolérance et le progrès/Moog Teeb Panpaasgo (MTP): BP 2364, Ouagadougou; tel. 50-36-45-35; f. 2000; Sankarist; contested 2002 legislative elections as part of the Coalition des forces démocratiques (CFD); Pres. CONGO EMMANUEL NAYABTIGUNGU KABORÉ.

Parti africain de l'indépendance (PAI): Ouagadougou; tel. 50-33-46-66; f. 1999; Sec.-Gen. SOUMANE TOURÉ.

Parti pour la démocratie et le progrès—Parti socialiste (PDP—PS): 11 BP 26, Ouagadougou 11; tel. and fax 50-31-14-10; e-mail pdp-ps@fasonet.bf; f. 2001 by merger of the Parti pour la démocratie et le progrès and the Parti socialiste burkinabè; Nat. Pres. Prof. ALI LANKOANDÉ.

Parti pour la démocratie et le socialisme (PDS): Ouagadougou; tel. 50-34-34-04; Pres. FÉLIX SOUBÉIGA.

Parti de la renaissance nationale (PAREN): Ouagadougou; tel. 50-43-12-26; f. 2000; social-democratic; Pres. KILACHIA LAURENT BADO.

Parti socialiste unifié: Ouagadougou; f. 2001 by mems of fmr Parti socialiste burkinabè; Leader BENOÎT LOMPO.

Rassemblement pour le développement du Burkina (RDB).

Rassemblement populaire des citoyens (RPC): Ouagadougou; f. 2006; promotes an alternative style of politics; Pres. ANTOINE OUARÉ.

Union des démocrates et progressistes indépendants (UDPI): BP 536, Ouagadougou; tel. 50-38-27-99; expelled from Groupe du 14 février in mid-2000; Leader LONGO DONGO.

Union pour la démocratie et le progrès social (UDPS): Ouagadougou; Leader FIDÈLE HIEN.

Union nationale pour la démocratie et le développement (UNDD): 03 BP 7114, Ouagadougou 03; tel. 50-31-15-15; f. 2003 by fmr mems of the ADF—RDA (q.v.); liberal; Pres. Me HERMANN YAMÉOGO.

Union des partis sankarist (UPS).

Union pour la renaissance—Mouvement sankariste (UNIR—MS): Ouagadougou; tel. 50-36-30-45; f. 2000; Pres. BÉNÉWENDÉ STANISLAS SANKARA.

Union pour la république (UPR): Ouagadougou; Leader TOUSSAINT ABEL COULIBALY.

Diplomatic Representation

EMBASSIES IN BURKINA FASO

Algeria: Secteur 13, Zone du Bois, 295 ave Babanguida, 01 BP 3893, Ouagadougou 01; tel. 50-36-81-81; fax 50-36-81-79; Ambassador MOHAMED EL AMINE BEN CHERIF.

Belgium: Immeuble Me Benoit Sawadogo, 994 rue Agostino Neto, Koulouba, 01 POB 1624, Ouagadougou 01; tel. 50-31-21-64; fax 50-31-06-60; e-mail ouagadougou@diplobel.org; internet www.diplomatie.be/ouagadougou; Ambassador JANSEN PAUL.

Canada: rue Agostino Neto, 01 BP 548, Ouagadougou 01; tel. 50-31-18-94; fax 50-31-19-00; e-mail ouaga@dfait-maeci.gc.ca; internet www.dfait-maeci.gc.ca/burkina_faso; Ambassador LOUIS-ROBERT DAIGLE.

BURKINA FASO

Chad: Ouagadougou; Ambassador AGNÈS MAÏMOUNA ALLAH.
China (Taiwan): 994 rue Agostino Neto, 01 BP 5563, Ouagadougou 01; tel. 50-31-61-95; fax 50-31-61-97; e-mail ambachine@fasonet.bf; Ambassador TAO WEN-LUNG.
Côte d'Ivoire: pl. des Nations Unies, 01 BP 20, Ouagadougou 01; tel. 50-31-82-28; fax 50-31-82-30; Ambassador RICHARD KODJO.
Cuba: rue 4/64, La Rotonde, Secteur 4, Ouagadougou; tel. 50-30-64-91; fax 50-31-73-24; e-mail embacuba.bf@fasonet.bf; Ambassador FERNANDO PRATS MARI.
Denmark: 316, ave Blaise Compaoré, 01 BP 1760, Ouagadougou 01; tel. 50-32-85-40; fax 50-32-85-77; e-mail ouaamb@um.dk; internet www.ambouagadougou.um.dk; Ambasssador MOGENS PEDERSEN.
Egypt: Zone du Conseil de L'Entente, blvd du Faso, 04 BP 7042, Ouagadougou 04; tel. 50-30-66-39; fax 50-31-38-36; e-mail egyptianembassy@liptinfor.bf; Ambassador MUHAMMAD MAMDOUH ALI EL-ASHMAWI.
France: ave du Trésor, 01 BP 504, Ouagadougou 01; tel. 50-49-66-66; fax 50-49-66-09; e-mail ambassade@ambafrance-bf.org; internet www.ambafrance-bf.org; Ambassador FRANÇOIS GOLDBLATT.
Germany: 399 ave Joseph Badoua, 01 BP 600, Ouagadougou 01; tel. 50-30-67-31; fax 50-31-39-91; e-mail amb.allemagne@fasonet.bf; Ambassador ULRICH HOCHSCHILD.
Ghana: 22 ave d'Oubritenga, 01 BP 212, Ouagadougou 01; tel. 50-30-76-35; e-mail embagna@fasonet.bf; Ambassador MOGTARI SAHANUN.
Korea, Democratic People's Republic: Ouagadougou; Ambassador KIL MUN YONG.
Libya: 01 BP 1601, Ouagadougou 01; tel. 50-30-67-53; fax 50-31-34-70; Ambassador ABD AN-NASSER SALEH MUHAMMAD YOUNES.
Mali: 2569 ave Bassawarga, 01 BP 1911, Ouagadougou 01; tel. 50-38-19-22; Ambassador Col TOUMANY SISSOKO.
Mauritania: Ouagadougou; Ambassador MOHAMED OULD SID AHMED LEKHAL.
Morocco: Ouaga 2000 Villa B04, place de la Cotière, 01 BP 3438, Ouagadougou 01; tel. 50-37-40-16; fax 50-37-41-72; e-mail maroc1@fasonet.bf; Ambassador ALI AHMAOUI.
Netherlands: 415 ave Dr Kwamé N'Krumah, 01 BP 1302, Ouagadougou 01; tel. 50-30-61-34; fax 50-30-76-95; e-mail oua@minbuza.nl; Ambassador Dr HAN GERARD DUIJFJES.
Nigeria: rue de l'Hôpital Yalgado, 01 BP 132, Ouagadougou 01; tel. 50-36-30-15; Ambassador AHMED KASHIM.
Saudi Arabia: Ouagadougou; Ambassador AID BIN MUHAMMAD ATH-THAKFI.
Senegal: Immeuble Espace Fadima, ave de la Résistance du 17 Mai, 01 BP 3226, Ouagadougou 01; tel. 50-31-14-18; fax 50-31-14-01; Ambassador CHEIKH SYLLA.
USA: 602 ave Raoul Follereau, Koulouba, 01 BP 35, Ouagadougou 01; tel. 50-30-67-23; fax 50-31-23-68; e-mail amembouaga@state.gov; internet ouagadougou.usembassy.gov; Ambassador JEANINE E. JACKSON.

Judicial System

In accordance with constitutional amendments approved by the Assemblée nationale in April 2000, the Supreme Court was abolished; its four permanent chambers were replaced by a Constitutional Council, a Council of State, a Court of Cassation and a National Audit Court, all of which commenced operations in December 2002. Judges are accountable to a Higher Council, under the chairmanship of the President of the Republic, in which capacity he is officially responsible for ensuring the independence of the judiciary. A High Court of Justice is competent to try the President and members of the Government in cases of treason, embezzlement of public funds, and other crimes and offences.

Constitutional Council: 11 BP 1114, Ouagadougou 11; tel. 50-31-06-24; internet www.conseil-constitutionnel.gov.bf; f. 2002 to replace Constitutional Chamber of fmr Supreme Court; Pres. IDRISSA TRAORÉ; Sec.-Gen. HONIBIPÈ MARIAM MARGUERITE OUÉDRAOGO.
Council of State: 01 BP 586, Ouagadougou 01; tel. 50-30-64-18; e-mail webmaster@conseil-etat.gov.bf; internet www.conseil-etat.gov.bf; f. 2002 to replace Administrative Chamber of fmr Supreme Court; comprises two chambers: a Consultative Chamber and a Chamber of Litigation; First Pres. HARIDIATA SERE DAKOURÉ; Pres. of Consultative Chamber THÉRÈSE SANOU TRAORÉ; Pres. of Chamber of Litigation SOULEYMANE COULIBALY.
Court of Cassation: 05 BP 6204, Ouagadougou 05; tel. 50-31-20-47; fax 50-31-02-71; e-mail cheick.ouedraogo@justice.gov.bf; internet www.cour-cassation.gov.bf; f. 2002 to replace Judicial Chamber of fmr Supreme Court; First Pres. CHEICK DIMKINSEDO OUÉDRAOGO.
High Court of Justice: Ouagadougou; f. 1998; comprises six deputies of the Assemblée nationale and three magistrates appointed by the President of the Court of Cassation; Pres. YARGA LARBA; Vice-Pres. DÉ ALBERT MILLOGO.
National Audit Court: 01 BP 2534, Ouagadougou 01; tel. 50-30-36-00; fax 50-30-35-01; e-mail infos@cour-comptes.gov.bf; internet www.cour-comptes.gov.bf; f. 2002 to replace Audit Chamber of fmr Supreme Court; comprises three chambers, concerned with: local government organs; public enterprises; and the operations of the State; First Pres. BOUREIMA PIERRE NEBIE; Procurator-Gen. THÉRÈSE TRAORÉ SANOU; Pres of Chambers PASCAL SANOU, SÉNÉBOU RAYMONDD MANUELLA OUILMA TRAORÉ, SABINE OUEDRAOGO YETA.

Religion

The Constitution provides for freedom of religion, and the Government respects this right in practice. The country is a secular state. Islam, Christianity and traditional religions operate freely without government interference. More than 50% of the population follow animist beliefs.

ISLAM

An estimated 30% of the population are Muslims.

Association Islamique Tidjania du Burkina Faso: Ouagadougou; Pres. CHEICK ABOUBACAR MAÏGA II.

CHRISTIANITY

The Roman Catholic Church

Burkina Faso comprises three archdioceses and 10 dioceses. At 31 December 2005 there were an estimated 1.6m. Roman Catholics in Burkina, comprising 12.7% of the total population.

Bishops' Conference

Conférence des Evêques de Burkina Faso et du Niger, 01 BP 1195, Ouagadougou 01; tel. 50-30-60-26; fax 50-31-64-81; e-mail ccbn@fasonet.bf.
f. 1966; legally recognized 1978; Pres. Rt Rev. PHILIPPE OUÉDRAOGO (Bishop of Ouahigouya).

Archbishop of Bobo-Dioulasso: Most Rev. ANSELME TITIANMA SANON, Archevêché, Lafiaso, 01 BP 312, Bobo-Dioulasso; tel. 20-97-00-35; fax 20-97-04-38; e-mail lafiaso@fasonet.bf.
Archbishop of Koupéla: Most Rev. SÉRAPHIN F. ROUAMBA, Archevêché, BP 51, Koupéla; tel. 40-70-00-30; fax 40-70-02-65; e-mail archevkou@fasonet.bf.
Archbishop of Ouagadougou: Most Rev. JEAN-MARIE UNTAANI COMPAORÉ, Archevêché, 01 BP 1472, Ouagadougou 01; tel. 50-30-67-04; fax 50-30-72-75; e-mail archidiocese.ouaga@liptinfor.bf.

Protestant Churches

Assemblées de Dieu du Burkina Faso: 01 BP 458, Ouagadougou 01; tel. 50-30-54-60; e-mail ad@adburkina.org; internet www.adburkina.org; f. 1921; Pres. Pastor JEAN PAWENTAORÉ OUÉDRAOGO.
Fédération des Eglises et Missions Evangéliques (FEME): BP 108, Ouagadougou; tel. 50-36-14-26; e-mail feme@fasonet.bf; f. 1961; 10 churches and missions, 82,309 adherents; Pres. Pastor FREEMAN KOMPAORÉ.

BAHÁ'Í FAITH

Assemblée spirituelle nationale: 01 BP 977, Ouagadougou 01; tel. 50-34-29-95; e-mail gnampa@fasonet.bf; Nat. Sec. JEAN-PIERRE SWEDY.

The Press

Direction de la presse écrite: Ouagadougou; govt body responsible for press direction.

DAILIES

24 Heures: 01 BP 3654, Ouagadougou 01; tel. 50-31-41-08; fax 50-30-57-39; f. 2000; privately owned; Dir BOUBAKAR DIALLO.
Bulletin de l'Agence d'Information du Burkina: 01 BP 2507, Ouagadougou 01; tel. 50-32-46-40; fax 50-33-73-16; e-mail infos@aib.bf; internet www.aib.bf; f. 1964 as L'Agence Voltaïque de Presse; current name adopted in 1984; Dir JAMES DABIRÉ.
L'Express du Faso: 01 BP 1, Bobo-Dioulasso 01; tel. 20-97-93-26; e-mail kami.express@caramail.com; f. 1998; privately owned; Dir of Publication KAMI MOUNTAMOU.
L'Observateur Paalga (New Observer): 01 BP 584, Ouagadougou 01; tel. 50-33-27-05; fax 50-31-45-79; e-mail lobservateur@zcp.bf; internet www.lobservateur.bf; f. 1973; privately owned; also a

BURKINA FASO

Sunday edn, *L'Observateur Dimanche*; Dir EDOUARD OUÉDRAOGO; circ. 7,000.

Le Pays: Cité 1200 logements, 01 BP 4577, Ouagadougou 01; tel. 50-36-20-46; fax 50-36-03-78; e-mail ed.lepays@cenatrin.bf; internet www.lepays.bf; f. 1991; independent; Dir-Gen. BOUREIMA JÉRÉMIE SIGUE; Editor-in-Chief MAHOROU KANAZOE; circ. 5,000.

Sidwaya Quotidien (Daily Truth): 5 rue du Marché, 01 BP 507, Ouagadougou 01; tel. 50-31-22-89; fax 50-31-03-62; e-mail daouda.ouedraogo@sidwaya.bf; internet www.sidwaya.bf; f. 1984; state-owned; Editor-in-Chief DAOUDA EMILE OUEDRAOGO; circ. 3,000.

PERIODICALS

L'Aurore: 01 BP 5104, Ouagadougou 01; tel. 70-25-22-81; e-mail enitiema@yahoo.fr; Dir of Publication ELIE NITIÈMA.

Bendré (Drum): 16.38 ave du Yatenga, 01 BP 6020, Ouagadougou 01; tel. 50-33-27-11; fax 50-31-28-53; e-mail bendrekan@hotmail.com; internet www.journalbendre.net; f. 1990; weekly; current affairs; Dir SY MOUMINA CHERIFF; circ. 7,000 (2002).

Les Echos: Ouagadougou; f. 2002; weekly; Editor DAVID SANHOUIDI.

Evasion: Cité 1200 logements, 01 BP 4577, Ouagadougou 01; tel. 50-36-17-30; fax 50-36-03-78; e-mail ed.lepays@cenatrin.bf; internet www.lepays.bf/hebdo; f. 1996; publ. by Editions le Pays; weekly; current affairs; Dir-Gen. BOUREIMA JÉRÉMIE SIGUE; Editor-in-Chief ABDOULAYE TAO.

L'Evènement: 01 BP 1860, Ouagadougou 01; tel. and fax 50-31-69-34; e-mail bangreib@yahoo.fr; internet www.cnpress-zongo.net/evenementbf; f. 2001; bimonthly; Editor-in-Chief NEWTON AHMED BARRY.

L'Hebdomadaire: Ouagadougou; tel. 50-31-47-62; e-mail hebdcom@fasonet.bf; internet www.hebdo.bf; f. 1999; Fridays; Dir ZÉPHIRIN KPODA; Editor-in-Chief DJIBRIL TOURÉ.

L'Indépendant: 01 BP 5663, Ouagadougou 01; tel. 50-33-37-75; e-mail sebgo@fasonet.bf; internet www.independant.bf; f. 1993 by Norbert Zongo; weekly; Tuesdays; Dir LIERMÉ DIEUDONNÉ SOMÉ; Editor-in-Chief TALATO SIID SAYA.

Le Journal du Jeudi (JJ): 01 BP 3654, Ouagadougou 01; tel. 50-31-41-08; fax 50-30-01-62; e-mail info@journaldujeudi.com; internet www.journaldujeudi.com; f. 1991; weekly; satirical; Dir BOUBAKAR DIALLO; Editor-in-Chief DAMIEN GLEZ; circ. 10,000.

Laabaali: Association Tin Tua, BP 167, Fada N'Gourma; tel. 40-77-01-26; fax 40-77-02-08; e-mail info@tintua.org; internet www.tintua.org/Liens/Laabali.htm; f. 1988; monthly; promotes literacy, agricultural information, cultural affairs, in Gourmanché; Dir of Publishing BENOÎT B. OUOBA; Editor-in-Chief SUZANNE OUOBA; circ. 3,500.

Le Marabout: 01 BP 3564, Ouagadougou 01; tel. 50-31-41-08; e-mail info@marabout.net; f. 2001; monthly; publ. by the Réseau africain pour la liberté d'informer; pan-African politics; satirical; Dir BOUBAKAR DIALLO; Editor-in-Chief DAMIEN GLEZ.

L'Opinion: 01 BP 6459, Ouagadougou 01; tel. and fax 50-30-89-49; e-mail zedcom@fasonet.bf; internet www.zedcom.bf; weekly; Dir of Publishing ISSAKA LINGANI.

Regard: 01 BP 4707, Ouagadougou 01; tel. 50-31-16-70; fax 50-31-57-47; weekly; Dir CHRIS VALÉA; Editor PATRICK ILBOUDO; circ. 4,000.

San Finna: Immeuble Photo Luxe, 12 BP 105, Ouagadougou 12; tel. and fax 50-35-82-64; e-mail sanfinna@yahoo.fr; internet www.sanfinna.com; f. 1999; Mondays; independent; current affairs, international politics; Editor-in-Chief MATHIEU N'DO.

Sidwaya Hebdo (Weekly Truth): 5 rue du Marché, 01 BP 507, Ouagadougou 01; tel. 50-31-22-89; fax 50-31-03-62; e-mail daouda.ouedraogo@sidwaya.bf; internet www.sidwaya.bf; f. 1997; state-owned; weekly; Editor-in-Chief DAOUDA EMILE OUEDRAOGO.

Sidwaya Magazine (Truth): 5 rue du Marché, 01 BP 507, Ouagadougou 01; tel. 50-31-22-89; fax 50-31-03-62; e-mail daouda.ouedraogo@sidwaya.bf; internet www.sidwaya.bf; f. 1989; state-owned; monthly; Editor-in-Chief DAOUDA E. OUÉDRAOGO; circ. 2,500.

La Voix du Sahel: 01 BP 5505, Ouagadougou 01; tel. 50-33-20-75; e-mail voixdusahel@yahoo.fr; privately owned; Dir of Publication PROMOTHÉE KASSOUM BAKO.

Votre Santé: Cité 1200 logements, 01 BP 4577, Ouagadougou 01; tel. 50-36-20-46; fax 50-36-03-78; e-mail ed.lepays@cenatrin.bf; internet www.lepays.bf/mensuel; f. 1996; publ. by Editions le Pays; monthly; Dir-Gen. BOUREIMA JÉRÉMIE SIGUE; Editor-in-Chief SÉNI DABO.

NEWS AGENCY

Agence d'Information du Burkina (AIB): 01 BP 2507, Ouagadougou 01; tel. 50-32-46-39; fax 50-33-73-16; e-mail aib.redaction@mcc.gov.bf; internet www.aib.bf; f. 1964; fmrly Agence Voltaïque de Presse; state-controlled; Dir JAMES DABIRÉ.

PRESS ASSOCIATIONS

Association Rayimkudemdé—Association Nationale des Animateurs et Journalistes en Langues Nationales du Burkina Faso (ARK): Sigh-Noghin, Ouagadougou; f. 2001; Pres. RIGOBERT ILBOUDO; Sec.-Gen. PIERRE OUÉDRAOGO.

Centre National de Presse—Norbert Zongo (CNP—NZ): 04 BP 8524, Ouagadougou 04; tel. and fax 50-34-37-45; internet www.cnpress-zongo.net; f. 1998 as Centre National de Presse; centre of information and documentation; provides journalistic training; incorporates Association des Journalistes du Burkina (f. 1988); Dir ABDOULAYE DIALLO.

Publishers

Editions Contact: 04 BP 8462, Ouagadougou 04; tel. 76-61-28-72; e-mail contact.evang@cenatrin.bf; f. 1992; evangelical Christian and other books in French.

Editions Découvertes du Burkina (ADDB): 06 BP 9237, Ouagadougou 06; tel. 50-36-22-38; e-mail jacques@liptinfor.bf; human and social sciences, poetry; Dir JACQUES GUÉGANÉ.

Editions Firmament: 01 BP 3392, Ouagadougou 01; tel. 50-38-44-25; e-mail brkabore@uemoa.int; f. 1994; literary fiction; Dir ROGER KABORÉ.

Editions Flamme: 04 BP 8921, Ouagadougou 04; tel. 50-34-15-31; fax 70-21-10-28; e-mail flamme@liptinfor.bf; f. 1999; owned by the Assembleés de Dieu du Burkina Faso; literature of Christian interest in French, in Mooré and in Dioula; Dir Pastor ZACHARIE DELMA.

Editions Gambidi: 01 BP 5743, Ouagadougou 01; tel. 50-36-59-42; e-mail jp.guingane@liptinfor.bf; politics, philosophy; Dir JEAN-PIERRE GUINGANÉ.

Graphic Technic International & Biomedical (GTI): 01 BP 3230, Ouagadougou 01; tel. and fax 50-31-67-69; medicine, literary, popular and children's fiction, poetry; Dir-Gen. SAWADOGO N. TASSERE.

Editions Hamaria: 01 BP 6788, Ouagadougou 01; tel. 50-34-38-04; sciences, fiction.

Presses Africaines SA: 01 BP 1471, Ouagadougou 01; tel. 50-30-71-75; fax 50-30-72-75; general fiction, religion, primary and secondary textbooks; Man. Dir A. WININGA.

Editions Sankofa et Gurli: 01 BP 3811, Ouagadougou 01; tel. 70-24-30-81; e-mail sankogur@hotmail.com; f. 1995; literary fiction, social sciences, African languages, youth and childhood literature; in French and in national languages; Dir JEAN-CLAUDE NABA.

Editions Sidwaya: BP 810, Ouagadougou; f. 1998 to replace Société Nationale d'Editions et de Presse; state-owned; transfer to private ownership proposed; general, periodicals; Pres. PIERRE WAONGO.

Broadcasting and Communications

TELECOMMUNICATIONS

Regulatory Authority

Autorité nationale de Régulation des Télécommunications du Burkina Faso (ARTEL): ave Dimdolobsom, Porte 43, Rue 3 angle Rue 48, 01 BP 6437, Ouagadougou 01; tel. 50-33-41-98; fax 50-33-50-39; e-mail secretariat@artel.bf; internet www.artel.bf; f. 2000 prior to the proposed liberalization of the telecommunications sector; Pres. of the Council of Administration BAZONA BERNARD BATIONO; Dir-Gen. LOUHOUN J. CLÉMENT DAKUYO.

Service Providers

Office National des Télécommunications (ONATEL): ave de la Nation, 01 BP 10000, Ouagadougou 01; tel. 50-49-44-02; fax 50-31-03-31; e-mail dcrp@onatel.bf; internet www.onatel.bf; 51% owned by Maroc Telecom (Morocco, Vivendi); 23% state owned; Pres. PAUL BALMA; Dir-Gen. MOHAMMED MORCHID.

TELMOB: tel. 49-42-41; fax 50-49-42-78; e-mail wema.d@onatel.bf; internet www.onatel.bf/telmob/index.htm; f. 2002; mobile cellular telephone operator in 19 cities; Dir DIEUDONNÉ WEMA; 400,000 subscribers (Dec. 2006).

Celtel Burkina Faso: ave du Général Aboubacar Sangoulé Lamizana, 01 BP 6622, Ouagadougou 01; tel. 50-33-14-00; fax 50-33-14-06; e-mail service_clientele@bf.celtel.com; internet www.bf.celtel.com; f. 2001; mobile cellular telephone operator in Ouagadougou, Bobo-Dioulasso and 19 other towns; subsidiary of Celtel International (United Kingdom); Dir-Gen. MOUHAMADOU NDIAYE; 55,000 subscribers (2003).

Telecel-Faso: ave de la Nation, 08 BP 11059, Ouagadougou 08; tel. 50-33-35-56; fax 50-33-35-58; e-mail infos@telecelfaso.bf; internet www.telecelfaso.bf; f. 2000; mobile cellular telephone operator in Ouagadougou, Bobo-Dioulasso and 19 other towns; 80% owned by Orascom Telecom (Egypt); Dir-Gen. AHMED CISSÉ; 80,000 subscribers (Dec. 2003).

BROADCASTING

Regulatory Authority

Higher Council of Communication (Conseil supérieur de la Communication): 290 ave Ho Chi Minh, 01 BP 6618, Ouagadougou 01; tel. 50-30-11-24; fax 50-30-11-33; e-mail info@csi.bf; internet www.csi.bf; f. 1995 as Higher Council of Information, present name adopted 2005; Pres. LUC ADOLPHE TIAO; Sec.-Gen. SONGRÉ ETIENNE SAWADOGO.

Radio

Radiodiffusion-Télévision du Burkina (RTB): 01 BP 2530, Ouagadougou 01; tel. 50-31-83-53; fax 50-32-48-09; internet www.rtb.bf; f. 2001; Dir-Gen. MARCEL TOE.

Radio Nationale du Burkina (La RNB): 03 BP 7029, Ouagadougou 03; tel. 50-32-43-02; fax 50-31-04-41; e-mail radio@rtb.bf; internet www.radio.bf; f. 1959; state radio service; comprises national broadcaster of informative and discussion programmes, music stations *Canal Arc-En-Ciel* and *Canal Arc-en-Ciel Plus*, and two regional stations, broadcasting in local languages, in Bobo-Dialasso and Gaoua; Dir MAFARMA SANOGO.

Radio Evangile Développement (RED): 04 BP 8050, Ouagadougou 04; tel. 50-43-51-56; e-mail redbf@laposte.net; internet www.red-burkina.org; f. 1993; broadcasts from Ouagadougou, Bobo-Dioulasso, Ouahigouya, Léo, Houndé, Koudougou and Yako; evangelical Christian; Dir-Gen. ETIENNE KIEMDE.

Horizon FM: 01 BP 2714, Ouagadougou 01; tel. 50-33-23-23; fax 50-30-21-41; e-mail hfm@grouphorizonfm.com; internet www.grouphorizonfm.com; f. 1990; private commercial station; broadcasts in French, English and eight vernacular languages; operates 10 stations nationally; Dir JUDITH IDA SAWADOGO.

Radio Locale-Radio Rurale: 03 BP 7029, Ouagadougou 03; tel. 50-31-27-81; fax 40-79-10-22; f. 1969; community broadcaster; local stations at Diapaga, Djibasso Gasson, Kongoussi, Orodara and Poura; Dir-Gen. BÉLIBIÉ SOUMAÏLA BASSOLE.

Radio Maria: BP 51, Koupela; tel. and fax 40-70-00-10; e-mail administration.bur@radiomaria.org; internet www.radiomaria.org; f. 1993; Roman Catholic; Dir BELEMSIGRI PIERRE CLAVER.

Radio Salankoloto-Association Galian: 01 BP 1095, Ouagadougou 01; tel. 50-31-64-93; fax 50-31-64-71; e-mail radiosalankoloto@cenatrin.bf; f. 1996; community broadcaster; Dir ROGER NIKIÉMA.

Radio Vive le Paysan: 05 BP 6274, Ouagadougou 05; tel. 50-31-16-36; fax 50-38-52-90; e-mail aeugene@fasonet.bf.

Radio la Voix du Paysan: BP 100, Ouahigouya; tel. 40-55-04-11; fax 40-55-01-62; community broadcaster; f. 1996; Pres. BERNARD LÉDÉA OUÉDRAOGO.

Television

La Télévision du Burkina: 955 blvd de la Révolution, 01 BP 2530, Ouagadougou 01; tel. 50-31-83-53; fax 50-32-48-09; e-mail television@rtb.bf; internet www.tnb.bf; branch of Radiodiffusion-Télévision du Burkina (q.v.); broadcasts 75 hours per week; Dir YACOUBA TRAORÉ.

Télévision Canal Viim Koéga—Fréquence Lumière: BP 108, Ouagadougou; tel. 50-30-76-40; e-mail cvktv@cvktv.org; internet www.cvktv.org; f. 1996; operated by the Fédération des Eglises et Missions Evangéliques; broadcasts six hours daily (Mon.–Fri.).

TV Canal 3: ave Kwamé N'Krumah, 11 BP 340, Ouagadougou 11; tel. 50-30-06-55; e-mail info@tvcanal3.com; internet www.tvcanal3.com; f. 2002.

Finance

(cap. = capital; res = reserves; dep. = deposits; m. = million; br(s). = branch(es); amounts in francs CFA)

BANKING

Central Bank

Banque centrale des états de l'Afrique de l'ouest (BCEAO): ave Bassawarga, BP 356, Ouagadougou; tel. 50-30-60-15; fax 50-31-01-22; e-mail webmaster@bceao.int; internet www.bceao.int; HQ in Dakar, Senegal; f. 1962; bank of issue for the mem. states of the Union économique et monétaire ouest-africaine (UEMOA, comprising Benin, Burkina Faso, Côte d'Ivoire, Guinea-Bissau, Mali, Niger, Senegal and Togo); cap. and res 859,313m., total assets 5,671,675m. (Dec. 2002); Resident Rep. JÉROME BRO GREBE; br. in Bobo-Dioulasso.

Other Banks

Bank of Africa—Burkina Faso (BOA—B): 770 ave de la Résistance du 17 mai, 01 BP 1319, Ouagadougou 01; tel. 50-30-88-70; fax 50-30-88-74; e-mail boadg@fasonet.bf; internet www.boaburkinafaso.com; f. 1998; cap. 2,000m., res 609.9m., dep. 69,324.7m. (Dec. 2005); Chair. LASSINÉ DIAWARA; 2 brs.

Banque Agricole et Commerciale du Burkina (BAC-B): 2 ave Gamal Abdel Nasser, Secteur 3, 01 BP 1644, Ouagadougou 01; tel. 50-33-33-33; fax 50-31-43-52; e-mail cncabf@cenatrin.bf; f. 1980; fmrly Caisse Nationale de Crédit Agricole du Burkina (CNCA-B); present name adopted 2002; 25% state-owned; cap. 3,500m., res 1,255m., dep. 56,417m. (Dec. 2003); Pres. TIBILA KABORE; Chair. and Gen. Man. LÉONCE KONÉ; 4 brs.

Banque Commerciale du Burkina (BCB): 653 ave Dr Kwamé N'Krumah, 01 BP 1336, Ouagadougou 01; tel. 50-30-78-78; fax 50-31-06-28; e-mail bcb@bcb.bf; internet www.bcb.bf; f. 1988; 50% owned by Libyan Arab Foreign Bank, 25% state-owned, 25% owned by Caisse Nationale de Sécurité Sociale; cap. 5,000m., res 1,041m., dep. 49,925m. (Feb. 2005); Pres. JACQUES ZIDA; Gen. Man. ABDULLA EL MOGADAMI; 4 brs.

Banque Internationale du Burkina (BIB): 1340 ave Dimdolobsom, 01 BP 362, Ouagadougou 01; tel. 50-30-00-00; fax 50-31-00-94; internet www.bib.bf; f. 1974; 25% owned by Fonds Burkina de Développement Economique et Social, 24.2% owned by Compagnie de Financement et de Participation (Rep. of the Congo), 22.8% state owned; cap. 4,800.0m., res 5,648.8m., dep. 127,749.3m. (Dec. 2005); Pres. and Dir-Gen. GASPARD-JEAN OUÉDRAOGO; 21 brs.

Banque Internationale pour le Commerce, l'Industrie et l'Agriculture du Burkina (BICIA—B): 479 ave Dr Kwamé N'Krumah, 01 BP 08, Ouagadougou 01; tel. 50-31-31-31; fax 50-31-19-55; e-mail info@biciab.bf; internet www.biciab.bf; f. 1973; affiliated to BNP Paribas (France); 25% state-owned; cap. 5,000m., res 6,028m., dep. 118,916m. (Dec. 2005); Pres. MICHEL KOMPAORÉ; Dir-Gen. JEAN-PIERRE BAJON-ARNAL; 11 brs.

Ecobank Burkina: Immeuble espace Fadima, 633 rue Maurice Bishop, 01 BP 145, Ouagadougou 01; tel. 50-32-83-28; fax 50-31-89-81; e-mail ecobank.bf@ecobank.com; internet www.ecobank.com; f. 1996; 59% owned by Ecobank Transnational Inc., 14.4% by private Burkinabè enterprises, 12% by Ecobank Benin, 12% by Ecobank Togo; cap. 1,500.0m., res 3,315.5m., dep. 61,337.0m. (Dec. 2004); Chair. ANDREA BAYALA; Dir-Gen. ASSIONGBON EKUÉ.

Société Générale de Banques au Burkina (SGBB): 248 rue de l'Hôtel de Ville, 01 BP 585, Ouagadougou 01; tel. 50-32-32-32; fax 50-31-05-61; e-mail sgbb@liptinfor.bf; internet www.sgbb.bf; f. 1998; 31% owned by Société Générale (France), 15% state-owned; cap. and res 5,510m., total assets 95,927m. (Dec. 2004); Dir-Gen. WILLIAM BERTHAULT.

Credit Institutions

Burkina Bail, SA: 1035 ave du Dr Kwamé N'krumah, Immeuble SODIFA, 01 BP 1913, Ouagadougou 01; tel. 50-33-26-33; fax 50-30-70-02; e-mail info@burkinabail.bf; internet www.burkinabail.bf; f. 1998; 47% owned by BIB, 34% owned by FMO and 18% owned by Cauris Investissement; cap. 1,000m., total assets 9,276m. (Dec. 2007); CEO KOUAFILANN ABDOULAYE SORY.

Réseau des Caisses Populaires du Burkina (RCPB): Ouagadougou; tel. 50-30-48-41; Dir-Gen. DAOUDA SAWADOGA; 276,966 mems (June 2002), 104 co-operatives.

Société Burkinabè de Financement (SOBFI): Immeuble Nassa, 1242 ave Dr Kwamé N'Krumah, 10 BP 13876, Ouagadougou 10; tel. 50-31-80-04; fax 50-33-71-62; e-mail sobfi@fasonet.bf; f. 1997; cap. 500.0m., total assets 2,850.9m. (Dec. 2002); Pres. DIAWAR DIACK.

Bankers' Association

Association Professionnelle des Banques et Etablissements Financiers (APBEF-B): 1021 ave Houari, 01 BP 6215, Boumedienne 01, Ouagadougou 01; tel. 50-31-20-65; fax 50-31-20-66; e-mail apbef-b@cenatrin.bf; f. 1967; Pres. MICHEL KAHN.

STOCK EXCHANGE

Bourse Régionale des Valeurs Mobilières (BRVM): s/c Chambre de Commerce, d'Industrie et d'Artisanat du Burkina, 01 BP 502, Ouagadougou 01; tel. 50-30-87-73; fax 50-30-87-19; e-mail louedraogo@brvm.org; internet www.brvm.org; f. 1998; national branch of BRVM (regional stock exchange based in Abidjan, Côte d'Ivoire, serving the member states of UEMOA); Man. LÉOPOLD OUÉDRAOGO.

INSURANCE

FONCIAS—TIARD: 99 ave Léo Frobénius, 01 BP 398, Ouagadougou 01; tel. 50-30-62-04; fax 50-31-01-53; e-mail groupe-foncias@foncias.bf; f. 1978; 51% owned by AGF (France), 20% state-owned;

non-life insurance and reinsurance; cap. 400m.; Dir-Gen. BERNARD GIRARDIN; also **Foncias-Vie**, life insurance; Dir-Gen. JOSEPH BARO.

Gras Savoye Burkina Faso: ave de la Résistance du 17 mai, 01 BP 1304, Ouagadougou 01; tel. 50-30-51-69; fax 50-30-51-73; affiliated to Gras Savoye (France); Dir-Gen. LAURENT SAWADOGO.

Société Nationale d'Assurances et de Réassurances (SONAR): 284 ave de Loudun, 01 BP 406, Ouagadougou 01; tel. 50-33-46-66; fax 50-30-89-75; e-mail sonarinfo@sonar.bf; internet www.sonar.bf; f. 1974; 42% owned by Burkinabè interests, 33% by French, Ivorian and US cos, 22% state-owned; life and non-life; cap. 720m. (SONAR-IARD, non-life), 500m. (SONAR-Vie, life); Dir-Gen. ANDRÉ B. BAYALA; 9 brs and sub-brs.

Union des Assurances du Burkina (UAB): 08 BP 11041, Ouagadougou 08; tel. 50-31-26-15; fax 50-31-26-20; e-mail uab@fasonet.bf; f. 1991; 42% owned by AXA Assurances Côte d'Ivoire; cap. 500m.; Pres. APPOLINAIRE COMPAORÉ; Dir-Gen. (non-life insurance) SI SALIFOU TRAORÉ; Dir-Gen. (life insurance) SOUMAÏLA SORGHO.

Trade and Industry

GOVERNMENT AGENCIES

Bureau des Mines et de la Géologie du Burkina (BUMIGEB): 4186 route de Fada N'Gourma, 01 BP 601, Ouagadougou 01; tel. 50-36-48-02; fax 50-36-48-88; e-mail bumigeb@cenatrin.bf; internet www.bumigeb.bf; f. 1978; restructured 1997; research into geological and mineral resources; Pres. S. KY; Dir-Gen. PASCALE DIENDÉRÉ.

Commission de Privatisation: 01 BP 6451, Ouagadougou 01; tel. 50-33-58-93; fax 50-30-77-41; Pres. PLACIDE SOME.

Comptoir Burkinabè des Métaux Précieux (CBMP): Ouagadougou; tel. 50-30-75-48; fax 50-31-56-34; promotes gold sector, liaises with artisanal producers; transfer to private management pending; Dir-Gen. YACOUBA BARRY.

Office National d'Aménagement des Terroirs (ONAT): 01 BP 3007, Ouagadougou 01; tel. 50-30-61-10; fax 50-30-61-12; f. 1974; fmrly Autorité des Aménagements des Vallées des Voltas; integrated rural development, including economic and social planning; Man. Dir ZACHARIE OUÉDRAOGO.

Office National des Barrages et des Aménagements Hydro-agricoles (ONBAH): 03 BP 7056, Ouagadougou 03; tel. 50-30-89-82; fax 50-31-04-26; f. 1976; control and development of water for agricultural use, construction of dams, water and soil conservation; state-owned; Dir-Gen. AÏZO TINDANO.

Office National du Commerce Extérieur (ONAC): 30 ave de l'UEMOA, 01 BP 389, Ouagadougou 01; tel. 50-31-13-00; fax 50-31-14-69; e-mail info@onac.bf; internet www.tradepoint.bf; f. 1974; promotes and supervises external trade; Man. Dir BAYA JUSTIN BAYILI; br. at Bobo-Dioulasso.

DEVELOPMENT ORGANIZATIONS

Agence Française de Développement (AFD): 52 ave de la Nation, 01 BP 529, Ouagadougou 01; tel. 50-30-60-92; fax 50-31-19-66; e-mail afdouagadougou@bf.groupe-afd.org; internet www.afd.fr; Country Dir LOUIS L'AOT.

Association Française des Volontaires du Progrès (AFVP): 01 BP 947, Ouagadougou 01; tel. 50-30-70-43; fax 50-30-10-72; e-mail eugene.some@afvp.org; internet www.afvp.org; f. 1973; supports small business; Nat. Delegate EUGÈNE SOME.

Bureau d'Appui aux Micro-entreprises (BAME): BP 610, Bobo-Dioulasso; tel. 20-97-16-28; fax 20-97-21-76; f. 1991; supports small business; Dir FÉLIX SANON.

Cellule d'Appui à la Petite et Moyenne Entreprise d'Ouagadougou (CAPEO): 01 BP 6443, Ouagadougou 01; tel. 50-31-37-62; fax 50-31-37-64; internet www.spid.com/capeo; f. 1991; supports small and medium-sized enterprises.

Promotion du Développement Industriel, Artisanal et Agricole (PRODIA): Secteur 8, Gounghin, 01 BP 2344, Ouagadougou 01; tel. 50-34-31-11; fax 50-34-71-47; f. 1981; supports small business; Dir MAMADOU OUÉDRAOGO.

CHAMBER OF COMMERCE

Chambre de Commerce, d'Industrie et d'Artisanat du Burkina Faso: 118/220 ave de Lyon, 01 BP 502, Ouagadougou 01; tel. 50-30-61-14; fax 50-30-61-16; e-mail ccia-bf@ccia.bf; internet www.ccia.bf; f. 1948; Pres. El Hadj OUMAROU KANAZOÉ; Dir-Gen. HAMADÉ OUÉDRAOGO; brs in Bobo-Dioulasso, Koupéla and Ouahigouya.

EMPLOYERS' ORGANIZATIONS

Club des Hommes d'Affaires Franco-Burkinabé: Ambassade de France au Burkina Faso, 01 BP 4382, Ouagadougou 01; tel. 50-31-32-73; fax 50-31-32-81; e-mail chafb@liptinfor.bf; internet www.chafb.bf; f. 1990; represents 65 major enterprises and seeks to develop trading relations between Burkina Faso and France; Pres. OUMAR YUGO.

Conseil National du Patronat Burkinabè (CNPB): 01 BP 1482, Ouagadougou 01; tel. 50-33-03-09; fax 50-30-03-08; e-mail cnpb@liptinfor.bf; f. 1974; comprises 27 professional groupings; Pres. El Hadj OUMAROU KANAZOE; Exec. Sec. EMILE KABORÉ.

    Groupement Professionnel des Industriels (GPI): Immeuble TELMOB, 447 ave de la Nation, 01 BP 5381, Ouagadougou 01; tel. and fax 50-30-11-59; e-mail gpi@fasonet.bf; internet www.gpi.bf; f. 1974; Pres. MARTIAL OUÉDRAOGO.

Fédération Nationale des Exportateurs du Burkina (FENEB): 01 BP 389, Ouagadougou 01; Permanent Sec. SEYDOU FOFANA.

Jeune Chambre du Burkina Faso: Ouagadougou; tel. 50-31-36-14; f. 1976; org. of entrepreneurs aged 18–40; affiliated to Junior Chambers International, Inc; Exec. Pres. J. P. L. AÏSHA TRAORÉ.

Maison de l'Entreprise du Burkina Faso (MEBF): rue 3-1119, porte 132, 11 BP 379, Ouagadougou 11; tel. 50-39-80-60; fax 50-39-80-62; e-mail info@me.bf; internet www.me.bf; f. 2002; promotes devt of the private sector; Pres. ALAIN ROGER COEFE.

Syndicat des Commerçants Importateurs et Exportateurs du Burkina (SCIMPEX): ave Kadiogo, Secteur 2, Immeuble CBC, 1er étage, 01 BP 552, Ouagadougou 01; tel. 50-31-18-70; fax 50-31-30-36; e-mail scimpex@fasonet.bf; internet www.scimpex-bf.com; f. 1959; Pres. LASSINÉ DIAWARA.

Union Nationale des Producteurs de Coton du Burkina Faso (UNPCB): 02 BP 1677, Bobo-Dioulasso 02; tel. 20-97-33-10; fax 20-97-20-59; e-mail unpcb@fasonet.bf; internet www.abcburkina.net/unpcb/unpcb_index.htm; f. 1998; Pres. FRANÇOIS TRAORÉ.

UTILITIES

Electricity

Société Générale de Travaux et de Constructions Electriques (SOGETEL): Zone Industrielle, Gounghin, 01 BP 429, Ouagadougou 01; tel. 50-30-23-45; fax 50-34-25-70; e-mail sogetel@cenatrin.bf; internet www.cenatrin.bf/sogetel; transport and distribution of electricity.

Société Nationale Burkinabè d'Electricité (SONABEL): 55 ave de la Nation, 01 BP 54, Ouagadougou 01; tel. 50-30-61-00; fax 50-31-03-40; e-mail info@sonabel.bf; internet www.sonabel.bf; f. 1984; state-owned; partial privatization proposed; production and distribution of electricity; Dir-Gen. SALIF LAMOUSSA KABORÉ.

Water

Office National de l'Eau et de l'Assainissement (ONEA): 01 BP 170, Ouagadougou 01; tel. 50-43-19-00; fax 50-43-19-11; e-mail onea@fasonet.bf; f. 1977; storage, purification and distribution of water; transferred to private management (by Veolia Water Burkina Faso) in 2001; Dir-Gen. MAMADOU LAMINE KOUATE.

Veolia Water Burkina Faso: 06 BP 9525, Ouagadougou 06; tel. and fax 50-34-03-00; manages operation of water distribution and sewerage services; subsidiary of Veolia Environnement (France).

CO-OPERATIVES

Union des Coopératives Agricoles et Maraîchères du Burkina (UCOBAM): 01 BP 277, Ouagadougou 01; tel. 50-30-65-27; fax 50-30-65-28; e-mail ucobam@zcp.bf; f. 1968; comprises 8 regional co-operative unions (6,500 mems, representing 35,000 producers); production and marketing of fruit, vegetables, jams and conserves; Dir-Gen. YASSIA OUEDRAOGO.

TRADE UNIONS

In 2001 there were more than 20 autonomous trade unions. The five trade-union syndicates were:

Confédération Générale du Travail Burkinabè (CGTB): 01 BP 547, Ouagadougou 01; tel. 50-31-36-71; f. 1988; confed. of several autonomous trade unions; Sec.-Gen. TOLÉ SAGNON.

Confédération Nationale des Travailleurs Burkinabè (CNTB): BP 445, Ouagadougou; tel. 50-31-23-95; e-mail cntb@fasonet.bf; f. 1972; Sec.-Gen. LAURENT OUÉDRAOGO; 10,000 mems.

Confédération Syndicale Burkinabè (CSB): 01 BP 1921, Ouagadougou 01; tel. and fax 50-31-83-98; e-mail cosybu2000@yahoo.fr; f. 1974; mainly public service unions; Sec.-Gen. JEAN MATHIAS LILIOU.

Organisation Nationale des Syndicats Libres (ONSL): 01 BP 99, Ouagadougou 01; tel. 50-34-34-69; fax 50-34-34-69; e-mail onslbf@yahoo.fr; f. 1960; 6,000 mems.

Union Syndicale des Travailleurs Burkinabè (USTB): BP 381, Ouagadougou; f. 1958; Sec.-Gen. BONIFACE SOMDAH; 35,000 mems in 45 affiliated orgs.

Transport

RAILWAY

SITARAIL—Transport Ferroviaire de Personnes et de Marchandises: rue Dioncolo, 01 BP 5699, Ouagadougou 01; tel. 50-31-07-35; fax 50-30-85-21; 67% owned by Groupe Bolloré, 15% state-owned, 15% owned by Govt of Côte d'Ivoire; national branch of SITARAIL (based in Abidjan, Côte d'Ivoire); responsible for operations on the railway line between Kaya, Ouagadougou and Abidjan (Côte d'Ivoire); Rep. in Burkina SOULEYMANE YAMÉOGO.

Société de Gestion du Patrimoine Ferroviaire du Burkina (SOPAFER—B): 01 BP 192, Ouagadougou 01; tel. 50-30-25-48; fax 50-31-35-94; railway network services; Dir-Gen. NÉBAMA KERE.

ROADS

In 2004 there were an estimated 15,272 km of roads, of which some 31% were paved. A major aim of current road projects is to improve transport links with other countries of the region. In 1999 a US $37m. project was begun to upgrade the road linking Ouagadougou with the Ghanaian border via the more isolated southern provinces.

Interafricaine de Transport et de Transit (IATT): 04 BP 8242, Ouagadougou 04; tel. 50-30-25-12; fax 50-30-37-04.

Société Africaine de Transit (SAT): 01 BP 4249, Ouagadougou 01; tel. 50-31-09-16.

Société Africaine de Transports Routiers (SATR): 01 BP 5298, Ouagadougou 01; tel. 50-34-08-62.

Société Nationale du Transit du Burkina (SNTB): 474 rue Ilboudo Waogyandé, 01 BP 1192, Ouagadougou 01; tel. 50-49-30-00; fax 50-30-85-21; f. 1977; 82% owned by Groupe SAGA (France), 12% state-owned; road haulage and warehousing; Dir-Gen. RÉGIS TISSIER.

CIVIL AVIATION

There are international airports at Ouagadougou and Bobo-Dioulasso, 49 small airfields and 13 private airstrips. Plans were announced in 2006 for the construction of a new international airport at Donsin, 35 km north east of the capital; the first phase of the project from 2007–11 was to cost some 115,000m. francs CFA. Two subsequent phases were projected to extend until 2023. Ouagadougou airport handled an estimated 2756,367 passengers and 4,105 metric tons of freight in 2005.

Air Burkina: 29 ave de la Nation, 01 BP 1459, Ouagadougou 01; tel. 50-30-76-76; fax 50-31-48-80; e-mail airburkina@wanadoo.fr; internet www.air-burkina.com; f. 1967 as Air Volta; 56% owned by Aga Khan Group, 14% state-owned; operates domestic and regional services; Dir MOHAMED GHELALA.

Tourism

Burkina Faso, which possesses some 2.8m. ha of nature reserves, is considered to provide some of the best opportunities to observe wild animals in West Africa. Some big game hunting is permitted. Several important cultural events are also held in Burkina Faso: the biennial pan-African film festival, FESPACO, is held in Ouagadougou, as is the biennial international exhibition of handicrafts, while Bobo-Dioulasso hosts the biennial week of national culture. In 2005 there were 244,728 foreign visitors. Receipts from tourism were estimated at US $25m. in 2001.

Office National du Tourisme Burkinabè (ONTB): ave Frobénius, BP 1318, Ouagadougou; tel. 50-31-19-59; fax 50-31-44-34; e-mail ontb@ontb.bf; internet www.ontb.bf; Dir-Gen. ISIDORE NABALOUM.

BURUNDI

Introductory Survey

Location, Climate, Language, Religion, Flag, Capital

The Republic of Burundi is a land-locked country lying on the eastern shore of Lake Tanganyika, in central Africa, a little south of the Equator. It is bordered by Rwanda to the north, by Tanzania to the south and east, and by the Democratic Republic of the Congo (formerly Zaire) to the west. The climate is tropical (hot and humid) in the lowlands, and cool in the highlands, with an irregular rainfall. The population is composed of three ethnic groups: the Hutu (85%), the Tutsi (14%) and the Twa (1%). The official languages are French and Kirundi, while Swahili is used, in addition to French, in commercial circles. More than 65% of the inhabitants profess Christianity, with the great majority of the Christians being Roman Catholics. A large minority still adhere to traditional animist beliefs. The national flag (proportions 3 by 5) consists of a white diagonal cross on a background of red (above and below) and green (hoist and fly), with a white circle, containing three green-edged red stars, in the centre. The capital is Bujumbura.

Recent History

Burundi (formerly Urundi) became part of German East Africa in 1899. In 1916 the territory was occupied by Belgian forces from the Congo (now the Democratic Republic of the Congo, DRC). Subsequently, as part of Ruanda-Urundi, it was administered by Belgium under a League of Nations mandate and later as a UN Trust Territory. Elections in September 1961, conducted under UN supervision, were won by the Union pour le progrès national (UPRONA). Internal self-government was granted in January 1962 and full independence on 1 July, when the two parts of the Trust Territory became separate states, as Burundi and Rwanda. Tensions between Burundi's two main ethnic groups, the Tutsi (traditionally the dominant tribe, despite representing a minority of the overall population) and the Hutu, escalated during 1965. Following an unsuccessful attempt by the Hutu to overthrow the Tutsi-dominated Government in October, nearly all the Hutu political élite were executed, eliminating any significant participation by the Hutu in Burundi's political life until the late 1980s (see below). In July 1966 the Mwami (King), Mwambutsa IV, was deposed, after a reign of more than 50 years, by his son Charles, and the Constitution was suspended. In November Charles, now Mwami Ntare V, was himself deposed by his Prime Minister, Capt. (later Lt-Gen.) Michel Micombero, who declared Burundi a republic.

Several alleged plots against the Government in 1969 and 1971 were followed by an abortive coup in 1972, during which Ntare V was killed. Hutu activists were held responsible for the attempted coup, and this served as a pretext for the Tutsi to conduct a series of large-scale massacres of the rival tribe, in which, it was estimated, about 100,000 were killed.

In 1972 Micombero began a prolonged restructuring of the executive, which resulted, in 1973, in the appointment of a seven-member Presidential Bureau, headed by himself. In July 1974 the Government introduced a new republican Constitution, which vested sovereignty in UPRONA, the sole legal political party. Micombero was elected Secretary-General of the party and re-elected for a seven-year presidential term.

In 1976 an army coup led by Lt-Col (later Col) Jean-Baptiste Bagaza deposed Micombero. Bagaza was appointed President by the Supreme Revolutionary Council (composed of army officers), and a new Council of Ministers was formed. The first national congress of UPRONA was held in December 1979, and a party Central Committee, headed by Bagaza, was elected to take over the functions of the Supreme Revolutionary Council in January 1980. A new Constitution, adopted by national referendum in November 1981, provided for the establishment of a unicameral legislature, the Assemblée nationale, to be elected by universal adult suffrage. The first legislative elections were held in October 1982. Having been re-elected President of UPRONA in July 1984, Bagaza, the sole candidate, was elected President of Burundi in August, winning 99.6% of the votes cast.

In September 1987 Bagaza was deposed in a military coup, led by Maj. Pierre Buyoya, who accused Bagaza of corruption. Buyoya immediately formed a Comité militaire pour le salut national (CMSN) to administer the country. The Constitution was suspended, and the Assemblée nationale was dissolved. On 2 October Buyoya was inaugurated as President of the Third Republic.

In August 1988 tribal tensions erupted into violence in the north of the country when groups of Hutus, claiming Tutsi provocation, slaughtered hundreds of Tutsis in the towns of Ntega and Marangara. The Tutsi-dominated army was immediately dispatched to the region to restore order, and large-scale tribal massacres occurred. In October Buyoya announced changes to the Council of Ministers, including the appointment of a Hutu, Adrien Sibomana, as Prime Minister, and established a committee to investigate the massacres; nevertheless, political tension persisted.

In May 1990, in response to a new draft charter on national unity, Buyoya announced plans to replace military rule with a 'democratic constitution under a one-party government'. In December, at an extraordinary national congress of UPRONA, the CMSN was abolished and its functions transferred to an 80-member Central Committee, with Buyoya as Chairman and with a Hutu, Nicolas Mayugi, as Secretary-General. At a referendum in February 1991 the draft charter on national unity was overwhelmingly approved. Later in the month a ministerial reorganization, in which Hutus received 12 of the 23 government portfolios, was viewed with scepticism by political opponents. In March a commission was established to prepare a report on the democratization of political structures, in preparation for the drafting of a new constitution. The commission's report, presented in September, recommended the establishment of a multi-party parliamentary system, which was to operate in conjunction with a renewable five-year presidential mandate. The proposals received the support of more than 90% of the voters in a referendum held on 9 March 1992, and the new Constitution was promulgated on 13 March.

In an extensive government reorganization in April 1992, Hutus were appointed to 15 of the 25 ministries, while Buyoya relinquished the defence portfolio. In the same month Buyoya approved legislation relating to the creation of new political parties in accordance with the new Constitution. New political parties were to be obliged to demonstrate impartiality with regard to ethnic or regional origin, gender and religion, and were to refrain from militarization. In October Buyoya announced the creation of the 33-member electoral commission, comprising representatives of the eight recognized political parties, together with administrative, judicial, religious and military officials.

A presidential election on 1 June 1993 was won, with 64.8% of the votes cast, by Melchior Ndadaye, the candidate of the Front pour la démocratie au Burundi (FRODEBU), who was supported by the Rassemblement du peuple burundien (RPB), the Parti du peuple and the Parti libéral; Buyoya received 32.4% of the vote as the UPRONA candidate, with support from the Rassemblement pour la démocratie et le développement économique et social (RADDES) and the Parti social démocrate. Elections for 81 seats in the Assemblée nationale were conducted on 29 June. FRODEBU again emerged as the most successful party, with 71% of the votes and 65 of the seats in the new legislature. UPRONA, with 21.4% of the votes, secured the remaining 16 seats. Ndadaye, Burundi's first Hutu Head of State, assumed the presidency on 10 July. A Tutsi, Sylvie Kinigi, became Prime Minister, while the new Council of Ministers included a further six Tutsi representatives.

On 21 October 1993 more than 100 army paratroopers swiftly overwhelmed supporters of the Government and occupied the presidential palace and the headquarters of the national broadcasting company. Ndadaye and several other prominent Hutu politicians and officials were detained and subsequently killed by the insurgents, who later proclaimed François Ngeze, one of the few Hutu members of UPRONA and a minister in the Government of former President Buyoya, as head of a Comité national du salut public (CNSP). While members of the Government sought refuge abroad and in the offices of foreign diplomatic missions in Bujumbura, the armed forces declared a state of emergency, closing national borders and the capital's airport. However, international condemnation of the coup, together with the scale and ferocity of renewed tribal violence, undermined support for the insurgents from within the armed forces, and precipitated the collapse of the CNSP, which was dissolved on 25 October. Kinigi ended the curfew, but remained in hiding and urged the deployment of an international force in Burundi to protect the civilian Government. On 28 October the UN confirmed that the Government had resumed control of the country. Ngeze and 10 coup leaders were arrested, while some 40 other insurgents were believed to have fled to Zaire (now the DRC). Meanwhile, following division within FRODEBU, a 'hardline' leader, Léonard Nyangoma, established a new party, Conseil national pour la défense de la démocratie (CNDD), with an armed wing, the Force pour la défense de la démocratie (FDD).

In early November 1993 several members of the Government, including the Prime Minister, had left the French embassy with a small escort of French troops, and on 8 November Kinigi met with 15 of the 17 surviving ministers, in an attempt to address the humanitarian crisis arising from the massacre and displacement of hundreds of thousands of Burundians following the failed coup. On the same day the Constitutional Court officially recognized the presidential vacancy resulting from the murder of both Ndadaye and his constitutional successor, Giles Bimazubute, the Speaker of the Assemblée nationale, and stated that presidential power should be exercised by the Council of Ministers, pending a presidential election, which was to be conducted within three months. However, the Minister of External Relations and Co-operation, Sylvestre Ntibantunganya (who succeeded Ndadaye as leader of FRODEBU), suggested that no electoral timetable should be considered before the resolution of internal security difficulties and the initiation of a comprehensive programme for the repatriation of refugees. In December Ntibantunganya was elected Speaker of the Assemblée nationale.

Meanwhile, in November 1993, following repeated requests by the Government for an international contribution to the protection of government ministers in Burundi, the Organization of African Unity (OAU—now the African Union—AU, see p. 164) agreed to the deployment of a protection force, to comprise some 180 civilian and military personnel. In December opposition parties, including UPRONA and the RADDES, organized demonstrations in protest at the deployment of the contingent, scheduled for January 1994, claiming that it infringed Burundi's sovereignty. As a compromise, in March the Government secured a significant reduction in the size of the mission, to comprise a military contingent of 47 and 20 civilian observers; it was finally deployed in February 1995.

In early January 1994 FRODEBU deputies in the Assemblée nationale approved a draft amendment to the Constitution, allowing a President of the Republic to be elected by the Assemblée nationale, in the event of the Constitutional Court's recognition of a presidential vacancy. UPRONA deputies, who had boycotted the vote, expressed concern that such a procedure represented election by indirect suffrage, in direct contravention of the terms of the Constitution. The continued boycott of the Assemblée nationale by UPRONA deputies forced the postponement, on 10 January, of an attempt by FRODEBU deputies to elect their presidential candidate, the Minister of Agriculture and Livestock, Cyprien Ntaryamira. Three days later, none the less, following the successful negotiation of a political truce with opposition parties, Ntaryamira was elected President by the Assemblée nationale. A Tutsi Prime Minister, Anatole Kanyenkiko, was appointed in early February, and the composition of a new multi-party Council of Ministers was subsequently agreed. During that month ethnic tension was renewed, as armed Hutu and Tutsi extremist factions attempted to establish territorial strongholds.

On 6 April 1994, returning from a regional summit meeting in Dar es Salaam, Tanzania, Ntaryamira and three government ministers were killed when the aircraft of the Rwandan President, Juvénal Habyarimana, in which they were travelling, was the target of a rocket attack above Kigali airport, Rwanda, and exploded on landing. Habyarimana, who was also killed, was widely acknowledged to have been the intended victim of the attack. In contrast to the violent chaos that erupted in Rwanda (q.v.) in the aftermath of the death of Habyarimana, Burundians responded positively to appeals for calm issued by Ntibantunganya, the Speaker of the Assemblée nationale, who, on 8 April, was confirmed (in accordance with the Constitution) as interim President for a three-month period.

Having discounted the possibility of organizing a general election, owing to security considerations, in June 1994 all major political parties joined lengthy negotiations to establish a procedure for the restoration of the presidency. The mandate of the interim President was extended for three months by the Constitutional Court in July, and by the end of August it had been decided that a new President would be elected by a broadly representative commission. A new power-sharing agreement, the Convention of Government, was announced on 10 September. Detailing the terms of government for a four-year transitional period (including the allocation of 45% of cabinet posts to opposition parties), it was incorporated into the Constitution on 22 September. The Convention also provided for the creation of a National Security Council (Conseil de sécurité nationale—CSN), which was formally inaugurated on 10 October. On 30 September the Convention elected Ntibantunganya to the presidency from a list of six candidates. Ntibantunganya's appointment was endorsed by the Assemblée nationale, and he was formally inaugurated on 1 October. Anatole Kanyenkiko was reappointed as Prime Minister, and a coalition Government was announced in accordance with the terms of the Convention. In December, however, UPRONA announced its intention to withdraw from the Government and from the legislature, following the election earlier that month of Jean Minani (a prominent FRODEBU member) to the post of Speaker of the Assemblée nationale. UPRONA members accused Minani of having incited Hutu attacks against Tutsis in the aftermath of the October 1993 attempted coup. In January 1995 the political crisis was averted by agreement on a compromise FRODEBU candidate, Léonce Ngendakumana, as Speaker. Minani subsequently assumed the FRODEBU party leadership. Later that month Kanyenkiko resisted attempts by the UPRONA leadership to expel him from the party, for having failed to comply with its demands for the withdrawal from the Government of all party members over the Minani affair. Two UPRONA ministers were subsequently dismissed from the Government, in apparent retaliation, prompting that organization to demand the resignation of the Prime Minister and to declare an indefinite general strike in support of this demand. In response to increased political opposition, Kanyenkiko acknowledged that he no longer commanded the necessary mandate to continue in office, and on 22 February Antoine Nduwayo, a UPRONA candidate selected in consultation with other opposition parties, was appointed Prime Minister by presidential decree. A new coalition Council of Ministers was announced on 1 March, but political stability was undermined immediately by the murder of the Hutu Minister of Energy and Mines, Ernest Kabushemeye.

An escalation in the scale and frequency of incidents of politically and ethnically motivated violence during 1995 prompted renewed concern that the security crisis would precipitate a large-scale campaign of ethnic massacres similar to that in Rwanda during 1994. Government-sponsored military initiatives were concentrated in Hutu-dominated suburbs of Bujumbura and in the north-east, where a campaign was waged against the alleged insurgent activities of the Parti de libération du peuple hutu (PALIPEHUTU—a small, proscribed, Hutu opposition group based in Tanzania), resulting in the deaths of hundreds of Hutu civilians. The Government accused Hutu extremist militias of conducting an intimidating and violent programme of recruitment in the region. In June 1995 a report published by the human rights organization Amnesty International claimed that national security forces in Burundi had collaborated with extremist Tutsi factions in the murder of thousands of Hutus since 1993. Increased security measures announced by Ntibantunganya in the same month included restrictions on a number of civil liberties.

By early 1996 reports of atrocities perpetrated against both Hutu and Tutsi civilians by dissident elements of the Tutsi-led armed forces (including militia known as the *Sans Echecs*) and by extremist Hutu rebel groups had become almost commonplace in rural areas. It was believed that the capital had been effectively 'cleansed' of any significant Hutu presence by the end of 1995. In late December the UN Secretary-General urged the Security Council to sanction some form of international military intervention in Burundi to address the crisis. However, the Burundian Government remained vehemently opposed to a foreign military presence.

In early April 1996 representatives of the US Agency for International Development and the Humanitarian Office of the European Union (EU, see p. 244) visited Burundi. Their findings, which were severely critical of the administration's failure to reconcile the country's various ethnic and political interests within the Government, prompted the USA and the EU immediately to suspend aid to Burundi. Despite pledges by Ntibantunganya in late April to undertake comprehensive reforms of the security forces and the judiciary, violence continued to escalate, prompting the suspension of French military co-operation with Burundi at the end of May.

Representatives of some 13 political parties (including FRODEBU and UPRONA) participated in discussions conducted in Mwanza, Tanzania, in April 1996, with mediation from the former President of Tanzania, Julius Nyerere. Talks resumed in Mwanza in early June; UPRONA, with support from an informal coalition of seven smaller, predominantly Tutsi parties (the Rassemblement unitaire), accused FRODEBU deputies of seeking to abrogate the Convention of Government, a charge that was strenuously denied by FRODEBU following the talks. At a conference of regional powers in Arusha, Tanzania, in late June, it was reported that Ntibantunganya and Nduwayo had requested foreign intervention to protect government installations. By early July a regional technical commission to examine the request for 'security assistance' (comprising regional defence ministers, but not representatives of the Burundian armed forces) had convened in Arusha and had reached preliminary agreement, with UN support, for an intervention force. Meanwhile, significant differences with regard to the mandate of such a force had emerged between Ntibantunganya and Nduwayo (who suggested that the President was attempting to neutralize the country's military capability). At a mass rally in Bujumbura of Tutsi-dominated opposition parties, the Prime Minister joined other leaders in rejecting foreign military intervention. Some days later, however, full endorsement of the Arusha proposal for intervention was recorded by member nations of the OAU at a summit meeting convened in Yaoundé, Cameroon.

Political and ethnic enmities intensified still further when reports of a massacre of more than 300 Tutsi civilians at Bugendana, allegedly committed by Hutu extremists, including heavily armed Rwandan Hutu refugees, emerged shortly after the UN accused the Burundian authorities of collaborating with the Rwandan administration in a new initiative of (largely enforced) repatriation of Rwandan refugees in Burundi. While FRODEBU members made an urgent appeal for foreign intervention to contain the increasingly violent civil and military reaction to these events, students (with the support of the political opposition) began a second week of protests against regional military intervention, and demonstrated in support of demands for the removal of the country's leadership.

In late July 1996 the armed forces were extensively deployed in the capital in a military coup. A statement made by the Minister of National Defence, Lt-Col Firmin Sinzoyiheba, criticized the failure of the administration to safeguard national security, and announced the suspension of the Assemblée nationale and all political activity, the imposition of a nationwide curfew and the closure of national borders and the airport at Bujumbura. Former President Buyoya was declared interim President of a transitional republic, and immediately sought to reassure former ministers and government officials that their safety would be guaranteed by the new regime. Ntibantunganya conveyed his refusal to relinquish office, but Nduwayo resigned, attributing his failure to effect national reconciliation principally to Ntibantunganya's ineffective leadership. In response to widespread external condemnation of the coup, Buyoya announced that a largely civilian government of national unity would be promptly installed, and that future negotiations with all Hutu groups would be considered. The forced repatriation of Rwandan Hutu refugees was halted with immediate effect.

Despite the appointment at the end of July 1996 of Pascal-Firmin Ndimira, a Hutu member of UPRONA, as Prime Minister, and an urgent attempt by Buyoya to obtain regional support, the leaders of Ethiopia, Kenya, Rwanda, Tanzania, Uganda and Zaire, meeting in Arusha, under OAU auspices, declared their intention to impose stringent economic sanctions against the new regime unless constitutional government was restored immediately. In early August the composition of a new 23-member, multi-ethnic Cabinet was announced. In mid-August Buyoya declared that an expanded transitional Assemblée nationale, incorporating existing elected deputies, would be inaugurated during September for a three-year period. Buyoya was formally sworn in as President on 27 September.

The regional sanctions that were imposed in early August 1996 resulted in the suspension of all significant trade and in Burundi's virtual economic isolation. However, the threat of a humanitarian crisis prompted the sanctions co-ordinating committee, meeting in Arusha in September, to authorize a relaxation of the embargo to facilitate the distribution of food and medical aid. An attempt by Buyoya later that month to secure the repeal of all sanctions by announcing an end to the ban on political parties and the restoration of the Assemblée nationale was received with scepticism by opponents, in view of the continued suspension of the Constitution and Buyoya's refusal to accept preconditions to the ending of sanctions that required the organization of unconditional peace negotiations. (In early October some 37 deputies attended the formal reopening of the Assemblée nationale, which was boycotted by the majority of FRODEBU deputies.) In October a meeting of regional leaders in Arusha decided that sanctions should be maintained until evidence emerged of constructive progress in the negotiations.

By late 1996 the military action in eastern Zaire had led to the repatriation of 30,000 Burundians and had severely weakened FDD fighting capacity, although some rebel activity continued from Tanzania. In January 1997 the office of the UN High Commissioner for Refugees (UNHCR) reported that the army had massed more than 100,000 (mainly Hutu) civilians in camps, as part of a 'regroupment' scheme, which the authorities claimed to be an initiative to protect villagers in areas of rebel activity.

Six ministers were replaced in a reorganization of Ndimira's Government in May 1997, and in August a new post of Minister of the Peace Process was created. Nevertheless, civil unrest continued and on 1 January 1998 an attack on Bujumbura airport by more than 1,000 Hutu rebels resulted in at least 250 deaths. Similar attacks, although on a smaller scale, continued during early 1998. On 18 February the second stage of the inter-Burundian peace talks was held. The discussions, which had been delayed following the death of the Minister of Defence in a helicopter crash, were attended by representatives of the Government, the political parties and the Assemblée nationale, and prominent civilians. The CNDD, however, suspended its participation in protest at human rights violations on the part of the Government. Following the announcement in late February that a regional summit, held in Kampala, Uganda, had voted to maintain the sanctions on Burundi, President Buyoya announced the impending repeal of travel restrictions that had been applied to former Presidents Bagaza and Ntibantunganya, and to the Speaker of the Assemblée nationale, Ngendakumana. In mid-March the courts dismissed a case against Ngendakumana, on charges of genocide.

Following negotiations between the Government and the Assemblée nationale concerning the expiry of FRODEBU's electoral mandate in June 1998, Buyoya and Ngendakumana publicly signed a political accord, and a new transitional Constitution was promulgated on 6 June. The new charter provided for institutional reforms, including the creation of two vice-presidencies to replace the office of Prime Minister, the enlargement of the Assemblée nationale from 81 to 121 seats, and the creation of a seven-member Constitutional Court. In accordance with the transitional Constitution, Buyoya was inaugurated as President on 11 June. On the following day the two Vice-Presidents were appointed: Frédérique Bavuginyumvira, a senior member of FRODEBU, who was allocated responsibility for political and administrative affairs, and Mathias Sinamenye (a Tutsi and hitherto the Governor of the Central Bank), with responsibility for economic and social issues. A new 22-member Council of Ministers included 13 Hutus and eight Tutsis. The newly enlarged Assemblée nationale, which was inaugurated in mid-July, incorporated nine representatives from smaller political parties (with four further seats remaining provisionally vacant), together with 27 civilian representatives and 21 new representatives of FRODEBU to replace those who had been killed or had fled into exile. On 22 July the inter-Burundian peace talks were adjourned at the request of the Government, as the parties were unable to reach agreement on the structure of the negotiations.

Meanwhile, little substantive progress was made in regional efforts to bring about direct peace talks between the Buyoya Government and its opponents. Consultations in Arusha in December 1996 were attended by representatives of the Buyoya administration, FRODEBU, the CNDD, PALIPEHUTU and other organizations. The first of a series of national discussions on the peace process began in January 1997, attended by academics, religious leaders, politicians and representatives of civil society. However, prominent political organizations, notably FRODEBU, refused to attend the talks. Buyoya attended the fourth Arusha summit meeting on the Burundi conflict in April. The leaders of the Great Lakes countries agreed to ease economic sanctions in the interest of alleviating conditions for the civilian population. The full revocation of sanctions was made dependent on the opening of direct, unconditional peace talks between the Burundian Government and opposition.

Initial optimism that inter-party discussions, commencing in Arusha in August 1997, would achieve progress in ending the political crisis diminished as the Buyoya Government became increasingly hostile to the mediation of Nyerere, claiming him to be biased in favour of the opposition. After it became evident that the sanctions would not be revoked immediately upon the opening of negotiations, the Buyoya Government announced that it would not be attending the Arusha talks, stating that it required more time to prepare, and the session was subsequently abandoned. Nyerere openly condemned the stance of the Buyoya regime, appealing for wider international assistance in resolving the crisis.

In May 1998 dissension between the political and military wings of the CNDD resulted in a division of the organization, into a faction headed by Nyangoma (which retained the name CNDD) and a larger faction comprising most of its armed forces, led by the FDD Chief of Staff, Jean-Bosco Ndayikengurukiye (which became known as the CNDD—FDD). In that month Nyerere conducted discussions with Burundian political leaders, in preparation for the peace negotiations, which commenced in mid-June in Arusha. At the talks, which were attended by 17 groupings involved in the conflict, it was agreed that the next round of discussions would take place on 20 July, and that all factions would suspend hostilities on that date. The Government, however, expressed reservations concerning the cease-fire, citing the need to maintain state security. The CNDD—FDD also refused to accept the cease-fire. It was agreed that the negotiations were to continue for three months, and that commissions would be established to negotiate each of the main issues of contention. At the July discussions, however, little progress was made. In October some moderate members of the UPRONA central committee elected a rival Chairman, Dr Luc Rukingama, the Minister of Information and a supporter of Buyoya. The commissions were duly established during further discussions in October and January 1999.

At a regional summit meeting, which took place in Arusha in January 1999, following an appeal from the UN Security Council earlier in the month, regional Heads of State voted to suspend the economic sanctions, in recognition of the progress made in the peace negotiations, although they emphasized that the eventual lifting of the sanctions would be dependent on the progress made at the peace talks. In May Buyoya announced his proposals for reconciliation; these included a 10-year transitional period during which he would occupy the presidency for the first five years and a Hutu representative would assume the post for the second five years. The plan also envisaged the extension of the Assemblée nationale to include Hutu rebel factions, the creation of an upper legislative chamber, the establishment of communal police forces, to resolve the issue of Tutsi-dominated defence and security forces, and the establishment of a national truth commission. Buyoya's opponents dismissed the proposals, citing his failure to honour his commitment to return the country swiftly to civilian rule in 1996 and the absence of any reference to elections in his plan. A round of discussions took place in Arusha in July; Nyerere criticized the lack of progress achieved at the negotiations, and the failure of the commissions to reach agreement. The absence from the negotiations of the two most significant rebel movements, the CNDD—FDD and an armed wing of PALIPEHUTU, known as Forces nationales de libération (FNL), was also viewed as a major impediment to agreement on a peace plan. Further talks at Arusha in September were impeded by the escalation of violence throughout the country, particularly around Bujumbura. Subsequent discussions were postponed, owing to the death of Nyerere in mid-October. All the participating parties expressed their commitment to the process, and nine organizations, including FRODEBU and UPRONA, created a movement for peace and solidarity, the Convergence nationale pour la paix et réconciliation (CNPR), which proposed that negotiations continue on neutral territory, owing to the alleged role of Tanzania in sheltering Hutu rebels. In December regional Heads of State, meeting in Arusha, nominated the former President of South Africa, Nelson Mandela, as the new mediator of the peace negotiations.

The escalation of Hutu-led attacks around the capital in the second half of 1999 led to the alleged rearming of Tutsi militias by the Tutsi-dominated security forces, and the enforced relocation of more than 320,000 Hutus into 'regroupment' camps. In mid-October, following an ambush in which two UN aid workers were killed, the UN announced that it was to restrict its operations and confine its staff to Bujumbura.

In January 2000 a major cabinet reorganization was effected. Peace negotiations (the first to be attended by Mandela) resumed in Arusha in late February. Mandela criticized Tutsi domination of public office and urged equal representation of Hutu and Tutsi in the armed forces, while also denouncing Hutu rebel attacks on civilians. At a further round of discussions, which commenced in Arusha in late March, agreement was reached on draft proposals for a new ethnically balanced armed force. (Nevertheless, government forces continued attacks against Hutu rebel positions, prompting fierce fighting south of Bujumbura.) In April Mandela visited Burundi for the first time, meeting government and militia leaders. Following a further meeting with Buyoya in Johannesburg, South Africa, in June, Mandela announced that the Burundian President had agreed to ensure equal representation of Hutu and Tutsi in the armed forces and the closure of 'regroupment' camps by the end of July.

In July 2000 Ndayikengurukiye, as leader of the CNDD—FDD, for the first time accepted an invitation by Mandela to participate in the peace negotiations. In the same month the drafting of a peace accord was finalized; the agreement stipulated the terms for the establishment of a transitional government for a period of three years, the integration of former Hutu rebels into the armed forces, and the creation of an electoral system that would ensure power-sharing between the Tutsi and the Hutu. At a summit meeting, which was attended by several regional Heads of State in Arusha, negotiating groups were presented with the draft peace agreement, which included compromise proposals on unresolved issues. However, the CNDD—FDD demanded the release by the authorities of political prisoners, the fulfilment of the pledge to dismantle the 'regroupment' camps, and bilateral negotiations with the armed forces, as a precondition to the cessation of hostilities. (The FNL had again failed to attend the discussions.) On 28 August the peace agreement was formally endorsed by representatives of the Government, the Assemblée nationale, seven Hutu political associations and seven Tutsi parties. The remaining three Tutsi groups that had attended the previous negotiations subsequently signed the accord at cease-fire discussions, which took place in Nairobi, Kenya, in late September, following assurances by Mandela that measures would be taken to ensure that the Hutu rebels cease hostilities. At the same time an Implementation and Monitoring Committee, comprising representatives of the negotiating parties, and international and civil society representatives, was established. Following the conclusion of these discussions, a statement was issued, demanding that the CNDD—FDD and FNL suspend rebel activity and sign the peace agreement.

In January 2001 14 of the 19 signatories of the peace accord agreed on the composition of a new Assemblée nationale, which would allocate Hutu parties 60% and Tutsi 40% representation in the legislature. Six candidates for the transitional presidency had emerged; however, the negotiating groups had failed to agree to return Buyoya to the office. Hostilities between government troops and Hutu rebels continued, and at the end of February the FNL launched an offensive on the northern outskirts of Bujumbura, which resulted in some 50,000 civilians fleeing to the centre of the capital. Government forces had regained control of Bujumbura by early March, but heavy fighting continued in regions outlying the capital. Later that month CNDD—FDD forces launched a major attack against the principal town of Gitega, 100 km east of Bujumbura, which was repelled by government troops. On 18 April, while Buyoya was attending peace negotiations with the CNDD—FDD leadership in Gabon, Tutsi army officers seized control of the state radio station in Bujumbura and announced that the Government had been overthrown. Troops loyal to Buyoya rapidly suppressed the coup attempt, and about 40 members of the armed forces were subsequently arrested in connection with the uprising.

In late July 2001 Mandela chaired a peace summit of regional Heads of State in Arusha at which the signatory groups to the Arusha accord finally reached agreement on the nature of the transitional leadership. A new multi-party transitional government, according the Hutu and Tutsi ethnic groups balanced representation, was to be installed on 1 November. The Secretary-General of FRODEBU, Domitien Ndayizeye, was nominated to the vice-presidency of the transitional administration. Buyoya was to continue in the office of President for 18 months (from 1 November), after which time he was to transfer the office to Ndayizeye. However, the CNDD—FDD and the FNL persisted in rejecting the peace accord and announced that they would continue hostilities against the transitional authorities, while one of the principal Tutsi opposition parties, the Parti pour le redressement national (PARENA), refused to join the proposed new government.

Following further negotiations in Arusha and in Pretoria, South Africa, in early October 2001, agreement was reached on the composition of the new 26-member transitional Government. FRODEBU and UPRONA were the most dominant parties in the new power-sharing administration, while portfolios were allocated to a further 13 parties that had signed the Arusha agreement. (In total, Hutus received 14 of the 26 ministerial posts.) On 29 October a transitional Constitution, which was drafted by a technical law commission and included principles incorporated in the previous Constitution of 1992 and the Arusha peace accord, was formally adopted by the Assemblée nationale. The new transitional Constitution provided for the establishment of an upper legislative chamber, the Sénat, and four new commissions to assist in the peace and reconciliation process. Former combatants belonging to political movements were to be integrated into the armed and security forces during the transitional period. Also at the end of October the South African Government dispatched troops to Burundi as part of a proposed 700-member contingent, in an effort, initiated by Mandela, to enforce national security and support the transitional authorities. In a reversal to the peace efforts, however, the CNDD—FDD had divided, with the emergence of a new faction, led by Jean-Pierre Nkurunziza, which commanded the support of most of the movement's combatants.

On 1 November 2001 the newly established transitional Government was officially installed, as scheduled. However, the FNL continued to launch attacks on the outskirts of Bujumbura, despite the deployment of the South African troops. In January 2002 the nomination to the transitional Assemblée nationale of a number of deputies, representing civil society and 14 of the political parties that had signed the peace agreement, was endorsed by the Constitutional Court. (FRODEBU and UPRONA retained their seats in the chamber.) Minani, the Chairman of FRODEBU, was subsequently elected Speaker of the Assemblée nationale. At the end of that month the Constitutional Court approved the establishment of a 51-member Sénat.

Efforts to bring about a cease-fire in the civil conflict continued, with a series of meetings in Pretoria in February 2002, which were attended by representatives of the Government and armed forces, and both factions of the CNDD—FDD (but not by the FNL). In March a further regional summit meeting was convened in Dar es Salaam, which the FNL and Nkurunziza's CNDD—FDD faction again boycotted. In response to the continued lack of progress in peace efforts, FRODEBU issued a statement in April condemning the Government's failure to suppress the rebel militia. The South African Deputy President, Jacob Zuma (who had replaced Mandela as the principal mediator), hosted a new series of consultations between the militia groups and the Burundi Government in Pretoria later that month. However, both the FNL and Nkurunziza's faction refused to participate, and Nkurunziza subsequently announced his opposition to Zuma's involvement in the cease-fire process. Further discussions between government and rebel delegations regarding the implementation of a cease-fire were scheduled to take place in Dar es Salaam in August. Early that month, following an attempt to remove the FNL 'hardline' leader, Agathon Rwasa, from his post, the movement divided: a new faction, led by Alain Mugabarabona, emerged, while Rwasa remained in control of most of the combatants. The peace negotiations, which commenced on 12 August, were attended for the first time by Mugabarabona's FNL faction and both CNDD—FDD factions. At the end of that month, however, renewed fighting between FNL supporters and government troops was reported on the outskirts of Bujumbura.

A summit meeting on Burundi (attended by regional Presidents), which was convened in Dar es Salaam on 7 October 2002, resulted in a cease-fire agreement between the Government, and Ndayikengurukiye's CNDD—FDD and Mugabarabona's FNL faction. Negotiations with the main CNDD—FDD continued, amid hostilities between government and rebel forces in central and northern Burundi. The authorities placed Bagaza (now the leader of PARENA) under house arrest, on suspicion of involvement with several attacks in Bujumbura. Also in November Maj.-Gen. Vincent Niyungeko, hitherto Chief of Staff of the armed forces, became the new Minister of Defence.

On 3 December 2002, following mediation from Uganda and South Africa, the Government finally reached a cease-fire agreement with the CNDD—FDD, which was scheduled to enter into effect at the end of that month. Under the Arusha agreement, the rebel factions were to be reconstituted as political parties, while Buyoya was to relinquish the presidency to Ndayizeye at the end of April 2003. However, the cease-fire agreement was not imposed at the end of December 2002, owing to delays in the arrival of observers from the AU. Hostilities between government and CNDD—FDD forces continued, particularly in Gitega, and Nkurunziza, attributing responsibility for the failure to implement the accord to the Government, suspended further discussions. In February 2003 the AU Cease-fire Observer Mission, comprising 35 monitors (from Burkina Faso, Mali, Togo and Tunisia), arrived in Bujumbura, with a mandate to monitor the peace agreement. In late April the first 100 members of an AU Mission in Burundi (AMIB) arrived in the country; the contingent (which was to comprise troops from South Africa, Ethiopia and Mozambique) was to assist in the enforcement of the cease-fire between the Government and the rebel factions. Despite the reported reluctance of Buyoya to relinquish the presidency, Ndayizeye was officially inaugurated as President for the scheduled period of 18 months on 30 April, thereby improving the prospects for sustained peace. On the same day Alphonse-Marie Kadege (who in December 2002 had replaced Rukingama as Chairman of the more moderate UPRONA faction) was appointed Vice-President. On 5 May Ndayizeye appointed a representative of Mugabarabona's FNL faction and Ndayikengurukiye's CNDD—FDD faction to the transitional Council of Ministers, as part of a government reorganization. In early May the Government announced that it had ended the ban on PARENA activities, imposed in November 2002.

On 7 July 2003 hostilities escalated into a major offensive by FNL forces against Bujumbura; by the time government troops had restored some control in the capital, four days later, some 170 people had been killed, and 6,000–7,000 civilians displaced, according to preliminary UN estimates. In mid-July the UN announced its decision to withdraw non-essential personnel from the capital, in response to the increasingly poor security situation. On 21 July, at further peace discussions in Dar es Salaam, the Government and Nkurunziza's CNDD—FDD faction reiterated their commitment to implementing the December 2002 cease-fire agreement. In late August the Assemblée nationale adopted legislation granting temporary immunity from prosecution (with regard to political crimes committed from July 1962) to political leaders returning from exile to participate in transitional organs of government. A regional summit meeting, convened in Dar es Salaam in mid-September, ended in failure, without agreement being reached between the Government and Nkurunziza's CNDD—FDD on political power-sharing.

On 8 October 2003 under the mediation of Zuma and the South African President, Thabo Mbeki, Ndayizeye signed an agreement with Nkurunziza on political, military and security power-sharing. The CNDD—FDD faction was to be allocated four ministerial portfolios, 40% of army officers' posts, the vice-presidency of the Assemblée nationale, three provincial governorships, and two ambassadorial posts, while former CNDD—FDD combatants were to be demobilized. Mugabarabona and Ndayikengurukiye issued a statement condemning the accord, which was finally approved by the legislature on 22 October. On 16 November the Government and Nkurunziza's CNDD—FDD signed a final comprehensive peace agreement, endorsing the accords of December 2002, and of October and November 2003. On the same day regional Heads of State issued an ultimatum to Rwasa (as leader of the only rebel faction to remain in conflict with the Government) to join the peace process. On 23 November Ndayizeye reorganized the Government of national unity to include four representatives of Nkurunziza's CNDD—FDD faction, including Nkurunziza himself, who was appointed to the third most senior post, Minister of State with responsibility for Good Governance and State Inspection.

On 7 January 2004 Ndayizeye established a 33-member Joint Military High Command, comprising 20 members of the existing armed forces and 13 of the former CNDD—FDD. In mid-January further fighting between government troops and FNL combatants in Bujumbura Rural province resulted in the displacement of some 10,000 civilians. Later that month negotiations between Ndayizeye and an FNL delegation, convened in Oisterwijk, Netherlands, ended without agreement on a cease-fire being reached. The FNL continued to refuse to recognize the transitional authorities, and clashes between government and rebel forces continued in early February. In late March the AU renewed the mandate of AMIB (which was due to expire at the beginning of April) for a further month, and urged the UN Security Council to authorize the deployment of UN peace-keeping troops in Burundi. In April Nkurunziza announced the suspension of CNDD—FDD participation in the transitional institutions, on the grounds that the Government had failed to implement the November 2003 power-sharing accord. On 21 May the UN Security Council approved the replacement of the AMIB mission with a UN contingent, the Opération des Nations Unies au Burundi (ONUB). With a maximum strength of 5,650 military personnel, ONUB officially commenced deployment on 1 June.

In July 2004 the International Monitoring Committee charged with overseeing the implementation of the power-sharing arrangements urged political parties to reach consensus in efforts to adopt a new constitution (necessary to allow elections to proceed). A draft power-sharing accord (which provided for a Government and Assemblée nationale of 60% Hutu and 40% Tutsi composition) was reached in Pretoria later that month, but was rejected by predominantly Tutsi parties. (Also in July the CNDD—FDD announced the resumption of its participation in the Government of national unity.) On 6 August the accord, which would allow elections to proceed on 31 October, was signed in Pretoria by 20 of the 30 delegations, with Tutsi parties, notably UPRONA, refusing to accept the proposed power-sharing arrangements. Despite continuing speculation that the elections would be postponed, a five-member Commission électorale nationale indépendante (CENI) was established at the end of August. In early September initial regional peace discussions were conducted in Bujumbura. Following the massacre of refugees at the Gatumba camp in August (see below), however, government forces launched attacks against FNL troop positions during that month.

In September 2004 the International Criminal Court (ICC, see p. 314) announced that Burundi had ratified the signatory treaty, allowing prosecutions for civilian massacres to proceed. Meanwhile, the main political groupings continued to fail to reach agreement on a proposed new constitution, with 11 Tutsi parties, including UPRONA, objecting to the parliamentary ethnic representation vested in the draft. In mid-October the CENI announced that legislative elections, scheduled to take place at the end of that month, were to be postponed until 22 April 2005. On 20 October 2004 a new interim 'post-transitional' Constitution was officially adopted by Ndayizeye, after its approval by both chambers of the legislature. The new Constitution, which was to extend the mandate of the transitional organs of government from 1 November until the elections in April 2005, was scheduled to be endorsed at a national referendum in late November. Although five Tutsi political parties had withdrawn opposition to the Constitution, six continued to protest that it favoured the Hutu. In mid-November Ndayizeye dismissed Kadege from the office of Vice-President, owing to his public opposition to the Constitution, replacing him with Frédéric Ngenzebuhoro, also of UPRONA. Later that month the CENI announced the postponement of the constitutional referendum until 22 December, citing lack of technical resources. (However, organization of the referendum was again delayed.) At the end of December the Government announced the creation of a new Forces de défense nationales and of a new police force, comprising equal numbers of the existing Tutsi-dominated armed forces and Hutu former rebel combatants (mainly CNDD—FDD); a Tutsi was appointed head of the new army, while the post of deputy commander was allocated to a Hutu. In January 2005 the CENI again rescheduled the referendum, for 28 February.

The new Constitution, which enshrined the power-sharing principles of a Government and Assemblée nationale of 60% Hutu and 40% Tutsi composition, was endorsed at a referendum on 28 February 2005 by some 92% of votes cast (with an estimated 88% of the electorate participating in the ballot). Adoption of the Constitution was expected to allow legislative elections to proceed on 22 April, to be followed by the election of a President by the new Assemblée nationale and Sénat. (Under the terms of the Constitution, subsequent Presidents were to be directly elected.) A meeting between the FNL leadership and the Tanzanian President, Benjamin Mkapa, in early April resulted in a declaration from the militia that it was prepared to cease hostilities and negotiate with the Government. The legislature failed to approve the new electoral code until late April, however, and the Government subsequently announced that Ndayizeye's mandate was to be extended to allow a further postponement of the elections. According to the new schedule, after local government elections in June, elections were to be conducted to the Assemblée nationale on 4 July, and to the Sénat on 19 July, followed by the election of a President by the new legislature on 19 August, with the inauguration to take place on 26 August.

On 3 June 2005 communal government elections were conducted under the transitional schedule; of the 3,225 contested seats, the CNDD—FDD secured 1,781, FRODEBU 822, and UPRONA 260 seats. In mid-June the Burundian Government approved a UN proposal for the establishment of a truth and reconciliation commission to investigate crimes perpetrated during the conflict from 1993. Elections to a reduced number of 100 seats in the Assemblée nationale took place, as scheduled, on 4 July 2005, and received the approval of international observers. According to official results, the CNDD—FDD won 59 seats, FRODEBU 25 and UPRONA 10 seats. A further 18 deputies were subsequently nominated in accordance with the constitutional requirements of balance of ethnic representation (60% Hutu and 40% Tutsi) and a minimum 30% representation of women; in effect, the Twa ethnic group was allocated three seats, while the CNDD—FDD, FRODEBU and UPRONA each received five additional seats. The CNDD—FDD won 30 of the 34 contested seats in elections to the Sénat, which followed on 29 July, while FRODEBU won only four seats; four former Presidents were subsequently allocated seats, and the Twa ethnic group was designated three seats. In early August the authorities and political parties agreed to expand the chamber to 49 deputies, in order to guarantee the stipulated minimum representation of women; the four political parties with the highest votes each nominated two women to the additional seats. On 19 August a joint session of the Assemblée nationale and the Sénat elected Nkurunziza as President; the sole candidate, he secured about 81.5% of votes cast. Nkurunziza was officially inaugurated on 26 August and subsequently formed a 20-member Government in accordance with the terms of the Constitution, comprising a 60% Hutu and 40% Tutsi balance of representation, with a minimum 30% of women.

In September 2005 the FNL leadership refused an offer by the new Government to enter into reconciliation negotiations. In following months the Government consequently increased military efforts to suppress rebel activity, particularly in the provinces of Bujumbura Rural and Bubanza where the movement was based, causing large displacement of civilians from these regions. As a result of increasing support within the FNL for reconciliation with the Government, Rwasa was ousted from the leadership in December, and was replaced by Jean-Bosco Sindayigaya, who announced that he was prepared to enter into unconditional negotiations with the authorities. However, Rwasa continued to head a smaller faction of the FNL opposed to negotiations and sporadic hostilities continued in early 2006. In December 2005 the UN Security Council extended the mandate of ONUB for a further six months, until July 2006, but envisaged a complete withdrawal of the mission by that time.

In January 2006 Nkurunziza ordered the provisional release of 'political prisoners' imprisoned in connection with the coup attempt of 1993, with the stated aim of promoting national reconciliation. In mid-March the President of FRODEBU, Léonce Ngendakumana, ordered its representatives to withdraw from the Government and legislature, in protest at the failure of the CNDD—FDD to consult with other coalition parties, and at decisions which he considered to be contrary to democratic principles; however, the three FRODEBU ministers refused to resign from their posts, and were subsequently expelled from the party. Raising concerns about the stability of the administration, in early March Nkurunziza announced that senior members of the armed and security forces had planned a coup attempt against him. No arrests were made, however, and the claims were dismissed by opposition parties. Later that month Nkurunziza replaced two CNDD—FDD ministers for alleged corruption and mismanagement. Also in March Rwasa agreed to enter into peace negotiations, providing that they constituted direct dialogue with Nkurunziza. In May, following a request from Nkurunziza that South Africa assist in the negotiations, Mbeki appointed the South African Minister of Safety and Security, Charles Nqakula, as mediator. (Zuma, who had mediated in previous discussions, had been dismissed from the South African Government in 2005, after being charged with corruption.) Negotiations commenced in Dar es Salaam in late May. In June government and FNL delegations signed a framework accord for a cessation of hostilities; however, discussions continued throughout July without agreement being reached on a cease-fire. On 30 June the UN Security Council adopted a resolution authorizing the extension of ONUB's mandate to the end of 2006, when the mission was to withdraw and be replaced by a UN office, the Bureau Intégré des Nations Unies au Burundi (BINUB).

In August 2006 several prominent politicians, including former President Ndayizeye, former Vice-President Kadege and FNL faction leader Mugabarabona were arrested on suspicion of involvement in a coup attempt, and subsequently charged. On 7 September, after Rwasa agreed to abandon demands for the restructured armed forces to comprise a higher proportion of Hutus, he and Nkurunziza signed a comprehensive cease-fire agreement, under the aegis of Mbeki, in Dar es Salaam. A Joint Verification and Monitoring Committee, composed of UN officials, together with representatives of the FNL and the Governments of Burundi, South Africa, Tanzania and Uganda, was established at the beginning of October to supervise the implementation of the cease-fire. (Owing to a boycott by the FNL members, however, the Committee subsequently failed to commence operations.)

In early September 2006 the Second Vice-President, Alice Nzomukunda, a member of the CNDD—FDD, tendered her resignation, citing her opposition to the arrests in connection with the alleged conspiracy to overthrow the Government. Later that month Nkurunziza reorganized several ministerial portfolios. At the end of 2006 ONUB duly withdrew and BINUB was installed for an initial period of one year, with authorization to continue the process of peace consolidation, including support for the demobilization and reintegration of former combatants and reform of the security sector. Some 850 South African peace-keeping troops previously belonging to ONUB were transferred to the authority of the AU, which announced plans to increase the size of the contingent deployed in the country to 1,700. In December 2007 BINUB's mandate was extended until the end of 2008.

Meanwhile, in mid-January 2007 Ndayizeye, Kadege and three other suspects were acquitted of the charges of conspiring to overthrow Nkurunziza's Government; however, Mugabarabona was convicted and sentenced to 20 years' imprisonment, while a further defendant received a term of 15 years. The outcome of Ndayizeye's trial precipitated political unrest, with ruling party leaders, particularly the Chairman of the CNDD—FDD, Hussein Radjabu, suspected of fabricating the conspiracy involving opposition figures in order to suppress dissent. The Minister of Development Planning and National Reconstruction (a member of the CNDD—FDD) was removed following an investigation into the sale of a presidential airplane, and subsequently fled abroad, causing further controversy. Later that month Radjabu briefly took refuge at the South African embassy in Bujumbura, after it was reported that the battalion in charge of his security was to be reduced considerably in size. At the end of January, after discussions in Dar es Salaam, the FNL leadership agreed, in principle, to accept the terms for the implementation of the cease-fire agreement.

In mid-February 2007 Marina Barampama, who had replaced Nzomukunda as Second Vice-President in September 2006, was dismissed from that post. Barampama had pledged her support to Radjabu, who had been removed from the chairmanship of the CNDD—FDD at a special congress of the party earlier in February 2007. Gabriel Ntiszerana, hitherto the Governor of the central bank, was appointed Second Vice-President and later that month Nkurunziza effected a minor reorganization of the Council of Ministers. In late April Radjabu was arrested and detained on charges of recruiting and arming demobilized troops and planning to launch an attack on state forces.

In March 2007 Nkurunziza announced proposals to move the country's capital from Bujumbura in the west to Burundi's second largest, more central city Gitega. However, no schedule was given for the relocation.

In consultation with international partners the Government developed a Priority Action Programme (PAP) aimed at enforcing the terms of a cease-fire agreement and supporting social and economic reconstruction projects. In May 2007 the UN hosted a donor conference at which participants pledged their financial support for the implementation of the PAP. In June Rwasa became the last of the rebel leaders to sign the cease-fire agreement drawn up in 2006. However, the following month FNL leaders deserted their roles in a joint monitoring group that had been established to oversee the implementation of the cease-fire, further delaying the peace process. It had been suggested that they had left the group owing to concerns for their safety, although the leaders had not offered an official statement. The FNL remained a threat to security despite the cease-fire agreement, and in September fighting resumed between rebel insurgents. In light of the continued impasse between the Government and opposition parties over the terms of a power-sharing agreement, and the increasing unrest among rebel groups, international observers appealed for renewed peace talks. In October Nkurunziza issued a statement announcing that a power-sharing compromise had been reached; the agreement pledged to guarantee the rights of political parties to meet freely and reinstate members of the opposition who had previously been dismissed from the Government.

President Nkurunziza installed a new, 21-member Council of Ministers in July 2007 in an effort to address concerns over allegations of corruption and human rights abuses. The new administration included eight new appointments, among them Clotilde Nizigama, who became Minister of the Economy, Finance and Co-operation and Development, and Immaculée Nahayo, who was named Minister of National Solidarity, Repatriation, National Reconstruction, Human Rights and Gender. The reorganization was, however, denounced by members of the opposition, who boycotted the inauguration ceremony, and who claimed that the move failed to resolve the issues of corruption. Several members of the ruling CNDD—FDD were also absent from the ceremony, indicating that divisions within the Government remained. The following month First Vice-President Martin Nduwimana was expelled from UPRONA amid allegations that he had been attempting to sabotage the party. In November Nduwimana resigned from the Government, and was replaced by Yves Sahinguvu. Later that month Nkurunziza announced a further changes to the composition of the Government; most notably, Vénant Kamana, hitherto Minister at the Presidency, in charge of Good Governance and General Inspection of the State and Local Administration, was appointed Minister of Interior and Communal Development. Positions for seven new assistant ministers were also created.

The cross-border movement of vast numbers of refugees, provoked by regional ethnic and political violence, has dominated recent relations with Rwanda, Tanzania and the DRC (formerly Zaire), and has long been a matter of considerable concern to the international aid community. The uprising by Laurent-Désiré Kabila's Alliance des forces démocratiques pour la libération du Congo-Zaïre (AFDL) in eastern Zaire in January 1997 resulted in the return of large numbers of refugees to Burundi, reportedly undermining the operations from Zaire of FDD combatants. Moreover, the seizure of power by the AFDL in May was welcomed by the Buyoya regime, which moved to forge close relations with Kabila's DRC. Burundi initially denied any involvement in the civil war that commenced in the DRC in August, but by May 1999 some 3,000 Burundian troops were reported to be stationed in the east of the country, with the aim of destroying CNDD—FDD camps. (The CNDD—FDD supported the DRC Government in the civil war and used the conflict as an opportunity to regroup and rearm.) In June the DRC instituted proceedings against Burundi, together with Rwanda and Uganda, at the International Court of Justice in The Hague, Netherlands, accusing them of acts of armed aggression in contravention of the terms of both the UN Charter and the Charter of the OAU. In early February 2001, however, the DRC abandoned proceedings against Burundi and Rwanda. In January 2002 the Burundian Government made a formal commitment to withdraw all troops (reported to number about 1,000) from the DRC, while the DRC authorities pledged to end their alliance with the CNDD—FDD. In mid-2004 intensified hostilities in eastern DRC resulted in the flight of a further 30,000 refugees to Burundi. In August some 160 Banyamulenge (Congolese Tutsi), numbering among those who had fled from Bukavu in June to take refuge in Burundi, were massacred at a refugee camp at Gatumba, near the border between the two countries.

BURUNDI

Although the FNL admitted responsibility for the atrocity (which prompted the further exodus of both Burundian Tutsis and Banyamulenge refugees to Rwanda), the Governments of Burundi and Rwanda maintained that Hutu militia operating within the DRC were involved and threatened to resume military engagement in the country.

The continued presence of large numbers of Burundian refugees in Tanzania, and increasingly strong accusations on the part of the Buyoya Government that Tanzania was supporting the Hutu rebellion, prompted tension between the two countries in mid-1997. In late August Tanzania announced that it had placed its armed forces on alert, stating that Burundian forces were mobilizing near the border in preparation for an invasion of the refugee camps. Meanwhile, the Buyoya Government's assertions that Nyerere was unduly biased in his role as mediator in the Burundian conflict further strained bilateral ties. In late 1997 Burundian allegations that the Tanzanian Government was involved in cross-border raids by Hutu militias, based in Tanzania, adversely affected relations, and in November there were reports of clashes between troops on the Tanzanian–Burundian border. In the same month Burundi's ambassador-designate to Tanzania was ordered to assume control of the Burundian embassy in Dar es Salaam, which was occupied by members of the CNDD and FRODEBU, but was arrested by the Tanzanian authorities and expelled. In 1998 bilateral relations improved slightly, and in July Tanzania agreed to the reopening of the Burundian embassy. Relations appeared to improve further in early 1999 and, following a meeting of the Burundian and Tanzanian ministers of foreign affairs, it was announced that a tripartite commission was to be established (with representatives from Burundi, Tanzania and UNHCR) to investigate allegations that armed militia groups had used Tanzania as a base from which to launch attacks on Burundi. In late 2001 Tanzania denied further accusations by the Government of Burundi that Burundian rebels were operating from Tanzanian territory. Following the installation of the elected Government in August 2005 (see above), UNHCR assisted the return of some 60,000 of the 400,000 Burundian refugees remaining in Tanzania. According to that organization, at the end of December 2006 some 352,000 Burundian refugees were still resident in Tanzania.

In December 2006 the Presidents of Burundi, Kenya, Uganda, the DRC and Rwanda signed a Pact of Security, Stability and Development in the Great Lakes Region, which was welcomed by the UN Security Council as a significant measure towards regional stabilization. In the same month the East African Community (EAC, see p. 412) officially accepted the membership applications of Burundi and Rwanda.

Government

Following the coup of 25 July 1996, the Constitution of March 1992 was suspended. A peace agreement, which was signed by representatives of the incumbent Government, the Assemblée nationale and 17 political groupings on 28 August 2000, provided for the installation of a transitional administration, in which power-sharing between the Hutu and Tutsi ethnic groups was guaranteed (see Recent History). Under an interim 'post-transitional' Constitution, which was officially adopted by the President on 20 October 2004, legislative elections were conducted in July 2005, and a President, elected by the new Assemblée nationale and the Sénat, was inaugurated on 26 August. The Assemblée nationale comprised 118 deputies, of whom 100 were elected, and the remainder nominated according to constitutional requirements for a proportion of 60% Hutu and 40% Tutsi representatives, and a minimum 30% of women, while three seats were allocated to the Twa ethnic group. The Sénat comprised 49 deputies, of whom 34 were elected (two deputies by ethnically balanced colleges from each of the country's provinces), and the remainder nominated according to constitutional requirements for balance of ethnic representation and minimum representation of women. The President, who is Head of State, appoints two Vice-Presidents, and, in consultation with them, the Government.

For the purposes of local government, Burundi comprises 17 provinces (administered by civilian Governors), each of which is divided into districts and further subdivided into communes. Each district has a council, which is directly elected for a term of five years.

Defence

Burundi's armed forces, as assessed at November 2007, comprised an army of 35,000 and a paramilitary force of 31,050 gendarmes (including a 50-strong marine police force). At the end of 2004 the Government had officially established a reconstituted armed forces (Forces de défense nationales—FDN—comprising equal proportions of Hutus and Tutsis), which incorporated some 23,000 former rebel combatants, and a new police force. In April 2003 the deployment of the first members of an AU Mission in Burundi (AMIB) commenced; the contingent (which comprised mainly South African troops, with reinforcements from Ethiopia and Mozambique) was mandated to assist in the enforcement of the cease-fire between the Government and rebel factions. In May 2004 the UN Security Council approved the deployment of the Opération des Nations Unies au Burundi (ONUB—with a maximum authorized strength of 5,650 military personnel), to replace AMIB. Under a resolution of 30 June 2006, the UN Security Council ended the mandate of ONUB at the end of December, when it was replaced by a UN office, the Bureau Intégré des Nations Unies au Burundi (BINUB). BINUB was established for an initial period of one year, with authorization to continue peace consolidation, including support for the demobilization and reintegration of former combatants and reform of the security sector. Some 850 South African peace-keeping troops previously belonging to ONUB were transferred to the authority of the AU, which announced plans to increase the size of the contingent deployed in the country to 1,700. In December 2007 BINUB's mandate was extended until 31 December 2008. Defence expenditure for 2007 was budgeted at 51,900m. Burundian francs.

Economic Affairs

In 2006, according to estimates by the World Bank, Burundi's gross national income (GNI), measured at average 2004–06 prices, was US $795m., equivalent to $100 per head (or $710 per head on an international purchasing-power parity basis). During 1996–2006, it was estimated, the population increased at an average annual rate of 2.3%, while gross domestic product (GDP) per head declined, in real terms, by an average of 0.6% per year. Overall GDP increased, in real terms, at an average annual rate of 1.7% in 1996–2006; growth was only 0.9% in 2005, but recovered to 5.1% in 2006.

Agriculture (including forestry and fishing) contributed an estimated 35.0% of GDP in 2005. According to FAO, an estimated 89.6% of the labour force were employed in the sector in mid-2005. The principal cash crop is coffee (which accounted for 67.7% of export earnings in 2006), followed by tea (80% of which is exported to Kenya every year). The main subsistence crops are cassava and sweet potatoes. Although Burundi is traditionally self-sufficient in food crops, population displacement, as a result of the political crisis resulted in considerable disruption in the sector. The livestock-rearing sector was also severely affected by the civil war. During 1996–2005, according to the World Bank, agricultural GDP decreased at an average annual rate of 1.2%; it declined by 6.6% in 2005.

Industry (comprising mining, manufacturing, construction and utilities) engaged 21.8% of the employed labour force in 1991 and contributed an estimated 20.1% of GDP in 2005. Industrial GDP declined at an average annual rate of 3.1% in 1996–2005; it declined by 6.2% in 2005.

Mining and power engaged 0.1% of the employed labour force in 1990 and, according to the IMF, contributed an estimated 1.1% of GDP in 2002. Together with electricity, gas and water, it contributed just 1.2% of GDP in 2005. Gold (alluvial), tin, tungsten and columbo-tantalite are mined in small quantities, although much activity has hitherto been outside the formal sector. Burundi has important deposits of nickel (estimated at 5% of world reserves), vanadium and uranium. In addition, petroleum deposits have been discovered. The GDP of the mining sector increased at an average annual rate of 3.4% in 1997–2001, according to IMF estimates; growth in 2001 was an estimated 14.3%.

Manufacturing engaged 1.2% of the employed labour force in 1990 and contributed an estimated 13.5% of GDP in 2005. The sector consists largely of the processing of foodstuffs and agricultural products (coffee, cotton, tea and the extraction of vegetable oils), and of textiles and leather products. Manufacturing GDP increased at an average annual rate of 2.5% in 1997–2001, according to IMF estimates. Manufacturing GDP increased by 3.2% in 2000 and remained constant in 2001.

Energy is derived principally from hydroelectric power (an estimated 38.6% of electricity consumed in 2001 was imported). Peat is also exploited as an additional source of energy. Imports of motor spirit and gas oils comprised 11.2% of the value of imports in 2006.

The services sector contributed an estimated 44.9% of GDP in 2005, but engaged only 4.4% of the employed labour force in 1990. According to the World Bank, the GDP of the services sector increased at an average annual rate of 7.0% in 1996–2005; it increased by 10.6% in 2005.

In 2006 Burundi recorded an estimated trade deficit of US $225.1m., and there was a deficit of $123.8m. on the current account of the balance of payments. In 2006 the principal source of imports (12.6%) was Saudi Arabia; other important suppliers in that year were Belgium, Kenya and Japan. The principal market for exports in 2004 (56.0%) was Switzerland and Liechtenstein; other important markets were Belgium, Rwanda and the United Kingdom. The main imports in 2006 were chemical products, gas oils, motor cars and motor spirit. The principal exports in that year were coffee and tea.

In 2006 the budget deficit was estimated at 43,400m. Burundian francs, equivalent to some 4.4% of GDP. Burundi's external debt at the end of 2004 was US $1,385m., of which $1,325m. was long-term public debt. In 2003 the cost of debt-servicing was equivalent to 66.0% of revenue from the export of goods and services. The annual rate of inflation averaged 12.7% in 1991–2005. Consumer prices increased by 19.2% in 2005. According to the Banque de la République du Burundi, the rate of inflation was only 0.1% in 2006.

Burundi, with its neighbours Rwanda and the Democratic Republic of the Congo, is a member of the Economic Community of the Great Lakes Countries (CEPGL, see p. 412). Burundi is also a member of the Common Market for Eastern and Southern Africa (COMESA, see p. 205), and of the International Coffee Organization (see p. 408). In December 2006 Burundi, together with Rwanda, was admitted to the East African Community (EAC, see p. 412).

Burundi's acute economic decline after 1993, owing to the severe political upheaval and accompanying population displacement, was further exacerbated by the regional economic sanctions imposed following the coup of July 1996. In addition, the decrease in the international price of coffee (the principal export crop) resulted in substantial losses in the sector from 1997. By early 1999, when sanctions were revoked, official reserves had become severely depleted, and the Government was obliged to borrow heavily in order to meet its financing requirements. As a result, domestic and foreign debts had accumulated at an unsustainable level, and Burundi was defaulting on its debt-servicing obligations. In May 2000 the IMF and the World Bank announced the resumption of international credit to Burundi. Following the signing of a peace agreement in August of that year (see Recent History), a transitional power-sharing Government was installed in November 2001. In January 2004 the IMF commended the Government's economic programme for 2002–03, which continued a strong recovery, and approved a three-year Poverty Reduction and Growth Facility (PRGF). The Government's main short-term objective under the PRGF-supported programme was to increase productivity in the agricultural sector, and, in particular, implement reforms within the coffee sector. In August 2005 the IMF and the World Bank's International Development Association officially agreed that, in view of progress demonstrated in economic stabilization and commitment to structural reforms, Burundi had qualified for interim debt relief under the enhanced initiative for heavily indebted poor countries, thereby enabling it to reduce the unsustainably high external debt-servicing burden. The World Bank, meanwhile, continued to offer loans for infrastructural development, but made them dependent on transparency in government. Burundi's admission to the EAC in December 2006, with the establishment of common external tariffs, was expected to benefit the country's industrial development, although some negative effects were reported; imports were expected to decrease by 23% in 2007 as a result of legislation adopted by neighbouring countries, limiting the weight that goods vehicles were permitted to transport across borders. Nevertheless, earnings from coffee exports rose by 400% in 2006/07 as a result of increased production. Conversely, export earnings from tea decreased by 13% in 2007, owing mainly to the inferior quality of the harvested crop. The Government has requested greater private investment in the tea processing factories, which rely on outdated equipment to produce their product, resulting in losses of around US $20m. every year. Ongoing political instability continued to impede the Government's privatization plans for those sectors and jeopardized further donor support; however, GDP was expected to increase by 3.5% in 2007 and growth of 6.0% was projected for 2008.

Education

Education is provided free of charge. Kirundi is the language of instruction in primary schools, while French is used in secondary schools. Primary education, which is officially compulsory, begins at seven years of age and lasts for six years. Secondary education begins at the age of 13 and lasts for up to seven years, comprising a first cycle of four years and a second of three years. In 2003/04, according to UNESCO estimates, 57% of children in the relevant age-group (males 60%; females 54%) were enrolled at primary schools. Enrolment at secondary schools in that year was equivalent to only an estimated 12% of the population in the appropriate age-group (males 14%; females 10%). In 2002/03 11,915 students were enrolled at the University of Bujumbura. There is also a private university at Ngozi. Public expenditure on education in 2004 was equivalent to 13% of total government expenditure.

Public Holidays

2008: 1 January (New Year's Day), 5 February (Unity Day), 24 March (Easter Monday), 1 May (Labour Day and Ascension Day), 1 July (Independence Day), 15 August (Assumption), 18 September (Victory of UPRONA Party), 1 October* (Id al-Fitr, end of Ramadan), 13 October (Rwagasore Day), 21 October (Ndadaye Day), 1 November (All Saints' Day), 25 December (Christmas).

2009: 1 January (New Year's Day), 5 February (Unity Day), 13 April (Easter Monday), 1 May (Labour Day), 21 May (Ascension Day), 1 July (Independence Day), 15 August (Assumption), 18 September (Victory of UPRONA Party), 20 September* (Id al-Fitr, end of Ramadan), 13 October (Rwagasore Day), 21 October (Ndadaye Day), 1 November (All Saints' Day), 25 December (Christmas).

* These holidays are dependent on the Islamic lunar calendar and may vary by one or two days from the dates given.

Weights and Measures

The metric system is in force.

BURUNDI

Statistical Survey

Area and Population

AREA, POPULATION AND DENSITY

Area (sq km)	27,834*
Population (census results)†	
15–16 August 1979	4,028,420
16–30 August 1990	
Males	2,473,599
Females	2,665,474
Total	5,139,073
Population (UN estimates at mid-year)‡	
2005	7,859,000
2006	8,173,000
2007	8,508,000
Density (per sq km) at mid-2007	305.7

* 10,747 sq miles.
† Excluding adjustment for underenumeration.
‡ Source: UN, *World Population Prospects: The 2006 Revision*.
Principal Towns: Bujumbura (capital), population 235,440 (census result, August 1990). *1978:* Gitega 15,943 (Source: Banque de la République du Burundi). *Mid-2005* (urban population, incl. suburbs, UN estimate): Bujumbura 447,000 (Source: UN, *World Urbanization Prospects: The 2005 Revision*).

BIRTHS AND DEATHS
(UN estimates, annual averages)

	1990–95	1995–2000	2000–05
Birth rate (per 1,000)	46.5	43.8	44.2
Death rate (per 1,000)	19.7	18.2	16.7

Source: UN, *World Population Prospects: The 2006 Revision*.

Expectation of life (years at birth, WHO estimates): 47.5 (males 46.3; females 48.4) in 2005 (Source: WHO, *World Health Statistics*).

ECONOMICALLY ACTIVE POPULATION*
(persons aged 10 years and over, 1990 census)

	Males	Females	Total
Agriculture, hunting, forestry and fishing	1,153,890	1,420,553	2,574,443
Mining and quarrying	1,146	39	1,185
Manufacturing	24,120	9,747	33,867
Electricity, gas and water	1,847	74	1,921
Construction	19,447	290	19,737
Trade, restaurants and hotels	19,667	6,155	25,822
Transport, storage and communications	8,193	311	8,504
Financing, insurance, real estate and business services	1,387	618	2,005
Community, social and personal services	68,905	16,286	85,191
Activities not adequately defined	8,653	4,617	13,270
Total labour force	**1,307,255**	**1,458,690**	**2,765,945**

* Figures exclude persons seeking work for the first time, totalling 13,832 (males 9,608, females 4,224), but include other unemployed persons.

Source: UN, *Demographic Yearbook*.

Mid-2005 (estimates in '000): Agriculture, etc. 3,591; Total labour force 4,008 (Source: FAO).

Health and Welfare

KEY INDICATORS

Total fertility rate (children per woman, 2005)	6.8
Under-5 mortality rate (per 1,000 live births, 2004)	190
HIV/AIDS (% of persons aged 15–49, 2005)	3.3
Physicians (per 1,000 head, 2004)	0.03
Hospital beds (per 1,000 head, 2006)	0.70
Health expenditure (2004): US $ per head (PPP)	16.2
Health expenditure (2004): % of GDP	3.2
Health expenditure (2004): public (% of total)	26.2
Access to water (% of persons, 2004)	79
Access to sanitation (% of persons, 2004)	36
Human Development Index (2005): ranking	167
Human Development Index (2005): value	0.413

For sources and definitions, see explanatory note on p. vi.

Agriculture

PRINCIPAL CROPS
('000 metric tons)

	2004	2005	2006
Wheat	7.5	7.5*	7.5*
Rice (paddy)	64.5	67.9	68.3
Maize	123.2	123.0*	123.0*
Millet	10.6	7.8	10.8
Sorghum	74.2	67.9	67.9*
Potatoes	26.1	26.0*	26.0*
Sweet potatoes	834.4	835.0*	835.0*
Cassava (Manioc)	709.6	710.0*	710.0*
Taro (Coco yam)	61.7	62.0*	62.0*
Yams	9.9	10.0*	10.0*
Sugar cane*	180.0	180.0	180.0
Dry beans	220.2	220.0*	220.0*
Dry peas*	33.5	32.8	32.8
Groundnuts (in shell)*	7.7	7.1	7.1
Oil palm fruit*	11.9	11.7	11.7
Bananas*	1,556.9	1,538.7	1,538.7
Coffee (green)	36.0	7.8†	31.0†
Tea (made)	7.7	7.5†	7.5*

* FAO estimate(s).
† Unofficial figure.

Aggregate production ('000 metric tons, may include official, semi-official or estimated data): Total cereals 280.0 in 2004, 274.1 in 2005, 277.5 in 2006; Total roots and tubers 1,641.7 in 2004, 1,643.0 in 2005, 1,643.0 in 2006; Total vegetables (incl. melons) 250.0 in 2004, 250.0 in 2005, 250.0 in 2006; Total fruits (excl. melons) 1,641.9 in 2004, 1,623.7 in 2005, 1,623.7 in 2006.

Source: FAO.

LIVESTOCK
('000 head, year ending September)

	2003	2004	2005
Cattle	355	374	396
Pigs*	70	70	70
Sheep	240	236	243
Goats*	750	750	750
Chickens*	4,300	4,300	4,300

* FAO estimates.

2006: Figures assumed to be unchanged from 2005 (FAO estimates).

Source: FAO.

BURUNDI

LIVESTOCK PRODUCTS
('000 metric tons)

	2003	2004	2005
Cattle meat	5.5	4.7	5.6
Sheep meat*	1.0	1.0	1.0
Goat meat*	2.9	2.9	2.9
Pig meat*	4.2	4.2	4.2
Chicken meat*	6.1	6.1	6.1
Cows' milk	14.8	14.3	16.2
Sheep's milk*	0.7	0.7	0.7
Goats' milk*	8.4	8.4	8.4
Hen eggs*	3.0	3.0	3.0

* FAO estimates.
2006: Figures assumed to be unchanged from 2005 (FAO estimates).
Source: FAO.

Forestry

ROUNDWOOD REMOVALS
('000 cubic metres, excl. bark, FAO estimates)

	2003	2004	2005
Sawlogs, veneer logs and logs for sleepers	266	266	266
Other industrial wood	67	67	67
Fuel wood	8,241	8,390	8,542
Total	8,574	8,723	8,875

2006: Production assumed to be unchanged from 2005 (FAO estimates).
Source: FAO.

SAWNWOOD PRODUCTION
('000 cubic metres, incl. railway sleepers, FAO estimates)

	1998	1999	2000
Coniferous (softwood)	7	17	18
Broadleaved (hardwood)	26	63	65
Total	33	80	83

2001–06: Figures assumed to be unchanged from 2000 (FAO estimates).
Source: FAO.

Fishing

(metric tons, live weight)

	2003	2004	2005*
Capture	14,697	13,855	14,000
Freshwater perches	1,323	4,643	4,000
Dagaas	13,080	8,876	9,600
Aquaculture	200	200	200
Total catch (incl. others)	14,897	14,055	14,200

* FAO estimates.
Source: FAO.

Mining

(metric tons, unless otherwise indicated)

	2004	2005	2006
Tin ore*	9	4	46
Tantalum and niobium (columbium) concentrates†	23.4	42.6	16.2
Gold (kilograms)*	3,229	3,905	4,313
Peat	4,643	4,871	4,000‡

* Figures refer to the metal content of ores.
† The estimated tantalum content (in metric tons) was 5.0 in 2004, 9.2 in 2005 and 2.9 in 2006.
‡ Estimate.
Source: US Geological Survey.

Industry

SELECTED PRODUCTS
('000 metric tons, unless otherwise indicated)

	2004	2005	2006
Beer ('000 hectolitres)	973.1	1,012.5	1,220.3
Soft drinks ('000 hectolitres)	119.6	143.6	257.7
Cottonseed oil ('000 litres)	157.9	135.9	101.2
Sugar	20.2	19.1	18.1
Cigarettes (million)	376.1	419.1	409.6
Paint	0.5	0.5	0.5
Polyethylene film (metric tons)	122.4	103.9	80.8
Soap (metric tons)	3,235.0	3,130.4	2,956.2
Plastic racks ('000)	233.0	112.0	234.9
Fabrics ('000 metres)	5,544.5	4,811.3	2,865.6
Blankets ('000)	106.8	43.3	n.a.
Fibro-cement products	0.4	0.4	—
Moulds (metric tons)	23.2	18.2	20.9
PVC tubing (metric tons)	91.9	114.9	137.1
Steel tubing (metric tons)	265.9	197.4	59.4
Electric energy (million kWh)	91.6	100.3	93.3

Source: Banque de la République du Burundi.

Finance

CURRENCY AND EXCHANGE RATES

Monetary Units
100 centimes = 1 Burundian franc.

Sterling, Dollar and Euro Equivalents (30 October 2007)
£1 sterling = 2,353.018 francs;
US $1 = 1,134.750 francs;
€1 = 1,639.374 francs;
10,000 Burundian francs = £4.25 = $8.81 = €6.10.

Average Exchange Rate (Burundian francs per US dollar)
2004   1,100.910
2005   1,081.580
2006   1,028.430

BURUNDI

Statistical Survey

GOVERNMENT FINANCE
(central government operations, '000 million Burundian francs)

Summary of balances	2005	2006*	2007†
Revenue	172.1	178.4	203.0
Less Expenditure and net lending	316.7	379.3	436.8
Overall balance (commitment basis)	–144.6	–200.9	–233.8
Change in arrears	–10.8	–23.2	–4.3
External (interest)	–10.7	–1.8	—
Domestic	–0.1	–21.4	–4.3
Overall balance (cash basis)	–155.1	–224.1	–238.1
Grants	90.6	180.7	245.0
Overall balance after grants	–64.5	–43.4	6.9

Revenue	2005	2006*	2007†
Tax revenue	158.9	162.2	185.2
Income tax	41.8	43.8	48.1
Taxes on goods and services	78.3	82.9	97.2
Taxes on international trade	38.4	33.2	37.4
Non-tax revenue	13.2	16.1	17.8
Total	172.1	178.4	203.0

Expenditure and net lending	2005	2006*	2007†
Current expenditure	200.6	226.9	268.2
Compensation of employees	72.6	96.6	121.7
Civilian	41.9	58.5	74.9
Military	24.0	23.0	27.1
New police force	6.7	15.1	19.7
Goods and services	65.7	62.2	71.3
Civilian	26.7	27.1	35.5
Military	29.6	23.0	23.0
New police force	9.5	12.1	12.8
Transfers and subsidies	30.3	40.6	46.5
Interest payments	32.0	27.5	28.7
DDR project‡	8.7	35.0	33.0
Elections	24.5	—	—
Project expenditure	84.1	119.4	137.6
Net lending	–1.4	–2.0	–2.0
Total	316.4	379.3	436.8

* Estimates.
† Budget forecast.
‡ Demobilization, disarmament and reintegration.

Source: IMF, *Burundi: Fifth Review Under the Arrangement Under the Poverty Reduction and Growth Facility and Request for Waiver of a Performance Criterion - Staff Report; Press Release on the Executive Board Discussion; and Statement by the Executive Director for Burundi* (March 2007).

INTERNATIONAL RESERVES
(US $ million at 31 December)

	2004	2005	2006
Gold*	0.42	0.49	0.61
IMF special drawing rights	0.35	0.27	0.33
Reserve position in IMF	0.56	0.51	0.54
Foreign exchange	64.84	99.30	129.66
Total	66.17	100.57	131.14

* Valued at market-related prices.

Source: IMF, *International Financial Statistics*.

MONEY SUPPLY
(million Burundian francs at 31 December)

	2004	2005	2006
Currency outside banks	57,153	67,856	68,437
Deposits at central bank	1,218	1,348	1,225
Demand deposits at commercial banks	91,079	104,871	145,068
Demand deposits at other monetary institutions	1,910	3,192	3,416
Total money	151,360	177,267	218,145

Source: IMF, *International Financial Statistics*.

COST OF LIVING
(Consumer Price Index for Bujumbura; base: January 1991 = 100)

	2003	2004	2005
Food	415.1	446.8	546.7
Clothing	449.9	547.3	576.6
Housing, heating and light	462.4	472.3	563.4
Transport	473.2	471.5	565.9
All items (incl. others)	427.3	452.8	539.9

Source: IMF, *Burundi: Selected Issues and Statistical Annex* (August 2006).

NATIONAL ACCOUNTS

Expenditure on the Gross Domestic Product
(million Burundian francs at current prices)

	2004	2005	2006
Government final consumption expenditure	163,470	204,900	290,000
Private final consumption expenditure	638,547	759,900	803,200
Gross fixed capital formation	84,139	133,800	245,400
Changes in inventories	176	—	—
Total domestic expenditure	886,332	1,098,600	1,338,600
Exports of goods and services	60,201	76,100	121,500
Less Imports of goods and services	198,047	312,600	473,500
GDP in purchasers' values	748,486	862,100	986,600

Source: IMF, *International Financial Statistics*.

Gross Domestic Product by Economic Activity
('000 million Burundian francs at current prices, estimates)

	2003	2004	2005
Agriculture, hunting, forestry and fishing	232.5	264.0	271.1
Mining and quarrying	6.6	7.4	9.1
Electricity, gas and water			
Manufacturing*	75.2	85.5	104.9
Construction	28.0	31.8	41.7
Trade, restaurants and hotels	30.7	34.8	44.7
Transport, storage and communications	32.2	36.6	46.9
Other services	174.9	198.7	256.0
GDP at factor cost	580.1	658.8	774.4
Indirect taxes, *less* subsidies	64.1	72.8	86.4
GDP in purchasers' values	644.2	731.5	860.8

* Including handicrafts ('000 million Burundian francs): 26.0 in 2003; 29.6 in 2004; 36.2 in 2005.

Source: IMF, *Burundi: Selected Issues and Statistical Appendix* (August 2006).

BURUNDI

Statistical Survey

BALANCE OF PAYMENTS
(US $ million)

	2005	2006*	2007†
Exports of goods f.o.b.	57.2	60.8	70.0
Imports of goods f.o.b.	−239.0	−285.9	−335.2
Trade balance	−181.8	−225.1	−265.2
Services (net)	−89.5	−107.6	−110.9
Balance on goods and services	−271.3	−332.7	−376.1
Other income (net)	−19.3	−20.7	−20.1
Balance on goods, services and income	−290.7	−353.4	−396.2
Current transfers (net)	207.6	229.6	236.3
Current balance	−83.1	−123.8	−159.9
Capital account (net)	26.2	75.7	118.8
Direct investment	15.0	8.0	15.0
Official loans (net)	37.7	−1.0	−11.1
Other investment	13.9	25.8	35.0
Net errors and omissions	12.5	—	—
Overall balance	22.2	−15.3	−2.2

*Estimates.
† Projections.

Source: IMF, *Burundi: Fifth Review Under the Arrangement Under the Poverty Reduction and Growth Facility and Request for Waiver of a Performance Criterion - Staff Report; Press Release on the Executive Board Discussion; and Statement by the Executive Director for Burundi* (March 2007).

External Trade

PRINCIPAL COMMODITIES
(million Burundian francs)

Imports c.i.f.	2004	2005	2006
Portland cement	11,296.0	14,529.7	15,418.7
Motor spirit (gasoline)	10,017.4	13,075.3	23,631.1
Gas oils	11,664.6	15,083.6	26,002.0
Chemical products	17,851.5	18,193.0	28,769.3
Iron and steel and castings thereof	8,056.8	10,720.3	12,890.2
Products in castings of iron and steel	3,032.4	9,430.3	5,910.1
Mechanical devices and spare parts	11,787.7	32,210.7	18,712.7
Other electrical apparatus	5,302.8	18,836.1	17,505.9
Motor cars	8,564.2	8,667.4	25,565.8
Trucks	5,324.1	8,083.3	20,224.3
Total (incl. others)	193,605.2	289,123.9	442,511.1

Exports f.o.b.	2004	2005	2006
Coffee	32,341.6	43,586.6	40,838.3
Tea	11,245.8	9,564.8	10,238.4
Sugar	3,272.3	969.7	466.0
Beer	2,067.3	1,432.8	603.6
Minerals	543.2	1,026.5	2,959.7
Other articles (excl. personal items)	646.5	2,421.6	690.8
Total (incl. others)	52,688.6	61,488.3	60,359.4

Source: Banque de la République du Burundi.

PRINCIPAL TRADING PARTNERS

Imports c.i.f. (million Burundian francs)	2004	2005	2006
Belgium-Luxembourg	26,359.0	35,451.4	51,820.5
China, People's Repub.	6,987.6	12,794.8	19,312.2
Denmark	4,553.7	5,354.7	9,890.7
France	12,431.1	15,115.5	19,597.8
Germany	7,755.2	15,505.8	10,421.4
India	10,073.9	11,318.2	15,243.8
Italy	6,701.3	15,592.6	14,085.1
Japan	11,600.2	19,802.9	34,338.9
Kenya	30,275.9	36,824.3	36,463.7
Netherlands	3,726.8	4,886.7	5,728.9
Russia	54.2	525.7	20,791.3
Saudi Arabia	466.0	10,724.1	55,862.0
South Africa	4,980.8	16,198.9	9,773.6
Tanzania	16,402.1	13,934.8	7,803.3
Uganda	12,155.5	12,297.0	17,405.1
United Kingdom	1,778.3	6,794.9	20,366.7
USA	2,092.7	7,451.3	10,251.2
Zambia	7,356.0	10,742.7	13,294.9
Total (incl. others)	193,605.2	289,123.9	442,511.1

Source: Banque de la République du Burundi.

Exports f.o.b. (US $ million)	2002	2003	2004
Belgium	6.2	4.5	8.5
Germany	0.9	0.8	1.9
Kenya	0.5	0.6	1.7
Netherlands	1.7	1.5	2.1
Rwanda	3.2	2.2	5.1
Switzerland and Liechtenstein	6.2	43.1	46.3
Tanzania	0.1	0.3	0.2
United Kingdom	5.8	5.0	4.1
Total (incl. others)	26.5	65.9	82.7

Source: UN, *International Trade Statistics Yearbook*.

2005 (million Burundian francs): Total exports 61,488.3 (Source: Banque de la République du Burundi).

2006 (million Burundian francs): Total exports 60,359.4 (Source: Banque de la République du Burundi).

Transport

ROAD TRAFFIC
('000 motor vehicles in use, estimates)

	1998	1999	2000
Passenger cars	6.6	6.9	7.0
Commercial vehicles	9.3	9.3	9.3

2001–03 ('000 motor vehicles in use): Figures assumed to be unchanged from 2000.

Source: UN, *Statistical Yearbook*.

LAKE TRAFFIC
(Bujumbura, '000 metric tons)

	2004	2005	2006
Goods:			
arrivals	169.1	188.5	172.1
departures	14.6	16.5	10.5

Source: Banque de la République du Burundi.

BURUNDI

CIVIL AVIATION
(traffic on scheduled services)

	1996	1997	1998
Passengers carried ('000)	9	12	12
Passenger-km (million)	2	8	8

Source: UN, *Statistical Yearbook*.

Tourism

TOURIST ARRIVALS BY REGION*

	2003	2004	2005
Africa	24,706	1,333	49,473
Americas	2,308	5,908	9,956
Asia	1,162	4,528	4,023
Europe	7,620	29,409	29,486
Unspecified	38,320	92,050	55,480
Total	74,116	133,228	148,418

* Including Burundian nationals residing abroad.

Tourism receipts (US $ million, incl. passenger transport): 1.2 in 2003; 1.8 in 2004; 1.9 in 2005.

Source: World Tourism Organization.

Communications Media

	2003	2004	2005
Telephones ('000 main lines in use)	23.9	27.7	31.1
Mobile cellular telephones ('000 subscribers)	64.0	100.6	153.0
Personal computers ('000 in use)	13	34	34
Internet users ('000)	14	25	40

Source: International Telecommunication Union.

Television receivers ('000 in use): 200 in 2001.
Radio receivers ('000 in use): 440 in 1997.
Facsimile machines (number in use): 4,000 in 1996.
Daily newspapers: 1 in 2004.
Non-daily newspapers: 5 in 1998 (circulation 8,000 copies).

Sources: International Telecommunication Union; UNESCO, *Statistical Yearbook*.

Education

(2004/05, unless otherwise indicated)

	Teachers	Males	Females	Total
Pre-primary	296	4,514*	4,384*	8,898*
Primary	21,289	557,983	478,876	1,036,859
Secondary: general	8,047*	92,225	67,015	159,240
technical and vocational		7,491	6,986	14,477
Higher	719	12,216	4,673	16,889

* 2003/04.

Institutions (1988/89): Primary 1,512; Secondary 400.

Source: UNESCO Institute for Statistics.

Adult literacy rate (UNESCO estimates): 59.3% (males 67.3; females 52.2%) in 2000 (Source: UNESCO Institute for Statistics).

Directory

The Constitution

On 20 October 2004 an interim 'post-transitional' Constitution was officially adopted by the President, after its approval by both chambers of the legislature. The new Constitution, which extended the mandate of the transitional organs of government from 1 November until elections, scheduled for 22 April 2005, was endorsed at a national referendum on 28 February 2005 (replacing the Constitution of 28 October 2001). In April 2005 the Government announced that the presidential mandate was to be extended to allow elections to be rescheduled. Under the new timetable, elections were conducted to the Assemblée nationale on 4 July, and to the Sénat on 19 July; the new legislative chambers elected the President on 19 August, and the inauguration took place on 26 August. The main provisions of the Constitution are summarized below:

PREAMBLE

The transitional Constitution upholds the rights of the individual, and provides for a multi-party political system. The Government is based on the will of the people, and must be composed in order to represent all citizens. The function of the political system is to unite and reconcile all citizens and to ensure that the established Government serves the people. The Government must recognize the separation of powers, the primacy of the law and the principles of good governance and transparency in public affairs. All citizens have equal rights and are assured equal protection by the law. The civic obligations of the individual are emphasized.

POLITICAL PARTY SYSTEM

Political parties may be established freely, subject to conformity with the law. Their organization and activities must correspond to democratic principles and membership must be open to all civilians. They are not permitted to promote violence, discrimination or hate on any basis, including ethnical, regional or religious or tribal affiliation. Members of defence and security bodies, and acting magistrates are prohibited from joining political parties. A five-member Commission électorale nationale indépendante guarantees the freedom, impartiality and independence of the electoral process.

EXECUTIVE POWER

Executive power is vested in the President, who is the Head of State. The President is elected by universal direct suffrage for a term of five years, which is renewable once. (The first post-transitional President is to be elected by a majority of two-thirds of members in both legislative chambers.) The President is assisted in the exercise of his powers by two Vice-Presidents, whom he appoints, and presides over the Government.

GOVERNMENT

The President appoints the Government in consultation with the Vice-Presidents. The Government is required to comprise a 60% proportion of Hutu ministers and deputy ministers and 40% of Tutsi ministers and deputy ministers, and to include a minimum 30% of women. Political parties that secured more than 5% of votes cast in legislative elections are entitled to nominate a proportionate number of representatives to the Government. The President is obliged to replace a minister in consultation with the political party that the minister represents.

LEGISLATURE

Legislative power is vested in the bicameral legislature, comprising a lower chamber, the Assemblée nationale, and an upper chamber, the Sénat. The Assemblée nationale has a minimum of 100 deputies, with a proportion of 60% Hutu and 40% Tutsi representatives, and including a minimum 30% of women. Deputies are elected by direct universal suffrage for a term of five years, while the Twa ethnic group nominates three representatives. If the election results fail to conform to the stipulated ethnic composition, additional deputies may be appointed in accordance with the electoral code. The Sénat comprises a minimum of two senators elected by ethnically balanced colleges from each of the country's provinces, and three Twa representatives, and includes a minimum 30% of women. Both chambers have a President and Vice-Presidents.

JUDICIARY

The President guarantees the independence of the judiciary, with the assistance of the Conseil Supérieur de la Magistrature. The highest judicial power is vested in the Cour Suprême. All appointments to these organs are made by the President, on the proposal of the Minister of Justice and in consultation with the Conseil Supérieur de la Magistrature, and are endorsed by the Sénat. The Cour Constitutionnelle interprets the provisions of the Constitution and ensures the conformity of new legislation. The Cour Constitutionnelle comprises seven members, who are appointed by the President, subject to the approval of the Sénat, for a six-year renewable term.

DEFENCE AND SECURITY FORCES

The establishment and operations of defence and security forces must conform to the law. Members of defence and security forces are prohibited from belonging to, participating in the activities of, or demonstrating prejudice towards, any political parties. All citizens are eligible to join the defence and security forces. During a period to be determined by the Sénat, defence and security forces are not permitted to comprise more than 50% of one single ethnic group, in order to ensure an ethnic balance and guard against acts of genocide and military coups.

The Government

HEAD OF STATE

President: Maj. JEAN-PIERRE NKURUNZIZA (elected 19 August 2005; inaugurated 26 August 2005).
First Vice-President: YVES SAHINGUVU.
Second Vice-President: GABRIEL NTISZERANA.

COUNCIL OF MINISTERS
(March 2008)

Minister of the Interior and Communal Development: VÉNANT KAMANA.
Minister of Public Security: ALAIN GUILLAUMME BUNYONI.
Minister of External Relations: ANTOINETTE BATUMUBWIRA.
Minister at the Presidency, in charge of Good Governance, Privatization, and General Inspection of the State and Local Administration: MARTIN NIVYABANDI.
Minister of Justice, Keeper of the Seals: JEAN BOSCO NDIKUMANA.
Minister of the Economy, Finance and Co-operation and Development: CLOTILDE NIZIGAMA.
Minister of National Defence and War Veterans: Lt-Gen. GERMAIN NIYOYANKANA.
Minister of National Education and Scientific Research: Dr SAÏDI KIBEYA.
Minister of Health and the Fight against AIDS: Dr EMMANUEL GIKORO.
Minister of Water, Energy and Mines: SAMUEL NDAYIRAGIJE.
Minister of Information, Communications and Relations with Parliament, and Government Spokesman: HAFSA MOSSI.
Minister of Agriculture and Livestock: FERDINAND NDERAGAKURA.
Minister of Commerce, Industry and Tourism: EUPHRASIE BIGIRIMANA.
Minister of the Environment, Territorial Development and Public Works: ANATOLE KANYENKIKO.
Minister of Transport, Posts and Telecommunications: PHILIPPE NJONI.
Minister of Civil Service, Labour and Social Security: CLOTILDE NIRAGIRA.
Minister of Youth, Sports and Culture: JEAN-JACQUES NYENIMIGABO.
Minister of National Solidarity, Repatriation, National Reconstruction, Human Rights and Gender: IMMACULÉE NAHAYO.
Minister of Regional Integration and East African Community Affairs: VENERAND BAKEVYUMUSAYA.

In addition, there are seven assistant ministers.

MINISTRIES

Office of the President: Bujumbura; tel. 22226063; e-mail ikiyago@burundi-gov.bi; internet presidence.burundi-gov.bi.
Ministry of Agriculture and Livestock: Bujumbura; tel. 22222087.
Ministry of Civil Service, Labour and Social Security: BP 1480, Bujumbura; tel. 22225645; fax 22228715.
Ministry of Commerce, Industry and Tourism: BP 492, Bujumbura; tel. 22225330; fax 22225595.
Ministry of the Economy, Finance and Co-operation and Development: BP 1830, Bujumbura; tel. 22225142; fax 22223128.
Minister of the Environment, Territorial Development and Public Works: Bujumbura.
Ministry of External Relations: Bujumbura; tel. 22222150.
Ministry of Health and the Fight against AIDS: Bujumbura.
Ministry of Information, Communications and Relations with Parliament: BP 2870, Bujumbura.
Ministry of the Interior and Communal Development: Bujumbura.
Ministry of Justice: Bujumbura; tel. 22222148.
Ministry of National Defence and War Veterans: Bujumbura.
Ministry of National Education and Scientific Research: Bujumbura.
Ministry of National Solidarity, Repatriation, National Reconstruction, Human Rights and Gender: BP 224, Bujumbura; tel. 22225394; fax 22224193; e-mail ministre@miniplan.bi; internet www.cslpminiplan.bi.
Ministry of Public Security: Bujumbura.
Ministry of Regional Integration and East African Community Affairs: Bujumbura.
Ministry of Transport, Posts and Telecommunications: BP 2000, Bujumbura; tel. 22222923; fax 22226900.
Ministry of Water, Energy and Mines: BP 745, Bujumbura; tel. 22225909; fax 22223337.
Ministry of Youth, Sports and Culture: Bujumbura; tel. 22226822.

President and Legislature

PRESIDENT

On 19 August 2005 the newly established Assemblée nationale and Sénat elected Jean-Pierre Nkurunziza, the leader of the Conseil national pour la défense de la démocratie—Force pour la défense de la démocratie (CNDD—FDD), as President; the sole candidate, he secured more than 81.5% of votes cast, according to provisional results.

SÉNAT

President: GERVAIS RUFYIKIRI (CNDD—FDD).
First Vice-President: ANATOLE MANIRAKIZA (CNDD—FDD).
Second Vice-President: GENEROSE BIMAZUBUTE (FRODEBU).
Elections, 29 July 2005

Party	Seats*
Conseil national pour la défense de la démocratie—Force pour la défense de la démocratie (CNDD—FDD)	30
Front pour la démocratie au Burundi (FRODEBU)	4
Total	**34**

* In accordance with constitutional requirements for balance of ethnic representation and a minimum 30% representation of women, a further four seats were allocated to former Presidents, three to the Twa ethnic group and eight to women, increasing the total number of senators to 49.

ASSEMBLÉE NATIONALE

President: PIE NTAVYOHANYUMA (CNDD—FDD).
First Vice-President: ALICE NZOMUKUNDA (CNDD—FDD).

BURUNDI

Second Vice-President: MARTIN NDUWIMANA (UPRONA).

Elections, 4 July 2005

Party	Votes	% of votes	Seats*
Conseil national pour la défense de la démocratie—Force pour la défense de la démocratie (CNDD—FDD)	1,417,800	58.55	59
Front pour la démocratie au Burundi (FRODEBU)	525,336	21.69	25
Union pour le progrès national (UPRONA)	174,575	7.21	10
Conseil national pour la défense de la démocratie (CNDD)	100,366	4.14	4
Mouvement pour la réhabilitation du citoyen—Rurenzangemero (MRC—Rurenzangemero)	51,730	2.14	2
Independents and others	151,619	6.26	—
Total	**2,421,426**	**100.00**	**100**

*In accordance with constitutional requirements for balance of ethnic representation and a minimum 30% representation of women, a further 18 seats were allocated, including three to members of the Twa ethnic group, increasing the total number of deputies to 118. CNDD—FDD, FRODEBU and UPRONA each received an additional five seats.

Election Commission

Commission électorale nationale indépendante (CENI): Bujumbura; f. 2004; independent; Chair. PAUL NGARAMBE.

Political Organizations

Political parties are required to demonstrate firm commitment to national unity, and impartiality with regard to ethnic or regional origin, gender and religion, in order to receive legal recognition. By 2005 the number of registered political parties had increased to 34; these included former rebel organizations.

Alliance burundaise-africaine pour le salut (ABASA): Bujumbura; f. 1993; Tutsi; Leader TÉRENCE NSANZE.

Alliance des Vaillants (AV—Intware) (Alliance of the Brave): Bujumbura; f. 1993; Tutsi; Leader ANDRÉ NKUNDIKIJE.

Alliance libérale pour le développement (ALIDE): f. 2001; Leader JOSEPH NTIDENDEREZA.

Alliance nouvelle pour la démocratie et le développement au Burundi: f. Aug. 2002; Leader JEAN-PAUL BURAFUTA.

Conseil national pour la défense de la démocratie (CNDD): Bujumbura; e-mail cndd_bur@usa.net; internet www.club.euronet.be/pascal.karolero.cndd.burundi; f. 1994; Hutu; Pres. LÉONARD NYANGOMA.

Conseil national pour la défense de la démocratie—Force pour la défense de la démocratie (CNDD—FDD): fmr armed wing of the Hutu CNDD; split into two factions in Oct. 2001, one led by JEAN-BOSCO NDAYIKENGURUKIYE and the other by JEAN-PIERRE NKURUNZIZA; Nkurunziza's faction incl. in Govt Nov. 2003, following peace agreement; registered as political org. Jan. 2005; Chair. JÉRÉMIE NGENDAKUMANA; Sec.-Gen. MANASSÉ NZOBONIMPA.

Forces nationales de libération (FNL): fmr armed wing of Hutu Parti de libération du peuple hutu (PALIPEHUTU, f. 1980); split in Aug. 2002 and in Dec. 2005; cease-fire with Govt announced Sept. 2006; Chair. JEAN-BOSCO SINDAYIGAYA; Leader SYLVESTRE NIYUNGEKO.

Front national de libération Icanzo (FNL Icanzo): reconstituted Dec. 2002 from fmr faction of Forces nationales de libération; Leader Dr ALAIN MUGABARABONA.

Front pour la démocratie au Burundi (FRODEBU): Bujumbura; f. 1992; split in June 1999; Hutu; Chair. LÉONCE NGENDAKUMANA.

KAZE—Force pour la défense de la démocratie (KAZE—FDD): f. May 2004; reconstituted as a political party from a faction of the armed CNDD—FDD (see above); Leader JEAN-BOSCO NDAYIKENGURUKIYE.

Mouvement pour la réhabilitation du citoyen—Rurenzangemero (MRC—Rurenzangemero): Bujumbura; f. June 2001; regd Nov. 2002; Leader Lt-Col EPITACE BAYAGANAKANDI.

Mouvement socialiste panafricaniste—Inkinzo y'Ijambo Ry'abarundi (MSP—Inkinzo) (Guarantor of Freedom of Speech in Burundi): Bujumbura; f. 1993; Tutsi; Pres. Dr ALPHONSE RUGAMBARARA.

Parti de la consensus nationale (PACONA): f. Feb. 2004; Leader JEAN-BOSCO NDAYIZAMBAYE.

Parti libéral (PL): BP 2167, Bujumbura; tel. 22214848; fax 22225981; e-mail liberalburundi@yahoo.fr; f. 1992; Hutu; Leader GAËTAN NIKOBAMYE.

Parti du peuple (PP): Bujumbura; f. 1992; Hutu; Leader MARORA SYLVESTRE.

Parti pour le développement et la solidarité des travailleurs (PML-Abanyamwete): Bujumbura; f. Oct. 2004; Leader PATRICIA NDAYIZEYE.

Parti pour la paix, la démocratie, la réconciliation et la reconstruction (PPDR): f. Dec. 2002 by fmr mems of FRODEBU (see above); regd March 2004; Leader JEAN-LÉOPOLD NZOBONIMPA.

Parti pour la réconciliation du peuple (PRP): Bujumbura; f. 1992; Tutsi; Leader MATHIAS HITIMANA.

Parti pour le redressement intégral du Burundi (PARIBU): Bujumbura; f. Sept. 2004; Leader BENOÎT NDORIMANA.

Parti pour le redressement national (PARENA): Bujumbura; f. 1994; Leader JEAN-BAPTISTE BAGAZA.

Parti social démocrate (PSD): Bujumbura; f. 1993; Tutsi; Leader GODEFROID HAKIZIMANA.

Rassemblement pour la démocratie et le développement économique et social (RADDES): Bujumbura; f. 1992; Tutsi; Chair. JOSEPH NZEYZIMANA.

Rassemblement pour le peuple du Burundi (RPB): Bujumbura; f. 1992; Hutu; Leader BALTHAZAR BIGIRIMANA.

Union pour la paix et le développement (Zigamibanga): f. Aug. 2002; Leader FREDDY FERUVI.

Union pour le progrès national (UPRONA): BP 1810, Bujumbura; tel. 22225028; f. 1958 following the 1961 elections; the numerous small parties which had been defeated merged with UPRONA, which became the sole legal political party in 1966; party activities were suspended following the coup of Sept. 1987, but resumed in 1989; Chair. ALOYS RUBUKA.

Diplomatic Representation

EMBASSIES IN BURUNDI

Belgium: 9 blvd de la Liberté, BP 1920, Bujumbura; tel. 22226176; fax 22223171; e-mail bujumbura@diplobel.org; Ambassador FRANÇOIS CORNET D'ELZIUS.

China, People's Republic: 675 sur la Parcelle, BP 2550, Bujumbura; tel. 22224307; fax 22213735; Ambassador ZENG XIANQI.

Egypt: 31 ave de la Liberté, BP 1520, Bujumbura; tel. 22223161; fax 22222918; Ambassador MUHAMMAD ABDUL EL-KHADER EL-KHASAB.

France: 60 ave de l'UPRONA, BP 1740, Bujumbura; tel. 22203000; fax 22203010; Ambassador JOËL LOUVET.

Germany: 22 rue 18 septembre, BP 480, Bujumbura; tel. 22226412; fax 22221004; e-mail info@buju.diplo.de; Ambassador THOMAS MANGARTZ.

Holy See: 46 ave des Travailleurs, BP 1068, Bujumbura; tel. 22225415; fax 22223176; e-mail nonciat@cbinf.com; Apostolic Nuncio Most Rev. PAUL RICHARD GALLAGHER (Titular Archbishop of Hodelm).

Kenya: Bujumbura; Ambassador BENJAMIN A. W. MWERI.

Korea, Democratic People's Republic: BP 1620, Bujumbura; tel. 22222881; Ambassador SOON CHUN LEE.

Russia: 78 blvd de l'UPRONA, BP 1034, Bujumbura; tel. 22226098; fax 22222984; Ambassador IGOR S. LIAKIN-FROLOV.

Rwanda: 24 ave du Zaïre, BP 400, Bujumbura; tel. 22223140; Ambassador JANVIER KANYAMASHULI.

Tanzania: 855 rue United Nations, BP 1653, Bujumbura; tel. 22248632; fax 22248637; e-mail tanzanrep@usan-bu.net; Ambassador FRANCIS MNDOLWA.

USA: ave des Etats-Unis, BP 1720, Bujumbura; tel. 22223454; fax 22222926; e-mail jyellin@bujumbura.us-state.gov; internet burundi.usembassy.gov; Ambassador PATRICIA N. MOLLER.

Judicial System

Constitutional Court: Bujumbura; comprises a minimum of seven judges, who are nominated by the President for a six-year term.

BURUNDI

Supreme Court: BP 1460, Bujumbura; tel. and fax 22213544; court of final instance; three divisions: ordinary, cassation and administrative; Pres. MARIE ANCILLA NTAKABURIMVO.

Courts of Appeal: Bujumbura, Gitega and Ngozi.

Tribunals of First Instance: There are 17 provincial tribunals and 123 smaller resident tribunals in other areas.

Religion

Some 67% of the population are Christians, the majority of whom are Roman Catholics. Anglicans number about 60,000. There are about 200,000 other Protestant adherents, of whom about 160,000 are Pentecostalists. About 23% of the population adhere to traditional beliefs, which include the worship of the god Imana. About 10% of the population are Muslims. The Bahá'í Faith is also active in Burundi.

CHRISTIANITY

Conseil National des Eglises Protestantes du Burundi (CNEB): BP 17, Bujumbura; tel. 22224216; fax 22227941; e-mail cneb@cbinf.com; f. 1935; 10 mem. churches; Pres. Rt Rev. JEAN NDUWAYO (Anglican Bishop of Gitega); Gen. Sec. Rev. OSIAS HABINGABWA.

The Anglican Communion

The Church of the Province of Burundi, established in 1992, comprises five dioceses.

Archbishop of Burundi and Bishop of Buye: Most Rev. SAMUEL NDAYISENGA, BP 94, Ngozi; fax 22302317.

Provincial Secretary: Rev. PASCAL BIGIRIMANA, BP 2098, Bujumbura; tel. 22224389; fax 22229129; e-mail eebprov@cbinf.com.

The Roman Catholic Church

Burundi comprises two archdioceses and five dioceses. At 31 December 2005 there were an estimated 4,871,295 adherents, equivalent to 66.1% of the total population.

Bishops' Conference

Conférence des Evêques Catholiques du Burundi, 5 blvd de l'UPRONA, BP 1390, Bujumbura; tel. 22223263; fax 22223270; e-mail cecab@cbinf.com.

f. 1980; Pres. Rt Rev. JEAN NTAGWARARA (Bishop of Bubanza).

Archbishop of Gitega: Most Rev. SIMON NTAMWANA, Archevêché, BP 118, Gitega; tel. 22402160; fax 22402620; e-mail archigi@bujumbura.ocicnet.net.

Other Christian Churches

Union of Baptist Churches of Burundi: Rubura, DS 117, Bujumbura 1; 87 mem. churches; Pres. PAUL BARUHENAMWO.

Other denominations active in the country include the Evangelical Christian Brotherhood of Burundi, the Free Methodist Church of Burundi and the United Methodist Church of Burundi.

BAHÁ'Í FAITH

National Spiritual Assembly: BP 1578, Bujumbura; tel. 79955840; e-mail bahaiburundi@yahoo.fr; Sec. YOLANDE KABERA.

The Press

National Communications Council (Conseil national de la communication—CNC): Bujumbura; f. 2001 under the terms of the transitional Constitution; responsible for ensuring press freedom; Pres. (vacant).

NEWSPAPER

Le Renouveau du Burundi: BP 2573, Bujumbura; tel. 22226232; f. 1978; daily; French; govt-owned; Dir THADDÉE SIRYUYUMUNSI; circ. 2,500 (2004).

PERIODICALS

Au Coeur de l'Afrique: Association des conférences des ordinaires du Rwanda et Burundi, BP 1390, Bujumbura; fax 22223027; e-mail cnid@cbinf.com; bimonthly; education; circ. 1,000.

Bulletin Économique et Financier: BP 482, Bujumbura; bi-monthly.

Bulletin Mensuel: Banque de la République du Burundi, Service des études, BP 705, Bujumbura; tel. 22225142; monthly.

In-Burundi: c/o Cyber Média, BP 5270, ave du 18 septembre, Bujumbura; tel. 2244464; current affairs internet publication; Editor-in-Chief EDGAR C. MBANZA.

Ndongozi Y'uburundi: Catholic Mission, BP 690, Bujumbura; tel. 22222762; fax 22228907; fortnightly; Kirundi.

Revue Administration et Juridique: Association d'études administratives et juridiques du Burundi, BP 1613, Bujumbura; quarterly; French.

PRESS ASSOCIATION

Burundian Association of Journalists (BAJ): Bujumbura; Pres. PAUL NDAYIZEYE.

NEWS AGENCY

Agence Burundaise de Presse (ABP): ave Nicolas Mayugi, BP 2870, Bujumbura; tel. 22213083; fax 22222282; e-mail abp@cbinf.com; internet www.abp.info.bi; f. 1975; publ. daily bulletin.

Publishers

BURSTA: BP 1908, Bujumbura; tel. 22231796; fax 22232842; f. 1986; Dir RICHARD KASHIRAHAMWE.

Editions Intore: 19 ave Matana, BP 2524, Bujumbura; tel. 22223499; e-mail anbirabuza@yahoo.fr; f. 1992; philosophy, history, journalism, literature, social sciences; Dir Dr ANDRÉ BIRABUZA.

IMPARUDI: ave du 18 septembre 3, BP 3010, Bujumbura; tel. 22223125; fax 22222572; e-mail imparudi@yahou.fr; f. 1950; Dir-Gen. THÉONESTE MUTAMBUKA.

Imprimerie la Licorne: 29 ave de la Mission, BP 2942, Bujumbura; tel. 22223503; fax 22227225; f. 1991.

Les Presses Lavigerie: 5 ave de l'UPRONA, BP 1640, Bujumbura; tel. 22222368; fax 22220318.

Régie de Productions Pédagogiques: BP 3118, Bujumbura II; tel. 22226111; fax 22222631; e-mail rpp@cbinf.com; f. 1984; school textbooks; Dir ABRAHAM MBONERANE.

GOVERNMENT PUBLISHING HOUSE

Imprimerie Nationale du Burundi (INABU): BP 991, Bujumbura; tel. 22224046; fax 22225399; f. 1978; Dir NICOLAS NIJIMBERE.

Broadcasting and Communications

TELECOMMUNICATIONS

Agence de Régulation et de Contrôle des Télécommunications (ARCT): 360 Ave Patrice Lumumba, BP 6702, Bujumbura; tel. 22210276; fax 22242832; Dir.-Gen. JOSEPH NSEGANA.

Direction Générale des Transports, Postes et Télécommunications: BP 2390, Bujumbura; tel. 22225422; fax 22226900; govt telecommunications authority; Dir-Gen. APOLLINAIRE NDAYIZEYE.

Office National des Télécommunications (ONATEL): BP 60, Bujumbura; tel. 22223196; fax 22226917; e-mail onatel@cbinf.com; f. 1979; service provider; privatization pending; Dir-Gen. AUGUSTIN NDABIHORE.

Téléphonie Cellulaire du Burundi (TELECEL): Bujumbura; e-mail clareher@telecel.bi; f. 1993; 40% govt-owned; mobile telephone service provider; Dir-Gen. MARTIN BAKA.

BROADCASTING

Radio

Radio Isanganiro: 27 ave. de l'Amitié, BP 810, Bujumbura; tel. 22246595; fax 22246600; e-mail isanganiro@isanganiro.org; internet www.isanganiro.org; f. Nov. 2002; controlled by Association Ijambo, f. by Studio Ijambo (see below); broadcasts on 89.7 FM frequency, in Kirundi, French and Swahili; services cover Bujumbura area, and were to be extended to all Great Lakes region; Dir MATHIAS MANIRAKIZA.

Radio Publique Africaine (RPA): Bujumbura; f. 2001 with the aim of promoting peace; independent; Dir ALEXIS SINDUHIJE.

Radio Umwizero/Radio Hope: BP 5314, Bujumbura; tel. 22217068; e-mail umwizero@cbinf.com; f. 1996; EU-funded, private station promoting national reconciliation, peace and devt projects; broadcasts nine hours daily in Kirundi, Swahili and French; Dir HUBERT VIEILLE.

BURUNDI

Studio Ijambo (Wise Words): Bujumbura; e-mail burundi@sfcg.org.bi; internet www.studioijambo.org; f. 1995 by Search for Common Ground; promotes peace and reconciliation.

Voix de la Révolution/La Radiodiffusion et Télévision Nationale du Burundi (RTNB): BP 1900, Bujumbura; tel. 22223742; fax 22226547; internet www.burundi-quotidien.com; f. 1960; govt-controlled; daily radio broadcasts in Kirundi, Swahili, French and English; Dir-Gen. INNOCENT MUHOZI; Dir (Radio) EMMANUEL NZEYIMANA.

Television

Voix de la Révolution/La Radiodiffusion et Télévision Nationale du Burundi (RTNB): BP 1900, Bujumbura; tel. 22223742; fax 22226547; internet www.burundi-quotidien.com; f. 1960; govt-controlled; television service in Kirundi, Swahili, French and English; Dir (Television) DAVID HICUBURUMAI.

Finance

(cap. = capital; res = reserves; dep. = deposits; m. = million; brs = branches; amounts in Burundian francs)

BANKING

Central Bank

Banque de la République du Burundi (BRB): BP 705, Bujumbura; tel. 22225142; fax 22223128; e-mail brb@brb.bi; internet www.brb.bi; f. 1964 as Banque du Royaume du Burundi; state-owned; bank of issue; total assets 389,762.8m. (Dec. 2005); Gov. SALVATOR TOYI; Vice-Gov. SPÉSIOSE BARANSATA; 2 brs.

Commercial Banks

Banque Burundaise pour le Commerce et l'Investissement SARL (BBCI): blvd du Peuple Murundi, BP 2320, Bujumbura; tel. 22223328; fax 22223339; e-mail bbci@cbinf.com; f. 1988; cap. and res 2,645.8m., total assets 14,016.2m. (Dec. 2003); Pres. CELESLIN MIZERO; Dir-Gen. CHARLES NIHANGAZA.

Banque Commerciale du Burundi SARL (BANCOBU): BP 990, Bujumbura; tel. 22222317; fax 22221018; e-mail bancobu@cbinf.com; f. 1988 by merger; cap. 1,100m., res 1,418.3m., dep. 39,506.6m. (Dec. 2004); Pres. PIERRE-CLAVER GAHUNGU; Man. Dir GASPARD SINDAYIGAYA; 8 brs.

Banque de Crédit de Bujumbura SM: ave Patrice Emery Lumumba, BP 300, Bujumbura; tel. 22201111; fax 22223007; e-mail direction@bcb.bi; internet www.bcb.bi; f. 1964; cap. 1,000.0m., res 6,236.7m., dep. 64,046.7m. (Dec. 2005); Pres. RÉNILDE BAZAHICA; 7 brs.

Banque de Financement et de Leasing S.A.: blvd de la Liberté, BP 2998, Bujumbura; tel. 22243206; fax 22225437; e-mail finalease@cbinf.com; cap. and res 1,400.5m., total assets 8,578.4m. (Dec. 2003); Pres. AUDACE BIREHA; Dir-Gen. ERIC BONANE RUBEGA.

Banque de Gestion et de Financement: 1 blvd de la Liberté, BP 1035, Bujumbura; tel. 22221352; fax 22221351; e-mail bgf@usan.bu.net; f. 1996; cap. 1,029.0m., res 860.6m., dep. 17,378.9m. (Dec. 2005); Pres. BÉDE BEDETSE; Gen. Man. MATHIAS NDIKUMANA.

Interbank Burundi SARL: 15 rue de l'Industrie, BP 2970, Bujumbura; tel. 22220629; fax 22220461; e-mail info@interbankbdi.com; internet www.interbankbdi.com; cap. and res 9,385.1m., total assets 117,387.0m. (Dec. 2006); Pres. GEORGES COUCOULIS.

Development Bank

Banque Nationale pour le Développement Economique SARL (BNDE): 3 ave du Marché, BP 1620, Bujumbura; tel. 22222888; fax 22223775; e-mail bnde@cbinf.com; f. 1966; cap. 3,241.9m., res 1,534.7m., dep. 6,045.6m. (Dec. 2005); Chair. and Man. Dir JEAN CIZA.

Co-operative Bank

Banque Coopérative d'Epargne et de Crédit Mutuel (BCM): BP 1340, Bujumbura; operating licence granted in April 1995; Vice-Pres. JULIEN MUSARAGANY.

Financial Institutions

Fonds de Promotion de L'Habitat Urbain (FPHU): BP 1996, Bujumbura; tel. 22227676; e-mail fphu@cbinf.com; cap. 818m. (2005); Dir-Gen. AUDACE BUKURU.

Société Burundaise de Financement: 6 rue de la Science, BP 270, Bujumbura; tel. 22222126; fax 22225437; e-mail sbf@cbinf.com; cap. and res 2,558.9m., total assets 11,680.4m. (Dec. 2003); Pres. ASTÈRE GIRUKWIGOMBA; Dir-Gen. DARIUS NAHAYO.

INSURANCE

Société d'Assurances du Burundi (SOCABU): 14–18 rue de l'Amitié, BP 2440, Bujumbura; tel. 22226520; fax 22226803; f. 1977; cap. 180m.; Man. Dir ONESIME NDUWIMANA.

Société Générale d'Assurances et de Réassurance (SOGEAR): BP 2432, Bujumbura; tel. 22222345; fax 22229338; f. 1991; Pres. BENOÎT NDORIMANA; Dir-Gen. L. SAUSSEZ.

Union Commerciale d'Assurances et de Réassurance (UCAR): BP 3012, Bujumbura; tel. 22223638; fax 22223695; f. 1986; cap. 150m.; Chair. Lt-Col EDOUARD NZAMBIMANA; Dir-Gen. PASCAL NTAMASHIMIKIRO.

Trade and Industry

GOVERNMENT AGENCIES

Agence de Promotion des Echanges Extérieurs (APEE): 27 rue de la Victoire, BP 3535, Bujumbura; tel. 22225497; fax 22222767; promotes and supervises foreign exchanges.

Office du Café du Burundi (OCIBU): 279 blvd de Tanzanie, BP 450, Bujumbura; tel. 22224017; fax 22225532; e-mail dgo@usan-bu.net; internet www.burundicoffee.com; f. 1964; supervises coffee plantations and coffee exports; Dir-Gen. BARTHÉLÉMY NIYIKIZA.

Office National du Commerce (ONC): Bujumbura; f. 1973; supervises international commercial operations between the Govt of Burundi and other states or private orgs; also organizes the import of essential materials; subsidiary offices in each province.

Office National du Logement (ONL): BP 2480, Bujumbura; tel. 22226074; f. 1974 to supervise housing construction.

Office du Thé du Burundi (OTB): 52 blvd de l'UPRONA, Bujumbura; tel. 22224228; fax 22224657; e-mail otb@cbinf.com; f. 1979; supervises production and marketing of tea; Man. Dir SALVATORE NIMUBONA.

DEVELOPMENT ORGANIZATIONS

Compagnie Financière pour le Développement SA: Bldg INSS, 1 Route Nationale, BP 139, Ngozi; tel. 22302279; fax 22302296; Pres. ABBÉ EPHREM GIRUKWISHAKA.

Fonds de Développement Communal SP: BP 2799, Bujumbura; tel. 22221963; fax 22243268; e-mail fdc@cbinf.com; Pres. BÉATRICE BUKWARE.

Fonds de Promotion de l'Habitat Urbain: 6 ave de la Liberté, BP 1996, Bujumbura; tel. 22227676; fax 22223225; e-mail fphu@cbinf.com; cap. 818m. Burundian francs; Pres. DIDACE BIRABISHA.

Institut des Sciences Agronomiques du Burundi (ISABU): BP 795, Bujumbura; tel. 22227349; fax 22225798; e-mail isabu@usan-bu.net; f. 1962 for the scientific development of agriculture and livestock.

Office National de la Tourbe (ONATOUR): BP 2360, Bujumbura; tel. 22226480; fax 22226709; f. 1977 to promote the exploitation of peat deposits.

Société d'Economie pour l'Exploitation du Quinquina au Burundi (SOKINABU): 16 blvd Mwezi Gisabo, BP 1783, Bujumbura; tel. 22223469; fax 22218160; e-mail chiastos@yahoo.fr; f. 1975 to develop and exploit cinchona trees, the source of quinine; Dir CHRISTIAN REMEZO.

CHAMBER OF COMMERCE

Chambre de Commerce, d'Industrie, d'Agriculture et d'Artisanat du Burundi: BP 313, Bujumbura; tel. 22222280; fax 22227895; f. 1923; Pres. DIDACE NZOHABONAYO; Sec.-Gen. CYRILLE SINGEJEJE; 130 mems.

UTILITY

Régie de Distribution d'Eau et d'Electricité (REGIDESO): Ngozi, Bujumbura; tel. 22302222; state-owned distributor of water and electricity services; Dir JÉRÔME CIZA.

TRADE UNIONS

Confédération des Syndicats du Burundi (COSYBU): ave du 18 Septembre, Ex Hôtel Central 8, BP 220, Bujumbura; tel. 22248190; fax 22248190; e-mail cosybu@yahoo.fr; Chair. Dr PIERRE-CLAVIER HAJAYANDI.

Union des Travailleurs du Burundi (UTB): BP 1340, Bujumbura; tel. 22223884; f. 1967 by merger of all existing unions; closely allied with UPRONA; sole authorized trade union prior to 1994, with 18 affiliated nat. professional feds; Sec.-Gen. MARIUS RURAHENYE.

Transport

RAILWAYS

There are no railways in Burundi. Plans have been under consideration since 1987 for the construction of a line passing through Uganda, Rwanda and Burundi, to connect with the Kigoma–Dar es Salaam line in Tanzania. This rail link would relieve Burundi's isolated trade position.

ROADS

In 2004 Burundi had a total of 12,322 km of roads, of which 5,012 km were national highways and 282 km secondary roads. A new crossing of the Ruzizi river, the Bridge of Concord (Burundi's longest bridge), was opened in early 1992.

Office des Transports en Commun (OTRACO): BP 1486, Bujumbura; tel. 22231313; fax 22232051; 100% govt-owned; operates public transport.

INLAND WATERWAYS

Bujumbura is the principal port for both passenger and freight traffic on Lake Tanganyika, and the greater part of Burundi's external trade is dependent on the shipping services between Bujumbura and lake ports in Tanzania, Zambia and the Democratic Republic of the Congo.

Société Concessionnaire de l'Exploitation du Port de Bujumbura (EPB): BP 59, Bujumbura; tel. 22226036; e-mail bujaport@cbinf.com; f. 1967; 43% state-owned; controls Bujumbura port; Dir-Gen. MÉTHODE SHIRAMBERE.

CIVIL AVIATION

The international airport at Bujumbura is equipped to take large jet-engined aircraft.

Air Burundi: 40 ave du Commerce, BP 2460, Bujumbura; tel. 22223460; fax 22223452; f. 1971 as Société de Transports Aériens du Burundi; state-owned; operates charter and scheduled passenger services to destinations throughout central Africa; CEO Col ANTOINE GATOTO; Dir C. KAGARI.

Tourism

Tourism is relatively undeveloped. The annual total of tourist arrivals declined from 125,000 in 1991 to only 10,553 in 1997. Total arrivals increased gradually thereafter, reaching 74,116 in 2003 and increasing to an estimated 148,418 in 2005. Tourism receipts amounted to an estimated US $1.9m. in 2005. However, continued failure fully to restore peace in the country effectively prevented any significant revival of tourism.

Office National du Tourisme (ONT): 2 ave des Euphorbes, BP 902, Bujumbura; tel. and fax 22229390; e-mail contact@burunditourisme.com; internet www.burunditourisme.com; f. 1972; responsible for the promotion and supervision of tourism; Dir DÉO NGENDAHAYO.

CAMBODIA

Introductory Survey

Location, Climate, Language, Religion, Flag, Capital

The Kingdom of Cambodia occupies part of the Indo-Chinese peninsula in South-East Asia. It is bordered by Thailand and Laos to the north, by Viet Nam to the east and by the Gulf of Thailand to the south. The climate is tropical and humid. There is a rainy season from June to November, with the heaviest rainfall in September. The temperature is generally between 20°C and 36°C (68°F to 97°F), with March and April usually the hottest months; the annual average temperature in Phnom-Penh is 27°C (81°F). The official language is Khmer, which is spoken by everybody except the Vietnamese and Chinese minorities. The state religion is Theravada Buddhism. The national flag (proportions 2 by 3) consists of three horizontal stripes, of dark blue, red (half the depth) and dark blue, with a stylized representation (in white) of the temple of Angkor Wat, showing three of its five towers, in the centre. The capital is Phnom-Penh.

Recent History

The Kingdom of Cambodia became a French protectorate in the 19th century and was incorporated into French Indo-China. In April 1941 Norodom Sihanouk, then aged 18, succeeded his grandfather as King. In May 1947 he promulgated a Constitution which provided for a bicameral Parliament, including an elected National Assembly. Cambodia became an Associate State of the French Union in November 1949 and attained independence on 9 November 1953. In order to become a political leader, King Sihanouk abdicated in March 1955 in favour of his father, Norodom Suramarit, and became known as Prince Sihanouk. He founded a mass movement, the Sangkum Reastr Niyum (Popular Socialist Community), which won all the seats in elections to the National Assembly in 1955, 1958, 1962 and 1966. King Suramarit died in April 1960, and in June Parliament elected Prince Sihanouk as Head of State. Prince Sihanouk's Government developed good relations with the People's Republic of China and with North Viet Nam, but it was highly critical of the USA's role in Asia. From 1964, however, the Government was confronted by an underground Marxist insurgency movement, the Khmers Rouges, while it also became increasingly difficult to isolate Cambodia from the war in Viet Nam.

In March 1970 Prince Sihanouk was deposed by a right-wing coup, led by the Prime Minister, Lt-Gen. (later Marshal) Lon Nol. The new Government pledged itself to the removal of foreign communist forces and appealed to the USA for military aid. Sihanouk went into exile and formed the Royal Government of National Union of Cambodia (GRUNC), supported by the Khmers Rouges. Sihanoukists and the Khmers Rouges formed the National United Front of Cambodia (FUNC). Their combined forces, aided by South Viet Nam's National Liberation Front and North Vietnamese troops, posed a serious threat to the new regime, but in October 1970 Marshal Lon Nol proclaimed the Khmer Republic. In June 1972 he was elected the first President. During 1973 several foreign states recognized GRUNC as the rightful government of Cambodia. In 1974 the republican regime's control was limited to a few urban enclaves, besieged by GRUNC forces, mainly Khmers Rouges, who gained control of Phnom-Penh on 17 April 1975. Prince Sihanouk became Head of State again but did not return from exile until September. The country was subjected to a pre-arranged programme of radical social deconstruction immediately after the Khmers Rouges' assumption of power; towns were largely evacuated, and their inhabitants forced to work in rural areas. During the following three years an estimated 1.7m. people died as a result of ill-treatment, hunger, disease and executions.

A new Constitution, promulgated in January 1976, renamed the country Democratic Kampuchea, and established a republican form of government; elections for a 250-member People's Representative Assembly were held in March 1976. In April Prince Sihanouk resigned as Head of State, and GRUNC was dissolved. The Assembly elected Khieu Samphan, formerly Deputy Prime Minister, to be President of the State Presidium (Head of State). The little-known Pol Pot (formerly Saloth Sar) became Prime Minister. In September 1977 it was officially disclosed that the ruling organization was the Communist Party of Kampuchea (CPK), with Pol Pot as the Secretary of its Central Committee.

After 1975 close links with China developed, while relations with Viet Nam deteriorated. In 1978, following a two-year campaign of raids across the Vietnamese border by the Khmers Rouges, the Vietnamese army launched a series of offensives into Kampuchean territory. In December the establishment of the Kampuchean National United Front for National Salvation (KNUFNS, renamed Kampuchean United Front for National Construction and Defence—KUFNCD—in December 1981, and United Front for the Construction and Defence of the Kampuchean Fatherland—UFCDKF—in 1989), a communist-led movement opposed to Pol Pot and supported by Viet Nam, was announced. Later in the month Viet Nam invaded Kampuchea, supported by the KNUFNS.

On 7 January 1979 Phnom-Penh was captured by Vietnamese forces, and three days later the People's Republic of Kampuchea was proclaimed. A People's Revolutionary Council was established, with Heng Samrin, leader of the KNUFNS, as President. It pledged to restore freedom of movement, freedom of association and of religion, and to restore the family unit. The CPK was replaced as the governing party by the Kampuchean People's Revolutionary Party (KPRP). The Khmer Rouge forces, however, remained active in the western provinces, near the border with Thailand, and conducted sporadic guerrilla activities elsewhere in the country. Several groups opposing both the Khmers Rouges and the Heng Samrin regime were established, including the Khmer People's National Liberation Front (KPNLF), headed by a former Prime Minister, Son Sann. In July, claiming that Pol Pot's regime had been responsible for 3m. deaths, the KPRP administration sentenced Pol Pot and his former Minister of Foreign Affairs, Ieng Sary, to death *in absentia*. In January 1980 Khieu Samphan assumed the premiership of the deposed Khmer Rouge regime, while Pol Pot became Commander-in-Chief of the armed forces. In 1981 the CPK was reportedly dissolved and was replaced by the Party of Democratic Kampuchea (PDK).

During the early years of the KPRP regime Viet Nam launched regular offensives on the Thai-Kampuchean border against the united armed forces of Democratic Kampuchea, the coalition Government-in-exile of anti-Vietnamese resistance groups formed in June 1982. As a result of the fighting, and the prevalence of starvation and disease, thousands of Kampuchean refugees crossed the border into Thailand; in turn, a large number of Vietnamese citizens subsequently settled on Kampuchean territory. The coalition Government-in-exile, of which Prince Sihanouk became President, Khieu Samphan (PDK) Vice-President and Son Sann (KPLNF) Prime Minister, received the support of China and of member states of the Association of South East Asian Nations (ASEAN, see p. 185), whilst retaining the Kampuchean seat in the UN General Assembly.

In the mid-1980s an increasingly conciliatory relationship between the USSR and China led to a number of diplomatic exchanges, aimed at reconciling the coalition Government-in-exile with the Government in Phnom-Penh, led by the General Secretary of the KPRP, Heng Samrin, but the Heng Samrin Government rejected peace proposals from ASEAN and the coalition Government-in-exile. In September 1987 the Chinese Government stated that it would accept a Kampuchean 'government of national reconciliation' under Prince Sihanouk, but that the presence of Vietnamese troops in Kampuchea remained a major obstacle. The USSR also declared that it was 'prepared to facilitate a political settlement' in Kampuchea. In October, having announced its readiness to conduct negotiations with some PDK leaders (but not Pol Pot), the Heng Samrin Government offered Prince Sihanouk a government post and issued a set of peace proposals, which included the complete withdrawal of Vietnamese troops, internationally observed elections and the formation of a coalition government. In December 1987 Prince Sihanouk and Hun Sen, the Chairman of the Council of Ministers in the Heng Samrin Government, met in France for private discussions. The meeting ended in a joint communiqué, stating that the conflict was to be settled politically by negotiations involving all the Kampuchean parties.

CAMBODIA

Introductory Survey

Under increasing pressure from the USSR and China, the four Kampuchean factions participated in a series of 'informal meetings', held in Indonesia, which were also attended by representatives of Viet Nam, Laos and the six ASEAN members. At the first of these meetings, in July 1988, Viet Nam advanced its deadline for a complete withdrawal of its troops from Kampuchea to late 1989. In April 1989 the National Assembly in Phnom-Penh ratified several constitutional amendments, whereby the name of the country was changed to the State of Cambodia, a new national flag, emblem and anthem were introduced, Buddhism was reinstated as the state religion, and the death penalty was abolished. In July 1989 the Paris International Conference on Cambodia (PICC) met for the first time. The PICC agreed to send a UN reconnaissance party to Cambodia to study the prospects for a cease-fire and the installation of a peace-keeping force.

The withdrawal of Vietnamese forces, completed on schedule in September 1989, was followed by renewed offensives into Cambodia by the resistance forces, particularly the PDK. In November, following substantial military gains by the PDK, the UN General Assembly adopted a resolution supporting the formation of an interim government in Cambodia, which would include members of the PDK but which retained a clause, introduced in 1988, relating to past atrocities committed by the organization. The resolution also cast doubt on the Vietnamese withdrawal (since it had not been monitored by the UN) and, in reference to the alleged presence of 1m. Vietnamese settlers in Cambodia, condemned 'demographic changes' imposed in the country. An Australian peace initiative was unanimously approved by the five permanent members of the UN Security Council in January 1990. In February Prince Sihanouk declared that the coalition Government-in-exile would henceforth be known as the National Government of Cambodia.

In July 1990 the USA withdrew its support for the National Government of Cambodia's occupation of Cambodia's seat at the UN. In August the UN Security Council endorsed the framework for a comprehensive settlement in Cambodia. The agreement provided for UN supervision of an interim government, military arrangements for the transitional period, free elections and guarantees for the future neutrality of Cambodia. A special representative of the Secretary-General of the UN was to control the proposed UN Transitional Authority in Cambodia (UNTAC). The UN would also assume control of the Ministries of Foreign Affairs, National Defence, Finance, the Interior and Information, Press and Culture. China and the USSR pledged to cease supplies of military equipment to their respective allies, the PDK and the Phnom-Penh Government.

At a fourth 'informal meeting' in Jakarta in September 1990 the four Cambodian factions accepted the UN proposals. They also agreed to the formation of the Supreme National Council (SNC), with six representatives from the Phnom-Penh Government and six from the National Government of Cambodia. SNC decisions were to be taken by consensus, effectively allowing each faction the power of veto, and the SNC was to occupy the Cambodian seat at the UN General Assembly. Prince Sihanouk was subsequently elected to the chairmanship of the SNC, and resigned as leader of the resistance coalition and as President of the National Government of Cambodia (positions to which Son Sann was appointed). Agreement was also reached on the four factions reducing their armed forces by 70% and the remaining 30% being placed in cantonments under UN supervision; the introduction of a system of multi-party democracy; the Phnom-Penh Government abandoning its demand for references to genocide to be included in a draft plan; and the holding of elections to a constituent assembly, which would subsequently become a legislative assembly comprising 120 seats.

Following the release of political prisoners by the Phnom-Penh Government in October 1991, including former 'reformist' associates of Hun Sen (who had been arrested in 1990 and replaced by supporters of the more conservative chairman of the National Assembly, Chea Sim), a congress of the KPRP was convened at which the party changed its name to the Cambodian People's Party (CPP). The communist insignia was removed from its emblem, Heng Samrin was replaced as Chairman of the Central Committee (formerly the Politburo) by Chea Sim and Hun Sen was elected as Vice-Chairman.

On 23 October 1991 the four factions signed the UN peace agreement in Paris, under the auspices of the PICC. The UN Advance Mission in Cambodia (UNAMIC), comprising 300 men, was in position by the end of 1991. The agreement also provided for the repatriation, under the supervision of the UN High Commissioner for Refugees, of the estimated 340,000 Cambodian refugees living in camps in Thailand. In November Prince Sihanouk returned to Phnom-Penh, accompanied by Hun Sen. The CPP and the United National Front for an Independent, Neutral, Peaceful and Co-operative Cambodia (FUNCINPEC), led by Prince Sihanouk, subsequently formed an alliance and announced their intention to establish a coalition government. (The alliance was abandoned in December, in response to objections from the KPNLF and the PDK.) The four factions endorsed the reinstatement of Prince Sihanouk as the Head of State of Cambodia. In late November, however, an attack by demonstrators on Khieu Samphan on his return to Phnom-Penh led senior PDK officials to flee to Bangkok where the SNC met and agreed that, henceforth, officials of the party would occupy the SNC headquarters in Phnom-Penh with members of UNAMIC. Further demonstrations took place in December and in January 1992 but, following an agreement with representatives of the UN Security Council, the Phnom-Penh Government released all remaining political prisoners between January and March 1992. The UN Security Council expanded UNAMIC's mandate to include mine-clearing operations, and in February authorized the dispatch of a 22,000-member peace-keeping force to Cambodia to establish UNTAC. In mid-March UNAMIC transferred responsibility for the implementation of the peace agreement to UNTAC.

The refugee repatriation programme, which began in March 1992, was threatened by continued cease-fire violations, which were concentrated in the central province of Kampong Thum. In June the continued obduracy of the PDK disrupted the implementation of the second phase of the peace-keeping operation, which comprised the placing in cantonments and disarmament of the four factions' forces. Although by mid-July about 12,000 troops from three of the factions had reported to the designated areas, the PDK intensified its violations of the cease-fire agreement, continued to deny the UN access to its zones and failed to attend meetings on the implementation of the peace agreement. At the Ministerial Conference on the Rehabilitation and Reconstruction of Cambodia, which was convened in Tokyo in late June, the application of economic sanctions against the PDK was considered. The PDK reiterated demands that power be transferred from the Phnom-Penh Government to the SNC and that both the SNC and UNTAC should co-operate in ensuring that all Vietnamese forces had withdrawn from Cambodia. During August Yasushi Akashi (who had been appointed UN Special Representative to Cambodia in charge of UNTAC in January 1992) affirmed that the legislative elections would proceed without the participation of the PDK if it continued to refuse to co-operate. The UN set a deadline for compliance of 15 November. By the end of November, however, no consensus had been reached, and the Security Council adopted a resolution condemning PDK obduracy. The Security Council approved an embargo on the supplies of petroleum products to the PDK and endorsed a ban on the export of timber (a principal source of income for the party) from 31 December. On the day the sanctions were adopted, however, the PDK announced the formation of a subsidiary party to contest the forthcoming elections, the Cambodian National Unity Party, led by Khieu Samphan and Son Sen.

By the final deadline at the end of January 1993 20 parties, excluding the PDK, had registered to contest the elections. The Phnom-Penh Government subsequently launched an offensive against the PDK in northern and western Cambodia, recovering much of the territory gained by the PDK since the signing of the peace agreement in October 1991. In early February 1993 Prince Sihanouk returned to Phnom-Penh from Beijing amidst intensifying politically motivated violence. There were also continuing attacks by the PDK on ethnic Vietnamese, and, following several rural massacres, thousands of Vietnamese took refuge in Viet Nam. Despite the violence, UNTAC's voter registration campaign, which ended in February, had been extremely successful; 4.7m. Cambodians were registered, constituting about 97% of the estimated eligible electorate. The repatriation programme for refugees on the Thai border was also successfully concluded; 360,000 refugees had been returned to Cambodia on schedule by the end of April.

On 23–28 May 1993 about 90% of the electorate participated in the elections to the Constituent Assembly. The PDK offered support to the FUNCINPEC Party but, owing to the massive voter participation in the election, Prince Sihanouk abandoned his proposals for the inclusion of the PDK in a future Government. Early results from the election, indicating a FUNCINPEC victory, prompted CPP allegations of irregularities. UNTAC, however, rejected CPP requests for fresh elections in at least four provinces. In early June, without prior consultation with the UN and disregarding the incomplete election results, Prince Sihanouk announced the formation of a new Government, with himself as Prime Minister and Prince Norodom Ranariddh and Hun Sen as joint Deputy Prime Ministers. The coalition was created and renounced within hours, owing to objections from Prince Ranariddh, who had not been consulted, and to suggestions by UN officials that it was tantamount to a coup. Two days later the official results of the election were released: the FUNCINPEC Party had secured 58 seats with 46% of the votes cast, the CPP 51 seats with 38% of the votes, the Buddhist Liberal Democratic Party (BLDP, founded by the KPNLF) 10 seats (3%) and a breakaway faction from the FUNCINPEC Party, MOLINAKA (National Liberation Movement of Cambodia), one seat. Despite the UN's endorsement of the election as fair, the CPP refused to dissolve the State of Cambodia Government in Phnom-Penh and announced that certain eastern provinces were threatening to secede unless demands for an independent examination of the results were met. Prince Norodom Chakrapong (a son of Prince Sihanouk who had been appointed to the Council of Ministers of the Phnom-Penh Government in December 1991) subsequently led a secessionist movement in seven provinces in the east and north-east of the country, which was reportedly sanctioned by the CPP leadership in an attempt to secure a power-sharing agreement with the FUNCINPEC Party.

On 14 June 1993, at the inaugural session of the Constituent Assembly, Prince Sihanouk was proclaimed Head of State, and 'full and special' powers were conferred on him. The Assembly adopted a resolution declaring null and void the overthrow of Prince Sihanouk 23 years previously and recognizing him retroactively as Head of State of Cambodia during that period. The secessionist movement in the eastern provinces collapsed, and on the following day an agreement was reached on the formation of an interim government, with Hun Sen and Prince Ranariddh as Co-Chairmen of the Provisional National Government of Cambodia. Prince Chakrapong returned to Phnom-Penh, where he was reconciled with Prince Sihanouk, and the CPP officially recognized the election results.

The PDK had immediately accepted the results of the election and supported the formation of a coalition government, but continued to engage in military action to support its demands for inclusion in a future government. In July 1993 the PDK offered to incorporate its forces into the newly formed Cambodian National Armed Forces (later restyled the Royal Cambodian Armed Forces), which had been created through the merger of the forces of the other three factions in June. PDK offensives escalated, however, after the party was denied a role in government, largely owing to US threats to withhold economic aid from Cambodia if the PDK were included prior to a renunciation of violence. In late August Cambodia's united armed forces initiated a successful offensive against PDK positions in north-western Cambodia. The Government rejected an appeal for urgent discussions by the PDK after government forces had captured PDK bases, insisting that the party surrender unconditionally the estimated 20% of Cambodian territory under its control.

In September 1993 the Constituent Assembly adopted a new Constitution, which provided for an hereditary monarchy. Prince Sihanouk duly promulgated the Constitution, thus terminating the mandate of UNTAC (whose personnel left the country by mid-November). The Constituent Assembly became the National Assembly, and Prince Sihanouk acceded to the throne of the new Kingdom of Cambodia. Chea Sim was re-elected Chairman of the National Assembly. Government ministers were to be chosen from parties represented in the National Assembly, thus precluding the involvement of the PDK. At the end of October the National Assembly approved the new Royal Government of Cambodia (previously endorsed by King Sihanouk), in which Prince Ranariddh was named First Prime Minister and Hun Sen Second Prime Minister. Subsequent initiatives to incorporate the PDK into the new Government failed, owing to objections from various parties. In May 1994 King Sihanouk threatened to stop negotiating with the PDK and the Government to end the fighting in the north-west of the country, which had reached a severity not witnessed since 1989, and forced the postponement of proposed peace talks in Pyongyang, the Democratic People's Republic of Korea (North Korea). Following the failure of peace talks held in May and June 1994, the Government ordered the PDK to leave Phnom-Penh and closed the party's mission in the capital.

In July 1994 the Government claimed to have suppressed a coup attempt led by Prince Chakrapong and Gen. Sin Song, a former Minister of National Security under the State of Cambodia. Following a personal appeal from King Sihanouk, Prince Chakrapong, who protested his innocence, was exiled from Cambodia, while Gen. Sin Song was placed under arrest. (Gen. Sin Song escaped from prison in September and was captured by Thai authorities in November.) Hun Sen also suspected his rival, Sar Kheng, a Deputy Prime Minister and Minister of the Interior, of involvement in the alleged revolt. Sar Kheng was, however, protected by his powerful brother-in-law, Chea Sim. The coup attempt was also used by the increasingly divided Government as a pretext to suppress criticism of the regime. Newspapers were closed, editors fined and imprisoned and in September an editor renowned as an outspoken critic of the Government was killed by unidentified assailants.

Despite King Sihanouk's continued advocacy of national reconciliation, in July 1994 legislation providing for the outlawing of the PDK was adopted by the National Assembly (whilst allowing for an immediate six-month amnesty for the lower ranks of the party). In response, the PDK announced the formation of a Provisional Government of National Unity and National Salvation of Cambodia (PGNUNSC), under the premiership of Khieu Samphan, which was to co-ordinate opposition to the Government in Phnom-Penh from its headquarters in Preah Vihear in the north of the country. In October Sam Rainsy was dismissed as Minister of Finance, apparently owing to his efforts to combat corruption at senior levels. Prince Sirivudh subsequently resigned as Minister of Foreign Affairs in protest at Rainsy's removal, which also demonstrated the decline in King Sihanouk's political influence; Prince Ranariddh and Hun Sen had jointly proposed Rainsy's dismissal in March, but King Sihanouk had withheld his consent. Prince Sirivudh also criticized the FUNCINPEC Party, of which he was Secretary-General, for submitting too readily to CPP demands, as it became increasingly apparent that real power lay with the former communists.

In May 1995 Rainsy was expelled from the FUNCINPEC Party and in April he was expelled from the National Assembly. Rainsy formed a new party, the Khmer Nation Party (KNP), which was officially launched in November. The Government declared the KNP illegal but refrained from action to disband it. Rainsy's expulsion from the National Assembly coincided with the adoption of the revised draft of a stringent press law, which imposed substantial fines and prison sentences for reporting issues affecting 'national security' or 'political stability'. In October Prince Sirivudh was also expelled from the National Assembly and charged with conspiring to assassinate Hun Sen. He was allowed to go into exile in France in December on condition that he refrain from political activity, and in January 1996 he was convicted and sentenced to 10 years' imprisonment *in absentia* on charges of criminal conspiracy and possession of unlicensed firearms. Also in January the Government began to adopt repressive measures against the KNP. In March Rainsy nominally merged the KNP with a defunct but still legally registered party, in an attempt to gain legal status. However, in April the Government ordered all parties without parliamentary representation to close their offices. Several KNP officials were assassinated during the year.

In August 1996 the prominent PDK leader, Ieng Sary, together with two military divisions that controlled the significant PDK strongholds of Pailin and Malai, defected from the movement and negotiated a peace agreement with the Government. Ieng Sary subsequently denied responsibility for the atrocities committed during Pol Pot's regime, and was granted a royal amnesty in September, at the request of both Hun Sen and Prince Ranariddh. Ieng Sary then formed a new political organization, the Democratic National United Movement (DNUM), while his supporters retained control of Pailin and Malai, despite efforts by troops loyal to the PDK leadership to recapture the region (where lucrative mineral and timber resources were situated). An estimated 2,500 PDK troops transferred allegiance to the Government in October. Former PDK troops (numbering about 4,000) were integrated into the national army in November.

Throughout 1996 political instability increased. In September the partial dissolution of the PDK increased tensions within the ruling coalition, as both the CPP and the FUNCINPEC Party attempted to attract former PDK troops. However, as the FUNCINPEC Party appeared more successful than the CPP at recruiting former PDK commanders and cadres, Hun Sen became concerned that the alliance between the royalists and the

PDK as former resistance forces would be re-established. In February 1997 Prince Ranariddh sent a helicopter mission to Anlong Veng to negotiate with the central PDK faction. However, PDK members opposed to peace talks ambushed the helicopter, killing the majority of the Prince's emissaries. Meanwhile, the two Prime Ministers were stockpiling weapons, violations of human and civil rights were becoming increasingly prevalent, corruption was rampant and labour unrest was widespread. In March Rainsy led a demonstration outside the National Assembly. The rally was attacked by assailants who threw four grenades, killing 19 and injuring more than 100 protesters. Rainsy accused Hun Sen of organizing the attack and expressed no confidence in the commission established to investigate the apparent assassination attempt against him.

In April 1997 Ung Phan, a former CPP member who had joined the FUNCINPEC Party in the early 1990s, led a rebellion against the party leadership of Prince Ranariddh, with the support of Hun Sen. The National Assembly, which was due to adopt legislation pertaining to local and national elections scheduled for 1998, was unable to convene, as the FUNCINPEC Party refused to attend until its dissident members were expelled from the Assembly, whereas the CPP insisted on their retention. In June the dissident FUNCINPEC members organized a party congress and formed a rival FUNCINPEC Party, with Toan Chhay, the Governor of Siem Reap, as its chairman.

In May 1997 Khieu Samphan announced the creation of a new political party, the National Solidarity Party, which would support the National United Front (an alliance founded in February by Prince Ranariddh) at the next election. Prince Ranariddh declared that, if the notorious former leadership of the PDK were excluded, he would welcome such an alliance. Hun Sen, however, deemed the potential alliance to be a threat to the CPP and, following the seizure of a shipment of weapons destined for Prince Ranariddh, accused the Prince of illegally importing weapons to arm PDK soldiers. The PDK was divided over the issue of peace negotiations. Pol Pot ordered the death of the Minister of National Defence, Son Sen, and also that of Ta Mok, the south-western regional army commander. Following the execution of Son Sen and his family, many PDK commanders rallied behind Ta Mok, and fighting erupted between the two factions. Pol Pot and his supporters fled into the jungle, with Khieu Samphan as a hostage, but were captured by Ta Mok's forces and returned to the PDK base at Anlong Veng, near the Thai border. In late July a US journalist, Nate Thayer, was invited by the PDK to Anlong Veng to witness the trial of Pol Pot. He was condemned by a 'people's court' for 'destroying national unity' and for the killing of Son Sen and his family. In October Thayer was permitted to interview the former leader, who denied that atrocities had occurred under his regime.

In June 1997 Prince Ranariddh claimed that Pol Pot was under arrest and that Khieu Samphan would surrender. Hun Sen, meanwhile, demanded that Ranariddh choose between himself and Khieu as a partner in government. Tensions between Prince Ranariddh and Hun Sen increased, as FUNCINPEC military forces were strengthened. Hun Sen continued to warn that PDK defectors were massing in Phnom-Penh. On 3 July, following several attempts by CPP troops to detect the presence of PDK soldiers in FUNCINPEC units, CPP forces disarmed a unit of Prince Ranariddh's bodyguards, on the grounds that they were allegedly PDK troops. On the following day Prince Ranariddh left the country. On 5 July serious fighting erupted in Phnom-Penh, and on 6 July, the day on which Khieu Samphan had been scheduled to broadcast the PDK's agreement with the FUNCINPEC Party to end its resistance and rejoin the political system, Hun Sen appeared on television to demand Prince Ranariddh's arrest (on charges of negotiating with the PDK, introducing proscribed PDK troops into Phnom-Penh and secretly importing weapons to arm those forces) and to urge FUNCINPEC officials to select another leader. More than 24 hours of pillaging then ensued. The UN subsequently claimed that it had documentary evidence showing that at least 43 people, principally from the royalist army structure, had been murdered by forces loyal to Hun Sen after the events of 5–6 July. Many more FUNCINPEC and KNP officials, as well as many FUNCINPEC members of the legislature, fled the country.

King Sihanouk's appeals for both sides to travel to China to negotiate a settlement were rejected by Hun Sen. Prince Ranariddh announced from Paris that a resistance movement was being organized in western Cambodia. Meanwhile, Hun Sen began negotiations with certain prominent members of the FUNCINPEC Party who remained in Phnom-Penh in an effort to attain the two-thirds' majority of the National Assembly necessary for the investiture of a new government. By the end of July 1997 the National Assembly had reconvened, with 98 of the 120 deputies present, including 40 of the 58 FUNCINPEC deputies. Hun Sen protested to the international community that his actions did not constitute a *coup d'état*, as he had not abolished the Constitution or the monarchy and had not dissolved the Government or the National Assembly. He also declared that he was in favour of free elections in 1998. The UN refused to condemn Hun Sen by name, although it expressed a 'grave preoccupation' with the situation in Cambodia. King Sihanouk, who had been in China since February, also insisted on remaining neutral and accepted that Chea Sim should continue to sign royal decrees in his absence. In August the National Assembly voted to remove Ranariddh's legal immunity (a warrant subsequently being issued for his arrest) and elected Ung Huot, the FUNCINPEC Minister of Foreign Affairs, to the post of First Prime Minister.

In July 1997 troops loyal to Prince Ranariddh, led by Gen. Nhiek Bun Chhay (the former military Deputy Chief of Staff and a principal negotiator with the PDK), were swiftly forced into the north-west of the country by CPP troops. They regrouped near the Thai border in an effective alliance with PDK troops under Ta Mok. Prolonged fighting took place for control of the town of O'Smach, about 70 km west of Anlong Veng, which was the last base for the resistance coalition led by Prince Ranariddh, the Union of Cambodian Democrats. At the end of August the King arrived in Siem Reap. Hun Sen rejected another proposal from the King to act as a mediator in peace talks, insisting that Ranariddh be tried for his alleged crimes.

In September 1997 Hun Sen announced a cabinet reorganization that effectively removed remaining supporters of Prince Ranariddh from the Government. However, in a secret ballot the National Assembly failed by 13 votes to approve the changes by the required two-thirds' majority. Hun Sen continued his efforts to encourage the return of all opposition representatives who had fled the country in July, except Ranariddh and Gen. Nhiek Bun Chhay. In late 1997 Rainsy returned to Cambodia and agreed to co-operate with Hun Sen. In December the National Assembly voted to postpone local and legislative elections from May until July 1998 and to increase the number of seats from 120 to 122. At the beginning of February 1998 Rainsy withdrew the KNP from the electoral process in protest at the unlawful methods allegedly employed by Hun Sen, including the registration of a breakaway faction of the KNP bearing an identical title and logo and the fatal shooting in January of a KNP official and his daughter. Rainsy subsequently restyled the KNP the Sam Rainsy Party.

Hun Sen and Ranariddh agreed to the terms of a Japanese peace proposal in February 1998, which provided for the severance of Ranariddh's links with the PDK, the implementation of a cease-fire in the north-west (which came into effect on 27 February), a royal pardon for Ranariddh if he were convicted *in absentia* of the charges against him and his guaranteed safe return to participate in the general election. Ranariddh was convicted in March of illegally importing weapons and of conspiring with the proscribed PDK, and sentenced to 30 years' imprisonment and a fine of US $54m. for damage caused on 5–6 July 1997. At the formal request of Hun Sen, Sihanouk granted Ranariddh a royal pardon, but no amnesty was accorded to Gen. Nhiek Bun Chhay or Serei Kosal, the commanders of Ranariddh's troops in the north-west, who were also found guilty. Ranariddh returned to Phnom-Penh at the end of March 1998, but the FUNCINPEC Party had been severely weakened by the killing of many of its senior personnel, the closure of its offices across the country and the defection of some principal officials.

In March 1998 two divisions of PDK troops mutinied against their leader, Ta Mok; further divisions rebelled in the following week, surrendering control of the PDK headquarters, Anlong Veng, to government troops. During the ensuing clashes thousands of civilians were evacuated to Thailand. Pol Pot died on 15 April, shortly after his comrades had offered to surrender him for trial by an international tribunal. It was later reported that he had committed suicide. Ta Mok announced that he was prepared to reach agreement with the Government but demanded autonomy for Anlong Veng. Sporadic clashes between the remnants of the PDK and government forces continued in late 1998. The grouping was practically defunct, however, by the end of the year, following further significant defections in October and December. In late December Nuon Chea (Pol Pot's former deputy) and Khieu Samphan defected to the Government, seeking sanctuary in Pailin, an area effectively controlled by Ieng Sary. In February 1999 a final 4,332 PDK troops surrendered to the Co-Ministers of National Defence in Anlong Veng. Ta Mok, however, remained in the border area.

The election campaign period was characterized by intimidation and violence. All demonstrations were banned, as was the dissemination of political information by private news media. Ranariddh and, more particularly, Rainsy (who did finally contest the election) sought to exploit traditional Cambodian hatred of the Vietnamese. Hun Sen refused to campaign, but the ruling CPP dominated the National Election Committee (NEC), the Constitutional Council, the armed forces and the judiciary, as well as central and local government. However, the general election, which took place on 26 July 1998, was deemed free and fair by the UN-co-ordinated Joint International Observer Group. Voting took place relatively peacefully, except for an attack on a polling station by PDK remnants, in which 10 people were killed; 90% of the 5,395,024 registered voters (representing 98% of the population of voting age) participated in the election, which was contested by 39 parties. Under a newly introduced modified system of proportional representation that favoured larger parties, the CPP secured 64 seats (with 41.4% of the popular vote), the FUNCINPEC Party 43 seats (31.7%) and the Sam Rainsy Party 15 seats (14.3%). At an audience with the King, Hun Sen proposed a three-party coalition, but this was rejected by Ranariddh and Rainsy

In August 1998 Rainsy was detained for questioning, following a grenade explosion at the Ministry of the Interior. Several thousand Cambodians took part in a demonstration in Phnom-Penh, organized by Sam Rainsy, to denounce electoral fraud and to demand the removal of Hun Sen. Despite a ruling by the Constitutional Court upholding the NEC's decision to reject allegations of electoral fraud, the peaceful demonstration outside the National Assembly lasted for more than two weeks. Discussions involving the three principal parties failed to produce a resolution. In September, however, following a grenade attack on a disused residence of Hun Sen, the protesters were violently dispersed by security forces, and Hun Sen ordered the arrest of Rainsy on charges of murder. The opposition accused Hun Sen of staging the incident in order to justify his suppression of the peaceful protest. Rainsy took refuge under the protection of the UN, and both Rainsy and Ranariddh abandoned their demands for a recount. Sporadic violence continued, and Hun Sen announced that the FUNCINPEC Party and the Sam Rainsy Party would be expelled from the National Assembly if they failed to attend its inauguration on 24 September. Tension was further heightened by a rocket-propelled grenade attack on a convoy of vehicles en route to the convening ceremony of the National Assembly. Hun Sen, who claimed to be the intended victim of the attack, issued retaliatory threats prompting Ranariddh and Rainsy to flee to Thailand. The situation continued to deteriorate in October 1998 with the arrest, torture and execution of many opposition supporters.

Ranariddh agreed to return to Cambodia to attend a meeting with Hun Sen, under the auspices of King Sihanouk, from which Rainsy was excluded. In November 1998 agreement was reached on the formation of a coalition Government, which would be supported by 107 of the 122 deputies, with Hun Sen as Prime Minister and Ranariddh as the Chairman of the National Assembly. The accord also provided for the creation of a Senate (to be presided over by Chea Sim), the reintegration of resistance soldiers into the armed forces, royal pardons for Gen. Nhiek Bun Chhay and Serei Kosal, as well as Prince Sirivudh and Prince Chakrapong, and restitution for property damaged during the fighting of July 1997. On 25 November the National Assembly convened, and Ranariddh was duly elected Chairman of the Assembly, with two CPP deputies. The new Royal Government was approved on 30 November and included Co-Ministers for the influential Ministries of Defence and of the Interior, while the CPP controlled the foreign affairs and finance portfolios and the FUNCINPEC Party assumed responsibility for information and health. Rainsy became the official leader of the opposition. The Senate, which was empowered to scrutinize and amend bills passed by the National Assembly, held its inaugural session on 25 March 1999. Representation in the 61-member upper chamber was proportionate to elected strength in the National Assembly; the CPP was allocated 31 seats, the FUNCINPEC Party 21 and the Sam Rainsy Party seven, whilst a further two members were appointed by the King. Chea Sim was duly elected as Chairman, and Gen. Nhiek Bun Chhay became one of the three Deputy Chairmen.

Reform of the Royal Cambodian Armed Forces began in January 1999 with Hun Sen's resignation as Commander-in-Chief, to demonstrate the neutrality of the armed forces. He was replaced by the former Chief of the General Staff, Gen. Ke Kimyan. By the end of September 15,551 'ghost' troops (soldiers who had been killed or had deserted, but whose pay continued to be collected by senior officers) had been removed from the army payroll. Plans announced in November 1999 provided for the demobilization of 11,500 troops in 2000, followed by a further 10,000 in both 2001 and 2002.

In March 1999 Ta Mok was captured near the Thai border and placed in detention. In May Kang Kek Ieu, known as Duch, the director of the Tuol Sleng detention centre where 16,000 detainees had been tortured and executed during the Democratic Kampuchean regime, was arrested and charged with belonging to a proscribed organization. These detentions intensified domestic and international pressure for the establishment of a tribunal to try former Khmer Rouge leaders for atrocities committed during 1975–79. Three jurists, commissioned by the UN to assess the evidence against the leaders of the PDK, recommended that 20–30 Khmer Rouge leaders be brought to trial and reparations be made to their victims. The Cambodian Government, however, in the interests of national reconciliation, was reluctant to indict former Khmer Rouge leaders who had surrendered to the Government, for fear that former PDK members might revert to armed insurrection. The Cambodian Government and the UN also differed as to the composition and structure of a tribunal. The UN favoured an international tribunal, whereas Hun Sen insisted that any trials take place within the existing Cambodian court structure. In April, however, Hun Sen conceded that UN-appointed foreign judges could take part in a trial in Cambodia, although he still favoured the nomination of a Cambodian prosecutor. Cambodia submitted draft legislation recommending a majority of Cambodian judges to the UN for approval in December. Hun Sen announced in January 2000 that the trials would begin on 17 April, with or without UN support. The Government approved draft legislation establishing a court in January, but the UN finally issued its rejection of the draft in February, stating that the legislation did not conform to international standards. In December 1999 the office of the UN Secretary-General's special envoy to Cambodia was closed at the request of the Cambodian Government, despite UN pleas that it remain open for a further year. The Cambodian Government had, however, agreed in August to extend the mandate of the representative of the UN High Commissioner for Human Rights based in Cambodia, Thomas Hammarberg. Following the delays in establishing a tribunal, in August 1999 the National Assembly approved legislation extending pre-trial detention for those accused of genocide and crimes against humanity from six months to three years, effectively postponing the trials of Ta Mok and Duch. In September both Ta Mok and Duch were formally charged with genocide under a 1979 decree of the People's Republic of Kampuchea, and in the first half of 2002 both were also charged with having committed crimes against humanity. In July 2006, however, Ta Mok died.

In June 1999 Gen. Nuon Paet, a senior Khmer Rouge commander, was convicted in connection with the abduction and murder of three foreign tourists (Australian, British and French nationals) in July 1994 and sentenced to life imprisonment. In July, however, Col Chhouk Rin, one of a number of other Khmer Rouge leaders charged in connection with the murder of the three tourists, was freed after it was announced that he was covered by the amnesty granted to Khmer Rouge cadres who surrendered to the Cambodian Government. However, in September 2002, following formal protests from the Australian, British and French Governments, his acquittal was reversed by the appeals court. Col Chhouk Rin was sentenced to life imprisonment, but remained free pending the outcome of his subsequent appeal to the Supreme Court. In February 2005 the verdict was upheld, and the court ordered that Chhouk Rin be imprisoned immediately; however, Chhouk Rin evaded the authorities until he was finally recaptured near the Thai border in October. Meanwhile, in May 2002 Gen. Sam Bith was arrested and charged in connection with the murder of the three tourists. In December Bith was convicted of the charges against him and also received a life sentence.

In April 2000 US Senator John Kerry announced that agreement had been reached on a formula for the establishment of a tribunal to try former Khmer Rouge leaders for the atrocities allegedly committed. The details of a draft accord on the establishment of the tribunal were finalized in July, whereupon the requisite legislation was submitted to the Cambodian National Assembly. Despite the opposition Sam Rainsy Party's support for the Government's agreement with the UN, significant delays ensued, but the National Assembly approved the draft legislation in January 2001. However, it specified that only those individuals deemed 'most responsible' for the atrocities would face the tribunal, thereby implicitly exempting significant numbers of middle- and lower-ranking former Khmer Rouge officials from prosecution. The legislation was approved by the Senate later in the same month.

In July 2001 the final version of legislation providing for the trial of Khmer Rouge leaders was passed by the National Assembly, and, in the following month, after receiving the approval of the Constitutional Council, it was signed into law by King Sihanouk. The UN was left to determine whether or not the trial framework would ensure the adequate implementation of international standards of justice. In June, following the departure of the UN Secretary-General's Special Representative for Human Rights in Cambodia, Peter Leuprecht, who had voiced doubts as to the efficacy of the proposed legislation, Prime Minister Hun Sen accused the UN of interfering with Cambodian sovereignty. His views were reiterated by Prince Ranariddh.

In February 2002 the UN unexpectedly announced that it had decided to abandon negotiations with the Cambodian Government over a UN role in the establishment of a joint tribunal to try former Khmer Rouge leaders. It claimed that the legal framework created by the Government did not conform to international standards of justice and that it would not ensure either the independence or impartiality of proceedings. In response, the Government stated that it intended to proceed with the trials and that it would make no further concessions to the UN in order to facilitate the establishment of a tribunal. In June Peter Leuprecht visited the country again and intimated that attempts were under way to facilitate the restarting of talks, with the possibility that the trials could be conducted in a Cambodian court but with the inclusion of foreign judges. In the following month Prime Minister Hun Sen announced that Cambodia was prepared to compromise with the UN by amending the laws that would govern the establishment of any tribunal. In November the UN voted in favour of a draft resolution submitted by Japan and France requesting that it resume negotiations with the Cambodian Government without further delay. Hun Sen affirmed his Government's intention to co-operate with the UN in the renewal of efforts to establish a satisfactory judicial framework for the tribunal.

Following a week of exploratory talks in January 2003, negotiations subsequently recommenced in March, resulting in the signing of a draft agreement concerning the tribunal. In June the two sides concluded a formal agreement providing for the establishment of a bicameral tribunal, composed of a Trial Chamber and a Supreme Court Chamber. Under the legislation approved in 2001, only those senior officials of the Khmers Rouges deemed to bear most responsibility for the atrocities of 1975–78 were to face trial. After a significant delay, owing to the prolonged political dispute that had arisen following the 2003 elections (see below), the legislation establishing the tribunal was finally ratified by the Cambodian legislature in October 2004 and promulgated by the King in the same month. In December 2004 a UN delegation arrived in the country to discuss funding. Of the estimated total budget of US $56.3m. for what was expected to be a three-year process, the Cambodian Government agreed to fund at least $13.3m.; however, following the announcement by UN Secretary-General Kofi Annan in late April 2005 that sufficient funds had been pledged by the international community for proceedings to commence, Hun Sen insisted that no action could be taken until the stipulated $56.3m. had been transferred, in its entirety, into Cambodian government coffers. Furthermore, in August Hun Sen claimed that his country could not afford its share of the projected cost of the tribunal, but the decision in June to reject proposals for a national fund-raising campaign to this very end had raised serious questions about the Cambodian premier's level of commitment to the carriage of justice. In December UN officials arrived in Cambodia to begin preparatory work.

In November 2000, meanwhile, dozens of armed men launched an attack on official buildings in Phnom-Penh. At least seven of the gunmen were killed in the raid, which government officials initially attributed to unspecified 'terrorists'; however, some of those involved alleged that they had been brought to Phnom-Penh under false pretences and forced to carry weapons. The leader of the US-based Cambodian Freedom Fighters organization, Chhun Yasith (a citizen of the USA), subsequently issued a statement claiming responsibility for the attack on behalf of his organization and alleging that its principal intention had been to disrupt the forthcoming visit of the President of Viet Nam, Tran Duc Luong (which had originally been scheduled for late November, but which was later postponed until November 2001). Forty-seven people, including two members of the Sam Rainsy Party, were subsequently reported to have been charged with terrorism in connection with the attack.

In late June and July 2001 the trial of 32 of those who had participated in the apparent coup attempt of November 2000 took place, amid accusations that the Government had played a part in fomenting the violence in order to facilitate the intimidation of political opponents by local leaders. Three US citizens, among those arrested, were sentenced to life imprisonment *in absentia*; 27 Cambodians were also given sentences ranging from three years to life. In November 2001 a further 26 nationals were imprisoned for terms of up to 15 years, following a second mass trial which had begun in October. Two people were released owing to lack of evidence. In February 2002 a further 20 people were tried in connection with the attempted coup and sentenced to prison terms; those convicted included one US citizen. In June 2005 Chhun Yasith was arrested in California, USA, and he was subsequently indicted on charges of conspiracy to kill, and to destroy property, in a foreign country, of conspiracy to use a weapon of mass destruction outside the USA and of engaging in a military expedition against a nation with which the USA was at peace. In April 2008 he was convicted on all four charges; he was to be sentenced later in the year.

In 2001 the Prime Minister continued to prevaricate on questions of democratic reform. The stagnation of democracy in the country was reflected by the violence that surrounded the registration period for Cambodia's first multi-party local elections (scheduled for February 2002), which ended in August 2001. At least 20 of the candidates planning to mount a challenge to Hun Sen and the ruling CPP were shot dead during the election campaign, during which the opposition was denied access to the state-controlled media.

In February 2002 polling for the 1,621 *khum* (communes) resulted in an overwhelming victory for the CPP, which secured control of 1,598 *khum*. The Sam Rainsy Party won control of 13 and the FUNCINPEC Party 10. Despite numerous allegations of intimidation and electoral irregularities, the opposition parties accepted the results; according to election monitors, however, the elections could be deemed neither free nor fair.

Following its disappointing performance in the local elections of 2002, a rift developed within the FUNCINPEC Party. As an indirect result, in May Prince Chakrapong, one of the sons of King Sihanouk, founded a new political party, the Prince Norodom Chakrapong Khmer Soul party. Meanwhile, in June the FUNCINPEC Party was weakened further by the defection of one of its founding members, Hang Dara, who announced the formation of the Hang Dara Movement Democratic Party to contest the next general election.

On 27 July 2003 23 political parties contested elections to the 123-member National Assembly. The CPP secured 73 seats, the FUNCINPEC Party 26 and the Sam Rainsy Party 24. However, the failure of the CPP to secure the two-thirds' majority necessary to form a single-party government raised the prospect of a further period of political instability in Cambodia. The FUNCINPEC Party and the Sam Rainsy Party both refused to enter into a multi-party government and, instead, agreed to form the Alliance of Democrats to oppose the CPP. Initially, the Alliance insisted that it would agree to form a tripartite government only if Hun Sen tendered his resignation as Prime Minister. The stalemate continued, angering King Sihanouk, who indicated his displeasure by failing to attend the inauguration of the newly elected National Assembly, an event also boycotted by both opposition parties. King Sihanouk subsequently attempted to secure a resolution to the dispute by convening a series of talks between leading figures in the CPP and the opposition. These resulted in the conclusion of a provisional agreement by the three parties in early November regarding the formation of a joint administration, although disagreement continued as to the details of the proposed arrangement. In December the three parties finally began negotiations on the formation of a new government, and the first session of the incoming National Assembly took place later that month. However, the CPP continued to reject opposition demands concerning the composition of a new administration, insisting that Hun Sen would continue as Prime Minister. In early 2004 King Sihanouk announced that he had approved a request by the Chairman of the Senate, Chea Sim, to extend the Senate's mandate by one year in order to avert a constitutional crisis; elections to the Senate had been scheduled to take place in March of that year. In January 2004 the FUNCINPEC Party and the Sam Rainsy Party announced that they intended to establish an alliance. The Alliance of Democrats was formally established in August.

Meanwhile, a series of shootings of prominent opposition supporters in the aftermath of the elections to the National Assembly was believed to have been co-ordinated by the CPP. In January 2004 the leader of the Free Trade Union of Workers of the Kingdom of Cambodia (FTUWKC), Chea Vichea, a prominent opponent of Hun Sen, was murdered in Phnom-Penh. His killing was believed to have been politically motivated. A few days subsequently, two men were arrested on suspicion of his murder. In March the criminal investigation against both suspects was abandoned by the investigating judge on the grounds of insufficient evidence; however, on the following day, the judge was dismissed and, in June, his ruling that the investigation be abandoned was overturned by the Court of Appeal. In August 2005 the two defendants were convicted of Chea Vichea's murder, following a trial during which no defence witnesses had been called and no forensic evidence had been admitted. Both men were sentenced to 20 years' imprisonment, and were also ordered to pay compensation to Chea Vichea's family. However, family members refused to accept any compensation, stating that they did not believe that the convicted men were the real murderers. The two men appealed against the verdict, but in April 2007 the convictions were upheld.

At the end of June 2004 the political deadlock that had resulted from the 2003 national elections ended when the CPP and the FUNCINPEC Party signed a power-sharing agreement, whereby the two parties could establish a coalition Government. The formation of a new, 207-member Government (in which the CPP held 136 posts and the FUNCINPEC Party 71) was ratified by the National Assembly in the following month, and Hun Sen was once again confirmed as Prime Minister by royal decree. Prince Ranariddh of the FUNCINPEC Party was appointed President of the National Assembly. Some controversy was generated by Parliament's approval of legislation permitting the appointments of new government officials to be confirmed together rather than approved separately, as had been the case previously. Chea Sim, President of the Senate and acting Head of State during King Sihanouk's absence from the country on medical grounds, refused to sign the new legislation and left the country, purportedly also for medical reasons. The Vice-President of the Senate, and a Deputy Prime Minister in the incoming Government, Gen. Nhiek Bun Chhay, subsequently approved the bill. The role of the Sam Rainsy Party remained unclear, and the party boycotted the National Assembly in protest at its exclusion from the new Government.

In October 2004 King Sihanouk unexpectedly announced his intention to abdicate, owing to ill health. As required by the Constitution, the Royal Council of the Throne was convened to appoint a successor. The Council subsequently announced that it had appointed one of Sihanouk's sons, Prince Norodom Sihamoni, to the throne. Sihamoni's coronation took place later in that month.

In February 2005 the National Assembly voted to strip Sam Rainsy and two other Sam Rainsy Party members—Cheam Channy and Chea Poch—of their parliamentary immunity, leaving them open to several defamation lawsuits. The Sam Rainsy Party conducted another parliamentary boycott in protest, which lasted until August, when 16 of the party's 24 National Assembly members resumed their seats, stating that they felt compelled to use the appropriate channels to challenge corruption within the Government and to speak out about other issues of concern to the Cambodian people. In the same month Cheam Channy was sentenced to seven years' imprisonment for attempting to form a military group with the aim of overthrowing the Government, on which charge he had been arrested in February.

In the latter stages of 2005 Prime Minister Hun Sen intensified his efforts to suppress political dissidence. In October seven people were charged with defamation and incitement against the Government after they criticized a proposed border treaty with Viet Nam; five of the accused fled the country to avoid arrest. In December Sam Rainsy was sentenced *in absentia* to 18 months' imprisonment for defaming leaders of the ruling coalition. In early January 2006 three prominent human rights activists were arrested on charges of defamation relating to a banner displayed during a rally to mark International Human Rights Day. However, one of the three men was released within a few days of his arrest as a 'gesture of good will' to the USA, which had deplored the Cambodian Government's stern policy against dissenters. The move appeared to mark the beginning of a relaxation of the ruling coalition's stance on political opposition; by the end of January a further four men imprisoned pending trial for defamation charges had been released and all charges against them had been abandoned. Furthermore, in February King Sihamoni granted royal pardons to both Sam Rainsy (who had sent conciliatory messages to the Prime Minister and to Prince Ranariddh, apologizing for past statements against both men and offering his assurance that he would endeavour to prevent any further political disharmony) and Cheam Channy, who had served just one year of his seven-year prison sentence. Rainsy's pardon prepared the way for his return to Cambodia in mid-February. Shortly after his return he met with Hun Sen, and a few days later with Prince Ranariddh, to discuss their political and personal differences. It was hoped that the pardons would prove to be indicative of a genuine easing of tension, and a greater spirit of tolerance, between the Prime Minister and his political opponents. However, critics of the Government suggested that the issuance of the pardons had been arranged merely to influence Cambodia's major international donors prior to the Consultative Group meeting—an annual bilateral and multilateral donor meeting—which took place in Phnom-Penh in March 2006 (see Economic Affairs).

Meanwhile, in January 2006 the country's first Senate elections were held. The ballot was open only to parliamentarians and members of local administrative bodies, with the general public being ineligible to vote. The CPP received 7,854 of the 11,352 votes cast, securing 45 of the 57 seats. The FUNCINPEC Party took 10 seats and the Sam Rainsy Party obtained just two; the fourth contending party, the Khmer Democratic Party, failed to win a single seat. A further four senators were appointed by the National Assembly and King Sihamoni. In May Nhem Bun Chin of the FUNCINPEC Party was dismissed as Minister of Vocational Training and Labour, owing to alleged 'irregularities', and was replaced by Vorng Soth of the CPP. In September the National Assembly approved a law whereby legislators would no longer be granted immunity from prosecution if they expressed opinions that threatened 'the good customs of society, law and order, and national security'.

In October 2006 Prince Ranariddh was ousted from office as President of the FUNCINPEC Party, amid allegations of corruption and bribery expressed by the Secretary-General of the party, Gen. Nhiek Bun Chhay. It was this involvement in crime, Nhiek Bun Chhay claimed, that had led to a recent disintegration of the working relationship between Prince Ranariddh and Prime Minister Hun Sen; Prince Ranariddh, however, adamantly denied any wrongdoing. Keo Puth Rasmey, the son-in-law of Norodom Sihanouk and at that time Cambodian ambassador to Germany, was elected as the new party President. Rasmey was subsequently also appointed to the position of Deputy Prime Minister of the Kingdom. In November the FUNCINPEC Party filed a lawsuit against Prince Ranariddh, accusing him of embezzling approximately US $3.6m. from party coffers. In the following month Prince Ranariddh lost his seat in the National Assembly, following his decision to assume control of the Khmer Front Party (KFP), now renamed the Norodom Ranariddh Party (NRP); according to laws governing the National Assembly, any member who left his or her political party was obliged to relinquish his or her Assembly seat. Two of Prince Ranariddh's supporters—Prince Chakrapong and Chhim Seak Leng—were also removed from their seats in the Senate and the National Assembly, respectively. In March 2007 Prince Ranariddh was found guilty *in absentia* of defrauding FUNCINPEC in a property transaction. In the same month, furthermore, he was formally charged with contravening a recently introduced monogamy law. Many observers regarded this new legislation, approved in 2006, as having been deliberately directed against the Prince's long-standing extra-marital relationship. The new criminal offence of adultery carried a maximum prison sentence of 12 months.

At the second *khum* elections, held on 1 April 2007, the CPP retained control of the majority of the local posts; the party secured a total of 7,993 local positions, including 1,591 of the available commune chief posts. The SRP won 2,660 posts, of which 28 were at the level of chief. The recently established NRP failed to win any of the senior positions of commune chief, and its candidates were elected to occupy only 425 other positions.

Although the local polls were conducted under more stable political conditions than in 2002, the level of voter participation declined to less than 68%, compared with more than 87% five years previously.

Efforts to establish the tribunal to prosecute crimes by former Khmer Rouge leaders (officially known as the Extraordinary Chambers in the Courts of Cambodia—ECCC) were accelerated from March 2006, in which month UN Secretary-General Kofi Annan submitted to the Cambodian Government a list of international candidates for judicial positions within the tribunal. In May the Cambodian Supreme Council of Magistracy, the national body responsible for all judicial and prosecutorial appointments, selected 17 national and 12 international judges and prosecutors from the UN-compiled list (leaving one further reserve international judge still to be appointed). In July those selected were formally sworn in by King Sihamoni at a ceremony held in the royal palace, and later that month the two newly appointed co-prosecutors began their formal investigations, with former King Sihanouk stating that he would be willing to testify against the Khmers Rouges. At a meeting held in November, however, Cambodian and international judges failed to agree on internal rules governing the operations of the ECCC, further delaying the proceedings. In December Human Rights Watch, a non-governmental organization (NGO) based in the USA, alleged that Cambodian government interference was responsible for halting the process; the NGO urged the ECCC's judicial personnel to revise the draft rules so as to ensure that all trials would be conducted publicly, that defendants could not be sentenced in absentia and that the defence counsel would remain independent. In March 2007 it was announced that most of the procedural disagreements between Cambodian and international judges had been resolved, although differences remained regarding the role of international lawyers: the Cambodian Bar Association demanded that foreign lawyers pay a registration fee of thousands of US dollars, while the judges nominated by the UN continued to insist upon the right of defendants and victims to choose their own legal counsel. In April, however, it was agreed that international lawyers would be obliged to pay a fee of just US $500. In June agreement was finally reached on the tribunal's rules of procedure, and at the end of July Duch became the first former leader of the Khmers Rouges to be formally charged with crimes against humanity.

In August 2007 the removal by royal decree of the President of the Court of Appeal, Ly Louch Leng, following allegations of bribery, and her replacement by You Bun Leng, a judge previously appointed to serve with the ECCC, was widely regarded as seriously jeopardizing the independence and efficiency of the judiciary. Yash Ghai, the Special Representative of the UN Secretary-General for Human Rights in Cambodia (a Kenyan professor of constitutional law who had replaced Peter Leuprecht in 2005) and Leandro Despouy, the UN's Special Rapporteur on the Independence of Judges and Lawyers, issued a statement questioning the Cambodian authorities' decision to make the appointment without due regard for the country's Constitution. Moreover, concerns relating to the composition of the Supreme Council of Magistracy were reiterated. The country's highest judicial body already included a government minister and an official of the ruling party, and the appointment in August of four new members, through executive rather than constitutional channels, further diminished confidence in the system.

In the latter part of 2007 former Khmer Rouge leaders Nuon Chea, Ieng Sary and Khieu Samphan were charged with war crimes and crimes against humanity. Ieng Thirith, former Minister of Social Affairs and wife of Ieng Sary, was also charged with crimes against humanity. In a report released in October, the UN criticized Cambodia's management of the proceedings, in particular the engagement of excessive numbers of apparently unqualified staff, warning that it would withdraw from the trials process if changes were not implemented. In November, in its first public session, the tribunal began its consideration of Duch's request for bail, his lawyers arguing that his detention without trial for eight years had been a breach of international standards of justice. The request was rejected in December. In the same month Buddhist monks and nuns, joined by members of the Muslim and Christian communities which had been similarly repressed during the 1970s, took part in a march to the tribunal building to demonstrate their support for an acceleration of the protracted process of bringing to justice those responsible for the atrocities of the late 1970s.

Also in December 2007, Buddhist monks were involved in a confrontation with riot police after they had tried to deliver a petition to the Vietnamese embassy in Phnom-Penh, in an attempt to draw attention to the plight of ethnic Cambodians resident in Viet Nam. In the same month Yash Ghai undertook his fourth visit to Cambodia. The Special Representative of the UN Secretary-General concluded that Cambodia's human rights situation was deteriorating, and he expressed particular concern with regard to the numerous land expropriations and illegal forced evictions that had left thousands of families homeless. Following Yash Ghai's comments, Prime Minister Hun Sen declared his determination never to meet the UN Special Representative, reportedly referring to him as a 'human rights tourist'. The weakness of the country's judicial system, the prevalence of corruption and the dearth of official land records (most of which had been destroyed by the Khmers Rouges) remained major issues. Five leading international human rights organizations, including Human Rights Watch, expressed their deep concern at recent developments, urging the Cambodian Government to fulfil its international obligations and to respect those UN officials charged with monitoring the situation.

International relations were severely affected by the events of July 1997. The USA, Germany and Japan suspended all but humanitarian assistance, and in October 1998 the US House of Representatives adopted a resolution accusing Hun Sen of genocide. Another serious consequence was the decision by ASEAN to postpone indefinitely Cambodia's admission to the grouping, which had been scheduled for July 1997. At the end of that month Hun Sen invited ASEAN to mediate in the Cambodian crisis and held discussions with the grouping in early August. Prior to the ASEAN summit meeting in Hanoi in December 1998, despite the formation of a Cambodian coalition Government in November, Singapore, Thailand and the Philippines remained opposed to Cambodia's immediate accession to the organization. However, the host country, Viet Nam, then announced that Cambodia had been accepted as the 10th member of ASEAN, although the formal admission was to take place later, at an unspecified date. Cambodia duly acceded to ASEAN on 30 April 1999. A further significant consequence of the events of July 1997 was the decision of the UN Accreditation Committee to leave Cambodia's seat at the UN vacant. However, following the formation of a coalition Government in November 1998, Cambodia regained its seat at the UN in December.

In August 2002, following a meeting of ASEAN in Brunei, Cambodia became a signatory to an anti-terrorism pact originally drawn up by Malaysia, Indonesia and the Philippines in May of that year; the pact was intended to increase regional co-operation on security issues. In November the country hosted the annual ASEAN summit meeting, which was also attended by the Republic of Korea, Japan and China, as well as India, which was present for the first time. During the meeting a framework agreement was signed to establish an ASEAN-China free trade area by 2010.

Relations between Cambodia and the People's Republic of China (which had formerly supported the PDK) improved from the mid-1990s. China continued to provide support, and in November 2000 President Jiang Zemin paid a two-day official visit to Cambodia, the first by a Chinese head of state in more than 35 years. China defended its support of the Khmers Rouges during the 1970s, claiming that its limited assistance had been intended to help maintain Cambodia's independence from foreign powers. In August 2005 King Sihamoni undertook an official visit to China, and Chinese Premier Wen Jiabao made a reciprocal visit to Phnom-Penh in April 2006.

In January 1994 Chuan Leekpai undertook the first-ever official visit to Cambodia by a Thai Prime Minister. Relations between Cambodia and Thailand had been strained by the Thai armed forces' unauthorized links with the PDK (which controlled illicit trade in gems and timber along the Thai border) and by Cambodian allegations of Thai involvement in the July 1994 coup attempt, but improved in September 1995 when the two countries signed an agreement to establish a joint border commission. Thailand remained neutral following the events of mid-1997, but extended humanitarian assistance to the estimated 35,000 refugees who crossed into Thailand to avoid the fighting in the north-west of Cambodia. In June 2001 the Thai Prime Minister, Thaksin Shinawatra, visited Cambodia, emphasizing the improved state of bilateral relations. However, in January 2003 demonstrators attacked the Thai embassy and several Thai-owned businesses in Phnom-Penh, having been provoked by comments, wrongly attributed to a Thai actress,

CAMBODIA

Introductory Survey

that implied that the temples at Angkor Wat had been stolen from Thailand. The violence escalated, prompting the Thai Government to withdraw its ambassador, together with more than 500 Thai nationals resident in Cambodia, and to downgrade diplomatic relations. Prime Minister Hun Sen subsequently issued a formal apology to the Thai Government. In April the Thai ambassador returned to Phnom-Penh, and in mid-2003 the Cambodian and Thai Cabinets held an unprecedented joint meeting. In September almost all of those Cambodians who had been imprisoned for their involvement in the riots were released, and in October 2004 the Thai embassy in Phnom-Penh reopened. Prime Minister Hun Sen visited Bangkok in May 2005 to commemorate the 55th anniversary of bilateral relations. A memorandum of understanding (MOU) pertaining to information and broadcasting was signed by the two countries in October of that year and a second MOU, which provided for a single tourist visa valid for both countries, was signed in the following month. Following the removal of Thaksin's Government by a military coup in September 2006 (see the chapter on Thailand), Hun Sen stated that relations between the two countries remained unchanged and that Cambodia respected the right of Thailand to resolve its domestic affairs without international interference.

In April 1995 Cambodia, Thailand, Viet Nam and Laos signed an agreement providing for the establishment of the Mekong River Commission (see p. 413), which was to co-ordinate the sustainable development of the resources of the Lower Mekong River Basin. In October 1999 the leaders of Cambodia, Laos and Viet Nam convened in the Laotian capital for their first 'unofficial' Indo-Chinese summit meeting. In November 2005 Prime Minister Hun Sen visited Viet Nam to discuss various bilateral issues, and the two countries signed a supplementary border treaty to complement an existing treaty signed by Cambodia and Viet Nam in 1985; the new agreement envisaged that the demarcation of the border between the two countries would be finalized by December 2008. In March 2006 King Sihamoni made his first official visit to Viet Nam.

In February 2007, for the first time in more than 30 years, a US navy frigate docked in Cambodia, visiting the port of Sihanoukville, where the crew assisted with local naval training, construction work and medical care. In the same month US President George W. Bush signed a congressional appropriations resolution for the forthcoming fiscal year. This contained 'no restrictions on direct US government funding of Cambodian government facilities' and followed the USA's decision to resume direct funding, which had remained suspended since 1997.

Cambodia's relations with Japan continued to improve, the latter having become a leading donor of development aid to the country. In 2005/06, in addition to its contribution of US $22m. towards the financing of the Khmer Rouge trials (see above), Japan provided aid totalling almost $115m., pledging a similar amount for the following fiscal year. In June 2007, during an official visit to Tokyo, Prime Minister Hun Sen and his Japanese counterpart signed an agreement to promote investment in Cambodia. The issue of North Korea's nuclear activity was also discussed, and Cambodia, previously a staunch ally of the North Korean regime, undertook to support the next resolution at the UN General Assembly relating to the human rights situation in North Korea. Nevertheless, in November the North Korean Prime Minister, Kim Yong Il, accompanied by a delegation that included various government ministers, paid a four-day official visit to Cambodia, where agreements relating to shipping links and trade were signed.

In June 2007 the inaugural session of the Cambodia Development Cooperation Forum (CDCF) was held in Phnom-Penh. Chaired solely by the Cambodian Government, the new forum replaced the Consultative Group and was to complement the implementation of the National Strategic Development Plan. Attended by about 25 delegations from the international community, the first meeting resulted in an annual total of US $689m. being pledged by overseas donors, for the first time including China. The second CDCF meeting was scheduled for December 2008.

Government

The Kingdom of Cambodia is a constitutional monarchy. The monarch is the Head of State and is selected by the Throne Council from among descendants of three royal lines. Legislative power is vested in the 123-member National Assembly, the lower chamber, which is elected for a term of five years by universal adult suffrage, and the 61-member Senate, the upper chamber, 57 of whose members are elected by parliamentarians and members of local administrative bodies, while the remaining four members are appointed by the National Assembly and the King. Executive power is held by the Cabinet (the Royal Government of Cambodia), headed by the Prime Minister, who is appointed by the King at the recommendation of the Chairman of the National Assembly from among the representatives of the majority party.

For local administration the Kingdom of Cambodia is divided into provinces, municipalities and districts, known as *khan*, *khum* and *sangkat*.

Defence

As assessed at November 2007, the total strength of the Royal Cambodian Armed Forces was estimated to be 124,300, comprising an army of 75,000, a navy of 2,800, an air force of 1,500 and provincial forces of about 45,000. There was also a paramilitary force numbering some 67,000 men and women. A system of conscription was officially in force, for those aged between 18 and 35, for five years; however, conscription has not been implemented since 1993. In 2007 government expenditure on defence was budgeted at an estimated 557,000m. riels.

Economic Affairs

In 2006, according to the World Bank, Cambodia's gross national income (GNI), measured at average 2004–06 prices, was US $6,906m., equivalent to $480 per head (or $2,920 per head on an international purchasing-power parity basis). During 1996–2006, it was estimated, the population increased at an average annual rate of 2.1%, while gross domestic product (GDP) per head increased, in real terms, by an average of 6.5% per year during the same period. Cambodia's overall GDP increased, in real terms, at an average annual rate of 8.8% during 1996–2006. According to the Asian Development Bank (ADB), GDP increased by 10.8% in 2006 and by 9.6% in 2007.

According to the IMF, agriculture (including forestry and fishing) contributed an estimated 31.7% of GDP in 2006. In that year the sector engaged an estimated 57.4% of the economically active population, but remained extremely vulnerable to adverse weather conditions, this problem being compounded by inadequate rural infrastructure and a lack of farm inputs such as fertilizers. In 1999 Cambodia announced its intention to resume exports of rice, which subsequently became a significant source of export revenue. In 2006 paddy rice production was estimated at 6.3m. tons. Other principal crops include cassava, maize, sugar cane and bananas. Rubber and timber are the two principal export commodities. The forestry sector accounted for only an estimated 3.2% of GDP in 2006, as reserves continued to be depleted and reafforestation remained inadequate. The fishing sector was also adversely affected by deforestation, which caused reductions in freshwater fishing catches, owing to the silting up of lakes and rivers. According to the IMF, however, the GDP of the fishing sector increased at an average annual rate of 2.0% in 2001–2006, and contributed an estimated 6.3% of GDP in 2006. According to figures from the ADB, agricultural GDP increased, in real terms, at an average annual rate of 4.1% during 1995–2006. The GDP of the agricultural sector rose by 5.5% in 2006 and by 4.5% in 2007.

Industry (including mining, manufacturing, construction and utilities) contributed an estimated 27.6% of GDP in 2006, and employed an estimated 14.5% of the labour force in the same year, according to the IMF. In real terms, according to figures from the ADB, industrial GDP increased at an average annual rate of 15.0% during 1995–2006. Sectoral GDP growth reached 18.3% in 2006 and 7.5% in 2007.

In 2006 mining and quarrying contributed only an estimated 0.4% of GDP and employed only an estimated 0.2% of the working population. Cambodia's mineral resources include phosphates, gemstones, iron ore, bauxite, silicon and manganese ore. In April 2005 plans were drafted to carry out exploratory activities in regions containing gold and other precious minerals. In the 1990s several agreements on petroleum exploration were signed with foreign enterprises. In early 2007 it was announced that Cambodia hoped to commence the exploitation of its petroleum reserves by 2010. Preliminary forecasts suggested that production in Block A alone might reach 12,000 barrels per day within 20 years, the petroleum deposits in this sector having been originally identified by a US company. Cambodia also has substantial reserves of natural gas. According to figures from the ADB, the GDP of the mining sector increased, in real terms, at an average annual rate of 12.5% during 1995–2006; growth in mining GDP reached 26.3% in 2005 and 16.0% in 2006.

The manufacturing sector contributed an estimated 19.6% of GDP in 2006 and employed 10.8% of the labour force in that year, according to the IMF. The sector is dominated by rice milling and the production of ready-made garments, household goods, textiles, tyres and pharmaceutical products. The manufacture of garments, mostly for export, grew rapidly during the 1990s, and by 2003 approximately 230,000 workers were engaged in garment manufacture. The total value of garment exports increased from US $2,261m. in 2005 to $2,727m. in 2006, in which year garment exports accounted for almost three-quarters of Cambodia's total exports. Although sectoral expansion did decelerate considerably in 2005, the expiry at the end of 2004 of the Multi-Fibre Arrangement (MFA—under which Cambodia had been granted quotas to export textiles to the USA and Europe) was less detrimental to the country than had been anticipated. According to ADB figures, the GDP of the manufacturing sector increased, in real terms, at an average annual rate of 17.3% during 1995–2006. Growth in manufacturing GDP was 9.7% in 2005 and 17.4% in 2006.

Household energy is derived principally from timber. All commercial energy used in Cambodia is imported. In 2003 only 17% of Cambodian households had access to electricity. In 2004 the country had an installed capacity of 190 MW, of which diesel generating units accounted for 84%, steam turbines 9% and hydropower 7%. In 2002 Cambodia signed an agreement with China, Thailand, Laos, Myanmar and Viet Nam to form a regional power distribution system, enabling hydropower development in the Mekong River area.

In 2006 the services sector contributed an estimated 40.7% of GDP and engaged 28.1% of the economically active population, according to the IMF. The tourism sector has become increasingly significant since 2000, as a result of improved political stability. Tourist arrivals totalled more than 1.3m. in 2006, when gross tourist receipts reached US $963m. The number of visitors was reported to have exceeded 2m. in 2007. In real terms, the GDP of the services sector increased at an average annual rate of 9.1% during 1995–2006. Growth in the sector reached 10.3% in 2006 and 10.0% in 2007.

In 2006 Cambodia recorded a visible trade deficit of US $1,056.1m., while there was a deficit of $337.4m. on the current account of the balance of payments. In 2006 the principal sources of imports were Hong Kong (32.5%), Thailand (18.1%), the People's Republic of China (14.5%) and Viet Nam (11.9%). Other major sources were France, the Republic of Korea and Singapore. In the same year the principal market for exports was the USA (63.3%); other important purchasers were Germany, the United Kingdom, France, Canada and Japan. The principal exports in 2006 were garments (accounting for 73.8% of the total), rice, rubber and fish, along with logs and sawn timber. The country's imports included petroleum products (accounting for 4.1% of the total), vehicles, cigarettes, motorcycles, cement and clothing.

Cambodia's overall budget deficit in 2007 was projected at 1,285m. riels. According to the ADB, Cambodia's external debt at the end of 2007 totalled US $2,464m. In that year the cost of debt-servicing was equivalent to 0.5% of revenue from exports of goods and services. According to figures from the ADB, the annual rate of inflation in Phnom-Penh averaged an estimated 4.7% during 1995–2006; consumer prices increased by 4.7% in 2006 and by 5.9% in 2007. The unemployment rate was estimated at 3.1% in 2004.

Cambodia is a member of the UN Economic and Social Commission for Asia and the Pacific (ESCAP, see p. 35), of the Asian Development Bank (ADB, see p. 182), of the Mekong River Commission (see p. 413) and of the Colombo Plan (see p. 411). Cambodia was formally admitted to the Association of South East Asian Nations (ASEAN, see p. 185) in April 1999. Following the implementation of the ASEAN Free Trade Area (AFTA, see p. 186) in January 2002, Cambodia was granted until 2007 to comply with the 0%–5% tariff agreement. Cambodia became a member of the World Trade Organization (WTO, see p. 396) in October 2004.

In mid-2004 the Cambodian Government announced the so-called 'Rectangular Strategy', focusing on the promotion of economic growth through: the development of agriculture; the expansion of the private sector; the repair and construction of physical infrastructure; and the development of human resources. According to a poverty assessment report published by the World Bank in early 2006, living standards for much of the Cambodian population had markedly improved since the mid-1990s. However, the economy remained narrowly based on the tourism and garment industries. In a report issued in 2006 Transparency International, a global organization committed to countering corruption, noted that the practice of corruption appeared 'to have permeated almost every aspect of Cambodian life'. Measures to improve and diversify agricultural production were outlined in the National Strategic Development Plan (NSDP) for 2006–10, which aimed to reduce the rate of poverty to 25%. The Cambodia Development Cooperation Forum (CDCF), which superseded the Consultative Group of international donors in 2007, held its first meeting in June, when it was announced that in that year aid from donor countries was to total $689m., with similar levels of support being envisaged for 2008–09; the Financial Sector Development Strategy 2006–2015 was also officially inaugurated. As plans for the exploitation of Cambodia's petroleum reserves proceeded (see above), initial assessments indicated that future oil and gas receipts might treble the Government's revenue, although some analysts expressed doubts with regard to the prudent management of future income from these resources. In February 2008 the ADB approved a series of loans and grants amounting to $71.8m., in support of a programme to improve secondary education facilities, to assist farmers in the area of Tonlé Sap Lake, to promote reform of the financial system and to rehabilitate major roads. The Cambodian Government was to contribute $30.5m. of the requisite total of $115.0m., with Australia providing a grant of $12.8m. towards the various projects. The ADB envisaged GDP growth of 7.5% in 2008.

Education

Education is compulsory for six years between the ages of six and 12. Primary education begins at the age of six and lasts for six years. In 2004/05 enrolment at pre-primary level included 10% of children in the relevant age group (males 9%; females 9%). Enrolment at primary level included 98.9% of children in the relevant age group (males 96%; females 97%), and enrolment at secondary level included 24.5% of children in the relevant age group (males 26%; females 22%). In 2003/04 there were 1,345 pre-primary institutions, and in 2002/03 there were 5,915 primary schools, 411 lower secondary schools and 183 upper secondary schools. In 2005 enrolment at tertiary level was equivalent to 4.0% of the relevant age-group (males 5.0%; females 2.0%). In 2003 the Ministry of Education, Youth and Sport was allocated 300,000m. riels (10.3% of total budgetary expenditure). In February 2008 the Asian Development Bank (ADB) agreed to grant the sum of US $27.1m. for the purposes of improving the quality of secondary education in Cambodia. The ADB was to provide funding for textbooks, the training of 14,400 teachers and equipment for teacher-training colleges.

Public Holidays

2008: 1 January (International New Year's Day), 7 January (Victory Day over the Genocide Regime), 21 February (Meak Bochea Day), 8 March (International Women's Day), 13–15 April (Cambodian New Year), 1 May (Labour Day), 13–15 May (King Sihamoni's Birthday), 19 May (Visaka Buchea Day), 23 May (Royal Ploughing Ceremony), 1 June (International Children's Day), 18 June (Former Queen's Birthday), 24 September (Constitution Day), 28–30 September (Bonn Pchum Ben), 23 October (Anniversary of Paris Peace Agreement on Cambodia), 31 October (Former King Sihanouk's Birthday), 9 November (Independence Day), 11–13 November (Water and Moon Festival), 10 December (Human Rights Day).

2009: 1 January (International New Year's Day), 7 January (Victory Day over the Genocide Regime), February* (Meak Bochea Day), 8 March (International Women's Day), April* (Cambodian New Year), 1 May (Labour Day), May* (Visaka Buchea Day), May* (Royal Ploughing Ceremony), 13–15 May (King Sihamoni's Birthday), 1 June (International Children's Day), 18 June (Former Queen's Birthday), 24 September (Constitution Day), September/October* (Bonn Pchum Ben), 23 October (Anniversary of Paris Peace Agreement on Cambodia), 31 October (Former King Sihanouk's Birthday), November* (Water and Moon Festival), 9 November (Independence Day), 10 December (Human Rights Day).

* Date to be confirmed.

Weights and Measures

The metric system is in force.

CAMBODIA

Statistical Survey

Source (unless otherwise stated): National Institute of Statistics, Ministry of Planning, Sangkat Boeung Keng Kang 1, blvd Monivong, Phnom-Penh; tel. (23) 216538; fax (23) 213650; e-mail census@camnet.com.kh; internet www.nis.gov.kh.

Area and Population

AREA, POPULATION AND DENSITY

Area (sq km)	181,035*
Population (census results)†	
17 April 1962	5,728,771
Prior to elections of 1 May 1981	6,682,000
3 March 1998	
Males	5,511,408
Females	5,926,248
Total	11,437,656
Population (official projections at mid-year)	
2006	14,080,653
2007	14,363,519
2008	14,655,950
Density (per sq km) at mid-2008	81.0

* 69,898 sq miles; figure includes Tonlé Sap lake (approximately 3,000 sq km).
† Excluding adjustments for underenumeration.

PROVINCES
(official population projections at mid-2008)

	Area (sq km)*	Population	Density (per sq km)
Banteay Mean Chey	6,679	839,037	125.6
Bat Dambang	11,702	1,057,263	90.3
Kampong Cham	9,799	1,944,031	198.4
Kampong Chhnang	5,521	551,472	99.9
Kampong Spueu	7,017	779,910	111.1
Kampong Thum	13,814	722,338	52.3
Kampot	4,873	627,974	128.9
Kandal	3,568	1,300,974	364.6
Kaoh Kong	11,160	215,674	19.3
Kracheh	11,094	360,691	32.5
Mondol Kiri	14,288	46,210	3.2
Phnom-Penh	290	1,441,692	4,971.4
Preah Vihear	13,788	164,764	11.9
Prey Veaeng	4,883	1,073,917	219.9
Pousat	12,692	451,141	35.5
Rotanak Kiri	10,782	131,835	12.2
Siem Reab	10,299	924,923	89.8
Krong Preah Sihanouk	868	231,184	266.3
Stueng Traeng	11,092	112,684	10.2
Svay Rieng	2,966	557,058	187.8
Takaev	3,563	937,556	263.1
Otdar Mean Chey	6,158	105,488	17.1
Krong Kaeb	336	41,589	123.8
Krong Pailin	803	36,545	45.5
Total	178,035	14,655,950	82.3

* Excluding Tonlé Sap lake (approximately 3,000 sq km).

PRINCIPAL TOWNS
(population at 1998 census)

Phnom-Penh (capital)	999,804	Bat Dambang (Battambang)	139,964
Preah Sihanouk (Sihanoukville)*	155,690	Siem Reab (Siem Reap)	119,528

* Also known as Kampong Saom (Kompong Som).

Mid-2005 ('000, incl. suburbs, UN estimate): Phnom-Penh 1,364 (Source: UN, *World Urbanization Prospects: The 2005 Revision*).

BIRTHS AND DEATHS
(annual averages, UN estimates)

	1990–95	1995–2000	2000–05
Birth rate (per 1,000)	41.0	32.0	27.5
Death rate (per 1,000)	11.6	10.4	10.0

Source: UN, *World Population Prospects: The 2006 Revision*.

2004: Live births 384,267; Deaths 124,391 (Source: UN, *Population and Vital Statistics Report*).

Expectation of life (years at birth, WHO estimates): 53.8 (males 50.7; females 56.8) in 2005 (Source: WHO, *World Health Statistics*).

EMPLOYMENT
('000 persons)

	2004	2005	2006
Agriculture, forestry and fishing	4,520	4,655	4,619
Mining and quarrying	17	19	20
Manufacturing	720	789	870
Electricity, gas and water	16	17	19
Construction	195	234	260
Wholesale and retail trade	1,042	1,104	1,140
Restaurants and hotels	30	43	61
Transport and communications	196	206	217
Financial intermediation	16	23	32
Real estate and renting	15	16	184
Public administration	180	185	18
Education	106	113	120
Health and social work	37	43	49
Other social services	78	89	108
Other services	327	341	336
Total employed	7,496	7,878	8,053

Source: IMF, *Cambodia: Selected Issues and Statistical Appendix* (August 2007).

Health and Welfare

KEY INDICATORS

Total fertility rate (children per woman, 2005)	3.9
Under-5 mortality rate (per 1,000 live births, 2005)	143
HIV/AIDS (% of persons aged 15–49, 2005)	1.6
Physicians (per 1,000 head, 2000)	0.16
Hospital beds (per 1,000 head, 2004)	0.57
Health expenditure (2004): US $ per head (PPP)	139.8
Health expenditure (2004): % of GDP	6.7
Health expenditure (2004): public (% of total)	25.8
Access to water (% of persons, 2004)	41
Access to sanitation (% of persons, 2004)	17
Human Development Index (2005): ranking	131
Human Development Index (2005): value	0.598

For sources and definitions, see explanatory note on p. vi.

Agriculture

PRINCIPAL CROPS
('000 metric tons)

	2004	2005	2006
Rice (paddy)	4,170.3	5,986.2	6,264.1
Maize	256.7	247.8	376.9
Sweet potatoes	35.1	39.1	45.3
Cassava (Manioc)	362.1	535.6	2,182.0
Dry beans	28.5	45.0	59.9
Soybeans (Soya beans)	82.3	179.1	98.3
Groundnuts (in shell)	21.5	22.6	23.8
Sesame seed*	10.3	10.4	10.4
Coconuts*	69.7	70.1	70.1
Sugar cane	130.4	118.2	141.7
Tobacco (leaves)	2.5	14.1	14.2
Natural rubber	26.1	20.3	21.4
Oranges	63.0	68.1	68.1
Guavas, mangoes and mangosteens*	37.8	39.5	39.5
Pineapples*	17.0	17.6	17.6
Bananas*	153.4	157.6	157.6

* FAO estimate(s).

Aggregate production ('000 metric tons, may include official, semi-official or estimated data): Total cereals 4,426.9 in 2004, 6,234.0 in 2005, 6,641.1 in 2006; Total roots and tubers 424.2 in 2004, 602.8 in 2005, 2,255.3 in 2006; Total vegetables (incl. melons) 475.0 in 2004, 481.3 in 2005, 481.3 in 2006; Total fruits (excl. melons) 334.3 in 2004, 346.1 in 2005, 346.1 in 2006.

Source: FAO.

LIVESTOCK
('000 head, year ending September)

	2004	2005	2006
Horses*	28	n.a.	28
Cattle	3,040	3,184	3,345
Buffaloes	651	677	724
Pigs	2,429	2,689	2,741
Chickens	13,991	15,086	15,136
Ducks*	7,000	7,000	7,000

* FAO estimates.
Source: FAO.

LIVESTOCK PRODUCTS
('000 metric tons, FAO estimates)

	2004	2005	2006
Cattle meat	54.7	57.4	60.2
Buffalo meat	9.1	9.4	10.1
Pig meat	122.5	126.7	126.7
Chicken meat	16.0	16.5	16.5
Cows' milk	20.7	21.7	22.7
Hen eggs	13.3	13.3	13.3
Other poultry eggs	3.8	3.8	3.8

Source: FAO.

Forestry

ROUNDWOOD REMOVALS
('000 cubic metres, excl. bark, FAO estimates)

	2003	2004	2005
Sawlogs, veneer logs and logs for sleepers	100	100	100
Other industrial wood	25	25	25
Fuel wood	9,558	9,386	9,221
Total	9,683	9,511	9,346

2006: Figures assumed to be unchanged from 2005 (FAO estimates).
Source: FAO.

SAWNWOOD PRODUCTION
('000 cubic metres, incl. railway sleepers)

	2001	2002	2003*
Total (all broadleaved)	5	10	4

* FAO estimate.
2004–06: Figures assumed to be unchanged from 2003 (FAO estimates).
Source: FAO.

Fishing

('000 metric tons, live weight)

	2003	2004	2005
Capture*	364.4	305.8	384.0
Freshwater fishes	308.3	249.6	323.5
Marine fishes*	33.7	34.3	37.0
Prawns and shrimps*	12.3	12.6	13.5
Aquaculture*	18.5	20.7	26.0
Total catch*	382.9	326.7	410.0

* FAO estimates.

Note: Figures exclude crocodiles, recorded by number rather than by weight. The total number of estuarine crocodiles caught was: 78,008 in 2003; 74,820 in 2004; 120,000 in 2005. Also excluded are aquatic plants (metric tons, aquaculture only): 7,800 in 2003; 16,840 in 2004; 16,000 in 2005 (FAO estimate).

Source: FAO.

Mining

('000 metric tons)

	2004	2005	2006*
Laterite (blocks)	118.4	62.4	65.0
Salt (unrefined)	40.0	—	—

* Estimates.
Source: US Geological Survey.

Industry

SELECTED PRODUCTS

	2004	2005	2006
Plywood ('000 cu m)*†	4	4	4
Electric energy (million kWh)‡	743.2	879.4	1,087.1

* Source: FAO.
† FAO estimate.
‡ Source: Electricity Authority of Cambodia.

Cigarettes (million): 4,175 in 1987; 4,200 annually in 1988–92 (estimates by US Department of Agriculture).

CAMBODIA

Statistical Survey

Finance

CURRENCY AND EXCHANGE RATES

Monetary Units
100 sen = 1 riel.

Sterling, Dollar and Euro Equivalents (30 November 2007)
£1 sterling = 8,269.740 riels;
US $1 = 4,002.000 riels;
€1 = 5,907.351 riels;
10,000 riels = £1.21 = $2.50 = €1.69.

Average Exchange Rate (riels per US $)
2004 4,016.250
2005 4,092.500
2006 4,103.250

BUDGET
('000 million riels)

Revenue	2005	2006	2007*
Tax revenue	1,948	2,372	2,602
Direct taxes	222	331	340
Trade tax	573	644	769
Value-added tax	677	836	907
Excise duties	380	418	475
Non-tax revenue	578	681	613
Forestry	3	2	20
Enterprises and immobile leases	28	35	28
Civil aviation	30	30	50
Tourism income	44	59	84
Casino royalties	44	77	62
Posts and telecommunications	123	83	92
Passports and visas	85	95	106
Capital revenue	127	377	45
Total	**2,653**	**3,431**	**3,261**

Expenditure	2005	2006	2007*
Current expenditure	2,073	2,378	2,861
Salaries	835	975	1,075
Operating costs	783	974	663
Economic transfers	85	137	530
Social transfers	28	34	306
Interest	55	50	50
Provincial expenditure	130	11	118
Other current expenditure	157	196	118
Capital expenditure	1,441	1,639	1,685
Locally financed	315	381	n.a.
Externally financed	1,126	1,258	n.a.
Total	**3,514**	**4,016**	**4,546**

* Budget projections.

Source: IMF, *Cambodia: Selected Issues and Statistical Appendix* (August 2007).

INTERNATIONAL RESERVES
(US $ million at 31 December)

	2004	2005	2006
IMF special drawing rights	0.08	0.24	0.19
Foreign exchange	943.13	952.74	1,157.07
Total	**943.21**	**952.98**	**1,157.26**

Source: IMF, *International Financial Statistics*.

MONEY SUPPLY
('000 million riels at 31 December)

	2004	2005	2006
Currency outside banks	1,132.45	1,283.83	1,603.11
Demand deposits at deposit money banks	20.94	24.60	50.35
Total money (incl. others)	**1,156.41**	**1,311.04**	**1,659.69**

Source: IMF, *International Financial Statistics*.

COST OF LIVING
(Consumer Price Index for Phnom-Penh; base: July–December 2000 = 100)

	2004	2005	2006
Food, beverages and tobacco	107.5	116.7	124.1
Clothing and footwear	86.6	89.8	93.3
Housing and utilities	113.1	116.4	119.2
Household furnishings and operations	95.0	94.4	96.4
Medical care and health expenses	102.2	102.2	103.5
Transport and communication	110.4	123.0	134.2
Recreation and education	109.4	110.3	111.6
Personal care and effects	104.7	107.3	113.1
All items	**108.9**	**115.2**	**120.6**

NATIONAL ACCOUNTS
('000 million riels at current prices)

Expenditure on the Gross Domestic Product

	2004	2005	2006
Government final consumption expenditure	961	1,048	1,033
Private final consumption expenditure	18,159	21,716	24,460
Change in stocks	–144	223	585
Gross fixed capital formation	3,932	4,936	5,820
Total domestic expenditure	**22,908**	**27,923**	**31,898**
Exports of goods and services	13,636	16,505	20,505
Less Imports of goods and services	15,201	18,736	22,594
GDP in purchasers' values	**21,343**	**25,693**	**29,809**
GDP at constant 2000 prices	19,351	21,956	24,334

Gross Domestic Product by Economic Activity

	2004	2005	2006
Agriculture, hunting, forestry and fishing	6,301	7,909	8,972
Mining and quarrying	74	97	115
Manufacturing	4,027	4,585	5,541
Electricity, gas and water	110	124	164
Construction	1,288	1,631	1,995
Trade	2,009	2,364	2,661
Hotels and restaurants	893	1,117	1,301
Transport, storage and communications	1,528	1,899	2,157
Finance	232	294	378
Public administration	419	464	515
Real estate and business	1,535	1,701	1,947
Other services	1,782	2,163	2,559
Sub-total	**20,197**	**24,348**	**28,305**
Less Imputed bank service charge	206	253	290
GDP at factor cost	**19,991**	**24,095**	**28,015**
Indirect taxes, *less* subsidies	1,352	1,598	1,795
GDP in purchasers' values	**21,343**	**25,693**	**29,809**

Source: IMF, *Cambodia: Selected Issues and Statistical Appendix* (August 2007).

BALANCE OF PAYMENTS
(US $ million)

	2004	2005	2006
Exports of goods f.o.b.	2,588.9	2,910.3	3,693.1
Imports of goods f.o.b.	–3,269.5	–3,927.8	–4,749.2
Trade balance	**–680.6**	**–1,017.6**	**–1,056.1**
Exports of services	804.9	1,118.1	1,296.3
Imports of services	–514.0	–647.1	–789.8
Balance on goods and services	**–390.1**	**–546.5**	**–549.6**
Other income received	48.6	67.7	90.0
Other income paid	–269.6	–321.8	–380.4
Balance on goods, services and income	**–611.1**	**–800.6**	**–840.0**
Current transfers received	443.7	460.8	527.2

CAMBODIA

—continued	2004	2005	2006
Current transfers paid	−15.5	−20.7	−24.5
Current balance	**−182.9**	**−360.5**	**−337.4**
Capital account (net)	68.1	94.9	267.6
Direct investment abroad	−10.2	−6.3	−8.4
Direct investment from abroad	131.4	381.2	483.2
Portfolio investment assets	−8.0	−7.2	−12.1
Other investment assets	−91.3	−302.8	−540.1
Other investment liabilities	197.3	270.0	398.8
Net errors and omissions	−45.8	5.1	−43.4
Overall balance	**58.5**	**74.5**	**208.2**

Source: IMF, *International Financial Statistics*.

External Trade

PRINCIPAL COMMODITIES
(US $ million)

Imports c.i.f.	2004	2005	2006
Cigarettes	81	80	103
Petroleum products	172	164	212
Motorcycles	45	55	93
Vehicles	65	90	105
Clothing	38	45	47
Cement	40	44	53
Total (incl. others)	**3,538**	**4,254**	**5,145**

Exports f.o.b.	2004	2005	2006
Crude rubber	115	119	175
Logs and sawn timber	16	16	18
Clothing	2,079	2,261	2,727
Fish	69	76	90
Rice	114	177	332
Total (incl. others)	**2,589**	**2,910**	**3,693**

Note: Totals include imports for re-export and estimates for unrecorded items.

Source: IMF, *Cambodia: Selected Issues and Statistical Appendix* (August 2007).

PRINCIPAL TRADING PARTNERS
(US $ million)

Imports c.i.f.	2004	2005	2006
China, People's Republic	413.1	204.2	612.1
France	77.7	42.0	119.2
Hong Kong	231.3	141.4	1,378.1
Indonesia	47.7	154.0	70.2
Japan	83.7	52.6	83.1
Korea, Republic	99.6	95.1	111.6
Malaysia	78.6	40.7	51.1
Singapore	168.7	90.1	105.7
Thailand	341.8	172.3	767.4
Viet Nam	144.6	62.5	505.6
Total (incl. others)	**2,074.6**	**1,268.3**	**4,235.5**

Exports f.o.b.	2004	2005	2006
Canada	25.1	47.6	103.2
France	94.5	62.8	124.8
Germany	237.7	77.3	335.4
Hong Kong	5.2	333.5	7.3
Japan	10.5	6.6	101.0
Malaysia	30.6	13.8	85.9
Singapore	42.4	18.1	21.2
United Kingdom	175.3	52.7	154.1
USA	1,312.0	665.9	2,116.6
Viet Nam	62.5	22.4	44.1
Total (incl. others)	**2,187.7**	**1,368.8**	**3,344.6**

Source: Asian Development Bank, *Key Indicators of Developing Asian and Pacific Countries*.

Transport

RAILWAYS
(traffic)

	1997	1998	1999
Freight carried ('000 metric tons)	16	294	259
Freight ton-km ('000)	36,514	75,721	76,171
Passengers ('000)	553	438	431
Passenger-km ('000)	50,992	43,847	49,894

Source: Ministry of Economy and Finance, Phnom-Penh.

2000: Passenger-km (million) 15; Freight ton-km ('000) 91 (Source: UN, *Statistical Yearbook*).

ROAD TRAFFIC
(estimated number of motor vehicles in use)

	2002	2003	2004
Passenger cars	209,128	219,602	235,298
Buses and coaches	3,196	3,269	3,502
Trucks	29,968	30,448	31,946
Other vehicles	421	428	440
Motorcycles and mopeds	586,278	619,748	646,944

Sources: Ministry of Public Works and Transport, Phnom-Penh, and Phnom-Penh Municipal Traffic Police.

SHIPPING
Merchant Fleet
(registered at 31 December)

	2004	2005	2006
Number of vessels	675	732	782
Displacement ('000 grt)	1,821.5	1,876.4	1,951.4

Source: Lloyd's Register-Fairplay, *World Fleet Statistics*.

International Sea-borne Freight Traffic
(estimates, '000 metric tons)

	1988	1989	1990
Goods loaded	10	10	11
Goods unloaded	100	100	95

Source: UN, *Monthly Bulletin of Statistics*.

Tourism

FOREIGN TOURIST ARRIVALS BY COUNTRY OF RESIDENCE

Country of residence	2004	2005	2006
Australia	38,211	47,465	26,543
Canada	20,680	24,110	14,235
China, People's Repub.	46,325	59,153	36,620
France	58,076	68,947	32,011
Germany	29,112	35,560	19,032
Japan	118,157	137,849	70,875
Korea, Republic	128,423	216,584	148,672
Malaysia	32,864	36,876	36,116
Philippines	32,910	40,261	24,382
Singapore	17,830	18,966	13,447
Taiwan	53,041	54,771	34,927
Thailand	55,086	63,631	35,698
United Kingdom	64,129	66,535	33,936
USA	94,951	109,419	60,296
Viet Nam	36,511	49,642	36,114
Total (incl. others)	**1,055,202**	**1,421,615**	**1,322,308**

Source: Ministry of Tourism, Phnom-Penh.

Tourism receipts (US $ million, excl. passenger transport): 603 in 2004; 840 in 2005; 963 in 2006 (Source: IMF, *Cambodia: Selected Issues and Statistical Appendix*—August 2007).

CAMBODIA *Directory*

Communications Media

	2003	2004	2005
Telephones ('000 main lines in use)	31.4	32.2	33.0
Mobile cellular telephones ('000 subscribers)	498.4	861.5	1,062.0
Personal computers ('000 in use)	32	38	n.a.
Internet users ('000)	31.4	41.0	44.0
Broadband subscribers ('000)	0.2	0.8	1.0

Telephones ('000 main lines in use): 32.8 in 2006.

Mobile cellular telephones ('000 subscribers): 1,140.0 in 2006.

Facsimile machines (number in use): 884 in 1995; 1,470 in 1996; 2,995 in 1997.

Television receivers ('000 in use): 98 in 1999; 99 in 2000.

Radio receivers ('000 in use): 1,120 in 1995; 1,300 in 1996; 1,340 in 1997.

Sources: UNESCO, *Statistical Yearbook* and International Telecommunication Union.

Education

(2004/05, unless otherwise indicated)

	Institutions*	Teachers	Students
Pre-primary	n.a.	3,869	88,294
Primary	5,915	50,654	2,695,372
Secondary	594	25,160†	631,508†
Lower secondary	411	18,724†	461,898†
Higher secondary	183	6,436†	169,610†
Tertiary	n.a.	2,498	56,810

* 2002/03 data.
† 2003/04 data.

Sources: IMF, *Cambodia: Statistical Appendix* (October 2004); UNESCO Institute for Statistics.

Adult literacy rate (UNESCO estimates): 73.6% (males 84.7%; females 64.1%) in 2004 (Source: UNESCO Institute for Statistics).

Directory

The Constitution

The Constitution was promulgated on 21 September 1993; various amendments were approved in March 1999 and in March 2006. The main provisions of the Constitution are summarized below:

GENERAL PROVISIONS

The Kingdom of Cambodia is a unitary state in which the King abides by the Constitution and multi-party liberal democracy. Cambodian citizens have full right of freedom of belief; Buddhism is the state religion. The Kingdom of Cambodia has a market economy system.

THE KING

The King is Head of State and the Supreme Commander of the Khmer Royal Armed Forces. The monarchist regime is based on a system of selection: within seven days of the King's death the Royal Council of the Throne (comprising the Chairman of the Senate, the Chairman of the National Assembly, the Prime Minister, the Supreme Patriarchs of the Mohanikay and Thoammayutikanikay sects, the First and Second Vice-Chairmen of the Senate and the First and Second Vice-Chairmen of the National Assembly) must select a King. The King must be at least 30 years of age and be a descendant of King Ang Duong, King Norodom or King Sisowath. The King appoints the Prime Minister and the Cabinet. In the absence of the King, the Chairman of the Senate assumes the duty of acting Head of State.

THE LEGISLATURE

Legislative power is vested in the National Assembly (the lower chamber) and the Senate (the upper chamber). The National Assembly has 123 members who are elected by universal adult suffrage. A member of the National Assembly must be a Cambodian citizen by birth, over the age of 25 years, and has a term of office of five years, the term of the National Assembly. The National Assembly may not be dissolved except in the case where the Royal Government (Cabinet) has been dismissed twice in 12 months. The National Assembly may dismiss cabinet members or remove the Royal Government from office by passing a censure motion through a two-thirds' majority vote of all the representatives in the National Assembly. The Senate comprises 61 members (the number not exceeding one-half of all of the members of the National Assembly). Two Senators are nominated by the King, two are elected by majority vote in the National Assembly and 57 are chosen by an electoral college comprising the 123 members of the National Assembly and more than 11,000 local councillors. A member of the Senate has a term of office of six years. The Senate reviews legislation passed by the National Assembly and acts as a co-ordinator between the National Assembly and the Royal Government. In special cases, the National Assembly and the Senate can assemble as the Congress to resolve issues of national importance. In March 2006 a constitutional amendment reduced the threshold required to form a government from a two-thirds' majority of the members of the National Assembly to a formula of 50% plus one of the votes of the Assembly.

THE CABINET

The Cabinet is the Royal Government of the Kingdom of Cambodia, which is led by a Prime Minister, assisted by Deputy Prime Ministers, with state ministers, ministers and state secretaries as members. The Prime Minister is designated by the King at the recommendation of the Chairman of the National Assembly from among the representatives of the winning party. The Prime Minister appoints the members of the Cabinet, who must be representatives in the National Assembly or members of parties represented in the National Assembly.

THE CONSTITUTIONAL COUNCIL

The Constitutional Council's competence is to interpret the Constitution and laws passed by the National Assembly and reviewed completely by the Senate. It has the right to examine and settle disputes relating to the election of members of the National Assembly and the Senate. The Constitutional Council consists of nine members with a nine-year mandate. One-third of the members are replaced every three years. Three members are appointed by the King, three elected by the National Assembly and three appointed by the Supreme Council of Magistracy.

The Government

HEAD OF STATE

King: HM King NORODOM SIHAMONI (appointed by the Royal Council of the Throne on 14 October 2004).

ROYAL GOVERNMENT OF CAMBODIA
(April 2008)

A coalition of the Cambodian People's Party (CPP) and the FUNCINPEC Party.

Prime Minister: HUN SEN (CPP).

Deputy Prime Minister and Minister of the Interior: SAR KHENG (CPP).

Deputy Prime Minister and Minister of National Defence: TEA BANH (CPP).

Deputy Prime Minister and Minister of Foreign Affairs and International Co-operation: HOR NAM HONG (CPP).

Deputy Prime Minister and Minister of Rural Development: LU LAY SRENG (FUNCINPEC).

Deputy Prime Minister and Minister in Charge of the Council of Ministers: SOK AN (CPP).

Deputy Prime Ministers without Portfolio: Gen. NHIEK BUN CHHAY (FUNCINPEC), KEO PUTH RASMEY (FUNCINPEC).

Senior Ministers: CHAM PRASIDH (CPP), CHHAY THON (CPP), KEAT CHHON (CPP), IM CHHUN LIM (CPP), MEN SAM ON (CPP), Dr MOK

CAMBODIA

Mareth (CPP), Nhim Vannda (CPP), Tav Senghuo (CPP), Hong Sun Huot (FUNCINPEC), Khun Haing (FUNCINPEC), Khy Taing Lim (FUNCINPEC), Kol Pheng (FUNCINPEC), Serei Kosal (FUNCINPEC), Veng Sereivuth (FUNCINPEC), You Hockry (FUNCINPEC).

Minister of Agriculture, Forestry and Fisheries: Dr Chan Sarun (CPP).
Minister of Commerce: Cham Prasidh (CPP).
Minister of Culture and Fine Arts: Prince Sisovat Panara Sirivudh (FUNCINPEC).
Minister of Economy and Finance: Keat Chhon (CPP).
Minister of Education, Youth and Sport: Kol Pheng (FUNCINPEC).
Minister of Environment: Dr Mok Mareth (CPP).
Minister of Health: Nuth Sokhom (FUNCINPEC).
Minister of Industry, Mines and Energy: Suy Sem (CPP).
Minister of Information: Khieu Kanharith (CPP).
Minister of Justice: Ang Vong Vattana (CPP).
Minister of Land Management, Urban Planning and Construction: Im Chhun Lim (CPP).
Minister of Parliamentary Affairs and Inspection: Men Sam On (CPP).
Minister of Planning: Chhay Thon (CPP).
Minister of Posts and Telecommunications: So Khun (CPP).
Minister of Public Works and Transport: Sun Chan Thol (FUNCINPEC).
Minister of Religions and Cults: Khun Haing (FUNCINPEC).
Minister of Social Affairs, Veterans and Youth Rehabilitation: Ith Sam Heng (CPP).
Minister of Tourism: Thong Khon (CPP).
Minister of Vocational Training and Labour: Vorng Soth (CPP).
Minister of Water Resources and Meteorology: Lim Kean Hor (CPP).
Minister of Women's Affairs: Ung Kantha Phavy (FUNCINPEC).
Secretary of State for Public Functions: Pich Bun Thin (CPP).
Secretary of State for Civil Aviation: Mao Hasvannal (FUNCINPEC).

There are also 133 further Secretaries of State.

MINISTRIES

Ministry of Agriculture, Forestry and Fisheries: 200 blvd Norodom, Sangkat Tonle Bassac, Khan Chamkarmon, Phnom-Penh; tel. (23) 211351; fax (23) 217320; e-mail maff@everyday.com.kh; internet www.maff.gov.kh.

Ministry of Commerce: 20A-B blvd Norodom, Phnom-Penh; tel. (23) 210365; fax (23) 217353; e-mail kunkoet@moc.gov.kh; internet www.moc.gov.kh.

Ministry of Culture and Fine Arts: 227 blvd Norodom, Phnom-Penh; tel. (23) 217645; fax (23) 725749; e-mail mcfa@cambodia.gov.kh; internet www.mcfa.gov.kh.

Ministry of Economy and Finance: 60 rue 92, Phnom-Penh; tel. and fax (23) 723164; e-mail mef@mef.gov.kh; internet www.mef.gov.kh.

Ministry of Education, Youth and Sport: 80 blvd Norodom, Phnom-Penh; tel. (23) 217253; fax (23) 212512; e-mail moeys@everyday.com.kh; internet www.moeys.gov.kh.

Ministry of Environment: 48 blvd Sihanouk Tonle Bassac, Khan Chamkarmon, Phnom-Penh; tel. (23) 427894; fax (23) 427844; e-mail moe-cabinet@camnet.com.kh; internet www.camnet.com.kh/moe.

Ministry of Foreign Affairs and International Co-operation: 3 rue Samdech Hun Sen, Khan Chamkarmon, Phnom-Penh; tel. (23) 214441; fax (23) 216144; e-mail mfaicinfo@mfaic.gov.kh; internet www.mfaic.gov.kh.

Ministry of Health: 151–153 blvd Kampuchea Krom, Phnom-Penh; tel. (23) 722873; fax (23) 426841; e-mail procure.pcu@bigpond.com.kh; internet www.moh.gov.kh.

Ministry of Industry, Mines and Energy: 45 blvd Preah Norodom, Phnom-Penh; tel. (23) 211141; fax (23) 428263; e-mail info@mime.gov.kh; internet www.mime.gov.kh.

Ministry of Information: 62 blvd Monivong, Phnom-Penh; tel. (23) 724159; fax (23) 427475; e-mail information@cambodia.gov.kh; internet www.information.gov.kh.

Ministry of the Interior: 275 blvd Norodom, Khan Chamkarmon, Phnom-Penh; tel. and fax (23) 721190; e-mail info@interior.gov.kh; internet www.interior.gov.kh.

Ministry of Justice: 240 blvd Sothearos, Phnom-Penh; tel. (23) 360327; fax (23) 364119; e-mail moj@cambodia.gov.kh; internet www.moj.gov.kh.

Ministry of Labour and Vocational Training: Phnom-Penh; e-mail mlv@cambodia.gov.kh; internet www.mlv.gov.kh.

Ministry of Land Management, Urban Planning and Construction: 771–773 blvd Monivong, Phnom-Penh; tel. (23) 215660; fax (23) 217035; e-mail gdadmin-mlmupc@camnet.com.kh; internet www.mlmupc.gov.kh.

Ministry of National Defence: blvd Confédération de la Russie, cnr rue 175, Phnom-Penh; tel. and fax (23) 883184; e-mail info@mond.gov.kh; internet www.mond.gov.kh.

Ministry of Parliamentary Affairs and Inspection: rue Jawaharlal Nehru, Phnom-Penh; tel. (23) 884261; fax (23) 884264; e-mail mnasrl@cambodia.gov.kh; internet www.mnasrl.gov.kh.

Ministry of Planning: 386 blvd Monivong, Sangkat Boeung Keng Kang 1, Phnom-Penh; tel. (23) 212049; fax (23) 210698; e-mail mop@cambodia.gov.kh; internet www.mop.gov.kh.

Ministry of Posts and Telecommunications: cnr rue Preah Ang Eng and rue Ang Non, Phnom-Penh; tel. (23) 426510; fax (23) 426011; e-mail mptc@cambodia.gov.kh; internet www.mptc.gov.kh.

Ministry of Public Works and Transport: 200 blvd Norodom, Phnom-Penh; tel. and fax (23) 427862; e-mail mpwt@online.com.kh; internet www.mpwt.gov.kh.

Ministry of Religions and Cults: Preah Sisowath Quay, cnr rue 240, Phnom-Penh; tel. (23) 725099; fax (23) 725699; e-mail morac@cambodia.gov.kh; internet www.morac.gov.kh.

Ministry of Rural Development: Jok Dimitrov, cnr rue 169, Phnom-Penh; tel. and fax (23) 880007; e-mail mrd@cambodia.gov.kh; internet www.mrd.gov.kh.

Ministry of Social Affairs, Veterans and Youth Rehabilitation: 788B blvd Monivong, Phnom-Penh; tel. (23) 726095; fax (23) 726086; e-mail mosalvy-gdlv@camnet.com.kh; internet www.mosalvy.gov.kh.

Ministry of Tourism: 3 blvd Monivong, Phnom-Penh 12258; tel. and fax (23) 212837; e-mail info@mot.gov.kh; internet www.mot.gov.kh.

Ministry of Water Resources and Meteorology: 47 blvd Norodom, Phnom-Penh; tel. (23) 724289; fax (23) 426345; e-mail mowram@cambodia.gov.kh; internet www.mowram.gov.kh.

Ministry of Women's Affairs: 3 blvd Norodom, Phnom-Penh; tel. and fax (23) 428965; e-mail mwva@online.com.kh; internet www.mwva.gov.kh.

Legislature

PARLIAMENT

National Assembly

National Assembly, blvd Samdech Sothearos, cnr rue 240, Phnom-Penh; tel. (23) 214136; fax (23) 217769; e-mail kimhenglong@cambodian-parliament.org; internet www.national-assembly.org.kh.

Chairman: Heng Samrin.

Election, 27 July 2003

	% of votes	Seats
Cambodian People's Party	47.35	73
FUNCINPEC Party	20.75	26
Sam Rainsy Party	21.87	24
Others	10.03	—
Total	100.00	123

Senate

Senate, Chamkarmon Palace, blvd Norodom, Phnom-Penh; tel. (23) 211441; fax (23) 211446; e-mail info@senate.gov.kh; internet www.senate.gov.kh.

President: Chea Sim (CPP).
First Vice-President: HRH Samdech Sisowath Chivan Monirak (FUNCINPEC).
Second Vice-President: Tep Ngorn (CPP).

CAMBODIA

Election, 22 January 2006

	Seats
Cambodian People's Party	45
FUNCINPEC Party	10
Sam Rainsy Party	2
King's appointees	2
National Assembly's appointees	2
Total	**61**

Note: 57 of the 61 Senators were chosen by means of an electoral college system (see The Constitution).

Election Commission

National Election Commission (NEC): blvd Norodom, Khan Chamkarmon, Phnom-Penh; tel. (12) 855018; fax (23) 214231; e-mail necinfo@forum.org.kh; internet www.necelect.org.kh; independent body, appointed by royal decree; Chair. IM SUOSDEY.

Political Organizations

Cambodian People's Party (CPP) (Kanakpak Pracheachon Kampuchea): 203 blvd Norodom, Sangkat Tonle Bassac, Khan Chamkarmon, Phnom-Penh; tel. and fax (23) 215801; internet www.thecpp.org; known as the Kampuchean People's Revolutionary Party 1979–91; 30-mem. Standing Cttee of the Cen. Cttee; Cen. Cttee of 268 full mems; Hon. Chair. of Cen. Cttee HENG SAMRIN; Chair. of Cen. Cttee CHEA SIM; Vice-Chair. HUN SEN; Chair. of Permanent Cttee SAY CHHUM.

Democratic National United Movement (DNUM): Pailin; f. 1996; est. by Ieng Sary, following his defection from the PDK; not a national political party, did not contest 1998 election; DNUM members are also free to join other political parties.

Farmers' Party: 21 rue 528, Sangkat Boeung Kak 1, Khan Chamkarmon, Phnom-Penh; tel. (16) 333200; Pres. PON PISITH.

FUNCINPEC Party (United National Front for an Independent, Neutral, Peaceful and Co-operative Cambodia Party): 11 blvd Monivong (93), Sangkat Sras Chak, Khan Daun Penh, BP 1444, Phnom-Penh; tel. (23) 428864; fax (23) 218547; e-mail funcinpec@funcinpec.org; internet www.funcinpec.org; FUNCINPEC altered its title to the FUNCINPEC Party when it adopted political status in 1992; the party's military wing was the National Army of Independent Cambodia (fmrly the Armée Nationale Sihanoukiste—ANS); merged with the Son Sann Party in Jan. 1999; Pres. KEO PUTH RASMEY; Sec.-Gen. Gen. NHIEK BUN CHHAY.

Hang Dara Movement Democratic Party: 16 rue 430, Sangkat Phsardoeum Thkov, Khan Chamkarmon, Phnom-Penh; tel. (12) 672007; f. 2002 to contest 2003 general election; breakaway faction of the FUNCINPEC Party; Pres. HANG DARA.

Human Rights Party (HRP): 72–74 rue 598, Boeng Kak Pir Subdistrict, Tuol Kok, Phnom-Penh; tel. (23) 884649; e-mail hrpcambodia@yahoo.com; internet www.hrpcambodia.org; f. 2007; Pres. KEM SOKHA.

Indra Buddra City Party: Commune, Chbarmon District, Kampong Spueu; tel. (12) 710331; Pres. NOREAK RATANAVATHANO.

Khmer Democratic Party (Kanakpak Pracheathippatei Khmer): 79A rue 186, Sangkat Touek Laak 3, Khan Tuol Kok, Phnom-Penh; tel. (12) 842947; Pres. OUK PHURIK.

Khmer Neutral Party (Kanakpak Kampuchea Appyeakroet): 14A rue Keo Chea, Phnom-Penh; tel. (23) 62365; fax (23) 27340; e-mail Masavang@datagraphic.fr; Pres. BUO HEL.

Khmer Republican Party (KRP): 282 rue 371, Phoum Obekaam, Sangkat Taek Thla, Khan Russey Keo, Phnom-Penh; tel. (23) 350842; e-mail krp2005@gmail.com; internet www.khmerrepublicanparty.org; f. 2007; Pres. LON RITH.

National Union Party (Kanakpak Ruop Ruom Cheat): Phnom-Penh; established by rebel mems of FUNCINPEC Party; Chair. (vacant); Sec.-Gen. UNG PHAN.

Norodom Ranariddh Party (NRP): Bldg 27, blvd Mao Tse Toung, Khan Chamkarmon, Phnom-Penh; tel. and fax (23) 756556; e-mail skpit@norodomranariddh.info; internet norodomranariddh.info; f. 2002 as Khmer Front Party in order to contest 2003 general election; name changed as above in 2006; Pres. Prince NORODOM RANARIDDH; Vice-Pres. Prince NORODOM CHAKRAPONG.

Rice Party (Svor): 69 blvd Sothearos, Sangkat Tonle Bassac, Khan Chamkarmon, Phnom-Penh 12301; tel. (11) 860060; e-mail riceparty@asia.com; f. 1992; Pres. NHOUNG SEAP.

Sam Rainsy Party (SRP): 71 blvd Sothearos, Sangkat Tonle Bassac, Khan Chamkarmon, Phnom-Penh; tel. (23) 217452; fax (23) 211336; e-mail srphqpp@forum.org.kh; internet www.samrainsyparty.org; f. 1995 as the Khmer Nation Party; name changed as above in 1998; 444,544 mems (Aug. 2001); Pres. KIM LY CHEA; Sec.-Gen. THA OUM.

Sangkum Jatiniyum Front Party: 40 rue 566, Boeungkak 1, Tuol Kok, Phnom-Penh; tel. (12) 762207; internet sjfparty.free.fr; f. 1997; fmrly the Khmer Unity Party; Delegate-Gen. HRH Samdech SISOWATH THOMICO; Sec.-Gen. SUTH DINA.

United Front for the Construction and Defence of the Kampuchean Fatherland (UFCDKF): Phnom-Penh; f. 1978 as the Kampuchean National United Front for National Salvation (KNUFNS), renamed Kampuchean United Front for National Construction and Defence (KUFNCD) in 1981, present name adopted in 1989; mass organization supporting policies of the CPP; an 89-mem. Nat. Council and a seven-mem. hon. Presidium; Chair. of Nat. Council CHEA SIM; Sec.-Gen. ROS CHHUN.

Diplomatic Representation

EMBASSIES IN CAMBODIA

Australia: Villa 11, R. V. Senei Vinnavaut Oum (rue 254), Sangkat Chaktomouk, Khan Daun Penh, Phnom-Penh; tel. (23) 213470; fax (23) 213413; e-mail australian.embassy.cambodia@dfat.gov.au; internet www.cambodia.embassy.gov.au; Ambassador MARGARET ANNE ADAMSON.

Brunei: 237 rue Pasteur 51, Sangkat Boeung Keng Kang 1, Khan Chamkarmon, Phnom-Penh; tel. (23) 211457; fax (23) 211456; e-mail brunei@bigpond.com.kh; Ambassador Pengiran Hajah BASMILLAH ABBAS.

Bulgaria: 227/229 blvd Norodom, Phnom-Penh; tel. (23) 217504; fax (23) 212792; e-mail bulgembpnp@online.com.kh; internet www.mfa.bg/phnom-penh; Chargé d'affaires KRASIMIR TULECHKI.

Canada: Villa 9, R. V. Senei Vinnavaut Oum (rue 254), Sangkat Chaktomouk, Khan Daun Penh, Phnom-Penh; tel. (23) 213470; fax (23) 211389; e-mail pnmpn@international.gc.ca; internet www.dfait-maeci.gc.ca/cambodia; Chargé d'affaires a.i. ERNEST LOIGNON.

China, People's Republic: 156 blvd Mao Tse Toung, Phnom-Penh; tel. (23) 720920; fax (23) 364738; e-mail chinaemb_kh@mfa.gov.cn; Ambassador ZHANG JINFENG.

Cuba: 96/98 rue 214, Sangkat Veal Vong, Khan 7 Makara, Phnom-Penh; tel. (23) 213212; fax (23) 217428; Ambassador BÁRBARA GILDA LÓPEZ ARMENTEROS.

France: 1 blvd Monivong, Phnom-Penh; tel. (23) 430020; fax (23) 430037; e-mail ambafrance.phnom-penh-amba@diplomatie.gouv.fr; internet www.ambafrance-kh.org; Ambassador JEAN-FRANÇOIS DESMAZIÈRES.

Germany: 76–78 rue Yougoslavie (rue 214), BP 60, Phnom-Penh; tel. (23) 216381; fax (23) 427746; e-mail germanembassy@everyday.com.kh; internet www.phnom-penh.diplo.de; Ambassador FRANK MANN.

India: 5 rue 466, Phnom-Penh; tel. (23) 210912; fax (23) 213640; e-mail embindia@online.com.kh; Ambassador ALOKE SEN.

Indonesia: 90 blvd Norodom, Phnom-Penh; tel. (23) 216148; fax (23) 216571; e-mail kukppenh@bigpond.com.kh; Ambassador NURRACHMAN OERIP.

Japan: 194 blvd Norodom, Sangkat Tonle Bassac, Khan Chamkarmon, Phnom-Penh; tel. (23) 217161; fax (23) 216162; e-mail eojc@online.com.kh; internet www.kh.emb-japan.go.jp; Ambassador KATSUHIRO SHINOHARA.

Korea, Democratic People's Republic: 39 rue 268, Phnom-Penh; tel. (15) 912567; fax (23) 426230; Ambassador RI IN SOK.

Korea, Republic: 50 rue 214, Sangkat Boeung Raing, Khan Daun Penh, BP 2433, Phnom-Penh; tel. (23) 211900; fax (23) 219200; e-mail cambodia@mofat.go.kr; internet khm.mofat.go.kr; Ambassador SHIN HYUN-SUK.

Laos: 15–17 blvd Mao Tse Toung, POB 19, Phnom-Penh; tel. (23) 997931; fax (23) 720907; e-mail laoembpp@camintel.com; Ambassador CHANTAVY BODHISANE.

Malaysia: 5 rue 242, Sangkat Chaktomouk, Khan Daun Penh, Phnom-Penh; tel. (23) 216176; fax (23) 216004; e-mail mwppenh@online.com.kh; internet www.kln.gov.my/perwakilan/phnompenh; Ambassador Dato' ADNAN Haji OTHMAN.

Myanmar: 181 blvd Norodom, Sangkat Boeung Keng Kang 1, Khan Chamkarmon, Phnom-Penh; tel. (23) 213663; fax (23) 213665; e-mail m.e.phnompenh@bigpond.com.kh; Ambassador HLA MIN.

CAMBODIA

Pakistan: 45 rue 310, Boeung Keng Kang 1, Phnom-Penh; tel. (23) 996890; fax (23) 992113; e-mail parep.cambodia@yahoo.com; Ambassador MOHAMMAD YOUNIS KHAN.

Philippines: 33 rue 294, Khan Chamkarmon, Sangkat Tonle Bassac, BP 2018, Phnom-Penh; tel. (23) 215145; fax (23) 215143; e-mail phnompenhpe@online.com.kh; Ambassador LOURDES G. MORALES.

Poland: 767 blvd Monivong, BP 58, Phnom-Penh; tel. (23) 217782; fax (23) 217781; e-mail emb.pol.pp@online.com.kh; internet www.phnompenh.polemb.net; Ambassador (vacant).

Russia: 213 blvd Sothearos, Phnom-Penh; tel. (23) 210931; fax (23) 216776; e-mail russemba@online.com.kh; internet www.embrusscambodia.mid.ru; Ambassador VALERY TERESHCHENKO.

Singapore: 129 blvd Norodom, Phnom-Penh; tel. (23) 221875; fax (23) 210862; e-mail singemb@online.com.kh; internet www.mfa.gov.sg/phnompenh; Ambassador TAN YEE WOAN.

Thailand: 196 Preah Norodom Blvd, Sangkat Tonle Bassac, Khan Chamkarmon, Phnom-Penh; tel. (23) 726306; fax (23) 726303; e-mail thaipnp@mfa.go.th; internet www.thaiembassy.org/phnompenh; Ambassador VIRAPHAND VACHARATHIT.

United Kingdom: 27–29 rue 75, Sangkat Sras Chak, Khan Daun Penh, Phnom-Penh; tel. (23) 427124; fax (23) 427125; e-mail britemb@online.com.kh; internet www.britishembassy.gov.uk/cambodia; Ambassador DAVID GEORGE READER.

USA: 1 rue 96, Sangkat Wat Phnom, Khan Daun Penh, Phnom-Penh; tel. (23) 728000; fax (23) 728600; internet phnompenh.usembassy.gov; Ambassador JOSEPH A. MUSSOMELI.

Viet Nam: 436 blvd Monivong, Phnom-Penh; tel. (23) 362741; fax (23) 427385; internet www.vietnamembassy-cambodia.org; Ambassador NGUYEN CHIEN THANG.

Judicial System

An independent judiciary was established under the 1993 Constitution. A council for legal and judicial reform was created in 2003 to co-ordinate the implementation of reforms. The highest judicial body is the Supreme Council of Magistracy.

Supreme Court: 222 rue 63, Sangkat Boeung Keng Kang 1, Khan Chamkarmon, Phnom-Penh; tel. and fax (23) 212826; Pres. DID MONTY.

Religion

BUDDHISM

The principal religion of Cambodia is Theravada Buddhism (Buddhism of the 'Tradition of the Elders'), the sacred language of which is Pali. A ban was imposed on all religious activity in 1975. By a constitutional amendment, which was adopted in April 1989, Buddhism was reinstated as the national religion and was retained as such under the 1993 Constitution. By 1992 2,800 monasteries (of a total of 3,369) had been restored and there were 21,800 Buddhist monks. In 2003 about 93% of the population were Buddhists.

Supreme Patriarchs: Ven. Patriarch TEP VONG, Ven. Patriarch BOU KRI.

Patriotic Kampuchean Buddhists' Association: Phnom-Penh; mem. of UFCDKF; Pres. LONG SIM.

CHRISTIANITY

The Roman Catholic Church

Cambodia comprises the Apostolic Vicariate of Phnom-Penh and the Apostolic Prefectures of Battambang and Kompong-Cham. At 31 December 2005 there were an estimated 23,437 adherents in the country, equivalent to about 0.2% of the population. An Episcopal Conference of Laos and Kampuchea was established in 1971. In 1975 the Government of Democratic Kampuchea banned all religious practice in Cambodia, and the right of Christians to meet to worship was not restored until 1990.

Vicar Apostolic of Phnom-Penh: Rt Rev. EMILE DESTOMBES (Titular Bishop of Altava), 787 blvd Monivong (rue 93), BP 123, Phnom-Penh; tel. and fax (23) 212462; e-mail evecam@forum.org.kh.

ISLAM

Islam is practised by a minority in Cambodia; in 2003 there were an estimated 700,000 Muslims. Islamic worship was also banned in 1975, but it was legalized in 1979, following the defeat of the Democratic Kampuchean regime.

The Press

According to Cambodia's Press Law, newspapers, magazines and foreign press agencies are required to register with the Department of Media at the Ministry of Information. In October 2002 160 Khmer language newspapers, 36 foreign language newspapers, 42 magazines, 19 bulletins and 12 foreign news agencies were registered.

NEWSPAPERS

In June 2004 Cambodia's first regional newspaper, *Somne Thmey*, was launched. It was to circulate in the country's four main provinces.

Areyathor (Civilization): 52 rue Lyuk Lay, Sangkat Chey, Chummneah, Phnom-Penh; tel. (23) 913662; f. 1994; 2 a week; Editor LEANG HI.

Business News: 28B rue 75, Sangkat Sraas Chak, Khan Daun Penh, Phnom-Penh 12201; tel. (23) 990110; fax (23) 990110; e-mail bizznews@camnet.com.kh; weekly; English; Editor-in-Chief BALA CHANDRAN.

Cambodge Nouveau: 58 rue 302, Sangkat Boeung Keng Kang 1, Khan Chamkarmon, Phnom-Penh 12302; tel. (23) 214610; e-mail cn@forum.org.kh; f. 1994; monthly; French; Editor-in-Chief ALAIN GASCUEL.

Cambodge Soir: 26CD rue 302, Sangkat Boeung Keng Kang 1, Khan Chamkarmon, Phnom-Penh 12302; tel. and fax (23) 362654; e-mail cambodgesoirpnh@online.com.kh; f. 1994; daily; French and Khmer; Editor-in-Chief PIERRE GILLETTE.

Cambodia Daily: 50B rue 240, Phnom-Penh; tel. (23) 426602; fax (23) 426573; e-mail aafc@camnet.com.kh; internet www.cambodiadaily.com; f. 1993; Mon.–Sat.; distributed free of charge within Cambodia; in English and Khmer; Editor-in-Chief KEVIN DOYLE; Publr BERNARD KRISHER; circ. 3,500.

Cambodia New Vision: BP 158, Phnom-Penh; tel. (23) 219898; fax (23) 360666; e-mail cabinet1b@camnet.com.kh; internet www.cnv.org.kh; f. 1998; official newsletter of the Cambodian Govt.

Cambodia Sin Chew Daily: 107 blvd Josep Broz Tito, rue 214, Sangkat Boeung Prolit, Khan 7 Makara, Phnom-Penh 12258; tel. (23) 215828; fax (23) 211728; e-mail sinchew_daily@online.com.kh; internet www.sinchew-i.com/cambodia; f. 1999; daily; Chinese; Editor-in-Chief PHANG KING YIANG.

Chakraval: 3 rue 181, Sangkat Tumnop Teuk, Khan Chamkarmon, Phnom-Penh; tel. (23) 211878; fax (23) 720141; e-mail chakraval@hotmail.com; f. 1992; daily; Khmer; Publr KEO SOPHORN; Editor NGOUN CHANMUNY.

Commercial News: 394 blvd Preah Sihanouk, Phnom-Penh; tel. (23) 721665; fax (23) 721709; e-mail tcnews@online.com.kh; internet www.thecommercialnews.com; f. 1993; Chinese; Chief Editor LIU XIAO GUANG; circ. 6,000.

Jian Hua Daily: 116–118 blvd Kampuchea Krom, Sangkat Monorom, Khan 7 Makara, Phnom-Penh 12251; tel. (23) 883801; fax (23) 883797; e-mail jianhuadaily@hotmail.com; daily; Chinese; Editor-in-Chief XENG ZUANG RONG.

Kampuchea Thmey (New Cambodia): 805 blvd Kampuchea Krom, Sangkat Tuk Laak 1, Khan Tuol Kok, Phnom-Penh 12156; tel. (23) 882990; fax (23) 882656; e-mail kampucheathmey@mail2world.com; daily; Editor-in-Chief KEV NAVY.

Kampuchea Thnai Nes (Cambodia Today Newspaper): 21 rue 163, Sangkat Veal Vong, Khan 7 Makara, Phnom-Penh 12253; tel. and fax (23) 364882; e-mail cambodiatoday@online.com.kh; daily; Editor-in-Chief HONG NARA.

Koh Santepheap (Island of Peace): 41E rue 338, Sangkat Boeung Tumpun, Khan Meanchey, Phnom-Penh 12351; tel. (23) 211818; fax (23) 220155; e-mail kohsantepheapdaily@gmail.com; internet www.kohsantepheapdaily.com.kh; daily; Khmer; Dir THONG UY PANG.

Mekong News: 11E rue 118, Sangkat Psah Thmei 2, Khan Daun Penh, Phnom-Penh 12206; tel. (12) 500872; fax (23) 994404; e-mail themekongnews@yahoo.com; f. 2005; fortnightly; English and Khmer; distributed free of charge; Editor and Publr M. NOOR ULLAH.

Moneaksekar Khmer (Khmer Conscience): 15A rue 293, Sangkat Boeung Kak 2, Khan Tuol Kok, Phnom-Penh 12152; tel. (12) 850690; daily; publ. by the Sam Rainsy Party; Editor DAM SITHI.

Neak Chea: 1 rue 158, Khan Daun Penh, Phnom-Penh; tel. (23) 428653; fax (23) 427229; e-mail adhoc@forum.org.kh; 2 a month; bulletin released by the Cambodia Human Rights and Development Association; Khmer.

Phnom Penh Post: 10A rue 264, Phnom-Penh; tel. and fax (23) 426568; e-mail editor.pppost@online.com.kh; internet www.phnompenhpost.com; f. 1992; fortnightly; English; Editor-in-Chief and Publr MICHAEL HAYES.

Pracheachon (The People): 101 blvd Norodom, Phnom-Penh; tel. (23) 723665; f. 1985; 2 a week; organ of the CPP; Editor-in-Chief SOM KIMSUOR; circ. 50,000.

CAMBODIA

Raja Bori News: 76 rue 57, Sangkat Boeung Kak 2, Khan Tuol Kok, Phnom-Penh 12152; tel. (12) 840993; weekly; Editor-in-Chief KIM SOMLOT.

Rasmei Angkor (Light of Angkor): 25/25z rue 372, Sangkat Boeung Salang, Khan Tuol Kok, Phnom-Penh 12160; tel. (11) 637609; f. 1992; 3 a week; Editor-in-Chief EN CHAN SIVUTHA.

Rasmei Kampuchea (Light of Cambodia): 474 blvd Preah Monivong, Sangkat Tonle Bassac, Khan Chamkarmon, Phnom-Penh 12301; tel. and fax (23) 362472; e-mail rasmei_kampuchea@yahoo.com; daily; f. 1993; local newspaper in northern Cambodia; Editor PEN SAMITHY.

Sahasa Wat Thmei (New Millennium): 48AE blvd Oknha Chun, Sangkat Chaktomuk, Khan Daun Penh, Phnom-Penh 12207; tel. (16) 719551; e-mail sahasawatthmey@mail2world.com; f. 2004; 3 a week; Editor-in-Chief UK SAMANG.

Samleng Thmei (New Voice): 91 rue 139, Sangkat Veal Vong, Khan 7, Phnom-Penh; tel. (15) 920589; Khmer; Editor KHUN NGOR.

Samleng Yuvachun (Voice of Khmer Youth): 251 rue 261, Sangkat Tuk Laak 2, Khan Tuol Kok 12200, Phnom-Penh 12309; tel. (12) 859142; e-mail khmeryouthnews@yahoo.com; f. 1993; Editor-in-Chief UK SUN HENG.

Somne Thmey (New Writing): 164B blvd Preah Norodom, Phnom-Penh; tel. (23) 224303; e-mail mcd.cambodia@online.com.kh; f. 2004; Khmer; weekly; publ. in Siem Reap, Preah Sihanouk, Kampong Cham and Bat Dambang; Editor-in-Chief PEN BONA.

Udomkate Khmer (Khmer Ideal): 17 blvd Samdech Sothearos, Sangkat Tuk Laak 3, Khan Tuol Kok, Phnom-Penh 12158; tel. (12) 851478; daily; Editor-in-Chief HOR SOK LEN.

PERIODICALS

Angkor Thom: 105 rue 324, Sangkat Boeung Salang, Khan Tuol Kok, Phnom-Penh 12253; tel. (23) 982817; f. 1997; fortnightly; Khmer; news, current affairs, arts and sport; Editor-in-Chief SENG SI THEANG.

Bayon Pearnik: 3 rue 174, Sangkat Psah Thmei 3, Khan Daun Penh, Phnom-Penh 312210; tel. (23) 211921; e-mail bp@forum.org.kh; internet www.bayonpearnik.com; monthly; English; tourism; Publr and Editor-in-Chief ADAM PARKER.

Cambodian Scene: 41 blvd Sang Kreach Tieng, rue 222, Sangkat Boeng Raing, Khan Daun Penh, Phnom-Penh 12211; tel. (23) 224488; fax (23) 222266; e-mail publisher@cambodianscene.com; internet www.cambodianscene.com; every 2 months; English; tourism, culture and entertainment guide; Publr and Editor-in-Chief MOEUN NHEAN.

L'Echo du Cambodge: 42 blvd Preah Norodom, Sangkat Psah Thmei 2, Khan Daun Penh, Phnom-Penh 12206; e-mail echoducambodge@yahoo.fr; monthly; French; Editor-in-Chief MARCEL ZARCA.

Indradevi: 167 blvd Mao Tse Toung, Sangkat Tuol Svay Prey 2, Khan Chamkarmon, Phnom-Penh 12309; tel. and fax (23) 215808; e-mail indradevi@camnet.com.kh; f. 2000; Editor-in-Chief CHHEM SARITH.

Kambuja: Kambuja Department, Agence Kampuchea Presse (AKP), Ministry of Information, 62 blvd Preah Monivong, Sangkat Wat Phnom, Khan Daun Penh, Phnom-Penh 12202; tel. and fax (23) 427945; e-mail akp@camnet.com.kh; monthly; Khmer; publ. by the Agence Kampuchea Presse; development, education and international affairs; Editor-in-Chief NERK SARAT.

Khmer Apsara: 143A Khum Pring Kang Cheung, Sangkat Chom Chao, Khan Dangkor, Phnom-Penh 12405; tel. (23) 890579; e-mail khmer_apsara01@yahoo.com; f. 2005; monthly; Khmer; entertainment, fashion, technology, health and culture; Editor-in-Chief EN SOPHANNA.

Pracheaprey (Popular): 77 Samdech Pann rue 214, Sangkat Boeung Pralit, Khan 7 Makara, Phnom-Penh 12258; tel. (23) 215741; fax (23) 216475; e-mail popularmagazine@online.com.kh; f. 2000; fortnightly; Khmer; news, current affairs, politics, arts, science and sport; Editor-in-Chief PRACH SIM.

Samay Thmei (Modern): 127 rue 357, Sangkat Chbar Ampheou 2, Khan Meanchey, Phnom-Penh 12355; tel. (23) 359969; fortnightly; Khmer; fashion, contemporary living, sports and entertainment; Editor-in-Chief EK SAMAT.

NEWS AGENCY

Agence Kampuchea Presse (AKP): 62 blvd Monivong, Phnom-Penh; tel. (23) 430564; fax (23) 427945; e-mail akp@camnet.com.kh; internet www.camnet.com.kh/akp; f. 1978; Dir-Gen. KIT-KIM HUON.

ASSOCIATIONS

Cambodian Association for the Protection of Journalists (CAPJ): BP 816, 58 rue 336, Sangkat Phsar Doeum Khor, Khan Tuol Kok, Phnom-Penh; tel. (15) 997004; fax (23) 215834; e-mail umsarin@hotmail.com; Pres. UM SARIN.

Club of Cambodian Journalists: 26A rue 336, Sangkat Phsar Doeum Kor, Khan Tuol Kok, Phnom-Penh 12159; tel. and fax (23) 884094; e-mail ccj@online.com.kh; internet www.ccj.com.kh; Pres. PEN SAMITHY; Sec.-Gen. PRACH SIM.

Khmer Journalists' Association: 170C rue 167, Sangkat Tuol Tom Poung 2, Khan Chamkarmon, Phnom-Penh 12311; tel. (23) 987622; e-mail mondulkeo@yahoo.com; f. 1979; mem. of UFCDKF; Pres. TATH LY HOK.

League of Cambodian Journalists (LCJ): 158 rue 132, Sangkat Tuk Laak 1, Khan Tuol Kok, Phnom-Penh 12156; tel. and fax (23) 864006; e-mail 012826802@mobitel.com.kh; f. 1995; Pres. OM CHANDARA.

Broadcasting and Communications

TELECOMMUNICATIONS

Applifone Co Ltd (Star-Cell): 173 rue 215, Sangkat Phsar Doeum Kor, Khan Tuol Kok, Phnom-Penh; tel. (23) 888 887; fax (23) 882492; e-mail info@star-cell.net; internet www.star-cell.net; f. 2006; operates GSM mobile telephone services; CEO DAMIR KARASSAYEV.

Cambodia Advance Communications Co Ltd (CADCOMMS): 825ABC blvd Preah Monivong, Sangkat Phsar Damthkov, Khan Chamkarmon, Phnom-Penh; tel. (23) 726680; fax (23) 726682; e-mail info@cadcomms.com; internet www.qbmore.com; f. 2006; operates mobile telephone services.

Cambodia Shinawatra Co Ltd (Camshin): 721 blvd Preah Monivong, Sangkat Boeung Keng Kang 3, Chamkarmorn, Phnom-Penh; tel. (23) 300667; fax (23) 365913; e-mail sales@camshin.com; internet www.camshin.com; f. 1993; a jt venture between the Ministry of Posts and Telecommunications and the Thai co, Shinawatra International Co Ltd; telephone communications co providing both fixed and mobile telephone services; CEO JIROJ SRINAMWONG.

CamGSM Co Ltd: 33 blvd Preah Sihanouk, Phnom-Penh; tel. (12) 812812; fax (12) 801801; e-mail helpline@cellcard.com.kh; internet www.mobitel.com.kh; f. 1996; operates national GSM 900 mobile telephone network under trade name Cellcard; CEO DAVID SPRIGGS.

Camintel: 1 cnr Terak Vithei Sisowath and Vithei Phsar Dek, Phnom-Penh; tel. (23) 986986; fax (23) 986277; e-mail support@camintel.com; internet www.camintel.com; f. 1995; jt venture between the Ministry of Posts and Telecommunications and the Indonesian co, Indosat; operates domestic telephone network; Chair. NHEK KORSOL VYTHYEA.

Telekom Malaysia International (Cambodia) Co Ltd: 56 blvd Norodom, Sangkat Chey Chumneah, Khan Daun Penh, Phnom-Penh; tel. (16) 810001; fax (16) 810004; e-mail casacom@hellogsm.com.kh; internet www.hellogsm.com.kh; f. 1992; est. as Cambodia Samart Communication; acquired by Telekom Malaysia Berhad in 2006; operates a national mobile telephone network; CEO MUHAMMED YUSOFF ZAMRI.

BROADCASTING

Radio

Apsara: 69 rue 57, Sangkat Boeung Keng Kang 1, Khan Chamkarmon, Phnom-Penh; tel. (12) 303002; fax (23) 214302; internet www.apsaratv.com.kh; f. 1996; broadcasts for 19 hours per day in Khmer; Head of Admin. KEO SOPHEAP; News Editor SIN SO CHEAT.

Bayon: 3 rue 466, Sangkat Tonle Bassac, Khan Chamkarmon, Phnom Penh; tel. (12) 682222; fax (23) 363795; internet www.bayontv.com.kh; Dir-Gen. KEM KUNNAVATH.

Beehive Radio (Sambok Khmoum): 949 rue 360, Boeung Keng Kang, Khan Chamkarmon, Phnom-Penh; tel. (23) 992939; fax (23) 240439; e-mail sok@online.com.kh; Dir-Gen. MAM SONANDO.

FM 90 MHZ: 65 rue 178, Phnom-Penh; tel. (23) 363699; fax (23) 368623; Dir-Gen. NHIM BUN THON; Dep. Dir-Gen. TUM VANN DET.

FM 99 MHZ: 41 rue 360, Phnom-Penh; tel. (23) 426794; Gen. Man. SOM CHHAYA.

FM 107 MHZ: 18 rue 562, Phnom-Penh; tel. (23) 880874; fax (23) 368212; e-mail tv9cambodia@hotmail.com; internet www.tv9.com.kh; Dir-Gen. KHUN HANG.

Krusa FM: Phnom-Penh; e-mail febcam@bigpond.com.kh; f. 2002; controlled by Far East Broadcasting; religious programmes; Dir SAMOEUN INTAL.

Phnom-Penh Municipality Radio: 131–132 blvd Pochentong, Phnom-Penh; tel. (23) 725205; fax (23) 360800; Gen. Man. KHAMPUN KEOMONY.

Radio WMC: 30 rue 488, Sangkat Phsar Dem Thkov, Khan Chamkarmon, Phnom-Penh; tel. and fax (12) 847854; e-mail wmc@forum

CAMBODIA

.org.kh; independent; radio station of Women's Media Centre of Cambodia; Dir CHEA SUDANETH.

Royal Cambodian Armed Forces Radio (RCAF Radio): c/o Borei Keila, rue 169, Phnom-Penh; tel. (23) 366061; fax (23) 366063; f. 1994; Dir THA TANA; News Editor SENG KATEKA.

Samlang Chivit Thmey (Voice of New Life Radio): BP 1426, Phnom-Penh; f. 1998; Christian programmes; broadcasts in Khmer, English and Vietnamese.

Ta Prohm Radio: 27B rue 472, Phnom-Penh; tel. (23) 213054; e-mail taprohm@yahoo.com; f. 2003; launched by FUNCINPEC Party as opposition radio station; broadcasts news programmes in Khmer to Phnom-Penh and surrounding area.

Vithyu Cheat Kampuchea (National Radio of Cambodia): 20 rue Preah Kossamak, Phnom-Penh; tel. (23) 722869; fax (23) 427319; f. 1978; fmrly Vithyu Samleng Pracheachon Kampuchea (Voice of the Cambodian People); controlled by the Ministry of Information; home service in Khmer; daily external services in English, French, Lao, Vietnamese and Thai; Dir-Gen. VANN SENG LY; Dep. Dir-Gen. TAN YAN.

Voice of Cambodia: Phnom-Penh; e-mail vocri@vocri.org; internet www.vocri.org; Cambodia's first international internet radio station.

There are also several private local radio stations.

Television

Apsara Television (TV11): 69 rue 57, Sangkat Boeung Keng Kang 1, Khan Chamkarmon, Phnom-Penh; tel. (23) 303002; fax (23) 214302; internet www.apsaratv.com.kh; broadcasts for 14 hours per day on weekdays, and for 16 hours per day at weekends, in Khmer; Dir-Gen. SOK EISAN.

Bayon Television (TV27): 3 rue 466, Sangkat Tonle Bassac, Khan Chamkarmon, Phnom Penh; tel. (12) 682222; fax (23) 363795; internet www.bayontv.com.kh; Dir-Gen. KEM KUNNAVATH.

National Television of Cambodia (TVK): 62 blvd Preah Monivong, Phnom-Penh; tel. and fax (12) 554535; e-mail tvk@camnet.gov.kh; internet www.tvk.gov.kh; f. 1983; broadcasts for 10 hours per day in Khmer; Dir-Gen. (Head of Television) KEM GUNAWADH.

Phnom-Penh Municipality Television (TV3): 2 blvd Russia, Phnom-Penh; tel. (12) 814323; fax (23) 360800; internet www.tv3.com.kh; Dir-Gen. KHAMPHUN KEOMONY.

Royal Cambodian Armed Forces Television (TV5) (RCAF TV): 165 rue 169, Borei Keila, Phnom-Penh; tel. (23) 366061; fax (23) 366063; e-mail mica.t.v.5@bigpond.com.kh; Editor-in-Chief PRUM KIM.

TV Khmer (TV9): 18 rue 562, Phnom-Penh; tel. (23) 880874; fax (23) 368212; e-mail tv9cambodia@hotmail.com; internet www.tv9.com.kh; f. 1992; Dir-Gen. KHOUN ELYNA; News Editor PHAN TITH.

Finance

(cap. = capital; res = reserves; dep. = deposits; brs = branches)

BANKING

At the end of July 2004 there were 17 banks (excluding the central bank) operating in Cambodia, comprising: one state-owned bank; three specialized banks; 10 locally incorporated private banks; and three branches of foreign banks.

Central Bank

National Bank of Cambodia (NBC): 22–24 blvd Preah Norodom, BP 25, Phnom-Penh; tel. (23) 722563; fax (23) 426117; e-mail nbc2@online.com.kh; f. 1954; est. as National Bank of Cambodia; name changed to People's National Bank of Cambodia in 1979; name reverted to above in 1992; cap. 100,000m. riels, res 6,537,600m. riels, dep. 3,875,862m. riels (June 2007); Gov. CHEA CHANTO; Dep. Gov. NEAVA CHANTHAN.

State Bank

Foreign Trade Bank: 3 rue Kramoun Sar, Khan Daun Penh, Phnom-Penh; tel. (23) 724466; fax (23) 426108; e-mail ftb@camnet.com.kh; internet www.ftbbank.com; f. 1979; removed from direct management of National Bank of Cambodia in 2000; scheduled for privatization; Man. TIM BO PHOL.

Specialized Banks

Cambodia Agriculture Industrial Specialized Bank: 87 blvd Preah Norodom, Sangkat Phsar Thmey III, Khan Daun Penh, Phnom-Penh; tel. (23) 218667; fax (23) 217751; e-mail kien@bigpond.com.kh; Man. CHHOR SANG.

Peng Heng SME Bank: 72 blvd Norodom, Phnom-Penh; tel. (23) 219243; fax (23) 219185; e-mail pengheng@camnet.com.kh; f. 2001.

Rural Development Bank: 9–13 rue 7, Sangkat Chaktomouk, Khan Daun Penh, Phnom-Penh; tel. (23) 220810; fax (23) 224628; e-mail rdb@online.com.kh; internet www.rdb.com.kh; f. 1998; provides credit to rural enterprises; Chair. and CEO SON KOUN THOR.

Private Banks

ACLEDA Bank PLC: 28 blvd Mao Tse Toung, Sangkat Boeung Trabek, Khan Chamkarmon, Phnom-Penh; tel. (23) 364619; fax (23) 364914; e-mail acledabank@acledabank.com.kh; internet www.acledabank.com.kh; f. 1993; became specialized bank in Oct. 2000 and was awarded commercial banking licence in Dec. 2003; provides financial services to all sectors; cap. US $30.0m., res US $5.9m., dep. US $123.1m. (2006); Chair. CHEA SOK; Pres. and CEO IN CHANNY; 137 brs.

Advanced Bank of Asia Ltd: 148 blvd Preah Sihanouk, Khan Chamkarmon, Phnom-Penh; tel. (23) 225333; fax (23) 216333; e-mail info@ababank.com; internet www.ababank.com.kh; Dir CHAE WAN CHO.

Cambodia Asia Bank Ltd: 439 blvd Monivong, Ground Floor, Phnom-Penh; tel. (23) 220000; fax (23) 426628; e-mail cab@cab.com.kh; internet www.cab.com.kh; incorporated in 1992; cap. US $13.0m., dep. US $3.2m.; Man. WONG TOW FOCK.

Cambodia Mekong Bank: 6 blvd Monivong, Khan Daun Penh, Phnom-Penh; tel. (23) 430980; fax (23) 430431; e-mail ho.mailbox@mekongbank.com; internet www.mekongbank.com.kh; f. 1994; cap. US $15.0m., dep. US $8.4m. (Dec. 2005); Chair. MICHAEL C. STEPHEN; Pres. and CEO KHOV BOUN CHHAY.

Cambodian Commercial Bank Ltd: 26 blvd Preah Monivong, Sangkat Phsar Thmey II, Khan Daun Penh, Phnom-Penh; tel. (23) 426145; fax (23) 426116; e-mail ccbpp@online.com.kh; internet www.ccb-cambodia.com; f. 1991; cap. (p.u.) US $17m., dep. US $91.8m. (Dec. 2005); Chair. NABHENGBHASANG KRISHNAMRA; Dir and Gen. Man. NATTHAWUT CHAKANAN; 4 brs.

Cambodian Public Bank (Campu Bank): Villa 23, rue Kramoun Sar, Sangkat Phsar Thmey II, Khan Daun Penh, Phnom-Penh; tel. (23) 214111; fax (23) 217655; e-mail campu@campubank.com.kh; f. 1992; cap. US $20m., dep. US $126.7m. (Dec. 2005); Pres. Tan Sri Dato' Dr HONG PIOW TEH; Gen. Man. PHAN YING TONG.

Canadia Bank PLC: 265–269 rue Preah Ang Duong, Sangkat Wat Phnom, Khan Daun Penh, Phnom-Penh; tel. (23) 215286; fax (23) 427064; e-mail canadia@camnet.com.kh; internet www.canadiabank.com; f. 1991 under the name Canadia Gold and Trust Corpn Ltd; name changed as above in 2004; cap. 50.6m. riels, res 32.3m. riels, dep. 411.6m. riels (2001); Exec. Dir and Gen. Man. PUNG KHEAV SE; 10 brs.

Singapore Banking Corporation Ltd: 68 rue Samdech Pan, Sangkat Boeung Raing, Khan Daun Penh, BP 688, Phnom-Penh; tel. (23) 211211; fax (23) 212121; e-mail info@sbc-bank.com; internet www.sbc-bank.com; f. 1992; cap. US $13m. (2003), dep. US $21.4m. (Dec. 2006); Pres. ANDY KUN SWEE TIONG; Chair. KUN KAY HONG.

Union Commercial Bank PLC: UCB Bldg, 61 rue 130, Sangkat Phsar Chas, Khan Daun Penh, Phnom-Penh; tel. (23) 427995; fax (23) 427997; e-mail ucbhq@ucb.com.kh; internet www.ucb.com.kh; f. 1994; cap. US $14.2m., dep. US $83m. (Dec. 2006); CEO YUM SUI SANG; Chair. and Pres. YIU KAI KWONG; 3 brs.

Vattanac Bank: 89 blvd Preah Norodom, Sangkat Boeung Raing, Khan Daun Penh, Phnom-Penh; tel. (23) 212727; fax (23) 216687; e-mail service@vattanacbank.com; internet www.vattanacbank.com; f. 2002; cap. US $13m. (Dec. 2005); Chair. SAM ANG; Pres. CHHUN LEANG.

INSURANCE

Asia Insurance (Cambodia) Ltd: 5 rue 13, Khan Daun Penh, Phnom-Penh; tel. (23) 427981; fax (23) 216969; e-mail email@asiainsurance.com.kh; internet www.asiainsurance.com.kh; f. 1996; Gen. Man. PASCAL BRANDT-GAGNON.

Cambodia National Insurance Company (CAMINCO): cnr rue 106 and rue 13, Sangkat Wat Phnom, Khan Daun Penh, Phnom-Penh; tel. (23) 722043; fax (23) 427810; internet www.caminco.com.kh; state-owned.

Forte Insurance (Cambodia) PLC: 325 blvd Mao Tse Toung, BP 565, Phnom-Penh; tel. (23) 885077; fax (23) 982907; e-mail info@forteinsurance.com; internet www.forteinsurance.com; f. 1996; Man. Dir CARLO CHEO; Gen. Man. YOUK CHAMROEUNRITH.

Infinity General Insurance PLC: 126 blvd Preah Norodom, Phnom-Penh; tel. (23) 999888; fax (23) 999123; e-mail cs@infinityinsurance.com.kh; internet www.infinityinsurance.com.kh.

Trade and Industry

DEVELOPMENT ORGANIZATIONS

Council for the Development of Cambodia (CDC): Government Palace, quai Sisowath, Wat Phnom, BP 1225, Phnom-Penh; tel. (23) 981154; fax (23) 428426; e-mail cdc.cib@bigpond.com.kh; internet www.cambodiainvestment.gov.kh; f. 1994; Chair. HUN SEN; Sec.-Gen. SOK CHENDA.

Cambodian Investment Board (CIB): Government Palace, quai Sisowath, Wat Phnom, Phnom-Penh; tel. (23) 981156; fax (23) 428426; e-mail cdc.cib@bigpond.com.kh; internet www.cambodiainvestment.gov.kh; f. 1993; part of CDC; sole body responsible for approving foreign investment in Cambodia; also grants exemptions from customs duties and other taxes; provides other facilities for investors; Chair. HUN SEN; Sec.-Gen. SUON SITTHY.

National Information Communications Technology Development Authority (NiDA): 3rd Floor, Satellite Bldg, Office of the Council of Ministers, blvd Confédération de la Russie, Phnom-Penh; tel. (23) 880635; fax (23) 880637; e-mail info@nida.gov.kh; internet www.nida.gov.kh; f. 2000; promotes information technology and formulates policy for its development; Chair. HUN SEN; Sec.-Gen. Dr PHU LEEWOOD.

CHAMBER OF COMMERCE

Cambodia Chamber of Commerce: Office Villa 7B, cnr rue 81 and rue 109, Sangkat Boeung Raing, Khan Daun Penh, Phnom-Penh; tel. (23) 212265; fax (23) 212270; e-mail admin@ppcc.org.kh; internet www.ppcc.org.kh; f. 1995; Pres. KITH MENG; Dir-Gen. Dr NANG SOTHY.

INDUSTRIAL AND TRADE ASSOCIATIONS

Export Promotion Department: Ministry of Commerce, 65–69 rue 136, Sangkat Phsar Kandal II, Khan Daun Penh, Phnom-Penh; tel. (23) 216948; fax (23) 217353; e-mail star@epd.gov.kh; internet www.moc.gov.kh; f. 1997; Dir SUTH DARA.

Garment Manufacturers' Association in Cambodia (GMAC): 175 blvd Jawaharlal Nehru (rue 215), Sangkat Phsar Doeum Kor, Khan Tuol Kork, Phnom-Penh; tel. (23) 301180; fax (23) 311181; e-mail info@gmac-cambodia.org; internet www.gmac-cambodia.org; Chair. VAN SOU IENG; First Vice-Chair. KONG SANG.

UTILITIES

Electricity

Electricité du Cambodge (EDC): EDC Bldg, rue 19, Wat Phnom, Khan Daun Penh, Phnom-Penh; tel. (23) 724771; fax (23) 426938; e-mail edchq@edc.com.kh; internet www.edc.com.kh; f. 1996; state-owned; Man. Dir Gen. TAN KIM VIN.

Electricity Authority of Cambodia (EAC): 2 rue 282, Boeng Keng Kang 1, Phnom-Penh; tel. (23) 217654; fax (23) 214144; internet www.eac.gov.kh; f. 2001; regulatory authority; Chair. Dr TY NORIN.

Water

Phnom-Penh Water Supply Authority: 45 rue 106, Phnom-Penh; tel. (23) 724046; fax (23) 428969; e-mail eksonnchan@ppwsa.com.kh; f. 1996 as an autonomous public enterprise; Dir-Gen. EK SONN CHAN.

TRADE UNIONS

Association of Independent Cambodian Teachers: 33 rue 432, Sangkat Boeng Trabaek, Khan Chamkarmon, Phnom-Penh; Pres. RUNG CHHUN; Gen. Sec. CHEA MUNI.

Cambodia Federation of Independent Trade Unions (CFITU): 45 rue 63, Boeung Keng Kang 1, Khan Chamkarmon, Phnom-Penh; tel. (23) 213356; e-mail CFITU@bigpond.com.kh; f. 1979 as Cambodia Federation of Trade Unions; changed name as above in 1999; Chair. ROS SOK.

Cambodia Labour Union Federation (CLUF): 78 rue 474, Sangkat Boeung Trabek, Khan Chamkarmon, Phnom-Penh; tel. (23) 866682; f. 1999; Pres. SOM AUN.

Cambodian Labor Organization (CLO): 425 rue 310, Sangkat Boeung Keng Kang II, Khan Chamkarmon, Phnom-Penh; tel. and fax (23) 218132; e-mail clo@forum.org.kh; f. 1995.

Cambodian Union Federation (CUF): 18 rue 112, Sangkat Phsar Depo III, Khan Tuol Kok, Phnom-Penh; tel. (23) 882453; fax (23) 427632; e-mail CUF@bigpond.com.kh; f. 1997 with the support of the CPP in response to the formation of the FTUWKC; Pres. RON CHHUN.

Cambodian Union Federation of Building and Wood Workers: 18A rue 112, Sangkat Phsar Depo III, Khan Tuol Kok, Phnom-Penh; tel. (23) 842382; fax (23) 882453; f. 2001; Pres. SAY SAM ON.

Coalition of Cambodia Apparel Workers' Democratic Union: 6c rue 476, Sangkat Tuol Tompoung I, Khan Chamkarmon, Phnom-Penh; tel. (23) 210481; e-mail c.cawdu@forum.org.kh; f. 2001; Pres. CHHORN SOKHA.

Free Trade Union of Workers of the Kingdom of Cambodia (FTUWKC): 28B Sangkat Boeung Raing, Khan Daun Penh, Phnom-Penh; tel. and fax (23) 216870; e-mail ftuwkc@cambodiaworkers.org; internet www.ftuwkc.org; fmrly Free Trade Union of Khmer Workers; f. 1996 by Mary Ou with the assistance of Sam Rainsy; Pres. CHEA MUNNY; Gen. Sec. MANN SENGHAK.

National Independent Federation Textile Union of Cambodia (NIFTUC): 29B rue 432, Sangkat Toul Tompoung II, Khan Chamkarmon, Phnom-Penh; tel. and fax (23) 219239; e-mail niftuc@forum.org.kh; f. 1999; Pres. MORM NHIM.

Transport

RAILWAYS

Royal Railway of Cambodia: Central Railway Station, Railway Sq., Sangkat Srach Chak, Khan Daun Penh, Phnom-Penh; tel. (12) 994168; fax (23) 430815; e-mail RRCcambodia@bigpond.com.kh; comprises two 1,000 mm-gauge single-track main lines with a total length of 650 km: the original 385-km Phnom-Penh to Poipet line, including the 48-km Sisophon to Poipet link, plans for the restoration of which were confirmed in early 2008; and the new line between Phnom-Penh and Sihanoukville, which was to be completed by 2010; Pres. and Dir-Gen. SOKHOM PHEAKAVANMONY.

ROADS

In 2004 the total road network was 38,257 km in length, of which 4,757 km were highways and 5,700 km were secondary roads. In the same year about 6.3% of the road network was paved. West and East Cambodia were linked by road for the first time in December 2001, with the opening of a bridge across the Mekong River.

INLAND WATERWAYS

The major routes are along the Mekong River, and up the Tonlé Sap River into the Tonlé Sap (Great Lake), covering, in all, about 2,400 km. The inland ports of Neak Luong, Kompong Cham and Prek Kdam have been supplied with motor ferries, and the ferry crossings have been improved.

SHIPPING

The main port is Sihanoukville, on the Gulf of Thailand, which has 11 berths and can accommodate vessels of 10,000–15,000 tons. Phnom-Penh port lies some distance inland. Steamers of up to 4,000 tons can be accommodated.

CIVIL AVIATION

There are international airports at Pochentong, near Phnom-Penh, and at Siem Reap. In mid-2003 construction of a new terminal at Phnom-Penh International Airport was completed. In mid-2004 renovation work to expand the runways at the airports in both Phnom-Penh and Siem Reap was completed. Additional refurbishment of the facilities at both airports was to be carried out by 2010, at an estimated cost of $20m. In 2008 the Government announced further investment in Phnom-Penh airport.

State Secretariat of Civil Aviation (SSCA): 62 blvd Norodom, Phnom-Penh; tel. (23) 360617; fax (23) 426169; e-mail civilaviation@cambodia.gov.kh; internet www.civilaviation.gov.kh; Dir-Gen. MAO HAS VANNAL.

Angkor Airways: 32 blvd Preah Norodom, Sangkat Phsar Kandal 2, Khan Daun Penh, Phnom-Penh; tel. (23) 222056; fax (23) 222057; e-mail service_pnh@angkorairways.com; internet www.angkorairways.com; f. 2004; flies between Siem Reap and Taiwan, Japan and South Korea.

PMT Air: 118, Street 2013, Sangkat Kakab, Khan Dong Kar, Phnom-Penh; tel. and fax (23) 23890322; e-mail tiket@pmtair.com; internet www.pmtair.com; f. 2003; domestic and international services.

President Airlines: 50 blvd Norodom, Phnom-Penh; tel. (23) 210338; fax (23) 219992; e-mail karna@presidentairlines.com; internet www.presidentairlines.com; f. 1998; domestic and international passenger services.

Royal Khmer Airlines: 36B, 245 blvd Mao Tse Toung, Sangkat Boeung Trabek, Khan Chamkarmon, Phnom-Penh; tel. (23) 994888; fax (23) 994508; e-mail pnhdzrk@royalkhmerairlines.com; internet www.royalkhmerairlines.com; f. 2000; jt venture with Indonesia; domestic and international services.

CAMBODIA

Royal Phnom-Penh Airways: 209 rue 19, Sangkat Chey Chumneah, Khan Daun Penh, Phnom-Penh; tel. (23) 215565; fax (23) 217420; e-mail ppenhairw@bigpond.com.kh; f. 1999; scheduled and charter passenger flights to domestic and regional destinations; Chair. Prince NORODOM CHAKRAPONG.

Siem Reap Airways International: 65 rue 214, Sangkat Boeung Raing, Khan Daun Penh, Phnom-Penh; tel. (23) 723962; fax (23) 720522; e-mail reservation@siemreapairways.com; internet www.siemreapairways.com; f. 2000; scheduled international and domestic passenger services; CEO PRASERT PRASARTTONG-OSOTH.

Tourism

Cambodia's attractions include the ancient temples of Angkor and the beaches of Sihanoukville. The number of tourist arrivals totalled 1.3m. in 2006, when receipts from tourism reached US $963m. More than 15% of tourists in 2007 were reported to have come from the Republic of Korea; other major sources of visitors are Japan and the USA.

Directorate-General of Tourism: 3 blvd Monivong, Phnom-Penh; tel. (23) 427130; fax (23) 426107; f. 1988; Dir SO MARA.

CAMEROON

Introductory Survey

Location, Climate, Language, Religion, Flag, Capital

The Republic of Cameroon lies on the west coast of Africa, with Nigeria to the west, Chad and the Central African Republic to the east, and the Republic of the Congo, Equatorial Guinea and Gabon to the south. The climate is hot and humid in the south and west, with average temperatures of 26°C (80°F). Annual rainfall in Yaoundé averages 4,030 mm (159 ins). The north is drier, with more extreme temperatures. The official languages are French and English; many local languages are also spoken, including Fang, Bamileke and Duala. Approximately 53% of Cameroonians profess Christianity, 25% adhere to traditional religious beliefs, and about 22%, mostly in the north, are Muslims. The national flag (proportions 2 by 3) has three equal vertical stripes, of green, red and yellow, with a five-pointed gold star in the centre of the red stripe. The capital is Yaoundé.

Recent History

In 1884 a German protectorate was established in Cameroon (Kamerun). In 1916, during the First World War, the German administration was overthrown by British and French forces. Under an agreement reached between the occupying powers in 1919, Cameroon was divided into two zones: a French-ruled area in the east and south, and a smaller British-administered area in the west. In 1922 both zones became subject to mandates of the League of Nations, with France and the United Kingdom as the administering powers. In 1946 the zones were transformed into UN Trust Territories, with British and French rule continuing in their respective areas.

French Cameroons became an autonomous state within the French Community in 1957. Under the leadership of Ahmadou Ahidjo, a northerner who became Prime Minister in 1958, the territory became independent, as the Republic of Cameroon, on 1 January 1960. The first election for the country's National Assembly, held in April 1960, was won by Ahidjo's party, the Union camerounaise. In May the new National Assembly elected Ahidjo to be the country's first President.

British Cameroons, comprising a northern and a southern region, was attached to neighbouring Nigeria, for administrative purposes, prior to Nigeria's independence in October 1960. Plebiscites were held, under UN auspices, in the two regions of British Cameroons in February 1961. The northern area voted to merge with Nigeria (becoming the province of Sardauna), while the south voted for union with the Republic of Cameroon, which took place on 1 October 1961.

The enlarged country was named the Federal Republic of Cameroon, with French and English as joint official languages. It comprised two states: the former French zone became East Cameroon, while the former British portion became West Cameroon. John Ngu Foncha, the Prime Minister of West Cameroon and leader of the Kamerun National Democratic Party, became Vice-President of the Federal Republic. Under the continuing leadership of Ahidjo, who (as the sole candidate) was re-elected President in May 1965, the two states became increasingly integrated. In September 1966 the two governing parties and several opposition groups combined to form a single party, the Union nationale camerounaise (UNC). Ahidjo was re-elected as President in March 1970, and Solomon Muna (who had replaced Foncha as Prime Minister of West Cameroon in 1968) became Vice-President.

In June 1972, following the approval by referendum of a new Constitution, the federal system was ended, and the country was officially renamed the United Republic of Cameroon. A centralized political and administrative system was rapidly introduced, and in May 1973 a new National Assembly was elected for a five-year term. After the re-election of Ahidjo as President in April 1975, the Constitution was revised, and a Prime Minister, Paul Biya (a bilingual Christian southerner), was appointed in June. In April 1980 Ahidjo was unanimously re-elected to the presidency for a fifth five-year term of office.

Ahidjo resigned as President in November 1982, and nominated Biya as his successor. In August 1983 Biya announced the discovery of a conspiracy to overthrow his Government, and simultaneously dismissed the Prime Minister and the Minister of the Armed Forces, both northern Muslims. Later in August Ahidjo resigned as President of the UNC, strongly criticizing Biya's regime. In September Biya was elected President of the ruling party, and in January 1984 he was re-elected as President of the Republic. The post of Prime Minister was subsequently abolished, and it was announced that the country's name was to revert to the Republic of Cameroon.

In February 1984 Ahidjo and two of his close military advisers were tried (Ahidjo *in absentia*) for their alleged complicity in the coup plot of August 1983, and received death sentences, which were, however, commuted to life imprisonment. On 6 April 1984 rebel elements in the presidential guard attempted to overthrow the Biya Government. After three days of intense fighting, in which hundreds of people were reported to have been killed, the rebellion was suppressed by forces loyal to the President; a total of 51 defendants subsequently received death sentences. Following extensive changes within the military hierarchy, the UNC Central Committee and the leadership of state-controlled companies, Biya reorganized his Government in July and introduced more stringent press censorship. In March 1985 the UNC was renamed the Rassemblement démocratique du peuple camerounais (RDPC).

Presidential and legislative elections were held in April 1988. Biya was re-elected unopposed to the presidency, securing 98.75% of the votes cast. In the elections to the National Assembly voters were presented with a choice of RDPC-approved candidates; 153 of the 180 deputies elected were new members.

In February 1990 11 people were arrested in connection with their alleged involvement in an unofficial opposition organization, the Social Democratic Front (SDF). In June, in response to mounting civil unrest, Biya stated that he envisaged the future adoption of a multi-party system and announced a series of reforms, including the abolition of laws governing subversion, the revision of the law on political associations, and the reinforcement of press freedom. In December the National Assembly adopted legislation whereby Cameroon officially became a multi-party state.

In January 1991 anti-Government demonstrators protested at Biya's failure to grant an amnesty to prisoners implicated in the 1984 coup attempt. In April 1991 the principal anti-Government groups created an informal alliance, the National Co-ordination Committee of Opposition Parties (NCCOP), which organized a widely observed general strike. Later in April, in response to increasing pressure for political reform, the National Assembly approved legislation granting a general amnesty for political prisoners and reintroducing the post of Prime Minister. Biya subsequently appointed Sadou Hayatou, hitherto Secretary-General at the Presidency, to the position. Hayatou named a transitional Government, principally composed of members of the former Cabinet. The Government's refusal to comply with the NCCOP's demands for an unconditional amnesty for all political prisoners (the existing provisions for an amnesty excluded an estimated 400 political prisoners jailed for allegedly non-political crimes) and for the convening of a national conference prompted the alliance to organize a campaign of civil disobedience, culminated in a general strike in June. The Government placed seven of Cameroon's 10 provinces under military rule, prohibited opposition gatherings, and later in June, following continued civil disturbances, banned the NCCOP and several opposition parties, alleging that the opposition alliance was responsible for terrorist activities. The observance of the general strike declined in subsequent months.

In October 1991 Biya announced that legislative elections were to be held in February 1992, and that a Prime Minister would be appointed from the party that secured a majority in the National Assembly. Following negotiations, in mid-November 1991 the Government and about 40 of the 47 registered opposition parties (including some parties belonging to the NCCOP) signed an agreement providing for the establishment of a committee to draft constitutional reforms. The opposition undertook to suspend the campaign of civil disobedience, while the Government agreed to end the ban on opposition meetings and to release all prisoners who had been arrested during anti-Government demonstrations. The Government revoked the ban on opposition gatherings later in November, and in December ended the military rule that had been imposed in seven provinces.

In January 1992 the Government postponed the legislative elections until March, in order to allow parties sufficient time for preparation. However, several opposition movements, including two of the principal parties, the SDF and the Union démocratique du Cameroun (UDC), refused to contest the elections, on the grounds that the scheduled date was still too early and benefited the RDPC. In February those opposition parties that had not accepted the tripartite agreement in November 1991 formed the Alliance pour le redressement du Cameroun (ARC), and announced that they were to boycott the elections.

At the legislative elections, which took place on 1 March 1992, the RDPC won 88 of the National Assembly's 180 seats, while the Union nationale pour la démocratie et le progrès (UNDP) obtained 68, the extreme left-wing Union des populations camerounaises (UPC) 18 and the Mouvement pour la défense de la République (MDR) six seats. The RDPC subsequently formed an alliance with the MDR, thereby securing an absolute majority in the National Assembly. In April Biya formed a 25-member Cabinet, principally comprising members of the previous Government and including five MDR members; Simon Achidi Achu, an anglophone member of the RDPC, was appointed Prime Minister.

In August 1992 Biya announced that the forthcoming presidential election, scheduled for May 1993, was to be brought forward to 11 October 1992. In September Biya promulgated legislation regulating the election of the President that prohibited the formation of electoral alliances. Shortly before the election two of the seven opposition candidates withdrew in favour of the Chairman of the SDF, John Fru Ndi, who received the support of the ARC. The presidential election, which took place as scheduled, immediately provoked opposition allegations of malpractice on the part of the Government. In mid-October Fru Ndi proclaimed himself President, following unconfirmed reports that he had won the election. Later that month, however, the Government announced that Biya had been re-elected by 39.9% of the votes cast, while Fru Ndi had secured 35.9%, prompting violent demonstrations by opposition supporters in many areas. The Supreme Court rejected a subsequent appeal by Fru Ndi that the results of the election be declared invalid. Biya was inaugurated as President on 3 November and pledged to implement further constitutional reforms. Later that month international condemnation of the Government increased, following the death by torture of a detained opposition member; the USA and Germany suspended economic aid to Cameroon in protest at the continued enforcement of the state of emergency. At the end of November Biya appointed a new 30-member Cabinet, which, in addition to three members of the MDR, included representatives of the UPC, the UNDP and the Parti national du progrès.

In March 1993 an informal alliance of opposition parties (led by the SDF), the Union pour le changement, organized a series of demonstrations and a boycott of French consumer goods (in protest at the French Government's involvement with Biya) in support of demands for a new presidential election. The Government accused the alliance of incitement to civil disorder and continued efforts to suppress opposition activity. In April a gathering organized by the Cameroon Anglophone Movement (CAM) in Buéa, in South-West Province, demanded the restoration of a federal system of government, in response to the traditional dominance of the French-speaking section of the population. In the following month the Government promulgated draft constitutional amendments that provided for the installation of a democratic political system, with the establishment of new organs of government, including an upper legislative chamber, to be known as the Senate, and restricted the power vested in the President (who was to serve a maximum of two five-year terms of office). The draft legislation retained a unitary state, but, in recognition of demands by supporters of federalism, envisaged a more decentralized system of local government.

In September 1994 an informal alliance of 16 opposition movements, the Front des alliés pour le changement (FAC), was established, effectively replacing the Union pour le changement. The UNDP and the UDC refused to join the alliance, however, on the grounds that it was dominated by the SDF. In November Biya announced that discussions on the revision of the Constitution were to resume, following the establishment of a Consultative Constitutional Review Committee, and that municipal elections were to take place in 1995. Constitutional discussions commenced in December 1994, but were boycotted by the opposition, which cited limitations in the agenda of the debate. In early 1995, however, the Consultative Constitutional Review Committee submitted revised constitutional amendments to Biya for consideration.

In July 1995 members of a new anglophone organization, the Southern Cameroons National Council (SCNC, which demanded that the former portion of the British Cameroons that had amalgamated with the Republic of Cameroon in 1961 be granted autonomy), staged a demonstration in Bamenda. In August representatives of anglophone movements, including the SCNC and the CAM, officially presented their demands for the establishment of an independent, English-speaking republic of Southern Cameroons at the UN; the organizations claimed that the plebiscite of 1961, whereby the former southern portion of British Cameroons had voted to merge with the Republic of Cameroon on terms of equal status, had been rendered invalid by subsequent francophone domination.

In October 1995 a special congress of the RDPC re-elected Biya as leader of the party for a further term of five years. In December the National Assembly adopted the revised constitutional amendments, submitted by Biya earlier that month, which increased the presidential mandate from five to seven years (while restricting the maximum tenure of office to two terms) and provided for the establishment of a Senate. In September Achu was replaced as Prime Minister by Peter Mafany Musonge, the General Manager of the Cameroon Development Corporation, and a new Cabinet was appointed.

In January 1997 the Government postponed the legislative elections (which had been scheduled to take place in March) owing to organizational difficulties. The elections, which were contested by 46 political parties, took place on 17 May. The announcement of provisional results (which attributed a large majority of seats to the RDPC) prompted opposition claims of widespread electoral malpractice; however, the Supreme Court rejected opposition appeals against RDPC victories and in early June the official election results were announced: the RDPC had secured 109 of the 180 seats in the legislature, while the SDF had obtained 43, the UNDP 13 and the UDC five seats. The Cabinet remained virtually unchanged from the previous administration. In August further polls were conducted in seven constituencies where the results had been annulled, owing to alleged irregularities; the RDPC won all of the seats, thus increasing its representation in the National Assembly to 116 seats.

It was announced in September 1997 that the presidential election would be held on 12 October. Shortly afterwards the SDF, the UNDP and the UDC declared a boycott of all elections, in protest at the absence of an independent electoral commission. In mid-September Biya was officially elected as the RDPC presidential candidate. At the election, which was contested by seven candidates, Biya was re-elected, winning 92.6% of the votes cast. The level of voter participation in the election was much disputed, with official sources asserting that 81.4% of the electorate took part, while opposition leaders claimed that the abstention rate was higher than 80%. Biya was formally inaugurated on 3 November. Following talks with various opposition groups, the RDPC reached an agreement with the UNDP on the creation of a coalition government; the SDF, however, refused to co-operate with the ruling party. In December, having re-appointed Musonge as Prime Minister, Biya effected a major cabinet reshuffle. The new Government included representatives from four of the country's many political groups, although the RDPC retained 45 of the 50 ministerial posts.

In September 1998 it was reported that some 60 English-speaking Cameroonians, who were alleged to be secessionists campaigning for the independence of Southern Cameroons, were being detained and tortured in Yaoundé, following attacks on police premises. There were counter-accusations made by the opposition, however, that the raids had been staged by government agents as a pretext for further suppression of demands for increased decentralization. In January 1999 the opposition condemned the Government for the alleged marginalization of the anglophone minority in Cameroon, noting that only three of the 2,000 soldiers recently recruited by the armed forces were English-speaking. In June the trial of the alleged anglophone secessionists (the majority of whom had been arrested in 1997) began in Yaoundé. In October three of the defendants were sentenced to life imprisonment, others received lengthy prison sentences, while 29 were acquitted. The human rights organization Amnesty International criticized the verdicts, alluding to the alleged bias of the military court and the reported torture of detainees, and in November the UN Human Rights Committee criticized Cameroon for its alleged failure to protect and to respect fundamental human rights.

A cabinet reshuffle effected in March 2000 was widely interpreted as a response to an escalation in urban crime (several foreign diplomats, including the ambassadors of the USA and the Netherlands, had been attacked). All ministers linked to security matters were involved in the reshuffle. Furthermore, some 70% of senior police-officers were reportedly replaced. In November deputies staged a sit-in outside the National Assembly after the security forces prevented a protest march, from the legislative building to the presidential palace, from proceeding. The march had been organized by the SDF in support of demands for the creation of an independent electoral commission. In the following month the National Assembly adopted legislation on the establishment of a National Elections Observatory (NEO) and on the regulation of state funding for political parties and electoral campaigns. However, five opposition parties boycotted the vote on the elections observatory, claiming that it would be unconstitutional, as it would perform the same functions as the Constitutional Council, and criticizing the President's role in appointing its 11 members. President Biya subsequently postponed municipal elections, due on 21 January 2001, until January 2002.

A reorganization of the cabinet was effected in April 2001, following accusations of corruption against several ministers. In October the NEO was inaugurated, amid opposition criticism that the 11 appointees were all supporters of the ruling RDPC. In December the municipal elections were postponed for a further six months.

Legislative and municipal elections were held concurrently on 30 June 2002, despite initial technical problems. Voting had been delayed by one week, owing to insufficient voting materials. Some 47 parties contested the elections to the National Assembly, at which the RDPC's majority increased to 133 seats, while its closest rival, the SDF, secured 21 seats, the UDC five, the UPC three and the UNDP only one seat. Electoral turn-out was reported to be less than 50%, and the elections were boycotted by the SCNC. Voting for the remaining 17 seats was cancelled by the Supreme Court, in response to complaints of various irregularities in the nine constituencies concerned. At the municipal elections, the RDPC also performed strongly, winning 286 of the 336 council seats contested. Opposition parties alleged widespread electoral fraud, however, and demanded that the elections be declared void. The SDF initially refused to participate in the newly elected legislature and municipal councils, although in mid-July Fru Ndi announced the end of the boycott, provoking internal conflict within his party. Several SDF senior officials subsequently resigned from the party and formed the Alliance des forces progressistes, claiming that Fru Ndi's unilateral decision to end the boycott had been inspired by covert plans to join the Government. In August there was an extensive cabinet reshuffle, in which 18 new members of government were appointed. On 15 September voting took place for the 17 legislative seats that had remained vacant since June; the RDPC secured a further 16 seats, increasing its majority to 149 of the 180 seats in the National Assembly, while the SDF won the remaining seat.

A total of 16 candidates were put forward by opposition parties (including the SDF and the UDC) to contest the presidential election, which took place on 11 October 2004. Despite a constitutional limit of two terms in office, Biya was again re-elected to the presidency, securing 75.2% of the vote. Fru Ndi (SDF) and Adamou Ndam Njoya (UDC) were attributed just 17.1% and 4.7% of the vote, respectively. Although opposition groups strongly contested the validity of the result, accusing Biya and his allies of large-scale electoral fraud, a delegation of electoral observers composed of former members of the US Congress declared the elections to have been fairly conducted.

In December 2004 President Biya appointed a new cabinet and, notably, an English-speaking Prime Minister, Ephraïm Inoni, hitherto Assistant Secretary-General of the Presidency. Despite the appointment of Inoni, representatives of Cameroon's anglophone community demanded increased representation in government to counterbalance what they perceived as a disproportionate number of francophone ministers. The new administration was again comprised largely of members of the RDPC.

In July 2005 the National Assembly approved legislation harmonizing the penal code in Cameroon. Hitherto, the anglophone and francophone regions of Cameroon had been subject to distinct penal codes based, respectively, on the Criminal Procedure Ordinance of 1958 and the Code d'instruction criminelle of 1938. The new, unique penal code was to combine elements of the Napoleonic, British and pre-colonial legal traditions. Although the measure was broadly welcomed as beneficial to national unity, unrest and secessionist sympathies grew throughout 2005 among anglophones of southern Cameroon. In October public celebrations in Bui County commemorating the anniversary of southern British Cameroons' union with the Republic of Cameroon in 1961 led to violent confrontations. Subsequently, more than 100 SCNC leaders and members, including the movement's National Chairman, Ette Otun Ayamba, were arrested.

In late September 2006 President Biya effected a minor reorganization of the Government; the key portfolios remained unchanged and Inoni retained the premiership. In December violence erupted at the University of Buéa after students accused the Government of imposing Francophones on a list of candidates for medical school. Two students were killed in clashes with the security forces. In January 2007 20 members of the SCNC were arrested when they attempted to hold a press conference led by Nfor Ngala Nfor, the movement's Vice-Chairman. At the conference he announced that he had sent a petition to the UN Human Rights Committee calling for it to investigate the clashes at the University of Buéa and to take a position on the question of the occupation of the Southern Cameroons by the Republic of Cameroon.

At legislative elections held in July 2007 the RDPC consolidated its majority in the National Assembly, winning 152 of the 180 seats available. However, opposition parties denounced the results, citing fraudulent activity and corruption. It was reported that in some areas no opposition party ballot papers were made available and that members of the RDPC had been observed bribing and intimidating voters. The results in five constituencies were subsequently annulled and, in accordance with the Constitution, voting was reheld on 30 September. Provisional results indicated that the RDPC had secured 13 of the 17 seats contested, thus its total number of seats in the final composition of the National Assembly was 153; the SDF retained its position as the second largest party with 16 seats, while the UNDP took six seats. However, the political opposition continued to dispute the results in several constituencies amid concerns that, having acquired the necessary two-thirds majority, the RDPC would proceed with plans for constitutional reforms that would allow President Biya to contest the next presidential election scheduled for 2011, at which his mandate was due to expire. Earlier in September 2007 a new Cabinet had been appointed, which included the nomination of a second Deputy Prime Minister, Jean Nkuete, who retained responsibility for agriculture and rural development. Henri Eyebe Ayissi was named as Minister of External Relations, while Essimi Menye assumed the finance portfolio.

In 1991 the Nigerian Government claimed that Cameroon had annexed nine Nigerian fishing settlements, following a longstanding border dispute, based on a 1913 agreement between Germany and the United Kingdom that ceded the Bakassi peninsula in the Gulf of Guinea (a region of strategic and economic significance) to Cameroon. Subsequent attempts by the Governments of Nigeria and Cameroon to resolve the dispute achieved little. In December 1993 some 500 Nigerian troops were dispatched to the region, in response to a number of incidents in which Nigerian nationals had been killed by Cameroonian security forces. Later that month the two nations agreed to establish a joint patrol in the disputed area, and to investigate the incidents. In February 1994, however, Cameroon announced that it was to submit the dispute for adjudication by the UN, the Organization of African Unity (OAU, now the African Union, see p. 164) and the International Court of Justice (ICJ, see p. 20), based in The Hague, Netherlands. Subsequent reports of clashes between Cameroonian and Nigerian forces in the region prompted fears of a full-scale conflict. In March Cameroon agreed to enter into negotiations with Nigeria (without the involvement of international mediators) to resolve the issue. In the same month the OAU issued a resolution urging the withdrawal of troops from the disputed region. In May negotiations between the two nations, with mediation by the Togolese Government, resumed in Yaoundé. In September the Cameroonian Government submitted additional claims to territory in north-eastern Nigeria to the ICJ.

In February 1996 renewed hostilities between Nigerian and Cameroonian forces in the Bakassi region resulted in several

CAMEROON

Introductory Survey

casualties. Later that month, however, Cameroon and Nigeria agreed to refrain from further military action, and delegations from the two countries resumed discussions, again with Togolese mediation. In March the ICJ ordered both nations to cease military operations in the region, to withdraw troops to former positions, and to co-operate with a UN investigative mission, which was to be dispatched to the area. In April, however, clashes continued, with each Government accusing the other of initiating the attacks. Claims by Nigeria that the Cameroonian forces were supported by troops from France were denied by the French Government. Diplomatic efforts to avoid further conflict increased. Nevertheless, both nations continued to reinforce their contingents in the region, and in December and again in May 1997 the Nigerian authorities claimed that Cameroonian troops had resumed attacks in the region. Further clashes were reported in late 1997 and early 1998.

Relations between Cameroon and Nigeria began to improve in late 1998, and in November the International Committee of the Red Cross organized an exchange of prisoners between the two sides. In April 1999 the President-elect of Nigeria, Gen. Olusegun Obasanjo, visited Cameroon, the first such visit since the beginning of the border conflict in 1994. The two countries reportedly agreed to resolve the dispute 'in a fraternal way'. It was, however, announced that ICJ proceedings would be continued, and in late May 1999 Nigeria filed its defence. Following the submission to the ICJ of various written counter-claims by Cameroon and Nigeria in 2000–01, both countries presented their evidence at public hearings in The Hague in February and March 2002.

In October 2002 the ICJ issued its final verdict on the demarcation of the land and maritime boundary between Cameroon and Nigeria, notably ruling in favour of Cameroon's sovereignty over the Bakassi peninsula, citing the 1913 Anglo-German partition agreement, while upholding Nigeria's offshore boundary claims. Despite having no option to appeal, Nigeria refused to accept the Court's decision, and troop deployments began to increase on both sides of the border. In mid-November, however, at a meeting in Geneva, Switzerland, mediated by the Secretary-General of the UN, Kofi Annan, the Presidents of Cameroon and Nigeria signed a joint communiqué announcing the creation of a bilateral commission, to be headed by a UN Special Representative, with a mandate to achieve a peaceful solution to the Bakassi peninsula dispute. At its inaugural meeting in Yaoundé in December, the commission agreed on a 15-point peace agenda and decided to establish a sub-committee to undertake the demarcation of the boundary. In August 2003 Nigeria and Cameroon adopted a framework for the demilitarization of the Bakassi region; the process of demarcation of boundaries between the two countries was expected to take up to three years to complete. In December the Nigerian Government ceded control of 32 villages on its north-eastern border to Cameroon, but sovereignty over the disputed territory with petroleum resources remained under discussion.

In January 2004 Presidents Biya and Obasanjo, meeting in Geneva, Switzerland, with UN mediation, agreed to establish joint security patrols in the disputed region. Following a meeting in Yaoundé in late July between Biya and Obasanjo, it was confirmed that Nigerian troops would withdraw from Bakassi by 15 September. However, the Nigerian Government subsequently reneged on this agreement following legal appeals by Bakassi residents regarding the constitutional legality of ceding land held by Nigerians. The Nigerian Federal High Court rejected this appeal in October but by the end of December the Nigerian Government had still not withdrawn troops from the disputed peninsula, citing difficulties over demarcating maritime boundaries. A new agreement for the withdrawal of Nigerian troops from the peninsula was reached in October 2005 by the bilateral commission. In December the UN Office in West Africa announced that 260 km of the disputed border had been demarcated. The 15th session of the bilateral commission, at which it was hoped a final settlement over the sovereignty of Bakassi would be reached, was scheduled for mid-January 2006, although it was postponed until both countries' presidents could meet in the presence of Annan. In June 2006, at a UN-mediated summit in New York, USA, it was agreed that Nigeria would withdraw its troops from the Bakassi peninsula within 60 days. In August a ceremony marked the transfer of the area to Cameroon after Nigeria completed its troop withdrawal from the disputed region. Nigerian police were to remain in control of the southern and eastern parts of the region until June 2008. In November 2007 the Nigerian Senate called into question the validity of the August 2006 agreement, claiming that former President Obasanjo had not presented the treaty to the National Assembly for ratification.

Government

Under the amended 1972 Constitution, the Republic of Cameroon is a multi-party state. Executive power is vested in the President, as Head of State, who is elected by universal adult suffrage for a term of seven years, and may serve a maximum of two terms. Legislative power is held by the National Assembly, which comprises 180 members and is elected for a term of five years. In December 1995 constitutional amendments provided for the establishment of an upper legislative chamber (to be known as the Senate). The Cabinet is appointed by the President. Local administration is based on 10 provinces, each with a governor who is appointed by the President.

Defence

As assessed at November 2007, Cameroon's armed forces were estimated to total 14,100 men (army 12,500, navy 1,300, air force 300). There was also a 9,000-strong paramilitary force. Cameroon has a bilateral defence agreement with France. The defence budget for 2007 was estimated at 150,000m. francs CFA.

Economic Affairs

In 2006, according to estimates by the World Bank, Cameroon's gross national income (GNI), measured at average 2004–06 prices, was US $18,054m., equivalent to $1,080 per head (or $2,370 per head on an international purchasing-power parity basis). During 1996–2006, it was estimated, the population increased at an average annual rate of 2.0%, while gross domestic product (GDP) per head increased, in real terms, by an average of 2.0% per year. Overall GDP increased, in real terms, at an average annual rate of 4.1% in 1996–2006; growth in 2006 was 3.9%.

Agriculture (including hunting, forestry and fishing) contributed 20.3% of GDP in 2006, according to the World Bank. An estimated 53.6% of the labour force were employed in agriculture in mid-2005, according to FAO. The principal cash crops are cocoa beans (which accounted for 9.3% of export earnings in 2004), cotton (5.8%) and coffee (3.1%). The principal subsistence crops are cassava, plaintains, maize and sorghum; Cameroon is not, however, self-sufficient in cereals. In 1995 an estimated 42% of the country's land area was covered by forest, but an inadequate transport infrastructure has impeded the development of the forestry sector. None the less, illegal logging and poaching in the country's forests remains a significant problem. During 1996–2006, according to the World Bank, the real GDP of the agricultural sector increased at an average annual rate of 4.7%; growth in 2006 was 3.4%.

Industry (including mining, manufacturing, construction and power) employed 8.9% of the labour force in 1990, and contributed 33.5% of GDP in 2006, according to the World Bank. During 1996–2006 industrial GDP grew at an average annual rate of 3.2%. However, it declined by 1.8% in 2005, before increasing by 5.5% in 2006.

Mining contributed 4.0% of GDP in 2000/01, but employed only 0.1% of Cameroon's working population in 1985. Receipts from the exploitation of the country's petroleum reserves constitute a principal source of government revenue. Deposits of limestone are also quarried. Significant reserves of natural gas, bauxite, iron ore, uranium and tin remain largely undeveloped. According to the IMF, the GDP of the mining sector increased by an average of 2.5% per year in 1995/96–2000/01; growth in 2000/01 was 0.6%.

Manufacturing contributed an estimated 18.5% of GDP in 2006, according to the World Bank. The sector employed an estimated 7% of the working population in 1995. The sector is based on the processing of both indigenous primary products (petroleum-refining, agro-industrial activities) and of imported raw materials (an aluminium smelter uses alumina imported from Guinea). According to the World Bank, manufacturing GDP increased at an average annual rate of 5.7% in 1996–2006; growth in 2006 was 4.6%.

In 2004 hydroelectric power installations supplied 95.4% of Cameroon's energy. In 2005 imports of mineral fuels accounted for 26.4% of the value of total imports.

Services contributed 46.2% of GDP in 2006. During 1996–2006, according to the World Bank, the GDP of the services sector increased at an average annual rate of 3.7%; growth in 2006 was 2.9%.

In 2005 Cameroon recorded a visible trade surplus of an estimated 112,700m. francs CFA, but there was an estimated deficit of 285,600m. francs CFA on the current account of the balance of payments. In 2004 the principal source of imports (22.4%) was France; other major suppliers were Nigeria (12.2%) and the USA (5.3%). France was also the principal market for exports in that year, taking 13.5% of total exports; other significant purchasers were Italy (11.5%), Spain (10.7%), the Netherlands (8.6%) and the USA (5.7%). The principal exports in 2004 were crude petroleum and oils, cocoa beans, raw cotton, aluminium and coffee. The principal imports in that year were machinery and transport equipment, food and live animals, manufactured goods, and chemicals and related products.

In 2006 there was a budget surplus of 3,108,000m. francs CFA. Cameroon's total external debt at the end of 2004 was US $9,496m., of which $7,924m. was long-term public debt. The annual rate of inflation averaged 2.5% in 2000–06; consumer prices increased by 5.2% in 2006. An estimated 7.5% of the labour force were unemployed in 2001.

Cameroon is a member of the Central African organs of the Franc Zone (see p. 307), of the Communauté économique des états de l'Afrique centrale (CEEAC, see p. 411), of the International Cocoa Organization (see p. 408) and of the International Coffee Organization (see p. 408).

Cameroon's potential for continued economic development has been hindered by its poor physical infrastructure, endemic fraud and corruption, and a consistent decline in petroleum production. The Cameroon Government has attempted to address this last issue, and it was hoped that revenue—projected to reach some US $500m. over a 25-year production period—from a 1,070-km pipeline from Chad to the southern Cameroonian port of Kribi, would partially offset the fall in direct earnings from petroleum, daily production of which decreased from a peak of 164,000 barrels in the mid-1980s to some 83,000 barrels in 2006. The decline in oil revenue was expected to reduce the budget surplus to just 1.1% of GDP in 2008; however, this was potentially to be offset by the increasing influence of, and investment by, the People's Republic of China in the country's petroleum, mining and forestry sectors. Furthermore, in assisting Cameroon with economic reforms the European Union (EU, see p. 244) was to invest €24m. in the cocoa and coffee sector, while in June 2006 France announced a substantial aid package, worth $627m. over a five-year period, for Cameroon. A special committee, involving French and Cameroonian officials and aid workers, was established to ensure that the French assistance was disbursed effectively. The market for cocoa demonstrated growth in the first half of 2007, with rising prices backed by increased demand and improved quality of product. This was attributed to some 2,500 drying ovens donated by the EU, concomitant with favourable weather conditions. However, the cotton sector in Cameroon continued to encounter difficulties as a result of declining world prices; in late 2007 it appeared unlikely that the Société de Dévelopment du Coton would continue to operate without significant governmental and external financial assistance. Despite having stated in December 2004 that Cameroon's public finances had significantly deteriorated in 2003–04, in October 2005 the IMF approved both a new three-year arrangement for Cameroon under the Poverty Reduction and Growth Facility, worth $26.8m., and funds totalling $8.2m. under the enhanced initiative for heavily indebted poor countries. Nevertheless, continued donor support and wide-ranging reforms were required in order to achieve the economic growth rates needed to significantly reduce poverty. GDP was estimated by the IMF to have increased by 3.8% in 2007, with further expansion projected in 2008, primarily as a result of the expanding non-petroleum sector. Low fuel prices were expected to reduce the rate of inflation to below 3.0%, while the 2008 budget was to provide tax breaks in agriculture and construction, in an attempt further to increase economic growth.

Education

Since independence, Cameroon has achieved one of the highest rates of school attendance in Africa, but provision of educational facilities varies according to region. Education, which is bilingual, is provided by the Government, missionary societies and private concerns. Education in state schools is available free of charge, and the Government provides financial assistance for other schools. Primary education begins at six years of age. It lasts for six years in Eastern Cameroon (where it is officially compulsory), and for seven years in Western Cameroon. Secondary education, beginning at the age of 12 or 13, lasts for a further seven years, comprising two cycles of four years and three years in Eastern Cameroon and five years and two years in Western Cameroon. In 2003/04 there were some 3.0m. pupils enrolled at the primary level, while the number of pupils enrolled at secondary schools totalled some 1.2m. There are seven universities, six of which are state-owned. There were 60,534 students enrolled at the state-owned universities in 1998/99 and they employed a total of 1,792 teachers in that academic year. Expenditure on education by the central Government in 2004 was estimated at 213,143m. francs CFA (26.3% of total spending).

Public Holidays

2008: 1 January (New Year), 11 February (Youth Day), 21 March (Good Friday), 24 March (Easter Monday), 1 May (Labour Day and Ascension Day), 20 May (National Day), 15 August (Assumption), 1 October* (Djoulde Soumae, end of Ramadan), 9 December* (Festival of Sheep), 25 December (Christmas).

2009: 1 January (New Year), 11 February (Youth Day), 10 April (Good Friday), 13 April (Easter Monday), 1 May (Labour Day), 20 May (National Day), 21 May (Ascension Day), 15 August (Assumption), 20 September* (Djoulde Soumae, end of Ramadan), 27 November* (Festival of Sheep), 25 December (Christmas).

* These holidays are dependent on the Islamic lunar calendar and may vary by one or two days from the dates given.

Weights and Measures

The metric system is in force.

CAMEROON

Statistical Survey

Source (unless otherwise stated): Direction de la Prévision, Ministère de l'Economie et des Finances, BP 18, Yaoundé; tel. 223-4040; fax 223-2150.

Area and Population

AREA, POPULATION AND DENSITY

Area (sq km)	475,442*
Population (census results)	
9 April 1976†	7,663,246
9 April 1987	
Males	5,162,878
Females	5,330,777
Total	10,493,655
Population (UN estimates at mid-year)‡	
2005	17,795,000
2006	18,175,000
2007	18,549,000
Density (per sq km) at mid-2007	39.0

* 183,569 sq miles.
† Including an adjustment for underenumeration, estimated at 7.4%. The enumerated total was 7,090,115.
‡ Source: UN, *World Population Prospects: The 2006 Revision.*

PROVINCES
(population at 1987 census)

	Urban	Rural	Total
Centre	877,481	774,119	1,651,600
Littoral	1,093,323	259,510	1,352,833
West	431,337	908,454	1,339,791
South-West	258,940	579,102	838,042
North-West	271,114	966,234	1,237,348
North	234,572	597,593	832,165
East	152,787	364,411	517,198
South	104,023	269,775	373,798
Adamaoua	178,644	316,541	495,185
Far North	366,698	1,488,997	1,855,695
Total	3,968,919	6,524,736	10,493,655

PRINCIPAL TOWNS
(population at 1987 census)

Douala	810,000	Bamenda	110,000
Yaoundé (capital)	649,000	Nkongsamba	85,420
Garoua	142,000	Kumba	70,112
Maroua	123,000	Limbé	44,561
Bafoussam	113,000		

Mid-2005 ('000, incl. suburbs, UN estimates): Douala 1,761; Yaoundé 1,485 (Source: UN, *World Urbanization Prospects: The 2005 Revision*).

BIRTHS AND DEATHS
(annual averages, UN estimates)

	1990–95	1995–2000	2000–05
Birth rate (per 1,000)	40.9	37.9	37.9
Death rate (per 1,000)	13.1	13.8	15.0

Source: UN, *World Population Prospects: The 2006 Revision.*

Expectation of life (years at birth, WHO estimates): 50.5 (males 50.0; females 51.0) in 2005 (Source: WHO, *World Health Statistics*).

ECONOMICALLY ACTIVE POPULATION
(persons aged six years and over, mid-1985, official estimates)

	Males	Females	Total
Agriculture, hunting, forestry and fishing	1,574,946	1,325,925	2,900,871
Mining and quarrying	1,693	100	1,793
Manufacturing	137,671	36,827	174,498
Electricity, gas and water	3,373	149	3,522
Construction	65,666	1,018	66,684
Trade, restaurants and hotels	115,269	38,745	154,014
Transport, storage and communications	50,664	1,024	51,688
Financing, insurance, real estate and business services	7,447	562	8,009
Community, social and personal services	255,076	37,846	292,922
Activities not adequately defined	18,515	17,444	35,959
Total in employment	2,230,320	1,459,640	3,689,960
Unemployed	180,016	47,659	227,675
Total labour force	2,410,336	1,507,299	3,917,635

Source: ILO, *Yearbook of Labour Statistics.*

Mid-2005 (estimates in '000): Agriculture, etc. 3,695; Total labour force 6,900 (Source: FAO).

Health and Welfare

KEY INDICATORS

Total fertility rate (children per woman, 2005)	4.4
Under-5 mortality rate (per 1,000 live births, 2005)	149
HIV/AIDS (% of persons aged 15–49, 2005)	5.4
Physicians (per 1,000 head, 2004)	0.19
Hospital beds (per 1,000 head, 1990)	2.55
Health expenditure (2004): US $ per head (PPP)	82.7
Health expenditure (2004): % of GDP	5.2
Health expenditure (2004): public (% of total)	28.0
Access to water (% of persons, 2004)	66
Access to sanitation (% of persons, 2004)	51
Human Development Index (2005): ranking	144
Human Development Index (2005): value	0.532

For sources and definitions, see explanatory note on p. vi.

Agriculture

PRINCIPAL CROPS
('000 metric tons)

	2004	2005	2006
Rice (paddy)	50	53	52*
Maize	966	1,023	850*
Millet	60†	52*	55*
Sorghum	608	523	550*
Potatoes	142	146	145*
Sweet potatoes	190	190*	190*
Cassava (Manioc)	2,093	2,139	2,100*
Yams	286	293*	300*
Taro (Coco yams)	1,128	1,152	1,200*
Other roots and tubers*	15	15	15
Sugar cane*	1,380	1,373	1,450
Dry beans	200	207	200*
Groundnuts (in shell)	226	234	160†
Oil palm fruit*	1,214	1,222	1,300
Melonseed*	57	57	58

CAMEROON

—continued	2004	2005	2006
Tomatoes	408	418	420*
Pumpkins, squash and gourds	125	128	130*
Dry onions	74	75	75*
Bananas	798	856	860*
Plantains	1,315	1,356	1,400*
Avocados*	54	56	55
Pineapples	48	50	50*
Coffee (green)†	54	44	41
Cocoa beans†	167	179	165
Natural rubber*	46	46	46

* FAO estimate(s).
† Unofficial figure(s).
Source: FAO.

LIVESTOCK
('000 head, year ending September, FAO estimates unless otherwise indicated)

	2003	2004	2005
Horses	17	17	17
Asses	39	40	40
Cattle	5,800	5,900	6,000*
Pigs	1,350	1,350	1,350
Sheep	3,800	3,800	3,800
Goats	4,400	4,400	4,400
Chickens	31,000	31,000	31,000

* Unofficial figure.

2006: Figures unchanged from 2005.

Source: FAO.

LIVESTOCK PRODUCTS
('000 metric tons, FAO estimates)

	2004	2005	2006
Cattle meat	93.0	94.0	94.0
Sheep meat	16.4	16.4	16.4
Goat meat	15.7	15.7	15.7
Pig meat	15.7	15.5	15.5
Chicken meat	31.8	33.1	30.0
Game meat	50.0	50.0	50.0
Cows' milk	130.0	130.0	130.0
Sheep's milk	17.2	17.2	17.2
Goats' milk	42.1	42.1	42.1
Hen eggs	13.4	13.4	13.4
Honey	3.0	3.1	3.0

Source: FAO.

Forestry

ROUNDWOOD REMOVALS
('000 cubic metres, excl. bark)

	2004	2005	2006
Sawlogs, veneer logs and logs for sleepers	1,450	1,450	1,450
Other industrial wood	350	350	350
Fuel wood	9,407	9,485	9,566
Total	11,207	11,285	11,366

Source: FAO.

SAWNWOOD PRODUCTION
('000 cubic metres, incl. railway sleepers)

	2003	2004	2005
Total (all broadleaved)	658	702	702*

* FAO estimate.

2006: Production assumed to be unchanged from 2005 (FAO estimate).

Source: FAO.

Fishing
('000 metric tons, live weight)

	2003	2004	2005
Capture	117.8	129.0	142.3
Freshwater fishes	55.0	65.0	75.0
Cassava croaker	1.3	0.9	0.4
Bobo croaker	1.5	2.0	2.4
Other croakers and drums	1.6	0.8	—
Sardinellas	21.8	11.8	1.8
Bonga shad	20.2	30.8	41.7
Aquaculture	0.3	0.3	0.3
Total catch	118.1	129.3	142.7

Source: FAO.

Mining

	2004	2005	2006
Crude petroleum (million barrels)	34.7	21.9	22.0
Gold (kilograms)*	1,500	18,895	20,000
Pozzolan ('000 metric tons)	600	600	600
Limestone ('000 metric tons)	103	103	100

* From artisanal mining.

Source: US Geological Survey.

Industry

SELECTED PRODUCTS
('000 metric tons, unless otherwise indicated)

	2002	2003	2004
Palm oil	153	162	172
Raw sugar	101	120	n.a.
Veneer sheets ('000 cu metres)	53	50	47
Plywood ('000 cu metres)	42	39	40
Jet fuels	69	69	69
Motor spirit (petrol)	232	290	402
Kerosene	140	217	258
Gas-diesel (distillate fuel) oil	370	446	607
Residual fuel oils	317	327	388
Lubricating oils	17	17	17
Petroleum bitumen (asphalt)	5	5	5
Liquefied petroleum gas	18	21	28
Cement	950	949	930
Aluminium (unwrought)	195	195	215
Electric energy (million kWh)	3,300	3,684	4,110

Veneer sheets: ('000 cu metres, FAO estimates) 47 in 2005–06.

Plywood: ('000 cu metres, FAO estimates) 40 in 2005–06.

Palm oil ('000 metric tons, unofficial estimates): 154 in 2005; 160 in 2006.

Sources: UN, *Industrial Commodity Statistics Yearbook*; FAO.

CAMEROON

Finance

CURRENCY AND EXCHANGE RATES

Monetary Units
100 centimes = 1 franc de la Coopération financière en Afrique centrale (CFA).

Sterling, Dollar and Euro Equivalents (31 December 2007)
£1 sterling = 892.702 francs CFA;
US $1 = 489.592 francs CFA;
€1 = 655.957 francs CFA;
10,000 francs CFA = £11.20 = $22.44 = €15.24.

Average Exchange Rate (francs CFA per US $)
2005   527.47
2006   522.89
2007   479.27

Note: An exchange rate of 1 French franc = 50 francs CFA, established in 1948, remained in force until January 1994, when the CFA franc was devalued by 50%, with the exchange rate adjusted to 1 French franc = 100 francs CFA. This relationship to French currency remained in effect with the introduction of the euro on 1 January 1999. From that date, accordingly, a fixed exchange rate of €1 = 655.957 francs CFA has been in operation.

BUDGET
('000 million francs CFA)

Revenue*	2004	2005	2006
Oil revenue	325	439	643
Non-oil revenue	942	1,104	1,165
Direct taxes	228	262	264
Taxes on international trade	179	189	206
Other taxes on goods and services	370	462	522
Value-added tax	331	385	445
Non-tax revenue (excluding privatization proceeds)	96	126	100
Total	**1,267**	**1,543**	**1,808**

Expenditure	2004	2005	2006
Current expenditure	1,169	1,055	1,097
Wages and salaries	450	414	419
Other goods and services	414	337	381
Interest on public debt	164	129	87
Subsidies and transfers	141	175	211
Capital expenditure	167	206	271
Externally financed investment	67	44	64
Domestically financed investment	90	159	177
Restructuring	10	3	31
Other	−5	17	−5
Total	**1,331**	**1,278**	**1,364**

* Excluding grants received ('000 million francs CFA): 19 in 2004; 47 in 2005; 2,664 in 2006.

Source: IMF, *Cameroon: Statistical Appendix* (August 2007).

INTERNATIONAL RESERVES*
(US $ million at 31 December)

	2004	2005	2006
IMF special drawing rights	0.67	2.13	4.63
Reserve position in IMF	1.01	1.00	1.08
Foreign exchange	827.63	946.25	1,710.51
Total	**829.31**	**949.38**	**1,716.22**

* Excluding reserves of gold (30,000 troy ounces each year).

Source: IMF, *International Financial Statistics*.

MONEY SUPPLY
('000 million francs CFA at 31 December)

	2004	2005	2006
Currency outside banks	324.04	273.48	265.67
Demand deposits at deposit money banks	492.14	550.03	632.35
Total money (incl. others)	**829.96**	**832.90**	**935.86**

Source: IMF, *International Financial Statistics*.

COST OF LIVING
(Consumer Price Index; base: 2000 = 100)*

	2004	2005	2006
Food	109.2	110.3	117.9
All items	108.4	110.5	116.2

* Data prior to 2004 for Douala and Yaoundé only.

Source: ILO.

NATIONAL ACCOUNTS
Expenditure on the Gross Domestic Product
('000 million francs CFA at current prices)

	2004	2005	2006
Government final consumption expenditure	847.1	872.1	901.3
Private final consumption expenditure	5,946.8	6,298.1	6,709.1
Gross capital formation	1,521.1	1,546.9	1,564.5
Change in inventories	54.8	121.5	2.7
Total domestic expenditure	**8,369.8**	**8,838.9**	**9,177.6**
Exports of goods and services	1,616.8	1,789.7	2,159.5
Less Imports of goods and services	1,652.7	1,878.6	1,967.0
GDP in purchasers' values	**8,333.9**	**8,749.6**	**9,370.1**
GDP at factor cost at constant 2000 prices	7,754.5	7,932.6	8,173.2

Gross Domestic Product by Economic Activity
('000 million francs CFA at current prices)

	2002	2003
Agriculture, hunting, forestry and fishing	2,075.2	2,144.9
Petroleum	512.2	487.5
Manufacturing	1,060.7	1,137.1
Electricity, gas and water	124.7	144.9
Construction	538.4	546.5
Services	3,054.7	3,243.9
GDP at factor cost	**7,365.9**	**7,704.8**
Indirect taxes, *less* subsidies	229.5	246.2
GDP in purchasers' values	**7,595.4**	**7,951.1**

Source: Banque des états de l'Afrique centrale.

2006 (US $ million at constant 2000 prices): Agriculture, etc. 2,533.59; Industry 3,443.77 (Manufacturing 2,226.03); Services 5,611.77; GDP at factor cost 11,589.14 (Source: African Development Bank, *Statistical Yearbook*).

BALANCE OF PAYMENTS
('000 million francs CFA)

	2003	2004	2005
Exports of goods f.o.b.	1,332.9	1,348.5	1,637.4
Imports of goods f.o.b.	−1,251.6	−1,383.8	−1,524.7
Trade balance	**81.3**	**−35.3**	**112.7**
Services (net)	−456.4	−392.8	−293.9
Balance on goods and services	**−375.1**	**−428.1**	**−181.2**
Other income (net)	−308.2	−274.6	−200.1
Balance on goods, services and income	**−683.3**	**−702.7**	**−381.3**
Current transfers (net)	126.2	96.5	95.7
Current balance	**−557.1**	**−606.2**	**−285.6**
Capital account (net)	44.5	44.6	48.1
Direct investment (net)	222.6	168.7	118.5
Portfolio investment (net)	0.3	0.4	0.4
Other investments (net)	−231.1	131.6	−44.4
Errors and omissions	159	63.7	79.9
Overall balance	**−361.8**	**−197.2**	**−83.1**

Source: Banque des états de l'Afrique centrale.

External Trade

PRINCIPAL COMMODITIES
(US $ million)

Imports c.i.f.	2002	2003	2004
Food and live animals	314.2	342.9	407.4
Cereals and cereal preparations	171.4	173.7	212.0
Mineral fuels, lubricants, etc.	274.4	249.7	427.8
Petroleum, petroleum products and related materials	270.5	243.6	423.4
Crude petroleum and oils	213.7	170.8	366.6
Chemicals and related products	247.0	291.3	312.5
Manufactured goods	290.8	324.2	327.4
Iron and steel	56.7	65.6	60.7
Tubes, pipes and fittings	24.2	14.9	12.8
Machinery and transport equipment	540.6	558.5	642.6
Road vehicles	160.5	199.3	198.8
Total (incl. others)	1,866.3	2,020.7	2,407.0

Exports f.o.b.	2002	2003	2004
Food and live animals	358.2	419.4	456.5
Coffee, tea, cocoa, spices, etc.	290.3	314.1	344.9
Cocoa and cocoa products	235.2	242.5	266.9
Cocoa beans (raw, roasted)	191.6	179.5	230.3
Coffee (green, roasted)	53.4	69.8	76.7
Crude materials, inedible, except fuels	349.8	440.3	599.7
Textile fibres and wastes	93.9	108.1	144.6
Raw cotton (not carded or combed)	93.9	108.1	144.6
Mineral fuels, lubricants, etc.	886.2	1,109.7	1,157.0
Petroleum, petroleum products and related materials	886.2	1,109.7	1,157.0
Crude petroleum and oils	824.6	999.3	1,019.4
Petroleum products (refined)	61.6	110.3	137.6
Manufactured goods	160.9	191.2	205.4
Aluminium	76.9	92.9	114.2
Total (incl. others)	1,801.7	2,245.8	2,478.4

Source: UN, *International Trade Statistics Yearbook*.

PRINCIPAL TRADING PARTNERS
(US $ million, estimates)

Imports c.i.f.	2002	2003	2004
Belgium	75	85	118
Brazil	17	28	36
Canada	21	16	15
China, People's Repub.	67	87	111
Côte d'Ivoire	29	34	32
Finland	9	11	63
France (incl. Monaco)	435	391	540
Germany	87	77	111
Guinea	31	35	38
India	25	31	27
Italy	62	68	69
Japan	85	122	111
Mauritania	14	19	28
Netherlands	52	64	55
Nigeria	200	170	293
South Africa	38	44	36
Spain	28	27	35
Thailand	26	22	55
Turkey	14	21	22
United Kingdom	60	40	50
USA	156	102	127
Total (incl. others)	1,866	2,021	2,407

Exports f.o.b.	2002	2003	2004
Belgium	38	56	96
Chad	39	46	28
China, People's Repub.	78	98	63
Congo, Democratic Repub.	11	29	21
Congo, Repub.	21	20	23
France (incl. Monaco)	234	244	335
Gabon	19	43	38
Germany	26	26	22
Guinea	11	33	30
India	27	8	17
Ireland	7	13	27
Italy	342	302	285
Netherlands	231	238	212
Nigeria	15	17	25
South Africa	4	53	20
Spain	359	491	264
Turkey	12	11	28
United Kingdom	26	43	98
USA	122	169	142
Total (incl. others)	1,802	2,246	2,478

Source: UN, *International Trade Statistics Yearbook*.

Transport

RAILWAYS
(traffic, year ending 30 June)

	2001	2002	2003
Freight ton-km (million)	1,159	1,179	1,090
Passenger-km (million)	303	308	322

Source: UN, *Statistical Yearbook*.

ROAD TRAFFIC
('000 motor vehicles in use, estimates)

	2001	2002	2003
Passenger cars	134.5	151.9	173.1
Commercial vehicles	51.1	37.4	57.4

Source: UN, *Statistical Yearbook*.

SHIPPING
Merchant Fleet
(registered at 31 December)

	2004	2005	2006
Number of vessels	64	66	66
Total displacement ('000 grt)	185.1	55.3	55.3

Source: Lloyd's Register-Fairplay, *World Fleet Statistics*.

International Sea-borne Freight Traffic
(freight traffic at Douala, '000 metric tons)

	1995	1996	1997
Goods loaded	1,841	1,967	2,385
Goods unloaded	2,317	2,211	2,497

Source: Banque des états de l'Afrique centrale, *Etudes et Statistiques*.

CIVIL AVIATION
(traffic on scheduled services)

	2001	2002	2003
Kilometres flown (million)	4	9	8
Passengers carried ('000)	157	235	225
Passenger-km (million)	423	585	562
Total ton-km (million)	84	73	70

Source: UN, *Statistical Yearbook*.

Tourism

FOREIGN VISITORS BY COUNTRY OF ORIGIN*

	2002	2004†	2005
Belgium	4,383	3,885	3,046
Canada	2,600	2,399	5,918
France	53,167	40,611	80,057
Italy	4,628	4,426	8,915
Netherlands	3,214	4,217	6,959
Switzerland	8,674	5,668	7,188
United Kingdom	6,069	5,818	11,618
USA	10,906	9,194	21,779
Total (incl. others)	226,019	189,856	176,372

* Arrivals at hotels and similar establishments.
† Figures not available for 2003.

Receipts from tourism (US $ million, incl. passenger transport): 182 in 2001; 124 in 2002; 162 in 2003.

Source: World Tourism Organization.

Education

(2004/05, unless otherwise indicated)

	Institutions	Teachers	Students ('000) Males	Females	Total
Pre-primary	1,371*	7,012	88.8†	87.2†	176.0†
Primary	9,459*	62,280	1,629	1,372	3,001
Secondary:					
general	700*	24,308	425.9	390.2	816.1
technical/ vocational	324*	24,189	242.9	138.6	381.4
Universities	6‡	3,173	60.5	39.4	99.9

* 1998 figure.
† 2003/04 figure.
‡ 1996/97 figure.

Source: UNESCO Institute for Statistics.

Adult literacy rate (UNESCO estimates): 67.9% (males 77.0%; females 59.8%) in 2001 (Source: UNESCO Institute for Statistics).

Communications Media

	2004	2005	2006
Telephones ('000 main lines in use)	99.4	100.3	n.a.
Mobile cellular telephones ('000 subscribers)	1,537	2,253	n.a.
Internet users ('000)	170	250	370

Broadband subscribers: 200 in 2005.

Personal computers ('000 in use): 160 in 2004.

Radio receivers ('000 in use): 2,270 in 1997.

2004: Daily newspapers 10; Non-daily newspapers 250.

Sources: mainly UNESCO, *Statistical Yearbook*; International Telecommunication Union.

Directory

The Constitution

In December 1995 the National Assembly formally adopted amendments to the 1972 Constiution that provided for a democratic system of government, with the establishment of an upper legislative chamber (to be known as the Senate), a Council of Supreme Judiciary Affairs, a Council of State, and a Civil Service High Authority, and restricted the power vested in the President, who was to serve a maximum of two seven-year terms. The restoration of decentralized local government areas was also envisaged. The main provisions of the 1972 Constitution, as amended, are summarized below:

The Constitution declares that the human being, without distinction as to race, religion, sex or belief, possesses inalienable and sacred rights. It affirms its attachment to the fundamental freedoms embodied in the Universal Declaration of Human Rights and the UN Charter. The State guarantees to all citizens of either sex the rights and freedoms set out in the preamble of the Constitution.

SOVEREIGNTY

1. The Republic of Cameroon shall be one and indivisible, democratic, secular and dedicated to social service. It shall ensure the equality before the law of all its citizens. Provisions that the official languages be French and English, for the motto, flag, national anthem and seal, that the capital be Yaoundé.

2–3. Sovereignty shall be vested in the people who shall exercise it either through the President of the Republic and the members returned by it to the National Assembly or by means of referendum. Elections are by universal suffrage, direct or indirect, by every citizen aged 21 or over in a secret ballot. Political parties or groups may take part in elections subject to the law and the principles of democracy and of national sovereignty and unity.

4. State authority shall be exercised by the President of the Republic and the National Assembly.

THE PRESIDENT OF THE REPUBLIC

5. The President of the Republic, as Head of State and Head of the Government, shall be responsible for the conduct of the affairs of the Republic. He shall define national policy and may charge the members of the Government with the implementation of this policy in certain spheres.

6–7. Candidates for the office of President must hold civic and political rights, be at least 35 years old and have resided in Cameroon for a minimum of 12 consecutive months, and may not hold any other elective office or professional activity. The President is elected for seven years, by a majority of votes cast by the people, and may serve a maximum of two terms. Provisions are made for the continuity of office in the case of the President's resignation.

8–9. The Ministers and Vice-Ministers are appointed by the President to whom they are responsible, and they may hold no other appointment. The President is also head of the armed forces, he negotiates and ratifies treaties, may exercise clemency after consultation with the Higher Judicial Council, promulgates and is responsible for the enforcement of laws, is responsible for internal and external security, makes civil and military appointments, provides for necessary administrative services.

10. The President, by reference to the Supreme Court, ensures that all laws passed are constitutional.

11. Provisions whereby the President may declare a state of emergency or state of siege.

THE NATIONAL ASSEMBLY

12. The National Assembly shall be renewed every five years, though it may at the instance of the President of the Republic legislate to extend or shorten its term of office. It shall be composed of 180 members elected by universal suffrage.

13–14. Laws shall normally be passed by a simple majority of those present, but if a bill is read a second time at the request of the

CAMEROON

President of the Republic a majority of the National Assembly as a whole is required.

15–16. The National Assembly shall meet twice a year, each session to last not more than 30 days; in one session it shall approve the budget. It may be recalled to an extraordinary session of not more than 15 days.

17–18. Elections and suitability of candidates and sitting members shall be governed by law.

RELATIONS BETWEEN THE EXECUTIVE AND THE LEGISLATURE

19. Bills may be introduced either by the President of the Republic or by any member of the National Assembly.

20. Reserved to the legislature are the fundamental rights and duties of the citizen; the law of persons and property; the political, administrative and judicial system in respect of elections to the National Assembly, general regulation of national defence, authorization of penalties and criminal and civil procedure etc., and the organization of the local authorities; currency, the budget, dues and taxes, legislation on public property; economic and social policy; the education system.

21. The National Assembly may empower the President of the Republic to legislate by way of ordinance for a limited period and for given purposes.

22–26. Other matters of procedure, including the right of the President of the Republic to address the Assembly and of the Ministers and Vice-Ministers to take part in debates.

27–29. The composition and conduct of the Assembly's programme of business. Provisions whereby the Assembly may inquire into governmental activity. The obligation of the President of the Republic to promulgate laws, which shall be published in both languages of the Republic.

30. Provisions whereby the President of the Republic, after consultation with the National Assembly, may submit to referendum certain reform bills liable to have profound repercussions on the future of the nation and national institutions.

THE JUDICIARY

31. Justice is administered in the name of the people. The President of the Republic shall ensure the independence of the judiciary and shall make appointments with the assistance of the Higher Judicial Council.

THE SUPREME COURT

32–33. The Supreme Court has powers to uphold the Constitution in such cases as the death or incapacity of the President and the admissibility of laws, to give final judgments on appeals on the Judgment of the Court of Appeal and to decide complaints against administrative acts. It may be assisted by experts appointed by the President of the Republic.

IMPEACHMENT

34. There shall be a Court of Impeachment with jurisdiction to try the President of the Republic for high treason and the Ministers and Vice-Ministers for conspiracy against the security of the State.

THE ECONOMIC AND SOCIAL COUNCIL

35. There shall be an Economic and Social Council, regulated by the law.

AMENDMENT OF THE CONSTITUTION

36–37. Bills to amend the Constitution may be introduced either by the President of the Republic or the National Assembly. The President may decide to submit any amendment to the people by way of a referendum. No procedure to amend the Constitution may be accepted if it tends to impair the republican character, unity or territorial integrity of the State, or the democratic principles by which the Republic is governed.

The Government

HEAD OF STATE

President: PAUL BIYA (took office 6 November 1982; elected 14 January 1984; re-elected 24 April 1988, 11 October 1992, 12 October 1997 and 11 October 2004).

CABINET
(March 2008)

A coalition of the Rassemblement démocratique du peuple camerounais (RDPC), the Union nationale pour la démocratie et le progrès (UNDP), the Union des populations camerounaises (UPC), the Mouvement pour la défense de la République (MDR) and the Alliance nationale pour la démocratie et le progrès (ANDP).

Prime Minister: EPHRAIM INONI (RDPC).
Deputy Prime Minister, in charge of Justice: AMADOU ALI (RDPC).
Deputy Prime Minister, in charge of Agriculture and Rural Development: JEAN NKUTE (RDPC).

Ministers of State

Minister of State in charge of Territorial Administration and Decentralization: MARAFA HAMIDOU YAYA (RDPC).
Minister of State and Secretary-General at the Presidency: LAURENT ESSO (RDPC).
Minister of State in charge of Posts and Telecommunications: BELLO BOUBA MAIGARI (UNDP).

Ministers

Minister of Labour and Social Security: ROBERT NKILI (RDPC).
Minister of Higher Education: JACQUES FAME NDONGO (RDPC).
Minister of Urban Development and Housing: CLOBERT TCHATAT (RDPC).
Minister of Secondary Education: LOUIS BAPES BAPES (RDPC).
Minister of Livestock, Fisheries and Animal Industries: Dr ABOUBAKARY SARKI (RDPC).
Minister of Communication: JEAN PIERRE BIYITI BI ESSAM.
Minister of Industry, Mines and Technological Development: BADEL NDANGA NDINGA (RDPC).
Minister of Transport: GOUNOKOU HAOUNAYE.
Minister of Energy and Water: JEAN BERNARD SINDEU.
Minister of Estates and Land Affairs: PASCAL ANONG ADIBIME (RDPC).
Minister of the Economy, Planning and Land Settlement: LOUIS PAUL MOTAZE (RDPC).
Minister of Trade: LUC MAGLOIRE MBANGA ATANGANA.
Minister of Culture: AMA TUTU MUNA (RDPC).
Minister of Youth: ADOUM GAROUA (RDPC).
Minister of Basic Education: HAMAN ADAMA (RDPC).
Minister of Tourism: BABA AMADOU (RDPC).
Minister of the Environment and the Protection of Nature: PIERRE HÉLÉ (RDPC).
Minister of Scientific Research and Innovation: MADELEINE TCHUENTÉ (RDPC).
Minister of Sports and Physical Education: EDJOA AUGUSTIN.
Minister of Forests and Wildlife: ELVIS NGOLLE NGOLLE (RDPC).
Minister of External Relations: HENRI EYEBE AYISSI (RDPC).
Minister of Small and Medium Businesses, Local Economy and Crafts: LAURENT ETOUNDI NGOA (RDPC).
Minister of Public Health: ANDRÉ MAMA FOUDA (RDPC).
Minister of Finance: ESSIMI MENYE (RDPC).
Minister of Social Affairs: CATHÉRINE BAKANG MBOCK (RDPC).
Minister of Employment and Professional Training: ZACHARIE PÉRÉVET (RDPC).
Minister of Public Works: BERNARD MESSENGUE AVOM (RDPC).
Minister of Women's Affairs and the Family: SUZANNE BOMBACK.
Minister of Public Service and Administrative Reform: EMMANUEL BONDE (RDPC).

Ministers-delegate

Minister-delegate at the Ministry of External Relations, in charge of Relations with the Commonwealth: JOSEPH DION NGUTÉ (RDPC).
Minister-delegate at the Ministry of Relations with Parliament and the Economic and Social Council: GRÉGOIRE OWONA (RDPC).
Minister-delegate at the Ministry of Justice: MAURICE KAMTO (RDPC).
Minister-delegate at the Ministry of the Economy, Planning and Land Settlement: ABDOULAYE YAOUBA.
Minister-delegate at the Ministry of Defence: RÉMY ZE MEKA (RDPC).
Minister-delegate at the Ministry of the Environment and the Protection of Nature: NANA ABOUBAKAR DJALLOH (UNDP).
Minister-delegate at the Ministry of Territorial Administration and Decentralization: EMMANUEL EDOU (RDPC).

Minister-delegate at the Ministry of External Relations, in charge of Relations with the Islamic World: Adoum Gargoum (RDPC).
Minister-delegate, in charge of the Supreme State Audit: Siegfried David Etamé Massoma (RDPC).
Minister-delegate at the Ministry of Finance: Pierre Titti.

Secretaries of State

Secretary of State for Public Works: Hans Nyetam Nyetam.
Secretary of State for Secondary Education: Cathérine Abena.
Secretary of State for Transport: Oumarou Mefiro.
Secretary of State for Forestry and Wildlife: Roland Mata Joseph.
Secretary of State for Basic Education: André Manga Ewolo.
Secretary of State for Justice, in charge of Prisons: Emmanuel Ngafeeson.
Secretary of State for Industry, Mines and Technological Development: Fuh Calistus Gentry.
Secretary of State for Defence, in charge of the National Gendarmerie: Jean Baptiste Bokam.
Secretary of State for Public Health: Alim Hayatou (RDPC).

Other Officials with the Rank of Minister

Ministers in charge of Special Duties at the Presidency: Hamadou Moustapha (ANDP), Mengot Victor Arrey Nkongho, Paul Atanga Nij.
Director of the Cabinet of the President of the Republic: Ngo'o Mebe (RDPC).

MINISTRIES

Correspondence to ministries not holding post boxes should generally be addressed c/o the Central Post Office, Yaoundé.

Office of the President: Palais de l'Unité, Yaoundé; tel. 2223-4025; internet www.camnet.cm/celcom/homepr.htm.
Office of the Prime Minister: Yaoundé; tel. 2223-8005; fax 2223-5735; e-mail spm@spm.gov.cm; internet www.spm.gov.cm.
Ministry of Agriculture and Rural Development: Quartier Administratif, Yaoundé; tel. 2223-1190; fax 2222-5091.
Ministry of Communication: Quartier Hippodrome, Yaoundé; tel. 2223-3467; fax 2223-3022; e-mail mincom@mincom.gov.cm; internet www.mincom.gov.cm.
Ministry of Culture: Quartier Hippodrome, Yaoundé; tel. 2222-6579; fax 2223-6579.
Ministry of Defence: Quartier Général, Yaoundé; tel. 2223-4055.
Ministry of the Economy, Planning and Land Settlement: Yaoundé.
Ministry of Employment and Professional Training: Yaoundé; tel. 2222-0186; fax 2223-1820.
Ministry of Energy and Water: Quartier Administratif, BP 955, Yaoundé; tel. 2223-3404; fax 2223-3400; e-mail minmee@camnet.cm; internet www.camnet.cm/investir/minmee.
Ministry of the Environment and the Protection of Nature: Yaoundé.
Ministry of Estates and Land Affairs: Yaoundé.
Ministry of External Relations: Yaoundé; tel. 2220-3850; fax 2220-1133; internet www.diplocam.gov.cm.
Ministry of Finance: BP 13750, Quartier Administratif, Yaoundé; tel. and fax 7723-2099; internet www.camnet.cm/investir/minfi/.
Ministry of Forests and Wildlife: BP 1341, Yaoundé; tel. 2220-4258; fax 2222-9487; e-mail onadef@camnet.cm; internet www.camnet.cm/investir/envforet/index.htm.
Ministry of Higher Education: 2 ave du 20 Mai, BP 1457, Yaoundé; tel. 2222-1770; fax 2222-9724; e-mail aowono@uycdc.uninet.cm; internet www.mineup.gov.cm.
Ministry of Industry, Mines and Technological Development: Quartier Administratif, BP 955, Yaoundé; tel. 2223-3404; fax 2223-3400; e-mail minmee@camnet.cm; internet www.camnet.cm/investir/minmee.
Ministry of Justice: Quartier Administratif, Yaoundé; tel. 2222-0189; fax 2223-0005.
Ministry of Livestock, Fisheries and Animal Industries: Yaoundé; tel. 2222-3311.
Ministry of National Education: Quartier Administratif, Yaoundé; tel. 2223-4050; fax 2223-1262.
Ministry of Posts and Telecommunications: Quartier Administratif, Yaoundé; tel. 2223-0615; fax 2223-3159; internet www.minpostel.gov.cm.
Ministry of Public Health: Quartier Administratif, Yaoundé; tel. 2222-2901; fax 2222-0233; internet www.camnet.cm/investir/hgy/index.htm.
Ministry of the Public Service and Administrative Reform: Yaoundé; tel. 2222-0356; fax 2223-0800.
Ministry of Public Works: Quartier Administratif, Yaoundé; tel. 2222-1916; fax 2222-0156.
Ministry of Relations with Parliament and the Economic and Social Council: Yaoundé.
Ministry of Scientific Research and Innovation: Yaoundé; tel. 2222-1331; fax 2222-1333; internet www.minrest.gov.cm.
Ministry of Secondary Education: Yaoundé.
Ministry of Small and Medium Businesses, Local Economy and Crafts: Yaoundé.
Ministry of Social Affairs: Quartier Administratif, Yaoundé; tel. 2222-5867; fax 2222-1121.
Ministry of Sports and Physical Education: Yaoundé; tel. 2223-1201.
Ministry of Technical and Professional Training: Yaoundé.
Ministry of Territorial Administration and Decentralization: Quartier Administratif, Yaoundé; tel. 2223-4090; fax 2222-3735.
Ministry of Trade: Yaoundé; tel. 2223-0216.
Ministry of Tourism: BP 266, Yaoundé; tel. 2222-4411; fax 2222-1295; e-mail mintour@camnet.cm; internet www.mintour.gov.cm.
Ministry of Transport: Quartier Administratif, Yaoundé; tel. 2222-8709; fax 2223-2238; e-mail mintrans@camnet.cm; internet www.camnet.cm/investir/transport.
Ministry of Urban Development and Housing: Yaoundé; tel. 2223-2282.
Ministry of Women's Affairs and the Family: Quartier Administratif, Yaoundé; fax 2223-3965.
Ministry of Youth: Quartier Administratif, Yaoundé; tel. 2223-3257; e-mail minjes@minjes.gov.cm; internet www.minjes.gov.cm.

President and Legislature

PRESIDENT

Election, 11 October 2004

Candidate	% of votes
Paul Biya (RDPC)	70.92
John Fru Ndi (SDF)	17.40
Adamou Ndam Njoya (UDC)	4.47
Garga Haman Adji (ADD)	3.37
Others*	3.84
Total	100.00

*There were 12 other candidates.

NATIONAL ASSEMBLY

President: Cavaye Yéguié Djibril.
General Election, 22 July 2007

Party	Seats
Rassemblement démocratique du peuple camerounais (RDPC)	140
Social Democratic Front (SDF)	14
Union démocratique du Cameroun (UDC)	4
Union nationale pour la démocratie et le progrès (UNDP)	4
Mouvement progressiste (MP)	1
Total	163*

*The results of voting in five constituencies (for 17 seats) were annulled, owing to irregularities. By-elections were held on 30 September 2007 at which the RDPC won 13 seats; the SDF and the UNDP secured two each.

Election Commission

Observatoire national des élections (ONEL) (National Elections Observatory): BP 13506, Yaoundé; tel. 2221-2543; internet www.onelcam.org; f. 2000; 11 dirs appointed by the Head of State; Pres. Enoch Kwayeb.

CAMEROON

Political Organizations

In early 2008 the Observatoire national des élections listed 197 legal political parties, of which the most important are listed below:

Action for Meritocracy and Equal Opportunity Party (AMEC): BP 20354, Yaoundé; tel. 9991-9154; fax 2223-4642; e-mail Tabijoachim@yahoo.fr; Leader JOACHIM TABI OWONO.

Alliance des forces progressistes (AFP): BP 4724, Douala; f. 2002; Leader MAIDADI SAIDOU YAYA.

Alliance pour la démocratie et le développement (ADD): BP 231, Garoua; Sec.-Gen. GARGA HAMAN ADJI.

Alliance nationale pour la démocratie et le progrès: BP 5019, Yaoundé; tel. and fax 220-9898; Pres. HAMADOU MOUSTAPHA.

Cameroon Anglophone Movement (CAM): advocates a federal system of govt.

Démocratie intégrale au Cameroun (DIC): BP 8282, Douala; tel. 7785-1712; f. 1991; Pres. GUSTAVE ESSAKA; Sec.-Gen. ANNETTE ESSAKA.

Mouvement africain pour la nouvelle indépendance et la démocratie (MANIDEM): BP 10298, Douala; tel. 3342-0076; fax 9996-0229; f. 1995; fmrly a faction of the UPC; Leader ANICET EKANE.

Mouvement démocratique pour la défense de la République (MDR): BP 6438, Yaoundé; tel. 2220-8982; f. 1991; Leader DAKOLE DAÏSSALA.

Mouvement des démocrates camerounais pour la paix (MDCP): BP 3274, Yaoundé; tel. 2220-8173; f. 2000; Leader GAMEL ADAMOU ISSA.

Mouvement pour la démocratie et le progrès (MDP): BP 8379, Douala; tel. 2239-1174; f. 1992; Pres. ARON MUKURI MAKA; Sec.-Gen. RENÉ MBANDA MANDENGUE.

Mouvement pour la jeunesse du Cameroun (MLJC): BP 26, Eséka; tel. 7714-8750; fax 2228-6019; Pres. DIEUDONNÉ TINA; Sec.-Gen. JEAN LÉONARD POM.

Mouvement pour la libération et le développement du Cameroun (MLDC): BP 886, Edéa; tel. 3346-4431; fax 3346-4847; f. 1998 by a breakaway faction of the MLJC; Leader MARCEL YONDO BLACK.

Mouvement progressiste (MP): BP 2500, Douala; tel. 9987-2513; e-mail djombyves@yahoo.fr; f. 1991; Pres. JEAN JACQUES EKINDI.

Nouvelle force populaire (NFP): BP 1139, Douala; f. 2002; Leader LÉANDRE DJINO.

Parti des démocrates camerounais (PDC): BP 6909, Yaoundé; tel. 2223-2842; f. 1991; Leader LOUIS-TOBIE MBIDA; Sec.-Gen. GASTON BIKELE EKANI.

Parti libéral-démocrate (PLD): BP 4764, Douala; tel. 3337-3792; f. 1991; Pres. JEAN ROBERT LIAPOE; Sec.-Gen. JEAN TCHUENTE.

Parti républicain du peuple camerounais (PRPC): BP 6654, Yaoundé; tel. 2222-2120; f. 1991; Leader ANDRÉ ATEBA NGOUA.

Parti socialiste camerounais (PSC): BP 12501, Douala; Sec.-Gen. EMMANUEL ELAME.

Rassemblement camerounais pour la république: BP 452, Bandjoun; tel. 3344-1349; f. 1992; Leader SAMUEL WAMBO.

Rassemblement démocratique du peuple camerounais (RDPC): Palais des Congrès, BP 867, Yaoundé; tel. and fax 2221-2417; e-mail rdpc@rdpc.cm; internet www.rdpc.cm; f. 1966 as Union nationale camerounaise by merger of the Union camerounaise, the Kamerun National Democratic Party and four opposition parties; adopted present name in 1985; sole legal party 1972–90; Pres. PAUL BIYA; Sec.-Gen. JOSEPH-CHARLES DOUMBA.

Social Democratic Front (SDF): BP 490, Mankon, Bamenda; tel. 3336-3949; fax 3336-2991; e-mail webmaster@sdfparty.org; internet www.sdfparty.org; f. 1990; Chair. NI JOHN FRU NDI; Sec.-Gen. Dr ELIZABETH TAMAJONG.

Social Democratic Movement (SDM): BP 7655, Yaoundé; tel. 9985-9372; f. 1995; breakaway faction of the Social Democratic Front; Leader SIGA ASANGA.

Southern Cameroons National Council (SCNC): f. 1995; supports the establishment of an independent republic in anglophone Cameroon; Chair. Chief ETTE OTUN AYAMBA.

Union démocratique du Cameroun (UDC): BP 1638, Yaoundé; tel. 2222-9545; fax 2222-4620; f. 1991; Leader ADAMOU NDAM NJOYA.

Union des forces démocratiques du Cameroun (UFDC): BP 7190, Yaoundé; tel. 2223-1644; f. 1991; Leader VICTORIN HAMENI BIELEU.

Union nationale pour la démocratie et le progrès (UNDP): BP 656, Douala; tel. 2220-9898; f. 1991; split in 1995; Chair. BELLO BOUBA MAIGARI; Sec.-Gen. PIERRE FLAMBEAU NGAYAP.

Union nationale pour l'indépendance totale du Cameroun (UNITOC): BP 1301, Yaoundé; tel. 2222-8002; f. 2002; Pres. DANIEL TATSINFANG; Sec.-Gen. JEAN CLAUDE TIENTCHEU FANSI.

Union des populations camerounaises (UPC): BP 1348 Yaoundé; tel. 2745-5043; f. 1948; split into two main factions in 1996: UPC (N), led by WINSTON NDEH NTUMAZAH and UPC (K), led by AUGUSTIN FRÉDÉRIC KODOCK.

Diplomatic Representation

EMBASSIES AND HIGH COMMISSIONS IN CAMEROON

Algeria: 433 rue 1828, Quartier Bastos, BP 1619, Yaoundé; tel. 2221-5351; fax 2231-5354; Ambassador BAALLAL AZZOUZ.

Belgium: rue 1792, Quartier Bastos, BP 816, Yaoundé; tel. 2220-0519; fax 2220-0521; e-mail yaounde@diplobel.org; internet www.diplomatie.be/yaounde/; Ambassador FRANCK CARRUET.

Brazil: rue 1828, Bastos, BP 16227, Yaoundé; tel. 2220-1085; fax 2220-2048; e-mail embiaunde@cameroun-online.com; Ambassador ROBERTO PESSOA DACOSTA.

Canada: Immeuble Stamatiades, pl. de l'Hôtel de Ville, BP 572, Yaoundé; tel. 2223-2311; fax 2222-1090; e-mail yunde@international.gc.ca; High Commissioner JULES SAVARIA.

Central African Republic: 41 rue 1863, Quartier Bastos, Montée du Carrefour de la Vallée Nlongkak, BP 396, Yaoundé; tel. and fax 2220-5155; Chargé d'affaires a.i. JEAN WENZOUÏ.

Chad: Quartier Bastos, BP 506, Yaoundé; tel. 2221-0624; fax 2220-3940; e-mail ambatchad_yaounde@yahoo.fr; Ambassador ANDRÉ SEKIMBAYE BESSANE.

China, People's Republic: Nouveau Bastos, BP 1307, Yaoundé; tel. 2221-0083; fax 2221-4395; e-mail chinaemb_cm@mfa.gov.cn; Ambassador HUANG CHANG QING.

Congo, Democratic Republic: BP 632, Yaoundé; tel. 2220-5103; Chargé d'affaires a.i. KUSAMBILA ZOLA WAY.

Congo, Republic: Rheinallée 45, BP 1422, Yaoundé; tel. 2221-2458; Chargé d'affaires a.i. JOSEPH NZIÉFÉ.

Côte d'Ivoire: BP 11354, Yaoundé; tel. 2221-3291; fax 2221-3295; Ambassador PAUL AYOMAN AMBOHALÉ.

Egypt: 718 rue 1828, Quartier Bastos, BP 809, Yaoundé; tel. 2220-3922; fax 2220-2647; Ambassador MOHAMED SA'AD M. AKL.

Equatorial Guinea: 82 rue 1851, Quartier Bastos, BP 277, Yaoundé; tel. and fax 2221-0804; Ambassador FLORENCIO MAYE ELA MANGUE.

France: Plateau Atémengué, BP 1631, Yaoundé; tel. 2222-7900; fax 2222-7909; e-mail chancellerie.yaounde-amba@diplomatie.gouv.fr; internet www.ambafrance-cm.org; Ambassador GEORGES SERRE.

Gabon: Quartier Bastos, Ekoudou, BP 4130, Yaoundé; tel. 2220-2966; fax 2221-0224; Ambassador MICHEL MANDOUGOUA.

Germany: Nouvelle Bastos, Bastos-Usine, BP 1160, Yaoundé; tel. 2221-0566; fax 2220-7313; e-mail info@jaun.diplo.de; internet www.jaunde.diplo.de; Ambassador VOLKER SEITZ.

Greece: Quartier Mont Fébé, BP 82, Yaoundé; tel. 2221-0195; fax 2220-3936; e-mail ambgrece@camnet.cm; Ambassador CHARAKAMBOUS PAUL.

Holy See: rue du Vatican, BP 210, Yaoundé (Apostolic Nunciature); tel. 2220-0475; fax 2220-7513; e-mail nonce.cam@sat.signis.net; Apostolic Pro-Nuncio Most Rev. ELISEO ANTONIO ARIOTTI (Titular Archbishop of Vibiana).

Israel: rue du Club Olympique à Bastos 154, Longkak, BP 5934, Yaoundé; tel. 2221-1291; fax 2221-0823; e-mail info@yaounde.mfa.gov.il; internet yaounde.mfa.gov.il; Ambassador AVRAHAM NIR.

Italy: Plateau Bastos, BP 827, Yaoundé; tel. 2220-3376; fax 2221-5250; e-mail ambasciata.yaounde@esteri.it; internet www.ambyaounde.esteri.it; Ambassador ANTONIO BELLAVIA.

Japan: 1513 rue 1828, Quartier Bastos, Ekoudou, BP 6868, Yaoundé; tel. 2220-6202; fax 2220-6203; Ambassador TSUZUKI KENSUKE.

Korea, Democratic People's Republic: Yaoundé; Ambassador KIM RYONG YONG.

Liberia: Quartier Bastos, Ekoudou, BP 1185, Yaoundé; tel. 2221-1296; fax 2220-9781; Ambassador MASSA JAMES.

Libya: Quartier Nylon Nlongkak, Quartier Bastos, BP 1980, Yaoundé; tel. 2220-4138; fax 2221-4298; Chargé d'affaires a.i. IBRAHIM O. AMAMI.

Morocco: 32 rue 1793, Quartier Bastos, BP 1629, Yaoundé; tel. 2220-5092; fax 2220-3793; e-mail ambmaroccam@yahoo.fr; Ambassador ABDELFATTAH AMOUR.

Nigeria: Quartier Bastos, BP 448, Yaoundé; tel. 2223-5551; High Commissioner EDWIN ENOSAKHARE EDOBOR.

Romania: Immeuble Dyna Immobilier, rue de Joseph Mballa Elounden, BP 6212, Yaoundé; tel. and fax 2221-3986; Chargé d'affaires a.i. MIRCEA BONCU.

Russia: Quartier Bastos, BP 488, Yaoundé; tel. 2220-1714; fax 2220-7891; e-mail consrusse@camnet.cm; Ambassador POULATE ABDOULAYEV.

Saudi Arabia: rue 1951, Quartier Bastos, BP 1602, Yaoundé; tel. 2221-2675; fax 2220-6689; Ambassador AHMED HUSSEIN ALBEDEWI.

Spain: blvd de l'URSS, Quartier Bastos, BP 877, Yaoundé; tel. 2220-3543; fax 2220-6491; e-mail embespcm@mail.mae.es; Ambassador MARÍA JESÚS ALONSO JIMÉNEZ.

Tunisia: rue de Rotary, Quartier Bastos, BP 6074, Yaoundé; tel. 2220-3368; fax 2221-0507; Chargé d'affaires a.i. MOHAMED NACER KORT.

United Kingdom: ave Winston Churchill, BP 547, Yaoundé; tel. 2222-0545; fax 2222-0148; e-mail BHC.yaounde@fco.gov.uk; internet www.britcam.org; High Commissioner DAVID SYDNEY MADDICOTT.

USA: rue Nachtigal, BP 817, Yaoundé; tel. 2223-1500; internet usembassy.state.gov/yaounde; Ambassador JANET E. GARVEY.

Judicial System

Supreme Court
Yaoundé; tel. 2222-0164; fax 2222-0576.
Consists of a president, nine titular and substitute judges, a procureur général, an avocat général, deputies to the procureur général, a registrar and clerks.
President: ALEXIS DIPANDA MOUELLE.

High Court of Justice
Yaoundé.
Consists of nine titular judges and six substitute judges, all elected by the National Assembly.
Attorney-General: MARTIN RISSOUCK MOULONG.

Religion

It is estimated that 53% of the population are Christians (an estimated 25.5% of those are Roman Catholics), 25% adhere to traditional religious beliefs, and 22% are Muslims.

CHRISTIANITY

Protestant Churches
There are about 1m. Protestants in Cameroon, with about 3,000 church and mission workers, and four theological schools.

Fédération des Eglises et missions évangéliques du Cameroun (FEMEC): BP 491, Yaoundé; tel. and fax 2223-8117; e-mail femec_org@yahoo.fr; internet www.wagne.net/femec; f. 1968; 10 mem. churches; Pres. Rev. Dr JEAN KOTTO (Evangelical Church of Cameroon); Admin. Sec. Rev. Dr GRÉGOIRE AMBADIANG DE MENDENG (Presbyterian Church of Cameroon).

Eglise évangélique du Cameroun (Evangelical Church of Cameroon): BP 89, Douala; tel. 3342-3611; fax 3342-4011; f. 1957; 1,200,000 mems; Pres. Rev. CHARLES E. NJIKE; Sec. Rev. HANS EDJENGUELE.

Eglise presbytérienne camerounaise (Presbyterian Church of Cameroon): BP 519, Yaoundé; tel. 3332-4236; independent since 1957; comprises four synods and 16 presbyteries; Gen. Sec. Rev. Dr MASSI GAM'S.

Eglise protestante africaine (African Protestant Church): BP 26, Lolodorf; e-mail epacameroun@yahoo.fr; f. 1934; Pres. Rev. FRANÇOIS PUASSE.

Presbyterian Church in Cameroon: BP 19, Buéa; tel. 3332-2487; fax 332-2754; e-mail pcc_modoffice19@yahoo.com; 1m. mems (2008); 302 ministers; Moderator Rt Rev. Dr NYANSAKO-NI-NKU.

Union des Eglises baptistes au Cameroun (Union of Baptist Churches of Cameroon): New Bell, BP 6007, Douala; tel. 3342-4106; e-mail mbangueeboa@yahoo.fr; autonomous since 1957; Gen. Sec. Rev. EMMANUEL MBANGUE EBOA.

Other Protestant churches active in Cameroon include the Cameroon Baptist Church, the Cameroon Baptist Convention, the Church of the Lutheran Brethren of Cameroon, the Evangelical Lutheran Church of Cameroon, the Presbyterian Church in West Cameroon and the Union of Evangelical Churches of North Cameroon.

The Roman Catholic Church
Cameroon comprises five archdioceses and 18 dioceses. At 31 December 2005 adherents represented some 25.5% of the total population. There are several active missionary orders, and four major seminaries for African priests.

Bishops' Conference
Conférence Episcopale Nationale du Cameroun, BP 1963, Yaoundé; tel. 2231-1592; fax 2231-2977; e-mail simonvita2000@yahoo.fr. f. 1989; Pres. Most Rev. SIMON-VICTOR TONYÉ BAKOT (Archbishop of Yaoundé).

Archbishop of Bamenda: Most Rev. CORNELIUS FONTEM ESUA, Archbishop's House, BP 82, Bamenda; tel. 3336-1241; fax 3336-3487; e-mail archbishopshouse@yahoo.com.

Archbishop of Bertoua: Most Rev. ROGER PIRENNE, Archevêché, BP 40, Bertoua; tel. 2224-1748; fax 2224-2585; e-mail pirenner@yahoo.fr.

Archbishop of Douala: Cardinal CHRISTIAN WIYGHAN TUMI, Archevêché, BP 179, Douala; tel. 3342-3714; fax 3343-1837; e-mail mikjp2004@yahoo.fr.

Archbishop of Garoua: Most Rev. ANTOINE NTALOU, Archevêché, BP 272, Garoua; tel. 2227-1353; fax 2227-2942.

Archbishop of Yaoundé: Most Rev. SIMON-VICTOR TONYÉ BAKOT, Archevêché, BP 207, Yaoundé; tel. 2220-2461; fax 2221-9735; e-mail simonvita2000@yahoo.fr.

BAHÁ'Í FAITH
National Spiritual Assembly: BP 145, Limbé; tel. 3333-2146; mems in 1,744 localities.

The Press

DAILIES
Cameroon Tribune: route de l'Aéroport, BP 1218, Yaoundé; tel. 2230-4147; fax 2230-4362; e-mail cameroon-tribune@cameroon-tribune.cm; internet www.cameroon-tribune.net; f. 1974; govt-controlled; French and English; Publr MARIE CLAIRE NNANA; Man. Editor ABUI MAMA ELOUNDOU; circ. 25,000.

Mutations: South Media Corporation, BP 12348, Yaoundé; tel. 2222-5104; fax 2222-9635; e-mail journalmutations@yahoo.fr; internet quotidienmutations.info; daily; French; independent; Publr ALAIN BLAISE BATONGUE.

The Post: POB 91, Buéa; tel. 3332-3287; fax 7773-8904; e-mail thepostnp@yahoo.com; internet www.postnewsline.com; weekly; independent; English; Publr FRANCIS WACHE; Editor CHARLY NDI CHIA.

Le Quotidien: BP 13088, Douala; tel. 3339-1189; fax 3339-1819; French; circ 29,000.

PERIODICALS
Accord Magazine: BP 3696, Messa, Yaoundé; tel. 9969-0600; e-mail accordmag@hotmail.com; popular culture.

Affaires Légales: BP 3681, Douala; tel. 3342-5838; fax 3343-2259; monthly; legal periodical.

Afrique en Dossiers: Yaoundé; f. 1970; French and English; Dir EBONGUE SOELLE.

L'Anecdote: Face collège Vogt, BP 25070, Yaoundé; tel. 2231-3395; e-mail journalanecdote@yahoo.com; weekly; conservative; Editor-in-Chief FRANÇOIS BIKORO.

Aurore Plus: BP 7042, Douala; tel. 3342-9261; fax 3342-4917; e-mail jouraurplus@yahoo.fr; twice weekly; Dir MICHEL MICHAUT MOUSSALA.

Cameroon Outlook: BP 124, Limbé; f. 1969; 3 a week; independent; English; Editor JÉRÔME F. GWELLEM; circ. 20,000.

Cameroon Panorama: BP 46, Buéa; tel. 3332-2240; e-mail cainsbuea@yahoo.com; f. 1962; monthly; English; Roman Catholic; Editor Rev. Fr MOSES TAZOH; circ. 4,500.

Cameroon Review: BP 408, Limbé; monthly; Editor-in-Chief JÉRÔME F. GWELLEM; circ. 70,000.

Cameroon Times: BP 408, Limbé; f. 1960; weekly; English; Editor-in-Chief JÉRÔME F. GWELLEM; circ. 12,000.

Challenge Hebdo: BP 1388, Douala; weekly; Editor BENJAMIN ZEBAZE.

Le Combattant: Yaoundé; weekly; independent; Editor BENYIMBE JOSEPH; circ. 21,000.

Courrier Sportif du Bénin: BP 17, Douala; weekly; Dir HENRI JONG.

Dikalo: BP 4320, Douala; tel. 3337-2122; fax 3337-1906; f. 1991; independent; 2 a week; French; Publications Dir TETTEH M. ARMAH; Editor HENRI EPEE NDOUMBE.

Ecovox: BP 1256, Bafoussam; tel. 3344-6668; fax 3344-6669; e-mail ecovox@cipcre.org; internet www.cipcre.org/ecovox; 2 a year; French; ecological news.

CAMEROON

L'Effort Camerounais: BP 15231, Douala; tel. 3343-2726; fax 3343-1837; e-mail leffortcamerounais@yahoo.com; internet www.leffortcamerounais.com; bi-monthly; Catholic; f. 1955; Editor-in-Chief ANTOINE DE PADOU CHONANG.

La Gazette: BP 5485, Douala; 2 a week; Editor ABODEL KARIMOU; circ. 35,000.

The Herald: BP 1218, Yaoundé; tel. 2231-5522; fax 2231-8497; 3 a week; English; Dir Dr BONIFACE FORBIN; circ. 1,568.

Al Houda: BP 1638, Yaoundé; quarterly; Islamic cultural review.

L'Indépendant Hebdo: Yaoundé; Chief Editor EVARISTE MENOUNGA.

Le Jeune Observateur: Yaoundé; f. 1991; Editor JULES KOUM (imprisoned for libel in January 2005).

J'informe: Yaoundé; tel. 9993-6605; fax 2220-5336; f. 2002; weekly; French; Editor DELOR MAGELLAN KAMGAING.

Journal Officiel de la République du Cameroun: BP 1603, Yaoundé; tel. and fax 2221-5218; weekly; official govt notices; Man. Editor JOSEPH MARCEL; circ. 4,000.

Le Messager: rue des écoles, BP 5925, Douala; tel. 3342-0214; fax 3342-0439; internet www.lemessager.net; f. 1979; 3 a week; independent; Man. Editor PIUS N. NJAWE; circ. 20,000.

The Messenger: BP 15043, Douala; English-language edn of Le Messager; Editor HILARY FOKUM.

Nleb Ensemble: Imprimerie Saint-Paul, BP 763, Yaoundé; tel. 2223-9773; fax 2223-5058; f. 1935; fortnightly; Ewondo; Dir Most Rev. JEAN ZOA; Editor JOSEPH BEFE ATEBA; circ. 6,000.

La Nouvelle Expression: 12 rue Prince de Galles, BP 15333, Douala; tel. 3343-2227; fax 3343-2669; internet www.lanouvelleexpression.net; independent; 3 a week; French; Man. Editor SÉVERIN TCHOUNKEU.

La Nouvelle Presse: Face mairie de Yaoundé VIème/Biyem-Assi, BP 2625, Messa, Yaoundé; tel. 9996-6768; e-mail lanvellepresse@iccnet.cm; f. 2001; weekly; Publications Dir JACQUES BLAISE MVIE.

Ouest Echos: BP 767, Bafoussam; tel. and fax 3344-1091; e-mail ouechos@wagne.net; internet www.wagne.net/ouestechos/; weekly; regional; Dir MICHEL ECLADOR PÉKOUA.

Recherches et Études Camerounaises: BP 193, Yaoundé; monthly; publ. by Office National de Recherches Scientifiques du Cameroun.

La Sentinelle: BP 24079, Douala; tel. and fax 3339-1627; weekly; lifestyle; circ. 3,200.

Le Serment: Yaoundé; newspaper; Editor-in-Chief ANSELME MBALLA.

Le Serviteur: BP 1405, Yaoundé; monthly; Protestant; Dir Pastor DANIEL AKO'O; circ. 3,000.

Le Travailleur/The Worker: BP 1610, Yaoundé; tel. 2222-3315; f. 1972; monthly; French and English; journal of Organisation Syndicale des Travailleurs du Cameroun/Cameroon Trade Union Congress; Sec.-Gen. LOUIS SOMBES; circ. 10,000.

Le Triomphe: BP 1862, Douala; tel. 3342-8774; f. 2002; weekly; Publications Dir SIPOWA CONSCIENCE PARFAIT.

L'Unité: BP 867, Yaoundé; weekly; French and English.

Weekly Post: Obili, Yaoundé; Publr Chief BISONG ETAHOBEN.

NEWS AGENCIES

CamNews: c/o SOPECAM, BP 1218, Yaoundé; tel. 2230-3830; fax 2230-4362; Dir JEAN NGANDJEU.

PRESS ASSOCIATIONS

Association des Journalistes Indépendants du Cameroun (AJIC): BP 2996, Yaoundé; tel. 2222-3572; independent journalists' asscn; Pres. CÉLESTIN LINGO.

Conseil Camerounais des Médias (CCM): Yaoundé; internet www.ccm-info.org; f. 2005; created by the UJC to strengthen the quality and independence of journalism in Cameroon; 9 mems; Pres. PIERRE ESSAMA ESSOMBA; Sec.-Gen. PIERRE-PAUL TCHINDJI.

Union des Journalistes du Cameroun (UJC): Yaoundé; Pres. CÉLESTIN LINGO.

Publishers

AES Presses Universitaires d'Afrique: BP 8106, Yaoundé; tel. 2222-0030; fax 2222-2325; e-mail aes@iccnet.cm; internet www.aes-pua.com; f. 1986; literature, social sciences and law; Dir-Gen. SERGE DONTCHUENG KOUAM.

Editions Akoma Mba: ave Germaine Ahidjo 20189, Yaoundé; tel. 9992-2955; fax 2222-4343; e-mail akomamba@hotmail.com; educational; Dir EDMOND VII MBALLA ELANGA.

Editions Clé (Centre de Littérature Evangélique): BP 1501, ave Maréchal Foch, Yaoundé; tel. 2222-3554; fax 2223-2709; e-mail editionscle@yahoo.fr; internet www.wagne.net/cle; f. 1963; African and Christian literature and studies; school textbooks; medicine and science; general non-fiction; Dir Dr MARCELIN VOUNDA ETOA.

Editions Le Flambeau: BP 113, Yaoundé; tel. 2222-3672; f. 1977; general; Man. Dir JOSEPH NDZIE.

Editions Ndzé: BP 647, Bertoua; tel. 9950-9295; fax 2224-2585; e-mail editions@ndze.com; internet www.ndze.com; fiction; Commercial Dir ALEXIS LIMBONA.

Editions Semences Africaines: BP 5329, Yaoundé-Nlongkak; tel. 9917-1439; e-mail renephilombe@yahoo.fr; f. 1974; fiction, history, religion, textbooks; Man. Dir RÉNÉ LÉA PHILOMBE.

New Times Publishing House: Presbook Compound, BP 408, Limbé; tel. 3333-3217; f. 1983; publishing and book-trade reference; Dir and Editor-in-Chief JÉRÔME F. GWELLEM.

Presses de l'Université catholique d'Afrique Centrale (PUCAC): BP 11628, Yaoundé; tel. 2230-5508; fax 2230-5501; e-mail p_ucac@yahoo.fr; internet www.pucac.com; Man. GABRIEL TSALA ONANA.

GOVERNMENT PUBLISHING HOUSES

Centre d'Edition et de Production pour l'Enseignement et la Recherche (CEPER): BP 808, Yaoundé; tel. 7723-1293; f. 1967; transfer pending to private ownership; general non-fiction, science and technology, tertiary, secondary and primary educational textbooks; Man. Dir JEAN CLAUDE FOUTH.

Imprimerie Nationale: BP 1603, Yaoundé; tel. 2223-1277; scheduled for transfer to private ownership; Dir AMADOU VAMOULKE.

Société de Presse et d'Editions du Cameroun (SOPECAM): route de l'Aéroport, BP 1218, Yaoundé; tel. 2230-4147; fax 2230-4362; e-mail mclairennana@yahoo.fr; f. 1977; under the supervision of the Ministry of Communication; Pres. PAUL TESSA; Dir-Gen. MARIE CLAIRE NNANA.

Broadcasting and Communications

TELECOMMUNICATIONS

A Telecommunications Regulation Agency was established in early 1999.

Cameroon Telecommunications (CAMTEL): BP 1571, Yaoundé; tel. 2223-4065; fax 2223-0303; e-mail camtel@camnet.cm; internet www.camtel.cm; f. 1999 by merger of INTELCAM and the Dept of Telecommunications; 51% privatization pending; Pres. NFON VICTOR MUKETE; Dir-Gen. DAVID NKOTO EMANE.

Cameroon Mobile Telecommunications Corporation: f. by CAMTEL in March 2006.

Mobile Telephone Networks (MTN) Cameroon Ltd: 360 rue Drouo, Bonamouti, Akwa, BP 15574, Douala; tel. 9900-9000; fax 9900-9040; internet www.mtncameroon.net; f. 1999 as CAMTEL Mobile; acquired by MTN in 2000; mobile cellular telephone operator; 70% owned by MTN Ltd, 30% owned by Broadband Telecom Ltd; CEO PHILIPPE VANDEBROUCK.

Société Camerounaise de Mobiles (SCM): BP 1864, Douala; tel. 3341-0111; fax 3342-7430; e-mail scm@scm.cm; f. 1999; mobile cellular telephone operator; operates in Yaoundé, Douala and Bafoussam; Dir-Gen. JEAN-PAUL GANDET.

BROADCASTING

Radio

Office de Radiodiffusion-Télévision Camerounaise (CRTV): BP 1634, Yaoundé; tel. 2221-4077; fax 2220-4340; internet www.crtv.cm; f. 1987; broadcasts in French and English; satellite broadcasts commenced in Jan. 2001, reaching some 80% of the national territory; Pres. of Council of Administration PIERRE MOUKOKO MBONJO (Minister of Communication); Dir-Gen. (vacant).

Radio Bertoua: BP 260, Bertoua; tel. 2224-1445; fax 2224-2275; Head of Station BAIVE NYONG PHILIP.

Radio Buéa: BP 86, Buéa; tel. 3332-2615; programmes in English, French and 15 vernacular languages; Man. PETERSON CHIA YUH; Head of Station GIDEON MULU TAKA.

Radio Douala: BP 986, Douala; tel. 3342-6060; programmes in French, English, Douala, Bassa, Ewondo, Bakoko and Bamiléké; Dir BRUNO DJEM; Head of Station LINUS ONANA MVONDO.

Radio Garoua: BP 103, Garoua; tel. 2227-1167; programmes in French, Hausa, English, Foulfouldé, Arabic and Choa; Dir BELLO MALGANA; Head of Station MOUSSA EPOPA.

Radio Ngaoundéré: BP 135, Ngaoundéré; tel. 2225-2148.

Radio Tam Tam: Yaoundé.

Radio Yaoundé FM 94: BP 1634, Yaoundé; tel. 2220-2502; Head of Station LOUISE POM.

There are also provincial radio stations at Abong Mbang, Bafoussam, Bamenda, Ebolowa and Maroua.

Television

Television programmes from France were broadcast by the Office de Radiodiffusion-Télévision Camerounaise from early 1990.

Office de Radiodiffusion-Télévision Camerounaise (CRTV): see Radio

Finance

(cap. = capital; res = reserves; dep. = deposits; m. = million; brs = branches; amounts in francs CFA)

BANKING

Central Bank

Banque des Etats de l'Afrique Centrale (BEAC): 736 ave Monseigneur Vogt, BP 1917, Yaoundé; tel. 2223-4030; fax 2223-3329; e-mail beac@beac.int; internet www.beac.int; f. 1973; bank of issue for mem. states of the Communauté économique et monétaire de l'Afrique centrale (CEMAC, fmrly Union douanière et économique de l'Afrique centrale): Cameroon, the Central African Repub., Chad, the Repub. of the Congo, Equatorial Guinea and Gabon; cap. 45,000m., res 326,675m., total assets 2,150,301m. (Dec. 2003); Gov. JEAN-FÉLIX MAMALEPOT; Dir in Cameroon SADOU HAYATOU; 5 brs in Cameroon.

Commercial Banks

Afriland First Bank: pl. de l'Indépendance, BP 11834, Yaoundé; tel. 2223-3068; fax 2222-1785; e-mail firstbank@afrilandfirstbank.com; internet www.afrilandfirstbank.com; SBF & Co. (36.62%), FMO (19.80%), private shareholders (43.58%); cap. and res 10,017m., total assets 161,293m. (Dec. 2003); Pres. Dr PAUL KAMMOGNE FOKAM; Gen. Man. ALAMINE OUSAMANE MEY.

Amity Bank Cameroon SA: BP 2705, Douala; tel. 3343-2055; fax 3343-2046; internet www.amitybank.cm; f. 1990; cap. and res –2,671m., total assets 24,717m. (June 2002); Pres. Prof. VICTOR ANOMAH NGU; Dir-Gen. MATHURIN NGASSA; 4 brs.

Banque Internationale du Cameroun pour l'Epargne et le Crédit (BICEC): ave du Général de Gaulle, BP 1925, Douala; tel. 3343-6000; fax 3343-1226; e-mail bicec@bicec.com; internet www.bicec.com; f. 1962 as Banque Internationale pour le Commerce et l'Industrie du Cameroun; name changed as above in 1997, following restructuring; 52.5% owned by Groupe Banques Populaires (France); cap. 3,000m., res 18,928m., dep. 258,615m. (Dec. 2003); Pres. JEAN-BAPTISTE BOKAM; Gen. Man. JEAN-PIERRE SCHIANO; 26 brs.

Citibank N.A. Cameroon: 96 rue Flatters, Bonanjo, BP 4571, Douala; tel. 3342-4272; fax 3342-4074; internet www.citigroup.com; f. 1997; Dir-Gen. ASIF ZAIDI; COO WILSON CHOLA.

Commercial Bank of Cameroon (CBC): ave du Général de Gaulle, BP 4004, Douala; tel. 3342-0202; fax 3343-3800; e-mail cbcbank@cbcbank.com; f. 1997; cap. and res. 12,596m., total assets 125,596m. (Dec. 2003); Pres. VICTOR FOTSO.

Crédit Lyonnais Cameroun SA: 530 rue du Roi George, BP 300, Douala; tel. 3343-5400; fax 3342-5413; e-mail scb_cl_cameroun@creditlyonnais.fr; f. 1989 as Société Commerciale de Banque—Crédit Lyonnais Cameroun; name changed as above in 2002; 35% state-owned; cap. and res 6,000m., total assets 258,316m. (Dec. 2004); Pres. MARTIN ARISTIDE OKOUDA; Gen. Man. FRANCIS DUBUS; Sec.-Gen. PIERRE SAM-NDOUMBE; 15 brs.

Ecobank Cameroun SA (Togo): blvd de la Liberté, BP 582, Douala; tel. 3343-8250; fax 3343-8487; e-mail ecobankcm@ecobank.com; internet www.ecobank.com; f. 2001; cap. 2,500m., res 2,953m., dep. 51,356m., total assets 72,038m. (Dec. 2005); Chair. ANDRÉ FOTSO; Man. Dir ABOU KABASSI KASSIMOU.

Highland Corporation Bank SA: Immeuble Hôtel Hilton, blvd du 20 mai, BP 10039, Yaoundé; tel. 2223-9287; fax 2232-9291; e-mail atnjp@camnet.cm; internet pcnet.ifrance.com/pcnet/hcb/; f. 1995; 100% privately owned; cap. 600m. (Dec. 1996); Exec. Pres. PAUL ATANGA NJI; Asst Dir-Gen. JOHANES MBATI.

Société Générale de Banques au Cameroun (SGBC): 78 rue Joss, BP 4042, Douala; tel. 3342-7010; fax 3343-0353; e-mail sgbcdla@camnet.cm; f. 1963; 25.6% state-owned; cap. and res 17,213m., total assets 301,391m. (June 2001); Chair. AMADOU NJIFENJOU MOULIOM; Dir-Gen. ALAIN BELLISSARD; 15 brs.

Standard Chartered Bank Cameroon SA: blvd de la Liberté, BP 1784, Douala; tel. 3343-5200; fax 3342-2789; internet www.standardchartered.com/cm/index.html; f. 1980 as Boston Bank Cameroon; name changed 1986; 100% owned by Standard Chartered Bank (United Kingdom); cap. 7,000m., total assets 143,619m. (June 2002); CEO PAUL SAGNIA; 3 brs.

Union Bank of Cameroon, Ltd (UBC): NWCA Ltd Bldg, 2nd Floor, Commercial Ave, BP 110, Bamenda, Douala; tel. 3336-2316; fax 3336-2310; e-mail ubc@unionbankcameroon.com; internet www.unionbankcameroon.com; total assets 7,278m. (June 2001); Pres. GABRIEL IKOMÉ NJOH; CEO ABRAHAM NDOFOR.

Development Banks

Banque de Développement des Etats de l'Afrique Centrale: see Franc Zone.

Crédit Foncier du Cameroun (CFC): 484 blvd du 20 mai 1972, BP 1531, Yaoundé; tel. 2223-5216; fax 2223-5221; f. 1977; 75% state-owned; cap. and res 7,835m., total assets 87,000m. (Dec. 2003); provides assistance for low-cost housing; Pres. ANDRÉ BOOTO A NGON; 10 brs.

Société Nationale d'Investissement du Cameroun (SNI): pl. Ahmadou Ahidjo, BP 423, Yaoundé; tel. 2222-4422; fax 2223-1332; e-mail sni@sni.cm; internet www.sni.cm; f. 1964; state-owned investment and credit agency; cap. 19,000m., res 20,980m., total assets 33,426m. (June 2000); Dir-Gen. ESTHER BELIBI DANG.

Financial Institutions

Caisse Autonome d'Amortissement du Cameroun: BP 7167, Yaoundé; tel. 2222-2226; fax 2222-0129; e-mail caa@caa.gov.cm; internet www.caa.gov.cm; f. 1985; cap. 5,000m. (1998); Dir-Gen. DIEUDONNÉ EVOU MEKOU.

Caisse Commune d'Epargne et d'Investissement (CCEI): pl. de l'Indépendance, BP 11834, Yaoundé; tel. 2223-3068; fax 2222-1785; total assets 88,551m. (June 2000); Pres. Dr PAUL KANMOGNE FOKAM; Dir-Gen. DANIEL POTOUONJOU TAPONZIÉ.

Fonds d'Aide et de Garantie des Crédits aux Petites et Moyennes Entreprises (FOGAPE): BP 1591, Yaoundé; tel. 2223-3859; fax 2222-3274; f. 1984; cap. 1,000m. (Oct. 1997); Pres. JOSEPH HENGA; Vice-Pres. ARMAND FIRMIN MVONDO.

National Financial Credit Company Cameroon (NFCC): BP 6578, Yaoundé; tel. 2222-4806; fax 2222-8781; e-mail national_financial_credit@yahoo.com; cap. and res 2,350m., total assets 9,338m.; Pres. ABEY JEROME ONGHER; Gen. Man. AWANGA ZACHARIA.

Société Camerounaise de Crédit Automobile (SOCCA): rue du Roi Albert, BP 554, Douala; tel. 3342-7478; fax 3342-1219; e-mail socca@socca-cm.cm; internet www.giefca.com/english/cameroun.htm; f. 1959; cap. and res 4,770m., total assets 23,748m. (Dec. 2003); Pres. VALENTIN MOUYOMBON; Dir-Gen. JOHANN BAUDOT.

Société Camerounaise de Crédit-Bail (SOCABAIL): rue du Roi Albert, BP 554, Douala; tel. 3342-7478; fax 3342-1219; e-mail soccabail@camnet.cm; cap. 500m., res 1,343m., total assets 5,880m. (June 1999); Pres. ALAIN GUYON.

STOCK EXCHANGE

Bourse des Valeurs de Douala (Douala Stock Exchange): 1450 blvd de la Liberté, BP 442, Douala; tel. 3343-8582; fax 3353-8584; e-mail dsx@dsx.cm; f. 2003; 23% state-owned; Chair. BÉNÉDICT BELIBI; Dir-Gen. PIERRE EKOULÉ MOUANGUÉ.

INSURANCE

Activa Assurances: Rue du Prince du Galles 1385, BP 12970, Douala; tel. 3343-4503; fax 3343-4572; e-mail activa.assur@camnet.cm; f. 1999; all branches except life insurance; cap. 400m.; 66% owned by Cameroonian investors, 33% by Ivorian investors; Chair. JEAN KACOU DIAGOU; Gen. Man. RICHARD LOWE.

AGF Cameroun Assurances: rue Manga Bell, BP 105, Douala; tel. 3342-9203; fax 3343-0324; e-mail agf.cameroun@agf-cm.com; internet www.agf-afrique.com/filiales/cameroun.htm; f. 1974; 71% owned by AGF Afrique; all classes of insurance; cap. 700m.; Dir-Gen. ADRIEN COZZA.

Assurances Mutuelles Agricoles du Cameroun (AMACAM): BP 962, Yaoundé; tel. 2222-4966; f. 1965; cap. 100m.; state-owned; privatization pending; Pres. SAMUEL NGBWA NGUELE; Dir-Gen. LUC CLAUDE NANFA.

Compagnie Camerounaise d'Assurances et de Réassurances (CCAR): 11 rue Franqueville, BP 4068, Douala; tel. 3342-3159; fax 3342-6453; f. 1974; cap. 499.5m.; Pres. YVETTE CHASSAGNE; Dir-Gen. CHRISTIAN LE GOFF.

Compagnie Nationale d'Assurances (CNA): BP 12125, Douala; tel. 3342-4446; fax 3342-4727; f. 1986; all classes of insurance; cap. 600m.; Chair. THÉODORE EBOBO; Man. Dir PROTAIS AYANGMA AMANG.

General and Equitable Assurance Cameroon Ltd (GEACAM): 56 blvd de la Liberté, BP 426, Douala; tel. 3342-5985; fax 3342-7103; cap. 300m.; Pres. V. A. NGU; Man. Dir J. CHEBAUT.

CAMEROON

Société Africaine d'Assurances et Réassurances (SAAR): BP 1011, Douala; tel. 3343-1765; fax 3343-1759; Dir-Gen. GEORGES LÉOPOLD KAGOU.

Société Camerounaise d'Assurances et de Réassurances (SOCAR): 1450 blvd de la Liberté, BP 280, Douala; tel. 3342-5584; fax 3342-1335; f. 1973; cap. 800m.; Chair. J. YONTA; Man. Dir R. BIOUELE.

Trade and Industry

GOVERNMENT AGENCY

Economic and Social Council: BP 1058, Yaoundé; tel. 2223-2474; advises the Govt on economic and social problems; comprises 150 mems, which serve a five-year term, and a perm. secr.; Pres. LUC AYANG; Sec.-Gen. FRANÇOIS EYOK.

DEVELOPMENT ORGANIZATIONS

Agence Française de Développement (AFD): Immeuble Flatters, rue de la Radio 2283, Douala; tel. 3342-5067; fax 3342-9959; e-mail afd.douala@camnet.cm; internet www.afd.fr; fmrly Caisse Française de Développement; Man. PASCAL COLLANGE.

Cameroon Development Corporation (CAMDEV): Bota Area, Limbé; tel. 3333-2251; fax 3343-2654; e-mail cdcbota@iccnet2000.com; f. 1947; reorg. 1982; cap. 15,626m. francs CFA; statutory corpn established to acquire and develop plantations of tropical crops for local and export markets; operates two oil mills, 11 banana-packing stations and seven rubber factories; Chair. Chief OKIAH NAMATA ELANGWE; Gen. Man. HENRY NJALLA QUAN.

Direction Générale des Grands Travaux du Cameroon (DGTC): BP 6604, Yaoundé; tel. 2222-1803; fax 2222-1300; f. 1988; commissioning, implementation and supervision of public works contracts; Chair. JEAN FOUMAN AKAME; Man. Dir MICHEL KOWALZICK.

Hévéa-Cameroun (HEVECAM): BP 1298, Douala and BP 174, Kribi; tel. 3346-1919; f. 1975; state-owned; development of 15,000 ha rubber plantation; 4,500 employees; transferred to private ownership in 1997; Pres. ELIE C. NYOKWEDI MALONGA; Man. Dir JEAN-MARC SEYMAN.

Institut de Recherche Agricole pour le Développement (IRAD): BP 2067, Yaoundé; tel. and fax 2222-3362; e-mail iradpnrua@yahoo.com; internet www.irad-cameroon.org; Dir SIMON ZOK.

Institut de Recherche pour le Développement (IRD): BP 1857, Yaoundé; tel. 2220-1508; fax 2220-1854; e-mail cameroun@ird.fr; internet www.ird.fr; f. 1984; Rep. in Cameroon Dr XAVIER GARDE.

Mission d'Aménagement et d'Equipement des Terrains Urbains et Ruraux (MAETUR): BP 1248, Yaoundé; tel. 2222-3113; fax 2223-3190; e-mail maetur@camnet.cm; internet www.maetur.gcnet.cm; f. 1977; Pres. LOUIS ABOGO NKONO; Dir-Gen. ANDRÉ MAMA FOUDA.

Mission d'Aménagement et de Gestion des Zones Industrielles: Yaoundé; state-owned industrial land authority; Dir GEORGES MANON CHRISTOL.

Mission de Développement de la Province du Nord-Ouest (MIDENO): BP 442, Bamenda; Gen. Man. JOHN B. NDEH.

Mission Française de Coopération et d'Action Culturelle: BP 1616, Yaoundé; tel. 2223-0412; fax 2222-5065; e-mail mission.coop@camnet.cm; administers bilateral aid from France; Dir LUC HALLADE.

Office Céréalier dans la Province du Nord: BP 298, Garoua; tel. 2227-1438; f. 1975 to combat effects of drought in northern Cameroon and stabilize cereal prices; Pres. Alhadji MAHAMAT; Dir-Gen. GILBERT GOURLEMOND.

Office National du Cacao et du Café (ONCC): BP 3018, Douala; tel. 3342-9482; fax 3342-0002; Dir-Gen. MICHAËL MONSIEUR NDOPING.

Société de Développement du Cacao (SODECAO): BP 1651, Yaoundé; tel. 2230-4544; fax 2230-3395; f. 1974; reorg. 1980; cap. 425m. francs CFA; development of cocoa, coffee and food crop production in the Littoral, Centre, East and South provinces; Pres. JOSEPH-CHARLES DOUMBA; Dir-Gen. JÉRÔME MVONDO.

Société de Développement du Coton (SODECOTON): BP 302, Garoua; tel. 2227-1556; fax 2227-2026; f. 1974; Chair. HAOUNAYE GOUNOKO; Man. MOHAMMED IYA.

Société de Développement de l'Elevage (SODEVA): BP 50, Kousseri; cap. 50m. francs CFA; Dir Alhadji OUMAROU BAKARY.

Société de Développement et d'Exploitation des Productions Animales (SODEPA): BP 1410, Yaoundé; tel. 2220-0810; fax 2220-0809; e-mail sodepa@iccnet.cm; f. 1974; cap. 375m. francs CFA; development of livestock and livestock products; Man. Dir BOUBA NDENGUE DIEUDONNÉ.

Société de Développement de la Haute-Vallée du Noun (UNVDA): BP 25, N'Dop, North-West Province; f. 1970; cap. 1,380m. francs CFA; rice, maize and soya bean cultivation; Dir-Gen. SAMUEL BAWE CHI WANKI.

Société d'Expansion et de Modernisation de la Riziculture de Yagoua (SEMRY): BP 46, Yagoua; tel. 2229-6213; f. 1971; cap. 4,580m. francs CFA; commercialization of rice products and expansion of rice-growing in areas where irrigation is possible; Pres. ALBERT EKONO; Dir-Gen. LIMANGANA TORI.

Société Immobilière du Cameroun (SIC): BP 387, Yaoundé; tel. 2223-3411; fax 2222-5119; f. 1952; cap. 1,000m. francs CFA; housing construction and development; Pres. ABDOULAYE HAMAN ADJI; Dir-Gen. BONIFACE NGOA NKOU.

CHAMBERS OF COMMERCE

Chambre d'Agriculture, d'Elevage et des Forêts du Cameroun: BP 6620, Yaoundé; tel. 2222-0441; fax 2222-2025; e-mail cfe_cameroun@yahoo.fr; f. 1955; 120 mems; Pres. PHILÉMON ADJIBOLO; Sec.-Gen. SOLOMON NFOR GWEI; other chambers at Yaoundé, Ebolowa, Bertoua, Douala, Ngaoundéré, Garoua, Maroua, Buéa, Bumenda and Bafoussam.

Chambre de Commerce, d'Industrie et des Mines du Cameroun (CCIM): rue de Chambre de Commerce, BP 4011, Douala; also at BP 36, Yaoundé; BP 211, Limbé; BP 59, Garoua; BP 944, Bafoussam; BP 551, Bamenda; tel. 7742-6855; fax 7742-5596; e-mail cride-g77@camnet.cm; internet www.g77tin.org/ccimhp.html; f. 1921; 138 mems; Pres. PIERRE TCHANQUE; Sec.-Gen. SAÏDOU ABDOULAYE BOBBOY.

EMPLOYERS' ORGANIZATIONS

Association Professionnelle des Établissements de Crédit (APECCAM): BP 133, Yaoundé; tel. 2223-5401; fax 2223-5402; Pres. BÉNÉDICT BELIBI.

Groupement des Femmes d'Affaires du Cameroun (GFAC): BP 1940, Douala; tel. 2223-4059; fax 2221-1041; e-mail gfacnational@yahoo.fr; Pres. FRANÇOISE FONING.

Groupement Interpatronal du Cameroun (GICAM): ave Nlongkak, BP 1134, Yaoundé; tel. 2220-0750; fax 2220-0752; e-mail gicam-yde@camnet.cm; internet www.legicam.org; f. 1957; Pres. ANDRÉ SIAKA; Sec.-Gen. FRANCIS SANZOUANGO.

Mouvement des Entrepreneurs du Cameroun (MECAM): BP 12443, Douala; tel. 3339-5000; fax 3339-5001; Pres. ALPHONSE BIBEHE.

Syndicat des Commerçants Importateurs-Exportateurs du Cameroun (SCIEC): 16 rue Quillien, BP 562, Douala; tel. 3342-0304; Pres. EMMANUEL UGOLINI; Treas. MICHEL CHUPIN.

Syndicat des Industriels du Cameroun (SYNDUSTRICAM): BP 673, Douala; tel. 3342-3058; fax 3342-5616; e-mail syndustricam@camnet.cm; f. 1953; Pres. CHARLES METOUCK; Sec.-Gen. BEKE BIHEGE.

Syndicat des Producteurs et Exportateurs de Bois du Cameroun: BP 570, Yaoundé; tel. 2220-2722; fax 2220-9694; f. 1939; Pres. CARLO ORIANI.

Syndicat Professionnel des Entreprises du Bâtiment, des Travaux Publics et des Activités Annexes: BP 1134, Yaoundé; BP 660, Douala; tel. and fax 2220-2722; Sec.-Gen. FRANCIS SANZOUANGOU.

Syndicats Professionnels Forestiers et Activités connexes du Cameroun: BP 100, Douala.

Union des Syndicats Professionnels du Cameroun (USPC): BP 829, Douala; Pres. MOUKOKO KINGUE.

West Cameroon Employers' Association (WCEA): BP 97, Tiko.

Utilities

Electricity

Société Nationale d'Electricité du Cameroun (SONEL): BP 4077, 63 ave de Gaulle, Douala; tel. 3342-5444; fax 3342-2209; e-mail sonel@camnet.cm; f. 1974; 44% state-owned; 56% stake acquired by AES Sirocco in 2001; Gen. Man. JEAN-DAVID BILE.

Water

Société Nationale des Eaux du Cameroun (SNEC): BP 4077, Douala; tel. 3342-5444; fax 3342-2247; e-mail contact@snec-cameroun.com; internet www.snec-cameroun.com; f. 1967; 73% state-owned; privatization suspended Dec. 2003; Pres. AMADOU ALI; Dir-Gen. BASILE ATANGANA KOUNA (acting).

PRINCIPAL CO-OPERATIVE ORGANIZATIONS

Centre National de Développement des Entreprises Coopératives (CENADEC): Yaoundé; f. 1970; promotes and organizes

CAMEROON

the co-operative movement; bureaux at BP 43, Kumba and BP 26, Bamenda; Dir JACQUES SANGUE.

Union Centrale des Coopératives Agricoles de l'Ouest (UCCAO): ave Samuel Wonko, BP 1002, Bafoussam; tel. 3344-4296; fax 3344-1845; e-mail uccao@uccao-cameroun.com; internet www.uccao-cameroun.com; f. 1958; marketing of cocoa and coffee; 120,000 mems; Pres. JACQUES FOTSO KANKEU; Gen. Man. FRANÇOIS MEFINJA FOKA.

West Cameroon Co-operative Association Ltd: BP 135, Kumba; founded as cen. financing body of the co-operative movement; provides short-term credits and agricultural services to mem. socs; policy-making body for the co-operative movement in West Cameroon; 142 mem. unions and socs representing c. 45,000 mems; Pres. Chief T. E. NJEA.

TRADE UNION FEDERATION

Confederation of Cameroon Trade Unions (CCTU): BP 1610, Yaoundé; tel. 2222-3315; f. 1985; fmrly the Union Nationale des Travailleurs du Cameroun (UNTC); Pres. ANDRE JULE MOUSSENI; Sec.-Gen. LOUIS SOMBES.

Transport

RAILWAYS

There are some 1,008 km of track—the West Line running from Douala to Nkongsamba (166 km), with a branch line leading southwest from Mbanga to Kumba (29 km), and the Transcameroon railway, which runs from Douala to Ngaoundéré (885 km), with a branch line from Ngoumou to Mbalmayo (30 km). In July 2002 the World Bank disbursed a loan of 15,600m. francs CFA to Cameroon to help rehabilitate the main line. In November the French Government approved a loan of US $12.5m. to Cameroon, primarily to improve rolling stock.

CAMRAIL S.A.: Gare Centrale de Bessengué, blvd de la Réunification, BP 766, Douala; tel. 3340-8247; fax 3340-8252; e-mail camrail.dg@iccnet2000.cm; internet www.camrail.net; f. 1999; passenger and freight transport; Pres. MICHEL ROUSSIN; Dir-Gen. BENOÎT DU SOUICH.

Office du Chemin de Fer Transcamerounais: BP 625, Yaoundé; tel. 2222-4433; supervises the laying of new railway lines and improvements to existing lines, and undertakes relevant research; Dir-Gen. LUC TOWA FOTSO.

ROADS

In 2004 there were an estimated 50,000 km of roads, of which 10.0% were paved.

SHIPPING

There are seaports at Kribi and Limbé-Tiko, a river port at Garoua, and an estuary port at Douala-Bonabéri, the principal port and main outlet, which has 2,510 m of quays and a minimum depth of 5.8 m in the channels and 8.5 m at the quays. Total handling capacity is 7m. metric tons annually. Plans are under way to increase the annual capacity of the container terminal. There are also plans to modernize Limbé-Tiko and to promote it internationally.

Office National des Ports/National Ports Authority: 81 rue de la Chambre de Commerce, BP 4023, Douala; tel. 3342-0133; fax 3342-6797; e-mail onpc@camnet.cm; internet www.camnet.cm/investir/transport/onpc; f. 1971; Chair. GOUNOKOU HAOUNAYE (Minister of Transport); Dir-Gen. ALPHONSE SIYAM SIVE.

Cameroon Shipping Lines SA (CAMSHIP): BP 4054, Douala; tel. 3342-0064; fax 3342-0114; f. 1975; scheduled for transfer to private-sector ownership; 6 vessels trading with Western Europe, USA, Far East and Africa; Chair. FRANÇOIS SENGAT KUO; Man. Dir RENÉ MBAYEN.

    Camafrica Liner Ltd: Centre des Affaires Maritimes, BP 4054, Douala; non-vessel owner container carrier co trading between West Africa and Europe.

Camtainer: Para-maratime Area, Douala Port, BP 4993, Douala; tel. 3342-7704; fax 3342-7173; e-mail camtainer@douala1.com; internet www.camnet.cm/investir/transpor/camtenair/sommaire.htm; f. 1984; Chair. JOSEPH TSANGA ABANDA; Man. ZACHARIE KUATE.

Compagnie Maritime Camerounaise SA (CMC): BP 3235, Douala; tel. 3342-8540; fax 3342-5842.

Conseil National des Chargeurs du Cameroun (CNCC): BP 1588, Douala; tel. 3342-3206; fax 3342-8901; e-mail info@cncc-cam.org; internet www.cncc-cam.org; f. 1975; promotion of the maritime sector; Gen. Man. AUGUSTE MBAPPE PENDA.

Delmas Cameroun: rue Kitchener, BP 263, Douala; tel. 3342-4750; fax 3342-8851; f. 1977; Pres. JEAN-GUY LE FLOCH; Dir-Gen. DANY CHUTAUX.

MAERSK CAMEROUN SA—Douala: BP 12414, Douala; tel. 3342-1185; fax 3342-1186.

Société Africaine de Transit et d'Affrètement (SATA): Douala; tel. 3342-8209; f. 1950; Man. Dir RAYMOND PARIZOT.

Société Agence Maritime de l'Ouest Africain Cameroun (SAMOA): 5 blvd de la Liberté, BP 1127, Douala; tel. 3342-1680; f. 1953; shipping agents; Dir JEAN PERRIER.

Société Camerounaise de Manutention et d'Acconage (SOCAMAC): BP 284, Douala; tel. 3342-4051; e-mail socamac@camnet.cm; internet www.camnet.cm/investir/transpor/socamac/socamac.htm; f. 1976; freight handling; Pres. MOHAMADOU TALBA; Dir-Gen. HARRY J. GHOOS.

Société Camerounaise de Transport et d'Affrètement (SCTA): BP 974, Douala; tel. 3342-1724; f. 1951; Pres. JACQUES VIAULT; Dir-Gen. GONTRAN FRAUCIEL.

Société Camerounaise de Transport Maritime: BP 12351, Douala; tel. 3342-4550; fax 3342-4946.

Société Ouest-Africaine d'Entreprises Maritimes—Cameroun (SOAEM—Cameroun): 5 blvd de la Liberté, BP 4057, Douala; tel. 3342-5269; fax 3342-0518; f. 1959; Pres. JACQUES COLOMBANI; Man. Dir JEAN-LOUIS GRECIET.

SOCOPAO Cameroun: BP 215, Douala; tel. 3342-6464; f. 1951; shipping agents; Pres. VINCENT BOLLORE; Man. Dir E. DUPUY.

Transcap Cameroun: BP 4059, Douala; tel. 3342-7214; f. 1960; Pres. RENÉ DUPRAZ; Man. Dir MICHEL BARDOU.

CIVIL AVIATION

There are international airports at Douala, Garoua and Yaoundé; there are, in addition, 11 domestic airports, as well as a number of secondary airfields.

Aéroports du Cameroun (ADC): Nsimalen, BP 13615, Yaoundé; tel. 2223-4521; fax 2223-4520; e-mail adc@iccnet.cm; internet aeroportsducameroun.com; f. 1999; manages major airports; 63% state-owned; Dir-Gen. ROGER NTONGO ONGUENE.

Air Affaires Afrique: BP 1225, Douala; tel. 3342-2977; fax 3342-9903; f. 1978; regional and domestic charter passenger services; CEO BYRON BYRON-EXARCOS.

Cameroon Airlines (CAMAIR): 3 ave du Général de Gaulle, BP 4092, Douala; tel. 3342-2525; fax 3342-3443; e-mail camair@camnet.cm; internet www.cameroon-airlines.com; f. 1971; domestic flights and services to Africa, North America and Europe; Dir-Gen. PAUL NGAMO HAMANI (interim); Inspector-Gen. of Administration and Finance ESTHER GOUETT.

Tourism

Tourists are attracted by Cameroon's cultural diversity and by its national parks, game reserves and sandy beaches. In 2005 176,372 tourists visited Cameroon. In 2003 receipts from tourism totalled US $162m.

Ministry of Tourism: see Ministries.

CANADA

Introductory Survey

Location, Climate, Language, Religion, Flag, Capital

Canada occupies the northern part of North America (excluding Alaska and Greenland) and is the second largest country in the world, after Russia. It extends from the Atlantic Ocean to the Pacific. Except for the boundary with Alaska in the north-west, Canada's frontier with the USA follows the upper St Lawrence Seaway and the Great Lakes, continuing west along latitude 49°N. The climate is an extreme one, particularly inland. Winter temperatures drop well below freezing but summers are generally hot. Rainfall varies from moderate to light and there are heavy falls of snow. The two official languages are English and French, the mother tongues of 57.2% and 21.8%, respectively, at the general census in 2006. About 45% of the population are Roman Catholics. The main Protestant churches are the United Church of Canada and the Anglican Church of Canada. Numerous other religious denominations are represented. The national flag (proportions 1 by 2) consists of a red maple leaf on a white field, flanked by red panels. The capital is Ottawa.

Recent History

The Liberals, led by Pierre Trudeau, were returned to office at general elections in 1968, 1972, 1974, and again in 1980 after a short-lived minority Progressive Conservative Party (PC) administration. Popular support for the Liberals, however, was undermined by an economic recession, and the PC, led by Brian Mulroney, obtained a substantial legislative majority at general elections held in September 1984.

During 1986 the persistence of high rates of unemployment, together with the resignations in discordant circumstances of five cabinet ministers, led to a fall in the PC Government's popularity. Popular support for the Government further declined, in response to criticism by the Liberals and the New Democratic Party (NDP) of the Government's negotiation of a new US-Canadian trade treaty, which the Liberals and the NDP viewed as overly advantageous to US business interests and potentially damaging to Canada's national identity, and which was approved by the House of Commons in August 1988. Nevertheless, in a general election in November the PC was re-elected, although with a reduced majority, and full legislative ratification of the free trade agreement followed in December. In February 1990 the federal Government opened negotiations with Mexico, to achieve a lowering of trade barriers. The US Government joined these discussions, and in December 1992 Canada, the USA and Mexico finalized terms for a tripartite North American Free Trade Agreement (NAFTA, see p. 338), with the aim of creating a free trade zone encompassing the whole of North America.

In the province of Québec, where four-fifths of the population speak French as a first language and which maintains its own cultural identity, the question of political self-determination has long been a sensitive issue. At provincial elections in 1976 the separatist Parti Québécois (PQ) came to power, and in 1977 made French the official language of education, business and government in Québec. In December 1985 the PQ was replaced by the Liberals as the province's governing party. The Liberals retained power at the next provincial elections, held in September 1989. However, political support for separatist aspirations was extended to the federal Parliament in May 1990, when seven PC members representing Québec constituencies, led by Lucien Bouchard (a former member of Mulroney's Cabinet), broke away from the party and formed the independent Bloc Québécois (BQ), with the object of acting in the interests of a 'sovereign Québec'. The BQ later expanded, with disaffected Liberal support, to nine members.

In 1982 the British Parliament transferred to Canada authority over all matters contained in British statutes relating to Canada, opening the way for institutional reform and the redistribution of legislative powers between Parliament and the provincial legislatures. All the provinces except Québec eventually accepted constitutional provisions that included a charter of rights and a formula for constitutional amendments, whereby such amendments would require the support of at least seven provinces representing more than 50% of the population. Québec, however, maintained that its legislature could exercise the right to veto constitutional provisions.

Following the return to office in 1985 of the Liberals in Québec, the federal Government adopted new initiatives to include Québec in the constitutional arrangements. In April 1987 Mulroney and the provincial premiers met at Meech Lake, Québec, to negotiate a constitutional accommodation for Québec. The resultant agreement, the Meech Lake Accord, recognized Québec as a 'distinct society' within the Canadian federation, and granted each of the provinces substantial new powers in the areas of federal parliamentary reform, judicial appointments and the creation of new provinces. The Accord was subject to ratification, not later than June 1990, by the federal Parliament and all provincial legislatures. By early 1990 the federal Parliament and each of the 10 provincial legislatures, except for New Brunswick and Manitoba, had approved the Accord.

Opposition to the Meech Lake arrangements, on the grounds that they afforded too much influence to Québec and failed to provide Inuit and Indian minorities with the same measure of protection as francophone groups, began to emerge in March 1990, when the Newfoundland legislature rescinded its earlier endorsement of the Accord. Following a meeting in June between Mulroney and the provincial premiers (at which a number of compromise amendments were adopted), the New Brunswick legislature agreed to accept the Accord, but the provinces of Manitoba and Newfoundland upheld their opposition. The Meech Lake Accord duly lapsed in late June, and the Québec Government, which had opposed any changes to the earlier terms of the Accord, responded by refusing to participate in future provincial conferences, and by appointing a commission to examine the province's political choices. In September 1991 the federal Government announced a new series of constitutional reform proposals, which, unlike the Meech Lake Accord, would require the assent of only seven provinces representing 50% of the total population. Under the new plan, Québec was to be recognized as a distinct society in terms of its language, culture and legal system, while each province would have full control of its cultural affairs. Native peoples were to receive full self-government within 10 years, inter-provincial trade barriers were to be abolished, and the federal Senate was to become an elected body with limited powers of legislative veto, except in matters involving natural resources, in which it would have full powers of veto. The reform proposals also included the creation of a Council of Federation to resolve disputes between the provinces and federal Government. A National Unity Committee, comprising an inter-party group of 30 federal legislators, was formed to ascertain public reaction to the plan, about which the Québec provincial government expressed initial reservations on economic grounds.

In March 1992 an all-party committee of the federal Parliament recommended new constitutional proposals providing for a system of 'co-operative federalism', which would grant Québec powers of veto over future constitutional changes, together with exclusive jurisdiction over the main areas of its provincial affairs. This plan was rejected by the Québec Government. Further, inconclusive, discussions among the provincial premiers (in which Québec refused to participate) took place in mid-1992. Mulroney's proposal to revive the Meech Lake proposals was opposed by the western provinces, which sought increased representation in a reformed Senate and were unwilling to concede a constitutional veto to Québec until after these changes were carried out. In late August 1992, following resumed consultations between Mulroney and the provincial premiers, a new programme of constitutional reforms, known as the Charlottetown Agreement, was finalized for submission to a national referendum. The proposals, which were endorsed by all of the provincial premiers as well as the leaders of the three main political parties, provided for an equal and elected Senate, a guarantee in perpetuity to Québec of one-quarter of the seats in the federal House of Commons (regardless of future movements in population), as well as three of the nine seats on the Supreme Court of Canada. There was also to be recognition of provincial jurisdiction in cultural affairs, and increased provincial powers over certain economic affairs and immigration. The inherent right to self-government of the Indian and Inuit population was also to be recognized.

Despite the apparent political consensus, considerable opposition to the Charlottetown Agreement became evident prior to the referendum, which took place in October 1992. Disagreements emerged on a regional basis, as well as among NDP and Liberal supporters, and aspects of the proposed constitution were opposed by the PQ and the BQ, and by the Reform Party (RP), a conservative-populist movement which led opposition in the western provinces. Nationally, the proposals were defeated by a margin of 54% to 45%; only four of the provinces (Ontario, New Brunswick, Newfoundland and Prince Edward Island) and the Northwest Territories endorsed the Agreement.

The defeat of the Charlottetown Agreement, together with the persistence of adverse economic conditions, led to a rapid erosion in the prestige of the Government, and in Mulroney's personal popularity. A reorganization of cabinet posts in January 1993 failed to restore public confidence, and in the following month Mulroney announced that he was to relinquish office in June. He was succeeded by the former Minister of Defence and Veterans' Affairs, Kim Campbell, who became Canada's first female Prime Minister.

The Campbell Government proved unable to restore the PC's political standing, and, faced with the expiry in November 1993 of its five-year parliamentary mandate, a general election was scheduled for October. The outcome of the election, which was contested primarily on domestic economic issues, resulted in a decisive victory for the Liberals, led by Jean Chrétien. A significant realignment of political forces was reflected in the new Parliament, in which PC representation was reduced to only two seats. The BQ, with 54 seats, became the official opposition party, and declared that it would pursue the achievement of full sovereignty for Québec. Campbell, who lost her seat in the federal Parliament, resigned as PC leader and was succeeded by Jean Charest.

The new Liberal Government set out to implement an economic recovery programme. Substantial reductions in defence expenditure were announced, as well as a C $6,000m. job-creation scheme, and in December 1993, following the renegotiation of certain treaty protocols with the US Government, NAFTA, which had received Canadian legislative ratification in June, was formally promulgated, to take effect from January 1994. The Liberals were re-elected at a general election held in June 1997, although with a reduced majority in the House of Commons. The RP replaced the BQ as the main opposition party.

The issue of separatism in Québec was reopened by provincial elections held in September 1994, in which the PQ, led by Jacques Parizeau, defeated the incumbent Liberal administration by a narrow margin. Parizeau, whose campaign had included an undertaking that a new referendum on independence would be held during 1995, was supported at federal level by the BQ, although the federal Government asserted that considerable uncertainty was felt within Québec over the possible economic consequences of secession. In June 1995 the PQ and the BQ, together with a smaller provincial nationalist group, the Action Démocratique du Québec, agreed a framework for the province's proposed independence and in mid-September the referendum received provincial legislative approval.

In the referendum, held on 30 October 1995, the sovereignty proposals were defeated by a margin of only 50,000 votes; in a turn-out of 93% of eligible voters, 49% were in favour of the sovereignty plan, and 51% opposed. Parizeau announced his intention to resign. In February 1996 Lucien Bouchard, having resigned from the federal House of Commons and relinquished the leadership of the BQ, succeeded Parizeau as Premier of Québec and leader of the PQ. Bouchard indicated that his administration viewed the sovereignty issue as less urgent than the resolution of Québec's immediate economic problems. In September 1997 Bouchard refused to attend a conference of provincial premiers and territorial commissioners, at which a seven-point framework on Canadian unity was agreed. The conference, held in Calgary, recognized the 'unique character' of Québec, but asserted that any future change in the constitutional powers of one province should be applicable to all provinces. By June 1998 the resultant 'Calgary Declaration' had been endorsed by the legislatures of all provinces except Québec.

The Supreme Court, which had been requested in February 1998 to rule on the legality of a unilateral secession by Québec, declared in August that no province had the right, in constitutional or international law, to leave the federation without prior negotiations with the federal and provincial governments, and that secession would require the approval of the federal legislature, together with that of seven of the 10 provinces. It was further stated that an obligation would exist for negotiation with Québec if a clear majority of its voters expressed a wish to leave the federation.

In March 1998 Jean Charest resigned as leader of the PC, to accept the leadership of the Liberal Party of Québec, which had been perceived as losing popular support for its anti-separatist policy. However, an unexpected rise in support for the Liberals meant they narrowly won the provincial legislative election in November. Following the election, Bouchard conceded that the PQ had failed to attract sufficient support to merit an early referendum.

In March 2000 members of the RP voted to form the Canadian Alliance (CA), an organization conceived at a convention held in September 1998 with the aim of uniting the major right-wing parties. The PC declined to join the CA, although a number of that party's prominent members chose to do so. In July Stockwell Day, a former PC member, was elected leader of the CA.

In October 2000 Chrétien announced that a general election would be held on 27 November, despite his Government's mandate being valid until June 2002. At the election, Chrétien's Liberals won 172 of the 301 seats in the House of Commons. The CA secured 66 parliamentary seats, while the BQ obtained 38 seats, the NDP 13 seats and the PC 12. The results demonstrated an increasing political polarization between the country's east and centre and its west—the CA won 50 of the 60 seats available in the two westernmost provinces, British Columbia and Alberta, but only two in Ontario (the Liberals being elected in 100 of the 103 constituencies in that province).

In January 2001 Bouchard announced his resignation as Premier of Québec, once a successor had been elected. He also resigned as a member of the provincial legislature and as leader of the PQ, stating that he had failed in his intention to achieve independence for the province and that he lacked both popular and party support. The BQ had lost several seats in Québec to the Liberals at the November 2000 federal general election and opinion polls continued to show a decline in support for the PQ's policy on independence. Also in January 2001 Lorne Calvert was elected Premier of Saskatchewan following the resignation of Roy Romanow. In the following month Roger Grimes succeeded Brian Tobin as Premier of Newfoundland, following Tobin's appointment to the federal Government. In early March Bernard Landry of the PQ, hitherto Minister of Finance in the province, was elected the new Premier of Québec. In May, in British Columbia, the NDP, which had been in government since 1991, was roundly defeated in provincial elections, retaining just two seats in the 79-seat Legislative Assembly. The Liberal Party secured the remaining 77 seats. The provincial party leader, Gordon Campbell, became Premier.

In mid-July 2001, following several months of internal dissent in the party owing to its poor performance in the 2000 legislative elections, 13 CA members resigned from the party in protest at Day's refusal to resign the leadership. Day had offered to step down temporarily if he could appoint his successor, an offer that had been rejected by CA members. Day eventually resigned in December, and stood for re-election in March 2002, but was defeated by Stephen Harper. In the same month Ernie Eves succeeded Mike Harris as Premier of Ontario.

Throughout 2002 the Government was subject to accusations of corruption. In May Chrétien dismissed the Minister of Defence, Art Eggleton, after it was revealed that Eggleton had awarded a C $36,000 contract in his ministry to a former girlfriend. At the same time, Don Boudria, who had been appointed Minister of Public Works and Services in January, was moved back to his former post as Leader of the Government in the House of Commons, a move widely regarded as a demotion, after he stayed in the holiday home of the head of a company that had been awarded lucrative government contracts. In June the Minister of Finance, Paul Martin, was dismissed and replaced by Deputy Prime Minister John Manley. It was widely believed that Martin, a long-time rival of Chrétien, was planning to launch a leadership challenge. In August Chrétien announced that he would stand down as Prime Minister in February 2004, and pass the premiership to another member of the Liberal Party. In October the Government faced further criticism when the Solicitor-General, Lawrence MacAulay, resigned following accusations that he had been involved in the awarding of federal grants to a community college headed by his brother.

Legislative elections were held in 10 of the 13 provinces and territories in late 2002 and throughout 2003. Following elections in the Yukon Territory in November 2002, Dennis Fentie of the Yukon Party replaced Pat Duncan of the Liberal Party as Premier. In April 2003 Charest became Premier of Québec when the Liberal Party secured 76 seats in the 125-member legislature in provincial elections, compared with 45 seats for the PQ. The NDP increased its majority in Manitoba at elections in June and Gary Doer retained the premiership. In the same month the PC was re-elected in New Brunswick, although with a reduced majority. In August the PC retained office in Nova Scotia, although Premier John Hamm presided over a minority Government. In September the PC won a third successive term in office in Prince Edward Island and Patrick Binns retained the premiership. In October the Liberals assumed control of Ontario from the PC, taking 72 seats, compared with 24 for the PC; Dalton McGuinty was appointed provincial Premier. Later in the same month the PC assumed power from the Liberals in elections in Newfoundland and Labrador (as the province had officially been renamed in December 2001); Danny Williams became Premier. Elections were also held in Saskatchewan and the Northwest Territories in November; in the former, the NDP retained a narrow majority in the provincial legislature, while in the latter, Joseph Handley was sworn in as Premier and Chairman of the territory's Executive Council in December.

In April 2003 the World Health Organization (WHO) declared that travel to Toronto was inadvisable as a result of an outbreak of Severe Acute Respiratory Syndrome (SARS), a previously unknown atypical pneumonia that had originated in eastern Asia. Although WHO rescinded its travel advice at the end of that month, the city remained on WHO's list of areas affected by the disease until early July. A total of 30 people died of SARS in the Toronto area in 2003.

In May 2003 British Columbia's Court of Appeal approved same-sex marriages. In June Ontario's Court of Appeal ruled that a definition of marriage which excluded same-sex couples was discriminatory and unconstitutional; one week later Prime Minister Chrétien announced that the federal Government would prepare draft legislation to define marriage as 'a heterosexual or homosexual union'. He also referred the issue to the federal Supreme Court, which ruled in favour of the Ontario ruling in December 2004, thus clearing the way for the Government to prepare draft legislation on the issue in February 2005. The proposed legislation was approved by the federal House of Commons in late June by 158 to 133 votes; the bill received senate approval in the following month. Thus, Canada became only the third country in the world to legalize same-sex marriages (after the Netherlands and Belgium).

In September 2003 the Liberal Party nominated Paul Martin as the successor to party leader Chrétien, who was scheduled to retire in early 2004. However, Chrétien stood down as premier early, and on 12 December 2004 Paul Martin succeeded him as Prime Minister and as party leader. Martin subsequently carried out a wide-ranging reallocation of government portfolios: notable appointments included Anne McLennan as Deputy Prime Minister and Ralph Goodale to the Ministry of Finance, while Bill Graham remained Minister of Foreign Affairs. Also in December the PC and CA announced that they had merged to form a new party, the Conservative Party of Canada; Stephen Harper was elected leader of the new party in March 2005.

Corruption allegations against the Liberal Government continued in 2004. In February a report by the office of the Auditor-General concluded that the Government had misappropriated funds during a state campaign intended to promote national unity in Québec in 1997–2001. It was alleged that contracts worth some C $100m. had been awarded to advertising companies in Québec with links to the Liberal Party, and that some of these contracts were false. Prime Minister Martin denied any involvement in the affair, which coincided with his time as Minister of Finance in the Chrétien Government, and ordered a public inquiry, to be headed by Justice John Gomery of the Superior Court of Québec. Nevertheless, the so-called 'sponsorship scandal' was widely believed to have affected support for the Liberal Party in the general election that was held on 28 June. The incumbent party failed to obtain a parliamentary majority, winning 135 seats in the newly enlarged 308-seat House of Commons, compared with the 172 seats it had secured in the previous election. The Conservatives won a total of 99 parliamentary seats, while the BQ increased its legislative representation to 54 seats (from 33 seats). The NDP secured 19 seats and the one remaining seat was won by an independent candidate. Voter turn-out was the lowest ever, at 60.9% of the electorate. Prime Minister Martin formed the first minority Government in Canada since 1979.

The Conservatives maintained their majority, albeit a reduced one, in a provincial election in Alberta in November 2004. Ralph Klein was returned to office as provincial Premier. At a provincial election in British Columbia in mid-May 2005 Gordon Campbell was re-elected to the premiership, although his Liberal Party's representation in the legislature was also reduced, to 46 seats. In contrast, the NDP increased its number of seats to 33, from only two in the previous legislature.

The Commission of Inquiry into the alleged misappropriation of campaign funds in Québec held two sets of public hearings in September 2004: the first hearing, in Ottawa, heard testimony from politicians and civil servants; while the second, in Montréal in early 2005, gathered statements from advertising and communications executives. As details emerged of alleged fraud and systemic mismanagement of sponsorship deals, the Government came under increasing pressure from opposition parties to hold a fresh election. In late April Prime Minister Martin announced that a general election would be held within 30 days of the publication of Justice Gomery's report, which was to be released in two parts. In mid-May the Government narrowly avoided a parliamentary defeat in a vote on the 2006 budget that was treated as a motion of confidence. The Government had been facing defeat until, on the eve of the crucial ballot, a Conservative member of Parliament, Belinda Stronach (who had contested the Conservative leadership against Stephen Harper in 2004), switched allegiances to the Liberal Party. (She was rewarded with a post in the federal Government.) Martin also obtained the support of the NDP in the vote in exchange for policy concessions in the proposed budget. The budget was finally approved by 153 votes to 152, the deciding vote cast by the Speaker of the House, Peter Milliken, a Liberal.

The first part of Justice Gomery's report of his Commission of Inquiry into the sponsorship scandal was published on 1 November 2005. The report concluded, *inter alia*, that the Liberal Party had obtained election funds illegally. Although there was no evidence to link former Prime Minister Chrétien to any wrongdoing, he was held politically accountable for the failures in management; Prime Minister Martin and the current Liberal Government were exonerated. Martin reiterated his pledge to hold a general election within 30 days of the release of the second part of Gomery's report, due in February 2006. However, in late November 2005 the Conservatives tabled a motion of 'no confidence' in the Government. Having lost the support of the NDP earlier in the month—according to the NDP, because of differences over health policy—the Government was defeated by 171 votes to 133, thus triggering a general election. Parliament was dissolved by the new Governor-General, Michaëlle Jean, who had succeeded Adrianne Clarkson in late September.

At the general election, held on 23 January 2006, the Conservative Party won 124 seats out of a total of 308 seats, an increase of 25 seats. As expected, the Liberals' parliamentary representation fell, by 32 seats to 103 seats. In contrast, the NDP increased its share of seats by 10, to 29 seats. The BQ, which was only represented in Québec, won 51 seats, a slight decrease from the 54 seats it held previously. There was one independent seat. Conservative leader Stephen Harper was declared Prime Minister-elect. However, as his party lacked the 155 seats required for a parliamentary majority, he was forced to form a minority Government. Voter turn-out was 14.8m., representing some 64.9% of the electorate.

Harper was sworn into office on 6 February 2006. His new Federal Ministry included Peter MacKay as Minister of Foreign Affairs and, controversially, David Emerson as Minister of International Trade. Emerson had been a member of the outgoing Liberal Government, but defected to the Conservatives following the election. The new Prime Minister pledged that his first piece of legislation on taking office would be the introduction of a Federal Accountability Act. The proposal reflected the conclusions of Justice Gomery's Commission of Inquiry, the second part of which was released on 1 February. The report made 19 recommendations towards improving executive answerability, including: reform of the Government's decision-making process; a curtailment of the powers of the Prime Minister; and an increase in the authority of the federal Parliament. In the same month Martin stood down as Liberal Party leader; Bill Graham held the post in an acting capacity until the election of Stéphane Dion at the Liberal Party conference in early December.

Legislative elections were held in several provinces and territories in 2006. At an election in Nova Scotia in June Rodney MacDonald of the Conservative Party was elected Premier. However, as previously, the Conservatives were forced to form a minority government, holding 23 of 52 legislative assembly seats. In New Brunswick in mid-September Shawn Graham of the Liberal Party was elected Premier under the 'first-past-the-post' voting system; although the Conservatives took a greater share of the popular vote, the Liberals won two more legislative seats. In the Yukon Territory in mid-October Dennis Fentie was returned for a second term as Premier.

In late November 2006 the House of Commons voted by an overwhelming margin (266 votes to 16) to approve legislation introduced by Prime Minister Harper recognizing Québec as a 'nation within a united Canada'. Although the resolution was largely seen as symbolic, the Minister for Intergovernmental Affairs, Michael D. Chong, resigned from the Cabinet in protest at the legislation's recognition of what he described as 'ethnic nationalism'. Chong's portfolio was assumed by Peter Van Loan.

In December 2006 Ed Stelmach succeeded Ralph Klein as Premier of Alberta following the latter's retirement. Stelmach was appointed to the post after being elected provincial leader of the PC.

In early January 2007 Harper announced a reallocation of cabinet portfolios. Rona Ambrose was replaced as Minister of the Environment by John Baird, while Robert D. Nicholson was appointed Minister of Justice. His previous cabinet role, as Leader of the Government in the House of Commons, was taken by Peter Van Loan. Meanwhile, Monte Solberg and Diane Finley, hitherto Minister of Citizenship and of Human Resources and Social Development, respectively, swapped responsibilities. In a further cabinet reshuffle in August, Minister of National Defence Gordon O'Connor, who had encountered criticism over Canada's continuing military involvement in the US-led 'war on terror' in Afghanistan (see below), was replaced by Peter MacKay. O'Connor assumed responsibility for the national revenue portfolio and Maxime Bernier was appointed as MacKay's successor as Minister of Foreign Affairs. The ministerial changes were believed by many to be an attempt by Prime Minister Harper to increase confidence in his Government in advance of a general election, which was widely expected to be held by the end of the year. However, in October, following Harper's annual Speech from the Throne, the Government survived three votes of confidence in the House of Commons. Defeat for any of Harper's legislative proposals might have precipitated an early general election.

A number of provinces and territories held legislative elections in 2007. In Québec on 26 March, Jean Charest, leader of the Québec Liberal Party, was re-elected Premier; however, the Liberals failed to secure a parliamentary majority, precipitating the formation of a minority government, the first in 129 years in that province. Action Démocratique du Québec defeated the PQ to become the official opposition, although the formation of government was almost equally divided between the three parties. The ruling NDP was returned to power in Manitoba in elections held on 22 May, allowing NDP leader Gary Doer to form a majority government for a third successive term. In Prince Edward Island the opposition Liberal Party defeated the ruling PC later in the same month, securing 23 of the 27 seats in the Legislative Assembly. The PC had governed the province since 1998, but its standing was reduced to four seats and the Liberal Party leader, Robert Ghiz, was duly sworn in as Premier in June. In Newfoundland and Labrador, however, the PC won an overwhelming majority in an election held on 9 October. Final results showed that Premier Danny Williams's PC had secured 44 of the 48 seats and a second successive term, while the Liberal Party won three mandates and the NDP one. The following day a provincial ballot in Ontario returned the Liberals to government when the party, led by Premier Dalton McGuinty, won 71 seats in the 107-member Legislative Assembly. In the same month Floyd Roland was elected the new Premier of the Northwest Territories by the Legislative Assembly following elections to that body at the beginning of the month, in which the 16 contested seats were won by independent candidates. Finally, in Saskatchewan, Brad Wall became Premier after his Saskatchewan Party won a majority in the provincial election of 7 November.

Former Prime Minister Brian Mulroney was the subject of corruption allegations in November 2007, regarding C $300,000 he reportedly received in payments from businessman Karlheinz Schreiber between 1993 and 1994. Mulroney denied receiving any money while still in office, and in January 2008 Harper announced that a formal government inquiry would take place after the House of Commons' ethics committee had concluded its own investigation. The findings of the ethics committee were released in early April and recommended a broad public inquiry, contrasting with the narrow focus counselled by president of the University of Waterloo, David Johnston, an independent third-party adviser whom the Government had commissioned in November 2007 to suggest appropriate parameters for the proposed investigation.

The question of land treaty claims by Canada's indigenous peoples came to prominence in the latter part of the 20th century, when disputes over land rights arose in Ontario, Manitoba and Québec. In September 1988, following 13 years of negotiations, the federal Government formally transferred to indigenous ownership an area covering 673,000 sq km in the Northwest Territories. In the Yukon Territory, an area of 41,000 sq km (representing 8.6% of the Territory's land) was transferred to indigenous control. At the same time, debate had begun to intensify in the formulation of a new constitutional status for the Northwest Territories, in which a population of only 58,000 (of which Inuit and other indigenous peoples comprised about one-half) occupied an area comprising one-third of Canada's land mass. In December 1991 specific terms for the creation of a semi-autonomous Nunavut Territory, covering an area of 2.2m. sq km, to the east of a boundary running northwards from the Saskatchewan–Manitoba border, were agreed by Inuit representatives and the federal Government, and in May 1992 a plebiscite on a proposal to divide the Northwest Territories into two self-governing units was approved by the territories' residents.

A formal agreement to settle all outstanding land treaty claims was finalized by the federal Government in May 1993, providing for Nunavut to come into official existence on 1 April 1999. Elections to a new, 17-seat Legislature for Nunavut, to be located at Iqaluit, were held in February 1999, and the new Territorial Government took office in April. In December 1997 the Supreme Court awarded legal title to 57,000 sq km of ancestral land to two native groups in British Columbia, and in the following month the federal Government offered a formal apology to all native groups for past mistreatment and injustices. The principle of 'aboriginal title', established by the Supreme Court ruling, was again exercised in April 1999 in British Columbia under the Nisga'a Agreement. The Agreement transferred some 2,000 sq km of land, together with substantial powers of self-government and C $196m., to 5,500 Nisga'a people; in return they ceded their wider aboriginal title. In August 2003 Chrétien signed an agreement that would transfer powers of self-government and 39,000 sq km of land to some 3,000 Tlicho people in the Northwest Territories; the agreement was ratified by the federal Parliament in February 2005. At a summit in British Columbia in late November, Prime Minister Martin pledged to spend C $4,300m. over the next 10 years on measures to reduce poverty and improve health, education and housing among the Indian and Inuit communities. An agreement worth C $350m., transferring powers of self-government to 5,300 Inuit people in north-west Labrador, came into effect on 1 December.

In early February 2006 an agreement was reached to protect some 1.8m. ha of land in British Columbia, incorporating the Great Bear rainforest. Negotiations on the issue had begun in 1997, and included representatives from the provincial government, indigenous First Nations, local communities, tourism and labour, and commercial resource companies. Ecosystem-based management would allow controlled resource development in 4.6m. ha of surrounding territory. In mid-June 2006 the Québec government announced that it would levy a 'carbon tax' on oil and gas companies with a view to fulfilling the province's commitment to the Kyoto Protocol (see below). An accord between the Government and the native Cree Indian communities of Québec was announced in July 2007; the agreement, which required ratification by both parties, would grant the communities increased powers of self-government, and guaranteed federal government investment in the region over the next 20 years.

Prime Minister Harper in June 2006 offered a formal apology to the Chinese Canadian community for the 'head tax' that was imposed on Chinese immigrants to Canada between 1885 and 1923. Cheap immigrant labour was encouraged from 1881 for the building of the Canadian Pacific Railway, but once completed the Government introduced the Chinese Immigration Act of 1885, which levied the charge. The Act was superseded by the Chinese Exclusion Act of 1923, which effectively prevented immigration from China until 1947. The Government agreed to pay compensation of C $20,000 each to survivors or their widows (around 400 people); some 81,000 Chinese immigrants had paid the tax, amounting to $23m.

Recent administrations have sought to emphasize Canada's independence from the USA in matters of foreign policy, while continuing the increased co-operation in areas such as trade and environmental protection. In the last two decades of the 20th century a number of bilateral environmental agreements were signed, including accords on gaseous emissions, both domestically and in the USA (which move northwards into Canada to produce environmentally destructive 'acid rain'), and the elimination of industrial pollution from the Great Lakes, in conjunction with the implementation of a number of domestic environmental-improvement programmes. In 1997, at the third Conference of the Parties to the Framework Convention on Climate Change (see World Meteorological Organization, see p. 155), held in Kyoto, Japan, Canada undertook to implement reductions of its emissions of 'greenhouse gases' to 6% below 1990 levels by the year 2012. In December 2002 the Government ratified the Protocol, despite opposition from the gas and petroleum industries and the province of Alberta, which threatened to challenge the legality of ratification in the Supreme Court. Canada assumed a leading role in the establishment, with seven other circumpolar countries, of the Arctic Council (see p. 411), which commenced operation in September 1996. The aims of the Council include the protection of the environment of the polar region, the formation of co-ordinated policies governing its future, and the safeguarding of the interests of its indigenous population groups. However, by April 2007 the country's 'greenhouse gas' emissions were reportedly 30% greater than those recorded in 1990 and the Martin administration conceded that Canada would be unable to satisfy its obligations prescribed under the Koyoto Protocol by 2012. The Prime Minister announced proposals in early February 2007 for the introduction of a C $1,500m. 'eco-trust' as part of the federal budget, intended to combat global warming and pollution, subject to legislative approval. Subsequently, legislation promulgated by the opposition 10 months earlier and intended to force governmental compliance with the terms of the Kyoto Protocol, was approved by the House of Commons in mid-February. The new law required that the Government formulate a detailed plan for the reduction of emissions within 60 days. An appeal to overturn the law was lodged by the Conservatives hours before voting commenced, but the attempt was dismissed by the Speaker of the House. Accordingly, on 26 April, John Baird, Minister of the Environment, announced a government initiative targeting a 20% reduction in current emissions by 2020. The opposition Liberal leader, Stephane Dion, denounced the Government's strategy as misleading.

There have been recurrent disagreements between Canada and France concerning the boundary of disputed waters near the French-controlled islands of Saint Pierre and Miquelon, off the southern coast of Newfoundland and Labrador. In June 1992 an international arbitration tribunal presented its report, generally regarded as favourable to Canada, and in December 1994 the two countries agreed a 10-year accord on the allocation of fishing rights around the islands. In September 2001 France and Canada held talks on energy exploration in the waters off Saint Pierre and Miquelon; geologists believed there were large petroleum and natural gas deposits between the islands and Newfoundland and Labrador and Nova Scotia.

In 1994 the Canadian Government vigorously contested a decision by the European Union (EU) unilaterally to award itself almost 70% of the internationally agreed quota of Greenland halibut caught in the north-west Atlantic fishing grounds. It declared that it would act to prevent EU fishing trawlers (principally from Spain and Portugal) from overfishing the already seriously depleted stocks of Greenland halibut and announced that Canada was extending its maritime jurisdiction beyond its Exclusive Economic Zone (EEZ), already extending 200 nautical miles (370 km) from the coastline. This action was rejected by the EU as contrary to international law. (In November 2003 Canada ratified the UN Convention on the Law of the Sea—UNCLOS—which establishes the limit of the EEZ as being 200 nautical miles from the coastline. In mid-July 2006 the Government announced that it would undertake an underwater survey to identify the outer edge of the continental shelf; under the terms of UNCLOS countries have the right to exploit natural resources on and under the seabed up to an identifiable shelf edge where it extends beyond the EEZ.)

In February 1995 the Canadian Government warned the EU that force would be used if necessary to ensure that total catches by EU vessels did not exceed the Northwest Atlantic Fishing Organization (NAFO)-agreed quota and, in the following month, its enforcement vessels impounded a Spanish trawler fishing in international waters. The EU responded by suspending all official political contacts with Canada, pending the trawler's release. The impasse was eased by the release of the trawler in the following month, when it was agreed to initiate quota allocation negotiations. A resolution was eventually reached in mid-April, under which Canada and EU countries each consented to accept 41% of the 1996 Greenland halibut quota. It was agreed that independent observers would monitor the activities of trawlers in the north-west Atlantic fishing zone. In early 2002 the Canadian Government imposed a ban on all vessels from Estonia and the Faeroe Islands from entering Canadian ports, accusing those fleets of violating NAFO-agreed shrimp quotas off the eastern coast of the country. In September the Government extended the ban to any foreign vessel which violated NAFO-agreed quotas. The ban on the Estonian fleet was lifted in December. In early July 2006 the EU and Canada announced that they would begin joint inspection patrols to combat illegal fishing and to enforce the NAFO Regulatory Area.

Canada, which maintains significant economic and commercial links with Cuba and operates a policy of 'constructive engagement' in its relations with that country, adopted a prominent role in international opposition to efforts, initiated by the US Government in March 1996, to penalize investors whose business in any way involves property in Cuba that was confiscated from US citizens following the 1959 revolution. The imposition of these measures, known as the Helms-Burton Act, led in July 1996 to the exclusion from the USA of nine Canadian businessmen involved in nickel-mining operations in Cuba. The Canadian Government responded by introducing legislation prohibiting Canadian companies from compliance with the Helms-Burton Act, and refused to recognize foreign court rulings arising from the Act. With Mexico, which also conducts significant trade with Cuba, Canada co-ordinated a joint challenge to the US Government through NAFTA dispute procedures. In November 1996 Canada actively promoted a resolution by the UN General Assembly condemning the US trade sanctions against Cuba and, in the same month, joined the EU in a complaint against the embargo to the World Trade Organization (WTO, see p. 396). In April 1998, following an official visit to Cuba by Chrétien, the Canadian Government signed a series of co-operation agreements with Cuba. However, relations between the two countries subsequently experienced a marked decline, owing to increasing official and public concern in Canada at the Cuban Government's human rights record, particularly in relation to the treatment of political prisoners. In July 1999 the Canadian Government stated that it would implement no further assistance programmes to Cuba that did not clearly further the protection of human rights, and it was indicated that Canada would not support, or encourage other countries to support, the admission of Cuba to the Organization of American States (see p. 360).

Relations with the USA improved in June 1999 following the resolution of a long-standing disagreement over the demarcation of salmon-fishing rights off the Pacific coast. However, in September 2000 a dispute arose over the USA's threat to impose export tariffs on Canadian timber which, the USA claimed, was subsidized by the Canadian Government, and which undercut the price of US timber. Canada requested a WTO investigation into US anti-subsidy policies, after the USA imposed duties of 32% on softwood lumber imports from Canada in response. In August 2001 Canada won a preliminary victory at the WTO, which adopted a report agreeing that the Government was not subsidizing exports. Canada hoped to remove US duties and replace an earlier quota agreement, which expired in March 2001, with a system based on free trade; however, the USA imposed tariffs of 27% on softwood lumber imports from Canada in May 2002 in order to protect its own timber industry. Negotiations to resolve the issue failed, and in January 2004 the Canadian Government rejected a US proposal to remove the duties in exchange for quotas limiting Canadian exports to the US market. The USA continued to refuse to remove the duties and in August the WTO ruled that Canada could retaliate with trade sanctions. In August 2005 a NAFTA panel ordered the USA to remove the duties on Canadian softwood and to refund some US $4,000m. already collected. However, the USA refused to comply and in this case received support from the WTO. The trade dispute was resolved in April 2006 when the USA agreed to remove its tariffs and refund the US $4,000m. in duties collected;

in return, Canada agreed to restrict its share of the US timber market to 34%.

Following the terrorist attacks on the USA on 11 September 2001 Canada and the USA increased co-operation on intelligence and security matters: under the 'Smart Border Declaration' signed by the two countries in December, 400 US National Guards were to be deployed at 43 crossings along both sides of the 6,400-km (4,000-mile) Canada–USA border. In the same month extensive anti-terrorist legislation was also introduced. Some 750 Canadian troops were deployed in Afghanistan in February 2002 as part of the US-led international forces present in that country, although all Canadian forces had returned home by November. However, in August 2003 around 1,900 Canadian troops were sent to Afghanistan as part of a NATO-led mission to protect the interim Government there and suppress militant resistance. By late 2006 Canada had committed C $1,000m. to fund reconstruction and poverty reduction and to strengthen governance in Afghanistan, over a 10-year period. In early 2008 there were some 2,500 Canadian armed forces personnel in Afghanistan; according to reports, 78 Canadian soldiers and one diplomat had been killed there since 2001.

In February 2007 Canada became embroiled in allegations relating to the abuse of Afghan detainees by military personnel similar to those that had already threatened the integrity of US and British coalition forces (see chapter on the USA). Under the Access to Information Act, the Department of National Defence released documents on 6 February apparently evidencing the violent mistreatment by military police officers of three prisoners held in Canadian custody near Qandahar, Afghanistan, during an interrogation exercise. A government inquiry into the scandal was immediately commenced and endorsed by NATO in April, although the controversy had adversely affected the minority Government's reputation and prompted opposition calls for the resignation of the Minister of Defence, Gordon O'Connor. In the same month the human rights organization Amnesty International alleged that Canadian military forces had been aware that prisoners transferred from Canadian custody into Afghan custody had been subject to abuse. An agreement allowing Canadian military access to any prisoner originally detained by Canadian forces was reached in the following month. Meanwhile, appeals launched in the Supreme Court by three suspected al-Qa'ida operatives, who had been detained in Canada between 2001 and 2003, returned a unanimous ruling in February 2007 that the Government had contravened Canada's Charter of Rights and Freedoms by ratifying legislation in 2002 that permitted the use of undisclosed evidence by the authorities to justify the indefinite detention, or deportation, of non-Canadian terrorist suspects without recourse to trial. The judgment had been suspended by one year to enable Parliament to amend the Immigration and Refugee Protection Act, while on 27 February the renewal of two further pieces of anti-terrorism legislation, due to expire on 1 March, was opposed by the federal legislature. The standing senate committee on National Security and Defence issued an interim report in the same month recommending that the Government announce a reassessment of its military involvement in Afghanistan subject to the deployment, within one year, of a 'larger and fully-engaged stability force' by NATO to the country. An increased Canadian military police presence in Afghanistan, of 60 officers, was also advised for the purpose of training the Afghan police force, while the Government was to enjoin its NATO allies to commit further troops to the region in an attempt to quell the violence and disorder perpetrated by Taliban forces still rife there.

The federal Government promised some C $300m. for the reconstruction of Iraq following the US-led invasion and occupation of that country and the fall of the Iraqi President, Saddam Hussain, in 2003. In January 2004 US President George W. Bush announced that Canadian companies would be allowed to tender bids for reconstruction projects in Iraq, worth an estimated US $18,600m.; the US Administration had previously declared that Canada, among other traditional allies, would not be invited to participate in such projects, following its opposition to the invasion of Iraq.

In late February 2005 Prime Minister Martin announced that Canada would not participate in a controversial US missile defence programme. However, in mid-2004 Martin's Government had acceded to a US request to allow installations of the North American Aerospace Defense Command (NORAD—a binational military organization established by the two countries in 1958) to be integrated into the anti-missile warning system, which was regarded as tantamount to Canadian participation. In mid-May 2006 the House of Commons voted to renew the NORAD agreement and to make it a permanent arrangement, subject to review every four years.

In July 2006 the Government assisted in evacuating some 15,000 Canadian nationals from Lebanon following Israeli military strikes in the south of that country against bases of the militant Shi'ite organization Hezbollah. The Government pledged some C $5.5m. in humanitarian aid to Lebanon and in mid-September announced the creation of a $25m. Lebanon Relief Fund.

In the mid-1990s Canada actively sought to obtain an international ban on the manufacture and use of landmines. At a conference held in Ottawa in December 1997, Canada became the first signatory of the Ottawa Convention, a treaty agreed by 121 countries, undertaking to discontinue the use of these armaments and providing for the destruction of existing stockpiles. However, by early 2006 the USA, the Russian Federation and the People's Republic of China had not become parties to the agreement. Humanitarian concerns remained at the forefront of Canadian foreign policy: in 2008 Canadian humanitarian or peace-keeping forces were deployed in the following countries: Afghanistan, Bahrain, Bosnia and Herzegovina, Cyprus, Democratic Republic of the Congo, Haiti, the Golan Heights, Sinai and East Jerusalem, Sierra Leone and Sudan.

Government

Canada is a federal parliamentary state. Under the Constitution Act 1982, executive power is vested in the British monarch, as Head of State, and may be exercised by her representative, the Governor-General, whom she appoints on the advice of the Canadian Prime Minister. The federal Parliament comprises the Head of State, a nominated Senate (a maximum of 112 members, appointed on a regional basis) and a House of Commons (308 members, elected by universal adult suffrage for single-member constituencies). A Parliament may last no longer than five years. The Governor-General appoints the Prime Minister and, on the latter's recommendation, other ministers to form the Federal Ministry. The Prime Minister should have the confidence of the House of Commons, to which the Cabinet is responsible. Canada comprises 10 provinces (each with a Lieutenant-Governor and a legislature, which may last no longer than five years, from which a Premier is chosen), and three territories constituted by Act of Parliament.

Defence

Canada co-operates with the USA in the defence of North America and is a member of NATO. Military service is voluntary. As assessed at November 2007, the armed forces numbered 64,000: army 33,300, navy 11,100, air force 19,600. There was also a paramilitary force of 9,350, comprising the Canadian Coast Guard and Fisheries and Oceans Canada. There were 65,773 reserve troops. The federal Government's defence budget for 2007 was C $17,800m.

Economic Affairs

In 2006, according to estimates by the World Bank, Canada's gross national income (GNI), measured at average 2004–06 prices, was US $1,177,445m., equivalent to US $36,170 per head (or $34,610 on an international purchasing-power parity basis). The country's population increased at an average annual rate of 0.9% in 1996–2006, while gross domestic product (GDP) per head increased, in real terms, by an average of 2.5% per year. Overall GDP increased, in real terms, at an average rate of 3.5% per year in 1996–2006. The economy grew by 2.8% in 2006.

Agriculture (including forestry and fishing) contributed 2.3% of GDP (in constant 2002 prices) in 2006 and the sector (excluding forestry and fishing) engaged 2.0% of the economically active population in 2007. In terms of farm receipts, the principal crops are wheat and canola (rapeseed), which, together with livestock production (chiefly cattle and pigs) and timber, provide an important source of export earnings. The cattle industry was affected in 2006 when several cases of bovine spongiform encephalopathy (BSE—commonly known as 'mad cow disease') were confirmed in Canada, leading to temporary bans on beef exports to several countries. Canada is a leading world exporter of forest products and of fish and seafood. The production of furs is also important. In real terms, the GDP of the agricultural sector increased at an average annual rate of 1.3% in 1996–2004; the sector increased by 2.7% in 2005, but decreased by 2.1% in 2006.

Industry (including mining, manufacturing, construction and power) provided 29.1% of GDP (in constant 2002 prices) in 2006 and the sector (including forestry and fishing) employed 19.7% of the economically active population in 2007. Industrial GDP increased, in real terms, at an average annual rate of 3.4% in 1996–2004. Industrial GDP increased by 6.5% in 2006.

Mining provided 4.8% of GDP (in constant 2002 prices) in 2006, and the sector (together with forestry, fishing, petroleum and gas) employed only 2.0% of the economically active population in 2007. Canada is a major world producer of zinc, asbestos, nickel, potash and uranium. Gold, silver, iron, copper, cobalt and lead are also exploited. There are considerable reserves of petroleum and natural gas in Alberta's oil sands, off the Atlantic coast and in the Canadian Arctic islands. In 2006 the country's proven natural gas reserves were estimated at 1,665,011m. cu m. Proven oil reserves were put at 17,100m. barrels in 2006 and crude oil production totalled 3.15m. barrels per day (b/d) in the same year. However, these figures did not include proven reserves in Alberta's oil sands, put at 163,500m. barrels in 2006. The GDP of the mining sector increased, in real terms, at an average rate of 1.7% in 2002–06. Mining GDP increased by 2.0% in 2006.

Manufacturing contributed 15.6% of GDP (in constant 2002 prices) and employed 12.1% of the economically active population in 2007. The principal branches of manufacturing in 2006, measured by the value of shipments, were transport equipment (accounting for 19.4% of the total), food products (11.8%), refined petroleum and coal industries (10.0%), chemical products (8.7%), primary metal industries (8.4%) and fabricated metal products (5.8%). The GDP of the sector increased, in real terms, at an average rate of 3.8% per year in 1996–2004. However, manufacturing GDP decreased by 1.0% in 2006.

Energy is derived principally from hydroelectric power (which provided 57.0% of the electricity supply in 2004) and from geothermal and nuclear power-stations. In 2006 Canada's total energy production (including nuclear energy) totalled an estimated 585,098m. kWh. In 2006 energy products accounted for 8.6% of imports.

Services provided 68.5% of GDP (in constant 2002 prices) and engaged 76.3% of the economically active population in 2007. The combined GDP of the service sectors increased, in real terms, at an average rate of 3.8% per year in 1996–2004. Services GDP increased by 3.8% in 2006.

In 2006 Canada recorded a visible trade surplus of US $45,146m., and there was a surplus of US $20,797m. on the current account of the balance of payments. In 2006 the USA accounted for 79.2% of Canada's total exports and 65.5% of total imports; the countries of the European Union (EU, see p. 244) and Japan were also important trading partners. The principal exports in that year were automotive products, energy products and industrial goods and materials. The principal imports were machinery and equipment, industrial goods and materials and automotive products. In January 1994 a free trade agreement with the USA and Mexico, the North American Free Trade Agreement (NAFTA, see p. 338), entered into force. Almost all restrictions on trade and investment between the three countries were to be removed over a 15-year period. Since the implementation of NAFTA, however, disagreements have persisted between Canada and the USA over alleged violations of the Agreement by the US Government in relation to bilateral trade in softwood lumber, wheat and other commodities. Since the mid-1990s the Canadian Government has implemented measures aimed at expanding trade in Latin America and the Caribbean: in 1996 Canada finalized a trade agreement with Chile, which phased out most customs duties by 2002. A similar agreement was signed with Costa Rica in 2001 and with the Dominican Republic in 2007, and negotiations towards a comparable accord with El Salvador, Guatemala, Honduras and Nicaragua were ongoing. In June 2007 talks began with Colombia and Peru with regard to establishing a free trade accord, and in January 2008 agreement on the matter was reached with Peru. In October 2007 negotiations towards a free trade agreement began with members of the Caribbean Community and Common Market (CARICOM, see p. 196) countries. A free trade accord was concluded with the members of the European Free Trade Association (EFTA, see p. 412) in January 2008, while Canada has also pursued efforts to develop similar arrangements with the EU. The Canadian Government has also expanded trade in the Far East, notably with the People's Republic of China, the Republic of Korea, Indonesia, Singapore and Viet Nam. A 12th round of negotiations between Canadian and Korean delegations was held in late 2007.

For the financial year 2006/07 there was a consolidated budget surplus of C $28,608m. The annual rate of inflation averaged 2.0% in 1995–2006. Consumer prices increased by an average of 2.0% in 2006. The rate of unemployment averaged 6.0% in 2007.

The sustained period of buoyancy enjoyed by the Canadian economy from the mid-1990s continued into the mid-2000s. The economic success was overseen by the Liberal Government and continued by its Conservative successor, with its emphasis on financial stringency, and was further aided by low rates of domestic inflation, high international commodity prices and by the beneficial effects of NAFTA on Canadian export sales to the USA. The fiscal year 2006/07 was the 10th successive year to record a consolidated budget surplus. As a result, Canada's debt as an equivalent of GDP fell to 32.3% in 2006/07, compared with 68.4% in 1995/06. The Government aimed to reduce this figure to 25.0% by 2014, and to eradicate it completely by 2021. The Government paid off C $13,200m. of the debt in September 2006. The 2006/07 budget planned for a further C $9,200m. reduction in the debt, which stood at C $778,272m. at the end of September 2007, compared with C $816,126m. at the same time the previous year. Nine of the 13 provinces and territories reported a budgetary surplus in 2006/07; however, of these, only Alberta's surplus (of C $6,968m.) was significant, owing to high prices for the province's abundant oil reserves. The economy was forecast to grow by 2.5% in 2008. The predominance of trade with the USA compensated for deficits with other major trading partners, including the EU and Japan, and allowed Canada to record substantial trade surpluses in the early 2000s. However, Canada was also vulnerable to failures in the economy of its largest trading partner: the economic downturn in the USA from the mid-2000s prompted concern that Canadian economic growth would be affected. Furthermore, in spite of its strong position, the Canadian economy remained susceptible to adverse movements in world prices for its major exports of raw materials, and many industrial sectors relied heavily on foreign investment. The strength of the Canadian dollar in 2007 continued to have a negative effect on exports.

Education

Education policy is a provincial responsibility, and the period of compulsory school attendance varies. French-speaking students are entitled by law, in some provinces, to instruction in French. Primary education is from the age of five or six years to 13–14, followed by three to five years at secondary or high school. In 2004/05 some 5,253,392 pupils attended primary and secondary schools. In 2006 there were 58 universities in the country. Total government budgetary expenditure on education totalled C $87,726m. (15.3% of total spending) in 2006/07.

Public Holidays*

2008: 1 January (for New Year's Day), 21 March (Good Friday), 24 March (Easter Monday), 19 May (Victoria Day), 1 July (Canada Day), 1 September (Labour Day), 13 October (Thanksgiving Day), 11 November (Remembrance Day), 25 December (Christmas Day), 26 December (Boxing Day).

2009: 1 January (New Year's Day), 10 April (Good Friday), 13 April (Easter Monday), 18 May (Victoria Day), 1 July (Canada Day), 7 September (Labour Day), 12 October (Thanksgiving Day), 11 November (Remembrance Day), 25 December (Christmas Day), 26 December (Boxing Day).

*Standard public holidays comprise the listed days, together with any other day so proclaimed by individual provinces or territories.

Weights and Measures

The metric system is in force.

Statistical Survey

Source (unless otherwise stated): Statistics Canada, Ottawa, ON K1A 0T6; tel. (613) 951-8116; fax (613) 951-0581; internet www.statcan.ca.

The following Statistics Canada resources have been adapted for use in this survey (with permission). [SC1]: *Land and freshwater area, by province and territory*; internet www.statcan.ca/english/Pgdb/phys01.htm. [SC2]: *Population and Dwelling Counts, for Canada, Provinces and Territories, 2006 and 2001 Censuses - 100% Data*; internet www12.statcan.ca/english/census06/data/popdwell/Table.cfm?T=101. [SC3]: *Population by year, by province and territory*; internet www40.statcan.ca/l01/cst01/demo02a.htm. [SC4]: *Population of census metropolitan areas (2001 Census boundaries)*; internet www40.statcan.ca/l01/cst01/demo05a.htm. [SC5]: *Births and birth rate, by province and territory*; internet www40.statcan.ca/l01/cst01/demo04a.htm. [SC6]: *Marriages by province and territory*; internet www40.statcan.ca/l01/cst01/famil04.htm. [SC7]: *Deaths and death rate, by province and territory*; internet www40.statcan.ca/l01/cst01/demo07a.htm. [SC8]: *Employment by industry* www40.statcan.ca/l01/cst01/econ40.htm. [SC9]: *Labour force characteristics*; internet www40.statcan.ca/l01/cst01/econ10.htm. [SC10]: *Field and speciality crops*; internet www40.statcan.ca/l01/cst01/prim11b.htm. [SC11]: *Fur production, by province and territory*; internet www40.statcan.ca/l01/cst01/prim46a.htm. [SC12]: *Manufacturing shipments, by subsector*; internet www40.statcan.ca/l01/cst01/manuf11.htm. [SC13]: *Consolidated government revenue and expenditures*; internet www40.statcan.ca/l01/cst01/govt48a.htm. [SC14]: *Gross domestic product, income-based*; internet www40.statcan.ca/l01/cst01/econ03.htm. [SC15]: *Gross domestic product, expenditure-based*; internet www40.statcan.ca/l01/cst01/econ04.htm. [SC16]: *Real gross domestic product, expenditure-based*; internet www40.statcan.ca/l01/cst01/econ05.htm. [SC17]: *Gross domestic product at basic prices by industry*; internet www40.statcan.ca/l01/cst01/econ41.htm. [SC18]: *Imports of goods on a balance-of-payments basis, by product*; internet www40.statcan.ca/l01/cst01/gblec05.htm. [SC19]: *Exports of goods on a balance-of-payments basis, by product*; internet www40.statcan.ca/l01/cst01/gblec04.htm. [SC20]: *Imports, exports and trade balance of goods on a balance-of-payments basis, by country or country grouping*; internet www40.statcan.ca/l01/cst01/gblec02a.htm. [SC21]: *Motor vehicle registrations, by province and territory*; internet www40.statcan.ca/l01/cst01/trade14a.htm. All data were retrieved January 2008.

Area and Population

AREA, POPULATION AND DENSITY

Area (sq km)	
Land	9,093,507
Inland water	891,163
Total	9,984,670*
Population (census results)†	
15 May 2001	30,007,094
16 May 2006	
Males‡	15,475,970
Females‡	16,136,925
Total	31,612,897
Population (official postcensal estimates at 1 July)	
2005	32,312,100
2006	32,649,500
2007	32,976,000
Density (per sq km) at 1 July 2007	3.6§

* 3,855,101 sq miles; area data prior to 2006 census, when land area was estimated at 9,017,699 sq km and population density of land area was estimated at 3.5 per sq km.
† Excluding census data for one or more incompletely enumerated Indian reserves or Indian settlements and excluding adjustment for underenumeration.
‡ Figures are rounded to nearest 5.
§ Land area only.

Sources: Statistics Canada, [SC1], [SC2], [SC3].

PROVINCES AND TERRITORIES
(official estimates as at 1 July 2007, rounded figures)

	Land area (sq km)	Population	Density (per sq km)	Capital
Provinces:				
Alberta	642,317	3,474,000	5.4	Edmonton
British Columbia	925,186	4,380,300	4.7	Victoria
Manitoba	553,556	1,186,700	2.1	Winnipeg
New Brunswick	71,450	749,800	10.5	Fredericton
Newfoundland and Labrador	373,872	506,300	1.4	St John's
Nova Scotia	53,338	934,100	17.5	Halifax
Ontario	917,741	12,803,900	14.0	Toronto
Prince Edward Island	5,660	138,600	24.5	Charlottetown
Québec	1,365,128	7,700,800	5.6	Québec
Saskatchewan	591,670	996,900	1.7	Regina
Territories:				
Northwest Territories	1,183,085	42,600	0.0	Yellowknife
Nunavut Territory*	1,936,113	31,100	0.0	Iqaluit
Yukon Territory	474,391	31,000	0.1	Whitehorse
Total	9,093,507	32,976,000	3.6	—

* Formerly part of Northwest Territories. Constituted as a separate Territory with effect from 1 April 1999.

Sources: Statistics Canada, [SC1], [SC3].

PRINCIPAL METROPOLITAN AREAS*
(official estimates as at 1 July 2006)

Toronto	5,406,300	London	465,700
Montréal	3,666,300	Kitchener	463,600
Vancouver	2,236,100	St Catharines–Niagara	396,800
Ottawa–Gatineau (capital)	1,158,300	Halifax	382,200
Calgary	1,107,200	Oshawa	344,400
Edmonton	1,050,000	Victoria	334,300
Québec	723,300	Windsor	332,100
Hamilton	716,200	Saskatoon	235,500
Winnipeg	706,700		

* Boundaries as at 2001 census.

Source: Statistics Canada, [SC4].

BIRTHS, MARRIAGES AND DEATHS
(year ending 30 June, unless otherwise indicated)

	Registered live births* Number	Rate (per 1,000)	Registered marriages† Number	Rate (per 1,000)	Registered deaths* Number	Rate (per 1,000)
2001/02	328,155	10.5	146,618	4.7	220,494	7.1
2002/03	330,523	10.5	146,738	4.7	223,905	7.1
2003/04	337,762	10.6	147,391	4.7	228,829	7.2
2004/05	339,270	10.6	148,585	4.6	229,372	7.1
2005/06	345,355	10.6	148,439	4.6	230,687	7.1
2006/07‡	352,848	10.8	149,792	4.6	237,931	7.3

* Including Canadian residents temporarily in the USA but excluding US residents temporarily in Canada.
† Figures refer to the first of the two years, from January to December.
‡ Preliminary figure(s).

Sources: Statistics Canada, [SC3], [SC5], [SC6], [SC7].

Expectation of life (years at birth, WHO estimates): 80.5 (males 78.0; females 82.7) in 2005 (Source: WHO, *World Health Report*).

CANADA

ECONOMICALLY ACTIVE POPULATION*
(annual averages, '000 persons aged 15 years and over)

	2005	2006	2007
Agriculture	343.7	346.4	337.2
Forestry, fishing, mining, petroleum and gas	306.4	330.1	339.3
Utilities	125.3	122.0	138.0
Construction	1,019.5	1,069.7	1,133.5
Manufacturing	2,207.4	2,117.7	2,044.9
Trade	2,574.6	2,633.5	2,682.4
Transportation and warehousing	793.6	802.2	822.8
Finance, insurance, real estate and leasing	987.8	1,040.5	1,060.4
Professional, scientific and technical services	1,050.0	1,089.9	1,136.9
Business, building and other support services	654.4	690.0	702.1
Educational services	1,106.1	1,158.4	1,183.2
Health care and social assistance	1,734.6	1,785.5	1,846.1
Information, culture and recreation	735.1	745.0	782.0
Accommodation and food services	1,004.5	1,015.0	1,069.4
Other services	693.4	701.0	723.5
Public administration	833.1	837.4	864.6
Total employed	16,169.7	16,484.3	16,866.4
Unemployed	1,172.8	1,108.4	1,079.4
Total labour force	17,342.6	17,592.8	17,945.8

* Figures exclude military personnel, inmates of institutions, residents of the Yukon, Northwest and Nunavut Territories, and Indian Reserves.

Sources: Statistics Canada, [SC8], [SC9].

Health and Welfare

KEY INDICATORS

Total fertility rate (children per woman, 2005)	1.5
Under-5 mortality rate (per 1,000 live births, 2005)	6
HIV/AIDS (% of persons aged 15–49, 2005, preliminary)	0.3
Physicians (per 1,000 head, 2000)	2.1
Hospital beds (per 1,000 head, 1999)	3.9
Health expenditure (2004): US $ per head (PPP)	3,173.0
Health expenditure (2004): % of GDP	9.8
Health expenditure (2004): public (% of total)	69.8
Human Development Index (2005): ranking	4
Human Development Index (2005): value	0.961

For sources and definitions, see explanatory note on p. vi.

Agriculture

PRINCIPAL CROPS
('000 metric tons)

	2005	2006	2007
Wheat	25,748.1	25,265.4	20,054.0
Barley	11,677.6	9,573.1	10,983.9
Corn for grain	9,332.2	8,989.8	11,648.7
Rye	330.4	382.9	233.0
Oats	3,282.7	3,852.2	4,696.3
Peas (dry)	2,993.6	2,519.9	2,934.8
Soybeans	3,155.6	3,465.5	2,695.7
Sunflower seed	84.4	157.3	124.8
Rapeseed (Canola)	9,483.3	9,000.3	8,750.7
Canary seed	227.2	132.8	162.0
Lentils	1,164.3	629.5	673.9
Linseed	990.6	988.8	633.5
Mustard seed	183.8	108.2	114.3
Tame hay	29,576.0	29,999.8	30,244.6

Source: Statistics Canada, [SC11].

LIVESTOCK
('000 head at 1 July)

	2004	2005	2006
Horses*	385	385	385
Cattle	14,653	15,063	14,830
Pigs	14,623	14,619	14,690
Sheep	997	980	919
Chickens*	160,000	160,000	160,000
Ducks*	1,150	1,150	1,150
Turkeys*	5,520	5,600	5,600

* FAO estimates.

Source: FAO.

LIVESTOCK PRODUCTS
('000 metric tons)

	2004	2005	2006
Cattle meat	1,496.0	1,523.0	1,391.2
Sheep meat	17.6	17.9	17.0
Pig meat	1,920.0	1,913.5	1,898.3
Horse meat*	18	18	18
Chicken meat	969.8	1,000.0	996.7
Turkey meat	145.0	155.4	163.4
Cows' milk	8,000†	8,100†	8,100*
Hen eggs	376.6	399.0	399.6

* FAO estimate(s).
† Unofficial figure.

Source: FAO.

Forestry

ROUNDWOOD REMOVALS
('000 cubic metres)

	2004	2005	2006
Sawlogs, veneer logs and logs for sleepers	172,749	173,154	167,974
Pulpwood	29,286	31,501	31,081
Other industrial wood	3,582	4,057	4,050
Fuel wood	2,789	2,789*	2,789*
Total	208,406	211,501	205,893

* Unofficial figure.

Source: FAO.

SAWNWOOD PRODUCTION
('000 cubic metres, incl. railway sleepers)

	2004	2005	2006
Coniferous (softwood)*	59,136	58,470	57,067
Broadleaved (hardwood)	1,816	1,717	1,642
Total	60,952	60,187	58,709

* Unofficial figures.

Source: FAO.

CANADA

Fur Industry

NUMBER OF PELTS PRODUCED
('000)

	2003	2004	2005
Alberta	148.8	n.a.	168.3
Manitoba	124.4	127.9	138.1
Northwest Territories	23.5	42.7	24.0
Nova Scotia	764.2	806.2	800.4
Nunavut Territory	12.3	6.6	12.0
Ontario	538.7	556.2	492.3
Prince Edward Island	40.6	41.5	34.1
Québec	261.7	252.9	276.7
Saskatchewan	84.8	62.6	67.7
Yukon Territory	4.0	3.5	5.8
Total (incl. others)	2,387.0	2,392.5	2,371.6

Note: Figures for British Columbia, New Brunswick and Newfoundland and Labrador are withheld due to confidentiality restrictions, but are included in the total.

Source: Statistics Canada, [SC11].

Fishing

(metric tons, live weight, preliminary)

	2003	2004	2005
Cod	22,768	24,729	32,915
Herring	200,333	183,432	107,027
Mackerel	44,913	53,612	53,462
Clams/quahaugs	39,284	33,704	24,925
Scallop*	93,864	82,486	77,571
Lobster	49,840	47,446	427,884
Shrimp	142,548	176,053	188,522
Queen Crab	96,898	103,354	121,840
Atlantic total (incl. others)	852,829	875,029	1,240,287
Hake	69,057	124,872	104,189
Salmon	38,605	25,566	27,068
Pacific total (incl. others)†	218,836	255,142	248,312
Canada total (incl. others)	1,071,665	1,130,171	1,488,598

* Includes meat with roe.
† British Columbia data only; includes quantities of tuna caught by Canadian fishermen in international waters and landed in Canada, and hake sold to foreign vessels under joint venture arrangements.

Note: Figures exclude landings of aquatic plants ('000 metric tons): 45,797 in 2003; 40,224 in 2004; 4 in 2005. Also excluded are miscellaneous other landings ('000 metric tons): 2,583 in 2003; 3,065 in 2004; 7,075 in 2005.

Source: Department of Fisheries and Oceans, Ottawa.

Mining

('000 metric tons, unless otherwise indicated)

	2004	2005	2006*
Metallic:			
Bismuth (metric tons)	180	141	184
Cadmium (metric tons)	740	634	475
Cobalt (metric tons)	2,085	2,391	2,793
Copper	545	577	595
Gold (kilograms)	129,478	119,549	103,402
Iron ore	28,596	30,387	34,094
Lead	73	73	82
Molybdenum (metric tons)	9,946	7,667	7,042
Nickel	177	193	226
Platinum group (kilograms)	26,164	22,709	22,878
Selenium (metric tons)	271	107	117
Silver (metric tons)	1,295	1,063	968
Uranium (metric tons)	11,548	12,597	9,781
Zinc	734	619	594
Non-metallic:			
Gypsum	9,205	8,570	9,072
Lime	2,386	2,289	2,211

—continued	2004	2005	2006*
Nepheline syenite	714	745	719
Potash (K$_2$O)	10,332	10,140	8,528
Salt	14,096	13,463	13,338
Sulphur, in smelter gas	678	653	693
Sulphur, elemental	7,834	7,757	8,296
Fuels:			
Coal	65,997	65,345	62,987
Structural materials:			
Cement	14,842	14,656	14,571
Stone	135,988	141,275	140,840

* Provisional figures.

2005: Natural gas (million cubic metres) 170,740; Crude petroleum ('000 cubic metres) 146,208.

Source: Natural Resources Canada.

Industry

VALUE OF SHIPMENTS
(C $ million)

	2004	2005	2006
Food industries	68,254.9	67,518.3	72,138.0
Beverage and tobacco products industries	12,567.7	12,643.5	11,196.7
Textile mills	3,731.2	3,381.3	2,561.6
Textile product mills	2,592.2	2,607.5	2,442.3
Leather and allied products industries	665.3	529.8	459.1
Paper industries	33,840.2	32,536.1	31,422.4
Printing, publishing and allied industries	11,701.7	12,224.7	10,868.4
Refined petroleum and coal products industries	45,736.1	57,073.5	61,219.4
Chemical and chemical products industries	47,266.6	51,432.2	53,046.1
Plastics and rubber products industries	25,791.5	27,329.3	27,808.9
Clothing industries	6,452.3	5,537.9	5,309.9
Wood product industries	36,020.3	33,704.4	29,465.4
Non-metallic mineral products industries	12,339.8	12,900.2	13,945.7
Primary metal industries	42,954.7	43,760.4	51,273.6
Fabricated metal products industries	33,255.7	35,393.9	35,411.5
Machinery industries (excl. electrical machinery)	28,143.2	30,694.6	31,424.7
Computer and electronic products industries	20,818.4	20,103.8	19,560.7
Electrical equipment, appliance and component industries	9,526.6	9,869.9	10,520.1
Transportation equipment industries	123,322.0	124,810.1	118,449.0
Furniture and fixture industries	13,374.3	13,407.6	13,358.9
Other manufacturing industries	8,424.6	8,795.3	9,161.9
Total	586,779.4	606,254.5	611,044.4

Source: Statistics Canada, [SC12].

Electric energy (net production, million kWh): 601,135 in 2002; 589,967 in 2003; 598,514 in 2004 (Source: UN, *Industrial Commodity Statistics Yearbook*).

CANADA

Finance

CURRENCY AND EXCHANGE RATES

Monetary Units
100 cents = 1 Canadian dollar (C $).

Sterling, US Dollar and Euro Equivalents (31 December 2007)
£1 sterling = C $1.9796;
US $1 = C $0.9881;
€1 = C $1.4546;
C $100 = £50.52 = US $101.20 = €68.75.

Average Exchange Rate (C $ per US $)
2005 1.2118
2006 1.1344
2007 1.0741

BUDGET
(C $ million, year ending 31 March)*

Revenue	2004/05	2005/06	2006/07
Income taxes	207,219	227,275	246,232
Property and related taxes	46,710	49,639	51,417
Consumption taxes	104,685	108,026	107,300
Health insurance premiums	3,206	3,258	3,327
Contributions to social security plans	69,039	71,441	74,369
Other taxes	17,788	18,747	19,702
Sales of goods and services	40,557	42,666	45,890
Investment income	40,327	47,514	47,468
Other revenue from own sources	8,129	7,447	5,562
Total own source revenue	537,660	576,012	601,266

Expenditure	2004/05	2005/06	2006/07
General government services	18,802	19,685	19,956
Protection of persons and property	41,175	43,725	45,301
Transport and communications	21,385	25,390	26,051
Health	94,565	99,017	106,850
Social services	156,706	165,167	172,374
Education	77,225	83,324	87,726
Resource conservation and industrial development	18,444	19,749	19,908
Environment	11,929	13,313	14,355
Recreation and culture	13,736	14,350	14,584
Labour, employment and immigration	2,328	2,514	2,582
Housing	3,900	4,525	4,782
Foreign affairs and international assistance	5,556	5,585	6,654
Regional planning and development	2,035	2,168	2,475
Research establishments	1,855	1,986	1,995
Debt charges	45,460	45,518	46,107
Other expenditures	1,662	1,688	960
Total expenditure	516,763	547,705	572,658

* Figures refer to the consolidated accounts of federal, provincial and territorial governments.

Source: Statistics Canada, [SC13].

INTERNATIONAL RESERVES
(US $ million at 31 December)

	2004	2005	2006
Gold*	48	56	69
IMF special drawing rights	924	897	963
Reserve position in IMF	3,338	1,401	833
Foreign exchange	30,166	30,664	33,198
Total	34,476	33,018	35,063

* National valuation.

Source: IMF, *International Financial Statistics*.

MONEY SUPPLY
(C $ million at 31 December*)

	2004	2005	2006
Currency outside banks	39,340	41,220	43,870
Demand deposits at deposit money banks	356,370	375,130	411,210
Total money (incl. others)	395,710	416,350	455,080

* Rounded to the nearest $10m.

Source: IMF, *International Financial Statistics*.

COST OF LIVING
(Consumer Price Index; base: 2000 = 100)

	2004	2005	2006
Food	111.3	114.1	116.8
Water, electricity, gas and other fuels	119.2	127.0	133.4
Clothing	97.7	97.3	95.5
Rent	106.3	107.1	108.2
All items	109.8	112.2	114.4

Source: ILO.

NATIONAL ACCOUNTS

National Income and Product
(C $ million at current prices)

	2004	2005	2006
Compensation of employees	654,957	694,041	737,382
Net operating surplus and mixed income	318,579	349,029	362,541
Domestic factor incomes	973,536	1,043,070	1,099,923
Consumption of fixed capital	168,274	176,338	184,750
Gross domestic product (GDP) at factor cost	1,141,810	1,219,408	1,284,673
Indirect taxes, less subsidies	148,836	156,181	161,582
Statistical discrepancy	182	–509	52
GDP at market prices	1,290,828	1,375,080	1,446,307

Gross national income (C $ '000 million): 1,270.81 in 2004; 1,344.21 in 2005; 1,422.19 in 2006 (Source: IMF, *International Financial Statistics*).

Gross national disposable income (C $ '000 million): 1,270.04 in 2004; 1,343.99 in 2005; 1,422.35 in 2006 (Source: IMF, *International Financial Statistics*).

Expenditure on the Gross Domestic Product
(C $ million at current prices)

	2004	2005	2006
Government final consumption expenditure	248,868	262,650	279,806
Private final consumption expenditure	720,401	760,701	803,502
Changes in inventories	5,610	9,669	7,783
Gross fixed capital formation	261,516	289,370	318,221
Total domestic expenditure	1,236,395	1,322,390	1,409,312
Exports of goods and services	495,347	520,379	524,706
Less Imports of goods and services	440,732	468,197	487,660
Statistical discrepancy	–182	508	–51
GDP at market prices	1,290,828	1,375,080	1,446,307
GDP at constant 2002 prices	1,210,656	1,247,780	1,282,204

CANADA

Gross Domestic Product by Economic Activity
(C $ million at constant 2002 prices)

	2004	2005	2006
Agriculture, hunting, forestry and fishing	27,685	28,437	27,847
Mining, petroleum and gas extraction	55,849	56,044	57,174
Manufacturing	185,504	188,478	186,631
Electricity, gas and water	29,131	30,550	30,128
Construction	63,592	68,527	74,087
Wholesale trade	60,283	63,879	68,383
Retail trade	62,870	65,132	69,015
Transportation and warehousing	51,960	53,802	55,501
Finance, insurance, real estate and leasing	215,098	221,951	230,362
Professional, scientific and technical services	52,349	53,793	55,377
Administration and support, waste management and remediation services	27,345	28,756	30,524
Education	53,807	55,008	56,221
Health care and social assistance	71,736	72,784	74,780
Information and cultural industries	40,232	41,848	43,147
Arts, entertainment and recreation	10,848	10,940	11,410
Accommodation and food services	25,721	26,418	27,365
Public administration	64,355	65,309	66,758
Other services	28,825	29,346	30,072
Statistical discrepancy	–388	–978	–877
GDP at basic prices	**1,126,802**	**1,160,024**	**1,193,905**

Sources: Statistics Canada, [SC14], [SC15], [SC16], [SC17].

BALANCE OF PAYMENTS
(US $ million)

	2004	2005	2006
Exports of goods f.o.b.	330,057	373,254	401,786
Imports of goods f.o.b.	–279,623	–320,575	–356,641
Trade balance	**50,434**	**52,679**	**45,146**
Exports of services	49,747	55,313	59,332
Imports of services	–58,990	–65,333	–72,649
Balance on goods and services	**41,191**	**42,659**	**31,829**
Other income received	29,431	39,860	54,344
Other income paid	–47,980	–58,397	–64,760
Balance on goods, services and income	**22,642**	**24,121**	**21,413**
Current transfers received	5,518	6,754	8,517
Current transfers paid	–5,839	–7,467	–9,133
Current balance	**22,321**	**23,408**	**20,797**
Capital account (net)	3,437	4,889	3,702
Direct investment abroad	–43,011	–33,584	–45,391
Direct investment from abroad	–660	29,142	69,068
Portfolio investment assets	–18,924	–44,072	–69,405
Portfolio investment liabilities	41,975	7,933	28,675
Other investment assets	–7,009	–16,567	–30,375
Other investment liabilities	–3,935	26,997	28,212
Net errors and omissions	2,972	3,189	–4,458
Overall balance	**–2,836**	**1,335**	**826**

Source: IMF, *International Financial Statistics*.

External Trade

PRINCIPAL COMMODITIES
(C $ million)

Imports f.o.b.	2004	2005	2006
Agricultural and fishing products	21,352.3	22,038.7	23,453.5
Energy products	24,781.6	33,668.9	34,578.4
Crude petroleum	16,439.0	21,581.9	22,512.3
Industrial goods and materials	73,503.5	78,556.2	83,981.1
Metals and metal ores	20,966.7	23,955.7	28,125.4
Chemicals and plastics	26,878.6	28,675.2	29,748.1
Machinery and equipment (excl. automotive products)	104,098.8	110,972.2	114,638.1
Industrial and agricultural machinery	27,277.7	29,690.1	31,734.3
Aircraft and other transportation equipment	12,962.6	14,968.5	14,800.2
Office machines and equipment	15,447.0	16,005.7	15,963.1
Automotive products	77,364.8	78,376.3	79,782.6
Passenger automobiles and chassis	22,347.4	23,476.7	25,103.8
Trucks and other motor vehicles	14,090.8	15,285.1	16,750.5
Motor vehicle parts	40,926.6	39,614.5	37,928.3
Other consumer goods	47,714.1	49,485.7	52,034.3
Total (incl. others)	**363,308.1**	**388,281.7**	**404,394.6**

Exports f.o.b.	2004	2005	2006
Agricultural and fishing products	30,691.1	30,107.1	31,327.0
Energy products	68,063.3	86,804.5	86,783.6
Crude petroleum	25,512.8	30,355.9	38,574.0
Natural gas	27,382.1	35,988.6	27,804.7
Forestry products	39,283.2	36,410.4	33,262.1
Lumber and sawmill products	20,525.1	18,789.0	16,221.3
Newsprint and other paper and paperboard products	12,025.1	11,814.6	11,075.3
Industrial goods and materials	77,966.9	84,257.7	93,959.0
Chemicals, plastics and fertilizers	27,105.7	30,181.5	30,980.8
Metals and alloys	24,953.5	27,037.1	33,530.3
Machinery and equipment (excl. automotive products)	91,122.3	94,110.6	94,672.6
Industrial and agricultural machinery	19,302.9	20,383.9	21,087.1
Aircraft and other transportation equipment	19,533.0	20,149.8	20,541.0
Automotive products	90,389.1	88,076.6	82,539.1
Passenger automobiles and chassis	47,239.6	44,574.3	42,375.5
Trucks and other motor vehicles	15,488.0	16,169.0	14,969.1
Motor vehicle parts	27,661.5	27,333.3	25,194.5
Other consumer goods	17,269.3	17,248.7	17,959.0
Total (incl. others)	**429,067.1**	**451,783.0**	**455,696.5**

Sources: Statistics Canada, [SC18], [SC19].

PRINCIPAL TRADING PARTNERS
(C $ million, balance of payments basis)

Imports	2004	2005	2006
Japan	10,087.2	11,215.9	11,882.5
United Kingdom	9,457.5	9,079.5	9,543.0
USA	250,290.7	259,795.4	264,889.2
Other European Union countries	26,992.7	29,455.2	32,494.7
Other OECD countries	22,237.7	24,314.5	23,683.1
Other countries	44,242.2	54,421.4	61,902.2
Total	**363,308.1**	**388,281.7**	**404,394.6**

Exports	2004	2005	2006
Japan	9,839.2	10,319.1	10,455.3
United Kingdom	9,358.6	9,522.4	11,559.9
USA	350,588.5	368,249.5	360,963.3
Other European Union countries	17,317.9	18,972.9	21,270.4
Other OECD countries	14,384.2	15,025.0	17,560.6
Other countries	27,578.7	29,694.1	33,887.0
Total	**429,067.1**	**451,783.0**	**455,696.5**

Source: Statistics Canada, [SC20].

Transport

RAILWAYS
(revenue traffic)

	2004	2005	2006
Passengers carried ('000)*	4,181	4,322	4,320
Passenger-km (million)*	1,439	1,479	1,458
Freight carried ('000 metric tons)	306,563	311,590	307,897
Net freight ton-km ('000)	343,232	352,912	355,831

* Intercity trains only.

Source: Railway Association of Canada, *Railway Trends*.

ROAD TRAFFIC
('000 vehicles registered at 31 December)

	2006
On-road motor vehicle registrations	20,065.2
Passenger cars and light trucks	18,738.9
Heavy trucks	760.9
Buses	80.4
Motorcycles and mopeds	484.9
Trailers	4,961.2
Other (off-road, construction, farm vehicles, etc.)	1,658.5
Total vehicle registrations	**26,684.8**

Note: Light trucks are defined as vehicles weighing less than 4,500 kilograms; heavy trucks are those weighing 4,500 kilograms and over.

Source: Statistics Canada, [SC21].

INLAND WATER TRAFFIC
(St Lawrence Seaway, '000 gross registered metric tons)

	2003	2004	2005
Montréal–Lake Ontario	28,900	30,801	31,273
Welland Canal	31,870	34,285	34,160

Source: St Lawrence Seaway Management Corpn.

SHIPPING
Merchant Fleet
(registered at 31 December)

	2004	2005	2006
Number of vessels	909	939	936
Total displacement ('000 grt)	2,663.6	2,742.0	2,787.8

Source: Lloyd's Register of Shipping, *World Fleet Statistics*.

CIVIL AVIATION
(scheduled services)

	2001	2002	2003
Kilometres flown (million)	567	885	870
Passengers carried ('000)	24,204	36,202	36,264
Passenger-km (million)	68,804	80,426	76,328
Total ton-km (million)	7,979	9,942	8,816

Source: UN, *Statistical Yearbook*.

Tourism

FOREIGN TOURIST ARRIVALS BY COUNTRY OF RESIDENCE

	2003	2004	2005
Australia	152,087	179,782	201,939
France	276,672	331,978	356,489
Germany	260,247	299,802	324,373
Hong Kong	91,632	115,449	111,415
Japan	262,182	414,057	423,881
Korea	138,563	169,866	179,961
Mexico	142,162	173,243	189,357
Netherlands	104,283	116,890	118,805
Taiwan	68,224	106,636	98,238
United Kingdom	708,092	824,758	906,179
USA	14,232,370	15,038,040	14,390,696
Total (incl. others)	17,534,298	19,095,342	18,770,444

Tourism receipts (US $ million, incl. passenger transport): 12,236 in 2003; 14,953 in 2004; 15,830 in 2005.

Source: World Tourism Organization.

Communications Media

	2003	2004	2005
Telephones ('000 main lines in use)	20,664.0	20,563.0	20,780.0
Mobile cellular telephones ('000 subscribers)	13,291.0	15,020.0	17,017.0
Personal computers ('000 in use)	16,485	22,390	22,390
Internet users ('000)	17,600	20,000	22,000
Broadband subscribers ('000)	4,513	5,416	6,429

Television receivers ('000 in use): 21,486 in 2002.

Facsimile machines (estimated number in use): 1,075,000 in 1998.

Daily newspapers: 103 in 2004 (circulation 5,578,000).

Book production (titles): 22,941 in 1999.

Sources: International Telecommunication Union; UN, *Statistical Yearbook*; UNESCO Institute for Statistics.

Education

(2001/02, UNESCO estimates)

	Teachers	Males	Females	Total
Pre-primary	28,624	262,785	249,000	511,785
Primary	141,045	1,264,585	1,196,358	2,460,943
Lower secondary	69,211	625,107	588,721	1,213,828
Upper secondary	78,679	767,401	727,796	1,495,197
General	67,662	714,416	677,638	1,392,054
Technical/vocational	11,017	52,985	50,158	103,143
Post-secondary	n.a.	52,640	73,171	125,811
Tertiary	132,230	547,146	707,687	1,254,833

Source: UNESCO Institute for Statistics.

Directory

The Constitution

Under the Constitution Act 1982, which was enacted as Schedule B to the Canada Act (UK) 1982, and which entered into force on 17 April 1982, executive authority is vested in the Sovereign, and exercised in her name by a Governor-General and Privy Council. Legislative power is exercised by a Parliament of two Houses, the Senate and the House of Commons. The Constitution includes a Charter of Rights and Freedoms, and provisions which recognize the nation's multi-cultural heritage, affirm the existing rights of native peoples, confirm the principle of equalization of benefits among the provinces and strengthen provincial ownership of natural resources.

THE GOVERNMENT

The national government operates through three main branches: Parliament (consisting of the Sovereign as represented by the Governor-General, the Senate and the House of Commons), which makes the laws; the Executive (the Cabinet or Ministry), which applies the laws; and the Judiciary, which interprets the laws.

The Prime Minister is appointed by the Governor-General and is habitually the leader of the political party commanding the confidence of the House of Commons. He chooses the members of his Cabinet from members of his party in Parliament, principally from those in the House of Commons. Each Minister or member of the Cabinet is usually responsible for the administration of a department, although there may be Ministers without portfolio whose experience and counsel are drawn upon to strengthen the Cabinet, but who are not at the head of departments. Each Minister of a department is responsible to Parliament for that department, and the Cabinet is collectively responsible before Parliament for government policy and administration generally.

Meetings of the Cabinet are presided over by the Prime Minister. From the Cabinet, signed orders and recommendations go to the Governor-General for his or her approval, and the Crown acts only on the advice of its responsible Ministers. The Cabinet takes the responsibility for its advice being in accordance with the support of Parliament and is held strictly accountable.

THE FEDERAL PARLIAMENT

Parliament must meet at least once a year, so that 12 months do not elapse between the last meeting in one session and the first meeting in the next. The duration of Parliament may not be longer than five years from the date of election of a House of Commons. Senators (normally a maximum of 104 in number) are appointed until age 75 by the Governor-General in Council. They must be at least 30 years of age, residents of the province they represent and in possession of C $4,000 of real property over and above their liabilities. Members of the House of Commons are elected by universal adult suffrage for the duration of a Parliament.

Under the Constitution, the federal Parliament has exclusive legislative authority in all matters relating to public debt and property; regulation of trade and commerce; raising of money by any mode of taxation; borrowing of money on the public credit; postal service, census and statistics; militia, military and naval service and defence; fixing and providing for salaries and allowances of the officers of the Government; beacons, buoys and lighthouses; navigation and shipping; quarantine and the establishment and maintenance of marine hospitals; sea-coast and inland fisheries; ferries on an international or interprovincial frontier; currency and coinage; banking, incorporation of banks, and issue of paper money; savings banks; weights and measures; bills of exchange and promissory notes; interest; legal tender; bankruptcy and insolvency; patents of invention and discovery; copyrights; Indians and lands reserved for Indians; naturalization and aliens; marriage and divorce; the criminal law, except the constitution of courts of criminal jurisdiction but including the procedure in criminal matters; the establishment, maintenance and management of penitentiaries; such classes of subjects as are expressly excepted in the enumeration of the classes of subjects exclusively assigned to the Legislatures of the provinces by the Act. Judicial interpretation and later amendment have, in certain cases, modified or clearly defined the respective powers of the federal Government and provincial governments.

Both the Parliament of Canada and the legislatures of the provinces may legislate with respect to agriculture and immigration, but provincial legislation shall have effect in and for the provinces as long and as far only as it is not repugnant to any Act of Parliament. Both Parliament and the provincial legislatures may legislate with respect to old age pensions and supplementary benefits, but no federal law shall affect the operation of any present or future law of a province in relation to these matters.

PROVINCIAL AND MUNICIPAL GOVERNMENT

In each of the 10 provinces the Sovereign is represented by a Lieutenant-Governor, appointed by the Governor-General in Council, and acting on the advice of the Ministry or Executive Council, which is responsible to the Legislature and resigns office when it ceases to enjoy the confidence of that body. The Legislatures are unicameral, consisting of an elected Legislative Assembly and the Lieutenant-Governor. The duration of a Legislature may not exceed five years from the date of the election of its members.

The Legislature in each province may exclusively make laws in relation to: amendment of the constitution of the province, except as regards the Lieutenant-Governor; direct taxation within the province; borrowing of money on the credit of the province; establishment and tenure of provincial offices and appointment and payment of provincial officers; the management and sale of public lands belonging to the province and of the timber and wood thereon; the establishment, maintenance and management of public and reformatory prisons in and for the province; the establishment, maintenance and management of hospitals, asylums, charities and charitable institutions in and for the province other than marine hospitals; municipal institutions in the province; shop, saloon, tavern, auctioneer and other licences issued for the raising of provincial or municipal revenue; local works and undertakings other than interprovincial or international lines of ships, railways, canals, telegraphs, etc., or works which, though wholly situated within the province are declared by the federal Parliament to be for the general advantage either of Canada or two or more provinces; the incorporation of companies with provincial objects; the solemnization of marriage in the province; property and civil rights in the province; the administration of justice in the province, including the constitution, maintenance and organization of provincial courts both in civil and criminal jurisdiction, and including procedure in civil matters in these courts; the imposition of punishment by fine, penalty or imprisonment for enforcing any law of the province relating to any of the aforesaid subjects; generally all matters of a merely local or private nature in the province. Further, provincial Legislatures may exclusively make laws in relation to education, subject to the protection of religious minorities; and to non-renewable natural resources, forestry resources and electrical energy, including their export from one province to another, and to the right to impose any mode or system of taxation thereon, subject in both cases to such laws not being discriminatory.

Under the Constitution Act, the municipalities are the creations of the provincial governments. Their bases of organization and the extent of their authority vary in different provinces, but almost everywhere they have very considerable powers of local self-government.

The Government

Head of State: HM Queen ELIZABETH II (succeeded to the throne 6 February 1952).

Governor-General: MICHAËLLE JEAN (took office on 27 September 2005).

FEDERAL MINISTRY
(March 2008)

Prime Minister: STEPHEN J. HARPER.

Leader of the Government in the House of Commons and Minister for Democratic Reform: PETER VAN LOAN.

Minister of International Trade and Minister for the Pacific Gateway and the Vancouver-Whistler Olympics: DAVID EMERSON.

Minister of Labour and Minister of the Economic Development Agency of Canada for the Regions of Québec: JEAN-PIERRE BLACKBURN.

Minister of Veterans' Affairs: GREGORY F. THOMPSON.

Leader of the Government in the Senate and Secretary of State (Seniors): MARJORY LEBRETON.

Minister of Citizenship and Immigration: DIANE FINLEY.

Minister of Agriculture and Agri-Food and Minister for the Canadian Wheat Board: GERRY RITZ.

Minister of Natural Resources: GARY LUNN.

Minister of Foreign Affairs: MAXIME BERNIER.

Minister of Fisheries and Oceans: LOYOLA HEARN.

Minister of Public Safety: STOCKWELL B. DAY.

Minister of National Revenue: GORDON O'CONNOR.

Minister of Justice and Attorney-General of Canada: ROBERT D. NICHOLSON.

Minister of the Environment: JOHN BAIRD.

President of the Queen's Privy Council for Canada, Minister of Intergovernmental Affairs and Minister of Western Economic Diversification: RONA AMBROSE.

Minister of Human Resources and Social Development: MONTE SOLBERG.

Minister of National Defence and Minister of the Atlantic Canada Opportunities Agency: PETER G. MACKAY.

Minister of Canadian Heritage, Status of Women and Official Languages: JOSÉE VERNER.

Minister of Indian Affairs and Northern Development and Federal Interlocutor for Métis and Non-Status Indians: CHARLES (CHUCK) STRAHL.

President of the Treasury Board: VIC TOEWS.

Minister of Industry: JIM PRENTICE.

Minister of Transport, Infrastructure and Communities: LAWRENCE CANNON.

Minister of Health and Minister for the Federal Economic Development Initiative for Northern Ontario: TONY CLEMENT.

Minister of Finance: JAMES M. (JIM) FLAHERTY.

Minister of International Co-operation: BEVERLEY J. ODA.

CANADA

Minister of Public Works and Government Services: MICHAEL FORTIER.
Secretary of State and Chief Government Whip: JAY D. HILL.
Secretary of State (Multiculturalism and Canadian Identity): JASON KENNEY.
Secretary of State (Small Business and Tourism): DIANE ABLONCZY.
Secretary of State (Foreign Affairs and International Trade and Sport): HELENA GUERGIS.
Secretary of State (Agriculture): CHRISTIAN PARADIS.

MINISTRIES

Office of the Prime Minister: Langevin Block, 80 Wellington St, Ottawa, ON K1A 0A2; tel. (613) 941-6888; fax (613) 941-6900; e-mail pm@pm.gc.ca; internet www.pm.gc.ca.

Agriculture and Agri-Food Canada: Sir John Carling Bldg, 930 Carling Ave, Ottawa, ON K1A 0C7; tel. (613) 759-1000; fax (613) 759-7977; e-mail info@agr.gc.ca; internet www.agr.gc.ca.

Atlantic Canada Opportunities Agency (ACOA): Blue Cross Centre, 3rd Floor, 644 Main St, POB 6051, Moncton, NB E1C 9J8; tel. (506) 851-2271; fax (506) 851-7403; internet www.acoa-apeca.gc.ca.

Canada Economic Development for the Regions of Québec: Tour de la Bourse 800, Sq. Victoria, bureau 3800, CP 247, Montréal, QC H4Z 1E8; tel. (514) 283-6412; fax (514) 283-3302; internet www.dec-ced.gc.ca.

Canada Revenue Agency: Office of the Minister of National Revenue, 7th Floor, 555 McKenzie Ave, Ottawa, ON K1A 0L5; tel. (613) 952-9184; internet www.cra-arc.gc.ca.

Canadian Heritage: 15 rue Eddy, Gatineau, QC K1A 0M5; tel. (819) 997-0055; fax (819) 953-5382; internet www.pch.gc.ca.

Citizenship and Immigration Canada: Jean Edmonds Towers, 21st Floor, 365 Laurier Ave West, Ottawa, ON K1A 1L1; tel. (613) 954-1064; fax (613) 957-2688; e-mail minister@cic.gc.ca; internet www.cic.gc.ca.

Department of Justice Canada: East Memorial Bldg, 284 Wellington St, Ottawa, ON K1A 0H8; tel. (613) 957-4222; fax (613) 954-0811; e-mail webadmin@justice.gc.ca; internet www.canada.justice.gc.ca.

Department of National Defence: National Defence Headquarters, Maj.-Gen. George R. Pearkes Bldg, 15 NT, 101 Colonel By Dr., Ottawa, ON K1A 0K2; tel. (613) 995-2534; fax (613)992-4739; e-mail information@forces.gc.ca; internet www.forces.gc.ca.

Environment Canada: 70 rue Crémazie, Gatineau, QC K1A 0H3; tel. (819) 997-2800; fax (819) 994-1412; e-mail enviroinfo@ec.gc.ca; internet www.ec.gc.ca.

Department of Finance Canada: East Tower, 19th Floor, 140 O'Connor St, Ottawa, ON K1A 0G5; tel. (613) 992-1573; fax (613) 996-0518; e-mail consltcomm@fin.gc.ca; internet www.fin.gc.ca.

Fisheries and Oceans Canada: Centennial Towers, 13th Floor, 200 Kent St, Station 13228, Ottawa, ON K1A 0E6; tel. (613) 993-0999; fax (613) 990-1866; e-mail info@dfo-mpo.gc.ca; internet www.dfo-mpo.gc.ca.

Foreign Affairs and International Trade Canada: Lester B. Pearson Bldg, 125 Sussex Dr., Ottawa, ON K1A 0G2; tel. (613) 944-4000; fax (613) 996-9709; e-mail enqserv@dfait-maeci.gc.ca; internet www.international.gc.ca.

Health Canada: Brooke Claxton Bldg, Tunney's Pasture, Ottawa, ON K1A 0K9; tel. (613) 957-2991; fax (613) 952-1154; e-mail info@hc-sc.gc.ca; internet www.hc-sc.gc.ca.

Human Resources and Social Development Canada: Phase IV, 140 promenade du Portage, Gatineau, QC K1A 0J9; tel. (819) 994-6313; fax (819) 953-7260; internet www.hrsdc.gc.ca; manages the Labour Program.

Indian and Northern Affairs Canada: Terrasses de la Chaudière, 10 Wellington, North Tower, Gatineau, ON K1A 0H4; tel. (819) 997-0811; fax (866) 817-3977; e-mail infopubs@ainc-inac.gc.ca; internet www.ainc-inac.gc.ca.

Industry Canada: C. D. Howe Bldg, 11th Floor, East Tower, 235 Queen St, Ottawa, ON K1A 0H5; tel. (613) 954-5031; fax (613) 954-2340; e-mail info@ic.gc.ca; internet www.ic.gc.ca.

Natural Resources Canada: 580 Booth St, Ottawa, ON K1A 0E4; tel. (613) 995-0947; fax (613) 996-9094; e-mail questions@nrcan.gc.ca; internet www.nrcan-rncan.gc.ca.

Public Safety Canada: 269 Laurier Ave West, Ottawa, ON K1A 0P8; tel. (613) 944-4875; fax (613) 954-5186; e-mail communications@ps-sp.gc.ca; internet www.ps-sp.gc.ca.

Public Works and Government Services Canada: 102 Corporate Communications, 16A1, Portage III, Gatineau, QC K1A 0S5; tel. (819) 956-3115; fax (819) 956-9062; e-mail questions@pwgsc.gc.ca; internet www.pwgsc.gc.ca.

Status of Women Canada: McDonald Bldg, 10th Floor, 123 Slater St, Ottawa, ON K1P 1H9; tel. (613) 995-7835; fax (613) 957-3359; e-mail communications@swc-cfc.gc.ca; internet www.swc-cfc.gc.ca.

Transport, Infrastructure and Communities Canada: Tower C, 29th Floor, pl. de Ville, 330 Sparks St, Ottawa, ON K1A 0N5; tel. (613) 990-2309; fax (613) 954-4731; e-mail webfeedback@tc.gc.ca; internet www.tc.gc.ca.

Treasury Board: Corporate Communications, l'Esplanade Laurier, 10th Floor, West Tower, 300 Laurier Ave West, Ottawa, ON K1A 0R5; tel. (613) 957-2400; fax (613) 998-9071; e-mail info@tbs-sct.gc.ca; internet www.tbs-sct.gc.ca.

Veterans Affairs Canada: 161 Grafton St, POB 7700, Charlottetown, PE C1A 8M9; tel. (613) 996-2242; fax (902) 566-8508; e-mail information@vac-acc.gc.ca; internet www.vac-acc.gc.ca.

Western Economic Diversification Canada: Canada Pl., 9700 Jasper Ave, Suite 1500, Edmonton, AB T5J 4H7; tel. (780) 495-4164; fax (403) 495-4557; e-mail donna.kinley@wd-deo.gc.ca; internet www.wd.gc.ca.

Federal Legislature

THE SENATE

Speaker: NOËL A. KINSELLA.
Seats at February 2008

Liberal Party	60
Conservative Party	22
Progressive Conservative	3
Independent	5
Independent New Democratic Party*	1
Vacant	14
Total	**105**

*The senator is an Independent member of the New Democratic Party.

HOUSE OF COMMONS

Speaker: PETER A. S. MILLIKEN.
General Election, 23 January 2006

	% of votes	Seats at election	Seats at April 2008
Conservative Party	36.3	124	127
Liberal Party	30.2	103	97
Bloc Québécois	10.5	51	48
New Democratic Party	17.5	29	30
Independent	0.3	1	4
Vacant	—	—	2
Total (incl. others)	100.0	308	308

Provincial Legislatures

ALBERTA

Lieutenant-Governor: NORMAN L. KWONG.
Premier: ED STELMACH.
Election, 3 March 2008

	Seats at election
Progressive Conservative	72
Liberal	9
New Democratic Party	2
Total	**83**

BRITISH COLUMBIA

Lieutenant-Governor: STEVEN L. POINT.
Premier: GORDON CAMPBELL.
Election, 17 May 2005

	Seats at election
Liberal	46
New Democratic Party	33
Total	**79**

CANADA

MANITOBA

Lieutenant-Governor: JOHN HARVARD.
Premier: GARY DOER.
Election, 22 May 2007

	Seats at election
New Democratic Party	36
Progressive Conservative	19
Liberal	2
Total	**57**

NEW BRUNSWICK

Lieutenant-Governor: HERMÉNÉGILDE CHIASSON.
Premier: SHAWN GRAHAM.
Election, 18 September 2006

	Seats at election	Seats at February 2008
Liberal	29	32
Progressive Conservative	26	23
Total	**55**	**55**

NEWFOUNDLAND AND LABRADOR

Lieutenant-Governor: JOHN CROSBIE.
Premier: DANNY WILLIAMS.
Election, 9 October 2007

	Seats at election	Seats at February 2008
Progressive Conservative	43	44
Liberal	3	3
New Democratic Party	1	1
Vacant	1	—
Total	**48**	**48**

NOVA SCOTIA

Lieutenant-Governor: MAYANN E. FRANCIS.
Premier: RODNEY J. MACDONALD.
Election, 13 June 2006

	Seats at election	Seats at February 2008
Progressive Conservative	23	22
New Democratic Party	20	20
Liberal	9	9
Independent	—	1
Total	**52**	**52**

ONTARIO

Lieutenant-Governor: DAVID ONLEY.
Premier: DALTON MCGUINTY.
Election, 10 October 2007

	Seats at election
Liberal	71
Progressive Conservative	26
New Democratic Party	10
Total	**103**

PRINCE EDWARD ISLAND

Lieutenant-Governor: BARBARA A. HAGERMAN.
Premier: ROBERT GHIZ.
Election, 28 May 2007

	Seats at election	Seats at February 2008
Liberal	23	24
Progressive Conservative	4	3
Total	**27**	**27**

QUÉBEC

Lieutenant-Governor: PIERRE DUCHESNE.
Premier: JEAN CHAREST.
Election, 26 March 2007

	Seats at election	Seats at February 2008
Liberal	48	48
Action Démocratique du Québec	41	41
Parti Québécois	36	35
Vacant	—	1
Total	**125**	**125**

SASKATCHEWAN

Lieutenant-Governor: Dr GORDON L. BARNHART.
Premier: BRAD WALL.
Election, 7 November 2007

	Seats at election	Seats at February 2008
New Democratic Party	38	38
Saskatchewan Party	20	19
Vacant	—	1
Total	**58**	**58**

Territorial Legislatures

NORTHWEST TERRITORIES

Commissioner: ANTHONY W. J. WHITFORD.
Premier and Minister of Finance: FLOYD ROLAND.
The Legislative Assembly consists of 19 independent members without formal party affiliation.

NUNAVUT TERRITORY

Commissioner: ANN M. HANSON.
Premier: PAUL OKALIK.
The Legislative Assembly consists of 19 independent members without formal party affiliation.

YUKON TERRITORY

Commissioner: GERALDINE VAN BIBBER.
Government Leader and Minister of the Executive Council Office: DENNIS FENTIE.
Election, 10 October 2006

	Seats at election
Yukon Party	10
Liberal	5
New Democratic Party	3
Total	**18**

Election Commission

Elections Canada: Jackson Bldg, 257 Slater St, Ottawa, ON K1A 0M6; tel. (613) 993-2975; fax (613) 954-8584; e-mail info@elections.ca; internet www.elections.ca; f. 1920; independent; Chief Electoral Officer MARC MAYRAND.

CANADA

Political Organizations

Action Démocratique du Québec: 740 rue Sainte-Maurice, bureau 108, Montréal, QC H3C 1L5; tel. (514) 270-4413; fax (514) 270-4469; e-mail adq@adq.qc.ca; internet www.adq.qc.ca; f. 1994; provincial nationalist; Leader Mario Dumont; Pres. Tom Pentefountas.

Alberta Alliance: 1303 44th Ave NE, Suite 3, Calgary, AB T2E 6L5; tel. (403) 769-0992; fax (866) 620-4791; e-mail info@albertaalliance.ca; internet www.albertaalliance.com; f. 2002; provincial; Leader Paul Hinman.

Bloc Québécois: 3730 Cremazie Est, bureau 307, Montréal, QC H2A 1B4; tel. (514) 526-3000; fax (514) 526-2868; internet www.blocquebecois.org; f. 1990 by group of seven Progressive Conservative MPs representing Québec constituencies in federal Parliament; seeks negotiated sovereignty for Québec; Leader Gilles Duceppe.

Canadian Action Party: 916 West Broadway Ave, Suite 385, Vancouver, BC V5Z 1K7; tel. (604) 708-3372; e-mail info@canadianactionparty.ca; internet www.canadianactionparty.ca; f. 1997; Leader Connie Fogal.

Christian Heritage Party of Canada: POB 4958, Station E, Ottawa, ON K1S 5J1; tel. (819) 281-6686; fax (819) 281-7174; e-mail nationaloffice@chp.ca; internet www.chp.ca; f. 1986; Pres. Larry Spencer (acting); Leader Ronald O. Gray.

Communist Party of Canada: 290A Danforth Ave, Toronto, ON M4K 1N6; tel. (416) 469-2446; fax (416) 469-4063; e-mail info@cpc-pcc.ca; internet www.communist-party.ca; f. 1921; Leader Miguel Figueroa.

Conservative Party of Canada: 130 Albert St, Suite 1204, Ottawa, ON K1P 5G4; tel. (613) 755-2000; fax (613) 755-2001; internet www.conservative.ca; f. 2003 by merger of Canadian Alliance and Progressive Conservative Party of Canada; Leader Stephen J. Harper.

Green Party of Canada: 204–396 Cooper St, Ottawa, ON K2P 2H7; tel. (613) 562-4916; fax (613) 482-4632; e-mail info@greenparty.ca; internet www.greenparty.ca; f. 1983; environmentalist; Leader Elizabeth May; Chair. Joe Foster.

Liberal Party of Canada: 81 Metcalfe St, Suite 400, Ottawa, ON K1P 6M8; tel. (613) 237-0740; fax (613) 235-7208; e-mail info@liberal.ca; internet www.liberal.ca; Leader Stéphane Dion; Pres. Marie-P. (Charette) Poulin.

Libertarian Party of Canada: 2938 East More Cres., Regina, SK S4V 0T7; tel. (613) 443-5423; e-mail info@libertarian.ca; internet www.libertarian.ca; f. 1974; supports the extension of individual freedoms; Leader Jean-Serge Brisson; Pres. Alan Mercer.

Marijuana Party: 3865 rue Bélanger, Suite 23, Montréal, QC H1X 1B4; tel. (514) 223-8517; e-mail info@marijuanaparty.ca; internet www.marijuanaparty.ca; f. 2000; revolutionary; campaigns for the legalization of marijuana; Leader Blair T. Longley.

Marxist-Leninist Party of Canada: 1867 Amherst St, Montréal, QC H2L 3L7; tel. and fax (514) 522-1373; e-mail info@mlpc.ca; internet www.mlpc.ca; f. 1970; publs The Marxist-Leninist Daily (English and French); Nat. Leader Sandra L. Smith.

New Democratic Party of Canada: 279 Laurier Ave West, Suite 300, Ottawa, ON K1P 5J9; tel. (613) 236-3613; fax (613) 230-9950; internet www.ndp.ca; f. 1961; social democratic; Leader Jack Layton; Pres. Anne McGrath.

Parti Québécois: 1200 ave Papineau, bureau 150, Montréal, QC H2K 4R5; tel. (514) 526-0020; fax (514) 526-0272; e-mail info@pq.org; internet www.pq.org; f. 1968; social democratic; seeks political sovereignty for Québec; Leader Pauline Marois; Pres. Monique Richard; 100,000 mems (2007).

Saskatchewan Party: 324 McDonald St, Regina, SK S4N 6P6; tel. (306) 359-1638; fax (306) 359-9832; e-mail info@saskparty.com; internet www.saskparty.com; f. 1997; provincial; Leader Brad Wall.

Socialist Party of Canada: POB 4280, Victoria, BC V8X 3X8; e-mail spc@worldsocialism.org; internet www.worldsocialism.org/canada; f. 1905; publ. journal, *Imagine*, on a sporadic basis; Gen. Sec. John Ayers; Treas. William Johnson.

Yukon Party: 211 Elliott St, POB 31113, Whitehorse, YT Y1A 5P7; tel. (867) 668-6505; e-mail info@yukonparty.ca; internet www.yukonparty.ca; provincial; Leader Dennis Fentie; Pres. Dan Macdonald.

Diplomatic Representation

EMBASSIES AND HIGH COMMISSIONS IN CANADA

Afghanistan: 240 Argyle Ave, Ottawa, ON K2P 1B9; tel. (613) 563-4223; fax (613) 563-4962; e-mail contact@afghanemb-canada.net; internet www.afghanemb-canada.net; Ambassador Omar Samad.

Albania: 130 Albert St, Suite 302, Ottawa, ON K1P 5G4; tel. (613) 236-4114; fax (613) 236-0804; e-mail embassyrepublicofalbania@on.aivn.com; Ambassador Besnik Konçi.

Algeria: 500 Wilbrod St, Ottawa, ON K1N 6N2; tel. (613) 789-8505; fax (613) 789-1406; e-mail ambalgcan@rogers.com; internet www.embassyalgeria.ca; Ambassador Smail Benamara.

Angola: 189 Laurier Ave East, Ottawa, ON K1N 6P1; tel. (613) 234-1152; fax (613) 234-1179; e-mail info@embangola-can.org; internet www.embangola-can.org; Ambassador Miguel Maria N'Zau Puna.

Antigua and Barbuda, Dominica, Grenada, Montserrat, Saint Christopher and Nevis, Saint Lucia and Saint Vincent and the Grenadines (Eastern Caribbean High Commission): 130 Albert St, Suite 700, Ottawa, ON K1P 5G4; tel. (613) 236-8952; fax (613) 236-3042; e-mail echcc@travel-net.com; High Commissioner Brendon Calvert Browne.

Argentina: 81 Metcalfe St, 7th Floor, Ottawa ON K1P 6K7; tel. (613) 236-2351; fax (613) 235-2659; e-mail embargentina@argentina-canada.net; internet www.argentina-canada.net; Ambassador Arturo G. Bothamley.

Armenia: 7 Delaware Ave, Ottawa, ON K2P 0Z2; tel. (613) 234-3710; fax (613) 234-3444; e-mail embottawa@rogers.com; internet www.armembassycanada.ca; Chargé d'affaires a.i. Arman Akopian.

Australia: 50 O'Connor St, Suite 710, Ottawa, ON K1P 6L2; tel. (613) 236-0841; fax (613) 236-4376; internet www.ahc-ottawa.org; High Commissioner William Norman Fisher.

Austria: 445 Wilbrod St, Ottawa, ON K1N 6M7; tel. (613) 789-1444; fax (613) 789-3431; e-mail ottawa-ob@bmeia.gv.at; internet www.austro.org; Ambassador Otto Ditz.

Azerbaijan: 275 Slater St, Suite 904, Ottawa, ON K1P 5H9; tel. (613) 288-0497; fax (613) 230-8089; e-mail azerbaijan@azembassy.ca; internet www.azembassy.ca; Chargé d'affaires Farid Shafiyev.

Bahamas: 50 O'Connor St, Suite 1313, Ottawa, ON K1P 6L2; tel. (613) 232-1724; fax (613) 232-0097; e-mail ottawa-mission@bahighco.com; High Commissioner Philip Patric Smith.

Bangladesh: 275 Bank St, Suite 302, Ottawa, ON K2P 2L6; tel. (613) 236-0138; fax (613) 567-3213; e-mail bangla@rogers.com; internet www.bdhc.org; High Commissioner Syed Masud Mahmood Khundoker (acting).

Barbados: 55 Metcalfe St, Suite 470, Ottawa, ON K1P 6L5; tel. (613) 236-9517; fax (613) 230-4362; e-mail ottawa@foreign.gov.bb; High Commissioner Glyne Samuel Murray.

Belarus: 130 Albert St, Suite 600, Ottawa, K1P 5G4; tel. (613) 233-9994; fax (613) 233-8500; e-mail belamb@igs.net; Ambassador Nina Nikolaevna Mazai.

Belgium: 360 Albert St, 8th Floor, Suite 820, Ottawa, ON K1R 7X7; tel. (613) 236-7267; fax (613) 236-7882; e-mail ottawa@diplobel.org; internet www.diplomatie.be/ottawa; Ambassador Jean L. A. Lint.

Benin: 58 Glebe Ave, Ottawa, ON K1S 2C3; tel. (613) 233-4429; fax (613) 233-8952; e-mail ambaben@benin.ca; internet www.benin.ca; internet www.benin.ca; Chargé d'affaires a.i. Awahou Labouda.

Bolivia: 130 Albert St, Suite 416, Ottawa, ON K1P 5G4; tel. (613) 236-5730; fax (613) 236-8237; e-mail bolivianembassy@bellnet.ca; Ambassador Edgar José Torrez-Mosqueira.

Bosnia and Herzegovina: 130 Albert St, Suite 805, Ottawa, ON K1P 5G4; tel. (613) 236-0028; fax (613) 236-1139; e-mail embassyofbih@bellnet.ca; internet www.bhembassy.ca; Ambassador Milenko Misić.

Brazil: 450 Wilbrod St, Ottawa, ON K1N 6M8; tel. (613) 237-1090; fax (613) 237-6144; e-mail mailbox@brasembottawa.org; internet www.brasembottawa.org; Ambassador Valdemar Carneiro Leão Neto.

Brunei: 395 Laurier Ave East, Suite 400, Ottawa, ON K1N 6R4; tel. (603) 234-5656; fax (603) 234-4397; e-mail bhco@bellnet.ca; High Commissioner Faizal Bahrin Haji Bakri (acting).

Bulgaria: 325 Stewart St, Ottawa, ON K1N 6K5; tel. (613) 789-3215; fax (613) 789-3524; e-mail mailmn@storm.ca; Ambassador Evgueni S. Stoytchev.

Burkina Faso: 48 Range Rd, Ottawa, ON K1N 8J4; tel. (613) 238-4796; fax (613) 238-3812; e-mail burkina.faso@sympatico.ca; internet www.burkinafaso.ca; Ambassador Juliette Bonkoungou-Yameogo.

Burundi: 325 Dalhousie St, Suite 815, Ottawa, ON K1N 7G2; tel. (613) 789-0414; fax (613) 789-9537; e-mail ambabucanada@infonet.ca; Ambassador Appolonie Simbizi.

Cameroon: 170 Clemow Ave, Ottawa, ON K1S 2B4; tel. (613) 236-1522; fax (613) 238-3885; e-mail cameroun@rogers.com; High Commissioner Martin Agbor Mbeng (acting).

Chile: 50 O'Connor St, Suite 1413, Ottawa, ON K1N 6L2; tel. (613) 235-4402; fax (613) 235-1176; e-mail echileca@chile.ca; internet www.chile.ca; Ambassador Eugenio Luis Ortega Riquelme.

CANADA

China, People's Republic: 515 St Patrick St, Ottawa, ON K1N 5H3; tel. (613) 789-3434; fax (613) 789-1911; e-mail chinaemb_ca@mfa.gov.cn; internet www.chinaembassycanada.org; Ambassador LU SHUMIN.

Colombia: 360 Albert St, Suite 1002, Ottawa, ON K1R 7X7; tel. (613) 230-3760; fax (613) 230-4416; e-mail embajada@embajadacolombia.ca; internet www.embajadacolombia.ca; Ambassador JAIME GIRÓN DUARTE.

Congo, Democratic Republic: 18 Range Rd, Ottawa, ON K1N 8J3; tel. (613) 230-6391; fax (613) 230-1945; e-mail info@ambassadesrdcongo.org; Chargé d'affaires a.i. LOUISE NZANGA RAMAZANI.

Costa Rica: 325 Dalhousie St, Suite 407, Ottawa, ON K1N 7G2; tel. (613) 562-2855; fax (613) 562-2582; e-mail embcr@costaricaembassy.com; internet www.costaricaembassy.com; Ambassador EMILIA MARÍA ALVAREZ NAVARRO.

Côte d'Ivoire: 9 Marlborough Ave, Ottawa, ON K1N 8E6; tel. (613) 236-9919; fax (613) 563-8287; e-mail acica@ambaci-ottawa.org; internet www.ambaci-ottawa.org; Ambassador DIÉNÉBOU KABA.

Croatia: 229 Chapel St, Ottawa, ON K1N 7Y6; tel. (613) 562-7820; fax (613) 562-7821; e-mail croemb.ottawa@mvpei.hr; internet ca.mfa.hr; Ambassador VESELA MRĐEN KORAĆ.

Cuba: 388 Main St, Ottawa, ON K1S 1E3; tel. (613) 563-0141; fax (613) 563-0068; e-mail cuba@embacubacanada.net; internet embacu.cubaminrex.cu/Default.aspx?tabid=73; Ambassador ERNESTO ANTONIO SENTÍ DARIAS.

Czech Republic: 251 Cooper St, Ottawa, ON K2P 0G2; tel. (613) 562-3875; fax (613) 562-3878; e-mail ottawa@embassy.mzv.cz; internet www.czechembassy.org; Ambassador PAVEL VOŠALÍK.

Denmark: 47 Clarence St, Suite 450, Ottawa, ON K1N 9K1; tel. (613) 562-1811; fax (613) 562-1812; e-mail ottamb@um.dk; internet www.ambottawa.um.dk; Ambassador POUL ERIK DAM KRISTENSEN.

Dominica: (see entry for Antigua and Barbuda).

Dominican Republic: 130 Albert St, Suite 418, Ottawa, ON K1P 5G4; tel. (613) 569-9893; fax (613) 569-8673; e-mail info@drembassy.org; internet www.drembassy.org; Ambassador LUIS ARIAS NUÑEZ.

Ecuador: 50 O'Connor St, Suite 316, Ottawa, ON K1P 6L2; tel. (613) 563-8206; fax (613) 235-5776; e-mail mecuacan@rogers.com; internet www.vivecuador.com; Ambassador FERNANDO RIBADENEIRA FERNÁNDEZ SALVADOR.

Egypt: 454 Laurier Ave East, Ottawa, ON K1N 6R3; tel. (613) 234-4931; fax (613) 234-9347; e-mail egyptemb@sympatico.ca; Ambassador MAHMOUD F. ES-SAEED.

El Salvador: 209 Kent St, Ottawa, ON K2P 1Z8; tel. (613) 238-2939; fax (613) 238-6940; e-mail embajada@elsalvador-ca.org; Ambassador MAURICIO ROSALES RIVERA.

Eritrea: 75 Albert St, Suite 610, Ottawa, ON K1P 5E7; tel. (613) 234-3989; fax (613) 234-6213; Ambassador AHFEROM BERHANE GHEBREMEDHIN.

Estonia: 260 Dalhousie St, Suite 210, Ottawa, ON K1N 7E4; tel. (613) 789-4222; fax (613) 789-9555; e-mail embassy.ottawa@mfa.ee; internet www.estemb.ca; Chargé d'affaires a.i. RASMUS LUMI.

Ethiopia: 151 Slater St, Suite 210, Ottawa, ON K1P 5H3; tel. (613) 235-6637; fax (613) 235-4638; internet www.ethiopia.ottawa.on.ca; Ambassador GETACHEW HAMUSSA HAILEMARIAM.

Finland: 55 Metcalfe St, Suite 850, Ottawa, ON K1P 6L5; tel. (613) 288-2233; fax (613) 288-2244; e-mail embassy@finland.ca; internet www.finland.ca; Ambassador PASI MIKAEL PATOKALLIO.

France: 42 Sussex Dr., Ottawa, ON K1M 2C9; tel. (613) 789-1795; fax (613) 562-3735; e-mail politique@ambafrance-ca.org; internet www.ambafrance-ca.org; Ambassador DANIEL JOUANNEAU.

Gabon: 4 Range Rd, Ottawa, ON K1N 8J5; tel. (613) 232-5301; fax (613) 232-6916; e-mail ambgabon@sprint.ca; Ambassador JOSEPH OBIANG NDOUTOUME.

Germany: 1 Waverley St, Ottawa, ON K2P 0T8; tel. (613) 232-1101; fax (613) 594-9330; e-mail germanembassyottawa@on.aibn.com; internet www.ottawa.diplo.de; Ambassador MATTHIAS MARTIN A. HÖPFNER.

Ghana: 1 Clemow Ave, Ottawa, ON K1S 2A9; tel. (613) 236-0871; fax (613) 236-0874; e-mail ghanacom@ghc-ca.com; internet www.ghanahighcommission-canada.com; High Commissioner MARGARET IVY AMOAKOHENE.

Greece: 76–80 MacLaren St, Ottawa, ON K2P 0K6; tel. (613) 238-6271; fax (613) 238-5676; e-mail embassy@greekembassy.ca; internet www.greekembassy.ca; Ambassador NIKOLAOS MATSIS.

Grenada: (see entry for Antigua and Barbuda).

Guatemala: 130 Albert St, Suite 1010, Ottawa, ON K1P 5G4; tel. (613) 233-7237; fax (613) 233-0135; e-mail embassy1@embaguate-canada.com; internet www.embaguate-canada.com; Ambassador MANUEL ESTUARDO ROLDÁN BARILLAS.

Guinea: 483 Wilbrod St, Ottawa, ON K1N 6N1; tel. (613) 789-8444; fax (613) 789-7560; e-mail ambassadedeguinea@bellnet.ca; Chargé d'affaires a.i. KABA HAWA DIAKITE.

Guyana: Burnside Bldg, 151 Slater St, Suite 309, Ottawa, ON K1P 5H3; tel. (613) 235-7249; fax (613) 235-1447; e-mail guyanahcott@rogers.com; High Commissioner RAJNARINE SINGH.

Haiti: 130 Albert St, Suite 1500, Ottawa, ON K1P 5G4; tel. (613) 238-1628; fax (613) 238-2986; e-mail bohio@bellnet.ca; Chargé d'affaires a.i. MARIE NATHALIE MENOS-GISSEL.

Holy See: Apostolic Nunciature, 724 Manor Ave, Rockcliffe Park, Ottawa, ON K1M 0E3; tel. (613) 746-4914; fax (613) 746-4786; e-mail nuntius@rogers.com; Nuncio Most Rev. LUIGI VENTURA (Titular Archbishop of Equilio).

Honduras: 151 Slater St, Suite 805, Ottawa, ON K1P 5H3; tel. (613) 233-8900; fax (613) 232-0193; e-mail embhonca@embassyhonduras.ca; internet www.embassyhonduras.ca; Ambassador DELIA BEATRIZ VALLE MARICHAL.

Hungary: 299 Waverley St, Ottawa, ON K2P 0V9; tel. (613) 230-2717; fax (613) 230-7560; e-mail mission.ott@kum.hu; internet www.mfa.gov.hu/emb/ottawa; Ambassador PAL VASTAGH.

Iceland: 360 Albert St, Suite 710, Ottawa, ON K1R 7X7; tel. (613) 482-1944; fax (613) 482-1945; e-mail icemb.ottawa@utn.stjr.is; internet www.iceland.org/ca; Ambassador MARKUS ORN ANTONSSON.

India: 10 Springfield Rd, Ottawa, ON K1M 1C9; tel. (613) 744-3751; fax (613) 744-0913; e-mail hicomind@hciottawa.ca; internet www.hciottawa.ca; High Commissioner RAJAMANI LAKSHMI NARAYAN.

Indonesia: 55 Parkdale Ave, Ottawa, ON K1Y 1E5; tel. (613) 724-1100; fax (613) 724-1105; e-mail info@indonesia-ottawa.org; internet www.indonesia-ottawa.org; Ambassador DJOKO HARDONO.

Iran: 245 Metcalfe St, Ottawa, ON K2P 2K2; tel. (613) 235-4726; fax (613) 232-5712; e-mail iranemb@salamiran.org; internet www.salamiran.org; Chargé d'affaires a.i. SEYED MAHDI MOHEBI.

Iraq: 215 McLeod St, Ottawa, ON K2P 0Z8; tel. (613) 236-9177; fax (613) 236-9641; e-mail media@iraqembassy.ca; internet www.iraqembassy.ca; Ambassador HOWAR M. ZIAD.

Ireland: 130 Albert St, Suite 1105, Ottawa, ON K1P 5G4; tel. (613) 233-6281; fax (613) 233-5835; e-mail embassyofireland@rogers.com; Ambassador DECLAN MICHAEL KELLY.

Israel: 50 O'Connor St, Suite 1005, Ottawa, ON K1P 6L2; tel. (613) 567-6450; fax (613) 567-9878; e-mail info@ottawa.mfa.gov.il; internet www.embassyofisrael.ca; Ambassador ALAN BAKER.

Italy: 275 Slater St, 21st Floor, Ottawa, ON K1P 5H9; tel. (613) 232-2401; fax (613) 233-1484; e-mail ambasciata.ottawa@esteri.it; internet www.ambottawa.esteri.it; Ambassador GABRIELE SARDO.

Jamaica: 275 Slater St, Suite 800, Ottawa, ON K1P 5H9; tel. (613) 233-9311; fax (613) 233-0611; e-mail hc@jhcottawa.ca; internet www.jhcottawa.ca; High Commissioner RUBY VIOLET EVADNE COYE.

Japan: 255 Sussex Dr., Ottawa, ON K1N 9E6; tel. (613) 241-8541; fax (613) 241-7415; e-mail infocul@embjapan.ca; internet www.ca.emb-japan.go.jp; Ambassador TSUNEO NISHIDA.

Jordan: 100 Bronson Ave, Suite 701, Ottawa, ON K1R 6G8; tel. (613) 238-8090; fax (613) 232-3341; e-mail jordan@on.aibn.com; internet www.embassyofjordan.ca; Ambassador NABIL ALI MOHAMED BARTO.

Kenya: 415 Laurier Ave East, Ottawa, ON K1N 6R4; tel. (613) 563-1773; fax (613) 233-6599; e-mail kenyahighcommission@rogers.com; internet www.kenyahighcommission.ca; High Commissioner Prof. JUDITH M. BAHEMUKA.

Korea, Republic: 150 Boteler St, Ottawa, ON K1N 5A6; tel. (613) 244-5010; fax (613) 244-5043; internet www.emb-korea.ottawa.on.ca; Ambassador SOO DONG KIM.

Kuwait: 333 Sussex Dr., Ottawa, ON K1N 1J9; tel. (613) 780-9999; fax (613) 780-9905; e-mail info@embassyofkuwait.ca; internet www.embassyofkuwait.ca; Ambassador MUSAED RASHED A. AL-HAROUN.

Latvia: 350 Sparks St, Suite 1200, Ottawa, ON K1R 7S8; tel. (613) 238-6014; fax (613) 238-7044; e-mail embassy.canada@mfa.gov.lv; internet www.ottawa.am.gov.lv; Ambassador MARGERS KRAMS.

Lebanon: 640 Lyon St, Ottawa, ON K1S 3Z5; tel. (613) 236-5825; fax (613) 232-1609; e-mail info@lebanonembassy.ca; internet www.lebanonembassy.ca; Chargé d'affaires a.i. MASSOUD MAALOUF.

Lesotho: 130 Albert St, Suite 1820, Ottawa, ON K1P 5G4; tel. (613) 234-0770; fax (613) 234-5665; e-mail lesotho.ottawa@bellnet.ca; High Commissioner MOTSEOSA PHILADEL SENYANE.

Libya: 81 Metcalfe St, Suite 1000, Ottawa, ON K1P 6K7; tel. (613) 230-0919; fax (613) 230-0683; e-mail info@libya-canada.org; internet www.libya-canada.org; Ambassador AHMED ALI JARRUD.

Lithuania: 130 Albert St, Suite 204, Ottawa, ON K1P 5G4; tel. (613) 567-5458; fax (613) 567-5315; e-mail litemb@storm.ca; internet www.lithuanianembassy.ca; Ambassador GINTĖ BERNADETA DAMUŠIS.

Macedonia, former Yugoslav republic: 130 Albert St, Suite 1006, Ottawa, ON K1P 5G4; tel. (613) 234-3882; fax (613) 233-1852; e-mail emb.macedonia.ottawa@sympatico.ca; Ambassador SASKO NASEV.

Madagascar: 3 Raymond St, Ottawa, ON K1R 1A3; tel. (613) 567-0505; fax (613) 567-2882; e-mail ambamadcanada@bellnet.ca; internet www.madagascar-embassy.ca; Ambassador SIMON CONSTANT HORACE.

Malaysia: 60 Boteler St, Ottawa, ON K1N 8Y7; tel. (613) 241-5182; fax (613) 241-5214; e-mail malottawa@kln.gov.my; High Commissioner Dato' DENNIS J. IGNATIUS.

Mali: 50 Goulburn Ave, Ottawa, ON K1N 8C8; tel. (613) 232-1501; fax (613) 232-7429; e-mail ambassadedumali@rogers.com; internet www.ambamalicanada.org; Ambassador MAMADOU BANDIOUGOU DIAWARA.

Mexico: 45 O'Connor St, Suite 1000, Ottawa, ON K1P 1A4; tel. (613) 233-8988; fax (613) 235-9123; e-mail info@embamexcan.com; internet www.sre.gob.mx/canada; Ambassador EMILIO RAFAEL JOSÉ GOICOECHEA LUNA.

Mongolia: 151 Slater St, Suite 503, Ottawa, ON K1P 5H3; tel. (613) 569-3830; fax (613) 569-3916; internet mail@mongolembassy.org; internet www.mongolembassy.org; Ambassador DUGERJAV GOTOV.

Montserrat: (see entry for Antigua and Barbuda).

Morocco: 38 Range Rd, Ottawa, ON K1N 8J4; tel. (613) 236-7391; fax (613) 236-6164; e-mail info@ambamaroc.ca; internet www.ambamaroc.ca; Ambassador MOHAMED TANGI.

Myanmar: 85 Range Rd, Suite 902/903, Ottawa, ON K1N 8J6; tel. (613) 232-6434; fax (613) 232-6435; e-mail meott@magma.ca; Chargé d'affaires a.i. U MAUNG MAUNG.

Netherlands: 350 Albert St, Suite 2020, Ottawa, ON K1R 1A4; tel. (613) 237-5030; fax (613) 237-6471; e-mail nlgovott@netcom.ca; internet www.netherlandsembassy.ca; Ambassador KAREL P. M. DE BEER.

New Zealand: Clarica Centre, 99 Bank St, Suite 727, Ottawa, ON K1P 6G3; tel. (613) 238-5991; fax (613) 238-5707; e-mail info@nzhcottawa.org; internet www.nzembassy.com/canada; High Commissioner KATHLEEN J. LACKEY.

Niger: 38 Blackburn Ave, Ottawa, ON K1N 8A3; tel. (613) 232-4291; fax (613) 230-9808; e-mail ambanigeracanada@rogers.com; internet www.ambanigeracanada.ca; Ambassador NANA AÏCHA MOUCTARI FOUMAKOYE.

Nigeria: 295 Metcalfe St, Ottawa, ON K2P 1R9; tel. (613) 236-0522; fax (613) 236-0529; e-mail chancery@nigeriahcottawa.com; internet www.nigeriahcottawa.com; High Commissioner IFEOMA JACINTE AKABOGU-CHINWUBA (acting).

Norway: 90 Sparks St, Suite 532, Ottawa, ON K1P 5B4; tel. (613) 238-6571; fax (613) 238-2765; e-mail emb.ottawa@mfa.no; internet www.emb-norway.ca; Ambassador TOR BERNTIN NAESS.

Pakistan: 10 Range Rd, Ottawa, ON K1N 8J3; tel. (613) 238-7881; fax (613) 238-7296; e-mail parepottawa@rogers.com; internet www.pakmission.ca; High Commissioner MUSA JAVED CHOHAN.

Panama: 130 Albert St, Suite 300, Ottawa, ON K1P 5G4; tel. (613) 236-7177; fax (613) 236-5775; e-mail embassyofpanama@gmail.com; Ambassador ROMY VÁSQUEZ DE GONZÁLEZ.

Papua New Guinea: 130 Albert St, Suite 300, Ottawa, ON K1A 5G4; fax (613) 236-5775; High Commissioner EVAN J. PAKI.

Paraguay: 151 Slater St, Suite 501, Ottawa, ON K1P 5H3; tel. (613) 567-1283; fax (613) 567-1679; e-mail consularsection@embassyofparaguay.ca; internet www.embassyofparaguay.ca; Ambassador JUAN ESTEBAN O. AGUIRRE MARTÍNEZ.

Peru: 130 Albert St, Suite 1901, Ottawa, ON K1P 5G4; tel. (613) 238-1777; fax (613) 232-3062; e-mail emperuca@bellnet.ca; internet www.embassyofperu.ca; Ambassador GUILLERMO JOSÉ MIGUEL RUSSO CHECA.

Philippines: 130 Albert St, Suite 606, Ottawa, ON K1P 5G4; tel. (613) 233-1121; fax (613) 233-4165; e-mail embassy@philippineembassy.ca; internet philippineembassy.ca; Ambassador JOSÉ S. BRILLANTES.

Poland: 443 Daly Ave, Ottawa, ON K1N 6H3; tel. (613) 789-0468; fax (613) 789-1218; e-mail ottawa@polishembassy.ca; internet www.polishembassy.ca; Ambassador PIOTR OGRODZINSKI.

Portugal: 645 Island Park Dr., Ottawa, ON K1Y 0B8; tel. (613) 729-0883; fax (613) 729-4236; e-mail embportugal@dgaccp.org; internet www.embportugal-ottawa.org; Ambassador JOÃO PEDRO DA SILVEIRA CARVALHO.

Romania: 655 Rideau St, Ottawa, ON K1N 6A3; tel. (613) 789-3709; fax (613) 789-4365; e-mail romania@romanian-embassy.com; internet ottawa.mae.ro; Ambassador ELENA STEFOI.

Russia: 285 Charlotte St, Ottawa, ON K1N 8L5; tel. (613) 235-4341; fax (613) 236-6342; e-mail rusemb@magma.ca; internet www.rusembcanada.mid.ru; Ambassador GEORGII MAMEDOV.

Rwanda: 121 Sherwood Drive, Ottawa, ON K1Y 3V1; tel. (613) 569-5420; fax (613) 569-5421; e-mail generalinfo@ambarwaottawa.ca; internet www.ambarwaottawa.ca; Ambassador EDDA MUKABAGWIZA.

Saint Christopher and Nevis: (see entry for Antigua and Barbuda).

Saint Lucia: (see entry for Antigua and Barbuda).

Saint Vincent and the Grenadines: (see entry for Antigua and Barbuda).

Saudi Arabia: 201 Sussex Dr., Ottawa, ON K1N 1K6; tel. (613) 237-4100; fax (613) 237-0567; e-mail caemb@mofa.gov.sa; Ambassador ABDUL AZIZ H. I. AS-SOWAYEGH.

Senegal: 57 Marlborough Ave, Ottawa, ON K1N 8E8; tel. (613) 238-6392; fax (613) 238-2695; e-mail ambassn@sympatico.ca; Ambassador ISSAKHA MBACKE.

Serbia: 17 Blackburn Ave, Ottawa, ON K1N 8A2; tel. (613) 233-6289; fax (613) 233-7850; e-mail diplomat@yuemb.ca; Ambassador DUŠAN BATAKOVIĆ.

Slovakia: 50 Rideau Terrace, Ottawa, ON K1M 2A1; tel. (613) 749-4442; fax (613) 749-4989; e-mail ottawa@slovakembassy.ca; internet www.ottawa.mfa.sk; Ambassador STANISLAV OPIELA.

Slovenia: 150 Metcalfe St, Suite 2200, Ottawa, ON K2P 1P1; tel. (613) 565-5781; fax (613) 565-5783; e-mail vot@gov.si; internet ottawa.embassy.si; Ambassador TOMAZ KUNSTELJ.

South Africa: 15 Sussex Dr., Ottawa, ON K1M 1M8; tel. (613) 744-0330; fax (613) 741-1639; e-mail rsafrica@southafrica-canada.ca; internet www.southafrica-canada.ca; High Commissioner ABRAHAM SOKAYA NKOMO.

Spain: 74 Stanley Ave, Ottawa, ON K1M 1P4; tel. (613) 747-2252; fax (613) 744-1224; e-mail emb@mae.es; internet www.embaspain.ca; Ambassador MARIANO ALONSO-BURÓN Y ABERASTURI.

Sri Lanka: 333 Laurier Ave West, Suite 1204, Ottawa, ON K1P 1C1; tel. (613) 233-8449; fax (613) 238-8448; e-mail slhcit@rogers.com; internet www.srilankahcottawa.org; High Commissioner WIJESINGHE JINASENA S. KARUNARATNE.

Sudan: 354 Stewart St, Ottawa, ON K1N 6K8; tel. (613) 235-4000; fax (613) 235-6880; e-mail sudanembassy-canada@rogers.com; internet www.sudanembassy.ca; Ambassador Dr FAIZA HASSAN TAHA ARMOUSA.

Sweden: 377 Dalhousie St, Ottawa, ON K1N 9N8; tel. (613) 244-8200; fax (613) 241-2277; e-mail sweden.ottawa@foreign.ministry.se; internet www.swedishembassy.ca; Ambassador INGRID M. IREMARK.

Switzerland: 5 Marlborough Ave, Ottawa, ON K1N 8E6; tel. (613) 235-1837; fax (613) 563-1394; e-mail ott.vertretung@eda.admin.ch; internet www.eda.admin.ch/canada; Ambassador WERNER BAUMANN.

Syria: 151 Slater St, Suite 1000, Ottawa, ON K1P 5H3; tel. (613) 569-5556; fax (613) 569-3800; e-mail info@syrianembassy.ca; internet www.syrianembassy.ca; Ambassador JAMIL SAKR.

Tanzania: 50 Range Rd, Ottawa, ON K1N 8J4; tel. (613) 232-1500; fax (613) 232-5184; e-mail tzottawa@synapse.net; High Commissioner PETER ALLAN KALLAGHE.

Thailand: 180 Island Park Dr., Ottawa, ON K1Y 0A2; tel. (613) 722-4444; fax (613) 722-6624; e-mail thaiott@magma.ca; internet www.thaiembottawa.org; Ambassador SNANCHART DEVAHASTIN.

Togo: 12 Range Rd, Ottawa, ON K1N 8J3; tel. (613) 238-5916; fax (613) 235-6425; e-mail ambatogoca@hotmail.com; Ambassador BAWOUMONDOM AMELETE.

Trinidad and Tobago: 200 First Ave, Ottawa, ON K1S 2G6; tel. (613) 232-2418; fax (613) 232-4349; e-mail ottawa@ttmissions.com; internet www.ttmissions.com; High Commissioner CAMILLE ROBINSON-REGIS.

Tunisia: 515 O'Connor St, Ottawa, ON K1S 3P8; tel. (613) 237-0330; fax (613) 237-7939; e-mail atottawa@comnet.ca; Ambassador MOULDI ESSAKRI.

Turkey: 197 Wurtemburg St, Ottawa, ON K1N 8L9; tel. (613) 789-4044; fax (613) 789-3442; e-mail turkishottawa@mfa.gov.tr; internet www.turkishembassy.com; Ambassador AYDEMIR ERMAN.

Uganda: 231 Cobourg St, Ottawa, ON K1N 8J2; tel. (613) 789-7797; fax (613) 789-8909; internet www.ugandahighcommission.com; High Commissioner GEORGE M. ABOLA.

Ukraine: 310 Somerset St West, Ottawa, ON K2P 0J9; tel. (613) 230-2961; fax (613) 230-2400; e-mail emb_ca@ukremb.ca; internet www.ukremb.ca; Ambassador Dr IHOR OSTASH.

United Arab Emirates: World Exchange Plaza, 45 O'Connor St, Suite 1800, Ottawa, ON K1P 1A4; tel. (613) 565-7272; fax (613) 5658007; e-mail safara@uae-embassy.com; internet www.uae-embassy.com; Ambassador HASSAN MOHAMMED OBAID AS-SUWAIDI.

United Kingdom: 80 Elgin St, Ottawa, ON K1P 5K7; tel. (613) 237-1530; fax (613) 237-7980; e-mail generalenquiries@britainincanada.org; internet www.britainincanada.org; High Commissioner ANTHONY JOYCE CARY.

USA: 490 Sussex Dr., POB 866, Station B, Ottawa, ON K1P 5T1; tel. (613) 238-5335; fax (613) 688-3080; internet ottawa.usembassy.gov; Ambassador DAVID HORTON WILKINS.

Uruguay: 130 Albert St, Suite 1905, Ottawa, ON K1P 5G4; tel. (613) 234-2727; fax (613) 233-4670; e-mail embassy@embassyofuruguay.ca; internet embassyofuruguay.ca; Ambassador ALVARO MARCELO MOERZINGER PAGANI.

Venezuela: 32 Range Rd, Ottawa, ON K1N 8J4; tel. (613) 235-5151; fax (613) 235-3205; e-mail info.canada@misionvenezuela.org; internet www.misionvenezuela.org; Chargé d'affaires a.i. JOSÉ ANTONIO RODRÍGUEZ DE LA SIERRA.

Viet Nam: 470 Wilbrod St, Ottawa, ON K1M 6M8; tel. (613) 236-0772; fax (613) 236-2704; e-mail vietem@istar.ca; internet www.vietnamembassy-canada.ca; Ambassador NGUYEN DUC HUNG.

Yemen: 54 Chamberlain Ave, Ottawa, ON K1S 1V9; tel. (613) 729-6627; fax (613) 729-8915; e-mail info@yemenincanada.ca; internet www.yemenincanada.ca; Ambassador Dr ABDULLA ABDULWALI NASHER.

Zambia: 151 Slater St, Suite 205, Ottawa, ON K1B 5H3; tel. (613) 232-4400; fax (613) 232-4410; e-mail embzamb@aol.com; High Commissioner DAVID CLIFFORD SAVIYE.

Zimbabwe: 332 Somerset St West, Ottawa, ON K2P 0J9; tel. (613) 237-4388; fax (613) 563-8269; e-mail zimembassy@bellnet.ca; internet www.zimbabweembassy.ca; Ambassador FLORENCE ZANO CHIDEYA.

Judicial System

FEDERAL COURTS

The Supreme Court of Canada: Supreme Court Bldg, 301 Wellington St, Ottawa, ON K1A 0J1; tel. (613) 995-4330; fax (613) 996-3063; e-mail reception@scc-csc.gc.ca; internet www.scc-csc.gc.ca; ultimate court of appeal in both civil and criminal cases throughout Canada. The Supreme Court is also required to advise on questions referred to it by the Governor-General in Council. Important questions concerning the interpretation of the Constitution Act, the constitutionality or interpretation of any federal or provincial law, the powers of Parliament or of the provincial legislatures, among other matters, may be referred by the Government to the Supreme Court for consideration.

In most cases, appeals are heard by the Court only if leave to appeal is given from any final judgment of the highest court of last resort in a province or territory, or of the Federal Court of Appeal. Such leave, or permission, will be given by the Court when a case involves a question of public importance. There are cases, however, where leave is not required. In criminal cases, for example, there may be an automatic right of appeal where one judge in the provincial court of appeal dissents on a question of law.

Chief Justice of Canada: BEVERLEY MCLACHLIN.

Puisne Judges: MICHEL BASTARACHE, WILLIAM I. CORNEIL BINNIE, LOUIS LEBEL, MARIE DESCHAMPS, MORRIS J. FISH, ROSALIE SIBERMAN ABELLA, LOUISE CHARRON, MARSHALL ROTHSTEIN.

The Federal Court: Supreme Court Bldg, Kent and Wellington Sts, Ottawa, ON K1A 0H9; tel. (613) 996-6795; fax (613) 952-7226; e-mail reception@cas-satj.gc.ca; internet www.fct-cf.gc.ca; has jurisdiction in claims against the Crown, claims by the Crown, miscellaneous cases involving the Crown, claims against or concerning crown officers and servants, relief against Federal Boards, Commissions, and other tribunals, interprovincial and federal-provincial disputes, industrial or industrial property matters, admiralty, income tax and estate tax appeals, citizenship appeals, aeronautics, interprovincial works and undertakings, residuary jurisdiction for relief if there is no other Canadian court that has such jurisdiction, jurisdiction in specific matters conferred by federal statutes.

Chief Justice: ALLAN LUTFY.

The Federal Court of Appeal

Supreme Court Bldg, Kent and Wellington Sts, Ottawa, ON K1A 0H9; tel. (613) 996-6795; fax (613) 952-7226; e-mail reception@cas-satj.gc.ca; internet www.fca-caf.gc.ca.

Has jurisdiction on appeals from the Trial Division, appeals from Federal Tribunals, review of decisions of Federal Boards and Commissions, appeals from Tribunals and Reviews under Section 28 of the Federal Court Act, and references by Federal Boards and Commissions. The Court has one central registry and consists of the principal office in Ottawa and local offices in major centres throughout Canada.

Chief Justice: JOHN D. RICHARD.

Trial Division Judges: JAMES K. HUGESSEN, YVON PINARD, FREDERICK E. GIBSON, SANDRA J. SIMPSON, DANIÈLE TREMBLAY-LAMER, DOUGLAS R. CAMPBELL, PIERRE BLAIS, FRANÇOIS LEMIEUX, JOHN A. O'KEEFE, ELIZABETH HENEGHAN, DOLORES HANSEN, ELEANOR R. DAWSON, EDMOND P. BLANCHARD, MICHAEL A. KELEN, MICHAEL BEAUDRY, LUC MARTINEAU, CAROLYN LAYDEN-STEVENSON, SIMON NOËL, JUDITH A. SNIDER, JAMES RUSSELL, JOHANNE GAUTHIER, JAMES O'REILLY, SEAN J. HARRINGTON, RICHARD MOSLEY, MICHEL M. J. SHORE, MICHAEL L. PHELAN, ANNE L. MACTAVISH, YVES DE MONTIGNY, ROGER T. HUGHES, ROBERT L. BARNES, LEONARD S. MANDAMIN.

Court of Appeal Judges: ALICE DESJARDINS, ROBERT DÉCARY, ALLEN M. LINDEN, GILLES LÉTOURNEAU, MARC NOËL, MARC NADON, J. EDGAR SEXTON, JOHN MAXWELL EVANS, KAREN SHARLOW, J. D. DENIS PELLETIER, C. MICHAEL RYER, JOHANNE TRUDEL.

PROVINCIAL AND TERRITORIAL COURTS

Alberta

Court of Appeal

Chief Justice of Alberta: CATHERINE A. FRASER (Edmonton).

Court of Queen's Bench

Chief Justice: ALLAN H. J. WACHOWICH (Edmonton).
Associate Chief Justice: N. C. WITTMANN (Calgary).

British Columbia

Court of Appeal

Chief Justice of British Columbia: LANCE SIDNEY GEORGE FINCH.

Supreme Court

Chief Justice: DONALD IAN BRENNER.
Associate Chief Justice: PATRICK DONALD DOHM.

Manitoba

Court of Appeal

Chief Justice of Manitoba: RICHARD J. SCOTT.

Court of Queen's Bench

Chief Justice: MARC M. MONNIN.
Associate Chief Justice: JEFFREY J. OLIPHANT.
Associate Chief Justice (Family Division): GERALD W. MERCIER.

New Brunswick

Court of Appeal

Chief Justice of New Brunswick: J. ERNEST DRAPEAU.

Court of Queen's Bench

Chief Justice: DAVID D. SMITH (Moncton).

Newfoundland and Labrador

Supreme Court—Court of Appeal

Chief Justice of Newfoundland and Labrador: CLYDE K. WELLS.

Trial Division

Chief Justice: J. DEREK GREEN.

Northwest Territories

Court of Appeal

Chief Justice: CATHERINE A. FRASER (Edmonton, Alberta).

Supreme Court

Judges of the Supreme Court: JOHN Z. VERTES (Sr Judge), J. EDWARD RICHARD, VIRGINIA A. SCHULER, LOUISE A. M. CHARBONNEAU.

Nova Scotia

Court of Appeal

Chief Justice of Nova Scotia: MICHAEL MACDONALD.

Supreme Court

Chief Justice: JOSEPH PHILLIP KENNEDY.
Associate Chief Justice: DEBORAH K. SMITH.

CANADA

Supreme Court (Family Division)

Associate Chief Justice (Family Division): ROBERT F. FERGUSON.

Nunavut Territory

Court of Appeal

Chief Justice: CATHERINE A. FRASER (Alberta).

Court of Justice

Judges of the Court of Justice: B. A. BROWNE, R. G. KILPATRICK, E. D. JOHNSON.

Ontario

Court of Appeal

Chief Justice of Ontario: WARREN K. WINKLER.
Associate Chief Justice of Ontario: DENNIS R. O'CONNOR.

Court of Justice

Chief Justice: ANNEMARIE E. BONKALO.
Associate Chief Justices: PETER D. GRIFFITHS, JOHN A. PAYNE.

Prince Edward Island

Supreme Court—Appeal Division

Chief Justice of Prince Edward Island: GERARD E. MITCHELL.

Supreme Court—Trial Division

Chief Justice: JACQUELINE R. MATHESON.

Québec

Court of Appeal

Chief Justice of Québec: J. J. MICHEL ROBERT.

Superior Court

Chief Justice: FRANÇOIS ROLLAND.
Associate Chief Justice: ROBERT PIDGEON.

Saskatchewan

Court of Appeal

Chief Justice of Saskatchewan: J. KLEBUC.

Court of Queen's Bench

Chief Justice: R. D. LAING (Saskatoon).

Yukon Territory

Court of Appeal

Chief Justice: LANCE S. G. FINCH (British Columbia).

Supreme Court

Judges of the Supreme Court: L. F. GOWER HUDSON, R. S. VEALE (both of Whitehorse).

Religion

CHRISTIANITY

According to the 2001 census, about 59% of the population belong to the three main Christian churches: Roman Catholic, United and Anglican. Numerous other religious denominations are active in Canada.

Canadian Council of Churches/Conseil canadien des églises: 47 Queen's Park Cres. East, Toronto, ON M5S 2C3; tel. (416) 972-9494; fax (416) 927-0405; e-mail admin@ccc-cce.ca; internet www.ccc-cce.ca; f. 1944; 21 mem. churches, one assoc. mem.; Pres. Rev. Dr JAMES CHRISTIE (United Church of Canada); Gen. Sec. Rev. Dr KAREN HAMILTON.

The Anglican Communion

The Anglican Church of Canada (L'Eglise anglicane du Canada) comprises 30 dioceses in four ecclesiastical provinces (each with a Metropolitan archbishop). The Church had about 800,000 members in 30 dioceses in 2007.

General Synod of the Anglican Church of Canada: 80 Hayden St, Toronto, ON M4Y 3G2; tel. (416) 924-9192; fax (416) 968-7983; e-mail info@national.anglican.ca; internet www.anglican.ca; f. 1893; Gen. Sec. The Venerable MICHAEL POLLESEL.

Primate of the Anglican Church of Canada: Most Rev. FRED HILTZ.
Province of British Columbia and Yukon: Metropolitan Most Rev. TERRENCE O. BUCKLE (Archbishop of Yukon) (until Dec. 2008).
Province of Canada: Metropolitan Most Rev. BRUCE A. STAVERT (Archbishop of Québec) (until early 2009).
Province of Ontario: Metropolitan Most Rev. CALEB J. LAWRENCE (Archbishop of Moosonee).
Province of Rupert's Land: Metropolitan Most Rev. JOHN CLARKE (Bishop of Athabasca).

The Orthodox Churches

According to census figures, there were some 479,620 members of Eastern Orthodox churches in Canada in 2001.

Greek Orthodox Metropolis of Toronto (Canada): 86 Overlea Blvd, Toronto, ON M4H 1C6; tel. (416) 429-5757; fax (416) 429-4588; e-mail greekomt@on.aibn.com; internet www.gocanada.org; 215,175 mems (2001); Metropolitan Archbishop SOTIRIOS ATHANASSOULAS.

Ukrainian Orthodox Church of Canada: 9 St John's Ave, Winnipeg, MB R2W 1G8; tel. (204) 586-3093; fax (204) 582-5241; e-mail consistory@uocc.ca; internet www.uocc.ca; f. 1918; 281 parishes; 32,720 mems (2001); Metropolitan of Winnipeg and of all Canada His Eminence JOHN; Presidium Chair. Fr BOHDAN HLADIO.

The Russian, Belarusian, Polish, Romanian, Serbian, Coptic, Antiochian and Armenian Churches are also represented in Canada.

The Roman Catholic Church

For Catholics of the Latin rite, Canada comprises 18 archdioceses (including one directly responsible to the Holy See), 46 dioceses and one territorial abbacy. There are also one archdiocese and four dioceses of the Ukrainian rite. In addition, the Maronite, Melkite and Slovak rites are each represented by one diocese (all directly responsible to the Holy See). In December 2005 the Roman Catholic Church had about 13.5m. adherents in Canada.

Canadian Conference of Catholic Bishops/Conférence des évêques catholiques du Canada: 2500 Don Reid Dr., Ottawa, ON K1H 2J2; tel. (613) 241-8117; fax (613) 241-9048; e-mail cecc@cccb.ca; internet www.cccb.ca; Pres. Most Rev. V. JAMES WEISGERBER (Archbishop of Winnipeg); Vice-Pres. Rt Rev. PIERRE MORISSETTE (Bishop of Baie-Comeau); Gen. Sec. MARIO PAQUETTE.

Latin Rite

Archbishop of Edmonton: Most Rev. RICHARD SMITH.
Archbishop of Gatineau: Most Rev. ROGER EBACHER.
Archbishop of Grouard-McLennan: Most Rev. GÉRARD PETTIPAS.
Archbishop of Halifax: Most Rev. ANTHONY MANCINI.
Archbishop of Keewatin-Le Pas: Most Rev. SYLVAIN LAVOIE.
Archbishop of Kingston: Most Rev. BRENDAN M. O'BRIEN.
Archbishop of Moncton: Most Rev. ANDRÉ RICHARD.
Archbishop of Montréal: Most Rev. Cardinal JEAN-CLAUDE TURCOTTE.
Archbishop of Ottawa: Most Rev. TERRENCE PRENDERGAST.
Archbishop of Québec: Cardinal MARC OUELLET.
Archbishop of Regina: Most Rev. DANIEL J. BOHAN.
Archbishop of Rimouski: Most Rev. BERTRAND BLANCHET.
Archbishop of St Boniface: Most Rev. EMILIUS GOULET.
Archbishop of St John's, NL: Most Rev. MARTIN WILLIAM CURRIE.
Archbishop of Sherbrooke: Most Rev. ANDRÉ GAUMOND.
Archbishop of Toronto: Most Rev. THOMAS COLLINS.
Archbishop of Vancouver: Most Rev. RAYMOND ROUSSIN.
Archbishop of Winnipeg: Most Rev. V. JAMES WEISGERBER.

Ukrainian Rite

Ukrainian Catholic Archeparchy of Winnipeg (Metropolitan See of Canada): 233 Scotia St, Winnipeg, MB R2V 1V7; tel. (204) 338-7801; fax (204) 339-4006; e-mail chancery@archeparchy.ca; internet www.archeparchy.ca; 126,200 mems (2001); Archeparch-Metropolitan of Winnipeg Most Rev. LAWRENCE HUCULAK.

The United Church of Canada

The United Church of Canada (l'Eglise Unie du Canada) was founded in 1925 with the union of Methodist, Congregational and 70% of Presbyterian churches in Canada. The Evangelical United Brethren of Canada joined in 1968. It is the largest Protestant denomination in Canada. In 2003 there were 3,584 congregations and 608,243 confirmed members (although, according to 2001 census figures, 2.8m. people identified themselves as adherents of the United Church).

Moderator: Rt Rev. DAVID GIULIANO.

CANADA   *Directory*

General Secretary: NORA SANDERS, 3250 Bloor St West, Suite 300, Toronto, ON M8X 2Y4; tel. (416) 231-5931; fax (416) 231-3103; e-mail info@united-church.ca; internet www.united-church.ca.

Other Christian Churches

Canadian Baptist Ministries: 7185 Millcreek Dr., Mississauga, ON L5N 5R4; tel. (905) 821-3533; fax (905) 826-3441; e-mail communications@cbmin.org; internet www.cbmin.org; more than 1,000 churches; 150,000 mems (2006); Gen. Sec. Rev. Dr GARY NELSON.

Christian Reformed Church in North America (Canadian Council): 3475 Mainway, POB 5070, Burlington, ON L7R 3Y8; tel. (905) 336-2920; fax (905) 336-8344; internet www.crcna.org; f. 1857; 246 congregations; 80,570 mems (2006); Dir in Canada Rev. BRUCE ADEMA.

Church of Jesus Christ of Latter-day Saints (Mormon): 28 St South, Suite 2410, Lethbridge, AB T1K 2V9; tel. (403) 328-8552; f. 1832; 481 congregations; 166,505 mems in Canada (2004); Dir GORDON GEDLAMAN.

Evangelical Lutheran Church in Canada (ELCIC): 393 Portage Ave, Suite 302, Winnipeg, MB R3B 3H6; tel. (204) 984-9150; fax (204) 984-9185; e-mail tgallop@elcic.ca; internet www.elcic.ca; f. 1986 by merger of the fmr Evangelical Lutheran Church of Canada and Lutheran Church in America—Canada Section; 624 congregations; 182,077 mems (2007); Nat. Bishop Rev. SUSAN JOHNSON, Vice-Pres. ROGER KINGSLEY.

Lutheran Church–Canada: 3074 Portage Ave, Winnipeg, MB R3K 0Y2; tel. (204) 895-3433; fax (204) 832-3018; e-mail info@lutheranchurch.ca; internet www.lutheranchurch.ca; f. 1988 by three Canadian congregations of the Lutheran Church-Missouri Synod; 329 congregations; 75,765 mems (2005); Pres. Rev. Dr RALPH MAYAN.

Pentecostal Assemblies of Canada: 2450 Milltower Court, Mississauga, ON L5N 5Z6; tel. (905) 542-7400; fax (905) 542-7313; e-mail info@paoc.org; internet www.paoc.org; f. 1919; 1,103 congregations; 245,279 mems (2005); Gen. Supt Dr WILLIAM D. MORROW.

Presbyterian Church in Canada: 50 Wynford Dr., Toronto, ON M3C 1J7; tel. (416) 441-1111; fax (416) 441-2825; e-mail pccweb@presbycan.ca; internet www.presbyterian.ca; f. 1875; 997 congregations; 125,509 mems (2003); Moderator Rev. Dr J. HANS KOUWENBERG; Prin. Clerk Rev. STEPHEN KENDALL.

Religious Society of Friends: 91A Fourth Ave, Ottawa, ON K1S 2L1; tel. (613) 235-8553; fax (613) 235-1753; e-mail cym-office@quaker.ca; internet www.quaker.ca; Clerk of Canadian Yearly Meeting BEVERLY SHEPHARD.

Seventh-day Adventist Church in Canada: 1148 King St East, Oshawa, ON L1H 1H8; tel. (905) 433-0011; fax (905) 433-0982; e-mail communications@sdacc.org; internet www.sdacc.org; 341 congregations; 57,431 (2007); f. 1901; Pres. DANIEL JACKSON; Sec. NILTON AMORIM.

BAHÁ'Í FAITH

Bahá'í Community of Canada: 7200 Leslie St, Thornhill, ON L3T 6L8; tel. (905) 889-8168; fax (905) 889-8184; e-mail info@ca.bahai.org; internet www.ca.bahai.org; f. 1902; 30,000 mems (2004); Sec.-Gen. KAREN MCKYE.

BUDDHISM

Buddhist Churches of Canada (Jodo Shinshu Buddhist Temples of Canada): 11786 Fentiman Pl., Richmond, BC V7E 6M6; tel. (604) 272-3330; fax (604) 272-6865; e-mail bccheadquarters@shaw.ca; internet www.bcc.ca; f. 1905; Bishop ORAI FUJIKAWA.

ISLAM

According to the Canadian Islamic Congress there were an estimated 750,000 Muslims in Canada in 2006.

Ahmadiyya Movement in Islam (Canada): 10610 Jane St, Maple, ON L6A 3A2; tel. (905) 303-4000; fax (905) 832-3220; e-mail info@ahmadiyya.ca; internet www.ahmadiyya.ca; f. 1965; Pres. LAL KHAN MALIK; Gen. Sec. Dr ASLAM DAUD.

Canadian Islamic Congress (CIC): 675 Queen St South, Suite 208, Kitchener, ON N2M 1A1; tel. (519) 746-1242; fax (519) 746-2929; e-mail np@canadianislamiccongress.com; internet www.canadianislamiccongress.com; f. 1998; Chair. and Nat. Pres. Dr MOHAMED I. ELMASRY; Nat. Exec. Dir Imam Dr ZIJAD DELIC.

Canadian Muslim Union (CMU): Toronto, ON; tel. (416) 558-4777; e-mail secretary@muslimunion.ca; internet www.muslimunion.ca; f. 2006 following split from the Muslim Canadian Congress; Sec.-Gen. EL-FAROUK KHAKI.

Council of Muslim Communities of Canada (CMCC): 1521 Trinity Dr., Unit 16, Mississauga, ON L5T1P6; tel. and fax (416) 512-2106; f. 1971; umbrella org. representing c. 30 communities nationwide; Pres. HANNY HASSAN.

Organization of North American Shi'a Itha-Asheri Muslim Communities (NASIMCO): 300 John St, POB 87629, Thornhill, ON L3T 7R3; tel. (905) 763-7512; fax (905) 763-7509; e-mail director@nasimco.org; internet www.nasimco.org; Pres. HUSSEIN WALJI; Sec. HABIB DHALLA.

JUDAISM

According to census figures, there were some 329,995 Jews in Canada in 2001.

Canadian Council for Reform Judaism (CCRJ): 3845 Bathurst St, Suite 301, Toronto, ON M3H 3N2; tel. (416) 630-0375; fax (416) 630-5089; e-mail ccrj@urj.org; internet urj.org/ccrj; f. 1988; Pres. ELLIOT JACOBSON; Exec. Dir Rabbi SHARON L. SOBEL.

Canadian Jewish Congress: 100 Sparks St, Suite 650, Ottawa, ON K1P 5B7; tel. (613) 233-8703; fax (613) 233-8748; e-mail canadianjewishcongress@cjc.ca; internet www.cjc.ca; f. 1919; 10 regional offices; CEO BERNIE M. FARBER; Co-Pres. Rabbi REUVEN BULKA, SYLVAIN ABITBOL.

United Synagogue of Conservative Judaism: 1000 Finch Ave West, Suite 508, Toronto, ON M3J 2V5; tel. (416) 667-1717; fax (416) 667-1818; e-mail canadian@uscj.org; internet www.uscj.org; Pres. Dr RAYMOND B. GOLDSTEIN.

SIKHISM

There were some 278,410 Sikhs in Canada, according to 2001 census figures.

Canadian Sikh Council (CSC): 4103 Sherbrooke St West, Montréal, QC H3Z1A7; tel. (416) 630-0375; fax (416) 630-5089; e-mail info@sikhcouncil.ca; internet www.sikhcouncil.ca; f. 2001; Dir Dr MANJIT SINGH.

World Sikh Organization of Canada (WSO Canada): 1183 Cecil Ave, Ottawa, ON K1H 7Z6; tel. (613) 521-1984; fax (613) 521-7454; e-mail wsopanth@gmail.com; internet worldsikh.org; f. 1984; Pres. GURPREET SINGH BAL; Exec. Dir ANNE LOWTHIAN.

The Press

The daily press in Canada is essentially local and regional in coverage, influence and distribution. Chain ownership has traditionally been predominant: at the beginning of 2000 63.4% of daily newspaper circulation was represented by two major groups: Hollinger Inc (42.0% of daily newspaper circulation) and Quebecor Inc (21.4%). However, in 2000 both Hollinger and the Thomson Corpn (10.5%) divested themselves of significant proportions of their newspaper interests; Thomson retained only the Toronto *Globe and Mail*, control of which was subsequently transferred to Bell Globemedia, Inc, a joint venture between companies including Thomson and the telecommunications operator, BCE, Inc. In November 2000 CanWest Global Communications Corpn acquired 14 daily metropolitan newspapers, a number of community newspapers and a 50% interest in the *National Post* (Canada's first national daily newspaper, launched by Hollinger's Southam Inc division in 1998). In 2001 CanWest acquired the remaining 50% interest in the *National Post*. In the process, CanWest acquired Hollinger's Southam Inc division. In late 2005 Osprey Media Group Inc owned 21 daily newspapers, Sun Media Corpn (a subsidiary of Quebecor Media Inc) owned 17, CanWest MediaWorks Publications 13, Transcontinental Media 11 and Hollinger Canadian Newspapers Limited Partnership 10. Torstar (which owned four daily newspapers, including the *Toronto Star*), accounted for 13.9% of total circulation in 2005. In mid-2007 Quebecor Media Inc acquired Osprey Media Group Inc, thus creating Canada's largest newspaper publishing enterprise.

In 2005 there were 100 daily newspapers with a combined circulation of almost 5.0m.; of these, only four were independent. In 2006 the Canadian Community Newspaper Association comprised 726 weekly and twice-weekly community newspapers, serving mainly the more remote areas of the country. A significant feature of the Canadian press is the number of newspapers catering for immigrant groups: there are over 80 of these daily and weekly publications appearing in over 20 languages.

There are numerous periodicals for business, trade, professional, recreational and special interest readership, although periodical publishing, particularly, encounters substantial competition from publications originating in the USA. In 2006 the principal industry association, Magazines Canada, comprised more than 300 consumer titles. Among periodicals, the only one that could be regarded as national in its readership and coverage was the weekly news magazine *Maclean's*.

The following are among the principal newspaper publishing groups:

CanWest MediaWorks Publications: 1450 Don Mills Road, Don Mills, ON M3B 3R5; tel. (416) 383-2300; internet www

CANADA

.canwestmediaworks.com; subsidiary of CanWest Global Communications Corpn; owns 12 English-language major metropolitan daily newspapers and 23 other newspapers in Canada; Pres. DENNIS SKULSKY.

Hollinger Canadian Newspapers Ltd Partnership: 120 Adelaide St West, Suite 512, Toronto, ON, M5H 1T1; tel. (416) 363-8721; fax (416) 363-4187; internet www.hollingerinc.com; f. 1985; publ. 10 daily newspapers; CEO G. WESLEY VOORHEIS.

Quebecor Media Inc: 612 rue St-Jacques, Montréal, QC H3C 4M8; tel. (514) 954-0101; e-mail webmaster@quebecor.com; internet www.quebecor.com; f. 1965; acquired Osprey Media Group Inc, which published 20 daily newspapers (daily circ. 325,249) and 34 non-dailies (weekly circ. 378,532), in mid-2007; together with its subsidiary Sun Media Corpn and prior to the acquisition of Osprey Media Group Inc, published 24 English- and French-language dailies (with a total average daily circulation of almost 1.3m.) and 171 community papers (with a total weekly circulation of more than 3.4m.); television, cable, telecommunications and publishing interests in 17 countries; Pres. and CEO PIERRE KARL PÉLADEAU.

    Sun Media Corpn: 333 King St East, Toronto, ON M5A 3X5; tel. (416) 947-2222; e-mail qi_info@quebecor.com; internet www.quebecor.com; f. 1965; Pres. and CEO PIERRE FRANCOEUR.

Torstar Corpn: 1 Yonge St, Toronto, ON M5E 1P9; tel. (416) 869-4010; fax (416) 869-4183; e-mail torstar@torstar.ca; internet www.torstar.com; f. 1958; incorporates the Star Media Group and Metroland Media Group; owns four daily newspapers (weekly circ. 4.5m.), 10 weekly publs and 95 community newspapers; Chair. FRANK IACOBUCCI; Pres. and CEO J. ROBERT PRITCHARD.

Transcontinental Media: 1100 René-Lévesque Blvd ouest, 24th Floor, Montréal, QC H3B 4X9; tel. (514) 392-9000; fax (514) 954-4016; internet www.medias-transcontinental.com; f. 1978; publ. 12 dailies (daily circ. 250,000) and more than 125 weekly, fortnightly and monthly newspapers (circ. 2.4m.); Chair. ANDRÉ PRÉFONTAINE; Pres. NATALIE LARIVIÈRE.

PRINCIPAL DAILY NEWSPAPERS

Alberta

Calgary Herald: 215 16th St, SE, POB 2400, Station M, Calgary, AB T2P 0W8; tel. (403) 235-7100; fax (403) 235-7379; e-mail calgaryherald@reachcanada.com; internet www.canada.com/calgaryherald; f. 1883; Publr PETER MENZIES; Exec. Editor RON NEWELL; circ. Mon. to Sat. 120,473, Sun. 121,445.

Calgary Sun: 2615 12th St, NE, Calgary, AB T2E 7W9; tel. (403) 410-1010; fax (403) 250-4180; e-mail callet@calgarysun.com; internet www.calgarysun.com; f. 1980; Publr and CEO GORDON NORRIE; Editor-in-Chief JOSE RODRIGUEZ; circ. Mon. to Sat. 62,975, Sun. 92,505.

Daily Herald-Tribune: 10604 100th St, Postal Bag 3000, Grande Prairie, AB T8V 6V4; tel. (780) 532-1110; fax (780) 532-2120; e-mail frinne@bowesnet.com; internet www.dailyheraldtribune.com; f. 1913; evening; Publr KENT KEEBAUGH; Man. Editor FRED RINNE; circ. 6,508.

Edmonton Journal: POB 2421, Edmonton, AB T5J 2S6; tel. (780) 429-5100; fax (780) 429-5536; e-mail letters@thejournal.canwest.com; internet www.canada.com/edmontonjournal; f. 1903; Pres. and Publr LINDA HUGHES; Editor-in-Chief ALLAN MAYER; circ. Mon. to Sat. 128,225, Sun. 126,052.

Edmonton Sun: 4990 92nd Ave, Suite 250, Edmonton, AB T6B 3A1; tel. (780) 468-0100; fax (780) 468-0128; internet www.edmontonsun.com; f. 1978; Publr and CEO GORDON NORRIE; Editor-in-Chief GRAHAM DALZIEL; circ. Mon. to Sat. 69,254, Sun. 95,880.

Fort McMurray Today: 8550 Franklin Ave, Bag 4008, Fort McMurray, AB T9H 3G1; tel. (403) 743-8186; fax (403) 715-3820; e-mail editorial@fortmcmurraytoday.com; internet www.fortmcmurraytoday.com; evening; Publr TIM O'ROURKE; Man. Editor MICHAEL HALL; circ. Mon. to Thur. 3,916, Fri. 5,870.

Lethbridge Herald: 504 Seventh St South, POB 670, Lethbridge, AB T1J 3Z7; tel. (403) 328-4411; fax (403) 328-4536; e-mail dawn.sugimoto@lethbridgeherald.com; internet www.lethbridgeherald.com; f. 1907; evening and Sun.; Publr MICHAEL J. HERTZ; Man. Editor DOYLE MACKINNON; circ. Mon. to Sat. 19,043, Sun. 17,659.

Medicine Hat News: 3257 Dunmore Rd, SE, POB 10, Medicine Hat, AB T1A 7E6; tel. (403) 527-1101; fax (403) 527-1244; e-mail apoirier@medicinehatnews.com; internet www.medicinehatnews.com; f. 1887; evening; Publr MICHAEL J. HERTZ; Man. Editor ALAN POIRIER; circ. 13,916.

Red Deer Advocate: 2950 Bremner Ave, Bag 5200, Red Deer, AB T4N 5G3; tel. (403) 314-4325; fax (403) 341-6560; e-mail editorial@reddeeradvocate.com; internet www.reddeeradvocate.com; f. 1894; Publr FRED GORMAN; Man. Editor JOE McLAUGHLIN; circ. Mon. to Sat. 18,171.

British Columbia

Alaska Highway News: 9916 98th St, Fort St John, BC V1J 3T8; tel. (250) 785-5631; fax (250) 785-3522; e-mail ahnews@awink.com; internet www.canada.com/fortstjohn; f. 1940; evening; Publr WILLIAM JULIAN; Man. Editor MIKE HEINTZMAN; circ. 3,880.

Alberni Valley Times: 4918 Napier St, POB 400, Port Alberni, BC V9Y 3H5; tel. and fax (250) 723-8171; fax (250) 723-0586; e-mail cduddy@nanaimodailynews.com; internet www.canada.com/vancouverisland/albernivalleytimes; Publr CURT DUDDY (acting); Man. Editor CALE COWAN; circ. Mon. to Sat. 5,806.

Daily Bulletin: 335 Spokane St, Kimberley, BC V1A 1Y9; tel. (250) 427-5333; fax (250) 427-5336; e-mail bulletin@cyberlink.bc.ca; f. 1932; evening; Publr STEEN JORGENSEN; Editor CHRIS DOUAN; circ. 2,000.

Daily Courier: 550 Doyle Ave, Kelowna, BC V1Y 7V1; tel. (250) 762-4445; fax (250) 763-0194; e-mail alison.yesilcimen@ok.bc.ca; internet www.kelownadailycourier.ca; f. 1904; morning; Publr ALISON YESILCIMEN; Man. Editor TOM WILSON; circ. Mon. to Sat. 18,252, Sun. 28,359.

Daily Townsman: 822 Cranbrook St North, Cranbrook, BC V1C 3R9; tel. (250) 426-5201; fax (250) 426-5003; e-mail townsman@cyberlink.bc.ca; evening; Publr STEEN JORGENSEN; Editor DAVID SANDS; circ. 4,000.

Kamloops Daily News: 393 Seymour St, Kamloops, BC V2C 6P6; tel. (250) 372-2331; fax (250) 374-3884; e-mail kamloopsnews@telus.net; internet www.kamloopsnews.ca; f. 1930; evening; Publr DON HERRON; Editor MEL ROTHENBURGER; circ. 8,532.

Nanaimo Daily News: 2575 McCullough Rd, Nanaimo, BC V9S 5W5; tel. (250) 7529-4200; fax (250) 729-4288; e-mail dnews@island.net; internet www.nanaimodailynews.com; f. 1874; evening; Publr CURT DUDDY; Man. Editor CALE COWAN; circ. 8,532.

Nelson Daily News: 266 Baker St, Nelson, BC V1L 4H3; tel. (250) 352-3552; fax (250) 352-2418; e-mail news@nelsondailynews.com; internet www.nelsondailynews.com; f. 1902; evening; Publr PETER HOWIE; Editor DREW EDWARDS; circ. 3,000.

Peace River Block News: 901 100th Ave, Dawson Creek, BC V1G 1W2; tel. (250) 782-4888; fax (250) 782-6770; e-mail news@prbn.ca; internet www.prbn.ca; f. 1930; afternoon; weekly regional edn; Publr BRIAN SIMS; Man. Editor BRAD LYON; circ. Mon. to Thur. 2,200, Fri. 2,600, weekly 10,000.

Penticton Herald: 186 Nanaimo Ave West, Suite 101, Penticton, BC V2A 1N4; tel. (250) 492-4002; fax (250) 492-2403; e-mail editor@pentictonherald.ca; internet www.pentictonherald.ca; morning; Publr ALISON YESILCIMEN; Man. Editor S. PAUL VARGA; Gen. Man. ANDRÉ MARTIN; circ. Mon. to Sat. 7,965, Sun. 7,048.

Prince George Citizen: 150 Brunswick St, POB 5700, Prince George, BC V2L 5K9; tel. (250) 562-2441; fax (250) 562-7453; e-mail news@princegeorgecitizen.com; internet www.princegeorgecitizen.com; f. 1916; morning; Publr DEL LAVERDURE; Man. Editor DAVE PAULSON; circ. 15,995.

The Province: 200 Granville St, Suite 1, Vancouver, BC V6C 3N3; tel. (604) 605-2000; fax (604) 605-2759; e-mail wmoriarty@png.canwest.com; internet www.canada.com/theprovince; f. 1898; Publr DENNIS SKULSKY; Editor-in-Chief WAYNE MORIARTY; circ. Mon. to Sat. 144,765, Sun. 178,636.

Sing Tao Daily News (Eastern Canada Edition): 8508 Ash St, Vancouver, BC V6P 3M2; tel. (416) 596-8140; fax (416) 599-6688; e-mail vanadmin@singtao.ca; internet singtao.ca; Chinese; Editor PAUL TSANG; circ. Mon. to Sat. 15,000.

Times Colonist: 2621 Douglas St, Victoria, BC V8T 4M2; tel. (250) 380-5211; fax (250) 380-5353; e-mail lchodan@tc.canwest.com; internet www.canada.com/victoriatimescolonist; f. 1980 by merger; Publr BOB McKENZIE; Editor-in-Chief LUCINDA CHODAN; circ. Mon. to Sat. 70,653–74,789, Sun. 72,808.

Trail Daily Times: 1163 Cedar Ave, Trail, BC V1R 4B8; tel. (250) 368-8551; fax (250) 368-8550; e-mail editor@trailtimes.ca; evening; Publr BARB BLATCHFORD; Editor TRACY GILCHRIST; circ. 5,500.

The Vancouver Sun: 200 Granville St, Suite 1, Vancouver, BC V6C 3N3; tel. (604) 605-2000; fax (604) 605-2720; e-mail info@png.canwest.com; internet www.canada.com/vancouversun; f. 1886; Pres. and Publr DENNIS SKULSKY; Editor-in-Chief PATRICIA GRAHAM; circ. Mon. to Fri. 167,483, Sat. 211,460.

World Journal (Vancouver): 2288 Clark Dr., Vancouver, BC V5N 3G8; tel. (604) 876-1338; fax (604) 876-9191; internet www.worldjournal.com; Chinese; Publr WILSON CHIEN; circ. 10,000.

Manitoba

Brandon Sun: 501 Rosser Ave, Brandon, MB R7A 0K4; tel. (204) 727-2451; fax (204) 725-0976; e-mail bchester@brandonsun.com; internet www.brandonsun.com; f. 1882; evening and Sun.; Publr EWAN POW; Man. Editor JAMES O'CONNOR; circ. Mon. to Fri. 14,393, Sat. 18,469, Sun. 12,625.

CANADA

Daily Graphic: 1941 Saskatchewan Ave West, POB 130, Portage La Prairie, MB R1N 3B4; tel. (204) 857-3427; fax (204) 239-1270; e-mail editor.dailygraphic@shawcable.com; internet www.portagedailygraphic.com; evening; Publr BARRY CLAYTON; Man. Editor CLARISE KLASSEN; circ. 2,869.

Flin Flon Reminder: 10 North Ave, Flin Flon, MB R8A 0T2; tel. (204) 687-3454; fax (204) 687-4473; f. 1946; evening; Publr RANDY DANELIUK; Editor RICH BILLY; circ. 4,000.

Winnipeg Free Press: 1355 Mountain Ave, Winnipeg, MB R2X 3B6; tel. (204) 697-7000; fax (204) 697-7375; e-mail bob.cox@freepress.mb.ca; internet www.winnipegfreepress.com; f. 1872; morning; Publr BOB COX; Editor MARGO GOODHAND; circ. Mon. to Fri. 121,198, Sat. 162,418, Sun. 118,699.

Winnipeg Sun: 1700 Church Ave, Winnipeg, MB R2X 3A2; tel. (204) 694-2022; fax (204) 632-8709; e-mail bbrennan@wpgsun.com; internet www.winnipegsun.com; f. 1980; Publr and CEO ED HUCULAK; Man. Editor MARK HAMM; circ. Mon. to Sat. 41,729, Sun. 50,941.

New Brunswick

L'Acadie Nouvelle: 476 blvd St-Pierre ouest, CP 5536, Caraquet, NB E1W 1B7; tel. (506) 727-4444; fax (506) 727-7620; e-mail infos@acadienouvelle.com; internet www.acadienouvelle.com; f. 1984; Publr GILLES GAGNÉ; Editor BRUNO GODIN; circ. 20,299.

Brunswick News: POB 3370, Fredericton, NB E3B 5A2; tel. (506) 452-6671; fax (506) 452-7405; e-mail news@dailygleaner.com; internet www.canadaeast.com/dg; f. 1881; fmrly the *Daily Gleaner*; morning; Publr ERIC LAWSON; Editor-in-Chief PETER HAGGERT; circ. 24,445.

New Brunswick Telegraph–Journal: 210 Crown St, POB 2350, Saint John, NB E2L 3V8; tel. (506) 632-8888; fax (506) 648-2654; e-mail newsroom@nbpub.com; internet www.telegraphjournal.com; Publr JAMES C. IRVING; Man. Editor DAVID SPRAGG; circ. Mon. to Fri. 40,549, Sat. 45,000.

St John Times–Globe: 210 Crown St, POB 2350, Saint John, NB E2L 3V8; tel. (506) 632-8888; fax (506) 648-2654; internet www.nbnews.com; evening; Publr VICTOR MLODECKI; circ. 23,000.

The Times and Transcript: 939 Main St, POB 1001, Moncton, NB E1C 8P3; tel. (506) 859-4900; fax (506) 859-4904; e-mail news@timestranscript.com; internet www.timestranscript.com; f. 1983; Mon. to Sat. evening, Sat. morning; Publr ERIC LAWSON; Man. Editor AL HOGAN; circ. Mon. to Fri. 36,899, Sat. 42,286.

Newfoundland and Labrador

Telegram: 1 Columbus Dr., POB 5970, St John's, NL A1C 5X7; tel. (709) 364-6300; fax (709) 364-9333; e-mail rwanger@thetelegram.com; internet www.thetelegram.com; f. 1879; evening; Publr MILLER H. AYRE; Exec. Editor KERRY HANN; circ. Mon. to Fri. 31,541, Sat. 55,031, Sun. 30,186.

Western Star: 106 West St, POB 460, Corner Brook, NL A2H 6E7; tel. (709) 634-4668; fax (709) 634-9824; e-mail rwilliams@thewesternstar.com; internet www.thewesternstar.com; f. 1900; Publr and Gen. Man. SHAWN WOODFORD; Man. Editor RICHARD WILLIAMS; circ. Mon. to Sat. 7,445.

Nova Scotia

Amherst Daily News: 147 South Albion St Town Sq., POB 280, Amherst, NS B4H 3Z2; tel. (902) 661-5426; fax (902) 667-0419; e-mail bworks@amherstdaily.com; internet www.amherstdaily.com; f. 1893; Publr RICHARD RUSSELL; Man. Editor BRAD WORKS; circ. Mon. to Sat. 3,038.

Cape Breton Post: 255 George St, POB 1500, Sydney, NS B1P 6K6; tel. (902) 563-3843; fax (902) 562-7077; e-mail fjackson@cbpost.com; internet www.capebretonpost.com; f. 1901; Publr ANITA DELAZZER; Man. Editor FRED JACKSON; circ. Mon. to Sat. 26,209.

Chronicle–Herald: 1650 Argyle St, POB 610, Halifax, NS B3J 2T2; tel. (902) 426-2811; fax (902) 426-1158; e-mail reception@herald.ca; internet thechronicleherald.ca; f. 1875; Publr GRAHAM W. DENNIS; Man. Editor TERRY O'NEIL; circ. Mon. to Sat. 108,777, Sun. 78,369.

Daily News: 1601 Lower Water St, Halifax, NS B3P 3J6, POB 8330, Station A, Halifax, NS B3K 5M1; tel. (902) 444-4444; e-mail info@hfxnews.ca; internet www.hfxnews.ca; f. 1974; Publr JAMIE THOMSON; Editor JACK ROMANELLI; circ. Mon. to Fri. 21,099, Sat. 23,208, Sun. 27,788.

The Evening News: 352 East River Rd, POB 159, New Glasgow, NS B2H 5E2; tel. (902) 752-3000; fax (902) 752-1945; e-mail news@ngnews.ca; internet www.ngnews.ca; f. 1910; evening; Publr RICHARD RUSSELL; Man. Editor DAVE GLENEN; circ. 7,970.

Mail–Star: 1650 Argyle St, POB 610, Halifax, NS B3J 2T2; tel. (902) 426-2811; fax (902) 426-3014; internet www.herald.ns.ca; evening; Publr GRAHAM W. DENNIS; Man. Editor TERRY O'NEIL; circ. 21,000.

Truro Daily News: 6 Louise St, POB 220, Truro, NS B2N 5C3; tel. (902) 893-9405; fax (902) 893-0518; e-mail news@trurodaily.com; internet www.trurodaily.com; f. 1891; evening; Publr RICHARD RUSSELL; Regional Man. Editor DAVE GLENEN; circ. Mon. to Fri. 6,583, Sat. 8,270.

Ontario

Barrie Examiner: 571 Bayfield St North, Barrie, ON L4M 4Z9; tel. (705) 726-6537; fax (705) 726-5414; internet www.thebarrieexaminer.com; f. 1864; evening; Publr RON LAURIN; Man. Editor MIKE BEAUDIN; circ. 10,925.

Beacon–Herald: 16 Packham Rd, POB 430, Stratford, ON N5A 6T6; tel. (519) 271-2220; fax (519) 271-1026; e-mail jkastner@bowesnet.com; internet www.stratfordbeaconherald.com; f. 1854; evening; Publr and Sales Man. DAVE CARTER; Man. Editor JOHN KASTNER; circ. Mon. to Sat. 10,764.

Brockville Recorder and Times: 1600 California Ave, POB 10, Brockville, ON K6V 5T8; tel. (613) 342-4441; fax (613) 342-4456; e-mail wb.raison@recorder.ca; internet www.recorder.ca; f. 1821; evening; Publr BOB PEARCE; Editor BARRY RAISON; circ. 11,914.

Cambridge Reporter: 26 Ainslie St South, POB 1510, Cambridge, ON N1R 5T2; tel. (519) 621-3810; fax (519) 621-8239; e-mail news@cambridge-reporter.com; internet www.cambridge-reporter.com; f. 1846; evening; Publr L. R. (VERNE) SHAULL; Editor CLYDE WARRINGTON; circ. 7,000.

Chatham Daily News: 45 Fourth St, POB 2007, Chatham, ON N7M 5M6; tel. (519) 354-2000; fax (519) 354-9489; internet www.chathamdailynews.ca; f. 1862; evening; Publr JIM BLAKE; Man. Editor BRUCE CORCORAN; circ. 13,355.

Chronicle–Journal: 75 Cumberland St South, Thunder Bay, ON P7B 1A3; tel. (807) 343-6200; fax (807) 345-5991; e-mail cj-editorial@cwconnect.ca; internet www.chroniclejournal.com; Publr and Gen. Man. COLIN J. BRUCE; News Editor JOANNE KUSHNIER; circ. Mon. to Sat. 28,925, Sun. 26,001.

Cobourg Daily Star: 99 King St West, POB 400, Cobourg, ON K9A 4L1; tel. (905) 372-0131; fax (905) 372-4966; internet www.northumberlandtoday.com; evening; Group Publr DON MACLEOD; Editorial Dir MANDY MARTIN; circ. 4,360.

Daily Observer: 186 Alexander St, Pembroke, ON K8A 4L9; tel. (613) 732-3691; fax (613) 732-2226; internet www.thedailyobserver.ca; f. 1855; evening; Publr STEVE GLOSTER; Man. Editor PETER LAPINSKIE; circ. 5,777.

The Daily Press: 187 Cedar South, Timmins, ON P4N 7G1; tel. (705) 268-5050; fax (705) 268-7373; internet www.timminspress.com; f. 1933; Publr and Gen. Man. BRUCE COWAN; Man. Editor TOM PERRY; circ. Mon. to Sat. 9,522.

Le Droit: 47 rue Clarence, bureau 222, CP 8860, succursale Terminus, Ottawa, ON K1G 3J9; tel. (613) 562-0111; fax (613) 562-6280; e-mail ledroit@ledroit.com; internet www.cyberpresse.ca; f. 1913; Publr JAQUES PRONOVOST; Man. Editor ANDRÉ LAROCQUE; circ. Mon. to Fri. 35,985, Sat. 40,494.

The Expositor: 53 Dalhousie St, POB 965, Brantford, ON N3T 5S8; tel. (519) 756-2020; fax (519) 756-4911; internet www.brantfordexpositor.ca; f. 1852; Publr MICHAEL PEARCE; Editor DAVE JUDD; circ. 21,905.

The Globe and Mail: 444 Front St West, Toronto, ON M5V 2S9; tel. (416) 585-5000; fax (416) 585-5085; e-mail newsroom@globeandmail.ca; internet www.globeandmail.com; f. 1844; Publr and CEO PHILLIP CRAWLEY; Editor-in-Chief EDWARD GREENSPON; circ. Mon. to Fri. 320,835, Sat. 410,266.

Guelph Mercury: 8–14 Macdonnell St, Guelph, ON N1H 6P7; tel. (519) 822-4310; fax (519) 767-1681; internet www.guelphmercury.com; f. 1854; evening; Group Publr DANA ROBBINS; Man. Editor PHIL ANDREWS; circ. 14,234.

Hamilton Spectator: 44 Frid St, Hamilton, ON L8N 3G3; tel. (905) 526-3333; fax (905) 526-1139; internet www.thespec.com; f. 1846; Publr and Exec. Vice-Pres. IAN OLIVER; Editor-in-Chief DAVID ESTOK; circ. Mon. to Fri. 105,765, Sat. 122,621.

Intelligencer: 45 Bridge St East, Belleville, ON K8N 5C7; tel. (613) 962-9171; fax (613) 962-9652; internet www.intelligencer.ca; f. 1870; evening; Publr MICHAEL A. POWER; Man. Editor NICK PALMER; circ. 14,958.

The Kingston Whig-Standard: 6 Cataraqui St, POB 2300, Kingston, ON K7K 1Z7; tel. (613) 544-5000; fax (613) 530-4118; internet www.thewhig.com; f. 1834; Publr FRED LAFLAMME; Man. Editor CHRISTINA SPENCER; circ. Mon. to Fri. 26,238, Sat. 34,242.

Lindsay Daily Post: 17 William St South, Lindsay, ON K9V 3A3; tel. (705) 324-2113; fax (705) 324-0174; internet www.thepost.ca; evening; Publr ANDY WHEELER; Man. Editor ANDREW CARROLL; circ. 4,831.

London Free Press: 369 York St, POB 2280, London, ON N6A 4G1; tel. (519) 679-6666; fax (519) 667-4503; e-mail letters@lfpress.com;

CANADA

internet www.lfpress.com; f. 1849; Publr SUSAN MUSZAK; Editor-in-Chief PAUL BERTON; circ. 95,792.

Ming Pao Daily News: 1355 Huntingwood Dr., Scarborough, ON M1S 3J1; tel. (416) 321-0093; fax (416) 321-3499; e-mail newsdesk@mingpaoca.com; Chinese; Editor-in-Chief RICHARD KWOK-KAI NG; circ. Mon. to Fri. 68,600, Sat. 97,000, Sun. 102,000.

National Post: 1450 Don Mills Rd, Suite 300, Don Mills, ON M3B 3R5; tel. (416) 383-2300; fax (416) 442-2212; e-mail queries@nationalpost.com; internet www.nationalpost.com; f. 1998; incorporates the *Financial Post* (f. 1907); national newspaper with printing centres in nine cities; owned by CanWest Global Communications Corpn; Publr GORDON FISHER; Editor-in-Chief DOUG KELLY; circ. Mon. to Fri. 228,187, Sat. 246,527.

Niagara Falls Review: 4801 Valley Way, POB 270, Niagara Falls, ON L2E 6T6; tel. (905) 358-5711; fax (905) 356-0785; internet www.niagarafallsreview.ca; f. 1879; morning; Publr DAVID A. BEATTIE; Man. Editor JOE WALLACE; circ. Mon. to Fri. 17,249, Sat. 19,782.

North Bay Nugget: 259 Worthington St, POB 570, North Bay, ON P1B 3B5; tel. (705) 472-3200; fax (705) 472-1438; e-mail news@nugget.ca; internet www.nugget.ca; f. 1909; evening; Publr DAN JOHNSON; Man. Editor JOHN SIZE; circ. Mon. to Fri. 17,358, Sat. 16,203.

Northern Daily News: 8 Duncan Ave, POB 1030, Kirkland Lake, ON P2N 3L4; tel. (705) 567-5321; fax (705) 567-6162; internet www.northernnews.ca; f. 1922; evening; Publr and Gen. Man. TIM CRESWELL; Man. Editor JOE O'GRADY; circ. 3,379.

Orillia Packet and Times: 31 Colborne St East, Orillia, ON L3V 1T4; tel. (705) 325-1355; fax (705) 325-4033; internet www.orilliapacket.com; f. 1926 by merger; evening; Publr TERRI-LYNN ROSE; Man. Editor MARK BISSET; circ. 8,039.

Ottawa Citizen: 1101 Baxter Rd, POB 5020, Ottawa, ON K2C 3M4; tel. (613) 829-9100; fax (613) 596-3755; e-mail sanderson@thecitizen.canwest.com; internet www.canada.com/ottawa/ottawacitizen; f. 1845; Publr and Gen. Man. JAMES ORBAN; Editor-in-Chief SCOTT ANDERSON; circ. Mon. to Fri. 132,236, Sat. 148,913, Sun. 138,306.

Ottawa Sun: 6 Antares Dr., Phase 3, Ottawa, ON K1G 5H7; tel. (613) 739-7000; fax (613) 739-9383; e-mail rick.gibbons@ott.sunpub.com; internet www.ottawasun.com; Publr RICK GIBBONS; Editor-in-Chief MIKE THERIEN; circ. Mon. to Fri. 50,107, Sat. 45,111, Sun. 52,688.

Peterborough Examiner: 730 Kingsway, Peterborough, ON K9J 8L4; tel. (705) 745-4641; fax (705) 743-4581; internet www.thepeterboroughexaminer.com; f. 1847; evening; Publr and Gen. Man. DARREN MURPHY; Man. Editor ED N. ARNOLD; circ. Mon. to Thur. 21,376, Fri. 22,224, Sat. 22,449.

The Record: 160 King St East, Kitchener, ON N2G 4E5; tel. (519) 894-2231; fax (519) 894-1241; e-mail business@therecord.com; internet www.therecord.com; f. 1878; evening; Publr DANA ROBBINS; Editor-in-Chief LYNN HADDRALL; circ. Mon. to Fri. 66,713, Sat. 73,111.

St Catharines Standard: 17 Queen St, St Catharines, ON L2R 5G5; tel. (905) 684-7251; fax (905) 684-6670; internet www.stcatharinesstandard.ca; f. 1891; evening; Publr PAUL MCCUAIG; Man. Editor ANDREA KRILUCK; circ. Mon. to Fri. 30,925, Sat. 38,864.

St Thomas Times–Journal: 16 Hincks St, St Thomas, ON N5R 5Z2; tel. (519) 631-2790; fax (519) 631-5653; e-mail news@stthomastimesjournal.com; internet www.stthomastimesjournal.com; f. 1882; evening; Publr BEV PONTON; Man. Editor ROSS PORTER; circ. 7,762.

Sarnia Observer: 140 Front St South, POB 3009, Sarnia, ON N7T 7M8; tel. (519) 344-3641; fax (519) 332-2951; internet www.theobserver.ca; f. 1853; evening; Publr DARYL C. SMITH; Man. Editor ROD HILTS; circ. Mon. to Fri. 19,243, Sat. 22,736.

Sault Star: 145 Old Garden River Rd, POB 460, Sault Ste Marie, ON P6A 5M5; tel. (705) 759-3030; fax (705) 759-0102; internet www.saultstar.com; f. 1912; evening; Publr LOU A. MAULUCCI; Man. Editor JOHN HALUCHA; circ. 18,957.

Sentinel–Review: 16 Brock St, POB 1000, Woodstock, ON N4S 3B4; tel. (519) 537-2341; fax (519) 537-3049; e-mail sentinelreview@bowesnet.com; internet www.woodstocksentinelreview.com; f. 1886; evening; Publr PAT LOGAN; Man. Editor BILL SCRIVEN; circ. 8,500.

Simcoe Reformer: 50 Gilbertson Dr., POB 370, Simcoe, ON N3Y 4L2; tel. (519) 426-5710; fax (519) 426-9255; e-mail refedit@bowesnet.com; internet www.simcoereformer.ca; f. 1858; evening; Group Publr CAM MCKNIGHT; Man. Editor KIM NOVAK; circ. 8,433.

Sing Tao Daily News: 417 Dundas St West, Toronto, ON M5T 1G6; tel. (416) 596-8140; fax (416) 599-6688; e-mail editor_toronto@singtao.ca; internet www.singtao.ca; Chinese; Editor-in-Chief ROBERT LEUNG; circ. Mon. to Sun. 160,693.

Standard-Freeholder: 44 Pitt St, Cornwall, ON K6J 3P3; tel. (613) 933-3160; fax (613) 933-7168; internet www.standard-freeholder.com; Publr and Gen. Man. MILTON S. ELLIS; Editor JACK ROMANELLI; circ. 14,393.

Sudbury Star: 33 MacKenzie St, Sudbury, ON P3C 4Y1; tel. (705) 674-5271; fax (705) 674-6834; internet www.thesudburystar.com; f. 1909; evening; Publr DAVID KILGOUR; Man. Editor BRIAN MACLEOD; circ. Mon. to Thur. 17,203, Fri. 19,883, Sat. 19,208.

Sun Times: 290 Ninth St East, POB 200, Owen Sound, ON N4K 1N7; tel. (519) 376-2250; fax (519) 376-7190; internet www.owensoundsuntimes.com; f. 1853 as *The Times*; evening; Publr CHERYL A. MCMENEMY; Man. Editor MICHAEL DEN TANDT; circ. 16,612.

Toronto Star: 1 Yonge St, Toronto, ON M5E 1E6; tel. (416) 367-2000; fax (416) 869-4328; e-mail lettertoed@thestar.com; internet www.thestar.com; f. 1892; Publr JAGODA S. PIKE; Editor-in-Chief J. FRED KUNTZ; circ. Mon. to Fri. 435,650, Sat. 640,367, Sun. 439,982.

Toronto Sun: 333 King St East, Toronto, ON M5A 3X5; tel. (416) 947-2222; fax (416) 947-3228; internet www.torontosun.com; f. 1971; Publr and CEO KIN-MAN LEE; Editor-in-Chief GLENN GARNETT; circ. Mon. to Fri. 178,326, Sat. 150,492, Sun. 309,615.

Welland-Port Colborne Tribune: 228 East Main St, POB 278, Welland, ON L3B 5P5; tel. (905) 732-2411; fax (905) 732-3660; e-mail tribme@wellandtribune.ca; internet www.wellandtribune.ca; f. 1863; Publr MIKE WALSH; Man. Editor ANGUS SCOTT; circ. 14,260.

Windsor Star: 167 Ferry St, Windsor, ON N9A 4M5; tel. (519) 255-5743; fax (519) 255-5515; e-mail letters@thestar.canwest.com; internet www.canada.com/windsorstar; f. 1918; Editor MARTY BENETEAU; circ. Mon. to Fri. 71,637, Sat. 80,791.

World Journal (Toronto): 415 Eastern Ave, Toronto, ON M4M 1B7; tel. (416) 778-0888; fax (416) 778-1037; internet www.worldjournal.com; Chinese; Pres. DAVID TING; Editor-in-Chief PAUL CHANG; circ. 38,000.

Prince Edward Island

Guardian: 165 Prince St, POB 760, Charlottetown, PE C1A 4R7; tel. (902) 629-6000; fax (902) 566-3808; e-mail letters@theguardian.pe.ca; internet www.theguardian.pe.ca; f. 1887; Publr DON BRANDER; Editor GARY MACDOUGALL; circ. Mon. to Sat. 20,746.

Journal–Pioneer: 316 Water St, POB 2480, Summerside, PE C1N 4K5; tel. (902) 436-2121; fax (902) 436-0784; e-mail newsroom@journalpioneer.com; internet www.journalpioneer.com; f. 1865; evening; Publr SANDY RUNDLE; Man. Editor MIKE TURNER; circ. 9,090.

Québec

Le Devoir: 2050 rue de Bleury, 9e étage, Montréal, QC H3A 3M9; tel. (514) 985-3333; fax (514) 985-3360; e-mail redaction@ledevoir.com; internet www.ledevoir.com; Publr BERNARD DESCÔTEAUX; Editor-in-Chief JEAN ROBERT SANSFAÇON; circ. Mon. to Fri. 26,676, Sat. 43,115.

The Gazette: 1010 rue Ste-Catherine ouest, Suite 200, Montréal, QC H3B 5L1; tel. (514) 987-2222; fax (514) 987-2270; e-mail letters@thegazette.canwest.com; internet www.canada.com/montrealgazette; f. 1778; English; Publr ALAN ALLNUTT; Editor-in-Chief ANDREW PHILLIPS; circ. Mon. to Fri. 142,213, Sat. 155,533, Sun. 135,614.

Le Journal de Montréal: 4545 rue Frontenac, Montréal, QC H2H 2R7; tel. (514) 521-4545; fax (514) 525-4542; e-mail transmission@journalmtl.com; f. 1964; Publr and Editor LYNE ROBITAILLE; Editor-in-Chief DANY DOUCET; circ. Mon. to Fri. 266,835, Sat. 314,575, Sun. 261,375.

Le Journal de Québec: 450 ave Béchard, Vanier, QC G1M 2E9; tel. (418) 683-1573; fax (418) 683-1027; e-mail commentaires@journaldequebec.com; internet www.journaldequebec.com; f. 1967; Publr PIERRE FRANCOEUR; Chief Editor SERGE GOSSELIN; circ. Mon. to Fri. 100,986, Sat. 124,717, Sun. 103,452 (2006).

Le Nouvelliste: 1920 rue Bellefeuille, CP 668, Trois Rivières, QC G9A 3Y2; tel. (819) 376-2501; fax (819) 376-0946; e-mail information@lenouvelliste.qc.ca; internet www.cyberpresse.ca/nouvelliste; f. 1920; Pres. and Publr RAYMOND TARDIF; Editor-in-Chief ALAIN TURCOTTE; circ. Mon. to Fri. 41,803, Sat. 44,601.

La Presse: 7 rue St-Jacques, Montréal, QC H2Y 1K9; tel. (514) 285-7070; fax (514) 285-6930; e-mail nouvelles@lapresse.ca; internet www.cyberpresse.ca/reseau; f. 1884; Pres. and Editor GUY CREVIER; circ. Mon. to Fri. 202,663, Sat. 277,935, Sun. 223,225.

Le Quotidien du Saguenay-Lac-St-Jean: 1051 blvd Talbot, Chicoutimi, QC G7H 5C1; tel. (418) 545-4474; fax (418) 690-8824; e-mail msimard@lequotidien.com; internet www.cyberpresse.ca/quotidien; f. 1973; Editor-in-Chief MICHEL SIMARD; circ. Mon. to Sat. 28,230, Sun. 38,475.

The Record: 1195 Galt St East, CP 1200, Sherbrooke, QC J1G 1Y7; tel. (819) 569-9511; fax (819) 569-3945; e-mail newsroom@sherbrookerecord.com; internet www.sherbrookerecord.com; f. 1897; Publr RANDY KINNEAR; Editor ELEANOR BROWN; circ. 4,875.

CANADA   *Directory*

Le Soleil: 410 blvd Charest est, CP 1547, succursale Terminus, Québec, QC G1K 7J6; tel. (418) 686-3394; fax (418) 686-3374; e-mail redaction@lesoleil.com; internet www.cyberpresse.ca/soleil; f. 1896; Publr CLAUDE GAGNON; Editor-in-Chief YVES BELLEFLEUR; circ. Mon. to Fri. 78,328, Sat. 110,746, Sun. 88,076.

La Tribune: 1950 rue Roy, Sherbrooke, QC J1K 2X8; tel. (819) 564-5454; fax (819) 564-8098; e-mail redaction@latribune.qc.ca; internet www.cyberpresse.ca/tribune; f. 1910; Pres. and Publr LOUISE BOISVERT; Editor-in-Chief MAURICE CLOUTIER; circ. Mon. to Fri. 31,556, Sat. 37,629.

La Voix de L'Est: 76 rue Dufferin, Granby, QC J2G 9L4; tel. (450) 375-4555; fax (450) 777-4865; e-mail redaction@lavoixdelest.qc.ca; internet www.cyberpresse.ca/vde; f. 1945; Pres. and Publr GUY GRANGER; circ. Mon. to Fri. 15,710, Sat. 18,595.

Saskatchewan

Daily Herald: 30 10th St East, Prince Albert, SK S6V 0Y5; tel. (306) 763-7202; fax (306) 763-3331; e-mail editorial@paherald.sk.ca; internet www.paherald.sk.ca; f. 1894; Publr IAN JENSEN; Man. Editor VERN FAULKNER; circ. Mon. to Sat. 7,600.

Leader–Post: 1964 Park St, POB 2020, Regina, SK S4P 3G4; tel. (306) 781-5211; fax (306) 781-5484; e-mail feedback@leaderpost.canwest.com; internet www.leaderpost.com; f. 1883; Publr GREG MCLEAN; Editor JANICE DOCKHAM; circ. Mon. to Thur. 48,999, Fri. 50,426, Sat. 52,858.

StarPhoenix: 204 Fifth Ave North, Saskatoon, SK S7K 2P1; tel. (306) 657-6231; fax (306) 657-6437; e-mail spnews@sp.canwest.com; internet www.canada.com/saskatoon/starphoenix; f. 1902; Publr DALE BRIN; Editor STEVE GIBB; circ. Mon. to Thur. 52,707, Fri. 60,499, Sat. 59,675.

Times–Herald: 44 Fairford St West, POB 3000, Moose Jaw, SK S6H 6E4; tel. (306) 692-6441; fax (306) 692-2101; e-mail editorial@mjtimes.sk.ca; internet www.mjtimes.sk.ca; f. 1889; evening; Publr and Gen. Man. ROB CLARK; Man. Editor LESLEY SHEPPARD; circ. 8,000.

Yukon Territory

Whitehorse Star: 2149 Second Ave, Whitehorse, Yukon, YT Y1A 1C5; tel. (867) 667-4481; fax (867) 668-7130; e-mail star@whitehorsestar.com; internet www.whitehorsestar.com; f. 1900; evening; Publr JACKIE PIERCE; Editor JIM BUTLER; circ. Mon. to Thur. 1,960, Fri. 3,739.

SELECTED PERIODICALS

Alberta

Oilweek: Suite 300, 5735 Seventh St, NE, Calgary, AB T2E 8V3 133; tel. (403) 265-3700; fax (403) 265-3706; internet www.oilweek.com; monthly magazine; f. 1948; Publr AGNES ZALEWSKI; Man. Editor DARRELL STONEHOUSE; circ. 7,500.

Ukrainski Visti (Ukrainian News): 12227 107th Ave, Suite 1, Edmonton, AB T5M 1Y9; tel. (780) 488-3693; fax (780) 488-3859; e-mail ukrnews@compusmart.ab.ca; f. 1929; fortnightly; Ukrainian and English; Publr and Editor MARCO LEVYTSKY; circ. 3,274.

British Columbia

BC Outdoors—Sport, Fishing and Outdoor Adventure: OP Publishing Ltd, 1080 Howe St, Suite 900, Vancouver, BC V6Z 2T1; tel. (604) 606-4644; fax (604) 687-1925; e-mail bcoutdoors@oppublishing.com; internet www.bcosportfishing.com; f. 1945; 6 a year; Editor MIKE MITCHELL; circ. 24,000.

Pacific Yachting: OP Publishing Ltd, 1080 Howe St, Suite 900, Vancouver, BC V6Z 2T1; tel. (604) 678-2589; fax (604) 687-1925; e-mail editor@pacificyachting.com; internet www.pacificyachting.com; f. 1968; monthly; Editor PETER A. ROBSON; circ. 17,069.

Vancouver Magazine: 2608 Granville St, Suite 560, Vancouver, BC V6H 3V3; tel. (604) 877-7732; fax (604) 877-4823; e-mail mail@vancouvermagazine.com; internet www.vancouvermagazine.com; f. 1957; 11 a year; Publr KIM PEACOCK; Editor-in-Chief GARY ROSS; circ. 60,000.

Western Living: 2608 Granville St, Suite 560, Vancouver, BC V6H 3V3; tel. (604) 877-7732; fax (604) 877-4838; e-mail wlmail@westernlivingmagazine.com; internet www.westernlivingmagazine.com; f. 1971; 10 a year; Editor JIM SUTHERLAND; circ. 195,500.

WestWorld BC: 4180 Lougheed Hwy, 4th Floor, Burnaby, BC V5C 6A7; tel. (604) 299-7311; fax (604) 299-9188; e-mail cwm@canadawide.com; internet www.canadawide.com/westworldbc_ad.htm; f. 1974; quarterly; travel and sport; Publr and Pres. PETER LEGGE; Editor ANNE ROSE; circ. 517,000.

Manitoba

The Beaver—Canada's History Magazine: 167 Lombard Ave, Suite 478, Winnipeg, MB R3B 0T6; tel. (204) 988-9300; fax (204) 988-9309; e-mail editors@historysociety.ca; internet www.beavermagazine.ca; f. 1920; 6 a year; Canadian history; Pres. and CEO DEBORAH MORRISON; Editor MARK REID; circ. 50,000.

Cattlemen: 1666 Dublin Ave, Winnipeg, MB R3H 0H1; tel. (204) 944-5753; fax (204) 944-5416; e-mail gren@fbcpublishing.com; internet www.canadiancattlemen.ca; f. 1938; 13 a year; animal husbandry; Editor GREN WINSLOW; circ. 28,000.

Country Guide: 1666 Dublin Ave, Winnipeg, MB R3H 0H1; tel. (204) 944-5754; fax (204) 942-8463; e-mail tbutton@twinbanks.com; internet www.country-guide.ca; f. 1882; 10 a year; agriculture; Editor TOM BUTTON; circ. 43,000.

Grainews: 1666 Dublin Ave, Winnipeg, MB R3H 0H1; tel. (204) 954-1450; fax (204) 944-5416; e-mail jay@fbcpublishing.com; internet www.grainews.ca; f. 1975; 17 a year; grain and cattle farming; Editor JAY WHETTER; circ. 43,000.

Kanada Kurier: 955 Alexander Ave, POB 1054, Winnipeg, MB R3C 2X8; tel. (204) 774-1883; fax (204) 783-5740; f. 1889; weekly; German; Editor RENATE ACHENBACH; circ. 25,000.

The Manitoba Co-operator: 1666 Dublin Ave, Winnipeg, MB R3H 0H1; tel. (204) 944-5767; fax (204) 954-1422; e-mail daveb@fbcpublishing.com; internet www.manitobacooperator.ca; f. 1925; owned by Farm Business Communications, a subsidiary of Glacier Ventures International Corpn; weekly; for the farming community; Man. Editor DAVE BEDARD; Editor LAURA RANCE; circ. 13,800.

New Brunswick

Brunswick Business Journal: 55 McKnight St, Suite 115, Fredericton, NB E3A 5W8; tel. (506) 472-4783; fax (506) 459-4189; f. 1984; monthly; Editor SUZANNE MCDONALD-BOYCE.

Newfoundland and Labrador

Atlantic Business Magazine: 251 Empire Ave, Suite 102, St John's, NL A1C 3H9; tel. (709) 726-9300; fax (709) 726-3013; e-mail dchafe@atlanticbusinessmagazine.com; internet www.atlanticbusinessmagazine.com; f. 1987; 6 a year; business; Publr HUBERT HUTTON; Editor DAWN CHAFE; circ. 29,060.

Northwest Territories

L'Aquilon: POB 1325, Yellowknife, NT X1A 2N9; tel. (867) 873-6603; fax (867) 873-2158; e-mail aquilon@internorth.com; internet www.aquilon.nt.ca; f. 1985; weekly; Editor ALAIN BESSETTE; circ. 1,000.

Hay River Hub: 8–4 Courtoreille St, Hay River, NT X0E 1G3; tel. (867) 874-6577; fax (867) 874-2679; e-mail editor@hayriverhub.com; internet www.hub.awna.com; f. 1973; weekly; Publr CHRIS BRODEUR; Man. Editor SEAN PERCY; circ. 3,000.

Northern News Services: 5108 50th St, Yellowknife, NT X1A 2R1; tel. (867) 873-4031; fax (867) 873-8507; e-mail nnsl@nnsl.com; internet www.nnsl.com; f. 1945 as *News/North*; weekly; Publr JACK SIGVALDASON; Man. Editor BRUCE VALPY; circ. 11,000.

Slave River Journal: 207 McDougal Rd, POB 990, Fort Smith, NT X0E 0P0; tel. (867) 872-3000; fax (867) 872-2754; e-mail reception@auroranet.nt.ca; internet www.srj.ca; f. 1978; weekly; Publr DON JAQUE; Editor LEA STORRY; circ. 1,750.

Yellowknifer: POB 2820, Yellowknife, NT X1A 2R1; tel. (867) 873-4031; fax (867) 873-8507; e-mail nnsl@nnsl.com; internet www.nnsl.com; weekly; Publr JACK SIGVALDASON; Man. Editor BRUCE VALPY; circ. 6,200.

Nova Scotia

Progress: 1660 Hollis St, Penthouse, Suite 1201, Halifax, NS B3J 1V7; tel. (902) 494-0999; fax (902) 494-0997; e-mail news@progresscorp.com; internet www.progresscorp.com; f. 1993; 8 a year; regional business; Editor PAMELA SCOTT-CRACE; circ. 25,800.

Canadian Forum: 5502 Atlantic St, Halifax, NS B3H 1G4; tel. (902) 421-7022; fax (902) 425-0166; f. 1920; 10 a year; political, literary and economic; Editor ROBERT CLUDOS; circ. 9,000.

Nunavut Territory

Kivalliq News: Rankin Inlet, NU; tel. (867) 645-3223; fax (867) 645-3225; e-mail kivalliqnews@nnsl.com; internet www.nnsl.com; f. 1994; weekly; owned by Northern News Services; English and Inuktitut; Publr JACK SIGVALDASON; Editor DARRELL GREER; circ. 1,400.

Nunatsiaq News: POB 8, Iqaluit, NU X0A 0H0; tel. (867) 979-5357; fax (867) 979-4763; e-mail editor@nunatsiaq.com; internet www.nunatsiaq.com; f. 1973; weekly; English and Inuktitut; Publr STEVEN ROBERTS; Editor JIM BELL; circ. 8,000.

Ontario

Anglican Journal: 80 Hayden St, Toronto, ON M4Y 3G2; tel. (416) 924-9192; fax (416) 921-4452; e-mail editor@national.anglican.ca; internet www.anglicanjournal.com; f. 1871; 10 a year; official publ. of the Anglican Church of Canada; Editor LEANNE LARMONDIN; circ. 200,000.

Better Farming: 21400 Service Rd, Vankleek Hill, ON K0B 1R0; tel. (613) 678-2232; fax (613) 678-5993; e-mail admin@betterfarming.com; internet www.betterfarming.com; f. 1999; monthly; Publr PAUL NOLAN; Man. Editor ROBERT C. IRWIN.

CAmagazine: The Canadian Institute of Chartered Accountants, 277 Wellington St West, Toronto, ON M5V 3H2; tel. (416) 977-3222; fax (416) 204-3409; e-mail christian.bellavance@cica.ca; internet www.camagazine.com; f. 1911; 10 a year; Editor-in-Chief CHRISTIAN BELLAVANCE; circ. 83,198 (63,667 in English; 19,531 in French).

Campus Canada: 5397 Eglington Ave West, Suite 101, Toronto, ON M9C 5K6; tel. (416) 928-2909; fax (416) 928-1357; internet www.campus.ca; f. 1983; quarterly; 30 campus edns; Man. Editor CHRISTIAN PEARCE; circ. 145,000.

Canada Gazette: Canada Gazette Directorate, Public Works and Govt Services Canada, 350 Albert St, Ottawa, ON K1A 0S5; tel. (613) 996-1268; fax (613) 991-3540; e-mail ncr.gazette@pwgsc.gc.ca; internet canadagazette.gc.ca; f. 1841; weekly; official newspaper of the Govt of Canada; English and French; Man. JOSÉE BOISVERT.

Canadian Architect: 12 Concorde Pl., Suite 800, Toronto, ON M3C 4J2; tel. (416) 442-3390; fax (416) 442-2214; e-mail ichodikoff@canadianarchitect.com; internet www.canadianarchitect.com; f. 1955; monthly; Editor IAN CHODIKOFF; circ. 13,000.

Canadian Art: 215 Spadina Ave, Suite 320, Toronto, ON M5T 2C7; tel. (416) 368-8854; fax (416) 368-6135; e-mail info@canadianart.ca; internet www.canadianart.ca; quarterly; Publr MELONY WARD; Editor RICHARD RHODES; circ. 21,000.

Canadian Bar Review/Revue du Barreau canadien: Canadian Bar Foundation, 500–865 Carling Ave, Ottawa, ON K1S 5S8; tel. (613) 237-2925; fax (613) 237-0185; e-mail review@cba.org; internet www.cba.org; f. 1923; quarterly, comprising 3 internet-publ. issues and 1 yearly consolidated vol.; Editor Prof. BETH BILSON; circ. 36,000.

Canadian Business: 1 Mount Pleasant Rd, 11th Floor, Toronto, ON M4Y 2Y5; tel. (416) 764-1200; fax (416) 764-1404; e-mail help@canadianbusiness.com; internet www.canadianbusiness.com; f. 1928; 24 a year; Publr DEBORAH ROSSER; Editor-in-Chief JOE CHIDLEY; circ. 88,278.

Canadian Chemical News: 130 Slater St, Suite 550, Ottawa, ON K1P 6E2; tel. (613) 232-6252; fax (613) 232-5862; e-mail info@accn.ca; internet www.accn.ca; f. 1949; 10 a year; Editor-in-Chief MICHELLE PIQUETTE; Man. Editor HEATHER DANA MUNROE; circ. 6,500.

Canadian Electronics: CLB Media Inc, 240 Edward St, Aurora, ON L4G 3S9; tel. (905) 727-0077; fax (905) 727-0017; e-mail tgouldson@clbmedia.com; internet www.electronicsincanada.com; f. 1986; 7 a year; Publr ROGER HERITAGE; Editor TIM GOULDSON; circ. 22,000.

Canadian Geographic: 39 McArthur Ave, Ottawa, ON K1L 8L7; tel. (613) 745-4629; fax (613) 744-0947; e-mail editorial@canadiangeographic.ca; internet www.canadiangeographic.ca; f. 1930; 6 a year; publ. of the Royal Canadian Geographical Soc; Editor RICK BOYCHUK; circ. 218,342.

Canadian Home Workshop: 25 Sheppard Ave, West Toronto, ON M2N 6S7; tel. (416) 733-7600; fax (905) 475-9246; e-mail editorial@canadianhomeworkshop.com; internet www.canadianhomeworkshop.com; f. 1977; monthly; home improvement; Editorial Dir DOUGLAS THOMPSON; Man. Editor JODI AVERY MACLEAN; circ. 125,015.

Canadian House & Home: 511 King St West, Suite 120, Toronto, ON M5V 2Z4; tel. (416) 593-0204; fax (416) 591-1630; e-mail chheditorial@hhmedia.com; internet www.canadianhouseandhome.com; f. 1982; 12 a year; Editor COBI LADNER; circ. 248,378.

Canadian Jewish News: 1500 Don Mills Rd, Suite 205, North York, ON M3B 3KY; tel. (416) 391-1836; fax (416) 391-0829; e-mail info@cjnews.com; internet www.cjnews.com; f. 1971; weekly; Gen. Man. GARY LAFORET; Editor MORDECHAI BEN-DAT; circ. 50,000.

Canadian Living: 25 Sheppard Ave West, Suite 100, North York, ON M2N 6S7; tel. (416) 733-7600; fax (416) 733-3398; e-mail letters@canadianliving.com; internet www.canadianliving.com; f. 1975; monthly; Editor-in-Chief SUSAN ANTONACCI; circ. 516,824.

Canadian Medical Association Journal: 1867 Alta Vista Dr., Ottawa, ON K1G 3Y6; tel. (613) 731-8610; fax (613) 565-7704; e-mail pubs@cma.ca; internet www.cmaj.ca; f. 1911; 25 a year; Editor Dr PAUL HÉBERT; circ. 69,700.

Canadian Musician: 23 Hannover Dr., Suite 7, St Catharines, ON L2W 1A3; tel. (905) 641-3471; fax (905) 641-1648; e-mail mail@nor.com; internet www.canadianmusician.com; f. 1979; 6 a year; Editor JEFF MACKAY; circ. 27,000.

Canadian Nurse/L'infirmière canadienne: 50 Driveway, Ottawa, ON K2P 1E2; tel. (613) 237-2133; fax (613) 237-3520; e-mail editor@canadian-nurse.com; e-mail redaction@cna-aiic.ca; internet www.canadian-nurse.com; f. 1905 as journal of the Canadian Nurses' Asscn; publ. in separate French and English edns since 2000; 9 a year; Editor-in-Chief LUCILLE AUFFREY; Man. Editor LISA BRAZEAU; circ. 126,000.

Canadian Pharmacists Journal: 1785 Alta Vista Dr., Ottawa, ON K1G 3Y6; tel. (613) 523-7877; fax (613) 523-2332; e-mail cpj@pharmacists.ca; internet www.pharmacists.ca/content/hcp/resource_centre/cpj/cpj_contacts.cfm; f. 1868; fmrly Canadian Pharmaceutical Journal; 6 a year; Publr LEESA BRUCE; Editor-in-Chief ROSEMARY KILLEEN; circ. 19,500.

Canadian Travel Press Weekly: 310 Dupont St, Toronto, ON M5R 1V9; tel. (416) 968-7252; fax (416) 968-2377; e-mail ctp@baxter.net; internet www.travelpress.com; 46 a year; Editor-in-Chief EDITH BAXTER; Man. Editor MIKE BAGINSKI; circ. 14,000.

Chatelaine: 1 Mount Pleasant Rd, 8th Floor, Toronto, ON M4Y 2Y5; tel. (416) 764-1888; fax (416) 764-2413; internet www.chatelaine.com; f. 1928; publ. by Rogers Publishing Inc; monthly; women's journal; Publr KERRY MITCHELL; Editor-in-Chief MARYAM SANATI; circ. 615,559.

ComputerWorld Canada: 55 Town Centre Ct, Suite 302, Scarborough, ON M1P 4X4; tel. (416) 290-0240; fax (416) 290-0238; e-mail sschick@itworldcanada.com; internet www.itworldcanada.com; f. 1984; 25 a year; Editor SHANE SCHICK; circ. 42,000.

Fashion: 111 Queen St East, Suite 320, Toronto, ON M5C 1S2; tel. (416) 364-3333; fax (416) 594-3374; internet www.fashionmagazine.com.ca; f. 1996 as Elm Street; ceased publication in 2004 but continued to publish quarterly fashion supplement Elm Street The Look until 2006 when magazine re-launched under above name; publ. by St Jospeh Media; monthly; women's interest; Editor-in-Chief LAURA deCARUFEL.

Flare: 1 Mount Pleasant Rd, 8th Floor, Toronto, ON M4Y 2Y5; tel. (416) 764-2863; fax (416) 764-2866; e-mail Raquel.Lowe@flare.rogers.com; internet www.flare.com; f. 1970; monthly; fashion, beauty and health; Editor-in-Chief LISA TANT; circ. 157,156.

The Hockey News: Transcontinental Publishing, 25 Sheppard Ave West, Suite 100, North York, ON M2N 6S7; tel. (416) 340-8000; fax (416) 340-2786; e-mail editorial@thehockeynews.com; internet www.thehockeynews.com; f. 1947; 42 a year; Man. Editor JASON KAY; circ. 102,599.

Holstein Journal: 30 East Beaver Creek Rd, Suite 210, Richmond Hill, ON L4B 1J2; tel. (905) 886-4222; fax (905) 886-0037; e-mail subs@holsteinjournal.com; internet www.holsteinjournal.com; f. 1938; publ. by The Holstein Journal Group, Inc; monthly; news and information pertaining to the Holstein dairy breed; Publr G. PETER ENGLISH; Editor BONNIE E. COOPER; circ. 4,223.

Journal of the Canadian Dental Association: 1815 Alta Vista Dr., Ottawa, ON K1G 3Y6; tel. (613) 523-1770; fax (613) 523-7736; e-mail rgalipeau@cda-adc.ca; internet www.cda-adc.ca/jcda; f. 1935; 11 a year; Editor Dr JOHN P. O'KEEFE; circ. 20,000.

Kanadai Magyarsag (Hungarian-Canadians): 74 Advance Rd, Etobicoke, ON M8Z 2T7; tel. (416) 233-3131; fax (416) 233-5984; e-mail magyarsag@wellerpublishing.com; internet canadahun.com; weekly; Publr IRENE VOROSVARY; Editor and Man. CSABA GAAL; circ. 9,800.

Legion Magazine: 86 Aird Pl., Kanata, ON K2L 0A1; tel. (613) 591-0116; fax (613) 591-0146; e-mail editor@legionmagazine.com; internet www.legionmagazine.com; f. 1926; 6 a year; publ. for Canadian veterans and Legionnaires; Gen. Man. JENNIFER MORSE; circ. 290,512.

Maclean's: 1 Mount Pleasant Rd, 11th Floor, Toronto, ON M4Y 2Y5; tel. (416) 764-1339; fax (416) 764-1332; e-mail michelle.farnopolsky@macleans.rogers.coma; internet www.macleans.ca; f. 1905 as The Business Magazine; present name adopted in 1911; weekly; Publr and Editor-in-Chief KENNETH WHYTE; Editor MARK STEVENSON; circ. 368,000.

Northern Miner: 12 Concorde Pl., Suite 800, Toronto, ON M3C 4J2; tel. (416) 442-2122; fax (416) 442-2191; e-mail tnm@northernminer.com; internet www.northernminer.com; f. 1915; owned by the Business Information Group; weekly; Publr DOUGLAS DONNELLY; Editor JOHN CUMMING; circ. 11,000.

Now: 189 Church St, Toronto, ON M5B 1Y7; tel. (416) 364-1300; fax (416) 364-1166; e-mail web@nowtoronto.com; internet www.nowtoronto.com; f. 1981; weekly; young adult; Publr and Editor MICHAEL HOLLETT; CEO and Editor ALICE KLEIN; circ. 406,000.

Ontario Medical Review: 525 University Ave, Suite 200, Toronto, ON M5G 2K7; tel. (416) 599-2580; fax (416) 340-2232; e-mail jeff_henry@oma.org; internet www.oma.org; f. 1922; monthly; publ. of the Ontario Medical Asscn; Editor JEFF HENRY; circ. 27,600.

Oral Health: 12 Concorde Pl., Suite 800, Toronto, ON M3C 4J2; tel. (416) 510-6785; fax (416) 510-5140; e-mail cwilson@

CANADA

oralhealthjournal.com; internet www.oralhealthjournal.com; f. 1911; monthly; dentistry; Editorial Dir CATHERINE WILSON; circ. 19,232.

Photo Life: 185 St Paul St, Québec, QC G1K 3W2; tel. (800) 905-7468; fax (800) 664-2739; e-mail editor@photolife.com; internet www.photolife.com; f. 1976; 6 a year; Editor-in-Chief ANITA DAMMER; circ. 55,000.

Quill & Quire: 111 Queen St East, 3rd Floor, Toronto, ON M5C 1S2; tel. (416) 364-3333; fax (416) 595-5415; e-mail info@quillandquire.com; internet www.quillandquire.com; f. 1935; 10 a year; book publishing industry; Editor DEREK WEILER; circ. 5,000.

Style: 555 Richmond St West, Suite 701, Toronto, ON M5V 3B1; tel. (416) 203-6737; fax (416) 203-1057; internet www.style.ca; f. 1888; monthly; fashion and clothing trade; Publr ROD MORRIS; Editor LESLIE WU; circ. 12,000.

Style at Home: 25 Sheppard Ave West, Suite 100, Toronto, ON M2N 6S7; tel. (416) 733-7600; fax (416) 218-3632; e-mail letters@styleathome.com; internet www.styleathome.com; f. 1997; 12 a year; Editor GAIL JOHNSTON HABS; circ. 231,023.

Sympatico Netlife: 25 Sheppard Ave West, Suite 100, North York, ON M2N 6S7; tel. (416) 733-7600; fax (416) 733-8272; e-mail giffen@sympatico.ca; internet www.ab.sympatico.ca/mags/netlife; 6 a year; computer technology; Man. Editor THERESA DILLON; Editor PETER GIFFEN; circ. 450,000.

Toronto Life Magazine: 111 Queen St East, Suite 320, Toronto, ON M5C 1S2; tel. (416) 364-3333; fax (416) 861-1169; e-mail editorial@torontolife.com; internet www.torontolife.com; f. 1966; monthly; Publr MARINA GLOGOVAC; Editor JOHN MACFARLANE; circ. 92,269.

Tribute Magazine: 71 Barber Greene Rd, Don Mills, Toronto, ON M3C 2A2; tel. (416) 445-0544; fax (416) 445-2894; e-mail sstewart@tribute.ca; internet www.tribute.ca; f. 1981; 9 a year; entertainment; Editor-in-Chief SANDRA I. STEWART; circ. 500,000.

TV Guide: POB 815, Markham Station, Markham ON L3P 7Z7; tel. (416) 733-7600; fax (416) 733-3632; e-mail tvguide@indas.on.ca; internet www.tvguide.ca; f. 1976; weekly; Editor CHRISTOPHER LOUDON; circ. 243,695.

TV Times: 1605 Main St West, Hamilton, ON L8S 1E6; tel. (289) 396-2070; fax (289) 396-2011; e-mail tvtimes@canwest.com; internet www.canada.com/entertainment/television/tvtimes.html; f. 1969; publ. by CanWest MediaWorks Publs Inc; weekly; 10 regional edns; Editor ERIC KOHANIK; circ. 1,941,000.

Québec

L'Actualité: 1200 ave McGill College, bureau 800, Montréal, QC H3B 4G7; tel. (514) 845-2564; fax (514) 845-7503; e-mail redaction@lactualite.rogers.com; internet www.lactualite.com; f. 1976; monthly; current affairs; Pres. MARC BLONDEAU; Editor PAULE BEAUGRAND-CHAMPAGNE; circ. 185,684.

Affaires Plus: 1100 blvd René-Lévesque ouest, 24e étage, Montréal, QC H3B 4X9; tel. (514) 392-9000; fax (514) 392-1586; e-mail daniel.germain@transcontinental.ca; internet www.affairesplus.com; f. 1978; monthly; Editor-in-Chief DANIEL GERMAIN; circ. 87,684.

Le Bulletin des Agriculteurs: 1200 ave McGill College, bureau 800, Montréal, QC H3B 4G7; tel. (514) 845-5141; fax (514) 843-2180; e-mail info@lebulletin.com; internet www.lebulletin.rogers.com; f. 1918; monthly; Editor-in-Chief YVON THÉRIEN; circ. 15,477.

Châtelaine: 1001 blvd de Maisonneuve ouest, bureau 800, Montréal, QC H3A 3E1; tel. (514) 843-2504; fax (514) 843-2185; internet redaction@chatelaine.rogers.com; internet www.chatelaine.qc.ca; f. 1960; monthly; circ. 202,744.

CIM Magazine: 3400 blvd de Maisonneuve ouest, bureau 855, Montréal, QC H3Z 3B8; tel. (514) 939-2710; fax (514) 939-2714; e-mail cim@cim.org; internet www.cim.org; monthly; fmrly *CIM Bulletin*; publ. by the Canadian Inst. of Mining, Metallurgy and Petroleum; Editor HEATHER EDNIE; circ. 10,460.

Il Cittadino Canadese: 5960 Jean-Talon est, bureau 209, Montréal, QC H1S 1M2; tel. (514) 253-2332; fax (514) 253-6574; e-mail journal@cittadinocanadese.com; internet www.cittadinocanadese.com; f. 1941; weekly; Italian; Editor BASILIO GIORDANO; circ. 38,500.

Commerce: 1100 blvd René-Lévesque ouest, 24e étage, Montréal, QC H3B 4X9; tel. (514) 392-9000; fax (514) 392-4726; e-mail commerce@transcontinental.ca; internet www.magazinecommerce.com; f. 1898; monthly; Editor-in-Chief DIANE BÉRARD; circ. 40,135.

Harrowsmith Country Life: 3100 Concorde East Blvd, Suite 213, Laval, QC H7E 2B8; tel. (450) 665-0271; fax (450) 665-2974; e-mail info@harrowsmithcountrylife.ca; internet www.harrowsmithcountrylife.ca; f. 1976; 6 a year; Editor TOM CRUICKSHANK; circ. 126,862.

Le Lundi: 7 chemin Bates, Outremont, QC H2V 1A6; tel. (514) 270-1100; fax (514) 270-5395; f. 1976; weekly; Editor MICHAEL CHOINIÈRE; circ. 25,037.

Le Producteur de Lait Québecois: 555 blvd Roland-Thérrien, Longueuil, QC J4H 3Y9; tel. (450) 679-8483; fax (450) 670-4788; internet www.lait.org/zone3/producteur/index.asp; f. 1980; 10 a year; dairy farming; publ. by Fédération des producteurs de lait du Québec; Publr DANIEL BOULANGER; Editor-in-Chief JEAN VIGNEAULT; circ. 12,000.

Progrès-Dimanche: 1051 blvd Talbot, Chicoutimi, QC G7H 5C1; tel. (418) 545-4474; fax (418) 690-8805; e-mail msimard@lequotidien.com; internet www.cyberpresse.ca/quotidien/progresdimanche; f. 1964; weekly; Editor-in-Chief MICHEL SIMARD; circ. 45,000.

Québec Science: 4388 rue St-Denis, bureau 300, Montréal, QC H2J 2L1; tel. (514) 843-6888; fax (514) 843-4897; e-mail courrier@quebecscience.qc.ca; internet www.quebecscience.qc.ca; internet www.cybersciences.com; f. 1969; 10 a year; Editor-in-Chief RAYMOND LEMIEUX; circ. 32,000.

Reader's Digest: 1100 blvd Réné-Lévesque ouest, Montréal, QC H3B 5H5; tel. (514) 934-0751; fax (514) 940-3637; internet www.readersdigest.ca; f. 1948; monthly; English edn; Editor-in-Chief PETER STOCKLAND; circ. 948,019.

Rénovation Bricolage: 7 chemin Bates, Outremont, QC H2V 4V7; tel. (514) 848-7164; fax (514) 848-0309; e-mail renobrico@tva-publications.com; f. 1976; 9 a year; Publr and Editor CLAUDE LECLERC; Editor-in-Chief VINCENT ROY; circ. 33,588.

Sélection du Reader's Digest: 1100 blvd Réne-Lévesque ouest, Montréal, QC H3B 5H5; tel. (514) 940-0751; fax (514) 940-7340; e-mail manon.sylvain@readersdigest.com; internet www.selection.ca; f. 1947; monthly; Editor ROBERT GOYETTE; circ. 249,843.

La Terre de Chez Nous: 555 blvd Roland-Therrien, Longueuil, QC J4H 3Y9; tel. (450) 679-8483; fax (450) 670-4788; e-mail laterre@laterre.ca; internet www.laterre.ca; f. 1929; weekly; agriculture and forestry; Editor-in-Chief MARC-ALAIN SOUCY; circ. 35,576.

TV Hebdo: 7 chemin Bates, Outremont, QC H2V 4V7; tel. (514) 848-7000; fax (514) 848-7070; e-mail tv@tvhebdo.com; internet www.tvhebdo.com; f. 1960; weekly; Editor-in-Chief JEAN-LOUIS PODLESAK; circ. 119,215.

Saskatchewan

Farm Light & Power: 2230 15th Ave, Regina, SK S4P 1A2; tel. (306) 525-3305; fax (306) 757-1810; f. 1959; monthly; Editor TOM BRADLEY; circ. 71,000.

Western Producer: 2310 Millar Ave, POB 2500, Saskatoon, SK S7K 2C4; tel. (306) 665-3544; fax (306) 934-2401; e-mail newsroom@producer.com; internet www.producer.com; f. 1923; weekly; agriculture; Editor BARB GLEN; circ. 74,000.

Yukon Territory

Yukon News: 211 Wood St, Whitehorse, YT Y1A 2E4; tel. (867) 667-6285; fax (867) 668-3755; e-mail plesniak@yukon-news.com; internet www.yukon-news.com; f. 1960; 3 a week; Editor RICHARD MOSTYN; circ. 8,000.

NEWS AGENCY

The Canadian Press: 36 King St East, Toronto, ON M5C 2L9; tel. (416) 364-0321; fax (416) 364-0207; internet www.cp.org; f. 1917; national news co-operative; 99 newspaper mems; Editor-in-Chief SCOTT WHITE.

PRESS ASSOCIATIONS

Canadian Business Press: 4195 Dundas St West, Suite 346, Toronto, ON M8X 1Y4; tel. (416) 239-1022; fax (416) 239-1076; e-mail admin@cbp.ca; internet www.cbp.ca; f. 1920; Chair. DAVID MCCLUNG; Pres. PHILIP BOYD; 168 mems.

Canadian Community Newspapers Association: 8 Market St, Suite 300, Toronto, ON M5E 1M6; tel. (416) 482-1090; fax (416) 482-1908; e-mail info@ccna.ca; internet www.communitynews.ca; f. 1919; Chair. CAM MCKNIGHT; CEO JOHN HINDS; 7 regional asscns; more than 700 mems.

Canadian Newspaper Association/Association Canadienne des Journaux (CNA/ACJ): 890 Yonge St, Suite 200, Toronto, ON M4W 3P4; tel. (416) 923-3567; fax (416) 923-7206; e-mail info@cna-acj.ca; internet www.cna-acj.ca; f. 1996; Chair. ALAN ALLNUTT; Vice-Chair. CLAUDE GAGNON.

Magazines Canada (The Magazine Asscn of Canada): 425 Adelaide St West, Suite 700, Toronto, ON M5V 3C1; tel. (416) 504-0274; fax (416) 504-0437; internet www.magazinescanada.ca; f. 1973 as the Canadian Magazine Publrs Asscn; present name adopted 2005; represents over 300 of the country's consumer titles; Chair. DEBORAH ROSSER; CEO MARK JAMISON.

CANADA *Directory*

Publishers

Editions d'Acadie: 236 rue St-Georges, Moncton, NB E1C 8N8; tel. (506) 857-8490; fax (506) 855-3130; f. 1972; Gen. Dir Marcel Ouellette.

Thomas Allen and Son Ltd: 390 Steelcase Rd East, Markham, ON L3R 1G2; tel. (416) 475-9126; fax (416) 475-4255; e-mail info@t-allen.com; internet www.thomas-allen.com; f. 1916; Pres. T. J. Allen.

Annick Press Ltd: 15 Patricia Ave, Toronto, ON M2M 1H9; tel. (416) 221-4802; fax (416) 221-8400; e-mail annickpress@annickpress.com; internet www.annickpress.com; f. 1975; children's; Dir Rick Wilks.

Arsenal Pulp Press Book Publishers Ltd: 341 Water St, Suite 200, Vancouver, BC V6B 1B8; tel. (604) 687-4233; fax (604) 687-4283; e-mail info@arsenalpulp.com; internet www.arsenalpulp.com; f. 1982; literary fiction and non-fiction, cultural studies, gay and lesbian; Publr Brian Lam.

Editions Bellarmin: 358 blvd Lebeau, Ville St-Laurent, QC H4N 1R5; tel. (514) 745-4290; fax (514) 745-4299; e-mail editions@fides.qc.ca; internet www.fides.qc.ca; f. 1891; religious, educational, politics, sociology, ethnography, history, sport, leisure; Dir-Gen. Antoine Del Busso.

Black Rose Books: CP 1258, succursale pl. du Parc, Montréal, QC H2X 4A7; tel. (514) 844-4076; fax (514) 849-4797; e-mail info@blackrosebooks.net; internet www.blackrosebooks.net; f. 1969; politics, social studies, humanities; Pres. Jacques Roux.

Borealis Press Ltd: 8 Mohawk Cres., Ottawa, ON K2H 7G6; tel. (613) 829-0150; fax (613) 829-7783; e-mail borealis@istar.ca; internet www.borealispress.com; f. 1972; Canadian fiction and non-fiction, drama, juvenile, poetry; Pres. Frank Tierney.

Breakwater Books: 100 Water St, POB 2188, St John's, NL A1C 6E6; tel. (709) 722-6680; fax (709) 753-0708; e-mail info@breakwater.nf.net; internet www.breakwaterbooks.com; f. 1973; fiction, non-fiction, children's, educational, folklore; Vice-Pres. Rebecca Rose.

Broadview Press: 280 Perry St, Unit 5, POB 1243, Peterborough, ON K9J 7H5; tel. (705) 743-8990; fax (705) 743-8353; e-mail customerservice@broadviewpress.com; internet www.broadviewpress.com; f. 1985; Pres. Don LePan.

Canada Law Book, Inc: 240 Edward St, Aurora, ON L4G 3S9; tel. (905) 841-6472; fax (905) 841-5085; e-mail w.moffatt@canadalawbook.ca; internet www.canadalawbook.ca; f. 1855; law reports, law journals, legal textbooks, etc.; Pres. Stuart Morrison.

Les Editions CEC, Inc: 8101 blvd Métropolitain est, Anjou, Montréal, QC H1J 1J9; tel. (514) 351-6010; fax (514) 351-1845; e-mail ressourceshumaines@ceceditions.com; f. 1956; textbooks; Pres. and Dir-Gen. Christian Jetté.

Chenelière Education: 7001 blvd St-Laurent, Montréal, QC H2S 3E3; tel. (514) 273-1066; fax (514) 276-0324; e-mail chene@dlcmcgrawhill.ca; internet www.cheneliere.ca; textbooks; Pres. Michel de la Chenelière.

Coach House Books: 401 Huron St, Toronto, ON M5S 2G5; tel. (416) 979-2217; fax (416) 977-1158; internet www.chbooks.com; f. 1965; fiction, poetry, drama; Publr Stan Bevington.

Crabtree Publishing Co, Ltd: 616 Welland Ave, St Catharines, ON L2M 5V6; tel. (905) 682-5221; fax (905) 682-7166; e-mail custserv@crabtreebooks.com; internet www.crabtreebooks.com; f. 1978; children's non-fiction; Pres. Peter A. Crabtree; Gen. Man. John Siemens.

Douglas & McIntyre Ltd: 2323 Québec St, Suite 201, Vancouver, BC V5T 4S7; tel. (604) 254-7191; fax (604) 254-9099; e-mail dm@douglas-mcintyre.com; internet www.douglas-mcintyre.com; f. 1964; imprints incl. Greystone Books; general non-fiction, literary fiction; Pres. Scott McIntyre.

The Dundurn Group: 3 Church St, Suite 200, Toronto, ON M5E 1M2; tel. (416) 214-5544; fax (416) 214-5556; e-mail info@dundurn.com; internet www.dundurn.com; f. 1972; drama and performing arts, history, reference, fiction and non-fiction; Pres. Kirk Howard.

Fenn Publishing Co Ltd: 34 Nixon Rd, Bolton, ON L7E 1W2; internet www.hbfenn.com; fiction and non-fiction; Pres. Harold Fenn; Publr C. Jordan Fenn.

Editions Fides: 306 rue Saint-Zotique Est, Montréal QC H2S 1L6; tel. (514) 745-4290; fax (514) 745-4299; e-mail editions@fides.qc.ca; internet www.fides.qc.ca; f. 1937; juvenile, history, theology, textbooks and literature; Dir-Gen. Antoine Del Busso.

Fifth House Publishers Ltd: 1511–1800 4th St, SW Calgary, AB T2S 2S5; tel. (403) 571-5241; fax (403) 571-5232; e-mail charlene@fifthhousepublishers.ca; internet www.fifthhousepublishers.ca; f. 1982; imprint of Fitzhenry & Whiteside Ltd; native, literary and non-fiction; Pres. Sharon Fitzhenry.

Fitzhenry & Whiteside Ltd: 195 Allstate Pkwy, Markham, ON L3R 4T8; tel. (905) 477-9700; e-mail godwit@fitzhenry.ca; internet www.fitzhenry.ca; f. 1966; children's fiction and non-fiction, textbooks, trade, educational, poetry; Pres. Sharon Fitzhenry.

General Publishing Co Ltd: 895 Don Mills Rd, Toronto, ON M3C 1W3; tel. (416) 445-3333; fax (416) 445-5967; f. 1934; fiction, history, biography, children's, general, textbooks.

Grolier Ltd: 12 Banigan Dr., Toronto, ON M4H 1A6; tel. (416) 425-1924; fax (416) 425-4015; internet www.scholasticlibrary.com; f. 1912; division of Scholastic Library Publishing; reference, children's; Gen. Man. Rob Furlonger.

Harcourt Assessment: 55 Horner Ave, Toronto, ON M8Z 4X6; tel. (416) 255-4491; fax (416) 255-1621; internet www.harcourtcanada.com; f. 1922; medical, educational, scholarly; Gen. Man. Scott Pawson.

Harlequin Enterprises Ltd: 225 Duncan Mill Rd, Don Mills, ON M3B 3K9; tel. (416) 445-5860; fax (416) 445-8655; e-mail customer_ecare@harlequin.ca; internet www.eharlequin.com; f. 1949; fiction, paperbacks; Chair. and CEO Donna M. Hayes.

HarperCollins Canada Ltd: 2 Bloor St East, Toronto, ON M4W 1A8; tel. (416) 975-9334; fax (416) 975-5223; internet www.harpercanada.com; f. 1989; trade, bibles, dictionaries, juvenile, paperbacks; Pres. and CEO David Kent.

Editions de l'Hexagone: 1010 rue de la Gauchetière est, Montréal, QC H2L 2N5; tel. (514) 523-1182; fax (514) 282-7530; e-mail vml@sogides.com; internet www.edhexagone.com; f. 1953; literature; Editorial Dir Jean-Yves Soucy.

Institut de Recherches Psychologiques, Inc/Institute of Psychological Research, Inc: 34 rue Fleury ouest, Montréal, QC H3L 1S9; tel. (514) 382-3000; fax (514) 382-3007; e-mail info@i-p-r.ca; internet www.i-p-r.ca; f. 1964; educational and psychological; Adviser Robert Chevrier.

Jesperson Publishing: 100 Water St, 3rd Floor, POB 2188, St John's, NL A1C 6E6; tel. (709) 757-2216; fax (709) 753-0708; e-mail info@jespersonpublishing.nf.net; internet www.jespersonpublishing.ca; f. 1974; educational and trade; Vice-Pres. Rebecca Rose.

Key Porter Books: 70 The Esplanade, 3rd Floor, Toronto, ON M5E 1R2; tel. (416) 862-7777; fax (416) 862-2304; e-mail marnie.ferguson@keyporter.com; internet www.keyporter.com; f. 1979; majority owned by H. B. Fenn and Co Ltd; general trade; Publr and Vice-Pres. Jordan Fenn.

Leméac Editeur: 4609 d'Iberville, 3e étage, Montréal, QC H2H 2L9; tel. (514) 525-5558; fax (514) 524-3145; e-mail lemeac@lemeac.com; f. 1957; literary, academic, general; Gen. Dir Lise P. Bergevin.

Lidec Inc: 4350 ave de l'Hôtel-de-Ville, Montréal, QC H2W 2H5; tel. (514) 843-5991; fax (514) 843-5252; e-mail lidec@lidec.qc.ca; internet www.lidec.qc.ca; f. 1965; educational, textbooks; Pres. Marc-Aimé Guérin.

James Lorimer & Co Ltd: 317 Adelaide St West, Suite 1002, ON M5V 1P9; tel. (416) 362-4762; fax (416) 362-3939; e-mail jlorimer@lorimer.ca; internet www.formac.ca/lorimer; f. 1971; urban and labour studies, children's, general non-fiction; Publr Chris Keen.

McClelland and Stewart Ltd: 75 Sherbourne St, 5th Floor, Toronto, ON M5A 2P9; tel. (416) 598-1114; fax (416) 598-7764; internet www.mcclelland.com; f. 1906; trade and illustrated; Pres. and Publr Doug Pepper; Chair. Avie J. Bennett.

McGill-Queen's University Press: 3430 rue McTavish, Montréal, QC H3A 1X9; tel. (514) 398-3750; fax (514) 398-4333; e-mail info@mcgill.ca; internet www.mqup.ca; f. 1960; scholarly and general interest; Exec. Dir Philip J. Cercone.

McGraw-Hill Ryerson Ltd: 300 Water St, Whitby, ON L1N 9B6; tel. (905) 430-5000; fax (905) 430-5191; internet www.mcgrawhill.ca; f. 1944; general; three divisions: educational publishing, higher education and professional publishing.

Editions du Noroît: CP 156, succursale de Lorimier, Montréal, QC H2H 2N6; tel. (514) 727-0005; fax (514) 723-6660; e-mail lenoroit@lenoroit.com; internet www.lenoroit.com; f. 1971; poetry; Dir Paul Bélanger.

Oberon Press: 145 Spruce St, Suite 205, Ottawa, ON K1R 6P1; tel. and fax (613) 238-3275; e-mail oberon@sympatico.ca; internet www.oberonpress.ca; f. 1966; poetry, fiction and general non-fiction; Pres. Michael Macklem.

Oxford University Press Canada: 70 Wynford Dr., Don Mills, ON M3C 1J9; tel. (416) 441-2941; fax (416) 444-0427; e-mail webmaster.ca@oup.com; internet www.oup.com/ca; f. 1904; general, education, scholarly, Canadiana; Pres. Joanna Gertler.

Pearson Education Canada, Inc: 26 Prince Andrew Pl., Toronto, ON M3C 2T8; tel. (416) 447-5101; fax (416) 443-0948; e-mail webinfo.pubcanada@pearsoned.com; internet www.pearsoned.ca; educational; Pres. Allan Reynolds.

Penguin Group (Canada): 90 Eglinton Ave East, Suite 700, Toronto, ON M4P 2Y3; tel. (416) 925-2249; fax (416) 925-0068;

CANADA

e-mail info@penguin.ca; internet www.penguin.ca; f. 1974; division of Pearson; Pres. ED CARSON; Publr DAVID DAVIDAR.

Pippin Publishing Corpn: POB 242, Don Mills, ON M3C 2S2; tel. (416) 510-2918; fax (416) 510-3359; e-mail jld@pippinpub.com; internet www.pippinpub.com; f. 1995; educational and trade; Pres. JONATHAN LOVAT DICKSON.

Pontifical Institute of Mediaeval Studies: 59 Queen's Park Cres. East, Toronto, ON M5S 2C4; tel. (416) 926-7144; fax (416) 926-7258; e-mail pontifex@chass.utoronto.ca; internet www.pims.ca; f. 1939; scholarly pubs concerning the Middle Ages; Pres. JAMES MCCONICA.

Prentice Hall Canada Inc: 1870 Birchmount Rd, Scarborough, ON M1P 2J7; tel. (416) 293-3621; fax (416) 299-2529; internet www.prenhall.com; f. 1960; trade, textbooks; Pres. BRIAN HEER.

Les Presses de l'Université Laval: Pavillon Maurice-Pollack, bureau 3103, Cité Universitaire, Québec, QC G1K 7P4; tel. (418) 656-2803; fax (418) 656-3305; e-mail presses@pul.ulaval.ca; internet www.pulaval.com; f. 1950; scholarly; Dir-Gen. DENIS DION.

Les Presses de l'Université de Montréal: 306 rue Saint-Zotique Est, Montréal, QC H2S 1L6; tel. (514) 343-6933; fax (514) 343-2232; e-mail pum@umontreal.ca; internet www.pum.umontreal.ca; f. 1962; scholarly and general; Dir-Gen. ANTOINE DEL BUSSO.

Les Presses de l'Université du Québec: Edif. le Delta I, 2875 blvd Laurier, Suite 450, Québec, QC G1V 2M2; tel. (418) 657-4399; fax (418) 657-2096; e-mail puq@puq.uquebec.ca; internet www.puq.ca; f. 1969; scholarly and general; Dir-Gen. CÉLINE FOURNIER.

Random House of Canada Ltd: 1 Toronto St, Unit 300, Toronto, ON M5C 2V6; tel. (416) 364-4449; fax (416) 364-6863; internet www.randomhouse.ca; f. 1944; merged with Doubleday Canada Ltd in 1999; Chair. JOHN NEALE; Pres. and CEO BRAD MARTIN.

Editions du Renouveau Pédagogique, Inc: 5757 rue Cypihot, St-Laurent, QC H4S 1R3; tel. (514) 334-2690; fax (514) 334-4720; e-mail info@erpi.com; internet www.erpi.com; f. 1965; textbooks; Pres. NORMAND CLÉROUX.

Scholastic Canada Ltd: 175 Hillmont Rd, Markham, ON L6C 1Z7; tel. (905) 887-7323; fax (905) 887-3643; e-mail custserv@scholastic.ca; internet www.scholastic.ca; f. 1957; wholly owned subsidiary of Scholastic, Inc; imprints include North Winds Press, Éditions Scholastic; Co-Pres LINDA GOSNELL, IOLE LUCCHESE.

Sélection du Reader's Digest (Canada) Ltée/The Reader's Digest Association (Canada) Ltd: 1125 Stanley St, Montréal, QC H3B 5H5; tel. (514) 940-0751; fax (514) 940-3637; e-mail customer.service@readersdigest.com; internet www.rd.ca; Pres. and CEO ANDREA MARTIN.

Editions du Septentrion: 1300 ave Maguire, Sillery, QC G1T 1Z3; tel. (418) 688-3556; fax (418) 527-4978; e-mail sept@septentrion.qc.ca; internet www.septentrion.qc.ca; f. 1988; history, essays, general; Man. GILLES HERMAN.

Simon & Schuster Canada: 625 Cochrane Dr., Suite 600, Markham, ON L3R 9R9; tel. (905) 943-9942; fax (905) 943-9026; e-mail info@simonandschuster.ca; internet simonsayscanada.com.

Thistledown Press Ltd: 633 Main St, Saskatoon, SK S7H 0J8; tel. (306) 244-1722; fax (306) 244-1762; e-mail editorial@thistledownpress.com; internet www.thistledownpress.com; f. 1975; Canadian fiction, non-fiction and poetry; Publr ALLAN FORRIE.

Thomson Carswell: 1 Corporate Plaza, 2075 Kennedy Rd, Toronto, ON M1T 3V4; tel. (416) 609-8000; fax (416) 298-5094; e-mail carswell.customerrelations@thomson.com; internet www.carswell.com; f. 1864; fmrly Carswell-Thomson Professional Publishing Canada; legal, financial, business; Pres. and CEO DON VAN MEER.

Thomson Nelson: 1120 Birchmount Rd, Scarborough, ON M1K 5G4; tel. (416) 752-9448; fax (416) 752-8101; e-mail inquire@nelson.com; internet www.nelson.com; f. 1914; retailing, consumer affairs, textbooks; Pres. GEORGE W. BERGQUIST.

Thompson Educational Publishing Inc: 20 Ripley Ave, Toronto, ON M6S 3N9; tel. (416) 766-2763; fax (416) 766-0398; e-mail publisher@thompsonbooks.com; internet www.thompsonbooks.com; f. 1989; textbooks; Pres. KEITH THOMPSON.

Turnstone Press Ltd: 100 Arthur St, Suite 607, Winnipeg, MB R3B 1H3; tel. (204) 947-1555; fax (204) 942-1555; internet www.turnstonepress.com; f. 1976; literary and regional; Man. Editor TODD BESANT.

University of Alberta Press (UAP): Ring House 2, Edmonton, AB T6G 2E1; tel. (780) 492-3662; fax (780) 492-0719; e-mail lindacameron@ualberta.ca; internet www.uap.ualberta.ca; f. 1969; scholarly, general non-fiction; Dir LINDA D. CAMERON.

University of British Columbia Press (UBC Press): 2029 West Mall, Vancouver, BC V6T 1Z2; tel. (604) 822-5959; fax (604) 822-6083; e-mail info@ubcpress.ca; internet www.ubcpress.ca; f. 1971; law, politics, history, environmental studies, anthropology, Canadian studies, sociology, military history; Dir R. PETER MILROY.

University of Calgary Press: 2500 University Dr., NW, Calgary, AB T2N 1N4; tel. (403) 220-7578; fax (403) 282-0085; e-mail whildebr@ucalgary.ca; internet www.uofcpress.com; f. 1981; Dir Dr GEOFFREY SIMMINS (acting).

University of Manitoba Press: 301 St John's College, University of Manitoba, Winnipeg, MB R3T 2M5; tel. (204) 474-9495; fax (204) 474-7566; e-mail uofm_press@umanitoba.ca; internet www.umanitoba.ca/uofmpress; f. 1967; native, Arctic and Canadian history; Icelandic and Canadian literature; Dir DAVID CARR; Man. Editor PAT SANDERS.

University of Ottawa Press/Les Presses de l'Université d'Ottawa: 542 King Edward, Ottawa, ON K1N 6N5; tel. (613) 562-5246; fax (613) 562-5247; e-mail press@uottawa.ca; internet www.uopress.uottawa.ca; f. 1936; university texts, scholarly and literary works in English and French; Man. Dir ERIC NELSON.

University of Toronto Press Inc: 10 St Mary St, Suite 700, Toronto, ON M4Y 2W8; tel. (416) 978-2239; fax (416) 978-4738; e-mail publishing@utpress.utoronto.ca; internet www.utpublishing.com; f. 1901; scholarly books and journals; Pres., Publr and CEO JOHN YATES.

John Wiley and Sons Canada Ltd: 6045 Freemont Blvd, Mississauga, ON L5R 4J3; tel. (416) 236-4433; fax (416) 236-8743; e-mail canada@wiley.com; internet ca.wiley.com; f. 1968; general and trade; CEO WILLIAM ZERTER.

Wilfrid Laurier University Press: Wilfrid Laurier University, 75 University Ave West, Waterloo, ON N2L 3C5; tel. (519) 884-0710; fax (519) 725-1399; e-mail brian@press.wlu.ca; internet www.wlupress.wlu.ca; f. 1974; academic and scholarly; Dir BRIAN HENDERSON.

GOVERNMENT PUBLISHING HOUSE

Government of Canada Publications: 350 Albert St, 5th Floor, Ottawa, ON K1A 0S5; tel. (613) 941-5995; fax (613) 954-5779; e-mail publications@pwgsc.gc.ca; internet publications.gc.ca; f. 1876; books and periodicals on numerous subjects, incl. agriculture, economics, environment, geology, history and sociology; Dir CHRISTINE LEDUC.

ORGANIZATIONS AND ASSOCIATIONS

Association of Canadian Publishers: 174 Spadina, Suite 306, Toronto, ON M5T 2C2; tel. (416) 487-6116; fax (416) 487-8815; e-mail admin@canbook.org; internet www.publishers.ca; f. 1976; trade asscn of Canadian-owned English-language book publrs; represents Canadian publishing internationally; 125 mems; Exec. Dir CAROLYN WOOD.

Association of Canadian University Presses/Association des Presses Universitaires Canadiennes: 10 St Mary St, Suite 700, Toronto, ON M4Y 2W8; tel. (416) 978-2239 (ext. 237); fax (416) 978-4738; e-mail clarose@utpress.utoronto.ca; internet www.acup.ca; f. 1965; Pres. LINDA CAMERON.

Canadian Copyright Institute: 192 Spadina Ave, Suite 107, Toronto, ON M5T 2C2; tel. (416) 975-1756; fax (416) 975-1839; e-mail info@thecci.ca; internet www.zvaios.com/cci; 83 mems; Admin. ANNE MCCLELLAND.

Canadian Publishers' Council: 250 Merton St, Suite 203, Toronto, ON M4S 1B1; tel. (416) 322-7011; fax (416) 322-6999; e-mail pubadmin@pubcouncil.ca; internet www.pubcouncil.ca; f. 1910; trade asscn of Canadian-owned publrs and Canadian-incorp. subsidiaries of British and US publrs; 24 mems; Pres. KEVIN HANSON.

Broadcasting and Communications

The 1968 Broadcasting Act established the Canadian Broadcasting Corporation (CBC) as the national, publicly owned, broadcasting service and created the Canadian Radio-Television and Telecommunications Commission (CRTC) as the agency regulating radio, television and cable television. The CRTC was constituted as an independent public body under the 1985 Canadian Radio-Television and Telecommunications Act. The CRTC derives its regulatory authority over broadcasting from the 1991 Broadcasting Act, and over telecommunications from the the 1987 Bell Canada Act and the 1993 Telecommunications Act, and their subsequent amendments.

Many privately owned television and radio stations have affiliation agreements with the CBC and help to distribute the national services. A number of the major private television networks (see below) also have affiliates.

Canadian Broadcasting Corporation/Société Radio Canada (CBC/SRC): 181 Queen St, Ottawa, ON K1P 1K9; tel. (613) 288-6000; fax (613) 724-5707; e-mail liaison@cbc.ca; internet www.cbc.radio-canada.ca; f. 1936; financed mainly by public funds, with supplementary revenue from commercial advertising on CBC Television; eight national radio and television networks, numerous regional stations and affiliates, a digital television channel (Country Canada) and music network (Galaxie); services in French, English, and eight native Canadian languages, incl. Dene and Inuktitut; production facilities and broadcast transmitters in many locations throughout Canada; Pres. and CEO ROBERT RABINOVITCH; Chair. TIMOTHY W. CASGRAIN.

French Networks: 1400 blvd René-Lévesque est, CP 6000, Montréal, QC H3C 3A8; tel. (514) 597-6000; e-mail auditoire@radio-canada.ca; internet www.cbc.radio-canada.ca; Exec. Vice-Pres. SYLVAIN LAFRANCE.

Radio Canada International: 1400 blvd René-Lévesque est, Montréal, QC H2L 2M2; tel. (514) 597-7500; fax 597-7760; e-mail info@rcinet.ca; internet www.rcinet.ca; f. 1945; operates short-wave, satellite and audio internet services; broadcasts in French, English, Spanish, Arabic, Russian, Ukrainian, Mandarin, Cantonese and Portuguese; Exec. Dir JEAN LARIN.

Station A: POB 500, Toronto, ON M5W 1E6; tel. (416) 205-3311; internet www.cbc.radio-canada.ca.

Canadian Radio-Television and Telecommunications Commission (CRTC): Ottawa, ON K1A 0N2; tel. (819) 997-0313; fax (819) 994-0218; internet www.crtc.gc.ca; f. 1968; offices in Dartmouth, Winnipeg and Vancouver; Chair. KONRAD VON FINCKENSTEIN; Vice-Chair. (Broadcasting) MICHAEL ARPIN; Vice-Chair. (Telecommunications) LEONARD KATZ; regulates c. 3,300 radio, television and cable broadcasters and 78 telecommunications carriers.

TELECOMMUNICATIONS
Principal Telecommunications Networks

Bell Aliant Regional Communications Income Fund: 6 South, Maritime Centre, 1505 Barrington St, Halifax, NS B3J 2W3; tel. (902) 487-4609; fax (902) 425-0708; internet bell.aliant.ca; f. 2006 by merger of Aliant and Bell operations; partly owned by Bell Canada and BCE Inc; operates as Aliant in Atlantic Canada and as Bell in central Canada; world-wide communications and information technology solutions; Pres. and CEO STEPHEN WETMORE.

Bell Canada Enterprises Inc (BCE Inc): 1000 rue de la Gauchetière ouest, bureau 3700, Montréal, QC H3B 4Y7; tel. (514) 870-8777; fax (514) 870-4385; e-mail bcecomms@bce.ca; internet www.bce.ca; f. 1880; privatization sale to consortium, led by Ontario Teachers' Pension Plan Board, agreed in Sept. 2007; provides fixed-line and mobile telecommunications, satellite and internet services; Chair. RICHARD J. CURRIE; Pres. and CEO MICHAEL SABIA.

Bell Canada: POB 8716, Station A, Montréal, QC H3C 4R5; e-mail bell.direct@bell.ca; internet www.bell.ca; 80% owned by BCE Inc; holds a monopoly in most of Québec and Ontario; CEO MICHAEL SABIA.

Bell Mobility: 105 rue Hotel de Ville, 5e étage, Hull, QC J8X 4H7; e-mail mobility@bell.ca; internet www.bellmobility.ca; mobile telecommunications; Pres. WADE OOSTERMAN.

Bell West: 111 Fifth Ave, SW, Calgary, AB T2P 3Y6; tel. (403) 410-8600; e-mail customercare@bell.ca; internet www.bell.ca; 100% owned by Bell Canada; Pres. (Western Region) PAUL HEALEY.

Manitoba Telecom Services Inc (MTS): 333 Main St, POB 6666, Winnipeg, MB R3C 3V6; tel. (204) 225-5687; fax (204) 772-6391; internet www.mts.ca; full-service (wireline voice, data, wireless and television services) telecommunications co for Manitoba; national broadband fibre optic network of 24,300 km; Allstream (National) Division serves business customers nationwide; Chair. THOMAS E. STEFANSON; CEO PIERRE BLOUIN.

Northwestel Inc: 301 Lambert St, POB 2727, Whitehorse, YT Y1A 4Y4; tel. (867) 668-5300; fax (867) 668-7079; internet www.nwtel.ca; f. 1979, bought by BCE Inc in 1988; provides fixed-line and mobile telecommunications services to 110,000 customers in Yukon Territory, Northwest Territories, Nunavut Territory and British Columbia; Chair. TERRY MOSEY; Pres. and CEO PAUL FLAHERTY.

Télébec: 555 ave Centrale, Val-d'Or, QC J9P 1P6; e-mail telebec@telebec.com; internet www.telebec.com; f. 1969; owned by Bell Nordiq Group Inc, subsidiary of BCE Inc; mobile telecommunications (Télébec Mobilité) and internet services (Télébec Internet).

Telesat Canada: 1601 Telesat Court, Gloucester, ON K1B 5P4; tel. (613) 748-0123; fax (613) 748-8712; e-mail info@telesat.ca; internet www.telesat.ca; f. 1969 by Act of Parliament; subsidiary of BCE Inc; owns eight satellites and operates a further seven on behalf of customers; carrier and distributor of more than 200 TV signals in North America; provides voice and data transmission services to telecommunication carriers in North and South America and wireless data business networks in Canada and the USA; Pres. and CEO DANIEL S. GOLDBERG.

Glentel: 8501 Commerce Ct, Burnaby, BC V5A 4N3; tel. (604) 415-6500; fax (604) 415-6565; internet www.glentel.com; f. 1963; wireless communications; Chair., Pres. and CEO THOMAS E. SKIDMORE.

Globalstar Canada Co: 115 Matheson Blvd West, Suite 100, Mississauga, ON L5R 3L1; tel. (905) 890-1377; fax (905) 890-2175; e-mail info@globalstar.ca; internet www.globalstar.ca; satellite voice and data communications; Chair. and CEO JAY MONROE.

Primus Telecommunications Canada Inc: 5343 Dundas St West, Suite 400, Etobicoke, ON M9B 6K5; tel. (416) 236-3636; fax (888) 865-1234; e-mail info@primustel.ca; internet www.primustel.ca; f. 1997; long-distance, international and internet services; Pres. and COO EDMUND (TED) CHISLETT.

Rogers Communications Inc: 333 Bloor St East, 9th Floor, Toronto, ON M4W 1G9; tel. (416) 935-8200; internet www.rogers.com; subsidiaries: Rogers Cable and Telecom provides fixed-line telephony, cable and internet services; Rogers Wireless Inc provides wireless and mobile cellular services; Chair. ALAN D. HORN; Pres. and CEO EDWARD S. ROGERS.

Fido: 333 Bloor St East, 10th Floor, Toronto, ON M4W 1G9; e-mail info.communications@fidomobile.ca; internet www.fido.ca; f. 1996; by Microcell Solutions Inc; subsidiary of Rogers Communications Inc since Nov. 2004; Vice-Pres. and Gen. Man. SYLVAIN ROY.

Saskatchewan Telecommunications International (SaskTel): 2121 Saskatchewan Dr., 12th Floor, Regina, SK S4P 3Y2; tel. (306) 777-4509; fax (306) 359-7475; internet www.sasktel.com; f. 1986; provides mobile, satellite and internet services for Saskatchewan; Chair. REGINALD BIRD; Pres. and CEO ROBERT WATSON.

SaskTel Mobility: 446 Second Ave North, Saskatoon, SK S7K 1W8; internet www.sasktel.com.

Sierra Wireless, Inc: 13811 Wireless Way, Richmond, BC V6V 3A4; tel. (604) 231-1100; fax (604) 231-1109; e-mail smyers@sierrawireless.com; internet www.sierrawireless.com; f. 1993; Chair. CHARLES LEVINE; CEO JASON W. COHENOUR.

SR Telecom Inc: 8150 Trans-Canada Hwy, Montréal, QC H4S 1M5; tel. (514) 335-1210; fax (514) 334-7783; e-mail info@srtelecom.com; internet www.srtelecom.com; f. 1981; Chair. PAUL GRISWOLD; Pres. and CEO SERGE FORTIN.

TELUS: TELUS Corpn, TELUS Plaza South, 32nd Floor, 10020 100 St, Edmonton, AB T5J 0N5; tel. (780) 493-6197; e-mail jim.johannsson@telus.com; internet www.telus.com; f. 2001 following merger of TELUS Communications and BC Telecom; Chair. BRIAN A. CANFIELD; Pres. and CEO DARREN ENTWISTLE.

TELUS Mobility: 200 Consilium Pl., Suite 1600, Scarborough, ON M1H 3J3; internet www.telusmobility.com; mobile telecommunications; incorporates Clearnet, QuébecTel and TELUS Mobility West; Acting Pres. and CEO DARREN ENTWISTLE.

TELUS Québec: 9 rue Jules-A.-Brillant, CP 2070, Rimouski, QC G5L 7E4; tel. (514) 977-8766; e-mail sacqt@telus.com; internet www.telusquebec.com; telecommunications for Québec; Pres. KAREN RADFORD.

RADIO

The CBC operates two AM and two FM networks, one each in English and French. The CBC's Northern Service provides both national network programming in English and French, and special local and short-wave programmes, some of which are broadcast in the eight principal languages of the Indian and Inuit peoples. In March 2004 there were 425 outlets for AM radio and 1,573 outlets for FM radio (including private affiliates and rebroadcasters). There were also 76 outlets for Digital Transitional Radio. The CBC radio service, which is virtually free of commercial advertising, is within reach of 99.5% of the population. Radio Canada International, the CBC's overseas short-wave service, broadcasts daily in nine languages and distributes recorded programmes for use world-wide.

TELEVISION

The CBC operates two television networks, one in English and one in French. CBC's Northern Service provides both radio and television service to 98% of the 90,000 inhabitants of northern Québec, the Northwest Territories, Nunavut and the Yukon. Almost 41% of these inhabitants are native Canadians, and programming is provided in Dene and Inuktitut languages as well as English and French. As of March 2004, CBC television was carried on 1,387 outlets. CBC television is available to approximately 99% of the English- and French-speaking population.

Canadian Satellite Communication Inc (Cancom) of Toronto has been licensed since 1981 by the CRTC to conduct a multi-channel television and radio broadcasting operation via satellite for the distribution of CTV programme output, Réseau de Télévision (TVA) and independent television and radio programmes to remote and under-served communities. Cancom also distributes by satellite the programme output of five US television networks. A second satellite broadcaster, Star Choice, was licensed by the CRTC in June 1998. A further satellite broadcaster, Anik F2, was launched in July 2004.

In March 2004 there were 663 licensed cable operators. There are five educational services: TV-Ontario in Ontario and Radio-Québec in Québec operate their own television stations and networks; the Learning and Skills Television of Alberta provides educational programming in that province; the Saskatchewan Communications

CANADA   *Directory*

Network Corporation distributes educational programming in Saskatchewan; and the Open Learning Agency (OLA) provides child and adult education by television in British Columbia.

Aboriginal Peoples Television Network (APTN): 339 Portage Ave, 2nd Floor, Winnipeg, MB R3B 2C3; tel. (204) 947-9331; fax (204) 947-9307; e-mail info@aptn.ca; internet www.aptn.ca; f. 1999; fmrly Television Northern Canada—TVNC; broadcasts in English, French and a number of aboriginal languages; Chair. SHIRLEY ADAMSON; CEO JEAN LaROSE.

Corus Entertainment Inc: 630 Third Ave, SW, Suite 501, Calgary, AB T2P 4L4; tel. (403) 444-4244; fax (403) 444-4242; e-mail investor.relations@corusent.com; internet www.corusent.com; f. 1999; operates 52 radio stations and 17 television channels, including 11 special interest television channels; Pres. and CEO JOHN M. CASSADAY.

W Network: 64 Jefferson Ave, Unit 18, Toronto, ON M6K 3H4; tel. (416) 534-1191; e-mail comments@wnetwork.com; internet www.wnetwork.com; f. 1995 as Women's Television Network; women's network; owned by Corus Entertainment Inc; Gen. Man. WENDY HERMAN.

CTV Television Network: 9 Channel Nine Court, POB 9, Station O, Scarborough, Toronto, ON M4A 2M9; tel. (416) 332-5000; fax (416) 299-2643; e-mail programming@ctv.ca; internet www.ctv.ca; 25 privately owned affiliated stations from coast to coast (including one satellite-to-cable service), with 247 rebroadcasters; covers 99% of English-speaking Canadian TV households; Pres. and CEO IVAN FECAN.

Global Television Network: 81 Barber Greene Rd, Don Mills, ON M3C 2A2; tel. (416) 446-5311; fax (416) 446-5447; internet www.canada.com/globaltv; 11 stations in eight provinces; a subsidiary of CanWest Global Communications Corpn; Pres. GERRY NOBLE.

Knowledge Network: 4355 Mathissi Pl., Burnaby, BC V5G 4S8; tel. (604) 431-3222; fax (604) 431-3387; e-mail knowline@ola.bc.ca; internet www.knowledgenetwork.ca; f. 1981; Pres. and CEO RUDY BUTTIGNOL; Chair. Dr RON BURNETT.

Réseau TVA: CP 170, succursale C, Montréal, QC H2L 4P6; tel. (514) 790-0461; fax (514) 598-6085; internet tva.canoe.com; f. 1960 as Corporation Télé-Métropole; runs the Canoë network; French-language network, with nine stations in Québec and 19 rebroadcasters serving 98% of the province and francophone communities in Ontario and New Brunswick; Pres. and CEO PIERRE DION.

RNC Media Inc: 171 rue Jean-Proulx, Gatineau, QC J8Z 1W5; tel. (819) 770-1040; fax (819) 770-0272; e-mail pbrosseau@rncmedia.ca; internet www.radionord.com; f. 1948 as radio Nord Communications Inc; 16 radio stations and five television stations; Pres. and CEO PIERRE R. BROSSEAU; Man. RAYNALD BRIÈRE.

Rogers Broadcasting Ltd (Rogers Media): 333 Bloor St East, 10th Floor, Toronto, ON M4W 1G9; tel. (416) 935-8200; fax (416) 935-8270; e-mail info@rogers.com; internet www.rogers.com; subsidiary of Rogers Communications Inc; 51 radio stations and eight television channels; Pres. RAEL MERSON.

Shaw Communications Inc: 630 Third Ave, SW, Suite 900, Calgary, AB T2P 4L4; tel. (403) 750-4500; fax (403) 750-4501; internet www.shaw.ca; f. 1966 as Capital Cable Television Co Ltd, present name adopted in 1993; Exec. Chair. J. R. SHAW; CEO JIM SHAW.

Shaw Satellite Services: 2055 Flavelle Blvd, Mississauga, ON L5K 1Z8; tel. (905) 403-2020; fax (905) 403-2022; e-mail gaston.dufour@sjrb.ca; internet www.cancom.ca; fmrly Canadian Satellite Communications Inc (Cancom); renamed as above 2006; a division of Shaw Communications Inc; responsible for providing and managing the distribution of television channels to cable companies via satellite; also operates StarChoice, a Canadian direct broadcast satellite service.

Taqramiut Nipingat Inc: 185 Dorval Ave, Suite 501, Dorval, QC H9S 5J9; tel. (514) 631-1394; fax (514) 631-6258; e-mail cgrenier@taqramiut.qc.ca; internet inuit.pail.ca/taqramiut-nipingat.htm; f. 1975; broadcasts programming in Inuktitut, French and English to Arctic regions of Québec (Nunavik); Pres. GEORGE KAKAYUK; Dir-Gen. CLAUDE GRENIER.

TQS Inc/Cogeco Radio-Télévision Inc: 612 rue St-Jacques, bureau 100, Montréal, QC H3C 5R1; tel. (514) 390-6035; fax (514) 390-6067; e-mail tvpublic@tqs.ca; internet www.tqs.ca; f. 1986 as Télévision Quatre Saisons; 60% owned by COGECO and 40% by CTVglobemedia; French-language; six television stations and one retransmitter in Québec; operates three French television stations in partnership with CTV Television; radio stations in Montréal, Québec City, Trois-Rivières and Sherbrooke; Pres. RENÉ GUIMOND.

TVOntario/TV Français Ontario: 2180 Yonge St, POB 200, Station Q, Toronto, ON M4T 2T1; tel. (416) 484-2600; fax (416) 484-6285; e-mail asktv@tvontario.org; internet www.tvo.org; f. 1970; Chair. PETER O'BRIAN; CEO LISA DE WILDE.

ASSOCIATIONS

Canadian Association of Broadcasters/L'Association canadienne des radiodiffuseurs: 350 Sparks St, Suite 306, Ottawa, ON K1R 7S8; tel. (613) 233-4035; fax (613) 233-6961; e-mail cab@cab-acr.ca; internet www.cab-acr.ca; f. 1926; over 600 mem. broadcasting stations; Pres. and CEO GLENN O'FARRELL; Chair. (Board of Dirs) CHARLOTTE BELL; Chair. (Radio Board) PAUL SKI; Chair. (Television Board) PIERRE LAMPRON.

Canadian Cable Television Association/Assocation canadienne de télévision par câble (CCTA/ACTC): 360 Albert St, Suite 1010, Ottawa, ON K1R 7X7; tel. (613) 232-2631; fax (613) 232-2137; internet www.ccta.com; represents 78 mem. cable cos; provides television services to 7.3m. subscribers and cable high-speed internet access to 2.8m. subscribers; Chair. PETER BISSONNETTE; Pres. MICHAEL HENNESSY.

Radio Advisory Board of Canada/Conseil consultatif canadien de la radio: 811–116 Albert St, Ottawa, ON K1P 5G3; tel. (613) 230-3261; fax (613) 728-3278; e-mail rabc.gm@on.aibn.com; internet www.rabc.ottawa.on.ca; 21 mem. asscns; Gen. Man. ROGER POIRIER.

Television Bureau of Canada: 160 Bloor St East, Suite 1005, Toronto, ON M4W 1B9; tel. (416) 923-8813; fax (416) 413-3879; e-mail tvb@tvb.ca; internet www.tvb.ca; f. 1962; 150 mems; Pres. and CEO THERESA TREUTLER.

Finance

(cap. = capital; auth. = authorized; res = reserves; dep. = deposits; m. = million; brs = branches; amounts in Canadian dollars)

BANKING

Since Confederation in 1867, the federal Government has exercised jurisdiction over banking operations throughout Canada. The Bank Act of 1980 created two categories of banking institution: Schedule I banks, in which no one interest is allowed to own more than 10% of the shares; and Schedule II banks, which are either subsidiaries of foreign financial institutions, or are banks controlled by Canadian non-bank financial institutions.

Major revisions to the Bank Act, the federal Trust and Loans Companies Act, the federal Insurance Companies Act and the Co-operative Credit Associations Act came into force in June 1992. This legislation permits federal financial institutions, with some restrictions, to diversify into each other's markets through subsidiaries. By 1 January 1995, following ratification of the North American Free Trade Agreement (NAFTA) and the enactment of the World Trade Organization Implementation Act, the domestic asset limitations on foreign-owned Schedule II banks in the Canadian market were removed.

In the past, the Bank Act was generally reviewed once every 10 years. As a result of extensive revisions to the federal financial institutions legislation in 1992, a further review of the Bank Act was carried out in 1997. In addition, a Task Force on the Future of the Canadian Financial Services Sector was appointed by the federal Government in 1996 to review the legislative framework of the financial services sector. The report of the Task Force, published in September 1998, recommended the abolition of existing barriers preventing financial institutions from providing unified services in banking, insurance and motor vehicle leasing. It was also proposed that commercial banks and trust companies (see below) be permitted to market all classes of insurance through their branch networks by 2002. The Task Force expressed support for the entry of foreign banks into the commercial loans market, and for the adoption of new regulations for consumer protection. In 1999 the Government adopted legislation permitting foreign banks to establish operations in Canada without their being obliged to establish Canadian-incorporated subsidiaries. Foreign bank branches (known as Schedule III banks) are prohibited from accepting deposits of less than C $150,000. The Bank Act Reform, a series of extensive changes to federal financial institutions, finally entered into effect in October 2001. This provided for much greater flexibility of the financial services system, as recommended by the Task Force, and also included an increase in the maximum level of single ownership in large banks from 10% to 20%, while any one interest was henceforth permitted to control as much as 65% of a medium-sized bank; the minimum amount of capital required to apply for a bank licence was halved to C $5m. In February 2008, according to the Office of the Superintendent of Financial Institutions, the banking industry included 20 domestic banks, 24 foreign bank subsidiaries and 22 full-service foreign bank branches. Although domestic banks continued to dominate the sector, foreign bank institutions increased their share of the financial services market to 8.4% in 2007 (compared with 5.7% in 1997). At August 2007 the combined assets of all banks (excluding foreign subsidiaries) totalled $2,548,219.4m.

Trust and loan companies, which were originally formed to provide mortgage finance and private customer loans, now occupy an import-

CANADA

ant place in the financial system, offering current account facilities and providing access to money transfer services. In February 2008, according to the Office of the Superintendent of Financial Institutions, 48 trust companies and 20 loan companies, which were regulated under the federal Trust and Loan Companies Act, were operating in Canada.

Central Bank

Bank of Canada: 234 Wellington St, Ottawa, ON K1A 0G9; tel. (613) 782-8111; fax (613) 782-8655; e-mail info@bankofcanada.ca; internet www.bankofcanada.ca; f. 1934; bank of issue; cap. and res 30m., dep. 2,981m. (Dec. 2007); Gov. MARK J. CARNEY.

Commercial Banks

Schedule I Banks

Bank of Montréal: 129 rue St-Jacques, Montréal, QC H2Y 1L6; tel. (514) 877-1285; fax (514) 877-6922; internet www.bmo.com; f. 1817; cap. 4,827m., dep. 203,848m. (Oct. 2006); Chair. DAVID A. GALLOWAY; Pres. and CEO WILLIAM DOWNE; 975 brs in Canada, 173 foreign brs.

Bank of Nova Scotia (Scotiabank): Scotia Plaza, 44 King St West, Toronto, ON M5H 1H1; tel. (416) 866-6161; fax (416) 866-3750; e-mail email@scotiabank.ca; internet www.scotiabank.com; f. 1832; acquired NBG Bank Canada (Greece) in Nov. 2005; cap. 4,025m., dep. 263,914m. (Oct. 2006); Chair. ARTHUR R. A. SCACE; Pres. and CEO RICHARD E. WAUGH; 1,272 brs in Canada, 143 foreign brs.

Canadian Imperial Bank of Commerce: Commerce Court, Toronto, ON M5L 1A2; tel. (416) 980-2211; fax (416) 368-8843; internet www.cibc.com; f. 1961 by merger of Canadian Bank of Commerce (f. 1867) and Imperial Bank of Canada (f. 1875); cap. 5,426m., dep. 202,891m. (Oct. 2006); Pres. and CEO GERALD T. McCAUGHEY; 1,061 brs in Canada.

Canadian Western Bank: 10303 Jasper Ave, Suite 2300, Edmonton, AB T5J 3X6; tel. (780) 423-8888; fax (780) 423-8897; internet www.cwbankgroup.com; f. 1988 by merger of the Bank of Alberta and the Western and Pacific Bank of Canada; cap. 215.3m., res 53.5m., dep. 6,297.0m. (Oct. 2006); Chair. JACK C. DONALD; Pres. and CEO LARRY M. POLLOCK; 34 brs.

Laurentian Bank of Canada/Banque Laurentienne du Canada: Laurentian Bank Tower, 1981 ave Collège McGill, Montréal, QC H3A 3K3; tel. (514) 284-4500; fax (514) 284-3396; internet www.laurentianbank.com; f. 1846 as Montreal City and District Savings Bank; name changed as above 1987; cap. 461.2m., dep. 13,094.5m. (Oct. 2006); Chair. DENIS DESAUTELS; Pres. and CEO REJEAN ROBITAILLE; 158 brs.

National Bank of Canada/Banque Nationale du Canada: 600 rue de la Gauchetière ouest, Montréal, QC H3B 4L2; tel. (514) 394-5000; fax (514) 394-8434; internet www.nbc.ca; f. 1859; cap. 1,966m., dep. 71,989m. (Oct. 2006); Chair. LOUIS VACHON; Pres. and CEO RÉAL RAYMOND; 451 brs.

Pacific and Western Bank of Canada: 140 Fullarton St, Suite 2002, London, ON N6A 5P2; tel. (519) 645-1919; fax (519) 645-2060; e-mail tellus@pwbank.com; internet www.pwbank.com; f. 1980 as Pacific and Western Trust Corpn; granted approval to become a Schedule I Bank in 2002 and name changed as above; subsidiary of Pacific and Western Credit Corpn; Pres. and CEO DAVID R. TAYLOR.

Royal Bank of Canada: 1 pl. Ville Marie, Montréal, QC H3C 3B5; tel. (514) 874-2110; fax (514) 974-4472; e-mail banks@rbc.com; internet www.rbc.com; f. 1869; bought RBTT Ltd in 2007; cap. 8,246m., dep. 343,523m. (Oct. 2006); Chair DAVID P. O'BRIEN; CEO GORDON M. NIXON; 1,443 brs.

Toronto-Dominion Bank: Toronto-Dominion Centre, 55 King St West and Bay St, Toronto, ON M5K 1A2; tel. (416) 982-8222; fax (416) 982-5671; e-mail customer.service@td.com; internet www.td.com; f. 1955 by merger of the Bank of Toronto (f. 1855) and the Dominion Bank (f. 1869); acquired Commerce Bancorp Inc in 2007; cap. 6,759m., dep. 260,907m. (Oct. 2006); Chair. JOHN M. THOMPSON; Pres. and CEO W. EDMUND CLARKE; 953 brs.

Principal Schedule II Banks

Amex Bank of Canada (USA): PO Box 7000, Station B, Willodale, ON M2K 2R6; tel. (905) 474-0870; fax (905) 940-7702; internet www.americanexpress.com/canada; f. 1990; Chair., Pres. and CEO DENISE PICKETT.

Bank of China (Canada) (People's Republic of China): Exchange Tower, Suite 2730, 130 King St West, POB 356, Toronto, ON M5X 1E1; tel. (416) 362-2991; fax (416) 362-3047; internet www.bank-of-china.com/canada; f. 1992; cap. 65.2m., dep. 162.1m. (Dec. 2006); Pres. and CEO DASHU ZHU; Chair. ZAOHANG LI.

Bank of Tokyo-Mitsubishi UFJ (Canada) (Japan): Suite 1700, South Tower, Royal Bank Plaza, POB 42, Toronto, ON M5J 2J1; tel. (416) 865-0220; fax (416) 865-9511; f. Jan. 2006 through merger of Bank of Tokyo-Mitsubishi (Canada) (f. 1996) and UFJ Bank Canada (f. 2001); cap. 335.6m., dep. 2,385.0m. (Oct. 2006); Pres. and CEO YOSHIO FURUHASHI.

BNP Paribas (Canada) (France): BNP Tower, 1981 McGill College Ave, Montréal, QC H3A 2W8; tel. (514) 285-6000; fax (514) 285-6278; e-mail bnpp.canada@americas.bnpparibas.com; internet www.bnpparibas.ca; f. 2000 by merger of Banque Nationale de Paris Canada (f. 1961) into Paribas Bank of Canada (f. 1981); cap. 345.6m., dep. 3,604.6m. (Dec. 2006); Chair. JACQUES H. WAHL; Pres. and CEO EDWARD SPEAL.

Citibank Canada (USA): Suite 1000, Citibank Pl., 123 Front St West, Toronto, ON M5J 2M3; tel. (416) 947-5500; fax (416) 947-5628; internet www.citibank.com/canada; f. 1981; subsidiary of Citibank NA (USA); cap. 123.0m., res 17.1m., dep. 6,837.0m. (Dec. 2006); Chair. and CEO KENNETH QUINN; 1 br.

HSBC Bank Canada: 300–885 West Georgia St, Vancouver, BC V6C 3E9; tel. (604) 685-1000; fax (604) 641-1849; e-mail info@hsbc.ca; internet www.hsbc.ca; f. 1981 as Hongkong Bank of Canada; merged with Barclays Bank of Canada in 1996; subsidiary of HSBC Holdings plc (United Kingdom); cap. 1,475m., res. 202m., dep. 44,173m. (Dec. 2006); Chair. MARTIN GLYNN; Pres. and CEO LINDSAY GORDON; c. 127 brs.

Mizuho Corporate Bank (Canada) (Japan): Suite 1102, 100 Yonge St, POB 29, Toronto, ON M5C 2W1; tel. (416) 874-0222; fax (416) 367-3452; f. 1982 following merger of Dai-Ichi Kangyo Bank and Industrial Bank of Japan; name changed as above in 2002; cap. 165.2m., dep. 1,398.3m. (Oct. 2006); Pres. TAKAHIKO UEDA; 1 br.

Société Générale (Canada): 1501 ave Collège McGill, bureau 1800, Montréal, QC H3A 3M8; tel. (514) 841-6000; fax (514) 841-6250; internet www.socgen.com; f. 1981; subsidiary of Société Générale SA (France); cap. 250.8m., res 30.0m., dep. 1,916.8m. (Dec. 2006); Chair. JEAN-JACQUES OGIER; Pres. and CEO EDOUARD-MALO HENRY; 3 brs.

Sumitomo Mitsui Banking Corpn of Canada (Japan): Toronto-Dominion Centre, Suite 1400, 222 Bay St, Toronto, ON M5K 1H6; tel. (416) 368-4766; fax (416) 367-3565; f. 2001 following merger of Sakura Bank and Sumitomo Bank of Canada; cap. 121.9m., dep. 1,410.2m. (Oct. 2006); Chair. TETSUYA KUBO; Pres. MINAMI AIDA.

Development Bank

Business Development Bank of Canada: 5 pl. Ville Marie, Suite 400, Montréal, QC H3B 5E7; tel. (514) 283-5904; fax (514) 283-2872; e-mail info-bdc@bdc.ca; internet www.bdc.ca; f. 1944; fed. govt corpn; auth. shareholders' equity 1,218.5m. (March 2004); Chair. JOHN A. MACNAUGHTON; Pres. and CEO JEAN-RENÉ HALDE; 94 brs.

Principal Trust and Loan Companies

Bank of Nova Scotia Trust Co: Scotia Plaza, 44 King St West, Toronto, ON M5H 1H1; tel. (416) 933-3000; fax (416) 933-3009; internet www.scotiabank.com; assets 878m. (Dec. 1999); Pres. RICHARD E. WAUGH.

Canadian Western Trust Corporation: 600–750 Cambie St, Vancouver, BC V6B 0A2; tel. (604) 685-2081; fax (604) 669–6069; e-mail informationservices@cwt.ca; internet www.cwt.ca/default2.htm; assets 285.0m. (Oct. 1999); Pres. and CEO LARRY M. POLLOCK.

CIBC Mellon: 320 Bay St, 4th Floor, POB 1, Toronto, ON M5H 4A6; tel. (416) 643-5000; e-mail generalinquiries@cibcmellon.com; internet www.cibcmellon.com; f. 1997; privately owned jt venture between CIBC and Mellon Financial; provides custody services (CIBC Mellon Global Securities Services Co) and trust services (CIBC Mellon Trust Co); Pres. and CEO THOMAS C. MACMILLAN.

Home Trust Co: 145 King St West, Suite 1910, Toronto, ON M5H 1J8; tel. (416) 360-4663; fax (416) 360-0401; internet www.hometrust.ca; f. 1977 as Home Savings and Loan Corpn; above name adopted in 2000; Pres. and CEO GERALD M. SOLOWAY.

ResMor Trust Co: 555 Fourth Ave, Suite 400, SW, Calgary, AB T2P 3E7; tel. (403) 539-4920; internet www.resmor.com; f. 1964 as Equisure Trust Co; acquired in 2003 by ResMor Capital Corpn; Pres. and CEO JAMES CLAYTON.

Royal Trust Corporation of Canada: Royal Bank Plaza, 200 Bay St, Toronto, ON M5W 1P9; tel. (416) 974-1400; fax (416) 861-9658; f. 1899; Chair. and CEO GEORGE LEWIS.

TD Canada Trust: Toronto-Dominion Centre, 55 King St West, 12th Floor, POB 1, Toronto, ON M5K 1H6; tel. (416) 982-6744; fax (416) 944-5853; internet www.tdcanadatrust.com; Co-Chairs BERNIE DORVAL, TIM HOCKEY.

Savings Institutions with Provincial Charters

ATB Financial: ATB Pl., 2nd Floor, 9888 Jasper Ave, Edmonton, AB T5J 1P1; tel. (780) 495-0667; fax (780) 422-4998; e-mail apm@atb.com; internet www.atb.com; f. 1938 as Alberta Treasury Branches; name changed as above in 2002; assets 17,600m. (March 2006); Pres. and CEO DAVID MOWAT; 154 brs.

CANADA

Desjardins Credit Union: 1615 Dundas St East, Whitby, ON L1N 2L1; tel. (905) 743-5790; fax (905) 743-6156; e-mail info@dcu.desjardins.com; internet www.desjardins.com/en/dcu; f. 1921, as Province of Ontario Savings Office; acquired by Desjardins Credit Union in 2003; dep. 2,300m. (Jan. 2003); Pres. and COO ALFRED PFEIFFER; 29 brs.

Bankers' Organizations

Canadian Bankers Association: Commerce Court West, Suite 3000, 199 Bay St, Box 348, Toronto, ON M5L 1G2; tel. (416) 362-6092; fax (416) 362-7705; e-mail inform@cba.ca; internet www.cba.ca; f. 1891; Chair. TIM HOCKEY; Pres. and CEO NANCY HUGHES ANTHONY; 51 mems.

Institute of Canadian Bankers: Tour Scotia, 1002 Sherbrooke St West, Suite 1000, Montréal, QC H3A 3M5; tel. (514) 282-9480; e-mail info@icb.org; internet www.icb.org; f. 1967; bought by CSI Global Education in 2007; provides financial training for the banking industry; Exec. Dir MARIE MULDOWNEY.

STOCK EXCHANGES

Bourse de Montréal/Montreal Exchange: Tour de la Bourse, CP 61, 800 sq. Victoria, Montréal, QC H4Z 1A9; tel. (514) 871-2424; fax (514) 871-3568; e-mail info@m-x.ca; internet www.m-x.ca; f. 1874; Chair. JEAN TURMEL; Pres. and CEO LUC BERTRAND; 91 approved participants.

Toronto Stock Exchange (TSX): The Exchange Tower, 130 King St West, Toronto, ON M5X 1J2; tel. (416) 947-4700; fax (416) 947-4662; e-mail info@tsx.com; internet www.tsx.com; f. 1861; volume of trade: 61,277m. shares (valued at some C $833,907m.) in 2004; Chair. WAYNE C. FOX; CEOs RIK PARKHILL, MICHAEL PTASZNIK; 121 mems.

TSX Venture Exchange: Fifth Ave SW, Suite 300, 10th Floor, Calgary, AB T2P 3C4; tel. (403) 218-2800; fax (403) 237-0450; e-mail info@tsx.com; internet www.tsx.ca; f. 1999 by merger of Alberta and Vancouver Stock Exchanges; incorporated Winnipeg Stock Exchange in 2000; acquired by Toronto Stock Exchange (TSX) in 2001; fmrly Canadian Venture Exchange; Pres. LINDA HOHOL; 68 mems.

INSURANCE

Principal Companies

AIG Life Insurance Co of Canada: 60 Yonge St, Toronto, ON M5E 1H5; tel. (416) 596-3900; fax (416) 596-4143; e-mail aiglifecainfo@aig.com; internet www.aiglife.ca; owned by American International Group (AIG) Inc; Pres. and CEO RODNEY O. MARTIN, Jr.

Assumption Life: Assumption Pl. Bldg, 770 Main St, POB 160, Moncton, NB E1C 8L1; tel. (506) 853-6040; e-mail e.business@assomption.ca; internet www.assomption.ca; f. 1903; Chair. PHILIPPE DESROSIERS; Pres. and CEO DENIS LOSIER.

Aviva Canada Inc: 2206 Eglinton Ave East, Scarborough, ON M1L 4S8; tel. (416) 288-1800; internet www.avivacanada.com; f. 1906; fmrly known as CGU Group Canada Ltd following merger of General Accident, Commerical Union and Canadian General Insurance Group in 1999; present name adopted 2003; commercial and personal insurance; Pres. and CEO IGAL M. MAYER.

Blue Cross Life Insurance Co of Canada: 644 Main St, POB 220, Moncton, NB E1C 8L3; tel. (506) 853-1811; fax (506) 853-4646; e-mail cabcpwebmaster@pac.bluecross.ca; internet www.bluecross.ca; life, accident and illness; Pres. and CEO JIM K. GILLIGAN.

The CUMIS Group Ltd: 151 North Service Rd, POB 5065, Burlington, ON L7R 4C2; tel. (905) 632-1221; e-mail customer.service@cumis.com; internet www.cumis.com; owns Cumis General Insurance Co (f. 1980) and Cumis Life Insurance Co (f. 1977); Chair. RUSS FAST; Pres. and CEO KENNETH W. LALONDE.

Desjardins sécurité financière/Desjardins Financial Security: 200 rue des Commandeurs, Lévis, QC G6V 6R2; tel. (418) 833-0529; fax (418) 647-5410; e-mail info@desjardinssecuritefinanciere.com; internet www.dsf-dfs.com; fmrly Assurance-vie Desjardins-Laurentienne, merged with Imperial Life Assurance in 2001; Pres. and CEO FRANÇOIS JOLY.

Dominion of Canada General Insurance Co: 165 University Ave, Toronto, ON M5H 3B9; tel. (416) 362-7231; fax (416) 362-9918; internet www.thedominion.ca; f. 1887; Chair. DUNCAN N. R. JACKMAN.

Empire Life Insurance Co: 259 King St East, Kingston, ON K7L 3A8; tel. (613) 548-1881; fax (613) 920-5868; e-mail buildingempires@empire.ca; internet www.empire.ca; f. 1923; Chair. DUNCAN N. R. JACKMAN; Pres. and CEO LESLIE (LES) C. HERR.

Equitable Life of Canada: 1 Westmount Rd North, POB 1603, Waterloo, ON N2J 4C7; tel. (519) 886-5110; fax (519) 886-5210; e-mail headoffice@equitable.ca; internet www.equitable.ca; f. 1920; Chair. DOUGLAS W. DODDS; Pres. and CEO RONALD E. BEETTAM.

Federation Insurance Co of Canada: 5 pl. Ville Marie, bureau 1400, Montréal, QC H3B 0A8; tel. (514) 875-5790; fax (514) 875-9769; f. 1947; Pres. NOEL WALPOLE.

GCAN Insurance Co: 181 University Ave, Suite 1000, Toronto, ON M5H 3M7; tel. (416) 682-5300; fax (416) 682-9213; internet www.gcan.ca; f. 1955; Pres. and CEO DAVID HUEBEL.

Great-West Life Assurance Co: 100 Osborne St North, POB 6000, Winnipeg, MB R3C 3A5; tel. (204) 946-1190; fax (204) 946-7838; e-mail contactus@gwl.ca; internet www.gwl.ca; f. 1891; owns London Life Insurance Co and Canada Life Assurance Co; Pres. and CEO RAYMOND L. MCFEETORS; COO (Canada) DENIS J. DEVOS.

Industrial Alliance Pacific Life Insurance Co: 2165 Broadway West, POB 5900, Vancouver, BC V6B 5H6; tel. (604) 734-1667; fax (604) 734-8221; e-mail intouch@iaplife.com; internet www.iaplife.com; f. 2000; Pres. GERRY BOUWERS.

ING Bank of Canada: 111 Gordon Baker Rd, Toronto, ON M2H 3R1; tel. (416)497-5157; fax (416) 941-0014; e-mail clientservices@ingdirect.ca; internet www.ingdirect.ca; Chair. ARKADI KUHLMANN; Pres. and CEO JOHANNE BROSSARD.

The Kings Mutual Insurance Co: POB 10, Berwick, NS B0P 1E0; tel. (902) 538-3187; fax (902) 538-7271; e-mail info@kingsmutual.ns.ca; internet www.kingsmutual.ns.ca; f. 1904; Chair. BARRY PHILLIP MAXNER.

Kingsway General Insurance Co: 5310 Explorer Dr., Suite 201, Mississauga, ON L4W 5H8; tel. (905) 629-7888; fax (905) 629-5008; e-mail caxford@kingsway-general.com; internet www.kingsway-general.com; f. 1986; incorporates York Fire and Casualty Insurance Co; Pres. and CEO JOHN L. MCGLYNN.

Manufacturers Life Insurance Co (Manulife): 200 Bloor St East, Toronto, ON M4W 1E5; e-mail manulife_bank@manulife.com; internet www.manulife.ca; f. 1887; acquired Commercial Union Life Assurance Co of Canada in 2001; merged in 2004 with Maritime Life Assurance's holding co, John Hancock Financial Services, creating the Manulife Financial Group; Pres. and CEO DOMINIC D'ALESSANDRO.

MetLife Insurance Ltd: Constitution Sq., 360 Albert St, Suite 1750, Ottawa, ON K1R 7X7; tel. (613) 237-7171; fax (613) 237-7585; internet www.metlife.com; CEO C. ROBERT HENRIKSON.

Optimum General Inc: 425 blvd de Maisonneuve ouest, bureau 1500, Montréal, QC H3A 3G5; tel. (514) 288-8725; fax (514) 288-0760; e-mail rdube@opsa.qc.ca; internet www.optimum-general.com; f. 1969; fmrly the Société National d'Assurance Inc; operates Optimum West Insurance Co, Optimum Insurance Co Inc and Optimum Farm Insurance Co; Chair. GILLES BLONDEAU; Pres. and CEO JEAN-CLAUDE PAGÉ.

Portage Mutual Insurance Co: 749 Saskatchewan Ave East, POB 340, Portage la Prairie, MB R1N 3B8; tel. (204) 857-3415; fax (204) 239-6655; e-mail info@portagemutual.com; internet www.portagemutual.com; f. 1884; Pres. and CEO THOMAS W. MCCARTNEY.

RBC Insurance Co of Canada: West Tower, 6880 Financial Dr., Mississauga, ON L5N 7Y5; internet www.rbcinsurance.com; fmrly Westbury Life; bought Unum Provident Canada and the Canadian operation of Provident Life and Accident Insurance Co in 2004; Pres. and CEO STANLEY W. SEGGIE.

Royal & Sun Alliance Insurance Co of Canada: 10 Wellington St East, Toronto, ON M5E 1L5; tel. (416) 366-7511; fax (416) 367-9869; internet www.royalsunalliance.ca; f. 1851; Pres. and CEO ROWAN SAUNDERS.

Sovereign General Insurance Co: 140 Sovereign Centre, 6700 Macleod Trail, SE, Calgary, AB T2H 0L3; tel. (403) 298-4200; fax (403) 298-4217; internet www.sovereigngeneral.com; f. 1894; COO ROB WESSELING.

Sun Life Financial Canada: 227 King St South, POB 1601, Station Waterloo, ON N2J 4C5; tel. (416) 979-9966; fax (416) 585-9546; e-mail service@sunlife.com; internet www.sunlife.ca; f. 1871; merged with Clarica in 2007; Pres. DEAN CONNOR.

Transamerica Life Canada: 5000 Yonge St, Toronto, ON M2N 7J8; tel. (416) 883-5000; e-mail webmaster.canada@aegoncanada.ca; internet www.transamerica.ca; f. 1927; wholly owned by Aegon NV (Netherlands); Chair., Pres. and CEO PAUL REABURN.

Unity Life of Canada: 100 Milverton Dr., Suite 400, Mississauga, ON L5R 4H1; tel. (905) 219-8000; fax (905) 219-8121; e-mail info@unitylife.ca; internet www.unitylife.ca; f. 1898; originally the Insurance Dept of Subsidiary High Court of the Ancient Order of Foresters, subsequently Toronto Mutual Life Insurance Co. until amalgamation with its subsidiary Western Life Assurance Co in 2002; Pres. and CEO ANTHONY W. POOLE.

Wawanesa Mutual Insurance Co: 191 Broadway, Winnipeg, MB R3C 3P1; tel. (204) 985-3923; fax (204) 942-7724; internet www.wawanesa.com; f. 1896; Pres. and CEO K. E. MCCREA.

Western Life Assurance Co: 717 Portage Ave, 7th Floor, Winnipeg, MB R3G 0M8; tel. (204) 784-6900; fax (204) 783-6913; e-mail

CANADA   *Directory*

info@westernlife.com; internet www.westernlifeassurance.net; f. 1851; fmrly Federated Life Insurance Company of Canada, present name adopted 2005; CEO Bruce Ratzlaff.

Zurich Canada: 400 University Ave, Toronto, ON M5G 1S7; tel. (416) 586-3000; fax (416) 586-2990; internet www.zurichcanada.com; CEO Alister Campbell.

Insurance Organizations

Advocis (Financial Advisors Association of Canada): 350 Bloor St East, 2nd Floor, Toronto, ON M4W 3W8; tel. (416) 444-5251; fax (416) 444-8031; e-mail info@advocis.ca; internet www.advocis.ca; f. 2002 by merger of the Canadian Assen of Insurance and Financial Advisors and Canadian Assen of Financial Planners; fmrly Life Underwriters Assen of Canada (f. 1906); Chair. Theresa Black Hughes; Pres and CEO Steve Howard; c. 12,000 mems.

Assuris: 1 Queen St East, Suite 1600, Toronto, ON M5C 2X9; tel. (416) 359-2001; fax (416) 955-9688; e-mail info@compcorp.ca; internet www.assuris.ca; fmrly Canadian Life and Health Insurance Compensation Corpn (CompCorp), name changed as above in Dec. 2005; total assets $122m. (Dec. 2006); Pres. and CEO Gordon M. Dunning; 190 mems.

Canadian Association of Mutual Insurance Companies: 311 McArthur Ave, Suite 205, Ottawa, ON K1L 6P1; tel. (613) 789-6851; fax (613) 789-7665; e-mail nflafreniere@camic.ca; internet www.camic.ca; Pres. Norman Lafrenière; 99 mems.

Canadian Life and Health Insurance Association Inc: 1 Queen St East, Suite 1700, Toronto, ON M5C 2X9; tel. (416) 777-2221; fax (416) 777-1895; internet www.clhia.ca; f. 1894; Chair. Yvon Charest; 74 mems.

Insurance Brokers Association of Canada: 155 University Ave, Suite 1230, Toronto, ON M5H 3B7; tel. (416) 367-1831; fax (416) 367-3687; e-mail ibac@ibac.ca; internet www.ibac.ca; f. 1921; Chair. Robert J. Kimball; Pres. Larry Kozakevich; 11 mem. asscns.

Insurance Bureau of Canada: 777 Bay St, Suite 2400, POB 121, Toronto, ON M5G 2C8; tel. (416) 362-2031; fax (416) 361-5952; internet www.ibc.ca; f. 1964; Pres. and CEO Mark Yakabuski.

Insurance Institute of Canada: 18 King St East, 6th Floor, Toronto, ON M5C 1C4; tel. (416) 362-8586; fax (416) 362-4239; e-mail genmail@insuranceinstitute.ca; internet www.insuranceinstitute.ca; f. 1952; Pres. Peter Hohman; 35,000 mems.

Chartered Insurance Professionals' Society (CIP Society): 18 King St East, 6th Floor, Toronto, ON M5C 1C4; tel. (416) 362-8586; fax (416) 362-4239; e-mail cips@insuranceinstitute.ca; internet www.insuranceinstitute.ca/cipsociety; a division of the Insurance Institute of Canada; represents c. 15,000 insurance professionals.

LOMA Canada: 1243 Islington Ave, Suite 505, Toronto, ON M8X 1Y9; tel. (416) 234-5661; fax (416) 233-5031; e-mail LOMACanada@loma.org; internet www.loma.org; f. 1924; Life Insurance Institute of Canada renamed LOMA Canada June 2006, following 2002 merger with LOMA; Pres. and CEO Thomas P. Donaldson; Exec. Dir Ross Turney; over 1,200 mem. cos in 84 countries.

Trade and Industry

CHAMBER OF COMMERCE

The Canadian Chamber of Commerce: 360 Albert St, Suite 420, Ottawa, ON K1R 7X7; tel. (613) 238-4000; fax (613) 238-7643; e-mail bzeiler-kligman@chamber.ca; internet www.chamber.ca; f. 1925; part of the Int. Chamber of Commerce, and of the Business and Industry Advisory Cttee to the Organisation for Economic Co-operation and Development (OECD); Chair. Sean Finn; Pres. and CEO Perrin Beatty; 170,000 mems.

INDUSTRIAL AND TRADE ASSOCIATIONS

Canadian Manufacturers and Exporters: 1 Nicholas St, Suite 1500, Ottawa, ON K1N 7B7; tel. (613) 238-8888; fax (613) 563-9218; internet www.cme-mec.ca; f. 1871 as the Ontario Manufacturers' Asscn, later renamed the Canadian Manufacturers' Asscn; merged with the Canadian Exporters' Asscn in 1943 to form the Alliance of Manufacturers and Exporters Canada; present name adopted in 2000; Chair. Larry Barrett; Pres. Jayson Myers; Gen. Man. Jack Radford; 3,500 mems.

Agriculture and Horticulture

Canada Beef Export Federation (Canada Beef): 6715 Eighth St, NE, Suite 235, Calgary, AB T2E 7H7; tel. (403) 274-0005; fax (403) 274-7275; e-mail canada@cbef.com; internet www.cbef.com; f. 1989; Chair. Arno Doerksen.

Canada Grains Council: 220 Portage Ave, Suite 1215, Winnipeg, MB R3C 0A5; tel. (204) 925-2130; fax (204) 925-2132; e-mail office@canadagrainscouncil.ca; internet www.canadagrainscouncil.ca; f. 1969; Chair. Richard Wansbutter; 34 mems.

Canadian Federation of Agriculture/Fédération Canadienne de l'agriculture (CFA/FCA): 75 Albert St, Suite 1101, Ottawa, ON K1P 5E7; tel. (613) 236-3633; fax (613) 236-5749; e-mail info@cfafca.ca; internet www.cfa-fca.ca; f. 1935; Exec. Dir Dr Justin To; 21 mems.

Canadian Horticultural Council: 9 Corvus Ct, Ottawa, ON K2E 7Z4; tel. (613) 226-4880; fax (613) 226-4497; e-mail question@hortcouncil.ca; internet www.hortcouncil.ca; f. 1922; Exec. Vice-Pres. Anne Fowlie.

Canadian Nursery Landscape Association/Association canadienne des pépiniéristes et des paysagistes: 7856 Fifth Line South, RR 4, Stn Main, Milton, ON L9T 2X8; tel. (905) 875-1399; fax (905) 875-1840; e-mail info@canadanursery.com; internet www.canadanursery.com; f. 1922 as the Eastern Canada Nurserymen's Asscn; present name adopted in 1999; Pres. Michael Murray; Exec. Dir Victor Santacruz; 3,200 mems.

Canadian Seed Growers' Association: 240 Catherine St, Suite 202, POB 8455, Ottawa, ON K1G 3T1; tel. (613) 236-0497; fax (613) 563-7855; e-mail seeds@seedgrowers.ca; internet www.seedgrowers.ca; f. 1904; Pres. Ed Lefsrud; Exec. Dir Dale Adolphe; 4,500 mems.

Canadian Wheat Board: 423 Main St, POB 816, Station Main, Winnipeg, MB R3C 2P5; tel. (204) 983-0239; fax (204) 983-3841; e-mail questions@cwb.ca; internet www.cwb.ca; sole marketing agency for western Canadian wheat and barley exports and for domestic sales of grains for human consumption; Chair. Ken Ritter; Pres. Greg Arason (acting).

National Farmers Union (NFU): 2717 Wentz Ave, Saskatoon, SK S7K 4B6; tel. (306) 652-9465; fax (306) 664-6226; e-mail nfu@nfu.ca; internet www.nfu.ca; f. 1969; Pres. Stewart Wells; 10,000 mems.

Union des producteurs agricoles: 555 blvd Roland-Therrien, bureau 100, Longueuil, QC J4H 3Y9; tel. (450) 679-0530; fax (450) 679-5436; e-mail upa@upa.qc.ca; internet www.upa.qc.ca; f. 1924; Pres. Christian Lacasse; 44,000 mems.

Building and Construction

Canadian Construction Association: 75 Albert St, Suite 400, Ottawa, ON K1P 5E7; tel. (613) 236-9455; fax (613) 236-9526; e-mail cca@cca-acc.com; internet www.cca-acc.com; f. 1918; Pres. Michael Atkinson; over 20,000 mems.

Canadian Institute of Steel Construction: 201 Consumers Rd, Suite 300, Willowdale, ON M2J 4G8; tel. (416) 491-4552; fax (416) 491-6461; e-mail info@cisc-icca.ca; internet www.cisc-icca.ca; f. 1930; Chair. Don Oborowsky; Pres. Mike Gilmor; 245 mems.

Canadian Paint and Coatings Association: 170 Laurier Ave West, Suite 1200, Ottawa, ON K1P 5V5; tel. (613) 231-3604; fax (613) 231-4908; e-mail cpca@cdnpaint.org; internet www.cdnpaint.org; f. 1913; Chair. Brian Edwards; 70 mems.

Canadian Precast/Prestressed Concrete Institute (CPCI): 196 Bronson Ave, Suite 100, Ottawa, ON K1R 6H4; tel. (613) 232-2619; fax (613) 232-5139; e-mail info@cpci.ca; internet www.cpci.ca; Pres. John R. Fowler; 26 active, 36 assoc., 12 supporting and 100 professional and student mems.

Ontario Painting Contractors Association: 211 Consumers Rd, Suite 305, Willowdale, ON M2J 4G8; tel. (416) 498-1897; fax (416) 498-6757; e-mail info@ontpca.org; internet www.ontpca.org; f. 1967; Pres. Gilbert Satov; Exec. Dir Andrew Sefton; 100 mems.

Clothing and Textiles

Apparel Quebec/Vêtement Québec (Institut des manufacturiers du vêtement du Québec—IMVQ): 555 rue Chabanel ouest, bureau 801, Montréal, QC H2N 2H8; tel. (514) 382-3846; fax (514) 383-1689; e-mail info@vetementquebec.com; internet www.apparelquebec.com; Dir-Gen. Agar Grinberg.

Canadian Apparel Federation: 124 O'Connor St, Suite 504, Ottawa, ON K1P 5M9; tel. (613) 231-3220; fax (613) 231-2305; e-mail info@apparel.ca; internet www.apparel.ca; f. 1977; Exec. Dir Bob Kirke.

Canadian Textiles Institute: 222 Somerset St West, Suite 500, Ottawa, ON K2P 2G3; tel. (613) 232-7195; fax (613) 232-8722; e-mail cti@textiles.ca; internet www.textiles.ca; f. 1935; Chair. Harvey L. Penner; Pres. Elizabeth Siwicki; 60 mems.

Textile Federation of Canada: c/o CTT, 3000 rue Boullé, St-Hyacinthe, QC J2S 1H9; tel. (450) 778-1870; fax (450) 778-9016; e-mail groupetextile@videotron.ca; Exec. Sec. Stephen Laramee; 1,250 mems.

Electrical and Electronics

Canadian Electrical Contractors' Association (CECA): 170 Attwell Dr., Suite 460, Toronto, ON M9W 5Z5; tel. (416) 675-3226; fax (416) 675-7736; e-mail ceca@ceca.org; internet www.ceca.org; f. 1955; Pres. RICK BRODHURST.

Corporation des maîtres électriciens du Québec/Corporation of Master Electricians of Québec (CMEQ): blvd Décarie, bureau 5925, Montréal, QC H3W 3C9; tel. (514) 738-2184; fax (514) 738-2192; e-mail webmestre@cmeq.org; internet www.cmeq.org; f. 1950; Pres. MICHEL BERGERON.

Electrical Contractors' Association of Alberta (ECCA): 11235 120 St, Edmonton, AB T5G 2X9; tel. (780) 451-2412; fax (780) 455-9815; e-mail ecaa@ecaa.ab.ca; internet www.ecaa.ab.ca; f. 1962; Exec. Dir SHERI MCLEAN; over 400 mems.

Electrical Contractors' Association of British Columbia (ECABC): 3989 Henning Dr., Suite 201, Burnaby, BC V5C 6N5; tel. (604) 294-4123; fax (604) 294-4120; e-mail eca@eca.bc.ca; internet www.eca.bc.ca; f. 1952; Exec. Dir RICHARD CAMPBELL.

Electrical Contractors' Association of New Brunswick, Inc: 850 Prospect St West, POB 322, Fredericton, NB E3B 4Y9; tel. (506) 452-7627; fax (506) 452-1786; e-mail dwe@eca.nb.ca; internet www.eca.nb.ca; Exec. Dir DAVID ELLIS.

Electrical Contractors' Association of Ontario: 170 Attwell Dr., Suite 460, Toronto, ON M9W 5Z5; tel. (416) 675-3226; fax (416) 675-7736; e-mail ecao@ecao.org; internet www.ecao.org; f. 1948; Exec. Vice-Pres. ERYL M. ROBERTS.

Electrical Contractors' Association of Saskatchewan: 1939 Elphinstone St, Regina, SK S4T 3N3; tel. (306) 525-0171; fax (306) 347-8595; e-mail michaelf@scaonline.ca; internet www.ecas.ca; Exec. Dir MICHAEL FOUGERE.

Canadian Electricity Association: see Utilities—Electricity.

Fisheries

Fisheries Council of Canada: 170 Laurier Ave West, Suite 900, Ottawa, ON K1P 5V5; tel. (613) 727-7450; fax (613) 727-7453; e-mail info@fisheriescouncil.org; internet www.fisheriescouncil.ca; f. 1915; Pres. PATRICK MCGUINNESS; six mem. asscns, over 110 mem. cos.

Food and Beverages

Baking Association of Canada: 7895 Tranmere Dr., Mississauga, ON L5S 1V9; tel. (905) 405-0288; fax (905) 405-0993; e-mail info@baking.ca; internet www.baking.ca; f. 1947; Pres. and CEO PAUL HETHERINGTON; 1,400 institutional mems, 200 assoc. mems.

Brewers Association of Canada/L'Association des brasseurs du Canada: 100 Queen St, Suite 650, Ottawa, ON K1P 1J9; tel. (613) 232-9601; fax (613) 232-2283; e-mail info@brewers.ca; internet www.brewers.ca; f. 1943; Chair. MICHAEL DOWNEY; Pres. and CEO IAN FARIS; 15 mems.

Canadian Council of Grocery Distributors: 6455 Jean-Talon East, Suite 402, St-Léonard, QC H1S 3E8; tel. (514) 982-0267; fax (514) 982-0659; internet www.ccgd.ca; f. 1919; Chair. ALEX A. CAMPBELL; Pres. and CEO NICK JENNERY; 69 institutional mems, 115 assoc. mems.

Canadian Association of Sales and Marketing Agencies/Association canadienne des agences en vente et marketing (CASMA/ACAVM): 885 Don Mills Rd, Suite 301, Toronto, ON M3C 1V9; tel. (416) 385-2322; fax (416) 510-8043; e-mail btordoff@casmaonline.ca; internet www.casmaonline.ca; f. 1942; fmrly the Canadian Food Brokers Asscn; mem. of the Asscn of Sales and Marketing Cos Int. (USA); Pres. KEITH BRAY; 70 mems, 60 assoc. mems.

Canadian Meat Council/Conseil des viandes du Canada (CMC/CVC): 955 Green Valley Cres., Suite 305, Ottawa, ON K2C 3V4; tel. (613) 729-3911; fax (613) 729-4997; e-mail info@cmc-cvc.com; internet www.cmc-cvc.com; f. 1919; Pres. BRIAN NILSSON; Exec. Dir JAMES M. LAWS; 45 regular and 60 assoc. mems.

Canadian National Millers' Association: 408 Queen St, Ottawa, ON K1R 5A7; tel. (613) 238-2293; fax (613) 235-5866; e-mail gharrison@canadianmillers.ca; internet www.canadianmillers.ca; f. 1920; Pres. GORDON HARRISON; 17 mems.

Canadian Pork Council/Conseil canadien du porc (CPC/CCP): 75 Albert St, Suite 1101, Ottawa, ON K1P 5E7; tel. (613) 236-9239; fax (613) 236-6658; e-mail info@cpc-ccp.com; internet www.cpc-ccp.com; Pres. CLARE SCHLEGEL; nine mems.

Confectionery Manufacturers Association of Canada/L'Association canadienne des fabricants confiseries (CMAC): 885 Don Mills Rd, Suite 301, Don Mills, ON M3C 1V9; tel. (416) 510-8034; fax (416) 510-8044; e-mail jrowsome@cmaconline.ca; internet www.confectionacanada.com; f. 1919; Pres. JOHN ROWSOME; 70 mems.

Food and Consumer Products of Canada: 885 Don Mills Rd, Suite 301, Don Mills, ON M3C 1V9; tel. (416) 510-8024; fax (416) 510-8043; internet www.fcpc.ca; Chair. MARC GUAY; Pres. and CEO NANCY CROITORU; 150 corporate mems.

Food Processors of Canada: 350 Sparks St, Suite 605, Ottawa, ON K1R 7S8; tel. (613) 722-1000; fax (613) 722-1404; e-mail fpc@foodprocessors.ca; internet www.foodprocessors.ca; f. 1989; fmrly Food Institute of Canada; Pres. CHRISTOPHER KYTE; 200 mems.

Forestry, Lumber and Allied Industries

Canadian Lumbermen's Association/Association canadienne de l'industrie du bois (CLA/ACIB): 2319 St Laurent Blvd, Suite 500, Ottawa, ON K1G 4JB; tel. (613) 233-6205; fax (613) 233-1929; e-mail info@cla-ca.ca; internet www.canadianlumbermen.com; f. 1907; Pres. and Exec. Dir JEAN-FRANÇOIS HOUDE; Chair. JEAN-PAUL LUPIEN; 206 mems.

Canadian Wood Council (CWC/CCB): 99 Bank St, Suite 400, Ottawa, ON K1P 6B9; tel. (613) 747-5544; fax (613) 747-6264; e-mail webmaster@cwc.ca; internet www.cwc.ca; f. 1959; Pres. PAULINE ROCHEFORT; Chair. YVES LAFLAMME; 14 mem. asscns.

Council of Forest Industries (COFI): I Business Bldg, Suite 1501, 700 West Pender St, Pender Pl., Vancouver, BC V6C 1G8; tel. (604) 684-0211; fax (604) 687-4930; e-mail info@cofi.org; internet www.cofi.org; f. 1960; Pres. and CEO JOHN ALLAN; Chair. BLAIR MAYES; 51 mems.

Forest Products Association of Canada/Association des produits forestiers du Canada (FPAC/APFC): 99 Bank St, Suite 410, Ottawa, ON KIP 6B9; tel. (613) 563-1441; fax (613) 563-4720; e-mail ottawa@fpac.ca; internet www.fpac.ca; f. 1913; fmrly the Canadian Pulp and Paper Asscn; Pres. and CEO AVRIM LAZAR; 20 mem. cos.

Ontario Forest Industries Association: 20 Toronto St West, Suite 950, Toronto, ON M5C 2B8; tel. (416) 368-6188; fax (416) 368-5445; e-mail info@ofia.com; internet www.ofia.com; f. 1943; Pres. and CEO JAMIE LIM; 20 mem. cos, 10 affiliate mems.

Hotels and Catering

Canadian Restaurant and Foodservices Association: 316 Bloor St West, Toronto, ON M5S 1W5; tel. (416) 923-8416; fax (416) 923-1450; e-mail info@crfa.ca; internet www.crfa.ca; f. 1944; Chair. ROBERT MCKELVIE; Pres. DOUGLAS NEEDHAM; 14,000 mems.

Hotel Association of Canada: 130 Albert St, Suite 1206, Ottawa, ON K1P 5G4; tel. (613) 237-7149; fax (613) 238-8928; e-mail info@hotelassociation.ca; internet www.hotelassociation.ca; f. 1913; Pres. IRWIN PRINCE; 10 provincial asscns; 28 corp. mems.

Hotel and Restaurant Suppliers Association, Inc/Association des fournisseurs d'hôtels et restaurants, inc: 9300 Henri Bourassa Blvd West, Suite 230, St-Laurent, QC H4S 1L5; tel. (514) 334-5161; fax (514) 334-1279; e-mail info@afhr.com; internet www.afhr.com; f. 1936; CEO VICTOR FRANCOEUR; Gen. Man. RICHARD MAINVILLE.

Mining

Canadian Association of Petroleum Producers (CAPP): 350 Seventh Ave, SW, Suite 2100, Calgary, AB T2P 3N9; tel. (403) 267-1100; fax (403) 261-4622; e-mail communication@capp.ca; internet www.capp.ca; f. 1952; represents the upstream petroleum and natural gas industry; Chair. GORDON J. KERR; Pres. PIERRE ALVAREZ; 150 mems, 125 assoc. mems.

Canadian Gas Association: See Utilities—Gas.

Mining Association of Canada (MAC): 350 Sparks St, Suite 1105, Ottawa, ON K1R 7S8; tel. (613) 233-9391; fax (613) 233-8897; e-mail info@mining.ca; internet www.mining.ca; f. 1935; Chair. PETER R. JONES; Pres. and CEO GORDON R. PEELING; 29 mems, 41 assoc. mems.

Northwest Territories and Nunavut Chamber of Mines: POB 2818, Yellowknife, NT X1A 2R1; tel. (867) 873-5281; fax (867) 920-2145; e-mail nwtmines@ssimicro.com; internet www.miningnorth.com; f. 1967 as Northwest Territories Chamber of Mines; present name adopted in 2000; Pres. LOUIS COVELLO; Gen. Man. MIKE VAYDIK; 600 mems.

Ontario Mining Association: 5775 Yonge St, Suite 520, North York, ON M2M 4J1; tel. (416) 364-9301; fax (416) 364-5986; internet www.oma.on.ca; f. 1920; Pres. CHRIS HODGSON; 55 mems.

Petroleum Services Association of Canada: 800 Sixth Ave, SW, Suite 1150, Calgary, AB T2P 3G3; tel. (403) 264-4195; fax (403) 263-7174; e-mail info@psac.ca; internet www.psac.ca; Chair. FRANK TIRPAK; Pres. and CEO ROGER SOUCY; over 260 mems.

Yukon Chamber of Mines: 3151B Third Ave, Whitehorse, YT Y1A 1G1; tel. (867) 667-2090; fax (867) 668-7127; e-mail info@ycmines.ca; internet www.ycmines.ca; f. 1947; Exec. Officer JOANNE HAINER; 500 mems.

Pharmaceutical

Canada's Research-Based Pharmaceuticals/Les compagnies de recherche pharmaceutique du Canada (Rx & D): 55 Metcalfe St, Suite 1220, Ottawa, ON K1P 6L5; tel. (613) 236-0455; fax (613) 236-6756; e-mail info@canadapharma.org; internet www.canadapharma.org; f. 1914 as Pharmaceutical Mfrs Asscn of Canada; Chair. RONNIE MILLER; Pres. RUSSELL WILLIAMS; c. 50 mems.

Canadian Generic Pharmaceutical Association (CGPA): 4120 Yonge St, Suite 409, Toronto, ON M2P 2B8; tel. (416) 223-2333; fax (416) 223-2425; e-mail info@canadiangenerics.ca; internet www.canadiangenerics.ca; fmrly Canadian Drug Mfrs' Asscn; Pres. JIM KEON; Chair. ALLAN OBERMAN; 18 mems.

Retailing

Retail Council of Canada: 1255 Bay St, Suite 800, Toronto, ON M5R 2A9; tel. (416) 922-6678; fax (416) 922-8011; e-mail mboydbonsu@retailcouncil.org; internet www.retailcouncil.org; f. 1963; Chair. KEVIN LAYDEN; Pres. and CEO DIANE J. BRISEBOIS; c. 9,000 mems.

Retail Merchants' Association of Canada (Ontario) Inc: 10 Milner Business Court, Suite 401, Scarborough, ON M1B 3C6; tel. (416) 293-2100; fax (416) 293-2103; internet www.rmacanada.com; f. 1948; Exec. Dir RALPH MOYAL.

Transport

Air Transport Association of Canada: see Transport—Civil Aviation.

Canadian Institute of Traffic and Transportation: 10 King St East, 4th Floor, Toronto, ON M5C 1C3; tel. (416) 363-5696; fax (416) 363-5698; internet www.citt.ca; f. 1958; Pres. CATHERINE VIGLAS; 2,000 mems.

Canadian Shippers' Council: see Transport—Shipping.

Canadian Trucking Alliance: 324 Somerset St West, Ottawa, ON K2P 0J9; tel. (613) 236-9426; fax (613) 563-2701; e-mail info@cantruck.com; internet www.cantruck.com; f. 1937; CEO DAVID BRADLEY.

Canadian Vehicle Manufacturers' Association: 170 Attwell Dr., Suite 400, Toronto, ON M9W 5Z5; tel. (416) 364-9333; fax (416) 367-3221; e-mail info@cvma.ca; internet www.cvma.ca; f. 1926; Pres. MARK A. NANTAIS; four mems.

Railway Association of Canada: see Transport—Railways.

Shipping Federation of Canada: see Transport—Shipping.

Miscellaneous

Canadian Association of Importers and Exporters (I. E. Canada): 160 Eglinton Ave East, Suite 300, Toronto, ON M4P 3B4; tel. (416) 595-5333; fax (416) 595-8226; e-mail info@iecanada.com; internet www.iecanada.com; f. 1932 as the Canadian Importers and Traders Asscn; name changed as above in 2000; Chair. ISABEL ALEXANDER; Pres. and CEO MARY ANDERSON; 650 mem. cos.

Canadian Printing Industries Association: 75 Albert St, Suite 906, Ottawa, ON K1P 5E7; tel. (613) 236-7208; fax (613) 236-8169; internet www.cpia-aci.ca; Chair. BOB ELLIOTT; Pres. and CEO SEAN MURRAY; 789 mems.

Shipbuilding Association of Canada: 222 Queen St, Ottawa, ON K1P 5V9; tel. (613) 232-7127; fax (613) 238-5519; e-mail pcairns@cfncon.com; internet www.shipbuilding.ca; f. 1995; Chair. ROLLIE WEBB; Pres. PETER CAIRNS; six mems, nine assoc. mems.

UTILITIES

Regulatory Authorities

Alberta Energy and Utilities Board: 640 Fifth Ave, SW, Calgary, AB T2P 3G4; tel. (403) 297-8311; fax (403) 297-8512; e-mail eub.inquiries@eub.ca; internet www.eub.ca; Chair. NEIL McCRANK.

British Columbia Utilities Commission: 900 Howe St, 6th Floor, Box 250, Vancouver, BC V6Z 2N3; tel. (604) 660-4700; fax (604) 660-1102; e-mail commission.secretary@bcuc.com; internet www.bcuc.com; Chair. ROBERT H. HOBBS.

Manitoba Public Utilities Board: 330 Portage Ave, Suite 400, Winnipeg, MB R3C 0C4; tel. (204) 945-2638; fax (204) 945-2643; e-mail publicutilities@gov.mb.ca; internet www.pub.gov.mb.ca; Chair. GRAHAM F. J. LANE.

National Energy Board: 444 Seventh Ave, SW, Calgary, AB T2P 0X8; tel. (403) 292-4800; fax (403) 292-5503; e-mail info@neb-one.gc.ca; internet www.neb-one.gc.ca; f. 1959; federal regulatory agency; Chair. and CEO GAÉTAN CARON; Sec. CLAUDINE DUTIL-BERRY.

New Brunswick Energy and Utilities Board: 15 Market Sq., Suite 1400, POB 5001, Saint John, NB E2L 4Y9; tel. (506) 658-2504; fax (506) 643-7300; e-mail rgorman@pub.nb.ca; internet www.pub.nb.ca; Chair. RAYMOND GORMAN.

Newfoundland and Labrador Board of Commissioners of Public Utilities: POB 21040, St John's, NL A1A 5B2; tel. (709) 726-8600; fax (709) 726-9604; e-mail ito@pub.nl.ca; internet www.pub.nf.ca; Chair. and CEO ROBERT NOSEWORTHY.

Nova Scotia Utility and Review Board: POB 1692, Postal Unit M, Halifax, NS B3J 3S3; tel. (902) 424-4448; fax (902) 424-3919; e-mail uarb.board@gov.ns.ca; internet www.nsuarb.ca; Chair. PETER W. GURNHAM.

Ontario Energy Board: 2300 Yonge St, 27th Floor, POB 2319, Toronto, ON M4P 1E4; tel. (416) 481-1967; fax (416) 440-7656; e-mail webmaster@oeb.gov.on.ca; internet www.oeb.gov.on.ca; Chair. HOWARD I. WETSTON.

Prince Edward Island Regulatory and Appeals Commission: 134 Kent St, Suite 501, POB 577, Charlottetown, PE C1A 7L1; tel. (902) 892-3501; fax (902) 566-4076; internet www.irac.pe.ca; f. 1991 as Public Utilities Commission; regulatory and appeal body for energy, utilities, etc.; Chair. and CEO MAURICE (MOE) RODGERSON; Vice-Chair. BRIAN J. McKENNA.

Québec Electricity and Gas Board (Régie de l'Énergie du Québec): Tour de la Bourse, bureau 2.55, 2e étage, 800 pl. Victoria, CP 001, Montréal, QC H4Z 1A2; tel. (514) 873-2452; fax (514) 873-2070; internet www.regie-energie.qc.ca.

Saskatchewan Municipal Board: 2151 Scarth St, 4th Floor, Regina, SK S4P 3V7; tel. (306) 787-6221; fax (306) 787-1610; internet www.smb.gov.sk.ca; Chair. B. G. McNAMEE.

Electricity

ATCO Electric: 10035 105th St, POB 2426, Edmonton, AB T5J 2V6; internet www.atcoelectric.com; fmrly Alberta Power Ltd; generates and distributes electricity in Alberta.

BC Hydro: 6911 Southpoint Dr., Burnaby, BC V3N 4X8; tel. (604) 224-9376; e-mail bob@bchydro.bc.ca; internet www.bchydro.com; serves 1.5m. customers in British Columbia; Chair. LARRY BELL; Pres. and CEO BOB ELTON.

Canadian Electricity Association, Inc: 350 Sparks St, Suite 907, Ottawa, ON K1R 7S8; tel. (613) 230-9263; fax (613) 230-9326; e-mail info@canelect.ca; internet www.canelect.ca; f. 1891; Pres. and CEO HANS KONOW.

Hydro-Québec: 75 blvd René-Lévesque ouest, Montréal, QC H2Z 1A4; tel. (514) 289-2211; fax (514) 289-3691; e-mail cote.flavie@hydro.qc.ca; internet www.hydro.qc.ca; f. 1944; govt-owned supplier to 3.8m. customer accounts in Québec; sold its largest international interest, HQI Transelec Chile SA, in 2006; Chair. MICHAEL L. TURCOTTE; Pres. and CEO THIERRY VANDAL.

Manitoba Hydro: 820 Taylor Ave, POB 815, Winnipeg, MB R3C 2P4; tel. (204) 474-3311; fax (204) 475-9044; e-mail publicaffairs@hydro.mb.ca; internet www.hydro.mb.ca; Pres. and CEO ROBERT B. BRENNAN.

Newfoundland and Labrador Hydro: Hydro Pl., 500 Columbus Dr., POB 12400, St John's, NL A1B 4K7; tel. (709) 737-1859; fax (709) 737-1816; e-mail hydro@nlh.nl.ca; internet www.nlh.nl.ca; publicly owned electricity wholesaler; Pres. and CEO ED MARTIN.

Northwest Territories Power Corporation: 4 Capital Dr., Hay River, NT X0E 1G2; tel. (867) 874-5200; fax (867) 874-5229; e-mail info@ntpc.com; internet www.ntpc.com; f. 1988; Chair. LEW VOYTILLA; Pres. and CEO LEON COURNEYA.

Nova Scotia Power Inc: POB 910, Halifax, NS B3J 2W5; tel. (902) 428-6230; fax (902) 428-6110; internet www.nspower.ca; fmrly Crown Corpn of Nova Scotia; privatized in 1992; distributes power to over 460,000 customers; utility subsidiary of Emera; CEO RALPH TEDESCO.

Ontario Power Generation, Inc (OPG): 700 University Ave, Suite 1900, Toronto, ON M5G 1X6; tel. (416) 592-2555; fax (416) 971-3691; e-mail webmaster@opg.com; internet www.opg.com; f. 1907 as Ontario Hydro, renamed as above in 1999; Canada's largest utility and main nuclear power producer; generating capacity of 22,000 MW; crown corpn; Pres. and CEO JAMES HANKINSON.

Prince Edward Island Energy Corporation: Jones Bldg, 11 Kent St, 4th Floor, POB 2000, Charlottetown, PE C1A 7N8; tel. (902) 894-0289; fax (902) 894-0290; e-mail dwmacquarrie@gov.pe.ca; internet www.gov.pe.ca/development/ec-info; CEO WAYNE MACQUARRIE.

SaskPower: 2025 Victoria Ave, Regina, SK S4P 0S1; tel. (306) 566-2121; fax (306) 566-3306; internet www.saskpower.com; f. 1930; conventional thermal, and alternative power; distributes power to over 439,000 customers; Pres. and CEO PATRICIA YOUZWA.

Gas

Canadian Gas Association (CGA): 350 Sparks St, Suite 809, Ottawa, ON K1R 7S8; tel. (613) 748-0057; fax (613) 748-9078; e-mail info@cga.ca; internet www.cga.ca; f. 1907; represents the natural gas delivery industry; Chair. RANDY L. JESPERSEN; Pres. and CEO SOPHIE BROCHU; 200 corporate mems.

Ontario Natural Gas Association: 77 Bloor St, Suite 1104, Toronto, ON M5S 1M2; tel. (416) 961-2339; fax (416) 961-1173; e-mail onga@sympatico.ca; Chair. BERNARD JONES.

TransCanada Pipelines Ltd: 111 Fifth Ave, SW, POB 1000, Station M, Calgary, AB T2P 4K5; tel. (403) 267-6100; fax (403) 267-6444; internet www.transcanada.com; production, storage, transmission and sale of natural gas through six subsidiary cos; Pres. and CEO DOUGLAS D. BALDWIN.

Westcoast Energy Inc: 666 Burrard St, Suite 3400, Park Place, Vancouver, BC V6C 3M8; tel. (604) 488-8000; fax (604) 488-8500; internet www.westcoastenergy.com; production, storage, transmission and sale of natural gas through four operating cos in British Columbia, Alberta and Manitoba; Chair. and CEO MICHAEL E. J. PHELPS.

Water

Northwest Territories Water Board: POB 1500, Yellowknife, NT X1A 2R3; tel. (867) 669-2772; fax (867) 669-2719; internet infosource.gc.ca/info_1/NTW-XI-e.html.

Nunavut Water Board: Gjoa Haven, NU X0E 1J0.

Resource Management and Environmental Protection Branch, Nova Scotia Department of Environment and Labour: 5151 Terminal Rd, 5th Floor, POB 2107, Halifax, NS B3J 3B7; tel. (902) 424-2554; fax (902) 424-0503; internet www.gov.ns.ca/enla/rmep.

Saskwater: 111 Fairford St East, 2nd Floor, Suite 200, Moose Jaw, SK S6H 1C8; tel. (306) 694-3098; fax (306) 694-3207; e-mail comm@saskwater.com; internet www.saskwater.com; Chair. MURRAY WESTBY; Pres. STUART KRAMER.

Water Branch, Manitoba Conservation: 200 Saulteaux Cres., POB 11, Winnipeg, MB R3J 3W3; tel. (204) 945-6398; e-mail wsd@gov.mb.ca; internet www.gov.mb.ca/waterstewardship; Minister of Water Stewardship CHRISTINE MELNICK.

Water Resources Branch, Ontario, Ministry of Environment and Energy: 135 St Clair Ave West, 1st Floor, Toronto, ON M4V 1P5; tel. (416) 325-4000; fax (416) 314-7337; e-mail picemail.moe@ontario.ca; internet www.ene.gov.on.ca/en/water/index.php; Dir Dr JAMES ASHMAN.

Water Resources Division, Prince Edward Island Department of the Environment: Jones Bldg, 11 Kent St, POB 2000, Charlottetown, PE C1A 7N8; tel. (902) 368-5000; fax (902) 368-5830; e-mail jjyoung@gov.pe.ca; Dir JIM YOUNG.

Water Resources Management Division, Newfoundland and Labrador Department of Environment and Conservation: Confederation Bldg, West Block, 4th Floor, POB 8700, St John's, NL A1B 4J6; tel. (709) 729-2563; fax (709) 729-0320; e-mail water@gov.nl.ca; internet www.env.gov.nl.ca/env/Env/water_resources.asp; f. 1949; Dir MARTIN GOEBEL.

Water Stewardship Division, British Columbia Ministry of Environment: 10470 152nd St, Surrey BC V3R 0Y3; tel. (604) 582-5200; fax (604) 582-5235; e-mail denise.moreau@gov.bc.ca; internet www.env.gov.bc.ca/wsd; Minister of Environment and Minister Responsible for Water Stewardship and Sustainable Communities BARRY PENNER.

TRADE UNIONS

At the beginning of 2007 there were 4,480,020 union members in Canada, representing 30.3% of the civilian (non-agricultural) labour force. In 2000 29.5% of union members belonged to unions with headquarters in the USA.

In 2007 unions affiliated to the Canadian Labour Congress represented 70.8% of total union membership.

Canadian Labour Congress: 2841 Riverside Dr., Ottawa, ON K1V 8X7; tel. (613) 521-3400; fax (613) 521-4655; e-mail sectreas@clc-ctc.ca; internet www.canadianlabour.ca; f. 1956; Pres. KENNETH V. GEORGETTI; Sec.-Treas. HASSAN YUSSUFF; 3.1m. mems (2006).

Affiliated unions with more than 15,000 members:

Amalgamated Transit Union: 61 International Blvd, Suite 210, Rexdale, ON M9W 6K4; tel. (416) 679-8846; fax (416) 679-9195; e-mail director@atucanada.ca; internet www.atucanada.ca; Dir ROBIN WEST; 25,000 mems (2007).

American Federation of Musicians of the United States and Canada: 75 The Donway West, Suite 1010, Don Mills, ON M3C 2E9; tel. (416) 391-5161; fax (416) 391-5165; e-mail afmcan@afm.org; internet www.afm.org; Vice-Pres. in Canada BOBBY HERRIOT; 15,000 mems (2006).

British Columbia Nurses' Union: 4060 Regent St, Burnaby, BC V5C 6P5; tel. (604) 433-2268; fax (604) 433-7945; internet www.bcnu.org; Pres. DEBRA MCPHERSON; 26,000 mems (2007).

Canadian Union of Postal Workers: 337 Bank St, Ottawa, ON K2P 1Y3; tel. (613) 236-7238; fax (613) 563-7861; e-mail feedback@cupw-sttp.org; internet www.cupw.ca; f. 1965; Nat. Pres. DEBORAH BOURQUE; 54,000 mems (2007).

Canadian Union of Public Employees (CUPE): 21 Florence St, Ottawa, ON K2P 0W6; tel. (613) 237-1590; fax (613) 237-5508; e-mail cupemail@cupe.ca; internet www.cupe.ca; Nat. Pres. PAUL MOIST; 550,000 mems (2006).

Communications, Energy and Paperworkers Union of Canada/Syndicat canadien des communications, de l'energie et du papier (CEP): 301 Laurier Ave West, Ottawa, ON K1P 6M6; tel. (613) 230-5200; fax (613) 230-5801; e-mail info@cep.ca; internet www.cep.ca; Pres. DAVE COLES; 150,000 mems (2006).

International Association of Fire Fighters: 350 Sparks St, Suite 403, Ottawa, ON K1R 7S8; tel. (613) 567-8988; fax (613) 567-8986; e-mail bglanz@iaff.org; internet www.iaff.org; Canadian Dir JIM LEE; 20,000 mems (2008).

International Association of Machinists and Aerospace Workers: 15 Gervais Dr., Suite 707, North York, ON M3C 1Y8; tel. (416) 386-1789; fax (416) 386-0210; e-mail info@iamaw.ca; internet www.iamaw.ca; Gen. Vice-Pres. in Canada DAVE L. RITCHIE; c. 47,000 mems (2007).

International Brotherhood of Electrical Workers: 1450 Meyerside Dr., Suite 300, Mississauga, ON L5T 2N5; tel. (905) 564-5441; fax (905) 564-8114; e-mail ivpd_01@ibew.org; internet www.ibew1st.org; Int. Vice-Pres. PHILLIP FLEMING; 54,780 mems (2005).

International Union of Operating Engineers: 28 Aberdeen St, Kentville, NS B4N 3X9; tel. (902) 678-9950; fax (902) 678-1838; internet www.iuoe.org; Canadian Pres. GARY LYNCH; 36,000 mems (2005).

IWA Canada (Industrial Wood and Allied Workers of Canada): 1285 Pender St, Suite 500, Vancouver, BC V6E 4B2; tel. (604) 683-1117; fax (604) 688-6416; internet www.iwa.ca; f. 1937; Pres. D. C. HAGGARD; 42,500 mems (2005).

Labourers' International Union of North America: 44 Hughson St South, Hamilton, ON L8N 2A7; tel. (905) 522-7177; fax (905) 522-9310; internet www.liuna.org; Canadian Dir and Vice-Pres. ENRICO H. MANCINELLI; 72,500 mems (2005).

National Automobile, Aerospace Transportation and General Workers Union of Canada (CAW–Canada): 205 Placer Court, North York, Willowdale, ON M2H 3H9; tel. (416) 497-4110; fax (416) 495-6559; e-mail caw@caw.ca; internet www.caw.ca; f. 1985; Nat. Pres. BUZZ HARGROVE; 250,000 mems (2006).

National Union of Public and General Employees: 15 Auriga Dr., Nepean, ON K2E 1B7; tel. (613) 228-9800; fax (613) 228-9801; e-mail national@nupge.ca; internet www.nupge.ca; Nat. Pres. JAMES CLANCY; 340,000 mems (2007).

Office and Professional Employees' International Union: 1200 ave Papineau, bureau 250, Montréal, QC H2K 4S6; tel. (514) 522-6511; fax (514) 522-9000; internet www.opeiu.org/canadian.html; Pres. MICHEL LAJEUNESSE; 35,000 mems (2005).

Ontario English Catholic Teachers' Association: 65 St Clair Ave East, Suite 400, Toronto, ON M4T 2Y8; tel. (416) 925-2493; fax (416) 925-7764; internet www.oecta.on.ca; Pres. ELAINE MAC NEIL; 36,000 mems (2007).

Ontario Secondary School Teachers' Federation: 60 Mobile Dr., Toronto, ON M4A 2P3; tel. (416) 751-8300; fax (416) 751-3394; internet www.osstf.on.ca; Pres. EARL MANNERS; 60,000 mems (2007).

Public Service Alliance of Canada: 233 Gilmour St, Ottawa, ON K2P 0P1; tel. (613) 560-4200; fax (613) 567-0385; internet www.psac-afpc.com; f. 1966; Nat. Pres. JOHN GORDON; 186,000 mems (2008).

Service Employees International Union: 75 The Donway West, Suite 810, North York, ON M3C 2E9; tel. (416) 447-2311; fax (416) 447-2428; e-mail stewarts@seiu.ca; internet www.seiu.ca; Int. Canadian Vice-Pres. SHARLEEN STEWART; 95,000 mems (2006).

Teamsters Canada: 2540 Daniel-Johnson, bureau 804, Laval, QC H7T 2S3; tel. (450) 682-5521; fax (450) 681-2244; internet www.teamsters-canada.org; Canadian Pres. ROBERT BOUVIER; 120,000 mems (2006).

UNITE-HERE: 460 Richmond St West, 2nd Floor, Toronto, ON M5V 1Y1; tel. (416) 510-0887; fax (416) 510-0891; e-mail info@unitehere.ca; internet www.unitehere.ca; f. 1995 by merger of Union of Needletrades, Industrial and Textile Employees and Hotel Employees and Restaurant Employees Union; Dirs ALEXANDRA DAGG, NICK WORHAUG; 50,000 mems (2006).

United Association of Journeymen and Apprentices of the Plumbing and Pipe Fitting Industry of the United States and Canada: 1959 152nd St, Suite 316, Surrey, BC V4A 9E3; tel.

(604) 531-0516; fax (604) 531-0547; internet www.ua.org; Vice-Pres. and Canadian Dir MICHEL GRENIER; 39,600 mems (2005).

United Brotherhood of Carpenters and Joiners of America (UBC): 5500 Canotek Rd, Suite 104, Ottawa, ON K1J 1K6; tel. (613) 741-2603; fax (613) 741-4421; e-mail gorc@on.aibn.com; internet www.carpenters.org; Gen. Exec. Bd Mem. JAMES E. SMITH; 53,000 mems (2005).

United Food and Commercial Workers Canada: 61 International Blvd, Suite 300, Rexdale, ON M9W 6K4; tel. (416) 675-1104; fax (416) 675-6919; e-mail ufcw@ufcw.ca; internet www.ufcw.ca; f. 1979; National Pres. WAYNE HANLEY; 240,000 mems (2000).

United Steel, Paper and Forestry, Rubber, Manufacturing, Energy, Allied Industrial and Service Workers International Union (United Steelworkers): 234 Eglinton Ave East, 8th Floor, Toronto, ON M4P 1K7; tel. (416) 487-1571; fax (416) 482-5548; e-mail usw@usw.ca; internet www.usw.ca; f. 1943; Nat. Dir for Canada KEN NEUMANN; 280,000 mems (2007).

Other Central Congresses

Centrale des syndicats du Québec: 9405 rue Sherbrooke est, Montréal, QC H1L 6P3; tel. (514) 356-8888; fax (514) 356-9999; internet www.csq.qc.net; f. 1974; name changed as above in 2000; Pres. RÉJEAN PARENT; 14 affiliated federations, 230 affiliated unions, more than 155,000 mems.

Affiliated union with more than 15,000 mems:

Fédération des syndicats de l'enseignement: 320 rue St-Joseph est, bureau 100, Québec, QC G1K 9E7; tel. (418) 649-8888; fax (418) 649-1914; internet www.fse.qc.net; Pres. JOHANNE FORTIER; 80,000 mems (2006).

Centrale des syndicats démocratiques: 801 4e rue, bureau 300, Québec, QC G1J 2T7; tel. (418) 529-2956; fax (418) 529-6323; e-mail info@csd.qc.ca; internet www.csd.qc.ca; f. 1972; Pres. FRANÇOIS VAUDREUIL; Sec. JEAN-CLAUDE DUFRESNE; 60,000 mems (2004).

Confederation of Canadian Unions: Station B, POB 1117, Ottawa, ON K1P 5R2; tel. (416) 736-5109; fax (416) 736-5519; e-mail ccucsc@ca.inter.net; f. 1969; Pres. JANE GRANT.

Confédération des syndicats nationaux: 1601 ave de Lorimier, Montréal, QC H2K 4M5; tel. (514) 598-2121; fax (514) 598-2052; e-mail csncommunications@csn.qc.ca; internet www.csn.qc.ca; f. 1921; Pres. CLAUDETTE CARBONNEAU; nine federated unions.

Federated unions with more than 15,000 members:

Fédération des employées et employés de services publics inc: 1601 ave de Lorimier, Montréal, QC H2K 4M5; tel. (514) 598-2231; fax (514) 598-2398; internet www.feesp.csn.qc.ca; Pres. GINETTE GUÉRIN; 46,368 mems (2006).

Fédération du commerce inc: 1601 ave de Lorimier, Montréal, QC H2K 4M5; tel. (514) 598-2181; fax (514) 598-2304; internet www.fc.csn.qc.ca; Pres. JEAN LORTIE; 38,000 mems (2005).

Fédération de la métallurgie: 2100 blvd de Maisonneuve est, bureau 204, Montréal, QC H2K 4S1; tel. (514) 529-4937; fax (514) 529-4935; e-mail metallurgie.executif@qc.aira.com; internet www.metallurgiecsn.ca; Pres. ALAIN LAMPRON; 21,500 mems (2005).

Fédération de la santé et des services sociaux: 1601 ave de Lorimier, Montréal, QC H2K 4M5; tel. (514) 598-2210; fax (514) 598-2223; internet www.fsss.qc.ca; Pres. FRANCINE LEVESQUE; 113,385 mems (2006).

Fédération nationale des enseignantes et des enseignants du Québec (FNEEQ): 1601 ave de Lorimier, Montréal, QC H2K 4M5; tel. (514) 598-2241; fax (514) 598-2190; internet www.fneeq.qc.ca; f. 1969; Pres. RONALD CAMERON; 23,500 mems (2006).

The American Federation of Labor and Congress of Industrial Organizations (AFL–CIO), with headquarters in Washington, DC, USA, represented 0.4% of the total union membership in Canada, at the beginning of 1997.

Affiliated union with over 15,000 members:

International Association of Bridge, Structural and Ornamental Iron Workers: 46 County Rd, Suite 4069, RR 3, Maidstone, ON N0R 1K0; tel. (519) 737-7110; fax (519) 737-7113; e-mail mdugallu700@kelcom.igs.net; internet www.ironworkerslocal700.com; Pres. WAYNE MCDONALD; 15,300 mems (2005).

Principal Unaffiliated Unions

Alberta Teachers' Association: 11010 142nd St, NW, Edmonton, AB T5N 2R1; tel. (780) 447-9400; fax (780) 455-6481; e-mail government@ata.ab.ca; internet www.teachers.ab.ca; Pres. FRANK BRUSEKER; Exec. Sec. GORDON R. THOMAS; 39,300 mems (2006).

British Columbia Teachers' Federation: 550 West Sixth Ave, Suite 100, Vancouver, BC V5Z 4P2; tel. (604) 871-2283; fax (604) 871-2294; internet www.bctf.bc.ca; f. 1917; Pres. IRENE LANZINGER; 41,000 mems (2007).

Canadian Telecommunications Employees' Association (CTEA): 1010 de La Gauchetière ouest (pl. du Canada), Suite 360, Montréal, QC H3B 2N2; tel. (514) 861-9963; fax (514) 861-5985; internet www.acet-ctea.com; f. 1943; Pres. BRENDA KNIGHT; 12,000 mems (2007).

Christian Labour Association of Canada (CLAC): 2335 Argentia Rd, Mississauga, ON L5N 5N3; tel. (905) 812-2855; fax (905) 812-5556; e-mail headoffice@clac.ca; internet www.clac.ca; Exec. Dir DICK HEINEN; 43,000 mems (2007).

Elementary Teachers' Federation of Ontario: 480 University Ave, Suite 1000, Toronto, ON M5G 1V2; tel. (416) 962-3836; fax (416) 642-2424; internet www.etfo.on.ca; f. 1998; Pres. DAVID CLEGG; 70,000 mems (2007).

Fédération interprofessionnelle de la santé du Québec: 2050 rue de Bleury, 4e étage, Montréal, QC H3A 2J5; tel. (514) 987-1141; fax (514) 987-7273; e-mail info@fiqsante.qc.ca; internet www.fiqsante.qc.ca; f. 1987; fmrly Fédération des infirmières et d'infirmiers du Québec; Pres. LINA BONAMIE; 56,500 mems (2006).

Ontario Nurses' Association: 85 Grenville St, Suite 400, Toronto, ON M5S 3A2; tel. (416) 964-8833; fax (416) 964-8864; e-mail onamail@ona.org; internet www.ona.org; Pres. LINDA HASLAM-STROUD; 53,000 mems (2007).

Professional Institute of the Public Service of Canada: 250 Tremblay Rd, Ottawa, ON K1G 3J8; tel. (613) 228-6310; fax (613) 228-9048; internet www.pipsc.ca; Pres. MICHÈLE DEMERS; 50,000 mems (2007).

Syndicat de la fonction publique Québec: 5100 blvd des Gradins, Québec, QC G2J 1N4; tel. (418) 623-2424; fax (418) 623-6109; e-mail communication@sfpq.qc.ca; internet www.sfpq.qc.ca; Gen. Pres. MICHEL SAWYER; 37,000 mems (2007).

United Nurses of Alberta: 10611 98th Ave, Suite 900, Edmonton, AB T5K 2P7; tel. (780) 425-1025; fax (780) 426-2093; e-mail provincialoffice@una.ab.ca; internet www.una.ab.ca; f. 1977; Pres. HEATHER SMITH; 19,280 mems (2005).

Transport

Owing to the size of the country, Canada's economy is particularly dependent upon its transport infrastructure. The St Lawrence Seaway allows ocean-going ships to reach the Great Lakes. In addition to an extensive railway network, the country's transport facilities are being increasingly augmented by new roads, air services and petroleum pipelines. The Trans-Canada Highway forms a main feature of a network of more than 900,000 km of roads and highways.

Canadian Transportation Agency (CTA): Ottawa, ON K1A 0N9; tel. (819) 994-0775; fax (819) 997-6727; e-mail cta.comment@cta-otc.gc.ca; internet www.cta.gc.ca; f. 1996 to replace the Nat. Transportation Agency; oversees the economic regulation of transport under federal jurisdiction; Chair. GEOFFREY C. HARE.

RAILWAYS

Canadian Pacific Railway Ltd (CPR): Gulf Canada Sq., 401 Ninth Ave, SW, Suite 500, Calgary, AB T2P 4Z4; tel. (403) 319-7000; e-mail ed_greenberg@cpr.ca; internet www.cpr.ca; f. 1881; 26,208 km (16,300 miles) of mainline track in Canada and the north-east and mid-west of the USA; Chair. JOHN E. CLEGHORN; Pres. and CEO FRED J. GREEN.

Ontario Northland Transportation Commission: 555 Oak St East, North Bay, ON P1B 8L3; tel. (705) 472-4500; fax (705) 476-5598; internet www.ontc.on.ca; agency of the Govt of Ontario; operates rail services over 1,120 km (696 miles) of track; Commr and Chair. TED HARGREAVES; Pres. and CEO STEVE CARMICHAEL.

VIA Rail Canada Inc: Station A, POB 8116, Montréal, QC H3C 3N3; tel. (514) 871-6000; fax (514) 871-6104; e-mail customer_relations@viarail.ca; internet www.viarail.ca; f. 1978; federal govt corpn; proposed transfer to private sector postponed Oct. 2007; operates passenger services over rail routes covering 13,822 km of track throughout Canada; Chair. DONALD A. WRIGHT; Pres. and CEO PAUL CÔTÉ.

Association

Railway Association of Canada: 99 Bank St, Suite 1401, Ottawa, ON K1P 6B9; tel. (613) 567-8591; fax (613) 567-6726; e-mail rac@railcan.ca; internet www.railcan.ca; f. 1917; Pres. and CEO CLIFF MACKAY; 60 mems.

ROADS

Provincial governments are responsible for roads within their boundaries. The federal Government is responsible for major roads in the Yukon, the Northwest Territories and Nunavut and in National Parks. In 2004 there were an estimated 1,408,800 km of roads (including 16,900 km of freeways and 200,400 km of highways). The Trans-Canada Highway extends from St John's, NL, to Victoria, BC.

INLAND WATERWAYS

The St Lawrence River and the Great Lakes provide Canada and the USA with a system of inland waterways extending from the Atlantic Ocean to the western end of Lake Superior, a distance of 3,769 km (2,342 miles). There is a 10.7-m (35-foot) navigation channel from Montréal to the sea and an 8.25-m (27-foot) channel from Montréal to Lake Erie. The St Lawrence Seaway (see below), which was opened in 1959, was initiated partly to provide a deep waterway and partly to satisfy the increasing demand for electric power. Power development has been undertaken by the provinces of Québec and Ontario, and by New York State. The navigation facilities and conditions are within the jurisdiction of the federal governments of the USA and Canada.

St Lawrence River and Great Lakes Shipping

St Lawrence Seaway Management Corpn: 202 Pitt St, Cornwall, ON K6J 3P7; tel. (613) 932-5170; fax (613) 932-7286; e-mail marketing@seaway.ca; internet www.greatlakes-seaway.com; f. 1998; responsible for management of the St Lawrence Seaway (f. 1959) allowing ocean-going vessels to enter the Great Lakes of North America; operated jtly with the USA; 47.2m. metric tons of freight in 2006; Chair. GUY C. VÉRONNEAU; Pres. and CEO RICHARD CORFE.

Algoma Central Corpn: 62 Church St, Suite 600, St Catharines, ON L2R 3C4; tel. (905) 687-7888; fax (905) 687-7882; internet www.algonet.com; f. 1899; Pres. and CEO T. S. DOOL; 24 bulk cargo vessels.

Canada Steamship Lines Inc (CSL Group): 759 square Victoria, Montréal, QC H2Y 2K3; tel. (514) 982-3800; fax (514) 982-3802; internet www.csl.ca; f. 1913; Pres. GERALD CARTER; 14 vessels.

SHIPPING

At 31 December 2006 the Canadian merchant fleet comprised 936 vessels, with a total displacement of 2,787,764 grt.

British Columbia Ferry Services Inc. (BC Ferries): 1112 Fort St, Victoria, BC V8V 4V2; tel. (250) 381-1401; fax (250) 381-5452; e-mail investor.relations@bcferries.com; internet www.bcferries.com; 36 passenger and car ferries; Chair. ELIZABETH HARRISON; Pres. and CEO DAVID HAHN.

Fednav Ltd: 1000 rue de la Gauchetière ouest, Montréal, QC H3B 4W5; tel. (514) 878-6500; fax (514) 878-6642; e-mail info@fednav.com; internet www.fednav.com; f. 1944; shipowners, operators, contractors, terminal operators; owned and chartered fleet of 85 vessels; Pres. LAURENCE PATHY.

Groupe Desgagnés Inc: 21 rue du Marché-Champlain, bureau 100, Québec, QC G1K 8Z8; tel. (418) 692-1000; fax (418) 692-6044; e-mail info@desgagnes.com; internet www.desgagnes.com; f. 1866; private co; 16 vessels; Chair. and CEO LOUIS-MARIE BEAULIEU.

Marine Atlantic Inc: 10 Fort William Pl., Suite 802, Baine Johnston Centre, St John's, NL A1C 1K4; tel. (709) 772-8957; fax (709) 772-8956; e-mail info@marine-atlantic.ca; internet www.marine-atlantic.ca; serves Atlantic coast of Canada; four vessels, incl. passenger, roll-on/roll-off and freight ferries; 405,336 passengers in 2006; Chair. ROB CROSBIE; Pres. and CEO ROGER FLOOD.

Associations

Canadian Shipowners Association (CSA): 350 Sparks St, Suite 705, Ottawa, ON K1R 7S8; tel. (613) 232-3539; fax (613) 232-6211; e-mail morrison@shipowners.ca; internet www.shipowners.ca; f. 1953; Pres. DONALD N. MORRISON; seven mem. cos.

Shipping Federation of Canada: 300 rue du St-Sacrement, bureau 326, Montréal, QC H27 1X4; tel. (514) 849-2325; fax (514) 849-8774; e-mail info@shipfed.ca; internet www.shipfed.ca; f. 1903; Chair. PAUL GOURDEAU; Pres. MICHAEL H. BROAD; 71 mems.

CIVIL AVIATION

Principal Company

Air Canada: Air Canada Centre, CP 14000, Dorval, Québec, QC H4Y 1H4; tel. (514) 422-5000; internet www.aircanada.com; f. 1937; fmrly Trans-Canada Air Lines; subsidiary of ACE Aviation Holdings Inc.; acquired Canadian Airlines in Jan. 2001; operates services to 170 cities world-wide; Chair. ROBERT MILTON; Pres. and CEO MONTIE R. BREWER.

Association

Air Transport Association of Canada (ATAC): 255 Albert St, Suite 1100, Ottawa, ON K1P 6A9; tel. (613) 233-7727; fax (613) 230-8648; e-mail atac@atac.ca; internet www.atac.ca; f. 1934 as the Commercial Air Transport and Mfrs' Asscn of Canada; present name adopted in 1962 following withdrawal of industrial mems; mems collectively account for more than 97% of national commercial air transport revenues; Chair. MIKE DOIRON; Pres. and CEO SAM BARONE.

Tourism

Most tourist visitors are from the USA accounting for an estimated 13.9m. of a total 18.1m. visitors in 2006. Receipts from tourism in that year were estimated to total C $16,598m.

Canadian Tourism Commission: Four Bentall Centre, 1055 Dunsmuir St, Suite 1400, Box 49230, Vancouver, BC V5P 1L2; tel. (604) 638-8300; e-mail ctx_feedback@ctc-cct.ca; internet www.canadatourism.com; Chair. CHARLES LAPOINTE; Pres. and CEO MICHELE MCKENZIE.

Tourism Industry Association of Canada: 116 Lisgar St, Suite 600, Ottawa, ON K2P 0C2; tel. (613) 238-3883; fax (613) 238-3878; e-mail info@tiac.travel; internet www.tiac.travel; f. 1931; private-sector asscn, encourages travel to and within Canada; promotes devt of travel services and facilities; Chair. KEN LAMBERT; Pres. and CEO RANDY WILLIAMS.

CAPE VERDE

Introductory Survey

Location, Climate, Language, Religion, Flag, Capital

The Republic of Cape Verde is an archipelago of 10 islands and five islets in the North Atlantic Ocean, about 500 km (300 miles) west of Dakar, Senegal. The country lies in a semi-arid belt, with little rain and an average annual temperature of 24°C (76°F). The official language is Portuguese, of which the locally spoken form is Creole (Crioulo). There were plans to make Crioulo an official language in 2005. Virtually all of the inhabitants profess Christianity, and more than 70% are Roman Catholics. The national flag, adopted in 1992 (proportions 3 by 5), comprises five horizontal stripes: blue (half the depth) at the top, white, red, white (each one-twelfth) and blue. Superimposed, to the left of centre, is a circle of 10 five-pointed gold stars (four on the white stripes and three each on the blue stripes above and below). The capital is Cidade de Praia.

Recent History

The Cape Verde Islands were colonized by the Portuguese in the 15th century. From the 1950s liberation movements in Portugal's African colonies campaigned for independence, and, in this context, the archipelago was linked with the mainland territory of Portuguese Guinea (now Guinea-Bissau) under one nationalist movement, the Partido Africano da Independência do Guiné e Cabo Verde (PAIGC). The independence of Guinea-Bissau was recognized by Portugal in September 1974, but the PAIGC leadership in the Cape Verde Islands decided to pursue its independence claims separately, rather than enter into a federation with Guinea-Bissau. In December 1974 a transitional Government, comprising representatives of the Portuguese Government and the PAIGC, was formed; members of other political parties were excluded. On 30 June 1975 elections for a legislative body, the Assembléia Nacional Popular (ANP—National People's Assembly) were held, in which only PAIGC candidates were allowed to participate. Independence was granted to the Republic of Cape Verde on 5 July 1975, with Aristides Pereira, Secretary-General of the PAIGC, becoming the country's first President. Cape Verde's first Constitution was approved in September 1980.

Although Cape Verde and Guinea-Bissau remained constitutionally separate, the PAIGC supervised the activities of both states. Progress towards the ultimate goal of unification was halted by the November 1980 coup in Guinea-Bissau. The Government of Cape Verde condemned the coup, and in January 1981 the Cape Verdean wing of the PAIGC was renamed the Partido Africano da Independência de Cabo Verde (PAICV). In February Pereira was re-elected as President by the ANP, and all articles concerning an eventual union with Guinea-Bissau were removed from the Constitution. Discussions concerning reconciliation were held in June 1982, however, and diplomatic relations between the two countries were subsequently normalized.

Meanwhile, elections to the ANP took place in December 1985. The candidates on the PAICV-approved list, not all of whom were members of the PAICV, obtained 94.5% of the votes cast. In January 1986 Pereira was re-elected for a further five-year term as President by the ANP. In April 1990 a newly formed political organization, the Movimento para a Democracia (MpD), issued a manifesto in Paris, France, which advocated the immediate introduction of a multi-party system. Pereira subsequently announced that the next presidential election would be held, for the first time, on the basis of universal suffrage.

In July 1990 a special congress of the PAICV reviewed proposals for new party statutes and the abolition of Article 4 of the Constitution, which guaranteed the supremacy of the PAICV. Pereira also resigned as Secretary-General of the PAICV, and was later replaced by the Prime Minister, Gen. Pedro Verona Rodrigues Pires. In September the ANP approved a constitutional amendment abolishing the PAICV's monopoly of power and permitting a multi-party system. The MpD subsequently received official recognition as a political party. On 13 January 1991 the first multi-party elections to take place in lusophone Africa resulted in a decisive victory for the MpD, which secured 56 of the 79 seats in the ANP. Later that month Dr Carlos Alberto Wahnon de Carvalho Veiga, the leader of the MpD, was sworn in as Prime Minister at the head of an interim Government, mostly comprising members of the MpD. The presidential election, held in mid-February, resulted in victory for António Mascarenhas Monteiro, supported by the MpD, who secured 73.5% of the votes cast. The first multi-party local elections, held in December, resulted in another decisive victory for the MpD, which secured control of 10 of the 14 local councils.

On 25 September 1992 a new Constitution of the Republic of Cape Verde (also referred to as the 'Second Republic') came into force, enshrining the principles of multi-party democracy. In August 1993 the opposition PAICV elected Aristides Lima to the post of Secretary-General of the party, replacing Pires, who was appointed party Chairman. At an extraordinary national convention of the MpD, which took place in February 1994, Veiga was re-elected Chairman. However, increasing conflict within the party resulted in some 30 party delegates boycotting the convention. That month Dr Eurico Correia Monteiro, the former Minister of Justice and Labour, announced the establishment of a new political party, the Partido da Convergência Democrática (PCD).

At legislative elections conducted in December 1995 the MpD secured an outright majority, taking 50 of the 72 seats in the Assembléia Nacional (AN, as the ANP had become in 1992). The PAICV won 21 seats, while the remaining seat was obtained by the PCD. At a presidential election conducted in February 1996 Mascarenhas, the sole candidate, was re-elected. However, the turn-out was only 45%. Veiga, meanwhile, expressed his intention to continue the policies of liberal economic and social reform that had been pursued in his previous term in office.

In March 1999 Veiga stated that he would not seek re-election as the Chairman of the MpD at the next party convention. Do Rosário and the Mayor of Praia, Jacinto Santos, subsequently announced their candidacies for the chairmanship of the party, and thus the premiership. In municipal elections held in February 2000 the MpD sustained substantial losses, retaining only eight of 17 local councils and losing the capital to the PAICV, which re-emerged as a credible political force. Following the resignation of Pedro Pires, who announced his candidacy for the presidential election, the PAICV elected José Maria Neves as its new President in June. In the following month do Rosário was elected Chairman of the MpD, and Santos subsequently formed a new political party, the Partido da Renovação Democrática (PRD).

In late July 2000 Veiga announced his resignation as Prime Minister and confirmed his candidacy for the presidential election scheduled to take place in early 2001; he was replaced by do Rosário. In October 2000 it was announced that the PCD, the União Caboverdiana Independente e Democrática and the Partido de Trabalho e Solidariedade were to form a coalition (the Aliança Democrática para a Mudança—ADM) to participate in the forthcoming legislative elections. At the legislative elections, held on 14 January 2001, the opposition PAICV secured 49.5% of the vote and 40 seats in the AN, compared with 40.5% (30 seats) for the MpD and 6.1% (two seats) for the ADM. A new Government, headed by Neves, was announced at the end of January. At the presidential election, conducted on 11 February, no candidate received an overall majority, necessitating a second round, held on 25 February, at which Pires narrowly defeated Veiga, receiving 50.01% of the valid votes cast. Appeals against the result by Veiga, who cited voting irregularities, were later rejected by the Supreme Court, which confirmed Pires as the new President. In December Agostinho Lopes was elected unopposed as the new Chairman of the MpD.

At local elections in March 2004, the MpD secured control of nine of the 17 municipalities, while the ruling PAICV won in only six. A government reshuffle was effected in April, with a new cabinet structure comprising 13 ministers and four secretaries of state. João Pinto Serra became Minister of Finance and Planning, while João Pereira Silva and Júlio Lopes Correia were appointed to the newly created portfolios of Economy, Growth and Competitiveness and Internal Affairs, respectively. In September this structure was amended to 14 ministers and three secretaries of state, with the creation of the Ministry of Social Communication.

At legislative elections, which were held on 22 January 2006, the PAICV won 52.3% of the valid votes cast, thus securing 41 seats in the AN, while the MpD won 44.0% of the votes and took 29 seats. The União Cristã, Independente e Democrática won two seats. The rate of voter participation was recorded at 54.5%. The MpD claimed that it had evidence of irregularities in the voting process and lodged an appeal with the Supreme Court, although international observers declared that the vote had been fair.

Meanwhile, in December 2005 President Pires announced that he would be standing for a second term in the presidential election, which was scheduled to take place on 12 February 2006. Former Prime Minister Veiga, who was supported by the MpD, also indicated his intention to contest the poll. According to final results published on 14 February, Pires secured 50.98% of the valid votes cast, while Veiga received 49.02%. It was notable that the votes of Cape Verdean citizens resident abroad, amounting to some 20% of registered voters, were crucial in ensuring Pires' re-election. An estimated 65% of overseas residents voted for Pires. The new Council of Ministers, again headed by Neves, was appointed on 8 March, with only minor alterations. At the end of that month Agostinho Lopes resigned as leader of the MpD; Jorge Santos was subsequently elected to that position.

In September 2006 the Minister of Finance and Public Administration, João Serra, resigned, owing to ill health, and was replaced by Cristina Duarte. In the following month the PCD voted at its fourth congress to disband—a first such occurrence in the country. In November unrest was caused following a ruling by the Supreme Court that the approval of decrees on value-added tax by the Council of Ministers in the preceding year had been unconstitutional, as they should have been approved by the legislature. Consequently the prices of fuel, electricity, water, telecommunications and transport escalated, owing to the suspension of protection from external price fluctuations, known as cross-subsidization. In November the Minister of the Economy, Growth and Competitiveness, João Pereira Silva, resigned following queries over the legality of certain tourism development contracts; he was succeeded by José Brito, a former ambassador to the USA.

In mid-February 2007 the PAICV and the MpD each nominated seven deputies to a new commission charged with reaching consensus on issues that required a two-thirds majority in the National Assembly, including constitutional reform. Under the remit of the new commission, deputies were to agree on changes to the electoral code, in particular the membership and structure of the Comissão Nacional de Eleições (National Election Commission). A new code was expected to be implemented prior to the municipal elections scheduled to take place in March 2008.

Cape Verde has traditionally professed a non-aligned stance in foreign affairs and maintains relations with virtually all the power blocs. On taking office in 1991, the MpD Government successfully sought to extend Cape Verde's range of international contacts, with special emphasis on potential new sources of development aid; substantial assistance has been received from both Israel and the Gulf states. The MpD Government enlarged the scope of Cape Verde's diplomatic contacts, establishing embassies in South Africa and Sweden, as well as diplomatic presences in Hong Kong, Macao, Singapore, Spain, the United Kingdom and the USA. In July 2001 the new PAICV administration established diplomatic relations at ambassadorial level with the People's Republic of China; as with numerous other African countries, these relations intensified considerably from the mid-2000s. In April 2002 the Government announced its intention to seek a 'special status' for Cape Verde with the European Union (EU), thereby increasing trade and investment, and in November 2003 Prime Minister Neves visited a number of European countries in an attempt to gain support for this aim. In early 2006 it was announced that a joint Cape Verdean-Portuguese working party to promote Cape Verde's bid for 'special status' with regard to the EU was to be created. The country has continued to maintain particularly close relations with Portugal and Brazil, and with other lusophone African former colonies—Angola, Guinea-Bissau, Mozambique and São Tomé and Príncipe, known collectively, with Cape Verde, as the Países Africanos da Língua Oficial Portuguesa (PALOP). In July 1996 a 'lusophone commonwealth', known as the Comunidade dos Países de Língua Portuguesa (CPLP), comprising the five PALOP countries together with Portugal and Brazil, was formed with the intention of benefiting each member state through joint co-operation on technical, cultural and social matters. In December 1996 Cape Verde became a full member of the Sommet francophone, a commonwealth comprising all the French-speaking nations of the world, and benefits in turn from membership of this body's Agence de coopération culturelle et technique.

Government

Under the 1992 Constitution, Cape Verde is a multi-party state, although the formation of parties on a religious or geographical basis is prohibited. Legislative power is vested in the Assembléia Nacional (AN—National Assembly), which comprises 72 deputies, elected by universal adult suffrage for a five-year term. The Head of State is the President of the Republic, who is elected by universal suffrage for a five-year term. Executive power is vested in the Prime Minister, who is nominated by the deputies of the AN, appointed by the President and governs with the assistance of a Council of Ministers.

Defence

The armed forces, initially formed from ex-combatants in the liberation wars, totalled about 1,200 (army 1,000, air force less than 100, coastguard 100), as assessed at November 2007. There is also a police force, the Police for Public Order, which is organized by the local municipal councils. National service is by selective conscription. In October 2002 the Government announced a programme of reform, involving the coastguard, the military police and special forces dealing with drugs-trafficking and terrorism offences. In June 2006 the country hosted a NATO Response Force training exercise for the first time. (In September 2006 an accord was signed with Portugal with regard to patrolling Cape Verde's territorial waters and assisting with the policing of drugs smuggling and illegal immigration.) Government defence expenditure in 2007 was budgeted at an estimated 640m. escudos.

Economic Affairs

In 2006, according to estimates from the World Bank, Cape Verde's gross national income (GNI), measured at average 2004–06 prices, was US $1,105m., equivalent to $2,130 per head (or $5.980 per head on an international purchasing-power parity basis). During 1996–2006, it was estimated, the population increased at an average annual rate of 2.4%, while gross domestic product (GDP) per head increased, in real terms, by an average of 3.5% per year. Overall GDP increased, in real terms, at an average annual rate of 5.9% in 1996–2006; growth in 2006 was 6.1%.

Agriculture (including forestry and fishing) contributed 7.0% of GDP in 2006, according to the World Bank, and employed an estimated 19.8% of the economically active population in mid-2005. The staple crop is maize; sugar cane, bananas, coconuts, tomatoes, mangoes, cabbages, sweet potatoes, potatoes and cassava are also cultivated. Drought and an invasion of locusts from mainland Africa severely reduced the harvest in 2004. Export earnings from fish and crustaceans declined from 262.0m. escudos (20.2% of the total value of exports, excluding fuel) in 1997 to 37.7m. escudos (1.9%) in 2001; however, earnings recovered to 635m. escudos (40.4%, excluding re-exports) in 2005. Lobster and tuna are among the most important exports. In 2005 the total fish catch was 7,742 metric tons. In late 2005 an agreement was reached with the European Union (EU) allowing EU vessels to fish in Cape Verdean waters; in return the EU would assist with the development of the local fishing industry. During 1996–2006 the GDP of the agricultural sector increased, in real terms, at an average annual rate of 3.6%, according to the African Development Bank; it declined by 0.7% in 2005, but grew by 5.8% in 2006.

Industry (including construction and power) contributed 16.4% of GDP in 2006, according to the World Bank and employed 30.6% of the labour force in 1990. During 1996–2006 industrial GDP increased, in real terms, at an average annual rate of 5.6%, according to the African Development Bank; growth in 2006 was 5.8%.

Mining employed 0.4% of the labour force in 1990 and contributed less than 1% of GDP in 1998. Salt and pozzolana, a volcanic ash used in cement manufacture, are the main non-fuel minerals produced.

Manufacturing contributed 4.8% of GDP in 2006, according to the World Bank, and employed about 6% of the labour force in 1995. The most important branches, other than fish-processing, are clothing, footwear, rum distilling and bottling. Legislation enacted in 1999 provided for the transformation of industrial parks at Mindelo and Praia into free-trade zones, and for the establishment of a further free-trade zone on Sal island. During

1996–2006 the GDP of the manufacturing sector increased, in real terms, at an average annual rate of 4.0%; an increase of 1.8% was recorded in 2006.

Energy is derived principally from hydroelectric power and gas. Imports of petroleum comprised 7.0% of the value of total estimated imports in 2005.

Services accounted for 70.7% of GDP in 2005. Tourism has been identified as the area with the most potential for economic development. A new international airport on Santiago, which was opened in 2005, was expected to give considerable impetus to the development of the tourism sector. The airport on São Vicente island was upgraded to international capacity in 2000. Plans were also under way for the construction of two further international airports, on São Vicente and Boa Vista. Tourist arrivals increased from 52,000 in 1998 to 197,844 in 2005. During 1996–2006 the combined GDP of the service sectors increased, in real terms, at an average annual rate of 7.5%, according to the African Development Bank; growth in 2006 was 5.8%.

In 2006 Cape Verde recorded a trade deficit of US $441.5m., and there was a deficit of $40.0m. on the current account of the balance of payments. In 2006 the principal source of imports was Portugal (50.2%); other major suppliers were the Netherlands (11.2%), Brazil (6.4%) and Spain (5.6%). Portugal was also the principal market for exports (53.2%) in that year; the other major purchaser was Spain (27.3%). The principal exports in 2005 were fish and crustaceans (40.4%), clothing (39.1%) and footwear (15.6%). The principal imports in that year were intermediate food products, construction materials, machinery, passenger vehicles and refined petroleum.

Budget figures for 2008 indicated a projected deficit of 5,481m. escudos. Cape Verde's total external debt at the end of 2004 was US $517m., of which $463m. was long-term public debt. In the previous year the cost of debt-servicing was equivalent to 5.3% of the value of exports of goods and services. The annual rate of inflation averaged 2.5% in 1996–2006. Consumer prices increased by an average of 4.9% in 2006. In 2003 unemployment affected some 21% of the labour force, according to official figures.

Cape Verde is a member of the Economic Community of West African States (ECOWAS, see p. 232), which promotes trade and co-operation in West Africa, and is a signatory to the Lomé Convention and subsequent Cotonou Agreement (see p. 301).

After a period of strong economic growth, combined with a consistent increase in per capita income and rising life expectancy and literacy rates, the UN announced in 2007 that Cape Verde was to relinquish its status as a least-developed country, becoming only the second nation (after Botswana in 1994) to graduate to medium-developed classification since the system's inception in 1971. While this was largely recognized as a positive development, it nevertheless provoked fears that levels of international aid would decline, although further significant assistance was pledged for the changeover period. Economic growth in recent years has been reinforced by increases in tourism and foreign-direct investment, and, in addition to significant external assistance, the country benefits from substantial remittances from emigrants. (There are about 700,000 Cape Verdeans living outside the country, principally in the USA, the Netherlands, Portugal, Italy and Angola.) GDP growth had been projected by the IMF to reach 6.5% in 2006, but this figure was significantly revised upwards to 10.8%, as a result of a strong performance by the tourism sector, which overtook the remittances of Cape Verdeans working abroad as the main contribution to the country's economy. The number of tourists visiting the islands increased by some 40% between 2000 and 2005, and the Government anticipated that by 2015 the islands would attract almost 1m. visitors per year. The Cape Verdean authorities also proposed to increase investment in skills, improve the commercial environment, simplify regulation in the financial sector and encourage the development of an offshore finance sector, in order further to enhance opportunities for economic development. Meanwhile, in March 1998 Cape Verde and Portugal signed an agreement providing for their respective currencies (now the euro for Portugal) to become linked through a fixed exchange rate, thus transforming the Cape Verde escudo into a convertible currency and promoting closer integration with the EU. Nevertheless, despite the recent improvements to many economic and social indicators, the country remains reliant on grants and loans, and it was estimated that 37% of the population were subsisting in poverty, while the vulnerability of the agricultural sector to severe periodic drought necessitates the import of approximately 85% of the country's total food requirements.

Education

Primary education, beginning at six or seven years of age and lasting for six years, is compulsory. Secondary education, beginning at 13 years of age, is divided into two cycles, the first comprising a three-year general course, the second a two-year pre-university course. There are three teacher-training units and two industrial and commercial schools of further education. A private university, the Universidade Jean Piaget de Cabo Verde, opened in Praia in 2002. According to UNESCO estimates, primary enrolment in 2003/04 included 91% of children in the relevant age-group (males 92%; females 91%), while secondary enrolment was equivalent to 55% of children in the relevant age-group (males 52%; females 58%). In 2002/03 there were 1,743 Cape Verdean students studying at overseas universities. In 2003 expenditure on education was budgeted at 4.8m. escudos, equivalent to 26% of the central Government's total public expenditure.

Public Holidays

2008: 1 January (New Year), 20 January (National Heroes' Day), 1 May (Labour Day), 5 July (Independence Day), 15 August (Assumption), 1 November (All Saints' Day), 25 December (Christmas Day).

2009: 1 January (New Year), 20 January (National Heroes' Day), 1 May (Labour Day), 5 July (Independence Day), 15 August (Assumption), 1 November (All Saints' Day), 25 December (Christmas Day).

Weights and Measures

The metric system is in force.

Statistical Survey

Sources (unless otherwise stated): Instituto Nacional de Estatística, Av. Amílcar Cabral, CP 116, Praia, Santiago; tel. 613960; e-mail inecv@mail.cvtelecom.cv; internet www.ine.cv; Statistical Service, Banco de Cabo Verde, Av. Amílcar Cabral 117, CP 101, Praia, Santiago; tel. 2607060; fax 2614447; e-mail apericles@bcv.cv; internet www.bcv.cv.

AREA AND POPULATION

Area: 4,036 sq km (1,558 sq miles).

Population: 341,491 (males 161,494, females 179,997) at census of 23 June 1990; 436,863 (males 211,479, females 225,384) at census of 16 June 2000. *2006:* 494,105 (official estimate). *By Island* (2000 census): Boa Vista 4,209; Brava 6,804; Fogo 37,421; Maio 6,754; Sal 14,816; Santo Antão 47,170; São Nicolau 13,661; Santiago 236,627; São Vicente 67,163. *2002* (official estimates): Boa Vista 4,661; Brava 6,678; Fogo 37,607; Maio 7,042; Sal 15,889; Santo Antão 47,312; São Nicolau 13,535; Santiago 247,947; São Vicente 69,837.

Density (2006): 122.4 per sq km.

Principal Towns (population at 2000 census): Praia (capital) 94,757; Mindelo 62,970. *Mid-2005* (incl. suburbs, UN estimate): Praia 117,000 (Source: UN, *World Urbanization Prospects: The 2005 Revision*).

Births and Deaths: Birth rate 30.9 per 1,000 (2000–05); Death rate 5.3 per 1,000 (2000–05) (Source: UN, *World Population Prospects: The 2006 Revision*). *2003:* Live births 13,334 (birth rate 28.9 per 1,000); Deaths 2,786 (death rate 7.0 per 1,000) (Source: UN, *Demographic Yearbook*).

Expectation of Life (years at birth, WHO estimates): 69.4 (males 66.6; females 71.9) in 2005. (Source: WHO, *World Health Statistics*).

Economically Active Population (persons aged 10 years and over, 1990 census): Agriculture, hunting, forestry and fishing 29,876;

CAPE VERDE

Mining and quarrying 410; Manufacturing 5,520; Electricity, gas and water 883; Construction 22,722; Trade, restaurants and hotels 12,747; Transport, storage and communications 6,138; Financial, insurance, real estate and business services 821; Community, social and personal services 17,358; Activities not adequately defined 24,090; *Total labour force* 120,565 (males 75,786, females 44,779), including 31,049 unemployed persons (males 19,712, females 11,337) (Source: ILO). *2000 Census* (persons aged 10 years and over): Total employed 144,310; Unemployed 30,334; Total labour force 174,644. *Mid-2005* (FAO estimates): Agriculture, etc. 41,000; Total (incl. others) 207,000 (Source: FAO).

HEALTH AND WELFARE
Key Indicators

Total Fertility Rate (children per woman, 2005): 3.6.

Under-5 Mortality Rate (per 1,000 live births, 2005): 35.

Physicians (per 1,000 head, 2004): 0.49.

Hospital Beds (per 1,000 head, 2000): 1.60.

Health Expenditure (2004): US $ per head (PPP): 225.1.

Health Expenditure (2004): % of GDP: 5.2.

Health Expenditure (2004): public (% of total): 75.8.

Access to Water (% of persons, 2002): 80.

Access to Sanitation (% of persons, 2002): 42.

Human Development Index (2005): ranking: 80.

Human Development Index (2005): 0.778.

For sources and definitions, see explanatory note on p. vi.

AGRICULTURE, ETC.

Principal Crops ('000 metric tons, 2006, FAO estimates): Maize 11.8; Potatoes 3.6; Sweet potatoes 4.5; Cassava 3.5; Sugar cane 14.0; Pulses 5.2; Coconuts 6.0; Cabbages 4.7; Tomatoes 4.8; Dry onions 1.9; Green beans 2.2; Cucumbers and gherkins 1.1; Bananas 6.6; Guavas, mangoes and mangosteens 4.5. *Aggregate Production* ('000 metric tons, may include official, semi-official or estimated data): Vegetables (incl. melons) 17.9; Fruits (excl. melons) 16.1; Roots and tubers 11.6.

Livestock ('000 head, 2006, FAO estimates): Cattle 23.0; Pigs 205.0; Sheep 10.0; Goats 112.8; Horses 0.5; Asses and mules 16.4; Chickens 460.

Livestock Products ('000 metric tons, 2006, FAO estimates): Pig meat 7.4; Other meat 1.4; Cows' milk 5.6; Goats' milk 5.7; Hen eggs 1.8.

Fishing (metric tons, live weight, 2005): Total catch 7,742 (Skipjack tuna 348; Yellowfin tuna 1,778).

Source: FAO.

MINING

Production (metric tons, 2006, estimates): Salt (unrefined) 1,600. Clay, gypsum, limestone and volcanic rock were also produced, at unreported levels. Source: US Geological Survey.

INDUSTRY

Production (metric tons, 2003, unless otherwise indicated): Canned fish 200; Frozen fish 900; Flour 15,901 (1999 figure); Beer 4,104,546 litres (1999 figure); Soft drinks 922,714 litres (1996 figure); Cigarettes and tobacco 77 kg (1999 figure); Paint 628,243 kg (1997 figure); Footwear 670,676 pairs (1996 figure); Soap 1,371,045 kg (1999 figure); Electric energy 220m. kWh (2004). Sources: mainly UN, *Industrial Commodity Statistics Yearbook*, and IMF, *Cape Verde: Statistical Appendix* (October 2001).

FINANCE

Currency and Exchange Rates: 100 centavos = 1 Cape Verde escudo; 1,000 escudos are known as a conto. *Sterling, Dollar and Euro Equivalents* (31 December 2007): £1 sterling = 150.068 escudos; US $1 = 74.907 escudos; €1 = 110.270 escudos; 1,000 Cape Verde escudos = £6.66 = $13.35 = €9.07. *Average Exchange Rate* (escudos per US dollar): 88.670 in 2005; 87.901 in 2006; 80.567 in 2007.

Budget (million escudos, 2008, proposed figures): *Revenue*: Taxation 28,059 (Taxes on income and profits 8,462, Taxes on international trade 5,583, Consumption taxes 13,177, Other tax revenue 837); Non-tax revenue 3,204; Net lending 23; Grants 7,265; Total 38,551. *Expenditure*: Recurrent 24,950 (Wages and salaries 14,245, Acquisition of goods and services 2,335, Transfers and other subsidies 4,453, Interest payments 2,053, Other recurrent expenditure 1,863); Capital 17,581; Other 1,500; Total 44,032. Source: IMF, *Third Review Under the Policy Support Instrument - Staff Report; Staff Supplement; Press Release on the Executive Board Discussion; and Statement by the Executive Director for Cape Verde* (January 2008).

International Reserves (US $ million at 31 December 2006): Reserve position in the IMF 0.02; Foreign exchange 254.43; Total 254.45. Source: IMF, *International Financial Statistics*.

Money Supply (million escudos at 31 December 2006): Currency outside banks 7,731.2; Demand deposits at commercial banks 31,186.1; Total money (incl. others) 38,917.3. Source: IMF, *International Financial Statistics*.

Cost of Living (Consumer Price Index; base: 1989 = 100): 184.9 in 2004; 185.7 in 2005; 195.7 in 2006.

Expenditure on the Gross Domestic Product (million escudos at current prices, 2005): Government final consumption expenditure 16,148; Private final consumption expenditure 67,648; Gross fixed capital formation (incl. increase in stocks) 33,019; *Total domestic expenditure* 116,815; Exports of goods and services 14,719; *Less* Imports of goods and services 44,363; *GDP in purchasers' values* 87,171. Source: IMF, *Cape Verde: Statistical Appendix* (September 2006).

Gross Domestic Product by Economic Activity (million escudos at current prices, 2005): Agriculture, forestry and livestock 7,869; Fishing 1,035; Industry and energy 7,530; Construction 9,112; Commerce 18,200; Hotels 2,088; Transport and communications 18,621; Banks and insurance 3,727; Housing 5,048; Public service 11,813; Other services 2,078; *Sub-total* 87,121; *Less* Imputed bank service charges 2,756; *Total value added** 84,366; Import taxes 13,773; *GDP at market prices* 98,139. Source: IMF, *Cape Verde: Statistical Appendix* (September 2006).

*Including indirect taxes, net of subsidies, with the exception of taxes on imports.

Balance of Payments (US $ million, 2006): Exports of goods f.o.b. 121.82; Imports of goods f.o.b. −563.33; *Trade balance* −441.50; Exports of services 397.45; Imports of services −245.33; *Balance on goods and services* −289.38; Other income received 18.54; Other income paid −63.77; *Balance on goods, services and income* −334.61; Current transfers (net) 294.64; *Current balance* −39.98; Capital account (net) 27.10; Direct investment from abroad 122.60; Portfolio investment liabilities 0.29; Other investment assets 14.78; Other investment liabilities −26.21; Net errors and omissions −40.59; *Overall balance* 57.99. Source: IMF, *International Finance Statistics*.

EXTERNAL TRADE

Principal Commodities (distribution by SITC, million escudos, 2005): *Imports c.i.f.*: Consumer goods 16,042 (Intermediate food products 8,819); Intermediary goods 9,553 (Construction materials 4,578); Capital goods 6,536 (Machines 3,296, Transportation 2,770); Petroleum imports 2,691 (Diesel oil 1,891); Other imports 3,422; Total 38,245. *Exports f.o.b.*: Fish and crustaceans 635.0; Footwear 245.0; Miscellaneous manufactured articles 691.4 (Articles of apparel and clothing accessories 614.3); Total (incl. others) 1,571.4; Re-exports 6,039.2. Source: IMF, *Cape Verde: Statistical Appendix* (September 2006).

Imports (distribution by SITC, US $ million, 2001): Food and live animals 63.4 (Milk and cream 12.0, Cereals and cereal preparations 16.5, Vegetables and fruit 9.1, Sugar, sugar preparations and honey 7.8); Beverages and tobacco 15.4 (Alcoholic beverages 8.9); Mineral fuels, lubricants, etc. 13.9 (Refined petroleum 13.4); Basic manufactures 40.5 (Cement 8.6, Manufactures of metals 9.4); Machinery and transport equipment 68.7 (Power generating machinery 9.7, General industrial machinery and parts 8.4, Electric machinery and apparatus 10.8, Passenger vehicles 12.8); Miscellaneous manufactured articles 21.3; Total (incl. others) 247.5. Source: UN, *International Trade Statistics Yearbook*.

Principal Trading Partners (million escudos, 2006): *Imports c.i.f.*: Brazil 3,024.7; Côte d'Ivoire 127.8; France 1,184.1; Germany 545.6; Italy 2,267.2; Netherlands 5,315.8; Portugal 23,878.1; Senegal 192.4; Spain 2,668.3; United Kingdom 649.5; USA 659.9; Total (incl. others) 47,578.9. *Exports f.o.b.*: Guinea-Bissau 75.9; Netherlands 10.5; Portugal 968.3; Spain 496.8; USA 25.0; Total (incl. others) 1,819.0.

TRANSPORT

Road Traffic (motor vehicles in use, 31 December 2003): Light vehicles 23,811; Heavy vehicles 5,032; Motorcycles 1,924.

Shipping: *Merchant Fleet* (registered at 31 December 2005): Number of vessels 45; Total displacement ('000 grt) 29.5 (Source: Lloyd's Register-Fairplay, *World Fleet Statistics*). *International Sea-borne Freight Traffic* (estimates, '000 metric tons, 1993): Goods loaded 144, goods unloaded 299 (Source: UN Economic Commission for Africa, *African Statistical Yearbook*).

CAPE VERDE

Civil Aviation (traffic on scheduled services, 2003): Kilometres flown 5,000,000; Passengers carried 253,000; Passenger-km 285,000,000; Total ton-km 27,000,000. (Source: UN, *Statistical Yearbook*.)

TOURISM

Tourist Arrivals by Country of Residence (2005): Belgium 5,121; France 14,284; Germany 21,121; Italy 69,728; Portugal 50,240; South Africa 9,432; Spain 7,626; Switzerland 1,976; USA 2,102; Total (incl. others) 197,844.

Tourism Receipts (US $ million, incl. passenger transport unless otherwise indicated): 137 in 2003; 164 in 2004; 177 in 2005 (excl. passenger transport).

Source: World Tourism Organization.

COMMUNICATIONS MEDIA

Radio Receivers* (1997): 73,000 in use.
Television Receivers† (2000): 2,000 in use.
Telephones† (2006): 71,600 main lines in use.
Mobile Cellular Telephones† (2006): 108,900 subscribers.
Facsimile Machines‡ (1996): 1,000 in use.
Personal Computers† (2005): 48,000 in use.
Internet Users† (2006): 29,000.
Broadband Subscribers† (2006): 1,800.
Non-daily Newspapers* (2004): 5 titles.
Book Production* (1989): 10 titles.

* Source: UNESCO, *Statistical Yearbook*.
† Source: International Telecommunication Union.
‡ Source: UN, *Statistical Yearbook*.

EDUCATION

Pre-primary (2004/05, unless otherwise stated): 446 schools (2003/04); 936 teachers; 20,507 pupils.

Primary (2004/05, unless otherwise indicated): 425 schools (2002/03); 3,190 teachers; 82,952 pupils.

Total Secondary (2004/05, unless otherwise stated): 33 schools (2003/04); 2,241 teachers; 51,672 pupils.

Higher (2004/05): 485 teachers; 3,910 pupils. Note: In 2002/03 a further 1,743 pupils were studying abroad.

Teacher Training (2003/04): 3 colleges; 52 teachers; 948 pupils.

Adult Literacy Rate (UNESCO estimates): 81.2% (males 87.8%; females 75.5) in 2004 (Source: UNESCO Institute for Statistics).

Source (unless otherwise indicated): Comunidade dos Países de Língua Portuguesa.

Directory

The Constitution

A new Constitution of the Republic of Cape Verde ('the Second Republic') came into force on 25 September 1992. The Constitution defines Cape Verde as a sovereign, unitary and democratic republic, guaranteeing respect for human dignity and recognizing the inviolable and inalienable rights of man as a fundament of humanity, peace and justice. It recognizes the equality of all citizens before the law, without distinction of social origin, social condition, economic status, race, sex, religion, political convictions or ideologies and promises transparency for all citizens in the practising of fundamental liberties. The Constitution gives assent to popular will, and has a fundamental objective in the realization of economic, political, social and cultural democracy and the construction of a society that is free, just and in solidarity.

The Head of State is the President of the Republic, who is elected by universal adult suffrage and must obtain two-thirds of the votes cast to win in the first round of the election. If no candidate secures the requisite majority, a new election is held within 21 days and contested by the two candidates who received the highest number of votes in the first round. Voting is conducted by secret ballot. Legislative power is vested in the Assembléia Nacional, which is also elected by universal adult suffrage. The Prime Minister is nominated by the Assembléia, to which he is responsible. On the recommendation of the Prime Minister, the President appoints the Council of Ministers, whose members must be elected deputies of the Assembléia. There are 17 local government councils, elected by universal suffrage for a period of five years.

A constitutional revision, adopted in July 1999, gave the President the right to dissolve the Assembléia Nacional, created a new advisory chamber (Conselho Económico e Social), and gave the State the right to adopt Crioulo as the country's second official language.

The Government

HEAD OF STATE

President: PEDRO DE VERONA RODRIGUES PIRES (elected 25 February 2001; re-elected 12 February 2006).

COUNCIL OF MINISTERS
(March 2008)

Prime Minister: JOSÉ MARIA PEREIRA NEVES.
Minister in Assistance to the Prime Minister and Minister of Qualifications, Employment and Parliamentary Affairs: SARA MARIA DUARTE LOPES.
Minister of State and of Infrastructure, Transport and the Sea: MANUEL INOCÊNCIO SOUSA.
Minister of State and of Health: BASÍLIO MOSSO RAMOS.
Minister of Foreign Affairs, Co-operation and Communities: VÍCTOR MANUEL BARBOSA BORGES.
Minister of Justice: JOSÉ MANUEL GOMES ANDRADE.
Minister of Internal Administration: LIVIO LOPES.
Minister of Culture: MANUEL MONTEIRO DA VEIGA.
Minister of the Environment and Agriculture: MARIA MADALENA BRITO NEVES.
Minister of Education and Higher Education: FILOMENA DE FÁTIMA RIBEIRO VIEIRA MARTINS.
Minister of Labour, Solidarity and the Family: SIDÓNIO FONTES LIMA MONTEIRO.
Minister of the Economy, Growth and Competitiveness: JOSÉ BRITO.
Minister of Finance and Public Administration: CRISTINA DUARTE.
Minister of Decentralization, Housing and Territorial Order: RAMIRO ANDRADE ALVES AZEVEDO.
Minister of the Presidency of the Council of Ministers, State Reform and National Defence: MARIA CRISTINA LOPES ALMEIDA FONTES LIMA.
Secretary of State in Assistance to the Minister of Finance and Public Administration: LEONESA MARIA LIMA FORTES.
Secretary of State for Public Administration: ROMEU FONSECA MODESTO.
Secretary of State for Education: OCTÁVIO RAMOS TAVARES.
Secretary of State for Youth and Sports: AMÉRICO SABINO SOARES NASCIMENTO.
Secretary of State for Foreign Affairs: (vacant).
Secretary of State for Agriculture: ROSA LOPES ROCHA.

MINISTRIES

Office of the President: Presidência da República, Palácio do Plateau, CP 100, Plateau, Praia, Santiago; tel. 2616555; fax 2614356; internet www.presidenciarepublica.cv.

Office of the Prime Minister: Gabinete do Primeiro Ministro, Palácio do Governo, Várzea, CP 16, Praia, Santiago; tel. 2610411; fax 2613099; e-mail gab.imprensa@gpm.gov.cv; internet www.primeiroministro.cv.

Ministry of Culture: Praia, Santiago; tel. 2610567.

Ministry of Decentralization, Housing and Territorial Order: Praia, Santiago.

Ministry of the Economy, Growth and Competitiveness: Praia, Santiago; tel. 2605300; fax 2617299; e-mail jorge.borges@gov1.gov.cv.

CAPE VERDE

Ministry of Education and Higher Education: Palácio do Governo, Várzea, CP 111, Praia, Santiago; tel. 2610509; fax 2612764; internet www.minedu.cv.
Ministry of the Environment and Agriculture: Ponta Belém, CP 115, Praia, Santiago; tel. 2615713; fax 2614054; internet www.maap.cv.
Ministry of Finance and Public Administration: 107 Av. Amílcar Cabral, CP 30, Praia, Santiago; tel. 2607400; e-mail aliciab@gov1.gov.cv; internet www.mf.cv.
Ministry of Foreign Affairs, Co-operation and Communities: Palácio das Comunidades, Achada de Santo António, Praia, Santiago; tel. 2615727; fax 2616262.
Ministry of Health: Palácio do Governo, Várzea, CP 47, Praia, Santiago; tel. 2610501.
Ministry of Infrastructure, Transport and the Sea: Ponta Belém, Praia, Santiago; tel. 2615709; fax 2611595; e-mail GSoares@mih.gov.cv.
Ministry of Internal Administration: Praia, Santiago.
Ministry of Justice: Rua Serpa Pinto, CP 205, Praia, Santiago; tel. 2623257; fax 2623261.
Ministry of Labour, Solidarity and the Family: Praia, Santiago.
Ministry of the Presidency of the Council of Ministers, State Reform and National Defence: Praia, Santiago.
Ministry of Qualifications, Employment and Parliamentary Affairs: Praia, Santiago.

President and Legislature

PRESIDENT

Presidential Election, 12 February 2006

Candidate	Votes	% of votes
Pedro de Verona Rodrigues Pires (PAICV)	86,583	50.98
Carlos Alberto de Carvalho Veiga (MpD)	83,241	49.02
Total	169,824	100.00

LEGISLATURE

Assembléia Nacional: Achada de Santo António, CP 20 A, Praia, Santiago; tel. 2608000; fax 2622660; e-mail an-cv@cvtelecom.cv; internet www.parlamento.cv.
Speaker: ARISTIDES RAIMUNDO LIMA.

Legislative Elections, 22 January 2006

Party	Votes	% of votes	Seats
Partido Africano da Independência de Cabo Verde (PAICV)	88,965	52.28	41
Movimento para a Democracia (MpD)	74,909	44.02	29
União Cristã, Independente e Democrática (UCID)	4,495	2.64	2
Partido da Renovação Democrática (PRD)	1,097	0.64	—
Partido Socialista Democrático (PSD)	702	0.41	—
Total	170,168	100.00	72

Election Commission

Comissão Nacional de Eleições (CNE): Praia; e-mail cne@cne.cv; internet www.cne.cv; Pres. BARTOLOMEU LOPES VARELA.

Political Organizations

Movimento para a Democracia (MpD): Av. Cidade Lisboa, 4° andar, CP 90 A, Praia, Santiago; tel. 2614122; e-mail mpd@mpd.cv; internet www.mpd.cv; f. 1990; advocates administrative decentralization; governing party from 1991 to 2001; formed alliance with the PCD to contest 2006 legislative and presidential elections; Chair. JORGE SANTOS.
Partido Africano da Independência de Cabo Verde (PAICV): Av. Amílcar Cabral, CP 22, Praia, Santiago; tel. 2612720; fax 2611410; internet www.paicv.org; f. 1956 as the Partido Africano da Independência do Guiné e Cabo Verde (PAIGC); name changed in 1981, following the 1980 coup in Guinea-Bissau; sole authorized political party 1975–90; governing party since 2001; Pres. JOSÉ MARIA NEVES; Sec.-Gen. ARISTIDES LIMA.
Partido da Renovação Democrática (PRD): Praia, Santiago; f. 2000 by fmr mems of the MpD; Pres. JOSÉ LUÍS BARBOSA.
Partido Socialista Democrático (PSD): Praia, Santiago; f. 1992; Sec.-Gen. JOÃO ALÉM.
Partido de Trabalho e Solidariedade (PTS): Praia, Santiago; f. 1998; Interim Leader ISAÍAS RODRIGUES.
União Cristã, Independente e Democrática (UCID): Achada Santo António-Frente, Restaurante "O Poeta", Praia, Santiago; tel. 2608134; fax 2624403.

Diplomatic Representation

EMBASSIES IN CAPE VERDE

Angola: Av. OUA, Achada de Santo António, CP 78A Praia, Santiago; tel. 2623235; fax 2623234; e-mail emb.angola@cv.telecom.cv; Ambassador JOSÉ AUGUSTO CÉSAR 'KILUANGE'.
Brazil: Chã de Areia 2, CP 93, Praia, Santiago; tel. 2615607; fax 2615609; e-mail contato@embrasilpraia.org; Ambassador MARIA DULCE SILVA BARROS.
China, People's Republic: Achada de Santo António, CP 8, Praia, Santiago; tel. 2623029; fax 2623047; e-mail chinaemb_cv@mfa.gov.cn; Ambassador WU YUANSHAN.
Cuba: Achada de Santo António, Praia, Santiago; tel. 2619048; fax 2617527; e-mail ecubacpv@cvtelecom.cv; Ambassador PEDRO EVELIO DORTA GONZÁLEZ.
France: Achada de Santo António, CP 192, Praia, Santiago; tel. 2615591; fax 2615590; internet www.ambafrance-cv.org; Ambassador BERNARD DEMANGE.
Korea, Democratic People's Republic: Praia; Ambassador RI IN SOK.
Portugal: Av. OUA, Achada de Santo António, CP 160, Praia, Santiago; tel. 2626097; fax 2613222; e-mail embport@cvtelecom.cv; internet www.consuladopt.cv; Ambassador Dr GRAÇA ANDERSEN GUIMARÃES.
Russia: Achada de Santo António, CP 31, Praia, Santiago; tel. 2622739; fax 2622738; e-mail embrus@cvtelecom.cv; Ambassador VLADIMIR E. PETUKHOV.
Senegal: Rua Abílio Macedo, Plateau, CP 269, Praia, Santiago; tel. 2615621; fax 2612838; e-mail silcarneyni@hotmail.com; Ambassador MARIÈME NDIAYE.
USA: Rua Abílio Macedo 6, Praia, Santiago; tel. 2608900; fax 2611355; internet praia.usembassy.gov; Ambassador ROGER DWAYNE PIERCE.

Judicial System

Supremo Tribunal de Justiça (STJ)

Gabinete do Juiz Presidente, Edif. dos Correios, Rua Cesário de Lacerda, CP 117, Praia, Santiago; tel. 2615810; fax 2611751; e-mail stj@supremo.gov.cv; internet www.stj.cv.
f. 1975; Pres. BENFEITO MOSSO RAMOS.
Attorney-General: FRANQUILIM AFONSO FURTADO.

Religion

CHRISTIANITY

At 31 December 2005 there were an estimated 332,114 adherents of the Roman Catholic Church in the country, equivalent to 73.7% of the population. Protestant churches, among which the Church of the Nazarene is the most prominent, represent about 1% of the population.

The Roman Catholic Church

Cape Verde comprises two dioceses, directly responsible to the Holy See. The Bishops participate in the Episcopal Conference of Senegal, Mauritania, Cape Verde and Guinea-Bissau, currently based in Senegal.
Bishop of Mindelo: Rt Rev. ARLINDO GOMES FURTADO, CP 447, 2110 Mindelo, São Vicente; tel. 2318870; fax 2318872; e-mail diocesemindelo@cvtelecom.cv.

CAPE VERDE

Bishop of Santiago de Cabo Verde: Rt Rev. PAULINO DO LIVRAMENTO ÉVORA, Av. Amílcar Cabral, Largo 5 de Outubro, CP 46, Praia, Santiago; tel. 2611119; fax 2614599; e-mail diocesecv@cvtelecom.cv.

The Anglican Communion

Cape Verde forms part of the diocese of The Gambia, within the Church of the Province of West Africa. The Bishop is resident in Banjul, The Gambia.

Other Christian Churches

Church of the Nazarene: District Office, Av. Amílcar Cabral, Plateau, CP 96, Praia, Santiago; tel. 2613611.

Other churches represented in Cape Verde include the Church of the Assembly of God, the Church of Jesus Christ of Latter-day Saints, the Evangelical Baptist Church, the Maná Church, the New Apostolic Church, the Seventh-day Adventist Church and the Universal Church of the Kingdom of God.

BAHÁ'Í FAITH

National Spiritual Assembly: Rua Madragoa, Plateau, Praia, Santiago; tel. 2617739.

The Press

Agaviva: Mindelo, São Vicente; tel. 2312121; f. 1991; monthly; Editor GERMANO ALMEIDA; circ. 4,000.

Boletim Oficial da República de Cabo Verde: Imprensa Nacional, CP 113, Praia, Santiago; tel. 2614150; e-mail incv@cvtelecom.cv; weekly; official announcements.

O Cidadão: Praça Dr António Aurélio Gonçalves 2, Mindelo, São Vicente; tel. 2325024; fax 2325022; e-mail cidadao@caboverde.zzn .com; weekly; Editor JOSÉ MÁRIO CORREIA.

Expresso das Ilhas: Santiago; internet www.expressodasilhas.cv; f. 2001 by the MpD; daily; Dir VLADEMIRO MARÇAL.

Horizonte: Achada de Santo António, CP 40, Praia, Santiago; tel. 2622447; fax 2623330; f. 1999; daily; pro-Govt; Editor FERNANDO MONTEIRO; circ. 5,000.

Raízes: CP 98, Praia, Santiago; f. 1977; quarterly; cultural review; Editor ARNALDO FRANÇA; circ. 1,500.

A Semana: Rotunda do Palmarejo, CP 36 C, Praia, Santiago; tel. 2629860; fax 2628661; e-mail asemana@cvtelecom.cv; internet www .asemana.cv; f. 1991; weekly; pro-PAICV; independent; Editor FILOMENA SILVA; circ. 5,000.

Terra Nova: Rua Guiné-Bissau 1, CP 166, Mindelo, São Vicente; tel. 2322442; fax 2321475; e-mail terranova@cabonet.cv; f. 1975; monthly; Roman Catholic; Editor P. ANTÓNIO FIDALGO BARROS; circ. 3,000.

There is also an online newspaper, Visão News (www.visaonews .com), based in the USA. Further news websites include Paralelo14 (www.paralelo14.com), AllCaboVerde.com (www.noscaboverde .com), Cabonet (www.cabonet.or) and Sport Kriolu (www .sportkriolu.com), dedicated to sport.

NEWS AGENCY

Inforpress: Achada de Santo António, CP 40 A, Praia, Santiago; tel. 2624313; fax 2622554; e-mail inforpress@mail.cvtelecom.cv; internet www.inforpress.cv; f. 1988 as Cabopress; Pres. JOSÉ AUGUSTO SANCHES.

PRESS ASSOCIATION

Associação de Jornalistas de Cabo Verde (AJOC): CP 1 A, Praia, Santiago; tel. 2622655; fax 2623054; f. 1993; Pres. PAULO JORGE LIMA; 11 media cos and 159 individual mems.

Publishers

Instituto Caboverdeano do Livro e do Disco (ICL): Centro Cultural, CP 158, Praia, Santiago; tel. 2612346; books, journals, music.

GOVERNMENT PUBLISHING HOUSE

Imprensa Nacional: CP 113, Praia, Santiago; tel. 2614209; Admin. JOÃO DE PINA.

Broadcasting and Communications

TELECOMMUNICATIONS

Cabo Verde Telecom: Rua Cabo Verde Telecom, Várzea, CP 220, Praia, Santiago; tel. 2609200; fax 2613725; e-mail cvtelecom@ cvtelecom.cv; internet www.nave.cv; f. 1995; 40% owned by Portugal Telecom; operates mobile network, Telemóvel; Chief Exec. ANTÓNIO PIRES CORREIA.

Cabo Verde Telecom was the sole telephone, cable and internet provider; however, in 2004 the Government announced plans to open the telecommunications market by 2010. There were plans to grant a licence for a second mobile provider.

Regulatory Authority

Agência Nacional das Comunicações (ANAC): Edifício do MIT, Ponta Belém, CP 892, Praia, Santiago; tel. 2604400; fax 2613069; e-mail info.anac@anac.cv; internet www.anac.cv; f. 2006; Pres. DAVID GOMES.

BROADCASTING

Rádio Televisão de Cabo Verde (RTC): Rua 13 de Janeiro, Achada de Santo António, CP 1 A, Praia, Santiago; tel. 2605200; fax 2605256; e-mail rtc@mail.cvtelecom.cv; internet www.rtc.cv; govt-controlled; 40 transmitters and relay transmitters; FM transmission only; radio broadcasts in Portuguese and Creole for 24 hours daily; one television transmitter and seven relay television transmitters; television broadcasts in Portuguese and Creole for eight hours daily with co-operation of RTP Africa (Portugal) and TV5 Honde; Pres. MARCOS OLIVEIRA.

Televisão de Cabo Verde: Praia, Santiago; sole television broadcaster; part of Radio Televisão de Cabo Verde; Dir DANIEL MEDINA.

Praia FM: Rua Visconde de S. Januario 19, 4° andar, CP 276 C, Praia, Santiago; tel. 2616356; fax 2613515; e-mail praiafm@ cvtelecom.cv; internet www.praiafm.biz; Dir GIORDANO CUSTÓDIO.

Rádio Comercial: Achada de Santo António, Prédio Gomes Irmãos, 3° esq., CP 507, Praia, Santiago; tel. 2623156; fax 2622413; e-mail multimedia.rc@cvtelecom.cv; f. 1997; Admin. HENRIQUE PIRES; Dir CARLOS FILIPE GONÇALVES.

Rádio Educativa de Cabo Verde: Achada de Santo António, Praia, Santiago; tel. 2611161.

Rádio Morabeza: Rua da Guiné Bissau 3A, CP 456, Mindelo, São Vicente; tel. 2324431; fax 2300069; e-mail radiomorabeza@cvtelecom .cv.

Rádio Nacional de Cabo Verde (RNCV): CP 26, Praia, Santiago; tel. 2613729.

Rádio Nova—Emissora Cristã de Cabo Verde: CP 166, Mindelo, São Vicente; tel. 2322082; fax 2321475; internet www .radionovaonline.com; f. 2002; Roman Catholic station; Dir ANTÓNIO FIDALGO BARROS.

Voz de São Vicente: CP 29, Mindelo, São Vicente; fax 2311006; f. 1974; govt-controlled; Dir JOSÉ FONSECA SOARES.

Radiotelevisão Portuguesa International and Canal Plus International began broadcasting in 1995. A further television channel, Pulu TV, began broadcasting in 2005, but was yet to be licensed. In 2005 there were estimated to be 12 radio stations.

Finance

(cap. = capital; res = reserves; dep. = deposits; m. = million; brs = branches; amounts in Cape Verde escudos, unless otherwise indicated)

BANKING

Central Bank

Banco de Cabo Verde (BCV): Av. Amílcar Cabral 117, CP 101, Praia, Santiago; tel. 2607000; fax 2607095; e-mail mcosta@bcv.cv; internet www.bcv.cv; f. 1976; bank of issue; cap. 200.0m., res 243.8m., dep. 16,630.4m. (Dec. 2005); Gov. CARLOS AUGUSTO DUARTE DE BURGO.

Other Banks

Banco Caboverdiano de Negócios (BCN): Av. Amílcar Cabral 97, CP 593, Praia, Santiago; tel. 2604250; fax 2614006; e-mail bcn@ bcdenegocios.cv; internet www.bcdenegocios.cv; f. 1996 as Banco Totta e Açores (Cabo Verde); renamed as above in 2004; owned by a Cape Verdean consortium; cap. €2.7m. (Oct. 2004); 3 brs; Pres. MANUEL J. CHANTRE.

Banco Comercial do Atlântico (BCA): Av. Amílcar Cabral, CP 474, Praia, Santiago; tel. 2600913; fax 2614955; e-mail bca@bca.cv; internet www.bca.cv; f. 1993; privatized in 2000; main commercial bank; cap. 1,000m., res 615.1m., dep. 43,663.1m. (Dec. 2005); Pres. and Gen. Man. João Henrique Real Pereira; 24 brs.

Banco Interatlântico: Av. Cidade de Lisboa, CP 131 A, Praia, Santiago; tel. 2614008; fax 2614752; e-mail bi@bi.cv; internet www.bi.cv; f. 1999; Pres. of Exec. Comm. Dr José Valentim Barbieri.

Caixa Económica de Cabo Verde, SA (CECV): Av. Cidade de Lisboa, CP 199, Praia, Santiago; tel. 2603603; fax 2612055; e-mail antonio.moreira@caixa.cv; internet www.caixa.cv; f. 1928; privatized in 1999; commercial bank; cap. 348.0m., res 926.4m., dep. 14,855.5m. (Dec. 2004); Exec. Dir António Carlos Moreira Semedo; 11 brs.

STOCK EXCHANGE

Bolsa de Valores de Cabo Verde, Sarl (BVC): Achada de Santo António, CP 115 A, Praia, Santiago; tel. 2603030; fax 2603038; e-mail bcv@bvc.cv; internet www.bvc.cv; f. 1998; reopened December 2005; Pres. Veríssimo Pinto.

INSURANCE

Companhia Caboverdiana de Seguros (IMPAR): Av. Amílcar Cabral, CP 469, Praia, Santiago; tel. and fax 2613765; e-mail impar@cvtelecom.cv; f. 1991; Pres. Dr Corsino António Fortes.

Garantia Companhia de Seguros: Chã d'Areia, CP 138, Praia, Santiago; tel. 26086221; fax 2616117; e-mail garantia@cvtelecom.cv; f. 1991; privatized in 2000; Pres. João Henrique Real Pereira.

Trade and Industry

GOVERNMENT AGENCIES

Agência Nacional de Segurança Alimentar (ANSA): Achada de Santo António, Praia, Santiago; e-mail ansa@cvtelecom.cv; food security agency; Pres. Miguel Monteiro.

Cabo Verde Investimentos (CI): Rotunda da Cruz do Papa 5, CP 89 C, Praia, Santiago; tel. 2604119; fax 2604870; e-mail Presidente@cvinvest.cv; f. 2004 to replace the Centro de Promoção Turística, de Investimento Externo e das Exportações (PROMEX); promotes public-private investment partnerships in infrastructure and tourism; Pres. Victor Fidalgo.

Comissão de Investimento Externo e Empresa Franca (CIEF): Praia, Santiago; foreign investment commission.

Gabinete de Apoio à Reestruturação do Sector Empresarial do Estado (GARSEE) (Cabo Verde Privatization): Largo do Tunis, Cruzeiro, CP 323, Praia, Santiago; tel. 2614748; fax 2612334; bureau in charge of planning and supervising restructuring and divestment of public enterprises; Project Dir Dr Sérgio Centeio.

DEVELOPMENT ORGANIZATION

Instituto Nacional de Investigação e Desenvolvimento Agrário (INIDA): CP 84, Praia, Santiago; tel. 2711147; fax 2711133; f. 1979; research and training on agricultural issues.

TRADE ASSOCIATION

Associação para a Promoção dos MicroEmpresários (APME): Fazenda, Praia, Santiago; tel. 2606056; f. 1988.

CHAMBERS OF COMMERCE

Câmara de Comércio, Indústria e Serviços de Barlavento (CCISB): Rua da Luz 31, CP 728, Mindelo, São Vicente; tel. 2328495; fax 2328496; e-mail camara.com@cvtelecom.cv; f. 1996; Pres. Manuel J. Monteiro.

Câmara de Comércio, Indústria e Serviços de Sotavento (CCISS): Rua Serpa Pinto 160, CP 105, Praia, Santiago; tel. 2617234; fax 2617235; e-mail cciss@cvtelecom.cv.

STATE INDUSTRIAL ENTERPRISES

Empresa Nacional de Avicultura, SARL (ENAVI): Tira Chapéu Zona Industrial, CP 135, Praia, Santiago; tel. 2627268; fax 2628441; e-mail enavi@cvtelecom.cv; poultry-farming.

Empresa Nacional de Combustíveis, SARL (ENACOL): Largo John Miller's, CP 1, Mindelo, São Vicente; tel. 2306060; fax 2323425; e-mail enacolsv@enacol.cv; internet www.enacol.cv; f. 1979; supervises import and distribution of petroleum; Dir Dr Mário A. Rodrigues.

Empresa Nacional de Produtos Farmacêuticos, SARL (EMPROFAC): Tira Chapéu Zona Industrial, CP 59, Praia, Santiago; tel. 2627895; fax 2627899; e-mail emprofac@cvtelecom.cv; f. 1979; due to be privatized by early 2007; state monopoly of pharmaceuticals and medical imports.

UTILITIES
Electricity and Water

Empresa de Electricidade e Água, SARL (Electra): Av. Baltasar Lopes Silva 10, CP 137, Mindelo, São Vicente; tel. 2303030; fax 2324446; e-mail comercial@electra.cv; internet www.electra.cv; f. 1982; 51% govt-owned; Pres. Rui Eduardo Ferreira Rodrigues Pena.

CO-OPERATIVE

Instituto Nacional das Cooperativas: Achada de Santo António, Praia, Santiago; tel. 2616376; central co-operative org.

TRADE UNIONS

Confederação Caboverdiana dos Sindicatos Livres (CCSL): Rua Dr Júlio Abreu, CP 155, Praia, Santiago; tel. and fax 2616319; e-mail ccsl@cvtelecom.cv; Sec.-Gen. José Manuel Vaz.

Federação Nacional dos Sindicatos dos Trabalhadores da Administração Pública (FNSTAP): CP 123, Praia; tel. 2614305; fax 2613629; Pres. Miguel Horta da Silva.

Sindicato dos Transportes, Comunicações e Turismo (STCT): Praia, Santiago; tel. 2616338.

União Nacional dos Trabalhadores de Cabo Verde—Central Sindical (UNTC—CS): Av. Cidade de Lisboa, CP 123, Praia, Santiago; tel. 2614305; fax 2613629; e-mail untc@cvtelecom.cv; internet www.untc-cs.org; f. 1978; Chair. Júlio Ascenção Silva.

Transport

ROADS

In 2004 there were an estimated 2,250 km of roads, of which 1,750 km were paved. In 2005 the Government planned to allocate €635m. to upgrade the road network, including building highways and a ring road around Praia.

Associação Apoio aos Reclusos e Crianças de Rua (AAPR): Achada de Santo António, CP 205 A, Praia, Santiago; tel. 2618441; fax 2619017; e-mail aapr@cvtelecom.cv; road development agency.

SHIPPING

Cargo-passenger ships call regularly at Porto Grande, Mindelo, on São Vicente, and Praia, on Santiago. There were plans to upgrade the ports at Praia, Sal, São Vicente and Porto Novo (Santo Antão). There are small ports on the other inhabited islands. Cape Verde's registered merchant fleet at 31 December 2005 consisted of 42 vessels, totalling 25,805 grt.

Comissão de Gestão dos Transportes Marítimos de Cabo Verde: CP 153, São Vicente; tel. 2314979; fax 2312055.

Empresa Nacional de Administração dos Portos, SA (ENAPOR, SA): Av. Marginal, CP 82, Mindelo, São Vicente; tel. 2324414; fax 2324337; e-mail enapor@cvtelecom.cv; internet www.enapor.cv; f. 1982; due to be privatized by early 2007; Chair. and Man. Dir Franklim do Rosário Spencer.

Arca Verde (Companhia Nacional de Navegação): Rua 5 de Julho, Plateau, Santiago; tel. 2615497; fax 2615496; e-mail cnnarcaverdepra@cvtelecom.cv; shipping co; undergoing privatization.

Cape Verde National Shipping Line, SARL (Cs Line): Rua Baltasar Lopez da Silva, CP 238, Mindelo, São Vicente.

Companhia Caboverdiana de Navegação: Rua Cristiano Sena Barcelos 3–5, Mindelo, São Vicente; tel. 2322852.

Companhia de Navegação Estrela Negra: Av. 5 de Julho 17, CP 91, Mindelo, São Vicente; tel. 2325423; fax 2315382.

Linhas Marítimas Caboverdianas (LINMAC): CP 357, Praia, Santiago; tel. 2614352; fax 2613715; Dir Esther Spencer.

Seage Agência de Navegação de Cabo Verde: Av. Cidade de Lisboa, CP 232, Praia, Santiago; tel. 2615758; fax 2612524; f. 1986; Chair. César Manuel Semedo Lopes.

Transnacional, a shipping company, operates a ferry service between some islands.

CIVIL AVIATION

The Amílcar Cabral international airport, at Espargos, on Sal island, can accommodate aircraft of up to 50 tons and 1m. passengers per year. The airport's facilities were expanded during the 1990s. A second international airport, Aeroporto da Praia, was opened in late 2005. There is also a small airport on each of the other inhabited islands. The airport on São Vicente was upgraded to international capacity in 2000. Plans were also under way for the construction of two further international airports, on Boa Vista and São Vicente. Transportes Aéreos de Cabo Verde (TACV) and the Portuguese carrier, TAP, operate flights to Cape Verde.

CAPE VERDE

Agência de Aviação Civil (AAC): Praia, Santiago; f. 2005; regulatory agency; Pres. VALDEMAR CORREIA.

Empresa Nacional de Aeroportos e Segurança AEREA, EP (ASA): Aeroporto Amílcar Cabral, CP 58, Ilha do Sal; tel. 2412626; fax 2411570; e-mail pca@asa.cv; internet www.asa.cv; airports and aircraft security; Pres. MÁRIO LOPES.

Transportes Aéreos de Cabo Verde (TACV): Av. Amílcar Cabral, CP 1, Praia, Santiago; tel. 2608200; fax 2617275; e-mail pferreira@tacv.aero; internet www.tacv.cv; f. 1958; internal services connecting the nine inhabited islands; also operates regional services to Senegal, The Gambia and Guinea-Bissau, and long-distance services to Europe and the USA; due to be privatized by 2007; Pres. and CEO JOÃO HIGINO SILVA; Gen. Man. PAULO FERREIRA.

A private company, Inter Island Airlines, offers flights between the islands of Cape Verde, and a new inter-island carrier, Halcyon Air, was established in early 2005.

Tourism

The islands of Santiago, Santo Antão, Fogo and Brava offer attractive mountain scenery. There are extensive beaches on the islands of Santiago, Sal, Boa Vista and Maio. Some 197,844 tourists visited Cape Verde in 2005. In 2005 tourism receipts totalled some US $177m. The sector is undergoing rapid expansion, with development in a number of Zonas de Desenvolvimento Turístico Integral. In late 2003 the Government began steps to have Fogo, which contains the only live volcano on Cape Verde, designated a UNESCO world heritage site. Plans were unveiled in March 2004 to promote the island of Santa Luzia as an eco-tourism destination. Construction of a large tourist resort on Santiago, expected to cost €550m., commenced in early 2005. Tourist arrivals are projected to increase to about 400,000 annually by 2008.

THE CENTRAL AFRICAN REPUBLIC

Introductory Survey

Location, Climate, Language, Religion, Flag, Capital

The Central African Republic is a land-locked country in the heart of equatorial Africa. It is bordered by Chad to the north, by Sudan to the east, by the Democratic Republic of the Congo (formerly Zaire) and the Republic of the Congo to the south and by Cameroon to the west. The climate is tropical, with an average annual temperature of 26°C (79°F) and heavy rainfall in the south-western forest areas. The national language is Sango, but French is the official language and another 68 languages and dialects have been identified. It is estimated that about one-half of the population are Christian; another 15% are Muslims, while animist beliefs are held by an estimated 24%. The national flag (proportions 3 by 5) has four equal horizontal stripes, of blue, white, green and yellow, divided vertically by a central red stripe, with a five-pointed yellow star in the hoist corner of the blue stripe. The capital is Bangui.

Recent History

The former territory of Ubangi-Shari (Oubangui-Chari), within French Equatorial Africa, became the Central African Republic (CAR) on achieving self-government in December 1958. David Dacko led the country to full independence and became its first President, on 13 August 1960. In 1962 a one-party state was established, with the ruling Mouvement d'évolution sociale de l'Afrique noire (MESAN) as the sole authorized party. Dacko was overthrown on 31 December 1965 by a military coup, which brought to power his cousin, Col (later Marshal) Jean-Bédel Bokassa, Commander-in-Chief of the armed forces.

In January 1966 Bokassa formed a new Government, rescinded the Constitution and dissolved the legislature. Bokassa became Life President in March 1972 and Marshal of the Republic in May 1974. In September 1976 the Council of Ministers was replaced by the Council for the Central African Revolution, and former President Dacko was appointed personal adviser to the President. In December the Republic was renamed the Central African Empire (CAE), and a new Constitution was instituted. Bokassa was proclaimed the first Emperor, and Dacko became his Personal Counsellor. However, in September 1979, while Bokassa was in Libya, Dacko deposed him in a bloodless coup, which received considerable support from France. The country was again designated a republic, with Dacko as its President and Henri Maidou as Vice-President.

President Dacko's principal concern was to establish order and economic stability, but his Government encountered opposition, particularly from students who objected to the continuation in office of CAE ministers. In August 1980 Dacko accepted demands for the dismissal of both Maidou and the Prime Minister, Bernard Christian Ayandho. Bokassa, at that time in exile in Côte d'Ivoire, was sentenced to death *in absentia* in December. In February 1981 a new Constitution, providing for a multi-party system, was approved by referendum and promulgated by Dacko. He won a presidential election in March, amid allegations of electoral malpractice, and was sworn in for a six-year term in April. Political tension intensified in subsequent months, and on 1 September the Chief of Staff of the Armed Forces, Gen. André Kolingba, deposed Dacko in a bloodless coup. Kolingba was declared President, and an all-military Government was formed. All political activity was suspended.

In March 1982 the exiled leader of the banned Mouvement pour la libération du peuple centrafricain (MLPC), Ange-Félix Patassé, returned to Bangui and was implicated in an unsuccessful coup attempt. Patassé, who had been Prime Minister under Bokassa in 1976–78 and who had contested the 1981 presidential election, sought asylum in the French embassy in Bangui, from where he was transported to exile in Togo.

In September 1985, for the first time since Kolingba's assumption of power, civilians were appointed to the Council of Ministers. In early 1986 a specially convened commission drafted a new Constitution, which provided for the creation of a sole legal political party, the Rassemblement démocratique centrafricain (RDC), and conferred extensive executive powers on the President, while defining a predominantly advisory role for the legislature. At a referendum in November some 91% of voters approved the draft Constitution and granted Kolingba a mandate to serve a further six-year term as President. The Council of Ministers was reorganized in December to include a majority of civilians. The RDC was officially established in February 1987, with Kolingba as founding President, and elections to the new Assemblée nationale took place in July, at which 142 candidates, all nominated by the RDC, contested the 52 seats.

In October 1986 Bokassa returned unexpectedly to the CAR and was immediately arrested. In June 1987 he was sentenced to death, having been convicted on charges of murder, conspiracy to murder, the illegal detention of prisoners and embezzlement. In February 1988 Kolingba commuted the sentence to one of life imprisonment with hard labour. (Bokassa was released from prison in September 1993 under a general amnesty for convicts; however, the former Emperor was banned for life from participating in elections and demoted from the military rank of marshal. He died in November 1996.)

The appointment during 1988 of former associates of Bokassa, Dacko and Patassé to prominent public offices appeared to represent an attempt by Kolingba to consolidate national unity. In August 1989, however, 12 opponents of his regime, including members of the Front patriotique oubanguien-Parti du travail and the leader of the Rassemblement populaire pour la reconstruction de la Centrafrique, Brig.-Gen. (later Gen.) François Bozizé Yangouvounda, were arrested in Benin, where they had been living in exile, and extradited to the CAR. Bozizé was subsequently found guilty of complicity in the 1982 coup attempt.

In 1990 opposition movements exerted pressure on the Government to introduce a plural political system. In December the Executive Council of the RDC recommended a review of the Constitution and the re-establishment of the premiership. Accordingly, in March 1991 Edouard Franck, a former Minister of State at the Presidency, was appointed Prime Minister, and in July the Assemblée nationale approved a constitutional amendment providing for the establishment of a multi-party political system. Kolingba resigned from the presidency of the RDC in the following month, in order to remain 'above parties'. In December Kolingba pardoned Bozizé.

Kolingba convened a Grand National Debate in August 1992, but it was boycotted by the influential Concertation des forces démocratiques (CFD), an alliance of opposition groupings, which announced that it would only participate in a multi-party national conference with sovereign powers. At the end of August the Assemblée nationale approved legislation in accordance with decisions taken by the Grand National Debate: constitutional amendments provided for the strict separation of executive, legislative and judicial powers, and Kolingba was granted temporary powers to rule by decree until the election of a new multi-party legislature. Concurrent legislative and presidential elections commenced in October, but were suspended by presidential decree and subsequently annulled by the Supreme Court, owing to alleged sabotage of the electoral process. In December Franck resigned as Prime Minister and was replaced by Gen. Timothée Malendoma, the leader of the Forum civique.

In February 1993 Malendoma, who had accused Kolingba of curtailing his powers, was dismissed from the premiership and replaced by Enoch Derant Lakoué, the leader of the Parti social-démocrate. Two rounds of concurrent legislative and presidential elections were held in late August and mid-September in which the MLPC won 34 of the 85 seats in the Assemblée nationale, while the RDC, in second place, secured 13 seats. Patassé, the MLPC leader and former Prime Minister, was elected President, winning 52.47% of the votes cast at a second round of voting. The seven other presidential candidates included Kolingba, Prof. Abel Goumba (the leader of the CFD) and former President Dacko. In October Patassé was inaugurated as President. Soon afterwards he appointed Jean-Luc Mandaba, the Vice-President of the MLPC, as Prime Minister; Mandaba formed a coalition Government, which had a working majority of 53 seats in the Assemblée nationale.

In December 1994 a draft Constitution was approved by 82% of voters in a national referendum. The new Constitution, which was adopted in January 1995, included provisions empowering

THE CENTRAL AFRICAN REPUBLIC

the President to nominate senior military, civil service and judicial officials, and requiring the Prime Minister to implement policies decided by the President. In addition, provision was made for the creation of directly elected regional assemblies and for the establishment of an advisory State Council, which was to deliberate on administrative issues. Several groups in the governing coalition (notably the Mouvement pour la démocratie et le développement—MDD, led by Dacko) expressed concern at the powers afforded to the President.

In April 1995 Mandaba resigned as Prime Minister, preempting a threatened vote of no confidence in his administration (initiated by his own party), following accusations of corruption and incompetence. Patassé appointed Gabriel Koyambounou, formerly a civil servant, as the new Prime Minister. Koyambounou subsequently nominated a new Council of Ministers, with an enlarged membership. In December several opposition movements (including the MDD, but not the RDC) united to form the Conseil démocratique des partis politiques de l'opposition (CODEPO), which aimed to campaign against alleged corruption and mismanagement by the Patassé regime.

In the mid-1990s the Government repeatedly failed to pay the salaries of public sector employees and members of the security forces, prompting frequent strikes and mounting political unrest. In mid-April 1996 CODEPO staged an anti-Government rally in Bangui. Shortly afterwards part of the national army mutinied in the capital and demanded the immediate settlement of all salary arrears. Patassé promised that part of the overdue salaries would be paid and that the mutineers would not be subject to prosecution. The presence of French troops (the Eléments français d'assistance opérationelle—EFAO) in Bangui, with a mandate to secure the safety of foreign nationals and (in accordance with a bilateral military accord) to protect the presidential palace and other key installations, contributed to the swift collapse of the rebellion. In late April Patassé appointed a new Chief of Staff of the Armed Forces, Col Maurice Regonessa, and banned all public demonstrations. In May, however, discontent resurfaced, and CODEPO organized another rally in Bangui, at which it demanded the resignation of the Government. Soon afterward the President ordered that control of the national armoury should be transferred from the regular army to the presidential guard. However, adverse reaction to this move within the ranks of the armed forces rapidly escalated into a second, more determined insurrection. Once again EFAO troops were deployed to protect the Patassé administration; some 500 reinforcements were brought in from Chad and Gabon to consolidate the resident French military presence (numbering 1,400). Five hostages were taken by the mutineers, including Col Regonessa, a government minister and the President of the Assemblée nationale. After five days of fierce fighting between dissident and loyalist troops, the French forces intervened to suppress the rebellion. France's military action (which allegedly resulted in civilian deaths) prompted intense scrutiny of the role of the former colonial power, and precipitated large pro- and anti-French demonstrations in Bangui. In total, 11 soldiers and 32 civilians were reported to have been killed in the second army mutiny. Following extended negotiations, the mutineers and government representatives eventually signed an accord, providing for an amnesty for the rebels (who were to return to barracks under EFAO guard), the immediate release of hostages, and the installation of a new government of national unity.

In June 1996 the Government and the opposition signed a protocol providing for the establishment of a government of national unity, led by a civilian Prime Minister with no official party ties. Following the publication of the protocol, Koyambounou's Government resigned. Jean-Paul Ngoupandé, hitherto ambassador to France and with no official political affiliation, was appointed as the new Prime Minister and immediately nominated a new Council of Ministers. National co-operation, however, remained elusive, as CODEPO, dissatisfied with the level of its ministerial representation, immediately withdrew from the Government.

At a conference on national defence held in August–September 1996, several resolutions were adopted regarding restructuring and improving conditions within the army. In mid-November a further mutiny erupted among troops who had been involved in the insurrections of April and May; a substantial part of Bangui was occupied by the rebels, and a number of hostages were taken. EFAO troops were deployed once again, ostensibly to maintain order and protect foreign residents; however, by guarding key installations and government buildings, they also effectively prevented the overthrow of the Patassé administration. More than 100 people were killed in the unrest during late November and early December.

In December 1996 the Presidents of Burkina Faso, Chad, Gabon and Mali negotiated a 15-day truce, which was supervised by the former transitional President of Mali, Gen. Amadou Toumani Touré; a one-month extension to the cease-fire was subsequently agreed. In January 1997, following the killing of two French soldiers in Bangui (reportedly by mutineers), EFAO troops retaliated by killing at least 10 members of the rebel forces; French military involvement in the CAR was condemned by the opposition, which also sought (without success) to initiate impeachment proceedings against Patassé. Subsequent to the renewal of violence, Touré again came to Bangui as mediator and helped to create a cross-party Committee of Consultation and Dialogue. The 'Bangui Accords', drawn up by this committee, were signed towards the end of January; these, as well as offering an amnesty to the mutineers, provided for the formation of a new government of national unity and for the replacement of the EFAO troops by peace-keeping forces from African nations. The opposition at first threatened to boycott the new Government, largely owing to the appointment of Michel Gbezera-Bria (a close associate of Patassé and hitherto the Minister of Foreign Affairs) as Prime Minister. However, with the creation of new ministerial posts for opposition politicians, a 'Government of Action' (which did not include Ngoupandé) was formed on 18 February; soon afterwards Gen. Bozizé replaced Gen. Regonessa as Chief of Staff of the Armed Forces.

In February 1997 responsibility for peace-keeping operations was transferred from the EFAO to forces of the newly formed Mission interafricaine de surveillance des accords de Bangui (MISAB), comprising some 700 soldiers from Burkina Faso, Chad, Gabon, Mali, Senegal and Togo (with logistical support from 50 French military personnel).

In May 1997, following the deaths in police custody of three former rebels suspected of criminal activities, nine ministers representing the G11 (a grouping of 11 opposition parties, including the MDD—which had left CODEPO in November 1996—and the RDC), as well as the two representatives of the former mutineers, suspended participation in the Government. In June violent clashes erupted between MISAB forces and former mutineers. In response to several attacks on the French embassy by the rebels, several hundred EFAO troops were redeployed on the streets of Bangui, and MISAB forces launched a major offensive in the capital, capturing most of the rebel-controlled districts. This assault led to the arrest of more than 80 former mutineers, but also to some 100 deaths, both of soldiers and of civilians. Subsequently, Touré returned to Bangui in his capacity as Chairman of MISAB, and negotiated a four-day truce, which took effect at the end of June, followed by a 10-day cease-fire agreement, signed at the beginning of July; all of the former mutineers were to be reintegrated into the regular armed forces, and their safety and that of the people living in the districts under their control was guaranteed; the rebels, for their part, were to relinquish their weaponry. Towards the end of July many of the people who had been held in custody in relation to the previous month's violence were released by the authorities, and the curfew in Bangui was eased, while it was reported that almost all of the former mutineers had rejoined the regular armed forces. In September the nine representatives of opposition parties in the Council of Ministers resumed their vacant posts.

In July 1997 France announced its intention to withdraw its troops from the CAR by April 1998; the first troops left the country in October 1997. France campaigned vigorously for the formation of a UN force, but encountered initial resistance from the USA. A National Reconciliation Conference, held in Bangui, in February 1998 led to the signing on 5 March of a National Reconciliation Pact by President Patassé and 40 representatives of all the country's political and social groups. The accord was countersigned by Gen. Touré and witnessed by many other African Heads of State. The Pact restated the main provisions of the Bangui Accords and of the political protocol of June 1996. It provided for military and political restructuring, to be implemented by a civilian Prime Minister, supported by all of the country's social and political groups. The powers and position of the President were, however, guaranteed, and a presidential election was scheduled for late 1999.

The signature of the Pact facilitated the authorization, later in March 1998, by the UN Security Council of the establishment of a peace-keeping mission, the UN Mission in the Central African Republic (MINURCA), to replace MISAB. MINURCA comprised

1,345 troops from Benin, Burkina Faso, Canada, Chad, Côte d'Ivoire, Egypt, France, Gabon, Mali, Portugal, Senegal and Togo, and was granted a mandate to remain in the country for an initial period of three months. The mission was subsequently extended until the end of February 1999.

Elections to the newly reorganized Assemblée nationale, which were contested by 29 parties, took place on 22 November and 13 December 1998. The MPLC won 47 of the 109 seats in the legislature, but secured the co-operation of seven independent members. The opposition won 55 seats; however, the defection, amid allegations of bribery, of a newly elected deputy belonging to the Parti social-démocrate (PSD) gave the ruling MPLC a majority in the Assemblée. Patassé's decision to call on a close associate, the nominally independent erstwhile Minister of Finance, Anicet Georges Dologuélé, to form a new Government provoked public demonstrations and caused the opposition formally to withdraw from the Assemblée (the boycott lasted until March 1999). Dologuélé announced the composition of a new coalition Council of Ministers in early January, but 10 opposition ministers immediately resigned in protest at the MPLC's alleged disregard for the results of the election. In mid-January Dologuélé announced the formation of another Council of Ministers, which included four members of the MDD, despite an earlier agreement made by the opposition not to accept posts in the new Government. The MDD leadership subsequently ordered its members to resign from their government positions; three of its four ministers did so.

In February 1999 the UN Security Council extended MINURCA's mandate until mid-November in order that it might assist in preparations for, and the conduct of, the presidential election, which was scheduled to be held on 29 August. France was reported to have opposed an extension of the mandate, and in February the French contingent withdrew from MINURCA (as did the troops from Côte d'Ivoire in April). The UN Secretary-General, Kofi Annan, called on all factions in the CAR to co-operate in preparations for the presidential election. In particular, Annan criticized delays in the appointment of the independent electoral commission, the Commission électorale mixte indépendante (CEMI), the 27 members of which were finally approved in May. In July the Constitutional Court authorized 10 candidates to stand in the election. President Patassé was to seek re-election, while other candidates included two former Presidents, Kolingba and Dacko, as well as Goumba, the opposition candidate in the 1993 presidential election. In August, at the request of bilateral creditors and the UN, a 45-member body was established to supervise the activities of the CEMI, which comprised members of both opposition and pro-Patassé parties. In the event, the election was not held until 19 September, owing to organizational problems. On 2 October the Constitutional Court announced that Patassé had been re-elected President, with 51.6% of the total votes cast. Patassé's nearest rivals were Kolingba, who won 19.4% of the votes, Dacko (11.2%), and Goumba (6.1%). On 22 October Patassé was sworn in as President for a further six-year term. In early November recently reappointed Prime Minister Dologuélé announced the formation of a new Council of Ministers, which included members of parties loyal to Patassé, as well as independents, three opposition representatives and two members of the armed forces. The Government stated that its main priorities were to improve human development in the CAR and to combat poverty; particular emphasis was also laid on the restructuring of the public sector and of the armed forces.

In October 1999 Kofi Annan requested that the UN Security Council authorize the gradual withdrawal of MINURCA from the CAR over a three-month period following the end of its mandate on 15 November. In December the UN announced proposals to establish a Bureau de soutien à la consolidation de la paix en Centrafrique (BONUCA), in Bangui, the role of which would be to monitor developments in the CAR in the areas of politics, socio-economics, human rights and security issues, as well as to facilitate dialogue between political figures. BONUCA began its operation on the same day as the final withdrawal of MINURCA, 15 February 2000, with a mandate for a one-year period. In September 2000 BONUCA's mandate was extended until the end of 2001, and in September 2001, following continued unrest, it was extended for a further one-year period.

In April 2001 Patassé dismissed the Dologuélé administration. Martin Ziguélé was appointed as Prime Minister, and a new Government was formed. In late May rebellious soldiers, thought to be supporters of Kolingba, attacked Patassé's official residence in an attempted coup. However, the insurgency was suppressed by troops loyal to Patassé, and at least 59 people were killed. Libya sent troops and helicopters, while a contingent of rebels from the Democratic Republic of the Congo (DRC) arrived to support the Patassé regime. Violence ensued throughout the country, with heavy fighting in Bangui resulting in some 300 deaths. Of an estimated 60,000–70,000 civilians who were reported to have fled the capital following the coup attempt, some 10,000 had returned by July, according to aid agencies. In August 2002 Kolingba and 21 associates were sentenced to death *in absentia* for their alleged involvement in the coup; a further 500 defendants were reported to have received prison terms of 10–20 years.

In August 2001 the Council of Ministers was reshuffled; most notably, the Minister of National Defence, Jean-Jacques Démafouth, was replaced, following allegations regarding his involvement in the attempted coup in May (he was, however, acquitted of all charges at his trial in October 2002). In October 2001 Gen. Bozizé was dismissed from the post of Chief of Staff of the Armed Forces because of similar allegations. However, in early November violence erupted in Bangui between supporters of Bozizé and the presidential guard (supported by forces from Libya) after attempts were made to arrest Bozizé, at the request of a judicial commission of inquiry into the failed coup attempt. Efforts to mediate between Bozizé and the CAR administration were unsuccessful, and later that month Bozizé fled to the town of Sarh in southern Chad, where he was granted refuge, with about 300 of his armed supporters. Tension reportedly increased between the CAR and Chad, as security forces pursued those loyal to Bozizé along the border between the two countries. At a meeting of the Communauté économique et monétaire de l'Afrique centrale (CEMAC) in Libreville, Gabon, in December, a commission was created, chaired by President Omar Bongo of Gabon, and also comprising Presidents Idriss Deby and Denis Sassou-Nguesso of Chad and the Republic of the Congo, respectively, to find a lasting solution to the crisis in the CAR. In late December the CAR judiciary abandoned legal proceedings against Bozizé, and in January 2002, during a meeting held in Chad, a government delegation invited Bozizé and his supporters to return to the CAR.

In April 2002, in consultation with political parties and development organizations, the Government announced a series of measures to reform public services and promote good governance. In July the Minister of State in charge of Finance and the Budget, Eric Sorongopé, was arrested on suspicion of embezzling government funds reportedly in excess of US $3m. More than 20 government officials were also detained on charges relating to the scandal. The subsequent withdrawal of IMF and World Bank representatives from Bangui also threatened to aggravate the ongoing budget crisis, and protests continued at the Government's failure to pay public sector wages. In September BONUCA's mandate was extended until December 2003.

On 25 October 2002 the northern suburbs of Bangui were invaded by forces loyal to Bozizé (who had been granted asylum in France earlier in the month, in accordance with an agreement reached at a CEMAC summit aimed at defusing tension between the CAR and Chad—see below). After five days of heavy fighting, pro-Government forces, supported by Libyan troops and some 1,000 fighters from a DRC rebel grouping, the Mouvement pour la libération du Congo (MLC), succeeded in repelling Bozizé's insurgents. Initial reports indicated that some 28 people had been killed during the fighting. None the less, by December the Patassé Government had failed fully to suppress the forces allied to Bozizé, and the CAR was effectively divided between loyalist areas in the south and east and rebel-held northern regions between the Chadian border and Bangui.

In December 2002 the first contingent of a CEMAC peace-keeping force (eventually to number 350) arrived in Bangui, and in January 2003 Libyan forces were withdrawn. Clashes were frequently claimed to have occurred between the regular CAR army and its allies, culminating in reports (denied by the CAR Government) of a massacre of MLC soldiers in December. In February, however, MLC fighters began to withdraw from the CAR, in response to international pressure on the Patassé Government. In late February Patassé announced the establishment of a new commission to rehabilitate officials returning from exile, and in March the RDC and other opposition parties resumed their participation in the Assemblée nationale. A ministerial reshuffle was effected in January.

On 15 March 2003 armed supporters of Bozizé entered Bangui, encountering little resistance from government troops. President Patassé, who had been attending a regional summit in

Niger, was forced to withdraw to the Cameroonian capital, Yaoundé, after shots were fired at his aeroplane as it attempted to land at Bangui. Reports suggested that casualties during the coup had numbered no more than 15 people. Following the surrender of the largely demoralized security forces in the capital, Bozizé declared himself Head of State, dissolved the Assemblée nationale and suspended the Constitution. Although the coup was condemned by the African Union (AU, see p. 164), the UN, CEMAC, France and the USA, Bozizé insisted that his actions constituted only a 'temporary suspension of democracy' and that a new consensus government would be formed in consultation with the former opposition, human rights groups and development agencies. Following this announcement, Bozizé secured the approval of the Governments of Gabon and the Republic of the Congo at a meeting with the foreign ministers of those countries. France deployed some 300 troops in Bangui in order to assist foreign nationals intending to leave the CAR. Bozizé also gained the support of opposition parties, which pledged to oppose any attempt by Patassé to return to power. In late March Abel Goumba, the leader of the Front patriotique pour le progrès, was appointed as Prime Minister, and a new, broad-based transitional Government was subsequently formed. Despite only receiving two positions in the new Council of Ministers, in mid-April the MLPC declared that it would adhere to the transitional arrangements decreed by Bozizé.

On 30 May 2003 Bozizé inaugurated a 98-member, advisory Conseil national de transition (CNT), which included representatives of political parties, trade unions, religious organizations and human rights groups, in order to assist him in exercising legislative power during the transitional period, which was to last 18–30 months. The CNT maintained its opposition to any involvement by former President Patassé in the political process, and elected Nicolas Tiangaye, a prominent human rights activist, as its Speaker. Meanwhile, Bozizé confirmed his intention to return the country to civilian rule in January 2005, and a timetable for the resumption of democracy was announced.

In June 2003 the Government announced plans for the demobilization or integration into the CAR army of 5,700 former fighters: 1,200 loyal to Bozizé, 3,500 loyal to Patassé and 1,000 returning from exile. Meanwhile, the Government continued its investigations into widely acknowledged corruption within the country's economic institutions and civil service. In June the executive boards of the state electricity and telecommunications companies were dismissed after the reported discovery of widespread accounting irregularities, and in July 866 non-existent workers were removed from the public sector payroll. Moreover, in the same month the judicial authorities began an investigation into the whereabouts of some 4,800m. francs CFA donated by the Japanese Government for the Patassé administration's reconciliation plans, and ordered the suspension of mineral and timber interests controlled by the former President, while the Government issued guidelines obliging government officials and politicians to declare their personal assets. In August the state prosecutor issued an international arrest warrant for Patassé, now in exile in Togo, on charges including murder and embezzlement. In September BONUCA's mandate was extended until December 2004.

In December 2003 Prime Minister Goumba was appointed Vice-President, and his previous post was allocated to Célestin-Leroy Gaombalet, a former financier. Gaombalet subsequently effected a government reshuffle, in which 14 ministers retained their portfolios; the changes mainly reflected popular dissatisfaction with deteriorating public security in Bangui, and new appointees also included several political figures linked to previous administrations. Also, in December a new mining code was promulgated, following the recommendations of a conference held in August. The legislation appeared to limit the President's discretion over awarding contracts for mineral exploitation, and strengthened the role of the security forces in monitoring illegal mining.

An eight-member interministerial committee, headed by Prime Minister Gaombalet, was established in January 2004 to oversee the forthcoming electoral process. According to a revised schedule, a referendum on a new constitution, which was to be drafted by the CNT, would be held in November, with municipal, presidential and legislative elections to follow between December and January 2005. Bozizé had earlier stated that he would not contest the presidential election but in mid-June 2004 he declared his candidature possible. In early December the newly appointed Transitional Constitutional Court (TCC) oversaw the planned referendum on a new constitution, which was approved by 87.2% of those who voted. The new Constitution provided for a presidential term of five years, renewable only once, and increased powers for the Prime Minister. Following the referendum Bozizé announced that presidential and legislative elections were to be rescheduled for mid-February 2005 and that he would stand as an independent candidate for the presidency. In late December 2004 the TCC disqualified nine presidential candidates including, notably, former President Patassé and former Prime Minister Ngoupandé. However, the TCC's decision provoked popular unrest and in early January 2005 Bozizé annulled the disqualification of Ngoupandé and two other candidates.

Following administrative delays, presidential and legislative elections were held concurrently on 13 March 2005. In the presidential election Bozizé secured 43.0% of the votes cast, while the former Prime Minister Ziguélé obtained 23.5% and Kolingba 16.0%. As no candidate had won an absolute majority, the two leading candidates, Bozizé and Ziguélé, proceeded to a second round of voting, held on 8 May, at which Bozizé took 64.67% of the vote. At the legislative elections the pro-Bozizé Convergence 'Kwa na kwa' (meaning 'Work and Only Work' in Sango) secured 42 of the 105 seats in the new Assemblée nationale, while the MLPC (the principal party supporting Ziguélé) won 11 seats; 34 independent candidates were also elected. Despite allegations by opposition groups of electoral malpractice, Ziguélé conceded defeat following the announcement of the results and appealed for calm from his supporters. In June Bozizé unveiled a new Council of Ministers headed by Elie Doté, who declared that the priorities of the new Government would be to implement large-scale institutional and infrastructural reform while achieving peace and macroeconomic stability in the country. Also in that month the AU's Peace and Security Council lifted sanctions that had been imposed on the CAR in the wake of Bozizé's seizure of power in March 2003.

The non-payment of public sector salaries led to strikes by teachers' and civil servants' unions throughout 2005, causing major disruption to the provision of key services. In November the Government reached an agreement with the Union Syndicale des Travailleurs de Centrafrique (USTC) providing for the payment of two months' salary arrears and three months' pension payments, in addition to a government commitment to ensure regular payments in the future. The USTC, for its part, agreed to suspend industrial action for six months to allow the agreement to be implemented. Meanwhile, in October an audit of government finances revealed that some 10% of civil servants had fraudulently claimed additional salary. In December BONUCA's mandate was extended until the end of 2006.

In late January 2006 Bozizé carried out a cabinet reshuffle, following the suspension of three ministers on corruption charges the previous October. Meanwhile, there were reports of unrest in the north of the country in the Paoua region, the birthplace of former President Patassé; many civilians were said to have fled armed rebels across the border into Chad. In April the Supreme Court confirmed that the CAR justice system was inadequate to try Patassé and his associates for the atrocities allegedly committed in the country following Bozizé's failed coup attempt of October 2002. The case was therefore referred to the International Criminal Court. In early June 2006 Doté conducted a peace mission to the Paoua region, during which he urged local leaders to encourage the population to return to their homes. In August Patassé and one of his advisers were found guilty of financial misconduct by the Criminal Court. They were sentenced to 20 years hard labour *in absentia* and fined 7,000m. francs CFA. (Two months earlier the former President had been ousted as leader of the MLPC and replaced by Ziguélé.) In late October the rebel coalition, the Union des forces démocratiques pour le changement (UFDR), took control of the north-eastern town of Birao. Bozizé, who returned early from a trip to the People's Republic of China at the onset of the crisis, travelled to Chad to meet with his counterpart, Deby Itno (as he had now become); the two heads of state subsequently blamed the unrest on the Sudanese Government which, they claimed, supported anti-Government forces in the CAR and Chad. In mid-November it was reported that the UFDR had also seized control of Ouanda Djalle and was heading south towards Bria, 600 km north of Bangui. Chadian forces were subsequently deployed to assist the CAR military in overcoming the rebels, while the French Government agreed to provide support in the form of logistics and aerial intelligence. In late November a major government counter-offensive was launched in which CEMAC forces were also involved resulted in the recapture of Birao. In mid-December

THE CENTRAL AFRICAN REPUBLIC

Ouanda Djalle, the last town to remain under rebel control, was reclaimed, following a series of French air strikes in the region.

In early February 2007 Abdoulaye Miskine, leader of the Front démocratique de libération du peuple centrafricain (FDPC—a faction of the UFDR), signed a peace deal with Bozizé, brokered by the Libyan leader, Col Muammar al-Qaddafi, in Sirte, Libya. Miskine was a former senior Chadian rebel leader and a close associate of Patassé who had been based in the CAR since 1998. Under the terms of the agreement FDPC rebels were to surrender their weapons and cease military activities in return for an amnesty. The agreement also committed the CAR Government to putting in place a programme for the rehabilitation of former rebels and their integration into the CAR military. Miskine called on all other rebel fighters to lay down their arms. The accord was also signed by André Ringui Le Gaillard, leader of the Armée populaire pour la restauration de la république et la démocratie (APRD), who had also served in the Government during Patassé's regime. In April an accord was signed by the CAR Government and the leader of the UFDR, Zakaria Damane, on behalf of the northern rebels, granting them an amnesty and providing for the implementation of an immediate cessation of hostilities. However, the cease-fire failed to hold and the violence continued, forcing thousands more people to flee their homes and seek refuge in neighbouring Cameroon and Chad. The UN encouraged the CAR Government to continue discussions with rebel leaders to restore peace and in July Damane was appointed as an adviser to the presidency. Shortly afterwards a government reshuffle was effected in which Gen. Raymond Paul Ndougou, a signatory to the April peace agreement, was named as Minister of the Interior and Public Security; Lt-Col Sylvain N'doutingaï assumed the position of Minister of Finance and the Budget, and of Mines, Energy and Hydraulics.

In September 2007, following the adoption of UN Resolution 1778, the UN Security Council approved the deployment for a period of one year of the United Nations Mission in the Central African Republic and Chad (MINURCAT), with the mandate to protect refugees, displaced persons and civilians adversely affected by the uprising in the Darfur region of Sudan. MINURCAT was also to facilitate the provision of humanitarian assistance in eastern Chad and the north-east of the CAR and create favourable conditions for the reconstruction and economic and social development of those areas. The multidimensional presence was to be supported by the European Union bridging military operation in Eastern Chad and North Eastern Central African Republic (EUFOR TCHAD/RCA) comprising some 4,300 troops. According to the office of the UN High Commissioner for Refugees (UNHCR), at the end of 2006 there were some 7,900 Sudanese refugees in the CAR; however, the number of Sudanese refugees in Chad was estimated at more than 230,000.

Prime Minister Elie Doté announced his resignation, and that of his Council of Ministers, in mid-January 2008 ahead of a planned parliamentary vote of no confidence in his leadership. The country had been experiencing civil unrest for several months and a number of trade unions had earlier in January commenced a general strike in protest at payment arrears owed to civil servants dating back some seven months. It was reported that the strike would continue despite the resignation, which trade union representatives maintained had no impact on their salary demands. Prof. Faustin-Archange Touadéra, the Rector of the University of Bangui who possessed no significant previous political experience, was named as Doté's successor and later in January a new Government was announced; many of the key portfolios remained unaltered, but three existing ministers were promoted to the status of Minister of State, including N'doutingaï, although he relinquished responsibility for finance and the budget. Among the most notable appointments was Dieudonné Kombo Yaya who was named as Minister of Foreign and Francophone Affairs and Regional Integration. Bernard Lalah Bonamna, hitherto Minister of Public Health, was moved to the Ministry of Education but resigned from the cabinet just one day after the appointment, objecting to the change in portfolio.

In May 1997 the CAR recognized the administration of President Laurent Kabila in the DRC (formerly Zaire). In the same month the CAR and the DRC signed a mutual assistance pact, which provided for permanent consultation on internal security and defence. The pact also sought to guarantee border security; however, during mid-1997 armed soldiers of what had been the Zairean army were reported to be fleeing troops loyal to Kabila and crossing the Oubangui river into the CAR. In January 1999 there was a further influx to the CAR of DRC civilians fleeing the fighting between government and rebel soldiers, who were occupying the northern part of the DRC. In August UNHCR estimated that the CAR was sheltering about 54,000 refugees from the DRC, Chad and Sudan. Following the attempted coup in the CAR in May 2001, UNHCR estimated that 23,000 people had escaped to the DRC; further movements were reported in the aftermath of the attempted coup of October 2002. In June 2003 Gen. Bozizé and President Joseph Kabila of the DRC agreed to re-establish existing bilateral security arrangements. In August 2004 officials from both countries met to discuss reopening the common border and, subsequently, an agreement was signed under the auspices of the UNHCR allowing some 10,000 Congolese refugees in the CAR to be repatriated.

In late 1994 the CAR and Chad agreed to establish a bilateral security structure to ensure mutual border security. In 1994 the CAR also became the fifth member of the Lake Chad Basin Commission (see p. 413). In December 1999 it was reported that some 1,500 Chadian refugees were preparing to leave the CAR, allegedly owing to fears for their security following the imminent departure of MINURCA forces. Relations between the CAR and Chad deteriorated when armed men, led by a Chadian rebel, raided southern Chad from the CAR on 29 and 31 December 2001; four people were killed during the raids. A further outbreak of violence in the border area was reported in April 2002, which resulted in at least one fatality. Despite pledges by both countries to increase co-operation, further clashes in August resulted in the deaths of 20 CAR soldiers. An emergency CEMAC summit took place later that month, chaired by the Gabonese President, Omar Bongo, and an observer mission was dispatched to examine the security situation along the common border. At the end of August the mission reported that, although tension remained high in the region, there was no concentration of troops on the border. The CAR's decision to appoint Col Martin Khoumtan-Madji (believed by the Chadian authorities to be an alias of Abdoulaye Miskine) as the head of a special unit in the CAR military, charged with securing the common border, further strained relations, as did Chad's reputed sponsorship of forces loyal to Bozizé. In early October a CEMAC summit in Libreville, Gabon, sought to defuse tensions between the two countries; in accordance with an accord reached at the summit, Bozizé and Khoumtan-Madji were subsequently granted asylum in France and Togo, respectively, and in December the first contingent of a CEMAC force was deployed in Bangui, initially to protect Patassé and later to monitor joint patrols of the border by Chadian and CAR troops. Relations between the two countries subsequently began to improve, and in January 2003 the Governments of the CAR, Chad and Sudan announced their intention to establish a tripartite committee to oversee the security and stability of their joint borders. Following Bozizé's assumption of power in the CAR in mid-March 2003, the Chadian Government dispatched some 400 troops to Bangui; 120 Chadian troops were subsequently integrated into CEMAC's operations in the CAR, which were initially scheduled to end in January 2005, with the remainder withdrawn. However, CEMAC troops remained in the CAR throughout 2005 as banditry and skirmishes between combatants from Chad continued to weaken security in the north of the country. In mid-2006 it was reported that rebels from Chad had attacked government forces and CEMAC units in the northeast of the CAR, close to the Sudanese border, although some sources blamed the violence in the region on CAR rebels.

Relations with Sudan have been strained in recent years, ostensibly owing to the instability in the west of that country, particularly in the Darfur region. In April 2006 the CAR closed the common border, after a number of incursions into its territory from Sudanese-based rebels. Furthermore, the CAR alleged Sudanese involvement in the UFDR's capture of Birao in October (see above) and President Bozizé accused his Sudanese counterpart, Omar Hassan Ahmad al-Bashir, of attempting to destabilize the CAR. These claims were refuted by the Sudanese authorities and in August 2007, following a visit by Bozizé to Khartoum, the two countries agreed to normalize bilateral relations and to improve border security through joint patrols.

The CAR maintains amicable relations with Nigeria, and in June 1999 the two countries signed a bilateral trade agreement. The CAR is also a close ally of Libya, and in April 1999 joined the Libyan-sponsored Community of Sahel-Saharan States (see p. 411). Diplomatic relations with Libya (which had been closely allied with the Patassé Government) were resumed in July 2003, following discussions between President Bozizé and the Libyan leader, Col Muammar al-Qaddafi.

Government

Following the overthrow of President Ange-Félix Patassé in mid-March 2003, the Constitution of January 1995 was suspended, and the Assemblée nationale dissolved. The self-proclaimed Head of State, Gen. François Bozizé, appointed a 63-member Conseil national de transition, to assist him in exercising legislative power, and a transitional Government. The transitional period was to last 18–30 months. A new constitution was approved by referendum on 5 December 2004. Bozizé was elected to the presidency after the second round of voting in a presidential election, held on 8 May 2005. Legislative elections to a new Assemblée nationale were held concurrently with the first round of the presidential election on 13 March.

For administrative purposes, the country is divided into 14 prefectures, two economic prefectures (Gribingui and Sangha), and one commune (Bangui). It is further divided into 67 sub-prefectures and two postes de contrôle administratif. At community level there are 65 communes urbaines, 102 communes rurales and seven communes d'élevage.

Defence

As assessed at November 2007, the armed forces numbered about 3,150 men (army 2,000, air force 150 and gendarmerie 1,000). Military service is selective and lasts for two years. The full withdrawal of the 1,345 troops of the United Nations Mission in the Central African Republic (MINURCA) was completed in mid-February 2000. In December 2002 the first contingent of a peace-keeping force from the Communauté économique et monétaire de l'Afrique centrale (CEMAC) arrived in Bangui. At November 2007 380 CEMAC troops were deployed in the CAR. Some 300 French troops also remained in the country, and were engaged in training CAR soldiers. France was also expected to provide some 1,500 members of the EUFOR TCHAD/RCA mission. Government expenditure on defence in 2007 was budgeted at 8,500m. francs CFA.

Economic Affairs

In 2006, according to estimates by the World Bank, the CAR's gross national income (GNI), measured at average 2004–06 prices, was US $1,493m., equivalent to $360 per head (or $1,280 per head on an international purchasing-power parity basis). During 1996–2006, it was estimated, the population increased at an average annual rate of 1.6%, while gross domestic product (GDP) per head, in real terms, remained constant. Overall GDP increased, in real terms, at an average annual rate of 1.5% in 1996–2006. It increased by 3.5% in 2006.

Agriculture (including hunting, forestry and fishing) contributed 57.1% of GDP in 2006. An estimated 68.2% of the economically active population were employed in the sector in mid-2005. The principal cash crops have traditionally been cotton (which accounted for 10.8% of export earnings in 2002, but decreased sharply to 1.4% in 2003) and coffee (only 1.2% of total exports in 2003, compared with 9.4% in 1999). In mid-2003 FAO warned that, although improved security would allow the 2003 cotton harvest to be sent to ginning complexes in Chad, there remained a severe shortage of seeds for the April–May 2004 planting season. In June 2004 the IMF reported that cotton production had largely ceased. However, it was subsequently reported that the French company Développement des Agro-industries du Sud (DAGRIS) would make substantial investments from March 2005 towards reconstructing the cotton industry. Livestock and tobacco are also exported. The major subsistence crops are cassava (manioc) and yams. The Government is encouraging the cultivation of horticultural produce for export. The exploitation of the country's large forest resources represents a significant source of export revenue. Rare butterflies are also exported. According to the World Bank, agricultural GDP increased at an average annual rate of 3.7% during 1996–2006. The sector's GDP increased by 3.2% in 2006.

Industry (including mining, manufacturing, construction and power) engaged 3.5% of the employed labour force in 1990 and provided 15.6% of GDP in 2006. According to the African Development Bank (ADB), industrial GDP increased at an average annual rate of 0.5% in 1996–2006; growth in 2006 was 0.3%.

Mining and quarrying engaged a labour force estimated at between 40,000 and 80,000 in the late 1990s, and contributed an estimated 7.6% of GDP in 2006. The principal activity is the extraction of predominantly gem diamonds (exports of diamonds totalled an estimated 415,000 carats in 2002 and provided some 36.1% of total export revenue in 2003). The introduction of gem-cutting facilities and the eradication of widespread 'black' market smuggling operations would substantially increase revenue from diamond mining. However, in the CAR diamonds are predominantly found in widely scattered 'alluvial' deposits (mainly in the south-west and west of the country), rather than Kimberlite deposits, which are concentrated and, thus, more easily exploited and policed. It was estimated that 50% of the potential revenue from taxes on diamond exports were lost to smuggling and corruption under the Patassé administration. The reopening in 1997 of the Bangui diamond bourse, which had been established in 1996, was intended to increase revenue by levying a 10% sales tax on transactions. In July 2003 the CAR became a participant in the Kimberley Process, an international certification scheme aimed at excluding diamonds from the world market that have been traded for arms by rebel movements in conflict zones. Deposits of gold are also exploited. The development of uranium resources may proceed, and reserves of iron ore, copper, tin and zinc have also been located, although the country's insecurity and poor infrastructure have generally deterred mining companies from attempting commercial exploitation of these reserves. Mining activity was largely suspended following Gen. François Bozizé's seizure of power in March 2003, pending an audit of companies involved in the sector. It was hoped that the adoption of a new mining code in December would revive the sector and increase transparency in licensing procedures. According to IMF estimates, the GDP of the mining sector increased by an average of 1.2% per year during 2002–06; growth in 2006 was 6.4%.

The manufacturing sector engaged 1.6% of the employed labour force in 1988. Manufacturing, which contributed 2.4% of GDP in 2006, is based on the processing of primary products. In real terms, the GDP of the manufacturing sector declined, according to the ADB, at an average annual rate of 1.8% during 1996–2006; however, it increased by 2.0% in 2005, and by 3.0% in 2006.

In 1999, according to preliminary figures, 97.7% of electrical energy generated within the CAR was derived from the country's two hydroelectric power installations. Imports of petroleum products comprised 16.9% of the cost of merchandise imports in 2005.

Services engaged 15.5% of the employed labour force in 1988 and provided 27.2% of GDP in 2006. In real terms, according to the ADB, the GDP of the services sector decreased at an average rate of 0.5% per year during 1996–2006; however, it increased by 1.6% in 2005, and by 4.4% in 2006.

In 2007 the CAR recorded a visible trade deficit of an estimated 16,700m. francs CFA and there was a deficit of an estimated 21,500m. francs CFA on the current account of the balance of payments. In 2003 the principal source of imports was France (providing 29.9% of the total), while the principal markets for exports were Belgium-Luxembourg (accounting for 70.2% of the total) and Germany (7.2%). Other major trading partners in that year were France, Cameroon and the Netherlands. The principal exports in 2006 were diamonds and wood products. The principal imports in 2003 were petroleum and petroleum products, cereals and cereal preparations, medicinal and pharmaceutical products and road vehicles and parts.

In 2006 there was an estimated budget surplus of 4,900m. francs CFA (equivalent to an estimated 0.6% of GDP). At the end of 2004 the CAR's external debt was US $1,078m., of which $926m. was long-term public debt. The annual rate of inflation averaged 3.0% in 2000–06; consumer prices increased by an estimated average of 6.6% in 2006, according to the ILO. In 1995 7.6% of the labour force were unemployed.

The CAR is a member of the Central African organs of the Franc Zone (see p. 307) and of the Communauté économique des états de l'Afrique centrale (CEEAC, see p. 411).

The CAR's land-locked position, the inadequacy of the transport infrastructure and the country's vulnerability to adverse climatic conditions and to fluctuations in international prices for its main agricultural exports have impeded sustained economic growth. Periodic reports of corruption, political instability and civil unrest have also severely disrupted economic activity and deterred foreign investment. Following his assumption of power in March 2003, President Bozizé and his new transitional Government attempted to reverse this trend and began efforts to secure financial assistance from international donors. Economic aid from the People's Republic of China has grown significantly in recent years, while in January 2006 the IMF authorized a disbursement to the CAR of US $10.2m. in Emergency Post-Conflict Assistance. Furthermore, the approval by the Fund in December of a Poverty Reduction and Growth Facility (PRGF) equivalent to $54.5m. was expected to assist with economic recovery. Following completion of the first review of the PRGF in September 2007, the IMF agreed to disburse additional funds of $4.8m. but advised the Government to implement more prudent fiscal policies. Bozizé's Government also introduced anti-corruption measures and in mid-2003 suspended mining and timber licences awarded under the previous administration, pending a review of the sectors. However, by late 2005 reports of large-scale graft had led to the suspension of many senior civil servants and, in November, of three cabinet ministers. The repeated failure of the CAR to meet conditions of structural adjustment and continuing incidences of corruption disrupted inflows of international aid, while the tax base remained limited in the absence of proper legislation pertaining to the lucrative mining and forestry sectors. Meanwhile, insecurity persisted in much of the country, particularly in rural areas, adversely affecting agricultural production. Some two-thirds of the population continued to live in acute deprivation, subsisting on less than $1 per day, and improvements in social provision and infrastructure to reduce poverty remained a government priority. Capital expenditure was expected to fall beneath the budgeted outlay for the 2007 financial year, largely as a result of costs associated with the re-capitalization of one of the CAR's commercial banks—a process which had cost the Government an estimated 2,700m. francs CFA. None the less, GDP growth of 4.0% was recorded in 2007, according to IMF estimates, and the economy was forecast to expand by 4.3% in 2008, while the rate of inflation was projected to be reduced to just 2.3%.

Education

Education is officially compulsory for eight years between six and 14 years of age. Primary education begins at the age of six and lasts for six years. Secondary education begins at the age of 12 and lasts for up to seven years, comprising a first cycle of four years and a second of three years. In 2003/04 enrolment at primary schools was equivalent to 56% of children in the relevant age-group (67% of boys; 44% of girls), according to UNESCO estimates, while in 2001/02 secondary enrolment was equivalent to only 12%. Current expenditure by the Ministry of Education in 1995 totalled 8,820m. francs CFA, equivalent to 1.6% of gross national income. The provision of state-funded education was severely disrupted during the 1990s and early 2000s, owing to the inadequacy of the Government's resources.

Public Holidays

2008: 1 January (New Year), 24 March (Easter Monday), 29 March (Anniversary of death of Barthélemy Boganda), 1 May (May Day and Ascension Day), 12 May (Whit Monday), 30 June (National Day of Prayer), 13 August (Independence Day), 15 August (Assumption), 1 November (All Saints' Day), 1 December (National Day), 25 December (Christmas).

2009: 1 January (New Year), 29 March (Anniversary of death of Barthélemy Boganda), 13 April (Easter Monday), 1 May (May Day), 21 May (Ascension Day), 1 June (Whit Monday), 30 June (National Day of Prayer), 13 August (Independence Day), 15 August (Assumption), 1 November (All Saints' Day), 1 December (National Day), 25 December (Christmas).

Weights and Measures

The metric system is officially in force.

Statistical Survey

Source (unless otherwise stated): Division des Statistiques et des Etudes Economiques, Ministère de l'Economie, du Plan et de la Coopération Internationale, Bangui.

Area and Population

AREA, POPULATION AND DENSITY

Area (sq km)	622,984*
Population (census results)	
8 December 1975	2,054,610
8 December 1988	
Males	1,210,734
Females	1,252,882
Total	2,463,616
Population (UN estimates at mid-year)†	
2005	4,191,000
2006	4,265,000
2007	4,343,000
Density (per sq km) at mid-2007	7.0

* 240,535 sq miles.
† Source: UN, *World Population Prospects: The 2006 Revision*.

PRINCIPAL TOWNS
(estimated population at mid-1994)

Bangui (capital)	524,000	Carnot		41,000
Berbérati	47,000	Bambari		41,000
Bouar	43,000	Bossangoa		33,000

Mid-2005 (incl. suburbs, UN estimate): Bangui 541,000 (Source: UN, *World Urbanization Prospects: The 2005 Revision*).

BIRTHS AND DEATHS
(annual averages, UN estimates)

	1990–95	1995–2000	2000–05
Birth rate (per 1,000)	41.6	40.0	37.9
Death rate (per 1,000)	16.6	18.0	19.4

Source: UN, *World Population Prospects: The 2006 Revision*.

Expectation of life (years at birth, WHO estimates): 42.3 (males 42.2; females 42.4) in 2005 (Source: WHO, *World Health Statistics*).

ECONOMICALLY ACTIVE POPULATION
(persons aged 6 years and over, 1988 census)

	Males	Females	Total
Agriculture, hunting, forestry and fishing	417,630	463,007	880,637
Mining and quarrying	11,823	586	12,409
Manufacturing	16,096	1,250	17,346
Electricity, gas and water	751	58	809
Construction	5,583	49	5,632
Trade, restaurants and hotels	37,435	54,563	91,998
Transport, storage and communications	6,601	150	6,751
Financing, insurance, real estate and business services	505	147	652
Community, social and personal services	61,764	8,537	70,301
Activities not adequately defined	7,042	4,627	11,669
Total employed	565,230	532,974	1,098,204
Unemployed	66,624	22,144	88,768
Total labour force	631,854	555,118	1,186,972

Source: ILO.

Mid-2005 (estimates in '000): Agriculture, etc. 1,281; Total labour force 1,878 (Source: FAO).

THE CENTRAL AFRICAN REPUBLIC

Health and Welfare

KEY INDICATORS

Total fertility rate (children per woman, 2005)	4.8
Under-5 mortality rate (per 1,000 live births, 2005)	193
HIV/AIDS (% of persons aged 15–49, 2005)	10.7
Physicians (per 1,000 head, 2004)	0.08
Hospital beds (per 1,000 head, 1991)	0.87
Health expenditure (2004): US $ per head (PPP)	54.3
Health expenditure (2004): % of GDP	4.1
Health expenditure (2004): public (% of total)	36.8
Access to water (% of persons, 2004)	75
Access to sanitation (% of persons, 2004)	27
Human Development Index (2005): ranking	171
Human Development Index (2005): value	0.384

For sources and definitions, see explanatory note on p. vi.

Agriculture

PRINCIPAL CROPS
('000 metric tons)

	2004	2005	2006
Rice (paddy)	30.7*	32.3*	30.0
Maize	110.0†	90.0†	90.0
Millet*	10.5	10.7	11.0
Sorghum*	44.2	45.8	43.0
Cassava (Manioc)*	543.7	547.4	565.0
Taro (Coco yam)*	100.0	100.0	100.0
Yams*	381.8	404.4	350.0
Sugar cane*	90.0	90.0	90.0
Groundnuts (in shell)	140.0†	140.0†	140.0
Oil palm fruit*	17.7	11.1	28.0
Sesame seed	44.2*	45.8*	43.0
Melonseed	27.9*	27.9*	28.0
Pumpkins, squash and gourds*	5.9	6.0	5.9
Bananas*	119.1	123.0	110.0
Plantains*	84.5	86.5	80.0
Oranges*	23.4	24.7	20.0
Pineapples*	14.6	15.0	14.0
Coffee (green)†	4.3	3.3	2.6
Cottonseed*	6.4	7.5	7.5
Cotton (lint)*	0.4	0.4	0.4

* FAO estimate(s).
† Unofficial figure(s).

Aggregate production ('000 metric tons, may include official, semi-official or estimated data): Total cereals 195.4 in 2004, 178.8 in 2005, 174.0 in 2006; Total roots and tubers 1,026.6 in 2004, 1,052.9 in 2005, 1,016.0 in 2006; Total pulses 27.0 in 2004, 27.0 in 2005, 27.0 in 2006; Total vegetables (incl. melons) 63.9 in 2004, 64.0 in 2005, 63.9 in 2006; Total fruits (excl. melons) 262.9 in 2004, 271.2 in 2005, 244.0 in 2006.

Source: FAO.

LIVESTOCK
('000 head, year ending September)

	2004	2005*	2006*
Cattle	3,423†	3,423	3,423
Goats	3,087*	3,087	3,087
Sheep	259*	259	259
Pigs	805†	805	805
Chickens	4,769†	4,769	4770

* FAO estimate.
† Unofficial figure.
Source: FAO.

LIVESTOCK PRODUCTS
('000 metric tons)

	2004	2005	2006
Cattle meat	74.0*	74.0†	74.0
Sheep meat†	1.5	1.5	1.5
Goat meat†	11.5	11.5	11.5
Pig meat	13.5*	14.1†	13.5
Chicken meat†	3.9	3.9	4.0
Game meat†	14.0	14.0	14.0
Cows' milk†	65.0	65.0	65.0
Hen eggs†	1.5	1.5	1.5
Honey†	13.8	14.2	13.0

* Unofficial figure.
† FAO estimate(s).
Source: FAO.

Forestry

ROUNDWOOD REMOVALS
('000 cubic metres, excluding bark)

	2003	2004	2005
Sawlogs, veneer logs and logs for sleepers	475	524	524*
Other industrial wood*	308	308	308
Fuel wood*	2,000	2,000	2,000
Total	2,783	2,832	2,832

* FAO estimate(s).

2006: Production assumed to be unchanged from 2005 (FAO estimates).
Source: FAO.

SAWNWOOD PRODUCTION
('000 cubic metres, including railway sleepers)

	2001	2002	2003
Total (all broadleaved)	150	97	69

2004–06: Figures assumed to be unchanged from 2003 (FAO estimate).
Source: FAO.

Fishing

('000 metric tons, live weight of capture, FAO estimates)

	2003	2004	2005
Total catch (freshwater fishes)	15.0	15.0	15.0

Source: FAO.

Mining

	2004	2005	2006
Gold (kg, metal content of ore)	12.2	10.4	10.3
Diamonds ('000 carats)	354.2	383.3	415.5

Source: IMF, *Central African Republic: Selected Issues and Statistical Appendix* (January 2008).

THE CENTRAL AFRICAN REPUBLIC

Industry

SELECTED PRODUCTS
('000 metric tons, unless otherwise indicated)

	2004	2005	2006
Beer ('000 hectolitres)	118.7	118.9	123.1
Sugar (raw, centrifugal)*	12	12	n.a.
Soft drinks ('000 hectolitres)	41.4	46.7	51.8
Cigarettes (million packets)	16.0	n.a.	n.a.
Palm oil*	1.7	1.7	1.7
Groundnut oil*	33.2	33.2	33.2
Plywood ('000 cubic metres)*	2.0	2.0	2.0

* FAO estimates.

Sources: IMF, *Central African Republic: Selected Issues and Statistical Appendix* (January 2008); FAO.

Electric energy (million kWh, estimates): 108 in 2002; 110 in 2003; 110 in 2004 (Source: UN, *Industrial Commodity Statistics Yearbook*).

Finance

CURRENCY AND EXCHANGE RATES

Monetary Units
100 centimes = 1 franc de la Coopération financière en Afrique centrale (CFA).

Sterling, Dollar and Euro Equivalents (31 December 2007)
£1 sterling = 892.702 francs CFA;
US $1 = 445.593 francs CFA;
€1 = 655.957 francs CFA;
10,000 francs CFA = £11.20 = $22.44 = €15.24.

Average Exchange Rate (francs CFA per US $)
2005   527.47
2006   522.89
2007   479.27

Note: An exchange rate of 1 French franc = 50 francs CFA, established in 1948, remained in force until January 1994, when the CFA franc was devalued by 50%, with the exchange rate adjusted to 1 French franc = 100 francs CFA. This relationship to French currency remained in effect with the introduction of the euro on 1 January 1999. From that date, accordingly, a fixed exchange rate of €1 = 655.957 francs CFA has been in operation.

BUDGET
('000 million francs CFA)

Revenue*	2005	2006†	2007‡
Tax revenue	50.6	60.3	71.2
Direct taxes	14.7	17.5	19.7
Indirect domestic taxes	26.4	27.7	34.1
Taxes on international trade	9.5	15.2	17.4
Taxes on imports	7.0	11.7	11.4
Non-tax revenue	8.0	12.9	14.0
Total	58.5	73.2	85.2

Expenditure§	2005	2006†	2007‡
Current primary expenditure	75.4	62.5	65.9
Wages and salaries	39.2	37.2	35.0
Other goods and services	22.2	15.2	16.7
Transfers and subsidies	14.0	10.2	14.2
Interest payments	6.6	13.1	6.6
Capital expenditure	38.4	34.1	38.4
Domestically financed	8.4	7.5	10.6
Externally financed	29.9	26.6	27.8
Total	120.4	109.8	110.9

* Excluding grants received ('000 million francs CFA): 29.5 in 2005; 91.5 in 2006 (estimate); 40.1 in 2007 (projected figure).
† Estimates.
‡ Projected figures.
§ Excluding adjustment for payment arrears ('000 million francs CFA): –26.9 in 2005; 50.0 in 2006 (estimate); 18.1 in 2007 (projected figure).

Source: IMF, *Central African Republic: Article IV Consultation, First Review Under the Three-Year Arrangement Under the Poverty Reduction and Growth Facility, Request for Waiver of Nonobservance and Modification of Performance Criteria, and Financing Assurances Review—Staff Report; Public Information Notice and Press Release on the Executive Board Discussion; and Statement by the Executive Director for the Central African Republic* (January 2008).

INTERNATIONAL RESERVES
(US $ million at 31 December)

	2004	2005	2006
Gold (national valuation)	4.88	5.71	7.06
IMF special drawing rights	2.46	0.12	0.71
Reserve position in IMF	0.25	0.23	0.24
Foreign exchange	145.62	138.87	124.40
Total	153.21	144.93	132.41

Source: IMF, *International Financial Statistics*.

MONEY SUPPLY
('000 million francs CFA at 31 December)

	2004	2005	2006
Currency outside banks	81.34	89.86	80.93
Demand deposits at commercial and development banks	16.38	23.85	24.53
Total money	97.72	113.70	105.46

Source: IMF, *International Financial Statistics*.

COST OF LIVING
(Consumer Price Index for Bangui; base: 2000 = 100)

	2003	2004	2005
Food	112.4	107.2	110.9
Fuel and light	n.a.	100.2	98.2
Clothing	n.a.	124.4	123.1
All items (incl. others)	110.9	108.6	111.7

2006: All items (incl. others) 119.1.

Source: ILO.

NATIONAL ACCOUNTS

Expenditure on the Gross Domestic Product
(US $ million at current prices)

	2004	2005	2006
Government final consumption expenditure	133.91	179.43	131.18
Private final consumption expenditure	1,180.04	1,162.58	1,317.65
Gross fixed capital formation	79.90	121.30	122.65
Total domestic expenditure	1,393.85	1,463.31	1,571.48
Exports of goods and services	154.74	164.08	177.59
Less Imports of goods and services	241.29	256.45	279.44
GDP in purchasers' values	1,307.30	1,370.94	1,469.63
GDP at constant 2000 prices	838.10	856.54	886.52

Source: African Development Bank, *Statistical Yearbook*.

THE CENTRAL AFRICAN REPUBLIC

Gross Domestic Product by Economic Activity
('000 million francs CFA at current prices)

	2004	2005	2006
Agriculture, hunting, forestry and fishing	372.3	384.5	421.8
Mining and quarrying	46.5	50.2	55.8
Manufacturing	16.3	17.7	18.0
Electricity, gas and water	5.6	5.8	6.4
Construction	30.6	32.4	35.2
Transport and communications	27.7	29.1	35.4
Commerce	75.3	79.9	86.5
Other merchant services	35.3	24.6	20.8
Government services	42.5	42.8	40.6
Technical assistance	5.9	20.0	17.7
GDP at factor cost	658.0	687.1	738.1
Indirect taxes	25.5	28.9	31.1
Customs duties	7.1	7.0	11.7
GDP in purchasers' values	690.6	723.0	781.0

Source: IMF, *Central African Republic: Selected Issues and Statistical Appendix* (January 2008).

BALANCE OF PAYMENTS
('000 million francs CFA)

	2005	2006*	2007†
Exports of goods	67.5	82.4	78.8
Imports of goods	−90.3	−106.2	−95.5
Trade balance	−22.9	−23.8	−16.7
Services (net)	−39.6	−37.0	−38.0
Balance on goods and services	−62.5	−60.8	−54.7
Income (net)	−1.1	−2.1	−0.4
Balance on goods, services, and income	−63.6	−62.9	−55.1
Current transfers (net)	16.2	42.2	33.5
Current balance	−47.3	−20.7	−21.5
Capital account (net)	15.4	82.1	25.5
Project disbursements	3.2	3.0	0.0
Program disbursements	4.0	0.0	0.0
Scheduled amortization	−11.8	−15.9	−13.2
Private sector (net)	28.6	−25.3	−2.3
Overall balance	−7.9	23.2	−11.5

* Estimates.
† Projections.

Source: IMF, *Central African Republic: Article IV Consultation, First Review Under the Three-Year Arrangement Under the Poverty Reduction and Growth Facility, Request for Waiver of Nonobservance and Modification of Performance Criteria, and Financing Assurances Review—Staff Report; Public Information Notice and Press Release on the Executive Board Discussion; and Statement by the Executive Director for the Central African Republic* (January 2008).

External Trade

PRINCIPAL COMMODITIES
(distribution by SITC, US $ million)

Imports c.i.f.	2001	2002	2003
Food and live animals	14.0	13.0	18.3
Cereals and cereal preparations	9.5	8.2	9.4
Flour of wheat or meslin	6.2	5.3	6.1
Beverages and tobacco	3.6	3.1	4.0
Tobacco and tobacco manufactures	2.7	2.4	3.1
Crude materials (inedible) except fuels	3.8	3.7	8.1
Textile fibres (excl. wool tops) and waste	2.4	2.7	3.5
Mineral fuels, lubricants, etc.	3.4	8.2	11.0
Petroleum, petroleum products, etc.	3.4	8.1	10.9
Chemicals and related products	9.2	10.1	17.5

Imports c.i.f.—continued	2001	2002	2003
Medicinal and pharmaceutical products	5.8	6.1	13.5
Medicaments	4.6	5.3	13.1
Manufactured goods	9.4	10.5	16.0
Non-ferrous metals	1.1	1.2	1.5
Machinery and transport equipment	19.3	18.3	18.9
Machinery specialized for particular industries	1.5	1.4	0.5
Civil engineering and contractors' plant and equipment	0.7	0.3	0.3
Construction and mining machinery	0.7	0.3	0.2
General industrial machinery, equipment and parts	2.3	2.3	4.7
Telecommunications and sound equipment	0.7	1.5	1.3
Road vehicles and parts*	10.2	8.6	8.4
Passenger motor cars (excl. buses)	3.0	2.3	1.3
Motor vehicles for goods transport and special purposes	2.5	2.1	0.9
Goods vehicles (lorries and trucks)	2.5	2.1	0.9
Parts and accessories for cars, buses, lorries, etc.*	1.1	1.2	0.5
Miscellaneous manufactured articles	4.5	7.3	4.7
Total (incl. others)	67.6	74.7	99.6

* Excluding tyres, engines and electrical parts.

Exports f.o.b.	2001	2002	2003
Food and live animals	1.9	1.2	0.8
Crude materials (inedible) except fuels	35.7	33.7	40.3
Cork and wood	13.8	11.1	15.6
Textile fibres (excl. wool tops) and waste	6.9	7.6	1.0
Cotton	6.9	7.5	0.9
Crude fertilizers and crude minerals (excl. coal, petroleum and precious stones)	15.0	15.1	23.7
Industrial diamonds (sorted)	15.0	15.0	23.7
Basic manufactures	34.2	33.2	23.9
Diamonds (excl. sorted industrial diamonds), unmounted	33.3	32.6	23.6
Sorted non-industrial diamonds, rough or simply worked	26.3	32.4	17.3
Machinery and transport equipment	1.2	0.8	0.2
Road vehicles	0.9	0.5	0.1
Total (incl. others)	74.3	69.5	65.7

Source: UN, *International Trade Statistics Yearbook*.

2004 ('000 million francs CFA): *Exports:* Diamonds 27.8; Coffee 1.0; Wood products 28.8; Cotton 1.8; Tobacco 0.1; Miscellaneous 7.3; Total 66.7 (Source: IMF, *Central African Republic: Selected Issues and Statistical Appendix*—January 2008).

2005 ('000 million francs CFA): *Exports:* Diamonds 32.8; Coffee 0.9; Wood products 25.8; Cotton 1.1; Tobacco 0.1; Miscellaneous 6.7; Total 67.5 (Source: IMF, *Central African Republic: Selected Issues and Statistical Appendix*—January 2008).

2006 ('000 million francs CFA, estimates): *Exports:* Diamonds 32.7; Coffee 0.8; Wood products 39.9; Cotton 0.7; Tobacco 0.1; Miscellaneous 8.2; Total 82.4 (Source: IMF, *Central African Republic: Selected Issues and Statistical Appendix*—January 2008).

THE CENTRAL AFRICAN REPUBLIC

PRINCIPAL TRADING PARTNERS
(US $ million)

Imports c.i.f.	2001	2002	2003
Belgium-Luxembourg	3.5	4.0	9.1
Brazil	—	0.5	1.1
Cameroon	8.5	8.5	10.0
Chad	1.0	0.5	0.6
China, People's Repub.	0.6	1.1	2.5
France (incl. Monaco)	27.1	25.9	29.8
Germany	1.1	2.6	1.5
Italy	1.3	1.0	0.8
Japan	6.8	7.3	2.9
Netherlands	0.9	0.7	8.8
USA	1.5	1.0	1.3
Total (incl. others)	67.6	74.7	99.6

Exports f.o.b.	2001	2002	2003
Belgium-Luxembourg	53.6	50.6	46.1
Cameroon	1.5	1.2	2.3
France (incl. Monaco)	2.1	1.8	4.3
Germany	4.1	4.1	4.7
Japan	0.5	0.7	0.2
Portugal	0.5	2.3	0.5
Spain	0.6	1.0	0.8
Sudan	1.3	0.5	0.4
Switzerland (incl. Liechtenstein)	0.9	1.1	0.9
Turkey	0.4	0.8	0.5
United Kingdom	—	0.8	2.0
Total (incl. others)	74.3	69.5	65.7

Source: UN, *International Trade Statistics Yearbook*.

Transport

ROAD TRAFFIC
(motor vehicles in use)

	1999	2000	2001
Passenger cars	4,900	5,300	5,300
Commercial vehicles	5,800	6,300	6,300

Source: UN, *Statistical Yearbook*.

SHIPPING
(international traffic on inland waterways, metric tons)

	1996	1997	1998
Freight unloaded at Bangui	60,311	56,206	57,513
Freight loaded at Bangui	5,348	5,907	12,524
Total	65,659	62,113	70,037

Source: Banque des états de l'Afrique centrale, *Etudes et Statistiques*.

CIVIL AVIATION
(traffic on scheduled services)*

	1999	2000	2001
Kilometres flown (million)	3	3	1
Passengers carried ('000)	84	77	46
Passenger-km (million)	235	216	130
Total ton-km (million)	36	32	19

* Including an apportionment of the traffic of Air Afrique.

Source: UN, *Statistical Yearbook*.

Tourism

FOREIGN VISITORS BY COUNTRY OF ORIGIN*

	2003	2004	2005
Cameroon	604	904	1,165
Chad	212	352	566
Congo, Democratic Rep.	103	142	248
Congo, Republic	411	418	468
Côte d'Ivoire	182	127	280
France	1,010	2,492	2,913
Gabon	32	166	251
Italy	130	383	475
Senegal	139	315	383
Total (incl. others)	5,687	8,156	11,969

* Arrivals at hotels and similar establishments.

Receipts from tourism (US $ million, incl. passenger transport): 4 in 2003; 4 in 2004; n.a. in 2005.

Source: World Tourism Organization.

Communications Media

	2003	2004	2005
Telephones ('000 main lines in use)	9.5	10.0	10.0
Mobile cellular telephones ('000 subscribers)	40.0	60.0	100.0
Personal computers ('000 in use)	10	11	n.a.
Internet users ('000)	6.0	9.0	11.0

2006: Figures assumed to be unchanged from 2005 (estimates).

Source: International Telecommunication Union.

Radio receivers: 283,000 in use in 1997 (Source: UNESCO, *Statistical Yearbook*).

Daily newspapers: 3 in 1996 (average circulation 6,000) (Source: UNESCO, *Statistical Yearbook*).

Non-daily newspapers: 1 in 1995 (average circulation 2,000) (Source: UNESCO, *Statistical Yearbook*).

Education

(2003/04, unless otherwise indicated)

Institutions[1]		Teachers	Males	Females	Total
Pre-primary[3]	162	572[2]	2,955	3,118	6,073
Primary[3]	930	4,004	220,118[4]	147,865[4]	367,983[4]
Secondary:					
general[3]	46	1,005	43,706[5]	22,786[5]	66,492[5]
vocational	n.a.		n.a.	n.a.	6,778[6]
Tertiary	n.a.	136	5,296[7]	1,027[7]	6,323[7]

[1] 1990/91 figures.
[2] 1987/88 figure.
[3] Estimates.
[4] 2004/05 figure.
[5] 2002/03 figure.
[6] 2001/02 figure.
[7] 1999/2000 figure.

Source: UNESCO Institute for Statistics.

Adult literacy rate (UNESCO estimates): 48.6% (males 64.8%; females 33.5%) in 2000 (Source: UNESCO Institute for Statistics).

THE CENTRAL AFRICAN REPUBLIC

Directory

The Constitution

Following the overthrow of President Ange-Félix Patassé in mid-March 2003, the Constitution of January 1995 was suspended. In December 2004 a new constitution was approved at a referendum by 87.2% of the electorate. The new Constitution provides for a presidential term of five years, renewable only once.

The Government

HEAD OF STATE

President of the Republic and Minister of National Defence, the Restructuring of the Armed Forces, Veterans and Disarmament: Gen. FRANÇOIS BOZIZÉ YANGOVOUNDA (assumed power 16 March 2003; elected by direct popular vote 8 May 2005).

COUNCIL OF MINISTERS
(March 2008)

Prime Minister and Head of Government: Prof. FAUSTIN-ARCHANGE TOUADÉRA.
Minister of State for Rural Development: JEAN-EUDES TEYA.
Minister of State for Planning, the Economy and International Co-operation: SYLVAIN MALICKO.
Minister of State for Mines, Energy and Hydraulics: Lt-Col SYLVAIN N'DOUTINGAÏ.
Minister of State for Transport and Civil Aviation: Lt-Col PARFAIT-ANICET M'BAYE.
Minister of the Interior and Public Security: Brig.-Gen. RAYMOND PAUL NDOUGOU.
Minister of Family and Social Affairs and National Solidarity: MARIE SOLANGE PAGONENDJI NDAKALA.
Minister of Youth, Sports, Arts and Culture: DÉSIRÉ ZANGA-KOLINGBA.
Minister of Finance and the Budget: EMMANUEL BIZOT.
Minister of Justice, Keeper of the Seals: THIERRY SAVONAROLE MALEYOMBO.
Minister of Posts and Telecommunications, responsible for New Technologies: FIDÈLE NGOUANDJIKA.
Minister in charge of the Secretariat-General of the Government and Relations with Parliament: LAURENT N'GON BABA.
Minister of Tourism Development and Artisanal Industries: BERNADETTE SAYO.
Minister of Foreign and Francophone Affairs and Regional Integration: DIEUDONNÉ KOMBO YAYA.
Minister of Equipment and Promotion of the Regions: CYRIAQUE SAMBA PANZA.
Minister of the Civil Service, Labour, Social Security and the Professional Integration of Youths: GASTON MACKOUZANGBA.
Minister of Water Resources, Forests, Hunting, Fishing and the Environment: YVONNE M'BOÏSSONA.
Minister of Public Health and the Fight against AIDS: FAUSTIN NTELNOUMBI.
Minister of National Education, Literacy, Higher Education and Research: (vacant).
Minister of Trade, Industry and Small and Medium-sized Enterprises: EMILIE BÉATRICE EPAYE.
Minister of Communication, Community Involvement, Dialogue and National Reconciliation: CYRIAQUE GONDA.
Minister of the Reconstruction of Public Buildings, Urban Planning and Housing: JEAN SERGE WAFIO.
Minister-delegate to the Minister of State for Rural Development, responsible for Agriculture: Dr DAVID BANZOKOU.
Minister-delegate to the Minister of State for Mines, Energy and Hydraulics: JEAN-CHRYSOSTOME MÉKONDONGO.
Minister-delegate to the Minister of State for Planning, the Economy and International Co-operation: MARIE REINE HASSEN.
Minister-delegate to the Minister of National Education, Literacy, Higher Education and Research, responsible for Primary and Secondary Education: AMBROISE ZAWA.
Minister-delegate to the Minister of National Defence, the Restructuring of the Armed Forces, Veterans and Disarmament: FRANCIS BOZIZÉ.
Minister-delegate to the Minister of State for Trade, Industry and Small and Medium-sized Enterprises, responsible for the Guichet Unique: AURÉLIEN SIMPLICE ZINGAS.
Minister-delegate to the Minister of Water Resources, Forests, Hunting, Fishing and the Environment: Dr DAVID BANZOKOU.

MINISTRIES

Office of the President: Palais de la Renaissance, Bangui; tel. 61-46-63.
Ministry of the Civil Service, Labour, Social Security and the Professional Integration of Youths: Bangui; tel. 61-21-88; fax 61-04-14.
Ministry of Community Involvement, Dialogue and National Reconciliation: BP 940, Bangui; tel. 61-27-66; fax 61-59-85.
Ministry of Equipment and Promotion of the Regions: Bangui.
Ministry of Family and Social Affairs and National Solidarity: Bangui; tel. 61-55-65.
Ministry of Finance and the Budget: BP 696, Bangui; tel. 61-38-05.
Ministry of Foreign and Francophone Affairs and Regional Integration: Bangui; tel. 61-54-67; fax 61-26-06.
Ministry of the Interior and Public Security: Bangui; tel. 61-14-77.
Ministry of Justice: Bangui; tel. 61-52-11.
Ministry of Mines, Energy and Hydraulics: Bangui; tel. 61-20-54; fax 61-60-76.
Ministry of National Defence, the Restructuring of the Armed Forces, Veterans and Disarmament: Bangui; tel. 61-00-25.
Ministry of National Education, Literacy, Higher Education and Research: BP 791, Bangui; tel. 61-08-38.
Ministry of Planning, the Economy and International Co-operation: BP 912, Bangui; tel. 61-70-55; fax 61-63-98.
Ministry of Posts and Telecommunications and New Technologies: Bangui; tel. 61-29-66.
Ministry of Public Health and the Fight against AIDS: Bangui; tel. 61-16-35.
Ministry of the Reconstruction of Public Buildings, Urban Planning and Housing: Bangui; tel. 61-69-54.
Ministry of Rural Development: Bangui; tel. 61-28-00.
Ministry of Tourism Development and Artisanal Industries: Bangui; tel. 61-04-16.
Ministry of Trade, Industry and Small and Medium-sized Enterprises: Bangui; tel. 61-10-69.
Ministry of Transport and Civil Aviation: BP 941, Bangui; tel. 61-70-49; fax 61-46-28.
Ministry of Water Resources, Forests, Hunting, Fishing and the Environment: Bangui; tel. 61-79-21.
Ministry of Youth, Sports, Arts and Culture: Bangui; tel. 61-39-69.

President and Legislature

PRESIDENT

Presidential Election, First Round, 13 March 2005

Candidate	Votes	% of votes
Gen. François Bozizé Yangovounda	382,241	42.97
Martin Ziguélé	209,357	23.53
André Kolingba	145,495	16.36
Jean-Paul Ngoupandé	45,182	5.08
Charles Massi	28,618	3.22
Abel Goumba	22,297	2.51
Henri Pouzère	18,647	2.10
Josué Binoua	13,559	1.52
Jean-Jacques Demafouth	11,279	1.27
Auguste Bouanga	7,085	0.80
Olivier Gabirault	5,834	0.66
Total*	**889,594**	**100.00**

* Excluding 57,022 invalid votes.

THE CENTRAL AFRICAN REPUBLIC

Presidential Election, Second Round, 8 May 2005

Candidate	Votes	% of votes
Gen. François Bozizé Yangovounda	610,903	64.67
Martin Ziguélé	333,716	35.33
Total	**944,619**	**100.00**

ASSEMBLÉE NATIONALE

Speaker: CÉLESTIN-LEROY GAOMBALET.

General Election, 13 March and 8 May 2005

Party	Seats
Convergence Kwa na kwa	42
MLPC	11
RDC	8
PSD	4
FPP	2
ADP	2
Löndö Association	1
Independents	34
Total	**104***

*Following the second round of elections, one seat remained undeclared.

Election Commission

Commission électorale mixte indépendante (CEMI): Bangui; f. 2004; Pres. JEAN WILLYBIRO SACKO.

Political Organizations

Alliance pour la démocratie et le progrès (ADP): Bangui; f. 1991; progressive; Leader JOSPEH THÉOPHILE DOUACLÉ.

Armée populaire pour la restauration de la république et la démocratie (APRD): Bangui; armed insurrectionary group; Leader ANDRÉ RINGUI LE GAILLARD.

Collectif des Centrafricains en France (CCF): Paris (France); f. 1984; umbrella org. for political representatives resident in France; Gen. Sec. ANDRÉ DOUNGOUMA-FOKY.

Concertation des partis politiques d'opposition (CPPO): Bangui; umbrella org. of 12 parties opposed to former President Patassé.

Conseil démocratique des partis politiques de l'opposition (CODEPO): Bangui; f. 1995; political alliance led by AUGUSTE BOUKANGA; comprises the following parties.

    Mouvement démocratique pour la renaissance et l'évolution de la République Centrafricaine (MDRERC): Bangui; Chair. JOSEPH BENDOUNGA; Sec.-Gen. LÉON SEBOU.

    Parti républicain centrafricain (PRC): Bangui.

Convention nationale (CN): Bangui; f. 1991; Leader DAVID GALIAMBO.

Coordination des patriotes centrafricains (CPC): Paris (France) and Bangui; f. 2003; umbrella org. for groups opposed to former President Patassé and affiliated to the uprising of March 2003; Sec.-Gen. ABDOU KARIM MÉCKASSOUA.

Forum démocratique pour la modernité (FODEM): ave Dejean, Sicai, Bangui; tel. 61-29-54; e-mail eric.neris@fodem.org; internet www.fodem.org; f. 1998; Pres. CHARLES MASSI.

Front démocratique de libération du peuple centrafricain (FDPC): Leader ABDOULAYE MISKINE.

Front patriotique pour le progrès (FPP): BP 259, Bangui; tel. 61-52-23; fax 61-10-93; f. 1972; aims to promote political education and debate; Leader ALEXANDRE GOUMBA.

G11: Bangui; f. 1997; alliance of 11 opposition parties led by Prof. ABEL GOUMBA; principal mems: ADP, FPP, MDD and RDC.

Mouvement d'évolution sociale de l'Afrique noire (MESAN): Bangui; f. 1949; comprises two factions, MESAN and MESAN-BOGANDA, led respectively by FIDÈLE OGBAMI and JOSEPH NGBANGADIBO.

Mouvement national pour le renouveau: Bangui; Leader PAUL BELLET.

Mouvement pour la démocratie et le développement (MDD): Bangui; f. 1993; aims to safeguard national unity and the equitable distribution of national wealth; Leader LOUIS PAPENIAH.

Mouvement pour la démocratie, l'indépendance et le progrès social (MDI-PS): BP 1404, Bangui; tel. 61-18-21; e-mail mdicentrafrique@chez.com; internet www.chez.com/mdicentrafrique; Sec.-Gen. DANIEL NDITIFEI BOYSEMBE.

Mouvement pour la libération du peuple centrafricain (MLPC): Bangui; f. 1979; leading party in govt Oct. 1993–March 2003; Pres. MARTIN ZIGUÉLÉ; Sec.-Gen. JEAN-MICHEL MANDABA.

Nouvelle alliance pour le progrès (NAP): Bangui; internet www.centrafrique-nap.com; Leader JEAN-JACQUES DEMAFOUTH.

Parti social-démocrate (PSD): BP 543, Bangui; tel. 61-59-02; fax 61-58-44; Leader ENOCH DERANT LAKOUÉ.

Rassemblement démocratique centrafricain (RDC): BP 503, Bangui; tel. 61-53-75; f. 1987; sole legal political party 1987–91; Leader Gen. ANDRÉ KOLINGBA.

Rassemblement populaire pour la reconstruction de la Centrafrique (RPRC): Bangui; Leader Gen. FRANÇOIS BOZIZÉ YANGOVOUNDA.

Union des démocrates pour le renouveau panafricain (UDRP): Bangui; Leader BENOÎT LIKITI.

Union des forces démocratiques pour le rassemblement (UFDR): Bangui; f. 2006; Leader ZAKARIA DAMANE.

    Front démocratique centrafricain (FDC): Bangui; Leader Commdt JUSTIN HASSAN.

    Groupe d'action patriotique de la libération de Centrafrique (GAPLC): Bangui; Leader MICHEL AM NONDROKO DJOTODIA.

    Mouvement des libérateurs centrafricains pour la justice (MLCJ): Bangui; Leader Capt. ABAKAR SABONE.

Union des forces républicaines de Centrafrique: Bangui; f. 2006; armed insurrectionary group; Leader Lt FRANÇOIS-FLORIAN N'DJADDER-BEDAYA.

Union pour un mouvement populaire de Centrafrique (UMPCA): Pres. YVONNE M'BOÏSSONA.

Union nationale démocratique du peuple centrafricain (UNDPC): Bangui; f. 1998; Islamic fundamentalist; based in south-east CAR; Leader MAHAMAT SALEH.

Union pour le progrès en Centrafrique (UPCA): Bangui; Leader FAUSTIN YERIMA.

Diplomatic Representation

EMBASSIES IN THE CENTRAL AFRICAN REPUBLIC

Cameroon: rue du Languedoc, BP 935, Bangui; tel. 61-18-57; fax 61-16-87; Chargé d'affaires a.i. GILBERT NOULA.

Chad: ave Valéry Giscard d'Estaing, BP 461, Bangui; tel. 61-46-77; fax 61-62-44; Ambassador MAHAMAT YAYA DAGACHE.

China, People's Republic: ave des Martyrs, BP 1430, Bangui; tel. 61-27-60; fax 61-31-83; e-mail chinaemb_cf@mfa.gov.cn; Ambassador SHI HU.

Congo, Democratic Republic: Ambassador EMBE ISEA MBAMBE.

Congo, Republic: BP 1414, Bangui; tel. 61-20-79; Ambassador LIKIBI TSIBA NOBERT.

Egypt: angle ave Léopold Sédar Senghor et rue Emile Gentil, BP 1422, Bangui; tel. 61-46-88; fax 61-35-45; e-mail ambassadedEgypt_Centreafrique@excite.com; Ambassador HANI RIAD MO'AWAD.

France: blvd du Général de Gaulle, BP 884, Bangui; tel. 61-30-05; fax 61-74-04; e-mail chancellerie.bangui-amba@diplomatie.gouv.fr; internet www.ambafrance-cf.org; Ambassador ALAIN-JEAN GIRMA.

Holy See: ave Boganda, BP 1447, Bangui; tel. 61-26-54; fax 61-03-71; e-mail nonrca@intent.cf; Apostolic Nuncio Most Rev. PIERRE NGUYÊN VAN TOT (Titular Archbishop of Rusticiana).

Japan: Temporarily closed; affairs handled through the Embassy of Japan, Yaoundé, Cameroon, since October 2003.

Libya: Bangui; tel. 61-46-62; fax 61-55-25; Ambassador (vacant).

Nigeria: ave des Martyrs, BP 1010, Bangui; tel. 61-40-97; fax 61-12-79; Ambassador A. A. ILEMIA.

Russia: ave du Président Gamal Abdel Nasser, BP 1405, Bangui; tel. 61-03-11; fax 61-56-45; e-mail ruscons@intent.cf; Ambassador IGOR P. LABUZOV.

Sudan: ave de France, BP 1351, Bangui; tel. 61-38-21; Ambassador Dr SULEIMA MOHAMED MUSTAPHA.

USA: ave David Dacko, BP 924, Bangui; tel. 61-02-00; fax 61-44-94; Ambassador FREDERICK B. COOK.

THE CENTRAL AFRICAN REPUBLIC — Directory

Judicial System

Supreme Court: BP 926, Bangui; tel. 61-41-33; highest judicial organ; acts as a Court of Cassation in civil and penal cases and as Court of Appeal in administrative cases; comprises four chambers: constitutional, judicial, administrative and financial; Pres. TAGBIA SANZIA.

There is also a Court of Appeal, a Criminal Court, 16 tribunaux de grande instance, 37 tribunaux d'instance, six labour tribunals and a permanent military tribunal. A High Court of Justice was established under the 1986 Constitution, with jurisdiction in all cases of crimes against state security, including high treason by the President of the Republic. The 1995 Constitution (which was suspended by Gen. François Bozizé in mid-March 2003) established a Constitutional Court, the judges of which were to be appointed by the President. In December 2004 Bozizé appointed a Transitional Constitutional Court that oversaw the referendum on a new constitution held in the same month.

Religion

It is estimated that 24% of the population hold animist beliefs, 50% are Christians (25% Roman Catholic, 25% Protestant) and 15% are Muslims. There is no official state religion.

CHRISTIANITY

The Roman Catholic Church

The Central African Republic comprises one archdiocese and eight dioceses. There were an estimated 853,345 adherents at 31 December 2006, representing some 23.8% of the population.

Bishops' Conference

Conférence Episcopale Centrafricaine, BP 1518, Bangui; tel. 50-27-46; fax 61-46-92; e-mail ceca_rca@yahoo.fr.
f. 1982; Pres. Most Rev. FRANÇOIS-XAVIER YOMBANDJE (Bishop of Bossangoa).
Archbishop of Bangui: Most Rev. PAULIN POMODIMO, Archevêché, BP 1518, Bangui; tel. 61-08-98; fax 61-46-92; e-mail archbangui@yahoo.fr.

Protestant Church

Eglise Protestante du Christ Roi: BP 608, Bangui; tel. 61-14-35.

The Press

The independent press is highly regulated. Independent publications must hold a trading licence and prove their status as a commercial enterprise. They must also have proof that they fulfil taxation requirements. There is little press activity outside Bangui.

DAILIES

E le Songo: Bangui; f. 1986.
Le Citoyen: BP 974, Bangui; tel. 61-89-16; independent; Dir MAKA GBOSSOKOTTO; circ. 3,000.
Le Confident: BP 427, Bangui; tel. 04-64-14; e-mail leconfident2000@yahoo.fr; internet www.leconfident.net; f. 2001; Mon.–Sat.; Dir MATHURIN C. N. MOMET.
Le Novateur: BP 913, Bangui; tel. 61-48-84; fax 61-87-03; e-mail ccea_ln@intnet.cf; independent; Publr MARCEL MOKWAPI; circ. 750.
Top Contact: Bangui; independent.

PERIODICALS

Bangui Match: Bangui; monthly.
Centrafrique-Presse: BP 1058, Bangui; tel. and fax 61-39-57; e-mail info@centrafrique-presse.com; internet www.centrafrique-presse.com; weekly; Publr PROSPER N'DOUBA.
Le Courrier Rural: BP 850, Bangui; publ. by Chambre d'Agriculture.
Le Délit d'Opinion: Bangui; independent.
Demain le Monde: BP 650, Bangui; tel. 61-23-15; f. 1985; fortnightly; independent; Editor-in-Chief NGANAM NÖEL.
Journal Officiel de la République Centrafricaine: BP 739, Bangui; f. 1974; fortnightly; economic data; Dir-Gen. GABRIEL AGBA.
Nations Nouvelles: BP 965, Bangui; publ. by Organisation Commune Africaine et Mauricienne; politics and current affairs.
Le Peuple: BP 569, Bangui; tel. 61-76-34; f. 1995; weekly; Editor-in-Chief VERMOND TCHENDO.

Le Progrès: BP 154, Bangui; tel. 61-70-26; f. 1991; monthly; Editor-in-Chief BELIBANGA CLÉMENT; circ. 2,000.
Le Rassemblement: Bangui; organ of the RDC; Editor-in-Chief MATHIAS GONEVO REAPOGO.
La Tortue Déchainée: Bangui; independent; satirical; Publr MAKA GBOSSOKOTTO.

PRESS ASSOCIATION

Groupement des Editeurs de la Presse Privée Indépendante de Centrafrique (GEPPIC): Bangui; Pres. MAKA GBOSSOKOTO.

NEWS AGENCY

Agence Centrafrique Presse (ACAP): BP 40, Bangui; tel. 61-22-79; internet www.acap-cf.info; f. 1960; Gen. Man. VICTOR DETO TETEYA.

Publisher

GOVERNMENT PUBLISHING HOUSE

Imprimerie Centrafricaine: ave David Dacko, BP 329, Bangui; tel. 61-72-24; f. 1974; Dir-Gen. SERGE BOZANGA.

Broadcasting and Communications

TELECOMMUNICATIONS

Société Centrafricaine de Télécommunications (SOCATEL): BP 939, Bangui; tel. 61-42-68; fax 61-44-72; e-mail dg-socatel@socatel.cf; internet www.socatel.cf; f. 1990; 60% state-owned; 40% owned by France Câbles et Radio (France Télécoms); further privatization suspended March 2003; Dir-Gen. VALENTIN NZAPAOKO.
CARATEL Entreprises: BP 2439, Bangui; tel. 61-44-10; fax 61-44-49; e-mail telecomp@intnet.cf; internet www.socatel.intnet.cf; mobile cellular telephone operator.
Centrafrique Telecom Plus: BP 2439, Bangui; tel. 61-44-10; fax 61-44-49; e-mail telecomp@intnet.cf; internet www.socatel.intnet.cf/index2.html; 40% owned by France Telecom; 22% owned by Socatel; f. 1996; supplies wireless and high-speed Internet services.
Telecel: BP 939, Bangui; tel. 61-19-30; fax 61-16-99; mobile cellular telephone operator; Dir-Gen. SERGES PSHISMIS.

BROADCASTING

Radiodiffusion-Télévision Centrafricaine: BP 940, Bangui; tel. 61-25-88; f. 1958 as Radiodiffusion Nationale Centrafricaine; govt-controlled; broadcasts in French and Sango; Sec.-Gen. DELPHINE ZOUTA.
Radio Rurale: community stations operating in Bouar, Nola, Berbérati and Bambari.
Radio Ndeke Luka: community station operated by UN.
Radio Nostalgie: commercial radio station in Bangui.
Radio Notre-Dame: radio station operated by Roman Catholic Church.

Finance

(cap. = capital; res = reserves; dep. = deposits; m. = million; br. = branch; amounts in francs CFA)

BANKING

Central Bank

Banque des Etats de l'Afrique Centrale (BEAC): BP 851, Bangui; tel. 61-40-00; fax 61-19-95; e-mail beacbgf@beac.int; HQ in Yaoundé, Cameroon; f. 1973; bank of issue for mem. states of the Communauté économique et monétaire de l'Afrique centrale (CEMAC, fmrly Union douanière et économique de l'Afrique centrale), comprising Cameroon, the CAR, Chad, the Repub. of the Congo, Equatorial Guinea and Gabon; cap. 45,000m., res 176,661m., total assets 2,144,626m. (Nov. 2003); Gov. JEAN-FÉLIX MAMALEPOT; Dir in CAR ENOCH DERANT LAKOUÉ.

Commercial Banks

Banque Internationale pour le Centrafrique (BICA): place de la République, BP 910, Bangui; tel. 61-00-42; fax 61-61-36; f. 1946; present name adopted 1996; 35% owned by Banque Belgolaise SA, Brussels, 15% by group of African investors (COFIPA), 40% by private citizens, 10% by Govt; cap. and res 1,117m., total assets

THE CENTRAL AFRICAN REPUBLIC

19,616m. (Dec. 2001); Pres. MARTIN BABA; Dir-Gen. JEAN-CLAUDE PORCHER; 1 br.

Banque Populaire Maroco-Centrafricaine (BPMC): rue Guérillot, BP 844, Bangui; tel. 61-31-90; fax 61-62-30; e-mail bpmc@intnet.cf; f. 1991; 57.5% owned by Groupe Banque Populaire (Morocco); cap. and res 4,183m., total assets 13,331m. (Dec. 2003); Gen. Man. MOHAMMED BENZIANI.

Commercial Bank Centrafrique (CBCA): rue de Brazza, BP 59, Bangui; tel. 61-29-90; fax 61-34-54; e-mail cbcabank@cbc-bank.com; internet www.cbc-bank.com/cb_centrafrique/page.php?langue=fr; f. 1962; 51% owned by Groupe Fotso; 39% owned by CAR private shareholders; 10% state-owned; cap. 1,500.m., res 1,856.3m., dep 22,941.2m. (Dec. 2005); Pres. SERGE PSIMHIS; Dir-Gen. RICHARD BORONG LIVE; 1 br.

Development Bank

Banque de Développement des Etats de l'Afrique Centrale: see Franc Zone.

Financial Institutions

Caisse Autonome d'Amortissement de la République Centrafricaine: Bangui; tel. 61-53-60; fax 61-21-82; management of state funds; Dir-Gen. JOSEPH PINGAMA.

Caisse Nationale d'Epargne (CNE): Office national des postes et de l'épargne, Bangui; tel. 61-22-96; fax 61-78-80; Pres. SIMONE BODEMO-MODOYANGBA; Dir-Gen. AMBROISE DAOUDA; Man. ANTOINE BEKOUANEBANDI.

Bankers' Association

Association Professionnelle des Banques: Bangui.

Development Agencies

Agence Française de Développement: rue de la Moyenne corniche, BP 817, Bangui; tel. 61-03-06; fax 61-22-40; e-mail afd@intnet.cf; e-mail afdbangui@yahoo.fr; internet www.afd.fr; administers economic aid and finances specific development projects; Man. DELPHINE DORBEAU.

Mission Française de Coopération et d'Action Culturelle: BP 934, Bangui; tel. 61-63-34; fax 61-28-24; administers bilateral aid from France; Dir HERVÉ CRONEL.

INSURANCE

Agence Centrafricaine d'Assurances (ACA): BP 512, Bangui; tel. 61-06-23; f. 1956; Dir R. CERBELLAUD.

Assureurs Conseils Centrafricains (ACCAF): ave Barthélemy Boganda, BP 743, Bangui; tel. 61-19-33; fax 61-44-70; e-mail centrafrique@ascoma.com; internet www.ascoma.com; f. 1968; owned by Ascoma (Monaco); Man. VENANT EBELA; Dir-Gen. SYLVAIN COUSIN.

Entreprise d'Etat d'Assurances et de Réassurances (SIRIRI): Bangui; tel. 61-36-55; f. 1972; Pres. EMMANUEL DOKOUNA; Dir-Gen. MARTIN ZIGUÉLÉ.

Union Centrafricaine d'Assurances et de Réassurances: rue du Général de Gaulle, BP 343, Bangui; tel. 61-36-66; fax 61-33-40; e-mail ucardg@intnet.cf; Dir-Gen. ALAIN BLANCHARD.

Trade and Industry

DEVELOPMENT ORGANIZATION

Société Centrafricaine de Développement Agricole (SOCADA): ave David Dacko, BP 997, Bangui; tel. 61-30-33; f. 1964; reorg. 1980; 75% state-owned, 25% Cie Française pour le Développement des Fibres Textiles (France); purchasing, transport and marketing of cotton, cotton-ginning, production of cottonseed oil and groundnut oil; Pres. MAURICE METHOT.

INDUSTRIAL AND TRADE ASSOCIATIONS

Agence de Développement de la Zone Caféière (ADECAF): BP 1935, Bangui; tel. 61-47-30; coffee producers' ascn; assists coffee marketing co-operatives; Dir-Gen. J. J. NIMIZIAMBI.

Agence Nationale pour le Développement de l'Elevage (ANDE): BP 1509, Bangui; tel. 61-69-60; fax 61-50-83; assists with development of livestock.

Bourse Internationale de Diamant de Bangui: BP 26, Bangui; tel. 61-58-63; fax 61-60-76; diamond exchange; supervised by the Ministry of Mines, Energy and Hydraulics.

Caisse de Stabilisation et de Péréquation des Produits Agricoles (CAISTAB): BP 76, Bangui; tel. 61-08-00; supervises marketing and pricing of agricultural produce; Dir-Gen. M. BOUNANDELE-KOUMBA.

Fédération Nationale des Eleveurs Centrafricains (FNEC): ave des Martyrs, BP 588, Bangui; tel. 61-23-97; fax 61-47-24.

Groupement des Industries Centrafricaines (GICA): BP 804, Bangui; umbrella group representing 12 principal companies of various industries; Pres. PATRICK DEJEAN.

Office National de la Forêts (ONF): BP 915, Bangui; tel. 61-38-27; f. 1969; reafforestation, development of forest resources; Dir-Gen. C. D. SONGUET.

CHAMBERS OF COMMERCE

Chambre d'Agriculture, d'Elevage, des Eaux, Forêts, Chasses, Pêches et du Tourisme: BP 850, Bangui; tel. 61-06-38; e-mail chagri_rca@hotmail.com; f. 1964; Sec.-Gen. HENRI OUIKON.

Chambre de Commerce, d'Industrie, des Mines et de l'Artisanat (CCIMA): blvd Charles de Gaulle, BP 823, Bangui; tel. 61-16-68; fax 61-35-61; e-mail ccima@intnet.cf; internet ccima-rca.com; f. 1935; Pres. ROBERT NGOKI; Treas. THÉODORE LAWSON.

EMPLOYERS' ORGANIZATION

Union Nationale du Patronat Centrafricain (UNPC): Immeuble Tropicana, 1°, BP 2180, Bangui; tel. and fax 61-16-79; e-mail unpc-rca@intnet.cf; Pres. FAUSTIN ZAGUI.

UTILITIES

Electricity

Société Energie de Centrafrique (ENERCA): ave de l'Indépendance, BP 880, Bangui; tel. 61-20-22; fax 61-54-43; e-mail enerca@intnet.cf; f. 1967; state-owned; production and distribution of electric energy; 119.1 GWh produced for the Bangui grid in 2003; Dir-Gen. SAMUEL TOZOUI.

Water

Société de Distribution d'Eau en Centrafrique (SODECA): BP 1838, Bangui; tel. 61-59-66; fax 61-25-49; e-mail sodeca@intnet.cf; f. 1975 as the Société Nationale des Eaux; state-owned co responsible for supply, treatment and distribution of water; Dir-Gen. SAMUEL RANGBA.

TRADE UNIONS

Confédération Chrétienne des Travailleurs de Centrafrique (CCTC): BP 939, Bangui; tel. 61-05-71; fax 61-55-81; Pres. LOUIS SALVADOR.

Confédération Nationale de Travailleurs de Centrafricains: BP 2141, Bangui; tel. 50-94-36; fax 61-35-61; e-mail cnt@intnet.cf; Sec.-Gen. JEAN-RICHARD SANDOS-OULANGA.

Confédération Syndicale des Travailleurs de Centrafrique (CSTC): BP 386, km 5, Bangui; tel. 61-38-69; Sec.-Gen. SABIN KPOKOLO.

Confédération Syndicale des Travailleurs de la Centrafrique: BP 386, Bangui; tel. and fax 61-38-69.

Organisation des Syndicats Libres du Secteur Public, Parapublic et Privé (OSLP): BP 1450, Bangui; tel. 61-20-00; Sec.-Gen. GABRIEL NGOUANDJI-TANGAS.

Union Générale des Travailleurs de Centrafrique (UGTC): BP 346, Bangui; tel. 61-05-86; fax 61-17-96; Pres. CÉCILE GUÉRÉ.

Union des Journalistes: Bangui; tel. 61-13-38.

Union Syndicale des Travailleurs de Centrafrique (USTC): BP 1390, Bangui; tel. 61-60-15; e-mail vvesfon@yahoo.fr; Sec. THÉOPHILE SONNY COLÉ.

Transport

RAILWAYS

There are no railways at present. There are long-term plans to connect Bangui to the Transcameroon railway. A line linking Sudan's Darfur region with the CAR's Vakaga province has also been proposed.

ROADS

In 1999 there were an estimated 23,810 km of roads. Only about 3% of the total network is paved. Eight main routes serve Bangui, and those that are surfaced are toll roads. Both the total road length and the condition of the roads are inadequate for current requirements. In 1997 the European Union provided 32,500m. francs CFA to improve infrastructure in the CAR. In September a vast road-improvement scheme was launched, concentrating initially on roads to the south and north-west of Bangui. The CAR is linked with

THE CENTRAL AFRICAN REPUBLIC

Cameroon by the Transafrican Lagos–Mombasa highway. Roads are frequently impassable in the rainy season (July–October).

Bureau d'Affrètement Routier Centrafricain (BARC): Gare routière, BP 523, Bangui; tel. 61-20-55; fax 61-37-44; Dir-Gen. J. M. LAGUEREMA-YADINGUIN.

Compagnie Nationale des Transports Routiers (CNTR): Bangui; tel. 61-46-44; state-owned; Dir-Gen. GEORGES YABADA.

Fonds Routier: BP 962, Bangui; tel. 61-62-95; fax 61-68-63; e-mail fondsroutier@admn.cf; f. 1981; Dir.-Gen. MARIE-CLAIR BITOUANGA.

Projet Sectoriel de Transports (PST): BP 941, Bangui; tel. 61-62-94; fax 61-65-79.

TBC Cameroun SARL: BP 637, Bangui; tel. 61-20-16; fax 61-13-19; e-mail rca@tbclogistics.com; internet www.tbclogistics.com; f. 1963.

INLAND WATERWAYS

There are some 2,800 km of navigable waterways along two main water courses. The first, formed by the Congo river and its tributary the Oubangui, can accommodate convoys of barges (of up to 800 metric tons load) between Bangui and Brazzaville and Pointe-Noire in the Republic of the Congo, except during the dry season, when the route is impassable. The second is the river Sangha, also a tributary of the Congo, on which traffic is again seasonal. There are two ports, at Bangui and Salo, on the rivers Oubangui and Sangha, respectively. Bangui port has a handling capacity of 350,000 tons, with 350 m of wharfs and 24,000 sq m of warehousing. Efforts are being made to develop the Sangha upstream from Salo, to increase the transportation of timber from this area and to develop Nola as a timber port.

Agence Centrafricaine des Communications Fluviales (ACCF): BP 822, Bangui; tel. 61-09-67; fax 61-02-11; f. 1969; state-owned; supervises development of inland waterways transport system; Chair. GUY MAMADOU MARABENA.

Société Centrafricaine de Transports Fluviaux (SOCATRAF): rue Parent, BP 1445, Bangui; tel. and fax 61-43-15; e-mail socatraf@intnet.cf; f. 1980; 51% owned by ACCF; Man. Dir FRANÇOIS TOUSSAINT.

CIVIL AVIATION

The international airport is at Bangui-M'Poko. There are also 37 small airports for internal services.

Agence pour la sécurité de la navigation aérienne en Afrique et Madagascar (ASECNA): 32–38, ave Jean Jaurès, BP 828, Bangui; tel. 61-33-80; fax 61-49-18; e-mail contact@asecna.aero; internet www.asecna.aero; Dir-Gen. YOUSSOUF MAHAMAT.

Centrafrican Airlines (CAL): Aéroport Bangui-M'Poko; f. 1999; privately owned; internal flights.

Mondial Air Fret (MAF): BP 1883, Bangui; tel. 61-14-58; fax 61-62-62; f. 1998; Dir THÉOPHILE SONNY COLÉ.

Tourism

Although tourism remains relatively undeveloped, the CAR possesses considerable scenic attractions in its waterfalls, forests and wildlife. In 2005 11,969 tourists arrived. In 2004 receipts from tourism were estimated at US $4m.

Fonds du Développement et Touristique: BP 2327, Bangui; tel. 61-13-51; fax 61-09-75.

Office National Centrafricain du Tourisme (OCATOUR): rue Roger Guérillot, BP 645, Bangui; tel. 61-45-66.

CHAD

Introductory Survey

Location, Climate, Language, Religion, Flag, Capital

The Republic of Chad is a land-locked country in north central Africa, bordered to the north by Libya, to the south by the Central African Republic, to the west by Niger, Nigeria and Cameroon, and to the east by Sudan. The climate is hot and arid in the northern desert regions of the Sahara but very wet, with annual rainfall of 5,000 mm (197 ins) in the south. The official languages are French and Arabic, and various African languages are also widely spoken. Almost one-half of the population are Muslims, living in the north. About 30% of the population are Christians. Most of the remainder follow animist beliefs. The national flag (proportions 2 by 3) has three equal vertical stripes, of dark blue, yellow and red. The capital is N'Djamena.

Recent History

Formerly a province of French Equatorial Africa, Chad achieved full independence on 11 August 1960. However, the sparsely populated northern territory of Borkou-Ennedi-Tibesti, accounting for some 47% of the area of Chad, remained under French military control until 1965. The first President of the independent republic was François (later Ngarta) Tombalbaye, a southerner and leader of the Parti progressiste tchadien. In 1965 a full-scale insurgency began, concentrated mainly in the north. The Muslims of northern Chad have historically been in conflict with their black southern compatriots, who are mainly Christians or animists. The banned Front de libération nationale du Tchad (FROLINAT, founded in Sudan in 1966) assumed leadership of the revolt. The rebellion was partially quelled in 1968, following French military intervention.

In 1973 several prominent figures in the regime, including Gen. Félix Malloum, the Army Chief of Staff, were imprisoned on charges of conspiracy. Also in that year Libyan troops occupied the so-called 'Aozou strip', an apparently mineral-rich region of some 114,000 sq km (44,000 sq miles) in northern Chad, over which Libya claimed sovereignty.

In April 1975 Tombalbaye was killed in a military coup. Malloum was released and appointed President, leading a military regime. In early 1978 FROLINAT, which received clandestine military assistance from Libya, seized control of a large area of the north before its advance was halted by French military intervention. In August, after negotiations with Malloum, Hissène Habré, a former leader of FROLINAT, was appointed Prime Minister. However, disagreements developed between Habré (a Muslim from the north) and Malloum over the status of Muslims in Chad.

In February 1979 armed conflict broke out between Habré's Forces armées du nord (FAN) and the government armed forces, the Forces armées tchadiennes (FAT). The FAN gained control of the capital, N'Djamena, and in March Malloum resigned and fled the country. In April a provisional Government was formed, comprising representatives of several groups, including FROLINAT, the FAN and the FAT, but sporadic fighting continued. In August 11 factions formed a Gouvernement d'union nationale de transition (GUNT), with Goukouni Oueddei, the leader of FROLINAT, as President and Lt-Col (later Gen.) Wadal Abdelkader Kamougué as Vice-President.

Goukouni's authority was undermined by continual disagreements with Habré, and in March 1980 fighting resumed. In October Libyan forces intervened directly in the hostilities, in support of Goukouni. By December Habré had been defeated, and a 15,000-strong Libyan force was established in the country. In November 1981 Libyan troops were withdrawn, and a peace-keeping force was installed under the auspices of the Organization of African Unity (OAU—now the African Union—AU, see p. 164). The conflict intensified, however, and in June 1982 Habré's forces captured N'Djamena. Habré was formally inaugurated as President in October, and Goukouni formed a rival administration in Bardai.

In January 1983 some members of the FAT joined Habré's FAN to form the Forces armées nationales tchadiennes (FANT). In August Goukouni's rebel forces, with Libyan support, captured the northern administrative centre of Faya-Largeau. France dispatched a further 3,000 troops to Chad and imposed an 'interdiction line' to separate the warring factions. In June 1984, in an attempt to consolidate his political support in the south, Habré replaced the FROLINAT-FAN movement with a new organization, the Union nationale pour l'indépendance et la révolution (UNIR). In September Libya and France agreed to withdraw their troops from Chad. By November all French troops had left the country; however, it was reported that some 3,000 Libyan troops remained. By the end of 1985 hostilities in southern Chad had ceased. In February 1986, however, GUNT forces, with support from Libya, attacked government positions south of the interdiction line. Habré appealed for French military assistance, and France agreed to establish a defensive air-strike force (designated Opération Epervier) in N'Djamena. The GUNT, meanwhile, began to disintegrate. Kamougué resigned as Vice-President in June, and in February 1987 declared his support for Habré. In August 1986, meanwhile, Acheikh Ibn Oumar's Conseil démocratique révolutionnaire (CDR) also withdrew support from Goukouni. In October, following armed clashes between the Libyan-supported CDR and his own Forces armées populaires (FAP), Goukouni declared himself willing to seek a reconciliation with Habré.

In December 1986 clashes began in the Tibesti region between Libyan forces and the (now pro-Habré) FAP. FANT troops moved into northern Chad and, with increased logistical support from France and the USA, forced Libya to withdraw from Faya-Largeau. In May 1987 Libyan troops retreated to the 'Aozou strip'. In August FANT troops attacked and occupied the town of Aozou, which was, however, recaptured by Libyan forces three weeks later. In September the FANT made an incursion into southern Libya. An OAU-brokered cease-fire took effect, but sporadic fighting continued, and the Chadian Government claimed that Libyan aircraft were repeatedly violating Chadian airspace.

Following negotiations in Gabon between the Ministers of Foreign Affairs of Chad and Libya, agreement was reached, in principle, to restore diplomatic relations. However, the issues of the sovereignty of the Aozou region, the fate of Libyan prisoners of war in Chad, and the security of common borders remained unresolved. In October 1988 diplomatic relations were resumed, and the September 1987 cease-fire agreement was reaffirmed, although Chad continued to accuse Libya of violating the conditions of the agreement.

The cohesion of the GUNT was undermined in 1988 by a dispute between Goukouni and Acheikh Ibn Oumar. Several former opposition groups transferred their support to Habré, and in November, following negotiations with UNIR, Acheikh Ibn Oumar and his supporters returned to Chad. He was appointed Minister of Foreign Affairs in March 1989. In April Mahamat Itno, the Minister of the Interior and Territorial Administration, was arrested following the discovery of an alleged plot to overthrow Habré. Idriss Deby (later Idriss Deby Itno), a former Commander-in-Chief of the Armed Forces, who was also implicated in the attempted coup, fled to Sudan, where he established a new opposition group.

In June 1989 the Government accused Libya of planning a military offensive against Chad, with the complicity of Sudan. In July the Libyan leader, Col Muammar al-Qaddafi, and Habré met for the first time, in Mali, but their negotiations were inconclusive. On 31 August, however, Acheikh Ibn Oumar met his Libyan counterpart in Algiers, where they signed an outline peace accord. Provision was made for the withdrawal of all armed forces from the Aozou region and the release of all prisoners of war. No agreement was reached at discussions between Habré and Qaddafi in Morocco in August 1990, and the territorial dispute was referred for adjudication by the International Court of Justice (ICJ) in The Hague, Netherlands.

In December 1989 a new Constitution was reportedly approved by 99.94% of voters in a national referendum. In endorsing the document, the electorate also approved Habré in the office of President for a further seven-year term. The new Constitution confirmed UNIR as the sole legal party, and provided for the establishment of an elected legislature. Elections to this 123-seat Assemblée nationale followed in July 1990.

In November 1990 the Mouvement patriotique du salut (MPS—previously styled the Forces patriotiques du salut) invaded Chad from Sudan and advanced rapidly towards N'Djamena. France reiterated its policy of non-interference in Chad's internal affairs, and on 30 November Habré and his associates fled Chad. Deby arrived in N'Djamena two days later. The Assemblée nationale was dissolved, and the Constitution suspended. Deby became interim Head of State. Several members of the former Habré regime, including Acheikh Ibn Oumar, were included in the new Government.

Following Deby's accession to power, many political organizations that had opposed Habré announced their support for the MPS. Deby announced that a smaller national army, the Armée nationale tchadienne (ANT), was to replace the FANT. The French Government responded favourably to the new administration, and the Libyan and Sudanese Governments declared their support for the MPS, undertaking not to allow forces hostile to Deby to operate on their territory. Deby, however, reiterated Chad's claim to the Aozou region, which remained under consideration by the ICJ. In February 1994 the ICJ ruled in favour of Chad in the issue of the sovereignty of the Aozou region. By May the withdrawal of Libyan troops from the region had been completed as scheduled; in the following month a co-operation agreement was signed by the two countries. Meanwhile, in March 1991 the Government promulgated a National Charter to operate for a 30-month transitional period, confirming Deby's appointment as President, Head of State and Chairman of the MPS, and creating a Council of Ministers (headed by Jean Bawoyeu Alingué) and a 31-member legislative Conseil de la République.

In September 1991 forces loyal to Habré apparently entered Chad from Niger and attacked military garrisons in the north of the country. In the following month disaffected ANT troops attacked an arsenal at N'Djamena airport in an attempt to seize power; some 40 people were killed in the ensuing fighting. Several officials, including the Minister of the Interior, were arrested on charges connected with the incident. France reaffirmed its support for the MPS and announced that an additional 300 troops would be dispatched to Chad. Following the coup attempt, Chad abrogated a recent co-operation agreement with Libya. In December some 3,000 pro-Habré rebels of the Libya-based Mouvement pour la démocratie et le développement (MDD) attacked towns in the Lake Chad region.

In April 1992 a number of amendments to the National Charter were adopted, and Joseph Yodoyman, a member of the opposition Alliance nationale pour la démocratie et le développement (ANDD), was appointed Prime Minister. A new Council of Ministers included, for the first time, members of several opposition parties and human rights organizations. In June an agreement between the Government and the Comité de sursaut national pour la paix et la démocratie (CSNPD), the dissident faction of the armed forces responsible for an abortive coup attempt in February, provided for the release of detained members of the CSNPD and their reintegration into the ANT. In June an agreement was signed in Libreville, Gabon, providing for a cessation of hostilities between government forces and the MDD. In July Yodoyman was expelled from the ANDD, and another member of the ANDD subsequently left the Government.

In September 1992 an agreement was reached by the Government and an opposition group based in Sudan, the Front national du Tchad (FNT), which granted the FNT the status of a political party. Later that month the Government signed further peace agreements with the MDD, which had resumed activities in the Lake Chad region, and with the CSNPD, which had engaged in clashes with government forces in Doba, in the south, in August. In October, however, the MDD was reported to have begun a renewed offensive against government forces near Lake Chad, and at the end of that month the MDD declared the peace agreement to be invalid, alleging that the Government was preparing to resume hostilities.

A national conference was convened in January 1993. In April the conference, which had been accorded sovereign status, adopted a Transitional Charter, elected Dr Fidel Moungar, hitherto Minister of National and Higher Education, as Prime Minister, and established a 57-member interim legislature, the Conseil supérieur de la transition (CST). The leader of the Rassemblement pour la démocratie et le progrès (RDP), Lol Mahamat Choua—who had briefly served as President in 1979—was elected Chairman of the CST. Under the terms of the Transitional Charter, Deby was to remain Head of State and Commander-in-Chief of the Armed Forces for a period of one year (with provision for one extension), while a Transitional Government, under the supervision of the CST, was to implement economic, political and social programmes as drafted by the conference.

In October 1993 the CST approved a motion expressing 'no confidence' in the Moungar administration, apparently initiated by supporters of Deby. Moungar resigned, and in November the CST elected Nouradine Kassiré Delwa Coumakoye, hitherto Minister of Justice, Keeper of the Seals, as Prime Minister. In December teachers and other government employees began strike action in protest at the Government's failure to pay salary arrears. The 50% devaluation of the CFA franc, in January 1994, precipitated further unrest.

In January 1994 members of the FNT (who were to have been integrated into the ANT) attacked a military garrison at Abéché, in the north-east. In February negotiations between the Chadian authorities and the CSNPD, with mediation by the Central African Republic (CAR), failed to secure a lasting peace, and further clashes were reported in southern Chad in late March.

In March 1994 an Institutional Committee submitted constitutional recommendations, which included provisions for the introduction of a five-year presidential term, the installation of a bicameral legislature and a Constitutional Court, and the establishment of a decentralized administrative structure. In April the CST extended the transitional period by one year. A new electoral timetable was adopted, whereby the Government was obliged to provide funds for the organization of the elections and, by June, to adopt an electoral code, to establish a national reconciliation council, and to appoint electoral and human rights commissions. In May Deby effected a comprehensive reorganization of the Government.

In August 1994 the Chadian authorities and the CSNPD signed a cease-fire agreement, providing for the recognition of the CSNPD as a political organization and the integration of its forces into the ANT. Later that month government troops were reported to have killed 26 civilians in the south, in reprisal for attacks by members of another rebel faction, the Forces armées pour la République fédérale (FARF). In September it was reported that the Minister of Mines and Energy, Lt-Col Mahamat Garfa (who had recently been dismissed as Chief of Army Staff), had fled N'Djamena with substantial government funds, and, together with some 600 members of the ANT, had joined rebel forces of the Conseil national de redressement du Tchad in eastern Chad; Garfa subsequently established a co-ordination of eight rebel groups operative in eastern Chad, the Alliance nationale de la résistance (ANR), while remaining in exile himself. In October Choua was replaced as Chairman of the CST by a member of the MPS, Mahamat Bachar Ghadaia.

Deby officially announced in November 1994 that the process of democratic transition would conclude on 9 April 1995, following presidential and legislative elections. In December 1994 Deby declared a general amnesty for political prisoners and opposition members in exile, notably excluding Habré. In early 1995 the CST adopted a new electoral code and approved the draft Constitution, which had been amended in accordance with recommendations made by a national conference in August 1994. In March 1995 the CST extended the transitional period for a further year and amended the National Charter to debar the incumbent Prime Minister from contesting the forthcoming presidential election or from belonging to a political party. In April the Court of Appeal annulled the results of an electoral census conducted in February, citing procedural irregularities. In the same month the CST, which had criticized the Government's lack of progress in organizing democratic elections, voted to remove Coumakoye from the premiership, electing Djimasta Koibla, a prominent member of the Union pour la démocratie et la République (UDR), as Prime Minister. In August security forces raided the home of Saleh Kebzabo, the leader of the opposition Union nationale pour le développement et le renouveau (UNDR). In protest, an informal alliance of opposition parties, to which the UNDR belonged, announced that it was to suspend participation in the CST and demanded the resignation of the head of the security forces.

In November 1995 the Government and the MDD agreed to a cease-fire, an exchange of prisoners and the integration of a number of MDD troops into the ANT. Reconciliation discussions between the Chadian Government and its opponents were convened in Franceville, Gabon, in January 1996. In March the Government and 13 opposition groups signed a cease-fire agreement. Although it appeared that the majority of the armed movements had rejected the agreement, the conclusion of the Franceville accord allowed the electoral programme to proceed. The new Constitution was endorsed by 63.5% of votes cast at a national referendum on 31 March.

In the first round of voting at the presidential election, held on 2 June 1996, Deby secured 43.9% of the votes cast, followed by Kamougué, with 12.4%, and Kebzabo, with 8.5%. Deby and Kamougué proceeded to a second round of voting on 3 July. Although most of the 13 unsuccessful first-round candidates urged a boycott of the vote, Kebzabo announced his support for Deby, who won a decisive victory, with 69.1% of votes cast. The rate of participation by voters exceeded 75% of the registered electorate. Following Deby's inauguration as President on 8 August, he reappointed Koibla as Prime Minister. Koibla named an interim Council of Ministers, which included several former opposition members, among them Kebzabo as Minister of Foreign Affairs. In September representatives of the Government and the MDD signed a peace agreement in Niger.

At legislative elections held on 5 January and 23 February 1997 the MPS secured an absolute majority in the 125-member Assemblée nationale, winning 65 seats, while Kamougué's Union pour le renouveau et la démocratie (URD) secured 29 seats, and Kebzabo's UNDR 15. In May Kamougué was elected as the President of the new Assemblée nationale. Nassour Guélengdouksia Ouaïdou, hitherto Secretary-General at the Presidency, was named as the new Prime Minister.

In April 1997 the Government and the FARF signed a conclusive peace agreement; the movement was to be legalized as a political party, and its civilian and armed members were to be integrated into the state apparatus. In August the Government was reported to have negotiated a peace agreement with the FAP, the military wing of Goukouni's FROLINAT. Agreement was reached on a general amnesty for the FNT, the Front national du Tchad rénové (FNTR—a breakaway group from the FNT) and the Mouvement pour la justice sociale et la démocratie at reconciliation talks with the Government in October. However, later that month fighting erupted in Logone Occidental prefecture between FARF rebels and government troops. Meanwhile, insecurity persisted. The Union des forces démocratiques (UFD) claimed responsibility for the kidnap, in February 1998, of four French nationals in Moyen Chari prefecture. Eleven rebels were reported to have been killed in an operation to liberate the hostages. French troops were mobilized in support of the Chadian security forces, although the military attaché at the French embassy in N'Djamena, said to be an associate of the UFD leader, Dr Mahamout Nahour, was declared persona non grata by the Chadian authorities after Nahour demanded only to negotiate with him. In May a presidential envoy and the FARF Chief of General Staff signed an agreement envisaging an immediate end to rebel activity; the Government undertook to withdraw élite elements of the National Nomadic Guard from the south, and there was to be a general amnesty for FARF militants. The terms of the April 1997 peace accord, whereby the FARF was to be legalized as a political party, were also to be renewed.

Reports emerged from late 1998 of a rebellion in the Tibesti region of northern Chad, led by the Mouvement pour la démocratie et la justice au Tchad (MDJT) of Youssouf Togoimi, who had been dismissed as Minister of the Armed Forces in 1997. In June 1999 FROLINAT announced that it was giving political and logistical support to the Tibesti rebellion. In November the MDJT announced that it had defeated ANT forces in Aozou, killing 80 and capturing 47 (a further 42 ANT troops were said to have defected to the rebellion).

Ouaïdou resigned as Prime Minister in December 1999. He was replaced by Nagoum Yamassoum, whose new Government included five UNDR members, among them Kebzabo as Minister of State, Minister of Agriculture. Also in that month it was announced that 13 'politico-military' groups, including FROLINAT and the FNTR, had formed a new anti-Government alliance led by Antoine Bangui, the Coordination des mouvements armés et partis politiques de l'opposition (CMAP). In February 2000 it was reported that the former armed wing of the MDD had renamed itself the Mouvement pour l'unité et la République and allied itself with the MDJT and the CDR.

In July 2000 the MDJT attacked a garrison in Bardaï and proclaimed its control of four towns in Tibesti. Official sources stated that 57 rebels and 13 government troops were killed during the fighting. The Prime Minister visited the region and invited MDJT negotiators to take part in peace discussions. In September it was reported that Moïse Ketté Nodji, the leader of the CSNPD, had been killed during clashes with ANT forces; it was subsequently reported that the CSNPD had been dissolved. In September Togoimi met with Deby for the first time, in Sirte, Libya. Togoimi's proposal for multilateral peace discussions, incorporating all opposition groups and Deby's administration, was followed later that month by a conference at which Deby met with representatives of some 30 organizations (including trade unions, civil society groups and political parties), styling themselves the Forces vives, who were reportedly united in their disapproval of a new electoral code (see below). However, renewed fighting broke out in October between members of the MDJT and government forces in the far north and subsequently intensified.

Meanwhile, in July 2000 the Assemblée nationale approved proposals for the creation of an independent electoral body, the Commission électorale nationale indépendante (CENI), which was to plan a reorganization of constituencies in advance of elections due to be held in 2001. An extensive reshuffle of the Government at the end of August 2000 followed the dismissal of ministers belonging to the URD, owing to their party's rejection of the new electoral code.

In February 2001 it was announced that a presidential election would take place on 20 May and that legislative elections, initially scheduled for April, would be postponed until March 2002 for financial reasons. Municipal and local elections, which would have elected the bodies that, in turn, were to elect the members of the proposed upper parliamentary chamber, the Sénat, were postponed indefinitely. In April 2001 Deby dismissed all UNDR ministers from the Government, following Kebzabo's announcement of his candidacy in the presidential election. The Secretary-General of the Parti pour la liberté et le développement (PLD), Ibn Oumar Mahamat Saleh, who was also a presidential candidate, subsequently ordered his party's three ministers to withdraw from the Government. In early May the six opposition presidential candidates, including Kamougué, Yorongar and former Prime Minister Alingué, signed an electoral pact, pledging to unite behind a single candidate in the event of a second round of voting. Meanwhile, in addition to the MDS, 27 political organizations, including the RDP, rallied behind Deby.

The presidential election took place, as scheduled, on 20 May 2001. Although international and national observers pronounced themselves largely satisfied with its conduct, the six opposition candidates alleged widespread fraud and malpractice. In late May, prior to the announcement of the results, eight members of the CENI resigned, in response to apparent irregularities in the vote counting. Following the CENI's announcement of preliminary results crediting Deby with 67.4% of the votes cast, all six opposition candidates were, on two occasions, briefly arrested for breaching a temporary ban on political meetings and for allegedly inciting violence and civil disobedience. Although the arrests were promptly rescinded, the Forces vives condemned the election result as fraudulent and called a general strike. Moreover, the opposition presented a petition to the Constitutional Council, requesting that the election be annulled. On 13 June the Constitutional Council issued the final results of the election, according to which Deby had won 63.2% of the valid votes cast, followed by Yorongar, with 16.4%. (Yorongar's supporters claimed that he had won more than one-half of the votes cast.) A turn-out of 61.4% was declared, compared with the 80.9% that had been announced initially. Following Deby's inauguration on 8 August, Yamassoum was reappointed as Prime Minister; the new Government comprised 20 representatives from the MPS, five from the RDP and 10 other allies of Deby.

Disagreements between the CMAP and the CPAL became apparent in late 2001, following a declaration by Deby in August that he was willing to engage in dialogue with the two groups. In September FROLINAT-Conseil provisoire de la révolution (FROLINAT-CPR), as the organization had been renamed, was expelled from the CMAP, which accused Goukouni's party of engaging in separate discussions with the Government. In late October, however, the CMAP expressed a willingness to enter into discussions with Deby and offered to send a delegation to N'Djamena if its security could be assured; the CPAL continued to oppose any negotiations. In December the CMAP presented the Government with proposals for a peace plan, and in the following month the Minister of Foreign Affairs, Mahamat Saleh Annadif, held discussions with CMAP members in France and with other exiled opposition members in Benin and Nigeria. In January 2002 Deby announced that the elections would be held on 21 April; according to the revised electoral code, the Assemblée nationale was to be enlarged to 155 members.

Meanwhile, reports emerged in December 2001 that the Libyan Government, which was mediating between MDJT rebels and the Chadian Government, had assured the rebels of its support. The involvement of Libya in the peace process was regarded as a major factor in the beneficial terms offered to the MDJT in a peace agreement, signed by the group's deputy leader, Adoum Togoi Abbo (a former Chadian ambassador to Libya), and the Chadian Government in early January 2002. According to the agreement, both sides would institute an immediate cease-fire and a general amnesty for prisoners. Moreover, the MDJT was to participate in the Chadian Government and other state institutions, while the rebel forces were to be regularized. The Libyan Government was to be responsible for monitoring the implementation of the agreement. However, Togoimi did not give his approval to the arrangements, and, as a split in the rebel group became evident, in early April the MDJT issued a statement accusing the Government of inhibiting the peace process by its refusal to postpone legislative elections in order to allow the appointment of MDJT representatives to the Government. In late April the CMAP also announced the suspension of peace negotiations with the Government.

Elections to the Assemblée nationale, which took place on 21 April 2002, were contested by 472 candidates, representing some 40 parties, although the UDR and PLD boycotted the polls. The MPS significantly increased its parliamentary representation, obtaining 110 seats. (The party's candidates were reportedly unopposed in around 50 constituencies.) The RDP became the second largest party, with 12 seats, while the Fédération action pour la République (FAR) became the largest opposition party, with nine seats. Coumakoye's VIVA—Rassemblement national pour la démocratie et le progrès and the UNDR each won five seats, and the URD's representation was significantly reduced, to only three seats. The Constitutional Council annulled the results of voting in two constituencies. In mid-June Ouaïdou was elected as President of the Assemblée nationale, and Deby appointed Haroun Kabadi, a senior official in the MPS, as Prime Minister, to head a 28-member Council of Ministers.

Meanwhile, in mid-May 2002 it was reported that Togoi was being held in detention by forces loyal to Togoimi, who had confirmed his rejection of the peace agreement signed in January; MDJT commanders denied that Togoi had been killed. None the less, in early July some 200 former MDJT fighters were reported to have joined government forces. In early June the FNTR announced the cessation of its armed struggle. An attack, in mid-September, on the eastern village of Tissi was attributed by the Chadian Government to troops supported by the CAR, although the ANR, which been dormant for several years, claimed responsibility for the raid and, amid heightened tension with the CAR (see below), emphasized that the perpetrators of the attack were resident in Chad.

The death of Togoimi, in Libya, in September 2002, while being treated for injuries sustained in a landmine explosion in Chad in August, raised hopes that peace talks between the Government and the MDJT would be reconvened, and Deby visited the north in order to encourage a resumption of negotiations. The leadership of the MDJT was assumed, in an acting capacity, by Adoum Maurice Hel-Bongo, although a split in the organization, between those loyal to Togoi and those loyal to Hel-Bongo became evident in subsequent months. In October renewed fighting broke out in the north; following an attack by the MDJT on an airport at Faya N'Gourma, in which some 20 ANT soldiers reportedly died, further clashes were reported near Fada, in which, according to official figures, 50 MDJT rebels were killed. In November rebels of the Forces des organisations nationales pour l'alternance et les libertés au Tchad (FONALT), one of the constituent groups of the ANR, claimed to have killed 116 ANT soldiers in clashes near Adré, close to the borders with Sudan and the CAR, although the Chadian Government made no official confirmation or denial of these reports.

In January 2003, following negotiations in Libreville, Gabon, the Government and the ANR signed a peace memorandum. Moreover, Garfa, the leader of the ANR, returned to Chad for the first time since 1994. However, the FONALT rejected the terms of the accord. During the first half of 2003 reports emerged of the formation of a new 'umbrella' grouping of 'politico-military' organizations opposed to the Deby regime, the Front uni pour la démocratie et la paix (FUDP). The initiative to establish the FUDP had apparently come from Chadian exiles in Benin, although, following pressure from the Beninois authorities, several influential members of the group left Benin for Togo. In April Hel-Bongo resigned as acting president of the MDJT. By mid-July, when Togoi was elected as President of the FUDP, at a congress reportedly held in Nigeria, several 'politico-military' organizations had announced their affiliation to the grouping, including the FNTR, the MDD and the faction of the MDJT loyal to Togoi. In August the faction of the MDJT that had remained outside the FUDP elected Col Hassan Abdallah Mardigué as its leader. In September more than 200 MDJT fighters were reported to have surrendered to government forces near Fada; following the signing of a peace accord between the Minister of National Defence, Veterans and Victims of War, Gen. Mahamat Nouri, and a local MDJT commander. None the less, later in the month clashes between MDJT rebels and government troops were reported around Bardai airport in the Tibesti region.

Meanwhile, in May 2003 15 deputies were elected to serve at the High Court of Justice, one of the institutions that had been established by the 1996 Constitution, but had hitherto remained in abeyance. Following a minor government reorganization in late May, a new Council of Ministers was formed in June, headed by a close ally of Deby, Moussa Mahamat Faki, and included 11 new members; the dismissal of Kabadi as Prime Minister followed his removal from the executive committee of the MPS. In late July it was reported that the Assemblée nationale had approved legislation delegating presidential prerogatives to Faki until October, while Deby received medical treatment in France.

In mid-December 2003 the Government signed a peace agreement with Togoi in Ouagadougou, Burkina Faso (where Togoi had been resident since 2000), providing for an immediate cease-fire, an amnesty for MDJT fighters and supporters, and for the eventual inclusion of an undisclosed number of MDJT ministers in the Chadian Government. However, 'hardline' factions of the MDJT rejected the terms of the agreement, claiming to have killed up to 30 government troops in renewed clashes in Tibesti shortly after the agreement had been signed.

In February 2004 Deby reorganized the Council of Ministers, making changes to seven government positions. Idriss Ahmed Idriss left the Ministry of the Economy and Finance to become the National Director of the regional bank, the Banque des états de l'Afrique centrale; he was replaced by Ahmat Awat Sakine, hitherto Director-General of the Treasury. Gen. Nouri retired as Minister of National Defence, Veterans and Victims of War, and was replaced by Gen. Allafouz Koni.

A number of new opposition coalitions were formed in 2004. In March six 'politico-military' organizations, including the MDD, the CDR and the MUR and a faction of the MDJT, formed the Union des forces pour le changement (UFC). Acheikh Ibn Oumar was named as Provisional National Co-ordinator of the new grouping, which declared itself committed to the development of national unity and the holding of fair and free elections. In April Ahmat Hassaballah Soubiane, a founder member of the MPS and the former Chadian ambassador to the USA and Canada, announced in Washington, DC, the formation of the Coalition pour la défense de la démocratie et des droits constitutionnels (CDDC). In May 25 opposition parties, including the URD, the UNDR and the RDP, announced that they had formed the Coordination des partis politiques pour la défense de la Constitution (CPDC), which, like the CDDC, sought to resist Deby's proposed constitutional modifications.

Eight constitutional amendments were approved by the Assemblée nationale in May 2004, the most notable of which removed the restriction limiting the President to serving two terms of office. The changes, which required endorsement in a national referendum, were vigorously criticized by opposition parties. In June the Constitutional Council rejected an opposition appeal to annul the constitutional revisions. In late July Deby effected a major reorganization of the Council of Ministers, dismissing nine ministers—among them Gen. Koni, who was replaced as Minister of National Defence, Veterans and Victims of War by Emmanuel Nadingar, hitherto Assistant Secretary-General to the Government—and creating a new Ministry of State Control and Moralization.

Faki resigned as Prime Minister on 3 February 2005; although no official reason for his departure was issued, speculation persisted that his resignation was in response to increasing tension between the Government and the President, and followed a series of strikes held by civil servants, teachers and health workers, protesting at unpaid wages. Deby nominated Pascal Yoadimnadji, hitherto the Minister of Agriculture, as the new premier, and new ministers responsible for the economy and for education were also appointed.

On 6 June 2005, according to official results, announced later in the month, some 77.8% of the votes cast in a referendum approved the proposed constitutional amendments, which thereby took effect. Some 71.0% of the registered electorate were reported to have participated in the plebiscite. The CPDC, which had called for a boycott of the referendum, denounced the results as fraudulent and announced its intention to call a general strike. In early August Deby implemented a major governmental reorganization; responsibility for defence affairs was transferred to the Office of the Presidency, with the nomination of Bichara Issa Djadallah as Minister-delegate at the Presidency, responsible for National Defence. This reinforcement of presidential control over the military coincided with heightened concern at divided loyalties among members of the armed forces, as well as widespread speculation that Deby's position as President had been weakened as a consequence of his alleged ill-health. In early August 15 senior army officers were arrested on charges of plotting a *coup d'état*, while mutinies in the armed forces were also reported.

In mid-October 2005 the Chadian authorities announced that at least 40 soldiers had deserted their posts in N'Djamena and fled to the east of the country (opposition sources put the number of deserters as high as 500). Some 30 of the deserters were reported to have surrendered to the Chadian armed forces following clashes at Adré. The deserters formed a new 'politico-military' organization, Socle pour le changement, l'unité nationale et la démocratie (SCUD), led by Yaya Dillo Djérou. A further rebel attack, in mid-December, on a barracks at Adré, was led by another recently formed rebel group, the Rassemblement pour la démocratie et les libertés (RDL), led by Capt. Mahamat Nour Adbelkerim, and apparently based in Sudan. In late December the RDL and SCUD were reported to have formed an alliance, the Front uni pour le changement démocratique (FUCD), under Nour's leadership. It was reported in February 2006 that Nour, who had previously called for the removal of Deby from office, had moderated his demands to include, principally, the convening of a national conference, to be held no later than mid-2006, to discuss the future political organization of Chad.

Considerable international controversy resulted following the approval of legislation by the Assemblée nationale, in late December 2005, that abolished conditions on the expenditure of petroleum revenues that had been agreed, following consultation with the World Bank in 1998, and which had guaranteed that 72% of state revenue from the sector would be dedicated to the development of health, education, agriculture and infrastructure, with a further 10% to be held in trust for future generations. (Chad had become a substantial producer and exporter of petroleum in 2003—see Economic Affairs section). In late January 2006 the Assemblée nationale voted to approve legislation introduced by Deby that extended its mandate by 18 months, apparently because the Government lacked funding required to hold the legislative elections that had been due to be held in April 2006. In late February a presidential election was, none the less, scheduled for 3 May.

In mid-March 2006 the Chadian authorities announced that an attempt to assassinate Deby had been prevented; two senior army officers were arrested, while it was alleged that the plot had been devised by several other former senior officers (including several relatives of Deby) who had recently defected to join the FUCD. At the end of the month the Chief of the Land Forces, Gen. Abakar Youssouf Mahamat Itno, was killed in clashes with rebels near the Sudanese border. In mid-April the forces of the FUCD advanced on N'Djamena, and on 13 April heavy fighting broke out in the city, although Government forces regained control of the city after several hours. More than 100 of the rebels (the majority of whom were reported to be Sudanese, according to official sources) were captured during the fighting, and Deby announced that Chad was to sever diplomatic relations with Sudan and work towards sealing the border between the two countries.

The presidential election proceeded as scheduled on 3 May 2006, although a boycott was urged by opposition parties. According to results released by the Constitutional Council some three weeks later, Deby secured 64.67% of the votes cast, comfortably defeating his nearest rival, Coumakoye, who took 15.13%. The rate of voter participation was recorded at 53.1%.

In late July 2006 President Deby effected a minor reorganization of the Government, dismissing two ministers who had been accused of embezzlement. Also in late July some 54 parties and civil society groups participated in a 'national dialogue' chaired by Prime Minister Yoadimnadji; however, the meeting was boycotted by the CPDC and the FAR. Deby was sworn in for a third elected term as President on 8 August and one week later announced the composition of an enlarged Council of Ministers, appointing three candidates who stood in the presidential election in May—Coumakoye, Pahimi Padacke Albert and Ibrahim Koullamallah—to ministerial posts. Yoadimnadji retained the premiership, while Adoum Younousmi was reappointed Minister of State, Minister of Infrastructure. At the end of August Deby replaced the Ministers of Economy, Planning and Co-operation, Petroleum and Stockbreeding.

In late November 2006 the Assemblée nationale approved the imposition of a six-month state of emergency in the regions of Borkou-Ennedi-Tibesti, Hadjer-Lamis, Moyen-Chari, Mandoul, N'Djamena, Ouaddaï, Salamat and Wadi Fira, after clashes between rival ethnic groups resulted in the deaths of at least 300 people. Heavy fighting also took place in that month between government troops and two rebel groups, the Union des forces pour la démocratie et le développement (UFDD), led by Nouri, and the Rassemblement des forces démocratique—Convention nationale Tchadienne (RAFD—CNT). The towns of Biltine and Abéché were reportedly briefly captured by the RAFD—CNT and the UFDD, respectively, before government forces re-established control. Clashes continued into December with several hundred people killed during renewed offensives; the UFDD also attacked the northern town of Ounianga Kebir in mid-January 2007. (The UFDD and the RAFD—CNT had announced the creation of a joint military command the previous month.)

Meanwhile, in late December 2006 the FUCD and the Government signed a peace agreement in Tripoli, Libya, which, *inter alia*, provided for the immediate cessation of hostilities between the two sides, the release of all prisoners of war and the integration of FUCD combatants into the Chadian security forces.

On 23 February 2007 Prime Minister Yoadimnadji died from a brain haemorrhage in Paris, France, where he had been transported for medical treatment. Younousmi became Prime Minister in an acting capacity and on 26 February Coumakoye was appointed as the permanent successor to Yoadimnadji. On 4 March Deby unveiled a new Government in which, most notably, Nour was awarded the national defence portfolio. Albert, hitherto Minister of Agriculture, was appointed Minister of Justice, Keeper of the Seals. In mid-March the legislature approved the new Government's programme, which included commitments to peace and security, and promises to bolster social spending and engage in political dialogue.

In August 2007 President Deby and several opposition party leaders signed an agreement on a code of conduct relating to electoral procedures. The electoral system was to be reviewed under the agreement and it was anticipated that legislative elections scheduled to be held in October 2009 would be postponed until the end of that year if reforms were implemented. On 25 October 2007 the Government and four rebel movements including the UFDD, the Rassemblement des forces pour le changement (RFC, as the RAFD—CNT had been restyled) and the Concord nationale Tchadienne concluded a peace agreement in Sirte, Libya, establishing a cease-fire. The accord granted an amnesty to all members of those organizations and permitted the rebel movements to reconstitute themselves as political parties. Under the agreement the disarmament of rebel movements was scheduled to take place in November and provision was made for their integration into the Chadian defence forces. However, in that month the cease-fire broke down following heavy fighting near Abéché between government forces and rebels from the UFDD and the RFD. Consequently, former rebel leader and hitherto Minister of National Defence Nour was dismissed from the Council of Ministers amid claims that he could no longer exert control over the rebel groups.

In early February 2008 the UFDD, the RFC and the UFDD—Fondemental (UFDD—F), which had formed an anti-Government coalition of forces, advanced on N'Djamena from bases in western Sudan with the aim of overthrowing President Deby. Government troops were deployed to the boundaries of the capital to intercept the militia, and it was feared that if rebel leaders Timane Erdemi of the RFC, Gen. Nouri of the UFDD and Adbelwahid Aboud Makaye of the UFDD—F did not enter into negotiations with the Government, the deployment of the

EUFOR peace-keeping mission in the region (see below) would be delayed. Heavy fighting broke out lasting for several days during which both sides claimed to be in control of the capital; however, by 6 February troops loyal to Deby, with the assistance of intelligence and logistical support provided by the French military, had succeeded in repelling the rebels from N'Djamena. The following day a curfew was imposed in many regions of the country and on 15 February a nation-wide state of emergency was declared. Some 20,000 Chadians were reported to have fled to Cameroon and relief agencies estimated that up to 150 people had been killed and at least 700 injured in the fighting. On 16 February a minor reorganization of the Government was carried out in which Gen. Mahamat Ali Abdallah, hitherto Minister of State, Minister of Mines and Energy was awarded the national defence portfolio.

Following the outbreak of a violent rebellion in the Darfur region of western Sudan in February 2003 (see the chapter on Sudan), Deby played a major role in promoting diplomatic measures intended to restore peace to the region, meeting the Sudanese President, Lt-Gen. Omar Hassan Ahmad al-Bashir, in April, August and December. In early November Sudanese and Chadian officials agreed to establish a joint force to patrol the countries' common border, amid rising concerns about cross-border banditry associated with the rebellion. Peace talks between representatives of the Sudanese Government and the rebel Sudan Liberation Movement (SLM) were held in N'Djamena in December, but were inconclusive. By March 2004 some 130,000 Sudanese citizens had sought refuge in eastern Chad, where many of the population belonged to the same tribe as the refugees from Darfur. At the end of that month indirect peace talks between the SLM, the Sudan Justice and Equality Movement (SJEM) and the Government, attended by international observers, commenced in Chad, and on 8 April a 45-day cease-fire was signed by representatives of the three parties. Further talks were held in Chad between the Government, the SLM and the SJEM later that month, but little progress was made. Furthermore, in late April and early May a series of clashes occurred between Chadian troops and Sudanese (principally Arab) militiamen, known as the *Janjaweed*, pursuing Sudanese rebels across the border; the Chadian Government denounced the incursions and protested to the Sudanese Government. In mid-June the Chadian Government announced that its troops had killed 69 *Janjaweed* fighters who had attacked the Chadian village of Birak, some 6 km from the Sudanese border. By December an estimated 200,000 Sudanese had fled to Chad, according to the office of the UN High Commissioner for Refugees, placing considerable strain on food and water resources in the border region. In that month the Sudanese Government concluded a ceasefire in N'Djamena with a previously unidentified rebel group, the National Movement for Reform and Development (NMRD), which described itself as a breakaway faction of the SJEM. Although it had been hoped that these negotiations would lead to the return of significant numbers of refugees to Sudan, little progress had been observed by late 2005 (by which time there were believed to be some 200,000 Sudanese refugees in Chad) and violent clashes in the border area continued.

Relations between Chad and Sudan became increasingly strained in 2005, and in April President Deby accused the Sudanese Government of providing support to a 3,000-strong rebel force operating near the two countries' mutual border. In late September at least two members of the Chadian armed forces were killed in clashes near Ouaddaï with a group of unidentified armed men wearing military uniforms, who had reportedly crossed into Chad from Sudan and killed at least 36 cattle herders. In early November, following defections from the Chadian army in the previous month by soldiers in eastern regions, the Minister-delegate at the Presidency, responsible for National Defence, Bichara Issa Djadallah, announced that the Chadian authorities did not rule out the pursuit of defectors who had entered Sudan. Moreover, in late November Deby accused the Sudanese Government of complicity in providing arms and logistical support to Chadian rebels, and the Government blamed Sudan for an attack on a barracks near Adré in mid-December, which resulted in some 300 deaths, mostly of rebel fighters, according to an official statement; although the Sudanese authorities denied any involvement in the attack, in late December Deby stated that he regarded a 'state of belligerence' as existing between the two countries. None the less, in January 2006 representatives of the Governments of both Chad and Sudan expressed a willingness to enter into negotiations to defuse tensions between the countries. Prior to agreeing to participate in any such discussions, however, the Chadian authorities demanded that Sudan conform to a number of conditions, including the disarmament of Chadian deserters in that country, the ending of Sudanese military incursions into Chadian territory, and the compensation of victims of cross-border raids. In early February Libya hosted a mini-summit on the conflict between Chad and Sudan, following which Deby, al-Bashir and al-Qaddafi signed an agreement, known as the Tripoli Accord, in which, *inter alia*, the leaders of Chad and Sudan agreed to cease supporting groups hostile to the other's Government. However, following a rebel attack on the Chadian capital, N'Djamena, in mid-April, Chad announced that it was to sever diplomatic relations with Sudan with immediate effect.

Relations improved in late July 2006 when the two countries signed an agreement in N'Djamena, according to which they agreed not to host each other's rebel groups on their territory. In August al-Bashir attended the swearing-in ceremony of Deby and it was announced that Chad and Sudan had re-established diplomatic relations with immediate effect, and that the border between the two countries would be reopened. There were, however, numerous reports of violent incidents in the border region during late 2006 and early 2007, and in November 2006 the Governments of both Chad and the CAR appealed for the dispatch of UN peace-keeping troops to the area. The Sudanese Government expressed its vehement opposition to any such moves. In late February 2007 the UN Secretary-General, Ban Ki-moon, proposed the deployment of an 11,000-strong UN peace-keeping mission to protect civilians and deter cross-border attacks. He also advocated the dispatch of a smaller contingent of UN military and police personnel to north-eastern CAR. However, the Chadian authorities stipulated that they would not accept a military force and requested that a civil force comprised solely of police officers be deployed to the area.

In early May 2007, following mediation by Saudi Arabia's King Abdallah, Presidents al-Bashir and Deby agreed to co-operate with the AU and the UN in their attempts to stabilize the Chad-Sudan border. Both countries approved the formation of a joint border force, and pledged to cease training and funding rebel groups and to stop all cross-border attacks. Furthermore, in June Deby announced that the Chadian Government had agreed in principle to the deployment of a European Union (EU, see p. 244) peace-keeping force along the border with Sudan. However, some rebel groups were concerned that French support for President Deby could unduly influence the force and warned that the EU troops could become a target for further violence if they did not remain impartial. In September, following the adoption of UN Resolution 1778, the UN Security Council approved the deployment for a period of one year of the United Nations Mission in the Central African Republic and Chad (MINURCAT), with the mandate to protect refugees, displaced persons and civilians adversely affected by the uprising in Darfur. MINURCAT was also to facilitate the provision of humanitarian assistance in eastern Chad and the north-east of the CAR and create favourable conditions for the reconstruction and economic and social development of those areas. The multidimensional presence was to be supported by the EU bridging military operation in Eastern Chad and North Eastern Central African Republic (EUFOR TCHAD/RCA) comprising some 4,300 troops. The deployment of the EU force was delayed by the rebel assault on N'Djamena in early February 2008; however, by mid-February EUFOR contingents had begun to arrive and the force was expected to be fully operational by the end of that month. Reports estimated that since the conflict in Sudan had spread across the border into Chad in 2005 some 180,000 Chadians had been displaced. Deby pledged that one-half of these should be assisted to return home by mid-2008, a target that could be achieved, according to UN officials, if sufficient security measures were implemented.

In early 1998 it was reported that Chad was to seek the extradition from Senegal of former President Habré, with a view to his prosecution in relation to human rights abuses and in connection with the embezzlement of state funds. A committee of inquiry, established by the Deby administration, held Habré's 'political police' responsible for the deaths of some 40,000 people and the torture of 200,000 others. In February 2000, following a ruling by a Senegalese court that he could be tried in that country, Habré was charged with complicity in acts of torture committed in Chad under his leadership, and placed under house arrest. The charges were dismissed in July, however, on the grounds that Senegal lacked the appropriate penal procedure to process such a case. In March 2001 the Senegalese Court of

Cassation upheld this ruling, and Habré remained in Senegal. In August 2005 Prime Minister Yoadimnadji announced that former members of Habré's security forces still working within state organizations would be removed from the their posts to face trial on suspected human-rights abuses, and also stated that the Government intended to introduce legislation that would provide compensation for the victims of torture and their families; this followed the publication of a report by the US-based organization Human Rights Watch, which stated that several officials suspected of complicity in humans rights abuses under Habré continued to hold senior positions in the Deby administration. In September a Belgian court issued a warrant for Habré's arrest, under a law that (as amended in 2003) gave that country's courts universal jurisdiction in cases of human rights abuses and war crimes, if Belgian citizens or long-term residents were among the plaintiffs. (Several of the alleged victims of abuses committed under Habré's regime had been granted Belgian citizenship) and in November he was remanded into custody in Dakar, Senegal, by a court investigating the request for extradition. However, in late November the court ruled that it had no jurisdiction to rule on Habré's extradition, and he was released. Habré was, however, re-arrested later in the month, and the Senegalese Minister of State, Minister of Foreign Affairs announced that a decision on which judicial body was competent to rule on Habré's extradition would be taken at a forthcoming summit of AU leaders. At the summit, held in Khartoum, Sudan, in January 2006, it was agreed that Habré should not be extradited to Belgium. Instead, a resolution calling for a panel of 'eminent African jurists' to rule on the appropriate venue for Habré's trial was approved. At an AU meeting held in Banjul, The Gambia, in July of that year it was announced that Habré was to be tried in Senegal. In January 2007 the Senegalese Minister of State, Minister of Foreign Affairs stated that Habré's trial was unlikely to commence before 2010.

In response to an attempted coup in the CAR in May 2001, Chad reportedly dispatched troops to defend the Government of President Ange-Félix Patassé. In early November heightened unrest broke out in the CAR, following an attempt to arrest the recently dismissed Chief of Staff of the Armed Forces, Gen. François Bozizé, in connection with the May coup attempt. Bozizé crossed into Chad, with an estimated 300 armed supporters, and was granted refuge in Sarh. Chad was subsequently involved in efforts by both the Libyan-sponsored Community of Sahel-Saharan States (see p. 411) and CEMAC to find a lasting solution to the crisis in the CAR. In late December the CAR judiciary abandoned legal proceedings against Bozizé. Meanwhile, repeated clashes were reported at the Chad–CAR border and an additional source of tension was the appointment of Col Martin Khoumtan-Madji (believed by the Chadian authorities to be an alias of Abdoulaye Miskine, a former senior member of the CSNPD based in the CAR since 1998) as the head of a special unit in the CAR military, comprising some 300 soldiers, including many former Chadian rebels, and answerable directly to the presidency, charged with securing the common border of the two countries.

In early August 2002 the CAR Prime Minister, Martin Ziguélé, accused Chadian troops of launching cross-border attacks in the CAR, precipitating an emergency CEMAC summit later that month. (Chadian sources stated that the troops that had launched the attacks in the CAR were loyal to Bozizé, and not affiliated to the ANT.) A report issued by a CEMAC observer mission, at the end of August, stated that, although tension remained high in the border region, there was no concentration of troops on the border, or of foreign troops in either country. An attack by the ANR in eastern Chad (see above), in early September, was attributed by the Chadian Government to troops supported by the CAR. In early October a CEMAC summit in Libreville, Gabon, sought to defuse tensions between the two countries; in accordance with an agreement reached at the summit, Bozizé and Khoumtan-Madji were granted asylum in France and Togo, respectively; a CEMAC force was subsequently deployed to monitor joint patrols of the border by Chadian and CAR troops. Tensions thereafter abated somewhat, and in late January 2003 the Governments of Chad, the CAR and Sudan announced their intention to establish a tripartite committee to oversee the security and stability of their joint borders. In mid-February the Presidents of Chad and the CAR met in Bangui in an attempt to normalize relations between the two countries. Later that month some 20,000 refugees (many of whom were Chadian nationals who had been resident in the CAR for many years) entered southern Chad, fleeing renewed fighting in the CAR. Following Bozizé's assumption of power in mid-March, some 400 Chadian troops were reportedly dispatched to the CAR; around 120 Chadian troops were subsequently integrated into the CEMAC force that had been deployed in the CAR in late 2002. Relations improved between the two countries during 2003, and in December Deby was a guest of honour at celebrations for the National Day of the CAR in Bangui. As a result of renewed unrest in the CAR, up to 13,000 refugees were believed to have fled the country for Chad during the second half of 2005. In late June 2006 clashes were reported between Chadian rebel forces and CAR and CEMAC troops near Tiroungoulou in which some 80 people were believed to have been killed.

Further concerns regarding regional security emerged in March 2004, when clashes at the Niger–Chad border between Islamist militants belonging to the Algerian-based Groupe salafiste pour la prédication et le combat (GSPC) and Chadian and Nigerien troops resulted in the deaths of some 43 GSPC fighters and three Chadian soldiers, according to the Chadian Government. It was announced that month that the Governments of Algeria, Chad, Mali and Niger were to reinforce security co-operation in the regions of their common borders. Meanwhile, the MDJT had reportedly captured a prominent GSPC leader, Amara Saïfi (also known as Abderrazak le Para). In July it was reported that the MDJT had released Saïfi, whose faction of the GSPC had apparently united with the Chadian rebel group to fight the Chadian army. In late October 2006 the Nigerien Government announced its intention to forcibly return to Chad some 150,000 Mahamid Arabs, who had migrated to Niger from Chad over a number of years. However, following protests from the Mahamids to the AU and the UN, the Nigerien authorities stated that only those without identification papers—estimated to number about 4,000—would be required to leave Niger.

In early August 2006 the People's Republic of China announced that it had resumed diplomatic relations with Chad, after bilateral ties between that country and Taiwan were severed.

Government

A new Constitution was adopted by national referendum on 31 March 1996. Under the terms of the Constitution, the Republic of Chad is a unitary state with a multi-party political system. Executive power is vested in the President, elected by direct universal suffrage, who is the Head of State and Commander-in-Chief of the Armed Forces. The President appoints the Prime Minister, who nominates the Council of Ministers. Legislative power is vested in a unicameral legislature, the 155-member Assemblée nationale, which is elected by direct universal suffrage for a four-year term. Constitutional amendments, approved by referendum in 2005, removed the restriction limiting the President to serving two five-year terms of office and abolished the Sénat. Chad is divided into 18 administrative regions, including the capital city, N'Djamena, which is a region of special status.

Defence

As assessed at November 2007, the Armée nationale tchadienne (ANT) numbered 25,350 (army approximately 20,000, air force 350, Republican Guard 5,000). In addition, there was a 4,500-strong gendarmerie. Military service is by conscription. Under defence agreements with France, the army receives technical and other aid: in February 2008 the number of troops deployed in Chad by France numbered 1,500, although in late 2005 a restructuring of French forces deployed in Africa was announced, in accordance with which all French troops would, eventually, be withdrawn from Chad. Direct aid from France to the Chadian army in 1999 was an estimated 6,160m. francs CFA. Defence expenditure for 2007 was budgeted at an estimated 33,300m. francs CFA.

Economic Affairs

In 2006, according to estimates by the World Bank, Chad's gross national income (GNI), measured at average 2004–06 prices, was US $4,745m., equivalent to $480 per head (or $1,230 on an international purchasing-power parity basis). During 1996–2006, it was estimated, the population increased at an average annual rate of 3.3%, while gross domestic product (GDP) per head increased, in real terms, by an average of 5.1% per year. Overall GDP increased, in real terms, at an average annual rate of 8.6% in 1996–2006, according to the World Bank; growth in 2006 was 1.3%.

Agriculture (excluding fishing) contributed 20.5% of GDP in 2006, according to the World Bank; some 70.4% of the labour force were employed in the sector in mid-2005. The principal cash crop is cotton (exports of which contributed an estimated 15.8% of total export revenue in 2003, a decline from 41.1% in 2001). The principal subsistence crops are sorghum, millet and groundnuts. Livestock-rearing, which contributed an estimated 21.0% of exports in 2003, also makes an important contribution to the domestic food supply. During 1996–2006 agricultural GDP increased at an average annual rate of 3.6%; growth in 2006 was 3.2%.

Industry (including mining and fishing) contributed 54.8% of GDP in 2006, according to the World Bank. About 4.2% of the population were employed in the sector in 1990. During 1996–2006 industrial GDP increased at an average annual rate of 20.3%; it increased by 144.5% in 2004, largely owing to the revenues from petroleum extraction (see below), but grew by just 5.0% in 2005, before declining by 3.7% in 2006.

The mining sector (including fishing, but excluding petroleum extraction) contributed 2.1% of GDP in 2005, according to the IMF. The petroleum sector contributed some 30.0% of GDP in that year, compared with 11.3% in 2003. For many years the only minerals exploited were natron (sodium carbonate), salt, alluvial gold and materials for the construction industry. However, long-delayed plans to develop sizeable petroleum reserves in the Doba Basin and at Sedigi, in the south of the country, were being pursued in the early 2000s, and production of petroleum at Doba commenced in mid-2003 (see below). There is believed to be considerable potential for the further exploitation of gold, bauxite and uranium. During 1998–2005 the GDP of the mining sector (including fishing) increased at an average annual rate of 4.3%, according to the IMF; growth of 6.8% was recorded in 2005.

The manufacturing sector (including handicrafts), which contributed 5.3% of GDP in 2006, operates mainly in the south of the country, and is dominated by agro-industrial activities, notably the processing of the cotton crop by the state-controlled Société Cotonnière du Tchad (COTONTCHAD). During 1998–2005 manufacturing GDP increased at an average annual rate of 0.9%, according to the IMF; the GDP of the sector declined by 6.3% in 2004, but increased by 16.6% in 2005.

Chad has historically been heavily dependent on imports of mineral fuels (principally from Cameroon and Nigeria) for the generation of electricity. Imports of fuel products comprised an estimated 17.5% of the total value of merchandise imports in 1995. The use of wood-based fuel products by most households has contributed to the severe depletion of Chad's forest resources. In November 2000 the Cameroonian Prime Minister announced the creation of a technical committee to instigate the export of electricity to Chad. None the less, by 2002 only 2% of households in Chad had access to electricity.

Services contributed 24.7% of GDP in 2006, according to the World Bank. The GDP of the sector increased at an average annual rate of 6.1% in 1999–2006; growth in 2006 was 4.9%.

In 2005 Chad recorded an estimated visible trade surplus of 1,211,100m. francs CFA, and there was a surplus of 26,500m. francs CFA on the current account of the balance of payments. In 1995 Chad's principal source of imports (41.3%) was France; other major suppliers were Cameroon, Nigeria and the USA. The principal markets for exports include Cameroon and France. The principal exports in 2003 were petroleum, livestock and cotton. The principal imports in 1995 were petroleum products, road vehicles and parts, sugar and cereals.

In 2005 Chad recorded an overall budgetary deficit of 64,300m. francs CFA (equivalent to 1.1% of GDP). Chad's external debt at the end of 2004 totalled US $1,701m., of which $1,582m. was long-term public debt. According to the IMF, external debt servicing (as a percentage of exports of goods and services) declined from 8.6% in 2005 to 5.7% in 2006, with the trend projected to continue in 2007, falling to 5.0%. Consumer prices increased by an annual average of 3.0% in 1996–2006; they increased by 8.0% in 2006.

Chad is a member of the Central African organs of the Franc Zone (see p. 307) and of the Communauté économique des états de l'Afrique centrale (CEEAC, see p. 411); the Lake Chad Basin Commission (see p. 413) is based in N'Djamena.

Traditionally, economic growth in Chad has been inhibited by a number of factors: conflict has deterred investment in the development of considerable mineral wealth and other resources, leaving the economy over-dependent on cotton, while the country's land-locked position has been compounded by infrastructural deficiencies. There was, however, considerable interest in Chad's petroleum deposits from the late 1990s, and in late 2000 a consortium led by the US ExxonMobil Corporation, and supported by Petronas of Malaysia and the US ChevronTexaco Corporation, began work to develop substantial petroleum resources in three fields in the Doba Basin, believed to contain reserves of approximately 900m. barrels. Operations commenced in July 2003, and a 1,070-km pipeline to transport petroleum from Doba to the port of Kribi in Cameroon was officially inaugurated in October. Output had reached some 225,000 barrels per day, by late 2005; production was expected to continue for 25–30 years and was projected to generate revenues of approximately US $120m. per year. Chad's proven total reserves of petroleum amounted to at least 1,500m. barrels. Nevertheless, provisions approved by the Assemblée nationale in 1998, whereby the majority of state revenue from the petroleum sector would be used to fund social, agricultural and infrastructural development, and which had been instrumental in generating international financial support for Chad, were abolished by parliamentary vote in late December 2005, as a result of which the World Bank suspended all financial assistance to the country, with effect from January 2006. Meanwhile, concern at the potential abuse of government revenues was heightened, following the publication, in mid-2005, of a report by a German-based NGO, Transparency International, which named Chad as having the joint-highest level (with Bangladesh) of perceived corruption of 159 countries surveyed. In July 2006 the Government announced plans to channel 70% of petroleum revenues into social development projects, and pledged to improve government efficiency and accountability. The former target was not achieved in the 2007 budget, owing to an increase in military expenditure, although the level of spending on poverty alleviation increased from $346m. in 2006, to $566m. in 2007. Despite the rapid growth in GDP that the production of petroleum was expected to generate, political instability continued to inhibit investment in the country; donor institutions warned the Government against over-reliance on the petroleum sector for future economic growth, and urged the improvement of expenditure management and further reforms to the cotton, domestic energy and financial sectors. The IMF projected GDP growth of 4.1% in 2008, while inflation was expected to decline to just 3.0%.

Education

Education is officially compulsory for six years between six and 12 years of age. Primary education begins at the age of six and lasts for six years. Secondary education, from the age of 12, lasts for seven years, comprising a first cycle of four years and a second of three years. In 2002/03 primary enrolment included 57% of children in the relevant age-group (males 68%; females 46%), while secondary enrolment in that year included only 11% of children in the appropriate age-group (males 16%; females 5%). The Université de N'Djamena was opened in 1971. In addition, there are several technical colleges. Some 5,901 students were enrolled at higher education institutions in 1999/2000. Total expenditure on education by the central Government (including foreign-financed investment) in 1996 was 32,196m. francs CFA (21.2% of total government expenditure).

Public Holidays

2008: 1 January (New Year), 20 March* (Maloud, Birth of the Prophet), 24 April (Easter Monday), 1 May (Labour Day), 12 May (Whit Monday), 25 May ('Liberation of Africa', anniversary of the OAU's foundation), 11 August (Independence Day), 15 August (Assumption), 1 October* (Id al-Fitr, end of Ramadan), 1 November (All Saints' Day), 28 November (Proclamation of the Republic), 1 December (Liberation and Democracy Day, anniversary of the 1990 coup d'état), 9 December* (Id al-Adha, Feast of the Sacrifice), 25 December (Christmas).

2009: 1 January (New Year), 9 March* (Maloud, Birth of the Prophet), 13 April (Easter Monday), 1 May (Labour Day), 25 May ('Liberation of Africa', anniversary of the OAU's foundation), 1 June (Whit Monday), 11 August (Independence Day), 15 August (Assumption), 20 September* (Id al-Fitr, end of Ramadan), 1 November (All Saints' Day), 28 November (Proclamation of the Republic), 27 November* (Id al-Adha, Feast of the Sacrifice), 1 December (Liberation and Democracy Day, anniversary of the 1990 coup d'état), 25 December (Christmas).

* These holidays are dependent on the Islamic lunar calendar and may vary by one or two days from the dates given.

Weights and Measures

The metric system is officially in force.

Statistical Survey

Source (unless otherwise stated): Institut national de la statistique, des études économiques et démographiques, BP 453, N'Djamena; tel. 52-31-64; fax 52-66-13; e-mail inseed@intnet.td; internet www.inseed-tchad.org.

Area and Population

AREA, POPULATION AND DENSITY

Area (sq km)	
Land	1,259,200
Inland waters	24,800
Total	1,284,000*
Population (sample survey)	
December 1963–August 1964	3,254,000†
Population (census result)	
8 April 1993‡	
Males	2,950,415
Females	3,208,577
Total	6,158,992
Population (UN estimates at mid-year)§	
2005	10,146,000
2006	10,468,000
2007	10,781,000
Density (per sq km) at mid-2007	8.4

* 495,800 sq miles.
† Including areas not covered by the survey.
‡ Figures are provisional. The revised total, including an adjustment for underenumeration (estimated at 1.4%), is 6,279,931.
§ Source: UN, *World Population Prospects: The 2006 Revision*.

ETHNIC GROUPS

1995 (percentages): Sara, Bongo and Baguirmi 20.1; Chadic 17.7; Arab 14.3; M'Bourn 6.3; Masalit, Maba and Mimi 6.1; Tama 6.1; Adamawa 6.0; Sudanese 6.0; Mubi 4.1; Hausa 2.1; Kanori 2.1; Massa 2.1; Kotoko 2.0; Peul 0.5; Others 4.5 (Source: La Francophonie).

PREFECTURES
(1993 census)

	Area (sq km)	Population*	Density (per sq km)	Principal city
Batha	88,800	288,458	3.2	Ati
Biltine	46,850	184,807	3.9	Biltine
Borkou-Ennedi-Tibesti (BET)	600,350	73,185	0.1	Faya-Largeau
Chari-Baguirmi†	82,910	1,251,906	15.1	N'Djamena
Guéra	58,950	306,253	5.2	Mongo
Kanem	114,520	279,927	2.4	Mao
Lac	22,320	252,932	11.3	Bol
Logone Occidental	8,695	455,489	52.4	Moundou
Logone Oriental	28,035	441,064	15.7	Doba
Mayo-Kebbi	30,105	825,158	27.4	Bongor
Moyen Chari	45,180	738,595	16.3	Sarh
Ouaddaï	76,240	543,900	7.1	Abéché
Salamat	63,000	184,403	2.9	Am-Timan
Tandjile	18,045	453,854	25.2	Laï
Total	**1,284,000**	**6,279,931**	**4.9**	

* Including adjustment for underenumeration.
† Including the capital district, N'Djamena (population 530,965).

Note: As a result of administrative reform, Chad's prefectures have been replaced by the following regions: Batha (principal city Ati), Borkou-Ennedi-Tibesti (Faya), Chari-Baguirmi (Massenya), Guéra (Mongo), Hadjer-Lamis (Massakory), Kanem (Mao), Lac (Bol), Logone Occidental (Moundou), Logone Oriental (Doba), Mandoul (Koumra), Mayo-Kebbi Est (Bongor), Mayo-Kebbi Ouest (Pala), Moyen-Chari (Sarh), Ouaddaï (Abéché) Salamat (Am-Timan), Tandjilé (Laï) and Wadi Fira (Biltine). The capital city, N'Djamena, also has the status of a region.

PRINCIPAL TOWNS
(population at 1993 census)

N'Djamena (capital)	530,965	Koumra	26,702
Moundou	99,530	Pala	26,115
Sarh	75,496	Am Timan	21,269
Abéché	54,628	Bongor	20,448
Kelo	31,319	Mongo	20,443

Mid-2005 (incl. suburbs, UN estimate): N'Djamena 888,000 (Source: UN, *World Urbanization Prospects: The 2005 Revision*).

BIRTHS AND DEATHS
(annual averages, UN estimates)

	1990–95	1995–2000	2000–05
Birth rate (per 1,000)	47.5	47.6	47.4
Death rate (per 1,000)	15.8	15.7	16.0

2001 (preliminary): Live births 397,896; Deaths 138,025.

Sources: UN, *World Population Prospects: The 2006 Revision* and *Population and Vital Statistics Report*.

Expectation of life (years at birth, WHO estimates): 46.7 (males 45.8; females 47.5) in 2005 (Source: WHO, *World Health Statistics*).

ECONOMICALLY ACTIVE POPULATION
('000 persons at mid-1990, ILO estimates)

	Males	Females	Total
Agriculture, hunting, forestry and fishing	1,179	1,102	2,281
Industry	105	9	115
Manufacturing	50	6	56
Services	245	100	344
Total labour force	**1,529**	**1,211**	**2,740**

Source: ILO.

1993 census (persons aged six years and over): Total employed 2,305,961; Unemployed 16,268; Total labour force 2,322,229.

Mid-2005 ('000, estimates): Agriculture, etc. 3,085; Total labour force 4,385 (Source: FAO).

Health and Welfare

KEY INDICATORS

Total fertility rate (children per woman, 2005)	6.7
Under-5 mortality rate (per 1,000 live births, 2005)	208
HIV/AIDS (% of persons aged 15–49, 2005)	3.5
Physicians (per 1,000 head, 2004)	0.04
Hospital beds (per 1,000 head, 2005)	0.40
Health expenditure (2004): US $ per head (PPP)	41.7
Health expenditure (2004): % of GDP	4.2
Health expenditure (2004): public (% of total)	36.9
Access to water (% of persons, 2004)	42
Access to sanitation (% of persons, 2004)	9
Human Development Index (2005): ranking	170
Human Development Index (2005): value	0.388

For sources and definitions, see explanatory note on p. vi.

Agriculture

PRINCIPAL CROPS
('000 metric tons)

	2004	2005	2006*
Rice (paddy)	91.1	148.7	106.6
Maize	107.4	201.3	183.9
Millet	297.5	578.3	589.8
Sorghum	449.4	582.6	693.6
Potatoes*	28	29	27
Sweet potatoes*	68	71	64
Cassava (Manioc)*	320	322	325
Taro (Coco yam)*	38	38	38
Yams*	231	231	230
Sugar cane*	n.a.	n.a.	389
Dry beans*	78	78	78
Groundnuts (in shell)†	450	450	450
Sesame seed†	35	35	35
Melonseed*	20	20	20
Cottonseed†	128	135	131
Dry onions*	14	14	14
Dates*	16	15	18
Mangoes*	32	32	32
Cotton (lint)†	81.6	76.2	86.0

* FAO estimate(s).
† Unofficial figures.

Aggregate production ('000 metric tons, may include official, semi-official or estimated data): Total cereals 1,213 in 2004, 1,853 in 2005, 1,913 in 2006; Total pulses 121 in 2004, 121 in 2005, 121 in 2006; Total roots and tubers 686 in 2004, 691 in 2005, 684 in 2006; Total vegetables (incl. melons) 95 in 2004, 95 in 2005, 95 in 2006; Total fruits (excl. melons) 111 in 2004, 110 in 2005, 113 in 2006.

Source: FAO.

LIVESTOCK
('000 head, year ending September)

	2003	2004*	2005*
Cattle	6,268†	6,400	6,540
Goats	5,588†	5,717	5,843
Sheep	2,511†	2,569	2,628
Pigs	24*	25	25
Horses	267†	273	275
Asses	380*	388	388
Camels	730*	735	740
Poultry	5,000*	5,200	5,200

* FAO estimate(s).
† Unofficial figure.

2006: Figures assumed to be unchanged from 2005 (FAO estimates).

Source: FAO.

LIVESTOCK PRODUCTS
('000 metric tons, FAO estimates)

	2004	2005	2006
Cattle meat	80.2	81.6	84.2
Sheep meat	13.3	13.6	14.0
Goat meat	21.4	21.9	22.2
Other meat	10.2	10.3	10.6
Cows' milk	172.8	176.6	180.4
Sheep's milk	9.6	9.9	10.1
Goats' milk	34.3	34.8	35.8
Poultry eggs	4.7	4.7	4.9

Source: FAO.

Forestry

ROUNDWOOD REMOVALS
('000 cubic metres, excl. bark, FAO estimates)

	2004	2005	2006
Sawlogs, veneer logs and logs for sleepers*	14	14	14
Other industrial wood†	747	747	747
Fuel wood	6,362	6,488	6,600
Total	7,123	7,249	7,361

* Output assumed to be unchanged since 1993.
† Output assumed to be unchanged since 1999.

Source: FAO.

SAWNWOOD PRODUCTION
('000 cubic metres, incl. railway sleepers)

	1994	1995	1996
Total (all broadleaved)	2.4*	2.4	2.4

* FAO estimate.

1997–2006: Annual production as in 1996 (FAO estimates).

Source: FAO.

Fishing

('000 metric tons, live weight, FAO estimates)

	2001	2002	2003
Total catch (freshwater fishes)	80.0	75.0	70.0

2004–05: Figure assumed to be unchanged from 2003 (FAO estimates).

Source: FAO.

Mining

	2004	2005	2006
Crude petroleum ('000 barrels)	61,400	63,300	55,900

Source: US Geological Survey.

Industry

SELECTED PRODUCTS

	2002	2003	2004
Sugar (centrifugal, raw, '000 metric tons)	23.1	38.0	40.0
Beer ('000 metric tons)	12.4	11.0	8.4
Cigarettes (million packs)	36.0	37.0	40.0
Electric energy (million kWh)	106.6	86.0	84.0

Source: IMF, *Chad: Selected Issues and Statistical Appendix* (January 2007).

Oil of groundnuts ('000 metric tons): 28.0 in 2006 (Source: FAO).

Finance

CURRENCY AND EXCHANGE RATES

Monetary Units
100 centimes = 1 franc de la Coopération financière en Afrique centrale (CFA).

Sterling, Dollar and Euro Equivalents (31 December 2007)
£1 sterling = 892.702 francs CFA;
US $1 = 445.593 francs CFA;
€1 = 655.957 francs CFA;
10,000 francs CFA = £11.20 = $22.44 = €15.24.

Average Exchange Rate (francs CFA per US $)
2005   527.47
2006   522.89
2007   479.27

Note: An exchange rate of 1 French franc = 50 francs CFA, established in 1948, remained in force until January 1994, when the CFA franc was devalued by 50%, with the exchange rate adjusted to 1 French franc = 100 francs CFA. This relationship to French currency remained in effect with the introduction of the euro on 1 January 1999. From that date, accordingly, a fixed exchange rate of €1 = 655.957 francs CFA has been in operation.

BUDGET
('000 million francs CFA)

Revenue*	2003	2004	2005
Non-petroleum revenue	124.6	140.3	159.2
Tax revenue	113.4	122.0	138.9
Taxes on income and profits	52.4	52.5	58.9
Companies	20.3	23.5	24.2
Individuals	30.2	26.9	32.4
Employers' payroll tax	1.9	2.1	2.3
Property tax	2.5	4.1	4.2
Taxes on goods and services	20.6	25.9	26.0
Turnover tax	14.4	15.4	17.9
Tax on petroleum products	4.7	5.1	5.4
Taxes on international trade	31.3	33.8	41.1
Import taxes	27.6	33.8	41.1
Export taxes	1.6	2.0	1.6
Other revenue	11.2	18.3	20.4
Property income	2.1	2.9	1.0
Administrative fees	1.9	1.2	2.3
Non-industrial sales	2.2	3.3	2.0
Petroleum-exploitation permits and share premium	—	8.3	13.6
Petroleum revenue	—	57.7	130.4
Total	124.6	198.0	289.7

Expenditure†	2003	2004	2005
Current expenditure	149.4	154.7	187.3
Wages and salaries	73.6	80.1	101.2
Civil service	56.2	60.9	73.3
Military	17.4	19.2	27.9
Goods and services	42.6	32.4	34.2
Transfers	19.2	30.1	37.1
Interest	9.5	10.2	10.4
External	8.6	8.2	7.2
Investment expenditure	198.6	182.1	217.7
Domestically financed	28.9	48.7	68.5
Foreign-financed	169.7	133.4	149.1
Total	348.0	336.8	404.9

* Excluding grants received ('000 million francs CFA): 122.7 in 2003; 69.4 in 2004; 104.2 in 2005.
† Excluding net lending ('000 million francs CFA): 76.6 in 2003; 68.0 in 2004; 53.3 in 2005.

Source: IMF, *Chad: Selected Issues and Statistical Appendix* (January 2007).

INTERNATIONAL RESERVES
(US $ million at 31 December)

	2004	2005	2006
Gold*	4.88	5.71	7.06
IMF special drawing rights	0.07	0.07	0.10
Reserve position in IMF	0.44	0.40	0.42
Foreign exchange	221.23	225.10	624.57
Total	226.62	231.28	632.15

* Valued at market-related prices.

Source: IMF, *International Financial Statistics*.

MONEY SUPPLY
('000 million francs CFA at 31 December)

	2004	2005	2006
Currency outside banks	110.11	154.10	217.21
Demand deposits at commercial and development banks	65.31	77.78	140.38
Total money (incl. others)	175.44	231.89	357.60

Source: IMF, *International Financial Statistics*.

COST OF LIVING
(Consumer Price Index for African households in N'Djamena; base: 2000 = 100)

	2004	2005	2006
All items	110.0	118.7	128.2

Source: IMF, *International Financial Statistics*.

NATIONAL ACCOUNTS

Expenditure on the Gross Domestic Product
(US $ million at current prices)

	2004	2005	2006
Government final consumption expenditure	474.3	585.1	612.5
Private final consumption expenditure	1,920.8	2,095.0	2,816.9
Gross capital formation	1,201.1	1,567.8	1,557.0
Total domestic expenditure	3,596.2	4,247.9	4,986.4
Exports of goods and services	2,227.6	3,204.2	3,636.2
Less Imports of goods and services	1,408.8	1,563.9	1,813.5
GDP in purchasers' values	4,415.0	5,888.1	6,809.1

Source: African Development Bank.

Gross Domestic Product by Economic Activity
('000 million francs CFA at constant 1995 prices)

	2003	2004	2005
Agriculture*	307.5	287.8	328.0
Mining and quarrying†	30.9	30.9	34.2
Electricity, gas and water	6.3	6.2	8.1
Manufacturing	97.9	91.9	107.2
Construction	20.4	23.5	26.9
Petroleum sector	123.5	485.0	486.9
Wholesale and retail trade, restaurants and hotels / Transport and communications	274.7	292.1	314.2
Public administration	128.6	143.8	160.6
Other services	104.7	85.6	157.8
GDP at factor cost	1,094.5	1,446.8	1,623.9
Indirect taxes, *less* subsidies	44.8	48.8	54.0
GDP in purchasers' values	1,139.3	1,495.6	1,677.9

* Excluding fishing.
† Including fishing.

Source: IMF, *Chad: Selected Issues and Statistical Appendix* (January 2007).

CHAD

BALANCE OF PAYMENTS
('000 million francs CFA)

	2003	2004	2005
Exports of goods f.o.b.	350.4	1,142.1	1,639.2
Imports of goods f.o.b.	−453.2	−462.3	−428.1
Trade balance	−102.8	679.8	1,211.1
Exports of services	41.4	47.6	66.4
Imports of services	−481.2	−721.6	−802.6
Balance on goods and services	−542.6	5.8	474.9
Factor income (net)	−265.3	−231.5	−543.2
Balance on goods, services and income	−807.9	−225.7	−68.3
Private unrequited transfers (net)	14.6	41.9	32.5
Official unrequited transfers (net)	43.0	72.9	62.3
Current balance	−750.3	−110.9	26.5
Public long- and medium-term capital	149.0	165.3	137.7
Direct investment	414.0	252.6	323.8
Other investments	−22.2	−27.3	−40.9
Fund for future generations	—	5.0	13.0
Short-term capital	−120.7	−233.4	−372.2
Net errors and omissions	303.5	−33.8	−64.5
Overall balance	−26.7	17.5	23.5

Source: IMF, *Chad: Selected Issues and Statistical Appendix* (January 2007).

External Trade

PRINCIPAL COMMODITIES

Imports c.i.f. (US $'000)	1995
Food and live animals	41,182
Cereals and cereal preparations	16,028
Wheat and meslin (unmilled)	8,945
Sugar, sugar preparations and honey	17,078
Refined sugars, etc.	16,825
Beverages and tobacco	7,175
Mineral fuels, lubricants, etc.	38,592
Refined petroleum products	38,551
Motor spirit (gasoline) and other light oils	6,490
Kerosene and other medium oils	8,456
Gas oils	23,318
Chemicals and related products	15,507
Medicinal and pharmaceutical products	7,789
Basic manufactures	26,190
Non-metallic mineral manufactures	7,654
Metal manufactures	8,804
Machinery and transport equipment	51,246
General industrial machinery, equipment and parts	8,175
Road vehicles (incl. air-cushion vehicles) and parts*	17,873
Parts and accessories for cars, lorries, buses, etc.*	8,253
Miscellaneous manufactured articles	27,335
Printed matter	13,565
Postage stamps, banknotes, etc.	11,622
Total (incl. others)	215,171

* Excluding tyres, engines and electrical parts.

Source: UN, *International Trade Statistics Yearbook*.

Exports ('000 million francs CFA)	2000	2001	2002*
Cotton	50.6	56.9	33.2
Livestock	48.8	49.5	52.0
Total (incl. others)	130.2	138.3	118.0

* Estimates.

Source: La Zone Franc, *Rapport Annuel 2002*.

Total imports c.i.f. (million francs CFA): 453,797 in 2004; 589,182 in 2005; 627,468 in 2006 (Source: IMF, *International Financial Statistics*).

Total exports c.i.f. (million francs CFA): 1,157,472 in 2004; 1,599,283 in 2005; 1,960,838 in 2006 (Source: IMF, *International Financial Statistics*).

PRINCIPAL TRADING PARTNERS

Imports c.i.f. (US $'000)	1995
Belgium-Luxembourg	4,771
Cameroon	33,911
Central African Repub.	3,010
China, People's Repub.	6,251
France	88,887
Germany	2,988
Italy	6,452
Japan	5,121
Malaysia	2,234
Netherlands	2,843
Nigeria	25,269
Spain	3,402
USA	13,966
Total (incl. others)	215,171

Source: UN, *International Trade Statistics Yearbook*.

Transport

ROAD TRAFFIC
(motor vehicles in use at 31 December)

	1994	1995*	1996*
Passenger cars	8,720	9,700	10,560
Buses and coaches	708	760	820
Lorries and vans	12,650	13,720	14,550
Tractors	1,413	1,500	1,580
Motorcycles and mopeds	1,855	2,730	3,640

* Estimates.

Source: International Road Federation, *World Road Statistics*.

2006: Passenger cars 18,867; Vans 24,874; Buses 3,278; Tractors 3,132; Motorcycles 63,036 (Source: Ministère de Travaux Publics et de Transport).

CIVIL AVIATION
(traffic on scheduled services*)

	1999	2000	2001
Kilometres flown (million)	3	3	1
Passengers carried ('000)	84	77	46
Passengers-km (million)	235	216	130
Total ton-km (million)	36	32	19

* Including an apportionment of the traffic of Air Afrique.

Source: UN, *Statistical Yearbook*.

Tourism

FOREIGN VISITORS BY NATIONALITY*

	2003	2004	2005
Belgium	164	219	241
Canada	1,044	1,942	1,935
Egypt	370	440	426
France	7,897	9,986	11,757
Germany	405	508	547
Italy	166	202	246
Libya	473	563	549
Saudi Arabia	121	143	149
Switzerland	303	381	458
United Kingdom	270	336	363
USA	3,206	3,433	3,693
Total (incl. others)	20,974	25,899	29,356

* Arrivals at hotels and similar establishments.

Receipts from tourism (US $ million, incl. passenger transport): 14 in 2000; 23 in 2001; 25 in 2002; 2003–05 n.a.

Source: World Tourism Organization.

CHAD *Directory*

Communications Media

	2004	2005	2006
Telephones ('000 main lines in use)	13.0	13.0	13.0
Mobile cellular telephones ('000 subscribers)	123.0	210.0	466.1
Personal computers ('000 in use)	15	15	n.a.
Internet users ('000)	35	40	60

Television receivers ('000 in use): 10.9 in 2000.

Radio receivers ('000 in use): 1,670 in 1997.

Facsimile machines (number in use): 182 in 1999.

Daily newspapers (national estimates): 2 in 1997 (average circulation 1,550 copies); 2 in 1998 (average circulation 1,560 copies).

Non-daily newspapers: 2 in 1995 (average circulation 10,000 copies); 14 in 1997; 10 in 1998.

Periodicals: 51 in 1997; 53 in 1998.

Sources: International Telecommunication Union; UNESCO, *Statistical Yearbook*; UNESCO Institute for Statistics; UN, *Statistical Yearbook*.

Education

(2004/05, unless otherwise indicated)

	Institutions	Teachers	Males	Females	Total
Pre-primary*	24	67	938	735	1,673
Primary	2,660†	19,989	755,748	506,645	1,262,393
Secondary	n.a.	6,921	174,836	58,597	233,433
Tertiary‡	n.a.	1,100	9,158	1,310	10,468

* 1994/95 figures; public education only.
† 1995/96.
‡ 2000/01.

Source: mainly UNESCO Institute for Statistics.

Adult literacy rate (UNESCO estimates): 25.7% (males 40.8%; females 12.8%) in 2000 (Source: UNESCO Institute for Statistics).

Directory

The Constitution

The Constitution of the Republic of Chad, which was adopted by national referendum on 31 March 1996, enshrines a unitary state. The President is elected for a term of five years by direct universal adult suffrage. The Prime Minister, who is appointed by the President, nominates the Council of Ministers. The legislature comprises a 155-member Assemblée nationale, which is elected by direct universal adult suffrage for a term of four years. The Constitution provides for an independent judicial system, with a High Court of Justice, and the establishment of a Constitutional Court and a High Council for Communication.

Constitutional amendments approved by the Assemblée nationale in May 2004 and confirmed by referendum in June 2005 provided for the abolition of the restriction on the number of terms that the President is permitted to serve (hitherto, the Head of State had been restricted to two terms in office), and for the abolition of an upper legislative chamber, the Sénat, provided for in the 1996 Constitution (which had not, however, been established). The amendments also provided for the establishment of a Conseil économique, social et culturel, the members of which would be appointed by the President of the Republic.

The Government

HEAD OF STATE

President: Gen. IDRISS DEBY ITNO (assumed office 4 December 1990; elected President 3 July 1996; re-elected 20 May 2001 and 3 May 2006).

COUNCIL OF MINISTERS
(April 2008)

Prime Minister: YOUSSOUF SALEH ABBAS.
Minister of National Defence: KAMOUGUE WADAL ABDELKADER.
Minister of External Relations: MOUSSA FAKI MAHAMAT.
Minister of Justice, Keeper of the Seals: JEAN BAWOYEU ALINGUE.
Minister of Communication and Government Spokesperson: MAHAMAT HISSEINE.
Minister of Infrastructure: ADOUM YOUNOUSMI.
Minister of the Interior and Public Security: AHMAT MAHAMAT BACHIR.
Minister of the Environment, Water and Fisheries: KHADIDJA ABDELKHADER.
Minister of Finance and the Budget: ABAKAR MALLAH MOURCHA.
Minister of the Economy and Planning: OUSMANE MATAR BREME.
Minister of Stockbreeding and Animal Resources: MAHAMAT ALI ABDALLAH.
Minister of Public Health: Prof. AVOKSOUMA DJONA.
Minister of National Education: ABDERAMANE KOKO.
Minister of Higher Education, Scientific Research and Professional Training: Dr OUMAR IDRISS AL-FAROUK.
Minister of Agriculture: NAIMBAYE LOSSIMIAN.
Minister of Mines and Energy: EMMANUEL NADINGAR.
Minister of Petroleum: MAHAMAT NASSER HASSANE.
Minister of Land Management, Town Planning and Housing: HAMID MAHAMAT DAHLOB.
Minister of Social Welfare, National Solidarity and Families: NGARMBATINA CARMEL SOU IV.
Minister in charge of Human Rights and the Promotion of Freedom: FATIMÉ ISSA RAMADAN.
Minister of the Civil Service and Labour: FATIMÉ TCHOMBI.
Minister of Posts and Information and Communications Technologies: PAHIMI PADACKE ALBERT.
Minister of Trade, Industry and Crafts: MAHAMAT ABDOULAYE MAHAMAT.
Minister of General State Control and the Promotion of Morality: MAHAMAT BECHIR OKORMI.
Minister of Culture, Youth and Sports: DJIBERT YOUNOUS.
Minister of the Development of Tourism: AHMAT BARKAI ANIMI.
Minister-delegate to the Prime Minister, responsible for Decentralization: ABDERAMAN DJASNABAYE.
Minister, Secretary-General of the Government, in charge of Relations with the National Assembly: KALZEUBE PAHIMI DEUBET.
Secretary of State for External Relations, responsible for International Co-operation and African Integration: DJIDDA MOUSSA OUTMAN.
Secretary of State for National Defence, responsible for War Veterans and Victims of War: HASAN SALEH AL-GADAM AL-DJINEDI.
Secretary of State for Agriculture, responsible for Professional Training and Food Security: Dr HAOUA OUTMAN DJAME.
Secretary of State for the Economy and Planning, responsible for Micro-credits and Poverty Prevention: AZZIZA BAROUD.
Secretary of State for Finance, responsible for the Budget: OUMAR BOUKAR GANA.
Secretary of State for Infrastructure, responsible for Transport: HASSAN TERAP.
Secretary of State for the Environment, responsible for Village and Rural Water Resources: TAHAR SOUGOUDI.
Secretary of State for National Education, responsible for Basic Education: HAPSITA ALBOUKHARI.
Secretary of State for the Secretary General of the Government, responsible for Relations with the National Assembly: YAYA DILLO.

MINISTRIES

Office of the President: Palais rose, BP 74, N'Djamena; tel. 51-44-37; fax 52-45-01; e-mail Contact@presidencedutchad.org; internet www.presidencedutchad.org.

Office of the Prime Minister: BP 463, N'Djamena; tel. 52-63-39; fax 52-69-77; e-mail cpcprimt@intnet.td; internet www.primature-tchad.com.

Ministry of Agriculture: BP 441, N'Djamena; tel. 52-65-66; fax 52-51-19; e-mail conacils@intnet.td.

Ministry of Associative Development, Micro-credits and Poverty Prevention: N'Djamena.

Ministry of the Civil Service and Labour: BP 637, N'Djamena; tel. and fax 52-21-98.

Ministry of Communication: BP 892, N'Djamena; tel. 52-40-97; fax 52-65-60.

Ministry of Culture and the Arts: BP 892, N'Djamena; tel. 52-40-97; fax 52-65-60.

Ministry of the Development of Tourism: BP 86, N'Djamena; tel. 52-44-21; fax 52-51-19.

Ministry of Economy and Planning: N'Djamena.

Ministry of the Environment, Quality of Life and National Parks: BP 905, N'Djamena; tel. 52-60-12; fax 52-38-39; e-mail facdrem@intnet.td.

Ministry of Finance and Information Technology: BP 816, N'Djamena; tel. 52-68-61; fax 52-49-08; e-mail d.dette@intnet.td.

Ministry of External Relations: BP 746, N'Djamena; tel. 51-80-50; fax 51-45-85.

Ministry of Fisheries, Water Resources and Villages: N'Djamena.

Ministry of General State Control and the Promotion of Morality: N'Djamena.

Ministry of Higher Education, Scientific Research and Professional Training: BP 743, N'Djamena; tel. 51-61-58; fax 51-92-31.

Ministry of Human Rights: N'Djamena.

Ministry of Infrastructure: N'Djamena.

Ministry of the Interior and Public Security: BP 916, N'Djamena; tel. 52-05-76.

Ministry of Justice: BP 426, N'Djamena; tel. 52-21-72; fax 52-21-39; e-mail justice@intnet.td.

Ministry of Land Management, Town Planning and Housing: BP 436, N'Djamena; tel. 52-31-89; fax 52-39-35.

Ministry of Mines and Energy: BP 816, N'Djamena; tel. 51-83-06; fax 52-75-60; e-mail cons.mines@intnet.td.

Ministry of National Defence: BP 916, N'Djamena; tel. 52-35-13; fax 52-65-44.

Ministry of National Education: BP 743, N'Djamena; tel. 51-92-65; fax 51-45-12.

Ministry of Petroleum: BP 816, N'Djamena; tel. 52-56-03; fax 52-36-66; e-mail mme@intnet.td; internet www.ministere-petrole.td.

Ministry of Posts and New Communications Technologies: BP 154, N'Djamena; tel. 52-15-79; fax 52-15-30; e-mail ahmatgamar1@yahoo.fr.

Ministry of Public Health: BP 440, N'Djamena; tel. 51-51-14; fax 51-58-00.

Ministry of Social Welfare, National Solidarity and Families: BP 80, N'Djamena; tel. 52-25-32; fax 52-48-88.

Ministry of Stockbreeding: BP 750, N'Djamena; tel. 52-89-43.

Ministry of Territorial Administration: BP 742, N'Djamena; tel. 52-56-09; fax 52-59-06.

Ministry of Youth and Sports: BP 519, N'Djamena; tel. 52-26-58.

President and Legislature

PRESIDENT

Election, 3 May 2006

Candidate	Votes	% of vote
Idriss Deby Itno	1,863,042	64.67
Kassiré Delwa Coumakoye	436,002	15.13
Pahimi Padacke Albert	225,368	7.82
Mahamat Abdoulaye	203,637	7.07
Ibrahim Koullamallah	152,940	5.31
Total	**2,880,989**	**100.00**

LEGISLATURE

Assemblée nationale

Palais du 15 janvier, BP 01, N'Djamena; tel. 53-00-15; fax 31-45-90; internet www.primature-tchad.org/ass.php.

President: NASSOUR GUÉLENDOUKSIA OUAÏDOU.

General Election, 21 April 2002

Party	Seats
Mouvement patriotique du salut (MPS)	110
Rassemblement pour la démocratie et le progrès (RDP)	12
Fédération action pour la République (FAR)	9
VIVA—Rassemblement national pour la démocratie et le progrès (VIVA—RNDP)	5
Union nationale pour le développement et le renouveau (UNDR)	5
Union pour le renouveau et la démocratie (URD)	3
Others*	9
Vacant†	2
Total	**155**

* There were nine other parties.
† The Constitutional Council annulled the results of voting in two constituencies, in which by-elections were subsequently to be held.

Election Commission

Commission électorale nationale indépendante (CENI): N'djamena; f. 2000; 31 mems, incl. 12 mems appointed by the Government, 16 by political parties represented in the Assemblée nationale, three by extra-parliamentary political parties.

Political Organizations

Legislation permitting the operation of political associations, subject to official registration, took effect in October 1991. In mid-2006 there were 78 officially registered political organizations, of which the following were among the most important:

Action tchadienne pour l'unité et le socialisme (ACTUS): N'Djamena; e-mail actus@club-internet.fr; f. 1981; Marxist-Leninist; Sec.-Gen. Dr DJIMADOUM LEY-NGARDIGAL.

Alliance nationale pour la démocratie et le développement (ANDD): BP 4066, N'Djamena; tel. 51-46-72; f. 1992; Leader SALIBOU GARBA.

Alliance tchadienne pour la démocratie et le développement (ATD): N'Djamena; e-mail info@atd-tchad.com; Leader ABDERAMAN DJASNABAILLE.

Concord nationale Tchadienne (CNT): Leader Col HASSANE SALEH AL GADAM AL JINEDI.

Convention pour la démocratie et le fédéralisme: N'Djamena; f. 2002; socialist; supports the establishment of a federal state; Leader ALI GOLHOR.

Convention nationale démocratique et sociale (CNDS): N'Djamena; Leader ADOUM DAYE ZERE.

Coordination des partis politiques pour la défense de la constitution (CPDC): f. 2004 to oppose President Deby's proposed constitutional modifications; mems include the RDP, the URD and the UNDR.

Fédération action pour la République (FAR): BP 4197, N'Djamena; tel. 51-79-67; fax 51-78-60; e-mail yorongarn@yahoo.fr; internet www.yorongar.com; supports the establishment of a federal republic; Leader NGARLEDJY YORONGAR.

Front pour le salut de la République (FSR): f. 2007 to unite opposition groups in attempt to oust President Deby; Pres. Col AHMAT HASSABALLAH SOUBIANE.

Mouvement patriotique du salut (MPS): Assemblée nationale, Palais du 15 janvier, BP 01, N'Djamena; e-mail administrateur@tchad-gpmps.org; internet www.tchad-gpmps.org; f. 1990 as a coalition of several opposition movements; other opposition groups joined during the Nov. 1990 offensive against the regime of Hissène Habré, and following the movement's accession to power in Dec. 1990; Pres. D'IDRISS NDELE MOUSSA.

Parti pour la liberté et le développement (PLD): N'Djamena; f. 1993; boycotted legislative elections in 2002; Sec.-Gen. IBN OUMAR MAHAMAT SALEH.

Rassemblement pour la démocratie et le progrès (RDP): N'Djamena; f. 1992; seeks to create a secure political environment by the establishment of a reformed national army; supported the re-election of Pres. Deby in 2001, but withdrew support from the Govt in Nov. 2003; Leader LOL MAHAMAT CHOUA.

Union pour la démocratie et la République (UDR): N'Djamena; f. 1992; supports liberal economic policies and a secular, decentralized republic; boycotted legislative elections in 2002; Leader Dr JEAN BAWOYEU ALINGUÉ.

Union nationale pour le développement et le renouveau (UNDR): N'Djamena; supports greater decentralization and increased limitations on the power of the state; Pres. SALEH KEBZABOH; Sec.-Gen. CÉLESTIN TOPONA.

Union pour le renouveau et la démocratie (URD): BP 92, N'Djamena; tel. 51-44-23; fax 51-41-87; f. 1992; Leader Gen. WADAL ABDELKADER KAMOUGUÉ.

VIVA—Rassemblement national pour la démocratie et le progrès (VIVA—RNDP): N'Djamena; f. 1992; supports a unitary, democratic republic; Pres. KASSIRÉ DELWA COUMAKOYE.

A number of unregistered dissident groups (some based abroad) are also active. In early 2008 these organizations, largely 'politico-military', included the following:

Alliance nationale de la résistance (ANR): f. 1996 as alliance of five movements; in early 2003 comprised eight rebel groups based in eastern Chad; signed peace agreement with Govt in Jan. 2003, although FONALT rejected this accord; Leader Col MAHAMAT GARFA.

> **Armée nationale tchadienne en dissidence (ANTD):** f. 1994; Leader Col MAHAMAT GARFA.
>
> **Forces des organisations nationales pour l'alternance et les libertés au Tchad (FONALT):** rejected cease-fire signed by ANR with Govt in Jan. 2003; Leader Col ABDOULAYE ISSAKA SARWA.

Coordination des mouvements armés et partis politiques de l'opposition (CMAP): internet www.maxpages.com/tchad/cmap2; f. 1999 by 13 'politico-military' orgs; a number of groups subsequently left, several of which later joined the FUDP (q.v.); Leader ANTOINE BANGUI.

> **Front extérieur pour la rénovation:** Leader ANTOINE BANGUI.

Front de libération nationale du Tchad-Conseil provisoire de la révolution (FROLINAT-CPR): f. 1968 in Sudan; based in Algeria; Leader GOUKOUNI OUEDDEI.

Front uni pour le changement démocratique (FUCD): f. 2005; signed a peace agreement with the Govt in Dec. 2006; Leader Capt. MAHAMAT NOUR ABDELKERIM.

> **Rassemblement pour la démocratie et les libertés (RDL):** f. 2005 in Eastern Chad; Leader Capt. MAHAMAT NOUR ABDELKERIM.
>
> **Socle pour le changement, l'unité nationale et la démocratie (SCUD):** f. 2005 in Eastern Chad; Leaders TOM ERDIMI, YAYA DILLO DJÉROU.

Front uni pour la démocratie et la paix (FUDP): f. 2003 in Benin; seeks by all possible means to establish a new constitution and a transitional govt in advance of free and transparent elections; faction of MDJT (q.v.) led by Adoum Togoi Abbo claims membership, but this is rejected by principal faction of MDJT; Pres. Brig.-Gen. ADOUM TOGOI ABBO.

> **Conseil national de résistance (CNR):** leadership of group forced to leave Benin for Togo in mid-2003; Pres. HISSÈNE KOTY YACOUB.
>
> **Convention populaire de résistance (CPR):** e-mail cpr60@voila.fr; f. 2001 by fmr mems of CNR (q.v.); Leader ABDEL-AZIZ ABDALLAH KODOK.

Front national du Tchad renové (FNTR): Dabo; e-mail yasaid2001@yahoo.fr; internet www.maxpages.com/tchad/fntr; f. 1996 in Sudan by fmr mems of FNT (q.v.); based in Dabo (France); announced abandonment of armed struggle in 2002; new leadership elected in early 2003; seeks establishment of semi-presidential and social-democratic system of govt; publishes monthly bulletin, *Al-Widha*, in French and Arabic; Hon. Pres. MAHAMAT MOUSSA; Sec.-Gen. SALAHADINE MAHADI.

Mouvement nationale des rénovateurs tchadiens (MNRT): e-mail fpls@romandie.com; democratic opposition in exile; Sec.-Gen. ALI MUHAMMAD DIALLO.

Rassemblement des forces pour le changement (RFC): internet www.rfctchad.com; f. 2006 as Rassemblement des forces démocratique (RAFC); Pres. TIMANE ERDIMI.

Union des forces pour le changement (UFC): f. 2004; advocates suspension of the 1996 Constitution and the composition of a new Charter of the Republic to develop national unity, free, transparent elections and the rule of law; National Co-ordinator ACHEIKH IBN OUMAR.

> **Conseil démocratique révolutionnaire (CDR):** Leader ACHEIKH IBN OUMAR.
>
> **Front démocratique populaire (FDP):** Leader Dr MAHAMOUT NAHOR.

Front populaire pour la renaissance nationale.

Mouvement pour la démocratie et le développement (MDD): tel. and fax 34-46-17; e-mail mdd@mdd-tchad.com; internet membres.lycos.fr/mddtchad; comprises two factions, led by ISSA FAKI MAHAMAT and BRAHIM MALLAH.

Mouvement pour la démocratie et la justice au Tchad (MDJT): based in Tibesti, northern Chad; e-mail admin@mdjt.net; internet www.mdjt.net; fmr deputy leader, Brig.-Gen. ADOUM TOGOI ABBO, signed a peace agreement with Govt in Jan. 2002, although this was subsequently rejected by elements close to fmr leader, YOUSSOUF TOGOIMI (who died in Sept. 2002); split into two factions in 2003; the faction led by Togoi claimed membership of the FUDP (q.v.) and signed a peace agreement with Govt in Dec. 2003, which was rejected by the faction led by Chair. Col HASSAN ABDALLAH MARDIGUÉ; announced a proposed merger with FROLINAT—CPR in December 2006.

Mouvement pour l'unité et la République (MUR): f. 2000 by faction of the MDD (q.v.); Leader GAILETH GATOUL BOURKOUMANDAH.

Union des forces pour la démocratie et le développement (UFDD): f. 2006; Leader Gen. MAHAMAT NOURI.

Union des forces pour la démocratie et le développement—Fondamentale (UFDD—F): Leader ABDELWAHID ABOUD.

Diplomatic Representation

EMBASSIES IN CHAD

Algeria: BP 178, rue de Paris, N'Djamena; tel. 52-38-15; fax 52-37-92; e-mail amb.algerie@intnet.td; Ambassador BOUBAKEUR OGAB.

Cameroon: rue des Poids Lourds, BP 58, N'Djamena; tel. 52-28-94; Chargé d'affaires a.i. ABBAS IBRAHIMA SALAHEDDINE.

Central African Republic: rue 1036, près du Rond-Point de la Garde, BP 115, N'Djamena; tel. 52-32-06; Ambassador DAVID NGUINDO.

China, People's Republic: BP 735, N'Djamena; tel. 52-29-49; fax 53-00-45; internet td.china-embassy.org; Ambassador WANG YINGWU.

Congo, Democratic Republic: ave du 20 août, BP 910, N'Djamena; tel. 52-21-83.

Egypt: Quartier Clemat, ave Georges Pompidou, auprès rond-point de la SONASUT, BP 1094, N'Djamena; tel. 51-09-73; fax 51-09-72; e-mail ambegyndj@africamail.com; Ambassador KHALED ABDALLAH SHEHATA.

France: rue du Lt Franjoux, BP 431, N'Djamena; tel. 52-25-75; fax 52-28-55; e-mail amba.france@intnet.td; internet www.ambafrance-td.org; Ambassador BRUNO FOUCHER.

Holy See: rue de Béguinage, BP 490, N'Djamena; tel. 52-31-15; fax 52-38-27; e-mail nonceapo@intnet.td; Apostolic Nuncio Most Rev. PIERRE NGUYÊN VAN TOT (Titular Archbishop of Rusticiana).

Korea, Democratic People's Republic: N'Djamena; Ambassador KIM PYONG GI.

Libya: BP 1096, N'Djamena; tel. 51-92-89; e-mail alibya1@intnet.td; Ambassador GHAYTH SALIM.

Nigeria: 35 ave Charles de Gaulle, BP 752, N'Djamena; tel. 52-24-98; fax 52-30-92; e-mail nigndjam@intnet.td; Ambassador M. ARGUNGU.

Russia: 2 rue Adjutant Collin, BP 891, N'Djamena; tel. 51-57-19; fax 51-31-72; e-mail amrus@intnet.td; Ambassador VLADIMIR N. MARTYNOV.

Saudi Arabia: Quartier Aéroport, rue Jander Miry, BP 974, N'Djamena; tel. 52-31-28; fax 52-33-28; e-mail najdiat.tchad@intnet.td.

Sudan: rue de la Gendarmerie, BP 45, N'Djamena; tel. 52-43-59; e-mail amb.soudan@intnet.td; Ambassador ABDALLAH CHEIKH.

USA: ave Félix Eboué, BP 413, N'Djamena; tel. 251-70-09; fax 251-56-54; e-mail YingraD@state.gov; internet chad.usembassy.gov; Ambassador LOUIS JOHN NIGRO, Jr.

Judicial System

The highest judicial authority is the Supreme Court, which comprises a Judicial Chamber, an Administrative Chamber and an Audit Chamber. There is also a Constitutional Council, with final jurisdiction in matters of state. The legal structure also comprises the Court of Appeal, and magistrate and criminal courts. A High Court of Justice, which is competent to try the President or members of the Government in cases of treason, embezzlement of public funds, and certain other crimes and offences, was inaugurated in June 2003.

CHAD

Supreme Court: rue 0221, Quartier Résidentiel, 1er arrondissement, BP 5495, N'Djamena; tel. 52-01-99; fax 52-51-81; e-mail ccsrp@intnet.td; internet www.coursupreme-tchad.org; Pres. ABDERAHIM BIREME HAMID; Pres. of the Judicial Chamber BELKOULAYE BEN COUMAREAUX; Pres. of the Administrative Chamber OUSMAME SALAH IDJEMI; Pres. of the Audit Chamber DOLOTAN NOUDJALBAYE; Prosecutor-Gen. EDOUARD NGARTA M'BAIOUROUM.

Constitutional Council: BP 5500, N'Djamena; tel. 52-03-41; e-mail conseil.sg@intnet.td; internet www.primature-tchad.org/cc.php; Pres. HOUDEÏNGAR DAVID NGARIMADEN.

Court of Appeal: N'Djamena; tel. 51-24-26; Pres. MAKI ADAM ISSAKA.

High Court of Justice: BP 1407, N'Djamena; tel. 52-33-54; fax 52-35-35; e-mail dchcj@intnet.td; internet www.primature-tchad.org/hdj.php; f. 2003; comprises 15 deputies of the Assemblée nationale, of whom 10 are titular judges and five supplementaries, who serve in the absence of a titular judge. All 15 are elected for the term of four years by their peers; competent to try the President and members of the Government in cases of treason, embezzlement of public funds, and certain other crimes and offences; Pres. ADOUM GOUDJA.

Religion

It is estimated that some 50% of the population are Muslims and about 30% Christians. Most of the remainder follow animist beliefs.

ISLAM

Conseil Suprême des Affaires Islamiques: POB 1101, N'Djamena; tel. 51-81-80; fax 52-58-84; Head of the Islamic Community Imam MOUSSA IBRAHIM.

CHRISTIANITY

The Roman Catholic Church

Chad comprises one archdiocese, six dioceses and one apostolic prefecture. At 31 December 2005 baptized Roman Catholics numbered approximately 803,646 (about 9.3% of the total population), most of whom resided in the south of the country and in N'Djamena.

Bishops' Conference

Conférence Episcopale du Tchad, BP 456, N'Djamena; tel. 51-74-44; fax 52-50-51; e-mail secreta.cet@intnet.td.

f. 1991; Pres. Most Rev. JEAN-CLAUDE BOUCHARD (Bishop of Pala).

Archbishop of N'Djamena: Most Rev. MATTHIAS N'GARTÉRI MAYADI, Archevêché, BP 456, N'Djamena; tel. 51-74-44; fax 52-50-51; e-mail archnja@intnet.td.

Protestant Churches

Entente des Eglises et Missions Evangéliques au Tchad (EEMET): BP 2006, N'Djamena; tel. 51-53-93; fax 51-87-20; e-mail eemet@intnet.td; asscn of churches and missions working in Chad; includes Assemblées Chrétiennes au Tchad (ACT), Assemblées de Dieu au Tchad (ADT), Eglise Evangélique des Frères au Tchad (EEFT), Eglise Evangélique au Tchad (EET), Eglise Fraternelle Luthérienne au Tchad (EFLT), Eglise Evangélique en Afrique Centrale au Tchad (EEACT), Eglise Evangélique Missionnaire au Tchad (EEMT); also five assoc. mems: Union des Jeunes Chrétiens (UJC), Groupe Biblique des Hôpitaux au Tchad (GBHT), Mission Evangélique contre la Lèpre (MECL), Croix Bleue du Tchad (CBT).

BAHÁ'Í FAITH

National Spiritual Assembly: BP 181, N'Djamena; tel. 51-47-05; e-mail ntirandaz@aol.com.

The Press

Al-Watan: N'Djamena; tel. 51-57-96; weekly; Editor-in-Chief MOUSSA NDORKOÏ.

Audy Magazine: BP 780, N'Djamena; tel. 51-49-59; f. 2000; 2 a month; women's interest; Dir TONGRONGOU AGOUNA GRÂCE.

Bulletin Mensuel de Statistiques du Tchad: BP 453, N'Djamena; monthly.

Carrefour: Centre al-Mouna, BP 456, N'Djamena; tel. 51-42-54; e-mail almouna@intnet.td; f. 2000; every 2 months; Dir Sister NADIA KARAKI; circ. 1,000 (2001).

Chronique: Association pour la Promotion des Libertés Fondamentales Tchad (APLFT), BP 4037, N'Djamena; tel. 51-91-14; monthly; promotes civic information and popular understanding of civic law; Dir MAOUNDONODJI GILBERT.

Comnat: BP 731, N'Djamena; tel. 51-46-75; fax 51-46-71; quarterly; publ. by Commission Nationale Tchadienne for UNESCO.

Grenier: BP 1128, N'Djamena; tel. 53-30-14; e-mail cedesep@intnet.td; monthly; economics; finance; Dir KOHOM NGAR-ONE DAVID.

Info-Tchad: BP 670, N'Djamena; tel. 51-58-67; news bulletin issued by Agence-Info Tchad; daily; French.

Informations Economiques: BP 458, N'Djamena; publ. by the Chambre de Commerce, d'Agriculture et d'Industrie; weekly.

La Lettre: BP 2037, N'Djamena; tel. and fax 51-91-09; e-mail ltdh@intnet.td; f. 1993; monthly; publ. by the Ligue Tchadienne des droits de l'Homme; Dir DOBIAN ASSINGAR.

N'Djamena Bi-Hebdo: BP 4498, N'Djamena; tel. 51-53-14; fax 52-14-98; e-mail ndjh@intnet.td; 2 a week; Arabic and French; f. 1989; Dir YALDET BÉGOTO OULATAR; Editor-in-Chief DIEUDONNÉ DJONABAYE; circ. 3,500 (2001).

Notre Temps: BP 4352, N'Djamena; tel. and fax 51-46-50; e-mail ntemps.presse@yahoo.fr; f. 2000; weekly; opposed to the Govt of Pres. Deby Itno; Editorial Dir NADJIKIMO BENOUDJITA; circ. 3,000 (2001).

L'Observateur: BP 2031, N'Djamena; tel. and fax 51-80-05; e-mail observer.presse@intnet.td; f. 1997; weekly; Dir NGARADOUMBE SAMBORY; circ. 4,000 (2001).

Le Progrès: 1976 ave Charles de Gaulle, BP 3055, N'Djamena; tel. 51-55-86; fax 51-02-56; e-mail progres@intnet.td; f. 1993; daily; Dir MAHAMAT HISSÈNE; circ. 3,000 (2001).

Revue Juridique Tchadienne: BP 907, N'Djamena; internet www.cefod.org/Droit_au_Tchad/Revuejuridique/Sommaire_rjt.htm; f. 1999; Dir MAHAMAT SALEH BEN BIANG.

Tchad et Culture: BP 907, N'Djamena; tel. 51-54-32; fax 51-91-50; e-mail cefod@intnet.td; internet www.cefod.org; f. 1961; monthly; Dir RONELNGUÉ TORIAÏRA; Editor-in-Chief NAYGOTIMTI BAMBÉ; circ. 4,500 (2002).

Le Temps: face Ecole Belle-vue, Moursal, BP 1333, N'Djamena; tel. 51-70-28; fax 51-99-24; e-mail temps.presse@intnet.td; f. 1995; weekly; Publishing Dir MICHAËL N. DIDAMA; circ. 6,000 (2001).

Victoire Al Nassr: N'Djamena; tel. 51-64-17; weekly; Dir ABOUBAKAR MAHAMAT BORGHO.

La Voix du Paysan: BP 1671, N'Djamena; tel. 51-82-66; monthly; Dir DJALDI TABDI GASSISSOU NASSER.

NEWS AGENCY

Agence-Info Tchad: BP 670, N'Djamena; tel. 52-58-67; f. 1966; Dir ABAKAR HASSAN ACHEICK.

Publisher

Imprimerie du Tchad (IDT): BP 456, N'Djamena; tel. 52-44-40; fax 52-28-60; Gen. Dir D. E. MAURIN.

Broadcasting and Communications

TELECOMMUNICATIONS

Société des Télécommunications du Tchad (SOTEL TCHAD): BP 1132, N'Djamena; tel. 52-14-36; fax 52-14-42; e-mail sotel@intnet.td; internet www.sotel.td; f. 2000 by merger of telecommunications services of fmr Office National des Postes et des Télécommunications and the Société des Télécommunications Internationales du Tchad; privatization proposed; Dir-Gen. ALI MAHAMAT ZÈNE ALI FADEL.

Celtel-Tchad: ave Charles de Gaulle, BP 5665, N'Djamena; tel. 52-04-18; fax 52-04-19; e-mail service_clientele@td.celtel.com; internet www.td.celtel.com; f. 2000; affiliated to Celtel International (United Kingdom); provides mobile cellular telecommunications in N'Djamena, Moundou and Abéché, with expansion to further regions proposed; Dir-Gen. TSHINSELE VAN BELLIGEN BESTON.

Millicom Tchad: N'Djamena; internet www.millicom.com; f. 2005; 87.% owned by Millicom International Cellular (Luxembourg/Sweden); operates mobile cellular telecommunications network in N'Djamena (with expansion to other cities proposed) under the brand name 'Tigo'.

BROADCASTING

Regulatory Authority

High Council of Communication (HCC): BP 1316, N'Djamena; tel. 52-36-00; fax 52-31-51; e-mail hcc@intnet.td; f. 1994; responsible for registration and regulation of radio and television stations, in addition to the printed press; funds independent radio stations; Pres. TIRENGAYE DEDJEBÉ BOB; Sec.-Gen. ADOUM GUEMESSOU.

Radio

Private radio stations have been permitted to operate in Chad since 1994, although private broadcasts did not begin until 1997. By mid-2002 15 private and community stations had received licences, of which nine had commenced broadcasts. There was, additionally, a state-owned broadcaster, with four regional stations.

Radio Nationale Tchadienne (RNT): BP 4589, N'Djamena; tel. and fax 51-60-71; f. 1955; state-controlled; programmes in French, Arabic and 11 vernacular languages; four regional stations; Dir ABBA ALI KAYA.

Radio Abéché: BP 36, Abéché, Ouaddaï; tel. 69-81-49.

Radio Faya-Largeau: Faya-Largeau, Borkou.

Radio Moundou: BP 122, Moundou, Logone Occidental; tel. 69-13-22; programmes in French, Sara and Arabic; Dir DIMANANGAR DJAÏNTA.

Radio Sarh: BP 270, Sarh, Bahr Kôh; tel. 68-13-61; programmes in French, Sara and Arabic; Dir BIANA FOUDA NACTOUANDI.

Union des radios privées du Tchad (URPT): N'Djamena; f. 2002; as a federation of nine private and community radio stations, including the following:

DJA FM: BP 1312, N'Djamena; tel. 51-64-90; fax 52-14-52; e-mail myzara@intnet.td; f. 1999; music, cultural and informative programmes in French, Arabic and Sara; Dir ZARA YACOUB.

Radio Brakoss (Radio de l'Agriculture): Moïssala, Mandoul; f. 1996; community radio station; operations suspended by the Govt in Feb. 2004, broadcasts resumed June 2004.

Radio Duji Lohar: BP 155, Moundou, Logone Occidental; tel. 69-17-14; fax 69-12-11; e-mail cdave@intnet.td; f. 2001.

Radio FM Liberté: BP 892, N'Djamena; tel. 51-42-53; f. 2000; financed by nine civil-society orgs; broadcasts in French, Arabic and Sara; Dir DOBIAN ASSINGAR.

Radio Lotiko: Diocese de Sarh, BP 87, Sahr; tel. 68-12-46; fax 68-14-79; e-mail lotiko@intnet.td; internet www.lotiko.org; f. 2001; community radio station; Dir FABRIZIO COLOMBO.

La Voix du Paysan: BP 22, Doba, Logone Oriental; f. 1996; Roman Catholic; Dir DJALDI TABDI GASSISSOU NASSER.

Television

Télévision nationale tchadienne (Télé Tchad): BP 274, N'Djamena; tel. 52-26-79; fax 52-29-23; state-controlled; broadcasts c. 38 hours per week in French and Arabic; Dir OUROUMADJI MOUSSA.

Broadcasts from Canal France International, TV5, CNN and seven Arabic television stations are also received in Chad.

Finance

(cap. = capital; res = reserves; dep. = deposits; m. = million; br(s). = branch(es); amounts in francs CFA)

BANKING

Central Bank

Banque des Etats de l'Afrique Centrale (BEAC): ave Charles de Gaulle, BP 50, N'Djamena; tel. 52-21-65; fax 52-44-87; e-mail beacndj@beac.int; internet www.beac.int; HQ in Yaoundé, Cameroon; f. 1973; bank of issue for mem. states of the Communauté économique et monétaire de l'Afrique centrale (CEMAC, fmrly Union douanière et économique de l'Afrique centrale), comprising Cameroon, the Central African Repub., Chad, the Repub. of the Congo, Equatorial Guinea and Gabon; cap. 45,000m., res 176,661m., total assets 2,144,626m. (Nov. 2003); Gov. JEAN-FÉLIX MAMALEPOT; Dir in Chad IDRISS AHMED IDRISS; brs at Moundou and Sarh.

Other Banks

Banque Agricole du Soudan au Tchad (BAST): ave el-Niméry, BP 1727, N'Djamena; tel. 51-90-41; fax 51-90-40; e-mail bast@intnet.td; cap. 1,200m. (2002), total assets 1,845m. (Dec. 1999); Pres. MOUHAMED OUSMAN AWAD; Dir-Gen. ABDELKADER OUSMAN HASSAN; 1 br.

Banque Commerciale du Chari (BCC): ave Charles de Gaulle, BP 757, N'Djamena; tel. 51-89-58; fax 51-62-49; e-mail bcc@intnet.td; 50% state-owned, 50% owned by Libya Arab Foreign Bank (Libya); cap. and res 3,567m., total assets 20,931m. (Dec. 2001); Pres. BIDJERE BINDJAKI; Dir-Gen. HAMED EL MISTIRI.

Banque Internationale pour l'Afrique au Tchad (BIAT): ave Charles de Gaulle, BP 87, N'Djamena; tel. 52-43-14; fax 52-23-45; e-mail biat@intnet.td; f. 1954; current name adopted 1981; 80.6% owned by Compagnie de Financement et de Participation (Bamako, Mali); cap. 3,000m. res 1,317m., dep. 24,876m. (Dec. 2003); Chair. BABER TOUNKARA; Dir-Gen. GUY MALLETT.

Banque Sahélo-Saharienne pour l'Investissement et le Commerce (BSIC): ave Charles de Gaulle, BP 81, N'Djamena; tel. 52-26-92; fax 62-26-93; e-mail bsic@bsic-tchad.com; internet www.bsic-tchad.com; f. 2004; Pres. and Dir-Gen. ALHADJI MOHAMED ALWARFALLI.

Commercial Bank Tchad (CBT): rue du Capitaine Ohrel, BP 19, N'Djamena; tel. 52-28-28; fax 52-33-18; e-mail expbdt@intnet.td; f. 1962; 50.7% owned by Groupe FOTSO (Cameroon), 17.5% state-owned; fmrly Banque de Développement du Tchad; cap. 4,020m., res 2,465m., dep. 38,624m. (Dec. 2005); Pres. YOUSSOUF ABBASALAH; Dir-Gen. GEORGES DJADJO; 1 br.

Financial Bank Tchad (FBT): BP 804, N'Djamena; tel. 52-33-89; fax 52-29-05; e-mail fbt@intnet.td; f. 1992; 67.8% owned by Financial BC (Togo); cap. and res 534m., total assets 22,216m. (Dec. 2003); Pres. RÉMY BAYSSET; Dir-Gen. MARC ATHIEL.

Société Générale Tchadienne de Banque (SGTB): 2–6 rue Robert Lévy, BP 461, N'Djamena; tel. 52-28-01; fax 52-37-13; e-mail sgtb@intnet.td; internet www.sgtb.td; f. 1963; 30% owned by Société Générale (France), 15% by Société Générale de Banque au Cameroun; cap. and res 3,603m., total assets 36,579m. (Dec. 2003); Pres. and Dir-Gen. CHEMI KOGRIMI; 3 brs.

Bankers' Organizations

Association Professionnelle des Banques au Tchad: 2–6 rue Robert Lévy, BP 461, N'Djamena; tel. 52-41-90; fax 52-17-13; Pres. CHEMI KOGRIMI.

Conseil National de Crédit: N'Djamena; f. 1965 to formulate a national credit policy and to organize the banking profession.

INSURANCE

Assureurs Conseils Tchadiens Cecar et Jutheau: rue du Havre, BP 139, N'Djamena; tel. 52-21-15; fax 52-35-39; e-mail biliou.alikeke@intnet.td; f. 1966; Dir BILIOU ALIKEKE.

Gras Savoye Tchad: rue du Général Thillo, BP 5620, N'Djamena; tel. 52-00-72; fax 52-00-71; e-mail gras.savoye@intnet.td; affiliated to Gras Savoye (France); Man. DOMKRÉO DJAMON.

Société Mutuelle d'Assurances des Cadres des Professions Libérales et des Indépendants (SMAC): BP 644, N'Djamena; tel. 51-70-19; fax 51-70-61.

Société de Représentation d'Assurances et de Réassurances Africaines (SORARAF): N'Djamena; Dir Mme FOURNIER.

Société Tchadienne d'Assurances et de Réassurances (La STAR Nationale): ave Charles de Gaulle, BP 914, N'Djamena; tel. 52-56-77; fax 52-51-89; e-mail star@intnet.td; internet www.lastarnationale.com; f. 1977; privatized in 1996; brs in N'Djamena, Moundou and Abéché; cap. 500m.; Dir-Gen. ALI ADOUM DJAYA.

Trade and Industry

DEVELOPMENT ORGANIZATIONS

Agence Française de Développement (AFD): route de Farcha, BP 478, N'Djamena; tel. 52-70-71; fax 52-78-31; e-mail afdndjamena@groupe-afd.org; internet www.afd.fr; Country Dir BENOÎT LEBEURRE.

Association Française des Volontaires du Progrès (AFVP): BP 448, N'Djamena; tel. 52-20-53; fax 52-26-56; e-mail afvptchd@intnet.td; internet www.afvp.org; f. 1965; Nat. Delegate ISMAÏLA DIAGNE.

Association Tchadienne pour le Développement: BP 470, Quartier Sabangali, N'Djamena; tel. 51-43-69; fax 51-89-23; e-mail darna.dnla@intnet.td; Dir DIGALI ZEUHINBA.

Mission Française de Coopération et d'Action Culturelle: BP 898, N'Djamena; tel. 52-42-87; fax 52-44-38; administers bilateral aid from France; Dir EDOUARD LAPORTE.

Office National de Développement Rural (ONDR): BP 896, N'Djamena; tel. 52-23-20; fax 52-29-60; e-mail psapdn@intnet.td; f. 1968; Dir HASSAN GUIHINI DADI.

Société de Développement du Lac (SODELAC): BP 782, N'Djamena; tel. 52-35-03; f. 1967 to develop the area of Lake Chad; cap. 179m. francs CFA; Pres. HASSANTY OUMAR CHAIB; Dir-Gen. ABBO YOUSSOUF.

CHAMBER OF COMMERCE

Chambre de Commerce, d'Industrie, d'Agriculture, des Mines et d'Artisanat: 13 rue du Col Moll, BP 458, N'Djamena; tel. 52-52-64; fax 52-52-63; e-mail cciama@intnet.td; f. 1935; brs at Sarh, Moundou, Bol and Abéché; Pres. Dr NICOLE FROUD; Dir-Gen. BEKOUTOU TAIGAM.

TRADE ASSOCIATIONS

Office National des Céréales (ONC): BP 21, N'Djamena; tel. 52-37-31; fax 52-20-18; e-mail onc1@intnet.td; f. 1978; production and marketing of cereals; Dir-Gen. MAHAMAT ALI HASSABALLAH; 11 regional offices.

Société Nationale de Commercialisation du Tchad (SONACOT): BP 630, N'Djamena; tel. 51-30-47; f. 1965; cap. 150m. francs CFA; 76% state-owned; nat. marketing, distribution and import-export co; Man. Dir MARBROUCK NATROUD.

EMPLOYERS' ORGANIZATIONS

Conseil National du Patronat Tchadien (CNPT): rue Bazelaire, angle ave Charles de Gaulle, BP 134, N'Djamena; tel. and fax 52-25-71; fax 51-60-65; Pres. RAKHIS MANNANY; Sec.-Gen. MARC MADENGAR BEREMADJI; 67 mem. enterprises with total work-force of 8,000 (2002).

Union des Transporteurs Tchadiens: N'Djamena; tel. 51-45-27.

UTILITIES

Veolia Water—STEE (Société Tchadienne d'Eau et d'Electricité): 11 rue du Col Largeau, BP 44, N'Djamena; tel. 51-28-81; fax 51-21-34; f. 1968; state-owned; managed privately by subsidiary of Veolia Environnement (France) since 2000; production and distribution of electricity and water; Pres. GOMON MAWATA WAKAG; Dir-Gen. ISMAEL MAHAMAT ADOUM.

TRADE UNIONS

Confédération Libre des Travailleurs du Tchad (CLTT): ave Charles de Gaulle, BP 553, N'Djamena; tel. 51-76-11; fax 52-44-56; Sec.-Gen. BRAHIM BAKAS; 22,500 mems (2001).

Union des Syndicats du Tchad (UST): BP 1114, N'Djamena; tel. 51-47-77; fax 51-44-40; f. 1988; federation of trade unions; Pres. DOMBAL DJIMBAGUE; Sec.-Gen. DJIBRINE ASSALI HAMDALLAH.

Transport

RAILWAYS

There are no railways in Chad. In 1962 the Governments of Chad and Cameroon signed an agreement to extend the Transcameroon railway from Ngaoundéré to Sarh, a distance of 500 km. Although the Transcameroon reached Ngaoundéré in 1974, its proposed extension into Chad remains indefinitely postponed.

ROADS

The total length of the road network in 1999 was an estimated 40,000 km, of which 3,100 km were principal roads and 1,400 km were secondary roads; only 412 km of the network was paved. There are also some 20,000 km of tracks suitable for motor traffic during the October–July dry season. The European Union is contributing to the construction of a highway connecting N'Djamena with Sarh and Léré, on the Cameroon border, and of a 400-km highway linking Moundou and Ngaoundéré.

Coopérative des Transportateurs Tchadiens (CTT): BP 336, N'Djamena; tel. 51-43-55; road haulage; Pres. SALEH KHALIFA; brs at Sarh, Moundou, Bangui (CAR), Douala and Ngaoundéré (Cameroon).

Société Générale d'Entreprise Routière (SGER): BP 175, N'Djamena; tel. and fax 51-55-12; e-mail itralu@intnet.td; devt and maintenance of roads; 95% owned by Arcory International (Sudan); Pres. PATRICK MORIN.

Société Tchadienne d'Affrètement et de Transit (STAT): 21 ave Félix Eboué, BP 100, N'Djamena; tel. 51-88-72; fax 51-74-24; e-mail stat.tchad@intnet.td; affiliated to Groupe Saga (France); road haulage.

INLAND WATERWAYS

The Chari and Logone rivers, which converge to the south of N'Djamena, are navigable. These waterways connect Sarh with N'Djamena on the Chari and Bongor and Moundou with N'Djamena on the Logone.

CIVIL AVIATION

The international airport is at N'Djamena. There are also more than 40 smaller airfields.

Air Affaires Tchad: BP 256, N'Djamena; tel. 51-06-20; e-mail airaffaires@yahoo.st; passenger and freight internal and charter flights.

Minair Tchad: ave Charles de Gaulle, BP 1239, N'Djamena; tel. 52-52-45; fax 51-07-80; e-mail abdel.ousman@intnet.td; passenger and freight air transport.

Toumaï Air Tchad (TAT): N'Djamena; tel. 52-28-29; fax 52-41-06; f. 2004; scheduled passenger and cargo flights on domestic routes, and between N'Djamena and destinations in central and West Africa; Pres. and Dir-Gen. MAHAMAT BABA ABATCHA.

Tourism

Chad's potential attractions for tourists include a variety of scenery from the dense forests of the south to the deserts of the north. Receipts from tourism in 2002 totalled an estimated US $25m. A total of 29,356 tourists visited Chad in 2005, compared with 20,974 in 2003.

Direction de la promotion touristique: BP 86, N'Djamena; tel. 52-44-16.

CHILE

Introductory Survey

Location, Climate, Language, Religion, Flag, Capital

The Republic of Chile is a long, narrow country lying along the Pacific coast of South America, extending from Peru and Bolivia in the north to Cape Horn in the far south. Isla de Pascua (Rapa Nui or Easter Island), about 3,780 km (2,350 miles) off shore, and several other small islands form part of Chile. To the east, Chile is separated from Argentina by the high Andes mountains. Both the mountains and the cold Humboldt Current influence the climate; between Arica in the north and Punta Arenas in the extreme south, a distance of about 4,000 km (2,500 miles), the average maximum temperature varies by no more than 13°C. Rainfall varies widely between the arid desert in the north and the rainy south. The language is Spanish. There is no state religion but the great majority of the inhabitants profess Christianity, and some 71% are adherents of the Roman Catholic Church. The national flag (proportions 2 by 3) is divided horizontally: the lower half is red, while the upper half has a five-pointed white star on a blue square, at the hoist, with the remainder white. The capital is Santiago.

Recent History

Chile was ruled by Spain from the 16th century until its independence in 1818. For most of the 19th century it was governed by a small oligarchy of landowners. Chile won the War of the Pacific (1879–83) against Peru and Bolivia. The greater part of the 20th century was characterized by the struggle for power between right- and left-wing forces.

In September 1970 Dr Salvador Allende Gossens, the Marxist candidate of Unidad Popular (a coalition of five left-wing parties, including the Partido Comunista de Chile—PCCh), was elected to succeed Eduardo Frei Montalva, a Christian Democrat who was President between 1964 and 1970. Allende promised to transform Chilean society by constitutional means, and imposed an extensive programme of nationalization. The Government failed to obtain a congressional majority in the elections of March 1973 and encountered a deteriorating economic situation as well as an intensification of violent opposition to its policies. Accelerated inflation led to food shortages and there were repeated clashes between pro- and anti-Government activists. The armed forces finally intervened in September 1973. President Allende died during the coup. The Congreso (Congress) was subsequently dissolved, all political activity banned and strict censorship introduced. The military Junta dedicated itself to the eradication of Marxism and the 'reconstruction' of Chile, and its leader, Gen. Augusto Pinochet Ugarte, became Supreme Chief of State in June 1974 and President in December. The Junta was widely criticized abroad for its repressive policies and violations of human rights. Critics of the regime were tortured and imprisoned, and several thousand were abducted or 'disappeared'. Some of those who had been imprisoned were released, as a result of international pressure, and sent into exile.

In September 1976 three constitutional acts were promulgated with the aim of creating an 'authoritarian democracy'. All political parties were banned in March 1977, when the state of siege was extended. Following a UN General Assembly resolution, adopted in December 1977, which condemned the Government for violating human rights, a referendum was held in January 1978 to seek endorsement of the regime's policies. Since more than 75% of the voters supported the President in his defence of Chile 'in the face of international aggression', the state of siege (in force since 1973) was ended and was replaced by a state of emergency.

At a plebiscite held in September 1980, 67% of voters endorsed a new Constitution, drafted by the Government, although dubious electoral practices were allegedly employed. Although the new Constitution was described as providing a 'transition to democracy' and President Pinochet ceased to be head of the armed forces, additional clauses allowed him to maintain his firm hold on power until 1989. The new Constitution became effective from March 1981. Political parties, which were still officially outlawed, began to re-emerge, and in mid-1983 five moderate parties formed a coalition, the Alianza Democrática, which advocated a return to democratic rule within 18 months. A left-wing coalition was also created.

In February 1984 the Council of State, a government-appointed consultative body, began drafting a law to legalize political parties and to prepare for elections in 1989. Despite the Government's strenuous attempts to eradicate internal opposition through the introduction of anti-terrorist legislation and extensive security measures, a campaign of explosions and public protests continued throughout 1984 and 1985. A number of protesters were killed in violent clashes with security forces, and many opposition leaders and trade unionists were detained and sent into internal exile.

Throughout 1986 President Pinochet's regime came under increasing attack from the Roman Catholic Church, guerrilla organizations (principally the Frente Patriótico Manuel Rodríguez—FPMR) and international critics, including the US Administration, which had previously refrained from condemning the regime's notorious record of violations of human rights. In September the FPMR made an unsuccessful attempt to assassinate Pinochet. The regime's immediate response was to impose a state of siege throughout Chile, under which leading members of the opposition were detained and strict censorship was introduced. One consequence of the state of siege was the reappearance of right-wing 'death squads', which were implicated in a series of murders following the assassination attempt.

President Pinochet clearly indicated his intention to remain in office beyond 1989 by securing, in mid-1987, the sole presidential candidacy, should it be approved by the same plebiscite that would decide the future electoral timetable. The referendum, to be held on 5 October 1988, asked if the sole candidate nominated by the Pinochet regime should be confirmed as President. If the Government lost the referendum, it would be obliged to hold open elections within one year. Several political parties and opposition groups established the Comando por el No campaign to co-ordinate the anti-Government vote. The official result recorded 55% of the votes cast for the anti-Pinochet campaign, and 43% for the President. Following the plebiscite, the opposition made repeated demands for changes to the Constitution, in order to accelerate the democratic process. However, Pinochet rejected the opposition's proposals, and affirmed his intention to remain in office until March 1990. Elections were to be held in December 1989.

In mid-1989 Patricio Aylwin Azócar, a lawyer and former senator who had been a vociferous supporter of the 'no' vote in the 1988 plebiscite, emerged as the sole presidential candidate for the centre-left Concertación de los Partidos de la Democracia (CPD, formerly the Comando por el No), an alliance of parties including the Partido Demócrata Cristiano (PDC), of which Aylwin had hitherto been President. Throughout 1989 the election campaign was dominated by demands from both the CPD and right-wing parties for constitutional reform. A document detailing 54 amendments (including the legalization of Marxist political parties) ratified by the Junta was finally accepted by the opposition, with some reservations, and the constitutional reforms were approved by 86% of voters in a national referendum in July. Uncertainty regarding President Pinochet's own intentions concerning the forthcoming elections was finally dispelled in mid-1989, when he dismissed the possibility of his candidacy as unconstitutional, but reiterated his intention to continue as Commander-in-Chief of the Army for at least four years.

The presidential and congressional elections were conducted on 14 December 1989. In the presidential ballot, Aylwin Azócar of the centre-left CPD won a clear victory over the government-supported candidate, former Minister of Finance Hernán Büchi Buc. The transfer of power took place on 11 March 1990. Two members of the outgoing Junta remained as commanders of the air force and police.

Having failed to obtain the support of the two-thirds' majority in the Congreso necessary to amend the 1981 Constitution significantly, Aylwin's new CPD administration was forced to reconcile attempts to fulfil campaign promises as quickly as possible with the need to adopt a conciliatory approach towards more right-wing parties in the Congreso. Agreement was reached almost immediately on a series of modifications to the tax laws, but attempts to amend existing legislation considered repressive by the new administration, including the death penalty and provisions for the censorship of the press, were less successful. (The death penalty was finally abolished in April 2001 and a press freedom law was approved in the following month.)

In April 1990 the Government created a national truth and reconciliation commission, the Comisión Nacional de Verdad y Reconciliación (CNVR), to document and investigate alleged violations of human rights during the previous administration. Although Pinochet, before leaving office, had provided for the impunity of the former military Junta with regard to abuses of human rights, it was suggested by human rights organizations that such safeguards might be circumvented by indicting known perpetrators of atrocities on charges of 'crimes against humanity', a provision which gained considerable public support following the discovery, during 1990, of a number of mass graves containing the remains of political opponents of the 1973–90 military regime. The army High Command condemned the Commission for undermining the prestige of the armed forces and attempting to contravene the terms of a comprehensive amnesty declared in 1978. Although a new accord between military leaders and the Government-elect had been negotiated in January 1990 (whereby the role of the armed forces was redefined as essentially subservient to the Ministry of Defence), relations between the new Government and the army High Command remained tense. Pinochet became the focus for widespread disaffection with the military élite, but resisted demands for his resignation, reiterating his intention to continue as Commander-in-Chief of the Army until 1997.

Escalating public and political antagonism towards the former military leadership was fuelled throughout 1990 and 1991 by further revelations of abuses of human rights and financial corruption, and erupted into widespread popular outrage and renewed political violence following the publication, in March 1991, of the findings of the CNVR. The report documented the deaths of 2,279 alleged political opponents of the former regime who were executed, died as a result of torture or disappeared (and were presumed to be dead) in 1973–90. Those responsible for the deaths were identified only by the institutions to which they belonged. However, Aylwin pledged full government co-operation for families wishing to pursue private prosecutions. The report concluded that the military Government had embarked upon a 'systematic policy of extermination' of its opponents through the illegal activities of the covert military intelligence agency, Dirección de Inteligencia Nacional (Dina), and was also highly critical of the Chilean judiciary for failing to protect the rights of individuals by refusing thousands of petitions for habeas corpus submitted by human rights lawyers. Pinochet publicly denounced the document and declared his opposition to government plans to make material reparation to the families of the victims named in the report.

In November 1993, following a prolonged investigation and a controversial trial, former Dina officials Gen. Manuel Contreras and Col Pedro Espinoza were convicted of the murder of Orlando Letelier, a former cabinet minister (and Chile's ambassador to the USA during the Government of Salvador Allende in the early 1970s), who was assassinated in 1976, together with a US associate, in Washington, DC. In April 2003 Contreras had been sentenced to 15 years' imprisonment for the kidnapping of Miguel Sandoval, a left-wing activist who had disappeared in 1975; the sentence was reduced to six years in 2004, and Contreras was released from prison. However, in November 2005 Contreras was sentenced to three years' imprisonment for involvement in the 'disappearance' in 1976 of schoolteacher Julia del Rosario Retamal Sepulveda. The judge in the case, Alejandro Solís, rejected the defendant's invocation of the amnesty law, ruling that it did not apply in cases of 'disappearance', on the grounds that such unresolved cases of abduction should be considered as ongoing. In November 2004 the Supreme Court had upheld this decision on appeal (see below). Nevertheless, proposals by President Aylwin to accelerate prosecution of military personnel were rejected by the Congreso in 1993.

A presidential election, held on 11 December 1993, was won by the CPD candidate Eduardo Frei Ruiz-Tagle, a PDC senator, with 58% of the votes cast, ahead of Arturo Alessandri Besa, the candidate of the right-wing coalition, the Unión para el Progreso de Chile (UPC), who received 24% of the votes. However, the ruling coalition failed to make significant gains at concurrently conducted congressional elections. In February 1994 formal congressional endorsement was secured for constitutional reform, whereby henceforth the length of the non-renewable presidential term would be fixed at six years.

On assuming the presidency in March 1994 Frei identified the immediate aims of his Government as the alleviation of poverty, the elimination of corrupt government, and the fostering of significant economic growth. In August Frei presented several constitutional reform proposals to the Congreso, including the abolition of appointed senators and the introduction of an electoral system based on proportional representation (to replace the unrepresentative binominal system). However, Frei encountered the same level of opposition to constitutional reform (particularly from the right and from the upper house), that had undermined most attempts at constitutional amendment made by the previous administration.

In November 1995 the Government secured the support of the opposition Renovación Nacional (RN) for revised proposals for new legislation relating to human rights and constitutional reform. However, the compromised nature of the agreement provoked considerable disaffection within the RN, and within the opposition UPC alliance in general, which was effectively dissolved following the departure of the Unión Demócrata Independiente (UDI) and the Unión de Centro-Centro (UCC) in protest at the actions of the RN. Concern was also expressed by members of the Partido Socialista (PS—within the ruling coalition) that the human rights legislation had been severely compromised.

During 1997 government efforts to abolish the designated seats in the Senado intensified in response to Pinochet's stated intention to assume one of the seats assigned to former Presidents on his retirement as Commander-in-Chief of the Army in March 1998. In July 1997 the Senado rejected the Government's latest petition for reform to the system of appointments. In October it was announced that Maj.-Gen. Ricardo Izurieta, previously chief of defence staff, was to succeed Pinochet as Commander-in-Chief of the Army. The announcement was made amid a number of changes in the military High Command, which appeared to confirm earlier predictions that military influence was henceforth to be concentrated in the Senado, where it would bolster the political right wing.

Legislative elections to renew all 120 seats in the Cámara de Diputados and 20 of the elective seats in the Senado were conducted on 11 December 1997. The governing Concertación secured 51% of the votes for deputies and retained a comfortable majority in the lower house. The elections revealed a shifting balance of power within the two major political groupings (support for the UDI, in particular, appeared to have superseded that for the RN within the Unión por Chile), and prompted renewed criticism of the country's binomial system of voting, the PCCh having failed to secure congressional representation despite attracting 8% and 7% of the votes to the upper and lower houses, respectively.

In January 1998 attempts were made by junior members of the Concertación and by the leadership of the PCCh to begin judicial proceedings against Pinochet on charges related to gross abuses of human rights. Pinochet responded by announcing that he would not retire as Commander-in-Chief of the Army on 26 January, as previously suggested, but would continue in office until 10 March, the day before he was scheduled to assume his ex-officio seat in the Senado, thereby preserving the immunity from prosecution provided by the position for as long as possible. On 6 March the military High Command announced that Pinochet had been named an honorary commander-in-chief—a position with no historical precedent. On 11 March Pinochet assumed his seat in the Senado. A largely symbolic, and unsuccessful, attempt by 11 Concertación deputies to initiate a formal impeachment action against Pinochet was initiated in the Cámara de Diputados in the same month.

At the presidential poll, held on 12 December 1999, the candidate of the ruling Concertación, Ricardo Lagos Escobar of the PS, and the nominee of the Alianza por Chile (formed by the RN and the UDI), Joaquín Lavín, both obtained 48% of the total votes cast. At the second round of voting, which took place on 16 January 2000, Lagos emerged victorious with 51% of the total votes, while Lavín received 49%. Lagos was sworn in as President on 11 March. He set out a reduction in unemployment and an increase in economic growth to be the main priorities for his new Government.

As the controversy surrounding the detention of former President Pinochet in the United Kingdom continued in 1999 (see below), domestic attention was once again focused on the actions of the security forces during the post-1973 military regime. In June the arrest of five retired army officers (former commanders of a notorious élite army unit popularly referred to as the 'caravan of death') was ordered by an appeal court judge following renewed investigation into the disappearance of 72 political prisoners in the immediate aftermath of the 1973 military coup. The decision to prosecute the five men on charges of aggravated kidnapping was considered a breakthrough in Chilean judicial practice, as the absence of physical or documented evidence of the deaths of the prisoners meant that the crimes were technically in continuance, and that the accused men were not protected by the 1978 amnesty which guaranteed the impunity of military personnel for crimes committed before that year. In July 1999 the legality of the arrests was confirmed by the Supreme Court. Attempts by the Government to stem the resurgence of popular resentment of the past actions of the armed forces included, in August, the first direct discussions of the fate of the 'disappeared' between representatives of the armed forces and human rights organizations. However, tensions were exacerbated by the US National Security Council's declassification, in June, of some 5,800 CIA documents which recorded abuses of human rights during 1973–78, and which appeared to support claims that the Chilean armed forces had falsified evidence purporting to demonstrate the threat posed by the Allende administration in order to justify the 1973 coup. In September 1999 the Supreme Court had ruled in favour of criminal proceedings being brought against two retired generals, Humberto Gordon Rubio and Roberto Schmied, earlier in the month for their alleged involvement in the murder of trade union leader Tucapel Jiménez in 1982. (In August 2002 12 former military officers, including four generals, were sentenced to terms of imprisonment for their involvement in the murder of Jiménez.) In the following month an arrest warrant was issued against Gen. (retd) Hugo Salas Wendel, a former Director of Dina, on charges of complicity in the killings in 1987 of 12 alleged members of a left-wing guerrilla group. In June 2000 the Mesa de Diálogo, a round-table discussion between human rights lawyers and the military, agreed to guarantee the anonymity of any military person offering information on the whereabouts of any 'disappeared' person. The first official report as a result of the agreement in January 2001 disclosed information on the fate of 200 people—151 were allegedly thrown into the sea, 20 were buried in a mass grave and 29 were scattered in graves around central Chile.

Proposed reforms to the Constitution under discussion in 2001 included the abolition of seats for non-elected senators and a revision of the electoral system. However, the results of legislative elections, held on 16 December, threatened progress on constitutional issues, as the right-wing UDI, a member of the Alianza por Chile (which opposed the reforms), made significant gains in the Senado and the Cámara de Diputados. In the Senado, where 18 of the 38 elective seats were contested, the CPD controlled 20 seats overall, but lost its one-seat majority, while the Alianza por Chile increased its representation to 16 seats (the UDI's total increased to nine seats). The remaining two seats were won by Independents. In the Cámara de Diputados the CPD won 62 seats, a substantially reduced majority, while the Alianza por Chile secured 57 seats (the UDI's representation increased to 35 deputies, replacing the PDC as Chile's largest party).

On 16 October 1998 former President Pinochet was arrested during a visit to London, United Kingdom, in response to a preliminary request that he should be extradited to Spain to answer charges of 'genocide and terrorism'. The Frei Government protested that Pinochet's diplomatic immunity had been infringed, while the British Government denied Pinochet's status as an accredited diplomat. Meanwhile, supporters and opponents of Pinochet clashed during demonstrations in Santiago, and there were concerns that Pinochet's detention was threatening to undermine the country's delicate political and military balance. The British House of Lords' hearing of the extradition appeal in late November overturned an earlier ruling that Pinochet was entitled to 'sovereign immunity' as a former head of state, and in December formal extradition proceedings commenced. President Frei reacted angrily to the decision, recalling the Chilean ambassador in London. Meanwhile, however, it had emerged that one of the three Law Lords who had rejected Pinochet's immunity in the November ruling had failed to declare potentially compromising personal links to the international human rights campaign group Amnesty International. As a result, the November pronouncement was suspended pending review by a new appellate committee, although in March 1999 the appellate committee upheld the pronouncement. However, it also found that only charges relating to events subsequent to December 1988 (at which time the 1984 UN Convention against Torture and Other Cruel, Inhuman or Degrading Treatment or Punishment had entered into British law) should be considered relevant, thus reducing the number of draft charges brought by Spain from 33 to three. Formal extradition proceedings were initiated in September 1999, and in October a court found that Pinochet, who remained under effective house arrest, could be lawfully extradited to Spain. However, in March 2000, after an independent doctors' report had concluded that he was physically unfit to undergo further legal proceedings, Pinochet was released, and on the following day the former dictator returned to Chile.

The return of Pinochet to Chile was interpreted as a triumph for the former President, and included a public welcome by the heads of the armed forces but no representation from the civilian Government. Initially, expectations that Pinochet would ever stand trial in Chile were very low; however, these were raised in June 2000 following the Santiago Appeal Court's ruling to lift the former dictator's political immunity. In August, in an historical judgment, the Supreme Court confirmed the decision. The judgment was made possible by changes to Chile's judiciary, several members of which had retired and had been replaced by more independent-minded judges. Foremost among these was Juan Guzmán Tapia, who vigorously took up the legal case against Pinochet and others accused of human rights' infringements. Over 200 lawsuits were filed against the former dictator. Pinochet's lawyers, meanwhile, argued that it would be too undignified for their client to submit to a medical examination to determine whether he was mentally fit to stand trial (compulsory in Chile for all citizens over the age of 70). In October an Argentine judge requested the extradition of Pinochet to stand trial for the 1974 killing, in Buenos Aires, of former Chilean army chief Carlos Prats and his wife. (In March 2005 the Supreme Court upheld Pinochet's immunity on charges relating to the killing of Prats and his wife). In November the Supreme Court ruled that Pinochet must not leave the country and on 1 December Judge Guzmán indicted Pinochet on charges of aggravated kidnapping and murder in the 'caravan of death' case (see above) and placed him under house arrest, a move which was subsequently suspended by the Santiago Appeals Court. The Supreme Court ruled that Pinochet must face interrogation by Judge Guzmán within 20 days, though not before undergoing the medical tests required by law. In early January 2001 Pinochet finally consented to the medical examination and was subsequently questioned. On 31 January Judge Guzmán issued an order for the former General's arrest on charges of kidnap and murder. However, following an appeal by Pinochet, in March the Santiago Appeals Court ruled that the charges should be reduced to conspiracy to cover up the events, as opposed to responsibility for the 'caravan of death', and in July the Court ruled that the former dictator was mentally unfit to stand trial. In July 2002 the Supreme Court voted to close the case against Pinochet permanently, as he was suffering from 'incurable' and 'irreversible' dementia. Within days Pinochet relinquished his position as senator-for-life. In October 2003, despite Pinochet's lucid demeanour in a television interview, the Supreme Court dismissed a further attempt to overturn the ruling. However, in May 2004 the Santiago Appeals Court voted to remove Pinochet's immunity from prosecution for the crimes allegedly committed as part of 'Plan Condor', an intelligence operation to eliminate opponents of the Latin American military dictatorships in the 1970s; on 26 October the Supreme Court voted to uphold this ruling.

In mid-July 2004 a US senate report on the accounts of the Washington, DC-based Riggs Bank alleged that, between 1985 and 2002, Pinochet and his wife had deposited up to US $12m. into secret accounts there. The Chilean authorities immediately initiated an investigation into the origin of the funds and, in response to separate, ongoing investigations by Spanish judge Baltazar Garzón, in early November the Attorney-General recommended that Pinochet's assets be 'frozen' while investigations continued. Meanwhile, in late August the Supreme Court upheld a decision by the appeals court in May to strip Pinochet of his immunity from prosecution. The decision allowed for Pinochet to be interrogated by Judge Guzmán on 25 September over his role in 'Plan Condor'. Despite Pinochet's lawyers claiming that he had recently suffered a significant deterioration in his mental condition, in mid-December Guzmán declared him to be of sufficiently sound mind to stand trial; the Supreme Court upheld this decision on 4 January 2005. The following day Pinochet was placed under house arrest pending trial, although one week later he was released on bail. In September the Penal Chamber of the Supreme Court ruled that the charges against Pinochet relating to 'Plan Condor' were inadmissible. Meanwhile, in August Pinochet's wife, Lucía Hiriart Rodríguez, and son, Marco Antonio, were arrested on tax-evasion charges. In the following month US financial investigators accused Pinochet of accepting bribes totalling more than US $3.5m., from European defence contractors through 'shell' companies. In October the Supreme Court removed Pinochet's immunity from prosecution on charges of embezzlement and the use of false passports to open foreign bank accounts. In November court-appointed psychiatrists reported that Pinochet had deliberately exaggerated his dementia in order to avoid prosecution. In December the Supreme Court stripped Pinochet of immunity from prosecution on charges relating to 'Operation Colombo', an operation allegedly undertaken during his dictatorship to abduct and murder 119 opponents of the regime. Also in that month, the Appeals Court of Santiago stripped Pinochet of immunity from prosecution on charges relating to misuse of public money. In January 2006 Pinochet was again placed under house arrest following charges being brought against him for involvement in 'Operation Colombo' (he was again released on bail later that month). Also in January, Pinochet's daughter, Inés Lucía, was arrested by the US Customs Service upon her arrival in Washington, DC, on charges of money-laundering and the use of a false passport; she initially applied for political asylum in that country, but later withdrew her claim and returned to Chile where she was arrested.

In late 2002 President Lagos encountered serious political difficulties when the Government became embroiled in a corruption scandal. A number of government officials were accused of accepting bribes to finance CPD election campaigns. Lagos was quick to announce plans to increase government accountability and improve the transparency of party funding, but allegations of corruption within the ruling CPD continued and two close associates of Lagos were subsequently arrested. In January 2003 the Supreme Court stripped five CPD congressmen of their parliamentary immunity in order that they too face corruption charges. As a result, Lagos's Concertación alliance was reduced to a one-seat majority in the Cámara de Diputados.

In August 2003 President Lagos announced a series of measures intended to resolve issues relating to human rights violations during the military dictatorship. These included increases in compensation paid to victims of political violence and their relatives, as well as measures to facilitate criminal prosecutions of former military personnel. However, he did not pledge to repeal the 1978 amnesty law, an omission that prompted criticism from relatives of the 'disappeared'. None the less, in November 2004 the Supreme Court—in reference to the prosecution, on charges of involvement in 'Plan Condor', of the former head of Dina, Manuel Contreras, and three other former secret policemen—again ruled against the invocation of the amnesty law in cases of 'disappearance', on the grounds that, until the body of the kidnapped person was found, such unresolved cases of abduction should be considered as ongoing. The Supreme Court's ruling opened the way for many other cases of human rights abuses during 1973–90 to be brought. Also in November 2004, the testimonies of some 35,000 victims of abuses under the Pinochet regime were published in a report by the National Commission on Political Imprisonment and Torture. Although victims' and human rights groups welcomed the report, many criticized it for omitting the names of those accused of the abuses. Prior to the report's publication, the Commander-in-Chief of the Chilean Army, Gen. Juan Emilio Cheyre Espinosa, issued on behalf of the armed forces a public apology, in which for the first time institutional responsibility was accepted for the systematic abuse of opponents of the Pinochet regime. On 29 November President Lagos announced that some 28,000 of the victims who gave testimony in the report would be eligible for a pension, equivalent to nearly US $200 per month.

In late October and early November 2004 the Senado finally approved a number of constitutional reforms. These included: the abolition of non-elected senators and of senators-for-life; the restoration of the President's power to dismiss the head of the armed forces and the police; and a reduction of the presidential term from six years to four. The constitutional reforms received final congressional approval in August 2005. Significantly, the reforms did not include changes to the binomial electoral system. Also in November 2004, a constitutional amendment legalizing divorce came into effect.

In September 2004 President Lagos carried out a cabinet reshuffle, in which, notably, the Minister of National Defence, Michelle Bachelet Jeria, and the Minister of Foreign Affairs, María Soledad Alvear Valenzuela, lost their portfolios. Both women subsequently announced their intention to stand as candidates in the forthcoming presidential election. In mid-January 2005 Alvear was chosen as the PDC's nominee; however, she withdrew from the contest in May, and Bachelet of the PS eventually secured the presidential nomination of the ruling Concertación. Alvear subsequently announced that she would support Bachelet's campaign. Joaquín Lavín of the Alianza por Chile was considered the main rival from the right-wing until the announcement in May that Sebastián Piñera Echeñique, a wealthy and charismatic businessman, would stand as a candidate of the Partido Renovación Nacional.

At the presidential election, held on 11 December 2005, Bachelet obtained 46.0% of valid votes cast, while Piñera received 25.4% of the ballot; Lavín came third with 23.2% of the votes. As no candidate obtained the requisite 50% of the ballot, a run-off election between the two leading candidates was held on 15 January 2006. Bachelet was elected President with 53.5% of valid votes cast, while Piñera secured 46.5% of the ballot. Following the legislative elections, held concurrently with the first round of the presidential ballot, the Concertación controlled 20 of the 38 seats in the Senado, while the Alianza por Chile held 17 seats; one Independent candidate was elected. In the election to the 120-seat Cámara de Diputados, the Concertación won a narrow majority, obtaining 65 seats overall (the PPD won 22 seats, the PDC 20 seats, the PS 16 seats, and the Partido Radical Socialdemócrata seven seats), while the Alianza por Chile secured 54 seats (34 seats were secured by the UDI, with the other 20 going to the RN). The Fuerza Regional Independiente alliance won the remaining seat.

Bachelet, who took office on 11 March 2006, declared her intention to continue many of the policies of the previous Government. Her Cabinet included Alejandro Foxley Rioseco, who had served in President Alywin's Government, as Minister of Foreign Affairs, and former President of the Senado, Andrés Zaldívar Larraín, as Minister of the Interior. One-half of the Cabinet was female. The new President stated that her priorities were to address the problem of income inequality and increase social spending, and to improve bilateral relations with neighbouring Argentina, Bolivia and Peru. In her first speech to the Congreso Nacional, in early May, Bachelet proposed establishing a pension fund and a stabilization fund, using profits from the higher than normal copper price. The new Government also planned to create 130,000 new jobs in 2006, through development of small businesses, to improve social housing and policing, and to provide universal nursery places.

In spite of the new Government's pledge to increase public spending on education, on 30 May 2006 some 600,000 high-school students, as well as 100,000 college students attended nation-wide demonstrations in protest at the education system. Protests had begun earlier in the month, when students demonstrated to demand transport subsidies and an end to fees for university entrance examinations. However, faced with no response from the Government, the protests escalated: although the demonstrations were largely peaceful, the police attempted to break up the protests using water cannons and tear gas, and some 700 arrests were made. The students pledged to resume the protests unless the Government met their requests by 2 June. In response, on 1 June the Government agreed to provide free transport for those attending school or college and to introduce grants to cover entrance examination fees for the poorest students. However, some protests continued into June, albeit on a smaller scale, as students occupied schools and colleges to demand greater representation on the education reform committee. The unrest damaged the new President's popularity ratings, and led to the dismissal in mid-July of Zaldívar Larraín as the Minister of the Interior, after the police handling of the demonstrations was criticized. He was replaced by Belisario Velasco Baraona, his erstwhile deputy. At the same time, the Ministers of Education and the Economy, Economic Promotion and Reconstruction were also removed from their cabinet posts.

In her first year in office President Bachelet also faced unrest from miners, teachers and health workers: in August 2006 workers at La Escondida copper mine went on strike to demand a higher pay increase in light of record copper prices. A settlement was reached at the end of the month, but in September teachers also instigated industrial action to demand a pay increase and in protest at the slow pace of education reform following the student protests earlier in the year. They were joined in their protests by health workers also demanding salary increases. In early October Baraona announced further rises in government spending, but teachers' unions maintained their threat to organize nation-wide protests unless the Government offered more specific pledges on education. President Bachelet pledged further expenditure on education in May 2007, and in November the Government and the opposition reached an agreement on reform of the education system; the proposal, however, had to be approved by the Congreso.

In October 2006 alleged widespread corruption in the government sports agency, Chiledeportes, came to light. The revelations centred on the agency's activities during the administration of President Lagos, but, nevertheless, were damaging to the Bachelet Government. Officials from the PPD, part of the ruling Concertación, were accused of diverting funds from Chiledeportes to the 2005 election campaign. In the same month the PPD Vice-President, Guido Girardi, was suspended from his post after it was revealed he had falsified invoices. The Alianza por Chile boycotted the legislative vote on the 2007 budget in early November in protest at the corruption revelations (although, as the coalition Government enjoyed a majority in the Congreso, the budget was still approved). A parliamentary investigation, headed by the Alianza por Chile, was immediately instigated and at the end of the month President Bachelet proposed the establishment of an all-party anti-corruption pact, a plan that was dismissed by the opposition.

Gen. Pinochet died on 10 December 2006 after suffering a heart attack a week earlier. The former dictator's death brought an end to the efforts by the judiciary and human rights organizations to bring him to trial on various charges of human rights abuses during his rule. In late October Pinochet had been indicted on human rights abuses and placed under house arrest after a court ruled that he was mentally fit to face trial: some 4,500 political opponents were alleged to have been detained at the notorious Villa Grimaldi detention centre during his regime, and more than 200 people murdered there. Pinochet was charged on one count of murder, 35 kidnappings and 24 cases of torture. However, several days later he was released on bail. At the end of November he was once again put under house arrest after being charged with involvement in the murder of former President Allende's bodyguards. Earlier in the same month the Appeals Court of Santiago also lifted his immunity from prosecution in the case of the 'disappearance' of a Spanish priest in 1974, and charges in the 'caravan of death' case (see above) were also once again brought. He was also due to face trial on fraud charges relating to his accounts at the US Riggs Bank (see above). Pinochet's widow and several members of his family were arrested in October 2007 on charges relating to the Riggs Bank case. Supporters of the former dictator charged that the arrests were an attempt by the Government to boost its flagging popularity.

In February 2007 a centralized public transport system was introduced in Santiago. The Transantiago network was intended to reduce congestion and simplify the transport system, replacing the myriad private concerns operating in the capital with a government-run scheme comprising 10 companies. However, in its first week of operation passengers protested that there were not enough services and that the new 'smart card' payment system did not work. In the same month members of the Transantiago trade union threatened industrial action over unequal pay scales. The Government responded by introducing measures to improve the system, including an increase in buses and extensions to routes, but protests continued. In late March President Bachelet dismissed Minister of Transport and Telecommunications Sergio Espejo, replacing him with René Cortázar Sanz. Espejo's sacking was part of a wider redistribution of cabinet portfolios intended to boost the administration's waning popularity: Isidro Solís Palma was replaced at the justice ministry with Carlos Maldonado Curti, José Goñi Carrasco took over from Vivianne Blanlot Soza as Minister of National Defence, while José Antonio Viera-Gallo was appointed Secretary-General of the Presidency in succession to Paulina Veloso Valenzuela.

In May 2007 the Government announced the creation of a metropolitan transport authority, aimed at improving management of Transantiago, which was operating at a loss. At the same time, the Ministry of Transport and Telecommunications proposed some US $290m. in extra funding be granted to the capital's bus and metro network. The monies were intended to guarantee the system's operations for the rest of the year as well as to cover the projected shortfall in financing. The proposal was approved by the Cámara de Diputados in June, but encountered fierce opposition in the upper house, where senators belonging to the ruling CPD threatened to vote against the Government unless amendments were introduced. The extra funding eventually received senate approval in mid-June, although not before the Government was forced to make several concessions to the legislation. These included ending guaranteed incomes to bus operators, irrespective of how many services they ran, which had led to a drastic reduction in the number of buses in operation and severe overcrowding on the metro system, and an increase in the transparency of Transantiago's operations via a monthly report to the Congreso. Some $100m. was also to be given to regional governments, who had objected to such substantial funding for the capital. In the same month industrial action by bus drivers compounded the Government's transport woes.

Industrial unrest continued throughout 2007: as well as intermittent strikes by bus drivers in Santiago protesting over the implementation of the Transantiago transport network (see above), in late June sub-contractors working at the state-owned copper company, Corporación Nacional del Cobre de Chile (CODELCO-Chile), withdrew their labour in protest at their poorer terms and conditions compared with miners employed directly by CODELCO-Chile. The dispute was discontinued at the end of July after an agreement was reached between the company and the copper workers' union, the Confederación de Trabajadores del Cobre (CUT). The CUT organized a general strike in late August to protest against the Bachelet Government's perceived neo-liberal economic policies. Demonstrations in Santiago descended into violence and led to almost 500 arrests. In the following month, on the anniversary of the 1973 coup, a march to commemorate those killed during the Pinochet regime degenerated into a riot that resulted in the death of one police officer and led to over 300 arrests.

A government request for a further US $92m. in funding for Transantiago was rejected by the Senado in November 2007. The vote was controversial because a PDC senator, Adolfo Zaldívar, voted with the opposition, which resulted in his expulsion from the party at the end of year. Following his exclusion, in January 2008 five other deputies also announced their departure from PDC, leaving the ruling coalition in a minority in both legislative chambers. In an attempt to restore confidence in her Government, in the same month President Bachelet carried out another extensive cabinet reshuffle. The reorganization was prompted by the resignation of the Minister of the Interior, Belisario Velasco; he was replaced by Edmundo Pérez Yoma, whose father had held the same post in the Allende administration. Among the other appointments, Karen Poniachik was replaced at the Ministry of Mining by Santiago González Larraín, while Hugo Lavados Montes succeeded Alejando Ferreiro as Minister of Economy, Economic Promotion and Reconstruction. None the less, in April the Minister of Education, Yasna Provoste Campillay, was forced to resign after the Senado convicted her of dereliction of duty and banned her from holding public office for five years, following the revelation of severe financial mismanagement in the Ministry of Education. She was replaced by Mónica Jiménez de la Jara.

In 2000 and 2001 a series of mining, dam and forestry projects prompted violent protests by the Mapuche indigenous peoples who were campaigning for the restitution of land they claimed under ancestral right. In May 2000 a Historical Truth and New Deal Commission was created to consider the demands and needs of indigenous communities. However, in October the Cámara de Diputados rejected legislation that would have granted constitutional recognition to the Mapuche peoples. In November 2003 the Commission produced its final report, which recommended the extension of constitutional and property rights to indigenous peoples and confirmation of their entitlement to participate in national politics. In early 2004 it was alleged that damage to timber-industry property and forest fires in the Biobío region were the acts of Mapuche activists opposed to the activities of the timber industry. In August five Mapuche activists were convicted under anti-terrorism legislation. In November seven Mapuche activists (and one non-Mapuche sympathizer) were acquitted on charges of conspiring to commit terrorist acts. Meanwhile, in August, after some eight years of legal dispute between the Spanish energy company Endesa, SA, and a coalition of ecological and indigenous groups of Pehuenche ethnicity, an agreement was finally reached that would allow construction of a major hydroelectric plant in the River Biobío basin. President Bachelet put forward to the Congreso a constitutional amendment in October 2007 that would recognize indigenous ancestral lands as well as promote the rights of the country's indigenous peoples. In mid-January 2008 the Government established a panel to address the issue of Mapuche rights; the move followed an increase in civil unrest among the indigenous population after a student was shot dead by a police officer during a demonstration at the beginning of the month.

In August 1991 Argentina and Chile reached a settlement regarding disputed territory in the Antarctic region. Responsibility for the contentious Laguna del Desierto region, however, was to be decided by international arbitration. In October 1994 Argentina's claim to the territory was upheld by a five-member international arbitration panel. In September 1997 it was agreed to proceed with the creation of a conciliation commission, originally envisaged within the terms of a peace and friendship treaty concluded in 1984. In December 1998 agreement on border demarcation of the still disputed 'continental glaciers' territory in the Antarctic region was reached by the Presidents of the two countries. In September 2000 both countries ratified the Mining and Co-operation Integration Treaty, which allowed joint exploitation of mineral deposits along their shared border. Relations between the two countries were strained in mid-2004, however, following the decision of Argentine President Néstor Carlos Kirchner to reduce exports of gas to Chile, which, the Lagos administration claimed, violated a 1995 agreement. Tensions were exacerbated following the appointment of Ignacio Walker Prieto as the Chilean Minister of Foreign Affairs in September; prior to his appointment Walker had criticized both President Kirchner for opportunism and Peronism in general for displaying 'authoritarian' and 'fascistic' traits. However, following Bachelet's election to the presidency in 2006, a bilateral group was established to resolve more effectively any future disagreements over energy matters. The two countries also agreed to establish a joint military force to participate in UN peacekeeping operations. The Senado approved legislation in May 2007 that allowed Chilean troops to be deployed overseas on peace-keeping or humanitarian missions.

Prospects for renewed diplomatic relations with Bolivia (which severed relations with Chile in 1978 over the issue of Bolivian access to the Pacific Ocean) improved following Bachelet's election to the presidency in 2006. The Bolivian Government had made repeated requests in the late 1990s for the renewal of discussions on Bolivian access to the sea, and sought Peru's assistance in the dispute; however, subsequent ministerial discussions failed to produce an effective formula for the restoration of diplomatic relations. The Lagos administration's decision in October 2003 to privatize the port of Arica elicited vehement objections from the Bolivian Government, which feared this would adversely affect Bolivia's external trade, owing to significant increases in port tariffs. However, bilateral discussions in July 2006 included Bolivian claims to Pacific access for the first time in more than a century. Furthermore, at an Ibero-American summit in November President Bachelet held sideline discussions with her Bolivian counterpart, Evo Morales Aima, on the issue. Negotiations continued throughout 2007, although in August Bolivia recalled its consul-general after he declared a conclusion to the issue of Bolivia's access to the sea to be imminent. In the same month Chile recalled its ambassador from Peru, after a government periodical had published a map appearing to lay claim to Chilean water. Relations improved in the following month after the two Presidents announced their commitment to a regional integration plan, but in January 2008 Chile again recalled its ambassador after the Peruvian legislature approved legislation revising the maritime border.

A free trade agreement with Colombia, the Acuerdo de Complementación Económica (ACE), took effect from 1 January 1994. However, tensions arose between the two countries in September 2004 following Chile's imposition of restrictions on imports of Colombian sugar, and Colombia's reciprocal imposition of tariffs on Chilean wine, fruit and vehicles. A free trade agreement with Ecuador came into effect on 1 January 1995. In December 1994 the signatory nations to the North American Free Trade Agreement (NAFTA) issued a formal invitation to Chile to join the group. However, 'fast track' authorization for Chile's accession to the Agreement was rejected by the US Congress, and in November 2000 it was announced that the USA would instead negotiate a bilateral trade deal with Chile. In the context of this delay, Chile intensified attempts to negotiate a bilateral free trade agreement with Canada and a formal trade agreement with the Mercado Común del Sur (Mercosur, see p. 391), of which Chile had become an associate member in October 1996. In November of that year agreement was reached with Canada on the removal of tariffs on three-quarters of bilateral trade, with the gradual removal of remaining duties over a five-year period. The agreement came into effect in July 1997 and its terms were modified and expanded in early 1998.

In April 1998 Chile and Mexico signed a free trade agreement, expanding the terms of an ACE in force since 1992. In June 1998 Chile signed a similar agreement with Peru, abolishing customs duties on 2,500 products. The agreement also envisaged the free passage of 50% of all products by 2003 and the creation of a free trade area within 18 years. With the exception of Bolivia, Chile has negotiated free trade agreements throughout the South American continent. In December 2002 Chile and the USA finally agreed on a free trade pact that would eliminate immediately all barriers on 85% of trade between the two countries, with the remaining trade restrictions being phased out within 12 years. The agreement came into effect in January 2004. In February 2003 an association agreement for political and economic co-operation between Chile and the European Union came into effect. In the same month a new free trade agreement was signed with the Republic of Korea. A free trade accord between Chile and the European Free Trade Association (EFTA, see p. 412) came into effect in February 2004. In December Chile was one of 12 countries that were signatories to the agreement, signed in Cusco, Peru, creating the South American Community of Nations (Comunidad Sudamericana de Naciones, which was renamed Union of South American Nations—Unión de Naciones Suramericanas, UNASUR, in April 2007), intended to promote greater regional economic integration. In November 2006 Chile rejoined the Andean Community of Nations (CAN, see p. 170) as an associate member; although the country had been a founding member of CAN, it had withdrawn from the organization in 1976 following a dispute.

Government

Chile is a republic, divided into 12 regions and a metropolitan area. Easter Island enjoys 'special territory' status within Chile. Under the terms of the Constitution, executive power is vested in the President, who is directly elected for a four-year term (reduced from six years in August 2005). The President is assisted by a Cabinet. Legislative power is vested in the bicameral Congreso Nacional (National Congress), comprising the 38-member Senado (Senate) and the 120-member Cámara de Diputados (Chamber of Deputies).

Defence

Military service is for one year (army) or 22 months (navy and air force) and is compulsory for men at 19 years of age. However, Michelle Bachelet Jeria, who took office as President in March 2006, pledged to end compulsory military service. As assessed at November 2007, the army had a strength of 36,016, the navy 20,450 and the air force 8,500. Paramilitary security forces numbered about 38,000 carabineros. Defence expenditure for 2007 was budgeted at 1,130,000m. pesos.

Economic Affairs

In 2006, according to estimates by the World Bank, Chile's gross national income (GNI), measured at average 2004–06 prices, was US $114,885m., equivalent to $6,980 per head (or $11,270 per head on an international purchasing-power parity basis). During 1996–2006, it was estimated, the population increased by an average of 1.2% per year, while gross domestic product (GDP) per head increased, in real terms, at an average annual rate of 2.6%. Overall GDP increased, in real terms, at an average annual rate of 3.9% in 1996–2006; real GDP increased by a preliminary 4.0% in 2006.

According to preliminary estimates, agriculture (including forestry and fishing) contributed an estimated 4.1% of GDP in 2006. The sector employed 13.2% of the employed labour force in late 2005. Important subsistence crops include wheat, oats, barley, rice, beans, lentils, maize and chick-peas. Industrial crops include sugar beet, sunflower seed and rapeseed. Fruit and vegetables are also important export commodities (together contributing 5.5% of total export revenues in 2006), particularly beans, asparagus, onions, garlic, grapes, citrus fruits, avocados, pears, peaches, plums and nuts. The production and export of wine increased significantly in recent years, although wine production decreased by an estimated 4.6% in 2006, compared with the previous year. Forestry and fishing, and derivatives from both activities, also make important contributions to the sector. During 1996–2003 agricultural GDP increased, in real terms, by an average of 4.3% per year; however, this rate increased to a preliminary 6.5% in 2003–06. Agricultural GDP increased by an estimated 5.4% in 2006.

According to preliminary figures, industry (including mining, manufacturing, construction and power) contributed an estimated 47.7% of GDP in 2006 and accounted for 23.0% of the employed labour force in late 2005. During 1996–2003 industrial GDP increased by an average of 2.5% per year, while in 2003–06 average annual growth in this sector reached 4.5%, according to preliminary figures. GDP growth in all industrial sectors was estimated at 2.6% in 2006.

Mining contributed an estimated 24.4% of GDP, according to preliminary estimates, in 2006 and engaged 1.3% of the employed labour force in late 2005. Chile, with some 20% of the world's known reserves, is the world's largest producer and exporter of copper. Copper accounted for 87.5% of Chile's total export earnings in 1970, but by 2006 the contribution of copper (including copper ore) to total export earnings stood at an estimated 56.5% (some US $33,340.3m.). Gold, silver, iron ore, nitrates, molybdenum, manganese, lead and coal are also mined. During 1996–2003 the sector increased by an average of 5.6% per year. In 2003–06 mining GDP grew at an average annual rate of 1.1%. In real terms, the sector's GDP increased by just 0.1% in 2006. Petroleum and natural gas deposits have been located in the south and, in 2004, offshore. Chile was a major producer of lithium carbonate, producing over one-third of global output.

According to preliminary estimates, manufacturing contributed 13.5% of GDP in 2006, and engaged 13.1% of the employed labour force in late 2005. The most important branches of manufacturing are food and non-ferrous metals. Manufacturing GDP increased by an average of 1.3% per year in 1996–2003, although in 2003–06 the GDP of this sector expanded at an average annual rate of 5.3%. According to preliminary figures, manufacturing GDP increased by 2.5% in 2006.

In 2004 electric energy was derived mainly from hydroelectric power (45.4%), natural gas (34.0%) and coal (16.1%). Chile produces some 40% of its national energy requirements. Plans are under consideration to exploit further Chile's vast hydroelectric potential (estimated at 18,700 MW—the largest in the world). In June 2007 the Government appropriated 32,000 sq km of land in the Magallanes region for oil and gas exploration. The area was to be divided into 10 blocks, which would then be put up for tender. The new venture was prompted by concerns that Chile had become increasingly reliant on imports to meet its energy needs. In 2005 Chile imported mineral fuels and lubricants equivalent to some 21.7% of the value of total merchandise imports.

The services sector, according to preliminary estimates, contributed an estimated 48.2% of GDP in 2006 and engaged 63.9% of the employed labour force in late 2005. The financial sector continued to expand in the early 21st century, fuelled, in part, by the success of private pension funds. During 1996–2003 overall services GDP increased by an average of 3.5% per year. In 2003–06 the sector's GDP rose at an average annual rate of 5.3%; manufacturing GDP increased, in real terms, by an estimated 4.6% in 2006.

In 2006 Chile recorded a visible trade surplus of US $21,291m., and there was a surplus of $5,256m. on the current account of the balance of payments. In that year Argentina was the principal source of imports (11.7%), while the USA was the principal market for exports (15.8%). Other major trading partners were Brazil, Japan, the People's Republic of China, South Korea and the Netherlands. In 2006 the principal exports were non-ferrous metals (40.0% of total export revenue), metalliferous ores and metal scrap (27.9%), vegetables and fruit (5.5%) and fish (5.1%). The principal imports in that year were machinery and transport equipment, and mineral and chemical products.

In 2006 there was a projected budgetary surplus of some 8,314.9m. pesos. Chile's external debt totalled some US $45,154m. at the end of 2005, of which $9,096m. was long-term public debt. Debt-servicing costs in that year were equivalent to some 15.4% of the value of exports of goods and services. The annual rate of inflation averaged 3.5% in 1996–2006, and stood at 3.4% in 2006. Some 6.9% of the labour force were unemployed in late 2005.

Chile is a member of the Latin American Integration Association (ALADI, see p. 331) and was admitted to the Rio Group (see p. 425) in 1990 and to the Asia-Pacific Economic Co-operation group (APEC, see p. 176) in 1994. Chile is also among the founding members of the World Trade Organization (WTO, see p. 396).

In spite of an expansion in the exports of fruit, seafoods and wines in the last two decades of the 20th century, in early 2008 Chile remained heavily dependent on exports of copper and on the stability of the world copper market. High international copper prices resulted in Chile recording its seventh successive trade surplus in 2006. Growth in trade was buoyed by foreign direct investment and tariff-cutting free trade agreements, particularly with the USA and the People's Republic of China. The strong copper prices, nevertheless, led to an appreciation in the Chilean peso, which, in turn, adversely affected other merchandise exports. Copper prices remained high through 2007 and the peso remained buoyant, fostering a rise in domestic demand. The Government continued to implement prudent fiscal and monetary policy to ensure stable growth. The level of investment remained strong in 2007 and external debt was estimated to have fallen to 32% of GDP. The IMF reported economic growth of 5.9% in that year. The 2008 budget, announced in May 2007, included a 15% increase in expenditure on education, housing and health services. The rises in spending by the administration of President Michelle Bachelet Jeria were intended to contain anti-Government feeling. This fiscal expansion was expected to reduce the budget surplus in 2008 and place upward pressure on consumer prices, which had been forecast to rise by 3.9% in 2008, the same rate of increase as in 2007. The IMF projected slower, albeit still healthy, economic growth of 5.0% in 2008.

Education

Pre-primary education is widely available for all children from five years of age. Primary education is officially compulsory, and is provided free of charge, for eight years, beginning at six or seven years of age. It is divided into two cycles: the first lasts for four years and provides a general education; the second cycle offers more specialized schooling. Secondary education, beginning at 13 or 14 years of age, is divided into the humanities-science programme (lasting for four years), with the emphasis on general education and possible entrance to university, and the technical-professional programme (lasting for between four and six years), designed to fulfil the requirements of specialist training. In 2004 enrolment at primary and secondary schools was equivalent to 96.2% of the total school-age population. Higher education is provided by three kinds of institution: universities, professional institutes and centres of technical information. The provision for education in the 2004 central government budget was 1,288,259m. pesos. In 2007 the Government announced a 15% increase in the education budget for 2008.

Public Holidays

2008: 1 January (New Year's Day), 21–22 March (Good Friday and Easter Saturday), 1 May (Labour Day), 21 May (Battle of Iquique), 15 August (Assumption), 18 September (Independence Day), 12 October (Day of the Race, anniversary of the discovery of America), 1 November (All Saints' Day), 8 December (Immaculate Conception), 25 December (Christmas Day).

2009: 1 January (New Year's Day), 10–11 April (Good Friday and Easter Saturday), 1 May (Labour Day), 21 May (Battle of Iquique), 15 August (Assumption), 18 September (Independence Day), 12 October (Day of the Race, anniversary of the discovery of America), 1 November (All Saints' Day), 8 December (Immaculate Conception), 25 December (Christmas Day).

Weights and Measures

The metric system is officially in force.

Statistical Survey

Sources (unless otherwise stated): Instituto Nacional de Estadísticas (INE), Avda Bulnes 418, Casilla 498-3, Correo 3, Santiago; tel. (2) 366-7777; fax (2) 671-2169; e-mail inesdadm@reuna.cl; internet www.ine.cl; Banco Central de Chile, Agustinas 1180, Santiago; tel. (2) 696-2281; fax (2) 698-4847; e-mail bcch@bcentral.cl; internet www.bcentral.cl.

Area and Population

AREA, POPULATION AND DENSITY*

Area (sq km)	756,096†
Population (census results)‡	
22 April 1992	13,348,401
24 April 2002	
Males	7,447,695
Females	7,668,740
Total	15,116,435
Population (official estimates at mid-year)	
2005	16,136,137
2006	16,432,674
2007	16,598,074
Density (per sq km) at mid-2007	22.0

* Excluding Chilean Antarctic Territory (approximately 1,250,000 sq km).
† 291,930 sq miles.
‡ Excluding adjustment for underenumeration.

REGIONS
(official estimates, mid-2007)

	Area (sq km)	Population	Density (per sq km)	Capital
De Tarapacá	59,099.1	481,729	8.2	Iquique
De Antofagasta	126,049.1	554,773	4.4	Antofagasta
De Atacama	75,176.2	274,436	3.7	Copiapó
De Coquimbo	40,579.9	687,659	16.9	La Serena
De Valparaíso	16,396.1	1,701,293	103.8	Valparaíso
Del Libertador Gen. Bernardo O'Higgins	16,387.0	857,677	52.3	Rancagua
Del Maule	30,296.1	983,396	32.5	Talca
Del Biobío	37,062.6	1,996,099	53.9	Concepción
De la Araucanía	31,842.3	945,544	29.7	Temuco
De Los Lagos	67,013.1	1,180,168	17.6	Puerto Montt
Aisén del Gen. Carlos Ibáñez del Campo	108,494.4	101,523	0.9	Coihaique
De Magallanes y Antártica Chilena	132,297.2	157,032	1.2	Punta Arenas
Metropolitan Region (Santiago)	15,403.2	6,676,745	433.5	—
Total	756,096.3	16,598,074	22.0	—

PRINCIPAL TOWNS
(2002 census)

Gran Santiago (capital)	4,668,473	Talca	201,797
Puente Alto	492,915	Arica	185,268
Antofagasta	296,905	Puerto Montt	175,938
Viña del Mar	286,931	Los Angeles	166,556
Valparaíso	275,982	Coquimbo	163,036
Talcahuano	250,348	Chillán	161,953
San Bernardo	246,762	La Serena	160,148
Temuco	245,347	Osorno	145,475
Iquique	216,419	Valdivia	140,559
Concepción	216,061	Calama	138,402
Rancagua	214,344		

BIRTHS, MARRIAGES AND DEATHS

	Registered live births*		Registered marriages		Registered deaths	
	Number	Rate (per 1,000)	Number	Rate (per 1,000)	Number	Rate (per 1,000)
1997	273,641	18.7	78,077	5.3	78,472	5.4
1998	270,637	18.3	73,456	5.0	80,257	5.4
1999	263,867	17.6	69,765	4.6	81,984	5.5
2000	261,993	17.2	66,607	4.4	78,814	5.2
2001	259,059	16.8	64,088	4.2	81,873	5.3
2002	251,559	16.1	60,971	3.9	81,079	5.2
2003	246,827	15.6	56,659	3.6	83,672	5.3
2004	230,352	15.1	53,403	3.3	86,138	5.4

* Adjusted for underenumeration.

Expectation of life (years at birth, WHO estimates): 77.5 (males 74.3; females 80.8) in 2005 (Source: WHO, *World Health Statistics*).

ECONOMICALLY ACTIVE POPULATION*
('000 persons aged 15 years and over, October–December)

	2003	2004	2005
Agriculture, hunting, forestry and fishing	771.8	783.2	777.1
Mining and quarrying	71.9	73.8	74.3
Manufacturing	797.2	805.1	775.0
Electricity, gas and water	31.2	31.9	34.8
Construction	427.4	473.0	471.3
Trade, restaurants and hotels	1,066.8	1,127.5	1,114.8
Transport, storage and communications	483.3	461.2	471.5
Financing, insurance, real estate and business services	453.5	472.6	521.2
Community, social and personal services	1,572.1	1,634.7	1,665.1
Total employed	5,675.1	5,862.9	5,905.0
Unemployed	453.1	494.7	440.4
Total labour force	6,128.2	6,357.6	6,345.4

* Figures are based on sample surveys, covering 36,000 households, and exclude members of the armed forces. Estimates are made independently, therefore totals are not always the sum of the component parts.

Health and Welfare

KEY INDICATORS

Total fertility rate (children per woman, 2005)	2.0
Under-5 mortality rate (per 1,000 live births, 2005)	10
HIV/AIDS (% of persons aged 15–49, 2005)	0.3
Physicians (per 1,000 head, 2003)	1.09
Hospital beds (per 1,000 head, 2004)	2.40
Health expenditure (2004): US $ per head (PPP)	720.3
Health expenditure (2004): % of GDP	6.1
Health expenditure (2004): public (% of total)	47.0
Access to water (% of persons, 2004)	95
Access to sanitation (% of persons, 2004)	94
Human Development Index (2005): ranking	40
Human Development Index (2005): value	0.867

For sources and definitions, see explanatory note on p. vi.

Agriculture

PRINCIPAL CROPS
('000 metric tons)

	2004	2005	2006
Wheat	1,922	1,852	1,404
Rice (paddy)	119	117	160
Barley	56	102	137
Maize	1,321	1,508	1,382
Oats	539	357	435
Potatoes	1,144	1,116	1,391
Sugar beet	2,278	2,598	2,200
Dry beans	49	45	50
Rapeseed	19	44	57
Cabbages*	61	62	62
Lettuce*	89	90	90
Tomatoes*	1,200	1,230	1,230
Pumpkins, squash and gourds*	100	103	103
Green chillies and peppers*	63	64	64
Dry onions*	365	380	380
Carrots*	100	101	101
Green corn*	252	255	255
Watermelons*	84	85	85
Cantaloupes and other melons*	67	70	70
Oranges	140	142*	142*
Lemons and limes	165	167*	167*
Apples	1,300	1,350*	1,350*
Pears	210	212*	212*
Peaches and nectarines	311	315*	315*
Plums	250	255*	255*
Grapes	1,900	2,250	2,250*
Avocados	160	163*	163*
Kiwi fruit	145	150*	150*

* FAO estimate(s).

Aggregate production ('000 metric tons, may include official, semi-official or estimated data): Total cereals 3,999 in 2004, 3,989 in 2005, 3,566 in 2006; Total roots and tubers 1,153 in 2004, 1,125 in 2005, 1,400 in 2006; Total vegetables (incl. melons) 2,726 in 2004, 2,793 in 2005, 2,793 in 2006; Total fruits (excl. melons) 4,735 in 2004, 5,171 in 2005, 5,171 in 2006.

Source: FAO.

LIVESTOCK
('000 head, year ending September)

	2003	2004	2005
Horses*	650	660	670
Cattle	3,932†	3,989†	4,200*
Pigs*	3,200	3,215	3,450
Sheep*	4,100	3,680	3,400
Goats*	715	725	735
Chickens*	78,000	88,000	95,000
Turkeys*	21,800	25,700	26,500

* FAO estimate(s).
† Unofficial figure.

2006: Figures assumed to be unchanged from 2005 (FAO estimates).
Source: FAO.

LIVESTOCK PRODUCTS
('000 metric tons)

	2004	2005	2006
Cattle meat	208.3	215.6	237.6
Sheep meat	9.5	9.2	11.1
Pig meat	372.8	410.7	467.9
Horse meat	9.6	8.8	9.4
Chicken meat	446.2	456.7	517.0
Cows' milk	2,250	2,300	2,400
Goats' milk*	9.8	9.9	9.9
Hen eggs†	1,195.5	1,265.4	1,265.4
Wool: greasy*	15.1	14.0	14.0

* FAO estimates.
† Unofficial figures.
Source: FAO.

Forestry

ROUNDWOOD REMOVALS
('000 cubic metres, excluding bark)

	2004	2005	2006
Sawlogs, veneer logs and logs for sleepers	15,985	17,921	18,725
Pulpwood	13,223	14,329	14,283
Other industrial wood	269	279	209
Fuel wood	13,111*	13,113	13,113
Total	42,588	45,642	46,330

* FAO estimate.
Source: FAO.

SAWNWOOD PRODUCTION
('000 cubic metres, including railway sleepers)

	2004	2005	2006
Coniferous (softwood)	7,754	7,978	8,378
Broadleaved (hardwood)	261	320	340
Total	8,015	8,298	8,718

Source: FAO.

Fishing

('000 metric tons, live weight)

	2003	2004	2005
Capture	3,612.9	4,918.7	4,330.3
Patagonian grenadier	85.9	71.2	79.8
Araucanian herring	304.0	356.1	289.5
Anchoveta (Peruvian anchovy)	823.2	1,859.6	1,548.8
Chilean jack mackerel	1,421.3	1,451.6	1,430.4
Chub mackerel	572.1	577.3	280.8
Jumbo flying squid	15.2	175.1	297.0
Aquaculture	563.4	645.7	682.7
Atlantic salmon	280.5	354.5	374.4
Coho (silver) salmon	95.3	88.6	102.9
Total catch	4,176.3	5,564.4	5,013.0

Note: Figures exclude aquatic plants ('000 metric tons): 349.1 in 2003 (capture 309.1, aquaculture 40.1); 410.3 in 2004 (capture 390.6, aquaculture 19.7); 425.3 in 2005 (capture 409.9, aquaculture 15.5).
Source: FAO.

Mining

('000 metric tons, unless otherwise indicated)

	2003	2004	2005
Copper (metal content)	4,904	5,413	5,321
Coal	347	238	732
Iron ore*	8,011	8,004	7,862
Calcium carbonate	5,905	6,516	6,783
Zinc—metal content (metric tons)	33,051	27,635	28,841
Molybdenum—metal content (metric tons)	33,375	41,883	47,748
Manganese (metric tons)†	19,641	25,801	39,786
Gold (kilograms)	38,954	39,986	40,447
Silver (kilograms)	1,313	1,360	1,400
Petroleum (crude)	1,319	1,292	1,208

* Gross weight. The estimated iron content is 61%.
† Gross weight. The estimated metal content is 32%.
Source: US Geological Survey.

Industry

SELECTED PRODUCTS
('000 metric tons, unless otherwise indicated)

	1999	2000	2001
Refined sugar	434	432	476
Beer (million litres)	334	322	337
Wine*	480.7	667.4	565.2
Soft drinks (million litres)	1,154	1,225	2,212
Cigarettes (million)	13,271	13,796	13,305
Non-rubber footwear ('000 pairs)	6,237	5,735	5,251
Particle board ('000 cu metres)	301	366	360
Mattresses ('000)	1,082	1,132	1,016
Sulphuric acid	2,436	2,363	2,736
Jet fuel	603	569	693
Motor spirit (petrol)	2,129	2,170	2,035
Kerosene	227	147	168
Distillate fuel oils	3,436	3,716	3,797
Residual fuel oils	1,425	1,592	1,574
Cement	2,508	2,686	3,145
Tyres ('000)	2,551	3,084	3,246
Glass sheets ('000 sq metres)	21,523	23,180	20,714
Blister copper	2,835	1,460	1,503
Refined copper, unwrought	2,666	2,668	2,882
Copper wire	5.8	5.9	5.7
Electric energy (million kWh)	38,389	41,268	43,918

2002 ('000 metric tons, unless otherwise indicated): Refined sugar 532; Wine 562.3*; Cigarettes (million) 13,839; Non-rubber footwear ('000 pairs) 5,280; Particle board ('000 cu metres) 448; Mattresses ('000) 1,126; Sulphuric acid 2,720; Jet fuel 126; Kerosene 152; Residual fuel oils 1,368; Cement 3,522; Blister copper 1,439; Refined copper, unwrought 2,850; Electric energy 45,983m. kWh.

2003 ('000 metric tons, unless otherwise indicated): Wine 668.2*; Cigarettes (million) 13,776; Non-rubber footwear ('000 pairs) 6,257; Mattresses ('000) 1,144; Sulphuric acid 2,866; Cement 3,550; Blister copper 1,542; Refined copper, unwrought 2,900; Electric energy 45,239m. kWh.

2004: Wine 729,723 metric tons*; Electric energy 45,239m. kWh.

2005: Wine 934,012 metric tons*; Electric energy 51,575m. kWh.

2006: Wine 977,087 metric tons*.

* Source: FAO.

Source (unless otherwise indicated): UN, *Industrial Commodity Statistics Yearbook*.

Finance

CURRENCY AND EXCHANGE RATES

Monetary Units
100 centavos = 1 Chilean peso.

Sterling, Dollar and Euro Equivalents (31 December 2007)
£1 sterling = 993.33 pesos;
US $1 = 495.82 pesos;
€1 = 729.90 pesos;
10,000 Chilean pesos = £10.07 = $20.17 = €13.70.

Average Exchange Rate (pesos per US $)
2005   560.090
2006   530.287
2007   522.501

GOVERNMENT FINANCE
(general government transactions, non-cash basis, million pesos)

Summary of Balances

	2004	2005	2006
Revenue	12,832,297	15,747,230	20,060,506
Less Expense	9,790,190	10,681,807	11,745,634
Net operating balance	3,042,107	5,065,423	8,314,872
Less Net acquisition of non-financial assets	1,797,639	2,043,679	2,330,764
Net lending/borrowing	1,244,468	3,021,744	5,984,108

Revenue

	2004	2005	2006
Net tax revenue	9,112,333	11,185,098	13,221,062
Gross copper revenue	1,767,108	2,440,441	4,431,123
Social security contributions	827,629	931,717	1,050,396
Grants	41,650	72,815	92,689
Property income	233,601	227,510	363,202
Operating revenue	386,569	416,132	440,315
Other revenue	463,407	473,517	461,719
Total	12,832,297	15,747,230	20,060,506

Expense

Expense by economic type	2004	2005	2006
Compensation of employees	2,301,577	2,517,513	2,760,449
Use of goods and services	998,037	1,217,319	1,397,872
Interest	560,977	556,028	539,103
Subsidies and grants	3,003,058	3,299,211	3,690,111
Social benefits	2,848,719	3,075,553	3,346,885
Other expense	77,822	16,183	11,214
Total	9,790,190	10,681,807	11,745,634

Source: Dirección de Presupuestos, Santiago.

INTERNATIONAL RESERVES
(US $ million at 31 December)

	2004	2005	2006
Gold (national valuation)	3.0	3.3	4.3
IMF special drawing rights	52.6	52.3	54.2
Reserve position in IMF	445.8	187.8	112.8
Foreign exchange	15,495.4	16,689.1	19,225.0
Total	15,996.8	16,932.5	19,396.3

Source: IMF, *International Financial Statistics*.

MONEY SUPPLY
('000 million pesos at 31 December)

	2004	2005	2006
Currency outside banks	1,626.6	1,876.9	2,149.4
Demand deposits at commercial banks	4,148.2	4,676.8	5,469.3
Total money	5,774.8	6,553.7	7,618.6

Source: IMF, *International Financial Statistics*.

COST OF LIVING
(Consumer Price Index for Santiago; base: 2000 = 100)

	2004	2005	2006
Food (incl. beverages)	104.4	107.4	110.6
Rent, fuel and light	118.4	122.1	127.5
Clothing (incl. footwear)	84.0	83.0	82.4
All items (incl. others)	110.3	113.6	117.5

Source: ILO.

NATIONAL ACCOUNTS
('000 million pesos at current prices)

Expenditure on the Gross Domestic Product

	2004*	2005*	2006†
Government final consumption expenditure	6,660.2	7,255.1	7,781.8
Private final consumption expenditure	34,695.2	38,772.5	42,527.1
Increase in stocks	568.4	1,160.0	875.6
Gross fixed capital formation	11,153.8	13,733.0	14,887.7
Total domestic expenditure	53,077.5	60,920.5	66,072.1
Exports of goods and services	23,739.2	27,332.5	35,129.7
Less Imports of goods and services	18,412.1	21,654.0	23,864.1
GDP in purchasers' values	58,404.6	66,599.0	77,337.7
GDP at constant 2003 prices	54,217.4	57,315.5	59,588.8

CHILE

Gross Domestic Product by Economic Activity

	2004*	2005*	2006†
Agriculture and forestry	1,906.1	2,104.5	2,279.7
Fishing	603.2	637.9	720.5
Mining and quarrying	7,491.5	10,536.8	17,799.4
Copper	6,717.6	9,496.4	16,695.7
Manufacturing	9,288.0	9,859.6	9,891.6
Electricity, gas and water	1,587.4	1,903.2	2,207.5
Construction	3,669.3	4,332.9	4,939.5
Trade, restaurants and hotels	5,333.2	5,863.6	6,041.3
Transport	4,116.7	4,275.7	4,285.9
Communications	1,241.7	1,348.3	1,484.9
Financial services‡	8,390.5	9,496.8	10,177.2
Sale of real estate	3,072.4	3,273.8	3,460.5
Personal services§	6,279.0	6,628.1	6,996.9
Public administration	2,362.0	2,610.5	2,780.7
Sub-total	55,341.1	62,871.9	73,065.6
Value-added tax	4,386.2	5,124.5	5,677.0
Import duties	472.8	545.9	635.0
Less Imputed bank service charge	1,795.4	1,943.6	2,039.9
GDP in purchasers' values	58,404.6	66,599.0	77,337.7

* Provisional figures.
† Preliminary data.
‡ Including insurance, renting of property and business loans.
§ Including education.

BALANCE OF PAYMENTS
(US $ million)

	2004	2005	2006
Exports of goods f.o.b.	32,520	41,297	58,116
Imports of goods f.o.b.	−22,935	−30,492	−35,903
Trade balance	9,585	10,805	22,213
Exports of services	6,034	7,020	7,504
Imports of services	−6,780	−7,656	−8,426
Balance on goods and services	8,839	10,169	21,291
Other income received	1,983	2,452	3,342
Other income paid	−9,820	−13,097	−22,734
Balance on goods, services and income	1,003	−476	1,900
Current transfers received	1,411	2,236	3,888
Current transfers paid	−339	−445	−532
Current balance	2,074	1,315	5,256
Capital account (net)	5	41	13
Direct investment abroad	−1,563	−2,209	−2,876
Direct investment from abroad	7,173	6,960	7,952
Portfolio investment assets	−4,430	−4,218	−10,851
Portfolio investment liabilities	1,122	1,594	843
Financial derivatives assets	639	1,244	1,501
Financial derivatives liabilities	−723	−1,307	−1,197
Other investment assets	−3,389	−2,399	−3,675
Other investment liabilities	−829	1,958	3,496
Net errors and omissions	−270	−1,268	1,537
Overall balance	−191	1,711	1,998

Source: IMF, *International Financial Statistics*.

External Trade

PRINCIPAL COMMODITIES
(distribution by SITC, US $ million)

Imports c.i.f.	2004	2005	2006
Food and live animals	1,446.1	1,630.3	2,100.2
Mineral fuels, lubricants, etc.	4,654.5	6,526.1	8,447.7
Petroleum, petroleum products, etc.	3,697.6	5,354.0	7,154.4
Gas, natural and manufactured	672.7	822.7	821.5
Chemicals and related products	2,869.5	3,435.3	3,921.5
Basic manufactures	2,916.3	3,504.1	4,034.9
Iron and steel	697.7	852.8	1,023.9
Machinery and transport equipment	7,440.1	10,749.2	11,705.4
Machinery specialized for particular industries	1,008.4	1,747.8	1,482.1
General industrial machinery equipment and parts	1,107.2	1,605.2	1,750.5
Office machines and automatic data-processing equipment	648.4	826.2	964.1
Telecommunications and sound equipment	1,035.7	1,303.6	1,783.4
Other electrical machinery apparatus, etc.	855.1	1,094.8	1,302.2
Road vehicles and parts*	2,159.4	3,254.7	3,436.2
Miscellaneous manufactured articles	2,184.2	2,574.3	3,154.0
Total (incl. others)	24,871.2	32,636.6	38,489.6

* Data on parts exclude tyres, engines and electrical parts.

Exports f.o.b.	2004	2005	2006
Food and live animals	6,090.4	6,967.3	7,971.3
Fish, crustaceans and molluscs and preparations thereof	2,136.4	2,502.6	2,998.8
Vegetables and fruit	2,663.8	2,861.7	3,246.6
Feeding-stuff for animals (excl. unmilled cereals)	374.8	499.8	550.6
Beverages and tobacco	873.3	920.3	1,011.1
Beverages	853.2	893.7	980.7
Crude materials (inedible) except fuels	9,419.4	12,955.9	19,476.0
Cork and wood	1,146.5	1,167.5	1,283.0
Pulp and waste paper	1,218.2	1,202.0	1,341.1
Metalliferous ores and metal scrap	6,709.2	10,189.2	16,444.9
Copper ores and concentrates, matte and cement copper	5,007.8	6,687.3	12,991.2
Chemicals and related products	1,648.1	2,102.5	2,455.8
Basic manufactures	11,261.6	14,151.1	23,636.4
Non-ferrous metals	9,693.4	12,032.7	21,209.9
Copper	9,332.8	11,616.4	20,349.1
Machinery and transport equipment	490.4	844.5	806.6
Total (incl. others)	32,024.9	40,573.9	58,995.5

CHILE

Statistical Survey

PRINCIPAL TRADING PARTNERS
(US $ million)

Imports c.i.f.	2004	2005	2006
Argentina	4,151.8	4,806.4	4,508.7
Brazil	2,781.3	3,779.5	4,242.6
Canada	347.7	406.1	482.4
China, People's Republic	1,847.3	2,542.3	3,490.3
Colombia	294.2	345.1	363.6
Finland	197.0	514.0	263.2
France	509.8	682.0	705.9
Germany	829.0	1,180.1	1,248.6
Italy	445.0	519.7	630.0
Japan	797.8	1,013.1	1,147.3
Korea, Republic	698.6	1,076.3	1,640.7
Mexico	620.2	763.9	1,003.0
Nigeria	376.3	259.6	454.1
Peru	695.1	1,108.4	1,427.1
Spain	515.4	619.9	708.7
Sweden	264.2	450.8	353.3
United Kingdom	219.3	266.4	295.4
USA	3,380.5	4,716.9	5,578.8
Venezuela	172.9	135.9	202.1
Total (incl. others)	24,871.2	32,636.6	38,489.6

Exports f.o.b.	2004	2005	2006
Argentina	423.7	604.1	731.8
Belgium	331.0	381.8	733.0
Brazil	1,410.6	1,773.4	2,875.9
Canada	776.5	1,079.0	1,299.9
China, People's Republic	3,222.2	4,595.9	5,297.1
Colombia	309.6	341.0	483.6
Ecuador	313.8	333.7	398.5
France	1,286.3	1,419.3	2,436.0
Germany	906.6	965.6	1,797.2
India	427.6	540.6	1,727.7
Italy	1,350.8	1,704.8	2,896.5
Japan	3,722.6	4,757.0	6,589.5
Korea, Republic	1,824.3	2,300.3	3,637.7
Mexico	1,291.4	1,568.5	2,269.8
Netherlands	1,696.9	2,356.5	3,931.7
Peru	498.0	681.7	880.4
Spain	743.4	991.4	1,408.3
United Kingdom	885.1	656.9	688.9
USA	4,863.4	6,600.8	9,294.6
Venezuela	261.4	345.4	484.6
Total (incl. others)	32,024.9	40,573.9	58,995.5

Transport

PRINCIPAL RAILWAYS

	2004	2005	2006
Passenger journeys ('000)	13,328	11,313	18,563
Passenger-kilometres ('000)	820,015	752,700	843,131
Freight ('000 metric tons)	25,305	25,330	25,747
Freight ton-kilometres (million)	3,898	3,848	3,660

ROAD TRAFFIC
(motor vehicles in use)

	2004	2005	2006
Passenger cars and jeeps (excl. taxis)	1,387,942	1,490,540	1,599,152
Buses and coaches (incl. taxis)	178,328	186,445	n.a.
Lorries and vans (excl. specialized vehicles)	694,376	724,124	n.a.
Motorcycles and mopeds	22,870	27,741	40,689

SHIPPING

Merchant Fleet
(registered at 31 December)

	2004	2005	2006
Number of vessels	539	543	549
Total displacement ('000 grt)	947.1	908.0	935.6

Source: Lloyd's Register-Fairplay, *World Fleet Statistics*.

International Sea-borne Shipping
(freight traffic, '000 metric tons)

	2003	2004	2005
Goods loaded	39,712	41,724	44,803
Goods unloaded	18,026	22,666	25,874

CIVIL AVIATION
(traffic on scheduled services)

	2003	2004	2005
Kilometres flown (million)	107	110	119
Passengers ('000)	6,319.2	6,618.9	7,222.3
Passenger-km (million)	17,363	17,702	19,006
Freight (million ton-km)	3,683	3,715	4,026

Tourism

ARRIVALS BY NATIONALITY

	2004	2005	2006
Argentina	576,817	606,567	684,406
Bolivia	134,709	177,278	231,062
Brazil	119,271	167,291	179,348
France	48,098	53,492	55,357
Germany	58,857	68,225	65,139
Peru	186,088	221,384	237,457
Spain	50,472	60,078	62,201
United Kingdom	50,286	53,021	58,512
USA	166,321	183,833	199,524
Total (incl. others)	1,785,024	2,027,082	2,252,952

Source: Servicio Nacional de Turismo.

Tourism receipts (US $ million, incl. passenger transport): 1,221 in 2002; 1,241 in 2003; 1,554 in 2004 (Source: World Tourism Organization).

CHILE   *Directory*

Communications Media

	2004	2005	2006
Telephones ('000 main lines in use)	3,318.3	3,435.9	3,326.4
Mobile cellular telephones ('000 subscribers)	9,566.6	10,569.6	12,450.8
Personal computers ('000 in use)	2,138	2,300	n.a.
Internet users ('000)	4,300	4,511	6,705

Radio receivers ('000 in use): 5,180 in 1997.

Facsimile machines: 40,000 in use in 1997.

Daily newspapers: 59 in 2004 (average circulation 816,000 copies).

Sources: mainly UNESCO, *Statistical Yearbook*; UN, *Statistical Yearbook*; International Telecommunication Union.

Education

(2004, unless otherwise indicated)

	Institutions	Teachers	Students
Pre-primary		16,528	287,454
Special primary		7,673	92,536
Primary	n.a.*	75,854	2,269,388
Secondary		49,144	989,039
Adult		1,897†	131,237
Higher (incl. universities)†	226	n.a.	567,114

* Many schools offer more than one level of education; a detailed breakdown is given below.
† Figure(s) for 2003.

Schools (2004): Pre-primary: 640; Special 766; Primary 3,679; Secondary 517; Adult 292; Pre-primary and special 10; Pre-primary and primary 3,172; Pre-primary and secondary 1; Special and primary 22; Special and adult 3; Primary and secondary 380; Primary and adult 82; Secondary and adult 156; Pre-primary, special and primary 52; Pre-primary, primary and secondary 1,070; Pre-primary, primary and adult 261; Special, primary and secondary 2; Primary, secondary and adult 49; Pre-primary, special, primary and secondary 13; Pre-primary, special, primary and adult 7; Pre-primary, primary, secondary and adult 106; Pre-primary, special, primary, secondary and adult 5.

Adult literacy rate (UNESCO estimates): 95.7% (males 95.8%; females 95.6%) in 2002 (Source: UNESCO Institute for Statistics).

Directory

The Constitution

The 1981 Constitution, described as a 'transition to democracy', separated the presidency from the Junta and provided for presidential elections and for the re-establishment of the bicameral legislature, consisting of an upper chamber (Senado) of both elected and appointed senators, who are to serve an eight-year term, and a lower chamber (Cámara de Diputados) of 120 deputies elected for a four-year term. There is a National Security Council consisting of the President of the Republic, the heads of the Armed Forces and the police, and the Presidents of the Supreme Court and the Senado.

In July 1989 a national referendum approved 54 reforms to the Constitution, including 47 proposed by the Government and seven by the Military Junta. Among provisions made within the articles were an increase in the number of directly elected senators from 26 to 38, the abolition of the need for the approval of two successive Congresos for constitutional amendments (the support of two-thirds of the Cámara de Diputados and the Senado being sufficient), the reduction in term of office for the President to be elected in 1989 from eight to four years, with no immediate re-election possible, and the redrafting of the provision that outlawed Marxist groups so as to ensure 'true and responsible political pluralism'. The President's right to dismiss the Congreso and sentence to internal exile were eliminated.

In November 1991 the Congreso approved constitutional changes to local government. The amendments provided for the replacement of centrally appointed local officials with directly elected representatives.

In February 1994 an amendment to the Constitution was approved whereby the length of the presidential term was reduced from eight to six years.

In September 2005 constitutional reforms came into force reducing the presidential term from six to four years, abolishing the positions of senators-for-life and appointed senators and providing for a presidential prerogative to dismiss the Commanders-in-Chief of the Armed Forces.

The Government

HEAD OF STATE

President: MICHELLE BACHELET JERIA (took office 11 March 2006).

THE CABINET
(April 2008)

A coalition of parties represented in the Concertación de los Partidos de la Democracia (CPD—including the Partido Demócrata Cristiano—PDC, the Partido Socialista de Chile—PS, the Partido por la Democracia—PPD, and the Partido Radical Socialdemócrata—PRSD).

Minister of the Interior: EDMUNDO PÉREZ YOMA (PDC).
Minister of Foreign Affairs: ALEJANDRO FOXLEY RIOSECO (PDC).
Minister of National Defence: JOSÉ GOÑI CARRACSO (PPD).
Minister of Finance: ANDRÉS VELASCO BRAÑES (Ind.).
Minister, Secretary-General of the Presidency: JOSÉ ANTONIO VIERA-GALLO QUESNEY (PS).
Minister, Secretary-General of the Government: FRANCISCO VIDAL SALINAS (PPD).
Minister of the Economy, Economic Promotion and Reconstruction: HUGO LAVADOS MONTES (PDC).
Minister of Mining: SANTIAGO GONZÁLEZ LARRAÍN (PRSD).
Minister of Planning: PAULA QUINTANA MELÉNDEZ (PS).
Minister of Education: MÓNICA JIMÉNEZ DE LA JARA (Ind.).
Minister of Justice: CARLOS MALDONADO CURTI (PRSD).
Minister of Labour and Social Security: OSVALDO ANDRADE LARA (PS).
Minister of Public Works: SERGIO BITAR CHACRA (PPD).
Minister of Health: MARÍA SOLEDAD BARRÍA IROUME (PS).
Minister of Housing and Urban Development: PATRICIA POBLETE BENNETT (PDC).
Minister of Agriculture: MARIGEN HORNKOHL VENEGAS (PDC).
Minister of the National Women's Service (Sernam): LAURA ALBORNOZ POLLMANN (PDC).
Minister of Transport and Telecommunications: RENÉ CORTÁZAR SANZ (PDC).
Minister of Territorial Management: ROMY SCHMIDT CRNOSIJA (PDC).
Minister of the National Commission for Culture and the Arts: PAULINA URRUTIA FERNÁNDEZ.
Minister of the National Energy Commission: MARCELO TOKMAN RAMOS.
Minister of the National Environment Commission: ANA LYA URIARTE RODRÍGUEZ.

MINISTRIES

Ministry of Agriculture: Teatinos 40, Santiago; tel. (2) 393-5000; fax (2) 393-5050; internet www.agricultura.gob.cl.

Ministry of the Economy, Economic Promotion and Reconstruction: Teatinos 120, 10°, Santiago; tel. (2) 672-5522; fax (2) 696-6305; e-mail economia@economia.cl; internet www.economia.cl.

Ministry of Education: Alameda 1371, 7°, Santiago; tel. (2) 390-4000; fax (2) 380-0317; e-mail consultas@mineduc.cl; internet www.mineduc.cl.

Ministry of Finance: Teatinos 120, 12°, Santiago; tel. (2) 675-5800; fax (2) 671-8064; e-mail webmaster@minhda.cl; internet www.minhda.cl.

Ministry of Foreign Affairs: Catedral 1158, Santiago; tel. (2) 679-4200; fax (2) 699-4202; internet www.minrel.gov.cl.

Ministry of Health: Enrique MacIver 541, 3°, Santiago; tel. (2) 639-4001; fax (2) 633-5875; e-mail consulta@minsal.cl; internet www.minsal.cl.

Ministry of Housing and Urban Development: Alameda 924, Santiago; tel. (2) 638-0801; fax (2) 633-3892; e-mail contactenos@minvu.cl; internet www.minvu.cl.

Ministry of the Interior: Palacio de la Moneda, Santiago; tel. (2) 690-4000; fax (2) 699-2165; internet www.interior.cl.

Ministry of Justice: Morandé 107, Santiago; tel. (2) 674-3100; fax (2) 698-7098; internet www.minjusticia.cl.

Ministry of Labour and Social Security: Huérfanos 1273, 6°, Santiago; tel. (2) 695-5133; fax (2) 698-8473; e-mail mintrab@mintrab.gob.cl; internet www.mintrab.gob.cl.

Ministry of Mining: Teatinos 120, 9°, Santiago; tel. (2) 473-3000; internet www.minmineria.cl.

Ministry of National Defence: Villavicencio 364, 22°, Edif. Diego Portales, Santiago; tel. (2) 222-1202; fax (2) 633-0568; internet www.defensa.cl.

Ministry of Planning (MIDEPLAN): Ahumada 48, 7°, Santiago; tel. (2) 675-1400; fax (2) 672-1879; internet www.mideplan.cl.

Ministry of Public Works: Morandé 59, Of. 545, Santiago; tel. (2) 361-2641; fax (2) 361-2700; internet www.mop.cl.

Ministry of Territorial Management: 6 Juan Antonio Rios, Santiago; tel. (2) 351-2100; fax (2) 351-2160; e-mail consultas@mbienes.cl; internet www.bienes.cl.

Ministry of Transport and Telecommunications: Amunátegui 139, 3°, Santiago; tel. (2) 421-3000; fax (2) 421-3552; e-mail mtt@mtt.cl; internet www.mtt.cl.

National Commission for Culture and the Arts: San Camilo 262, Santiago; tel. (2) 589-7824; internet www.consejodelacultura.cl.

National Energy Commission: Teatinos 120, 7°, Segundo Hall, Santiago; tel. (2) 365-6800; fax (2) 361-1118; internet www.cne.cl.

National Environment Commission: Teatinos 254/258, Santiago; tel. (2) 241-1800; fax (2) 240-5758; internet www.conama.cl.

National Women's Service (Sernam): Teatinos 950, 5°, Santiago; tel. (2) 549-6100; fax (2) 549-6148; e-mail mlobos@sernam.gov.cl; internet www.sernam.gov.cl.

Office of the Minister, Secretary-General of the Government: Palacio de la Moneda, Santiago; tel. (2) 690-4160; fax (2) 697-1756; e-mail cmladini@segegob.cl; internet www.segegob.cl.

Office of the Minister, Secretary-General of the Presidency: Palacio de la Moneda, Santiago; tel. (2) 690-4218; fax (2) 690-4329.

President and Legislature

PRESIDENT

Election, 11 December 2005 and 15 January 2006

	% of votes cast First round	% of votes cast Second round*
Michelle Bachelet Jeria (CPD)	45.95	53.49
Sebastián Piñera Echeñique (RN)	25.41	46.50
Joaquín Lavín Infante (Alianza por Chile)	23.22	—
Tomás Hirsch Goldschmidt (PH)	5.40	—
Total	100.00	100.00

* Official preliminary figures.

CONGRESO NACIONAL

Senado
(Senate)

President: ADOLFO ZALDÍVAR LARRAÍN (Ind.).

General Election, 11 December 2005*

	% of valid votes	Seats
Concertación de Partidos por la Democracia (CPD)†	55.7	20
Alianza por Chile‡	37.2	17
Juntos Podemos Más§	6.0	—
Fuerza Regional Independiente¶	0.6	—
Independents	0.4	1
Total	100.0	38

A total of 4,715,108 valid votes were cast. In addition, there were 151,373 blank and 254,712 spoiled votes
* Results of an election to renew 20 of the 38 seats in the Senado.
† Including the Partido Demócrata Cristiano (PDC), the Partido Socialista (PS), the Partido por la Democracia (PPD) and the Partido Radical Socialdemócrata (PRS).
‡ Including the Partido Unión Demócrata Independiente (UDI) and the Partido Renovación Nacional (RN).
§ Including the Partido Comunista de Chile (PCCh) and the Partido Humanista (PH).
¶ Including la Alianza Nacional de Independientes (ANI) and the Partido de Acción Regionalista (PAR).

Cámara de Diputados
(Chamber of Deputies)

President: JUAN BUSTOS RAMÍREZ (PS).

General Election, 11 December 2005

Legislative bloc	Valid votes	% of valid votes	Seats
Concertación de Partidos por la Democracia (CPD)*	3,374,865	51.77	65
Alianza por Chile†	2,522,558	38.70	54
Juntos Podemos Más‡	482,507	7.40	—
Fuerza Regional Independiente§	76,582	1.17	1
Independents	61,489	0.94	—
Total	6,518,001	100.00	120

In addition, there were 218,242 blank and 379,377 spoiled votes
* Including the Partido por la Democracia (PPD), which won 22 seats, the Partido Demócrata Cristiano (PDC), which won 20 seats, the Partido Socialista (PS), with 16 seats, and the Partido Radical Socialdemócrata (PRSD), with seven seats.
† Including the Partido Unión Demócrata Independiente (UDI), which won 34 seats, and the Partido Renovación Nacional (RN), which won 20 seats.
‡ Including the Partido Comunista de Chile (PCCh) and the Partido Humanista (PH).
§ Including la Alianza Nacional de Independientes (ANI) and the Partido de Acción Regionalista (PAR).

Election Commission

Tribunal Calificador de Elecciones (TCE): Teatinos 391, Santiago; tel. (2) 463-8500; fax (2) 699-4464; e-mail secretaria@tribunalcalificador.cl; internet www.tribunalcalificador.cl; f. 1980; Pres. RICARDO GÁLVEZ BLANCO.

Political Organizations

Alianza por Chile: Santiago; f. 1996 as the Unión por Chile; name changed to above in 1999; right-wing alliance; Leader JOAQUÍN LAVÍN INFANTE.

Partido Renovación Nacional (RN): Antonio Varas 454, Providencia, Santiago; tel. (2) 373-8740; fax (2) 373-8704; e-mail cmonckeberg@rn.cl; internet www.rn.cl; f. 1987; right-wing; Pres. CARLOS LARRAÍN PEÑA; Sec.-Gen. LILY PÉREZ SAN MARTÍN.

Partido Unión Demócrata Independiente (UDI): Suecia 286, Providencia, Santiago; tel. (2) 241-4200; fax (2) 233-6189; e-mail udi@caudi.cl; internet www.udi.cl; f. 1989; right-wing; Pres. HERNÁN LARRAÍN FERNÁNDEZ; Sec.-Gen. DARÍO PAYA MIRA.

Chile Primero: Santiago; e-mail contacto@chileprimero.cl; internet www.chileprimero.cl; f. 2007 by fmr mems of the PPD (q.v.); independent; Pres. FERNANDO FLORES; Vice-Pres. ESTEBAN VALENZUELA.

Concertación de Partidos por la Democracia (CPD): Londres 57, Santiago; tel. and fax (2) 639-7170; f. 1988 as the Comando por el No, an opposition front to campaign against the military regime in the plebiscite of 5 October 1988; name changed to above following plebiscite.

Partido Demócrata Cristiano (PDC): Alameda 1460, 2°, Santiago; tel. and fax (2) 757-4400; e-mail info@pdc.cl; internet www.pdc.cl; f. 1957; Pres. SOLEDAD ALVEAR VALENZUELA; Sec. MOISÉS VALENZUELA MARTÍNEZ.

Partido por la Democracia (PPD): Erasmo Escala 2154, Santiago; tel. (2) 735-2824; fax (2) 735-1692; internet www.ppd.cl; f. 1989; Pres. SERGIO BITAR CHACRA; Sec.-Gen. PEPE AUTH STEWART.

Partido Radical Socialdemócrata (PRSD): Miraflores 495, Santiago; tel. and fax (2) 632-2161; e-mail rnavarreteb@yahoo.com; internet www.partidoradical.cl; centre-left; allied to CPD; Pres. JOSÉ ANTONIO GÓMEZ URRUTIA; Sec.-Gen. ERNESTO VELASCO RODRÍGUEZ.

Partido Socialista de Chile (PS): Paris 873, Santiago; tel. (2) 630-6900; fax (2) 672-0507; e-mail redes@pschile.cl; internet www.pschile.cl; f. 1933; left-wing; mem. of Socialist International; Pres. CAMILO ESCALONA MEDINA.

Izquierda Cristiana (IC): Compañía 2404, Santiago; tel. (2) 672-9897; e-mail contacto@izquierdacristiana.cl; f. 1971; Pres. MANUEL JACQUES; Sec.-Gen. BERNARDA PÉREZ.

Juntos Podemos Más: Avda Brasil 23, 2°, Santiago; tel. (2) 688-8323; e-mail info@podemos.cl; internet www.podemos.cl; electoral alliance comprising:

Partido Comunista de Chile (PCCh): Avda Vicuña Mackenna 31, Santiago; tel. and fax (2) 222-2750; e-mail www@pcchile.cl; internet www.pcchile.cl; f. 1912; achieved legal status in Oct. 1990; Pres. GUILLERMO TELLIER; Sec.-Gen. LAUTARO CARMONA.

Partido Humanista (PH): Livingstone 72, Santiago; tel. (2) 634-2614; e-mail Info@partidohumanista.cl; internet www.partidohumanista.cl; Pres. EFREN OSORIO JARA; Sec.-Gen. MARILEN CABRERA OLMOS.

Partido Militar Metropolitano: Santiago; f. 2007 by fmr mems of the military during the Pinochet regime; Leader GABRIEL FUENTES CAMPUZANO.

Partido Regionalista de los Independientes (PRI): Avda Constitución 218, Of. 2, Santiago; tel. and fax (2) 738-0886; e-mail contacto@partido-ani.cl; internet www.partido-ani.cl; f. 2006 following merger of Alianza National de Independientes and Partido de Acción Regionalista de Chile; contested 2005/06 elections as the Fuerza Regional Independiente electoral alliance; Pres. JUAN CARLOS MORAGA DUQUE.

Wallmapuwen: Santiago; e-mail wallmapuwen@gmail.com; internet www.wallmapuwen.cl; f. 2006; campaigns for Mapuche rights; Sec.-Gen. PEDRO GUSTAVO QUILAQUEO.

Diplomatic Representation

EMBASSIES IN CHILE

Argentina: Miraflores 285, Santiago; tel. (2) 582-2500; fax (2) 639-3321; e-mail embajador@embargentina.cl; internet www.embargentina.cl; Ambassador CARLOS ENRIQUE ABIHAGGLE.

Australia: Isidora Goyenechea 3621, 12° y 13°, Casilla 33, Correo 10 Las Condes, Santiago; tel. (2) 550-3500; fax (2) 331-5960; e-mail consular.santiago@dfat.gov.au; internet www.chile.embassy.gov.au; Ambassador CRISPIN CONROY.

Austria: Barros Errazuriz 1968, 3°, Santiago; tel. (2) 223-4774; fax (2) 204-9382; e-mail santiago-de-chile-ob@bmaa.gv.at; Ambassador WOLFGANG ANGERHOLZER.

Belgium: Edif. Forum, Providencia 2653, 11°, Of. 1103, Santiago; tel. (2) 232-1070; fax (2) 232-1073; e-mail santiago@diplobel.org; internet www.diplomatie.be/santiago; Ambassador FRANCIS DE SUTTER.

Brazil: Alonso Ovalle 1665, Casilla 1497, Santiago; tel. (2) 698-2486; fax (2) 671-5961; e-mail embrasil@brasembsantiago.cl; internet www.brasembsantiago.cl; Ambassador MARIO VILALVA.

Bulgaria: Rodolfo Bentjerodt 4895, Vitacura, Santiago; tel. (2) 228-3110; fax (2) 208-0404; e-mail embul@entelchile.net; Chargé d'affaires a.i. PETER D. ATANASSOV.

Canada: Edif. World Trade Center, Torre Norte, 12°, Nueva Tajamar 481, Santiago; tel. (2) 362-9660; fax (2) 362-9663; e-mail stago@international.gc.ca; internet geo.international.gc.ca/latin-america/chile; Ambassador NORBERT KALISCH.

China, People's Republic: Pedro de Valdivia 550, Santiago; tel. (2) 233-9880; fax (2) 335-2755; e-mail embajadachina@entelchile.net; internet cl.china-embassy.org/esp; Ambassador LI CHANGHUA.

Colombia: Presidente Errázuriz 3943, Las Condes, Santiago; tel. (2) 206-1314; fax (2) 208-0712; e-mail esantiag@cancilleria.gov.co; Ambassador JESÚS ALBERTO VALLEJO MEJÍA.

Costa Rica: Calle Zurich 255, Dpto 85, Las Condes, Santiago; tel. (2) 334-9486; fax (2) 334-9490; e-mail embacostarica@adsl.tie.cl; Ambassador EDGAR GARCÍA MIRANDA.

Croatia: Ezequias Alliende 2370, Providencia, Santiago; tel. (2) 269-6141; fax (2) 269-6092; e-mail embajada@croacia.cl; Ambassador BORIS MARUNA.

Cuba: Avda Los Leones 1346, Providencia, Santiago; tel. (2) 494-1485; fax (2) 494-1495; e-mail afragap@vtr.net; Ambassador ALFONSO FRAGA PÉREZ.

Czech Republic: Avda El Golf 254, Santiago; tel. (2) 232-1066; fax (2) 232-0707; e-mail santiago@embassy.mzv.cz; internet www.mfa.cz/santiago; Ambassador LUBOMÍR HLADÍK.

Denmark: Jacques Cazotte 5531, Casilla 13430, Vitacura, Santiago; tel. (2) 941-5100; fax (2) 218-1736; e-mail sclamb@um.dk; internet www.ambsantiago.um.dk/la; Ambassador KIM HØJLUND CHRISTENSEN.

Dominican Republic: Candelaria Goyenechea 4153, Vitacura, Santiago; tel. (2) 953-7570; e-mail mvelazquez@serex.gov.do; Ambassador CÉSAR MEDINA ABREU.

Ecuador: Avda Providencia 1979 y Pedro Valdivia, 5°, Santiago; tel. (2) 231-5073; fax (2) 232-5833; e-mail embajadaecuador@adsl.tie.cl; internet www.embajadaecuador.cl; Ambassador FRANCISCO BORJA CEVALLOS.

Egypt: Roberto del Río 1871, Providencia, Santiago; tel. (2) 274-8881; fax (2) 274-6334; e-mail egipto@ctcinternet.cl; Ambassador ASHRAF YOSSEF ZA'ZA.

El Salvador: Coronel 2330, 5°, Of. 51, Santiago; tel. (2) 233-8324; fax (2) 231-0960; e-mail embasalva@adsl.tie.cl; internet www.rree.gob.sv/embajadas/chile.nsf; Ambassador AIDA ELENA MINERO REYES.

Finland: Alcántara 200, Of. 201, Las Condes, Santiago; tel. (2) 263-4917; fax (2) 263-4701; e-mail sanomat.snt@formin.fi; Ambassador IIVO SALMI.

France: Condell 65, Casilla 38D, Providencia, Santiago; tel. (2) 470-8000; fax (2) 470-8050; e-mail ambassade@ambafrance-cl.org; internet www.france.cl; Ambassador ELISABETH BETON-DÉLÈGUE.

Germany: Las Hualtatas 5677, Vitacura, Santiago; tel. (2) 463-2500; fax (2) 463-2525; e-mail reg1@santi.diplo.de; internet www.santiago.diplo.de; Ambassador Dr PETER SCHOLZ.

Greece: Jorge Sexto 306, Las Condes, Santiago; tel. (2) 212-7900; fax (2) 212-8048; e-mail embassygr@tie.cl; internet www.grecia.cl; Ambassador CHRYSSOULA KARYKOPOULOU-VLAVIANOU.

Guatemala: Séptimo de Línea 1262, Providencia, Santiago; tel. (2) 264-0525; fax (2) 264-1146; e-mail embajada@guatemala.cl; internet www.embajadadeguatemala.cl; Ambassador ANTONIO R. CASTELLANOS LÓPEZ.

Haiti: Zurich 255, Of. 21, Las Condes, Santiago; tel. (2) 650-8180; fax (2) 334-0384; e-mail embhai@terra.cl; Ambassador GUY G. LAMOTHE.

Holy See: Calle Nuncio Sótero Sanz 200, Casilla 16.836, Correo 9, Santiago (Apostolic Nunciature); tel. (2) 231-2020; fax (2) 231-0868; e-mail nunciatu@entelchile.net; Nuncio Most Rev. ALDO CAVALLI (Titular Archbishop of Vibo Valentia).

Honduras: Zurich 255, Of. 51, Las Condes, Santiago; tel. (2) 234-4069; fax (2) 334-7946; e-mail honduras@entelchile.net; Ambassador FRANCISCO MARTÍNEZ.

Hungary: Avda Los Leones 2279, Providencia, Santiago; tel. (2) 247-2210; fax (2) 234-1227; e-mail huembstg@entelchile.net; internet www.mfa.gov.hu/kulkepviselet/CL/HU; Ambassador JÓZSEF KOSÁRKA.

India: Triana 871, Casilla 10433, Santiago; tel. (2) 235-2005; fax (2) 235-9607; e-mail info@embajadaindia.cl; internet www.embajadaindia.cl; Ambassador SUSMITA GONGULEE THOMAS.

Indonesia: Nueva Costanera 3318, Vitacura, Santiago; tel. (2) 207-6266; fax (2) 207-9901; e-mail kbristgo@mi-mail.cl; Ambassador IBRAHIM AMBONG.

Israel: San Sebastián 2812, 5°, Las Condes, Santiago; tel. (2) 750-0500; fax (2) 750-0555; e-mail info@santiago.mfa.gov.il; internet santiago.mfa.gov.il; Ambassador DAVID COHEN.

Italy: Clemente Fabres 1050, Providencia, Santiago; tel. (2) 470-8400; fax (2) 223-2467; e-mail info.santiago@esteri.it; internet www.ambsantiago.esteri.it; Ambassador PAOLO CASARDI.

Japan: Avda Ricardo Lyon 520, Santiago; tel. (2) 232-1807; fax (2) 232-1812; e-mail embajada.dejap001@chilnet.cl; internet www.cl.emb-japan.go.jp; Ambassador WATARU HAYASHI.

Jordan: Rosa O' Higgins 287, Las Condes, Santiago; tel. (2) 325-7748; fax (2) 325-7754; e-mail jordanem@vtr.net; Ambassador NABIL MASARWEH.

CHILE

Korea, Democratic People's Republic: Santiago; Ambassador YU CHANG UN (resident in Peru).

Korea, Republic: Alcántara 74, Casilla 1301, Santiago; tel. (2) 228-4214; fax (2) 206-2355; e-mail corembad@tie.cl; Ambassador SHIN JANG-BUM.

Lebanon: Alianza 1728, Casilla 1950, Santiago; tel. (2) 219-9724; fax (2) 219-3502; e-mail libano@netline.cl; Ambassador MOURAD JAMMAL.

Malaysia: Tajamar 183, 10° y 11°, Of. 1002, Correo 35, Las Condes, Santiago; tel. (2) 233-6698; fax (2) 234-3853; e-mail mwstg@embdemalasia.cl; internet www.kln.gov.my/perwakilan/santiago; Ambassador ABDULLAH FAIZ MOHD ZAIN.

Mexico: Félix de Amesti 128, Las Condes, Santiago; tel. (2) 583-8400; fax (2) 583-8484; e-mail info@emexico.cl; internet www.emexico.cl; Ambassador RICARDO VILLANUEVA HALLAL.

Morocco: Avda Luis Pasteur 5850, Of. 203, Vitacura, Santiago; tel. (2) 218-0311; fax (2) 219-4280; e-mail ambmarch@terra.cl; Ambassador ABDELHADI BOUCETTA.

Netherlands: Las Violetas 2368, Casilla 56-D, Santiago; tel. (2) 756-9200; fax (2) 756-9226; e-mail stg@minbuza.nl; internet www.holanda-paisesbajos.cl; Ambassador HERO DE BOER.

New Zealand: El Golf 99, Of. 703, Las Condes, Santiago; tel. (2) 290-9800; fax (2) 458-0940; e-mail embajada@nzembassy.cl; internet www.nzembassy.com/home.cfm?c=16; Ambassador NIGEL FYFE.

Nicaragua: Zurich 255, Of. 111, Las Condes, Santiago; tel. (2) 234-1808; fax (2) 234-5170; e-mail embanic@vtr.net; Ambassador MARÍA LUISA ROBLETO AGUILAR.

Norway: San Sebastián 2839, Of. 509, Casilla 2431, Santiago; tel. (2) 234-2888; fax (2) 234-2201; e-mail emb.santiago@mfa.no; internet www.noruega.cl; Ambassador PÅL MOE.

Panama: La Reconquista 640, Las Condes, Santiago; tel. (2) 202-6318; fax (2) 202-5439; e-mail embajada@panamachile.tie.cl; Ambassador ALEJANDRO YOUNG DOWNEY.

Paraguay: Huérfanos 886, 5°, Ofs 514–515, Santiago; tel. (2) 639-4640; fax (2) 633-4426; e-mail epychemb@entelchile.net; Ambassador JUAN ANDRÉS CARDOZO DOMÍNGUEZ.

Peru: Avda Andrés Bello 1751, Casilla 16277, Providencia, Santiago; tel. (2) 235-2356; fax (2) 235-8139; e-mail embstgo@entelchile.net; Ambassador HUGO OTERO LANZAROTTI.

Philippines: Félix de Amesti 367, Santiago; tel. (2) 208-1313; fax (2) 208-1400; e-mail santiagope@dfa.gov.ph; Ambassador MARÍA CONSUELO PUYAT-REYES.

Poland: Mar del Plata 2055, Santiago; tel. (2) 204-1213; fax (2) 204-9332; e-mail embajador.polonia@entelchile.net; internet www.polonia.cl; Ambassador JAROSŁAW SPYRA.

Portugal: Nueva Tajamar 555, Torre Norte 16°, Las Condes, Santiago; tel. (2) 203-0542; fax (2) 203-0545; e-mail embaixada.portugal@entelchile.net; Ambassador LUÍS FILIPE DE MENDONÇA CRISTINA DE BARROS.

Romania: Benjamín 2955, Las Condes, Santiago; tel. (2) 231-1893; fax (2) 232-3441; e-mail embajada@rumania.tie.cl; internet www.rumania.cl; Ambassador VALENTIN FLOREA.

Russia: Cristobal Colón 4152, Las Condes, Santiago; tel. (2) 208-6254; fax (2) 206-8892; e-mail embajada@rusia.tie.cl; internet www.chile.mid.ru; Ambassador YURIY A. FILÁTOV.

South Africa: Avda 11 de Septiembre 2353, 16°, Torre San Ramón, Santiago; tel. (2) 231-2860; fax (2) 231-3185; e-mail info@embajada-sudafrica.cl; internet www.embajada-sudafrica.cl; Ambassador VICTOR ZAZERAJ.

Spain: Avda Andrés Bello 1895, Casilla 16456, Providencia, Santiago; tel. (2) 235-2755; fax (2) 235-1049; e-mail embespcl@correo.mae.es; internet www.mae.es/embajadas/santiagodechile; Ambassador JOSÉ ANTONIO MARTÍNEZ DE VILLAREAL Y BAENA.

Sweden: Avda 11 de Septiembre 2353, 4°, Providencia; tel. (2) 940-1700; fax (2) 940-1730; e-mail ambassaden.santiago-de-chile@foreign.ministry.se; internet www.embajadasuecia.cl; Ambassador MARIA CHRISTINA LUNDQVIST.

Switzerland: Avda Américo Vespucio Sur 100, 14°, Las Condes, Santiago; tel. (2) 263-4211; fax (2) 263-4094; e-mail vertretung@san.rep.admin.ch; internet www.eda.admin.ch/santiago; Ambassador ANDRÉ REGLI.

Syria: Carmencita 111, Casilla 12, Correo 10, Santiago; tel. (2) 232-7471; Ambassador FARES CHAINE.

Thailand: Avda Américo Vespucio 100, 15°, Las Condes, Santiago; tel. (2) 263-0710; fax (2) 263-0803; e-mail rte.santiago@vtr.net; internet www.thaiembassy.org/santiago; Ambassador VIMON KIDCHOP.

Turkey: Edif. Montolin, Of. 71, Monseñor Sotero Sanz 55, Providencia, Santiago; tel. (2) 231-8952; fax (2) 231-7762; e-mail embturquia@123.cl; Ambassador AYSENUR ALPASLAN.

United Kingdom: Avda el Bosque Norte 0125, Casilla 72-D, Santiago; tel. (2) 370-4100; fax (2) 370-4180; e-mail embsan@britemb.cl; internet www.britemb.cl; Ambassador HOWARD DRAKE.

USA: Avda Andrés Bello 2800, Las Condes, Santiago; tel. (2) 232-2600; fax (2) 330-3710; internet www.usembassy.cl; Ambassador PAUL E. SIMONS.

Uruguay: Avda Pedro de Valdivia 711, Santiago; tel. (2) 204-7988; fax (2) 274-4066; e-mail urusgo@uruguay.cl; internet www.uruguay.cl; Ambassador JUAN CARLOS PITA ALVARIZA.

Venezuela: Bustos 2021, Providencia, Santiago; tel. (2) 225-0021; fax (2) 223-1170; e-mail emvenchi@entelchile.net; Ambassador MARÍA LOURDES URBANEJA DURANT.

Judicial System

The Supreme Court consists of 21 members.

There are Courts of Appeal (in the cities or departments of Arica, Iquique, Antofagasta, Copiapó, La Serena, Valparaíso, Santiago, San Miguel, Rancagua, Talca, Chillán, Concepción, Temuco, Valdivia, Puerto Montt, Coyhaique and Punta Arenas) whose members are appointed from a list submitted to the President of the Republic by the Supreme Court. The number of members of each court varies. Judges of the lower courts are appointed in a similar manner from lists submitted by the Court of Appeal of the district in which the vacancy arises. Judges and Ministers of the Supreme Court do not continue in office beyond the age of 75 years.

Corte Suprema
Bandera 344, 2°, Santiago; tel. (2) 873-5258; fax (2) 873-5276; e-mail mgonzalezp@poderjudicial.cl; internet www.poderjudicial.cl.

President of the Supreme Court: ENRIQUE EDMUNDO TAPIA WITTING.

Ministers of the Supreme Court: MARCOS LIBEDINSKY TSCHORNE, SERGIO MANUEL MUÑOZ GAJARDO, ALBERTO ANÍBAL CHAIGNEAU DEL CAMPO, ORLANDO ANTONIO ALVAREZ HERNÁNDEZ, URBANO MARÍN VALLEJO, MILTON IVAN JUICA ARANCIBIA, NIBALDO SEGURA PEÑA, ADALIS SALVADOR OYARZUN MIRANDA, JAIME DEL CARMEN RODRÍGUEZ ESPOZ, RUBEN ALBERTO BALLESTEROS CARCAMO, MARGARITA ELIANA HERRREROS MARTÍNEZ, HUGO ENRIQUE DOLMESTCH URRA, JUAN ARAYA ELIZALDE, RAÚL PATRICIO VALDES ALDUNATE, HÉCTOR GUILLERMO CARREÑO SEAMAN, PEDRO PIERRY ARRAU, GABRIELA PÉREZ PAREDES, SONIA MIREYA ARANEDA BRIONES, CARLOS GUILLERMO KÜNSEMÜLLER LOEBENFELDER.

Public Prosecutor: MÓNICA EUGENIA MALDONADO CROQUEVIELLE.

Secretary of the Court: CARLOS ADRIAN MENESES PIZARRO.

Religion

CHRISTIANITY

The Roman Catholic Church

Some 71% of the population are Roman Catholics; there were an estimated 11.4m. adherents at 31 December 2005. Chile comprises five archdioceses, 18 dioceses, two territorial prelatures and one apostolic vicariate.

Bishops' Conference

Conferencia Episcopal de Chile, Echaurren 4, 6°, Casilla 517-V, Correo 21, Santiago; tel. (2) 671-7733; fax (2) 698-1416; e-mail secretariageneral@episcopado.cl; internet www.iglesia.cl.

f. 1955 (statutes approved 2000); Pres. Mgr ALEJANDRO GOIĆ KARMELIĆ (Bishop of Rancagua).

Archbishop of Antofagasta: PABLO LIZAMA RIQUELME, San Martín 2628, Casilla E, Antofagasta; tel. and fax (55) 26-8856; e-mail antofagasta@episcopado.cl; internet www.iglesiadeantofagasta.cl.

Archbishop of Concepción: RICARDO EZZATI ANDRELLO, Calle Barros Arana 544, Casilla 65-C, Concepción; tel. (41) 22-8173; fax (41) 23-2844; e-mail amoreno@episcopado.cl; internet www.arzobispadodeconcepcion.cl.

Archbishop of La Serena: MANUEL GERARDO DONOSO DONOSO, Los Carrera 450, Casilla 613, La Serena; tel. (51) 21-2325; fax (51) 22-5886; e-mail laserena@episcopado.cl; internet www.iglesia.cl/laserena.

Archbishop of Puerto Montt: CRISTIÁN CARO CORDERO, Calle Benavente 385, Casilla 17, Puerto Montt; tel. (65) 25-2215; fax (65) 27-1861; e-mail puertomontt@episcopado.cl; internet www.arzobispadodepuertomontt.cl.

Archbishop of Santiago de Chile: Cardinal FRANCISCO JAVIER ERRÁZURIZ OSSA, Erasmo Escala 1884, Casilla 30-D, Santiago; tel. (2) 696-3275; fax (2) 671-2042; e-mail curiasantiago@arzobispado.tie.cl; internet www.iglesiadesantiago.cl.

CHILE   *Directory*

The Anglican Communion

Anglicans in Chile come within the Diocese of Chile, which forms part of the Anglican Church of the Southern Cone of America, covering Argentina, Bolivia, Chile, Paraguay, Peru and Uruguay.

Bishop of Chile: Rt Rev. H. F. ZAVALA M., Iglesia Anglicana, José Miguel de la Barra 480, Of. 205, Casilla 50675, Correo Central, Santiago; tel. (2) 639-1509; fax (2) 639-4581; e-mail fzavala@evangel.cl; internet www.iglesiaanglicana.cl.

Other Christian Churches

Evangelical Lutheran Church: Pedro de Valdivia 3420-H, Dpto 33, Ñuñoa, Casilla 167–11, Santiago; tel. (2) 223-3195; fax (2) 205-2193; e-mail secretaria@ielch.cl; f. 1937 as German Evangelical Church in Chile; present name adopted in 1959; Pres. GLORIA ROJAS; 3,000 mems.

Jehovah's Witnesses: Avda Concha y Toro 3456, Casilla 267, Puente Alto; tel. (2) 288-1264; fax (2) 288-1257; Dir PEDRO J. LOVATO GROSSO.

Methodist Church of Chile: Sargento Aldea 1041, Casilla 67, Santiago; tel. (2) 556-6074; fax (2) 554-1763; e-mail info@gbgm-umc.org; autonomous since 1969Bishop NEFTALÍ ARAVENA BRAVO; 7,317 mems.

Orthodox Church of the Patriarch of Antioch: Avda Perú 502, Recoleta, Santiago; tel. and fax (2) 737-4697; internet www.chileortodoxo.com; Archbishop Mgr SERGIO ABAD.

Pentecostal Church of Chile: Calle Pena 1103, Casilla de Correo 2, Curicó; tel. (75) 1035; f. 1945; Bishop ENRIQUE CHÁVEZ CAMPOS; 90,000 mems.

Pentecostal Mission Church: Calle Passy 32, Santiago; tel. (2) 634-6785; fax (2) 634-6786; f. 1952; Sec. Rev. DANIEL GODOY FERNÁNDEZ; Pres. Rev. ERASMO FARFÁN FIGUEROA; 12,000 mems.

Unión de Iglesias Evangélicas Bautistas de Chile: Casilla 41-22, Santiago; tel. (2) 264-1208; fax (2) 431-8012; e-mail centrobautista@ubach.cl; internet www.ubach.cl; f. 1908; Pres. RAQUEL CONTRERAS EDDINGER; Vice-Pres. HERNÁN MULATO H.

JUDAISM

Comité Representativo de las Entidades Judías en Chile (CREJ): Avda Padre Hurtado Norte 1880, Vitacura, Santiago; tel. and fax (2) 211-6399; Pres. GABRIEL ZALIASNIK; Exec. Dir MARCELO ISAACSON.

Comunidad Israelita Sefardi de Chile: Avda Ricardo Lyon 812, Providencia, Santiago; tel. (2) 209-8086; fax (2) 204-7382; e-mail contacto@sefardies.cl; internet www.sefaradies.cl; Pres. MERY NACHARI GALVANI; Sec.-Gen. LEÓN HASSÓN T.

ISLAM

Centro Islámico de Chile: Mezquita As-Salam, Campoamor 2975, esq. Chile-España, Ñuñoa, Santiago; tel. (2) 343-1376; fax (2) 343-1378; e-mail contacto@islamenchile.cl; internet www.islamenchile.cl; f. 1925 as the Sociedad Unión Musulmana; Sec. MOHAMED RUMIE.

BAHÁ'Í FAITH

National Spiritual Assembly: Manuel de Salas 356, Casilla 3731, Ñuñoa, Santiago; tel. (2) 269-2005; fax (2) 225-8276; e-mail secretaria@bahai.cl; internet www.bahai.cl.

The Press

Most newspapers of nation-wide circulation in Chile are published in Santiago.

DAILIES

Santiago

La Cuarta: Diagonal Vicuña Mackenna 1842, Casilla 2795, Santiago; tel. (2) 555-0034; fax (2) 555-1017; internet www.lacuarta.cl; morning; Gen. Man. JUAN CARLOS LARRAÍN WORMALD.

Diario Financiero: San Crescente 81, 2°, Las Condes, Santiago; tel. (2) 339-1000; fax (2) 231-3340; e-mail suscripciones@diariofinanciero.cl; internet www.diariofinanciero.cl; f. 1988; morning; Dir FRANCISCO JOSE COVARRUBIAS PORZIO; Gen. Man. EDUARDO POOLEY P.; circ. 20,000.

Diario Oficial de la República de Chile: Casilla 81-D, Agustinas 1269, Santiago; tel. (2) 698-3969; fax (2) 698-1059; e-mail fceballos@anfitrion.cl; internet www.diarioficial.cl; f. 1877; Dir FLORENCIO CEBALLOS BUSTOS; circ. 10,000.

Estrategia: Luis Carrera 1298, Vitacura, Santiago; tel. (2) 655-6228; fax (2) 655-6256; e-mail estrategia@edgestion.cl; internet www.estrategia.cl; f. 1978; morning; Editor MÓNICA HABERLAND.

El Mercurio: Avda Santa María 5542, Casilla 13-D, Santiago; tel. (2) 330-1111; fax (2) 242-1131; e-mail redaccion@mercurio.cl; internet www.elmercurio.cl; f. 1827; morning; conservative; Gen. Man. FERNANDO CISTERNAS BRAVO; circ. 120,000 (weekdays), 280,000 (Sun.).

La Nación: Agustinas 1269, Casilla 81-D, Santiago; tel. (2) 787-0100; fax (2) 698-1059; e-mail mpmoya@lanacion.cl; internet www.lanacion.cl; f. 1917 to replace govt-subsidized *El Cronista*; morning; financial; Propr Soc. Periodística La Nación; Dir JUAN WALKER EDWARDS; Sub-Dir RODRIGO DE CASTRO; circ. 45,000.

Santiago Times: Avda Santa María 227, Of. 12, Santiago; tel. (2) 738-0150; fax (2) 735-2267; e-mail editor@santiagotimes.cl; internet www.santiagotimes.cl; daily; national news in English; Editor STEPHEN ANDERSON; 10,000 subscribers.

La Segunda: Avda Santa María 5542, Casilla 13-D, Santiago; tel. (2) 330-1111; fax (2) 228-9289; e-mail opinion@lasegunda.cl; internet www.lasegunda.com; f. 1931; owned by proprs of *El Mercurio*; evening; Dir CRISTIÁN ZEGERS ARIZTÍA; circ. 40,000.

La Tercera: Avda Vicuña Mackenna 1962, Ñuñoa, Santiago; tel. (2) 550-7000; fax (2) 550-7999; e-mail latercera@latercera.cl; internet www.latercera.cl; f. 1950; morning; Dir CRISTIÁN BOFILL RODRÍGUEZ; circ. 200,000.

Las Ultimas Noticias: Bellavista 0112, Providencia, Santiago; tel. (2) 730-3000; fax (2) 730-3331; e-mail rodolfo.gambetti@lun.cl; internet www.lun.cl; f. 1902; owned by the proprs of El Mercurio; morning; Dir AGUSTÍN EDWARDS DEL RÍO; Gen. Man. JUAN ENRIQUE CANALES BESA; circ. 150,000 (except Sat. and Sun.).

Antofagasta

La Estrella del Norte: Manuel Antonio Matta 2112, Antofagasta; tel. (55) 45-3600; internet www.estrellanorte.cl; f. 1966; evening; Dir CAUPOLICÁN MÁRQUEZ VERGARA; circ. 5,000.

El Mercurio: Manuel Antonio Matta 2112, Antofagasta; tel. (55) 425-3600; fax (55) 425-3612; e-mail cronicafta@mercurio.cl; internet www.mercurioantofagasta.cl; f. 1906; morning; conservative independent; Proprs Soc. Chilena de Publicaciones; Dir ARTURO ROMÁ HERRERA; circ. 9,000.

Arica

La Estrella de Arica: San Marcos 580, Arica; tel. (58) 20-0261; fax (58) 25-2890; internet www.estrellaarica.cl; f. 1976; Dir REINALDO NEIRA RUIZ; circ. 10,000.

Atacama

Chañarcillo: Los Carrera 801, Casilla 198, Chañaral, Atacama; tel. and fax (52) 21-9044; internet www.chanarcillo.cl; f. 1992; morning; Dir LUIS CERPA HIDALGO.

Calama

El Mercurio: Abaroa 2051, Calama; tel. (55) 34-1604; fax (55) 36-4255; e-mail cronicacalama@mercurio.cl; internet www.mercuriocalama.cl; f. 1968; propr Soc. Chilena de Publicaciones; Dir ROBERTO GAETE; circ. 4,500 (weekdays), 7,000 (Sun.).

Chillán

La Discusión de Chillán, SA: Calle 18 de Septiembre 721, Casilla 479, Chillán; tel. (42) 21-2650; fax (42) 21-3578; internet www.diarioladiscusion.cl; f. 1870; morning; independent; Dir TITO CASTILLO PERALTA; circ. 5,000.

Concepción

El Sur: Calle Freire 799, Casilla 8-C, Concepción; tel. (41) 23-5825; internet www.elsur.cl; f. 1882; morning; independent; Dir RAFAEL MAIRA LAMAS; circ. 28,000 (weekdays), 45,000 (Sun.).

Copiapó

Atacama: Atacama 724A, Copiapó; tel. (52) 21-8509; fax (52) 23-2212; internet www.diarioatacama.cl; morning; independent; Dir SAMUEL SALGADO; circ. 6,500.

Coyhaique

El Diario de Aysén: 21 de Mayo 410, Coyhaique; tel. (67) 234-850; fax (67) 232-318; e-mail contacto@diarioaysen.cl; internet www.diarioaysen.cl; Dir ALDO MARCHESSE COMPODÓNICO.

Curicó

La Prensa: Merced 373, Curicó; tel. (75) 31-0453; fax (75) 31-1924; e-mail laprensa@entelchile.net; internet diariolaprensa.cl; f. 1898; morning; right-wing; Pres. CARLOS LAZCANO ALFONSO; Man. Dir MANUEL MASSA MAUTINO; Editor CARLOS POZO CARVACHO; circ. 6,000.

1187

CHILE

Iquique

La Estrella de Iquique: Luis Uribe 452, Iquique; tel. (57) 39-9311; fax (57) 42-7975; internet www.estrellaiquique.cl; f. 1966; evening; Dir SERGIO MONTIVERA BRUNA; circ. 10,000.

El Nortino: Baquedano 1470, Iquique; tel. (57) 41-6666; fax (57) 41-2997; f. 1992; morning; Dir-Gen. REYNALDO BERRÍOS GONZÁLEZ.

La Serena

El Día: Brasil 431, La Serena; tel. (51) 22-2863; fax (51) 22-2844; internet www.diarioeldia.cl; f. 1944; morning; Dir ANTONIO PUGA RODRÍGUEZ; circ. 10,800.

Los Angeles

La Tribuna: Colo Colo 464, Casilla 15-D, Los Angeles; tel. (43) 31-3315; fax (43) 31-4987; internet www.diariolatribuna.cl; independent; Dir CIRILO GUZMÁN DE LA FUENTE; circ. 4,500.

Osorno

El Diario Austral: Yungay 499, Valdivia; tel. (63) 23-2200; fax (63) 24-2209; e-mail vpineda@australvaldivia.cl; internet www.australvaldivia.cl; f. 1982; Dir VERÓNICA MORENO AGUILERA; circ. 6,500 (weekdays), 7,300 (Sun.).

Ovalle

El Ovallino: Victoria 323-B, Ovalle; tel. and fax (53) 627-557; internet www.diarioelovallino.cl; Dir JORGE CONTADOR ARAYA.

Puerto Montt

El Llanquíhue: Antonio Varas 167, Puerto Montt; tel. (65) 432-400; fax (65) 432-401; internet www.diariollanquihue.cl; f. 1885; Dir ERNESTO MONTALBA; circ. 4,800 (weekdays), 5,700 (Sun.).

Punta Arenas

La Prensa Austral: Waldo Seguel 636, Casilla 9-D, Punta Arenas; tel. (61) 20-4000; fax (61) 24-7406; e-mail direccion@laprensaaustral.cl; internet www.laprensaaustral.cl; f. 1941; morning; independent; Dir MANUEL GONZÁLEZ ARAYA; circ. 10,000, Sunday (El Magallanes; f. 1894) 12,000.

Quillota

El Observador: La Concepción 277, Casilla 1-D, Quillota; tel. (33) 312-096; fax (33) 311-417; e-mail elobser@entelchile.net; internet www.diarioelobservador.cl; f. 1970; Tuesdays and Fridays; Man. Dir ROBERTO SILVA BIJIT.

Rancagua

El Rancagüino: O'Carroll 518, Casilla 50, Rancagua; tel. (72) 23-0358; fax (72) 22-1483; e-mail prensaelrancaguino@adsl.tie.cl; internet www.elrancaguino.cl; f. 1915; independent; Dir ALEJANDRO GONZÁLEZ; Gen. Man. FERNANDO REYES; circ. 10,000.

Talca

El Centro: Tres Oriente 798, Talca; tel. (71) 51-5300; e-mail diario@elcentrosa.cl; internet www.diarioelcentro.cl; f. 1989; Dir ANTONIO FAUNDES MERINO.

Temuco

El Diario Austral: Antonio Varas 945, Casilla 1-D, Temuco; tel. (45) 29-2929; fax (45) 23-9189; internet www.australtemuco.cl; f. 1916; propr Soc. Periodística Araucanía, SA; morning; commercial, industrial and agricultural interests; Dir MARCO ANTONIO PINTO ZEPEDA; circ. 15,100 (weekdays), 23,500 (Sun.).

Tocopilla

La Prensa de Tocopilla: Bolívar 1244, Tocopilla; tel. (83) 81-3036; internet www.prensatocopilla.cl; f. 1924; morning; independent; Gen. Man. JORGE LEIVA CONCHA; circ. 3,000.

Valdivia

El Diario Austral: Yungay 499, Valdivia; tel. (63) 24-2200; fax (63) 24-2209; internet www.australvaldivia.cl; f. 1982; Dir VERONICA MORENO AGUILERA; circ. 5,600.

Valparaíso

La Estrella: Esmeralda 1002, Casilla 57-V, Valparaíso; tel. (32) 26-4230; fax (32) 26-4241; internet www.estrellavalpo.cl; f. 1921; evening; independent; Dir ALFONSO CASTAGNETO; owned by the proprs of *El Mercurio*; circ. 28,000 (weekdays), 35,000 (Sat.).

El Mercurio: Esmeralda 1002, Casilla 57-V, Valparaíso; tel. (32) 26-4264; fax (32) 26-4138; internet www.mercuriovalp.cl; f. 1827; owned by the proprs of El Mercurio in Santiago; morning; Dir MARCO ANTONIO PINTO ZEPADA; circ. 65,000.

PERIODICALS

Santiago

América Economía: Apoquindo 4499, 10°, Las Condes, Santiago; tel. (2) 290-9400; fax (2) 206-6005; e-mail rferro@aeconomia.cl; internet www.americaeconomia.com; f. 1986; monthly; business; CEO ELÍAS SELMAN; Publr NILS STRANDBERG; Editorial Dir RAÚL FERRO ISAKAZ.

CA (Ciudad/Arquitectura) Revista Oficial del Colegio de Arquitectos de Chile AG: Manuel Montt 515, Santiago; tel. (2) 235-3368; fax (2) 235-8403; internet www.revistaca.cl; f. 1964; 4 a year; architects' magazine; Dir PAULINA VILLALOBOS; circ. 3,500.

Caras: Reyes Lavalle 3194, Las Condes, Santiago; tel. (2) 399-6399; fax 399-6299; internet www.caras.cl; e-mail revista@caras.cl; women's interest; Dir PATRICIA GUZMÁN.

Chile Agrícola: Teresa Vial 1170, Casilla 2, Correo 13, Santiago; tel. and fax (2) 522-2627; e-mail chileagricola@hotmail.com; f. 1975; 6 a year; organic farming; Dir RAÚL GONZÁLEZ VALENZUELA; circ. 7,000.

Chile Forestal: Avda Bulnes 285, Of. 601, Santiago; tel. (2) 390-0213; fax (2) 696-6724; e-mail mespejo@conaf.cl; internet www.conaf.cl; f. 1974; 10 a year; state-owned; technical information and features on forestry sector; Editor RICARDO SAN MARTÍN; Dir MARIELA ESPEJO SUAZO; circ. 4,000.

Cinegrama: Avda Holanda 279, Providencia, Santiago; tel. (2) 422-8500; fax (2) 422-8570; internet www.cinegrama.cl; e-mail cinegrama@holanda.cl; monthly; cinema; Dir JAIME GODOY; Editor LEYLA LÓPEZ.

The Clinic: Santo Domingo 550, Santiago; tel. (2) 633-9584; fax (2) 639-6584; internet www.theclinic.cl; fortnightly; political and social satire; Dir JUAN ANDRÉS GUZMÁN; Gen. Man. PABLO DITTBORN.

Conozca Más: Reyes Lavalle 3193, Las Condes, Santiago; tel. (2) 366-7100; fax (2) 246-2810; e-mail viamail@conozcamas.cl; internet www.conozcamas.cl; monthly; science; Dir PAULA AVILES; circ. 90,000.

Cosas: Almirante Pastene 329, Providencia, Santiago; tel. (2) 364-5100; fax (2) 235-8331; internet www.cosas.com; f. 1976; fortnightly; entertainment and lifestyle; Dir MÓNICA COMANDARI KAISER; circ. 40,000.

Creces: Luis Uribe 2610, Ñuñoa, Santiago; tel. and fax (2) 341-5829; e-mail crecesnwebmaster@entelchile.net; internet www.creces.cl; monthly; science and technology; Dir FERNANDO MÖNCKEBERG BARROS; circ. 12,000.

Ercilla: Avda Holanda 279, Providencia, Santiago; tel. (2) 422-8500; fax (2) 422-8570; e-mail ercilla@holanda.cl; internet www.ercilla.cl; f. 1936; weekly; general interest; conservative; Dir JUAN IGNACIO OTO; circ. 28,000.

Mujer a Mujer: Vicuña McKenna 1870, Ñuñoa, Santiago; tel. (2) 550-7000; fax (2) 550-7379; e-mail mujer@latercera.cl; internet www.mujeramujer.cl; weekly; women's interest; Dir JACKELINE OTEY.

Paula: Avda Santa María 0120, Providencia, Santiago; tel. (2) 200-0407; fax (2) 200-0490; e-mail paula@paulacom.cl; internet www.paula.cl; f. 1967; monthly; women's interest; Dir PAULA RECART; circ. 85,000.

Punto Final: San Diego 31, Of. 606, Casilla 13954, Correo 21, Santiago; tel. and fax (2) 697-0615; e-mail punto@interaccess.cl; internet www.puntofinal.cl; f. 1965; fortnightly; politics; left-wing; Dir MANUEL CABIESES DONOSO; circ. 15,000.

¿Qué Pasa?: Vicuña Mackenna 1870, Ñuñoa, Santiago; tel. (2) 550-7523; fax (2) 550-7529; e-mail quepasa@copesa.cl; internet www.quepasa.cl; f. 1971; weekly; general interest; Dir BERNADITA DEL SOLAR VERA; circ. 30,000.

Revista Mensaje: Almirante Barroso 24, Casilla 10445, Santiago; tel. (2) 696-0653; fax (2) 671-7030; e-mail rrpp@mensaje.cl; internet www.mensaje.cl; f. 1951; monthly; national, church and international affairs; Dir ANTONIO DELFAU; circ. 6,000.

Semanario Datos Sur: Avda Urmeneta 231, Puerto Montt; tel. (65) 26-6700; e-mail info@datossur.cl; internet www.datossur.cl; weekly; regional, national and business news; Dir ALEX BERKHOFF ALCARRAZ.

Semanario El Siglo: Diagonal Paraguay 458, Of. 1, Casilla 13479, Correo 21, Santiago; tel. and fax (2) 633-0074; e-mail elsiglo@elsiglo.cl; internet www.elsiglo.cl; f. 1940; fortnightly; publ. by the Communist Party of Chile (PCCh); Dir CLAUDIO DE NEGRI QUINTANA; circ. 15,000.

Vea: Avda Holanda 279, Providencia, Santiago; tel. (2) 422-8500; fax (2) 422-8572; e-mail revistavea@holanda.cl; internet www.vea.cl; f. 1939; weekly; general interest, illustrated; Dir JAIME GODOY CARTES; circ. 150,000.

CHILE *Directory*

PRESS ASSOCIATION

Asociación Nacional de la Prensa: Carlos Antúnez 2048, Santiago; tel. 232-1004; fax 232-1006; e-mail info@anp.cl; internet www.anp.cl; f. 1951; Pres. JUAN LUIS SOMMERS COMANDARI; Sec.-Gen FERNANDO SILVA VARGAS.

NEWS AGENCIES

Agencia Chile Noticias (ACN): Carlos Antúnez 1884, Of. 104, Providencia, Santiago; tel. and fax (2) 223-0205; e-mail prensa@chilenoticias.cl; internet www.chilenoticias.cl; f. 1993; Dir NORBERTO PARRA H.

Agencia Orbe: Avda Phillips 56, Of. 66, Santiago; tel. (2) 251-7800; fax (2) 251-7901; e-mail prensa@orbe.cl; internet www.orbe.cl; Bureau Chief PATRICIA ESCALONA CÁCERES.

UPI Chile: Avda Nataniel Cox 47, 9°, Santiago; tel. (2) 657-0874; fax (2) 698-6605; internet www.upi.cl; Bureau Chief FRANCISCO JARA ARANCIBIA.

Business News Americas: San Patricio 2944, Las Condes, Santiago; tel. (2) 232-0302; fax (2) 232-9376; e-mail info@bnamericas.com; internet www.bnamericas.com; internet-based business information; CEO GREGORY BARTON.

Chile Information Project (CHIP): Avda Santa María 227, Of. 12, Recoleta, Santiago; tel. (2) 735-9044; fax (2) 735-2267; internet www.chipsites.com; English language; Dir STEPHEN J. ANDERSON.

Association

Asociación de Corresponsales de la Prensa Extranjera en Chile: Coronel Santiago Bueras 188, Santiago; tel. (2) 688-0424; fax (2) 633-6130; Pres. OMAR RUZ.

Publishers

Arrayán Editores: Bernarda Morin 435, Providencia, Santiago; tel. (2) 431-4200; fax (2) 274-1041; e-mail web@arrayan.cl; internet www.arrayan.cl; f. 1982; general; Gen. Man. PABLO MARINKOVIC M.

Carlos Quiroga Editorial: La Concepción 56, Of. 206, Providencia, Santiago; tel. and fax (2) 202-9825; e-mail cquiroga@carlosquiroga.cl; internet www.carlosquiroga.cl; children's and educational; Gen. Man. MARIANELLA MEDINA.

Edebé—Editorial Don Bosco: Avda Libertador B. O'Higgins 2373, Santiago; tel. (2) 437-8050; e-mail contacto@edebe.cl; internet www.edebe.cl; f. 1904 as Editorial Salesiana; adopted present name in 1996; general, political, biography, religious, children's; Dir JORGE RIVERA SMITH.

Ediciones B Chile: Monseñor Sótero Sanz 55, Of. 600, Providencia, Santiago; tel. (2) 231-6200; fax (2) 231-6300; e-mail mansieta@edicionesbchile.cl; children's and fiction; Gen. Man. MARILÉN WOOD.

Ediciones Mil Hojas: Avda Antonio Varas 1480, Providencia, Santiago; tel. (2) 274-3172; fax (2) 223-7544; e-mail milhojas@terra.cl; internet www.milhojas.cl; educational and reference.

Ediciones San Pablo: Avda Libertador B. O'Higgins 1626, Santiago; tel. (2) 698-9145; fax (2) 671-6884; internet www.san-pablo.cl; Catholic texts; Dir-Gen. BRUNO BRESSAN.

Ediciones Universitarias de Valparaíso: Universidad Católica de Valparaíso, 12 de Febrero 187, Casilla 1415, Valparaíso; tel. (32) 27-3087; fax (32) 27-3429; e-mail euvsa@ucv.cl; internet www.euv.cl; f. 1970; literature, social and general sciences, engineering, education, music, arts, textbooks; Gen. Man. ALEJANDRO DAMIÁN VILARREAL.

Ediciones Urano: Avda Francisco Bilbao 2809, Providencia, Santiago; tel. (2) 341-6731; fax (2) 225-3896; e-mail infoch@edicionesurano.cl; internet www.edicionesurano.cl; f. 1983 in Spain, f. 1996 in Chile; self-help, mystical and scholarly.

Editec (Ediciones Técnicas Ltda): El Condor 844, Of. 205, Ciudad Empresarial, Huechuraba, Santiago; tel. (2) 757-4200; fax (2) 757-4201; e-mail editec@editec.cl; internet www.editec.cl; Pres. RICARDO CORTES DONOSO; Gen. Man. ROLY SOLIS SEPÚLVEDA.

Editorial Antártica, SA: San Francisco 116, Santiago; tel. (2) 639-3476; fax (2) 633-3402; e-mail plaborde@antartica.cl; internet www.antartica.cl; f. 1978; Gen. Man. PAUL LABORDE U.

Editorial Borlando: Avda Victoria 151, Santiago; tel. (2) 555-9566; fax (2) 555-9564; internet www.editorialborlando.cl; f. 1984; scholarly, juvenile, educational and reference; Dir-Gen. SERGIO BORLANDO PORTALES.

Editorial Cuatro Vientos Ltda: Maturana 19, Metro República, entre Brasil y Cumming, Santiago; tel. (2) 672-9226; fax (2) 673-2153; e-mail editorial@cuatrovientos.cl; internet www.cuatrovientos.net; f. 1980; Man. Editor JUAN FRANCISCO HUNEEUS COX.

Editorial y Distribuidora Lenguaje y Pensamiento Ltda: Avda Apoquindo 6275, Of. 36, Las Condes, Santiago; tel. (2) 245-2909; fax (2) 202-8263; e-mail info@editoriallenguajeypensamiento.cl; internet www.editoriallenguajeypensamiento.cl/www.

Editorial Evolución, SA: Avda Alameda 171, Of. 307, Santiago; tel. (2) 638-9717; fax (2) 236-4796; e-mail info@evolucion.cl; internet www.evolucion.cl; business and management; Dir JUAN BRAVO CARRASCO.

Editorial Fondo de Cultura Económica Chile, SA: Paseo Bulnes 152, Santiago; tel. (2) 697-2644; fax (2) 696-2329; e-mail miriam.morales@fcechile.cl; internet www.fcechile.com.

Editorial Jurídica de Chile: Ahumada 8, 4°, Santiago; tel. (2) 461-9500; fax (2) 461-9501; e-mail covalle@editorialjuridica.cl; internet www.editorialjuridica.cl; f. 1945; law; Dir RAÚL TAVOLARI OLIVEROS.

Editorial Patris: José Manuel Infante 132, Providencia, Santiago; tel. (2) 235-1343; fax (2) 235-8674; e-mail edit.patris@entelchile.net; internet www.patris.cl; f. 1982; Catholic.

Editorial Planeta Grandes Publicaciones de Chile: Orrego Luco 0140, Providencia, Santiago; tel. (2) 472-8200; fax (2) 231-5048; internet www.barsa.com; fmrly Barsa Planeta; reference.

Editorial Renacimiento: Huérfanos 623, Santiago; tel. (2) 632-7334; fax (2) 633-9374; e-mail pedidos@editorialrenacimiento.com; internet www.editorialrenacimiento.com; f. 1977; Gen. Man. MANUEL VILCHES.

Editorial Terra Chile: E. Pinto Lagarrigue 156, 1°, Santiago; tel. (2) 735-0059; fax (2) 738-0445; Gen. Man. ORLANDO MILESI.

Editorial Texido: Manuel Antonio Tocornal 1487, Santiago; tel. (2) 555-5534; f. 1969; Gen. Man. ELSA ZLATER.

Editorial Tiempo Presente Ltda: Almirante Pastene 329, Providencia, Santiago; tel. (2) 364-5100; fax (2) 235-8331; e-mail info@cosas.com; internet www.cosas.com; Gen. Man. MATÍAS PFINGSTHORN.

Editorial Universitaria, SA: Avda Libertador Bernardo O'Higgins 1050, Santiago; tel. (2) 487-0700; fax (2) 487-0702; e-mail comunicaciones@universitaria.cl; internet www.universitaria.cl; f. 1947; general literature, social science, technical, textbooks; Man. Dir RODRIGO CASTRO.

Empresa Editora Zig-Zag SA: Los Conquistadores 1700, 10°, Providencia, Santiago; tel. (2) 810-7400; fax (2) 810-7452; e-mail zigzag@zigzag.cl; internet www.zigzag.cl; f. 1905; general publrs of literary works, reference books and magazines; Pres. GONZALO VIAL C.; Gen. Man. RAMÓN OLACIREGUI.

Grupo Planeta: Avda 11 de Septiembre 2353, 16°, Providencia, Santiago; tel. (2) 652-9000; fax (2) 652-2912; e-mail info@planeta.cl; internet www.planeta.cl; non-fiction, philosophy, psychology; Dir-Gen. OSCAR M. ENRIQUE CORNÚ.

Lexis-Nexis Chile: Miraflores 383, 11°, Santiago; tel. (2) 510-5000; fax (2) 510-5110; e-mail informacion@lexisnexis.cl; internet www.lexisnexis.cl; legal, business, government and academic; f. 1973.

McGraw-Hill/Interamericana de Chile Ltda: Carmencita 25, Of. 51, Las Condes, Santiago; tel. (2) 661-3000; fax (2) 661-3000; e-mail christian_mendez@mcgraw-hill.com; internet www.mcgraw-hill.cl; educational and technical.

Norma de Chile, SA: Avda Providencia 1760, Of. 502, Santiago; tel. (2) 236-3355; fax (2) 236-3362; e-mail ventasnorma@carvajal.cl; internet www.norma.com; f. 1960; part of Editorial Norma of Colombia; Gen. Man. ELSY SALAZAR CAMPO.

Pearson Educación de Chile: José Ananias 505, Macul, Santiago; tel. (2) 237-2387; fax (2) 237-3297; e-mail infopear@pearsoned.cl; internet www.pearsoneducacion.cl; Gen. Man. JAIME VALENZUELA S.

Pehuen Editores Ltda: María Luisa Santander 537, Providencia, Santiago; tel. (2) 225-6264; fax (2) 204-9399; e-mail epehuen@entelchile.net; internet www.pehuen.cl; f. 1983; literature and sociology; Pres. JORGE BARROS TORREALBA; Gen. Man. SEBASTIÁN BARROS CERDA.

RIL Editores: Alférez Real 1464, Providencia, CP 750-0960, Santiago; tel. (2) 223-8100; fax (2) 225-4269; e-mail ril@rileditores.com; internet www.rileditores.com; literature, poetry, scholarly and political; f. 1991 as Red Internacional del Libro Ltda; Dir ELEONORA FINKELSTEIN; Dir of Publications DANIEL CALABRESE.

PUBLISHERS' ASSOCIATION

Cámara Chilena del Libro AG: Avda Libertador B. O'Higgins 1370, Of. 501, Casilla 13526, Santiago; tel. (2) 672-0348; fax (2) 698-9226; e-mail prolibro@tie.cl; internet www.camlibro.cl; Pres. EDUARDO CASTILLO GARCÍA.

Broadcasting and Communications

TELECOMMUNICATIONS

Regulatory Authority

Subsecretaría de Telecomunicaciones (Department of Telecommunications, Ministry of Public Works): Amunátegui 139, 5°, Casilla 120, Correo 21, Santiago; tel. (2) 421-3000; fax (2) 421-3553; e-mail subtel@subtel.cl; internet www.subtel.cl; f. 1977; Under-Sec. Pablo Bello Arellano.

Major Operators

AT&T Chile: Málaga 89, 7°, Santiago; tel. (2) 582-5000; fax (2) 585-5079; e-mail info@firstcom.cl; internet www.attla.cl; Pres. Alejandro Rojas; Dir-Gen. Jaime Chico Pardo.

Claro: Santiago; internet www.clarochile.cl; acquired in Aug. 2005 by América Móvil, SA de CV (Mexico); fmrly known as Smartcom.

CMET Telecomunicaciones: Avda Los Leones 1412, Providencia, Santiago; tel. (2) 251-3333; fax (2) 274-9573; internet www.cmet.cl; f. 1978.

Empresa Nacional de Telecomunicaciones, SA—ENTEL Chile, SA: Andrés Bello 2687, 14°, Casilla 4254, Las Condes, Santiago; tel. (2) 360-0123; fax (2) 360-3424; internet www.entel.cl; f. 1964; operates the Chilean land satellite stations of Longovilo, Punta Arenas and Coihaique, linked to INTELSAT system; 52% owned by Telecom Italia; Pres. Juan José Hurtado Vicuña.

Grupo GTD: Santiago; e-mail soporte@gtdinternet.com; internet www.grupogtd.com; f. 1979; internet and telephone service provider; Pres. Juan Manuel Casanueva.

Telefónica CTC Chile: Providencia 111, Santiago; tel. (2) 691-2020; fax (2) 691-2018; internet www.telefonicadechile.cl; fmrly Compañia de Telecomunicaciones de Chile, SA; privatized in 1988; owned by Telefónica, SA (Spain); Pres. Emilio Gilolmo López.

   Movistar: Miraflores 130, Santiago; tel. (2) 661-6000; internet www.movistar.cl; f. 1996 as Telefónica Móvil de Chile, present name adopted in 2005 following merger of Telefónica Móvil de Chile with BellSouth (USA); mobile cellular telephone services; Gen. Man. Oliver Flögel.

Telmex: Rinconada El Salto 202, Huechuraba, Casilla 12, Santiago; tel. (2) 380-0171; fax (2) 382-5142; internet www.telmex.com.cl; Dir-Gen. Jaime Chico Pardo.

VTR GlobalCom: Reyes Lavalle 3340, 9°, Las Condes, Santiago; tel. (2) 310-1000; fax (2) 310-1560; internet www.vtr.cl; f. 1928 as Vía Transradio Chilena; present name adopted in 1999; 80% owned by UnitedGlobalCom of Liberty Media International (USA), 20% owned by Cristalerías Chile of the Claro group; Pres. Blas Tomic; Gen. Man. Pedro Gutiérrez Sánchez.

BROADCASTING

Regulatory Authority

Asociación de Radiodifusores de Chile (ARCHI): Pasaje Matte 956, Of. 801, Casilla 10476, Santiago; tel. (2) 639-8755; fax (2) 639-4205; e-mail archi@archiradios.cl; internet www.archiradios.cl; f. 1936; 455 broadcasting stations; Pres. Jaime Bellolio.

Radio

In 2004 there were 1,445 radio stations (1,271 FM and 174 AM) transmitting in Chile.

Agricultura (AM y FM): Avda Manuel Rodríguez 15, Santiago; tel. (2) 695-3088; fax (2) 672-2749; internet www.radioagricultura.cl; owned by Sociedad Nacional de Agricultura; Pres. Manuel Valdés Valdés; Gen. Man. Guido Errázuriz Moreno.

Aurora FM: Eliodoro Yáñez 1783, Providencia, Santiago; tel. (2) 390-2112; fax (2) 632-5860; f. 1982; part of Ibero American media group; Pres. Ernesto Corona Bozzo; Gen. Man. Juan Carrasco Hernández.

Beethoven FM: Garibaldi 1620, Ñuñoa, Santiago; tel. (2) 225-0222; fax (2) 274-3323; e-mail director@redfm.cl; internet www.beethovenfm.cl; f. 1981; mainly classical music; affiliate stations in Viña del Mar and Temuco; Exec. Dir Ricardo Gutiérrez Gatica.

Belén AM: Benavente 385, 3°, Casilla 17, Puerto Montt; tel. (65) 25-8048; fax (65) 25-8097; e-mail radiobel.en001@chilnet.cl; f. 1990; owned by Archbishopric of Puerto Montt; Dir Nelson González Andrade; Gen. Man. Carlos Wagner Catalán.

Bío Bío La Radio: Avda Libertador B. O'Higgins 680, Concepción; tel. (41) 225-660; fax (41) 226-742; e-mail pandrade@laradio.cl; internet www.radiobiobio.cl; affiliate stations in Concepción, Los Angeles, Temuco, Ancud, Castro, Osorno, Puerto Montt, Santiago and Valdivia; Man. Patricio Andrade.

La Clave FM: Monjitas 454, Of. 406, Santiago; tel. (2) 633-1621; fax (2) 639-2914; f. 1980; Pres. Miguel Nasur Allel; Gen. Man. Víctor Ibarra Negrete.

Compañía Radio Chilena: Phillips 40, 2°, Casilla 10277, Santiago; tel. (2) 463-5000; fax (2) 463-5050; e-mail radio@radiochilena.cl; internet www.radiochilena.com; f. 1922; news; FM, AM and satellite; Exec. Dir Juan Luis Silva Dibarrart.

Duna FM: Eliodoro Yáñez 1804, Providencia, Santiago; tel. (2) 225-5494; fax (2) 225-6013; e-mail aholuigue@duna.cl; internet www.duna.cl; affiliate stations in Viña del Mar and Concepción; Pres. Felipe Lamarca Claro; Dir A. Holuigue.

Estrella del Mar AM: Eleuterio Ramírez 207, Ancud-Isla de Chiloé; tel. (65) 63-2900; fax (65) 63-2900; f. 1982; affiliate stations in Castro and Quellón; Dir Miguel Angel Millar Silva.

Festival AM: Quinta 124A, Viña del Mar; tel. (32) 68-9328; fax (32) 68-0266; e-mail schiesa@festival.cl; internet www.festival.cl; f. 1976; Pres. Luis Muñoz Ahumada; Dir-Gen. Santiago Chiesa Howard.

Finísima FM: Luis Thayer Ojeda 1145, Santiago; tel. (2) 233-5771; fax (2) 231-0611; affiliate stations in Santiago, Arica, Iquique, Calama, Copiapó, La Serena, Ovalle, Isla de Pascua, Quilpe, San Antonio, San Felipe, Villa Alemana, Viña del Mar, Rancagua, Talca, Chillán, Concepción, Los Angeles, Temuco, Puerto Montt, Coihayque, Puerto Aysen and Punto Arenas; Gen. Man. Cristián Wagner Muñoz.

FM-Hit: Eliodoro Yáñez 1783, Providencia, Santiago; tel. (2) 274-6737; fax (2) 274-8928; internet www.concierto.cl; f. 1999; part of Ibero American media group; affiliate stations in Santiago, Iquique, Antofagasta, San Antonio, La Serena, Viña del Mar, Concepción, Temuco, Osorno and Puerto Montt; Gen. Man. Jaime Vega de Kuyper.

Horizonte: Avda Los Leones 1625, Providencia, Santiago; tel. (2) 274-6737; fax (2) 410-5400; internet www.horizonte.cl; f. 1985; affiliate stations in Arica, Antofagasta, Iquique, La Serena, Viña del Mar, Concepción, San Antonio, Temuco, Villarrica, Puerto Montt, Punta Arenas and Osorno.

Infinita FM: Avda Los Leones 1285, Providencia, Santiago; tel. (2) 754-4400; fax (2) 341-6727; internet www.infinita.cl; f. 1977; affiliate stations in Santiago, Viña del Mar, Concepción and Valdivia; Gen. Man. Carlos Alberto Peñafiel Guarachi.

Para Ti FM: El Conquistador del Monte 4644, Huechuraba, Santiago; tel. (2) 740-9393; fax (2) 740-0405; internet www.fmparati.cl; 16 affiliate stations throughout Chile; Gen. Man. Felipe Molfino Burkert.

Pudahuel FM: Eliodoro Yáñez 1783, Providencia, Santiago; tel. (2) 223-0704; fax (2) 223-7589; e-mail radio@pudahuel.cl; internet www.pudahuel.cl; f. 1966; part of Ibero American media group; affiliate stations in Arica, Iquique, Antofagasta, Calama, Copiapó, Coquimbo, La Serena, Ovalle, San Felipe, Valparaíso, Viña del Mar, Rancagua, Curico, Linares, Talca, Chillán, Concepción, Los Angeles, Talcahuano, Pucón, Temuco, Villarrica, Ancud-Castro, Osorno, Puerto Montt, Valdivia and Punta Arenas; Pres. Susana Mutinelli Anchubidart; Gen. Man. Joaquín Blaya Barrios.

Radio El Conquistador FM: El Conquistador del Monte 4644, Huechuraba, Santiago; tel. (2) 740-0000; fax (2) 740-0259; e-mail rconquis@entelchile.net; internet www.elconquistadorfm.cl; f. 1962; affiliate stations in Santiago, Iquique, Antofagasta, La Serena, Viña del Mar, Rancagua, Talca, Chillán, Concepción, Talcahuano, Pucón, Temuco, Villarrica, Lago Llanquihue, Osorno, Puerto Montt, Puerto Varas, Valdivia and Punta Arenas; Pres. Joaquín Molfino.

Radio Cooperativa (AM y FM): Antonio Bellet 353, Casilla 16367, Correo 9, Santiago; tel. (2) 364-8000; fax (2) 236-0535; e-mail info@cooperativa.cl; internet www.cooperativa.cl; f. 1936; affiliate stations in Copiapó, Arica, Coquimbo, La Serena, Valparaíso, Concepción, Calama, Temuco and Castro; Pres. Luis Ajenjo Isasi; Gen. Man. Sergio Parra Godoy.

Radio Nacional de Chile: Argomedo 369, Santiago; tel. (2) 638-1348; fax (2) 632-1065; internet www.radionacionaldechile.cl; affiliate stations in Arica and Punta Arenas; Gen. Man. Santiago Agliati.

Radio Polar: Bories 871, 3°, Punta Arenas; tel. (61) 24-1909; fax (61) 24-9001; internet www.radiopolar.com; f. 1940; Pres. René Venegas Olmedo.

Santa María de Guadalupe: Miguel Claro 161, Casilla 2626, Santiago; tel. (2) 235-7996; fax (2) 235-8527; e-mail radio@santamariadeguadalupe.com; internet www.santamariadeguadalupe.com; religious broadcasting; affiliate stations in Arica, Iquique, Antofagasta, La Serena, Viña del Mar, Temuco, Puerto Varas, Coihayque and Punta Arenas; Dir Alfonso Chadwick.

Superandina FM: Santa Rosa 441, Of. 34–36, Casilla 401, Los Andes; tel. (34) 42-2515; fax (34) 90-4091; e-mail radio@superandina.cl; internet www.superandina.cl; f. 1987; Dir José Andrés Gálvez.

Universo FM: Félix de Amesti 124, 8°, Las Condes, Santiago; tel. (2) 206-6065; fax (2) 206-6049; e-mail alfredo@universo.cl; internet www.universo.cl; affiliate stations in 18 cities, including Iquique, Copiapó, La Serena, Ovalle, Concepción, Temuco, Puerto Montt, Coihayque and Punta Arenas; Asst Gen. Man. ALFREDO URETA Q.

Television

Corporación de Televisión de la Universidad Católica de Chile—Canal 13: Inés Matte Urrejola 0848, Casilla 14600, Providencia, Santiago; tel. (2) 251-4000; fax (2) 630-2040; e-mail dasein@reuna.cl; internet www.canal13.cl; f. 1959; non-commercial; Exec. Dir ELEODORO RODRÍGUEZ MATTE; Gen. Man. JAIME BELLOLIO RODRÍGUEZ.

Corporación de Televisión de la Universidad Católica de Valparaíso: Agua Santa Alta 2455, Casilla 247, Viña del Mar; tel. (32) 616-000; fax (32) 610-505; e-mail tv@ucv.cl; f. 1957; Dir JORGE A. BORNSCHEUER.

Megavisión, SA—Canal 9: Avda Vicuña Mackenna 1348, Ñuñoa, Santiago; tel. (2) 810-8000; fax (2) 551-8369; e-mail mega@mcl.cl; internet www.mega.cl; f. 1990; Pres. RICARDO CLARO VALDÉS; Gen. Man. CRISTÓBAL BULNES SERRANO.

Red de Televisión SA/Chilevisión—Canal 11: Inés Matte Urrejola 0825, Casilla 16547, Correo 9, Providencia, Santiago; tel. (2) 461-5100; fax (2) 461-5371; e-mail info@chilevision.cl; internet www.chilevision.cl; part of Ibero American media group; News Dir FELIPE POZO.

La Red Televisión, SA/TV Azteca Chile, SA: Manquehue Sur 1201, Las Condes, Santiago; tel. (2) 385-4000; fax (2) 385-4020; internet www.redtv.cl; e-mail administracion@lared.cl; f. 1991; Pres. JUAN CARLOS LATORRE; Gen. Man. JOSÉ MANUEL LARRAÍN.

Televisión Nacional de Chile—Canal 7: Bellavista 0990, Casilla 16104, Providencia, Santiago; tel. (2) 707-7777; fax (2) 707-7766; e-mail rrpp@tvn.cl; internet www.tvn.cl; govt network of 140 stations and an international satellite signal; Chair. LUIS ORTIZ QUIROGA; Exec. Dir PABLO PIÑEIRA ECHENIQUE.

Finance

(cap. = capital; res = reserves; dep. = deposits; m. = million; brs = branches; amounts in pesos, unless otherwise specified)

BANKING

Supervisory Authority

Superintendencia de Bancos e Instituciones Financieras: Moneda 1123, 6°, Casilla 15-D, Santiago; tel. (2) 442-6200; fax (2) 441-0914; e-mail superintendente@sbif.cl; internet www.sbif.cl; f. 1925; affiliated to Ministry of Finance; Supt GUSTAVO ARRIAGADA MORALES.

Central Bank

Banco Central de Chile: Agustinas 1180, Santiago; tel. (2) 670-2000; fax (2) 670-2099; e-mail bcch@bcentral.cl; internet www.bcentral.cl; f. 1926; under Ministry of Finance until Dec. 1989, when autonomy was granted; bank of issue; cap. and res −2,152,068.4m., dep. 12,604,880.6m. (Dec. 2006); Gov. VITTORO CORBO LIOI.

State Bank

BancoEstado: Avda Libertador B. O'Higgins 1111, Casilla 240V, Santiago; tel. (2) 970-7000; fax (2) 970-5711; internet www.bancoestado.cl; f. 1953 as Banco del Estado de Chile; state bank; cap. 4,000m., res 401,214m., dep. 9,500,642m. (Dec. 2005); Pres. JOSÉ LUIS MARDONES SANTANDER; Gen. Man. JOSÉ MANUEL MENA VALENCIA; 214 brs.

Commercial Banks

Banco BICE: Teatinos 220, Santiago; tel. (2) 692-2000; fax (2) 696-5324; e-mail webmaster@bice.cl; internet www.bice.cl; f. 1979 as Banco Industrial y de Comercio Exterior; name changed as above in 1988; cap. 27,481m., res 97,635.3m., dep. 1,474,358.2m. (Dec. 2006); Pres. and Chair. BERNARDO MATTE LARRAÍN; Gen. Man. RENÉ LÉHUEDÉ FUENZALIDA; 15 brs.

Banco Bilbao Vizcaya Argentaria Chile: Pedro de Valdivia 100, 17°, Providencia, Santiago; tel. (2) 679-1000; fax (2) 698-5640; e-mail ascarito@bbva.cl; internet www.bbva.cl; f. 1883; merged with Banco Nacional in 1989; acquired Banesto Chile Bank in 1995; controlling interest acquired by Banco Bilbao Vizcaya (Spain) in 1998; name changed as above in 2003; cap. 166,312m., res 100,592m., dep. 4,381,868m. (Dec. 2006); Chair. JOSÉ SAID SAFFIE; Gen. Man. and CEO IGNACIO LACASTA CASADO; 92 brs.

Banco de Chile: Ahumada 251, Casilla 151-D, Santiago; tel. (2) 637-1111; fax (2) 637-3434; internet www.bancochile.cl; f. 1894; 42% owned by SAOS, SA; cap. 554,765.9m., res 84,617.0m., dep. 10,990,197.7m. (Dec. 2006); Chair. FERNANDO CAÑAS BERKOWITZ; Pres. and CEO PABLO GRANIFO LAVÍN; 248 brs in Chile, 2 brs in USA.

Banco de Crédito e Inversiones (Bci): Huérfanos 1134, Casilla 136-D, Santiago; tel. (2) 692-7000; fax (2) 695-3775; e-mail webmaster@bci.cl; internet www.bci.cl; f. 1937; cap. 248,223m., res 219,222m., dep. 6,984,110m. (Dec. 2006); Pres. and Chair. LUIS ENRIQUE YARUR REY; 112 brs.

Banco del Desarrollo: Avda Libertador B. O'Higgins 949, 3°, Casilla 320-V, Casilla 1, Santiago; tel. (2) 674-5000; fax (2) 671-5547; e-mail bdd@bandes.cl; internet www.bdd.cl; f. 1983; cap. 142,502m., res 4m., dep. 1,623,328m. (Dec. 2005); Chair. VICENTE CARUZ MIDDLETON; Gen. Man. DANIEL ALBARRÁN RUIZ-CLAVIJO; 83 brs.

Banco Internacional: Moneda 818, Casilla 135-D, Santiago; tel. (2) 369-7000; fax (2) 369-7367; e-mail banco@binter.cl; internet www.bancointernacional.cl; f. 1944; cap. 8,547.4m., res 7,307.4m., dep. 145,506.9m. (Dec. 2006); Chair. ALEJANDRO L. FURMAN SIHMAN; Gen. Man. ALVARO ACHONDO GONZÁLEZ.

Banco Santander Chile: Bandera 140, 13°, Casilla 57-D, Santiago; tel. (2) 320-2000; fax (2) 320-8877; e-mail webmaster@santander.cl; internet www.santandersantiago.cl; f. 1926; cap. 761,853m., res 197,903m., dep. 12,378,506m. (Dec. 2006); subsidiary of Banco de Santander (Spain); incorporated Banco Osorno y La Unión in 1996; Chair. MAURICIO LARRAÍN GARCES; 72 brs.

Banco Security: Apoquindo 3150, Las Condes, Santiago; tel. (2) 584-4000; fax (2) 270-4001; e-mail banco@security.cl; internet www.security.cl; f. 1981; fmrly Banco Urquijo de Chile; cap. 101,190m., res 31,355m., dep. 1,690,827m. (Dec. 2006); Pres. and Chair. FRANCISCO SILVA S.; Gen. Man. RAMÓN ELUCHANS OLIVARES; 13 brs.

Corpbanca: Rosario Norte 660, 10°, Santiago; tel. (2) 660-2365; fax (2) 660-2366; e-mail ggeneral@corpbanca.cl; internet www.corpbanca.cl; f. 1871 as Banco de Concepción, current name adopted in 1997; cap. 433,249m., res 39,104m., dep. 2,596,663m. (Dec. 2006); Chair. and Pres. CARLOS ABUMOHOR TOUMA; CEO MARIO CHAMORRO; 80 brs.

HSBC Bank (Chile): Avda Andrés Bello 2711, 9°, Las Condes, Santiago; tel. (2) 299-7320; fax (2) 299-7391; e-mail ricardo.navarrete@cl.hsbc.com; internet www.hsbc.cl; f. 2003 as HSBC Bank Chile; present name adopted in 2004; cap. 91,803m., res −2,354m., dep. 252,197m. (Dec. 2006); Pres. FRANK LAWSON; CEO and Gen. Man. ROBERT A. UNDERWOOD.

Scotiabank Sud Americano: Morandé 226, Casilla 90-D, Santiago; tel. (2) 692-6000; fax (2) 698-6008; e-mail scotiabank@scotiabank.cl; internet www.scotiabank.cl; f. 1944; cap. 71,578m., res 72,066m., dep. 1,318,890m. (Dec. 2006); Pres. and Chair. PETER C. CARDINAL; CEO and Gen. Man JAMES CALLAHAN; 52 brs.

Banking Association

Asociación de Bancos e Instituciones Financieras de Chile AG: Ahumada 179, 12°, Santiago; tel. (2) 636-7100; fax (2) 698-8945; e-mail general@abif.cl; internet www.abif.cl; f. 1945; Pres. HERNÁN SOMERVILLE SENN; Gen. Man. ALEJANDRO ALARCÓN PÉREZ.

Other Financial Supervisory Bodies

Superintendencia de Administradoras de Fondos de Pensiones (SAFP) (Superintendency of Pension Funds): Teatinos 317, Santiago; tel. (2) 753-0100; fax (2) 753-0122; internet www.safp.cl; f. 1981; Supt SOLANGE BERSTEIN JÁUREGUI.

Superintendencia de Seguridad Social (Superintendency of Social Security): Huérfanos 1376, 5°, Santiago; tel. (2) 620-4500; fax (2) 696-4672; e-mail secgral@suseso.cl; internet www.suseso.gov.cl; f. 1927; Supt JAVIER FUENZALIDA SANTANDER.

STOCK EXCHANGES

Bolsa de Comercio de Santiago: La Bolsa 64, Casilla 123-D, Santiago; tel. (2) 399-3000; fax (2) 318-1961; e-mail chathaway@bolsadesantiago.com; internet www.bolsadesantiago.com; f. 1893; 32 mems; Pres. PABLO YRARRÁZAVAL VALDÉS.

Bolsa de Corredores—Valores de Valparaíso: Prat 798, Casilla 218-V, Valparaíso; tel. (32) 25-0677; fax (32) 21-2764; e-mail bolsadec.orred001@chilnet.cl; internet www.bovalpo.com; f. 1905; Pres. CARLOS F. MARÍN ORREGO; Man. ARIE JOEL GELFENSTEIN FREUNDLICH.

Bolsa Electrónica de Chile: Huérfanos 770, 14°, Santiago; tel. (2) 484-0100; fax (2) 484-0101; e-mail contactoweb@bolchile.cl; internet www.bolchile.cl; Gen. Man. JUAN CARLOS SPENCER OSSA.

INSURANCE

In 2002 there were 55 general, life and reinsurance companies operating in Chile.

CHILE *Directory*

Supervisory Authority

Superintendencia de Valores y Seguros: Avda Libertador B. O'Higgins 1449, Casilla 834-0518, Santiago; tel. (2) 473-4000; fax (2) 473-4102; internet www.svs.cl; f. 1931; under Ministry of Finance; Supt GUILLERMO LARRAÍN RÍOS.

Principal Companies

ABN Amro (Chile) Seguros Generales, SA: Avda Apoquindo 3039, Las Condes, Santiago; tel. (2) 396-6600; fax (2) 396-6666; e-mail ccm.clientservice.santiago@cl.abnamro.com; internet www.abnamro.cl; Pres. CECILIA STAGNARO FRÍAS.

Ace Seguros de Vida, SA: Miraflores 222, 17°, Santiago; tel. (2) 549-8300; fax (2) 632-6289; e-mail juan.ortega@ace-ina.com; internet www.acelimited.com; Gen. Man. JUAN LUIS ORTEGA GARTERAS.

Aseguradora Magallanes, SA: Agustinas 1022, Of. 722; tel. (2) 365-4848; fax (2) 365-4860; e-mail fvarela@magallanes.cl; internet www.magallanes.cl; f. 1957; general; Pres. EDUARDO DOMINGUEZ COVARRUBIAS; Gen. Man. FERNANDO VARELA VILLAROEL.

Axa Assistance Chile: Josué Smith Solar 390, 6650378 Providencia, Santiago; tel. (2) 941-8900; fax (2) 941-8951; e-mail asistencia@axa-assistance.cl; internet www.axa-assistance.cl; f. 1936; general; Gen. Man. BERNARDO SERRANO LÓPEZ.

Chilena Consolidada, SA: Pedro de Valdivia 195, Casilla 16587, Correo 9, Providencia, Santiago; tel. (2) 200-7000; fax (2) 274-9933; internet www.chilena.cl; f. 1853; owned by Zurich group; general and life; Pres. GASTÓN AGUIRRE SILVA; Gen. Man. JOSÉ MANUEL CAMPOSANO LARRAECHEA.

Chubb de Chile Compañía de Seguros Generales, SA: Gertrudis Echeñique 30, 4°, Santiago; tel. (2) 398-7000; fax (2) 398-7090; e-mail chileinfo@chubb.com; internet www.chubb.com/international/chile; f. 1992; general; Gen. Man. CLAUDIO M. ROSSI.

Cía de Seguros de Crédito Continental, SA: Avda Isidora Goyenechea 3162, 6°, Edif. Parque 1 Golf, Santiago; tel. (2) 636-4000; fax (2) 636-4001; e-mail comer@continental.cl; internet www.continental.cl; f. 1990; general; Gen. Man. FRANCISCO ARTIGAS CELIS.

Cardif Chile: Vitacura 2771, 14°, Vitacura, Santiago; tel. (2) 370-4800; fax (2) 370-4877; internet www.cardif.cl; f. 1997; owned by BNP Paribas (France); Gen. Man. FRANCISCO VALENZUELA CORNEJO.

Cía de Seguros Generales Consorcio Nacional de Seguros, SA: El Bosque Sur 130, Santiago; tel. (2) 230-4000; fax (2) 250-2525; internet www.consorcio.cl; f. 1992; general; Gen. Man. NICOLÁS GELLONA AMUNATEGUI.

Cía de Seguros Generales Cruz del Sur, SA: Avda El Golf 150, Santiago; tel. (2) 461-8000; fax (2) 461-8715; internet www.cruzdelsur.cl; f. 1974; general; Pres. JOSÉ TOMÁS GUZMÁN DUMAS; Gen. Man. MIKEL URIARTE PLAZAOLA.

Cía de Seguros Generales Euroamérica, SA: Agustinas 1127, 2°, Casilla 180-D, Santiago; tel. (2) 672-7242; fax (2) 696-4086; internet www.euroamerica.cl; f. 1986; general; Gen. Man. PATRICIA JAIME VÉLIZ.

Cía de Seguros de Vida Consorcio Nacional de Seguros, SA: Avda El Bosque Sur 180, 3°, Casilla 232, Correo 35, Providencia, Santiago; tel. (2) 230-4000; fax (2) 230-4050; internet www.consorcio.cl; f. 1916; life; Pres. JUAN BILBAO HORMAECHE; Gen. Man. NICOLÁS GELLONA AMUNATEGUI.

Cía de Seguros de Vida La Construcción, SA: Avda Providencia 1806, 11°–18°, Providencia, Santiago; tel. (2) 340-3000; fax (2) 340-3024; f. 1985; life; Pres. VÍCTOR MANUEL JARPA RIVEROS; Gen. Man. MANUEL ZEGERS IRARRÁZAVAL.

Cía de Seguros de Vida Cruz del Sur, SA: El Golf 150, Santiago; tel. (2) 461-8000; fax (2) 334-7250; internet www.cruzdelsur.cl; f. 1992; life; Pres. ROBERTO ANGELINI; Gen. Man. MIKEL URIARTE PLAZAOLA.

Santander Seguros: Bombero Ossa 1068, 4°, Santiago; tel. (2) 676-4100; fax (2) 676-4220; internet www.santandersantiago.cl/santander_seguros/index.asp; life.

Euroamérica Seguros de Vida, SA: Agustinas 1127, 3°, Casilla 21-D, Santiago; tel. (2) 479-9000; fax (2) 479-9428; internet www.euroamerica.cl; f. 1962; life; Pres. BENJAMIN I. DAVIS CLARKE; Gen. Man. CLAUDIO ASECIO FULGERI.

ING Seguros de Vida, SA: Avda Suecia 211, Providencia, Casilla 13224, Santiago; tel. (2) 252-1464; fax (2) 364-2060; internet www.ingvida.cl; f. 1989; life; Gen. Man. RODRIGO GUZMÁN LEYTON.

ISE Chile Compañía de Seguros Generales, SA: Encomenderos 113, Casilla 185-D, Centro 192, Las Condes, Santiago; tel. (2) 422-9000; fax (2) 232-8209; internet www.isechile.cl; f. 1989 in Chile; general; Gen. Man. PATRICIO ALDUNATE BOSSAY.

Mapfre Garantías y Crédito, SA: Avda Isadora Goyenechea, 14°, Casilla 7550071, Las Condes, Santiago; tel. (2) 870-1500; fax (2) 870-1501; internet www.mapfregc.cl; f. 1991; general; Pres. RAFAEL CASAS GUTIÉRREZ; Gen. Man. RODRIGO CAMPERO PETERS.

Renta Nacional Compañías de Seguros, SA: Amunátegui 178, 2°, Santiago; tel. (2) 670-0200; fax (2) 670-0039; e-mail fbeytia@rentanac.cl; internet www.rentanac.cl; f. 1982; life; Pres. FRANCISCO JAVIER ERRÁZURIZ OVALLE.

Royal & Sun Alliance Seguros (Chile), SA: Providencia 1760, 4°, Santiago; tel. (2) 661-1000; fax (2) 661-1413; e-mail lacwebmaster@lacrso.royalsun.com; internet www.royalsunalliance.cl; f. 2000; Pres. VÍCTOR MANUEL JARPA RIVEROS.

Seguros Interamericana: Agustinas 640, 9°, Casilla 111, Correo Central, Santiago; tel. (2) 630-3000; fax (2) 633-2239; internet www.interamericana.cl; f. 1980; life; Exec. Pres. RICARDO GARCÍA; Gen. Man. EDUARDO BUSTAMENTE.

Vida Security, SA: Apoquindo 3150, 8°, Las Condes, Santiago; tel. (2) 584-2400; internet www.vidasecurity.cl; f. 2002 through merger of Seguros Security and Seguros Previsión Vida; Pres. FRANCISCO SILVA SILVA; Gen. Man. ALEJANDRO ALZÉRRECA LUNA.

Insurance Association

Asociación de Aseguradores de Chile, AG: La Concepción 322, Of. 501, Providencia, Santiago; tel. (2) 236-2596; fax (2) 235-1502; e-mail seguros@aach.cl; internet www.aach.cl; f. 1931; Pres. MIKEL URIARTE PLAZAOLA.

Trade and Industry

GOVERNMENT AGENCIES

National Energy Commission (Comisión Nacional de Energía—CNE): see The Government—Ministries.

National Environment Commission (Comisión Nacional del Medio Ambiente—CONAMA): Teatinos 254–258, Santiago; tel. (2) 240-5600; fax (2) 244-1262; e-mail informacion@conama.cl; internet www.conama.cl; f. 1994; environmental regulatory body; Minister ANA LYA URIARTE RODRÍGUEZ.

Corporación de Fomento de la Producción (CORFO): Moneda 921, Casilla 3886, Santiago; tel. (2) 631-8200; e-mail info@corfo.cl; internet www.corfo.cl; f. 1939; holding group of principal state enterprises; grants loans and guarantees to private sector; responsible for sale of non-strategic state enterprises; promotes entrepreneurship; Pres. HUGO LAVADOS MONTES (Minister of the Economy, Economic Promotion and Reconstruction); Exec. Vice-Pres. CARLOS ALVAREZ VOULLIÈME; 13 brs.

PROCHILE (Dirección General de Relaciones Económicas Internacionales): Alameda 1315, 2°, Casilla 14087, Correo 21, Santiago; tel. (2) 565-9000; fax (2) 696-0639; e-mail info@prochile.cl; internet www.prochile.cl; f. 1974; bureau of international economic affairs; Dir ALICIA FROHMANN.

Servicio Nacional de Capacitación y Empleo (SENCE) (National Training and Employment Service): Teatinos 333, 8°, Santiago; tel. (2) 870-6222; fax (2) 696-7103; internet www.sence.cl; attached to Ministry of Labour and Social Security; Dir FERNANDO ROULIEZ FLECK.

STATE CORPORATIONS

Corporación Nacional del Cobre de Chile (CODELCO-Chile): Huérfanos 1270, Casilla 150-D, Santiago; tel. (2) 690-3000; fax (2) 690-3059; e-mail comunica@codelco.cl; internet www.codelco.com; f. 1976 as a state-owned enterprise with copper-producing operational divisions at Chuquicamata, Radomiro Tomić, Salvador, Andina, Salvador, Talleres Rancagua and El Teniente; attached to Ministry of Mining; Pres. SANTIAGO GONZÁLEZ LARRAÍN (Minister of Mining); Exec. Pres. JOSÉ PABLO ARELLANO MARÍN; 18,496 employees.

Empresa Nacional de Petróleo (ENAP): Vitacura 2736, 10°, Las Condes, Santiago; tel. (2) 280-3000; fax (2) 280-3199; e-mail webenap@enap.cl; internet www.enap.cl; f. 1950; state-owned petroleum and gas exploration and production corporation; Pres. SANTIAGO GONZÁLEZ LARRAÍN (Minister of Mining); Gen. Man. ENRIQUE DÁVILA ALVEAL; 3,286 employees.

DEVELOPMENT ORGANIZATIONS

Comisión Chilena de Energía Nuclear: Amunátegui 95, Santiago; tel. (2) 470-2500; fax (2) 470-2570; e-mail oirs@cchen.cl; internet www.cchen.cl; f. 1965; govt body to develop peaceful uses of atomic energy; concentrates, regulates and controls all matters related to nuclear energy; Pres. ROBERTO HOJMAN GUIÑERMAN; Exec. Dir LORETO VILLANUEVA Z.

Corporación Nacional de Desarrollo Indígena (Conadi): Aldunate 620, 8°, Temuco, Chile; tel. (45) 641-500; fax (45) 641-520; e-mail ctranamil@conadi.gov.cl; internet www.conadi.cl; promotes the economic and social development of indigenous communities; Nat. Dir AROLDO CAYUN ANTICURA.

Corporación Nacional Forestal (CONAF): Región Metropolitana, Valenzuela Castillo 1868, Santiago; tel. (2) 225-0428; fax (2) 225-0641; e-mail consulta@conaf.cl; internet www.conaf.cl; f. 1970 to promote forestry activities, enforce forestry law, promote afforestation, administer subsidies for afforestation projects and to increase and preserve forest resources; manages 13.97m. ha designated as National Parks, Natural Monuments and National Reserves; under Ministry of Agriculture; Dir MARÍA CATALINA BAU.

Empresa Nacional de Minería (ENAMI): MacIver 459, 2°, Casilla 100-D, Santiago; tel. (2) 637-5278; fax (2) 637-5452; e-mail eiturra@enami.cl; internet www.enami.cl; promotes the devt of small and medium-sized mines; attached to Ministry of Mining; partially privatized; Exec. Vice-Pres. JAIME PÉREZ DE ARCE ARAYA.

CHAMBERS OF COMMERCE

Cámara de Comercio de Santiago: Edif. Del Comercio, Monjitas 392, Santiago; tel. (2) 360-7000; fax (2) 633-3595; e-mail cpn@ccs.cl; internet www.ccs.cl; f. 1919; 1,300 mems; Pres. PETER HILL D.

Cámara de Comercio, Servicios y Turismo de Antofagasta: Latorre 2580, Of. 21, Antofagasta; tel. (55) 225-175; fax (55) 222-053; e-mail info@camaracomercioantofagasta.cl; internet www.camaracomercioantofagasta.cl; f. 1924; Pres. GONZALO SANTOLAYA GOICOVIC.

Cámara de Comercio, Servicios y Turismo de Temuco, AG: Vicuña Mackenna 396, Temuco; tel. (45) 210-556; fax (45) 237-047; e-mail info@camaratemuco.cl; internet www.camaratemuco.cl; Pres. MAX HENZI IBARRA; Sec. GERARDO DONOSO URREJOLA.

Cámara Nacional de Comercio, Servicios y Turismo de Chile: Merced 230, Santiago; tel. (2) 365-4000; fax (2) 365-4001; internet www.cnc.cl; f. 1858; Pres. PEDRO CORONA BOZZO; Pres., Int. Cttee ALEX THIERMANN I.; 120 mems.

Cámara de la Producción y del Comercio de Concepción: Cauplicán 567, 2°, Concepción; tel. (41) 241-121; fax (41) 227-903; e-mail lmandiola@cpcc.cl; internet www.cpcc.cl; f. 1927; Pres. PEDRO SCHLACK HARNECKER; Gen. Man. LEONCIO TORO ARAYA.

INDUSTRIAL AND TRADE ASSOCIATIONS

Servicio Agrícola y Ganadero (SAG): Avda Bulnes 140, Santiago; tel. (2) 345-1100; fax (2) 345-1102; e-mail dirnac@sag.gob.cl; internet www.sag.cl; under Ministry of Agriculture; responsible for the protection and devt of safe practice in the sector; Nat. Dir FRANCISCO JAVIER BAHAMONDE MEDINA.

Servicio Nacional de Pesca (SERNAPESCA): Victoria 2832, Valparaíso; tel. (32) 81-9100; fax (32) 25-6311; e-mail informaciones@sernapesca.cl; internet www.sernapesca.cl; f. 1978; govt regulator of the fishing industry; Dir INÉS MONTALVA RODRÍGUEZ.

Sociedad Agrícola y Servicios Isla de Pascua (SASIPA): Alfredo Calle Hotu Matu'a s/n, Hanga Roa, Isla De Pascua; tel. (32) 10-0212; f. 1966; administers agriculture and public services on Easter Island; Pres. ROBERTO IPINZA CARMONA.

EMPLOYERS' ORGANIZATIONS

Confederación del Comercio Detallista y Turismo de Chile, AG (CONFEDECH): Merced 380, 8°, Of. 74, Santiago; tel. (2) 639-1264; fax (2) 638-0338; e-mail comerciodetallista@confedech.cl; internet www.comerciodetallista.cl; f. 1938; retail trade; Nat. Pres. RAFAEL CUMSILLE ZAPAPA; Sec.-Gen. ROBERTO ZUÑIGA BELAUZARÁN.

Confederación Gremial Nacional Unida de la Mediana y Pequeña Industria, Servicios y Artesanado (CONUPIA): General Parra 703, Providencia, Santiago; tel. (2) 235-8022; internet www.conupia.cl; e-mail gerencia@conupia.cl; small and medium-sized industries and crafts; Pres. IVÁN VUSKOVIC V; Sec.-Gen. JOSÉ LUIS RAMÍREZ.

Confederación de la Producción y del Comercio: Monseñor Sótero Sanz 182, Providencia, Santiago; tel. (2) 231-9764; fax (2) 231-9808; e-mail procomer@entelchile.net; internet www.cpc.cl; f. 1936; Pres. ALFREDO OVALLE RODRÍGUEZ.

Affiliated organizations:

Asociación de Bancos e Instituciones Financieras de Chile AG: see Finance (Banking Association).

Cámara Nacional de Comercio, Servicios y Turismo de Chile: see Chambers of Commerce.

  Cámara Chilena de la Construcción: Marchant Pereira 10, 3°, Providencia, CP 6640721, Santiago; tel. (2) 376-3300; fax (2) 371-3430; internet www.camaraconstruccion.cl; f. 1951; Pres. LUIS NARIO MATUS; Sec.-Gen. ARTURO DEL RÍO LEYTON; 17,442 mems.

  Sociedad de Fomento Fabril, FG (SOFOFA): Avda Andrés Bello 2777, 3°, Las Condes, Santiago; tel. (2) 391-3100; fax (2) 391-3200; internet www.sofofa.cl; f. 1883; largest employers' org.; Pres. BRUNO PHILIPPI IRARRÁZABAL; Sec.-Gen. ANDRÉS CONCHA RODRÍGUEZ; 2,500 mems.

Sociedad Nacional de Agricultura—Federación Gremial (SNA): Tenderini 187, 2°, CP 6500978, Santiago; tel. (2) 639-6710; fax (2) 633-7771; e-mail info@sna.cl; internet www.sna.cl; f. 1838; landowners' asscn; controls Radio Stations CB 57 and XQB8 (FM) in Santiago, CB-97 in Valparaíso, CD-120 in Los Angeles, CA-144 in La Serena, CD-127 in Temuco; Pres. LUIS SCHMIDT MONTES.

Sociedad Nacional de Minería (SONAMI): Avda Apoquindo 3000, 5°, Santiago; tel. (2) 335-9300; fax (2) 334-9700; e-mail monica.cavallini@sonami.cl; internet www.sonami.cl; f. 1883; Pres. ALFREDO OVALLE RODRÍGUEZ; Gen. Man. ALBERTO SALAS MUÑOZ; 48 mem. cos.

There are many federations of private industrialists, organized by industry and region.

UTILITIES

Comisión Nacional de Energía: Teatinos 120, 7°, Clasificador 14, Correo 21, Santiago; tel. (2) 460-6800; fax (2) 365-6800; e-mail energia@cne.cl; internet www.cne.cl; Pres. MARCELO TOKMAN RAMOS (Minister of the CNE); Exec. Sec. RODRIGO IGLESIAS ACUÑA.

Superintendencia de Electricidad y Combustibles (SEC): Avda Libertador B. O'Higgins 1449, 13°, Santiago; internet www.sec.cl; Supt PATRICIA CHOTZEN GUTIÉRREZ.

Electricity

The four national power grids are SING (operated by CODELCO and EDELNOR), SIC, Aysén and Magallanes.

AES Gener, SA: Mariano Sánchez Fontecilla 310, 3°, Santiago; tel. (2) 686-8900; fax (2) 686-8991; e-mail gener@gener.cl; internet www.gener.cl; f. 1981 as Chilectra Generación, SA, following the restructuring of Compañía Chilena de Electricidad, SA; privatized in 1988 and name Chilgener, SA, adopted in 1989; current name adopted in 1998; owned by AES Corpn (USA); responsible for operation of power plants Renca, Ventanas, Laguna Verde, El Indio, Altalfal, Maitenes, Queltehues and Volcán; total output 10,169.0 GWh (Dec. 2002); also operates subsidiaries in Argentina and Colombia; Pres. ANDRÉS GLUSKI; Gen. Man. LUIS FELIPE CERÓN CERÓN; 1,121 employees (group).

  Eléctrica Santiago: Jorge Hirmas 2964, Renca, Santiago; tel. (2) 680-4760; fax (2) 680-4743; operates the Renca and the Nueva Renca thermoelectric plants in Santiago; installed capacity of 379 MW.

  Empresa Eléctrica Guacolda, SA: Miraflores 222, 16°, Santiago; tel. (2) 362-4000; fax (2) 360-1675; internet www.guacolda.cl; operates a thermoelectric power-station in Huasco; installed capacity of 304 MW; Pres. JOSÉ FLORENCIO GUZMÁN.

  Energía Verde: O'Higgins 940, Of. 90, Concepción; tel. (41) 240-1900; fax (41) 225-3227; internet www.energiaverde.cl; operates two co-generation power-stations at Constitución and Laja and a steam plant at Nacimiento; supplies the Cabrero industrial plant; CEO JAIME ZUAZAGOITÍA.

  Norgener, SA: Jorge Hirmas 2964, Renca, Santiago; tel. (2) 680-4870; fax (2) 680-4895; northern subsidiary supplying the mining industry; Exec. Dir JUAN CARLOS OLMEDO.

Arauco Generación: Vitacura 2771, 9°, Las Condes, Santiago; tel. (2) 560-6700; fax (2) 236-5090; e-mail gic@arauco.cl; internet www.arauco.cl; f. 1994 to commercialize surplus power from pulp processing facility; Pres. JOSÉ TOMÁS GUZMÁN; Gen. Man. MATÍAS DOMEYKO.

Chilquinta Energía, SA: General Cruz 222, Valparaíso; tel. (32) 502-000; fax (32) 231-171; e-mail contactoweb@chiquinta.cl; internet www.chilquinta.cl; f. 1997 as Energas, SA; present name adopted in 2001; owned by Inversiones Sempra and PSEG of the USA; Pres. GEORGE LIPARIDIS; Gen. Man. CRISTIÁN ARNOLDS.

Compañía Eléctrica del Litoral, SA: Avda Peñablanca 540, Algarrobo, Santiago; tel. (2) 481-195; fax (2) 483-313; internet www.litoral.cl; e-mail fmartine@litoral.cl; f. 1949; Gen. Man. LUIS CONTRERAS IGLESIAS.

Compañía General de Electricidad, SA (CGE): Teatinos 280, Santiago; tel. (2) 624-3243; fax (2) 680-7104; e-mail cge@cge.cl; internet www.cge.cl; installed capacity of 662 MW; Pres. JORGE EDUARDO MARÍN CORREA; Gen. Man. PABLO GUARDA BARROS.

Compañía Nacional de Fuerza Eléctrica, SA (CONAFE): Norte 13, Of. 810, Viña del Mar; tel. (32) 220-6100; fax (32) 227-1593; e-mail serviciocliente@conafe.cl; internet www.conafe.cl; f. 1945; Pres. JOSÉ LUIS HORNAUER HERRMANN; Gen. Man. RAÚL RIVERAS BANDERAS.

Empresa Eléctrica de Magallanes, SA (Edelmag, SA): Croacia 444, Punta Arenas; tel. (71) 40-00; fax (71) 40-77; e-mail edelmag@edelmag.cl; internet www.edelmag.cl; f. 1981; 55% owned by CGE; Pres. JORGE JORDAN FRANULIC; Gen. Man. CARLOS YÁÑEZ ANTONUCCI.

Empresa Eléctrica del Norte Grande, SA (EDELNOR): El Bosque Norte 500, 9°, Vitacura, Santiago; tel. (2) 353-3200; fax (2)

353-3210; e-mail contacto@edelnor.cl; internet www.edelnor.cl; f. 1981; acquired by Codelco and Tractebel SA of Belgium in Dec. 2002; Pres. JAN FLACHET; Gen. Man. JUAN CLAVERÍA A.

Empresas Emel, SA: Avda Libertador B. O'Higgins 886, Central Post Office, 5° y 6°, Santiago; tel. (2) 376-6500; fax (2) 633-3849; internet www.emel.cl; holding co for the Emel group of electricity cos, bought by CGE in Nov. 2007; output in 2000 totalled 18,6124 MWh; Gen. Man. RICARDO CRUZAT OCHAGAVÍA; Emel group includes:

ELECDA (Empresa Eléctrica de Antofagasta, SA): José Miguel Carrera 1587, Antofagasta 1250; tel. (55) 649-100; Regional Man. FELINDO CONCHA HENRÍQUEZ.

ELIQSA (Empresa Eléctrica de Iquique, SA): Zegeres 469, Iquique; tel. (57) 40-5400; fax (57) 42-7181; e-mail eliqsa@eliqsa.cl; Regional Man. MARCO ANTONIO SANQUEA RAMOS.

EMELAT (Empresa Eléctrica Atacama, SA): Circunvalación Ignacio Carrera Pinto 51, Copiapó; tel. (52) 205-100; fax (52) 205-103; f. 1981; distribution co; Pres. MICHAEL FRIEDLANDER; Regional Man. GABRIEL BARRAZA ALCAYAGA.

EMELARI (Empresa Eléctrica de Arica, SA): Baquedano 731, Arica; tel. (58) 201-100; fax (58) 23-1105; Regional Man. MARCO ANTONIO SANQUEA RAMOS.

EMELECTRIC (Empresa Eléctrica de Melipilla, Colchagua y Maule): Regional Mans MARCO ANTONIO CARVAJAL, SERGIO QUIROZ ARIAS.

ENERSIS, SA: Avda Kennedy 5454, Casilla 1557, Vitacura, Santiago; tel. (2) 353-4400; fax (2) 378-4768; e-mail comunicacion@e.enersis.cl; internet www.enersis.com; f. 1981; holding co for Spanish group generating and distributing electricity through its subsidiaries throughout South America; 60.62% owned by Endesa, SA; Pres. PABLO YRARRÁZAVAL V.; Gen. Man. IGNACIO ANTOÑANZAS ALVEAR; 10,957 employees.

Chilectra, SA: Santo Domingo 789, Casilla 1557, Santiago; tel. (2) 632-2000; fax (2) 639-3280; e-mail rrpp@chilectra.cl; internet www.chilectra.cl; f. 1921; transmission and distribution arm of ENERSIS; supplies distribution cos, including the Empresa Eléctrica Municipal de Lo Barnechea, Empresa Municipal de Til-Til, and the Empresa Eléctrica de Colina, SA; holds overseas distribution concessions in Argentina, Peru and Brazil; acquired by ENERSIS of Spain in 1999; Pres. JORGE ROSENBLUT; Gen. Man. RAFAEL LÓPEZ R.

Endesa Chile: Santa Rosa 76, Casilla 1392, Santiago; tel. (2) 630-9000; fax (2) 635-4720; e-mail comunicacion@endesa.cl; internet www.endesa.cl; f. 1943; installed capacity 4,035 MW (Feb. 2002); ENERSIS obtained majority control of Endesa Chile in April 1999; operates subsidiaries Pehuenche, Pangue, San Isidro y Celta; Pres. MARIO VALCARCE DURÁN; Gen. Man. RAFAEL MATEA ALCALÁ.

SAESA (Sociedad Austral de Electricidad, SA): Manuel Bulnes 441, Osorno; tel. (64) 20-6200; fax (64) 20-6209; e-mail saesa@saesa.cl; internet www.saesa.cl; owned by PSEG Corpn of the USA; Pres. ROBERT DOUGHERTY, Jr; Gen. Man. EDUARDO NOVOA CASTELLÓN.

Gas

Abastecedora de Combustible (Abastible, SA): Avda Vicuña Mackenna 55, Providencia, Santiago; tel. (2) 693-0000; fax (2) 693-9304; internet www.abastible.cl; f. 1956; owned by COPEC; Pres. FELIPE LAMARCA CLARO; Gen. Man. JOSÉ ODONE.

AGA Chile, SA: Juan Bautista Pistene 2344, Santiago; tel. (2) 907-6888; internet www.aga.cl; f. 1920; natural and industrial gases utility; owned by Linde Gas Corpn of Germany.

Compañía de Consumidores de Gas de Santiago (GASCO, SA): 1061 Santo Domingo, Casilla 8-D, Santiago; tel. (2) 694-4444; fax (2) 694-4370; e-mail info@gasco.cl; internet www.gasco.cl; natural gas utility; supplies Santiago and Punta Arenas regions; owned by CGE; Pres. MATÍAS PÉREZ CRUZ; Vice-Pres. JORGE MARÍN CORREA.

Electrogas: Evaristo Lillo 78, Of. 41, Las Condes, Santiago; tel. (2) 377-1458; fax (2) 233-4931; f. 1998; subsidiary of Endesa Chile.

GasValpo, SA: Camino Internacional 1420, Viña del Mar; tel. (32) 27-7000; fax (32) 21-3092; e-mail info@gasvalpo.cl; internet www.gasvalpo.cl; f. 1853; owned by AGL of Australia.

GasAndes: Avda. Isidora Goyenechea 3600, Las Condes, Santiago; tel. (2) 362-4200; fax (2) 334-3676; internet www.gasandes.com; distributes gas transported from the Argentine province of Mendoza via a 463-km pipeline.

GasAtacama Generación: Costanera Oriente s/n, Km 2.5, Barrio Industrial, Mejillones; tel. (55) 357-200; fax (55) 623-170; natural gas producer and transporter; Man. LUIS CAHUE.

Lipigas: Las Urbinas 53, 13°, Of. 131, Providencia, Santiago; tel. (32) 656-500; fax (32) 656-595; e-mail info@lipigas.cl; internet www.lipigas.cl; f. 1950; Pres. JAIME SANTA CRUZ; Gen. Man. MARIO FERNÁNDEZ.

Agrogas: Lo Ovalle 1321, Santiago; tel. (2) 511-0904; f. 1977; supplier of liquid gas.

Industrias Codigas: Las Urbinas 53, 9°, Providencia, Santiago; tel. (2) 520-4700; fax (2) 520-4733; f. 1959; Pres. HUGO YACONI MERINO; Gen. Man. JOSÉ LUIS MEIER.

Enagas: f. 1975 as Empresa Nacional del Gas, present name adopted in 1981; gas distribution.

Water

Aguas Andinas, SA: Avda Presidente Balmaceda 1398, Santiago; tel. (2) 688-1000; fax (2) 698-5871; e-mail info@aguasandinas.cl; internet www.aguasandinas.cl; water supply and sanitation services to Santiago and the surrounding area; sold to a French-Spanish consortium in June 1999; Pres. ALFREDO NOMAN.

Empresa de Obras Sanitarias de Valparaíso, SA (Esval): Cochrane 751, Valparaíso; tel. (32) 209-000; fax (32) 209-502; e-mail infoesval@entelchile.net; internet www.esval.cl; f. 1989; sanitation and irrigation co serving Valparaíso; Pres. JUAN HURTADO VICUÑA; Gen. Man. GUSTAVO GONZÁLEZ DOORMAN; 377 employees.

Sigsig Ltda (Tecnagent) (Servicios de Ingeniería Sigren y Sigren Ltda): Presidente Errázuriz 3262, Casilla 7550295, Las Condes, Santiago; tel. (2) 335-2001; fax (2) 334-8466; e-mail tecnagent@tecnagent.cl; internet www.tecnagent.cl; f. 1986; Pres. RAÚL SIGREN BINDHOFF; Gen. Man. RAÚL A. SIGREN ORFILA.

TRADE UNIONS

There are more than 50 national labour federations and unions.

Union Confederations

There are 37 union confederations, of which the following are among the most important:

Agrupación Nacional de Empleados Fiscales (ANEF): Edif. Tucapel Jiménez, Alameda 1603, Santiago; tel. (2) 696-2957; fax 699-3806; internet www.anef.cl; f. 1943; affiliated to CUT; public-service workers; Pres. RAÚL DE LA PUENTE PEÑA; Sec.-Gen. JORGE CONSALES CARVAJAL.

Colegio de Profesores de Chile: Moneda 2394, Santiago; tel. (2) 470-4200; fax (2) 470-4290; e-mail cpch@colegiodeprofesores.cl; internet www.colegiodeprofesores.cl; 80,000 mems; Pres. JAIME GAJARDO ORELLANA; Sec.-Gen. PEDRO CHULAK PIZARRO.

Confederación Nacional Campesina: Eleuterio Ramírez 1471, Santiago; tel. and fax (2) 696-2673; affiliated to CUT; Pres. EUGENIO LEÓN GAJARDO; Sec.-Gen. RENÉ ASTUDILLO R.

Confederación Nacional de Federaciones y Sindicatos de Empresas e Interempresas de Trabajadores del Transporte Terrestre y Afines (CONATRACH): Concha y Toro 2A, 2°, Santiago; tel. and fax (2) 698-0810; Vice-Pres. WILLY RAMÍREZ.

Confederación Nacional de Federaciones y Sindicatos de Gente de Mar, Portuarios y Pesqueros de Chile (CONGEMAR): Tomás Ramos 158–172, Valparaíso; tel. (32) 255-430; fax (32) 257-580; affiliated to CUT; Pres. WALTER ASTORGA LOBOS; Sec.-Gen. JUAN GUZMÁN CARRASCO.

Confederación Nacional de Federaciones y Sindicatos de Trabajadores Textiles y Ramos Similares (CONTEXTIL): Serrano 14, Of. 203, 2°, Santiago; tel. and fax (2) 638-6379; e-mail contextil@yahoo.es; affiliated to CUT; Pres. PATRICIA COÑOMÁN CARRILLO; Sec.-Gen. MARÍA FELISA GARAY ASTUDILLO.

Confederación Nacional de Sindicatos Agrícolas—Unidad Obrero Campesina (UOC): Eleuterio Ramírez 1463, Santiago; tel. and fax (2) 696-6342; e-mail confe.uocchile@uocchile.cl; affiliated to CUT; Pres. OSCAR VALLADARES GONZÁLEZ.

Confederación Nacional de Sindicatos, Federaciones y Asociaciones de Trabajadores del Sector Privado de Chile (CEPCH): Valentín Letelier 18, Santiago; tel. (2) 695-2252; trade union for workers in private sector; affiliated to CUT; Pres. ANGÉLICA CARVALLO PRENAFETA; Sec.-Gen. ISABEL GONZÁLEZ C.

Confederación Nacional de Sindicatos de Trabajadores de la Construcción, Maderas, Materiales de Edificación y Actividades Conexas: Almirante Hurtado 2069, Santiago; tel. and fax (2) 696-4536; e-mail cntc@chile.com; affiliated to CUT; Pres. JULIO ARANCIBIA.

Confederación Nacional de Suplementeros de Chile (CONASUCH): Tucapel Jiménez 26, Santiago; tel. (2) 695-7639; fax (2) 699-1646; f. 1942; trade union for newspaper vendors; Pres. IVÁN ENCINA CARO.

Confederación Nacional de Trabajadores del Comercio (CONSFECOVE): Santiago; tel. (2) 632-2950; fax (2) 632-2884; affiliated to CUT; Pres. JOSÉ LUIS ORTEGA; Sec.-Gen. SUSANA ROSAS VALDEBENITO.

Confederación Nacional de Trabajadores del Cuero y Calzado (FONACC): Arturo Prat 1490, Santiago; tel. (2) 556-9602; affiliated to CUT; Pres. MANUEL JIMÉNEZ TORRES.

CHILE   *Directory*

Confederación Nacional de Trabajadores Electrometalúrgicos, Mineros y Automotrices de Chile (CONSFETEMA): Vicuña Mackenna 3101, San Joaquín, Santiago; tel. (2) 238-1732; fax (2) 553-6494; e-mail consfetema@123mail.cl; Pres. LUIS SEPÚLVEDA DEL RÍO.

Confederación Nacional de Trabajadores Forestales (CTF): Rengo 884, Casilla 2717, Concepción; tel. and fax (41) 220-0407; Pres. JORGE GONZÁLEZ CASTILLO.

Confederación Nacional de Trabajadores de la Industria del Pan (CONAPAN): Tucapel Jiménez 32, 2°, Santiago; tel. and fax (2) 672-1622; affiliated to CUT; Pres. GUILLERMO CORTES MUÑOZ.

Confederación Nacional de Trabajadores de la Industria Textil (CONTEVECH): Agustinas 2349, Santiago; tel. (2) 699-3442; fax (2) 687-3269; affiliated to CUT; Pres. MARIANO AHUMADA CORREA.

Confederación Nacional de Trabajadores Metalúrgicos (CONSTRAMET): Santa Rosa 101, esq. Alonso Ovalle, Santiago; tel. (2) 664-8581; fax (2) 638-3694; e-mail contrame@ctcinternet.cl; affiliated to CUT and the International Metalworkers' Federation; Pres. MIGUEL SOTO ROA; Sec.-Gen. ROBERTO BUSTAMENTE.

Confederación de Sindicatos Bancarios y Afines: Santiago; tel. (2) 699-5597; internet www.bancaria.cl; affiliated to CUT; Pres. ANDREA RIQUELME BELTRÁN; Sec.-Gen. LUIS MESINA MARÍN.

Confederación de Trabajadores del Cobre (CTC): Santiago; copper workers' union; Pres. CRISTIÁN CUEVAS.

There are also 45 union federations and over 100 individual unions.

Transport

RAILWAYS

State Railways

Empresa de los Ferrocarriles del Estado: Avda Libertador B. O'Higgins 3170, Santiago; tel. (2) 376-8500; fax (2) 776-2609; e-mail contacto@efe.cl; internet www.efe.cl; f. 1851; 3,977 km of track (2000); the State Railways are divided between the Ferrocarril Arica–La Paz, La Calera Puerto Montt, and Metro Regional de Valparaíso (passenger service only); several lines scheduled for privatization; Pres. JORGE RODRÍGUEZ GROSSI; Gen. Man. JORGE INOSTROZA.

Parastatal Railways

Ferrocarril del Pacífico, SA (FEPASA): Málaga 120, 5°, Las Condes, Santiago; tel. (2) 412-1000; fax (2) 412-1040; e-mail oguevara@fepasa.cl; internet www.fepasa.cl; f. 1993; privatized freight services; Pres. RAMÓN ABOITIZ MUSATADI; Gen. Man. GAMALIEL VILLALOBOS ARANDA.

Metro de Santiago: Empresa de Transporte de Pasajeros Metro, SA, Avda Libertador B. O'Higgins 1414, Santiago; tel. (2) 250-3000; fax (2) 699-2475; internet www.metrosantiago.cl; started operations 1975; 40.2 km (2003); 3 lines; Pres. CLEMENTE PÉREZ ERRÁZURIZ; Gen. Man. HERNÁN VEGA MOLINA.

Private Railways

Empresa de Transporte Ferroviario, SA (Ferronor): Huérfanos 587, Ofs 301 y 302, Santiago; tel. (2) 638-0430; e-mail ferronor@ferronor.cl; internet www.ferronor.cl; 2,300 km of track (2002); established as a public/private concern, following the transfer of the Ferrocarril Regional del Norte de Chile to the then Ministry of Production Development (CORFO) as a *Sociedad Anónima* in 1989; operates cargo services only; Commercial Man. PABLO ARRANZ; Pres. ROBERTO PIRAZZOLI.

Ferrocarril Codelco-Chile: Barquito, Region III, Atacama; tel. (52) 48-8521; fax (52) 48-8522; Gen. Man. B. BEHN THEUNE.

  Diego de Almagro a Potrerillos: transport of forest products, minerals and manufactures; 99 km.

  Ferrocarril Rancagua–Teniente: transport of forest products, livestock, minerals and manufactures; 68 km.

Ferrocarril de Antofagasta a Bolivia (FCAB): Bolívar 255, Casillas ST, Antofagasta; tel. (55) 20-6700; fax (55) 20-6220; e-mail webmaster@fcab.cl; internet www.fcab.cl; f. 1888; owned by Luksic conglomerate (Quiñenco); operates an international railway to Bolivia and Argentina; cargo forwarding services; total track length 934 km; Chair. ANDRÓNICO LUKSIC ABAROA; Gen. Man. M. V. SEPÚLVEDA.

Ferrocarril Tocopilla–Toco: Calle Arturo Prat 1060, Casilla 2098, Tocopilla; tel. (55) 81-2139; fax (55) 81-2650; owned by Sociedad Química y Minera de Chile, SA; 117 km (1995); Gen. Man. SEGISFREDO HURTADO GUERRERO.

Association

Asociación Chilena de Conservación de Patrimonio Ferroviario (ACCPF—Chilean Railway Society): Concha y Toro 10, Barrio Brasil, Santiago; tel. (2) 699-4607; fax (2) 280-0252; e-mail rsandoval@ucinf.cl; internet www.accpf.cl; Pres. SERGIO CARMONA MALATESTA; Sec.-Gen. CLAUDIO CURELLI MANN.

ROADS

The total length of roads in Chile in 2001 was an estimated 79,605 km (49,464 miles), of which some 6,279 km were highways and some 16,410 km were secondary roads. The road system includes the entirely paved Pan-American Highway, extending 3,455 km from north to south. Toll gates exist on major motorways. The 1,200-km Carretera Austral (Southern Highway), linking Puerto Montt and Puerto Yungay, was completed in 1996, at an estimated total cost of US $200m.

SHIPPING

As a consequence of Chile's difficult topography, maritime transport is of particular importance. In 1997 90% of the country's foreign trade was carried by sea (51m. metric tons). The principal ports are Valparaíso, Talcahuano, Antofagasta, San Antonio, Arica, Iquique, Coquimbo, San Vicente, Puerto Montt and Punta Arenas. Most port operations were privatized in the late 1990s.

Chile's merchant fleet amounted to 935,594 grt (comprising 549 vessels) at December 2006.

Supervisory Authorities

Asociación Nacional de Armadores: Blanco 869, 3°, Valparaíso; tel. (32) 21-2057; fax (32) 21-2017; e-mail info@armadores-chile.cl; internet www.armadores-chile.cl; f. 1931; shipowners' asscn; Pres. EUGENIO VALENZUELA CARVALLO.

Cámara Marítima y Portuaria de Chile, AG: Blanco 869, 2°, Valparaíso; tel. (32) 25-3443; fax (32) 25-0231; e-mail info@camport.cl; internet www.camport.cl; Pres. VICTOR PINO TORCHE; Vice-Pres. EDUARDO HARTWIG ITURRIAGA.

Dirección General de Territorio Marítimo y Marina Mercante: Errázuriz 537, 4°, Valparaíso; tel. (32) 20-8000; fax (32) 25-2539; e-mail webmaster@directemar.cl; internet www.directemar.cl; maritime admin. of the coast and national waters, control of the merchant navy; ship registry; Dir-Gen. FRANCISCO MARTÍNEZ VILLARROEL.

Cargo Handling Companies

Empresa Portuaria Antofagasta: Grecia s/n, Antofagasta; tel. (55) 25-1737; fax (55) 22-3171; e-mail afernandez@puertoantofagasta.cl; internet www.puertoantofagasta.cl; Pres. BLAS ENRIQUE ESPINOZA SEPÚLVEDA; Gen. Man. ALVARO FERNÁNDEZ SLATER.

Empresa Portuaria Arica: Máximo Lira 389, Arica; tel. (58) 25-5078; fax (58) 23-2284; e-mail puertoarica@puertoarica.cl; internet www.puertoarica.cl; Pres. FRANCISCO JAVIER GONZÁLEZ; Gen. Man. ALDO SIGNORELLI BONOMO.

Empresa Portuaria Austral: Avda B. O'Higgins 1385, Punta Arenas; tel. (61) 24-1111; fax (61) 24-1111; e-mail portspuq@epa.co.cl; internet www.epa.co.cl; Pres. YANKO VILICIC RASMUSSEN; Gen. Man. EDUARDO MANZANARES CASTESC.

Empresa Portuaria Chacabuco: Avda B. O'Higgins s/n, Puerto Chacabuco; tel. (67) 35-1198; fax (67) 35-1174; e-mail gerencia@chacabucoport.cl; internet www.portchacabuco.cl; Pres. ENRIQUE RUNÍN Z.

Empresa Portuaria Coquimbo: Melgareja 676, Coquimbo; tel. (51) 31-3606; fax (51) 32-6146; e-mail ptoqq@entelchile.net; internet www.puertocoquimbo.cl; Pres. HUGO MIRANDA RAMÍREZ.

Empresa Portuaria Iquique: Jorge Barrera 62, Iquique; tel. (57) 40-0100; fax (57) 41-3176; e-mail epi@epi.cl; internet www.epi.cl; f. 1998; Pres. MARCO ANTONIO BLAVIA BEYA.

Empresa Portuaria Puerto Montt: Angelmó 1673, Puerto Montt; tel. (65) 25-2247; e-mail info@empormontt.cl; internet www.empormontt.cl; Gen. Man. PATRICIO CAMPAÑA CUELLO.

Empresa Portuaria San Antonio: Alan Macowan 0245, San Antonio; tel. (35) 58-6000; fax (35) 58-6015; e-mail correo@saiport.cl; internet www.saiport.cl; f. 1998; Pres. PATRICIO ARRAU PONS; Gen. Man. ALVARO ESPINOSA ALMARZA.

Empresa Portuaria Talcahuano-San Vicente: Blanco Encalada 547, Talcahuano; tel. (41) 79-7600; fax (41) 79-7626; e-mail eportuaria@puertotalcahuano.cl; internet www.ptotalsve.cl; Pres. ELIANA CARABALL MARTINEZ; Gen. Man. LUIS ALBERTO ROSENBERG NESBET.

Empresa Portuaria Valparaíso: Errázuriz 25, 4°, Of. 1, Valparaíso; tel. (2) 244-8800; fax (2) 223-4427; e-mail comercial@epv.cl;

internet www.epv.cl; Pres. GERMÁN CORREA DIAZ; Gen. Man. HARALD JAEGER KARL.

Principal Shipping Companies

Santiago

Naviera Magallanes, SA (NAVIMAG): Avda El Bosque, Norte 0440, 11°, Of. 1103/1104, Las Condes, Santiago; tel. (2) 442-3150; fax (2) 442-3156; internet www.navimag.com; f. 1979; Chair. PEDRO LECAROS MENÉNDEZ; Gen. Man. HÉCTOR HENRÍQUEZ NEGRÓN.

Nisa Navegación, SA: Avda El Bosque Norte 0440, 11°, Casilla 2829, Santiago; tel. (2) 442-3100; fax (2) 203-5190; internet www.nisa.cl; Chair. PEDRO LECAROS MENÉNDEZ; Fleet Man. C. SALINAS.

Sociedad Anónima de Navegación Petrolera (SONAP): Moneda 970, 20°, Casilla 13-D, Santiago; tel. (2) 630-1009; fax (2) 630-1041; e-mail valsonap@sonap.cl; f. 1954; tanker services; Chair. FELIPE VIAL C.; Gen. Man. JOSÉ THOMSEN Q.

Transmares Naviera Chilena Ltda: Moneda 970, 20°, Edif. Eurocentro, Casilla 193-D, Santiago; tel. (2) 630-1000; fax (2) 698-9205; e-mail transmares@transmares.cl; f. 1969; dry cargo service Chile–Uruguay–Brazil; Chair. WOLF VON APPEN; Gen. Man. C. KUHLENTHAL.

Valparaíso

Agencias Universales, SA (AGUNSA): Edif. del Pacífico, 15°, Avda Andrés Bello 2687, Casilla 2511, Las Condes, Santiago; tel. (2) 203-9000; fax (2) 203-9009; e-mail agunsascl@agunsa.cl; internet www.agunsa.cl; f. 1960; maritime transportation and shipping, port and docking services; owned by Empresas Navieras, SA; Chair. JOSÉ MANUEL URENDA SALAMANCA; Gen. Man. LUIS MANCILLA PÉREZ.

Broom Valparaíso: Almirante Señoret 70, 10°, Valparaíso; tel. (32) 226-8200; fax (32) 221-3308; e-mail info@ajbroom.cl; internet www.broomgroup.com; f. 1920; ship owners and brokers; Pres. JAMES C. WELLS M; CEO ANDRÉS NUÑEZ SORENSEN.

Cía Chilena de Navegación Interoceánica, SA: Plaza de la Justicia 59, Valparaíso; tel. (32) 275-500; fax (32) 255-949; e-mail info@ccni.cl; internet www.ccni.cl; f. 1930; regular sailings to Japan, Republic of Korea, Taiwan, Hong Kong, USA, Mexico, South Pacific, South Africa and Europe; bulk and dry cargo services; owned by Empresas Navieras, SA; Pres. CARLOS ALLIMANT; 116 employees.

Cía Sud Americana de Vapores: Plaza Sotomayor 50, Casilla 49-V, Valparaíso; also Hendaya 60, 12°, Santiago; tel. (32) 20-3000; tel. (2) 330-7000; fax (32) 20-3333; e-mail info@csav.com; internet www.csav.com; f. 1872; regular service between South America and US/Canadian ports, US Gulf ports, North European, Mediterranean, Scandinavian and Far East ports; bulk carriers, tramp and reefer services; part of Cristalchile group; Chair. RICARDO CLARO VALDÉS; Gen. Man. JOAQUÍN BARROS FONTAINE.

Empresa Marítima, SA (Empremar Chile): Encomenderos 260, Piso 7°, Las condes, Santiago; tel. (2) 469-6100; fax (2) 469-6199; internet www.empremar.cl; f. 1953; international and coastal services; Chair. LORENZO CAGLEVIC; Gen. Man. E. ESPINOZA.

Naviera Chilena del Pacífico, SA (Nachipa): Almirante Señoret 70, 6°, Casilla 370, Valparaíso; also Serrano 14, Of. 502, Casilla 2290, Santiago; tel. (32) 50-0300; e-mail valparaiso@nachipa.com; internet www.nachipa.cl; cargo; Pres. PABLO SIMIAN ZAMORANO.

Sudamericana Agencias Aéreas y Marítimas, SA (SAAM): Blanco 895, Valparaíso; tel. (32) 20-1000; fax (32) 20-1481; e-mail gerenciavap@saamsa.com; internet www.saam.cl; f. 1961; cargo services; Pres. RICARDO DE TEZANOS PINTO D.; Gen. Man. ALEJANDRO GARCÍA-HUIDOBRO O.

Several foreign shipping companies operate services to Valparaíso.

Punta Arenas

Cía Marítima de Punta Arenas, SA: Avda Independencia 830, Casilla 337, Punta Arenas; tel. (61) 22-1871; fax (61) 22-7514; f. 1949; shipping agents and owners operating in the Magellan Straits; Pres. PEDRO LECAROS MENÉNDEZ; Gen. Man. ARTURO STORAKER MOLINA.

Puerto Montt

Transporte Marítimo Chiloé-Aysén, SA: Angelmo 2187, Puerto Montt; tel. (65) 27-0419; Deputy Man. PEDRO HERNÁNDEZ LEHMAN.

CIVIL AVIATION

There are 325 airfields in the country, of which eight have long runways. Arturo Merino Benítez, 20 km north-east of Santiago, and Chacalluta, 14 km north-east of Arica, are the principal international airports.

Aerocardal: Aeropuerto Internacional Arturo Merino Benítez, Avda Diego Barros Ortiz s/n, Pudahuel, Santiago; tel. (2) 377-7400; fax (2) 377-7402; e-mail aerocard@aerocardal.com; internet www.aerocardal.cl; f. 1991; executive, charter and tourist services.

Aerovías DAP: Avda B. O'Higgins 891, Casilla 406, Punta Arenas; tel. (61) 61-6100; fax (61) 22-1693; e-mail ventas@aeroviasdap.cl; internet www.aeroviasdap.cl; f. 1980; domestic services; CEO ALEX PISCEVIC.

Línea Aérea Nacional de Chile (LAN-Chile): Américo Vespucio 901, Renca, Santiago; tel. (2) 565-2525; fax (2) 565-1729; internet www.lanchile.com; f. 1929; operates scheduled domestic passenger and cargo services, also Santiago–Easter Island; international services to French Polynesia, Spain, and throughout North and South America; under the Govt's privatization programme, 99% of LAN-Chile shares have been sold to private interests since 1989; Pres. JORGE AWAD MEHECH; Gen. Man. IGNACIO CUETO PLAZA.

Tourism

Chile has a wide variety of attractions for the tourist, including fine beaches, ski resorts in the Andes, lakes, rivers and desert scenery. There are many opportunities for hunting and fishing in the southern archipelago, where there are plans to make an integrated tourist area with Argentina, requiring investment of US $120m. Isla de Pascua (Easter Island) may also be visited by tourists. In 2006 there were an estimated 2,252,952 tourist arrivals. In 2004 receipts from tourism totalled $1,554m.

Servicio Nacional de Turismo (SERNATUR): Avda Providencia 1550, 2°, Santiago; tel. (2) 731-8419; fax (2) 236-1417; e-mail pcasanova@sernatur.cl; internet www.sernatur.cl; f. 1975; Dir Dr OSCAR SANTELICES ALTAMIRANO.

Asociación Chilena de Empresas de Turismo (ACHET): Moneda 973, Of. 647, Santiago; tel. (2) 699-2140; fax (2) 699-4245; e-mail achet@achet.cl; internet www.achet.cl; f. 1945; 155 mems; Pres. GUILLERMO CORREA SANFUENTES; Man. LORENA ARRIAGADA GÁLVEZ.

THE PEOPLE'S REPUBLIC OF CHINA

Introductory Survey

Location, Climate, Language, Religion, Flag, Capital

The People's Republic of China covers a vast area of eastern Asia, with Mongolia and Russia to the north, Tajikistan, Kyrgyzstan and Kazakhstan to the north-west, Afghanistan and Pakistan to the west, and India, Nepal, Bhutan, Myanmar (formerly Burma), Laos and Viet Nam to the south. The country borders the Democratic People's Republic of Korea (North Korea) in the north-east, and has a long coastline on the Pacific Ocean. The climate ranges from subtropical in the far south to an annual average temperature of below 10°C (50°F) in the north, and from the monsoon climate of eastern China to the aridity of the north-west. The principal language is Northern Chinese (Mandarin, known as Putonghua or common speech); in the south and south-east local dialects are spoken. The Xizangzu (Tibetans), Wei Wuer (Uygurs), Menggus (Mongols) and other groups have their own languages. The traditional religions and philosophies of life are Confucianism, Buddhism and Daoism. There are also Muslim and Christian minorities. The national flag (proportions 2 by 3) is plain red, with one large five-pointed gold star and four similar but smaller stars, arranged in an arc, in the upper hoist. The capital is Beijing (Peking).

Recent History

The People's Republic of China was proclaimed on 1 October 1949, following the victory of Communist forces over the Kuomintang (KMT) Government, which fled to the island province of Taiwan. The new Communist regime received widespread international recognition, but it was not until 1971 that the People's Republic was admitted to the United Nations, in place of the KMT regime, as the representative of China. Most countries now recognize the People's Republic.

With the establishment of the People's Republic, the leading political figure was Mao Zedong, who was Chairman of the Chinese Communist Party (CCP) from 1935 until his death in 1976. Chairman Mao, as he was known, also became Head of State in October 1949, but he relinquished this post in December 1958. His successor was Liu Shaoqi, First Vice-Chairman of the CCP, who was elected Head of State in April 1959. Liu was dismissed in October 1968, during the Cultural Revolution (see below), and died in prison in 1969. The post of Head of State was left vacant, and was formally abolished in January 1975, when a new Constitution was adopted. The first Premier (Head of Government) of the People's Republic was Zhou Enlai, who held this office from October 1949 until his death in 1976. Zhou was also Minister of Foreign Affairs from 1949 to 1958.

The economic progress of the early years of Communist rule enabled China to withstand the effects of the industrialization programmes of the late 1950s (called the 'Great Leap Forward'), the drought of 1960–62 and the withdrawal of Soviet aid in 1960. To prevent the establishment of a ruling class, Chairman Mao launched the Great Proletarian Cultural Revolution in 1966. The ensuing excesses of the Red Guards caused the army to intervene; Liu Shaoqi and Deng Xiaoping, General Secretary of the CCP, were disgraced. In 1971 an attempted coup by the Defence Minister, Marshal Lin Biao, was unsuccessful, and by 1973 it was apparent that Chairman Mao and Premier Zhou Enlai had retained power. In 1975 Deng Xiaoping re-emerged as first Vice-Premier and Chief of the General Staff. Zhou Enlai died in January 1976. Hua Guofeng, hitherto Minister of Public Security, was appointed Premier, and Deng was dismissed. Mao died in September 1976. His widow, Jiang Qing, tried unsuccessfully to seize power, with the help of three radical members of the CCP's Political Bureau (Politburo). The 'Gang of Four' and six associates of Lin Biao were tried in November 1980. All were found guilty and were given long terms of imprisonment. (Jiang Qing committed suicide in May 1991.) The 10th anniversary of Mao's death was marked in September 1986 by an official reassessment of his life; while his accomplishments were praised, it was now acknowledged that he had made mistakes, although most of the criticism was directed at the 'Gang of Four'.

In October 1976 Hua Guofeng succeeded Mao as Chairman of the CCP and Commander-in-Chief of the People's Liberation Army (PLA). The 11th National Congress of the CCP, held in August 1977, restored Deng Xiaoping to his former posts. In September 1980 Hua Guofeng resigned as Premier, but retained his chairmanship of the CCP. The appointment of Zhao Ziyang, a Vice-Premier since April 1980, to succeed Hua as Premier confirmed the dominance of the moderate faction of Deng Xiaoping. In June 1981 Hua Guofeng was replaced as Chairman of the CCP by Hu Yaobang, former Secretary-General of the Politburo, and as Chairman of the Party's Central Military Commission by Deng Xiaoping. A sustained campaign by Deng to purge the Politburo of 'leftist' elements led to Hua's demotion to a Vice-Chairman of the CCP and, in September 1982, to his exclusion from the Politburo.

In September 1982 the CCP was reorganized and the post of Party Chairman abolished. Hu Yaobang became, instead, General Secretary of the CCP. A year later a 'rectification' (purge) of the CCP was launched, aimed at expelling 'Maoists', who had risen to power during the Cultural Revolution, and those opposed to the pragmatic policies of Deng. China's new Constitution, adopted in December 1982, restored the office of Head of State, and in June 1983 Li Xiannian, a former Minister of Finance, became President of China. In September 1986 the sixth plenary session of the 12th CCP Central Committee adopted a detailed resolution on the 'guiding principles for building a socialist society', which redefined the general ideology of the CCP, to provide a theoretical basis for the programme of modernization and the 'open door' policy of economic reform.

In January 1986 an 'anti-corruption' campaign was launched, to investigate reports that many officials had exploited the programme of economic reform for their own gain. A significant cultural liberalization took place in 1986, with a revival of the 'Hundred Flowers' movement of 1956–57, which had encouraged the development of intellectual debate. However, a series of student demonstrations in major cities in late 1986 was regarded by China's leaders as an indication of excessive 'bourgeois liberalization'. In January 1987 Hu Yaobang unexpectedly resigned as CCP General Secretary, being accused of 'mistakes on major issues of political principles'. Zhao Ziyang became acting General Secretary. At the 13th National Congress of the CCP, which opened in October, Deng Xiaoping retired from the Central Committee, but amendments to the Constitution of the CCP permitted him to retain the influential positions of Chairman of the State Military Commission and of the CCP Central Military Commission. A new Politburo was appointed by the Central Committee in November. The majority of its 18 members were relatively young officials, who supported Deng Xiaoping's policies. The membership of the new Politburo also indicated a decline in military influence in Chinese politics. The newly appointed Standing Committee of the Politburo (the highest decision-making body) was regarded, on balance, as being 'pro-reform'. In late November Li Peng was appointed Acting Premier of the State Council, in place of Zhao Ziyang. At the first session of the Seventh National People's Congress (NPC), held in March–April 1988, Li Peng was confirmed as Premier, and Yang Shangkun (a member of the CCP Politburo) was elected President.

Following the death of Hu Yaobang in April 1989, students criticized the alleged prevalence of corruption and nepotism within the Government, seeking a limited degree of Soviet-style *glasnost* (openness) in public life. When negotiations between government officials and the students' leaders had failed to satisfy the protesters' demands, workers from various professions joined the demonstrations in Tiananmen Square, Beijing, which had now become the focal point of the protests. At one stage more than 1m. people congregated in the Square, as demonstrations spread to more than 20 other Chinese cities. In mid-May some 3,000 students began a hunger strike in Tiananmen Square, while protesters demanded the resignation of both Deng Xiaoping and Li Peng, and invited President Gorbachev of the USSR, who was visiting Beijing, to address them. The students ended their hunger strike at the request of Zhao Ziyang. On 20 May martial law was declared in Beijing. Within days, some 300,000 troops had assembled. At the end of

May the students erected a 30 m-high replica of the US Statue of Liberty in the Square.

On 3 June 1989 a further unsuccessful attempt was made to dislodge the demonstrators, but on the following day troops of the PLA attacked protesters on and around Tiananmen Square, killing an unspecified number of people. Television evidence and eye-witness accounts estimated the total dead at between 1,000 and 5,000. The Government immediately rejected these figures and claimed, furthermore, that the larger part of the casualties had been soldiers and that a counter-revolutionary rebellion had been taking place. Arrests and executions ensued, although some student leaders eluded capture and fled to Hong Kong. Zhao Ziyang was dismissed from all his party posts and replaced as General Secretary of the CCP by Jiang Zemin, hitherto the secretary of the Shanghai municipal party committee. Zhao was accused of participating in a conspiracy to overthrow the CCP and placed under house arrest. In November Deng resigned as Chairman of the CCP Central Military Commission, his sole remaining party position, and was succeeded by Jiang Zemin, who was hailed as the first of China's 'third generation' of communist leaders (Mao being representative of the first, and Deng of the second). In January 1990 martial law was removed in Beijing, and it was announced that a total of 573 prisoners, detained following the pro-democracy demonstrations, had been freed. Further groups of detainees were released subsequently. In March Deng Xiaoping resigned from his last official post, that of Chairman of the State Central Military Commission, and was succeeded by Jiang Zemin. An extensive military reorganization ensued. At the CCP's 14th National Congress, held in October 1992, a new 319-member Central Committee was elected. The Politburo was expanded and a new Secretariat was chosen by the incoming Central Committee. Many opponents of Deng Xiaoping's support for a 'socialist market economy' were replaced.

At the first session of the Eighth NPC, convened in March 1993, Jiang Zemin was elected as the country's President, remaining CCP General Secretary. Li Peng was reappointed as Premier, and an extensive reorganization of the State Council was announced. The Congress also approved amendments to the 1982 Constitution. Changes included confirmation of the State's practice of a 'socialist market economy'. During 1993, however, the Government became concerned at the growing disparity between urban and rural incomes. In June thousands of peasants took part in demonstrations in Sichuan Province to protest against excessive official levies. In response to the ensuing riots, the central Government banned the imposition of additional local taxes.

In March 1995, at the third session of the Eighth NPC, the appointment of Wu Bangguo and of Jiang Chunyun as Vice-Premiers of the State Council was approved. In an unprecedented display of opposition, however, neither nominee received the NPC's full endorsement. Nevertheless, the position of Jiang Zemin, now regarded by many as the eventual successor to the 'paramount' leadership of the ailing Deng Xiaoping, appeared to have been strengthened. Personnel changes in the military hierarchy later in the year were also viewed as favourable to Jiang Zemin. In April 1996 the Government initiated 'Strike Hard', a new campaign against crime, executing hundreds of people.

The death of Deng Xiaoping in February 1997 precipitated a period of uncertainty regarding China's future direction. President Jiang Zemin declared that the economic reforms would continue, and this was reiterated in Premier Li Peng's address to the fifth session of the Eighth NPC in March. Delegates at the Congress approved legislation reinforcing the CCP's control over the PLA, and revisions to the criminal code were also promulgated, whereby statutes concerning 'counter-revolutionary' acts (under which many of the pro-democracy demonstrators had been charged in 1989) were removed from the code, but were replaced by 11 crimes of 'endangering state security'. Financial offences were also included for the first time.

At the 15th National Congress of the CCP, convened in September 1997, emphasis was placed on radical reform of the 370,000 state-owned enterprises (SOEs). Delegates approved amendments to the party Constitution, enshrining the 'Deng Xiaoping Theory' of socialism with Chinese characteristics alongside 'Mao Zedong Thought' as the guiding ideology of the CCP. The Congress elected a new 344-member Central Committee, which re-elected Jiang Zemin as General Secretary of the CCP, and appointed a 22-member Politburo. The composition of the new Politburo appeared to confirm Jiang Zemin's enhanced authority: Qiao Shi, a reformist and Jiang's most influential rival, who was ranked third in the party hierarchy, was excluded, reportedly because of his age, as was Gen. Liu Huaqing, China's most senior military figure. Zhu Rongji, a former mayor of Shanghai, replaced Qiao Shi. Gen. Liu was replaced by a civilian, Wei Jinxiang, who was responsible for combating corruption within the CCP. The absence of the military from the Politburo, and the composition of the new Central Military Commission, confirmed Jiang's increased authority over the PLA.

At the first session of the Ninth NPC, which was held in March 1998, the number of ministry-level bodies was reduced from 40 to 29, mainly through mergers. Jiang Zemin was re-elected President, and Hu Jintao was elected Vice-President. Li Peng resigned as Premier and was replaced by Zhu Rongji, who received overwhelming support from the NPC delegates. Li Peng replaced Qiao Shi as Chairman of the NPC. Zhu's appointments to a new 39-member State Council included a number of associates of Jiang Zemin.

In March 1999, at the second session of the Ninth NPC, a number of constitutional amendments were ratified, including the elevation in status of private-sector and other non-state enterprises to 'important components of the socialist market economy', a recommendation for adherence to the rule of law, and the incorporation of Deng Xiaoping's ideology into the Constitution alongside Marxism-Leninism and 'Mao Zedong Thought'. At celebrations of the 50th anniversary of the foundation of the People's Republic of China in October, in a highly symbolic gesture, a picture of Jiang Zemin was paraded alongside portraits of Mao Zedong and Deng Xiaoping: the first time that the current President had been publicly placed on a par with his predecessors. In the same month Hu Jintao was appointed a Vice-Chairman of the Central Military Commission.

In February 2000, in an attempt to refute the growing belief that China would eventually be obliged to abandon one-party rule, Jiang Zemin had launched a new political theory entitled 'The Three Represents', which declared that the CCP would 'always represent the development needs of China's advanced social productive forces, always represent the onward direction of China's advanced culture and always represent the fundamental interests of the largest number of Chinese people'. It appeared, however, that with the advent of significant social change the CCP was finding it increasingly difficult to maintain control over its members. In the following months there was harsh repression of provincial labour unrest.

The third session of the Ninth NPC, which convened in Beijing in March 2000, focused mainly on economic issues. At its plenary session in October, the CCP announced a new five-year plan, under which China was to concentrate on rural development, the creation of employment, economic modernization and combating corruption. During the fourth session of the Ninth NPC, held in March 2001, Premier Zhu Rongji outlined plans for economic restructuring in preparation for China's membership of the World Trade Organization (WTO). From April 2001 the authorities renewed their action against dissent, as part of the latest nation-wide 'Strike Hard' campaign. The campaign was co-ordinated by Luo Gan, a protégé of Li Peng, with the approval of Jiang Zemin. In April 2001 Jin Ruchao was sentenced to death for his alleged role in setting off a series of bombs in Hebei in March, which killed a total of 108 people.

In May 2001 Pan Yue, a prominent intellectual who also served as a deputy director of economic reform, presented to President Jiang a plan to transform the CCP into a more broadly representative body; the plan was subsequently discussed by the Politburo Standing Committee. Pan's plan was believed to reflect the views of an increasing number of party cadres, as a means to prolong CCP rule without effecting democratization. In a report released in June, the CCP acknowledged that its rule might be undermined by social discontent arising from the country's free-market reforms, warning that inequality and corruption were issues of increasing importance. On 1 July 2001, in a speech to mark the 80th anniversary of the foundation of the CCP, President Jiang urged the modernization of the Party and for the first time stated that business people would be welcome as party members. However, Jiang's rightward shift was not universally welcomed. The left-wing forces, which included orthodox Communists, supporters of moderate socialism, the agricultural lobby and liberals, all opposed the transformation of the CCP into a more business-orientated party. In mid-July the International Olympic Committee (IOC) awarded the 2008 Olympic Games to Beijing, resulting in mass celebrations across the country. Some residential areas of the capital were subsequently demolished. as part of a modernization programme in preparation for the Games.

In July 2002 senior CCP officials met to determine the new positions to be allocated at the Congress. The 16th CCP Congress was finally held in early November, having been postponed from September, and resulted in the long-awaited transfer of power to the 'fourth generation' leadership headed by the incoming General Secretary, Hu Jintao. A new 356-member Central Committee was elected, as well as a 24-member Politburo, the Standing Committee of which was expanded from seven to nine members, of whom Hu was the only incumbent to be retained. Jiang retained the chairmanship of the CCP Central Military Commission, which again contained several important military allies of his. Another Jiang associate, Gen. Liang Guanglie, hitherto Commander of the Nanjing Military Region, was appointed Chief of the PLA's General Staff. Jiang thus retained full control of the powerful PLA. The Congress stressed continuity in policy, but introduced some economic reforms. Although state ownership would remain dominant, private businesses would be able to compete on a more equal basis. Discriminatory regulations on investment, financing, taxation, land use and foreign trade would be revised, and private property would be granted greater legal protection.

The final stage of the transfer of power to the 'fourth generation' of Chinese leadership took place during the 10th NPC, held in March 2003. Hu Jintao was appointed President, succeeding Jiang Zemin. Zeng Qinghong, who had become a full member of the Politburo in December 1999, was appointed Vice-President. Wen Jiabao succeeded Zhu Rongji as Premier, and Huang Ju, Wu Yi, Zeng Peiyan, and Hui Liangyu were appointed as Vice-Premiers. The new State Council also included Ma Kai as Minister of State Development and Reform Commission, Jin Renqing as Minister of Finance, and Lu Fuyuan as Minister of Commerce. Both Ma and Jin were known to have economic backgrounds. Li Zhaoxing, a former ambassador to the USA and the UN and hitherto a Vice-Minister of Foreign Affairs, was appointed Minister of Foreign Affairs, replacing Tang Jiaxuan, who became one of five state councillors. Gen. Cao Gangchuan was appointed Minister of National Defence. Hua Jianmin, an ally of Jiang, was appointed Secretary-General of the State Council. The new Chairman of the NPC was Wu Bangguo, replacing Li Peng. The incoming leadership immediately confronted a new challenge with the outbreak of Severe Acute Respiratory Syndrome (SARS), a previously unknown illness (see below).

In August 2003 government directives banning media discussion of political and constitutional reform were issued. There were, none the less, some signs of reform in the second half of 2003. In district elections in Beijing in December two seats were secured by independent candidates, this being the first time that independent candidates had won seats in the District People's Congress for more than 20 years. Also in December, a constitutional amendment to provide protection of private property was introduced by members of the NPC. This significant amendment represented the first formal initiative to provide legal protection of private property rights in China since 1949. The changes were endorsed at the second session of the 10th NPC in March 2004. Detailed amendments to the Constitution were subsequently made, stating in Article 13 that 'citizens' lawful private property is inviolable'. Another important constitutional change approved at the NPC session was a new reference to the 'Three Represents' theory (see above) as a guiding ideology. Premier Wen Jiabao also outlined plans for eliminating agricultural taxation and reducing economic inequalities. (In March 2007, following several years of discussion of the contentious issue, the NPC finally approved new legislation to afford greater legal protection for private property and assets.) At the fourth plenary session of the 16th CCP Congress in September 2004 former President Jiang Zemin relinquished his last official post, that of Chairman of the Central Military Commission, to Hu Jintao.

In January 2005 the death of former Premier and CCP leader Zhao Ziyang, who had been removed from his post and placed under house arrest following the student protests of 1989, prompted speculation about a revival of pro-democracy protests, with security around Tiananmen Square being reinforced. Following Zhao's death, the Government reiterated its refusal to reassess the events of 1989, emphasizing that suppression of the democracy movement had been necessary to ensure the social stability upon which China's economic successes since 1989 had depended. In November 2005 an official event was held to commemorate the 90th anniversary of the birth of Hu Yaobang, the former CCP General Secretary whose death had initiated the Tiananmen Square protests of 1989.

In April 2007 President Hu effected a reorganization of the State Council. The Minister of Foreign Affairs, Li Zhaoxing, was replaced by Yang Jiechi, a former ambassador to the USA, while Chen Lei succeeded Wang Shucheng as Minister of Water Resources. Also of note was the appointment of Wan Gang, a non-member of the CCP, as Minister of Science and Technology. (A second non-member, Chen Zhu, joined the State Council in June as Minister of Health, following the departure of Gao Qiang.) Huang Ju, a Vice-Premier of the State Council and member of the Standing Committee of the CCP Politburo, died of cancer in June. In view of Huang's position as an ally of Jiang Zemin, his death prompted speculation about the consolidation of President Hu's power base within the party. Further changes were announced in August, including the appointment of Xie Xuren as successor to Minister of Finance Jin Renqing, and the selection of Ma Wen as Minister of Supervision, following Li Zhilun's death in April.

At the 17th CCP Congress, held in October 2007, President Hu outlined plans to address the disparity between rich and poor and to amend property laws; Hu acknowledged continuing problems such as corruption (see below) and drew attention to the 'wide-ranging and deep transformation' China was undergoing. Elections to the CCP Central Committee were followed by a plenary session of the new Committee, during which President Hu was re-elected General Secretary of the party and the composition of the Politburo and Standing Committee was determined. New appointees to the latter included Xi Jinping, Secretary of the Shanghai Municipal Committee, and Li Keqiang, Chairman of the Standing Committee of the Provincial People's Congress of Liaoning.

At the first session of the 11th NPC held in March 2008 President Hu Jintao was re-elected for a second five-year term of office. Xi Jinping was elected as Vice-President, in succession to Zeng Qinghong. Wen Jiabao was confirmed as Premier for a further five-year term. A subsequent reorganization of the State Council included the appointment of Gen. Liang Guanglie as Minister of National Defence, and the elevation of the State Environmental Protection Agency to the status of ministry (one of four so-called 'super-ministries'), under Zhou Shengxian.

In other domestic affairs, the increasing disquiet over corruption within the CCP, the state bureaucracy and economic enterprises was acknowledged in August 1993, when the Party initiated an anti-corruption campaign. Hundreds of executions of officials were subsequently reported, and in April 1995, following allegations of corruption, Wang Baosen, a deputy mayor of Beijing, committed suicide. In the same month Chen Xitong, Secretary of the Beijing Municipality Committee, was arrested. An extensive inquiry concluded that Wang Baosen, a protégé of Chen Xitong, had been responsible for serious irregularities, including the embezzlement of the equivalent of millions of US dollars. In September, having been similarly disgraced, Chen Xitong was expelled from the Politburo and from the Central Committee of the CCP, later being removed from the CCP itself. The mayor of Beijing, Li Qiyan, resigned in October 1996. The campaign against corruption intensified in 1997 with the sentencing in August of Chen Xiaotong, son of Chen Xitong, to 12 years' imprisonment for the misappropriation of public funds. In August 1998 Chen Xitong was sentenced to 16 years' imprisonment for corruption and dereliction of duty. It was reported that between October 1992 and June 1997 121,000 people had been expelled from the CCP for corruption, while 37,500 others had faced criminal charges.

Corruption appeared to be rife in many areas of government. Among the most notable cases was that of a former Vice-Chairman of the Standing Committee of the NPC, Cheng Kejie, who was executed in September 2000 for accepting large bribes. Also in September, Maj.-Gen. Ji Shengde, the former head of military intelligence of the PLA, was formally charged with taking bribes while in office. His trial formed part of the biggest corruption and smuggling investigation in the history of the People's Republic, with several senior officials in various Chinese cities facing prosecution. Fourteen were executed, while other defendants received sentences of life imprisonment. In October, following a two-year investigation, government auditors reported the embezzlement or serious misuse of the equivalent of more than US $11,000m. of public funds by government officials. Further revelations of corruption emerged in January 2001 when the official media reported that Liu Yong, a municipal party official in Shenyang, had operated a criminal gang and used the proceeds to support his business activities. In June more than 100 officials from Shenyang, including the city's mayor, Mu Suixin, were detained in connection with their links to Liu.

In January 2002 Wang Xuebing, the president of China Construction Bank and an ally of Zhu Rongji, was placed under investigation for alleged financial mismanagement, and in November he was expelled from the CCP following bribery charges. In March a money-laundering and illegal loans scandal emerged at the Bank of China, the perpetrators having fled overseas. As various other financial scandals continued to emerge, in September three officials from CITIC Industrial Bank were arrested on suspicion of massive fraud. In August Zhao Keming, a former deputy mayor of Xiamen, was sentenced to death, with a two-year reprieve, for accepting bribes. In February 2003 one of the perpetrators involved in the Bank of China scandal, branch manager Yu Zhendong, was arrested in the USA. In May the Governor of Yunnan Province, Li Jiating, received a suspended death sentence for taking bribes totalling more than the equivalent of US $2,200m. Also in May, Zhou Zhengyi, chairman of a Shanghai property company, Nongkai Development Group, was placed under investigation amid allegations of fraudulent loan-taking. One of these loans, for $270m., had been received from the Bank of China in 2002. Speculation over the Bank of China's involvement in the scandal intensified following the removal of the chief executive of the bank's Hong Kong branch, Liu Jinbao, in late May. Zhou Zhengyi was formally arrested in September 2003 on charges of fabricating documents and manipulating his company's trading price on the stock market (he was found guilty in June 2004 and sentenced to three years' imprisonment). Meanwhile, in July 2003 Yang Bin, who had been the proposed governor of the Sinuiju free trade area on China's border with the Democratic People's Republic of Korea (DPRK or North Korea—see below), was sentenced to 18 years' imprisonment for fraud and corruption. In another development in October, China's Minister of Land and Natural Resources, Tian Fengshan, was removed from office as a result of allegations of corruption.

In February 2004 the CCP announced the introduction of new regulations for the supervision of its officials, intended to reduce corruption within the Party. Also in February Liu Jinbao, former chief executive of the Bank of China in Hong Kong (see above), was arrested. (Liu was sentenced to death with a two-year suspension in August 2005 for embezzlement and accepting bribes.) A report issued by the Government in August 2004 stated that approximately 4,000 officials had left China after appropriating public funds since the mid-1980s, and that the total sum embezzled had amounted to around 5,000m. yuan during that time. In March 2005 the Procurator-General, Jia Chunwang, announced that 30,788 government officials had been prosecuted in 2004 for work-related offences such as corruption, embezzlement and abuse of power. In the same month two prominent corruption cases emerged: Zhang Enzhao, the Chairman of China Construction Bank, resigned, reportedly as a result of an investigation into allegations of corruption; and Ma De, a former senior official from Heilongjiang Province, pleaded guilty to accepting some 6m. yuan in bribes between 1992 and 2002 in exchange for helping officials to secure promotions.

Further action against corruption was instigated during 2006. A prominent case involved the Shanghai pension fund, from which more than 3,000m. yuan was said to have been misappropriated for the purposes of speculative investments. Those dismissed in connection with the scandal included the Secretary of the Shanghai Municipal Committee of the CCP, Chen Liangyu (who was later expelled from the party), as well as the director of the National Bureau of Statistics, Qiu Xiaohua. The head of Shanghai's Formula One motor-racing circuit likewise faced questioning. In September 2007 several senior officials received long prison sentences for their involvement in the scandal, and in April 2008 Chen was sentenced to 18 years' imprisonment.

In January 2007 auditors revealed that US $34.8m. had been misappropriated from funds allocated to assist the millions of villagers displaced by the construction of the Three Gorges Dam on the Changjiang (River Yangtze) in Hubei Province, upon which work had commenced in 1994. The world's largest hydro-electric project had provoked much criticism from environmentalists and others, which intensified following reports that cracks had appeared in the dam. In October 2007, after reported acknowledgement from officials of the dam's potentially disastrous impact on the environment, it was announced that a further 4m. people were to be relocated. The funding in question, which should have financed housing and other resettlement schemes, had allegedly been used instead by corrupt local officials to pay staff salaries and to clear the debts of local government departments. In the following month a senior member of the CCP Central Commission for Discipline Inspection announced plans to establish an anti-corruption agency, which would report directly to the State Council; the Minister of Supervision, Ma Wen, was appointed to chair the newly formed National Corruption Prevention Bureau in September. In March further reforms to address the problem of corruption were announced. More than 1,000 senior officials were believed to have been disciplined in corruption-related cases between January and May alone. In June, as part of a limited period of leniency initiated by the authorities, some 1,800 officials reportedly admitted to taking part in corrupt practices. One of the most significant trials in 2007 was that of Zheng Xiaoyu, the former director of the State Food and Drug Administration. Zheng was convicted of accepting bribes and of dereliction of duty; he was executed in July. According to the charges against him, he had received approximately US $850,000 in exchange for his approval of various sub-standard drugs. The case highlighted other important issues, such as product safety and the inadequacies of food and pharmaceutical regulations in China. By October, in response to several international scandals involving the safety standards of Chinese exports, an extensive government campaign had resulted in hundreds of arrests.

Meanwhile, the suppression of dissident activity continued, while the issue of media freedom remained an area of much contention. In January 1991 the trials of many of those arrested during the pro-democracy protests of 1989 commenced. Most activists received relatively short prison sentences. In July 1992 Bao Tong, a senior aide of Zhao Ziyang, the former General Secretary of the CCP, was found guilty of involvement in the pro-democracy unrest of mid-1989. In February 1994 Asia Watch, an independent New York-based human rights organization, issued a highly critical report of the situation in China, detailing the cases of more than 1,700 detainees, imprisoned for their political, ethnic or religious views. In July the trial on charges of counter-revolutionary activity of 14 members of a dissident group, in detention since 1992, commenced. In December 1994 nine of the defendants received heavy prison sentences.

In February 1993 Wang Dan and Guo Haifeng, leading student activists in the 1989 demonstrations, were freed. In late 1994, however, complaining of police harassment, Wang Dan filed a lawsuit against the authorities. He was rearrested in May 1995. The imposition of an 11-year sentence on Wang Dan at the conclusion of his cursory trial on charges of conspiracy, in October 1996, drew international condemnation. In April 1998 he was released on medical parole and sent into exile in the USA. In May 1993, having served 12 years of a 15-year sentence, dissident activist Xu Wenli was released from prison. He was rearrested in April 1994, but released shortly afterwards. In August 1993 the arrest and expulsion from China of Han Dongfang, a trade union activist who had attempted to return to his homeland after a year in the USA, attracted much international attention.

In 1997 there was increasing pressure on the CCP to reconsider its assessment of the 1989 pro-democracy demonstrations as a 'counter-revolutionary rebellion'. In June 1997, in an unprecedented decision, a court in Liaoning Province overruled convictions of 'counter-revolution' against four dissidents imprisoned for their role in the 1989 pro-democracy movement. However, an appeal to the CCP National Congress by Zhao Ziyang (who remained under house arrest) to reassess the official verdict was dismissed. In mid-1997 the Chinese Government refuted reports by the human rights organization Amnesty International that several pro-democracy activists remained among the numerous political prisoners in China, classifying as criminals the estimated 2,000 people imprisoned on charges of 'counter-revolution'.

China's treatment of political dissidents attracted international attention in November 1997, with the release on medical grounds into exile in the USA of Wei Jingsheng. Wei had been imprisoned in 1979, but was released on parole in September 1993. He was rearrested, however, in April 1994, and detained incommunicado until December 1995, when he was convicted of conspiring to overthrow the Government. His sentencing to 14 years' imprisonment provoked an international outcry, and he was released shortly after Jiang Zemin's visit to the USA in 1997 (see below). Bao Ge, a prominent Shanghai dissident and campaigner for compensation for Chinese victims of Japanese war aggression, was released from three years' imprisonment without trial in June 1997.

In September 1998 Amnesty International released a report stating that China had executed 1,876 people in 1997, more than the rest of the world combined. Also in September 1998, the UN High Commissioner for Human Rights, Mary Robinson, made an unprecedented official visit to China, including Tibet, and Hong Kong. Following the visit, in October China signed the International Covenant on Civil and Political Rights in New York, guaranteeing freedom of expression, a fair trial and protection against arbitrary arrest.

Attempts by dissidents in Beijing and the provinces to create and register an opposition party, the Chinese Democratic Party (CDP), with the principal aim of democratic elections, were suppressed by the Government. In November the Government published a judicial interpretation of the crimes of political subversion (thereby expanding existing punishable offences), specifying that 'incitement to subvert state power' would result in imprisonment for between three years and life for any publisher, musician, author, artist or film-maker found guilty of the charge. In December 1998 at least 30 members of the CDP were detained, and three veteran activists, Xu Wenli, Qin Yongmin and Wang Youcai, were sentenced to 13, 12 and 11 years' imprisonment, respectively, provoking strong international condemnation. Human rights groups declared the release on medical parole and subsequent exile to the USA of the prominent dissident, Liu Nianchun, shortly before the conviction of the CDP activists, to be an attempt to deflect criticism of their trials. By November 1999 a further 18 CDP leaders had been convicted of subverting state power and sentenced to long terms of imprisonment.

In February 1999 two dissidents, Gao Yu (a journalist) and Sun Weibang, who had received substantial prison sentences, were released ahead of schedule, prompting speculation that the Government was attempting to counter criticism before the imminent visit to the People's Republic by the US Secretary of State and the forthcoming meeting of the UN Commission on Human Rights in Geneva. None the less, China continued its suppression of dissent. In late April, however, a US-sponsored resolution at the aforementioned UN Commission meeting, condemning China's human rights record, was defeated. The resolution was again defeated in April 2000. In August 2000 a group of Chinese dissidents filed a lawsuit in the USA accusing Li Peng of crimes against humanity for sanctioning the events of June 1989 in Tiananmen Square.

Attempts were made by the Government in February and in November 2000 to regulate the publication of material on the internet, with the issuing of new rules first granting the regime the right to 'reorganize' or close down offending websites, and then requiring government approval prior to the posting of news bulletins. In February 2001 the trial began of the first webmaster to have been prosecuted for publishing subversive material on the internet, and between April and November 2001 some 17,000 internet cafés were shut down in a nation-wide campaign against pornographic and subversive websites.

The killings in Tiananmen Square in 1989 attracted renewed attention in early January 2001 following the 'leak' of papers and transcripts of government meetings at the time, which had been smuggled out of China by a reformist civil servant and subsequently published abroad as 'The Tiananmen Papers'. The papers, which were immediately denounced by the Government as forgeries, appeared to show a division in the leadership over how to deal with the protesters, with Zhao Ziyang having favoured a conciliatory approach, while Li Peng supported decisive action against the students, regarding them as part of a 'counter-revolutionary rebellion'. Deng Xiaoping had taken the decision to suppress the protesters, with the support of a group of semi-retired elders. The papers also indicated that Jiang Zemin had been appointed to his positions directly by Deng, thus circumventing the Party's rules of selection. In June 2002 the authorities reportedly detained at least 23 people in connection with the publication of 'The Tiananmen Papers' following a protracted investigation into the matter.

Targets of the Government's continuing suppression reportedly included ethnic separatists, 'underground' churches, unregistered internet cafés, tax-evading peasants and Chinese scholars returning from overseas. In August 2002 the US-based group Human Rights Watch reported that growing numbers of political dissidents were being detained in mental institutions, estimating that at least 3,000 people had been subjected to psychiatric detention for political activity in the preceding two decades. Attempts by the authorities to maintain order prior to the Party Congress resulted in renewed measures to curb access to the internet during 2002. In June three leading internet providers were punished for disseminating harmful content and were forced to suspend a number of services. This was accompanied by a campaign to close down illegal internet cafés, after a fire at one such facility killed 24 people. By August 2002 it had been announced that 14,000 'cybercafés' had been shut down, 3,100 of which were permanent closures, ostensibly for safety reasons.

In late December 2002 the authorities acknowledged that they had again arrested the US-based activist, Wang Bingzhang. Wang had disappeared in mid-2002 in Viet Nam, where he had travelled with two other Chinese dissidents, Yue Wu and Zhang Qi, in order to hold meetings with other activists. Wang was charged with espionage on behalf of Taiwan, and with terrorism—charges condemned by the CDP—and he went on trial in late January 2003. In early February he was sentenced to life imprisonment, and at the end of that month he lost his appeal. Also in late December 2002 the authorities released, on the basis of 'medical parole', Xu Wenli, who immediately left for the USA. Xu's release was widely seen as a goodwill gesture towards the USA, Xu himself describing his release as 'political'. In January 2003 the authorities expelled another prominent dissident, Fang Jue, to exile in the USA. He had been released from prison in July 2002, but had subsequently been detained during the CCP Congress in November. Zhang Qi had also been detained, and upon her release in March 2003 she immediately returned to the USA, where she was based.

Press freedom was further restricted from mid-2003, with lists of banned topics being issued to journalists, and in August an order was issued restraining public debate on political reform and on constitutional amendments, as well as on reassessment of historical events (the latter was believed to refer to the 1989 student protests). Despite increasing privatization of the media sector, with newspapers being required to become financially independent of the State, there were few signs that the Government was relinquishing its control over the reporting of sensitive issues. The Government also continued to exercise strict control over the internet, reportedly employing a large police force employed to monitor web activities.

In February 2004 it was announced that foreign investment in Chinese media companies was to be allowed; however, this would be permitted only on the condition that foreign investors agreed to adhere to government regulations on media content. In March pro-democracy activist Wang Youcai (see above) was released and permitted to travel to the USA on medical grounds. Also in March, several members of the staff of *Nanfang Dushi Bao* (*Southern Metropolis Daily*) were arrested, reportedly in connection with articles published by the newspaper on the SARS epidemic (editor-in-chief Cheng Yizhong was released in August). Again in March, the second session of the NPC approved an amendment to the Constitution that introduced an explicit reference to human rights. Some observers, however, criticized the amendment as vague and ineffectual. In April a resolution condemning China's human rights record was rejected at a meeting of the UN Commission on Human Rights for the 11th time. In July a new campaign for censorship of text messages was announced, with telephone companies being required to use filtering technology to identify words and numbers that were considered suspicious. In October Zhao Yan, a Chinese national working as a researcher for the *New York Times*, was arrested and charged with providing state secrets to foreigners, following the newspaper's publication of a report stating Jiang Zemin's intention to resign as head of China's military (see below) before this had been officially announced. (In March 2006 espionage charges against Zhao Yan were reportedly abandoned, only to be revived in May. He was acquitted of those charges in August, but was sentenced to three years' imprisonment on charges of fraud; he lost his appeal in December. Zhao was released in September 2007.) In December 2004 three leading intellectuals, Yu Jie, Liu Xiaobo and Zhang Zhuhua, who were known to have expressed critical views, were detained for questioning.

The exact number of executions in China remained a state secret; Amnesty International estimated that 3,400 people were executed in 2004, although the true figure remained unknown and was thought possibly to be far higher, with some estimates suggesting that as many as 15,000 executions a year were being carried out. In September 2005 the UN High Commissioner for Human Rights, Louise Arbour, made a five-day visit to Beijing and declared herself to be 'guardedly optimistic' about China's progress on human rights and the possibility of imminent ratification of the International Covenant on Civil and Political Rights, although she expressed concern over the continued use of the death penalty.

Strong state reactions to real and perceived dissent continued in 2005. In late April Shi Tao, a journalist with the Changsha-based newspaper *Dangdai Shang Bao* (*Contemporary Business News*), was sentenced to 10 years' imprisonment for 'leaking state secrets'. Shi had reportedly e-mailed to a New York website editor his notes on government instructions regarding coverage of the 15th anniversary of the suppression of the Tiananmen Square demonstrations. The internet company Yahoo! was condemned by human rights groups for apparently assisting the Chinese prosecutors in connecting the 'leaked' information to Shi's e-mail address. Also in April Ching Cheong, the Hong Kong-based China correspondent for *The Straits Times*, a Singapore newspaper, was arrested, reportedly while attempting to obtain a manuscript connected to former Premier Zhao Ziyang, who had died under house arrest in January (see below). In the following month the Ministry of Foreign Affairs announced that Ching had confessed to charges of espionage, and in August he was charged with spying for Taiwan. Also in August, a petition for his release, signed by more than 13,000 people, was rejected by the Government. (Ching filed an appeal in September 2006; this appeal was postponed, and the imprisoned reporter was told that he would not be allowed to defend himself. The appeal was dismissed by the court in November. Ching was released in February 2008.) In October 2005 it was reported that Peng Ming, a dissident based in the USA who had been arrested in Myanmar in May 2004, had been sentenced to life imprisonment on charges of terrorism and espionage. Peng, the founder of the China Federation Party, was one of the few Chinese pro-democracy activists to advocate the use of force to overthrow the CCP.

In February 2005 it was reported that some 12,500 internet cafés had been shut down by the authorities in the last three months of 2004, to create a 'safer environment for young people'. Despite previous access issues with the authorities, in May 2005 the internet search company Google obtained a licence to operate in the People's Republic. In June the Government ordered all websites and weblogs in the country to register with the authorities or risk fines and possible closure. In October the Government announced a general ban on internet material inciting 'illegal demonstrations', apparently in response to the increasing number of public protests around the country (see below). Further internet restrictions were announced in November, prohibiting the dissemination of 'information that goes against state security and public interest'. In January 2006 Google provoked criticism from advocates of free speech, including the international media organization Reporters Without Borders, when the company announced that it would comply with the Chinese Government's demands by restricting access to certain websites from its Chinese search engine, in order to maintain a presence in the fast-expanding Chinese media market.

In October 2006 China provoked an outcry from international media rights groups when two internet writers, Li Jianping and Guo Qizhen, were sentenced to two and four years in prison, respectively. Both were accused of having criticized China's national leaders. Reporters Without Borders estimated that in 2006 around 50 internet writers were serving sentences in Chinese prisons. Also in October, the Ministry of Information Industry was reported to have established a new team to study the regulation of the estimated 17.5m. weblog users in the People's Republic. The team was said to have been considering new registration requirements, which would ensure that new weblog users could only register new 'blog' accounts using their real names.

In October 2006, following a series of miscarriages of justice, the NPC approved a law allowing only the Supreme Court to authorize death sentences. In the following month the Deputy Procurator-General, Wang Zhenchuan, made a rare admission that illegal interrogation and torture had been used in China's judicial system (despite the official outlawing of torture in 1996) and that at least 30 wrongful verdicts were handed down annually as a result of the use of torture. Meanwhile, in August a blind human rights activist, Chen Guangcheng, had been sentenced to more than four years' imprisonment for allegedly 'damaging property and organizing a mob to disturb traffic'. Chen had attracted much international media attention in 2005 when he had accused health workers in Linyi, Shandong Province, of forcing some 7,000 people to have late-term abortions or sterilizations. Having been tried again and convicted in a different court, Chen's final appeal was rejected in January 2007. In December 2006 media reports in the West suggested that, in advance of the removal from provincial courts of the power to authorize capital punishment, the Sichuan authorities had secretly executed a protester who had taken part in a mass demonstration against a hydroelectric dam in the province in 2004. According to lawyers for Chen Tao, one of four demonstrators arrested, he was executed for 'deliberately killing' a riot police officer during the protest.

As the holding of the 2008 Olympic Games in Beijing approached, China's human rights situation came under increased international scrutiny. The authorities' regulation of the internet continued to be a major issue, with the number of internet users in China having exceeded an estimated 220m. by early 2008 In April 2007 CCP officials were reportedly instructed to combat the 'spread of decadent and backward ideological and cultural material online'. The proliferation of weblogs drew attention to the power of the internet and its application in attempts to gain greater freedom of expression: in May the Government was forced to suspend plans to register names and contact details of 'bloggers' following widespread opposition to the proposed measures. However, weblogs remained subject to censorship. Meanwhile, in an unusual development in January, President Hu demanded an investigation into the murder of a journalist outside an illegal coal mine in Shanxi Province. Lan Chengzhang had been working for the *China Trade News* at the time of his death; in June the mine's owner was given a life sentence for his involvement in the killing. In March activist Zhang Jianhong was sentenced to six years' imprisonment on charges of incitement to subversion of the State's authority, in relation to articles posted on the internet. Another prominent activist, Hu Jia, was detained in late December. His trial on similar charges of inciting subversion commenced in March 2008. Media restrictions were increased as part of a reported campaign in advance of the 17th CCP Congress, held in October 2007. With frequent reports of surveillance, harassment and arrests, critics maintained that, contrary to official assertions, the human rights situation in China had shown few signs of improvement.

In religious affairs, the emergence of Falun Gong in the late 1990s posed new challenges to the supremacy of the CCP, which banned the popular religious sect in July 1999 on the grounds that it constituted a threat to society. The group, which was also known as Falun Dafa, had been established in 1992 by Li Hongzhi, who was based in the USA, and from 1999 it attracted increasing attention in China and abroad, claiming tens of millions of adherents, mainly in China. The ban imposed in 1999 was prompted by demonstrations, attended by tens of thousands of supporters in numerous towns and cities, in protest at the arrest of more than 100 adherents of the religious sect. Particularly concerned by the high level of Falun Gong membership among CCP and PLA officials, the authorities embarked on a campaign of harsh persecution of those who refused to renounce their faith. Despite condemnation and prosecution by the full force of the law, Falun Gong members continued to make quiet protests. In October 2000 Falun Gong was declared to be a political rival to the CCP and an enemy of the nation. The suppression of Falun Gong continued, with dispersals of rallies, arrests and detentions in 're-education camps'. In August 2001 the authorities sentenced 45 'die-hard' members to long prison sentences for organizing resistance. In early 2002 Falun Gong succeeded in infiltrating Chinese television broadcasts in several different cities, and in September 15 Falun Gong members were sentenced to between four and 20 years' imprisonment for violating anti-cult laws and damaging broadcasting equipment. In 2005 the US-based Falun Gong Information Center asserted that 2,300 practitioners had died in custody in China since the banning of the sect in 1999.

In January 2000 five Catholic bishops were consecrated in a display of strength by the state-controlled Chinese Catholic Church, impeding any improvement in relations with the Vatican, which opposed the consecration. In August 1999 the Chinese Government had refused to grant permission for the Pope to visit Hong Kong, owing to the Vatican's links with Taiwan. According to a US-based Catholic organization, the arrest of an archbishop belonging to the clandestine Roman Catholic Church (recognized by the Vatican) in February 2000 was part of an attempt by China to undermine allegiance to the Vatican. During the year there was substantial evidence of the CCP's intensification of repression of all non-official religious movements. In October, on

China's National Day, the Pope canonized 120 missionary and Chinese Roman Catholic martyrs, and in the following October Catholic scholars from around the world gathered in Beijing to commemorate the 400th anniversary of the arrival of Italian Jesuit Matteo Ricci in Beijing in 1601. Pope John Paul II expressed regret for past Vatican actions and appealed for the establishment of diplomatic relations. In December 2001 the increasing importance of religion in China was acknowledged at a conference on religion attended by all seven members of the Politburo Standing Committee. It was planned to bring independent churches under state control, thereby obviating the need for clandestine churches. Nevertheless, in October 2002 the US State Department's annual report on religious freedom continued to designate China as a country engaged in widespread repression of religion.

By early 2003 China and the Vatican had held several rounds of informal discussions on improving bilateral relations. However, China was in confrontation with Bishop Joseph Zen Zekiun, the head of the Roman Catholic Church in Hong Kong, who had become increasingly critical of the central Government's administration in Hong Kong and its religious policies on the mainland. China was one of the few countries not represented at the funeral of Pope John Paul II in April 2005. In June, according to the US-based China Aid Association, police forcibly entered 100 'underground' churches in Jilin Province, detaining some 600 worshippers. The detention of members of the unofficial Catholic church in Hebei Province, apparently the most significant 'underground' church in China, also continued in 2005. In October 2006 a prominent human rights lawyer who had campaigned for religious freedom, Gao Zhisheng, was arrested on charges of 'inciting subversion of state power'. He was convicted in December and received a three-year prison sentence, suspended for five years. Relations with the Vatican were further strained in 2006 when, without papal approval, China's state-controlled Catholic church consecrated three bishops, two of whom were subsequently excommunicated by the Vatican. In July hundreds of police officers in Zhejiang were reported to have been engaged in violent clashes with around 3,000 protesters from the 'underground' Christian movement who were demonstrating against the demolition of a church claimed by the Government to be an illegal structure. Eight Christians were accused of inciting the protesters and were put on trial in December. Xu Shuangfu, the founder of another 'underground' Christian sect, who had been convicted of murdering members of a rival group, was executed in November, along with two other leaders. None the less, in August Bishop An Shuxin, who had spent more than 10 years in prison for being a member of the 'underground' Catholic Church loyal to the Pope was freed. Furthermore, the Archbishop of Canterbury, Dr Rowan Williams, head of the Anglican Communion, was able to pay an official visit to China in October.

Relations between China and the Vatican showed an improvement in January 2007, when the Pope announced that he would make efforts to restore full diplomatic links with the People's Republic. Following a meeting in Rome to review the Roman Catholic Church's strategy towards China, the Pope stated that the Vatican was willing to engage in dialogue to overcome the 'incomprehension of the past'. In June Pope Benedict XVI released an open letter to all Chinese Catholics, appealing for the unity of the faith and the strengthening of links between followers of the state-controlled church and those loyal to the Vatican. Moreover, the Pope expressed a willingness to enter negotiations with the Chinese Government over issues such as the appointment of bishops. At the same time the Vatican press office acknowledged the possibility of the nunciature's transfer to Beijing from Taiwan under certain circumstances. In September Father Joseph Li Shan was consecrated as Bishop of Beijing; although formal approval by the Vatican was not given, the Chinese authorities' choice was reportedly praised by a senior Vatican official.

Meanwhile, social unrest continued to increase. Official statistics released in 2005 estimated that in the previous year 3.7m. people had taken part in 74,000 'mass incidents' of one form or another, including labour strikes and riots, an increase of more than 20% in comparison with 2003. Many public protests were related to land disputes, reflecting the tensions between the country's rapid industrial construction and urban expansion and the attempts of peasants to preserve their homes and farmland.

In the early 21st century the Chinese authorities confronted three serious issues of public health. First, there was increasing concern about the spread of HIV/AIDS in China. During 2001 the authorities acknowledged the seriousness of the problem, and in January new legislation was introduced in Chengdu that forbade infected people to marry; compulsory tests were to be carried out on high-risk groups such as prostitutes and drug addicts. In early June it was reported that as many as 500,000 people in Henan Province had been infected with HIV after selling their blood plasma to companies that had employed unhygienic practices. The authorities announced an increase in funds to counter the spread of the virus and to improve the safety of blood banks. In June 2002 a UN report warned that China was on the brink of an AIDS catastrophe, estimating that the total number of cases could rise to 10m. by 2010. The authorities subsequently admitted that as many as 1m. citizens might be infected with HIV. However, there were signs that the Chinese Government was attempting to provide improved access to health information and to affordable health care. Measures included the supply of free drugs to HIV/AIDS sufferers who were on a low income and the provision of AIDS training to doctors at provincial level. In December 2003 Premier Wen Jiabao publicly associated himself with the campaign against HIV/AIDS by visiting AIDS patients in a Beijing hospital on World Aids Day. Nevertheless, according to a report published by Human Rights Watch in September 2003, official government figures continued to conceal the true extent of the spread of the virus, whilst HIV/AIDS sufferers experienced employment discrimination and were sometimes denied access to treatment. In November 2006 the Ministry of Public Health announced that HIV cases in China had risen by 30% within a year, with a total of 183,733 cases having been reported. The authorities stressed that this apparent rise in the number of cases was largely due to improved testing and better reporting. In November of the following year figures released by the Ministry showed an apparent increase in confirmed cases to 223,501, while the estimated total number of cases stood at 700,000. It was reported in the same month that the Ministry was planning to remove a long-standing ban on the entry of HIV-positive foreign citizens to the country.

Second, by the end of April 2003 the oubreak of SARS, a hitherto unknown virus, had affected almost 3,500 people and resulted in more than 150 deaths in the People's Republic alone. The Minister of Public Health, Zhang Wenkang, and the mayor of Beijing, Meng Xuenong, were accused of having concealed the extent of the disease and were relieved of their party and state positions. The SARS epidemic was officially declared to be over in mid-June, and the World Health Organization (WHO) removed its ban on travel to Beijing. A committee was established in April under NPC Standing Committee Chairman Wu Bangguo to discuss various issues of constitutional change, including workers' rights and direct election of officials above the village level.

Third, in November 2005 China became the fifth country to register human fatalities resulting from the epidemic of avian influenza ('bird flu') that had spread across East Asia since 2003, when two women from Anhui Province were reported to have died after contracting the virus. Earlier in the month, 6m. poultry had been culled in Liaoning Province, while the central Government had announced that it would endeavour to vaccinate all of China's 14,000m. poultry, following a series of outbreaks throughout the year. By January 2007 China had confirmed its 22nd human case of the disease; 14 of these had proved fatal.

In the area of space research, in late 2001 the authorities announced plans to accelerate the development of China's programme. In March 2002 China successfully launched and returned to Earth an unmanned space capsule, *Shenzhou III*, and in January 2003 achieved the same results with *Shenzhou IV*, both of which could be used to carry astronauts into orbit. Also in January 2003 China announced plans to launch its first manned space flight later in that year, thereby becoming the third nation, after the former USSR and the USA, to launch such missions. The long-term goal was to develop a space station and moon base. In October 2003 a spacecraft carrying 'taikonaut' Yang Liwei was successfully launched into orbit. A second manned space mission was successfully completed in October 2005, when 'taikonauts' Fei Junlong and Nie Haishen orbited the Earth for five days aboard *Shenzhou VI* before landing safely in Inner Mongolia. The expedition generated widespread popular enthusiasm. In January 2007, however, China drew international criticism when it apparently used a ground-based medium-range ballistic missile to destroy a weather satellite about 865 km above Earth. The test—the first of its kind since the 1980s—renewed concerns about China's growing military strength. Indeed, China was reported to have surpassed Japan in military funding in mid-2007, ranking fourth internationally. China launched the *Chang'e 1* satellite in October 2007, the country's first spacecraft to orbit the Moon.

Tibet (Xizang), hitherto a semi-independent region of western China, was occupied in October 1950 by Chinese Communist forces. In March 1959 there was an unsuccessful armed uprising by Tibetans opposed to Chinese rule. The Dalai Lama, the head of Tibet's Buddhist clergy and thus the region's spiritual leader, fled with some 100,000 supporters to Dharamsala, northern India, where a government-in-exile was established. The Chinese ended the former dominance of the lamas (Buddhist monks) and destroyed many monasteries. Tibet became an 'Autonomous Region' of China in September 1965, but the majority of Tibetans have continued to regard the Dalai Lama as their 'god-king', and to resent the Chinese presence. In October 1987 violent clashes occurred in Lhasa (the regional capital) between the Chinese authorities and Tibetans seeking independence. Similar demonstrations followed, and in 1988 the Dalai Lama proposed that Tibet become a self-governing Chinese territory, in all respects except foreign affairs.

On 7 March 1989 martial law was imposed in Lhasa for the first time since 1959, after further violent clashes between separatists and the Chinese police, which resulted in the deaths of 16 protesters. In October 1989 the Chinese Government condemned as an interference in its internal affairs the award of the Nobel Peace Prize to the Dalai Lama. In May 1990 martial law was ended in Lhasa. Human rights groups claimed that during the last six months of the period of martial law as many as 2,000 persons had been executed. In May 1992 a report issued by Amnesty International was critical of the Chinese authorities' violations of the human rights of the monks and nuns of Tibet. In May 1993 several thousand Tibetans were reported to have demonstrated in Lhasa against Chinese rule. A number of protesters were believed to have been killed by the security forces.

In April 1994 China condemned the Dalai Lama's meeting with US President Bill Clinton during the former's lecture tour of the USA. In May 1995 the Dalai Lama's nomination of the 11th incarnation of the Panchen Lama (the second position in the spiritual hierarchy, the 10th incumbent having died in 1989) was condemned by the Chinese authorities, which banned the six-year old nominee, Gedhun Choekyi Nyima, from travelling to Dharamsala. In September 1995 it was reported that independence activists had carried out two bombings in Lhasa.

China lodged a strong protest following an informal meeting between the Dalai Lama and US President Clinton in Washington, DC, in September 1995. In November the Chinese Government announced Gyaltsen (Gyaincain) Norbu as its own nominee as Panchen Lama. The boy was enthroned at a ceremony in Lhasa in December, the whereabouts of the Dalai Lama's choice remaining unknown until mid-1996, when China's ambassador to the UN in Geneva admitted that the boy was in detention in Beijing. There were violent confrontations in Tibet in May 1996, following the banning of any public display of images of the Dalai Lama. During the latter part of 1996 visits by the Dalai Lama to the United Kingdom and Australia aroused further protests from the Chinese Government. A series of minor explosions during 1996 culminated in late December with the detonation of a powerful bomb outside a government office in Lhasa, which injured several people.

The Chinese leadership condemned the Dalai Lama's visit to Taiwan in March 1997, despite assurances that he was visiting in his capacity as a spiritual leader. In May it was reported that Chadrel Rinpoche, an official in the Tibetan administration and one of Tibet's most senior monks, had been sentenced to six years' imprisonment for allegedly revealing information to the Dalai Lama about the Chinese Government's search for the new Panchen Lama. The USA's decision in mid-1997 to appoint a special co-ordinator for Tibet was criticized by the Chinese authorities. In October the Dalai Lama appealed to the Chinese Government to reopen negotiations over the status of Tibet, confirming that he did not seek full independence for the region. In December the Geneva-based International Commission of Jurists (see p. 430) published a report accusing China of suppressing nationalist dissent in Tibet and attempting to extinguish Tibetan culture, and appealed for a referendum, under the auspices of the UN, to decide the territory's future status. In April 1998 China agreed to allow envoys of the European Union (EU) to make a one-week investigatory visit to Tibet. In May the EU adopted two resolutions relating to China, condemning the sale of organs of executed prisoners and calling for a UN committee to investigate the transactions and, furthermore, urging the UN to appoint a rapporteur for Tibet issues.

During his visit to China and Hong Kong in late June 1998 (see below), US President Clinton discussed Tibet with Chinese leaders, with the Dalai Lama's support. The Chinese Government proclaimed its readiness to open negotiations if the Dalai Lama first declared both Tibet and Taiwan to be inalienable parts of China. In October the Dalai Lama admitted that since the 1960s he had received US $1.7m. annually from the US Central Intelligence Agency (CIA) to support the Tibetan separatist movement. Whilst visiting the USA in early November, the Dalai Lama had an unofficial meeting with President Clinton, and in January 1999 a new US special co-ordinator for Tibetan affairs was appointed. In May the Dalai Lama visited the United Kingdom and met the British Prime Minister, Tony Blair, who was reported to have received the religious leader in a spiritual capacity.

In January 2000 the Chinese Government was embarrassed by the flight from Tibet to Dharamsala of the third-ranking Lama, the Karmapa, who had, unusually, been recognized both by the Dalai Lama and by the Chinese Government. The Karmapa's request for political asylum placed the Indian authorities in a difficult position. China continued to exert great influence over the Dalai Lama's movements in 2000. Following the UN's decision to exclude him from a summit meeting of world religious leaders in August, in October the Republic of Korea refused to grant a visa to the Dalai Lama, on the grounds that it would be 'inappropriate'.

In April 2001 the Dalai Lama paid a 10-day visit to Taiwan, which was largely religious in nature, but he none the less met President Chen Shui-bian and addressed the legislature, thus antagonizing China, which opposed any co-operation between the two 'renegade provinces'. In May the CCP organized commemorative ceremonies in Tibet to mark the 50th anniversary of the 'peaceful liberation' of the region. On the anniversary the Dalai Lama had a meeting with US President George W. Bush in Washington, DC.

In July 2001 China's chosen Panchen Lama visited Shanghai and Zhejiang Province at the invitation of the central Government. Later in the month, the Government announced that it would build a monument to commemorate Chinese rule over Tibet in the grounds of the Potala Palace, the former winter residence of the Dalai Lama. The monument was completed in early 2002. In August 2001 the Chinese Government declared that, upon the death of the current incumbent, it would appoint its own Dalai Lama. In the same month Chinese troops seized the largest Tibetan monastery, Serthar, and forced thousands of monks and nuns to denounce the Dalai Lama. In late 2001, during a visit to China, the UN High Commissioner for Human Rights, Mary Robinson, urged Chinese leaders not to use the USA's 'war on terror' as a pretext for suppressing ethnic minorities.

In January 2002 Ngawang Choephel, a Tibetan music scholar serving an 18-year sentence on spying charges, was released, and in April the authorities freed, on medical grounds, Tanag Jigme Sangpo, who had first been imprisoned in 1965, and again since 1983, for campaigning against Chinese rule. He was believed to be the country's longest-serving political prisoner, having endured a total of 32 years in detention. In June CCP officials in Tibet formally welcomed Gyaltsen Norbu as the new Panchen Lama. In September 2002 exiled Tibetan officials travelled to China (including Tibet—the first such visit there since 1985) on a 16-day tour arranged by the elder brother of the Dalai Lama, Gyalo Thondup, who had visited Beijing in August. During the tour, the Dalai Lama's envoy to the USA, Lodi Gyaltsen Gyari, and the envoy to Europe, Kelsang Gyaltsen, held the first meetings with government officials since 1993, amid hopes of a more conciliatory attitude on the part of China. In November 2002 the Dalai Lama finally visited Mongolia, although the Chinese Government denounced the visit. In the same month China revealed that the Dalai Lama's chosen Panchen Lama, in detention since 1995, was 'very happy' and living with his family in Tibet. In December 2002 the authorities sentenced to death two Tibetans for their alleged role in a series of bombings in Sichuan Province during 1998–2002. In January 2003 10 more people were arrested in connection with the bombings, and one of the two men sentenced earlier was executed.

In June 2003 discussions between Chinese officials and envoys of the Dalai Lama were held. The delegation to Beijing was led by the Dalai Lama's representative in the USA, Lodi Gyaltsen

Gyari. Also in June, Indian Prime Minister Atal Bihari Vajpayee acknowledged Tibet as part of China in writing for the first time. In the same month 18 Tibetans were deported to China from Nepal, despite condemnation of this action by the UN. In September US President George W. Bush held talks with the Dalai Lama. In February 2004 Phuntsog Nyidron, a Tibetan Buddhist nun believed to have received the longest sentence ever given to a female political prisoner in China, was released after 15 years in prison. In May the Chinese Government issued a document entitled 'Regional Ethnic Autonomy in Tibet', requiring the Dalai Lama to abandon any attempts to control developments there, even though he had expressed willingness to accept limited autonomy rather than full Tibetan independence. In August Gyaltsen Norbu, the boy nominated by the Chinese Government as the new Panchen Lama in 1995, made a visit to Tibet. In September 2004 a third round of talks between Chinese officials and envoys of the Dalai Lama were held in Beijing.

In September 2005 celebrations were held in Lhasa to commemorate the 40th anniversary of the founding of the Tibet Autonomous Region. In October the construction of the 1,118-km railway link from Golmud in Qinghai Province to Lhasa was completed. While the rail connection strengthened possibilities for economic development in Tibet, it compounded fears that such development schemes, and the considerable influx of Han Chinese (who dominated the new economy) from neighbouring provinces, were irreversibly transforming the character and culture of the region. President Hu Jintao formally inaugurated the new link on 1 July 2006. The first passenger services departed on the same day, and by October services were also being offered from Shanghai and Guangzhou. However, negative global media attention was focused on the region in October, when mountaineers climbing Everest reported having seen Chinese border guards open fire on a group of Tibetans attempting to cross into Nepal. In December a local human rights group reported that government officials and students in Tibet had been officially banned from observing an annual Buddhist festival. The announcement of the ban in the official *Lhasa Evening News* demonstrated, according to analysts, that the political situation in Tibet was becoming increasingly repressive following the appointment in the previous May of the uncompromising Zhang Qingli as the region's CCP secretary.

In March 2007 the central Government's announcement of substantial funding to develop the region provoked a mixed reaction. The disclosure that 100,000m. yuan was to be spent on various projects, including the construction of an airport and the extension of the Lhasa railway line, prompted renewed concern in some quarters about the potential exploitation of resources, the eradication of indigenous culture and increased central control over the region. In October the presentation of the Congressional Gold Medal to the Dalai Lama in the USA precipitated violent confrontations in Tibet, between monks celebrating the occasion and police officers. In March 2008, in the largest protests against Chinese rule since 1989, hundreds of monks attended rallies in Lhasa. The ensuing violence was reported to have resulted in dozens of deaths. In April nine monks were arrested in connection with a bomb attack on a government building in eastern Tibet in the previous month.

Anti-Chinese sentiment in the Xinjiang Uygur Autonomous Region intensified in the 1990s, resulting in the initiation of a new, often brutal, campaign by the authorities to repress the Islamist separatist movement, whose goal was to establish an independent 'East Turkestan'. The region had been conquered by the Chinese Manchus in the mid-18th century, and it had subsequently enjoyed brief periods of independence. Since 1949, however, Han Chinese had been encouraged or forced to move to the region by the Government, thereby reducing the proportion of the indigenous Uygur population and compounding resentment. The Han Chinese and the Uygur communities often had little contact with one another, with the Han occupying the higher-status jobs, and forming majorities in the cities. Separatist movements such as the Xinjiang Liberation Front and the Uygur Liberation Organization (ULO) often had the support of the Uygur diaspora in Kyrgyzstan and Uzbekistan. Suppression of separatism increased in 1996, following a number of violent incidents. Hundreds of people were detained for their part in rioting and bomb attacks, and many were subsequently executed or imprisoned. Reports in late 1997 indicated that there had been a renewal of armed separatist activity, in which more than 300 people had been killed. In January 1998 13 people were executed in Xinjiang, allegedly for robbery and murder, although unofficial reports suggested that those executed were Muslim separatist demonstrators. Muslim separatists were believed to be responsible for an incendiary device deposited on a bus in Wuhan in February, which killed 16 people. Two leading activists, Yibulayin Simayi and Abudureyimu Aisha, were executed in January 1999, and a further 10 separatists were reportedly executed in May. Three Muslims were sentenced to death in September for participating in the separatist campaign, whilst six others received long prison sentences. In October 2000 Abduhelil Abdulmejit, a leading organizer of resistance to Chinese rule in Xinjiang who had been imprisoned three years previously, was reported to have died of pneumonia while in custody; international groups alleged that he had been tortured and murdered.

During 2001 the authorities continued the 'Strike Hard' campaign against separatists, with multiple executions reported. In August the PLA conducted large-scale military exercises involving 50,000 troops in the region. China's fears of Islamist separatism were heightened after the terrorist attacks in the USA on 11 September 2001. China stated that as many as 1,000 Uygur Islamist fighters had been trained in terrorist camps in Afghanistan operated by the al-Qa'ida network of the Saudi-born dissident, Osama bin Laden. Stability in Xinjiang remained crucial to China's 'go west' programme of developing the country's remote inner regions, and in late September Chinese troops began anti-guerrilla operations in the Afghan border region of Xinjiang, aimed at preventing Islamist infiltration. In November the Minister of Foreign Affairs, Tang Jiaxuan, likened China's anti-separatist campaign to the USA's 'war on terror'. In December, following the collapse of Afghanistan's ruling Taliban regime, China urged the USA to surrender captured Uygur Islamist fighters; the USA refused to comply.

In January 2002 the Government released a new report alleging links between the separatists and Osama bin Laden. In March Amnesty International reported that thousands of Muslim Uygurs had been detained since 11 September 2001, and that up to 8,000 had been given 'political education' courses. In June 2002 the authorities announced that from September Xinjiang University would no longer teach courses in the Uygur language; for 50 years students had had a choice of studying in Uygur or Mandarin. In August the USA designated the East Turkestan Islamic Movement (ETIM) a terrorist group and 'froze' the organization's assets, in a conciliatory gesture towards the Chinese Government. The UN also added the organization to its list of terrorist organizations in September. In 2003 China continued to portray its suppression of Uygur separatism in Xinjiang, previously considered an internal affair, as part of the war on global terrorism. In December China issued a 'terrorist' list that named the Eastern Turkestan Liberation Organization, the World Uygur Youth Congress and the East Turkestan Information Center, as well as the ETIM, as 'terrorist' organizations. Of these, only the ETIM was considered a terrorist movement by the USA.

In March 2004 it was reported that Rebiya Kadeer, a Uygur businesswoman and rights activist who had been imprisoned in 1999 for sending newspaper articles to her husband in the USA, would be released in 2006 (in the event she was freed in 2005, prior to a visit by US Secretary of State Condoleezza Rice, although her son was imprisoned for seven years in November 2006, having been found guilty of tax evasion). In July 2004, during a visit by President Hu to Tashkent (see below), a statement was signed by China and Uzbekistan whereby Uzbekistan agreed to co-operate with China in suppressing separatist activities in Xinjiang as part of a wider effort to combat terrorist activities. During 2004 Erkin Alptekin (son of Isa Yusuf Alptekin, who had been head of a brief Uygur government in the 1940s), reportedly emerged as leader of a Uygur exile movement committed to achieving independence for Xinjiang, or East Turkestan, by peaceful means. In September 2004 an East Turkestan government-in-exile was proclaimed by Anwar Yusuf Turani, head of the East Turkestan National Freedom Center. Many Uygur groups, however, did not recognize the government-in-exile. In October, celebrations in the regional capital, Urumqi, to commemorate the 50th anniversary of the founding of the Xinjiang Uygur Autonomous Region passed without incident.

Tension in the Xinjiang region recurred in January 2007 when 18 terrorist suspects were killed in a police operation against an alleged militants' training camp close to the Chinese border with Afghanistan and Pakistan, reportedly supervised by members of the ETIM. A few days previously the Vice-Secretary of the region's Communist Party Committee had denounced Rebiya

Kadeer as a separatist, determined to 'destroy the peace and stability of Chinese society'. Kadeer, who now lived in exile in the USA, had been nominated for the 2006 Nobel Peace Prize. In February Ismail Semed, a Uygur activist who had previously been accused of ETIM membership, was executed, having been convicted in 2005 of trying to 'split the motherland' and possession of arms. In January 2008 two militants, suspected of planning an attack on the forthcoming Olympic Games, were killed in a police operation in Urumqi, and 15 others were arrested. In March it was announced that an attempted attack on an aircraft, en route from Xinjiang to Beijing in the previous week, had been similarly thwarted.

In September 1984, following protracted negotiations, China reached agreement with the British Government over the terms of the future administration of Hong Kong upon the territory's return to Chinese sovereignty, scheduled for mid-1997. The transfer of Hong Kong from British to Chinese administration was effected at midnight on 30 June 1997, whereupon some 4,000 troops of the PLA were deployed in the territory. In December 36 deputies from Hong Kong were directly elected to the Ninth NPC in Beijing. In June 2007 President Hu Jintao travelled to Hong Kong to attend the celebration of the 10th anniversary of the territory's transfer to Chinese sovereignty. However, tensions with regard to the pace of democratic reform in Hong Kong remained. (See the chapter on Hong Kong for further information.)

In June 1986 China and Portugal opened formal negotiations for the return of the Portuguese overseas territory of Macao to full Chinese sovereignty, and agreement was reached in January 1987. The agreement was based upon the 'one country, two systems' principle, which had formed the basis of China's negotiated settlement regarding the return of Hong Kong. China duly resumed sovereignty of Macao at midnight on 19 December 1999, whereupon a PLA garrison was established in the territory. President Jiang Zemin visited Macao in December 2000. During 2001 and 2002 China, Hong Kong, and Macao increased co-operation in combating cross-border crime. President Hu Jintao visited Macao in December 2004 to mark the fifth anniversary of the territory's return to Chinese rule. (See the chapter on Macao for further information.)

Taiwan has continued to reject China's proposals for reunification, whereby the island would become a 'special administrative region' along the lines of Hong Kong and Macao. China has never relinquished its claim to sovereignty over the island and has repeatedly threatened to use military force against Taiwan in the event of any formal declaration of independence from the mainland. In July 2003 a US military report claimed that China was increasing its short-range missile capacity in preparation for possible conflict with Taiwan. Concurrently with the Taiwanese presidential election of March 2004, a referendum on the issue of the island's response to the deployment of Chinese missiles was held, but this failed to produce a valid result. In March 2005 the third plenum of the 10th NPC approved anti-secession legislation aimed at preventing Taiwan from declaring independence. In April–May, during an historic visit to the mainland by Lien Chan, leader of the opposition KMT, President Hu Jintao and the former Premier of Taiwan agreed to uphold their opposition to Taiwanese independence. A defence policy document published in December 2006 (in which the Chinese Government pledged to strengthen the country's naval and air forces) identified the issue of Taiwan as one of several regional security concerns. At the 17th CCP Congress in October 2007, President Hu reiterated an appeal for negotiations leading to reunification. Despite intermittent political tensions, however, cross-Straits business links flourished as Taiwanese investment continued to flow to the mainland. (See the chapter on Taiwan for further information.)

In foreign relations following the establishment of the People's Republic in 1949, China was dependent on the USSR for economic and military aid. Chinese planning was initially based on the Soviet model, with highly centralized control, but from 1955 Mao Zedong began to develop a distinctively Chinese form of socialism. As a result, the USSR withdrew all technical aid to China in August 1960. Chinese hostility to the USSR increased, in what became known as the 'Sino-Soviet Split', and was exacerbated by territorial disputes, and by the Soviet invasion of Afghanistan and the Soviet-supported Vietnamese invasion of Cambodia in the late 1970s. Sino-Soviet relations remained strained until 1987, when representatives of the two countries signed a partial agreement concerning the exact demarcation of the disputed common border at the Amur River. The withdrawal of Soviet troops from Afghanistan (completed in February 1989) and Viet Nam's assurance that it would end its military presence in Cambodia by September 1989 resulted in a further *rapprochement*. In May 1989 a full summit meeting was held in Beijing, at which normal state and party relations between China and the USSR were formally restored. During the next two years senior Chinese officials visited the USSR. In December 1991, upon the dissolution of the USSR, China recognized the newly independent states of the former union. The President of Russia, Boris Yeltsin, visited China in December 1992. In May 1994, in Beijing, Premier Li Peng and his Russian counterpart signed various co-operation agreements. In September President Jiang Zemin travelled to Moscow, the first visit to Russia by a Chinese Head of State since 1957. The two sides reached agreement on the formal demarcation of the western section of the border (the eastern section having been delimited in May 1991), and each pledged not to aim nuclear missiles at the other. In June 1995 the Chinese Premier paid an official visit to Russia, where several bilateral agreements were signed.

Sino-Russian relations continued to improve, and in April 1996 in Beijing Presidents Jiang and Yeltsin signed a series of agreements, envisaging the development of closer co-operation in areas such as energy, space research, environmental protection, and the combating of organized crime. Together with their counterparts from Kazakhstan, Kyrgyzstan and Tajikistan, the two Presidents also signed a treaty aimed at reducing tension along their respective borders. Progress on the Sino-Russian border question, and also on matters such as trade, was made during the Chinese Premier's visit to Moscow in December 1996. A further treaty on military co-operation and border demilitarization was signed by the Presidents of China, Russia, Kazakhstan, Kyrgyzstan and Tajikistan in April 1997, during a visit by President Jiang Zemin to Russia. An agreement signed during President Yeltsin's visit to Beijing in November formally ended the border dispute. In November 1998, in Moscow, representatives from Russia, China and the DPRK signed an inter-governmental agreement on the delimitation of their borders along the Tumannaya River.

In February 1999 11 agreements on bilateral economic and trade co-operation were signed during a visit to Russia by Zhu Rongji. In June, following a visit to China by the Russian Minister of Foreign Affairs, it was announced that a final accord on the demarcation of a common border between the two countries had been agreed after seven years of negotiations. During a summit meeting of China, Russia, Kazakhstan, Kyrgyzstan and Tajikistan (collectively known as the 'Shanghai Five'—see below) in the Kyrgyz capital, Bishkek, agreements were signed on the China–Kazakhstan–Kyrgyzstan and the Chinese–Kyrgyz borders. In November it was announced that all Chinese–Kazakh border issues had been completely resolved.

Following the resignation of Boris Yeltsin as Russian President in December 1999, his successor, Vladimir Putin, confirmed his commitment to maintaining and improving links with China. Putin visited Beijing in July 2000, and in September NPC Chairman Li Peng visited Russia. In July 2001 Presidents Jiang and Putin signed a new 20-year Sino-Russian 'Good-neighbourly Treaty of Friendship and Co-operation' in Moscow and reaffirmed their opposition to the USA's plans for a national missile defence (NMD) system. Since the 1990s Russia had sold between 70 and 100 advanced fighter aircraft, many of which were jointly produced by the two countries in Shenyang. In August 2001 the Russian gas monopoly, Gazprom, indicated that it would help build new pipelines connecting Siberia with northern China. In September Prime Minister Zhu Rongji visited Russia and signed several trade agreements, and in late October Vice-President Hu Jintao visited Moscow, where he met Putin.

In June 2002 China and Russia submitted a joint proposal to the UN Conference on Disarmament for a new international treaty to ban space weapons—a move aimed at preventing the USA from militarizing outer space. Russian Prime Minister Mikhail Kasyanov visited Beijing in late August to discuss strategic issues, and President Putin visited China at the beginning of December to meet Jiang Zemin and Hu Jintao. The two countries issued a joint declaration on a number of global strategic issues; they also sought to increase bilateral trade and economic co-operation, although there were disagreements regarding plans for a pipeline that would export Russian oil to Daqing, in north-eastern China. Hu Jintao visited Russia during his first overseas trip in his capacity as China's President in May 2003. During the visit President Hu and President Putin discussed the use of Siberian oil resources in China. President Putin's visit to China in October 2004 was dominated by the

Chinese Government's wish to reach an agreement on the Daqing oil pipeline. The proposed construction of the first section of the pipe to Skovorodino, Amur Oblast, near the border with China, raised the possibility that China might be the first to benefit from deliveries through the new pipeline, and during a visit to Beijing in March 2006 President Putin appeared to favour the Daqing route as Russia's first priority. In August 2007 it was reported that construction of a pipeline extending from Daqing to the Chinese province of Heilongjiang, on the Russian border, was scheduled to begin in 2008.

In June 2005 the final border dispute between Russia and China was settled. In August the Chinese and Russian armed forces conducted joint military exercises for the first time. To promote better bilateral relations, 2006 was declared the 'Year of Russia in China'. In November Russian Prime Minister Mikhail Fradkov paid an official visit to China, and together with Chinese officials signed eight agreements designed to expand bilateral investment, trade and technical co-operation. In particular, the two sides pledged fresh co-operation in the energy sector, agreeing to a joint venture whereby Russian oil supplier Rosneft and China National Petroleum Corporation (CNPC) would establish 300 new petrol stations in the People's Republic. Further commitments were made to strengthen co-operation in the fields of oil and nuclear energy. President Hu paid an official visit to Russia in March 2007, marking the beginning of the 'Year of China in Russia'. Hu and President Putin signed a major agreement on bilateral trade, and declared their joint commitment to increased co-operation in a number of fields, including technology and security.

During the 1990s China steadily consolidated its relations with the former Soviet republics of Central Asia. China shared with these republics a fear of the spread of Islamist terrorism, along with a common interest in developing and transporting the petroleum and gas deposits of the Caspian Sea-Central Asia region. In the late 1990s China, along with Russia, Kazakhstan, Kyrgyzstan, and Tajikistan, established the 'Shanghai Five' group (renamed the Shanghai Co-operation Organization—SCO at their annual meeting in June 2001, when Uzbekistan became the sixth member). The grouping aimed to stabilize the region in order to promote development. Both China and Russia hoped that the SCO would help counter US influence in Central Asia. During 2000–01 China also gradually began improving relations with the Taliban regime in Afghanistan, signing several economic and technical agreements in the expectation that the Taliban would cease supporting Islamist Uygur fighters in Xinjiang. Following the collapse of the Taliban regime in late 2001, the new Afghan Prime Minister, Hamid Karzai, visited Beijing in January 2002 to discuss Chinese aid towards the reconstruction of his country. In May of that year Kyrgyzstan ratified a 1999 border treaty that ceded nearly 95,000 ha of disputed territory to China, and in October 2002 the two countries conducted their first-ever joint military exercises, under the auspices of the SCO. Further agreements were signed in June 2006, including an accord on continuing work on a China–Kyrgyzstan–Uzbekistan railway link. In December 2002 the President of Kazakhstan, Nursultan Nazarbayev, visited Beijing, where he reached an agreement to construct a pipeline from Kazakhstan to western China. The first phase of the pipeline opened in 2006, and construction was due to be completed in 2011.

On his first state visit as China's President, Hu Jintao visited Kazakhstan in June 2003. In June 2004 President Hu visited Uzbekistan to attend an SCO summit meeting, and signed an agreement with Uzbek President Islam Karimov to co-operate in combating 'terrorism, separatism and extremism'. Further bilateral agreements between Uzbekistan and the People's Republic were concluded during President Karimov's visit to Beijing in May 2005. In December a 1,000-km oil pipeline from Atasu in Kazakhstan to Alashankou in the Xinjiang Uygur Autonomous Region was inaugurated by President Nazarbayev. In October 2006, at a meeting of the Central Asia Regional Economic Co-operation forum (CAREC—linking the Xinjiang region of China with Afghanistan, Azerbaijan, Kazakhstan, Kyrgyzstan, Mongolia, Tajikistan and Uzbekistan), China alluded to further economic and technological co-operation with Central Asia. In December the Chinese and Kazakh Presidents met in Beijing, where they agreed to expand co-operation in oil and gas exploration and to increase bilateral trade.

From the 1970s there was an improvement in China's relations with the West and also with Japan. Almost all Western countries had recognized the Government of the People's Republic as the sole legitimate government of China, and had consequently withdrawn recognition from the 'Republic of China', which had been confined to Taiwan since 1949. For many years, however, the USA refused to recognize the People's Republic, regarding the Taiwan administration as the legitimate Chinese Government. In February 1972 President Richard Nixon of the USA visited the People's Republic and acknowledged that 'Taiwan is a part of China'. In January 1979 the USA recognized the People's Republic and severed diplomatic relations with Taiwan.

Following the suppression of the pro-democracy movement in 1989, all senior-level government exchanges were suspended by the USA, and the export of weapons to China was prohibited, but in November 1990 President George Bush received the Chinese Minister of Foreign Affairs in Washington. Sino-US relations deteriorated in September 1992, upon President Bush's announcement of the sale of fighter aircraft to Taiwan. In August 1993 the USA imposed sanctions on China, in response to the latter's sales of technology for nuclear-capable missiles to Pakistan, in alleged violation of international non-proliferation guidelines. The sanctions remained in force until October 1994. China condemned the USA's decision, in September 1994, to expand its official links with Taiwan. In June 1995, following President Clinton's highly controversial decision to grant him a visa, President Lee of Taiwan embarked upon an unofficial visit to the USA, where he met members of the US Congress. The visit resulted in the withdrawal of the Chinese ambassador from Washington. In October, at a meeting in New York, Presidents Jiang Zemin and Bill Clinton agreed to resume dialogue on various issues, the USA reaffirming its commitment to the 'one China' policy. In November the two countries reached agreement on the resumption of bilateral military contacts. In March 1996, as China began a new series of missile tests, the USA stationed two naval convoys east of Taiwan, its largest deployment in Asia since 1975. President Clinton's decision to sell anti-aircraft missiles and other defensive weapons to Taiwan was condemned by China. In February 2000 the US House of Representatives approved the Taiwan Security Enhancement Act (TSEA), establishing direct military links between the USA and Taiwan.

President Jiang Zemin visited the USA in October 1997, the first such visit by a Chinese Head of State since 1985. Measures to reduce the US trade deficit with China and to accelerate China's entry into the WTO were negotiated. In addition, the Chinese Government agreed to control the export of nuclear-related materials, in return for the removal of sanctions on the sale of nuclear-reactor technology to the People's Republic. In April 1998 the US Secretary of State, Madeleine Albright, visited China to prepare for an official visit by President Clinton in late June and early July. Prior to his visit it was announced that China's most favoured nation (MFN, subsequently restyled normal trading relations—NTR) status would be renewed for a further year. Although Clinton continued to be criticized for his constructive engagement policy, the visit was a diplomatic success, being notable for an unprecedented live broadcast in which Presidents Clinton and Jiang debated various issues

Sino-US relations deteriorated significantly during 1999, owing to continued differences over China's human rights record, Tibet, trade relations, espionage and US plans for a missile defence system for Asia. During an official visit by Albright to the People's Republic at the end of February, she reiterated US disapproval at the suppression of organized dissent in China and urged the release of a number of political prisoners. Further acrimonious exchanges concerned demands from the US Congress that the USA's proposed Theater Missile Defense (TMD) system, which was principally designed to protect Japan and the Republic of Korea, be extended to include Taiwan. During a visit to the USA by Zhu Rongji in April, despite the Chinese Premier's offer of a number of economic concessions in return for a bilateral trade agreement to facilitate WTO entry, no agreement was reached. At a final press conference, however, the two sides affirmed their commitment to signing an agreement by the end of 1999. Although China suspended bilateral negotiations in May, following the NATO bombing of the Chinese embassy in Yugoslavia (see below), China's normal trade relations status was renewed in July. China agreed to resume talks in September, and in November (following 13 years of negotiations) a bilateral trade agreement was concluded, which would allow for China's eventual accession to the WTO. The agreement with the USA facilitated the conclusion of bilateral trade agreements with the EU and other WTO members during 2000.

It was widely believed that the failure to reach a trade agreement in April 1999 was, in part, due to popular US anti-Chinese sentiment, which had been exacerbated by US claims in March that a Chinese spy had stolen important nuclear data during the 1980s. A further disclosure of Chinese espionage (which had allegedly taken place in 1995), involving information relevant to the construction of a 'neutron' bomb, emerged during Zhu's visit to the USA. The findings of a select committee of the US House of Representatives, which were released in May 1999, confirmed that Chinese spies had systematically stolen US nuclear technology from the late 1970s until the mid-1990s. China denounced the document as a plot to encourage anti-Chinese sentiment and to deflect attention from events in Yugoslavia. China had vigorously opposed the NATO bombing of Yugoslavia in May 1999, when the Chinese embassy had been severely damaged, leading to the deaths of three people and injuring 20 others. The USA subsequently agreed to pay compensation to the families of those killed and injured by the bombing and also for the damage caused to the Chinese embassy building.

In June 2000, during a visit to China, US Secretary of State Madeleine Albright criticized the People's Republic's human rights record and urged China to increase its efforts for peace with Taiwan. In retaliation, the Chinese Government insisted that US military aid to Taiwan be immediately suspended. In October the situation improved upon the signature of a law granting China the status of permanent NTR. In the following month Bill Clinton announced the waiving of penalties against China for supplying missile parts to Iran and Pakistan. There were initial fears that the election of George W. Bush to the presidency of the USA in late 2000 would lead to the termination of that country's recent policy of engagement with China. Bush, and his Republican Party in particular, had been critical of Clinton's policy on China. In February 2001 the US State Department's annual report on human rights stated that China's situation had deteriorated for the third consecutive year, particularly owing to the campaign against Falun Gong practitioners. China responded by releasing, for the second year, its own report on human rights abuses in the USA. The USA at the same time announced that it would sponsor a resolution condemning China's human rights record at a UN meeting in March. Vice-Premier Qian Qichen visited the USA in March, when he met several senior officials to discuss bilateral links and cautioned against the sale of advanced weapons to Taiwan. Relations quickly became strained following the revelation that Senior Colonel Xu Junping of the PLA had defected while visiting the USA in December 2000. A US-based Chinese scholar, Gao Zhan, was detained in China along with her husband and son, the latter a US citizen. Gao was accused of spying, although her husband and son were released.

A major test for Sino-US relations came at the beginning of April 2001, when a US surveillance plane was forced to make an emergency landing at an airbase on Hainan Island, off the coast of southern China, following its collision with a Chinese fighter aircraft over the South China Sea. The Chinese pilot was killed in the incident, while the spy plane's crew of 24 was detained by the Chinese authorities. Intense negotiations followed, and the crew was released later in the month, after a partial apology from the US ambassador. In the immediate aftermath of the incident, the USA announced that it would sell Taiwan a US $4,000m. armaments 'package', consisting of navy destroyers, anti-submarine aircraft, diesel submarines, amphibious assault vehicles, and surface-to-air missiles and torpedoes. Bush also announced that the USA would do whatever was necessary to defend Taiwan from China. However, the transaction stopped short of selling an advanced combat-radar system, which had been requested by Taiwan. In early May the USA resumed reconnaissance flights near the Chinese coast, and stated that military exchanges with China would be downgraded. At the same time, China reiterated its warnings against the USA's planned NMD system, fearing that it would also protect Taiwan.

Relations between China and the USA were further strained by a meeting between President Bush and the Dalai Lama in Washington, DC, in late May 2001, and by a stopover by Taiwanese President Chen Shui-bian in New York during the same week. However, in June the USA and China reached new trade accords, facilitating China's entry into the WTO. The USA reacted negatively, however, to the conviction of Gao Zhan and another US-based Chinese academic, Qin Guangguang, for espionage in late July. Gao, Qin and another academic, Li Shaomin, were freed prior to a visit by the US Secretary of State, Colin Powell. In August a US aircraft carrier made a visit to Hong Kong; however, two US Navy aircraft carrier battle groups staged a one-day exercise in the South China Sea, coinciding with Chinese military exercises in the Taiwan Straits.

In early September 2001 the USA sought to reduce China's fears over its NMD programme by promising to keep China informed of its development and by abandoning its objections to China's build-up of its nuclear forces, in return for China's acceptance of NMD. The USA also urged China not to transfer ballistic missile technology to countries it considered 'rogue states'. The terrorist attacks against the USA on 11 September 2001 were strongly condemned by China, which pledged co-operation in the US-led 'war on terror'. In late October Bush made his first official visit to China to attend the summit meeting of Asia-Pacific Economic Co-operation (APEC, see p. 176), which was dominated by the issue of terrorism. However, the USA did not share China's view that Uygur and Tibetan separatists in Xinjiang and Tibet respectively were terrorists. Disagreements also remained over the USA's successful NMD interceptor test in December. At the end of 2001 President Bush signed proclamations granting China the status of permanent NTR commencing on 1 January 2002, and also ended the Jackson-Vanik regulation preventing communist states from having normal trading relations with the USA if they restricted emigration.

US President Bush visited Beijing in February 2002. Discussions with President Jiang were candid: the two sides disagreed on the issues of human rights, China's close relations with Iran, Iraq and North Korea (countries the US President had described as forming an 'axis of evil'), the USA's planned missile defence system, China's export of nuclear technology to Pakistan and US support for Taiwan. In March, for the third consecutive year, China released a report on human rights abuses in the USA, in response to the latter's annual report on the human rights situation in China. More significantly, the Taiwanese Minister of National Defense made a non-transit visit to the USA to attend a private security conference, and it was revealed that the USA maintained contingency plans for a nuclear attack on seven states, including China.

In April 2002 President Hu Jintao made his first official visit to the USA, where he held discussions with President Bush. Hu emphasized the importance of Taiwan as a major determinant of bilateral relations. The former US President, Bill Clinton, made a private visit to China in May. In late June military officials from both countries began discussions to restore bilateral military relations, and in July the US Department of Defense sent a team to China to discover the remains of several US servicemen who had disappeared in the course of espionage missions conducted during the protracted period of mutual hostility known as the Cold War. Despite this progress, the release of two new reports in the USA in mid-July highlighted remaining concerns about China. The first report, issued by the US Department of Defense, warned that China was increasing its defence spending in order to intimidate Taiwan. The second, issued by the Congressional US-China Security Review Commission, warned that China had become a leading proliferator of missile technology to countries opposed to the USA, and that US corporations and their investments in China were assisting its emergence as a major economic power, to the detriment of the US trade balance. In late August China introduced the 'Regulations on Export Control of Missiles and Missile-related Items and Technologies' to curb the export of missiles and related technology, in an apparent goodwill gesture to the visiting US Deputy Secretary of State, Richard Armitage. In return, the USA designated the East Turkestan Islamic Movement a terrorist group (see above).

In October 2002 Jiang Zemin visited the USA and was hosted by President George W. Bush at his ranch in Texas, a gesture of hospitality conferred on few other world leaders. The major issues discussed were the emerging diplomatic crises over Iraq and North Korea. However, Jiang was keen to avoid confrontation with the USA, regarding the improvement in bilateral relations as a major accomplishment of his presidency. In November a US warship arrived in Qingdao, the first such visit since the Hainan aircraft incident of April 2001. In December 2002, in Washington, DC, China and the USA held their first formal senior-level military talks since Bush assumed office, and days later the commander of US forces in the Pacific, Adm. Thomas Fargo, visited Beijing.

There was strong opposition in China to the US military intervention in Iraq in March 2003, but public protests in China against the war were banned. Tensions over trade issues also increased, and during a visit to Beijing in September US

Secretary of the Treasury John Snow criticized China's refusal to revalue its currency, amid US concerns that undervaluation of the yuan was having an adverse effect on the US economy. China in turn expressed strong criticism of the USA's imposition of quotas on Chinese textile exports in November 2003. In December the issue of Taiwan dominated a visit by Chinese Premier Wen Jiabao to Washington.

The US State Department's annual report on human rights for 2003, published in February 2004, contained especially strong criticism of human rights protection in China, accusing the Chinese Government of 'back-sliding' on a number of issues. In March 2004 dialogue between China and the USA was suspended following the latter's decision to sponsor a resolution condemning China's human rights record. The resolution was rejected at a UN meeting in April (see above). Also in April, US Vice-President Dick Cheney visited Beijing, where he had discussions with the Chinese leadership on issues relating to Taiwan and North Korea, as well as on economic matters. In the same month Chinese Vice-Premier Wu Yi made an official visit to the USA in an attempt to resolve ongoing trade disputes. In May China rejected renewed criticism by the USA of its human rights record, and accused the US Government of failing to investigate alleged abuse of Iraqi prisoners by US soldiers in its annual human rights report. An official US report on China's military capability, published in June, claimed that there was evidence that the country was preparing for military conflict over Taiwan. In July, during a visit to Beijing by US National Security Adviser Condoleezza Rice, a US official expressed his country's intention to continue selling advanced military equipment to Taiwan, despite strong Chinese opposition.

Increasing US concerns over China's economic strength and the trade deficit between the two countries (to the detriment of the USA) were illustrated in mid-2005 when a bid by the China National Offshore Oil Corporation (CNOOC) to take control of Unocal, a California-based oil and gas company, encountered vocal opposition within the US House of Representatives. The bid was regarded as potentially damaging to the economic and national security of the USA, and in the event Unocal accepted the lower bid of a US firm, Chevron. Diplomatic tension likewise arose over the huge increase in Chinese textile exports to the USA following the expiry of the WTO's Multi-Fibre Arrangement (MFA) in January 2005. Negotiations resulted in an agreement in November whereby limits were imposed on the rate at which the volume of Chinese clothing exports to the USA could increase. There was also marked US anxiety over the issue of China's increasing military spending. In July an annual report from the US Department of Defense claimed that China might have as many as 730 ballistic missiles aimed at Taiwan (an increase of 230 compared with the previous year's estimate), and assessed China's annual military spending at US $90,000m., three times the official estimate given by the Chinese Government. In October Donald Rumsfeld, visiting China for the first time since his appointment as US Secretary of Defense, expressed concerns at China's broadening ballistic capabilities in the Pacific region. In September, meanwhile, Hu Jintao paid his first visit as Head of State to the USA, and in November President Bush reciprocated by visiting Beijing.

Trade issues formed the focus of Sino-US relations in 2006, following the establishment in February of a US task force aimed at ensuring that China complied with global trading requirements. US companies had continued to accuse China of 'flooding' the USA with artificially cheap imports. In April President Hu Jintao paid a visit to Washington, DC, where trade was once again the main topic of discussion. While President George W. Bush continued to press China on the revaluation of its currency, and Hu promised that the Government would 'continue to take steps' in this regard, no significant advance was made. A US Treasury report issued in May accused China of making 'too little progress' on the adjustment of its exchange rate. In December a team led by US Treasury Secretary Henry Paulson visited China for a 'Strategic Economic Dialogue' aimed at curbing the growing trade imbalance between the two nations, as well as focusing on long-term issues such as environmental protection. The visit took place just days after the publication of a US report assessing China's implementation of WTO requirements, which described China's record in the organization as 'decidedly mixed'.

Relations between the two nations did not improve significantly in 2007. In January the USA announced that it would allow Taiwanese President Chen Shui-bian to stop off in California en route to Nicaragua, prompting the Chinese Government to accuse Chen of trying to damage Sino-US relations. In March the Chinese Ministry of Foreign Affairs protested against reported US plans to sell missiles to Taiwan. China's increase in military spending (the country's budgetary defence allocation had risen by 17.8% in 2007) was a source of concern for the US Government: a US Department of Defense report circulated in May drew attention to the transformation of China's armed forces, the processes of which, it was suggested, were not sufficiently transparent. The quality of China's exports was also a point of contention between the two countries. A notable example of this was the discovery of the use of lead paint on toys manufactured in China, an issue that the Chinese Government agreed to address in September.

China's relations with Japan began to deteriorate in 1982, after China complained that passages in Japanese school textbooks sought to justify the Japanese invasion of China in 1937. In June 1989 the Japanese Government criticized the Chinese Government's suppression of the pro-democracy movement and suspended (until late 1990) a five-year aid programme to China. In April 1992 Jiang Zemin travelled to Japan, the first visit by the General Secretary of the CCP for nine years. In October Emperor Akihito made the first ever imperial visit to the People's Republic. Japan was one of many countries to criticize China's resumption of underground nuclear testing, at Lop Nor in Xinjiang Province, in October 1993. Relations were seriously strained in May 1994, when the Japanese Minister of Justice referred to the 1937 Nanjing massacre (in which more than 300,000 Chinese citizens were killed by Japanese soldiers) as a 'fabrication', and again in August, when a second Japanese minister was obliged to resign, following further controversial remarks about his country's war record. In May 1995, during a visit to Beijing, the Japanese Prime Minister expressed his deep remorse for the wartime atrocities, but offered no formal apology.

China's continuation of its nuclear-testing programme, in defiance of international opinion, prompted Japan to announce a reduction in financial aid to China. In August 1995 Japan suspended most of its grant aid to China. Following China's 'final' nuclear test in July 1996, and the declaration of a moratorium, Japan resumed grant aid in March 1997. (China signed the Comprehensive Nuclear Test Ban Treaty in September 1996.) In July 1996, however, Sino-Japanese relations were affected by a territorial dispute relating to the Diaoyu (or Senkaku) Islands, a group of uninhabited islets in the East China Sea, which China had claimed as its own since ancient times, and Japan since 1895, and to which Taiwan also laid claim. The construction of a lighthouse on one of the islands by a group of Japanese nationalists led to strong protests from the Governments of both the People's Republic and Taiwan. The Japanese Government sought to defuse the tension by withholding recognition of the lighthouse. At a meeting with President Jiang Zemin during the APEC conference in November 1996, the Japanese Prime Minister apologized for Japanese aggression during the Second World War, and emphasized his desire to resolve the dispute over the Diaoyu Islands. In May 1997, following the landing on one of the islands by a member of the Japanese Diet, the Japanese Government distanced itself from the incident.

Following the normalization of relations between the Japanese Communist Party (JCP) and its Chinese equivalent after a period of more than 30 years, the Chairman of the JCP, Tetsuzo Fuwa, paid an official visit to China in July 1998. During a visit by Jiang Zemin to Japan in November, the first of its kind by a Chinese Head of State, relations were strained by Japan's failure to issue an unequivocal apology for its invasion and occupation of China during 1937–45. The summit meeting between Jiang and the Japanese Prime Minister, Keizo Obuchi, was, nevertheless, deemed to have been successful. Keizo Obuchi paid a reciprocal visit to the People's Republic in July 1999, during which he held summit talks with Zhu Rongji and Jiang Zemin. Tensions remained, but a number of co-operation agreements were reached.

In April 2001 NPC Chairman Li Peng cancelled a trip to Japan, apparently in response to the Japanese decision to permit former Taiwanese President Lee Teng-hui to visit Japan, and the publication of a new history textbook that attenuated Japan's wartime atrocities in China and South-East Asia. By mid-2001 China and Japan had become embroiled in trade disputes involving tariffs on imported goods. China was further antagonized by the visit of the Japanese Prime Minister, Junichiro Koizumi, to the Yasukuni Shrine, a controversial war memorial in Tokyo that glorified Japan's war dead, including several prominent war criminals. Li Peng finally visited Japan in early April 2002, when he met Koizumi. Later that month, Koizumi visited China to attend the Boao Forum, where he met Zhu Rongji. Relations were strained in May, however, when Chinese security forces forcibly removed North Korean refugees seeking asylum at a number of foreign diplomatic missions, including the Japanese consulate in Shenyang, thus violating international protocol. A diplomatic impasse was resolved in June when China agreed to release the asylum-seekers to a third country. In August, meanwhile, a Tokyo court finally admitted that Japan had conducted biological warfare in China during the Second World War, but rejected the demands by 180 Chinese plaintiffs for individual compensation. In January 2003 the Diaoyu/Senkaku Islands dispute re-emerged when Japan announced plans to lease the islands to a private owner, prompting protests from China. Also in January, Prime Minister Koizumi made a further visit to the Yasukuni Shrine (see above). Two further incidents related to Japan's wartime atrocities caused tensions in the Sino-Japanese relationship in 2003. In August 29 people were poisoned by chemical weapons that had been left buried in north-eastern China after the Japanese invasion of the area during the war. In September an incident involving the use of Chinese prostitutes by Japanese tourists also caused deep offence in China, especially as the event coincided with an anniversary of the Japanese occupation.

In January 2004 there was renewed conflict over the Diaoyu/Senkaku Islands when a Japanese ship fired a water cannon at a Chinese boat. In March there were protests in China following the arrest by Japanese police of seven Chinese activists who had landed on the islands. Strong anti-Japanese sentiment was evident in rioting by Chinese football supporters after Japan's football team defeated China in the Asia Cup final in August. Japanese officials made a complaint to the Chinese Government following an incident in which a Chinese submarine was found to have entered Japanese waters. China later apologized for the intrusion.

In April 2005 violent demonstrations took place across China in protest at Japan's bid for a permanent seat on the UN Security Council, as well as at the Japanese Government's approval for use in schools of history textbooks reportedly omitting mention of Japanese atrocities in China (and Korea) during the Second World War. In May Chinese Vice-Premier Wu Yi cancelled a scheduled meeting with Prime Minister Koizumi while visiting Japan, prompting speculation that this action was motivated by comments made by Koizumi denying the political significance of his visits to the controversial Yasukuni Shrine. In July the Teikoku Oil Company, a Japanese firm, was granted drilling rights by the Japanese Government for an area of the East China Sea that was also claimed by China; conversely, in October the Japanese Government asserted that, according to their reconnaissance information, Chinese oil companies were extracting natural gas from disputed waters.

A meeting between Minister of Foreign Affairs Li Zhaoxing and his Japanese counterpart, Taro Aso, in April 2006 resulted in a pledge to further Sino-Japanese co-operation and a promise to expedite negotiations on disputed gas exploration in the East China Sea. In June Japan agreed to resume low-interest loans to China, which had earlier been suspended as a result of the Chinese Government's criticisms of the Yasukuni Shrine visits. Sino-Japanese relations sharply deteriorated in August, however, following the publication of a Japanese defence policy document that was deemed to have exaggerated China's military strength and, more crucially, by Prime Minister Koizumi's visit to the Yasukuni Shrine on 15 August (the anniversary of Japan's surrender in the Second World War). The appointment of Shinzo Abe as Japanese Prime Minister in the following month resulted in a marked improvement in relations between the two countries, not least owing to Abe's decision to visit Beijing, his first destination for an official overseas trip. During the trip, which took place in October, President Hu and Abe agreed to expand bilateral links in the areas of trade, investment and technology.

Sino-Japanese relations developed further in 2007. The Chinese Minister of Foreign Affairs, Li Zhaoxing, visited Japan in February 2007, attending talks with Prime Minister Abe and Minister for Foreign Affairs Taro Aso. This was followed by a much-anticipated visit from Wen Jiabao, who thus became the first ever Chinese Premier to address the Diet (the Japanese legislature); in his speech he emphasized the suffering caused by the Japanese occupation and the need for amends, but also looked forward to increased co-operation between the two countries. Discussions between Wen and Abe resulted in an agreement to co-operate in fields such as the economy, defence, energy and the environment. In April it was reported that trade between the two countries had increased to such a level that China had overtaken the USA to become Japan's principal trading partner.

The long-standing border dispute with India, which gave rise to a short military conflict in 1962, remained unresolved. Discussions on the issue were held in 1988 and 1991, and in September 1993 the two countries signed an agreement to reduce their troops along the frontier and to resolve the dispute by peaceful means. In December 1994 China and India agreed to hold joint military exercises in mid-1995. In August 1995 it was confirmed that the two countries were to disengage their troops from four border posts in Arunachal Pradesh. Further progress was made at the ninth round of Sino-Indian border discussions, held in October 1996, and during the visit of President Jiang Zemin to India (the first by a Chinese Head of State) in November. In May 1998, immediately prior to India's nuclear tests, the Indian Minister of Defence, George Fernandes, stated that China constituted India's main long-term security threat, citing its aid to Pakistan's nuclear programme and its military facilities in the Andaman Sea. However, the Indian Minister of External Affairs, Jaswant Singh, denied that India viewed China as a threat, when he visited Beijing in June 1999. Li Peng visited India in January 2001, and discussions were held with a view to the restoration of normal relations. Outstanding Indian concerns included the increasing levels of imports of cheap Chinese goods and the question of China's nuclear co-operation with Pakistan, while China resented India's decades-long hosting of Tibetan separatist organizations. However, in early January 2002 Prime Minister Zhu Rongji led a business delegation to India, and in April officials from the two countries held discussions in New Delhi, aimed at establishing joint counter-terrorism measures.

In April 2003 George Fernandes began a week-long visit to Beijing, to discuss outstanding bilateral issues, including China's support for Pakistan and Chinese observation posts in the Bay of Bengal. In June Atal Bihari Vajpayee visited Beijing, the first visit by an Indian Prime Minister in over a decade. The Indian Prime Minister officially recognized Tibet as part of China, and China agreed to trade with India's north-eastern state of Sikkim, thus implicitly recognizing India's control of that area. In November China and India held joint naval exercises, representing the first ever joint military exercises between the two countries. Further negotiations took place in 2004 in an attempt to move towards resolution of remaining border disputes, with Chinese Minister of National Defence Cao Gangchuan making an official visit to India in March (the first such visit by a Chinese defence minister), and a further round of talks taking place in July. During an historic visit to India in March 2005, Chinese Premier Wen Jiabao signed an agreement aimed at resolving the border dispute. In July 2006 the two sides reopened the Nathu La border pass connecting the Indian state of Sikkim with Tibet. The reopening of the historic pass, which had been closed in 1962 during the Sino-Indian war and which was the only direct land link between the two countries, was a formal recognition by India of China's claim to Tibet and by China of India's claim to Sikkim. However, shortly before a visit to India by President Hu Jintao in November (the first visit by a Chinese head of state for 10 years), China's ambassador to India reiterated his country's claim to the Indian state of Arunachal Pradesh; the statement was rapidly refuted by the Indian Minister of External Affairs. The Chinese President's visit, nevertheless, was hailed as a success. President Hu and Indian Prime Minister Manmohan Singh pledged to double bilateral trade to US $40,000m. by 2010, to encourage bilateral investment, to expedite feasibility studies on a joint trade agreement and to continue to work together to resolve joint border issues. In January 2008 Prime Minister Singh paid a visit to China, attending talks with President Hu and Premier Wen Jiabao and signing agreements on bilateral trade and military exercises.

In December 2001 China hosted Pakistani President Pervez Musharraf, who arrived to mark the 50th anniversary of relations between the two countries. China and Pakistan had long been close allies, and co-operated in economic and military issues. Musharraf visited Beijing again in August 2002 and reaffirmed the close relations between the two countries. In October 2003 the Chinese and Pakistani navies conducted joint military exercises. In November President Musharraf made another visit to Beijing during which various agreements were concluded, including trade accords and an extradition treaty. Although plans for Chinese assistance to Pakistan in building a nuclear plant were not finalized, an agreement for the construction of a second nuclear plant was signed in May 2004. Chinese Premier Wen Jiabao visited Pakistan in April 2005. Relations between the two nations were strengthened further in November 2006, when President Hu Jintao signed a free trade agreement (FTA) with President Musharraf during a visit to the Pakistani capital of Islamabad. The visit, the first by a Chinese head of state for a decade, was widely regarded as an attempt to reassure Pakistan of the continuing strength of bilateral links, particularly in view of China's growing relationship with India. Co-operation agreements signed by the two leaders aimed to treble the value of bilateral trade within five years.

The question of the sovereignty of the Spratly (Nansha) Islands, situated in the South China Sea and claimed by six countries (Brunei, China, Malaysia, the Philippines, Taiwan and Viet Nam), remained unresolved in the early 21st century. The strategic importance of the islands was due to the major international shipping routes passing through the area, and China's claim to the islands and the surrounding sea raised concerns about its possible expansionist ambitions. By 1994 both China and Viet Nam had awarded petroleum exploration concessions to US companies, leading to increased tension among the claimants. In February 1995 it emerged that Chinese forces had occupied a reef to which the Philippines laid claim, resulting in a formal diplomatic protest from Manila. More than 60 Chinese fishermen and several vessels were subsequently detained by the Philippine authorities. Following consultations in August, China and the Philippines declared their intention to resolve peacefully their claims to the Spratly Islands. In January 1996 the Chinese Government denied any involvement in a naval skirmish in Philippine waters, during which a ship flying the Chinese flag and a Philippine patrol boat exchanged gunfire. In November 1998 China angered the Philippine Government by building permanent structures on the disputed Mischief Reef. In late November 20 Chinese fishermen were arrested near Mischief Reef by the Philippine navy. Following Chinese protests, the men were released. In December China reiterated both its claim to sovereignty over the Spratly Islands and surrounding waters and its commitment to pursuing a peaceful solution through negotiation. Discussions between the two countries in April 1999 were unsuccessful, and relations deteriorated further in May when a Chinese fishing vessel sank following a collision with a Philippine navy boat, which was claimed to be accidental by the Philippines but deliberate by the People's Republic. Another Chinese fishing vessel sank in a collision with a Philippine navy vessel in July. A similar territorial dispute relating to the Paracel (Xisha) Islands, which had been seized by China from South Vietnamese forces in 1974, also remained unresolved. In May 1996, despite having agreed to abide by the UN Convention on the Law of the Sea, China declared an extension of its maritime boundaries in the South China Sea. Other claimants to the Paracel Islands, in particular Indonesia, the Philippines and Viet Nam, expressed grave concern at China's apparent expansionism. In November 2002, in Phnom-Penh, Cambodia, Prime Minister Zhu Rongji signed a landmark 'declaration on the conduct of parties in the South China Sea' with members of the Association of South East Asian Nations (ASEAN, see p. 185), which aimed to avoid conflict in the area. Under this agreement, which was similar to one drafted in late 1999 but not implemented, claimants would practise self-restraint in the event of potentially hostile action (such as inhabiting the islands), effect confidence-building measures and give advance notice of military exercises in the region. However, the agreement did not include the Paracel Islands, and disagreements continued among the signatories on what the accord should encompass. Additionally, China introduced a provision requiring consensus to resolve outstanding issues, thereby allowing for future indecision among ASEAN members. In September 2003 China proposed a joint development and petroleum exploration strategy for the Spratly Islands. In November the Philippines Government complained that China had violated the 2002 accord by installing markers in parts of the islands. There were a number of similar disputes in 2004, with China protesting at a move by Viet Nam to conduct tourist boat tours of the islands. In March 2005 CNOOC, the Philippine National Oil Company and the Vietnam Oil and Gas Corporation (Petrovietnam) signed an accord pledging to conduct joint marine seismic experiments in the Spratly Islands region.

In August and October 1990 diplomatic relations were established with Indonesia and Singapore respectively. In late 1991, following many years of mutual hostility resulting from a border dispute and from the Vietnamese intervention in Kampuchea (now Cambodia) in 1978, the restoration of normal relations between China and Viet Nam was announced. In February 2002 President Jiang Zemin began his second official visit to Viet Nam. In November 2000 President Jiang Zemin toured Laos, Cambodia and Brunei, the tour culminating in his attendance at the APEC conference in Brunei. His visit to Cambodia was the first by a Chinese Head of State for more than 30 years. In December 2001 Jiang visited Myanmar, seeking to increase China's influence there with regard to India and promising US $100m. in finance towards investment projects. From 2000 China also increased links with a number of South Pacific island nations, providing aid and investment. At the ASEAN summit meeting in Phnom-Penh, Cambodia, in November 2002, China and 10 South-East Asian nations signed an agreement to establish the world's largest free trade area by 2010. In January 2003 the head of Myanmar's ruling State Peace and Development Council, Gen. Than Shwe, visited Beijing, where he was promised US $200m. in development loans. In August, in defiance of US attempts to isolate Myanmar's leadership, 32 members of Myanmar's military junta visited Beijing to hold discussions with the Chinese authorities. In October China's links with ASEAN were strengthened when China signed ASEAN's Treaty of Amity and Co-operation, a pact for the promotion of regional stability, at an ASEAN summit meeting in Bali. China and ASEAN also agreed to work towards an FTA. In November 2004 a trade agreement was signed between China and ASEAN members committing countries to lower tariffs on goods trade by 2010. Also in November 2004, Soe Win, Myanmar's new Prime Minister, made an official visit to China. In April 2007 plans were announced to construct an oil pipeline from Yunnan Province in China to a port in Myanmar.

During 1992 China established diplomatic relations with the Republic of Korea. China remained committed to the achievement of peace on the Korean peninsula, and in June 1996 it was reported that secret discussions between representatives of the Republic and of the DPRK had been held in Beijing. In late 1997 China participated in quadripartite negotiations, together with the USA, the DPRK and the Republic of Korea, to resolve the Korean issue. Further quadripartite negotiations took place during 1999. In May 2000 the North Korean leader, Kim Jong Il, visited China, on his first trip abroad for 17 years. In the following month China welcomed the holding of the first ever inter-Korean presidential summit meeting in the DPRK. Regular inter-Korean meetings followed. Kim Jong Il visited China again in January 2001, and President Jiang visited North Korea in September. During 2001, however, China increased measures to counter the growing number of North Korean refugees entering the country. Premier Zhu Rongji made his first trip to the Republic of Korea in October 2000.

During 2002 China continued to play an important role on the Korean peninsula, its main interest being a reduction of tensions and the reconnection of the inter-Korean railway lines and their subsequent connection with China's own railway system. However, there were tensions with South Korea over the introduction of a bill that would grant special rights to ethnic Koreans in China and also over China's forcible removal of North Korean refugees from South Korean embassies in the People's Republic. In late June the Chinese Government allowed 24 North Korean refugees who had been concealed in the embassy of South Korea to leave for that country. After the incident, the authorities began an operation against South Korean activists and missionaries who had been helping North Koreans to flee via China. In October North Korea appointed a Chinese businessman of Dutch citizenship, Yang Bin, as the new governor of its recently created Sinuiju Special Administrative Region; however, the Chinese authorities arrested him on charges of bribery and fraud, thereby preventing him from assuming the post. By early 2003 China was becoming increasingly concerned about the growing diplomatic crisis between North Korea and the USA over the former's decision formally to restart its nuclear programme. In January 2003 the vice-ministers of foreign affairs of China and South Korea met to discuss the crisis. In July South Korean President Roh Moo-Hyun visited Beijing for discussions with Hu Jintao on the subject of North Korea. Later in the month a Chinese envoy delivered a letter from Hu Jintao to North Korean leader Kim Jong Il. Chinese diplomatic efforts played a major role in ensuring North Korean participation in the six-party talks on the nuclear issue attended by North Korea, South Korea, China, the USA, Japan and Russia, which were held in Beijing in August 2003. Chinese Minister of Foreign Affairs Li Zhaoxing paid his first visit to the North Korean capital of

THE PEOPLE'S REPUBLIC OF CHINA

Pyongyang in March 2004. Kim Jong Il made an unofficial visit to Beijing in April 2004, which became public following a major railway accident that coincided with Kim's return journey from China. Relations with South Korea were affected in 2004 by a dispute over the ancient kingdom of Koguryo, believed by Koreans to have been ruled by their own ancestors, but which China claimed had been ruled by one of its own ethnic groups. In August references to Koguryo were deleted from the Chinese Ministry of Foreign Affairs website. In November 2006 relations between the two countries were strengthened when China and South Korea announced that they were to begin official negotiations on an FTA in 2007. The announcement followed an official visit to Beijing by South Korean President Roh Moo-Hyun in the previous month. Talks were held between the two countries in 2007 in order to prepare for the commencement of formal negotiations.

Following the North Korean Government's declaration in February 2005 that it possessed nuclear weapons, the delayed fourth round of six-party disarmament talks was hosted by China, with discussions commencing in Beijing in July. China was credited with having played an important role in the conclusion of a framework agreement at the talks in September, under which the DPRK agreed to disarm in exchange for various concessions; however, the agreement subsequently faltered (see the chapter on the Democratic People's Republic of Korea for further information). In October President Hu Jintao made his first official visit to the DPRK as Head of State, in advance of the fifth round of talks, which began in Beijing in November. In January 2006 Chinese and North Korean media belatedly confirmed that Kim Jong Il had made an unofficial visit to the People's Republic, following a week of speculation to that effect in the international media. Soon after Kim's departure, US Assistant Secretary of State Christopher Hill, the US chief negotiator in the six-party nuclear talks, also paid an unscheduled visit to Beijing.

Throughout 2006 the Chinese Government continued to urge the DPRK to revoke its nuclear weapons programme. The perception that China wielded any real influence over the DPRK was ended in July when, in defiance of international opinion, North Korea proceeded with a test of a long-range missile, and again in October when it carried out its long-held threat to conduct its first test of a nuclear device. Embarrassed by the DPRK's blatant disregard for its entreaties, China surprised international observers by agreeing, albeit with reservations, to the imposition of UN sanctions against the regime of Kim Jong Il. Amid North Korean fears that China would cut off its vital oil supplies if any further tests were to be conducted, a Chinese envoy who visited Pyongyang later that month returned with assurances that no tests were planned. By the end of October China was once more exerting its influence, with an announcement that North Korea had agreed during discussions in Beijing to return to the six-party talks on the issue of its nuclear weapons programme. By way of encouragement, China was reported to have removed its 'freeze' on North Korean assets held in the Macao-based Banco Delta Asia (BDA, which had allegedly been involved in corrupt financial activities on behalf of the Government of the DPRK). In February 2007 the six-party talks, with considerable Chinese input, resulted in a multi-faceted agreement, the terms of which included the closure of the DPRK's Yongbyon nuclear site in exchange for substantial amounts of aid. Following a delay of several months owing to a dispute over the release of North Korean funds held in BDA, Yongbyon was declared closed in July. With further negotiations taking place later in the year, some observers were hopeful that the immobilization of the DPRK's nuclear facilities and eventual denuclearization were attainable objectives.

Following the reversion of Hong Kong to Chinese sovereignty, relations between China and the United Kingdom improved significantly from 1998. The British Secretary of State for Foreign and Commonwealth Affairs, Robin Cook, paid a visit to China and Hong Kong in January. The first China-EU summit meeting, which was scheduled to become an annual event, took place in London in April, prior to the Asia-Europe Meeting (ASEM). China and the EU committed themselves to greater mutual co-operation in the area of trade and economic relations. The Chinese Premier also had talks with his British counterpart, Tony Blair, who visited China and Hong Kong in October. He declared his intention to broach the issue of human rights through 'persuasion and dialogue'. The two sides pledged to increase co-operation in a number of areas, and in October 1999 Jiang Zemin became the first Chinese Head of State to visit the United Kingdom. This visit was part of a six-nation tour, which also included France, Portugal, Morocco, Algeria and Saudi Arabia. In the United Kingdom and France, however, Jiang's visit prompted protests by supporters of human rights, resulting in complaints from the Chinese authorities. In December, during a China-EU summit meeting in Beijing, the Chinese Government rejected criticism of its human rights record, reiterating its previous position that economic development would precede an improvement in human rights. In October 2000 China concluded bilateral trade agreements with the EU necessary for WTO accession. In May 2001 Beijing hosted an EU delegation, seeking a new comprehensive partnership with China, particularly in the area of commerce. The fourth annual China-EU summit meeting took place in Brussels in early September, and discussed access by EU companies to China's insurance market, the last obstacle to China's admission to the WTO (which took place in December 2001). In late October–early November Vice-President Hu Jintao made his first official trip to the EU, visiting the United Kingdom, France, Germany and Spain. Jiang Zemin visited Germany in April 2002. In July 2003 Tony Blair made a diplomatic visit to China during which he sought to enhance trade links between China and the United Kingdom. In October there were developments towards greater economic co-operation between China and the EU at a China-EU summit meeting in Beijing. A new visa system was agreed to give Chinese tourists easier access to European countries. China also agreed to work with the EU on the Galileo satellite project, which once completed would represent a more advanced alternative to the US Global Positioning System. In January 2004 President Hu Jintao held talks in Paris with French President Jacques Chirac, who expressed his support for China's opposition to a proposed referendum in Taiwan (see above). President Chirac's support of China on this issue provoked anger in Taiwan. President Hu's visit to Paris also provoked protests by French government members and human rights activists. Likewise, human rights activists and Tibetan independence groups staged demonstrations during President Hu's official visit to the United Kingdom in November 2005, as part of a trip in which he also visited Germany and Spain.

Premier Wen Jiabao made his first official visit to EU headquarters in Brussels shortly after the expansion of the Union in May 2004. In the same month Wen visited the United Kingdom and had discussions with Tony Blair on various issues, including human rights in the context of reported abuse of prisoners by British soldiers deployed in Iraq, as well as of political developments in Hong Kong and mainland China. In June Chinese and British fleets carried out the first ever joint navy exercises. During 2004 the EU continued to resist demands for the removal of a ban on weapons trade with China, which had been in place since 1989, but some EU countries, including France and Germany, expressed their disapproval of the ban. There was renewed opposition to the removal of the ban within both the EU and the USA, following the approval of an anti-secession law by the Chinese NPC in March 2005, and in April plans to remove the embargo were apparently abandoned.

The termination of the WTO's 10-year MFA in January 2005 resulted in a huge increase in the volume of Chinese exports of clothing to the EU, prompting the Union's Trade Commissioner, Peter Mandelson, to impose new quotas in June. These quotas were quickly exceeded, however, leading to the accumulation of large quantities of Chinese garments in European ports. After several unsuccessful rounds of negotiations, an agreement was reached in early September, whereby 50% of the goods held up in ports were released and the remaining 50% were to be offset against the quotas for 2006. However, in 2006 a fresh trade dispute arose, this time over the issue of shoe exports. In April the EU announced that it would begin imposing import duties of up to 20% on shoes from China and Viet Nam, which it accused of giving unfair subsidies to their domestic shoe manufacturers. By November, with no sign of either side making any concession, the Chinese Government announced that it would support the nation's shoemakers in mounting a legal challenge to the imposition of the new tariff structure in an EU court. None the less, an EU-China summit meeting held in Helsinki, Finland, in September resulted in broad agreements to extend co-operation, including the opening of negotiations on a new Partnership and Co-operation Agreement, to replace the original Trade and Co-operation Agreement signed in 1985. In the following month the European Commission adopted a revised policy on China, urging closer engagement. In January 2007, however, the EU reiterated that its conditions for the removal of its weapons

THE PEOPLE'S REPUBLIC OF CHINA

embargo on China (see above) remained unchanged. A number of European leaders visited China during 2006, including French President Jacques Chirac, German Chancellor Angela Merkel and Italian Prime Minister Romano Prodi. In July the President of the European Parliament, Josep Borrell Fontelles, paid an official visit to Beijing, the first such visit by a senior European Parliament official in 13 years. In September Premier Wen Jiabao visited both the United Kingdom and Germany. Relations between China and Germany appeared to grow tense in September 2007 when, against China's wishes, Chancellor Merkel met with the Dalai Lama.

China established diplomatic relations with Israel in 1992, and during the 1990s co-operated in several military technology projects, including China's indigenous fighter aircraft programme. However, the USA, fearing that this would strengthen China's position against Taiwan, exerted pressure on Israel to cancel a lucrative contract to supply airborne warning and control (AWACS) aircraft to China in early 2000. Initially, Israel refused to comply, particularly after Jiang Zemin had made the first official trip to the country by a Chinese Head of State, in April. In July, however, Israel was obliged to yield to pressure, as it could not risk losing the USA as a major ally. In January 2003 Israel ceased exports of weapons to China. China also maintained good relations with a number of Middle Eastern nations, including Iran and Iraq, and in June 2000 hosted Iranian President Muhammad Khatami, who was seeking closer economic links. President Hosni Mubarak of Egypt visited Beijing in January 2002. In April 2002 Zhu Rongji visited Turkey and Egypt, and Jiang made a tour of Libya, Nigeria, Tunisia and Iran. The issues discussed included business and energy, defence co-operation, and the war against global terrorism. China did not support the US-led military action against Iraq in March 2003, but the Chinese Government did provide humanitarian assistance to Iraqi refugees. During 2004 there was also a strengthening of relations between China and Iran, China's second largest source of oil imports. In November China signed a deal for the development of Iran's Yadavaran oil field, the value of which was estimated at US $70,000m. During a visit to Tehran in November 2004 the Chinese Minister of Foreign Affairs indicated that he did not support US plans to exert pressure on Iran over the issue of its nuclear programme. As the diplomatic altercation over Iran's nuclear aspirations intensified from 2005, China consistently opposed the imposition of sanctions against Tehran. Following the conflict between Lebanon and Israel in mid-2006, in September China announced that it was to increase its force in Lebanon to 1,000 peace-keepers, its largest single such deployment since China first began contributing to UN-mandated peace-keeping forces in the 1980s. Many interpreted this deployment as China's way of bolstering its standing in the Middle East and of signalling its peaceful credentials to Western countries increasingly alarmed by China's rapid rise as a major economic power.

China continued to pursue closer relations with African nations. The first Forum on China-Africa Co-operation (FOCAC) was held in Beijing in October 2000, when the People's Republic announced its decision to reduce or cancel outstanding debt totalling US $1,200m. During a state visit to China by Nigerian President Olusegun Obasanjo in April 2005 a series of economic agreements between the two countries was concluded. In July President Hu Jintao signed a co-operation agreement with Robert Mugabe, President of Zimbabwe, during a visit by the latter to China. Trade links between China and Africa were further strengthened in November 2006 when Beijing successfully hosted a summit meeting of FOCAC, which was attended by senior representatives from 48 African nations. China pledged to ensure that by 2010 its trade with Africa would more than double to reach $100,000m., while its aid to Africa in the form of preferential loans and export credits was projected to reach $5,000m. by 2009. In addition, China announced the immediate implementation of various trade and investment agreements, including plans for a new aluminium production plant in Egypt, the upgrading of a Nigerian highway and a copper project in Zambia. However, the summit meeting drew widespread opprobrium from international critics, many of whom questioned China's lack of commitment to human rights and democracy among African nations. In particular, they deplored China's continued support for the Government of Sudan despite growing international condemnation of its conduct in the province of Darfur (see the chapter on Sudan) and accused China of depleting African resources. It was also alleged that the rapid expansion in Africa's imports from China was curbing indigenous

Introductory Survey

manufacturing. China's increasingly strong strategic interests in Africa were demonstrated by the fact that in 2005 crude petroleum from Africa accounted for more than 30% of China's total oil imports. In the first six months of 2006, furthermore, Angola displaced Saudi Arabia as the largest exporter of petroleum to China. Premier Wen Jiabao visited seven African countries in June 2006, and in February 2007 President Hu Jintao embarked on an eight-nation African tour, with South Africa and Sudan included in his itinerary. In May Liu Guijin was appointed as China's envoy to Africa, specifically to engage in attempts to resolve the issue of Darfur.

In April 2001 President Jiang visited several Latin American nations, including Argentina, Brazil, Chile, Cuba, Uruguay and Venezuela, attempting to foster economic links. In August the Minister of National Defence, Gen. Chi Haotian, also visited Venezuela, and discussed energy and security issues with President Hugo Chávez. In February 2003 China hosted the visiting Cuban President, Fidel Castro. There were developments towards close economic co-operation with Brazil in 2004, when in May President Lula da Silva visited Beijing to discuss possibilities for increasing trade between the two countries, and President Hu visited Brazil in November for talks on trade deals. In July 2006 China concluded an FTA with Chile, aimed at giving China access to the latter's natural resources. The agreement, which took effect in October, was expected eventually to exempt nearly all goods from import tariffs. The arrangement represented China's first FTA with a Latin American country. China also strengthened its relations with Venezuela in 2006, with President Hugo Chávez announcing during a six-day visit to the Chinese capital in August that Venezuelan sales of crude petroleum to China were projected to double in 2007.

Government

China is a unitary state. Directly under the Central Government there are 22 provinces, five autonomous regions, including Xizang (Tibet), and four municipalities (Beijing, Chongqing, Shanghai and Tianjin). The highest organ of state power is the National People's Congress (NPC). In March 2008 the first session of the 11th NPC was attended by 2,967 deputies, indirectly elected for five years by the people's congresses of the provinces, autonomous regions, municipalities directly under the Central Government, and the People's Liberation Army. The NPC elects a Standing Committee to be its permanent organ. The current Constitution, adopted by the NPC in December 1982 and amended in 1993, was China's fourth since 1949. It restored the office of Head of State (President of the Republic). Executive power is exercised by the State Council (Cabinet), comprising the Premier, Vice-Premiers and other ministers heading ministries and commissions. The State Council is appointed by, and accountable to, the NPC.

Political power is held by the Chinese Communist Party (CCP). The CCP's highest authority is the Party Congress, convened every five years. In October 2007 the CCP's 17th National Congress elected a Central Committee of 204 full members and 167 alternate members. To direct policy, the Central Committee elected a 25-member Politburo. The incoming Standing Committee of the Politburo comprised nine members.

Provincial people's congresses are the local organs of state power. Local revolutionary committees, created during the Cultural Revolution, were abolished in January 1980 and replaced by provincial people's governments.

Defence

China is divided into seven major military units. All armed services are grouped in the People's Liberation Army (PLA). As assessed at November 2007 by Western sources, the regular forces totalled 2,105,000, of whom approximately 800,000 were believed to be conscripts, and of whom some 136,000 were women: the army numbered 1,600,000, the navy 255,000 (including a naval air force of 26,000), and the air force 250,000. Reserves numbered some 800,000, and the People's Armed Police comprised an estimated 1.5m. Military service is by selective conscription, and lasts for two years in all services. Defence expenditure for 2007 was budgeted at 350,000m. yuan.

Economic Affairs

In 2006, according to estimates by the World Bank, China's gross national income (GNI), measured at average 2004–06 prices, was US $2,641,587m., equivalent to some $2,010 per head (or $7,740 on an international purchasing-power parity basis). During 1996–2006, it was estimated, the population increased at an average annual rate of 0.7%, while gross domestic product (GDP) per head increased, in real terms, by an average annual rate of 8.3%, one of the highest growth rates in the world. Overall GDP increased, in real terms, at an average annual rate of 9.1% in 1996–2006. According to official figures, compared with the previous year GDP expanded by 11.1% in 2006 and by 11.9% in 2007.

Agriculture (including forestry and fishing) contributed 11.7% of GDP in 2006, and in the same year accounted for 42.6% of total employment. China's principal crops are rice (production of which accounted for an estimated 29% of the total world harvest in 2006), maize, sweet potatoes, wheat, soybeans, sugar cane, tobacco, cotton and jute. According to the World Bank, agricultural GDP increased at an average annual rate of 3.6%, in real terms, in 1996–2006. Growth in agricultural GDP was 4.5% in 2006, compared with the previous year. The Asian Development Bank (ADB) estimated the sector's growth at 3.7% in 2007.

Industry (including mining, manufacturing, construction and power) contributed 48.9.% of GDP and engaged 25.2% of the employed labour force in 2006. According to the World Bank, industrial GDP increased at an average annual rate of 10.1%, in real terms, in 1996–2006. Growth in industrial GDP was 10.0% in 2006, compared with the previous year. The sector's growth in 2007 was estimated by the ADB at 13.4%.

The mining sector accounted for less than 0.9% of total employment in 2002. Output in the sector accounted for some 5.3% of total industrial production in 2002. China has enormous mineral reserves and is the world's largest producer of natural graphite, antimony, tungsten and zinc. Other important minerals include coal, iron ore, molybdenum, tin, lead, mercury, bauxite, phosphate rock, diamonds, gold, manganese, crude petroleum and natural gas.

According to the World Bank, the manufacturing sector contributed an estimated 30.9% of GDP in 2006, and the sector accounted for 13.0% of total employment in 2002. China is a leading world producer of chemical fertilizers, cement and steel. From the early 2000s industries such as information technology, electronics and motor vehicles expanded rapidly. The GDP of the manufacturing sector increased at an average annual rate of 9.9%, in real terms, during 1996–2006, according to the World Bank. Growth in the GDP of the manufacturing sector was 7.9% in 2006, compared with the previous year.

Energy is derived principally from coal (76.7% in 2006); other sources are petroleum (11.9%), hydroelectric, nuclear and wind power (7.9%) and natural gas (3.5%). China is a major importer of crude petroleum. The 18,200-MW Three Gorges Dam hydroelectric power project on the Changjiang (River Yangtze) was scheduled for completion in 2009; its 26 generators will have a potential annual output of 84,700m. kWh. China's national grid was also scheduled for completion in 2009. Imports of mineral fuels comprised 9.7% of the cost of total merchandise imports in 2005.

Services contributed 39.3% of GDP in 2006 and in that year engaged 32.2% of the employed labour force. Tourism, along with retail and wholesale trade, has continued to expand rapidly. Receipts from international tourism reached US $33,949m. in 2006, with revenue from domestic tourism in that year estimated at the equivalent of almost $82m. The number of foreign visitor arrivals (including travellers from Hong Kong, Macao and Taiwan, who accounted for about 82% of the total in 2006) was reported to have risen from 124m. in 2006 to almost 132m. in 2007. The 2008 Olympic Games were to be held in Beijing in August. During 1996–2006, according to the World Bank, the GDP of the services sector increased at an average annual rate of 10.1% in real terms. Growth in the GDP of the services sector was 12.6% in 2006, compared with the previous year. The ADB estimated the sector's growth at 11.4% in 2007.

In 2006 China recorded a trade surplus of US $217,746m., and there was a surplus of $249,866m. on the current account of the balance of payments. In 2006 the principal source of imports was Japan (which provided 14.6% of total imports). Other important suppliers were the Republic of Korea (11.3%), Taiwan (11.0%), and the USA (7.5%). The principal markets for exports in 2006 were the USA (21.0% of total exports), Hong Kong (16.0%) and Japan (9.4%). Most of the goods exported to Hong Kong are subsequently re-exported. In 2006 the European Union (EU) replaced the USA as China's biggest export market. The principal imports in 2004 were machinery and transport equipment, basic manufactures such as textiles, and chemicals and related products. The principal exports in that year were machinery and transport equipment and textiles and clothing.

In 2006 China's overall budget deficit was 148,231m. yuan, equivalent to 0.7% of GDP. China's total external debt at the end of 2005 stood at US $281,612m., of which $82,853m. was long-term public debt. In 2005 the cost of debt-servicing was equivalent to 3.1% of the value of exports of goods and services. The annual rate of deflation averaged 0.6% in 1996–2006. In 2007, however, consumer prices rose by an estimated 4.8%. The official rate of urban unemployment decreased from 4.1% in December 2006 to 4.0% at the end of 2007. However, as these statistics did not include workers who had been made redundant through reform of state-owned enterprises, or unemployed persons from rural areas who had migrated to urban areas in search of work, many observers estimated the urban unemployment rate to be at least 10%. In the mid-2000s the number of rural unemployed was unofficially estimated to be at least 150m.

China joined the Asian Development Bank (ADB, see p. 182) in 1986 and the Asia-Pacific Economic Co-operation forum (APEC, see p. 176) in 1991. In 1994 China became a member of the Association of Tin Producing Countries (ATPC). China joined the Bank for International Settlements (BIS, see p. 194) in 1996. In the same year the secretariat of the Tumen River Economic Development Area (TREDA) was established in Beijing by the Governments of China, North and South Korea, Mongolia and Russia. China became a full member of the World Trade Organization (WTO, see p. 396) in December 2001. China is also a member of the UN Economic and Social Commission for Asia and the Pacific (ESCAP, see p. 35) and became an observer member of the South Asian Association for Regional Co-operation (SAARC, see p. 384) in 2005.

Following the introduction in 1978 of the 'open door' reform policy, which aimed to decentralize the economic system and to attract overseas investment, the Chinese economy subsequently became one of the fastest-growing in the world. The process of reforming the state-owned enterprises (SOEs) continued in the 21st century. Following China's accession to the WTO in 2001, both external trade and foreign direct investment showed strong expansion. China's membership of the WTO obliged the country to liberalize its banking sector, and in December 2006 all restrictions on the activities of foreign banks in the People's Republic were removed. In a preliminary ruling in February 2008, however, the WTO upheld a complaint from the EU, Canada and the USA in a dispute regarding China's imports of car components. In 2007 the emergence of various scandals relating to the sub-standard quality of China's manufactured goods resulted in an international crisis of confidence in the safety of Chinese products. Despite this, in that year the value of Chinese exports reportedly rose by almost 26% in comparison with 2006, while the trade surplus was estimated to have increased by nearly 48%, to reach a record $262,200m. In early 2008, however, China's trade surplus began to decline. The fixed exchange rate of 8.3 yuan to the US dollar was removed in July 2005, and by early 2008 the yuan had appreciated by about 13% against the US currency. China was placed under renewed pressure, notably from the USA and the European Union, to accelerate its programme of currency reform. Meanwhile, economic conditions had forced millions of people to move from rural areas to cities since the 1980s, this migrant population being estimated at as many as 200m. by the early 21st century. The Eleventh Five-Year Plan (2006–10), announced in October 2005, projected annual GDP growth of 7.5%. GDP increased by almost 12% in 2007, despite six increases in interest rates during the year. In February 2008 the rate of inflation reached 8.7%, its highest level for many years. The Government anticipated economic growth of around 8% in 2008.

Education

The education system expanded rapidly after 1949. Fees are charged at all levels. Much importance is attached to kindergartens. Primary education begins for most children at seven years of age and lasts for five years. Secondary education usually begins at 12 years of age and lasts for a further five years, comprising a first cycle of three years and a second cycle of two years. Free higher education was abolished in 1985; instead, college students have to compete for scholarships, which are awarded according to academic ability. As a result of the student disturbances in 1989, college students were required to complete one year's political education, prior to entering college. Since 1979 education has been included as one of the main priorities for modernization. The whole educational system was being reformed in the late 1990s and early 2000s, with the aim of introducing nine-year compulsory education. According to official statistics, 90% of the population had been covered by the

THE PEOPLE'S REPUBLIC OF CHINA

compulsory education scheme by 2002. The establishment of private schools has been permitted since the early 1980s. In 2003/04 enrolment at pre-primary school was equivalent to 36% of pupils in the relevant age group (males 37%; females 35%). In 2005/06 enrolment in secondary education was equivalent to 76% of the relevant age group (males 75%; females 76%). The 2003 budget allocated an estimated 349,140m. yuan to education. The numbers of Chinese students studying abroad were increasing in the early 21st century, with around 50,000 Chinese students reported to have been studying in British higher education institutions alone in 2005/06.

Public Holidays

2008: 1 January (Solar New Year), 6–8 February* (Lunar New Year), 8 March (International Women's Day, women only), 4 April (Qingming Festival), 1 May (Labour Day), 8 June (Dragon Boat Festival), 1 August (Army Day), 14 September (Mid-Autumn Festival), 1–3 October (National Days).

2009: 1 January (Solar New Year), 26–28 January* (Lunar New Year, provisional), 8 March (International Women's Day), 4 April (Qingming Festival), 1 May (Labour Day), 28 May (Dragon Boat Festival), 1 August (Army Day), 1–3 October (National Days), 3 October (Mid-Autumn Festival).

* From the first to the fourth day of the first moon of the lunar calendar.

Weights and Measures

The metric system is officially in force, but some traditional Chinese units are still used.

Statistical Survey

Source (unless otherwise stated): National Bureau of Statistics of China, 38 Yuetan Nan Jie, Sanlihe, Beijing 100826; tel. (10) 68515074; fax (10) 68515078; e-mail service@stats.gov.cn; internet www.stats.gov.cn/english/.

Note: Wherever possible, figures in this Survey exclude Taiwan. In the case of unofficial estimates for China, it is not always clear if Taiwan is included or excluded. Where a Taiwan component is known, either it has been deducted from the all-China figure or its inclusion is noted. Figures for the Hong Kong Special Administrative Region (SAR) and for the Macao SAR are listed separately. Transactions between the SARs and the rest of the People's Republic continue to be treated as external transactions.

Area and Population

AREA, POPULATION AND DENSITY

Area (sq km)	9,572,900*
Population (census results)	
1 July 1990	1,130,510,638
1 November 2000	
Males	640,275,969
Females	602,336,257
Total	1,242,612,226
Population (official estimates at 31 December)	
2005	1,307,560,000
2006	1,314,480,000†
2007	1,321,290,000†
Density (per sq km) at 31 December 2007	138.0

* 3,696,100 sq miles.
† Preliminary.

PRINCIPAL ETHNIC GROUPS
(at census of 1 November 2000)

	Number	%
Han (Chinese)	1,137,386,112	91.53
Zhuang	16,178,811	1.30
Manchu	10,682,262	0.86
Hui	9,816,805	0.79
Miao	8,940,116	0.72
Uygur (Uigur)	8,399,393	0.68
Tujia	8,028,133	0.65
Yi	7,762,272	0.63
Mongolian	5,813,947	0.47
Tibetan	5,416,021	0.44
Bouyei	2,971,460	0.24
Dong	2,960,293	0.24
Yao	2,637,421	0.21
Korean	1,923,842	0.16
Bai	1,858,063	0.09
Hani	1,439,673	0.12
Kazakh	1,250,458	0.10
Li	1,247,814	0.10
Dai	1,158,989	0.09
She	709,592	0.06
Lisu	634,912	0.05
Gelao	579,357	0.05
Dongxiang	513,805	0.04
Others	3,568,237	0.29
Unknown	734,438	0.06
Total	**1,242,612,226**	**100.00**

THE PEOPLE'S REPUBLIC OF CHINA

Statistical Survey

ADMINISTRATIVE DIVISIONS
(previous or other spellings given in brackets)

	Area ('000 sq km)	Population at 1 November 2000 Total	Density (per sq km)	Capital of province or region	Estimated population ('000) at mid-2000*
Provinces					
Sichuan (Szechwan)	487.0	82,348,296	169	Chengdu (Chengtu)	3,294
Henan (Honan)	167.0	91,236,854	546	Zhengzhou (Chengchow)	2,070
Shandong (Shantung)	153.3	89,971,789	587	Jinan (Tsinan)	2,568
Jiangsu (Kiangsu)	102.6	73,043,577	712	Nanjing (Nanking)	2,740
Guangdong (Kwangtung)	197.1	85,225,007	432	Guangzhou (Canton)	3,893
Hebei (Hopei)	202.7	66,684,419	329	Shijiazhuang (Shihkiachwang)	1,603
Hunan (Hunan)	210.5	63,274,173	301	Changsha (Changsha)	1,775
Anhui (Anhwei)	139.9	58,999,948	422	Hefei (Hofei)	1,242
Hubei (Hupeh)	187.5	59,508,870	317	Wuhan (Wuhan)	5,169
Zhejiang (Chekiang)	101.8	45,930,651	451	Hangzhou (Hangchow)	1,780
Liaoning (Liaoning)	151.0	41,824,412	277	Shenyang (Shenyang)	4,828
Jiangxi (Kiangsi)	164.8	40,397,598	245	Nanchang (Nanchang)	1,722
Yunnan (Yunnan)	436.2	42,360,089	97	Kunming (Kunming)	1,701
Heilongjiang (Heilungkiang)	463.6	36,237,576	78	Harbin (Harbin)	2,928
Guizhou (Kweichow)	174.0	35,247,695	203	Guiyang (Kweiyang)	2,533
Shaanxi (Shensi)	195.8	35,365,072	171	Xian (Sian)	3,123
Fujian (Fukien)	123.1	34,097,947†	277	Fuzhou (Foochow)	1,397
Shanxi (Shansi)	157.1	32,471,242	207	Taiyuan (Taiyuan)	2,415
Jilin (Kirin)	187.0	26,802,191	143	Changchun (Changchun)	3,093
Gansu (Kansu)	366.5	25,124,282	69	Lanzhou (Lanchow)	1,730
Hainan	34.3	7,559,035	220	Haikou	438‡
Qinghai (Tsinghai)	721.0	4,822,963	7	Xining (Hsining)	692
Autonomous regions					
Guangxi Zhuang (Kwangsi Chuang)	220.4	43,854,538	199	Nanning (Nanning)	1,311
Nei Monggol (Inner Mongolia)	1,177.5	23,323,347	20	Hohhot (Huhehot)	978
Xinjiang Uygur (Sinkiang Uighur)	1,646.9	18,459,511	11	Urumqi (Urumchi, Wulumuqi)	1,415
Ningxia Hui (Ninghsia Hui)	66.4	5,486,393	83	Yinchuan (Yinchuen)	592
Tibet (Xizang)	1,221.6	2,616,329	2	Lhasa (Lhasa)	134
Municipalities					
Shanghai	6.2	16,407,734	2,646	—	12,887
Beijing (Peking)	16.8	13,569,194	808	—	10,839
Tianjin (Tientsin)	11.3	9,848,731	872	—	9,156
Chongqing (Chungking)	82.0	30,512,763	372	—	4,900
Total	9,572.9	1,242,612,226§	130		

* UN estimates, excluding population in counties under cities' administration.
† Excluding islands administered by Taiwan, mainly Jinmen (Quemoy) and Mazu (Matsu), with 49,050 inhabitants according to figures released by the Taiwan authorities at the end of March 1990.
‡ December 1998 figure.
§ Including 2,500,000 military personnel and 1,050,000 persons with unregistered households.

PRINCIPAL TOWNS
(Wade-Giles or other spellings in brackets)

Population at mid-2005
('000, incl. suburbs, UN estimates)

Shanghai (Shang-hai)	14,503	Shijiazhuang (Shih-chia-chuang or Shihkiachwang)	2,275	Zibo	2,982
Beijing (Pei-ching or Peking, the capital)	10,717	Jinxi	2,268	Kunming (K'un-ming)	2,837
Guangzhou (Kuang-chou or Canton)	8,425	Jilin	2,255	Hangzhou (Hang-chou or Hangchow)	2,831
Shenzhen	7,233	Wenzhou	2,212	Qingdao (Ch'ing-tao or Tsingtao)	2,817
Wuhan (Wu-han or Hankow)	7,093	Nanchang (Nan-ch'ang)	2,188	Taiyuan (T'ai-yüan)	2,794
Tianjin (T'ien-chin or Tientsin)	7,040	Zaozhuang	2,096	Jinan (Chi-nan or Tsinan)	2,743
Chongqing (Ch'ung-ch'ing or Chungking)	6,363	Nanchong	2,046	Zhengzhou (Cheng-chou or Chengchow)	2,590
Shenyang (Shen-yang or Mukden)	4,720	Nanning	2,040	Fuzhou	2,453
Dongguan	4,320	Linyi	2,035	Changsha (Chang-sha)	2,451
Chengdu (Chengtu)	4,065	Urumqi (Wulumuqi)	2,025	Lanzhou (Lan-chou or Lanchow)	2,411
Xian (Hsi-an or Sian)	3,926	Yantai	1,991	Xiamen	2,371
Harbin (Ha-erh-pin)	3,695	Xuzhou	1,960	Tangshan	1,825
Nanjing (Nan-ching or Nanking)	3,621	Baotou	1,920	Ningbo	1,810
Guiyang	3,447	Hefei	1,916	Datong	1,763
Dalian (Ta-lien or Dairen)	3,073	Suzhou	1,849	Tianmen	1,676
Changchun (Ch'ang-ch'un)	3,046	Nanyang	1,830	Shangqiu	1,650
				Liuan	1,647
				Wuxi	1,646
				Luoyang	1,644
				Hohhot	1,625
				Anshan	1,611

Source: UN, *World Urbanization Prospects: The 2005 Revision*.

THE PEOPLE'S REPUBLIC OF CHINA

BIRTHS AND DEATHS
(sample surveys)

	2004	2005	2006
Birth rate (per 1,000)	12.29	12.40	12.09
Death rate (per 1,000)	6.42	6.51	6.81

2006 (rounded number): Births 15,840,000; Deaths 8,920,000.

Marriages (number registered): 8,035,000 in 2003; 8,608,000 in 2004; 8,166,000 in 2005.

Expectation of life (years at birth, WHO estimates): 72.4 (males 70.8; females 74.1) in 2005 (Source: WHO, *World Health Statistics*).

EMPLOYMENT*
('000 persons at 31 December, official estimates)

	2000	2001	2002
Agriculture, forestry and fishing	333,550	329,740	324,870
Mining	5,970	5,610	5,580
Manufacturing	80,430	80,830	83,070
Electricity, gas and water	2,840	2,880	2,900
Construction	35,520	36,690	38,930
Geological prospecting and water conservancy	1,100	1,050	980
Transport, storage and communications	20,290	20,370	20,840
Wholesale and retail trade and catering	46,860	47,370	49,690
Banking and insurance	3,270	3,360	3,400
Real estate	1,000	1,070	1,180
Social services	9,210	9,760	10,940
Health care, sports and social welfare	4,880	4,930	4,930
Education, culture, art, radio, film and television broadcasting	15,650	15,680	15,650
Scientific research and polytechnic services	1,740	1,650	1,630
Government agencies, etc.	11,040	11,010	10,750
Others	56,430	58,520	62,450
Total	**629,780**	**630,520**	**637,790**

* In addition to employment statistics, sample surveys of the economically active population are conducted. On the basis of these surveys, the total labour force ('000 persons at 31 December) was: 760,750 in 2003; 768,230 in 2004; 778,770 in 2005. Of these totals, the number of employed persons ('000 at 31 December) was: 744,320 (agriculture, etc. 365,460, industry 160,770, services 218,090) in 2003; 752,000 (agriculture, etc. 352,690, industry 169,200, services 230,111) in 2004; 758,250 (agriculture, etc. 339,700, industry 180,840, services 237,710) in 2005; 764,000 (agriculture, etc. 325,610, industry 192,250, services 246,140) in 2006.

Health and Welfare

KEY INDICATORS

Total fertility rate (children per woman, 2005)	1.7
Under-5 mortality rate (per 1,000 live births, 2005)	27
HIV/AIDS (% of persons aged 15–49, 2005)	0.1
Physicians (per 1,000 head, 2002)	1.64
Hospital beds (per 1,000 head, 2004)	2.31
Health expenditure (2004): US $ per head (PPP)	276.7
Health expenditure (2004): % of GDP	4.7
Health expenditure (2004): public (% of total)	38.0
Access to water (% of persons, 2004)	77
Access to sanitation (% of persons, 2004)	44
Human Development Index (2005): ranking	81
Human Development Index (2005): value	0.777

For sources and definitions, see explanatory note on p. vi.

Agriculture

(FAO data are assumed to include Hong Kong, Macao and Taiwan; may include official, semi-official or estimated data)

PRINCIPAL CROPS
('000 metric tons)

	2004	2005	2006
Wheat	91,956	97,449	104,470
Rice (paddy)	180,529	181,999	184,070
Barley	3,225	3,447	3,430
Maize	130,438	139,502	145,625
Rye	603	554	783
Oats	604	704	1,160
Millet	1,816	1,789	1,821
Sorghum	2,344	2,558	2,490
Buckwheat	900	750	893
Triticale (wheat-rye hybrid)	748	559	600
Potatoes	72,259	73,460	70,338
Sweet potatoes	105,837	100,465	100,222
Cassava (Manioc)	4,218	4,186	4,318
Taro (Coco yam)	1,638	1,633	1,540
Sugar cane	90,978	87,513	100,684
Sugar beet	5,860	7,884	10,536
Dry beans	1,758	1,607	2,007
Dry broad beans	1,809	1,804	2,100
Dry peas	1,063	1,103	1,140
Chestnuts	808	828	850
Walnuts	440	503	499
Soybeans (Soya beans)	17,407	16,803	15,500
Groundnuts (in shell)	14,413	14,399	14,722
Coconuts	292	298	290
Oil palm fruit	678	690	650
Sunflower seed	1,555	1,833	1,820
Rapeseed	13,182	13,052	12,649
Sesame seed	708	630	666
Linseed	463	483	480
Cottonseed	12,650	11,403	13,460
Cabbages and other brassicas	32,322	33,817	34,826
Asparagus	5,807	5,906	6,106
Lettuce and chicory	10,504	11,003	11,605
Spinach	10,813	11,013	11,612
Tomatoes	30,145	31,626	32,540
Cauliflower and broccoli	7,330	7,369	8,083
Pumpkins, squash and gourds	5,669	5,760	6,060
Cucumbers and gherkins	25,560	26,553	27,357
Aubergines (Eggplants)	16,532	17,028	17,530
Green chillies and peppers	12,033	12,529	13,031
Green onions and shallots	709	746	777
Dry onions	18,047	19,040	19,600
Garlic	10,597	11,084	11,587
Green beans	2,310	2,376	2,431
Green peas	2,111	2,210	2,408
Carrots and turnips	8,298	8,385	8,700
Mushrooms and truffles	1,362	1,411	1,510
Watermelons	57,832	69,214	71,220
Cantaloupes and other melons	14,280	15,062	15,525
Grapes	5,776	6,592	6,375
Apples	23,685	24,020	26,066
Pears	10,767	11,437	11,988
Peaches and nectarines	7,043	7,833	7,510
Plums and sloes	4,438	4,632	4,535
Oranges	2,335	2,447	2,765
Tangerines, mandarins, clementines and satsumas	10,996	11,826	13,240
Lemons and limes	653	701	783
Grapefruit and pomelos	445	428	505

THE PEOPLE'S REPUBLIC OF CHINA

—continued	2004	2005	2006
Guavas, mangoes and mangosteens	3,585	3,676	3,550
Pineapples	1,269	1,442	1,400
Persimmons	2,034	2,081	1,987
Bananas	6,249	6,670	7,053
Tea (made)	855	954	1,050
Chillies and peppers, dry	238	243	245
Ginger	297	314	279
Tobacco (leaves)	2,411	2,689	2,750
Jute and jute-like fibres	87	83	87
Natural rubber	575	513	538

Aggregate production ('000 metric tons, may include official, semi-official or estimated data): Total cereals 413,193.0 in 2004, 429,340.8 in 2005, 445,355.1 in 2006; Total vegetable fibres 7,096.0 in 2004, 6,515.5 in 2005, 7,552.5 in 2006; Total nuts 1,517.8 in 2004, 1,606.7 in 2005, 1,625.0 in 2006; Total oilcrops 82,846.6 in 2004, 79,325.0 in 2005, 83,328.3 in 2006; Total pulses 4,942.8 in 2004, 4,792.8 in 2005, 5,556.5 in 2006; Total roots and tubers 183,970.2 in 2004, 179,761.4 in 2005, 176,433.1 in 2006; Total spices 747.4 in 2004, 778.3 in 2005, 729.3 in 2006; Total vegetables (incl. melons) 412,610.0 in 2004, 434,331.8 in 2005, 448,445.9 in 2006; Total fruits (excl. melons) 84,838.8 in 2004, 89,354.9 in 2005, 93,409.5 in 2006.

Source: FAO.

LIVESTOCK
('000 head at 31 December)

	2004	2005	2006
Horses	7,902	7,641	7,402
Asses, mules or hinnies	12,164	11,659	11,376
Cattle	112,540	115,604	117,766
Buffaloes	22,287	22,366	22,813
Camels	265	262	266
Pigs	472,896	488,812	510,625
Sheep	157,330	170,882	173,899
Goats	183,363	195,759	199,027
Rabbits and hares	196,641	202,196	205,037
Chickens	4,214,748	4,297,343	4,356,968
Ducks	710,361	720,018	732,019
Geese and guinea fowls	260,878	267,819	273,000

Source: FAO.

LIVESTOCK PRODUCTS
('000 metric tons)

	2004	2005	2006
Cattle meat	6,449	6,791	7,173
Buffalo meat	330	346	351
Sheep meat	2,240	2,431	2,540
Goat meat	1,756	1,927	2,161
Pig meat	48,118	51,202	52,927
Horse meat	192	204	200
Rabbit meat	470	518	600
Chicken meat	9,944	10,377	10,701
Duck meat	2,262	2,599	2,673
Goose and guinea fowl meat	2,026	2,306	2,383
Other meat	263	273	276
Cows' milk	22,929	27,838	32,249
Buffaloes' milk	2,750	2,800	2,850
Sheep's milk	1,078	1,295	1,091
Goats' milk	252	256	262
Hen eggs	23,501	24,316	25,326
Other poultry eggs	4,111	4,328	4,529
Honey	301	303	307
Wool: greasy	374	393	389

Source: FAO.

Statistical Survey

Forestry

ROUNDWOOD REMOVALS
('000 cubic metres, excl. bark, FAO estimates)

	2004	2005	2006
Sawlogs, veneer logs and logs for sleepers	52,230	52,231	52,227
Pulpwood	6,678	6,678	6,678
Other industrial wood	35,760	35,760	35,760
Fuel wood	211,255	207,359	203,505
Total	305,923	302,028	298,170

Source: FAO.

Timber production (official figures, '000 cubic metres): 47,460 in 2005; 78,000 in 2006.

SAWNWOOD PRODUCTION
('000 cubic metres, incl. railway sleepers, FAO estimates)

	2004	2005	2006
Coniferous (softwood)	6,495	5,270	7,984
Broadleaved (hardwood)	9,741	2,054	2,261
Total	16,236	7,324	10,245

Source: FAO.

Fishing

('000 metric tons, live weight)

	2003	2004	2005
Capture	17,051.8	17,271.4	17,361.6
Freshwater fishes	1,730.8	1,724.0	1,830.4
Aquaculture	28,883.6	30,612.6	32,414.1
Common carp	2,267.3	2,366.8	2,474.7
Crucian carp	1,789.0	1,945.8	2,083.5
Bighead carp	1,906.0	2,079.6	2,182.0
Grass carp (White amur)	3,492.6	3,698.4	3,857.1
Silver carp	3,382.0	3,466.8	3,524.8
Pacific cupped oyster	3,668.2	3,750.9	3,826.4
Japanese carpet shell	2,546.1	2,799.0	2,857.4
Total catch	45,935.5	47,884.0	49,775.7

Note: Figures exclude aquatic plants ('000 metric tons, wet weight): 10,098.0 (capture 296.2, aquaculture 9,801.8) in 2003; 11,093.2 (capture 378.6, aquaculture 10,714.6) in 2004; 11,163.7 (capture 308.4, aquaculture 10,855.3) in 2005.

Source: FAO.

Aquatic products (official figures, '000 metric tons): 45,645 (marine 26,463, freshwater 19,182) in 2002; 47,046 (marine 26,858, freshwater 20,188) in 2003; 49,018 (marine 27,678, freshwater 21,340) in 2004. The totals include artificially cultured products ('000 metric tons): 29,058 (marine 12,128, freshwater 16,930) in 2002; 30,253 (marine 12,533, freshwater 17,720) in 2003; 32,087 (marine 13,167, freshwater 18,920) in 2004. Figures include aquatic plants on a dry-weight basis ('000 metric tons): 1,333 in 2002; 1,413 in 2003; 1,505 in 2004. Freshwater plants are not included.

Mining

('000 metric tons, unless otherwise indicated, estimates)

	2003	2004	2005
Coal*	1,722,000	1,992,000	2,205,000
Crude petroleum*	169,600	175,900	181,350
Natural gas (million cu m)*	35,015	41,460	50,944
Iron ore: gross weight	261,000	320,000	420,000
Copper ore†	610	742	762
Nickel ore (metric tons)†	61,000	75,600	77,000
Bauxite	13,000	15,000	18,000
Lead ore†	955	998	1,000
Zinc ore†	2,030	2,390	2,450
Tin concentrates (metric tons)†	102,000	118,000	120,000

THE PEOPLE'S REPUBLIC OF CHINA

—continued

	2003	2004	2005
Manganese ore†	920	1,100	1,200
Tungsten concentrates (metric tons)†	55,500	60,000	61,000
Molybdenum ore (metric tons)†	31,000	38,500	40,000
Vanadium (metric tons)†	35,000	40,000	42,500
Antimony ore (metric tons)†	100,000	125,000	120,000
Cobalt ore (metric tons)†	700	1,260	1,300
Mercury (metric tons)†	610	1,140	1,100
Silver (metric tons)†	2,400	2,450	2,500
Uranium (metric tons)†‡	750	750	750
Gold (metric tons)†	205	215	225
Magnesite	4,600	4,650	4,700
Phosphate rock§	7,550	7,650	9,130
Potash‖	500	550	600
Native sulphur	700	820	900
Fluorspar	2,650	2,700	2,700
Barite (Barytes)	3,600	3,900	4,200
Salt (unrefined)*	34,377	40,434	46,611
Gypsum (crude)	6,850	7,000	7,300
Graphite (natural)	710	700	720
Asbestos	500	400	350
Talc and related materials	3,000	3,000	3,050

* Official figures. Figures for coal include brown coal and waste. Figures for petroleum include oil from shale and coal. Figures for natural gas refer to gross volume of output.
† Figures refer to the metal content of ores, concentrates or (in the case of vanadium) slag.
‡ Data are estimates from the World Nuclear Association (London, United Kingdom).
§ Figures refer to phosphorous oxide (P_2O_5) content.
‖ Potassium oxide (K_2O) content of potash salts mined.

2006 ('000 metric tons, unless otherwise indicated, official figures): Coal (incl. brown coal and waste) 2,380,000; Crude petroleum (incl. oil from shale and coal) 184,000; Natural gas (million cu m, gross volume of output) 58,600.

Source: mainly US Geological Survey.

Industry

SELECTED PRODUCTS
Unofficial Figures
('000 metric tons, unless otherwise indicated)*

	2002	2003	2004
Plywood ('000 cu m)†‡	12,163	21,835	21,797
Mechanical wood pulp†‡§	565	565	565
Chemical and semi-chemical wood pulp†‡§	3,495	3,500	3,500
Other fibre pulp†‡§	11,546	12,146	12,146
Sulphur§‖¶(a)	2,200	2,400	2,600
Sulphur§‖¶(b)	3,240	3,400	3,730
Kerosene	8,261	8,553	9,622
Residual fuel oil	18,455	20,048	20,293
Lubricating oils	3,202	3,509	5,326
Paraffin wax	1,537	1,723	2,619
Petroleum coke	5,123	5,735	8,855
Petroleum bitumen (asphalt)	4,269	4,787	9,026
Liquefied petroleum gas	10,368	12,117	14,170
Refined aluminium (primary and secondary)‖	4,510	5,970	6,900
Refined copper (primary and secondary)‖	1,650	1,850	2,200
Refined lead (primary and secondary)‖	1,330	1,580	1,940
Tin (unwrought, Sn content)‖	82	98	115
Refined zinc (primary and secondary)‖	2,100	2,320	2,720

* Figures include Hong Kong and Macao SARs, but exclude Taiwan, except where otherwise specified.
† Data from FAO.
‡ Including Taiwan.
§ Provisional or estimated figure(s).
‖ Data from the US Geological Survey.
¶ Figures refer to (a) sulphur recovered as a by-product in the purification of coal-gas, in petroleum refineries, gas plants and from copper, lead and zinc sulphide ores; and (b) the sulphur content of iron and copper pyrites, including pyrite concentrates obtained from copper, lead and zinc ores.

Source: mainly UN, *Industrial Commodity Statistics Yearbook*.

Official Figures
('000 metric tons, unless otherwise indicated)

	2004	2005	2006
Edible vegetable oils	16,826.3	20,709.6	23,352.3
Refined sugar	10,337.0	9,123.7	9,490.7
Beer	29,485.9	31,260.5	35,435.8
Cigarettes ('000 million)	187,363.5	193,890.1	202,181.3
Cotton yarn (pure and mixed)	12,913	14,505	17,430
Woven cotton fabrics—pure and mixed (million metres)	48,100	48,439	59,855
Chemical fibres	16,998.0	16,647.9	20,731.8
Paper and paperboard	54,132.7	62,054.2	68,630.2
Rubber tyres ('000)	327,093.7	343,900.6	435,470.8
Sulphuric acid	39,289.0	45,446.6	50,331.7
Caustic soda (Sodium hydroxide)	10,411.2	12,399.8	15,117.8
Soda ash (Sodium carbonate)	13,347.0	14,210.8	15,600.3
Insecticides	820.8	1,147.3	1,384.6
Nitrogenous fertilizers (a)*	33,577.3	38,090.3	39,115.4
Phosphate fertilizers (b)*	12,467.8	12,062.0	12,254.6
Potash fertilizers (c)*	2,003.1	1,626.3	2,080.5
Synthetic rubber	1,840.4	1,811.1	1,998.1
Plastics	23,665.0	23,088.6	26,026.0
Motor spirit (gasoline)	52,779.9	54,092.2	55,947.6
Distillate fuel oil (diesel oil)	101,786.6	110,794.2	116,555.4
Coke	206,186.3	254,117.0	297,683.1
Cement	966,820	1,068,848	1,236,765
Pig-iron	268,309.9	343,751.9	412,451.9
Crude steel	282,910.9	353,239.8	419,148.5
Internal combustion engines ('000 kw)	318,935.6	365,634.6	452,673.4
Tractors—over 20 horse-power (number)	1,138,000	1,633,000	1,993,000
Railway freight wagons (number)	31,700	39,200	39,300
Road motor vehicles ('000)	5,091.1	5,704.9	7,278.9
Bicycles ('000)	79,062.2	69,006.4	78,866.3
Electric fans ('000)	141,696.7	120,223.9	144,658.5
Mobile telephones ('000 units)	237,515.8	303,542.1	480,137.9
Microcomputers ('000)	59,749	80,849	93,364
Integrated circuits (million)	23,551	26,997	33,575
Colour television receivers ('000)	74,318	82,832	83,754
Cameras ('000)	78,914.0	81,990.0	85,515.1
Electric energy (million kWh)	2,203,309	2,500,260	2,865,726

* Production in terms of (a) nitrogen; (b) phosphorous oxide; or (c) potassium oxide.

Finance

CURRENCY AND EXCHANGE RATES
Monetary Units
100 fen (cents) = 10 jiao (chiao) = 1 renminbiao (People's Bank Dollar), usually called a yuan.

Sterling, Dollar and Euro Equivalents (31 December 2007)
£1 sterling = 14.634 yuan;
US $1 = 7.305 yuan;
€1 = 10.753 yuan;
100 yuan = £6.83 = $13.69 = €9.30.

Average Exchange Rate (yuan per US $)
2005   8.1943
2006   7.9734
2007   7.6075

Note: Since 1 January 1994 the official rate has been based on the prevailing rate in the interbank market for foreign exchange.

THE PEOPLE'S REPUBLIC OF CHINA

STATE BUDGET
(million yuan)*

Revenue	2004	2005	2006
Taxes	2,416,568	2,877,854	3,480,972
Company income tax	395,733	534,392	703,960
Tariffs	104,377	106,617	114,178
Agricultural and animal husbandry taxes	90,219	93,640	108,404
Business tax	358,197	423,246	512,871
Consumption tax	150,190	163,381	188,569
Value-added tax	901,794	1,079,211	1,278,481
Other receipts	244,872	306,401	413,070
Sub-total	2,661,440	3,184,255	3,894,042
Less Subsidies for losses by enterprises	21,793	19,326	18,022
Total	2,639,647	3,164,929	3,876,020
Central Government	1,450,310	1,654,853	2,045,662
Local authorities	1,189,337	1,510,076	1,830,358

Expenditure†	2004	2005	2006
Capital construction	343,750	404,134	439,038
Circulation of capital	1,244	1,817	1,658
Agriculture, forestry and water conservancy	169,379	179,240	216,135
Culture, education, science and health care‡	514,365	610,418	742,598
National defence	220,001	247,496	297,938
Administration	405,991	483,543	563,905
Social security	311,608	369,886	436,178
Subsidies to compensate price increases	79,580	99,847	138,752
Promotion of innovation, science and technology	124,394	149,459	174,456
Operating expenses of industry, transport and commerce	36,821	44,415	58,125
Geological prospecting	11,545	13,270	14,182
Total (incl. others)	2,848,689	3,393,028	4,042,273
Central Government	789,408	877,597	999,140
Local authorities	2,059,281	2,515,431	3,043,133

* Figures represent a consolidation of the regular (current) and construction (capital) budgets of the central Government and local administrative organs. The data exclude extrabudgetary transactions, totalling (in million yuan): Revenue 456,680 (central 37,937, local 418,743) in 2003; 469,918 (central 35,069, local 434,849) in 2004; 554,416 (central 40,258, local 514,158) in 2005. Expenditure 415,636 (central 32,932, local 382,704) in 2003; 435,173 (central 38,950, local 396,223) in 2004; 524,248 (central 45,834, local 478,414) in 2005. Note: Figures for extrabudgetary revenue and expenditure in 2006 were not available.
† Excluding payments of debt interest.
‡ Current expenditure only.

INTERNATIONAL RESERVES
(US $ million at 31 December)

	2004	2005	2006
Gold (national valuation)	4,074	4,074	4,074
IMF special drawing rights	1,247	1,251	1,068
Reserve position in IMF	3,320	1,391	1,081
Foreign exchange*	609,932	818,872	1,066,344
Total*	618,574	825,588	1,072,567

* Excluding the Bank of China's holdings of foreign exchange.
Source: IMF, *International Financial Statistics*.

MONEY SUPPLY
(million yuan at 31 December)*

	2004	2005	2006
Currency outside banking institutions	2,131,290	2,365,610	2,707,260
Demand deposits at banking institutions	7,442,320	8,314,920	9,880,260
Total money (incl. others)	9,581,540	10,690,320	12,603,510

* Figures are rounded to the nearest 10 million yuan.
Source: IMF, *International Financial Statistics*.

COST OF LIVING
(General Consumer Price Index; base: previous year = 100)

	2004	2005	2006
Food	109.9	102.9	102.3
Clothing	98.5	98.3	99.4
Housing*	104.9	105.4	104.6
All items (incl. others)	103.9	101.8	101.5

* Including water, electricity and fuels.

NATIONAL ACCOUNTS
('000 million yuan at current prices)

Expenditure on the Gross Domestic Product

	2004	2005	2006
Government final consumption expenditure	2,319.9	2,660.5	3,029.3
Private final consumption expenditure	6,383.4	7,121.8	8,012.1
Increase in stocks	405.1	334.2	395.2
Gross fixed capital formation	6,511.8	7,730.5	9,015.1
Total domestic expenditure	15,620.2	17,847.0	20,451.7
Exports of goods and services; Less Imports of goods and services	407.9	1,022.3	1,665.4
Sub-total	16,028.1	18,869.2	22,117.1
Statistical discrepancy*	−40.2	−482.4	−1,030.0
GDP in purchasers' values	15,987.8	18,386.8	21,087.1

* Referring to the difference between the sum of the expenditure components and official estimates of GDP, compiled from the production approach.

Gross Domestic Product by Economic Activity

	2004	2005	2006
Agriculture, forestry and fishing	2,141.3	2,307.0	2,473.7
Construction	869.4	1,013.4	1,185.1
Other industry*	6,521.0	7,723.1	9,131.1
Transport, storage and communications	930.4	1,083.6	1,203.2
Wholesale and retail trade	1,245.4	1,353.5	1,515.8
Hotels and restaurants	366.5	419.3	483.3
Financial intermediation	539.3	630.7	758.7
Real estate	717.4	824.4	948.4
Other services	2,657.1	3,031.8	3,387.8
Total	15,987.8	18,386.8	21,087.1

* Includes mining, manufacturing, electricity, gas and water.

THE PEOPLE'S REPUBLIC OF CHINA

BALANCE OF PAYMENTS
(US $ million)

	2004	2005	2006
Exports of goods f.o.b.	593,393	762,484	969,682
Imports of goods f.o.b.	−534,410	−628,295	−751,936
Trade balance	58,982	134,189	217,746
Exports of services	62,434	74,404	91,999
Imports of services	−72,133	−83,795	−100,833
Balance on goods and services	49,284	124,798	208,912
Other income received	20,544	38,959	51,240
Other income paid	−24,067	−28,324	−39,485
Balance on goods, services and income	45,761	135,433	220,667
Current transfers received	24,326	27,735	31,578
Current transfers paid	−1,428	−2,349	−2,378
Current balance	68,659	160,818	249,866
Capital account (net)	−69	4,102	4,020
Direct investment abroad	−1,805	−11,306	−17,830
Direct investment from abroad	54,936	79,127	78,095
Portfolio investment assets	6,486	−26,157	−110,419
Portfolio investment liabilities	13,203	21,224	42,861
Other investment assets	1,980	−48,947	−31,809
Other investment liabilities	35,928	44,921	45,118
Net errors and omissions	26,834	−16,441	−13,047
Overall balance	206,153	207,342	246,855

Source: IMF, *International Financial Statistics*.

External Trade

PRINCIPAL COMMODITIES
(distribution by SITC, US $ million)

Imports c.i.f.	2002	2003	2004
Food and live animals	5,237.8	5,960.0	9,154.4
Crude materials (inedible) except fuels	22,736.2	34,121.3	55,357.6
Metalliferous ores and metal scrap	7,273.9	11,794.9	25,189.5
Mineral fuels, lubricants, etc.	19,284.6	29,188.9	47,993.1
Petroleum, petroleum products, etc.	17,224.7	26,679.6	44,500.7
Crude petroleum oils, etc.	12,757.3	19,782.4	33,911.7
Chemicals and related products	39,035.9	48,975.3	65,473.5
Organic chemicals	10,978.2	15,849.9	23,718.9
Basic manufactures	48,488.7	63,902.3	73,985.8
Textile yarn, fabrics, etc.	13,059.8	14,217.4	15,304.2
Iron and steel	13,599.1	22,033.9	23,386.9
Machinery and transport equipment	137,009.7	192,825.6	252,830.1
Machinery specialized for particular industries	15,647.0	21,012.1	26,286.8
General industrial machinery, equipment and parts	12,202.0	16,566.7	22,662.0
Office machines and automatic data-processing equipment	17,094.0	24,223.4	29,631.5
Telecommunications and sound equipment	14,149.9	19,512.0	24,627.3
Other electrical machinery, apparatus, etc.	55,381.5	79,799.1	110,738.8
Thermionic valves, tubes, etc.	35,167.4	52,523.0	74,455.2
Electronic microcircuits	25,644.1	41,108.4	61,047.2
Road vehicles and transport equipment *	11,482.6	17,452.9	19,403.0
Miscellaneous manufactured articles	19,800.9	33,011.5	50,143.4
Total (incl. others)	295,170.1	412,759.7	561,228.7

Exports f.o.b.	2002	2003	2004
Food and live animals	14,620.7	17,531.1	18,864.2
Mineral fuels, lubricants, etc.	8,435.2	11,114.2	14,480.3
Chemicals and related products	15,324.9	19,580.8	26,359.7
Basic manufactures	52,954.5	69,018.4	100,646.1
Textile yarn, fabrics, etc.	20,562.0	26,900.2	33,427.9
Machinery and transport equipment	126,976.0	187,772.5	268,260.3
Office machines and automatic data-processing equipment	36,227.8	62,506.2	87,101.1
Automatic data-processing machines and units	20,132.3	41,017.3	59,911.3
Telecommunications and sound equipment	32,016.8	45,032.5	68,496.7
Other electrical machinery, apparatus, etc.	31,898.3	42,314.3	59,488.1
Road vehicles and transport equipment*	10,137.3	15,051.0	20,398.5
Miscellaneous manufactured articles	101,152.5	126,088.4	156,398.1
Clothing and accessories (excl. footwear)	41,301.5	52,060.8	61,856.4
Footwear	11,090.1	12,954.8	15,202.6
Baby carriages, toys, games and sporting goods	12,628.9	14,455.4	16,320.2
Children's toys	5,574.1	5,979.4	6,379.5
Total (incl. others)	325,595.9	438,227.6	593,325.4

* Data on parts exclude tyres, engines and electrical parts.

Source: UN, *International Trade Statistics Yearbook*.

2005 (distribution by harmonized system, US $ million): *Imports:* Animals and animal products 4,258; Vegetable products 11,161; Animal or vegetable fats 3,311; Prepared foodstuffs 3,458; Mineral products 92,293; Chemical products 50,583; Plastics and rubber 38,893; Hides and skins 5,424; Wood and wood products 5,746; Wood pulp products 11,003; Textiles and textile articles 23,445; Footwear and headgear 671; Articles of stone, plaster, cement and asbestos 3,384; Pearls, precious or semi-precious stones, metals 3,470; Base metals and articles thereof 56,593; Machinery, mechanical appliances and electrical equipment 271,119; Transportation equipment 19,835; Instruments (measuring, musical) 51,188; Arms and ammunition 3; Miscellaneous manufactured articles 2,103; Works of art 7; Total (incl. others) 660,218. *Exports:* Animals and animal products 6,700; Vegetable products 8,282; Animal or vegetable fats 284; Prepared foodstuffs 11,196; Mineral products 20,920; Chemical products 31,853; Plastics and rubber 23,286; Hides and skins 15,602; Wood and wood products 7,570; Wood pulp products 5,114; Textiles and textile articles 107,661; Footwear and headgear 22,773; Articles of stone, plaster, cement and asbestos 12,257; Pearls, precious or semi-precious stones, metals 5,533; Base metals and articles thereof 57,086; Machinery, mechanical appliances and electrical equipment 322,008; Transportation equipment 28,410; Instruments (measuring, musical) 28,398; Arms and ammunition 28; Miscellaneous manufactured articles 47,023; Works of art 45; Total (incl. others) 762,337.

2006 (distribution by harmonized system, US $ million): *Imports:* Animals and animal products 4,663; Vegetable products 10,976; Animal or vegetable fats 3,921; Prepared foodstuffs 4,074; Mineral products 123,544; Chemical products 56,221; Plastics and rubber 46,277; Hides and skins 6,276; Wood and wood products 6,495; Wood pulp products 11,893; Textiles and textile articles 25,678; Footwear and headgear 775; Articles of stone, plaster, cement and asbestos 3,963; Pearls, precious or semi-precious stones, metals 4,616; Base metals and articles thereof 59,795; Machinery, mechanical appliances and electrical equipment 328,185; Transportation equipment 29,720; Instruments (measuring, musical) 60,075; Arms and ammunition 2; Miscellaneous manufactured articles 2,423; Works of art 12; Total (incl. others) 791,793. *Exports:* Animals and animal products 7,120; Vegetable products 8,897; Animal or vegetable fats 391; Prepared foodstuffs 13,802; Mineral products 21,398; Chemical products 37,753; Plastics and rubber 29,638; Hides and skins 15,382; Wood and wood products 9,912; Wood pulp products 6,896; Textiles and textile articles 138,102; Footwear and headgear 26,253; Articles of stone, plaster, cement and asbestos 15,544; Pearls, precious or semi-precious stones, metals 6,894; Base metals and articles thereof 85,317; Machinery, mechanical appliances and electrical equipment 414,065; Transportation equipment 38,431; Instruments (measuring, musical) 35,630; Arms and ammunition 39; Miscellaneous manufactured articles 55,160; Works of art 65; Total (incl. others) 969,284.

Source: Asian Development Bank, *Key Indicators of Developing Asian and Pacific Countries*.

THE PEOPLE'S REPUBLIC OF CHINA

PRINCIPAL TRADING PARTNERS
(US $ million)*

Imports c.i.f.	2003	2004	2005
Australia	7,300.1	11,552.5	16,193.6
Brazil	5,842.3	8,672.9	9,992.5
Canada	4,374.5	7,353.0	7,511.2
France	6,098.7	7,648.2	9,006.8
Germany	24,291.9	30,356.0	30,722.9
Hong Kong	11,118.7	11,796.7	12,224.8
Indonesia	5,747.0	7,215.7	8,437.0
India	4,251.4	7,678.0	9,766.2
Iran	3,307.4	4,490.7	6,786.7
Italy	5,080.6	6,451.4	6,925.3
Japan	74,148.1	94,326.7	100,407.7
Korea, Republic	43,128.1	62,234.1	76,820.4
Malaysia	13,986.4	18,174.7	20,093.2
Philippines	6,306.8	9,059.4	12,869.7
Russia	9,728.1	12,127.4	15,889.9
Saudi Arabia	5,172.3	7,522.7	12,245.7
Singapore	10,484.9	13,994.4	16,514.6
Taiwan	49,360.4	64,759.3	74,680.3
Thailand	8,826.8	11,540.5	13,991.9
USA	33,866.1	44,656.6	48,621.8
Total (incl. others)	412,759.8	561,228.8	659,952.8

Exports f.o.b.	2003	2004	2005
Australia	6,263.6	8,838.3	11,061.5
Belgium	3,933.7	5,859.7	7,738.8
Canada	5,632.2	8,161.2	11,653.7
France	7,293.5	9,921.4	11,639.4
Germany	17,442.1	23,755.7	32,527.1
Hong Kong†	76,274.4	100,868.6	124,473.3
India	4,251.4	5,936.0	8,934.3
Indonesia	4,481.9	6,256.4	8,350.4
Italy	6,652.3	9,223.8	11,688.9
Japan	59,408.7	73,509.0	83,986.3
Korea, Republic	20,094.8	27,811.6	35,107.8
Malaysia	6,140.9	8,086.1	10,606.4
Netherlands	13,501.2	18,518.8	25,875.7
Russia	6,029.9	9,098.1	13,211.3
Singapore	8,863.8	12,687.6	16,632.3
Spain	3,890.8	5,475.7	8,439.7
Taiwan	9,004.1	13,544.4	16,549.6
United Kingdom	10,823.7	14,967.0	18,976.5
USA	92,466.8	124,942.0	162,890.8
Total (incl. others)	438,227.8	593,325.6	761,953.4

* Imports by country of origin; exports by country of consumption.
† The majority of China's exports to Hong Kong are re-exported.

2006 (US $ million, rounded figures): *Imports:* Association of South East Asian Nations (ASEAN) 89,500; European Union (EU) 90,300; Hong Kong 10,800; Japan 115,700; Korea, Republic 89,800; Russia 17,600; Taiwan 87,100; USA 59,200; Total (incl. others) 791,600. *Exports:* Association of South East Asian Nations (ASEAN) 71,300; European Union (EU) 182,000; Hong Kong 155,400; Japan 91,600; Korea, Republic 44,500; Russia 15,800; Taiwan 20,700; USA 203,500; Total (incl. others) 969,100.

Transport

SUMMARY

	2004	2005	2006
Freight (million ton-km):			
railways	1,928,880	2,072,600	2,195,400
roads	784,090	869,320	964,700
waterways	4,142,870	4,967,230	5,390,780
Passenger-km (million):			
railways	571,220	606,200	662,200
roads	874,840	929,210	1,013,590
waterways	6,630	6,780	7,490

ROAD TRAFFIC
('000 motor vehicles in use)*

	2003	2004	2005
Passenger cars and buses	14,788.1	17,359.1	21,324.6
Goods vehicles	8,535.1	8,930.0	9,555.5
Total (incl. others)	23,829.3	26,937.1	31,596.6

*Excluding military vehicles.

SHIPPING

Merchant Fleet
(registered at 31 December)

	2004	2005	2006
Number of vessels	3,497	3,590	3,695
Total displacement ('000 grt)	20,369.2	22,284.1	23,488.4

Source: Lloyd's Register-Fairplay, *World Fleet Statistics*.

Sea-borne Shipping
(freight traffic, '000 metric tons)

	2003	2004	2005
Goods loaded and unloaded	2,011,260	2,460,740	2,927,770

CIVIL AVIATION

	2004	2005	2006
Passenger traffic (million)	121.2	138.3	159.7
Passenger-km (million)	178,277.9	204,492.9	237,066.0
Freight traffic ('000 metric tons)	2,767.0	3,067.2	3,494.3
Freight ton-km (million)	7,180.4	7,899.5	9,427.5
Total ton-km (million)	23,099.9	26,127.2	30,579.8

Tourism

FOREIGN VISITORS
(arrivals, '000)

Country of origin	2004	2005	2006
Australia	376.3	483.0	538.1
Canada	348.0	429.8	499.1
France	281.1	372.0	402.2
Germany	365.3	454.9	500.6
Indonesia	349.8	377.6	433.0
Japan	3,334.3	3,390.0	3,745.9
Korea, Republic	2,844.9	3,545.3	3,924.0
Malaysia	741.9	899.6	910.6
Mongolia	553.8	642.0	631.2
Philippines	549.4	654.0	704.2
Russia	1,792.2	2,223.9	2,405.1
Singapore	636.8	755.9	827.9
Thailand	464.2	586.3	592.0
United Kingdom	418.1	499.6	552.6
USA	1,308.6	1,555.5	1,710.3
Total (incl. others)*	16,932.5	20,255.1	22,210.3

* Excluding visitors from Hong Kong, Macao and Taiwan.

Tourism receipts (US $ million): 25,739 in 2004; 29,296 in 2005; 33,949 in 2006.

Communications Media

	2004	2005	2006
Telephones ('000 main lines in use)*	311,756	350,445	367,786
Mobile cellular telephones ('000 subscribers)*	334,824	393,406	461,058
Personal computers ('000 in use)*	52,990	52,990	n.a.
Internet users ('000)*	94,000	111,000	137,000
Broadband subscribers ('000)*	24,940	37,417	50,916
Book production:			
titles	208,294	222,473	233,971
copies (million)	6,413	6,465	6,408
Newspaper production:			
titles	1,922	1,931	1,938
copies (million)	402,400	412,600	424,500
Magazine production:			
titles	9,490	9,468	9,468
copies (million)	2,830	2,760	2,850

* Source: International Telecommunication Union.

1997 ('000 in use): Radio receivers 417,000; Facsimile machines 2,000 (Sources: UNESCO, *Statistical Yearbook*, and UN, *Statistical Yearbook*).

2000 ('000 in use): 380,000 television receivers (Source: International Telecommunication Union).

Education

(2006)

	Institutions	Full-time teachers ('000)	Students ('000)
Kindergartens	130,495	776	22,639
Primary schools	341,639	5,588	107,115
Regular secondary schools	76,703	4,851	84,519
Junior secondary schools	60,550	3,463	59,374
Senior secondary schools	16,153	1,387	25,145
Vocational secondary schools	6,100	307	6,762
Special schools	1,605	33	363
Higher education	1,867	1,076	17,388

Adult literacy rate (based on census data): 90.9% (males 95.1%; females 86.5%) in 2000 (Source: UNESCO Institute for Statistics).

Directory

The Constitution

A new Constitution was adopted on 4 December 1982 by the Fifth Session of the Fifth National People's Congress. Its principal provisions, including amendments made in 1993, 1999 and 2004, are detailed below. The Preamble, which is not included here, states that 'Taiwan is part of the sacred territory of the People's Republic of China'. The seventh paragraph of the Preamble was amended in 1993 and 1999 to state: 'The basic task of the nation is to concentrate its efforts on socialist modernization by following the road of building socialism with Chinese characteristics. Under the leadership of the Communist Party of China and the guidance of Marxism-Leninism, Mao Zedong Thought and Deng Xiaoping Theory, the Chinese people of all nationalities will continue to adhere to the people's democratic dictatorship.' The paragraph was further amended in 2004 to refer to 'Chinese-style socialism' and to 'the important thought of the Three Represents'.

GENERAL PRINCIPLES

Article 1: The People's Republic of China is a socialist state under the people's democratic dictatorship led by the working class and based on the alliance of workers and peasants.

The socialist system is the basic system of the People's Republic of China. Sabotage of the socialist system by any organization or individual is prohibited.

Article 2: All power in the People's Republic of China belongs to the people.

The organs through which the people exercise state power are the National People's Congress and the local people's congresses at different levels.

The people administer state affairs and manage economic, cultural and social affairs through various channels and in various ways in accordance with the law.

Article 3: The state organs of the People's Republic of China apply the principle of democratic centralism.

The National People's Congress and the local people's congresses at different levels are instituted through democratic election. They are responsible to the people and subject to their supervision.

All administrative, judicial and procuratorial organs of the State are created by the people's congresses to which they are responsible and under whose supervision they operate.

The division of functions and powers between the central and local state organs is guided by the principle of giving full play to the initiative and enthusiasm of the local authorities under the unified leadership of the central authorities.

Article 4: All nationalities in the People's Republic of China are equal. The State protects the lawful rights and interests of the minority nationalities and upholds and develops the relationship of equality, unity and mutual assistance among all of China's nationalities. Discrimination against and oppression of any nationality are prohibited; any acts that undermine the unity of the nationalities or instigate their secession are prohibited.

The State helps the areas inhabited by minority nationalities speed up their economic and cultural development in accordance with the peculiarities and needs of the different minority nationalities.

Regional autonomy is practised in areas where people of minority nationalities live in compact communities; in these areas organs of self-government are established for the exercise of the right of autonomy. All the national autonomous areas are inalienable parts of the People's Republic of China.

The people of all nationalities have the freedom to use and develop their own spoken and written languages, and to preserve or reform their own ways and customs.

Article 5: The People's Republic of China shall be governed according to law and shall be built into a socialist country based on the rule of law.

The State upholds the uniformity and dignity of the socialist legal system.

No law or administrative or local rules and regulations shall contravene the Constitution.

All state organs, the armed forces, all political parties and public organizations and all enterprises and undertakings must abide by the Constitution and the law. All acts in violation of the Constitution and the law must be looked into.

No organization or individual may enjoy the privilege of being above the Constitution and the law.

Article 6: The basis of the socialist economic system of the People's Republic of China is socialist public ownership of the means of production, namely, ownership by the whole people and collective ownership by the working people.

The system of socialist public ownership supersedes the system of exploitation of man by man; it applies the principle of 'from each according to his ability, to each according to his work.'

In the initial stage of socialism, the country shall uphold the basic economic system in which the public ownership is dominant and diverse forms of ownership develop side by side, and it shall uphold the distribution system with distribution according to work remaining dominant and a variety of modes of distribution coexisting.

Article 7: The state-owned economy, namely the socialist economy under the ownership of the whole people, is the leading force in the national economy. The State ensures the consolidation and growth of the state-owned economy.

Article 8: The rural collective economic organizations shall implement a two-tier operations system that combines unified operations with independent operations on the basis of household contract operations and different co-operative economic forms in the rural areas—the producers', supply and marketing, credit, and consumers' co-operatives—are part of the socialist economy collectively owned by the working people. Working people who are all members of rural economic collectives have the right, within the limits prescribed by law, to farm plots of cropland and hilly land allotted for their private use, engage in household sideline production and raise privately-owned livestock.

The various forms of co-operative economy in the cities and towns, such as those in the handicraft, industrial, building, transport, commercial and service trades, all belong to the sector of socialist economy under collective ownership by the working people.

The State protects the lawful rights and interests of the urban and rural economic collectives and encourages, guides and helps the growth of the collective economy.

Article 9: Mineral resources, waters, forests, mountains, grassland, unreclaimed land, beaches and other natural resources are owned by the State, that is, by the whole people, with the exception of the forests, mountains, grassland, unreclaimed land and beaches that are owned by collectives in accordance with the law.

The State ensures the rational use of natural resources and protects rare animals and plants. The appropriation or damage of natural resources by any organization or individual by whatever means is prohibited.

Article 10: Land in the cities is owned by the State.

Land in the rural and suburban areas is owned by collectives except for those portions which belong to the State in accordance with the law; house sites and private plots of cropland and hilly land are also owned by collectives.

The State may, in the public interest and in accordance with the provisions of law, expropriate or requisition land for its use and shall make compensation for the land expropriated or requisitioned.

No organization or individual may appropriate, buy, sell or lease land, or unlawfully transfer land in other ways.

All organizations and individuals who use land must make rational use of the land.

Article 11: The non-public sector of the economy comprising the individual and private sectors, operating within the limits prescribed by law, is an important component of the socialist market economy.

The State protects the lawful rights and interests of the non-public sectors of the economy such as the individual and private sectors of the economy. The State encourages, supports and guides the development of the non-public sectors of the economy and, in accordance with the law, exercises supervision and control over the non-public sectors of the economy.

Article 12: Socialist public property is sacred and inviolable.

The State protects socialist public property. Appropriation or damage of state or collective property by any organization or individual by whatever means is prohibited.

Article 13: Citizens' lawful private property is inviolable.

The State, in accordance with the law, protects the rights of citizens to private property and to its inheritance.

The State may, in the public interest and in accordance with the law, expropriate or requisition private property for its use and shall make compensation for private property expropriated or requisitioned.

Article 14: The State continuously raises labour productivity, improves economic results and develops the productive forces by enhancing the enthusiasm of the working people, raising the level of their technical skill, disseminating advanced science and technology, improving the systems of economic administration and enterprise operation and management, instituting the socialist system of responsibility in various forms and improving organization of work.

The State practises strict economy and combats waste.

The State properly apportions accumulation and consumption, pays attention to the interests of the collective and the individual as well as of the State and, on the basis of expanded production, gradually improves the material and cultural life of the people.

The State establishes a sound social security system compatible with the level of economic development.

Article 15: The State practises a socialist market economy. The State strengthens economic legislation and perfects macro-control. The State prohibits, according to the law, disturbance of society's economic order by any organization or individual.

Article 16: State-owned enterprises have decision-making power in operations within the limits prescribed by law.

State-owned enterprises practise democratic management through congresses of workers and staff and in other ways in accordance with the law.

Article 17: Collective economic organizations have decision-making power in conducting economic activities on the condition that they abide by the relevant laws. Collective economic organizations practise democratic management, elect and remove managerial personnel, and decide on major issues in accordance with the law.

Article 18: The People's Republic of China permits foreign enterprises, other foreign economic organizations and individual foreigners to invest in China and to enter into various forms of economic co-operation with Chinese enterprises and other economic organizations in accordance with the law of the People's Republic of China.

All foreign enterprises and other foreign economic organizations in China, as well as joint ventures with Chinese and foreign investment located in China, shall abide by the law of the People's Republic of China. Their lawful rights and interests are protected by the law of the People's Republic of China.

Article 19: The State develops socialist educational undertakings and works to raise the scientific and cultural level of the whole nation.

The State runs schools of various types, makes primary education compulsory and universal, develops secondary, vocational and higher education and promotes pre-school education.

The State develops educational facilities of various types in order to wipe out illiteracy and provide political, cultural, scientific, technical and professional education for workers, peasants, state functionaries and other working people. It encourages people to become educated through self-study.

The State encourages the collective economic organizations, state enterprises and undertakings and other social forces to set up educational institutions of various types in accordance with the law.

The State promotes the nation-wide use of Putonghua (common speech based on Beijing pronunciation).

Article 20: The State promotes the development of the natural and social sciences, disseminates scientific and technical knowledge, and commends and rewards achievements in scientific research as well as technological discoveries and inventions.

Article 21: The State develops medical and health services, promotes modern medicine and traditional Chinese medicine, encourages and supports the setting up of various medical and health facilities by the rural economic collectives, state enterprises and undertakings and neighbourhood organizations, and promotes sanitation activities of a mass character, all to protect the people's health.

The State develops physical culture and promotes mass sports activities to build up the people's physique.

Article 22: The State promotes the development of literature and art, the press, broadcasting and television undertakings, publishing and distribution services, libraries, museums, cultural centres and other cultural undertakings that serve the people and socialism, and sponsors mass cultural activities.

The State protects places of scenic and historical interest, valuable cultural monuments and relics and other important items of China's historical and cultural heritage.

Article 23: The State trains specialized personnel in all fields who serve socialism, increases the number of intellectuals and creates conditions to give full scope to their role in socialist modernization.

Article 24: The State strengthens the building of socialist spiritual civilization through spreading education in high ideals and morality, general education and education in discipline and the legal system, and through promoting the formulation and observance of rules of conduct and common pledges by different sections of the people in urban and rural areas.

The State advocates the civic virtues of love for the motherland, for the people, for labour, for science and for socialism; it educates the people in patriotism, collectivism, internationalism and communism and in dialectical and historical materialism; it combats capitalist, feudalist and other decadent ideas.

Article 25: The State promotes family planning so that population growth may fit the plans for economic and social development.

Article 26: The State protects and improves the living environment and the ecological environment, and prevents and remedies pollution and other public hazards.

The State organizes and encourages afforestation and the protection of forests.

Article 27: All state organs carry out the principle of simple and efficient administration, the system of responsibility for work and the system of training functionaries and appraising their work in order constantly to improve quality of work and efficiency and combat bureaucratism.

All state organs and functionaries must rely on the support of the people, keep in close touch with them, heed their opinions and suggestions, accept their supervision and work hard to serve them.

Article 28: The State maintains public order and suppresses treasonable and other criminal activities that endanger national security; it penalizes activities that endanger public security and disrupt the socialist economy as well as other criminal activities; and it punishes and reforms criminals.

Article 29: The armed forces of the People's Republic of China belong to the people. Their tasks are to strengthen national defence, resist aggression, defend the motherland, safeguard the people's peaceful labour, participate in national reconstruction, and work hard to serve the people.

The State strengthens the revolutionization, modernization and regularization of the armed forces in order to increase the national defence capability.

Article 30: The administrative division of the People's Republic of China is as follows:

(1) The country is divided into provinces, autonomous regions and municipalities directly under the central government;

(2) Provinces and autonomous regions are divided into autonomous prefectures, counties, autonomous counties and cities;

(3) Counties and autonomous counties are divided into townships, nationality townships and towns.

Municipalities directly under the central government and other large cities are divided into districts and counties. Autonomous prefectures are divided into counties, autonomous counties, and cities.

All autonomous regions, autonomous prefectures and autonomous counties are national autonomous areas.

Article 31: The State may establish special administrative regions when necessary. The systems to be instituted in special administrative regions shall be prescribed by law enacted by the National People's Congress in the light of the specific conditions.

Article 32: The People's Republic of China protects the lawful rights and interests of foreigners within Chinese territory, and while on Chinese territory foreigners must abide by the law of the People's Republic of China.

The People's Republic of China may grant asylum to foreigners who request it for political reasons.

FUNDAMENTAL RIGHTS AND DUTIES OF CITIZENS

Article 33: All persons holding the nationality of the People's Republic of China are citizens of the People's Republic of China.

All citizens of the People's Republic of China are equal before the law.

Every citizen enjoys the rights and at the same time must perform the duties prescribed by the Constitution and the law.

The State respects and preserves human rights.

Article 34: All citizens of the People's Republic of China who have reached the age of 18 have the right to vote and stand for election, regardless of nationality, race, sex, occupation, family background, religious belief, education, property status, or length of residence, except persons deprived of political rights according to law.

Article 35: Citizens of the People's Republic of China enjoy freedom of speech, of the press, of assembly, of association, of procession and of demonstration.

Article 36: Citizens of the People's Republic of China enjoy freedom of religious belief.

No state organ, public organization or individual may compel citizens to believe in, or not to believe in, any religion; nor may they discriminate against citizens who believe in, or do not believe in, any religion.

The State protects normal religious activities. No one may make use of religion to engage in activities that disrupt public order, impair the health of citizens or interfere with the educational system of the state.

Religious bodies and religious affairs are not subject to any foreign domination.

Article 37: The freedom of person of citizens of the People's Republic of China is inviolable.

No citizen may be arrested except with the approval or by decision of a people's procuratorate or by decision of a people's court, and arrests must be made by a public security organ.

Unlawful deprivation or restriction of citizens' freedom of person by detention or other means is prohibited; and unlawful search of the person of citizens is prohibited.

Article 38: The personal dignity of citizens of the People's Republic of China is inviolable. Insult, libel, false charge or frame-up directed against citizens by any means is prohibited.

Article 39: The home of citizens of the People's Republic of China is inviolable. Unlawful search of, or intrusion into, a citizen's home is prohibited.

Article 40: The freedom and privacy of correspondence of citizens of the People's Republic of China are protected by law. No organization or individual may, on any ground, infringe upon the freedom and privacy of citizens' correspondence except in cases where, to meet the needs of state security or of investigation into criminal offences, public security or procuratorial organs are permitted to censor correspondence in accordance with procedures prescribed by law.

Article 41: Citizens of the People's Republic of China have the right to criticize and make suggestions to any state organ or functionary. Citizens have the right to make to relevant state organs complaints and charges against, or exposures of, violation of the law or dereliction of duty by any state organ or functionary; but fabrication or distortion of facts with the intention of libel or frame-up is prohibited.

In case of complaints, charges or exposures made by citizens, the state organ concerned must deal with them in a responsible manner after ascertaining the facts. No one may suppress such complaints, charges and exposures, or retaliate against the citizen making them.

Citizens who have suffered losses through infringement of their civic rights by any state organ or functionary have the right to compensation in accordance with the law.

Article 42: Citizens of the People's Republic of China have the right as well as the duty to work.

Using various channels, the State creates conditions for employment, strengthens labour protection, improves working conditions and, on the basis of expanded production, increases remuneration for work and social benefits.

Work is the glorious duty of every able-bodied citizen. All working people in state-owned enterprises and in urban and rural economic collectives should perform their tasks with an attitude consonant with their status as masters of the country. The State promotes socialist labour emulation, and commends and rewards model and advanced workers. The State encourages citizens to take part in voluntary labour.

The State provides necessary vocational training to citizens before they are employed.

Article 43: Working people in the People's Republic of China have the right to rest.

The State expands facilities for rest and recuperation of working people, and prescribes working hours and vacations for workers and staff.

Article 44: The State prescribes by law the system of retirement for workers and staff in enterprises and undertakings and for functionaries of organs of state. The livelihood of retired personnel is ensured by the State and society.

Article 45: Citizens of the People's Republic of China have the right to material assistance from the State and society when they are old, ill or disabled. The State develops the social insurance, social relief and medical and health services that are required to enable citizens to enjoy this right.

The State and society ensure the livelihood of disabled members of the armed forces, provide pensions to the families of martyrs and give preferential treatment to the families of military personnel.

The State and society help make arrangements for the work, livelihood and education of the blind, deaf-mute and other handicapped citizens.

Article 46: Citizens of the People's Republic of China have the duty as well as the right to receive education.

The State promotes the all-round moral, intellectual and physical development of children and young people.

Article 47: Citizens of the People's Republic of China have the freedom to engage in scientific research, literary and artistic creation and other cultural pursuits. The State encourages and assists creative endeavours conducive to the interests of the people that are made by citizens engaged in education, science, technology, literature, art and other cultural work.

Article 48: Women in the People's Republic of China enjoy equal rights with men in all spheres of life, political, economic, cultural and social, including family life.

The State protects the rights and interests of women, applies the principle of equal pay for equal work for men and women alike and trains and selects cadres from among women.

Article 49: Marriage, the family and mother and child are protected by the State.

Both husband and wife have the duty to practise family planning.

Parents have the duty to rear and educate their minor children, and children who have come of age have the duty to support and assist their parents.

Violation of the freedom of marriage is prohibited. Maltreatment of old people, women and children is prohibited.

Article 50: The People's Republic of China protects the legitimate rights and interests of Chinese nationals residing abroad and protects the lawful rights and interests of returned overseas Chinese and of the family members of Chinese nationals residing abroad.

Article 51: The exercise by citizens of the People's Republic of China of their freedoms and rights may not infringe upon the interests of the State, of society and of the collective, or upon the lawful freedoms and rights of other citizens.

Article 52: It is the duty of citizens of the People's Republic of China to safeguard the unity of the country and the unity of all its nationalities.

Article 53: Citizens of the People's Republic of China must abide by the Constitution and the law, keep state secrets, protect public property and observe labour discipline and public order and respect social ethics.

Article 54: It is the duty of citizens of the People's Republic of China to safeguard the security, honour and interests of the motherland; they must not commit acts detrimental to the security, honour and interests of the motherland.

Article 55: It is the sacred obligation of every citizen of the People's Republic of China to defend the motherland and resist aggression.

It is the honourable duty of citizens of the People's Republic of China to perform military service and join the militia in accordance with the law.

Article 56: It is the duty of citizens of the People's Republic of China to pay taxes in accordance with the law.

STRUCTURE OF THE STATE

The National People's Congress

Article 57: The National People's Congress of the People's Republic of China is the highest organ of state power. Its permanent body is the Standing Committee of the National People's Congress.

Article 58: The National People's Congress and its Standing Committee exercise the legislative power of the State.

Article 59: The National People's Congress is composed of deputies elected from the provinces, autonomous regions, municipalities directly under the Central Government, and the special administrative regions, and of deputies elected from the armed forces. All the minority nationalities are entitled to appropriate representation.

Election of deputies to the National People's Congress is conducted by the Standing Committee of the National People's Congress.

The number of deputies to the National People's Congress and the manner of their election are prescribed by law.

Article 60: The National People's Congress is elected for a term of five years.

Two months before the expiration of the term of office of a National People's Congress, its Standing Committee must ensure that the election of deputies to the succeeding National People's Congress is completed. Should exceptional circumstances prevent such an election, it may be postponed by decision of a majority vote of more than two-thirds of all those on the Standing Committee of the incumbent National People's Congress, and the term of office of the incumbent National People's Congress may be extended. The election of deputies to the succeeding National People's Congress must be completed within one year after the termination of such exceptional circumstances.

Article 61: The National People's Congress meets in session once a year and is convened by its Standing Committee. A session of the National People's Congress may be convened at any time the Standing Committee deems this necessary, or when more than one-fifth of the deputies to the National People's Congress so propose.

When the National People's Congress meets, it elects a presidium to conduct its session.

Article 62: The National People's Congress exercises the following functions and powers:

(1) to amend the Constitution;

(2) to supervise the enforcement of the Constitution;

(3) to enact and amend basic statutes concerning criminal offences, civil affairs, the state organs and other matters;

(4) to elect the President and the Vice-President of the People's Republic of China;

(5) to decide on the choice of the Premier of the State Council upon nomination by the President of the People's Republic of China, and to decide on the choice of the Vice-Premiers, State Councillors, Ministers in charge of Ministries or Commissions and the Auditor-General and the Secretary-General of the State Council upon nomination by the Premier;

(6) to elect the Chairman of the Central Military Commission and, upon his nomination, to decide on the choice of all the others on the Central Military Commission;

(7) to elect the President of the Supreme People's Court;

(8) to elect the Procurator-General of the Supreme People's Procuratorate;

(9) to examine and approve the plan for national economic and social development and the reports on its implementation;

(10) to examine and approve the state budget and the report on its implementation;

(11) to alter or annul inappropriate decisions of the Standing Committee of the National People's Congress;

(12) to approve the establishment of provinces, autonomous regions, and municipalities directly under the Central Government;

(13) to decide on the establishment of special administrative regions and the systems to be instituted there;

(14) to decide on questions of war and peace; and

(15) to exercise such other functions and powers as the highest organ of state power should exercise.

Article 63: The National People's Congress has the power to recall or remove from office the following persons:

(1) the President and the Vice-President of the People's Republic of China;

(2) the Premier, Vice-Premiers, State Councillors, Ministers in charge of Ministries or Commissions and the Auditor-General and the Secretary-General of the State Council;

(3) the Chairman of the Central Military Commission and others on the Commission;

(4) the President of the Supreme People's Court; and

(5) the Procurator-General of the Supreme People's Procuratorate.

Article 64: Amendments to the Constitution are to be proposed by the Standing Committee of the National People's Congress or by more than one-fifth of the deputies to the National People's Congress and adopted by a majority vote of more than two-thirds of all the deputies to the Congress.

Statutes and resolutions are adopted by a majority vote of more than one-half of all the deputies to the National People's Congress.

Article 65: The Standing Committee of the National People's Congress is composed of the following:

the Chairman;
the Vice-Chairmen;
the Secretary-General; and
members.

Minority nationalities are entitled to appropriate representation on the Standing Committee of the National People's Congress.

The National People's Congress elects, and has the power to recall, all those on its Standing Committee.

No one on the Standing Committee of the National People's Congress shall hold any post in any of the administrative, judicial or procuratorial organs of the State.

Article 66: The Standing Committee of the National People's Congress is elected for the same term as the National People's Congress; it exercises its functions and powers until a new Standing Committee is elected by the succeeding National People's Congress.

The Chairman and Vice-Chairmen of the Standing Committee shall serve no more than two consecutive terms.

Article 67: The Standing Committee of the National People's Congress exercises the following functions and powers:

(1) to interpret the Constitution and supervise its enforcement;

(2) to enact and amend statutes with the exception of those which should be enacted by the National People's Congress;

(3) to enact, when the National People's Congress is not in session, partial supplements and amendments to statutes enacted by the National People's Congress provided that they do not contravene the basic principles of these statutes;

(4) to interpret statutes;

(5) to examine and approve, when the National People's Congress is not in session, partial adjustments to the plan for national economic and social development and to the state budget that prove necessary in the course of their implementation;

(6) to supervise the work of the State Council, the Central Military Commission, the Supreme People's Court and the Supreme People's Procuratorate;

(7) to annul those administrative rules and regulations, decisions or orders of the State Council that contravene the Constitution or the statutes;

(8) to annul those local regulations or decisions of the organs of state power of provinces, autonomous regions and municipalities directly under the Central Government that contravene the Constitution, the statutes or the administrative rules and regulations;

(9) to decide, when the National People's Congress is not in session, on the choice of Ministers in charge of Ministries or Commissions or the Auditor-General and the Secretary-General of the State Council upon nomination by the Premier of the State Council;

(10) to decide, upon nomination by the Chairman of the Central Military Commission, on the choice of others on the Commission, when the National People's Congress is not in session.

(11) to appoint and remove the Vice-Presidents and judges of the Supreme People's Court, members of its Judicial Committee and the President of the Military Court at the suggestion of the President of the Supreme People's Court;

(12) to appoint and remove the Deputy Procurators-General and Procurators of the Supreme People's Procuratorate, members of its Procuratorial Committee and the Chief Procurator of the Military Procuratorate at the request of the Procurator-General of the Supreme People's Procuratorate, and to approve the appointment and removal of the Chief Procurators of the People's Procuratorates of provinces, autonomous regions and municipalities directly under the Central Government;

(13) to decide on the appointment and recall of plenipotentiary representatives abroad;

(14) to decide on the ratification and abrogation of treaties and important agreements concluded with foreign states;

(15) to institute systems of titles and ranks for military and diplomatic personnel and of other specific titles and ranks;

(16) to institute state medals and titles of honour and decide on their conferment;

(17) to decide on the granting of special pardons;

(18) to decide, when the National People's Congress is not in session, on the proclamation of a state of war in the event of an armed attack on the country or in fulfilment of international treaty obligations concerning common defence against aggression;

(19) to decide on general mobilization or partial mobilization;

(20) to decide on entering the state of emergency throughout the country or in particular provinces, autonomous regions, or municipalities directly under the Central Government; and

(21) to exercise such other functions and powers as the National People's Congress may assign to it.

Article 68: The Chairman of the Standing Committee of the National People's Congress presides over the work of the Standing Committee and convenes its meetings. The Vice-Chairmen and the Secretary-General assist the Chairman in his work.

Chairmanship meetings with the participation of the Chairman, Vice-Chairmen and Secretary-General handle the important day-to-day work of the Standing Committee of the National People's Congress.

Article 69: The Standing Committee of the National People's Congress is responsible to the National People's Congress and reports on its work to the Congress.

Article 70: The National People's Congress establishes a Nationalities Committee, a Law Committee, a Finance and Economic Committee, an Education, Science, Culture and Public Health Committee, a Foreign Affairs Committee, an Overseas Chinese Committee and such other special committees as are necessary. These special committees work under the direction of the Standing Committee of the National People's Congress when the Congress is not in session.

The special committees examine, discuss and draw up relevant bills and draft resolutions under the direction of the National People's Congress and its Standing Committee.

Article 71: The National People's Congress and its Standing Committee may, when they deem it necessary, appoint committees of inquiry into specific questions and adopt relevant resolutions in the light of their reports.

All organs of State, public organizations and citizens concerned are obliged to supply the necessary information to those committees of inquiry when they conduct investigations.

Article 72: Deputies to the National People's Congress and all those on its Standing Committee have the right, in accordance with procedures prescribed by law, to submit bills and proposals within the scope of the respective functions and powers of the National People's Congress and its Standing Committee.

Article 73: Deputies to the National People's Congress during its sessions, and all those on its Standing Committee during its meetings, have the right to address questions, in accordance with procedures prescribed by law, to the State Council or the Ministries and Commissions under the State Council, which must answer the questions in a responsible manner.

Article 74: No deputy to the National People's Congress may be arrested or placed on criminal trial without the consent of the presidium of the current session of the National People's Congress or, when the National People's Congress is not in session, without the consent of its Standing Committee.

Article 75: Deputies to the National People's Congress may not be called to legal account for their speeches or votes at its meetings.

Article 76: Deputies to the National People's Congress must play an exemplary role in abiding by the Constitution and the law and keeping state secrets and, in production and other work and their public activities, assist in the enforcement of the Constitution and the law.

Deputies to the National People's Congress should maintain close contact with the units which elected them and with the people, listen to and convey the opinions and demands of the people and work hard to serve them.

Article 77: Deputies to the National People's Congress are subject to the supervision of the units which elected them. The electoral units have the power, through procedures prescribed by law, to recall the deputies whom they elected.

Article 78: The organization and working procedures of the National People's Congress and its Standing Committee are prescribed by law.

The President of the People's Republic of China

Article 79: The President and Vice-President of the People's Republic of China are elected by the National People's Congress.

Citizens of the People's Republic of China who have the right to vote and to stand for election and who have reached the age of 45 are eligible for election as President or Vice-President of the People's Republic of China.

The term of office of the President and Vice-President of the People's Republic of China is the same as that of the National People's Congress, and they shall serve no more than two consecutive terms.

Article 80: The President of the People's Republic of China, in pursuance of decisions of the National People's Congress and its Standing Committee, promulgates statutes; appoints and removes the Premier, Vice-Premiers, State Councillors, Ministers in charge of Ministries or Commissions, and the Auditor-General and the Secretary-General of the State Council; confers state medals and titles of honour; issues orders of special pardons; proclaims entering the state of emergency; proclaims a state of war; and issues mobilization orders.

Article 81: The President of the People's Republic of China, on behalf of the People's Republic of China, engages in activities involving State affairs and receives foreign diplomatic representatives and, in pursuance of decisions of the Standing Committee of the National People's Congress, appoints and recalls plenipotentiary representatives abroad, and ratifies and abrogates treaties and important agreements concluded with foreign states.

Article 82: The Vice-President of the People's Republic of China assists the President in his work.

The Vice-President of the People's Republic of China may exercise such parts of the functions and powers of the President as the President may entrust to him.

Article 83: The President and Vice-President of the People's Republic of China exercise their functions and powers until the new President and Vice-President elected by the succeeding National People's Congress assume office.

Article 84: In case the office of the President of the People's Republic of China falls vacant, the Vice-President succeeds to the office of President.

In case the office of the Vice-President of the People's Republic of China falls vacant, the National People's Congress shall elect a new Vice-President to fill the vacancy.

In the event that the offices of both the President and the Vice-President of the People's Republic of China fall vacant, the National People's Congress shall elect a new President and a new Vice-President. Prior to such election, the Chairman of the Standing Committee of the National People's Congress shall temporarily act as the President of the People's Republic of China.

The State Council

Article 85: The State Council, that is, the Central People's Government, of the People's Republic of China is the executive body of the highest organ of state power; it is the highest organ of state administration.

Article 86: The State Council is composed of the following: the Premier; the Vice-Premiers; the State Councillors; the Ministers in charge of ministries; the Ministers in charge of commissions; the Auditor-General; and the Secretary-General.

The Premier has overall responsibility for the State Council. The Ministers have overall responsibility for the respective ministries or commissions under their charge.

The organization of the State Council is prescribed by law.

Article 87: The term of office of the State Council is the same as that of the National People's Congress.

The Premier, Vice-Premiers and State Councillors shall serve no more than two consecutive terms.

Article 88: The Premier directs the work of the State Council. The Vice-Premiers and State Councillors assist the Premier in his work.

Executive meetings of the State Council are composed of the Premier, the Vice-Premiers, the State Councillors and the Secretary-General of the State Council.

The Premier convenes and presides over the executive meetings and plenary meetings of the State Council.

Article 89: The State Council exercises the following functions and powers:

(1) to adopt administrative measures, enact administrative rules and regulations and issue decisions and orders in accordance with the Constitution and the statutes;

(2) to submit proposals to the National People's Congress or its Standing Committee;

(3) to lay down the tasks and responsibilities of the ministries and commissions of the State Council, to exercise unified leadership over the work of the ministries and commissions and to direct all other administrative work of a national character that does not fall within the jurisdiction of the ministries and commissions;

(4) to exercise unified leadership over the work of local organs of state administration at different levels throughout the country, and to lay down the detailed division of functions and powers between the Central Government and the organs of state admin-

istration of provinces, autonomous regions and municipalities directly under the Central Government;

(5) to draw up and implement the plan for national economic and social development and the state budget;

(6) to direct and administer economic work and urban and rural development;

(7) to direct and administer the work concerning education, science, culture, public health, physical culture and family planning;

(8) to direct and administer the work concerning civil affairs, public security, judicial administration, supervision and other related matters;

(9) to conduct foreign affairs and conclude treaties and agreements with foreign states;

(10) to direct and administer the building of national defence;

(11) to direct and administer affairs concerning the nationalities, and to safeguard the equal rights of minority nationalities and the right of autonomy of the national autonomous areas;

(12) to protect the legitimate rights and interests of Chinese nationals residing abroad and protect the lawful rights and interests of returned overseas Chinese and of the family members of Chinese nationals residing abroad;

(13) to alter or annul inappropriate orders, directives and regulations issued by the ministries or commissions;

(14) to alter or annul inappropriate decisions and orders issued by local organs of state administration at different levels;

(15) to approve the geographic division of provinces, autonomous regions and municipalities directly under the Central Government, and to approve the establishment and geographic division of autonomous prefectures, counties, autonomous counties and cities;

(16) in accordance with the provisions of law, to decide on entering the state of emergency in parts of provinces, autonomous regions, and municipalities directly under the Central Government;

(17) to examine and decide on the size of administrative organs and, in accordance with the law, to appoint, remove and train administrative officers, appraise their work and reward or punish them; and

(18) to exercise such other functions and powers as the National People's Congress or its Standing Committee may assign it.

Article 90: The Ministers in charge of ministries or commissions of the State Council are responsible for the work of their respective departments and convene and preside over their ministerial meetings or commission meetings that discuss and decide on major issues in the work of their respective departments.

The ministries and commissions issue orders, directives and regulations within the jurisdiction of their respective departments and in accordance with the statutes and the administrative rules and regulations, decisions and orders issued by the State Council.

Article 91: The State Council establishes an auditing body to supervise through auditing the revenue and expenditure of all departments under the State Council and of the local government at different levels, and those of the state financial and monetary organizations and of enterprises and undertakings.

Under the direction of the Premier of the State Council, the auditing body independently exercises its power to supervise through auditing in accordance with the law, subject to no interference by any other administrative organ or any public organization or individual.

Article 92: The State Council is responsible, and reports on its work, to the National People's Congress or, when the National People's Congress is not in session, to its Standing Committee.

The Central Military Commission

Article 93: The Central Military Commission of the People's Republic of China directs the armed forces of the country.

The Central Military Commission is composed of the following: the Chairman; the Vice-Chairmen; and members.

The Chairman of the Central Military Commission has overall responsibility for the Commission.

The term of office of the Central Military Commission is the same as that of the National People's Congress.

Article 94: The Chairman of the Central Military Commission is responsible to the National People's Congress and its Standing Committee.

Regional Administration

Two further sections, not included here, deal with the Local People's Congresses and Government and with the Organs of Self-Government of National Autonomous Areas, respectively.

The People's Courts and the People's Procuratorates

Article 123: The people's courts in the People's Republic of China are the judicial organs of the State.

Article 124: The People's Republic of China establishes the Supreme People's Court and the local people's courts at different levels, military courts and other special people's courts.

The term of office of the President of the Supreme People's Court is the same as that of the National People's Congress; he shall serve no more than two consecutive terms.

The organization of people's courts is prescribed by law.

Article 125: All cases handled by the people's courts, except for those involving special circumstances as specified by law, shall be heard in public. The accused has the right of defence.

Article 126: The people's courts shall, in accordance with the law, exercise judicial power independently and are not subject to interference by administrative organs, public organizations or individuals.

Article 127: The Supreme People's Court is the highest judicial organ.

The Supreme People's Court supervises the administration of justice by the local people's courts at different levels and by the special people's courts; people's courts at higher levels supervise the administration of justice by those at lower levels.

Article 128: The Supreme People's Court is responsible to the National People's Congress and its Standing Committee. Local people's courts at different levels are responsible to the organs of state power which created them.

Article 129: The people's procuratorates of the People's Republic of China are state organs for legal supervision.

Article 130: The People's Republic of China establishes the Supreme People's Procuratorate and the local people's procuratorates at different levels, military procuratorates and other special people's procuratorates.

The term of office of the Procurator-General of the Supreme People's Procuratorate is the same as that of the National People's Congress; he shall serve no more than two consecutive terms.

The organization of people's procuratorates is prescribed by law.

Article 131: People's procuratorates shall, in accordance with the law, exercise procuratorial power independently and are not subject to interference by administrative organs, public organizations or individuals.

Article 132: The Supreme People's Procuratorate is the highest procuratorial organ.

The Supreme People's Procuratorate directs the work of the local people's procuratorates at different levels and of the special people's procuratorates; people's procuratorates at higher levels direct the work of those at lower levels.

Article 133: The Supreme People's Procuratorate is responsible to the National People's Congress and its Standing Committee. Local people's procuratorates at different levels are responsible to the organs of state power at the corresponding levels which created them and to the people's procuratorates at the higher level.

Article 134: Citizens of all nationalities have the right to use the spoken and written languages of their own nationalities in court proceedings. The people's courts and people's procuratorates should provide translation for any party to the court proceedings who is not familiar with the spoken or written languages in common use in the locality.

In an area where people of a minority nationality live in a compact community or where a number of nationalities live together, hearings should be conducted in the language or languages in common use in the locality; indictments, judgments, notices and other documents should be written, according to actual needs, in the language or languages in common use in the locality.

Article 135: The people's courts, people's procuratorates and public security organs shall, in handling criminal cases, divide their functions, each taking responsibility for its own work, and they shall co-ordinate their efforts and check each other to ensure correct and effective enforcement of law.

THE NATIONAL FLAG, THE NATIONAL ANTHEM, THE NATIONAL EMBLEM AND THE CAPITAL

Article 136: The national flag of the People's Republic of China is a red flag with five stars.

The National Anthem of the People's Republic of China is the March of the Volunteers.

Article 137: The national emblem of the People's Republic of China is the Tiananmen (Gate of Heavenly Peace) in the centre, illuminated by five stars and encircled by ears of grain and a cogwheel.

Article 138: The capital of the People's Republic of China is Beijing (Peking).

THE PEOPLE'S REPUBLIC OF CHINA

The Government

HEAD OF STATE

President: Hu Jintao (re-elected by the 11th National People's Congress on 15 March 2008).
Vice-President: Xi Jinping.

STATE COUNCIL
(April 2008)

Premier: Wen Jiabao.
Vice-Premiers: Li Keqiang, Hui Liangyu, Zhang Dejiang, Wang Qishan.
State Councillors: Liu Yandong, Liang Guanglie, Ma Kai, Meng Jianzhu, Dai Bingguo.
Secretary-General: Ma Kai.
Minister of Foreign Affairs: Yang Jiechi.
Minister of National Defence: Gen. Liang Guanglie.
Minister of State Development and Reform Commission: Zhang Ping.
Minister of Education: Zhou Ji.
Minister of Science and Technology: Wan Gang.
Minister of Industry and Information: Li Yizhong.
Minister of State Ethnic Affairs Commission: Yang Jing.
Minister of Public Security: Meng Jianzhu.
Minister of State Security: Geng Huichang.
Minister of Supervision: Ma Wen.
Minister of Civil Affairs: Li Xueju.
Minister of Justice: Wu Aiying.
Minister of Finance: Xie Xuren.
Minister of Human Resources and Social Security: Yin Weimin.
Minister of Land and Resources: Xu Shaoshi.
Minister of Housing and Urban-Rural Construction: Jiang Weixin.
Minister of Railways: Liu Zhijun.
Minister of Transport: Li Shenglin.
Minister of Water Resources: Chen Lei.
Minister of Agriculture: Sun Zhengcai.
Minister of Environmental Protection: Zhou Shengxian.
Minister of Commerce: Chen Deming.
Minister of Culture: Cai Wu.
Minister of Health: Chen Zhu.
Minister of State Population and Family Planning Commission: Li Bin.
Governor of the People's Bank of China: Zhou Xiaochuan.
Auditor-General of the National Audit Office: Liu Jiayi.

MINISTRIES

Ministry of Agriculture: 11 Nongzhanguan Nanli, Chao Yang Qu, Beijing 100026; tel. (10) 64192293; fax (10) 64192468; e-mail webmaster@agri.gov.cn; internet www.agri.gov.cn.
Ministry of Civil Affairs: 147 Beiheyan Dajie, Dongcheng Qu, Beijing 100721; tel. (10) 65135333; fax (10) 65135332; internet www.mca.gov.cn.
Ministry of Commerce: 2 Dongchangan Jie, Dongcheng Qu, Beijing 100731; tel. (10) 65121919; fax (10) 65599340; e-mail webmaster@mofcom.gov.cn; internet www.mofcom.gov.cn.
Ministry of Culture: 10 Chaoyangmen Bei Jie, Dongcheng Qu, Beijing 100020; tel. (10) 65551432; fax (10) 65551433; e-mail webmaster@whb1.ccnt.com.cn; internet www.ccnt.com.cn.
Ministry of Education: 37 Damucang Hutong, Xidan, Beijing 100816; tel. (10) 66096114; fax (10) 66011049; e-mail webmaster@moe.edu.cn; internet www.moe.edu.cn.
Ministry of Environmental Protection: 115 Xizhimennei Nan Xiao Jie, Xicheng Qu, Beijing 100035; internet english.sepa.gov.cn.
Ministry of Finance: 3 Nansanxiang, Sanlihe, Xicheng Qu, Beijing 100820; tel. (10) 68551888; fax (10) 68533635; e-mail webmaster@mof.gov.cn; internet www.mof.gov.cn.
Ministry of Foreign Affairs: 225 Chaoyangmen Nan Dajie, Chaoyang Qu, Beijing 100701; tel. (10) 65961114; fax (10) 65962146; e-mail webmaster@mfa.gov.cn; internet www.fmprc.gov.cn.
Ministry of Health: 1 Xizhinenwai Bei Lu, Xicheng Qu, Beijing 100044; tel. (10) 68792114; fax (10) 64012369; e-mail zxc@szhealth.gov.cn; internet www.moh.gov.cn.

Directory

Ministry of Housing and Urban-Rural Construction: 9 Sanlihe Dajie, Xicheng Qu, Beijing 100835; tel. (10) 58933575; fax (10) 58934114; e-mail cin@mail.cin.gov.cn; internet www.cin.gov.cn.
Ministry of Human Resources and Social Security: 12 Hepinglizhong Jie, Dongcheng Qu, Beijing 100716; tel. (10) 84201114; fax (10) 64218350; internet www.molss.gov.cn.
Ministry of Industry and Information: 13 Xichangan Jie, Beijing 100804; tel. (10) 66014249; fax (10) 66034248; e-mail webmaster@mii.gov.cn; internet www.mii.gov.cn.
Ministry of Justice: 10 Chaoyangmennan Dajie, Chao Yang Qu, Beijing 100020; tel. (10) 65205114; fax (10) 65205316.
Ministry of Land and Resources: 64 Funei Dajie, Xisi, Beijing 100812; tel. (10) 66558407; fax (10) 66127247; e-mail webmaster@mail.mlr.gov.cn; internet www.mlr.gov.cn.
Ministry of National Defence: 20 Jingshanqian Jie, Beijing 100009; tel. (10) 66730000; fax (10) 65962146.
Ministry of Personnel: 12 Hepinglizhong Jie, Dongcheng Qu, Beijing 100716; tel. (10) 84223240; fax (10) 64211417; internet www.mop.gov.cn.
Ministry of Public Security: 14 Dongchangan Jie, Dongcheng Qu, Beijing 100741; tel. (10) 65122831; fax (10) 65136577; internet www.mps.gov.cn.
Ministry of Railways: 10 Fuxing Lu, Haidian Qu, Beijing 100844; tel. (10) 63244150; fax (10) 63242150; e-mail webmaster@ns.chinamor.cn.net; internet www.chinamor.cn.net.
Ministry of Science and Technology: 15B Fuxing Lu, Haidian Qu, Beijing 100862; tel. (10) 68515050; fax (10) 68515006; e-mail officemail@mail.most.gov.cn; internet www.most.gov.cn.
Ministry of State Security: 14 Dongchangan Jie, Dongcheng Qu, Beijing 100741; tel. (10) 65244702.
Ministry of Supervision: 4 Zaojunmiao, Haidian Qu, Beijing 100081; tel. (10) 62256677; fax (10) 62254181.
Ministry of Transport: Beijing.
Ministry of Water Resources: 2 Baiguang Lu, Ertiao, Xuanwu Qu, Beijing 100053; tel. (10) 63203069; fax (10) 63202650; internet www.mwr.gov.cn.

STATE COMMISSIONS

State Development and Reform Commission: 38 Yuetannan Jie, Xicheng Qu, Beijing 100824; tel. (10) 68504409; fax (10) 68512929; e-mail news@sdpc.gov.cn; internet www.sdpc.gov.cn.
State Economic and Trade Commission: 26 Xuanwumenxi Dajie, Xuanwumen Qu, Beijing 100053; tel. (10) 63192334; fax (10) 63192348; e-mail iecc@setc.gov.cn; internet www.setc.gov.cn.
State Ethnic Affairs Commission: 252 Taipingqiao Dajie, Xicheng Qu, Beijing 100800; tel. and fax (10) 66017375; fax (10) 66017375; e-mail webmaster@www.seac.gov.cn; internet www.seac.gov.cn.
State Population and Family Planning Commission: 14 Zhichun Lu, Haidian Qu, Beijing 100088; tel. (10) 62046622; fax (10) 62051865; e-mail sfpcdfa@public.bta.net.cn; internet www.sfpc.gov.cn.

People's Governments

PROVINCES

Governors: Wang Sanyun (acting—Anhui), Huang Xiaoxing (Fujian), Xu Shouseng (Gansu), Huang Huahua (Guangdong), Lin Shusen (Guizhou), Luo Baoming (Hainan), Hu Chunhua (acting—Hebei), Li Zhanshu (Heilongjiang), Guo Gengmao (acting—Henan), Li Hongzhong (acting—Hubei), Zhou Qiang (Hunan), Luo Zhijun (acting—Jiangsu), Wu Xinxiong (Jiangxi), Han Changfu (Jilin), Chen Zhenggao (acting—Liaoning), Song Xiuyan (Qinghai), Yuan Chunqing (acting—Shaanxi), Jiang Daming (Shandong), Meng Xuenong (acting—Shanxi), Jiang Jufeng (Sichuan), Qin Guangrong (Yunnan), Lu Zushan (Zhejiang).

SPECIAL MUNICIPALITIES

Mayors: Guo Jinlong (Beijing), Wang Hongju (Chongqing), Han Zheng (Shanghai), Huang Xingguo (Tianjin).

AUTONOMOUS REGIONS

Chairmen: Ma Biao (Guangxi Zhuang), Bagatur (acting—Nei Monggol), Wang Zhengwei (Ningxia Hui), Qiangba Puncog (Tibet—Xizang), Nur Bekri (acting—Xinjiang Uygur).

THE PEOPLE'S REPUBLIC OF CHINA

Legislature

QUANGUO RENMIN DAIBIAO DAHUI
(National People's Congress)

The National People's Congress (NPC) is the highest organ of state power, and is indirectly elected for a five-year term. The first plenary session of the 11th NPC was convened in Beijing in March 2008, and was attended by 2,967 deputies. The first session of the 11th National Committee of the Chinese People's Political Consultative Conference (CPPCC, www.cppcc.gov.cn, Chair. JIA QINGLIN), a revolutionary united front organization led by the Communist Party, took place simultaneously. The CPPCC holds discussions and consultations on the important affairs in the nation's political life. Members of the CPPCC National Committee or of its Standing Committee may be invited to attend the NPC or its Standing Committee as observers.

Standing Committee

In March 2008 161 members were elected to the Standing Committee, in addition to the following:

Chairman: WU BANGGUO.

Vice-Chairmen: WANG ZHAOGUO, LU YONGXIANG, UYUNQIMG, HAN QIDE, HUA JIANMIN, CHEN ZHILI, ZHOU TIENONG, LI JIANGUO, ISMAIL TILIWALDI, JIANG SHUSHENG, CHEN CHANGZHI, YAN JUNQI, SANG GUOWEI.

Secretary-General: LI JIANGUO.

Political Organizations

COMMUNIST PARTY

Zhongguo Gongchan Dang (Chinese Communist Party—CCP): Beijing; f. 1921; 73.4m. mems in June 2007; at the 17th Nat. Congress of the CCP in Oct. 2007, a new Cen. Cttee of 204 full mems and 167 alternate mems was elected; at its first plenary session the 17th Cen. Cttee appointed a new Political Bureau.

Seventeenth Central Committee

General Secretary: HU JINTAO.

Political Bureau (Politburo)

Members of the Standing Committee: HU JINTAO, WU BANGGUO, WEN JIABAO, JIA QINGLIN, LI CHANGCHUN, XI JINPING, LI KEQIANG, HE GUOQIANG, ZHOU YONGKANG.

Other Full Members: BO XILAI, Gen. GUO BOXIONG, HUI LIANGYU, LI YUANCHAO, LIU QI, LIU YANDONG, LIU YUNSHAN, WANG GANG, WANG LEQUAN, WANG QISHAN, WANG YANG, WANG ZHAOGUO, XU CAIHOU, YU ZHENGSHENG, ZHANG DEJIANG, ZHANG GAOLI, ZHOU YONGKANG.

Alternate Member: (vacant).

Secretariat: XI JINPING, LIU YUNSHAN, LI YUANCHAO, HE YONG, LING JIHUA, WANG HUNING.

OTHER POLITICAL ORGANIZATIONS

China Association for Promoting Democracy: 98 Xinanli Guloufangzhuangchang, Beijing 100009; tel. (10) 64033452; f. 1945; 65,000 mems, drawn mainly from literary, cultural and educational circles; Chair. XU JIALU; Sec.-Gen. ZHAO GUANGHUA.

China Democratic League: 1 Beixing Dongchang Hutong, Beijing 100006; tel. (10) 65137983; fax (10) 65125090; internet www.dem-league.org.cn; f. 1941; formed from reorganization of League of Democratic Parties and Organizations of China; 131,300 mems, mainly intellectuals active in education, science and culture; Chair. JIANG SHUSHENG; Sec.-Gen. ZHANG BAOWEN.

China National Democratic Construction Association: 208 Jixiangli, Chaowai Lu, Beijing 100020; tel. (10) 65523229; fax (10) 65523518; e-mail bgt@cndca.org.cn; internet www.cndca.org.cn; f. 1945; 99,260 mems, mainly industrialists and business executives; Chair. CHENG SIWEI; Sec.-Gen. ZHANG JIAO.

China Zhi Gong Dang (Party for Public Interests): Beijing; e-mail zhigong@public2.east.net.cn; f. 1925; reorg. 1947; 15,000 mems, mainly returned overseas Chinese and scholars; Chair. LUO HAOCAI; Sec.-Gen. QIU GUOYI.

Chinese Communist Youth League: 10 Qianmen Dongdajie, Beijing 100051; tel. (10) 67018132; fax (10) 67018131; e-mail guoji3acyt@yahoo.com; f. 1922; 68.5m. mems; First Sec. of Cen. Cttee HU CHUNHUA.

Chinese Peasants' and Workers' Democratic Party: f. 1930; est. as the Provisional Action Cttee of the Kuomintang; took present name in 1947; more than 65,000 mems, active mainly in public health and medicine; Chair. JIANG ZHENGHUA; Sec.-Gen. JIAO PINGSHENG (acting).

Directory

Jiu San (3 September) Society: f. 1946; fmrly Democratic and Science Soc; 68,400 mems, mainly scientists and technologists; Chair. HAN QIDE; Sec.-Gen. XU GUOQUAN.

Revolutionary Committee of the Chinese Kuomintang: tel. (10) 6550388; f. 1948; over 53,000 mems, mainly fmr Kuomintang mems, and those in cultural, educational, health and financial fields; Chair. HE LULI; Sec.-Gen. LIU MINFU.

Taiwan Democratic Self-Government League: f. 1947; 1,600 mems; recruits Taiwanese living on the mainland; Chair. ZHANG KEHUI; Sec.-Gen. ZHANG HUAJUN.

Diplomatic Representation

EMBASSIES IN THE PEOPLE'S REPUBLIC OF CHINA

Afghanistan: 8 Dong Zhi Men Wai Dajie, Chao Yang Qu, Beijing 100600; tel. (10) 65321532; fax (10) 653226603; e-mail afgemb.beijing@gmail.com; Ambassador AHMAD EKLIL HAKIMI.

Albania: 28 Guang Hua Lu, Jian Guo Men Wai, Beijing 100600; tel. (10) 65321120; fax (10) 65325451; e-mail embassy.beijing@mfa.gov.al; Ambassador MAXHUN PEKA.

Algeria: 2 Dong Zhi Men Wai Dajie, Chao Yang Qu, Beijing 100600; tel. (10) 65321231; fax (10) 65321648; Ambassador DJAMEL EDDINE GRINE.

Angola: 1-8-1 Tayuan Diplomatic Office Bldg, Beijing 100600; tel. (10) 65326968; fax (10) 65326992; internet www.angolaembassychina.com; Ambassador JOÃO MANUEL BERNARDO.

Argentina: Bldg 11, 5 Dong Wu Jie, San Li Tun, Beijing 100600; tel. (10) 65322090; fax (10) 65322319; e-mail echin@public.bta.net.cn; Chargé d'affaires a.i. MARÍA ISABEL RENDÓN.

Armenia: 9-2-62 Tayuan Diplomatic Compound, Beijing 100600; tel. (10) 65325677; fax (10) 65325654; e-mail armemb@public3.bta.net.cn; Ambassador MOVSISIAN VAHAGN.

Australia: 21 Dong Zhi Men Wai Dajie, San Li Tun, Beijing 100600; tel. (10) 51404111; fax (10) 51404450; e-mail pubaff.beijing@dfat.gov.au; internet www.china.embassy.gov.au; Ambassador GEOFFREY WILLIAM RABY.

Austria: 5 Xiu Shui Nan Jie, Jian Guo Men Wai, Beijing 100600; tel. (10) 65322061; fax (10) 65321505; e-mail peking-ob@bmaa.gv.at; internet www.aussenministerium.at/peking; Ambassador MARTIN SAJDIK.

Azerbaijan: 3-2-31 San Li Tun Diplomatic Compound, Beijing 100600; tel. (10) 65324614; fax (10) 65324615; e-mail mailbox@azerbembassy.org.cn; internet www.azerbembassy.org.cn; Ambassador YASHAR TOFIGI ALIYEV.

Bahamas: 4/F, Tayuan Diplomatic Office Bldg, 14 Liang Ma He Lu, Beijing 100600; tel. (10) 65322922; fax (10) 65322304; e-mail pmiller@mfabahamas.org; internet www.bahamasembassy.cn; Chargé d'affaires a.i. PHILIP MILLER.

Bahrain: 10-06 Liangmaqiao Diplomatic Residence Compound, 22 Dong Fang Dong Lu, Chao Yang Qu, Beijing; tel. (10) 65326483; fax (10) 65326393; e-mail beijing.mission@mofa.gov.bh; Ambassador BIBI SHARAF AL-ALALAWI.

Bangladesh: 42 Guang Hua Lu, Beijing 100600; tel. (10) 65321819; fax (10) 65324346; e-mail bdemb@public3.bta.net.cn; internet www.bangladeshembassy.com.cn; Ambassador MUNSHI FAIZ AHMAD.

Belarus: 1 Dong Yi Jie, Ri Tan Lu, Beijing 100600; tel. (10) 65321691; fax (10) 65326417; e-mail china@belembassy.org; internet www.belembassy.com; Ambassador ANATOLY AFANASYEVICH TOZIK.

Belgium: 6 San Li Tun Lu, Beijing 100600; tel. (10) 65321736; fax (10) 65325097; e-mail Beijing@diplobel.org; internet www.diplomatie.be/beijing; Ambassador BERNARD PIERRE.

Benin: 38 Guang Hua Lu, Jian Guo Men Wai, Beijing 100600; tel. (10) 65323054; fax (10) 65325103; Ambassador SEDOZAN APITHY.

Bolivia: 2-3-2 Tayuan Diplomatic Office Bldg, Beijing 100600; tel. (10) 65323074; fax (10) 65324686; e-mail embolch@public3.bta.net.cn; Ambassador LUIS FERNANDO RODRÍGUEZ UREÑA.

Bosnia and Herzegovina: 1-5-1 Tayuan Diplomatic Office Bldg, Beijing 100600; tel. (10) 65326587; fax (10) 65326418; Ambassador PERO BARUNČIĆ.

Botswana: Unit 811, IBM Tower, Pacific Century Place, 2A Gong Ti Bei Lu, Beijing 100027; tel. (10) 65391616; fax (10) 65391199; Ambassador NAOMI E. MAJINDA.

Brazil: 27 Guang Hua Lu, Jian Guo Men Wai, Beijing 100600; tel. (10) 65322881; fax (10) 65322751; e-mail empequim@public.bta.net.cn; internet www.brazil.org.cn; Ambassador LUIZ CASTRO NEVES.

Brunei: 1 Liang Ma Qiao Bei Jie, Chao Yang Qu, Beijing 100600; tel. (10) 65329773; fax (10) 65324097; e-mail beb@public.bta.net.cn; Ambassador MAGDALENE TEO CHEE SIONG.

THE PEOPLE'S REPUBLIC OF CHINA

Bulgaria: 4 Xiu Shui Bei Jie, Jian Guo Men Wai, Beijing 100600; tel. (10) 65321946; fax (10) 65324502; e-mail bulemb@public.bta.net.cn; internet www.mfa.bg/beijing; Ambassador ANGEL ORBETSOV.

Burundi: 25 Guang Hua Lu, Jian Guo Men Wai, Beijing 100600; tel. (10) 65321801; fax (10) 65322381; e-mail ambbubei@yahoo.fr; Ambassador GABRIEL SABUSHIMIKE.

Cambodia: 9 Dong Zhi Men Wai Dajie, Beijing 100600; tel. (10) 65321889; fax (10) 65323507; e-mail cambassybeijing@sohu.com; Ambassador KHEK CAIMEALY.

Cameroon: 7 Dong Wu Jie, San Li Tun, Beijing 100600; tel. (10) 65321771; fax (10) 65321761; e-mail acpk71@hotmail.com; Ambassador ELEIH-ELLE ETIAN.

Canada: 19 Dong Zhi Men Wai Dajie, Chao Yang Qu, Beijing 100600; tel. (10) 65323536; fax (10) 65324311; internet www.beijing.gc.ca; Ambassador ROBERT WRIGHT.

Cape Verde: 6-2-121 Tayuan Diplomatic Office Bldg, Beijing; tel. (10) 65327547; fax (10) 65327546; e-mail ecvb@163bj.com; internet www.embcvchina.com; Ambassador JULIO CESAR FREIRE DE MORAIS.

Central African Republic: 1-1-132 Tayuan Diplomatic Office Bldg, No. 1 Xin Dong Lu, Chao Yang Qu, Beijing; tel. 65327353; fax 65327354; e-mail centra_chine@yahoo.fr; Ambassador (vacant).

Chad: 21 Guanghua Lu, Beijing 100600; tel. (10) 65321296; fax (10) 5323638; e-mail ambatchad.beijing@yahoo.fr; Ambassador AHMED SOUNGUI.

Chile: 1 Dong Si Jie, San Li Tun, Beijing 100600; tel. (10) 65321591; fax (10) 65323170; e-mail embachile@echilecn.com; Ambassador FERNANDO REYES MATTA.

Colombia: 34 Guang Hua Lu, Jian Guo Men Wai, Beijing 100600; tel. (10) 65321713; fax (10) 65321969; e-mail ebeijing@minrelext.gov.co; Ambassador GUILLERMO RICARDO VÉLEZ LONDOÑO.

Congo, Democratic Republic: 6 Dong Wu Jie, San Li Tun, Beijing 100600; tel. (10) 65320321; fax (10) 65321360; Ambassador CHARLES MUMBALA NZANKU.

Congo, Republic: 7 Dong Si Jie, San Li Tun, Beijing 100600; tel. (10) 65321658; fax (10) 65322915; Ambassador PIERRE PASSI.

Costa Rica: Jian Guo Men Wai, 1-5-41 Jiao Gong Lu, Beijing 100600; tel. (10) 65324157; fax (10) 65324546; e-mail embajadacrchina@gmail.com; Ambassador ANTONIO BURGUÉS TERÁN.

Côte d'Ivoire: 9 San Li Tun, Bei Xiao Jie, Beijing 100600; tel. (10) 65321223; fax (10) 65322407; Ambassador COFFIE ALAIN NICAISE PAPATCHI.

Croatia: 2-72 San Li Tun Diplomatic Office Bldg, Beijing 100600; tel. (10) 65326241; fax (10) 65326257; e-mail vrhpek@public.bta.net.cn; Ambassador BORIS VELIĆ.

Cuba: 1 Xiu Shui Nan Jie, Jian Guo Men Wai, Beijing 100600; tel. (10) 65321714; fax (10) 65322656; e-mail earufe@public3.bta.net.cn; Ambassador CARLOS MIGUEL PEREIRA.

Cyprus: 2-13-2 Tayuan Diplomatic Office Bldg, Liang Ma He Nan Lu, Chao Yang Qu, Beijing 100600; tel. (10) 65325057; fax (10) 65324244; e-mail cyembpek@public3.bta.net.cn; Ambassador MARIOS IERONYMIDES.

Czech Republic: Ri Tan Lu, Jian Guo Men Wai, Beijing 100600; tel. (10) 85329500; fax (10) 65325653; e-mail beijing@embassy.mzv.cz; internet www.mzv.cz/beijing; Ambassador Dr VITESLAV GREPL.

Denmark: 1 Dong Wu Jie, San Li Tun, Beijing 100600; tel. (10) 85329900; fax (10) 85329916; e-mail bjsamb@um.dk; internet www.ambbeijing.um.dk; Ambassador JEPPE TRANHOLM-MIKKELSEN.

Djibouti: 2-2-102 Tayuan Diplomatic Office Bldg, Beijing; tel. (10) 65327857; fax (10) 65327858; Ambassador MOUSSA BOUH ODOWA.

Dominica: 1-12-1, Tayuan Diplomatic Office Bldg, 14 Liangmahe Lu, Chao Yang Qu, Beijing; e-mail dominica@dominicaembassy.com; Ambassador DAVID KING HSIU.

Ecuador: 2-62 San Li Tun Office Bldg, Chaoyang Qu, 100600 Beijing; tel. (10) 65323158; fax (10) 65324371; e-mail embecuch@public3bta.net.cn; Ambassador WASHINGTON HAGO.

Egypt: 2 Ri Tan Dong Lu, Jian Guo Men Wai, Beijing 100600; tel. (10) 65321825; fax (10) 65325365; Ambassador MAHMOUD ALLAM.

Equatorial Guinea: 2 Dong Si Jie, San Li Tun, Beijing; tel. (10) 65323709; fax (10) 65323805; e-mail ntugabeso@hotmail.com; Ambassador NARCISO NTUGU ABESO OYANA.

Eritrea: 2-10-1 Tayuan Diplomatic Office Bldg, Beijing 100600; tel. (10) 65326534; fax (10) 65326532; Ambassador TSEGGAI TESFATSION SEREKE.

Estonia: Office Building C-617/618, Kempinski Hotel, Beijing Lufthansa Center, Beijing 100016; tel. (10) 64637913; fax (10) 64637908; e-mail embassy.beijing@mfa.ee; internet www.peking.vm.ee; Ambassador ANDRES UNGA.

Ethiopia: 3 Xiu Shui Nan Jie, Jian Guo Men Wai, Beijing 100600; tel. (10) 65325258; fax (10) 65325591; e-mail ethchina@public3.bta.net.cn; internet www.ethiopiaemb.org.cn; Ambassador HAILEKIROS GESSESSE.

Fiji: 1-15-2 Tayuan Diplomatic Office Bldg, Beijing 100600; tel. (10) 65327305; fax (10) 65327253; e-mail info@fijiembassy.org.cn; internet www.fijiembassy.org.cn; Ambassador Sir JAMES AH KOY.

Finland: Beijing Kerry Centre, 26/F South Tower, 1 Guanghua Lu, Beijing 100020; tel. (10) 85298541; fax (10) 85298547; e-mail sanomat.pek@formin.fi; internet www.finland.cn; Ambassador ANTTI KUOSMANEN.

France: 3 Dong San Jie, San Li Tun, Chao Yang Qu, Beijing 100600; tel. (10) 65321331; fax (10) 65324841; e-mail secretariat@ambafrance-cn.org; internet www.ambafrance-cn.org; Ambassador HERVÉ LADSOUS.

Gabon: 36 Guang Hua Lu, Jian Guo Men Wai, Beijing 100600; tel. (10) 65322810; fax (10) 65322621; Ambassador EMMANUEL MBA-ALLO.

Georgia: LA 03-02, Section A, Liangmaqiao Diplomatic Compound, Beijing; tel. (10) 65327518; fax (10) 65327519; e-mail geobeijing@gmail.com; internet www.china.mfa.gov.ge; Ambassador MIKHEIL UKLEBA.

Germany: 17 Dong Zhi Men Wai Dajie, San Li Tun, Beijing 100600; tel. (10) 85329000; fax (10) 65325336; e-mail embassy@peki.diplo.de; internet www.beijing.diplo.de; Ambassador Dr MICHAEL SCHAEFER.

Ghana: 8 San Li Tun Lu, Beijing 100600; tel. (10) 65321319; fax (10) 65323602; Ambassador AFARE APEADU DONKOR.

Greece: 19 Guang Hua Lu, Jian Guo Men Wai, Beijing 100600; tel. (10) 65321588; fax (10) 65321277; e-mail gremb.pek@mfa.gr; internet www.grpressbeijing.com; Ambassador MICHEL KAMBANIS.

Grenada: T5-2-52, Tayuan Diplomatic Office Building, Chaoyang Qu, Beijing 100600; tel. (10) 65321208; fax (10) 65321015; e-mail grenembbeijing@yahoo.com; Ambassador JOSLYN R. WHITEMAN.

Guinea: 2 Xi Liu Jie, San Li Tun, Beijing 100600; tel. (10) 65323649; fax (10) 65324957; Ambassador DIARE MAMADY.

Guinea-Bissau: 2-2-101 Tayuan Diplomatic Compound, Beijing; tel. (10) 65327393; fax (10) 65327106; Chargé d'affaires CARRINGTON CA.

Guyana: 1 Xiu Shui Dong Jie, Jian Guo Men Wai, Beijing 100600; tel. (10) 65321601; fax (10) 65325741; e-mail guyemb@public3.bta.net.cn; Chargé d'affaires CECIL POLLYDORE.

Hungary: 10 Dong Zhi Men Wai Dajie, San Li Tun, Beijing 100600; tel. (10) 65321431; fax (10) 65325053; e-mail titkarsag.pek@kum.hu; internet www.huemb.org.cn; Ambassador SÁNDOR MÉSZÁROS.

Iceland: Landmark Tower 1, 802, 8 North Dongsanhuan Lu, Beijing 100004; tel. (10) 65907795; fax (10) 65907801; e-mail icemb.beijing@utn.stjr.is; internet www.iceland.org/cn; Ambassador GUNNAR SNORRI GUNNARSSON.

India: 1 Ri Tan Dong Lu, Jian Guo Men Wai, Beijing 100600; tel. (10) 65321908; fax (10) 65324684; internet www.indianembassy.org.cn; Ambassador NIRUPAMA RAO.

Indonesia: 4 Dong Zhi Men Wai Dajie, Beijing 100600; tel. (10) 65325486; fax (10) 65325368; e-mail kombei@public3.bta.net.cn; internet www.indonesianembassy-china.com; Ambassador SUDRADJAT.

Iran: 13 Dong Liu Jie, San Li Tun, Beijing 100600; tel. (10) 65322040; fax (10) 65321403; Ambassador JAVAD MANSOURI.

Iraq: 25 Xiu Shui Bei Jie, Jian Guo Men Wai, Beijing 100600; tel. (10) 65324355; fax (10) 65321599; e-mail iraqbeijing@yahoo.com; Ambassador MOHAMMAD SABIR ISMAIL.

Ireland: 3 Ri Tan Dong Lu, Jian Guo Men Wai, Beijing 100600; tel. (10) 65322691; fax (10) 65326857; e-mail beijingembassy@dfa.ie; internet www.embassyofireland.cn; Ambassador DECLAN KELLEHER.

Israel: 17 Tian Ze Lu, Chao Yang Qu, Beijing 100600; tel. (10) 65327788; fax (10) 65327781; e-mail israemb@public3.bta.net.cn; internet beijing.mfa.gov.il; Ambassador AMOS NADAI.

Italy: 2 Dong Er Jie, San Li Tun, Beijing 100600; tel. (10) 85327600; fax (10) 65324676; e-mail ambasciata.pechino@esteri.it; internet www.ambpechino.esteri.it; Ambassador RICCARDO SESSA.

Jamaica: Office 6-2-72, Jian Guo Men Wai Diplomatic Compound, 1 Xiu Shui Jie, Beijing 100600; tel. (10) 65320667; fax (10) 65320669; e-mail embassy@jamaicagov.cn; internet www.jamaicagov.cn; Ambassador WAYNE MCCOOK.

Japan: 7 Ri Tan Lu, Jian Guo Men Wai, Beijing 100600; tel. (10) 65322361; fax (10) 65324625; e-mail info@eoj.cn; internet www.cn.emb-japan.go.jp; Ambassador YUJI MIYAMOTO.

Jordan: 5 Dong Liu Jie, San Li Tun, Beijing 100600; tel. (10) 65323906; fax (10) 65323283; e-mail beijingmission@jordan-embassy.com; Ambassador ANMAR ABDULHALIM NAMIR HARMUD.

THE PEOPLE'S REPUBLIC OF CHINA

Kazakhstan: 9 Dong Liu Jie, San Li Tun, Beijing 100600; tel. (10) 65324189; fax (10) 65326183; e-mail kz@kazembchina.org; internet www.kazembchina.org; Ambassador IKRAM ADYRBEKOV.

Kenya: 4 Xi Liu Jie, San Li Tun, Beijing 100600; tel. (10) 65323381; fax (10) 65321770; e-mail kenrepbj@hotmail.com; Ambassador RUTH SERETI SOLITEI.

Korea, Democratic People's Republic: Ri Tan Bei Lu, Jian Guo Men Wai, Beijing 100600; tel. (10) 65321186; fax (10) 65326056; Ambassador CHOE JIN SU.

Korea, Republic: 3rd–4th Floors, China World Trade Centre, 1 Jian Guo Men Wai Dajie, Beijing 100600; tel. (10) 65053171; fax (10) 65053458; e-mail consul@koreanembassy.cn; internet www.koreaemb.org.cn; Ambassador (vacant).

Kuwait: 23 Guang Hua Lu, Jian Guo Men Wai, Beijing 100600; tel. (10) 65322216; fax (10) 65321607; Ambassador FAISAL RASHED AL-GHAIS.

Kyrgyzstan: 2-4-1 Tayuan Diplomatic Office Bldg, Beijing 100600; tel. (10) 65326458; fax (10) 65326459; e-mail tianshan@kyrgyzstan.link263.com; Ambassador KADYRBEK T. SARBAYEV.

Laos: 11 Dong Si Jie, San Li Tun, Chao Yang Qu, Beijing 100600; tel. (10) 65321224; fax (10) 65326748; e-mail laoemcn@public.east.cn.net; Ambassador VICHIT XINDAVONG.

Latvia: Unit 71, Green Land Garden, No. 1A Green Land Rd, Chao Yang Qu, Beijing 100016; tel. (10) 64333863; fax (10) 64333810; e-mail embassy.china@mfa.gov.lv; internet www.latvianembassy.org.cn; Ambassador JANIS LOVNIKS.

Lebanon: 10 Dong Liu Jie, San Li Tun, Beijing 100600; tel. (10) 65322197; fax (10) 65322770; e-mail lebanon@public.bta.net.cn; Ambassador SLEIMAN RASSI.

Lesotho: 302 Dongwai Diplomatic Office Bldg, 23 Dong Zhi Men Wai Dajie, Chaoyang Qu, Beijing 100600; tel. (10) 65326843; fax (10) 65326845; e-mail boemeli@public.bta.net.en; Ambassador RACHOBOKOANE ANTHONY THIBELI.

Liberia: Rm 013, Gold Island Diplomatic Compound, 1 Xi Ba He Nanlu, Beijing 100028; tel. (10) 64403007; fax (10) 64403918; Ambassador NEH RITA SANGAI DUKULY TOLBERT.

Libya: 3 Dong Liu Jie, San Li Tun, Beijing 100600; tel. (10) 65323666; fax (10) 65323391; Secretary of the People's Bureau MUSTAFA M. EL-GUELUSHI.

Lithuania: B30 King's Garden, 18 Xiaoyun Lu, Chao Yang Qu, Beijing 100016; tel. (10) 84518520; fax (10) 84514442; e-mail amb.cn@urm.lt; internet cn.mfa.lt; Ambassador ROKAS BERNOTAS.

Luxembourg: 21 Nei Wu Bu Jie, Beijing 100600; tel. (10) 65135937; fax (10) 65137268; e-mail pekin.amb@mae.etat.lu; Ambassador CARLO KRIEGER.

Macedonia, former Yugoslav republic: 3-2-21 San Li Tun Diplomatic Office Bldg, Beijing 100600; tel. (10) 65327846; fax (10) 65327847; e-mail macdesch@public3.bta.net.cn; internet www.macedonianembassy.com.cn; Ambassador FATMIR DZELADINI.

Madagascar: 3 Dong Jie, San Li Tun, Beijing 100600; tel. (10) 65321353; fax (10) 65322102; e-mail ambpek@public2.bta.net.cn; Ambassador VICTOR SIKONINA.

Malawi: Beijing; Ambassador THENGO MALOYA.

Malaysia: 2 Liang Ma Qiao Bei Jie, Chao Yang Qu, San Li Tun, Beijing 100600; tel. (10) 65322531; fax (10) 65325032; e-mail mwbjing@kln.gov.my; Ambassador Dato' SYED NORULZAMAN.

Maldives: 1-5-31 Jian Guo Men Wai Diplomatic Compound, Jianwai Xiushui Lu, Chao Yang Qu, Beijing 100600; tel. (10) 85323847; fax (10) 85323746; e-mail admin@maldivesembassy.cn; Ambassador AHMED LATHEEF.

Mali: 8 Dong Si Jie, San Li Tun, Beijing 100600; tel. (10) 65321704; fax (10) 65321618; e-mail ambamali@163bj.com; Ambassador N'TJI LAICO TRAORÉ.

Malta: 1-52 San Li Tun Diplomatic Compound, Beijing 100600; tel. (10) 65323114; fax (10) 65326125; e-mail maltamembassy.beijing@gov.mt; Ambassador KARL XUEREB.

Mauritania: 9 Dong San Jie, San Li Tun, Beijing 100600; tel. (10) 65321346; fax (10) 65321685; Ambassador OULD TALEB AMAR SIDI MOHAMED.

Mauritius: 202 Dong Wai Diplomatic Office Bldg, 23 Dong Zhi Men Wai Dajie, Chao Yang Qu, Beijing 100600; tel. (10) 65325695; fax (10) 65325706; e-mail mebj@public.bta.net.cn; Ambassador PAUL REYNOLD LIT FONG CHONG LEUNG.

Mexico: 5 Dong Wu Jie, San Li Tun, Beijing 100600; tel. (10) 65321717; fax (10) 65323744; e-mail embmxchn@public.bta.net.cn; internet www.sre.gob.mx/china; Ambassador JORGE EUGENIO GUAJARDO GONZÁLEZ.

Micronesia, Federated States: 1-1-11 Jian Guo Men Wai Diplomatic Compound, Chao Yang Qu, Beijing 100010; e-mail embassy@fsmembassy.cn; Chargé d'affaires CARLSON D. APIS.

Moldova: 2-9-1 Tayuan Diplomatic Office Bldg, Beijing 100600; tel. (10) 65325494; fax (10) 65325379; e-mail beijing@mfa.md; Ambassador IACOV TIMCIUC.

Mongolia: 2 Xiu Shui Bei Jie, Jian Guo Men Wai, Beijing 100600; tel. (10) 65321203; fax (10) 65325045; e-mail mail@mongolembassychina.org; internet www.mongolembassychina.org; Ambassador GALSANGIIN BATSÜKH.

Montenegro: 3-1-12 San Li Tun Diplomatic Compound, Beijing 100600; tel. (10) 65327610; fax (10) 65327690; e-mail embmontenegro@yahoo.com; Chargé d'affaires a.i. LJILJANA TOSKOVIĆ.

Morocco: 16 San Li Tun Lu, Beijing 100600; tel. (10) 65321489; fax (10) 65321453; e-mail embmor@public.bta.net.cn; Ambassador MOHAMED CHERTI.

Mozambique: 1-7-2 Tayuan Diplomatic Office Bldg, Beijing 100600; tel. (10) 65323664; fax (10) 65325189; e-mail embamoc@public.bta.net.cn; Ambassador ANTÓNIO INÁCIO JÚNIOR.

Myanmar: 6 Dong Zhi Men Wai Dajie, Chao Yang Qu, Beijing 100600; tel. (10) 65321425; fax (10) 65321344; e-mail info@myanmarembassy.com; internet www.myanmarembassy.com; Ambassador U THEIN LWIN.

Namibia: 2-9-2 Tayuan Diplomatic Office Bldg, Beijing 100600; tel. (10) 65324810; fax (10) 65324549; e-mail namemb@eastnet.com.cn; Ambassador LEONARD NAMBAHU.

Nepal: 1 Xi Liu Jie, San Li Tun Lu, Beijing 100600; tel. (10) 65322739; fax (10) 65323251; e-mail beijing@nepalembassy.org.cn; internet www.nepalembassy.org.cn; Ambassador TANKA KARKI.

Netherlands: 4 Liang Ma He Nan Lu, Beijing 100600; tel. (10) 65321131; fax (10) 65324689; e-mail pek-cdp@minbuza.nl; internet www.hollandinchina.org; Ambassador DIRK JAN VAN DEN BERG.

New Zealand: 1 Ri Tan, Dong Er Jie, Chao Yang Qu, Beijing 100600; tel. (10) 65322731; fax (10) 65324317; e-mail nzemb@eastnet.com.cn; internet www.nzembassy.com/china; Ambassador ANTHONY PATRICK F. BROWNE.

Niger: 1-21 San Li Tun, Beijing 100600; tel. (10) 65324279; fax (10) 65327041; e-mail nigerbj@public.bta.net.cn; Ambassador ADAMOU BOUBAKAR.

Nigeria: 2 Dong Wu Jie, San Li Tun, Beijing; tel. (10) 65323631; fax (10) 65321650; Ambassador JONATHAN OLUWOLE COKER.

Norway: 1 Dong Yi Jie, San Li Tun, Beijing 100600; tel. (10) 65322261; fax (10) 65322392; e-mail emb.beijing@mfa.no; internet www.norway.cn; Ambassador SVEIN OLE SAETHER.

Oman: 6 Liang Ma He Nan Lu, San Li Tun, Beijing 100600; tel. (10) 65323692; fax (10) 65327185; Ambassador ABDULLAH SALEH AL-SAADII.

Pakistan: 1 Dong Zhi Men Wai Dajie, San Li Tun, Beijing 100600; tel. (10) 65322504; fax (10) 65322715; e-mail pakrepbeijing@yahoo.com; internet www.embassyofpakistan-beijing.org.cn; Ambassador SALMAN BASHIR.

Papua New Guinea: 2-11-2 Tayuan Diplomatic Office Bldg, Beijing 100600; tel. (10) 65324312; fax (10) 65325483; e-mail kundu_beijing@pngembassy.org.cn; internet www.pngembassy.org.cn; Ambassador JOHN MOMIS.

Peru: 1-91 San Li Tun, Bangonglou, Beijing 100600; tel. (10) 65323477; fax (10) 65322178; e-mail embaperu-pekin@rree.gob.pe; internet www.embperu.cn.net; Ambassador JESÚS J. WU LUY.

Philippines: 23 Xiu Shui Bei Jie, Jian Guo Men Wai, Beijing 100600; tel. (10) 65321872; fax (10) 65323761; e-mail main@philembassy-china.org; internet www.philembassy-china.org; Ambassador SONIA BRADY.

Poland: 1 Ri Tan Lu, Jian Guo Men Wai, Chao Yang Qu, Beijing 100600; tel. (10) 65321235; fax (10) 65321745; e-mail polska@public2.bta.net.cn; internet www.pekin.polemb.net; Ambassador KRZYSZTOF SZUMSKI.

Portugal: 8 San Li Tun Dong Wu Jie, Beijing 100600; tel. (10) 65323242; fax (10) 65324637; e-mail embport@public2.bta.net.cn; Ambassador RUI QUARTIN SANTOS.

Qatar: A7 Liang Maqiao Diplomatic Compound, Chao Yang Qu, Beijing 100600; tel. (10) 6532231; fax (10) 65325274; e-mail beijing@mofa.gov.qa; Ambassador ABDULLA A. AL-MUFTAH.

Romania: Ri Tan Lu, Dong Er Jie, Beijing 100600; tel. (10) 65323442; fax (10) 65325728; e-mail ambasada@roamb.link263.com; Ambassador VIOREL ISTICIOAIA-BUDURA.

Russia: 4 Dong Zhi Men Nei, Bei Zhong Jie, Beijing 100600; tel. (10) 65322051; fax (10) 65324851; e-mail embassy@russia.org.cn; internet www.russia.org.cn; Ambassador SERGEI SERGEEVICH RAZOV.

Rwanda: 30 Xiu Shui Bei Jie, Jian Guo Men Wai, Beijing 100600; tel. (10) 65322193; fax (10) 65322006; e-mail ambrwda@public3.bta.net.cn; Ambassador BEN MATHIAS RUGANGAZI.

THE PEOPLE'S REPUBLIC OF CHINA

Saudi Arabia: 1 Bei Xiao Jie, San Li Tun, Beijing 100600; tel. (10) 65324825; fax (10) 65325324; Ambassador SALEH BIN ABDUL-AZIZ AL-HUJYLAN.

Senegal: Diplomatic Office Bldg, 23 Dong Zhi Men Wai Da Jie, Beijing 100600; tel. (10) 65325035; fax (10) 65323730; Ambassador Gen. PAPE KHALILOU FALL.

Serbia: 1 Dong Liu Jie, San Li Tun, Beijing 100600; tel. (10) 65323516; fax (10) 65321207; e-mail ambjug@netchina.com.cn; internet www.embserbia.cn; Ambassador MIOMIR UDOVICKI.

Sierra Leone: 7 Dong Zhi Men Wai Dajie, Beijing 100600; tel. (10) 65322174; fax (10) 65323752; e-mail sejohnny@163bj.com; Ambassador SAHR E. JOHNNY.

Singapore: 1 Xiu Shui Bei Jie, Jian Guo Men Wai, Beijing 100600; tel. (10) 65323926; fax (10) 65322215; e-mail singemb_bej@sgmfa.gov.sg; internet www.mfa.gov.sg/beijing; Ambassador CHIN SIAT-YOON.

Slovakia: Ri Tan Lu, Jian Guo Men Wai, Beijing 100600; tel. (10) 65321531; fax (10) 65324814; e-mail slovak.emb.bj@svkmofabeijing.com; Ambassador ZIGMUND BERTÓK.

Slovenia: Block F, 57 Ya Qu Yuan, King's Garden Villas, 18 Xiao Yun Lu, Chao Yang Qu, Beijing 100016; tel. (10) 64681030; fax (10) 64681040; e-mail vpe@gov.si; internet beijing.embassy.si; Ambassador MARJAN CENCEN.

Somalia: 2 San Li Tun Lu, Beijing 100600; tel. and fax (10) 65321752; Ambassador MOHAMMED AHMED AWIL.

South Africa: 5 Dong Zhi Men Wai Dajie, Chao Yang Qu, Beijing 100600; tel. (10) 65320171; fax (10) 65327319; e-mail safrican@163bj.com; Ambassador NDUMISO NDIMA NTSHINGA.

Spain: 9 San Li Tun Lu, Beijing 100600; tel. (10) 65323629; fax (10) 65323401; e-mail embesp@public.bta.net.cn; internet www.mae.es/embajadas/pekin; Ambassador CARLOS BLASCO VILLA.

Sri Lanka: 3 Jian Hua Lu, Jian Guo Men Wai, Beijing 100600; tel. (10) 65321861; fax (10) 65325426; e-mail lkembj@public3.bta.cn.net; internet www.slemb.com; Ambassador KARUNATILAKA AMUNUGAMA.

Sudan: Bldg 27, San Li Tun, Beijing 100600; tel. (10) 65323715; fax (10) 65321280; e-mail mail@sudanembassychina.com; internet www.sudanembassychina.com; Ambassador MIRHGANI MOHAMED SALIH.

Suriname: 1-3-31 Diplomatic Compound, Jian Guo Men Wai, Beijing 100600; tel. (10) 65322938; fax (10) 65322941; e-mail surembchina@hotmail.com; Ambassador MOHAMED ISAAK SOEROKARSO.

Sweden: 3 Dong Zhi Men Wai Dajie, San Li Tun, Beijing 100600; tel. (10) 65329790; fax (10) 65325008; e-mail ambassaden.peking@foreign.ministry.se; internet www.swedenabroad.com/peking; Ambassador MIKAEL LINDSTRÖM.

Switzerland: 3 Dong Wu Jie, San Li Tun, Beijing 100600; tel. (10) 65322736; fax (10) 65324353; e-mail vertretung@bei.rep.admin.ch; Ambassador DANTE CANDIDO MARTINELLI.

Syria: 6 Dong Si Jie, San Li Tun, Beijing 100600; tel. (10) 65321563; fax (10) 65321575; e-mail sy@syria.org.cn; internet www.syria.org.cn; Ambassador MOHAMMED KHEIR AL-WADI.

Tajikistan: 5-1-41 Tayuan Diplomatic Office Bldg, Beijing 100600; tel. (10) 65322598; fax (10) 65323039; e-mail tjkemb@public2.bta.net.cn; Ambassador RASHID ALIMOV.

Tanzania: 8 Liang Ma He Nan Lu, San Li Tun, Beijing 100600; tel. (10) 65321491; fax (10) 65324351; e-mail tzrep@tanzaniaembassy.org.cn; internet www.tanzaniaembassy.org.cn; Ambassador OMAR RAMADHAN MAPURI.

Thailand: 40 Guang Hua Lu, Jian Guo Men Wai, Beijing 100600; tel. (10) 65321903; fax (10) 65321748; e-mail thaibej@public.bta.net.cn; internet www.thaiembbeij.org; Ambassador RATHAKIT MANATHAT.

Timor-Leste: Rm 156, Gold Island Diplomatic Compound, 1 Xi Ba He Nan Lu, Beijing 100028; tel. (10) 64403072; fax (10) 64403071; e-mail rdtlemb_beijing@yahoo.com; Ambassador OLIMPIO MARIA ALVES GOMES MIRANDA BRANCO.

Togo: 11 Dong Zhi Men Wai Dajie, Beijing 100600; tel. (10) 65322202; fax (10) 65325884; Ambassador NOLANA TA-AMA.

Tonga: Suite 3002, Embassy House, No. 18, Dong Zhi Men Wai Xiao Jie, Beijing 100027; tel. (10) 84499757; fax (10) 84499758; Ambassador EMELINE UHEINA TUITA.

Tunisia: 1 Dong Jie, San Li Tun, Beijing 100600; tel. (10) 65322435; fax (10) 65325818; e-mail at_beijing@public.netchina.com.cn; Ambassador Dr MOHAMED SAHBI BASLI.

Turkey: 9 Dong Wu Jie, San Li Tun, Beijing 100600; tel. (10) 65322490; fax (10) 65325480; e-mail embassy@turkey.org.cn; internet www.turkey.org.cn; Ambassador OKTAY ÖZÜYE.

Turkmenistan: King's Garden, Villa D-26, 18 Xiao Yuan Lu, Beijing; tel. (10) 65326975; fax (10) 65326976; e-mail China@a-1.net.cn; Ambassador (vacant).

Uganda: 5 Dong Jie, San Li Tun, Beijing 100600; tel. (10) 65321708; fax (10) 65322242; e-mail info@ugandaembassycn.org; internet www.ugandaembassycn.org; Ambassador CHARLES MADIBO WAGIDOSO.

Ukraine: 11 Dong Liu Jie, San Li Tun, Beijing 100600; tel. (10) 65324013; fax (10) 65326359; e-mail ukrembcn@public3.bta.net.cn; internet www.ukremb.cn; Ambassador SERHIY OLEKSIYOVYCH KAMYSHEV.

United Arab Emirates: 1-9-1, Ta Yuan Diplomatic Office Bldg, Beijing; tel. (10) 65322112; Ambassador MOHAMMED RASHID ALI AL-BOOT.

United Kingdom: 11 Guang Hua Lu, Jian Guo Men Wai, Beijing 100600; tel. (10) 65321961; fax (10) 65321937; internet www.uk.cn; Ambassador WILLIAM GEOFFREY EHRMAN.

USA: 3 Xiu Shui Bei Jie, Jian Guo Men Wai, Beijing 100600; tel. (10) 65323831; fax (10) 65323178; internet beijing.usembassy-china.org.cn; Ambassador CLARK THORP RANDT, Jr.

Uruguay: 1-11-2 Tayuan Diplomatic Office Bldg, Beijing 100600; tel. (10) 65324445; fax (10) 65327375; e-mail urubei@public.bta.net.cn; Ambassador LUIS LEONARDO ALMAGRO LEMES.

Uzbekistan: 11 Bei Xiao Jie, San Li Tun, Beijing 100600; tel. (10) 65326305; fax (10) 65326304; e-mail Embassy@uzbekistan.cn; internet www.uzbekistan.cn; Ambassador ALISHER A. SALAHITDINOV.

Vanuatu: 3-1-11 San Li Tun Diplomatic Compound, Beijing; tel. (10) 65320337; fax (10) 65320336; e-mail vanuatuembassybj@yahoo.com.cn; internet www.vanuatuembassy.org.cn; Ambassador LO CHI WAI.

Venezuela: 14 San Li Tun Lu, Beijing 100600; tel. (10) 65321295; fax (10) 65323817; e-mail embvenez@public.bta.net.cn; internet www.venezuela.org.cn; Ambassador ROCÍO MANEIRO GONZÁLEZ.

Viet Nam: 32 Guang Hua Lu, Jian Guo Men Wai, Beijing 100600; tel. (10) 65321155; fax (10) 65325720; Ambassador TRAN VAN LUAT.

Yemen: 5 Dong San Jie, San Li Tun, Beijing 100600; tel. (10) 65321558; fax (10) 65324305; e-mail info@embassyofyemen.net; internet www.embassyofyemen.net; Ambassador ABDULMALEK SULAIMAN M. AL-MUALEMI.

Zambia: 5 Dong Si Jie, San Li Tun, Chao Yang Qu, Beijing 100600; tel. (10) 65321554; fax (10) 65321891; e-mail admin@zambiaembassy-beijing.com; internet www.zambiaembassy-beijing.com; Ambassador DAVID SAVIYE.

Zimbabwe: 7 Dong San Jie, San Li Tun, Beijing 100600; tel. (10) 65323795; fax (10) 65325383; e-mail zimbei@163.bj.com; Ambassador CHRISTOPHER HATIKURI MUTSVANGWA.

Judicial System

The general principles of the Chinese judicial system are laid down in Articles 123–135 of the December 1982 Constitution (q.v.).

PEOPLE'S COURTS

Supreme People's Court: 27 Dongjiaomin Xiang, Beijing 100745; tel. (10) 65136195; e-mail info@court.gov.cn; internet www.court.gov.cn; f. 1949; the highest judicial organ of the State; handles first instance cases of national importance; handles cases of appeals and protests lodged against judgments and orders of higher people's courts and special people's courts, and cases of protests lodged by the Supreme People's Procuratorate in accordance with the procedures of judicial supervision; reviews death sentences meted out by local courts, supervises the administration of justice by local people's courts; interprets issues concerning specific applications of laws in judicial proceedings; its judgments and rulings are final; Pres. WANG SHENGJUN (five-year term of office coincides with that of National People's Congress, by which the President is elected).

Local People's Courts: comprise higher courts, intermediate courts and basic courts.

Special People's Courts: include military courts, maritime courts and railway transport courts.

PEOPLE'S PROCURATORATES

Supreme People's Procuratorate: 147 Beiheyan Dajie, Beijing 100726; tel. (10) 65126655; e-mail webmaster@spp.gov.cn; internet www.spp.gov.cn; acts for the National People's Congress in examining govt depts, civil servants and citizens, to ensure observance of the law; prosecutes in criminal cases; Procurator-Gen. CAO JIANMING (elected by the National People's Congress for a five-year term).

Local People's Procuratorates: undertake the same duties at the local level; ensure that the judicial activities of the people's courts, the execution of sentences in criminal cases and the activities of departments in charge of reform through labour conform to the law; institute, or intervene in, important civil cases that affect the interest of the State and the people.

Religion

The 1982 Constitution states that citizens enjoy freedom of religious belief and that legitimate religious activities are protected. Since 1994 all religious organizations have been required to register with the Bureau of Religious Affairs. In the late 1990s a new religious sect, Falun Gong (also known as Falun Dafa), emerged and quickly gained new adherents. However, the authorities banned the group, describing it as an 'evil cult'.

State Administration for Religious Affairs: 32 Beisantiao, Jiaodaokou, Dongcheng Qu, Beijing 100007; tel. (10) 64023355; fax (10) 66013565; Dir YE XIAOWEN.

ANCESTOR WORSHIP

Ancestor worship is believed to have originated with the deification and worship of all important natural phenomena. The divine and human were not clearly defined; all the dead became gods and were worshipped by their descendants. The practice has no code or dogma and the ritual is limited to sacrifices made during festivals and on birth and death anniversaries.

BUDDHISM

Buddhism was introduced into China from India in AD 67, and flourished during the Sui and Tang dynasties (6th–8th century), when eight sects were established. The Chan and Pure Land sects are the most popular. The dominant religion of Tibet (Xizang) is Tibetan Buddhism or Lamaism, a branch of Vajrayana Buddhism. According to official sources, in 1998 there were 9,500 Buddhist temples in China. There were 100m. believers in 1997.

Buddhist Association of China (BAC): f. 1953; Pres. YI CHENG; Sec.-Gen. XUE CHENG.

Tibetan Institute of Lamaism: Pres. BUMI JANGBALUOZHU; Vice-Pres. CEMOLIN DANZENGCHILIE.

14th Dalai Lama: His Holiness the Dalai Lama TENZIN GYATSO; spiritual and temporal leader of Tibet; fled to India following the failure of the Tibetan national uprising in 1959; resident at: Thekchen Choeling, McLeod Ganj, Dharamsala 176 219, Himachal Pradesh, India; tel. (91) 1892-21343; fax (91) 1892-21813; e-mail ohhdl@cta.unv.ernet.ind; internet www.tibet.com.

CHRISTIANITY

During the 19th century and the first half of the 20th century large numbers of foreign Christian missionaries worked in China. According to official sources, there were 10m. Protestants and more than 4m. Catholics in China in 2000, although unofficial sources estimate that the Christian total could be as high as 90m. The Catholic Church in China operates independently of the Vatican, although there is also an 'underground' Catholic Church, which is recognized by the Vatican. In addition, there is an increasing number of Christian sects in China.

Three-Self Patriotic Movement Committee of Protestant Churches of China: 219 Jiujiang Lu, Shanghai 200002; tel. (21) 63210806; fax (21) 63232605; internet www.chineseprotestantchurch.org; Pres. and acting Sec.-Gen. JI JIANHONG.

China Christian Council: 219 Jiujiang Lu, Shanghai 200002; tel. (21) 63210806; fax (21) 63232605; e-mail tspmccc@online.sh.cn; f. 1980; comprises provincial Christian councils; Pres. and acting Sec.-Gen. Rev. CAO SHENGJIE.

The Catholic Church: Catholic Mission, Si-She-Ku, Beijing; Bishop of Beijing JOSEPH LI SHAN.

Chinese Patriotic Catholic Association: Pres. MICHAEL FU TIESHAN; Sec.-Gen. LIU BAINIAN; c. 3m. mems (1988).

CONFUCIANISM

Confucianism is a philosophy and a system of ethics, without ritual or priesthood. The respect that adherents accord to Confucius is not bestowed on a prophet or god, but on a great sage whose teachings promote peace and good order in society and whose philosophy encourages moral living.

DAOISM

Daoism was founded by Zhang Daoling during the Eastern Han dynasty (AD 125–144). Lao Zi, a philosopher of the Zhou dynasty (born 604 BC), is its principal inspiration, and is honoured as Lord the Most High by Daoists. According to unofficial sources, there were 1,600 Daoist temples in China in 2005.

China Daoist Association: Temple of the White Cloud, Xi Bian Men, Beijing 100045; tel. (10) 6367179; e-mail chinadaosim@yahoo.com.cn; internet www.taoist.org.cn; f. 1957; Pres. REN FARONG; Sec.-Gen. YUAN BINGDONG.

ISLAM

According to Muslim history, Islam was introduced into China in AD 651. There were some 20.3m. adherents in China in 2000 according to official sources, mainly among the Wei Wuer (Uygur) and Hui people, although unofficial sources estimate that the total is far higher.

Beijing Islamic Association: Dongsi Mosque, Beijing; f. 1979; Chair. Imam Al-Hadji CHEN GUANGYUAN.

China Islamic Association: Beijing 100053; tel. (10) 63546384; fax (10) 63529483; f. 1953; Chair. Imam Al-Hadji CHEN GUANGYUAN; Sec.-Gen. YU ZHENGUI.

The Press

In 2006 China had 1,938 newspaper titles (including those below provincial level) and 9,468 periodicals. Each province publishes its own daily newspaper. The major newspapers and periodicals only are listed below.

PRINCIPAL NEWSPAPERS

Anhui Ribao (Anhui Daily): 206 Jinzhai Lu, Hefei, Anhui 230061; tel. (551) 2832626; fax (551) 2832534; e-mail ahch2005@163.com; internet www.anhuinews.com; Editor-in-Chief SUN BANGKUN.

Beijing Ribao (Beijing Daily): 34 Xi Biaobei Hutong, Dongdan, Beijing 100734; tel. (10) 85201155; fax (10) 65136522; internet www.bjd.com.cn; f. 1952; organ of the Beijing municipal cttee of the CCP; Dir WAN YUNLAI; Editor-in-Chief LIU ZONGMING; circ. 700,000.

Beijing Wanbao (Beijing Evening News): 34 Xi Biaobei Hutong, Dongdan, Beijing 100743; tel. (10) 65132233; fax (10) 65126581; internet www.ben.com.cn; f. 1958; Editor-in-Chief REN HUANYING; circ. 800,000.

Beijing Youth Daily: Beijing; internet www.bjyouth.com; national and local news; promotes ethics and social service; circ. 3m.–4m.

Changsha Wanbao (Changsha Evening News): 161 Caie Zhong Lu, Changsha, Hunan 410005; tel. (731) 4424457; fax (731) 4445167.

Chengdu Wanbao (Chengdu Evening News): Qingyun Nan Jie, Chengdu 610017; tel. (28) 664501; fax (28) 666597; circ. 700,000.

China Business Times: Beijing; f. 1989; Editor HUANG WENFU; circ. 500,000.

China Economic Times: tel. (10) 81785356; fax (10) 81787260; e-mail zgjjxww@vip.163.com; internet www.jjxww.com; economic news; publ. by the Development Research Centre of the State Council.

Chongqing Ribao (Chongqing Daily): Chongqing; Dir and Editor-in-Chief LI HUANIAN.

Chungcheng Wanbao (Chungcheng Evening News): 51 Xinwen Lu, Kunming, Yunnan 650032; tel. (871) 4144642; fax (871) 4154192.

Dazhong Ribao (Dazhong Daily): 46 Jinshi Lu, Jinan, Shandong 250014; tel. (531) 2968989; fax (531) 2962450; internet www.dzdaily.com.cn; f. 1939; Dir XU XIYU; Editor-in-Chief LIU GUANGDONG; circ. 2,100,000.

Fujian Ribao (Fujian Daily): Hualin Lu, Fuzhou, Fujian; tel. (591) 57756; e-mail fjdailya@163.com; internet www.fjdaily.com; daily; Dir HUANG SHIYUN; Editor-in-Chief HUANG ZHONGSHENG.

Gansu Ribao (Gansu Daily): Gansu; tel. (931) 8157213; fax (931) 8158955; e-mail gsdaily@vip.sohu.net; internet www.gansudaily.com.cn.

Gongren Ribao (Workers' Daily): Liupukang, Andingmen Wai, Beijing 100718; tel. (10) 64211561; fax (10) 64214890; f. 1949; trade union activities and workers' lives; also major home and overseas news; Dir LIU YUMING; Editor-in-Chief SHENG MINGFU; circ. 2.5m.

Guangming Ribao (Guangming Daily): 106 Yongan Lu, Beijing 100050; tel. (10) 63017788; fax (10) 63039387; internet www.guangmingdaily.com.cn; f. 1949; literature, art, science, education, history, economics, philosophy; Editor-in-Chief YUAN ZHIFA; circ. 920,000.

Guangxi Ribao (Guangxi Daily): Guangxi Region; Dir and Editor-in-Chief CHENG ZHENSHENG; circ. 650,000.

Guangzhou Ribao (Canton Daily): 10 Dongle Lu, Renmin Zhonglu, Guangzhou, Guangdong; tel. (20) 81887294; fax (20) 81862022; internet www.gzdaily.com; f. 1952; daily; social, economic and current affairs; Editor-in-Chief LI YUANJIANG; circ. 600,000.

Guizhou Ribao (Guizhou Daily): Guiyang, Guizhou; tel. (851) 627779; f. 1949; Dir GAO ZONGWEN; Editor-in-Chief GAN ZHENGSHU; circ. 300,000.

Hainan Ribao (Hainan Daily): 7 Xinhua Nan Lu, Haikou, Hainan 570001; tel. (898) 6222021; e-mail hnrb@hndaily.com.cn; internet hnrb.hinews.com; Dir ZHOU WENZHANG; Editor-in-Chief CHANG FUTANG.

THE PEOPLE'S REPUBLIC OF CHINA

Harbin Ribao (Harbin Daily): Harbin; internet www.harbindaily.com.

Hebei Ribao (Hebei Daily): 210 Yuhuazhong Lu, Shijiazhuang, Hebei 050013; tel. (311) 6048901; fax (311) 6046969; e-mail webmaster@hebeidaily.com; internet www.hebeidaily.com.cn; f. 1949; Dir GUO ZENGPEI; Editor-in-Chief PAN GUILIANG; circ. 500,000.

Heilongjiang Ribao (Heilongjiang Daily): Heilongjiang Province; Dir JIA HONGTU; Editor-in-Chief AI HE.

Henan Ribao (Henan Daily): 1 Weiyi Lu, Zhengzhou, Henan; tel. (371) 5958319; fax (371) 5955636; e-mail hnbynews@gmail.com; internet www.hnby.com.cn; f. 1949; Dir YANG YONGDE; Editor-in-Chief GUO ZHENGLING; circ. 390,000.

Huadong Xinwen (Eastern China News): f. 1995; published by Renmin Ribao.

Huanan Xinwen (South China News): Guangzhou; f. 1997; published by Renmin Ribao.

Hubei Ribao (Hubei Daily): 65 Huangli Lu, Wuhan, Hubei 430077; tel. (27) 6833522; fax (27) 6813989; f. 1949; Dir ZHOU NIANFENG; Editor-in-Chief SONG HANYAN; circ. 800,000.

Hulunbeir Ribao (Hulunbeir Daily): Hulunbeir; tel. (470) 8258009; fax (470) 8258035; e-mail hlbrdaily@163.com; internet www.hlbrdaily.com.cn.

Hunan Ribao (Hunan Daily): 18 Furong Zhong Lu, Changsha, Hunan 410071; tel. (731) 4312999; fax (731) 4314029; Dir JIANG XIANLI; Editor-in-Chief WAN MAOHUA.

Jiangxi Ribao (Jiangxi Daily): 175 Yangming Jie, Nanchang, Jiangxi; tel. (791) 6849888; fax (791) 6772590; f. 1949; Dir ZHOU JINGUANG; circ. 300,000.

Jiefang Ribao (Liberation Daily): 300 Han Kou Lu, Shanghai 200001; tel. (21) 63521111; fax (21) 63516517; e-mail info@jfdaily.com; internet www.jfdaily.com.cn; f. 1949; Editor-in-Chief JIA SHUMEI; circ. 1m.

Jiefangjun Bao (Liberation Army Daily): 34 Fuchengmenwai Dajie, Xicheng Qu, Beijing 100832; tel. (10) 68577779; fax (10) 68577779; e-mail feedback@pladaily.com.cn; internet www.chinamil.com.cn; f. 1956; official organ of the Central Military Comm; Dir Maj.-Gen. ZHANG SHIGANG; Editor-in-Chief WANG MENGYUN; circ. 800,000.

Jilin Ribao (Jilin Daily): Jilin Province; Dir and Editor-in-Chief YI HONGBIN.

Jingji Ribao (Economic Daily): 2 Bai Zhi Fang Dong Jie, Beijing 100054; tel. (10) 63559988; fax (10) 63539408; e-mail jjrbtg@ced.com.cd; internet www.economicdaily.com.cn; f. 1983; financial affairs, domestic and foreign trade; administered by the State Council; Editor-in-Chief TUO ZHEN; circ. 1.2m.

Jinrong Shibao (Financial News): 44 Taipingqiao Fengtaiqu, Beijing 100073; tel. (10) 63269233; fax (10) 68424931.

Liaoning Ribao (Liaoning Daily): Liaoning Province; e-mail dudan@lndaily.com.cn; internet www.lndaily.com.cn; Dir XIE ZHENGQIAN.

Nanfang Ribao (Nanfang Daily): 289 Guangzhou Da Lu, Guangzhou, Guangdong 510601; tel. (20) 87373998; fax (20) 87375203; internet www.nanfangdaily.com.cn/southnews; f. 1949; Nanfang Daily Group also publishes *Nanfang Dushi Bao* (Southern Metropolis Daily), *Ershiyi Shiji Jingji Baodao* (21st Century Economic Herald), and weekly edn *Nanfang Zhoumou* (Southern Weekend); circ. 1m.

Nanjing Ribao (Nanjing Daily): 53 Jiefang Lu, Nanjing, Jiangsu 210016; tel. (25) 4496564; fax (25) 4496544; e-mail bwdh@longhoo.net; internet www.njrb.com.cn.

Nongmin Ribao (Peasants' Daily): Shilipu Beili, Chao Yang Qu, Beijing 100025; tel. (10) 65005522; fax (10) 65071154; f. 1980; 6 a week; circulates in rural areas nation-wide; Dir ZHANG DEXIU; Editor-in-Chief ZHANG WENBAO; circ. 1m.

Renmin Ribao (People's Daily): 2 Jin Tai Xi Lu, Chao Yang Qu, Beijing 100733; tel. (10) 65368971; fax (10) 65368974; e-mail info@peopledaily.com.cn; internet www.people.com.cn; f. 1948; organ of the CCP; also publishes overseas edn; Pres. WANG CHEN; Editor-in-Chief ZHANG YANNONG; circ. 2.15m.

Shaanxi Ribao (Shaanxi Daily): Shaanxi Province; tel. (29) 82267114; fax (29) 82268082; e-mail sxdaily@tom.com; internet www.sxdaily.com.cn; Dir LI DONGSHENG; Editor-in-Chief DU YAO-FENG.

Shanxi Ribao (Shanxi Daily): 24 Shuangtasi Jie, Taiyuan, Shanxi; tel. (351) 446561; fax (351) 441771; internet www.sxrb.com; Dir ZHAO WENBIN; Editor-in-Chief LI DONGXI; circ. 300,000.

Shenzhen Tequ Bao (Shenzhen Special Economic Zone Daily): 4 Shennan Zhonglu, Shenzhen 518009; tel. (755) 3902688; fax (755) 3906900; internet www.sznews.com/tqb; f. 1982; reports on special economic zones, as well as mainland, Hong Kong and Macao; Editor-in-Chief HUANG YANGLUE.

Sichuan Ribao (Sichuan Daily): Sichuan Daily Press Group, 70 Hongxing Zhong Lu, Erduan, Chengdu, Sichuan 610012; tel. and fax (28) 86968000; e-mail 028@scol.com.cn; internet www.scol.com.cn; internet www.sichuandaily.com.cn; f. 1952; Chair. of Bd YU CHANGQIU; Editor-in-Chief LUO XIAOGANG; circ. 8m.

Tianjin Ribao (Tianjin Daily): 873 Dagu Nan Lu, Heri Qu, Tianjin 300211; tel. (22) 7301024; fax (22) 7305803; e-mail info@tjrb.com.cn; internet www.tianjindaily.com.cn; f. 1949; Dir and Editor-in-Chief ZHANG JIANXING; circ. 600,000.

Wenhui Bao (Wenhui Daily): 50 Huqiu Lu, Shanghai 200002; tel. (21) 63211410; fax (21) 63230198; internet wenhui.news365.com.cn; f. 1938; Editor-in-Chief WU ZHENBIAO; circ. 500,000.

Xin Jing Bao (The Beijing News): Beijing; tel. (10) 67106666; e-mail webmaster@thebeijingnews.com; internet news.thebeijingnews.com; f. 2003 as jt venture by owners of Guangming Ribao and Nanfang Ribao; Editor-in-chief (vacant).

Xin Min Wan Bao (Xin Min Evening News): 839 Yan An Zhong Lu, Shanghai 200040; tel. (21) 62791234; fax (21) 62473220; e-mail newmedia@wxjt.com.cn; internet xmwb.news365.com.cn; f. 1929; specializes in public policy, education and social affairs; Editor-in-Chief HU JINGJUN; circ. 1.8m.

Xinhua Ribao (New China Daily): 55 Zhongshan Lu, Nanjing, Jiangsu 210005; tel. (21) 741757; fax (21) 741023; internet www.xinhua.org; Editor-in-Chief ZHOU ZHENGRONG; circ. 900,000.

Xinjiang Ribao (Xinjiang Daily): Xinjiang Region; tel. (991) 5593359; fax (991) 5859962; e-mail info@xjdaily.com; internet www.xjdaily.com; Editor-in-Chief HUANG YANCAI.

Xizang Ribao (Tibet Daily): Tibet; Editor-in-Chief LI ERLIANG.

Yangcheng Wanbao (Yangcheng Evening News): 733 Dongfeng Dong Lu, Guangzhou, Guangdong 510085; tel. (20) 87776211; fax (20) 87664985; internet www.ycwb.com; f. 1957; Editor-in-Chief PAN WEIWEN; circ. 1.3m.

Yunnan Ribao (Yunnan Daily): 51 Xinwen Lu, Kunming 650032; tel. (871) 5031269; fax (871) 5031264; e-mail ynrb-zbs@yndaily.com; internet www.yndaily.com; Editor-in-Chief SUN GUANSHENG.

Zhejiang Ribao (Zhejiang Daily): Zhejiang Province; e-mail zjrb@zjnews.com.cn; internet zjdaily.zjol.com.cn; f. 1949; Dir CHEN MINER; Editor-in-Chief YANG DAJIN.

Zhongguo Qingnian Bao (China Youth Daily): 2 Haiyuncang, Dong Zhi Men Nei, Dongcheng Qu, Beijing 100702; tel. (10) 64098088; fax (10) 64098077; e-mail cehuabu@cyol.com; internet www.cyol.net; f. 1951; daily; aimed at 14–40 age-group; Dir XU ZHUQING; Editor-in-Chief CHEN XIAOCHUAN; circ. 1.0m.

Zhongguo Ribao (China Daily): 15 Huixin Dongjie, Chao Yang Qu, Beijing 100029; tel. (10) 64995000; fax (10) 64918377; internet www.chinadaily.com.cn; f. 1981; English; China's political, economic and cultural developments; world, financial and sports news; also publishes Business Weekly (f. 1985), Beijing Weekend (f. 1991), Shanghai Star (f. 1992), Reports from China (f. 1992), 21st Century (f. 1993), China Daily Hong Kong Edition; Editor-in-Chief ZHU LING; circ. 300,000.

Zhongguo Xinwen (China News): 12 Baiwanzhuang Nanjie, Beijing 10037; tel. (10) 88387443; fax (10) 68327649; e-mail zhangqinghua@chinanews.com.cn; internet www.chinanews.com.cn; f. 1952; daily; current affairs; Editor-in-Chief WANG XIJIN.

SELECTED PERIODICALS

Ban Yue Tan (China Comment): Beijing; tel. (10) 6668521; internet www.xinhuanet.com/banyt; f. 1980; in Chinese and Wei Wuer (Uygur); Editor-in-Chief DONG RUISHENG; circ. 6m.

Beijing Review: 24 Baiwanzhuang Lu, Beijing 100037; tel. (10) 68326085; fax (10) 68326628; e-mail bjreview@public3.bta.net.cn; internet www.bjreview.com.cn; f. 1958; weekly; edns in English, French, Spanish, Japanese and German; also *Chinafrica* (monthly in English and French); Publr WANG GANGYI; Editor-in-Chief LII HAIBO.

BJ TV Weekly: 2 Fu Xing Men Wai Zhenwumiao Jie, Beijing 100045; tel. (10) 6366036; fax (10) 63262388; circ. 1m.

Caijing: 10th Floor, Prime Tower 22 Chaoyangmenwai Lu, Beijing 100020; tel. (10) 65885047; fax (10) 65885046; e-mail money1@homeway.com.cn; internet www.caijing.com.cn/english/; f. 1998; business and finance; 2 a month; Editor HU SHULI.

China TV Weekly: 15 Huixin Dong Jie, Chao Yang Qu, Beijing 100013; tel. (10) 64214197; circ. 1.7m.

Chinese Literature Press: 24 Baiwanzhuang Lu, Beijing 100037; tel. (10) 68326010; fax (10) 68326678; e-mail chinalit@public.east.cn.net; f. 1951; monthly (bilingual in English); quarterly (bilingual in French); contemporary and classical writing, poetry, literary criticism and arts; Exec. Editor LING YUAN.

Dianying Xinzuo (New Films): 796 Huaihai Zhong Lu, Shanghai; tel. (21) 64379710; f. 1979; bi-monthly; introduces new films.

Dianzi yu Diannao (Compotech China): Beijing; internet www.compotech.com.cn; f. 1985; popular information on computers and microcomputers.

Elle (China): 14 Lane 955, Yan'an Zhong Lu, Shanghai; tel. (21) 62790974; fax (21) 62479056; internet www.ellechina.com; f. 1988; monthly; fashion; Pres. YANG XINCI; Chief Editor WU YING; circ. 300,000.

Family Magazine: 14 Siheng Lu, Xinhepu, Dongshan Qu, Guangzhou 510080; tel. (20) 7777718; fax (20) 7185670; monthly; circ. 2.5m.

Feitian (Fly Skywards): 50 Donggan Xilu, Lanzhou, Gansu; tel. (931) 25803; f. 1961; monthly.

Guoji Xin Jishu (New International Technology): Zhanwang Publishing House, Beijing; f. 1984; also publ. in Hong Kong; international technology, scientific and technical information.

Guowai Keji Dongtai (Recent Developments in Science and Technology Abroad): Institute of Scientific and Technical Information of China, 54 San Li He Lu, Beijing 100045; tel. (10) 68570713; fax (10) 68511839; e-mail kjdt@istic.ac.cn; internet www.wanfang.com.cn; f. 1962; monthly; scientific journal; Editor-in-Chief GUO YUEHUA; circ. 40,000.

Hai Xia (The Strait): 27 De Gui Xiang, Fuzhou, Fujian; tel. (10) 33656; f. 1981; quarterly; literary journal; CEOs YANG YU, JWO JONG LIN.

Huasheng Monthly (Voice for Overseas Chinese): 12 Bai Wan Zhuang Nan Jie, Beijing 100037; tel. (10) 68311578; fax (10) 68315039; internet www.hsm.com.cn; f. 1995; monthly; intended mainly for overseas Chinese and Chinese nationals resident abroad; Editor-in-Chief FAN DONGSHENG.

Jianzhu (Construction): Baiwanzhuang, Beijing; tel. (10) 68992849; f. 1956; monthly; Editor FANG YUEGUANG; circ. 500,000.

Jinri Zhongguo (China Today): 24 Baiwanzhuang Lu, Beijing 100037; tel. (10) 68326037; fax (10) 68328338; e-mail chinahoy@chinatoday.com; internet www.chinatoday.com.cn; f. 1952; fmrly China Reconstructs; monthly; edns in English, Spanish, French, Arabic and Chinese; economic, social and cultural affairs; illustrated; Pres. and Editor-in-Chief HUANG ZU'AN.

Liaowang (Outlook): 57 Xuanwumen Xijie, Beijing; tel. (10) 63073049; internet news.sohu.com/liaowang; f. 1981; weekly; current affairs; Gen. Man. ZHOU YICHANG; Editor-in-Chief JI BIN; circ. 500,000.

Luxingjia (Traveller): Beijing; tel. (10) 6552631; f. 1955; monthly; Chinese scenery, customs, culture.

Meishu Zhi You (Chinese Art Digest): 32 Beizongbu Hutong, East City Region, Beijing; tel. (10) 65591404; f. 1982; every 2 months; art review journal, also providing information on fine arts publs in China and abroad; Editors ZONGYUAN GAO, PEI CHENG.

Nianqingren (Young People): 169 Mayuanlin, Changsha, Hunan; tel. (731) 23610; f. 1981; monthly; general interest for young people.

Nongye Zhishi (Agricultural Knowledge): 21 Ming Zi Qian Lu, Jinan, Shandong 250100; tel. (531) 8932238; e-mail sdnyzs@jn-public.sd.cninfo.net; internet www.sdny.com.cn; f. 1950; fortnightly; popular agricultural science; Dir YANG LIJIAN; circ. 410,000.

Qiushi (Seeking Truth): 2 Shatan Beijie, Beijing 100727; tel. (10) 64037005; fax (10) 64018174; f. 1988; succeeded Hong Qi (Red Flag); 2 a month; theoretical journal of the CCP; Editor-in-Chief LI BAOSHAN; circ. 1.83m.

Renmin Huabao (China Pictorial): 33 Chegongzhuang Xilu, Haidian Qu, Beijing 10004; tel. (10) 68411144; fax (10) 68413023; e-mail xubu61@163.com; internet www.chinapictorial.com.cn; f. 1950; monthly; edns: two in Chinese, one in Tibetan and 12 in foreign languages; Dir and Editor-in-Chief ZHANG JIAHUA.

Shufa (Calligraphy): 81 Qingzhou Nan Lu, Shanghai 200233; tel. (21) 64519008; fax (21) 64519015; f. 1977; every 2 months; journal on ancient and modern calligraphy; Chief Editor LU FUSHENG.

Tiyu Kexue (Sports Science): 11 Tiyuguan Lu, Beijing 100061; tel. (10) 87182588; fax (10) 67181293; f. 1981; sponsored by the China Sports Science Soc; monthly; in Chinese; summary in English; Chief Officer TIAN YE; circ. 5,000.

Wenxue Qingnian (Youth Literature Journal): 27 Mu Tse Fang, Wenzhou, Zhejiang; tel. (577) 3578; f. 1981; monthly; Editor-in-Chief CHEN YUSHEN; circ. 80,000.

Women of China English Monthly: 15 Jian Guo Men Dajie, Beijing 100730; tel. (10) 65134616; fax (10) 65225380; e-mail geo@womenofchina.com.cn; internet www.womenofchina.com.cn; f. 1956; monthly; in English; administered by All-China Women's Federation; women's rights and status, views and lifestyle, education and arts, etc.; Editor-in-Chief YUN PENGJU.

Xian Dai Faxue (Modern Law Science): Southwest University of Political Science and Law, Chongqing, Sichuan 400031; tel. (23) 65382256; fax (23) 65382527; e-mail lsp57120@163.com; internet www.swupl.edu.cn; f. 1979; bi-monthly; with summaries in English; Editor-in-Chief SUN CHANGYONG.

Yinyue Aihaozhe (Music Lovers): 74 Shaoxing Lu, Shanghai 200020; tel. (21) 64372608; fax (21) 64332019; f. 1979; every 2 months; music knowledge; illustrated; Editor-in-Chief CHEN XUEYA; circ. 50,000.

Zhongguo Duiwai Maoyi Ming Lu (Directory of China's Foreign Trade): CCPIT Bldg, 1 Fuxingmen Wai Dajie, Beijing 100860; tel. (10) 68022948; fax (10) 68510201; e-mail inform@press-media.com; f. 1974; monthly; edns in Chinese and English; information on Chinese imports and exports, foreign trade and economic policies; Editor-in-Chief YANG HAIQING.

Zhongguo Ertong (Chinese Children): 21 Xiang 12, Dongsi, Beijing; tel. (10) 6444761; f. 1980; monthly; illustrated journal for elementary school pupils.

Zhongguo Guangbo Dianshi (China Radio and Television): 12 Fucheng Lu, Beijing; tel. (10) 6896217; f. 1982; monthly; reports and comments.

Zhongguo Sheying (Chinese Photography): 61 Hongxing Hutong, Dongdan, Beijing 100005; tel. (10) 65252277; fax (10) 65257623; e-mail cphoto@public.bta.net.cn; internet www.cphoto.com.cn; f. 1957; monthly; photographs and comments; Editor WEN DANQING.

Zhongguo Zhenjiu (Chinese Acupuncture and Moxibustion): China Academy of Traditional Chinese Medicine, Dongzhimen Nei, Beijing 100700; tel. (10) 84014607; fax (10) 84046331; e-mail webmaster@cjacupuncture.com; internet www.cjacupuncture.com; f. 1981; monthly; publ. by Chinese Soc. of Acupuncture and Moxibustion; abstract in English; Editor-in-Chief Prof. DENG LIANGYUE.

Other popular magazines include *Gongchandang Yuan* (Communists, circ. 1.63m.) and *Nongmin Wenzhai* (Peasants' Digest, circ. 3.54m.).

NEWS AGENCIES

Xinhua (New China) News Agency: 57 Xuanwumen Xi Dajie, Beijing 100803; tel. (10) 63071114; fax (10) 63071210; internet www.xinhuanet.com; f. 1931; offices in all Chinese provincial capitals, and about 100 overseas bureaux; news service in Chinese, English, French, Spanish, Portuguese, Arabic and Russian, feature and photographic services; Pres. TIAN CONGMING; Editor-in-Chief HE PING.

Zhongguo Xinwen She (China News Service): POB 1114, Beijing; e-mail xiansuo@chinanews.com.cn; internet www.chinanews.cn; f. 1952; office in Hong Kong; supplies news features, special articles and photographs for newspapers and magazines in Chinese printed overseas; services in Chinese; Dir WANG SHIGU.

PRESS ORGANIZATIONS

All China Journalists' Association: Xijiaominxiang, Beijing 100031; tel. (10) 66023981; fax (10) 66014658; Chair. SHAO HUAZE.

China Newspapers Association: Beijing; Chair. WANG CHEN.

The Press and Publication Administration of the People's Republic of China (State Copyright Bureau): 85 Dongsi Nan Dajie, East District, Beijing 100703; tel. (10) 65124433; fax (10) 65127875; Dir SHI ZONGYUAN.

Publishers

In 2003 there were 570 publishing houses in China. A total of 233,971 titles (and 6,465m. copies) were published in 2006. In 2004 it was announced that foreign companies were to be allowed to enter the book distribution market. However, direct involvement by foreign companies in the publishing business remained restricted.

Beijing Chubanshe Chuban Jituan (Beijing Publishing House Group): 6 Bei Sanhuan Zhong Lu, Beijing 100011; tel. (10) 62016699; fax (10) 62012339; e-mail public@bphg.com.cn; internet www.bph.com.cn; f. 1956; politics, history, law, economics, geography, science, literature, art, etc.; Dir ZHU SHUXIN; Editor-in-Chief TAO XINCHENG.

Beijing Daxue Chubanshe (Beijing University Press): 205 Chengfu Lu, Zhongguancun, Haidian Qu, Beijing 100871; tel. (10) 62752024; fax (10) 62556201; internet cbs.pku.edu.cn; f. 1979; academic and general.

China International Book Trading Corpn: POB 399, 35 Chegongzhuang Xilu, Beijing 100044; tel. (10) 68433113; fax (10) 68420340; e-mail bk@mail.cibtc.co.cn; internet www.cibtc.com.cn; f. 1949; foreign trade org. specializing in publs, including books, periodicals, art and crafts, microfilms, etc.; import and export distributors; Pres. QI PINGJIN.

China Publishing Group (CPG): Beijing; e-mail zq@cnpubg.com; internet www.cnpubg.com; f. 2002; aims to restructure and consolidate publishing sector; comprises 29 major publishing houses, including the People's Publishing House, the Commercial Press, Zhonghua Book Co, Encyclopedia of China Publishing House, China Fine Arts Publishing Group, People's Music Publishing House, SDX Joint Publishing Co, China Translation and Publishing Corpn, Orient Publishing Centre; also includes three publications wholesalers: Xinhua Bookstore Head Office, China National Publishing Industry Trading Corpn and China National Publications Import & Export (Group) Corpn; Pres. of the Bd YANG MUZHI.

CITIC Publishing House: Tayuan Diplomatic Office Bldg, 14 Liangmahe Lu, Chao Yang Qu, Beijing 100600; tel. (10) 85323366; fax (10) 85322505; e-mail liyinghong@citicpub.com; internet www.publish.citic.com; f. 1988; finance, investment, economics and business; Pres. WANG BIN.

Dianzi Gongye Chubanshe (Publishing House of the Electronics Industry—PHEI): 288 Jin Jia Cun, Wanshou Nan Lu, Beijing 100036; tel. (10) 68159028; fax (10) 68159025; internet www.phei.com.cn; f. 1982; electronic sciences and technology; Pres. LIANG XIANGFENG; Vice-Pres. WANG MINGJUN.

Dolphin Books: 24 Baiwanzhuang Lu, Beijing 100037; tel. (10) 68997480; fax (10) 68326642; internet www.dolphin-books.com.cn; f. 1986; children's books in Chinese and foreign languages; Dir WANG YANRONG.

Falü Chubanshe (Law Publishing House): Lianhuachi Xili, Fengtai Qu, Beijing 100073; tel. (10) 63939796; fax 63939622; e-mail international@lawpress.com.cn; internet www.lawpress.com.cn; f. 1980; current laws and decrees, legal textbooks, translations of important foreign legal works; Dir LAN MINGLIANG.

Foreign Languages Press: 19 Chegongzhuang Xi Lu, Fu Xing Men Wai, Beijing 100044; tel. (10) 68413344; fax (10) 68424931; e-mail info@flp.com.cn; internet www.flp.com.cn; f. 1952; books in 20 foreign languages reflecting political and economic developments in People's Republic of China and features of Chinese culture; Dir GUO JIEXIN; Editor-in-Chief XU MINGQIANG.

Gaodeng Jiaoyu Chubanshe (Higher Education Press): 4 Dewai Dajie, Xicheng Qu, Beijing 100011; tel. (10) 82085550; fax (10) 82085552; e-mail international@hep.edu.cn; internet www.hep.edu.cn; f. 1954; academic, textbooks; Pres. LIU ZHIPENG; Editor-in-Chief ZHANG ZENGSHUN.

Gongren Chubanshe (Workers' Publishing House): Liupukeng, Andingmen Wai, Beijing; tel. (10) 64215278; f. 1949; labour movement, trade unions, science and technology related to industrial production.

Guangdong Keji Chubanshe (Guangdong Science and Technology Press): 11 Shuiyin Lu, Huanshidong Lu, Guangzhou, Guangdong 510075; tel. and fax (20) 37607770; e-mail gdkjzbb@21cn.com; internet www.gdstp.com.cn; f. 1978; natural sciences, technology, agriculture, medicine, computing, English language teaching; Dir HUANG DAQUAN.

Heilongjiang Kexue Jishu Chubanshe (Heilongjiang Science and Technology Press): 41 Jianshe Jie, Nangang Qu, Harbin 150001, Heilongjiang; tel. and fax (451) 3642127; f. 1979; industrial and agricultural technology, natural sciences, economics and management, popular science, children's and general.

Huashan Wenyi Chubanshe (Huashan Literature and Art Publishing House): 45 Bei Malu, Shijiazhuang, Hebei; tel. (0311) 22501; f. 1982; novels, poetry, drama, etc.

Kexue Chubanshe (Science Press): 16 Donghuangchenggen Beijie, Beijing 100717; tel. (10) 64034313; fax (10) 64020094; e-mail webmaster@mail.sciencep.com; internet www.sciencep.com; f. 1954; books and journals on science and technology.

Lingnan Meishu Chubanshe (Lingnan Art Publishing House): 11 Shuiyin Lu, Guangzhou, Guangdong 510075; tel. (20) 87771044; fax (20) 87771049; f. 1981; works on classical and modern painting, picture albums, photographic, painting techniques; Pres. CAO LIXIANG.

Minzu Chubanshe (The Ethnic Publishing House): 14 Anwai Hepingli Beijie, Beijing 100013; tel. and fax (10) 64211126; e-mail e56@e56.com.cn; internet www.e56.com.cn; f. 1953; books and periodicals in minority languages, e.g. Mongolian, Tibetan, Uygur, Korean, Kazakh, etc.; Editor-in-Chief HUANG ZHONGCAI.

Qunzhong Chubanshe (Masses Publishing House): Bldg 15, Part 3, Fangxingyuan, Fangzhuan Lu, Beijing 100078; tel. (10) 67633344; f. 1956; politics, law, judicial affairs, criminology, public security, etc.

Renmin Chubanshe (People's Publishing House): 8 Hepinglidongjie, Andingmenwai, Beijing; tel. (10) 4213713; f. 1950; managed by the Ministry of Communications; publishes works on Marxism-Leninism, Mao Zedong Thought and Deng Xiaoping Theories, compilations of CCP and government documentation and laws, collected works and biographies of CCP and government leaders, and academic works in such fields as philosophy, social sciences, arts and culture and biography; Dir and Editor-in-Chief XUE DEZHEN.

Renmin Jiaoyu Chubanshe (People's Education Press): 55 Sha Tan Hou Jie, Beijing 100009; tel. (10) 58758866; fax (10) 58758833; e-mail pep@pep.com.cn; internet www.pep.com.cn; f. 1950; school textbooks, guidebooks, teaching materials, etc.

Renmin Meishu Chubanshe (People's Fine Arts Publishing House): Beijing; tel. (10) 65122371; fax (10) 65122370; f. 1951; works by Chinese and foreign painters, sculptors and other artists, picture albums, photographic, painting techniques; Dir GAO ZONGYUAN; Editor-in-Chief CHENG DALI.

Renmin Weisheng Chubanshe (People's Medical Publishing House): 3, 3 Qu, Fang Qun Yuan, Fang Zhuang, Beijing 100078; tel. (10) 67616688; fax (10) 67617314; e-mail pmph@pmph.com; internet www.pmph.com; f. 1953; medicine (Western and traditional Chinese), pharmacology, dentistry, public health; Pres. HU GUOCHEN.

Renmin Wenxue Chubanshe (People's Literature Publishing House): 166 Chaoyangmen Nei Dajie, Beijing 100705; tel. and fax (10) 65138394; e-mail rwbq@sina.com; internet www.rw-cn.com; f. 1951; largest publr of literary works and translations into Chinese; Dir LIU YUSHAN; Editor-in-Chief GUAN SHIGUANG.

Shanghai Guji Chubanshe (Shanghai Classics Publishing House): 272 Ruijin Erlu, Shanghai 200020; tel. (21) 64370011; fax (21) 64339287; e-mail guji1@guji.com.cn; internet www.guji.com.cn; f. 1956; classical Chinese literature, history, art, philosophy, geography, linguistics, science and technology.

Shanghai Jiaoyu Chubanshe (Shanghai Education Publishing House): 123 Yongfu Lu, Shanghai 200031; tel. (21) 64377165; fax (21) 64339995; e-mail webmaster@seph.com.cn; internet www.seph.com.cn; f. 1958; academic; Dir and Editor-in-Chief NAN-LINE BAO.

Shanghai Yiwen Chubanshe (Shanghai Translation Publishing House): 193 Fujian Lu, Shanghai 200001; tel. (21) 53594508; fax (21) 63914291; e-mail info@yiwen.com.cn; internet www.yiwen.com.cn; f. 1978; translations of foreign classic and modern literature; philosophy, social sciences, dictionaries, etc.

Shangwu Yinshuguan (The Commercial Press): 36 Wangfujing Dajie, Beijing 100710; tel. (10) 65252026; fax (10) 65134942; e-mail billyhu@sohu.com; internet www.cp.com.cn; f. 1897; dictionaries and reference books in Chinese and foreign languages, translations of foreign works on social sciences; Editor HU LONGBIAO; Pres. YANG DEYAN.

Shaonian Ertong Chubanshe (Juvenile and Children's Publishing House): 1538 Yan An Xi Lu, Shanghai 200052; tel. (21) 62823025; fax (21) 62821726; e-mail forwardz@public4.sta.net.cn; f. 1952; children's educational and literary works, teaching aids and periodicals; Gen. Man. ZHOU SHUNPEI.

Shijie Wenhua Chubanshe (World Culture Publishing House): Dir ZHU LIE.

Wenwu Chubanshe (Cultural Relics Publishing House): 29 Wusi Dajie, Beijing 100009; tel. (10) 64048057; fax (10) 64010698; e-mail web@wenwu.com; internet www.wenwu.com; f. 1956; books and catalogues of Chinese relics in museums and those recently discovered; Dir SU SHISHU.

Wuhan Daxue Chubanshe (Wuhan University Press): Luojia Hill, Wuhan, Hubei; tel. (27) 68752069; fax (27) 68754094; e-mail wdp3@whu.edu.cn; internet www.wdp.com.cn; f. 1981; reference books, academic works, maps, audio-visual works, etc.; Pres. Prof. CHEN QINGHUI.

Xiandai Chubanshe (Modern Press): 504 Anhua Li, Andingmenwai, Beijing 100011; tel. (10) 64263515; fax (10) 64214540; f. 1981; directories, reference books, etc.; Dir ZHOU HONGLI.

Xinhua Chubanshe (Xinhua Publishing House): 8 Jungyuan Lu, Shijingshan, Beijing 100000; tel. (10) 63074407; fax (10) 63073880; e-mail wjybox@xinhuanet.com; f. 1979; social sciences, economy, politics, history, geography, directories, dictionaries, etc.; Dir LUO HAIYUAN.

Xuelin Chubanshe (Scholar Books Publishing House): 120 Wenmiao Lu, Shanghai 200010; tel. and fax (21) 63768540; f. 1981; academic, including personal academic works at authors' own expense; Dir LEI QUNMING.

Zhongguo Caizheng Jingji Chubanshe (China Financial and Economic Publishing House): 8 Dafosi Dongjie, Dongcheng Qu, Beijing; tel. (10) 64011805; internet www.cfeph.cn; f. 1961; finance, economics, commerce and accounting.

Zhongguo Dabaike Quanshu Chubanshe (Encyclopaedia of China Publishing House): 17 Fu Cheng Men Bei Dajie, Beijing 100037; tel. (10) 88390738; fax (10) 88390680; e-mail jxh@ecph.com.cn; internet www.ecph.com.cn; f. 1978; specializes in encyclopaedias; Dir SHAN JIFU.

Zhongguo Ditu Chubanshe (SinoMaps Press): 3 Baizhifang Xijie, Beijing 100054; tel. (10) 63529243; fax (10) 63529403; e-mail chenping@sinomaps.com; internet www.sinomaps.com; f. 1954; cartographic publr; Dir ZHAO XIAOMING.

Zhongguo Funü Chubanshe (China Women Publishing House): 24A Shijia Hutong, Beijing 100010; tel. (10) 65224637; fax (10)

65133162; e-mail service@womenbooks.com.cn; internet www.womenbooks.com.cn; f. 1981; women's movement, marriage and family, child-care, etc.; Editor-in-chief YANG GUANGHUI.

Zhongguo Qingnian Chubanzongshe (China Youth Publishing Group): 21 Dongsi Shiertiao, Beijing 100708; tel. (10) 84015396; fax (10) 64031803; e-mail rightscenter@cyp.com.cn; internet www.cyp.com.cn; f. 1950; state-owned; literature, social and natural sciences, youth work, autobiography; also periodicals; Pres. ZHANG JINGYAN; Editor-in-Chief WEN YUXIN.

Zhongguo Shehui Kexue Chubanshe (China Social Sciences Publishing House): 158A Gulou Xidajie, Beijing 100720; tel. (10) 84029453; fax (10) 84002041; internet www.csspw.com.cn; f. 1978; Dir MENG ZHAOYU.

Zhongguo Xiju Chubanshe (China Theatrical Publishing House): 52 Dongsi Batiao Hutong, Beijing; tel. (10) 64015815; f. 1957; traditional and modern Chinese drama.

Zhongguo Youyi Chuban Gongsi (China Friendship Publishing Corpn): e-mail tmdoxu@public.east.cn.net; Dir YANG WEI.

Zhonghua Shuju (Zhonghua Book Co): 38 Taipingqiao Xili, Fenglai Qu, Beijing; tel. (10) 63458226; f. 1912; general; Pres. SONG YIFU.

PUBLISHERS' ASSOCIATION

Publishers' Association of China: Beijing; tel. (10) 65212827; internet www.pac.org.cn; f. 1979; arranges academic exchanges with foreign publrs; Chair. YU YOUXIAN.

Broadcasting and Communications

TELECOMMUNICATIONS

Ministry of Information Industry: see under Ministries.

China Mobile Communications Corpn (China Mobile): 53A Xibianmen Nei Dajie, Xuanwu Qu, Beijing 100053; tel. (10) 63604988; fax (10) 63600364; internet www.chinamobile.com; controlled by Ministry of Information Industry; controlling shareholder in China Mobile (Hong Kong) Ltd; f. 2000; Pres. WANG JIANZHOU.

China Netcom Group Corpn (Hong Kong) Ltd: Bldg C, 156, Fuxingmeinei Dajie, Xicheng Qu, Beijing 100031; tel. (10) 88093588; fax (10) 88091446; e-mail cnc@china-netcom.com; internet www.china-netcom.com; f. 1999; internet and telephone service provider; incorporated in Hong Kong; merged with China Telecom northern operations (10 provinces) in May 2002; 115.33m. fixed-line telephone subscribers, 11.48m. broadband subscribers (2005); Chair. ZHANG CHUNJIANG; CEO ZUO XUNSHENG.

China Satellite Communications Corpn (CHINA SATCOM): 42 Xueyuan Lu, Haidian Qu, Beijing 100083; tel. and fax (10) 62026997; internet www.chinasatcom.com; f. 2001; provides internet, telephone and related services; Pres. ZHANG HAINAN.

China Telecom Corpn Ltd: 31 Jinrong Jie, Xicheng Qu, Beijing 100032; tel. (10) 66428166; fax (10) 66010728; e-mail ir@chinatelecom.com.cn; internet www.chinatelecom-h.com; f. 1997; est. as a vehicle for foreign investment in telecommunications sector; restructured as a jt-stock limited company in 2002 with responsibility for fixed-line networks, via its subsidiaries, in 20 provinces, municipalities and autonomous regions; Chair. and CEO WANG XIAOCHU; Pres. LENG RONGQUAN.

China United Telecommunications Corpn (UNICOM): 1/F, Hongji Centre Office Bldg, 18 Jianguomenei Dajie, Beijing; tel. (10) 65181800; fax (10) 65183405; e-mail webmaster@chinaunicom.com.cn; internet www.chinaunicom.com.cn; f. 1994; cellular telecommunications; Chair. and CEO CHANG XIAOBING.

Netease.com: Rm 1901, Tower E3, The Towers, Oriental Plaza No. 1, East Chang An Jie, Dong Cheng Qu, Beijing 100738; tel. (10) 85180163; fax (10) 85183618; e-mail bjsales@service.netease.com; internet corp.163.com; f. 1997; Nasdaq-listed internet portal; Founder and CEO WILLIAM DING LEI.

Sina.com: Soho New Town, 16F Bldg C, 88 Jianguo Lu, Chao Yang Qu, Beijing 100022; tel. (10) 65665009; fax (10) 85801740; internet www.sina.com.cn; Nasdaq-listed internet portal; Pres. and CEO CHARLES CHAO.

Sohu.com: 15th Floor, Tower 2, Bright China Chang An Bldg, 7 Jianguomen Nei Jie, Beijing 100005; tel. (10) 65102160; fax (10) 65101377; internet www.sohu.com; Nasdaq-listed internet portal; Chair. CHARLES ZHANG.

BROADCASTING

In 2006 there were 267 radio broadcasting stations, 17,457 radio transmitting and relay stations (covering 95.4% of the population). In the same year there were 296 television stations and 27,163 television transmitting and relay stations (covering 96.2% of the population).

Regulatory Authority

State Administration of Radio, Film and Television (SARFT): 2 Fu Xing Men Wai Dajie, POB 4501, Beijing 100866; tel. (10) 68513409; fax (10) 68512174; e-mail sarft@chinasarft.gov.cn; internet www.sarft.gov.cn; controls the Central People's Broadcasting Station, the Central TV Station, Radio Beijing, China Record Co, Beijing Broadcasting Institute, Broadcasting Research Institute, the China Broadcasting Art Troupe, etc.; Dir WANG TAIHUA.

Radio

China National Radio (CNR): 2 Fu Xing Men Wai Dajie, Beijing 100866; tel. (10) 68045630; fax (10) 68045631; e-mail cn@cnr.cn; internet www.cnradio.com; f. 1941; domestic service in Chinese, Zang Wen (Tibetan), Min Nan Hua (Amoy), Ke Jia (Hakka), Hasaka (Kazakh), Wei Wuer (Uygur), Menggu Hua (Mongolian) and Chaoxian (Korean); Dir-Gen. YANG BO.

Zhongguo Guoji Guangbo Diantai (China Radio International): 16A Shijingshan Lu, Beijing 100040; tel. (10) 68891123; fax (10) 68891232; internet www.cri.cn; f. 1941; fmrly Radio Beijing; foreign service in 38 languages incl. Arabic, Burmese, Czech, English, Esperanto, French, German, Indonesian, Italian, Japanese, Lao, Polish, Portuguese, Russian, Spanish, Turkish and Vietnamese; Dir WANG GENGNIAN.

Television

China Central Television (CCTV): Media Centre, 11B Fuxing Lu, Haidian Qu, Beijing 100038; tel. (10) 68508381; fax (10) 68513025; e-mail cctv-international@cctv.com; internet www.cctv.com; operates under Bureau of Broadcasting Affairs of the State Council, Beijing; f. 1958; operates eight networks; 24-hour global satellite service commenced in 1996; Pres. ZHAO HUAYONG.

Anhui Television (AHTV): 355 Tong Cheng Nan Lu, Hefei 230066; tel. (551) 2615582; fax (551) 2615582; e-mail webmaster@ahtv.com.cn; internet www.ahtv.com.cn; f. 1960; broadcasts two television channels.

China Beijing Television Station (BTV): tel. (10) 68419922; fax (10) 68429120; e-mail webmaster@btv.com.cn; internet www.btv.org; broadcasts nine television channels; state-owned.

Chongqing Television: tel. (23) 68812609; fax (23) 63850485; e-mail webmaster@ccqtv.com; internet www.ccqtv.com; f. 1961; broadcasts nine television channels.

Fujian Television: 2 Gu Tian Lu, Fuzhou 350001; tel. (591) 83313789; internet www.fjtv.net; f. 1960; broadcasts two television channels; part of the Fujian Media Group.

Gansu Television (GSTV): 226 Dong Gang Xi Lu, Lanzhou 370000; tel. (931) 8416419; fax (931) 8416499; internet www.gstv.com.cn; f. 1970; broadcasts three television channels.

Guangdong Television: Guangdong Television Centre, 331 Huan Shi Dong Lu, Guangzhou 510066; tel. (20) 83355188; e-mail gdtv@gdtv.com.cn; internet www.gdtv.com.cn; f. 1959; broadcasts two television channels; programmes in Mandarin, Cantonese and English; state-owned; broadcasts three channels.

Guangxi Television (GXTV): Nanning; tel. (771) 2196666; fax (771) 5854039; e-mail gxtv@gxtv.com.cn; internet www.gxtv.com.cn; f. 1970; broadcasts two television channels.

Guizhou Television (GZTV): e-mail webmaster@gztv.com; internet www.gztv.com.cn; f. 1968; broadcasts three television channels.

Hainan Television (HNTV): f. 1982; broadcasts three television channels.

Hebei Television (HEBTV): internet www.hebtv.com.cn; f. 1969; broadcasts two television channels.

Henan Television (HNTV): 2 Jing Wu Lu, Zhengzhou 450008; tel. (371) 5726212; fax (371) 5726285; e-mail hntv@hntv.ha.cn; internet www.hntv.ha.cn; f. 1969; broadcasts three television channels.

Hubei Television (HBTV): 1 Zi Jin Cun Liang Dao Jie, Wuchang, Wuhan 430071; tel. (27) 7839223; fax (27) 7816130; e-mail webmaster@hbtv.com.cn; internet www.hbtv.com.cn; f. 1960; broadcasts two television channels.

Hunan Television (HNTV): 314 De Ya Lu, Changsha 410003; tel. (731) 4250525; fax (731) 4250525; e-mail web@hunantv.com; internet www.hunantv.com; f. 1960; broadcasts two television channels.

Jiangsu Broadcasting Corpn: 8 Xi Ci Tang Xiang, Zhong Shan Dong Lu, Nanjing 210002; tel. (25) 84454436; e-mail public@jsbc.com.cn; internet www.jsbc.com; f. 1960; broadcasts two television channels.

Liaoning Television (LNTV): 10 Guang Rong Jie, Shenyang 110003; tel. (24) 23232945; fax (24) 22913733; e-mail lntv@lntv.com.cn; internet www.lntv.com.cn; f. 1959; broadcasts two television channels.

THE PEOPLE'S REPUBLIC OF CHINA

Nei Monggol Television (NMGTV): 19 Xinhua Dajie, Hohhot 010058; tel. (471) 6962288; fax (471) 6963805; e-mail info@nmtv.cn; internet www.nmtv.cn; f. 1969; broadcasts two television channels.

Ningxia Television (NXTV): internet www.nxtv.com.cn; f. 1970; broadcasts two television channels.

Shaanxi Television (SXTV): 76 Chang An Nan Jie, Xian 710061; tel. (29) 83145678; fax 5218553; e-mail webmaster@sxtvs.com; internet www.sxtvs.com; f. 1970; broadcasts four television channels.

Shandong Television (SDTV): 81 Jingshi Lu, Jinan 250001; tel. (531) 2951295; fax (531) 2953809; e-mail webmaster@sdtv.com.cn; internet www.sdtv.com.cn; f. 1960; broadcasts six television channels.

Shanghai Media Group: internet www.smg.sh.cn; f. 2001; est. from merger of Radio Shanghai, Eastern Radio Shanghai, Shanghai Television, Oriental Television Station and Shanghai Cable TV; broadcasts 13 television channels and 11 radio channels.

Shanxi Television (SXTV): tel. (575) 8658877; fax (575) 8658807; e-mail sxtv@sxtv.com.cn; internet www.shtv.com.cn; f. 1960; broadcasts two television channels.

Sichuan Television (SCTV): 40 Dong Sheng Jie, Chengdu 610015; tel. (28) 86636065; fax (28) 86635195; e-mail webmaster@sctv.com; f. 1960; broadcasts nine television channels.

Xinjiang Television (XJTV): tel. (991) 2577531; fax (991) 2871947; e-mail XJTVS@96669.net; internet www.xjtvs.com.cn; f. 1970; broadcasts 12 television channels; broadcasts in Mandarin, Uygur and Kazakh.

Xizhang Television (XZTV): tel. (891) 6820611; fax (891) 683 5729; e-mail xztv@xztv.com.cn; internet www.xztv.com.cn; f. 1985; broadcasts two television channels; Mandarin and Tibetan.

Yunnan Television: tel. (871) 5357842; fax (871) 5350586; internet www.yntv.cn; f. 1969; broadcasts six television channels.

Zhejiang Television (ZJTV): internet www.zjtv.com.cn; f. 1960; broadcasts two television channels.

In October 1993 the Government approved new regulations, attempting to restrict access to foreign satellite broadcasts. In April 1994 foreign companies were prohibited from establishing or operating cable TV stations in China. By mid-1996 there were more than 3,000 cable television stations in operation, with networks covering 45m. households. The largest subscriber service is Beijing Cable TV (Dir GUO JUNJIN). Satellite services are available in some areas: millions of satellite receivers are in use. In September 2001 the Government signed a deal that would allow News Corpn and AOL Time Warner to become the first foreign broadcasters to have direct access to China's markets, although broadcasts would be restricted to Guangdong Province. In February 2004 it was announced that restrictions on foreign investment in TV and film production companies were to be removed. However, foreign media companies would be required to comply with government regulations on media content.

Finance

(cap. = capital; auth. = authorized; p.u. = paid up; res = reserves; dep. = deposits; m. = million; amounts in yuan unless otherwise stated)

BANKING

Radical economic reforms, introduced in 1994, included the strengthening of the role of the central bank and the establishment of new commercial banks. The Commercial Bank Law took effect in July 1995.

Regulatory Authority

China Banking Regulatory Commission: 15 Financial St, Xicheng Qu, Beijing 100800; tel. (10) 66279113; internet www.cbrc.gov.cn; f. 2003; Chair. LIU MINGKANG.

Central Bank

People's Bank of China: 32 Chengfang Jie, Xicheng Qu, Beijing 100800; tel. (10) 66194114; fax (10) 66015346; e-mail master@pbc.gov.cn; internet www.pbc.gov.cn; f. 1948; bank of issue; decides and implements China's monetary policies; Gov. ZHOU XIAOCHUAN; 2,204 brs.

Other Banks

Agricultural Bank of China: 23A Fuxing Lu, Haidian Qu, Beijing 100036; tel. (10) 68216807; fax (10) 68297160; e-mail webmaster@intl.abocn.com; internet www.abchina.com; f. 1951; serves mainly China's rural financial operations, providing services for agriculture, industry, commerce, transport, etc. in rural areas; cap. and res 79,607m., dep. 4,387,793m. (Dec. 2005); Pres. XIANG JUNBO; 28,111 brs (domestic).

Agricultural Development Bank of China: 2A Yuetanbei Jie, Xicheng Qu, Beijing 100045; tel. (10) 68081557; fax (10) 68081773; internet www.adbc.com.cn; f. 1994; cap. 165,800m. (2006); Pres. ZHENG HUI.

Bank of Beijing Co Ltd: 2nd Floor, Tower B, Beijing International Financial Bldg, 156 Fu Xing Men Nei Jie, Beijing 100031; tel. (10) 66426928; fax (10) 66426691; internet www.bankofbeijing.com.cn; f. 1996; est. as Beijing City United Bank Corpn, changed name to Beijing City Commercial Bank Corpn. Ltd in 1998, assumed present name in 2004; cap. 5,027.6m., res 3,219.6m., dep. 221,501.9m. (Dec. 2005); Chair. YAN BINGZHU; Pres. YAN XIAOYAN.

Bank of China Ltd: 1 Fu Xing Men Nei Dajie, Beijing 100818; tel. (10) 66596688; fax (10) 66016869; internet www.boc.cn; f. 1912; handles foreign exchange and international settlements; operates Orient AMC (asset management corporation) since 1999; fmrly Bank of China, became shareholding company in Aug. 2004; 10% stake acquired in 2005 by a consortium headed by Royal Bank of Scotland PLC (UK); further 10% acquired by Temasek Holdings (Private) Ltd; cap. 209,427m., res 11,830m., dep. 4,345,337m. (Dec. 2005); Chair. XIAO GANG; Pres. LI LIHUI; 117 brs.

Bank of Communications Ltd: 188 Yin Cheng Lu, Shanghai 200120; tel. (21) 58408478; fax (21) 58408476; e-mail webmaster@hq.bankcomm.com; internet www.bankcomm.com; f. 1908; commercial bank; cap. 45,804m., res 28,095m., dep. 1,314,488m. (Dec. 2005); a 19.9% stake was acquired by HSBC in Aug. 2004; Chair. JIANG CHAOLIANG; Pres. LI JUN; 93 brs.

Bank of Jiangsu Co Ltd: 55 Hongwu Lu, Nanjing, Jiangsu Province; tel. (25) 58588050; fax (25) 58588055; internet www.jsbchina.cn; f. 2007; est. by merger of 13 banks; Chair. and Pres. HUANG ZHIWEI.

Bank of Ningbo Co Ltd: 294 Zhongshan Dong Lu, Ningbo 315040, Zhejiang; tel. (574) 87050028; fax (574) 87050027; internet www.nbcb.com.cn; f. 1997; cap. 2,050m., res 555.7m., dep. 51,329m. (Dec. 2006); Chair. LU HUAYU; Pres. YU FENGYING.

Bank of Shanghai Co Ltd: 585 Zhongshan Lu (E2), Shanghai 200010; tel. (21) 63370888; fax (21) 63370777; e-mail shenjie@bankofshanghai.com.cn; internet www.bankofshanghai.com; f. 1995; est. as Shanghai City United Bank, assumed present name in 1998; cap. 2,600m., res 4,983m., dep. 222,107.7m. (Dec. 2005); Chair. JIANHUA FU; Pres. CHEN XIN; 208 brs.

BNP Paribas (China) Ltd: 13th Floor, North Tower, Shanghai Stock Exchange Bldg, 528 Pudong Nan Lu, Shanghai 200120; tel. (21) 58405500; fax (21) 58889232; internet www.bnpparibas.com.cn; f. 1992; fmrly International Bank of Paris and Shanghai; name changed as above 2004; 100% owned by BNP Paribas SA, Paris; cap. US $72.5m., res US $3.2m., dep. US $215.4m. (Dec. 2005); Chair. and Pres. DIDIER BALME.

Changsha City Commercial Bank: 1 Furong Zhong Lu, Changsha, Hunan; tel. (73) 14305570; fax (73) 14305560; e-mail changsaguoji@163.com; internet www.cscb.cn; f. 1997; cap. 606.3m., res 218.3m., dep. 34,472.4m. (Dec. 2005); Chair. ZHI YONG ZHANG; Pres. YU GUO ZHU.

Changsu Rural Commercial Bank: 100 Xinynan Lu, Changsu 215500; tel. (512) 52779881; fax (512) 52717720; internet www.csrcbank.com; f. 1953; cap. 319.9m., res. 517.4m., dep. 17,193.8m. (Dec. 2005); Chair. WU JIANYA; Pres. SONG JIANMING.

China Bohai Bank: Tianjin; internet www.cbhb.com.cn; f. 2004; 20% stake owned by Standard Chartered Bank; Chair. YANG ZILIN.

China Citic Bank: Block C, Fuhua Mansion, 8 Chao Yang Men Bei Dajie, Dongcheng Qu, Beijing 100027; tel. (10) 65542388; fax (10) 65541671; e-mail webmaster@citicib.com.cn; internet www.citicib.com.cn; f. 1987; est. as Citic Industrial Bank; name changed as above in July 2005; cap. 26,660.7m., res 1,517m., dep. 530,597.5m. (Dec. 2005); Chair. KONG DAN; Pres. CHEN XIAOXIAN; 26 brs.

China Construction Bank Corpn (CCBC): 25 Jinrong Jie, Beijing 100032; tel. (10) 67597114; fax (10) 66212862; e-mail ccb@bj.china.com; internet www.ccb.com; f. 1954; fmrly People's Construction Bank of China; makes payments for capital construction projects in accordance with state plans and budgets; issues medium- and long-term loans to enterprises and short-term loans to construction enterprises and others; also handles foreign-exchange business; housing loans; operates Cinda AMC (asset management corporation) since 1998 and China Great Wall AMC since 1999; in 2005 became the first mainland Chinese bank to have its shares publicly traded on the Hong Kong Stock Exchange; cap. 224,689m., res 62,890m., dep. 4,176,020m. (Dec. 2005); 44 brs; Pres. GUO SHUQING.

China Development Bank (CDB): 29 Fuchengmenwai Dajie, Xicheng Qu, Beijing 100037; tel. (10) 68306688; fax (10) 68306699; e-mail webmaster@cdb.com.cn; internet www.cdb.com.cn; f. 1994; merged with China Investment Bank 1998; handles low-interest loans for infrastructural projects and basic industries; Gov. CHEN YUAN; 32 brs.

THE PEOPLE'S REPUBLIC OF CHINA

China Everbright Bank: Everbright Bldg, 6 Fu Xing Men Wai Lu, Beijing 100045; tel. (10) 68098000; fax (10) 68561260; e-mail eb@cebbank.com; internet www.cebbank.com; f. 1992; est. as Everbright Bank of China; acquired China Investment Bank and assumed present name in 1999; cap. 8,216.9m., res 4,144.9m., dep. 300,410.3m. (Dec. 2004); Pres. GUO YOU; Chair. WANG MINGQUAN; 30 brs.

China International Capital Corporation (CICC): 28th Floor, China World Tower 2, 1 Jian Guo Men Wai Dajie, Beijing 100004; tel. (10) 65051166; fax (10) 65051156; e-mail info@cicc.com.cn; internet www.cicc.com.cn; f. 1995; international investment bank; 43.4% owned by China Jianyin Investment Limited, 34.3% owned by Morgan Stanley; registered cap. US $100m.; CEO LEVIN ZHU.

China Merchants Bank: China Merchants Bank Tower, 7088 Shennan Blvd, Shenzhen 518040; tel. (755) 83198888; fax (755) 83195112; e-mail office@cmbchina.com; internet www.cmbchina.com; f. 1987; cap. 10,374.3m., res 10,591.9m., dep. 680,344.7m. (Dec. 2005); Chair. QIN XIAO; Pres. and CEO MA WEIHUA; 35 brs.

China Minsheng Banking Corporation: 8/F, 2 Fuxingmen Nei Dajie, Xicheng Qu, Beijing 100031; tel. (10) 58560666; fax (10) 58560635; internet www.cmbc.com.cn; first non-state national commercial bank, opened Jan. 1996; cap. 10,167.1m., res 7,316.8m., dep. 675,566.1m. (Dec. 2006); Chair. DONG WENBIAO; Pres. EDDIE T. S. WANG; 20 brs.

China Zheshang Bank Co Ltd: 288 Qingchun Lu, Hangzhou, Zhejiang 310006; tel. (574) 87252668; fax (574) 87245409; e-mail zcbho@mail.nbptt.zj.cn; internet www.czbank.com; f. 1993; fmrly Zhejiang Commercial Bank; cap. 1,500.7m., res 129.4m., dep. 34,212.1m. (Dec. 2006); Chair. ZHANG DAYANG; Pres. GONG FANGLE.

Chinese Mercantile Bank: Ground and 23rd Floors, Dongfeng Bldg, 2 Yannan Lu, Futian Qu, Shenzhen 518031; tel. (755) 83786833; fax (755) 83788435; e-mail szcmbank@public.szptt.net.cn; f. 1993; wholly owned by ICBC (Asia); CEO PANG KOON KWAI.

Chongqing Commercial Bank Ltd: 153 Zou Rong Lu, Zou Rong Sq., Yu Zhong Qu, Chongqing; tel. (23) 63836229; fax (23) 63792176; e-mail intdept@cta.cq.cn; internet www.cqcbank.com.cn; f. 1996; cap. 1,607.7m., res 149.3m., dep. 28,195.8m. (Dec. 2005); Pres. CHONG YI WANG; Chair. FU ZHANG.

CITIC Group: Capital Mansion, 6 Xianyuannan Lu, Chao Yang Qu, Beijing 100004; tel. (10) 64660088; fax (10) 64661186; e-mail g-office@citic.com.cn; internet www.citic.com; f. 1979; name changed from China International Trust and Investment Corporation in 2003; economic and technological co-operation; finance, banking, investment and trade; registered cap. 3,000m.; total assets 935,720m. (Dec. 2006); Chair. KONG DAN; Pres. CHANG ZHENMING.

Export and Import Bank of China (China Exim Bank): 77 Beiheyan Jie, Dongcheng Qu, Beijing 100009; tel. (10) 64099988; fax (10) 64005186; internet www.eximbank.gov.cn; f. 1994; provides trade credits for export of large machinery, electronics, ships, etc.; Chair. and Pres. LI RUOGU.

Guangdong Development Bank: 83 Nonglinxia Lu, Dongshan Qu, Guangzhou, Guangdong 510080; tel. (20) 87310888; fax (20) 87310779; internet www.gdb.com.cn; f. 1988; 85% stake acquired by a consortium led by Citigroup Inc (USA) in Nov. 2006; cap. 3,585.7m., res 1,397.4m., dep. 288,528.7m. (Dec. 2003); Chair. LI RUOHONG; Pres. ZHANG GUANGHUA; 24 brs.

Hua Xia Bank: 22 Hua Xia Bank Mansions, Jianguomennei Dajie, Dongcheng Qu, Beijing 100005; tel. (10) 85238000; fax (10) 85239000; e-mail zhgjb@hxb.cc; internet www.hxb.com.cn; f. 1992; est. as part of Shougang Corpn; cap. 4,200.0m., res 4,142.9m., dep. 286,716.9m. (Dec. 2004); Chair. ZAI HONGXIANG; Pres. WU JIAN.

Industrial and Commercial Bank of China: 55 Fuxingmennan Dajie, Xicheng Qu, Beijing 100031; tel. (10) 66106070; fax (10) 66106053; e-mail webmaster@icbc.com.cn; internet www.icbc.com.cn; f. 1984; handles industrial and commercial credits and international business; operates Huarong AMC (asset management corporation) since 1999; cap. 248,000m., res 1,803m., dep. 5,925.6m. (Dec. 2005); Chair. and Pres. JIANG JIANQING; Gen. Man. CHEN AIPING.

Industrial Bank Co Ltd: Zhong Shang Bldg, 154 Hudong Lu, Hualin, Fuzhou, Fujian 350003; tel. (591) 7839338; fax (591) 7841932; e-mail fjib@pub3.fz.fj.cn; internet www.cib.com.cn; f. 1982; fmrly Fujian Industrial Bank; cap. 3,999m., res 6,238.9m., dep. 449,771.1m. (Dec. 2005); Chair. GAO JIANPING; Pres. LI RENJIE; 19 brs.

Laiwu City Commercial Bank Co Ltd: 36 Pengquan Dong Dajie, Laicheng Qu, Laiwu, Shanddong; tel. (634) 8861182; fax (634) 8681177; internet www.lwccb.com.cn; f. 1987; cap. 414.8m., res 110.8m., dep. 6,434.9m. (Dec. 2006); Chair LI MINSHI; Pres. TAN LEQING.

Linyi City Commercial Bank Co Ltd: 336 Yimeng Lu, Linyi, Shandong; tel. (539) 8309052; fax (539) 8309052; internet www.lyccb.com.cn; f. 1998; cap. 375.5m., res 86.7m., dep. 8,472.8m. (Dec. 2004); Pres. MA LEI; Chair. WANG JIAYU.

Qingdao International Bank: Full Hope Mansion C, 12 Hong Kong Middle Rd, Qingdao, Shandong 266071; tel. (532) 85026230; fax (532) 85026221; e-mail service@qibank.net; internet www.qibank.net; f. 1996; jt venture between Industrial and Commercial Bank of China and Hana Bank (South Korea); cap. 400.0m., dep. 495.0m., (Dec. 2006); Chair. KIM JONG JUN; Pres. CHUNG OUAN CHUL.

Shanghai Pudong Development Bank: 12 Zhongshan Dong Yi Lu, Shanghai 200002; tel. (21) 63296188; fax (21) 63232036; e-mail bdo@spdb.com.cn; internet www.spdb.com.cn; f. 1993; cap. 4,354.9m., res 18,642.5m., dep. 629,945.7m. (Dec. 2006); Chair. JIN YUN; Pres. FU JIANHUA; 28 brs.

Shaoxing City Commercial Bank Co Ltd: 20 Lao Dong Lu, Shaoxing, Zhejiang 312000; tel. (575) 5138588; fax (575) 5131190; e-mail sxsyyh@mail.sxpttt.zj.cn; internet www.sxccb.com; f. 1997; cap. 556.0m., res 71.2m., dep. 17,789.3m. (Dec. 2006); Pres. CHEN FANG XIAO; Chair. CHEN JUN QUAN.

Shenzhen Development Bank Co Ltd: 5047 Shennan Dong Lu, Shenzhen 518001; tel. (755) 2088888; fax (755) 2081069; e-mail shudi@sdb.com.cn; internet www.sdb.com.cn; f. 1987; 18% acquired by Newbridge Capital (USA) in 2004; cap. 1,945.8m., res 3,782.7m., dep. 250,528.4m. (Dec. 2006); Chair. FRANK NEWMAN; Pres. XIAO SUINING.

Shenzhen Ping An Bank: Shenzhen Ping An Bank Bldg, 1099 Shennan Lu, Central, Shenzhen 518031; tel. (755) 25198888; fax (755) 25878189; e-mail ibd@bankofshenzhen.com; internet www.18ebank.com; f. 1995; fmrly Shenzhen Commercial Bank; cap. 5,502m., res 1,011.8m., dep. 75,665.1m. (Dec. 2006); Chair. HUANG LIZHE; Pres. RICHARD JACKSON; 45 brs.

Xiamen International Bank: 8–10 Jiang Lu, Xiamen, Fujian 361001; tel. (592) 2078888; fax (592) 2988788; e-mail xib@public.xm.fj.cn; internet www.xib.com.cn; f. 1985; cap. 1,068m., res 537m., dep. 28,036m. (Dec. 2006); Chair. CHEN GUI ZONG; Pres. LU YAO MING; 3 brs.

Foreign Banks

Before mid-1995 foreign banks were permitted only to open representative offices in China. The first foreign bank established a full branch in Beijing in mid-1995, and by March 1998 there were 51 foreign banks in China. In March 1997 foreign banks were allowed for the first time to conduct business in yuan. However, they are only entitled to accept yuan deposits from joint-venture companies. Representative offices totalled 519 in December 1996. In March 1999 the Government announced that foreign banks, hitherto restricted to 23 cities and Hainan Province, were to be permitted to open branches in all major cities.

STOCK EXCHANGES

Several stock exchanges were in the process of development in the mid-1990s, and by early 1995 the number of shareholders had reached 38m. By 1995 a total of 15 futures exchanges were in operation, dealing in various commodities, building materials and currencies. The number of companies listed on the Shanghai and Shenzhen Stock Exchanges rose from 323 in 1995 to 1,434 in 2006. In August 1997, in response to unruly conditions, the Government ordered the China Securities Regulatory Commission (see below) to assume direct control of the Shanghai and Shenzhen exchanges.

Stock Exchange Executive Council (SEEC): Beijing; tel. (10) 64935210; f. 1989; oversees the development of financial markets in China; mems comprise leading non-bank financial institutions authorized to handle securities; Vice-Pres. WANG BOMING.

Securities Association of China (SAC): Olympic Hotel, 52 Baishiqiao Lu, Beijing 100081; tel. (10) 68316688; fax (10) 68318390; internet www.sac.net.cn; f. 1991; non-governmental org. comprising 122 mems (stock exchanges and securities cos) and 35 individual mems; Chair. HUANG XIANGPING.

Beijing Securities Exchange: 5 Anding Lu, Chao Yang Qu, Beijing 100029; tel. (10) 64939366; fax (10) 64936233.

Shanghai Stock Exchange: 528 Pudong Nan Lu, Shanghai 200120; tel. (21) 68808888; fax (21) 68807813; e-mail webmaster@sse.com.cn; internet www.sse.com.cn; f. 1990; 837 listed companies (Dec. 2004); Chair. GENG LIANG; Pres. ZHU CONGJIU.

Shenzhen Stock Exchange: 5045 Shennan Dong Lu, Shenzhen, Guangdong 518010; tel. (755) 20833333; fax (755) 2083117; internet www.szse.cn/main/en; f. 1991; Chair. ZHENG KELIN; Pres. GUI MINJIE.

Regulatory Authorities

Operations are regulated by the State Council Securities Policy Committee and by the following:

China Securities Regulatory Commission (CSRC): Bldg 3, Area 3, Fangqunyuan, Fangzhuang, Beijing 100078; tel. (10) 67617343; fax (10) 67653117; e-mail csrcweb@publicf.bta.net.cn; internet www.csrc.gov.cn; f. 1993; Chair. SHANG FULIN.

INSURANCE

A new Insurance Law, formulated to standardize activities and to strengthen the supervision and administration of the industry, took effect in October 1995. Changes included the separation of life insurance and property insurance businesses. By the end of 2006 the number of insurance institutions operating in China totalled 107, of which seven were insurance group corporations, 41 were joint-venture corporations and 50 were domestically funded insurance corporations. Total premiums rose from 44,000m. yuan in 1994 to some 564,000m. yuan in 2006. Of the latter figure, property insurance accounted for 157,900m. yuan and life insurance for 406,100m. yuan.

Aegon-CNOOC Life Insurance Co Ltd: 15/F Pufa Tower, 588 Pudong Nan Lu, Shanghai 200120; internet www.aegon-cnooc.com; f. 2002; jt venture between Aegon (The Netherlands) and China National Offshore Oil Corpn.

Anbang Property and Casualty Insurance Co Ltd: Beijing; tel. (10) 65309999; e-mail webmaster@ab-insurance.com; internet www.ab-insurance.com; f. 2004.

AXA-Minmetals Assurance Co: 12/F China Merchants Tower, 161 Jia Zui Dong Lu, Pudong, Shanghai 200120; tel. (21) 58792288; fax (21) 58792299; internet www.axa-minmetals.com.cn; f. 1999; jt venture by Groupe AXA (France) and China Minmetals Group; CEO ALLAN LAM.

China Continent Property and Casualty Insurance Co Ltd: Shanghai; tel. (21) 58369588; internet www.ccic-net.com.cn; f. 2003; Chair. DAI FENGJU; CEO JIANG MING.

China Insurance (Holdings) Co Ltd: 28 Xuanwumen Xi Lu, Xuanwu Qu, Beijing; tel. (10) 63600601; fax (10) 63600605; internet www.chinainsurance.com; f. 1931; fmrly China Insurance Co, renamed Aug. 2002; cargo, hull, freight, fire, life, personal accident, industrial injury, motor insurance, reinsurance, etc.; Chair. FENG XIAO ZENG; Pres. LIN FAN.

China Insurance Group: 410 Fu Cheng Men Nei Dajie, Beijing; tel. (10) 66016688; fax (10) 66011869; internet www.china-insurance.com; f. 1996; fmrly People's Insurance Co of China (PICC), f. 1949; hull, marine cargo, aviation, motor, life, fire, accident, liability and reinsurance, etc.; 300m. policy-holders (1996); Chair. and Pres. MA YONGWEI.

China Life Insurance Co: 16 Chaowai Dajie, Chao Yang Qu, Beijing 10020; tel. (10) 85659999; e-mail serve@e-chinalife.com; internet www.chinalife.com.cn; f. 1999; formed from People's Insurance (Life) Co, division of fmr People's Insurance Co of China—PICC; restructured into a parent company and a shareholding company Aug. 2003; initial public offering Dec. 2003; Chair. YANG CHAO; Exec. Dir WU YAN.

China Pacific Insurance Co Ltd (CPIC): 1226 Zhongshan Lu (Bei 1), Shanghai; tel. (21) 65367846; internet www.cpic.com.cn; f. 1991; jt-stock co; Chair. GAO GUOFU; Pres. YANG XIANGHAI.

China United Property Insurance Co: Shanghai; tel. (21) 53554600; fax (21) 63276000; internet www.cicsh.com; f. 1986; fmrly Xinjiang Corpn Property Insurance Co.

Huatai Insurance Co of China Ltd: Gaoxin Mansion, 1 Nanbinhe Lu, Guanganmenwai, Xuanwu Qu, Beijing 100055; tel. (10) 63370088; fax (10) 63370081; e-mail beijing@ehuatai.com; internet www.ehuatai.com; f. 1996; est. by 63 industrial cos; Chair. and CEO WANG ZIMU.

Manulife Sinochem Life Insurance Co Ltd: Shanghai 200121; tel. (21) 50492288; fax (21) 50473329; internet www.manulife-sinochem.com; f. 1996; jt venture between Manulife (Canada) and Sinochem.

New China Life Insurance: Beijing; internet www.newchinalife.com; f. 1996.

PICC Property and Casualty Co Ltd: : 69 Dongheyan Jie, Xuanwu Men, Beijing 100052; tel. (10) 63156688; fax (10) 63033589; e-mail webmaster@piccnet.com.cn; internet www.picc.com.cn; f. 2003; fmrly the People's Insurance Company of China; Chair. WU YAN; CEO YI WANG.

Ping An Insurance (Group) Co of China (Ping An): Ping An Bldg, Bagua San Lu, Bagualing, Shenzhen 518029; tel. (755) 82262888; fax (755) 82431019; internet www.pa18.com; f. 1988; 19.9% owned by HSBC Bank PLC (UK); total assets 292,519m. (June 2005); Chair. and CEO MA MINGZHE.

Sino Life Insurance: 6/F, Sino Life Tower, 707 Zhangyang Lu, Pudong New Area, Shanghai 200120; tel. (21) 58773333; fax (21) 58880099; internet www.sino-life.com; f. 2000.

Sunlife Everbright Insurance Co Ltd: 37/F, Tianjin International Bldg, 75 Nanjing Lu, Heping Qu, Tianjin 300050; tel. (22) 23391188; internet www.sunlife-everbright.com; f. 1999; jt venture between Sunlife Financial (Canada) and China Everbright Group; Pres. and CEO JANET DE SILVA.

Sunshine Property and Casualty Insurance Co Ltd: 28/F, Kuntai International Mansion, 12B Chao Wai Dajie, Beijing 100020; tel. (10) 58289999; fax (10) 58289688; internet www.csic.cc; Pres. and Dir-Gen. ZHANG WEIGONG.

Tai Ping Insurance Co Ltd: 410 Fu Cheng Men Nei Dajie, Beijing 100034; tel. (10) 66016688; fax (10) 66011869; internet www.tplic.com; marine freight, hull, cargo, fire, personal accident, industrial injury, motor insurance, reinsurance, etc.; Pres. SUN XIYUE.

Taikang Life Insurance Co Ltd: Zhongyi Bldg, 6 Xizhimenwai Lu, Xicheng Qu, Beijing 100044; tel. (10) 68330586; internet www.taikang.com; f. 1996; Chair. CHEN DONGSHENG.

Tianan Insurance Co Ltd: Shanghai 200120; tel. (21) 61017878; internet www.tianan-insurance.com; f. 1994.

Yongan Insurance: Xian; tel. (29) 87233888; fax (29) 88231200; internet www.yaic.com.cn.

Regulatory Authority

China Insurance Regulatory Commission (CIRC): 410 Fu Cheng Men Nei Dajie, Beijing 100034; tel. (10) 66016688; fax (10) 66018871; internet www.circ.gov.cn; f. 1998; under direct authority of the State Council; Chair. WU DINGFU.

Trade and Industry

GOVERNMENT AGENCIES

China Council for International Investment Promotion (CCIIP): Rm 406-409, Jing Guang Centre, Hujia Lu, Chaoyang Qu, POB 8806, Beijing 100020; tel. (10) 65978801; fax (10) 85226257; e-mail msc@cciip.org.cn; internet www.cciip.org.cn; f. 2006 by the State Council; aims to promote China's inward and outward investment; Pres. MIAO GENGSHU; Sec.-Gen. ZHOU MING.

China Investment Corpn (CIC): Beijing; f. 2007; sovereign wealth fund; manages China's foreign-exchange reserves; Chair. LOU JIWEI.

China National Light Industry Council: 22B Fuwai Dajie, Beijing 100833; tel. (10) 68396613; fax (10) 68396264; e-mail webmaster@clii.com.cn; internet www.clii.com.cn; under supervision of State Council; Chair. CHEN SHINENG; Sec. Gen. WANG SHICHENG.

China National Textile Industry Council (CNTIC): 12 Dong Chang An Jie, Beijing 100742; tel. (10) 65129545; under supervision of State Council; Chair. SHI WANPENG.

Ministry of Commerce: see under Ministries.

State Administration for Industry and Commerce: 8 San Li He Dong Lu, Xicheng Qu, Beijing 100820; tel. (10) 68013447; fax (10) 68020848; e-mail dfa@saic.gov.cn; internet www.saic.gov.cn; responsible for market supervision and administrative execution of industrial and commercial laws; functions under the direct supervision of the State Council.

State Administration of Foreign Exchange (SAFE): Huanrong Hotel, 18 Fucheng Lu, Beijing 100037; tel. (10) 68402265; internet www.safe.gov.cn; drafts foreign-exchange regulations, designs and implements balance of payments statistical system, manages foreign-exchange reserves; brs in Hong Kong, Singapore, London and New York; Administrator HU XIAOLIAN.

State Economic and Trade Commission: see under State Commissions.

State-owned Assets Supervision and Administration Commission: Beijing; e-mail iecc@sasac.gov.cn; internet www.sasac.gov.cn; f. 2003; supervision and administration of state-owned assets, regulation of ownership transfers of state-owned enterprises; Chair. LI RONGRONG.

Takeover Office for Military, Armed Police, Government and Judiciary Businesses: Beijing; f. 1998; est. to assume control of enterprises formerly operated by the People's Liberation Army.

CHAMBERS OF COMMERCE

All-China Federation of Industry and Commerce (All-China General Chamber of Industry and Commerce): 93 Beiheyan Dajie, Beijing 100006; tel. (10) 65136677; fax (10) 65131769; e-mail acfic@acfic.org.cn; internet www.acfic.com.cn (Chinese); www.chinachamber.org.cn (English); f. 1953; Chair. HUANG MENGFU.

China Chamber of Commerce for the Import and Export of Foodstuffs, Native Produce and Animal By-products (CFNA): Talent International Bldg, 80 Guanqumennei Jie, Chongwen Qu, Beijing 100062; tel. (10) 87109881; fax (10) 87109885; e-mail cfna@cccfna.org.cn; internet www.cccfna.org.cn; f. 1988; over 5,400 mems; Pres. CAO XUMIN.

China Chamber of Commerce for Import and Export of Light Industrial Products and Arts-Crafts (CCCLA): 10/F, Pan Jia Yuan Da Sha Bldg, 12 Pan Jia Yuan Nanli, Chao Yang Qu, Beijing

100021; tel. (10) 67732707; fax (10) 67732698; e-mail xxb@cccla.org.cn; internet www.cccla.org.cn; f. 1988; over 6,000 mems; Chair. WANG HANJIANG.

China Chamber of Commerce for Import and Export of Machinery and Electronic Products (CCCME): Rm 904, 9/F, Bldg 12, Pan Jia Yuan Nanli, Chao Yang Qu, Beijing; tel. (10) 58280863; fax (10) 58280860; e-mail international@cccme.org.cn; internet www.cccme.org.cn; f. 1988; more than 6,500 mems; Exec. Vice-Pres. and Sec.-Gen. ZHANG YUJING.

China Chamber of Commerce for Import and Export of Medicines and Health Products (CCCMHPIE): 8/F, 12 Pan Jia Yuan Nanli, Chao Yang Qu, Beijing 100021; tel. (10) 87789677; fax (10) 67734768; internet www.cccmhpie.org.cn; f. 1989; more than 1,500 mems; Pres. ZHOU XIAOMING.

China Chamber of Commerce for Import and Export of Textiles (CCCT): 12 Pan Jia Yuan Nanli, Chao Yang Qu, Beijing 100021; tel. (10) 67739246; fax (10) 67719235; e-mail info@ccct.org.cn; internet www.ccct.org.cn; f. 1988; Chair. WANG SHENYANG; over 6,300 mems.

China Council for the Promotion of International Trade (CCPIT)—China Chamber of International Commerce (CCOIC): 1 Fuxingmenwai Lu, Beijing 100860; tel. (10) 88075000; fax (10) 68030747; e-mail info@ccpit.org; internet www.ccpit.org; Chair. WAN JIFEI.

TRADE AND INDUSTRIAL ORGANIZATIONS

Beijing Urban Construction Group Co Ltd: 62 Xueyuannan Lu, Haidian, Beijing 100081; tel. (10) 62255511; fax (10) 62256027; e-mail cjp@mail.bucg.com; internet www.bucg.com; construction of civil and industrial buildings and infrastructure; Chair. LIU LONGHUA.

China Aerospace Science and Industry Corpn (CASIC): tel. (10) 68373522; fax (10) 68383626; e-mail bgt@casic.com.cn; internet www.casic.com.cn; f. 1999; Gen. Man. YIN XINGLIANG.

China Aerospace Science and Technology Corpn: 9 Fucheng Lu, Haidian Qu, Beijing 100830; tel. (10) 68370043; e-mail casc@spacechina.com; internet www.spacechina.com; f. 1999; Gen. Man. ZHANG QINGWEI.

China Aviation Industry Corporation I: AVIC1 Plaza, 128, Jianguo Lu, Beijing 100022; tel. (10) 65665922; fax (10) 65666518; e-mail lixm@avic1.com.cn; internet www.avic1.com.cn; f. 1999; Pres. LIN ZUOMING.

China Aviation Industry Corporation II: 67 Jiao Nan Dajie, Beijing 100712; tel. (10) 64094013; fax (10) 64032109; e-mail international@avic2.com; internet www.avic2.com.cn; Pres. ZHANG HONGBIAO.

China Aviation Supplies Import and Export Group Corpn (CASC): 25 Yong An Li Dajie, Jian Guo Men Wai, Beijing 100022; tel. (10) 65682255; internet www.casc.com.cn; f. 1980; Pres. LI HAI.

China Certification and Inspection Group Co Ltd (CCIC): 15 Fanghuadi Xi Jie, Chao Yang Qu, Beijing 100020; tel. (10) 65013951; fax (10) 65004625; e-mail inspect@ccic.com; internet www.ccic.com; fmrly China National Import and Export Commodities Inspection Corpn; inspects, tests and surveys import and export commodities for overseas trade, transport, insurance and manufacturing firms; Pres. ZHOU WENHUI.

China Civil Engineering Construction Corpn (CCECC): 4 Beifeng Wo, Haidian Qu, Beijing 100038; tel. (10) 63263392; fax (10) 63263864; e-mail zongban@ccecc.com.cn; internet www.ccecc.com.cn; f. 1979; general contracting, provision of technical and labour services, consulting and design, etc.; Pres. LIN RONGXIN.

China Construction International Inc: 9 Sanlihe Lu, Haidian Qu, Beijing; tel. (10) 68394086; fax (10) 68394097; Pres. FU RENZHANG.

China Electronics Corpn: 27 Wanshou Lu, Haidian Qu, Beijing 100846; tel. (10) 68218529; fax (10) 68213745; e-mail webmaster@cec.com.cn; internet www.cec.com.cn; Pres. CHEN ZHAOXIONG.

China Garment Industry Corpn: 9A Taiyanggong Beisanhuandong Lu, Chao Yang Qu, Beijing 100028; tel. (10) 64216660; fax (10) 64239134; Pres. DONG BINGGEN.

China General Technology (Group) Holding Ltd (Genertec): 23/F Genertec Plaza, 90 Xi San Huan Zhong Lu, Feng Tai Qu, Beijing 100055; tel. (10) 63348889; fax (10) 63348118; e-mail genertec@genertec.com.cn; internet www.genertec.com.cn; f. 1998; est. through merger of China National Technical Import and Export Corpn, China National Machinery Import and Export Corpn, China National Instruments Import and Export Corpn and China National Corpn for Overseas Economic Co-operation; total assets 16,000m. yuan; Chair. HE TONGXIN; Dir and Pres. LI DANG.

China Great Wall Computer Group: 38A Xueyuan Lu, Haidian Qu, Beijing 100083; tel. (10) 68342714; fax (10) 62011240; internet www.gwssi.com.cn; f. 1988; Chair. CHEN ZHAOXIONG; Pres. LU MING.

China Great Wall Industry Corpn: 67 Beisihuan Xilu, Haidian Qu, Beijing 100080; tel. (10) 88102188; fax (10) 88102107; e-mail cgwic@cgwic.com; internet www.cgwic.com.cn; f. 1980; international commercial wing of China Aerospace Science and Technology Corpn (CASC); registered cap. 200m. yuan; Pres. WANG HAIBO.

China Guangdong Nuclear Power Holding Co Ltd (CGNPC): Science Bldg, 1001 Shangbu Zhong Lu, Shenzhen 518031; internet www.cgnpc.com.cn; f. 1994; operates nuclear power plants; develops hydropower and wind power stations; more than 20 subsidiaries.

China International Book Trading Corpn: see under Publishers.

China International Contractors Association: 10/F, South Wing, CSCEC Mansion, 15 San Li He Lu, Beijing 100037; tel. (10) 64211159; fax (10) 64213959; e-mail wailian@chinca.org; internet www.chinca.org; f. 1988; Chair. DIAO CHUNHE.

China International Futures Co Ltd (CIFCO): 20/F, 1050 Huaqiang Bei Lu, Shenzhen 518031; tel. (755) 83281693; fax (755) 83281807; e-mail lizongping@cifco.net.cn; internet www.szcifco.com; f. 1992; Chair. TIAN YUAN.

China International Telecommunication Construction Corpn (CITCC): 56 Nan Fang Zhuang, Fengtai Qu, Beijing 100078; tel. (10) 67668689; fax (10) 67668732; internet www.citcc.cn; f. 1983; Pres. LI RUI.

China International Water and Electric Corpn (CWE): 3 Liupukang Yiqu Zhongjie, Xicheng Qu, Beijing 100011; tel. (10) 64015511; fax (10) 64014075; e-mail cwe@cwe.com.cn; internet www.cwe.com.cn; f. 1956; est. as China Water and Electric International Corpn, name changed 1983; imports and exports equipment for projects in the field of water and electrical engineering; undertakes such projects; provides technical and labour services; Pres. LU GUOJUN.

China Iron and Steel Industry and Trade Group Corpn (Sinosteel): Sinosteel Plaza, 8 Hai Dian Lu, Beijing 100080; tel. (10) 62686689; fax (10) 62686688; e-mail support@sinosteel.com.cn; internet www.sinosteel.com; f. 1999; formed by merger of China National Metallurgical Import and Export Corpn, China Metallurgical Raw Materials Corpn and China Metallurgical Steel Products Processing Corpn; Pres. HUANG TIANWEN.

China Minmetals Corpn (Minmetals): 5 San Li He, Haidian Qu, Beijing 100044; tel. (10) 68495888; fax (10) 68335570; e-mail zc@minmetals.com.cn; internet www.minmetals.com.cn; f. 1950; fmrly China National Metals and Minerals Import and Export Corpn, current name adopted 2004; imports and exports steel, antimony, tungsten concentrates and ferro-tungsten, zinc ingots, tin, mercury, pig-iron, cement, etc.; Pres. ZHOU ZHONGSHU.

China National Aerotechnology Import and Export Corpn: Catic Plaza, 18 Beichen Dong Lu, Chao Yang Qu, Beijing 100101; tel. (10) 84972255; fax (10) 84971088; e-mail catic-jl@catic.com.cn; internet www.catic.com.cn; f. 1979; exports signal flares, electric detonators, tachometers, parachutes, general purpose aircraft, etc.; Pres. SHULA FU.

China National Animal Breeding Stock Import and Export Corpn (CABS): 5/F Beijing News Plaza, 26 Jian Guo Men Nei Dajie, Beijing 100005; tel. (10) 65228866; fax (10) 85201555; e-mail www.cabs.com.cn; internet www.cabs.com.cn; sole agency for import and export of stud animals including cattle, sheep, goats, swine, horses, donkeys, camels, rabbits, poultry, etc., as well as pasture and turf grass seeds, feed additives, medicines, etc.; Gen. Man. LIU XIAOFENG.

China National Arts and Crafts Import and Export Corpn: Arts and Crafts Bldg, 103 Jixiangli, Chao Yang Men Wai, Chao Yang Qu, Beijing 100020; tel. (10) 65931075; fax (10) 65931036; e-mail po@mbox.cnart.com.cn; internet www.cnart-group.com; deals in jewellery, ceramics, handicrafts, embroidery, pottery, wicker, bamboo, etc.; Pres. CHEN KUN.

China National Automotive Industry Corpn (CNAIC): 46 Fucheng Lu, Haidian Qu, Beijing 100036; tel. (10) 88123968; fax (10) 68125556; Pres. CHEN XULIN.

China National Automotive Industry Import and Export Corpn (CAIEC): 265 Beisihuan Zhong Lu, Beijing 100083; tel. (10) 82379009; fax (10) 82379088; e-mail info@caiec.cn; internet www.caiec.cn; Pres. ZHANG FUSHENG; 1,100 employees.

China National Cereals, Oils and Foodstuffs Import and Export Corpn (COFCO): 7th–13th Floors, Tower A, COFCO Plaza, Jian Guo Men Nei Dajie, Beijing 100005; tel. (10) 65268888; fax (10) 65278612; e-mail minnie@cofco.com.cn; internet www.cofco.com.cn; f. 1952; imports, exports and processes grains, oils, foodstuffs, etc.; also hotel management and property development; Chair. NING GAONING; Pres. YU XUBO.

China National Chartering Corpn (SINOCHART): Rm 1601/1602, 1607/1608, Jiu Ling Bldg, 21 Xisanhuan Bei Lu, Beijing 100081; tel. (10) 68405601; fax (10) 68405628; e-mail sinochrt@public.intercom.co.cn; internet www.sinotransgroup.com; f. 1950; subsidiary of SINOTRANS (see below); arranges chartering of ships,

THE PEOPLE'S REPUBLIC OF CHINA

reservation of space, managing and operating chartered vessels; Pres. LIU SHUNLONG; Gen. Man. ZHANG JIANWEI.

China National Chemical Construction Corpn: Bldg No. 15, Songu, Anzhenxili, Chao Yang Qu, Beijing 100029; tel. (10) 64429966; fax (10) 64419698; e-mail cnccc@cnccc.com.cn; internet www.cnccc.com.cn; Pres. CHEN LIHUA.

China National Chemicals Import and Export Corporation (SINOCHEM): SINOCHEM Tower, A2 Fu Xing Men Wai Dajie, Beijing 100045; tel. (10) 68568888; fax (10) 68568890; internet www.sinochem.com; f. 1950; import and export, domestic trade and entrepôt trade of oil, fertilizer, rubber, plastics and chemicals; Pres. LIU DESHU.

China National Coal Industry Import and Export Corpn (CNCIEC): 88B An Ding Men Wai, Dongcheng Qu, Beijing 100011; tel. (10) 64287188; fax (10) 64287166; e-mail cnciec@chinacoal.com; internet www.chinacoal.com; f. 1982; imports and exports coal and tech. equipment for coal industry, joint coal development and compensation trade; Chair. and Pres. WANG CHANGCHUN.

China National Coal Mine Corpn: 21 Bei Jie, Heipingli, Beijing 100013; tel. (10) 64217766; Pres. WANG SENHAO.

China National Complete Plant Import and Export Corpn (Group) (Complant): 9 Xi Bin He Lu, An Ding Men, Beijing; tel. (10) 64253388; fax (10) 64211382; e-mail info@complant.com; internet www.complant.com; Chair. LI ZHIMIN; Gen. Man. TANG JIANGUO.

China National Electronics Import and Export Corpn: 8th Floor, Electronics Bldg, 23A Fuxing Lu, Beijing 100036; tel. (10) 68219550; fax (10) 68212352; e-mail ceiec@ceiec.com.cn; internet www.ceiec.com.cn; f. 1980; imports and exports electronics equipment, light industrial products, ferrous and non-ferrous metals; advertising; consultancy; Pres. and CEO CONG YADONG.

China National Export Bases Development Corpn: Bldg 16–17, District 3, Fang Xing Yuan, Fang Zhuang Xiaoqu, Fengtai Qu, Beijing 100078; tel. (10) 67628899; fax (10) 67628803; Pres. XUE ZHAO.

China National Foreign Trade Transportation Corpn (Group) (SINOTRANS): 12/F, Sinotrans Plaza, Xizhimen Beidajie, Beijing 100044; tel. (10) 62296666; fax (10) 62296600; e-mail info@sinotrans.com; internet www.sinotransgroup.com; f. 1950; agents for China's import and export corpns; arranges customs clearance, deliveries, forwarding and insurance for sea, land and air transportation; registered cap. 4,249m. yuan, sales 28,580m. yuan (2005); Chair. MIAO GENGSHU; Pres. ZHAO HUXIANG.

China National Gold Group Corpn (China Gold): Qingnianhu, Beijie Anwai, Beijing 100011; tel. (10) 84123187; fax (10) 84113355; e-mail cngc@chinagoldgroup.com; internet www.chinagoldgroup.com; gold mining, research and trade; Pres. SUN ZHAOXUE.

China National Instruments Import and Export Corpn (Instrimpex): Instrimpex Bldg, 6 Xi Zhi Men Wai Jie, Beijing 100044; tel. (10) 68330618; fax (10) 68330528; e-mail zcb@instrimpex.com.cn; internet www.instrimpex.com.cn; f. 1955; imports and exports; technical service, real estate, manufacturing, information service, etc.; Pres. ZHANG GUIXIU.

China National Light Industrial Products Import and Export Corpn: 910, 9th Section, Jin Song, Chao Yang Qu, Beijing 100021; tel. (10) 67766688; fax (10) 67747246; e-mail info@chinalight.com.cn; internet www.chinalight.com.cn; imports and exports household electrical appliances, audio equipment, photographic equipment, films, paper goods, building materials, bicycles, sewing machines, enamelware, glassware, stainless steel goods, footwear, leather goods, watches and clocks, cosmetics, stationery, sporting goods, etc.; Pres. XU LIEJUN.

China National Machine Tool Corpn: 19 Fang Jia Xiaoxiang, An Nei, Beijing 100007; tel. (10) 64033767; fax (10) 64015657; internet cnmtc.net.cn; f. 1979; imports and exports machine tools and tool products, components and equipment; supplies apparatus for machine-building industry; Pres. QUAN YILU.

China National Machinery and Equipment Import and Export Corpn (Group) (CMEC): 178 Guang An Men Wai Dajie, Beijing 100055; tel. (10) 63451188; fax (10) 63261865; e-mail cmec@mail.cmec.com; internet www.cmec.com; f. 1978; imports and exports machine tools, all kinds of machinery, automobiles, hoisting and transport equipment, electric motors, photographic equipment, etc.; Pres. XIE BIAO.

China National Medicine and Health Products Import and Export Corpn (Meheco): Meheco Plaza, 18 Guangming Zhong Jie, Chongwen Qu, Beijing 100061; tel. (10) 67116688; fax (10) 67021579; e-mail webmaster@meheco.cn; internet www.meheco.cn; Pres. ZHANG BEN ZHI.

China National Native Produce and Animal By-Products Import and Export Corpn (TUHSU): Sanli Bldg, 208 An Ding Men Wai Jie, Beijing 100011; tel. (10) 64248899; fax (10) 64204099; e-mail tuhsu@tuhsu.com.cn; internet www.tuhsu.com.cn; f. 1949;

Directory

imports and exports include tea, coffee, cocoa, fibres, etc.; 9 tea brs; 23 overseas subsidiaries; Pres. LIU YONGFU.

China National Non-Ferrous Metals Import and Export Corpn (CNIEC): 12B Fuxing Lu, Beijing 100814; tel. (10) 63975588; fax (10) 63964424; Chair. WU JIANCHANG; Pres. XIAO JUNQING.

China National Nuclear Corpn: 1 Nansanxiang, Sanlihe, Beijing; tel. (10) 68512211; fax (10) 68533989; internet www.cnnc.com.cn; Pres. KANG RIXIN.

China National Oil Development Corpn: Liupukang, Beijing 100006; tel. (10) 6444313; subsidiary of China National Petroleum Corpn; Pres. WANG DONGJIN.

China National Packaging Import and Export Corpn: Xinfu Bldg B, 3 Dong San Huan Bei Lu, Chao Yang Qu, Beijing 100027; tel. (10) 64611166; fax (10) 64616437; e-mail info@chinapack.net; internet www.chinapack.net; handles import and export of packaging materials, containers, machines and tools; contracts for the processing and converting of packaging machines and materials supplied by foreign customers; Pres. ZHENG CHONGXIANG.

China National Petroleum Corpn (CNPC): 6 Liupukang Jie, Xicheng Qu, Beijing 100724; tel. (10) 62094538; fax (10) 62094806; e-mail admin@hq.cnpc.com.cn; internet www.cnpc.com.cn; responsible for petroleum extraction and refining in northern and western China, and for setting retail prices of petroleum products; restructured mid-1998, transferring to PetroChina Co Ltd (a publicly listed subsidiary) domestic operations in the areas of petroleum and gas exploration and devt, petroleum refining and petrochemical production, marketing, pipeline transport, and natural gas sales and utilization; acquired PetroKazakhstan in 2005; Pres. JIANG JIEMIN.

China National Publications Import and Export Corpn: 16 Gongrentiyuguandong Lu, Chao Yang Qu, Beijing; tel. (10) 65066688; fax (10) 65063101; e-mail info-center@cnpeak.com; internet www.cnpeak.com; imports and exports books, newspapers and periodicals, records, CD-ROMs, etc.; Pres. JIAO GUOYING.

China National Publishing Industry Trading Corpn: POB 782, 504 An Hua Li, An Ding Men Wai, Beijing 100011; tel. (10) 64215031; fax (10) 64214540; internet www.cnpitc.com.cn; f. 1981; imports and exports publications, printing equipment technology; holds book fairs abroad; undertakes joint publication; Pres. WU JIANGJIANG.

China National Seed Group Corpn: An Zhen Xi Li, Chao Yang Qu, Beijing 100029; tel. (10) 64436699; fax (10) 64423338; e-mail webmaster@chinaseeds.com.cn; internet www.chinaseeds.com.cn; f. 1978; imports and exports crop seeds, including cereals, cotton, oil-bearing crops, teas, flowers and vegetables; seed production for foreign seed companies etc.; Pres. SONG XIAOMING.

China National Silk Import and Export Corpn: 105 Bei He Yan Jie, Dongcheng Qu, Beijing 100006; tel. (10) 65123338; fax (10) 65125125; e-mail cnsiec@public.bta.net.cn; internet www.chinasilk.com; Pres. CHEN YIQING.

China National Technical Import and Export Corpn: 16/F, Genertec Plaza, 90 Xi San Huan Zhong Lu, Fengtai Qu, Beijing 100055; tel. (10) 63349205; fax (10) 63349187; e-mail info@cntic.com.cn; internet www.cntic.com.cn; f. 1952; imports all kinds of complete plant and equipment, acquires modern technology and expertise from abroad, undertakes co-production and jt ventures, and technical consultation and updating of existing enterprises; Pres. JIANG XINSHENG.

China National Textiles Import and Export Corpn: Chinatex Mansion, 19 Jian Guo Men Nei Lu, Beijing 100005; tel. (10) 65281122; fax (10) 65124711; e-mail info@chinatex.net; internet www.chinatex.com; f. 1951; imports synthetic fibres, raw cotton, wool, garment accessories, etc.; exports cotton yarn, cotton fabric, knitwear, woven garments, etc.; over 30 subsidiaries; Pres. ZHAO BOYA.

China National Tobacco Import and Export Group Corpn: 9 Guang An Men Wai Dajie, Xuan Wu Qu, Beijing 100055; tel. (10) 63605290; fax (10) 63605915; internet www.cntiegc.com.cn; Chair. ZHANG HUI.

China North Industries Group Corpn (CNGC): 46 Sanlihe Lu, Beijing 100821; tel. (10) 68594210; fax (10) 68594232; e-mail webmaster@cngc.com.cn; internet www.cngc.com.cn; exports vehicles and mechanical products, light industrial products, chemical products, opto-electronic products, building materials, military products, etc.; Pres. MA ZHIGENG.

China Railway Construction Corpn: 40 Fuxing Lu, Beijing 100855; tel. (10) 51888114; fax (10) 68217382; e-mail webmaster@crccg.com; internet www.crccg.com; f. 1948; state-owned; over 30 subsidiaries; design, construction, equipment installation and maintenance of railways and highways; Gen. Man. WANG ZHENHOU.

China Railway Group Ltd: 1 Xinghuo Lu, Fengtai Qu, Beijing 100070; tel. (10) 51845717; fax (10) 51842057; internet www.crec.cn; f. 2007; est. as jt stock co; 46 subsidiaries; infrastructure construction, design, survey and consulting services; mfr of engineering equipment; Chair. SHI DAHUA; Pres. LI CHANGJIN.

China Road and Bridge Corpn: Zhonglu Bldg, 88C, An Ding Men Wai Dajie, Beijing 100011; tel. (10) 64285616; fax (10) 64285686; e-mail crbc@crbc.com; internet www.crbc.com; overseas and domestic building of highways, urban roads, bridges, tunnels, industrial and residential buildings, airport runways and parking areas; contracts to do surveying, designing, pipe-laying, water supply and sewerage, building, etc., and/or to provide technical or labour services; Chair. MA GUODONG; Pres. ZHOU JICHANG.

China Shipbuilding Trading Corpn Ltd: 26/F, Fangyuan Mansion, 56 Zhongguancun Nan Dajie, Haidian Qu, Beijing 100044; tel. (10) 88026030; fax (10) 88026000; e-mail webmaster@cstc.com.cn; internet www.chinaships.com; f. 1982; Pres. LI ZHUSHI.

China State Construction Engineering Corpn: CSCEC Mansion, 15 San Li He Dajie, Haidian Qu, Beijing 100037; tel. (10) 88082888; fax (10) 68314326; e-mail cscec-us@worldnet.att.net; internet www.cscec.com.cn; f. 1982; Pres. SUN WENJIE.

China State Shipbuilding Corpn (CSSC): 5 Yuetan Bei Jie, Beijing 100861; tel. (10) 68038833; fax (10) 68034592; e-mail cssc@cssc.net.cn; internet www.cssc.net.cn; f. 1999; naval and civil shipbuilding; Pres. CHEN XIAOJIN.

China Tea Import and Export Corpn: Zhongtuchu Bldg, 208 Andingmenwai Jie, Beijing 100011; tel. (10) 64204127; fax (10) 64204101; e-mail info@teachina.com; internet www.chinatea.com.cn; Chair. ZHU FUTANG; Gen. Man. SUN YUEHUA.

China Xinshidai (New Era) Co: Xinshidai Plaza, 7 Huayuan Lu, Haidian Qu, Beijing 100088; tel. (10) 82803388; fax (10) 82803688; e-mail xsd@xsd.com.cn; internet www.xsd.com.cn; f. 1980; imports and exports defence industry and civilian products; Pres. WANG XINGYE.

Daqing Petroleum Administration Bureau: Sartu Qu, Daqing, Heilongjiang; tel. (459) 814649; fax (459) 322845; Gen. Man. WANG ZHIWU.

Maanshan Iron and Steel Co (Masteel): 8 Hongqibei Lu, Maanshan 243003, Anhui Province; tel. (555) 2888158; fax (555) 2324350; internet www.magang.com.cn; sales 34,319.9m. yuan (2006); Chair. GU JIANGUO; Pres. ZHU CHANGQUI.

PetroChina International Co Ltd (China National United Oil Corporation—Chinaoil): 27 Chengfang Lu, Xicheng Qu, Beijing 100032; tel. (10) 66227001; fax (10) 66227002; internet www.chinaoil.com.cn; international trading subsidiary of PetroChina Co Ltd; imports and exports petroleum, natural gas and refined petroleum products; Chair. DUAN WENDE; Pres. WANG LIHUA.

Shanghai International Trust Trading Corpn: 201 Zhaojiabang Lu, Shanghai 200032; tel. (21) 64033866; fax (21) 64034722; f. 1979; present name adopted 1988; handles import and export business, international mail orders, processing, assembling, compensation, trade, etc.

State Bureau of Non-Ferrous Metals Industry: 12B Fuxing Lu, Beijing 100814; tel. (10) 68514477; fax (10) 68515360; under supervision of State Economic and Trade Commission; Dir ZHANG WULE.

Wuhan Iron and Steel (Group) Co (WISCO): Qingshan Qu, Wuhan, Hubei Province; tel. (27) 6892004; fax (27) 6862325; internet www.wisco.com.cn; proposals for merger with two other steel producers in Hubei announced late 1997; Pres. DENG QILIN.

Xinxing Oil Co (XOC): Beijing; f. 1997; exploration, development and production of domestic and overseas petroleum and gas resources; Gen. Man. ZHU JIAZHEN.

UTILITIES

Regulatory Authority

State Electricity Regulatory Commission: 86 Xichangan Dajie, Beijing 100031; tel. (10) 66058800; e-mail manager@serc.gov.cn; internet www.serc.gov.cn; f. 2003; Chair. CHAI SONGYUE.

Electricity

Anhui Province Energy Group Co Ltd (Wenergy): 81 Wuhu Lu, Hefei 230001; tel. (551) 2225588; fax (551) 4669573; e-mail service@wenergy.com.cn; internet www.wenergy.com.cn.

Beijing Electric Power Corpn: Qianmen Xi Dajie, Beijing 100031; tel. (10) 63129201; internet www.bjpsc.com.

Central China Electric Power Group Co: 47 Xudong Lu, Wuchang, Wuhan 430077; tel. (27) 6813398.

Changsha Electric Power Bureau: 162 Jiefang Sicun, Changsha 410002; tel. (731) 5912121; fax (731) 5523240.

China Atomic Energy Authority: e-mail webmaster@caea.gov.cn; internet www.caea.gov.cn; Chair. SUN QIN.

China Guodian Corpn: transfer of Jianbi power plant from fmr State Power Corpn completed Sept. 2003.

China Northwest Electric Power Group Co: 57 Shangde Lu, Xian 710004; tel. (29) 7275061; fax (29) 7212451; Chair. LIU HONG.

China Power Grid Development (CPG): 4 Xueyuang Nanli, Haidan Qu, Beijing; manages transmission and transformation lines for the Three Gorges hydroelectric scheme; Pres. ZHOU XIAOQIAN.

China Power Investment Corpn: Bldg 3, 28 Financial St, Xicheng Qu, Beijing 100032; tel. (10) 66298000; fax (10) 66298095; e-mail engweb@cpicorp.com.cn; internet www.zdt.com.cn; f. 2002; formed from part of the constituent businesses of fmr State Power Corpn; parent company of China Power International; Pres. WANG BINGHUA.

China Southern Power Grid Co: 6 Huasui Lu, Zhujiang Xincheng, Tianhe Qu, Guangzhou, Guangdong 510623; tel. (20) 38121080; fax (20) 38120189; e-mail international@csg.net.cn; internet eng.csg.cn; f. 2002; est. from power grids in southern provinces of fmr State Power Corpn; Chair. YUAN MAOZHEN; Pres. WANG YEPING.

China Three Gorges Project Corpn (CTGPC): 1 Jianshe Dajie, Yichang 443002, Hubei Province; tel. (717) 6762899; fax (717) 6270248; internet www.ctgpc.com; Pres. LI YONGAN.

China Yangtze Power Co Ltd: Block B, Focus Place, 19 Financial St, Xicheng Qu, Beijing 100032; tel. (10) 58688999; fax (10) 58688888; e-mail cypc@cypc.com.cn; internet www.cypc.com.cn; f. 2002; generation of power from the Yangtze river; manages power-generating assets on behalf of China Yangtze Three Gorges Project Development Corpn; initial public offering on the Shanghai Stock Exchange Nov. 2003; Gen. Man. LI YONGAN.

Chongqing Jiulong Electric Power Co Ltd: 8 Qianjinzhi Lu, Yangjiaping, Jiulongpo Qu, Chongqing 400050; tel. (23) 68787910; fax (23) 68787944; internet www.jiulongep.com; Chair. LIU WEIQING.

Chongqing Three Gorges Water Conservancy and Electric Power Co Ltd: 12/F, Yide Bldg, 183 Bayi Lu, Yuzhong Qu, Chongqing 400010; tel. (23) 87509622; fax (23) 58237588; internet www.cqsxsl.com; Chair. YE JIANQIAO.

Dalian Power Supply Co: 102 Zhongshan Lu, Dalian 116001; tel. (411) 2637560; fax (411) 2634430; Chief Gen. Man. LIU ZONGXIANG.

Datang International Power Generation Co Ltd: 8/F, 482 Guanganmennei Dajie, Xuanwu Qu, Beijing 100053; internet www.dtpower.com; one of China's largest independent power producers; Chair. ZHAI RUOYU; Exec. Dir ZHANG YI.

Fujian Electric Power Co Ltd: 4 Xingang Dao, Taijrang Qu, Fuzhou 350009; tel. and fax (591) 3268514; Gen. Man. LI WEIDONG.

Fujian Mindong Electric Power Co Ltd: 8–10/F, Hualong Bldg, 143 Huancheng Lu, Jiaocheng Qu, Ningde 352100; tel. (593) 2096666; f. 2000; Chair. ZHOU DUNBIN.

Gansu Electric Power Co: Lanzhou 730050; tel. (931) 2334311; fax (93) 2331042; e-mail webmaster@gsepc.com; internet www.gsepc.com; Dir ZHANG MINGXI.

GD Power Development Co Ltd: 9/F, International Investment Plaza Tower B, 6–8 Fu Cheng Men Bei Dajie, Xicheng Qu, Beijing; tel. (10) 58682200; fax (10) 583553800; e-mail gdd1@600795.com.cn; internet www.600795.com.cn; manufacture and sale of electricity and heat, and the operation of power grids in northern, eastern, north-eastern and north-western China, as well as Yunnan and Sichuan Provinces; Chair. ZHOU DABING.

Guangdong Electric Power Bureau: 757 Dongfeng Dong Lu, Guangzhou 510600; tel. (20) 87767888; fax (20) 87770307.

Guangdong Electric Power Development Co Ltd: 23–26/F, South Tower, Yuedian Plaza, 2 Tian He Dong Lu, Guangzhou 510630; tel. (20) 87570251; internet www.ged.com.cn; Chair. LI PAN.

Guangdong Yudean Group: Guangzhou; tel. (20) 85138888; fax (20) 85138666; internet www.gdyd.com; Chair. LI SHIZHUANG.

Guangxi Guiguan Electric Power Co Ltd: 6 Minzhu Lu, Nanning 530023; tel. (771) 5636271; fax (771) 5656215; e-mail ggep@ggep.com.cn; internet www.ggep.com.cn; Chair. YANG QING; Gen. Man. DAI BO.

Guangzhou Electric Power Co: 9th Floor, Huale Bldg, 53 Huale Lu, Guangzhou 510060; tel. (20) 83821111; fax (20) 83808559.

Guodian Changyuan Electric Power Co Ltd: Huazhong Electric Finance Bldg, 117 Xu Dong Jie, Wuchang Qu, Wuhan, Hubei 430067; tel. (27) 86610545; fax (27) 86786970; e-mail cyzqb01@cydl.com.cn; internet www.cydl.com.cn; Chair. LI QINGKUI.

Hainan Electric Power Industry Bureau: 34 Haifu Dadao, Haikou 570203; tel. (898) 5334777; fax (898) 5333230.

Huadian Energy Co Ltd: 209 Dacheng Jie, Harbin 150001; tel. (451) 2308810; fax (451) 2525878; Chair. SHUHUI REN.

Huadian Power International Corpn Ltd: 14 Jingsan Lu, Jinan, Shandong 250001; tel. (531) 82366608; fax (531) 8236 6090; e-mail hdpi@hdpi.com.cn; internet www.hdpi.com.cn; f. 1994; fmrly Shandong International Power Development, renamed as above 2003; Chair. HE GONG; Dir CHEN JIANHUA.

Huadong Electric Power Group Corpn: 201 Nanjing Dong Lu, Shanghai; tel. (21) 63290000; fax (21) 63290727; power supply.

THE PEOPLE'S REPUBLIC OF CHINA

Huaneng Power International: West Wing, Building C, Tianyin Mansion, 2c Fuxingmennan Lu, Xicheng, Beijing; tel. (10) 66491999; fax (10) 66491888; e-mail ir@hpi.com.cn; internet www.hpi.com.cn; f. 1998; transfer of generating assets from fmr State Power Corpn completed Sept. 2003; Chair. LI XIAOPENG; Pres. NA XIZHI.

Huazhong Electric Power Group Corpn: Liyuan, Donghu, Wuhan, Hubei Province; tel. (27) 6813398; fax (27) 6813143; electrical engineering; Gen. Man. LIN KONGXING.

Hunan Chendian International Development Share-holding: 15/F, Wanguo Bldg, Minsheng Lu, Intersection Qingnian Dajie, Chenzhou 423000; tel. (735) 2339232; internet www.chinacdi.com; f. 2000; electricity and gas supply and generation; Chair. FU GUO.

Hunan Huayin Electric Power Co Ltd: 255, Third Section, Central Furong Lu, Changsha 410007; tel. (731) 5388028; internet www.hypower.com.cn; Chair. LIU SHUNDA.

Inner Mongolia Electric Power Co: 28 Xilin Nan Lu, Huhehaose 010021; tel. (471) 6942222; fax (471) 6924863.

Jiangmen Electric Power Supply Bureau: 87 Gangkou Lu, Jiangmen 529030; tel. and fax (750) 3360133.

Jiangxi Electric Power Corpn: 13 Yongwai Zheng Jie, Nanchang 330006; tel. (791) 6224701; fax (791) 6224830; internet www.jepc.com.cn; f. 1993.

National Grid Construction Co: established to oversee completion of the National Grid by 2009.

North China Grid Company Ltd: 482 Guanganmen Nei Dajie, Xuanwu Qu, Beijing 100053; tel. and fax (10) 63263377; internet www.ncpg.com.cn; Pres. ZHU GUOZHEN.

Northeast China Electric Power Group: 11 Shiyiwei Lu, Heping Qu, Shenyang 110003; tel. (24) 3114382; fax (24) 3872665.

Shandong Electric Power Group Corpn: 150 Jinger Lu, Jinan 250001; tel. (531) 6911919.

Shandong Rizhao Power Co Ltd: 1st Floor, Bldg 29, 30 Northern Section, Shunyu Xiaoqu, Jinan 250002; tel. (531) 2952462; fax (531) 2942561; subsidiary of Huaneng Power International.

Shanghai Electric Power Co Ltd: 268 Zhongshou Nan Lu, 36F, Shanghai 200010; tel. (21) 51156666; e-mail sepco@shanghaipower.com; internet www.shanghaipower.com; Chair. ZHOU SHIPING.

Shanghai Municipal Electric Power Co (SMEPC): 1122 Yuanshen Lu, Shanghai 200122; tel. (21) 28925222; fax (21) 28926512; e-mail smepc@smepc.com; internet www.smepc.com.cn.

Shantou Electric Power Development Co: 23 Zhuchi Lu, Shantou 515041; tel. (754) 8857191; Chair. LIN WEIGUANG.

Shanxi Zhangze Electric Power Co Ltd: 197 Wuyi Lu, Taiyuan 030001; tel. (351) 4265120; internet www.zhangzepower.com; Chair. WANG QINGWEN.

Shenergy Co Ltd: 1 Fuxing Zhong Lu, Shanghai 200021; tel. (621) 63900888; fax (621) 63900119; internet www.shenergy.com.cn; f. 1992; supply and distribution of electricity and natural gas; Chair. WU JIAHUA.

Shenzhen Power Supply Co: 2 Yanhe Xi Lu, Luohu Qu, Shenzhen 518000; tel. (755) 5561920.

Sichuan Electric Power Co: Room 1, Waishi Bldg, Dongfeng Lu, Chengdu 610061; tel. (28) 444321; fax (28) 6661888.

Sichuan Mingxing Electric Power Co Ltd: 88 Ming Yue Lu, Sui Ning 629000; tel. (825) 2210076; fax (825) 2210017; internet www.mxdl.com.cn; f. 1988; distribution of electric power and gas; Chair. QIN GANG.

State Grid Corpn of China: No. 1 Lane 2, Baiguang Lu, Beijing 100761; tel. (10) 63416475; fax (10) 63548152; e-mail sgcc-info@sgcc.com.cn; internet www.sgcc.com.cn; f. 1997 from holdings of Ministry of Electric Power; fmrly State Power Corpn of China; became a grid company following division of State Power Corpn into 11 independent companies (five generating companies, four construction companies and two transmission companies) in Dec. 2002; generating assets to be transferred to Huaneng Group, Huadian Group, Guodian Group, China Power Investment Corpn and Datang Group; GPres. and CEO LIU ZHENYA.

Tianjin Electric Power Corpn: 29 Jinbu Dao, Hebei Qu, Tianjin 300010; tel. (22) 24406326; fax (22) 22346327; internet www.tepco.com.cn.

Top Energy Co Ltd: V-6 Section, Taiyuan Xue-Fu High-Tech Industrial Park, Shanxi Province 030006; tel. (351) 7032515; fax (351) 7021077; e-mail top600780@sina.com; internet www.600780.net; f. 1992; Chair. CHANG XIAOGANG.

Wuhan Power Supply Bureau: 981 Jiefang Dadao, Hankou, Wuhan 430013; tel. (27) 2426455; fax (27) 2415605.

Wuxi Power Supply Bureau: 8 Houxixi, Wuxi 214001; tel. (510) 2717678; fax (510) 2719182.

Xiamen Power Transformation and Transmission Engineering Co: 67 Wenyuan Lu, Xiamen 361004; tel. (592) 2046763.

Xian Power Supply Bureau: Huancheng Dong Lu, Xian 710032; tel. (29) 7271483.

Xinjiang Tianfu Thermoelectric Co Ltd: 54 Hongxing Lu, Shihezi 832000; tel. (993) 2901128; e-mail yj@tfrd.com.cn; internet www.tfrd.com.cn; f. 1999; generation and distribution of electricity in Shihezi, Xinjiang Uygur Autonomous Region; Chair. CHENG FENG.

Zhejiang Southeast Electric Power Co: ; tel. (51) 85774567; fax (51) 85774321; internet www.zsepc.com; Chair. SHEN ZHIYUN.

Gas

Beijing Gas Group Co Ltd: e-mail bjgas@bjgas.com; internet www.bjgas.com; owned by the Hong Kong-based Beijing Enterprises Holdings Ltd.

Beijing Natural Gas Co: Bldg 5, Dixingju, An Ding Men Wai, Beijing 100011; tel. (10) 64262244.

Changchun Gas Co: 30 Tongzhi Jie, Changchun 130021; tel. (431) 8926479; internet www.ccrq.com.cn.

Changsha Gas Co: 18 Shoshan Lu, Changsha 410011; tel. (731) 4427246.

Qingdao Gas Co: 399A Renmin Lu, Qingdao 266032; tel. (532) 4851945; fax (532) 4858653; e-mail gasoffice@qdgas.com.cn; internet www.qdgas.com.cn.

Shanghai Dazhong Public Utilities: 8/F, 1515 Zhongshan Xi Lu, Shanghai 200235; tel. (21) 64288888; fax (21) 64288727; internet www.dzug.cn; Chair. YANG GUOPING.

Shenzhen Energy Investment Co Ltd: ; tel. (755) 83680288; fax (755) 83680298; e-mail sec@sec.com.cn; internet www.sec.com.cn; f. 1992; Chair. YANG HAIXIAN.

Wuhan Gas Co: Qingnian Lu, Hankou, Wuhan 430015; tel. (27) 5866223.

Xiamen Gas Corpn: Ming Gong Bldg, Douxi Lukou, Hubin Nan Lu, Xiamen 361004; tel. (592) 2025937; fax (592) 2033290.

Xinao Gas Holdings Ltd: Huaxiang Lu, Langfang Economic and Technical Development Zone, Hebei 065001; tel. (316) 6079983; fax (316) 6088199; e-mail xinao@xinaogas.com; internet www.xinaogas.com; Chair. WANG YUSUO.

Water

Beijing Municipal Water Works Bureau: 83 Cuiwei Lu, Haidian Qu, Beijing 100036; tel. (10) 68213366; fax (10) 68130728.

Changchun Water Group Co Ltd: 53 Dajing Lu, Changchun 130000; tel. (431) 88974423; e-mail ccws@changchunwater.com; internet www.changchunwater.com.

Chengdu Municipal Waterworks Co Ltd: 16 Shierqiao Jie, Shudu Dadao, Chengdu 610072; tel. (28) 77663122; fax (28) 7776876; internet www.cdwater.chengdu.gov.cn.

The China Water Company: Unit 13, 11/F, Pos Plaza, 1600 Century Ave, Pudong New Area, Shanghai; e-mail cwcsha@chinawater.com.hk; internet www.chinawater.com.hk; f. 1996 to develop investment opportunities for water projects; 48.8% owned by Thames Water Utilities Ltd (United Kingdom).

Guangzhou Water Supply Co: 12 Zhongshan Yi Lu, Yuexiu Qu, Guangzhou 510600; fax (20) 87159099; internet www.gzwatersupply.com.

Haikou Water Group Co Ltd: tel. (898) 66269271; fax (898) 66269696; internet www.haikouwater.com.

Harbin Water Co: 49 Xi Shidao Jie, Daoli Qu, Harbin 150010; tel. (451) 4610522; fax (451) 4611726.

Jiangmen Water Supply Co Ltd: 44 Jianshe Lu, Jiangmen 529000; tel. (750) 3286358; fax (750) 3286368; e-mail webmaster@jmwater.com; internet www.jmwater.com.

Qinhuangdao Pacific Water Co: Hebei; f. 1998; Sino-US water supply project.

Shanghai Water Authority: 100 Da Gu Lu, Shanghai 200003; tel. (21) 23111111; internet www.shanghaiwater.gov.cn; service provider for municipality of Shanghai.

Shenzhen Water Supply Group Co: Water Bldg, 1019 Shennan Zhong Lu, Shenzhen 518031; tel. (755) 2137836; fax (755) 2137888; e-mail webmaster@waterchina.com; internet www.waterchina.com.

Tianjin Waterworks Group: 54 Jianshe Lu, Heping Qu, Tianjin 300040; tel. (22) 3393887; fax (22) 3306720; e-mail sonic356@sohu.com; internet www.jinnanwater.com.

Xian Water Co: Huancheng Xi Lu, Xian 710082; tel. (29) 4244881.

Zhanjiang Water Co: 20 Renmin Dadaonan, Zhanjiang 524001; tel. (759) 2286394.

Zhongshan Water Supply Co: 23 Yinzhu Jie, Zhuyuan Lu, Zhongshan 528403; tel. (760) 8312969; fax (760) 6326429.

Zhoushan Water Supply Co Ltd: Zhoushan; tel. (580) 2022769; e-mail webmaster@zswater.com; internet www.zswater.com.

THE PEOPLE'S REPUBLIC OF CHINA

Zhuhai Water Supply Co Ltd: tel. (756) 8899110; e-mail zhgsdnzx@pub.zhuhai.gd.cn; internet www.zhuhai-water.com.cn.

TRADE UNIONS

All-China Federation of Trade Unions (ACFTU): 10 Fu Xing Men Wai Jie, Beijing 100865; tel. (10) 68592114; fax (10) 68562030; e-mail webmaster@acftu.org.cn; internet www.acftu.org.cn; f. 1925; organized on an industrial basis; 15 affiliated national industrial unions, 30 affiliated local trade union councils; membership is voluntary; trade unionists enjoy extensive benefits; 134m. mems; Chair. WANG ZHAOGUO; First Sec. SUN CHUNLAN.

Principal affiliated unions:

All-China Federation of Railway Workers' Unions: f. 1924; Chair. GUO YIMIN; 3.1m. mems (2006).

Chinese Agricultural, Forestry and Water Conservancy Workers' Union: f. 1933; Chair. SHENG MINGFU; 10m. mems (2008).

Chinese Aviation Workers' Union: f. 2003; Chair. GAO HONGFENG; 360,000 mems.

Chinese Defence Industry, Postal and Telecommunications Workers' Union: f. 2001; Chair. DONG XUIBIN; 6.41m. mems (2007).

Chinese Educational, Scientific, Cultural, Health and Sports Workers' Union: f. 2001; Chair. WANG XIAOLONG; 25m. mems (2007).

Chinese Energy and Chemical Workers' Union.

Chinese Financial, Commercial, Light Industry, Textile and Tobacco Workers' Union: f. 2001; Chair. JIA YANMIN; 48m. mems (2007).

Chinese Financial Workers' Union: f. 1951; Chair. HE JIESHENG; 2m. mems (2007).

Chinese Machinery, Metallurgy and Building Materials Workers' Union: f. 2001; Chair. LIU HAIHUA; 35m. mems (2007).

Chinese Seamen and Construction Workers' Union: f. 2003; Chair. WU ZIHENG; 40m. mems (2008).

Transport

RAILWAYS

Ministry of Railways: see under Ministries; controls most railways through regional divisions; total length in operation in Dec. 2006 was almost 77,084 km, of which about 23,435 km were electrified; major routes include Beijing–Guangzhou, Tianjin–Shanghai, Manzhouli–Vladivostok, Jiaozuo–Zhicheng and Lanzhou–Badou.

A new 2,536-km line from Beijing to Kowloon (Hong Kong) was completed in 1995. China's first high-speed service, linking Guangzhou and Shenzhen, commenced in 1994, and a direct service between Shanghai and Hong Kong commenced in 1997. A new 1,142-km railway linking Tibet (Xizang) with the rest of China, via Qinghai Province was completed in October 2005. The Government then announced plans to extend the line to Xigaze, the region's second largest city. Regular services on the new magnetic-levitation ('maglev') railway linking Shanghai to Pudong International airport, built in co-operation with a German consortium, began in March 2004. In 2006 China and Germany reportedly reached consensus on the construction of a 200-km 'maglev' line from Shanghai to Hangzhou, which was expected to be operational by 2010. In 2006 China's first private railway was initiated, following the sale of a 138-km line between Guangdong Province and Guanxi Zhuang Autonomous Region to Shenzhen Zhongji Industrial Group. In September of the same year the Ping An Insurance Group won government approval to invest in the construction of a railway linking Guangzhou and Wuhan, expected to be completed in 2010. In 2008 plans were announced to expedite construction on railway lines linking Yunnan Province with Viet Nam, Myanmar and Thailand; the link between the Yunnanese capital of Kunming and Ho Chi Minh City in Viet Nam was scheduled for completion in 2009. The construction of a 1,318-km line between Beijing and Shanghai, which upon completion would be the longest high-speed railway in the world, commenced in 2008. A high-speed link between Beijing and Guangzhou was also planned.

City Underground Railways

Beijing Mass Transit Railway Operation Corpn Ltd: 2 Beiheyan Lu, Xicheng, Beijing 100044; tel. (10) 68340565; e-mail service@bjsubway.com; internet www.bjsubway.com; f. 1969; total length 142 km; projected to expand to 440 km by 2012; Gen. Man. XIE ZHENGGUANG.

Chongqing Metro: internet www.cqmetro.cn; f. 2005; China's first monorail system; one operating line of 19.15 km, with further developments planned.

Guangzhou Metro: 204 Huanshi Lu, Guangzhou 510010; tel. (20) 83289033; e-mail ServiceCenter@21cn.com; internet www.gzmtr.com; opened June 1997; total length 36.6 km; network expected to comprise 9 lines and 225 km of track by 2010; Pres. LU GUANGLIN.

Nanjing Metro: internet www.nj-dt.com; f. 2005; one line of 17 km; Line 2 due to be completed in 2009.

Shanghai Shentong Metro Group Co Ltd: Level 31, Jiu Shi Bldg, 28 Zhongshan Nan Lu, Shanghai 200010; tel. (21) 58308595; fax (21) 63300065; internet www.shtmetro.com; f. 1995; 228.4 km; network planned to exceed 500 km by 2010; Gen. Man. GU CHENG.

Shenzhen Metro: Shenzhen; internet www.szmc.net; f. 2004; currently two lines with a total distance of 21.9 km.

Tianjin Metro General Corpn: 97 Jiefangbei Lu, Heping, Tianjin 300041; tel. (22) 23395410; fax (22) 23396194; internet www.ditie.cc; f. 1984; total planned network 154 km; closed in 2001 for reconstruction and extension, reopened in 2006; Gen. Man. WANG YUJI.

Wuhan Metro: f. 2004; currently one 10.2-km line, with six more lines being planned.

Underground systems are also planned for Chengdu (scheduled for completion in 2010) and Qingdao.

ROADS

At the end of 2006 China had 3,456,999 km of highways. Four major highways link Lhasa (Tibet) with Sichuan, Xinjiang, Qinghai Hu and Kathmandu (Nepal). A programme of expressway construction began in the mid-1980s. By 2006 there were 45,339 km of expressways, routes including the following: Shenyang–Dalian, Beijing–Tanggu, Shanghai–Jiading, Guangzhou–Foshan and Xian–Lintong. Expressway construction was to continue, linking all main cities and totalling 55,000 km by 2020. A new 123-km highway linking Shenzhen (near the border with Hong Kong) to Guangzhou opened in 1994. A 58-km road between Guangzhou and Zhongshan connects with Zhuhai, near the border with Macao. Construction of a bridge, linking Zhuhai with Macao was completed in 1999. A bridge connecting the mainland with Hong Kong and Macao was also under consideration.

INLAND WATERWAYS

At the end of 2006 there were some 123,388 km of navigable inland waterways in China. The main navigable rivers are the Changjiang (Yangtze River), the Zhujiang (Pearl River), the Heilongjiang, the Grand Canal and the Xiangjiang. The Changjiang is navigable by vessels of 10,000 tons as far as Wuhan, more than 1,000 km from the coast. Vessels of 1,000 tons can continue to Chongqing upstream.

There were 5,142 river ports at the end of 1996. In 1997 there were some 5,100 companies involved in inland waterway shipping.

SHIPPING

China has a network of more than 2,000 ports, of which more than 130 are open to foreign vessels. In May 2001 plans were announced for the biggest container port in the world to be built on the Yangshan Islands, off shore from Shanghai. The main ports include Dalian, Qinhuangdao, Tianjin, Yantai, Qingdao, Rizhao, Lianyungang, Shanghai, Ningbo, Guangzhou and Zhanjiang. In December 2006 China's merchant fleet comprised 3,695 ships, totalling 23.5m. grt.

Bureau of Water Transportation: Beijing; controls rivers and coastal traffic.

China International Marine Containers (Group) Co Ltd (CIMC): 2 Gangwan Dajie, Shekou Industrial Zone, Shenzhen, Guangdong 518067; tel. (755) 26691130; fax (755) 26692707; e-mail email@cimc.com; internet www.cimc.com; f. 1980; jt venture between China Merchants Holdings, the East Asiatic Co Ltd (EAC) and China Ocean Shipping (Group) Co (COSCO); manufacture and supply of containers, trailers and airport equipment; cap. 2,017.0m., res 7,596.8m., sales 30,938.5m. (2005); Chair. LI JIANHONG; Pres. MAI BOLIANG.

China National Chartering Corpn (SINOCHART): see Trade and Industrial Organizations.

China Ocean Shipping (Group) Co (COSCO): 11th and 12th Floors, Ocean Plaza, 158 Fu Xing Men Nei, Xi Cheng Qu, Beijing 100031; tel. (10) 66493388; fax (10) 66492288; internet www.cosco.com.cn; reorg. 1993, re-est. 1997; head office transferred to Tianjin late 1997; br. offices: Shanghai, Guangzhou, Tianjin, Qingdao, Dalian; 200 subsidiaries (incl. China Ocean Shipping Agency—PENAVIC) and joint ventures in China and abroad, engaged in ship-repair, container-manufacturing, warehousing, insurance, etc.; merchant fleet of 600 vessels; 47 routes; Pres. WEI JIAFU.

China Shipping (Group) Co: Shanghai; e-mail cscas@cnshipping.com; internet www.cnshipping.com/english; f. 1997; state-owned shipping conglomerate; incorporates five specialized shipping fleets of oil tankers, tramps, passenger ships, container vessels and special cargo ships respectively; a total of 440 vessels with an aggregate deadweight of 15m. metric tons; Pres. LI SHAODE.

China Shipping Container Lines Co Ltd: 5th Floor, Shipping Tower, 700 Dong Da Ming Lu, Shanghai 200080; tel. (21) 65966833; fax (21) 65966498; e-mail braingui@cnshipping.com; internet www.cscl.com.cn; container shipping company; 151 vessels (Jan. 2008); Chair. LI SHAODE.

China Shipping Development Co Ltd: 168 Yuanshen Lu, Pudong New Area, Shanghai 200120; tel. (21) 68757170; fax (21) 68757929; internet www.cnshipping.com/encsd; 50.51% owned by China Shipping (Group) Co; operates oil tankers and dry bulk cargo vessels; Chair. LI SHAODE.

Fujian Shipping Co: 151 Zhong Ping Lu, Fuzhou 350009; tel. (591) 3259900; fax (591) 3259716; e-mail fusco@pub2.fz.fj.cn; internet www.fusco-cn.com; f. 1950; transport of bulk cargo, crude petroleum products, container and related services; Gen. Man. LIU QIMIN.

Guangzhou Maritime Transport (Group) Co: 22 Shamian Nan Jie, Guangzhou 510131; tel. (20) 81861255; fax (20) 84428954; internet www.gzmaritime.com.

CIVIL AVIATION

Air travel continues to expand very rapidly. In 2006 a total of 142 civil airports were in operation. In October 2002 the Government announced that the nine largest airlines were to be merged into three groups, based in Guangzhou, Shanghai and Beijing. Air China incorporated China National Aviation Corpn (which also controlled Zhejiang Airlines and 43% of Hong Kong's Dragonair) and China Southwest Airlines; China Eastern Airlines incorporated China Northwest Airlines and Yunnan Airlines; and China Southern Airlines incorporated China Northern Airlines and China Xinjiang Airlines. In 2004 the establishment of private airlines was approved.

Air China Ltd: Beijing International Airport, POB 644, Beijing 100621; tel. (10) 64582211; e-mail master@mail.airchina.com.cn; internet www.airchina.com.cn; 51% owned by state-owned China National Aviation Holding Co (CNAC); international and domestic scheduled passenger and cargo services; in process of joining Star Alliance group of airlines in 2006; Chair. LI JIAXIANG; Pres. MA XULUN.

China Eastern Airlines: 2550 Hongqiao Rd, Hongqiao Airport, Shanghai 200335; tel. (21) 95108; fax (21) 62686116; e-mail web_service@ce-air.com; internet www.ce-air.com; f. 1987; domestic services; overseas destinations include USA, Europe, Japan, Sydney, Singapore, Seoul and Bangkok; Pres. LI FENGHUA.

China Eastern Airlines Wuhan (CEAW): 435 Jianshe Dajie, Wuhan 430030; tel. (87) 63603888; fax (87) 83625693; e-mail wuhanair@public.wh.hb.cn; f. 1986; fmrly Wuhan Air Lines; became China's first partly privately owned airline upon refounding on 2002; 96% owned by China Eastern Airlines; domestic services; Pres. CHENG YAOKUN.

China Eastern Xi Bei Airlines: Laodong Nan Lu, Xian, Shaanxi 710082; tel. (29) 88792299; fax (29) 84261622; e-mail webcnwa@mail.cnwa.com; internet www.cnwa.com; f. 1992; fmrly China Northwest Airlines; renamed following acquisition of assets by China Eastern Airlines in 2005; domestic services and flights to Macao, Singapore and Japan; Pres. GAO JUNQUI.

China Eastern Yunnan Airlines: Wujaba Airport, Kunming 650200; tel. (871) 7113007; fax (871) 7151509; internet www.c3q.com.cn; f. 1992; est. as Yunnan Airlines; renamed following acquisition of assets by China Eastern Airlines in 2005; 49 domestic services; also serves Bangkok (Thailand), Singapore, and Vientiane (Laos); Pres. XUE XIAOMING.

China General Aviation Corpn: Wusu Airport, Taiyuan, Shanxi 030031; tel. (351) 7040600; fax (351) 7040094; f. 1989; 34 domestic routes; Pres. ZHANG CHANGJING.

China Southern Airlines: 278 Jichang Lu, Guangzhou, Guangdong 510405; tel. (20) 86128473; fax (20) 86658989; e-mail webmaster@cs-air.com; internet www.cs-air.com; f. 1991; merged with Zhong Yuan Airlines, 2000; acquired operations and assets of China Northern Airlines and China Xinjiang Airlines in 2004; domestic services; overseas destinations include Bangkok, Fukuoka, Hanoi, Ho Chi Minh City, Kuala Lumpur, Penang, Pyongyang, Singapore, Manila, Vientiane, Jakarta and Surabaya; Chair. LIU SHAOYONG; Pres. SI XIANMIN.

Xiamen Airlines: Gaoqi International Airport, Xiamen, Fujian 361009; tel. (592) 5739888; fax (592) 5739777; internet www.xiamenair.com.cn; f. 1992; 60% owned by China Southern Airlines, 40% owned by Xiamen Construction and Development Corpn; domestic services; also serves Bangkok (Thailand); Pres. YANG GUANGHUA.

China United Airlines: Beijing; tel. (10) 67978899; internet www.cu-air.com; f. 2005; originally est. in 1986 as part of the People's Liberation Army civil transport division; closed down in 2002; resumed operations in 2005; 80% owned by Shanghai Airlines; Pres. LAN DINGSHOU.

Hainan Airlines (HNA): HNA Devt Bldg, 29 Haixiu Lu, Haikou, Hainan 570206; tel. (898) 66739801; fax (898) 66739807; e-mail webmaster@hnair.com; internet www.hnair.com; f. 1993; leading air transport enterprise of HNA Group; 300 domestic services; international services to Korea; 14.8% owned by financier George Soros; Chair. CHEN FENG; Pres. ZHU YIMIN.

Changan Airlines: 16/F, Jierui Bldg, 5 South Er Huan Rd, Xian, Shaanxi 710068; tel. (29) 8378027; fax (29) 8707911; f. 1992; subsidiary of HNA Group; local passenger and cargo services; Pres. SHE YINING.

China Xinhua Airlines: 1 Jinsong Nan Lu, Chao Yang Qu, Beijing 100021; tel. (10) 66766027; fax (10) 67740126; e-mail infocxh@homeway.com.cn; internet www.chinaxinhuaair.com; f. 1992; subsidiary of HNA Group; Chair. LIU JIAXU; Pres. YANG JINGLIN.

Shanxi Airlines: Customs Bldg, Wusu Airport, Taiyuan, Shanxi 030031; subsidiary of HNA Group; Chair. QIN JIANMIN, LI QING.

Okay Airways: Tianjin Binhai International Airport, Dongli Qu, Tianjin 300300; internet www.okair.net; f. 2004; inaugural flight 2005; the People's Republic of China's first privately owned airline; Pres. LIU JIEYIN.

Shandong Airlines: Shandong Aviation Mansion, 5746 Er Huan Dong Lu, Lixia Qu, Jinan, Shandong 250014; tel. (531) 85698666; fax (531) 85698668; e-mail webmaster@shandongair.com.cn; internet www.shandongair.com; f. 1994; domestic services; Pres. SUN YUDE.

Shanghai Air Lines: 212 Jiangming Lu, Shanghai 200040; tel. (21) 62558888; fax (21) 62558885; e-mail liw@shanghai-air.com; internet www.shanghai-air.com; f. 1985; domestic services; also serves Phnom-Penh (Cambodia); applied to join Star Alliance international group of airlines in 2006; Chair. ZHOU CHI; Pres. FAN HONGXI.

Shenzhen Airlines: Lingtian Tian, Lingxiao Garden, Shenzhen Airport, Shenzhen, Guangdong 518128; tel. (755) 7771999; fax (755) 7777242; internet shenzhenair.com; f. 1993; previously state-owned; now owned by Guangdong Development Bank (65%), Air China (25%) and Shenzhen Investment Management (10%); domestic services; Pres. LI KUN.

Sichuan Airlines: Chengdu Shuangliu International Airport, Chengdu, Sichuan 610202; tel. (28) 5393001; fax (28) 5393888; e-mail scaloi@public.cd.sc.cn; internet www.scal.com.cn; f. 1986; domestic services; Pres. LAN XINGGUO.

Spring Airlines: Shanghai Hongqiao Airport, Shanghai; tel. (21) 62520000; fax (21) 62523734; e-mail webmaster@china-sss.com; internet www.china-sss.com; privately owned; low-cost airline; inaugural flight July 2005; Chair. and Pres. WANG ZHENGHUA.

United Eagle Airlines: Chengdu Shuangliu International Airport, Chengdu, Sichuan Province 610202; tel. (28) 66006333; fax (28) 85706199; internet www.ueair.com; f. 2004; privately owned; Chair. LI JINING.

Tourism

The tourism sector has continued to develop rapidly. Attractions include dramatic scenery and places of historical interest such as the Temple of Heaven and the Forbidden City in Beijing, the Great Wall, the Ming Tombs and the terracotta warriors at Xian. In 2005 there were 11,828 tourist hotels in operation. The number of tourists (including visitors from Hong Kong, Macao and Taiwan, who accounted for about 82% of the total in 2006) rose from 124m. in 2006 to almost 132m. in 2007. Receipts from international tourism totalled US $33,949m. in 2006. The 2008 Olympic Games were to be held in Beijing in August.

China International Travel Service (CITS): 103 Fu Xing Men Nei Dajie, Beijing 100800; tel. (10) 85228888; fax (10) 65226855; e-mail mktng@cits.com.cn; internet www.cits.net; f. 1954; makes travel arrangements for foreign tourists; 10 subsidiary overseas cos; Pres. YAO YUECAN.

China National Tourism Administration (CNTA): 9A Jian Guo Men Nei Dajie, Beijing 100740; tel. (10) 65138866; fax (10) 65122096; e-mail webmaster@cnta.gov.cn; internet www.cnta.gov.cn; Chair. SHAO QIWEI.

Chinese People's Association for Friendship with Foreign Countries: 1 Tai Ji Chang Dajie, Beijing 100740; tel. (10) 65122474; fax (10) 65128354; internet www.cpaffc.org.cn; f. 1954; Chair. QI HUAIYUAN.

CHINESE SPECIAL ADMINISTRATIVE REGIONS
HONG KONG

Introductory Survey

Location, Climate, Language, Religion, Flag, Capital

The Special Administrative Region (SAR) of Hong Kong, as the territory became on 1 July 1997, lies in eastern Asia, off the south coast of the People's Republic of China. The SAR consists of the island of Hong Kong, Stonecutters Island, the Kowloon Peninsula and the New Territories, which are partly on the mainland. The climate is sunny and dry in winter, and hot and humid in summer. The average annual rainfall is 2,214 mm (87 ins), of which about 80% falls between May and September. The official languages are Chinese and English. Cantonese is spoken by the majority of the Chinese community, while Putonghua (Mandarin) is widely understood and of increasing significance. The main religion is Buddhism. Confucianism, Islam, Hinduism and Daoism are also practised, and there is a large Christian community. The flag of the Hong Kong SAR (proportions 2 by 3), flown subordinate to the flag of the People's Republic of China, displays a bauhinia flower consisting of five white petals, each bearing a red line and a red five-pointed star, at the centre of a red field. The administrative and business centre is Central District.

Recent History

Hong Kong Island was ceded to the United Kingdom under the terms of the Treaty of Nanking (Nanjing) in 1842. The Kowloon Peninsula was acquired by the Convention of Peking (Beijing) in 1860. The New Territories were leased from China in 1898 for a period of 99 years. From the establishment of the People's Republic in 1949, the Chinese Government asserted that the 'unequal' treaties giving Britain control over Hong Kong were no longer valid.

Japanese forces invaded Hong Kong in December 1941, forcing the British administration to surrender. In August 1945, at the end of the Second World War, the territory was recaptured by British forces. Colonial rule was restored, with a British military administration until May 1946. Upon the restoration of civilian rule, the territory was again administered in accordance with the 1917 Constitution, which vested full powers in the British-appointed Governor. In 1946 the returning Governor promised a greater measure of self-government but, after the communist revolution in China in 1949, plans for constitutional reform were abandoned. Thus, unlike most other British colonies, Hong Kong did not proceed, through stages, to democratic rule. The essential features of the colonial regime remained unaltered until 1985, when, following the Sino-British Joint Declaration (see below), the first changes were introduced into the administrative system. Prior to 1985 the Executive and Legislative Councils consisted entirely of nominated members, including many civil servants in the colonial administration. There were, however, direct elections for one-half of the seats on the Urban Council, responsible for public health and other amenities, but participation was low.

Between 1949 and 1964 an estimated 1m. refugees crossed from the People's Republic to Hong Kong, imposing serious strains on Hong Kong's housing and other social services. More than 460,000 Chinese immigrants arrived, many of them illegally, between 1975 and 1980. Strict measures, introduced in October 1980, reduced the continuous flow of refugees from China, but the number of legal immigrants remained at a high level.

During the 1980s the influx of large numbers of refugees from Viet Nam, most of whom lived for substantial periods in detention camps, was problematic. The Hong Kong authorities, meanwhile, exerted pressure on the British Government to end its policy of granting first asylum to these refugees. In response, legislation was introduced in June 1988 to distinguish between political refugees and 'economic migrants'. The latter were to be denied refugee status, and in October the British and Vietnamese Governments agreed terms for their voluntary repatriation. In March 1989 the first group of co-operative 'economic migrants' flew back to Viet Nam. The number of Vietnamese arrivals increased sharply in the late 1980s, despite the unpleasant conditions in the camps where they were confined on arrival, and the restricting of the definition of refugee status. The relative paucity of those who agreed to return to Viet Nam (totalling 1,225 by February 1990) prompted the British Government to attempt, unsuccessfully, to gain general international endorsement for a policy of compulsory repatriation (which, it was claimed, would discourage further large-scale immigration). The Vietnamese Government announced in December 1989 that an agreement had been concluded between the United Kingdom and Viet Nam on a programme of 'involuntary' repatriation, whereby 'economic migrants' could be returned to Viet Nam against their will, on condition that no physical force was used. Reports of forcible repatriation caused violent disturbances in many of the camps. The programme was subsequently halted. At a meeting in January 1990, the UN steering committee for the Comprehensive Plan of Action on Indo-Chinese refugees failed to agree upon a policy. By May 1990 no further cases of the involuntary repatriation of Vietnamese had been reported. At an international conference held in that month, Hong Kong and the member countries of the Association of South East Asian Nations (ASEAN) threatened to refuse asylum to Vietnamese refugees altogether, unless the USA and Viet Nam gave approval to the policy of involuntary repatriation. In September Hong Kong, Viet Nam and the United Kingdom reached an agreement, supported by the UN High Commissioner for Refugees (UNHCR), to allow the repatriation of a new category of refugees—those who were not volunteering to return but who had indicated that they would not actively resist repatriation. This policy had little success, and the number of refugees increased.

In October 1991, following protracted negotiations, it was announced that Viet Nam had agreed to the mandatory repatriation of refugees from Hong Kong. The first forcible deportation (mainly of recent arrivals) under the agreement was carried out in November. Tension and violence in the camps continued. In May 1992 an agreement between the United Kingdom and Viet Nam provided for the forcible repatriation of all economic migrants. By the end of 1995 the detention camp population had been greatly reduced, with only 1,479 being classified as refugees. Unrest in the camps continued intermittently. The People's Republic of China, meanwhile, continued to insist that all camps be cleared prior to the transfer of sovereignty in mid-1997. The Whitehead Detention Centre was closed in January 1997, and the refugees were transferred to other camps. Despite an acceleration in the repatriation programme, some 1,200 Vietnamese migrants remained in Hong Kong in December 1997. In January 1998 the SAR administration (see below) announced that it was abolishing the 'port of asylum' policy which had been applied to Vietnamese refugees. Those arriving illegally would no longer be given time to apply for asylum. At the end of May 2000 the last Vietnamese refugee camp, at Pillar Point, was closed. Most of the refugees were granted residency in the SAR.

Meanwhile, following a visit to Hong Kong by the British Prime Minister in September 1982, discussions between the United Kingdom and China were held regarding the territory's future status. In 1984 the United Kingdom conceded that in mid-1997, upon the expiry of the lease on the New Territories, China would regain sovereignty over the whole of Hong Kong. In September 1984 British and Chinese representatives met in Beijing and initialled a legally binding agreement, the Sino-British Joint Declaration, containing detailed assurances on the future of Hong Kong. China guaranteed the continuation of the territory's capitalist economy and life-style for 50 years after 1997. The territory, as a Special Administrative Region of the People's Republic, would be designated 'Hong Kong, China', and would continue to enjoy a high degree of autonomy, except in matters of defence and foreign affairs. It was agreed that Hong Kong would retain its identity as a free port and separate customs territory, and its citizens would be guaranteed freedom of speech, of assembly, of association, of travel and of religious belief. In December 1984, after being approved by the National People's Congress (NPC—the Chinese legislature) and the British Parliament, the agreement was signed in Beijing by the British and Chinese Prime Ministers, and in May 1985 the two Governments exchanged documents ratifying the agreement. A Joint Liaison Group (JLG), comprising British and Chinese representatives, was established to monitor the provisions of the agreement, and this group held its first meeting in July 1985. A 58-member Basic Law Drafting Committee (BLDC), including 23 representatives from Hong Kong, was formed in Beijing in June, with the aim of drawing up a new Basic Law (Constitution) for Hong Kong.

The majority of the population reportedly accepted the terms of the Joint Declaration, but the sensitive issue of the future nationality of Hong Kong residents proved controversial. The 1981 British Nationality Act had already caused alarm in the territory, where the reclassification of 2.3m. citizens was perceived as a downgrading of their status. As holders of Hong Kong residents' permits, they had no citizenship status under British laws. Following the approval of the Hong Kong agreement, the British Government announced a new form of nationality, to be effective from 1997, designated 'British National (Overseas)', which would not be transferable to descendants and would confer no right of abode in the United Kingdom.

In September 1985 indirect elections were held for 24 new members of an expanded Legislative Council (Legco), to replace the former appointees and government officials. The participation rate among the very small proportion of the population eligible to vote in the elections was low. In March 1986 municipal elections were held for the urban and regional councils, which were thus, for the first time, wholly directly elected. A new Governor, Sir David Wilson (who had played a prominent part in the Sino-British negotiations on the territory's future), formally assumed office in April 1987, following the death of his predecessor, Sir Edward Youde, in December 1986. In May 1987 the Hong Kong Government published proposals regarding the development of representative government during the final decade of British rule. Among the options that it proposed was the introduction, in 1988, of direct elections to the Legislative Council, based upon universal adult suffrage. In spite of the disapproval of the Chinese Government, in February 1988 the Hong Kong Government published, with the support of the majority of the population, a policy document on the development of representative government; the principal proposal was the introduction, in 1991, of 10 (subsequently increased) directly elected members of the Legislative Council.

In April 1988 the first draft of the Basic Law for Hong Kong was published, and a Basic Law Consultative Committee (BLCC) was established in Hong Kong, initially with 176 members, to collect public comments on its provisions, over a five-month period; the draft was to be debated by the Legislative Council and by the Parliament of the United Kingdom, but no referendum was to be held in Hong Kong, and final approval of the Basic Law rested with the NPC of China. The draft offered five options for the election of a chief executive and four regarding the composition of the future Legislative Council, none of which, however, proposed that the Council should be elected entirely by universal suffrage. Although the legislature would be empowered to impeach the chief executive for wrongdoing, the Chinese Government would have final responsibility for his removal.

In November 1988 the UN Commission on Human Rights criticized the British attitude to the transfer of Hong Kong, with particular reference to the lack of direct elections. A second draft of the Basic Law was approved by the Chinese NPC in February 1989, which ignored all five options previously proposed for the election of a chief executive. In May there were massive demonstrations in Hong Kong in support of the anti-Government protests taking place in China. In June, following the killing of thousands of protesters by the Chinese armed forces in Tiananmen Square in Beijing, further demonstrations and a general strike took place in Hong Kong, expressing revulsion at the massacres. The British Government refused to consider renegotiating the Sino-British Joint Declaration but, in response to demands that the British nationality laws should be changed to allow Hong Kong residents the right to settle in the United Kingdom after 1997, it announced in December 1989 that the British Parliament would be asked to enact legislation enabling as many as 50,000 Hong Kong residents (chosen on a 'points system', which was expected to favour leading civil servants, business executives and professional workers), and an estimated 175,000 dependants, to be given the right of abode in the United Kingdom. The measure was intended to 'maintain confidence' in the colony during the transition to Chinese sovereignty, by curbing the emigration of skilled personnel. The Hong Kong authorities cautiously welcomed the announcement, but China warned prospective applicants that it would not recognize their British nationality after 1997. Despite widespread protests in Hong Kong against the scheme, the relevant legislation was approved in the United Kingdom's House of Commons in April 1990.

Among other recommendations made by the parliamentary select committee were the introduction of a Bill of Rights for Hong Kong and an increase in the number of seats subject to direct election in the Hong Kong Legislative Council, to one-half of the total in 1991, leading to full direct elections in 1995. A draft Bill of Rights, based on the UN International Covenant on Civil and Political Rights, was published by the Hong Kong Government in March 1990. The draft was criticized in principle because its provisions would have been subordinate, in the case of conflict, to the provisions of the Basic Law. Nevertheless, the Bill of Rights entered into law in June 1991.

In April 1990 China's NPC approved a final draft of the Basic Law for Hong Kong: 24 of the 60 seats in the Legislative Council would be subject to direct election from 1999, and 30 seats from 2003; a referendum, to be held after 2007, would consult public opinion on the future composition of the Council, although the ultimate authority to make any changes would rest with the NPC. The British Government had agreed to co-operate with these measures by offering 18 seats for direct election in 1991 and 20 seats in 1995. Under the Basic Law, the Chief Executive of the Hong Kong Special Administrative Region (SAR), as the territory was to be designated in 1997, would initially be elected for a five-year term by a special 800-member election committee; a referendum was to be held during the third term of office in order to help to determine whether the post should be subject to a general election. However, no person with the right of residence in another country would be permitted to hold an important government post. Particular concern was expressed over a clause in the Law that would 'prohibit political organizations and groups in the Hong Kong SAR from establishing contacts with foreign political organizations or groups'.

Liberal groups founded Hong Kong's first formal political party, the United Democrats of Hong Kong (UDHK), with Martin Lee as its Chairman, in April 1990. The party subsequently became the main opposition to the conservatives, and achieved considerable success in local elections in March and May 1991, and in the territory's first direct legislative elections in September. Of the 18 seats in the Legislative Council subject to election by universal suffrage, 17 were won by members of the UDHK and like-minded liberal and independent candidates. Only 39% of registered electors, however, reportedly voted. Despite the party's electoral success, the Governor nominated only one of the UDHK's 20 suggested candidates when selecting his direct appointees to the Legislative Council. Changes in the membership of the Executive Council were announced in October, liberal citizens again being excluded by the Governor.

In April 1992 Christopher Patten, hitherto Chairman of the Conservative Party in the United Kingdom, was appointed Governor to replace Sir David Wilson upon his retirement. Patten took office in July. Plans for democratic reform in the territory, announced by the Governor in October, included the separation of the Executive Council from the Legislative Council. The former was reorganized to include prominent lawyers and academics. At the 1995 elections to the latter, the number of directly elected members was to be increased to the maximum permissible of 20; the franchise for the existing 21 'functional constituencies', representing occupational and professional groups, was to be widened and nine additional constituencies were to be established, in order to encompass all categories of workers. Various social and economic reforms were also announced. In the same month Patten paid his first visit to China.

The proposed electoral changes were denounced by China as a contravention of the Basic Law and of the 1984 Joint Declaration. Although Patten's programme received the general support of the Legislative Council, many conservative business leaders were opposed to the proposals. In November 1992, following Hong Kong's announcement that it was to proceed with the next stage of preparations for the disputed construction of a new airport (without, as yet, the Chinese Government's agreement to the revised financing of the project), China threatened to cancel, in 1997, all commercial contracts, leases and agreements between the Hong Kong Government and the private sector that had been signed without its full approval. The dispute continued in early 1993, China's criticism of the territory's Governor becoming increasingly acrimonious. In February China announced plans to establish a 'second stove', or alternative administration for Hong Kong, if the Governor's proposed reforms were implemented. In April, however, the impasse was broken when the United Kingdom and China agreed to resume negotiations. In July the 57-member Preliminary Working Committee (PWC), established to study issues relating to the forthcoming transfer of sovereignty and chaired by the Chinese Minister of Foreign Affairs, held its inaugural meeting in Beijing. Negotiations between the United Kingdom and China continued intermittently throughout 1993. In December, however, no progress having been made, proposed electoral reforms were submitted to the Legislative Council. The Governor's decision to proceed unilaterally was denounced by China, which declared that it would regard as null and void any laws enacted in Hong Kong.

In February 1994 the Legislative Council approved the first stage of the reform programme, which included the lowering of the voting age from 21 to 18 years. China confirmed that all recently elected bodies would be disbanded in 1997. The second stage was presented to the Legislative Council in March 1994. Relations with China deteriorated further in April, upon the publication of a British parliamentary report endorsing Patten's democratic reforms. In the same month the UDHK and Meeting Point, a smaller party, merged and formed the Democratic Party of Hong Kong. In April the trial in camera of a Beijing journalist (who worked for a respected Hong Kong newspaper) on imprecise charges of 'stealing state secrets' and his subsequent severe prison sentence aroused widespread concern in the territory over future press freedom. Hundreds of journalists took part in a protest march through the streets of Hong Kong.

In June 1994, in an unprecedented development that reflected growing unease with Patten's style of government, the Legislative Council approved a motion of censure formally rebuking the Governor for refusing to permit a debate on an amendment to the budget. Nevertheless, at the end of the month the Legislative Council endorsed further constitutional reforms, entailing an increase in the number of its directly elected members and an extension of the franchise. Despite China's strong opposition to these reforms, shortly afterwards the People's Republic and the United Kingdom concluded an agreement on the transfer of defence sites, some of which were to be retained for military purposes and upgraded prior to 1997, while others were to be released for redevelopment. At the end of August 1994, following the issuing of a report by the PWC in the previous month, the Standing Committee of the NPC in Beijing approved a decision on the abolition, in 1997, of the current political structure of Hong Kong.

In September 1994, at elections to the 18 District Boards (the first to be held on a fully democratic basis), 75 of the 346 seats were won by the Democratic Party. The pro-Beijing Democratic Alliance for the Betterment of Hong Kong (DAB) won 37 seats, the progressive Association for Democracy and People's Livelihood (ADPL) 29 seats, and the pro-Beijing Liberal Party and Liberal Democratic Foundation 18 seats and 11 seats, respectively. Independent candidates secured 167 seats. The level of voter participation was a record 33.1%. In December 1994 the director of the State Council's Hong Kong and Macao Affairs Office and secretary-general of the PWC, Lu Ping, formally confirmed that the Legislative Council would be disbanded in 1997. Elections for the 32 seats on the Urban Council and the 27 seats on the Regional Council took place in March 1995. The Democratic Party took 23 seats, the DAB eight seats and the ADPL also eight seats. Fewer than 26% of those eligible voted in the polls. In the same month Donald Tsang Yam-kuen was nominated as Financial Secretary; his predecessor, along with other expatriate senior officials, had been requested to take early retirement to allow for the appointment of a local civil servant. Tsang took office in September.

Following a redrafting of the legislation, in June 1995 the United Kingdom and China reached agreement on the establishment of the Court of Final Appeal. Contrary to the Governor's original wishes, this new body would not now be constituted until after the transfer of sovereignty in mid-1997. The agreement was approved by the Legislative Council in July 1995. In the same month an unprecedented motion of no confidence in the Governor was defeated at a session of the Legislative Council. At elections to the Legislative Council in September, for the first time all 60 seats were determined by election. The Democratic Party won 19 seats in total, including 12 of the 20 seats open to direct election on the basis of geographical constituencies and two of the 10 chosen by an electoral committee. The Liberal Party took nine of the 60 seats, the pro-Beijing DAB six, and the ADPL four. Independent candidates won 17 seats.

The Governor aroused much controversy in September 1995, when he urged the United Kingdom to grant the right of abode to more than 3m. citizens of Hong Kong. The proposals were rebuffed by the British Home Secretary. In October, however, an improvement in Sino-British relations was confirmed by the visit of the Chinese Minister of Foreign Affairs to London. The two sides reached agreement on the establishment of a liaison office to improve bilateral contacts between civil servants. China's disclosure of a plan to establish a parallel administration six months prior to the transfer of sovereignty provoked outrage in Hong Kong.

In January 1996 the 150-member Preparatory Committee of the Hong Kong SAR was formally established in Beijing to succeed the PWC. The 94 Hong Kong delegates included representatives of the territory's business and academic communities. The Democratic Party was excluded from the new body, which was to appoint a 400-member Selection Committee responsible for the choice of the territory's future Chief Executive. During a visit to the territory in March, the British Prime Minister announced that more than 2m. holders of the forthcoming Hong Kong SAR passports would be granted visa-free access to (but not residency in) the United Kingdom. The Preparatory Committee in Beijing approved a resolution to appoint a provisional body to replace the Legislative Council. As the final deadline approached, thousands of Hong Kong residents rushed to submit applications for British Dependent Territories Citizenship (BDTC) which, although conferring no right of abode in the United Kingdom, would provide an alternative travel document to the new SAR passports. In April the territory's, Chief Secretary, Anson Chan, travelled to Beijing for discussions with Lu Ping. A visit to Hong Kong by Lu Ping earlier in the month had been disrupted by pro-democracy demonstrators. In early July eight pro-democracy politicians from Hong Kong, including five members of the Legislative Council, were refused entry to China to deliver a petition of 60,000 signatures against the proposed establishment of a provisional legislative body for Hong Kong. In mid-August nominations opened for candidacy for the 400-member Selection Committee. In the same month a new pro-democracy movement, The Frontier, comprising teachers, students and trade unionists, was established. In October 1996 the Chinese Minister of Foreign Affairs declared that from mid-1997 the annual protests against the Tiananmen Square massacre of 1989 (and similar demonstrations) would not be tolerated in Hong Kong; furthermore, criticism of the Chinese leadership by the territory's press would not be permitted.

In December 1996 the second ballot for the selection of Hong Kong's Chief Executive (the first having been held in November) resulted in the choice of Tung Chee-hwa, a shipping magnate and former member of the territory's Executive Council, who obtained 320 of the 400 votes. Later in the month the Selection Committee chose the 60 members of the SAR's controversial Provisional Legislative Council (PLC). More than 30 of the new appointees were members of the existing Legislative Council, belonging mainly to the DAB and to the Liberal Party. Despite much criticism of the PLC's establishment, the new body held its inaugural meeting in Shenzhen in January 1997, and elected Rita Fan as its President.

In early 1997 the Chief Executive-designate announced the composition of the Executive Council, which was to comprise three ex-officio members (as previously) and initially 11 non-official members. Anson Chan was to remain as Chief Secretary, while Donald Tsang was to continue as Financial Secretary; Elsie Leung was to become Justice Secretary, replacing the incumbent Attorney General. China's approval of Tung Chee-hwa's recommendations that senior civil servants be retained did much to enhance confidence in the territory's future. In February, however, relations with the outgoing administration deteriorated when the Preparatory Committee voted overwhelmingly in favour of proposals to repeal or amend 25 laws, thereby reducing the territory's civil liberties.

Meanwhile, Lawrence Leung had abruptly resigned as Director of Immigration in July 1996 for 'personal reasons'. In January 1997 he cast doubt on the integrity of the Hong Kong Government when he appeared before a hearing of the Legislative Council and claimed that he had in fact been dismissed, thus denying the official version of his departure from office. The scandal deepened with the revelation that Leung had been found to possess undisclosed business interests. Newspaper reports alleged that Leung had been involved in espionage activities on behalf of China. The Government finally admitted that Leung had indeed been dismissed, but denied the reports of espionage.

In May 1997 the PLC approved its first legislation (a bill on public holidays), despite protests from the British Government and pro-democracy groups in Hong Kong that the PLC was not entitled to pass laws during the transition period. The PLC declared, however, that the legislation would come into effect only on 1 July. Following the circulation in April of a public consultation document on proposed legislation governing civil liberties and social order, a series of amendments, relating to the holding of public demonstrations and the funding of political organizations, was announced in May.

Shortly after the transfer of Hong Kong from British to Chinese sovereignty at midnight on 30 June 1997, the inauguration of the SAR Executive Council, the PLC and members of the judiciary was held. Some 4,000 dignitaries attended the ceremonies, although the British Prime Minister and Foreign Secretary, and the US Secretary of State, did not attend the inauguration of the PLC, to register their disapproval at the undemocratic nature of its formation. Pro-democracy groups and members of the former legislature staged peaceful demonstrations in protest at the abolition of the Legislative Council. More than 4,000 Chinese troops of the People's Liberation Army entered Hong Kong shortly after the handover ceremony, joining the small number of Chinese military personnel that had been deployed in the territory in April, following protracted negotiations with the British Government; a further 500 had entered the territory on 30 June, immediately prior to the handover.

Details of the procedure for elections to a new Legislative Council, which would replace the PLC, were announced by the SAR Government in early July 1997. The elections were scheduled to take place in May 1998 and were to be conducted under a new system of voting. Of the 60 seats in the legislature, 20 were to be directly elected by means of a revised system of proportional representation, 30 were to be elected by 'functional constituencies' (comprising professional and special interest groups) and 10 by an 800-member electoral college. Legislative amendments governing the electoral arrangements were approved by the PLC in late September 1997. The significant reduction of the franchise, by comparison with the 1995 legislative elections, was condemned by the Democratic Party. The appointment by indirect election of 36 Hong Kong delegates to the Chinese NPC, in December 1997, also attracted criticism.

Following the transfer of sovereignty to China, concerns continued about freedom of expression in the SAR. In March 1998 a prominent publisher and a member of the Chinese People's Political Consultative Conference (CPPCC), Xu Simin, challenged the right of the public broadcaster, Radio Television Hong Kong, to criticize government policy, while Tung stated on the same day that government policies should be positively presented by the media. Following expressions of popular discontent, Tung issued a denial that Xu's position reflected government policy. In the same month the Secretary of Justice, Elsie Leung, was criticized following the Government's decision not to prosecute another prominent publisher, CPPCC member and a friend of Tung's, Sally Aw Sian, for corruption, despite a ruling against her by the Independent Commission Against Corruption. Pro-democracy groups expressed fears regarding the independence of the Justice Department. This occurred two weeks after Leung had declined to prosecute the official Chinese news agency, Xinhua, for an alleged breach of privacy laws, after it took 10 months (despite a legal 40-day limit) to issue a denial that it possessed information pertaining to Emily Lau, the leader of The Frontier. (In March 1999 a motion of no confidence in Elsie Leung, prompted by these controversial legal decisions, was defeated in the Legislative Council.) In May 1998 two pro-democracy activists were found guilty of defacing flags of China and the Hong Kong SAR at a rally in January, the first such conviction since Hong Kong's transfer to Chinese sovereignty. In March 1999 the Court of Final Appeal ruled that the law prohibiting the defacing of the SAR flag was an unconstitutional restriction of freedom of expression. In December, however, under pressure from Beijing, the Court rescinded its own decision, and the conviction was confirmed, provoking protests from civil rights organizations. In January 1998 a demonstration coincided with the visit of the former Chinese President, Yang Shangkun, who was regarded as one of those responsible for the Tiananmen Square massacre in 1989. Similar protests were conducted during a visit by Qiao Shi, the Chairman of the Standing Committee of the Eighth Chinese NPC, in February 1998, and in June a commemoration of the 1989 massacre took place without incident. In the following year, the 10th anniversary of the massacre was marked by a peaceful demonstration, attended by 70,000 protesters. On the second anniversary of the resumption of Chinese sovereignty, on 1 July 1999, more than 2,000 pro-democracy demonstrators protested against Chinese control. Tung Chee-hwa's unpopular policies were the subject of similar demonstrations on 1 July 2000.

Following the sudden removal in October 1999 of Cheung Man-yee, Director of Broadcasting of the government-owned Radio Television Hong Kong and an advocate of editorial independence, there were renewed fears for the freedom of the Hong Kong media in April 2000 when China warned against the reporting of any remarks advocating Taiwanese independence. The statement was issued following the broadcast in Hong Kong of an interview with Taiwanese Vice-President-elect Annette Lu, during which she made 'separatist' remarks. China's interference was widely condemned, prompting an assurance by Tung Chee-hwa that freedom of the press and freedom of speech continued to be guaranteed under the provisions of the Basic Law. In October, in Beijing, relations between the Hong Kong media and the People's Republic were further damaged when Hong Kong reporters were accused by Chinese President Jiang Zemin of being 'naïve' for implying that China's support for the Chief Executive would lead to Tung Chee-hwa's reappointment without election. A number of unprecedented personal criticisms of the Chinese President subsequently appeared in the Hong Kong media, and in the following month journalists from the SAR were banned from attending celebrations in China to mark the 20th anniversary of the establishment of the Shenzhen Special Economic Zone. Those who attempted to contravene the ban were detained until after the ceremony. In November Willy Wo-Lap Lam, a prominent journalist and critic of mainland policy, resigned from the *South China Morning Post*. Also in November, students held the latest in a series of protests against the Public Order Ordinance, which stipulated that permission for demonstrations had to be obtained from the security forces at least seven days in advance. Earlier in the month the Government had postponed until December a debate on the Ordinance in the Legislative Council, after opposition politicians protested that the administration was trying to enact the law by forcible means.

Fears concerning the SAR's autonomy were exacerbated by the rapid adoption by the PLC in April 1998 of the Adaptation of Laws Bill. The Bill was ostensibly simply to replace references to the British crown in existing legislation but in practice it exempted Xinhua, the office of the Chinese Ministry of Foreign Affairs and the garrison of the People's Liberation Army from all laws unless otherwise stated. Concerns about the territory's legal autonomy were also raised by the conviction and execution, in November and December respectively, of five criminals from Hong Kong in the People's Republic.

At the elections to the first Legislative Council of the SAR on 24 May 1998, participation (53.3% of registered voters) was the highest since the introduction of direct elections in Hong Kong. The Democratic Party and other pro-democracy parties suffered a reduction in their overall political strength in the legislature, despite the fact that they won 14 of the 20 directly elective seats. A total of 19 seats were secured by pro-democracy candidates, including 13 by the Democratic Party (nine directly elected), led by Martin Lee, which became the largest party in the Legislative Council. Lee advocated direct elections by universal suffrage for all 60 seats in the next poll, to be held in 2000. Pro-Beijing supporters dominated the functional constituencies and the election committee ballot. The pro-business Liberal Party, led by Allen Lee, failed to win a single seat in the direct elections but obtained nine in the other constituencies. The DAB also won nine seats, five of which were directly elective.

The powers of the new legislature were curbed by the Basic Law. Legislative Councillors were not permitted to introduce bills related to political expenditure, the political structure or the operation of the government. The passage of private members' bills or motions also required a majority of votes of both groups of councillors—those elected directly and those returned through functional constituencies and the election committee. At its first session in July 1998 the Legislative Council elected Rita Fan as its President. The division between the Chief Executive, who rarely consulted the legislature, and the Legislative Council became more apparent after Tung Chee-hwa's second annual policy address in October. He announced the abolition of urban and regional councils, a decision opposed by many members of the legislature.

In March 1999 Anson Chan agreed to continue serving as Chief Secretary for two years beyond her normal retirement age, until 2002, when Tung Chee-hwa's term of office was to end. In April 1999 the administration decided to abolish the municipal and regional councils, while existing district boards were to be replaced by district councils. Although the public had been dissatisfied with the performance of the municipal councils, there was resentment at the restructuring of local democracy, which was perceived as a regressive step. In November the Democratic Party threatened legal action if the plan was not abandoned, as it contravened the Basic Law. The first district elections in the Hong Kong SAR took place on 28 November. The Democratic Party won the largest number of elected seats (86), but the pro-Beijing DAB substantially increased its representation, from 37 seats to 83.

Popular support for the SAR Government declined substantially throughout 2000, and public unrest increased. In February Tung Chee-hwa effected a reshuffle of senior officials following the retirement of three officials from the civil service. In May the controversial Elsie Leung was reappointed Secretary of Justice for an additional two years. In June Tung Chee-hwa's administration was embarrassed by the resignation of Rosanna Wong as Secretary for Housing. Three days later the Legislative Council approved a vote of no confidence in Wong and one of her senior officials, holding them responsible for a series of scandals relating to sub-standard construction works. Wong, however, remained a member of the Executive Council. This affair appeared to justify the resignation in April of the prominent opposition politician, Christine Loh, from the Legislative Council. Loh had cited her frustration with the Government's reluctance to share power with the legislature. In September one of Tung Chee-hwa's aides and two officials of Hong Kong University resigned after an independent inquiry found them guilty of attempting to suppress the results of unfavourable public opinion polls conducted by a university researcher.

The second elections to the Legislative Council took place on 10 September 2000. Twenty-four (increased from 20 in the previous legislature) of the seats were directly elective, with 30 seats elected by 'functional constituencies' and six (reduced from 10) by an 800-member electoral college. The level of voter participation was 43.6%. The Democratic Party won the highest number of seats, with 12 (of which nine were directly elected), just ahead of the DAB, which obtained 11 seats. The Democratic Party's share of the votes cast, however, was inferior to that obtained in the 1998 elections. Public apathy was attributed to dissatisfaction with the Government and to the main political parties' failure to publicize coherent manifestos. Nine days later a DAB legislator-elect, Gary Cheng, resigned from the Legislative Council following a scandal over his failure to declare business interests. (A by-election held in December was won by an independent candidate.) At the first session of the new Legislative Council, Rita Fan was re-elected President.

The Government suffered a reverse in January 2001, when Anson Chan unexpectedly announced that she was to resign, for 'personal reasons'. The widely respected Chan was succeeded in April by Donald Tsang; the latter was replaced as Financial Secretary by Antony Leung, a former banker and member of the Executive Council, who was known to be close to Tung Chee-hwa.

In March 2001 the Hong Kong Government presented the new Chief Executive Election Bill, proposing the recognition of the powers of the central Government in Beijing to remove the Chief Executive and providing details of the procedure for the next election for that post, scheduled for 24 March 2002 (but see below). The new incumbent was to serve a five-year term commencing on 30 June 2002. The Bill was approved by the Legislative Council by 36 votes to 18 in July 2001 after minor amendments, but critics of the Bill regarded it as a set-back for the democratic process.

In early 2001 the Chinese Government warned that it would not allow Hong Kong to become a centre for the activities of Falun Gong, a religious sect banned on the mainland since mid-1999, and in May 2001 the Hong Kong Government increased its efforts to prevent the movement's followers from congregating in the territory in advance of a business forum. The conference was to be attended by President Jiang Zemin, former US President Bill Clinton, Thai Prime Minister Thaksin Shinawatra and hundreds of business leaders. Prior to Jiang's visit, scores of Falun Gong followers were prevented from entering Hong Kong; however, a small demonstration by followers was permitted to take place some 300 m from the forum venue. At the conference itself, President Jiang promised to guarantee Hong Kong's autonomy, and praised Tung Chee-hwa's work. At the same time, however, more than 100 Hong Kong academics urged the People's Republic to release Chinese scholars detained on the mainland in previous months (some of whom were citizens or residents of the USA, or residents of Hong Kong), including Li Shaomin and Gao Zhan, who had both been convicted for espionage.

The two were freed in late July, and Li was allowed to resume his academic duties.

In October 2001 the Hong Kong authorities proposed to the Chinese Government draft legislation that would allow mainland citizens to invest legally in the SAR's stock market, as part of a plan to develop closer financial links with the mainland. Tung Chee-hwa's fifth annual policy address to the Legislative Council, delivered in the same month, however, was criticized for lacking bold initiatives needed to improve the economy. In November opposition groups and trade unions, led by Emily Lau, announced the formation of a coalition aimed at preventing the re-election of Tung Chee-hwa as Chief Executive. In early December Lau strongly criticized the procedures for the election of the Chief Executive as undemocratic, and accused Tung of cronyism and of being an unsuitable leader, adding that greater checks and balances were needed. Despite his growing unpopularity, in mid-December Tung announced his intention to stand for a second five-year term as Chief Executive, and was quickly endorsed by President Jiang Zemin. Tung was also endorsed by the convenor of the Executive Council, Leung Chun-ying, Liberal Party leader James Tien and the director of the Beijing Liaison Office, Jiang Enzhu. However, Martin Lee and his Democratic Party boycotted the reception at which Tung formally announced his re-election bid. In late December the Chief Executive visited Beijing, where he discussed the establishment of a free trade arrangement between Hong Kong and the mainland. At the end of February 2002 Tung was nominated for re-election by 714 members of the 800-member Election Committee, thereby securing him a second term in office without challenge. He was formally sworn in for a second term on 1 July.

In March 2002 police charged 16 Falun Gong members (11 locals, one New Zealander and four Swiss nationals) with obstruction following demonstrations outside the Beijing Liaison Office—the first time that legal action had been taken against the group in the SAR. The 16 went on trial in mid-June and were convicted in mid-August. Members of the group also demonstrated on 13 May 2002 to mark the 10th anniversary of the creation of the sect, and the birthday of its founder, Li Hongzhi.

In mid-April 2002 Harry Wu Hongda, a prominent US-based human rights activist, was prevented from entering Hong Kong. His detention on arrival at Chek Lap Kok airport, and deportation the following day, prompted concerns that Hong Kong's freedoms were increasingly under threat, particularly since Wu did not require a visa to enter the SAR, and had visited unimpeded on numerous occasions. Wu was again denied permission to enter the SAR in late June. In late April, the dismissal of the China correspondent of the *South China Morning Post*, Jasper Becker, led to fears that critical coverage of mainland issues would be suppressed.

Plans for a major reorganization of government structures were announced in mid-April 2002. Under the new system, the Executive Council would be expanded into a cabinet-style body consisting of 14 ministers, all appointed by the Chief Executive, and which would administer the 184,000-member civil service. Critics of the proposals warned that the new system would strengthen Tung's (and therefore China's) control over the territory and compromise the independence of the professional civil service. The Legislative Council none the less adopted the changes, and a new cabinet was appointed in late June. However, the mainland's influence was highlighted by the fact that Tung's appointments were delayed by a few days while the Chinese Government subjected them to scrutiny. When finally announced on 24 June 2002, the new Executive Council notably incorporated five appointees from the private sector, including Henry Tang Ying-yen, the new Secretary for Commerce, Industry and Technology and Patrick Ho, the Secretary for Home Affairs. The portfolios of several leading officials, such as Donald Tsang, the Chief Secretary for Administration and Antony Leung, the Financial Secretary, remained unchanged.

Hong Kong observed the fifth anniversary of its reversion to the People's Republic on 1 July 2002, amid exhortations from President Jiang Zemin to Hong Kong's citizens to identify more closely with the mainland. Jiang, who was visiting the SAR, also issued a rare note of criticism of the territory's Government, urging it to improve its performance. At the same time, Vice-Premier Qian Qichen seemingly ruled out democratic reforms in 2007, as promised by the Basic Law, instead emphasizing the need for stability. Tung had described the priority of economic recovery as his greatest challenge during his second term. However, by July 2002 there were also increasing tensions between Tung and the civil service following new legislation that allowed the Government to reduce civil service pay by 4.42%, owing to the growing budget deficit. Some 30,000 public servants marched in protest at the decreases, in the largest demonstrations in Hong Kong since 1989.

In late September 2002 the Government revealed proposals for new anti-subversion laws, which it was required to introduce under Article 23 of the Basic Law, but which had thus far remained unimplemented. Chinese Vice-Premier Qian Qichen had, in June, specifically urged the SAR Government to introduce these laws, giving the impression that the mainland was seeking to extend its laws into the SAR. Critics immediately warned that the new laws would undermine civil liberties and freedom of speech. Suspicions were increased by the fact that a draft of the laws was not made available to the public. The proposals specifically sought to criminalize treason, secession, sedition and subversion, and would also give police the powers to conduct emergency 'search and entry' acts without a warrant. 'Secession' referred to attempts to break away from China, while 'subversion' was defined as threatening or using force to intimidate or overthrow the Government. The Government would also be able to ban any groups affiliated with a mainland organization that had been proscribed in the mainland by the central authorities on national security grounds. Furthermore, the laws could also ban any 'seditious publications' that incited treason, secession or subversion, or disclosed state secrets. A maximum penalty of life imprisonment would be imposed on violators of the new laws. The Secretary for Security, Regina Ip, stated that the laws would not be used to target specific groups such as Falun Gong, or specific individuals, and that existing freedoms would not be affected. In November 10 human rights groups, including the local branches of Amnesty International and Human Rights Watch, urged the Government to abandon the proposed laws.

On 1 December 2002 Martin Lee retired from the leadership of the Democratic Party, after completing four two-year terms (the maximum allowed), and was succeeded by a former party vice-chairman, Yeung Sum. Lee remained a member of the Legislative Council, however, and was expected to continue pressing for greater democratization of the SAR. In early December the Hong Kong Bar Association condemned the anti-subversion laws, describing them as unacceptable and harmful to the territory's freedoms. In mid-December between 20,000 and 60,000 people from a broad section of society demonstrated against the planned anti-subversion laws, and demonstrations in late December by those in favour of the laws attracted 10,000 people. By late January 2003 the Government indicated that, following the end of a three-month public consultation period, some aspects of the laws would be modified, namely provisions dealing with the possession of seditious publications, and a ban on access to state secrets.

The outbreak of Severe Acute Respiratory Syndrome (SARS, a hitherto unknown pneumonia-like illness) in Hong Kong in early 2003, which killed almost 300 people in the territory before the disease was brought under control in June, led to further problems for the Government. There were demands for Tung Chee-hwa to resign, following accusations that the Chief Executive had mishandled the SARS crisis. Meanwhile, there was continuing public disquiet over the proposed security legislation, which was due to be introduced in early July. At the beginning of July, on the sixth anniversary of Hong Kong's reversion to Chinese sovereignty, 500,000 people took part in a demonstration against the proposed new laws. Following the protests, the Liberal Party chairman, James Tien, resigned from his position in the Government, stating that his party would not support the bill in the Legislative Council vote. Tung Chee-hwa subsequently delayed the introduction of the legislation. In late July two government ministers, Secretary for Security Regina Ip and Financial Secretary Antony Leung, resigned from their positions. Both officials had been a target of criticism in the protests at the beginning of the month, and both were known to have close ties with the Chinese Government in Beijing. In early September the controversial anti-subversion bill was withdrawn by Tung Chee-hwa owing to popular opposition; this represented an indirect challenge to the authority of the Chinese Government in Hong Kong. In November Chinese Vice-Premier Zeng Peiyan visited Hong Kong and expressed China's continuing support for Tung Chee-hwa. At local government elections held in Hong Kong at the end of November the pro-Beijing DAB suffered heavy losses, prompting the resignation of the alliance's chairman, Tsang Yok-sing.

In January 2004 there were further popular protests demanding the direct election of Hong Kong's Chief Executive and for all members of the Legislative Council. In February a group of Hong Kong politicians, led by Chief Secretary for Administration Donald Tsang, visited Beijing for discussions with the Chinese Government on the future political development of Hong Kong. Chinese officials stated that any decisions on changes to the procedures for election of the Chief Executive and the Legislative Council would be made by the mainland Chinese leadership. In April the Standing Committee of the NPC in Beijing ruled that the SAR's next Chief Executive would not be chosen by direct election in 2007. The introduction of direct elections for all members of the Legislative Council in 2008 was similarly ruled out. The NPC ruling prompted protests by democracy campaigners in Hong Kong, who claimed that the decision contravened Hong Kong's Basic Law. At the end of April 2004 eight Chinese ships entered Hong Kong harbour, representing the strongest show of force by the Chinese navy since 1997. In May 2004 there were renewed concerns over the freedom of the media after two well-known radio broadcasters, Albert Cheng and Raymond Wong, left Hong Kong, citing attempts to limit their freedom of speech and threats of violence by pro-Beijing groups. The Chinese Government denied having had any part in threatening the broadcasters. Shortly after the departures of Cheng and Wong, a third broadcaster, Allen Lee, who had replaced Cheng as host of a popular radio talk show, resigned as well, claiming to have been subjected to similar instances of intimidation. Lee also resigned from his position as a Hong Kong delegate to China's NPC. In June Chief Executive Tung held discussions with pro-democracy leaders and reiterated the promise that universal suffrage would eventually be realized in Hong Kong. At the beginning of July, on the seventh anniversary of Hong Kong's return to Chinese sovereignty, as many as 500,000 people, according to one estimate, took part in a demonstration demanding universal suffrage. In the same month the Secretary for Health, Welfare and Food, Yeoh Eng-kiong, resigned following publication of a report on the 2003 SARS epidemic. In August 2004 a Chinese military parade, involving some 3,000 troops, took place in Hong Kong. Also in August there were reports of voter intimidation by pro-Beijing factions in advance of the forthcoming legislative elections.

At the elections to the Legislative Council held on 12 September 2004, in which 30 of the total of 60 members were directly elected, support for the pro-democracy faction was less evident than had been widely expected. Of the directly elective seats, 18 were won by democratic parties and 12 by pro-Beijing parties, despite pre-election polls having suggested that the democratic parties might secure as many as 21 of these seats. In the Legislative Council as a whole, pro-Beijing parties held 34 of 60 seats after the election, thus retaining their majority. Voter participation in the election was comparatively high, at 55.6%. There was speculation that following the election the mainland Chinese Government would attempt to expand its influence in the SAR.

On 10 March 2005 Tung Chee-hwa resigned from the post of Chief Executive, two years before his term of office was due to end, citing ill health. However, there was speculation that the Chief Executive had been removed from his post by the central Government in Beijing owing to his unpopularity in the SAR and his perceived poor handling of the pro-democracy movement. Tung was to become Vice-Chairman of a body of the mainland Chinese Government, the CPPCC (see above). Chief Secretary for Administration Donald Tsang took the role of acting Chief Executive until 25 May, whereupon he resigned in order to present his candidacy in the election for a new Chief Executive, due to be held in July. Financial Secretary Henry Tang replaced Tsang as acting Chief Executive. Meanwhile, in a controversial ruling in April, the NPC had decreed that Tung's successor would serve out only the remaining two years of his predecessor's second term, rather than being appointed to the position for a full five-year term. Legislators and legal experts protested that this apparent establishment of a probationary period for Hong Kong's new leader was a contravention of the SAR's Basic Law.

In addition to Tsang, two other politicians decided to present their candidacy for the July 2005 election: Lee Wing-tat, Chairman of the Democratic Party, and legislator Chim Pui-chung. Tsang, however, was widely considered to have the support of the central Government. In the event, Lee and Chim both failed to secure the required 100 nominations from among the 800-member Election Committee, and as a result their candidacies were rejected. Consequently Donald Tsang, whose candidacy was endorsed by 674 of the 800 Committee members, was elected unopposed to the post of Chief Executive on 16 June. Despite protests from Lee and Chim that the election had been unfairly weighted because of Tsang's superior access to the media and his refusal to debate with them during the campaign, together with more general complaints about the undemocratic electoral system employed, Tsang's lengthy experience of public office under both the British and Chinese administrations, and his reputation for decisiveness and financial acumen, were thought to make him a popular choice among Hong Kong residents.

In June 2005 tens of thousands of protesters attended a vigil in Hong Kong to mark the 16th anniversary of the suppression of the Tiananmen Square protests. However, the annual pro-democracy march in July (on the anniversary of the return of Hong Kong to Chinese rule) attracted far fewer demonstrators than in previous years. In August Hong Kong reporter Ching Cheong, detained since April, was charged with espionage by the Chinese Government. In late September all the members of Hong Kong's Legislative Council, notably including several pro-democracy legislators whose political stance had prompted the central Government to impose a ban preventing them from travelling in mainland China, were invited on a tour of the Zhujiang (Pearl River) Delta region, in what was widely regarded as a conciliatory gesture towards the SAR's pro-democratic movement. In October Elsie Leung, Secretary for Justice since 1997, resigned, as had been widely expected following the resignation of Tung earlier in the year. Chief Executive Tsang nominated Wong Yan Lung, a barrister with reported links to the pro-democratic Article 45 Concern Group, as her replacement, and the central Government approved the nomination. In the same month a series of electoral reform proposals was published, officially the result of extensive public consultation but generally viewed as representing the compromise that the central Government was prepared to offer in exchange for ruling out universal suffrage in 2007/08 (see above). These proposals included the doubling of the membership of the Election Committee from 800 to 1,600 members and increasing the size of the Legislative Council from 60 to 70 members. Chief Executive Tsang endorsed the proposals, which were nevertheless criticized by the pro-democracy movement for failing to set out a definite timetable for the adoption of universal suffrage. As the vote on the proposals drew near, in early December 2005 a number of pro-democracy legislators were invited to cross into mainland China to meet with senior representatives of the central Government. Two days later a large pro-democracy march (estimates of attendance varied from 63,000 to more than 250,000) took place in Hong Kong, demanding universal suffrage. On 21 December the Legislative Council voted to reject the set of electoral reform proposals published in October. Following the vote, Chief Executive Tsang announced that he would not pursue further the question of constitutional reform during his current term and would be concentrating instead on economic issues.

Increasing dissatisfaction with the reform process led, in March 2006, to the establishment of a new political party in the SAR. Founded by members of the Article 45 Concern Group, intellectuals and democracy activists, the new Civic Party became the fourth largest party in the Legislative Council. According to the leader of the new grouping, Audrey Eu, the Civic Party advocated the early introduction of full democracy to Hong Kong, although the party's manifesto contained no time frame for this process. In May, however, democracy activists were thwarted once again when the Legislative Council endorsed by 31 votes to 22 a bill to alter the term of office of the Chief Executive. Under the new legislation, the term of any Chief Executive who took office prior to the expiry of the mandate of his or her predecessor would end upon the expiry of the predecessor's term. The term of office of Donald Tsang, therefore, would end in 2007 (completing that begun by Tung in 2002), after which he would be eligible to stand for one further term only. Pro-reform activists described the bill as a 'missed opportunity for democracy' and continued to demand a change in the law to allow the Chief Executive to belong to a political party.

This continued wish for full democracy was clearly demonstrated on 1 July 2006, when thousands took to the streets of Hong Kong for the SAR's fourth annual pro-democracy march. Although estimates of the number of demonstrators varied widely, from 28,000 (according to police sources) to 58,000 (according to the organizers), even the lower estimate suggested that the march had attracted around 10,000 more protesters than the similar rally of mid-2005. Particularly notable was the participation of former Chief Secretary Anson Chan, who, while stressing that she did not intend to challenge the Government, demanded the introduction of universal suffrage. None the less, there were many in the SAR who opposed the activists' demands; a pro-China rally, conducted earlier the same day, attracted a reported 40,000 demonstrators.

Democracy activists were further angered in August 2006 when the Legislative Council approved a controversial surveillance law granting new powers to the authorities. The Interception of Communications and Surveillance Bill provided for measures such as the monitoring of e-mails and telephone lines, including private communications in both homes and offices. Under the new legislation, surveillance operations would require approval by judges appointed by the Hong Kong leadership, thus raising concerns about political bias. Pro-democracy legislators (who had tabled proposals for about 200 amendments to the bill, all of which were defeated), believed that the legislation would allow police officers to spy on anyone opposing the Government, in particular politicians, journalists and lawyers. The bill was approved by 32 votes to none, after pro-democracy legislators abandoned the proceedings. The environment was another major topic of debate in 2006, amid increasing concern over Hong Kong's deteriorating air quality. A 'Lights Out' campaign, launched at 8 p.m. on 8 August, persuaded residents to turn off their lights for three minutes. In his second Policy Address, made in October, Donald Tsang admitted that air quality was a problem, and pledged to address the issue over the coming year. Tsang also envisaged further economic liberalization measures to consolidate Hong Kong's position as an international financial centre, the establishment of more economic and trade arrangements with overseas partners, and better support for families.

Elections to determine the membership of the committee that would choose the SAR's next leader were held on 10 December 2006. Once again the ballot was restricted to the business and community sectors, with only about 5% of Hong Kong's registered electorate being eligible to vote and the level of participation being declared at 27.4%. Nevertheless, the results improved the prospects of the pro-reform camp, which unexpectedly secured 114 of the 427 contested seats on the 800-member Election Committee; the remaining 373 seats were uncontested. Having surpassed the threshold of 100 seats required to present an opposition candidate for the post of Chief Executive, the democrats were thus able to nominate Alan Leong of the Civic Party as their candidate for the forthcoming election.

Alan Leong duly received 132 formal nominations in February 2007, while Donald Tsang received 641. The unprecedented challenge mounted by Leong and the reformists, combined with the novelty of two televised debates between the candidates, contributed to an atmosphere of change, however marginal. At the same time, members of the pro-democracy movement criticized Leong for participating in an essentially undemocratic process, thereby lending it legitimacy. On 25 March Tsang was re-elected as Chief Executive, by an increased margin of 649–123. Leong protested against the outcome, alleging that the system had been manipulated. Meanwhile, Tsang had expressed hopes of establishing a timetable for full democracy in the SAR by 2012, but he acknowledged that he would need the support of China in order to secure this objective.

In April 2007 Tsang was formally appointed to the position of Chief Executive by Chinese Premier Wen Jiabao, and in June the composition of the Executive Council was announced. The new Council, which was sworn in during the following month, retained former Financial Secretary Henry Tang, who was promoted to Chief Secretary for Administration. The erstwhile Director of the Chief Executive's Office, John Tsang Chun-wah, was appointed to replace Tang, while Wong Yan-lung remained Secretary for Justice. New appointees included Tsang Tak-sing as Secretary for Home Affairs, and two women members, Secretary for Development Carrie Lam and Secretary for Transport and Housing Eva Cheng.

Having outlined his intentions for the Government to continue with a 'people-based' approach, in July 2007 Tsang again promised to work towards democratic reform. Speaking during the 10th anniversary of Hong Kong's transfer to Chinese sovereignty, Tsang also stressed the importance of Chinese rule. The occasion, which was attended by Chinese President Hu Jintao, was marked by festivities and, subsequently, by pro-reform demonstrations that drew between 20,000 and 68,000 participants. In mid-July the Government presented a Green Paper on Constitutional Development, which was to be subject to a three-month public consultation period. Options proposed in the document included the implementation of universal suffrage for elections to the post of Chief Executive, by 2012 at the earliest. Following the completion of the consultation, it was revealed that the majority of those polled supported the introduction of direct elections to the Legislative Council as well as for the post of Chief Executive, upon the expiry of the current Government's term in 2012. Tsang's recommendations to the central Chinese Government in December 2007 were criticized for weakening these proposals to a certain extent, suggesting the holding of elections for the Chief Executive as a preliminary phase in 2012 or, perhaps preferably, 2017. The decision of the central Government to consider Tsang's proposal, albeit with any implementation to be deferred until 2017, followed by the possibility of direct elections for the Legislative Council in 2020, was hailed as a positive development by Tsang, but the slow pace of reform was greeted with disappointment in some quarters.

Meanwhile, the Chairman of the DAB, Ma Lik, died in August 2007. In the following month Anson Chan announced that she would come out of retirement to contest Ma's former seat in the Legislative Council; Chan's victory at the by-election in December was regarded by some as a further indication of popular support for the pro-democracy movement.

Legislation approved by the PLC in July 1997 had included the introduction of measures to restrict the immigration into the territory of mainland-born children of Hong Kong residents. However, in January 1998 a judge ruled that this new legislation contravened the Basic Law. The Court of Final Appeal ruled against the SAR Government in January 1999, upholding the judgment that the legislation was unconstitutional, prompting condemnation of the Court by the People's Republic of China. Fearing that the ruling on the right of abode by the Court of Final Appeal would result in an influx of more than 1.6m. mainland Chinese, the SAR administration asked the Court in February to clarify its judgment, which apparently asserted the Court's right to overrule decisions relating to the Basic Law made by the NPC in Beijing. The Court of Final Appeal declared that it recognized the authority of the Standing Committee of the Chinese NPC. In May the Legislative Council voted to request the Standing Committee of the NPC to interpret the relevant articles of the Basic Law, to the dissatisfaction of lawyers and democrats, who protested that the SAR's autonomy was being undermined. The NPC published its interpretation, which was not retroactive, in June, stating that the Court of Final Appeal had failed to adhere to the Basic Law in not requesting an interpretation before delivering its judgment. The NPC stipulated that mainlanders were to be granted the right of abode in Hong Kong only if at least one parent had been permanently resident in the territory at the time of their birth and that mainland children of Hong Kong parents who wished to settle in the territory had to apply for mainland approval before entering the SAR. In December 17 immigrants with parents resident in Hong Kong were denied the right of abode by the Court of Final Appeal, which recognized China's unrestricted powers to interpret the Basic Law (three subsequently obtained permission to reside in the territory). Violent clashes between demonstrators and the security forces followed the ruling.

In August 2000 disaffected mainland Chinese immigrants seeking the right of abode in Hong Kong firebombed the Immigration Department building. Two people were killed, including one immigration officer; 22 people were subsequently arrested and charged with murder. In July 2001 Hong Kong's Court of Final Appeal ruled that a three-year-old boy born in Hong Kong while his mother was visiting the territory had the right to reside there, in a decision praised as a triumph of the rule of law. However, in early August the same court ordered the deportation of a 14-year-old girl to the mainland owing to the fact that she had been born there and subsequently adopted by Hong Kong parents. In June 2001 the Government planned to deport 5,000 migrants to the mainland, pending the outcome of a court case. The Court of Final Appeal in January 2002 announced that all except about 200 of these 5,000 people would be returned to the mainland by the end of March. Although some 400 people returned to the mainland before the 31 March deadline, approximately 4,300 refused to do so. In April, therefore, the authorities began forcibly deporting the remaining abode-seekers. The actions were particularly criticized because they resulted in children being separated from their parents and families being split up. Scores began legal proceedings against the deportations, amid strong protests by those concerned, and Bishop Joseph Zen Ze-kiun, the outspoken head of the Roman Catholic Church in Hong Kong, personally intervened on behalf of several mentally ill or sick abode-seekers who were facing expulsion. It was reported in January 2003 that some 2,302 child abode-seekers had been deported to the mainland during 2002. In February 2003 plans were announced to ease immigration restrictions for skilled workers and business people from the Chinese mainland wishing to enter Hong Kong. This policy, the so-called Admission Scheme for Mainland Professionals, was introduced in July, and by December 1,545 applications for residence in Hong Kong had been received under the Scheme, of which 1,143 had been approved. Under new regulations introduced in the same month, persons holding a dependant visa were no longer entitled to take up employment in Hong Kong. Meanwhile, there were continuing efforts to prevent illegal immigration from mainland China, with 18,621 mainland Chinese being refused entry to Hong Kong in 2003. The total number of illegal immigrants intercepted by the authorities notably declined, from 25,651 in 1995/96 to 3,926 in 2003/04, a reduction of nearly 85%. In February 2007 new rules came into effect to limit the number of pregnant women from the mainland travelling to Hong Kong in order to give birth there. Reports suggested that as many as 12,000 mainland women had given birth in the SAR in 2006, in order to gain Hong Kong residency rights for their children and to circumvent the mainland's 'one child' policy.

In September 1998 the Sino-British JLG met in Hong Kong, for the first time since Hong Kong's transfer to China, to resolve outstanding issues. The most significant problem was that of the 1,100 Vietnamese refugees remaining in Hong Kong; China requested funds from the United Kingdom to facilitate their repatriation.

Despite the tensions surrounding the transfer of sovereignty, many citizens of Hong Kong supported the Government of the People's Republic of China in its territorial dispute with Japan regarding the Diaoyu (or Senkaku) Islands. In September 1996 a Hong Kong activist, David Chan, was accidentally drowned during a protest against Japan's claim to the islands. As issues of patriotism assumed greater significance in Hong Kong, more than 10,000 people attended a demonstration to mourn the death of David Chan and to denounce Japan. In October protesters from Hong Kong joined a flotilla of small boats from Taiwan and Macao, which successfully evaded Japanese patrol vessels and raised the flags of China and Taiwan on the disputed islands.

In July 2001 Tung Chee-hwa visited Washington, DC, and held a meeting with US President George W. Bush, at which Hong Kong's handling of Falun Gong and other issues of freedom were discussed. In August a US aircraft carrier made a visit to Hong Kong. However, in March 2002 China refused permission for a US warship to make a routine visit to Hong Kong, mainly in protest at the increasing links between the USA and Taiwan. In April, however, the ban was removed. In November, following an undercover operation by the US Federal Bureau of Investigation (FBI), three men were arrested for allegedly seeking to sell drugs in exchange for anti-aircraft missiles for the Islamist al-Qa'ida group. They agreed in January 2003 to be extradited to the USA. During a visit to Hong Kong in July British Prime Minister Tony Blair expressed his support for movement towards greater democracy in Hong Kong, following mass protests earlier in the month (see above), but also stated that it was important to maintain stability in the territory. In March 2004 a group of democracy activists, led by Martin Lee, visited the USA in order to discuss with representatives of the US Government their concerns over human rights in Hong Kong. Also in March, Chan Yu-lam, a resident of Hong Kong and a British citizen who had formerly been employed at the Hong Kong branch of the Xinhua state news agency of China, was accused of having spied on behalf of the United Kingdom and sentenced to life imprisonment by a court in Guangzhou. (Two other Hong Kong officials, Wei Pinguan and Cai Xiaohong, were imprisoned later in the year after also having been charged with spying for the United Kingdom.) Following the ruling of the Standing

Committee of China's NPC in April, vetoing direct elections in Hong Kong (see above), the British Foreign and Commonwealth Office issued a statement claiming that the ruling had broken the promise of a high degree of autonomy for Hong Kong which been made by the Chinese Government in 1997. In May 2004 Bishop Joseph Zen Zekiun, who had been banned from visiting the mainland in 1998, was permitted to make a three-day visit to Shanghai. In March 2006 Zen was elevated to the rank of Cardinal by Pope Benedict XVI, in a potentially significant development for relations between China and the Vatican.

Government

Since 1 July 1997 the Hong Kong SAR has been administered by a Chief Executive, who is accountable to the State Council of the People's Republic of China and serves a five-year term, there being a limit of two consecutive terms. The first incumbent was chosen by a 400-member Selection Committee in December 1996. Upon the expiry of his first term in 2002, the Chief Executive was chosen by an 800-member Election Committee, which also oversaw the selection of his successor in 2005. In July 2002 a new government structure was introduced, which expanded the Executive Council into a cabinet-style body comprising 14 ex-officio members known as principal officials (each with an individual portfolio) and five non-official members, all accountable to the Chief Executive. In October 2005 the number of non-official Council members was increased to 15. Elections to the third four-year term of the 60-member Legislative Council took place in September 2004; 30 of the seats (compared with 24 in the previous legislature) were directly elective (under a system of proportional representation), with 30 seats being determined by 'functional constituencies' (comprising professional and special interest groups).

Defence

In December 1996 the Standing Committee of the National People's Congress in Beijing adopted the Hong Kong Garrison Law, which provided for the stationing in Hong Kong of troops of the People's Liberation Army (PLA). The Garrison Law defined the duties and obligations of the troops, jurisdiction over them and also the relationship between the troops and the Government of the Hong Kong SAR. The legislation took effect on 1 July 1997. The garrison may intervene in local matters only at the request of the Hong Kong Government, which remains responsible for internal security. In November 2007 an estimated total of 7,000 Chinese troops were stationed in Hong Kong.

Economic Affairs

In 2006, according to estimates by the World Bank, Hong Kong's gross national income (GNI), measured at average 2004–06 prices, was US $199,509m., equivalent to US $28,460 per head (or US $38,200 on an international purchasing-power parity basis). During 1996–2006, it was estimated, the population increased at an average annual rate of 0.9%, while gross domestic product (GDP) per head increased, in real terms, at an average rate of 3.3% per year over the same period. Overall GDP increased, in real terms, at an average annual rate of 4.2% in 1996–2006. Compared with the previous year, a growth rate of 7.0% was recorded in 2006. GDP growth was officially estimated at 6.3% in 2007.

Agriculture and fishing together contributed less than 0.1% of GDP and employed only 0.3% of the working population in 2005. Crop production is largely restricted to vegetables, while cattle, pigs and poultry are the principal livestock. Hong Kong relies heavily on imports for its food supplies. According to figures from the World Bank, the GDP of the agricultural sector decreased at an average annual rate of 1.0% in 2000–06. It was estimated that agricultural GDP declined by 3.4% in 2006. The Asian Development Bank (ADB) estimated that the agricultural sector contracted by 8.8% in 2007.

Industry (including mining, manufacturing, construction and utilities) provided an estimated 8.7% of GDP in 2006 and employed 15.2% of the working population in 2005. According to the World Bank, industrial GDP declined at an average annual rate, in real terms, of 3.2% in 2000–06. The GDP of the industrial sector was estimated to have decreased by 1.6% in 2006. The ADB estimated that the industrial sector contracted by 0.9% in 2007.

Manufacturing contributed an estimated 3.1% of GDP in 2006. According to the 2006 census, the manufacturing sector employed 9.7% of the working population. In real terms the GDP of the sector declined at an average annual rate of 4.1% in 2000–06, according to World Bank figures. Compared with the previous year, however, manufacturing GDP expanded by 2.2% in 2006, before decreasing by an estimated 2.0% in the first three quarters of 2007. The principal branches of manufacturing include textiles and clothing, plastic products, metal products and electrical machinery (particularly radio and television sets).

Electricity production is derived mainly from coal, which accounted for 68.5% of output in 2004. Total production of electricity reached 38,613m. kWh in 2006. Fuel imports accounted for 2.7% of the cost of Hong Kong's total merchandise imports in 2005.

The services sector plays the most important role in the economy, accounting for an estimated 91.3% of GDP in 2006. According to the 2006 census, services employed 82.7% of the working population. According to World Bank figures the GDP of the services sector increased at an average annual rate, in real terms, of 6.2% in 2000–06. The sector's GDP increased by 7.2% in 2006. The ADB estimated growth in the services sector at 7.2% in 2007. The value of Hong Kong's invisible exports (notably financial services, tourism and shipping) was US $72,734m. in 2006. Revenue from tourism totalled an estimated US $13,546m. in 2005. The number of visitors to the territory rose to a record 28.2m. (of whom 15.5m. were from mainland China) in 2007. The region's first Disney theme park opened in Hong Kong in September 2005. The territory's banking and mercantile houses have branches throughout the region, and Hong Kong is regarded as a major financial centre, owing partly to the existence of an excellent international telecommunications network and to the absence of restrictions on capital inflows.

In 2006 Hong Kong recorded a visible trade deficit of US $14,033m., and there was a surplus of US $20,575m. on the current account of the balance of payments. Re-exports constituted 95.9% of total exports in 2007. The principal sources of Hong Kong's imports in 2007 were the People's Republic of China (46.4%) and Japan (10.0%); the principal markets for exports (including re-exports) were the People's Republic of China (48.7%) and the USA (13.7%). Other major trading partners included Taiwan, Singapore, the Republic of Korea, Germany and the United Kingdom. In 2006 the principal domestic exports were electrical machinery, telecommunications equipment, office machines, clothing and photographic equipment. The principal imports in that year were electrical machinery, telecommunications equipment, office machines and automatic data-processing equipment, and clothing.

Preliminary figures for the fiscal year 2007/08 indicated a consolidated budgetary surplus of HK $115,675m., the largest ever recorded. A small deficit of around HK $7,543m. was predicted for 2008/09. The Asian Development Bank estimated Hong Kong's external debt at US $491,224m. in 2006. Following a long period of deflation, Hong Kong returned to inflationary conditions for the first time in 68 months in mid-2004. The annual rate of inflation averaged just 0.2% in 1995–2006. The consumer price index rose by 2.0% in 2006 and by the same percentage in 2007. The census of mid-2006 recorded an unemployment rate of 5.8%. The seasonally adjusted rate of unemployment decreased in 2007, to stand at an estimated 3.4% in the final quarter of that year. The shortage of skilled labour in certain areas has continued.

Hong Kong is a member of the Asian Development Bank (ADB, see p. 182) and an associate member of the UN Economic and Social Commission for Asia and the Pacific (ESCAP, see p. 35). The territory became a member of Asia-Pacific Economic Co-operation (APEC, see p. 176) in 1991. Hong Kong joined the Bank for International Settlements (BIS, see p. 194) in 1996, and in early 1997 announced its participation in the IMF's New Arrangements to Borrow (NAB) scheme. After mid-1997 Hong Kong remained a separate customs territory, within the World Trade Organization (WTO, see p. 396).

Hong Kong's financial system remained unchanged following the territory's transfer to Chinese sovereignty in mid-1997. The rapid economic growth of China, combined with the closer integration of the SAR with the mainland, has given rise to increased demand for services in Hong Kong. China is the SAR's principal trading partner, as well as a growing source of tourism revenue. After a period of relatively weak performance in the early 2000s, Hong Kong's economy subsequently improved. By 2004/05, following several years of successive deficits, the budget had returned to surplus, and the property and stock markets began to recover. However, the economy remained vulnerable to the volatility of sources of revenue such as duties on properties and stocks. Proposals to introduce a 5% goods-and-services tax, as a means of expanding Hong Kong's narrow tax base, were abandoned in early 2007 following widespread public opposition. The Hong Kong stock market, as measured by the Hang Seng Index, expanded by 39% in 2007 compared with the previous year (reaching a record closing level of 31,638 points on 30 October), while the value of annual market turnover increased by 159%, to reach HK $21,665,500m. In the longer term Hong Kong's position as a leading international financial centre, as well as a conduit to mainland Chinese business, was believed to be threatened by rising competition from Shanghai and other Chinese cities. Environmental degradation, furthermore, had become an issue of major concern, with increasing levels of air pollution (much of it generated by the rapid industrialization of neighbouring Guangdong Province on the mainland) being recorded. By 2007, amid reports that a number of companies had already relocated from Hong Kong as a direct consequence of the city's deteriorating air quality, fears that foreign investment in the SAR might be thus jeopardized were increasingly being expressed. Nevertheless, following the strong GDP growth of 2007, the Government expressed cautious optimism in early 2008, anticipating that the year's economic growth would reach about 4%–5%.

Hong Kong

CHINESE SPECIAL ADMINISTRATIVE REGIONS

Education

In 2006/07 an estimated 140,783 children attended kindergarten. Full-time education is compulsory between the ages of six and 15. Primary education has been free in all government schools and in nearly all aided schools since 1971 and junior secondary education since 1978. There are three main types of secondary school: grammar, technical and pre-vocational. The four government-run teacher-training colleges merged to form the Hong Kong Institute of Education in 1994. The Hong Kong Institute of Vocational Education (IVE), which was founded in 1999, incorporates seven government-funded technical institutes and two colleges. In 2003/04 total enrolment at primary and secondary schools was equivalent to 94.9% of the school-age population. Primary enrolment in that year included 93% of children in the relevant age-group (males 96%, females 90%), while the comparable ratio for secondary enrolment was 78% (males 79%, females 77%). An education reform programme was in progress from 2000, including reform of curriculum and education management, and the establishment of Project Yi Jin, a life-long learning initiative. In 2006/07 the seven universities (including Lingnan University, formerly Lingnan College, renamed in July 1999) and the Hong Kong Institute of Education had an estimated combined enrolment of 91,675 full-time and part-time students. The Open University of Hong Kong (founded in 1989 as the Open Learning Institute of Hong Kong) had 27,496 students in 2006/07. Budgetary expenditure on general education was an estimated HK $25,757m. in the financial year 2006/07, with a further $11,240m. being allocated to universities and polytechnics.

Public Holidays

2008: 1 January (first weekday in January), 7–10 February (Chinese Lunar New Year), 21–24 March (Easter), 5 April (Ching Ming), 1 May (Labour Day), 12 May (Buddha's birthday), 8 June (Tuen Ng, Dragon Boat Festival), 1 July (SAR Establishment Day), 15 September (Chinese Mid-Autumn Festival), 1 October (National Day), 7 October (Chung Yeung Festival), 25–26 December (Christmas).

2009: 1 January (first weekday in January), 26–28 January (Chinese Lunar New Year), 4 April (Ching Ming), 10–13 April (Easter), 1 May (Labour Day), 2 May (Buddha's Birthday), 28 May (Tuen Ng, Dragon Boat Festival), 1 July (SAR Establishment Day), 3 September (Chinese Mid-Autumn Festival), 1 October (National Day), 26 October (Chung Yeung Festival), 25–26 December (Christmas).

Weights and Measures

The metric system is in force. Chinese units include: tsün (37.147 mm), chek or ch'ih (37.147 cm); kan or catty (604.8 grams), tam or picul (60.479 kg).

Statistical Survey

Source (unless otherwise stated): Census and Statistics Department, 19/F Wanchai Tower, 12 Harbour Rd, Hong Kong; tel. 25825073; fax 28271708; e-mail gen-enquiry@censtatd.gov.hk; internet www.censtatd.gov.hk.

Area and Population

AREA, POPULATION AND DENSITY

Land area (sq km)	1,104*
Population (census and by-census results)†	
15 March 2001	6,708,389
14 July 2006	
Males	3,272,956
Females	3,591,390
Total	6,864,346
Usual residents	6,645,220
Present at census	6,416,124
Absent at census	229,096
Mobile residents	219,126
Present at census	43,632
Absent at census	175,494
Population (official estimate at mid-year)	
2007	6,925,900
Density (per sq km) at mid-2007	6,273.5

* 426 sq miles.

† All residents (including mobile residents) on the census date, including those who were temporarily absent from Hong Kong. In 2006 the census recorded population by place of birth as follows: Hong Kong 4,138,844, China (other than Hong Kong) 2,298,956, Other 426,546.

DISTRICTS AND DISTRICT COUNCILS
(2006 census)

	Area (sq km)*	Population	Density (per sq km)†
Hong Kong Island	80.47	1,268,112	15,759
Central and Western	—	250,064	20,102
Wan Chai	—	155,196	15,788
Eastern	—	587,690	31,664
Southern	—	275,162	7,083
Kowloon	46.93	2,019,533	43,033
Yau Tsim Mong	—	280,548	40,136
Sham Shui Po	—	365,540	39,095
Kowloon City	—	362,501	36,178
Wong Tai Sin	—	423,521	45,540
Kwun Tong	—	587,423	52,123
New Territories	976.57	3,573,635	3,659
Kwai Tsing	—	523,300	22,421
Tsuen Wan	—	288,728	4,679
Tuen Mun	—	502,035	6,057
Yuen Long	—	534,192	3,858
North	—	280,730	2,055
Tai Po	—	293,542	2,156
Sha Tin	—	607,544	8,842
Sai Kung	—	406,442	3,135
Islands	—	137,122	783
Total	**1,103.97**	**6,864,346‡**	**6,218**

* Data at 31 December 2006.

† Data for district councils are not strictly comparable with the district aggregates and the territory total as calculations were based on area distribution at mid-2006.

‡ Including marine population (3,066).

PRINCIPAL TOWNS
(population at 1996 census)

Kowloon*	1,988,515	Tai Po	271,661
Victoria (capital)	1,011,433	Tseun Wan	268,659
Tuen Mun	445,771	Sheung Shui	192,321
Sha Tin	445,383	Tsing Yu	185,495
Kwai Chung	285,231	Aberdeen	164,439

* Including New Kowloon.

BIRTHS, MARRIAGES AND DEATHS
(numbers rounded to nearest 100 persons)

	Known live births		Registered marriages		Known deaths	
	Number	Rate (per 1,000)	Number	Rate (per 1,000)	Number	Rate (per 1,000)
2000	54,100	8.1	30,900	4.6	33,800	5.1
2001	48,200	7.2	32,800	4.8	33,400	5.0
2002	48,200	7.1	32,100	4.7	34,300	5.0
2003	47,000	6.9	35,400	5.2	37,000	5.4
2004	49,800	7.2	41,400	6.0	36,900	5.3
2005	57,100	8.4	43,000	6.3	38,800	5.7
2006	65,600	9.6	50,300	7.3	37,500	5.5
2007*	69,600	10.1	47,200	6.8	38,900	5.6

* Provisional figures.

Expectation of life (years at birth, 2007, provisional): Males 79.3; Females 85.4.

CHINESE SPECIAL ADMINISTRATIVE REGIONS
Hong Kong

EMPLOYMENT
('000 persons aged 15 years and over, excl. armed forces)

	2003	2004	2005
Agriculture and fishing	7.5	8.9	9.5
Mining and quarrying	0.4	0.3	0.4
Manufacturing	272.0	235.5	227.7
Electricity, gas and water	16.2	14.5	15.4
Construction	265.9	268.2	270.1
Wholesale, retail and import/export trades, restaurants and hotels	991.8	1,074.3	1,110.6
Transport, storage and communications	346.4	360.1	362.4
Financing, insurance, real estate and business services	469.7	482.2	506.1
Community, social and personal services	849.5	864.5	883.5
Total	3,219.1	3,308.6	3,385.5
Males	1,779.4	1,820.9	1,848.8
Females	1,439.6	1,487.6	1,536.8

Unemployment ('000 persons aged 15 years and over, excl. armed forces): 277.2 in 2003; 242.5 in 2004; 200.7 in 2005.

Source: ILO.

2006 census (persons aged 15 years and over): Manufacturing 325,066; Construction 230,227; Wholesale, retail and import/export trades, restaurants and hotels 916,217; Transport, storage and communications 391,285; Financing, insurance, real estate and business services 571,378; Community, social and personal services 905,425; Other (incl. agriculture and fishing, mining and quarrying, electricity, gas and water and activities not adequately defined) 26,138; *Total employed* 3,365,736; Unemployed 206,648; *Total labour force* 3,572,384 (males 1,930,331, females 1,642,053).

Health and Welfare

KEY INDICATORS

Total fertility rate (children per woman*, 2004)	0.9
Under-5 mortality rate (per 1,000 live births, provisional, 2005)	2.4
HIV/AIDS (% of persons aged 15–49, 2003)	0.1
Physicians (per 1,000 head, provisional, 2005)†	1.7
Hospital beds (per 1,000 head, provisional, 2005)	4.9
Human Development Index (2005): ranking	21
Human Development Index (2005): value	0.937

* Excluding female domestic helpers.
† Excluding practitioners of Chinese medicine.

For sources and definitions, see explanatory note on p. vi.

Agriculture

PRINCIPAL CROPS
('000 metric tons, FAO estimates)

	2000	2001	2002
Lettuce	5	5	5
Spinach	11	11	11
Onions and shallots (green)	4	4	4
Other vegetables	24	14	34
Fruit	4	4	4

2003–04: Figures assumed to be unchanged from 2001 (FAO estimates).

2005–06: Separate data not available for Hong Kong (see the chapter on the People's Republic of China).

Source: FAO.

Total vegetables ('000 metric tons): 25 in 2005; 21 in 2006 (Source: Asian Development Bank, *Key Indicators of Developing Asian Pacific Countries*).

LIVESTOCK
('000 head, year ending September, FAO estimates)

	2002	2003	2004
Cattle (head)	1,500	1,500	1,500
Pigs	100	100	100
Chickens	1,000	1,000	1,000
Ducks	250	230	250

2005–06: Separate data for Hong Kong not available (see the chapter on the People's Republic of China).

Source: FAO.

LIVESTOCK PRODUCTS
('000 metric tons)

	2002	2003	2004
Beef and veal*	14	13	13
Pig meat*	147	145	194
Poultry meat	61	58	29
Game meat†	6	6	6
Cattle hides (fresh)†	2	2	2

* Unofficial figures.
† FAO estimates.

2005–06: Separate data for Hong Kong not available (see the chapter on the People's Republic of China).

Source: FAO.

Chicken meat ('000 metric tons): 13 in 2004; 21 in 2005; 17 in 2006 (Source: Asian Development Bank, *Key Indicators of Developing Asian Pacific Countries*).

Fishing
('000 metric tons, live weight, FAO estimates)

	2003	2004	2005
Capture	157.4	167.5	162.0
Lizardfishes	5.8	6.2	6.0
Threadfin breams	17.0	18.1	17.5
Shrimps and prawns	4.6	4.9	4.7
Squids	7.3	7.8	7.5
Aquaculture	4.9	4.6	4.1
Total catch	162.3	172.1	166.1

Source: FAO.

Industry

SELECTED PRODUCTS
('000 metric tons, unless otherwise indicated)

	2001	2002	2003
Uncooked macaroni and noodle products	62	20*	99
Cotton yarn (pure and mixed)	90.9	94.9	67.9
Cotton woven fabrics (million sq m)	378	333	221
Knitted sweaters ('000)	151,965	113,685	143,143
Men's and boys' jackets ('000)	1,838	1,285	1,087
Men's and boys' trousers ('000)	14,139	22,696	11,293
Women's and girls' blouses ('000)	187,209	20,712†	46,037
Women's and girls' dresses ('000)	2,242	1,078	851
Women's and girls' skirts, slacks and shorts ('000)	23,823‡	42,011	66,394
Men's and boys' shirts ('000)	105,254	47,136	76,365
Watches ('000)§	14,796	8,938	11,518

* Instant macaroni and noodles only.
† Calculated according to different criteria from previous years.
‡ Excluding women's and girls' slacks and shorts made of corduroy.
§ Excluding quartz digital-analogue and pen watches.

Source: UN, *Industrial Commodity Statistics Yearbook*.

Cement ('000 metric tons): 1,039 in 2004; 1,005 in 2005; 1,255 in 2006 (Source: Asian Development Bank, *Key Indicators of Developing Asian and Pacific Countries*).

Electric energy (million kWh): 37,129 in 2004; 38,448 in 2005; 38,613 in 2006 (Source: Asian Development Bank, *Key Indicators of Developing Asian and Pacific Countries*).

Finance

CURRENCY AND EXCHANGE RATES

Monetary Units
100 cents = 1 Hong Kong dollar (HK $).

Sterling, US Dollar and Euro Equivalents (31 December 2007)
£1 sterling = HK $15.630;
US $1 = HK $7.802;
€1 = HK $11.485;
HK $100 = £6.40 = US $12.82 = €8.71.

Average Exchange Rate (HK $ per US $)
2005   7.7773
2006   7.7678
2007   7.8014

BUDGET
(HK $ million, year ending 31 March)

Revenue	2004/05	2005/06	2006/07
Direct taxes:			
Earnings and profits tax	96,709	111,752	115,318
Indirect taxes:			
Bets and sweeps tax	12,057	11,938	12,047
Duties on petroleum products, beverages, tobacco and cosmetics	6,603	6,424	7,023
General rates (property tax)	12,640	14,146	15,467
Motor vehicle taxes	3,417	3,895	4,335
Royalties and concessions	775	616	610
Others (stamp duties, hotel accommodation tax and air passenger departure tax)	17,449	19,617	26,992
Fines, forfeitures and penalties	949	988	1,009
Receipts from properties and investments	8,710	9,815	11,280
Loans, reimbursements, contributions and other receipts	3,025	2,791	2,740

Revenue—continued	2004/05	2005/06	2006/07
Operating revenue from utilities	3,401	3,374	3,336
Fees and charges	10,793	11,109	11,672
Investment income:			
General revenue account	4,916	3,857	10,560
Land Fund	6,560	4,226	12,031
Capital Works Reserve Fund (land sales and interest)	59,428	30,977	41,484
Capital Investment Fund	8,406	2,943	2,307
Loan Fund	1,688	1,972	2,009
Other capital revenue	6,065	6,595	7,794
Total government revenue	263,591	247,035	288,014

Expenditure	2004/05	2005/06	2006/07
Operating expenditure	196,906	192,462	193,985
Recurrent expenditure	115,944	112,202	113,893
Personal emoluments	46,531	44,665	44,434
Pensions	14,900	12,834	13,654
Departmental expenses	14,803	15,294	16,746
Other recurrent expenditure	39,710	39,419	38,999
Subventions	76,351	74,950	75,609
Education	25,488	25,606	25,757
Health	27,844	27,075	27,583
Universities and polytechnics	11,872	11,326	11,240
Other subventions	11,147	10,943	11,029
Non-recurrent operating expenditure	4,611	5,300	4,483
Capital expenditure	45,329	40,609	35,440
Plant, equipment and works	823	676	720
Subventions	722	680	821
Capital Works Reserve Fund	33,725	28,954	26,725
Other funds	10,059	10,299	7,174
Total government expenditure	242,235	233,071	229,425

2007/08 (HK $ million, year ending 31 March, estimates): Total government revenue 273,845; Total government expenditure 248,437.

INTERNATIONAL RESERVES
(US $ million at 31 December)

	2004	2005	2006
Gold (national valuation)	29	34	42
Foreign exchange*	123,540	124,240	133,170
Total	123,569	124,274	133,212

* Including the foreign-exchange reserves of the Hong Kong Special Administrative Region Government's Land Fund.

Source: IMF, *International Financial Statistics*.

MONEY SUPPLY
(HK $ '000 million at 31 December)

	2004	2005	2006
Currency outside banks	140.6	142.1	150.0
Demand deposits at banking institutions	231.8	173.6	197.2
Total money	372.4	315.7	347.2

Source: IMF, *International Financial Statistics*.

COST OF LIVING
(Consumer Price Index; base: 2000 = 100)

	2004	2005	2006
Food	96.7	98.4	100.1
Housing	82.5	82.5	86.4
Electricity, gas and other fuels	103.1	107.3	109.6
Clothing and footwear	99.6	101.5	102.5
All items (incl. others)	92.6	93.6	95.5

Source: ILO.

CHINESE SPECIAL ADMINISTRATIVE REGIONS

Hong Kong

NATIONAL ACCOUNTS
(HK $ million at current prices)

Expenditure on the Gross Domestic Product

	2004	2005	2006
Government final consumption expenditure	127,327	121,435	123,436
Private final consumption expenditure	767,923	804,936	866,095
Change in stocks	7,076	−4,761	−926
Gross fixed capital formation	275,034	289,224	316,968
Total domestic expenditure	1,177,360	1,210,834	1,305,573
Exports of goods and services	2,456,594	2,747,543	3,028,904
Less Imports of goods and services	2,342,052	2,575,328	2,860,148
GDP in purchasers' values	1,291,902	1,383,049	1,474,329
GDP at chained 2005 prices	1,291,139	1,383,049	1,476,430

Gross Domestic Product by Economic Activity

	2004	2005	2006*
Agriculture and fishing	886	847	849
Mining and quarrying	72	100	93
Manufacturing	44,455	45,547	44,247
Electricity, gas and water	39,726	39,924	40,180
Construction	40,376	38,538	39,106
Wholesale, retail and import/export trades, restaurants and hotels	345,092	386,726	399,179
Transport, storage and communications	126,820	135,119	137,081
Financing, insurance, real estate and business services	266,834	294,666	355,761
Community, social and personal services	257,630	253,312	255,722
Ownership of premises	122,906	138,455	152,544
Gross domestic product at factor cost	1,244,798	1,333,235	1,424,761
Taxes on production and imports	58,729	62,891	71,270
Statistical discrepancy	−11,625	−13,077	−21,703
GDP in purchasers' values	1,291,902	1,383,049	1,474,329

* Preliminary figures.

BALANCE OF PAYMENTS
(US $ million)

	2004	2005	2006
Exports of goods f.o.b.	260,263	289,579	317,600
Imports of goods f.o.b.	−269,575	−297,206	−331,634
Trade balance	−9,312	−7,627	−14,033
Exports of services	55,157	63,761	72,734
Imports of services	−31,138	−33,979	−36,560
Balance on goods and services	14,708	22,156	22,140
Other income received	52,003	64,806	82,792
Other income paid	−48,997	−64,604	−82,135
Balance on goods, services and income	17,713	22,357	22,797
Current transfers received	626	943	940
Current transfers paid	−2,611	−3,067	−3,161
Current balance	15,728	20,233	20,575
Capital account (net)	−329	−634	−286
Direct investment abroad	−45,715	−27,201	−43,459
Direct investment from abroad	34,032	35,618	42,891
Portfolio investment assets	−43,214	−40,723	−50,563
Portfolio investment liabilities	3,882	9,256	17,376
Financial derivatives assets	20,605	20,797	18,376
Financial derivatives liabilities	−14,912	−16,877	−13,373
Other investment assets	−32,609	−18,750	−50,351
Other investment liabilities	57,838	18,432	59,443
Net errors and omissions	7,980	3,227	5,386
Overall balance	3,286	1,378	6,016

Source: IMF, *International Financial Statistics*.

External Trade

PRINCIPAL COMMODITIES
(HK $ million)

Imports c.i.f.	2004	2005	2006
Food and live animals	54,993	56,551	61,497
Chemicals and related products	127,655	144,233	155,536
Basic manufactures	326,888	344,268	372,067
Textile yarn, fabrics, made-up articles, etc.	109,918	107,273	108,552
Machinery and transport equipment	1,072,722	1,216,931	1,401,055
Office machines and automatic data-processing equipment	209,170	250,312	284,995
Telecommunications and sound recording and reproducing apparatus and equipment	264,596	295,713	335,208
Electrical machinery, apparatus and appliances n.e.s., and electrical parts thereof	459,762	530,197	629,143
Miscellaneous manufactured articles	442,529	471,044	496,257
Clothing (excl. footwear)	133,436	143,392	146,439
Photographic apparatus, equipment and supplies, optical goods, watches and clocks	63,199	64,045	61,433
Baby carriages, toys, games and sporting goods	63,331	68,332	79,157
Total (incl. others)	2,111,123	2,329,469	2,599,804

Exports f.o.b.*	2004	2005	2006
Chemicals and related products	101,563	109,833	121,060
Basic manufactures	262,142	275,406	297,018
Textile yarn, fabrics, made-up articles, etc.	111,364	107,561	108,052
Machinery and transport equipment	1,011,120	1,188,155	1,347,588
Office machines and automatic data-processing equipment	220,355	288,544	315,235
Telecommunications and sound recording and reproducing apparatus and equipment	286,860	325,629	358,948
Electrical machinery, apparatus and appliances n.e.s., and electrical parts thereof	396,937	461,014	554,495
Miscellaneous manufactured articles	596,721	629,930	643,537
Clothing (excl. footwear)	195,507	212,267	220,529
Photographic apparatus, equipment and supplies, optical goods, watches and clocks	186,589	195,905	199,560
Baby carriages, toys, games and sporting goods	89,412	92,190	90,631
Total (incl. others)	2,019,114	2,250,173	2,461,027

* Including re-exports (HK $ million): 1,893,132 in 2004; 2,114,143 in 2005; 2,326,500 in 2006.

2007: *Imports:* Electrical machinery, apparatus and appliances, and electrical parts thereof 740,115; Telecommunications and sound recording and reproducing apparatus and equipment 385,444; Office machines and automatic data processing machines 249,433; Miscellaneous manufactured articles 205,240; Articles of apparel and clothing accessories 149,387; Textile yarn, fabrics, made-up articles and related products 105,775; Non-metallic mineral manufactures 101,903; Plastics in primary forms 81,318; Petroleum, petroleum products and related materials 73,859; Photographic apparatus, equipment and supplies, optical goods, watches and clocks 71,966; Total (incl. others) 2,868,011. *Exports:* Total 2,687,513 (re-exports 2,578,392).

# CHINESE SPECIAL ADMINISTRATIVE REGIONS — Hong Kong

PRINCIPAL TRADING PARTNERS
(HK $ million, excl. gold)

Imports	2005	2006	2007
China, People's Repub.	1,049,335	1,192,952	1,329,652
Germany	41,054	44,428	48,048
Japan	256,501	268,140	287,329
Korea, Repub.	103,035	119,647	119,393
Malaysia	57,153	60,339	62,818
Philippines	38,278	40,847	47,788
Singapore	135,190	164,837	194,775
Taiwan	168,227	194,917	205,102
Thailand	46,455	53,081	57,373
USA	119,252	123,569	138,768
Total (incl. others)	2,329,469	2,599,804	2,868,011

Domestic exports	2005	2006	2007
Australia	1,869	2,478	1,764
China, People's Repub.	44,643	40,268	40,610
Germany	4,353	4,910	3,022
Japan	4,320	4,931	2,864
Korea, Republic	1,650	1,789	1,453
Netherlands	5,386	7,958	2,922
Singapore	4,076	4,128	3,047
Taiwan	5,142	4,461	4,032
United Kingdom	7,304	7,859	5,847
USA	37,767	33,159	23,878
Total (incl. others)	136,030	134,527	109,122

Re-exports	2005	2006	2007
China, People's Repub.	967,923	1,115,941	1,267,722
France	30,341	31,841	34,190
Germany	68,367	70,753	78,096
Japan	114,258	115,490	116,703
Korea, Repub.	46,591	50,084	51,477
Netherlands	37,252	33,082	41,498
Singapore	42,465	44,484	47,403
Taiwan	45,285	47,645	48,902
United Kingdom	61,944	65,773	69,015
USA	322,872	337,971	344,324
Total (incl. others)	2,114,143	2,326,500	2,578,392

Transport

RAILWAYS
(traffic)

	2003	2004	2005
Passenger train journeys ('000)	3,188	n.a.	n.a.
Freight ('000 metric tons):			
loaded	76,000	64,000	49,000
unloaded	253,000	208,000	166,000

ROAD TRAFFIC
('000 registered motor vehicles at 31 December)

	2004	2005	2006
Private cars	345	351	360
Buses (private and public)	13	13	13
Light buses (private and public)	6	6	6
Taxis	18	18	18
Goods vehicles	110	111	112
Motorcycles	33	34	36
Government vehicles (excl. military vehicles)	6	6	6
Total (incl. others)	533	541	553

Note: Figures do not include tramcars.

SHIPPING
Merchant Fleet
(registered at 31 December)

	2004	2005	2006
Number of vessels	1,058	1,128	1,179
Total displacement ('000 grt)	26,085.1	29,808.9	32,684.9

Source: Lloyd's Register-Fairplay, *World Fleet Statistics*.

Traffic
(2006, unless otherwise indicated, provisional)

	Ocean-going vessels	River vessels
Total capacity (million nrt)	700	181*
Cargo landed ('000 metric tons)	107,500	37,400
Cargo loaded ('000 metric tons)*	56,200	38,400

*Figure for 2003.

Passenger traffic ('000, arrivals and departures by sea, 2006): Passengers landed 10,903; Passengers embarked 12,390.

Note: Includes passengers travelling to and from Macao by helicopter.

CIVIL AVIATION

	2004	2005	2006
Passengers ('000):			
arrivals	12,366	13,265	14,382
departures	11,847	12,700	13,683
Freight ('000 metric tons):			
landed	1,166	1,246	1,301*
loaded	1,937	2,156	2,279*

*Provisional figure.

Tourism

VISITOR ARRIVALS BY COUNTRY OF RESIDENCE

	2003	2004	2005
Australia	196,900	325,800	422,200
Canada	141,800	211,200	236,000
China, People's Repub.	5,692,500	7,793,900	8,029,700
Germany	88,100	131,500	157,500
Indonesia	133,200	190,900	206,800
Japan	563,300	746,500	810,900
Korea, Repub.	225,200	322,300	379,300
Macao	156,100	187,100	193,200
Malaysia	148,000	244,300	284,800
Philippines	178,700	257,400	301,100
Singapore	184,200	352,200	428,300
Taiwan	407,100	546,800	619,900
Thailand	140,100	237,000	276,700
United Kingdom	235,100	345,200	387,700
USA (incl. Guam)	532,500	825,800	877,900
Total (incl. others)	9,676,300	13,655,100	14,773,200

Note: Figures are rounded to the nearest 100 persons.

Receipts from tourism (US $ million, incl. passenger transport): 9,004 in 2003; 11,815 in 2004; 13,546 in 2005.

Source: World Tourism Organization.

2006 ('000 persons): Total arrivals 25,251 (mainland China 13,591; Taiwan 2,177; Macao 578).

CHINESE SPECIAL ADMINISTRATIVE REGIONS

Hong Kong

Communications Media

	2004	2005	2006
Telephones ('000 in use)	3,763.4	3,797.8	3,849.7
Mobile cellular telephones ('000 subscribers)	8,214.0	8,639.4	9,356.4
Personal computers ('000 in use)	4,187	4,172	n.a.
Internet users ('000)	3,479.7	3,526.2	3,770.4
Broadband subscribers ('000)	1,517.7	1,659.1	1,796.2

1997 ('000 in use): Radio receivers 4,450.

2000 ('000 in use): Television receivers 3,105.

2004 (unless otherwise indicated): Daily newspapers 46; Non-daily newspapers 23; Periodicals 864 (2003).

2004 ('000 in use): Facsimile machines 456.

Sources: partly UNESCO, *Statistical Yearbook*; UN, *Statistical Yearbook*; International Telecommunication Union.

Education

(2006/07)

	Institutions	Teachers	Students
Kindergartens	1,015	10,384	140,783
Primary schools	668	23,695	410,516
Secondary schools	528	26,984	480,775
Special schools	62	1,403	7,720
Institute of Vocational Education*	1	2,135	61,270†
Approved post-secondary college	2	123	1,381†
Other post-secondary colleges	17	n.a.	8,163†
UGC-funded institutions‡	8	5,813†	91,675
Open University of Hong Kong	1	130	27,496
Adult education institutions	2,222	n.a.	186,763

* Formed by merger of two technical colleges and seven technical institutes in 1999.
† Provisional figure.
‡ Funded by the University Grants Committee.

Adult literacy rate (UNESCO estimates): 94.6% in 2003 (Source: UN Development Programme, *Human Development Report*).

Directory

The Constitution

Under the terms of the Basic Law of the Hong Kong Special Administrative Region, the Government comprises the Chief Executive, the Executive Council and the Legislative Council. The Chief Executive must be a Chinese citizen of at least 40 years of age; is appointed for a five-year term, with a limit of two consecutive terms; is chosen by an 800-member Election Committee; is accountable to the State Council of the People's Republic of China, and has no military authority; appoints the Executive Council, judges and the principal government officials; makes laws with the advice and consent of the legislature; has a veto over legislation, but can be overruled by a two-thirds' majority; may dissolve the legislature once in a term, but must resign if the legislative impasse continues with the new body. The Legislative Council has 60 members; in September 2004 candidates for 30 seats were directly elected under a system of proportional representation and 30 seats were determined by elections within 'functional constituencies' (comprising professional and special interest groups). The Legislative Council is responsible for enacting, revising and abrogating laws, for approving the budget, taxation and public expenditure, for debating the policy address of the Chief Executive and for approving the appointment of the judges of the Court of Final Appeal and of the Chief Justice of the High Court.

The Government

Chief Executive: DONALD TSANG YAM-KUEN (elected unopposed 16 June 2005; re-elected 25 March 2007).

EXECUTIVE COUNCIL
(April 2008)

Chairman: The Chief Executive.

Ex-Officio Members (Principal Officials)

Chief Secretary for Administration: HENRY TANG YING-YEN.
Financial Secretary: JOHN TSANG CHUN-WAH.
Secretary for Justice: WONG YAN-LUNG.
Secretary for Education: MICHAEL SUEN MING-YEUNG.
Secretary for Commerce and Economic Development: FREDERICK MA SI-HANG.
Secretary for Constitutional and Mainland Affairs: STEPHEN LAM SUI-LUNG.
Secretary for Security: AMBROSE LEE SIU-KWONG.
Secretary for Food and Health: Dr YORK CHOW.
Secretary for the Civil Service: DENISE YUE CHUNG-YEE.
Secretary for Home Affairs: TSANG TAK-SING.
Secretary for Labour and Welfare: MATTHEW CHEUNG KIN-CHUNG.
Secretary for Financial Services and the Treasury: Prof. K. C. CHAN.
Secretary for Development: CARRIE LAM CHENG YUET-NGOR.
Secretary for the Environment: EDWARD YAU TANG-WAH.
Secretary for Transport and Housing: EVA CHENG.

In addition to the above ex-officio members of the Executive Council, in 2008 there were also 15 non-official members.

GOVERNMENT OFFICES

Executive Council: Central Government Offices, Lower Albert Rd, Central; tel. 28102545; fax 28450176.
Office of the Chief Executive: 5/F Main Wing, Central Government Offices, Lower Albert Rd, Central; tel. 28783300; fax 25090577.
Government Secretariat: Central Government Offices, Lower Albert Rd, Central; tel. 28102900; fax 28457895.
Government Information Services: Murray Bldg, Garden Rd, Central; tel. 28428777; fax 28459078; internet www.info.gov.hk.

Legislature

LEGISLATIVE COUNCIL

The third Legislative Council to follow Hong Kong's transfer to Chinese sovereignty was elected on 12 September 2004. The Legislative Council comprises 60 members: 30 chosen by functional constituencies and 30 (increased from 24 in the previous legislature) by direct election in five geographical constituencies. The term of office of the Legislative Council was to last for four years.

President: RITA FAN HSU LAI-TAI.

Election, 12 September 2004

Party	Directly elective seats	Functional Constituency seats	Total seats
Democratic Alliance for the Betterment of Hong Kong	9	3	12
Liberal Party	2	8	10
Democratic Party of Hong Kong	8	1	9
Article 45 Concern Group	3	1	4
Hong Kong Confederation of Trade Unions	2	—	2
The Frontier	1	—	1
Association for Democracy and People's Livelihood	1	—	1
Neighbourhood and Worker's Service Centre	1	—	1
April Fifth Action	1	—	1
Hong Kong Federation of Trade Unions	—	1	1
Independents	2	16	18
Total	**30**	**30**	**60**

Election Commission

Electoral Affairs Commission: 10/F, Harbour Centre, 25 Harbour Rd, Wanchai; tel. 28911001; fax 28274644; e-mail eacenq@reo.gov.hk; internet www.eac.gov.hk; f. 1997; Chair. PANG KIN-KEE.

1261

Political Organizations

April Fifth Action: e-mail april5action@yahoo.com.hk; socialist group; anti-Beijing; Spokesperson Leung Kwok-hung.

Association for Democracy and People's Livelihood (ADPL): Sun Beam Commercial Bldg, Rm 1104, 469–471 Nathan Rd, Kowloon; tel. 27822699; fax 27823137; e-mail info@adpl.org.hk; internet www.adpl.org.hk; advocates democracy; Chair. Frederick Fung Kin-kee; Gen. Sec. Tam Kwok-kiu.

Citizens' Party: GPOB 321, Central; tel. 28930029; e-mail enquiry@citizensparty.org; internet www.citizensparty.org; f. 1997; urges mass participation in politics; Chair. Dr Joe Wong.

Civic Party: Unit B, 16/F, Wing Hang Finance Centre, 60 Gloucester Rd, Wanchai; tel. 28657111; fax 28652771; e-mail contact@civicparty.hk; internet www.civicparty.hk; f. 2006; pro-democracy; Chair. Prof. Kuan Hsin-chi; Leader Audrey Eu Yuet-mee.

Democratic Alliance for the Betterment and Progress of Hong Kong (DAB): SUP Tower, 12/F, 83 King's Rd, North Point; tel. 25280136; fax 25284339; e-mail info@dab.org.hk; internet www.dab.org.hk; f. 2005; pro-Beijing; formed by merger of the Democratic Alliance for the Betterment of Hong Kong (f. 1992, supported return of Hong Kong to the motherland and implementation of the Basic Law) and the Hong Kong Progressive Alliance (f. 1994, supported by business and professional community); Chair. Tam Yiu-chung; Sec.-Gen. Kan Chi-ho.

Democratic Party: Hanley House, 4/F, 776–778 Nathan Rd, Kowloon; tel. 23977033; fax 23978998; e-mail waiyin@dphk.ecoffiz.com; internet www.dphk.org; f. 1994; formed by merger of United Democrats of Hong Kong (UDHK—declared a formal political party in 1990) and Meeting Point; liberal grouping; advocates democracy; Chair. Albert Ho Chun-yan; Sec.-Gen. Cheung Yin-tung.

The Frontier: Rm 228 Kwong Yau Block, Kwong Fuk Estate, Tai Po; tel. 25249899; fax 25245310; e-mail frontier@frontier.org.hk; internet www.frontier.org.hk; f. 1996; pro-democracy movement, comprising teachers, students and trade unionists; Spokesperson Emily Lau.

Hong Kong Democratic Foundation: POB 35588, King's Road Post Office, North Point; tel. 28696443; fax 28696318; e-mail secretariat@hkdf.org; internet www.hkdf.org; advocates democracy and an open society; Chair. Alan Lung Ka-Lun.

Liberal Party: 4/F Dina House, Ruttonjee Centre, 11 Duddell St, Central; tel. 28696833; fax 25334239; e-mail liberal@liberal.org.hk; internet www.liberal.org.hk; f. 1993; est. by mems of Co-operative Resources Centre (CRC); business-orientated; pro-Beijing; Chair. James Tien Pei-chun.

Neighbourhood and Worker's Service Centre: e-mail nwsc@netvigator.com; internet www.nwsc.org.hk.

New Hong Kong Alliance: 4/F, 14–15 Wo On Lane, Central; fax 28691110; pro-China.

At the elections of September 2004, the Hong Kong Confederation of Trade Unions and the Hong Federation of Trade Unions also secured seats in the Legislative Council (see Trade and Industry section for details of these organizations).

The Chinese Communist Party (based in the People's Republic) and the Kuomintang (Nationalist Party of China, based in Taiwan) also maintain organizations.

Judicial System

The Court of Final Appeal was established on 1 July 1997 upon the commencement of the Hong Kong Court of Final Appeal Ordinance. It replaced the Privy Council in London as the highest appellate court in Hong Kong to safeguard the rule of law. The Court comprises five judges—the Chief Justice, three permanent judges and one non-permanent Hong Kong judge or one judge from another common-law jurisdiction.

The High Court consists of a Court of Appeal and a Court of First Instance. The Court of First Instance has unlimited jurisdiction in civil and criminal cases, while the District Court has limited jurisdiction. Appeals from these courts lie to the Court of Appeal, presided over by the Chief Judge or a Vice-President of the Court of Appeal with one or two Justices of Appeal. Appeals from Magistrates' Courts are heard by a Court of First Instance judge.

Court of Final Appeal

1 Battery Path, Central; tel. 21230123; fax 21210300; internet www.judiciary.gov.hk.

Chief Justice of the Court of Final Appeal: Andrew K. N. Li.
Permanent Judges of the Court of Final Appeal: K. Bokhary, Patrick S. O. Chan, R. A. V. Ribeiro.

High Court

38 Queensway; tel. 28690869; fax 28690640; internet www.judiciary.gov.hk.

Chief Judge of the High Court: Geoffrey T. L. Ma.
Justices of Appeal: K. H. Woo, M. Stuart-Moore, F. Stock, D. Le Pichon, P. C. Y. Cheung, A. G. Rogers, M. C. K. N. Yuen, W. C. K. Yeung, R. C. Tang.
Judges of the Court of First Instance: D. Y. K. Yam, W. S. Y. Waung, M. P. Burrell, V. S. Bokhary, K. K. Pang, W. D. Stone, C. M. Beeson, P. V. T. Nguyen, M. J. Hartmann, A. R. Suffiad, A. H. Sakhrani, A O. T. Chung, C. F. L. Chu, L. P. S. Tong, S. S. H. Kwan, M. A. McMahon, J. M. H. Lam, A. K. N. Cheung, M. V. Lunn, A. T. Barma, A. F. T. Reyes, B. W. Fung, J. W. L. Barnes, A. R. Wright, S. C. Poon, J. L. Saunders, D. G. Saw.

OTHER COURTS

District Courts: There are 32 District Judges.
Magistrates' Courts: There are 59 Magistrates and 11 Special Magistrates, sitting in 9 magistracies.

Religion

The population is predominantly Buddhist. The number of active Buddhists is estimated at between 650,000 and 700,000, and there were more than 600 temples in 2005. Confucianism and Daoism are widely practised. The three religions are frequently found in the same temple. In 2005 there were some 660,000 Christians, approximately 90,000 Muslims, 40,000 Hindus, and 8,000 Sikhs. Judaism, the Bahá'í faith and Zoroastrianism are also represented.

BUDDHISM

Hong Kong Buddhist Association: 1/F, 338 Lockhart Rd; tel. 25749371; fax 28340789; e-mail enquiry@hkbuddhist.org; internet www.hkbuddhist.org; Pres. Ven. Kok Kwong.

CHRISTIANITY

Hong Kong Christian Council: 9/F, 33 Granville Rd, Kowloon; tel. 23687123; fax 27242131; e-mail hkcc@hkcc.org.hk; internet www.hkcc.org.hk; f. 1954; 22 mem. orgs; Chair. Rev. Dr Thomas Soo Yee-po; Gen. Sec. Rev. Ralph Lee Ting Sun.

The Anglican Communion

Primate of Hong Kong Sheng Kung Hui and Bishop of Hong Kong Island and Macao: Most Rev. Peter K. K. Kwong, Bishop's House, 1 Lower Albert Rd, Central; tel. 25265355; fax 25212199; e-mail office1@hkskh.org; internet www1.hkskh.org.

Bishop of Eastern Kowloon: Rt Rev. Louis Tsui, Holy Trinity Bradbury Centre, 4/F, 139 Ma Tau Chung Rd, Kowloon; tel. 27139983; fax 27111609; e-mail ekoffice@ekhkskh.org.hk; internet www.ekhkskh.org.hk.

Bishop of Western Kowloon: Rt Rev. Thomas Soo, Ultra Grace Commercial Bldg, 15/F, 5 Jordan Rd, Kowloon; tel. 27830811; fax 27830799; e-mail dwk@hkskh.org.

The Lutheran Church

Evangelical Lutheran Church of Hong Kong: 50A Waterloo Rd, Kowloon; tel. 23885847; fax 23887539; e-mail info@elchk.org.hk; internet www.elchk.org.hk; f. 1954; 13,000 mems; Bishop Rev. Nicholas Tai Ho-fai.

The Roman Catholic Church

For ecclesiastical purposes, Hong Kong forms a single diocese, nominally suffragan to the archdiocese of Canton (Guangzhou), China. According to Vatican sources, in December 2005 there were an estimated 344,166 adherents in the territory, representing more than 5% of the total population.

Bishop of Hong Kong: Cardinal Joseph Zen Ze-kiun, Catholic Diocese Centre, 12/F, 16 Caine Rd; tel. 257652; fax 254707; e-mail bishophk@pacific.net.hk.

The Press

Hong Kong has a thriving press. At the end of 2005, according to government figures, there were 49 daily newspapers, including 23 Chinese-language and 13 English-language dailies, and 722 periodicals.

CHINESE SPECIAL ADMINISTRATIVE REGIONS   Hong Kong

PRINCIPAL DAILY NEWSPAPERS
English Language

China Daily: internet www.chinadaily.com.cn/en/hk; Hong Kong edition of China's official English-language newspaper; launched 1997; Editor-in-chief ZHU LING; circ. 20,000.

International Herald Tribune: 1201 K Wah Centre, 191 Java Rd, North Point; tel. 29221188; fax 29221190; internet www.iht.com; Correspondent SYLVIA HUI.

South China Morning Post: 16/F, Somerset House, Taikoo Place, 979 King's Rd, Quarry Bay; tel. 25652222; fax 28111048; e-mail info@scmp.com; internet www.scmp.com; f. 1903; Editor-in-chief MARK CLIFFORD; Editor C. K. LAU; circ. 106,000.

The Standard: Sing Tao News Corporation Bldg, 3 Tung Wong Rd, Shau Kei Wan; tel. 27982798; fax 27953009; e-mail editor@thestandard.com.hk; internet www.thestandard.com.hk; f. 1949; publ. as free newspaper since Jan. 2007; Editor-in-Chief IVAN TONG; circ. 45,000.

Target Intelligent Report: Suite 2901, Bank of America Tower, 12 Harcourt Rd, Central; tel. 25730379; fax 28381597; e-mail info@targetnewspapers.com; internet www.targetnewspapers.com; f. 1972; financial news, commentary, politics, property, litigations, etc.

Wall Street Journal Asia: 25/F Central Plaza, 18 Harbour Rd; tel. 25737121; fax 28345291; e-mail wsja.publisher@dowjones.com; internet www.wsj-asia.com; f. 1976; business; Editor JOHN BUSSEY; circ. 80,393.

Chinese Language

Hong Kong Commercial Daily: 1/F, 499 King's Road, North Point; tel. 25905322; fax 25658947; internet www.hkcd.com.hk; f. 1952; Chair. and CEO HUANG YANG LUE; Editor CHENG XI TIAN.

Hong Kong Daily News: All Flats, Hong Kong Industrial Bldg, 17/F, 444–452 Des Voeux Rd West; tel. 28555111; fax 28198717; e-mail edit@hkdailynews.com.hk; internet www.hkdailynews.net; f. 1958; morning; CEO RODDY YU; Chief Editor K. K. YEUNG; circ. 120,000.

Hong Kong Economic Journal: North Point Industrial Bldg, 22/F, 499 King's Rd; tel. 28567567; fax 28111070; e-mail info@hkej.com; internet www.hkej.com; Dir CHO CHI-MING; circ. 30,000.

Hong Kong Economic Times: Kodak House, Block 2, 6/F, 321 Java Rd, North Point; tel. 28802888; fax 28111926; internet www.etpress.com.hk; f. 1988; Publr MAK PING LEUNG; Chief Editor CHAN CHO BIU; circ. 80,371.

Ming Pao Daily News: Block A, Ming Pao Industrial Centre, 15/F, 18 Ka Yip St, Chai Wan; tel. 25953111; fax 28982534; e-mail mingpao@mingpao.com; internet www.mingpao.com; f. 1959; morning; Chief Editor PAUL CHEUNG; circ. 78,258.

Oriental Daily News: Oriental Press Centre, 23 Dai Cheong St, Tai Po Industrial Estate, New Territories; tel. 36000000; fax 36001100; internet www.orientaldaily.com.hk; Chair. C. F. MA; Editor-in-Chief LIU KOU CHOUAN; circ. 650,000.

Ping Kuo Jih Pao (Apple Daily): Hong Kong; tel. 29908388; fax 27410830; e-mail adnews@appledaily.com; internet appledaily.atnext.com; f. 1995; published by Next Media; Propr JIMMY LAI; Publr LOH CHAN; circ. 309,261.

Sing Pao Daily News: Sing Pao Bldg, 101 King's Rd, North Point; tel. 25702201; fax 28870348; e-mail dailynews@singpao.com.hk; internet www.singpao.com.hk; f. 1939; morning; Chief Editor ALVIN POON HEI-CHUNG; circ. 229,250.

Sing Tao Daily: Sing Tao Bldg, 3/F, 1 Wang Kwong Rd, Kowloon Bay, Kowloon; tel. 27982575; fax 27953022; e-mail info@singtao.com; internet www.singtao.com; f. 1938; morning; Editor-in-Chief LUK KAM WING; circ. 60,000.

The Sun: internet the-sun.on.cc; f. 1999; publ. by the Oriental Press Group.

Ta Kung Pao: 342 Hennessy Rd, Wanchai; tel. 25757181; fax 28345104; e-mail tkp@takungpao.com; internet www.takungpao.com; f. 1902; morning; supports People's Republic of China; Editor T. S. TSANG; circ. 150,000.

Wen Wei Po: Hing Wai Centre, 3/F, 7 Tin Wan Praya Rd, Aberdeen; tel. 28738288; fax 28730657; internet www.wenweipo.com; f. 1948; morning; Dir ZHANG GUO-LIANG; First Editor-in-Chief CHEUNG CHING-WAN; Editor-in-Chief WONG BAK YAO; circ. 200,000.

SELECTED PERIODICALS
English Language

Asia Money: 5/F Printing House, 6 Duddell St, Central; tel. 29128081; fax 28656225; e-mail richard.morrow@asiamoney.com; internet www.asiamoney.com; 10 a year; Publr ANDREW COVER; Editor RICHARD MORROW.

Business Traveller Asia/Pacific: Suite 405, 4/F, Chinachem Exchange Square, 1 Hoi Wan St, Quarry Bay; tel. 25949399; fax 25196846; e-mail enquiry@businesstravellerasia.com; internet www.businesstravellerasia.com; f. 1982; consumer business travel; 10 a year; Publr PEGGY TEO; Editor-in-Chief TOM OTLEY; circ. 32,439.

Hong Kong Electronics: 31/F, Wu Chung House, 213 Queen's Rd East, Wanchai; tel. 28924672; fax 25750303; e-mail hktdc@tdc.org.hk; internet www.tdctrade.com; f. 1985; 4 a year (April, June, Oct. and Dec.); publ. by the Hong Kong Trade Development Council; Editor GEOFF PICKEN; circ. 90,000.

Hong Kong Enterprise: Office Tower, Convention Plaza, 38/F, 1 Harbour Rd; tel. 25844333; fax 28240249; e-mail hktdc@tdc.org.hk; internet www.tdctrade.com; f. 1967; monthly; publ. by the Hong Kong Trade Development Council; Editor GEOFF PICKEN; circ. 150,000.

Hong Kong Household: Office Tower, Convention Plaza, 38/F, 1 Harbour Rd, Wanchai; tel. 25844333; fax 28240249; e-mail hktdc@tdc.org.hk; internet www.tdctrade.com; f. 1983; publ. by the Hong Kong Trade Development Council; household and hardware products; 2 a year; Editor GEOFF PICKEN; circ. 90,000.

Hong Kong Industrialist: Federation of Hong Kong Industries, Hankow Centre, 4/F, 5–15 Hankow Rd, Tsimshatsui, Kowloon; tel. 27323188; fax 27213494; e-mail fhki@fhki.org.hk; internet www.fhki.org.hk; monthly; publ. by the Federation of Hong Kong Industries; Editor LIM SIONG HOON; circ. 6,000.

Hong Kong Special Administrative Region Government Gazette: Printing Division, Government Logistics Department, Cornwall House, Taikoo Place, 979 King's Rd, Quarry Bay; tel. 25649500; internet www.gld.gov.hk; weekly.

Official Hong Kong Guide: c/o HKTB, Citicorp Centre, 9–11/F, 18 Whitfield Rd, North Point; f. 1982; monthly; information on sightseeing, shopping, dining, etc. for overseas visitors; published by the Hong Kong Tourism Board.

Orientations: 815, 8/F, Zung Fu Industrial Bldg, 1067 King's Rd, Quarry Bay; tel. 25111368; fax 25074620; e-mail omag@netvigator.com; internet www.orientations.com.hk; f. 1970; 8 a year; arts of East Asia, the Indian subcontinent and South-East Asia; Publr and Editorial Dir ELIZABETH KNIGHT.

Reader's Digest (Asia Edn): Reader's Digest Association Far East Ltd, 19/F Cyber Centre, 3 Tung Wong Rd, Shau Kei Wan; tel. 96906381; fax 96906389; e-mail friends@rdasia.com.hk; internet www.readersdigest.com.hk; f. 1963; general topics; monthly; Editor PETER DOCKRILL; circ. 332,000.

Sunday Examiner: Catholic Diocese Centre, 11/F, 16 Caine Rd; tel. 25220487; fax 25369939; internet sundayex.catholic.org.hk; f. 1946; religious; weekly; Editor-in-Chief Sister TERESA YUEN; Deputy Editor-in-Chief Fr JIM MULRONEY; circ. 6,500.

Textile Asia: c/o Business Press Ltd, California Tower, 11/F, 30–32 D'Aguilar St, GPOB 185, Central; tel. 25233744; fax 28106966; e-mail texasia@biznetvigator.com; internet www.textileasia-businesspress.com; f. 1970; monthly; textile and clothing industry; Publr and Editor-in-Chief KAYSER W. SUNG; circ. 17,000.

Travel Business Analyst: GPO Box 12761, Hong Kong; tel. 2507-2310; fax (33-4) 9449-0949; e-mail TBAoffice@gmail.com; internet www.travelbusinessanalyst.com; f. 1982; travel trade; monthly; Editor MURRAY BAILEY.

Chinese Language

Affairs Weekly: Hong Kong; tel. 28950801; fax 25767842; f. 1980; general interest; Editor WONG WAI MAN; circ. 130,000.

Cheng Ming Monthly: Hennessy Rd, POB 20370; tel. 25740664; e-mail editor@chengmingmag.com; internet www.chengmingmag.com; current affairs; Chief Editor WAN FAI.

City Magazine: Hang Seng Bldg, 7/F, 200 Hennessy Rd, Wanchai; tel. 28931393; fax 28388761; f. 1976; monthly; fashion, wine, cars, society, etc.; Publr JOHN K. C. CHAN; Chief Editor PETER WONG; circ. 30,000.

East Touch: Sing Tao Bldg, 1 Wang Kwong Rd, Kowloon Bay; f. 1995; weekly; fashion, celebrity and entertainment news.

East Week: 4/F, Sing Tao Bldg, 1 Wang Kwong Rd, Kowloon Bay; tel. 27982323; fax 29604610; f. 1992; weekly; publication halted in 2002; relaunched in 2003; general interest; Chair. LAI TING YIU.

Kung Kao Po (Catholic Chinese Weekly): 16 Caine Rd; tel. 25220487; fax 25213095; internet kkp.catholic.org.hk; f. 1928; religious; weekly; Editor-in-Chief Sister TERESA YUEN.

Ming Pao Monthly: Ming Pao Industrial Centre, 15/F, Block A, 18 Ka Yip St, Chai Wan; tel. 25155107; fax 28982566; e-mail www.mingpaomonthly.com; Chief Editor KOO SIU-SUN.

Next Magazine: 8 Chun Ying St, T. K. O. Industrial Estate West, Tseung Kwan O, Kowloon; tel. 27442733; fax 29907210; internet www.nextmedia.com; internet next.atnext.com; f. 1989; weekly;

news, business, lifestyle, entertainment; Editor-in-Chief CHEUNG KIM HUNG; circ. 172,708.

Open Magazine: Causeway Bay, POB 31429; tel. 28939197; fax 28915591; e-mail open@open.com.hk; internet www.open.com.hk; f. 1990; monthly; Chief Editor JIN CHONG; circ. 15,000.

Oriental Sunday: Oriental Press Centre, Wang Tai Rd, Kowloon Bay, Kowloon; tel. 27951111; fax 27952299; e-mail os@newmediagroup.com.hk; internet www.orientalsunday.com.hk; f. 1991; weekly; leisure magazine; Chair. C. F. MA; circ. 120,000.

Reader's Digest (Chinese Edn): Reader's Digest Association Far East Ltd, 19/F Cyber Centre, 3 Tung Wong Rd, Shau Kei Wan; tel. 25681117; fax 25690370; internet www.readersdigest.com.hk; f. 1965; monthly; Editor-in-Chief JOEL POON; circ. 200,000.

Today's Living: 1801–1802, 18/F, Westlands Center, 20 Westlands Rd, Quarry Bay; tel. 28822230; fax 28823949; e-mail magazine@todaysliving.com; internet www.todaysliving.com; f. 1987; monthly; interior design; Publr and Editor-in-Chief KENNETH LI; circ. 35,000.

Yazhou Zhoukan: Block A, Ming Pao Industrial Centre, 15/F, 18 Ka Yip St, Chai Wan; tel. 25155358; fax 25059662; e-mail yzzk@mingpao.com; internet www.yzzk.com; f. 1987; international Chinese news weekly; Chief Editor YAU LOP-POON; circ. 110,000.

Yuk Long TV Weekly: Hong Kong; tel. 25657883; fax 25659958; f. 1977; entertainment, fashion, etc.; Publr TONY WONG; circ. 82,508.

NEWS AGENCIES

International News Service: 2E Cheong Shing Mansion, 33–39 Wing Hing St, Causeway Bay; tel. 25665668; Rep. AU KIT MING.

Xinhua (New China) News Agency, Hong Kong SAR Bureau: 387 Queen's Rd East, Wanchai; tel. 28314126; f. 2000; est. from fmr news dept of branch office of Xinhua (responsibility for other activities assumed by Liaison Office of the Central People's Govt in the Hong Kong SAR); Dir ZHANG GUOLIANG.

PRESS ASSOCIATIONS

Chinese Language Press Institute: 3/F, Sing Tao News Corpn Bldg, 3 Tung Wong Rd, Shau Kei Wan; tel. 27982501; fax 27953017; e-mail clpi68@yahoo.com.hk; f. 1968; Pres. TIONG HIEW KING.

Hong Kong Chinese Press Association: Rm 2208, 22/F, 33 Queen's Rd, Central; tel. 28613622; fax 28661933; 13 mems; Chair. HUE PUE-YING.

Hong Kong Journalists Association: GPOB 11726, Henfa Commercial Bldg, Flat 15A, 348–350 Lockhart Rd, Waichai; tel. 25910692; fax 25727329; e-mail hkja@hkja.org.hk; internet www.hkja.org.hk; f. 1968; 413 mems; Chair. FAN HO TSAI.

Newspaper Society of Hong Kong: Rm 904, 75–83 King's Rd, North Point; tel. 25713102; fax 25712676; e-mail secretariat@nshk.com.hk; internet www.nshk.org.hk; f. 1954; Chair. KEITH KAM; Pres. LEE CHO-JAT.

Publishers

Art House of Collectors HK Ltd: 37 Lyndhurst Terrace, Ground Floor, Central; tel. 28818026; fax 28904304; Dir LI LAP FONG.

Asia 2000 Ltd: Rm A, 18/F, Hollywood Centre, 77–91 Queen's Rd West; tel. 25301409; fax 25261107; e-mail sales@asia2000.com.hk; internet www.asia2000.com.hk; Asian studies, politics, photography, fiction; Man. Dir MICHAEL MORROW.

Asian Research Service: GPOB 2232; tel. 25707227; fax 25128050; f. 1972; maps, atlases, monographs on Asian studies and journals; Dir NELSON LEUNG.

Chinese University Press: Chinese University of Hong Kong, Sha Tin, New Territories; tel. 29465300; fax 26036692; e-mail cup@cuhk.edu.hk; internet www.chineseupress.com; f. 1977; studies on China and Hong Kong and other academic works; Dir QI GAN.

Chung Hwa Book Co (HK) Ltd: 7/F, Kati It Bldg; tel. 7150176; fax 7658468; internet www.chunghwabook.com.hk.

Commercial Press (Hong Kong) Ltd: Eastern Central Plaza, 8/F, 3 Yiu Hing Rd, Shau Kei Wan; tel. 25651371; fax 25645277; e-mail webmaster@commercialpress.com.hk; internet www.commercialpress.com.hk; f. 1897; trade books, dictionaries, textbooks, Chinese classics, art, etc.; Chair. and Man. Dir CHAN MAN HUNG.

Excerpta Medica Asia Ltd: 1601, 16/F, Leighton Centre, 77 Leighton Rd, Causeway Bay; tel. 29651300; fax 29760778; e-mail emal@excerptahk.com; internet www.excerptahk.com; subsidiary of Elsevier; f. 1980; sponsored medical publications, abstracts, journals, etc.

Hoi Fung Publisher Co: 125 Lockhart Rd, 2/F, Wanchai; tel. 25286246; fax 25286249; Dir K. K. TSE.

Hong Kong University Press: Hing Wai Centre, 14/F, 7 Tin Wan Praya Rd, Aberdeen; tel. 25502703; fax 28750734; e-mail hkupress@hkucc.hku.hk; internet www.hkupress.org; f. 1956; Publr COLIN DAY.

Ismay Publications Ltd: C. C. Wu Bldg; tel. 25752270; internet www.ismaychina.com; Man. Dir MINNIE YEUNG.

Joint Publishing (HK) Co Ltd: 1304 Eastern Centre; tel. 28069233; internet www.jointpublishing.com.

Ling Kee Publishing Co Ltd: Zung Fu Industrial Bldg, 1067 King's Rd, Quarry Bay; tel. 25616151; fax 28111980; e-mail admin@lingkee.com; internet www.lingkee.com; f. 1956; educational and reference; Chair. B. L. AU; Man. Dir K. W. AU.

Oxford University Press (China) Ltd: Warwick House East, 18/F, 979 King's Rd, Taikoo Place, Quarry Bay; tel. 25163222; fax 25658491; e-mail oupchina@oupchina.com.hk; internet www.oupchina.com.hk; f. 1961; school textbooks, reference, academic and general works relating to Hong Kong, Taiwan and China; Regional Dir SIMON LI.

Taosheng Publishing House: Lutheran Bldg, 3/F, 50A Waterloo Rd, Yau Ma Tei, Kowloon; tel. 23887061; fax 27810413; e-mail taosheng@elchk.org.hk; Dir CHANG CHUN WA.

Textile Asia/Business Press Ltd: California Tower, 11/F, 30–32 D'Aguilar St, GPOB 185, Central; tel. 25233744; fax 28106966; e-mail texasia@netvigator.com; internet www.textileasia-businesspress.com; f. 1970; textile magazine; Man. Dir KAYSER W. SUNG.

The Woods Publishing Co: Li Yuen Building, 2/F, 7 Li Yuen St West, Central; tel. 25233002; fax 28453296; e-mail tybook@netvigator.com; Production Man. TONG SZE HONG.

Times Publishing (Hong Kong) Ltd: Seaview Estate, Block C, 10/F, 2–8 Watson Rd, North Point; tel. 25668381; fax 25080255; e-mail abeditor@asianbusiness.com.hk; internet www.asianbusinessnet.com; trade magazines and directories; CEO COLIN YAM; Executive Editor JAMES LEUNG.

GOVERNMENT PUBLISHING HOUSE

Government Information Services: see Government Offices.

PUBLISHERS' ASSOCIATIONS

Hong Kong Publishers' and Distributors' Association: Flat C, 4/F, 240–246 Nathan Rd, Kowloon; tel. 23674412; 45 mems; Chair. HO KAM-LING; Sec. HO NAI-CHI.

Hong Kong Publishing Federation Ltd: Room 904, SUP Tower, 75-83 King's Road, North Point; tel. 25786000; fax 25786838.

Hong Kong Publishing Professionals Society Ltd: 8/F, Eastern Central Plaza, 3 Yiu Hing Rd, Shaukeiwan; tel. 29766804; fax 25645270; Chair. Dr CHAN MAN HUNG.

The Society of Hong Kong Publishers: 23/F, Henan Building, 90 Jaffe Rd, Wanchai.

The Society of Publishers in Asia: c/o Perfect Promotion Ltd, Rm 702, 7/F Tak Woo House, 17–19 D'Aguilar St, Central; tel. 28822555; fax 28824673; e-mail mail@sopasia.com; internet www.sopasia.com; Chair. ALAN LAMMIN.

Broadcasting and Communications

TELECOMMUNICATIONS

Asia Satellite Telecommunications Co Ltd (AsiaSat): 19/F, Sunning Plaza, 10 Hysan Ave, Causeway Bay; tel. 25000888; fax 25000895; e-mail as-mkt@asiasat.com; internet www.asiasat.com; f. 1988; CEO PETER JACKSON.

China Mobile Ltd: 60th Floor, The Center, 99 Queen's Rd, Central; tel. 31218888; fax 25119092; internet www.chinamobileltd.com; f. 1997; leading mobile services provider in mainland China, operating through its 31 subsidiaries in all 31 provinces, autonomous regions and municipalities in the People's Republic; subsidiary of China Mobile Communications Corpn; 301.2m. subscribers (Dec. 2006); Chair. and CEO WANG JIANZHOU.

China Netcom Group Corpn (Hong Kong) Ltd: Rm 6701, 67/F, The Centre, 99 Queen's Rd, Central; tel. 26268888; fax 26268862; internet www.china-netcom.com; f. 1999; internet and telephone service provider; operations focused in northern and southern China; 115.33m. fixed-line telephone subscribers, 11.48m. broadband subscribers (2005); Chair. ZHANG CHUNJIANG; CEO ZUO XUNSHANG.

Pacific Century CyberWorks (PCCW): 39/F PCCW Tower, Taikoo Place, 979 King's Rd, Quarry Bay; tel. 28882888; fax 28778877; e-mail general@pccw.com; internet www.pccw.com; fmrly Cable and Wireless HKT Ltd, acquired by PCCW August 2000; 20% owned by China Netcom; telecommunications/internet services provider; Chair. RICHARD LI TZAR KAI.

CHINESE SPECIAL ADMINISTRATIVE REGIONS   Hong Kong

Regulatory Authority

Office of the Telecommunications Authority: tel. 29616333; fax 28035110; e-mail webmaster@ofta.gov.hk; internet www.ofta.gov.hk; statutory regulator, responsible for implementation of the Govt's pro-competition and pro-consumer policies; Dir-Gen. M. H. AU. Hutchison Telecom, New T and T Hong Kong Ltd, and New World Telecom also operate local services. At November 2007 there were five companies licensed to provide mobile telecommunications services, serving 10.5m. customers in Hong Kong.

BROADCASTING
Regulatory Authority

Broadcasting Authority: 39/F Revenue Tower, 5 Gloucester Rd, Wanchai; tel. 25945721; fax 25072219; e-mail ba@tela.gov.hk; internet www.hkba.hk; regulatory body; administers and issues broadcasting licences; Chair. DANIEL R. FUNG.

Radio

Hong Kong Commercial Broadcasting Co Ltd: 3 Broadcast Drive, KCPOB 73000; tel. 23365111; fax 23380021; e-mail comradio@crhk.com.hk; internet www.crhk.com.hk; f. 1959; broadcasts in English and Cantonese on three radio frequencies; Chair. G. J. HO; Dir and CEO RITA CHING-HAN CHAN.

Metro Broadcast Corpn Ltd (Metro Broadcast): Basement 2, Site 6, Whampoa Garden, Hunghom, Kowloon; tel. 21239877; fax 21239888; e-mail webmaster@metroradio.com.hk; internet www.metroradio.com.hk; f. 1991; broadcasts on three channels in English, Cantonese and Mandarin; Gen. Man. CRAIG B. QUICK.

Radio Television Hong Kong: Broadcasting House, 30 Broadcast Drive, Kowloon; tel. 23396300; fax 23380279; e-mail admin@rthk.org.hk; internet www.rthk.org.hk; f. 1928; govt-funded; 24-hour service in English, Cantonese and Mandarin on seven radio channels; Dir GRACIE FOO (acting).

Television

Asia Television Ltd (ATV): 25–31 Dai Shing St, Tai Po Industrial Estate, Tai Po; tel. 29928888; fax 23380438; e-mail atv@hkatv.com; internet www.hkatv.com; f. 1973; operates two commercial television services (English and Chinese) and produces television programmes; Chair. WONG PO-YAN; Dir and CEO CHAN WING-KEE.

Hong Kong Cable Television Ltd: Cable TV Tower, 9 Hoi Shing Rd, Tsuen Wan; tel. 21126868; fax 21127878; e-mail info@hkce.com; internet www.cabletv.com.hk; f. 1993; 24-hour subscription service of news, sport and entertainment on 35 channels; carries BBC World Service Television; Chair. and CEO STEPHEN NG.

Phoenix Satellite Television: No. 9, Tower 1, Seashore Square, 18 Defeng St, Kowloon; tel. 26219888; fax 26219898; internet www.phoenixtv.com; f. 1995; partly owned by News Corpn (USA); broadcasts worldwide in Mandarin; CEO LIU CHANGLE.

Radio Television Hong Kong: see Radio; produces drama, documentary and public affairs programmes; also operates an educational service for transmission by two local commercial stations; Dir CHU PUI-HING.

STAR Group Ltd: One Harbourfront, 8/F, 18 Tak Fung St, Hunghom, Kowloon; tel. 26218888; fax 26213050; e-mail corp_aff@startv.com; internet www.startv.com; f. 1990; subsidiary of News Corpn; broadcasts over 40 channels in English, Hindi, Tamil, Mandarin, Cantonese, Korean and Thai, including a range of sports programmes, music, movies, news, entertainment and documentaries; reaches more than 300m. people in 53 countries across Asia, India and the Middle East, with a daily audience of about 100m. people; has interests in cable systems in India and Taiwan; services also extend to interactive cable TV, radio, wireless and digital media platforms; CEO PAUL AIELLO; COO LAUREEN ONG.

Television Broadcasts Ltd (TVB): TVB City, 77 Chun Choi St, Tseung Kwan O Industrial Estate, Kowloon; tel. 23352288; fax 23581300; e-mail external.affairs@tvb.com.hk; internet www.tvb.com; f. 1967; operates Chinese and English language television programme services; Exec. Chair. Sir RUN RUN SHAW.

Finance

(cap. = capital; res = reserves; dep. = deposits; m. = million; brs = branches; amounts in Hong Kong dollars unless otherwise stated)

BANKING

In December 2006 there were 138 licensed banks operating in Hong Kong. There were also 31 restricted licence banks (formerly known as licensed deposit-taking companies), 33 deposit-taking companies, and 84 foreign banks' representative offices.

Hong Kong Monetary Authority (HKMA): 55/F, Two International Finance Centre, 8 Finance St, Central; tel. 28788196; fax 28788197; e-mail hkma@hkma.gov.hk; internet www.hkma.gov.hk; f. 1993; est. by merger of Office of the Commissioner of Banking and Office of the Exchange Fund; government authority responsible for maintaining monetary and banking stability; manages official reserves in the Exchange Fund; Chief Exec. JOSEPH YAM; Deputy Chief Execs PETER PANG, EDDIE YUE, Y. K. CHOI.

Banks of Issue

Bank of China (Hong Kong) Ltd (People's Repub. of China): Bank of China Tower, 1 Garden Rd, Central; tel. 28266888; fax 28105963; internet www.bochk.com; f. 1917; became third bank of issue in May 1994; merged in Oct. 2001 with the local branches of 11 mainland banks (incl. Kwangtung Provincial Bank, Sin Hua Bank Ltd, China and the South Sea Bank Ltd, Kincheng Banking Corpn, China State Bank, National Commercial Bank Ltd, Yien Yieh Commercial Bank Ltd, Hua Chiao Commercial Bank Ltd and Po Sang Bank Ltd), to form the Bank of China (Hong Kong); cap. 43,043m., res 35,958m., dep. 798,579m. (Dec. 2006); CEO HE GUANGBEI; 217 brs.

The Hongkong and Shanghai Banking Corporation Ltd: 1 Queen's Rd, Central; tel. 28221111; fax 28101112; internet www.asiapacific.hsbc.com; f. 1865; personal and commercial banking; cap. 22,494m., res 116,456m., dep. 1,989,467m. (Dec. 2006); Chair. VINCENT CHENG; CEO SANDY FLOCKHART; more than 600 offices world-wide.

Standard Chartered Bank: Standard Chartered Bank Bldg, 4–4A Des Voeux Rd, Central; tel. 28203333; fax 28569129; internet www.standardchartered.com.hk; f. 1859; cap. 3,901m., res 12,737m., dep. 344,363m.; CEO BENJAMIN HUNG.

Other Commercial Banks

Bank of East Asia Ltd: Bank of East Asia Bldg, 16/F, 10 Des Voeux Rd, Central; tel. 36083608; fax 36086000; internet www.hkbea.com; inc in Hong Kong in 1918, absorbed United Chinese Bank Ltd in Aug. 2001, and First Pacific Bank (FPB) in April 2002; cap. 3,875.4m., res 16,288.1m., dep. etc. 249,424.4m. (Dec. 2006); Chair. and Chief Exec. DAVID K. P. LI; 87 brs in Hong Kong and 19 overseas brs.

China Construction Bank (Asia) Ltd: 44–45/F, Tower One Lippo Centre, 89 Queensway, Admiralty; tel. 28684438; fax 25377182; internet www.ccbhk.com; fmrly known as Jian Sing Bank Ltd; wholly owned subsidiary of China Construction Bank Corpn; cap. 310m., res 42.2m., dep. 3,073.9m. (Dec. 2006); Chair. LUO ZHEFU.

Chiyu Banking Corpn Ltd: 74–78 Des Voeux Rd, Central; tel. 28430111; fax 25267420; f. 1947; cap. 300m., res 432m., dep. 28,534.8m. (Dec. 2006); Chair. HE GUANGBEI; 22 brs.

Chong Hing Bank Ltd: POB 2535, G/F, New World Tower, 16–18 Queen's Rd, Central; tel. 28417417; fax 28459134; e-mail info@lchbank.com; internet www.lchbank.com; f. 1948; fmrly Liu Chong Hing Bank; cap. 217.5m., res 5,834.2m., dep. 22,205.9m. (Dec. 2006); Chair. and Man. Dir LIU LIT-MAN; 39 domestic brs, 3 overseas brs.

CITIC Ka Wah Bank Ltd: 232 Des Voeux Rd, Central; tel. 22876767; fax 25417029; e-mail info@citickawahbank.com; internet www.citickawahbank.com; f. 1922; cap. 3,083.3m., res 632.7m., dep. 76,784.8m. (Dec. 2006); acquired Hong Kong Chinese Bank Ltd Jan. 2002; Chair. DOU JIANZHONG; CEO DOREEN CHAN HUI DOR LAM; 30 domestic brs.

Dah Sing Bank Ltd: Dah Sing Financial Centre, 36/F, 108 Gloucester Rd, Central; tel. 25078866; fax 25985052; e-mail ops@dahsing.com.hk; internet www.dahsing.com; f. 1947; cap. 2,300.0m., res 1,332.6m., dep. 85,051.7m. (Dec. 2006); Chair. DAVID S. Y. WONG; Man. Dir DEREK H. H. WONG; 39 domestic brs.

DBS Bank (Hong Kong) Ltd: 11/F, The Center, 99 Queen's Rd, Central; tel. 22188822; fax 21678222; e-mail hkcs@dbs.com; internet www.dbs.com.hk; f. 1938; inc in 1954 as Kwong On Bank, name changed 2000; subsidiary of the Development Bank of Singapore; cap. 5,200m., res 2,872.8m., dep. 178,838.5m. (Dec. 2006); acquired Dao Heng Bank and Overseas Trust Bank July 2003; Chair. FRANK WONG; CEO RANDOLPH GORDON SULLIVAN; 32 brs.

Hang Seng Bank Ltd: 83 Des Voeux Rd, Central; tel. 21981111; fax 28684047; e-mail ccdca@hangseng.com; internet www.hangseng.com; f. 1933; a principal member of the HSBC group, which has an ownership of 62.14%; cap. 9,559m., res 33,789m., dep. 540,303m. (Dec. 2006); Chair. MICHAEL R. P. SMITH; Vice-Chair. and CEO RAYMOND OR; 149 brs in Hong Kong, 17 in mainland China and 1 in Macao; also rep. office in Taipei.

Industrial and Commercial Bank of China (Asia): 33/F, ICBC Tower, 3 Garden Rd, Central; tel. 25881188; fax 28051166; e-mail enquiry@icbcasia.com; internet www.icbcasia.com; f. 1964; fmrly Union Bank of Hong Kong; cap. 2,242.5m., res 6,108.5m., dep. 125,671.1m. (Dec. 2006); Chair. JIANG JIANQING; 38 brs.

Mevas Bank: 33/F, Dah Sing Financial Centre, 108 Gloucester Rd; tel. 31013286; fax 31013298; e-mail contactus@mevas.com; internet www.mevas.com; cap. 400m., res 0.6m., dep. 6,104.2m. (Dec. 2006); Chair. DAVID S. Y. WONG; CEO HO MAN-CHAN.

Nanyang Commercial Bank Ltd: Nanyang Commercial Bank Bldg, 151 Des Voeux Rd, Central; tel. 28520888; fax 28153333; e-mail nanyang@ncb.com.hk; internet www.ncb.com.hk; f. 1949; cap. 600m., res 13,270.3m., dep. 83,247.1m. (June 2007); Chair. HE GUANGBEI; 41 brs, 1 overseas br.

Public Bank (Hong Kong) Ltd: Asia Financial Centre, 120 Des Voeux Rd, Central; tel. 25419222; fax 25410009; e-mail contact@afh.com.hk; internet www.publicbank.com.hk; f. 1934; fmrly Asia Commercial Bank; name changed as above June 2006; cap. 810.0m., res 698.9m., dep. 14,727m. (Dec. 2006); Chair. and CEO ROBIN Y. H. CHAN; Gen. Man. and CEO STEPHEN TAN; 12 domestic brs, 1 overseas.

Shanghai Commercial Bank Ltd: 12 Queen's Rd, Central; tel. 28415415; fax 28104623; e-mail contact@shacombank.com.hk; internet www.shacombank.com.hk; f. 1950; cap. 2,000m., res 7,433.6m., dep. 79,128.3m. (Dec. 2006); CEO, Man. Dir and Gen. Man. JOHN KAM-PAK YAN; 41 domestic brs, 5 overseas brs.

Standard Bank Asia Ltd: 36/F, Two Pacific Place, 88 Queensway; tel. 28227888; fax 28227999; e-mail askbanking@standardbank.com.hk; internet www.standardbank.com; f. 1970; est. as Jardine Fleming & Company Ltd; renamed Jardine Fleming Bank Ltd in 1993; absorbed by Standard Bank Investment Corpn Ltd; name changed as present in July 2001; cap. US $72m., res US $113.4m., dep. US $2,071.9m. (Dec. 2006); Chair. ROB A. G. LEITH.

Tai Yau Bank Ltd: 29/F, Tai Tung Bldg, 8 Fleming Rd, Wanchai; tel. 25223296; f. 1947; cap. 300.0m., res 146.1m., dep. 1,229.3m. (Dec. 2005); Chair. KO FOOK KAU.

Wing Hang Bank Ltd: 161 Queen's Rd, Central; tel. 28525111; fax 25410036; e-mail whbpsd@whbhk.com; internet www.whbhk.com; f. 1937; cap. 294.2m., res 9,002.5m., dep. 108,066.0m. (Dec. 2006); acquired Chekiang First Bank Ltd in Aug. 2004; Chair. and Chief Exec. PATRICK Y. B. FUNG; 38 domestic brs, 13 overseas brs.

Wing Lung Bank Ltd: 45 Des Voeux Rd, Central; tel. 28268333; fax 28100592; e-mail wlb@winglungbank.com; internet www.winglungbank.com; f. 1933; cap. 1,160.9m., res 1,529.4m., dep. 69,954.7m. (Dec. 2006); Chair. MICHAEL PO-KO WU; Exec. Dir and Gen. Man. CHE-SHUM CHUNG; 33 domestic brs, 4 overseas brs, 2 rep. offices in China.

Principal Foreign Banks

ABN AMRO Bank NV (Netherlands): 37/F, Cheung Kong Center 2, Queens Rd, Central; tel. 28429211; fax 28459049; internet www.abnamro.com/hk; CEO (Asia) JEREON DROST; 3 brs.

American Express Bank Ltd (USA): 17/F, One Pacific Place, 88 Queensway, Central; tel. 28440688; fax 28453637; internet www.americanexpress.com/hk; Senior Country Exec. DOUGLAS H. SHORT III; 3 brs.

Australia and New Zealand Banking Group Ltd: 27/F, One Exchange Square, 8 Connaught Place, Central; tel. 28437111; fax 28680089; internet www.anz.com.au/hongkong; Gen. Man. PHAITHUL TEJASAKULSIN.

Bangkok Bank Public Co Ltd (Thailand): Bangkok Bank Bldg, 28 Des Voeux Rd, Central; tel. 28016688; fax 28451805; e-mail bangkokbank@bbl.com.hk; Gen. Man. LEO KUNG YIN CHENG; 2 brs.

Bank Negara Indonesia: G/F, Far East Finance Centre, 16 Harcourt Rd; tel. 28618600; fax 28656500; Gen. Man. BRAMONO DWIEDJANTO.

Bank of Communications, Hong Kong Branch: 20 Pedder St, Central; tel. 28419611; fax 28106993; e-mail enquiry@bankcomm.com.hk; internet www.bankcomm.com.hk; f. 1934; Gen. Man. FANG LIANKUI; 41 brs.

Bank of India: Ruttonjee House, 2/F, 11 Duddell St, Central; tel. 25240186; fax 28106149; e-mail boihk@netvigator.com; internet www.bankofindia.com.hk; Chief Exec. B. G. KURUP.

Bank of Scotland: Jardine House, 15/F, 1 Connaught Place, Central; tel. 25212155; fax 28459007; e-mail hicoperations@bankofscotlandint.com; internet www.bankofscotlandinternational.com; Regional Dir A. MCMULLIN; 1 br.

Bank of Tokyo-Mitsubishi UFJ Ltd (Japan): 8/F, AIG Tower, 1 Connaught Rd, Central; tel. 28236666; fax 25293821.

Barclays Capital Asia Ltd: Citibank Tower, 42/F, 3 Garden Rd, Central; tel. 29032000; fax 29032999; internet www.barclayscapital.com; f. 1972; Chair. and CEO ROBERT A. MORRICE.

BNP Paribas (France): 59–63/F, Two International Finance Centre, 8 Finance St, Central; tel. 29098888; fax 25302707; e-mail didier.balme@bnpgroup.com; internet www.bnpparibas.com; f. 1958; Chief Exec. MIGNONNE CHENG; 2 brs.

Calyon (France): 27/F, Two Pacific Place, 88 Queensway; tel. 28267333; fax 228261270; CEO GILLES ALLEIN; 1 br.

China Construction Bank (Asia) Corpn Ltd: 16/F, York House, The Landmark, 15 Queen's Rd Central, Central; tel. 25973333; fax 25972500; internet www.asia.ccb.com; fmrly Bank of America (Asia); wholly owned subsidiary of China Construction Bank Corpn; commercial banking and retail banking; cap. 310m., res 7,713m., dep. 27,561m. (Dec. 2006); Pres. and CEO SAMUEL N. TSIEN; 14 brs in Hong Kong; 2 brs in Macao.

Citibank, NA (USA): Citibank Tower, 39–40/F and 44–50/F, Citibank Plaza, 3 Garden Rd, Central; tel. 28688888; fax 23068111; internet www.citibank.com.hk; 20 brs.

Commerzbank AG (Germany): Hong Kong Club Bldg, 21/F, 3A Chater Rd, Central; tel. 28429666; fax 28681414; internet www.commerzbank.com.hk; 1 br.

Crédit Suisse (Switzerland): 23/F, Three Exchange Square, 8 Connaught Place, Central; tel. 28414888; fax 28400012; internet www.credit-suisse.com/hk.

Deutsche Bank AG (Germany): 51–56/F, Cheung Kong Center, 2 Queen's Rd, Central; tel. 22038888; fax 28459056; internet www.db.com/hongkong; Gen. Mans Dr MICHAEL THOMAS, REINER RUSCH; 1 br.

Equitable PCI Bank (Philippines): 7/F, No. 1, Silver Fortune Plaza, Wellington St; tel. 28680323; fax 28100050; Vice-Pres. PAUL LANG; 1 br.

Fortis Bank (Belgium): Fortis Bank Tower, 26/F, 77–79 Gloucester Rd, Wanchai; tel. 28230456; fax 25276851; e-mail info@fortisbank.com.hk; internet www.fortisbank.com.hk; Gen. Man. DAVID YU; 28 brs.

Indian Overseas Bank: POB 182, Ruttonjee House, 3/F, 11 Duddell St, Central; tel. 25227249; fax 28450159; 2 brs.

JP Morgan Chase Bank (USA): 39/F, One Exchange Square, Connaught Place, Central; tel. 28431234; fax 28414396.

Malayan Banking Berhad (Malaysia): 21/F, Man Yee Bldg, 68 Des Voeux Rd, Central; tel. 35188888; fax 35188890; trades in Hong Kong as Maybank; Gen. Man. AMOS ONG SEET JOON; 2 brs.

Mizuho Corporate Bank Ltd (Japan): 17/F, Two Pacific Place, 88 Queensway, Admiralty; tel. 21033040; fax 28101326; Man. Dir and CEO NOBORU AKATSUKA; 1 br.

National Bank of Pakistan: POB 99006, 1103 Fourseas Bldg, 208–212 Nathan Rd, Kowloon; tel. 23697355; fax 27245622; e-mail nbphkkm@netvigator.com; CEO GHULAM HUSSAIN AZHAR.

Oversea-Chinese Banking Corpn Ltd (Singapore): 9/F, 9 Queen's Rd, Central; tel. 28682086; fax 28453439; Gen. Man. BENJAMIN YEUNG; 3 brs.

Philippine National Bank: 2/F, Wings Bldg, 110–116 Queen's Rd, Central; tel. 25253638; fax 25253107; e-mail pnbhkgrp@pnbhk.com; Gen. Man. DANILO T. FLORES; 1 br.

N. M. Rothschild and Sons (Hong Kong) Ltd: 16/F, Alexandra House, 16–20 Chater Rd, Central; tel. 25255333; fax 28681728; e-mail jackson.woo@rothschild.com.hk; cap. 207.6m., dep. 9.5m. (Dec. 2006); Chair. RUSSELL EDEY.

Société Générale Asia Ltd (France): Level 38, Three Pacific Place, 1 Queen's Rd East; tel. 21665388; fax 28682368; internet www.sgcib.com; CEO JACKSON CHEUNG.

Sumitomo Mitsui Banking Corpn (SMBC) (Japan): 7–8/F, One International Finance Centre, 1 Harbour View St, Central; tel. 22062000; fax 22062888; Gen. Man. TOSHIO MORIKAWA; 1 br.

UBAF (Hong Kong) Ltd (France): The Sun's Group Centre, 21/F, 200 Gloucester Rd, Wanchai; tel. 25201361; fax 25274256; e-mail info@ubafhk.com; internet www.ubafhk.com; Man. Dir G. ALEJANDRO.

United Overseas Bank Ltd (Singapore): 25/F, Gloucester Tower, 11 Pedder St, Central; tel. 29108888; fax 28105506; internet www.uobgroup.com/hk; Sr Vice-Pres. and CEO ROBERT CHAN TZE LEUNG; 5 brs.

Banking Associations

The Chinese Banks' Association Ltd: South China Bldg, 5/F, 1–3 Wyndham St, Central; tel. 25224789; fax 28775102; 1,666 mems; chaired by Bank of East Asia.

The DTC Association (The Hong Kong Association of Restricted Licence Banks and Deposit-Taking Companies): Unit 2404, 24/F, Bonham Trade Centre, 50 Bonham Strand East, Sheung Wan; tel. 25264079; fax 25230180; e-mail dtca@dtca.org.hk; internet www.dtca.org.hk; f. 1981; Sec. PUI CHONG LUND; 50 mem. banks.

The Hong Kong Association of Banks: Rm 525, Prince's Bldg, Central; tel. 25211169; fax 28685035; e-mail info@hkab.org.hk; internet www.hkab.org.hk; f. 1981; est. to succeed The Exchange Banks' Asscn of Hong Kong; all licensed banks in Hong Kong are required by law to be mems of this statutory body, the function of which is to represent and further the interests of the banking sector; 132 mems; chaired by HSBC; Sec. EVA WONG.

CHINESE SPECIAL ADMINISTRATIVE REGIONS   Hong Kong

STOCK EXCHANGE

Hong Kong Exchanges and Clearing Ltd: 12/F, One International Finance Centre, Harbour View St, Central; tel. 25221122; fax 22953106; e-mail info@hkex.com.hk; internet www.hkex.com.hk; f. 2000; est. by merger of the Stock Exchange of Hong Kong, the Hong Kong Futures Exchange and the Hong Kong Securities Clearing Co; Chair. RONALD ARCULLI; CEO PAUL CHOW.

SUPERVISORY BODY

Securities and Futures Commission (SFC): 8/F, Chater House, 8 Connaught Rd, Central; tel. 28409222; fax 25217836; e-mail enquiry@sfc.hk; internet www.sfc.hk; f. 1989; supervises the securities and futures markets; CEO MARTIN WHEATLEY; Exec. Dir and COO PAUL KENNEDY.

INSURANCE

In December 2007 there were 178 authorized insurance companies, of which 112 were pure general insurers, 47 were pure long-term insurers and the remaining 19 were composite insurers. The following are among the principal companies:

ACE Insurance Ltd: 25/F, Shui On Centre, 6–8 Harbour Rd, Wanchai; tel. 31916800; fax 25603565; e-mail contact.acehk@ace-ina.com; internet www.aceinsurance.com.hk; CEO JOHN FRENCH.

American Home Assurance Co: AIA Bldg, 1 Stubbs Rd, Wanchai; tel. 28321800; e-mail cs@aiu.com.hk; internet www.aiu.com.hk.

Asia Insurance Co Ltd: Worldwide House, 16/F, 19 Des Voeux Rd, Central; tel. 28677988; fax 28100218; e-mail kclau@asiainsurance.com.hk; internet www.asiainsurance.com.hk; Chair. SEBASTIAN KI CHIT LAU.

Aviva Life Insurance Co Ltd: Suite 1701, Cityplaza One, 1111 King's Rd, Taikoo Shing; tel. 35509600; fax 29071787; e-mail enquiry@aviva-asia.com; internet www.aviva-asia.com.

AXA General Insurance Hong Kong Ltd: 30/F, PCCW Tower, Taikoo Place, 979 King's Rd, Quarry Bay; tel. 25233061; fax 28100706; e-mail axahk@axa-insurance.com.hk; internet www.axa-insurance.com.hk.

Bank of China Group Insurance Co Ltd: 9/F, Wing On House, 71 Des Voeux Rd Central; tel. 28670888; fax 25221705; e-mail administration_ins@bocgroup.com; internet www.bocgroup.com/bocg-ins.

Hong Kong Export Credit Insurance Corpn: South Seas Centre, Tower I, 2/F, 75 Mody Rd, Tsim Sha Tsui East, Kowloon; tel. 27329988; fax 27226277; internet www.hkecic.com; f. 1966; est. by govt to encourage and support trade; Commr K. K. CHEUNG; Gen. Man. CYNTHIA CHIN.

HSBC Insurance (Asia-Pacific) Holdings Ltd: 18/F, Tower 1, HSBC Centre, 1 Sham Mong Road, Kowloon; tel. 22886688; fax 28277636; e-mail insurance@hsbc.com.hk; CEO Dr VICTOR KUK.

Ming An Insurance Co (HK) Ltd: Ming An Plaza, 19/F, 8 Sunning Rd, Causeway Bay; tel. 28151551; fax 25416567; e-mail mai@mingan.com.hk; internet www.mingan.com; CEO PENG WEI.

MSIG Insurance (Hong Kong) Ltd: 9/F, Cityplaza One, 1111 King's Rd, Taikoo Shing; tel. 28940555; fax 28905741; e-mail hk_hotline@hk.msig-asia.com; internet www.msig.com.hk; CEO KENNETH J. REID.

Prudential Assurance Co Ltd: 23/F, One Exchange Square, Central; tel. 29778311; fax 21648445; internet www.prudential.com.hk; life and general; CEO JAMES C. K. WONG.

QBE Hongkong and Shanghai Insurance Ltd: 17/F, Warwick House, West Wing, Taikoo Place, 979 King's Rd, Quarry Bay; tel. 28778488; fax 36070300; e-mail general@qbe.com.hk; internet www.qbe.com.hk.

Royal and Sun Alliance (Hong Kong) Ltd: Dorset House, 32/F, Taikoo Place, 979 King's Rd, Quarry Bay; tel. 29683000; fax 29685111; e-mail willum.richards@royalsunalliance.com.hk; internet www.royalsunalliance.com.hk.

Swiss Re Hong Kong Branch: 61/F, Central Plaza, 18 Harbour Rd, Wanchai; tel. 25825608; acquired Mercantile and General Reinsurance in 1996; Gen. Man. DARRYL PIDCOCK; Gen. Man. DAVID ALEXANDER.

Zurich Insurance Group (Hong Kong): Levels 15–17 Cityplaza 3, 14 Taikoo Wan Road, Taikoo Shing; tel. 29682222; fax 29680988; e-mail zhk@zurich.com.hk; internet www.zurich.com.hk.

Insurance Associations

Hong Kong Federation of Insurers (HKFI): 29/F, Sunshine Plaza, 353 Lockhart Rd, Wanchai; tel. 25201868; fax 25201967; e-mail hkfi@hkfi.org.hk; internet www.hkfi.org.hk; f. 1988; 87 general insurance and 47 life insurance mems; Chair. MICHAEL HUDDART.

Insurance Institute of Hong Kong: Rm 1705, Beverly House, 93–107 Lockhart Rd, Wanchai; tel. 25200098; fax 22953939; e-mail enquiry@iihk.org.hk; internet www.iihk.org.hk; f. 1967; Pres. MICHAEL HAYNES.

Trade and Industry

Hong Kong Trade Development Council: Office Tower, 38/F, Convention Plaza, 1 Harbour Rd, Wanchai; tel. 1830668; fax 28240249; e-mail hktdc@tdc.org.hk; internet www.hktdc.com; f. 1966; Chair. JACK SO CHAK-KWONG; Exec. Dir FREDERICK LAM.

Trade and Industry Department: Trade and Industry Department Tower, 700 Nathan Rd, Kowloon; tel. 23985333; fax 27892491; e-mail enquiry@tid.gov.hk; internet www.tid.gov.hk; Dir-Gen. JOSEPH LAI.

DEVELOPMENT ORGANIZATIONS

Hong Kong Housing Authority: 33 Fat Kwong St, Homantin, Kowloon; tel. 27122712; fax 27114111; e-mail hkha@housingauthority.gov.hk; internet www.housingauthority.gov.hk; f. 1973; plans, builds and manages public housing; Chair. EVA CHENG; Dir of Housing THOMAS CHAN CHUN-YUEN.

Hong Kong Productivity Council: HKPC Bldg, 78 Tat Chee Ave, Yau Yat Chuen, Kowloon Tong, Kowloon; tel. 27885678; fax 27885900; e-mail justina@hkpc.org; internet www.hkpc.org; f. 1967; aims to promote increased productivity of industry in order to achieve optimum utilization of resources, enhance the value-added content of products and services, and increase international competitiveness; governed by a Council comprising a Chair and 22 mems appointed by the Govt, representing managerial, labour, academic and professional interests, and govt depts associated with productivity matters; Chair. ANDREW LEUNG KWAN-YUEN; Exec. Dir WILSON FUNG.

Kadoorie Agricultural Aid Loan Fund: c/o Director of Agriculture, Fisheries and Conservation, Cheung Sha Wan Govt Offices, 5/F, 303 Cheung Sha Wan Rd, Kowloon; tel. 21506666; fax 23113731; e-mail mailbox@afcd.gov.hk; f. 1954; provides low-interest loans to farmers; HK $9.3m. was loaned in 2006/07; Chair. THOMAS CHAN CHUN-YUEN.

J. E. Joseph Trust Fund: c/o Director of Agriculture, Fisheries and Conservation, Cheung Sha Wan Govt Offices, 5/F, 303 Cheung Sha Wan Rd, Kowloon; tel. 21506666; fax 23113731; e-mail mailbox@afcd.gov.hk; f. 1954; grants low-interest credit facilities to farmers and farmers' co-operative socs; HK $3.8m. was loaned in 2006/07.

CHAMBERS OF COMMERCE

Chinese Chamber of Commerce, Kowloon: 2/F, 8–10 Nga Tsin Long Rd, Kowloon; tel. 23822309; f. 1936; 234 mems; Chair. and Exec. Dir YEUNG CHOR-HANG.

The Chinese General Chamber of Commerce: 4/F, 24–25 Connaught Rd, Central; tel. 25256385; fax 28452610; e-mail cgcc@cgcc.org.hk; internet www.cgcc.org.hk; f. 1900; 6,000 mems; Chair. IAN FOK CHUN-WAN.

Hong Kong General Chamber of Commerce: United Centre, 22/F, 95 Queensway, POB 852; tel. 25299229; fax 25279843; e-mail chamber@chamber.org.hk; internet www.chamber.org.hk; f. 1861; 4,000 mems; Chair. DAVID ELDON; CEO ALEX FONG.

Kowloon Chamber of Commerce: KCC Bldg, 3/F, 2 Liberty Ave, Homantin, Kowloon; tel. 27600393; fax 27610166; e-mail kcc02@hkkcc.biz.com.hk; internet www.hkkcc.org.hk; f. 1938; 1,600 mems; Chair. LAU CHI WAI; Sec. of Gen. Affairs CHENG PO-WO.

FOREIGN TRADE ORGANIZATIONS

Hong Kong Chinese Importers' and Exporters' Association: Champion Bldg, 7–8/F, 287–291 Des Voeux Rd, Central; tel. 25448474; fax 25444677; e-mail info@hkciea.org.hk; internet www.hkciea.org.hk; f. 1954; 3,000 mems; Pres. WONG TING KWONG.

Hong Kong Exporters' Association: Rm 825, Star House, 3 Salisbury Rd, Tsimshatsui, Kowloon; tel. 27309851; fax 27301869; e-mail exporter@exporters.org.hk; internet www.exporters.org.hk; f. 1955; 680 mems (March 2007) comprising leading merchants and manufacturing exporters; Chair. TOM TANG; Exec. Dir SHIRLEY SO.

INDUSTRIAL AND TRADE ASSOCIATIONS

Chinese Manufacturers' Association of Hong Kong: CMA Bldg, 64 Connaught Rd, Central; tel. 25456166; fax 25414541; e-mail info@cma.org.hk; internet www.cma.org.hk; f. 1934; promotes and protects industrial and trading interests; operates testing and certification laboratories; 3,700 mems; Pres. PAUL T. S. YIN.

Communications Association of Hong Kong: GPOB 13461; tel. 25042732; fax 25042752; e-mail info@cahk.hk; internet www.cahk.hk; 108 mems; Chair. HUBERT CHAN.

CHINESE SPECIAL ADMINISTRATIVE REGIONS

Federation of Hong Kong Garment Manufacturers: Cheung Lee Commercial Bldg, Rm 401–3, 25 Kimberley Rd, Tsimshatsui, Kowloon; tel. 27211383; fax 23111062; e-mail info@garment.org.hk; internet www.garment.org.hk; f. 1964; 120 mems; Pres. YEUNG FAN; Sec.-Gen. MICHAEL LEUNG.

Federation of Hong Kong Industries (FKHI): Hankow Centre, 4/F, 5–15 Hankow Rd, Tsimshatsui, Kowloon; tel. 27323183; fax 27213494; e-mail fhki@fhki.org.hk; internet www.fhki.org.hk; f. 1960; 3,000 mems; Chair. CLEMENT CHEN; Dir-Gen. DENNIS T. W. YAU.

Federation of Hong Kong Watch Trades and Industries Ltd: Peter Bldg, Rm 604, 58–62 Queen's Rd, Central; tel. 25233232; fax 28684485; e-mail hkwatch@hkwatch.org; internet www.hkwatch.org; f. 1947; 650 mems; Chair. JERRY TSANG.

Hong Kong Association for the Advancement of Science and Technology Ltd: 2A, Tak Lee Commercial Bldg, 113–17 Wanchai Rd, Wanchai; tel. 28913388; fax 28381823; e-mail info@hkaast.org.hk; internet www.hkaast.org.hk; f. 1985; 170 mems; Pres. AARON W. K. TONG.

Hong Kong Biotechnology Association Ltd: Rm 789, HITEC, 1 Trademart Drive, Kowloon Bay, Kowloon; tel. 26209955; fax 26201238; e-mail etang@hkbta.org.hk; internet www.hkbta.org.hk; f. 1999; 100 mems; Chair. FRANK WAN.

Hong Kong Chinese Enterprises Association: Harbour Centre, Rm 2104–6, 25 Harbour Rd, Wanchai; tel. 28272831; fax 28272606; e-mail info@hkcea.com; internet www.hkcea.com; f. 1991; 960 mems; Chair. QIN XIAO.

Hong Kong Chinese Textile Mills Association: 11/F, 38–40 Tai Po Rd, Sham Shiu Po, Kowloon; tel. 27778236; fax 27881836; f. 1921; 150 mems; Pres. Dr ROGER NG KENG-PO.

Hong Kong Construction Association Ltd: 3/F, 180–182 Hennessy Rd, Wanchai; tel. 25724414; fax 25727104; e-mail admin@hkca.com.hk; internet www.hkca.com.hk; f. 1920; 372 mems; Pres. CONRAD WONG.

Hong Kong Electronic Industries Association Ltd: Rm 1201, 12/F, Harbour Crystal Centre, 100 Granville Rd, Tsimshatsui, Kowloon; tel. 27788328; fax 27882200; e-mail hkeia@hkeia.org; internet www.hkeia.org; 310 mems; Chair. Dr K. B. CHAN; Exec. Dir CHARLES CHAPMAN.

Hong Kong Garment Manufacturers Association: 401–3, Cheung Lee Commercial Bldg, 25 Kimberley Rd, Tsimshatsui, Kowloon; tel. 23052893; fax 23052493; e-mail sec@textilecouncil.com; f. 1987; 40 mems; Chair. PETER WANG.

Hong Kong Information Technology Federation Ltd: 2505–6, 25/F, Stelux House, 698 Prince Edward Rd East, San Po Kong, Kowloon; tel. 31018197; fax 30074728; e-mail info@hkitf.com; internet www.hkitf.org.hk; 316 mems; f. 1980; Pres. DANIEL NG; over 300 mems.

Hong Kong Jewellery and Jade Manufacturers Association: Flat A, 12/F, Kaiser Estate Phase 1, 41 Man Yue St, Hunghom, Kowloon; tel. 25430543; fax 28150164; e-mail hkjja@hkstar.com; internet www.jewellery-hk.org; f. 1965; 227 mems; Pres. CHARLES CHAN; Chair. KING LI; Gen. Man. CATHERINE CHAN.

Hong Kong Jewelry Manufacturers' Association: Unit G, 2/F, Kaiser Estate Phase 2, 51 Man Yue St, Hunghom, Kowloon; tel. 27663002; fax 23623647; e-mail hkjma@jewelry.org.hk; internet www.jewelry.org.hk; f. 1988; 345 mems; Chair. ADDY WONG.

Hong Kong Knitwear Exporters and Manufacturers Association: Cheung Lee Commercial Bldg, Rm 401–03, Tsimshatsui, Kowloon; tel. 27552621; fax 27565672; f. 1966; 70 mems; Chair. LAWRENCE LEUNG; Exec. Sec. KARINA TSUI.

Hong Kong and Kowloon Footwear Manufacturers' Association: Kam Fung Bldg, 3/F, Flat D, 8 Cleverly St, Sheung Wan; tel. and fax 25414499; 88 mems; Pres. LOK WAI-TO; Sec. LEE SUM-HUNG.

Hong Kong Optical Manufacturers' Association Ltd: 2/F, 11 Fa Yuen St, Mongkok, Kowloon; tel. 23326505; fax 27705786; e-mail hkoma@netvigator.com; internet www.hkoptical.org.hk; f. 1982; 111 mems; Pres. HUI LEUNG WAH.

Hong Kong Plastics Manufacturers Association Ltd: Rm 3, 10/F, Asia Standard Tower, 59–65 Queen's Rd, Central; tel. 25742230; fax 25742843; f. 1957; 200 mems; Chair. CLIFF SUN; Pres. JEFFREY LAM.

Hong Kong Printers Association: 1/F, 48–50 Johnston Rd, Wanchai; tel. 25275050; fax 28610463; e-mail printers@hkprinters.org; internet www.hkprinters.org; f. 1939; 400 mems; Chair. YEUNG KAM KAI.

Hong Kong Rubber and Footwear Manufacturers' Association: Kar Tseuk Bldg, Block A, 2/F, 185 Prince Edward Rd, Kowloon; tel. 23812297; fax 23976927; e-mail hkrfma@netvigator.com; f. 1948; 180 mems; Chair. CHEUNG KAM; Pres. BENJAMIN KO.

Hong Kong Sze Yap Commercial and Industrial Association: Cosco Tower, Unit 1205–6, 183 Queen's Rd, Central; tel. 25438095; fax 25449495; e-mail gahk_ltd@hotmail.com; f. 1909; 1,082 mems; Chair. LOUIE CHICK-NAN; Sec. WONG KA CHUN.

Hong Kong Toys Council: Hankow Centre, 4/F, 5–15 Hankow Rd, Tsimshatsui, Kowloon; tel. 27323188; fax 27213494; e-mail hktc@fhki.org.hk; internet www.toyshk.org; f. 1986; 200 mems; Chair. LAWRENCE W. L. CHAN; Sec.-Gen. JOSEPH LI.

Hong Kong Watch Manufacturers' Association: Yu Wing Bldg, 3/F and 11/F, Unit A, 64–66 Wellington St, Central; tel. 25225238; fax 28106614; e-mail hkwma@netvigator.com; internet www.hkwma.org; 650 mems; Pres. TOMMY LEUNG; Sec.-Gen. KENNETH WONG.

Information and Software Industry Association Ltd: 4/F HKPC Bldg, 78 Tat Chee Ave, Yau Yat Chuen, Kowloon; tel. 26222867; fax 26222731; e-mail info@isia.org.hk; internet www.isia.org.hk; f. 1999; 76 mems; Chair. ALDOUS NG.

New Territories Commercial and Industrial General Association Ltd: Cheong Hay Bldg, 2/F, 107 Hoi Pa St, Tsuen Wan; tel. 24145316; fax 24934130; e-mail ntciga@netvigator.com; f. 1973; 2,663 mems; Pres. LAU YUE SUN; Chair. WAN HOK LIM; Sec.-Gen. NGAN KAM CHUEN.

Real Estate Developers Association of Hong Kong: Worldwide House, Rm 1403, 19 Des Voeux Rd, Central; tel. 28260111; fax 28452521; f. 1965; 829 mems; Pres. Dr STANLEY HO; Chair. KEITH KERR; Sec.-Gen. LOUIS LOONG.

Textile Council of Hong Kong Ltd: 401–3, Cheung Lee Commercial Bldg, 25 Kimberley Rd, Tsimshatsui, Kowloon; tel. 23052893; fax 23052493; e-mail sec@textilecouncil.com; internet www.textilecouncil.com; f. 1989; 11 mems; Chair. HARRY LEE; Exec. Dir MICHAEL LEUNG.

Toys Manufacturers' Association of Hong Kong Ltd: Rm 1302, Metroplaza, Tower 2, 223 Hing Fong Rd, Kwai Chung, New Territories; tel. 24221209; fax 24221639; e-mail tm_hk@hotmail.com; internet www.tmhk.net; f. 1996; 250 mems; Pres. SAMSON CHAM.

EMPLOYERS' ORGANIZATIONS

Employers' Federation of Hong Kong: Suite 2004, Sino Plaza, 255–257 Gloucester Rd, Causeway Bay; tel. 25280033; fax 28655285; e-mail efhk@efhk.org.hk; internet www.efhk.org.hk; f. 1947; 504 mems; Chair. JAMES C. NG; Exec. Dir LOUIS PONG.

Hong Kong Factory Owners' Association Ltd: Wing Wong Bldg, 11/F, 557–559 Nathan Rd, Kowloon; tel. 23882372; fax 23857129; f. 1982; 1,261 mems; Pres. HWANG JEN; Sec. CHA KIT YEN.

UTILITIES
Electricity

CLP Power Ltd: 147 Argyle St, Kowloon; tel. 26788111; fax 27604448; internet www.clpgroup.com; f. 1918; fmrly China Light and Power Co Ltd; generation and supply of electricity to Kowloon and the New Territories; Chair. Sir MICHAEL D. KADOORIE; CEO ANDREW BRANDLER.

The Hongkong Electric Co Ltd: 44 Kennedy Rd; tel. 28433111; fax 28100506; e-mail mail@hec.com.hk; internet www.heh.com; generation and supply of electricity to Hong Kong Island, and the islands of Ap Lei Chau and Lamma; Chair. CANNING FOK KIN-NING; Man. Dir TSO KAI SUM.

Gas

Gas Authority: all gas supply cos, gas installers and contractors are required to be registered with the Gas Authority. At the end of 2003 there were seven registered gas supply cos.

Chinese People Gas Holdings Co Ltd: Unit 2113, 21/F, China Merchants Tower, Shun Tak Centre, 168–200 Connaught Rd, Central; tel. 29022008; fax 28030108; e-mail info@681hk.com; internet www.681hk.com; distributes and supplies natural gas in mainland China; Chair. LIU JING; Man. Dir MO SHIKANG.

Hong Kong and China Gas Co Ltd (Towngas): 23/F, 363 Java Rd, North Point; tel. 29633388; fax 25616182; internet www.towngas.com; f. 1862; production, distribution and marketing of gas, water and related activities in Hong Kong and mainland China; operates two plants; Chair. LEE SHAU KEE; Man. Dir ALFRED CHAN WING KIM.

Water

Drainage Services Department: responsible for planning, designing, constructing, operating and maintaining the sewerage, sewage treatment and stormwater drainage infrastructures.

Water Supplies Department: 48/F, Immigration Tower, 7 Gloucester Rd, Wanchai; tel. 28294500; fax 28240578; e-mail wsdinfo@wsd.gov.hk; internet www.wsd.gov.hk; responsible for water supplies for some 7m. people living within 1,100 sq km of the Hong Kong SAR; Dir MA LEE TAK.

CHINESE SPECIAL ADMINISTRATIVE REGIONS   *Hong Kong*

TRADE UNIONS

In December 2005 there were 729 trade unions in Hong Kong, comprising 686 employees' unions, 21 employers' associations and 22 mixed organizations.

Hong Kong and Kowloon Trades Union Council (TUC): 12/F, Kam Shek Commercial Bldg, 17 Waterloo Rd, Mongkok, Kowloon; tel. 23845150; fax 27705396; f. 1949; 66 affiliated unions, mostly covering the catering and building trades; 30,000 mems; supports Taiwan; affiliated to ITUC; Pres. TONG WOON FAI; Gen. Sec. LIEW NAN KIEM.

Hong Kong Confederation of Trade Unions: Wing Wong Commercial Bldg, 19/F, 557–559 Nathan Rd, Kowloon; tel. 27708668; fax 27707388; e-mail hkctu@hkctu.org.hk; internet www.hkctu.org.hk; registered Feb. 1990; 79 affiliated independent unions and federations; 170,000 mems; affiliated to ITUC; Pres. LAU CHIN-SHEK; Gen. Sec. LEE CHEUK-YAN.

The Hong Kong Federation of Trade Unions (HKFTU): 12 Ma Hang Chung Rd, Tokwawan, Kowloon; tel. 36525700; fax 27608477; e-mail info@ftu.org.hk; internet www.ftu.org.hk; f. 1948; 221 affiliated and associated unions, mostly in textiles, printing, insurance, construction, transportation, manufacturing, civil service, wholesale & retail, public transport and public utilities; approx. 300,000 mems; Chair. WONG KWOK KIN.

Also active are the Federation of Hong Kong and Kowloon Labour Unions (31 affiliated unions with 21,700 mems) and the Federation of Civil Service Unions (29 affiliated unions with 12,000 mems).

Transport

Transport Department: Immigration Tower, 41/F, 7 Gloucester Rd, Wanchai; tel. 28042600; fax 28240433; e-mail tdeng@td.gov.hk; internet www.td.gov.hk; Commr ALAN C. K. WONG.

RAILWAYS

Kowloon–Canton Railway Corpn: 8/F, Fo Tan Railway House, 9 Lok King St, Fo Tan, New Territories; tel. 26881333; fax 31241073; internet www.kcrc.com; f. 1982; operated by the Kowloon–Canton Railway Corpn, a public statutory body; assets controlled by MTR Corpn since 2007; operates both heavy and light rail systems over a 133-km network; the 34-km East Rail runs north–south from East Tsim Sha Tsui to the frontier at Lo Wu; West Rail, a domestic passenger line, opened in 2003, extending rail services to the northwest New Territories; Ma On Shan Rail and the Tsim Sha Tsui Extension was completed in 2004; also provides train passenger and freight services to and from various cities on the mainland; the Lok Ma Chau Spur Line, completed in 2007, provides a second railway link to the mainland, branching off the existing East Rail line north of Sheung Shui Station and terminating at Lok Ma Chau; the Kowloon Southern Link was to join East Rail and West Rail by connecting West Rail Nam Cheong Station to East Tsim Sha Tsui Station; construction began in 2005, scheduled for completion in 2009; a new 17-km railway linking Sha Tin and Central via a new cross-harbour tunnel, thereby providing the first direct rail route from the Chinese border to Hong Kong Island, was planned; CEO Ir JAMES BLAKE.

MTR Corporation: MTR Tower, Telford Plaza, Kowloon Bay; tel. 29932111; fax 27988822; internet www.mtr.com.hk; f. 1975; privatized in 2000, shares commenced trading on Hong Kong Stock Exchange in Oct. 2000; plans for merger with Kowloon–Canton Railway Corpn announced in 2004; network of 87.7 km of railway lines and 50 stations; the first section of the underground mass transit railway (MTR) system opened in 1979; a 15.6-km line from Kwun Tong to Central opened in 1980; a 10.5-km Tsuen Wan extension opened in 1982; the 12.5-km Island Line opened in 1985–86; in 1989 a second harbour crossing between Cha Kwo Ling and Quarry Bay, known as the Eastern Harbour Crossing, commenced operation, adding 4.6 km to the railway system; 34-km link to new airport at Chek Lap Kok and to Tung Chung New Town opened in 1998; an additional line, the Tseung Kwan O Extension, was completed in 2002; a new line serving the Disneyland theme park opened in 2005; CEO C. K. CHOW; Chair. Dr RAYMOND K. F. CH'IEN.

TRAMWAYS

Hong Kong Tramways Ltd: Whitty Street Tram Depot, Connaught Rd West, Western District; tel. 21186338; fax 21186038; e-mail enquiry@hktramways.com; internet www.hktramways.com; f. 1904; operates six routes and 161 double-deck trams between Kennedy Town and Shaukeiwan; Gen. Man. JAMES YU.

ROADS

At the end of 2005 there were 1,955 km of public roads in Hong Kong. Almost all of them are concrete or asphalt surfaced. Owing to the hilly terrain, and the density of building development, the scope for substantial increase in the road network is limited. A new 29-km steel bridge linking Hong Kong's Lantau Island with Macao and Zhuhai City, in the Chinese province of Guangdong, was being planned in the early 21st century, with studies being carried out to determine the project's financial and technological feasibility.

Highways Department: Ho Man Tin Government Offices, 5/F, 88 Chung Hau St, Ho Man Tin, Kowloon; tel. 27623304; fax 27145216; e-mail ts.tau@hyd.gov.hk; internet www.hyd.gov.hk; f. 1986; planning, design, construction and maintenance of the public road system; co-ordination of major highway and railway projects; Dir WAI CHI-SING.

FERRIES

Conventional ferries, hoverferries and catamarans operate between Hong Kong, China and Macao. There is also an extensive network of ferry services to outlying districts.

Hongkong and Yaumati Ferry Co Ltd: 98 Tam Kon Shan Rd, Ngau Kok Wan, North Tsing Yi, New Territories; tel. 23944294; fax 27869001; e-mail hkferry@hkf.com; internet www.hkf.com; licensed routes on ferry services, incl. excursion, vehicular and dangerous goods; Chair. COLIN K. Y. LAM.

Shun Tak-China Travel Ship Management Ltd (TurboJET): 83 Hing Wah St West, Lai Chi Kok, Kowloon; tel. 23070880; fax 27865125; e-mail com@turbojet.com.hk; internet www.turbojet.com.hk; f. 1999; operates hydrofoil services between Hong Kong, Macao and Shenzhen.

The Star Ferry Co Ltd: Star Ferry Pier, Kowloon Point, Tsimshatsui, Kowloon; tel. 21186223; fax 21186028; e-mail sf@starferry.com.hk; internet www.starferry.com.hk; f. 1898; operates 8 passenger ferries between Tsimshatsui and Central, the main business district of Hong Kong; between Central and Hung Hom; between Tsimshatsui and Wanchai; and between Wanchai and Hung Hom; also a licensed harbour tour ferry service at Victoria Harbour; Gen. Man. JOHNNY LEUNG.

SHIPPING

Hong Kong is one of the world's largest shipping centres and among the busiest container ports. Hong Kong was a British port of registry until the inauguration of a new and independent shipping register in December 1990. Following Hong Kong's reunification with the People's Republic of China, Hong Kong maintains full autonomy in its maritime policy. At the end of 2006 the register comprised a fleet of 1,179 vessels, totalling 32.7m. grt. The container terminals at Kwai Chung are privately owned and operated. The construction of a ninth terminal (CT9) at Kwai Chung was completed in 2004, bringing the total number of berths to 24. Lantau Island has been designated as the site for any future expansion.

Marine Department, Hong Kong Special Administrative Region Government: Harbour Bldg, 22/F, 38 Pier Rd, Central, GPOB 4155; tel. 25423711; fax 25449241; e-mail mdenquiry@mardep.gov.hk; internet www.mardep.gov.hk; Dir ROGER TUPPER.

Shipping Companies

Anglo-Eastern Ship Management Ltd: Universal Trade Centre, 14/F, 3 Arbuthnot Rd, Central, POB 11400; tel. 28636111; fax 28612419; e-mail dbarlow@angloeasterngroup.com; internet www.aesm.com.hk; f. 1974; merged with Denholm Ship Management in 2001; Chair. PETER CREMERS; Man. Dir MARCEL LIEDTS.

COSCO (Hong Kong) Shipping Co Ltd (CHS): 50–51/F, Cosco Tower, 183 Queen's Rd, Central; tel. 28098688; fax 25461041; internet www.coscochs.com.hk; established by merger of former Ocean Tramping Co Ltd and Yick Fung Shipping and Enterprise Co; Chair. of Bd LIU GUOYUAN; Man. Dir LI ZHENYU.

Fairmont Shipping (HK) Ltd: Fairmont House, 21/F, 8 Cotton Tree Drive; tel. 25218338; fax 28104560; e-mail fsahkginfo@fairmontshipping.com; Pres. ROBERT HO.

Hong Kong Ming Wah Shipping Co: Unit 3701, China Merchants Tower, 37/F, Shun Tak Centre, 168–200 Connaught Rd, Central; tel. 25172128; fax 25473482; e-mail mwex@hkmw.com.hk; internet www.hkmw.com.hk; f. 1980.

Island Navigation Corpn International Ltd: Harbour Centre, 28–29/F, 25 Harbour Rd, Wanchai; tel. 28333222; fax 28270001; Man. Dir F. S. SHIH.

Jardine Shipping Services: 18/F, Tower Two, Ever Gain Plaza, 88 Container Port Rd, Kwai Chung; tel. 25793388; fax 28569927; e-mail terence.sit@jsa.com.hk; internet www.jardine-shipping.com; Pres. TERENCE SIT.

Oak Maritime (HK) Inc Ltd: 2301 China Resources Bldg, 26 Harbour Rd, Wanchai; tel. 25063866; fax 25063563; Chair. STEVE G. K. HSU; Pres. FRED C. P. TSAI.

Orient Overseas Container Line Ltd: Harbour Centre, 31/F, 25 Harbour Rd, Wanchai; tel. 28333888; fax 25318122; e-mail hkgcsd@oocl.com; internet www.oocl.com; member of the Grand Alliance of shipping cos (five partners); Chair. C. C. TUNG; CEO PHILIP CHOW.

CHINESE SPECIAL ADMINISTRATIVE REGIONS

Teh-Hu Cargocean Management Co Ltd: Unit B, Fortis Bank Tower, 15/F, 77–79 Gloucester Rd, Wanchai; tel. 25988688; fax 28249339; e-mail tehhuhk@on-nets.com; f. 1974; Man. Dir Kenneth K. W. Lo.

Wah Kwong Shipping Agency Co Ltd: Shanghai Industrial Investment Bldg, 26/F, 48–62 Hennessy Rd, POB 283; tel. 25279227; fax 28656544; e-mail wk@wahkwong.com.hk; internet www.wahkwong.com.hk; Chair. George S. K. Chao.

Wallem Shipmanagement Ltd: Hopewell Centre, 46/F, 183 Queen's Rd East; tel. 28768200; fax 28761234; e-mail wsmhk@wallem.com; internet www.wallem.com; Man. Dir Jim Nelson.

Associations

Hong Kong Cargo-Vessel Traders' Association: 21–23 Man Wai Bldg, 2/F, Ferry Point, Kowloon; tel. 23847102; fax 27820342; e-mail info@cvta.com.hk; internet www.cvta.com.hk; 978 mems; Chair. Chow Yat-tak; Sec. Chan Bak.

Hong Kong Shipowners' Association: Queen's Centre, 12/F, 58–64 Queen's Rd East, Wanchai; tel. 25200206; fax 25298246; e-mail hksoa@hksoa.org.hk; internet www.hksoa.org.hk; f. 1957; 160 mems; Chair. Peter Cremers; Man. Dir Arthur Bowring.

Hong Kong Shippers' Council: Rm 2407, Hopewell Centre, 183 Queen's Rd East; tel. 28340010; fax 28919787; e-mail shippers@hkshippers.org.hk; internet www.hkshippers.org.hk; 63 mems; Chair. Willy Lin; Exec. Dir Sunny Ho.

CIVIL AVIATION

At the end of 2007 Hong Kong was served by more than 85 airlines. A new international airport, on the island of Chek Lap Kok, near Lantau Island, opened in July 1998. The airport has two runways; the second runway commenced operations in May 1999. In 2007 Hong Kong International Airport handled 47.8m. passengers (an increase of 7.5% in comparison with 2006) and 3.74m. metric tons of cargo (4.5% more than in 2006). A helicopter link with Macao was established in 1990.

Airport Authority of Hong Kong: Cheong Yip Rd, Hong Kong International Airport, Lantau; tel. 21887111; fax 28240717; internet www.hongkongairport.com; scheduled for privatization; f. 1995; Chair. Dr Victor Fung Kwok-king; CEO Stanley H. C. Hui.

Civil Aviation Department: Queensway Government Offices, 46/F, 66 Queensway; tel. 28674203; fax 28690093; e-mail enquiry@cad.gov.hk; internet www.cad.gov.hk; Dir-Gen. Norman Lo Shung-man.

AHK Air Hong Kong Ltd: 4/F, South Tower, Cathay Pacific City, 8 Scenic Rd, Hong Kong International Airport; tel. 27618588; fax 27618586; e-mail ahk.hq@airhongkong.com.hk; internet www.airhongkong.com.hk; f. 1986; regional cargo carrier; COO Richard Cater.

Cathay Pacific Airways Ltd: South Tower, 5/F, Cathay Pacific City, 8 Scenic Rd, Hong Kong International Airport, Lantau; tel. 27475000; fax 28106563; internet www.cathaypacific.com; f. 1946; services to more than 40 major cities in the Far East, Middle East, North America, Europe, South Africa, Australia and New Zealand; Chair. Christopher D. Pratt; CEO Tony Tyler.

Heli Express Ltd: Hong Kong; e-mail info@heliexpress.com; internet www.helihongkong.com; f. 1990; fmrly East Asia Airlines; merged with Helicopters Hong Kong Ltd in 1998; renamed as Heli Express Ltd in 2005; operates helicopter services between Hong Kong, Macao and Shenzhen (China); Chair. Stanley Ho.

Hong Kong Dragon Airlines Ltd (Dragonair): Dragonair House, 11 Tung Fai Rd, Hong Kong International Airport, Lantau; tel. 31933193; fax 31933194; internet www.dragonair.com; f. 1985; scheduled and charter flights to destinations throughout mainland China and to Bangladesh, Thailand, Cambodia, Brunei, Malaysia, Taiwan and Japan; wholly owned subsidiary of Cathay Pacific Airways Ltd; Dir and CEO Kenny Tang.

Hong Kong Express Airways Ltd: 7/F, One Citygate, 20 Tat Tung Rd, Tung Chung, Lantau; tel. 31511800; internet www.hongkongexpress.com; f. 2004; flights to mainland China and Thailand; Pres. Ronnie Choi.

Tourism

Tourism is a major source of foreign exchange, tourist receipts reaching US $13,546m. in 2005. Almost 28.2m. people visited Hong Kong in 2007, compared with 25.3m. in the previous year. In 2007 there were 650 hotels, hostels and guesthouses, and the number of rooms available totalled 56,573. The first phase of a new Disneyland theme park opened in September 2005.

Hong Kong Tourism Board: Citicorp Centre, 9–11/F, 18 Whitfield Rd, North Point; tel. 28076543; fax 28076595; e-mail info@discoverhongkong.com; internet www.DiscoverHongKong.com; f. 1957; reconstituted as Hong Kong Tourism Board 1 April 2001; co-ordinates and promotes the tourist industry; has govt support and financial assistance; up to 20 mems of the Board represent the Govt, the private sector and the tourism industry; Chair. James Tien; Exec. Dir Clara Chong.

MACAO

Introductory Survey

Location, Climate, Language, Religion, Flag, Capital

The Special Administrative Region (SAR) of Macao comprises the peninsula of Macao, an enclave on the mainland of southern China, and two nearby islands, Taipa, which is linked to the mainland by three bridges, and Coloane. The latter island is connected to Taipa by a causeway and by an area of reclaimed land. The territory lies opposite Hong Kong on the western side of the mouth of the Xijiang (Sikiang) River. The climate is subtropical, with temperatures averaging 15°C in January and 29°C in July. There are two official languages, Chinese (Cantonese being the principal dialect) and Portuguese. English is also widely spoken. The predominant religions are Roman Catholicism, Chinese Buddhism, Daoism and Confucianism. The flag of the Macao SAR (proportions 2 by 3), introduced upon the territory's reversion to Chinese sovereignty in December 1999 and flown subordinate to the flag of the People's Republic of China, displays a stylized white flower below an arc of one large and four small yellow stars, above five white lines, on a green background. The executive and legislative bodies of Macao are based in the city of Macao, which is situated on the peninsula.

Recent History

Established by Portugal in 1557 as a permanent trading post with China, Macao became a Portuguese Overseas Province in 1951. After the military coup in Portugal in April 1974, Col José Garcia Leandro was appointed Governor of the province. A new statute, promulgated in February 1976, redefined Macao as a 'Special Territory' under Portuguese jurisdiction, but with a great measure of administrative and economic independence. Proposals to enlarge the Legislative Assembly from 17 to 21 members, thus giving the Chinese population an increased role in the administration of Macao, were abandoned when they did not receive the approval of the Government of the People's Republic of China in March 1980. China and Portugal established diplomatic relations in February 1979. In the same month Col Leandro was replaced as Governor by Gen. Nuno de Melo Egídio, deputy chief of staff of Portugal's armed forces. In June 1981 Gen. Egídio was, in turn, replaced by Cdre (later Rear-Adm.) Vasco Almeida e Costa, a Portuguese former minister and naval commander. Following a constitutional dispute in March 1984 over the Governor's plans for electoral reform (extending the franchise to the ethnic Chinese majority), the Legislative Assembly was dissolved. Elections for a new Assembly were held in August, at which the Chinese majority were allowed to vote for the first time, regardless of their length of residence in the territory. Following the elections, the Assembly was for the first time dominated by ethnic Chinese deputies.

In January 1986 Governor Almeida e Costa resigned. In May he was replaced by Joaquim Pinto Machado, whose appointment represented a break in the tradition of military governors for Macao. His political inexperience, however, placed him at a disadvantage. In May 1987 he resigned, citing 'reasons of institutional dignity' (apparently referring to the problem of corruption in the Macao administration). He was replaced in August by Carlos Melancia, a former Socialist deputy in the Portuguese legislature, who had held ministerial posts in several Portuguese governments.

The first round of negotiations between the Portuguese and Chinese Governments on the future of Macao took place in June 1986 in Beijing. Portugal's acceptance of China's sovereignty greatly simplified the issue. On 13 April 1987, following the conclusion of the fourth round of negotiations, a joint declaration was formally signed in Beijing by the Portuguese and Chinese Governments, during an official visit to China by the Prime Minister of Portugal. According to the agreement (which was formally ratified in January 1988), Macao was to become a 'special administrative region' (SAR) of the People's Republic (to be known as Macao, China) on 20 December 1999. Macao was thus to have the same status as that agreed (with effect from 1997) for Hong Kong, and was to enjoy autonomy in most matters except defence and foreign policy. A Sino-Portuguese Joint Liaison Group (JLG), established to oversee the transfer of power, held its inaugural meeting in Lisbon in April 1988. In 1999 a Chief Executive for Macao was to be appointed by the Chinese Government, following 'elections or consultations to be held in Macao', and the territory's legislature was to contain 'a majority of elected members'. The inhabitants of Macao were to become citizens of the People's Republic of China. The Chinese Government refused to allow the possibility of dual Sino-Portuguese citizenship, although Macao residents in possession of Portuguese passports were apparently to be permitted to retain them for travel purposes. The agreement guaranteed a 50-year period during which Macao would be permitted to retain its free capitalist economy, and to be financially independent of China.

In August 1988 a Macao Basic Law Drafting Committee was formed. Comprising 30 Chinese members and 19 representatives from Macao, the Committee was to draft a law determining the territory's future constitutional status within the People's Republic of China. Elections to the Legislative Assembly were held in October 1988. Low participation (fewer than 30% of the electorate) was recorded, and a 'liberal' grouping secured three of the seats reserved for directly elected candidates, while a coalition of pro-Beijing and conservative Macanese (lusophone Eurasian) groups, won the other three.

In January 1989 it was announced that Portuguese passports were to be issued to about 100,000 ethnic Chinese inhabitants, born in Macao before October 1981, and it was anticipated that as many as a further 100,000 would be granted before 1999. Unlike their counterparts in the neighbouring British dependent territory of Hong Kong, therefore, these Macao residents (but not all) were to be granted the full rights of a citizen of the European Community (EC, now European Union—EU, see p. 244). In February 1989 President Mário Soares of Portugal visited Macao, in order to discuss the transfer of the territory's administration to China.

Following the violent suppression of the pro-democracy movement in China in June 1989, as many as 100,000 residents of Macao participated in demonstrations in the enclave to protest against the Chinese Government's action. The events in the People's Republic caused great concern in Macao. In August, however, China assured Portugal that it would honour the agreement to maintain the capitalist system of the territory after 1999.

In March 1990 the implementation of a programme to grant permanent registration to parents of 4,200 Chinese residents, the latter having already secured the right of abode in Macao, developed into chaos when other illegal immigrants demanded a similar concession. The authorities decided to declare a general amnesty, but were unprepared for the numbers of illegal residents, some 50,000 in total, who rushed to take advantage of the scheme, thereby revealing the true extent of previous immigration from China. Border security was subsequently increased, in an effort to prevent any further illegal immigration.

In late March 1990 the Legislative Assembly approved the final draft of the territory's revised Organic Law. The Law was approved by the Portuguese Assembly of the Republic in mid-April, and granted Macao greater administrative, economic, financial and legislative autonomy, in advance of 1999. The powers of the Governor and of the Legislative Assembly, where six additional seats were to be created, were therefore increased. The post of military commander of the security forces was abolished, responsibility for the territory's security being assumed by a civilian Under-Secretary.

Meanwhile, in February 1990, it was alleged that Carlos Melancia had accepted a substantial bribe from a foreign company in connection with a contract for the construction of the new airport in Macao. In September Melancia was served with a summons relating to the alleged bribery. Although he denied any involvement in the affair, the Governor resigned, and was replaced on an acting basis by the Under-Secretary for Economic Affairs, Dr Francisco Murteira Nabo. In September 1991 it was announced that Melancia and five others were to stand trial on charges of corruption. Melancia's trial opened in April 1993. In August the former Governor was acquitted on the grounds of insufficient evidence. In February 1994, however, it was announced that Melancia was to be retried, owing to irregularities in his defence case.

Meanwhile, many observers believed that the enclave was being adversely affected by the political situation in Lisbon, as differences between the socialist President and centre-right Prime Minister were being reflected in rivalries between officials in Macao. In an attempt to restore confidence, therefore, President Soares visited the territory in November 1990. In January 1991, upon his re-election as Head of State, the President appointed Gen. Vasco Rocha Vieira (who had previously served as the territory's Chief of Staff and as Under-Secretary for Public Works and Transport) Governor of Macao. In March 1991 the Legislative Assembly was expanded from 17 to 23 members. All seven Under-Secretaries were replaced in May.

Following his arrival in Macao, Gen. Rocha Vieira announced that China would be consulted on all future developments in the territory. The 10th meeting of the Sino-Portuguese JLG took place in Beijing in April 1991. Topics under regular discussion included the participation of Macao in international organizations, progress towards an increase in the number of local officials employed in the civil service (hitherto dominated by Portuguese and Macanese personnel) and the status of the Chinese language. The progress of the working group on the translation of local laws from Portuguese into Chinese was also examined, a particular problem being the lack of suitably qualified bilingual legal personnel. It was agreed that Portuguese was to remain an official language after 1999. The two sides also reached agreement on the exchange of identity cards for those Macao residents who would require them in 1999. Regular meetings of the JLG continued.

In July 1991 the Macao Draft Basic Law was published by the People's Republic of China. Confidence in the territory's future was enhanced by China's apparent flexibility on a number of issues. Unlike the Hong Kong Basic Law, that of Macao did not impose restrictions on holders of foreign passports assuming senior posts in the territory's administration after 1999, the only exception being the future Chief Executive. Furthermore, the draft contained no provision for the stationing of troops from China in Macao after the territory's return to Chinese administration.

In November 1991 the Governor of Macao visited the People's Republic of China, where it was confirmed that the 'one country, two systems' policy would operate in Macao from 1999. In March 1993 the final draft of the Basic Law of the Macao SAR was ratified by the National People's Congress (NPC) in Beijing, which also approved the design of the future SAR's flag. The adoption of the legislation was welcomed by the Governor of Macao, who reiterated his desire for a smooth transfer of power in 1999. The Chief Executive of the SAR was to be selected by local representatives. The SAR's first Legislative Council was to comprise 23 members, of whom eight would be directly elected. Its term of office would expire in October 2001, when it would be expanded to 27 members, of whom 10 would be directly elected.

Meanwhile, elections to the Legislative Assembly were held in September 1992. The level of participation was higher than on previous occasions, with 59% of the registered electorate (albeit only 13.5% of the population) attending the polls. Fifty candidates contested the eight directly elective seats, four of which were won by members of the main pro-Beijing parties, the União Promotora para o Progresso (UPP) and the União para o Desenvolvimento (UPD).

Relations between Portugal and China remained cordial. In June 1993 the two countries reached agreement on all outstanding issues regarding the construction of the territory's airport and the future use of Chinese air space. Furthermore, Macao was to be permitted to negotiate air traffic agreements with other countries. Later in the year visits by President Soares of Portugal to Macao and by the Chinese President, Jiang Zemin, to Lisbon took place. In February 1994 the Chinese Minister of Communications visited Macao to discuss with the Governor the progress of the airport project.

In April 1994, during a visit to China, the Portuguese Prime Minister received an assurance that Chinese nationality would not be imposed on Macanese people of Portuguese descent, who would be able to retain their Portuguese passports. Speaking in Macao itself, the Prime Minister expressed confidence in the territory's future. In July a group of local journalists dispatched a letter, alleging intimidation and persecution in Macao, to President Soares, urging him to intervene to defend the territory's press freedom. The journalists' appeal followed an incident involving the director of the daily *Gazeta Macaense*, who had been fined for reproducing an article from a Lisbon weekly newspaper, and now faced trial. The territory's press had been critical of the Macao Supreme Court's decision to extradite ethnic Chinese to the mainland (despite the absence of any extradition treaty) to face criminal charges and a possible death sentence.

The draft of the new penal code for Macao did not incorporate the death penalty. In January 1995, during a visit to Portugal, Vice-Premier Zhu Rongji of China confirmed that the People's Republic would not impose the death penalty in Macao after 1999, regarding the question as a matter for the authorities of the future SAR. The new penal code, prohibiting capital punishment, took effect in January 1996.

On another visit to the territory in April 1995, President Soares emphasized the need for Macao to assert its identity, and stressed the importance of three issues: the modification of the territory's legislation; the rights of the individual; and the preservation of the Portuguese language. Travelling on to Beijing, accompanied by Gen. Rocha Vieira, the Portuguese President had successful discussions with his Chinese counterpart on various matters relating to the transition.

In May 1995, during a four-day visit to the territory, Lu Ping, the director of the mainland Hong Kong and Macao Affairs Office, proposed the swift establishment of a preparatory working committee (PWC) to facilitate the transfer of sovereignty. He urged that faster progress be made on the issues of the localization of civil servants and of the law, and on the use of Chinese as the official language. Lu Ping also expressed his desire that the reorganized legislative and municipal bodies to be elected in 1996–97 conform with the Basic Law.

In December 1995, while attending the celebrations to mark the inauguration of the territory's new airport, President Soares had discussions with the Chinese Vice-President, Rong Yiren. During a four-day visit to Beijing in February 1996, the Portuguese Minister of Foreign Affairs, Jaime Gama (who urged that the rights and aspirations of the people of Macao be protected), met President Jiang Zemin and other senior officials, describing the discussions as positive. While acknowledging the sound progress of recent years, Gama and the Chinese Minister of Foreign Affairs agreed on an acceleration in the pace of work of the Sino-Portuguese JLG. In the same month Gen. Rocha Vieira was reappointed Governor of Macao by the newly elected President of Portugal, Jorge Sampaio. António Guterres, the new Portuguese Prime Minister, confirmed his desire for constitutional consensus regarding the transition of Macao.

At elections to the Legislative Assembly in September 1996 the pro-Beijing UPP received 15.2% of the votes and won two of the eight directly elective seats, while the UPD won 14.5% and retained one of its two seats. The business-orientated groups were more successful: the Associação Promotora para a Economia de Macau took 16.6% of the votes and secured two seats; the Convergência para o Desenvolvimento de Macau (CODEM) and the União Geral para o Desenvolvimento de Macau each won one seat. The pro-democracy Associação de Novo Macau Democrático (ANMD) also won one seat. The level of voter participation was 64%. The 23-member legislature was to remain in place beyond the transfer of sovereignty in 1999.

From 1996 there were numerous bomb attacks and brutal assaults, including several serious attacks on local casino staff. Many attributed the alarming increase in organized crime to the opening of the airport in Macao, which was believed to have facilitated the entry of rival gangsters from mainland China, Taiwan and Hong Kong. In May 1997, following the murder of three men believed to have associations with one such group of gangsters, the Chinese Government expressed its concern at the deterioration of public order in Macao and urged Portugal to observe its responsibility, as undertaken in the Sino-Portuguese joint declaration of 1987, to maintain the enclave's social stability during the transitional period, whilst pledging the enhanced co-operation of the Chinese security forces in the effort to curb organized crime in Macao.

The freedom of Macao's press was jeopardized in June 1997, when several Chinese-language newspapers, along with a television station, received threats instructing them to cease reporting on the activities of the notorious 14K triad, a 10,000-member secret society to which much of the violence had been attributed. In July an explosive device was detonated in the grounds of the Governor's palace, although it caused no serious damage. In the following month China deployed 500 armed police officers to reinforce the border with Macao in order to intensify its efforts to combat illegal immigration, contraband and the smuggling of arms into the enclave. Despite the approval in July of a law further to restrict activities such as extortion and 'protection rackets', organized crime continued unabated. In early October the police forces of Macao and China initiated a joint campaign against illegal immigration.

Meanwhile, the slow progress of the 'three localizations' (civil service, laws and the implementation of Chinese as an official language) continued to concern the Government of China. In mid-1996 almost 50% of senior government posts were still held by Portuguese expatriates. In January 1997 the Governor pledged to accelerate the process with regard to local legislation, the priority being the training of the requisite personnel. In February President Sampaio travelled to both Macao and China, where he urged respect for Macao's identity and for the Luso-Chinese declaration regarding the transfer of sovereignty. In December 1997 details of the establishment in Macao of the office of the Chinese Ministry of Foreign Affairs, which was to commence operations in December 1999, were announced. In January 1998 the Macao Government declared that the vast majority of senior civil service posts were now held by local officials.

In March 1998 the Chinese authorities reiterated their concern at the deteriorating situation in Macao. In April, by which month none of the 34 triad-related murders committed since January 1997 had been solved, the Portuguese and Chinese Governments agreed to co-operate in the exchange of information about organized criminal activities. Also in April 1998 the trial, on charges of breaching the gaming laws, of the head of the 14K triad, Wan Kuok-koi ('Broken Tooth'), was adjourned for two months, owing to the apparent reluctance of witnesses to appear in court. In early May Wan Kuok-koi was rearrested and charged with the attempted murder of Macao's chief of police, António Marques Baptista, in a car-bomb attack. The case was dismissed by a judge three days later on the grounds of insufficient evidence. Wan Kuok-koi remained in prison, charged with other serious offences. His renewed detention led to a spate of arson attacks. The Portuguese Government was reported to have dispatched intelligence officers to the enclave to reinforce the local security forces. In June Marques Baptista travelled to Beijing and Guangzhou for discussions on the problems of cross-border criminal activity and drugs-trafficking.

The Preparatory Committee for the Establishment of the Macao SAR, which was to oversee the territory's transfer to Chinese sovereignty and was to comprise representatives from both the People's Republic and Macao, was inaugurated in Beijing in May 1998. Four subordinate working groups (supervising administrative, legal, economic, and social and cultural affairs) were subsequently established. The second plenary session of the Preparatory Committee was convened in July 1998, discussions encompassing issues such as the 'localization' of civil servants, public security and the drafting of the territory's fiscal budget for 2000. In July 1998, during a meeting with the Chinese Premier, the Governor of Macao requested an increase in the mainland's investment in the territory prior to the 1999 transfer of sovereignty.

In July 1998, as abductions continued and as it was revealed, furthermore, that the victims had included two serving members of the Legislative Assembly, President Jiang Zemin of China urged the triads of Macao to cease their campaign of intimidation. The police forces of Macao, Hong Kong and Guangdong Province launched 'S Plan', an operation aiming to curb the activities of rival criminal gangs. In August, in an apparent attempt to intimidate the judiciary, the territory's Attorney-General and his wife were shot and slightly wounded. In the following month five police officers and 10 journalists who were investigating a bomb attack were injured when a second bomb exploded.

In August 1998 representatives of the JLG agreed to intensify Luso-Chinese consultations on matters relating to the transitional period. In September, in response to the increasing security problems, China unexpectedly announced that, upon the transfer of sovereignty, it was to station troops in the territory. This abandonment of a previous assurance to the contrary caused much disquiet in Portugal, where the proposed deployment was deemed unnecessary. Although the Basic Law made no specific provision for the stationing of a mainland garrison, China asserted that it was to be ultimately responsible for the enclave's defence. By October, furthermore, about 4,000 soldiers of the People's Liberation Army (PLA) were on duty at various Chinese border posts adjacent to Macao. During a one-week visit to Beijing, the territory's Under-Secretary for Public Security had discussions with senior officials, including the Chinese Minister of Public Security. In mid-October four alleged members of the 14K triad were detained without bail in connection with the May car-bombing and other incidents.

In November 1998 procedures for the election of the 200 members of the Selection Committee were established by the Preparatory Committee. Responsible for the appointment of the members of Macao's post-1999 Government, the delegates of the Selection Committee were required to be permanent residents of the territory: 60 members were to be drawn from the business and financial communities, 50 from cultural, educational and professional spheres, 50 from labour, social service and religious circles and the remaining 40 were to be former political personages.

In November 1998 raids on casinos believed to be engaged in illegal activities, conducted by the authorities, resulted in several arrests. Further violence took place in December. At the end of that month it was confirmed that Macao residents of wholly Chinese origin would be entitled to full mainland citizenship, while those of mixed Chinese and Portuguese descent would be obliged to decide between the two nationalities. In January 1999 several protesters were arrested during demonstrations to draw attention to the plight of numerous immigrant children, who had been brought illegally from China to Macao to join their legitimately resident parents. The problem had first emerged in 1996 when, owing to inadequate conditions, the authorities had closed down an unofficial school attended by 200 children, who because of their irregular status were not entitled to the territory's education, health and social services.

In January 1999 details of the composition of the future PLA garrison were disclosed. The troops were to comprise solely ground forces, totalling fewer than 1,000 soldiers and directly responsible to the Commander of the Guangzhou Military Unit. They would be permitted to intervene to maintain social order in the enclave only if the local police were unable to control major triad-related violence or if street demonstrations posed a threat of serious unrest. In March, during a trip to Macao (where he had discussions with the visiting Portuguese President), Qian Qichen, a Chinese Vice-Premier, indicated that an advance contingent of PLA soldiers would be deployed in Macao prior to the transfer of sovereignty. Other sources of contention between China and Portugal remained the unresolved question of the post-1999 status of those Macao residents who had been granted Portuguese nationality and also the issue of the court of final appeal.

In April 1999, at the first plenary meeting of the Selection Committee, candidates for the post of the SAR's Chief Executive were elected. Edmund Ho received 125 of the 200 votes, while Stanley

Au garnered 65 votes. Three other candidates failed to secure the requisite minimum of 20 votes. Edmund Ho and Stanley Au, both bankers and regarded as moderate pro-business candidates, thus proceeded to the second round of voting by secret ballot, held in May. Edmund Ho received 163 of the 199 votes cast, and confirmed his intention to address the problems of law and order, security and the economy. The Chief Executive-designate also fully endorsed China's decision to deploy troops in Macao.

During 1999, in co-operation with the Macao authorities, the police forces of Guangdong Province, and of Zhuhai in particular, initiated a new offensive against the criminal activities of the triads, which had been in regular evidence with further murders throughout the year. China's desire to deploy an advance contingent of troops prior to December 1999, however, reportedly continued to be obstructed by Portugal. Furthermore, the announcement that, subject to certain conditions, the future garrison was to be granted law-enforcement powers raised various constitutional issues. Many Macao residents, however, appeared to welcome the mainland's decision to station troops in the enclave. In a further effort to address the deteriorating security situation, from December 1999 Macao's 5,800-member police force was to be restructured.

In July 1999 the penultimate meeting of the JLG took place in Lisbon. In August, in accordance with the nominations of the Chief Executive-designate, the composition of the Government of the future SAR was announced by the State Council in Beijing. Appointments included that of Florinda da Rosa Silva Chan as Secretary for Administration and Justice. Also in August an outspoken pro-Chinese member of the Legislative Assembly was attacked and injured by a group of unidentified assailants in an apparently random assault. In September the Governor urged improved co-operation with the authorities of Guangdong Province in order to combat organized crime, revealing that the majority of the inmates of Macao's prisons were not residents of the territory. In the same month it was reported that 90 former Gurkhas of the British army were being drafted in as prison warders, following the intimidation of local officers. Also in September the Chief Executive-designate announced the appointment of seven new members of the Legislative Council, which was to succeed the Legislative Assembly in December. While the seven nominees of the Governor in the existing Legislative Assembly were thus to be replaced, 15 of the 16 elected members (one having resigned) were to remain in office as members of the successor Legislative Council. (In practice, however, the new Legislative Council continued to be known by its former name.) At the same time the composition of the 10-member Executive Council was also announced.

In October 1999 President Jiang Zemin paid a two-day visit to Portugal, following which it was declared that the outstanding question of the deployment of an advance contingent of Chinese troops in Macao had been resolved. The advance party was to be restricted to a technical mission, which entered the territory in early December. In November the 37th and last session of the JLG took place in Beijing, where in the same month the Governor of Macao held final discussions with President Jiang Zemin.

Meanwhile, in April 1999 Wan Kuok-koi had been acquitted of charges of coercing croupiers. In November his trial on other serious charges concluded: he was found guilty of criminal association and other illegal gambling-related activities and sentenced to 15 years' imprisonment. Eight co-defendants received lesser sentences. In a separate trial Artur Chiang Calderon, a former police officer alleged to be Wan Kuok-koi's military adviser, received a prison sentence of 10 years and six months for involvement in organized crime. While two other defendants were also imprisoned, 19 were released on the grounds of insufficient evidence. As the transfer of the territory's sovereignty approached, by mid-December almost 40 people had been murdered in triad-related violence since January 1999.

In late November 1999 representatives of the JLG reached agreement on details regarding the deployment of Chinese troops in Macao and on the retention of Portuguese as an official language. At midnight on 19 December 1999, therefore, in a ceremony attended by the Presidents and heads of government of Portugal and China, the sovereignty of Macao was duly transferred; 12 hours later (only after the departure from the newly inaugurated SAR of the Portuguese delegation), 500 soldiers of the 1,000-strong force of the PLA, in a convoy of armoured vehicles, crossed the border into Macao, where they were installed in a makeshift barracks. Prior to the ceremony, however, it was reported that the authorities of Guangdong Province had detained almost 3,000 persons, including 15 residents of Macao, suspected of association with criminal gangs. The celebrations in Macao were also marred by the authorities' handling of demonstrations by members of Falun Gong, a religious movement recently outlawed in China. The expulsion from Macao of several members of the sect in the days preceding the territory's transfer and the arrest of 30 adherents on the final day of Portuguese sovereignty prompted strong criticism from President Jorge Sampaio of Portugal. Nevertheless, in an effort to consolidate relations with the EU, in May 2000 the first official overseas visit of the SAR's Chief Executive was to Europe, his itinerary including Portugal. The EU agreed in principle in December to grant residents of Hong Kong and Macao visa-free access to member states, subject to final approval by the European Parliament.

In March 2000, in an important change to the immigration rules, it was announced that children of Chinese nationality whose parents were permanent residents of Macao would shortly be allowed to apply for residency permits. A monthly quota of 420 successful applicants was established, while the youngest children were to receive priority. In May hundreds of demonstrators participated in a march to protest against Macao's high level of unemployment. This shortage of jobs was attributed to the territory's use of immigrant workers, mainly from mainland China and South-East Asia, who were estimated to total 28,000. During the ensuing clashes several police officers and one demonstrator were reportedly injured. Trade unions continued to organize protests, and in July (for the first time since the unrest arising from the Chinese Cultural Revolution of 1966) tear gas and water cannon were used to disperse about 200 demonstrators who were demanding that the immigration of foreign workers be halted by the Government. In the same month it was announced that, in early 2001, an office of the Macao SAR was to be established in Beijing, in order to promote links between the two Governments. In Guangzhou in August 2000, as cross-border crime continued to increase, senior officials of Macao's criminal investigation unit met with their counterparts from China and Hong Kong for discussions on methods of improving co-operation. It was agreed that further meetings were henceforth to be held twice a year, alternately in Beijing and Macao.

Celebrations to mark the first anniversary of the reversion to Chinese sovereignty were attended by Jiang Zemin, who made a speech praising Macao's local administration, but warning strongly against those seeking to use either of the SARs as a base for subversion. A number of Falun Gong adherents from Hong Kong who had attempted to enter Macao for the celebrations were expelled. The same fate befell two Hong Kong human rights activists who had hoped to petition Jiang Zemin during his stay in Macao about the human rights situation in the People's Republic. A group of Falun Gong members in Macao, who held a protest the day before the Chinese President's arrival, were detained in custody and subsequently alleged that they had suffered police brutality.

In January 2001 China urged the USA to cease interfering in its internal affairs, following the signature by President Bill Clinton of the US Macao Policy Act, which related to the control of Macao's exports and the monitoring of its autonomy. The Governor of Guangdong Province, Lu Ruihua, made an official visit to Macao in February to improve links between the two regions. At the same time, the Legislative Council announced plans to strengthen ties with legislative bodies in the mainland, and the President of the Legislative Council, Susana Chou, visited Beijing, where she held discussions with Vice-Premier Qian Qichen. Also in February, a Macao resident was charged with publishing on-line articles about Falun Gong.

Edmund Ho visited Beijing in early March 2001 to attend the fourth session of the Ninth NPC, and held talks with President Jiang Zemin, who praised the former's achievements since the reversion of Macao to Chinese rule. On returning to Macao, Ho received the President of Estonia, Lennart Meri, who was touring the mainland and who thus became the first head of state to visit the SAR since its reversion to China. The two leaders discussed co-operation in the fields of tourism, trade, information technology and telecommunications, with Ho apparently seeking to learn from Estonia's experience in opening the telecommunications market. The EU announced in mid-March that SAR passport holders would, from May 2001, no longer require visas to enter EU countries. In the same month Jorge Neto Valente, a prominent lawyer and reputedly the wealthiest Portuguese person in Macao, was kidnapped by a gang, but freed in a dramatic police operation.

The Macao, Hong Kong and mainland police forces established a working group in mid-March 2001 to combat cross-border crime, with a special emphasis on narcotics, and in late March the Macao, Hong Kong and Guangdong police forces conducted a joint anti-drugs operation, 'Spring Thunder', resulting in the arrest of 1,243 suspected traffickers and producers, and the seizure of large quantities of heroin, ecstasy and marijuana. As part of the growing campaign against crime, a Shanghai court sentenced to death a Macao-based gangster, Zeng Jijun, on charges of running a debt-recovery group, members of which had committed murder. Three of Zeng's associates were given long prison sentences.

In May 2001 Macao and Portugal signed an agreement to strengthen co-operation in the fields of economy, culture, public security and justice during the visit of the Portuguese Minister of Foreign Affairs, Jaime Gama, the highest-ranking Portuguese official to visit Macao since its reversion to Chinese rule. In June Macao's Secretary for Security, Cheong Kuoc Va, visited Beijing and signed new accords aimed at reducing the trafficking of drugs, guns and people. In the same month Chief Executive Edmund Ho made his first official visit to the headquarters of the EU in Brussels, where he sought to promote contacts and exchanges between the SAR and the EU.

China's most senior representative in Macao, Wang Qiren, died of cancer at the beginning of July 2001. Later in the month, another major campaign against illegal activities related to the triads was conducted by the Macao, Hong Kong and Guangdong police forces, and formed part of ongoing attempts to eradicate organized crime. At the end of the month, the Secretary for Security reported that cases of violent crime had declined by 37.3% year-on-year in the first half of 2001, and murders, robberies, arson, drugs-trafficking and kidnapping had all decreased significantly over the same period. In a further sign of co-operation between Macao and the mainland against crime, the two sides signed an agreement on mutual judicial co-operation and assistance in late August, the first of its kind.

Elections to the Legislative Council were held on 23 September 2001, the first since Macao's reversion to Chinese rule. The number of seats was increased from 23 to 27: seven members were appointed by the Chief Executive, 10 elected directly and 10 indirectly. Of the 10 directly elective seats, two seats each were won by the business-orientated CODEM, the pro-Beijing factions UPP and UPD and the pro-democracy ANMD. Two other factions won one seat each. Of the 10 indirectly elective seats, four were won by the OMKC (a group representing business interests), and two seats each were one by the DCAR (a group representing welfare, cultural, educational, and sports interests), the Comissão Conjunta da Candidatura das Associações de Empregados—CCCAE—a group representing labour interests), and the OMCY (a group representing professionals).

In October 2001 China appointed Bai Zhijian as director of its liaison office in Macao, and later in the month Cui Shiping was selected as Macao's representative in the NPC, replacing the late Wang Qiren. At the same time, Edmund Ho attended the summit meeting of Asia-Pacific Economic Co-operation (APEC, see p. 176) in Shanghai, and the EU-Macao Joint Committee held a meeting in the SAR, aimed at improving trade, tourism and legal co-operation between the two entities. During late 2001, meanwhile, Macao increased co-operation with Hong Kong and the mainland in fighting crime and combating terrorism, amid reports that Russian mafias were becoming increasingly active in the SARs, and in mid-November the three police departments held an anti-drugs forum in Hong Kong. Later in the month, Edmund Ho announced that personal income tax would be waived and industrial and commercial taxes reduced for 2002, in order to alleviate the impact of the economic downturn. Ho also pledged to create 6,000 new jobs and invest more in infrastructure, and urged employers to avoid staff reductions.

In December 2001 the Government finally acted to end the 40-year monopoly on casinos and gambling held by Stanley Ho and his long-established company, the Sociedade de Turismo e Diversões de Macau (STDM). Under the new arrangements, some 21 companies, none of which was Chinese-owned, were to be permitted to bid for three new operating licences for casinos in the SAR. The intention was to improve the image of the gambling industry, ridding the territory of its reputation for vice and making it more business- and family-orientated. Meanwhile, Stanley Ho's daughter Pansy was playing an increasingly prominent role in managing the family businesses (which included the shipping, property and hotel conglomerate, Shun Tak Holdings); in December the group opened a new convention and entertainment centre.

Also in December 2001 Edmund Ho paid a visit to Beijing, where he and President Jiang Zemin discussed the situation in Macao. In early January 2002 Ho visited the mainland city of Chongqing, seeking to reinforce economic ties between the two places, and stating that Macao would play a more active role in developing the region. Also in January, the Government granted permission to the Taipei Trade and Cultural Office (TTCO) to issue visas for Taiwan-bound visitors from Macao and the mainland. In February Li Peng, Chairman of the Standing Committee of the NPC, paid an official visit to Macao, where he held discussions with the Chief Executive of the SAR. During Li's visit, a leading Macao political activist, along with several activists from the Hong Kong-based 'April Fifth Action Group', were arrested for planning to stage protests against Li for his role in the Tiananmen Square suppression of 1989 and in favour of the release of mainland political dissidents. The Hong Kong activists were immediately deported. At the same time the Hong Kong media reported that a Hong Kong-based cameraman had been beaten and had his camera destroyed by a Macao policeman when he attempted to film the interception of the activists. Other journalists also claimed to have been treated aggressively, their allegations being disputed by the Macao police.

In early March 2002 a new representative office of the Macao SAR was established in Beijing, with the aim of enhancing ties between the SAR and the central Government and mainland. Wu Beiming was named as its director. At its inaugural ceremony, Edmund Ho and Chinese Vice-Premier Qian Qichen praised the 'one country, two systems' model, and the director of the central government liaison office in Macao, Bai Zhijian, suggested that Macao might become a model for Taiwan's eventual reunification with the mainland.

On 1 April 2002 Stanley Ho's STDM formally relinquished its 40-year monopoly on casinos. However, Ho retained influence in the gambling sector after his Sociedade de Jogos de Macau (SJM) won an 18-year licence to operate casinos (see Economy, below). Also in early April, Edmund Ho attended the first annual conference of the Boao Forum for Asia (BFA—a non-profit NGO), held on Hainan Island, China, where he met Hong Kong Chief Executive Tung Chee-hwa and Chinese Premier Zhu Rongji, as well as business leaders from both places.

The US Government in early April 2002 issued its second annual 'United States-Macao Policy Act Report'. This stated that the SAR continued to develop in a positive direction, citing its support for the USA's anti-terrorism campaign, the opening of the economy, the reorganization of its customs services, efforts to counter organized crime and the preservation of its own identity, including maintaining basic civil and human rights. As a result, Macao would continue to be accorded a special status distinct from mainland China under US law and policy. In the middle of the month the United Kingdom announced that it was granting visa-free access to holders of Macao SAR passports, and in late May the visiting Portuguese Minister of Foreign Affairs, António Martins da Cruz, also expressed confidence in Macao's future. In early June Macao hosted the Euro-China Business meeting, aimed at promoting small- and medium-sized enterprises in China to European investors. Also at this time, the Taiwanese Government eased restrictions on residents of Hong Kong and Macao applying for landing visas, essentially allowing those persons to obtain such visas on their first visit to Taiwan. However, in late July a Macao official criticized Taiwanese President Chen Shui-bian and accused him of seeking independence from the mainland. In June the Procurator-General, Ho Chio Meng, visited Portugal to promote judicial co-operation between the two territories, the first such visit by a Macao delegation since the territory's return to Chinese rule.

In July 2002 Beijing appointed Wan Yongxiang as the special commissioner at the Office of the Special Commissioner of the Chinese Ministry of Foreign Affairs in the Macao SAR, succeeding Yuan Tao, who had held that post since 1999, when the office was established. At the end of July the Government announced the introduction of new identity cards, to be introduced from December 2002 over a period of four years. The cards were expected to function additionally as driving licences, border and medical access passes, and electronic payment methods.

The Russian Minister of Foreign Affairs, Igor Ivanov, visited Macao in late July 2002, mainly seeking to consolidate bilateral economic and trading relations, and to encourage Macao businesses to invest in Russia. In early August Edmund Ho visited the Chinese Autonomous Region of Nei Monggol (Inner Mongolia) to examine the possibility of developing links with the Sino-Russian border region, and later in the month he visited Guangzhou, in southern China, to discuss further economic co-operation and the joint development of Hengqin island (which is under the jurisdiction of Zhuhai City but located very close to Macao). In late September Ho visited Mozambique, where he and President Joaquim Alberto Chissano agreed to strengthen bilateral economic relations. At the same time, Secretary for Security Cheong Kuoc Va visited Portugal and signed security co-operation agreements aimed at combating transnational crime. In mid-October Edmund Ho visited the Republic of Korea (South Korea) and met President Kim Dae-Jung. While there, Ho sought to increase Korean investment and to promote tourism from South Korea. The two leaders also agreed to extend reciprocal visa-free visits from a maximum of 30 days to 90 days, effective from January 2003.

In early December 2002 Macao selected its 12 candidates for the 10th NPC, to be held in Beijing in March 2003. At the same time, Edmund Ho paid a routine visit to Beijing, where he held discussions with Jiang Zemin and Vice-President Hu Jintao. The Macao SAR and the EU signed a four-year legal co-operation programme in early December, aimed at consolidating Macao's legal system. In early January 2003 the Chairman of the National Committee of the Chinese People's Political Consultative Conference (CPPCC), Li Ruihuan, visited Macao and praised the way in which the territory had been administered. Observers noted that Beijing was more satisfied with the governance of the Macao SAR than with that of Hong Kong. In March deputies from Macao duly attended the first plenary session of the 10th NPC in Beijing. In the same month Edmund Ho held a meeting with the new Chinese Premier, Wen Jiabao, at which the future development of Macao under the policy of 'one country, two systems' was discussed.

In October 2003 Chinese Vice-President Zeng Qinghong visited Macao to attend the signing ceremony of the Closer Economic Partnership Arrangement (CEPA) between Macao and the Chinese mainland. Also in October, Chinese Vice-Premier Wu Yi attended a trade forum in Macao relating to China's trade relations with Portuguese-speaking countries.

In November 2003, Edmund Ho outlined plans for administrative reform of Macao's Government, alongside legal reform, to begin in 2004. In June 2004 it was announced that the re-election of the Chief Executive would take place in late August. Edmund Ho began his election campaign in mid-August, and was duly re-elected on 29 August, securing 296 of the 300 votes of the members of the Election Committee. In December 2004 Chinese President Hu Jintao visited Macao to mark the fifth anniversary of Macao's reunification with the People's Republic. During his visit Hu praised the successful implementation of 'one country, two systems' in Macao. In January 2005 President Sampaio of Portugal visited Macao, at the conclusion of an official visit to China.

In mid-2005 it was reported that the number of voters registered for the legislative election scheduled for September had reached 220,653, almost one-half of the population of the SAR and an increase of some 35% compared with the number registered for the elections of 2001. During the period prior to the election, the Macao Commission Against Corruption, established in 1999, announced that it had uncovered a series of schemes involving electoral malpractice. (Subsequently, in early October it was reported that 36 residents of the SAR were being charged with electoral fraud.) At the elections, held on 25 September, the number of seats allocated by direct suffrage was increased from 10 to 12, bringing the total number of seats in the Legislative Council to 29. The pro-democracy ANMD received the highest proportion of votes cast (18.8%) and secured two of the 12 directly elective seats. The Associação dos Cidadãos Unidos de Macau (ACUM), which reportedly drew a large degree of its support from immigrants from Fujian Province and their families, also obtained two seats, while the pro-Beijing UPD and UPP retained their representation of two seats each in the legislature. Angela Leong On Kei, wife of influential businessman and casino owner Stanley Ho, was elected on the list of the Aliança para o Desenvolvimento de Macau (AMD). The remaining three seats were divided among Nova Esperança (NE), supported by civil servants and the ethnic Portuguese community, the União Geral para o Bem-querer de Macau (UBM) and CODEM. The turn-out was evaluated at 58.4% of registered voters. The 10 indirectly elective seats, meanwhile, were distributed as in 2001: four were allocated to representatives of business interests (OMKC), and two each to representatives of labour interests (CCCAE), the interests of professionals (OMCY) and welfare, cultural, educational, and sports interests (União Excelente).

In September 2005 the US Administration asserted that the Government of the Democratic People's Republic of Korea (DPRK—North Korea) had been 'laundering' and counterfeiting money through a Macao bank, Banco Delta Asia (BDA). The Macao authorities took control of the bank pending an inquiry into its activities, and the assets held within these accounts, believed to total US $25m., were 'frozen'. A three-month investigation by Chinese officials reportedly concluded in January 2006 that the allegations were accurate. In February it was announced that BDA was terminating its links with the DPRK and that independent accountants had been appointed to monitor the bank's clients. In October an independent audit conducted by Ernst and Young, an international accounting company, reported that it had found no evidence to suggest that the bank had knowingly facilitated money-laundering activities. However, following the completion of an 18-month investigation, in March 2007 US Treasury officials concluded that the bank had deliberately disregarded illicit activities and ordered US banks and companies to terminate all links with BDA. The Monetary Authority of Macao expressed deep regret at this conclusion. Nevertheless, the North Korean assets in question were to be released and transferred to a mainland Chinese bank, thus apparently removing a major obstacle to progress at the forthcoming round of six-nation negotiations, to be held in Beijing, on the issue of the DPRK's nuclear programme. In the following week, however, an apparent delay in the bank transfer process resulted in the failure of these discussions. A Russian bank subsequently agreed to act as intermediary for the transfer of the funds, which was carried out in late June (see the chapter on the Democratic People's Republic of Korea). In September the Monetary Authority of Macao announced that control of BDA was being restored to its Chairman, Stanley Au, partly because the bank had shown an improvement in its practices. The US Treasury's measures, despite a legal challenge filed by the bank, remained in effect.

In December 2006 a corruption scandal emerged in Macao when the Chief Executive ordered the arrest of Ao Man Long, Secretary for Transport and Public Works, and that of 11 others. Ao, who had served as a government official for 20 years, was accused of bribery and involvement in irregular financial activities, including the transfer of millions of patacas from bank accounts in Hong Kong to the United Kingdom. Various members of his family were also said to be involved in the affair. Ao was alleged to have worked with his relatives to register a number of bogus companies abroad in order to 'launder' the bribes that he had reportedly received. Ao was subsequently charged on 76 corruption-related counts, including accepting bribes and money-laundering; he was alleged to have misappropriated some 800m. patacas. The trial at the Court of Final Appeal, to which about 100 witnesses were summoned, began in November 2007. In January 2008, having been found guilty of 57 of the charges against him, Ao was sentenced to 27 years' imprisonment. Four of Ao's family members were also charged with various money-laundering offences and went on trial in January.

At a May Day labour rally in 2007, demonstrators protesting against alleged corruption and the use of illegal workers in the SAR proceeded to demand the resignation of Edmund Ho as Chief Executive. In this unusual display of civil unrest, there were violent clashes between thousands of protesters and several hundred police officers, armed with batons and pepper spray. The police also fired blank shots into the air to disperse the demonstrators. However, one man was reportedly shot and injured during the clashes, although the police denied the use of live ammunition. A number of protesters were arrested by the authorities. Another demonstration took place in October. Amid increasing popular concern about the rapid pace of change and the perceived deterioration in the quality of life in Macao, in December hundreds attended a further protest against corruption, this time coinciding with the eighth anniversary of the establishment of the SAR. Meanwhile, in August 2007 it was alleged in the media that Edmund Ho owned shares in Many Town Company, a Hong Kong-based business with interests in STDM; the Government issued a denial, claiming that Ho's shares had been transferred to his brother in 1995.

Although the next elections for Macao's Legislative Council were not due to take place until 2009, it was reported in 2006 that bogus associations were already being established in an apparent attempt to influence the outcome of the future poll. The majority of these newly founded nominal organizations were sports groups, part of the category representing culture, education and sporting interests, which together with local charities would form the constituency responsible for choosing two of the Legislative Council's 10 indirectly elected members. (The three constituencies of labour, employer and professional interests were entitled to determine the remaining eight indirectly elective seats.) The legitimacy of the SAR's Election Committee, responsible for choosing Macao's next Chief Executive, was also believed to be in serious jeopardy, with 80 of its 300 members due to be selected by the constituency of culture, education and sport. A total of 207 bogus associations had reportedly been created between January and April 2006 alone, compared with 234 for the whole of 2005. Under electoral rules, such associations were required to have been established for at least three years in order to be eligible to vote, hence the proliferation of these organizations prior to the deadline in 2006.

Government

The Macao Special Administrative Region (SAR) is governed by a Chief Executive, who was first chosen by a 200-member Selection Committee in May 1999. The incumbent Chief Executive was re-elected in August 2004 by a Selection Committee of 300 members. The Chief Executive is accountable to the State Council of China, the term of office being five years, with a limit of two consecutive terms. Upon the territory's transfer to Chinese sovereignty in December 1999, a 10-member Executive Council, appointed by the Chief Executive to assist in policy-making, assumed office. The Chief Executive is assisted in administration by five Secretaries, who hold individual portfolios. In 2001 the Legislative Council (commonly referred to as the Legislative Assembly) was expanded from 23 to 27 members, of whom 10 were directly elected, 10 indirectly elected and seven appointed by the Chief Executive, all with a mandate of four years. In 2005 the membership of the Legislative Council was increased to 29, to incorporate two additional deputies to be chosen by direct election. For the purposes of local government, the islands of Taipa and Coloane are administered separately.

Defence

The 1998 budget allocated 1,200m. patacas to Macao's security. Upon the territory's transfer of sovereignty in December 1999, troops of the People's Liberation Army (PLA) were deployed in Macao. The force comprises around 1,000 troops: a maximum of 500 soldiers are stationed in Macao, the remainder being positioned in China, on the border with the SAR. The unit is directly responsible to the Commander of the Guangzhou Military Region and to the Central Military Commission. The Macao garrison is composed mainly of ground troops. Naval and air defence tasks are performed by the naval vessel unit of the PLA garrison in Hong Kong and by the airforce unit in Huizhou. Subject to certain conditions, the garrison was granted law-enforcement powers, to assist the maintenance of public security.

Economic Affairs

In 2001, according to estimates by the World Bank, Macao's gross national income (GNI), measured at average 1999–2001 prices, was US $6,336m., equivalent to $14,150 per head. In 2002 GNI was $21,880 per head on an international purchasing-power parity basis. During 1996–2006, it was estimated, the population increased at an average annual rate of 1.0%, when gross domestic product (GDP) per head increased, in real terms, at an average annual rate of 6.3%. According to the World Bank, overall GDP rose, in real terms, at an average annual rate of 11.8% in 1999–2006. GDP increased by by 17.0% in 2006 and was estimated to have expanded by 27.3% in 2007.

Agriculture is of minor importance. The main crops are rice and vegetables. Cattle, pigs and chickens are reared.

Industry (including mining, manufacturing, construction and public utilities) accounted for 14.2% of total GDP in 2005, according to provisional figures, and in 2006 employed 23.2% of the economically active population. The mining sector is negligible.

According to provisional figures, the manufacturing sector contributed 4.1% of total GDP in 2005, and it engaged 11.1% of the economically active population in 2006. The most important manufacturing industry is the production of textiles and garments. Exports of textiles and garments decreased from 15,334.5m. patacas in 2005 to 14,660.1m. patacas in 2006. Other industries include footwear and furniture.

Macao possesses few natural resources. Energy is derived principally from imported petroleum. Imports of fuels and lubricants accounted for 10.9% of total import costs in 2006. The territory receives some of its electricity and water supplies from mainland China.

The services sector accounted for 85.8% of GDP in 2005 and employed 76.8% of the economically active population in 2006. Tourism and related gambling activities make a substantial contribution to the territory's economy. In December 2001 STDM lost its long-standing monopoly of the gambling industry (see Recent History). The Government subsequently awarded casino-operating licences to various other companies, and by early 2008 the number of casinos in the SAR had reached 29. In March 2008, however, a moratorium on the issuing of new gaming licences and on the building of new casinos was announced. The gross revenue of the casino business rose from 57,521m. patacas in 2006 to a record 83,847m. patacas in 2007. In 2006 the Government's revenue from gambling taxes was estimated to total 20,747.6m. patacas, representing more than 75% of public revenue. Tourist arrivals increased steadily from the 1990s, with the number of visitors from the People's Republic of China rising particularly rapidly. In 2006 arrivals rose by 17.6% to reach nearly 22.0m., and in 2007 they increased by 22.8% to exceed 27.0m. The number of visitors from mainland China rose by 14.6% in 2006, increasing by a further 24.1% in 2007, when they represented 55.1% of total tourist arrivals. Visitors from Hong Kong accounted for 30.3% of total arrivals in 2007.

Legislation regulating offshore banking was introduced in 1987. It was hoped that the territory would develop as an international financial centre. The Financial System Act, which took effect in September 1993, aimed to improve the reputation of Macao's banks by curbing the unauthorized acceptance of deposits. A law enacted in April 1995 aimed to attract overseas investment by offering the right of abode in Macao to entrepreneurs with substantial funds (at least US $250,000) at their disposal. From December 1999, upon the territory's reversion to Chinese sovereignty, Macao administered its own finances and was exempt from taxes imposed by central government. The pataca was retained, remaining freely convertible.

In 2005 Macao recorded a preliminary visible trade deficit of US $2,792m., but there was a surplus of US $3,367m. on the current account of the balance of payments. The principal sources of imports in 2006 were the People's Republic of China (which supplied 45.1% of the total), followed by Hong Kong (10.1%) and Japan (8.3%). The principal market for exports was the USA (which purchased 44.1%), followed by the People's Republic of China (14.8%) and Hong Kong (11.2%). The main exports were textiles and garments (which accounted for 71.6% of the total in 2006), machinery and apparatus, and footwear. The principal imports were raw materials for industry, notably textiles, fuels, foodstuffs and other consumer goods. After December 1999 Macao retained its status as a free port and remained a separate customs territory.

In 2006 a provisional budgetary surplus of 9,838.7m. patacas was recorded. The average annual rate of inflation (including rents) between 1998 and 2006 was 0.5%. Consumer prices rose by almost 5.6% in 2007. The level of unemployment decreased from 3.8% of the labour force in 2006 to 3.1% in 2007. There is a shortage of skilled labour in Macao.

In 1991 Macao became a party to the General Agreement on Tariffs and Trade (GATT, subsequently superseded by the World Trade Organization—WTO, see p. 396) and an associate member of the UN Economic and Social Commission for Asia and the Pacific (ESCAP, see p. 35). In June 1992 Macao and the European Community (now the European Union) signed a five-year trade and economic co-operation agreement, granting mutual preferential treatment on tariffs and other commercial matters. The agreement was extended in December 1997. Macao remained a 'privileged partner' of the EU after December 1999. Macao also retained its membership of WTO after December 1999. The Multi-Fibre Arrangement (MFA), which for many years had governed Macao's exports of textiles and garments through a preferential system of quotas, ended in January 2005, when the integration of the relevant regulations into the WTO framework was completed.

Despite various attempts to diversify, gambling and tourism have increasingly dominated the economy of Macao. As the casino sector continued to expand, in January 2006 Fisherman's Wharf, a new amusement park, opened to the public. The Venetian Macao Resort, constructed at a cost of US $2,400m., opened in August 2007. The 980,000 sq m complex incorporates the world's largest hotel, with 3,000 suites. the mainland Chinese authorities envisaged closer integration of Macao within the Zhujiang (Pearl River) Delta region, particularly with regard to infrastructural development. The Macao SAR and the Zhuhai Special Economic Zone (SEZ) jointly developed a new industrial zone, which was officially inaugurated in December 2003. The projected Hong Kong–Zhuhai–Macao bridge was expected greatly to increase regional integration. In September 2006, however, officials admitted that the cost of the bridge was expected to reach 55,000m. yuan and that the project was unlikely to be completed before 2015. Since the 1990s various land-reclamation programmes, most notably the 470,000-sq m Nam Van Lakes project incorporating residential and business accommodation for 60,000 people, have substantially enlarged the territory's area. Such major infrastructural projects, along with the rapid expansion of the tourism industry, have resulted in the creation of thousands of new jobs. Foreign direct investment in Macao reached 51,940m. patacas in 2006, representing a 39.5% increase compared with the previous year. In terms of GDP per head in 2005, Macao was ranked third among 23 developing Asian countries in a survey conducted by the Asian Development Bank. By 2007, however, local residents were beginning to express fears for the quality of life in Macao, particularly with regard to issues such as rising property prices and increasing traffic congestion.

Education

The education system in Macao comprises: pre-school education (lasting two years); primary preparatory year (one year); primary education (six years); secondary education (five–six years, divided into junior secondary of three years and senior secondary of two–three years). Schooling normally lasts from the ages of three to 17. In 2005/06 schools enrolled a total of 89,154 pupils (including kindergarten 10,216; primary 35,187; secondary 43,751). From 1995/96 free education was extended from government schools to private schools. Private schools provide education for more than 90% of children. The majority of these schools have joined the free education system, and together with the government schools they form the public school system, in which all pupils from primary preparatory year up to the junior secondary level (10 years) receive free tuition. Based on the four years of free education, compulsory education was implemented from 1999/2000. In 2003/04 the enrolment rate at pre-primary level included 85% of pupils in the relevant age-group. In the same year enrolment at primary schools included 89% of pupils in the relevant age-group, while enrolment at secondary level included 76.8% of pupils. In higher learning, there are 12 public and private universities, polytechnic institutes and research centres. Some 15,927 students attended courses offered by those institutions in the academic year 2005/06, ranging from the bacharelato (three-year courses) to doctorate programmes. The University of Macao was inaugurated, as the University of East Asia, in 1981 (passing from private to government control in 1988), and had 5,589 students, with 336 academic staff, in 2003/04. The languages of instruction are primarily English, Cantonese and Portuguese. The 2003 budget allocated 1,886.6m. patacas to education and training (including administration costs and equal to 16.23% of total government expenditure).

Public Holidays

2008: 1 January (New Year), 7–9 February (Chinese Lunar New Year), 21–22 March (Easter), 4 April (Ching Ming), 1 May (Labour Day), 12 May (Feast of Buddha), 8 June (Dragon Boat Festival), 15 September (day following Chinese Mid-Autumn Festival), 1–2 October (National Day of the People's Republic of China and day following), 7 October (Festival of Ancestors—Chung Yeung), 2 November (All Souls' Day), 8 December (Immaculate Conception), 20 December (SAR Establishment Day), 22 December (Winter Solstice), 24–25 December (Christmas).

2009: 1 January (New Year), 26–28 January (Chinese Lunar New Year), 5 April (Ching Ming, provisional), 10–12 April (Easter), 1 May (Labour Day), 2 May (Feast of Buddha), 28 May (Dragon Boat Festival), 4 September (day following Chinese Mid-Autumn Festival), 1–2 October (National Day of the People's Republic of China and day following), 26 October (Festival of Ancestors—Chung Yeung), 2 November (All Souls' Day), 8 December (Immaculate Conception), 20 December (SAR Establishment Day), 22 December (Winter Solstice), 24–25 December (Christmas).

Weights and Measures

The metric system is in force.

CHINESE SPECIAL ADMINISTRATIVE REGIONS *Macao*

Statistical Survey

Source (unless otherwise indicated): Direcção dos Serviços de Estatística e Censos, Alameda Dr Carlos d'Assumpção 411–417, Dynasty Plaza, 17° andar, Macao; tel. 3995311; fax 28307825; e-mail info@dsec.gov.mo; internet www.dsec.gov.mo.

AREA AND POPULATION

Area (2006): 28.6 sq km (11.04 sq miles), comprising Macao peninsula 9.3, Taipa island 6.5, Coloane island 7.6, Co Tai 5.2.

Population: 435,235 (males 208,865, females 226,370) at census of 23 August 2001 (414,200 inhabitants were of Chinese nationality and 8,793 inhabitants were of Portuguese nationality); 502,113 (males 245,167, females 256,946) according to results of by-census of 19 August 2006 (491,482 were classed as usual residents and 10,631 as mobile residents).

Density (2006 census): 17,556 per sq km.

Population by Parish (resident population at 2006 census, '000, preliminary): Santo António 113; São Lázaro 31; São Lourenço 48; Sé 41; Nossa Senhora de Fátima 201; Taipa 63; Coloane 3; Maritime 2; Total 502.

Births, Marriages and Deaths (2006): Registered live births 4,058 (birth rate 8.1 per 1,000); Registered marriages 2,100 (marriage rate 4.2 per 1,000); Registered deaths 1,566 (death rate 3.1 per 1,000).

Expectation of Life (years at birth, 2002–05 average): 79.4 (males 77.6; females 82.3).

Economically Active Population (2006): Manufacturing 29,548; Production and distribution of electricity, gas and water 886; Construction 31,072; Wholesale and retail trade, repair of motor vehicles, motorcycles and personal and household goods 36,375; Hotels, restaurants and similar activities 30,003; Transport, storage and communications 16,751; Financial services 6,914; Real estate, renting and services to companies 16,267; Public administration, defence and compulsory social security 20,319; Education 11,333; Health and social work 5,422; Other community, social and personal service activities 52,532; Private households with employed persons 6,929; Others 703; *Total employed* 265,054; Unemployed 10,410; *Total labour force* 275,464.

HEALTH AND WELFARE
Key Indicators

Under-5 Mortality Rate (per 1,000 live births, 2006): 3.1.
HIV/AIDS (% persons aged 15–49, 2006): 0.000.
Physicians (per 1,000 head, 2006): 2.24.
Hospital Beds (per 1,000 head, 2006): 1.91.
Human Development Index (2004): value 0.909.

For definitions, see explanatory note on p. vi.

AGRICULTURE, ETC.

(separate data for 2005 and 2006 not available for livestock—see the chapter on the People's Republic of China)

Livestock ('000 head, 2004): Poultry 700 (FAO estimate).

Livestock Products ('000 metric tons, 2004): Beef and veal 1.1; Pig meat 9.6; Poultry meat 6.5 (FAO estimate); Hen eggs 1.0 (FAO estimate).

Fishing (metric tons, live weight, 2005, FAO estimates): Marine fishes 1,020; Shrimps and prawns 230; Other marine crustaceans 210; Total catch (incl. others) 1,500.

Source: FAO.

INDUSTRY

Production (2003, unless otherwise indicated): Wine 700,745 litres; Knitwear 36.18m. units; Footwear 12.13m. pairs; Clothing 230.73m. units; Furniture 5,253 units; Electric energy 1,668.4 million kWh (2006).

FINANCE

Currency and Exchange Rates: 100 avos = 1 pataca. *Sterling, Dollar and Euro Equivalents* (31 December 2007): £1 sterling = 16.096 patacas; US $1 = 8.034 patacas; €1 = 11.827 patacas; 100 patacas = £6.21 = $12.45 = €8.46. *Average Exchange Rate* (patacas per US dollar): 8.011 in 2005; 8.001 in 2006; 8.036 in 2007. Note: The pataca has a fixed link with the value of the Hong Kong dollar (HK $1 = 1.030 patacas).

Budget (million patacas, 2006, provisional): *Revenue:* Direct taxes 21,715.4; Indirect taxes 1,402.6; Other revenue 14,070.5; Total 37,188.5. *Expenditure:* Total 27,349.8.

International Reserves (US $ million at 31 December 2006): Total (all foreign exchange) 9,132.1.

Money Supply (million patacas at 31 December 2006): Currency outside banks 3,403.6; Demand deposits at commercial banks 14,851.5; Total money 18,255.2.

Cost of Living (Consumer Price Index; base: July 2004–June 2005 = 100): All items 98.77 in 2004; 103.11 in 2005; 108.42 in 2006.

Gross Domestic Product (million patacas at current prices): 82,966 in 2004; 92,951 in 2005; 114,364 in 2006.

Expenditure on the Gross Domestic Product (million patacas at current prices, 2006): Government final consumption expenditure 8,772.3; Private consumption expenditure 27,940.0; Changes in inventories 720.7; Gross fixed capital formation 38,366.3; *Total domestic expenditure* 75,799.4; Exports of goods and services 104,796.5; *Less* Imports of goods and services 66,231.6; *GDP in purchasers' values* 114,364.4.

Gross Domestic Product by Economic Activity (million patacas at current prices, 2005, provisional): Mining and quarrying 9.9; Manufacturing 3,129.1; Electricity, gas and water supply 1,340.1; Construction 6,300.9; Wholesale, retail, repair, restaurants and hotels 8,848.0; Transport, storage and communications 3,405.4; Financial intermediation, real estate, renting and business activities 16,475.9; Public administration, other community, social and personal services (incl. gaming services) 36,199.7; *Sub-total* 75,709.0; *Less* Financial intermediation services indirectly measured 2,549.2; *GDP at basic prices* 73,159.9; Taxes on products (net) 19,320.2; Statistical discrepancy 270.9; *GDP at market prices* 92,751.0.

Balance of Payments (US $ million, 2005): Exports of goods f.o.b. 2,478; Imports of goods f.o.b. –5,271; *Trade balance* –2,792; Exports of services 8,614; Imports of services –1,576; *Balance on goods and services* 4,246; Other income received 801; Other income paid –1,580; *Balance on goods, services and income* 3,466; Current transfers received 84; Current transfers paid –184; *Current balance* 3,367; Capital account (net) 515; Direct investment abroad –47; Direct investment from abroad 1,848; Portfolio investment assets –617; Financial derivatives assets –522; Other investment assets –4,396; Other investment liabilities 3,318; Net errors and omissions –2,230; *Overall balance* 1,234. Source: IMF, *International Financial Statistics*.

EXTERNAL TRADE

Principal Commodities (million patacas, 2006): *Imports c.i.f.* (distribution by SITC): Food and live animals 2,187.8; Beverages and tobacco 1,945.3 (Beverages 1,287.9); Mineral fuels, lubricants, etc. 4,005.6 (Petroleum, petroleum products, etc. 3,169.1); Chemicals and related products 1,723.5; Basic manufactures 8,925.1 (Textile yarn, fabrics, etc. 4,947.6); Machinery and transport equipment 8,947.6 (Electrical machinery, apparatus, etc. 1,339.5; Transport equipment and parts 1,798.1); Miscellaneous manufactured articles 8,454.8 (Clothing and accessories 3,518.5); Total (incl. others) 36,527.3. *Exports f.o.b.:* Textile yarn and thread 393.2; Textile fabrics 1,319.5; Machinery and mechanical appliances 1,400.5; Clothing 12,855.6; Footwear 399.0; Total (incl. others) 20,461.3 (incl. re-exports 6,088.4). *2007:* Total imports 43,113.9; Total exports 20,430.6.

Principal Trading Partners (million patacas, 2006): *Imports c.i.f.:* Australia 584.8; China, People's Republic 16,469.5; France 1,472.7; Germany 1,172.8; Hong Kong 3,722.6; Japan 3,049.2; Korea, Republic 716.1; Singapore 1,517.1; Taiwan 1,173.5; United Kingdom 684.4; USA 1,997.4; Total (incl. others) 36,527.3. *Exports f.o.b.:* Canada 142.4; China, People's Republic 3,035.4; France 677.9; Germany 1,497.1; Hong Kong 2,292.1; The Netherlands 258.7; United Kingdom 837.8; USA 9,021.3; Total (incl. others) 20,461.3 (incl. re-exports 6,088.4). *2007:* Total imports 43,113.9; Total exports 20,430.6.

TRANSPORT

Road Traffic (motor vehicles in use, December 2006): Light vehicles 71,726 (Private passenger cars 67,384); Heavy vehicles 5,780; Motorcycles 85,368.

Shipping (international sea-borne containerized freight traffic, '000 metric tons, 2007): Goods loaded 230.1; Goods unloaded 54.9.

Civil Aviation (2006, unless otherwise indicated): Passenger arrivals 1,400,595; Passenger departures 1,421,439; Goods loaded (metric tons) 22,758 (2007); Goods unloaded (metric tons) 69,625 (2007).

CHINESE SPECIAL ADMINISTRATIVE REGIONS

TOURISM

Visitor Arrivals by Country of Residence ('000 persons, 2007): China, People's Republic 14,873.5; Hong Kong 8,177.0; Taiwan 1,444.3; Total (incl. others) 27,003.4.

Receipts from Tourism (US $ million): 7,452 in 2004; 7,943 in 2005; 9,778 in 2006.

COMMUNICATIONS MEDIA

Radio Receivers (1997): 160,000 in use.

Television Receivers (2000): 125,115 in use.

Daily Newspapers (2006): 12.

Telephones (2007): 178,013 main lines in use.

Facsimile Machines (1999): 6,290 in use.

Mobile Cellular Telephones (2007): 794,323 subscribers.

Personal Computers (2006): 108,338 households.

Internet Users (2007): 119,913.

Broadband Subscribers (2006): 92,200.

Sources: partly International Telecommunication Union and UNESCO, *Statistical Yearbook*.

EDUCATION
(2005/06)

Kindergarten: 56 schools; 448 teachers; 10,216 pupils.

Primary: 77 schools; 1,632 teachers; 35,187 pupils.

Secondary: 58 schools; 2,307 teachers; 43,751 pupils.

Vocational/Technical: 5 schools; 139 teachers; 2,244 pupils.

Higher: 12 institutes; 1,547 teachers; 15,927 students.

Adult Literacy Rate: 93.5% at 2006 by-census.

Notes: Figures for schools and teachers refer to all those for which the category is applicable. Some schools and teachers provide education at more than one level. Institutions of higher education refer to those recognized by the Government of Macao Special Administrative Region.

Directory

The Constitution

Under the terms of the Basic Law of the Macao Special Administrative Region (SAR), which took effect on 20 December 1999, the Macao SAR is an inalienable part of the People's Republic of China. The Macao SAR, which comprises the Macao peninsula and the islands of Taipa and Coloane, exercises a high degree of autonomy and enjoys executive, legislative and independent judicial power, including that of final adjudication. The executive authorities and legislature are composed of permanent residents of Macao. The socialist system and policies shall not be practised in the Macao SAR, and the existing capitalist system and way of life shall not be changed for 50 years. In addition to the Chinese language, the Portuguese language may also be used by the executive, legislative and judicial organs.

The Central People's Government is responsible for foreign affairs and for defence. The Government of Macao is responsible for maintaining social order in the SAR. The Central People's Government appoints and dismisses the Chief Executive, principal executive officials and Procurator-General.

The Chief Executive of the Macao SAR is accountable to the Central People's Government. The Chief Executive shall be a Chinese national of no less than 40 years of age, who is a permanent resident of the region and who has resided in Macao for a continuous period of 20 years. He or she is elected locally by a broadly representative Selection Committee and appointed by the Central People's Government.

The Basic Law provides for a 300-member Election Committee, which serves a five-year term. The Election Committee shall be composed of 300 members from the following sectors: 100 members from industrial, commercial and financial sectors; 80 from cultural, educational and professional sectors; 80 from labour, social welfare and religious sectors; and 40 from the Legislative Council, municipal organs, Macao deputies to the National People's Congress (NPC), and representatives of Macao members of the National Committee of the Chinese People's Political Consultative Conference (NCCPPCC). The term of office of the Chief Executive of the Macao SAR is five years; he or she may serve two consecutive terms. The Chief Executive's functions include the appointment of a portion of the legislative councillors and the appointment or removal of members of the Executive Council.

With the exception of the first term (which expired on 15 October 2001), the term of office of members of the Legislative Council (commonly known as the Legislative Assembly) shall be four years. The second Legislative Council shall be composed of 27 members, of whom 10 shall be returned by direct election, 10 by indirect election and seven by appointment. The third and subsequent Legislative Councils shall comprise 29 members, of whom 12 shall be returned by direct election, 10 by indirect election and seven by appointment.

The Macao SAR shall maintain independent finances. The Central People's Government shall not levy taxes in the SAR, which shall practise an independent taxation system. The Macao pataca shall remain the legal currency. The Macao SAR shall retain its status as a free port and as a separate customs territory.

The Government

Chief Executive: EDMUND HO HAU WAH (assumed office 20 December 1999; re-elected 29 August 2004).

SECRETARIES
(April 2008)

Secretary for Administration and Justice: FLORINDA DA ROSA SILVA CHAN.

Secretary for Economy and Finance: FRANCIS TAM PAK YUEN.

Secretary for Security: CHEONG KUOC VA.

Secretary for Social and Cultural Affairs: FERNANDO CHUI SAI ON.

Secretary for Transport and Public Works: LAU SI IO.

GOVERNMENT OFFICES

Office of the Chief Executive: Headquarters of the Government of the Macao Special Administrative Region, Av. da Praia Grande; tel. 28726886; fax 28726665; internet www.gov.mo.

Executive Council: Headquarters of the Government of the Macao Special Administrative Region, Av. da Praia Grande; tel. 28726886; fax 9895704; Sec.-Gen. HO VENG ON.

Office of the Secretary for Administration and Justice: 28 Rua de S. Lourenço, Sede do Governo, 4° andar; tel. 28726886; fax 28726880; internet www.gov.mo.

Office of the Secretary for Economy and Finance: H28 Rua de S. Lourenço, Sede do Governo, 3° andar; tel. 28726886; fax 28726665; internet www.gov.mo.

Office of the Secretary for Security: Calçada dos Quartéis, Quartel de S. Francisco; tel. 7997501; fax 28580702; internet www.gov.mo.

Office of the Secretary for Social and Cultural Affairs: 28 Rua de S. Lourenço, Sede do Governo, 2° andar; tel. 28726886; fax 28727594; internet www.gov.mo.

Office of the Secretary for Transport and Public Works: 1° andar, Edif. dos Secretários, Rua de S. Lourenço 28; tel. 28726886; fax 28727566; internet www.gov.mo.

Macao Government Information Bureau: Gabinete de Comunicação Social do Governo de Macau, Av. da Praia Grande 762–804, Edif. China Plaza, 15° andar; tel. 28332886; fax 28355426; e-mail info@gcs.gov.mo; internet www.gcs.gov.mo; Dir VICTOR CHAN CHI PING.

Economic Services Bureau: Direcção dos Serviços de Economia, Rua Dr Pedro José Lobo 1–3, Edif. Luso Internacional, 25/F; tel. 28386937; fax 28590310; e-mail info@economia.gov.mo; internet www.economia.gov.mo; Dir SOU TIM PENG (acting).

Legislature

LEGISLATIVE COUNCIL (LEGISLATIVE ASSEMBLY)

Following the election of 25 September 2005, the Legislative Assembly comprised 29 members (compared with 27 in its previous term): seven appointed by the Chief Executive, 12 elected directly and 10 indirectly. Members serve for four years. The Assembly chooses its President from among its members, by secret vote. At this election, the pro-democracy Associação de Novo Macau Democrático (ANMD) received the highest proportion of votes cast (18.8%) to secure two of the 12 directly elective seats. The Associação dos Cidadãos Unidos de Macau (ACUM), thought to be supported by immigrants from Fujian Province, took two seats, as did the União para o Desenvolvimento (UPD) and the União Promotora para o Progresso (UPP), both considered to be pro-Beijing groupings. Angela Leong On Kei, wife of influential businessman and casino owner Stanley Ho, was elected on the list of the Aliança para o Desenvolvimento de Macau (AMD). The remaining three seats were divided among Nova Esperança

(NE), supported by civil servants and the ethnic Portuguese community, the União Geral para o Bem-querer de Macau (UBM) and the Convergência para o Desenvolvimento de Macau (CODEM). Four of the 10 indirectly elective seats were taken by the OMKC, a group representing business interests. The CCCAE, representing labour interests, the OMCY, representing professionals, and União Excelente, representing welfare, cultural, educational, and sports interests, each occupied two of the remaining six seats. The Legislative Assembly was superseded, under the terms of the Basic Law, by the Legislative Council. In practice, however, the legislature continues to be referred to as the Legislative Assembly.

Legislative Council (Legislative Assembly): Edif. da Assembléia Legislativa, Praça da Assembléia Legislativa, Aterros da Baía da Praia Grande; tel. 28728377; fax 28727857; e-mail info@al.gov.mo; internet www.al.gov.mo.

President: SUSANA CHOU.

Political Organizations

There are no formal political parties, but a number of registered civic associations exist and may participate in elections for the Legislative Assembly by presenting a list of candidates. The following groupings contested the legislative election of September 2005: Um Novo Vigor de Macau (UNVM), Associação pela Democracia e Bem-Estar Social de Macau (ADBSM), União dos Operários (UO), União dos Trabalhadores da Indústria de Jogos de Fortuna e Azar de Macau (UTJM), Nova Esperança (NE), União Geral para o Bem-querer de Macau (UBM), União Promotora para o Progresso (UPP), Associação de Novo Macau Democrático (ANMD), União para o Desenvolvimento (UPD), Associação Visão de Macau (AVM), Nova Juventude de Macau (NJM), Convergência para o Desenvolvimento de Macau (CODEM), Associação Direitos dos Cidadãos (ADDC), Aliança para o Desenvolvimento de Macau (AMD), Associação dos Cidadãos Unidos de Macau (ACUM), Associação de Activismo para a Democracia (AAD), Por Macau and Associação de Apoio à Comunidade e Proximidade do Povo (AACPP).

Judicial System

Formal autonomy was granted to the territory's judiciary in 1993. A new penal code took effect in January 1996. Macao operates its own five major codes, namely the Penal Code, the Code of Criminal Procedure, the Civil Code, the Code of Civil Procedure and the Commercial Code. In 1999 the authority of final appeal was granted to Macao. The judicial system operates independently of the mainland Chinese system.

Court of Final Appeal

Praçeta 25 de Abril, Edif. dos Tribunais de Segunda Instância e Ultima Instância; tel. 3984117; fax 28326744; e-mail ptui@court.gov.mo; internet www.court.gov.mo; Pres. SAM HOU FAI.

Procurator-General: HO CHIO MENG.

Religion

The majority of residents profess Buddhism, and there are numerous places of worship, Daoism and Confucianism also being widely practised. The Christian community numbers about 30,000. There are small Muslim and Hindu communities.

CHRISTIANITY

The Roman Catholic Church

Macao forms a single diocese, directly responsible to the Holy See. At 31 December 2005 there were 27,661 adherents in the territory, comprising nearly 6% of the population.

Bishop of Macao: Rt Rev. JOSÉ LAI HUNG SENG, Paço Episcopal, Largo da Sé s/n, POB 324; tel. 28309954; fax 28309861; e-mail mdiocese@macau.ctm.net.

The Anglican Communion

Macao forms part of the Anglican diocese of Hong Kong (q.v.).

The Press

A new Press Law, prescribing journalists' rights and obligations, was enacted in August 1990.

PORTUGUESE LANGUAGE

O Clarim: Rua Central 26-A; tel. 28573860; fax 28307867; e-mail clarim@macau.ctm.net; internet www.oclarim.com.mo; f. 1948; weekly; Editor ALBINO BENTO PAIS; circ. 1,500.

Hoje Macau: Av. Dr Rodrigues 600E, Edif. Centro Comercial First National, 14° andar, Sala 1408; tel. 28752401; fax 28752405; e-mail hoje@macau.ctm.net; internet www.hojemacau.com; f. 2001; daily; Dir JOÃO COSTEIRA VARELA; circ. 1,200.

Jornal Tribuna de Macau: Av. Almeida Ribeiro 99, Edif. Comercial Nam Wah, 6° andar, Salas 603–05; tel. 28378057; fax 28337305; internet www.jtm.com.mo; f. 1998 through merger of Jornal de Macau (f. 1982) and Tribuna de Macau (f. 1982); daily; Dir JOSÉ FIRMINO DA ROCHA DINIS; circ. 1,000.

Ponto Final: Alameda Dr Carlos d'Assumpção; tel. 28339566; fax 28339563; e-mail editor@pontofinalmacau.com; internet www.pontofinalmacau.com; Dir RICARDO PINTO; circ. 1,500.

CHINESE LANGUAGE

Cheng Pou: Av. da Praia Grande, 63, Edif. Hang Cheong, E–F; tel. 28965972; fax 28965741; internet www.chengpou.com.mo; daily; Dir KUNG SU KAN; Editor-in-Chief LEONG CHI CHUN; circ. 5,000.

Correio Sino-Macaense: tel. 28717569; fax 28717572; f. 1989.

Jornal Informação (Son Pou): Rua de Francisco 22, 1° C, Edif. Mei Fun; tel. 28561557; fax 28566575; internet www.sonpou.com.mo; weekly; Dir CHAO CHONG PENG; circ. 8,000.

Jornal San Wa Ou: Av. Venseslau de Morais 221, Edif. Ind. Nam Fong, 2a Fase, 15°, Bloco E; tel. 28717569; fax 28717572; e-mail correiro@macau.ctm.net; internet www.waou.com.mo; daily; Dir LAM CHONG; circ. 1,500.

Jornal 'Si-Si': Rua de Brás de Rosa, Cheong Meng Garden, Meng Seng Kwok, 10° andar B; tel. and fax 28974354; internet www.jornalsisi.com; weekly; Dir and Editor-in-Chief CHEANG VENG PENG; circ. 3,000.

Jornal Va Kio: Rua da Alfândega 7–9; tel. 28345888; fax 28513724; e-mail vakio@macau.ctm.net; internet www.jornalvakio.com; f. 1937; daily; Publr ALICE CHIANG SAO MENG; Editor-in-Chief LEONG CHI SANG; circ. 28,000.

O Pulso de Macau: Rua Oito do Bairro Iao Hon S/N, Edif. Hong Tai, Apt F058 R/C; tel. 28400194; fax 28400284; e-mail pulsomo@yahoo.com.hk; internet www.pulso.com.mo; weekly; Dir HO SI VO.

Ou Mun Iat Pou (Macao Daily News): Rua Pedro Nolasco da Silva 37; tel. 28371688; fax 28331998; internet www.macaodaily.com; f. 1958; daily; Dir PANG CHU LEI; Editor-in-Chief PO LOK; circ. 100,000.

Semanário Desportivo de Macau: Estrada D. Maria II, Edif. Kin Chit Garden, 2 G–H; tel. 28718259; fax 28718285; e-mail info_macausports@macaustreet.com; internet www.macausports.com.mo; weekly; sport; Dir FONG NIM LAM; Editor-in-Chief FONG NIM SEONG; circ. 2,000.

Semanário Recreativo de Macau: Av. Sidónio Pais 31 D, 3/F A; tel. 28553216; fax 28516792; weekly; Dir IEONG CHEOK KONG; Editor-in-Chief TONG IOK WA.

Seng Pou (Star): Travessa da Caldeira 9; tel. 28938387; fax 28388192; e-mail sengpou@macau.ctm.net; f. 1963; daily; Dir and Editor-in-Chief KUOK KAM SENG; Deputy Editor-in-Chief TOU MAN KUM; circ. 6,000.

Si Man Pou (Jornal do Cidadão): Rua dos Pescadores, Edif. Ind. Ocean, Bl. 2, 2/F–B; tel. 28722111; fax 28722133; e-mail shemin@macau.ctm.net; internet www.shimindaily.com.mo; f. 1944; daily; Dir and Editor-in-Chief KUNG MAN; circ. 8,000.

Tai Chung Pou: Rua Dr Lourenço P. Marques 7 A, 2/F; tel. 28939888; fax 28934114; e-mail taichung@macau.ctm.net; f. 1933; daily; Portuguese supplement; Dir VONG U. KONG; Editor-in-Chief CHAN TAI PAC; circ. 8,000.

Today Macau Journal: Pátio da Barca 20, R/C; tel. 28215050; fax 28210478; e-mail todaymac@macau.ctm.net; daily; Dir LAM VO I; Editor-in-Chief IU VENG ION; circ. 6,000.

ENGLISH LANGUAGE

Macau Post Daily: Av. de Almeida Ribeiro 99, Edif. Nam Wah Centre, 10° F; tel. 28331050; fax 28331104; e-mail macaupost@macau.ctm.net; internet www.macaupostdaily.com; f. 2004; Dir HARALD BRUNING.

SELECTED PERIODICALS

Agora Macau: Av. 1° de Maio, Kam Hoi San; tel. 28762763; fax 28762766; e-mail agora@macau.ctn.net; internet www.agoramacau.com; weekly; Chinese; Dir NG KUOK SAO.

Boletim Associação Budista Geral de Macau: Estrada de Lou Lim Ieok 2, Pou Tai Un, Ilha da Taipa; tel. 28811038; bi-monthly; Dir LEI SENG VO.

Business Intelligence: Av. da Amizade, Edif. Chong Yu 12 D; tel. 28331258; fax 28331487; e-mail prego@macaubusiness.com; internet www.bizintelligenceonline.com; monthly; Chinese; Dir PAULO ALEXANDRE TEIXEIRA DE AZEVEDO.

Cáritas Ligação: Largo de Santo Agostinho 1A; tel. 28573297; bimonthly; Dir PUN CHI MENG.

CHINESE SPECIAL ADMINISTRATIVE REGIONS   *Macao*

Chinese Cross Currents: Av. Conselheiro Ferreira de Almeida 95E; tel. 28532536; fax 28568274; e-mail currents@riccimac.org; internet www.riccimac.org/eng/ccc; f. 2004; quarterly; Chinese and English; cultural studies; published by the Macau Ricci Institute; Dir of Publs ARTUR WARDEGA.

Macau Business: 16/F, Office 1605, 600E, First National Commercial Centre, Av. Dr Rodrigo Rodrigues; tel. 28331258; fax 28331487; e-mail editor@macaubusiness.com; internet www.macaubusiness.com; f. 2004; monthly; Publr PAULO A. AZEVEDO; Editor-in-Chief AJAY SHAMDASANI; circ. 32,500.

Macau Manager: Rua de Santa Clara 9, Edif. Ribeiro, 6° andar; tel. 28323233; quarterly; Chinese; published by the Macau Management Asscn; Dir CHUI SAI CHEONG.

Macau Times: Rua Almirante Costa Cabral 11, Edif. Iau Fai, 11° andar; e-mail mail@macautimes.net; internet www.macautimes.net; monthly; Chinese; published by the Macau Christian Literature Asscn; Dir WONG TAI WAI.

Revista Mensal de Macau: Av. Dr Rodrigo Rodrigues 600E, Edif. Centro Comercial First International, 14° andar, Rm 1404; tel. 28323660; fax 28323601; e-mail contacto@revistamacau.com; internet www.revistamacau.com; f. 1987; quarterly; Portuguese; govt publication; Dir VICTOR CHAN CHI PING; Editor LUIS ORTET.

Saúde de Macau: Rua Ferreira do Amaral 9, 2° andar; tel. 28307271; quarterly; health issues; Dir KUOK HONG NENG.

x1 Week: Av. do Infante D. Henrique 43-53A, Edif. The Macau Square, 7° andar; tel. 28710566; fax 28710565; e-mail info@x1week.com; internet www.x1week.com; computing; Dir CHAN SAO SEONG.

NEWS AGENCIES

China News Service: Rua de Londres, Edif. Zhu Kuan, 14/F, Y/Z; tel. 28594585; fax 28594586; Correspondent HUANG HONGBIN.

Xinhua (New China) News Agency Macao SAR Branch: Av. Gov. Jaime Silvério Marques, Edif. Zhu Kuan, 13° andar-V; tel. 28727710; fax 28700548; e-mail xinhua@macau.ctm.net; Dir WANG HONGYU.

PRESS ASSOCIATIONS

Associação de Jornalistas da Região Administrativa Especial de Macau: Av. do Dr Rodrigo Rodrigues, 600E, Centro Comercial First National, 14° andar, Sala 1407; f. 2005; Pres. JOÃO COSTEIRA VARELA.

Macao Chinese Media Workers Association: Travessa do Matadouro, Edif. 3, 3B; tel. 28939486; e-mail mcju@macau.ctm.net; Pres. LEI PANG CHU.

Macao Journalists Association: Rua de Jorge Alvares, 7–7B, Viva Court, 17F, Flat A; tel. 28569819; fax 28569819; e-mail macauja@macau.ctm.net; internet hk.myblog.yahoo.com/macaujournalist; f. 1999; Pres. PANG OI CHI.

Macao Journalists Club: Estrada do Repouso, Edif. Tak Fai 18B; tel. 28921395; fax 28921395; e-mail cjm@macau.ctm.net; Pres. LO SONG MAN.

Macao Media Club: Rua de Santa Clara 5–7E, Edif. Ribeiro, 4B; tel. 28330035; fax 28330036; e-mail mmedia@macau.ctn.net; Pres. CHEONG CHI SENG.

Macao Sports Press Association: Av. Olímpica, Estádio de Macau 33; tel. 28838206, ext. 151; fax 28718285; e-mail macsport@macau.ctm.net; Pres. LAO LU KONG.

Publishers

Associação Beneficência Leitores Jornal Ou Mun: Nova-Guia 339; tel. 28711631; fax 28711630.

Fundação Macau: Av. República 6; tel. 28966777; fax 28968658; e-mail info@fm.org.mo; internet www.fmac.org.mo.

Instituto Cultural de Macau: publishes literature, social sciences and history; see under Tourism.

Livros do Oriente: Av. Amizade 876, Edif. Marina Gardens, 15E; tel. 28700320; fax 28700423; e-mail livros.macau@loriente.com; internet www.loriente.com; f. 1990; publishes in Portuguese, English and Chinese on regional history, culture, etc.; Gen. Man. ROGÉRIO BELTRÃO COELHO; Exec. Man. CECÍLIA JORGE.

Universidade de Macau—Centro de Publicações: Av. Padre Tomás Pereira, SJ, Taipa; tel. 3974504; fax 3974506; e-mail pub_enquiry@umac.mo; internet www.umac.mo/pub; f. 1993; art, economics, education, political science, history, literature, management, social sciences, etc.; Head Dr RAYMOND WONG.

GOVERNMENT PUBLISHER

Imprensa Oficial: Rua da Imprensa Nacional s/n; tel. 28573822; fax 28596802; e-mail info@imprensa.macau.gov.mo; internet www.imprensa.macau.gov.mo.

Broadcasting and Communications

TELECOMMUNICATIONS

The Government initiated a liberalization of the mobile telecommunications market in 2001. In October 2006 the Government awarded an eight-year licence for 3G operations to Hutchison Telephone (Macau) Co Ltd, and to China Unicom (Macao) Ltd, a subsidiary of the Hong Kong-based China Unicom Ltd. These services commenced in October 2007.

Companhia de Telecomunicações de Macau, SARL (CTM): Rua de Lagos, Edif. Telecentro, Taipa; tel. 28833833; fax 28913031; e-mail comm@macau.ctm.net; internet www.ctm.net; holds local telecommunications monopoly; shareholders include Cable and Wireless (51%), Portugal Telecom (28%), and CITIC Pacific (20%); Chair. JAMES CHEESEWRIGHT; CEO VANDY POON; 900 employees.

Hutchison Telephone (Macau) Co Ltd (3 Macau): Av. Xian Xing Hai, Zhu Kuan Bldg, 8/F; tel. 8933388; fax 781282; e-mail feedback@three.com.mo; internet www.three.com.mo; f. 2001; mobile telecommunications operator; subsidiary of Hutchison Whampoa Group (Hong Kong); local capital participation; CEO ELIZABETE FONG.

SmarTone Mobile (Macau) Ltd: Macao; e-mail enquiry@smartone.com.mo; internet www.smartone.com.mo; mobile telecommunications provider; subsidiary of SmarTone Mobile Communications Ltd (Hong Kong); local capital participation; CEO ALEX IP.

Regulatory Authority

Office for the Development of Telecommunications and Information Technology (GDTTI): Av. da Praia Grande 789, 3/F; tel. 28356328; fax 83969166; e-mail ifx@gdtti.gov.mo; internet www.gdtti.gov.mo.

BROADCASTING

Radio

Rádio Vilaverde: Macao Jockey Club, Taipa; tel. 28822163; internet www.am738.com; private radio station; programmes in Chinese; Man. KOK HOI.

Television

Teledifusão de Macau, SARL (TDM): Rua Francisco Xavier Pereira 157-A, POB 446; tel. 28335888 (Radio), 28519188 (TV); fax 28520208; internet www.tdm.com.mo; f. 1982; owned by the Govt of the Macao SAR ; two radio channels: Rádio Macau (Av. Dr Rodrigo Rodrigues, Edif. Nam Kwong, 7/F; tel. 28335888; fax 28343220; rmacau@tdm.com.mo), broadcasting 24 hours per day in Portuguese on TDM Canal 1 (incl. broadcasts from RTP International in Portugal) and 17 hours per day in Chinese on TDM Channel 2; Chair. Dr STANLEY HO; Exec. Vice-Chair. Dr MANUEL GONÇALVES.

Macau Cable TV Ltd: Alameda Dr Carlos d'Assumpção 411–417, Edif. Dynasty Plaza, 21° andar; e-mail enquiry@macaucabletv.com; internet www.macaucabletv.com; f. 2000; offers 70 channels from around the world.

Macao Satellite Television: c/o Cosmos Televisão por Satélite, Av. Infante D. Henrique 29, Edif. Va Iong, 4/F A; commenced transmissions in 2000; operated by Cosmos Televisão por Satélite, SARL; domestic and international broadcasts in Chinese aimed at Chinese-speaking audiences world-wide.

Macao is within transmission range of the Hong Kong television stations.

Cosmos Televisão por Satélite, SARL: Av. Infante D. Henrique 29, Edif. Va Iong, 4/F A; tel. 28785731; fax 28788234; commenced trial satellite transmissions in 1999, initially for three hours per day; by the year 2003 the company planned to provide up to six channels; Chair. NG FOK.

Finance

(cap. = capital; res = reserves; dep. = deposits; m. = million; brs = branches; amounts in patacas unless otherwise indicated)

BANKING

Macao has no foreign-exchange controls, its external payments system being fully liberalized on current and capital transactions. The Financial System Act, aiming to improve the reputation of the territory's banks and to comply with international standards, took effect in September 1993.

CHINESE SPECIAL ADMINISTRATIVE REGIONS   *Macao*

Issuing Authority

Autoridade Monetária de Macau (AMCM) (Monetary Authority of Macao): Calçada do Gaio 24–26, POB 3017; tel. 28568288; fax 28325432; e-mail general@amcm.gov.mo; internet www.amcm.gov.mo; f. 1989; est. as Autoridade Monetária e Cambial de Macau (AMCM), to replace the Instituto Emissor de Macau; cap. 2,140.3m., res 1,788.0m., dep. 50,319.0m. (Dec. 2005); govt-owned; Pres. Anselmo L. S. Teng.

Banks of Issue

Banco Nacional Ultramarino (BNU), SA: Av. Almeida Ribeiro 22, POB 465; tel. 28355111; fax 28355653; e-mail markt@bnu.com.mo; internet www.bnu.com.mo; f. 1864; est. in Macao 1902; subsidiary of Caixa Geral de Depósitos since 2001; agent of Macao Government; agreement whereby the Bank remains an agent of the treasury signed with the administration of the Macao SAR in 2000; to remain a note-issuing bank until 2010; CEO Dr Herculano J. Sousa; 11 brs.

Bank of China: Bank of China Bldg, Av. Dr Mário Soares; tel. 28781828; fax 28781833; e-mail bocmacau@macau.ctm.net; internet www.bocmacau.com; f. 1950 as Nan Tung Bank, name changed 1987; authorized to issue banknotes from Oct. 1995; Gen. Man. Ye Yixin; 24 brs.

Other Commercial Banks

Banco Comercial de Macau, SA: Av. da Praia Grande 572, POB 545; tel. 7910000; fax 28595817; e-mail bcmbank@bcm.com.mo; internet www.bcm.com.mo; f. 1974; cap. 225m., res 248.1m., dep. 7,939.0m. (Dec. 2005); Chair. and Pres. David Shou-Yeh Wong; CEO Chiu Lung-Man; 17 brs.

Banco Delta Asia (BDA), SARL: Av. Conselheiro Ferreira de Almeida 79; tel. 28559898; fax 28570068; e-mail contact@bdam.com; internet www.delta-asia.com; f. 1935; fmrly Banco Hang Sang; cap. 210.0m., res 173.2m., dep. 3,323.1m. (Dec. 2004); Chair. Stanley Au; Exec. Dir Miron Mushkat; 9 brs.

Banco Tai Fung, SARL: Tai Fung Bank Headquarters Bldg, Av. Alameda Dr Carlos d'Assumpção 418; tel. 28322323; fax 28570737; e-mail tfbsecr@taifungbank.com; internet www.taifungbank.com; f. 1971; cap. 1,000m., dep. 29,487m. (Dec. 2007); Chair. Fung Ka York; Gen. Man. Liu Daguo; 21 brs.

Banco Weng Hang, SA: Av. Almeida Ribeiro 241; tel. 28335678; fax 28576527; e-mail bwhhrd@whbmac.com; internet www.whbmac.com; f. 1973; subsidiary of Wing Hang Bank Ltd, Hong Kong; cap. 120m., res 998.4m., dep. 16,414.4m. (Dec. 2006); Chair. Patrick Fung Yuk-bun; Gen. Man. Lee Tak Lim; 12 brs.

China Construction Bank (Macau) Corpn Ltd: Av. Almeida Ribeiro 70–76, POB 165; tel. 28568821; fax 28570386; internet www.asia.ccb.com; f. 1937; fmrly Banco da América (Macau); cap. 200m., res 64.3m., dep. 2,543.9m. (Dec. 2006); Chair. Samuel Ng Tsien; Man. Dir Kin Hong Cheong.

Luso International Banking Ltd: Av. Dr Mário Soares 47; tel. 28378977; fax 28711100; e-mail lusobank@lusobank.com.mo; internet www.lusobank.com.mo; f. 1974; cap. 315.6m., res 240.2m., dep. 11,052.6m. (Dec. 2005); Chair. Lu Yao Ming; Gen. Man. Ip Kai Ming; 11 brs.

Macau Chinese Bank Ltd: Av. da Praia Grande 811; tel. 28322678; fax 28322680; fmrly Finibanco (Portugal).

Seng Heng Bank Ltd: Av. da Amizade 555, 18/F Macau Landmark, Torre Banco Seng Heng; tel. 28555222; fax 28338064; e-mail sengheng@macau.ctm.net; internet www.senghengbank.com; f. 1972; cap. 150.0m., res 1,430.7m., dep. 19,563.7m. (Dec. 2005); Chair. and Man. Dir Dr Stanley Ho; CEO Patrick Huen Wing Ming; 6 brs.

Banking Association

Associação de Bancos de Macau (ABM) (The Macau Association of Banks): Av. da Praia Grande 575, Edif. 'Finanças', 15/F; tel. 28511921; fax 28346049; e-mail abm@macau.ctm.net; f. 1985; Chair. Ye Yixin.

INSURANCE

ACE Seguradora, SA: Rua Dr Pedro José Lobo 1–3, Luso Bank Bldg, 17/F, Apt 1701–02; tel. 28557191; fax 28570188; Rep. Andy Au.

American Home Assurance Co: Av. Almeida Ribeiro 61, Central Plaza, 15/F, 'G'; non-life insurance.

American International Assurance Co (Bermuda) Ltd: 601 AIA Tower, Nos. 251A–301, Av. Comercial de Macau; tel. 9881817; fax 28315900; e-mail salina-if.ieong@aig.com; life insurance; Rep. Alexandra Foo Cheuk Ling.

Asia Insurance Co Ltd: Rua do Dr Pedro José Lobo 1–3, Luso International Bank Bldg, 11/F, Units 1103–04; tel. 28570439; fax 28570438; e-mail asiamc@macau.ctm.net; non-life insurance; Rep. S. T. Chan.

AXA China Region Insurance Company: Av. do Infante D. Henrique 43–53a, 20° andar, The Macau Square; life insurance; Rep. Wrestly Wong.

China Insurance (Macau) Co Ltd: Av. Alameda Dr Carlos D'Assumpção 398, Edif. CNAC, 10° andar; tel. 28785578; fax 28787218; e-mail cic@macau.ctm.net; internet www.cicmacau.com.mo; non-life insurance.

China Life Insurance Co Ltd: Av. Dr Rodrigo Rodrigues Quarteirão 11, Lote A, Zape, China Insurance Bldg, 15/F; tel. 28558918; fax 28787287; e-mail cic@macau.ctm.net; Rep. Cheng Mingjin.

Companhia de Seguros Fidelidade: Av. da Praia Grande 567, 14°; tel. 28374072; fax 28511085; life and non-life insurance; Gen. Man. Eduardo Clarisseau Mesquita D'Abreu.

Crown Life Insurance Co: Av. da Praia Grande 287, Nam Yuet Commercial Centre, Bl. B, 8/F; tel. 28570828; fax 28570844; Rep. Steven Siu.

Delta Asia Insurance Company Ltd: Av. da Praia Grande, 369–371, Edif. Keng Ou, 13/F; e-mail contact@bdam.com; internet www.delta-asia.com/macau.

HSBC Insurance (Asia) Ltd: Av. da Praia Grande 619, Edif. Comercial Si Toi, 1/F; tel. 28212323; fax 28217162; non-life insurance; Rep. Nora Chio.

Ing Life Insurance Co (Macao) Ltd: Av. Almeida Ribeiro 61, 11/F, Unit C and D; tel. 9886060; fax 9886100; internet www.ing.com.mo; Deputy Gen. Man. Tony Poon Chi Fai.

Insurance Co of North America: Av. Almeida Ribeiro 32, Tai Fung Bank Bldg, Rm 806–7; tel. 28557191; fax 28570188; Rep. Joseph Lo.

Luen Fung Hang Insurance Co Ltd (Luen Fung Hang Life Ltd): 398 Alameda Dr Carlos d'Assumpção, Edif. CNAC, 4° andar; tel. 28700033; fax 28700088; e-mail info@luenfunghang.com; internet www.luenfunghang.com; life (Luen Fung Hang Life Ltd) and non-life insurance; Rep. Si Chi Hok.

Macao Life Insurance Co (Macao Insurance Company): Av. da Praia Grande 574, Edif. BCM, 10–11F; tel. 28555078; fax 28551074; e-mail mic@bcm.com.mo; internet www.macauinsurance.com.mo; life and non-life insurance (Macao Insurance Company); Rep. Si Chi Hok.

Manulife (International) Ltd: Av. da Praia Grande 517, Edif. Comercial Nam Tung, 8/F, Unit B & C; tel. 3980388; fax 28323312; internet www.manulife.com.hk; Rep. Daniel Tang.

MassMutual Asia Ltd: Av. da Praia Grande 517, Edif. Nam Tung 16, 6/F; life insurance.

Min Xin Insurance Co Ltd: Rua do Dr Pedro José Lobo 1–3, Luso International Bank Bldg, 27/F, Rm 2704; tel. 28305684; fax 28305600; non-life insurance; Rep. Peter Chan.

Mitsui Sumitomo Insurance Co Ltd: Rua Dr Pedro José Lobo 1–3, Edif. Banco Luso, 11/F, Apartment 1202; tel. 28385917; fax 28596667; non-life insurance; Rep. Takao Yasukochi.

MSIG Insurance (Hong Kong) Ltd: Av. da Praia Grande 693, Edif. Tai Wah, 13° andar; tel. 28923329; fax 28923349; internet www.msig.com.hk.

QBE Insurance (International) Ltd: Av. da Praia Grande 369–71, Edif. Keng On 'B', 9/F; tel. 28323909; fax 28323911; non-life insurance; Rep. Sally Siu.

The Wing On Fire & Marine Insurance Co Ltd: Av. Almeida Ribeiro 61, Central Plaza, 7/F, Block E; tel. 28356688; fax 28333710; non-life insurance; Rep. Chiang Ao Lai Lai.

Winterthur Swiss Insurance (Macao) Ltd: Av. da Praia Grande 369–371, Edif. Keng Ou, 13/F, C; tel. 28356618; fax 28356800; non-life insurance; Man. Allan Yu Kin Nam.

Insurers' Associations

Federation of Macao Professional Insurance Intermediaries: Rua de Pequim 244–46, Macao Finance Centre, 6/F, G; tel. 28703268; fax 28703266; Rep. David Kong.

Macao Insurance Agents and Brokers Association: Av. da Praia Grande 309, Nam Yuet Commercial Centre, 8/F, D; tel. 28378901; fax 28570848; Rep. Jack Li Kwok Tai.

Macao Insurers' Association: Av. da Praia Grande 575, Edif. 'Finanças', 15/F; tel. 28511923; fax 28337531; e-mail mia@macau.ctm.net; Pres. Jiang Yidao.

Trade and Industry

CHAMBER OF COMMERCE

Associação Comercial de Macau (Macao Chamber of Commerce): Rua de Xangai 175, Edif. ACM, 5/F; tel. 28576833; fax 28594513; internet www.acm.org.mo; Pres. MA MAN KEI.

INDUSTRIAL AND TRADE ASSOCIATIONS

Associação dos Construtores Civis e Empresas de Fomento Predial de Macau (Macao Association of Building Contractors and Developers): Rua do Campo 9–11; tel. 28323854; fax 28345710; Pres. TOMMY LAU.

Associação dos Exportadores e Importadores de Macau (Macau Importers and Exporters Association): Av. Infante D. Henrique 60–62, Centro Comercial 'Central', 3/F; tel. 28375859; fax 28512174; e-mail aeim@macau.ctm.net; internet www.macauexport.com; exporters' and importers' asscn; Chair. TUSI WAI KUAN.

Associação dos Industriais de Tecelagem e Fiação de Lã de Macau (Macao Weaving and Spinning of Wool Manufacturers' Asscn): Av. da Amizade 271, Edif. Kam Wa Kok, 6/F–A; tel. 28553378; fax 28511105; Pres. WONG SHOO KEE.

Associação Industrial de Macau (Industrial Association of Macau): Rua Dr Pedro José Lobo 34–36, Edif. AIM, 17/F, POB 70; tel. 28574125; fax 28578305; e-mail aim@macau.ctm.net; internet www.madeinmacau.net; f. 1959; Pres. PETER PAN.

Centro de Produtividade e Transferência de Tecnologia de Macau (Macao Productivity and Technology Transfer Centre): Rua de Xangai 175, Edif. ACM, 6/F; tel. 28781313; fax 28788233; e-mail cpttm@cpttm.org.mo; internet www.cpttm.org.mo; vocational or professional training; Pres. Dr ERIC YEUNG; Dir-Gen. VICTOR KUAN.

Euro-Info Centre Relay of Macao: Alameda Dr Carlos d'Assumpção No. 263, Edif. China Civil Plaza, 20°andar; tel. 28713338; fax 28713339; e-mail eic@macau.ctm.net; internet www.ieem.org.mo/eic/eicmacau.html; f. 1992; promotes trade with European Union; Man. VIOLET NG; Pres. JOSÉ LUÍS DE SALES MARQUES.

Instituto de Promoção do Comércio e do Investimento de Macau (IPIM) (Macao Trade and Investment Promotion Institute): Av. da Amizade 918, World Trade Center Bldg, 1°–4° andares; tel. 28710300; fax 28590309; e-mail ipim@ipim.gov.mo; internet www.ipim.gov.mo; Pres. LEE PENG HONG.

SDPIM (Macao Industrial Parks Development Co Ltd): Av. da Amizade 918, World Trade Center Bldg, 13° andar A & B; tel. 28786636; fax 28785374; e-mail sdpim@macau.ctm.net; internet www.sdpim.com.mo; f. 1993; Pres. of the Bd PAULINA Y. ALVES DOS SANTOS.

World Trade Center Macao, SARL: Av. da Amizade 918, Edif. World Trade Center, 16/F–19/F; tel. 28727666; fax 28727633; e-mail wtcmc@macau.ctm.net; internet www.wtc-macau.com; f. 1995; trade information and business services, office rentals, exhibition and conference facilities; Man. Dir ALBERTO EXPEDITO MARÇAL.

UTILITIES

Electricity

Companhia de Electricidade de Macau, SARL (CEM): Estrada D. Maria II 32–36, Edif. CEM; tel. 28339933; fax 28719760; internet www.cem-macau.com; f. 1972; sole distributor; 6% owned by China Power International Holding Ltd; Chair. JOSÉ VAZ MARCELINO.

Water

Sociedade de Abastecimento de Aguas de Macau, SARL (SAAM) (Macao Water): Av. do Conselheiro Borja 718; tel. 28233332; fax 28220150; e-mail mwater@macau.ctm.net; internet www.macaowater.com; f. 1985; jt venture with Suez Lyonnaise des Eaux; Chair. STEPHEN CLARK; Man. Dir CHAN KAM LENG.

TRADE UNIONS

Macao Federation of Trade Unions: Rua Ribeira do Patane 2; tel. 28576231; fax 28553110; Pres. PUN IOK LAN.

Macao Labour Union: Pres. HO HEN KUOK.

Transport

RAILWAYS

There are no railways in Macao. A plan to connect Macao with Zhuhai and Guangzhou (People's Republic of China) is under consideration. Construction of the Zhuhai–Guangzhou section was under way in mainland China in the early 21st century. In October 2006 the Government announced plans to invest 4,200,000m. patacas in the construction of an elevated light rail system. According to local media reports, the project would span around 22 km, with 26 stations.

ROADS

In 2000 the public road network extended to 341 km. The peninsula of Macao is linked to the islands of Taipa and Coloane by three bridges and by a 2.2-km causeway respectively. The first bridge (2.6 km) opened in 1974. In conjunction with the construction of an airport on Taipa (see Civil Aviation), a 4.4-km four-lane bridge to the Macao peninsula was opened in April 1994. A third link between Macao and Taipa, a double-deck bridge, was inaugurated in late 2004. A second connection to the mainland, the 1.5-km six-lane road bridge (the Lotus Bridge) linking Macao with Hengqin Island (in Zhuhai, Guangdong Province), opened to traffic in December 1999. The financing of a new 29-km steel bridge linking Macao with Hong Kong's Lantau Island and Zhuhai City, Guangdong Province, was under discussion in 2006.

SHIPPING

There are representatives of shipping agencies for international lines in Macao. There are passenger and cargo services to the People's Republic of China. Regular services between Macao and Hong Kong are run by the Hong Kong-based New World First Ferry and Shun Tak-China Travel Ship Management Ltd companies. A new terminal opened in late 1993. The port of Kao-ho (on the island of Coloane), which handles cargo and operates container services, entered into service in 1991.

Agência de Navegação Ka Fung: tel. 28553311; fax 28569233; e-mail info@kafung-shipping.com; internet www.kafung-shipping.com; f. 1984.

CTS Parkview Holdings Ltd: Av. Amizade, Porto Exterior, Terminal Marítimo de Macau, Sala 2006B; tel. 28726789; fax 28727112; purchased by Sociedade de Turismo e Diversões de Macau (STDM) in 1998.

DHC Logistics (Macau) Ltd: Av. Dr Rodrigo Rodrigues 338, 21° andar, Edif. do Grupo de Seguros de Chian; tel. 28788063; fax 28788093; e-mail pollywong@dhclogistics.com; internet www.dhclogistics.com.

New Line Shipping Ltd: 1-3 Rua do Dr Pedro José Lobo, Edif. Banco Luso, Rm 1707-1708; tel. 28710250; fax 28710252; e-mail newline@macau.ctm.net; internet www.newline.com.mo; f. 2001.

STDM Shipping Dept: Av. da Amizade Terminal Marítimo do Porto Exterior; tel. 28726111; fax 28726234; e-mail shpgdept@macau.ctm.net; affiliated to STDM; Gen. Man. ALAN HO; Office Man. TERENCE LEI.

Association

Associação de Agências de Navegação e Congêneres de Macau (Macau Shipping Association): Rua de Xanghai 175, Edif. ACM, 8F; tel. 28528207; fax 28302667; e-mail macshpg@yahoo.com.hk; Pres. VONG KOK SENG.

Port Authority

Capitania dos Portos de Macau: Rampa da Barra, Quartel dos Mouros, POB 47; tel. 28559922; fax 28511986; e-mail webmaster@marine.gov.mo; internet www.marine.gov.mo; Dir WONG SOI MAN.

CIVIL AVIATION

Macao International Airport was officially opened in December 1995. The terminal has the capacity to handle 6m. passengers a year. By 2007 a total of 14 airlines operated flights to 25 destinations, mostly in China, but also to the Democratic People's Republic of Korea, the Philippines, Singapore, Taiwan and Thailand. Between January and December 2007 Macau International Airport handled a total of 5,498,879 passengers and 180,935 metric tons of cargo. A helicopter service between Hong Kong and Macao was put into operation in 1990 by Heli Express Ltd (formerly East Asia Airlines), and a scheduled helicopter service between Macao and Shenzhen, provided by the same company, commenced in January 2003. In late 2003 Air Macau launched direct flights between Macao and Chengdu, capital of Sichuan Province.

Autoridade de Aviação Civil (AACM) (Civil Aviation Authority of Macao): Alameda Dr Carlos D'Assumpção, 336–342, Centro Comercial Cheng Feng, 18 andar; tel. 28511213; fax 28338089; e-mail aacm@aacm.gov.mo; internet www.aacm.gov.mo; f. 1991; Pres. SIMON CHAN WENG HONG.

Administração de Aeroportos, Lda (ADA): Macau International Airport, Taipa; tel. 28861111; fax 28862222; e-mail directoraeroporto@ada.com.mo; internet www.ada.com.mo; CEO JOSÉ CARLOS ANGEJA.

CAM (Sociedade do Aeroporto Internacional de Macau, SARL): CAM Office Bldg, 4/F, Av. Wai Long, Macao International Airport; tel. 5988888; fax 28785465; e-mail cam@macau-airport.com; internet www.macau-airport.com; f. 1989; airport owner, responsible for design, construction, development and international marketing of Macao International Airport; Chair. DENG JUN.

Air Macau: 398 Alameda Dr Carlos d'Assumpção, 12°–18° andar; tel. 3966888; fax 3966866; e-mail airmacau@airmacau.com.mo; internet www.airmacau.com.mo; f. 1994; controlled by China National Aviation Corporation (Group) Macao Co Ltd; services to several cities in the People's Republic of China, the Republic of Korea, the Philippines, Taiwan and Thailand; other destinations planned; Chair. GU TIEFEI; CEO DAVID H. J. FEI.

Viva Macau: Alameda Dr Carlos d' Assumpção, 181–187 Edif. Jardim Brilhantismo, 9° andar; tel. 28718882; fax 28718803; e-mail inquiry@flyvivamacau.com; internet www.flyvivamacau.com; f. 2004; low-cost airline; operates flights to destinations incl. Sydney (Australia), Jakarta (Indonesia) and Tokyo (Japan); CEO CON KORFIATIS; Pres. NGAN IN LENG.

Tourism

Tourism is now a major industry, a substantial portion of the Government's revenue being derived from the territory's casinos. The other attractions are the cultural heritage and museums, dog-racing, horse-racing, and annual events such as Chinese New Year (January/February), the Macao Arts Festival (February/March), Dragon Boat Festival (May/June), the Macao International Fireworks Festival (September/October), the International Music Festival (October), the Macao Grand Prix for racing cars and motorcycles (November) and the Macao International Marathon (December). At the end of 2005 there were 44 hotels of the designation of two-stars and above. A total of 10,832 hotel rooms were available in December 2005. Average per caput visitor spending (excluding gambling) in 2006 was 1,610 patacas. Total visitor arrivals rose from 22.0m. in 2006 to 27.0m. in 2007, the majority of visitors travelling from the People's Republic of China and from Hong Kong. Receipts from tourism reached US $9,778m. in 2006.

Macao Government Tourist Office (MGTO): Alameda Dr Carlos d'Assumpção, 335–341, Edif. Hot Line, 12° andar; tel. 28315566; fax 28510104; e-mail mgto@macautourism.gov.mo; internet www.macautourism.gov.mo; Dir Eng. JOÃO MANUEL COSTA ANTUNES.

Instituto Cultural de Macau: Praça do Tap Seac, Edif. do Instituto Cultural,; tel. 28366866; fax 28366899; e-mail postoffice@icm.gov.mo; internet www.icm.gov.mo; f. 1982; organizes performances, concerts, exhibitions, festivals, etc.; library facilities; Pres. HEIDI HO.

Macau Hotel Association: Rua Luís Gonzaga Gomes s/n, Bl. IV, r/c, Centro de Actividades Turísticas, Cabinet A; tel. 28703416; fax 28703415; e-mail nhacmo@macau.ctm.net; internet www.macauhotel.org; Chair. JOHNSON CHAN.

Sociedade de Turismo e Diversões de Macau (STDM), SARL: Hotel Lisboa, 9F, Avda de Lisboa; tel. 28574266; fax 28562285; e-mail stdmmdof@macau.ctm.net; fmrly operated 11 casinos; since STDM's monopoly franchise ended in 2002, operation of the casinos has been handled by STDM's subsidiary Sociedade de Jogos de Macau (SJM); Man. Dir Dr STANLEY HO.

CHINA (TAIWAN)

Introductory Survey

Location, Climate, Language, Religion, Flag, Capital

The Republic of China has, since 1949, been confined mainly to the province of Taiwan (comprising one large island and several much smaller ones), which lies off the south-east coast of the Chinese mainland. The territory under the Republic's effective jurisdiction consists of the island of Taiwan (also known as Formosa) and nearby islands, including the P'enghu (Pescadores) group, together with a few other islands which lie just off the mainland and form part of the province of Fujian (Fukien), west of Taiwan. The largest of these is Kinmen (Jinmen), also known as Quemoy, which (with three smaller islands) is about 10 km from the port of Xiamen (Amoy), while five other islands under Taiwan's control, mainly Matsu (Mazu), lie further north, near Fuzhou. Taiwan itself is separated from the mainland by the Taiwan (Formosa) Strait, which is about 130 km (80 miles) wide at its narrowest point. The island's climate is one of rainy summers and mild winters. Average temperatures are about 15°C (59°F) in the winter and 26°C (79°F) in the summer. The average annual rainfall is 2,580 mm (102 in). The official language is Northern Chinese (Mandarin), but Taiwanese, a dialect based on the language of Fujian Province, is widely spoken. The predominant religions are Buddhism and Daoism (Taoism), but there are also adherents of I-kuan Tao, Christianity (mainly Roman Catholics and Protestants) and Islam. The philosophy of Confucianism has a large following. The national flag (proportions 2 by 3) is red, with a dark blue rectangular canton, containing a white sun, in the upper hoist. The capital is Taipei.

Recent History

China ceded Taiwan to Japan in 1895. The island remained under Japanese rule until the end of the Second World War in 1945, when it was returned to Chinese control, becoming a province of the Republic of China, then ruled by the Kuomintang (KMT, Nationalist Party). The leader of the KMT was Gen. Chiang Kai-shek, President of the Republic since 1928. The KMT Government's forces were defeated in 1949 by the Communist revolution in China. President Chiang and many of his supporters withdrew from the Chinese mainland to Taiwan, where they established a KMT regime in succession to their previous all-China administration. This regime continued to assert that it was the rightful Chinese Government, in opposition to the People's Republic of China, proclaimed by the victorious Communists in 1949. The Nationalists successfully resisted attacks by their Communist rivals, and declared that they intended to recover control of mainland China.

Although its effective control was limited to Taiwan, the KMT regime continued to be dominated by politicians who had formerly been in power on the mainland. Unable to replenish their mainland representation, the National Assembly (last elected fully in 1947) and other legislative organs extended their terms of office indefinitely, although fewer than one-half of the original members were alive on Taiwan by the 1980s. The political domination of the island by immigrants from the mainland caused some resentment among native Taiwanese, and led to demands for increased democratization and for the recognition of Taiwan as a state independent of China. The KMT consistently rejected demands for independence, restating the party's long-standing policy of seeking political reunification, although under KMT terms, with the mainland.

The KMT regime continued to represent China at the United Nations (and as a permanent member of the UN Security Council) until October 1971, when it was replaced by the People's Republic. After 1971 a number of countries broke off diplomatic relations with Taiwan and recognized the People's Republic. In mid-2007 the Taiwan Government was recognized by 25 countries. After its removal from the UN in 1971, Nationalist China was subsequently expelled from several other international organizations. In November 1991, however, as 'Chinese Taipei', Taiwan joined the Asia-Pacific Economic Co-operation (APEC) forum. In September 1992, under the name of the 'Separate Customs Territory of Taiwan, P'enghu, Kinmen and Matsu', Taiwan was granted observer status at the General Agreement on Tariffs and Trade (GATT) and was finally approved for membership of the successor body in September 2001: on 1 January 2002 Taiwan formally became a member of the World Trade Organization (WTO, see p. 396). In June 1995 Taiwan offered to make a donation of US $1,000m., to be used for the establishment of an international development fund, if the island were permitted to rejoin the UN. In February 2004 it was announced that Taiwan would become a member of the Commission for the Conservation and Management of Highly Migratory Fish Stocks in the Western and Central Pacific Ocean (responsible for implementing the 1995 UN Fish Stocks Agreement). Following its admission to the WTO, therefore, this represented the second recognition of Taiwan by an international organization. In September 2006, for the 14th consecutive year, the General Committee of the UN General Assembly rejected a proposal urging Taiwan's participation in the UN. Taiwan's leaders pledged to continue the island's campaign to gain re-entry, stating that henceforth they would make their application under the name of Taiwan, rather than the 'Republic of China'. In September 2007, however, the island's membership application, as Taiwan, was again rejected. The issue was submitted to Taiwanese voters in two referendums held in March 2008, but the results were declared invalid owing to the low level of voter participation (see below). In May 2003, meanwhile, the People's Republic of China strongly opposed a US proposal that Taiwan be permitted to participate in WHO. The People's Republic strongly reiterated its view in May 2007, when the World Health Assembly rejected for the 11th time the proposal by the Pacific nation of Palau that Taiwan be granted observer status in WHO.

In 1973 the Government of Taiwan rejected an offer from the People's Republic to hold secret discussions on the reunification of China. In October 1981 Taiwan rejected China's suggested terms for reunification, whereby Taiwan would become a 'special administrative region' and would have a substantial degree of autonomy, including the retention of its own armed forces. In 1983 China renewed its offer, including a guarantee to maintain the status quo in Taiwan for 100 years if the province agreed to reunification. In 1984, following the agreement between the People's Republic of China and the United Kingdom that China would regain sovereignty over the British colony of Hong Kong in 1997, mainland Chinese leaders urged Taiwan to accept similar proposals for reunification on the basis of 'one country—two systems'. The island's Government insisted that Taiwan would never negotiate with the People's Republic until the mainland regime renounced communism. In May 1986, however, the Government was forced to make direct contact with the Chinese Government for the first time, over the issue of a Taiwanese pilot who had defected to the mainland. In October 1987 the Government announced the repeal of the 38-year ban on visits to the mainland by Taiwanese citizens, with the exception of civil servants and military personnel. These regulations were relaxed in November 1998.

In April 1989 the Government announced that it was considering a 'one China, two governments' formula, whereby China would be a single country under two administrations, one in Beijing and one in Taipei. In May a delegation led by the Minister of Finance attended a meeting of the Asian Development Bank (ADB) in Beijing, as representatives of 'Taipei, China', demonstrating a considerable relaxation in Taiwan's stance. Reconciliation initiatives were abruptly halted, however, by the violent suppression of the pro-democracy movement in Beijing in June. In May 1990 a proposal by the President of Taiwan to open direct dialogue on a government-to-government basis with the People's Republic was rejected by China, which continued to maintain that it would negotiate only on a party-to-party basis with the KMT.

In February 1991 the recently formed National Unification Council (NUC), under the chairmanship of the President of Taiwan, put forward radical new proposals, whereby Taiwan and the People's Republic of China might recognize each other as separate political entities. In March a national unification programme, which incorporated the demand that Taiwan be acknowledged as an independent and equal entity, was approved by the Central Standing Committee of the KMT. The programme also included a proposal for direct postal, commercial and shipping links with the mainland.

In April 1991 a delegation from the Straits Exchange Foundation (SEF), established in late 1990 to deal with bilateral issues, travelled to Beijing for discussions, the first such delegation ever to visit the People's Republic. Also in April President Lee announced the end of the state of war with the People's Republic; 10 amendments to the Constitution adopted earlier that month by the National Assembly were promulgated on the following day. As the mainland Chinese Government continued to warn against independence for Taiwan, in September 1991 the island's President asserted that conditions were not appropriate for reunification with the mainland and that Taiwan was a de facto sovereign and autonomous country. In December the non-governmental Association for Relations across the Taiwan Straits (ARATS) was established in Beijing. In January 1992 the SEF protested to the People's Republic over the detention of a former pilot of the mainland air force who had defected to Taiwan in 1965 and, upon returning to his homeland for a family reunion in December 1991, had been arrested. He subsequently received a 15-year prison sentence.

In July 1992 the Taiwanese Government reiterated that it would not consider party-to-party talks with the mainland. In the same month President Lee Teng-hui urged the establishment of 'one country, one good system'. In mid-July statutes to permit the further expansion of economic and political links with the People's Republic were adopted by the Legislative Yuan. In August the vice-president of the mainland Red Cross travelled to the island, thus becoming the most senior representative of the People's Republic to visit Taiwan since 1949. Delegates from the SEF and ARATS met in Hong Kong in October 1992 for discussions. However, the Chairman of the Mainland Affairs Council insisted that the People's Republic renounce the use of military force prior to any dialogue on the reunification question.

In 1993 divisions between Taiwan's business sector and political groupings (the former advocating much closer links with the People's Republic, the latter urging greater caution) became evident. In January, and again later in the year, the Secretary-General of the SEF resigned, following disagreement with the Mainland Affairs Council. Historic talks between the Chairman of the SEF and of the ARATS were held in Singapore in April. Engaging in the highest level of contact since 1949, Taiwan and the People's Republic agreed on the establishment of a formal structure for future negotiations on economic and social issues.

Following a series of aircraft hijackings to Taiwan from the mainland, an SEF-ARATS meeting was held in Taiwan in December 1993, in an attempt to address the issue of the repatriation of hijackers. Further meetings between delegates of the SEF and ARATS were held in early 1994. In April, however, 24 Taiwanese tourists were among those robbed and killed on board a pleasure boat plying Qiandao Lake, in mainland China. In June three men were convicted of the murders and promptly executed.

In August 1994 the SEF-ARATS talks were resumed when Tang Shubei, Vice-Chairman and Secretary-General of the ARATS, flew to Taipei for discussions with his Taiwanese counterpart, Chiao Jen-ho. Tang thus became to date the most senior Communist Chinese official to visit the island. Although the visit was marred by opposition protesters, the two sides reached tentative agreement on several issues, including the repatriation of hijackers and illegal immigrants from Taiwan to the mainland. Procedures for the settlement of cross-Straits fishing disputes were also established. In mid-November relations were strained once again when, in an apparent accident during a training exercise, Taiwanese anti-aircraft shells landed on a mainland village, injuring several people. Nevertheless, in late November a further round of SEF-ARATS talks took place in Nanjing, at which agreement in principle on the procedure for the repatriation of hijackers and illegal immigrants was confirmed. Further progress was made at meetings in Beijing in January 1995. It was announced in March that the functions of the SEF were to be enhanced. To improve co-ordination, the SEF board of directors would henceforth include government officials, while meetings of the Mainland Affairs Council would be attended by officials of the SEF. In the same month the Mainland Affairs Council approved a resolution providing for the relaxation of restrictions on visits by mainland officials and civilians.

In 1995 President Jiang Zemin's Lunar New Year address, incorporating the mainland's 'eight-point' policy on Taiwan, was regarded as more conciliatory than hitherto. In April, in response, President Lee proposed a 'six-point' programme for cross-Straits relations: unification according to the reality of separate rules; increased exchanges on the basis of Chinese culture; increased economic and trade relations; admission to international organizations on an equal footing; the renunciation of the use of force against each other; and joint participation in Hong Kong and Macao affairs.

In May 1995 the SEF Chairman, Koo Chen-fu, and his mainland counterpart, Wang Daohan, formally agreed to meet in Beijing in July. In June, however, this proposed second session of senior-level negotiations was postponed by the ARATS, in protest at President Lee's recent visit to the USA. Tension between the two sides increased in July, when the People's Republic unexpectedly announced that it was about to conduct an eight-day programme of guided missile and artillery-firing tests off the northern coast of Taiwan. A second series of exercises took place in August. In January 1996 the Taiwanese Premier again urged the early resumption of cross-Straits dialogue. In February there were unconfirmed reports of the extensive mobilization of mainland troops. In the same month, upon his appointment as Chairman of the Mainland Affairs Council, Chang King-yuh pledged to attempt to improve relations with the mainland. In March the People's Republic began a new series of missile tests, including the firing of surface-to-surface missiles into coastal areas around Taiwan. Live artillery exercises continued in the Taiwan Strait until after the island's presidential election, arousing international concern.

In November 1996 the Mainland Affairs Council announced that the permanent stationing of mainland media representatives in Taiwan was to be permitted. President Lee's renewed offer to travel to the People's Republic was rejected and, despite repeated SEF requests, Tang Shubei of the ARATS continued to assert that Taiwan's pursuit of its 'two Chinas' policy (a reference to President Lee's attempts to raise the diplomatic profile of the island) prevented the resumption of cross-Straits discussions. In January 1997, however, as the reversion of the entrepôt of Hong Kong to Chinese sovereignty approached, shipping representatives of Taiwan and of the People's Republic reached a preliminary consensus on the establishment of direct sea links. Limited services resumed in April, thus ending a ban of 48 years. In July 1997, upon the reversion to Chinese sovereignty of the British colony of Hong Kong, President Lee firmly rejected the concept of 'one country, two systems' and any parallel with Taiwan.

The declaration by an ARATS official in January 1998 that Taiwan did not need to recognize the Government of the People's Republic as the central Government as a precondition for dialogue was regarded as a significant concession on the part of the mainland authorities. However, Taiwan continued to insist that China abandon its demand that talks be conducted under its 'one China' principle. In February the ARATS sent a letter to the SEF requesting the resumption of political and economic dialogue between the two sides, and inviting a senior SEF official to visit the mainland. The SEF responded positively to the invitation in March, and proposed that a delegation be sent to the People's Republic to discuss procedural details, prior to a visit to the mainland by the SEF Chairman.

In April 1998 a delegation of the SEF visited the People's Republic. Following negotiations with the ARATS, it was announced that the Chairman of the SEF would visit the People's Republic later in 1998 formally to resume the dialogue, which had been suspended since 1995. The arrest on the mainland in May 1998 of four Taiwanese business executives on charges of espionage, and their subsequent conviction, and the visit to Malaysia by the Taiwanese Premier, in April, threatened to reverse the recent improvement in relations. However, in July the Chinese Minister of Science and Technology visited Taiwan, the first such visit by a mainland Minister since the civil war. This was followed later in the month by a formal visit to Taiwan by the Deputy Secretary-General of the ARATS. The kidnap and murder in August in the People's Republic of a Taiwanese local government official caused serious concern for the Taiwanese authorities. In October Koo Chen-fu, the SEF Chairman, duly travelled to the People's Republic, where he held several meetings with his ARATS counterpart, Wang Daohan, met with President Jiang Zemin (the highest level of bilateral contact since 1949) and had discussions with other senior officials. A four-point agreement was reached, allowing for increased communications between the two sides.

In April 1999 President Lee reaffirmed that the People's Republic should recognize Taiwan as being of equal status, that cross-Straits negotiations should concentrate on practical issues and that reunification could take place only if the mainland were to become a democracy. An SEF group went to Beijing in March, and preliminary agreement was reached that the ARATS Chairman would visit Taiwan in either mid-September or mid-October. In August, however, the ARATS suspended contacts with the SEF, following President Lee's insistence on the 'two-state theory' (see below), and it was confirmed in October that Wang Daohan would not visit Taiwan while the island continued to adhere to the theory.

Meanwhile, China was becoming increasingly demonstrative in its opposition to Taiwan's inclusion in the US-led Theater Missile Defense (TMD) anti-missile system. Ballistic missiles were deployed in mainland coastal regions facing Taiwan, and fears were heightened within the international community in July 1999 when the People's Republic announced that it had developed a neutron bomb, after declaring itself ready for war should Taiwan attempt to gain independence. This declaration was prompted by a radio interview given by President Lee, during which he asserted that relations with the People's Republic were 'state-to-state'. Chinese military exercises took place in the Taiwan Strait later that month, following which Taiwan promised that it would not amend its Constitution to enshrine its claim to statehood in law. In August the USA reaffirmed its readiness to defend Taiwan against Chinese military action. Tension increased in late August when the KMT incorporated the 'two-state theory' into the party resolution, claiming that this would henceforth become the administrative guide-line and priority of the Taiwanese authorities. Later that month the Mainland Affairs Council announced that former Taiwan government officials involved in affairs related to national intelligence or secrets were not to be permitted to travel to China within three years of leaving their posts. In September, following a severe earthquake in Taiwan that killed or injured several thousand people, China was among the many countries to offer emergency assistance to the island, but Taiwan accused the People's Republic of contravening humanitarian principles by trying to force other countries to seek its approval before offering help. Relations became increasingly strained following the reversion of the Portuguese territory of Macao to Chinese sovereignty in December 1999. The People's Republic announced that reunification of the two sides of the Taiwan Strait would also be on the basis of 'one country, two systems'.

In February 2000 the People's Republic threatened to attack Taiwan if it indefinitely postponed reunification talks. The approval in the Legislative Yuan in March of a law providing for the first direct transport links between Taiwan's outlying islands and mainland China for 50 years did not substantially improve matters, and in April the Vice-President-elect, Annette Lu, was denounced by the Chinese media after she made 'separatist' remarks, televised in Hong Kong, declaring that Taiwan was only a 'remote relative and close neighbour' of China. A Taiwanese opposition group subsequently endorsed a motion to dismiss Lu for putting the island at risk by provoking China. President Chen Shui-bian offered to compromise and to reopen negotiations on the basis that each side was free to interpret the 'one China' formula as it saw fit. Chinese Premier Zhu Rongji rejected the suggestion, effectively dispelling all hopes of restarting negotiations in the near future.

In October 2000 China published a policy document on its national defence, which confirmed that the People's Republic would use force to prevent Taiwanese secession, to stop occupation of the island, and also in the event of Taiwan indefinitely postponing reunification with the mainland. In November, however, there were signs of an improvement in relations when Wu Po-hsiung, the Vice-Chairman of the KMT, travelled to Beijing and met unofficially with Chinese Vice-Premier Qian Qichen. Wu was the most senior KMT official to visit mainland China for more than 50 years. During the meeting both sides agreed to hold important academic forums to discuss cross-Straits relations. However, Qian emphasized the importance of Taiwan's recognition of the 'one China' principle before official negotiations could resume.

Also in November 2000, Taiwan announced that journalists from the People's Republic were to be granted permission to stay in Taiwan for periods of up to one month, during which time they would be invited to attend any press conferences called by the President's office and the Executive Yuan. In the following month plans were announced for 'mini three links' with China, providing for direct trade, transport and postal links between Kinmen and Matsu islands and the mainland, albeit subject to rigorous security checks. In early January 2001 groups sailed from Kinmen and Matsu to Xiamen and Fuzhou, respectively, in the People's Republic. China's response toward the initiative was guarded.

Cross-Straits relations were strained in April 2001 by a visit to Taiwan by the Dalai Lama, the exiled spiritual leader of Tibet. Despite such tensions, economic links between Taiwan and the mainland continued to develop, with many Taiwanese companies investing in the mainland. In August President Chen endorsed a plan by a special advisory committee to expand commercial links with the People's Republic, a reversal of the previous Government's 'no haste, be patient' policy of limiting trade with the mainland for fear of becoming over-dependent on exchanges with Taiwan. In September the Taiwanese Government approved a proposal allowing Chinese investment in Taiwan's land and property market, as part of the new opening to the mainland. The limit on individual investments in the mainland was formally removed in November; restrictions on direct remits to and from the mainland via Taiwanese banks were also abolished.

In October 2001 Taiwan boycotted the APEC summit meeting in Shanghai, following China's refusal to allow Taiwan's chosen delegate, former Vice-President Li Yuan-tsu, to attend, on the grounds that he was not an 'economic' official. Despite this, the opposition Democratic Progressive Party (DPP—see below) deleted from its charter a vow to achieve the island's formal independence, since it was already a de facto separate entity. The change indicated a growing acceptance of the status quo by the DPP. It was hoped that the acceptance of China and Taiwan into the WTO in mid-November would improve cross-Straits relations, by enhancing communications in the field of trade.

In January 2002 the Government announced a new passport design incorporating the words 'issued in Taiwan' on the cover, ostensibly to differentiate clearly Taiwanese passports from mainland ones. Also in January the Government announced a list of more than 2,000 items that would thenceforth be legally importable from the mainland, mostly consumer but also agricultural goods, and at the same time facilitated direct transport links with the mainland. Later in the month, Chinese Vice-Premier Qian Qichen invited members of the DPP to visit the mainland, stating that most DPP members were not independence activists. President Chen welcomed Qian's remarks. In March China announced that, for the first time, two Taiwanese banks would be allowed to open offices on the mainland. Taiwan would also allow mainland banks to establish offices on the island. The Taiwanese Government also eased restrictions on the island's companies investing in computer-chip manufacturing on the mainland, although controls would remain on the number of plants established and type of chips produced, owing to fears that Taiwan's valuable electronics industry might become dependent on the mainland, and that the mainland might gain access to advanced semiconductor technology used to guide missiles.

In May 2002 an official Chinese newspaper published the mainland's strongest criticism to date of President Chen, describing him as a 'troublemaker' who sought to damage bilateral relations, and criticizing his efforts to promote a separate 'Taiwanese' identity. None the less, Taiwan reluctantly allowed China to ship more than 2,300 metric tons of water to its outlying islands in order to help relieve the worst drought in many years, an arrangement that would have been unthinkable a few years previously. Furthermore, two state-owned oil companies from both sides agreed upon a joint venture to explore petroleum and gas deposits in the straits. Taiwan's arrest in June of one of its own military officers for passing military secrets to China failed to damage these improving commercial links.

In July 2002 the Taiwanese Ministry of National Defense warned in a biannual report that China's military spending was accelerating rapidly and that it would possess 600 short-range missiles targeting the island by 2005. President Chen further incensed the mainland in early August 2002 by supporting demands for a referendum to determine the island's future, and referring to China and Taiwan as two countries. Taiwan then cancelled planned military exercises as a gesture of good faith, but Chen's comments delayed the introduction of direct transport links. At the end of July the Government announced that Chinese products could be advertised on the island and that Chinese employees of Taiwanese or foreign companies would be allowed to work in Taiwan. A Taiwanese semiconductor manufacturer, the world's largest, also announced plans to build a new factory on the Chinese mainland, in Shanghai.

Bilateral relations remained volatile, however, and in September 2002 Chen described China's threats against the island as a form of 'terrorism'. China accused Taiwan of allowing the banned Falun Gong sect to use the island as a base for disrupting Chinese television and satellite broadcasts. A Chinese official stated that the source of the sect's propaganda transmissions had been traced to the island, but a Taiwanese investigation revealed no evidence of such activity, and the unofficial leader of Falun Gong in Taiwan, Chang Ching-hsi, emphasized that the sect had no desire to exacerbate the tensions in cross-Straits relations.

Attempts to restore direct transport links between China and Taiwan gained momentum in October 2002 when the People's Republic abandoned the 'one China' principle as a condition for such links and agreed that these could be described as 'cross-Straits' rather than 'domestic'. However, two weeks later President Chen seemingly retreated from the proposal. During 2002 Taiwan and China acquired advanced weaponry from the USA and Russia respectively. In October two Chinese ships and a submarine sailed around the east coast of Taiwan en route to the South China Sea, where the Chinese navy was conducting military exercises. The voyage served to warn Taiwan that Chinese forces were in a position to encircle the island if necessary.

In January 2003 President Chen stated that Taiwan was a sovereign state, and would never accept a Hong Kong-style solution nor federate with the mainland. Vice-President Lu described China as being of a 'terrorist nature', referring to its missile build-up across the Taiwan Strait and to its coercive diplomacy. In late January, none the less, the first Taiwanese airliner in more than 50 years flew to mainland China, via Hong Kong, landing in Shanghai. The flight was one of 16 charter operations organized by the Taiwanese carrier, China Airlines (CAL), to transport Taiwanese visitors in China home for Chinese New Year celebrations. In February the Minister of National Defense stated that Taiwan would not reduce weapons purchases from the USA in return for the dismantling of Chinese missiles targeting the island. His remarks came in response to Chinese President Jiang Zemin's offer of such an arrangement, made to US President George W. Bush in October 2002.

An outbreak on the mainland of a pneumonia-like virus, Severe Acute Respiratory Syndrome (SARS), spread to Taiwan in early 2003. Taiwan accused the Chinese authorities of concealing the seriousness of the outbreak, thereby endangering Taiwan and neighbouring countries. In May Taiwan formally rejected an aid programme offered by China to assist in countering the SARS epidemic on the island. Also in May, China continued to stress its opposition to Taiwan's membership of WHO at a meeting of the World Health Assembly in Geneva, Switzerland. However, China did agree to Taiwan's participation in a global conference on SARS in June 2003.

Despite increased trade and educational links, cross-Straits relations continued to be dominated by political tensions. In August 2003 the island's authorities arrested two Taiwanese citizens and a Taiwanese American on charges of spying for China. Also in August, a Chinese surveillance vessel was seen to the north of Taiwan, in advance of large-scale military exercises in that area. Military exercises simulating an attack on Taiwan by China were conducted in September. Taiwan's announcement in the same month that it was to issue new passports for its citizens, which for the first time would have the word 'Taiwan' printed on the front (see above) heightened cross-Straits tensions, as did mass protests in Taipei demanding that the name 'Taiwan' be used officially by government agencies and private companies (see below). In October the island's legislature approved the so-called Act Governing Relations between Peoples of the Taiwan Area and the Mainland Area, which was to provide a framework for the regulation of travel and business links between Taiwan and the mainland.

In November 2003 tensions between Taiwan and the mainland were further exacerbated after Taiwan's legislature approved a bill allowing referendums to take place on the island (see below). Although the legislation in its final version prohibited a vote on Taiwan's sovereignty except in the event of an external attack, China feared that the new law might lead to the holding of a vote on Taiwan's independence. An official at China's Taiwan Affairs Office warned that President Chen would be 'risking war' should he initiate any move towards Taiwanese independence. In December the issue of Taiwan dominated a visit by Chinese Premier Wen Jiabao to Washington, DC, with Wen seeking assurance from the USA that it would not support moves towards Taiwanese independence, following the introduction of the new referendum law. President Chen defended plans to hold a referendum in March 2004 on the subject of a proposed request to China that it remove hundreds of missiles aimed at the island. In January 2004 President Chen suggested that the referendum might be presented as an opportunity to reduce bilateral tensions. He stated that the referendum might include 'counter-proposals' such as direct transport links between Taiwan and China if the latter were to withdraw its missiles. In February, furthermore, President Chen suggested the establishment of a demilitarized zone between the mainland and Taiwan in order to facilitate joint discussions. Chen also stated that he would not declare Taiwanese independence, were he to win the forthcoming presidential election, although his attitude to relations with the Chinese mainland, for example in rejecting the 'one country, two systems' model advocated by China, was regarded by some as tantamount to stating that independence already existed.

The Chinese Government did not attempt directly to influence the presidential election held in March 2004, resulting in a narrow victory for Chen. However, following widespread controversy and protests over the election result, the Chinese Government stated that it would not tolerate social instability in Taiwan. In the event, President Chen's referendum, held concurrently with the presidential election, did not produce a valid result (see below). In July a senior Chinese official warned of an attack on Taiwan by 2008, if Chen were to proceed with constitutional reforms outlined in the Taiwanese President's inaugural speech in May 2004, despite pledges from Chen that the amendments would not address the question of Taiwan's sovereignty. In August President Chen cancelled a military exercise scheduled for September after China removed 3,000 troops from the island of Dongshan owing to a typhoon threat. In December the Standing Committee of China's NPC approved a draft of anti-secession legislation aimed at preventing Taiwan from declaring independence. The legislation was approved by the third plenum of the 10th NPC in March 2005.

In January 2005 it was announced that for the first time direct flights between Taipei and the Chinese mainland would be permitted over the forthcoming Lunar New Year period. The first direct commercial flights between Taipei and Beijing duly took place at the end of the month. In late April, in the first such visit since 1949, the Chairman of the opposition KMT, Lien Chan, embarked upon an official visit to the mainland, where he and Chinese President Hu Jintao agreed to remain opposed to Taiwanese independence. Following Chan's visit, in May 2005 the Government of the People's Republic offered the Taiwanese Government a pair of pandas (traditionally China's most esteemed diplomatic gift), along with a series of concessions that included the removal of fruit import tariffs and the easing of restrictions for mainland Chinese tourists visiting Taiwan. (The fruit tariffs were abolished by the Chinese Government in August.) Concern was voiced by the island's Government, however, that acceptance of the pandas might compromise Taiwanese sovereignty and might be misinterpreted as a move towards unification; nevertheless, a significant proportion of the island's population, supported by the opposition 'pan-blue' alliance (see below), was believed to want Taiwan to receive the pandas. (The offer was eventually rejected by Taiwan's Council of Agriculture in March 2006, on the grounds that the pandas would not receive the necessary care in Taiwan.) Also in May 2005 James Soong, leader of the People First Party (PFP), another opposition party and an ally of the KMT within the 'pan-blue' alliance, visited the People's Republic and met with President Hu. In June the Chinese Government announced that regulations restricting employment by Chinese companies of residents of Taiwan (and Hong Kong and Macao) were to be relaxed. The approval of a series of constitutional amendments by the Taiwanese National Assembly in June (see below) enabled future constitutional changes, including any declaration of independence, to be endorsed by referendum.

In a New Year speech on 1 January 2006 President Chen reiterated his commitment to achieving a new constitution, ratified by referendum, by 2008, with the implication that this would enshrine Taiwan's independence and sovereignty. This objective was repeated in further remarks by Chen later that month, this time on the occasion of the Chinese Lunar New Year, in which Chen also proposed the abolition of the National Unification Council, along with the guidelines for unification proposed by the council and accepted by the Executive Yuan in

1991. He also stated his intention of reapplying for membership of the UN under the name of 'Taiwan', instead of the 'Republic of China'. In response, a spokesman for China's Taiwan Affairs Office described President Chen as a 'troublemaker and saboteur'. In mid-March 2006 tens of thousands of protesters participated in a rally in Taipei to protest against the perceived threat of domination by the People's Republic. In April former KMT Chairman Lien Chan made a further controversial trip to Beijing to meet with President Hu Jintao, who publicly urged the restoration of talks at the highest level between the People's Republic and Taiwan. In June it was announced that up to 168 charter passenger flights would operate between the island and the mainland at four key holiday periods every year and that cargo and humanitarian flights would be licensed on an individual basis. (One month later the first non-stop cargo charter flight was made from Taiwan to Shanghai.) At a two-day Conference on Sustaining Taiwan's Economic Development, held in July, it was decided that investment limits might be relaxed for some Taiwanese companies operating on the mainland. However, during the economic forum President Chen stressed the importance of Taiwan's national development and declared that cross-Straits trade should be viewed as part of the 'entire framework of international trade'. In August the Mainland Affairs Council established the Taiwan Strait Tourism and Travel Association, in response to China's foundation earlier in the month of the Cross-Strait Tourism Exchange Association.

Meanwhile, bilateral economic and trading links continued to expand unabated; by mid-2006 official Chinese statistics showed that 70,256 Taiwanese companies had invested on the mainland (excluding companies that had invested via third territories, such as Hong Kong). This investment was estimated to have reached a total of US $50,800m., despite measures introduced by the Taiwanese Government in May to tighten the management of cross-Straits investment links. As concerns remained that many of the island's business people were contravening existing Taiwanese investment regulations, the Government continued to face heavy pressure from the business community, which was becoming increasingly frustrated at the inability of Taiwanese companies to deal more directly with China. In September the Mainland Affairs Council announced that it was to raise the limit on the number of Chinese visitors attending business meetings in Taiwan from 30 to 50. By the end of the year, furthermore, tourists from the mainland would be able to visit Taiwan without first passing through a third location. Despite these conciliatory overtures, Taiwan continued to express concern over the increase in Chinese military strength; in early September President Chen was quoted as declaring that Taiwan would be in a position to win a 'decisive battle' over China by 2015, despite an increase in the number of missiles being deployed by the mainland against Taiwan, rising at the rate of 120 annually. The Chinese Government, meanwhile, continued to encourage the development of closer relations with Taiwan, particularly in the fields of tourism and financial exchanges. In November 2006 a spokesman from the mainland's Taiwan Affairs Office urged the island to loosen its control over cross-Straits tourism and also to ensure that financial exchanges improved. Nevertheless, in a defence document published in December China described Taiwan as a 'major threat'.

Cross-Straits relations suffered further in January 2007, when President Chen used his New Year speech to reiterate his views on Taiwan's status, declaring that the island's sovereignty belonged to its people. He was immediately accused by a Chinese government spokesman of attempting to damage relations with the mainland. In the same month bilateral tensions were renewed when Taiwan announced revisions to school history textbooks, in which references to 'the mainland' and 'our country' were to be replaced by simply 'China', thus implying that Taiwan and China were not part of the same country, with a common history. Furthermore, in February the name of the island's postal service, Chunghwa Post, was changed to Taiwan Post; two other state-owned companies were reported to be including 'Taiwan' in their names. In March the Taiwanese President's confirmation that he wished the island to pursue independence, draft a new constitution and change its official designation from the 'Republic of China' to Taiwan prompted the mainland Chinese Minister of Foreign Affairs to refer to such statements as 'criminal'. On the same day the Chinese Premier, Wen Jiabao, expressed a willingness to open a dialogue with Taiwan on the condition that the latter recognized the 'one China' principle. Soon after, it was reported that in early February Taiwan had test-fired a missile that had a range of 1,000 km and was therefore capable of reaching Shanghai or Hong Kong. However, the Taiwanese Government declined to confirm reports that such a missile test had been conducted. In a further development, Taiwan's National Day celebrations in October featured a parade that displayed its military capabilities, including a ship-to-ship missile and anti-ballistic missile. The event, the first of its kind since the early 1990s, appeared to constitute a response to the perceived threat of military action from the mainland. Members of the political opposition were reported to be planning a boycott of events in protest at Chen's attempts to alter the island's designation to Taiwan (see below). Also in October, at the 17th CCP Congress, the Chinese President, Hu Jintao, reaffirmed Premier Wen's position, stressing the need for a dialogue to attain 'peaceful reunification'. Meanwhile, preparations in Beijing for the 2008 Olympic Games were a source of further tension, with Taiwan refusing to accept the proposed route of the Olympic torch in April 2007, based on the implications of an itinerary that sent the torch to Hong Kong and Macao after Taiwan; for Taiwan's Olympic Committee, this 'domestic route' represented an 'attempt to downgrade (Taiwan's) sovereignty'. After several months of difficult discussions, the International Olympic Committee (IOC, see p. 315) announced in September that the route would omit Taiwan completely. In January 2008 the DPP presidential candidate, Frank Hsieh, stated that the matter of the expansion of direct cross-Straits flights would be resolved shortly, regardless of the outcome of the forthcoming presidential election.

In domestic affairs, in December 1972 legislative elections were held, for the first time in 24 years, to fill 53 seats in the National Assembly. The new members, elected for a fixed term of six years, joined 1,376 surviving 'life-term' members of the Assembly. President Chiang Kai-shek remained in office until his death in April 1975. He was succeeded as leader of the ruling KMT by his son, Gen. Chiang Ching-kuo, who had hitherto been Premier. Dr Yen Chia-kan, Vice-President since 1966, became the new President. In 1978 President Yen retired and was succeeded by Gen. Chiang. At elections for 71 seats in the Legislative Yuan in December 1983, the KMT won an overwhelming victory, confirming its dominance over the independent 'Tangwai' (non-party) candidates. In March 1984 President Chiang was re-elected for a second six-year term, and Lee Teng-hui, a former mayor of Taipei and a native Taiwanese, became Vice-President. President Chiang died in January 1988 and was succeeded by Lee Teng-hui.

In September 1986 135 leading opposition politicians formed the DPP, in defiance of the KMT's ban on the formation of new political parties. Partial elections to the National Assembly and the Legislative Yuan were held in December. The KMT achieved a decisive victory, but the DPP received about one-quarter of the total votes, and more than doubled the non-KMT representation. In February 1987 the KMT began to implement a programme of political reform. Martial law (in force since 1949) was replaced by the National Security Law in July and, under the terms of the new legislation, political parties other than the KMT were permitted, and civilians were removed from the jurisdiction of military courts. In April seven major posts in a reorganization of the Executive Yuan were allocated to reformist members of the KMT. In November 1987 the second annual Congress of the DPP approved a resolution declaring that Taiwanese citizens had the right to advocate independence. In January 1988, however, two opposition activists were imprisoned, on charges of sedition, for voicing such demands.

In February 1988 a plan to restructure the legislative bodies was approved by the Central Standing Committee of the KMT. Voluntary resignations were to be sought from 'life-term' members of the Legislative Yuan and National Assembly, and seats were no longer to be reserved for representatives of mainland constituencies. The 13th national Congress of the KMT was held in July. Following a decision to hold free elections for two-thirds of the members of the KMT's Central Committee, numerous new members were elected, and the proportion of native Taiwanese increased sharply. In January 1989 three legislative measures were enacted: a revision of regulations concerning the registration of political parties; a retirement plan for those members of the three legislative assemblies who had been elected by mainland constituencies in 1947; and a new law aiming to give greater autonomy to the Taiwan Provincial Government (which retained responsibility for the general administration of the island, with the exception of the cities of Taipei and Kaohsiung) and the Provincial Assembly. In the following month the KMT became the first political party to register under the new legislation.

Despite objections to the new laws, regarding the size of the retirement pensions being offered and the terms of the Civic Organizations Law (under which political parties were obliged to reject communism and any notion of official political independence for Taiwan), the DPP applied for official registration in April.

Partial elections to the Legislative Yuan and the Taiwan Provincial Assembly were held on 2 December 1989. A total of 101 seats in the Legislative Yuan were contested, with the KMT obtaining 72 seats and the DPP winning 21, thus securing the prerogative to propose legislation in the Legislative Yuan. In February 1990 the opening of the National Assembly's 35-day plenary session, convened every six years to elect the country's President, was disrupted by DPP members' violent action in a protest against the continuing domination of the Assembly by elderly KMT politicians, who had been elected on the Chinese mainland prior to 1949 and who had never been obliged to seek re-election. Many injuries resulted from clashes between riot police and demonstrators. In March 1990 DPP members were barred from the National Assembly for refusing to swear allegiance to the 'Republic of China', attempting instead to substitute 'Taiwan' upon taking the oath. Various amendments to the Temporary Provisions, which for more than 40 years had permitted the effective suspension of the Constitution, were approved by the National Assembly in mid-March. Revisions included measures to strengthen the position of the mainland-elected KMT members, who were granted new powers to initiate and veto legislation, and also an amendment to permit the National Assembly to meet annually. The revisions were opposed not only by the DPP but also by more moderate members of the KMT, and led to a large protest rally in Taipei, demanding the abolition of the National Assembly and the holding of direct presidential elections. Nevertheless, President Lee was duly re-elected, unopposed, by the National Assembly for a six-year term, two rival KMT candidates having withdrawn.

The National Affairs Conference (NAC) convened in June 1990 to discuss proposals for reform. A Constitutional Reform Planning Group was subsequently established. The NAC reached consensus on the issue of direct presidential elections, which would permit the citizens of Taiwan, rather than the members of the National Assembly, to select the Head of State. Meanwhile, the Council of Grand Justices had ruled that elderly members of the National Assembly and of the Legislative Yuan should step down by the end of 1991.

In October 1990 the NUC, chaired by President Lee, was formed. In the same month the Mainland Affairs Council, comprising heads of government departments and led by the Vice-Premier of the Executive Yuan, was founded. In December President Lee announced that Taiwan would formally end the state of war with the mainland; the declaration of emergency was to be rescinded by May 1991. Plans were announced for gradual constitutional reform, to be implemented in 1991–93. Meanwhile, in early December 1990 Huang Hwa, the leader of a faction of the DPP and independence activist, had received a 10-year prison sentence upon being found guilty of 'preparing to commit sedition'.

In April 1991 the National Assembly was convened, the session again being marred by violent clashes between KMT and DPP members. The DPP subsequently boycotted the session, arguing that a completely new constitution should be introduced and that elderly KMT delegates, who did not represent Taiwan constituencies, should not have the right to make amendments to the existing Constitution. Some 20,000 demonstrators attended a DPP-organized protest march. Nevertheless, the National Assembly duly approved the constitutional amendments, and at midnight on 30 April the 'period of mobilization for the suppression of the Communist rebellion' and the Temporary Provisions were formally terminated. The existence, but not the legitimacy, of the Government of the People's Republic was officially acknowledged by President Lee. Furthermore, Taiwan remained committed to its 'one China' policy. In May 1991 widespread protests following the arrest of four advocates of independence for Taiwan led to the abolition of the Statute of Punishment for Sedition. The law had been adopted in 1949 and had been frequently employed by the KMT to suppress political dissent.

A senior UN official visited the island in August 1991, the first trip by such a representative since Taiwan's withdrawal from the organization in 1971. Large-scale rallies to demand the holding of a referendum on the issue of Taiwan's readmission to the UN as an independent state took place in September and October, resulting in clashes between demonstrators and the security forces.

In August 1991 the opposition DPP officially announced its alternative draft constitution for 'Taiwan', rather than for the 'Republic of China', thus acknowledging the de facto position regarding sovereignty. In September, after being reinstated in the Legislative Yuan, Huang Hsin-chieh, the Chairman of the DPP, relinquished his seat in the legislature and urged other senior deputies to do likewise. Huang had been deprived of his seat and imprisoned in 1980, following his conviction on charges of sedition. At the party congress in October 1991, Huang was replaced as DPP Chairman by Hsu Hsin-liang. The DPP congress adopted a resolution henceforth to advocate the establishment of 'the Republic of Taiwan', and urged the Government to declare the island's independence.

Elections to the new 405-member National Assembly, which was to be responsible for amending the Constitution, were held in December 1991. The 225 seats open to direct election were widely contested. The campaign was dominated by the issue of Taiwan's possible independence. The opposition's independence proposal was overwhelmingly rejected by the electorate, the DPP suffering a humiliating defeat. The KMT secured a total of 318 seats (179 of which were won by direct election), while the DPP won 75 seats (41 by direct election). All elderly mainland-elected delegates were obliged to relinquish their seats. In February 1992 20,000 demonstrators protested against the sedition laws and demanded a referendum on the issue of independence.

In March 1992, at a plenary session of the KMT Central Committee, it was agreed to reduce the President's term of office from six to four years. The principal question of arrangements for future presidential elections, however, remained unresolved. In April street demonstrations were organized by the DPP to support demands for direct presidential elections. In May the National Assembly adopted eight amendments to the Constitution, one of which empowered the President to appoint members of the Control Yuan.

Taiwan's first full elections since the establishment of Nationalist rule in 1949 were held in December 1992. The KMT retained 102 of the 161 seats in the Legislative Yuan. The DPP, however, garnered 31% of the votes and more than doubled its representation in the legislature, winning 50 seats. Following this set-back, the Premier and the KMT Secretary-General resigned. In February 1993 Lien Chan, hitherto Governor of Taiwan Province, became the island's first Premier of Taiwanese descent.

In May 1993 about 30 conservative rebels resigned from the KMT, and formed the New Alliance Nationalist Party. Furthermore, in June the Government was defeated in the Legislative Yuan, when a group of KMT deputies voted with the opposition to approve legislation on financial disclosure requirements for elected and appointed public officials. The unity of the KMT was further undermined in August, when six dissident legislators belonging to the New Kuomintang Alliance, which had registered as a political group in March, announced their decision to leave the ruling party in order to establish the New Party (NP). Nevertheless, in August 1993, at the 14th KMT Congress, Lee Teng-hui was re-elected Chairman of the party. A new 31-member Central Standing Committee and 210-member Central Committee, comprising mainly Lee's supporters, were selected. In a conciliatory gesture by the KMT Chairman, four vice-chairmanships were created, the new positions being filled by representatives of different factions of the party.

In September 1993, following a series of bribery scandals, the Executive Yuan approved measures to combat corruption. The administrative reform plan included stricter supervision of public officials and harsher penalties for those found guilty of misconduct. In the same month a KMT member of the Legislative Yuan was sentenced to 14 years' imprisonment for bribery of voters during the 1992 election campaign; similar convictions followed. At local government elections held in November 1993, although its share of the votes declined, the KMT secured 15 of the 23 posts at stake. The DPP, which accused the KMT of malpractice, won only six posts, despite receiving a substantial proportion of the votes; it retained control of Taipei County. Following allegations of extensive bribery at further local polls in early 1994 (at which the DPP and independent candidates made strong gains), the Ministry of Justice intensified its campaign against corruption. Proposals for constitutional amendments to permit the direct election in 1996 of the Taiwanese President by popular vote (rather than by electoral college) and to limit the powers of the Premier were approved by the National Assembly in July 1994.

At gubernatorial and mayoral elections in December 1994 the DPP took control of the Taipei mayoralty, in the first such direct polls for 30 years, while the KMT succeeded in retaining the provincial governorship of Taiwan, in the first ever popular election for the post, and the mayoralty of Kaohsiung. The NP established itself as a major political force, its candidate for the mayoralty of Taipei receiving more votes than the KMT incumbent.

Elections to the Legislative Yuan were held on 2 December 1995. A major campaign issue was that of corruption, allegations of malpractice and indictments having reached alarming levels. The KMT's strength declined to 84 of the 164 seats, the party faring particularly badly in Taipei. The DPP increased its representation to 53 seats. The NP, which favoured reconciliation with the mainland, secured 21 seats. In mid-March a DPP demonstration on the streets of Taipei, in support of demands for Taiwan's independence, was attended by 50,000 protesters. At Taiwan's first direct presidential election, held on 23 March 1996, the incumbent President Lee received 54.0% of the votes cast, thus securing his re-election for a four-year term. At the concurrent elections for the National Assembly, the KMT took 183 of the 334 seats. The DPP won 99 seats and the NP 46 seats. The Chairman of the DPP, Shih Ming-teh, resigned and Hsu Hsin-liang, who had resigned in November 1993, subsequently returned to the post.

In June 1996 the President's announcement of the composition of the new Executive Yuan aroused much controversy. Although several members retained their previous portfolios, the President (apparently under pressure from within the KMT and disregarding public concern at the rising levels of corruption and organized crime) demoted the popular Ministers of Justice, and of Transportation and Communications, who had exposed malpractice and initiated campaigns against corruption. Other changes included the replacement of the Minister of Foreign Affairs by John Chang, the grandson of Chiang Kai-shek. The most controversial nomination, however, was the reappointment as Premier of Lien Chan, despite his recent election as the island's Vice-President. As fears of a constitutional crisis grew, opposition members of the Legislative Yuan, along with a number of KMT delegates, demanded that the President submit the membership of the Executive Yuan to the legislature for approval, and threatened to boycott the chamber.

In December 1996 the multi-party National Development Conference (NDC), established to review the island's political system, held its inaugural meeting. The convention approved KMT proposals to abolish the Legislative Yuan's right to confirm the President's choice of Premier, to permit the legislature to introduce motions of no confidence in the Premier and to empower the President to dismiss the legislature. The Provincial Governor, (James) Soong Chu-yu, subsequently tendered his resignation in protest at the NDC's recommendations that elections for the provincial governorship and assembly be abolished, as the first stage of the dissolution of the provincial apparatus. In January 1997 President Lee refused to accept the Governor's resignation, but the affair drew attention to the uneasy relationship between the island's President and its Governor, and brought to the fore the question of reunification with the mainland. In July the National Assembly approved a series of constitutional reforms, implementing the NDC's recommendations.

In early May 1997 more than 50,000 demonstrators, protesting against the problem of increasing crime (particularly crimes of violence), demanded the resignation of President Lee. Three members of the Executive Yuan subsequently resigned. The appointment of Yeh Chin-feng as Minister of the Interior (the first woman to oversee Taiwan's police force) did little to appease the public, which remained highly suspicious of the alleged connections between senior politicians and the perpetrators of organized crime. In mid-May thousands of protesters, despairing of the rapid deterioration in social order, again took to the streets of Taipei, renewing their challenge to President Lee's leadership and demanding the immediate resignation of Premier Lien Chan. In late June a 'Say No to China' rally attracted as many as 70,000 supporters.

In August 1997 Vincent Siew, former Chairman of the Council for Economic Planning and Development and also of the Mainland Affairs Council, replaced Lien Chan as Premier (Lien Chan retained the post of Vice-President), and John Chang was appointed Vice-Premier. In the same month President Lee was re-elected unopposed as Chairman of the ruling KMT. The KMT experienced a serious set-back in elections at mayoral and magistrate levels, held in November 1997. The DPP, which had campaigned on a platform of more open government, won 12 of the 23 constituency posts contested, while the KMT achieved only eight posts. Consequently, more than 70% of Taiwan's population was to come under DPP administration. Following the KMT's poor performance in the ballot, the Secretary-General of the party resigned, and was replaced by John Chang. A major reorganization of the party followed.

At local elections held in January 1998, the KMT won an overwhelming majority of the seats contested, while the DPP, in a reversal of fortune, performed badly. In April the Minister of Justice tendered, and then subsequently withdrew, his resignation, claiming that lawmakers with connections to organized crime were exerting pressure on the Government to dismiss him. However, in July he was forced to resign, following his mishandling of an alleged scandal concerning the acting head of the Investigation Bureau.

In June 1998 the first-ever direct election for the leadership of the DPP was held. Lin Yi-hsiung won a convincing victory, assuming the chairmanship of the party in August. Meanwhile, in local elections in June, the KMT suffered a set-back, winning fewer than 50% of the seats contested. Independent candidates performed well. In August 17 new members were elected to the KMT Central Standing Committee, the 16 others being appointed by President Lee.

Elections to the newly expanded 225-member Legislative Yuan took place on 5 December 1998. The KMT won 46.4% of the votes cast, securing 125 seats, the DPP received 29.6% of the votes and won 72 seats, while the pro-unification NP secured only 7.1% of the votes and 11 seats. The New Nation Alliance, a breakaway group from the DPP (formed in September), won only one seat (with 1.6% of the votes cast). The KMT's victory was widely attributed to its management of the economy, in view of the Asian financial crisis, the developments in cross-Straits dialogue and a decline in factionalism within the party in 1998. In the election (held simultaneously) to select the mayor of Taipei, the KMT candidate, Ma Ying-jeou, a popular former Minister of Justice, defeated the DPP incumbent, Chen Shui-bian. However, Frank Hsieh, the DPP candidate, won the office of mayor of Kaohsiung. The KMT retained control of both city councils.

Chiou I-jen resigned as Secretary-General of the DPP in December 1998 and was replaced by Yu Shyi-kun. Later that month Chao Shu-po, a Minister without Portfolio, was appointed Governor of Taiwan Province, replacing the elected incumbent, James Soong, as part of the plans to dismantle the provincial government, agreed in 1997. In March 1999 an unprecedented vote of no confidence in the leadership of Premier Vincent Siew was defeated in the Legislative Yuan. The motion was presented by the opposition following Siew's reversal of his earlier position and his decision to reduce the tax on share transactions, apparently as a result of pressure from President Lee. The National Assembly approved a controversial constitutional amendment on 4 September, which, *inter alia*, extended the terms of the deputies from May 2000 to June 2002. Election to the Assembly was henceforth to be on the basis of party proportional representation. Shortly afterwards, the KMT leadership expelled the Speaker of the National Assembly, Su Nan-cheng, from the party on the grounds that he had violated its policy on the tenure extension, thereby also removing him from his parliamentary seat and the post of Speaker. There was widespread dissatisfaction regarding the National Assembly's action, and in March 2000 the Council of Grand Justices of the Judicial Yuan ruled it to be unconstitutional. Later that month the DPP and the KMT reached an agreement on the abolition of the National Assembly and the cancellation of elections scheduled for early May. In April the National Assembly convened, and approved a series of constitutional amendments, which effectively deprived the body of most of its powers, and reduced it to an *ad hoc* institution. The powers to initiate constitutional amendments, to impeach the President or Vice-President and to approve the appointment of senior officials were transferred to the Legislative Yuan. The National Assembly was to retain the functions of ratifying constitutional amendments and impeachment proceedings, in which case 300 delegates, appointed by political parties according to a system of proportional representation, would convene for a session of a maximum duration of one month.

In November 1999 it was announced that a presidential election was to be held in March 2000. Five candidates registered: Lien Chan (with Vincent Siew as candidate for Vice-

President) was the KMT nominee, while Chen Shui-bian, a former mayor of Taipei, was to stand for the DPP (with the feminist Annette Lu as vice-presidential candidate), and Li Ao was to represent the NP; the former DPP Chairman, Hsu Hsin-liang, qualified as an independent candidate, as did James Soong who, along with a number of his supporters, was consequently expelled from the KMT, his prospects being jeopardized by charges of embezzlement. In January 2000 Lien Chan, in an attempt to regain the support of disillusioned voters, proposed that the KMT's extensive business holdings be placed in trust and that the party terminate its direct role in the management of the numerous companies in which it owned shares. The KMT adopted the proposal shortly afterwards. In a reflection of the tense political situation between Taiwan and China, Chen Shui-bian of the DPP modified the party's stance and pledged not to declare formal independence for the island unless Chinese forces attacked.

The presidential election, held on 18 March 2000, was won by Chen Shui-bian, who obtained 39.3% of the votes cast. James Soong, his closest rival, received 36.8% of the vote. (On the day after the election he founded the PFP, in an attempt to take advantage of his popularity.) Lien Chan of the KMT secured only 23.1% of the votes. The remaining candidates obtained less than 1%. (Upon his inauguration in May, Chen would thus become Taiwan's first non-KMT President since 1945.) Violence erupted as disappointed KMT supporters besieged the party's head-quarters, attributing the KMT's defeat to the leadership's expulsion of James Soong and the resultant division of the party. Lee Teng-hui subsequently accepted responsibility for the defeat and resigned from the chairmanship of the party. Lien Chan assumed the leadership. As the KMT continued to dominate the Legislative Yuan, however, the party did not entirely relinquish its influence, and in April 2000 it gave permission for Tang Fei, a KMT member and hitherto Minister of National Defense, to serve as Premier, although he was to be suspended from party activities while in the post. Following protracted negotiations, the membership of the new Executive Yuan, which incorporated 11 DPP members and 13 KMT members, was approved in early May. The incoming Government largely lacked ministerial experience. Furthermore, the DPP's lack of a legislative majority impeded the passage of favourable legislation. The size of the budget deficit also made it difficult for the DPP to fulfil specific electoral pledges on health, housing and education. In July Frank Hsieh replaced Lin Yi-hsiung as Chairman of the DPP.

In October 2000 Tang Fei resigned as Premier, ostensibly owing to ill health. It was suggested that his departure from the post was due to the Government's failure to agree upon the fate of Taiwan's fourth nuclear power plant, the DPP being opposed to the project. Vice-Premier Chang Chun-hsiung was appointed Premier, and a minor reorganization of the Executive Yuan was effected. Changes included the appointment of Yen Ching-chang as Minister of Finance, his predecessor having resigned following a sharp decline in the stock market.

Political disputes over the construction of Taiwan's fourth nuclear power plant intensified later in October 2000. The Minister of Economic Affairs, Lin Hsin-yi, was expelled from the KMT for 'seriously opposing KMT policies and impairing the people's interests' after he had demonstrated his support for the cancellation of the project. At the end of the month Chang Chun-hsiung announced that the Executive Yuan had decided to halt construction of the plant for financial and economic reasons. Although environmentalists were pleased, citing Taiwan's inability to process nuclear waste and to cope with accidents, the KMT reacted furiously, rejecting the Government's right to cancel a project approved by the legislature, and, together with the NP and the PFP, immediately began collecting legislators' signatures for the recall (censure) of Chen Shui-bian. The opposition was not mollified by a subsequent apology from Chen, and shortly afterwards the Legislative Yuan approved revised legislation on the process for presidential impeachment. Owing to the controversy, KMT member Vincent Siew refused to act as the President's representative to the annual APEC forum in Brunei in November and was replaced by Perng Fai-nan, the Governor of the Central Bank. The dispute became so serious that the business community issued an unprecedented public message that economic recovery should take priority over political differences, but in December some 10,000 protesters in Taipei demanded that Chen resign. In November the Government requested a constitutional interpretation on the issue from the Council of Grand Justices, which it agreed to be bound by.

The Council ruled in mid-January 2001 that the Government should have sought the legislature's approval before terminating the project, and in mid-February the Government decided immediately to resume construction of the plant. In March a minor government reorganization was effected. The most notable change was the appointment of Hu Ching-piao, hitherto a Minister without Portfolio, as Chairman of the Atomic Energy Council, replacing Hsia Der-yu.

In July 2001 the KMT issued a policy document arguing that Taiwan's best option in terms of its relations with China was to form a 'confederation' with the mainland—the furthest that any political party had moved in urging union with China. However, the KMT's Central Standing Committee refrained from adopting the proposal, reflecting the party's uncertainty over mainland policy. In August the Taiwan Solidarity Union (TSU) was formally established with the support of former President Lee Teng-hui, consisting of breakaway members of the KMT and DPP, led by the former Minister of the Interior, Huang Chu-wen. The party was formed in an attempt to secure for President Chen a majority in December's elections, an important goal given that the KMT had used its majority to block many of Chen's reforms during the previous one-year period. However, there were fears that the new party would drain support from Chen's DPP. Lee himself was expelled from the KMT in late September for supporting the TSU.

The last months of 2001 were dominated by campaigning for the legislative election. The KMT and PFP drew their support from those who had fled the mainland in 1949 and their descendants (approximately 15% of the population), while native Taiwanese (who comprised 65% of the population) supported the DPP and the TSU. Despite the economic recession, Chen's popularity rose in the period prior to the elections, amid rumours that the DPP would form a coalition to secure a majority.

At the elections held on 1 December 2001 the DPP emerged as the biggest single party in the new legislature, having won 36.6% of the votes cast and 87 seats, but failed to win a majority. The KMT won 31.3% of votes and 68 seats, thereby losing its dominance of the Legislative Yuan for the first time in its history. The PFP came third, winning 20.3% of the votes and 46 seats, while the newly formed TSU came fourth, with 8.5% of the votes and 13 seats. The NP won only 2.9% of the votes and one seat, while independents took nine seats. The level of voter participation was registered as 66.2%.

In the immediate aftermath of the elections, political manoeuvring to establish a coalition began, as the DPP and KMT sought to have their candidate elected as Vice-President of the Legislative Yuan. On 21 January 2002 President Chen reorganized the Executive Yuan, appointing his Secretary-General, Yu Shyi-kun, as Premier. The move was seen as a consolidation of the President's power, aimed at improving his prospects for re-election in 2004; the new Premier was also thought to be a more efficient administrator than his predecessor. Other notable appointments included Chen Shih-meng, hitherto deputy governor of the Central Bank, as the Secretary-General to the President, replacing Yu. Lin Hsin-i, hitherto Minister of Economic Affairs, was appointed Vice-Premier and Chairman of the Council for Economic Planning and Development, Eugene Chien, hitherto Deputy Secretary-General to the President, as Minister of Foreign Affairs, and Gen. Tang Yao-ming, hitherto Chief of the General Staff, as the new Minister of National Defense. Tang was the first native-born Taiwanese to hold the newly augmented defence post in a military dominated by mainlanders, and he was to oversee military reforms in early 2002. Lee Yung-san, Chairman of the International Commercial Bank of China, was appointed Minister of Finance, while Lee Ying-yuan, hitherto deputy representative in Washington, DC, was appointed Secretary-General of the Executive Yuan; however, the ministers in charge of mainland and overseas Chinese affairs were retained, suggesting a desire for continuity in relations with China.

In late January 2002 elections were held for provincial city and township councillors. Although the KMT won the largest number of seats in these elections, it failed to expand its popularity on a national level, with the results reflecting the KMT's competent organizational mobilization methods. At the beginning of February an alliance of the KMT and PFP ('pan-blue' camp) successfully blocked the DPP-TSU ('pan-green' camp) candidate for the post of Vice-President of the Legislative Yuan, electing Chiang Ping-kun of the KMT to that position. At the same time, the incumbent President of the legislature, Wang Jin-pyng of the KMT, was re-elected to his post.

In February 2002 the KMT-PFP alliance immediately challenged the new Government by attempting to force it to accept revisions to legislation concerning local budget allocations, which had been approved by the outgoing Legislative Yuan in December 2001. However, in the decisive vote in the new Legislative Yuan, the KMT and PFP failed to secure the majority necessary to accomplish this, thereby giving the Government a minor victory. An early set-back for the Government came in late March 2002 when the Minister of Economic Affairs, Christine Tsung, resigned, citing a hostile political environment, particularly in the Legislative Yuan. She was replaced by her deputy, Lin Yi-fu.

A major political scandal erupted in late March 2002 when one daily and one weekly newspaper reported that the Government of former President Lee Teng-hui had, in co-operation with the island's intelligence service (National Security Bureau—NSB), clandestinely established an unauthorized fund worth US $100m. to finance covert operations on the mainland and to further Taiwanese interests among influential lobby groups abroad, including the USA. Prosecutors immediately raided the offices of the two newspapers and seized the offending copies, accusing the editors of revealing state secrets. The scandal threatened to damage Lee's position, as well as jeopardize intelligence-gathering missions on the mainland and Taiwan's reputation for maintaining confidentiality; it was widely believed that the source of the 'leaks' was a former NSB colonel who had embezzled US $5.5m. and then fled the island. Following the revelations, President Chen reiterated his commitment to press freedom and proposed new supervision for the NSB.

In early April 2002 the Executive Yuan approved plans to abolish the posts of Speaker and Deputy Speaker of the National Assembly, and replace them with that of a chairman of the session. In early May the Government revealed proposals to reform the electoral system, which would reduce the number of seats in the Legislative Yuan from 225 to 150 and extend the term of legislators from three to four years. Some 90 seats would be filled from single-seat constituencies (thereby eliminating the need for candidates from the same party to compete against each other, as in the existing multi-seat constituencies), with the remaining seats divided proportionally among parties that received more than 5% of the total vote. It was hoped that such reforms would make government more efficient and less dependent upon the availability of finance. A disadvantage of the system of multi-seat constituencies was that it required the participation of larger numbers of candidates and thus greater funding, thereby encouraging corruption.

Also in early May 2002, KMT Chairman Lien Chan announced that his party would form an official alliance with the PFP in order to strengthen opposition to the ruling DPP. However, plans for a joint candidacy in the 2004 presidential elections were hampered by regulations stipulating that the presidential and vice-presidential candidates should belong to the same party. Meanwhile, in mid-May thousands of people demonstrated in favour of changing Taiwan's official name from the 'Republic of China' to 'Taiwan'—an initiative that was supported by 70% of respondents in an opinion poll conducted by the Ministry of Foreign Affairs in 2001.

In mid-June 2002 Premier Yu Shyi-kun appointed Liu Shyh-fang as the first female Secretary-General of the Executive Yuan, replacing Lee Ying-yuan, who was standing as the DPP's candidate in elections for the mayoralty of Taipei, in December. In late July President Chen Shui-bian formally assumed the chairmanship of the DPP, in a move designed to bring party policy into line with the Government. In mid-September the Executive Yuan approved drafts of the new Political Party Law, which would ban political parties from operating or investing in profit-making enterprises, and allow the Government to investigate and confiscate assets unlawfully obtained by political parties. Although ostensibly aimed at creating greater political fairness and financial openness, the draft legislation was viewed as being directed at the KMT which, during the decades of its rule, had amassed a vast commercial fortune worth an estimated NT $53,750m. (US $1,600m.) in 2001. As a result, the KMT would be obliged to sell many of its assets.

A new political dispute emerged in late September 2002 over planned reforms of the debt-ridden agricultural and fishermen's credit co-operatives. The Government sought to reduce the activities of these local financial bodies, which had traditionally been used as a source of funds and influence for local KMT politicians. However, opposition to the reforms from farmers, KMT politicians and also Lee Teng-hui and the TSU was so intense that by late November President Chen was forced to suspend the plans. At the same time, more than 120,000 farmers and fishermen marched through Taipei to protest against the reforms, in what was the largest demonstration on the island since Chen took office. The protesters also demanded the establishment of a new agricultural development fund to alleviate the difficulties caused by Taiwan's entry into the WTO. Premier Yu Shyi-kun offered to resign, but was retained by Chen, who instead accepted the resignations of the Minister of Finance, Lee Yung-san, and the Chairman of the Council of Agriculture, Fan Chen-tsung. They were replaced by Lin Chuan and Lee Chin-lung, respectively. The departure of the respected Lee Yung-san, and the appointment of the third finance minister in as many years, raised concerns about political stability.

Meanwhile, Taiwan's political forces were also increasingly focused on elections for the mayoralties of Taipei and Kaohsiung, which took place in early December 2002, and were widely regarded as a preparation for the 2004 presidential elections. In Taipei the incumbent mayor, Ma Ying-jeou of the KMT, defeated his DPP rival, Lee Ying-yuan, winning 64.1% of the votes cast. Thus, he immediately emerged as a potential presidential candidate. His popularity complicated efforts by the KMT and PFP ('pan-blue' camp) to select one of respective party chairmen Lien Chan and James Soong as their joint presidential candidate. In mid-December the two formally committed themselves to this goal. In Kaohsiung the incumbent mayor, Frank Hsieh of the DPP, narrowly defeated his KMT rival Huang Chun-ying, by 50.0% to 46.8% of the votes cast.

In January 2003 the release from 'death row' of three men accused of a double murder in 1991 prompted fresh demands for a substantial reform of the judicial system. The men were released on the grounds of insufficient evidence, and human rights activists and lawyers hoped that the case would set a precedent for establishing a clearer burden of proof in future capital cases. New legislation was to take effect from September 2003, which would give a greater role for defence counsels in courts. Also on the agenda were reforms aimed at divesting political parties of their media interests, namely in radio and television stations. During the decades of KMT rule, the party had amassed control or ownership of various media outlets, which the DPP now sought to dismantle.

In early February 2003 President Chen appointed Chiou I-jen, hitherto Secretary-General of the National Security Council, as Secretary-General to the President, while Kang Ning-hsiang, hitherto Vice-Minister of National Defense, succeeded Chiou in his former position. Later that month the leaders of the KMT and PFP again pledged to present a joint candidate for the presidency of Taiwan in 2004, with KMT Chairman Lien Chan as the presidential candidate and PFP Chairman James Soong as the vice-presidential candidate.

Following the outbreak of SARS in early 2003, in April the Executive Yuan issued a bill containing urgent measures to prevent the spread of the disease, including restrictions on travel between Taiwan and Hong Kong. In May the Taiwanese Minister of Health, Twu Shiing-jer, resigned over the SARS crisis, and the Legislative Yuan announced that US $3,100m. would be spent on combating the effects of the disease, which by June had killed more than 80 people on the island. The epidemic was under control by mid-2003.

The issue of Taiwan's very identity came to the fore once again in early September 2003, when as many as 150,000 independence activists, led by former President Lee Teng-hui, rallied in Taipei to demand that the island's name be formally changed from the 'Republic of China' to 'Taiwan'. The continued use of the former had remained the source of much international confusion and diplomatic tensions, and it was believed that the adoption of 'Taiwan' would facilitate wider diplomatic recognition. On the following day a rival rally, attended mainly by descendants of Chiang Kai-shek and veterans of the civil war (who continued to favour eventual reunification with the mainland), attracted several thousand supporters. The two rallies highlighted divisions on the island over the issue of Taiwanese independence. Also in September, President Chen made proposals for the drafting of a new Taiwanese constitution to replace the operative constitution that had been introduced by Chiang Kai-shek and the KMT, declaring Taiwan to be a part of China. President Chen stated that he wanted a new constitution to be drafted by 2006, then approved by referendum and enacted by 2008.

In November 2003 Taiwan's legislature approved a new law to allow referendums to be held on the island, prompting strong criticism from China (see above). The approval of the legislation came shortly after President Chen formally declared his intention to stand for re-election in the March 2004 presidential election. In December 2003 President Chen announced plans to hold a referendum on the issue of China's deployment of missiles against Taiwan (see above), to coincide with the forthcoming presidential poll. Also in December, President Chen confirmed that Vice-President Annette Lu, a vocal supporter of Taiwanese independence, would stand alongside him in the presidential election. Opposition presidential candidate Lien Chan and vice-presidential candidate James Soong, of the KMT and of the allied PFP respectively, as well as the popular mayor of Taipei, Ma Ying-jeou of the KMT, voiced strong opposition to the proposed referendum. In February 2004 popular demonstrations involving more than 70,000 people took place in southern Taiwan in support of the referendum, amid demands for China's removal of the missiles aimed at the island. At the end of February, in Taiwan's largest ever demonstration, an estimated 1.5m. people formed a 500-km 'human chain', linking hands across the island to protest against China's deployment of missiles. Meanwhile, the wording of the referendum question had been modified to ask voters whether, in the event of China's refusal to withdraw its missiles, they would favour a strengthening of Taiwan's defence system.

In a dramatic development on the day prior to the presidential election, scheduled for 20 March 2004, while campaigning in Tainan both President Chen and Vice-President Lu were wounded in a shooting incident. Neither was critically injured in the apparent assassination attempt, and the poll proceeded as planned. President Chen was re-elected by a narrow margin of 29,518 votes, equivalent to only 0.2% of valid votes, with 337,297 ballot papers being declared invalid. A turn-out of 80.28% of the electorate was recorded. In the concurrent referendum on the issue of Taiwan's response to the deployment of mainland missiles, however, the majority of citizens declined to vote on President Chen's proposals, thus indicating widespread division within Taiwan on the issue of the island's relationship with China. President Chen's re-election was immediately challenged by opposition candidate Lien Chan, who claimed that there had been irregularities in the electoral process, and demanded a recount of the votes. Supporters of Lien rioted in Taipei and other cities. There was also some speculation that the assassination attempt on President Chen had been deliberately staged in order to further his election prospects. Ballot papers were subsequently reported to have been seized by the judicial authorities. President Chen's re-election was none the less officially confirmed by Taiwan's Central Election Commission, amid further protests by supporters of Lien Chan.

In April 2004 the Minister of the Interior, Yu Cheng-hsien, resigned, citing the failure to prevent the shooting of Chen during the election campaign as the reason for his departure. In the same month the Minister of Foreign Affairs, Eugene Y. H. Chien, resigned in connection with the resignation of the head of the American Institute in Taiwan (see below). A recount of votes cast in the presidential election was completed on 19 May. It was estimated that 38,000 ballots were controversial, and that of these 23,000 were votes for Chen. This conclusion was not likely to reverse Chen's re-election, however; in addition to the controversial ballots, there remained unanswered questions surrounding the apparent attempt to assassinate Chen on the day before his re-election. In July US forensic expert Henry Lee, who had been investigating the shooting, stated that the truth about the incident might never be established, although the likelihood that the attack had been staged was reportedly believed to be minimal. Also in July remarks by Vice-President Annette Lu suggesting a resettlement of Taiwan's aboriginal communities to South America caused widespread offence among the island's indigenous population. Meanwhile, President Chen was inaugurated for his second term on 20 May, despite ongoing controversy over the election result, and on the same day he announced appointments to the new Executive Yuan. Yu Shyi-kun was retained as Premier. In June the Executive Yuan approved a special defence budget of NT $610,800m. for the purchase of weapons from the USA (first agreed in 2001). In July a new political party, the pro-independence Formosa Party, was inaugurated. In the same month it was announced that the remains of former President Chiang Kai-shek would be permanently buried in Taiwan, despite his wish to be buried on the mainland. In August the Legislative Yuan approved a bill on constitutional changes, which included plans for a reduction in the number of legislators and for reform of the electoral system. Also in August there was controversy surrounding the establishment of an independent committee to investigate the March shooting of President Chen, with the President of the Judicial Yuan claiming that the investigatory powers being given to this body were unconstitutional. In September protests took place in Taipei against the proposed special budget for the purchase of US weapons, which had been approved by the Executive Yuan in June. Protesters feared that the purchase would exacerbate tensions with mainland China and also objected to the Government's plan to finance the weapons by privatizing state assets, claiming that the money should instead be spent on public welfare.

In an election to the Legislative Yuan held in December 2004 the 'pan-green' alliance, consisting of the DPP and the TSU, secured 101 seats, whereas the 'pan-blue' alliance, comprising the KMT, the PFP and NP, secured 114 seats. The resulting opposition majority in the legislature was expected to hinder President Chen's proposals on constitutional changes and on relations with mainland China. President Chen resigned as DPP Chairman after the election, taking responsibility for the party's failure to gain a larger number of seats. Meanwhile, disputes over the legitimacy of President Chen's victory in March continued, with a High Court rejecting two opposition attempts, in November and December respectively, to nullify the presidential election result. There was a suggestion during 2004 of a merger between the KMT and the PFP, with plans for this being announced in advance of President Chen's inauguration in May; however, in December PFP Chairman James Soong stated that such a merger was no longer a possibility. Following the DPP's disappointing election performance in December, there was speculation that instead a coalition between the PFP and the DPP might be formed.

In January 2005 the Executive Yuan approved a draft amendment to the referendum law (see above), requiring any changes to Taiwan's boundaries to be approved by the population. This was seen by some as an attempt to counter the anti-secession law introduced by the Standing Committee of China's NPC in late 2004 (see above). Later in January Premier Yu Shyi-kun and all ministers of the Executive Yuan resigned prior to the first meeting of the new Legislative Yuan, according to tradition. President Chen subsequently appointed Frank Hsieh, mayor of Kaohsiung and a leading member of the DPP, as Premier. New government appointments were made later in the month. Also in January Secretary-General Su Tseng-chang was appointed Chairman of the DPP, replacing Chen; former Premier Yu Shyi-kun was subsequently appointed Secretary-General in his place. In February Premier Hsieh appointed Wu Rong-i as the new Vice-Premier and Minister of the Consumer Protection Commission.

In March 2005 a large rally, attended by President Chen, took place in Taipei in protest at the approval of anti-secession legislation by China's NPC (see above). On 14 May elections were held for an ad-hoc National Assembly, which was to convene in order to ratify or reject the range of constitutional amendments approved by the Legislative Yuan in August 2004. The DPP secured 127 of the Assembly's 300 seats, receiving 42.5% of votes cast, while the KMT won 117 seats. When the Assembly came to vote in the following month, 248 members voted in favour of the amendments, 23 more than the two-thirds' majority required for ratification. The amendments to the Constitution were thus passed into law. They included a reduction in the number of seats in the Legislative Yuan (from 225 to 113), reforms to the electoral system, the transfer of the power to impeach the President and Vice-President from the National Assembly to the Judicial Yuan, and the ratification of all future constitutional amendment proposals by popular referendum (requiring the approval of 50% of eligible voters, following approval by 75% of the Legislative Yuan). These reforms were due to come into effect before the next legislative elections, scheduled for 2007. Meanwhile, in mid-June and again in mid-September 2005 the Supreme Court rejected the appeals of the 'pan-blue' alliance to have the results of the 2004 presidential election declared invalid. In July 2005 Ma Ying-jeou, the mayor of Taipei, was elected Chairman of the KMT, in the party's first leadership election. Ma received 72.4% of votes cast by party members to defeat Wang Jin-pyng, President of the Legislative Yuan. In August the Supreme Prosecutor's Office announced that it was closing its investigation into the shooting of President Chen and Vice-President Lu in the previous year, having concluded that the attack was carried out by a retired construction worker, Chen Yi-hsiung, who had committed suicide shortly after the incident. It was stated that Chen Yi-hsiung had considered President Chen and his Government responsible for his personal financial difficulties.

The mid-term elections for city and county magistrates held in December 2005 resulted in significant gains for the KMT, which took 14 of the 23 contested constituencies, and led to considerable embarrassment for the DPP, which won in only six. The KMT also outperformed the DPP in elections for county councillors, township governors and magistrates. Following the elections, Su Tseng-chang resigned from the post of Chairman of the DPP. Yu Shyi-kun, the former Premier and latterly Secretary-General to the President, was elected as his replacement in January 2006. In the same month, Frank Hsieh resigned as Premier, citing the failure of the legislature to approve his proposed budget for 2006 as the prime motive for his departure, while also hinting at policy disagreements with President Chen, over cross-Straits relations in particular; in his farewell speech Hsieh warned Chen that the policy of a separate sovereign identity for Taiwan was not supported by the majority of the population. The DPP's poor electoral performance was also regarded by some as a contributory factor in his resignation (Hsieh had offered his resignation to President Chen on two occasions in December 2005 following the defeat), as was a scandal over allegations of corruption and exploitation surrounding the construction of the metro system in the city of Kaohsiung, where hundreds of Thai construction workers had reportedly rioted in August 2005 in protest at their poor living and working conditions. President Chen appointed Su Tseng-chang to replace Hsieh (thereby becoming Chen's fifth Premier since the President's accession to power in 2000). The new Executive Yuan was sworn in on 25 January 2006. Tsai Ing-wen became Vice-Premier and Minister of the Consumer Protection Commission, Lee Yi-yang was appointed Minister of the Interior, Huang Chih-fang was the new Minister of Foreign Affairs, and Joseph J. C. Lyu took the post of Minister of Finance. In all, 14 new appointments were made, while the remaining 29 members of the Executive Yuan were retained from the previous administration. Meanwhile, President Chen appointed the former Minister of Foreign Affairs, Dr Tan Sun Chen, as presidential Secretary-General, after the post was reportedly refused by Hsieh, who stated his intention to withdraw from politics.

President Chen's reiteration in January 2006 of his commitment to the ratification by referendum of a new constitution by 2008, his proposed abolition of the NUC and his declaration that he intended to reapply for membership of the UN under the name of 'Taiwan' (see above) drew strong criticism from the opposition, with KMT Chairman Ma Ying-jeou remarking that such a move would contradict election promises made by Chen in 2000 and 2004, as well as risk damaging relations with China. In response, Joseph Wu, Minister of the Mainland Affairs Council, noted that the NUC had not in fact convened since 1999 and was so poorly funded as to be effectively useless.

Chen and the DPP continued to antagonize the opposition: in February 2006 the party announced its intention to change Taiwan's official name, its flag, its national anthem and the definition of its territory; in the following month it was reported that all statues of Chiang Kai-shek were to be removed from public places (this was later denied by a government spokesperson). None the less, in April Chen participated in an unprecedented televised meeting with Ma Ying-jeou. On the following day the special defence budget proposed in June 2004 was opposed for the 50th time by the 'pan-blue' alliance in the Legislative Yuan.

President Chen's authority was greatly undermined in May 2006 by the Taipei District Court's detention of his son-in-law, Chao Chien-ming, with four members of his family (who were later released) on charges of insider dealing. It was alleged that in 2005 Chao had purchased 20m. shares of the Taiwan Development Corporation, a state-owned property company, in his mother's name, having learned from an inside source that the value of the company's stock was about to increase. Chao relinquished his membership of the DPP in an attempt to protect the party's image. (Chao was indicted, along with his father and three others, and released on bail in July 2006. In December he was sentenced to six years' imprisonment by the Taipei District Court; his appeal was rejected by the High Court in June 2007.) Chen, whose popularity was already at its lowest level ever, had apologized to the nation for his family's involvement in the affair earlier in May; this was reiterated by a spokesperson of the DPP on the day that Chao was arrested, and the opposition was urged not to create instability by attempting to oust the President. However, the PFP immediately instigated a campaign to recall the President but initially failed to gain the support of the KMT.

In May 2006 former DPP legislator Shen Fu-hsiung confirmed an allegation that in the 1990s, during his campaign for the mayoralty of Taipei, Chen had received no fewer than six political donations from the fugitive tycoon Chen You-hao. (Chen You-hao, former head of the Tuntex group, had fled Taiwan in 2002 when Tuntex was in financial difficulties and was subsequently accused of embezzling funds from the group and incurring bank debts of some US $1,800m.) Shen also claimed that he had accompanied Chen You-hao on a visit to the President's wife, Wu Shu-jen (a former legislator), to whom the tycoon had given nearly US $200,000, an accusation that Wu had previously denied. Two days later the 'pan-blue' alliance submitted a recall motion to the legislature.

On 1 June 2006, under intense political pressure, President Chen ceded much of his authority to Premier Su Tseng-chang. Henceforth the President would no longer have the power to dictate policy or appoint members of the Executive Yuan, but would remain in charge of foreign and defence policy and would oversee relations with the People's Republic. The President also announced that he would play no further active role within the DPP. Opposition politicians declared Chen's move insufficient and demanded his resignation; protest rallies were held in the days that followed in an effort to increase pressure on the President to stand down. In a live televised speech later in the month Chen defended his administration and denied the allegations that had been made against his family, including a claim that his wife had accepted gift vouchers from a department store (see below). The motion of recall was voted upon in late June: despite gaining some support from the KMT (90 votes, including that of Wang Jin-pyng, the President of the Legislative Yuan, who was supposed to remain neutral), the 'pan-blue' alliance received just 119 votes, thus falling short of the number of votes (two-thirds of the seats currently occupied) required to submit the motion to a national referendum.

At the end of June 2006 it was announced that Ho Chih-chin, an academic, would succeed Joseph J. C. Lyu as Minister of Finance. Lyu, who had come under criticism for his handling of negotiations over the management of Mega Financial Holding, retained a position within the Executive Yuan, as Minister without Portfolio. In early July party factions within the DPP unanimously approved the candidacy of former Premier Frank Hsieh in the forthcoming Taipei mayoral election. Hsieh agreed to stand in the election on 15 June, and it was hoped by his supporters that he would promote unity within the DPP and help to restore the party's declining reputation.

Controversy surrounding President Chen continued: in July 2006 prosecutors questioned Wu Shu-jen in relation to allegations that the President's wife and her family doctor, Huang Fang-yen, had acted on behalf of certain businessmen who wished to acquire the Sogo department store and that in return Wu had accepted vouchers worth about US $185,000. A report in the *China Times* claimed that forged receipts to the value of around US $600,000 had been submitted for reimbursement under the special allowances budget of the Office of the President. This was confirmed by a KMT legislator, Chiu Yi, who accused the President of having embezzled the money, although Chiu failed to provide any evidence to support his allegation. High court prosecutors were reported to be investigating the claim. The Office of the President also came under scrutiny for the alleged improper use of taxpayers' money from May 2000 to pay the wages of the housekeeper at an apartment occupied by the President before his move to his official residence in January 2001, and which subsequently became the home of his daughter. Following these charges, DPP legislators in turn accused KMT Chairman Ma Ying-jeou of remitting a proportion of his official allowance as mayor of Taipei into his personal account for private use, and reported their suspicions to the National Audit Office. Meanwhile, Premier Su Tseng-chang appeared to be consolidating his position within the DPP after the Conference on Sustaining Taiwan's Economic Development, held in late July 2006, during which he gained the support of local business groups and trade unions. At the DPP convention, also held in July 2006, the party voted by a small majority to dissolve its factions in an attempt to promote unity.

In August 2006 the Executive Yuan underwent a further reorganization when the Minister of Economic Affairs, Hwang In-san, who had resigned on the grounds of ill health, was replaced by his deputy, Chen Ruey-long. Also in August, the Minister of Transportation and Communications, Kuo Yao-chi, offered to resign, in order to take responsibility for a scandal that had arisen from the controversial awarding of a contract for an electronic motorway toll collection system. She was replaced later in the month by Tsai Duei. At the same time prosecutors began to question President Chen over the alleged misuse of public funds, although they did not immediately release their findings. Meanwhile, the President continued to antagonize the KMT (and mainland China) by reiterating that he intended to draft a new constitution, and that Taiwan should apply to join the UN as an observer under the name of 'Taiwan'. These moves came despite considerable popular support for efforts to force the President to resign. In early August the PFP announced that it would begin an attempt to impeach Chen, and Shih Ming-teh, a former DPP chairman, subsequently announced the formation of a 'one million people' mass movement to remove him from office. Within six working days his campaign had attracted more than 1m. supporters, each of whom donated NT $100 to show their commitment to the cause. The former ally of Chen vowed that he and his supporters would stage a round-the-clock protest outside the presidential office in the following month and that they would not disperse until the President resigned. While the KMT expressed support for Shih's campaign, neither the KMT nor the PFP was prepared to participate in the name of their respective parties, instead merely encouraging their members to attend the rallies.

In September 2006 at least 100,000 demonstrators took to the streets of Taipei, wearing red to signify their anger at Chen's alleged corruption. Despite inclement weather conditions, around 4,000 spent the night in front of the presidential office, and many stayed for several days until a march in mid-September. In an attempt to increase public support for the President, the DPP organized a rival rally the next day. Encouraged by Chen's declining popularity, the PFP again attempted to initiate a recall motion against the President, and in late September the Legislative Yuan voted by 106 to 82 to refer the motion for review by a parliamentary committee prior to a full legislative debate in October. By mid-October the momentum against the President had grown, with violent skirmishes (including a scuffle between two rival legislators from the DPP and KMT) marring the official National Day celebrations. Demonstrators caused serious disruption of the events, obstructing Chen's motorcade, blocking roads and effectively besieging the presidential office. None the less, the next recall motion against Chen again failed when the opposition secured only 116 votes, still short of the requisite two-thirds' majority. Later in October the opposition once more blocked a controversial arms bill involving multi-million dollar weapons purchases from the USA (see above); in an attempt to halt the debate, one independent legislator sprayed tear gas and brandished a stun gun during a parliamentary committee hearing.

In early October 2006 President Chen's wife, Wu Shu-jen, had been cleared by prosecutors of wrongdoing during the takeover of the Sogo department store (see above) on the basis of lack of evidence. In early November, however, prosecutors declared that they had sufficient evidence to charge Chen with misuse of public funds and that they were prevented from doing so only by his presidential immunity. However, no such immunity surrounded Wu Shu-jen, who was indicted along with three former presidential aides on charges of forgery and corruption. According to the prosecutors, Wu and the three senior aides had misappropriated around US $448,484 from the 'state affairs fund'. While the prosecutors accepted Chen's explanation that in two out of the six cases being investigated the funds had been used for secret diplomatic missions, they concluded that the use of such assets in four other cases could not be verified. Prosecutor Eric Chen, in charge of the case, even claimed that Wu had purchased a NT $1.3m. ring using receipts from the fund. Immediately after the charges were brought, opposition members demanded Chen's resignation and urged the DPP to join them in approving a motion of recall against the embattled President. None the less, the DPP insisted that Chen retained its full support, noting that he had promised to resign if his wife were to be convicted and that he had attributed the apparent irregularities in the use of the state affairs fund to poorly defined regulations. Meanwhile, thousands of protesters once more descended on Taipei, again demanding the President's resignation. The demonstration was spurned by the PFP and the KMT; however, the latter warned that the President could be impeached only by formal legal proceedings. The revelations against Chen prompted the opposition to initiate a third recall motion against the President, which was scheduled for the end of November. Furthermore, disagreements began to emerge within the ranks of the DPP, when two members resigned from the Legislative Yuan in order to demonstrate dissatisfaction with their party's handling of the scandal. At the same time, DPP legislators filed a lawsuit against Ma Ying-jeou, accusing him of embezzling public funds.

When the crucial recall vote was held in late November 2006, the DPP again rallied to support its leader, boycotting the vote and thus preventing the motion from obtaining the requisite two-thirds' majority. Moreover, at mayoral elections held in Taipei and Kaohsiung in December the DPP performed better than anticipated. Although the DPP candidate in Taipei, Frank Hsieh, lost to his KMT rival, Hau Long-bin, the former nevertheless garnered almost 40.9% of the votes, an increase of 5.0% in comparison with the mayoral election of 2002, and in Kaohsiung the DPP candidate, Chen Chu, won by a narrow margin of 0.14%, to become the island's first female mayor. The KMT in Kaohsiung immediately demanded a recount of the votes, declaring that too many ballots had been invalidated, and in February 2007 judges in Kaohsiung announced that a recount would take place. This was held in mid-March. In June the Kaohsiung District Court nullified the election results, but this decision was revoked by the High Court in November.

Party differences were temporarily, and somewhat unexpectedly, put aside in late December 2006 when the KMT voted with the Government to place the long-delayed arms procurement bill (see above) on the legislative agenda. The proposed legislation, which the KMT had previously boycotted along with the PFP, would ensure that the purchase of US weapons would be funded from the annual budget of the Ministry of National Defense, rather than from a special budget. However, the passage of the legislation remained uncertain, as the KMT voted against a motion providing for the bill to be referred directly for a second reading. In June 2007 budget legislation, which encompassed funding for military procurement that had been debated and altered by the Legislative Yuan, was finally approved after a delay of six months.

In January 2007 the KMT and PFP formalized a party alliance, undertaking to present a single candidate in each district in the legislative election scheduled for the end of the year. In March Lee Jye, the Minister of National Defense, was expelled from the KMT as a result of a dispute regarding a government order to remove statues of Chiang Kai-shek from military premises, a decision with which Lee had complied. Ma Ying-jeou had resigned from the chairmanship of the KMT in February following accusations of forgery and of the embezzlement of NT $11.2m. during his tenure of the mayoralty of Taipei. Ma denied the allegations and reiterated his intention to stand as presidential candidate in 2008. Although he was replaced as KMT Chairman in April by Wu Poh-hsi, in May the party confirmed his candidacy for the presidency of Taiwan, and in August 2007 he was cleared of all charges (prosecutors appealed against the decision in January 2008). Meanwhile, in May 2007, following his defeat by former Premier Frank Hsieh in the contest for the nomination of the DPP presidential candidate, Su Tseng-chang resigned as Premier. President Chen appointed Chang Chun-hsiung, who had served as Premier in 2000–02, to replace Su. Premier Chang Chun-hsiung subsequently effected a government reorganization, although many of the incumbent members of the Executive Yuan were retained; notable exceptions included Tsai Ing-wen, who was succeeded by Chiou I-jen as Vice-Premier and Minister of the Consumer Protection Commission, and Lee Jye, who was replaced by Lee Tien-yu in the position of Minister of National Defense.

In September 2007 several prominent members of the DPP, including Chairman Yu Shyi-kun, Vice-President Annette Lu and former Minister of Foreign Affairs (Mark) Chen Tan-sun, were indicted on charges of corruption and forgery. Yu Shyi-kun, who resigned from the DPP chairmanship with immediate effect, was charged with the misuse of some US $172,000, which he claimed had been spent on public, rather than private, affairs. Meanwhile, the DPP's presidential candidate, Frank Hsieh, and his vice-presidential candidate, Su Tseng-Chang, were both cleared of similar charges. President Chen returned to the position of DPP Chairman in October. In September the DPP had adopted a resolution affirming Taiwan's separate identity and appealing for a new constitution and a referendum on the issue of sovereignty; the name of Taiwan, it was stated, should enter into common usage without necessarily abolishing the official designation of the 'Republic of China'. The DPP continued its campaign against the commemoration of Chiang Kai-shek, cancelling two public holidays honouring the former President in August, and removing Chiang's name from a prominent memorial hall in Taipei in December.

CHINA (TAIWAN)

Legislative elections held on 12 January 2008 resulted in a resounding victory for the KMT, which secured 81 seats (out of a reduced total of 113 seats in accordance with the constitutional amendments of 2005); the DPP, with only 27 seats, was thus defeated by a considerable margin. The Non-Partisan Solidarity Union (NPSU) won three seats and the KMT's alliance partner, the PFP, only one. Turn-out was extremely low in comparison with previous elections, at approximately 58%. Voters were also presented with two proposals at referendums, both of which were rejected: the first proposed measure was the seizure of state assets allegedly appropriated by the KMT during and after its assumption of power in 1945; the second, submitted by the KMT, involved additional anti-corruption measures. The results were widely regarded as an indication of public opposition to the DPP's forceful stance on sovereignty and Taiwan's status, as well as of the fear of jeopardizing relations with the mainland and of alienating the island's strategic allies. Following the DPP's defeat, Chen resigned as the party's Chairman and was replaced by Frank Hsieh. Later in the month, Premier Chang Chun-hsiung and the other members of the Executive Yuan submitted their resignations, but President Chen refused to accept these, citing a need for stability. Meanwhile, the election pledges of presidential candidate Ma Ying-jeou included an undertaking to pursue neither unification nor independence.

On 22 March 2008 Ma Ying-jeou of the KMT was elected the island's President, having received almost 58.5% of the votes cast, thus defeating Frank Hsieh, who subsequently announced that he would resign as Chairman of the DPP. At 76.3%, the level of participation by voters in the presidential election was high. However, the results of two concurrent referendums on the issue of the island's application for membership of the UN were declared invalid: although the number of votes in favour of each proposal exceeded 50% of the ballots cast, the total number of votes exercised failed to reach the requisite threshold of 50% of the registered electorate. The first proposal, which sought approval for the island's application under the name of Taiwan, was supported by the DPP; the KMT urged that this referendum be boycotted. The second referendum, initiated by the KMT, asked voters if they supported an application to return to the UN as 'the Republic of China' or alternatively as Taiwan or under any other suitable designation. Liu Chao-shiuan, a former Vice-Premier and hitherto President of Soochow University, was subsequently nominated as the island's Premier by the President-elect. Ma Ying-Jeou and his new Government were scheduled to take office on 20 May.

In foreign relations, meanwhile, in January 1979 Taiwan suffered a serious set-back when the USA established full diplomatic relations with the People's Republic of China and severed relations with Taiwan. The USA also terminated the 1954 mutual security treaty with Taiwan. Commercial links are still maintained, however, and Taiwan's purchase of armaments from the USA has remained a controversial issue. In August 1982 a joint Sino-US communiqué was published, in which the USA pledged to reduce gradually its sale of armaments to Taiwan. In September 1992 President George Bush announced the sale of up to 150 F-16 fighter aircraft to Taiwan. The announcement was condemned by the People's Republic. In December the US trade representative became the first senior US government official to visit the island since 1979. In September 1994 the USA announced a modification of its policy towards Taiwan, henceforth permitting senior-level bilateral meetings to be held in US government offices. In December the US Secretary of Transportation visited the Ministry of Foreign Affairs in Taipei, the first US official of cabinet rank to visit Taiwan for more than 15 years. In June 1995 President Lee was permitted to make a four-day unofficial visit to the USA, where he gave a speech at Cornell University, and met members of the US Congress. This visit provoked outrage in China, and the Chinese ambassador to Washington was recalled. During 1996 the Taiwanese Vice-President was granted transit visas permitting him to disembark in the USA on a number of occasions.

In March 1996, as mainland China began a new series of missile tests off the Taiwanese coast (see above), the USA stationed two naval convoys in waters east of the island, representing the largest US deployment in Asia since 1975. The sale of defensive weapons to Taiwan was agreed. In September 1996 President Lee and the US Deputy Treasury Secretary met in Taipei for discussions, the most senior-level contact between the two sides since 1994. In late 1996, however, Taiwanese donors were implicated in reported irregularities in the financing of President Bill Clinton's re-election campaign and in a large illicit contribution to the US Democratic Party. In early 1997 the first of the Patriot anti-missile air defence systems, purchased from the USA under an arrangement made in 1993, were reported to have been deployed on the island. The first of the F-16s were delivered to Taiwan in April 1997. The Taiwanese Government expressed satisfaction at the USA's continued commitment to Taiwan's security, confirmed following the visit to the USA of the President of the People's Republic, Jiang Zemin, in October and again in June 1998, during President Clinton's visit to the People's Republic. However, a statement by Clinton affirming that the USA would not support Taiwan's membership of the UN was sharply criticized in Taiwan. In late October 1998 the Taiwanese Chief of Staff, Gen. Tang Fei, made a secret two-week visit to the USA. This was regarded as an extremely sensitive matter, in view of the fact that the SEF Chairman had recently met with Jiang Zemin. In the following month the People's Republic complained to the USA following the US Energy Secretary's visit to Taiwan.

In January 1999 the People's Republic was antagonized by Taiwan's proposed inclusion in the US-led TMD system (see above). Tensions continued throughout the year, and in August the USA reaffirmed its commitment to defend Taiwan against Chinese military action. In the following month, however, the USA again refused to support Taiwan's application for UN membership. In October of that year the island welcomed the adoption, albeit in modified form, of the Taiwan Security Enhancement Act (TSEA), establishing direct military ties, by the International Relations Committee of the US House of Representatives, despite opposition from the Clinton Administration. Reaction from the People's Republic was unfavourable, and its displeasure increased in early February 2000 when the House of Representatives overwhelmingly approved the Act. In April of that year the US Senate postponed consideration of the Act at the behest of the Taiwanese President-elect, Chen Shui-bian, in order not to antagonize China during the sensitive period preceding his inauguration. In the same month the US Government announced that it had decided to defer the sale of four naval destroyers to Taiwan, although it was prepared to supply long-range radar and medium-range air-to-air missiles. In September the USA granted a transit visa to Taiwanese Vice-President Annette Lu to stay in New York en route to Central America. Lu subsequently declared that the stopover had marked a breakthrough in talks between the USA and Taiwan. In October China was angered by a resolution approved by the US Congress supporting Taiwan's participation in the UN and other international organizations.

The election of George W. Bush to the US Presidency in late 2000 was widely expected to boost US-Taiwan relations at the expense of the USA's relations with the mainland, since Bush had used uncompromising rhetoric against the latter in his election campaign. This became more apparent after the crisis over the detention of a US reconnaissance plane and its crew following its collision with a Chinese fighter aircraft on 1 April 2001 (see the chapter on the People's Republic of China). Following that incident, in late April the USA agreed to sell Taiwan military equipment and armaments worth a total of US $4,000m. President Bush declared that the USA would do whatever was necessary to defend Taiwan, in the event of an invasion by mainland forces. The People's Republic was further antagonized by the visit of President Chen Shui-bian to the USA in May 2001, when he met business leaders and members of the US Congress. Chen's visit was followed by that of his predecessor, Lee Teng-hui, in June, as well as by a group of Taiwanese military and intelligence officials on an exchange programme, the first such exchange since 1979.

In August 2001 two US Navy aircraft carrier battle groups staged a one-day exercise in the South China Sea coinciding with Chinese military exercises in the Taiwan Strait. In October the Minister of National Defense, Wu Shih-wen, began finalizing the purchase of the naval destroyers offered earlier in the year, and the USA also offered Taiwan anti-tank missiles. In December the US House of Representatives approved the 2002 Defense Authorization Act, which included weapons sales to Taiwan and the promise of US help in acquiring submarines.

In January 2002 the Bush Administration rejected demands by a former US State Department official, Richard Holbrooke, that a fourth communiqué on US-Taiwan relations was needed, stating that the existing 1982 communiqué was satisfactory. A delegation from a US 'think tank', consisting of retired generals and officials, visited the mainland, and subsequently Taiwan, where they met President Chen and other senior officials and discussed the island's security. Also in January, Vice-President Annette Lu made a brief stopover in New York, en route to South America, and former President Lee Teng-hui announced that he planned to visit the USA in May. During his visit to Beijing in late February 2002, President Bush pledged to adhere to the 1979 Taiwan Relations Act.

There were indications that the USA's long-standing 'strategic ambiguity' regarding Taiwan was gradually coming to an end in early 2002. In March the Minister of National Defense, Gen. (retd) Tang Yao-ming visited the USA to attend a private three-day defence and security conference in Florida, where he met the US Deputy Secretary of Defense, Paul Wolfowitz, and Assistant Secretary of State James Kelly. During the conference, Wolfowitz reportedly stated that the USA would assist in training Taiwan's military in areas of command and doctrine. Tang was the first incumbent to make a non-transit visit to the USA since 1979, and the event emphasized the increasingly important security links between the two sides. China condemned Tang's visit as interference in its affairs and responded by denying permission for a US warship to visit Hong Kong in April. Meanwhile, the scandal in late March concerning former President Lee Teng-hui's co-operation with the island's intelligence services in secretly establishing an unauthorized fund (see below) embarrassed Taiwan and several US lobbying groups, which had received sums of this money. Lee subsequently postponed his planned visit to the USA. In April, however, the US Under-Secretary of Commerce for International Trade, Grant Aldonas, became the highest-ranking official of George W. Bush's Administration to visit Taiwan, where he met Chen Shui-bian.

Reflecting the occasional political aspects of commercial relations with the USA, in September 2002 the Taiwanese Government urged the state-owned airline, CAL, to place a US $2,000m. order for 12 aircraft for its fleet with Boeing (of the USA) rather than the rival European-manufactured Airbus. However, in October CAL awarded the contract to Airbus, while also purchasing 10 Boeing aircraft. Also in September, the US Congress approved the Foreign Relations Authorization Act, Fiscal Year 2003, which for the first time allowed staff of the US State Department and other government agencies to work at the American Institute in Taiwan, the unofficial US mission to the island. Previously, US officials were required to embark upon sabbatical leave before serving at the institute. US military officers would also be allowed to work there, albeit not in uniform. Furthermore, the bill recognized Taiwan as a major non-NATO ally of the USA.

In August 2003 plans for Taiwan's purchase of four naval destroyers from the USA, first discussed in September 2002, were finalized. Taiwan also made an advance payment towards the acquisition of eight new diesel-submarines from the USA. Also in August 2003, again reflecting the political influences on Taiwan's trade relations with the USA, CAL purchased 12 aircraft engines from US company General Electric, rejecting an alternative purchase from European company Rolls-Royce. At the end of August the USA expressed concern that China's increased military capability could pose a threat to Taiwan and reaffirmed US willingness to sell weapons to the island.

In November 2003 President Chen made a visit to New York, in the course of which he was permitted to make a public speech. However, during a visit by Chinese Premier Wen Jiabao to Washington, DC, in December the Bush Administration appeared to support China's opposition to referendum plans in Taiwan, reaffirming its 'one China' policy and opposing any unilateral decision by either China or Taiwan to change the status quo. In January 2004 President Chen attempted to placate US concerns over his proposed referendum on Chinese missiles (see above) by suggesting that the referendum might be presented as an opportunity to reduce tensions between Taiwan and mainland China.

In April 2004 Therese Shaheen, head of the American Institute in Taiwan, resigned after reportedly having misrepresented US policy on Taiwanese independence. Her departure prompted the resignation of Taiwan's Minister of Foreign Affairs, Eugene Y. H. Chien. In June the Executive Yuan approved a special defence budget for the purchase of weapons from the USA, which had been agreed in April 2001 (see above). In October 2004 comments made in Beijing by US Secretary of State Colin Powell, suggesting that Taiwan was not an independent country and that it would eventually be reunified with China, caused concern on the island. Following public opposition in Taiwan to a special defence budget for purchase of US weapons (see above), the USA warned that there would be serious implications if the armaments purchase was not approved by the Legislative Yuan. However, in late 2005 the opposition parties in the Legislative Yuan continued to oppose the special defence budget, blocking its progress for the 42nd time in December, despite significant reductions in the overall size of the proposed purchase. In January 2006 the US Government described as 'inflammatory' President Chen's proposals on the occasion of the Chinese Lunar New Year, which included the abolition of the NUC and the reunification guidelines established by it (see above). The US State Department emphasized in a statement that it supported the maintenance of the status quo in cross-Straits relations, within the overall framework of a 'one China' policy.

In May 2006 the Deputy US Trade Representative, Karan Bhatia, visited Taiwan to discuss trade issues. In the following month the USA reacted positively to the announcement of a programme of direct charter flights to the mainland (see below). Although Bhatia had rejected requests by President Chen to begin negotiations on a bilateral trade agreement between Taiwan and the USA, in July it was reported that Chen had secured a commitment from Henry Hyde, Chairman of the International Relations Committee of the US House of Representatives, to support Taiwan's campaign to reopen negotiations on free trade. Meanwhile, the USA continued to press Taiwan to purchase its weapons, with US officials expressing 'grave concern' over Taiwan's defence capabilities when two DPP legislators visited Washington, DC, in August. (The remarks followed the opposition's rejection in April, for the 50th time, of a defence budget that included the procurement of US weapons—see above. Despite these comments, however, in early September it was reported that President Bush had been advised by his security staff to deny the sale of F-16 jets, estimated to be worth US $3,100m., to Taiwan, for fear of antagonizing China.) The two legislators also received a sharp rebuttal over a proposal to negotiate a Taiwan-USA free trade agreement (FTA), with US officials stating that there could be no FTA in the near future. However, the two sides were to continue to focus on discussions under the Taiwan-US Trade and Investment Framework Agreement (TIFA). While the USA had initially expressed alarm over President Chen's isolationist stance, it did not want Taiwan to descend into a period of political uncertainty. As Chen became increasingly embroiled in various scandals, the director of the American Institute in Taiwan, Stephen Young, very publicly entered the fray to state that the USA wished Chen to remain in power for the sake of the stability of the island. The USA's commitment to the security of Taiwan was confirmed in February 2007 when the US Department of Defense announced the sale of more than 450 missiles to the island. In May, furthermore, Young reiterated his appeal to the Taiwanese legislature to grant approval to the outstanding defence budget that would permit the purchase of weaponry from the USA (aspects of the sale were expected to proceed following the legislature's approval of an amended budget in June 2007). Opposition legislators accused Young of interfering in Taiwan's internal affairs, with some demanding his expulsion from the island.

The USA continued to exert pressure on Taiwan to give up its efforts to join the UN under the proposed name of Taiwan, claiming that this new policy (see above) would threaten the stability of the region. In August 2007 the US Deputy Secretary of State, John Negroponte, declared that it would be 'a mistake' if Taiwan were to proceed with a proposal to submit to referendum the issue of UN membership concurrently with the 2008 presidential election, urging the Government to respect the status quo.

Taiwan severed diplomatic relations with Japan in 1972, following Tokyo's rapprochement with China. Mainland displeasure was incurred in February 1993, however, when, for the first time in two decades, the Taiwanese Minister of Foreign Affairs paid a visit to Japan. In September 1994 pressure from China resulted in the withdrawal of President Lee's invitation to attend the forthcoming Asian Games in Hiroshima. Instead, however, the Taiwanese Vice-Premier was permitted to visit Japan. Similarly, in July 1995 Japan announced that the Taiwanese Vice-Premier would not be permitted to attend a meeting of APEC members to be held in Osaka in November. Instead, President Lee was represented by Koo Chen-fu, the SEF Chairman. The latter also attended the APEC meeting in the Philippines in November 1996. At the Kuala Lumpur APEC summit in November 1998 President Lee was represented by a Minister without Portfolio, Chiang Ping-kun, who also attended the 1999 APEC conference, held in September in Auckland, New

Zealand. Perng Fai-nan, the Governor of the Central Bank, represented President Chen Shui-bian at the APEC meeting in Brunei in November 2000.

In 1996 Taiwan's relations with Japan continued to be strained by the issue of adequate compensation for the thousands of Asian (mostly Korean) women used by Japanese troops for sexual purposes during the Second World War. In October Taiwan rejected a Japanese offer of nominal compensation for Taiwanese women. Relations deteriorated further during 1996 on account of a dispute relating to a group of uninhabited islets in the East China Sea: known as the Tiaoyutai (Diaoyu Dao) in Chinese, or Senkaku in Japanese, the islands were claimed by Taiwan, China and Japan. In July, following the construction of a lighthouse on one of the islands by a Japanese right-wing group, the Taiwanese Ministry of Foreign Affairs lodged a strong protest over Japan's decision to incorporate the islands within its 200-mile (370-km) exclusive economic zone. In early October further discussions with Japan on the question of Taiwanese fishing rights within the disputed waters ended without agreement. In the same month a flotilla of small boats, operated by activists from Taiwan, Hong Kong and Macao, succeeded in evading Japanese patrol vessels. Having reached the disputed islands, protesters raised the flags of Taiwan and of China. In May 1997 the Taiwanese Minister of Foreign Affairs expressed grave concern, following the landing and planting of their national flag on one of the disputed islands by a Japanese politician and three aides. A number of protesters and journalists from Taiwan and Hong Kong set sail from the port of Shenao, ostensibly to participate in an international fishing contest. They were intercepted by Japanese coastguard vessels and failed to gain access to the islands. Reports in October that Japanese patrol boats were forcibly intercepting Taiwanese fishing vessels were a further cause for concern for the Taiwanese authorities. There was a significant development in bilateral relations in November 1999, when the Governor of Tokyo paid an official visit to Taiwan, the most senior Japanese official to do so since the severing of diplomatic relations. The People's Republic condemned the visit, claiming that it undermined Sino-Japanese relations. The former President of Taiwan, Lee Teng-hui, made a private visit to Japan in late April 2001, ostensibly for medical treatment. In order to minimize tensions with China, the Japanese authorities forbade Lee to make political statements while in Japan. In March 2002 it was revealed that Japanese politicians, including former Prime Minister Ryutaro Hashimoto, had received money from an unauthorized fund established by Lee in order to procure influence in Japan. However, the incident failed to damage bilateral relations, and in late 2001–early 2002 officials from both sides were investigating the possibility of establishing a free trade agreement. In November 2002 the Japanese Government refused Lee a visa to visit Keio University, which subsequently withdrew its invitation for him to deliver a speech there. In January 2003 Taiwan, along with China, condemned Japan's moves to assert sovereignty over the Tiaoyutai islands in the East China Sea by renting them out to private companies. In May Japan's Minister of Foreign Affairs reportedly told a Chinese official that Japan supported Taiwan's application to join WHO with observer status. Discussions on a free trade agreement between Japan and Taiwan remained unresolved in 2003; this was thought to have been due partly to China's opposition to such an agreement. In September 2003 the second Taiwan-Japan Forum opened in Tokyo, at which issues of mutual concern were discussed. In February 2005, as part of a revised strategic understanding with the USA, Japan identified Taiwan's security as a 'common strategic objective' for the first time, thereby drawing criticism from the Chinese mainland. In January 2007, as China prepared to mark the 35th anniversary of Japan's transfer of diplomatic recognition from Taiwan to the People's Republic, the island's Government announced that it would mark 2007 as 'Taiwan-Japan Cultural Exchange Year'. In the same month it was reported that Japan and the USA were preparing to discuss contingency plans for their troops to deal jointly with any potential confrontation between Taiwan and China, a suggestion that drew immediate condemnation from the mainland. In June, furthermore, a visit by former Taiwanese President Lee Teng-hui to the Yasukuni Shrine, a controversial war memorial in Japan, further antagonized the mainland.

The dispute over the sovereignty of the Tiaoyutai islands, and the corresponding right to fish in the waters around the islands, continued in 2005, with Taiwanese fishermen repeatedly complaining of harassment by Japanese patrol boats. In June an armed naval frigate, carrying the Taiwanese Minister of National Defense, the President of the Legislative Yuan and 15 legislators, was dispatched to the region, reportedly in response to these complaints of harassment. Subsequent negotiations between Taiwan and Japan over fishing rights, the 15th round of talks on the issue since 1996, concluded without agreement in July, and in August President Chen reiterated Taiwan's claim to sovereignty over the Tiaoyutai islands. In September Taiwanese Secretary-General Yu Shyi-kun attended a forum on relations between Taiwan and Japan in Tokyo, thus becoming the highest-ranking Taiwanese official to visit Japan since the withdrawal of diplomatic recognition in 1972.

In March 1989, meanwhile, President Lee paid a state visit to Singapore, the first official visit overseas by a President of Taiwan for 12 years. In a further attempt to end diplomatic isolation, Lee said that he would visit any foreign country, even if it maintained diplomatic relations with China. In January 1993 official confirmation of Taiwan's purchase of 60 Mirage fighter aircraft from France provoked strong protest from China. In January 1994 Taiwan suffered a reverse when (following pressure from the People's Republic) France recognized Taiwan as an integral part of Chinese territory and agreed not to sell weapons to the island. In February President Lee embarked upon an eight-day tour of South-East Asia. His itinerary incorporated the Philippines, Indonesia and Thailand, all three of which maintained diplomatic relations with the People's Republic of China. Although the tour was described as informal, President Lee had meetings with the three heads of state, leading to protests from China. In May the Taiwanese President visited Nicaragua, Costa Rica, South Africa (the island's only remaining major diplomatic ally) and Swaziland. In March 1995 it was reported that Taiwan was to purchase shoulder-fired anti-aircraft missiles from a French company, despite France's previous assurances to the People's Republic that it would not sell weapons to Taiwan (the purchase was confirmed in 1996). In April 1995 President Lee travelled to the United Arab Emirates and to Jordan. Although accompanied by senior members of the Executive Yuan, the visits were described as private (Taiwan having no diplomatic relations with these countries). In June the Taiwanese Premier visited Austria, Hungary and the Czech Republic, where he had private meetings with his Czech counterpart and with President Václav Havel. Again, the visits provoked a strong protest from China.

In August 1996 Vice-Premier Hsu Li-teh led a delegation of government and business representatives to South Africa. In September, however, the Taiwanese Minister of Foreign Affairs was obliged to curtail an ostensibly private visit to Jakarta (where he was reported to have had discussions with his Indonesian counterpart), following protests from the People's Republic of China. Also in 1996, the first delivery of Mirage aircraft to Taiwan from France (first announced in 1993) took place. At the same time, it was confirmed that France would sell six frigates to Taiwan (delivery of these was completed in March 1998). In January 1997 the Vice-President was received by the Pope during a visit to the Holy See, the only European state that continued to recognize Taiwan. In the same month the Minister of Foreign Affairs embarked upon a tour of seven African nations, in order to consolidate relations. His itinerary included South Africa, despite that country's recent announcement of its intention to sever diplomatic relations with Taiwan. In March 1997 a six-day visit to Taiwan by the Dalai Lama was strongly condemned by the People's Republic of China, which denounced a meeting between President Lee and the exiled spiritual leader of Tibet as a 'collusion of splittists'. A second visit by the Dalai Lama, scheduled for July 1998, was postponed, following mainland China's criticism of the opening of a representative office of the Dalai Lama's religious foundation in Taiwan.

In July 1997, following the Bahamas' withdrawal of recognition from Taiwan and establishment of diplomatic relations with the People's Republic of China, the Taiwanese Minister of Foreign Affairs undertook an extensive tour of the countries of Central America and the Caribbean, in an effort to maintain their support. In September, during a tour of Central America (the six nations of the region having become the core of Taiwan's remaining diplomatic allies), President Lee attended an international conference on the development of the Panama Canal. The USA granted a transit visa to the Taiwanese President, enabling him to stop over in Hawaii en route to and from Central America. A visit to Europe in October by Vice-President Lien Chan was curtailed when pressure from China forced the Spanish Government to withdraw an invitation. The Malaysian and Singaporean Prime Ministers met their Taiwanese counterpart in Taiwan in November, on their return from the APEC forum in Canada. The People's Republic expressed concern at the meetings.

In January 1998 the Taiwanese Premier, Vincent Siew, met senior officials during a visit to the Philippines and Singapore. It was believed that discussions had focused on the possibility of Taiwan extending economic assistance to those countries. Moreover, the Taiwanese Government expressed its intention to pursue the creation of a multilateral Asian fund, under the auspices of APEC, to support the ailing Asian economies. Relations with Taiwan's Asian neighbours were further strengthened in February, when a leading member of the KMT visited the Republic of Korea, again, it was understood, to discuss financial assistance in the wake of the Asian economic crisis. Negotiations between the Malaysian Deputy Prime Minister and Finance Minister and the Taiwanese Premier, held in Taiwan in February, also concentrated on economic and financial issues. Vincent Siew made a return visit to Malaysia in April. China was highly critical of these visits, accusing Taiwan of seeking to gain political advantage from the regional economic crisis.

In August 1999 the Taiwanese Government threatened to refuse entry to the island to Philippine labourers in retaliation for Manila's unilateral termination of its aviation agreement with Taipei. In October the Philippine authorities decided to close the country to Taiwanese aircraft. Access was, however, temporarily granted in November during talks on the renewal of the agreement. Negotiations faltered in December, but reached a successful conclusion in early 2000, thus permitting flights to the Philippines to resume. In March, however, flights were suspended again. In June the Taiwanese Government imposed a three-month ban on new work permits for Philippine nationals, citing interference by the Philippines' representative office in Taiwan concerning labour disputes. Any connection with the aviation dispute was denied. In September a new aviation agreement, enabling flights between Taipei and Manila to restart, was signed.

Following the withdrawal of diplomatic recognition by South Africa, in 1998 Taiwan made extensive efforts to maintain relations with the island's other allies. The Minister of Foreign Affairs visited eight African countries in February, and in April it was announced that Taiwan's overseas aid budget was to be substantially increased, in an attempt to retain diplomatic support. In May the Vice-President, Lien Chan, visited Taiwan's Central American and Caribbean allies. China expressed serious concern in November at New Zealand's decision to grant Taiwanese officials in Wellington privileges accorded to accredited diplomats. Following the loss of four allies during 1998, relations were established with the Marshall Islands in November of that year, and with the former Yugoslav republic of Macedonia in January 1999. The latter rapidly benefited from its contacts with Taiwan, receiving extensive aid following the Kosovo conflict. The Prime Minister of Papua New Guinea initiated diplomatic relations with Taiwan in early July 1999. Following his resignation later that month, recognition was withdrawn from Taiwan, allegedly because of a failure to adhere to correct procedures for the establishment of relations. Full diplomatic relations were established with Palau in December of that year, and Taiwan opened an embassy on the island in March 2000. In August 2000 the new Taiwanese President, Chen Shui-bian, embarked upon a tour of diplomatic allies in Central America and West Africa. In October Taiwan was concerned that it might lose a diplomatic ally when the Minister of Foreign Affairs of Solomon Islands unexpectedly cancelled a visit to Taipei and travelled instead to Beijing. The Premier of Solomon Islands did not attend a regional forum, instead visiting Taipei to make amends and to reiterate his commitment to maintaining relations.

Throughout 2001 Taiwan continued to seek a higher diplomatic profile. President Chen in late May began a tour of five Latin American nations—El Salvador, Guatemala, Panama, Paraguay, and Honduras—as part of Taiwan's 'dollar diplomacy'—a practice of giving aid and bringing investment in return for diplomatic recognition. While in El Salvador, Chen met eight regional leaders, who pledged support for Taiwan. Taiwan and the People's Republic of China were increasingly vying for support in this region to boost their overall global standing. Taiwan was also in competition with China for support from Pacific island nations, five of which (Marshall Islands, Nauru, Palau, Solomon Islands and Tuvalu) recognized Taiwan. Two of these nations, Solomon Islands and the Marshall Islands, were thought to be wavering in their support of Taiwan. The Dalai Lama visited Taiwan in March–April 2001 and held talks with President Chen, much to the anger of China. In June the former Yugoslav republic of Macedonia announced that it would recognize the People's Republic of China, thus leading to a break in relations with Taiwan. In November Wu Shu-chen, wife of President Chen, travelled to Strasbourg, France, to accept the 'Prize for Freedom' awarded to her husband by Liberal International, a world grouping of liberal parties. Chen himself had been refused a visa by the European Union (EU).

In January 2002 it was reported that Taiwan had secretly been developing military and intelligence links with India, through mutual co-operation including bilateral visits of military personnel and the exchange of intelligence data. Also in January, Vice-President Lu visited Nicaragua and Paraguay, having visited The Gambia in December 2001. Vice-President Lu also visited Indonesia in mid-August 2002 and met several ministers, but not President Megawati Sukarnoputri, owing to pressure on the latter by China. While in Indonesia, Lu discussed possible liquefied natural gas projects, investment and migrant labour. Taiwanese companies had in previous years invested US $17,000m. in Indonesia, the home of some 100,000 of Taiwan's migrant workers. President Chen completed a four-nation tour of Africa in early July 2002, having visited Senegal, São Tomé and Príncipe, Malawi and Swaziland. While en route to Swaziland, he was refused permission to land in South Africa. Diplomatic relations between Taiwan and Nauru were terminated in late July 2002 after the latter established relations with the People's Republic of China. In September 2002 Taiwan announced the opening of a trade and economic affairs representative office in Mongolia. In late 2002 Taiwan and the Democratic People's Republic of Korea (North Korea) were planning to open economic liaison offices in the respective capitals, the latter keen to attract new sources of investment. President Chen was forced to cancel a trip to Indonesia in December after the South-East Asian country came under heavy pressure from China.

In March 2003 President Chen was again refused a visa by the EU, and was thus unable to address members of the European Parliament in Brussels. Also in March, the Taiwanese Government issued a warning that several Pakistani citizens with links to terrorist networks might be attempting to enter Taiwan. Taiwan expressed concern over the political situation in the West African state of São Tomé and Príncipe following a military coup there in July 2003. In October 2003 Liberia transferred its diplomatic recognition to the People's Republic of China. In August, meanwhile, Taiwan signed a free trade agreement with Panama. In November Kiribati granted diplomatic recognition to Taiwan, and a Taiwanese embassy opened on the Pacific island in January 2004. Also in January, there were tensions in Taiwan's relations with France after French President Jacques Chirac expressed his support for China's opposition to a proposed referendum in Taiwan (see above) during a visit by Chinese President Hu Jintao to Paris. Two visits by Taiwanese ministers to France were subsequently cancelled. Joint military exercises between the French and Chinese navies were held in March off Taiwan's northern coast. Also in March, Dominica withdrew its diplomatic recognition of Taiwan.

In November 2004 the Prime Minister of Vanuatu, Serge Vohor, announced that his country had established diplomatic relations with Taiwan, despite also maintaining formal relations with the People's Republic of China; the resulting controversy concluded in the dismissal of Vohor in a parliamentary vote of no confidence, and his successor announced that his Government was to withdraw recognition from Taiwan. In January 2005 Grenada withdrew recognition from Taiwan. Also in January, President Chen undertook an official visit to Palau, thus becoming the first Taiwanese President to visit the Pacific nation. He also travelled to Solomon Islands, where he strenuously denied accusations of 'money diplomacy', and to the US territory of Guam. The President of the Marshall Islands visited Taipei in late 2004, and in May 2005 President Chen became the first head of any foreign state to visit the Marshall Islands in an official capacity, as part of a diplomatic tour of Pacific nations, during which he also became the first foreign head of state to visit Kiribati and Tuvalu and controversially altered his published itinerary to visit Fiji, a country that maintained diplomatic relations with the People's Republic of China. Also in May, diplomatic relations with Nauru, terminated in 2002, were re-established. In October 2005 Senegal re-established diplomatic links with the People's Republic of China and terminated its full relations with Taiwan. Despite this relative lack of formal recognition in the international community, Taiwan's commercial relations with numerous countries continued to flourish, and in 2006 about 50 countries without full diplomatic relations with Taiwan maintained representative offices or visa-issuing centres on the island. In August 2006, however, Chad transferred diplomatic recognition to the People's Republic, announcing this decision less than 24 hours before Premier Su Tseng-chang was due to embark upon an official visit to the African nation. Following Saint Lucia's restoration of recognition in May 2007 and Costa Rica's termination of diplomatic links in June, the total number of countries retaining full diplomatic relations with Taiwan stood at 24, prompting senior members of the Government to renew diplomatic campaigns. Vice-President Annette Lu travelled to Central and South America, while Minister of Foreign Affairs Huang Chih-fang visited several African states. In January 2008, however, it was announced that Malawi had severed diplomatic relations with Taiwan.

In September 2006 a summit meeting attended by Taiwan and its six Pacific allies was convened in Palau; this was followed by the second Taiwan-Pacific Allies Summit, which was held in Majuro, the Marshall Islands, in October 2007. In April, meanwhile, a similar event had been hosted in Fiji by the People's Republic, which had invited the participation of the Pacific Islands with which it maintained diplomatic relations. These developments underlined the increasingly intense competition between Taiwan and the mainland for dominance in the Pacific region.

The question of the sovereignty of the Spratly Islands, situated in the South China Sea and to which five countries as well as Taiwan laid claim, remained unresolved. Believed to possess petroleum and gas resources, in addition to encompassing rich fishing areas, the grouping comprises more than 100 small islands and reefs. A contingent of Taiwanese marines is maintained on Taiping Island, the largest of the disputed islands, located some 1,574 km south-west of Taiwan. A satellite telecommunications link between Taiping and Kaohsiung was inaugurated in October 1995. In December 1998 the Legislative Yuan approved the first legal definition of Taiwan's sea borders. The Spratly Islands were claimed, as were the disputed Tiaoyutai Islands, within the 12- and 24-nautical mile zones. In November 2002, in Phnom-Penh, Cambodia, members of the Association of South East Asian Nations (ASEAN, see p. 185) signed a landmark 'declaration on the conduct of parties in the South China Sea', which aimed to avoid conflict in the area. Under this agreement, which was similar to one drafted in late 1999 but not implemented, claimants would practise self-restraint in the event of potentially hostile action (such as inhabiting the islands), effect confidence-building measures and give advance notice of military exercises in the region. However, the agreement did not include the Paracel Islands, and disagreements continued among the signatories on what the accord should encompass. Additionally, China introduced a provision requiring consensus to resolve outstanding issues, thereby allowing for future indecision among ASEAN members. It was unclear how the declaration affected Taiwan, since it was not a member of ASEAN. In August 2003 Minister of the Interior Yu Cheng-hsien visited Taiping Island and reaffirmed Taiwanese sovereignty. In February 2008 President Chen Shui-bian visited Taiwanese forces stationed on Taiping, where he inaugurated a new airstrip and proposed a 'Spratly Initiative', urging claimant countries to disregard the issue of sovereignty and to co-operate in the protection of the islands' environment and resources. The Philippines and Viet Nam had been particularly critical of the construction of the airstrip.

Government

Under the provisions of the amended 1947 Constitution, the Head of State is the President, who is elected by popular vote for a four-year term. There are five Yuans (governing bodies), the highest legislative organ being the Legislative Yuan, to which the Executive Yuan (the Council of Ministers) is responsible. Since the elections of January 2008, the Legislative Yuan has comprised 113 members; 73 chosen by direct election, most of the remainder being appointed from separate lists of candidates on the basis of proportional representation. The Legislative Yuan serves a four-year term. There are also Control, Judicial and Examination Yuans. Their respective functions are: to investigate the work of the executive; to interpret the Constitution and national laws; and to supervise examinations for entry into public offices. In April 2000 the role of the National Assembly was revised. The powers to initiate constitutional amendments, to impeach the President or Vice-President, and to approve the appointment of senior officials were transferred to the Legislative Yuan. The National Assembly retained the functions of ratifying constitutional amendments and responsibility for impeachment proceedings, in which case 300 delegates appointed by political parties according to a system of proportional representation were to convene for a session of a maximum duration of one month. The Taiwan Provincial Government handles the general administrative affairs of the island (excluding the cities of Taipei and Kaohsiung). Its policy-making body is the Taiwan Provincial Government Council. In July 1997 the National Assembly approved a series of constitutional amendments, including the suspension of elections at local government level, as the first stage of the dissolution of the provincial apparatus. Accordingly, the elected Governor of Taiwan was replaced by an appointed Governor in December 1998. The Taiwan Provincial Assembly exercises the province's legislative power. The Fukien (Fujian) Provincial Government is responsible for the administration of Quemoy and Matsu.

Defence

As assessed at November 2007, the armed forces totalled an estimated 290,000: army 200,000 (with deployments of 15,000–20,000 and 8,000–10,000, respectively, on the islands of Quemoy and Matsu), air force 45,000 and navy 45,000 (including 15,000 marines). Paramilitary forces numbered 17,000. Reserves totalled 1,657,000. Military service lasts for 20 months. Defence expenditure, including special procurements, for 2008 was budgeted at NT $341,000m.

Economic Affairs

In 2006, according to official figures, Taiwan's gross national income (GNI), at current prices, totalled US $375,085m., equivalent to US $16,494 per head. During 1996–2006, it was estimated, the population increased at an average annual rate of 0.6%, while in real terms on the basis of figures in US dollars gross domestic product (GDP) per head increased by an average of 1.9% per year in 1996–2006. In terms of New Taiwan dollars, overall GDP increased at an average annual rate of 4.4% in 1996–2006. Compared with the previous year, GDP increased by 4.9% in 2006. In 2007, according to the Asian Development Bank (ADB), GDP expanded by 5.7%.

Agriculture (including hunting, forestry and fishing) contributed 1.7% of GDP in 2006. It engaged 5.3% of the employed labour force in 2007. The principal crops are vegetables, rice, sugar cane and citrus fruits. Agricultural GDP decreased at an average annual rate of 0.9%, in real terms, during 1996–2006. Compared with the previous year, agricultural GDP decreased by 6.1% in 2006. The sector contracted by 2.9% in 2007, according to the ADB.

Industry (comprising mining, manufacturing, construction and utilities) engaged 36.8% of the employed labour force in 2007 and provided 27.7% of GDP in 2006. Industrial GDP increased, in real terms, at an average rate of 4.4% per year in 1996–2006. Compared with the previous year, industrial GDP increased by 7.0% in 2006. The industrial sector expanded by 9.2% in 2007, according to the ADB.

Mining contributed 0.3% of GDP in 2006, employing a negligible percentage of the labour force. Marble, sulphur and dolomite are the principal minerals extracted. The GDP of the mining sector decreased at an average rate of 7.5% per year in 1996–2006. Mining GDP decreased by 10.9% in 2006.

Manufacturing contributed 23.6% of GDP in 2006 and engaged 27.6% of the employed labour force in 2007. The most important branches, measured by gross value of output, are electronics (particularly personal computers), plastic goods, synthetic yarns and the motor vehicle industry. The sector's GDP grew at an average annual rate of 5.4%, in real terms, in 1996–2006. Manufacturing GDP increased by 7.5% in 2006, compared with the previous year.

In 2006 50.9% of Taiwan's energy supply was derived from imported petroleum. Imports of crude petroleum accounted for 11.6% of total import expenditure in 2006. In that year nuclear power supplied 7.2% of Taiwan's energy requirements. Taiwan has substantial reserves of natural gas.

The services sector contributed 70.7% of GDP in 2006, while engaging 42.8% of the employed labour force in 2007. The number of tourist arrivals rose to more than 3.7m. in 2007. Visitors from Japan account for most tourist arrivals. Tourism receipts increased by 3.2% in 2006, to reach US $5,136m. In 1996–2006 the GDP of the services sector increased, in real terms, at an average annual rate of 4.5%. In 2006 services GDP increased by 4.1%, compared with the previous year. In 2007, according to the ADB, the services sector expanded by 4.3%.

In 2006 Taiwan recorded a visible trade surplus of US $23,404m., and there was a surplus of US $24,661m. on the current account of the balance of payments. In 2006 the principal sources of imports were Japan (accounting for 22.8%), the People's Republic of China (12.2%) and the USA (11.2%). The principal markets for exports in that year were the People's Republic of China (accounting for 23.1% of exports), Hong Kong (16.7%) and the USA (14.4%). Trade with the People's Republic of China (mainly via Hong Kong) has expanded rapidly in recent years. The value of exports to mainland China increased from US $4,217.5m. in 2000 to US $51,808.6m. in 2006. Taiwan's principal imports in 2006 were mineral products, electronic products, chemical products and base metals. The principal exports in that year were electrical equipment, electronic products, base metals and plastics.

The 2008 budget envisaged expenditure of NT $2,471,500m. and revenue of NT $2,244,900m. The Government anticipated the budget deficit to be the equivalent of 1.4% of projected GDP. Taiwan's long-term external public debt stood at US $190m. at the end of 2006, when the cost of debt-servicing reached the equivalent of 3.6% of the value of exports of goods and services, declining to US $182m. in mid-2007. The annual rate of inflation averaged 0.8% during the period 1996–2006. Consumer prices rose by 1.8% in 2007. Some 3.9% of the labour force were unemployed in 2007 (compared with an average of 4.1% in 2005). There is a shortage of labour in certain sectors.

Taiwan became a member of the Asian Development Bank (ADB, see p. 182) in 1966, and of the Asia-Pacific Economic Co-operation (APEC, see p. 176) forum in late 1991. In September 1992 Taiwan was granted observer status at the General Agreement on Tariffs and Trade (GATT), and was finally granted membership of the successor World Trade Organization (WTO, see p. 396) in November 2001, effective from 1 January 2002.

Taiwan's economic growth has been substantial, mainly owing to the versatility of its manufacturing base and the strength of its export sector. The island has held consistently large reserves of foreign exchange, which were estimated to stand at US $286,900m. in March 2008. In May 2002 the Government announced a new six-year national development plan, Challenge 2008, envisaging expenditure of US $75,000m. on infrastructure and public construction projects. The opening in January 2007 of a new high-speed railway linking Taipei and Kaohsiung, reducing travel time between Taiwan's two largest cities to 90 minutes, was expected to help integrate the island's western seaboard into a single commercial zone. Direct investment from abroad increased by 356.9% in 2006 in comparison with the previous year, while Taiwan's direct investment abroad rose by 22.7% in that year. The island's privatization programme (first introduced in 1989) continued intermittently, having been delayed by opposition from labour unions and vested interest groups. Chunghwa Telecom completed its privatization in 2005. Other companies scheduled for transfer to the private sector included Chinese Petroleum, China Shipbuilding, Taiwan Sugar Corporation, Tang Eng Iron Works and Taiwan Power. Despite political tensions, economic links with the People's Republic of China were becoming increasingly significant, with the value of Taiwan's exports to the mainland rising from just 7.6% of total exports in 2002 to 23.1% in 2006. Furthermore, in anticipation of the conclusion of a bilateral accord on foreign-exchange settlements, in early 2007 Taiwan agreed to provide direct currency exchanges between the New Taiwan dollar and the yuan for mainland Chinese tourists. The rate of GDP growth was forecast to decelerate to 4.3% in 2008, with the weakening in the US export market being partially offset by the continued strength of the island's sales to mainland China.

Education

Education at primary schools and junior high schools is free and compulsory between the ages of six and 15 years. Secondary schools consist of junior and senior middle schools, normal schools for teacher-training and vocational schools. There are also a number of private schools. Higher education is provided in universities, colleges, junior colleges and graduate schools. The Government's budgetary expenditure on education in 2006 was NT $452,991m. In 2006/07 there were 1,798,436m. pupils enrolled in state primary schools, and there were 1,707,336m. children in secondary schools. The net enrolment ratio for children between the ages of six and 14 was 97.6% in 2006. There were 163 universities and other institutes of higher education in 2006/07. The adult literacy rate in 2006 was 97.5%.

Public Holidays

2008: 1–2 January (Founding of the Republic/New Year), 7–10 February (Chinese New Year), 5 April (Ching Ming/Tomb Sweeping Day and Death of President Chiang Kai-shek), 8 June (Dragon Boat Festival), 15 September (Mid-Autumn Moon Festival), 28 September (Teachers' Day/Birthday of Confucius), 10 October (Double Tenth Day, anniversary of 1911 revolution), 25 October (Retrocession Day, anniversary of end of Japanese occupation), 12 November (Birthday of Sun Yat-sen), 25 December (Constitution Day).

2009: 1–2 January (Founding of the Republic/New Year), 26–29 January (Chinese New Year), 5 April (Ching Ming/Tomb Sweeping Day and Death of President Chiang Kai-shek), 28 May (Dragon Boat Festival), 3 October (Mid-Autumn Moon Festival), 28 September (Teachers' Day/Birthday of Confucius), 10 October (Double Tenth Day, anniversary of 1911 revolution), 25 October (Retrocession Day, anniversary of end of Japanese occupation), 12 November (Birthday of Sun Yat-sen), 25 December (Constitution Day).

Weights and Measures

The metric system is officially in force, but some traditional Chinese units are still used.

Statistical Survey

Source (unless otherwise stated): Bureau of Statistics, Directorate-General of Budget, Accounting and Statistics (DGBAS), 1, Section 1, Jhongsiao East Rd, Taipei 10058; tel. (2) 23803542; fax (2) 23803547; e-mail sicbs@dgbas.gov.tw; internet www.dgbas.gov.tw.

Area and Population

AREA, POPULATION AND DENSITY

Area (sq km)	36,188*
Population (census results)	
16 December 1990	20,393,628
16 December 2000	
Males	11,386,084
Females	10,914,845
Total	22,300,929
Population (official figures at 31 December)	
2005	22,770,383
2006	22,876,527
2007	22,958,360
Density (per sq km) at 31 December 2007	634.4

* 13,972 sq miles.

PRINCIPAL TOWNS
(population at 31 December 2006)

Taipei (capital)	2,632,242	Taoyuan	384,803
Kaohsiung	1,514,706	Sanchong	383,636
Taichung	1,044,392	Jhongli	355,707
Tainan	760,037	Fongshan	338,596
Banciao	544,292	Sindian	289,366
Jhunghe	411,011	Chiayi	272,364
Hsinchu	394,757	Tucheng	237,000
Sinjhuang	392,472	Yonghe	235,679
Keelung	390,633	Jhanghua	235,322

CHINA (TAIWAN)

BIRTHS, MARRIAGES AND DEATHS
(registered)

	Live births Number	Rate (per 1,000)	Marriages Number	Rate (per 1,000)	Deaths Number	Rate (per 1,000)
2000	305,312	13.76	181,642	8.19	125,958	5.68
2001	260,354	11.65	170,515	7.63	127,647	5.71
2002	247,530	11.02	172,655	7.69	128,636	5.73
2003	227,070	10.06	171,483	7.60	130,801	5.80
2004	216,419	9.56	131,453	5.80	135,092	5.97
2005	205,854	9.06	141,140	6.21	139,398	6.13
2006	204,459	8.96	142,669	6.25	135,839	5.95
2007	204,414	8.92	135,041	5.89	141,111	6.16

Expectation of life (years at birth, 2006): Males 74.57; Females 80.81.

ECONOMICALLY ACTIVE POPULATION
(annual averages, '000 persons aged 15 years and over)*

	2005	2006	2007
Agriculture, forestry and fishing	590	554	543
Mining and quarrying	7	7	6
Manufacturing	2,732	2,777	2,845
Construction	791	829	846
Electricity and gas supply	28	28	28
Water supply and remediation services	61	60	65
Trade	1,726	1,759	1,782
Hotels and restaurants	634	665	681
Transport and storage	412	417	415
Information and communication	199	209	206
Finance and insurance	406	407	404
Education	556	563	588
Public administration, defence and compulsory social	336	334	332
Total employed (incl. others)	9,942	10,111	10,294
Unemployed	428	411	419
Total labour force	10,371	10,522	10,713
Males	6,012	6,056	6,116
Females	4,359	4,467	4,597

* Excluding members of the armed forces and persons in institutional households.

Health and Welfare

KEY INDICATORS

Total fertility rate (children per woman, 2006)	1.1
Under-5 mortality rate (per 1,000 live births, 2006)	6.06
HIV/AIDS (% of persons aged 15–49, 2006)	0.03
Physicians (per 1,000 head, 2006)	1.73
Hospital beds (per 1,000 head, 2006)	6.51
Health expenditure (2005): US $ per head (PPP)	n.a.
Health expenditure (2005): % of GDP	6.02
Health expenditure (2005): public (% of total)	62.90
Human Development Index (2004): value	0.925

For definitions, see explanatory note on p. vi.

Agriculture

PRINCIPAL CROPS
('000 metric tons)

	2004	2005	2006
Potatoes	36.3	41.7	49.6
Rice*	1,164.6	1,187.6	1,261.8
Sweet potatoes	175.4	214.0	235.2
Sorghum	12.8	8.3	4.7
Maize	144.3	133.5	128.4
Tea	20.2	18.8	19.3
Tobacco	5.5	2.7	2.2
Groundnuts	68.3	53.9	71.6
Sugar cane	1,129.4	875.5	651.0
Bananas	189.9	148.7	214.3
Pineapples	458.5	439.9	491.6
Citrus fruit	547.8	471.6	549.0
Vegetables	3,064.6	2,654.6	2,878.0

* Figures are in terms of brown rice. The equivalent in paddy rice (in '000 metric tons) was: 1,433.6 in 2004, 1,467.1 in 2005; 1,558.0 in 2006.

LIVESTOCK
('000 head at 31 December)

	2004	2005	2006
Cattle	144.8	137.9	134.8
Buffaloes	5.0	4.1	3.5
Pigs	6,819.0	7,171.5	7,068.6
Sheep and goats	249.4	263.5	267.4
Chickens	108,443	105,018	109,633
Ducks	9,768	11,769	11,912
Geese	2,819	3,038	2,841
Turkeys	197	179	163

LIVESTOCK PRODUCTS

	2004	2005	2006
Beef (metric tons)	5,120	6,048	5,626
Pig meat (metric tons)	1,088,737	911,449	930,609
Goat meat (metric tons)	6,323	3,234	3,896
Chickens ('000 head)*	377,960	337,632	346,153
Ducks ('000 head)*	32,255	33,596	37,741
Geese ('000 head)*	6,402	6,449	6,723
Turkeys ('000 head)*	386	376	335
Milk ('000 metric tons)	322	304	323
Duck eggs ('000)	417,126	487,549	466,232
Hen eggs ('000)	6,998,992	6,314,144	6,620,415

* Figures refer to numbers slaughtered.

Forestry

ROUNDWOOD REMOVALS
('000 cubic metres)

	2004	2005	2006
Industrial wood	30.4	31.4	27.0
Fuel wood	9.6	12.7	9.2
Total	40.0	44.1	36.2

CHINA (TAIWAN)

Fishing

('000 metric tons, live weight)

	2004	2005	2006
Tilapias	81.0	83.5	72.6
Other freshwater fishes	13.5	12.3	10.2
Japanese eel	29.6	28.5	23.8
Milkfish	56.9	50.1	56.1
Pacific saury	60.8	111.5	60.6
Skipjack tuna	189.8	170.3	194.4
Albacore	46.1	39.9	40.1
Yellowfin tuna	95.2	122.0	77.7
Bigeye tuna	99.9	73.7	59.1
Chub mackerel	60.6	77.8	54.8
Sharks, rays, skates, etc.	43.8	39.9	49.4
Marine shrimps and prawns	38.1	40.2	37.7
Other crustaceans	11.1	9.4	63.8
Pacific cupped oyster	29.8	28.4	28.5
Common squids	13.7	14.2	8.9
Argentine shortfin squid	58.3	59.9	148.1
Total catch (incl. others)	1,278.1	1,311.6	1,271.3

Note: Figures exclude aquatic plants, totalling (in '000 metric tons): 9.4 in 2004; 2.7 in 2005; 12.3 in 2006.

Mining

(metric tons, unless otherwise indicated)

	2004	2005	2006
Crude petroleum ('000 litres)	44,563	32,389	23,564
Natural gas ('000 cu m)	796,038	548,457	462,958
Sulphur	222,760	267,790	245,789
Marble (raw material)	22,970,546	24,069,551	25,492,633
Dolomite	114,598	173,986	61,224

Industry

SELECTED PRODUCTS
('000 metric tons, unless otherwise indicated)

	2004	2005	2006
Wheat flour	796.7	801.6	784.3
Granulated sugar and molasses	482.1	487.6	392.3
Carbonated beverages ('000 litres)	399,334	403,999	362,933
Alcoholic beverages—excl. beer ('000 hectolitres)	447.2	397.5	371.4
Cigarettes (million)	26,175.6	27,522.5	22,073.3
Cotton yarn	287.4	270.9	286.1
Paper	837.2	847.0	836.0
Paperboard	3,555.0	3,378.0	3,350.6
Sulphuric acid	1,188.2	1,182.9	1,264.9
Spun yarn	279.8	237.4	208.3
Cement	19,049.9	19,891.0	19,293.8
Steel ingots	18,211.7	17,150.8	19,203.3
Sewing machines ('000 units)	246.2	214.1	161.4
Electric fans ('000 units)	11,586.8	9,177.0	7,410.1
Personal computers ('000 units)	6,789.8	4,560.1	3,150.1
Monitors ('000 units)	3,876.7	2,802.9	1,874.6
Television sets and VCRs ('000 units)	1,662.2	2,141.8	1,829.0
Audio units for cars ('000 units)	1,023.3	904.9	682.1
Loudspeakers and microphones ('000 units)	67,269.0	52,070.0	49,038.0

—continued	2004	2005	2006
Electronic tubes ('000 units)	4,755	555	—
Integrated circuits (million units)	7,915.7	8,620.0	10,576.4
Electronic condensers (million units)	264,213.1	237,568.0	218,290.2
Telephone sets ('000 units)	1,904.0	646.3	872.6
Passenger motor cars (units)	423,303	439,090	299,401
Trucks and buses (units)	5,937	5,610	6,301
Bicycles ('000 units)	4,948.5	4,867.9	4,415.4
Ships (value of sales, NT $ million)	22,811.7	25,802.0	26,435.5
Electric energy (million kWh)	206,084	214,215	221,993
Refined petroleum (million litres)	58,561.5	61,830.0	59,460.2

2007 (metric tons, unless otherwise indicated): Carbonated beverages ('000 litres) 354,331; Cement 18,957; Steel ingots 20,879; Personal computers ('000 units) 1,303; Monitors ('000 units) 1,462; Passenger cars, trucks and buses (units) 284,490; Electrical energy (million kWh) 228,803.

Finance

CURRENCY AND EXCHANGE RATES

Monetary Units
100 cents = 1 New Taiwan dollar (NT $).

Sterling, US Dollar and Euro Equivalents (30 November 2007)
£1 sterling = NT $66.683;
US $1 = NT $32.270;
€1 = NT $47.634;
NT $1,000 = £15.00 = US $30.99 = €20.99.

Average Exchange Rate (NT $ per US $)
2004   33.422
2005   32.167
2006   32.531

GENERAL GOVERNMENT BUDGET
(NT $ million, year ending 31 December)

Revenue	2004	2005	2006
Current revenue	1,865,612	2,017,145	2,079,647
Taxes	1,353,410	1,531,297	1,556,652
Public enterprise	306,699	281,568	311,112
Fees	85,286	88,860	91,126
Capital revenue	106,036	98,082	72,459
Total	1,971,648	2,115,227	2,152,106

Expenditure	2004	2005	2006
General administration	334,143	343,015	346,045
National defence	248,910	248,547	237,101
Education, science and culture	461,886	472,005	489,816
Economic development	425,992	465,478	385,364
Social welfare	344,503	353,255	369,421
Community development and environmental protection	90,152	87,372	76,357
Pensions and survivors' benefits	179,874	191,323	196,954
Obligations	139,461	132,661	138,415
Subsidies to provincial and municipal governments	13,993	15,909	12,456
Total	2,238,914	2,309,565	2,251,929
Current	1,700,598	1,734,862	1,759,316
Capital	538,315	574,702	492,613

2007 (NT $ million, year ending 31 December, preliminary estimate): Total revenue 2,258.0; Total expenditure 2,356.2.

2008 (NT $ million, year ending 31 December, budget proposals): Total revenue 2,244.9; Total expenditure 2,471.5.

INTERNATIONAL RESERVES
(US $ million at 31 December)

	2004	2005	2006
Gold (national valuation)	4,822	4,662	4,692
Foreign exchange	241,738	253,290	266,148
Total	246,560	257,952	270,840

CHINA (TAIWAN)

MONEY SUPPLY
(NT $ '000 million at 31 December)

	2004	2005	2006
Currency outside banks	669.8	730.4	758.7
Demand deposits at deposit money banks	6,698.2	7,140.8	7,463.9
Total money	7,368.0	7,871.2	8,222.6

COST OF LIVING
(Consumer Price Index; base: 2001 = 100)

	2005	2006	2007
Food	111.84	111.09	114.27
Clothing	105.08	102.55	105.63
Housing	98.08	98.91	99.84
Transport and communications	101.73	103.44	105.22
Medicines and medical care	110.97	114.63	119.11
Education and entertainment	98.69	98.86	99.46
All items (incl. others)	103.46	104.08	105.95

NATIONAL ACCOUNTS
(NT $ million in current prices)

National Income and Product

	2004	2005	2006
Domestic factor incomes	8,922,326	9,240,979	9,620,418
Consumption of fixed capital	1,436,485	1,485,187	1,541,999
Gross domestic product (GDP) at factor cost	10,358,811	10,726,166	11,162,417
Indirect taxes, less subsidies	706,737	728,561	727,406
GDP in purchasers' values	11,065,548	11,454,727	11,889,823
Factor income from abroad	517,602	559,722	629,123
Less Factor income paid abroad	145,503	268,856	317,424
Gross national product (GNP)	11,437,647	11,745,593	12,201,522
Less Consumption of fixed capital	1,436,485	1,485,187	1,541,999
National income in market prices	10,001,162	10,260,406	10,659,523
Other current transfers from abroad	105,960	111,436	124,829
Less Other current transfers paid abroad	233,815	248,647	252,847
National disposable income	9,873,307	10,123,195	10,531,505

Expenditure on the Gross Domestic Product

	2004	2005	2006
Government final consumption expenditure	1,465,293	1,498,304	1,503,349
Private final consumption expenditure	6,718,928	7,022,565	7,182,821
Increase in stocks	86,840	10,838	11,678
Gross fixed capital formation	2,420,150	2,438,435	2,517,565
Total domestic expenditure	10,691,211	10,970,142	11,215,413
Exports of goods and services	6,978,144	7,358,019	8,304,602
Less Imports of goods and services	6,603,807	6,873,434	7,630,192
GDP in purchasers' values	11,065,548	11,454,727	11,889,823
GDP at constant 2001 prices	11,337,829	11,809,552	12,386,799

Gross Domestic Product by Economic Activity

	2004	2005	2006
Agriculture, hunting, forestry and fishing	181,475	189,759	193,142
Mining and quarrying	37,096	35,375	38,358
Manufacturing	2,624,232	2,658,475	2,718,392
Construction	211,830	227,548	257,757
Electricity, gas and water	177,465	177,336	176,308
Transport, storage and communications	697,265	704,576	716,393
Trade, restaurants and hotels	2,111,492	2,275,302	2,438,209
Finance, insurance and real estate*	2,066,013	2,120,020	2,169,385
Government services	1,230,357	1,256,082	1,275,326
Other services	1,389,090	1,458,979	1,555,899
Sub-total	10,726,315	11,103,452	11,539,169
Value-added tax	213,086	215,892	214,968
Import duties	126,147	135,383	135,686
GDP in purchasers' values	11,065,548	11,454,727	11,889,823

* Including imputed rents of owner-occupied dwellings.

BALANCE OF PAYMENTS
(US $ million)

	2004	2005	2006
Exports of goods f.o.b.	182,362	198,456	223,789
Imports of goods f.o.b.	−166,249	−180,559	−200,385
Trade balance	16,113	17,897	23,404
Exports of services	25,789	25,827	29,272
Imports of services	−30,731	−32,480	−33,661
Balance on goods and services	11,171	11,244	19,015
Other income received	15,485	17,394	19,338
Other income paid	−4,353	−8,355	−9,757
Balance on goods, services and income	22,303	20,283	28,596
Current transfers received	3,170	3,463	3,837
Current transfers paid	−6,995	−7,727	−7,772
Current balance	18,478	16,019	24,661
Capital account (net)	−77	−117	−118
Direct investment abroad	−7,145	−6,028	−7,399
Direct investment from abroad	1,898	1,625	7,424
Portfolio investment assets	−21,823	−33,902	−40,783
Portfolio investment liabilities	17,154	31,045	21,814
Financial derivatives assets	888	909	1,930
Financial derivatives liabilities	−1,731	−1,912	−2,895
Other investment assets	408	−6,254	−1,266
Other investment liabilities	17,520	16,819	1,551
Net errors and omissions	1,025	1,852	1,167
Overall balance	26,595	20,056	6,086

CHINA (TAIWAN) — Statistical Survey

External Trade

PRINCIPAL COMMODITIES
(US $ million)

Imports c.i.f.	2004	2005	2006
Mineral products	22,965.7	29,858.9	38,808.9
Crude petroleum	13,107.7	18,207.0	23,528.5
Products of chemical or allied industries	17,593.0	19,495.1	22,468.4
Organic chemicals	7,621.4	8,566.7	9,742.3
Base metals and articles thereof	18,478.9	18,808.3	23,158.6
Iron and steel products	10,814.8	10,597.3	10,234.3
Machinery and mechanical appliances; electrical equipment; sound and television apparatus	66,855.3	68,832.6	72,541.2
Electronic products	30,896.8	33,345.9	36,773.3
Machinery	17,668.8	17,305.0	17,907.4
Electrical machinery products	6,275.6	6,632.7	6,631.4
Information and communication products	5,552.8	5,546.1	4,957.3
Vehicles, aircraft, vessels and associated transport equipment	5,320.7	6,976.6	4,949.8
Optical, photographic, cinematographic, measuring, precision and medical apparatus; clocks and watches; musical instruments	12,594.5	11,334.7	12,376.5
Total (incl. others)	168,757.5	182,614.4	202,698.3

Exports f.o.b.	2004	2005	2006
Chemicals	7,969.5	10,126.4	11,268.6
Plastics, rubber and articles thereof	12,647.3	14,732.8	15,908.3
Textiles and textile articles	12,572.3	11,840.1	11,788.8
Fibre and yarn	8,962.8	8,651.0	8,664.6
Base metals and articles thereof	18,429.3	20,467.8	24,010.7
Iron and steel	12,022.1	13,238.1	14,742.4
Machinery and mechanical appliances; electrical equipment; sound and television apparatus	94,783.7	98,268.6	111,592.2
Electronic products	45,578.2	51,008.1	62,822.9
Machinery	12,591.4	13,397.4	14,269.3
Electrical machinery products	8,406.3	9,449.9	10,882.8
Information and communication products	13,204.6	10,973.9	9,883.9
Vehicles, aircraft, vessels and associated transport equipment	6,532.6	7,307.7	7,378.6
Total (incl. others)	182,370.9	198,431.7	224,017.4

2007 (excluding trade with People's Republic of China): Total imports 219,346.7; Total exports 246,722.7.

PRINCIPAL TRADING PARTNERS
(US $ million)

Imports c.i.f.	2004	2005	2006
Australia	3,429.6	4,726.4	5,349.5
Canada	1,204.3	1,324.1	1,373.8
China, People's Republic	16,792.3	20,093.7	24,783.1
France	2,099.9	2,544.4	2,220.0
Germany	5,852.0	6,180.3	6,135.2
Hong Kong	2,309.2	2,109.7	1,880.6
Indonesia	4,114.5	4,543.0	5,204.3
Italy	1,349.3	1,451.6	1,545.2
Japan	43,717.8	46,053.3	46,284.4
Korea, Republic	11,663.6	13,239.2	14,999.6
Malaysia	5,425.0	5,217.2	6,051.6
Netherlands	2,202.6	2,068.7	2,342.6
Philippines	3,063.8	2,794.8	2,775.5
Russia	2,473.1	2,196.4	1,903.0
Saudi Arabia	5,559.0	7,437.2	9,760.2
Singapore	4,330.7	4,960.7	5,105.6
Switzerland	1,343.0	1,338.2	1,256.3
Thailand	2,784.7	2,887.1	3,317.5
United Kingdom	1,745.0	1,714.1	1,781.0
USA	21,780.4	21,170.8	22,664.5
Total (incl. others)	168,757.6	182,614.4	202,698.1

Exports f.o.b.	2004	2005	2006
Australia	2,268.6	2,392.6	2,723.0
Canada	1,651.9	1,690.3	1,770.3
China, People's Republic	36,349.4	43,643.7	51,808.6
France	1,591.5	1,452.9	1,565.7
Germany	4,607.1	4,463.1	5,007.0
Hong Kong*	32,896.2	34,035.6	37,381.2
Indonesia	1,895.9	2,358.6	2,499.5
Italy	1,739.0	1,797.5	2,194.7
Japan	13,808.0	15,110.8	16,300.3
Korea, Republic	5,629.8	5,877.4	7,154.2
Malaysia	4,218.3	4,282.6	4,941.5
Netherlands	4,807.2	4,396.2	4,411.6
Philippines	4,035.5	4,324.9	4,484.4
Singapore	6,747.3	8,042.2	9,279.6
Thailand	3,317.9	3,820.3	4,576.6
United Kingdom	3,430.2	3,262.8	3,510.6
USA	28,751.0	29,113.9	32,360.7
Viet Nam	3,451.7	4,102.8	4,869.4
Total (incl. others)	182,370.4	198,431.7	224,017.3

* The majority of Taiwan's exports to Hong Kong are re-exported.

2007: *Imports:* Hong Kong 1,824.9; Japan 45,943.5; Korea, Republic 15,159.6; Malaysia 6,184.2; Singapore 4,792.6; Thailand 3,613.4; Total (incl. others, but excluding People's Republic of China) 219,346.7. *Exports:* Hong Kong 37,978.2; Japan 15,936.2; Korea, Republic 7,794.6; Malaysia 5,390.2; Singapore 10,501.4; Thailand 5,199.0; Total (incl. others, but excluding People's Republic of China) 246,722.7.

Transport

RAILWAYS
(traffic)

	2005	2006	2007
Passengers ('000)	531,446	554,194	586,750
Passenger-km ('000)	12,255,347	12,352,488	12,239,082
Freight ('000 metric tons)	19,251	19,060	16,807
Freight ton-km ('000)	981,575	996,527	888,183

ROAD TRAFFIC
(motor vehicles in use at 31 December)

	2005	2006	2007
Passenger cars	5,634,362	5,698,324	5,712,842
Buses and coaches	26,967	27,522	27,361
Goods vehicles	953,470	971,801	975,650
Motorcycles and scooters	13,195,265	13,557,028	13,943,473

SHIPPING

Merchant Fleet
(at 31 December)

	2004	2005	2006
Number of vessels	639	636	628
Total displacement ('000 grt)	3,556.3	3,222.3	2,785.7

Source: Lloyd's Register-Fairplay, *World Fleet Statistics*.

Sea-borne freight traffic
('000 metric tons)

	2004	2005	2006
Goods loaded	277,114	273,389	279,718
Goods unloaded	419,127	414,538	426,788

CHINA (TAIWAN)

CIVIL AVIATION
(traffic on scheduled services)

	2004	2005	2006
Passengers carried ('000)	44,116.5	44,267.8	43,725.1
Freight carried ('000 metric tons)	1,823.1	1,818.8	1,809.6

Tourism

TOURIST ARRIVALS BY COUNTRY OF ORIGIN

	2004	2005	2006
Hong Kong and Macao	417,087	432,718	431,884
Indonesia	44,161	88,464	90,870
Japan	887,311	1,124,334	1,161,489
Korea, Republic	148,095	182,517	196,260
Malaysia	92,760	107,549	115,202
Philippines	87,005	92,074	79,993
Singapore	116,885	166,179	184,160
Thailand	103,089	93,568	95,643
USA	382,822	390,929	394,802
Overseas Chinese*	522,045	579,908	664,198
Total (incl. others)	2,950,342	3,378,118	3,519,827

* i.e. those bearing Taiwan passports.

2007: Total arrivals 3,716,063.

Tourism receipts (US $ million): 4,053 in 2004; 4,977 in 2005; 5,136 in 2006.

Communications Media

	2004	2005	2006
Book production (titles)	39,882	41,966	42,281
Magazines	890	944	939
Telephone subscribers ('000)	13,530	13,615	13,473
Mobile telephones ('000 in use)	22,760	22,171	23,249
Publishing industries	3,290	3,443	3,453
Internet users ('000)	8,036	7,271	7,037
Broadband subscribers ('000)*	3,751	4,341	4,506

* Source: International Telecommunication Union.

Television receivers (2006): Colour television receivers per 100 households: 152.29; Cable television receivers per 100 households: 79.92.

Education

(2006/07)

	Schools	Full-time teachers	Students
Pre-school	3,329	19,037	201,815
Primary	2,651	100,692	1,798,436
Secondary (incl. vocational)	1,210	100,498	1,707,336
Higher	163	50,388	1,313,993
Special	24	1,736	6,588
Supplementary	877	1,620	259,058
Total (incl. others)	8,254	273,971	5,287,226

Adult literacy rate (official estimate): 97.5% in 2006.

Directory

Note: the issue of the implementation of a uniform system of romanization of Taiwanese names remained unresolved in 2007; the central Government favours the use of a system of Pinyin similar to that employed in mainland China but with certain differences (Tongyong), while local authorities in Taiwan remain divided between usage of the standard mainland Pinyin system (Hanyu) and a form of the traditional Wade-Giles system.

The Constitution

On 1 January 1947 a new Constitution was promulgated for the Republic of China. When the Chinese Communist Party established the People's Republic of China on the Chinese mainland in 1949, the Government of the Republic of China, led by the Kuomintang (KMT), relocated to Taiwan, where it maintained jurisdiction over Taiwan, Penghu, Kinmen, Matsu and numerous other islets. The two sides of the Taiwan Strait have since been governed as separate territories. The form of government that was incorporated in the Constitution is based on a five-power system and has the major features of both cabinet and presidential government. A process of constitutional reform, initiated in 1991, continued in the early 21st century. The following is a summary of the Constitution, as subsequently amended:

PRESIDENT

The President shall be directly elected by popular vote for a term of four years. Both the President and Vice-President are eligible for re-election to a second term. The President represents the country in all state functions, including foreign relations; commands land, sea and air forces, promulgates laws, issues mandates, concludes treaties, declares war, makes peace, declares martial law, grants amnesties, appoints and removes civil and military officers, and confers honours and decorations. The President, subject to certain limitations, may issue emergency orders to deal with national calamities and ensure national security; may dissolve the Legislative Yuan; and also appoints the Premier and the officials of the Judicial Yuan, the Examination Yuan and the Control Yuan.

EXECUTIVE YUAN

The Executive Yuan is the highest administrative organ of the nation and is responsible to the Legislative Yuan; it has two categories of subordinate organization:

Executive Yuan Council (policy-making organization)

Ministries and Commissions (executive organizations), of which there are currently 37, including other agencies.

LEGISLATIVE YUAN

The Legislative Yuan is the highest legislative organ of the State, empowered to hear administrative reports of the Executive Yuan, and to advise on government policy, statutory and budgetary issues. It may hold a binding vote of no confidence in the Executive Yuan. It comprises 113 members: 73 are chosen by direct election from single-member constituencies; 34 members are elected on the basis of proportional representation from a nation-wide constituency, with seats being allocated only to parties that have garnered more than 5% of the total votes in this second, supplementary ballot; the remaining six members are elected from and by aborigines. Members serve for a term of four years and are eligible for re-election.

JUDICIAL YUAN

The Judicial Yuan is the highest judicial organ of state and has charge of civil, criminal and administrative cases, and of cases concerning disciplinary measures against public functionaries (see Judicial System).

EXAMINATION YUAN

The Examination Yuan supervises examinations for entry into public offices, and deals with personnel matters of the civil service, implements training and protection measures for public functionaries, and supervises the public service pension fund. The Examination Yuan is also responsible for certification examinations for professionals and technologists.

CONTROL YUAN

The Control Yuan is the highest control organ of the State, exercising powers of impeachment, censure and audit, comprising 29 members serving a six-year term. (According to the Additional Articles of the Constitution of the Republic of China as amended in April 2000, the

CHINA (TAIWAN)

members of the Control Yuan shall be nominated by the President of the State, and with the consent of the Legislative Yuan.) The Control Yuan may impeach or censure a public functionary at central or local level, who is deemed guilty of violation of law or dereliction of duty, and shall refer the matter to the civil courts for action in cases involving a criminal offence; the Control Yuan may propose corrective measures to the Executive Yuan or to its subordinate organs.

The Government

HEAD OF STATE

President: CHEN SHUI-BIAN (inaugurated 20 May 2000; re-elected 20 March 2004; President-elect MA YING-JEOU; to take office 20 May 2008).
Vice-President: ANNETTE LU HSU-LIEN.
Secretary-General: YEH CHU-LAN.

EXECUTIVE YUAN
(April 2008)

Premier: CHANG CHUN-HSIUNG (Premier-designate LIU CHAO-SHIUAN; to take office 20 May 2008).
Vice-Premier and Minister of the Consumer Protection Commission: CHIOU I-JEN.
Secretary-General: CHEN CHIN-JUN.
Deputy Secretary-General: CHEN MEI-LING.
Ministers without Portfolio: LIN SI-YAO, WU TSE-CHENG (Minister of the Public Construction Commission), LIN FERNG-CHING, HO MEI-YEUH, LIU YUH-SAN, HUANG HWEI-CHEN, LIU SHI-FAN.
Minister of the Interior: LEE YI-YANG.
Minister of Foreign Affairs: HUANG CHIH-FANG.
Minister of National Defense: MICHAEL TSAI.
Minister of Finance: LEE RUEY-TSANG (acting).
Minister of Education: TU CHENG-SHENG.
Minister of Justice: SHIH MAO-LIN.
Minister of Economic Affairs: STEVE CHEN RUEY-LONG.
Minister of Transportation and Communications: TSAI DUEI.
Minister of the Mongolian and Tibetan Affairs Commission: HSU CHIH-HSIUNG.
Minister of the Overseas Compatriot Affairs Commission: CHANG FU-MEI.
Governor of the Central Bank of China: PERNG FAI-NAN.
Minister of the Directorate-General of Budget, Accounting and Statistics: HSU JAN-YAU.
Minister of Central Personnel Administration: CHOU HUNG-HSIEN.
Minister of the Government Information Office: SHIEH JHY-WEY.
Minister of the Department of Health: HOU SHENG-MOU.
Minister of the Environmental Protection Administration: WINSTON DANG.
Director of the National Palace Museum: LIN MUN-LEE.
Minister of the Mainland Affairs Council: CHEN MING-TONG.
Minister of the Council for Economic Planning and Development: HO MEI-YUEH.
Minister of the Veterans' Affairs Commission: HU CHEN-PU.
Minister of the National Youth Commission: LIN TAI-HUA.
Minister of the Atomic Energy Council: SU SHIAN-JANG.
Minister of the National Science Council: CHEN CHIEN-JEN.
Minister of the Research, Development and Evaluation Commission: SHIH NING-JYE.
Minister of the Council of Agriculture: SU JIA-CHYUAN.
Minister of the Council for Cultural Affairs: WANG TUOH.
Minister of the Council of Labor Affairs: LU TIEN-LIN.
Chairperson of the Fair Trade Commission: TANG JINN-CHUAN.
Minister of the Sports Affairs Council: YANG JONG-HER.
Minister of the Council of Indigenous Peoples: ICYANG PAROD.
Minister of the Coast Guard Administration: WANG GINN-WANG.
Minister of the Council for Hakka Affairs: LEE YUNG-TE.
Chairperson of the Central Election Commission: MASA J. S. CHANG.
Chairperson of the Co-ordination Council for North American Affairs: LIN FANG-MEI.
Minister of the Financial Supervisory Commission: HU SHENG-CHENG.

MINISTRIES, COMMISSIONS, ETC.

Office of the President: 122 Chungking South Rd, Sec. 1, Taipei 10048; tel. (2) 23113731; fax (2) 23311604; e-mail public@mail.oop.gov.tw; internet www.president.gov.tw.

Ministry of Economic Affairs: 15 Foo Chou St, Taipei 10015; tel. (2) 23212200; fax (2) 23919398; e-mail service@moea.gov.tw; internet www.moea.gov.tw.

Ministry of Education: 5 Chung Shan South Rd, Taipei 10051; tel. (2) 23566051; fax (2) 23976978; internet www.moe.gov.tw.

Ministry of Finance: 2 Ai Kuo West Rd, Taipei 10066; tel. (2) 23228000; fax (2) 23965829; e-mail root@mof.gov.tw; internet www.mof.gov.tw.

Ministry of Foreign Affairs: 2 Kaitakeland Blvd, Taipei 10048; tel. (2) 23482999; fax (2) 23812703; e-mail eyes@mofa.gov.tw; internet www.mofa.gov.tw.

Ministry of the Interior: 5–9/F, 5 Hsu Chou Rd, Taipei 10055; tel. (2) 23565005; fax (2) 23566201; e-mail service@mail.moi.gov.tw; internet www.moi.gov.tw.

Ministry of Justice: 130 Chungking South Rd, Sec. 1, Taipei 10048; tel. (2) 23146871; fax (2) 23896759; internet www.moj.gov.tw.

Ministry of National Defense: 2/F, 164 Po Ai Rd, Taipei 10048; tel. (2) 23116117; fax (2) 23144221; internet www.mnd.gov.tw.

Ministry of Transportation and Communications: 2 Chang Sha St, Sec. 1, Taipei 10048; tel. (2) 23492900; fax (2) 23896009; e-mail motceyes@motc.gov.tw; internet www.motc.gov.tw.

Mongolian and Tibetan Affairs Commission: 4/F, 5 Hsu Chou Rd, Sec. 1, Taipei 10055; tel. (2) 23566467; fax (2) 23416186; e-mail mtacserv@mtac.gov.tw; internet www.mtac.gov.tw.

Overseas Compatriot Affairs Commission: 4/F, 5 Hsu Chou Rd, Taipei 10055; tel. (2) 23566166; fax (2) 23566323; e-mail ocacinfo@mail.ocac.gov.tw; internet www.ocac.gov.tw.

Directorate-General of Budget, Accounting and Statistics: 1, Sec. 1, Jhongsiao East Rd, Taipei 10058; tel. (2) 33566500; fax (2) 23825267; e-mail sicbs@dgbas.gov.tw; internet www.dgbas.gov.tw.

Government Information Office: 2 Tientsin St, Taipei 10051; tel. (2) 33568888; fax (2) 23568733; e-mail service@mail.gio.gov.tw; internet www.gio.gov.tw.

Council of Indigenous Peoples: 7/F, 3 Songren Rd, Sec. 1, Taipei 11010; tel. (2) 87891800; fax (2) 23454323; e-mail minister@apc.gov.tw; internet www.apc.gov.tw.

Council of Agriculture: see under Trade and Industry—Government Agencies.

Atomic Energy Council (AEC): 80 Cheng Kung Rd, Sec. 1, Yonghe City, Taipei County 23452; tel. (2) 82317919; fax (2) 82317804; e-mail public@aec.gov.tw; internet www.aec.gov.tw.

Central Personnel Administration: 11/F, 2-2 Jinan Rd, Taipei 10051; tel. (2) 23979298; fax (2) 23975505; internet www.cpa.gov.tw.

Consumer Protection Commission: 1 Jihe Rd, Taipei 11166; tel. (2) 28863200; fax (2) 28866646; e-mail tcpc@ms1.hinet.net; internet www.cpc.gov.tw.

Council for Hakka Affairs: 8/F, 3 Songren Rd, Taipei 11010; tel. (2) 87894567; fax (2) 87894620; e-mail src@mail.hakka.gov.tw; internet www.hakka.gov.tw.

Council for Cultural Affairs: 30-1 Beiping East Rd, Taipei 10051; tel. (2) 23434000; fax (2) 23222937; e-mail adm@cca.gov.tw; internet www.cca.gov.tw.

Council for Economic Planning and Development: 3 Baocing Rd, Taipei 10020; tel. (2) 23165300; fax (2) 23700415; internet www.cepd.gov.tw.

Environmental Protection Administration: 41 Chung Hua Rd, Sec. 1, Taipei 10042; tel. (2) 23117722; fax (2) 23116071; e-mail www@sun.epa.gov.tw; internet www.epa.gov.tw.

Public Construction Commission: 9/F, 3 Songren Rd, Taipei 11010; tel. (2) 87897500; fax (2) 87897800; e-mail secr@mail.pcc.gov.tw; internet www.pcc.gov.tw.

Fair Trade Commission: 12–14/F, 2-2 Chi Nan Rd, Sec. 2, Taipei 10054; tel. (2) 23517588; fax (2) 23974997; e-mail ftcpub@ftc.gov.tw; internet www.ftc.gov.tw.

Department of Health: 12/F, 100 Ai Kuo East Rd, Taipei 10092; tel. (2) 23210151; fax (2) 23122907; internet www.doh.gov.tw.

Council of Labor Affairs: 3 Yangping North Rd, Sec. 2, Taipei 10346; tel. (2) 85902866; fax (2) 85902959; internet www.cla.gov.tw.

Mainland Affairs Council: 15/F, 2-2 Chi Nan Rd, Sec. 1, Taipei 10054; tel. (2) 23975589; fax (2) 23975300; e-mail macst@mac.gov.tw; internet www.mac.gov.tw.

National Science Council: 17–22/F, 106 Ho Ping East Rd, Sec. 2, Taipei 10622; tel. (2) 27377992; fax (2) 27377608; e-mail nsc@nsc.gov.tw; internet www.nsc.gov.tw.

CHINA (TAIWAN)

National Youth Commission: 14/F, 5 Hsu Chou Rd, Taipei 10055; tel. (2) 23566232; fax (2) 23566307; e-mail nycn@nyc.gov.tw; internet www.nyc.gov.tw.

National Council on Physical Fitness and Sports: 20 Jhulun St, Taipei 10481; tel. (2) 87711800; fax (2) 27523600; e-mail public@ncpfs.gov.tw; internet www.ncpfs.gov.tw.

Research, Development and Evaluation Commission: 6/F, 2-2 Chi Nan Rd, Sec. 1, Taipei 10051; tel. (2) 23419066; fax (2) 23969990; e-mail service@rdec.gov.tw; internet rdec.gov.tw.

Veterans' Affairs Commission: 222 Chung Hsiao East Rd, Sec. 5, Taipei 11075; tel. (2) 27255749; fax (2) 27230170; e-mail eyes@mail.vac.gov.tw; internet vac.gov.tw.

Co-ordination Council for North American Affairs: 133 Po-ai Rd, Taipei 10048; tel. (2) 23119212; fax (2) 23822651; e-mail sgccnaa@mofa.gov.tw; headquarters for Taipei Economic and Cultural Representative Office (TECRO) in the USA.

Financial Supervisory Commission: 18/F, No.7, Sec. 2, Hsien Ming Blvd, Panchiao City, Taipei County 22041; tel. (2) 89680899; fax (2) 89681215; e-mail fscey@fscey.gov.tw; internet www.fscey.gov.tw.

Coast Guard Administration: 296 Singlong Rd, Taipei 11687; tel. (2) 22399201; fax (2) 22399258; e-mail master@cga.gov.tw; internet www.cga.gov.tw.

President and Legislature

PRESIDENT

Election, 22 March 2008

Candidate*	Votes	% of votes
Ma Ying-jeou (Kuomintang—KMT)	7,659,014	58.45
Frank C. T. Hsieh (Democratic Progressive Party—DPP)	5,444,949	41.55
Total	13,103,963†	100.00

* The vice-presidential candidates were respectively Vincent V. C. Siew of the KMT and Su Tseng-chang of the DPP.
† Not including invalid or spoiled ballot papers.

LI-FA YUAN
(Legislative Yuan)

President: WANG JIN-PYNG.

Election, 12 January 2008

Party	Seats
Kuomintang (KMT)	81
Democratic Progressive Party (DPP)	27
Non-Partisan Solidarity Union (NPSU)	3
People First Party (PFP)	1
Independents	1
Total	113

Election Commission

Central Election Commission: 10/F, 5 Hsu Chou Rd, Taipei 10055; tel. (2) 23565484; e-mail cec13@cec.gov.tw; internet www.cec.gov.tw; f. 1980; Chairperson and 11–19 commissioners nominated by Premier and approved by President; Chairperson is also a member of the Executive Yuan; Chair. MASA J. S. CHANG.

Political Organizations

Legislation adopted in 1989 permitted political parties other than the KMT to function. At August 2006 a total of 109 parties were registered with the Ministry of the Interior.

China Democratic Socialist Party (CDSP): 6/F, 7 Heping East Rd, Sec. 3, Taipei 10670; tel. (2) 27072883; f. 1932 by merger of National Socialists and Democratic Constitutionalists; aims to promote democracy, protect fundamental freedoms, and improve public welfare and social security; Chair. I BUH-LUEN; Sec.-Gen. SUEN SHANN-HAUR.

China Young Party: 12/F, 2 Sinsheng South Rd, Sec. 3, Taipei 10660; tel. (2) 23626715; f. 1923; aims to recover sovereignty over mainland China, safeguard the Constitution and democracy, and foster understanding between Taiwan and the non-communist world; Chair. JEAN JYI-YUAN.

Democratic Progressive Party (DPP): 10/F, 30 Beiping East Rd, Taipei 10051; tel. and fax (2) 23929989; e-mail foreign@dpp.org.tw; internet www.dpp.org.tw; f. 1986; advocates 'self-determination' for the people of Taiwan and UN membership; supports establishment of independent Taiwan following plebiscite; 530,975 mems (2004); Chair. (vacant); Sec.-Gen. LEE YING-YUAN.

Green Party Taiwan: 2/F, 148, Sec. 3, Musin Rd, Wunshan District, Taipei 11660; tel. (2) 29384710; fax (2) 29383402; e-mail contact@greenparty.org.tw; internet www.greenparty.org.tw; f. 1996; est. by breakaway faction of the DPP.

Jiann Gwo Party (Taiwan Independence Party—TAIP): 9/F, 15–8 Nanjing East Rd, Sec. 5, Taipei 10564; tel. (2) 22800879; f. 1996 by dissident mems of DPP; Chair. HUANG CHIEN-MING; Sec.-Gen. LI SHENG-HSIUNG.

Kuomintang (KMT) (Nationalist Party of China): 232, Sec. 2, Bade Rd, Taipei 10492; tel. (2) 87711234; fax (2) 23434561; internet www.kmt.org.tw; f. 1894; aims to supplant communist rule in mainland China; supports democratic, constitutional government, and advocates the unification of China; aims to promote market economy and equitable distribution of wealth; 1.1m. mems; Chair. WU POH-HSIUNG; Sec.-Gen. WU TUN-YI.

New Party (NP): 4/F, 65 Guangfu South Rd, Taipei 10563; tel. (2) 27562222; fax (2) 27565750; e-mail webmaster@mail.np.org.tw; internet www.np.org.tw; f. 1993 by dissident KMT legislators (hitherto mems of New Kuomintang Alliance faction); merged with China Social Democratic Party in late 1993; advocates co-operation with the KMT and DPP in negotiations with the People's Republic, the maintenance of security in the Taiwan Straits, the modernization of the island's defence systems, measures to combat government corruption, the support of small and medium businesses and the establishment of a universal social security system; 80,000 mems; Chair. YOK MU-MING.

Non-Partisan Solidarity Union: 3/F, 5–1 Zhenjiang St, Taipei 10051; tel. (2) 23585066; internet www.npsu.org.tw; f. 2004; Chair. CHANG PO-YA.

People First Party (PFP): 1/F, 63 Chang-an East Rd, Sec. 2, Taipei 10455; tel. (2) 25068555; internet www.pfp.org.tw; f. 2000; plans for merger with KMT announced May 2004; Chair. JAMES C. Y. SOONG; Sec.-Gen. CHIN CHIN-SHENG.

Taiwan Solidarity Union (TSU): 9/F, 65 Guancian Rd, Taipei 11047; tel. (2) 23706686; fax (2) 23706616; internet www.tsu.org.tw; f. 2001 by a breakaway faction of the Kuomintang (KMT); Chair. HUANG HUN-KUI; Sec.-Gen. CHEN CHIEN-MING.

Diplomatic Representation

EMBASSIES IN THE REPUBLIC OF CHINA

Belize: 11/F, 9 Lane 62, Tien Mou West Rd, Taipei 11156; tel. (2) 28760894; fax (2) 28760896; e-mail embelroc@ms41.hinet.net; internet www.embassyofbelize.org.tw; Ambassador WILLIAM QUINTO.

Burkina Faso: 6/F, 9-1 Lane 62, Tien Mou West Rd, Taipei 11156; tel. (2) 28733096; fax (2) 28733071; e-mail abftap94@ms17.hinet.net; Ambassador JACQUES Y. SAWADOGO.

Dominican Republic: 6/F, Lane 62, Tien Mou West Rd, Taipei 11156; tel. (2) 28751357; fax (2) 28752661; e-mail embajada_dom_entaipei@hotmail.com; Ambassador VÍCTOR MANUEL SÁNCHEZ.

El Salvador: 2/F, 9 Lane 62, Tien Mou West Rd, Shih Lin, Taipei 11156; tel. (2) 28763606; fax (2) 28763514; e-mail embasal.taipei@msa.hinet.net; Ambassador FRANCISCO RICARDO SANTANA BERRÍOS.

The Gambia: 9/F, 9-1 Lane 62, Tien Mou West Rd, Taipei 11156; tel. (2) 28753911; fax (2) 28752775; e-mail gm.roc@msa.hinet.net; Ambassador MAWDO CORAJIKI JUWARA.

Guatemala: 3/F, 9-1 Lane 62, Tien Mou West Rd, Taipei 11156; tel. (2) 28756952; fax (2) 28740699; e-mail embaguat.tw@iname.com; internet www.geocities.com/WallStreet/Floor/8227; Ambassador FRANCISCO BERMÚDEZ AMADO.

Haiti: 8/F, 9-1 Lane 62, Tien Mou West Rd, Taipei 11156; tel. (2) 28766718; fax (2) 28766719; e-mail haiti@ms26.hinet.net; Ambassador PAUL RAYMOND PERODIN.

Holy See: 87 Ai Kuo East Rd, Taipei 10642 (Apostolic Nunciature); tel. (2) 23216847; fax (2) 23911926; Chargé d'affaires a.i. Mgr AMBROSE MADTHA.

Honduras: 9/F, 9 Lane 62, Tien Mou West Rd, Taipei 11156; tel. (2) 28755507; fax (2) 28755726; e-mail honduras@ms9.hinet.net; Ambassador MARLENE VILLELA-TALBOTT.

CHINA (TAIWAN)

Marshall Islands: 4/F, 9-1 Lane 62, Tien Mou West Rd, Shi-lin, Taipei 111; tel. (2) 28734884; fax (2) 28734904; e-mail rmiembtp@ms41.hinet.net; Ambassador ALEXANDER CARTER BING.

Nauru: Room C, 9/F, 247 Chung Cheng Rd, Sec. 2 Shi-lin, Taipei; tel. (2) 8736121; fax (2) 8736125; Ambassador LUDWIG D. KEKE.

Nicaragua: 3/F, Lane 62, Tien Mou West Road, Taipei 11156; tel. (2) 28749034; fax (2) 28749080; e-mail icaza@ms13.hinet.net; Ambassador WILLIAM TAPIA.

Palau: 5/F, 9 Lane 62, Tien Mou West Rd, Taipei 11156; tel. (2) 28765415; fax (2) 28760436; e-mail palau.embassy@msa.hinet.net; Chargé d'affaires a.i. LYDIA NGIRABLOSCH.

Panama: 6/F, 111 Sung Kiang Rd, Taipei 10486; tel. (2) 25099189; fax (2) 25099801; Ambassador JULIO MOCK CÁRDENAS.

Paraguay: 7/F, 9-1 Lane 62, Tien Mou West Rd, Taipei 11156; tel. (2) 28736310; fax (2) 28736312; e-mail eptaipei@seed.net.tw; Ambassador RAMÓN ANTERO DÍAZ PEREIRA.

São Tomé and Príncipe: 10/F, 9-1 Lane 62, Tien Mou West Rd, Taipei 11156; tel. (2) 28766824; fax (2) 28766984; e-mail ladislaualmeida@yahoo.co.uk; Ambassador LADISLAU D'ALMEIDA.

Solomon Islands: 7/F, 9-1 Lane 62, Tien Mou West Rd, Taipei 11156; tel. (2) 28731168; fax (2) 28735224; e-mail embassy@solomons.org.tw; internet www.solomons.org.tw; Ambassador BERAKI JINO.

Saint Christopher and Nevis: 5/F, 9-1 Lane 62, Tien Mou West Rd, Taipei 11156; tel. (2) 28738252; fax (2) 28733246; Chargé d'affaires JASMINE HUGGINS.

Swaziland: 10/F, 9 Lane 62, Tien Mou West Rd, Taipei 11156; tel. (2) 28725934; fax (2) 28726511; e-mail swazitpi@ms41.hinet.net; Ambassador NJABULISO GWEBU.

Judicial System

Under Articles 78 and 79 of the Constitution and Article 5 of the Constitutional Amendments, 15 Justices of the Constitutional Court (including the President and Vice-President of the Judicial Yuan) have the authority to interpret the Constitution, to render uniform interpretations of statutes and regulations whenever they are in conflict, and to declare the dissolution of any political party in violation of the Constitution. All of the Justices of the Constitutional Court are nominated and, with the consent of the Legislative Yuan (Congress), appointed by the President of the Republic of China. Owing to a transition to a staggered system of appointment, of 15 Justices appointed in 2003, eight, including the President and Vice-President of the Judicial Yuan, serve a four-year term, while the others serve an eight-year term.

Judicial Yuan: 124 Chungking South Rd, Sec. 1, Taipei 10048; tel. (2) 23618577; fax (2) 23898923; e-mail judicial@mail.judicial.gov.tw; internet www.judicial.gov.tw; Pres. LAI IN-JAW; Vice-Pres. HSIEH TSAY-CHUAN; Sec.-Gen. FAN KUANG-CHUN; the highest judicial organ, and the interpreter of the constitution and national laws and ordinances; supervises the following:

Supreme Court: 6 Chang Sha St, Sec. 1, Taipei 10048; tel. (2) 23141160; fax (2) 23114246; e-mail tpsemail@mail.judicial.gov.tw; Court of third and final instance for civil and criminal cases; Pres. WU CHII-PIN.

High Courts: Courts of second instance for appeals of civil and criminal cases.

District Courts: Courts of first instance in civil, criminal and non-contentious cases.

Supreme Administrative Court: 1 Lane 126, Chungking South Rd, Sec. 1, Taipei 10048; tel. (2) 23113691; fax (2) 23111791; e-mail jessie@judicial.gov.tw; Court of final resort in cases brought against govt agencies; Pres. CHANG DENG-KE.

High Administrative Courts: Courts of first instance in cases brought against govt agencies.

Commission on Disciplinary Sanctions Against Functionaries: 124 Chungking South Rd, 3/F, Sec. 1, Taipei 10036; tel. (2) 23111639; fax (2) 23826255; decides on disciplinary measures against public functionaries impeached by the Control Yuan; Chief Commissioner LIN KUO-HSIEN.

Religion

According to the Ministry of the Interior, in 2004 35% of the population were adherents of Buddhism, 33% of Daoism (Taoism), 3.5% of I-kuan Tao and 2.6% of Christianity.

BUDDHISM

Buddhist Association of Taiwan: Mahayana and Theravada schools; 1,613 group mems and more than 5.4m. adherents; Leader Ven. CHIN-HSIN.

CHRISTIANITY

The Roman Catholic Church

Taiwan comprises one archdiocese, six dioceses and one apostolic administrative area. In December 2005, according to official figures, there were 307,612 adherents.

Bishops' Conference

Chinese Regional Bishops' Conference, 3 Lane 85, Linsen North Rd, Taipei 10443; tel. (2) 23571776; fax (2) 25231078; e-mail bishconf@ms1.hinet.net; internet www.catholic.org.tw.

f. 1967; Pres. Cardinal PAUL SHAN KUO-HSI (Bishop of Kaohsiung).

Archbishop of Taipei: Most Rev. JOSEPH CHENG TSAI-FA, Archbishop's House, 94 Loli Rd, Taipei 10587; tel. (2) 27371311; fax (2) 27373710.

The Anglican Communion

Anglicans in Taiwan are adherents of the Protestant Episcopal Church. In 2004 the Church had 1,000 members.

Bishop of Taiwan: Rt Rev. DAVID JUNG-HSIN LAI, 7 Lane 105, Hangchow South Rd, Sec. 1, Taipei 10060; tel. (2) 23411265; fax (2) 23962014; e-mail skhtpe@ms12.hinet.net; internet www.episcopalchurch.org/taiwan.htm.

Presbyterian Church

Tai-oan Ki-tok Tiu-Lo Kau-Hoe (Presbyterian Church in Taiwan): No. 3, Lane 269, Roosevelt Rd, Sec. 3, Taipei 10647; tel. (2) 23625282; fax (2) 23628096; e-mail pct@mail.pct.org.tw; internet www.pct.org.tw; f. 1865; Gen. Sec. Rev. CHANG TE-CHIEN; 224,679 mems (2000).

DAOISM (TAOISM)

In 2004 there were about 7.6m. adherents. Temples numbered 18,274, and clergy totalled 33,850.

I-KUAN TAO

Introduced to Taiwan in the 1950s, this 'Religion of One Unity' is a modern, syncretic religion, drawn mainly from Confucian, Buddhist and Daoist principles and incorporating ancestor worship. In 2004 there were 3,260 temples. Adherents totalled 810,000.

ISLAM

Leader MOHAMMED NI GUO-AN; 58,000 adherents in 2004.

The Press

In 2008 the number of active registered newspapers stood at 100. The majority of newspapers are privately owned.

PRINCIPAL DAILIES

Taipei

Apple Daily News: 38, 141 Lane, Sinyi Rd, Taipei 11494; tel. (2) 66013456; fax (2) 66019995; e-mail enquiry@appledaily.com.tw; internet www.appledaily.com.tw; jt venture between Hong Kong-based Next Media and several Singapore companies.

The China Post: 8 Fu Shun St, Taipei 10452; tel. (2) 25969971; fax (2) 25957962; e-mail cpost@msl.hinet.net; internet www.chinapost.com.tw; f. 1952; morning; English; Publr and Editor JACK HUANG; readership 250,000.

China Times: 132 Da Li St, Taipei 10801; tel. (2) 23087111; fax (2) 23063312; internet www.chinatimes.com.tw; f. 1950; morning; Chinese; Chair. YU JIANXIN; Editor-in-Chief HUANG QINGLONG; circ. 1.2m.

Commercial Times: 132 Da Li St, Taipei; tel. (2) 23087111; fax (2) 23069456; e-mail commercialtimes@mail.chinatimes.com.tw; f. 1978; morning; Chinese; Publr PENG CHWEI-MING; Editor-in-Chief SIMON CHENG; circ. 300,000.

Economic Daily News: 555 Chung Hsiao East Rd, Sec. 4, Taipei 11003; tel. (2) 27681234; fax (2) 27600129; f. 1967; morning; Chinese; Publr WANG PI-CHEN.

Liberty Times: 399 Rueiguang Rd, Nei-Hu District, Taipei 11492; tel. (2) 26562828; fax (2) 26561034; e-mail newstips@libertytimes.com.tw; internet www.libertytimes.com.tw; f. 1980; Publr WU A-MING; Editor-in-Chief ROGER CHEN.

CHINA (TAIWAN)

Mandarin Daily News: 2 Foo Chou St, Taipei 10078; tel. (2) 23921133; fax (2) 23410203; e-mail feedback@mail.mdnkids.com; internet www.mdnkids.com; f. 1948; children's newspaper; morning; Publr LIN LIANG.

Taipei Times: 14/F, 399 Ruiguang Rd, Neihu District, Taipei 11492; tel. (2) 26561000; fax (2) 26561070; e-mail letters@taipeitimes.com; internet www.taipeitimes.com; f. 1999; English; circ. 700,000 (2007).

Taiwan Daily News: 361 Wen Shin Rd, Sec. 3, Taichung 407; tel. (4) 22958511; fax (4) 2958950; internet www.taiwandaily.net; f. 1964; morning; Publr ANTONIO CHIANG; Editor-in-Chief LIU CHIH TSUNG; circ. 250,000.

Taiwan News: 7/F, 88 Hsin Yi Rd, Sec. 2, Taipei 10641; tel. (2) 23517666; fax (2) 23518389; e-mail editor@etaiwannews.com; internet www.etaiwannews.com; f. 1949; morning; English; Chair. T. C. KAO; Publr LUIS KO.

United Daily News: 555 Chung Hsiao East Rd, Sec. 4, Taipei 11003; tel. (2) 27681234; fax (2) 27632303; e-mail secretariat@udngroup.com.tw; internet www.udn.com; f. 1951; morning; Publr WANG SHAW-LAN; Editor-in-Chief HUANG SHU-CHUAN; circ. 1.2m.

Provincial

China Daily News (Southern Edn): 57 Hsi Hwa St, Tainan 70449; tel. (6) 2202691; fax (6) 2201804; f. 1946; morning; Publr LIU CHZ-SHIEN; circ. 670,000.

The Commons Daily: 180 Min Chuan 2 Rd, Kaohsiung 80661; tel. (7) 3363131; fax (7) 3363604; f. 1950; fmrly Min Chung Daily News; morning; Executive-in-Chief WANG CHIN-HSIUNG; circ. 148,000.

Keng Sheng Daily News: 36 Wuchuan St, Hualien 97048; tel. (38) 340131; fax (38) 329664; e-mail leader.hsieh@gmail.com; f. 1947; morning; Publr HSIEH LEADER; circ. 50,000.

Taiwan Hsin Wen Daily News: 3 Woo Fu I Rd, Kaohsiung 80252; tel. (7) 2226666; f. 1949; morning; Publr CHANG REI-TE.

Taiwan Times: 32 Kaonan Rd, Renwu Township, Kaohsiung 81453; tel. (7) 3428666; fax (7) 3102828; f. 1978; Publr WANG YUH-FA.

SELECTED PERIODICALS

Artist Magazine: 6/F, 147 Chung Ching South Rd, Sec. 1, Taipei 10048; tel. (2) 23866715; fax (2) 23317096; e-mail artvenue@seed.net.tw; f. 1975; monthly; Publr HO CHENG KUANG; circ. 37,600.

Better Life Monthly: 11 Lane 199, Hsin-yih Rd, Sec. 4, Taipei 10685; tel. (2) 27549488; fax (2) 27001516; e-mail bettlife@ms14.hinet.net; f. 1987; Publr JACK S. LIN.

Brain: 9/F, 47 Nanking East Rd, Sec. 4, Taipei 10550; tel. (2) 27132644; fax (2) 27137318; e-mail askbrain@brain.com.tw; internet www.brain.com.tw; f. 1977; media industry; monthly; Publr JOHNSON WU.

Business Next: e-mail service@bxnext.com.tw; internet www.bxnext.com.tw; f. 1999; bi-weekly; circ. 160,000.

Business Weekly: 12/F, 141, Sec. 2, Minsheng East Rd, Taipei 10483; tel. (2) 25056789; fax (2) 27364620; e-mail mailbox@bwnet.com.tw; internet www.businessweekly.com.tw; f. 1987; Publr JIN WEI-TSUN.

Car Magazine: 1/F, 3 Lane 3, Tung Shan St, Taipei 10014; tel. (2) 23218168; fax (2) 23935614; e-mail carguide@ms13.hinet.net; f. 1982; monthly; Publr H. K. LIN; Editor-in-Chief TA-WEI LIN; circ. 85,000.

China Times Weekly: 5/F, 25 Min Chuan East Rd, Sec. 6, Taipei 11494; tel. (2) 27936000; fax (2) 87918589; internet www.chinatimes.com; f. 1978; weekly; Chinese; Publr CHANG KUO-LI.

Commonwealth Monthly: 11/F, 139, Sec. 2, Nanking East Rd, Taipei 10553; tel. (2) 26620332; fax (2) 25082941; e-mail cwadmin@cw.com.tw; internet www.cw.com.tw; f. 1981; monthly; business; Pres. CHARLES H. C. KAO; Publr and Editor DIANE YING; circ. 110,000.

CompoTech Asia: Room 3B07, 5, Sec. 5, Shin-yi Rd, Taipei; tel. (2) 27201789; e-mail carol_liao@computechasia.com; internet www.compotech.com.tw; f. 1999; monthly; computing; Editor-in-Chief CAROL LIAO.

Cosmopolitan: 5/F, 8 Lane 181, Jiou-Tzung Rd, Taipei 11494; tel. (2) 28797890; fax (2) 287978990; e-mail hwaker@ms13.hinet.net; f. 1992; monthly; Publr MINCHUN CHANG.

Crown Magazine: 50 Alley 120, Tun Hua North Rd, Sec. 4, Taipei; tel. (2) 27168888; fax (2) 25148285; internet www.crown.com.tw; f. 1954; monthly; literature and arts; Publr PING HSIN TAO; Editor CHEN LIH-HWA; circ. 76,000.

Defense Technology Monthly: 6/F, 6 Nanking East Rd, Sec. 5, Taipei 10564; tel. (2) 27669628; fax (2) 27666092; e-mail service@dtm.com.tw; internet www.dtmonline.com; f. 1894; Publr J. D. BIH.

Elle Taiwan: 5/F, 9 Lane 130, Sec. 3, Min Sheng East Rd, Taipei 10596; tel. (2) 67706168; fax (2) 87706170; e-mail newmedia@hft.com.tw; internet www.elle.com.tw; f. 1991; monthly; women's magazine; Publr JEAN DE WITT; Editors-in-Chief CINDY HU, DORIS LEE; circ. 50,000.

Evergreen Monthly: 11/F, 2 Pa Teh Rd, Sec. 3, Taipei 10558; tel. (2) 25782321; fax (2) 25786838; f. 1983; health care knowledge; Publr LIANG GUANG-MING; circ. 50,000.

Excellence Magazine: 3/F, 15 Lane 2, Sec. 2, Chien Kuo North Rd, Taipei 10487; tel. (2) 25093578; fax (2) 25173607; f. 1984; monthly; business; Man. LIN HSIN-JYH; Editor-in-Chief LIU JEN; circ. 70,000.

Families Monthly: 11/F, 2 Pa Teh Rd, Sec. 3, Taipei 10558; tel. (2) 25785078; fax (2) 25786838; f. 1976; family life; Editor-in-Chief THELMA KU; circ. 155,000.

Foresight Investment Weekly: 7/F, 52 Nanking East Rd, Sec. 1, Taipei 10450; tel. (2) 25512561; fax (2) 25119596; f. 1980; weekly; Dir and Publr SUN WUN HSIUNG; Editor-in-Chief WU WEN SHIN; circ. 55,000.

Global Views Monthly: 2/F, 1 Lane 93, Sungkiang Rd, Taipei 10455; tel. (2) 25173688; fax (2) 25082941; e-mail gvm@cgvm.com.tw; internet www.gvm.com.tw; f. 1986; Editor-in-Chief TIAO MING-FANG.

Gourmet World: 3/F, 53, Sec. 1, Jen-Ai Rd, Taipei 10052; tel. (2) 23972215; fax (2) 23412184; f. 1992; Publr HSU TANG-JEN.

Harvest Farm Magazine: 14 Wenchow St, Taipei 10648; tel. (2) 23628148; fax (2) 23636724; e-mail h3628148@ms15.hinet.net; internet www.harvest.org.tw; f. 1951; every 2 weeks; Publr HU FU-HSIUNG; Editor-in-Chief YU SHU-LIEN.

Issues and Studies: A Social Science Quarterly on China, Taiwan and East Asian Affairs: Institute of International Relations, National Chengchi University, 64 Wan Shou Rd, Taipei 11666; tel. (2) 82377377; fax (2) 82377231; e-mail issues@nccu.edu.tw; internet http://iir.nccu.edu.tw/english/dirkinde4.htm; f. 1965; quarterly; English; contemporary Chinese studies and East Asian affairs; Editor CHEN-SHEN J. YEN.

The Journalist: 16/F, 218 Tun Hua South Rd, Sec. 2, Taipei 10669; tel. (2) 23779977; fax (2) 23775850; f. 1987; weekly; Publr WANG SHIN-CHING.

Ladies Magazine: 11/F, 3, 187 Shin Yi Rd, Sec. 4, Taipei 10681; tel. (2) 27026908; fax (2) 27014090; f. 1978; monthly; Publr CHENG CHIN-SHAN; Editor-in-Chief THERESA LEE; circ. 60,000.

Madame Figaro Taiwan: e-mail service@heritage.com.tw; internet www.figaro.tw; f. 2001; fashion; published by Stone Media.

Management Magazine: 5/F, 220 Ta Tung Rd, Sec. 3, Hsichih City, Taipei County 22103; tel. (2) 86471828; fax (2) 86471466; e-mail frankhung@mail.chinamgt.com; internet www.harment.com; f. 1973; monthly; Chinese; Publr and Editor FRANK L. HUNG; Pres. KATHY T. KUO; circ. 65,000.

Money Monthly: 10/F, 289 Chung Hsiao East Rd, Taipei 10696; tel. (2) 25149822; fax (2) 27154657; f. 1986; monthly; personal financial management; Publr PATRICK SUN; Man. Editor JENNIE SHUE; circ. 55,000.

National Geographic/The Earth: 4/F, 319, Sec. 4, Bade Rd, Taipei 10565; tel. (2) 27485988; fax (2) 27480188.

National Palace Museum Monthly of Chinese Art: 221, Sec. 2, Jishan Rd, Taipei 11143; tel. (2) 28821230; fax (2) 28821440; f. 1983; monthly in Chinese; Publr TU CHENG-SHENG; circ. 10,000.

Nong Nong Magazine: 11/F, 141, Sec. 2, Minsheng East Rd, Taipei 10483; tel. (2) 2502689; fax (2) 25051989; e-mail group@nongnong.com.tw; f. 1984; monthly; women's interest; Publr ANTHONY TSAI; Editor VIVIAN LIN; circ. 70,000.

PC Home: 4/F, 141, Sec. 2, Minsheng East Rd, Taipei 10483; tel. (2) 25000888; fax (2) 25001920; internet www.pchome.com.tw; f. 1996; monthly; Chair. HUNG-TZE JANG; CEO ARTHUR LEE.

PC Office: 11/F, 8 Tun Hua North Rd, Taipei 10547; tel. (2) 25007779; fax (2) 25007903; internet www.pcoffice.com.tw; f. 1997; monthly; Publr HUNG-TZE JANG.

Reader's Digest (Chinese Edn): 2/F, 2 Ming Sheng East Rd, Sec. 5, Taipei 10572; tel. (2) 82531198; fax (2) 82531211; internet www.readersdigest.com.tw; monthly; Editor-in-Chief VICTOR FUNG.

Studio Classroom: 10 Lane 62, Ta-Chih St, Taipei 10462; tel. (2) 25338082; fax (2) 25326406; internet www.studioclassroom.com; f. 1962; monthly; English teaching magazine; Publr DORIS BROUGHAM.

Taiwan Journal: 2 Tientsin St, Taipei 10051; tel. (2) 23970180; fax (2) 23568233; e-mail tj@mail.gio.gov.tw; internet taiwanjournal.nat.gov.tw; f. 1964; fmrly Free China Journal; weekly; English; news review; Publr SHIEH JHY-WEY; Editor-in-Chief VIRGINIA SHENG; circ. 30,000.

Taiwan Panorama: 5/F, 54 Chung Hsiao East Rd, Sec. 1, Taipei 10049; tel. (2) 23922256; fax (2) 23970655; e-mail service@mail.taiwan-panorama.com; internet www.sinorama.com.tw; f. 1976; fmrly *Sinorama*; monthly; bilingual cultural magazine, with edns in Chinese with Japanese or English; Publr PASUYA WEN-CHIH YAO; Editor-in-Chief LAURA LEE; circ. 70,000.

CHINA (TAIWAN) *Directory*

Taiwan Review: 2 Tientsin St, Taipei 100; tel. (2) 23516419; fax (2) 23510829; e-mail tr@mail.gio.gov.tw; internet taiwanreview.nat.gov.tw; f. 1951; fmrly *Taipei Review*, renamed as above March 2003; monthly; English; illustrated; Publr CHENG WEN-TSANG; Editor-in-Chief CHANG HUI-JHEN.

Time Express: B1/F, 205–1 Beisin Rd, Sec. 3, Sinolian City, Taipei County 23143; tel. (2) 89131717; fax (2) 89132332; e-mail timeex@ccw.com.tw; f. 1973; monthly; Publr RICHARD C. C. HUANG.

Unitas: 10/F, 180 Keelung Rd, Sec. 1, Taipei 11006; tel. (2) 27666759; fax (2) 27491208; e-mail unitas@udngroup.com.tw; monthly; Chinese; literary journal; Publr CHANG PAO-CHING; Editor-in-Chief HSU HUI-CHIH.

Vi Vi Magazine: 7/F, 550 Chung Hsiao East Rd, Sec. 5, Taipei 11081; tel. (2) 27275336; fax (2) 27592031; f. 1984; monthly; women's interest; Pres. TSENG CHING-TANG; circ. 60,000.

Vogue/GQ Conde Nast Interculture: 15/F, 51, Sec. 2, Keelung Rd, Sinyi District, Taipei 11082; tel. (2) 27328899; fax (2) 27390504; e-mail vogueeditor@mail.condenast.com.tw; internet www.vogue.com.tw; f. 1996; monthly; Publr BENTHAM LIU.

Wealth Magazine: 7/F, 52 Nanking East Rd, Sec. 1, Taipei 10444; tel. (2) 25816196; fax (2) 25316438; internet www.wealth.com.tw; f. 1974; monthly; finance; Pres. TSHAI YEN-KUEN; Editor ANDY LIAN; circ. 75,000.

Win Win Weekly: 7/F, 52 Nanking East Rd, Taipei 10444; tel. (2) 25816196; fax (2) 25119596; f. 1996; Publr GIN-HO HSHIE.

Youth Juvenile Monthly: 3/F, 66-1 Chung Cheng South Rd, Sec. 1, Taipei 10045; tel. (2) 23112836; fax (2) 23115368; e-mail customer@youth.com.tw; internet www.youth.com.tw; f. 1965; Publr LEE CHUNG-GUAI.

NEWS AGENCY

Central News Agency (CNA): 209 Sung Chiang Rd, Taipei 10485; tel. (2) 25000919; fax (2) 25051180; e-mail cnamark@mail.cna.com.tw; internet www.cna.com.tw; e-mail charlie@mail.cna.com.tw; f. 1924; news service in Chinese, English and Spanish; feature and photographic services; 25 domestic and 32 overseas bureaux; Pres. SU TZEN-PING; Chair. LIU CHIH-TSUNG.

Publishers

There are more than 8,000 publishing houses in Taiwan. In 2006 a total of 42,281 titles were published.

Art Book Co: 1/F, 18 Lane 283, Roosevelt Rd, Sec. 3, Taipei 10647; tel. (2) 23620578; fax (2) 23623594; e-mail artbook@ms43.hinet.net; Publr HO KUNG SHANG.

Cheng Wen Publishing Co: 3/F, 277 Roosevelt Rd, Sec. 3, Taipei 10647; tel. (2) 23628032; fax (2) 23660806; e-mail ccicncwp@ms17.hinet.net; Publr LARRY C. HUANG.

Children's Publication Co Ltd: 7F-1, 314 Nei-Hu Rd, Sec. 1, Taipei 11444; tel. (2) 87972799; fax (2) 87972700; e-mail jay@012book.com.tw; internet www.012book.com.tw; f. 1994.

China Times Publishing Co: 2/F, 240 Hoping West Rd, Sec. 3, Taipei 10803; tel. (2) 23087111; fax (2) 23027844; e-mail jess@readingtimes.com.tw; internet www.readingtimes.com.tw; f. 1975; Pres. MO CHAO-PING.

Chinese Culture University Press: 55 Hua Kang Rd, Yangmingshan, Taipei 11114; tel. (2) 28610511 ext. 17503; fax (2) 28617164; e-mail euca@staff.pccu.edu.tw; internet www2.pccu.edu.tw/cuca/ad3.htm; Publr LEE FU-CHEN.

Cite Publishing Ltd: 2/F, 141 Mingsheng East Rd, Sec. 2, Taipei 10482; tel. (2) 25007088; fax (2) 25007579; e-mail regina@hmg.com.tw; internet www.cite.com.tw; f. 1996.

The Commercial Press Ltd: 37 Chungking South Rd, Sec. 1, Taipei 10046; tel. (2) 23116118; fax (2) 23710274; e-mail ecptw@cptw.com.tw; internet www.cptw.com.tw; f. 1897; Editor SYLVIA WEN-I CHEN.

Commonwealth Publishing Co: 2/F, 1 Lane 93, Sung Chiang Rd, Taipei; tel. (2) 25173686; fax (2) 25173688; e-mail cwpc@cwgv.com.tw; internet www.bookzone.com.tw; f. 1982.

Crown Publishing Group: 50 Lane 120, Tun Hua North Rd, Taipei 10547; tel. (2) 27168888; fax (2) 27133422; e-mail edit3@crown.com.tw; internet www.crown.com.tw; f. 1954; Publr PHILIP PING; 90 employees.

The Eastern Publishing Co Ltd: 4/F, 121 Chungking South Rd, Sec. 1, Taipei 100; tel. (2) 23114514; fax (2) 23317402; internet www.1945.co.tw; e-mail lola@1945.com.tw; f. 1945; Publr CHENG SI-MING.

Elite Publishing Co: 1/F, 33-1 Lane 113, Hsiamen St, Taipei 10048; tel. (2) 23671021; fax (2) 23657047; e-mail elite113@ms12.hinet.net; internet www.elitebooks.com.tw; f. 1975; Publr KO CHING-HWA.

Far East Book Co: 66 Chungking South Rd, Sec. 1, Taipei 10045; tel. (2) 23118740; fax (2) 23114184; e-mail service@mail.fareast.com.tw; internet eng.fareast.com.tw; art, education, history, physics, mathematics, law, literature, dictionaries, textbooks, language tapes, Chinese-English dictionaries; Publr GEORGE C. L. PU.

Global Group Holding Ltd: 10/F, 15 Lane 174, Hsin Ming Rd, Neihu District, Taipei; tel. (2) 27911197, ext. 208; fax (2) 27918606; e-mail readers@gobooks.com.tw; internet www.gobooks.com.tw; Publr CHU PAO-LOUNG; Dir KELLY CHU.

Hsin Yi Foundation: 75 Chungking South Rd, Sec. 2, Taipei 10015; tel. (2) 23965303; fax (2) 23965015; e-mail arni@hsin-yi.org.tw; internet www.hsin-yi.org.tw; f. 1971; children's education and devt; Exec. Dir SING-JU CHANG.

Kwang Hwa Publishing Co: 5/F, 54 Chung Hsiao East Rd, Sec. 1, Taipei 10049; tel. (2) 23922256; fax (2) 23970655; e-mail service@mail.sinorama.com.tw; internet www.sinorama.com.tw; Publr CHENG WEN-TSANG.

Li-Ming Cultural Enterprise Co: 3/F, 49 Chungking South Rd, Sec. 1, Taipei 10045; tel. (2) 23314046; fax (2) 23817230; e-mail liminglf@ms15.hinet.net; internet www.limingco.com.tw; f. 1971; Pres. SHEN FANG-SHIN.

Linking Publishing Co Ltd: 555, Sec. 4, Jhongsiao East Rd, Taipei 100; tel. (2) 27634300; fax (2) 27567688; e-mail sheh.chang@udngroup.com; internet www.linkingbooks.com.tw/linkingp; Publr LIU KUO-JUEI.

Locus Publishing Co: 11/F, 25 Nanking East Rd, Sec. 4, Taipei 10550; tel. (2) 87123898; fax (2) 25453927; e-mail locus@locuspublishing.com; internet www.locuspublishing.com; f. 1996.

San Min Book Co Ltd: 386 Fusing North Rd, Taipei 10476; tel. (2) 25006600; fax (2) 25064000; e-mail editor@sanmin.com.tw; internet www.sanmin.com.tw; f. 1953; literature, history, philosophy, social sciences, dictionaries, art, politics, law; Publr LIU CHEN-CHIANG.

Ta Chien Publishing Co Ltd: 19 Sinheheng Rd, Tainan 70248; tel. (6) 2917489; fax (6) 2921618; e-mail tachiens@ms16.hinet.net; internet www.tachien.com.tw.

Tung Hua Book Co Ltd: 105 Emei St, Taipei 10844; tel. (2) 23114027; fax (2) 23116615; e-mail service@bookcake.com.tw; internet www.bookcake.com.tw; f. 1965; Publr CHARLES CHOH.

The World Book Co: 6/F, 99 Chungking South Rd, Sec. 1, Taipei 10045; tel. (2) 23113834; fax (2) 23317963; e-mail wbc.ltd@msa.hinet.com; internet www.worldbook.com.tw; f. 1921; literature, textbooks; Chair. YEN FENG-CHANG; Publr YEN ANGELA CHU.

Youth Cultural Enterprise Co Ltd: 3/F, 66-1 Chungking South Rd, Sec. 1, Taipei 10045; tel. (2) 23112836; fax (2) 23115368; e-mail customer@youth.com.tw; internet www.youth.com.tw; f. 1958; Publr LEE CHUNG-KUEI.

Yuan Liou Publishing Co Ltd: 6/F, 81, Sec. 2, Nanchang Rd, Taipei 10084; tel. (2) 23926899; fax (2) 23926658; e-mail ylib@ylib.com; internet www.ylib.com; f. 1975; fiction, non-fiction, children's; Publr WANG JUNG-WEN.

Broadcasting and Communications

TELECOMMUNICATIONS

Directorate-General of Telecommunications: Ministry of Transportation and Communications, 16 Chinan Rd, Sec. 2, Taipei 10054; tel. (2) 23433969; fax (2) 23433728; internet www.dgt.gov.tw; regulatory authority.

Chunghwa Telecommunications Co Ltd: 21 Hsinyi Rd, Sec. 1, Taipei 10048; tel. (2) 23445385; fax (2) 23919166; e-mail chtir@cht.com.tw; internet www.cht.com.tw; f. 1996; previously state-controlled company, privatization completed in 2005; Chair. HO-CHEN TAN.

Far EasTone Telecom: 468 Ruei Guang Rd, Nei Hu District, Taipei 11492; tel. (2) 87935000; e-mail ir@fareastone.com.tw; internet www.fareastone.com.tw; mobile telephone services; Pres. JAN NILSSON.

KG Telecom: 43 Kuan Chien Rd, Taipei 10047; tel. (2) 23888800; e-mail kgtweb@kgt.com.tw; internet www.kgt.com.tw; merged with Far EasTone Telecom in 2003; mobile telephone services.

Taiwan Mobile Co Ltd: 18/F, 172–1, Ji-Lung Rd, Sec. 2, Taipei 106; fax (2) 66368669; e-mail ir@taiwanmobile.com; internet www.taiwanmobile.com; f. 1998; est. as Pacific Cellular Corpn; merged with Taiwan Tele-Shop in 2005; mobile telephone and internet services; Chair. RICHARD TSAI; Pres. HARVEY CHANG.

BROADCASTING

Broadcasting stations are mostly commercial. The Ministry of Transportation and Communications determines power and frequencies, and the Government Information Office supervises the operation of all stations, whether private or governmental.

CHINA (TAIWAN)

Radio

In July 2006 there were 172 radio broadcasting corporations in operation.

Broadcasting Corpn of China (BCC): 10/F, 375 Sung Chiang Rd, Taipei 10482; tel. (2) 25019688; fax (2) 25018545; internet www.bcc.com.tw; f. 1928; domestic (5 networks and 1 channel) services; 9 local stations, 131 transmitters; Pres. LEE CHING-PING; Chair. CHAO SHOU-PO.

Central Broadcasting System (CBS): 55 Pei An Rd, Tachih, Taipei 10464; tel. (2) 28856168; fax (2) 28850023; e-mail rtm@cbs.org.tw; internet www.cbs.org.tw; f. 1928; national broadcasting system of Taiwan; broadcasts internationally in 13 languages via medium and short wave under the call sign Radio Taiwan International (RTI); Chair LIN FENG-JENG.

Cheng Sheng Broadcasting Corpn Ltd: 7/F, 66-1 Chungking South Rd, Sec. 1, Taipei 10045; tel. (2) 23617231; fax (2) 23715665; internet www.csbc.com.tw; f. 1950; 6 stations, 3 relay stations; Chair. WENG YEN-CHING; Pres. PANG WEI-NANG.

International Community Radio Taipei (ICRT): 2/F, 373 Sung Chiang Rd, Taipei 10482; tel. (2) 25184899; fax (2) 25183666; internet www.icrt.com.tw; predominantly English-language broadcaster; Chair. NELSON CHANG; Gen. Man. JANET CHU.

Kiss Radio: 34/F, 6 Min Chuan 2 Rd, Kaohsiung 80658; tel. (7) 3365888; fax (7) 3364931; e-mail helena@kiss.com.tw; internet www.kiss.com.tw; Pres. HELENA YUAN.

M-radio Broadcasting Corpn: 810/F-1, 1-18 Taichung Kang Rd, Sec. 2, Taichung City 40751; tel. (4) 23235656; fax (4) 23231199; e-mail jason@mradio.com.tw; internet www.mradio.com.tw; Pres. CHEN WEI-LIANG; Gen. Man. JASON C. LIN.

UFO Broadcasting Co Ltd: 25/F, 102 Roosevelt Rd, Sec. 2, Taipei 10084; tel. (2) 23636600; fax (2) 23673083; internet www.ufo.net.tw; Pres. CHANG HSIAO-YEN.

Voice of Taipei Broadcasting Co Ltd: 10/F, B Rm, 15-1 Han Chou South Rd, Sec. 1, Taipei 10050; tel. (2) 23957255; fax (2) 23947855; internet www.vot.com.tw; Pres. NITA ING.

Television

Legislation to place cable broadcasting on a legal basis was adopted in mid-1993, and by June 2004 63 cable television companies were in operation. A non-commercial station, Public Television (PTV), went on air in July 1998. Legislation to place satellite broadcasting on a legal basis was adopted in February 1999, and by mid-2006 141 satellite broadcasting channels (provided by 57 domestic and 17 international companies) and 5 domestic Digital Broadcasting System (DBS) channels were in operation. In July 2006 Chinese Television System (CTS) and Public Television Service Foundation (PTS), along with six other channels—CTS Education and Culture, CTS Recreation, Dimo TV, Hakka TV, Taiwan Indigenous Television and Taiwan Macroview TV—combined to form the Taiwan Broadcasting Service (TBS). The two principal channels, CTS and PTS (see below), merged some services following an agreement to share some of their entertainment and educational programmes.

China Television Co (CTV): 120 Chung Yang Rd, Nan Kang District, Taipei 11523; tel. (2) 27838308; fax (2) 27826007; e-mail prog@mail.chinatv.com.tw; internet www.chinatv.com.tw; f. 1969; Chinatimes Group; Pres. CHOU SHENG-YUAN; Chair. ALBERT YU.

Chinese Television System (CTS): 100 Kuang Fu South Rd, Taipei 10694; tel. (2) 27510321; fax (2) 27775414; e-mail public@mail.cts.com.tw; internet www.cts.com.tw; f. 1971; Chair. LOUIS CHEN; Pres. LI YUAN.

Formosa Television Co (FTV): 14/F, 30 Pa Teh Rd, Sec. 3, Taipei 10551; tel. (2) 25702570; fax (2) 25773170; internet www.ftv.com.tw; f. 1997; Chair. TIEN TZAI-TING; Pres. CHEN KANG-HSING.

Public Television Service Foundation (PTS): 50 Lane 75, Sec. 3, Kang Ning Rd, Neihu, Taipei 11460; tel. (2) 26338037; fax (2) 26301895; e-mail pub@mail.pts.org.tw; internet www.pts.org.tw; some services merged with Chinese Television System July 2006, as part of plans to create Taiwan Broadcasting System (see above); Chair. LOUIS CHEN; Pres. HU YUAN-HUI.

Taiwan Television Enterprise (TTV): 10 Pa Teh Rd, Sec. 3, Taipei 10502; tel. (2) 25781515; fax (2) 25799657; internet www.ttv.com.tw; f. 1962; Pres. and Chair. LAI KUO-CHOU.

Finance

(cap. = capital; dep. = deposits; m. = million; brs = branches; amounts in New Taiwan dollars unless otherwise stated)

BANKING

In May 2005 there were 47 banks operating in Taiwan. In September 2002 the Ministry of Finance announced plans to privatize state banks by 2006, and to sell the Government's stake in commercial banks by 2010. The Financial Supervisory Commission (see under Ministries) was established in 2004.

Central Bank

Central Bank of the Republic of China (Taiwan): 2 Roosevelt Rd, Sec. 1, Taipei 100; tel. (2) 23936161; fax (2) 23571500; e-mail adminrol@mail.cbc.gov.tw; internet www.cbc.gov.tw; f. 1928; fmrly Central Bank of China; name changed as above in 2007; bank of issue; cap. and res 1,087,690m., dep. 6,838,405m. (Dec. 2006); Gov. PERNG FAI-NAN; Dir-Gen. CHEN HSIN-SHENG.

Domestic Banks

Bank of Taiwan: 120 Chungking South Rd, Sec. 1, Taipei 10036; tel. (2) 23493456; fax (2) 23315840; e-mail botservice@mail.bot.com.tw; internet www.bot.com.tw; f. 1946; cap. 48,000m., res 154,152.7m., dep. 2,452,411.1m. (Dec. 2006); Chair. TSAI JER-SHYONG; Pres. LO TSE-CHENG; 147 domestic brs, 6 overseas brs.

Export-Import Bank of the Republic of China (Eximbank): 8/F, 3 Nan Hai Rd, Taipei 100; tel. (2) 23210511; fax (2) 23940630; e-mail eximbank@eximbank.com.tw; internet www.eximbank.com.tw; f. 1979; cap. 12,000m., res 804m., dep. 51,777.7m. (Dec. 2006); Chair. PAULINE FU; Pres. JOSEPH N. TSAI; 3 brs.

Land Bank of Taiwan: 46 Kuan Chien Rd, Taipei 100; tel. (2) 23483456; fax (2) 23757023; e-mail lbot@imail.landbank.com.tw; internet www.landbank.com.tw; f. 1946; to be privatized or merged with the Bank of Taiwan; cap. 25,000m., res 71,423.9m., dep. 1,729,306.7m. (Dec. 2006); Chair. TSAI JER-SHYONG; Pres. YI-HSIUNG CHANG; 136 brs.

Taiwan Co-operative Bank: 77 Kuan Chien Rd, Taipei 10038; tel. (2) 23118811; fax (2) 23890704; e-mail tacbid01@14.hinet.net; internet www.tcb.com.tw; f. 1946; acts as central bank for co-operatives, and as major agricultural credit institution; merged with Farmers Bank of China in May 2006; cap. 45,000.0m., res 43,331.0m., dep. 2,251,758.9m. (Dec. 2006); Chair. SEAN C. CHEN; Pres. FAN-CHIH WU; 183 brs.

Commercial Banks

Bank of Kaohsiung: 168 Po Ai 2nd Rd, Kaohsiung 813; tel. (7) 5570535; fax (7) 5580529; e-mail service@mail.bok.com.tw; internet www.bok.com.tw; f. 1982; cap. 5,034.2m., res 4,891.9m., dep. 140,226.4m. (Dec. 2005); Chair. KAO-CHIN WANG; Pres. S. H. CHUANG; 36 brs.

Bank of Overseas Chinese: 8 Hsiang Yang Rd, Taipei 100; tel. (2) 23317201; fax (2) 23715181; e-mail plan@mail.booc.com.tw; internet www.booc.com.tw; f. 1961; purchased by Citigroup (USA) in 2007; cap. 11,944.8m., res 326.4m., dep. 255,853.6m. (Dec. 2005); Chair. MIKE S. E. CHANG; Pres. JOHNSON C. H. SHIH; 55 brs.

Bank of Panhsin: 18 Cheng Tu St, Ban Chiau City, Taipei County 220; tel. (2) 29629170; fax (2) 29572011; internet www.bop.com.tw; f. 1997; cap. 8,198m., res 689m., dep. 162,957.4m. (Dec. 2005); Chair. PING-HUI LIU; Pres. MING-JIN SHIEH; 37 brs.

Bank SinoPac Co Ltd: 6/F, 306 Sec. 2, Bade Rd, Jhongshan District, Taipei 10492; tel. (2) 25082288; fax (2) 81618485; internet www.banksinopac.com.tw; f. 1992; cap. 19,728.1m., res 6,208.8m., dep. 477,263.0m. (Dec. 2005); Chair. PAUL C. LO; Pres. and CEO ANGUS CHEN; 46 brs, including 2 overseas.

Bowa Commercial Bank: 1/F–5/F, 161, Sec. 5, Chung Hsiao East Rd, Taipei 105; tel. (2) 27568000; fax (2) 27699990; e-mail bowa605@bowabank.com; internet www.bowabank.com; f. 1992; cap. 13,570m., res 1,567.2m., dep. 179,592.6m. (Dec. 2005); Chair. HERBERT S. S. CHUNG; Pres. WEN-KE WU; 39 brs.

Cathay United Bank: 1/F, 7, Sungren Rd, Taipei, 110; tel. (2) 87226666; fax (2) 87895759; internet www.cathaybk.com.tw; f. 1974; cap. 46,420.5m., res 29,509.9m., dep. 1,102,226.4m. (Dec. 2006); merged with United World Chinese Commercial Bank in 2003; Chair. GREGORY K. H. WANG; Pres. TSU PEI CHEN; 140 domestic brs, 2 overseas brs.

Chang Hwa Commercial Bank Ltd: 38 Zihyou Rd, Sec. 2, Central District, Taichung 40045; tel. (4) 2222001; fax (4) 2231170; e-mail webmaster@chb.com.tw; internet www.chb.com.tw; f. 1905; cap. 62,094.8m., res 8,712.8m., dep. 1,262,441.8m. (Dec. 2006); Chair. PO-SHIN CHANG; Pres. JULIUS CHEN; 184 brs, 7 overseas.

China Development Industrial Bank: F/3, 125 Nanking East Rd, Sec. 5, Taipei 105; tel. (2) 27638800; fax (2) 27562144; internet www.cdibank.com.tw; f. 1959; cap. 83,854.0m., res 36,230.8m., dep. 61,984.3m. (Dec. 2005); Chair. ANGELO J. Y. KOO; Pres. JEFFREY SUZN; 3 brs.

Chinatrust Commercial Bank: 3 Sung Shou Rd, Taipei 110; tel. (2) 27222002; fax (2) 27251499; internet www.chinatrust.com.tw; f. 1966; cap. 51,771m., dep. 1,409,734m. (Dec. 2005); Chinatrust Financial Holding Co; Chair. CHARLES L. F. LO; 111 brs.

CHINA (TAIWAN)

The Chinese Bank: 6 Chung Hsiao West Rd, Sec. 1, Taipei 100; tel. (2) 55586666; fax (2) 55584556; e-mail tcb018@mail.chinesebank.com.tw; internet www.chinesebank.com.tw; f. 1992; acquired by HSBC in April 2008; cap. 14,214m., res 1,858m., dep. 194,574m. (Dec. 2005); Pres. L. H. WEI (acting); 39 brs.

Chinfon Commercial Bank: 1 Nanyang St, Taipei 100; tel. (2) 23114881; fax (2) 23712395; e-mail ibd@chinfonbank.com.tw; internet www.chinfonbank.com.tw; f. 1971; cap. 11,128m., res 52.0m., dep. 136,088.2m. (Dec. 2006); Chair. HUANG SHI-HUI; Pres GREGORY C. P. CHANG; 34 brs, 2 overseas.

Cosmos Bank: 5–10/F, 39 Tun Hua South Rd, Sec. 2, Taipei 106; tel. (2) 27011777; fax (2) 27849848; e-mail bbb@cosmosbank.com.tw; internet www.cosmosbank.com.tw; f. 1992; cap. 17,710m., res 2,576m., dep. 234,091.2m. (Dec. 2005); Chair. HSUI SHENG-FA; Pres. C. C. HU; 66 brs.

Cota Commercial Bank: 32–1, Shih Fu Rd, Taichung 400; tel. (4) 22245161; fax (4) 22275237; internet www.cotabank.com.tw; f. 1999; cap. 3,431m., dep. 95,737m. (Dec. 2006); Chair. LIAO CHUN-TSE; Pres. CHANG YING-CHE; 18 brs.

E. Sun Commercial Bank: 3/F, 115 Minsheng East Rd, Sec. 3, Taipei; tel. (2) 21751313; fax (2) 27193013; e-mail wulin@email.esunbank.com.tw; internet www.esunbank.com.tw; f. 1992; cap. 28,909.9m., res 11,097.4m., dep. 638,522.5m. (Dec. 2006); Chair. YUNG-JEN HUANG; Pres. YUNG-HSUNG HOU; 94 domestic brs, 2 overseas brs.

Entie Commercial Bank: 158 Min Sheng East Rd, Sec. 3, Taipei 105; tel. (2) 27189999; fax (2) 27187843; internet www.entiebank.com.tw; f. 1993; cap. 17,093m., res 1,398m., dep. 296,739.5m. (Dec. 2005); Chair. CHIU CHIENG HSIUNG; Pres. and Gen. Man. ALEX JIUNN-CHIH WANG; 53 brs.

Far Eastern International Bank: 207 Tun Hua South Rd, Sec. 2, Taipei; tel. (2) 23786868; fax (2) 23779000; e-mail service@feib.com.tw; internet www.feib.com.tw; f. 1992; cap. 18,708.5m., res 2,598.5m., dep. 323,177.3m. (Dec. 2006); Chair. DOUGLAS TONG HSU; Pres. ELI HONG; 36 brs.

First Commercial Bank: 30, Sec. 1, Chung King South Rd, Taipei 100; tel. (2) 23481111; fax (2) 23892967; e-mail fcb@mail.firstbank.com.tw; internet www.firstbank.com.tw; f. 1899; cap. 46,216m., res 26,748.6m., dep. 1,475,924.1m. (Dec. 2006); Chair. MICHAEL CHANG; Pres. CHIN-YUN WU; 179 domestic brs, 11 overseas brs.

Fuhwa Commercial Bank: 4, Sec. 1, Chung Hsiao West Rd, Taipei 100; tel. (2) 23801888; fax (2) 23801700; e-mail service@fuhwabank.com.tw; internet www.fuhwabank.com.tw; f. 1992; cap. 18,000m., res 680m., dep. 289,987m. (Dec. 2005); Chair. JIA SHYONG CHIOU; 49 brs.

Hua Nan Commercial Bank: 38 Chung Ching South Rd, Sec. 1, Taipei 100; tel. (2) 23713111; fax (2) 23821060; e-mail service@ms.hncb.com.tw; internet www.hncb.com.tw; f. 1919; cap. 37,091m., res 28,565.0m., dep. 1,504,280.6m. (Dec. 2006); Chair. LIN MING-CHEN; Pres. DAVID J. Y. LEE; 182 brs, 4 overseas.

Hwatai Commercial Bank: 246 Chang An E. Rd, Sec. 2, Taipei 104; tel. (2) 27525252; fax (2) 87725177; e-mail h0014@hwataibank.com.tw; internet www.hwataibank.com.tw; f. 1999; cap. 4,499m., res 1,719m., dep. 73,236m. (Dec. 2004); Chair. M. H. LIN; Pres. THOMAS C. W. LEE; 30 brs.

Industrial Bank of Taiwan: 99, Tiding Blvd, Sec. 2, Taipei; tel. (2) 87527000; fax (2) 27989609; internet www.ibt.com.tw; Chair. KENNETH C. M. LO; Pres. HENRY PENG.

Jih Sun International Bank: 10 Chung King South Rd, Sec. 1, Taipei 100; tel. (2) 23119888; fax (2) 23613988; e-mail planning@jsun.com; internet www.jihsunbank.com.tw; f. 1992 as Baodao Commercial Bank, assumed present name in Dec. 2001; cap. 19,247.6m., res 250.2m., dep. 270,081.7m. (Dec. 2005); Chair. KUO-HO CHEN; Pres. BRENDA HUANG; 34 brs.

King's Town Bank: 506 His Men Rd, Sec. 1, Tainan 700; tel. (6) 2139171; fax (6) 2136885; e-mail tnb@ms5.hinet.net; internet www.tnb.com.tw; fmrly Tainan Business Bank; name changed as above in April 2006; Chair. CHEN PING-CHUN; Pres. J. C. SU.

Mega International Commercial Bank Co Ltd (Megabank): 100 Chi Lin Rd, Taipei 104; tel. (2) 25633156; fax (2) 25611216; e-mail service@megabank.com.tw; internet www.megabank.com.tw; f. 2006; est. from merger of International Commercial Bank of China and Chiao Tung Bank; cap. 64,109.8m., res 69,085.9m., dep. 1,576,861.1m. (Dec. 2006); Chair. Y. T. (MCKINNEY) TSAI; Pres. SHIU KUANG-SI; 105 domestic brs, 17 overseas brs.

Shanghai Commercial and Savings Bank: 2 Min Chuan East Rd, Sec. 1, Taipei 104; tel. (2) 25817111; fax (2) 25318501; internet www.scsb.com.tw; f. 1915; cap. 19,626.8m., dep. 405,814.9m. (Dec. 2006); Chair. H. C. YUNG; Pres. E. J. CHIOU; 58 brs.

Standard Chartered Bank (Taiwan) Ltd: 106 Chung Yang Rd, Hsinchu 300; tel. (3) 5245131; fax (3) 5250977; internet www.standardchartered.com.tw; f. 1948; fmrly Hsinchu International Bank; acquired by Standard Chartered Bank in October 2006; cap. 16,545.1m., res 3,451.5m., dep. 389,986.1m. (Dec. 2006); Chair. CHIH-WEI WU; 86 brs.

Sunny Bank: 90 Shih Pai Rd, Sec. 1, Taipei 112; tel. (2) 28208166; fax (2) 28233414; internet www.esunnybank.com.tw; f. 1997; absorbed Kao Shin Bank in Nov. 2005; cap. 10,915m., res 1,334m., dep. 222,624.2m. (Dec. 2005); Chair. SHENG-HONG CHEN; Pres. JERRY YEH; 66 brs.

Ta Chong Bank Ltd: 2 Sinyi Rd, 2/F, Sec. 5, Sinyi District, Taipei 11049; tel. (2) 87869888; fax (2) 87869800; e-mail service@tcbank.com.tw; internet www.tcbank.com.tw; f. 1992; cap. 20,793m., res 248m., dep. 315,792m. (Dec. 2005); Chair. EDMUND KOH; 52 brs.

Taichung Commercial Bank: 87 Min Chuan Rd, Taichung 403; tel. (4) 22236021; fax (4) 22240748; e-mail service@ms2.tcbbank.com.tw; internet www.tcbbank.com.tw; f. 1953; cap. 15,380m., res 160.5m. (Dec. 2005), dep. 250,434.5m. (Dec. 2006); Chair. SHIU-NAN HUANG; Pres. CHUNG YU-YING; 79 brs.

Taipei Fubon Commercial Bank Co Ltd: 169 Jenai Rd, Sec. 4, Taipei 106; tel. (2) 27716999; fax (2) 27780065; internet www.taipeifubon.com.tw; f. 1969; fmrly City Bank of Taipei; acquired by Fubon Financial Holding in Aug. 2002; official merger of Taipei Bank and Fubon Commercial Bank in Jan. 2005, renamed as above; cap. 28,131m., res 41,608m., dep. 912,697m. (Dec. 2005); Chair. DANIEL M. TSAI; Pres. JESSE Y. DING; 124 brs, 3 overseas.

Taishin International Bank: 44 Chung Shan North Rd, Sec. 2, Taipei 104; tel. (2) 25683988; fax (2) 25230539; e-mail pr@taishinbank.com.tw; internet www.taishinbank.com.tw; f. 1992; absorbed Dah An Commercial Bank in Feb. 2002; cap. 33,635m., res 17,362.4m., dep. 617,423.3m. (Dec. 2004); Chair. THOMAS T. L. WU; Pres. CHARLES WANG; 24 brs.

Taiwan Business Bank: 30 Tacheng St, Taipei 103; tel. (2) 25597171; fax (2) 25507942; e-mail tbb@mail.tbb.com.tw; internet www.tbb.com.tw; f. 1915; reassumed present name 1976; cap. 38,735.9m., res 223m., dep. 1,005,921.9m. (Dec. 2006); Chair. MICHAEL C. S. CHANG; Pres. HWANG SHIU-NAN; 128 brs.

Taiwan Shin Kong Commercial Bank: 27–28/F, 66, Jhongsiao West Rd, Sec. 1, Taipei 100; tel. (2) 23895858; fax (2) 23120164; e-mail service@mail.skbank.com.tw; internet www.skbank.com.tw; f. 2000; cap. 21,577.7m., res 5,598.3m., dep. 329,951.9m. (Dec. 2006); Chair. PATRICK C. J. LIANG; Pres. TSENG-CHANG LEE; 28 brs.

Union Bank of Taiwan: 109 Ming Sheng East Rd, Sec. 3, Taipei 105; tel. (2) 27180001; fax (2) 27174093; e-mail 014_0199@email.ubot.com.tw; internet www.ubot.com.tw; f. 1992; cap. 18,277.9m., res 99.6m., dep. 341,699.0m. (Dec. 2006); Chair. SHIANG-CHANG LEE; Pres. JEFF LIN; 76 brs.

There are also a number of Medium Business Banks throughout the country.

Community Financial System

The community financial institutions include both credit co-operatives and credit departments of farmers' and fishermen's associations. These local financial institutions focus upon providing savings and loan services for the community. At the end of 2007 there were 27 credit co-operatives in Taiwan.

Foreign Banks

In February 2008 a total of 32 foreign banks had branches in Taipei.

STOCK EXCHANGE

Under new regulations introduced in 2003, foreign investors were divided into two categories: foreign institutional investors (FINIs) and foreign individual investors (FIDIs). While FIDIs were subject to a US $5m. investment quota, FINIs could benefit from an investment quota with no upper limit. However, some industries continued to impose investment 'ceilings' for foreign investors.

Taiwan Stock Exchange Corpn: 3/F, No. 7, Sec. 5, Xinyi Rd, Taipei 11049; tel. (2) 81013101; fax (2) 81013066; internet www.tse.com.tw; f. 1961; Chair. WU RONG-I; Pres. SU SONG-CHIN.

Supervisory Body

Securities and Futures Bureau: 85 Hsin Sheng South Rd, Sec. 1, Da-an District, Taipei 106; tel. (2) 87735100; fax (2) 87734143; e-mail sfbmail@sfb.gov.tw; internet www.sfb.gov.tw; Dir-Gen. WU TANG-CHIEH.

INSURANCE

Aegon Life Insurance (Taiwan) Inc: 15/F, 238 Jianguo North Rd, Sec. 2, Taipei 104; tel. (2) 25068800; fax (2) 25030585; internet www.aegon.com.tw; f. 2001; Chair. JAMES H. C. LIU.

AIG General Insurance: 16/F, 200 Kee-Lung Rd, Sec. 1, Taipei 110; tel. (2) 37251827; fax (2) 87884338; e-mail aiggeneral@aig.com; internet www.aiggeneral.com.tw.

CHINA (TAIWAN)

Allianz President General Insurance Co Ltd: 8/F, 178 Ming Chuan East Rd, Sec. 3, Taipei; tel. (2) 27155888; fax (2) 27176616; e-mail azpl@ms2.seeder.net; internet www.allianz.com.tw; f. 1995; Chair. BRUCE BOWERS.

Bank Taiwan Life Insurance Co Ltd: 6/F, 69 Tun Hua South Rd, Sec. 2, Taipei 105; tel. (2) 27849151; fax (2) 27052214; internet www.twfhclife.com.tw; f. 1941; life insurance; Dir WEI HAO-DING; Gen. Man. FU DENG-HSIEH.

Cathay Life Insurance Co Ltd: 296 Jen Ai Rd, Sec. 4, Taipei 10650; tel. (2) 27551399; fax (2) 27551222; e-mail master@cathlife.com.tw; internet www.cathlife.com.tw; f. 1962; Chair. HONG-TU TSAI; Pres. T. K. HUANG.

Central Reinsurance Corpn: 12/F, 53 Nanking East Rd, Sec. 2, Taipei 104; tel. (2) 25115211; fax (2) 25235350; e-mail centralre@centralre.com; internet www.crc.com.tw; f. 1968; Chair. CHENG-TUI YANG; Pres. C. T. JUANG.

China Life Insurance Co Ltd: 5/F, 122 Tun Hua North Rd, Taipei; tel. (2) 27196678; fax (2) 27125966; e-mail services@mail.chinalife.com.tw; internet www.chinalife.com.tw; f. 1963; Chair. CHANG CHING-WANG; Gen. Man. ALAN WANG.

Chung Kuo Insurance Co Ltd: 58 Wucheng St, Sec. 1, Taipei 104; tel. (2) 23812727; fax (2) 23713576; internet www.cki.com.tw; f. 1931; Chair. S. Y. LIU; Pres. C. Y. LIU.

Far Glory Life Insurance Co Ltd: 18/F, 200 Keelung Rd, Sec. 1, Taipei 110; tel. (2) 27583099; fax (2) 23451635; internet www.fglife.com.tw; f. 1993; Chair. T. S. CHAO; Pres. C. S. TU.

The First Insurance Co Ltd: 54 Chung Hsiao East Rd, Sec. 1, Taipei 100; tel. (2) 23913271; fax (2) 23412864; internet www.firstins.com.tw; f. 1962; Chair. CHENG HANG LEE; Pres. JAMES LAI.

Fubon Insurance Co Ltd: 237 Chien Kuo South Rd, Sec. 1, Taipei 106; tel. (2) 27067890; fax (2) 27042915; internet www.518fb.com; f. 1961; Chair. T. M. SHIH; Gen. Man. T. H. CHEN.

Fubon Life Assurance Co Ltd: 14/F, 108 Tun Hua South Rd, Sec. 1, Taipei 105; tel. (2) 87716699; fax (2) 87715522; internet www.fubonlife.com.tw; f. 1993; Chair. RICHARD M. TSAI; Pres. PEN-YUAN CHENG.

Global Life Insurance Co Ltd: 3/F, 303, Fusing South Rd, Sec. 1, Taipei; tel. (2) 27089985; fax (2) 66381175; e-mail jimbolin@globallife.com.tw; internet www.globallife.com.tw; f. 1993; Chair. JOHN TSENG; Pres. LAI YI-MING.

Hontai Life Insurance Co Ltd: 4/F, 156 Minsheng East Rd, Sec. 3, Taipei; tel. (2) 27166888; fax (2) 27166887; internet www.hontai.com.tw; f. 1994; fmrly Hung Fu Life Insurance Co; Chair. DAVID JOU.

Kuo Hua Insurance Co Ltd: 166 Chang An East Rd, Sec. 2, Taipei 104; tel. (2) 27514225; fax (2) 27817802; e-mail kh11601@kuohua.com.tw; internet www.kuohua.com.tw; f. 1962; Chair. and Pres. J.B. WANG.

Kuo Hua Life Insurance Co Ltd: 277 Song-Ren Rd, Xinyi District, Taipei; tel. (2) 21765166; fax (2) 55519707; internet www.khltw.com; f. 1963; Chair. M. S. HSIA; Pres. CHING JIANG-CHEN.

Massmutual Mercuries Life Insurance Co Ltd: 6/F, 2 Lane 150, Hsin-Yi North Rd, Sec. 5, Taipei 110; tel. (2) 23455511; fax (2) 23456616; internet www.mli.com.tw; f. 1993; Chair. HENRY CHEN; Pres. CHUNG-SHIN LU.

Mingtai Fire and Marine Insurance Co Ltd: 1 Jen Ai Rd, Sec. 4, Taipei; tel. (2) 27725678; fax (2) 27726666; internet www.mingtai.com.tw; f. 1961; Chair. LARRY P. C. LIN; Pres. H. T. CHEN.

Nan Shan Life Insurance Co Ltd: 168 Zhuangjing Rd, Xinyi District, Taipei 11049; tel. (2) 87588888; fax (2) 87867087; internet www.nanshanlife.com.tw; f. 1963; Chair. EDMUND TSE; Pres. FRANK CHAN.

Prudential Life Assurance Co Ltd: 10/F, 161 Nanking East Rd, Sec. 5, Taipei; tel. (2) 27678866; fax (2) 27679299; internet www.pcalife.com.tw; f. 1962; Chair. STEPHEN D. JIN.

Shinkong Insurance Co Ltd: 13 Chien Kuo North Rd, Sec. 2, Taipei 104; tel. (2) 25075335; fax (2) 25074580; internet www.skinsurance.com.tw; f. 1963; Chair. ANTHONY T. S. WU; Pres. YIH HSIUNG LEE.

Shin Kong Life Insurance Co Ltd: 37/F, 66 Chung Hsiao West Rd, Sec. 1, Taipei 100; tel. (2) 23895858; fax (2) 23758688; internet www.skl.com.tw; f. 1963; Chair. EUGENE T. C. WU; Pres. PO TSENG PAN.

Singfor Life Insurance Co Ltd: 8/F, 6 Chung Hsiao West Rd, Sec. 1, Taipei; tel. (2) 23817172; fax (2) 23917176; e-mail sc_lin@singforlife.com.tw; internet www.singforlife.com.tw; f. 1993; Chair. JOHN HUANG; Gen. Man. WEN YEN-CHEN.

Sinon Life Insurance Co Ltd: 11-2/F, 155 Tsu Chih St, Taichung; tel. (4) 3721653; fax (4) 3722008; e-mail sinonlife@mail.sinonlife.com.tw; internet www.sinonlife.com.tw; f. 1993; Chair. WEN BEN-YANG; Gen. Man. CHUNG SHIN-LIU.

South China Insurance Co Ltd: 5/F, 560 Chung Hsiao East Rd, Sec. 4, Taipei 106; tel. and fax (2) 27588418; internet www.south-china.com.tw; f. 1963; Chair. C. F. LIAO; Pres. ALLAN I. R. HUANG.

Taian Insurance Co Ltd: 59 Kwantsien Rd, Taipei; tel. (2) 23819678; fax (2) 23315332; e-mail taian@mail.taian.com.tw; internet www.taian.com.tw; f. 1961; Chair. C. H. CHEN; Gen. Man. PATRICK S. LEE.

Taiwan Fire and Marine Insurance Co Ltd: 8–9/F, 49 Kuan Chien Rd, Jungjeng Chiu, Taipei 100; tel. (2) 23821666; fax (2) 23892374; e-mail tfmi@mail.tfmi.com.tw; internet www.tfmi.com.tw; f. 1946; Chair. K. L. LAI; Pres. HERBERT YOUNG.

Taiwan Life Insurance Co Ltd: 16–19/F, 17 Hsu Chang St, Taipei; tel. (2) 23116411; fax (2) 23759714; e-mail service1@twlife.com.tw; internet www.twlife.com.tw; f. 1947; Chair. PING-YU CHU; Pres. CHENG-TAO LIN.

Tokio Marine Newa Insurance Co Ltd: 7–12/F, 130 Nanking East Rd, Sec. 3, Taipei 104; tel. (2) 27205522; fax (2) 87891190; f. 1999; Chair. KENNETH K. T. YEN; Pres. CHUNG-KENG CHEN.

Union Insurance Co Ltd: 4/F, 219 Chung Hsiao East Rd, Sec. 4, Taipei; tel. (2) 27765567; fax (2) 27737199; internet www.unionins.com.tw; f. 1963; Chair. S. H. CHIN; Gen. Man. FRANK S. WANG.

Zurich Insurance Taiwan Ltd: 56 Tun Hua North Rd, Taipei; tel. (2) 27752888; fax (2) 27416004; internet www.zurich.com.tw; f. 1961; CEO DANIEL RAYMOND.

Trade and Industry

GOVERNMENT AGENCIES

Bureau of Foreign Trade (Ministry of Economic Affairs): 1 Houkow St, Taipei 10066; tel. (2) 23510271; fax (2) 23513603; e-mail boft@trade.gov.tw; internet www.trade.gov.tw; Dir-Gen. HUANG CHIH-PENG.

Council of Agriculture (COA): 37 Nan Hai Rd, Taipei 10014; tel. (2) 23812991; fax (2) 23719233; e-mail coa@mail.coa.gov.tw; internet www.coa.gov.tw; f. 1984; govt agency directly under the Executive Yuan, with ministerial status; a policy-making body in charge of national agriculture, forestry, fisheries, the animal industry and food administration; promotes technology and provides external assistance; Chair. SU JIA-CHYUAN.

Department of Investment Services (Ministry of Economic Affairs): 8/F, 71 Guancian Rd, Taipei 10047; tel. (2) 23892111; fax (2) 23820497; e-mail dois@moea.gov.tw; internet www.dois.moea.gov.tw; f. 1959 to assist investment and planning; Dir-Gen. BERTON CHIU.

Industrial Development Bureau (Ministry of Economic Affairs): 41-3 Hsin Yi Rd, Sec. 3, Taipei 10651; tel. (2) 27541255; fax (2) 27030160; e-mail service@moeaidb.gov.tw; internet www.moeaidb.gov.tw; Dir-Gen. CHEN CHAO-YIEH.

CHAMBERS OF COMMERCE

General Chamber of Commerce of the Republic of China: 6/F, 390 Fu Hsing South Rd, Sec. 1, Taipei 10665; tel. (2) 27012671; fax (2) 27555493; e-mail moonkuo@roccoc.org.tw; internet www.roccoc.org.tw; f. 1946; 86 group mems, incl. 43 nat. feds of trade asscns, 18 nat. commercial asscns, 22 district export asscns and district chambers of commerce; Chair. CHANG PEN-TSAO; Sec.-Gen. PETER LEE.

Taiwan Chamber of Commerce: 13/F, 168 Sung Chiang Rd, Taipei; tel. (2) 25365455; fax (2) 25211980; e-mail tcoc@tcoc.org.tw; internet www.tcoc.org.tw; f. 1946; 110 mems, comprising 89 provincial trade asscns and 21 local chambers of commerce; Chair. CHANG PEN-TSAO.

INDUSTRIAL AND TRADE ASSOCIATIONS

China Productivity Center: 2/F, 79 Hsin Tai 5 Rd, Sec. 1, Hsichih, Taipei County 22101; tel. (2) 26982989; fax (2) 26982976; internet www.cpc.org.tw; f. 1956; management, technology, training, etc.; Pres. CHEN MING-CHANG.

Chinese National Association of Industry and Commerce: 13/F, 390 Fu Hsing South Rd, Sec. 1, Taipei; tel. (2) 27070111; fax (2) 27070977; e-mail servcie@nfict.org; internet www.cnaic.org; f. 1975; private, independent, non-profit organization comprising major commercial and industrial firms, financial institutions, business asscns, industrialists and business people; Chair. THEODORE M. H. HUANG.

Chinese National Federation of Industries (CNFI): 12/F, 390 Fu Hsing South Rd, Sec. 1, Taipei 10665; tel. (2) 27033500; fax (2) 27033982; e-mail cnfi@cnfi.org.tw; internet www.cnfi.org.tw; f. 1948; 148 mem. asscns; Chair. PRESTON W. CHEN; Sec.-Gen. TSAI LIEN-SHENG.

Taiwan External Trade Development Council: 5–7/F, 333 Keelung Rd, Sec. 1, Taipei 11003; tel. (2) 27255200; fax (2)

CHINA (TAIWAN)   Directory

27576653; e-mail taitra@taitra.org.tw; internet www.taitra.org.tw; trade promotion body; Chair. C. J. HSU; Pres. and CEO CHAO YUEN-CHUAN.

Taiwan Handicraft Promotion Centre: 1 Hsu Chou Rd, Taipei 10055; tel. (2) 23933655; fax (2) 23937330; e-mail thpc@handicraft.org.tw; internet www.handicraft.org.tw; f. 1957; Pres. J. H. LIN.

Trading Department of Central Trust of China: 49 Wuchang St, Sec. 1, Taipei 10006; tel. (2) 23111511; fax (2) 23821047; f. 1935; export and import agent for private and govt-owned enterprises.

UTILITIES

Electricity

Taiwan Power Co (Taipower): 242 Roosevelt Rd, Sec. 3, Taipei 10016; tel. (2) 23651234; fax (2) 23650037; e-mail service@taipower.com.tw; internet www.taipower.com.tw; f. 1946; electricity generation; Chair. EDWARD K. M. CHEN; Pres. C. Y. TU.

Gas

The Great Taipei Gas Corpn: 5/F, Lane 11, 35 Kwang Fu North Rd, Taipei 10577; tel. (2) 27684999; fax (2) 27630480; e-mail k2@taipeigas.com.tw; internet www.taipeigas.com.tw; supply of gas and gas equipment; Chair. LI FENG-YAO.

Hsin Kao Gas Co Ltd: 56 Ta-Yi St, Yen Cheng, Kaohsiung; tel. (7) 5315701; fax (7) 5312932; internet www.hkgas.com.tw; Chair. CHEN TIEN-MIAO; Gen. Man. CHEN CHIEN-TONG.

Shin Shin Natural Gas Co Ltd: 100 Yungho Rd, Sec. 1, Yungho, Taipei; tel. (2) 2921-7811; fax (2) 2928-2829; internet www.shinshingas.com.tw; f. 1971; supplies natural gas to non-industrial users; Chair. CHEN HO-CHIA; Pres. WEI YU-HUI.

Water

Taiwan Water Corpn: 2–1 Shuangshih Rd, Sec. 2, Taichung 40425; tel. (4) 2224191; fax (4) 2224201; e-mail service@mail.water.gov.tw; internet www.water.gov.tw; f. 1974; supplies water throughout Taiwan Province and Kaohsiung City; Chair. HSU SHIANG-KUEEN; Pres. HUANG CHING-SZU.

CO-OPERATIVES

In December 2004 there were 5,555 co-operatives, with a total membership of 5,195,265 and total capital of NT $23,524m. Of the specialized co-operatives the most important was the consumers' co-operative (3,928 co-ops).

The Co-operative League (f. 1940) is a national organization responsible for co-ordination, education and training and the movement's national and international interests (Chair. T. C. HWANG).

TRADE UNIONS

Chinese Federation of Labour: 4F, No. 177, Section 3, Roosevelt Rd, Taipei 10647; tel. (2) 23660111; fax (2) 23696111; e-mail cfl.labor@msa.hinet.net; internet www.cfl.org.tw; f. 1948; mems: 53 federations of unions representing more than 1,000,000 workers; Pres. CHIEH CHEN.

National Federations

Chunghwa Postal Workers' Union: 9/F, 45 Chungking South Rd, Sec. 2, Taipei 10076; tel. (2) 23921380; fax (2) 23414510; e-mail cpwu8331@ms78.hinet.net; internet www.cpwu.org.tw; f. 1930; fmrly Chinese Federation of Postal Workers; restructuring completed July 2003; 24,000 mems; Pres. TSAI LIANG-CHUAN.

National Chinese Seamen's Union: 8/F, 25 Nanking East Rd, Sec. 3, Taipei 10487; tel. (2) 25150259; fax (2) 25078211; e-mail ncsu.seamen@msa.hinet.net; internet www.ncsu.org.tw; f. 1913; 21,520 mems (June 2005); Pres. FANG FU-LIANG.

Taiwan Railway Labor Union: Rm 6044, 6/F, 3 Peiping West Rd, Taipei 10041; tel. (2) 23896115; fax (2) 23896134; e-mail service@trlu.org.tw; internet www.trlu.org.tw; f. 1947; 15,579 mems; Pres. CHEN HAN-CHIN.

Regional Federations

Taiwan Federation of Textile and Dyeing Industry Workers' Unions (TFTDWU): 2 Lane 64, Chung Hsiao East Rd, Sec. 2, Taipei 10053; tel. (2) 23415627; fax (2) 23413748; f. 1958; 6,600 mems (July 2005); Chair. ING-JIE CHEN.

Taiwan Provincial Federation of Labour: 92 Sungann Rd, Sec.1, Taichung 40650; tel. (4) 22309009; fax (2) 22309012; e-mail tpfl@ms39.hinet.net; internet www.tpfl.org.tw; f. 1948; 45 mem. unions and 1,060,000 mems; Pres. CHEN JEA; Sec.-Gen. JING-HUNG CHEN.

Transport

RAILWAYS

Taiwan Railway Administration (TRA): 3 Peiping West Rd, Taipei 10026; tel. (2) 23815226; fax (2) 23831367; internet www.railway.gov.tw; f. 1891; a public utility under the Ministry of Transportation and Communications; operates both the west line and east line systems, with a route length of 1,101.5 km; the west line is the main trunk line from Keelung, in the north, to Fangliao, in the south, with several branches; electrification of the main trunk line was completed in 1979; the east line runs along the east coast, linking Hualien with Taitung; the north link line, with a length of 86.6 km from Suao Sing to Hualien, was opened in 1980; the south link line, with a length of 98.2 km from Taitung to Fangliao, opened in late 1991, completing the round-the-island system; Dir-Gen. N. H. HO.

Taipei Rapid Transit Corpn (TRTC): 7 Lane 48, Zhong Shan North Rd, Sec. 2, Taipei 10450; tel. (2) 21812345; fax (2) 25115003; internet www.trtc.com.tw; f. 1994; 74.4 km (incl. 10.5 km medium-capacity rail) open, with further lines under construction; also operates the Maokong Gondola cable car system; Chair. RICHARD C. L. CHEN; Pres. Dr HUEI-SHENG TSAY.

Taiwan High Speed Rail Corpn (THSRC): 3/F, 100 Hsin Yi Rd, Taipei 110; tel. (2) 87892000; internet www.thsrc.com.tw; f. 1996; operates 345-km high-speed rail link between Taipei and Kaohsiung; Chair. NITA ING; CEO OU CHIN-DER.

An Airport Rail System linking Taipei with Taiwan Taoyuan International Airport is under construction by the Ministry of Transportation and Communications; this is due for completion in 2012.

ROADS

There were 36,698 km of highways in 2005, most of them asphalt-paved. The Sun Yat-sen Freeway was completed in 1978. Construction of a 505-km Second Freeway, which was to extend to Pingtung, in southern Taiwan, began in July 1987 and was completed in late 2004. The Nantou branch, from the Wufeng system interchange of the Second Freeway to Puli in central Taiwan, with a length of 38 km, was scheduled for completion in 2008. Work on the Taipei–Ilan freeway began in 1991. The 31-km freeway and its 24.1-km extension, from Toucheng to Suao, were completed in 2005.

Directorate-General of Highways: 70 Chung Hsiao West Rd, Sec. 1, Taipei 10047; tel. (2) 23113456; fax (2) 23111644; internet www.thb.gov.tw; Dir-Gen. JAMES J. Y. CHEN.

Kuo-Kuang Motor Transport Co Ltd: 4/F, 17 Hsu Chang St, Taipei 10047; tel. (2) 23810731; fax (2) 23810268; internet www.kingbus.com.tw; f. 2001; operates national bus service; Chair. HONG-SEN LEE.

Taiwan Area National Expressway Engineering Bureau: 1 Lane 1, Hoping East Rd, Sec. 3, Taipei 10669; tel. (2) 27078808; fax (2) 27017818; e-mail neebeyes@taneeb.gov.tw; internet www.taneeb.gov.tw; f. 1990; responsible for planning, design, construction and maintenance of provincial and county highways; Dir-Gen. BANE L. B. CHJOU.

Taiwan Area National Freeway Bureau: 70 Banshanya, Liming Village, Taishan Township, Taipei County 234; tel. (2) 29096141; fax (2) 29093218; e-mail tanfb1@freeway.gov.tw; internet www.freeway.gov.tw; f. 1970; Dir-Gen. LEE THAY-MING.

SHIPPING

Taiwan has seven international ports: Anping, Kaohsiung, Keelung, Taichung, Hualien, Suao and Taipei. In December 2006 the merchant fleet comprised 628 vessels, with a total displacement of more than 2.7m. grt. Some of the main shipping companies are as follows:

Evergreen International Storage & Transport Corpn: 899, Ching Kuo Rd, Taoyuan 3305; tel. (3) 3252060; fax (3) 3252059; e-mail bcd@evergreen-eitc.com.tw; internet www.evergreen-eitc.com.tw; Chair. YE JIONG-CHAO.

Evergreen Marine Corpn (Taiwan) Ltd: Evergreen Bldg, 166 Ming Sheng East Rd, Sec. 2, Taipei 10423; tel. (2) 25057766; fax (2) 25058159; e-mail mgt@evergreen-marine.com; internet www.evergreen-marine.com; f. 1968; world-wide container liner services; Chair. CHANG YUNG-FA; Pres. LONG-SHUNG WANG.

Taiwan Navigation Co Ltd: 2–6/F, 29 Chi Nan Rd, Sec. 2, Taipei 10054; tel. (2) 23941769; fax (2) 23936578; e-mail tnctpe@taiwanline.com.tw; internet www.taiwanline.com.tw; Chair. RICHARD HUANG; Pres. I. Y. CHANG.

U-Ming Marine Transport Corpn: 29/F, Taipei Metro Tower, 207 Tun Hua South Rd, Sec. 2, Taipei 10602; tel. (2) 27338000; fax (2) 27359900; e-mail uming@metro.feg.com.tw; internet www.uming.com.tw; world-wide transportation services; Chair. DOUGLAS TONG HSU; Pres. C. K. ONG.

Wan Hai Lines Ltd: 10/F, 136 Sung Chiang Rd, Taipei 10485; tel. (2) 25677961; fax (2) 25216000; e-mail serv@wanhai.com.tw; internet

CHINA (TAIWAN)

www.wanhai.com.tw; f. 1965; regional container liner services; Chair. C. H. CHEN; Pres. P. T. CHEN.

Yang Ming Marine Transport Corpn (Yang Ming Line): 271 Ming De 1st Rd, Keelung 20646; tel. (2) 24559988; fax (2) 24559958; e-mail tara@yml.com.tw; internet www.yml.com.tw; f. 1972; worldwide container liner services, bulk carrier and supertanker services; Chair. FRANK LU; Pres. HUANG WONG-HSIU.

CIVIL AVIATION

There are two international airports, Taiwan Taoyuan International Airport—formerly known as Chiang Kai-shek—near Taipei, which opened in 1979 (a second passenger terminal and expansion of freight facilities being completed in 2000), and Kaohsiung International Airport (which also offers domestic flight services). There are also 16 domestic airports, three of which offer international charter flight services. In March 2004 Air Macau opened a new passenger air route between Shenzhen Airport, on the mainland, and Taipei, via Macao.

Civil Aeronautics Administration: 340 Tun Hua North Rd, Taipei 10548; tel. (2) 23496000; fax (2) 23496277; e-mail gencaa@mail.caa.gov.tw; internet www.caa.gov.tw; Dir-Gen. BILLY K. C. CHANG.

China Airlines Ltd (CAL): 131 Nanking East Rd, Sec. 3, Taipei 10410; tel. (2) 25062345; fax (2) 25145754; e-mail ju-reng_chen@email.china-airlines.com; internet www.china-airlines.com; f. 1959; international services to destinations in the Far East, Europe, the Middle East, the USA and Australia; Chair. and Pres. K. S. CHAO.

EVA Airways (EVA): Eva Air Bldg, 376 Hsin-nan Rd, Sec. 1, Luchu Township, Taoyuan County, 33801; tel. (3) 3515151; fax (3) 3510023; e-mail sammykao@evaair.com; internet www.evaair.com.tw; f. 1989; subsidiary of Evergreen Group; commenced flights in 1991; services to destinations in Asia, the Middle East, Europe, North America, Australia and New Zealand; Chair. LIN BOU-SHIU; Pres. CHEN HSING-TE.

Far Eastern Air Transport Corpn (FAT): 5 Alley 123, Lane 405, Tun Hua North Rd, Taipei 10592; tel. (2) 27121555; fax (2) 27122428; internet www.fat.com.tw; f. 1957; domestic services and regional international services; Chair. STEPHEN J. TSUEI; Pres. M. W. CHENG.

Mandarin Airlines (MDA): 13/F, 134 Ming Sheng East Rd, Sec. 3, Taipei 10596; tel. (2) 27171188; fax (2) 27170716; e-mail mandarin@mandarin-airlines.com; internet www.mandarin-airlines.com; f. 1991; subsidiary of CAL; merged with Formosa Airlines 1999; domestic and regional international services; Pres. HARRIS WANG.

TransAsia Airways (TNA): 9/F, 139 Chengchou Rd, Taipei 10341; tel. (2) 25575767; fax (2) 25570643; internet www.tna.com.tw; f. 1951; fmrly Foshing Airlines; domestic flights and international services; Chair. FAN CHIEH-CHIANG; Pres. SUN HUANG-HSIANG.

UNI Airways Corpn (UIA): 9/F, 100 Chang An East Rd, Sec. 2, Taipei 10491; tel. (2) 25135533; fax (2) 25133202; internet www.uniair.com.tw; f. 1989; fmrly Makung Airlines; merged with Great China Airlines and Taiwan Airlines 1998; domestic flights and international services (to Bali, Indonesia; Seoul, South Korea; Bangkok, Thailand; and Hanoi, Viet Nam); Chair. SU HOMNG-YIH; Pres. PETER CHEN.

Tourism

The principal tourist attractions include the island scenery and cultural heritage. In 2006 there were 3,519,827 visitor arrivals (including 579,908 overseas Chinese) in Taiwan. Revenue from tourism in 2006 totalled US $5,136m. The number of visitor arrivals increased to 3,716,063 in 2007. To strengthen the development of the tourism industry, a 'Doubling Tourist Arrivals Plan', targeting 5m. arrivals in 2008, was inaugurated in September 2002. In order to raise Taiwan's international profile, the Tourism Bureau also launched the 'Tourism Flagship Plan' in 2006. In advance of the restarting of negotiations with the People's Republic on the removal of the official restrictions on the numbers of mainland Chinese visitors to the island, the Taiwan Strait Tourism and Travel Association was established in August 2006.

Tourism Bureau, Ministry of Transportation and Communications: 9/F, 290 Chung Hsiao East Rd, Sec. 4, Taipei 10694; tel. (2) 23491500; fax (2) 27717036; e-mail tbroc@tbroc.gov.tw; internet taiwan.net.tw; f. 1972; Dir-Gen. JANICE LAI.

Taiwan Visitors Association: 5/F, 9 Min Chuan East Rd, Sec. 2, Taipei 10470; tel. (2) 25943261; fax (2) 25943265; internet www.tva.org.tw; f. 1956; promotes domestic and international tourism; Chair. CHANG SHUO LAO.

COLOMBIA

Introductory Survey

Location, Climate, Language, Religion, Flag, Capital

The Republic of Colombia lies in the north-west of South America, with the Caribbean Sea to the north and the Pacific Ocean to the west. Its continental neighbours are Venezuela and Brazil to the east, and Peru and Ecuador to the south, while Panama connects it with Central America. The coastal areas have a tropical rainforest climate, the plateaux are temperate, and in the Andes mountains there are areas of permanent snow. The language is Spanish. Almost all of the inhabitants profess Christianity, and almost 90% are Roman Catholics. There are small Protestant and Jewish minorities. The national flag (proportions 2 by 3) has three horizontal stripes, of yellow (one-half of the depth) over dark blue over red. The capital is Bogotá.

Recent History

Colombia was under Spanish rule from the 16th century until 1819, when it achieved independence as part of Gran Colombia, which included Ecuador, Panama and Venezuela. Ecuador and Venezuela seceded in 1830, when Colombia (then including Panama) became a separate republic. In 1903 the province of Panama successfully rebelled and became an independent country. For more than a century, ruling power in Colombia has been shared between two political parties, the Conservatives (Partido Conservador Colombiano, PCC) and the Liberals (Partido Liberal Colombiano, PL), whose rivalry has often led to violence. President Laureano Gómez of the PCC, who was elected 'unopposed' in November 1949, ruled as a dictator until his overthrow by Gen. Gustavo Rojas Pinilla in a coup in June 1953. President Rojas established a right-wing dictatorship but, following widespread rioting, he was deposed in May 1957, when a five-man military junta took power. According to official estimates, lawlessness during 1949–58, known as 'La Violencia', caused the deaths of about 280,000 people.

In an attempt to restore peace and stability, the PCC and the PL agreed to co-operate in a National Front. Under this arrangement, the presidency was to be held by the PCC and the PL in rotation, while cabinet portfolios would be divided equally between the two parties and both would have an equal number of seats in each house of the bicameral Congreso (Congress). In December 1957, in Colombia's first vote on the basis of universal adult suffrage, this agreement was overwhelmingly approved by a referendum and was subsequently incorporated in Colombia's Constitution, dating from 1886.

In May 1958 the first presidential election under the amended Constitution was won by the National Front candidate, Dr Alberto Lleras Camargo, a PL member who had been President in 1945–46. He took office in August 1958, when the ruling junta relinquished power. As provided by the 1957 agreement, he was succeeded by a member of the PCC, Dr Guillermo León Valencia, who was, in turn, succeeded by a PL candidate, Dr Carlos Lleras Restrepo, in 1966.

At the presidential election in April 1970, the National Front candidate, Dr Misael Pastrana Borrero (PCC), narrowly defeated Gen. Rojas, the former dictator, who campaigned as leader of the Alianza Nacional Popular (ANAPO), with policies that had considerable appeal for the poor. At concurrent elections to the Congreso the National Front lost its majority in each of the two houses, while ANAPO became the main opposition group in each. The result of the presidential election was challenged by supporters of ANAPO, and an armed wing of the party, the Movimiento 19 de Abril (M-19), began to organize guerrilla activity against the Government. It was joined by dissident members of a pro-Soviet guerrilla group, the Fuerzas Armadas Revolucionarias de Colombia—Ejército del Pueblo (FARC—EP, commonly known as the FARC), established in 1966.

The bipartisan form of government ended formally with the presidential and legislative elections of April 1974, although the 1974–78 Cabinet remained subject to the parity agreement. The PCC and the PL together won an overwhelming majority of seats in the Congreso, and support for ANAPO was greatly reduced. The presidential election was won by the PL candidate, Dr Alfonso López Michelsen.

At elections to the Congreso in February 1978, the PL won a clear majority in both houses, and in June the PL candidate, Dr Julio César Turbay Ayala, won the presidential election. President Turbay continued to observe the National Front agreement, and attempted to address the problems of urban terrorism and drugs-trafficking. In 1982 the guerrillas suffered heavy losses after successful counter-insurgency operations, combined with the activities of a new anti-guerrilla group associated with drugs-smuggling enterprises, the Muerte a Secuestradores (MAS, Death to Kidnappers), whose targets later became trade union leaders, academics and human rights activists.

At congressional elections in March 1982, the PL maintained its majority in both houses. In May the PCC candidate, Dr Belisario Betancur Cuartas, won the presidential election, benefiting from a division within the PL. President Betancur, who took office in August, declared a broad amnesty for guerrillas in November, reconvened the Peace Commission (first established in 1981) and ordered an investigation into the MAS. Despite the Peace Commission's successful negotiation of cease-fire agreements with the FARC, the M-19 (now operating as a left-wing guerrilla movement) and the Ejército Popular de Liberación (EPL) during 1984, factions of all three groups which were opposed to the truce continued to conduct guerrilla warfare against the authorities. The assassination of the Minister of Justice in May 1984 prompted the Government to declare a nation-wide state of siege and announce its intention to enforce its hitherto unobserved extradition treaty with the USA.

Relations between the M-19 and the armed forces deteriorated during 1985, and in June the M-19 formally withdrew from the cease-fire agreement. In November a dramatic siege by the M-19 at the Palace of Justice in the capital, during which more than 100 people were killed, resulted in severe public criticism of the Government and the armed forces for their handling of events. Negotiations with the M-19 were suspended indefinitely.

At congressional elections in March 1986 the traditional wing of the PL secured a clear victory over the PCC, and the PL's candidate, Dr Virgilio Barco Vargas, was elected President in May. The large majority secured by the PL at both elections obliged the PCC to form the first formal opposition to a government for 30 years.

Hopes that an indefinite cease-fire agreement, concluded between the FARC and the Government in March 1986, would facilitate the full participation of the Unión Patriótica (UP), formed by the FARC, in the political process were largely frustrated by the Government's failure to respond effectively to a campaign of assassinations of UP members, conducted by paramilitary 'death squads'. The crisis was compounded in October 1987 by the decision of six guerrilla groups, including the FARC, the Ejército de Liberación Nacional (ELN) and the M-19, to form a joint front, the Coordinadora Guerrillera Simón Bolívar (CGSB). Although in 1987 the Government extended police powers against drugs dealers, its efforts were severely hampered by the Supreme Court's ruling that Colombia's extradition treaty with the USA was unconstitutional.

In January 1989 the Government and the M-19 concluded an agreement to initiate talks between the Government, all political parties in the Congreso and the CGSB. In March the M-19 and the Government signed a document providing for the reintegration of the guerrillas into society. In the same month, the ELN, the EPL and the FARC publicly confirmed their willingness to participate in peace talks with the Government. In September the M-19 announced that it had reached agreement with the Government on a peace treaty, under which its members were to demobilize and disarm in exchange for a full pardon. In addition, the movement was to enter the political mainstream; in October the M-19 was formally constituted as a political party and by March 1990 all M-19 guerrilla forces had surrendered their weapons. In exchange for firm commitments from the Barco administration that a referendum would be held to decide the question of constitutional reform and that proposals for comprehensive changes to the electoral law would be introduced in the

Congreso, members of the M-19 were guaranteed a general amnesty, reintegration into civilian life and full political participation in forthcoming elections.

A presidential election was scheduled to be held in May 1990. In March Bernardo Jaramillo, the UP presidential candidate, was assassinated, and in April Carlos Pizarro of the M-19 became the third presidential candidate to be killed by hired assassins since August 1989. Antonio Navarro Wolff became the M-19 presidential candidate, in conjunction with the recently established Convergencia Democrática (later Alianza Democrática—AD), a mainly left-wing alliance. César Gaviria Trujillo of the PL was proclaimed the winner of the election. Some 90% of voters approved proposals for the creation of a National Constituent Assembly in a de facto referendum held simultaneously. The new President formed a Cabinet of 'national unity', and confirmed his commitment to continuing the strenuous efforts to combat drugs-trafficking.

In October 1990 the creation of the National Constituent Assembly was declared constitutionally acceptable by the Supreme Court. Candidates for the AD—M-19 secured 19 of the 70 contested Assembly seats, forcing the ruling PL and the Conservatives to seek support from them for the successful enactment of reform proposals. In February 1991 the five-month session of the National Constituent Assembly was inaugurated. The composition of the Assembly had been expanded from 70 to 73 members in order to incorporate three invited members of former guerrilla groupings (two from the EPL and one from the Partido Revolucionario de Trabajadores—PRT) and was later expanded to accommodate a representative of the Comando Quintín Lame. By June an agreement was reached between President Gaviria and representatives of the PL, the AD—M-19 and the conservative Movimiento de Salvación Nacional (MSN) that, in order to facilitate the process of political and constitutional renovation, the Congreso should be dissolved prematurely. The Assembly subsequently voted to dismiss the Congreso, pending new congressional and gubernatorial elections to be conducted in October (although congressional elections had not been scheduled to take place until 1994).

The new Constitution became effective on 6 July 1991. The state of siege, imposed in 1984 in response to the escalation in political and drugs-related violence, also was ended. The Constitution placed considerable emphasis upon provisions to encourage greater political participation and to eradicate electoral corruption and misrepresentation. Controversially, it also sought to prohibit the extradition of Colombian nationals (see below). While the Constitution was welcomed enthusiastically by the majority of the population, reservations were expressed that clauses relating to the armed forces remained largely unchanged and that provisions which recognized the democratic rights of indigenous groups did not extend to their territorial claims.

Relations with the Medellín cartel improved considerably following the release, in May 1991, of two remaining hostages, and in June, following the decision to prohibit constitutionally the practice of extradition, the Government's efforts were rewarded with the surrender of Pablo Escobar, the supposed head of the Medellín drugs cartel. Charges brought against Escobar included several of murder, kidnapping and terrorism. In July spokesmen for the Medellín cartel announced that its military operations were to be suspended and that the 'Extraditables' were to be disbanded. Hopes that Escobar's surrender might precipitate a decline in drugs-related violence were frustrated by reports that Escobar was continuing to direct cocaine cartel operations from his purpose-built prison at Envigado, and by the emergence of the powerful Cali drugs cartel, which was expected to compensate for any shortfall in the supply of illicit drugs resulting from the demise of the Medellín cartel.

The Liberals were most successful in the congressional elections of October 1991, with a clear majority of seats in both chambers. The traditional Conservative opposition suffered from a division in their support between the PCC, the MSN and the Nueva Fuerza Democrática, securing around one-quarter of the seats in both houses between them. The AD—M-19 received only 10% of the votes cast, equivalent to nine seats in the Senado and 15 seats in the Cámara de Representantes.

Meanwhile, in February 1990 the Government had established the National Council for Normalization, in an attempt to repeat the success of recent peace initiatives with the M-19 in negotiations with other revolutionary groups. The EPL announced the end of its armed struggle in August and joined the political mainstream (retaining the initials EPL as Esperanza, Paz y Libertad), along with the Comando Quintín Lame and the PRT, in 1991. Attempts to negotiate with the FARC and the ELN, however, proved fruitless, and violent clashes between the remaining guerrilla groups (now co-ordinating actions as the Coordinadora Nacional Guerrillera Simón Bolívar—CNGSB) and security forces persisted.

An escalation in guerrilla activity in 1992 prompted the Government to intensify anti-insurgency measures. In October the Congreso approved proposals for an increased counter-insurgency budget and for the creation of new armed units to combat terrorism. The Government's rejection of any agenda for renewed negotiations provoked an intensification of the conflict, leading Gaviria to declare a 90-day state of internal disturbance in November. As a result, the M-19 announced that it was to withdraw from the Government and resume an active opposition role.

As the security situation continued to deteriorate, in February 1993 the Government announced a significant increase in its budget allocation for security, and in April doubled the length of prison terms for terrorist acts. The state of internal disturbance was also extended twice. Attempts by the Government and the ELN to negotiate a truce were frustrated by mutual perceptions of intransigence. In April 1994 the Corriente de Renovación Socialista (CRS), a dissident faction of the ELN more disposed to political assimilation, surrendered its weapons, under the supervision of international observers, and subsequently was awarded two seats in the newly elected Cámara de Representantes (see below).

An intensification of drugs-related violence in the capital during early 1993 was attributed to an attempt by Pablo Escobar (who had escaped from prison in mid-1992) to force the Government to negotiate more favourable conditions for his surrender, and prompted the formation of a vigilante group, Pepe (Perseguidos por Pablo Escobar—those Persecuted by Pablo Escobar), which launched a campaign of retaliatory violence against Escobar's family, associates and property. A simultaneous and sustained assault by Pepe and by the security forces against the remnants of the Medellín cartel resulted in the death or surrender of many notable cartel members, culminating in the death of Escobar himself, in December, during an exchange of fire with security forces attempting to effect his arrest.

The results of congressional and local elections conducted in March 1994 represented a serious blow for the political left in Colombia, and re-established the traditional two-party dominance of the PL and the PCC. The PL candidate, Ernesto Samper Pizano, was elected to the presidency in June and inaugurated on 7 August.

Shortly after taking office, allegations emerged that Samper's election campaign had been funded partly by contributions from the Cali cartel. Tape recordings of conversations were dismissed by the Prosecutor-General as insufficient proof of such contributions actually having been made. In July 1994 a similar recording, which appeared to implicate the Colombian Chief of National Police in the payment of a bribe by the Cali cartel, prompted the US Senate to vote to make the disbursement of future aid to Colombia dependent on an assessment of the level of its co-operation in anti-drugs programmes.

A CNGSB offensive during the weeks preceding the transfer of power from Gaviria to Samper in August 1994 resulted in numerous deaths on both sides and considerable damage inflicted on power installations and the transport infrastructure. Guerrilla activities further intensified after the new administration took office. In September, under intense international pressure, and following a series of revelations in which the security forces were implicated in abuses of human rights, the new Government announced an initiative to address allegations of human rights abuses by the security forces; these included reforming the National Police and disbanding all paramilitary units. In November President Samper complied with a guerrilla request that imprisoned rebel leaders be moved from military installations to civilian prisons, and declared the Government's willingness to enter into unconditional dialogue with the guerrillas.

In February 1995 President Samper reiterated his commitment to combating all illegal drugs-related activities in the country, a precondition to the disbursement of US financial aid to Colombia. A number of initiatives were launched in Cali, resulting in the capture of the head of the Cali drugs cartel, Gilberto Rodríguez Orejuela, and four other cartel leaders in mid-1995 (Rodríguez Orejuela was extradited to the USA to face charges of drugs-trafficking in December 2004). Meanwhile, in

April 1995 nine prominent PL politicians were suspended from the party pending investigation by the office of the Prosecutor-General into allegations of their maintaining links with the Cali cartel. In the following months it was confirmed that the Comptroller-General and the Attorney-General were also to be the subject of investigation as a result of similar allegations, while Samper's former election campaign treasurer, Santiago Medina, was arrested on charges related to the processing of drugs cartel contributions through Samper's election fund. In August the Minister of National Defence, Fernando Botero Zea, resigned, having been implicated in the affair by evidence submitted to the authorities by Medina. Medina maintained that Samper had been fully aware of the origin of the funds, an accusation denied by the President.

In May 1995 the Government extended an offer of participation in legislative and consultative processes to the FARC, in the hope of securing their commitment to surrender arms. While the FARC responded positively to the initial proposal, further progress was to be dependent on the Government's successful execution of its stated intention to demilitarize the sensitive north-eastern region of La Uribe. However, negotiations were hampered by renewed FARC and ELN offensives in late May. An escalation in the number of acts of violence perpetrated by guerrilla forces and by paramilitary defence groups prompted Samper to declare a state of internal disturbance for a 90-day period. In October, however, the Constitutional Court rejected the terms of the state of emergency. Following the assassination in November of a prominent Conservative politician, the President declared a new 90-day state of internal disturbance.

In December 1995 the congressional accusations committee voted against the initiation of a full-scale inquiry into allegations of Samper's impropriety in the use of funds proceeding from drugs cartels, on the grounds of insufficient evidence. The repercussions of the scandal, however, were considered to have severely undermined the political integrity of the Government. Relations between the US Government and the Samper administration deteriorated dramatically during 1995, culminating in allegations that the US Government was attempting to destabilize the administration through the covert actions of the US Drugs Enforcement Agency. In January 1996 the PCC announced an immediate suspension of co-operation with the Government and the resignation of two of the four incumbent PCC cabinet members. Evidence collected by the Prosecutor-General was submitted to the accusations committee in February, together with four formal charges to be brought against the President, including that of illegal enrichment. Later in the month congressional commissions of both parliamentary chambers decided to launch a new and public investigation into the matter. In March Samper testified before a new parliamentary investigation into the affair; he denied allegations that he had contrived the plan to solicit funding from the Cali cartel, but conceded that the cartel had part-financed the campaign, albeit without his knowledge. In June the Congreso voted to acquit Samper of charges of having been aware of the part-financing of his election campaign by drugs-traffickers. The US Administration condemned the result and in the following month revoked Samper's visa to travel to the USA.

In April 1996 the Supreme Court took the unprecedented step of requesting that the Senado suspend the Attorney-General, Orlando Vásquez Velásquez, in order that he face charges of obstructing the course of justice (he had allegedly fabricated evidence to discredit the Prosecutor-General). In October Vásquez Velásquez was found guilty of the charges; he was dismissed as Attorney-General and banned from holding public office for a five-year period. In December 1997 he was sentenced to eight years' imprisonment on drugs charges. During 1996 Botero, Medina and María Izquierdo, a former PL senator, were all sentenced to terms of imprisonment for their involvement in the Samper affair.

Civil unrest and guerrilla activity continued during 1996. The state of internal disturbance was extended for a further 90 days in January, and also in April following a CNGSB-organized nation-wide 'armed industrial strike', which occasioned as many as 40 deaths. A major offensive launched in August by FARC and ELN rebels (resulting in as many as 100 fatalities) coincided with large-scale protests by coca growers demanding a review of the coca-eradication programme, particularly the use of aerial spraying. In early 1997 the Samper administration encountered increasing pressure from the USA to combat drugs-trafficking and corruption. The USA again refused to 'certify' Colombia, claiming that there had been a substantial increase in the production of illicit drugs in that country during 1996. Legislation passed in November permitting the extradition of Colombian nationals sought for criminal offences abroad was strongly criticized by the US Administration as it would not have retroactive effect. (In March 2005 Samper was cleared of allegations by a US Federal Attorney that he had accepted US $5m. from the Cali cartel to ensure that the legislation would not have retroactive effect.)

In the months preceding the October 1997 local elections the activities of guerrilla and paramilitary groups intensified. More than 40 candidates were killed, some 200 were kidnapped and as many as 1,900 withdrew after receiving death threats. In May the Government had agreed to the temporary demilitarization of part of the Caquetá department in order to secure the release of 70 members of the armed forces captured by the FARC. Voting was cancelled in numerous municipalities, while reports of secret preliminary peace negotiations between government representatives and the FARC were undermined by a major military offensive in September, in which 652 FARC guerrillas were killed and a further 1,600 were captured.

The PL retained a narrow overall majority in both chambers of the legislature at congressional elections in March 1998. The ballot was preceded by a period of violent attacks on the security forces by guerrilla groups; in one incident 80 counter-insurgency troops were killed by the FARC, and a further 43 were taken prisoner. The first round of the presidential election was held in May of that year. The PL candidate, Horacio Serpa Uribe, secured 35% of the valid votes cast, followed by the PCC nominee, Andrés Pastrana Arango (34%). Serpa's candidacy had been strongly opposed by the US Administration as he was alleged to have links with drugs-traffickers. Pastrana emerged victorious in the second ballot in June, and was inaugurated President in August.

In July 1998 President-elect Pastrana announced that he had held secret talks with Manuel Marulanda Vélez (alias 'Tirofijo'), the FARC leader, and that he had agreed to demilitarize five southern municipalities for a 90-day period (commencing in November) in order to facilitate negotiations with the guerrillas. Pastrana subsequently recognized the political status of the FARC, thereby allowing the Government to negotiate with an outlawed group. None the less, FARC attacks on the security forces continued. Shortly before the negotiations between the Government and the FARC began in January 1999, it was revealed that in December the FARC had held informal talks in Costa Rica with government officials from the USA and Colombia. (Relations between Colombia and the USA had improved notably under the Pastrana administration: in October Pastrana made an official visit to the USA—the first by a Colombian Head of State in 23 years—and in December the two countries agreed on measures to improve military co-operation in the fight against the drugs trade.) In mid-January 1999 the FARC suspended talks until the authorities provided evidence that they were taking action against paramilitary groups, which claimed responsibility for the massacre of more than 130 civilians earlier in the month. In February Pastrana announced the extension of the period of demilitarization by three months.

The ELN, meanwhile, made tentative moves to negotiate a peace settlement during 1998, and in February signed an accord with government peace negotiators in Madrid, Spain, on the holding of preliminary peace talks. In April the ELN disclosed that its leader, Gregorio Manuel Pérez Martínez, had died shortly afterwards; a collective leadership was appointed subsequently. In July, at a meeting in Mainz, Germany, between the ELN and representatives of Colombian 'civil society' (grouped in the National Peace Council—Consejo Nacional de Paz—CNP), the ELN agreed to facilitate talks between its members and the Government. The guerrillas subsequently postponed a meeting with the CNP in protest at its signing of an agreement with the Autodefensas Unidas de Colombia (AUC), an organization representing most of Colombia's paramilitary groups, to hold parallel peace talks. Nevertheless, in October representatives of the ELN, the CNP and the Government agreed on a timetable for preliminary peace talks, beginning in February 1999, which would culminate in the assembling of a national convention. The Government recognized the political status of the ELN, but the group did not cease hostilities. The planned peace negotiations failed to begin in February 1999, not least because of the Government's refusal to agree to the ELN's request that four districts in the department of Bolívar be demilitarized. The ELN intensified its operations, in an apparent attempt to increase pressure on the Government to accede to its demands. The guerrillas hijacked an Avianca domestic flight in April, kidnapping all 46 people on board, and abducted some 140 members of the congregation of a church in Cali in May. In June Pastrana withdrew political recognition of the ELN and made the release of hostages a precondition for future peace talks. A civilian commission was appointed subsequently by the Government to negotiate towards this end. The ELN freed the last hostage in November 2000.

Little progress was achieved in negotiations with the FARC until April 1999, as the guerrillas continued to insist that the Government demonstrate some success in its actions against paramilitary groups prior to a resumption of talks. The enforced resignation in that month of two senior army officers, alleged to have collaborated with paramilitary groups, appeared to appease the FARC, however, and in early May talks between Marulanda and President Pastrana resulted in an agreement on a comprehensive agenda for future peace negotiations; the period of demilitarization was again extended. Pastrana's strategy was not supported entirely by his administration and in May Rodrigo Lloreda, the Minister of National Defence, resigned in protest at concessions granted to the FARC. Pastrana's position was further undermined by the Congreso's rejection of legislation aimed at increasing the President's power concerning the peace process. Furthermore, the FARC continued to pursue its military campaign. The talks were subsequently postponed indefinitely, with the Government insisting that international monitors be allowed to investigate abuses allegedly committed by the FARC in the demilitarized zone. As negotiations resumed in October in La Uribe, after Pastrana had apparently withdrawn his demand for international observers, demonstrations for peace were attended by some 10m. people throughout the country.

Relations with the US Government continued to improve under President Pastrana. In March 1999 the USA decided to 'certify' Colombia's efforts to combat drugs-trafficking and in September Pastrana announced the establishment of a new antinarcotics battalion, to be trained and financed by the USA. Collaboration between the Colombian and US authorities led to the arrest of more than 60 suspected drugs-traffickers in two major operations conducted in October and December. However, the most important progress in Colombian-US relations came in 2000 with the development of Pastrana's so-called 'Plan Colombia'. This was an ambitious, US $7,500m. project intended to strengthen the Colombian state by increasing the efficiency of the security forces and the judicial system, eliminating drugs production through both crop eradication and crop substitution, and by reducing unemployment. In July 2000 the US Congress approved a contribution to the Plan of $1,300m., including a military component of $1,000m. and significant sums for judicial reform and human rights education. Human rights organizations warned of an escalation of human rights abuses following the Plan's implementation, as the main aid component was allocated to strengthening the security forces, whose links to paramilitary groups were, allegedly, yet to be severed. At the same time, Colombia's Andean neighbours feared that an escalation in violence would force thousands of refugees onto their territory, and subsequently reinforced their borders.

At negotiations in September 2000 the FARC threatened to halt the peace process if plans for the US military component of Plan Colombia, to be directed against coca-growing areas of Putumayo, were implemented. The FARC effectively blockaded Putumayo from the end of that month, and succeeded in delaying the aerial spraying of coca plantations. (The military offensive against the plantations began in December, although in February 2001 the aerial spraying of crops was suspended in the Putumayo region after local authorities warned of the adverse effects the herbicides used could have on people and licit crops.) In October the Government dismissed 388 members of the armed forces in a move designed to improve military efficiency as well as to allay accusations of corruption and violations of human rights. However, the dismissals did not prevent the FARC from withdrawing from peace talks in November in order to demand greater government action in combating the AUC. By the end of the year President Pastrana was under increasing pressure to regain control of the demilitarized zone; a report released in December estimated a 30% increase in FARC military capacity since the zone was created. The murder in late December of Diego Turbay Cote, President of the congressional peace commission, allegedly by members of the FARC, further heightened tensions. However, following threats by the FARC that failure to prolong the demilitarized zone would lead to 'total war', Pastrana extended the deadline until the end of January 2001. A further extension was granted in February, after which the FARC leadership met the President in the demilitarized zone and signed a 13-point accord, including an agreement to revive the stalled negotiations, to expedite an exchange of sick prisoners, and to begin discussions on a cease-fire. In March diplomats representing governments from Latin America, Europe, Japan and Canada met with FARC leaders to monitor the peace process. The new US Administration of George W. Bush refused an invitation to join the peace process, preferring instead to focus on drugs-eradication policies. In July the US House of Representatives approved a US $670m. aid package, known as the Andean Regional Initiative, to support Plan Colombia and to promote stability in the rest of the Andean region.

In the first four months of 2001 an estimated 760 people were killed, and in the first seven months 1,700 were kidnapped, a significant increase on the previous year. However, in June progress was made in peace negotiations when the FARC signed a prisoner-exchange agreement with the Government; about 300 prisoners were released by the FARC at the end of the month. Nevertheless, in August President Pastrana signed legislation granting new powers to the military to combat guerrilla forces. The legislation was controversial as it allowed for less scrutiny from government investigators, and was opposed by human rights organizations. None the less, in October the Government extended the existence of the demilitarized zone until January 2002, after the FARC agreed to reduce the number of kidnappings and to begin cease-fire negotiations. However, it refused demands by the FARC to remove military controls around the demilitarized zone. This impasse effectively prevented any progress on substantive issues such as cease-fire negotiations during the rest of the year. Then, in a move that signalled the end of the peace process, on 9 January 2002 Pastrana gave the FARC just 48 hours to leave the demilitarized zone. Hours before the expiry of the deadline the FARC rescinded demands for relaxed security around the demilitarized zone and agreed to recommence negotiations; as a result the guerrillas were able to continue their occupation of the zone. On 20 January, with the help of representatives from 10 facilitating countries and UN envoy James LeMoyne, agreement was reached on an extension, to early April, to the deadline for a cease-fire agreement. However, on 20 February, following the hijacking of an aeroplane and the kidnapping of a prominent senator, Pastrana terminated peace talks and ordered the armed forces to regain control of the demilitarized zone.

In April 2000 an agreement was reached with the ELN on the establishment of a demilitarized zone, similar to that granted to the FARC, in southern Bolívar. However, the Government encountered much local opposition to the proposed zone, including roadblocks and demonstrations. In July informal discussions on a national convention, as demanded by the guerrilla movement as a precursor to peace talks, were held with the ELN in Geneva, Switzerland, with envoys from Cuba, France, Norway, Spain and Switzerland present. These ended without agreement. In response, the ELN continued to sabotage Colombia's oil industry by attacking pipeline transport. Tentative moves towards peace recommenced in December after the ELN released 42 hostages. Negotiations in Havana, Cuba, at the end of the year resulted in a preliminary agreement on the terms and conditions of the demilitarized zone in Bolívar, although it was conditional on the acceptance by the ELN of the presence of an international verification committee in the region, as well as representatives from local and judicial institutions and one civilian police agency. The agreement was strongly opposed by the AUC and by residents of the proposed region. The prospects for a demilitarized zone were reduced after the ELN suspended negotiations with the Government in March in protest at the aerial spraying of coca in the Bolívar region. At the same time, the AUC began an offensive in the area in order to prevent the establishment of the demilitarized zone. The ELN resumed peace negotiations in April, but these faltered in August when President Pastrana suspended unofficial talks, which had been taking place in Venezuela, accusing the ELN of inflexibility. Although contact between the two sides resumed in December in Cuba, and in January 2002, following a Christmas truce, negotiations on a permanent cease-fire were initiated, the ELN withdrew from talks with the Pastrana administration in May. In mid-2004 the ELN expressed interest in re-entering negotiations, under Mexican mediation; however, the group again withdrew from talks in early 2005, allegedly in protest at Mexican criticism of Cuba. Nevertheless, in November the ELN accepted a government offer to resume negotiations. In December talks towards a possible framework for peace began in Havana, attended by delegations representing the peace commission, the ELN (including spokesman Francisco Galán, who was released from prison for the duration), local government and civil society groups, as well as foreign representatives overseeing the negotiations.

In legislative elections, held on 10 March 2002, the most significant gains were made by independents and parties allied to Alvaro Uribe Vélez, the former Governor of Antioquia and a candidate in the forthcoming presidential election. The PL remained the largest single party in the Senado and the Cámara de Representantes, with 29 and 54 seats, respectively. However, its representation was substantially reduced, while that of the PCC diminished to 13 seats in the Senado and 21 seats in the lower house.

A presidential election was held on 26 May 2002, amid a climate of increased intimidation by both guerrilla and paramilitary groups. (Voter participation was estimated at only 46% of the electorate.) Alvaro Uribe, a dissident member of the PL, was elected President with 54% of the votes cast, compared with 32% secured by his nearest rival, Horacio Serpa, again the PL's official candidate. The PCC had withdrawn its candidate following the party's disappointing results in the legislative elections; the PCC, the PL and a number of independents subsequently declared their support for the President-elect and his pledge to impose 'democratic security', thus giving him an overwhelming majority in both parliamentary chambers.

Upon taking office in August 2002, Uribe resolved to strengthen the capacity of the Government to achieve a lasting victory over the rebel groups. To this end, the new President issued a decree establishing a 'state of internal disturbance' and introducing a war tax in September (intended to raise US $750m.). The decree extended police powers to military units and designated two 'Rehabilitation and Consolidation Zones' in the north-eastern departments of Sucre, Bolívar and Arauca, within which media access and civil liberties were to be drastically curtailed. Uribe pledged to double the size of the army (to some 100,000 professional soldiers), recruit a further 100,000 police officers, create localized militias of 'peasant soldiers' and establish a network of 'informants' to ensure public security along the road network. As a result of the measures, the President's popularity soared. In November the internal disturbance decree was renewed for a further 90-day period, despite a Constitutional Court ruling against it in July. In December the Congreso approved labour, pension and fiscal reforms that provided for an increase in military spending. Notwithstanding concerns over reports of human rights infringements by the security forces, throughout 2003 and 2004 the Government achieved apparent progress in its campaign against the rebel groups. According to the US Department of State, between May 2002 and September 2004 the murder rate in the country decreased by 17.6%, while that of acts of terrorism fell by 18.4%, kidnappings by 35.1% and the massacre rate by 55.4%.

In December 2002 agreement was reached in the Congreso on some 15 proposed economic and political reforms, which were to be included in a national referendum. In July 2003 the Constitutional Court approved the terms of the so-called 'austerity referendum' (the first in Colombia's history), to be held on 25 October. The proposals included: a two-year 'freeze' on public-sector salaries, and reductions in civil service pensions; the transfer of responsibility for regional finances to the federal authorities; the reduction in the number of seats in the Congreso; and an increase in prison terms for those convicted of corruption. However, despite President Uribe's pledge that popular endorsement of the measures would improve governability and avert possible financial disaster, the necessary 25% of the electorate failed to vote. This was, in part, owing to the complexity of the referendum document, but also to widespread fears of violence and to the scheduling of the referendum one day before local elections. The failure of the proposals meant that the Uribe administration had to gain congressional approval for its reforms. The following day President Uribe suffered a further reverse when left-wing opposition groups performed well in the regional elections, at the expense of the pro-Government parties.

The Government's referendum defeat led to the resignations, in November 2003, of several members of the Cabinet, including the Minister of the Interior and Justice, Fernando Londoño Hoyos. In the same month President Uribe dismissed both the head of the national police force following corruption allegations, and the Chief of the Armed Forces, Jorge Mora Rangel, after becoming increasingly frustrated at the military's lack of progress in the civil war. In December the Congreso approved a series of anti-terrorism measures, granting extensive powers to the police and military. However, in late August 2004 the Constitutional Court ruled that the measures were unconstitutional, owing to irregularities in the congressional voting procedure. Earlier in the month the Court had also overturned parts of the Government's proposed reform to the pension system. Following these defeats, a controversial clause was added to a proposed amendment to the Constitution, to allow a President to serve two consecutive terms in office. The provision stated that the Constitutional Court was not empowered to overturn the legislation. The constitutional amendment was approved by the Congreso in December, and by the Constitutional Court in October 2005. Legislation on the framework for implementation of the amendment, known as the *Ley de Garantías* (Electoral Guarantees Law), was approved by the Constitutional Court in November. Although the new law allowed for presidential re-election, it was intended to prevent the incumbent head of state enjoying an unfair advantage over his rivals. Later that month Uribe formally announced his candidacy in the presidential election that was scheduled for May 2006.

Legislative elections were held on 12 March 2006, at which turn-out was around 40%. The Partido Social de la Unidad Nacional (Partido de la U), formed prior to the elections by some former members of the PL and which supported Uribe and presidential re-election, won significant representation in both houses, taking 28 seats in the Cámara de Respresentantes and 20 in the Senado. Of the two traditional parties, the PCC, which also supported Uribe's administration, won 29 lower-house seats and 18 senate seats, while the PL secured 36 and 17 seats in each chamber, respectively. Cambio Radical, another pro-Uribe party, fared well, garnering 20 seats in the Cámara and 15 in the Senado.

At the presidential election held on 28 May 2006 President Uribe secured an even bigger majority than the results of the parliamentary elections might have suggested, winning 63.6% of the valid votes cast. The second placed candidate, Carlos Gaviria Díaz of the left-wing Polo Democrático Alternative (PDA), won a higher than expected 22.5% of the ballot, while Horacio Serpa, representing the PL, won just 12.1% of the votes. Uribe's new administration included a few changes in personnel, with Juan Manuel Santos, leader of the Partido de la U, appointed Minister of National Defence. In its first few months the Government was beset by disputes by Uribe's supporters over minor cabinet posts, with coalition parties threatening to withdraw support for the President if they were not represented adequately within the Cabinet.

In November 2006 the Supreme Court ordered the arrest of three members of the Congreso, all supporters of the President, on charges of promoting the creation of paramilitary groups in the department of Sucre to fight left-wing rebels. The following week Salvador Arana, a former ambassador to Chile and erstwhile Governor of Sucre, was also implicated, and later in the month other legislators were wanted for questioning over alleged links with right-wing paramilitary groups. In February 2007 six pro-Uribe members of the legislature were arrested on charges of having links with paramilitary organizations; the Minister of Foreign Affairs, María Consuelo Araújo, was forced to resign from office as her brother was among those arrested. The reputation of the Uribe administration was further diminished later in February after the President's former intelligence adviser, and close ally, Jorge Noguera, was arrested on charges of supplying information on left-wing sympathizers to the AUC. By late 2007 some 37 congressmen, primarily from pro-Uribe parties, were being investigated by the Supreme Court in the so-called 'para-politics' scandal.

Local and regional elections were held in late October 2007. Notwithstanding the assassination of 29 aspiring candidates prior to the elections, no serious violence was reported on the day and polling took place in all but two of the 1,098 municipalities. The results were mixed, with pro-Uribe parties securing one-half of the governorships available and approximately 63% of the municipalities. Most significant, however, was the decisive victory of Samuel Moreno Rojas of the PDA over Enrique Peñalosa (openly supported by President Uribe) in the contest for the mayor of Bogotá, regarded as the most important elected post after the presidency.

In May 2006, in Jamundí, 300 km south of Bogotá, 10 police officers involved in an anti-drugs operation and a civilian were killed by the military. The deaths initially appeared to be an accidental shooting, but nevertheless President Uribe called for an immediate investigation into the incident, in the course of which alleged links emerged between the troops and local drugs gangs: eight people were arrested the following week, including the commander, Col Bayron Carvajal. In September, moreover, it was reported that army officers had staged the discovery of car bombs in Bogotá that they themselves had planted, in order to claim reward money for preventing attacks by guerrillas. Uribe was prompted to give a nation-wide address, urging the country not to lose faith in its security forces. According to official police figures, 17,206 people suffered violent deaths in 2006, 517 fewer than in 2005. Kidnappings also fell from 329 in 2005 to 200 in 2006.

Following the declaration of a cease-fire in December 2002, in mid-July 2003 the leaders of the AUC declared that their federation, which totalled some 13,000 fighters, would proceed with peace talks and disband by December 2005. Formal negotiations towards a settlement began in July 2004. In late October proposals by AUC adviser Carlos Alonso Lucio that AUC combatants be incorporated into the Colombian military were rejected following vociferous objections by human rights organizations and senior military officials. In late November AUC leader Salvatore Mancuso began the demobilization of AUC combatants under the Government-sponsored programme of reinsertion to civilian society. In that month the Supreme Court ruled that Mancuso should be extradited to the USA to face charges of drugs-trafficking. However, it was widely understood that President Uribe would spare Mancuso extradition, conditional upon the continued demobilization of AUC combatants. In June 2005 the Cámara de Representantes approved legislation, known as the *Ley de Justicia y Paz* (Peace and Justice Law), according the status of political prisoners to demobilized paramilitaries and allowing for reduced prison sentences for demobilized paramilitaries subsequently convicted of human rights abuses, including rape and murder. Although opposition and human rights groups were vociferous in their condemnation of the legislation, the Government maintained that such concessions were necessary to ensure the success of the peace process. In early October the European Union (see p. 244) offered its support for the demobilization process, although it expressed concern that the *Ley de Justicia y Paz* would offer effective impunity to perpetrators of violent and non-political crimes. (Sustained criticism of the law, at home as well as abroad, resulted in its amendment by the Constitutional Court to strengthen provisions for the punishment of crimes committed by paramilitaries; it was finally approved by the Court in June 2006.) In mid-2005 the AUC announced the indefinite suspension of demobilization, owing to concerns over the possible extradition of its leaders to the USA on drugs-trafficking charges. In November the Government issued an ultimatum that any AUC combatants not demobilized by the end of the year would be engaged in combat by the armed forces. Following protracted negotiations, the Government granted a deferral, to mid-February 2006, of the deadline for demobilization. The AUC resumed demobilization of its 30,000 members in December 2005; the process was formally completed in March 2006.

Meanwhile, in November 2005 the US Congress approved a contribution of US $20m. towards the demobilization process, on condition that the Colombian Government co-operate fully with extradition requests. In August 2006, in an effort to accelerate the paramilitary peace process, the arrest was ordered of Vicente Castaño, one of the few leaders of the AUC who had not surrendered to the authorities, for the murder of his brother, Carlos, in 2004. (It was believed that Carlos was killed after he had initiated negotiations with the Government.) In December 2006 AUC leaders announced their withdrawal from the peace process in protest at their transfer to the high-security Itagüí prison. Later that month the trial began in Medellín of Mancuso, who had surrendered under the terms of the *Ley de Justicia y Paz*. In July 2007 AUC leaders temporarily suspended their testimonials in protest at the ruling by the Supreme Court that former paramilitaries should be tried with common crimes rather than the pardonable offence of sedition. In August, in an apparent attempt to appease the AUC, President Uribe's Government presented legislation to the Congreso under which some 19,000 paramilitaries would be charged with simple criminal conspiracy, thereby making them eligible for parole, probation and early release. In November Ramón María Isaza Arango (alias 'El Viejo'), the founder of one of the first armed paramilitary forces, was sentenced to 11 years' imprisonment; however, under the terms of the *Ley de Justicia y Paz* the sentence could be reduced to eight years' detention should he confess to all of his crimes and make restitution to his victims.

In 2003–04 the Colombian military continued to mount offensives against the FARC (which forged an alliance with the ELN in August 2003, the month in which the aerial spraying of coca plantations resumed in Putumayo). In April 2004 the Government announced the initiation of the so-called 'Plan Patriota', a largely US-funded military campaign in which some 17,000 troops were to be deployed in the traditional FARC strongholds of Caquetá, Guaviare, Meta and Putumayo. However, the announcement met with some opposition: in May the UN Special Envoy to Colombia, Jan Egeland, expressed concerns that Plan Patriota could lead to increased numbers of internally displaced refugees and human rights abuses. Nevertheless, in September the Government announced the capture of nearly 6,000 alleged insurgents and the death of some 1,500 others as a result of Plan Patriota. In February 2005 the FARC launched a large-scale counter-offensive against the army. In early August the Government declared that, since the beginning of the year, during Plan Patriota operations 1,322 irregular combatants (mainly of the FARC) had been killed and nearly 4,000 had been captured. In spite of this, in December President Uribe agreed to demilitarize 180 sq km of a south-eastern department in order to facilitate an exchange of FARC prisoners for hostages held by the guerrillas. (An estimated 3,000 civilians had been kidnapped, among them foreigners and politicians, including Ingrid Betancourt, a former presidential candidate captured in February 2002.) In January 2006 the FARC rejected the possibility of such an exchange while Uribe remained head of state; however, in June, following the President's re-election, the FARC announced that it was prepared to negotiate with the Government if Uribe agreed to suspend US-backed operations against the organization. In October the rebels offered a cease-fire on condition that a zone be demilitarized for 45 days. Uribe immediately authorized negotiations to proceed on the creation of the 'safe haven'; within days, however, in the wake of a car bomb attack outside a military school in Bogotá, the Goverment had withdrawn from talks and Uribe made a public pledge to free the hostages held by the FARC by military means. In July some 450 FARC fighters stormed a police station, killing 17 officials, while on 27 December the group launched its most lethal attack on the armed forces since Uribe took office, killing almost 30 soldiers who had been deployed to destroy coca crops in the south of the country.

In an effort to re-engage the FARC in the peace process and revive the possibility of exchanging prisoners for hostages, in early June 2007 President Uribe ordered the release of some 150 imprisoned members of the group, including Rodrigo Granda Escobar, the supposed international spokesperson of the FARC, who had been arrested in December 2004 (see below). Weeks later, however, the FARC announced that 11 of 12 deputies from Valle del Cauca, kidnapped in 2002, had been killed in crossfire in a battle with an 'unidentified military group'. Widely attended nation-wide protests ensued in July to denounce the use of kidnapping. Although the FARC appeared to implicate either the armed forces or a paramilitary group in the deputies' deaths, their delay in releasing the bodies led many to believe that they wished to conceal that the hostages had been killed in cold blood.

In August 2007 President Uribe agreed to allow the Venezuelan President, Lt-Col (retd) Hugo Chávez Frías, to mediate in the proposed prisoner exchange between the Colombian Government and the FARC. Despite considerable optimism that Chávez might succeed in this endeavour (the Venezuelan leader was said to be revered by the FARC), the agreement was cancelled abruptly by Uribe in November. President Nicolas Sarkozy of France—who was keen to secure the release of Betancourt (see above), who also held French citizenship—appealed to Uribe to reinstate Chávez, who had previously been given until 31 December to facilitate the humanitarian exchange. It was reported that Uribe had been angered by Chávez's dealings with Colombian military leaders, contrary to their agreement. In mid-December, however, the FARC announced its intention to hand over three of the hostages (including Clara Rojas—Betancourt's running mate in the 2002 presidential election—and her captive-born son, Emmanuel) to Chávez, and at the end of the month the Colombian Government allowed Venezuelan helicopters to enter Colombia in order to retrieve the hostages. The FARC promptly suspended the planned hand-over, blaming Colombian military operations; however, it subsequently emerged that Emmanuel was not held by the guerrillas but had been placed in foster care in Bogotá some years previously. Rojas and the other hostage, former senator Consuelo González, were released to Venezuelan officials in early January 2008. At the end of February the FARC liberate four further captives; the announcement appeared to be in response to a planned series of anti-FARC demonstrations, held earlier in the month in Colombia and throughout the world, in which several million people participated. However, the released hostages' testimonies of the appalling conditions in which they had been kept resulted in further widespread denunciation of the FARC's methods.

Meanwhile, in October 2004 the US Congress approved an increase in the number of US troops in Colombia from 400 to 800. The US budget for 2005, the last year of Plan Colombia, provided for some US $463m. of aid for Colombia, including at least $100m. for Plan Patriota. In September 2005 the USA renewed and extended the Andean Trade Promotion and Drug Eradication Act (ATPDEA) with Colombia. The ATPDEA offered commercial incentives to those Andean countries deemed cooperative in US counter-narcotics policy. US funding to Colombia for counter-narcotics operations was budgeted at US $465m. in both 2006 and 2007. The same level of financing was requested for 2008; in late February the US legislature approved an extension to the ATPDEA for a further 10 months.

Colombia has a long-standing border dispute with Venezuela. Relations between the countries improved following the signing, in October 1989, of a border integration agreement, which included a provision on joint co-operation in the campaign to eradicate drugs-trafficking. In March 1990 the San Pedro Alejandrino agreement, signed by the two countries, sought to initiate the implementation of recommendations made by existing bilateral border commissions and to establish a number of new commissions, including one to examine the territorial claims of both sides. Colombia's efforts to improve relations with Venezuela were hampered by the activities of FARC guerrillas in the border region, leading the two countries to sign an agreement to improve border co-operation in February 1997; however, in April Venezuela deployed 5,000 troops along its frontier with Colombia in an attempt to halt repeated incursions by Colombian guerrillas. Agreements were subsequently signed by the two countries to strengthen military co-operation and intelligence sharing. In 2000 relations deteriorated, owing to Venezuelan President Chávez's opposition to Plan Colombia and accusations by Colombia that Venezuela was covertly aiding the guerrilla forces. Relations deteriorated further in 2001, after Venezuela refused to allow the extradition to Colombia of a suspect in the April 1999 hijack of an Avianca flight (see above). Following the appointment of President Uribe, relations improved: in November 2002 Chávez and Uribe held a meeting at which they agreed on measures to promote bilateral trade and, notably, to establish a system to deal with problems on their common border. Despite repeated incursions into Venezuelan territory by Colombian combatants and drugs-traffickers in 2004 (including an incident in September that resulted in the death of five Venezuelan soldiers), in a public demonstration of amity, Uribe and Chávez met in Cartagena in November to discuss border security and economic co-operation. However, relations were severely strained in December following the arrest of Rodrigo Granda of the FARC. It was subsequently alleged by the Venezuelan Government that Granda, although ultimately arrested in Cúcuta, Colombia, was first kidnapped in Caracas by Venezuelan and Colombian agents in the pay of the Colombian Government and with the collusion of US intelligence services. Chávez repeatedly demanded an apology for this perceived violation of Venezuelan sovereignty, but both the Uribe Government and the US Administration denied all accusations of wrongdoing. Although Chávez recalled the Venezuelan ambassador to Colombia in January 2005 and imposed restrictions on trade and passage between the two countries, bilateral relations were normalized in February. In August 2007 Chávez was invited to mediate between the Colombian Government and the FARC to effect an exchange of prisoners and hostages (see above), although the initiative was cancelled by President Uribe in November. Bilateral relations deteriorated rapidly, and later in the month Chávez recalled Venezuela's ambassador to Colombia. Uribe congratulated Chávez for his successful efforts to secure the release of two hostages in January 2008, but relations between the two countries deteriorated further after Chávez requested that the Colombian guerrilla groups be accorded belligerent, rather than terrorist, status.

Ecuador has repeatedly objected to incursions by Colombian combatants into its territory, and to the Colombian Government's policy of aerial spraying of drugs crops in departments on the border between the two countries. Tensions increased in September 2005 after the Ecuadorean Minister of National Defence, Gen. (retd) Oswaldo Jarrín, refused to classify the FARC as a terrorist group. None the less, in November the Uribe administration agreed to a temporary cessation of aerial fumigation in border areas from January 2006. In that month, at a meeting in Bogotá of the defence ministers of both countries, Jarrín pledged increased co-operation in policing the common border. In December, however, Colombia resumed its cropspraying programme along the border, which Ecuador described as a hostile act. Following intervention by the Organization of American States (OAS, see p. 360), the diplomatic crisis was resolved after Colombia agreed to give notice of any aerial fumigation conducted in the border area.

At the beginning of March 2008 Colombian forces launched a raid on a FARC training camp in Ecuador, killing 17 rebels, including the guerrilla grouping's second-in-command, Raúl Reyes. The raid was a major success for the Colombian Government; however, the Ecuadorean administration reacted to the incursion by expelling the Colombian ambassador in Quito, withdrawing its own ambassador from Bogotá, and sending troops to the Colombian–Ecuadorean border. Tensions were further exacerbated by the Colombian Government's claim that documents seized in the raid proved that the Ecuadorean President, Rafael Correa, was interested in establishing official relations with FARC and that a member of his Government had met Reyes for discussions. President Correa dismissed the claims, asserting that his Government's involvement had been solely on humanitarian grounds as part of efforts to secure the release of hostages. Uribe also claimed that computers taken from the camp indicated that President Chávez had pledged some US $30m.-worth of petroleum to the FARC. In protest at the allegations, and at Colombia's military incursion, Chávez expelled the Colombian ambassador to Venezuela and dispatched troops to the Venezuelan–Colombian border. The stand-off between the three countries was ended a week later following a Rio Group summit in Santo Domingo, Dominican Republic, at which the three heads of state agreed to abide by an OAS resolution that included a clause that Colombian troops would not launch any further incursions into Ecuadorean territory. Colombia and Venezuela restored diplomatic relations after Colombia announced it would not pursue charges against Chávez in the International Criminal Court over his connections with the FARC; however, Colombian–Ecuadorean relations remained suspended.

In 1980 Nicaragua laid claim to the Colombian-controlled islands of Providencia and San Andrés. Colombia has a territorial dispute with Honduras over cays in the San Andrés and Providencia archipelago. In October 1986 the Colombian Senado approved a delimitation treaty of marine and submarine waters in the Caribbean Sea, which had been signed by the Governments of Colombia and Honduras in August. In late 1999 the Honduran National Assembly finally ratified the treaty, strengthening Colombia's claim to the islands of Providencia and San Andrés, and thus angering Nicaragua, which filed a complaint with the International Court of Justice (ICJ). In December 2007 the ICJ dismissed Nicaragua's claim to the San Andrés archipelago, although it had yet to rule on jurisdiction on the other disputed waters.

On 1 January 1994 a 10-year trade liberalization programme came into effect between Colombia, Mexico and Venezuela. A free trade agreement with Chile, the Acuerdo de Complementación Económica (ACE), also took effect on the same day. Negotiations on a free trade agreement between the USA and Colombia, Ecuador and Peru were originally scheduled to conclude in late January 2005. However, negotiations became protracted—owing to disagreements between the countries over matters including agriculture, textiles and intellectual property, together with protests by public service workers and indigenous groups in late 2004 in the three Andean countries concerned—and in November 2005 Colombia withdrew from talks. In November 2006 a free trade agreement between Colombia and the USA was signed, although US congressional approval had yet to be received in late 2007, not least because of concerns regarding the ramifications of Colombia's 'para-politcs' scandal.

Government

Executive power is exercised by the President (assisted by a Cabinet), who is elected for a four-year term by universal adult suffrage. Legislative power is vested in the bicameral Congress, consisting of the Senate (102 members elected for four years) and the House of Representatives (161 members elected for four years). The country is divided into 32 Departments and one Capital District.

Defence

At 18 years of age, every male (with the exception of students) must present himself as a candidate for military service of between one and two years. As assessed at November 2007, the strength of the army was an estimated 216,921 (including 173,000 conscripts), the navy 27,605 (including 14,000 marines and 7,000 conscripts) and the air force 9,373. In addition there were some 61,900 reservists, of whom 54,700 were in the army, 4,800 in the navy and 1,200 in the air force. The paramilitary police force numbers 144,097 men. The budget allocated a projected 16,100,000m. pesos on defence in 2008.

Economic Affairs

In 2006, according to estimates by the World Bank, Colombia's gross national income (GNI), measured at average 2004–06 prices, was US $125,032m., equivalent to $2,740 per head (or $7,620 per head on an international purchasing-power parity basis). During 1996–2006, it was estimated, the population increased at an average annual rate of 1.6%; however, average annual growth of gross domestic product (GDP) per head, in real terms, was 1.0% in 1996–2006. Colombia's overall GDP increased, in real terms, by an average of 2.6% per year in 1996–2006; GDP grew by a provisional 6.8% in 2006.

Agriculture (including hunting, forestry and fishing) contributed a provisional 11.5% of GDP and employed 19.4% of the labour force in 2006. The principal cash crops are coffee (which accounted for 6.0% of official export earnings in 2006), cocoa, sugar cane, bananas, tobacco, cotton and cut flowers. Rice, cassava, plantains and potatoes are the principal food crops. Timber and beef production are also important. During 1996–2006 agricultural GDP increased at an average annual rate of 1.7%. Agricultural GDP increased by 3.0% in 2006.

Industry (including mining, manufacturing, construction and power) employed 19.3% of the labour force and contributed a provisional 34.2% of GDP in 2006. During 1996–2006 real industrial GDP increased at an average annual rate of 2.9%. Industrial GDP increased by 9.0% in 2006.

Mining employed 0.7% of the labour force and, according to provisional figures, contributed 6.6% of GDP in 2006. Petroleum, natural gas, coal, nickel, emeralds and gold are the principal minerals exploited. Silver, platinum, iron, lead, zinc, copper, mercury, limestone and phosphates are also mined. During 1996–2006 the real GDP of the mining sector increased at an average annual rate of 3.6%. Mining GDP increased by a provisional 0.1% in 2006.

Manufacturing contributed a provisional 16.0% of GDP and employed 13.1% of the labour force in 2006. During 1996–2006 manufacturing GDP increased at an average annual rate of 3.2%. Manufacturing GDP increased by 10.8% in 2006. Based on the value of output, the most important branches of manufacturing were food products, beverages, chemical products, textiles and transport equipment.

Hydroelectricity provided 79.8% of Colombia's electricity requirements in 2004. In the early 1990s a rapid expansion programme of thermal power-stations was undertaken in order to increase electricity output in line with demand, and to reduce reliance on hydroelectric power. Natural gas provided some 12.9% of electricity requirements in 2004. The country is self-sufficient in petroleum and coal, and these minerals together accounted for 37.9% of export revenues in 2006.

The services sector contributed a provisional 54.3% of GDP and engaged 61.0% of the labour force in 2006. During 1996–2006 the combined GDP of the service sectors increased, in real terms, at an estimated average rate of 2.3% per year. The GDP of the services sector increased by 4.9% in 2006.

In 2006 Colombia recorded a visible trade surplus of US $322m. and there was a deficit of $3,057m. on the current account of the balance of payments. The country's principal trading partner in 2005 was the USA, which provided 28.3% of imports and took 40.0% of exports. Other important trading partners in that year were Brazil, Mexico, Venezuela and Ecuador. The principal exports in 2006 were petroleum and its derivatives, coal, metal manufactures, and foodstuffs, beverages and tobacco. The principal imports in the same year were mechanical and electrical equipment, and vehicles and transport equipment. A significant amount of foreign exchange is believed to be obtained from illegal trade in gold, emeralds and, particularly, the drug cocaine.

In 2006 there was an estimated general central budgetary deficit of 11,955.6m. pesos. Colombia's external debt amounted to US $37,656m. at the end of 2005, of which $22,491m. was long-term public debt. Debt-servicing was equivalent to 35.3% of the value of exports of goods and services. In 1996–2006 the average annual rate of inflation was 9.7%; consumer prices increased by an annual average of 4.0% in 2006. Some 12.7% of the labour force were unemployed in 2006.

Colombia is a member of Latin American Integration Association (see p. 331) and of the Andean Community (see p. 170). Both organizations attempt to increase trade and economic co-operation within the region. In December 2004 Colombia was one of 12 countries that were signatories to the agreement, signed in Cusco, Peru, creating the South American Community of Nations (Comunidad Sudamericana de Naciones, which was renamed Union of South American Nations—Unión de Naciones Suramericanas, UNASUR, in April 2007), intended to promote greater regional economic integration.

Since taking office in 2002 the Government of President Alvaro Uribe has overseen steady growth in the Colombian economy. Although not without its set-backs, the Government's uncompromising policy towards domestic security issues, particularly its campaign against rebel groups, greatly improved investor confidence. Reforms, albeit limited, of the tax, pensions and labour sectors led to the IMF and the World Bank announcing new loans to Colombia of US $2,200m. and $3,300m., respectively in January 2003. Further loans, of $145m. and $610m., were made available by the IMF in 2004 and 2005, respectively. Uribe's re-election in May 2006 further increased much-needed foreign investment, and an increased pro-Uribe legislative majority from March made it more likely that the Government could implement further-reaching reforms in its second term. Indeed, the Uribe administration's privatization plan accelerated from 2006, with the sale of Colombia Telecomunicaciones completed in March; banking and energy sector assets were also sold off in the last quarter of the year. Divestment of state-owned enterprises continued in 2007, when 10% of the state petroleum concern, Empresa Colombiana de Petróleos (ECOPETROL), was sold off. Nevertheless, government expenditure on security-related activities increased substantially in 2007 as the long-running civil war continued. The so-called 'para-politics' scandal (see Recent History) in early 2007 prompted a partial severance of US military aid to Colombia in that year, and in early 2008 a free trade agreement between the two countries still awaited ratification by the US Congress. Nevertheless, direct foreign investment in the country remained strong, reaching, according to preliminary figures, some US $7,600m. in 2007. The petroleum sector absorbed much of this investment, although the manufacturing and service sectors also benefited. Structural reforms in the financial sector were expected further to improve the business climate in 2008. The Government hoped that the greater levels of security would also facilitate the promotion of Colombia as a tourist destination; in 2007 the Ministry of Trade, Industry and Tourism announced that up to 11,000 luxury hotel rooms would be constructed in 2007–10. The IMF put economic growth at 6.6% in 2007, while consumer prices were estimated to have increased by 5.5%. Economic downturn in the USA was likely to adversely affect Colombian exports in 2008, and slower growth of 4.8% was projected for that year, although the rate of inflation was also expected to fall, to 4.6%.

Education

Primary education is free and compulsory for five years, to be undertaken by children between six and 12 years of age. No child may be admitted to secondary school unless these five years have been successfully completed. Secondary education, beginning at the age of 11, lasts for up to six years. Following completion of a first cycle of four years, pupils may pursue a further two years of vocational study, leading to the Bachiller examination. In 2004 enrolment at primary schools included 83.2% of pupils in the relevant age-group, while the comparable ratio for secondary education was 54.9%. In 2007 there were 32 public universities in Colombia. Government expenditure on education in the 1999 budget was 5,789,000m. pesos, representing 19.7% of total spending.

Public Holidays

2008: 1 January (New Year's Day), 6 January (Epiphany), 19 March (St Joseph's Day), 20 March (Maundy Thursday), 21 March (Good Friday), 1 May (Labour Day and Ascension Day), 22 May (Corpus Christi), 23 June (Sacred Heart of Jesus), 29 June (SS Peter and Paul), 20 July (Independence), 7 August

COLOMBIA

(Battle of Boyacá), 15 August (Assumption), 12 October (Discovery of the Americas), 1 November (All Saints' Day), 11 November (Independence of Cartagena), 8 December (Immaculate Conception), 25 December (Christmas Day).
2009: 1 January (New Year's Day), 6 January (Epiphany), 19 March (St Joseph's Day), 9 April (Maundy Thursday), 10 April (Good Friday), 1 May (Labour Day), 21 May (Ascension Day), 11 June (Corpus Christi), 22 June (for Sacred Heart of Jesus), 29 June (SS Peter and Paul), 20 July (Independence), 7 August (Battle of Boyacá), 15 August (Assumption), 12 October (Discovery of the Americas), 1 November (All Saints' Day), 11 November (Independence of Cartagena), 8 December (Immaculate Conception), 25 December (Christmas Day).

Weights and Measures

The metric system is in force.

Statistical Survey

Sources (unless otherwise stated): Departamento Administrativo Nacional de Estadística (DANE), Transversal 45 No 26-70, Interior I-CAN, Bogotá, DC; tel. (1) 597-8300; fax (1) 597-8399; e-mail dane@dane.gov.co; internet www.dane.gov.co; Banco de la República, Carrera 7A, No 14-78, 5°, Apdo Aéreo 3531, Bogotá, DC; tel. (1) 343-1111; fax (1) 286-1686; e-mail wbanco@banrep.gov.co; internet www.banrep.gov.co.

Area and Population

AREA, POPULATION AND DENSITY

Area (sq km)	1,141,748*
Population (census results)	
24 October 1993†	37,635,094
30 June 2005‡	
Males	21,169,835
Females	21,718,757
Total	42,888,592
Population (official projections at mid-year)	
2006	43,405,387
2007	43,926,034
Density (per sq km) at mid-2007	38.5

* 440,831 sq miles.
† Revised figure, including adjustment for underenumeration. The enumerated total was 33,109,840 (males 16,296,539, females 16,813,301) in 1993.
‡ A 'census year' was conducted between 22 May 2005 and 22 May 2006, and a 'conciliated' total for 30 June 2005 was finally published in May 2007 (the original enumerated total was 41,298,706) incorporating adjustments for underenumeration, geographical undercoverage and underlying natural growth trends.

DEPARTMENTS
(census of 30 June 2005)*

Department	Area (sq km)	Population	Capital (with population†)
Amazonas	109,665	67,726	Leticia (32,450)
Antioquia	63,612	5,682,276	Medellín (2,233,660)
Arauca	23,818	232,118	Arauca (74,385)
Atlántico	3,388	2,166,156	Barranquilla (1,113,016)
Bolívar	25,978	1,878,993	Cartagena (895,400)
Boyacá	23,189	1,255,311	Tunja (152,419)
Caldas	7,888	968,740	Manizales (368,433)
Caquetá	88,965	420,337	Florencia (142,123)
Casanare	44,640	295,353	Yopal (103,754)
Cauca	29,308	1,268,937	Popayán (258,653)
César	22,905	903,279	Valledupar (348,990)
Chocó	46,530	454,030	Quibdó (110,032)
Córdoba	25,020	1,467,929	Montería (381,525)
Cundinamarca	22,623	2,280,037	Bogotá‡
Guainía	72,238	35,230	Puerto Inírida (15,827)
La Guajira	20,848	681,575	Riohacha (169,311)
Guaviare	42,327	95,551	San José del Guaviare (45,573)
Huila	19,890	1,011,418	Neiva (315,332)
Magdalena	23,188	1,149,917	Santa Marta (414,387)
Meta	85,635	783,168	Villavicencio (384,131)
Nariño	33,268	1,541,956	Pasto (383,846)
Norte de Santander	21,658	1,243,975	Cúcuta (585,919)
Putumayo	24,885	310,132	Mocoa (36,185)
Quindío	1,845	534,552	Armenia (272,574)
Risaralda	4,140	897,509	Pereira (428,397)
San Andrés y Providencia Islands	44	70,554	San Andrés (55,426)
Santander del Sur	30,537	1,957,789	Bucaramanga (509,918)
Sucre	10,917	772,010	Sincelejo (236,780)
Tolima	23,562	1,365,342	Ibagué (495,246)
Valle del Cauca	22,140	4,161,425	Cali (2,075,380)
Vaupés	65,268	39,279	Mitú (17,641)
Vichada	100,242	55,872	Puerto Carreño (12,897)
Capital District			
Bogotá, DC	1,587	6,840,116	—
Total	1,141,748	42,888,592	—

* A 'census year' was conducted between 22 May 2005 and 22 May 2006, and a 'conciliated' total for 30 June 2005 was finally published in May 2007 (the original enumerated total was 41,298,706) incorporating adjustments for underenumeration, geographical undercoverage and underlying natural growth trends.
† These amended figures for 11 November 2005 include an adjustment for geographical undercoverage and were announced in November 2006, prior to the publication of the final conciliated figures for 30 June 2005.
‡ The capital city, Bogotá, exists as the capital of a department as well as the Capital District. The city's population is included only in Bogotá, DC.

PRINCIPAL TOWNS
(estimated population at mid-1999)

Bogotá, DC (capital)	6,260,862	Neiva	300,052
Cali	2,077,386	Soledad	295,058
Medellín	1,861,265	Armenia	281,422
Barranquilla	1,223,260	Villavicencio	273,140
Cartagena	805,757	Soacha	272,058
Cúcuta	606,932	Valledupar	263,247
Bucaramanga	515,555	Montería	248,245
Ibagué	393,664	Itagüí	228,985
Pereira	381,725	Palmira	226,509
Santa Marta	359,147	Buenaventura	224,336
Manizales	337,580	Floridablanca	221,913
Bello	333,470	Sincelejo	220,704
Pasto	332,396	Popayán	200,719

COLOMBIA

BIRTHS, MARRIAGES AND DEATHS*

	Registered live births	Registered deaths
1999	746,194	183,553
2000	752,834	187,432
2001	724,319	191,513
2002	700,455	192,262
2003	710,702	192,121
2004	723,099	188,933
2005	719,968	189,022
2006	711,457	189,760

* Data are tabulated by year of registration rather than by year of occurrence, although registration is incomplete. According to UN estimates, the average annual rates in 1990–95 were: births 26.1 per 1,000; deaths 6.3 per 1,000; in 1995–2000: births 23.6 per 1,000; deaths 5.7 per 1,000; and in 2000–05: births 21.2 per 1,000; deaths 5.6 per 1,000 (Source: UN, *World Population Prospects: The 2006 Revision*).

Registered marriages: 102,448 in 1980; 95,845 in 1981; 70,350 in 1986.

Expectation of life (years at birth, WHO estimates): 74.1 (males 70.6; females 77.7) in 2005 (Source: WHO, *World Health Statistics*).

EMPLOYMENT
(household survey, '000 persons aged 10 years and over, July–September)

	2004	2005	2006
Agriculture, hunting, forestry and fishing	3,578	4,074	3,414
Mining and quarrying	198	131	116
Manufacturing	2,421	2,351	2,312
Electricity, gas and water	71	84	72
Construction	779	859	897
Trade, restaurants and hotels	4,375	4,431	4,421
Transport, storage and communications	1,293	1,201	1,266
Financial intermediation	228	240	220
Real estate, renting and business activities	778	835	890
Community, social and personal services	3,928	4,009	3,949
Activities not adequately described	5	1	53
Total	17,654	18,217	17,609

Unemployed('000): 2,767 in 2004; 2,406 in 2005; 2,568 in 2006.

Source: ILO.

Health and Welfare

KEY INDICATORS

Total fertility rate (children per woman, 2005)	2.5
Under-5 mortality rate (per 1,000 live births, 2005)	21
HIV/AIDS (% of persons aged 15–49, 2005)	0.6
Physicians (per 1,000 head, 2002)	1.35
Hospital beds (per 1,000 head, 2004)	1.20
Health expenditure (2004): US $ per head (PPP)	570
Health expenditure (2004): % of GDP	7.8
Health expenditure (2004): public (% of total)	86.0
Access to water (% of persons, 2004)	93
Access to sanitation (% of persons, 2004)	86
Human Development Index (2005): ranking	75
Human Development Index (2005): value	0.791

For sources and definitions, see explanatory note on p. vi.

Agriculture

PRINCIPAL CROPS
('000 metric tons)

	2004	2005	2006
Rice (paddy)	3,016	2,502	2,250*
Maize	1,746	1,876	1,340*
Sorghum	267	253	159*
Potatoes	1,847	1,754	1,754*
Cassava (Manioc)	1,919	2,050	2,000*
Yams	310	333	333*
Sugar cane	39,205	39,849	39,849*
Dry beans	130	138	138*
Soybeans (Soya beans)	73	62	70†
Coconuts	103	108	108*
Oil palm fruit	3,107	3,273	3,273*
Cottonseed	81	60	60†
Cabbages	140	143	143*
Tomatoes	389	375	375*
Green chillies and peppers	48	49	49*
Dry onions	465	478	478*
Carrots	184	197	197*
Watermelons	91	92	92*
Bananas	1,577	1,765	1,765*
Plantains	3,274	3,457	3,457*
Oranges	88	96	96*
Mangoes	153	149	149*
Avocados	174	186	186*
Pineapples	391	420	420*
Papayas	103	138	138*
Coffee (green)	681	693	696*

* FAO estimate.
† Unofficial figure.

Aggregate production ('000 metric tons, may include official, semi-official or estimated data): Total cereals 5,085 in 2004, 4,688 in 2005, 3,789 in 2006; Total roots and tubers 4,172 in 2004, 4,231 in 2005, 4,181 in 2006; Total vegetables (incl. melons) 1,557 in 2004, 1,567 in 2005, 1,567 in 2006; Total fruits (excl. melons) 7,291 in 2004, 7,910 in 2005, 7,910 in 2006.

Source: FAO.

LIVESTOCK
('000 head, year ending September)

	2003	2004	2005
Horses	2,592	2,591	2,554
Asses, mules or hinnies	728	658	571
Cattle	24,799	24,922	25,699
Pigs	1,500*	1,892	1,724
Sheep	2,500*	2,831	3,333
Goats	3,200*	3,771	4,105
Chickens*	140,000	145,000	150,000

* FAO estimate(s).

2006: Figures assumed to be unchanged from 2005 (FAO estimates).

Source: FAO.

LIVESTOCK PRODUCTS
('000 metric tons)

	2003	2004	2005
Cattle meat	642	717	792
Sheep meat*	6.5	6.7	7.0
Goat meat*	6.5	6.6	6.7
Pig meat	123.9	129.9	127.7
Horse meat*	5.7	5.8	6.0
Chicken meat	678	709	763
Cows' milk	6,652	6,700	6,770
Hen eggs	449	449	492

* FAO estimates.

2006: Figures assumed to be unchanged from 2005 (FAO estimates).

Source: FAO.

COLOMBIA   Statistical Survey

Forestry

ROUNDWOOD REMOVALS
('000 cu metres, excl. bark)

	2004	2005	2006
Sawlogs, veneer logs and logs for sleepers	1,077	706	674
Pulpwood	836	839	842
Other industrial wood	80	82	121
Fuel wood	8,469	8,021*	8,021*
Total	10,462	9,647	9,658

* FAO estimate.
Source: FAO.

SAWNWOOD PRODUCTION
('000 cu metres, incl. railway sleepers)

	2004	2005	2006
Coniferous (softwood)	149	98	93
Broadleaved (hardwood)	473	309	296
Total	622	407	389

Source: FAO.

Fishing

('000 metric tons, live weight, FAO estimates)

	2003	2004	2005
Capture	129.8	111.9	121.0
Characins	14.8	13.7	14.0
Freshwater siluroids	9.1	8.5	9.0
Other freshwater fishes	6.6	6.1	6.0
Pacific anchoveta	25.3	5.7	10.0
Skipjack tuna	12.6	5.8	12.3
Yellowfin tuna	48.5	21.4	23.4
Aquaculture	60.9	60.1	60.1
Tilapias	15.6	19.1	19.1
Pirapatinga	1.3	1.2	1.2
Rainbow trout	4.2	4.1	4.1
Whiteleg shrimp	16.5	18.0	18.0
Total catch	190.7*	172.0*	181.1

* FAO estimate.
Note: Figures exclude crocodiles, recorded by number rather than by weight. The number of spectacled caimans caught was: 555,719 in 2003; 612,041 in 2004; 601,958 in 2005.
Source: FAO.

Mining

('000 metric tons, unless otherwise indicated)

	2003	2004	2005
Gold (kilograms)	46,515	37,739	35,785
Silver (kilograms)	9,511	8,533	7,142
Salt	447	526	474
Hard coal	50,028	53,693	59,064
Iron ore*	625	508	499
Crude petroleum ('000 barrels)	197,586	192,866	191,990

* Figures refer to the gross weight of ore. The estimated iron content is 46%.
Source: US Geological Survey.

Industry

SELECTED PRODUCTS
('000 metric tons, unless otherwise indicated)

	2001	2002	2003
Sugar	2,242	2,531	2,646
Cement	6,776	6,633	7,300
Crude steel ingots (incl. steel for casting)*	638.3	663.7	668.4
Semi-manufactures of iron and steel (hot-rolled)*	552	575	550
Gas-diesel (distillate fuel) oils	3,312	3,275	3,308
Residual fuel oils	2,986	3,136	2,932
Motor spirit (petrol)	5,092	4,676	4,756

* Source: US Geological Survey.
Source: mostly UN, *Industrial Commodity Statistics Yearbook*.

2004 ('000 metric tons): Crude steel ingots (incl. steel for casting) 730.0; Semi-manufactures of iron and steel (hot-rolled) 575 (Source: US Geological Survey).

Finance

CURRENCY AND EXCHANGE RATES

Monetary Units
  100 centavos = 1 Colombian peso.

Sterling, Dollar and Euro Equivalents (31 December 2007)
  £1 sterling = 3,982.38 pesos;
  US $1 = 1,987.81 pesos;
  €1 = 2,926.3 pesos;
  10,000 Colombian pesos = £2.51 = $5.03 = €3.42.

Average Exchange Rate (pesos per US $)
  2005   2,320.83
  2006   2,361.14
  2007   2,078.29

CENTRAL GOVERNMENT BUDGET
('000 million pesos)

Revenue	2003	2004	2005
Tax revenue	31,372.9	36,735.5	42,288.4
Tax on earnings	11,729.5	15,181.7	17,348.6
Value-added tax (domestic)	8,887.9	10,073.7	11,411.7
Value-added tax (external)	4,183.5	4,881.9	6,016.2
Levies	2,158.9	2,233.1	2,822.5
Tax on petrol	1,025.0	1,057.4	1,143.3
Tax on financial transactions	1,621.5	2,237.6	2,401.2
Other taxes	1,776.4	1,070.1	1,144.8
Non-tax revenue	205.8	201.7	229.5
Special funds	321.0	380.9	471.9
Capital revenue	2,419.0	2,508.3	2,811.8
Total	34,318.6	39,826.4	45,801.5

Expenditure*	2003	2004	2005
Interest payments	9,655.5	10,263.9	9,856.7
Foreign	4,355.3	4,222.4	4,469.2
Domestic	5,306.3	5,944.0	5,589.0
Operational expenditures	32,566.4	37,435.0	44,925.7
Personal services	6,130.1	6,586.3	7,331.5
General expenditure	2,162.7	2,227.2	2,838.4
Transfers	24,273.5	28,621.5	34,755.9
Investment	2,882.8	3,126.5	4,372.5
Total	45,104.7	50,825.4	59,155.0

* Excluding net lending ('000 million pesos): 864.8 in 2003; 298.2 in 2004; 122.8 in 2005.

Budgetary central government ('000 million pesos): *Revenue:* 40,629.2 in 2004; 46,207.4 in 2005; 57,076.8 in 2006. *Expenditure (incl. lending minus repayments):* 52,111.5 in 2004; 60,465.2 in 2005; 69,032.4 in 2006.

COLOMBIA

Statistical Survey

INTERNATIONAL RESERVES
(US $ million at 31 December)

	2004	2005	2006
Gold (national valuation)	143	168	141
IMF special drawing rights	181	173	193
Reserve position in IMF	444	408	430
Foreign exchange	12,769	14,206	14,673
Total	13,537	14,955	15,437

Source: IMF, *International Financial Statistics*.

MONEY SUPPLY
('000 million pesos at 31 December)

	2004	2005	2006
Currency outside banks	13,784.5	16,376.6	20,119.7
Demand deposits at commercial banks	13,781.7	16,363.8	18,748.2
Total money (incl. others)	27,601.9	32,756.2	38,884.2

Source: IMF, *International Financial Statistics*.

COST OF LIVING
(Consumer Price Index for low-income families; base: 2000 = 100)

	2004	2005	2006
Food and beverages	134.6	143.1	150.5
Clothing and footwear	108.9	109.6	109.7
Rent, fuel and light*	112.7	117.0	121.1
All items (incl. others)	132.5	139.6	145.2

* Including certain household equipment.

Source: ILO.

NATIONAL ACCOUNTS
('000 million pesos at current prices, rounded figures)

Composition of the Gross National Product

	2003	2004	2005*
Compensation of employees	77,772	84,770	92,204
Operating surplus	54,053	61,425	64,585
Consumption of fixed capital	73,761	84,432	97,925
Gross domestic product (GDP) at factor cost	205,586	230,627	254,714
Indirect taxes	26,258	30,368	34,284
Less Subsidies	3,327	3,247	3,685
GDP in purchasers' values	228,517	257,746	285,313
Net factor income from abroad	−9,917	−11,377	−12,910
Gross national product (GNP)	218,600	246,370	272,403

* Provisional figures.

Expenditure on the Gross Domestic Product

	2004	2005	2006*
Final consumption expenditure	209,885	228,344	253,441
Households†	161,392	175,842	196,509
General government	48,493	52,501	56,932
Gross capital formation	49,525	59,304	75,574
Total domestic expenditure	259,410	287,648	329,016
Exports of goods and services	55,381	61,372	71,956
Less Imports of goods and services	57,045	63,707	79,841
GDP in market prices	257,746	285,313	321,130
GDP at constant 1994 prices	83,772	87,728	93,722

* Provisional figures.
† Including non-profit institutions serving households.

Gross Domestic Product by Economic Activity

	2004	2005	2006*
Agriculture, hunting, forestry and fishing	28,627	32,005	34,749
Mining and quarrying	15,613	17,715	20,035
Manufacturing	38,685	42,475	48,236
Electricity, gas and water	11,081	11,950	12,588
Construction	13,521	16,763	22,125
Wholesale and retail trade; repair of motor vehicles, motorcycles, and personal and household goods; hotels and restaurants	26,741	29,611	34,192
Transport, storage and communications	19,912	22,038	23,706
Financial intermediation, insurance, real estate, renting and business activities	37,985	41,265	43,707
Other community, social and personal service activities	53,204	57,317	62,165
Sub-total	245,369	271,139	301,503
Less Financial intermediation services indirectly measured	10,965	12,381	12,068
Gross value added in basic prices	234,403	258,758	289,435
Taxes on products	23,419	26,639	31,793
Less Subsidies on products	76	84	97
GDP in market prices	257,746	285,313	321,130

* Provisional figures.

BALANCE OF PAYMENTS
(US $ million)

	2004	2005	2006
Exports of goods f.o.b.	17,224	21,729	25,181
Imports of goods f.o.b.	−15,878	−20,134	−24,859
Trade balance	1,346	1,595	322
Exports of services	2,255	2,664	3,373
Imports of services	−3,935	−4,766	−5,493
Balance on goods and services	−334	−507	−1,798
Other income received	671	1,074	1,525
Other income paid	−4,970	−6,539	−7,528
Balance on goods, services and income	−4,633	−5,972	−7,800
Current transfers received	3,994	4,342	5,037
Current transfers paid	−270	−260	−293
Current balance	−909	−1,890	−3,057
Direct investment abroad	−142	−4,662	−1,098
Direct investment from abroad	3,082	10,240	6,463
Portfolio investment assets	−1,565	−1,689	−3,332
Portfolio investment liabilities	1,306	−53	902
Financial derivatives liabilities	−190	−62	−9
Other investment assets	432	−181	−723
Other investment liabilities	212	−366	607
Net errors and omissions	241	379	279
Overall balance	2,470	1,726	32

Source: IMF, *International Financial Statistics*.

COLOMBIA

External Trade

PRINCIPAL COMMODITIES
(US $ million, revised figures)

Imports c.i.f.	2004	2005	2006
Agricultural, livestock, hunting and forestry products	1,082	1,019	1,241
Prepared foodstuffs, beverages and tobacco	884	991	1,261
Textiles, clothing and leather products	781	892	1,110
Chemical products	3,831	4,498	5,280
Rubber and plastic goods	546	709	876
Metals and metal manufactures	1,429	1,888	2,447
Mechanical, electrical telecommunications and medical equipment	4,567	6,346	7,597
Vehicles and transport equipment	2,523	3,260	4,370
Total (incl. others)	16,764	21,204	26,162

Exports f.o.b.	2004	2005	2006
Coffee	956	1,471	1,461
Coal	1,859	2,598	2,913
Petroleum and its derivatives	4,227	5,559	6,328
Prepared foodstuffs, beverages and tobacco	1,222	1,393	1,574
Textiles, clothing and leather products	1,366	1,440	1,555
Paper and publishing	500	554	633
Chemicals	1,373	1,595	1,806
Metal manufactures	1,116	1,367	1,877
Mechanical, electrical and transport equipment	478	572	n.a.
Total (incl. others)	16,788	21,190	24,391

PRINCIPAL TRADING PARTNERS
(US $ million, provisional figures)

Imports c.i.f.	2003	2004	2005
Argentina	257.1	321.9	411.7
Bolivia	198.3	170.3	191.7
Brazil	769.0	970.3	1,383.4
Canada	313.5	384.5	389.3
Chile	299.9	359.1	377.1
China, People's Rep.	688.7	1,067.7	1,616.8
Ecuador	409.7	412.4	529.0
France	381.3	303.2	384.1
Germany	611.7	661.2	773.7
Italy	289.5	319.2	331.5
Japan	642.9	643.7	705.3
Korea, Rep.	337.8	453.0	593.7
Mexico	744.4	1,038.8	1,757.1
Peru	193.4	260.9	350.1
Spain	255.5	258.8	333.3
Switzerland	171.0	207.3	208.0
Taiwan	164.5	197.2	226.8
United Kingdom	164.3	197.3	190.3
USA	4,081.2	4,838.1	6,005.6
Venezuela	727.4	1,081.8	1,219.1
Total (incl. others)	13,880.6	16,744.8	21,204.2

Exports f.o.b.	2003	2004	2005
Belgium-Luxembourg	227.8	288.9	368.2
Canada	176.5	155.8	298.0
Chile	188.2	254.3	296.2
Costa Rica	193.7	235.2	219.4
Ecuador	779.0	1,010.7	1,324.4
France	146.9	199.5	174.7
Germany	264.4	264.9	339.2
Italy	285.2	361.1	439.0
Japan	201.5	262.1	330.2
Mexico	358.2	525.1	610.9
Netherlands	301.1	386.2	439.7
Panama	170.5	216.5	264.1
Peru	395.4	544.2	209.9
Puerto Rico	362.6	444.5	371.9
Spain	196.9	211.9	346.6
United Kingdom	184.4	279.7	320.0
USA	5,797.6	6,597.5	8,479.0
Venezuela	694.3	1,623.0	2,097.6
Total (incl. others)	13,092.2	16,729.7	21,187.1

Source: Dirección de Impuestos y Aduanas Nacionales.

Transport

RAILWAYS
(traffic)

	1996	1997	1998
Freight ('000 metric tons)	321	348	281
Freight ton-km ('000)	746,544	736,427	657,585

Source: Sociedad de Transporte Ferroviario, SA.

ROAD TRAFFIC
(motor vehicles in use)

	1997	1998	1999
Passenger cars	1,694,323	1,776,100	1,803,201
Buses	126,362	131,987	134,799
Goods vehicles	179,530	183,335	184,495
Motorcycles	385,378	450,283	479,073

Source: IRF, *World Road Statistics*.

SHIPPING

Merchant Fleet
(registered at 31 December)

	2004	2005	2006
Number of vessels	126	137	144
Total displacement ('000 grt)	75.1	94.0	96.2

Source: Lloyd's Register-Fairplay, *World Fleet Statistics*.

Domestic Sea-borne Freight Traffic
('000 metric tons)

	1987	1988	1989
Goods loaded and unloaded	772.1	944.8	464.6

International Sea-borne Freight Traffic
('000 metric tons)

	1999	2000	2001
Goods loaded	4,111	3,543	3,832
Goods unloaded	1,274	1,114	1,399

COLOMBIA

CIVIL AVIATION
(traffic)

	2001	2002	2003
Domestic			
Passengers carried ('000)	7,560	7,732	7,438
Freight carried (metric tons)	103,826	121,636	131,187
International			
Passengers ('000):			
arrivals	1,446	1,429	1,460
departures	1,605	1,455	1,484
Freight (metric tons):			
loaded	129,557	127,688	146,142
unloaded	242,780	257,293	299,463

Source: Departamento Administrativo de Aeronáutica Civil.

Tourism

TOURIST ARRIVALS

Country of origin	2003	2004	2005
Argentina	16,028	23,059	34,025
Brazil	16,938	21,910	27,209
Canada	16,292	20,147	24,471
Costa Rica	18,410	24,478	25,002
Ecuador	64,431	91,682	95,816
France	16,545	20,458	23,060
Germany	14,163	15,881	18,130
Italy	14,899	17,936	19,955
Mexico	26,998	34,016	42,580
Panama	18,764	24,363	28,811
Peru	25,732	36,654	44,490
Spain	32,525	45,239	57,064
USA	171,906	203,603	235,386
Venezuela	73,567	92,523	113,674
Total (incl. others)	624,909	790,940	933,243

Tourism receipts (US $ million, incl. passenger transport): 1,191 in 2003; 1,366 in 2004; 1,570 in 2005.

Source: World Tourism Organization.

Communications Media

	2004	2005	2006
Telephones ('000 main lines in use)	8,768.1	7,678.8	7,865.3
Mobile cellular telephones ('000 subscribers)	10,400.6	21,850.0	29,762.7
Personal computers ('000 in use)	2,996	1,892	n.a.
Internet users ('000)	3,587.7	4,738.5	6,705.0
Broadband subscribers ('000)	127.1	318.7	627.8

2004: 24 daily newspapers.

1997 ('000 in use): Radio receivers 21,000; Facsimile machines 173.

2000: Television receivers ('000 in use) 11,936.

Book production: 5,302 titles in 1997.

Sources: UN, *Statistical Yearbook*; UNESCO, *Statistical Yearbook*; International Telecommunication Union.

Education

(2004/05 unless otherwise indicated)

	Institutions*	Teachers	Students ('000) Males	Females	Total
Pre-primary	32,432	49,926	509.7	489.6	999.3
Primary	55,869	186,898	2,729.3	2,569.0	5,298.3
Secondary general	} 12,921	151,813†	1,952.2	2,062.2	4,014.3
technical/vocational		12,527†	129.2	153.7	282.9
Higher (incl. universities)	321	93,673	595.6	628.0	1,223.6

* 2001/02.
† 2003/04.

Sources: Ministerio de Educación Nacional and UNESCO Institute for Statistics.

Adult literacy rate (UNESCO estimates): 92.8% (males 92.8%; females 92.9%) in 2005 (Source: UNESCO Institute for Statistics).

Directory

The Constitution

A new, 380-article Constitution, drafted by a 74-member National Constituent Assembly, took effect from 6 July 1991. The new Constitution retained the institutional framework of a directly elected President with a non-renewable four-year term of office, together with a bicameral legislature composed of an upper house or Senate (with 102 directly elected members) and a lower house or House of Representatives (to include at least two representatives of each national department). On 14 December 2004 both chambers of the Congreso approved a constitutional amendment to allow re-election of the President for a second term in office. The reform was approved by the Constitutional Court in October 2005, taking force prior to the presidential election scheduled for May 2006. A Vice-President is elected at the same time as the President, and also holds office for a term of four years.

The new Constitution also contained comprehensive provisions for the recognition and protection of civil rights, and for the reform of the structures and procedures of political participation and of the judiciary.

The fundamental principles upon which the new Constitution is based are embodied in articles 1–10.

Article 1: Colombia is a lawful state, organized as a single Republic, decentralized, with autonomous territorial entities, democratic, participatory and pluralist, founded on respect for human dignity, on the labour and solidarity of its people and on the prevalence of the general interest.

Article 2: The essential aims of the State are: to serve the community, to promote general prosperity and to guarantee the effectiveness of the principles, rights and obligations embodied in the Constitution, to facilitate the participation of all in the decisions which affect them and in the economic, political, administrative and cultural life of the nation; to defend national independence, to maintain territorial integrity and to ensure peaceful coexistence and the validity of the law.

The authorities of the Republic are instituted to protect the residents of Colombia, in regard to their life, honour, goods, beliefs and other rights and liberties, and to ensure the fulfilment of the obligations of the State and of the individual.

Article 3: Sovereignty rests exclusively with the people, from whom public power emanates. The people exercise power directly or through their representatives in the manner established by the Constitution.

Article 4: The Constitution is the highest authority. In all cases of incompatability between the Constitution and the law or other juridical rules, constitutional dispositions will apply.

It is the duty of nationals and foreigners in Colombia to observe the Constitution and the law, and to respect and obey the authorities.

Article 5: The State recognizes, without discrimination, the primacy of the inalienable rights of the individual and protects the family as the basic institution of society.

Article 6: Individuals are solely responsible to the authorities for infringements of the Constitution and of the law. Public servants are equally accountable and are responsible to the authorities for failure to fulfil their function or abuse of their position.

Article 7: The State recognizes and protects the ethnic diversity of the Colombian nation.

Article 8: It is an obligation of the State and of the people to protect the cultural and natural riches of the nation.

Article 9: The foreign relations of the State are based on national sovereignty, with respect for self-determination of people and with recognition of the principles of international law accepted by Colombia.

Similarly, Colombia's external politics will be directed towards Caribbean and Latin American integration.

Article 10: Spanish (Castellano) is the official language of Colombia. The languages and dialects of ethnic groups are officially recognized within their territories. Education in communities with their own linguistic traditions will be bilingual.

The Government

HEAD OF STATE

President: ALVARO URIBE VÉLEZ (took office 7 August 2002; re-elected 28 May 2006).
Vice-President: FRANCISCO SANTOS CALDERÓN.

CABINET
(March 2008)

A coalition of the Partido Conservador Colombiano, the Partido Liberal Colombiano and Independents.

Minister of the Interior and Justice: CARLOS HOLGUÍN SARDI.
Minister of Foreign Affairs: FERNANDO ARAÚJO PERDOMO.
Minister of Finance and Public Credit: OSCAR IVÁN ZULUAGA.
Minister of National Defence: JUAN MANUEL SANTOS CALDERÓN.
Minister of Agriculture and Rural Development: ANDRÉS FELIPE ARIAS LEYVA.
Minister of Social Protection: DIEGO PALACIO BETANCOURT.
Minister of Mines and Energy: HERNÁN MARTÍNEZ TORRES.
Minister of Trade, Industry and Tourism: LUIS GUILLERMO PLATA PÁEZ.
Minister of National Education: CECILIA MARÍA VÉLEZ WHITE.
Minister of the Environment, Housing and Territorial Development: JUAN LOZANO.
Minister of Communications: MARÍA DEL ROSARIO GUERRA DE LA ESPRIELLA.
Minister of Transport: ANDRÉS URIEL GALLEGO HENAO.
Minister of Culture: PAULA MARCELA MORENO ZAPATA.

MINISTRIES

Office of the President: Palacio de Nariño, Carrera 8A, No 7-26, Bogotá, DC; tel. (1) 562-9300; fax (1) 286-8063; internet www.presidencia.gov.co.
Ministry of Agriculture and Rural Development: Avda Jiménez, No 7-65, Bogotá, DC; tel. (1) 334-1199; fax (1) 284-1775; e-mail minagric@colomsat.net.co; internet www.minagricultura.gov.co.
Ministry of Communications: Edif. Murillo Toro, Carrera 7 y 8, Calle 12 y 13, Apdo Aéreo 14515, Bogotá, DC; tel. (1) 286-6911; fax (1) 344-3434; internet www.mincomunicaciones.gov.co.
Ministry of Culture: Calle 8, No 6-97, Bogotá, DC; tel. (1) 342-4100; fax (1) 342-1721; e-mail servicioalcliente@mincultura.gov.co; internet www.mincultura.gov.co.
Ministry of the Environment, Housing and Territorial Development: Calle 37, No 8-40, Bogotá, DC; tel. (1) 288-9897; fax (1) 288-9892; internet www.minambiente.gov.co.
Ministry of Finance and Public Credit: Carrera 8A, No 6-64, Of. 305, Bogotá, DC; tel. (1) 381-1700; fax (1) 350-9344; internet www.minhacienda.gov.co.
Ministry of Foreign Affairs: Palacio de San Carlos, Calle 10A, No 5-51, Bogotá, DC; tel. (1) 282-7811; fax (1) 341-6777; internet www.minrelext.gov.co.
Ministry of the Interior and Justice: Palacio Echeverry, Carrera 8A, No 8-09, Bogotá, DC; tel. (1) 334-0630; fax (1) 341-9583; internet www.mij.gov.co.
Ministry of Mines and Energy: Centro Administrativo Nacional (CAN), Avda El Dorado, Bogotá, DC; tel. (1) 222-4555; fax (1) 222-3651; internet www.minminas.gov.co.
Ministry of National Defence: Centro Administrativo Nacional (CAN), 2°, Avda El Dorado, Bogotá, DC; tel. (1) 220-4999; fax (1) 222-1874; internet www.mindefensa.gov.co.
Ministry of National Education: Centro Administrativo Nacional (CAN), Of. 501, Calle 45, Avda El Dorado, Bogotá, DC; tel. (1) 222-2800; fax (1) 222-4578; e-mail dci@mineducacion.gov.co; internet www.mineducacion.gov.co.
Ministry of Social Protection: Carrera 7A, No 34-50, Bogotá, DC; tel. (1) 287-3434; fax (1) 285-7091; e-mail oaai@tutopia.com; internet www.minproteccionsocial.gov.co.
Ministry of Trade, Industry and Tourism: Edif. Centro de Comercio Internacional, Calle 28, No 13A-15, 18°, Bogotá, DC; tel. (1) 606-7676; fax (1) 606-7522; internet www.mincomercio.gov.co.
Ministry of Transport: Centro Administrativo Nacional (CAN), Of. 409, Avda El Dorado, Bogotá, DC; tel. (1) 222-4411; fax (1) 222-1647; e-mail mintrans@mintransporte.gov.co; internet www.mintransporte.gov.co.

President and Legislature

PRESIDENT

Presidential Election, 28 May 2006

	Votes	% of votes cast
Alvaro Uribe Vélez	7,397,835	63.56
Carlos Gaviria Díaz	2,613,157	22.45
Horacio Serpa Uribe	1,404,235	12.07
Antanas Mockus Sivickas	146,583	1.26
Others	76,303	0.66
Total*	**11,638,113**	**100.00**

* Excluding 271,292 blank and 132,332 invalid ballots.

CONGRESO

Senado
(Senate)

President: CLAUDIA BLUM.

General Election, 12 March 2006, provisional results

	Seats	% of votes cast
Partido Social de la Unidad Nacional (Partido de la U)	20	17.49
Partido Conservador Colombiano (PCC)	18	16.13
Partido Liberal Colombiano (PL)	17	15.52
Partido Cambio Radical	15	13.36
Polo Democrático Alternativo	11	9.74
Partido Convergencia Ciudadana	7	6.25
Alas Equipo Colombia	5	4.68
Partido Colombia Democrática	3	2.85
Movimiento Colombia Viva	2	2.46
Movimiento Mira	2	2.35
Indigenous groups*	2	—
Total	**102**	**100.00†**

* Under the reforms of the Constitution in 1991, at least two Senate seats are reserved for indigenous groups.
† Including others.

Cámara de Representantes
(House of Representatives)

President: JULIO E. GALLARDO ARCHBOLD.

General Election, 12 March 2006, provisional results

	Seats
Partido Liberal Colombiano (PL)	36
Partido Conservador Colombiano (PCC)	29
Partido Social de Unidad Nacional (Partido de la U)	28
Partido Cambio Radical	20
Polo Democrático Alternativo	9
Partido Convergencia Ciudadana	8
Alas Equipo Colombia	7
Movimiento Apertura Liberal	5
Movimiento de Integración Regional	4
Movimiento Nacional	2
Movimiento Popular Unido (MPU)	2
Partido Colombia Democrático	2
Other parties*	14
Total	**166**

* Includes two seats reserved for Afro-Colombian groupings and one seat for indigenous groupings.

Election Commission

Consejo Nacional Electoral (CNE): Avda El Dorado 46–20, 6°, Bogotá, DC; tel. (1) 220-0800; internet www.cne.gov.co; f. 1888 as

COLOMBIA

Gran Consejo Electoral, re-founded as above in 1985; Pres. CIRO MUÑOZ OÑATE.

Political Organizations

Alas Equipo Colombia: Calle 34, No 28A-18, Bogotá, DC; tel. (1) 244-1213; fax (1) 269-7034; e-mail contactenos@alasequipocolombia.org; internet www.alasequipocolombia.org; f. 2005 following merger of Partido ALAS and Movimiento Equipo Colombia; conservative; Pres. JAIME ARIAS RAMÍREZ; Sec.-Gen. JAVIER PINILLA PALACIO.

Colombia Viva: Edif. Corkidi, Of. 303, 5-32 Calle 12, Bogotá, DC; tel. (1) 282-9691; e-mail info@movimientocolombiaviva.org; internet www.movimientocolombiaviva.org; f. 2005; Pres. HABIB MERHEG; Sec.-Gen. LILIANA TÁMARA.

Movimiento Apertura Liberal: 5-70 Avda 3B, Latino, Cúcuta, Norte de Santander; tel. (0975) 834-555; Leader Dr MIGUEL ANGEL FLORES RIVERA.

Movimiento de Integración Regional (IR): 4-140 Avda 20 de Julio, San Andres, Isla; tel. (1) 512-2193; e-mail ir@latinmail.com; Leader DORKY JAY JULIO.

Movimiento Mira: 35A-44, Transversal 29, Bogotá, DC; tel. (1) 337-9339; internet www.webmira.com; Leader ALEXANDRA MORENO PIRAQUIVE.

Movimiento Nacional (MN): Carrera 16, No 33-24, Bogotá, DC; tel. (1) 245-4418; fax (1) 284-8529; e-mail movimientonacional@movimientonacional.org; Sec.-Gen. JUAN PABLO CEPERA MÁRQUEZ.

Movimiento Nacional de Autodefensas Desmovilizadas (MNAD): internet www.colombialibre.org; f. 2007 by mems of fmr right-wing paramilitary org., Autodefensas Unidas de Colombia (AUC); AUC announced cease-fire in Dec. 2002; demobilization began in Nov. 2004, completed in 2006; Spokesperson ANTONIO LÓPEZ.

Movimiento Nacional Progresista (MNP): Carrera 10, No 19-45, Of. 708, Bogotá, DC; tel. (1) 286-7517; fax (1) 341-9368; Sec.-Gen. EDUARDO AISAMAK LEÓN BELTRÁN.

Movimiento Obrero Independiente Revolucionario (MOIR): Calle 39, No 21-30, Bogotá, DC; tel. (1) 245-9647; e-mail moir@moir.org.co; internet www.moircolombia.org; left-wing workers' movt; Maoist; affiliated to the Polo Democrático Alternativo (q.v.); Sec.-Gen. HÉCTOR VALENGA.

Movimiento Popular Unido (MPU): 13N-85 Avda 4 Norte, Cali, Valle del Cauca; tel. (2) 661-2493; e-mail amc50@latinmail.com; internet www.movimientopopularunido.com; f. 1994; conservative; Leader ALBERTO MACHADO CEBALLOS.

Movimiento de Salvación Nacional (MSN): Carrera 24, No 21-16, Manizales, Caldas; tel. (87) 884-0180; internet www.salvacionnacional.com; f. 1990; split from the Partido Conservador Colombiano (q.v.).

Organización Nacional Indígena de Colombia (ONIC): Calle 13, No 4-38, Bogotá; tel. (1) 284-2168; fax (1) 284-3465; e-mail onic@onic.org.co; internet www.onic.org.co; f. 1982; asscn of indigenous political and devt groups.

Partido Cambio Radical: Carrera 7, No 26-20, 20°, Bogotá, DC; tel. (1) 210-7373; fax (1) 210-6868; e-mail cambioradical1@etb.net.co; internet www.partidocambioradical.org; f. 2002; Leader GERMÁN VARGAS LLERAS.

Partido Colombia Democrático: Calle 40A, No 13-09, Bogotá, DC; tel. (1) 287-0600; fax (1) 338-2310; internet www.colombiademocratica.com; f. 2003; conservative; Nat. Dir MARIO URIBE ESCOBAR.

Partido Comunista Colombiano (PC): Calle 18A, No 14-56, Apdo Aéreo 2523, Bogotá, DC; tel. (1) 334-1947; fax (1) 281-8259; e-mail notipaco@pacocol.org; internet www.pacocol.org; f. 1930; Marxist-Leninist party; Sec.-Gen. ALVARO VÁSQUEZ DEL REAL.

Partido Conservador Colombiano (PCC): Avda 22, No 37-09, Bogotá, DC; tel. (1) 369-3923; fax (1) 369-0053; e-mail presidencia@partidoconservador.com; internet www.partidoconservador.com; f. 1849; 2.9m. mems; Pres. EFRAÍN JOSÉ CEPEDA SARABIA; Sec.-Gen. BENJAMÍN HIGUITA RIVERA.

Partido Convergencia Ciudadana: 48-33 Carrera 27A, Bucaramanga, Santander; tel. (7) 647-6411; e-mail convergencia@intercable.net.co; internet www.convergencia.org.co; f. 1997; supports AUC paramilitary grouping; Pres. SAMUEL ARRIETA BUELVAS.

Partido Liberal Colombiano (PL): Avda Caracas, No 36-01, Bogotá, DC; tel. (1) 593-4500; fax (1) 288-1138; e-mail direcciondecomunicaciones@partidoliberal.org.co; internet www.partidoliberal.org.co; f. 1848; Pres. CÉSAR GAVIRIA TRUJILLO; Sec.-Gen. JOSÉ NOO RIOS.

Partido Social de la Unidad Nacional (Partido de la U): 32-16 Carrera 7, 21°, Bogotá, DC; tel. (1) 340-1394; internet www.partidodelau.com; f. 2005; conservative; supports Pres. Uribe; Pres. CARLOS GARCÍA ORJUELA.

Polo Democrático Alternativo (PDA): Carrera 17A, No 37-27, Bogotá; tel. (1) 288-6188; internet www.polodemocratico.net; f. 2002 as electoral alliance, constituted as a political party in July 2003; founded by fmr mems of the Movimiento 19 de Abril; name changed to above in 2006 from Polo Democrático Independiente; left-wing; Pres. GUSTAVO PETRO; Sec-Gen. ANTONIO NAVARRO.

The following are the principal guerrilla groups in operation in Colombia:

Ejército de Liberación Nacional (ELN): internet www.nodo50.org/patrialibre; Castroite guerrilla movt; f. 1964; 3,500 mems; political status recognized by the Govt in 1998; mem. of the Coordinadora Nacional Guerrilla Simón Bolívar; Leader NICOLÁS RODRÍGUEZ BAUTISTA.

Fuerzas Armadas Revolucionarias de Colombia—Ejército del Pueblo (FARC—EP): f. 1964, although mems active from 1949; name changed from Fuerzas Armadas Revolucionarias de Colombia to the above in 1982; fmrly military wing of the Communist Party; composed of 39 armed fronts and about 6,000–8,000 mems; political status recognized by the Govt in 1998; mem. of the Coordinadora Nacional Guerrilla Simón Bolívar; C-in-C PEDRO ANTONIO MARÍN (alias Manuel Marulanda Vélez or 'Tirofijo').

Diplomatic Representation

EMBASSIES IN COLOMBIA

Algeria: Carrera 11, No 93-53, Of. 302, Bogotá, DC; tel. (1) 635-0520; fax (1) 635-0531; e-mail ambalgbg@cable.net.co; Ambassador OMAR BENCHEHIDA.

Argentina: Avda 40A, No 13-09, 16°, Apdo Aéreo 53013, Bogotá, DC; tel. (1) 288-0900; fax (1) 288-8868; e-mail embargentina@etb.net.co; Ambassador MARTÍN ANTONIO BALZA.

Austria: Edif. Fiducafe, 4°, Carrera 9, No 73-44, Bogotá, DC; tel. (1) 326-2680; fax (1) 317-7639; e-mail bogota-ob@bmeia.gv.at; internet www.embajadadeaustria.org.co; Ambassador HANS PETER GLANZER.

Belgium: Calle 26, No 4A-45, 7°, Apdo Aéreo 3564, Bogotá, DC; tel. (1) 380-0370; fax (1) 380-0340; e-mail bogota@diplobel.org; internet www.diplobel.org/colombia; Ambassador JEAN-LUC BODSON.

Bolivia: Transversal 14A, No 118A-26, Apdo Aéreo 96219, Santa Barbara, Bogotá, DC; tel. (1) 629-8237; fax (1) 619-4940; e-mail embolivia-bogota@rree.gov.bo; Ambassador CARLOS VLADIMIR SCHMIDT COLQUE.

Brazil: Calle 93, No 14-20, 8°, Bogotá, DC; tel. (1) 218-0800; fax (1) 218-8393; internet www.brasil.org.co; Ambassador VALDEMAR CARNEIRO LEÃO.

Canada: Carretera 7, No 115-33, 14°, Apdo Aéreo 110067, Bogotá, DC; tel. (1) 657-9800; fax (1) 657-9912; e-mail bgota@dfait-maeci.gc.ca; internet www.bogota.gc.ca; Ambassador MATTHEW LEVIN.

Chile: Calle 100, No 11B-44, Bogotá, DC; tel. (1) 214-7990; fax (1) 619-3863; e-mail embajadachile@cable.net.co; Ambassador GASPAR TAPIA GABRIEL.

China, People's Republic: Carrera 16, No 98-30, Bogotá, DC; tel. (1) 622-3215; fax (1) 622-3114; e-mail chinaemb_co@mfa.gov.cn; internet co.china-embassy.org/chn; Ambassador WU CHANGSHENG.

Costa Rica: Carrera 8, No 95-48, Bogotá, DC; tel. (1) 623-0205; fax (1) 691-8558; e-mail embacosta@andinet.com; internet www.embajadacostarica.netfirms.com/funcionarios.htm; Ambassador MELVIN ALFREDO SÁENZ BIOLLEY.

Cuba: Carrera 9, No 92-54, Bogotá, DC; tel. (1) 621-7054; fax (1) 611-4382; e-mail embacuba@cable.net.co; internet embacu.cubaminrex.cu/colombia; Ambassador JOSÉ ANTONIO PÉREZ NOVOA.

Czech Republic: Carrera 7, No 114-33, Ofs 603 y 604, Bogotá, DC; tel. (1) 640-0600; fax (1) 640-0599; e-mail bogota@embassy.msv.cz; internet www.mzv.cz/bogota; Ambassador ZDENĚK KREJČÍ.

Dominican Republic: Calle 100, No 19-61, Of. 402, Bogotá, DC; tel. (1) 635-3627; fax (1) 635-3884; e-mail embajado@cable.net.co; Ambassador RAÚL FERNANDO DE JESÚS BARRIENTO LARA.

Ecuador: Edif. Fernando Mazuera, 7°, Calle 72, No 6-30, Bogotá, DC; tel. (1) 212-6549; fax (1) 212-6536; e-mail eecucolombia@mmrree.gov.ec; internet www.embajadaecuacol.net; Ambassador FRANCISCO SUÉSCUM OTTATI.

Egypt: Transversal 19A 101-10, Bogotá, DC; tel. (1) 256-2940; fax (1) 256-9255; e-mail embegyptbta@unete.com; Ambassador MOHAMED AHDY KHAIRAT.

El Salvador: Edif. El Nogal, Of. 503, Carrera 9A, No 80-15, Bogotá, DC; tel. (1) 349-6765; fax (1) 349-6670; e-mail elsalvador@supercable.net.co; Ambassador JOAQUÍN ALEXANDER MAZA MARTELLI.

COLOMBIA

France: Carrera 11, No 93-12, Bogotá, DC; tel. (1) 638-1400; fax (1) 638-1430; internet www.ambafrance-co.org; Ambassador JEAN-MICHEL MARLAUD.

Germany: Apdo 98833, Bogotá, DC; tel. (1) 423-2600; fax (1) 429-3145; e-mail info@bogota.diplo.de; internet www.bogota.diplo.de; Ambassador MICHAEL GLOTZBACH.

Guatemala: Diagonal 145A, No 32-37, Bogotá, DC; tel. (1) 636-1724; fax (1) 274-1196; e-mail embcolombia@minex.gob.gt; Ambassador MANLIO FERNANDO SESENNA OLIVERO.

Holy See: Carrera 15, No 36-33, Apdo Aéreo 3740, Bogotá, DC (Apostolic Nunciature); tel. (1) 320-0289; fax (1) 285-1817; e-mail nunciatura@cable.net.co; Apostolic Nuncio Most Rev. BENIAMINO STELLA.

Honduras: Calle 121, No 11D-23, Bogotá, DC; tel. (1) 215-4259; fax (1) 637-0686; e-mail info@embajadadehonduras.org.co; internet www.embajadadehonduras.org.co; Ambassador RAFAEL MURILLO SELVA RENDÓN.

India: Edif. Bancafe, Torre B, Carrera 7, No 71-21, Of. 1001, Bogotá, DC; tel. (1) 317-4865; fax (1) 317-4976; e-mail indembog@cable.net.co; internet www.embajadaindia.org; Ambassador DEEPAK BHOJWANI.

Indonesia: Carrera 9, No 76-27, Bogotá, DC; tel. (1) 217-6738; fax (1) 326-2165; e-mail info@indonesiabogota.org.co; internet www.indonesiabogota.org.co; Chargé d'affaires a.i. MEITY SUHARIAH ICHWANU.

Iran: Calle 96, No 11A-16/20, Apdo 93854, Bogotá, DC; tel. (1) 610-3064; fax (1) 610-2556; e-mail embajadairan@andinet.com.co; Ambassador ABDOULAZIM HASHEMINIK.

Israel: Calle 35, No 7-25, 14°, Bogotá, DC; tel. (1) 327-7500; fax (1) 327-7555; e-mail info@bogota.mfa.gov.il; internet bogota.mfa.gov.il; Ambassador MERON REUBEN.

Italy: Calle 93B, No 9-92, Apdo Aéreo 50901, Bogotá, DC; tel. (1) 218-6604; fax (1) 610-5886; e-mail ambbogo.mail@esteri.it; internet www.ambbogota.esteri.it; Ambassador ANTONIO TARELLI.

Japan: Carrera 7A, No 71-21, 11°, Torre B, Bogotá, DC; tel. (1) 317-5001; fax (1) 317-5007; e-mail info@embjp-colombia.com; internet www.colombia.emb-japan.go.jp; Ambassador TATSUMARO TERAZAWA.

Korea, Republic: Calle 94, No 9-39, Bogotá, DC; tel. (1) 616-7200; fax (1) 610-0338; e-mail embcorea@mofat.go.kr; internet col.mofat.go.kr/index.jsp; Ambassador SONG KI-DO.

Lebanon: Calle 74, No 11-88, CP 51084, Bogotá, DC; tel. (1) 212-8360; fax (1) 347-9106; e-mail emblibanco@hotmail.com; Chargé d'affaires a.i. HASSAN MUSLIMANI.

Mexico: Edif. Teleport Business Park, Calle 114, No 9-01, Of. 204, Torre A, Bogotá, DC; tel. (1) 629-4989; fax (1) 629-5121; e-mail emcolmex@etb.net.co; internet www.sre.gob.mx/colombia; Ambassador (vacant).

Morocco: Carrera 6A, No 113-37, Bogotá, DC; tel. (1) 620-5888; fax (1) 634-9477; e-mail embamarruecost@etb.net.co; Ambassador MOHAMED KHATTABI.

Netherlands: Carrera 13, No 93-40, 5°, Apdo Aéreo 43585, Bogotá, DC; tel. (1) 638-4200; fax (1) 623-3020; e-mail bog@minbuza.nl; internet colombia.nlembajada.org; Ambassador FRANS B. A. M. VAN HAREN.

Nicaragua: Calle 108A, No 25-42, Bogotá, DC; tel. (1) 619-8934; fax (1) 612-6050; e-mail embnicaragua@007mundo.com; Chargé d'affaires a.i. EDGARD JOSÉ GENIE AREVALO.

Norway: Edif. Fiducafé, 8°, Carrera 9, No 73-44, 8°, Bogotá, DC; tel. (1) 317-7851; fax (1) 317-7858; e-mail emb.bogota@mfa.no; internet www.noruega.org.co; Ambassador MARTIN TORE BJØRNDAL (resident in Venezuela).

Panama: Calle 92, No 7A-40, Bogotá, DC; tel. (1) 257-5058; fax (1) 257-5067; e-mail embpacol@cable.net.co; internet www.empacol.org; Ambassador CARLOS R. OZORES TYPALDOS.

Paraguay: Carrera 7, No 72-28, Of. 302, Bogotá, DC; tel. (1) 347-0322; e-mail emboy@etb-net-co; Ambassador FELIPE ROBERTTI.

Peru: Calle 80A, No 6-50, Bogotá, DC; tel. (1) 257-0505; fax (1) 249-8581; e-mail embajadaperu@supercabletv.net.co; internet www.embajadadelperu.org.co; Ambassador JOSÉ ANTONIO MEIER ESPINOZA.

Poland: Calle 104A, No 23-48, Bogotá, DC; tel. (1) 214-0400; fax (1) 214-0854; e-mail polemb@cable.net.co; internet www.bogota.polemb.net; Ambassador HENRYK KOBIEROWSKI.

Portugal: Carrera 12, No 93-37, Of. 302, Bogotá, DC; tel. (1) 622-1334; fax (1) 622-1134; e-mail embporbo@andinet.com; Ambassador AUGUSTO JOSÉ PESTANA SARAIVA PEIXOTO.

Romania: Carrera 7A, No 92-58, Bogotá, DC; tel. (1) 256-6438; fax (1) 256-6158; e-mail ambrombogota@etb.net.co; Ambassador MARIA SIPOS.

Russia: Carrera 4, No 75-02, Apdo Aéreo 90600, Bogotá, DC; tel. (1) 212-1881; fax (1) 210-4694; e-mail embajadarusia@cable.net.co; internet www.colombia.mid.ru; Ambassador VLADIMIR V. TRUJANOVSKI.

Spain: Calle 92, No 12-68, Apdo 90355, Bogotá, DC; tel. (1) 622-0090; fax (1) 621-0809; e-mail embespco@correo.mae.es; Ambassador ANDRÉS COLLADO GONZÁLEZ.

Sweden: Calle 72-bis, No 5-83, 8°, Bogotá, DC; tel. (1) 325-6180; fax (1) 325-6181; e-mail embsueca@cable.net.co; internet www.swedenabroad.com/bogota; Ambassador LENA NORDSTRÖM.

Switzerland: Carrera 9, No 74-08/1101, 11°, Bogotá, DC; tel. (1) 349-7230; fax (1) 349-7195; e-mail bog.vertretung@eda.admin.ch; internet www.eda.admin.ch/bogota; Ambassador THOMAS KUPFER.

United Kingdom: Edif. ING Barings, Carrera 9, No 76-49, 9°, Bogotá, DC; tel. (1) 317-6690; fax (1) 317-6265; e-mail ppa.bogota@fco.gov.uk; internet www.britain.gov.co; Ambassador HAYDON WARREN-GASH.

USA: Calle 22D-bis, No 47-51, Apdo Aéreo 3831, Bogotá, DC; tel. (1) 315-0811; fax (1) 315-2197; internet bogota.usembassy.gov; Ambassador WILLIAM R. BROWNFIELD.

Uruguay: Carrera 9A, No 80-15, 11°, Apdo Aéreo 101466, Bogotá, DC; tel. (1) 235-2748; fax (1) 248-3734; e-mail urucolom@007mundo.com; Ambassador SILVIA LOURDES IZQUIERDO VILA.

Venezuela: Carrera 11, No 87-51, 5°, Bogotá, DC; tel. (1) 640-1213; fax (1) 640-1242; e-mail embajada@embaven.org.co; internet www.embaven.org.co; Ambassador JOSÉ PÁVEL RONDÓN DAZA (recalled for consultations in Nov. 2007).

Judicial System

The constitutional integrity of the State is ensured by the Constitutional Court. The Constitutional Court is composed of nine judges who are elected by the Senate for eight years. Judges of the Constitutional Court are not eligible for re-election.

President of the Constitutional Court: Dr RODRIGO ESCOBAR GIL.

Judges of the Constitutional Court: NILSON PINILLA PINILLA, MANUEL JOSÉ CEPEDA ESPIÑOSA, JAIME CÓRDOBA TRIVIÑO, RODRIGO ESCOBAR GIL, MARCO GERARDO MONROY CABRA, HUMBERTO SIERRA PORTO, ALVARO TAFUR GAVIS, CLARA INÉS VARGAS HERNÁNDEZ, JAIME ARAUJO RENTERIA.

The ordinary judicial integrity of the State is ensured by the Supreme Court of Justice. The Supreme Court of Justice is composed of the Courts of Civil and Agrarian, Penal and Laboral Cassation. Judges of the Supreme Court of Justice, of which there are 23, are selected from the nominees of the Higher Council of Justice and serve an eight-year term of office which is not renewable.

Director of Public Prosecutions: MARIO IGUARÁN ARANA.

SUPREME COURT OF JUSTICE

Corte Suprema de Justicia

Edif. de Palacio de Justicia, Calle 12, No 7-65, Bogotá, DC; tel. (1) 562-2000; internet www.ramajudicial.gov.co.

President: Dr CÉSAR JULIO VALENCIA COPETE.

Court of Civil and Agrarian Cassation (seven judges): Pres. Dr RUTH MARINA DÍAZ RUEDA.

Court of Penal Cassation (nine judges): Pres. Dr ALFREDO GÓMEZ QUINTERO.

Court of Laboral Cassation (seven judges): Pres. Dr GUSTAVO JOSÉ GNECCO MENDOZA.

COUNCIL OF STATE

The Council of State serves as the supreme consultative body to the Government in matters of legislation and administration. It also serves as the supreme tribunal for administrative litigation (*Contencioso Administrativo*). It is composed of 27 magistrates, including a President.

Council of State

Edif. del Palacio de Justicia, 7-65 Calle 12, Bogotá, DC; tel. (1) 350-6700; internet www.ramajudicial.gov.co

President: Dr GUSTAVO APONTE SANTOS.

Religion

CHRISTIANITY

The Roman Catholic Church

Colombia comprises 13 archdioceses, 52 dioceses and 10 apostolic vicariates. An estimated 87.1% of the population were adherents at 31 December 2005.

COLOMBIA

Bishops' Conference

Conferencia Episcopal de Colombia, Carrera 47, No 84-85, Apdo Aéreo 7448, Bogotá, DC; tel. (1) 311-4277; fax (1) 311-5575; e-mail colcec@cable.net.co.

f. 1978; statutes approved 1996; Pres. Cardinal LUIS AUGUSTO CASTRO QUIROGA (Archbishop of Tunja).

Archbishop of Barranquilla: RUBÉN SALAZAR GÓMEZ, Carrera 45, No 53-122, Apdo Aéreo 1160, Barranquilla 4, Atlántico; tel. (5) 349-1145; fax (5) 349-1530; e-mail arquidio@arquidiocesibaq.org.co.

Archbishop of Bogotá: Cardinal PEDRO RUBIANO SÁENZ, Carrera 7A, No 10-20, Bogotá, DC; tel. (1) 350-5511; fax (1) 350-7290; e-mail cancilleria@arquidiocesisbogota.org.co.

Archbishop of Bucaramanga: VÍCTOR MANUEL LÓPEZ FORERO, Calle 33, No 21-18, Bucaramanga, Santander; tel. (7) 642-4387; fax (7) 642-1361; e-mail sarqdbu@col1.telecom.com.

Archbishop of Cali: JUAN FRANCISCO SARASTI JARAMILLO, Carrera 4, No 7-17, Apdo Aéreo 8924, Cali, Valle del Cauca; tel. (2) 889-0562; fax (2) 883-7980; e-mail jsarasti@andinet.com.

Archbishop of Cartagena: JOSÉ ENRIQUE JIMÉNEZ CARVAJAL, Apdo Aéreo 400, Cartagena; tel. (5) 664-5308; fax (5) 664-4974; e-mail arzoctg@telecartagena.com.

Archbishop of Ibagué: FLAVIO CALLE ZAPATA, Calle 10, No 2-58, Ibagué, Tolima; tel. (8) 261-1680; fax (8) 263-2681; e-mail arguibague@hotmail.com.

Archbishop of Manizales: FABIO BETANCUR TIRADO, Carrera 23, No 19-22, Manizales, Caldas; tel. (6) 884-0114; fax (6) 882-1853; e-mail arquiman@epm.net.co.

Archbishop of Medellín: ALBERTO GIRALDO JARAMILLO, Calle 57, No 49-44, 3°, Medellín; tel. (4) 251-7700; fax (4) 251-9395; e-mail arquidiomed@epm.net.co.

Archbishop of Nueva Pamplona: GUSTAVO MARTÍNEZ FRÍAS, Carrera 5, No 4-87, Nueva Pamplona; tel. (7) 568-1329; fax (7) 568-4540; e-mail gumafri@hotmail.com.

Archbishop of Popayán: IVÁN ANTONIO MARÍN-LÓPEZ, Calle 5, No 6-71, Apdo Aéreo 593, Popayán; tel. (2) 824-1710; fax (2) 824-0101; e-mail ivanarzo@emtel.net.co.

Archbishop of Santa Fe de Antioquia: ORLANDO ANTONIO CORRALES GARCÍA, Plazuela Martínez Pardo, No 12-11, Santa Fe de Antioquia; tel. (4) 853-1155; fax (4) 853-1596; e-mail arquistafe@edatel.net.co.

Archbishop of Tunja: LUIS AUGUSTO CASTRO QUIROGA, Calle 17, No 9-85, Apdo Aéreo 1019, Tunja, Boyacá; tel. (8) 742-2093; fax (8) 743-3130; e-mail arquidio@telecom.com.co.

Archbishop of Villavicencio: OSCAR URBINA ORTEGA, Carrera 39, No 34-19, Apdo Aéreo 2401, Villavicencio, Meta; tel. (8) 663-0337; fax (8) 665-3200; e-mail diocesisvillavicencio@andinet.com.

The Anglican Communion

Anglicans in Colombia are members of the Episcopal Church in the USA.

Bishop of Colombia: Rt Rev. FRANCISCO JOSÉ DUQUE GÓMEZ, Carrera 6, No 49-85, Apdo Aéreo 52964, Bogotá, DC; tel. (1) 288-3167; fax (1) 288-3248; e-mail iec@iglesiaepiscopal.org.co; internet www.iglesiaepiscopal.org.co; there are 3,500 baptized mems, 2,000 communicant mems, 29 parishes, missions and preaching stations; 5 schools and 1 orphanage; 8 clergy.

Protestant Church

Iglesia Evangélica Luterana de Colombia: Calle 75, No 20C-54, Apdo Aéreo 51538, Bogotá, DC; tel. (1) 212-5735; fax (1) 212-5714; e-mail ofcentral@ielco.org; 3,000 mems; Pres. Bishop SIGIFREDO DANIEL BUITRAGO PACHÓN.

BAHÁ'Í FAITH

National Spiritual Assembly of the Bahá'ís of Colombia: Apdo Aéreo 51387, Bogotá, DC; tel. and fax (1) 268-1658; e-mail bahaicol@colombianet.net; internet www.bahaicol.org; adherents in 1,013 localities.

JUDAISM

There is a community of about 25,000 with 66 synagogues.

The Press

DAILIES

Bogotá, DC

El Espacio: Carrera 61, No 45-35, Avda El Dorado, Apdo Aéreo 80111, Bogotá, DC; tel. (1) 425-1570; fax (1) 410-4595; internet www.elespacio.com.co; f. 1965; evening; Dir JAIME ARDILA CASAMITJANA; Editor ALBERTO URIBE GÓMEZ; circ. 159,000.

El Nuevo Siglo: Calle 45A, No 102-02, Apdo Aéreo 5452, Bogotá, DC; tel. (1) 413-9200; fax (1) 413-8547; internet www.elnuevosiglo.com.co; f. 1925; Conservative; Dirs JUAN PABLO URIBE, JUAN GABRIEL URIBE; circ. 68,000.

La República: Calle 25 Bis, 102A-63, Bogotá, DC; tel. (1) 413-5077; fax (1) 413-3725; e-mail diario@larepublica.com.co; internet www.la-republica.com.co; f. 1953; morning; finance and economics; Co-ordinator JORGE HERRERA; Editor JORGE EMILIO SIERRA M.; circ. 55,000.

El Tiempo: Avda El Dorado, No 59-70, Apdo Aéreo 3633, Bogotá, DC; tel. (1) 294-0100; fax (1) 410-5088; e-mail julguz@eltiempo.com.co; internet www.eltiempo.com; f. 1911; morning; Liberal; Dir ENRIQUE SANTOS CALDERÓN; Editor FRANCISCO SANTOS; circ. 265,118 (weekdays), 536,377 (Sundays).

Barranquilla, Atlántico

El Heraldo: Calle 53B, No 46-25, Barranquilla, Atlántico; tel. (5) 371-5000; fax (5) 371-5091; internet www.elheraldo.com.co; f. 1933; morning; Liberal; Gen. Editor HUGO PENTON; circ. 70,000.

La Libertad: Carrera 53, No 55-166, Barranquilla, Atlántico; tel. (5) 349-1175; e-mail libertad@metrotel.net.co; internet www.lalibertad.com.co; Liberal; Dir ROBERTO ESPER REBAJE; circ. 25,000.

El Tiempo Caribe: Carrera 50B, No 41-18, Barranquilla, Atlántico; tel. (5) 379-1510; fax (5) 341-7715; e-mail orlgam@eltiempo.com.co; internet www.eltiempo.com; f. 1956; daily; Liberal; Dir ORLANDA GAMBOA; circ. 45,000.

Bucaramanga, Santander del Sur

El Frente: Calle 35, No 12-22, Apdo Aéreo 665, Bucaramanga, Santander del Sur; tel. (7) 42-5319; fax (7) 33-4541; internet www.elfrente.com.co; f. 1942; morning; Conservative; Dir RAFAEL SERRANO PRADA; circ. 10,000.

Vanguardia Liberal: Calle 34, No 13-42, Bucaramanga, Santander del Sur; tel. (7) 680-0700; fax (7) 630-2443; e-mail erodriguez@vanguardialiberal.com.co; internet www.vanguardia.com; f. 1919; morning; Liberal; Sunday illustrated literary supplement and women's supplement; Dir EDUARDO MUÑOZ SERPA; Editor MARCO ANTONIO IBARRA PENALOSA; circ. 48,000.

Cali, Valle del Cauca

Diario Occidente: Centro Comercial Chipichape, Bodega 2, 2°, Of. 220, Cali, Valle del Cauca; tel. (2) 680-2002; e-mail direccion@diariooccidente.com.co; internet www.diariooccidente.com.co; f. 1961; morning; Conservative; Man. SERGIO SANTA SANDOVAL; circ. 25,000.

El País: Carrera 2A, No 24-46, Apdo Aéreo 4766, Cali, Valle del Cauca; tel. (2) 898-7000; e-mail diario@elpais.com.co; internet www.elpais.com.co; f. 1950; Conservative; Dir EDUARDO FERNÁNDEZ DE SOTO; Gen. Man. MARÍA ELVIRA DOMÍNGUEZ; circ. 60,000 (weekdays), 120,000 (Saturdays), 108,304 (Sundays).

El Pueblo: Avda 3A, Norte 35-N-10, Cali, Valle del Cauca; tel. (2) 68-8110; morning; Liberal; Dir LUIS FERNANDO LONDOÑO CAPURRO; circ. 50,000.

Cartagena, Bolívar

El Universal: Pie del Cerro Calle 30, No 17-36, Cartagena, Bolívar; tel. (5) 650-1050; fax (5) 650-1057; e-mail director@eluniversal.com.co; internet www.eluniversal.com.co; f. 1948; daily; Liberal; Editor-in-Chief LEDIZ CALO; Dir PEDRO LUIS MOGOLÓN; circ. 167,000.

Cúcuta, Norte de Santander

La Opinión: Avda 4, No 16-12, Cúcuta, Norte de Santander; tel. (75) 82-9999; e-mail gerencialaopinion@coll.telecom.com.co; internet www.laopinion.com.co; f. 1960; morning; Liberal; Dir Dr JOSÉ EUSTORGIO COLMENARES OSSA; circ. 27,000.

Manizales, Caldas

La Patria: Carrera 20, No 46-35, Manizales, Caldas; e-mail lapatria@lapatria.com; internet www.lapatria.com; f. 1921; morning; independent; Dir Dr LUIS JOSÉ RESTREPO RESTREPO; circ. 22,000.

Medellín, Antioquia

El Colombiano: Carrera 48, No 30 sur-119, Apdo Aéreo 80636, Medellín, Antioquia; tel. (4) 331-5252; fax (4) 331-4858; e-mail elcolombiano@elcolombiano.com.co; internet www.elcolombiano.com; f. 1912; morning; Conservative; Dir ANA MERCEDES GÓMEZ MARTÍNEZ; circ. 90,000.

El Mundo: Calle 53, No 74-50, Apdo Aéreo 53874, Medellín, Antioquia; tel. (4) 264-2800; fax (4) 264-3729; e-mail direccion@elmundo

COLOMBIA

.com; internet www.elmundo.com; f. 1979; Dir GUILLERMO GAVIRIA ECHEVERRI; Editor IRENE GAVIRIA CORREA; circ. 20,000.

Montería, Córdoba

El Meridiano de Córdoba: Avda Circunvalar, No 38-30, Montería, Córdoba; tel. (4) 782-6888; fax (4) 782-6996; e-mail publicidad@elmeridianodecordoba.com; internet www.elmeridianodecordoba.com.co; f. 1995; morning; Dir WILLIAM ENRIQUE SALLEG TABOADA; circ. 18,000.

Neiva

Diario del Huila: Calle 8A, No 6-30, Neiva; tel. (8) 871-2542; fax (8) 871-2543; e-mail prensa@diariodelhuila.com; internet www.diariodelhuila.com; f. 1966; Gen. Editor ALFREDO RUBIO; circ. 12,000.

Pasto, Nariño

El Derecho: Calle 20, No 26-20, Pasto, Nariño; tel. (2) 77-2170; f. 1928; Conservative; Pres. Dr JOSÉ ELÍAS DEL HIERRO; Dir EDUARDO F. MAZUERA; circ. 12,000.

Pereira, Risaralda

Diario del Otún: Carrera 8A, No 22-75, Apdo Aéreo 2533, Pereira, Risaralda; tel. (6) 335-1313; fax (6) 325-4878; e-mail eldiario@interco.net.co; internet www.eldiario.com.co; f. 1982; Financial Dir JAVIER IGNACIO RAMÍREZ MÚNERA; circ. 30,000.

El Imparcial: Km 11, Vía Pereira-Armenia, El Jordán, Pereira, Risaralda; tel. (6) 325-9935; fax (6) 325-9934; f. 1948; morning; Dir ZAHUR KLEMATH ZAPATA; circ. 15,000.

La Tarde: Carrera 9A, No 20-54, Pereira, Risaralda; tel. (6) 313-7676; fax (6) 335-5187; internet www.latarde.com; f. 1975; evening; Dir SONIA DÍAZ MANTILLA; circ. 30,000.

Popayán, Cauca

El Liberal: Carrera 3, No 2-60, Apdo Aéreo 538, Popayán, Cauca; tel. (28) 24-2418; fax (28) 23-3888; e-mail liberal@emtel.net.co; internet www.colombiavirtual.com/elliberal; f. 1938; Man. ANA MARIA LONDOÑO R.; circ. 6,500.

Santa Marta, Magdalena

El Informador: Calle 21, No 5-06, Santa Marta, Magdalena; e-mail elinformador@qhubonet.net.co; internet www.el-informador.com; f. 1921; Liberal; Dir JOSÉ B. VIVES; circ. 9,000.

Villavicencio, Meta

Clarín del Llano: Villavicencio, Meta; tel. (8) 662-3207; Conservative; Dir ELÍAS MATUS TORRES; circ. 5,000.

PERIODICALS

Antena: Bogotá, DC; television, cinema and show business; circ. 10,000.

Arco: Carrera 6, No 35-39, Apdo Aéreo 8624, Bogotá, DC; tel. (1) 285-1500; f. 1959; monthly; history, philosophy, literature and humanities; Dir ALVARO VALENCIA TOVAR; circ. 10,000.

ART NEXUS/Arte en Colombia: Carrera 5, No 67-19, Apdo Aéreo 90193, Bogotá, DC; tel. (1) 312-9435; fax (1) 312-9252; e-mail artnexus@artnexus.com; internet www.artnexus.com; f. 1976; quarterly; Latin American art, photography, visual arts; editions in English and Spanish; Pres. and Chief Editor CELIA SREDNI DE BIRBRAGHER; CEO SUSANNE BIRBRAGHER; circ. 26,000.

El Campesino: Carrera 39A, No 15-11, Bogotá, DC; f. 1958; weekly; cultural; Dir JOAQUÍN GUTIÉRREZ MACÍAS; circ. 70,000.

Consigna: Diagonal 34, No 5-11, Bogotá, DC; tel. (1) 287-1157; fortnightly; Turbayista; Dir (vacant); circ. 10,000.

Coyuntura Económica: Calle 78, No 9-91, Apdo Aéreo 75074, Bogotá, DC; tel. (1) 312-5300; fax (1) 212-6073; e-mail administrador@fedesarrollo.org; internet www.fedesarrollo.org; f. 1970; twice yearly; economics; published by Fundación para Educación Superior y el Desarrollo; Editor CAROLINA MEJÍA; circ. 500.

Cromos Magazine: Avda El Dorado 69-76, Bogotá, DC; tel. (1) 423-2300; fax (1) 423-7641; e-mail internet@cromos.com.co; internet www.cromos.com.co; f. 1916; weekly; illustrated; general news; Dir ALBERTO ZALAMEA; circ. 102,000.

As Deportes: Calle 20, No 4-55, Bogotá, DC; f. 1978; sports; circ. 25,000.

Economía Colombiana: Dirección Economía y Finanzas, San Agustín 6-45, Of. 126A, Bogotá, DC; tel. (1) 282-4597; fax (1) 282-3737; f. 1984; published by Contraloría General de la República; 6 a year; economics.

El Espectador: Avda El Dorado 69-76, Bogotá, DC; tel. and fax (1) 423-2300; e-mail editorweb@elespectador.com.co; internet www.elespectador.com; f. 1887 as a daily paper; published weekly from 2001; Editor FIDEL CANO; circ. 200,000.

Estrategia: Carrera 4A, 25A-12B, Bogotá, DC; monthly; economics; Dir RODRIGO OTERO.

Guión: Carrera 16, No 36-89, Apdo Aéreo 19857; Bogotá, DC; tel. (1) 232-2660; f. 1977; weekly; general; Conservative; Dir JUAN CARLOS PASTRANA; circ. 35,000.

Hit: Calle 20, No 4-55, Bogotá, DC; cinema and show business; circ. 20,000.

Informe Financiero: Dirección Economía y Finanzas, San Agustín 6-45, Of. 126A, Bogotá, DC; tel. (1) 282-4597; fax (1) 282-3737; published by Contraloría General de la República; monthly; economics.

Insurrección: internet www.eln-voces.com; f. 1998; fortnightly; fmrly Correo de Magdalena; organ of the Ejército de Liberación Nacional.

Menorah: Apdo Aéreo 9081, Bogotá, DC; tel. (1) 611-2014; f. 1950; independent monthly review for the Jewish community; Dir ELIÉCER CELNIK; circ. 10,000.

Nueva Frontera: Carrera 7A, No 17-01, 5°, Bogotá, DC; tel. (1) 334-3763; f. 1974; weekly; politics, society, arts and culture; Liberal; Dir CARLOS LLERAS RESTREPO; circ. 23,000.

Pluma: Apdo Aéreo 12190, Bogotá, DC; monthly; art and literature; Dir (vacant); circ. 70,000.

Que Hubo: Bogotá, DC; weekly; general; Editor CONSUELO MONTEJO; circ. 15,000.

Resistencia: e-mail elbarcinocolombia@yahoo.com; internet www.farcep.org/resistencia; f. 1993; quarterly; organ of the Fuerzas Armadas Revolucionarias de Colombia—Ejército del Pueblo; Dir RAÚL REYES.

Revista Diners: Calle 85, No 18-32, 6°, Bogotá, DC; tel. (1) 636-0508; fax (1) 623-1762; e-mail diners@cable.net.co; internet www.revistadiners.com.co; f. 1963; monthly; Dir GERMÁN SANTAMARÍA; circ. 110,000.

Revista Escala: Calle 30, No 17-752, Bogotá, DC; tel. (1) 287-8200; fax (1) 285-9882; e-mail escala@col-online.com; internet www.revistaescala.com; f. 1962; fortnightly; architecture; Dir DAVID SERNA CÁRDENAS; circ. 18,000.

Semana: Calle 93B, No 13-47, Bogotá, DC; tel. (1) 646-8400; fax (1) 621-9526; internet www.semana.com; general; Pres. FELIPE LÓPEZ CABALLERO.

Síntesis Económica: Calle 70A, No 10-52, Bogotá, DC; tel. (1) 212-5121; fax (1) 212-8365; f. 1975; weekly; economics; Dir FÉLIX LAFAURIE RIVERA; circ. 16,000.

Tribuna Médica: Calle 8B, No 68A-41, y Calle 123, No 8-20, Bogotá, DC; tel. (1) 262-6085; fax (1) 262-4459; internet www.tribunamedica.com; f. 1961; monthly; medical and scientific; Editor JACK ALBERTO GRIMBERG; circ. 50,000.

Tribuna Roja: Bogotá, DC; tel. (1) 243-0371; e-mail tribojar@moir.org.co; internet www.moir.org.co/tribuna/tribuna.htm; f. 1971; quarterly; organ of the MOIR (pro-Maoist Communist party); Dir CARLOS NARANJO; circ. 300,000.

Vea: Calle 20, No 4-55, Bogotá, DC; weekly; popular; circ. 90,000.

Voz La Verdad del Pueblo: Carrera 8, No 19-34, Ofs 310–311, Bogotá, DC; tel. (1) 284-5209; fax (1) 342-5041; weekly; left-wing; Dir CARLOS A. LOZANO G.; circ. 45,000.

NEWS AGENCIES

Ciep—El País: Carrera 16, No 36-35, Bogotá, DC; tel. (1) 232-6816; fax (1) 288-0236; Dir JORGE TÉLLEZ.

Colprensa: Diagonal 34, No 5-63, Apdo Aéreo 20333, Bogotá, DC; tel. (1) 287-2200; fax (1) 285-5915; e-mail colpre@elsitio.net.co; internet www.colprensa.com; f. 1980; Dir ROBERTO VARGAS GALVIS.

PRESS ASSOCIATIONS

Asociación Colombiana de Periodistas: Avda Jiménez, No 8-74, Of. 510, Bogotá, DC; tel. (1) 243-6056.

Asociación Nacional de Diarios Colombianos (ANDIARIOS): Calle 61, No 5-20, Apdo Aéreo 13663, Bogotá, DC; tel. (1) 212-8694; fax (1) 212-7894; internet www.andiarios.com; f. 1962; 30 affiliated newspapers; Pres. Dr EDUARDO GARCÉS; Exec. Dir Dr NORA SANÍN DE SAFFON.

Asociación de la Prensa Extranjera: Pedro Meléndez, No 87-93, Bogotá, DC; tel. (1) 288-3011.

Círculo de Periodistas de Bogotá, DC (CPB): Calle 26, No 13A-23, 23°, Bogotá, DC; tel. (1) 282-4217; e-mail cpb@circulodeperiodistasdebogota.org; internet www.circulodeperiodistasdebogota.org; Pres. MARÍA TERESA HERRÁN.

COLOMBIA

Publishers

Comunicadores Técnicos Ltda: Carrera 18, No 46-58, Apdo Aéreo 28797, Bogotá, DC; technical; Dir PEDRO P. MORCILLO.

Ediciones Aula XXI: Calle 19, No 44-10, Bogotá, DC; tel. (1) 574-3990; fax (1) 244-6129; e-mail gerencia@edicionesaulaxxi.com; internet www.edicionesaulaxxi.com; general interest, reference, fiction and educational; Legal Rep. CARLOS MARIO ESCOBAR BRAVO.

Ediciones Cultural Colombiana Ltda: Calle 72, No 16-15 y No 16-21, Apdo Aéreo 6307, Bogotá, DC; tel. (1) 217-6529; fax (1) 217-6570; f. 1951; textbooks; Dir JOSÉ PORTO VÁSQUEZ.

Ediciones Gaviota: Transversal 43, No 99-13, Bogotá, DC; tel. (1) 613-6650; fax (1) 613-9117; e-mail gaviotalibros@edicionesgaviota.com.co.

Ediciones Lerner Ltda: Calle 8A, No 68A-41, Apdo Aéreo 8304, Bogotá, DC; tel. (1) 420-0650; fax (1) 262-4459; f. 1959; general; Commercial Man. FABIO CAICEDO GÓMEZ.

Ediciones Modernas: Carrera 41A, No 22F, Bogotá, DC; tel. (1) 269-0072; fax (1) 244-0706; e-mail edimodernas@edimodernas.com.co; internet www.empresario.com.co/edimodernas; f. 1991; juvenile.

Editora Cinco, SA: Calle 61, No 13-23, 7°, Apdo Aéreo 15188, Bogotá, DC; tel. (1) 285-6200; e-mail presidencia@editoracinco.com; recreation, culture, textbooks, general; Man. PEDRO VARGAS G.

Editorial Cypres Ltda: Carrera 15, No 80-36, Of. 302, Bogotá, DC; tel. (1) 691-0578; fax (1) 636-3824; e-mail cypres@etb.net.co; general interest and educational.

Editorial El Globo, SA: Calle 16, No 4-96, Apdo Aéreo 6806, Bogotá, DC.

Editorial Hispanoamérica: Carrera 56B, No 45-27, Bogotá, DC; tel. (1) 221-3020; fax (1) 315-5587; e-mail info@hispanoamerica.com.co; internet www.hispanoamerica.com.co; f. 1984; materials for primary education; Man. GABY TERESA CORTÉS; Editor ALVARO PINZÓN.

Editorial Paulinas: Calle 161A, No 31-50, Bogotá, DC; tel. (1) 522-0828; fax (1) 671-0992; e-mail ventasp@paulinas.org.co; internet www.paulinas.org.co; Christian and self-help.

Editorial Presencia, Ltda: Calle 23, No 24-20, Apdo Aéreo 41500, Bogotá, DC; tel. (1) 269-2188; fax (1) 269-6830; textbooks, tradebooks; Gen. Man. MARÍA UMAÑA DE TANCO.

Editorial San Pablo: Carrera 46, No 22A-90, Quintaparedes, Apdo Aéreo 080152, Bogotá, DC; tel. (1) 368-2099; fax (1) 244-4383; e-mail editorial@sanpablo.com.co; internet www.sanpablo.com.co; f. 1914; religion (Catholic); Editorial Dir Fr P. VICENTE MIOTTO.

Editorial Temis, SA: Calle 17, No 68D, Apdo Aéreo 46, Bogotá, DC; tel. (1) 424-7855; fax (1) 292-5801; e-mail editorial@editorialtemis.com; internet www.editorialtemis.com; f. 1951; law, sociology, politics; Man. Dir JORGE GUERRERO.

Editorial Voluntad, SA: Carrera 7A, No 24-89, 24°, Bogotá, DC; tel. (1) 241-0444; fax (1) 241-0439; e-mail voluntad@voluntad.com.co; internet www.voluntad.com.co; f. 1930; school books; Pres. GASTÓN DE BEDOUT.

Fondo de Cultura Económica: Calle 16, No 80-18, Bogotá, DC; tel. (1) 531-2288; fax (1) 531-1322; internet www.fce.com.co; f. 1934; academic; Dir CONSUELO SÁIZAR GUERRERO.

Fundación Centro de Investigación y Educación Popular (CINEP): Carrera 5A, No 33A-08, Apdo Aéreo 25916, Bogotá, DC; tel. (1) 245-6181; fax (1) 287-9089; internet www.cinep.org.co; f. 1977; education and social sciences; Man. Dir FRANCISCO DE ROUX.

Instituto Caro y Cuervo: Calle 10, No 4-69, Bogotá, DC; tel. (1) 342-2121; e-mail direcciongeneral@caroycuervo.gov.co; internet www.caroycuervo.gov.co; f. 1942; philology, general linguistics and reference; Man. Dir HERNANDO CABARCAS ANTEQUERA; Gen. Sec. LILIANA RIVERA OREJUELA.

Inversiones Cromos, SA: Avda El Dorado No 69-76, Bogotá, DC; tel. (1) 423-2300; fax (1) 423-7641; internet internet@cromos.com.co; f. 1916; Dir ALBERTO ZALAMEA; Gen. Man. JORGE EDUARDO CORREA ROBLEDO.

Legis, SA: Avda El Dorado, No 81-10, Apdo Aéreo 98888, Bogotá, DC; tel. (1) 425-5200; e-mail servicio@legis.com.co; internet www.legis.com.co; f. 1952; economics, law, general; Man. JUAN ALBERTO CASTRO.

McGraw Hill Interamericana, SA: Carrera 11, No 93-46, Oficina 301, Bogotá, DC; tel. (1) 600-3800; fax (1) 600-3822; internet www.mcgraw-hill.com.co; university textbooks; Dir-Gen. CARLOS G. MÁRQUEZ.

Publicar, SA: Avda 68, No 75A-50, 4°, Centro Comercial Metrópolis, Apdo Aéreo 8010, Bogotá, DC; tel. (1) 225-5555; fax (1) 225-4015; e-mail m-navia@publicar.com; internet www.publicar.com; f. 1959; directories; CEO MARÍA SOL NAVIA.

Siglo del Hombre Editores, SA: Carrera 31A, No 25B-50, Bogotá, DC; tel. (1) 337-7700; fax (1) 337-7665; e-mail info@siglodelhombre.com; f. 1992; arts, politics, anthropology, history, humanities; Gen. Man. EMILIA FRANCO DE ARCILA.

Tercer Mundo Editores, SA: Transversal 2A, No 67-27, Apdo Aéreo 4817, Bogotá, DC; tel. (1) 255-1539; fax (1) 212-5976; e-mail tmundoed@polcola.com.co; f. 1963; social sciences; Pres. SANTIAGO POMBO VEJARANO.

Thomson PLM: Calle 98, No 19A-21, Apdo Aéreo 52998, Bogotá, DC; tel. (1) 257-4400; fax (1) 616-7620; internet www.plmlatina.com; medical; Commerical Dir DANILO SÁNCHEZ.

Villegas Editores: Avda 82, No 11-50, Interior 3, Bogotá, DC; tel. (1) 616-1788; fax (1) 616-0020; internet www.villegaseditores.com; f. 1985; illustrated and scholarly.

ASSOCIATIONS

Cámara Colombiana del Libro: Calle 35, No. 5A-05, Bogotá, DC; tel. (1) 323-0111; fax (1) 285-1082; e-mail camlibro@camlibro.com.co; internet www.camlibro.com.co; f. 1951; Pres. ENRIQUE GONZÁLEZ VILLA; Exec. Dir JULIANA CÁLAD; 120 mems.

Colcultura: Biblioteca Nacional de Colombia, Calle 24, No 5-60, Apdo Aéreo 27600, Bogotá, DC; tel. (1) 282-8656; fax (1) 341-4028; e-mail mgiraldo@mincultura.go.co; Dir ISADORA DE NORDEN.

Fundalectura: Avda 40, No 16-46, Bogotá, DC; tel. (1) 320-1511; fax (1) 287-7071; e-mail contactenos@fundalectura.org.co; internet www.fundalectura.org.co; Exec. Dir CARMEN BARVO.

Broadcasting and Communications

GOVERNMENT AGENCIES

Comisión de Regulación de Telecomunicaciones (CRT): 28-01, Carrera 13, 8°, Bogotá, DC; tel. (1) 327-7000; fax (1) 327-7001; e-mail atencioncliente@crt.gov.co; internet www.crt.gov.co; f. 2000; regulatory body; Exec. Dir GABRIEL ADOLFO JURADO.

Ministerio de Comunicaciones, Dirección de Telecomunicaciones: Edif. Murillo Toro, Carreras 7A y 8A, entre Calle 12A y 13, Apdo Aéreo 14515, Bogotá, DC; tel. (1) 344-3460; fax (1) 286-1185; internet www.mincomunicaciones.gov.co; broadcasting authority; Dir MARÍA DEL ROSARIO GUERRA (Minister of Communications).

TELECOMMUNICATIONS

AT&T Colombia, SA: Calle 100, No 7-33, Edif. Capital Tower, Bogotá, DC; tel. (1) 650-0000; internet www.att.com.co; f. 1994; known as BellSouth Colombia until Dec. 2006; owned by Telefónica Móviles, SA (Spain); mobile telephone services.

Celumóvil, SA: Calle 71A, No 6-30, 18°, Bogotá, DC; tel. (1) 346-1666; fax (1) 211-2031; Sec.-Gen. CARLOS BERNARDO CARREÑO R.

COMCEL: Bogotá, DC; internet www.comcel.com.co; f. 1994 as Occidente y Caribe Celular, SA (Occel); present name adopted in 2000; merged with Celcaribe in 2003; owned by América Móvil, SA de CV (Mexico); cellular mobile telephone operator.

Colombia Telecomunicaciones, SA (TELECOM): Calle 23, No 13-49, Bogotá, DC; tel. (1) 286-0077; fax (1) 282-8768; internet www.telecom.com.co; f. June 2003 following dissolution of Empresa Nacional de Telecomunicaciones (f. 1947); 50% bought by Telefónica (Spain) in April 2006; fmr state telecommunications enterprise; Pres. ALFONSO GÓMEZ PALACIO.

Empresa de Telecomunicaciones de Bogotá, SA (ETB): Carrera 8, No 20-56, 3°–9°, Bogotá, DC; tel. (1) 242-3483; fax (1) 242-2127; e-mail adrimara@etb.com.co; internet www.etb.com.co; Bogotá telephone co; partially privatized in May 2003; Pres. RAFAEL ANTONIO ORDUZ MEDINA; Gen. Man. ADRIANA MARTÍNEZ MENDIETA.

BROADCASTING

Radio

The principal radio networks are as follows:

Cadena Melodía de Colombia: Calle 45, No 13-70, Bogotá, DC; tel. (1) 323-1500; fax (1) 288-4020; internet www.cadenamelodia.com; Pres. EFRAÍN PÁEZ ESPITIA.

Cadena Radial Auténtica: Calle 2, 9-53-67, Bogotá, DC; tel. (1) 246-5311; fax (1) 285-2505; e-mail cra@cmb.org.co; internet www.cmb.org.co/cra; f. 1983; stations include Radio Auténtica and Radio Mundial; Religious (Roman Catholic); Pres. JORGE ENRIQUE GÓMEZ MONTEALEGRE.

Cadena Radial La Libertad Ltda: Carrera 53, No 55-166, Apdo Aéreo 3143, Barranquilla; tel. (5) 31-1517; fax (5) 32-1279; news and music programmes for Barranquilla, Cartagena and Santa Marta; stations include Emisora Ondas del Caribe (youth programmes), Radio Libertad (classical music programmes) and Emisora Fuentes.

Cadena Super: Calle 16A, No 86A-78, Bogotá, DC; tel. (1) 618-1371; fax (1) 618-1360; internet www.cadenasuper.com; f. 1971; stations

COLOMBIA   *Directory*

include Radio Super and Super Stereo FM; Pres. JAIME PAVA NAVARRO.

CARACOL, SA (Primera Cadena Radial Colombiana, SA): Edif. Caracol Radio, Calle 67, No 7-37, Bogotá, DC; tel. (1) 348-7600; fax (1) 337-7126; internet www.caracol.com.co; f. 1948; 107 stations; Pres. JOSÉ MANUEL RESTREPO FERNÁNDEZ DE SOTO.

Circuito Todelar de Colombia: Avda 13, No 84-42, Apdo Aéreo 27344, Bogotá, DC; tel. (1) 616-1011; fax (1) 616-0056; f. 1953; 74 stations; Pres. BERNARDO TOBÓN DE LA ROCHE.

Colmundo Radio, SA ('La Cadena de la Paz'): Diagonal 58, 26A-29, Apdo Aéreo 36750, Bogotá, DC; tel. (1) 217-8911; fax (1) 348-2746; internet www.colmundo.com; f. 1989; Pres. Dr NÉSTOR CHAMORRO P.

Organización Radial Olímpica, SA (ORO, SA): Calle 72, No 48-37, 2°, Apdo Aéreo 51266, Barranquilla; tel. (5) 358-0500; fax (5) 345-9080; internet www.oro.com.co; programmes for the Antioquia and Atlantic coast regions.

Radio Cadena Nacional, SA (RCN Radio): Carrera 13A, No 37-32, Bogotá, DC; tel. (1) 314-7070; fax (1) 288-6130; e-mail rcn@impsat.net.co; internet www.rcn.com.co; 116 stations; official network; Pres. RICARDO LONDOÑO LONDOÑO.

Radiodifusora Nacional de Colombia: Centro Administrativo Nacional (CAN), Avda El Dorado 46, Bogotá, DC; tel. (1) 222-0925; fax (1) 222-2765; e-mail presidencia@inravision.gov.co; internet www.rtvc.gov.co; f. 1940; national public radio; Dir ATHALA MORRIS.

Radiodifusores Unidos, SA (RAU): Carrera 13, No 85-51, Of. 705, Bogotá, DC; tel. (1) 617-0584; commercial network of independent local and regional stations throughout the country.

Television

Television services began in 1954, and the NTSC colour television system was adopted in 1979. The government-run broadcasting network, INRAVISION, controls three national stations. Two national, privately run stations began broadcasts in mid-1988. There are also two regional stations and one local, non-profit station. Broadcasting time is distributed among competing programmers through a public tender.

Canal Uno: Centro Administrativo Nacional (CAN), Avda El Dorado, Bogotá, DC; tel. (1) 342-3777; fax (1) 341-6198; e-mail administrativa@telecolombia.com; internet www.telecolombia.com; formerly Cadena Uno; f. 1992; Dir FERNANDO BARRERO CHÁVEZ.

Canal 3: Centro Administrativo Nacional (CAN), Avda El Dorado, Bogotá, DC; tel. (1) 222-1640; fax (1) 222-1514; f. 1970; Exec. Dir RODRIGO ANTONIO DURÁN BUSTOS.

Canal A: Calle 35, No 7-51, CENPRO, Bogotá, DC; tel. (1) 232-3196; fax (1) 245-7526; f. 1966; Gen. Man. ROCÍO FERNÁNDEZ DEL CASTILLO.

Caracol Televisión, SA: Calle 76, No 11-35, Apdo Aéreo 26484, Bogotá, DC; tel. (1) 319-0860; fax (1) 321-1720; internet www.canalcaracol.com; f. 1969; Pres. RICARDO ALARCÓN GAVIRIA.

Teleantioquia: Edif. Anexo a EDATEL, 3°, Calle 41, No 52-28, Apdo Aéreo 8183, Medellín, Antioquia; tel. (4) 261-2222; fax (4) 262-0832; e-mail comunicaciones@teleantioquia.com.co; internet www.teleantioquia.com.co; f. 1985.

Telecafé: Carrera 19A, Calle 43, Sacatín contiguo Universidad Autónoma, Manizales, Caldas; tel. (68) 86-2949; fax (68) 86-3009; e-mail telecafe2004@epm.net.co; f. 1986; Gen. Man. ALBERTO LÓPEZ MARÍN.

TeleCaribe: Carrera 54, No 72-142, 4°, Barranquilla, Atlántico; tel. (5) 368-0183; fax (5) 360-7300; e-mail info@telecaribe.com.co; internet www.telecaribe.com.co; f. 1986; Pres. ARTURO SARMIENTO; Gen. Man. EDGAR REY SINNING.

Telepacífico: Calle 5A, No 38A-14, 3°, esq. Centro Comercial Imbanaco, Cali, Valle del Cauca; tel. (2) 518-4000; fax (2) 588-281; e-mail infotv@telepacifico.com; internet www.telepacifico.com; Gen. Man. LUIS GUILLERMO RESTREPO.

TV Cúcuta: tel. (7) 574-7874; fax (7) 575-2922; f. 1992; Pres. JOSÉ A. ARMELLA.

ASSOCIATION

Asociación Nacional de Medios de Comunicación (ASOMEDIOS): Carrera 19C, No 85-72, Bogotá, DC; tel. (1) 611-1300; fax (1) 621-6292; e-mail asomedio@cable.net.co; internet www.asomedios.com; f. 1978; merged with ANRADIO (Asociación Nacional de Radio, Televisión y Cine de Colombia) in 1980; Pres. SERGIO ARBOLEDA CASAS.

Finance

(cap. = capital; res = reserves; dep. = deposits; m. = million; amounts in pesos)

Contraloría General de la República: Carrera 10, No 17-18, Torre Colseguros, 27°, Bogotá, DC; tel. (1) 353-7700; fax (1) 353-7616; e-mail ahernandez@contraloriagen.gov.co; internet www.contraloriagen.gov.co; f. 1923; Controller-Gen. JULIO CÉSAR TURBAY QUINTERO.

BANKING

Supervisory Authority

Superintendencia Financiera de Colombia: Calle 7, No 4-49, 11°, Apdo Aéreo 3460, Bogotá, DC; tel. (1) 594-0200; fax (1) 350-7999; e-mail super@superfinanciera.gov.co; internet www.superfinanciera.gov.co; f. 2006 following merger of the Superintendencia Bancaria and the Superintendencia de Valores; Supt CÉSAR PRADO VILLEGAS.

Central Bank

Banco de la República: Carrera 7A, No 14-78, 5°, Apdo Aéreo 3531, Bogotá, DC; tel. (1) 343-1111; fax (1) 286-1686; e-mail wbanco@banrep.gov.co; internet www.banrep.gov.co; f. 1923; sole bank of issue; cap. 12,711.4m., res 15,009,002.4m., dep. 5,343,714.8m. (Dec. 2006); Gov. JOSÉ DARÍO URIBE ESCOBAR; 17 brs.

Commercial Banks

Bogotá, DC

ABN AMRO Bank (Colombia), SA (fmrly Banco Real de Colombia): Carrera 7A, No 115-33, 17°, Bogotá, DC; tel. (1) 521-9100; fax (1) 640-0675; internet www.abnamro.com; f. 1997; Pres. FABIO CASTELLANOS; 9 brs.

Bancafé: Calle 28, No 13A-15, 6°, Apdo Aéreo 240332, Bogotá, DC; tel. (1) 606-7614; fax (1) 606-7727; e-mail c.gaona@bancafe.com.co; internet www.bancafe.com; f. 1953; fmrly Banco Cafetero, SA; 99% owned by Fondo de Garantías de Instituciones Financieras de Colombia; cap. 108,794.0m., res 75,750.2m., dep. 5,015,437.5m. (Dec. 2003); Pres. ALVARO CARILLO BUITRAGO; 283 brs.

Banco Agrario de Colombia (Banagrario): Carrera 8, No 15-43, Bogotá, DC; tel. (1) 382-1400; fax (1) 599-5509; e-mail presidencia@bancoagrario.gov.co; internet www.banagrario.gov.co; f. 1999; state-owned; Pres. DAVID GUERRERO PÉREZ; 732 brs.

Banco de Bogotá: Calle 36, No 7-47, 15°, Apdo Aéreo 3436, Bogotá, DC; tel. (1) 332-0032; fax (1) 338-3302; internet www.bancodebogota.com.co; f. 1870; cap. 2,253.8m., res 1,714,939.0m., dep. 11,716,869.1m. (Dec. 2005); Pres. Dr ALEJANDRO FIGUEROA JARAMILLO; 286 brs.

Banco de Comercio Exterior de Colombia, SA (BANCOLDEX): Calle 28, No 13A-15, 40°, Apdo Aéreo 240092, Bogotá, DC; tel. (1) 382-1515; fax (1) 336-6984; internet www.bancoldex.com; f. 1992; provides financing alternatives for Colombian exporters; affiliate trust company FIDUCOLDEX, SA, manages PROEXPORT (Export Promotion Trust); cap. 855,670m., res 313,412m., dep. 845,976m. (Dec. 2006); Pres. JORGE HUMBERTO BOTERO ANGULO.

Banco de Crédito—Helm Financial Services: Calle 27, No 6-48, Bogotá, DC; tel. (1) 286-8400; fax (1) 251-8381; internet www.bancodecredito.com; f. 1963 as Banco de Crédito; present name adopted in 2000; cap. 138,001.7m., res 276,288.2m., dep. 3,067,820.7m. (Dec. 2006); Man. LUIS FERNANDO MESA PRIETO; 24 brs.

Banco GNB Sudameris Colombia, SA: Carrera 7, No 71-52, 19°, Torre B, Bogotá, DC; tel. (1) 325-5000; fax (1) 313-3259; internet www.sudameris.com.co; f. 2005 following merger of Banco Sudameris Colombia, SA and Banco Tequendama; cap. 40,459.8m., res 171,707.1m., dep. 2,782,195.1m. (Dec. 2006); Pres. and Chair. JORGE RAMÍREZ OCAMPO; 6 brs.

Banco Popular, SA: Calle 17, No 7-43, 3°, Apdo Aéreo 6796, Bogotá, DC; tel. (1) 339-5449; fax (1) 281-9448; e-mail vpinternacional@bancopopular.com.co; internet www.bancopopular.com.co; f. 1950; cap. 77,253m., res 628,424m., dep. 5,480,596m. (Dec. 2006); Int. Man. HERNANDO VIVAS V.; 190 brs.

Banistmo Colombia, SA: Carrera 7, No 71-21, Of. 1601, Torre B, 16°, Apdo Aéreo 3532, Bogotá, DC; tel. (1) 286-3155; fax (1) 281-8646; e-mail contactenos@hsbc.com.co; internet www.banistmo.com.co; f. 1976 as Banco Anglo Colombiano; present name adopted in 2005; bought by HSBC Bank PLC (United Kingdom) in 2006; cap. 129,046m., res 16,224m., dep. 1,055,743m. (Dec. 2005); 52 brs.

BBVA Colombia: Carrera 9A, No 72-21, 11°, Apdo Aéreo 53859, Bogotá, DC; tel. (1) 312-4666; fax (1) 347-1600; internet www.bbvaganadero.com.co; f. 1956 as Banco Ganadero; name changed as above in 2004; 73.7% owned by Banco Bilbao Vizcaya Argentaria, SA (Spain); cap. 89,779m., res 951,000m., dep. 11,041,704m. (Dec. 2006); Exec. Pres. LUIS B. JUANGO FITERO; 279 brs.

COLOMBIA   Directory

Citibank Colombia, SA: Carrera 9A, No 99-02, 3°, Bogotá, DC; tel. (1) 638-2420; fax (1) 618-2606; internet www.citibank.com.co; wholly owned subsidiary of Citibank (USA); Pres. STEVEN JOSÉ PUIG; 23 brs.

Cali

Banco de Occidente: Carrera 4, No 7-61, 12°, Apdo Aéreo 7607, Cali, Valle del Cauca; tel. (2) 886-1111; fax (2) 886-1298; e-mail dinternacional@bancodeoccidente.com.co; internet www.bancodeoccidente.com.co; f. 1965; cap. 3,821m., res 513,113m., dep. 4,818,272m. (Dec. 2004); 78.2% owned by Grupo Aval Acciones y Valores; Pres. EFRAÍN OTERO ÁLVAREZ; 122 brs.

Medellín

Bancolombia, SA: Carrera 52, No 50-20, Medellín, Antioquia; tel. (4) 576-6060; fax (4) 513-4827; e-mail mcarvaj@bancolombia.com.co; internet www.bancolombia.com.co; f. 1945; renamed 1998 following merger with Banco de Colombia; cap. 393,914m., res 2,430,986m., dep. 19,581,645m. (Dec. 2006); Pres. JORGE LONDOÑO SALDARRIAGA; Chair. JUAN CAMILO OCHOA; 385 brs.

Banco Santander: Edif. Bavaria, 16°, Carrera 46, No 52-36, Medellín, Antioquia; tel. (1) 284-3100; fax (1) 281-0311; internet www.bancosantander.com.co; f. 1961; fmrly Banco Comercial Antioqueño, SA; subsidiary of Banco Santander (Spain); cap. 198,731.1m., res 193,821m., dep. 3,536,562m. (Dec. 2006); Pres. MÓNICA IÑES MARÍA APARICIO SMITH; 30 brs.

Development Bank

BCSC: Carrera 7, No 77-65, 11°, Bogotá, DC; tel. (1) 313-8000; fax (1) 321-6912; e-mail csgarzon@fundacion-social.com.co; internet www.bcsc.com.co; f. 1911 as Banco Caja Social; name changed to above in 2005; cap. 185,392m., dep. 4,420,000m. (Dec. 2006); Pres. EULALIA ARBOLEDA DE MONTES; 260 brs.

Banking Associations

Asociación Bancaria y de Entidades Financieras de Colombia (Asobancaria): Carrera 9A, No 74-08, 9°, Bogotá, DC; tel. (1) 326-6612; fax (1) 326-6604; e-mail info@asobancaria.com; internet www.asobancaria.com; f. 1936; 56 mem. banks; Pres. MARÍA MERCEDES CUÉLLAR LÓPEZ.

Asociación Nacional de Instituciones Financieras (ANIF): Calle 70A, No 7-86, Bogotá, DC; tel. (1) 310-1500; fax (1) 235-5947; internet www.anif.org; f. 1974; Pres. Dr SERGIO CLAVIJO.

STOCK EXCHANGE

Bolsa de Valores de Colombia: Carrera 8A, No 13-82, 4°–8°, Apdo Aéreo 3584, Bogotá, DC; tel. (1) 243-6501; fax (1) 243-7327; internet www.bvc.com.co; f. 2001 following merger of stock exchanges of Bogotá, Medellín and Occidente; Pres. AUGUSTO ACOSTA TORRES; Sec.-Gen. MARÍA FERNANDA TORRES.

INSURANCE

Principal Companies

ACE Seguros, SA: Calle 72, No 10-51, 6°, 7° y 8°, Apdo Aéreo 29782, Bogotá, DC; tel. (1) 319-0300; fax (1) 319-0304; internet www.ace-ina.com; fmrly Cigna Seguros de Colombia, SA; Pres. MIGUEL SIERRA.

Afianzamiento y Seguros: Avda 3N, Suite 13N-09, Cali; tel. (2) 667-4401; fax (2) 668-2232; Man. ALDEMAR SARRIA.

Aseguradora Colseguros, SA: Carrera 13A, No 29-24, Parque Central Bavaria, Apdo Aéreo 3537, Bogotá, DC; tel. (1) 560-0600; fax (1) 561-6695; internet www.colseguros.com; f. 1874; Pres. MAX THIERMANN.

Aseguradora El Libertador, SA: Carrera 13, No 26-45, 9°, Apdo Aéreo 10285, Bogotá, DC; tel. (1) 281-2427; fax (1) 286-0662; e-mail aselib@impsat.net.co; Pres. FERNANDO ROJAS CÁRDENAS.

Aseguradora Solidaria de Colombia: Carrera 12, No 93-30, Apdo Aéreo 252030, Bogotá, DC; tel. (1) 621-4330; fax (1) 621-4321; e-mail eguzman@solidaria.com.co; internet www.solidaria.com.co; Pres. CARLOS GUZMÁN PÉREZ.

Chubb de Colombia Cía de Seguros, SA: Carrera 7A, No 71-52, Torre B, 10°, Bogotá, DC; tel. (1) 326-6200; fax (1) 326-6210; e-mail informaciongeneral@chubb.com; internet www.chubb.com.co; f. 1972; Pres. MANUEL OBREGÓN; 4 brs.

Cía Agrícola de Seguros, SA: Edif. Agrícola de Seguros, Suite 7-94, Calle 67, Bogotá, DC; tel. (1) 212-1100; fax (1) 635-5876; internet www.agricoladeseguros.com; f. 1952; Pres. Dr JOSÉ F. JARAMILLO HOYOS.

Cía Aseguradora de Fianzas, SA (Confianza): Calle 82, No 11-37, 7°, Apdo Aéreo 056965, Bogotá, DC; tel. (1) 617-0899; fax (1) 610-8866; e-mail correos@confianza.com.co; internet www.confianza.com.co; f. 1979; Pres. JOAQUÍN VEGA GARZÓN.

Cía Central de Seguros, SA: Carrera 7A, No 76-07, 9°, Apdo Aéreo 5764, Bogotá, DC; tel. (1) 319-0730; fax (1) 319-0749; e-mail francisco.arciniegas@qbecentral.com.co; internet www.centralseguros.com.co; f. 1956; Pres. SYLVIA LUZ RINCÓN LEMA.

Cía de Seguros Atlas, SA: Calle 21, No 23-22, 3°-11°, Apdo Aéreo 413, Manizales, Caldas; tel. (6) 884-1500; fax (6) 884-1447; e-mail satlas@andi.org.co; internet www.andi.org.co/seguros_atlas.htm; Pres. JORGE HOYOS MAYA.

Cía de Seguros Bolívar, SA: Carrera 10A, No 16-39, Apdo Aéreo 4421, Bogotá, DC; tel. (1) 341-0077; fax (1) 281-8262; internet www.segurosbolivar.com.co; f. 1939; Dir RAMÓN MENESES.

Cía de Seguros Colmena, SA: Calle 72, No 10-07, 7° y 8°, Apdo Aéreo 6774, Bogotá, DC; tel. (1) 211-4971; fax (1) 211-4952; internet www.colmena-arp.com.co; Dir-Gen. JUAN MANUEL DÍAZ-GRANADOS.

Cía de Seguros de Créditos Comerciales (CREDISEGURO): Calle 49, 63-110, 1°, Bogotá, DC; tel. (1) 435-5355; fax (1) 260-1773; e-mail marivere@suramericana.com.co; internet www.crediseguro.com.co.

Cía Mundial de Seguros, SA: Calle 33, No 6–24, 2° y 3°, Bogotá, DC; tel. (1) 285-5600; fax (1) 285-1220; internet www.mundialseguros.com.co; f. 1995; Dir-Gen. CAMILO FERNÁNDEZ ESCOVAR.

Cía Suramericana Administradora de Riesgos Profesionales y Seguros de Vida, SA (SURATEP): Centro Suramericana, Edif. Torre Suratep, Calle 49A, No. 63-55, Bogotá, DC; tel. (1) 430-7100; fax (1) 231-8080; e-mail servicioalcliente@suratep.com.co; internet www.suratep.com; f. 1996.

Cía Suramericana de Seguros, SA: Centro Suramericana, Carrera 64B, No 49A-30, Apdo Aéreo 780, Medellín, Antioquia; tel. (4) 260-2100; fax (4) 260-3194; e-mail contactenos@suramericana.com.co; internet www.suramericana.com.co; f. 1944; Pres. GONZALO ALBERTO PÉREZ ROJAS.

Condor, SA, Cía de Seguros Generales: Calle 119, No 16-59, Apdo Aéreo 57018, Bogotá, DC; tel. (1) 612-0666; fax (1) 215-6121; Pres. EUDORO CARVAJAL IBÁÑEZ.

La Equidad Seguros, Organización Cooperativa: Torre La Equidad Seguros, 1°, Carrera 9A, 99-07, Bogotá, DC; tel. (1) 592-2929; fax (1) 592-2910; e-mail equidad@laequidad.com.co; internet www.laequidad.com.co; Dir ALBERTO MORA.

Generali Colombia—Seguros Generales, SA: Carrera 7A, No 72-13, 8°, Apdo Aéreo 076478, Bogotá, DC; tel. (1) 346-8888; fax (1) 255-1164; e-mail presidencia@generali.com.co; internet www.generali.com.co; f. 1937; Pres. EDUARDO SARMIENTO.

La Interamericana Cía de Seguros Generales, SA: Calle 78, No 9-57, 4° y 5°, Apdo Aéreo 92381, Bogotá, DC; tel. (1) 322-0304; fax (1) 210-0765; Pres. DIDIER SERRANO.

La Previsora, SA, Cía de Seguros: Calle 57, No 8-93, Apdo Aéreo 52946, Bogotá, DC; tel. (1) 211-2880; fax (1) 211-8717; internet www.previsora.com; f. 1914; Pres. ALBERTO QUINTANA; Exec. Pres. JUAN CARLOS MALDONADO.

Liberty Seguros, SA: Calle 71A, No 6-30, 2°, 3°, 4° y 14°, Apdo Aéreo 100327, Bogotá, DC; tel. (1) 212-4900; fax (1) 212-7706; e-mail lhernandez@impsat.net.co; internet www.libertycolombia.com.co; f. 1954; fmrly Latinoamericana de Seguros, SA; Pres. MAURICIO GARCÍA ORTIZ.

Mapfre Seguros Generales de Colombia, SA: Carrera 7A, No 74-36, 2°, Apdo Aéreo 28525, Bogotá, DC; tel. (1) 343-6180; fax (1) 346-8793; internet www.mapfre.com.co; f. 1995; Pres. JOSÉ MANUEL INCHAUSTI.

Pan American de Colombia Cía de Seguros de Vida, SA: Carrera 7A, No 75-09, Apdo Aéreo 76000, Bogotá, DC; tel. (1) 212-1300; fax (1) 217-8799; internet www.panamericanlife.com; Gen. Man. ALFONSO PONTÓN.

Royal and Sun Alliance Seguros (Colombia), SA: Carrera 7A, No 32-33, 6°, 7°, 11° y 12°, Bogotá, DC; tel. (1) 561-0380; fax (1) 320-3726; internet www.royalsunalliance.com.co; fmrly Seguros Fénix, SA; Pres. DINAND BLOM.

Segurexpo de Colombia, SA: Calle 72, No 6-44, 12°, Apdo Aéreo 75140, Bogotá, DC; tel. (1) 326-6969; fax (1) 211-0218; e-mail bogota@segurexpo.com; internet www.segurexpo.com; f. 1993; Pres. JUAN PABLO LUQUE LUQUE.

Seguros Alfa, SA: Carrera 13, No 27-47, 22° y 23°, Apdo Aéreo 27718, Bogotá, DC; tel. (1) 344-4720; fax (1) 344-6770; e-mail presidencia@segurosalfa.com.co; internet www.segurosalfa.com.co; Pres. ANGELA MENDOZA.

Seguros Colpatria, SA: Carrera 7A, No 24-89, 9°, Apdo Aéreo 7762, Bogotá, DC; tel. (1) 241-7430; e-mail uinversion@banco.colpatria.com.co; internet www.colpatria.com; Pres. Dr FERNANDO QUINTERO.

Seguros del Estado, SA: Carrera 11, No 90-20, Apdo Aéreo 6810, Bogotá, DC; tel. (1) 218-6977; fax (1) 218-0971; e-mail generales-dhernandez@segurosdelestado.com; internet www.segurosdelestado.com; Gen. Man. DANILO HERNÁNDEZ AZULA.

COLOMBIA
Directory

Skandia Seguros de Vida, SA: Avda 19, No 113-30, Apdo Aéreo 100327, Bogotá, DC; tel. (1) 620-5566; fax (1) 214-0038; e-mail cwills@skandia.com.co; internet www.skandia.com.co; Pres. CAMILO WILLS FRANCO.

Insurance Association

Federación de Aseguradores Colombianos (FASECOLDA): Carrera 7A, No 26-20, 11° y 12°, Apdo Aéreo 5233, Bogotá, DC; tel. (1) 210-8080; fax (1) 210-7041; e-mail fasecolda@fasecolda.com; internet www.fasecolda.com; f. 1976; 30 mems; Exec. Pres. ROBERTO JUNGUITO BONNET.

Trade and Industry

GOVERNMENT AGENCIES

Agencia Nacional de Hidrocarburos (ANH): Calle 99, No 9A-54, 14°, Bogotá, DC; tel. (1) 593-1717; fax (1) 593-1718; e-mail info@anh.gov.co; internet www.anh.gov.co; f. 2003; govt agency responsible for regulation of the petroleum industry; Dir-Gen. JOSÉ ARMANDO ZAMORA REYES.

Departamento Nacional de Planeación: Calle 26, No 13-19, 14°, Bogotá, DC; tel. (1) 336-1600; fax (1) 281-3348; e-mail vgonzalez@dnp.gov.co; internet www.dnp.gov.co; f. 1958; supervises and administers devt projects; approves foreign investments; Dir-Gen. CAROLINA RENTERÍA RODRÍGUEZ.

Superintendencia de Industria y Comercio (SUPERINDUSTRIA): Carrera 13, No 27-00, 5°, Bogotá, DC; tel. (1) 382-0840; fax (1) 382-2696; e-mail info@sic.gov.co; internet www.sic.gov.co; supervises chambers of commerce; controls standards and prices; Supt GUSTAVO VALBUENA QUIÑONES.

Superintendencia de Sociedades (SUPERSOCIEDADES): Avda El Dorado, No 46-80, Apdo Aéreo 4188, Bogotá, DC; tel. (1) 324-5777; fax (1) 324-5000; e-mail webmaster@supersociedades.gov.co; internet www.supersociedades.gov.co; f. 1931; oversees activities of local and foreign corpns; Supt HERNANDO RUIZ LÓPEZ.

DEVELOPMENT AGENCIES

Agencia Presidencial para la Acción Social y la Cooperación Internacional: Calle 7, No 6-54, Bogotá, DC; tel. (1) 352-6666; fax (1) 284-4120; internet www.accionsocial.gov.co; f. 2005 following merger of Red de Solidaridad Social (RSS) y la Agencia Colombiana de Cooperación Internacional (ACCI); govt agency intended to channel domestic and international funds into social programmes.

Asociación Colombiana de Ingeniería Sanitaria y Ambiental (ACODAL): Calle 39, No 14-75, Bogotá, DC; tel. (1) 245-9539; fax (1) 323-1407; internet www.acodal.org.co; f. 1956 as Asociación Colombiana de Acueductos y Alcantarillados; asscn promoting sanitary and environmental engineering projects; Pres. MARYLUZ MEJÍA DE PUMAREJO; Man. JOSÉ FERNANDO CÁRDENAS.

Asociación Colombiana de las Micro, Pequeñas y Medianas Empresas (ACOPI): Carrera 15, No 36-70, Bogotá, DC; tel. and fax (1) 320-4783; e-mail comunicaciones@acopi.org.co; internet www.acopi.org.co; f. 1951; promotes small and medium-sized industries; Pres. Dr NORMAN CORREA CALDERÓN.

Centro Internacional de Educación y Desarrollo Humano (CINDE): Edif. Las Tres Carabelas, El Laguito, Cartagena; tel. (5) 665-5100; fax (5) 665-0319; e-mail cinde@cinde.org.co; internet www.cinde.org.co; education and social devt; f. 1977; Pres. JAIME OLARTE RESTREPO.

Corporación para la Investigación Socioeconómica y Tecnológica de Colombia (CINSET): Carrera 48, No 91-94, La Castellana, Bogotá, DC; tel. (1) 256-0961; fax (1) 218-6416; e-mail cinset@cinset.org.co; internet www.cinset.org.co; f. 1987; social, economic and technical devt projects; Pres. NORMAN CORREA CALDERÓN; Exec. Dir JUAN CARLOS GUTIÉRREZ ARIAS.

Corporación Región: Calle 55, No 41-10, Medellín; tel. (4) 216-6822; fax (4) 239-5544; e-mail coregion@region.org.co; internet www.region.org.co; f. 1989; environmental, political and social devt; Pres. RUBÉN HERNANDO FERNÁNDEZ ANDRADE.

Fondo Financiero de Proyectos de Desarrollo (FONADE): Calle 26, No 13-19, 19°-22°, Apdo Aéreo 24110, Bogotá, DC; tel. (1) 594-0407; fax (1) 282-6018; e-mail fonade@colomsat.net.co; internet www.fonade.gov.co; f. 1968; responsible for channelling loans towards economic devt projects; administered by a cttee under the head of the Departamento Nacional de Planeación; FONADE works in close asscn with other official planning orgs; Gen. Man. Dr ELVIRA FORERO HERNÁNDEZ.

Fundación para el Desarrollo Integral del Valle del Cauca (FDI): Calle 8, No 3-14, 3°, Apdo Aéreo 7482, Cali, Valle del Cauca; tel. (2) 886-1300; f. 1969; industrial devt org.; Pres. JULIAN DOMÍNGUEZ RIVERA.

Instituto Colombiano de Desarrollo Rural: Centro Administrativo Nacional (CAN), Avda Eldorado, Calle 43, No 57–41, Bogotá, DC; e-mail incoder@incoder.gov.co; internet www.incoder.gov.co; rural devt agency.

CHAMBERS OF COMMERCE

Confederación Colombiana de Cámaras de Comercio (CONFECAMARAS): Of. 502, Carrera 13, No 27-47, Apdo Aéreo 29750, Bogotá, DC; tel. (1) 346-7055; fax (1) 346-7026; e-mail confecamaras@confecamaras.org.co; internet www.confecamaras.org.co; f. 1969; 56 mem. orgs; Exec. Pres. EUGENIO MARULANDA GÓMEZ.

Cámara Colombo Japonesa de Comercio e Industria: Calle 72, No 7-82, 7°, Bogotá, DC; tel. (1) 210-0383; fax (1) 349-0736; internet www.camaracolombojaponesa.com.co; f. 1988; Colombian-Japanese trade asscn; Pres. JAIME ROA DREWS.

Cámara Colombo Venezolana: Calle 72, No 8-24, Of. 503, Edif. Suramericana, Bogotá, DC; tel. (1) 211-6224; fax (1) 211-6089; e-mail info@comvenezuela.com; internet www.comvenezuela.com; f. 1977; Colombian-Venezuelan trade asscn; 19 mem. cos; Pres. MARÍA LUISA CHIPPE.

Cámara de Comercio de Bogotá: Avda Eldorado, 68D-35, Bogotá, DC; tel. (1) 383-0300; fax (1) 284-7735; e-mail webmaster@ccb.org.co; internet www.ccb.org.co; f. 1878; 3,650 mem. orgs; Pres. SERGIO MUTIS CABALLERO.

Cámara de Comercio Colombo Americano (Colombian-American Chamber of Commerce): Of. 1209, Calle 98, No 22-64, Bogotá, DC; tel. (1) 623-7088; fax (1) 621-6838; e-mail website@amchamcolombia.com.co; internet www.amchamcolombia.com.co; f. 1955; Colombian–US trade asscn.

Cámara de Comercio Colombo Británica (British-Colombian Chamber of Commerce): Of. 409, Calle 95, No 13-55, Bogotá, DC; tel. (1) 621-2401; fax (1) 621-2431; e-mail britcham@colombobritanica.com; internet www.colombobritanica.com.

There are also local Chambers of Commerce in the capital towns of all the Departments and in many of the other trading centres.

INDUSTRIAL AND TRADE ASSOCIATIONS

Corporación de la Industria Aeronáutica Colombiana, SA (CIAC SA): Avda Calle 26, No 103-08, Entrada 1, Bogotá, DC; tel. (1) 413-8312; e-mail info@ciac.gov.co; internet www.ciac.gov.co; Gen. Man. ALBERTO MELÉNDEZ.

Industria Militar (INDUMIL): Calle 44, No 51-11, Apdo Aéreo 7272, Bogotá, DC; tel. (1) 220-7800; fax (1) 222-4889; internet www.indumil.gov.co; attached to Ministry of National Defence; Man. Adm. (retd) MANUEL F. AVENDAÑO.

Instituto Colombiano Agropecuario (ICA): Calle 37, No 8-43, 4° y 5°, Bogotá, DC; tel. (1) 285-5520; fax (1) 232-4689; e-mail info@ica.gov.co; internet www.ica.gov.co; f. 1962; attached to the Ministry of Agriculture and Rural Devt; institute for promotion, co-ordination and implementation of research into and teaching and devt of agriculture and animal husbandry.

Instituto de Hidrología, Meteorología y Estudios Ambientales (IDEAM): Diagonal 97, No 17-60, 1°, 2°, 3° y 7°, Bogotá, DC; tel. (1) 283-6927; fax (1) 635-6218; internet www.ideam.gov.co; f. 1995; responsible for irrigation, flood control, drainage, hydrology and meteorology; Dir PABLO LEYVA.

Instituto de Investigación e Información Geocientífica, Mineroambiental y Nuclear (INGEOMINAS): Diagonal 53, No 34-53, Apdo Aéreo 4865, Bogotá, DC; tel. (1) 222-1811; fax (1) 220-0582; e-mail henciso@ingeominas.gov.co; internet www.ingeominas.gov.co; f. 1968; responsible for mineral research, geological mapping and research including hydrogeology, remote sensing, geochemistry, geophysics and geological hazards; Dir Dr ADOLFO ALARCÓN GUZMÁN.

There are several other agricultural and regional development organizations.

EMPLOYERS' AND PRODUCERS' ORGANIZATIONS

Asociación Colombiana de Cooperativos (ASCOOP): Transversal 29, No 35-29, Bogotá, DC; tel. (1) 368-3500; fax (1) 268-4230; e-mail comunicaciones@ascoop.coop; internet www.ascoop.coop; promotes co-operatives; Exec. Dir CARLOS E. ACERO.

Asociación de Cultivadores de Caña de Azúcar de Colombia (ASOCAÑA): Calle 58N, No 3N-15, Apdo Aéreo 4448, Cali, Valle del Cauca; tel. (2) 64-7902; fax (2) 64-5888; internet www.asocana.com.co; f. 1959; sugar planters' asscn; Pres. MAURICIO IRAGORRI RIZO.

Asociación Nacional de Comercio Exterior (ANALDEX): Carrera 10, No 27, Int. 137, Of. 902, Apdo Aéreo 29812, Bogotá, DC; tel. (1) 342-0788; fax (1) 284-6911; e-mail analdex@analdex.org; internet www.analdex.org; exporters' asscn; Pres. JAVIER DÍAZ MOLINA.

Asociación Nacional de Empresarios (ANDI) (National Asscn of Manufacturers): Calle 52, No 47-48, Apdo Aéreo 997, Medellín, Antioquia; tel. (4) 511-1177; fax (4) 511-7575; e-mail comercial@

andi.com.co; internet www.andi.com.co; f. 1944; Pres. LUIS CARLOS VILLEGAS ECHEVERRI; 9 brs; 756 mems.

Asociación Nacional de Exportadores de Café de Colombia: Calle 72, No 10-07, Of. 1101, Bogotá, DC; tel. (1) 347-8419; fax (1) 347-9523; e-mail asoexport@asoexport.org; internet www.asoexport.org; f. 1933; private asscn of coffee exporters; Pres. JORGE E. LOZANO MANCERA.

Federación Colombiana de Ganaderos (FEDEGAN): Carrera 14, No 36-65, Apdo Aéreo 9709, Bogotá, DC; tel. (1) 245-3041; fax (1) 232-7153; e-mail fedegan@fedegan.org.co; internet www.fedegan.org.co; f. 1963; cattle raisers' asscn; about 350,000 affiliates; Pres. JORGE VISBAL MARTELO.

Federación Nacional de Cacaoteros: Carrera 17, No 30-39, Apdo Aéreo 17736, Bogotá, DC; tel. (1) 288-7188; fax (1) 288-4424; e-mail f_cacaoteros@hotmail.com; internet www.fedecacao.com.co; fed. of cocoa growers; Gen. Man. Dr JOSÉ OMAR PINZÓN USECHE.

Federación Nacional de Cafeteros de Colombia (FEDERACAFE) (National Federation of Coffee Growers): Calle 73, No 8-13, Apdo Aéreo 57534, Bogotá, DC; tel. (1) 217-0600; fax (1) 217-1021; internet www.cafedecolombia.com; f. 1927; totally responsible for fostering and regulating the coffee economy; Gen. Man. Dr GABRIEL SILVA LUJÁN; 203,000 mems.

Federación Nacional de Comerciantes (FENALCO): Carrera 4, No 19-85, 7°, Bogotá, DC; tel. (1) 350-0600; fax (1) 350-9424; e-mail fenalco@fenalco.com.co; internet www.fenalco.com.co; business fed; Pres. GUILLERMO BOTERO NIETO.

Federación Nacional de Cultivadores de Cereales y Leguminosas (FENALCE): Carrera 14, No 97-62, Apdo Aéreo 8694, Bogotá, DC; tel. (1) 218-2114; fax (1) 218-9463; e-mail fenalce@cable.net.co; internet www.fenalce.org; f. 1960; fed. of grain growers; Pres. CARLOS ADEL KAFRUNI; 30,000 mems.

Sociedad de Agricultores de Colombia (SAC) (Colombian Farmers' Society): Carrera 7A, No 24-89, 44°, Apdo Aéreo 3638, Bogotá, DC; tel. (1) 281-0263; fax (1) 284-4572; e-mail socdeagr@impsat.net.co; internet www.sac.org.co; f. 1871; Pres. RAFAEL MEJÍA LÓPEZ.

There are several other organizations, including those for rice growers, engineers and financiers.

UTILITIES
Electricity

Corporación Eléctrica de la Costa Atlántica (Corelca): Calle 55, No 72-109, 9°, Barranquilla, Atlántico; tel. (5) 356-0200; fax (5) 356-2370; internet www.corelca.gov.co; responsible for supplying electricity to the Atlantic departments; generates more than 2,000m. kWh annually from thermal power-stations; Man. Dir HERNÁN CORREA NOGUERA.

Empresa de Energía de Bogotá, SA (EEB): Avda El Dorado, No 55-51, Bogotá, DC; tel. (1) 221-1665; fax (1) 221-6858; e-mail jpacheco@eeb.com.co; internet www.eeb.com.co; provides electricity for Bogotá area by generating capacity of 680 MW, mainly hydroelectric; Man. Dir LUIS EDUARDO GARZÓN.

Instituto Colombiano de Energía Eléctrica (ICEL): Carrera 13, No 27-00, 3°, Apdo Aéreo 16243, Bogotá, DC; tel. (1) 342-0181; fax (1) 286-2934; formulates policy for the devt of electrical energy; constructs systems for the generation, transmission and distribution of electrical energy; Man. DOUGLAS VELÁSQUEZ JACOME; Sec.-Gen. PATRICIA OLIVEROS LAVERDE.

Interconexión Eléctrica, SA (ISA): Calle 12 Sur, No 18-168, El Poblado, Apdo Aéreo 8915, Medellín, Antioquia; tel. (4) 325-2270; fax (4) 317-0848; e-mail isa@isa.com.co; internet www.isa.com.co; f. 1967; created by Colombia's principal electricity production and distribution cos to form a national network; installed capacity of 2,641m. kWh; operates major power-stations at Chivor and San Carlos; public co; Gen. Man. LUIS FERNANDO ALARCÓN MANTILLA.

Isagen: Medellín, Antioquia; e-mail isagen@isagen.com.co; internet www.isagen.com.co; f. 1995 following division of ISA (q.v.); state-owned; generates electricity from three hydraulic and two thermal power plants; Gen. Man. Ing. LUIS FERNANDO RICO PINZÓN.

Gas

Empresa Colombiana de Gas (Ecogás): Of. 209, Centro Internacional de Negocios La Triada, Calle 35, No 19-41, Bucaramanga, Santander; tel. (7) 642-1000; fax (7) 642-6446; e-mail lparra@ecogas.com.co; internet www.ecogas.com.co; f. 1997; operation and maintenance of gas-distribution network; sold in 2006 to Empresa de Energía de Bogotá, SA; Dir FEDERICO ARANGO TORO.

Gas Natural, SA ESP: Avda 40A, No 13-09, 9°, Bogotá, DC; tel. (1) 338-1199; fax (1) 288-0807; internet portal.gasnatual.com; f. 1987; owned by Gas Natural of Spain; distributes natural gas in Bogotá and Soacha; Pres. MARÍA EUGENIA CORONADO.

TRADE UNIONS

Central Unitaria de Trabajadores (CUT): Calle 35, No 7-25, 9°, Apdo Aéreo 221, Bogotá, DC; tel. (1) 323-7550; fax (1) 323-7550; e-mail cut@cut.org.co; internet www.cut.org.co; f. 1986; comprises 50 feds and 80% of all trade-union members; Pres. CARLOS RODRÍGUEZ DÍAZ; Sec.-Gen. BORIS MONTES DE OCA ANAYA.

Federación Colombiana de Educadores (FECODE): Carrera 13A, No 34-54, Bogotá, DC; tel. (1) 338-1711; fax (1) 285-3245; internet fecode.edu.co; Pres. WITNEY CHÁVEZ SÁNCHEZ.

Federación Nacional de Loteros (FECOLOT): Cale 27, No 25-38, Bogotá, DC; tel. (1) 232-1041; fax (1) 232-1045; lottery ticket sellers' union; Pres. ALBERTO TARRIBA.

Federación Nacional Sindical Unitaria Agropecuaria (FENSUAGRO): Calle 17, No 10-16, Of. 104, Bogotá, DC; tel. (1) 282-8871; e-mail fensuagro@hotmail.com; f. 1976 as Federación Nacional Sindical Agropecuaria (FENSA); comprises 37 unions, 7 peasant asscns, with 80,000 mems; Pres. EVERTO DÍAZ.

Federación Nacional Sindicatos Bancarios Colombianos (FENASIBANCOL): Calle 30A, No 6-22, Of. 1601, Bogotá, DC; tel. (1) 287-5728; fax (1) 288-0235; e-mail fena@colomsat.net.co; Pres. EDUARDO CALA FLÓREZ.

Federación Nacional de Sindicatos de Trabajadores de Empresas y Entidades de Servicios Públicos y Oficiales (FENASINTRAP): Carrera 19, No 1C-47, Bogotá, DC; tel. (1) 246-4327; Pres. ROBERTO RUBIANO BORJA.

Federación Nacional de Trabajadores de Alimentación, Bebidas, Afines y Similar (Fentralimentación): Calle 8 sur, 68B-60, Bogotá, DC; tel. (1) 414-6505; fax (1) 290-0390; represents the food and drink industry; Pres. ALFONSO LÓPEZ FREYLE.

Federación Nacional de Trabajadores al Servicio del Estado (FENALTRESE): Calle 17, No 5-21, Of. 502, Bogotá DC; tel. (1) 334-4815; e-mail fenaltrese@hotmail.com; Pres. ROBERTO CHAMUCERO.

FUNTRAENERGETICA: Calle 16, No 13-49, Of. 201, Bogotá, DC; tel. (1) 334-0447; fax (1) 286-5459; e-mail funtraenergetica@007mundo.com; f. 2001 following merger of Funtrammetal and Fedepetrol; represents workers in the energy sector; Pres. JOAQUÍN ROMERO.

Unión Sindical Obrera de la Indústria del Petróleo (USO): Calle 38, No 13-37, Of. 302, Bogota; e-mail medios@usofrenteobrero.org; internet www.usofrenteobrero.org; f. 1922; petroleum workers' union; affiliated to CUT; Sec.-Gen. (vacant); 3,200 mems.

Unión de Trabajadores de Colombia (UTRAMMICOL): tel. (1) 288-5728; fax (1) 285-0663; e-mail utrammicol@multiphone.net.co; Pres. LUIS CARLOS VELÁSQUEZ.

Confederación General del Trabajo (CGT): Calle 39A, No 14-52, Bogotá, DC; tel. (1) 288-1504; fax (1) 573-4021; e-mail cgt@etb.net.co; internet www.cgtcolombia.org; Sec.-Gen. JULIO ROBERTO GÓMEZ ESGUERRA.

Confederación de Trabajadores de Colombia (CTC) (Colombian Confederation of Workers): Calle 39, No 26A-23, 5°, Apdo Aéreo 4780, Bogotá, DC; tel. (1) 269-7119; e-mail ctc1@etb.net.co; internet www.ctc-colombia.com.co; f. 1934; mainly Liberal; 600 affiliates, including 6 national orgs and 20 regional feds; admitted to the International Trade Union Confederation; Pres. APECIDES ALVIS FERNÁNDEZ; 400,000 mems.

Transport

Land transport in Colombia is rendered difficult by high mountains, so the principal means of long-distance transport is by air.

Superintendencia de Puertos y Transporte: Ministerio de Transporte, Edif. Estación de la Sabana. 3°, Calle 13, No 18-24, Bogotá, DC; tel. (2) 352-6700; e-mail info@superpuertos.gov.co; internet www.supertransporte.gov.co; f. 1992 as Superintendencia General de Puertos, present name adopted in 1998; part of the Ministry of Transport; oversees transport sector; Supt ALVARO HERNANDO CARDONA GONZÁLEZ.

Instituto Nacional de Concesiones (INCO): Edif. Ministerio de Transporte, Centro Administrativo Nacional (CAN), 3°, Avda El Dorado, Bogotá, DC; tel. (1) 324-0800; e-mail contactenos@inco.gov.co; internet www.inco.gov.co; govt agency charged with devt of transport infrastructure; part of the Ministry of Transport; Gen. Man. ALVARO JOSÉ SOTO GARCÍA.

RAILWAYS

In 2000 there were 3,304 km of track. The Instituto Nacional de Concesiones (q.v.) operates the Red Ferrea del Atlántico and the Red Ferrea del Pacífico.

COLOMBIA																																				Directory

Instituto Nacional de Vías (INVIAS): Edif. INVIAS, Centro Administrativo Nacional (CAN), Transversal 45, No 26-60, Bogotá, DC; internet www.invias.gov.co; govt agency responsible for railway infrastructure; part of the Ministry of Transport; Dir-Gen. DANIEL ANDRÉS GARCÍA ARIZABALETA.

El Cerrejón Mine Railway: International Colombia Resources Corpn, Carrera 54, No 72-80, Apdo Aéreo 52499, Barranquilla, Atlántico; tel. (5) 350-5389; fax (5) 350-2249; internet www.elcerrejoncoal.com; f. 1989 to link the mine and the port at Puerto Bolívar; 150 km.

Ferrocarriles del Norte de Colombia, SA (FENOCO, SA): Calle 94A, No 11A-27, Bogotá, DC; tel. (1) 622-0505; operates the Concesión de la Red Férrea del Atlántico.

Metro de Medellín: Calle 44, No 46-001, Apdo Aéreo 9128, Medellín, Antioquia; tel. (4) 452-6000; fax (4) 452-4450; internet www.metrodemedellin.org.co; f. 1995; five-line metro system; Gen. Man. Dr RAMIRO MÁRQUEZ RAMÍREZ.

Sociedad de Transporte Férreo de Occidente, SA: Avda Vásquez Cobo, Estación Ferrocarril, 2°, Cali; tel. (2) 660-3314; fax (2) 660-3320; runs freight services between Cali and the port of Buenaventura.

Tren de Occidente, SA: Carrera 14, No 94A-24, Of. 202, Bogotá, DC; tel. (1) 635-9208; operates the Concesión de la Red Férrea del Pacífico.

ROADS

In 2002 there were 110,000 km of roads, of which 26,000 km was paved. The country's main highways are the Caribbean Trunk Highway, the Eastern and Western Trunk Highways, the Central Trunk Highway and there are also roads into the interior. There are plans to construct a Jungle Edge highway to give access to the interior, a link road between Turbo, Bahía Solano and Medellín, a highway between Bogotá and Villavicencio and to complete the short section of the Pan-American Highway between Panama and Colombia.

Transmilenio: Edif. Ministerio de Transporte, Centro Administrativo Nacional (CAN), 3°, Avda El Dorado, No 66-63, Bogotá, DC; tel. (1) 220-3000; fax (1) 324-9870; internet www.transmilenio.gov.co; f. 2000; bus-based mass transit system in Bogotá.

INLAND WATERWAYS

The Magdalena–Cauca river system is the centre of river traffic and is navigable for 1,500 km, while the Atrato is navigable for 687 km. The Orinoco system has more than five navigable rivers, which total more than 4,000 km of potential navigation (mainly through Venezuela); the Amazon system has four main rivers, which total 3,000 navigable km (mainly through Brazil). There are plans to connect the Arauca with the Meta, and the Putumayo with the Amazon, and also to construct an Atrato–Truandó inter-oceanic canal.

SHIPPING

The four most important ocean terminals are Buenaventura on the Pacific coast and Santa Marta, Barranquilla and Cartagena on the Atlantic coast. The port of Tumaco on the Pacific coast is gaining in importance and there are plans for construction of a deep-water port at Bahía Solano. In December 2006 Colombia's merchant fleet totalled 96,167 grt.

Port Authorities

Sociedad Portuaria Regional de Barranquilla: Carrera 38, Calle 1A, Barranquilla, Atlántico; tel. (5) 371-6200; fax (5) 371-6310; e-mail info@sprb.com.co; internet www.sprb.com.co; privatized in 1993; Port Man. ERNESTO DURÁN GONZÁLEZ.

Sociedad Portuaria Regional de Buenaventura: Edif. de Administración, Avda Portuaria, Apdo 478-10765, Buenaventura; tel. 241-0700; internet www.puertobuenaventura.com; Port Man. VÍCTOR GONZÁLEZ.

Sociedad Portuaria Regional de Cartagena: Manga, Terminal Marítimo, Cartagena, Bolívar; tel. (5) 660-8071; fax (5) 650-2239; e-mail comercial@sprc.com; internet www.puertocartagena.com; f. 1993; Port Man. ALFONSO SALAS TRUJILLO; Harbour Master VICTOR D. HURTADO.

Sociedad Portuaria de Santa Marta: Carrera 1, 10A-12, Apdo 655, Santa Marta; tel. (5) 421-1311; fax (5) 421-2161; e-mail spsm@spsm.com.co; internet www.spsm.com.co; Port Man. JULIÁN PALACIOS.

Principal Shipping Companies

Colombiana Internacional de Vapores, Ltda (Colvapores): Avda Caracas, No 35-02, Apdo Aéreo 17227, Bogotá, DC; e-mail colvabao@metrotel.net.co; internet www.colvapores.com; cargo services mainly to the USA.

Flota Mercante Grancolombiana, SA: Edif. Grancolombiana, Carrera 13, No 27-75, Apdo Aéreo 4482, Bogotá, DC; tel. (1) 286-0200; fax (1) 286-9028; f. 1946; owned by the Colombian Coffee Growers' Federation (80%) and Ecuador Development Bank (20%); one of Latin America's leading cargo carriers serving 45 countries world-wide; Pres. LUIS FERNANDO ALARCÓN MANTILLA.

Líneas Agromar, Ltda: Calle 73, Vía 40-350, Apdo Aéreo 3259, Barranquilla, Atlántico; tel. (5) 345-1111; fax (5) 345-9634; Pres. MANUEL DEL DAGO FERNÁNDEZ.

Petromar Ltda: Bosque, Diagonal 23, No 56-152, Apdo Aéreo 505, Cartagena, Bolívar; tel. (5) 662-7208; fax (5) 662-7592; internet www.petromar.com; Pres. Capt. ALEX KOUTSAKIS.

Naviera Blancamar, SA: El Bosque, No 20-05, Cartagena; tel. (5) 669-0197; fax (5) 662-3531.

Transportadora Colombiana de Graneles, SA (NAVESCO, SA): Avda 19, No 118-95, Of. 214-301, Bogotá, DC; tel. (1) 620-9035; fax (1) 620-8801; e-mail navesco@colomsat.net.co; Gen. Man. GUILLERMO SOLANO VARELA.

Several foreign shipping lines call at Colombian ports.

CIVIL AVIATION

Colombia has more than 100 airports, including 11 international airports: Bogotá, DC (El Dorado International Airport), Medellín, Cali, Barranquilla, Bucaramanga, Cartagena, Cúcuta, Leticia, Pereira, San Andrés and Santa Marta.

Airports Authority

Aeronaútica Civil (Aerocivil): Aeropuerto El Dorado, 4°, Bogotá, DC; tel. (1) 425-1000; e-mail quejasyreclamos@aerocivil.gov.co; internet www.aerocivil.gov.co; f. 1967 as Departamento Administrativo de Aeronáutica Civil, reorganized in 1992; part of the Ministry of Transport; develops and regulates the civil aviation industry; Pres. ANDRÉS URIEL GALLEGO.

National Airlines

AIRES (Aerovías de Integración Regional): El Dorado International Airport, Bogotá, DC; internet www.aires.com.co; f. 1981; domestic and international passenger services, domestic cargo services; CEO FRANCISCO JOSÉ MENDEZ GARCÍA.

AVIANCA (Aerovías Nacionales de Colombia, SA): Avda El Dorado, No 93-30, 5°, Bogotá, DC; tel. (1) 413-9511; fax (1) 413-8716; internet www.avianca.com; f. 1919; operates domestic services to all cities in Colombia and international services to the USA, France, Spain and throughout Central and Southern America; merged with Aerolíneas Centrales de Colombia, SA (ACES) and Sociedad Aeronáutica de Medellín Consolidada, SA (SAM) in 2002; Chair. ANDRÉS OBREGÓN SANTO DOMINGO; Pres. FABIO VILLEGAS.

Satena (Servicio de Aeronavegación a Territorios Nacionales): Avda El Dorado, Entrada 1, Interior 11, Apdo Aéreo 11163, Bogotá, DC; tel. (1) 423-8530; e-mail gerencia@satena.com; internet www.satena.com; f. 1962; commercial enterprise attached to the Ministry of National Defence; internal services; CEO and Gen. Man. Maj.-Gen. HECTOR CAMPO.

Tampa Cargo, SA: Terminal Internacional de Carga, Bodega 1, Avda El Dorado, No 116-87, Bogotá, DC; tel. (1) 439-7900; fax (1) 439-7998; e-mail info@tampacargo.com.co; internet www.tampacargo.com.co; f. 1973; operates international cargo services to destinations throughout the Americas; COO MAURICIO LONDOÑO.

In addition, Aerosucre and Líneas Aéreas Suramericanas (LAS) operate international and domestic charter cargo services).

Tourism

The principal tourist attractions are the Caribbean coast (including the island of San Andrés), the 16th-century walled city of Cartagena, the Amazonian town of Leticia, the Andes mountains rising to 5,700m above sea-level, the extensive forests and jungles, pre-Columbian relics and monuments of colonial art. In 2005 there were 933,243 visitors (compared with 790,940 in 2004), most of whom came from the USA, Ecuador and Venezuela. In 2005 tourism receipts were US $1,570m.

Ministry of Trade, Industry and Tourism: Edif. Centro de Comercio Internacional, Calle 28, No 13A-15, 18°, Bogota, DC; tel. (1) 606-7676; fax (1) 696-7521; internet www.mincomercio.gov.co; Dir of Tourism CARLOS ALBERTO VIVES PACHECO.

Asociación Colombiana de Agencias de Viajes y Turismo (ANATO): Carrera 21, No 83-63, Apdo Aereo 7088, Bogotá, DC; tel. (1) 610-7099; fax (1) 236-2424; e-mail direccionejecutiva@anato.org; internet www.anato.com.co; f. 1949; Pres. Dr OSCAR RUEDA GARCÍA; Exec. Dir LUIS BETANCUR.

THE COMOROS*

Introductory Survey

Location, Climate, Language, Religion, Flag, Capital

The Union of the Comoros (formerly the Federal Islamic Republic of the Comoros) is an archipelago in the Mozambique Channel, between the island of Madagascar and the east coast of the African mainland. The group comprises four main islands (Ngazidja, Nzwani and Mwali, formerly Grande-Comore, Anjouan and Mohéli respectively, and Mayotte, which is a French overseas possession) and numerous islets and coral reefs. The climate is tropical, with average temperatures ranging from 23°C (73.4°F) to 28°C (82.4°F). Average annual rainfall is between 1,500 mm (59 ins) and 5,000 mm (197 ins). The official languages are Comorian (a blend of Swahili and Arabic), French and Arabic. Islam is the state religion. The flag (proportions 2 by 3) has four equal horizontal stripes, of yellow, white, red and blue, with a green triangle at the hoist depicting a white crescent moon and a vertical row of four five-pointed white stars. The capital, which is situated on Ngazidja, is Moroni.

Recent History

Formerly attached to Madagascar, the Comoros became a separate French Overseas Territory in 1947. The islands achieved internal self-government in December 1961, with a Chambre des députés and a Government Council responsible for local administration.

On 6 July 1975 the Chambre des députés voted for immediate independence, elected the President of the Government Council, Ahmed Abdallah, to be first President of the Comoros and reconstituted itself as the Assemblée nationale. Although France made no attempt to intervene, it maintained control of the island of Mayotte. Abdallah was deposed in August, and the Assemblée nationale was abolished. A National Executive Council was established, with Prince Saïd Mohammed Jaffar, leader of the opposition party, the Front national uni, as its head, and Ali Soilih, leader of the coup, among its members. In November the Comoros was admitted to the UN, as a unified state comprising the whole archipelago. In December France officially recognized the independence of Ngazidja, Nzwani and Mwali, but relations between France and the Comoros were effectively suspended. In February 1976 Mayotte voted overwhelmingly to retain its links with France.

In January 1976 Ali Soilih was elected Head of State, and adopted extended powers under the terms of a new Constitution. In May 1978 Soilih was killed, following a coup by a group of European mercenaries, led by a Frenchman, Col Robert Denard, on behalf of Abdallah, and the Comoros was proclaimed a Federal Islamic Republic. Shortly afterwards diplomatic relations with France were restored. In October a new Constitution was approved in a referendum, on the three islands excluding Mayotte, by 99.3% of the votes cast. Abdallah was elected President in the same month, and in December elections for a new legislature, the Assemblée fédérale, took place. In January 1979 the Assemblée fédérale approved the formation of a one-party state (unofficial opposition groups, however, continued to exist). In September 1984 Abdallah was re-elected President.

In February 1987 Abdallah indicated that independent opposition candidates would be permitted to contest legislative elections scheduled for March. In the event, however, opposition candidates were only allowed to contest 20 seats on Ngazidja, where they received 35% of the total votes, and pro-Government candidates retained full control of the 42-seat Assemblée fédérale. There were allegations of widespread fraud and intimidation of opposition candidates. In November 1989 a constitutional amendment permitting Abdallah to remain in office for a third six-year term was approved by 92.5% of votes cast in a popular referendum. The result of the referendum, however, was disputed by the President's opponents. Violent demonstrations followed, and opposition leaders were detained. On the night of 26–27 November Abdallah was assassinated by members of the presidential guard, under the command of Denard. The President of the Supreme Court, Saïd Mohamed Djohar, was appointed interim Head of State; however, Denard and his supporters defeated the regular army in a coup. The mercenaries' action provoked international condemnation, despite denials by Denard of complicity in Abdallah's death. (In May 1999 Denard stood trial in Paris, France, in connection with the assassination. Both Denard and his co-defendant, Dominique Malacrino, were acquitted of the murder charge.) In mid-December Denard agreed to relinquish power and, following the arrival of French paratroops in Moroni, was transported to South Africa, together with the remaining mercenaries. Djohar subsequently announced that the French troops were to remain in the Comoros for up to two years in order to train local security forces.

At the end of December 1989 the main political groups formed a provisional Government of National Unity. An amnesty for all political prisoners was proclaimed, and an inquiry into the death of Abdallah was instigated. In March 1990 Djohar, the official candidate for the Union comorienne pour le progrès (Udzima), secured victory at a multi-candidate presidential election taking 55.3% of the votes cast, and defeating Mohamed Taki Abdulkarim, the leader of the Union nationale pour la démocratie aux Comores (UNDC).

In August 1991 Djohar established a new coalition Government, which included two members of the Front démocratique (FD) and, in an attempt to appease increasing discontent on Mwali, two members of the Mwalian opposition. However, the two leading political associations represented in the coalition Government, Udzima and the Parti comorien pour la démocratie et le progrès (PCDP), objected to the reshuffle, and shortly afterwards the ministers belonging to the two parties resigned. In November Udzima (which had been officially renamed Parti Udzima) withdrew its support for Djohar and joined the opposition. Later in November agreement was reached between Djohar and the principal opposition leaders to initiate a process of national reconciliation, which would include the formation of a government of national unity and the convening of a constitutional conference. The accord also guaranteed the legitimacy of Djohar's election as President. In January 1992 a new transitional Government of National Unity was formed, under the leadership of Taki as its Co-ordinator, pending legislative elections.

At a constitutional referendum, held on 7 June 1992, reform proposals, which had been submitted in April, were approved by 74.3% of the votes cast. The new Constitution limited the presidential tenure to a maximum of two five-year terms of office and provided for a bicameral legislature, comprising an Assemblée fédérale, elected for a term of four years, and a 15-member Sénat, selected for a six-year term by the regional Councils. In early July Djohar dismissed Taki, following the latter's appointment of a former mercenary to a financial advisory post in the Government. Later that month Djohar formed a new Government.

The first round of voting in legislative elections, which had originally been scheduled to take place in October 1992, took place on 22 November. Numerous electoral irregularities and violent incidents were reported and several opposition parties demanded that the results be declared invalid. Election results in six constituencies were subsequently annulled, while the second round of voting on 29 November took place in only 34 of the 42 constituencies. Following partial elections on 13 and 30 December, reports indicated that candidates supporting Djohar—including seven members of the Union des démocrates pour la démocratie (UDD), a pro-Government organization based on Nzwani—had secured a narrow majority in the Assemblée fédérale. The leader of the UDD, Ibrahim Abdérémane Halidi, was appointed Prime Minister on 1 January 1993 and formed a new Council of Ministers.

In May 1993 eight supporters of the Minister of Finance, Commerce and Planning (and Djohar's son-in-law), Mohamed Saïd Abdallah M'Changama, allied with a number of opposition

---

*Some of the information contained in this chapter refers to the whole Comoros archipelago, which the independent Comoran state claims as its national territory. However, the island of Mayotte (Mahoré) is, in fact, administered by France. Separate information on Mayotte may be found in the chapter on French Overseas Possessions.

deputies, proposed a motion of 'no confidence' in the Government (apparently with the tacit support of Djohar), which was approved by 23 of the 42 deputies. Shortly afterwards, Djohar appointed an associate of M'Changama, Saïd Ali Mohamed, as Prime Minister, and a new Council of Ministers was formed. In June, in view of the continued absence of a viable parliamentary majority, Djohar dissolved the Assemblée fédérale and announced legislative elections. He subsequently dismissed Mohamed and appointed a former presidential adviser, Ahmed Ben Cheikh Attoumane, as Prime Minister. Shortly afterwards an interim Council of Ministers was formed (although two of the newly appointed ministers immediately resigned).

Following the dissolution of the Assemblée fédérale, opposition parties declared Djohar unfit to hold office, in view of the increasing political confusion, and demanded that legislative elections take place within the period of 40 days stipulated in the Constitution. In July 1993, however, Djohar announced that the legislative elections (which were to take place concurrently with local elections) were to be postponed until October—they were later postponed until November. In response, opposition parties organized a one-day strike, in support of demands that Djohar bring forward the date of the legislative elections or resign. In September a number of opposition movements, notably Udzima and the UNDC, established an informal electoral alliance, known as the Union pour la République et le progrès, while the FD, the PCDP, CHUMA (Islands' Fraternity and Unity Party) and the Mouvement pour la démocratie et le progrès (MDP) agreed to present joint candidates. In October Djohar established a political organization, the Rassemblement pour la démocratie et le renouveau (RDR), principally comprising supporters of M'Changama and several prominent members of the Government. In November the legislative elections were rescheduled for December, while the local elections were postponed indefinitely. Later in November Djohar reorganized the Council of Ministers and established a new national electoral commission, in response to opposition demands.

At the first round of the legislative elections, which took place on 12 December 1993, four opposition candidates secured seats in the Assemblée fédérale. Following a second round of voting on 20 December, the electoral commission declared the results in several constituencies to be invalid. Opposition candidates refused to participate in further elections in these constituencies, on the grounds that voting was again to be conducted under the supervision of the authorities, rather than that of the commission; RDR candidates consequently won all 10 contested seats, and 22 seats overall, thereby securing a narrow majority in the Assemblée fédérale. In January 1994 Djohar appointed the Secretary-General of the RDR, Mohamed Abdou Madi, as Prime Minister. The new Council of Ministers included several supporters of M'Changama, who was elected Speaker of the Assemblée fédérale. Later in January 12 principal opposition parties, which claimed that the RDR had assumed power illegally, formed a new alliance, the Forum pour le redressement national (FRN). In October Djohar dismissed Abdou Madi and appointed Halifa Hamoudi as premier.

In January 1995 the Government announced that elections to the regional councils were to take place in April (later postponed until July) and were to be followed by the establishment of an upper legislative chamber, the Sénat, and a Constitutional Council. The opposition, however, accused Djohar of acting unconstitutionally in the preparation for elections and claimed that he planned to assume control of the electoral process.

In April 1995 reports emerged of a widening rift between Djohar and Houmadi, after the Prime Minister apparently claimed that Djohar and M'Changama had engaged in financial malpractice. At the end of that month Djohar dismissed Houmadi from the premiership and appointed a former Minister of Finance, Mohamed Caabi El Yachroutu, as his successor. A 13-member Council of Ministers, which included only five members of the previous administration, was established. In May three former Prime Ministers (Mohamed, Abdou Madi and Houmadi) conducted a series of political meetings urging public support for the removal of M'Changama (who, they claimed, exerted undue influence over Djohar) and demanded the dissolution of the Assemblée fédérale.

In September 1995 about 30 European mercenaries, led by Denard, staged a military coup, seizing control of the garrison at Kandani and capturing Djohar. The mercenaries, who were joined by some 300 members of the Comoran armed forces, released a number of prisoners and installed a former associate of Denard, Capt. Ayouba Combo, as leader of a Transitional Military Committee. The French Government denounced the coup and suspended economic aid to the Comoros, but initially refused to take military action, despite requests for assistance from El Yachroutu, who had taken refuge in the French embassy. In October Combo announced that he had transferred authority to Mohamed Taki Abdulkarim and the leader of CHUMA, Saïd Ali Kemal, (who had both welcomed the coup) as joint civilian Presidents, apparently in an attempt to avert military repercussions by the French Government. The FRN, however, rejected the new leadership and entered into negotiations with El Yachroutu. Following a further appeal for intervention from El Yachroutu, who invoked a defence co-operation agreement that had been established between the two countries in 1978, some 900 French military personnel landed on the Comoros and surrounded the mercenaries at Kandani. Shortly afterwards Denard and his associates, together with the disaffected members of the Comoran armed forces, surrendered to the French troops. (In October 1996, following his release from imprisonment in France in July, Denard claimed that the coup attempt had been planned at the request of several Comoran officials, including Taki. In mid-2006 Denard was given a suspended sentence of five years by a French court for his involvement in the coup. Denard died in France in October 2007.)

Following the French military intervention, El Yachroutu declared himself interim President, in accordance with the Constitution, and formed a Government of National Unity, which included members of the constituent parties of the FRN. Djohar (who had been transported to Réunion by the French in order to receive medical treatment) rejected El Yachroutu's assumption of power and announced the reappointment of Saïd Ali Mohamed as Prime Minister. Later in October 1995 a National Reconciliation Conference decided that El Yachroutu would remain interim President, pending the forthcoming election, which was provisionally scheduled for early 1996. The incumbent administration opposed Djohar's stated intention to return to the Comoros and announced that measures would be taken to prevent him from entering the country. At the end of October El Yachroutu granted an amnesty to all Comorans involved in the coup attempt and appointed representatives of the UNDC and Udzima (which had supported the coup) to the new Council of Ministers. In November Djohar announced the formation of a rival Government, headed by Mohamed. El Yachroutu, who was supported by the Comoran armed forces, refused to recognize the legitimacy of Djohar's appointments, while opposition parties equally opposed his return to power; only elements of the RDR continued to support Djohar's authority. There was also widespread speculation that the French Government had believed Djohar's authority to be untenable and had tacitly supported his removal from power. Political leaders on Mwali rejected the authority of both rival Governments, urged a campaign of civil disobedience and established a 'citizens' committee' to govern the island; discontent with the central administration also emerged on Nzwani.

A presidential election took place, in two rounds, on 6 and 16 March 1996. At the first round, which was contested by some 15 candidates, Taki obtained the highest number of votes, with 21%, while the leader of the FRN, Abbas Djoussouf, secured about 15% of the votes. Taki was elected to the presidency on 16 March, obtaining 64% of the vote. International observers were satisfied with the electoral process; officials reported that 62% of the electorate had participated in the second round. The new Head of State was sworn in on 25 March. Taki appointed a new Council of Ministers, which included five of the presidential candidates who had supported him in the second round of the election.

In April 1996 Taki dissolved the Assemblée fédérale and announced that legislative elections would take place in October, despite the constitutional requirement that elections be held within a period of 40 days following the dissolution of the legislature. New Governors, all belonging to the UNDC, were appointed to each of the three islands. In August Taki issued a decree awarding himself absolute powers. This measure was widely criticized in the media and by opposition groups as being in violation of the Constitution.

In September 1996 Taki established a constitutional consultative committee, comprising 42 representatives of political parties and other organizations, which was to provide advice concerning the drafting of a new constitution; the FRN refused to participate in the committee. Also in that month the legislative elections were postponed until November. A national referendum to endorse a new draft Constitution was scheduled for

20 October. In order to comply with a constitutional proposal, which effectively restricted the number of political parties to a maximum of three, 24 pro-Taki political organizations merged to form one presidential party, the Rassemblement national pour le développement (RND). The new Constitution, which was approved by 85% of votes cast, vested legislative power in a unicameral parliament, the Assemblée fédérale, (thereby abolishing the Sénat) and extended the presidential term to six years, with an unrestricted number of consecutive mandates. Political parties were required to have two parliamentary deputies from each island (following legislative elections) to be considered legal; organizations that did not fulfil these stipulations were to be dissolved. Extensive executive powers were vested in the President, who was to appoint the Governors of the islands and gained the right to initiate constitutional amendments.

Following unsuccessful negotiations with the Government, the opposition parties (having formed a new alliance) refused to participate in the electoral process. Consequently, the legislative elections, which took place after a further delay, in two rounds, in December 1996, were only contested by the RND and the Front national pour la justice (FNJ), a fundamentalist Islamic organization, together with 23 independent candidates (in apparent contravention of a stipulation in the new Constitution that only legally created political parties were entitled to participate in national elections). The RND secured 36 of the 43 seats in the Assemblée fédérale, while the FNJ won three, with four seats taken by independent candidates. Taki nominated Ahmed Abdou, who had served in the administration of former President Ahmed Abdallah, as Prime Minister to head a new Council of Ministers.

During early 1996 separatist leaders declared their intention to seek the restoration of French rule and in March established a 'political directorate' on Nzwani, chaired by Abdallah Ibrahim, the leader of the Mouvement populaire anjouanais, a grouping of separatist movements on Nzwani. (The relative prosperity of neighbouring Mayotte appeared to have prompted the demand for a return to French rule; it was reported that up to 200 illegal migrants a day attempted to enter Mayotte from Nzwani.) Military reinforcements were sent to Nzwani and the Governor of the island was replaced once again.

On 3 August 1997 the 'political directorate' unilaterally declared Nzwani's secession from the Comoros. The separatists subsequently elected Ibrahim as president of a 13-member 'politico-administrative co-ordination', which included Abdou Madi, a former Prime Minister during Djohar's presidency, as spokesperson. The declaration of independence was condemned by Djoussouf, who appealed for French mediation in the crisis. However, France, while denouncing the secession, declared itself in favour of the intervention of the Organization of African Unity (OAU, now the African Union—AU, see p. 164), which dispatched a special envoy to the Comoros. Meanwhile, separatist agitation intensified on Mwali, culminating on 11 August, when secessionists declared Mwali's independence from the Comoros, appointed a president and a prime minister to head a 12-member government, and called for reattachment to France.

As OAU mediation efforts continued, it was announced in mid-August 1997 that secessionist leaders on Mwali and Nzwani had agreed to negotiate with the authorities in Moroni, although those on Nzwani had insisted on the immediate withdrawal of the military reinforcements that had been sent to the island in July. By late August the Government had complied with this demand, and the OAU announced its intention to hold a reconciliation conference in September in Addis Ababa, Ethiopia, while maintaining that secession was unacceptable. Nzwani's Governor resigned and was not replaced. In early September Taki dispatched some 300 troops to Nzwani in an attempt forcibly to suppress the separatist insurrection. After two days of heavy fighting between secessionist and government forces, the OAU declared that the government troops had failed to quash the rebellion. The Government claimed that the separatists had been aided by foreign elements and expressed regret at France's refusal to support the military operation. As it emerged that some 40 Comoran soldiers and 16 Nzwani residents had been killed in the fighting, with many more injured, demonstrators demanding Taki's resignation clashed violently with the security forces in Moroni. The separatists on Nzwani reaffirmed their independence and empowered Ibrahim to rule by decree. Taki subsequently declared a state of emergency, assumed absolute power and dismissed the Government of Ahmed Abdou and his military and civilian advisers. (Abdou had reportedly resigned his position in late August, although this had not been announced publicly.) Shortly afterwards, Taki established a State Transition Commission, which included representatives from Nzwani and Mwali. The reconciliation conference was postponed indefinitely by the OAU. The League of Arab States (Arab League, see p. 332) agreed to a request from Taki for assistance, and following talks with the OAU regarding the co-ordination of the mediation effort, all three islands hosted discussions in late September, which were convened by envoys from both organizations. The opposition continued to call for Taki's resignation, the decentralization of power through constitutional reform and the organization of new elections.

In September 1997 Ibrahim announced his decision to hold a referendum on self-determination for Nzwani on 26 October, prior to a reconciliation conference sponsored by both the OAU and the Arab League. Despite international opposition, the referendum was conducted as scheduled; according to separatist officials, 99.9% of the electorate voted in favour of independence for Nzwani. The following day Ibrahim dissolved the 'politico-administrative co-ordination' and appointed a temporary government, which was charged with preparing a constitution and organizing a presidential election. Taki responded by severing Nzwani's telephone lines, suspending air and maritime links. In November the OAU announced plans to deploy a force of military observers in the Comoros, despite the separatists' insistence that the force would not be allowed to land on Nzwani; an initial eight-member contingent, which arrived that month, was subsequently to be increased to 25 and was to receive logistical support from France.

In early December 1997 Taki formed a new Council of Ministers, appointing Nourdine Bourhane as Prime Minister. An inter-Comoran reconciliation conference was held later that month; some agreement was reached on proposals for the establishment of an international commission of inquiry to investigate September's military intervention and on the holding of a Comoran inter-island conference to discuss institutional reform. In January 1998 the OAU announced that both the Comoran Government and the Nzwani separatists had agreed to a number of conciliatory measures, including the restoration of air and maritime links and the release of federal soldiers still detained on Nzwani.

In February 1998 tension increased further on Nzwani, where several rival separatist factions had emerged; fighting broke out between Ibrahim's supporters and followers of Abdou Madi with the apparent support of both Taki and the OAU, in an abortive attempt to mount resistance to the secessionists. Later in February a separatist constitution was approved by a reported 99.5% of voters in a referendum on Nzwani. Ibrahim subsequently appointed a new separatist government. OAU mediation efforts effectively broke down in March, following an unsuccessful visit to Nzwani by a ministerial delegation.

In May 1998 Taki acted to break the political deadlock, forming a committee to re-establish dialogue with the opposition, appointing a new Council of Ministers, and releasing a prominent separatist from detention in Moroni. Abdou Madi returned to federal government, and, seemingly as a conciliatory gesture to the secessionists, the premiership (a position traditionally held by a Nzwanian) was left vacant.

In July 1998, as social unrest on Nzwani escalated, a dispute over the future aims of the secessionist movement led to the dismissal of the island's government, provoking violent clashes between islanders loyal to Ibrahim, who favoured independence within the framework of an association of the Comoran islands, and supporters of the outgoing prime minister of the island, Chamassi Saïd Omar, who continued to advocate reattachment to France.

Meanwhile, as social and economic conditions deteriorated further, with salaries still unpaid and strike action ongoing, Taki sought overseas assistance in resolving the crisis. In August 1998 the Government provisionally suspended transport links with both Nzwani and Mayotte. France later refused the Government's request for a suspension of links between Mayotte and Nzwani, thus worsening the already fragile relations between the two countries. At meetings with Djoussouf and the leadership of his own party in October, Taki proposed the establishment of a government of public salvation, an idea opposed by many members of the RND and several government ministers.

On 6 November 1998 President Taki died unexpectedly, reportedly having suffered a heart attack, although several senior officials expressed serious doubts about the cause of death. Tadjidine Ben Saïd Massoundi, the President of the High Council of the Republic and a former Prime Minister, was designated acting President, in accordance with the Constitution, pending an election, which would be held after 30–90 days. Massoundi immediately revoked the ban on the movement of people and goods to Nzwani and proceeded with Taki's project for the formation of a government of public salvation. Djoussouf, the main opposition leader, was subsequently appointed Prime Minister, to head a Council of Ministers composed of members of the FRN and the RND. In January 1999 Massoundi extended his presidential mandate, which was soon to expire, pending a resolution of the crisis dividing the islands. Also in that month Ibrahim agreed to relinquish some of his powers to a five-member 'politico-administrative directorate', as meetings commenced between the rival separatist factions. No consensus was reached in the following months, however, and when Ibrahim replaced the directorate with a 'committee of national security' in March, the new administration was immediately rejected by rival leaders.

At an OAU-sponsored inter-island conference, held in Antananarivo, Madagascar, in April 1999, an agreement was reached that envisaged substantial autonomy for Nzwani and Mwali, the changing of the country's name to the Union of the Comoran Islands and the rotation of the presidency among the three islands. However, the delegates from Nzwani refused to sign the agreement, insisting on the need to consult the Nzwani population prior to a full endorsement. On 30 April the Chief of Staff of the Comoran armed forces, Col Assoumani Azali, seized power in a bloodless coup, deposing Massoundi and dissolving the Government, the Assemblée fédérale and all other constitutional institutions. Azali promulgated a new constitutional charter and proclaimed himself head of state and of government and Commander-in-Chief of the armed forces. Full legislative functions were also vested in Azali, who announced his intention to stay in power for one year only, during which time he pledged to oversee the creation of the new institutions envisaged in the Antananarivo accord. The appointment of a State Committee (composed of six members from Ngazidja, four from Mwali and two from Nzwani) was followed by that of a State Council, which was to supervise the activities of the State Committee and comprised eight civilians and 11 army officers. The coup was condemned by the OAU; the UN, however, sent representatives to Azali's inauguration.

In June 1999 Lt-Col Saïd Abeid Abdérémane, who had previously held the role of 'national mediator' on Nzwani, formed a government of national unity on the island and assumed the role of 'national co-ordinator'. In July delegates from the three islands, including Azali and Abeid, met on Mwali for talks aimed at resolving the political crisis. The negotiations represented the most senior-level contact between the islands since the secessions of August 1997.

In August 1999 elections to establish an Assemblée nationale on Nzwani were held. No official results were released, but reports indicated that separatists won the majority of seats. In December the OAU threatened to impose sanctions on Nzwani should its leaders not have signed the peace accord by 1 February 2000. In response, Abeid announced that a referendum would be held on Nzwani in January 2000 regarding the signing of the Antananarivo accord. According to the separatist authorities of Nzwani, the results of the referendum revealed an overwhelming majority (94.47%) in favour of full independence for the island; the OAU, however, announced that it did not recognize the outcome of the ballot, following allegations of intimidation and repression of those in favour of reconciliation.

Meanwhile, following a series of meetings between Azali and a number of political parties from all three islands regarding the establishment of a more representative and decentralized government in Moroni, the State Committee underwent an extensive reorganization in December 1999, including the appointment of a Prime Minister, Bianrifi Tarmidi (from Mwali). Although Mwali was well represented in the new executive, only one Nzwanian minister was appointed. In March 2000 army units, led by Capt. Abdérémane Ahmed Abdallah (the son of former President Ahmed Abdallah), reportedly attempted, unsuccessfully, to overthrow Azali; Abdallah was subsequently arrested. In the following month demonstrations were organized by a number of political parties in protest at Azali's failure to transfer the country to civilian rule by 14 April, as he had promised following the April 1999 coup (see above). Azali later claimed that the conditions set for the holding of elections, namely the signing of the Antananarivo accord by the Nzwanian separatists, had not been met.

In February 2000, as threatened, the OAU imposed economic sanctions on Nzwani; the overseas assets of the separatist leaders were 'frozen' and they themselves were confined to the island. Furthermore, as part of the OAU sanctions, the federal Government suspended sea and air transport links, as well as telephone communications with Nzwani. In May the OAU announced that the lifting of sanctions against Nzwanian separatists was dependent on a return to constitutional order on the Comoros; it advocated the restoration of the October 1996 Constitution, the reinstatement of Massoundi as Head of State, as well as the appointment of an interim government and Prime Minister. The possibility of armed intervention on Nzwani was rejected at an OAU summit, held in July, although it was agreed to establish a total maritime blockade of the island.

In August 2000 an agreement, known as the Fomboni Accord, was reached by Azali and Abeid following negotiations on Mwali. The agreement provided for the establishment of a new Comoran entity and granted the three islands considerable control over internal matters. A new constitution was to be drafted and approved, by referendum, within 12 months. Moreover, Abeid and Azali called for the sanctions imposed on Nzwani to be lifted. The declaration was rejected by the OAU, however, on the grounds that it contravened the Antananarivo accord and threatened the integrity of the Comoros. Nevertheless, a tripartite commission, comprising delegates from Ngazidja, Nzwani and Mwali, was established to define the terms of the new constitution. In November Bianrifi Tarmidi was replaced as Prime Minister by Hamada Madi 'Boléro', who subsequently formed a new Government. Despite attempts to include them in the new Government and the tripartite commission, opposition members refused to participate, instead presenting to international mediators their own proposals for a resolution to the crisis.

With the mediation of the OAU and the Organisation internationale de la francophonie (OIF), negotiations between opposition and government members continued throughout late 2000 and early 2001. In February the Framework Agreement for Reconciliation in the Comoros was signed in Fomboni by representatives of the Comoran Government, the Nzwani administration, opposition parties and civil society. The OAU, the OIF and the European Union (EU, see p. 244) were to be guarantors of the peace accord, which provided for the establishment of a new Comoran entity. Under the provisions of the agreement, an independent tripartite commission (comprising equal numbers of delegates from each of the islands, representing all the signatory groups) was to draft a new constitution, which would be subject to approval in a national referendum. The new constitution was to define the areas of jurisdiction of the new entity and the individual islands, although the central administration would retain control over religion, nationality, currency, foreign affairs and defence. An independent national electoral commission was also to be created. Following the constitutional referendum, a transitional government of national union was to be formed and charged with creating the new institutions by 31 December. However, in March, following disagreements over the composition of a follow-up committee intended to monitor the implementation of the Fomboni accord, the opposition withdrew from the reconciliation process. Nevertheless, the OAU suspended sanctions against Nzwani in May.

On 8–9 August 2001 a bloodless military coup on Nzwani resulted in the removal from power of Saïd Abeid Abdérémane. Abeid was replaced by a collective presidency, comprising Maj. Mohamed Bacar, Maj. Hassane Ali Toihili and Maj. Charif Halidi; a government of eight civilian commissioners (none of whom had been members of the previous government) was appointed. The new leadership stated its commitment to the Fomboni agreement. However, on 24 September a further bloodless military coup was instigated by the deputy head of the Comoran army and close ally of Col Azali, Maj. Ayouba Combo. Although Combo was initially declared leader of the army, and Ahmed Aboubakar Foundi was installed as leader of Nzwani, they were captured the following day, before subsequently escaping the island. In November Abeid attempted unsuccessfully to regain control of Nzwani, but was defeated by forces loyal to Bacar and fled the island; the attempted coup was strongly condemned by the Government, which reaffirmed its support for the island's authorities.

At the constitutional referendum, which took place on 23 December 2001, 76.4% of the electorate voted in favour of the proposed new constitution. The country, which was to change its name to the Union of the Comoros, was to be led by the

President of the Union, at the head of a Council of the Union, and governed by a legislative assembly, the Assemblée de l'Union. The position of President was to rotate between the islands, while the Vice-Presidents, who were also members of the Council of the Union, were to be inhabitants of the two remaining islands; the first President was to come from Ngazidja. Each of the three islands was to become financially autonomous and was to be ruled by its own local government and institutions. The Union was to be responsible for matters of religion, nationality, currency, foreign affairs and external defence, while shared responsibilities between the Union and the islands were to be determined at a later date. A transitional government was to be installed to monitor the implementation of the new institutions.

In January 2002 a transitional Government of National Unity (GNU) was installed, with 'Boléro' reappointed as Prime Minister, and included members of the former Government, opposition representatives and two of Nzwani's separatist leaders. However, on the following day the GNU collapsed, after the withdrawal of the opposition representatives, as a result of a disagreement over the allocation of ministerial portfolios. Meanwhile, Col Azali resigned as Head of State and announced his intention to stand as an independent candidate in the forthcoming presidential election; 'Boléro' was to serve as President *ad interim*. In February the GNU was re-established.

In March and April 2002 voters on Nzwani, Mwali and Ngazidja approved new local Constitutions. In a first round of voting in the federal presidential election on 17 March, contested by nine candidates, Col Azali secured 39.8% of the vote. Mahamoud Mradabi won 15.7% and Saïd Ali Kemal 10.7%; however, both Mradabi and Kemal boycotted the second round. Consequently, on 14 April Col Azali was elected unopposed as Federal President of the Union of the Comoros, reportedly securing more than 75% of the votes cast. Although the result was declared invalid by the electoral commission, on the grounds that the election had not been free and fair, following the dissolution of the electoral commission, and the appointment of an independent electoral body, Col Azali was declared Federal President. Meanwhile, in late March and early April, Maj. Mohamed Bacar and Mohamed Saïd Fazul were elected as regional Presidents of Nzwani and Mwali, respectively; on 19 May Abdou Soule Elbak was elected regional President of Ngazidja. The regional Presidents subsequently formed local Governments. Col Azali appointed a new federal Government in early June.

In July 2002 Col Azali declared his intention to bring forward the process of national reconciliation, holding legislative elections in September. As a result of a meeting in August, Ngazidja was also granted its own internal security forces by Azali. Nevertheless, at the end of August street barricades were erected in Moroni, in protest at incomplete devolution on Ngazidja, which left Elbak with less authority than the other islands' Presidents. Later in the year Col Azali postponed the legislative elections until March-April 2003, despite assertions from international representatives that the absence of institutions for dialogue was a threat to the national reconciliation process. In September 2002 supporters of Azali formed a new political party, the Convention pour le renouveau des Comores (CRC).

In January 2003 the follow-up committee on the implementation of the reconciliation agreement proposed that elections to the islands' local assemblies be held in April and elections to the Assemblée de l'Union in May. In early March Elbak and Bacar denounced Azali's failure to implement measures to resolve the institutional crisis and accused the federal President of repeated constitutional violations, requesting that the EU temporarily delay payment for fishing rights to the federal Government. In March the federal Government announced the indefinite postponement of the legislative elections.

In August 2003, at an AU-sponsored meeting in Pretoria, South Africa, representatives of the federal and island governments signed a memorandum, according to which the federal Government would retain control of the army, but the administration of the police force would be devolved to the island Governments. Agreement was also reached that, during a transitional period leading to legislative elections, the customs services would be managed by a joint board, with taxes shared between the federal and island administrations. In December, following further mediation by the AU, the agreement reached in August was ratified by Azali and the three island Presidents at a ceremony in Moroni. A follow-up committee was appointed to monitor the implementation of the accord.

Elections to the three island assemblies were held on 14 and 21 March 2004. Pro-Azali candidates won an overall total of only 12 seats in the assemblies, while candidates allied to Elbak secured 14 of the 20 seats in the Ngazidja assembly, supporters of Bacar were reported to have won 19 of the 25 seats available on Nzwani, and nine allies of Fazul were elected to the 10-member assembly on Mwali. Elections to the Assemblée de l'Union took place on 18 and 25 April. According to final results, declared on 28 April, the CRC won only six of the 18 directly elected seats, while a loose coalition supporting the three island Presidents secured 11 seats and CHUMA took one seat. The rate of participation by eligible voters at the second round was 68.5%. The remaining 15 seats in the 33-member federal assembly were taken by five nominees each from the island legislatures. The inauguration of the Assemblée took place on 4 June at which Saïd Dhuffur Bounnou was elected Speaker. In mid-July President Azali unveiled his new ministerial team, granting responsibility for co-ordinating Union affairs on their home islands to the two Vice-Presidents. The new cabinet comprised the two Vice-Presidents, seven ministers of state and two secretaries of state, and included a member of CHUMA, and representatives nominated by the island Presidents of Nzwani and Mwali. President Bacar declined to participate in the creation of the Government.

The Constitutional Court was inaugurated in September 2004, and Abdallah Ahmed Sourette was elected President in October. In November legislation on the division of power between the national and island authorities was approved by the Assemblée de l'Union. The bill granted authority over the gendarmerie to the island Presidents, precipitating a demonstration by the armed forces. The island Presidents also expressed their dissatisfaction with the bill, which they claimed had been amended by the Assemblée de l'Union without their consent. It was subsequently declared invalid by the Constitutional Court and returned to the Assemblée.

Despite the submission of draft legislation in April 2005 which would have permitted President Azali to stand for a second term as President of the Union, in June the Assemblée de l'Union officially approved a rotating presidency among the three islands, thus ensuring that the next President of the Union would be from Nzwani. In October the Assemblée de l'Union approved legislation granting Comorans living abroad the right to vote. It was estimated that some 200,000 Comorans were resident in France. In early 2006 the Commission nationale des élections aux Comores announced that the presidential elections would be held on 14 May.

Meanwhile, in July 2005 President Azali effected a reorganization of the Union Government. Most notably, Oubeidi Mze Cheik, hitherto the Director of the Customs Office, became Minister of Finance and the Budget, while Aboudou Soefo was appointed Minister of Foreign Affairs, Co-operation, the Francophonie, with responsibility for Comorans Abroad.

The 2006 presidential elections were the first in which the principle of the office rotating between alternating islands of the Union was enacted. In the first round of the presidential election, held on 16 April 2006, three of the 13 candidates from the island of Nzwani received sufficient votes cast to proceed to the nationwide second ballot; this took place on 14 May at which Ahmed Abdullah Sambi, a businessman and the founder of the FNJ, secured 99,112 (58.02%) of the votes cast. The elections were observed to have been free, fair and credible by international monitors. The former Prime Minister, Ibrahim Halidi, was placed second with 48,378 (28.32%) of the votes, while Mohammad Djaanfari received 23,322 votes (13.65%). Sambi officially assumed the presidency on 26 May and a new Cabinet of Ministers was appointed within three days, considerably reduced in size, consisting of two Vice-Presidents and six ministers. Notably the defence portfolio was allocated to the President's office and the army was to be reunified under single command. National troops were confined to barracks for the duration of the election and the AU contributed over 400 troops to ensure the first peaceful transition of power since independence.

The new Government was swift to pursue corruption charges against former officials, to recommence the payment of salaries to civil servants (which had been suspended from the beginning of the year), and to reduce the price of rice—a staple food. Economic issues were paramount on the agenda of the new administration. However, conflicts over the competencies of the Union and island Governments persisted, with negotiations over legislation on the division of powers regarding justice, internal security and management of state companies (including ports and airports), reaching stalemate in early December 2006. Later in that month President Sambi flew to Nzwani with the aim of installing a regional branch of the Armée nationale de développement (AND) and ensuring its representation at the island's port and airport. However, he was obstructed in the latter goal by the island Government's own armed forces. Negotiations resumed in early 2007, following international mediation.

In March 2007 President Sambi carried out a reorganization of the Government and created four new portfolios, increasing the number of ministers to 12. Most notably, Mohamed Ali Solihi was appointed Minister of Finance, Budget and Planning, while the newly created departments included a Ministry of Energy, headed by Houmadi Abdallah, and a Ministry of Islamic Affairs, Human Rights and Information.

The period prior to the island presidential elections in mid-2007 was marred by violence and allegations of corruption and intimidation. Elections took place on Ngazidja and Mwali on 10 June as scheduled, while the election on Nzwani was postponed until 17 June at the request of President Sambi and the AU. However, Bacar proceeded to hold the election despite the AU's demands for it to be rescheduled and subsequently claimed victory with 73.22% of the vote, declaring himself President of Nzwani for a second term. Both the AU and the Union Government announced that the election was null and void. While unrest continued on Nzwani, a second round of voting took place on Ngazidja and Mwali on 25 June. Mohamed Abdouloihabi was elected to the presidency on Ngazidja and Mohamed Ali Said secured victory on Mwali in what were largely deemed to be free and fair elections. Meanwhile, a meeting between President Sambi and the AU was convened on 24 June to attempt to resolve the issue on Nzwani; a statement was issued demanding that a new election be held on the island.

The impasse continued and in October 2007 the AU imposed sanctions on Nzwani, which included restrictions on the movements of the self-proclaimed President and his supporters and the freezing of their assets. These attempts to regain control of the island and restore peace failed and Bacar dismissed threats of military force. The Union Government conceded that a military intervention by the AND would be unlikely to succeed given the limited strength of the Union's armed forces compared to the contingent of armed militia on Nzwani.

In mid-February 2008, following the failure of further negotiations aimed at breaking the deadlock, the AU Peace and Security Council mandated the deployment of a Mission d'assistance électorale et sécuritaire (MAES) to 'facilitate the restoration of the authority of the Union' on Nzwani by use of military force. The MAES was to comprise some 1,500 members, including troops from Senegal, Sudan, and Tanzania, as well as logistical support staff from Libya, and represented the first occasion that the AU had approved military intervention to enforce peace in a member country. On 25 March some 450 Sudanese, Tanzanian and Comoran troops landed on Nzwani and succeeded in regaining control of the island. The following day President Sambi announced that Union Vice-President Ikililou Dhoinine had been appointed interim President of Nzwani, pending the formation of a transitional government, and confirmed that the presidential election on the island would be reheld within two months. Bacar was reported to have fled Nzwani, initially taking refuge on Mayotte where he requested political asylum. The Comoran authorities immediately sought his extradition from Mayotte; however, on 28 March Bacar was transported by the French military to Réunion where he was, according to French officials, to be investigated for landing illegally on Mayotte in possession of weapons. That charge was dismissed, although Bacar and 22 of his supporters remained in custody on Réunion. On 31 March Laili Zamane Abdou, hitherto President of the Nzwani Court of Appeal, was sworn in as interim President.

Diplomatic relations between the Comoros and France, suspended in December 1975, were restored in July 1978; in November of that year the two countries signed agreements on military and economic co-operation, apparently deferring any decision on the future of Mayotte. In subsequent years, however, member countries of the UN General Assembly repeatedly voted in favour of a resolution affirming the Comoros' sovereignty over Mayotte, with only France dissenting. Following Djohar's accession to power, diplomatic relations were established with the USA in June 1990. In September 1993 the Arab League accepted an application for membership from the Comoros. In mid-1999, following the military coup headed by Col Azali, France and the USA suspended all military co-operation with the Comoros; France resumed military co-operation in September 2002. In September 2004 the USA claimed that the Comoros was harbouring a militant Islamist group, Al Haramain. In mid-2004 a joint commission with Sudan was created, and in early 2005 President Azali visited France, and the Franco-Comoran commission resumed, after a hiatus of 10 years. In November 2006 a framework partnership agreement was signed by the French Minister-Delegate for Co-operation, Development and La Francophonie, allocating a grant of €88m. to the Union for 2006–10. Following the accession of President Sambi, relations with and funding from Iran increased significantly, owing to his personal historical connections with that country.

Government

Under the Constitution of 23 December 2001, each of the islands in the Union of the Comoros is headed by a local government and is partially autonomous. The Head of State of the Union of the Comoros is the President, who appoints the members of the Government and heads the Council of the Union, which also comprises the two Vice-Presidents. The members of the Council are elected for a four-year term, and the position of President rotates between the islands, while the Vice-Presidents are inhabitants of the two remaining islands. Federal legislative power is vested in the Assemblée de l'Union, which serves a five-year term and is composed of 33 deputies, 18 of whom are directly elected (nine on Ngazidja, seven on Nzwani and two on Mwali), with the remaining 15 seats divided equally among representatives of the three islands. Each island also elects its own legislative local assembly and president. A final transition to a federalized system was achieved in June 2004.

Defence

The national army, the Armée nationale de développement (AND), comprised about 1,100 men in early 2000. Government expenditure on defence in 1994 was an estimated US $3m. In December 1996 an agreement was ratified with France, which provided for the permanent presence of a French military contingent in the Comoros, which was to be renewed by rotation. French military co-operation with the Comoros was suspended after the coup of April 1999, but resumed in September 2002.

Economic Affairs

In 2006, according to estimates from the World Bank, the gross national income (GNI) of the Comoros (excluding Mayotte), measured at average 2004–06 prices, was US $406m., equivalent to $660 per head (or $2,010 per head on an international purchasing-power parity basis). During 1996–2006, it was estimated, the population increased at an average annual rate of 2.1%, while gross domestic product (GDP) per head declined, in real terms, by an average of 0.2% per year. Overall GDP increased, in real terms, at an average annual rate of 2.3% in 1996–2006; growth in 2006 was 0.5%.

Agriculture (including hunting, forestry and fishing) contributed an estimated 48.5% of GDP in 2005. According to FAO, approximately 71.3% of the labour force were employed in the agricultural sector in mid-2005. In 2004 the sector accounted for some 98% of export earnings. The principal cash crops are vanilla, ylang ylang and cloves. In 2005 export earnings for vanilla declined to an estimated 1,166m. Comoran francs, a 58.5% decrease from 2004 (and of some 98% from 2003). The Comoros produces an estimated 80% of the ylang ylang consumed globally. Cassava, taro, rice, maize, pulses, coconuts and bananas are also cultivated. In late 2005 an agreement on fishing rights in Comoran waters, which would extend until 2010, was reached with the European Union (EU). (Moroni was selected to host a new Indian Ocean Commission Centre for Fishing Surveillance, largely funded by the EU.) According to the World Bank, the real GDP of the agricultural sector increased at an average annual rate of 2.8% in 1996–2006; agricultural GDP grew by 4.4% in 2005, but declined by 10.3% in 2006.

Industry (including manufacturing, construction and power) contributed an estimated 10.5% of GDP in 2005. Some 9.4% of the labour force were employed in the industrial sector in 1990. According to the World Bank, the Comoros' industrial GDP increased at an average annual rate of 1.8% in 1996–2006; industrial GDP declined by 5.9% in 2005, but increased by 8.6% in 2006.

The manufacturing sector contributed an estimated 4.1% of GDP in 2005. The sector consists primarily of the processing of agricultural produce, particularly of vanilla and essential oils. According to the World Bank, manufacturing GDP increased at an average annual rate of 1.6% in 1996–2006; manufacturing GDP grew by 3.1% in 2005, but decreased by 3.0% in 2006.

Electrical energy is derived from wood (some 80%), and from thermal installations. Imports of petroleum products comprised an estimated 11.9% of the total cost of imports in 2005 and some 36m. kWh hours of electricity were produced in the Comoros in 2005.

The services sector contributed an estimated 41.0% of GDP in 2005. Strong growth in tourism from 1991 led to a significant expansion in trade, restaurant and hotel activities, although political instability inhibited subsequent growth and there remained much potential for development. In 2007 a new facility at Moroni airport was completed; the project was financed by the Government of the People's Republic of China and was expected to precipitate a three-fold increase in annual passenger turnover. Furthermore, it was hoped that the additional capacity would provide a stimulus to the tourism sector. According to the World Bank, the GDP of the services sector decreased at an average rate of 1.9% per year in 1996–2006. However, it increased by 7.1% in 2005, and by 12.6% in 2006.

In 2005, according to the IMF, the Comoros recorded a visible trade deficit of US $76.8m. and there was a deficit of $12.3m. on the current account of the balance of payments. In 2005, according to the IMF, the principal source of imports was South Africa (accounting for some 15.4% of the total); other major sources were France (13.8%), Mauritius and Pakistan. France was the principal market for exports (73.3%); Germany was another important purchaser (10.4%). The leading exports in that year were vanilla (providing 54.0% of the total), ylang ylang (34.6%) and cloves (6.8%). The principal imports in that year were petroleum products (11.9%), meat and fish (10.7%), rice (9.7%), and cement (7.6%).

The Comoran budget deficit, excluding grants received, was estimated at 748m. Comoros francs in 2007. The Comoros' external public debt at the end of 2004 totalled US $305.8m., of which $275.2m. was long-term public debt. The annual rate of inflation averaged 4.2% during 1999–2005. In 2005 the rate was 2.0%. According to the IMF, an estimated 13.3% of the labour force were unemployed in 2005.

In 1985 the Comoros joined the Indian Ocean Commission (IOC, see p. 412). The country is also a member of the Common Market for Eastern and Southern Africa (COMESA, see p. 205) and of the Franc Zone (see p. 306).

The Comoros has a relatively undeveloped economy, with high unemployment, a limited transport system, a severe shortage of natural resources and heavy dependence on foreign aid, particularly from France. An intensification of political instability on the islands, following the seizure of power by the army in April 1999, had a particularly adverse effect on maritime trade and tourism, as well as compromising vital donor assistance. Following the conclusion of an agreement on national reconciliation in February 2001 (see above), in November 2002 the federal Government and the EU signed a National Indicator Programme on co-operation during 2002–07; the Comoros was to receive €27.3m. under the Programme, mostly for education. However, the Union maintained a particularly high level of external debt. In 2004 production of vanilla, the Comoros' main export, declined substantially, while the price for that commodity also fell, largely owing to the availability of increased supplies from other vanilla producing countries and the rising use by food producers of synthetic flavour substitutes. By late 2006 the price per kilo had declined to some US $30, compared with $600 per kilo in 2003, and Comoran vanilla remained more expensive internationally than that from its competitor Madagascar, owing to the pegging of the Comoros franc to the euro. Both the value and production of cloves also declined dramatically in 2005, although a recovery was experienced in 2006. Production of ylang ylang, of which the Comoros was the world's major producer, continued to increase, however. The Union Government was seeking a Poverty Reduction and Growth Facility programme—vital as a step towards obtaining international debt relief—and to that end a monitoring programme was undertaken by the IMF during 2005–06. Among the proposals made by the IMF were the reform of the tax system and the privatization of inefficient public monopolies such as the state-owned telecommunications and petroleum companies. Economic growth was described as having been weak and narrowly based and, as with many neighbouring countries, was highly dependent on emigrant remittances (among the highest in the world, according to the IMF). Although membership of the Franc Zone was credited with maintaining relatively low levels of inflation and fiscal deficit, the large public wage bill and weak institutional capacity inhibited fiscal progress and the financial conditions were discouraging to private sector investment. The presidential election of 2006 was regarded as having been severely disruptive to the economy, as the revenue-sharing mechanism between the islands faltered, expenditure escalated and borrowing from the Central Bank increased notably, thus undoing some of the progress achieved in the mid-2000s. However, the new administration demonstrated its willingness to improve the situation, ensuring greater transparency in joint revenue arrangements and introducing revenue-enhancing and expenditure-limiting measures in the supplementary budget in August 2006. The IMF estimated that GDP rose, in real terms, by just 1% in 2007. However, more substantial economic growth of 3% was projected for 2008.

Education

Education is officially compulsory for 10 years between six and 16 years of age. Primary education begins at the age of six and lasts for six years. Secondary education, beginning at 12 years of age, lasts for seven years, comprising a first cycle of four years and a second of three years. According to UNESCO estimates, enrolment at primary schools in 2003/04 included 86% of children in the relevant age-group (males 91%; females 80%), while enrolment at secondary schools in that year was equivalent to 35% of children in the relevant age-group (males 40%; females 30%), according to UNESCO estimates. Children may also receive a basic education through traditional Koranic schools, which are staffed by Comoran teachers. The Comoros' first university opened in December 2003, with an enrolment of 1,200 students. Current expenditure by the Ministry of Education in 1995 was 3,381m. Comoros francs, representing 21.1% of total current government expenditure.

Public Holidays

2008: 1 January (New Year's Day), 10 January*† (Muharram, Islamic New Year), 19 January* (Ashoura), 20 March* (Mouloud, Birth of the Prophet), 1 May (International Labour Day), 6 July (Independence Day), 30 July* (Leilat al-Meiraj, Ascension of the Prophet), 1–3 October* (Id al-Fitr, end of Ramadan), 27 November (Anniversary of President Abdallah's assassination), 9 December* (Id al-Adha, Feast of the Sacrifice), 29 December*† (Muharram, Islamic New Year).

2009: 1 January (New Year's Day), 7 January*‡ (Ashoura), 9 March* (Mouloud, Birth of the Prophet), 1 May (International Labour Day), 6 July (Independence Day), 19 July* (Leilat al-Meiraj, Ascension of the Prophet), 20–22 September* (Id al-Fitr, end of Ramadan), 27 November* (Anniversary of President Abdallah's assassination and Id al-Adha, Feast of the Sacrifice), 18 December* (Muharram, Islamic New Year), 27 December*‡ (Ashoura).

* These holidays are dependent on the Islamic lunar calendar and may differ by one or two days from the dates given.

† This festival occurs twice (marking the start of the Islamic years AH 1429 and 1430) within the same Gregorian year.

‡ This festival occurs twice (in the Islamic years AH 1430 and 1431) within the same Gregorian year.

Weights and Measures

The metric system is in force.

THE COMOROS

Statistical Survey

Sources (unless otherwise stated): *Rapport Annuel*, Banque Centrale des Comores, place de France, BP 405, Moroni; tel. (73) 1814; fax (73) 0349; e-mail bancecom@comorestelecom.km; internet www.bancecom.com.

Note: Unless otherwise indicated, figures in this Statistical Survey exclude data for Mayotte.

AREA AND POPULATION

Area: 1,862 sq km (719 sq miles). *By Island*: Ngazidja (Grande-Comore) 1,146 sq km, Nzwani (Anjouan) 424 sq km, Mwali (Mohéli) 290 sq km.

Population: 335,150 (males 167,089, females 168,061), excluding Mayotte (estimated population 50,740), at census of 15 September 1980; 446,817 (males 221,152, females 225,665), excluding Mayotte, at census of 15 September 1991; 527,900 in 1998; 575,660, excluding Mayotte, at census of 1 September 2003. *Mid-2007* (UN estimate): 839,000 (Source: UN, *World Population Prospects: The 2006 Revision*). *By Island* (1991 census): Ngazidja (Grande-Comore) 233,533; Nzwani (Anjouan) 188,953; Mwali (Mohéli) 24,331.

Density (per sq km, mid-2007): 450.6.

Principal Towns ('000, incl. suburbs, mid-2005, UN estimate): Moroni (capital) 44,000. Source: UN, *World Urbanization Prospects: The 2005 Revision*.

Births and Deaths (including figures for Mayotte, UN estimates, 2000–05): Average annual birth rate 36.5 per 1,000; average annual death rate 7.4 per 1,000. Source: UN, *World Population Prospects: The 2006 Revision*.

Expectation of Life (years at birth, including Mayotte, WHO estimates): 64.4 (males 62.2; females 66.7) in 2005. Source: WHO, *World Health Statistics*.

Economically Active Population (ILO estimates, '000 persons at mid-1980, including figures for Mayotte): Agriculture, forestry and fishing 150; Industry 10; Services 20; Total 181 (males 104, females 77) (Source: ILO, *Economically Active Population Estimates and Projections, 1950–2025*). *1991 Census* (persons aged 12 years and over, excluding Mayotte): Total labour force 126,510 (males 88,034, females 38,476) (Source: UN, *Demographic Yearbook*). Mid-2005 (official estimates in '000): Agriculture, etc. 271; Total labour force 380 (Source: FAO).

HEALTH AND WELFARE
Key Indicators

Total Fertility Rate (children per woman, 2005): 4.6.
Under-5 Mortality Rate (per 1,000 live births, 2005): 71.
HIV/AIDS (% of persons aged 15–49, 2005): 0.1.
Physicians (per 1,000 head, 2004): 0.15.
Hospital Beds (per 1,000 head, 2006): 2.20.
Health Expenditure (2004): US $ per head (PPP): 24.9.
Health Expenditure (2004): % of GDP: 2.8.
Health Expenditure (2004): public (% of total): 56.9.
Access to Water (% of persons, 2004): 86.
Access to Sanitation (% of persons, 2004): 33.
Human Development Index (2005): ranking: 134.
Human Development Index (2005): value: 0.561.

For sources and definitions, see explanatory note on p. vi.

AGRICULTURE, ETC.

Principal Crops ('000 metric tons, unless otherwise indicated, 2006, FAO estimates): Rice (paddy) 17.0; Maize 4.0; Potatoes 0.5; Sweet potatoes 5.0; Cassava (Manioc) 58.0; Taro 9.0; Yams 4.0; Pulses 14.3; Groundnuts (in shell) 0.9; Coconuts 77.0; Tomatoes 0.6; Bananas 65.0; Vanilla (dried, metric tons) 60; Cloves 1.5. *Aggregate Production* ('000 metric tons, may include official, semi-official or estimated data): Total vegetables (incl. melons) 3.7; Total fruits (excl. melons) 68.

Livestock ('000 head, year ending September 2006, FAO estimates): Asses 5.0; Cattle 45.0; Sheep 21.0; Goats 115.0; Chickens 500.

Livestock Products (metric tons, 2006, FAO estimates): Cattle meat 1,100; Sheep and goat meat 434; Chicken meat 561; Cow milk 4,550; Hen eggs 776.

Fishing ('000 metric tons, live weight, 2005): Total catch 15.1 (Sardinellas 1.0; Anchovies, etc. 1.0; Seerfishes 0.6; Skipjack tuna 3.2; Yellowfin tuna 5.9; Carangids 0.6; Indian mackerels 0.2).

Source: FAO.

INDUSTRY

Electric Energy (million kWh): 35.2 in 2003; 35.8 in 2004; 36.0 in 2005. Source: IMF, *Union of the Comoros: Selected Issues and Statistical Appendix* (October 2006).

FINANCE

Currency and Exchange Rates: 100 centimes = 1 Comoros franc. *Sterling, Dollar and Euro Equivalents* (31 December 2007): £1 sterling = 732.632 Comoros francs; US $1 = 365.694 Comoros francs; €1 = 491.968 Comoros francs; 1,000 Comoros francs = £1.36 = $2.73 = €2.03. *Average Exchange Rate* (Comoros francs per US $): 395.601 in 2005; 392.168 in 2006; 359.450 in 2007. Note: The Comoros franc was introduced in 1981, replacing (at par) the CFA franc. The fixed link to French currency was retained, with the exchange rate set at 1 French franc = 50 Comoros francs. This remained in effect until January 1994, when the Comoros franc was devalued by 33.3%, with the exchange rate adjusted to 1 French franc = 75 Comoros francs. This relationship to French currency remained in effect with the introduction of the euro on 1 January 1999. From that date, accordingly, a fixed exchange rate of €1 = 491.968 Comoros francs has been in operation.

Budget (million Comoros francs, 2007, projected): *Revenue*: Tax revenue 22,163; Other revenue 4,089; Total 26,252 (excluding grants received 13,419). *Expenditure*: Budgetary current expenditure 29,298 (Wages and salaries 12,784, Goods and services 6,591, Transfers 3,463, Interest payments 859, Foreign-financed project assistance 2,340, Technical assistance programmes 3,296); Capital expenditure 11,121 (Externally financed 9,421, Domestically financed 1,700); Total 40,419.

International Reserves (US $ million at 31 December 2006): Gold 0.33; Reserve position in IMF 0.82; Foreign exchange 92.70; Total 93.85. Source: IMF, *International Financial Statistics*.

Money Supply (million Comoros francs at 31 December 2006): Currency outside deposit money banks 12,765; Demand deposits at deposit money banks 10,199; Total money (incl. others) 24,652. Source: IMF, *International Financial Statistics*.

Cost of Living (Consumer Price Index; base: 1999 = 100): All items 120.1 in 2003; 125.5 in 2004; 128.0 in 2005. Source: IMF, *Union of the Comoros: Selected Issues and Statistical Appendix* (October 2006).

Expenditure on the Gross Domestic Product (million Comoros francs at current prices, 2005): Government final consumption expenditure 18,678; Private final consumption expenditure 154,245; Gross fixed capital formation 14,253; Total domestic expenditure 187,176; Exports of goods and services 19,102; *Less* Imports of goods and services 53,166; *GDP in purchasers' values* 153,112. Source: IMF, *Union of the Comoros: Selected Issues and Statistical Appendix* (October 2006).

Gross Domestic Product by Economic Activity (million Comoros francs at current prices, 2005, estimates): Agriculture, hunting, forestry and fishing 78,110; Manufacturing 6,666; Electricity, gas and water 2,292; Construction and public works 7,876; Trade, restaurants and hotels 27,261; Transport and communications 14,111; Finance, insurance, real estate and business services 8,698; Government services 15,854; Other services 130; *Sub-total* 160,998; *Less* Imputed bank service charge 7,886; *GDP in purchasers' values* 153,112. Source: IMF, *Union of the Comoros: Selected Issues and Statistical Appendix* (October 2006).

Balance of Payments (US $ million, 2005, estimates): Exports of goods f.o.b. 13.8; Imports of goods f.o.b. −90.6; *Trade balance* −76.8; Services (net) −5.3; *Balance on goods and services* −82.1; Income (net) −2.3; *Balance on goods, services and income* −84.4; Private transfers (net) 65.0; Government transfers (net) 7.1; *Current balance* −12.3; Net capital account (incl. errors and omissions) 4.7; *Overall balance* −7.6. Source: IMF, *Union of the Comoros: Selected Issues and Statistical Appendix* (October 2006).

EXTERNAL TRADE

Principal Commodities (million Comoros francs, 2005): *Imports c.i.f.*: Meat and fish 3,771; Rice 3,417; Petroleum products 4,196; Cement 2,686; Iron and steel 1,373; Total (incl. others) 35,344. *Exports f.o.b.*: Cloves 146; Ylang ylang 747; Vanilla 1,166; Total (incl. others) 2,160. Source: IMF *Union of the Comoros: Selected Issues and Statistical Appendix* (October 2006).

Principal Trading Partners (US $ million, 2000): *Imports*: Belgium 1.3; France-Monaco 13.9; Indonesia 1.5; Kenya 3.9; Pakistan 4.9; South Africa 39.0; United Arab Emirates 1.8; Total (incl. others) 71.9. *Exports*: Canada 0.3; France-Monaco 3.0; Germany 0.5; Israel 0.2; Singapore 1.1; United Kingdom 0.6; USA 1.1; Total (incl. others) 6.9. Source: UN, *International Trade Statistics Yearbook*.

TRANSPORT

Road Traffic (motor vehicles in use, 1999, estimates): Passenger cars 692; Total 790. Source: International Road Federation, *World Road Statistics*.

Shipping: *Merchant Fleet* (registered at 31 December 2006): Number of vessels 252; Total displacement (grt) 727,185 (Source: Lloyd's Register-Fairplay, *World Fleet Statistics*). *International Sea-borne Freight Traffic* (estimates, '000 metric tons, 1991): Goods loaded 12; Goods unloaded 107 (Source: UN Economic Commission for Africa, *African Statistical Yearbook*).

Civil Aviation (traffic at Prince Said Ibrahim international airport, 1999): Passengers carried ('000) 130.4; Freight handled 1,183 metric tons.

TOURISM

Tourist Arrivals (2004): France 9,460; Madagascar 656; Réunion 1,429; Zimbabwe 786; Total (incl. others) 17,603. *2005:* Total arrivals 19,551.

Receipts from Tourism (US $ million, incl. passenger transport): 11 in 2002; 8 in 2003; 10 in 2004.

Source: partly World Tourism Organization.

COMMUNICATIONS MEDIA

Radio Receivers (1997): 90,000 in use. Source: UNESCO, *Statistical Yearbook*.

Television Receivers (1997): 1,000 in use. Source: UNESCO, *Statistical Yearbook*.

Telephones (2005): 16,900 main lines in use. Source: International Telecommunication Union.

Mobile Cellular Telephones (2005): 16,100 in use. Source: International Telecommunication Union.

Facsimile Machines (1998): 173 in use. Source: UN, *Statistical Yearbook*.

Personal Computers (2004): 5,000 in use. Source: International Telecommunication Union.

Internet Users (2006): 21,000. Source: International Telecommunication Union.

EDUCATION

Pre-primary (2003/04): 483 teachers; 2,279 pupils. Source: UNESCO Institute for Statistics.

Primary: 348 schools (1998); 3,050 teachers (2004/05); 106,700 pupils (2004/05). Sources: UNESCO Institute for Statistics and IMF, *Comoros: Statistical Appendix* (August 2005).

Secondary: Teachers: general education 3,118 (2004/05); teacher training 11 (1991/92); vocational 20 (2004/05). Pupils: 43,349 (2004/05). Sources: UNESCO Institute for Statistics and IMF, *Comoros: Statistical Appendix* (August 2005).

Post-secondary Vocational (2003/04): 51 teachers; 734 pupils. Source: UNESCO Institute for Statistics.

Tertiary (2003/04): 130 teachers; 1,779 pupils. Source: UNESCO Institute for Statistics.

Adult Literacy Rate: 56.2% (males 63.5%; females 49.1%) in 2002. Source: UN Development Programme, *Human Development Report*.

Directory

The Constitution

In accordance with an agreement on national reconciliation, signed on 17 February 2001 by representatives of the Government, the separatist administration on Nzwani, opposition parties and civil society, a new Constitution was presented in August and approved by referendum on 23 December. Under the terms of the new Constitution, the country was renamed the Union of the Comoros, and each of the three islands, Ngazidja, Nzwani and Mwali, were to be granted partial autonomy and were to be headed by a local government. The Union, governed by a central government, was to be headed by the President. The main provisions of the Constitution are summarized below.

PREAMBLE

The preamble affirms the will of the Comoran people to derive from the state religion, Islam, inspiration for the principles and laws that the State and its institutions govern; to guarantee the pursuit of a common future; to establish new institutions based on the rule of law, democracy and good governance, which guarantee an equal division of power between the Union and those islands that compose it; to adhere to the principles laid down by the Charters of the UN, the Organization of African Unity (now the African Union) and the Organization of the Islamic Conference and by the Treaty of the League of Arab States; and to guarantee the rights of all citizens, without discrimination, in accordance with the UN Declaration of Human Rights and the African Charter of Human Rights.

The preamble guarantees solidarity between the Union and the islands, as well as between the islands themselves; equality amongst the islands and their inhabitants, regardless of race, origin, or religion; the right to freedom of expression, education, health and justice; the freedom and security of individuals; the inviolability of an individual's home or property; and the right of children to be protected against abandonment, exploitation and violence.

THE UNION OF THE COMOROS

The Comoros archipelago constitutes a republic. Sovereignty belongs to the people, and is exercised through their elected representatives or by the process of referendum. There is universal secret suffrage, which can be direct or indirect, for all citizens who are over the age of 18 and in full possession of their civil and political rights. Political parties and groups operate freely, respecting national sovereignty, democracy and territorial integrity.

COMPETENCIES OF THE UNION AND THE ISLANDS

Each island freely administers its own affairs, while respecting the unity of the Union and its territorial integrity. Each island establishes its own fundamental laws, which must respect the Constitution. All Comorans within the Union have equal rights, freedoms and duties. All the islands are headed by an elected executive and assembly. The Union has ultimate authority over the individual islands and legislates on matters of religion, nationality, currency, foreign affairs, external defence and national identity. As regards those competencies shared by both the Union and the islands, the Union has ultimate jurisdiction only if the issue concerned affects more than one island, if the matter cannot be resolved by one island alone, or if the judicial, economic or social integrity of the Union may be compromised. The islands are responsible for those matters not covered by the Union, or by shared responsibility. The islands are financially autonomous.

THE UNION'S INSTITUTIONS

Executive Power

The President of the Union is the symbol of national unity. He is the guarantor of national independence, the unity of the Republic, the autonomy of the islands, territorial integrity and adherence to international agreements. He is the Head of State and is responsible for external defence and security, foreign affairs and negotiating and ratifying treaties.

The Council of the Union is composed of the President and two Vice-Presidents, selected from each island. The members of the Council are elected for a four-year term, and the position of President rotates between the islands, while the Vice-Presidents are inhabitants of the two remaining islands. The President appoints the members of the Government (ministers of the Union) and determines their respective portfolios. The composition of the Government must represent all of the islands equally.

Legislative Power

Legislative power is vested in the Assembly of the Union (Assemblée de l'Union), which is composed of 33 deputies, elected for a period of five years. Fifteen of the deputies are selected by the islands' local assemblies (five deputies per island) and 18 are directly elected by universal suffrage. L'Assemblée de l'Union sits for two sessions each year and, if necessary, for extraordinary sessions.

Judicial Power

Judicial power is independent of executive and legislative power. The President of the Union is the guarantor of the independence of the judicial system and is assisted by the Higher Council of the Magistracy (Conseil Supérieur de la Magistrature). The Supreme Court (Cour Suprême) is the highest ruling authority in judicial, administrative and fiscal matters, and its rulings are final and binding. A Constitutional Court (Cour Constitutionelle) was created in 2004.

THE HIGH COUNCIL

The High Council considers constitutional matters, oversees the results of elections and referendums and guarantees basic human rights and civil liberties. Moreover, the High Council is responsible for ruling on any conflicts regarding the separate competencies of the Union and the islands. The President of the Union, the Vice-Presidents, the President of the Assemblée de l'Union, and each President of the local island executives appoint one member to the High Council. Members are elected for a six-year mandate, renewable once; the President of the High Council is appointed by the members for a six-year term.

REVISION OF THE CONSTITUTION

The power to initiate constitutional revision is jointly vested in the President of the Union and the members of the Assemblée de l'Union. Constitutional revision must be approved by a majority of two-thirds of the deputies in the Assemblée de l'Union and by two-thirds of the members of the islands' local assemblies. However, the organizational structure of the Union cannot be revised, and any revision that may affect the unity and territorial boundaries of the Union is not permitted.

PROVISIONAL ARRANGEMENTS

The Union's institutions, as defined in the Constitution, are to be established in accordance with the terms laid out in the agreement on national reconciliation of 17 February 2001. Institutions on the island of Mayotte will be established within a maximum period of six months following the island's decision to rejoin the Union of the Comoros.

The Government

HEAD OF STATE

Federal President: AHMED ABDALLAH SAMBI (elected 14 May 2006).

REGIONAL PRESIDENTS

Mwali: MOHAMED ALI SAID.
Ngazidja: MOHAMED ABDOULOIHABI.
Nzwani: LAILI ZAMANE ABDOU.

GOVERNMENT OF THE UNION OF THE COMOROS
(March 2008)

Vice-President, with responsibility for Transport, Post, Telecommunications and Tourism: IDI NADHOIM.
Vice-President, with responsibility for Health, Solidarity and Gender Empowerment: IKILILOU DHOININE.
Minister of Finance, Budget and Planning: MOHAMED ALI SOLIHI.
Minister of Justice, the Civil Service, Penitentiary Administration and Administrative Reforms and Keeper of the Seals: MOURAD SAID IBRAHIM.
Minister of External Relations and Co-operation, with responsibility for the Diaspora and Francophone and Arab Relations: AHMED BEN SAÏD DJAFFAR.
Minister of Agriculture, Fisheries and the Environment: SITI KASSIM.
Minister of Territorial Management, Infrastructure, Urban Planning and Housing: NAÏLANE MHADJI.
Minister of National Education, Research, the Arts, Culture, Youth and Sports and Government Spokesperson: ABDOURAHIM SAÏD BACAR.
Minister of Islamic Affairs, Communication and Human Rights, responsible for Relations with Parliament and the Island Institutions: M'MADI ALI.
Minister of Energy, Mining and Crafts: HOUMADI ABDALLAH.
Minister of the Economy, Labour, Employment and the Promotion of Female Entrepreneurs: HASSANI HAMADI.
Minister of Investment Promotion, Micro-Finance and Decentralized Co-operation: SAID ATTOUMANI.

MINISTRIES

Office of the Head of State: Palais de Beit Salam, BP 521, Moroni; tel. (74) 4808; fax (74) 4829; e-mail presidence@comorestelecom.km; internet www.beit-salam.km.
Ministry of Agriculture, Fisheries and the Environment: Moroni.
Ministry of the Economy, Foreign Trade, Industrial Promotion and Employment: Moroni; tel. (73) 0951; fax (73) 1981.
Ministry of Energy, Mining and Crafts: Moroni.
Ministry of External Relations and Co-operation, with responsibility for the Diaspora and Francophone and Arab Relations: BP 428, Moroni; tel. (73) 2306; fax (73) 2108; e-mail mirex@snpt.km.
Ministry of Finance, Budget and Planning: BP 324, Moroni; tel. (74) 4140; fax (74) 4141.
Ministry of Health, Solidarity and Gender Empowerment: Moroni.
Ministry of Investment Promotion, Micro-Finance and Decentralized Co-operation: Moroni.
Ministry of Islamic Affairs, Communication and Human Rights: Moroni.
Ministry of Justice, the Civil Service, Penitentiary Administration and Administrative Reforms: BP 2028, Moroni; tel. (74) 4040; fax (73) 4045.
Ministry of National Education, Research, the Arts, Culture, Youth and Sports: BP 73, Moroni; tel. (74) 4180; fax (74) 4181.
Ministry of Territorial Management, Infrastructure, Urban Planning and Housing: BP 12, Moroni; tel. (74) 4500; fax (73) 2222.
Ministry of Transport, Post, Telecommunications and Tourism: BP 1315, Moroni; tel. (73) 4266; fax (73) 2222.

President and Legislature

PRESIDENT

Presidential Election, 14 May 2006

Candidate	Votes cast	% of votes
Ahmed Abdallah Sambi	99,112	58.02
Ibrahim Halidi	48,378	28.32
Mohamed Djaanfari	23,322	13.65
Total	**170,812**	**100.00**

LEGISLATURE

Assemblée de l'Union: BP 447, Moroni; tel. (74) 4000; fax (74) 4011.
President: SAÏD DHIUFFUR BOUNOU.
Elections, 18 and 25 April 2004

Party	Seats
Convention pour le renouveau des Comores (CRC)	6
CHUMA	1
Coalition supporting the three regional Presidents*	11
Total	**33†**

* A loose coalition supporting the three regional Presidents.
† The remaining 15 seats were filled by nominees from the islands' local assemblies, members of which had been elected on 14 and 21 March 2004.

Election Commission

Commission électorale nationale indépendante aux Comores (CENI): Moroni; f. 2007 to succeed the Commission nationale des élections aux Comores; 10–13 mems; each island has a Commission électorale insulaire, consisting of 7 mems; Pres. ALI SAID M'DAHOMA.

Political Organizations

CHUMA (Islands' Fraternity and Unity Party): Moroni; e-mail chuma@pourlescomores.com; f. 1985; Leader SAÏD ALI KEMAL.
Convention pour le renouveau des Comores (CRC): f. 2002; Leader Col ASSOUMANI AZALI; Sec.-Gen. ABOUDOU SOEFOU.
Djawabu: Leader YOUSSOUF SAÏD SOILIHI.

Forces pour l'action républicaine (FAR): Leader Col ABDOU-RAZAK ABDULHAMID.

Front de l'action pour la démocratie et le développment (FADD): Nzwani; main opposition party on Nzwani.

Front démocratique (FD): BP 758, Moroni; tel. (73) 3603; e-mail idriss@snpt.km; f. 1982; Chair. MOUSTOIFA SAÏD CHEIKH; Sec.-Gen. ABDALLAH HALIFA.

Front national pour la justice (FNJ): Islamic fundamentalist orientation; Leader AHMED RACHID.

Mouvement des citoyens pour la République (MCR): f. 1998; Leader MAHAMOUD MRADABI.

Mouvement populaire anjouanais (MPA): f. 1997 by merger of Organisation pour l'indépendance d'Anjouan and Mouvement séparatiste anjouanais; principal separatist movement on Nzwani (Anjouan).

Mouvement pour la démocratie et le progrès (MDP—NGDC): Moroni; Leader ABBAS DJOUSSOUF.

Mouvement pour la République, l'ouverture et l'unité de l'archipel des Comores (Mouroua) (Movement for the Republic, Openness and the Unity of the Comoran Archipelago): Moroni; f. 2005; advocates institutional reform; Pres. SAÏD ABBAS DAHALANI.

Mouvement pour le socialisme et la démocratie (MSD): Moroni; f. 2000 by splinter group of the FD; Leader ABDOU SOEFOU.

Parti comorien pour la démocratie et le progrès (PCDP): Route Djivani, BP 179, Moroni; tel. (73) 1733; fax (73) 0650; Leader ABDOU SOULE ELBAK.

Parti républicain des Comores (PRC): BP 665, Moroni; tel. (73) 3489; fax (73) 3329; e-mail prc@online.fr; internet www.chez.com/prc; f. 1998; Leader MOHAMED SAÏD ABDALLAH M'CHANGAMA.

Parti socialiste des Comores (Pasoco): tel. (73) 1328; Leader AHMED AFFANDI ALI.

Rassemblement pour une initiative de développement avec une jeunesse avertie (RIDJA): BP 1905, Moroni; tel. and fax (73) 3356; f. 1999; Leader SAÏD LARIFOU; Sec.-Gen. AHAMED ACHIRAFI.

Rassemblement national pour le développement (RND): f. 1996; Chair. OMAR TAMOU; Sec. Gen. ABDOULHAMID AFFRAITANE.

Shawiri: Moroni; Leader Col MAHAMOUD MRADABI.

Shawiri—Unafasiya (SU): Moroni; f. 2003 following a split in Shawiri; Sec.-Gen. HADJI BEN SAÏD.

Union nationale pour la démocratie aux Comores (UNDC): Moroni; f. 1986; Pres. KAMAR EZZAMANE MOHAMED.

There are also a number of Islamist groups.

Diplomatic Representation

EMBASSIES IN THE COMOROS

China, People's Republic: Coulée de Lave, C109, BP 442, Moroni; tel. (73) 2521; fax (73) 2866; e-mail chinaemb_km@mfa.gov.cn; Ambassador TAO WEIGUANG.

France: blvd de Strasbourg, BP 465, Moroni; tel. (73) 0615; fax (73) 3347; e-mail pierre.lanners@snpt.km; internet www.ambafrance-km.org; Ambassador CHRISTIAN JOB.

South Africa: Itsandra Royal Hotel, Rm 112, Moroni; Ambassador MASILO MABETA.

Judicial System

Under the terms of the Constitution, the President is the guarantor of the independence of the judicial system, and is assisted by the Higher Council of the Magistracy (Conseil Supérieur de la Magistrature). The highest ruling authority in judicial, administrative and fiscal matters is the Supreme Court (Cour Suprême). The High Council considers constitutional matters. A Constitutional Court (Cour Constitutionelle), comprising seven members, appointed by the President of the Union of the Comoros, the two Vice-Presidents and the three regional Presidents, was established in 2004.

Constitutional Court: Moroni; Pres. ABDALLAH AHMED SOURETTE.

Religion

The majority of the population are Muslims, mostly Sunni. At 31 December 2004 there were an estimated 4,300 adherents of the Roman Catholic Church, equivalent to 0.5% of the total population.

ISLAM

Organisation Islamique des Comores: BP 596, Coulée, Moroni; tel. (73) 2071.

CHRISTIANITY

The Roman Catholic Church

Office of Apostolic Administrator of the Comoros: Mission Catholique, BP 46, Moroni; tel. and fax (76) 1996; e-mail mcatholique@comorestelecom.km; Apostolic Admin. Fr JOHAN GEERITS.

The Press

Al Watwan: Nagoudjou, BP 984, Moroni-Coulée; tel. and fax (73) 4448; fax (73) 3340; e-mail alwatwan@snpt.km; internet www.comores-online.com/al-watwan; f. 1985; weekly; state-owned; Dir-Gen. MOHAMED ABDOU SOIMADOU; Editor-in-Chief AHMED ALIAMIR; circ. 1,500.

L'Archipel: Moroni; f. 1988; privately owned; monthly; French; Editor-in-Chief ABOUBACAR MCHANGAMA.

Comores Aujourd'hui: Moroni; Dir HAMADA MADI.

La Gazette des Comores: BP 2216, Moroni; tel. (73) 5234; e-mail la_gazette@snpt.km; weekly; Publication Dir ALLAOUI SAÏD OMAR.

Kashkazi: BP 5311, Moroni; internet www.kashkazi.com; f. 2005; weekly; French.

Le Matin des Comores: BP 1040, Moroni; tel. (73) 2995; fax (73) 2939; daily; Dir ALILOIAFA MOHAMED SAÏD.

NEWS AGENCY

Agence comorienne de presse (HZK-Presse): BP 2216, Moroni; tel. (73) 9121; e-mail hzk_presse2@yahoo.fr; internet www.hzk-presse.com; f. 2004; Dir EL-HAD SAID OMAR.

PRESS ASSOCIATION

Organisation comorienne de la presse écrite (OCPE): Moroni; f. 2004; Pres. ABOUBACAR MCHANGAMA.

Publisher

KomÉdit: BP 535, Moroni; e-mail edition@komedit.com; f. 2000; general.

Broadcasting and Communications

TELECOMMUNICATIONS

Comores Télécom (Comtel): BP 7000, Moroni; tel. (74) 4300; fax (73) 1079; e-mail webmaster@comorestelecom.km; internet www.comorestelecom.km; formerly Société Nationale des Postes et des Télécommunications; post and telecommunications operations separated in 2004; scheduled for privatization; there were further plans to divide the mobile telecommunications and fixed-line branches of Comtel; Dir-Gen. CHARIKANAE BOUCHRANE.

BROADCASTING

Transmissions to the Comoros from Radio France Internationale commenced in early 1994. A number of privately owned radio and television stations also broadcast in the Comoros. In 2004 a Comoran television station was being established with funds from the People's Republic of China.

Office de la Radio Télévision des Comores (ORTC): Moroni; Comoran state broadcasting company; broadcasts Radio Comoros (f. 1960) and Télévision Nationale Comorienne (TNC; f. 2006); Dir-Gen. RADHUIA WAHAB.

Radio-Télévision Anjouanaise (RTA): Mbouyoujou-Ouani, Nzwani; tel. (71) 0124; e-mail contact@rtanjouan.org; internet www.rtanjouan.org; f. 1997; television station f. 2003; owned by the Nzwani regional government; Dir (Radio) FAHARDINE ABDOULBAY; Dir (Television) AMIR ABDALLAH.

Radio

Radio-Comoro: BP 250, Moroni; tel. (73) 2531; fax (73) 0303; govt-controlled; domestic programmes in Comoran and French; international broadcasts in Swahili, Arabic and French; Dir-Gen. ISMAIL IBOUROI; Tech. Dir ABDULLAH RADJAB.

Radio Dzialandzé Mutsamudu (RDM): Mutsamudu, Nzwani; f. 1992; broadcasts on Nzwani; Co-ordinator SAÏD ALI DACAR MGAZI.

Radio KAZ: Mkazi, BP 1933; tel. (73) 5201.
Radio Ngazidja: Moroni; broadcasts on Ngazidja; also known as Radio Mdjidjengo; represents Ngazidja regional government; Man. ABDOU DJIBABA.

Television

Djabal TV: Iconi, BP 675, Moroni; tel. (73) 6767.
Mtsangani Television (MTV): Mtsangani, BP 845, Moroni; tel. (73) 3316; f. 1996; owned by Centre d'Animation Socio-culturelle de Matsangani; cultural and educational programmes.
TV—SHA: Shashagnogo; tel. (73) 3636.

Finance

BANKING

(cap. = capital; res = reserves; dep. = deposits; m. = million; brs = branches; amounts in Comoros francs)

Central Bank

Banque Centrale des Comores: pl. de France, BP 405, Moroni; tel. (73) 1814; fax (73) 0349; e-mail bancecom@snpt.km; internet www.bancecom.com; f. 1981; bank of issue; cap. 1,100m., res 10,305m., dep. 17,606m. (Dec. 2006); Gov. AHAMADI ABDOULBASTOI.

Commercial Bank

Banque pour l'Industrie et le Commerce—Comores (BIC): pl. de France, BP 175, Moroni; tel. (73) 0243; fax (73) 1229; e-mail bic@snpt.km; f. 1990; 51% owned by Le Groupe Banque Populaire (France); 34% state-owned; cap. 300.0m., res 1,673.0m., dep. 20,247.9m. (Dec. 2004); Dir-Gen. CHRISTIAN GOULT; 6 brs.

There are a number of offshore financial institutions based in the Comoros. In 2005 the Madagascar-based bank BNI–Crédit Lyonnais announced plans to open a branch in the Comoros. In 2006 it was announced that EXIM Bank (Tanzania) would open a subsidiary in Moroni and that a merchant bank would open during that year.

Savings Bank

Société Nationale de la Poste et des Services Financiers (SNPSF): Moroni; internet www.snpsf.km; f. 2004.

Development Bank

Banque de Développement des Comores: pl. de France, BP 298, Moroni; tel. (73) 0818; fax (73) 0397; e-mail bdc.moroni@snpt.km; f. 1982; provides loans, guarantees and equity participation for small- and medium-scale projects; 50% state-owned; cap. and res 1,242.0m., total assets 3,470.5m. (Dec. 2002); Pres. MZE CHEI OUBEIDI; Gen. Man. SAÏD ABDILLAHI.

Trade and Industry

GOVERNMENT AGENCIES

Office National du Commerce: Moroni; state-operated agency for the promotion and development of domestic and external trade.
Office National d'Importation et de Commercialisation du Riz (ONICOR): BP 748, Itsambouni, Moroni; tel. (73) 5566; fax (73) 0144; e-mail onicor_moroni@snpt.km; Gen. Man. MUSLIME MOUSSA.
Société de Développement de la Pêche Artisanale des Comores (SODEPAC): Moroni; state-operated agency overseeing fisheries development programme.

DEVELOPMENT ORGANIZATION

Centre Fédéral d'Appui au Développement Rural (CEFADER): Moroni; rural development org. with branches on each island.

CHAMBERS OF COMMERCE

Union des Chambres de Commerce des Comores: BP 763, Moroni; tel. (73) 0958; fax (73) 1983; privatized in 1995; Pres. AHMED BAZI.

TRADE ASSOCIATION

Organisation Comorienne de la Vanille (OCOVA): BP 472, Moroni; tel. (73) 2709; fax (73) 2719.
There is a further association, the **Fédération du secteur privé comorien (FSPC)**.

EMPLOYERS' ORGANIZATIONS

Club d'Actions des Promoteurs Economiques: Moroni; f. 1999; Head SAÏD HASSANE DINI.
Organisation Patronale des Comores (OPACO): Oasis, BP 981, Moroni; tel. (73) 0848; f. 1991; Pres. CHAMSOUDINE AHMED.

UTILITIES

MA-MWE—Gestion de l'Eau et de l'Electricité aux Comores: BP 1762, Moroni; tel. (73) 3130; fax (73) 2359; e-mail cee@snpt.km; f. as Electricité et Eau des Comores; transferred to private management and renamed Comorienne de l'Eau et de l'Electricité in 1997; renationalized and renamed Service Public de l'Eau et de l'Electricité in 2001; reprivatized in Jan. 2002 and renamed as above; responsible for the production and distribution of electricity and water; Dir-Gen. ALLOUI SAÏD ABASSE.
Société d'Electricité d'Anjouan (EDA): Nzwani; Technical Dir YOUSSOUF ALI OICHEH.

STATE-OWNED ENTERPRISE

Comores Hydrocarbures: BP 3840, Moroni; tel. (73) 0490; fax (73) 1818; imports petroleum products; scheduled for privatization; Man. Dir MOHAMED EL-AMINE SOEFOU.

TRADE UNION

Confédération des Travailleurs/euses des Comores (CTC): BP 1199, Moroni; tel. and fax (73) 5143; e-mail syndicatctcomores@yahoo.fr; f. 1996; Sec.-Gen. IBOUROI ALI TABIBOU.

Transport

ROADS

In 1999 there were an estimated 880 km of classified roads. About 76.5% of the network was paved in that year.

SHIPPING

The port of Mutsamudu, on Nzwani, can accommodate vessels of up to 11 m draught. Goods from Europe are routed via Madagascar, and coastal vessels connect the Comoros with the east coast of Africa. The country's registered merchant fleet at 31 December 2006 numbered 252 vessels, totalling 727,185 grt. Mayotte suspended ferry services to the other islands in the archipelago in late 2004 due to safety issues.
Société Comorienne de Navigation: Moroni; services to Madagascar.

CIVIL AVIATION

The international airport is at Moroni-Hahaya on Ngazidja. Work began on the upgrading of the airport in late 2004. Each of the other islands has a small airfield. International services were operated by Air Austral (Réunion), Air Mayotte, Air Tanzania, Sudan Airways, Precision Air (Tanzania) and Yemenia. Blue Line (France) also offered charter flights between June and September. Kenya Airways commenced flying to the Comoros and Mayotte in November 2006.
Comores Air Services: Moroni; tel. (73) 3366; internal services and international flights to Madagascar.
Comores Aviation International: Moroni; tel. (73) 3400; fax (73) 3401; internet www.comores-aviation.com; f. 1999; twice-weekly charter flights between Moroni and Mayotte; Dir JEAN-MARC HEINTZ.

Tourism

The principal tourist attractions are the beaches, underwater fishing and mountain scenery. Increasing numbers of Comorans resident abroad were choosing to visit the archipelago; in 2004 it was estimated that 58.3% of visitors to the Comoros were former Comoran residents. In 2005 hotel capacity amounted to an estimated 836 beds. Receipts from tourism totalled US $26m. in 1997, but had decreased to $10m. by 2004. Tourist arrivals increased to 27,474 in 1998, but had decreased to 19,551 by 2005. In late 2004 the ferry service to Mayotte was suspended, disrupting the tourism sector as many tourists travel via Mayotte.
Société Comorienne de Tourisme et d'Hôtellerie (COMOTEL): Itsandra Hotel, BP 1027, Moroni; tel. (73) 2365; national tourist agency; Dir-Gen. SITTI ATTOMANE.

THE DEMOCRATIC REPUBLIC OF THE CONGO

Introductory Survey

Location, Climate, Language, Religion, Flag, Capital

The Democratic Republic of the Congo (formerly Zaire) lies in central Africa, bordered by the Republic of the Congo to the north-west, by the Central African Republic and Sudan to the north, by Uganda, Rwanda, Burundi and Tanzania to the east and by Zambia and Angola to the south. There is a short coastline at the outlet of the River Congo. The climate is tropical, with an average temperature of 27°C (80°F) and an annual rainfall of 150 cm–200 cm (59 ins–97 ins). French is the official language. More than 400 Sudanese and Bantu dialects are spoken; Kiswahili, Kiluba, Kikongo and Lingala being the most widespread. An estimated 50% of the population is Roman Catholic, and there is a smaller Protestant community. Many inhabitants follow traditional (mostly animist) beliefs. The national flag (proportions 2 by 3) is light blue, with a yellow star in the upper left corner and a diagonal red stripe edged in yellow. The capital is Kinshasa.

Recent History

The Democratic Republic of the Congo (DRC), formerly the Belgian Congo, became independent from Belgium as the Republic of the Congo on 30 June 1960. Five days later the armed forces mutinied, and the UN subsequently dispatched troops to the region to maintain order. In July 1964 President Joseph Kasavubu appointed Moïse Tshombe, the former leader of a group supporting the secession of the Katanga region, as interim Prime Minister, pending elections, and in August the country was renamed the Democratic Republic of the Congo. In November 1965 Col (subsequently Marshal) Joseph-Désiré Mobutu seized power and proclaimed himself head of the 'Second Republic'. In late 1970 Mobutu, as sole candidate, was elected President. (From January 1972, as part of a national policy of 'authenticity', he became known as Mobutu Sese Seko.) In November 1970 elections to a new National Assembly (subsequently renamed the National Legislative Council, NLC) took place. In October 1971 the DRC was renamed the Republic of Zaire, and one year later the Government of Zaire and the Executive Committee of the Mouvement populaire de la révolution (MPR), the sole legal political party, merged into the National Executive Council (NEC).

In March 1977, and again in May 1978, Katangan separatists invaded Zaire from Angola, taking much of Shaba (formerly Katanga) region; however, the separatists were repulsed on both occasions by the Zairean army, with armed support from a number of Western Governments. Legislative elections took place in October 1977, and, at a presidential election in December, Mobutu (again the sole candidate) was re-elected for a further seven-year term. In early 1982 opponents of Zaire's one-party system of government formed the Union pour la démocratie et le progrès social (UDPS). This was followed by the formation of the Front congolais pour le rétablissement de la démocratie (FCD), a coalition of opposition parties.

In April 1990 Mobutu announced that a plural political system, initially to comprise three parties, would be introduced after a transitional period of one year; the UDPS was immediately granted legal status. At the same time Mobutu declared the inauguration of the 'Third Republic' and relinquished the posts of Chairman of the MPR and State Commissioner for National Defence in the NEC, although remaining Head of State. The NEC was dissolved and Prof. Lunda Bululu, previously an adviser to Mobutu, was appointed First State Commissioner (Prime Minister). In May 1990 a new, smaller, transitional NEC was formed, and Mobutu announced the imminent 'depoliticization' of the security forces and of the administration in general. In June Mobutu relinquished presidential control of the NEC and of foreign policy, and authorized the formation of independent trade unions. In October it was announced that a full multi-party political system would be established, and in November the necessary legislation was introduced.

By February 1991 a large number of new parties had emerged. Prominent among them was the Union des fédéralistes et républicains indépendants (UFERI), led by Nguza Karl-I-Bond. An enlarged transitional Government, appointed in March and reshuffled in April, included members of minor opposition groups. None of the major opposition parties, including the UDPS and the UFERI, agreed to join the new Government. Prof. Mulumba Lukoji, an economist who had served in previous administrations, was appointed First State Commissioner.

In July 1991 some 130 opposition movements formed a united front, the Union sacrée. A National Conference was convened at the beginning of August, with the aim of drafting a new constitution, but was repeatedly suspended, initially owing to the dissatisfaction of the Union sacrée with the composition of its participants, prompting renewed civil unrest and the dispatch of French and Belgian troops to Zaire to evacuate nationals of those countries. In November Karl-I-Bond was appointed to the premiership. The Union sacrée denounced the appointment and expelled UFERI members from its ranks. Despite the expiry of his mandate as President in early December, Mobutu remained in office.

In April 1992 the National Conference reopened and declared its status to be sovereign and its decisions to be binding. Mobutu reacted with cautious opposition to the erosion of his powers. In mid-August the National Conference elected Etienne Tshisekedi Wa Mulumba, the leader of the UPDS, as First State Commissioner, following the resignation of Karl-I-Bond. A 'transition act', adopted by the Conference in early August, afforded Tshisekedi a mandate to govern, pending the promulgation of a new constitution that would curtail the powers of the President. Later that month Tshisekedi appointed a transitional 'Government of National Union', which included opponents of Mobutu.

The political interests of Tshisekedi and Mobutu clashed when the President declared his intention to promote the adoption of a 'semi-presidential constitution', rather than the parliamentary system favoured by the Conference. In November 1992 the National Conference (without the participation of Mobutu's supporters) adopted a draft Constitution, providing for the establishment of a 'Federal Republic of the Congo', the introduction of a bicameral legislature and the election of a President (who would fulfil a largely ceremonial function) by universal suffrage. In early December the National Conference dissolved itself and was succeeded by a 453-member High Council of the Republic (HCR), headed by Archbishop Monsengwo, which, as the supreme interim executive and legislative authority, was empowered to amend and adopt the new Constitution and to organize elections. At the same time Monsengwo declared that the report of a special commission, established by the Conference in order to examine allegations of corruption brought against Mobutu and his associates, would be considered by the HCR. Mobutu responded by ordering the suspension of the HCR and the Government. Attempts by the presidential guard to obstruct the convening of the HCR ended, following the organization of a public rally in Kinshasa by Monsengwo and other members of the HCR. With support from the USA, Belgium and France, Monsengwo reiterated the HCR's recognition of Tshisekedi as head of Zaire's Government.

In mid-January 1993 the HCR declared Mobutu to be guilty of treason, on account of his mismanagement of state affairs, and threatened impeachment proceedings unless he recognized the legitimacy of the 'Government of National Union'. In March, in an attempt to reassert his political authority, Mobutu convened a special 'conclave' of political forces to debate the country's future, which appointed Faustin Birindwa, a former UDPS member and adviser to Tshisekedi, as Prime Minister, charged with the formation of a 'Government of National Salvation'. The NLC was also reconvened to operate within the terms of the previous Constitution introduced by Mobutu. Birindwa's Cabinet, appointed in April, included Karl-I-Bond as First Deputy Prime Minister in charge of Defence. While the Birindwa administration was denied widespread official international recognition,

Tshisekedi became increasingly frustrated at the weakness of his Government and the deteriorating stability of the country. During April the army embarked upon a campaign of intimidation of opposition members, while tribal warfare re-emerged in Shaba and also erupted in the north-eastern region of Kivu. Tshisekedi urged the intervention of the UN to address these problems, and in July the Secretary-General of the UN appointed a Special Envoy to Zaire.

At the end of September 1993 an agreement was concluded between representatives of President Mobutu and of the principal opposition groups, providing for the adoption of a single constitutional text for the transitional period, which would be subject to approval by a national referendum. During October, however, attempts to finalize the terms of the agreement were complicated by the insistence of Tshisekedi's supporters that he should continue in the office of Prime Minister, despite the objections of Mobutu's representatives that Tshisekedi's mandate had been superseded by the September agreement.

In early January 1994, in an attempt to end the political impasse, an agreement to form a government of national reconciliation was signed by all major political parties, with the notable exception of Tshisekedi's own UDPS. Encouraged by the unexpected level of political support for the initiative, in mid-January Mobutu announced the dissolution of the HCR and the NLC, the dismissal of the Government of National Salvation, headed by Birindwa, and the candidacy for the premiership of two contestants, Tshisekedi and Lukoji, to be decided by the transitional legislature (to be known as the Haut Conseil de la République—Parlement de Transition, HCR—PT). The HCR—PT promptly rejected Mobutu's procedure for the selection of a new Prime Minister. Subsequent attempts by the legislature to formulate a new procedure were frustrated by the increasingly divergent interests of the member parties of the USOR, and by Tshisekedi's insistence of his legitimate claim to the office.

On 8 April 1994 the HCR—PT endorsed a new Transitional Constitution Act, reiterating the provisions of previous accords for the organization of a constitutional referendum and presidential and legislative elections, and defining the functions of transitional institutions during a 15-month period. The Government, to be accountable to the HCR—PT, was to assume some former powers of the President, including the control of the Central Bank and the security forces. A new Prime Minister was to be appointed from opposition candidates, to be nominated within 10 days of the President's promulgation of the Act (on 9 April). Widening divisions within the USOR frustrated attempts to unite the opposition behind Tshisekedi as sole candidate, prompting the expulsion, in May, of 10 dissident parties from the USOR.

In June 1994 the HCR—PT ratified the candidature of seven opposition representatives for the premiership, rejecting that of Tshisekedi on a technicality. On 14 June it was reported that Léon Kengo Wa Dondo had been elected Prime Minister by 322 votes to 133 in the HCR—PT. However, Kengo Wa Dondo's election was immediately denounced as illegitimate, under the terms of the April Constitution Act, by the opposition. A new transitional Government, announced on 6 July, was similarly rejected by the radical opposition. On 11 July, during a motion of confidence, the Government received overwhelming support from the HCR—PT. In October an expanded radical opposition grouping (the Union sacrée de l'opposition radicale et ses alliés, USORAL) resumed its participation in the HCR—PT, having boycotted proceedings since the election of Kengo Wa Dondo in June.

In late June 1995 the HCR—PT adopted a constitutional amendment (approved by Mobutu), whereby the period of national transition (due to end on 9 July) was to be extended by two years, owing to a shortage of government resources. Meanwhile, opposition frustration at the Government's failure to publish an electoral timetable intensified. In December opposition groups unanimously rejected a government offer to participate in a national coalition administration and reiterated their demands for the prompt announcement of a timetable for multi-party elections. An electoral commission, comprising 44 members (22 from both of the major political groupings) and headed by Bayona Bameya (a close political associate of President Mobutu), was formally installed in April 1996. A draft of the new Constitution, which provided for a federal state with a parliamentary system of government and a president with limited powers, was approved by the Government in late May.

In the mid-1990s existing ethnic tensions in eastern Zaire were heightened by the inflow of an estimated 1m. Hutu refugees from Rwanda (see below). The plight of the region's Zairean Tutsis (Banyamulenge) aroused international concern in late 1996, following reports of the organized persecution of Banyamulenge communities by elements of the Zairean security forces and by extremist Hutu refugees. In October the Sud-Kivu regional administration ordered all Banyamulenge to leave the area within one week or risk internment or forced expulsion. Although the order was subsequently rescinded, this threat provoked the mobilization of armed Banyamulenge rebels, who launched a violent counter-offensive, allegedly supported by the Tutsi-dominated authorities in Rwanda and Burundi. Support for the rebels from dissidents of diverse ethnic origin (including Shaba and Kasaï secessionists, and local Mai-Mai warriors) increased during the month, and later in October the rebels announced the formation of the Alliance des forces démocratiques pour la libération du Congo-Zaïre (AFDL), under the leadership of Laurent-Désiré Kabila (hitherto leader of the Parti de la révolution populaire, and a known opponent of the Mobutu regime since the 1960s). AFDL forces made rapid territorial gains, and the movement soon gathered momentum, emerging as a national rebellion aimed at overthrowing Mobutu. Counter-attacks by Zairean troops from January 1997 failed to recapture any significant area of territory. In March the AFDL entered the strategically important northern town of Kisangani (which had served as the centre of military operations for the Government), and in early April Mbuji-Mayi fell to the rebels. AFDL troops, entering Lubumbashi on 9 April, were welcomed as liberators, while government troops withdrew from the city. The Zairean Government continued to make allegations that the AFDL offensive was being supported by government troops from Rwanda, Uganda, Burundi and Angola, while the AFDL, in turn, claimed that the Zairean army had been reinforced by forces of the União Nacional para a Independência Total de Angola (UNITA).

Meanwhile, in August 1996 Mobutu had travelled to Switzerland to receive medical treatment. His absence, and uncertainties as to the state of his health, contributed to the poor co-ordination of the Zairean Government's response to the AFDL, which by the end of November was in control of most of Kivu. In that month the HCR—PT urged the expulsion of all Tutsis from Zairean territory; following attacks on Tutsis and their property, many Tutsi residents of Kinshasa fled to Brazzaville (Republic of the Congo). In the same month repeated public demonstrations demanded the resignation of Kengo Wa Dondo (himself part Tutsi in origin) for having failed to respond effectively to the insurrection. In December Mobutu returned to Zaire, appointed Gen. Mahele Bokungu as Chief of General Staff and reorganized the Government, retaining Kengo Wa Dondo as Prime Minister.

The continued exclusion of Tshisekedi from the Government prompted his supporters to mount a campaign of civil disobedience, and in January 1997 his faction of the UDPS announced its support for the AFDL. In March, following the capture of Kisangani, the HCR—PT voted to dismiss Kengo Wa Dondo, who tendered his resignation as Prime Minister later that month. He was replaced at the beginning of April by Tshisekedi, who, having offered government posts to members of the AFDL (which they refused), announced that he was dissolving the HCR—PT. Parliament, in turn, voted to dismiss Tshisekedi, whose supporters organized a demonstration of support in Kinshasa, only to come under attack from the security forces. On 8 April Mobutu declared a national state of emergency, dissolving the Government and ordering the deployment of security forces throughout Kinshasa. Gen. Likulia Bolongo was appointed Prime Minister at the head of a new 28-member 'Government of National Salvation', in which USORAL refused to participate. An arrest warrant was subsequently issued for Kengo Wa Dondo, who was alleged to have fled to Switzerland with funds from the national treasury.

After peace talks between Mobutu and Kabila, mediated by the South African President, Nelson Mandela, ended in failure in early May 1997, Kabila reiterated his intention to take the capital by force. On 16 May Mobutu left Kinshasa (travelling to Togo, and then to Morocco, where he died in September), while many of his supporters and family fled across the border to Brazzaville. On 17 May AFDL troops entered Kinshasa (encountering no resistance), and Kabila declared himself President of the DRC (the name in use during 1964–71), which swiftly gained international recognition. On 20 May 1997 Kabila arrived in Kinshasa and on 23 May he formed a transitional Government, which, while dominated by members of the AFDL, also included members of the UDPS and of the Front patriotique. No Prime

Minister was appointed, and Tshisekedi was not offered a cabinet post. On 26 May, following a number of protests, Kabila issued a decree indefinitely banning all political parties and public demonstrations. On 28 May Kabila issued a constitutional decree (which was to remain in force pending the adoption of a new constitution), investing the President with virtually absolute legislative and executive power, as well as control over the armed forces and the treasury. Of the previously existing state institutions, only the judiciary was not dissolved.

On 29 May 1997 Kabila was inaugurated as President of the DRC, assuming full executive, legislative and military powers. Despite concern regarding the new administration's treatment of refugees, Kabila's assumption of power was well received internationally. In August a military Court of Justice was established by decree, and at the end of October two statutory orders were signed by Kabila; one redesignated the administrative areas and local authorities of the DRC (the nine former regions were reorganized into 11 provinces), while the other created a paramilitary force (the Service national), which, under the control of the President, was to monitor and facilitate national reconstruction. In late October Kabila appointed a 42-member Constitutional Commission, which was to draft a new constitution by March 1998. In the following month Kabila reaffirmed that the activities of political parties were suspended, pending presidential and legislative elections, scheduled to take place in 1999.

Following accusations of financial malpractice against several members of the Cabinet, in June 1998 Kabila announced a cabinet reorganization, in which five ministers were dismissed. Eight new posts were created, increasing the number of ministers to 37. In July a UN investigative team, which, despite continued obstruction by the Government, had conducted enquiries in the DRC between November 1997 and early 1998, published its report, concluding that the AFDL had massacred a large number of Rwandan Hutu refugees in 1996 and 1997; these findings were rejected by the Government on the grounds that they were based on an incomplete investigation.

In late July 1998 Kabila issued a decree expelling Rwandan troops from the country. In early August an armed insurrection was launched in Nord-Kivu province, in the east of the DRC, reportedly with Rwandan and French support. Western Governments advised their citizens to leave the country, and several diplomatic missions were closed. The rebels advanced quickly in the east of the country and were soon reported to have captured Bukavu and Goma. Shortly afterwards a second front was opened from Kitona, in the west of the country, where further advances resulted in the rebels gaining control of Boma, Banana and Matadi. The Inga Dam, which supplies both electricity and water to Kinshasa and the Katanga mining region, was also captured, enabling the rebels to interrupt power supplies. At that time the rebel forces announced that they had formed a political organization, the Rassemblement congolais démocratique (RCD), with the aim of introducing political democracy in the DRC. The RCD leadership included Z'ahidi Ngoma, together with a former Prime Minister, Lunda Bululu, and Ernest Wamba dia Wamba.

Other countries in the region were, meanwhile, becoming involved in the conflict. While Rwanda had initially denied accusations that it was supporting the rebels, it quickly became evident that the anti-Kabila insurgents had the support of both Rwanda and Uganda, and that Kabila was receiving support from Angola, Namibia and Zimbabwe. Angolan troops, in particular, were instrumental in recapturing rebel-held towns in the western DRC, and in early September 1998 had expelled the rebels from that part of the country. Regional divisions were clearly evident in August at a meeting of Ministers of Defence of the Southern African Development Community (SADC, see p. 386) to mobilize support for Kabila; only one-half of the participating delegates favoured intervention in the conflict. Regional efforts to reach a political solution to the civil conflict continued in September. The Government refused to negotiate with the RCD and a newly formed rebel grouping, the Mouvement pour la libération du Congo (MLC), however, on the grounds that their activities were supported by Rwanda and Uganda, respectively.

Although their advance had been halted in the west, the rebels continued to make progress in the east, capturing towns in Kasaï Oriental and Katanga. Despite their continued military successes, however, the rebels lacked popular support, and the movement was widely perceived as a Rwandan-backed Tutsi invasion. In January 1999 the ongoing civil war led to the declaration of a state of siege in six of the 11 provinces of the DRC. On 29 January Kabila issued a decree ending the ban on political parties. However, the new system was widely criticized for continuing restrictions, which effectively prevented many existing parties from registering. Kabila also announced that the AFDL was to be transformed into People's Power Committees to encourage involvement in the political process at a local level. Following Kabila's dissolution of the Cabinet on 20 February, a new Government was formed in March.

In May 1999 the RCD announced changes to its executive committee; Wamba dia Wamba was replaced as President by Dr Emile Ilunga. (Z'ahidi Ngoma had resigned in February.) However, a number of the RCD's founding members opposed this move, and Wamba dia Wamba denounced it as a coup. Following clashes in Kisangani between supporters of Wamba dia Wamba and those of Ilunga, two factions emerged; one of these, led by Ilunga, was based in Goma, with the support of Rwanda, while the other, led by Wamba dia Wamba, was based in Kisangani and supported by Uganda. In June the DRC began proceedings at the International Court of Justice (ICJ, see p. 20), in The Hague, Netherlands, against Burundi, Rwanda and Uganda for acts of armed aggression, which it claimed to have been in contravention of both the charters of the Organization of African Unity (OAU, now the African Union, see p. 164) and the UN. (In February 2001 the DRC abandoned the proceedings against Burundi and Rwanda.)

Despite a number of regional initiatives to end the civil war in late 1998 and early 1999, no lasting cease-fire agreement was negotiated, largely owing to Kabila's continued insistence that the rebels were supported by Rwanda and Uganda, and that they, therefore, be excluded from any talks. Although Col Muammar al-Qaddafi, the Libyan leader, hosted two rounds of regional talks in Sirte (Libya), it was in Lusaka, Zambia, under the mediation of Zambia's President Chiluba, that the rebels were first accorded a place at the negotiations, during a summit held in late June. Following this meeting, a cease-fire agreement was signed by the Heads of State of the DRC, Angola, Namibia, Zimbabwe, Rwanda and Uganda on 10 July (witnessed by the OAU, SADC, the UN and Zambia), by the leader of the MLC, Jean-Pierre Bemba Gombo, on 1 August and, following the resolution of a dispute (owing to the divisions within the RCD), by all 50 founding members of the RCD on 31 August. The agreement provided for an immediate cease-fire, the establishment of a Joint Military Commission (JMC), which was to investigate cease-fire violations, disarm militia groups and monitor the withdrawal of foreign troops, the deployment of a UN peace-keeping force and the organization of a national debate within the DRC. However, the UN stressed that authorization for a full peace-keeping force would have to be preceded by a 90-member military liaison mission and a subsequent 500-strong military observer mission. In July a general amnesty for rebels within the DRC was announced, and in that month the JMC was formed, comprising representatives of the rebel groups and the six Lusaka signatory states (the DRC, Angola, Namibia, Rwanda, Uganda and Zimbabwe). In mid-August the UN military liaison mission received official approval.

In August 1999 further fighting erupted in Kisangani between forces from Rwanda and Uganda and their respective factions of the RCD. A cease-fire was negotiated in late August, and at the end of the month the Ilunga faction of the RCD (known as RCD—Goma) announced a new executive committee. An investigation into the causes of the fighting recommended that all fighting forces be removed from Kisangani; as a result, the MLC transferred its headquarters to Gbadolite, while the Wamba dia Wamba faction of the RCD, known as the RCD—Mouvement de libération (RCD—ML), withdrew from Bunia. In early September the rebels raised objections to the composition of the cease-fire commission and voiced doubts over the neutrality of the mediators. At the end of the month, however, the rebels and the Government agreed that the national debate would be facilitated by the Italian Sant'Egidio Roman Catholic Community, although differences remained over the location for the conference and over OAU involvement.

In November 1999 both factions of the RCD announced that they no longer respected the cease-fire (having previously denied violations), and the Ilunga faction of the movement accused the Government of openly breaching the agreement. In that month the UN Security Council voted to extend the mandate of the military liaison mission until mid-January 2000, owing to the difficulties experienced in obtaining security assurances and permission to deploy throughout the DRC. On 30 November 1999 the Council approved the establishment of a UN Mission in the Democratic Republic of the Congo (MONUC), to comprise some 5,000 troops, together with up to 500 military observers and liaison and technical assessment officers, with an initial mandate until March 2000. At a meeting of the UN Security Council concerning the conflict in the DRC, which took place in New York, USA, in January 2000, regional Heads of State expressed support for the rapid deployment of MONUC forces to support the Lusaka peace accord. In late February the UN Security Council authorized the expansion of MONUC to number 5,537 and the extension of its mandate to the end of August.

Also in late February 2000 the national debate was convened in Kinshasa, but was boycotted by opposition politicians, as well as by representatives of the rebel groups. Participants in the discussions subsequently submitted a final report, urging the establishment of a new legislature and the revision of the Lusaka accord. The rebel groups rejected an offer by Kabila of a general amnesty in return for the cessation of hostilities, and fierce fighting between government and rebel forces continued in the east of the country, particularly in Kasaï Occidental. In early April participants at a meeting of the JMC signed a new cease-fire agreement, whereby all the forces involved in the conflict were to suspend hostilities and remain in position for a period of three months, pending the deployment of MONUC personnel to form a neutral zone between them.

In July 2000 240 deputies of a new 300-member transitional Parliament were elected by a commission under the supervision of the Ministry of Internal Affairs, while the remaining 60 were nominated by Kabila. A presidential decree, adopted in that month, provided for the decentralization of the Government, with the transferral of the legislature to Lubumbashi. On 22 August the new transitional Parliament was inaugurated in Lubumbashi, despite criticism from the international community, which accused Kabila of acting in contravention of the Lusaka accord.

In August 2000 the UN Security Council adopted a resolution extending the mandate of MONUC until mid-October to allow further time for the implementation of the cease-fire agreement. Kabila subsequently informed the UN that he authorized the immediate deployment of MONUC troops throughout the DRC. In October, in a reorganization of the RCD—Goma leadership, Ilunga was replaced by Adolphe Onusumba. In the same month an attempt to oust Wamba dia Wamba from the leadership of the RCD—ML was suppressed by Ugandan troops. The RCD—ML subsequently divided, following the establishment of a dissident breakaway faction, led by Roger Lumbala, which became known as RCD—National (RCD—N). In early December, following renewed fierce fighting, RCD—Goma, supported by Rwandan troops, succeeded in gaining control of the significant town of Pweto, in the south-eastern province of Katanga. The six countries and three rebel groups involved in the conflict subsequently signed an agreement in Harare, Zimbabwe, pledging to withdraw forces 15 km from positions of military engagement, prior to the deployment of MONUC troops (which was scheduled to take place within 45 days). Nevertheless, hostilities subsequently continued at Pweto, and in other eastern regions, while RCD—Goma refused to withdraw its forces in accordance with the agreement until the Government entered into bilateral discussions with the rebels and permitted the complete deployment of MONUC troops. In mid-December the UN Security Council adopted a resolution in favour of extending the mandate of MONUC to mid-June 2001.

On 16 January 2001 Kabila was assassinated by a member of his presidential guard at his private residence in Kinshasa. The transitional Parliament approved the nomination by the political leadership of his son, Maj.-Gen. Joseph Kabila Kabange (hitherto Chief of Staff), as interim President. Following his inauguration on 26 January, Joseph Kabila immediately engaged in international diplomatic efforts to resolve the conflict and urged rebel leaders to attend peace discussions with him. Following a meeting with Kabila in early February, the President of Rwanda, Maj.-Gen. Paul Kagame, announced that Rwandan troops would be withdrawn from Pweto on condition that control of the town was transferred to MONUC. However, the UN Security Council continued to demand that the DRC Government demonstrate its commitment to peace prior to the deployment of MONUC troops and insisted that the implementation of the disengagement plan agreed in December was essential to this end. At a meeting of the UN Security Council in mid-February Kabila accepted the former Botswanan President, Sir Ketumile Masire, as mediator to the conflict. Following a further meeting of the UN Security Council later that month, attended by representatives of the six countries and three rebel factions involved in the conflict, it was agreed that the 15 km withdrawal of forces was to commence by mid-March.

The withdrawal from positions of military engagement duly commenced in mid-March 2001, in accordance with the UN-sponsored agreement, with the retreat from Pweto of the RCD—Goma and allied Rwandan troops. The first contingents of MONUC troops arrived in the DRC, and by the end of the month were stationed in the north-east of the country. At the beginning of April, however, the Ugandan-supported Forces pour la libération du Congo (FLC, which had been formed earlier that year by breakaway members of the MLC and the RCD—ML) refused to proceed with the withdrawal from military positions near Kisangani until MONUC guaranteed security in the region. The deployment of MONUC troops in the east of the country was delayed, after RCD forces initially prevented the peace-keeping forces from entering Kisangani. In mid-April Kabila appointed a new, enlarged Cabinet, which included only four members of the previous administration.

In April 2001 a UN commission of experts issued a report, which accused Rwandan and Ugandan troops of systematic illegal exploitation of the DRC's mineral resources, and urged the Security Council to impose a trade embargo against the two countries. The Ugandan Government pledged to investigate the allegations of corruption (which implicated close members of the Ugandan President's family) and to complete the withdrawal of its forces from the DRC. In early May representatives of the DRC Government and the rebel factions, meeting in Lusaka, under the aegis of the OAU, SADC and the UN, signed a declaration establishing the principles for an 'Inter-Congolese National Dialogue' (a formal process of national consultation, with the aim of reaching a permanent peace settlement). It was decided that Masire would gather public opinion for a proposed agenda, prior to further preparatory discussions. Later in May Kabila ended the remaining restrictions on political activity (thereby removing a major impediment to conducting the Inter-Congolese National Dialogue) and ordered the release of a number of detained human rights activists.

In late May 2001 a report by the state prosecutor claimed that forces opposing the Government (the RCD factions, and Rwandan and Ugandan troops) had conspired in the assassination of Laurent-Désiré Kabila, with the aim of seizing power. In June the UN Security Council approved a resolution extending the mandate of MONUC until mid-2002; the Council welcomed the progress towards negotiating a peace settlement, but reiterated demands that all foreign forces complete their withdrawal from the country. In early August, however, Kagame insisted that Kabila fulfil pledges to demobilize Rwandan Hutu militia, known as Interahamwe (who had become allied with DRC government forces, after participating in the genocide in Rwanda in 1994), as a precondition to withdrawing the Rwandan troops deployed in the country. Also in August Wamba dia Wamba was ousted as the RCD—ML leader by Mbusa Nyamwisi.

Preparatory discussions between Kabila and the leaders of the FLC and the RCD factions, mediated by Masire, which were for the first time attended by unarmed opposition groups and civic associations, were conducted in Gaborone, Botswana, in late August 2001. Agreement was reached on a number of significant issues for the organization of the Inter-Congolese National Dialogue, which was to commence in the Ethiopian capital, Addis Ababa, in mid-October. In early September the Namibian Government announced that it had withdrawn its troops (numbering some 1,850) from the DRC.

In mid-October 2001 the Inter-Congolese National Dialogue was convened in Addis Ababa; however, negotiations were suspended one week later, after the Government withdrew in protest at the absence of the allied Mai-Mai delegation. At the beginning of 2002, however, international donors pledged considerable development aid to support further efforts, in recognition of the progress achieved.

The Inter-Congolese National Dialogue was reconvened in Sun City, South Africa, in February 2002, but was initially boycotted by Bemba. In April it was announced that the Government and the MLC had reached a compromise agreement, providing for the establishment of an administration of national unity: Kabila was to remain President and Bemba became Prime Minister for a transitional period, prior to general elections. Signatories to the agreement commenced discussions in Matadi in May to draft a new constitution, while RCD—Goma and the UDPS announced their intention to form a political alliance to oppose the accord between Kabila and Bemba. At the end of July a peace agreement was signed by Kabila and President Kagame of Rwanda in Pretoria, South Africa. Under the accord, Kabila pledged to arrest and disarm the Interahamwe militia in the DRC, while the Rwandan Government was to withdraw all troops from the country (thereby also providing for the integration of RCD—Goma into the peace process). President Robert Mugabe of Zimbabwe subsequently announced his intention of withdrawing the remaining Zimbabwean troops supporting the DRC Government. In August, however, following further fighting between Rwandan troops and armed groups in Sud-Kivu province, the DRC accused Rwanda of violating the cease-fire, while Rwanda, in turn, accused the Kabila Government of continuing to provide armaments to the Interahamwe militia. In early September the DRC and Uganda reached an accord in the Angolan capital, Luanda, providing for the normalization of relations between the two countries, and the full withdrawal of Ugandan troops in the DRC. The Ugandan and Zimbabwean Governments subsequently commenced the withdrawal of forces from the DRC (although the UN permitted some Ugandan troops provisionally to remain near Bunia to assist in the maintenance of security). At the end of September the withdrawal of Rwandan forces commenced, and it was announced that all 23,400 Rwandan troops had left the country by early October.

In mid-October 2002 Mai-Mai militia attacked RCD—Goma forces in the east of the country, following the departure of the Rwandan forces supporting the rebels. Later that month a five-member Panel of Experts on the illicit exploitation of the DRC's mineral resources submitted a report to the UN Security Council. Kabila subsequently suspended six ministers and a number of senior officials (including the head of the National Security Agency) who had been implicated in the report, and reorganized the Council of Ministers. On 4 December the UN Security Council approved a resolution providing for the enlargement of MONUC to 8,700 personnel. Following the convening of a peace conference in early December in Pretoria, the Government and rebels signed an extensive power-sharing agreement later that month. Under the terms of this accord, Kabila was to remain as President, while four vice-presidential posts were to be allocated, respectively, to the incumbent Government, opposition parties, RCD—Goma and the MLC. The new 36-member transitional administration, to remain in power for a two-year period, was to comprise representatives of the Government, all three RCD factions, the MLC, the opposition and civil society. At the end of December the MLC and the RCD factions signed a cease-fire agreement in Gbadolite, which was to allow the transportation of humanitarian assistance in the region. (However, all rebel factions subsequently failed to observe the cease-fire, and continued hostilities near the border with Uganda were reported.)

In early January 2003 a military court in Kinshasa imposed death sentences on 26 defendants, and custodial terms on a further 64, for their involvement in the assassination of President Laurent-Désiré Kabila. Later in January the UN Security Council adopted a resolution extending the mandate of the Panel of Experts on the exploitation of the DRC's resources for a further six months. In early March a coalition of three militia established with Ugandan support, the Front de l'intégration pour la paix en Ituri, succeeded in taking control of Bunia from a militia of the Hema ethnic group, known as Union des patriotes congolais (UPC). A further agreement to restore peace in the region was signed by the DRC and Ugandan Governments and the local rebel groups later that month. Meanwhile, further discussions on constitutional and security issues for the transitional period were conducted in Pretoria; agreement was reached on the adoption of a draft constitution and the deployment of a neutral international force in the country, pending the establishment of a new national army (which would include former rebel combatants). All measures agreed by the participating groups under the December 2002 settlement were to be ratified at a final session of the Inter-Congolese National Dialogue. However, the Rwandan Government renewed threats to resume military engagement in eastern DRC if the UN failed to secure the total withdrawal of Ugandan forces. On 20 March 2003, in response to continuing violence near Bunia, in contravention of the cease-fire agreement, the UN Security Council adopted a resolution urging an increase in the number of military and humanitarian observers stationed in the DRC under the MONUC mandate, and an immediate withdrawal of the Ugandan troops. At the final peace conference, which was convened at Sun City on 2 April, government and rebel representatives endorsed the establishment of the two-year transitional administration. The official adoption of the Constitution on 4 April was followed by Kabila's inauguration as interim Head of State on 7 April. The Ugandan Government subsequently pledged to withdraw forces from the DRC, in accordance with the peace agreement, and the departure of some 7,000 from the north-east commenced at the beginning of May. Despite the deployment of some 700 (mainly Uruguayan) MONUC troops at Bunia to compensate for the Ugandan withdrawal, UPC forces recaptured the town following intensive fighting, during which large numbers of civilians were massacred. On 30 May, in response to the developing humanitarian crisis, the UN Security Council authorized the establishment of a 1,500-member Interim Emergency Multinational Force, with a three-month mandate to restore order. Deployment of the contingent (which comprised troops from several European Union—EU, see p. 244—nations, principally France) commenced in early June despite protests from the various factions at French involvement in the conflict. Later that month it was announced that the UPC leadership was prepared to withdraw forces from Bunia.

In early May 2003 the nomination of the four Vice-Presidents to the new transitional Government was announced: these were Bemba; the new leader of RCD—Goma, Azarias Ruberwa; a former minister (representing the incumbent administration), Abdoulaye Yerodia Ndombasi; and the former UNESCO official detained in 1997–98, Z'ahidi Ngoma, as the representative of the political opposition. On 29 June all former combatant groups finally signed an agreement on power-sharing in the future integrated transitional armed forces. This final stage in the peace process allowed Kabila on the following day to nominate a transitional Government, in which portfolios were divided between representatives of the former rebel factions, the incumbent administration, political opposition and civil society organizations. While Kabila's Government, RCD—Goma, and the MLC were allocated the most significant portfolios, the new administration also included Nyamwisi (representing the RCD—ML), and Lumbala (representing RCD—N). The four Vice-Presidents were finally inaugurated on 17 July, after the arrival of the rebel representatives in Kinshasa. The inauguration of some ministers belonging to RCD—Goma was also delayed, owing to their reluctance to pledge allegiance to Kabila, but the new power-sharing Government was finally installed on 24 July. At the end of that month the UN Security Council approved a one-year extension of MONUC's mandate, and increased the contingent's military strength significantly; it was envisaged that these MONUC reinforcements would replace the Interim Emergency Multinational Force at the beginning of September. The new International Criminal Court (ICC, see p. 314), which had been established on 1 July 2002 in The Hague, Netherlands, announced that it was to initiate investigations into alleged atrocities committed in the Ituri region. On 20 August 2003 Kabila announced nominations to the military leadership of the new unified armed forces, which was to incorporate elements of all the former rebel groups and the Mai-Mai militia; former RCD—Goma and MLC commanders were appointed to senior posts, including those of services Chiefs of Staff. On 22 August the inaugural session of the new bicameral transitional Parliament was conducted in Kinshasa; representation in the 500-member Assemblée nationale and 120-member Sénat was likewise divided between the former rebel groups, the Mai-Mai, the incumbent Government, political opposition and civil society. At the beginning of September the Interim Emergency Multinational Force officially transferred control of the Ituri region to MONUC reinforcements; the remaining French troops belonging to the contingent were finally withdrawn by the end of that month.

In November 2003, following a final report by the Panel of Experts, the UN Security Council issued a statement condemning the widespread illicit exploitation of the DRC's natural resources, which had financed the activities of former combatant groups, and urged the imposition of state authority throughout the country. Some 85 companies, including many large multinationals, were cited as having contravened Organisation for Economic Co-operation and Development (OECD, see p. 347) regulations through their involvement in mining operations in the country. Meanwhile, following continued ethnic hostilities near Bunia, most of the MONUC contingent had been dispatched to the region, and to the more southern town of Uvira, by the end of that month. In early December the new unified military was officially established, following the integration of former rebel combatants and Mai-Mai into the existing armed forces. In early

February 2004 unidentified combatants attacked a MONUC convoy, killing a Kenyan military observer belonging to the contingent. In mid-May, following dialogue with the Government and MONUC, the ethnic rebel groups active in the Ituri region signed a peace agreement in Kinshasa.

At the end of May 2004 some 2,000 dissident troops, led by former RCD—Goma commanders who had been integrated into the national army, Brig.-Gen. Laurent Nkunda and Col Jules Mutebutsi, attacked forces loyal to the Government deployed in Bukavu, and by 2 June had seized control of the town. Both Banyamulenge officers claimed to have initiated military action in order to prevent further human rights abuses being perpetrated by government forces in the region against their ethnic group. The failure of MONUC troops to prevent the capture of Bukavu caused protest riots in Kinshasa. The Rwandan Government denied accusations by Kabila that Rwandan troops had been redeployed on DRC territory. Rebel forces began to withdraw from Bukavu about two days later, and troops loyal to Kabila succeeded in regaining control of the town by 9 June. Nkunda, together with some 300 supporters, fled to Rwanda, and were subsequently disarmed. In mid-June Kabila dispatched some 10,000 troop reinforcements to the eastern border with Rwanda, prompting Kagame to warn that Rwanda would take any necessary measures to protect national security. (Later in June, however, the two Heads of State reached agreement to abide by the 2002 peace agreement.)

In August 2004 some 160 Banyamulenge, numbering among 20,000 who had fled from Bukavu to Burundi in June, were massacred at a refugee camp at Gatumba, near the border between the two countries. A Burundian Hutu rebel faction, Forces nationales de libération, admitted responsibility for the atrocity; however, the Governments of Rwanda and Burundi believed that the Interahamwe militia operating within the DRC were also implicated and threatened to resume military engagement in the country. Nkunda denounced the massacre and also warned that he would take retaliatory action if the DRC Government failed to protect the Banyamulenge refugees. Ruberwa announced that RCD—Goma, in view of the collapse of the peace process, was to suspend participation in the transitional Government. At the end of August the Governments of the DRC, Uganda and Rwanda agreed to co-operate in the disarmament of the militia continuing to operate in the country, including the Interahamwe and members of the Ugandan rebel organization, the Alliance of Democratic Forces. At the beginning of September, following a visit by Mbeki to Kinshasa for mediation, Ruberwa announced that RCD—Goma had rejoined the Government. During that month the UN Security Council subsequently considered a proposal for the expansion of MONUC, then numbering some 10,800, to about 24,000 military personnel. Resolution 1565, approved on 1 October, authorized the expansion of the mission to 16,700 (while renewing the contingent's mandate for a further six months); the UN Secretary-General expressed concern that the approved increase in strength failed to meet his recommendations.

In late November 2004 Kabila suspended from office six cabinet ministers and 12 senior managers of state enterprises, who were accused of extensive financial malpractice. At the beginning of December, after MONUC troops confirmed the presence of Rwandan forces in the DRC, Kabila requested that the UN Security Council impose sanctions against Rwanda. Kagame protested that Rwandan forces had responded to rebel bombardments launched from DRC territory. Heavy fighting continued in Nord-Kivu between government forces and dissident army units reportedly supported by Rwanda, and later in December MONUC announced that its troops were to establish a temporary 'buffer zone' between the factions engaged in conflict. In early January 2005 Kabila replaced the six ministers who had been suspended from office and reorganized the Government. Indications from the Commission électorale nationale indépendante (CENI) that, owing to the intensified hostilities, the elections due to be conducted by the end of June would be postponed until later that year prompted opposition protests (which were violently dispersed by the security forces), while Bemba threatened to withdraw from the transitional administration in response to lack of progress in the peace process. In mid-February the Front des nationalistes et intégrationistes (FNI), an ethnic Lendu rebel group fighting the UPC in Ituri, killed nine MONUC personnel, prompting an ultimatum from MONUC that all Ituri militia disarm by the end of March or face military action. Several militia leaders were subsequently arrested, including the leader of the UPC, Thomas Lubanga Dyilo, and Floribert Ndjabu Ngabu of the FNI.

At the end of March 2005 the mandate of MONUC was extended for a further six months, while in mid-April the UN Security Council voted to adopt the recommendation of the UN panel of experts investigating implementation of the armaments embargo in eastern DRC, that the embargo be extended to the entire country, and provided for an imposition of a travel ban and 'freeze' of assets on those who violated the sanctions. Meanwhile, inter-party disputes over the provisions of a draft constitution, particularly over the extent of provincial self-government, caused protracted delays to the electoral schedule. On 13 May the transitional Assemblée nationale finally approved by a large majority a new Constitution, which was to be submitted for endorsement at a national referendum. The new Constitution provided for the election of a president by popular vote for a maximum of two five-year terms, a balanced distribution of power between the executive and legislature and the granting of citizenship to members of all ethnic groups resident in the country since 1960. In June Parliament approved the extension of the transitional period for six months (in accordance with the provisions of the April 2003 Constitution). In September 2005, in response to the continuing instability in eastern DRC, the UN Security Council authorized the temporary reinforcement of MONUC by 841 mainly police personnel; on 28 October a further increase in military strength of 300 for the period of the elections was approved and the mandate of the contingent was extended until the end of September 2006. In November 2005 several ministers, including those responsible for the economy and finance portfolios, were replaced in a government reorganization. At the end of November the Assemblée nationale adopted legislation, granting amnesty for political crimes committed during 1996–2003, despite opposition from Kabila on the grounds that it would include those responsible for the assassination of his father.

According to official results of the national referendum, which was conducted on 18 December 2005, the draft Constitution was adopted by 84.3% of votes cast, subject to its approval by the country's Supreme Court. The minimum age for a presidential candidate was reduced from 35 to 30 years, thereby allowing Kabila to contest the forthcoming elections. (Kabila was subsequently officially nominated as the candidate of the Parti du peuple pour la reconstruction et la démocratie—PPRD, which he had formed in 2002.) The new Constitution also provided for an increase in the number of provinces from 11 to 26 (including Kinshasa), and granted them significant powers of self-government. The Supreme Court endorsed the results of the referendum on 3 February, having rejected a number of legal challenges by opposition parties and non-governmental organizations. The new Constitution was signed into effect by Kabila on 18 February. (A new national flag was adopted at the same time.) New electoral legislation was approved by Parliament on 21 February, when the CENI also announced that the presidential and legislative elections were again to be postponed, to 18 June, to allow the completion of preparations, including voter registration, throughout the country. The electoral legislation entered into effect on 9 March; by the expiry of the two-week deadline 33 presidential candidates, including Kabila, Bemba and Ruberwa, had emerged, while some 9,000 had registered to contest the 500 seats in the Assemblée nationale. In March Lubanga was transferred from MONUC custody to the ICC on charges of war crimes, becoming the first indictee to be extradited to the Court.

In May 2006 government and MONUC troops intensified operations in Ituri, in an effort to ensure that elections there were conducted peacefully. Later that month one Nepalese member of MONUC was killed and seven others were captured by the FNI; the hostages were released following negotiations between the FNI, the Government and MONUC, after which the FNI also pledged to cease hostilities. In return, the Government announced in mid-July that it would integrate FNI units into its forces. Also in July a militia group engaged in hostilities in the Ituri region, known as the Mouvement Révolutionnaire Congolais (MRC), agreed also to end hostilities in return for integration into the armed forces. In an attempt to ensure peaceful elections in the capital, on 26 April the UN Security Council authorized the temporary deployment of an EU military force (EUFOR RD Congo). The European Council of Ministers gave its approval in mid-June and the troops began arriving shortly afterwards. In early July some 20 of the 33 presidential candidates demanded a further postponement of the elections, on the grounds that organization was inadequate. On 27 July the Government reached a UN-mediated peace agreement with the MRC, whereby the militia coalition, in return for an amnesty from prosecution, undertook to end hostilities in the Ituri region, to allow the free movement of displaced civilians for the elections and to eventually become integrated into the armed forces.

The presidential and legislative elections took place on 30 July 2006. Despite reports of some procedural irregularities and violent incidents in the Kasaï region, where Tshisekedi received most support, a South African observer mission announced that the elections had been conducted fairly. However, a number of presidential candidates subsequently accused the authorities of perpetrating mass falsification of the results, and in early August six poll officials were arrested on suspicion of malpractice. The announcement of partial results of the presidential election on 20 August precipitated fighting between members of the security forces and Bemba's supporters in Kinshasa, in which a total of 23 people were killed. According to the CENI, Kabila secured 44.81% and Bemba 20.03% of votes cast; about 70.5% of the electorate had participated in the ballot. Consequently, a second round of the presidential election was scheduled for 29 October (when deputies were also to be elected to the provincial Assemblies).

Hostilities between forces loyal to Kabila and Bemba's supporters continued in Kinshasa following the CENI's announcement, and MONUC troops were obliged to intervene to rescue from Bemba's residence 14 foreign diplomats, who had attempted to mediate between the factions. EUFOR RD Congo reinforcements were dispatched to Kinshasa from Gabon, in an effort to restore peace in the capital. After three days of fighting, Kabila and Bemba reached an agreement to withdraw their forces from central Kinshasa. Results of the legislative elections were released in early September 2006; the PPRD secured 111 seats, Bemba's Mouvement de libération du Congo (MLC) won 64, the revived Parti lumumbiste unifié (PALU) 34, the Mouvement social pour le renouveau 27, the Forces du renouveau (FR) 26 and the RCD 15. More than 70 other parties also secured parliamentary representation. The new Assemblée nationale was officially inaugurated on 22 September; however, in December petitions were raised against the election of 18 deputies and in July 2007 the results of those seats were annulled. Meanwhile, Kabila conclusively won the second presidential round on 29 October 2006 by 58.05% of votes cast, according to official results. Bemba subsequently submitted an appeal against the election results at the Supreme Court, and violent clashes ensued in Kinshasa between security forces and Bemba's supporters (who set fire to the Supreme Court building), until Bemba complied with a presidential ultimatum to withdraw his militia from the capital. Bemba's legal challenge was rejected on 28 November.

Kabila was inaugurated as President on 6 December 2006. At the end of that month the leader of PALU, Antoine Gizenga, was nominated Prime Minister-Designate. Owing to delays in selecting traditional chiefs for 58 seats reserved in the provincial Assemblies, indirect elections to the Sénat were rescheduled for 19 January 2007 and gubernatorial elections for 27 and 30 January. Gizenga commenced inter-party discussions to form a new coalition administration. Meanwhile, following negotiations mediated by the Rwandan Government, the DRC authorities reached a peace agreement with Nkunda, whereby his forces were to be integrated into the national army.

On 19 January 2007 the provincial Assemblies, comprising 690 deputies, elected the 108-member Sénat. According to official results, the PPRD secured 22 seats in the chamber, the MLC 14, while the FR and the RCD each received seven seats. A further 22 parties were represented in the Sénat, while Bemba himself became one of eight senators representing the capital. The Sénat was installed on 3 February and two days later a new 60-member Government was unveiled. The most notable appointments included Denis Kalume Numbi as Minister of State, in charge of the Interior, Decentralization and Security and Antipas Mbusa Nyamwisi as Minister of State, in charge of Foreign Relations and International Co-operation, while Athanse Matenda Kyelu assumed the post of Minister of Finance.

The uneasy peace accords signed in early 2007 were short-lived. In mid-February the holding of local elections precipitated violent clashes in the west of the country in which some 130 people were killed, while it was reported that as many as 600 people died in the capital in March when troops who remained loyal to Bemba refused to disarm and fighting broke out between the rebels and members of the armed forces. Bemba was threatened with an arrest warrant for failing to command his troops to withdraw and he subsequently sought refuge in the South African embassy in Kinshasa. In April he was granted permission to leave the country to receive medical treatment in Portugal. In June he extended his stay in that country, continuing to cite medical reasons, although the move also allowed him additional time to negotiate guarantees for his safety on his return.

Fighting escalated in Nord-Kivu in mid-2007, prompting the UN to extend the mandate of MONUC until the end of 2007. (This was subsequently further extended until the end of 2008.) Nkunda had consolidated his influence over the region and rebels under his command had reportedly formed 'mixed brigades' by joining with fighters who remained outside of an agreement to demobilize and integrate into the national armed forces signed earlier in 2007. There was an increasing imbalance in the strength of the rebel forces compared to that of the government troops and fighting in the east of the country intensified. Furthermore, Nkunda withdrew his forces from the national army just months after they had been integrated into it. In August, under pressure from Rwandan officials, the DRC Government announced it would deploy troops to Nord-Kivu, agreeing that the combined rebel forces demanded a more sophisticated approach to reconciliation. Meanwhile, MONUC increased diplomatic pressure on the warring factions and national forces to reach a comprehensive peace agreement.

On 5 September 2007 the UN brokered a fragile cease-fire under which Nkunda ordered the withdrawal of his troops to areas outside Kivu, while President Kabila entered into talks with Nkunda to negotiate the reintegration of his fighters into the national army. Nkunda subsequently declared that his forces would only integrate when his demands for Rwandan rebel forces to be removed from the DRC were met. Just weeks after the cease-fire was agreed Nkunda claimed that his troops had been attacked by Interahamwe and Hutu militia groups and fighting resumed.

At a meeting on 9 November 2007 in Nairobi, Kenya, mediated by the UN, the USA and the EU, the Governments of the DRC and Rwanda reached a mutual agreement on their commitments to ending the violence that had beset the eastern region of the DRC. That country pledged to develop a detailed plan for the disarmament of militia groups in Kivu to be presented in December. In response Rwanda agreed that no support would be given to armed rebels and controls would be enforced to prevent the groups crossing the border in either direction. International diplomatic representatives later met in Goma to agree details of a task force mandated with implementing the new agreement. However, renewed attacks by Nkunda's forces on the national army were launched just days after the agreement, and hopes of a peaceful resolution of the conflict once again diminished. It was estimated that during 2007 some 375,000 people in the DRC had been displaced.

In late November 2007 Kabila announced a major governmental reorganization, which was intended to improve efficiency within the Cabinet. The number of ministers was reduced from 60 to 32, with the number of ministers of state also reduced from six to three.

In December 2007 Nkunda announced a unilateral cease-fire ahead of a conference scheduled to begin on 27 December aimed at fostering peace and stability in the DRC. The official opening was later postponed until 6 January 2008, but, following several weeks of negotiations, an official cease-fire was signed on 24 January. Among the terms of the peace deal was an agreement by the DRC Government not to renew an arrest warrant for war crimes charges against Nkunda, thus granting him an amnesty. Fighting broke out between Tutsi rebels and rival factions just days later, contravening the terms of the accord, but government officials maintained that the cease-fire was still in place and that the rebels would comply with the agreement.

The DRC Government has maintained strong relations with its former allies in the civil conflict, Zimbabwe, Angola and Namibia, but Zimbabwe's political and economic influence has been overtaken by that of South Africa, owing to President Mbeki's strong involvement in the domestic and regional peace process. Following Kabila's agreement with Kagame in Pretoria in July 2002, relations improved between the Rwandan and DRC Governments, although the two continued to support opposing forces engaged in hostilities in Nord-Kivu. The DRC Government's relations with Uganda also improved, despite ongoing tensions between Kabila and Uganda's main ally in the DRC, the MLC. The occupation of Bukavu by dissident troops in mid-2004 again increased concerns of conflict between the DRC and Rwanda and prompted the mass flight of civilians to neighbouring countries. Following the massacre of Banyamulenge refugees from the DRC in Burundi in August (see above), MONUC confirmed later that year that Rwandan troops had re-engaged in hostilities in DRC territory. According to UNHCR, some 314,039 DRC refugees remained in neighbouring countries at the end of 2006. In December 2005 the ICJ upheld an appeal by the DRC against Uganda, submitted in April, and ordered the Ugandan Government to pay reparations for violations against international law perpetrated by its forces deployed in the country during 1998–2003. In February 2006, however, the ICJ ruled that it was unable to issue a decision in a similar case brought by the DRC against the Rwandan Government (which had refused to accept the jurisdiction of the Court).

Government
According to the new Constitution, which entered into effect in February 2006, the President is the Head of State and Commander-in-Chief of the armed forces and is elected by direct universal suffrage for a term of five years, which is renewable once. Legislative power is vested in a bicameral Parlement, comprising a lower chamber, the Assemblée nationale, and an upper chamber, the Sénat. The 500 members of the Assemblée nationale are elected by direct universal suffrage for a renewable term of five years, while the 108 members of the Sénat are indirectly elected by the Assemblies of each of the country's 26 provinces for a renewable term of five years.

Defence
As assessed at November 2007, the armed forces of the Democratic Republic of the Congo numbered an estimated 134,484, comprising an army of 125,233, a navy of 6,703 and an air force of 2,548. A civil war began in August 1998 in the east of the country, with troops from a number of neighbouring countries becoming involved. Although peace was partially restored following a power-sharing agreement reached by the Government and rebel groups in December 2002, hostilities continued in the east of the country, and from late 2004 Rwandan troops were reported to have been redeployed in the region. As part of the power-sharing agreement between the Government and former rebel factions, a new unified armed forces, which incorporated former rebel combatants and militia, was officially established in December 2003. Under a military co-operation agreement, signed in June 2004, South Africa was to assist in the integration and training of the new armed forces; the Belgian Government was also to support the programme. The UN Mission in the Democratic Republic of the Congo (MONUC), which had been officially established in November 1999, had a total authorized strength of 16,700 military personnel and 475 civilian police (with a provisional increase in personnel for the duration of the electoral period and a further temporary increase in military strength approved in December 2006). At mid-February 2007 MONUC comprised 17,498 total uniformed personnel, including 16,475 troops, 719 military observers and 304 police, supported by 1,026 international civilian personnel, 2,114 local civilian staff and 585 UN volunteers. A European Union (see p. 244) force (EUFOR RD Congo) was temporarily deployed in the country during the electoral period. The defence budget for 2007 was US $181m.

Economic Affairs
In 2006, according to estimates by the World Bank, the gross national income (GNI) of the DRC, measured at average 2004–06 prices, was US $7,742m., equivalent to $130 per head (or $720 per head on an international purchasing-power parity basis). During 1996–2006, it was estimated, the population increased at an average annual rate of 2.6%, while gross domestic product (GDP) per head declined, in real terms, by an average of –1.9% per year. Overall GDP increased, in real terms, at an average annual rate of 0.6% in 1996–2006; it increased by an estimated 5.1% in 2006.

Agriculture (including forestry, livestock, hunting and fishing) contributed an estimated 44.8% of GDP in 2006. About 60.8% of the working population were employed in agriculture in mid-2005. The principal cash crops are coffee (which accounted for 8.8% of export earnings in 1999, although its contribution declined to an estimated 1.6% in 2006), palm oil and palm kernels, sugar, tea, cocoa, rubber and cotton. Agricultural GDP declined at an average annual rate of 1.1% in 1996–2006, but, according to the World Bank, increased by 2.9% in 2005 and by 2.5% in 2006.

Industry (including mining, manufacturing, construction and public works, and power) contributed an estimated 22.4% of GDP in 2006. Some 15.9% of the working population were employed in industry in 1991. Industrial GDP declined at an average annual rate of 3.1% in 1996–2006, but, according to the World Bank, increased by 8.9% in 2005 and by an estimated 9.8% in 2006.

Mining (including mineral processing) contributed an estimated 8.4% of GDP in 2006. Diamonds, of which the DRC has rich deposits, are the most important source of foreign exchange, accounting for an estimated 38.1% of export earnings in 2006. Other main minerals are copper, cobalt (of which the country has 65% of the world's reserves) and zinc. Cadmium, cassiterite, gold and silver are also mined on a small scale. Columbite-tantalite (coltan) has become a principal export in eastern regions previously under rebel control. By the mid-2000s the partial restoration of peace and the adoption of new mining and investment codes had prompted renewed investment interest in the sector. There are extensive offshore reserves of petroleum (revenue from petroleum accounted for an estimated 25.0% of export earnings in 2006). Mining GDP (including the processing of minerals) decreased at an average annual rate of 22.5% in 1990–95, but increased by an average of 2.1% per year in 1996–2001, and by 9.6% per year during 2001–06. According to the IMF, growth was 18.4% in 2004 and 8.9% in 2005, although in 2006 mining GDP was estimated to have remained constant.

Manufacturing contributed an estimated 5.4% of GDP in 2006. The most important sectors are textiles, building materials, agricultural processing and industrial chemicals. In 2004 manufacturing plants were operated at far below capacity. According to the World Bank, manufacturing GDP declined at an average annual rate of 1.3% in 1996–2006; however, it increased by 8.0% in 2006.

Energy is derived principally from hydroelectric power. In 2004 an estimated 99.7% of electricity production was generated by hydroelectric plants. In 2006 imports of petroleum comprised an estimated 5.8% of the value of total merchandise imports.

The services sector contributed an estimated 32.8% of GDP in 2006, and employed some 19.0% of the working population in 1991. The GDP of the services sector decreased at an average annual rate of 0.1% in 1996–2006, but, according to the World Bank, increased by an estimated 8.5% in 2006.

In 2006 the DRC recorded an estimated trade deficit of US $421m., while there was a deficit of $644m. on the current account of the balance of payments. In 1995 the principal source of imports (an estimated 16.6%) was Belgium-Luxembourg; other major suppliers were South Africa, Nigeria, Ecuador, the United Kingdom and Germany. In that year South Africa was the principal market for exports (taking an estimated 29.6% of the total); the USA, Belgium-Luxembourg and Angola were also important markets for exports. According to estimates, the principal exports in 2006 were mineral products (mainly industrial diamonds, crude petroleum, cobalt and copper) and agricultural products (primarily coffee). The principal import was petroleum.

In 2006 the estimated overall budget deficit was 27,107,000m. new Congolese francs. At the end of 2004 external debt totalled US $11,841m., of which $10,532m. was long-term public debt. In 2003 the cost of scheduled debt-servicing was equivalent to 8.5% of the value of exports of goods and services. Annual inflation averaged 224.5% in 1995–2006. Consumer prices increased by 21.7% in 2005 and by 13.2% in 2006.

The DRC maintains economic co-operation agreements with its neighbours, Burundi and Rwanda, through the Economic Community of the Great Lakes Countries (see p. 412). The DRC is also a member of the International Coffee Organization (see p. 408) and of the Common Market for Eastern and Southern Africa (COMESA, see p. 205). In September 1997 the DRC became a member of the Southern African Development Community (SADC, see p. 386).

Potentially one of Africa's richest states, the DRC has extensive agricultural, mineral and energy resources. During the early 1990s, however, most foreign investment in the country was withdrawn, and by June 1994 government revenues had declined to such an extent that it was suspended from the IMF. The outbreak of civil war in August 1997 resulted in a further deterioration in the financial situation, and rebel factions, supported by Ugandan and Rwandan forces, gained control of much of the east of the country, where they systematically exploited mineral resources. Following the succession to the presidency of Joseph Kabila in January 2001, significant progress in peace negotiations was achieved, and a UN embargo on trade in unlicensed diamonds was imposed in May. In the same month the new Government implemented an IMF-monitored plan for the rehabilitation of public finances and the Fund subsequently approved a three-year rehabilitation and reconstruction programme, supported by a Poverty Reduction and Growth Facility (PRGF) arrangement (officially commencing in April 2002). An extensive power-sharing accord, which incorporated the principal rebel factions, was reached in December, and a new transitional Government of national unity was installed in July 2003. Government priorities were to reduce corruption, rehabilitate infrastructure and introduce further reform of government institutions and state-owned enterprises. In November, at a meeting of 'Paris Club' donors, convened under the auspices of the IMF and World Bank, the Kabila Government presented a new economic plan for 2005–07; the 'minimum partnership programme for transition and recovery', which was designed to consolidate the level of recovery reached under the poverty reduction strategy, received considerable pledges of financial support. However, intensified fighting in the east of the country from mid-2004, divisions within the transitional Government, and the logistical difficulties in organizing elections in the absence of infrastructure resulted in protracted delays to the transitional process. In February 2006 the UN and European Commission convened a donor conference in Brussels, Belgium, to secure financing for a US $681m. Humanitarian Action Plan for the DRC. The sixth and final PRGF review was abandoned by the IMF in mid-2006, following excessive budgetary expenditure earlier that year, although the Fund agreed to consider a new arrangement once a new government was installed. Despite the suspension of formal lending by the IMF, international donors remained strongly engaged in the country, not least in funding the elections, which were expected to cost more than $460m. In September 2007 the Chinese Government agreed to provide some $500m. in development aid to the DRC, to facilitate the rehabilitation and reconstruction of the country's roads and railways, as well as to increase capacity in the health sector. The deal was promulgated by China as a means to secure greater access to the mineral wealth of the DRC, and consequently omitted the structural adjustment conditions that had characterized aid programmes proffered by the IMF. However, there remained concerns that the new agreement would complicate ongoing negotiations between the DRC and international credit organizations regarding the cancellation of outstanding debt. Moreover, donors had previously been urged by international pressure groups to take stronger action against apparently systemic corruption and graft, particularly in customs and the mining and forestry sectors. GDP was estimated to have increased by 6.5% in 2007 and further growth, of 8.4%, was projected in 2008.

Education

Primary education, beginning at six years of age and lasting for six years, is officially compulsory. Secondary education, which is not compulsory, begins at 12 years of age and lasts for up to six years, comprising a first cycle of two years and a second of four years. In 2002/03, according to UNESCO estimates, primary enrolment was equivalent to 62% of pupils in the relevant age-group (69% of boys; 54% of girls), while the comparable ratio for secondary enrolment was 22% (28% of boys; 16% of girls). The country has four universities, situated at Kinshasa, Kinshasa/Limete, Kisangani and Lubumbashi. In the budget for 1997 a total of 144,000m. new zaires (0.2% of total expenditure by the central Government) was allocated to education. In 2002 an emergency programme for education, with an estimated cost of US $101m., was introduced to restore access to basic education throughout the country.

Public Holidays

2008: 1 January (New Year's Day), 4 January (Commemoration of the Martyrs of Independence), 17 January (National Hero's Day), 1 May (Labour Day), 17 May (National Liberation Day), 30 June (Independence Day), 1 August (Parents' Day), 14 October (Youth Day), 17 November (Army Day), 24 November (Anniversary of the Second Republic), 25 December (Christmas Day).
2009: 1 January (New Year's Day), 4 January (Commemoration of the Martyrs of Independence), 17 January (National Hero's Day), 1 May (Labour Day), 17 May (National Liberation Day), 30 June (Independence Day), 1 August (Parents' Day), 14 October (Youth Day), 17 November (Army Day), 24 November (Anniversary of the Second Republic), 25 December (Christmas Day).

Weights and Measures

The metric system is in force.

Statistical Survey

Sources (unless otherwise stated): Département de l'Economie Nationale, Kinshasa; Institut National de la Statistique, Office Nationale de la Recherche et du Développement, BP 20, Kinshasa; tel. (12) 31401.

Area and Population

AREA, POPULATION AND DENSITY

Area (sq km)	2,344,885*
Population (census result)	
1 July 1984	
Males	14,543,800
Females	15,373,000
Total	29,916,800
Population (UN estimates at mid-year)†	
2005	58,741,000
2006	60,644,000
2007	62,636,000
Density (per sq km) at mid-2007	26.7

* 905,365 sq miles.
† Source: UN, *World Population Prospects: The 2006 Revision*.

REGIONS*

	Area (sq km)	Population (31 Dec. 1985)†
Bandundu	295,658	4,644,758
Bas-Zaïre	53,920	2,158,595
Équateur	403,293	3,960,187
Haut-Zaïre	503,239	5,119,750
Kasaï Occidental	156,967	3,465,756
Kasaï Oriental	168,216	2,859,220
Kivu	256,662	5,232,442
Shaba (formerly Katanga)	496,965	4,452,618
Kinshasa (city)‡	9,965	2,778,281
Total	**2,344,885**	**34,671,607**

* In October 1997 a statutory order redesignated the regions as provinces. Kivu was divided into three separate provinces, and several of the other provinces were renamed. The Constitution of February 2006 increased the existing 11 provinces to 26: Bas-Uele, Équateur, Haut-Lomami, Haut-Katanga, Haut-Uele, Ituri, Kasaï, Kasaï Oriental, Kongo Central, Kwango, Kwilu, Lomami, Lualaba, Lulua, Mai-Ndombe, Maniema, Mongala, Nord-Kivu, Nord-Ubangi, Sankuru, Sud-Kivu, Sud-Ubangi, Tanganyika, Tshopo, Tshuapa and Kinshasa (city).
† Provisional.
‡ Including the commune of Maluku.

Source: Département de l'Administration du Territoire.

THE DEMOCRATIC REPUBLIC OF THE CONGO

PRINCIPAL TOWNS
(population at census of July 1984)

Kinshasa (capital)	2,664,309	Likasi		213,862
Lubumbashi	564,830	Boma		197,617
Mbuji-Mayi	486,235	Bukavu		167,950
Kolwezi	416,122	Kikwit		149,296
Kisangani	317,581	Matadi		138,798
Kananga	298,693	Mbandaka		137,291

Source: UN, *Demographic Yearbook*.

Mid-2005: ('000, incl. suburbs, UN estimates) Kinshasa 6,049; Kolwezi 1,270; Lubumbashi 1,179; Mbuji-Mayi 1,024 (Source: UN, *World Urbanization Prospects: The 2005 Revision*).

BIRTHS AND DEATHS
(annual averages, UN estimates)

	1990–95	1995–2000	2000–05
Birth rate (per 1,000)	48.7	49.2	49.6
Death rate (per 1,000)	19.0	21.1	19.3

Source: UN, *World Population Prospects: The 2006 Revision*.

Expectation of life (years at birth, WHO estimates): 46.0 (males 44.4; females 47.6) in 2005 (Source: WHO, *World Health Statistics*).

Economically Active Population (mid-2005, estimates in '000): Agriculture, etc. 14,433; Total labour force 23,736 (Source: FAO).

Health and Welfare

KEY INDICATORS

Total fertility rate (children per woman, 2005)	6.7
Under-5 mortality rate (per 1,000 live births, 2005)	205
HIV/AIDS (% of persons aged 15–49, 2005)	3.2
Physicians (per 1,000 head, 2004)	0.11
Hospital beds (per 1,000 head, 1990)	1.43
Health expenditure (2004): US $ per head (PPP)	15.3
Health expenditure (2004): % of GDP	4.0
Health expenditure (2004): public (% of total)	28.1
Access to water (% of persons, 2004)	58
Access to sanitation (% of persons, 2004)	27
Human Development Index (2005): ranking	168
Human Development Index (2005): value	0.411

For sources and definitions, see explanatory note on p. vi.

Agriculture

PRINCIPAL CROPS
('000 metric tons)

	2004	2005	2006
Rice (paddy)	315	315	316
Maize	1,155	1,155	1,155
Millet	37	37	38
Sorghum	6	6	6
Potatoes	92	93	93
Sweet potatoes	224	230	233
Cassava (Manioc)	14,951	14,974	14,974
Taro (Coco yam)	66	66	66
Yams	85	85	86
Sugar cane	1,551	1,552	1,522
Dry beans	109	110	113
Dry peas	1	1	1
Groundnuts (in shell)	364	368	369
Oil palm fruit	1,079	1,092	1,106
Melonseed*	40	40	40
Cottonseed*	20	20	20
Cabbages*	23	23	23
Tomatoes*	40	40	40

—continued	2004	2005	2006
Onions (dry)*	53	53	53
Pumpkins, squash and gourds	30	30	30
Bananas	313	314	314
Plantains	1,199	1,193	1,203
Oranges	180	180	180
Avocados	62	63	63
Mangoes	202	203	205
Pineapples	195	195	196
Papayas	214	216	218
Coffee (green)	32	32	32

* FAO estimates.

Aggregate production ('000 metric tons, may include official, semi-official or estimated data): Total cereals 1,522 in 2004, 1,526 in 2005, 1,525 in 2006; Total roots and tubers 15,488 in 2004, 15,518 in 2005, 15,523 in 2006; Total vegetables (incl. melons) 4,423 in 2004, 4,413 in 2005, 4,447 in 2006; Total fruits (excl. melons) 2,442 in 2004, 4,413 in 2005, 4,447 in 2006.

Source: FAO.

LIVESTOCK
('000 head, year ending September)

	2004	2005	2006*
Cattle	758	757	757
Sheep	899	900	900
Goats	4,016	4,022	4,022
Pigs	957	959	960
Chickens	19,710	19,769	20,000

* FAO estimates.
Source: FAO.

LIVESTOCK PRODUCTS
('000 metric tons)

	2004	2005	2006
Cattle meat	12.4	12.4	12.5
Goat meat	18.5	18.5	18.5
Pig meat	23.8	23.9	24.0
Chicken meat	10.6	10.6	10.7
Game meat	88.0	88.7	89.0
Sheep meat	2.8	2.8	2.8
Cows' milk*	5.0	5.0	5.0
Hen eggs*	6.0	6.0	6.0

* FAO estimates.
Source: FAO.

Forestry

ROUNDWOOD REMOVALS
('000 cubic metres, excl. bark, FAO estimates)

	2003	2004	2005
Sawlogs, veneer logs and logs for sleepers	170	170	170
Other industrial wood	3,483	3,483	3,483
Fuel wood	68,517	69,777	71,066
Total	72,170	73,430	74,719

2006: Production assumed to be unchanged from 2005 (FAO estimates).
Source: FAO.

SAWNWOOD PRODUCTION
('000 cubic metres, incl. railway sleepers)

	2003	2004	2005
Total (all broadleaved)	15	15	15

2006: Production assumed to be unchanged from 2005 (FAO estimates).
Source: FAO.

THE DEMOCRATIC REPUBLIC OF THE CONGO

Fishing

('000 metric tons, live weight)

	2000	2001	2002
Capture*	209.3	214.6	220.0
Aquaculture	2.1	2.7	3.0
Total catch*	211.4	217.3	223.0

* FAO estimates.

2003–05: Figures assumed to be unchanged from 2002 (FAO estimates).

Source: FAO.

Mining

(metric tons, unless otherwise indicated)

	2003	2004	2005*
Hard coal*	1,000	1,000	1,000
Crude petroleum ('000 barrels)	9,200	10,100	10,000
Copper ore†	59,800	73,300	92,000
Tantalum and niobium (columbium) concentrates	71‡	42‡	45
Cobalt concentrates†*	14,500‡	20,500‡	22,000
Gold (kilograms)*	4,100	5,700	4,200
Silver (kilograms)	35,501	32,953	53,553
Germanium (kilograms)	2,500	2,500	2,500
Diamonds ('000 carats)§	26,981	30,880	30,300

* Estimated production.
† Figures refer to the metal content of mine output.
‡ Revised figure.
§ An estimated 20% of the diamond is gem quality; the majority of production is from artisanal mining.

Source: US Geological Survey.

Industry

SELECTED PRODUCTS

('000 metric tons, unless otherwise indicated)

	2004	2005	2006*
Maize flour	14	14	14
Wheat flour	185	184	186
Sugar	81	89	91
Cigarettes ('000 cartons)	2,922	3,087	3,048
Beer (million litres)	203	252	301
Soft drinks (million litres)	130	156	162
Soaps	19	21	24
Acetylene	8	13	10
Tyres ('000 units)	49	50	53
Cement	402	511	530
Steel	145	110	104
Explosives	30	28	26
Bottles ('000 units)	19	19	18
Cotton fabrics ('000 sq metres)	263	1,079	852
Printed fabrics ('000 sq metres)	4,730	8,514	6,411
Footwear ('000 pairs)	3,393	5,878	1,432
Blankets ('000 units)	14	15	12
Electric energy (million kWh)	6,922	7,128	7,633

* Estimates.

Source: IMF, *Democratic Republic of the Congo: Selected Issues and Statistical Appendix* (September 2007).

Finance

CURRENCY AND EXCHANGE RATES

Monetary Units
100 centimes = 1 new Congolese franc.

Sterling, Dollar and Euro Equivalents (28 February 2007)
£1 sterling = 1,100.88 new Congolese francs;
US $1 = 562.62 new Congolese francs;
€1 = 743.28 new Congolese francs;
1,000 new Congolese francs = £0.91 = $1.78 = €1.35.

Average Exchange Rate (new Congolese francs per US $)
2004   395.93
2005   473.91
2006   468.28

Note: In June 1967 the zaire was introduced, replacing the Congolese franc (CF) at an exchange rate of 1 zaire = CF 1,000. In October 1993 the zaire was replaced by the new zaire (NZ), equivalent to 3m. old zaires. On 30 June 1998 a new Congolese franc, equivalent to NZ 100,000, was introduced. The NZ was withdrawn from circulation on 30 June 1999. Some of the figures in this survey are still given in terms of a previous currency.

BUDGET

('000 million new Congolese francs)*

Revenue†	2004	2005	2006‡
Taxes on income and services	53,076	54,763	74,935
Corporations and enterprises	32,087	26,465	36,214
Individuals	18,324	24,243	33,173
Taxes on goods and services	72,071	107,218	146,711
Turnover taxes	49,466	79,573	108,883
Selective excises	22,207	27,067	37,037
Beer	6,640	6,791	9,293
Tobacco	6,247	6,519	8,920
Taxes on international trade	83,818	119,554	163,591
Import duties and taxes	77,464	110,408	151,076
Export duties and taxes	6,324	9,039	12,375
Others	28	107	140
Other revenue	39,038	107,421	143,461
Total	**248,003**	**388,956**	**528,698**

Expenditure	2004	2005	2006‡
Wages and salaries	93,223	146,776	218,898
Goods and services (incl. off-budget)	119,855	143,842	133,194
Interest on public debt	93,647	125,008	138,986
Transfers and subsidies	26,590	43,937	87,102
Exceptional expenditure	398	97,071	171,706
Investment	72,059	113,878	134,050
Total	**405,772**	**670,512**	**883,936**

* Figures refer to the consolidated accounts of the central Government.
† Excluding grants received ('000 million new Congolese francs): 51,354 in 2004; 175,942 in 2005; 328,131 in 2006 (estimate).
‡ Estimates.

Source: IMF, *Democratic Republic of Congo: Selected Issues and Statistical Appendix* (September 2007).

INTERNATIONAL RESERVES

(US $ million at 31 December)

	1993	1994	1995
Gold	8.59	10.71	10.83
Foreign exchange	46.20	120.69	146.60
Total	**54.79**	**131.40**	**157.43**

1996 (US $ million at 31 December): Foreign exchange 82.50.
1997 (US $ million at 31 December): Gold 15.80.
2002 (US $ million at 31 December): IMF special drawing rights 8.32.
2003 (US $ million at 31 December): IMF special drawing rights 7.96.
2004 (US $ million at 31 December): IMF special drawing rights 5.50.
2005 (US $ million at 31 December): IMF special drawing rights 1.38.
2006 (US $ million at 31 December): IMF special drawing rights 0.26.

Source: IMF, *International Financial Statistics*.

THE DEMOCRATIC REPUBLIC OF THE CONGO

Statistical Survey

MONEY SUPPLY
(million new Congolese francs at 31 December)

	2004	2005	2006
Currency outside banks	101,467	119,937	182,234
Demand deposits at deposit money banks	15,364	18,952	29,426
Total money (incl. others)	117,078	139,097	211,983

Source: IMF, *International Financial Statistics*.

COST OF LIVING
(Consumer Price Index for Kinshasa; base: August 1995 = 100)

	2004	2005	2006
Food	434,306	546,165	635,950
Rent	535,268	622,109	683,064
Clothing	857,806	930,811	1,002,694
All items (incl. others)	529,126	644,137	729,096

Source: IMF, *Democratic Republic of the Congo: Selected Issues and Statistical Appendix* (September 2007).

NATIONAL ACCOUNTS

Expenditure on the Gross Domestic Product
(US $ million at current prices)

	2004	2005	2006
Government final consumption expenditure	537.89	588.96	661.16
Private final consumption expenditure	5,770.90	6,054.38	7,659.96
Gross capital formation	840.22	1,008.34	1,465.90
Total domestic expenditure	7,149.01	7,651.68	9,787.02
Exports of goods and services	1,993.72	2,242.47	2,760.96
Less Imports of goods and services	2,573.39	2,792.36	3,750.29
GDP in purchasers' values	6,569.34	7,101.80	8,797.69

Source: African Development Bank.

Gross Domestic Product by Economic Activity
('000 million new Congolese francs at current prices)

	2004	2005	2006*
Agriculture, forestry, livestock, hunting, and fishing	1,275	1,571	1,796
Mining†	222	296	337
Manufacturing	137	183	216
Construction and public works	105	140	182
Electricity and water	79	138	164
Wholesale and retail trade	396	521	620
Transport and telecommunications	94	127	162
Trade and commerce	136	170	198
Public administration	91	121	167
Other services	93	120	168
GDP at factor cost	2,626	3,386	4,009
Import duties	67	100	159
GDP at market prices	2,692	3,486	4,168

* Estimates.
† Including processing.

Source: IMF, *Democratic Republic of the Congo: Selected Issues and Statistical Appendix* (September 2007).

BALANCE OF PAYMENTS
(US $ million)

	2004*	2005†	2006†
Exports of goods f.o.b.	1,813	2,071	2,319
Imports of goods f.o.b.	−1,753	−2,473	−2,740
Trade balance	60	−402	−421
Exports of services	172	343	390
Imports of services	−494	−770	−851
Balance on goods and services	−262	−829	−882
Other income received	91	105	18
Other income paid	−377	−518	−487
Balance on goods, services and income	−548	−1,242	−1,351
Current transfers (net)	392	487	708
Current balance	−157	−755	−644
Capital and financial account (net)	−129	218	143
Net errors and omissions	29	168	70
Overall balance	−257	−368	−431

* Estimates.
† Projections.

Source: IMF, *Democratic Republic of the Congo: Staff-Monitored Program* (September 2007).

External Trade

PRINCIPAL COMMODITIES
(US $ million)

Imports c.i.f.	2004	2005	2006*
Petroleum	96	115	158
Total (incl. others)	1,753	2,473	2,740

Exports f.o.b.	2004	2005	2006*
Copper	57	113	257
Cobalt	407	260	373
Diamonds	1,009	1,158	884
Crude petroleum	360	453	580
Coffee	18	8	38
Total (incl. others)	1,813	2,071	2,319

* Estimates.

Source: IMF, *Democratic Republic of the Congo: Selected Issues and Statistical Appendix* (September 2007).

SELECTED TRADING PARTNERS
(US $ million)

Imports c.i.f.	1995
Belgium-Luxembourg	147.2
Canada	9.8
China, People's Repub.	26.8
Côte d'Ivoire	35.5
Ecuador	65.1
Germany	48.2
India	9.9
Iran	10.3
Italy	26.5
Japan	11.8
Kenya	22.5
Morocco	9.2
Netherlands	36.5
Nigeria	72.5
South Africa	89.3
Togo	22.5
United Kingdom	50.2
Zambia	9.4
Total (incl. others)	889.2

THE DEMOCRATIC REPUBLIC OF THE CONGO

Exports f.o.b.	1995
Angola	51.0
Belgium-Luxembourg	90.9
Canada	11.6
Germany	8.7
Israel	17.2
Italy	29.6
Philippines	30.2
Senegal	9.5
South Africa	219.7
Switzerland	29.7
United Kingdom	29.7
USA	107.6
Total (incl. others)	**742.8**

Source: UN, *International Trade Statistics Yearbook*.

Transport

RAILWAYS
(traffic)*

	1999	2000	2001†
Passenger-km (million)	145.2	187.9	222.1
Freight (million ton-km)	386.5	429.3	459.1

* Figures refer to Société Nationale des Chemins de Fer Congolaise (SNCC) services only.
† Estimates.

Source: IMF, *Democratic Republic of the Congo: Selected Issues and Statistical Appendix* (June 2003).

ROAD TRAFFIC
(motor vehicles in use at 31 December)

	1994	1995*	1996*
Passenger cars	698,672	762,000	787,000
Buses and coaches	51,578	55,000	60,000
Lorries and vans	464,205	495,000	538,000
Total vehicles	**1,214,455**	**1,312,000**	**1,384,000**

* Estimates.

Source: IRF, *World Road Statistics*.

1999: Passenger cars 172,600; Commercial vehicles 34,600 (Source: UN, *Statistical Yearbook*).

SHIPPING

Merchant Fleet
(registered at 31 December)

	2004	2005	2006
Number of vessels	20	21	21
Total displacement ('000 grt)	12.9	13.9	13.9

Source: Lloyd's Register-Fairplay, *World Fleet Statistics*.

International Sea-borne Freight Traffic
(estimates, '000 metric tons)

	1988	1989	1990
Goods loaded	2,500	2,440	2,395
Goods unloaded	1,400	1,483	1,453

Source: UN, *Monthly Bulletin of Statistics*.

Statistical Survey

CIVIL AVIATION
(traffic on scheduled services)

	1992	1993	1994
Kilometres flown (million)	4	4	6
Passengers carried ('000)	116	84	178
Passenger-km (million)	295	218	480
Total ton-km (million)	56	42	87

Source: UN, *Statistical Yearbook*.

Tourism

FOREIGN TOURIST ARRIVALS BY ORIGIN

	2003	2004	2005
Africa	20,380	14,531	36,489
Congo, Republic	121	109	437
America	2,568	4,592	3,824
East Asia	3,156	3,998	5,943
Europe	9,037	13,117	14,751
Belgium	2,337	4,446	4,788
France	2,012	3,348	3,245
Germany	384	637	951
Italy	475	785	1,038
Total	**35,141**	**36,238**	**61,007**

Tourism receipts (US $ million): 2 in 1998.

Source: World Tourism Organization.

Communications Media

	2004	2005	2006
Telephones ('000 main lines in use)	10.5	10.6	9.7
Mobile cellular telephones ('000 subscribers)	1,990.7	2,746.0	4,415.5
Internet users ('000)	112.5	140.6	180.0

Radio receivers ('000 in use): 18,030 in 1997.

Television receivers ('000 in use): 100 in 1998.

Facsimile machines (estimated number in use): 5,000 in 1995.

Personal computers ('000 in use): 200 in 1998; 500 in 1999.

Book production (titles published): 112 in 1996.

Daily newspapers: 9 in 1998 (estimated average circulation 129,000).

Sources: International Telecommunication Union; UNESCO Institute for Statistics.

Education

(2002/03, unless otherwise indicated)

	Teachers	Students Males	Students Females	Students Total
Pre-primary*	3,075	34,335	34,787	69,122
Primary	162,797	2,116,752†	1,905,659†	4,022,411†
General secondary*	113,904	772,225	439,959	1,212,184
Technical and vocational*		275,903	166,936	442,839
Tertiary†	3,788	n.a.	n.a.	60,341*

* Estimate(s).
† 1998/99.

Institutions (1998/99): Primary 17,585; Secondary 6,007.

Source: UNESCO Institute for Statistics.

Adult literacy rate (UNESCO estimates): 67.2% (males 80.9%; females 54.1%) in 2001 (Source: UNESCO Institute for Statistics).

Directory

The Constitution

A new Constitution was approved by the transitional legislature in May 2005, and endorsed by a national referendum in December. The Constitution officially entered into effect on 18 February 2006; its main provisions are summarized below:

GENERAL PROVISIONS

The state of the Democratic Republic of the Congo is divided for the purposes of administration into 25 provinces and the capital of Kinshasa (which has the status of a province). The provinces are granted autonomous powers for managing local resources, and also powers that are exercised in conjunction with the central Government, including control of between 40% and 60% of public funds. Each province has a Government and Assembly. The Constitution reaffirms the principle of democracy, guarantees political pluralism, and protects fundamental human rights and freedoms. The establishment of a one party system is prohibited and punishable by law as an act of treason.

PRESIDENT

The President is the Head of State and Commander-in-Chief of the armed forces. He is elected by direct universal suffrage for a term of five years, which is renewable once. Presidential candidates must be of Congolese nationality and a minimum of 30 years of age. The President nominates a Prime Minister from the political party that commands a majority in the legislature and other members of the Government on the proposal of the Prime Minister. He exercises executive powers in conjunction with the Government and subject to the approval of the legislature. The areas of defence, security and foreign affairs are conducted jointly by the President and the Government.

GOVERNMENT

The Government comprises the Prime Minister and a number of ministers and deputy ministers. The Government is responsible for conducting national politics, which it determines in conjunction with the President. The Government is accountable to the Assemblée nationale, which is empowered to adopt a motion of censure against it.

LEGISLATURE

Legislative power is vested in a bicameral Parlement, comprising a lower chamber, the Assemblée nationale, and an upper chamber, the Sénat. Members of the Assemblée nationale are elected by direct universal suffrage for a renewable term of five years. The number of deputies is determined by electoral law. Members of the Sénat are indirectly elected by the Assemblies of each of the country's provinces for a renewable term of five years. Both chambers have a President and two Vice-Presidents.

JUDICIARY

The Constitution guarantees the independence of the judicial system. Members of the judiciary are under the authority of the Conseil Supérieur de la Magistrature. The Cour de Cassation has jurisdiction over legal decisions and the Conseil d'État over administrative decisions. The Cour Constitutionnelle interprets the provisions of the Constitution and ensures the conformity of new legislation. The system also comprises a Haute Cour Militaire, and lower civil and military courts and tribunals. The Conseil Supérieur de la Magistrature has 18 members, including the Presidents and Chief Prosecutors of the main courts. The Cour Constitutionnelle comprises nine members, who are appointed by the President (three nominated by Parlement and three by the Conseil Supérieur de la Magistrature) for a term of nine years. The Head of State appoints and dismisses magistrates, on the proposal of the Conseil Supérieur de la Magistrature.

The Government

HEAD OF STATE

President: Maj.-Gen. JOSEPH KABILA KABANGE (inaugurated 26 January 2001, 7 April 2003 and 6 December 2006).

CABINET
(March 2008)

Prime Minister: ANTOINE GIZENGA.
Minister of State, in charge of Agriculture: FRANÇOIS JOSEPH MOBUTU NZANGA NGBANGAWE.
Minister of State, in charge of the Interior, Decentralization and Security: DENIS KALUME NUMBI.
Minister of State at the Presidency: NKULU MITUMBA KILOMBO.
Minister in Assistance to the Prime Minister: GODEFROID MAYOBO MPWENE NGANTIEN.
Minister of Foreign Affairs and International Co-operation: ANTIPAS MBUSA NYAMWISI.
Minister of National Defence and War Veterans: CHIKEZ DIEMU.
Minister of Justice and Human Rights: MUTOMBO BAKAFUA NSENDA.
Minister of Relations with Parliament: ADOLPHE LUMANU MULENDA BWANA SEFU.
Minister of Planning: OLIVIER KAMITATU ETSU.
Minister of Finance: ATHANASE MATENDA KYELU.
Minister of the Budget: ADOLPHE MUZITO.
Minister without Portfolio: JEANNINE MABUNDA LIOKO.
Minister of the National Economy and Trade: ANDRÉ PHILIPPE FUTA.
Minister of Communications and Media: EMILE BONGELI.
Minister of Infrastructure, Public Works and Reconstruction: PIERRE LUMBI OKONGO.
Minister of Industry and Small and Medium-sized Enterprises: SIMON MBOSO KIAMPUTU.
Minister of Transport and Communication Routes: CHARLES MWANDO NSIMBA.
Minister of Gender, Family and Children: PHILOMÈNE OMATUKU ATSHAKAWO.
Minister of Higher and University Education and Scientific Research: LÉONARD MASUGA RUGAMIRA.
Minister of Primary and Secondary Education and Professional Training: MAKER MWANGU FAMBA.
Minister of Mines: MARTIN KABWELULU LABILO.
Minister of Energy: SALOMON BANAMUHERE BALIENE.
Minister of Hydrocarbons: LAMBERT MENDE OMALANGA.
Minister of Posts, Telephones and Telecommunications: LOUISE MUNGA.
Minister of the Environment, the Protection of Nature and Tourism: JOSÉ ENDUNDU.
Minister of Public Health: VICTOR MAKWENGE KAPUT.
Minister of Town Planning and Housing: SYLVAIN NGABU CHUMBU.
Minister of Land Affairs: EDOUARD KABUKAPUA.
Minister of Labour and Social Security: MARIE ANGE LUKIANA MUFWANKOL.
Minister of the Civil Service: LAURENT-SIMON IKENGE LISAMBOLA.
Minister of Social and Humanitarian Affairs and National Solidarity: JEAN-CLAUDE MUYAMBO KYASSA.
Minister of Culture and the Arts: ESDRAS KAMBALE.
Minister of Youth and Sports: WILLY BAKONGA.

MINISTRIES

Office of the President: Hôtel du Conseil Exécutif, ave de Lemera, Kinshasa-Gombe; tel. (12) 30892; internet www.presidentrdc.cd.
Office of the Prime Minister: Kinshasa.
Ministry of Agriculture: Kinshasa.
Ministry of the Budget: Kinshasa.
Ministry of the Civil Service: Kinshasa.
Ministry of Communications and Media: ave du 24 novembre, BP 3171, KIN I, Kinshasa-Kabinda; tel. (12) 23171.
Ministry of Culture and the Arts: BP 8541, Kinshasa 1; tel. (12) 31005.
Ministry of Energy: Immeuble Snel, 239 ave de la Justice, BP 5137 KIN I, Kinshasa-Gombe; tel. (12) 22570.
Ministry of the Environment, the Protection of Nature and Tourism: 76 ave des Cliniques, Kinshasa-Gombe; internet www.minenv.itgo.com.
Ministry of Finance: blvd du 30 juin, BP 12998 KIN I, Kinshasa-Gombe; tel. (12) 33232; internet www.minfinrdc.cd.
Ministry of Foreign Affairs and International Co-operation: Kinshasa.
Ministry of Gender, Family and Children: Kinshasa.

THE DEMOCRATIC REPUBLIC OF THE CONGO

Ministry of Higher and University Education and Scientific Research: Kinshasa.

Ministry of Hydrocarbons: Kinshasa.

Ministry of Industry and Small and Medium-sized Enterprises: Kinshasa.

Ministry of Infrastructure, Public Works and Reconstruction: Kinshasa.

Ministry of the Interior, Decentralization and Security: ave de Lemera, Kinshasa-Gombe; tel. (12) 23171.

Ministry of Justice and Human Rights: 228 ave de Lemera, BP 3137, Kinshasa-Gombe; tel. (12) 32432.

Ministry of Labour and Social Security: blvd du 30 juin, BP 3840, Kinshasa-Gombe.

Ministry of Land Affairs: Kinshasa.

Ministry of Mines: Kinshasa; internet www.miningcongo.cd.

Ministry of National Defence and War Veterans: BP 4111, Kinshasa-Gombe; tel. (12) 59375.

Ministry of the National Economy and Trade: Kinshasa.

Ministry of Planning: 4155 ave des Côteaux, BP 9378, Kinshasa-Gombe 1; tel. (12) 31346.

Ministry of Posts, Telephones and Telecommunications: Immeuble Kilou, 4484 ave des Huiles, BP 800 KIN I, Kinshasa-Gombe; tel. (12) 24854.

Ministry of Primary and Secondary Education and Professional Training: Enceinte de l'Institut de la Gombe, BP 3163, Kinshasa-Gombe; tel. (12) 30098.

Ministry of Public Health: blvd du 30 juin, BP 3088 KIN I, Kinshasa-Gombe; tel. (12) 31750.

Ministry of Relations with Parliament: Kinshasa.

Ministry of Social and Humanitarian Affairs and National Solidarity: Kinshasa.

Ministry of Town Planning and Housing: 15 ave des Cliniques, BP 12348 KIN I, Kinshasa-Gombe; tel. (12) 31252.

Ministry of Transport and Communication Routes: Immeuble Onatra, blvd du 30 juin, BP 3304, Kinshasa-Gombe; tel. (12) 23660.

Ministry of Youth and Sports: 77 ave de la Justice, BP 8541 KIN I, Kinshasa-Gombe.

President and Legislature

PRESIDENT

Presidential Election, First Round, 30 July 2006

Candidate	Votes	% of votes
Joseph Kabila Kabange (Independent)	7,590,485	44.81
Jean-Pierre Bemba Gombo (Mouvement de libération du Congo)	3,392,592	20.03
Antoine Gizenga (Parti lumumbiste unifié)	2,211,280	13.06
François Joseph Mobutu Nzanga Ngbangawe (Union des démocrates mobutistes)	808,397	4.77
Oscar Kashala Lukumuenda (Union pour la reconstruction du Congo)	585,410	3.46
Azarias Ruberwa (Rassemblement congolais pour la démocratie)	285,641	1.69
Pierre wa Syakassighe Pay-Pay (Coalition des démocrates congolais)	267,749	1.58
Vincent de Paul Lunda Bululu (Rassemblement des forces sociales et fédéralistes)	237,257	1.40
Others	1,558,723	9.20
Total	**16,937,534**	**100.00**

Presidential Election, Second Round, 29 October 2006

Candidate	Votes	% of votes
Joseph Kabila Kabange (Independent)	9,436,779	58.05
Jean-Pierre Bemba Gombo (Mouvement de libération du Congo)	6,819,822	41.95
Total	**16,256,601**	**100.00**

LEGISLATURE

The bicameral Parlement of the Democratic Republic of the Congo comprises a lower chamber, or Assemblée nationale, and an upper chamber, or Sénat, members of which are elected by the deputies of the provincial Assemblées.

Assemblée nationale

President: VITAL KAMERHE.

General Election, 30 July 2006

Party	Seats
Parti du peuple pour la reconstruction et la démocratie	111
Mouvement de libération du Congo	64
Parti lumumbiste unifié	34
Mouvement social pour le renouveau	27
Forces du renouveau	26
Rassemblement congolais pour la démocratie	15
Coalition des démocrates congolais	10
Convention des démocrates chrétiens	10
Union des démocrates mobutistes	9
Camp de la patrie	8
Démocratie chrétienne fédéraliste—Convention des fédéralistes pour la démocratie	8
Parti démocrate chrétien	8
Union des nationalistes fédéralistes du Congo	7
Others*	100
Independents	63
Total	**500**

* Comprising 56 political parties that won less than five seats.

Sénat

President: LÉON KENGO WA DONDO.

Election, 19 January 2007

Party	Seats
Parti du peuple pour la reconstruction et la démocratie	22
Mouvement de libération du Congo	14
Forces du renouveau	7
Rassemblement congolais pour la démocratie	7
Parti démocrate chrétien	6
Convention des démocrates chrétiens	3
Mouvement social pour le renouveau	3
Parti lumumbiste unifié	2
Others*	18
Independents	26
Total	**108**

* Comprising 18 political parties that each won one seat.

Election Commission

Commission électorale indépendante (CEI): 4471 blvd du 30 juin, Commune de la gombe, Kinshasa; tel. (81) 10613; e-mail ceirdc@yahoo.fr; internet www.cei-rdc.cd; f. 2004; Chair. ABBÉ APOLLINAIRE MALU-MALU.

Political Organizations

In January 1999 a ban on the formation of political associations was officially ended, and in May 2001 remaining restrictions on the registration and operation of political parties were removed. Despite a peace agreement between the Government and rebel factions, reached in December 2002 and the subsequent installation of power-sharing institutions in 2003, heavy fighting continued in the east of the country. Some 260 political parties registered to contest presidential and legislative elections on 30 July 2006.

Camp de la patrie: Kinshasa; Leader ARTHUR NGOMA Z'AHIDI.

Coalition des démocrates congolais (CODECO): f. 2006; Leader PIERRE WA SYAKASSIGHE PAY-PAY.

Convention des démocrates chrétiens: Kinshasa; FLORENTIN MOKONDA BONZA.

Démocratie chrétienne fédéraliste—Convention des fédéralistes pour la démocratie chrétienne (DCF—COFEDEC): 2209 ave des Etoiles, Kinshasa-Gombe; Leader VENANT TSHIPASA VANGI.

Forces du renouveau: Kinshasa; Leader ANTIPAS MBUSA NYAMWISI.

Forces novatrices pour l'union et la solidarité (FONUS): 13 ave de l'Enseignement, Kasa-Vubu, Kinshasa; f. 2004; advocates political pluralism; Pres. JOSEPH OLENGHANKOY; Sec.-Gen. JOHN KWET.

Front des nationalistes intégrationnistes (FNI): Bunia; f. 2003 in Uganda; ethnic Lendu rebel group, in conflict with Union des patriotes congolais in north-east; Leader FLORIBERT NDJABU NGABU.

Mouvement de libération du Congo (MLC): 6 ave du Port, Kinshasa-Gombe; f. 1998; fmr Ugandan-supported rebel movement; incl. in Govt in July 2003; Leader JEAN-PIERRE BEMBA GOMBO; Sec.-Gen. THOMAS LUHAKA.

Mouvement populaire de la révolution (MPR): 5448 ave de la Justice, Immeuble Yoko, Kinshasa-Gombe; f. 1966 by Pres. Mobutu; sole legal political party until Nov. 1990; advocates national unity and opposes tribalism; Leader Prof. VUNDWAWE TE PEMAKO; Sec.-Gen. KITHIMA BIN RAMAZANI.

Mouvement social pour le renouveau (MSR): Kinshasa; f. 2006; Leader PIERRE LUMBI.

Parti démocrate chrétien: Leader JOSÉ ENDUNDO BONONGE.

Parti démocrate et social chrétien (PDSC): 3040 route de Matadi, C/Ngaliema, Kinshasa; tel. (12) 21211; f. 1990; centrist; Pres. ANDRÉ BOBOLIKO; Sec.-Gen. TUYABA LEWULA.

Parti lumumbiste unifié (PALU): 9 rue Cannas, C/Limete, Kinshasa; Leader ANTOINE GIZENGA.

Parti du peuple pour la reconstruction et la démocratie (PPRD): Croisement des aves Pumbu et Batetela, Kinshasa-Gombe; f. March 2002 by Pres. Joseph Kabila; Sec.-Gen. VITAL KAMERHE.

Parti pour l'unité et la sauvegarde de l'intégrité du Congo (PUSIC): Bunia; coalition of four tribal militia groups, led by Hema; Leader ROBERT PIMBU.

Rassemblement congolais pour la démocratie (RCD—Goma): 26 ave Lukusa, Kinshasa-Gombe; f. 1998; rebel movement until Dec. 2002 peace agreement; incl. in Govt July 2003; main Ilunga faction; supported by Rwanda; Leader AZARIAS RUBERWA; Sec.-Gen. FRANCIS BEDY MAKHUBU MABELE.

Rassemblement congolais pour la démocratie—Mouvement de libération (RCD—ML): 290 ave Libenge, Lingwala; broke away from main RCD in 1999; supported by Uganda; a number of groups were merged into the FLC (see above) in Jan. 2001; Pres. MBUSA NYAMWISI.

Rassemblement congolais pour la démocratie—National (RCD—N): blvd du 30 juin, S.V./64 Haut-Uélé (Isiro); broke away from RCD—ML in Oct. 2000; Leader ROGER LUMBALA.

Rassemblement des forces sociales et fédéralistes (RSF): 98 rue Poto-poto, Kimbanseke; Leader VINCENT DE PAUL LUNDA BULULU.

Rassemblement pour une nouvelle société (RNS): 1 bis rue Lufu, C/Bandalungwa; e-mail info@congozaire.org; Leader Dr ALAFUELE M. KALALA.

Union des démocrates mobutistes (UDEMO): f. by son of fmr Pres. Mobutu; Leader FRANÇOIS JOSEPH MOBUTU NZANGA NGBANGAWE.

Union des nationalistes fédéralistes du Congo (UNAFEC): 5 ave Citronniers, Kinshasa-Gombe; Leader GABRIEL KYUNGA WA KUMWANZA.

Union des patriotes congolais (UPC): 25 blvd de la Libération, Bunia; rebel group of Hema ethnic group, fmrly in conflict with Lendu in north-east; registered as political org. 2004, after peace agreement with Govt; Leader THOMAS LUBANGA.

Union pour la démocratie et le progrès social (UDPS): 546 ave Zinnia, Limete, Kinshasa; tel. (81) 3140685; e-mail udps@udps.net; internet www.udps.net; f. 1982; Leader Dr ETIENNE TSHISEKEDI WA MULUMBA; Sec.-Gen. RÉMY MASSAMBA.

Union pour la reconstruction du Congo (UREC): Leader OSCAR LUKUMWENA KASHALA.

Union pour la République (UPR): 622 ave Monts des Arts, Kinshasa-Gombe; f. 1997; by fmr mems of the MPR; Leader BOBOY NYABAKA.

Union pour la République—Mouvement National (UNIR—MN): Immeuble VeVe center, 2 rue de Bongandanga, c/Kasa-Vubu, Kinshasa; tel. (81) 2431078; e-mail info@unir-mn.org; internet www.unir-mn.org; f. 2001; officially registered as a political party in 2005; Pres. FRÉDÉRIC BOYENGA-BOFALA.

Diplomatic Representation

EMBASSIES IN THE DEMOCRATIC REPUBLIC OF THE CONGO

Angola: 4413–4429 blvd du 30 juin, BP 8625, Kinshasa; tel. (12) 32415; fax (13) 98971; e-mail consangolakatanga@voila.fr; Ambassador MAWETE JOÃO BAPTISTA.

Belgium: Immeuble Le Cinquantenaire, pl. du 27 octobre, BP 899, Kinshasa; tel. (12) 20110; fax (12) 21058; e-mail kinshasa@diplobel.org; internet www.diplobel.org/congo; Ambassador JOHAN SWINNEN.

Benin: 3990 ave des Cliniques, BP 3265, Kinshasa-Gombe; tel. (98) 128659; e-mail abkin@raga.net; Ambassador GEORGES S. WHANNOU DE DRAVO.

Cameroon: 171 blvd du 30 juin, BP 10998, Kinshasa; tel. (12) 34787; Chargé d'affaires a.i. DOMINIQUE AWONO ESSAMA.

Canada: 17 ave Pumbu, Commune de la gombe, BP 8341, Kinshasa 1; tel. (89) 50310; fax (99) 75403; e-mail kinshasa@international.gc.ca; Ambassador SIGRID JOHNSON.

Central African Republic: 11 ave Pumbu, BP 7769, Kinshasa; tel. (12) 30417; Ambassador BERNARD LE SISSA.

Chad: 67–69 ave du Cercle, BP 9097, Kinshasa; tel. (12) 22358; Ambassador (vacant).

Congo, Republic: 179 blvd du 30 juin, BP 9516, Kinshasa; tel. (12) 34028; Ambassador EDOUARD ROGER OKOULA.

Côte d'Ivoire: 68 ave de la Justice, BP 9197, Kinshasa; tel. (12) 21208; Ambassador GUILLAUME AHIPEAU.

Cuba: 4660 ave Cateam, BP 10699, Kinshasa; tel. (12) 8803823; Ambassador LUIS CASTILLO.

Egypt: 519 ave de l'Ouganda, BP 8838, Kinshasa; tel. (51) 10137; fax (88) 03728; Ambassador MORTDA ALY MOHAMED LASHIN.

Ethiopia: BP 8435, Kinshasa; tel. (12) 23327; Ambassador DIEUDEONNE A. GANGA.

France: 97 ave de la République du Tchad, BP 3093, Kinshasa; tel. (81) 5559999; fax (81) 5559937; e-mail ambafrance@ic.cd; internet www.ambafrance-cd.org; Ambassador BERNARD PREVOST.

Gabon: ave du 24 novembre, BP 9592, Kinshasa; tel. (12) 68325; Ambassador MICHEL MADOUNGOU.

Germany: 82 ave Roi Baudouin, BP 8400, Kinshasa-Gombe; tel. (81) 5561380; e-mail amballemagne@ic.cd; internet www.kinshasa.diplo.de; Ambassador KARL-ALBRECHT RICHARD WOKALEK.

Greece: Immeuble de la Communauté Hellénique, 3ème étage, blvd du 30 juin, BP 478, Kinshasa; tel. (99) 70521; e-mail gremb.kin@mfa.gr; Ambassador IOANNIS CHRISTOPHILIS.

Holy See: 81 ave Goma, BP 3091, Kinshasa; tel. (88) 08814; fax (88) 48483; e-mail nuntius@raga.net; Apostolic Nuncio Most Rev. GIOVANNI D'ANIELLO (Titular Archbishop of Paestum).

Israel: 141 blvd du 30 juin, BP 8343, Kinshasa; tel. (99) 87218; fax (88) 07494; e-mail daniel.saada@mfa.gov.il; Ambassador DANIEL SAADA.

Japan: Immeuble Citibank, 2ème étage, ave Colonel Lukusa, BP 1810, Kinshasa; tel. (81) 8845305; fax (satellite) 871-761-21-41-42; e-mail ambassadedujapon@yahoo.co.jp; internet www.rdc.emb-japan.go.jp; Ambassador YASUO TAKANO.

Kenya: 4002 ave de l'Ouganda, BP 9667, Kinshasa; tel. (81) 5554797; fax (81) 5554805; e-mail kinshasa@mfa.go.ke; Ambassador KARUCHU SYLVESTER GAKUMU.

Korea, Democratic People's Republic: 168 ave de l'Ouganda, BP 16597, Kinshasa; tel. (81) 8801443; fax (81) 5300194; e-mail ckc.kin168@yahoo.com; Ambassador RI WON SON.

Korea, Republic: 65 blvd Tshatshi, BP 628, Kinshasa; tel. (81) 9820302; e-mail amb-rdc@mofat.go.kr; Ambassador KIM YOUNG-JUN.

Lebanon: 3 ave de l'Ouganda, Kinshasa; tel. (12) 82469; Chargé d'affaires a.i. CHEHADE MOUALLEM.

Liberia: 3 ave de l'Okapi, BP 8940, Kinshasa; tel. (12) 82289; Ambassador JALLA D. LANSANAH.

Mauritania: BP 16397, Kinshasa; tel. (12) 59575; Ambassador Lt-Col M'BARECK OULD BOUNA MOKHTAR.

Netherlands: 11 ave Zongontolo, 55 Immeuble Residence, BP 10299, Kinshasa; tel. (99) 8001140; fax (99) 9975326; e-mail kss@minbuza.nl; Ambassador E. C. W. VAN DER LAAN.

Nigeria: 141 blvd du 30 juin, BP 1700, Kinshasa; tel. (81) 7005142; fax (81) 2616115; e-mail nigemb@jobantech.cd; Ambassador Dr ONUORAH JONIKUL OBODOZIE.

Portugal: 270 ave des Aviateurs, BP 7775, Kinshasa; tel. (81) 5161277; e-mail ambassadeportugal@micronet.net; Ambassador ALFREDO MANUEL SILVA DUARTE COSTA.

Russia: 80 ave de la Justice, BP 1143, Kinshasa 1; tel. (12) 33157; fax (12) 45575; Ambassador VALERII GAMAIVNE.

South Africa: 77 ave Ngongo Lutete, BP 7829, Kinshasa-Gombe; tel. (88) 48287; fax (88) 04152; e-mail ambasud@ckt.cd; Ambassador Rev. Dr MOLEFE S. TSELE.

Spain: blvd du 30 juin, Bldg Communauté Hellénique, Commune de la gombe, BP 8036, Kinshasa; tel. (81) 8843195; e-mail emb.kinshasa@mae.es; Dr MIGUEL FERNÁNDEZ-PALACIOS MARTÍNEZ.

Sudan: 24 ave de l'Ouganda, Kinshasa; tel. (99) 37396; Chargé d'affaires a.i. ABDEL RA'OUF AMIR.

Sweden: 93 ave Roi Baudouin, Commune de la gombe, BP 11096, Kinshasa; tel. (99) 8174289; fax (satellite) 870-600-147849; e-mail

THE DEMOCRATIC REPUBLIC OF THE CONGO

ambassaden.kinshasa@foreign.ministry.se; internet www.swedenabroad.com/kinshasa; Ambassador MAGNUS WERNSTEDT.

Tanzania: 142 blvd du 30 juin, BP 1612, Kinshasa; tel. (12) 81700; fax (12) 88081; e-mail amb.tanzanie@ic.cd; Ambassador GORDON LUHWANO NGILANGWA.

Togo: 3 ave de la Vallée, BP 10117, Kinshasa; tel. (12) 30666; Ambassador MAMA GNOFAM.

Tunisia: 67–69 ave du Cercle, BP 1498, Kinshasa; tel. (12) 33167; e-mail atkinshasa@yahoo.fr; Ambassador (vacant).

Turkey: 18 ave Pumbu, BP 7817, Kinshasa; tel. (88) 01207; fax (88) 04740; e-mail tckinsbe@raga.net; Ambassador MEHMET ÖZYILDIZ.

United Kingdom: 83 ave Roi Baudouin, BP 8049, Kinshasa; tel. (81) 7150761; fax (81) 3464291; e-mail ambrit@ic.cd; Ambassador NICHOLAS KAY.

USA: 310 ave des Aviateurs, BP 397, Kinshasa; tel. (81) 5560151; fax (81) 5560173; e-mail AEKinshasaConsular@state.gov; internet kinshasa.usembassy.gov; Ambassador WILLIAM JOHN GARVELINK.

Zambia: 54–58 ave de l'Ecole, BP 1144, Kinshasa; tel. (81) 9999437; fax (88) 45106; e-mail ambazambia@ic.cd; Ambassador (vacant).

Judicial System

Under the Constitution that entered into effect in February 2006, the judicial system is independent. Members of the judiciary are under the authority of the Conseil Supérieur de la Magistrature. The Cour de Cassation has jurisdiction over legal decisions and the Conseil d'État over administrative decisions. The Cour Constitutionnelle interprets the provisions of the Constitution and ensures the conformity of new legislation. The judicial system also comprises a Haute Cour Militaire, and lower civil and military courts and tribunals. The Conseil Supérieur de la Magistrature has 18 members, including the Presidents and Chief Prosecutors of the main courts. The Cour Constitutionnelle comprises nine members, who are appointed by the President (three nominated by the legislature and three by the Conseil Supérieur de la Magistrature) for a term of nine years. The Head of State appoints and dismisses magistrates, on the proposal of the Conseil Supérieur de la Magistrature.

Cour de Cassation
cnr ave de la Justice and ave de Lemera, BP 3382, Kinshasa-Gombe; tel. (12) 25104.
President of the Cour de Cassation: LWAMBA BINDU.
Procurator-General of the Republic: MONGULU T'APANGANE.

Religion

Many of the country's inhabitants follow traditional beliefs, which are mostly animistic. A large proportion of the population is Christian, predominantly Roman Catholic, and there are small Muslim, Jewish and Greek Orthodox communities.

CHRISTIANITY

The Roman Catholic Church
The Democratic Republic of the Congo comprises six archdioceses and 41 dioceses. An estimated 50% of the population are Roman Catholics.

Bishops' Conference
Conférence Episcopale de la République Démocratique du Congo, BP 3258, Kinshasa-Gombe; tel. (12) 34528; fax (88) 44948; e-mail conf.episc.rdc@ic.cd.
f. 1981; Pres. Most Rev. LAURENT MONSENGWO PASINYA (Archbishop of Kisangani).

Archbishop of Bukavu: FRANÇOIS-XAVIER MAROY RUSENGO, Archevêché, ave Mbaki 18, BP 3324, Bukavu, Kivu; tel. (81) 3180621; e-mail archevechebk@yahoo.fr.

Archbishop of Kananga: Most Rev. MARCEL MADILA BASANGUKA, Archevêché, BP 70, Kananga; tel. (81) 5013942; e-mail archidiocesekananga@yahoo.fr.

Archbishop of Kinshasa: Most Rev. LAURENT MONSENGWO PASINYA, Archevêché, ave de l'Université, BP 8431, Kinshasa 1; tel. (12) 3723546; e-mail archikin@ic.cd.

Archbishop of Kisangani: (vacant), Archevêché, ave Mpolo 10B, BP 505, Kisangani; tel. (81) 2006715; fax (761) 608336.

Archbishop of Lubumbashi: Most Rev. FLORIBERT SONGASONGA MWITWA, Archevêché, BP 72, Lubumbashi; tel. (99) 7031991; e-mail archidiolub@mwangaza.cd.

Archbishop of Mbandaka-Bikoro: Most Rev. JOSEPH KUMUONDALA MBIMBA, Archevêché, BP 1064, Mbandaka; tel. (98) 849988; e-mail mbandakabikoro@yahoo.fr.

The Anglican Communion
The Church of the Province of the Congo comprises six dioceses.

Archbishop of the Province of the Congo and Bishop of Boga: Most Rev. PATRICE BYANKYA NJOJO, CAC-Boga, POB 25586, Nairobi, Kenya.

Bishop of Bukavu: Rt Rev. FIDÈLE BALUFUGA DIROKPA, CAC-Bukavu, POB 53435, Nairobi, Kenya.

Bishop of Katanga: Rt Rev. ISINGOMA KAHWA, BP 16482, Kinshasa; tel. (88) 06533; e-mail peac_isingoma@yahoo.fr.

Bishop of Kindu: Rt Rev. ZACHARIA MASIMANGE KATANDA, CAC-Kindu, POB 53435, Nairobi, Kenya; e-mail angkindu@antenna.nl.

Bishop of Kisangani: Rt Rev. SYLVESTRE MUGERA TIBAFA, CAC-Kisangani, BP 861, Kisangani.

Bishop of Nord Kivu: Rt Rev. METHUSELA MUNZENDA MUSUBAHO, CAC-Butembo, POB 21285, Nairobi, Kenya; fax (satellite) 871-166-1121.

Kimbanguist
Eglise de Jésus Christ sur la Terre par le Prophète Simon Kimbangu: BP 7069, Kinshasa; tel. (12) 68944; f. 1921; officially est. 1959; c. 5m. mems (1985); Spiritual Head HE SALOMON DIALUNGANA KIANGANI; Sec.-Gen. Rev. LUNTADILLA.

Protestant Churches
Eglise du Christ au Congo (ECC): ave de la Justice 75, BP 4938, Kinshasa-Gombe; f. 1902; a co-ordinating agency for all the Protestant churches, with the exception of the Kimbanguist Church; 62 mem. communities and a provincial org. in each province; c. 10m. mems (1982); Pres. Bishop MARINI BODHO; includes:

Communauté Baptiste du Congo-Ouest: BP 4728, Kinshasa 2; f. 1970; 450 parishes; 170,000 mems (1985); Gen. Sec. Rev. LUSAKWENO-VANGU.

Communauté des Disciples du Christ: BP 178, Mbandaka; tel. 31062; f. 1964; 250 parishes; 650,000 mems (1985); Gen. Sec. Rev. Dr ELONDA EFEFE.

Communauté Episcopale Baptiste en Afrique: 2 ave Jason Sendwe, BP 2809, Lubumbashi 1; tel. and fax (2) 348602; e-mail kitobokabwe@yahoo.fr; f. 1956; 1,300 episcopal communions and parishes; 150,000 mems (2001); Pres. Bishop KITOBO KABWEKA-LEZA.

Communauté Evangélique: BP 36, Luozi; f. 1961; 50 parishes; 33,750 mems (1985); Pres. Rev. K. LUKOMBO NTONTOLO.

Communauté Lumière: BP 10498, Kinshasa 1; f. 1931; 150 parishes; 220,000 mems (1985); Patriarch KAYUWA TSHIBUMBU WA KAHINGA.

Communauté Mennonite: BP 18, Tshikapa; f. 1960; 40,000 mems (1985); Gen. Sec. Rev. KABANGY DJEKE SHAPASA.

Communauté Presbytérienne: BP 117, Kananga; f. 1959; 150,000 mems (1985); Gen. Sec. Dr M. L. TSHIHAMBA.

Eglise Missionaire Apostolique: 375 ave Commerciale, BP 15859, Commune de N'Djili, Kinshasa 1; tel. (98) 165927; e-mail buzi4@hotmail.com; f. 1986; 5 parishes; 2,600 mems; Apostle for Africa Rev. LUFANGA-AYIMOU NANANDANA.

The Press

DAILIES

L'Analyste: 129 ave du Bas-Congo, BP 91, Kinshasa-Gombe; tel. (12) 80987; Dir and Editor-in-Chief BONGOMA KONI BOTAHE.

L'Avenir: Immeuble Ruzizi, 873 ave Bas-Congo Kinshasa-Gombe; tel. (99) 9942485; internet www.groupelavenir.net; owned by Groupe de l'avenir; Chair. PIUS MUABILU.

Boyoma: 31 blvd Mobutu, BP 982, Kisangani; Dir and Editor BADRIYO ROVA ROVATU.

Elima: 1 ave de la Révolution, BP 11498, Kinshasa; tel. (12) 77332; f. 1928; evening; Dir and Editor-in-Chief ESSOLOMWA NKOY EA LINGANGA.

Mjumbe: BP 2474, Lubumbashi; tel. (2) 25348; f. 1963; Dir and Editor TSHIMANGA KOYA KAKONA.

Le Palmarès: 220 ave Mpolo, BP 63, Kinshasa-Gombe; supports Union pour la démocratie et le progrès social; Editor MICHEL LADELUYA.

Le Phare: bldg du 29 juin, ave Col Lukusa 3392, BP 15662, Kinshasa-Gombe; tel. (12) 45896; e-mail info@le-phare.com; f. 1983; Editor POLYDOR MUBOYAYI MUBANGA; circ. 4,000.

Le Potentiel: Immeuble Ruzizi, 873 ave du Bas-Congo, BP 11338, Kinshasa; tel. (12) 891053; e-mail potentiel@ic.cd; f. 1982; Editor MODESTE MUTINGA MUTUISHAYI; circ. 8,000.

La Référence Plus: BP 22520, Kinshasa; tel. (12) 45783; f. 1989; Dir ANDRÉ IPAKALA.

PERIODICALS

Afrique Editions: Kinshasa; tel. (88) 43202; e-mail bpongo@raga.net.

Allo Kinshasa: 3 rue Kayange, BP 20271, Kinshasa-Lemba; monthly; Editor MBUYU WA KABILA.

L'Aurore Protestante: Eglise du Christ au Congo, BP 4938, Kinshasa-Gombe; French; religion; monthly; circ. 10,000.

BEA Magazine de la Femme: 2 ave Masimanimba, BP 113380, Kinshasa 1; every 2 weeks; Editor MUTINGA MUTWISHAYI.

Cahiers Economiques et Sociaux: BP 257, Kinshasa XI, (National University of the Congo); sociological, political and economic review; quarterly; Dir Prof. NDONGALA TADI LEWA; circ. 2,000.

Cahiers des Religions Africaines: Faculté de Théologie Catholique de Kinshasa, BP 712, Kinshasa/Limete; tel. (12) 78476; f. 1967; English and French; religion; 2 a year; circ. 1,000.

Le Canard Libre: Kinshasa; f. 1991; Editor JOSEPH CASTRO MULEBE.

Circulaire d'Information: Association Nationale des Entreprises du Congo, 10 ave des Aviateurs, BP 7247, Kinshasa 1; tel. (12) 22565; f. 1959; French; legal and statutory texts for the business community; monthly.

La Colombe: 32B ave Tombalbaye, Kinshasa-Gombe; tel. (12) 21211; organ of Parti démocrate et social chrétien; circ. 5,000.

Congo-Afrique: Centre d'Etudes pour l'Action Sociale, 9 ave Père Boka, BP 3375, Kinshasa-Gombe; tel. (12) 34245; e-mail cepas@raga.net; f. 1961; economic, social and cultural; monthly; Editors FRANCIS KIKASSA MWANALESSA, RENÉ BEECKMANS; circ. 2,500.

Le Conseiller Comptable: 51 rue du Grand Séminaire, Quartier Nganda, BP 308, Kinshasa; tel. (88) 01216; fax (88) 00075; f. 1974; French; public finance and taxation; quarterly; Editor TOMENA FOKO; circ. 2,000.

Documentation et Information Protestante (DIP): Eglise du Christ au Congo, BP 4938, Kinshasa-Gombe; tel. and fax (88) 46387; e-mail eccm@ic.cd; French and English; religion.

Documentation et Informations Africaines (DIA): BP 2598, Kinshasa 1; tel. (12) 33197; fax (12) 33196; e-mail dia@ic.cd; internet www.peacelink.it/dia/index.html; Roman Catholic news agency reports; 3 a week; Dir Rev. Père VATA DIAMBANZA.

L'Entrepreneur Flash: Association Nationale des Entreprises du Congo, 10 ave des Aviateurs, BP 7247, Kinshasa 1; tel. (12) 22565; f. 1978; business news; monthly; circ. 1,000.

Etudes d'Histoire Africaine: National University of the Congo, BP 1825, Lubumbashi; f. 1970; French and English; history; annually; circ. 1,000.

JuriCongo: coin des aves Commerce et Plateau, Galerie du 24 Novembre, Kinshasa; fax (12) 20320; e-mail cavas@ic.cd; guide to judicial affairs; Pres. EMERY MUKENDI WAFWANA.

Les Kasaï: 161 9e rue, BP 575, Kinshasa/Limete; weekly; Editor NSENGA NDOMBA.

Kin-Média: BP 15808, Kinshasa 1; monthly; Editor ILUNGA KASAMBAY.

KYA: 24 ave de l'Equateur, BP 7853, Kinshasa-Gombe; tel. (12) 27502; f. 1984; weekly for Bas-Congo; Editor SASSA KASSA YI KIBOBA.

Libération: Kinshasa; f. 1997; politics; supports the AFDL; weekly; Man. NGOYI KABUYA DIKATETA M'MIANA.

Mambenga 2000: BP 477, Mbandaka; Editor BOSANGE YEMA BOF.

Le Moniteur de l'Economie (Economic Monitor): Kinshasa; Man. Editor FÉLIX NZUZI.

Mwana Shaba: Générale des Carrières et des Mines, BP 450, Lubumbashi; monthly; circ. 25,000.

Ngabu: Société Nationale d'Assurances, Immeuble Sonas Sankuru, blvd du 30 juin, BP 3443, Kinshasa-Gombe; tel. (12) 23051; f. 1973; insurance news; quarterly.

Njanja: Société Nationale des Chemins de Fer Congolais, 115 pl. de la Gare, BP 297, Lubumbashi; tel. (2) 23430; fax (2) 61321; railways and transportation; annually; circ. 10,000.

NUKTA: 14 chaussée de Kasenga, BP 3805, Lubumbashi; weekly; agriculture; Editor NGOY BUNDUKI.

Post: Immeuble Linzadi, 1538 ave de la Douane, Kinshasa-Gombe; e-mail thepostrdc@yahoo.com; internet www.congonline.com/thepost; 2 a week; Editor-in-Chief MUKEBAYI NKOSO.

Problèmes Sociaux Zaïrois: Centre d'Exécution de Programmes Sociaux et Economiques, Université de Lubumbashi, 208 ave Kasa-vubu, BP 1873, Lubumbashi; f. 1946; quarterly; Editor N'KASHAMA KADIMA.

Promoteur Congolais: Centre du Commerce International du Congo, 119 ave Colonel Tshatshi, BP 13, Kinshasa; f. 1979; international trade news; six a year.

Sciences, Techniques, Informations: Centre de Recherches Industrielles en Afrique Centrale (CRIAC), BP 54, Lubumbashi.

Le Sport Africain: 13è niveau Tour adm., Cité de la Voix du Congo, BP 3356, Kinshasa-Gombe; monthly; Pres. TSHIMPUMPU WA TSHIMPUMPU.

Taifa: 536 ave Lubumba, BP 884, Lubumbashi; weekly; Editor LWAMBWA MILAMBU.

Telema: Faculté Canisius, Kimwenza, BP 3724, Kinshasa-Gombe; f. 1974; religious; quarterly; edited by the Central Africa Jesuits; circ. 1,200.

Umoja: 23 Bunkeye Matonge, Kinshasa; weekly; Publr LÉON MOUKANDA LUNYAMA.

Vision: Kinshasa; 2 a week; independent; Man. Editor XAVIER BONANE YANGANZI.

La Voix des Sans-Voix: ave des Ecuries 3858, commune de Ngaliema, BP 11445, Kinshasa-Gombe; tel. (88) 40394; fax (88) 01826; e-mail vsv@ic.cd; internet www.congonline.com/vsv.

NEWS AGENCIES

Agence Congolaise de Presse (ACP): 44–48 ave Tombalbaye, BP 1595, Kinshasa 1; tel. (12) 22035; e-mail acpresse@rd-congo.com; internet www.rd-congo.com/acp.html; f. 1957; state-controlled; Dir-Gen. ALI KALONGA.

Digital Congo: 3335 ave Kabasele Tshiamala, Kinshasa-Gombe; tel. (88) 06269; e-mail info@multimediacongo.net; internet www.digitalcongo.net; news service owned by Multimedia Congo.

Documentation et Informations Africaines (DIA): BP 2598, Kinshasa 1; tel. (12) 34528; f. 1957; Roman Catholic news agency; Dir Rev. Père VATA DIAMBANZA.

Press Association

Union de la Presse du Congo: BP 4941, Kinshasa 1; tel. (12) 24437.

Publishers

Aequatoria Centre: BP 276, Mbandaka; f. 1980; anthropology, biography, ethnicity, history, language and linguistics, social sciences; Dir HONORÉ VINCK.

CEEBA Publications: BP 246, Bandundu; f. 1965; humanities, languages, fiction; Man. Dir (Editorial) Dr HERMANN HOCHEGGER.

Centre de Linguistique Théorique et Appliquée (CELTA): BP 4956, Kinshasa-Gombe; tel. (81) 8129998; e-mail anyembwe@yahoo.fr; f. 1971; language arts and linguistics; Dir-Gen. ANDRÉ NYEMBWE NTITA.

Centre de Documentation Agricole: BP 7537, Kinshasa 1; tel. (12) 32498; agriculture, science; Dir PIERTE MBAYAKABUYI; Chief Editor J. MARCELLIN KAPUKUNGESA.

Centre de Recherches Pédagogiques: BP 8815, Kinshasa 1; f. 1959; accounting, education, geography, language, science; Dir P. DETIENNE.

Centre de Vulgarisation Agricole: BP 4008, Kinshasa 2; tel. (12) 71165; fax (12) 21351; agriculture, environment, health; Dir-Gen. KIMPIANGA MAHANIAH.

Centre International de Sémiologie: 109 ave Pruniers, BP 1825, Lubumbashi.

Centre Protestant d'Editions et de Diffusion (CEDI): 209 ave Kalémie, BP 11398, Kinshasa 1; tel. (12) 22202; fax (12) 26730; f. 1935; fiction, poetry, biography, religious, juvenile; Christian tracts, works in French, Lingala, Kikongo, etc.; Dir-Gen. HENRY DIRKS.

Commission de l'Education Chrétienne: BP 3258, Kinshasa-Gombe; tel. (12) 30086; education, religion; Man. Dir Abbé MUGADJA LEHANI.

Connaissance et Pratique du Droit Congolais Editions (CDPC): BP 5502, Kinshasa-Gombe; f. 1987; law; Editor DIBUNDA KABUINJI.

Editions Lokole: BP 5085, Kinshasa 10; state org. for the promotion of literature; Dir BOKEME SHANE MOLOBAY.

Editions Saint Paul: BP 8505, Kinshasa; tel. (99) 4657188; e-mail fspkin10@ic.cd; f. 1988; fiction, general non-fiction, poetry, religion; Dir Sister MASTAKI GODELIEVE; Sec. Sister M. ROSARIO ZAMBELLO.

THE DEMOCRATIC REPUBLIC OF THE CONGO   *Directory*

Facultés Catholiques de Kinshasa: 2 ave de l'Université, Kinshasa-Limete; tel. and fax (12) 46965; e-mail facakin@ic.cd; f. 1957; anthropology, art, economics, history, politics, computer science; Rector Prof. Mgr HIPPOLYTE NGIMBI NSEKA.

Les Editions du Trottoir: BP 1800, Kinshasa; tel. (12) 9936043; e-mail smuyengo@yahoo.fr; f. 1989; communications, fiction, literature, drama; Pres. CHARLES DJUNJU-SIMBA.

Librairie les Volcans: 22 ave Pres. Mobutu, BP 400, Goma, Nord-Kivu; f. 1995; social sciences; Man. Dir RUHAMA MUKANDOLI.

Presses Universitaires du Congo (PUC): 290 rue d'Aketi, BP 1800, Kinshasa 1; tel. (12) 9936043; e-mail smuyengo@yahoo.fr; f. 1972; science, arts and communications; Dir Abbé SÉBASTIEN MUYENGO.

GOVERNMENT PUBLISHING HOUSE

Imprimerie du Gouvernement Central: BP 3021, Kinshasa-Kalina.

Broadcasting and Communications

REGULATORY AUTHORITY

Autorité de Régulation de la Poste et des Télécommunications du Congo (AARPTC): blvd du 30 juin, BP 3000, Kinshasa 1; tel. (13) 92491; e-mail info.arptc@arptc.cd; internet www.arptc.cd.

Telecommunications

Celtel: croisement des aves Tchad et Bas-Congo, Kinshasa; tel. (99) 6000555; e-mail info@cd.celtel.com; internet www.cd.celtel.com; mobile cellular telephone network; Dir-Gen. ANTOINE PAMBORO; 1.83m. subscribers (Dec. 2006).

Congo Chine Telecom (CCT): ave du Port, Kinshasa; mobile cellular telephone network; covers Kinshasa and Bas-Congo, Kasaï, Katanga and Oriental provinces; 51% owned by ZTE (People's Republic of China), 49% state-owned; 466,000 subscribers (Dec. 2006).

Oasis Telecom (Tigo): 372 ave Col Mondjiba, Kinshasa; tel. (89) 8901000; fax (89) 8901001; internet www.tigo.cd; 100% owned by Millicom; 50,000 subscribers (Dec. 2006).

Supercell: 99 ave des Tulipiers, BP 114, Goma; tel. (80) 8313010; e-mail rogern@supercell.cd; 69,000 subscribers.

Vodacom Congo: Immeuble Mobil–Oil, 2ème étage, 3157 blvd du 30 juin, BP 797, Kinshasa 1; tel. (81) 3131000; fax (81) 3131351; e-mail vodacom@vodacom.cd; internet www.vodacom.cd; 51% owned by Vodacom (South Africa); 2.33m. subscribers (Dec. 2006).

BROADCASTING

Radio-Télévision Nationale Congolaise (RTNC): BP 3171, Kinshasa-Gombe; tel. (12) 23171; state radio, terrestrial and satellite television broadcasts; Dir-Gen. JOSE KAJANGUA.

Radio

Several private radio broadcasters operate in Kinshasa.

Radio Candip: Centre d'Animation et de Diffusion Pédagogique, BP 373, Bunia.

La Voix du Congo: Station Nationale, BP 3164, Kinshasa-Gombe; tel. (12) 23175; state-controlled; operated by RTNC; broadcasts in French, Swahili, Lingala, Tshiluba, Kikongo; regional stations at Kisangani, Lubumbashi, Bukavu, Bandundu, Kananga, Mbuji-Mayi, Matadi, Mbandaka and Bunia.

Television

Several private television broadcasters operate in Kinshasa.

Antenne A: Immeuble Forescom, 2e étage, ave du Port 4, POB 2581, Kinshasa 1; tel. (12) 21736; private and commercial station; Dir-Gen. IGAL AVIVI NEIRSON.

Canal Z: ave du Port 6, POB 614, Kinshasa 1; tel. (12) 20239; commercial station; Dir-Gen. FRÉDÉRIC FLASSE.

Tele Kin Malebo (TKM): 32B route de Matadi, Ngaliema, Kinshasa; tel. (12) 2933338; e-mail malebokin@hotmail.com; private television station; nationalization announced 1997; Dir-Gen. NGONGO LUWOWO.

Télévision Congolaise: BP 3171, Kinshasa-Gombe; tel. (12) 23171; govt commercial station; operated by RTNC; broadcasts two channels.

Finance

(cap. = capital; res = reserves; dep. = deposits; m. = million; br(s). = branch(es); amounts in new Congolese francs unless otherwise indicated)

BANKING

The introduction as legal tender of a new currency unit, the new Congolese franc (CF), was completed on 30 June 1998. However, as a result of the civil conflict, its value immediately declined dramatically. In late 2003, following the restoration of relative peace and installation of new transitional authorities, the Central Bank introduced new notes in an effort to revive the national currency and nation-wide operations were gradually restored.

Central Bank

Banque Centrale du Congo: 563 blvd Colonel Tshatshi au nord, BP 2697, Kinshasa; tel. (12) 20704; fax (12) 8805152; e-mail cabgouv@bcc.cd; internet www.bcc.cd; f. 1964; res 1,030m. (2002); Gov. JEAN-CLAUDE MASANGU MULONGO; 8 brs.

Commercial Banks

Banque Commerciale du Congo SARL (BCDC): blvd du 30 juin, BP 2798, Kinshasa; tel. (81) 8845704; fax (99) 631048; e-mail dir@bcdc.cd; internet www.bcdc.cd; f. 1952; as Banque du Congo Belge, name changed as above 1997; cap. 3,544.9m., res 1,733.0m., dep. 61,141.6m. (Dec. 2004); Pres. GUY ROBERT LUKAMA; Man. Dir YVES CUYPERS; 29 brs.

Banque Congolaise SARL: Immeuble Flavica 14/16, ave du Port, BP 9497, Kinshasa 1; tel. (12) 819982003; fax (12) 1398801; e-mail bank@rayventures.com; f. 1988; cap. and res NZ 3,000.2m., total assets NZ 9,579.1m. (Dec. 2003); Pres. BEYA KALAMBA; Admistrator-Delegate ROGER A. YAGHI.

Banque Internationale de Crédit SARL (BIC): 191 ave de l'Equateur, BP 1299, Kinshasa 1; tel. (81) 3330730; fax (81) 2616000; e-mail bic@ic.cd; f. 1994; cap. and res 946.2m., dep. 12,352.7m. (Dec. 2003); Pres. PASCAL KINDUELO LUMBU.

Banque Internationale pour l'Afrique au Congo (BIAC): Immeuble Nioki, ave de la Douane, BP 8725, Kinshasa 1; tel. (81) 7004001; e-mail com@biac.cd; internet www.biac.cd; cap. and res 945.6m., total assets 5,248.5m. (Dec. 2002); Pres. CHARLES SANLAVILLE.

Citibank (Congo) SARL Congo: Immeuble Citibank Congo, angle aves Col Lukusa et Ngongo Lutete, BP 9999, Kinshasa 1; tel. (81) 8840015; fax (12) 40015; e-mail singa.boyenge@citicorp.com; f. 1971; cap. and res NZ 199,425.2m., total assets NZ 1,928,804.9m. (Dec. 1996); Pres. ROBERT THORNTON; 1 br.

Rawbank Sarl: 3487 blvd du 30 juin, Immeuble Concorde Commune de la Gombe, Kinshasa; tel. (99) 8320000; fax (89) 240224; e-mail contact@rawbank.cd; internet www.rawbank.cd; f. 2002; cap. 1,233.6m., res 507.0m., dep. 12,056.3m. (Dec. 2004); Chair. MAZHAR RAWJI.

Société Financière de Développement SARL (SOFIDE): Immeuble SOFIDE, 9–11 angle aves Ngabu et Kisangani, BP 1148, Kinshasa 1; tel. (12) 816601531; e-mail sofide2001@yahoo.fr; f. 1970; partly state-owned; provides tech. and financial aid, primarily for agricultural devt; cap. and res 285.3m., total assets 1,202.0m. (Dec. 2003); Pres. and Dir-Gen. RAPHAËL SENGA KITENGE; 4 brs.

Stanbic Bank Congo SARL: 12 ave de Mongala, BP 16297, Kinshasa 1; tel. (12) 817006000; fax (12) 813013848; e-mail sbiccongo@raga.net; internet www.stanbicbank.cg; f. 1973; subsidiary of Standard Bank Investment Corpn (South Africa); cap. and res 59.3m., total assets 11,415.8m. (Dec. 2003); Chair. M. MUMBA; Administrator Delegate LOUIS NALLET; 1 br.

INSURANCE

INTERAFF: Bldg Forescom, ave du Port 4, Kinshasa-Gombe; tel. (88) 01618; fax (320) 2091332; e-mail interaff@raga.net; internet www.ic.cd/interaff.

Société Nationale d'Assurances (SONAS): 3443 blvd du 30 juin, Kinshasa-Gombe; tel. (12) 5110503; e-mail sonask@hotmail.com; f. 1966; state-owned; cap. US $5m.; 9 brs.

Trade and Industry

GOVERNMENT AGENCY

Bureau Central de Coordination (BCECO): ave Colonel Mondjiba 372, Complexe Utex Africa, Kinshasa; tel. (81) 9999180; e-mail bceco@bceco.cd; internet www.bceco.cd; f. 2001; manages projects funded by the African Development Bank and the World Bank; Dir-Gen. Mapon Matata Ponyo.

DEVELOPMENT ORGANIZATIONS

Bureau pour le Développement Rural et Urbain: Mont Ngafula, Kinshasa; e-mail bdru_kin@yahoo.fr.

Caisse de Stabilisation Cotonnière (CSCo): BP 3058, Kinshasa-Gombe; tel. (12) 31206; f. 1978 to replace Office National des Fibres Textiles; acts as an intermediary between the Govt, cotton ginners and textile factories, and co-ordinates international financing of cotton sector.

La Générale des Carrières et des Mines (GÉCAMINES): 450 blvd Kamanyola, BP 450, Lubumbashi; tel. (2) 222118; fax (2) 223655; f. 1967 to acquire assets of Union Minière du Haut-Katanga; state-owned corpn engaged in mining and marketing of copper, cobalt, zinc and coal; also has interests in agriculture; Exec. Chair. Yuma Monga (acting).

Institut National pour l'Etude et la Recherche Agronomiques: BP 1513, Kisangani; f. 1933; agricultural research.

Office National du Café: ave Général Bobozo, BP 8931, Kinshasa 1; tel. (12) 77144; f. 1979; state agency for coffee and also cocoa, tea, quinquina and pyrethrum; Pres. Feruza wa Ghenda.

Pêcherie Maritime Congolaise: Kinshasa; DRC's only sea-fishing enterprise.

CHAMBER OF COMMERCE

Chambre de Commerce, d'Industrie et d'Agriculture du Congo: 10 ave des Aviateurs, BP 7247, Kinshasa 1; tel. (12) 22286.

INDUSTRIAL AND TRADE ASSOCIATION

Association Nationale des Entreprises du Congo: 10 ave des Aviateurs, BP 7247, Kinshasa; tel. (12) 24623; f. 1972; represents business interests for both domestic and foreign institutions; Man. Dir Edouard Luboya Diyoka; Gen. Sec. Athanase Matenda Kyelu.

EMPLOYERS' ASSOCIATION

Fédération des Entreprises du Congo (FEC): Kinshasa; e-mail feccongo@hotmail.com; Pres. Pascal Kinduel Lumbu; Sec.-Gen. Joseph Mukadula Kabue.

UTILITIES

Electricity

Société Nationale d'Electricité (SNEL): 2831 ave de la Justice, BP 500, Kinshasa; tel. (12) 26893; fax (12) 33735; f. 1970; state-owned; Dir-Gen. Muyumba Kalembe.

Water

Régie de Distribution d'Eau (REGIDESO): 65 blvd du 30 juin, BP 12599, Kinshasa; tel. (12) 22792; water supply admin; Pres. Lubungu Pene Shako.

TRADE UNIONS

The Union Nationale des Travailleurs was founded in 1967 as the sole trade-union organization. In 1990 the establishment of independent trade unions was legalized, and by early 1991 there were 12 officially recognized trade-union organizations.

Confédération Démocratique du Travail: BP 10897, Quartier Industriel, C/Limete, Kinshasa 1; tel. 8804573; e-mail cdtcongo@yahoo.fr.

Confédération Syndicale du Congo: 81 ave Tombalbaye, Kinshasa-Gombe; tel. (89) 8922090; fax (13) 98126; e-mail csc_congo@hotmail.com; internet http://www.csc.cd; f. 1991.

Union Nationale des Travailleurs du Congo: Commune de la Gombe, BP 8814, 5 ave Mutombo Katshi, Kinshasa; tel. (81) 3288290; e-mail untcrdc@yahoo.fr; internet www.untc.org; f. 1967; comprises 16 unions; Pres. Katalay Moleli Sangol.

Transport

Compagnie des Transports du Congo: ave Muzu 52/75, Kinshasa; tel. (88) 46249; fax (322) 7065718; e-mail ros@ic.cd; road transport; Dir Roger Senger.

Office National des Transports (ONATRA): BP 98, Kinshasa 1; tel. (12) 21457; fax (12) 1398632; e-mail onatradf@ic.cd; f. 1935; operates 12,674 km of waterways, 366 km of railways and road and air transport; administers ports of Matadi, Boma and Banana; Pres. of Admin. Council Nestor Mwemena.

RAILWAYS

The main line runs from Lubumbashi to Ilebo. International services run to Dar es Salaam (Tanzania) and Lobito (Angola), and also connect with the Zambian, Zimbabwean, Mozambican and South African systems. In May 1997 the railway system was nationalized. In late 2003, under a major government programme, the rehabilitation of 500 km of railway linking northern and southern regions of the country commenced.

Kinshasa–Matadi Railway: BP 98, Kinshasa 1; 366 km operated by ONATRA; Pres. Jacques Mbelolo Bitwemi.

Société Nationale des Chemins de Fer du Congo (SNCC): 115 pl. de la Gare, BP 297, Lubumbashi; tel. (2) 346306; fax (2) 342254; e-mail sncc01@ic-libum.cd; f. 1974; 3,606 km (including 858 km electrified); administers all internal railway sections as well as river transport and transport on Lakes Tanganyika and Kivu; man. contract concluded with a Belgian-South African corpn, Sizarail, in 1995 for the man. of the Office des Chemins de Fer du Sud (OCS) and the Société des Chemins de Fer de l'Est (SFE) subsidiaries, with rail networks of 2,835 km and 1,286 km, respectively; assets of Sizarail nationalized and returned to SNCC control in May 1997; Dir-Gen. Medard Ilunga.

ROADS

In 1999 there were an estimated 157,000 km of roads, of which some 33,000 km were main roads. Following the installation of transitional authorities in July 2003, an extensive infrastructure rehabilitation programme, financed by external donors, including the World Bank, was initiated. Work on a principal road, connecting the south-western town of Moanda with Kinshasa and Lubumbashi, commenced late that year.

Office des Routes: Direction Générale, ave Ex-Descamp, BP 10899, Kinshasa-Gombe; tel. (12) 32036; construction and maintenance of roads.

INLAND WATERWAYS

The River Congo is navigable for more than 1,600 km. Above the Stanley Falls the Congo becomes the Lualaba, and is navigable along a 965-km stretch from Ubundu to Kindu and Kongolo to Bukama. The River Kasai, a tributary of the River Congo, is navigable by shipping as far as Ilebo, at which the line from Lubumbashi terminates. The total length of inland waterways is 14,935 km.

Régie des voies fluviales: 109 ave Lumpungu, Kinshasa-Gombe, BP 11697, Kinshasa 1; tel. (12) 26526; fax (12) 42580; administers river navigation; Gen. Man. Ngiam Kipoy.

Société Congolaise des Chemins de Fer des Grands Lacs: River Lualaba services: Bubundu–Kindu and Kongolo–Malemba N'kula; Lake Tanganyika services: Kamina–Kigoma–Kalundu–Moba–Mpulungu; Pres. and Gen. Man. Kibwe Mbuyu Kakudji.

SHIPPING

The principal seaports are Matadi, Boma and Banana on the lower Congo. The port of Matadi has more than 1.6 km of quays and can accommodate up to 10 deep-water vessels. Matadi is linked by rail with Kinshasa. The country's merchant fleet numbered 21 vessels and amounted to 13,922 gross registered tons at 31 December 2006.

Compagnie Maritime du Congo SARL: USB Centre, pl. de la Poste, BP 9496, Kinshasa; tel. (88) 20396; fax (88) 26234; e-mail cmdckin@ic.cd; f. 1946; services: North Africa, Europe, North America and Asia to West Africa, East Africa to North Africa; Gen. Man. Alex Mukendi Kamama.

CIVIL AVIATION

International airports are located at Ndjili (for Kinshasa), Luano (for Lubumbashi), Bukavu, Goma and Kisangani. There are smaller airports and airstrips dispersed throughout the country.

Blue Airlines: BP 1115, Barumbu, Kinshasa 1; tel. (12) 20455; f. 1991; regional and domestic charter services for passengers and cargo; Man. T. Mayani.

Business Aviation: 1345 ave de la Plaine, Kingabwa-Kinshasa; tel. (88) 45588; fax (99) 42260; e-mail businessaviation@ic.cd; internet www.businessaviation.cd; regional services.

Compagnie Africaine d'Aviation: 6ème rue, Limete, Kinshasa; tel. (88) 43072; fax (88) 41048; e-mail ltadek@hotmail.com; f. 1992; Pres. David Blattner.

Hewa Bora Airways (HWA): 1928 ave Kabambare, BP 1284, Kinshasa; tel. (81) 7005015; internet www.hba.cd; f. 1994 following merger of Zaire Airlines, Zaire Express and Congo Airlines; international, regional and domestic scheduled services for passengers and cargo; Chair. and CEO Stavros Papaioannou.

THE DEMOCRATIC REPUBLIC OF THE CONGO

Lignes Aériennes du Congo (LAC): 4 ave du Port, Kinshasa-Gombe, BP 8552, Kinshasa 1; tel. 819090001; Pres. LOUISE L. LONGANGE; Man. Dir PROSPER MAZIMPAKA FAATY.

Malila Airlift: ave Basoko 188, Kinshasa-Gombe; tel. (88) 46428; fax (satellite) 1-5304817707; e-mail malila.airlift@ic.cd; internet www.malila.cd; f. 1996; regional services; Man. VÉRONIQUE MALILA.

Waltair Aviation: 9ème rue 206, Limete, Kinshasa; tel. (88) 48439; fax (satellite) 1-3094162616; e-mail waltair.rdc@ic.cd; regional services; Dir VINCENT GILLET.

Tourism

The country offers extensive lake and mountain scenery, although tourism remains largely undeveloped. In 2005 tourist arrivals totalled 61,007. Receipts from tourism amounted to an estimated US $2m. in 1998.

Office National du Tourisme: 2A/2B ave des Orangers, BP 9502, Kinshasa-Gombe; tel. (12) 30070; f. 1959; Man. Dir BOTOLO MAGOZA.

Société Congolaise de l'Hôtellerie: Immeuble Memling, BP 1076, Kinshasa; tel. (12) 23260; Man. N'JOLI BALANGA.

THE REPUBLIC OF THE CONGO

Introductory Survey

Location, Climate, Language, Religion, Flag, Capital

The Republic of the Congo is an equatorial country on the west coast of Africa. It has a coastline of about 170 km on the Atlantic Ocean, from which the country extends northward to Cameroon and the Central African Republic. The Republic of the Congo is bordered by Gabon to the west and the Democratic Republic of the Congo to the east, while in the south there is a short frontier with the Cabinda exclave of Angola. The climate is tropical, with temperatures averaging 21°C–27°C (70°F–80°F) throughout the year. The average annual rainfall is about 1,200 mm (47 ins). The official language is French; Kituba, Lingala and other African languages are also used. Almost one-half of the population follow traditional animist beliefs and about 54% are Roman Catholics. There are small Protestant and Muslim minorities. The national flag (proportions 2 by 3) comprises a yellow stripe running diagonally from lower hoist to upper fly, separating a green triangle at the hoist from a red triangle in the fly. The capital is Brazzaville.

Recent History

Formerly part of French Equatorial Africa, Middle Congo became the autonomous Republic of the Congo, within the French Community, in November 1958, with Abbé Fulbert Youlou as Prime Minister, and subsequently as President when the Congo became fully independent on 15 August 1960. Youlou relinquished office in August 1963, following a period of internal unrest, and was succeeded by Alphonse Massamba-Débat, initially as Prime Minister, and from December as President. In July 1964 the Mouvement national de la révolution (MNR) was established as the sole political party. In August 1968 Massamba-Débat was overthrown in a military coup, led by Capt. (later Maj.) Marien Ngouabi, who was proclaimed President in January 1969. A new Marxist-Leninist party, the Parti congolais du travail (PCT), replaced the MNR, and in January 1970 the country was renamed the People's Republic of the Congo. In March 1977 Ngouabi was assassinated, and in April Col (later Brig.-Gen.) Jacques-Joachim Yhombi-Opango, the head of the armed forces, became the new Head of State. In February 1979 Yhombi-Opango surrendered his powers to a Provisional Committee appointed by the PCT. In March the head of the Provisional Committee, Col (later Gen.) Denis Sassou-Nguesso, became Chairman of the PCT Central Committee and President of the Republic. In July 1989 Sassou-Nguesso, the sole candidate, was re-elected Chairman of the PCT and President of the Republic for a third five-year term. At legislative elections in September the PCT-approved single list of 133 candidates was endorsed by 99.2% of voters. The list included, for the first time, non-party candidates.

Progress towards political reform dominated the latter half of 1990. In August several political prisoners were released, among them Yhombi-Opango, and in September the Central Committee of the PCT agreed to the immediate registration of new political parties. During an extraordinary Congress of the PCT the party abandoned Marxism-Leninism as its official ideology and formulated constitutional amendments legalizing a multi-party system, which took effect in January 1991. Gen. Louis Sylvain Goma was appointed Prime Minister (a position he had held between 1975 and 1984), to lead an interim Government.

A National Conference, chaired by the Roman Catholic Bishop of Owando, Ernest N'Kombo, was convened in February 1991; opposition movements were allocated seven of the 11 seats on the Conference's governing body. Having voted to establish itself as a sovereign body, in April the Conference announced proposals to abrogate the Constitution and abolish the Assemblée nationale populaire. In June a 153-member legislative Haut conseil de la République (HCR) was established, chaired by N'Kombo; this was empowered to supervise the implementation of the resolutions made by the Conference. From June the Prime Minister replaced the President as Chairman of the Council of Ministers, and the country's official name reverted to the Republic of the Congo. A new Prime Minister, André Milongo (a former World Bank official), was appointed in June. In December the HCR adopted a draft Constitution, which provided for legislative power to be vested in an elected Assemblée nationale and Sénat and for executive power to be held by an elected President.

The draft Constitution was approved by 96.3% of voters at a national referendum in March 1992. At elections to the Assemblée nationale, held in June and July, the Union panafricaine pour la démocratie social (UPADS) won 39 of the 125 seats, the Mouvement congolais pour la démocratie et le développement intégral (MCDDI) 29 seats and the PCT 18 seats. At indirect elections to the Sénat, held in July, the UPADS won the largest share (23) of the 60 seats, followed by the MCDDI, with 13 seats. At the first round of presidential voting, in August, Pascal Lissouba, the leader of the UPADS (and Prime Minister in 1963–66), won the largest share of the votes cast (35.9%); of the 15 other candidates, his closest rival was Bernard Kolélas of the MCDDI (22.9%). Sassou-Nguesso took 16.9% of the votes cast. At a second round of voting, two weeks later, Lissouba defeated Kolélas, with 61.3% of the votes cast.

Lissouba took office as President in August 1992. Maurice-Stéphane Bongho-Nouarra, of the UPADS, was appointed as Prime Minister. Meanwhile, the Union pour le renouveau démocratique (URD), a new alliance of seven parties, including the MCDDI, formed a coalition with the PCT (thereby establishing a parliamentary majority), which succeeded in winning a vote of 'no confidence' against the Government in October. In November the Government resigned, and shortly afterwards Lissouba dissolved the Assemblée nationale and announced that fresh legislative elections would be held. In December Claude Antoine Dacosta, a former World Bank official, was appointed Prime Minister and formed a transitional Government, comprising members of all the main political parties.

At the first round of elections to the Assemblée nationale, which took place in May 1993, the Mouvance présidentielle (MP), an electoral coalition of the UPADS and its allies, won 62 of the 125 seats, while the URD-PCT coalition secured 49. Protesting that serious electoral irregularities had occurred, the URD-PCT refused to contest the second round of elections in June (for seats where a clear majority had not been achieved in the first round) and demanded the repetition of some of the first-round polls. After the second round the MP had secured an absolute majority (69) of seats in the legislature. In June President Lissouba appointed a new Council of Ministers, with Yhombi-Opango as Prime Minister. In late June the Supreme Court ruled that electoral irregularities had occurred at the first round of elections, and in August, following external mediation, the Government and the opposition agreed to rerun the second round of elections.

Following the repeated elections, held in October 1993, the MP retained its majority in the Assemblée nationale, with 65 seats. In September six opposition parties formed an alliance, the Forces démocratiques unies (FDU), headed by Sassou-Nguesso and affiliated with the URD. In December Lissouba and the two main opposition leaders—Sassou-Nguesso and Kolélas—signed an agreement seeking a permanent end to hostilities between their supporters.

In February 1997 some 19 opposition parties issued a number of demands, including the expedited establishment of republican institutions, the creation of an independent electoral commission, the disarmament of civilians and the deployment of a multinational peace-keeping force. In May further unrest erupted, and in June an attempt by the Government, in preparation for legislative and presidential elections scheduled for July and August, to disarm the 'Cobra' militia group associated with Sassou-Nguesso precipitated a fierce national conflict along ethnic and political lines, involving the militias and opposing factions within the regular armed forces. Barricades were erected in Brazzaville, which was divided into three zones, controlled by supporters of Lissouba, Sassou-Nguesso and Kolélas, respectively. Despite mediation, none of the numerous cease-fire agreements signed during mid-1997 endured. In June French troops assisted in the evacuation of foreign residents from Brazzaville, and later in the month themselves departed. In September Lissouba appointed a Government of National Unity, under the premiership of Kolélas, thereby compromising the latter's role as a national mediator.

In October 1997 Sassou-Nguesso's forces, assisted by Angolan government troops, won control of Brazzaville and the strategic port of Pointe-Noire. Lissouba and Kolélas both found refuge abroad. Sassou-Nguesso was inaugurated as President on 25 October; he appointed a new transitional Government in November. It was later announced that a Conseil national de transition (CNT) was to hold legislative power, pending the approval of a new constitution by referendum (scheduled for 2001), and subsequent legislative elections. It was reported that some 10,000 people had been killed during the civil war, while the national infrastructure had been severely disrupted.

Throughout 1998 clashes continued in the southern Pool region, a stronghold of the militia loyal to Kolélas, causing thousands to flee the area. In December a battle for control of Brazzaville broke out between forces loyal to Kolélas (who remained in exile), reputedly supported by Angolan rebel groups, and Congolese government forces, augmented by Sassou-Nguesso's militia and Angolan government troops. More than 8,000 refugees were reported to have fled into the neighbouring Democratic Republic of the Congo (DRC). In late December government forces, aided by Angolan troops, launched offensives against Kolélas' forces in the south and west of the country. By March 1999 the rebel militias had been obliged to withdraw to Pool, and by mid-1999 the further advance of government forces permitted residents to return to evacuated districts. In November the Government announced that it had reached agreement with the militias loyal to Lissouba and Kolélas, although the two rebel leaders rejected the agreement, which included provision for a cease-fire and for a general amnesty. In December the CNT adopted legislation providing for an amnesty for those militiamen who surrendered their weapons to the authorities before 15 January 2000. In May Kolélas and his nephew, Col Philippe Bikinkita, the Minister of the Interior in the previous Lissouba administration, were convicted, *in absentia*, of operating personal prisons in Brazzaville and of mistreating prisoners and causing their deaths during the 1997 civil war. Kolélas and Bikinkita, both in exile abroad, were sentenced to death and ordered to pay compensation to their victims.

In December 1999 President Omar Bongo of Gabon was designated the official mediator in negotiations between the Government and the militias. Following discussions in Libreville, Gabon, representatives of the armed forces and of the rebel militias subsequently signed a second peace agreement, in the presence of Bongo and Sassou-Nguesso. In February 2000 the committee in charge of observing the implementation of the peace process announced, at a meeting with Bongo, that the civil war was definitively over. By that month it was estimated that around one-half of the estimated 810,000 people displaced by the conflict had returned to their homes.

In November 2000 the Government adopted a draft Constitution, which included provisions for the institution of an executive presidency and a bicameral legislature. The Head of State would be elected for a term of seven years, renewable only once. In December it was announced that some 13,000 weapons had been surrendered and 12,000 militiamen disarmed in the past year, although UN sources suggested that this represented less than one-half of the total number of militiamen in the Congo. Also in December, the PCT rejected demands by the MCDDI for an amnesty for Lissouba and Kolélas.

Internal and exiled opposition groups boycotted the opening ceremony of a period of national dialogue in March 2001. Some 2,200 delegates from public institutions, civic associations and political parties attended a series of regional debates, reportedly reaching a consensus on the draft Constitution, despite concerns that the President would have the power to appoint and dismiss ministers at will, and that there would be no provision for a vote of censure against the Government.

In September 2001 the CNT approved the text of the proposed Constitution to be submitted to referendum, pending the compilation of an electoral census. Concerns were, however, expressed at the low level of opposition representation on the Commission nationale d'organisation des élections (CONEL), which was, moreover, to be responsible to the Ministry of the Interior, Security and Territorial Administration.

The new Constitution was approved by 84.5% of votes cast at the referendum, which took place on 20 January 2002, with a participation rate of 77.5% of the electorate. In February the Supreme Court approved 10 presidential candidates, including Sassou-Nguesso and Milongo. Six political parties supportive of Milongo, including Yhombi-Opango's Rassemblement pour la démocratie et le développement, formed an opposition alliance, the Convention pour la démocratie et le salut (CODESA). In early March three opposition candidates, including Milongo, who had been widely regarded as the sole credible challenger to Sassou-Nguesso, and who now headed the Union pour la démocratie et la République (UDR—Mwinda), withdrew from the election. Milongo urged his supporters to boycott the poll, stating that his concerns about the transparency of electoral procedures and the impartiality of the CONEL remained unresolved. With all the major opposition candidates thereby excluded, Sassou-Nguesso won an overwhelming victory at the presidential election, which was held on 10 March, securing 89.41% of the votes cast. According to official figures, 69.4% of the electorate participated in the election.

Meanwhile, in late March 2002 renewed violence erupted in the Pool region, apparently instigated by members of a 'Ninja' militia group, led by Rev. Frédéric Bitsangou Ntumi (who had been a co-signatory of the peace agreement reached in 1999), which attacked the town of Kindamba, prompting several thousand civilians to flee. The conflict widened in early April, when two people were killed in an attack on a train on the Congo-Océan railway by members of the militia. By mid-April the unrest had spread to southern Brazzaville, and by late May some 50,000 people were reported to have been displaced. In late April government forces announced that they had regained control of the railway, facilitating a normalization in the supply of fuel and food to Brazzaville, although fighting continued in Pool. At the end of May government troops regained control of the rebel stronghold of Vindza, and in early June humanitarian assistance was finally permitted to reach the region.

The first round of elections to the 137-member Assemblée nationale, held on 26 May 2002, was contested by some 1,200 candidates from more than 100 parties; although more than one-half of the candidates had no party affiliation, it was reported that many of these nominally independent candidates were allies of Sassou-Nguesso. As a result of the unrest in Pool, voting was postponed indefinitely in eight constituencies, while disruption caused by protesters and administrative irregularities necessitated a rerun of polling in a further 12 constituencies on 28–29 May. Moreover, the CONEL subsequently announced the disqualification of 15 candidates. Turn-out in the first round, at which the PCT and its allies in the FDU won 38 of the 51 seats decided, was around 65%. Prior to the second round, the security situation in Brazzaville deteriorated markedly. In mid-June, while Sassou-Nguesso was in Italy, Ninja troops attacked the capital's main military base resulting in the deaths of 72 rebels, three army officers and 15 civilians. Despite requests by the UDR—Mwinda for a postponement of the elections in those areas where fighting had occurred, voting went ahead on 23 June, although the rate of participation, at an estimated 30% nationwide, was appreciably lower than in the first round, and was as low as 10% in some constituencies in Brazzaville and in Pointe-Noire. Following the polls, supporters of Sassou-Nguesso held an absolute majority in the new Assemblée; the PCT emerged as the largest party, with 53 seats, while the FDU alliance, by this stage comprising some 29 parties, held a total of 30 seats. The UDR—Mwinda became the largest opposition party, with six seats, while the UPADS held four seats. Notably, the MCDDI failed to secure representation in the Assemblée.

The local and municipal elections, held on 30 June 2002, were marked by a low turn-out and further entrenched Sassou-Nguesso's power; the success of the PCT and of constituent parties of the FDU ensured that supporters of the President held more than two-thirds of the elective seats. As the councillors elected on 30 June were those who would, in turn, elect the members of the Sénat on 7 July, the victory of those loyal to Sassou-Nguesso in the upper parliamentary chamber was also to be expected. Following these elections, the Sénat comprised 56 supporters of the President (44 from the PCT and 12 from the FDU), two representatives of civil society organizations, one independent and one member of the opposition. In early August Jean-Pierre Thystère Tchicaya, the leader of the Rassemblement pour la démocratie et le progrès social, one of the constituent parties of the FDU, was elected as President of the Assemblée nationale, and the Secretary-General of the PCT, Ambroise-Edouard Noumazalay, was elected as President of the Sénat. Sassou-Nguesso was inaugurated as elected President on 14 August; later in the month he announced the formation of a new Government, which, notably, included no representatives of the opposition (although several representatives from civil society were appointed to ministerial positions).

During the second half of 2002 sporadic attacks by Ninja militias in the Pool region, in particular against freight trains on the Congo-Océan railway, continued. In October unrest intensified, and several deaths of civilians were reported in clashes; up to 10,000 civilians were reported to have fled Pool, for Brazzaville, or the neighbouring Bouenza region, between early October and mid-November. In mid-November Sassou-Nguesso announced that a 'safe passage' would be provided from Pool to Brazzaville until mid-December for fighters who surrendered their arms, reiterating that the terms of the peace agreement concluded in 1999 remained valid. Fighting subsequently intensified, however, and despite an extension of the amnesty offered by Sassou-Nguesso, less than 500 rebels had surrendered by January 2003 (estimates of the number of rebels at large varied from 3,000–10,000), some 15 civilians were killed in an attack in Pool in January, and in February the first outbreak of violence in the Bouenza region since 1999 was reported. None the less, in March 2003 the Government and Ntumi's Ninja militia group signed a peace agreement. It was reported that at least 2,300 rebels had surrendered their weapons by April. In August the Assemblée nationale formally approved an amnesty for former Ninja fighters, to cover the period from January 2000. By September 2003 the situation in Pool had stabilized sufficiently to allow an electoral commission to be formed in the region; the delayed local and legislative elections were due to be held in 2005. None the less, in October 2003 renewed clashes between Ninja fighters and government forces near Mindouli, in Pool, resulted in at least 13 deaths.

In April 2004 divisions emerged within the FDU after five constituent parties issued a statement denouncing the alliance's inaction and demanding that a convention be held in an effort to address issues such as state reform, the consolidation of peace, and combating corruption and fraud. In June the European Commission extended a grant of €2m. to finance a programme of disarmament and reintegration in all areas of the Congo affected by civil war, to be conducted over a period of between two and three years by the UN Development Programme. In August the Government announced its intention to allocate 201m. francs CFA for the disarmament, demobilization and reintegration of 450 former combatants. Also in that month some 20 opposition parties and associations, including the MCDDI, formed a coalition, the Coordination de l'opposition pour une alternance démocratique (CODE-A), with the stated aim of fostering non-violent political change in the Congo.

Meanwhile, in July 2004 the Congo was suspended from the Kimberley Process, an international initiative to eliminate the illegal trade in diamonds to fund conflicts, after a report identified irregularities in the country's diamond exports. Sassou-Nguesso subsequently pledged to halt diamond trading pending the implementation of reforms in the sector aimed at securing recertification by the Process.

In mid-October 2004 the rail service between Brazzaville and Pointe-Noire was suspended following a series of attacks on trains in the Pool region. Ntumi denied claims that the attacks had been perpetrated by his Ninja rebel group, by now also known as the Conseil national de la résistance (CNR), and demanded an independent inquiry into the incidents. Meanwhile, displaced persons who had fled hostilities in Pool continued to return gradually during 2004 with government assistance, although reports suggested that armed fighters continued to intimidate civilians, despite the peace agreement signed in March 2003. (It was estimated that between 100,000 and 147,000 people had fled Pool between 1998 and 2002, and that by late 2004 most towns and villages in the region had regained no more than two-thirds of their original populations.)

In January 2005 President Sassou-Nguesso effected a reorganization of the Council of Ministers. The new Government comprised 35 ministers, all of whom were members of the PCT. The post of Prime Minister was created, and awarded to Isidore Mvouba, hitherto Minister of State, Minister of Transport and Privatization, responsible for the Co-ordination of Government Action and a native of the Pool region. The hitherto deputy Governor of the Banque des états de l'afrique centrale, Pacifique Issoïbeka, was appointed as Minister for the Economy, Finance and the Budget, while Bruno Itoua, hitherto Managing Director of the Société Nationale des Pétroles du Congo, was appointed Minister of Energy and Hydraulics. Opposition figures, including the leader of CODE-A, Herve Ambroise Malonga, criticized the creation of the post of Prime Minister, claiming that it was in violation of the 2002 Constitution, which had enshrined presidential control over the executive.

During 2005 the Pool region continued to be a source of instability. In early March 2005 clashes between the security forces and the Ninja militia, which followed the arrest of a member of the rebel group, resulted in the temporary closure of businesses and schools in southern districts of Brazzaville. Also in early March the Government initiated a new programme for the disarmament, demobilization and reintegration of 450 former combatants in Pool. Earlier programmes had reportedly resulted in the reintegration of some 8,000 former militiamen. The Government condemned an attack on a convoy of UN officials tasked with evaluating the humanitarian situation in Pool in April, blaming the Ninja militia group for the incident. It was later reported that the CNR had disarmed the attackers and recovered property that had been seized from the UN officials. In May it was announced that the Government had commenced power-sharing talks with the CNR with the aim of bringing members of the movement into 'all national institutions'. Meanwhile, the CNR also declared its intention of participating in future elections in the region (although it remained unclear as to when the holding of legislative elections in the region, postponed since 2002, would be feasible: the Government had intended that the polls be held in late 2005).

Indirect partial elections to renew one-half of the seats in the Sénat were held, as scheduled, on 2 October 2005, after which the PCT continued to hold an absolute majority of seats in the chamber, although its representation was reduced from 44 senators to 39. Most opposition parties, including those of CODE-A, boycotted these election, and, partly in consequence, several independent representatives were elected.

In mid-October 2005 at least six people were killed in clashes in southern Brazzaville between Ninja fighters and pro-Government troops. The outbreak of violence followed the return of Kolélas to the Congo, to attend the funeral of his wife (who had died in Paris, France). President Sassou-Nguesso subsequently requested that the legislature grant amnesty to Kolélas, in the interests of national reconciliation; legislation to that end was duly approved on 6 December, and the death sentence issued *in absentia* against the former Prime Minister in May 2000 was overturned. The Minister of Justice and Human Rights, Gabriel Entcha Ebia, stated that private citizens would none the less retain the right to file lawsuits against Kolélas. Several days after the granting of amnesty, Kolélas issued a solemn apology to the Congolese people for the harm that he had caused during the 1997 civil war, and acknowledged his role in instigating the conflict.

Unrest in the south of the country continued into 2006; in January the International Committee of the Red Cross (ICRC, see p. 319) and the international aid organization Médecins sans frontières suspended their operations after attacks on their staff by armed bandits. (The ICRC resumed its activities in the region in mid-February.) By this time some 43,000 members of rebel militias were thought to have been disarmed; however, in March Ntumi insisted on the creation of an agreement on 'political partnership' between the Government and the CNR as a condition for complete disarmament of his troops. In March the acting President of UPADS, Pascal Gamassa, asked that the party be pardoned, in the name of former President Lissouba, for the role it played in the civil war of 1997.

In early January 2007 Sassou-Nguesso resigned from the presidency of the PCT, citing Article 72 of the Constitution which rendered incompatible the functions of the Head of State with those of a party leader. At the end of that month the Rassemblement pour la démocratie et la république, one of the constituent parties of the FDU, announced that it was withdrawing from the governing coalition, citing disillusionment with the PCT. (The party occupied one seat in the Assemblée nationale and had never been represented in government or any key national institutions.) In February it was announced that the first and second rounds of legislative elections would be held on 24 June and 22 July, respectively. In early March the President carried out a minor cabinet reshuffle.

Despite several opposition parties opting to boycott the ballot, the first round of legislative elections took place as scheduled on 24 June 2007 at which the PCT claimed 23 of the initial 44 seats available. However, allegations of widespread malpractice and procedural irregularities threatened to undermine the legitimacy of the poll and the results in 19 constituencies were annulled. A new ballot was held in those areas, although the announcement of the results was delayed until 19 July, prompting the postponement (until 5 August) of the second round of the elections. Following the second round of voting, official results indicated that the PCT had retained control of the Assemblée nationale, securing 46 of the 137 seats; the MCDDI and UPADS each secured 11 seats. Observers from the African Union (AU, see p. 164) subsequently urged that a new independent electoral commission be established, following claims from opposition parties that the recently inaugurated supervisory body comprised a disproportionate number of government supporters.

In early December 2007 André Obami Itou was elected President of the Sénat, following the death the previous month of Noumazalay. In late December Sassou-Nguesso effected a minor reorganization of the Government; no changes were made to the key portfolios and Mvouba retained the premiership.

Since the 1997 civil war the principal aims of Congolese foreign policy have been to gain international recognition for the legitimacy of the Sassou-Nguesso Government and to ensure the continued support of the country's bilateral and multilateral donors. During the 1997 civil war President Lissouba accused France of favouring the rebel forces of Sassou-Nguesso (who was reported to have allied himself with French petroleum interests) over the elected administration. In May 1998 France extended its formal recognition to the Sassou-Nguesso Government, and in June resumed aid payments that had been suspended since the 1997 conflict. Relations between France and the Congo deteriorated from mid-2002, as a result of an investigation by a French court into several Congolese officials, including Sassou-Nguesso, in connection with the reported disappearance of 353 Congolese citizens, following their return from asylum in the DRC to the Congo in 1999 (see above). In December 2002 the Congo filed a case against France at the International Court of Justice (ICJ) in The Hague, Netherlands, claiming that the investigations represented a violation of Congolese sovereignty and disregarded Sassou-Nguesso's immunity as a Head of State. The ICJ ruled in June 2003 that investigations into the Inspector-General of the Congolese armed forces, Gen. Norbert Dabira, could continue, while noting that no action that warranted the intervention of the ICJ had yet been undertaken against Sassou-Nguesso or other government ministers. However, the ICJ was not expected to issue a ruling on the legitimacy of the jurisdiction of French courts over actions that were alleged to have occurred on Congolese territory; the ICJ also stated that the ruling would not prevent the Court conducting further investigations into the case. The head of Congo's national police force, Col Jean-François Ndenguet, was detained briefly during a visit to France at the beginning of April 2004 in connection with the investigation into the disappearances, but was released after claiming diplomatic immunity.

Prior to Sassou-Nguesso's seizure of power in 1997, relations with Angola were strained, as a result of the existence in the Congo of bases of an Angolan secessionist group, the Frente de Libertação do Enclave de Cabinda (FLEC). Angolan government troops facilitated Sassou-Nguesso's victory in the 1997 conflict by providing significant tactical support, and also played a role in the defeat of the rebel attack on Brazzaville in December 1998. In January 1999 the Heads of State of Angola, the Congo and the DRC met to agree a common policy on the conflicts in their countries. In December the interior ministers of the three countries met in Luanda, Angola, and signed a co-operation accord. The accord created a tripartite commission to ensure border security, the free movement of people and goods, the training of personnel, and the provision of assistance to displaced persons. Angolan troops assisted the Congolese Government in the renewed insurgency in the Pool region from early 2002, but the last contingent of Angolan soldiers was withdrawn from the Congo in December of that year.

Relations between the Republic of the Congo and the DRC steadily improved from the late 1990s. In December 1998 the two countries signed a non-aggression pact and agreed to establish a joint force to guarantee border security. In December 1999 Sassou-Nguesso met President Laurent-Désiré Kabila in order to discuss bilateral co-operation and the implementation of the tripartite Luanda accord, and further discussion on issues of common interest subsequently took place regularly between the two countries. In May 2001 some 19 DRC nationals suspected of involvement in the assassination of Laurent-Désiré Kabila in January were extradited from the Republic of the Congo to Kinshasa. In September 2002 Congolese authorities announced that, in accordance with a programme established in association with the International Organization for Migration (see p. 317), up to 4,000 soldiers from the DRC who had sought refuge or deserted in the Congo were to be repatriated. In October a formal repatriation agreement for the 62,000 refugees from the DRC in the Congo was signed by representatives of both countries, in collaboration with the office of the UN High Commissioner for Refugees (UNHCR). Moreover, some 400 Congolese refugees were believed to have been repatriated from the Kimaza refugee camp in southwestern DRC during 2004. In April 2005 the repatriation of some 57,000 refugees from the Congo to the DRC's Equateur province commenced under an agreement signed in September 2004 by officials from the two countries and UNHCR; by October 2007 a total of 36,000 refugees had returned to Equateur province since the programme began, including almost 18,000 since the beginning of 2007. The voluntary repatriation programme was expected to be completed by mid-2008.

By the mid-2000s Sassou-Nguesso's attempts to obtain international legitimacy for his regime had been largely successful. In 2003 Sassou-Nguesso served as President of the Communauté économique des états de l'Afrique centrale (CEEAC, see p. 411) for the period of one year, and also became President of the Communauté économique et monétaire de l'Afrique centrale (see p. 307). In January 2006 Sassou-Nguesso was elected as head of the AU, following the withdrawal of the candidacy of President Lt-Gen. Omar Hassan Ahmad al-Bashir of Sudan, as a result of controversy regarding the support of that country's Government for *Janjaweed* militia in the conflict in the western region of Darfur. The Republic of the Congo was also elected as a non-permanent member of the UN Security Council for a period of two years, with effect from September 2005.

Government

Following the assumption of power by Gen. Denis Sassou-Nguesso on 15 October 1997, the 1992 Constitution was suspended. A new Constitution, which was approved by referendum on 20 January 2002, took effect following a presidential election in March–April and legislative elections in May–June. Under the terms of the 2002 Constitution, executive power is vested in a President, who is directly elected for a seven-year term, renewable only once. The President appoints a Council of Ministers. (Although the President appointed a Prime Minister in early 2005, no explicit constitutional provision for such a post exists.) Legislative power is vested in a bicameral Parliament, comprising a 137-member Assemblée nationale, which is directly elected for a five-year term, and a 66-member Sénat, which is indirectly elected by local councils for a six-year term (with one-half of the membership renewable every three years).

For administrative purposes the country is divided into 10 regions, consisting of 76 districts (sous-préfectures) and six municipalities (communes urbaines).

Defence

As assessed at November 2007, the army numbered 8,000, the navy about 800 and the air force 1,200. In addition, there was a 2,000-strong Gendarmerie. The estimated defence budget for 2007 was 45,000m. francs CFA.

Economic Affairs

In 2005, according to estimates by the World Bank, the Congo's gross national income (GNI), measured at average 2003–05 prices, was US $3,806m., equivalent to $950 per head (or $940 on an international purchasing-power parity basis). During 1996–2006, it was estimated, the population increased at an average annual rate of 3.1%, while gross domestic product (GDP) per head increased, in real terms, by an average of 0.4% per year. Overall GDP increased, in real terms, at an average annual rate of 3.6% in 1996–2006; growth in 2006 was 6.4%.

Agriculture (including forestry and fishing) contributed an estimated 4.2% of GDP in 2006, according to the World Bank, and employed about 36.4% of the total labour force in mid-2005, according to FAO estimates. The staple crops are cassava, bananas and plantains, while the major cash crops are sugar cane, oil palm, cocoa and coffee. Forests cover about 57% of the country's total land area, and forestry is a major economic activity. Sales of timber provided an estimated 8.4% of export earnings in 1995, but in February 1998, to encourage local processing of wood, forestry companies were prohibited from exporting rough timber. Following the implementation of liberalization measures in the sector, output of timber was expected to increase significantly in the early 2000s. In 2003 exports of wood provided 9.7% of export earnings. According to the African Development Bank (ADB), during 1996–2006 agricultural

GDP increased at an average annual rate of 3.7%; growth in 2006 was 5.3%.

Industry (including mining, manufacturing, construction and power) contributed an estimated 73.5% of GDP in 2006, according to the World Bank, and employed an estimated 14.7% of the labour force in 1990. During 1996–2006, according to the ADB, industrial GDP increased at an average annual rate of 3.3%; it grew by 6.9% in 2006.

Mining and manufacturing contributed an estimated 67.3% of GDP in 2005, according to the IMF. The hydrocarbons sector is the only significant mining activity. In 2003 sales of petroleum and petroleum products provided 83.1% of export earnings, according to preliminary figures. Annual petroleum production (an estimated 93.3m. barrels in 2006, according to the US Geological Survey) was expected to continue to increase, as a result of major exploration and development planned at various offshore deposits, in particular near to the maritime border with Angola. Deposits of natural gas are also exploited. Lead, zinc, gold and copper are produced in small quantities. There are also exploitable reserves of diamonds, phosphate, iron ore, bauxite and potash. In October 2001 the Government issued the Portuguese company Escom a licence to prospect for diamonds in the far north of the country.

Manufacturing contributed 4.9% of GDP in 2006, according to the World Bank. The most important industries, the processing of agricultural and forest products, were adversely affected by the civil conflict in the late 1990s, but began to recover in the early 2000s, as political stability was restored. The textile, chemical and construction materials industries are also significant. According to the ADB, during 1996–2006 manufacturing GDP increased at an average annual rate of 5.8%; growth of 7.8% was recorded in 2006.

In 2004 all of the country's electricity production was generated by hydroelectric plants. The construction of a new hydroelectric dam at Imboulou, some 200 km north of Brazzaville, commenced in late 2003, with an anticipated completion date of 2009.

The services sector contributed 22.3% of GDP in 2006, according to the World Bank. During 1996–2006, according to the ADB, the GDP of the services sector increased at an average annual rate of 3.1%; the GDP of the sector increased by 4.7% in 2006.

In 2005 the Congo recorded a visible trade surplus of an estimated US $3,373.7m., when there was an estimated surplus of $903.2m. on the current account of the balance of payments. In 2002 the principal source of imports (25.9%) was France. In 2003 the People's Republic of China was the principal market for exports (21.8%). The Republic of Korea, the USA and the Democratic People's Republic of Korea are also important export-trading partners. The principal exports in 2003 were petroleum and petroleum products, and wood. The principal imports in that year were machinery and transport equipment, food and live animals and basic manufactures.

The budget surplus for 2005, according to estimates, was 501,000m. francs CFA (equivalent to 15.9% of GDP). The country's external debt totalled US $5,829m. at the end of 2004, of which $5,051m. was long-term public debt. In 2003 the cost of debt-servicing was equivalent to 4.0% of the value of exports of goods and services. In December 2004 the ADB approved a grant of $50m. to allow the Congo to clear one-third of its debt to that organization. The annual rate of inflation in Brazzaville during 1996–2006 was 3.3%. Consumer prices increased by an average of 6.6% in 2006.

The Republic of the Congo is a member of the Central African organs of the Franc Zone (see p. 307) and of the Communauté économique des états de l'Afrique centrale (CEEAC, see p. 411).

Civil conflict and ensuing instability adversely affected the Congo's economic performance in the late 1990s and, to a lesser extent, in the first half of the 2000s. The World Bank suspended relations with the Congo in November 1997 in response to the non-payment of debt arrears, while the outbreak of further hostilities in December 1998 led to the suspension of all donor activity. In recent years the high relative level of debt has remained a major impediment to the resumption of aid. None the less, in November 2000 the IMF approved a credit of some US $14m. for the Congo in emergency post-conflict assistance, and in August 2001 the World Bank declared that the Congo was again eligible for credit, having cleared all its overdue service payments. The Government's seven-year post-conflict economic reconstruction programme, which took effect from 2003, emphasized major infrastructural improvements, including the construction of a year-round river port at Lékéti and a new international airport in the north of the country. The Congo is the fifth-largest producer of petroleum in sub-Saharan Africa, and the Government's publication of an independent audit of the state-owned petroleum company, the Société Nationale des Pétroles du Congo, was a contributing factor in the IMF's decision, in December 2004, to approve a three-year Poverty Reduction and Growth Faciltity (PRGF), equivalent to some $84.4m.; the high international prices for petroleum prevailing in the mid-2000s also benefited the Congo's economy, although the country's external debt-service ratio continued to prevent it from qualifying for relief under the Bretton Woods institutions' initiative for heavily indebted poor countries. As of February 2008 the Congo had yet to qualify for the initiative. Petroleum production was reported to have declined slightly in 2007 to 87m. barrels (with an average of just 255,000 barrels per day); however, production was expected to recover significantly in 2008, to around 105m. barrels, owing to the discovery of new deposits. Meanwhile, the third review of the PRGF was delayed and missed reform targets under the most recent IMF staff-monitored programme further postponed the disbursement of funds from that organization. Although draft anti-corruption legislation was approved in mid-2007, international donors remained concerned at the lack of transparency in the national accounts, particularly with regard to the recording of transactions in the petroleum sector. GDP growth of 6.1% was recorded in 2006, while more modest growth, of 3.7%, was projected for 2007.

Education

Education is officially compulsory for 10 years between six and 16 years of age. Primary education begins at the age of six and lasts for six years. Secondary education, from 12 years of age, lasts for seven years, comprising a first cycle of four years and a second of three years. According to UNESCO estimates, enrolment at primary schools in 2003/04 was equivalent to 89% of children in the relevant age-group (boys 92%; girls 85%). In that year, enrolment at secondary schools was equivalent to 39% of children in the relevant age-group (boys 35%; girls 42%). In 1999/2000 13,403 students were attending tertiary institutions. In 2000 there were some 20,000 students enrolled in the Marien Ngouabi University in Brazzaville. Some Congolese students also attend further education establishments abroad. Expenditure on education by all levels of government was 52,274m. francs CFA in 1995. In September 2004 the World Bank approved a grant of US $20m. to assist with the reconstruction of the country's educational sector, which had been severely damaged by years of civil conflict.

Public Holidays

2008: 1 January (New Year's Day), 21 March (Good Friday), 24 March (Easter Monday), 1 May (Labour Day), 12 May (Whit Monday), 15 August (Independence Day), 25 December (Christmas).

2009: 1 January (New Year's Day), 10 April (Good Friday), 13 April (Easter Monday), 1 May (Labour Day), 1 June (Whit Monday), 15 August (Independence Day), 25 December (Christmas).

Weights and Measures

The metric system is in force.

THE REPUBLIC OF THE CONGO

Statistical Survey

Source (unless otherwise stated): Direction Générale, Centre National de la Statistique et des Etudes Economiques, Immeuble du Plan, Rond point du Centre Culturel Français, BP 2031, Brazzaville; tel. and fax 81-59-09; e-mail cnsee@hotmail.com; internet www.cnsee.org.

Area and Population

AREA, POPULATION AND DENSITY

Area (sq km)	342,000*
Population (census results)	
22 December 1984	1,909,248
30 July 1996	2,591,271
Population (UN estimates at mid-year)†	
2005	3,610,000
2006	3,689,000
2007	3,768,000
Density (per sq km) at mid-2007	11.0

* 132,047 sq miles.
† Source: UN, *World Population Prospects: The 2006 Revision*.

ETHNIC GROUPS

1995 (percentages): Kongo 51.4; Téké 17.2; Mbochi 11.4; Mbédé 4.7; Punu 2.9; Sanga 2.5; Maka 1.8; Pygmy 1.4; Others 6.7 (Source: La Francophonie).

REGIONS
(population at 1996 census)

	Area (sq km)	Population	Capital
Bouenza	12,260	189,839	Madingou
Cuvette	} 74,850 {	112,946	Owando
Cuvette ouest		49,422	Ewo
Kouilou	13,650	77,048	Pointe-Noire
Lékoumou	20,950	75,734	Sibiti
Likouala	66,044	66,252	Impfondo
Niari	25,925	103,678	Loubomo (Dolisie)
Plateaux	38,400	139,371	Djambala
Pool	33,955	265,180	Kinkala
Sangha	55,795	39,439	Ouesso
Total*	341,829	1,118,909	

*Excluding the municipalities of Brazzaville (100 sq km, population 856,410), Pointe-Noire (45 sq km, population 455,131), Loubomo (Dolisie—18 sq km, population 79,852), Nkaya (8 sq km, population 46,727), Ouesso (population 17,784) and Mossendjo (population 16,458).

PRINCIPAL TOWNS
(population at 1996 census)

Brazzaville (capital)	856,410	Loubomo (Dolisie)	79,852
Pointe-Noire	455,131	Nkaya	46,727

BIRTHS AND DEATHS
(annual averages, UN estimates)

	1990–95	1995–2000	2000–05
Birth rate (per 1,000)	38.5	37.2	35.1
Death rate (per 1,000)	11.1	12.6	12.7

Source: UN, *World Population Prospects: The 2006 Revision*.

Expectation of life (years at birth, WHO estimates): 54.4 (males 53.6; females 55.1) in 2005 (Source: WHO, *World Health Statistics*).

EMPLOYMENT
('000 persons at 1984 census)

	Males	Females	Total
Agriculture, etc.	105	186	291
Industry	61	8	69
Services	123	60	183
Total	289	254	543

Mid-2005 (estimates in '000): Agriculture, etc. 584; Total labour force 1,603 (Source: FAO).

Health and Welfare

KEY INDICATORS

Total fertility rate (children per woman, 2005)	6.3
Under-5 mortality rate (per 1,000 live births, 2005)	108
HIV/AIDS (% of persons aged 15–49, 2005)	5.3
Physicians (per 1,000 head, 2004)	0.20
Hospital beds (per 1,000 head, 1990)	3.35
Health expenditure (2004): US $ per head (PPP)	30.1
Health expenditure (2004): % of GDP	2.5
Health expenditure (2004): public (% of total)	49.2
Access to water (% of persons, 2004)	58
Access to sanitation (% of persons, 2004)	27
Human Development Index (2005): ranking	139
Human Development Index (2005): value	0.548

For sources and definitions, see explanatory note on p. vi.

Agriculture

PRINCIPAL CROPS
('000 metric tons)

	2004	2005	2006
Maize	9.2	8.0*	8.0*
Sweet potatoes†	5.8	5.6	6.0
Cassava (Manioc)	932.2	900.0†	1,000.0†
Cassava leaves	50.3	52.0†	50.0†
Yams	11.4	11.0†	11.0
Sugar cane	616.8	550.0	550.0†
Groundnuts (in shell)†	22.2	21.3	25.0
Oil palm fruit†	90.9	91.5	90.0
Bananas†	92.5	96.9	87.0
Plantains	61.4	65.0†	64.0†
Guavas, mangoes and mangosteens†	26.0	26.8	25.0
Avocados	6.6	6.5†	6.3†

* Unofficial figure.
† FAO estimate(s).

Aggregate production ('000 metric tons, may include official, semi-official or estimated data): Total cereals 10.4 in 2004, 9.4 in 2005, 9.4 in 2006; Total roots and tubers 991.6 in 2004, 959.6 in 2005, 1,059.3 in 2006; Total vegetables (incl. melons) 98.1 in 2004, 99.9 in 2005, 97.7 in 2006; Total fruits (excl. melons) 227.3 in 2004, 236.0 in 2005, 223.1 in 2006.

Source: FAO.

LIVESTOCK
('000 head, year ending September, FAO estimates)

	2003	2004	2005
Cattle	100	110	115
Pigs	46.3	46.3	46.5
Sheep	98	98	99
Goats	294.2	294.2	295.0
Chickens	2,230	2,300	2,400

2006: Figures assumed to be unchanged from 2005 (FAO estimates).

Source: FAO.

THE REPUBLIC OF THE CONGO

LIVESTOCK PRODUCTS
('000 metric tons, FAO estimates)

	2003	2004	2005
Cattle meat	1.9	2.0	2.2
Pig meat	2.1	2.1	2.1
Chicken meat	5.2	5.4	5.6
Game meat	18.0	20.0	20.0
Sheep and goat meat	1.1	1.1	1.1
Cows' milk	1.1	1.1	1.1
Hen eggs	1.2	1.2	1.2

2006: Figures assumed to be unchanged from 2005 (FAO estimates).
Source: FAO.

Forestry

ROUNDWOOD REMOVALS
('000 cubic metres, excluding bark)

	2004	2005	2006
Sawlogs, veneer logs and logs for sleepers	165	165*	165*
Pulpwood*	361	361	361
Other industrial wood*	370	370	370
Fuel wood*	1,448	1,369	1,256
Total*	2,344	2,265	2,152

* FAO estimate(s).
Source: FAO.

SAWNWOOD PRODUCTION
('000 cubic metres, including railway sleepers)

	2004	2005	2006
Total (all broadleaved)	200.0	209.0	267.6

Source: FAO.

Fishing

('000 metric tons, live weight)

	2003	2004	2005
Capture	54.7	54.2	58.4
Freshwater fishes	31.2	30.3	32.5
West African croakers	3.0	2.3	2.8
Sardinellas	7.3	7.9	9.7
Aquaculture	0.0	0.0	0.0
Total catch	54.7	54.3	58.4

Source: FAO.

Mining

	2004	2005	2006
Crude petroleum ('000 barrels)	82,069	92,550	93,261
Gold (kg)*	160	120	100

* Estimated metal content of ore.
Source: US Geological Survey.

Industry

SELECTED PRODUCTS
('000 metric tons, unless otherwise indicated)

	2002	2003	2004
Raw sugar	56	45	65
Veneer sheets ('000 cu metres)	23	3	8
Jet fuels	43	38	47
Motor gasoline (petrol)	41	53	49
Kerosene	19	21	19
Distillate fuel oils	75	119	120
Residual fuel oils	228	287	295
Electric energy (million kWh)	397	343	399

Source: UN, *Industrial Commodity Statistics Yearbook*.

Finance

CURRENCY AND EXCHANGE RATES

Monetary Units
100 centimes = 1 franc de la Coopération financière en Afrique centrale (CFA).

Sterling, Dollar and Euro Equivalents (31 May 2007)
£1 sterling = 964.12 francs CFA;
US $1 = 487.59 francs CFA;
€1 = 655.957 francs CFA;
10,000 francs CFA = £10.37 = $20.51 = €15.24.

Average Exchange Rate (francs CFA per US $)
2004   528.29
2005   527.47
2006   522.89

Note: The exchange rate of 1 French franc = 50 francs CFA, established in 1948, remained in force until January 1994, when the CFA franc was devalued by 50%, with the exchange rate adjusted to 1 French franc = 100 francs CFA. The relationship to French currency remained in effect with the introduction of the euro on 1 January 1999. From that date, accordingly, a fixed exchange rate of €1 = 655.957 francs CFA has been in operation.

BUDGET
('000 million francs CFA)

Revenue*	2003	2004	2005†
Petroleum revenue	422	530	1,020
Royalties	149	n.a.	n.a.
Government profit share sold by SNPC	251	n.a.	n.a.
Other revenue	182	208	220
Domestic taxes	134	149	168
Direct	64	72	43
Indirect	70	78	125
Customs receipts	43	50	43
Non-tax revenue	5	9	10
Total	604	738	1,240

Expenditure‡	2003	2004	2005†
Current expenditure	471	496	575
Wages and salaries	120	123	130
Materials and supplies	50	55	62
Transfers	131	123	142
Common charges	43	52	66
Interest payments	118	128	158
External	94	111	128
Domestic	23	17	30
Local authorities	9	15	17
Capital expenditure	135	161	170
Externally financed	24	32	16
Domestically financed	111	128	154
Total	605	656	745

* Excluding grants received ('000 million francs CFA): 10 in 2003; 8 in 2004; 6 in 2005 (estimate).
† Estimates.
‡ Excluding net lending ('000 million francs CFA): 1 in 2003; 0 in 2004; 0 in 2005 (estimate).

Source: IMF, *Republic of Congo: Statistical Appendix* (June 2007).

THE REPUBLIC OF THE CONGO

INTERNATIONAL RESERVES
(US $ million at 31 December)

	2004	2005	2006
Gold (national valuation)	4.88	5.71	7.06
IMF special drawing rights	7.23	2.43	0.19
Reserve position in IMF	0.83	0.77	0.81
Foreign exchange	111.54	728.63	429.08
Total	124.48	737.54	437.14

Source: IMF, *International Financial Statistics*.

MONEY SUPPLY
('000 million francs CFA at 31 December)

	2004	2005	2006
Currency outside banks	155.89	207.24	271.24
Demand deposits at active commercial banks	110.72	159.98	273.02
Total money (incl. others)	278.79	396.19	584.61

Source: IMF, *International Financial Statistics*.

COST OF LIVING
(Consumer Price Index for Brazzaville; base: 2000 = 100)

	2004	2005	2006
Food	90.8	95.6	105.3
Clothing	106.7	106.6	101.8
Fuel and electricity	110.3	112.5	127.4
All items (incl. others)	106.4	109.6	116.8

Source: ILO.

NATIONAL ACCOUNTS
('000 million francs CFA at current prices)
Expenditure on the Gross Domestic Product

	2003	2004	2005*
Final consumption expenditure	1,008	1,118	1,300
Households	656	751	883
Non-profit institutions serving households			
General government	353	368	417
Gross capital formation	532	556	707
Gross fixed capital formation	520	541	692
Changes in inventories			
Acquisitions, less disposals, of valuables	12	15	15
Total domestic expenditure	1,540	1,774	2,007
Exports of goods and services	1,642	1,935	2,722
Less Imports of goods and services	1,112	1,315	1,579
GDP in market prices	2,072	2,294	3,150
GDP at constant 1990 prices	961	995	1,072

* Estimates.

Gross Domestic Product by Economic Activity

	2003	2004	2005*
Agriculture, hunting, forestry and fishing	133	136	148
Mining and manufacturing†	1,170	1,349	2,073
Electricity, gas and water	19	20	23
Construction	86	91	105
Trade, restaurants and hotels	184	197	225
Transport, storage and communications	130	140	163
Government services	148	152	173
Other services	138	147	170
GDP at factor cost	2,009	2,230	3,080
Import duties	63	65	69
GDP in purchasers' values	2,072	2,294	3,150

* Estimates.
† Including petroleum sector ('000 million francs CFA): 1,036 in 2003; 1,205 in 2004; 1,902 in 2005 (estimate).

Source: IMF, *Republic of Congo: Statistical Appendix* (June 2007).

BALANCE OF PAYMENTS
(US $ million)

	2003	2004	2005
Exports of goods f.o.b.	2,636.5	3,433.2	4,729.8
Imports of goods f.o.b.	−831.1	−969.0	−1,356.1
Trade balance	1,805.4	2,464.2	3,373.7
Exports of services	194.1	196.7	234.7
Imports of services	−875.4	−1,016.3	−1,560.5
Balance on goods and services	1,124.1	1,644.6	2,047.9
Other income received	10.3	13.3	15.4
Other income paid	−596.4	−961.8	−1,137.7
Balance on goods, services and income	538.0	696.0	925.6
Current transfers received	26.5	34.5	31.5
Current transfers paid	−44.0	−56.0	−53.8
Current balance	520.5	674.4	903.2
Capital account (net)	16.9	12.7	5.7
Direct investment abroad	−1.7	−4.5	n.a.
Direct investment from abroad	323.1	−8.5	724.0
Portfolio investment liabilities	−0.2	2.1	−13.1
Other investment assets	−180.3	−440.7	n.a.
Other investment liabilities	−842.4	−323.3	−1,534.1
Net errors and omissions	−116.0	−92.8	325.8
Overall balance	−280.1	−180.7	411.5

Source: IMF, *International Financial Statistics*.

External Trade

PRINCIPAL COMMODITIES
(distribution by SITC, US $ million)

Imports c.i.f.	2003
Food and live animals	144.3
Meat and meat preparations	39.0
Fish, crustaceans, molluscs and preparations thereof	29.3
Cereals and cereal preparations	36.2
Chemicals and related products	97.2
Medicinal and pharmaceutical products	39.0
Basic manufactures	134.2
Non-metallic mineral manufactures	22.7
Iron and steel	47.6
Machinery and transport equipment	196.7
Road vehicles and parts*	41.5
Miscellaneous manufactured articles	62.7
Total (incl. others)	681.5

Exports f.o.b.	2001	2002	2003
Crude materials (inedible) except fuels	111.9	140.7	216.3
Cork and wood	111.9	140.7	216.3
Wood in the rough or roughly squared	71.7	108.8	167.6
Wood, simply worked and railway sleepers of wood	40.2	31.9	48.7
Mineral fuels, lubricants, etc.	1,177.4	2,252.6	1,465.2
Petroleum, petroleum products, etc.	1,177.4	2,148.8	1,418.3
Crude petroleum oils, etc.	1,129.9	2,102.6	1,418.3
Refined petroleum oils, etc	47.5	46.2	n.a.
Total (incl. others)	1,313.1	2,423.2	1,722.0

* Data on parts exclude tyres, engines and electrical parts.

Source: UN, *International Trade Statistics Yearbook*.

THE REPUBLIC OF THE CONGO

PRINCIPAL TRADING PARTNERS
(US $ million)

Imports c.i.f.	2000	2001	2002
Belgium	23.5	24.3	31.8
Cameroon	19.7	22.2	23.0
China, People's Rep.	4.1	6.8	26.0
Côte d'Ivoire	7.1	6.9	7.0
France (incl. Monaco)	139.4	127.2	166.4
Gabon	8.1	9.0	2.9
Germany	11.4	16.3	23.3
India	6.1	6.0	11.9
Indonesia	4.2	6.2	5.6
Italy	41.2	79.7	53.2
Japan	21.0	27.6	21.4
Lebanon	0.2	0.6	38.1
Netherlands	29.3	29.2	29.0
Saudi Arabia	3.0	3.6	9.1
Senegal	5.7	5.1	5.7
South Africa	10.8	14.7	11.8
Thailand	7.2	7.2	7.5
United Kingdom	19.7	21.5	24.1
USA	66.6	59.2	66.4
Total (incl. others)	517.6	564.2	643.5

Exports f.o.b.	2001	2002	2003
Brazil	21.7	16.5	56.5
Cameroon	1.1	26.7	10.2
Chile	10.9	33.6	—
China, People's Rep.	78.0	168.8	375.8
France (incl. Monaco)	25.1	175.5	68.4
Germany	4.4	142.7	8.8
Iceland	1.5	63.0	47.5
India	20.6	18.8	—
Indonesia	—	21.3	24.9
Israel	0.8	36.7	2.9
Italy	38.0	39.3	21.9
Japan	1.7	97.1	0.4
Korea, Democratic People's Rep.	207.0	271.5	131.0
Korea, Rep.	20.6	174.7	239.1
Netherlands	21.2	35.3	8.6
Portugal	17.7	24.9	38.9
Singapore	0.3	44.3	0.1
Spain	15.8	18.2	26.7
USA	273.3	252.4	165.3
Total (incl others)	1,313.1	2,423.2	1,722.0

Source: UN, *International Trade Statistics Yearbook*.

Transport

RAILWAYS
(traffic)

	1999	2000	2001
Passengers carried ('000)	56.5	546.0	742.0
Freight carried ('000 metric tons)	65.7	236.0	548.0

Passenger-km (million): 9 in 1999.

Freight ton-km (million): 21 in 1999.

Sources: UN, *Statistical Yearbook*; IMF, *Republic of Congo: Selected Issues and Statistical Appendix* (July 2004).

ROAD TRAFFIC
(estimates, '000 motor vehicles in use)

	1999	2000	2001
Passenger cars	26.2	29.7	29.7
Commercial vehicles	20.4	23.1	23.1

Source: UN, *Statistical Yearbook*.

SHIPPING
Merchant Fleet
(registered at 31 December)

	2004	2005	2006
Number of vessels	18	19	19
Total displacement ('000 grt)	3.4	3.6	3.6

Source: Lloyd's Register-Fairplay, *World Fleet Statistics*.

Freight Traffic at Pointe-Noire
(metric tons)

	1996	1997	1998
Goods loaded	670,150	708,203	n.a.
Goods unloaded	584,376	533,170	724,000*

*Rounded figure.

Source: mainly Banque des états de l'Afrique centrale, *Etudes et Statistiques*.

CIVIL AVIATION
(traffic on scheduled services)*

	2001	2002	2003
Kilometres flown (million)	3	1	1
Passengers carried ('000)	95	47	52
Passenger-km (million)	157	27	31
Total ton-km (million)	22	3	3

*Including an apportionment of the traffic of Air Afrique.

Source: UN, *Statistical Yearbook*.

Tourism

FOREIGN VISITORS BY COUNTRY OF RESIDENCE*

	2000	2001	2002
Angola	1,747	1,767	2,169
Belgium	230	443	477
Cameroon	591	832	950
Central African Republic	238	208	172
Congo, Democratic Rep.	2,172	2,481	2,402
Côte d'Ivoire	401	1,380	633
France	4,831	8,576	6,196
Gabon	906	1,192	907
Germany	230	119	103
Italy	869	841	382
Senegal	354	379	253
Togo	270	86	58
United Kingdom	640	584	505
USA	518	408	414
Total (incl. others)	18,797	27,363	21,611

*Arrivals at hotels and similar establishments.

Receipts from tourism (US $ million, incl. passenger transport): 25.6 in 2002; 30.0 in 2003; 23.1 in 2004.

Source: World Tourism Organization.

Communications Media

	2003	2004	2005
Telephones ('000 main lines in use)	7.0	13.8	15.9
Mobile cellular telephones ('000 subscribers)	330.0	383.7	490.0
Personal computers ('000 in use)	15	17	n.a.
Internet users ('000)	15	36	50

Source: International Telecommunication Union.

Radio receivers ('000 in use): 341 in 1997 (Source: UNESCO Institute for Statistics).

Television receivers ('000 in use): 33 in 1997 (Source: UNESCO Institute for Statistics).

Daily newspapers (national estimates): 6 in 1997 (average circulation 20,500 copies) (Source: UNESCO, *Statistical Yearbook*).

Non-daily newspapers (national estimates): 15 in 1995 (average circulation 38,000 copies) (Source: UNESCO, *Statistical Yearbook*).

Education

(2004/05, except where otherwise indicated)

	Institutions*	Teachers	Males	Females	Total
Pre-primary	95	1,070	11,515	11,805	23,320
Primary	1,168	7,214	311,078	286,226	597,304
Secondary†	n.a.	6,866	128,149	107,145	235,294
Tertiary‡	n.a.	894	10,487	1,969	12,456

* 1998/99.
† 2003/04.
‡ 2002/03.

Sources: mostly UNESCO Institute for Statistics.

Adult literacy rate (UNESCO estimates): 84.7% (males 90.5%; females 79.0%) in 2004 (Source: UNESCO Institute for Statistics).

Directory

The Constitution

The 1992 Constitution was suspended following the assumption of power by Gen. Denis Sassou-Nguesso on 15 October 1997. A new Constitution, which was approved by the Conseil national de transition (interim legislative body) on 2 September 2001 and endorsed by a public referendum on 20 January 2002, took effect following presidential and legislative elections in March–July 2002. Its main provisions are summarized below:

PREAMBLE

The Congolese people, having chosen a pluralist democracy as the basis for the development of the country, condemn the tyrannical use of power and political violence and declare that the fundamental principles proclaimed and guaranteed by the UN Charter, the Universal Declaration of Human Rights and other international treaties form an integral part of the present Constitution.

I. THE STATE AND SOVEREIGNTY

Articles 1–6: The Republic of the Congo is a sovereign, secular, social and democratic State. The principle of the Republic is government of the people, by the people and for the people. National sovereignty belongs to the people, who exercise it through universal suffrage by their elected representatives or by referendum. The official language of the Republic is French. The national languages of communication are Lingala and Kituba.

II. FUNDAMENTAL RIGHTS AND LIBERTIES

Articles 7–42: All citizens are equal before the law. Arbitrary arrest and all degrading forms of punishment are prohibited, and all accused are presumed innocent until proven guilty. Incitement to ethnic hatred, violence or civil war and the use of religion to political ends are forbidden. Equal access to education, which is compulsory until the age of 16, is guaranteed to all. The State is obliged to create conditions that enable all citizens to enjoy the right to work. All citizens, excluding members of the police and military forces, may participate in trade union activity. Slavery is forbidden, and forced labour permitted only as a judicial punishment.

III. DUTIES

Articles 43–50: All citizens have duties towards their family, society, the State and other legally recognized authorities. All citizens are obliged to conform to the Constitution, the laws of the Republic and to fulfil their obligations towards the State and society.

IV. POLITICAL PARTIES

Articles 51–55: Political parties may not be identified with an ethnic group, a region, a religion or a sect. They must protect and promote fundamental human rights, the rule of law, democracy, individual and collective freedoms, national territorial integrity and sovereignty, proscribe intolerance, ethnically based extremism, and any recourse to violence, and respect the secular form of the State.

V. EXECUTIVE POWER

Articles 56–88: The President of the Republic is the Head of State, Head of the Executive and Head of Government. The President is directly elected by an absolute majority of votes cast, for a term of seven years, renewable once. Presidential candidates must be of Congolese nationality and origin, aged between 40 and 70 years and have resided on national territory for at least 24 successive months prior to registering as a candidate. If required, a second round of voting takes place between the two highest-placed candidates in the first ballot. In the event of the death, resignation, or long-term incapacity of the President of the Republic, the President of the Sénat assumes limited executive functions for up to 90 days, pending an election, which he may not contest.

The President appoints ministers, senior civil servants, military staff and ambassadors. Ministers may not hold a parliamentary mandate or civic, public or military post, and their professional activity is restricted. The President of the Republic is the Supreme Head of the armed forces and the President of the Higher Council of Magistrates, and possesses the right of pardon. The President of the Republic chairs the Council of Ministers.

VI. LEGISLATIVE POWER

Articles 89–113: The Parliament is bicameral. Deputies are directly elected to the Assemblée nationale for a renewable term of five years. Senators are elected indirectly to the Sénat by local councils for a term of six years. One-half of the Sénat is elected every three years. Deputies and senators must be Congolese nationals, aged over 25 years in the case of deputies, or over 45 years in the case of senators, residing in national territory. A deputy or senator elected as a member of a political grouping may not resign from the grouping without simultaneously resigning his parliamentary position.

VII. RELATIONS BETWEEN THE LEGISLATIVE AND EXECUTIVE INSTITUTIONS

Articles 114–132: The President of the Republic may not dissolve the Assemblée nationale. The Assemblée nationale may not remove the President of the Republic. The legislative chambers consider proposed legislation in succession, with a view to adopting an identical text. If necessary, the President of the Republic may convene a joint commission to present a revised text to the two chambers. The President of the Republic may then call the Assemblée nationale to make a final decision. Special conditions apply to the passage of certain laws, including the national budget, and to a declaration of war or state of emergency.

VIII. JUDICIAL POWER

Articles 133–143: Judicial power is exercised by the Supreme Court, the Revenue and Budgetary Discipline Court, appeal courts and other national courts of law, which are independent of the legislature. The President of the Republic chairs a Higher Council of Magistrates, which guarantees the independence of the judiciary. The President of the Republic nominates judges to the Supreme Court and to the other courts of law, at the suggestion of the Higher Council of Magistrates. Judges of the Supreme Court may not be removed from office.

IX. CONSTITUTIONAL COURT

Articles 144–151: The Constitutional Court consists of nine members, each with a renewable mandate of nine years. One-third of the Court is renewed every three years. The President of the Republic nominates three members of the Constitutional Court independently, and the others at the suggestion of the President of each legislative chamber and of the Bureau of the Supreme Court. The President of the Republic nominates the President of the Constitutional Court. The Court ensures that laws, treaties and international agreements conform to the Constitution and oversees presidential elections.

X. HIGH COURT OF JUSTICE

Articles 152–156: The High Court of Justice is composed of an equal number of deputies and senators elected by their peers, and of members of the Supreme Court elected by their peers. It is chaired by the First President of the Supreme Court and is competent to try the President of the Republic in case of high treason. Members of the legislature, the Supreme Court and the Constitutional Court and government ministers are accountable to the High Court of Justice for crimes or offences committed in the execution of their duties, subject to a two-thirds' majority in a secret vote at a joint session of Parliament.

XI. ECONOMIC AND SOCIAL COUNCIL

Articles 157–160: The Economic and Social Council is a consultative assembly, which may become involved in any economic or social problem concerning the Republic, either of its own will or at the request of the President of the Republic or the President of either legislative chamber.

XII. HIGHER COUNCIL FOR THE FREEDOM OF COMMUNICATION

Articles 161–162: The Higher Council for the Freedom of Communication ensures freedom of information and communication, formulating recommendations on applicable issues.

XIII. MEDIATOR OF THE REPUBLIC

Articles 163–166: The Mediator of the Republic is an independent authority responsible for simplifying and humanizing relations between government and citizens, and may be addressed by any person dissatisfied with the workings of any public organization.

XIV. NATIONAL COMMISSION FOR HUMAN RIGHTS

Articles 167–169: The National Commission for Human Rights seeks to promote and protect human rights.

XV. POLICE AND MILITARY FORCES

Articles 170–173: The police and military bodies consist of the national police force, the national gendarmerie and the Congolese armed forces. These bodies are apolitical and subordinate to the civil authority. The creation of militia groups is prohibited.

XVI. LOCAL AUTHORITIES

Articles 174–177: The local administrative bodies of the Republic of the Congo are the department and the commune, and any others created by law.

XVII. INTERNATIONAL TREATIES AND AGREEMENTS

Articles 178–184: The President of the Republic negotiates, signs and, with the approval of Parliament, ratifies international treaties and agreements. Any proposed change to the territorial boundaries of the Republic must be submitted to popular referendum.

XVIII. ON REVISION

Articles 185–187: The Constitution may be revised at the initiative of the President of the Republic or members of Parliament. The territorial integrity of the Republic, the republican form of government, the secular nature of the State, the number of presidential terms of office permitted and the rights outlined in sections I and II (above) may not be the subject of any revision. Any constitutional amendments proposed by the President of the Republic are submitted directly to a referendum. Any constitutional changes proposed by Parliament must be approved by two-thirds of the members of both legislative chambers convened in congress, before being submitted to referendum. In both cases the Constitutional Court must have declared the acceptability of the proposals.

The Government

HEAD OF STATE

President: Gen. DENIS SASSOU-NGUESSO (assumed power 15 October 1997; inaugurated 25 October 1997; elected 10 March 2002).

COUNCIL OF MINISTERS
(March 2008)

Prime Minister, responsible for the Co-ordination of Government Action and Privatization: ISIDORE MVOUBA.

Minister at the Presidency, responsible for National Defence, Veterans and the War Disabled: Gen. JACQUES YVON NDOLOU.

Minister at the Presidency, responsible for Co-operation, Humanitarian Action and Solidarity: CHARLES ZACHARIE BOWAO.

Minister at the Presidency, responsible for Regional Integration and NEPAD: JUSTIN BALLAY MEGOT.

Minister of State, Keeper of the Seals, Minister of Justice and Human Rights: AIMÉ EMMANUEL YOKA.

Minister of State, Minister of Planning and Land Management: PIERRE MOUSSA.

Minister of State, Minister of the Civil Service and the Reform of the State: JEAN-MARTIN MBEMBA.

Minister of State, Minister of Hydrocarbons: JEAN-BAPTISTE TATI LOUTARD.

Minister of the Economy, Finance and the Budget: PACIFIQUE ISSOÏBEKA.

Minister of Mining, Extractive Industry and Geology: Gen. PIERRE OBA.

Minister of Equipment and Public Works: Gen. FLORENT NTSIBA.

Minister of Foreign Affairs and the Francophonie: BASILE IKOUÉBÉ.

Minister of Agriculture and Stockbreeding: RIGOBERT MABOUNDOU.

Minister of the Forest Economy: HENRI DJOMBO.

Minister of Construction, Town Planning and Living Conditions: CLAUDE ALPHONSE NSILOU.

Minister of Territorial Administration and Decentralization: RAYMOND MBOULOU.

Minister of Transport and Civil Aviation: EMILE OUSSO.

Minister of Land Reform and the Preservation of the Public Domain: LAMYR NGUELÉ.

Minister of Technical Education and Vocational Training: PIERRE MICHEL NGUIMBI.

Minister of Higher Education: HENRI OSSEBI.

Minister of Industrial Development and the Promotion of the Private Sector: EMILE MABONZOT.

Minister of Trade, Consumption and Supplies: JEANNE DAMBENDZET.

Minister of Posts and Telecommunications, responsible for New Technologies: THIERRY MOUNGALA.

Minister of Primary and Secondary Education, responsible for Literacy: ROSALIE KAMA-NIAMAYOUA.

Minister of Culture and the Arts: JEAN-CLAUDE GAKOSSO.

Minister of Labour, Employment and Social Security: GILBERT ONDONGO.

Minister of Energy and Water Resources: BRUNO JEAN-RICHARDS ITOUA.

Minister of Communication, responsible for Relations with Parliament, Government Spokesperson: ALAIN AKOUALA-ATIPAULT.

Minister of Security and Public Order: Gen. PAUL MBOT.

Minister of Scientific Research and Technical Innovation: HELLOT MAMPOUYA MATSON.

Minister of Sports and Youth: SERGE MICHEL ODZOCKI.

Minister of Health, Social Affairs and Families: EMILIENNE RAOUL.

Minister of Maritime Transport and the Merchant Navy: MARTIN PARFAIT AIMÉ COUSSOU-MAVOUNGOU.

Minister of Fisheries, responsible for Aquaculture: GUY BRICE PARFAIT KOLÉLAS.

Minister of the Promotion of Women and the Integration of Women into Development: JEANNE FRANÇOISE LÉKOMBA LOUMÉTO-POMBO.

Minister of Small and Medium-sized Enterprises and Crafts: ADÉLAÏDE MOUNDÉLÉ-NGOLLO.

THE REPUBLIC OF THE CONGO

Minister of Tourism and the Environment: André Okombi Salissa.

Minister-delegate to the Minister of State, Minister of Planning and Land Management: Gaston Gapo.

MINISTRIES

Office of the President: Palais du Peuple, Brazzaville; tel. 81-17-11; internet www.presidence.cg.

Office of the Prime Minister: Brazzaville; tel. 81-10-67; internet www.congo-site.net.

Office of the Minister at the Presidency, responsible for Co-operation, Humanitarian Action and Solidarity: Brazzaville; tel. 81-10-89.

Office of the Minister at the Presidency, responsible for National Defence, Veterans and the War Disabled: Brazzaville; tel. 81-22-31.

Office of the Minister at the Presidency, responsible for Regional Integration and NEPAD: Brazzaville.

Ministry of Agriculture and Stockbreeding: BP 2453, Brazzaville; tel. 81-41-31; fax 81-19-29.

Ministry of Equipment and Public Works: BP 2099, Brazzaville; tel. 81-59-41; fax 81-59-07.

Ministry of the Civil Service and the Reform of the State: BP 12151, Brazzaville; tel. 81-41-68; fax 81-41-49.

Ministry of Communication, responsible for Relations with Parliament: BP 114, Brazzaville; tel. 81-41-29; fax 81-41-28; e-mail depcompt@congonet.cg.

Ministry of Construction, Town Planning and Living Conditions: BP 1580, Brazzaville; tel. 81-34-48; fax 81-12-97.

Ministry of Culture and the Arts: BP 20480, Brazzaville; tel. 81-02-35; fax 81-40-25.

Ministry of the Economy, Finance and the Budget: ave de l'Indépendance, croisement ave Foch, BP 2083, Brazzaville; tel. 81-45-24; fax 81-43-69; internet www.mefb-cg.org.

Ministry of Energy and Water Resources: Brazzaville.

Ministry of Fisheries: Brazzaville.

Ministry of Foreign Affairs and the Francophonie: BP 2070, Brazzaville; tel. 81-10-89; fax 81-41-61.

Ministry of the Forest Economy: Immeuble de l'Agriculture, Face à Blanche Gomez, BP 98, Brazzaville; tel. 81-41-37; fax 81-41-34; e-mail ajdbosseko@minifor.com; internet www.minifor.com.

Ministry of Health, Social Affairs and Families: BP 20101, Brazzaville; tel. 81-30-75; fax 81-14-33.

Ministry of Higher Education: Ancien Immeuble de la Radio, BP 169, Brazzaville; tel. 81-08-15; fax 81-52-65.

Ministry of Hydrocarbons: BP 2120, Brazzaville; tel. 81-10-86; fax 81-10-85.

Ministry of Industrial Development and the Promotion of the Private Sector: Centre Administratif, Quartier Plateau, BP 2117, Brazzaville; tel. 81-30-09; fax 81-06-43.

Ministry of Justice and Human Rights: BP 2497, Brazzaville; tel. and fax 81-41-49.

Ministry of Labour, Employment and Social Security: Immeuble de la BCC, ave Foch, BP 2075, Brazzaville; tel. 81-41-43; fax 81-05-50.

Ministry of Land Reform and the Preservation of the Public Domain: Brazzaville; tel. 81-34-48.

Ministry of Maritime Transport and the Merchant Navy: Brazzaville; tel. 81-10-67; fax 82-55-14.

Ministry of Mining, Extractive Industry and Geology: BP 2124, Brazzaville; tel. 81-02-64; fax 81-50-77.

Ministry of Planning and Land Management: BP 64, Brazzaville; tel. 81-06-56; fax 81-58-08.

Ministry of Posts and Telecommunications: BP 44, Brazzaville; tel. 81-41-18; fax 81-19-34.

Ministry of Primary and Secondary Education: BP 5253, Brazzaville; tel. 81-24-52; fax 81-25-39.

Ministry of the Promotion of Women and the Integration of Women into Development: Brazzaville; tel. 81-19-29.

Ministry of Scientific Research and Technical Innovation: Ancien Immeuble de la Radio, Brazzaville; tel. 81-03-59.

Ministry of Security and Public Order: BP 2474, Brazzaville; tel. 81-41-73; fax 81-34-04.

Ministry of Small and Medium-sized Enterprises and Crafts: Brazzaville.

Ministry of Sports and Youth: BP 2061, Brazzaville; tel. 60-89-24.

Ministry of Technical Education and Vocational Training: BP 2076, Brazzaville; tel. 81-17-27; fax 81-56-82; e-mail metp_cab@yahoo.fr.

Ministry of Territorial Administration and Decentralization: BP 880, Brazzaville; tel. 81-40-60; fax 81-33-17.

Ministry of Tourism and Environment: Brazzaville.

Ministry of Trade, Consumption and Supplies: BP 2965, Brazzaville; tel. 81-41-16; fax 81-41-57; e-mail mougany@yahoo.fr.

Ministry of Transport and Civil Aviation: Immeuble Mafoua Virgile, BP 2066, Brazzaville; tel. 81-53-39; fax 81-57-56.

President and Legislature

PRESIDENT

Presidential Election, 10 March 2002

Candidate	Votes	% of votes
Denis Sassou-Nguesso	1,075,247	89.41
Joseph Kignoumbi Kia Mbougou	33,154	2.76
Angèle Bandou	27,849	2.32
Jean-Félix Demba Ntello	20,252	1.68
Luc Adamo Matéta	19,074	1.59
Côme Mankassa	15,054	1.25
Bonaventure Mizidi Bavouenza	11,981	1.00
Total	**1,202,611**	**100.00**

LEGISLATURE

The legislature, Parlement, comprises two chambers: a directly elected lower house, the Assemblée nationale; and an indirectly elected upper house, the Sénat.

Assemblée nationale

Palais du Parlement, BP 2106, Brazzaville; tel. 81-11-12; fax 81-41-28; e-mail dsancongo@yahoo.fr.

President: Justin Koumba.

General Election, 24 June and 5 August 2007

Party	Seats
Parti congolais du travail (PCT)	46
Mouvement congolais pour la démocratie et le développement intégral (MCDDI)	11
Union panafricaine pour la démocratie sociale (UPADS)	11
Mouvement d'action pour le renouveau (MAR)	5
Mouvement pour la solidarité et la démocratie (MSD)	5
Club 2002-Parti pour l'unité et la République (PUR)	3
Action pour le Congo (APC)	3
Forces démocratiques nouvelles (FDN)	2
Rassemblement pour la démocratie et le progrès social (RDPS)	2
Union pour la République (UR)	2
Union patriotique pour la démocratie et le progrès (UPDP)	2
Union pour le progrès (UP)	2
Jeunesse en mouvement (JEM)	1
Mouvement pour la démocratie et le progrès (MDP)	1
Parti la vie	1
Rassemblement citoyen (RC)	1
Union des forces démocratiques (UFD)	1
Union pour la démocratie et la République—Mwinda (UDR—Mwinda)	1
Independents	37
Total	**137**

Sénat

Palais du Parlement, Brazzaville; tel. and fax 81-18-34.

President: André Obami Itou.

The upper chamber comprises 66 members, elected by representatives of local, regional and municipal authorities for a six-year term. After the most recent elections to the Sénat, held on 2 October 2005, the strength of the parties was as follows:

Party	Seats
Parti congolais du travail (PCT)	39
Forces démocratiques unies (FDU) *	12
Parti pour la reconstruction du Congo	1
Civil society organizations	1
Independent	6
Vacant†	7
Total	**66**

* An alliance of 29 parties.
† Six seats remained vacant, as unrest had led to the postponement, in June 2002, of local elections in the Pool region and continued insecurity there. Additionally, one seat remained vacant, following irregularities in voting in the elections held in October 2005, pending a new election to that seat.

Election Commission

Commission nationale d'organisation des élections (CONEL): Brazzaville; f. 2001; reorganized in 2007; mems appointed by President of the Republic, Commission is responsible to the Ministry of the Interior, Security and Territorial Administration; Pres. HENRI BOUKA.

Advisory Council

Economic and Social Council: Brazzaville; f. 2003; 75 mems, appointed by the President of the Republic; Pres. AUGUSTE-CÉLESTIN GONGARAD NKOUA.

Political Organizations

In early 2004 there were more than 100 political parties and organizations in the Republic of the Congo. The following were among the most important of those believed to be active in early 2008.

Action pour le Congo (APC): Brazzaville.

Alliance pour la Démocratie et le Développement National (ADDN): Brazzaville; f. 2005; supports Govt of Pres. Sassou-Nguesso; Pres. BRUNO MAZONGA.

Club 2002: Brazzaville; f. 2002; Pres. WILFRID NGUESSO.

Conseil national de la résistance (CBR): formed as political wing of 'Ninja' rebel group; Leader Rev. FRÉDÉRIC BITSANGOU (NTUMI).

Coordination de l'opposition pour une alternance démocratique (CODE-A): Brazzaville; f. 2005; opposition alliance; Leader HERVE AMBROISE MALONGA.

Forces démocratiques nouvelles (FDN): Brazzaville.

Jeunesse en mouvement (JEM): Brazzaville; f. 2002.

Mouvement d'action pour le renouveau (MAR): BP 1287, Pointe-Noire; Leader JEAN BAPTISTE TATI LOUTARD.

Mouvement congolais pour la démocratie et le développement intégral (MCDDI): 744 route de Djoué, Brazzaville; e-mail info@mcddi.net; internet www.mcddi.org; f. 1990; Leader BERNARD KOLÉLAS.

Mouvement pour la démocratie et le progrès (MDP): Brazzaville; f. 2007; Leader JEAN-CLAUDE IBOVI.

Mouvement pour la solidarité et la démocratie (MSD): Brazzaville; Leader RENÉ SERGE BLANCHARD OBA.

Parti congolais du travail (PCT): BP 80, Brazzaville; f. 1969; sole legal political party 1969–90; Pres. DENNIS SASSOU-NGUESSO; Sec.-Gen. AMBROISE-EDOUARD NOUMAZALAY.

Parti pour l'unité et la République (PUR): Brazzaville.

Parti de la sauvegarde des valeurs républicaines (PSVR): Brazzaville; f. 2006 by fmr mems of MCDDI (q.v.); Pres. MICHEL MAMPOUYA.

Parti la vie: Brazzaville.

Rassemblement citoyen (RC): route du Djoué, face Centre Sportif de Bacongo, Brazzaville; Pres. CLAUDE ALPHONSE NSILOU.

Rassemblement pour la démocratie et le progrès social (RDPS): Pointe-Noire; f. 1990; Pres. JEAN-PIERRE THYSTÈRE TCHIKAYA.

Union pour la démocratie et la République—Mwinda (UDR—Mwinda): Brazzaville; e-mail journalmwinda@presse-ecrite.com; internet www.mwinda.org; f. 1992; Leader (vacant).

Union des forces démocratiques (UFD): Brazzaville; supports Govt; Pres. DAVID CHARLES GANOU.

Union panafricaine pour la démocratie sociale (UPADS): BP 1370, Brazzaville; e-mail courrier@upads.org; internet www.upads.org; Pres. PASCAL LISSOUBA; Sec.-Gen. PASCAL TSATY MABIALA.

Union patriotique pour la démocratie et le progrès (UPDP): 112 rue Lamothe, Brazzaville; Pres. GONGARA KOUA.

Union pour le progrès (UP): 965 rue Sounda, pl. des 15 ans, Brazzaville; Pres. JEAN-MARTIN MBEMBA; Sec.-Gen. OMER DEFOUNDOUX.

Union pour la République (UR): 5 Impasse de Brazza, Brazzaville; Pres. BENJAMIN BOUNKOULOU.

Diplomatic Representation

EMBASSIES IN THE REPUBLIC OF THE CONGO

Algeria: rue Col Brisset, BP 2100, Brazzaville; tel. 81-17-37; fax 81-54-77; Ambassador ABDELAH LAOUARI.

Angola: BP 388, Brazzaville; tel. 81-47-21; fax 81-52-87; e-mail miranotom@yahoo.fr; Ambassador Dr PEDRO FERNANDO MAVUNZA.

Belgium: ave Patrice Lumumba, BP 225, Brazzaville; tel. 81-37-12; fax 81-37-04; e-mail brazzaville@diplobel.org; internet www.diplomatie.be/brazzaville; Ambassador MICHEL TILEMANS.

Cameroon: BP 2136, Brazzaville; tel. 81-10-08; fax 81-56-75; Chargé d'affaires a.i. GUILLAUME NSEKE.

Central African Republic: BP 10, Brazzaville; tel. 83-40-14.

China, People's Republic: blvd du Marechal Lyauté, BP 213, Brazzaville; tel. 81-11-32; fax 81-11-35; e-mail chinaemb_cg@mfa.gov.cn; Ambassador LI SHULI.

Congo, Democratic Republic: Brazzaville; tel. 83-29-38; Ambassador FÉLIX MUMENGUI OTTHUW.

Cuba: 28 rue Lacien Fourneaux, BP 80, Brazzaville; tel. 81-03-79; e-mail embacuba@congonet.cg; Ambassador SIDENIO ACOSTA ADAY.

Egypt: 7 bis ave Bayardelle, BP 917, Brazzaville; tel. 81-07-94; fax 81-15-33; Ambassador MEDHAT KAMAL ABD EL-RAOF EL-KADI.

France: rue Alfassa, BP 2089, Brazzaville; tel. 81-55-41; e-mail webmestre@mail.com; internet www.ambafrance-cg.org; Ambassador NICHOLAS NORMAND.

Guinea: Brazzaville; tel. 81-24-66.

Holy See: rue Col Brisset, BP 1168, Brazzaville; tel. 81-55-80; fax 81-55-81; e-mail nonapcg@yahoo.com; Apostolic Nuncio Most Rev. ANDRES CARRASCOSA COSO (Titular Archbishop of Elo).

Italy: 2 blvd Lytautey, BP 2484, Brazzaville; tel. 81-58-41; fax 81-11-52; e-mail ambasciata.brazzaville@esteri.it; internet www.ambbrazzaville.esteri.it/Ambasciata_Brazzaville; Ambassador ANGELO TRAVAGLINI.

Korea, Democratic People's Republic: Brazzaville; tel. 83-41-98; Ambassador RI WON SON.

Libya: BP 920, Brazzaville.

Nigeria: 11 blvd Lyauté, BP 790, Brazzaville; tel. 83-13-16; Ambassador GREG MBADIWE.

Russia: ave Félix Eboué, BP 2132, Brazzaville; tel. 81-19-23; fax 81-50-85; e-mail amrussie@ic.cd; internet www.congo.mid.ru; Ambassador MIKHAIL S. TSVIGUN.

Judicial System

The 2002 Constitution provides for the independence of the judiciary from the legislature. Judges are to be accountable to the Higher Council of Magistrates, under the chairmanship of the President of the Republic. The constituent bodies of the judiciary are the Supreme Court, the Revenue and Budgetary Discipline Court and the appeal courts. The High Court of Justice is chaired by the First President of the Supreme Court and is competent to try the President of the Republic in case of high treason, and to try members of the legislature, the Supreme Court, the Constitutional Court and government ministers for crimes or offences committed in the execution of their duties.

Supreme Court: BP 597, Brazzaville; tel. 83-01-32; First Pres. PLACIDE LENGA.

High Court of Justice: Brazzaville; f. 2003; Pres. PLACIDE LENGA (First Pres. of the Supreme Court); Chief Prosecutor GEORGES AKIERA.

Constitutional Court: Brazzaville; Pres. GÉRARD BITSINDOU; Vice-Pres. AUGUSTE ILOKI; Mems SIMON-PIERRE NGOUONIMBA NCZARY, THOMAS DHELLO, MARC MASSAMBA-NDILOU, JACQUES BOMBÈTE,

THE REPUBLIC OF THE CONGO

Jean-Pierre Berri, Delphine-Emmanuelle Adouki, Jean-Bernard Anaël Samory.

Religion

Almost one-half of the population follow traditional animist beliefs. Most of the remainder are Christians (of whom a majority are Roman Catholics).

CHRISTIANITY

The Roman Catholic Church

The Congo comprises one archdiocese, five dioceses and an apostolic prefecture. At 31 December 2005 there were an estimated 2.3m. Roman Catholics in the Republic of the Congo, accounting for some 54.1% of the population.

Bishops' Conference

Conférence Episcopale du Congo, BP 200, Brazzaville; tel. 63-83-91; fax 81-18-28; e-mail confepiscongo@yahoo.fr.
f. 1992; Pres. Most Rev. Louis Portella Mbuyu (Bishop of Kinkala).

Archbishop of Brazzaville: Most Rev. Anatole Milandou, Archevêché, BP 2301, Brazzaville; tel. 538-20-84; fax 81-26-15; e-mail archibrazza@yahoo.fr.

Protestant Church

Eglise Evangélique du Congo: BP 3205, Bacongo-Brazzaville; tel. and fax 81-04-54; f. 1909; Presbyterian; autonomous since 1961; 145,000 mems (2005); 105 parishes (1998); Pres. (vacant).

ISLAM

In 1997 an estimated 2% of the population were Muslims.

Comité Islamique du Congo: 77 Makotipoko Moungali, BP 55, Brazzaville; tel. 82-87-45; f. 1988; Leaders Habibou Soumare, Bachir Gatsongo, Bouilla Guibidanesi.

BAHÁ'Í FAITH

Assemblée spirituelle nationale: BP 2094, Brazzaville; tel. 81-36-93; e-mail congolink1@aol.com.

The Press

In July 2000 legislation was adopted on the freedom of information and communication. The legislation, which confirmed the abolition of censorship and reduced the penalty for defamation from imprisonment to a fine, specified three types of punishable offence: the encouragement of social tension (including incitement to ethnic conflict), attacks on the authorities (including libels on the Head of State or on the judiciary), and libels against private individuals. The terms of the legislation were to be guaranteed by a regulatory body, the Higher Council for the Freedom of Communication.

DAILIES

ACI Actualité: BP 2144, Brazzaville; tel. and fax 81-01-98; publ. by Agence Congolaise d'Information; Dir-Gen. Théodore Kiamossi.

Aujourd'hui: Brazzaville; tel. and fax 83-77-44; f. 1991; Man. Dir and Editor-in-Chief Fylla di Fua di Sassa.

Mweti: BP 991, Brazzaville; tel. 81-10-87; national news; Dir Matongo Aveley; Editor-in-Chief Hubert Madouaba; circ. 7,000.

PERIODICALS

L'Arroseur: Immeuble Boulangerie ex-Léon, BP 15021, Brazzaville; tel. 58-65-51; fax 58-37-60; e-mail larroseur@yahoo.fr; f. 2000; weekly; satirical; Dir Gerry-Gérard Mangondo; Editor-in-Chief Jean-Marie Kanga.

L'Autre Vision: 48 rue Assiéné-Mikalou, BP 5255, Brazzaville; tel. 51-57-06; e-mail lautrevision@yahoo.fr; 2 a month; Dir Jean Paulin Itoua.

Capital: 3 ave Charles de Gaulle, Plateau Centre Ville, BP 541, Brazzaville; tel. 58-95-10; fax 51-37-48; e-mail capital@hotmail.com; 2 a month; economics and business; Dir Serge-Denis Matondo; Editor-in-Chief Hervé Sampa.

Le Choc: BP 1314, Brazzaville; tel. 666-42-96; fax 82-04-25; e-mail groupejustinfo@yahoo.fr; internet www.lechoc.info; weekly, news concerning several African states; Dir-Gen. and Publr Asie Dominique de Marseille; Dir of Publication Marien Ngapili.

Le Coq: Brazzaville; e-mail sosolecoq@yahoo.fr; f. 2000; weekly; Editor-in-Chief Malonga Bouka.

Le Défi Africain: Brazzaville; f. 2002; Dir of Publication Jean Romuald Mbepa.

Les Dépêches de Brazzaville: Résidence Méridien, BP 15457, Brazzaville; tel. and fax 81-28-13; e-mail redaction@brazzaville-adiac.com; internet www.brazzaville-adiac.com; 6 a year; publ. by Agence d'Information de l'Afrique Centrale; Dir-Gen. Jean-Paul Pigasse; Dir and Editor-in-Chief Belinda Ayessa.

Les Echos du Congo: Immeubles Fédéraux 036, Centre-ville, Brazzaville; tel. 51-57-09; e-mail wayiadrien@yahoo.fr; weekly; pro-govt; Dir-Gen. Adrien Wayi-Lewy; Editor-in-Chief Innocent Olivier Taty.

Epanza Makita: Brazzaville; f. 2004.

Le Flambeau: BP 1198, Brazzaville; tel. 66-35-23; e-mail congolink1@aol.com; weekly; independent; supports Govt of Pres. Sassou-Nguesso; Dir and Man. Editor Prince-Richard Nsana.

La Lettre de Brazzaville: Résidence Méridien, BP 15457, Brazzaville; tel. and fax 81-28-13; e-mail redaction@adiac.com; f. 2000; weekly; publ. by Agence d'Information de l'Afrique Centrale; Man. Dir Jean-Paul Pigasse; Editor-in-Chief Belinda Ayessa.

Le Nouveau Stade: BP 2159, Brazzaville; tel. 68-45-52; 2 a month; sports; Dir-Gen. Louis Ngami; Editor-in-Chief S. F. Kimina Makumbu.

La Nouvelle République: 3 ave des Ambassadeurs, BP 991, Brazzaville; tel. 81-00-20; state-owned; 2 a week; Dir-Gen. Gaspard Nwan; Editorial Dir Henri Boukoulou.

L'Observateur: 165 ave de l'Amitié, BP 13370, Brazzaville; tel. 66-33-37; fax 81-11-81; e-mail lobservateur_2001@yahoo.fr; f. 1999; weekly; independent; opposes Govt of Pres. Sassou-Nguesso; Dir Gislin Simplice Ongouya; circ. 2,000 (2004).

Le Pays: BP 782, Brazzaville; tel. 61-06-11; fax 82-44-50; e-mail heblepays@yahoo.fr; f. 1991; weekly; Editorial Dir Sylvère-Arsène Samba.

La Référence: BP 13778, Brazzaville; tel. 56-11-37; fax 62-80-13; 2 a month; supports Govt of Pres. Sassou-Nguesso; Dir Philippe Richet; Editor-in-Chief R. Assebako Amaidjore.

La Rue Meurt (Bala-Bala): BP 1258, Brazzaville; tel. 66-39-80; fax 81-02-30; e-mail laruemeurt@yahoo.fr; f. 1991; weekly; satirical; opposes Govt of Pres. Sassou-Nguesso; Publr Matthieu Gayele; Editorial Dir Jean-Claude Bongolo; circ. 2,000 (2004).

La Semaine Africaine: blvd Lyautey, face Chu, BP 2080, Brazzaville; tel. 678-76-94; e-mail contact@lasemaineafricaine.com; internet www.lasemaineafricaine.com; f. 1952; weekly; Roman Catholic; general news and social comment; circulates widely in francophone equatorial Africa; Editor-in-Chief Joachim Mbanza; circ. 7,500.

Le Stade: BP 114, Brazzaville; tel. 81-47-18; f. 1985; weekly; sports; Dir Hubert-Trésor Madouaba-Ntoualani; Editor-in-Chief Lelas Paul Nzolani; circ. 6,500.

Tam-Tam d'Afrique: 97 rue Moussana, Ouenzé, BP 1675, Brazzaville; tel. 51-03-95; e-mail gouala@yahoo.fr; weekly; economics, finance; circ. 1,500 (2004).

Le Temps: BP 2104, Brazzaville; e-mail kiala_matouba@yahoo.fr; weekly; owned by supporters of former Pres. Lissouba; Editor-in-Chief Henri Boukoulou.

Vision pour Demain: 109 rue Bakongo Poto-Poto, BP 650, Brazzaville; tel. 41-14-22; 6 a year; Dir Saint Eudes Mfumu Fylla.

NEWS AGENCIES

Agence Congolaise d'Information (ACI): ave E. P. Lumumba, BP 2144, Brazzaville; tel. and fax 81-01-98; e-mail agencecongoinfo@yahoo.fr; Gen. Man. Bernard Mantele.

Agence d'Information d'Afrique Centrale (ADIAC): Les Manguiers, 76 ave Paul Doumer, Brazzaville; tel. 532-01-09; fax 532-01-10; e-mail belie@congonet.cg; internet www.brazzaville-adiac.com; f. 1997; Dirs Jean-Paul Pigasse, Belinda Ayessa; br. in Paris (France).

Publishers

Editions ADIAC—Agence d'Information d'Afrique Centrale: Hôtel Méridien, BP 15457, Brazzaville; tel. and fax 81-28-13; e-mail redaction@brazzaville-adiac.com; internet www.brazzaville-adiac.com; f. 1997; publishes chronicles of current affairs; Dirs Jean-Paul Pigasse, Belinda Ayessa.

Editions 'Héros dans l'Ombre': BP 1678, Brazzaville; tel. 768-11-49; e-mail leopold_mamo@yahoo.fr; f. 1980; literature, criticism, poetry, essays, politics, drama, research; Chair. Léopold Pindy Mamonsono.

Editions Lemba: BP 2351, Brazzaville; tel. 67-65-58; fax 81-00-17; e-mail editions_lemba@yahoo.fr; literature; Dir Apollinaire Singou-Basseha.

THE REPUBLIC OF THE CONGO

Editions PAARI—Pan African Review of Innovation: BP 1622 Brazzaville; tel. 51-86-49; e-mail edpaari@yahoo.fr; f. 1991; social and human sciences, philosophy.

Editions Renaissance Congolaise: Brazzaville.

Imprimerie Centrale d'Afrique (ICA): BP 162, Pointe-Noire; f. 1949; Man. Dir M. SCHNEIDER.

Mokandart: BP 939, Brazzaville; tel. 68-46-69; e-mail mokandart@yahoo.fr; adult and children's literature; Pres. ANNICK VEYRINAUD MAKONDA.

GOVERNMENT PUBLISHING HOUSE

Imprimerie Nationale du Congo (INC): BP 58, Brazzaville; Dir JULES ONDZEKI.

Broadcasting and Communications

Higher Council for the Freedom of Communication: Brazzaville; f. 2003; 11 mems, nominated by the President of the Republic; Pres. JACQUES BANANGANZALA.

TELECOMMUNICATIONS

Celtel Congo: blvd Charles de Gaulle, angle allée Makimba, BP 1267, Pointe-Noire; tel. 520-00-00; fax 94-88-75; internet www.cg.celtel.com; f. 1999; mobile cellular telephone operator; network covers Brazzaville, Pointe-Noire, Loubomo (Dolisie), Ouesso, Owando and other urban areas; subsidiary of Celtel International (United Kingdom); Dir-Gen. ANTOINE PAMBORO; 30,000 subscribers (Dec. 2000).

Cyrus International (CYRTEL): Brazzaville; mobile cellular telephone operator; operates as jt venture between Nexus International (70%), a subsidiary of France Telecom and SOTELCO.

Libertis: 22 rue Behagle, BP 1150, Brazzaville; tel. 81-47-70; fax 81-44-16; f. 2000; mobile cellular telephone operator; network covers Brazzaville and Pointe-Noire; subsidiary of Orascom Telecom (Egypt).

Société des Télécommunications du Congo (SOTELCO): BP 39, Brazzaville; tel. 81-16-66; f. 2001 by division of postal and telecommunications services of the fmr Office National des Postes et Télécommunications; mobile cellular telephone system introduced in 1996; majority Govt-owned, part-owned by Atlantic TeleNetwork; further transfer to private ownership pending; Dir-Gen. RENÉ-SERGE BLANCHARD OBA (acting).

RADIO AND TELEVISION

Radio Brazzaville: face Direction Générale, SOTELCO, Brazzaville; tel. 51-60-73; f. 1999; official station; Man. JEAN-PASCAL MONGO SLYM.

Canal FM: BP 60, Brazzaville; tel. 83-03-09; f. 1977 as Radio Rurales du Congo; present name adopted 2002; community stations established by the Agence de coopération culturelle et technique; transmitters in Brazzaville, Sembé, Nkayi, Etoumbi and Mossendjo; Dir ETIENNE EPAGNA-TOUA.

Radio Liberté: BP 1660, Brazzaville; tel. 81-57-42; f. 1997; operated by supporters of Pres. Sassou-Nguesso.

Radiodiffusion-Télévision Congolaise (RTC): BP 2241, Brazzaville; tel. 81-24-73; state-owned; Pres. JEAN-GILBERT FOUTOU; Dir-Gen. GILBERT-DAVID MUTAKALA.

Radio Congo: BP 2241, Brazzaville; tel. 81-50-60; radio programmes in French, Lingala, Kikongo, Subia, English and Portuguese; transmitters at Brazzaville and Pointe-Noire; Gen. Man. ALPHONSE BOUYA DIMI; Dir of Broadcasting THÉOPHILE MIETE LIKIBI.

Télé Pointe Noire: BP 769, Pointe Noire; tel. 94-02-65; f. 1988.

TV Congo: Brazzaville; f. 1960; formerly Télé Congo; operated by Radiodiffusion Télévision Congolaise.

Finance

(cap. = capital; res = reserves; dep. = deposits; m. = million; br(s). = branch(es); amounts in francs CFA)

BANKING

Central Bank

Banque des Etats de l'Afrique Centrale (BEAC): BP 126, Brazzaville; tel. 81-10-73; fax 81-10-94; e-mail beacbzv@beac.int; internet www.beac.int; HQ in Yaoundé, Cameroon; f. 1973; bank of issue for mem. states of the Communauté économique et monétaire en Afrique centrale (CEMAC, fmrly Union douanière et économique de l'Afrique centrale) comprising Cameroon, the Central African Repub., Chad, the Repub. of the Congo, Equatorial Guinea and Gabon; cap. 45,000m., res 176,661m., total assets 2,144,626m. (Nov. 2003); Gov. JEAN-FÉLIX MAMALEPOT; Dir in Repub. of the Congo MATHIAS DZON; br. at Pointe-Noire.

Commercial Banks

BGFI Bank Congo: BP 14579, Angle rue Reims, face à paierie de France, Brazzaville; tel. 81-40-50; fax 81-50-89; e-mail agence_brazzaville@bgfi.com; internet www.bgfi.com; subsidiary of BGFIBANK Group (Gabon); cap. 5,000m. (2007); Dir-Gen. NARCISSE OBIANG ONDO; 2 brs.

COFIPA—Compagnie de Financement et de Participation: ave Amílcar Cabral, BP 147, Brazzaville; tel. 81-58-34; fax 81-03-73; e-mail cofipabzv@caramail.com; f. 2001 on privatization of Union Congolaise de Banques; cap. and res 2,868.2m., total assets 57,523.9m. (Dec. 2003); Dir-Gen. XAVIER ALIBERT; 14 brs.

La Congolaise de Banque (LCB): ave Amílcar Cabral, BP 2889, Brazzaville; tel. 81-09-78; fax 81-09-77; e-mail caic20@calva.com; f. 2004 on privatization of Crédit pour l'Agriculture, l'Industrie et le Commerce (CAIC); Dir-Gen. GILBERT BOPOUNZA; 4 brs.

Crédit Lyonnais-Congo (CL Co): ave Emmanuel Daddet, BP 1312, Pointe-Noire; tel. 94-24-00; fax 94-16-65; f. 2002 to replace Banque Internationale du Congo; 81% owned by Crédit Lyonnais (France), 9% state-owned; cap. and res 2,868.2m., total assets 57,523.9m. (Dec. 2003); Dir-Gen. PASCAL PETRIS; 2 brs.

Société Congolaise de Financement (SOCOFIN): BP 899, Pointe-Noire; tel. 67-10-44; fax 94-37-93; e-mail socofin.pnr@cg.celtelplus.com; f. 2001; cap. and res 370.0m., total assets 7,993.6m. (Dec. 2002); Dir-Gen. ERIC LECLERE.

Co-operative Banking Institution

Mutuelle Congolaise d'Epargne et de Crédit (MUCODEC): ave Paul Doumer, BP 13237, Brazzaville; tel. 81-07-57; fax 81-01-68; e-mail mucodec@wanadoo.fr; f. 1994; cap. and res 2,080m., total assets 29,000m. (Dec. 2003); Pres. JULIEN BOBOUNNGA; 45 brs.

Development Bank

Banque de Développement des Etats de l'Afrique Centrale: BP 1177, Brazzaville; tel. 81-17-61; fax 81-18-80; e-mail bdeac@bdeac.org; internet www.bdeac.org; cap. 22,240.0m., res 6,935.1m., dep. 11,536.6m. (Dec. 2006); Pres. and Chair. ANICET G. DOLOGUÉLÉ.

Financial Institution

Caisse Congolaise d'Amortissement (CCA): ave Foch, BP 2090, Brazzaville; tel. 81-57-35; fax 81-52-36; f. 1971; management of state funds; Dir-Gen. GEORGES NGUEKOUMOU.

INSURANCE

Assurances et Réassurances du Congo (ARC): BP 1033, Pointe-Noire; tel. 94-08-00; f. 1973; 50% state-owned; privatization pending; Dir-Gen. RAYMOND IBATA; brs at Brazzaville, Loubomo and Ouesso.

Gras Savoye Congo: 13 rue Germain Bikouma, angle Route de la Radio, Immeuble Guenin, BP 1901, Pointe-Noire; tel. 94-79-72; fax 94-79-74; e-mail grassavoye.congo@cg.celtelplus.com; affiliated to Gras Savoye (France); insurance brokers and risk managers; Man. PHILIPPE BAILLÉ.

Société de Courtage d'Assurances et de Réassurances (SCDE): BP 13177, Immeuble Foch, ave Foch, Brazzaville; tel. 81-17-63.

Trade and Industry

GOVERNMENT AGENCY

Comité des Privatisations et de Renforcement des Capacités Locales: Immeuble ex-SCBO, 7ème étage, BP 1176, Brazzaville; tel. 81-46-21; fax 81-46-09; e-mail privat@aol.com; oversees and co-ordinates transfer of state-owned enterprises to the private sector.

DEVELOPMENT ORGANIZATIONS

Agence Française de Développement (AFD): rue Béhagle, BP 96, Brazzaville; tel. 81-53-30; fax 81-29-42; e-mail afdbrazzaville@groupe-afd.org; internet www.afd.fr; French fund for economic co-operation; Country Dir ALAIN DALHEM.

Mission Française de Coopération et d'Action Culturelle: BP 2175, Brazzaville; tel. 83-15-03; f. 1959; administers bilateral aid from France; Dir JEAN-BERNARD THIANT.

Société Nationale d'Elevage (SONEL): BP 81, Loutété, Massangui; f. 1964; development of semi-intensive stock-rearing; exploitation of cattle by-products; Man. Dir THÉOPHILE BIKAWA.

THE REPUBLIC OF THE CONGO

CHAMBERS OF COMMERCE

Chambre de Commerce, d'Agriculture, d'Industrie et des Métiers de Brazzaville: BP 92, Brazzaville; tel. and fax 81-16-08; f. 1935; Pres. PAUL OBAMBI; Sec.-Gen. GÉRARD DONGO.

Chambre de Commerce, d'Agriculture et d'Industrie de Kouilou: BP 665, Pointe-Noire; tel. 94-12-80; fax 94-07-13; f. 1948; fmrly Chambre de Commerce, d'Industrie et des Métiers de Pointe-Noire; Chair. NARCISSE POATY PACKA; Sec.-Gen. JEAN-BAPTISTE SOUMBOU.

Chambre de Commerce, d'Agriculture et d'Industrie de Loubomo: BP 78, Loubomo; tel. 91-00-17.

Chambre Nationale d'Industrie et d'Agriculture du Congo: BP 1119, Brazzaville; tel. 83-29-56; fmrly Conférence Permanente des Chambres de Commerce du Congo; Pres. PAUL OBAMBI.

EMPLOYERS' ORGANIZATIONS

Forum des Jeunes Entreprises du Congo (FJEC): BP 2080, Brazzaville; tel. 81-56-34; e-mail fjec@inmarsat.francetelecom.fr; f. 1996; Sec.-Gen. PAUL KAMPAKOL.

Union Nationale des Opérateurs du Congo (UNOC): BP 5187, Brazzaville; tel. 81-54-32; operates a professional training centre; Pres. El Hadj DJIBRIL ABDOULAYE BOPAKA.

Union Patronale et Interprofessionnelle du Congo (UNICONGO): BP 42, Brazzaville; tel. 81-47-68; fax 81-47-66; f. 1958; Nat. Pres. JEAN-CHRISTOPHE TRANCEPAIN; Sec.-Gen. JEAN-JACQUES SAMBA; membership of 10 feds, representing 400 enterprises, with a total work-force of 25,000 (2001).

UTILITIES

Electricity

Société Nationale d'Electricité (SNE): 95 ave Paul Doumer, BP 95, Brazzaville; tel. 81-05-66; fax 81-05-69; e-mail snecongo@caramail.com; f. 1967; transfer to private management proposed; operates hydroelectric plants at Bouenza and Djoué; Pres. ALBERT CAMILLE PELLA; Dir-Gen. ALPHONSE BOUDONESA.

Water

Société Nationale de Distribution d'Eau (SNDE): rue du Sergent Malamine, BP 229, Brazzaville; tel. 94-22-16; fax 94-28-60; f. 1967; transferred to private-sector management by Bi-Water (United Kingdom) in 2002; water supply and sewerage; holds monopoly over wells and import of mineral water; Dir-Gen. YOKA ONIKA.

TRADE UNION FEDERATIONS

Independent trade unions were legalized in 1991.

Confédération Générale des Travailleurs du Congo (CGTC): Brazzaville; f. 1995; Chair. PAUL DOUNA.

Confédération Nationale des Syndicats Libres (CNASYL): Brazzaville; f. 1994; Sec.-Gen. MICHEL KABOUL MAOUTA.

Confédération Syndicale Congolaise (CSC): BP 2311, Brazzaville; tel. 83-19-23; f. 1964; 80,000 mems.

Confédération Syndicale des Travailleurs du Congo (CSTC): BP 14743, Brazzaville; tel. 61-47-35; f. 1993; fed. of 13 trade unions; Chair. MICHEL SOUZA; 40,000 mems.

Confédération des Syndicats Libres Autonomes du Congo (COSYLAC): BP 14861, Brazzaville; tel. 82-42-65; fax 83-42-70; e-mail b.oba@congonet.cg; Pres. RENÉ BLANCHARD SERGE OBA.

Fédération nationale des travailleurs du Congo (FENATRAC): Brazzaville; f. 2001 by split from CSTC (q.v.); Sec. JULIEN NGOULOU.

Transport

RAILWAYS

In 1999 there were 1,152 km of railway track in the Congo. A 286-km section of privately owned line was used until 1991 to link the manganese mines at Moanda (in Gabon) with the main line to Pointe-Noire. Rail traffic has been severely disrupted since the 1997 civil war. The main line (of some 518 km) between Brazzaville and Pointe-Noire reopened briefly in November 1998 for freight traffic, but was subsequently closed following further unrest and sabotage. In early 2000 the Government signed two agreements with the Société Nationale des Chemins de Fer Français (France) relating to the repair of the line and associated infrastructure, and to the management of the network. Freight services resumed in August 2000, followed by passenger services in January 2001, although there was further disruption to the railways during unrest in mid-2002. In May 2004 the rail service linking Brazzaville to the Pool region resumed operations.

Chemin de Fer Congo-Océan (CFCO): BP 651, Pointe-Noire; tel. 94-11-84; fax 94-12-30; f. 1969; entered partnership with Rail Afrique International in June 1998; transfer to private management proposed; Dir-Gen. JACKY TRIMARDEAU.

ROADS

In 2004 there were an estimated 17,289 km of roads. Only about 5.0% of the total network was paved. The principal routes link Brazzaville with Pointe-Noire, in the south, and with Ouesso, in the north. A number of major construction projects initiated by President Sassou-Nguesso in 2000 and 2001 have involved the highways from Brazzaville to Kinkala, and from Brazzaville to the Pool region.

Régie Nationale des Transports et des Travaux Publics: BP 2073, Brazzaville; tel. 83-35-58; f. 1965; civil engineering, maintenance of roads and public works; Man. Dir HECTOR BIENVENU OUAMBA.

INLAND WATERWAYS

The Congo and Oubangui rivers form two axes of a highly developed inland waterway system. The Congo river and seven tributaries in the Congo basin provide 2,300 km of navigable river, and the Oubangui river, developed in co-operation with the Central African Republic, an additional 2,085 km.

Coordination Nationale des Transports Fluviaux: BP 2048, Brazzaville; tel. 83-06-27; Dir MÉDARD OKOUMOU.

Transcap—Congo: BP 1154, Pointe-Noire; tel. 94-01-46; f. 1962; Chair. J. DROUAULT.

SHIPPING

The deep-water Atlantic seaport at Pointe-Noire is the most important port in Central Africa and Brazzaville is one of the principal ports on the Congo river. A major rehabilitation programme began in October 1999, with the aim of establishing Pointe-Noire as a regional centre for container traffic and as a logistics centre for offshore oil exploration. In 1997 708,203 metric tons of goods were loaded at the port of Pointe-Noire, and 533,170 tons were unloaded.

La Congolaise de Transport Maritime (COTRAM): Pointe-Noire; f. 1984; national shipping co; state-owned.

Maersk Congo: 10 rue Massabi, Zone Portuaire, Pointe-Noire; tel. 94-21-41; fax 94-23-25; f. 1997; represents Maersk Sealand (Denmark).

Port Autonome de Brazzaville: BP 2048, Brazzaville; tel. 83-00-42; f. 2000; port authority; Dir JEAN-PAUL BOCKONDAS.

Port Autonome de Pointe-Noire (PAPN): BP 711, Pointe-Noire; tel. 94-00-52; fax 94-20-42; e-mail info@papn-cg.com; internet www.papn-cg.com; f. 2000; port authority; Dir-Gen. JEAN-MARIE ANIÉLÉ.

SAGA Congo: 18 rue du Prophète Lasse Zephirin, BP 674, Pointe-Noire; tel. 94-10-16; fax 94-34-04.

Société Congolaise de Transports Maritimes (SOCOTRAM): BP 4922, Pointe-Noire; tel. 94-49-21; fax 94-49-22; e-mail info@socotram.com; internet www.socotram.fr; f. 1990.

CIVIL AVIATION

There are international airports at Brazzaville (Maya-Maya) and Pointe-Noire (Agostinho Neto). There are also five regional airports, at Loubomo (Dolisie, Ngot-Nzounzoungou), Nkaye, Owando, Ouesso and Impfondo, as well as 12 smaller airfields. In early 2001 the construction of a new international airport at Ollombo, some 500 km north of Brazzaville, began; the airport was expected to open by 2008. The refurbishment of Brazzaville airport commenced in 2001.

Aéro-Service: ave Charles de Gaulle, BP 1138, Pointe-Noire; tel. 94-23-80; fax 94-14-41; e-mail info@aero-service.net; internet www.aero-service.net; f. 1967; scheduled and charter passenger and freight services; operates nationally and to regional destinations; Pres. and Dir-Gen. R. GRIESBAUM.

Trans Air Congo: Immeuble City Center, ave Amílcar Cabral, BP 2422, Brazzaville; tel. 81-10-46; fax 81-10-57; e-mail info@flytransaircongo.com; internet www.transaircongo.org; f. 1994; private airline operating internal scheduled and international charter flights; Pres. and Dir-Gen. BASSAM ELHAGE.

Tourism

The tourism sector was severely disrupted in the late 1990s by political instability and internal unrest. Tourist visitors numbered 4,753 in 1999 (compared with tourist arrivals of 25,082 in 1998). In 2001, however, the number of tourist arrivals increased to 27,363, but declined slightly, to 21,611 in 2002. In 2004 earnings from tourism were estimated at US $23m.

Direction Générale du Tourisme et des Loisirs: BP 456, Brazzaville; tel. 83-09-53; f. 1980; Dir-Gen. ANTOINE KOUNKOU-KIBOUILOU.

COSTA RICA

Introductory Survey

Location, Climate, Language, Religion, Flag, Capital

The Republic of Costa Rica lies in the Central American isthmus, with Nicaragua to the north, Panama to the south, the Caribbean Sea to the east and the Pacific Ocean to the west. The climate is warm and damp in the lowlands (average temperature 27°C (81°F)) and cooler on the Central Plateau (average temperature 22°C (72°F)), where two-thirds of the population live. The language spoken is Spanish. Almost all of the inhabitants profess Christianity, and the majority adhere to the Roman Catholic Church, the state religion. The national flag (proportions 3 by 5) has five horizontal stripes, of blue, white, red, white and blue, the red stripe being twice the width of the others. The state flag, in addition, has on the red stripe (to the left of centre) a white oval enclosing the national coat of arms, showing three volcanic peaks between the Caribbean and the Pacific. The capital is San José.

Recent History

Costa Rica was ruled by Spain from the 16th century until 1821, when independence was declared. The only significant interruption in the country's constitutional government since 1920 occurred in February 1948, when the victory of the opposition candidate, Otilio Ulate Blanco, in the presidential election was disputed. The legislature annulled the election in March but a civil war ensued. The anti-Government forces, led by José Figueres Ferrer, were successful, and a revolutionary junta took power in April. Costa Rica's army was abolished in December. After the preparation of a new Constitution, Ulate took office as President in January 1949.

Figueres, who founded the socialist Partido de Liberación Nacional (PLN), dominated national politics for decades, holding presidential office in 1953–58 and 1970–74. Under his leadership, Costa Rica became one of the most democratic countries in Latin America. Since the 1948 revolution, there have been frequent changes of power, all achieved by constitutional means. Figueres's first Government nationalized the banks and instituted a comprehensive social security system. The presidential election of 1958, however, was won by a conservative, Mario Echandi Jiménez, who reversed many PLN policies. His successor, Francisco Orlich Bolmarich (President from 1962 to 1966), was supported by the PLN but continued the encouragement of private enterprise. Another conservative, José Joaquín Trejos Fernández, held power in 1966–70. In 1974 the PLN candidate, Daniel Oduber Quirós, was elected President. He continued the policies of extending the welfare state and of establishing amicable relations with communist states. Communist and other left-wing parties were legalized in 1975. In 1978 Rodrigo Carazo Odio of the conservative Partido Unidad Opositora (PUO) coalition (subsequently the Coalición Unidad) was elected President. During Carazo's term of office increasing instability in Central America led to diplomatic tension, and in 1981 the President was criticized for his alleged involvement in illegal arms-trafficking between Cuba and El Salvador.

At presidential and legislative elections in February 1982, Luis Alberto Monge Alvarez of the PLN won a comfortable majority when his party secured 33 of the 57 seats in the Asamblea Legislativa (Legislative Assembly). Following his inauguration in May, President Monge announced a series of emergency economic measures, in an attempt to rescue the country from near-bankruptcy. A policy of neutrality towards the left-wing Sandinista Government of Nicaragua was continued. However, following a number of cross-border raids, a national alert was declared in May. The rebel Nicaraguan leader, Edén Pastora Gómez, was expelled in order to reduce Costa Rican involvement in the Nicaraguan conflict. Relations with Nicaragua deteriorated as guerrilla activity spread to San José. In November Monge declared Costa Rica's neutrality in an attempt to elicit foreign support for his country. This declaration was opposed by the USA and led to the resignation of the Costa Rican Minister of Foreign Affairs.

In early 1984 there were increasing reports of incursions into Costa Rica by the Sandinista forces. Public opposition to any renunciation of neutrality was emphasized by a demonstration in support of peace and neutrality, held in San José and attended by over 20,000 people. An attempt was made to defuse the tension with the establishment of a commission, supported by the Contadora group (Colombia, Mexico, Panama and Venezuela), to monitor events in the border area. In late May, however, the attempted assassination of Pastora near the Costa Rican border exacerbated the rift within the Cabinet concerning government policy towards Nicaragua. In December, following an incident involving a Nicaraguan refugee at the Costa Rican embassy in Managua, diplomatic relations with Nicaragua were reduced to a minimal level. Reports of clashes between Costa Rican Civil Guardsmen and Sandinista forces along the joint border became increasingly frequent. In 1985 the Government's commitment to neutrality was disputed when it decided to establish an anti-guerrilla battalion, trained by US military advisers.

At presidential and legislative elections in February 1986 Oscar Arias Sánchez, the candidate of the PLN, was elected President, with 52% of the votes cast. The PLN also obtained a clear majority in the Asamblea Legislativa. The new Government was committed to the development of a welfare state, the renegotiation of the country's external debt, and the conclusion of a social pact with the trade unions. Furthermore, Arias was resolved to maintain and reinforce Costa Rica's policy of neutrality. Diplomatic relations with Nicaragua were fully restored, and it was decided to establish a permanent inspection commission at the common border. The Government embarked on a series of arrests and expulsions of Contras resident in Costa Rica. A degree of Costa Rican complicity in anti-Sandinista activity became apparent, however, in 1986, when the existence of a secret airstrip in Costa Rica, which was used as a supply base for the Contras, was made public.

Throughout 1986 and 1987 Arias became increasingly involved in the quest for peace in Central America. In August 1987 the Presidents of El Salvador, Nicaragua, Guatemala, Honduras and Costa Rica signed a peace agreement based on proposals presented by Arias, who was subsequently awarded the Nobel Peace Prize. In January 1988 Arias brought Nicaraguan government officials and Contra leaders together in San José for their first discussions concerning the implementation of a cease-fire. Prior to this meeting, Arias ordered three Contra leaders to leave Costa Rica or cease their military activities. Arias maintained his independent position by supporting discussions between the Contras and Sandinistas, held in Nicaragua in March, and by condemning any continuation of aid to the Contras. In November a border agreement was signed with Nicaragua.

At presidential and legislative elections in February 1990, Rafael Angel Calderón Fournier, the candidate of the Partido Unidad Social Cristiana (PUSC), was elected President, with 51% of the votes cast. The PUSC also obtained a clear majority in the Asamblea Legislativa. The defeat of the PLN was widely attributed to popular dissatisfaction at the Government's economic policies in 1988 and 1989, which appeared to have been designed to appease the IMF and World Bank. Calderón inherited a large fiscal deficit and was therefore forced to renege on his pre-election promise of improvements in welfare and income distribution. In an attempt to reduce the deficit, the Government introduced an adjustment programme of austerity measures. In October 70,000–100,000 public and private-sector employees participated in a one-day national strike to protest against the new Government's economic policies.

In August 1991 the Minister of Public Security and the Minister of National Planning and Economic Policy resigned following disagreements with President Calderón. The Minister of the Interior and Police, Luis Fishman, was subsequently appointed acting Minister of Public Security. The Civil Guard and the Rural Guard therefore came under the sole charge of Fishman. Opposition groups expressed concern at this concentration of power, in view of the continuing decline in popular support for Calderón and the level of public unrest. In November, in response to pressure from student and public-sector unions, Calderón abandoned austerity measures involving a reduction in the education budget and the dismissal of thousands of public employees. This decision prompted the resignation of the Minister of Finance, who claimed that the President's action would make it impossible to curb the rapidly increasing fiscal deficit and thus attain IMF-agreed targets.

In January 1992 Calderón was summoned before the Asamblea Legislativa's commission on drugs-trafficking to answer allegations that the PUSC had been the recipient of the proceeds of illegal drugs-trafficking during its election campaign in 1990. The President denied any knowledge of such payments. Following the decision made by the Government in March 1992 to remove foreign-exchange controls, there was mounting concern that Costa Rican banking institutions were being used increasingly for the purposes of laundering money obtained from illegal drugs-trafficking. Concern about security in the country also increased in 1993 after Nicaraguan embassy staff and members of the Supreme Court were temporarily taken hostage in March and April, respectively. The hostage-takers later released their captives unharmed in exchange for a ransom and safe passage out of the country.

Presidential and legislative elections were held in February 1994. The presidential ballot was narrowly won by José María Figueres Olsen, the PLN candidate. The PLN failed to obtain an outright majority in the Asamblea Legislativa, securing only 28 of the 57 seats, while the PUSC won 25 seats. Figueres assumed office in early May.

Industrial unrest increased in 1994 and 1995. In May 1994 industrial action by employees of the Geest banana company resulted in violent clashes with the security forces. The strike was organized in protest at the dismissal of some 400 workers for attempting to join a union. The dispute, which was resolved following government intervention, came in the wake of allegations by the American Federation of Labor and Congress of Industrial Organizations, of violations of labour rights in Costa Rica. In July 1995 some 50,000 teachers also began strike action in protest at proposed reforms to the state pension system. Growing dissatisfaction among other public-sector employees at government economic policy, in particular proposals for the deregulation and privatization of state enterprises, culminated in a 100,000-strong demonstration in the capital in August. Following the protest, the Government reached an accord with the teachers, under which it agreed to establish a commission, to include representatives of the teachers' unions, to debate the proposed reform of the pension system and to review certain other of the Government's economic policies.

At the presidential election of February 1998 Miguel Angel Rodríguez Echeverría, again the candidate of the PUSC, secured a narrow victory over the PLN candidate, José Miguel Corrales Bolaños. The PUSC failed to obtain an outright majority in the concurrently held legislative election, securing only 27 of the 57 seats, while the PLN won 23. On 8 May Rodríguez was sworn in as President.

The new President's attempts to alleviate the budget deficit through economic reform met with considerable opposition in 2000. In May of that year the Government was forced to withdraw proposed legislation on the privatization of the telecommunications and energy sectors, after the largest popular protests in the country in 30 years.

In June 2001 a constitutional commission was appointed to recommend a process of transformation from the presidential system of government to a semi-parliamentary one, in an attempt to improve the political decision-making process. In early July the Asamblea Legislativa approved legislation designed to improve tax efficiency: the new law would reduce tax on basic goods, while increasing duties on some luxury goods and services.

Presidential and legislative elections were held on 3 February 2002. As no candidate gained 40% of the votes cast, for the first time in Costa Rican history a further round of voting was held between the two leading candidates, Abel Pacheco de la Espriella of the ruling PUSC and Rolando Araya of the PLN, on 7 April. At this ballot Pacheco won 58% of the votes cast. In the legislative election, also held on 3 February, the recently formed Partido Acción Ciudadana (PAC) secured 14 seats at the expense of the two main parties: the number of PUSC deputies in the 57-seat Asamblea Legislativa fell from 27 to 19, while the PLN's parliamentary representation fell from 23 to 17.

Pacheco was inaugurated as President on 8 May 2002. Upon assuming office, he pledged to reform the tax system and to seek ways to curb public-sector expenditure in order to reduce the budget deficit. However, extensive damage caused by heavy flooding in the previous month, which had left an estimated 5,100 people homeless, meant that the Government was forced to divert revenue to the subsequent reconstruction effort.

In mid-May 2003 employees at the state electricity and telecommunications company, the Instituto Costarricense de Electricidad (ICE), began industrial action in an attempt to force the Government to issue a US $100m. bond to finance the company, after that year's budget had reduced funding to the electricity and telecommunications sector. In early June ICE employees returned to work, having secured the Government's agreement on most demands. Industrial action by teachers, which began in late May, continued until the end of June, when the Government agreed to revise proposed pension reforms.

In October 2003 there was further conflict in the telecommunications sector as trade unions organized a demonstration in the capital to coincide with a round of negotiations towards the proposed Central American Free Trade Agreement (CAFTA). The protesters were concerned that the Government would agree to end the ICE's monopoly. President Pacheco insisted his Government was opposed to such a move; however, in January 2004 the administration agreed to certain concessions on liberalization of the sector.

In August 2004 the deteriorating economic situation prompted public-sector unions to organize a week-long general strike. In particular, the industrial action was in protest at the Government's offer of a 4.5% salary increase, which was lower than the monthly rate of inflation (which reached 8.5% in that month). The unrest escalated later in the month when drivers' associations began protests around the country against the monopoly on vehicle inspections held by the Spanish company Riteve SyC. On 31 August the Government agreed to increase the pay offer and to review Riteve SyC's contract. The concessions provoked the resignation of the Minister of Finance, Alberto Dent. On 7 September Ricardo Toledo, who had brokered the controversial increase, submitted his resignation as Minister of the Presidency. The following day two other ministers also resigned. In the ensuing cabinet reorganization, Dent was succeeded by Federico Carrillo Zürcher, while Manuel Antonio González Sanz became Minister of Foreign Commerce.

Throughout 2004 a series of disclosures of alleged corruption within the public sector tarnished the country's reputation for transparency. In May an investigation was begun into a loan in 2001 by the Government of Finland to the Costa Rican health service. The inquiry revealed that a number of executives at the Costa Rican social security institute, the Caja Costarricense de Seguro Social (CCSS) had received payments from Corporación Fischel, the company contracted to supply the medical equipment. The former head of the CCSS and former PUSC deputy, Elisio Vargas, and the President of Corporación Fischel, Walter Reiche, were both subsequently imprisoned in connection with the case. Then, in September, former President Calderón was charged with accepting illegal payments from Corporación Fischel; he was placed under house arrest in October. His apprehension came just one week after another former PUSC President, Miguel Angel Rodríguez, had resigned as Secretary-General of the Organization of American States after being accused of accepting payments from a French communications company, Alcatel, in connection with a contract with the ICE; he was later placed under house arrest. Furthermore, in late September President Pacheco admitted to having received an illegal contribution of US $100,000 from Alcatel during his 2002 election campaign. In the following month it was revealed that two Taiwanese firms had also donated $350,000 to the President's election campaign (foreign contributions and those over $28,000 were prohibited). Pacheco was beleaguered by further accusations of corrupt practices in 2005: in June of that year he submitted to a parliamentary inquiry into a number of undisclosed gifts, including free flights, and in connection with two allegedly private trips to Spain that were partially state-funded. The President declined to renounce his immunity from prosecution.

The corruption scandals prompted a protest march, attended by thousands of people, in the capital in mid-October 2004. Nevertheless, later that month another former President, this time from the PLN, José María Figueres, was accused of receiving illegal payments totalling US $900,000 from a sub-contractor of Alcatel. Figueres was subsequently expelled from the PLN. On 12 November four other members of the PLN, including the Secretary-General, Carmen María Valverde Acosta, resigned from the party to avoid internal investigations into allegations of corruption. In mid-October 2005 former Presidents Calderón and Rodríguez were released from house arrest; however, following an investigation prosecutors presented formal charges against Calderón in mid-March 2007 and against Rodríguez in late July.

In early August 2005 some 5,000 industrial workers held a demonstration in San José to demand that the Asamblea Legislativa approve DR-CAFTA (as CAFTA had been renamed following the inclusion of the Dominican Republic in negotiations in 2004). However, President Pacheco had refused to submit the Agreement for ratification until the legislature had approved his proposed reform of the tax system, which had been under legislative discussion for over two years. The proposals included the replacement of sales tax with value-added tax for some goods and services and the extension of profits tax to export zones. The first reading of the tax reform bill was finally approved by the Asamblea Legislativa on 16 February 2006. However, on 22 March the Constitutional Court ruled that the proposed legislation was unconstitutional. The proposed DR-CAFTA was eventually submitted for discussion by a congressional committee in October 2005, but it too had yet to be ratified by the time the legislature was dissolved in preparation for the general election in early 2006.

In December 2006 the Asamblea Legislativa approved stringent immigration legislation that proposed to penalize those who provided accommodation or employment for illegal immigrants, and to establish a division of the police force dedicated to immigration. The law increased tensions with neighbouring Nicaragua, whose Government protested that the law unfairly targeted Nicaraguan migrant workers. Despite the efforts of the incoming PLN administration (see below) to overturn the legislation, the measures took effect in August 2006.

Presidential and legislative elections were held on 5 February 2006. Former President Oscar Arias Sánchez was the PLN's presidential nominee. He was eligible to contest the election after an April 2003 supreme court ruling in favour of former heads of state standing for re-election. Ricardo Toledo, the former Minister of the Presidency under Pacheco, was the representative of the incumbent PUSC, while Ottón Solís Fallas was again the PAC's presidential candidate. Although, according to opinion polls, Arias seemed most likely to win the election, Solís Fallas proved an unexpectedly strong competitor: according to provisional results, both candidates secured 40% of the ballot. Nevertheless, following a manual recount, on 7 March it was declared that Arias had secured the presidency with 40.9% of the votes cast, ahead of Solís Fallas, who obtained 39.8% of the ballot. Otto Guevara Guth, representing the Movimiento Libertario (ML), received 8.5% of the ballot, while Toledo obtained only 3.6% of the votes cast. Voter turn-out was just 65.2%. The PLN also performed well in the concurrently held legislative election, winning 25 of the 57 seats in the Asamblea Legislativa, while the PAC secured 18. The ML's parliamentary representation stayed the same (with six seats); however, the PUSC obtained just four seats, far fewer than anticipated. The remaining four seats were won by small, independent parties.

Arias was inaugurated as President on 8 May 2006 and a new Cabinet installed. The President's brother, Rodrigo Arias Sánchez, was appointed Minister of the Presidency, while Alfredo Volio was designated Minister of Production, assuming the new portfolio that replaced the Ministry of Economy, Industry, and Commerce. Upon assuming office, Arias negotiated an alliance with the ML and the PAC to secure a legislative majority. In return for their support, Arias undertook to introduce legislation granting property rights to residents in marginal urban areas, and to restrict political patronage by abolishing the executive presidencies and the boards of directors of a number of public institutions.

Intermittent protests against the proposed DR-CAFTA continued in 2006 and 2007. On 23 October 2006 ICE employees were joined by workers from the health, education and finance sectors to participate in two days of industrial action. Some 9,000 protesters gathered in San José at demonstrations organized by the Coordinadora Nacional de Lucha contra el Tratado de Libre Comercio to signal their opposition to the putative trade agreement with the USA. The opposition was particularly opposed to proposed legislation, necessary for DR-CAFTA to take effect, that would liberalize the telecommunications and insurance industries, as well as privatizing the ICE. Nevertheless, President Arias reiterated his electoral pledge to ratify DR-CAFTA and on 12 December the legislative committee studying the accord voted to submit the bill for ratification to the Asamblea Legislativa. In January 2007 the Government succeeded in gaining approval for imposition of a time limit on discussion of legislation necessary for the passage of DR-CAFTA in the Asamblea. The opposition PAC reacted by submitting a complaint to the Constitutional Court over the legality of the move. Then, in early April, in what was viewed by the Government as a further delaying tactic, the opposition submitted a request to the Tribunal Supremo de Elecciones (TSE) that a referendum on implementation of DR-CAFTA be held; the request was granted, subject to the opposition providing 132,000 signatures (equivalent to 5% of the electorate) in favour of a vote. The time limit for the collection of signatures was 10 months, which would have made implementation of the accord almost impossible before the 1 March 2008 deadline. However, President Arias appeared to pre-empt the opposition tactic by announcing, in mid-April, his intention to ask the Asamblea to approve his request for a binding plebiscite on ratification to be held within 90 days instead. This was duly approved later in the month.

In July 2007 the Supreme Court ruled against an opposition claim that DR-CAFTA would be unconstitutional and set a date for the referendum of 7 October. The referendum campaign was bitterly fought: in late September the Second Vice-President (and Minister of Planning), Kevin Casas Zamora, was forced to resign after it was revealed he had written a memo to the President recommending aggressive tactics be used by the 'yes' campaign to win the plebiscite (Roberto Gallardo Núñez succeeded him in both roles in the following month). Despite this scandal, supporters of the free trade agreement secured a narrow victory in the referendum, winning 51.6% of the total votes cast, compared with 48.4% garnered by the 'no' campaign, led by the PAC. Turn-out was put at 59.2% of the electorate. The opposition initially demanded a recount, owing to the closeness of the result, and accused the Government of campaigning after the agreed deadline of 4 October. Nevertheless, at the end of November President Arias signed into law the proposed DR-CAFTA. However, the legislature still had to approve the 13 measures necessary to implement the treaty by the February 2008 deadline. The first of these measures, which included liberalization of the telecommunications and insurance sectors, was approved by the Asamblea on the same day. Although it agreed not to obstruct passage of the enabling laws, the PAC refused to attend congressional sessions to discuss the reforms, rendering many sessions inquorate. By early February 2008 only one-half of the necessary laws had been approved, forcing Arias to appeal to the DR-CAFTA signatories for an extension of the deadline, which was granted until 1 October.

In August 1989, at a summit meeting in Honduras, the Presidents of Costa Rica, El Salvador, Guatemala, Honduras and Nicaragua ratified a plan, known as the Tela Agreement, to remove the Contra forces from base camps in Honduras, in exchange for the introduction of political reforms and the holding of free elections in Nicaragua. Peace proposals for El Salvador and Guatemala were also elaborated, as was an agreement on co-operation in the campaign against the trafficking and use of illicit drugs. In November, however, the conflicts in Nicaragua and El Salvador intensified. In December the deadline for the disbanding of Contra forces, agreed at Tela, passed unfulfilled. In February 1990, after being defeated in an election, Nicaragua's Sandinista Government decreed an immediate cease-fire. The Contras accepted this, and a cease-fire agreement was concluded in April.

In 1995 relations with Nicaragua became strained, following a series of incidents concerning immigration and the policing of the countries' joint border. A tightening of immigration policy in Costa Rica, prompted in part by a downturn in the country's economy, had led to the automatic expulsion of illegal immigrants who had previously been tolerated. In July 1998 further antagonism developed between the two countries when Nicaragua prohibited Costa Rican civil guards from carrying arms while navigating the San Juan river, part of Nicaraguan territory which forms the border between the two countries. In June 2000 both Governments agreed a procedure that would allow armed Costa Rican police officers to patrol the river. Nevertheless, in September 2001 Nicaragua disputed a ruling by the Costa Rican Constitutional Court that armed police officers were entitled to use the San Juan river without seeking prior permission from Nicaragua. In July 2002 the two Governments came into conflict over a separate issue when Nicaragua announced that it was to award concessions for petroleum exploration in an area of the Caribbean Sea and Pacific Ocean claimed by Costa Rica. Bilateral discussions aimed at solving the issue within three years began in October. Failure to resolve the dispute within the allotted time prompted Costa Rica, on 28 September

2005, to refer the matter to the International Court of Justice (ICJ). In response, the President of Nicaragua, Enrique Bolaños, increased the number of troops patrolling the border area. Furthermore, in November the Nicaraguan Government declared an interest in reclaiming the province of Guanacaste, annexed by Costa Rica in 1825.

In October 2000 Costa Rica ratified a maritime boundaries treaty with Colombia, recognizing their control over 500,000 sq km of the Pacific Ocean, including the Isla del Coco.

Costa Rica severed diplomatic relations with Taiwan in June 2007 in favour of establishing relations with the People's Republic of China, which provided US $20m. in immediate aid for victims of severe floods that occurred in September, and a further $27m. for longer term projects.

Government

Under the Constitution of 1949, executive power is vested in the President, assisted by two Vice-Presidents (or, in exceptional circumstances, one Vice-President) and an appointed Cabinet. The President is elected for a four-year term by compulsory adult suffrage, and a successful candidate must receive at least 40% of the votes. The legislative organ is the unicameral Asamblea Legislativa, with 57 members who are similarly elected for four years.

Defence

There have been no Costa Rican armed forces since 1948. As assessed at November 2007, Rural and Civil Guards totalled 2,000 and 4,500 men, respectively. In addition, there were 2,500 Border Security Police. The paramilitary budget was put at 68,700m. colones in 2007.

Economic Affairs

In 2006, according to estimates by the World Bank, Costa Rica's gross national income (GNI), measured at average 2004–06 prices, was US $21,844m., equivalent to $4,980 per head (or $10,770 per head on an international purchasing-power parity basis). During 1996–2006, it was estimated, the population increased by an average of 2.1% per year, while gross domestic product (GDP) per head increased, in real terms, by an average of 3.1% per year. Overall GDP increased, in real terms, by an average annual rate of 5.2% in 1996–2006; GDP increased by an estimated 3.8% in 2007.

Agriculture (including hunting, forestry and fishing) contributed an estimated 8.0% of GDP and employed 13.2% of the economically active population in 2007. The principal cash crops are bananas (which accounted for a preliminary 7.2% of export earnings in 2007) and coffee (2.7%). Seafood exports were also significant, providing an estimated 10.3% of export earnings in 2007. Sugar cane is also cultivated. According to the World Bank, the real GDP of the agricultural sector increased at an average annual rate of 2.5% during 1996–2005. According to official estimates, real agricultural GDP increased by 12.6% in 2006 and by a further 6.8% in 2007.

Industry (including mining, manufacturing, construction and power) employed 22.2% of the economically active population and provided an estimated 28.2% of GDP in 2007. According to the World Bank, real industrial GDP increased at an average annual rate of 5.6% during 1996–2005. According to official figures, the real GDP of the sector increased by an estimated 11.0% in 2006 and by a further estimated 7.3% in 2007. Mining employed less than 0.2% of the economically active population and contributed an estimated 0.2% of GDP in 2007.

The manufacturing sector employed 13.1% of the employed work-force and contributed an estimated 20.4% of GDP in 2007. The principal branches of manufacturing were food products, chemical products, beverages and paper and paper products. Production of computer components by the US manufacturer Intel began in 1998, and by 2005 as many as 15 other high-technology manufacturers had opened factories in the country. In 2007 the manufacturing sector accounted for some 20.2% of total export earnings. According to the World Bank, the real GDP of the manufacturing sector increased at an average annual rate of 5.6% during 1996–2005. According to official estimates, the sector's GDP increased by 10.0% in 2006 and by a further 5.7% in 2007.

Energy is derived principally from petroleum and hydroelectric power. The Arenal hydroelectricity project was inaugurated in 1979; however, its full generating capacity of 1,974 MW did not fulfil Costa Rica's electricity requirements, and in 1993 the state electricity company, Instituto Costarricense de Electricidad (ICE), began its third electricity development programme. The programme included a US $300m. hydroelectric power project on the Río Reventazón, completed in 2000, and the country's first wind-generated power plant. In 2000 the ICE announced plans to build a 1,250 MW hydroelectric plant at Boruca by 2011. In November 2007 China National Petroleum Corporation announced that it planned to help modernize Costa Rica's oil refining facilities. The Chinese firm was also scheduled to commence oil and gas exploration in areas off the country's Caribbean coast. In 2004 hydroelectric power accounted for 79% of total electrical energy generation. Imports of mineral products accounted for an estimated 12.4% of the total value of imports in 2006.

The services sector employed 64.6% of the economically active population and provided an estimated 63.8% of GDP in 2007. According to the World Bank, the real GDP of this sector increased at an average annual rate of 5.3% during 1996–2005. According to official estimates, sectoral GDP increased by 7.1% in 2006 and by a further 6.8% in 2007. Tourism is the country's most important source of foreign-exchange earnings. Receipts from tourism totalled an estimated US $1,804m. in 2005 and tourist arrivals numbered 1,679,051 in the same year. Of these, some 45.2% came from the USA. In December 2004 a second cruise-ship terminal was inaugurated at Puerto Limón to cater for the increasing number of visiting cruise ships.

In 2006 Costa Rica recorded a visible trade deficit of US $2,743.3m. and there was a deficit of $1,118.3m. on the current account of the balance of payments. In 2006 the principal source of imports (38.1%) was the USA; other major suppliers were Mexico (5.2%), Venezuela (5.2%) and Japan (4.7%). The USA was also the principal market for exports (39.1%); other significant purchasers were the People's Republic of China (6.6%), the Netherlands (6.0%), Guatemala (3.8%) and Nicaragua (3.5%). China became the second largest market for Costa Rican exports (mostly microprocessors) in 2007, after bilateral relations were established. The principal exports in 2006 were machinery and electrical equipment (particularly computer components), food and live animals (particularly bananas), basic manufactures and optical and topographical equipment. The principal imports in that year were machinery and electrical equipment, mineral products and chemicals and related products.

In 2004 there was an estimated budgetary deficit of 161,775m. colones (equivalent to some 2.0% of GDP). Costa Rica's estimated total external debt at the end of 2005 was US $6,223m., of which $3,470m. was long-term public debt. The cost of debt-servicing in that year was equivalent to 5.9% of the value of exports of goods and services. The annual rate of inflation averaged 11.3% in 1996–2006. Consumer prices increased by 11.5% in 2006. Some 6.0% of the labour force were unemployed in that year.

Costa Rica is a member of the Central American Common Market (CACM, see p. 201) and the Inter-American Development Bank (IDB, see p. 308). In May 2000 legislation was passed enhancing the Caribbean Basin Initiative, first introduced in 1983, granting North American Free Trade Agreement parity to products from 24 states, including Costa Rica. In November 2002 a free trade agreement with Canada was promulgated, and in August 2007 President Oscar Arias Sánchez signed a free trade agreement with Panama.

Negotiations towards a Central American Free Trade Agreement (CAFTA) between Costa Rica, El Salvador, Guatemala, Honduras, Nicaragua and the USA began in January 2003 (the Dominican Republic joined negotiations in the following year, when the proposed agreement was restyled DR-CAFTA). However, disagreement emerged over US demands that Costa Rica liberalize its telecommunications industry, over which the ICE enjoyed a monopoly. Following negotiations in January 2004 the two countries reached an agreement whereby the Costa Rican Government would partially privatize the telecommunications and insurance sectors in return for agricultural subsidies. DR-CAFTA was signed in May and ratified by the US Senate in 2005. Nevertheless, the proposed accord faced continued opposition in Costa Rica (see Recent History). The Arias Government, which took office in May 2006, pledged to ratify DR-CAFTA, and the social reforms promised by the new President were dependent on a programme of economic liberalism. Ratification was impeded by both the Asamblea and by industrial action, but in October 2007 the accord was approved in a referendum; however, the Government still faced legislative opposition to the free trade agreement, and it was unlikely that the necessary 'implementation agenda' necessary for DR-CAFTA's implementation would be passed by the February 2008 deadline. If implemented, DR-

COSTA RICA

CAFTA was expected to increase export revenue as the USA removed tariffs on Costa Rican goods, although there remained concerns that cheaper US commodities would adversely affect the agricultural sector. Furthermore, continued popular opposition to the accord would affect foreign investment. The budget for 2008 envisaged a further rise in taxation and increased expenditure on education, infrastructure, public housing and social welfare programmes, although much of President Arias's planned reform agenda depended on implementation of DR-CAFTA.

Education

Education at all levels is available free of charge, and is officially compulsory for children between six and 15 years of age. Primary education begins at six years of age and lasts for six years. Secondary education consists of a three-year basic course, followed by a more highly specialized course of two years. In 2002/03 primary enrolment included an estimated 90.4% of children in the relevant age-group (males 89.7%; females 91.2%), while the comparable ratio for secondary enrolment was 52.7% (males 50.3%; females 55.1%). There are four public universities, one of which is an open university and an increasing number of private ones. In 2002/03 total enrolment at primary, secondary and tertiary levels was 68.0% (males 67.2%; females 68.9%). Costa Rica has the highest adult literacy rate in Central America. Government expenditure on education in 2004 was 440,157.4m. colones, equivalent to 11.1% of total government spending.

Public Holidays

2008: 1 January (New Year's Day), 19 March (Feast of St Joseph, San José only), 20 March (Maundy Thursday), 21 March (Good Friday), 11 April (Anniversary of the Battle of Rivas), 1 May (Labour Day), 25 July (Anniversary of the Annexation of Guanacaste Province), 2 August (Our Lady of the Angels), 15 August (Mothers' Day), 15 September (Independence Day), 13 October (Columbus Day), 25 December (Christmas Day), 28–31 December (San José only).

2009: 1 January (New Year's Day), 19 March (Feast of St Joseph, San José only), 9 April (Maundy Thursday), 10 April (Good Friday), 11 April (Anniversary of the Battle of Rivas), 1 May (Labour Day), 25 July (Anniversary of the Annexation of Guanacaste Province), 2 August (Our Lady of the Angels), 15 August (Mothers' Day), 15 September (Independence Day), 12 October (Columbus Day), 25 December (Christmas Day), 28–31 December (San José only).

Weights and Measures

The metric system is in force.

Statistical Survey

Sources (unless otherwise stated): Instituto Nacional de Estadística y Censos, Edif. Ana Lorena, Calle Los Negritos, de la Rotonda de la Bandera 450 m oeste, Mercedes de Montes de Oca, San José; tel. 280-9280; fax 224-2221; e-mail informacion@inec.go.cr; internet www.inec.go.cr; Banco Central de Costa Rica, Avdas Central y Primera, Calles 2 y 4, Apdo 10.058, 1000 San José; tel. 233-4233; fax 223-4658; internet www.bccr.fi.cr.

Area and Population

AREA, POPULATION AND DENSITY

Area (sq km)	
Land	51,060
Inland water	40
Total	51,100*
Population (census results)	
11 June 1984†	2,416,809
28 June 2000	
Males	1,996,350
Females	1,928,981
Total	3,925,331
Population (official estimate at mid-year)	
2005	4,215,569
2006	4,269,884
2007	4,325,540
Density (per sq km) at mid-2007	84.6

* 19,730 sq miles.
† Excluding adjustment for underenumeration.

PROVINCES
(official estimates at mid-2007)

	Area (sq km)	Population (estimates)	Density (per sq km)	Capital (with population)
Alajuela	9,757.5	815,386	83.6	Alajuela (252,358)
Cartago	3,124.7	486,733	155.8	Cartago (148,065)
Guanacaste	10,140.7	301,082	29.7	Liberia (54,813)
Heredia	2,657.0	401,391	151.1	Heredia (117,492)
Limón	9,188.5	395,625	43.1	Limón (104,763)
Puntarenas	11,265.7	411,424	36.5	Puntarenas (117,269)
San José	4,965.9	1,513,899	304.9	San José (348,558)
Total	51,100.0	4,325,540	84.6	—

PRINCIPAL TOWNS
(official estimates at mid-2005)

San José	342,977		Heredia	115,426
Alajuela	247,588		Puntarenas	114,824
Cartago	145,748			

BIRTHS, MARRIAGES AND DEATHS

	Registered live births Number	Rate (per 1,000)	Registered marriages Number	Rate (per 1,000)	Registered deaths Number	Rate (per 1,000)
1999	78,526	21.9	25,613	7.1	15,052	4.2
2000	78,178	20.5	24,436	6.2	14,944	3.9
2001	76,401	19.2	23,790	6.0	15,609	4.0
2002	71,144	17.6	23,926	5.9	15,004	3.7
2003	72,938	17.8	24,448	6.0	15,800	3.9
2004	72,247	17.4	25,370	6.1	15,949	3.8
2005	71,548	17.0	25,631	6.1	16,139	3.8
2006	71,291	16.7	26,575	6.2	16,766	3.9

Expectation of life (years at birth, WHO estimates): 77.3 (males 75.3; females 79.5) in 2005 (Source: WHO, *World Health Statistics*).

ECONOMICALLY ACTIVE POPULATION*
('000 persons aged 12 years and over, household survey, July)

	2005	2006	2007
Agriculture, hunting and forestry	260.49	246.91	244.75
Fishing	9.49	9.27	9.85
Mining and quarrying	3.99	4.69	2.61
Manufacturing	242.68	243.90	251.57
Electricity, gas and water supply	20.55	22.04	21.06
Construction	115.73	126.70	151.79
Wholesale and retail trade	332.16	352.15	366.51
Hotels and restaurants	98.02	97.83	108.27
Transport, storage and communications	111.86	118.48	125.72
Financial intermediation	36.24	38.21	49.47
Real estate, renting and business activities	103.00	108.41	121.62

COSTA RICA

—continued	2005	2006	2007
Public administration activities	81.36	86.49	88.68
Education	104.08	108.41	110.74
Health and social work	62.73	62.47	64.01
Other community, social and personal service activities	64.85	65.87	72.70
Private households with employed persons	121.17	131.15	128.56
Extra-territorial organizations and bodies	2.01	2.60	1.12
Not classifiable by economic activity	6.51	4.57	6.61
Total employed	1,776.90	1,829.93	1,925.65
Unemployed	126.17	116.03	92.79
Total labour force	1,903.07	1,945.96	2,018.44

* Figures for activities are rounded to the nearest 10 persons, and totals may not be equivalent to the sum of component parts as a result.

Health and Welfare

KEY INDICATORS

Total fertility rate (children per woman, 2005)	2.2
Under-5 mortality rate (per 1,000 live births, 2005)	12
HIV/AIDS (% of persons aged 15–49, 2005)	0.3
Physicians (per 1,000 head, 2000)	1.32
Hospital beds (per 1,000 head, 2004)	1.4
Health expenditure (2004): US $ per head (PPP)	592
Health expenditure (2004): % of GDP	6.6
Health expenditure (2004): public (% of total)	77.0
Access to water (% of persons, 2004)	97
Access to sanitation (% of persons, 2004)	92
Human Development Index (2005): ranking	48
Human Development Index (2005): value	0.846

For sources and definitions, see explanatory note on p. vi.

Agriculture

PRINCIPAL CROPS
('000 metric tons)

	2004	2005	2006
Rice (paddy)	197.2	183.3	151.0
Potatoes	76.4	74.9	53.1
Cassava (Manioc)	295.0	300.0*	300.0*
Sugar cane	3,804.6	3,615.6	4,220.0†
Watermelons*	86.7	92.6	92.6
Cantaloupes and other melons	226.8	243.9	243.9*
Oil palm fruit	670.0	780.0	780.0
Bananas*	2,249.2	2,352.6	2,352.6
Plantains*	70.0	45.2	76.6
Oranges	250.0	326.4	326.4*
Pineapples	1,077.3	1,605.2	1,200.0
Coffee (green)	126.0†	131.9*	131.9*

* FAO estimate(s).
† Unofficial figure.
Source: FAO.

LIVESTOCK
('000 head, year ending September)

	2004	2005	2006
Horses*	115	115	115
Asses, mules or hinnies*	13	13	13
Cattle	1,081	1,000	1,000
Pigs*	550	550	550
Sheep*	3	3	3
Goats*	5	5	5
Chickens*	19,500	19,500	19,500

* FAO estimates.
Source: FAO.

LIVESTOCK PRODUCTS
('000 metric tons)

	2004	2005	2006
Cattle meat	70.0	80.7	80.7*
Pig meat	37.9	39.1	38.7
Chicken meat	84.5	91.0	91.0*
Cows' milk	752.3	779.5	779.5*
Hen eggs	49.9	48.2	48.2*
Honey*	1.3	1.3	1.3

* FAO estimate(s).
Source: FAO.

Forestry

ROUNDWOOD REMOVALS
('000 cubic metres, excl. bark, FAO estimates)

	2004	2005	2006
Sawlogs, veneer logs and logs for sleepers	828	952	952
Other industrial wood	246	246	246
Fuel wood	3,445	3,438	3,424
Total	4,519	4,636	4,622

Source: FAO.

SAWNWOOD PRODUCTION
('000 cubic metres, incl. railway sleepers)

	2003	2004	2005
Coniferous (softwood)*	12	12	12
Broadleaved (hardwood)	800*	414	476
Total*	812	426	488

* FAO estimate(s).
2006: Figures assumed to be unchanged from 2005 (FAO estimates).
Source: FAO.

Fishing

('000 metric tons, live weight)

	2003	2004	2005
Capture*	29.4	20.9	22.3
Clupeoids	2.6	2.1	2.2
Marlins, sailfishes, etc.	1.0	0.7	1.1
Tuna-like fishes	1.4	1.7	1.8
Common dolphinfish	4.0	2.3	3.2
Sharks, rays, skates, etc.	10.2	3.9	4.4
Other marine fishes	3.7	3.9	3.8
Aquaculture	20.5	24.7	24.0
Tilapias	14.9	19.0	17.6
Whiteleg shrimp	5.1	5.1	5.7
Total catch*	49.9	45.6	46.4

* FAO estimates.
Source: FAO.

Industry

SELECTED PRODUCTS
('000 metric tons, unless otherwise indicated)

	2002	2003	2004
Raw sugar	361	358	—
Kerosene	5	0	1
Distillate fuel oils	143	173	157
Residual fuel oils	240	224	127
Bitumen	4	32	25
Cement	1,200	1,320	1,300
Electric energy (million kWh)	7,485	7,566	8,210

Source: UN, *Industrial Commodity Statistics Yearbook*.

Finance

CURRENCY AND EXCHANGE RATES

Monetary Units
100 céntimos = 1 Costa Rican colón.

Sterling, Dollar and Euro Equivalents (31 December 2007)
£1 sterling = 997.894 colones;
US $1 = 498.100 colones;
€1 = 733.253 colones;
10,000 Costa Rican colones = £10.02 = $20.08 = €13.64.

Average Exchange Rate (colones per US $)
2005 477.787
2006 511.302
2007 516.617

GENERAL BUDGET
(million colones)

Revenue*	2002	2003	2004
Current revenue	1,349,078	1,562,667	1,794,630
Taxation	1,227,910	1,413,526	1,633,393
Income tax	185,613	233,103	268,079
Social security contributions	400,750	444,834	505,521
Taxes on property	29,567	43,114	53,748
Taxes on goods and services	541,147	620,191	713,261
Taxes on international trade	60,271	71,942	92,360
Other taxes	10,561	342	424
Other current revenue	132,069	146,941	160,648
Current transfers	−10,901	2,200	589
Capital revenue	−2,920	7,692	−3,387
Total	1,346,158	1,570,359	1,791,243

Expenditure†	2002	2003	2004
Current expenditure	1,404,855	1,579,434	1,813,270
Wages and salaries	566,892	648,913	736,421
Social security contributions	2,480	1,956	3,316
Other purchases of goods and services	192,865	197,655	234,256
Interest payments	261,863	299,148	334,995
Internal	213,044	239,064	261,342
External	48,817	60,085	73,653
Current transfers	380,755	431,762	504,283
Capital expenditure	149,954	160,821	138,121
Investment	114,462	125,300	98,242
Capital transfers	35,492	35,521	39,879
Total	1,554,810	1,740,254	1,951,392

* Excluding grants received (million colones): 58,924 in 2002; 64,150 in 2003; 69,745 in 2004.
† Excluding lending minus repayments (million colones): 3,483 in 2002; 3,705 in 2003; 1,627 in 2004.

Note: Figures represent the consolidated accounts of central and local government activities.

INTERNATIONAL RESERVES
(US $ million at 31 December)

	2004	2005	2006
Gold (national valuation)	0.02	0.02	0.02
IMF special drawing rights	0.13	0.04	0.04
Reserve position in IMF	31.06	28.59	30.09
Foreign exchange	1,890.61	2,284.02	3,084.45
Total	1,921.82	2,312.67	3,114.60

Source: IMF, *International Financial Statistics*.

MONEY SUPPLY
('000 million colones at 31 December)

	2004	2005	2006
Currency outside banks	205.6	247.1	305.1
Demand deposits at commercial banks	837.6	1,058.8	1,489.9
Total money (incl. others)	1,046.7	1,310.4	1,963.2

Source: IMF, *International Financial Statistics*.

COST OF LIVING
(Consumer Price Index; base: January 1995 = 100)

	2004	2005	2006
Food, beverages and tobacco	287.0	329.9	379.1
Clothing and footwear	176.7	185.8	197.4
Housing	257.1	301.8	326.2
Medical care	349.2	380.0	415.8
Transport	338.5	393.3	470.5
Leisure and education	244.5	267.6	293.6
All items (incl. others)	276.4	319.0	354.8

NATIONAL ACCOUNTS
(million colones at current prices)

National Income and Product

	2005	2006*	2007*
GDP in purchasers' values	9,511,600	11,515,368	13,554,148
Net primary incomes from abroad	−377,996	−377,778	−412,728
Gross national income	9,133,604	11,137,590	13,141,420
Less consumption of fixed capital	588,023	703,364	827,894
Net national income	8,545,581	10,434,226	12,313,527
Net current transfers	129,381	178,663	243,543
Gross national disposable income	8,674,962	10,612,888	12,557,070

* Preliminary figures.

Expenditure on the Gross Domestic Product

	2005	2006*	2007*
Government final consumption expenditure	1,316,361	1,561,470	1,829,833
Private final consumption expenditure	6,362,388	7,652,758	8,880,881
Increase in stocks	567,806	745,585	537,658
Gross fixed capital formation	1,787,194	2,299,332	2,926,828
Total domestic expenditure	10,033,749	12,259,145	14,175,200
Exports of goods and services	4,626,382	5,629,361	6,563,345
Less Imports of goods and services	5,148,531	6,373,137	7,184,396
GDP in purchasers' values	9,511,600	11,515,368	13,554,148
GDP at constant 1991 prices	1,892,473	2,021,410	2,099,060

* Preliminary figures.

COSTA RICA

Gross Domestic Product by Economic Activity

	2005	2006*	2007*
Agriculture, hunting, forestry and fishing	752,769	929,268	1,020,589
Mining and quarrying	14,578	23,725	26,661
Manufacturing	1,871,922	2,236,136	2,592,820
Electricity, gas and water	235,866	241,458	284,060
Construction	390,989	512,680	681,898
Trade, restaurants and hotels	1,687,027	2,046,324	2,378,351
Transport, storage and communications	841,952	1,025,485	1,209,706
Finance and insurance	532,161	649,189	790,322
Real estate	315,425	344,042	381,727
Other business services	399,041	521,888	650,759
Public administration	354,477	414,794	480,593
Other community, social and personal services	1,603,559	1,896,801	2,226,174
Sub-total	8,999,766	10,841,790	12,723,660
Less Imputed bank service charge	405,828	489,484	582,522
GDP at basic prices	8,593,938	10,352,304	12,141,138
Taxes, *less* subsidies, on products	917,662	1,163,063	1,413,011
GDP in purchasers' values	9,511,600	11,515,368	13,554,148

* Preliminary figures.

BALANCE OF PAYMENTS
(US $ million)

	2004	2005	2006
Exports of goods f.o.b.	6,369.7	7,099.6	8,067.5
Imports of goods f.o.b.	−7,791.0	−9,242.0	−10,810.8
Trade balance	−1,421.3	−2,142.4	−2,743.3
Exports of services	2,241.8	2,621.2	2,955.4
Imports of services	−1,384.5	−1,505.3	−1,611.6
Balance on goods and services	−563.9	−1,026.5	−1,399.5
Other income received	144.5	234.5	340.0
Other income paid	−588.8	−449.4	−408.0
Balance on goods, services and income	−1,008.2	−1,241.4	−1,467.5
Current transfers received	371.2	470.6	586.1
Current transfers paid	−158.7	−200.1	−237.0
Current balance	−795.8	−971.0	−1,118.3
Capital account (net)	11.5	—	0.4
Direct investment abroad	−60.6	43.0	−98.1
Direct investment from abroad	793.8	861.0	1,469.1
Portfolio investment assets	53.1	−680.7	−509.3
Portfolio investment liabilities	−239.5	—	—
Other investment assets	−308.7	141.4	654.6
Other investment liabilities	233.5	507.9	323.1
Net errors and omissions	63.7	155.7	293.1
Overall balance	−248.8	57.2	1,014.7

Source: IMF, *International Financial Statistics*.

External Trade

PRINCIPAL COMMODITIES
(US $ million)

Imports c.i.f.	2004	2005	2006
Food and live animals	436.9	422.8	583.5
Mineral products	782.9	1,015.3	1,583.6
Basic manufactures	279.8	301.0	482.3
Chemicals and related products	929.9	1,062.7	1,321.3
Plastic materials and manufactures	566.1	676.8	933.2
Leather, hides and furs	59.7	73.6	61.4
Paper, paperboard and manufactures	26.9	32.1	48.5
Wood pulp and other fibrous materials	386.1	409.0	677.3
Silk, cotton and textile fibres	587.0	568.8	607.3
Footwear, hats, umbrellas, etc.	58.2	66.2	83.6
Stone manufactures, etc.	99.7	107.7	187.7
Natural and cultured pearls	34.8	46.4	56.4
Common metals and manufactures	615.0	652.0	1,114.4
Machinery and electrical equipment	2,615.0	3,300.6	3,905.5
Transport equipment	446.5	498.8	608.6
Optical and topographical apparatus and instruments etc.	245.2	265.6	295.4
Total (incl. others)	8,292.2	9,640.1	12,740.2

Exports f.o.b.	2004	2005	2006
Food and live animals	1,419.0	1,774.4	2,026.6
Mineral products	16.5	49.7	57.6
Basic manufactures	526.7	577.3	726.3
Chemicals and related products	409.7	429.3	472.9
Plastic materials and manufactures	292.9	355.7	392.0
Leather, hides and furs	83.7	88.2	79.9
Paper, paperboard and manufactures	34.4	45.7	46.1
Wood pulp and other fibrous materials	123.9	142.4	172.9
Silk, cotton and textile fibres	550.2	530.1	514.5
Stone manufactures, etc.	67.5	72.8	87.4
Natural and cultured pearls	32.3	53.7	83.3
Common metals and manufactures	180.9	223.1	306.2
Machinery and electrical equipment	1,771.8	2,127.5	2,690.3
Transport equipment	18.2	24.7	31.6
Optical and topographical apparatus and instruments, etc.	546.5	580.6	685.4
Total (incl. others)	6,439.8	7,150.7	8,453.2

PRINCIPAL TRADING PARTNERS
(US $ million)

Imports c.i.f.	2004	2005	2006
Brazil	351.1	405.8	490.0
China, People's Rep.	282.8	411.8	543.0
Colombia	287.8	271.3	332.6
Germany	184.3	165.6	190.9
Guatemala	158.7	182.9	289.5
Japan	515.1	569.2	602.8
Korea, Republic	125.3	174.4	242.7
Mexico	418.5	470.9	664.4
USA	3,717.3	3,833.3	4,860.3
Venezuela	327.9	466.8	663.6
Total (incl. others)	8,292.2	9,641.0	12,740.2

COSTA RICA

Exports f.o.b.	2004	2005	2006
China, People's Rep.	161.7	240.7	557.7
El Salvador	188.9	198.1	235.0
Germany	270.5	213.1	198.4
Guatemala	257.2	283.5	319.1
Honduras	186.3	220.1	258.9
Mexico	190.1	193.4	189.3
Netherlands	331.8	450.4	509.6
Nicaragua	228.6	275.1	298.9
USA	2,848.2	2,872.6	3,304.9
Total (incl. others)	6,439.8	7,150.7	8,453.2

Transport

ROAD TRAFFIC
(motor vehicles in use at 31 December)

	2002	2003	2004
Private cars	367,832	581,247	620,992
Buses and coaches	12,891	18,516	20,950
Goods vehicles	191,315	195,449	199,506
Road tractors	25,842	n.a.	n.a.
Motorcycles and mopeds	91,883	61,273	64,947

Source: IRF, *World Road Statistics*.

SHIPPING
Merchant Fleet
(registered at 31 December)

	2004	2005	2006
Number of vessels	14	16	15
Total displacement ('000 grt)	4.6	4.9	3.6

Source: Lloyd's Register-Fairplay, *World Fleet Statistics*.

International Sea-borne Freight Traffic
('000 metric tons)

	1996	1997	1998
Goods loaded	3,017	3,421	3,721
Goods unloaded	3,972	4,522	5,188

Source: Ministry of Public Works and Transport.

CIVIL AVIATION
(scheduled services)

	2003	2004	2005
Kilometres flown (million)	19.7	24.4	26.9
Passengers carried ('000)	584	n.a.	n.a.
Passenger-km (million)	1,671.3	2,173.0	2,305.8
Total ton-km (million)	120	n.a.	n.a.

Source: UN, mostly Economic Commission for Latin America and the Caribbean, *Statistical Yearbook*.

Tourism

FOREIGN TOURIST ARRIVALS BY COUNTRY OF ORIGIN

	2003	2004	2005
Canada	54,656	74,212	86,906
Colombia	26,645	26,786	27,130
El Salvador	33,892	38,264	44,873
France	23,606	23,467	24,365
Germany	29,151	34,154	38,523
Guatemala	35,174	40,166	37,771
Honduras	23,004	25,540	27,719
Italy	18,361	19,483	20,726
Mexico	46,113	47,130	50,330
Netherlands	24,665	21,905	24,173
Nicaragua	163,632	191,398	231,712
Panama	56,490	63,956	72,730
Spain	34,442	42,381	49,218
United Kingdom	23,019	24,158	26,917
USA	510,751	633,640	758,134
Total (incl. others)	1,238,692	1,452,926	1,679,051

Tourism receipts (US $ million, incl. passenger transport): 1,424 in 2003; 1,586 in 2004; 1,804 in 2005 (Source: World Tourism Organization).

Communications Media

	2004	2005	2006
Telephones ('000 main lines in use)	1,343.2	1,388.5	1,351.2
Mobile cellular telephones ('000 subscribers)	923.1	1,101.0	1,443.7
Personal computers ('000 in use)	1,014	930*	n.a.
Internet users	885	922.5	1,214.4
Broadband subscribers ('000)	27.9	46.7	59.1

* Estimate.

Radio receivers ('000 in use): 3,045 in 1999.
Television receivers ('000 in use): 930 in 2000.
Facsimile machines (number in use): 8,500 in 1997.
Daily newspapers: 7 in 2004.
Non-daily newspapers: 42 in 2004.
Book production: 1,464 titles (excluding pamphlets) in 1998.

Sources: UNESCO, *Statistical Yearbook*, UN, *Statistical Yearbook*, International Telecommunication Union.

Education

(2005, unless otherwise indicated)

	Institutions*	Teachers	Males	Females	Total
Pre-primary	2,705	6,741	52,205†	50,134†	102,339†
Primary	4,007	25,399	280,527	261,560	542,087
Secondary	708	16,355‡	173,529	173,715	347,244
General	n.a.	14,100‡	143,649	142,765	286,414
Vocational	n.a.	2,594	29,880	30,950	60,830
Tertiary	52§	4,494‡	50,573	60,144	110,717

* 2005.
† 2004.
‡ 2003, estimated figure.
§ 1999.

Source: mainly UNESCO Institute for Statistics.

Adult literacy rate (UNESCO estimates): 94.9% (males 94.7%; females 95.1%) in 2000 (Source: UNESCO Institute for Statistics).

Directory

The Constitution

The present Constitution of Costa Rica was promulgated in November 1949. Its main provisions are summarized below:

GOVERNMENT

The government is unitary: provincial and local bodies derive their authority from the national Government. The country is divided into seven Provinces, each administered by a Governor who is appointed by the President. The Provinces are divided into Cantons, and each Canton into Districts. There is an elected Municipal Council in the chief city of each Canton, the number of its members being related to the population of the Canton. The Municipal Council supervises the affairs of the Canton. Municipal government is closely regulated by national law, particularly in matters of finance.

LEGISLATURE

The government consists of three branches: legislative, executive and judicial. Legislative power is vested in a single chamber, the Legislative Assembly (Asamblea Legislativa), which meets in regular session twice a year—from 1 May to 31 July, and from 1 September to 30 November. Special sessions may be convoked by the President to consider specified business. The Assembly is composed of 57 deputies elected for four years. The chief powers of the Assembly are to enact laws, levy taxes, authorize declarations of war and, by a two-thirds' majority, suspend, in cases of civil disorder, certain civil liberties guaranteed in the Constitution.

Bills may be initiated by the Assembly or by the Executive and must have three readings, in at least two different legislative periods, before they become law. The Assembly may override the presidential vote by a two-thirds' majority.

EXECUTIVE

The executive branch is headed by the President, who is assisted by the Cabinet. If the President should resign or be incapacitated, the executive power is entrusted to the First Vice-President; next in line to succeed to executive power are the Second Vice-President and the President of the Legislative Assembly.

The President sees that the laws and the provisions of the Constitution are carried out, and maintains order; has power to appoint and remove cabinet ministers and diplomatic representatives, and to negotiate treaties with foreign nations (which are, however, subject to ratification by the Legislative Assembly). The President is assisted in these duties by a Cabinet, each member of which is head of an executive department.

ELECTORATE

Suffrage is universal, compulsory and secret for persons over the age of 18 years.

DEFENCE

The Costa Rican Constitution has a clause outlawing a national army. Only by a continental convention or for the purpose of national defence may a military force be organized.

The Government

HEAD OF STATE

President: Oscar Arias Sánchez (took office 8 May 2006).
First Vice-President: Laura Chincilla Miranda.

THE CABINET
(April 2008)

Minister of the Presidency: Rodrigo Arias Sánchez.
First Vice-President and Minister of Justice: Laura Chincilla Miranda.
Minister of Planning: Roberto Javier Gallardo Núñez.
Minister of Finance: Guillermo Zúñiga.
Minister of Foreign Relations: Bruno Stagno Ugarte.
Minister of Foreign Commerce: Marco Vinicio Ruiz.
Minister of Public Security: Jeanina del Vecchio.
Minister of Production: Marco Vargas Díaz.
Minister of the Environment and Energy: Dr Roberto Dobles Mora.
Minister of Labour: Francisco Morales.
Minister of Public Education: Leonardo Garnier.
Minister of Public Health: Dr María Luisa Avila Agüero.
Minister of Housing and Poverty: Fernando Zumbado Jiménez.
Minister of Public Works and Transport: Karla González Carvajal.
Minister of Science and Technology: Eugenia Flores Vindas.
Minister of Culture, Youth and Sport: María Elena Carballo.
Minister of Tourism: Carlos Ricardo Benavides.
Minister of Agriculture and Livestock: Marco Vargas Díaz.

MINISTRIES

Ministry of Agriculture and Livestock: Antigüo Colegio La Salle, Sabana Sur, Apdo 10094, 1000 San José; tel. 231-5311; fax 232-2103; e-mail sunii@mag.go.cr; internet www.mag.go.cr.
Ministry of Culture, Youth and Sport: Avdas 3 y 7, Calles 11 y 15, frente al parque España, San José; tel. 255-3188; fax 233-7066; e-mail mincjd@mcjd.go.cr; internet www.mcjdcr.go.cr.
Ministry of the Environment and Energy: Avdas 8 y 10, Calle 25, Apdo 10104, 1000 San José; tel. 233-4533; fax 257-0697; e-mail prensa@minae.go.cr; internet www.minae.go.cr.
Ministry of Finance: Edif. Antigüo Banco Anglo, Avda 2a, Calle 3a, San José; tel. 257-9333; fax 255-4874; e-mail webmaster1@hacienda.go.cr; internet www.hacienda.go.cr.
Ministry of Foreign Commerce: Apdo 28, 1007 Centro Colón, San José; tel. 299-4700; fax 255-3281; e-mail pep@comex.go.cr; internet www.comex.go.cr.
Ministry of Foreign Relations: Avda 7 y 9, Calle 11 y 13, Apdo 10027, 1000 San José; tel. 223-7555; fax 257-6597; e-mail despacho.ministro@rree.go.cr; internet www.rree.go.cr.
Ministry of Housing and Poverty: Paseo de los Estudiantes, Apdo 222, 1002 San José; tel. 202-7900; fax 202-7910; e-mail info@mivah.go.cr; internet www.mivah.go.cr.
Ministry of Justice: 50 m norte de la Clínica Bíblica, frente a la Escuela M. García Flamenco, 1000 San José; tel. 280-9054; fax 234-7959; e-mail justicia@gobnet.go.cr; internet www.mj.go.cr.
Ministry of Labour: Edif. Benjamín Núñez, 4°, Barrio Tournón, Apdo 10133, 1000 San José; tel. 257-8211; internet www.ministrabajo.go.cr.
Ministry of Planning: Avdas 3 y 5, Calle 4, Apdo 10.127, 1000 San José; tel. 281-2700; fax 253-6243; e-mail pnd@ns.mideplan.go.cr; internet www.mideplan.go.cr.
Ministry of Production: Del Restaurante Princesa Marina 100 m sur, 100 m oeste y 50 m norte, Barrio La Guaria, Moravia, San José; tel. 240-5222; fax 297-1741; e-mail informacion@meic.go.cr; internet www.meic.go.cr.
Ministry of Public Education: Edif. Antigua Embajada, Apdo 10087, 1000 San José; tel. 256-8132; fax 248-1763; e-mail minieduc@sol.racsa.co.cr; internet www.mep.go.cr.
Ministry of Public Health: Calle 16, Avda 6 y 8, Apdo 10123, 1000 San José; tel. 223-0333; fax 255-4997; e-mail prensams@netsalud.sa.cr; internet www.ministeriodesalud.go.cr.
Ministry of Public Security: Apdo 55, 4874 San José; tel. 227-4866; fax 226-6581; internet www.msp.go.cr.
Ministry of Public Works and Transport: Plaza González Víquez, Calles 9 y 11, Avda 20 y 22, Apdo 10176, 1000 San José; tel. 523-2000; fax 255-0242; internet www.mopt.go.cr.
Ministry of Science and Technology: 1.3 km al norte de la Embajada Americana, Apdo 5589, 1000 San José; tel. 290-1790; fax 290-4967; e-mail micit@micit.go.cr; internet www.micit.go.cr.
Ministry of Tourism: San José.

President and Legislature

PRESIDENT

Election, 5 February 2006

Candidate	Votes cast	% of votes
Oscar Arias Sánchez (PLN)	664,551	40.92
Ottón Solís Fallas (PAC)	646,382	39.80
Otto Guevara Guth (ML)	137,710	8.48
Ricardo Toledo (PUSC)	57,655	3.55
Antonio Alvarez Desanti (UPC)	39,557	2.44
Total (incl. others)*	1,623,992	100.00

* In addition, there were 30,422 spoiled votes and 8,834 blank votes cast.

COSTA RICA

ASAMBLEA LEGISLATIVA
General Election, 5 February 2006

Party	% of votes cast	Seats
Partido Liberación Nacional (PLN)	36.54	25
Partido Acción Ciudadana (PAC)	25.34	18
Movimiento Libertario (ML)	9.17	6
Partido Unidad Social Cristiana (PUSC)	7.82	4
Others*	21.13	4
Total	**100.00**	**57**

*The remaining seats were allocated to four small, independent parties.

Election Commission

Tribunal Supremo de Elecciones (TSE): Apdo 2163, 1000 San José; tel. 287-5555; e-mail secretariatse@tse.go.cr; internet www.tse.go.cr; f. 1949; independent; Pres. Luis Antonio Sobrado González; Exec. Dir Fernando Víquez Jiménez.

Political Organizations

The following parties contested the February 2006 election at a national level.

Alianza Democrática Nacionalista (ADN): Contiguo a casa 37, Barrio La Favorita, Pavas, San José; tel. 232-8762; fax 220-3041; e-mail info@adn.co.cr; internet www.adn.co.cr; f. 2005; Pres. José Miguel Villalobas Umaña; Sec. Emilia María Rodríguez Arias.

Movimiento Libertario (ML): Of. de Cabinas San Isidro, Barrio Los Yoses Sur, Apdo 4674, 1000 San José; tel. 280-0044; fax 281-0044; internet www.libertario.org; f. 1994; Pres. Otto Guevara Guth; Sec.-Gen. Ronaldo Alfaro García.

Partido Acción Ciudadana (PAC): 25 San Pedro, 425 m sur del Templo Parroquial, San José; tel. 281-2727; fax 280-6640; e-mail pac2002@racsa.co.cr; internet www.pac.or.cr; f. 2000; centre party; Pres. Epsy Campbell Barr.

Partido Fuerza Democrática (FD): Edif. Colón, Apdo 1129, 1007 San José; tel. 258-7207; fax 258-7204; f. 1992 as coalition; later became national party; Pres. Marco Nuñez González; Sec.-Gen. Vladimir de la Cruz de Lemos.

Partido Integración Nacional (PIN): Edif. Nortesa, Of. 1, 3°, 100 m sur del Museo de Arte, Formas y Sonidos, San Pedro de Montes de Oca, San José; tel. 220-3300; fax 225-5091; e-mail waltermunoz@costarricense.cr; f. 1996; Pres. Dr Walter Muñoz Céspedes; Sec.-Gen. Marlyn Bendaña Valverde.

Partido Liberación Nacional (PLN): Mata Redonda, 125 m oeste del Ministerio de Agricultura y Ganadería, Casa Liberacionista José Figueres Ferrer, Apdo 10051, 1000 San José; tel. 232-5133; fax 231-4097; e-mail secregeneralpln@ice.co.cr; internet www.pln.or.cr; f. 1952; social democratic party; affiliated to the Socialist International; 500,000 mems; Pres. Francisco Antonio Pacheco Fernández; Sec.-Gen. Dr René Castro Salazar.

Partido Patria Primero: 400 m norte de la Toyota Purdy Motor, Paseo Colón, San José; tel. 221-5353; fax 258-7475; Pres. Juan José Vargas Fallas; Sec. Wilberth Hernández Vargas.

Partido Renovación Costarricense (PRC): Centro Educativo Instituto de Desarrollo de Inteligencia, Hatillo 1, Avda Villanea, Apdo 31, 1300 San José; tel. 254-3651; fax 252-3270; e-mail jimmysos@costarricense.cr; f. 1995; Pres. Justo Orozco Alvarez; Vice-Pres. Rafael Matamoros Mesén.

Partido Rescate Nacional: De la Iglesia Católica de San Pedro de Montes de Oca 150 m al oeste, contiguo al restaurante El Farolito, San José; tel. 234-9569; fax 285-3282; e-mail delgadorojas@racsa.co.cr; f. 1996; Pres. Fabio Enrique Delgado Hernández; Sec.-Gen. Alejandro López Martínez.

Partido Unidad Social Cristiana (PUSC): Del Restaurante Kentucky Fried Chicken 75 m al sur, frente a la Embajada de España, Paseo Colón, Apdo 10095, 1000 San José; tel. 248-2470; fax 280-2998; e-mail partidounidad@racsa.co.cr; f. 1983; Pres. Luis Fishman Zonzinski; Sec.-Gen. Xinia Carvajal Salazar.

Partido Vanguardia Popular: 11 Calle Fallas, 50 m sur de la plaza de deportes, Ciudadela Cucubres, Apdo 585, 2400 San José; tel. 225-8300; fax 259-4106; e-mail upvargas@sol.racsa.co.cr; internet www.vanguardiapopular.org; f. 1995 as Partido Pueblo Unido; Pres. Trino Barrantes Araya; Sec.-Gen. Humberto Elías Vargas Carbonell.

Unión Para el Cambio (UPC): Ultima casa a la izquierda, 675 m sur del Banco Nacional, Barrio Roosevelt, Montes de Oca, San José; tel. 280-0006; fax 524-0534; e-mail info@upc.or.cr; internet www.upc.or.cr; f. 2005; Pres. Antonio Alvarez Desanti; Sec.-Gen. Rocío Alvarez Olaso.

Unión Nacional: Frente a la Asociación China, Barrio Francisco Peralta, San José; tel. 256-1125; fax 253-8248; Pres. Arturo Acosta Mora; Sec.-Gen. Hernán Ricardo Zamora Rojas.

Unión Patriótica (UP): 200 m norte del Centro Cultural Costarricense Norteamericano, Barrio Escalante, San José; tel. 243-2050; fax 551-0542; Pres. José Miguel Corrales Bolaños; Sec.-Gen. Rafael Angel Varela Granados.

Diplomatic Representation

EMBASSIES IN COSTA RICA

Argentina: Curridabat, Apdo 1963, 1000 San José; tel. 234-6520; fax 283-9983; e-mail embarg@racsa.co.cr; Ambassador Juan José Arcuri.

Belgium: Los Yoses, 4a entrada, 25 m sur, Apdo 3725, 1000 San José; tel. 225-6633; fax 225-0351; e-mail sanjose@diplobel.be; internet www.diplobel.org/costarica; Ambassador Baron Olivier Gilles de Pélichy.

Bolivia: Barrio Rohrmoser 669, Apdo 84810, 1000 San José; tel. 296-3747; fax 232-7292; e-mail embocr@racsa.co.cr; Ambassador Martín Callisaya Coaquira.

Brazil: Edif. Torre Mercedes, 6°, Apdo 10132, 1000 San José; tel. 295-6875; fax 295-6874; e-mail embajador@embrasil.co.cr; Ambassador Hildebrando Tadeu Nascimento Valadares.

Canada: Oficentro Ejecutivo La Sabana, Edif. 5, 3°, detrás de la Contraloría, Centro Colón, Apdo 351, 1007 San José; tel. 242-4400; fax 242-4410; e-mail sjcra@international.gc.ca; internet www.sanjose.gc.ca; Ambassador Neil Reeder.

Chile: Los Yoses, del Automercado Los Yoses 225 m sur, Apdo 10102, 1000 San José; tel. 280-0037; fax 253-7016; e-mail echilecr@racsa.co.cr; internet www.embachile.co.cr; Ambassador Mendoza Negri Gonzalo.

China, People's Republic: De la casa de D. Oscar Arias, 100 m sur y 50 m este, Rohrmoser, Pavas, Apdo 1518, 1200 San José; tel. 291-4811; fax 291-4820; Ambassador Wang Xiaoyuan.

Colombia: Barrio Dent de Taco Bell, San Pedro, Apdo 3154, 1000 San José; tel. 283-6871; fax 283-6818; e-mail esanjose@cancilleria.gov.co; Ambassador Luis Guillermo de San Francisco Fernández Correa.

Czech Republic: 75 m oeste de la entrada principal del Colegio Humboldt, Apdo 12041, 1000 San José; tel. 296-5671; fax 296-5595; e-mail sanjose@embassy.mzv.cz; internet www.mzv.cz/sanjose; Ambassador Milan Jakobec.

Dominican Republic: McDonald's de Curridabat 400 sur, 90 m este, Apdo 4746, 1000 San José; tel. 283-8103; fax 280-7604; e-mail embdominicanacr@racsa.co.cr; Ambassador Adonaida Medina Rodríguez.

Ecuador: Edif. de la esq. sureste del Museo Nacional, 125 m al este, Avda 2, Calles 19 y 21, Apdo 1374, 1000 San José; tel. 232-1503; fax 232-1503; e-mail cecusanjose@mmrree.gov.ec; internet www.consuladoecuadorsj.com; Ambassador Dr Juan Leoro Almeida.

El Salvador: Paseo Colón, Calle 30, Avda 1, No 53, Apdo 1378, 1000 San José; tel. 257-7855; fax 257-7683; e-mail embasacr@sol.racsa.co.cr; Ambassador Milton José Colindres Uceda.

France: Carretera a Curridabat, del Indoor Club 200 m sur y 25 m oeste, Apdo 10177, 1000 San José; tel. 234-4167; fax 234-4195; e-mail sjfrance@sol.racsa.co.cr; internet www.ambafrance-cr.org; Ambassador Jean-Paul Monchau.

Germany: Barrio Rohrmoser, de la Casa de Oscar Arias 200 m norte, 75 m este, Apdo 4017, 1000 San José; tel. 290-9091; fax 231-6403; e-mail info@embajada-alemana-costarica.org; internet www.embajada-alemana-costarica.org; Ambassador Volker Fink.

Guatemala: De Pops Curridabat 500 m sur y 30 m este, 2a Casa Izquierda, Apdo 328, 1000 San José; tel. 291-6208; fax 290-4111; e-mail costarica@minex.gob.gt; Ambassador Juan José Barrios Taracena.

Holy See: Urb. Rohrmoser, Sabana Oeste, Centro Colón, Apdo 992, 1007 San José (Apostolic Nunciature); tel. 232-2128; fax 231-2557; e-mail nuapcr@racsa.co.cr; Apostolic Nuncio Most Rev. Osvaldo Padilla (Titular Archbishop of Pia).

Honduras: Pavas, del Parque de la Amistad en Rohrmoser, 100 m sur y 50 m este, Apdo 2239, 1000 San José; tel. 231-1642; fax 253-2209; e-mail embhoncr@embajadahonduras.co.cr; internet www.sre.hn/costarica.html; Ambassador Gen. (retd) Alvaro Romero.

Israel: Edif. Centro Colón, 11°, Calle 38 Paseo Colón, Apdo 5147, 1000 San José; tel. 221-6444; fax 257-0867; e-mail ambassador.sec@

COSTA RICA

sanjose.mfa.gov.il; internet sanjose.mfa.gov.il; Ambassador EHUD MOSHE EITAM.

Italy: Los Yoses, 5a entrada, Apdo 1729, 1000 San José; tel. 224-6574; fax 225-8200; e-mail ambasciata.sanjose@esteri.it; internet www.ambsanjose.esteri.it; Ambassador LEONARDO SAMPOLI.

Japan: Oficentro Ejecutivo La Sabana, Edif. 7, 3°, detrás de la Contraloría, Sabana Sur, Apdo 501, 1000 San José; tel. 232-1255; fax 231-3140; e-mail embjapon@sol.racsa.co.cr; internet www.cr.emb-japan.go.jp; Ambassador HIDEKAZU YAMAGUCHI.

Korea, Republic: Oficentro Ejecutivo La Sabana, Edif. 2, 3°, Sabana Sur, Apdo 838, 1007 San José; tel. 220-3160; fax 220-3168; e-mail koreasec@sol.racsa.co.cr; internet cri.mofat.go.kr; Ambassador CHO BYOUNG-LIP.

Mexico: Avda 7, No 1371, Apdo 10107, 1000 San José; tel. 257-0633; fax 258-2437; e-mail residencia@embamexico.or.cr; internet portal.sre.gob.mx/costarica; Ambassador MARÍA CARMEN OÑATE MUÑOZ.

Netherlands: Los Yoses, Avda 8, Calles 35 y 37, Apdo 10285, 1000 San José; tel. 296-1490; fax 296-2933; e-mail nethemb@racsa.co.cr; internet www.nethemb.or.cr; Ambassador S. T. BLANKHART.

Nicaragua: Edif. Trianón, Avda Central 250, Barrio la California, Apdo 1382, 1000 San José; tel. 221-2884; fax 221-3036; e-mail embanic@sol.racsa.co.cr; Ambassador HAROLD FERNANDO RIVAS REYES.

Panama: Del San Pedro de Montes de Oca, Apdo 103, 2050 San José; tel. 257-3241; fax 257-4864; e-mail panaembacr@racsa.co.cr; Ambassador LUIS E. VERGARA.

Peru: Del Colegio de Igenieros y Arquitectos, 350 m al norte, Urb. Freses, Curridabat, Apdo 4248, 1000 San José; tel. 253-4671; fax 253-0457; e-mail embajadaperu.costarrica@gmail.com; Ambassador OSCAR ALBERTO GUTIÉRREZ LA MADRID.

Poland: De la Iglesia Santa Teresita 300 m este, 3307, Barrio Escalante, Apdo 664, 2010 San José; tel. 234-7411; fax 234-7900; e-mail embajpolonia1@racsa.co.cr; internet www.polonia-emb-cr.com/indes.php; Ambassador ANDRZEJ BRAITER.

Russia: Curridabat, Lomas de Ayarco Sur, de la carretera a Cartago, 1a entrada, 100 m sur, Apdo 6340, 1000 San José; tel. 256-9181; fax 221-2054; e-mail emrusa@racsa.co.cr; Ambassador VALERII DMITRIEVICH NIKOLAYENKO.

Spain: Calle 32, Paseo Colón, Avda 2, Apdo 10150, 1000 San José; tel. 222-1933; fax 222-4180; e-mail embespcr@correo.mae.es; Ambassador ARTURO REIG TAPIA.

Switzerland: Paseo Colón, Centro Colón, Apdo 895, 1007 San José; tel. 221-4829; fax 255-2831; e-mail sjc.vertretung@eda.admin.ch; Ambassador GABRIELA NÜTZI SULPIZIO.

United Kingdom: Edif. Centro Colón, 11°, Apdo 815, 1007 San José; tel. 258-2025; fax 233-9938; e-mail britemb@racsa.co.cr; internet www.britishembassycr.com; Ambassador TOM KENNEDY.

Uruguay: Avda 14, Calles 35 y 37, Apdo 3448, 1000 San José; tel. 288-3424; fax 288-3070; e-mail embajrou@racsa.co.cr; Ambassador BRUGNINI GARCÍA LAGOS.

USA: Calle 120 Avda 0, Pavas, Apdo 920, 1200 San José; tel. 519-2000; fax 220-2305; e-mail info@usembassy.or.cr; internet sanjose.usembassy.gov; Ambassador MARK LANGDALE.

Venezuela: Barrio Escalante, de la Iglesia de Santa Teresita 300 m este y 50 m norte, de la rotonda del Farolito 50 m sur, San José; tel. 234-0728; fax 253-1453; e-mail info@embavencr.com; internet www.embajadadevenezuelaencostarica.org; Ambassador (vacant).

Judicial System

Ultimate judicial power is vested in the Supreme Court, the justices of which are elected by the Assembly for a term of eight years, and are automatically re-elected for an equal period, unless the Assembly decides to the contrary by a two-thirds vote. The Supreme Court justices sit in four courts, the First Court (civil, administrative, agrarian and commercial matters), the Second Court (employment and family), the Third Court (penal) and the Constitutional Court.

There are, in addition, appellate courts, criminal courts, civil courts and special courts. The jury system is not used. Judges of the lower courts are appointed by the Supreme Court's administrative body, the Supreme Council. The Supreme Council's members are elected by the Supreme Court.

The Supreme Court
Sala Constitucional de la Corte Suprema de Justicia, Apdo 5, 1003 San José; tel. 295-3000; fax 257-0801; e-mail sala4-informacion@poder-judicial.go.cr; internet www.poder-judicial.go.cr.

President of the Supreme Court: LUIS PAULINO MORA MORA.

Supreme Council
Members: MIRIAM ANCHÍA PANIAGUA, MARVIN MARTÍNEZ FERNÁNDEZ, MILENA CONEJO AGUILAR, ROCÍO CERVANTES BARRANTES.

Justices of the First Court: Dr ANABELLE LEÓN FEOLI, Dr OSCAR GONZÁLEZ CAMACHO, Dr ROMÁN SOLÍS ZELAYA, Dr CARMENMARÍA ESCOTO FERNÁNDEZ, LUIS GUILLERMO RIVAS LOÁICIGA.

Justices of the Second Court: ORLANDO AGUIRRE GÓMEZ, Dr BERNARDO VAN DER LAAT ECHEVERRÍA, ZARELA VILLANUEVA MONGE, Dr JULIA VARELA ARAYA, ROLANDO VEGA ROBERT.

Justices of the Third Court: JOSÉ MANUEL ARROYO GUTIÉRREZ, JESÚS RAMÍREZ QUIRÓS, RODRIGO CASTRO MONGE, ALFONSO CHAVES RAMÍREZ, MAGDA PEREIRA VILLALOBOS.

Justices of the Constitutional Court: Dr LUIS FERNANDO SOLANO CARRERA, ANA VIRGINIA CALZADA MIRANDA, LUIS PAULINO MORA MORA, Dr FERNANDO CRUZ CASTRO, ADRIÁN VARGAS BENAVIDES, Dr ERNESTO JINESTA LOBO, Dr GILBERT ARMIJO SANCHO.

Religion

Under the Constitution, all forms of worship are tolerated. Roman Catholicism is the official religion of the country. Various Protestant churches are also represented.

CHRISTIANITY
The Roman Catholic Church
Costa Rica comprises one archdiocese and seven dioceses. At 31 December 2005 Roman Catholics represented some 83.0% of the total population.

Bishops' Conference
Conferencia Episcopal de Costa Rica, Apdo 7288, 1000 San José; tel. 221-3053; fax 221-6662; e-mail seccecor@racsa.co.cr; internet www.iglesiacr.org.

f. 1977; Pres. Most Rev. JOSÉ FRANCISCO ULLOA ROJAS.

Archbishop of San José de Costa Rica: Most Rev. HUGO BARRANTES UREÑA, Arzobispado, Apdo 497, 1000 San José; tel. 258-1015; fax 221-2427; e-mail curiam@racsa.co.cr.

The Anglican Communion
Costa Rica comprises one of the five dioceses of the Iglesia Anglicana de la Región Central de América.

Bishop of Costa Rica: Rt Rev. HÉCTOR MONTERROSO, Apdo 10520, 1000 San José; tel. 225-0790; fax 253-8331; e-mail iarca@amnet.co.cr.

Other Churches
Federación de Asociaciones Bautistas de Costa Rica: Apdo 1631, 2100 Guadalupe; tel. 253-5820; fax 253-4723; e-mail fabcr2@icc.co.cr; internet www.fabcr.org; f. 1946; represents Baptist churches; Pres. JOSÉ ARMANDO SOTO VILLEGAS.

Iglesia Evangélica Luterana de Costa Rica (Evangelical Lutheran Church of Costa Rica): Apdo 1512, Pavas, 1200 San José; tel. 231-3345; fax 291-0986; e-mail iglevlutcostarica@gmail.com; internet www.ielcor.org; f. 1955; 600 mems; Pres. Rev. RENÉ LAMMER.

Iglesia Evangélica Metodista de Costa Rica (Evangelical Methodist Church of Costa Rica): Apdo 5481, 1000 San José; tel. 236-2171; fax 236-5921; e-mail iglesiametodistacr@yahoo.com; internet www.geocities.com/iglesiametodistacr; autonomous since 1973; affiliated to the United Methodist Church; 6,000 mems; Pres. Bishop LUIS F. PALOMO.

BAHÁ'Í FAITH
National Spiritual Assembly of the Bahá'ís of Costa Rica: Apdo 553, 1150 La Uruca; tel. 520-2127; fax 296-1033; e-mail secretaria.nacional@bahaicr.org; f. 1942.

The Press
DAILIES
Al Día: Llorente de Tibás, Apdo 10138, 1000 San José; tel. 247-4640; fax 247-4665; e-mail aldia@nacion.co.cr; internet www.aldia.co.cr; f. 1992; morning; independent; Dir EDGAR FONSECA; Editor MÓNICA GÓMEZ; circ. 60,000.

Boletín Judicial: La Uruca, Apdo 5024, San José; tel. 231-5222; internet www.boletinjudicial.go.cr; f. 1878; journal of the judiciary; circ. 2,500.

Diario Extra: Calle 4, Avda 4, Apdo 177, 1009 San José; tel. 223-6666; fax 223-6101; internet www.diarioextra.com; e-mail dzuniga@

COSTA RICA

diarioextra.com; f. 1978; morning; independent; Dir WILLIAM GÓMEZ VARGAS; circ. 120,000.

La Gaceta: La Uruca, Apdo 5024, San José; tel. 231-5222; internet www.imprenal.go.cr; f. 1878; official gazette; Dir NELSON LOAIZA; circ. 5,300.

El Heraldo: 400 m al este de las oficinas centrales, Apdo 1500, San José; tel. 222-6665; fax 222-3039; e-mail info@elheraldo.net; internet www.elheraldo.net; f. 1994; morning; independent; Chief Editor FRANCISCO GAMBOA; Dir ERWIN KNOHR; circ. 30,000.

La Nación: Llorente de Tibás, Apdo 10138, 1000 San José; tel. 247-4747; fax 247-5002; e-mail cacortes@nacion.com; internet www.nacion.com; f. 1946; morning; independent; Dir ALEJANDRO URBINA; circ. 120,000.

La Prensa Libre: Calle 4, Avda 4, Apdo 177, 1009 San José; tel. 223-6666; fax 233-6831; e-mail plibre@prensalibre.co.cr; internet www.prensalibre.co.cr; f. 1889; evening; independent; Dir ANDRÉS BORRASÉ SANOU; circ. 56,000.

La República: Barrio Tournón, Guadalupe, Apdo 2130,1000 San José; tel. 522-3300; fax 257-0401; e-mail info@larepublica.co.cr; internet www.larepublica.co.cr; f. 1950; reorganized 1967; morning; independent; Dir ALBERTO MUÑOZ; Pres. FRED BLASER; circ. 61,000.

PERIODICALS

Abanico: Calle 4, Avda 4, Apdo 177, 1009 San José; tel. 223-6666; fax 223-4671; internet www.prensalibre.co.cr; weekly supplement of La Prensa Libre; women's interests; circ. 50,000.

Actualidad Económica: San José; tel. 224-2411; fax 224-1528; e-mail jcarvajal@actualidad.co.cr; internet www.actualidad.co.cr; Dir NORA RUIZ.

Contrapunto: La Uruca, Apdo 7, 1980 San José; tel. 231-3333; f. 1978; fortnightly; publ. of Sistema Nacional de Radio y Televisión; Dir-Gen. BELISARI SOLANO; circ. 10,000.

Eco Católico: Calle 22, Avdas 3 y 5, Apdo 1064, San José; tel. 222-8391; fax 256-0407; e-mail info@ecocatolico.com; internet www.ecocatolico.org; f. 1931; Catholic weekly; Dir ARMANDO ALFARO; circ. 20,000.

El Financiero: Grupo Nación, Edif. Subsidiarias, Llorente de Tibás, 185-2120 Guadalupe; tel. 247-5555; fax 247-5177; e-mail capital@financiero.co.cr; internet www.financiero.co.cr; f. 1995; Dir YANANCY NOGUERA CALDERÓN; Chief Editor JOSÉ DAVID GUEVARA MUÑOZ.

INCAE Business Review: Campus Walter Kissling Gam, Alajuela; tel. 224-6598; internet www.incae.ac.cr/ES/publicaciones; f. 2002; publ. by INCAE business school; Editorial Dir JOHN STANHAM; Dir MARLENE DE ESTRELLA LÓPEZ.

Perfil: Llorente de Tibás, Apdo 1517, 1100 San José; tel. 247-4345; fax 247-5110; e-mail perfil@nacion.co.cr; f. 1984; fortnightly; women's interest; Dir CAROLINA CARAZO BARRANTES; circ. 16,000.

Revista Comunicación: Escuela de Ciencias del Lenguaje, Instituto Tecnológico de Costa Rica, Apdo 159-7050, Cartago; tel. 550-2015; fax 550-2034; e-mail recom@itcr.ac.cr; internet www.itcr.ac.cr/revistacomunicacion; f. 1977; 2 a year; publ. by Instituto Tecnológico de Costa Rica; Dir TERESITA ZAMORA PICADO.

Revista Medicina Vida y Salud: Colegio de Médicos y Cirujanos de Costa Rica, Sabana Sur, Apdo 548, 1000 San José; tel. 232-3433; fax 232-2406; e-mail medicos@racsa.co.cr; internet www.medicos.sa.cr; f. 1957; journal of the Colegio de Médicos; monthly; Pres. Dr MINOR VARGAS BALDARES; Dir and Editor Dr ILSE CERDA MONTERO; circ. 5,000.

Semanario Universidad: San José; tel. 207-5355; fax 207-4774; e-mail semana@cariari.ucr.ac.cr; internet www.semanario.ucr.ac.cr; f. 1970; weekly; general; Dir LAURA MARTÍNEZ QUESADA; circ. 15,000.

The Tico Times: Calle 15, Avda 8, Apdo 4632, 1000 San José; tel. 258-1558; fax 223-6378; e-mail info@ticotimes.net; internet www.ticotimes.net; f. 1956; weekly; in English; Dir DERY DYER; circ. 15,210.

Tiempos de Costa Rica: 100 m sur de Ferretería El Mar, San Pedro, San José; tel. 280-2332; fax 280-6840; e-mail admin@tdm.com; internet www.tdm.com; f. 1996; Costa Rican edition of the international Tiempos de Mundo; Dir and Publr FRANK I. GROW; Editor-in-Chief CARLOS VERDECIA.

PRESS ASSOCIATIONS

Colegio de Periodistas de Costa Rica: Sabana Este, Calle 42, Avda 4, Apdo 5416, San José; tel. 233-5850; fax 223-8669; e-mail ejecutiva@colegiodeperiodistas.org; internet www.colper.or.cr; f. 1969; 1,447 mems; Pres. HERIBERTO VALVERDE.

Sindicato Nacional de Periodistas: Sabana Este, Calle 42, Avda 4, Apdo 5416, San José; tel. 222-7589; fax 258-3229; e-mail sindicato@colper.or.cr; f. 1970; 200 mems; Sec.-Gen. SERGIO FERNÁNDEZ SOLANO.

Publishers

Alef Editores: Apdo 146, 1017 San José; tel. 255-0202; fax 222-7878; e-mail alefreading@racsa.co.cr; Dir JOSÉ SUCCAR.

Caribe-Betania Editores: Apdo 1.307, San José; tel. 222-7244; e-mail info@editorialcaribe.com; internet www.caribebetania.com; f. 1949 as Editorial Caribe; merged with Editorial Betania in 1992 and name changed as above; division of Thomas Nelson Publrs; religious textbooks; Exec. Vice-Pres. TAMARA L. HEIM; Dir JOHN STROWEL.

Editorial Costa Rica: Costado oeste del cementerio, Guadalupe de Goicoechea, Apdo 10010, San José; tel. 255-2323; fax 253-5091; e-mail difusion@editorialcostarica.com; internet www.editorialcostarica.com; f. 1959; govt-owned; cultural; Gen. Man. MARÍA ISABEL BRENES; Dir Dr CLAUDIO MONGE PEREIRA.

Editorial Fernández Arce: 50 este de Sterling Products, la Paulina de Montes de Oca, Apdo 2410, 1000 San José; tel. 224-5201; fax 225-6109; internet www.fernandez-arce.com; f. 1967; textbooks for primary, secondary and university education; Dir Dr MARIO FERNÁNDEZ LOBO.

Editorial INBio: San José; tel. 507-8183; e-mail editorial@inbio.ac.cr; internet www.inbio.ac.cr/editorial; part of Instituto Nacional de Biodiversidad; Man. FABIO ROJAS.

Editorial de la Universidad Autónoma de Centro América (UACA): Apdo 7637, 1000 San José; tel. 234-0701; fax 224-0391; e-mail info@uaca.ac.cr; internet www.uaca.ac.cr; f. 1981; Editor GUILLERMO MALAVASSI.

Editorial de la Universidad Estatal a Distancia (EUNED): Apdo 474, 2050 San Pedro; tel. 253-2121; fax 234-9138; e-mail editoria@uned.ac.cr; internet www.uned.ac.cr; f. 1979; Pres. Dr LUIS ALBERTO CAÑAS ESCALANTE; Dir RENÉ MUIÑOZ GUAL.

Editorial Universitaria Centroamericana (EDUCA): Ciudad Universitaria Rodrigo Facio, San Pedro, Montes de Oca, Apdo 64, 2060 San Pedro; tel. 224-3727; fax 253-9141; e-mail educa@sp.cusa.ac.cr; f. 1969; organ of the CSUCA; science, literature, philosophy; Dir ANITA DE FORMOSO.

Grupo Editorial Norma: Zona Franca Metropolitana Local 7B, Barreal de Heredia, Heredia; tel. 293-1333; fax 239-3947; e-mail gerencia@farben.co.cr; internet www.norma.com; Man. Editor ALEXANDER OBONAGA.

Grupo Santillana: La Uruca 78, 1150 San José; tel. 220-4242; fax 220-1320; e-mail santilla@santillana.co.cr; internet www.gruposantillana.com; Dir ELSA MORALES CORDERO.

Imprenta Nacional: San José; tel. 296-9570; Dir-Gen. NELSON LOAIZA.

Librería Lehmann, Imprenta y Litografía, Ltda: Calles 1 y 3, Avda Central, Apdo 10011, San José; tel. 522-4848; fax 233-0713; e-mail servicio@librerialehman.com; internet www.librerialehmann.com; f. 1896; general fiction, educational, textbooks; Man. Dir ANTONIO LEHMANN STRUVE.

Trejos Hermanos Sucesores, SA: Curridabat, Apdo 10096, San José; tel. 224-2411; e-mail henry@trejoshnos.com; internet www.trejoshnos.com; f. 1912; general and reference; Pres. ALVARO TREJOS; Man. HENRY CHAMBERLAIN.

PUBLISHING ASSOCIATION

Cámara Costarricense del Libro: Paseo de los Estudiantes, Apdo 1571, 1002 San José; tel. 225-1363; fax 252-4297; e-mail ccl@libroscr.com; internet www.libroscr.com; f. 1978; Pres. OSCAR CASTILLO.

Broadcasting and Communications

TELECOMMUNICATIONS

Autoridad Reguladora de los Servicios Públicos (ARESEP): regulatory body for the telecommunications industry, public utilities and transport (see Trade and Industry—Utilities).

Cámara Costarricense de Telecomunicaciones (CCTEL): Edif. Centro Colón, Apdo 591, 1007 San José; tel. and fax 255-3422; e-mail cctel@cctel.org; internet cctel.org; Pres. MIGUEL LEÓN S.

Instituto Costarricense de Electricidad (ICE): govt agency for power and telecommunications (see Trade and Industry—Utilities).

Radiográfica Costarricense, SA (RACSA): Avda 5, Calle 1, Frente a Edif. Numar, Apdo 54, 1000 San José; tel. 287-0087; fax 287-0379; e-mail racsaenlinea@racsa.co.cr; internet www.racsa.co.cr; f. 1921; state telecommunications co, owned by ICE; Gen. Man. ROGER CARVAJAL BONILLA.

COSTA RICA
Directory

RADIO

Asociación Costarricense de Información y Cultura (ACIC): Apdo 365, 1009 San José; f. 1983; independent body; controls private radio stations; Pres. JUAN FEDERICO MONTEALEGRE MARTÍN.

Cámara Nacional de Radio (CANARA): Paseo de los Estudiantes, Apdo 1583, 1002 San José; tel. 256-2338; fax 255-4483; e-mail info@canara.org; internet www.canara.org; f. 1947; Pres. JAVIER CASTRO VARGAS; Exec. Dir JUAN SEPÚLVEDA TRONCOSO.

Control Nacional de Radio (CNR): Edif. García Pinto, 2°, Calle 33, Avdas Central y Primera, Barrio Escalante, Apdo 1344, 1011 San José; tel. 524-0455; fax 524-0454; e-mail controlderadio@ice.co.cr; internet www.controlderadio.go.cr; f. 1954; governmental supervisory department; Dir MELVIN MURILLO ALVAREZ.

Non-commercial

Faro del Caribe: Apdo 2710, 1000 San José; tel. 286-1755; fax 227-1725; e-mail juntadirectiva@farodelcaribe.org; internet www.farodelcaribe.org; f. 1948; religious and cultural programmes in Spanish and English; Man. GEOVANNY CALDERÓN CASTRO.

Radio FCN Sonora (Family Christian Network): Apdo 60-2020, Zapote, San José; tel. 209-8000; fax 293-7993; e-mail info@fcnradio.com; internet www.fcnradio.com; Dir Dr DECAROL WILLIAMSON; Man. ALEXANDER PORRAS.

Radio Fides: Avda 4, Curia Metropolitana, Apdo 5079, 1000 San José; tel. 258-1415; fax 233-2387; e-mail emilliom@radiofides.co.cr; internet www.radiofides.co.cr; f. 1952; Roman Catholic station; Dir EMILIO OTÁROLA.

Radio Nacional: 1 km oeste del Parque Nacional de Diversiones, La Uruca, Apdo 7, 1980 San José; tel. 231-7983; fax 220-0070; e-mail rnacional@sinart.go.cr; internet www.sinart.co.cr; f. 1978; Exec. Pres. JUAN CARLOS CHAVARRÍA; Dir ANA JANE CAMACHO.

Radio Santa Clara: Santa Clara, San Carlos, Apdo 221, Ciudad Quesada, Alajuela; tel. and fax 460-6666; e-mail radio@radiosantaclara.org; internet www.radiosantaclara.org; f. 1984; Roman Catholic station; Dir Rev. MARCO A. SOLÍS V.

Radio Universidad: Ciudad Universitaria Rodrigo Facio, San Pedro, Montes de Oca, Apdo 2060, 1000 San José; tel. 207-4727; fax 207-4832; e-mail radiouncr@cariari.ucr.ac.cr; internet www.radiouniversidad.ucr.ac.cr; f. 1949; classical music; Dir CARLOS MORALES.

Commercial

There are about 80 commercial radio stations, including:

Grupo Columbia: 200 m oeste de la Casa Presidencial, Zapote, Apdo 168-2020, San José; tel. 224-7272; fax 225-9275; e-mail columbia@columbia.co.cr; internet www.radiodos.com; operates Radio Columbia, Radio Dos, Radio 955 Jazz; Dir YASHÍN QUESADA ARAYA; Gen. Man. MIGUEL MONGE.

Cadena Musical: Apdo 854, 1000 San José; tel. 257-2789; fax 233-9975; internet www.radiomusical.com; f. 1954; operates Radio Musical, Radio Bomba; Gen. Man. JORGE JAVIER CASTRO.

Grupo Centro: Apdo 6133, San José; tel. 240-7591; fax 236-3672; e-mail rcentro@racsa.co.cr; f. 1971; operates Radio Centro 96.3 FM, Radio 820 AM, Televisora Guanacasteca Channels 16 and 28; Dir ROBERTO HERNÁNDEZ RAMÍREZ.

Radio Chorotega: Conferencia Episcopal de Costa Rica, Casa Cural de Santa Cruz, Apdo 92, 5175 Guanacaste; tel. and fax 680-0447; f. 1983; Roman Catholic station; Dir Rev. HUGO BRENES VILLALOBOS.

Radio Eco: Apdo 585, 1007 Centro Colón, San José; tel. 220-1001; fax 290-0970; e-mail info@radioeco.com; internet www.radioeco.com; Dir RICARDO ZAMORA; Gen. Man. LUIS ENRIQUE ORTIZ VAGLIO.

Radio Emaús: San Vito, Coto Brus; tel. and fax 773-3101; e-mail radioemaus@racsa.co.cr; f. 1962; Roman Catholic station; religious programmes; Dir Rev. MIGUEL ANGEL BERGANZA.

Radio Monumental: Avda Central y 2, Calle 2, Apdo 800, 1000 San José; tel. 296-6093; fax 231-1210; e-mail ventas@monumental.co.cr; internet www.monumental.co.cr; f. 1929; operates 8 radio stations: Radio Monumental, Radio ZFM, Radio Reloj, Punto Cinco, EXA FM, Radio Fabulosa, Radio Favorita and 670 AM; Gen. Man. TERESA MARÍA CHÁVES ZAMORA.

Radio Musical: Apdo 854, 1000 San José; tel. 257-2789; fax 233-9975; e-mail info@radiomusical.com; internet www.radiomusical.com; f. 1951.

Radio Sendas de Vida: San José; tel. 248-1148; fax 233-1259; e-mail info@radiosendas.com; internet www.radiosendas.com; f. 1982; Christian station; Pres. CARLOS UMAÑA R.

TELEVISION
Government-owned

Sistema Nacional de Radio y Televisión Cultural (SINART): 1 km al oeste del Parque Nacional de Diversiones La Uruca, Apdo 7, 1980 San José; tel. 231-3333; fax 231-6604; e-mail sinart@racsa.co.cr; internet www.sinart.go.cr; f. 1977; cultural; Dir-Gen. BELISARI SOLANO.

Commercial

Alphavisión (Canal 19): Detrás de la Iglesia de Santa María y Griega, Carretera a Desamparados, Apdo 1490, San José; tel. 226-9333; fax 226-9095; f. 1987; Gen. Man. CECILIA RAMÍREZ.

Canal 54: Detrás de la Iglesia Santa Marta, Carretera a Desamparados, San José; tel. 286-3344; fax 231-3408; e-mail canalcr@sol.racsa.co.cr; f. 1996; Pres. ANTONIO ALEXANDRE GARCÍA.

Multivisión de Costa Rica, Ltda (Canal 9): 150 m oeste del Centro Comercial de Guadalupe, Apdo 4666, 1000 San José; tel. 233-4444; fax 221-1734; f. 1961; operates Radio Sistema Universal AM (f. 1956), Channel 9 (f. 1962), and FM (f. 1980); sold Channel 4 (f. 1964) to Repretel in 2000; Gen. Man. ARNOLD VARGAS.

Televisora de Costa Rica (Canal 7), SA (Teletica): Costado oeste Estadio Nacional, Apdo 3876, San José; tel. 232-2222; fax 231-6258; e-mail info@teletica.com; internet www.teletica.com; f. 1960; operates Channel 7; Pres. OLGA COZZA DE PICADO; Gen. Man. RENÉ PICADO COZZA.

Representaciones Televisivas Repretel (Canales 4, 6 y 11): Edif. Repretel, La Uruca del Hospital México, 300 m al oeste, Apdo 2869, 1000 San José; tel. 299-7200; fax 232-4203; e-mail info@repretel.com; internet www.repretel.com; f. 1993; Pres. FERNANDO CONTRERAS LÓPEZ; Gen. Man. JULIO MENA RIVERA; News Dir MARCELA ANGULO.

Finance

(cap. = capital; res = reserves; dep. = deposits; m. = million; brs = branches; amounts in colones, unless otherwise indicated)

BANKING
Central Bank

Banco Central de Costa Rica: Avdas Central y Primera, Calles 2 y 4, Apdo 10058, 1000 San José; tel. 243-3333; fax 243-4566; internet www.bccr.fi.cr; f. 1950; total assets 1,411,859.2m. (Nov. 2005); state-owned; Pres. Dr FRANCISCO DE PAULA GUTIÉRREZ GUTIÉRREZ; Man. ROY GONZÁLEZ ROJAS.

State-owned Banks

Banco de Costa Rica (BCR): Avdas Central y 2da, Calles 4 y 6, Apdo 10035, 1000 San José; tel. 287-9000; fax 255-0991; e-mail bancobcr@bancobcr.com; internet www.bancobcr.com; f. 1877; responsible for industry; cap. 53,323.6m., res 102,024.1m., dep. 1,176,153.0m. (Dec. 2006); Pres. VICTOR EMILIO HERRERA ARAUZ; Gen. Man. (vacant); 136 brs.

Banco Nacional de Costa Rica: Avda 1–3, Calle 4, Apdo 10015, 1000 San José; tel. 212-2000; fax 255-0270; e-mail bncr@bncr.fi.cr; internet www.bncr.fi.cr; f. 1914; responsible for the agricultural sector; cap. 39,765.4m., res 115,849.9m., dep. 1,905,220.4m. (Dec. 2006); state-owned; Pres. RODOLFO BRENES GÓMEZ; Gen. Man. GUILLERMO ENRIQUE HEYDEN QUINTERO; 125 brs.

Banco Popular y de Desarrollo Comunal: Calle 1, Avda 2, Apdo 10190, San José; tel. 257-5797; fax 255-1966; e-mail popularenlinea@bp.fi.cr; internet www.bancopopular.fi.cr; f. 1969; cap. 24,991.2m. (2003); Pres. ANA ISABEL SOLANO BRENES; Vice-Pres. OLGA QUIRÓS MCTAGGART.

Private Banks

Banco BAC San José, SA: Calle Central, Avdas 3 y 5, Apdo 5445, 1000 San José; tel. 295-9595; fax 222-7103; e-mail info@bancosanjose.fi.cr; internet www.bacsanjose.com; f. 1968; fmrly Bank of America, SA; cap. 22,289.0m., res 6,209.0m., dep. 402,736.2m. (Dec. 2006); Pres. ERNESTO CASTEGNARO ODIO; Gen. Man. GERARDO CORRALES BRENES.

Banco Banex, SA: Barrio Tournón, Diagonal a Ulacit, Apdo 7983, 1000 San José; tel. 287-1000; fax 287-1020; e-mail interna@banex.co.cr; internet www.banex.co.cr; f. 1981 as Banco Agroindustrial y de Exportaciones, SA; adopted present name in 1987; incorporated Banco Metropolitano in 2001 and Banco Bancrecen in 2002; cap. 19,127.4m., res 6,273.6m., dep. 345,587.6m. (Dec. 2006); Pres. ALBERTO VALLARINO; Gen. Man. SERGIO RUIZ; 33 brs.

Banco BCT, SA: 160 Calle Central, Apdo 7698, San José; tel. 212-8000; fax 222-3706; e-mail info@bct.fi.cr; internet www.bct.fi.cr; f. 1984; total assets 13,794m. (1999); merged with Banco del Comercio, SA in 2000; Pres. ANTONIO BURGUÉS; Gen. Man. LEONEL BARUCH.

Banco Cuscatlan de Costa Rica, SA: De La Rotonda Juan Pablo II, 150 m norte, Cantón Central, La Uruca, Apdo 6531, 1000 San José; tel. 299-0299; fax 296-0026; e-mail cuscatlan@cuscatlancr.com;

internet www.bancocuscatlan.com; f. 1984 as Banco de Fomento Agrícola; changed name to Banco BFA in 1994; changed name to above in 2000; cap. 12,698.9m., res 2,612.2m., dep. 226,216.7m. (Dec. 2006); Pres. ERNESTO ROHRMOSER GARCIA; Gen. Man. ALVARO ENRIQUE SABORIO LEGERS.

Banco Improsa, SA: 2985 Calle 29 y 31, Avda 5, Carmen, San José; tel. 257-0689; fax 223-7319; e-mail banimpro@sol.racsa.co.cr; internet www.improbank.com; Pres. JORGE MONGE.

Banco Interfin, SA: Calle 3, Avdas 2 y 4, Apdo 6899, San José; tel. 210-4000; fax 210-4510; e-mail webmaster@interfin.fi.cr; internet www.interfin.fi.cr; f. 1982; bought by Scotiabank in 2006; dep. 15,450.0m., res 2,312.1m., total assets 23,786.3m. (Dec. 2004); Pres. LUIS LUKOWIECKI; Gen. Man. Dr LUIS LIBERMAN.

Banco Lafise: De la Rotonda la Bandera, Barrio Escalante, 50 m oeste, Apdo 5099, 1000 San José; tel. 280-5555; fax 280-5090; e-mail info@lafise.fi.cr; internet www.lafise.fi.cr; f. 1974; owned by Grupo Lafise; cap. 3,403.6m., res 258.0m., total assets 3,983.1m. (Dec. 2004); Pres. ROBERTO J. ZAMORA LLANES; Gen. Man. GILBERTO SERRANO.

Banco Promérica, SA: Edif. Promérica, Sabana Oeste Carretera Principal a Pava, Apdo 1289, 1200 San José; tel. 519-8090; fax 232-5727; e-mail solucion@promerica.fi.cr; internet www.promerica.fi.cr; 21 brs; Chief Financial Officer GUSTAVO SALAZAR.

Banco Uno, SA: Blvd Rohrmoser, 30 m este de Plaza Mayor, San José; tel. 290-4001; fax 290-4000; e-mail bunocr@grupo-uno.com; internet www.bancouno.fi.cr; cap. 2,673.9m., res 171.3m. (Dec. 2005); Pres. Dr ERNESTO FERNÁNDEZ HOLMANN.

Citibank (Costa Rica), SA: Oficentro Plaza Roble, Edif. El Patio, 4°, Guachipelín de Escazú; tel. 201-0800; fax 201-8311; e-mail citibab@sol.racsa.co.cr; internet www.latam.citibank.com/corporate/lacrco/spanish/index.htm.

Scotiabank Costa Rica: Avda 1 Calles Central y 2, Apdo 5395, 1000, San José; tel. 287-8700; fax 255-3076; e-mail scotiacr@scotiabank.com; internet www.scotiabankcr.com; f. 1995; Gen. Man. BRIAN W. BRADY; 13 brs.

Banking Association

Asociación Bancaria Costarricense: San José; tel. 253-2889; fax 225-0987; e-mail abc@abc.fi.cr; internet www.abc.fi.cr; Pres. MARIO CASTILLO LARA.

STOCK EXCHANGE

Bolsa Nacional de Valores, SA: Edif. Cartagena, 4°, Calle Central, Avda Primera, Santa Ana, Apdo 6155, 1000 San José; tel. 204-4848; fax 204-4749; e-mail bnv@bnv.co.cr; internet www.bnv.co.cr; f. 1976; Pres. Dr ORLANDO SOTO ENRÍQUEZ; Gen. Man. JOSÉ RAFAEL BRENES.

INSURANCE

In 1998 the Legislative Assembly approved legislative reform effectively terminating the state monopoly of all insurance activities.

Caja Costarricense de Seguro Social: Apdo 10105, San José; tel. 295-2000; fax 222-1217; e-mail edoryan@ccss.sa.cr; internet www.info.ccss.sa.cr; accident and health insurance, state-owned; Exec. Pres. Dr EDUARDO DORYAN GARRÓN.

Instituto Nacional de Seguros: Calles 9 y 9 bis, Avda 7, Apdo 10061, 1000 San José; tel. 287-6000; fax 255-3381; e-mail contactenos@ins-cr.com; internet www.ins.go.cr; f. 1924; administers the state monopoly of insurance; services of foreign insurance companies may be used only by authorization of the Ministry of Finance, and only after the Instituto has certified that it will not accept the risk; Exec. Pres. Dr GUILLERMO CONSTENLA UMAÑA; Gen. Man. MARIANO CAMPOS SALAS.

Trade and Industry

GOVERNMENT AGENCIES

Instituto Nacional de Vivienda y Urbanismo (INVU): Apdo 2534, San José; tel. 221-5266; fax 223-4006; internet www.invu.go.cr; housing and town planning institute; Exec. Pres. ELADIO PRADO CASTRO; Vice-Pres. JOSÉ MANUEL JIMÉNEZ GÓMEZ.

Promotora del Comercio Exterior de Costa Rica (PROCOMER): Calle 40, Avdas Central y 3, Centro Colón, Apdo 1278, 1007 San José; tel. 299-4700; fax 299-4881; e-mail info@procomer.com; internet www.procomer.com; f. 1997 to improve international competitiveness by providing services aimed at increasing, diversifying and expediting international trade; Pres. MARCO VINICIO RUIZ; Dir ROBERTO CALVO.

DEVELOPMENT ORGANIZATIONS

Cámara de Azucareros: Calle 3, Avda Fernández Güell, Apdo 1577, 1000 San José; tel. 221-2103; fax 222-1358; e-mail crazucar@racsa.co.cr; internet www.camaraazucarera.org.mx; f. 1949; sugar growers; 16 mems; Pres. FEDERICO CHAVARRÍA K.

Cámara Nacional de Bananeros: Edif. Urcha, 3°, Calle 11, Avda 6, Apdo 10273, 1000 San José; tel. 222-7891; fax 233-1268; e-mail canaba@racsa.co.cr; f. 1967; banana growers; Pres. DIANA GUZMÁN CALZADA; Exec. Dir MARÍA DE LOS ANGELES VINDAS.

Cámara Nacional de Cafetaleros: Condominio Oroki 4D, La Uruca, Apdo 1310, San José; tel. and fax 296-8334; e-mail camcafe@ice.co.cr; f. 1948; 35 mems; coffee millers and growers; Pres. RODRIGO VARGAS RUÍZ; Exec. Dir GABRIELA LOBO H.

Central de Trabajadores de Costa Rica (CTCR): De Acueductos y Alcantarillados 175 m este, entre calles 11 y 13, Barrio Estudiante, San José; tel. 221-5697; fax 280-1187; f. 1984.

Corporación Bananera Nacional, SA (CORBANA): Zapote frente casa Presidencial, Apdo 6504, 1000 San José; tel. 224-4111; fax 234-9421; e-mail corbana@racsa.co.cr; internet www.corbana.co.cr; f. 1971; public company; cultivation and wholesale of agricultural produce, incl. bananas; Man. ROMANO ORLICH.

Costa Rican Investment and Development Board (CINDE): Edif. Los Balcones, Plaza Roble, 4°, Guachipelin, Ezcazú; tel. 201-2800; fax 201-2867; e-mail invest@cinde.org; internet www.cinde.or.cr; f. 1983; coalition for development of initiatives to attract foreign investment for production and export of new products; Chair. ALBERTO TREJOS; CEO EDNA CAMACHO.

Instituto del Café de Costa Rica: Calle 1, Avdas 18 y 20, Apdo 37, 1000 San José; tel. 243-7812; fax 222-2838; internet www.icafe.go.cr; e-mail promo@icafe.go.cr; f. 1933 to develop the coffee industry, to control production and to regulate marketing; Dir. GABRIEL GONZÁLEZ BEJARANO.

Sistema de Información del Sector Agropecuario: San José; tel. 296-2579; fax 296-1652; e-mail infoagro@mag.go.cr; internet www.infoagro.go.cr; dissemination of information to promote the agricultural sector.

CHAMBERS OF COMMERCE

Cámara de Comercio de Costa Rica: Urb. Tournón, 150 m noroeste del parqueo del Centro Comercial El Pueblo, Apdo 1.114, 1000 San José; tel. 221-0005; fax 223-157; e-mail servicio@camara-comercio.com; internet www.camara-comercio.com; f. 1915; 900 mems; Pres. CARLOS A. FEDERSPIEL PINTO; Sec. JULIO UGARTE TATUM.

Cámara de Industrias de Costa Rica: 350 m sur de la Fuente de la Hispanidad, San Pedro de Montes de Oca, Apdo 10003, San José; tel. 281-0006; fax 234-6163; e-mail cicr@cicr.com; internet www.cicr.com; Pres. JACK LIBERMAN GINSBURG; Vice-Pres. MAYI ANTILLÓN.

Unión Costarricense de Cámaras y Asociaciones de la Empresa Privada (UCCAEP): De McDonalds en Sabana Sur, 400 m al sur, 100 m al este, 25 m al sur, San José; tel. 290-5595; fax 290-5596; internet www.uccaep.or.cr; f. 1974; business fed; Pres. RAFAEL CARRILLO; Exec. Dir SHIRLEY SABORÍO.

INDUSTRIAL AND TRADE ASSOCIATIONS

Asociación de Empresas de Zonas Francas (AZOFRAS): Plaza Mayor, 2°, Pavas, San José; tel. 520-1635; fax 520-1636; e-mail azofras@racsa.co.cr; internet www.azofras.com; f. 1990; Pres. JORGE BRENES; Exec. Dir TIMOTHY SCOTT HALL.

Cámara Nacional de Agricultura y Agroindustria: 300 metros sur y 50 metros este de McDonalds, Plaza del Sol, Curridabat, San José; tel. 225-8245; fax 280-0969; e-mail cnaacr@sol.racsa.co.cr; internet www.cnaacr.com; f. 1947; Pres. ALVARO SÁENZ SABORÍO; Exec. Dir MÓNICA NAVARRO DEL VALLE.

Consejo Nacional de Producción: 125 m al sur de Yamuni La Sabana en Avda 10, Apdo 2205, San José; tel. 255-0056; fax 256-9625; e-mail sim@cnp.go.cr; internet www.mercanet.cnp.go.cr; f. 1948 to encourage agricultural and fish production and to regulate production and distribution of basic commodities; Pres. (vacant); Gen. Man. ZORAIDA FALLAS CORDERO.

Instituto de Desarrollo Agrario (IDA): Apdo 5054, 1000 San José; tel. 224-6066; internet www.ida.go.cr; Exec. Pres. MARCO VINICIO CORDERO QUESADA.

Instituto Mixto de Ayuda Social (IMAS): Calle 29, Avdas 2 y 4, Apdo 6213, San José; tel. 255-5555; fax 224-8783; e-mail gerencia_general@imas.go.cr; internet www.imas.go.cr; Pres. DIEGO VÍQUEZ LIZANO; Vice-Pres. MARÍA ISABEL CASTRO DURÁN.

Instituto Nacional de Fomento Cooperativo: Apdo 10103, 1000 San José; tel. 256-2944; fax 255-3835; e-mail info@infocoop.go.cr; internet www.infocoop.go.cr; f. 1973 to encourage the establishment of co-operatives and to provide technical assistance and credit facilities; Pres. VÍCTOR HUGO MORALES ZAPATA; Exec. Dir ANA PATRICIA JIMÉNEZ GÓMEZ.

COSTA RICA

UTILITIES

Regulatory Body

Autoridad Reguladora de los Servicios Públicos (ARESEP): Sabana Sur, 400 m oeste de la Contraloría General de la República, Apdo 936, 1000 San José; tel. 220-0102; fax 290-0374; internet www.aresep.go.cr; f. 1996; oversees telecommunications, public utilities and transport sectors; Regulator FERNANDO HERRERO ACOSTA.

Electricity

Cía Nacional de Fuerza y Luz, SA (CNFL): Calle Central y 1, Avda 5, Apdo 10026, 1000 San José; tel. 296-4608; fax 296-3950; internet www.cnfl.go.cr; f. 1941; electricity co; mem. of ICE Group; Pres. TEÓFILO DE LA TORRE ARGUELLO.

Instituto Costarricense de Electricidad (ICE) (Costa Rican Electricity Institute): Apdo 10032, 1000 San José; tel. 220-7720; fax 220-1555; e-mail ice-si@ice.co.cr; internet www.ice.co.cr; f. 1949; govt agency for power and telecommunications; Exec. Pres. PEDRO PABLO QUIRÓS CORTÉZ; Dir TEÓFILO DE LA TORRE ARGUELLO.

JASEC (Junta Administrativa del Servicio Eléctrico Municipal de Cartago): Apdo 179, 7050 Cartago; tel. 550-6800; fax 551-2115; e-mail agomez@jasec.co.cr; internet www.jasec.co.cr; f. 1964; Pres. ROLANDO RODRÍGUEZ BRENES.

Water

Instituto Costarricense de Acueductos y Alcantarillados: Avda Central, Calle 2, Apdo 5120, 1000 San José; tel. 257-8822; fax 222-2259; e-mail administrador@aya.go.cr; internet www.aya.go.cr; water and sewerage; Pres. RAFAEL VILLALTA.

TRADE UNIONS

Asociación Nacional de Empleados Públicos (ANEP): Apdo 5152, 1000 San José; tel. 257-8233; fax 257-8859; e-mail info@anep.or.cr; internet www.anep.or.cr; f. 1958; Sec.-Gen. ALBINO VARGAS BARRANTES.

Central del Movimiento de Trabajadores Costarricenses (CMTC) (Costa Rican Workers' Union): Calle 20, 75 m este de la Cinta Amarilla, Apdo 4137, 1000 San José; tel. 222-5893; fax 221-3353; e-mail cmtccr@racsa.co.cr; internet cmtcr.org; Pres. DENNIS CABEZAS BADILLA; Sec.-Gen. JOSÉ ANGEL OBANDO.

Central de Trabajadores de Costa Rica (CTCR): De Acueductos y Alcantarillados 175 m este, entre calles 11 y 13, Barrio Estudiante, San José; tel. 221-5697; fax 280-1187; f. 1984.

Confederación Costarricense de Trabajadores Democráticos (Costa Rican Confederation of Democratic Workers): Ofs Centrales del Banco Nacional, 13°, Apdo 2167, San José; tel. 223-7903; fax 212-2745; f. 1966; mem. of ITUC and ORIT; Sec.-Gen. OLGER CHAVES; 50,000 mems.

Confederación de Trabajadores Rerum Novarum (CTRN): Barrio Escalante, de la Rotonda el Farolito 250 m este, Apdo 31100, San José; tel. 283-4244; fax 234-2282; e-mail ctrnovan@racsa.co.cr; internet www.rerumnovarum.or.cr; Pres. RODRIGO AGUILAR; Sec.-Gen. GILBERT BROWN YOUNG.

Confederación Unitaria de Trabajadores (CUT): Calles 1 y 3, Avda 12, Casa 142, Apdo 186, 1009 San José; tel. 233-4188; fax 221-4709; e-mail mcalde@racsa.co.cr; f. 1980 from a merger of the Federación Nacional de Trabajadores Públicos and the Confederación General de Trabajadores; 53 affiliated unions; Sec.-Gen. MIGUEL MARÍN CALDERÓN; c. 75,000 mems.

The Consejo Permanente de los Trabajadores, formed in 1986, comprises six union organizations and two teachers' unions.

Transport

Autoridad Reguladora de los Servicios Públicos (ARESEP): regulatory body for the telecommunications industry, public utilities and transport (see Trade and Industry—Utilities).

Cámara Nacional de Transportes: 50 m norte y 15 m este de la antigua Embajada China, San Pedro de Montes de Oca, 2958-1000, San José; tel. 283-1820; fax 283-1712; e-mail canatram@racsa.co.cr; national chamber of transport; Exec. Dir JAVIER REYNA.

RAILWAYS

AmericaTravel: Edif. INCOFER, Avda 20, Calle 2, Apdo 246, San José; tel. 233-3300; fax 223-3311; e-mail americatravel@ice.co.cr; internet www.americatravelcr.com; operates weekend tourist trains between San José and Caldera; Gen. Man. JUAN PANIAGUA ZELEDÓN.

Instituto Costarricense de Ferrocarriles (INCOFER): Calle Central, Avda 22 y 24, Apdo 1, 1009 San José; tel. 222-8857; fax 222-6998; e-mail incofer@sol.racsa.co.cr; f. 1985; govt-owned; Pres. MIGUEL CARABAGUÍAZ; 471 km, of which 388 km are electrified.

INCOFER comprised:

División I: Atlantic sector running between Limón, Río Frío, Valle la Estrella and Siquirres. Main line of 109 km, with additional 120 km of branch lines, for tourists and the transport of bananas; services resumed in 1999.

División II: Pacific sector running from San José to Puntarenas and Caldera; 116 km of track, principally for transport of grain, iron and stone.

Note: In 1995 INCOFER suspended most operations, pending privatization, although some cargo transport continued. In 2006 commuter trains ran between San José and San Pedro (4 km) and San José and Pavas (6 km), while freight trains operated between San José and Caldera (91 km).

ROADS

In 2006 there were 35,332 km of roads, of which 24% were paved. In 2001 the construction of four major roads across the country began; the first road to be built was 74 km long, running from San José to San Ramón.

SHIPPING

Local services operate between the Costa Rican ports of Puntarenas and Limón and those of Colón and Cristóbal in Panama and other Central American ports. The multi-million dollar project at Caldera on the Gulf of Nicoya is now in operation as the main Pacific port; Puntarenas is being used as the second port. The Caribbean coast is served by the port complex of Limón/Moín. International services are operated by various foreign shipping lines. The Caldera and Puntarenas ports were opened up to private investment and operation from 2002.

Junta de Administración Portuaria y de Desarrollo Económico de la Vertiente Atlántica (JAPDEVA): Calle 17, Avda 7, Apdo 5.330, 1000 San José; tel. 795-4747; fax 795-0728; e-mail cthomas@japdeva.go.cr; internet www.japdeva.go.cr; state agency for the development of Atlantic ports; Exec. Pres. WALTER ROBINSON DAVIS; Gen. Man. DANNY MORRIS BRAUMLEY.

Instituto Costarricense de Puertos del Pacífico (INCOP): Calle 36, Avda 3, Apdo 543, 1000 San José; tel. 223-7111; fax 223-4348; e-mail pnd@ns.mideplan.go.cr; internet www.mideplan.go.cr/pnd/actores/sector_publico/incop; f. 1972; state agency for the development of Pacific ports; Exec. Pres. ENRIQUE MONTEALEGRE MARTÍ.

CIVIL AVIATION

Costa Rica has four international airports: Juan Santamaría Airport, the largest, 16 km from San José at El Coco, Tobías Bolaños Airport in Pavas, Daniel Oduber Quirós Airport, at Liberia, and Limón International.

Fly Latin America: San José; e-mail info@flylatinamerica.net; internet www.flylatinamerica.com; operates services to 9 destinations in Central and South America; Pres. CHARLES STRATFORD; Man. GERMAN NAVARRO.

Líneas Aéreas Costarricenses, SA (LACSA) (Costa Rican Airlines): Edif. Lacsa, La Uruca, Apdo 1.531, San José; tel. 290-2727; fax 232-4178; internet centralamerica.com/cr/lacsa/lacsa.htm; f. 1945; operates international services within Latin America and to North America.

Nature Air: Tobias Bolaños Airport, San José; tel. 299-6000; e-mail info@natureair.com; internet www.natureair.com; flights from San José to 18 domestic destinations.

Servicios Aéreos Nacionales, SA (SANSA): Paseo Colón, Centro Colón, Apdo 999, 1007 San José; tel. 248-1124; fax 255-2176; e-mail info@flysansa.com; internet www.flysansa.com; subsidiary of TACA; international, regional and domestic scheduled passenger and cargo services; Man. Dir CARLOS MANUEL DELGADO AGUILAR.

Tourism

Costa Rica boasts a system of nature reserves and national parks unique in the world, covering one-third of the country. The main tourist features are the Irazú and Poás volcanoes, the Orosí valley and the ruins of the colonial church at Ujarras. Tourists also visit San José, the capital, the Pacific beaches of Guanacaste and Puntarenas, and the Caribbean beaches of Limón. Some 1,679,051 tourists visited Costa Rica in 2005, while tourism receipts totalled US $1,804m. Most visitors came from the USA (53%). There were 379 hotels in Costa Rica in 2003.

Cámara Nacional de Turismo (Canatur): San José; tel. 234-6222; fax 253-8102; e-mail info@tourism.co.cr; internet www.canatur.org; Pres. GONZALO VARGAS.

Instituto Costarricense de Turismo (ICT): La Uruca, Costado Este del Puente Juan Pablo II, Apdo 777, 1000 San José; tel. 299-5880; fax 291-5675; internet www.visitcostarica.com; f. 1955; Exec. Pres. CARLOS RICARDO BENAVIDES; Gen. Man. ALLAN RENÉ FLORES MOYA.

CÔTE D'IVOIRE
(THE IVORY COAST)

Introductory Survey

Location, Climate, Language, Religion, Flag, Capital

The Republic of Côte d'Ivoire lies on the west coast of Africa, between Ghana to the east and Liberia to the west, with Guinea, Mali and Burkina Faso to the north. Average temperatures vary between 21°C and 30°C (70°F and 86°F). The main rainy season, May–July, is followed by a shorter wet season in October–November. The official language is French, and a large number of African languages are also spoken. At the time of the 1998 census it was estimated that some 34% of the population were Christians (mainly Roman Catholics), 27% Muslims, 15% followed traditional indigenous beliefs, and 3% practised other religions, while 21% had no religious affiliation. (However, it was thought that the proportion of Muslims was, in fact, significantly higher, as the majority of unregistered foreign workers in Côte d'Ivoire were believed to be Muslims.) The national flag (proportions 2 by 3) has three equal vertical stripes, of orange, white and green. The political and administrative capital is Yamoussoukro, although most government ministries and offices remain in the former capital, Abidjan, which is the major centre for economic activity.

Recent History

Formerly a province of French West Africa, Côte d'Ivoire achieved self-government, within the French Community, in December 1958. Dr Félix Houphouët-Boigny, leader of the Parti démocratique de la Côte d'Ivoire—Rassemblement démocratique africain (PDCI—RDA), became Prime Minister in 1959. The country became fully independent on 7 August 1960; a new Constitution was adopted in October 1960, and Houphouët-Boigny became President in November.

Until 1990 the PDCI—RDA was Côte d'Ivoire's only legal political party, despite constitutional provision for the existence of other political organizations. A high rate of economic growth, together with strong support from France, contributed, until the late 1980s, to the stability of the regime. However, the announcement in early 1990 of austerity measures precipitated an unprecedented level of unrest. In April Houphouët-Boigny appointed Alassane Ouattara, the Governor of the Banque centrale des états de l'Afrique de l'ouest (BCEAO, the regional central bank), to chair a special commission to formulate economic and political reforms. From May it was announced that hitherto unofficial political organizations were to be formally recognized.

Côte d'Ivoire's first contested presidential election was held on 28 October 1990. Houphouët-Boigny—challenged by Laurent Gbagbo, the candidate of the socialist Front populaire ivoirien (FPI)—was re-elected for a seventh term with the support of 81.7% of votes cast. In November the legislature, the Assemblée nationale, approved two constitutional amendments. The first authorized the President of the legislature to assume the functions of the President of the Republic, in the event of the presidency becoming vacant, until the expiry of the previous incumbent's mandate (an arrangement that had existed, on an interim basis, since October 1985, following the abolition of the post of Vice-President of the Republic). The second amendment provided for the appointment of a Prime Minister, who would be accountable to the President; Ouattara was subsequently designated premier. At legislative elections that month the PDCI—RDA returned 163 deputies to the 175-member Assemblée nationale; the FPI won nine seats, the Parti ivoirien des travailleurs (PIT) one, and two independent candidates were elected. Henri Konan Bédié, who had held the presidency of the legislature since 1980, was re-elected to that post.

The Government's response to the report of a commission of inquiry into student disturbances in May–June 1991, in which one student died, provoked renewed violence in early 1992, led by the outlawed Fédération estudiantine et scolaire de Côte d'Ivoire (FESCI). Houphouët-Boigny refused to subject the armed forces Chief of General Staff, Brig.-Gen. Robert Gueï, to disciplinary proceedings, despite the commission's conclusion that Gueï was ultimately responsible for violent acts perpetrated by forces under his command. In February Gbagbo was among more than 100 people arrested during a violent anti-Government demonstration in Abidjan, and in March was one of nine opposition leaders imprisoned under a new presidential ordinance that rendered political leaders responsible for violent acts committed by their supporters.

Houphouët-Boigny left Côte d'Ivoire in May 1993 to receive medical treatment in Europe. As the President's health failed, controversy arose over the issue of succession. Many senior politicians, including Ouattara and Gbagbo (both of whom were known to have presidential aspirations), asserted that the process defined in the Constitution effectively endorsed an 'hereditary presidency', since Bédié, like Houphouët-Boigny, was a member of the Akan ethnic group. Houphouët-Boigny died on 7 December. Bédié assumed the duties of President of the Republic with immediate effect. Ouattara initially refused to recognize Bédié's right of succession, but tendered his resignation two days later. Daniel Kablan Duncan, hitherto Minister-delegate to the Prime Minister, with responsibility for the Economy, Finance and Planning, was appointed as Prime Minister. Bédié's position was consolidated by his election to the chairmanship of the PDCI—RDA in April 1994. Disaffected members of the PDCI—RDA left the party in June to form what they termed a moderate, centrist organization, the Rassemblement des républicains (RDR); Ouattara formally announced his membership of the RDR in early 1995.

A new electoral code, adopted in December 1994, imposed new restrictions on eligibility for public office, notably stipulating that candidates for the presidency or for the Assemblée nationale be of direct Ivorian descent. The RDR protested that these restrictions would prevent Ouattara from contesting the presidency, since the former Prime Minister was of Burkinabè descent and would also be affected by the code's requirement that candidates had been continuously resident in Côte d'Ivoire for five years prior to seeking election.

In October 1995 the FPI (which was to have been represented by Gbagbo) and the RDR (whose Secretary-General, Djény Kobina, was to have replaced Ouattara as the party's candidate) announced their boycott of the forthcoming presidential election as long as the conditions were not 'clear and open'. Subsequent negotiations involving Bédié and opposition groups made no effective progress, and the presidential election took place, as scheduled, on 22 October 1995, following a week of violence in several towns. Bédié, with 95.3% of the valid votes cast, secured an overwhelming victory.

Prior to the legislative elections in November 1995, representatives of both the FPI and the RDR were appointed to the electoral commission, and both parties abandoned their threatened boycott of the poll. However, ongoing disturbances resulted in the postponement of polling in five constituencies, including the constituency that was to have been contested by Gbagbo; moreover, Kobina's candidacy was disallowed, on the grounds that he had been unable to prove direct Ivorian descent. In December the Constitutional Council annulled the results of the elections in three constituencies. The PDCI—RDA thus held 146 seats, the RDR 14, and the FPI nine, indicating a notable loss of support for the PDCI—RDA in the north in favour of the RDR.

In October 1995, shortly before the presidential election, Brig.-Gen. Gueï was replaced in his armed forces command and appointed as Minister of Employment and the Civil Service. The departures of Gueï and the former Minister of Defence, Léon Konan Koffi, from the Government in August 1996 were interpreted as an indication of Bédié's desire to remove from positions of influence figures connected with the insecurity prior to the 1995 elections. In January 1997 Gueï was dismissed from the army, having been found to have committed serious disciplinary offences in the discharge of his duties.

In June 1998 RDR and FPI deputies boycotted a vote in the Assemblée nationale that approved substantial amendments to the Constitution. The opposition objected, in particular, to provisions conferring wider powers on the Head of State, whose mandate was to be extended to seven years. Henceforth, candidates for public office were required to be Ivorian by birth, of direct Ivorian descent, and to have been continuously resident in Côte d'Ivoire for 10 years. The amendments included provisions for the establishment of an upper legislative chamber, the Sénat.

In August 1999 Ouattara was appointed to the newly created post of President of the RDR. Although he declared his intention to contest the 2000 presidential election, in October 1999 it was announced that his nationality certificate (which had been issued in September) had been annulled. In December a warrant was issued for Ouattara's arrest on charges of fraudulently procuring identity papers, although he had recently returned to France.

In December 1999 a mutiny by soldiers demanding salary increases, the payment of outstanding arrears and the reinstatement of Gueï as armed forces Chief of General Staff rapidly escalated into a *coup d'état*. On 24 December Gueï announced that he had assumed power at the head of a Comité national de salut public (CNSP), and that the Constitution and its institutions had been suspended. In January 2000 Bédié left Côte d'Ivoire; he subsequently sought refuge in France.

Gueï encountered considerable difficulty in achieving his stated objective of forming a broad-based government. The CNSP was at first perceived as being supportive of Ouattara. Consequently, the FPI (which had become increasingly distanced from the RDR) withdrew its nominees from the coalition Government appointed in early January 2000, although subsequent negotiations resulted in the party attaining a larger number of ministerial posts than any other. The PDCI—RDA declined to approve Gueï's appointment of two ministers from the party.

A draft Constitution, presented in May 2000, provoked considerable controversy, as it demanded that presidential candidates be of only Ivorian nationality and parentage. Seydou Elimane Diarra, an experienced diplomat and technocrat, and Minister of State, responsible for Governmental Co-ordination and the Planning of Development since January, was appointed as Prime Minister in mid-May. The revised Constitution was endorsed by 86.5% of votes cast in a referendum on 23–24 July, with turn-out estimated at 56%. Notably, all those involved in the *coup d'état* and members of the CNSP were granted immunity from prosecution.

In August 2000 Gueï announced that he would contest the forthcoming presidential election as an independent. In October the Supreme Court announced that 14 of the 19 presidential candidates—including Ouattara and Bédié—did not comply with the conditions of eligibility. Of the five candidates permitted to stand, only Gueï and Gbagbo were regarded as capable of eliciting popular support; allegations that the two men had undertaken a private agreement of co-operation had been encouraged by the increasingly prominent role of the FPI in Gueï's Council of Ministers. (In late September, following a further ministerial reorganization, the FPI had become the sole political party to be represented in the Government.)

The two weeks preceding the presidential election were characterized by heightened unrest, and a state of emergency was imposed. Nevertheless, voting proceeded on 22 October 2000. Preliminary results indicated that Gbagbo had received a greater percentage of votes cast than Gueï; however, on 24 October the Ministry of the Interior and Decentralization dissolved the national electoral commission and declared Gueï the winner of the election. The Government claimed that certain, unspecified, political parties had perpetrated electoral fraud, and announced that, following the readjustment of the results, Gueï, with 52.7% of the votes cast, had defeated Gbagbo, with 41.0%. Prime Minister Diarra resigned in protest at alleged fraudulence on 23 October. Two days later the head of the presidential guard withdrew his support for Gueï, after pro-Gbagbo demonstrations were held across the country. Following clashes between rival army factions in the military barracks in Abidjan, and a declaration of support for Gbagbo by the Chief of Staff of the Armed Forces, Gueï fled, and Gbagbo declared himself President.

According to official figures released by the electoral commission, and confirmed by the Supreme Court, Gbagbo had secured 59.4% of the valid votes cast, while Gueï had received 32.7%. However, a low rate of participation (an estimated 33.2% overall, but markedly lower in the largely Muslim and RDR-supporting regions in the north, as well as in Yamoussoukro and other strongholds of the PDCI—RDA) cast doubt on the legitimacy of Gbagbo's victory. Concern was raised that Gbagbo had voiced support, during his campaign, for the notion of strengthening national identity, or '*ivoirité*', in potentially inflammatory terms, similar to those used previously by Bédié. Gbagbo was inaugurated as President on 26 October 2000. In the following three days violent clashes between the security forces and RDR demonstrators demanding the annulment of the election resulted in 203 deaths, according to official figures.

On 27 October 2000 Gbagbo appointed a new Council of Ministers, comprising members of the FPI, the PDCI—RDA and the PIT. (The RDR stated that it would await legislative elections before participating in a coalition government.) Pascal Affi N'Guessan, the manager of Gbagbo's electoral campaign and a minister in the outgoing Government, was named as Prime Minister.

In early December 2000 the Supreme Court ruled that the candidacy of Ouattara in the forthcoming legislative elections was invalid. The RDR urged an 'active boycott' of the elections in protest. An estimated 30 people died in clashes between supporters of Ouattara and the police, and following the death of his personal secretary, who had reportedly been beaten by police-officers, Ouattara fled to France. The UN, the Organization of African Unity (now the African Union—AU, see p. 164) and the European Union (EU, see p. 244) announced that they would withdraw their observers from the elections in response to the unrest and the exclusion of Ouattara. The legislative elections proceeded on 10 December, although violent clashes between RDR supporters and the security forces, in which 85 people were killed, prevented voting in 28 northern constituencies. Electoral turn-out was low, at 31.5%. The FPI won 96 of the 225 seats in the Assemblée nationale, the PDCI—RDA 77, the PIT four, and independent candidates 17, while a 'moderate' faction of the RDR secured one seat.

At the remaining legislative elections, held in mid-January 2001, the PDCI—RDA secured 17 of the 26 contested seats, increasing its overall representation in the Assemblée nationale to 94 seats, only two less than the FPI. Independent candidates won five seats and the RDR faction four. Two seats in Kong, Ouattara's native town, remained uncontested. Only 13.3% of eligible voters participated in the elections. The legislative balance of power remained unclear, and soon emerged that seven of the 22 nominally independent deputies had been financed by the PDCI—RDA and were to return to the party. A further 14 independents, PDCI—RDA dissidents who had left the party to support Gueï, formed a parliamentary alliance with the FPI and, in February, created a new centre-right party with some 50 other former members of the PDCI—RDA, the Union pour la démocratie et la paix de la Côte d'Ivoire (UDPCI).

N'Guessan was retained as Prime Minister in a new Council of Ministers appointed on 24 January 2001; of the 28 ministers, 18 were members of the FPI, while six were from the PDCI—RDA. Meanwhile, tensions between native Ivorians and Burkinabè migrants heightened, and, following a number of violent incidents, several thousand Burkinabè were reported to have returned to Burkina Faso from Côte d'Ivoire in January–February. In July N'Guessan was elected as President of the FPI, replacing Gbagbo.

In late 2001 a national reconciliation forum, chaired by Diarra, was attended by some 700 representatives of political, religious and civil society organizations. Bédié returned to Côte d'Ivoire from France to participate, while Gueï also returned from self-imposed seclusion in the west of Côte d'Ivoire to address the forum. At the beginning of December 2001 Ouattara addressed the forum, calling for the introduction of a new constitution and reiterating his determination to be elected to the presidency. When the forum closed, in mid-December, it recommended, *inter alia*, that Ouattara be granted a nationality certificate and that a committee of legal experts be created to examine certain clauses in the Constitution. In January 2002 a meeting took place in Yamoussoukro between Gbagbo, Bédié, Gueï and Ouattara. In a joint statement, issued in mid-February, the four leaders reviewed the resolutions of the reconciliation forum and made further recommendations. In April Bédié was re-elected as President of the PDCI—RDA.

Ouattara was finally granted Ivorian citizenship in June 2002, although, having held Burkinabè citizenship, he remained barred from contesting the presidency. In a further attempt at reconciliation, four RDR ministers were appointed to a reshuffled Government of National Unity, under N'Guessan's premiership, in August. However, discontent at the composition of the Government became evident almost immediately; in particular, opposition parties expressed their dissatisfaction at the overruling of their preferred candidates for ministerial appointments by Gbagbo. Consequently, the UDPCI withdrew its support from the Government, although its sole minister remained in his post, in an independent capacity. Moreover, the PDCI—RDA alleged that Gbagbo had sought to portray the party as representing factional interests by overruling its nomination of seven ministerial candidates from various ethnic groups in favour of a list including six members of the Akan ethnic group, to which Bédié belonged.

In the early hours of 19 September 2002, while Gbagbo was on a state visit to Italy, an apparently meticulously planned armed rebellion broke out, almost simultaneously, in Bouaké, Korhogo and Abidjan. The unrest in Abidjan culminated in an attack on a military barracks and the assassination of Emile Boga Doudou, the Minister of State, Minister of the Interior and Decentralization. Gueï, who had recently gained in prominence as a critic of the Government, was also killed. Although some 300 people were killed in the city, government troops rapidly regained control of Abidjan. However, two ministers were held hostage for several days in the north, which remained under rebel control. The exact motivation and identity of the rebels was initially obscure. Gbagbo, following his return to Côte d'Ivoire on 20 September, implied that an unnamed foreign country (widely understood to refer to Burkina Faso) was implicated in the insurgency, which he described as an attempted *coup d'état*.

Continuing unrest in the north prompted widespread concern across West Africa. In late September 2002 an emergency summit of the Economic Community of West African States (ECOWAS, see p. 232) resolved to dispatch a military mission to act as a 'buffer' between government and rebel troops, and mandated a 'contact group', comprising six Heads of State, to undertake negotiations between Gbagbo and the insurgents. In early October Master-Sgt Tuo Fozié emerged as a spokesman for the rebels, who identified themselves as the Mouvement patriotique de la Côte d'Ivoire (MPCI) and stated as their principal demand the removal of Gbagbo from the presidency and the holding of fresh elections. Negotiations between the MPCI and ECOWAS mediators took place in early October. Meanwhile, Gbagbo announced that the Government was prepared to enter into a cease-fire with the rebels, subject to their disarmament and the nation-wide restoration of government authority. However, the signature of the proposed cease-fire accord by the Government was delayed on two occasions, and subsequently cancelled, precipitating the departure of the ECOWAS 'contact group' from Côte d'Ivoire.

In mid-October 2002 Gbagbo effectively assumed personal responsibility for defence. On 17 October Fozié signed a cease-fire agreement on behalf of the MPCI, to take effect from the following day; Gbagbo announced his acceptance of the accord. In late October, outside their base in Abidjan, French soldiers used tear gas to disperse pro-Government demonstrators, who were demanding the expulsion of Ouattara from the French embassy; both this demand, and calls for the rejection of government compromise with rebel groups, were increasingly expressed by the Coordination des jeunes patriotes (CJP), a movement led by Charles Blé Goudé, a former leader of the FESCI and an ally of Gbagbo. At the end of October the Government and the MPCI entered into further negotiations in Lomé, Togo, under the aegis of ECOWAS; another former leader of the FESCI, Guillaume Soro Kigbafori, now the Secretary-General of the recently formed political wing of the MPCI, led the rebel delegation.

In early November 2002 the Government announced an amnesty for the rebels and its acceptance of their eventual reintegration into the armed forces. Later in the month the four RDR representatives resigned from the Government, in protest at alleged human rights abuses in which the Government was implicated. At the end of November Ouattara left Côte d'Ivoire and sought refuge in Gabon.

In late November 2002 national security deteriorated further, with the emergence of two new rebel groups, apparently unconnected to the MPCI, in western regions. The Mouvement populaire ivoirien du grand ouest (MPIGO) and the Mouvement pour la justice et la paix (MJP) both announced their intention of taking vengeance for the death of Gueï, and by the end of the month had gained control of the cities of Man and Danane, near the border with Liberia. It was reported that the western rebel groups included mercenaries from Liberia. In early December Ivorian government forces attacked Danane and Man; in the ensuing clashes more than 150 people were killed. In mid-December the French Minister of Defence announced that French troops in Côte d'Ivoire were henceforth to be permitted to use force to enforce the cease-fire; France was to increase its contingent of troops in the country to number some 2,500, while the deployment of the ECOWAS mission remained in abeyance.

During January 2003 French-led diplomatic efforts to broker and maintain an enduring cease-fire intensified; following a visit to Côte d'Ivoire by the French Minister of Foreign Affairs, Dominique de Villepin, it was announced that a summit was to be convened in Marcoussis, France. Despite ongoing clashes in the west of Côte d'Ivoire, on 13 January a peace treaty was signed in Lomé by the leaders of the MPIGO and the MPJ, and, on behalf of the Government, by Laurent Dona Fologo, the President of the Economic and Social Council. Representatives of the Ivorian Government, seven political parties and the three rebel groups attended the Marcoussis summit, which commenced on 15 January. On 18 January the first contingent of the ECOWAS military mission (ECOMICI) arrived in Côte d'Ivoire. Although unrest continued, on 24 January unanimous agreement on a peace plan was reached by all parties involved in the negotiations. In accordance with this plan, Gbagbo was to remain as President until the expiry of his term of office in 2005, but was to share power with a new Prime Minister, appointed by consensus, at the head of a government of national reconciliation; the premier was to be forbidden from contesting the subsequent presidential election. Rebel groups and opposition parties were to receive government posts, while, under proposed constitutional reforms, candidates for public office were to be required to have only one Ivorian parent, rather than two, as had hitherto been the case. They were, however, to be of solely Ivorian nationality, and the minimum age qualification was to be reduced from 40 to 35 years. (These proposed constitutional amendments were subject to approval by a two-thirds' majority of the Assemblée nationale and by referendum.)

The terms of the Marcoussis Accords, although welcomed internationally, provoked widespread protests in areas of Côte d'Ivoire under government control. Blé Goudé became a leading spokesman for those opposed to the sharing of power with rebel groups, and numerous attacks on French interests in Abidjan occurred. Moreover, the MPCI's assertion (which was not, however, substantiated by the text of the accords) that it was to gain control of the ministries responsible for defence and security was a particular source of grievance. Further delays in the formation of the proposed government of national reconciliation resulted from the deteriorating security situation, although Diarra was officially appointed as Prime Minister on 10 February 2003.

On 8 March 2003 an ECOWAS summit in Accra, Ghana, resulted in an agreement on the allocation of ministerial portfolios; the FPI was to be given 10 posts, the PDCI—RDA eight, the RDR and the MPCI seven each, and the MJP and the MPIGO one each, while four smaller parties were to receive a total of six posts. The defence and security portfolios were to be excluded from these arrangements. Instead, a 15-member Conseil de la securité nationale (CSN), comprising the President, the Prime Minister, the Chief of Staff of the Armed Forces, the leaders of the gendarmerie and the police force, and representatives of the political parties and groups in the Government of National Reconciliation, was to be established to monitor the operations of these ministries, and to approve Diarra's nominees to these posts.

Further difficulties were encountered prior to the inaugural session of the Council of Ministers on 13 March 2003. The RDR announced that insecurity in Côte d'Ivoire continued to prevent its ministerial candidates from returning to the country from abroad. The MPCI, the MPIGO and the MJP also announced that they would not attend the meeting. Following the session, the appointment of eight ministers of state and 15 ministers, from among those parties that attended, was announced. Prior to a further meeting of the Council of Ministers on 20 March, the appointees to 15 of the 18 unfilled posts were announced; however, representatives of the MPCI, the MPIGO and the MJP again failed to attend the meeting in Abidjan, and a delegation of the groups met the Prime Minister in Yamoussoukro to express their concerns regarding security and the functioning of the CSN. In late March Gbagbo issued a decree confirming a CSN decision that two existing ministers, from the FPI and the RDR, were to assume additional responsibilities for the security and defence ministries, on an interim basis. These interim appointments were denounced by the MPCI, which denied that its representative on the CSN had consented to the measures. In mid-April the first full meeting of the Council of Ministers was held; among the former rebels appointed to the

Government were Soro, as Minister of State, Minister of Communication, and Fozié, as Minister of Youth and Public Service, while the military leader of the MPCI, Col Michel Gueu, was appointed as Minister of Sports and Leisure.

In early May 2003 the Chief of Staff of the Armed Forces, Gen. Mathias Doué, and Gueu signed a cease-fire agreement, which was intended to apply to all rebel groups operating within the country. However, violence continued, with more than 100 deaths reported in renewed clashes in western regions. Later in May Soro confirmed that the MPCI's military activities had ceased. In mid-June the national army and rebel forces agreed to the eventual confinement of troops, and by the end of the month it was reported that order had been restored in western regions. In late June the UN Mission in Côte d'Ivoire (MINUCI), authorized by the UN Security Council in May and charged with overseeing the implementation of the Marcoussis Accords, commenced operations in Abidjan, and on 4 July, in a ceremony held at the presidential palace, MPCI leaders formally announced the end of the conflict. In August the Assemblée nationale approved legislation providing for an amnesty for those involved in political unrest between 17 September 2000 and 19 September 2002, excluding those involved in abuses of human rights or violations of international humanitarian law. By the end of August 2003 more than 50 political prisoners had been released. Meanwhile, the MPCI effectively absorbed the MPIGO and MJP, and announced that the organization was henceforth to be known as the Forces nouvelles (FN).

In mid-September 2003 René Amani, a close associate of Diarra, was appointed as Minister of Defence, and Martin Bleou, a human rights activist and professor of law, was named as Minister of Security. However, the FN and the RDR rejected these nominations. The FN suspended its participation in the Government, accusing Gbagbo of delaying the process of reconciliation, although one of its nine ministers announced his intention to remain in his post. Moreover, the former rebels declared that they would not co-operate with the proposals for the disarmament and reintegration of former combatants. In late September, after an attack on a branch of the BCEAO and an outbreak of fighting in which at least 23 people were killed, French troops entered Bouaké and restored order, with the approval of the FN. In mid-October the Government prohibited demonstrations for a period of three months, and also resolved to dissolve the CJP; these measures followed several violent demonstrations in Abidjan, led by the CJP, which had demanded the expedited disarmament of the FN and had criticized the peace-keeping role of French troops in the conflict.

Ongoing diplomatic efforts, under the aegis of ECOWAS, to advance the peace process appeared to have little short-term success. Negotiations between Diarra and Soro, convened in Accra in November 2003 by the Ghanaian President, John Kufuor, and attended by six heads of state from the region, failed to satisfy FN demands for greater security and increased devolution of powers from the President to the Prime Minister. At the end of the month several hundred supporters of the proscribed CJP attacked and besieged the French military base in Abidjan, demanding that French troops permit government forces to march into FN-controlled territory.

In early December 2003 Gbagbo announced that the former rebel forces in the north of the country would commence disarmament later that month, several months later than had been initially planned. In the event the disarmament process was further delayed, although some 40 government soldiers that had been held as prisoners-of-war in FN-controlled areas were, none the less, released. Also that month the Council of Ministers approved legislation that permitted presidential candidates to have only one parent of Ivorian origin, rather than two; as a constitutional amendment, this measure would require the approval of a two-thirds' majority of the Assemblée nationale and endorsement by public referendum before it could enter into force. Gbagbo announced that two other items of legislation, intended to grant greater security to migrant workers in Côte d'Ivoire, with regard to the right to apply for Ivorian citizenship, and to own agricultural land, would also be subject to approval by referendum, although without having been presented to the Assemblée nationale.

In late December 2003 the FN announced that its ministers were to resume their governmental responsibilities. In January 2004 French peace-keeping troops began to enter regions of northern Côte d'Ivoire, with the agreement of the FN, reportedly in order to assist in the provision of humanitarian aid, although tensions persisted. In late February the UN Security Council established the UN Operation in Côte d'Ivoire (UNOCI, see p. 87); with an authorized military strength of 6,240, the peace-keeping operation was to be deployed for an initial period of 12 months from 4 April, on which date authority was to be transferred from MINUCI and ECOMICI to UNOCI. Nevertheless, the process of national reconciliation appeared to be stalling, with Soro's announcement that former rebel fighters would not disarm prior to legislative and presidential elections scheduled for 2005. In early March 2004 the PDCI—RDA announced that its ministers were to suspend their participation in the Government with immediate effect, in response to what it termed acts of humiliation and aggression against the party by supporters of Gbagbo; notably, all parties represented in the Government, with the exceptions of Gbagbo's FPI and the PIT, expressed support for the action of the PDCI—RDA.

In late March 2004 clashes occurred between members of the security forces and protesters following a demonstration in Abidjan, organized by seven of the 10 signatory parties of the Marcoussis Accords (known collectively as the G7). According to official figures, 37 people were killed, although opposition sources estimated the number of deaths at more than 300. An inquiry, conducted by the office of the UN High Commissioner for Human Rights (see p. 12), later reportedly concluded that the security forces had been responsible for the killings of at least 120 civilians in a 'carefully planned operation' organized by 'the highest authorities of the state'. Following the outbreak of violence, the RDR, the FN and the Mouvement des forces d'avenir (MFA) announced that they were to suspend their participation in the Government. The first contingent of UNOCI forces arrived in Côte d'Ivoire in early April.

In mid-April 2004 President Gbagbo acceded to the G7's principal demands in an attempt to restore some stability, agreeing to allow equal access to the state media to all political organizations, to respect the right to demonstrate and to ensure the security of the people. The peace process remained stalled, however, and in mid-May Gbagbo dismissed three opposition ministers from the Government, including Soro, replacing them, in an acting capacity, with members of the FPI. Soro had previously urged FN ministers to return to Bouaké from Abidjan, after Gbagbo had threatened to suspend their salaries and restrict their freedom to travel in response to their boycott of government meetings. In early June the French embassy came under attack from the CJP and other Gbagbo loyalists, who accused France of favouring the rebel movements; UN vehicles were also vandalized during the attacks, which were condemned by Gbagbo.

In late July 2004 all parties to the conflict attended a meeting of West African heads of state in Accra, convened by the UN Secretary-General and the President of Ghana, at which they signed an agreement on means of implementing the Marcoussis Accords. The agreement, which was to be monitored by UNOCI, ECOWAS and the AU, stated that disarmament of the rebels was to commence by 15 October and progress on amending the Constitution as regards presidential eligibility and on other political reforms was to be made by the end of September. In mid-August, in accordance with the agreement, Gbagbo reinstated the three government ministers dismissed in May, and all ministers from opposition parties and rebel groups resumed participation in the Government. Shortly afterwards Gbagbo delegated some of his powers to the Prime Minister pending a presidential election scheduled for October 2005. However, the disarmament deadline was not observed by the former rebels, who declared that insufficient progress had been made towards the realization of the proposed political reforms.

In early November 2004 the 18-month cease-fire was broken when the Ivorian air force launched bombing raids on Bouaké and other targets in the north of the country, reportedly resulting in the deaths of more than 80 civilians. On the third day of the renewed offensive, nine French peace-keeping troops, together with a US aid consultant, were killed when a French military base in Bouaké was bombed. In retaliation, French forces, acting on the direct orders of President Jacques Chirac, destroyed the Ivorian air force on the ground (see Defence, below). This precipitated several days of violence in Abidjan and elsewhere, with thousands of Ivorians, in particular members of Blé Goudé's CJP, rioting, looting and attacking French and other foreign targets. French troops intervened to take control of Abidjan's airport and major thoroughfares and to protect French and other foreign nationals, clashing with rioters and protesters in the process (see below). On 15 November the UN Security Council voted unanimously in favour of imposing a 13-month arms embargo, drafted by France, on Côte d'Ivoire (the embargo was reinforced by a further Security Council resolution in February 2005, although additional sanctions regarding the assets and travel movements of specific political figures were not enforced). Meanwhile, Soro and eight other opposition ministers announced that they would not attend meetings of the Government, claiming that their security in Abidjan could not be guaranteed.

In November and December 2004 the South African President, Thabo Mbeki, designated as mediator by the AU, held talks with both the Ivorian Government and the FN aimed at re-establishing the Marcoussis Accords as the basis for solution of the crisis. Following concessions made by Gbagbo during these talks, a series of political reforms proposed by the Accords were submitted to the legislature for approval, and in mid-December the Assemblée nationale voted in favour of amending the Constitution to permit persons with only one Ivorian parent to contest the presidency (thus allowing Ouattara to stand against Gbagbo in the election scheduled for October 2005). Gbagbo, however, insisted that any constitutional change would require ratification at a referendum, while the G7 objected that such a plebiscite was unnecessary. Soro and his fellow opposition ministers continued their boycott of government meetings in early 2005, declining to attend a special meeting arranged in Yamoussoukro at which Mbeki was also present, while the FN failed to observe another proposed disarmament deadline on 15 January. Unrest intensified in February–March and on 4 April the mandate of the UNOCI and French peace-keeping troops was extended for one month. (The mandate was extended for a further month on 4 May, and for an interim period of 21 days on 3 June, pending a reassessment of the mandate of UNOCI.)

In early April 2005 Mbeki hosted a summit in Pretoria, South Africa, attended by Bédié, Diarra, Gbagbo, Ouattara and Soro, as a result of which an agreement was signed, on 6 April, committing all parties to the disbandment of militia groups and to the disarmament of the former rebel troops. Conditions for eligibility of presidential candidates at the election due to be held in October were to be decided separately by Mbeki, following consultation with the UN Secretary-General, Kofi Annan, and the Chairman of the AU, the President of Nigeria, Olusegun Obasanjo. One week later, in a letter to the signatories of the Pretoria agreement, Mbeki ruled that the Ivorian Constitutional Council should confirm the candidates of those parties that signed the Marcoussis Accords; this was interpreted as permitting Ouattara's eventual candidacy. Two of the FN ministers subsequently resumed participation in the Government. The first moves towards resolving the military aspects of the conflict commenced on 21 April, when both parties moved heavy weaponry away from the 'buffer zone' dividing the country. Later that month Gbagbo declared that he would accept Ouattara as a legitimate candidate at the presidential election, but implied that, in so doing, normal constitutional provisions would be temporarily lifted. The Government subsequently announced that the first round of the election would take place on 30 October.

In mid-May 2005 the FN and the Ivorian armed forces agreed that disarmament of the former rebel forces would commence on 27 June and be completed by 10 August, and that a new republican army would be established to incorporate members of the existing armed forces and former rebel fighters. Later that month the PDCI—RDA, the RDR, the MFA and the UDPCI formed a new alliance, known as the Rassemblement des Houphouëtistes pour la démocratie et la paix (RHDP), and agreed that, in the event of the presidential election progressing to a second round (which would occur if no candidate received an absolute majority of votes cast in the first round), all four parties would support a common candidate in opposition to Gbagbo. In early June at least 100 people were reported to have been killed in a further outbreak of fighting near Duékoué; although most reports attributed the violence to a dispute between the Dioula and Gouro ethnic groups, Gbagbo made a speech implying that elements of the FN were responsible for instigating the violence. The President subsequently appointed a military governor for the region around Duékoué, and announced plans to deploy special military units in Abidjan in an effort to improve security in the city.

On 24 June 2005 the UN Security Council extended the mandate of UNOCI and the French peace-keeping forces for a further seven months, until January 2006, broadening the mandate granted to UNOCI to include an active role in disarmament, support for the organization of elections and the establishment of the rule of law and increasing its authorized military strength to 7,090. At the end of June 2005, following two days of talks in Pretoria, chaired by Mbeki and attended by Bédié, Diarra, Gbagbo, Ouattara and Soro, it was agreed that the dismantlement of pro-Government militias would commence immediately and be completed by 20 August, while legislation providing for the establishment of an independent electoral commission would be approved by mid-July. The South African authorities also stated that they would press for the imposition of sanctions against any parties perceived to be inhibiting the peace process. In mid-July, following further negotiations, the timetable for disarmament was revised again: some 40,500 former rebels and 15,000 pro-Government troops were to assemble at cantonment sites from 31 July and surrender their weapons between 26 September and 3 October. Later that month Gbagbo approved a number of legislative reforms, notably concerning nationality, citizenship rights and the establishment of an independent electoral commission, using his exceptional constitutional powers to override the requirement for parliamentary approval.

The FN refused to begin the disarmament process on 31 July 2005, stating that the terms of the legislation recently adopted by decree by Gbagbo differed from those that had been agreed at Pretoria in April. The G7 had also criticized the new legislation, claiming that the proposed electoral commission had not been provided with sufficient powers and that the amended law on nationality would restrict the number of people eligible to vote. However, in August South African mediators judged that the legislation conformed to the provisions of the peace agreement, prompting the FN to express doubts about the impartiality of Mbeki. Later that month the FN and the main opposition parties declared that it would be impossible for a free and fair election to be held within two months and called for Gbagbo's resignation to allow a transitional administration to organize the poll at a later date. At the beginning of September the FN rejected South Africa's mediation, after the South African Government blamed the movement for hindering the peace process in a briefing to the UN Security Council, and urged the AU and ECOWAS to assume control of efforts to resolve the crisis. Later that month Annan acknowledged that it was no longer feasible to hold the presidential election on 30 October, given that the electoral commission had still to be established and the voters' register updated. Moreover, there had been no progress on the disarmament of pro-Government militias and former rebels. At the end of September Gbagbo refused to attend an extraordinary ECOWAS summit held in Abuja, the Nigerian capital, to discuss the situation in Côte d'Ivoire, accusing some member states of having supported the rebellion. The President, meanwhile, insisted that it was his constitutional right to remain in office until an election could be held.

In early October 2005, on the basis of recommendations made by ECOWAS, the Peace and Security Council (PSC) of the AU proposed the extension by up to 12 months of President Gbagbo's term of office following its expiry at the end of the month and the appointment of a new Prime Minister with more extensive powers, acceptable to all signatories of the Marcoussis Accords. The Council supported the continued involvement of South Africa in mediation efforts, and also recommended the establishment of an international working group to monitor the implementation of the peace plan. Chaired by the Nigerian Minister of Foreign Affairs, the working group was to comprise high-ranking officials from Benin, Ghana, Guinea, Niger, Nigeria, South Africa, France, the United Kingdom, the USA, the UN, the AU, ECOWAS, the EU, La Francophonie, the World Bank and the IMF. The UN Security Council adopted a resolution endorsing the AU proposals later that month, despite calls from the RHDP and the FN for Gbagbo's removal from the presidency.

In November 2005 Obasanjo led efforts to reach a consensus on the nomination of a new Prime Minister, holding talks with all sides. However, the FN repeatedly insisted that, if Gbagbo were to remain in office, Soro or one of his deputies should assume the premiership on the grounds that the FN controlled one-half of the country. In late November mediation by Obasanjo, Mbeki and Mamadou Tandja, the President of Niger and serving Chairman of ECOWAS, failed to break the stalemate over the choice of Prime Minister. Finally, on 4 December, Obasanjo, Mbeki and Tandja designated Charles Konan Banny, hitherto Governor of the BCEAO, as interim Prime Minister. The appointment of Banny, who was sworn in to replace Diarra on 7 December, was broadly welcomed; the new Prime Minister was to be responsible for ensuring the disarmament of former rebel fighters and pro-Gbagbo militias and organizing a presidential election (which he would not be permitted to contest) by October 2006.

On 15 December 2005 the UN Security Council unanimously adopted a resolution to ban imports of rough diamonds from Côte d'Ivoire and to renew for a further year the arms embargo and the possibility of imposing sanctions on individuals deemed to have impeded the peace process. The Security Council also reiterated demands that the FN produce a comprehensive list of weapons in their possession. Later that month, after three weeks of negotiations, Banny announced the formation of a 32-member transitional Council of Ministers, which comprised seven ministers from the FPI, six from the FN, five each from the PDCI—RDA and the RDR and one each from the MFA, the PIT, the UDPCI and the Union démocratique citoyenne, as well as four representatives of civil society. Banny assumed personal responsibility for the economy and finance (as well as communication), while Soro was appointed as Minister of State for the Programme of Reconstruction and Reintegration, the most senior position in the Government after that of Prime Minister. Antoine Bohoun Bouabré of the FPI, an ally of Gbagbo and hitherto Minister of State, Minister of the Economy and Finance, became Minister of State for Planning and Development. The portfolios of defence and the interior were, notably, allocated to independents.

In mid-January 2006 tensions in Abidjan intensified, as up to 2,000 supporters of Gbagbo and the ruling FPI, many claiming membership of the CJP, protested in front of the UN's headquarters in the city, while others demonstrated outside the French embassy, demanding the departure of UN and French peace-keeping troops. Protesters erected barricades on major routes in Abidjan, paralysing economic activity, and assumed control of state television, broadcasting calls for viewers to join the demonstrations. An estimated 1,000 people occupied a UN military base in the western town of Guiglo, where subsequent violent clashes reportedly led to five deaths and the withdrawal of UN troops from Guiglo and nearby Duékoué. Despite a government ban on demonstrations, it was reported that the security forces did little to suppress the protests, which were prompted by the recommendation of the international working group that the Assemblée nationale be dissolved, following the expiry of its mandate a month earlier. The FPI rejected this recommendation, questioning the competency of the working group to rule on the matter, and announced the withdrawal of its ministers from the Government. After three days of rioting Obasanjo, Banny and Gbagbo issued a joint statement urging an end to the protests and insisting that the working group did not have the power itself to dissolve the legislature. On the following day Blé Goudé called on the demonstrators to dismantle the barricades and disperse, and relative calm returned to Abidjan (although at the end of the month the leader of the CJP stated that the protests would resume if Banny failed to produce a timetable for disarming former rebel fighters within two weeks). A few days later the FPI announced its decision to resume its participation in the Government. UN officials warned that the provision of humanitarian assistance to refugees and displaced persons in western Côte d'Ivoire had been severely disrupted owing to damage to UN facilities (estimated at US $3.5m.) and the evacuation of staff.

On 24 January 2006 the UN Security Council extended the mandate of UNOCI and the French troops until 15 December. Ouattara returned to Côte d'Ivoire in late January after three years in exile; a few days earlier he had announced his intention to stand in the presidential election due to be held by October. Nearly 400 of the 2,000 civilian staff working for the UN and UN humanitarian agencies in Côte d'Ivoire were temporarily relocated to The Gambia and Senegal at the end of January, amid continued concerns over their safety. Meanwhile, Annan criticized a decree issued unilaterally by Gbagbo prolonging the mandate of the Assemblée nationale. In early February the UN Security Council agreed to redeploy some 200 soldiers from the UN Mission in Liberia to Côte d'Ivoire and approved the imposition of sanctions against three individuals: Blé Goudé, Eugène Djué, also a leader of the CJP, and Martin Kouakou Fofié, an FN commander accused of human rights abuses, were to be subject to a 12-month travel ban and a freeze on their assets. In late February negotiations were held, chaired by Banny, between Gbagbo, Soro, Bédié and Ouattara, in Yamoussoukro, representing the first occasion on which the four leaders had met in Côte d'Ivoire since the de facto division of the country between opposing forces in late 2002. It was agreed, in principle, that further discussions between the parties would take place, with a particular view to establishing a new schedule for the disbanding of the rival militia and paramilitary groups. In mid-March 2006 Soro returned to Abidjan for the first time in more than one year, to assume his ministerial responsibilities.

In March 2006 a fresh crisis arose after Banny announced his intention to recommence the identification campaign for the registration of voters. Gbagbo strongly opposed the proposals, and argued that the existing voter registers from 2000 were adequate and merely required updating. However, the opposition supported Banny's initiative, arguing that up to 3m. Ivorians had no identification papers, preventing them from voting. Following mediation in early April 2006 by the Chairman of the AU, Denis Sassou-Nguesso President of the Republic of the Congo, a compromise was reached stipulating that the disarmament and identification processes would occur at the same time and in a co-ordinated manner, along with the redeployment of the public administration in the north. The agreement was rejected, however, by the FPI and the CJP leaders. In mid-May Banny announced that a one-week pilot phase of voter identification would begin in seven areas across the country on 18 May, to be followed by a national programme of identification and disarmament. Meanwhile, the military authorities on both sides took the first steps towards redeploying their forces in preparation for disarmament. This was followed in late May by the resumption of talks between government and FN forces on the sequencing of the disarmament process. However, the disarmament, initially scheduled to take place in early June, was delayed until mid-July.

In early September 2006 a further meeting between Banny, Gbagbo, Soro, Bédié and Ouattara took place, although no agreement could be reached on the issues of disarmament, the elections and voter identification. The following day the entire Ivorian Government resigned after three people were killed and some 1,500 others were taken ill as a result of the illegal unloading of toxic waste from a Panamanian-registered vessel at Abidjan port in mid-August; the waste was subsequently deposited at numerous sites around the city. Gbagbo requested that Banny form a new administration and in mid-September, by which time a further four people had been killed and some 30,000 people had reportedly sought medical attention, Banny unveiled a new Council of Ministers. The key positions remained unaltered, but the Minister of Transport and the Minister of the Environment, Water and Forestry were both replaced. Later in September the UN confirmed that the presidential election would not take place in October after a meeting in New York, USA, between a number of African mediators and the main parties involved in the crisis ended in deadlock. Gbagbo had refused to attend the talks and subsequently stated that he intended to remain as President, despite the expiry of his mandate at the end of October.

Following a meeting in Addis Ababa, Ethiopia, on 17 October 2006, the PSC recommended that a new transitional period, with a maximum duration of 12 months, commence on 1 November. The mandates of Gbagbo and Banny were to be extended until 31 October 2007 and the Prime Minister was to assume 'all the necessary powers, and all appropriate financial, material and human resources' to ensure, *inter alia*, that credible electoral rolls were compiled, and that the disarmament, demobilization and reintegration (DDR) programme was carried out, with a view to holding transparent elections by the expiry of his mandate. The granting to the Prime Minister of the power to introduce legislation by decree was contrary to the 2000 Constitution, which vested legislative authority in the President, and Banny was also to take control of the country's defence and security forces. The FN stated that it would refuse to recognize any arrangement whereby Gbagbo remained head of state, while Gbagbo, for his part, was reported to have maintained that any recommendations that did not comply with the Ivorian Constitution would not be applied. Nevertheless, on 1 November 2006 the UN Security Council adopted a resolution (No. 1721) endorsing the PSC's decision. On 15 December the Security Council extended the mandate of UNOCI until 10 January 2007 and on that date UNOCI's mandate was further extended until 30 June.

Meanwhile, in mid-December 2006 senior military figures announced that they had uncovered an attempt to stage a coup; the leaders of the plot, reportedly with the assistance of an unnamed foreign military force, had intended to assassinate both Gbagbo and the Chief of Staff of the Armed Forces, Brig.-Gen. Phillipe Mangou. Later that month the President unveiled a new initiative aimed at resolving the stalled peace process and offered to commence direct dialogue with the FN. Under Gbagbo's proposals the 'buffer zone' dividing the country would be removed, a new amnesty law would be enacted, and he also announced his intention to create a national civic service to aid young people with the development of skills and a programme that would assist displaced persons to return to their homes. At an ECOWAS summit held in Ougadougou, Burkina Faso, in mid-January 2007 the Burkinabè President and newly appointed Chairman of ECOWAS, Blaise Compaoré, was entrusted with facilitating dialogue between Gbagbo and the FN. Both Soro, on behalf of the FN, and Gbagbo attended separate meetings with Compaoré in Burkina Faso later that month and representatives from both sides attended discussions with the Burkinabè President in early February. Ouatarra, on behalf of the RDR, and Alphonse Djédjé Mady, the Secretary-General of the PCDI–RCA, met with Compaoré later that month.

On 4 March 2007 Gbagbo and Soro signed an agreement in Ougadougou, which provided a detailed timetable for the resolution of the ongoing political crisis in Côte d'Ivoire. According to the schedule, a joint armed forces command, the Centre de commandement integré (CCI), was to be established within two weeks, to be headed by Mangou and the Chief of Staff of the FN and to comprise an equal number of troops from both sides, while a power-sharing government was to be formed by mid-April. The signatories to the accord also agreed to undertake a nation-wide identification programme, scheduled to last for up to three months, which would result in the issuing of identity cards and the compilation of a definitive electoral list. The DDR programme was scheduled to commence two weeks after the formation of the new administration. In mid-March President Gbagbo announced the creation of the CCI, and on 29 March Soro was appointed Prime Minister. A 33-member Government, which featured six new appointees, was installed on 7 April. Most notably, the former presidential spokesman, Asségnini Désiré Tagro, assumed the newly created position of Minister of the Interior, and a senior member of the FN, Sidiki Konaté became Minister of Tourism and Crafts, while N'Guessan Michel Amani, hitherto Minister of National Education, replaced René Aphing Kouassi as Minister of Defence. On 16 April the 'buffer zone' was officially abolished.

In June 2007 an aircraft carrying Prime Minister Soro came under fire as it landed at Bouaké airport; four people were killed in the incident but Soro escaped unharmed. The perpetrators of the attack were not identified, although there were concerns regarding the potential involvement of a pro-Government militia group, which intended to destabilize the peace process. A national inquiry into the attempted assassination was initiated and in July the Government announced that it would request support from the UN Secretary-General in investigating the case. In June UNOCI's mandate was extended until 16 July and on that date it was further extended, until 15 January 2008.

In late July 2007 Gbagbo and Soro attended a ceremony in Bouaké at which stockpiled weapons were set alight in a gesture symbolizing the end of the five-year conflict. It was hoped that the destruction of the weapons would increase momentum towards achieving nation-wide reconciliation. However, political unrest was reported in the west of the country and the day before the ceremony in Bouaké Gbagbo's supporters held protests in Abidjan at the lack of transport to take them to Bouaké.

The reconciliation and disarmament process continued to progress at a slow pace, owing to ongoing disagreements between the signatories to the Ouagadougou Agreement. In August 2007 it was announced that elections, previously scheduled to be held in January 2008, were to be postponed until later that year. In September 2007 the much-delayed process of issuing identification papers to Ivorians without documents was officially launched, thus granting all citizens the right to enrol on the electoral register. This was deemed the precursor to establishing a full electoral list ahead of the planned legislative and presidential elections the following year. In November the country's major political parties adopted an electoral code, under the aegis of the Commission électorale indépendante, which aimed to ensure the free and fair conduct of future polls. Although Gbagbo had abandoned talks with the FN at the end of that month, at which a draft agreement aimed at accelerating the reconciliation process and scheduling elections for mid-2008 had been presented, he subsequently agreed to hold elections in June 2008. In December 2007 the disarmament of former rebel forces began. It was anticipated that some 5,000 government soldiers and 33,000 members of the rebel forces were to assemble at disarmament sites and barracks by the end of March 2008. Meanwhile, in January the UN Security Council approved the extension of UNOCI's mandate until 30 July.

Relations with France, the country's principal trading partner and provider of bilateral assistance, have been close since independence. French reaction to Gbagbo's election as President in October 2000 was divided, largely along party lines. President Chirac demanded that the election be rerun, incorporating those candidates who had been excluded from participating, while the leading party in the Government, the Parti socialiste, generally welcomed the accession to power of Gbagbo and the FPI. Following meetings between Gbagbo and Chirac in January 2001, France announced that full co-operation with Côte d'Ivoire, which had been suspended following the December 1999 *coup d'état*, would be restored. From late 2002 France dispatched additional troops to Côte d'Ivoire to supplement the 550 already stationed in the country and by late 2004 there were some 4,000 French troops stationed in Côte d'Ivoire, independent of the 6,000 UNOCI troops also deployed there. The French Government also played an active role in the diplomatic efforts that led to the signature of the Marcoussis Accords in late January 2003 (see above). However, France stated that it regarded the civil conflict as an internal Ivorian matter, disregarding Gbagbo's statements relating to the alleged involvement of external forces in the rebellion; such involvement would have resulted in the invocation of a clause in a defence treaty between the two countries, necessitating the active military support of France for the Ivorian authorities. None the less, there was widespread anti-French feeling, particularly in Abidjan, following the conclusion of the Marcoussis Accords, and several thousand French citizens resident in Côte d'Ivoire reportedly left the country.

Following the destruction of the Ivorian air force by the French military on 6 November 2004, in retaliation for an Ivorian bombing raid that had resulted in the deaths of nine French peace-keeping troops (see above), numerous French targets in Abidjan, including schools, businesses and homes, were attacked. French troops entered Abidjan to secure the international airport and protect French citizens, airlifting many of them out of the city. (In total it was estimated that 9,000 foreign citizens, the majority of them French, were evacuated from Abidjan during the crisis; the embassies of several European countries in the city suspended their operations in subsequent months.) Some 600 French troops were dispatched to reinforce that country's military presence in Côte d'Ivoire, while diplomatic relations between the two countries remained tense. The French Government subsequently admitted that its forces had killed some 20 Ivorian civilians during clashes with rioters in Abidjan; the Ivorian authorities claimed the number was significantly higher.

The emphasis on '*ivoirité*', or national identity, in the domestic policies of Bédié, Gueï and Gbagbo, has strained Côte d'Ivoire's relations with other West African states, particularly Burkina Faso; Burkinabè migrants in Côte d'Ivoire increasingly suffered from discrimination and became the victims of inter-ethnic violence, causing several thousand to flee the country in early 2001. As the process of national reconciliation advanced, tensions eased somewhat, and Gbagbo made his first visit as President to Burkina in December. However, following the onset of widespread civil unrest in Côte d'Ivoire in September 2002, thousands of citizens of Burkina and Mali left the country, and the common border of Côte d'Ivoire and Burkina Faso was closed until early September 2003, when stability appeared to be returning to the region. In July 2004, at a meeting in Abidjan, representatives of the two countries pledged to combat 'destabilizing acts' against their respective countries and agreed to increase co-operation in security and defence matters.

The protracted civil war in neighbouring Liberia resulted in the presence of large numbers of Liberian refugees in Côte d'Ivoire in the 1990s; the office of the UN High Commissioner for Refugees (UNHCR) estimated the total number at 327,288 at the end of 1996. The possible infiltration of refugee groups by Liberian fighters, together with sporadic incursions into eastern Côte d'Ivoire by Liberian armed factions, proved a significant security concern of the Ivorian authorities at this time. By 2002, following the installation of elected organs of state in Liberia in 1997, and the outbreak of civil conflict in Côte d'Ivoire in September 2002, the number of Liberian refugees in the country registered with UNHCR had declined to 43,000, although it rose again to 74,180 over the course of 2003, following the deterioration of the security situation in eastern Liberia. Conversely, some 25,000 Ivorian nationals were thought by UNHCR to have fled to Liberia in 2002 to escape fighting in western Côte d'Ivoire, while in 2004 some 10,000 Ivorians were reported to have sought refuge in Liberia following the renewed outbreak of violence in Côte d'Ivoire in November. In July 2005 UNHCR reported that some 6,000 refugees had returned from Côte d'Ivoire to Liberia since the beginning of the year, most within the previous month, owing to improved conditions in Liberia and the deteriorating security situation in western Côte d'Ivoire. By January 2006 some 25,600 Liberian refugees remained in Côte d'Ivoire; an estimated 15,000 had returned to Liberia during that year. There were some 12,600 Ivorian refugees in Liberia in December 2006.

Government

Under the terms of the Constitution of July 2000, executive power is vested in the President, as Head of State, who is appointed by direct universal suffrage for a term of five years, renewable only once. The mandate of President Laurent Gbagbo, which had been due to expire in October 2005, was extended by a further 12 months and in November 2006 was again extended, until 31 October 2007. The President appoints a Prime Minister, and on the latter's recommendation, a Council of Ministers. Legislative power is held by the Assemblée nationale, which is elected for a term of five years. (However, in early 2006 the term of the legislature elected in December 2000 was extended indefinitely and it remained uncertain as to when legislative elections would be held.) The country is divided into 19 regions, and further sub-divided into 57 departments and 197 communes, each with its own elected council.

Defence

As assessed at November 2007, Côte d'Ivoire's active armed forces comprised an army of 6,500 men, a navy of 900, an air force of 700, a presidential guard of 1,350 and a gendarmerie of 7,600. There was also a 1,500-strong militia. Reserve forces numbered 10,000 men. Military service is by selective conscription and lasts for 18 months. France supplies equipment and training, and had increased its military presence in Côte d'Ivoire from 550 to some 3,800 by August 2004, in order to monitor and enforce the cease-fire agreed in October 2002 between the Ivorian Government and rebels of the Mouvement patriotique de Côte d'Ivoire. The deployment by the Economic Community of West African States of a military mission (ECOMICI) commenced in Côte d'Ivoire in January 2003; by August an estimated 1,300 ECOMICI troops, of an authorized maximum of 3,411, were in Côte d'Ivoire. In June 2003 the UN Mission in Côte d'Ivoire (MINUCI) commenced operations in Abidjan, comprising 26 military liaison officers and 30 international civilian personnel. In late February 2004 the UN Security Council established the UN Operation in Côte d'Ivoire (UNOCI, see p. 87); with an authorized military strength of 6,240, the peace-keeping operation was deployed for an initial period of 12 months from early April, when authority was transferred from MINUCI and ECOMICI to UNOCI. In June 2005 the authorized military strength of UNOCI was increased to 7,090 troops, and in January 2006 the mandate of the operation was extended until December of that year. The mandate was subsequently extended until June 2007 and a further 1,500 additional personnel were authorized. The defence budget for 2007 was an estimated 139,000m. francs CFA. In November 2004, following the death of nine French troops in an airstrike conducted by Ivorian military aircraft, the entire Ivorian air force, reportedly consisting of two Sukhoi-25 warplanes and five helicopters, was destroyed on the ground by French retaliatory action. Later that month the UN imposed a 13-month arms embargo on Côte d'Ivoire.

Economic Affairs

In 2006, according to estimates by the World Bank, Côte d'Ivoire's gross national income (GNI), measured at average 2004–06 prices, was US $16,002m., equivalent to $870 per head (or $1,550 on an international purchasing-power parity basis). During 1996–2006, it was estimated, the population increased at an average annual rate of 2.0%, while gross domestic product (GDP) per head declined, in real terms, by an average of 0.9% per year. Overall GDP increased, in real terms, by an average annual rate of 1.1% in 1996–2006; real GDP decreased by 0.3% in 2005, but grew by 4.1% in 2006.

Agriculture (including forestry and fishing) contributed 20.9% of GDP in 2006, according to the World Bank, and employed about 43.7% of the labour force in mid-2005, according to FAO estimates. Côte d'Ivoire is the world's foremost producer of cocoa, responsible for some 38% of global cocoa bean production in 2005/06. In 2003 cocoa and related products contributed 40.6% of the country's total export earnings. Côte d'Ivoire also produces and exports coffee, although output declined markedly during the early 2000s. Other major cash crops include cotton, rubber, bananas and pineapples. The principal subsistence crops are yams, cassava, plantains, rice (although large quantities of the last are still imported) and maize. Excessive exploitation of the country's forest resources has led to a decline in the importance of this sector. Abidjan is among sub-Saharan Africa's principal fishing ports; however, the participation of Ivorian fishing fleets is minimal. During 1996–2006 agricultural GDP increased at an average annual rate of 1.7%. Agricultural GDP decreased by 1.5% in 2005, but grew by 2.1% in 2006.

Industry (including mining, manufacturing, construction and power) contributed 23.7% of GDP in 2006, according to the World Bank. According to UN estimates, 11.5% of the labour force were employed in the sector in 1994. During 1996–2006 industrial GDP increased by an average annual rate of 0.8%; industrial GDP decreased by 0.6% in 2005, but grew by 11.1% in 2006.

Mining and quarrying contributed only 1.9% of GDP in 2005. Commercial exploitation of important offshore reserves of petroleum and natural gas commenced in the mid-1990s, and output of crude petroleum amounted to some 14.6m. barrels in 2005. Gold and diamonds are also mined, although illicit production of the latter has greatly exceeded commercial output. There is believed to be significant potential for the development of nickel deposits, and there are also notable reserves of manganese, iron ore and bauxite.

The manufacturing sector, which, according to the World Bank contributed 16.9% of GDP in 2006, is dominated by agro-industrial activities (such as the processing of cocoa, coffee, cotton, palm kernels, pineapples and fish). Crude petroleum is refined at Abidjan, while the tobacco industry uses mostly imported tobacco. During 1996–2006 manufacturing GDP decreased by an average of 0.5% per year. The GDP of the sector decreased by 1.4% in 2005, but grew by 1.8% in 2006.

Some 67.5% of Côte d'Ivoire's electricity generation in 2004 was derived from natural gas, while 32.4% was derived from hydroelectric installations, and 0.1% from petroleum (a major decline from 1994, when 50.3% of the country's electricity had been generated from petroleum combustion). Since 1995 the country has exploited indigenous reserves of natural gas, with the intention of becoming not only self-sufficient in energy, but also a regional exporter; the first stage of a major gas-powered turbine and power station in Abidjan commenced operations in 1999. Imports of fuel products accounted for 17.1% of the value of total merchandise imports in 2003.

According to the World Bank, the services sector contributed 55.4% of GDP in 2006, and (according to UN estimates) employed 37.4% of the labour force in 1994. The transformation of Abidjan's stock market into a regional exchange for the member states of the Union économique et monétaire ouest-africaine (UEMOA, see p. 307) was expected to enhance the city's status as a centre for financial services. Abidjan's position as a major hub of regional communications and trade has been threatened by political unrest since the late 1990s, particularly following the rebel uprising of 2002–03. The GDP of the services sector increased by an average of 0.9% per year in 1996–2006. The GDP of the sector increased by 2.6% in 2006.

In 2006 Côte d'Ivoire recorded a visible trade surplus of US $3,151.9m., and there was a surplus of $529.2m. on the current account of the balance of payments. In 2003 the principal source of imports was France (which supplied 32.6% of total imports); Nigeria (14.4%) and the United Kingdom (7.0%) were also notable suppliers. France was the principal market for exports in 2003 (taking 19.1% of total exports), followed by the Netherlands, the USA and Spain. The principal exports in 2003 were food and live animals (amounting to 54.3% of total exports) and mineral fuels and lubricants (12.8%). The principal imports in the same year were machinery and transport equipment (representing 21.4% of total imports), food and live animals (18.5%), mineral fuels and lubricants (17.1%) and chemicals and related products (14.1%).

Côte d'Ivoire recorded an estimated overall budget deficit of 162,100m. francs CFA in 2006 (equivalent to 1.8% of GDP). The country's total external debt was US $11,739m. at the end of 2004, of which $10,837m. was long-term public debt. In that year the cost of debt-servicing was equivalent to 6.9% of the value of exports of goods and services. The annual rate of inflation averaged 2.7% in 1990–93. Consumer prices increased by an average of 26.1% in 1994 (following the devaluation of the

CÔTE D'IVOIRE

currency at the beginning of the year); the inflation rate slowed to an annual average of 14.3% in 1995, and averaged 3.0% in 1996–2006. Consumer prices increased by 4.4% in 2005 and by 2.4% in 2006. An estimated 216,158 persons were registered as unemployed in 2006, representing 2.7% of the labour force.

Côte d'Ivoire is a member of numerous regional and international organizations, including the Economic Community of West African States (ECOWAS, see p. 232), the West African organs of the Franc Zone (see p. 307), the African Petroleum Producers' Association (APPA, see p. 407), the International Cocoa Organization (ICCO, see p. 408), the International Coffee Organization (see p. 408) and the Conseil de l'Entente (see p. 412). The African Development Bank (see p. 162) has its headquarters in Abidjan; however, in February 2003 the bank temporarily relocated to Tunis, Tunisia, as a result of heightened instability in Côte d'Ivoire.

From the late 1990s the economy of Côte d'Ivoire was adversely affected by international economic and domestic political developments, including a sharp fall in international prices for cocoa, the country's principal export and major cash crop. By the time of the *coup d'état* of December 1999 Côte d'Ivoire's financial situation was precarious. In late 2000 the World Bank suspended assistance to Côte d'Ivoire, following a failure to repay debt totalling US $39.8m., while continuing political instability resulted in a decline in GDP in 2000. The World Bank resumed full co-operation in February 2002, after all outstanding debt had been paid, as did the European Union, which had suspended assistance in mid-1999, following revelations of the misappropriation of aid. However, the rebellion that commenced in September 2002 and the loss of government control over the northern half of the country (as well as certain western regions) inhibited the economic growth that, it had been hoped, the normalization of relations with external creditors might otherwise encourage. The international trade of the country was severely disrupted, particularly as a result of the closure of the border with Burkina Faso for a period of 12 months. Abidjan's status as an *entrepôt* for trade with land-locked neighbouring countries was challenged by the effects of this closure, and that of the Abidjan–Ouagadougou railway line, and consequently much trade was lost to Accra, Ghana; Cotonou, Benin; and Lomé, Togo. A good cocoa crop and a sharp increase in international prices for the commodity at the end of 2002 were among the principal factors that prevented a dramatic economic decline in that year. Outbreaks of violence in November 2004 prompted some 8,000 French nationals to depart Côte d'Ivoire, depriving the economy of a valuable section of its consumption base, as well as the capital's many French-owned businesses. Although the World Bank indicated strong growth in 2006, there was concern that the economy was becoming over-reliant on the production of petroleum. (Revenue from that sector was estimated by some sources to have increased four-fold in 2006.) In July 2007 the World Bank approved an International Development Association grant of $120m. to support the Government's crisis recovery programme under the Ougadougou Agreement, signed in March. The IMF projected GDP growth of 1.7% in 2007, with growth of 3% forecast for 2008, while budget revenue in 2007 was judged satisfactory; lower revenue from taxes on petroleum were to be offset by improved collection of value-added and corporate taxes. None the less, overall prospects in the country remained dependent on the long-term restoration of political order.

Education

Education at all levels is available free of charge. Primary education, which is officially compulsory for six years between the ages of seven and 13 years, begins at six years of age and lasts for six years. According to UNESCO estimates, enrolment at primary schools in 2002/03 included 56% of children in the relevant age-group (males 62%; females 50%). Secondary education, from the age of 12, lasts for up to seven years, comprising a first cycle of four years and a second cycle of three years. In 2001/02 total enrolment at secondary level included 20% of children in the relevant age-group (males 26%; females 15%), according to UNESCO estimates. The Université de Cocody (formerly the Université Nationale de Côte d'Ivoire), in Abidjan, has six faculties, and there are two other universities, at Abodo-Adjamé (also in Abidjan) and at Bouaké, in the north. Some 47,187 students were enrolled at university-level institutions in 1997/98. Expenditure on education in 1999 was estimated at 303,700m. francs CFA, equivalent to 25.3% of total government expenditure (excluding spending on the public debt). Education in the north of the country was badly disrupted following the failed coup in 2002.

Public Holidays

2008: 1 January (New Year's Day), 21 March (Good Friday), 24 March (Easter Monday), 1 May (Labour Day and Ascension Day), 12 May (Whit Monday), 7 August (National Day), 15 August (Assumption), 1 October* (Id al-Fitr, end of Ramadan), 1 November (All Saints' Day), 7 December (Félix Houphouët-Boigny Remembrance Day), 9 December* (Id al-Adha, Feast of the Sacrifice), 25 December (Christmas).

2009: 1 January (New Year's Day), 10 April (Good Friday), 13 April (Easter Monday), 1 May (Labour Day), 21 May (Ascension Day), 1 June (Whit Monday), 7 August (National Day), 15 August (Assumption), 20 September* (Id al-Fitr, end of Ramadan), 1 November (All Saints' Day), 27 November* (Id al-Adha, Feast of the Sacrifice), 7 December (Félix Houphouët-Boigny Remembrance Day), 25 December (Christmas).

* These holidays are dependent on the Islamic lunar calendar and may vary by one or two days from the dates given.

Weights and Measures

The metric system is in force.

Statistical Survey

Source (unless otherwise stated): Institut National de la Statistique, BP V55, Abidjan; tel. 20-21-05-38; fax 20-21-44-01; e-mail site-ins@globeaccess.net; internet www.ins.ci.

Area and Population

AREA, POPULATION AND DENSITY

Area (sq km)	322,462*
Population (census results)	
1 March 1988	10,815,694
20 December 1998	
Males	7,844,621
Females	7,522,050
Total	15,366,671
Population (official estimates at December)	
2005	19,096,988
2006	19,657,738
2007	20,227,876
Density (per sq km) at December 2007	62.7

* 124,503 sq miles.

ETHNIC GROUPS

1998 census (percentages, residents born in Côte d'Ivoire): Akan 42*; Voltaïque 18†; Mandé du nord 17‡; Krou 11; Mandé du sud 10§; Naturalized Ivorians 1; Others 1.

* Comprising the Baoulé, Agni, Abrou, Ebrié, Abouré, Adioukrou and Appollonien groupings.
† Comprising the Sénoufo, Lobi and Koulango groupings.
‡ Comprising the Malinké and Dioula groupings.
§ Comprising the Yacouba and Gouro groupings.

CÔTE D'IVOIRE

NATIONALITY OF POPULATION
(numbers resident in Côte d'Ivoire at 1998 census)

Country of citizenship	Population	%
Côte d'Ivoire	11,366,625	73.97
Burkina Faso	2,238,548	14.57
Mali	792,258	5.16
Guinea	230,387	1.50
Ghana	133,221	0.87
Liberia	78,258	0.51
Other	527,375	3.43
Total	**15,366,672**	**100.00**

POPULATION BY REGION
(1998 census)

Region	Population
Centre	1,001,264
Centre-Est	394,758
Centre-Nord	1,189,424
Centre-Ouest	2,169,826
Nord	929,686
Nord-Est	696,292
Nord-Ouest	740,175
Ouest	1,445,279
Sud	5,399,220
Sud-Ouest	1,400,748
Total	**15,366,672**

Note: In January 1997 the Government adopted legislation whereby Côte d'Ivoire's regions were to be reorganized. Further minor reorganizations were effected in April and July 2000. The new regions (with their regional capitals) are: Agnéby (Agboville), Bas-Sassandra (San-Pédro), Bafing (Touba), Denguélé (Odienné), 18 Montagnes (Man), Fromager (Gagnoa), Haut-Sassandra (Daloa), Lacs (Yamoussoukro), Lagunes (Abidjan), Marahoué (Bouaflé), Moyen-Cavally (Guiglo), Moyen-Comoé (Abengourou), N'zi-Comoé (Dimbokro), Savanes (Korhogo), Sud-Bandama (Divo), Sud-Comoé (Aboisso), Vallée du Bandama (Bouaké), Worodougou (Mankono) and Zanzan (Bondoukou).

PRINCIPAL TOWNS
(population at 1998 census)

Abidjan*	2,877,948	Korhogo	142,093
Bouaké	461,618	San-Pédro	131,800
Yamoussoukro*	299,243	Man	116,657
Daloa	173,107	Gagnoa	107,124

* The process of transferring the official capital from Abidjan to Yamoussoukro began in 1983.

2005 ('000, official estimates): Abidjan 3,576.0; Bouaké 573.7; Daloa 215.1.

BIRTHS AND DEATHS
(annual averages, official estimates)

	2005	2006	2007
Birth rate (per 1,000)	38.3	37.9	37.5
Death rate (per 1,000)	14.3	14.0	13.8

Expectation of life (years at birth, WHO estimates): 44.4 (males 41.8; females 47.4) in 2005 (Source: WHO, *World Health Statistics*).

ECONOMICALLY ACTIVE POPULATION*
(persons aged 6 years and over, 1988 census)

	Males	Females	Total
Agriculture, hunting, forestry and fishing	1,791,101	836,574	2,627,675
Mining and quarrying	} 78,768	6,283	85,051
Manufacturing			
Electricity, gas and water	13,573	1,092	14,665
Construction	82,203	2,313	84,516
Trade, restaurants and hotels	227,873	302,486	530,359
Transport, storage and communications	114,396	3,120	117,516
Other services	434,782	156,444	591,226
Activities not adequately defined	998	297	1,295
Total labour force	**2,743,694**	**1,308,609**	**4,052,303**

* Figures exclude persons seeking work for the first time, totalling 210,450 (males 142,688; females 67,762).

Source: UN, *Demographic Yearbook*.

1988 census (revised figures): Total employed 4,025,478; Unemployed 237,275; Total labour force 4,262,753.

1998 census: Total employed 6,084,487; Unemployed 163,647; Total labour force 6,248,134.

Mid-2005 ('000, estimates): Agriculture, etc. 3,224; Total labour force 7,379 (Source: FAO).

2006 (official estimates): Total employed 7,787,952; Unemployed 216,158; Total labour force 8,004,110.

Health and Welfare

KEY INDICATORS

Total fertility rate (children per woman, 2005)	4.8
Under-5 mortality rate (per 1,000 live births, 2005)	196
HIV/AIDS (% of persons aged 15–49, 2005)	7.1
Physicians (per 1,000 head, 2004)	0.12
Hospital beds (per 1,000 head, 1990)	0.81
Health expenditure (2004): US $ per head (PPP)	63.6
Health expenditure (2004): % of GDP	3.8
Health expenditure (2004): public (% of total)	23.8
Access to water (% of persons, 2004)	84
Access to sanitation (% of persons, 2004)	37
Human Development Index (2005): ranking	166
Human Development Index (2005): value	0.432

For sources and definitions, see explanatory note on p. vi.

Agriculture

PRINCIPAL CROPS
('000 metric tons)

	2004	2005	2006
Rice (paddy)	673.0	703.9	700.0*
Maize	608.0	640.2	600.0†
Millet	60	50	60†
Sorghum	75	80	30*
Sweet potatoes	45	50	50*
Cassava (Manioc)	2,128	2,198	2,200*
Taro (Coco yam)	360	355	360*
Yams	4,970.9	5,160.3	4,800.0*
Sugar cane*	1,000	1,100	1,100
Cashew nuts*	88.2	94.0	94.0
Kolanuts	65.2	73.8	73.8*
Groundnuts (in shell)†	88	82	85
Coconuts*	223	213	213
Oil palm fruit	1,564.3	1,881.9	1,881.9*
Cottonseed†	161.0	140.0	140.0
Tomatoes	25.4	26.2	26.2*
Aubergines (Eggplants)	70.0	72.4	72.4*
Chillies and green peppers*	23.4	23.9	23.9

CÔTE D'IVOIRE

—continued	2004	2005	2006
Green corn (Maize)*	240	240	240
Bananas	241.2	222.0	222.0*
Plantains	1,520	1,900	1,500*
Oranges*	30	30	30
Pineapples	249.0	194.5	194.5*
Guavas, mangoes and mangosteens	121	125	125*
Cotton (lint)	79	139	114†
Coffee (green)	251	230	166†
Cocoa beans	1,407.2	1,360.0	1,400†
Natural rubber (dry weight)	136.8	134.8	134.8*

* FAO estimate(s).
† Unofficial figure(s).

Aggregate production ('000 metric tons, may include official, semi-official or estimated data): Total cereals 1,425.0 in 2004, 1,483.2 in 2005, 1,399.0 in 2006; Total roots and tubers 7,509.4 in 2004, 7,768.6 in 2005, 7,415.0 in 2006; Total vegetables (incl. melons) 615.9 in 2004, 624.3 in 2005, 624.3 in 2006; Total fruits (excl. melons) 2,223.0 in 2004, 2,534.8 in 2005, 2,134.8 in 2006.

Source: FAO.

LIVESTOCK
('000 head, year ending September)

	2003	2004	2005*
Cattle	1,460*	1,500*	1,500
Pigs	336	343	345
Sheep	1,523*	1,523*	1,523
Goats	1,192*	1,192*	1,192
Poultry	33,000*	33,000*	33,000

* FAO estimate(s).

2006: Figures assumed to be unchanged from 2005 (FAO estimates).
Source: FAO.

LIVESTOCK PRODUCTS
('000 metric tons)

	2003	2004	2005*
Cattle meat	51.1	52.2	51.8
Sheep meat	5.1	5.1	5.0
Goat meat	3.9*	4.3*	4.3
Pig meat	12.3*	11.8*	11.8
Chicken meat	69.3*	69.3*	69.3
Game meat	13*	13*	13
Other meat	15*	15*	15
Cows' milk	25.9*	25.9*	25.9
Hen eggs	34.6	29.4	32.0

* FAO estimate(s).

2006: Figures assumed to be unchanged from 2005 (FAO estimates).
Source: FAO.

Forestry

ROUNDWOOD REMOVALS
('000 cubic metres, excluding bark)

	2003	2004	2005
Sawlogs, veneer logs and logs for sleepers	1,556	1,678	1,347
Fuel wood*	8,615	8,655	8,700
Total*	10,171	10,333	10,047

* FAO estimates.

2006: Figures assumed to be unchanged from 2005 (FAO estimates).
Source: FAO.

SAWNWOOD PRODUCTION
('000 cubic metres, including railway sleepers)

	2003	2004	2005
Total (all broadleaved)	503	503	363

2006: Production assumed to be unchanged from 2005 (FAO estimate).
Source: FAO.

Fishing

('000 metric tons, live weight)

	2003	2004	2005*
Capture*	68.9	54.4	55.0
Freshwater fishes	21.0*	4.9	5.0
Bigeye grunt	2.1	2.4	2.4
Round sardinella	8.3	10.6	9.7
Madeiran sardinella	0.4	6.0	5.0
Bonga shad	8.5*	7.5*	8.0
Aquaculture	0.9	0.9	0.9
Total catch*	69.8	55.3	55.9

* FAO estimate(s).
Source: FAO.

Mining

	2003	2004	2005
Diamonds ('000 carats)	230.0*	300.0	300.0*
Gold (kg)	1,313	1,219	1,638
Natural gas (million cubic metres)	1,457	2,000	2,200
Crude petroleum ('000 barrels)	7,506	8,125	14,574

* Estimate.
Source: US Geological Survey.

Industry

SELECTED PRODUCTS
('000 metric tons, unless otherwise indicated)

	2002	2003	2004
Beer of barley*†	205	205	205
Canned fish*	121.8	n.a.	n.a.
Palm oil—unrefined*	265.0‡	321.8	200.0
Raw sugar*‡	175	170	175
Plywood ('000 cubic metres)	76	76	n.a.
Jet fuel	92	104	88
Motor gasoline (petrol)	487	359	589
Kerosene	547	612	940
Gas-diesel (distillate fuel) oils	1,084	745	1,313
Residual fuel oils	337	318	209
Cement§	650	650	650
Electric energy (million kWh)	5,308	5,093	5,411

Cotton yarn (pure and mixed, '000 metric tons): 24.7† in 1989.

Electric energy (million kWh): 5,531 in 2005.

Cement ('000 metric tons, estimates): 650 in 2003–05 (Source: mainly US Geological Survey).
* Data from FAO.
† Provisional or estimated figures.
‡ Unofficial figure(s).
§ Data from the US Geological Survey.

Source: mainly UN, *Industrial Commodity Statistics Yearbook*.

Finance

CURRENCY AND EXCHANGE RATES

Monetary Units
100 centimes = 1 franc de la Communauté financière africaine (CFA).

Sterling, Dollar and Euro Equivalents (31 May 2007)
£1 sterling = 964.116 francs CFA;
US $1 = 487.592 francs CFA;
€1 = 655.957 francs CFA;
10,000 francs CFA = £10.37 = $20.51 = €15.24.

Average Exchange Rate (francs CFA per US $)
2004   528.29
2005   527.47
2006   522.89

Note: An exchange rate of 1 French franc = 50 francs CFA, established in 1948, remained in force until January 1994, when the CFA franc was devalued by 50%, with the exchange rate adjusted to 1 French franc = 100 francs CFA. This relationship to French currency remained in effect with the introduction of the euro on 1 January 1999. From that date, accordingly, a fixed exchange rate of €1 = 655.957 francs CFA has been in operation.

BUDGET
('000 million francs CFA)

Revenue*	2004	2005	2006†
Tax revenue	1,240.4	1,251.1	1,399.8
Direct taxes	288.6	360.3	441.1
Indirect taxes‡	951.8	890.8	958.7
Social security contributions	113.5	116.8	122.1
Oil and gas revenue	37.7	47.9	68.6
Other	40.0	55.6	81.6
Total	1,431.6	1,471.4	1,672.1

Expenditure§	2004	2005	2006†
Current expenditure	1,310.6	1,382.0	1,520.1
Wages and salaries	545.8	563.4	589.0
Social security benefits	135.6	149.2	167.6
Subsidies and other current transfers	84.7	93.5	178.0
Other current expenditure	363.0	398.3	423.5
Interest due	181.4	177.5	162.1
Internal	29.5	26.0	29.5
External	151.9	151.5	132.6
Capital expenditure	228.2	235.3	279.4
Domestically funded	121.8	133.7	211.3
Funded from abroad	106.4	101.6	78.7
Crisis-related expenditure	94.2	76.4	68.1
Total	1,633.0	1,693.7	1,867.6

* Excluding grants received ('000 million francs CFA): 75.9 in 2004; 94.6 in 2005; 55.5 in 2006 (estimate).
† Estimates.
‡ Excluding taxes on petroleum products.
§ Excluding net lending ('000 million francs CFA): 10.6 in 2004; 20.3 in 2005; 22.1 in 2006 (estimate).

Source: IMF, *Côte d'Ivoire: 2007 Article IV Consultation and Request for Emergency Post-Conflict Assistance-Staff Report; Staff Statement; Staff Supplement; Public Information Notice and Press Release on the Executive Board Discussion* (September 2007).

INTERNATIONAL RESERVES
(excluding gold, US $ million at 31 December)

	2004	2005	2006
IMF special drawing rights	0.2	0.6	1.0
Reserve position in IMF	0.9	0.9	1.0
Foreign exchange	1,692.5	1,320.0	1,795.7
Total	1,693.6	1,321.5	1,797.7

Source: IMF, *International Financial Statistics*.

MONEY SUPPLY
('000 million francs CFA at 31 December)

	2004	2005	2006
Currency outside banks	671.5	754.1	815.2
Demand deposits at deposit money banks*	619.0	628.3	710.7
Total money (incl. others)	1,300.4	1,397.3	1,551.0

* Excluding the deposits of public establishments of an administrative or social nature.

Source: IMF, *International Financial Statistics*.

COST OF LIVING
(Consumer Price Index for African households in Abidjan; base: 1996 = 100)

	2004	2005	2006
Food, beverages and tobacco	111.6	114.3	117.5
Clothing and footwear	100.2	101.9	101.4
Electricity, gas and other fuel	110.7	113.6	114.0
Rent	116.3	126.1	128.3
All items (incl. others)	112.7	117.1	119.9

Source: ILO.

NATIONAL ACCOUNTS
('000 million francs CFA at current prices)

Expenditure on the Gross Domestic Product

	2003	2004	2005
Final consumption expenditure	6,335.3	6,528.8	6,839.0
Households	} 5,241.8	} 5,400.3	} 5,770.4
Non-profit institutions serving households			
General government	1,093.5	1,128.5	1,068.6
Gross capital formation	779.8	818.8	773.9
Change in stocks	32.0	78.2	102.0
Total domestic expenditure	7,147.1	7,425.8	7,714.9
Exports of goods and services	3,749.6	3,741.6	4,184.8
Less Imports of goods and services	2,912.4	2,955.7	3,449.0
Statistical discrepancy	—	−33.2	—
GDP in purchasers' values	7,984.3	8,178.5	8,450.7

Gross Domestic Product by Economic Activity

	2003	2004	2005
Agriculture, livestock-rearing, forestry and fishing	2,039.9	1,896.0	1,965.4
Mining and quarrying	89.4	116.4	145.9
Manufacturing	1,246.0	1,331.3	1,341.0
Electricity, gas and water	179.5	190.4	196.3
Construction and public works	214.0	248.9	254.4
Trade	1,054.0	1,141.1	1,175.6
Transport, storage and communications	356.4	381.2	395.6
Non-market services	1,147.0	1,113.3	1,261.7
Other services	1,079.7	1,065.7	1,088.0
Sub-total	7,405.9	7,484.3	7,823.9
Import duties and taxes	578.4	694.3	626.8
GDP in purchasers' values	7,984.3	8,178.5	8,450.7

Source: Banque centrale des états de l'Afrique de l'ouest.

CÔTE D'IVOIRE

BALANCE OF PAYMENTS
(US $ million)

	2004	2005	2006
Exports of goods f.o.b.	6,919.3	7,697.4	8,190.8
Imports of goods f.o.b.	−4,291.4	−5,251.1	−5,038.9
Trade balance	2,627.9	2,446.3	3,151.9
Exports of services	762.7	832.4	818.7
Imports of services	−2,032.6	−2,123.5	−2,217.5
Balance on goods and services	1,358.0	1,155.2	1,753.1
Other income received	189.7	193.9	197.9
Other income paid	−841.3	−847.1	−926.0
Balance on goods, services and income	706.3	502.0	1,025.1
Current transfers received	187.4	194.8	204.4
Current transfers paid	−652.8	−657.2	−700.3
Current balance	240.9	39.6	529.2
Capital account (net)	145.9	185.2	27.5
Direct investment from abroad	283.0	311.9	315.0
Portfolio investment assets	−37.5	−50.0	−40.7
Portfolio investment liabilities	8.9	48.1	48.2
Financial derivatives assets	−6.0	−5.2	—
Financial derivatives liabilities	10.2	0.9	—
Other investment assets	−402.5	−374.4	−568.0
Other investment liabilities	−119.6	−400.3	−195.5
Net errors and omissions	26.6	−57.5	52.1
Overall balance	149.9	−301.6	167.8

Source: IMF, *International Financial Statistics*.

External Trade

PRINCIPAL COMMODITIES
(distribution by SITC, US $ million)

Imports c.i.f.	2000	2002*	2003
Food and live animals	377.9	523.0	655.1
Fish, crustaceans and molluscs, and preparations thereof	131.4	180.4	202.1
Fish, frozen, excl. fillets	127.9	175.3	196.5
Cereals and cereal preparations	153.4	218.4	250.2
Rice	97.5	134.3	157.7
Rice, semi-milled or wholly milled	91.2	130.6	156.7
Rice, semi-milled or wholly milled (unbroken)	76.5	102.0	122.3
Mineral fuels, lubricants, etc.	838.0	534.8	606.3
Petroleum, petroleum products, etc.	837.7	534.5	605.8
Crude petroleum and oils obtained from bituminous materials	679.5	419.2	537.8
Petroleum products, refined	154.9	109.9	61.5
Fuel oils, etc.	132.9	88.6	22.1
Chemicals and related products	352.1	447.6	499.7
Medical and pharmaceutical products	94.8	100.6	123.5
Medicaments (incl. veterinary medicaments)	89.3	91.6	114.7
Artificial resins and plastic materials, cellulose esters, etc.	90.7	101.0	118.4
Polymerization and copolymerization products	79.4	87.0	102.8
Basic manufactures	319.1	359.0	360.8
Iron and steel	64.7	84.1	74.9
Machinery and transport equipment	406.6	524.9	756.2
Road vehicles	104.7	115.9	249.2
Other transport equipment	7.0	138.6	191.3
Special purpose vessels, floating docks, etc.	—	134.5	174.1
Miscellaneous manufactured articles	84.6	88.9	119.0
Total (incl. others)†	2,482.2	2,599.0	3,536.3

Exports f.o.b.	2000	2002*	2003
Food and live animals	1,744.3	2,843.9	2,982.9
Fish, crustaceans and molluscs, and preparations thereof	128.9	139.7	141.0
Fish, prepared or preserved	120.1	135.7	136.2
Vegetables and fruit	179.5	183.9	189.0
Fruit and nuts, fresh, dried	171.6	179.6	183.4
Coffee, tea, cocoa, spices and manufactures thereof	1,327.2	2,353.7	2,418.8
Coffee and coffee substitutes	303.0	119.4	142.3
Coffee, green, roasted; coffee substitutes containing coffee	257.8	73.2	79.0
Coffee, not roasted; coffee husks and skins	244.1	72.1	77.8
Cocoa	1,017.9	2,203.0	2,230.4
Cocoa beans, raw, roasted	845.6	1,757.1	1,735.4
Cocoa butter and paste	160.7	390.1	409.1
Cocoa paste	98.2	244.7	233.9
Cocoa butter	62.5	145.4	175.2
Crude materials (inedible) except fuels	511.6	427.9	522.2
Cork and wood	271.7	190.0	198.1
Wood, simply worked and railway sleepers of wood	239.8	160.9	164.4
Wood, non-coniferous species, sawn, planed, tongued, grooved, etc.	237.2	158.1	162.8
Wood, non-coniferous species, sawn lengthwise, slices or peeled	218.0	135.5	131.1
Textile fibres (not wool tops) and their wastes (not in yarn)	148.9	134.6	178.4
Raw cotton, excl. linters, not carded or combed	148.0	133.8	177.6
Mineral fuels, lubricants, etc.	737.5	564.8	703.4
Petroleum, petroleum products, etc.	735.0	563.5	703.3
Crude petroleum and oils obtained from bituminous materials	69.7	90.9	195.9
Petroleum products, refined	644.7	457.5	489.9
Gasoline and other light oils	294.2	204.2	395.1
Motor spirit, incl. aviation spirit	61.3	47.8	313.6
Sprit type jet fuel	232.9	156.3	81.5
Gas oils	211.0	139.1	52.6
Chemicals and related products	142.9	234.3	215.2
Basic manufactures	244.3	258.6	240.4
Machinery and transport equipment	37.4	441.3	532.1
Road vehicles	13.6	13.2	364.1
Passenger motor vehicles (excl. buses)	3.4	3.1	189.4
Other transport equipment	4.7	409.3	113.2
Ships, boats and floating structures	2.4	407.6	109.0
Special purpose vessels, floating docks, etc.	1.9	407.5	108.8
Total (incl. others)	3,627.9	4,971.9	5,493.4

* No data were available for 2001.
† Including commodities and transactions not classified elsewhere in the SITC (US $ million): 0.2 in 2000, 0.0 in 2002, 382.4 in 2003 (Armoured fighting vehicles, war firearms, ammunition, parts, etc. 0.2 in 2000, 0.0 in 2002, 377.2 in 2003; Tanks and other armoured fighting vehicles, motorized, parts, etc. 0.2 in 2000, 0.0 in 2002, 368.6 in 2003).

Source: UN, *International Trade Statistics Yearbook*.

CÔTE D'IVOIRE

PRINCIPAL TRADING PARTNERS
(US $ million)

Imports c.i.f.	2000	2002*	2003
Bahrain	45.5	9.2	—
Belgium	100.3	62.6	80.2
Brazil	23.2	28.8	31.7
China, People's Republic	66.6	62.4	123.4
France (incl. Monaco)	504.7	555.6	1,152.6
Germany	89.5	93.6	100.4
India	17.6	72.3	70.3
Indonesia	8.0	17.5	36.3
Italy	90.5	121.7	111.3
Japan	72.2	71.1	58.3
Korea, Republic	24.6	38.2	39.1
Netherlands	76.0	93.1	117.2
Nigeria	659.8	366.8	509.8
Russia	62.5	77.1	57.6
Senegal	16.1	26.7	43.0
Singapore	1.2	141.2	7.3
South Africa	38.1	48.4	53.1
Spain	81.4	83.7	82.8
Thailand	54.6	64.1	74.1
United Kingdom	56.3	64.7	247.6
USA	89.0	89.8	114.1
Venezuela	25.8	11.1	8.3
Total (incl. others)	2,482.2	2,599.0	3,536.3

Exports f.o.b.	2000	2002*	2003
Belgium	138.7	128.9	147.1
Benin	43.2	41.7	74.3
Burkina Faso	129.5	146.6	112.8
Cameroon	34.1	41.0	59.7
Equatorial Guinea	19.0	17.3	130.9
France (incl. Monaco)	540.5	653.5	1,047.0
Germany	110.0	137.8	119.9
Ghana	134.9	106.0	124.4
India	93.3	85.8	75.3
Indonesia	33.5	57.0	57.2
Italy	172.5	189.0	188.4
Liberia	41.2	24.9	18.7
Mali	207.8	179.3	97.9
Netherlands	353.4	940.2	974.3
Niger	40.2	51.9	49.8
Nigeria	68.8	465.8	164.4
Poland	43.9	78.0	91.8
Russia	62.2	137.1	116.5
Senegal	145.8	57.3	95.7
Spain	136.5	246.8	309.5
Togo	88.6	80.9	121.2
United Kingdom	89.4	131.1	169.1
USA	301.3	374.7	389.3
Total (incl. others)	3,627.9	4,971.9	5,493.4

* No data were available for 2001.

Source: UN, *International Trade Statistics Yearbook*.

Transport

RAILWAYS
(traffic)

	2001	2002	2003
Passengers ('000)	399.5	320.0	87.5
Freight carried ('000 metric tons)	1,016.3	900.7	149.7

Passenger-km (million): 93.1 in 1999 (Source: SITARAIL—Transport Ferroviaire de Personnel et de Marchandises, Abidjan).

Freight ton-km (million): 537.6 in 1999 (Source: SITARAIL—Transport Ferroviaire de Personnel et de Marchandises, Abidjan).

ROAD TRAFFIC
('000 motor vehicles in use)

	1998	1999	2000
Passenger cars	98.4	109.6	113.9
Commercial vehicles	45.4	54.1	54.9

2001–02 ('000 motor vehicles in use): Figures assumed to be unchanged from 2000.

Source: UN, *Statistical Yearbook*.

SHIPPING
Merchant Fleet
(registered at 31 December)

	2004	2005	2006
Number of vessels	34	35	35
Total displacement ('000 grt)	9.1	9.2	9.2

Source: Lloyd's Register-Fairplay, *World Fleet Statistics*.

International Sea-borne Freight Traffic
(freight traffic at Abidjan, '000 metric tons)

	2001	2002	2003
Goods loaded	5,787	5,710	6,108
Goods unloaded	9,858	9,018	8,353

Source: Port Autonome d'Abidjan.

Freight traffic at San-Pédro ('000 metric tons, 2000): Goods loaded 1,102; Goods unloaded 251.

CIVIL AVIATION
(traffic on scheduled services)*

	1999	2000	2001
Kilometres flown (million)	6	3	1
Passengers carried ('000)	260	108	46
Passenger-km (million)	381	242	130
Total ton-km (million)	50	34	19

* Including an apportionment of the traffic of Air Afrique.

Source: UN, *Statistical Yearbook*.

Tourism

ARRIVALS BY COUNTRY OF RESIDENCE
('000)

	1996*	1997†	1998†
Belgium	4.3	4.2	4.5
Benin	12.5	11.1	14.3
Burkina Faso	11.0	11.9	17.1
Congo, Repub.	6.0	n.a.	7.6
France	66.7	69.0	73.2
Gabon	3.0	n.a.	5.4
Germany	3.2	3.8	3.9
Ghana	5.4	n.a.	6.7
Guinea	8.1	n.a.	12.5
Italy	5.0	14.0	7.6
Mali	10.7	n.a.	15.2
Niger	5.0	n.a.	5.4
Nigeria	7.9	n.a.	14.1
Senegal	13.0	12.1	16.6
Togo	8.7	8.2	10.8
United Kingdom	5.1	4.5	5.6
USA	15.3	17.0	18.8
Total (incl. others)	236.9	274.1	301.0

* Figures refer only to air arrivals at Abidjan—Félix Houphouët-Boigny airport.

† Figures refer to air arrivals at Abidjan—Félix Houphouët-Boigny airport and to arrivals at land frontiers.

Receipts from tourism (US $ million, excl. passenger transport): 317 in 1997; 331 in 1998; 337 in 1999; 291 in 2000; 289 in 2001; 490 in 2002.

Source: World Tourism Organization.

Communications Media

	2004	2005	2006
Telephones ('000 main lines in use)	257.9	258.5	260.9
Mobile cellular telephones ('000 subscribers)	1,674.3	2,349.4	4,065.4
Personal computers ('000 in use)	262	n.a.	n.a.
Internet users ('000)	160	200	300
Broadband subscribers ('000)	0.8	1.2	n.a.

Source: International Telecommunication Union.

Television receivers ('000 in use): 887 in 2000 (Source: UNESCO, *Statistical Yearbook*).

Radio receivers ('000 in use): 2,260 in 1997 (Source: UNESCO, *Statistical Yearbook*).

Daily Newspapers (national estimates): 12 (average circulation 235,000 copies) in 1997; 12 (average circulation 238,000 copies) in 1998; 21 in 2004 (Source: UNESCO Institute for Statistics).

Non-daily Newspapers: 15 in 1996 (average circulation 251,000 copies) (Source: UNESCO, *Statistical Yearbook*).

Education

(2002/03, unless otherwise indicated)

		Students		
	Teachers	Males	Females	Total
Pre-primary	2,179	24,786	23,861	48,647
Primary	48,308	1,141,762	904,403	2,046,165
Secondary	20,124*	474,203†	262,446†	736,649†
Tertiary*	n.a.	71,283	25,398	96,681

* 1998/99.
† 2001/02.

Institutions: 207 pre-primary in 1995/96; 7,599 primary in 1996/97.

Source: mostly UNESCO Institute for Statistics.

Adult literacy rate (UNESCO estimates): 48.7% (males 60.8%; females 38.6%) in 2000 (Source: UNESCO Institute for Statistics).

Directory

The Constitution

Following the *coup d'état* of 24 December 1999, the Constitution that had been in force, with amendments, since 1960 was suspended. A new Constitution was subsequently prepared by a consultative committee, and was approved by referendum in July 2000. The main provisions of the Constitution are summarized below:

PREAMBLE

The people of Côte d'Ivoire recognize their diverse ethnic, cultural and religious backgrounds, and desire to build a single, unified and prosperous nation based on constitutional legality and democratic institutions, the rights of the individual, cultural and spiritual values, transparency in public affairs, and the promotion of sub-regional, regional and African unity.

FREEDOMS, RIGHTS AND DUTIES

Articles 1–28: The State guarantees the implementation of the Constitution and guarantees to protect the rights of each citizen. The State guarantees its citizens equal access to health, education, culture, information, professional training, employment and justice. Freedom of thought and expression are guaranteed to all, although the encouragement of social, ethnic and religious discord is not permitted. Freedom of association and demonstration are guaranteed. Political parties may act freely within the law; however, parties must not be created solely on a regional, ethnic or religious basis. The rights of free enterprise, the right to join a trade union and the right to strike are guaranteed.

NATIONAL SOVEREIGNTY

Articles 29–33: Côte d'Ivoire is an independent and sovereign republic. The official language is French. Legislation regulates the promotion and development of national languages. The Republic of Côte d'Ivoire is indivisible, secular, democratic and social. All its citizens are equal. Sovereignty belongs to the people, and is exercised through referendums and the election of representatives. The right to vote freely and in secret is guaranteed to all citizens over 18 years of age.

HEAD OF STATE

Articles 34–57: The President of the Republic is the Head of State. The President is elected for a five-year mandate (renewable once only) by direct universal suffrage. Candidates must be aged between 40 and 65, and be Ivorian citizens holding no other nationality, and resident in the country, with Ivorian parents. If one candidate does not receive a simple majority of votes cast, a second round of voting takes place between the two most successful candidates. The President holds executive power, and appoints a Prime Minister to co-ordinate government action. The President appoints the Government on the recommendation of the Prime Minister. The President presides over the Council of Ministers, is the head of the civil service and the supreme head of the armed forces. The President may initiate legislation and call referendums. The President may not hold any other office or be a leader of a political party.

ASSEMBLÉE NATIONALE

Articles 58–83: The Assemblée nationale holds legislative power. The Assemblée nationale votes on the budget and scrutinizes the accounts of the nation. Deputies are elected for periods of five years by direct universal suffrage. Except in exceptional cases, deputies have legal immunity during the period of their mandate.

INTERNATIONAL AGREEMENTS

Articles 84–87: The President negotiates and ratifies treaties and international agreements. International agreements, which modify internal legislation, must be ratified by further legislation. The Constitution must be amended prior to the ratification of certain agreements if the Constitutional Council deems this necessary.

CONSTITUTIONAL COUNCIL

Articles 88–100: The Constitutional Council rules on the constitutionality of legislation. It also regulates the functioning of government. It is composed of a President, of the former Presidents of Côte d'Ivoire and of six councillors named by the President and by the President of the Assemblée nationale for mandates of six years. The Council supervises referendums and announces referendum and election results. It also examines the eligibility of candidates to the presidency and the legislature. There is no appeal against the Council's decisions.

JUDICIAL POWER

Articles 101–112: The judiciary is independent, and is composed of the High Court of Justice, the Court of Cassation*, the Council of State, the National Audit Court, and regional tribunals and appeals courts. The Higher Council of Magistrates examines questions relating to judicial independence and nominates and disciplines senior magistrates. The High Court of Justice judges members of the Government in cases relating to the execution of their duties. The High Court, which is composed of deputies elected by the Assemblée nationale, may only judge the President in cases of high treason.

* Although the Constitution of 2000 refers to the highest court of appeal as the Court of Cassation, in early 2004 this court retained its previous designation, as the Supreme Court.

THE ECONOMIC AND SOCIAL COUNCIL

Articles 113–114: The Economic and Social Council gives its opinion on proposed legislation or decrees relating to its sphere of competence. The President may consult the Council on any economic or social matter.

THE MEDIATOR OF THE REPUBLIC

Articles 115–118: The Mediator is an independent mediating figure, appointed for a non-renewable six-year mandate by the President, in consultation with the President of the Assemblée nationale. The Mediator, who may not hold any other office or position, receives immunity from prosecution during the term of office.

CÔTE D'IVOIRE

OTHER ISSUES

Articles 119–133: Only the President or the Assemblée nationale, of whom a two-thirds' majority must be in favour, may propose amending the Constitution. Amendments relating to the nature of the presidency or the mechanism whereby the Constitution is amended must be approved by referendum; all other amendments may be enacted with the agreement of the President and of a four-fifths' majority of the Assemblée nationale. The form and the secular nature of the republic may not be amended. Immunity from prosecution is granted to members of the Comité national de salut public and to all those involved in the change of government of December 1999.

The Government

HEAD OF STATE

President of the Republic: LAURENT GBAGBO (took office 26 October 2000).

COUNCIL OF MINISTERS
(March 2008)

Prime Minister: GUILLAUME SORO KIGBAFORI.
Minister of State for Planning and Development: ANTOINE BOHOUN BOUABRÉ.
Minister of Defence: N'GUESSAN MICHEL AMANI.
Minister of the Interior: ASSÉGNINI DÉSIRÉ TAGRO.
Keeper of the Seals, Minister of Justice and Human Rights: MAMADOU KONÉ.
Minister of Foreign Affairs: YOUSSOUF BAKAYOKO.
Minister of the Economy and Finance: KOFFI CHARLES DIBY.
Minister of Agriculture: AMADOU GON COULIBALY.
Minister of Mines and Energy: LÉON-EMMANUEL MONNET.
Minister of Construction, Town Planning and Housing: MARCEL BENOÎT AMON TANOH.
Minister of National Reconciliation and Relations with the Institutions: SÉBASTIEN DANO DJÉ DJÉ.
Minister of Economic Infrastructure: PATRICK ACHI.
Minister of Health and Public Hygiene: RÉMI ALLAH KOUADIO.
Minister of National Education: GILBERT BLEU-LAINE.
Minister of Higher Education and Scientific Research: IBRAHIMA CISSÉ.
Minister of Technical Education and Professional Training: MOUSSA DOSSO.
Minister of the Civil Service and Employment: HUBERT OULAYE.
Minister of Transport: TOIKEUSSE MABRI.
Minister of African Integration: AMADOU KONÉ.
Minister of Culture and Francophone Affairs: KOMOÉ AUGUSTIN KOUADIO.
Minister of Solidarity and the Victims of War: LOUIS ANDRÉ DAKOURY-TABLEY.
Minister of Animal Production and Fisheries: ALPHONSE DOUATI.
Minister of the Environment, Water and Forestry: DANIEL AHIZI AKA.
Minister of the Family, Women and Social Affairs: JEANNE BROU PEUHMOND ADJOUA.
Minister of the Struggle against AIDS: CHRISTINE NEBOUT ADJOBI.
Minister of Industry and the Promotion of the Private Sector: MARIE TÉHOUA AMAH.
Minister of Trade: YOUSSOUF SOUMAHORO.
Minister of Tourism and Crafts: SIDIKE KONATÉ.
Minister of Information and Communication Technology: HAMED BAKAYOKO.
Minister of Youth, Sport and Leisure: BANZIO DAGOBERT.
Minister of Reconstruction and Reintegration: FATOUMATA BAMBA.
Minister of Communication: IBRAHIM SY SAVANE.
Minister of Cities and Urban Health: THÉODORE MEL EG.

MINISTRIES

Office of the President: 01 BP 1354, Abidjan 01; tel. 20-22-02-22; fax 20-21-14-25; internet www.presidence.ci.
Office of the Prime Minister: blvd Angoulvant, 01 BP 1533, Abidjan 01; tel. 20-31-50-00; fax 20-22-18-33; internet www.premierministre.ci.
Ministry of African Integration: 5e–6e étages, Immeuble AMCI, 15 ave Joseph Anoma, Plateau, Abidjan; tel. 20-33-90-09.
Ministry of Agriculture: 25e étage, Immeuble Caisse de Stabilisation, BP V82, Abidjan; tel. 20-21-38-58; fax 20-21-46-18; e-mail minagra@cimail.net.
Ministry of Animal Production and Fisheries: 11e étage, Immeuble Caisse de Stabilisation, Plateau, Abidjan; tel. 20-21-33-94.
Ministry of Cities and Urban Health: Abidjan.
Ministry of the Civil Service and Employment: Immeuble Fonction Public, blvd Angoulvand, BP V93, Abidjan; tel. 20-21-42-90; fax 20-21-12-86.
Ministry of Communication: 22e étage, Tour C, Tours Administratives, Plateau, Abidjan; tel. 20-21-07-84; internet www.communication.gouv.ci.
Ministry of Construction, Town Planning and Housing: 26e étage, Tour D, Tours Administratives, 20 BP 650, Abidjan; tel. 20-21-82-35; fax 20-21-35-68.
Ministry of Culture and Francophone Affairs: 22e étage, Tour E, Tours Administratives, BP V39, Abidjan; tel. 20-21-40-34; fax 20-21-33-59; e-mail culture.ci@ci.refer.org.
Ministry of Defence: Camp Galliéni, côté Bibliothèque nationale, BP V241, Abidjan; tel. 20-21-02-88; fax 20-22-41-75.
Ministry of Economic Infrastructure: 23e étage, Immeuble Postel 2001, BP V6, Plateau, Abidjan; tel. 20-34-73-01; fax 20-21-37-30; e-mail minie@aviso.ci.
Ministry of the Economy and Finance: 16e étage, Immeuble SCIAM, ave Marchand, BP V163, Abidjan; tel. 20-20-08-42; fax 20-21-32-08.
Ministry of the Environment, Water and Forestry: 10e étage, Tour D, Tours Administratives, BP V06, Abidjan; tel. 20-22-61-35; fax 20-22-20-50.
Ministry of the Family, Women and Social Affairs: Tour E, Tours Administratives, BP V200, Abidjan; tel. 20-21-76-26; fax 20-21-44-61.
Ministry of Foreign Affairs: Bloc Ministériel, blvd Angoulvand, BP V109, Abidjan; tel. 20-22-71-50; fax 20-33-23-08; e-mail infos@mae.ci; internet www.mae.ci.
Ministry of Health and Public Hygiene: 16e étage, Tour C, Tours Administratives, Plateau, Abidjan; tel. 20-21-52-40.
Ministry of Higher Education and Scientific Research: 20e étage, Tour C, Tours Administratives, BP V151, Abidjan; tel. 20-21-57-73; fax 20-21-22-25.
Ministry of Industry and the Promotion of the Private Sector: 15e étage, Immeuble CCIA, rue Jean-Paul II, BP V65, Abidjan; tel. 20-21-64-73.
Ministry of Information and Communication Technology: 21e étage, Immeuble Postel 2001, BP V138, Abidjan; tel. 22-34-73-65; fax 22-44-78-47.
Ministry of the Interior: Immeuble SETU, en face de la préfecture, BP V241, Abidjan; tel. 20-22-38-16; fax 20-22-36-48.
Ministry of Justice and Human Rights: Bloc Ministériel, blvd Angoulvand A-17, BP V107, Plateau, Abidjan; tel. 20-21-17-27; fax 20-33-12-59.
Ministry of Mines and Energy: 15e étage, Immeuble SCIAM, ave Marchand, BP V40, Abidjan; tel. 20-21-66-17; fax 20-21-37-30.
Ministry of National Education: 28e étage, Tour D, Tours Administratives, BP V120, Abidjan; tel. 20-21-85-27; fax 20-22-93-22; e-mail menfb@ci.refer.org.
Ministry of National Reconciliation and Relations with the Institutions: Cocody, 08 BP 590, Abidjan 08; tel. 22-48-89-82; fax 22-48-92-82.
Ministry of Planning and Development: 23e étage, Immeuble CCIA, rue Jean-Paul II, Abidjan; tel. 20-22-20-04.
Ministry of Reconstruction and Reintegration: Abidjan.
Ministry of Solidarity and the Victims of War: Cité administrative, Tour B, 14e étage, Abidjan; tel. 20-21-33-20; e-mail info@solidarite.gouv.ci; internet www.solidarite.gouv.ci.
Ministry of the Struggle against AIDS: 7e étage, Immeuble Caisse de Stabilisation, Plateau, Abidjan; tel. 20-21-08-46.
Ministry of Technical Education and Professional Training: 10e étage, Tour C, Tours Administratives, Plateau, Abidjan; tel. 20-21-17-02.
Ministry of Tourism and Crafts: 15e étage, Tour D, Tours Administratives, BP V184, Abidjan 01; tel. 20-34-79-13; fax 20-44-55-80; internet www.tourisme.gouv.ci.
Ministry of Trade: 26e étage, Immeuble CCIA, rue Jean-Paul II, BP V65, Abidjan; tel. 20-21-76-35; fax 20-21-64-74.
Ministry of Transport: 14e étage, Immeuble Postel 2001, BP V06, Abidjan; tel. 20-34-48-58; fax 20-21-37-30.

CÔTE D'IVOIRE

Ministry of Youth, Sport and Leisure: 8e étage, Tour B, Tours Administratives, BP V136, Abidjan; tel. 20-21-92-64; fax 20-22-48-21.

President and Legislature

PRESIDENT

Presidential Election, 22 October 2000

Candidate	Votes	% of votes
Laurent Gbagbo (FPI)	1,065,597	59.36
Robert Gueï (Ind.)	587,267	32.72
Francis Wodié (PIT)	102,253	5.70
Théodore Mel-Eg (UDCY)	26,331	1.47
Nicolas Dioulo (Ind.)	13,558	0.76
Total*	**1,795,006**	**100.00**

* Excluding invalid votes (25,413).

LEGISLATURE

Assemblée nationale
01 BP 1381, Abidjan 01; tel. 20-21-60-69; fax 20-22-20-87.
President: MAMADOU KOULIBALY.

General Election, 10 December 2000*

Party	Seats
Front populaire ivoirien (FPI)	96
Parti démocratique de la Côte d'Ivoire—Rassemblement démocratique africain (PDCI—RDA)	94
Rassemblement des républicains (RDR) †	5
Parti ivoirien des travailleurs (PIT)	4
Union démocratique citoyenne (UDCY)	1
Mouvement des forces d'avenir (MFA)	1
Independents	22
Total‡	**223**

* These figures include the results of voting in 26 constituencies where elections were postponed until 14 January 2001, owing to unrest.
† The RDR officially boycotted the elections, and these seats were won by a faction within the party that did not participate in the boycott.
‡ Voting for the remaining two seats was postponed indefinitely.

Election Commission

Commission électorale indépendant: 08 BP 2648, Adidjan; tel. 21-30-58-01; f. 2001; 13 mems; Pres. ROBERT MAMBÉ BEUGRÉ.

Advisory Councils

Constitutional Council: blvd Carde, BP 4642, Abidjan 01; tel. 20-25-38-50; fax 20-21-21-68; internet www.gouv.ci/conseilconstitutionnel.php; f. 2000 to replace certain functions of the fmr Constitutional Chamber of the Supreme Court; Pres. YANON YAPO GERMAIN.

Economic and Social Council: 04 BP 301, Abidjan 04; tel. 20-21-14-54; internet ces-ci.org; Pres. LAURENT DONA-FOLOGO; Vice-Pres. DIGBEU HILAIRE ANY, ETIENNE KOUDOU BOTI, NICOLE DEIGNA, MARTIN KOUAKOU N'GUESSA, VAKABA DEMOVALY TOURÉ; 120 mems.

Political Organizations

In mid-2007 there were more than 100 registered political organizations.

Alliance pour la paix, le progrès et la souveraineté (APS): Abidjan; f. 2003 by fmr members of the UDPCI (q.v.); Pres. HILAIRE DIGBEU ANI.

Forces nouvelles (FN): Bouaké; tel. 20-20-04-04; e-mail senacom@fnci.info; internet www.fnci.info; f. 2003 by the Mouvement patriotique de Côte d'Ivoire (MPCI), following its absorption of the Mouvement populaire ivoirien du grand ouest (MPIGO) and the Mouvement pour la justice et la paix (MJP), both of which were based in Man, in the west of Côte d'Ivoire; representatives of these three 'politico-military' groups, which had emerged following the outbreak of civil conflict in September 2002, were included in the Government of National Reconciliation formed in March 2003; Sec.-Gen. GUILLAUME SORO KIGBAFORI.

Front populaire ivoirien (FPI): Marcory Zone 4C, 22 BP 302, Abidjan 22; tel. 21-24-36-76; fax 21-35-35-50; internet www.fpi.ci; f. 1990; socialist; Pres. PASCAL AFFI N'GUESSAN; Sec.-Gen. SYLVAIN MIAKA OURETO.

Mouvement des forces d'avenir (MFA): 15 BP 794, Abidjan 15; tel. 21-24-42-02; e-mail contact@mfa-ci.com; internet mfaci.hostarea.org; f. 1995; mem. of alliance, Rassemblement des Houphouëtistes pour la démocratie et la paix, formed in advance of proposed (but subsequently postponed) presidential elections in 2005; Pres. INNOCENT KOBENA ANAKY.

Parti africain pour la renaissance ivoirienne (PARI): Abidjan; f. 1991; Sec.-Gen. DANIEL ANIKPO.

Parti démocratique de la Côte d'Ivoire—Rassemblement démocratique africain (PDCI—RDA): 05 BP 36, Abidjan 05; e-mail sg@pdcirda.org; internet www.pdcirda.org; f. 1946; mem. of alliance, Rassemblement des Houphouëtistes pour la démocratie et la paix, formed in advance of proposed (but subsequently postponed) presidential elections in 2005; Pres. HENRI KONAN BÉDIÉ; Sec.-Gen. ALPHONSE DJÉDJÉ MADY.

Parti ivoirien des travailleurs (PIT): 20 BP 43, Abidjan 20; tel. 20-37-29-00; fax 20-37-29-00; e-mail pit.ci@africaonline.co.ci; social-democratic; f. 1990; First Nat. Sec. FRANCIS WODIÉ.

Parti pour le progrès et le socialisme (PPS): Abidjan; f. 1993; Sec.-Gen. Prof. BAMBA MORIFÉRÉ.

Rassemblement des républicains (RDR): 8 rue Lepic, Cocody, 06 BP 1440, Abidjan 06; tel. 22-44-33-51; fax 22-41-55-73; e-mail le-rdr@yahoo.fr; internet www.le-rdr.org; f. 1994 following split from PDCI—RDA (q.v.); officially boycotted the general election of Dec. 2000, except for a faction of some 60 candidates, led by ALPHONSE OULAÏ TOUSSÉA; mem. of alliance, Rassemblement des Houphouëtistes pour la démocratie et la paix, formed in advance of proposed (but subsequently postponed) presidential elections in 2005; Pres. Dr ALASSANE DRAMANE OUATTARA; Sec.-Gen. HENRIETTE DAGRI-DIABATÉ.

Union démocratique citoyenne (UDCY): 37 bis rue de la Canebière—PISAM, 01 BP 1410, Abidjan 01; tel. 22-47-12-94; e-mail udcy_ci@hotmail.com; internet www.udcy.com; f. 2000 following split from PDCI—RDA (q.v.); Pres. THÉODORE MEL-EG.

Union des sociaux-démocrates (USD): 08 BP 1866, Abidjan 08; tel. 22-44-06-70; Pres. BERNARD ZADI ZAOUROU; Sec.-Gen. Me JÉRÔME CLIMANLO COULIBALY.

Union pour la démocratie et pour la paix de la Côte d'Ivoire (UDPCI): 06 BP 1481, Abidjan 06; tel. 22-41-60-94; e-mail info@udpci.org; internet www.udpci.org; f. 2001 following split from PDCI—RDA by supporters of fmr head of state Gen. Robert Gueï; mem. of alliance, Rassemblement des Houphouëtistes pour la démocratie et la paix, formed in advance of proposed (but subsequently postponed) presidential elections in 2005; Pres. PAUL AKOTO YAO; Sec.-Gen. ALASSANE SALIF N'DIAYE.

Diplomatic Representation

EMBASSIES IN CÔTE D'IVOIRE

Following the onset of civil conflict in 2002 and subsequent unrest in Abidjan, many diplomatic missions have suspended or terminated their operations, or have transferred to other countries of the region.

Algeria: 53 blvd Clozel, 01 BP 1015, Abidjan 01; tel. 20-21-23-40; fax 20-22-37-12; Ambassador SALEH LEBDIOUI.

Angola: Lot 2461, rue des Jardins, Cocody-les-Deux-Plateaux, 01 BP 1734, Abidjan 01; tel. 22-41-38-79; fax 22-41-28-89; Ambassador GILBERTO BUTA LUTUKUTA.

Belgium: Immeuble Alliance, ave Terrasson des Fougères, 01 BP 1800, Abidjan 01; tel. 20-21-00-88; fax 20-22-41-77; e-mail abidjan@diplobel.org; internet www.diplomatie.be/abidjan; Ambassador DIRK VERHEYEN.

Benin: rue des Jasmins, Lot 1610, Cocody-les-Deux-Plateaux, 09 BP 283, Abidjan 09; tel. 22-41-44-13; fax 22-42-76-07; Ambassador OMER JEAN-GILLES DE SOUZA.

Brazil: Immeuble Alpha 2000, rue Gourgas, 01 BP 3820, Abidjan 01; tel. 20-22-23-41; fax 22-22-64-01; e-mail brascote@aviso.ci; Ambassador FAUSTO CARMELLO.

Burkina Faso: Immeuble SIDAM, 5e étage, 34 ave Houdaille, 01 BP 908, Plateau, Abidjan 01; tel. 20-21-15-01; fax 20-21-66-41; e-mail amba.bf@africaonline.ci; Ambassador EMILE ILBOUDO.

Cameroon: Immeuble le Général, blvd Botreau Roussel, 06 BP 326, Abidjan 06; tel. 20-21-33-31; fax 20-21-66-11; Ambassador (vacant).

Canada: Immeuble Trade Center, 23 ave Noguès, 01 BP 4104, Abidjan 01; tel. 20-30-07-00; fax 20-30-07-20; e-mail abdjn@

CÔTE D'IVOIRE

dfait-maeci.gc.ca; internet www.dfait-maeci.gc.ca/abidjan; Ambassador MARIE-ISABELLE MASSIP.

Central African Republic: 9 rue des Jasmins, Cocody Danga Nord, 01 BP 3387, Abidjan 01; tel. 20-21-36-46; fax 22-44-85-16; Ambassador YAGAO-N'GAMA LAZARE.

China, People's Republic: Lot 45, ave Jacques Aka, Cocody, 01 BP 3691, Abidjan 01; tel. 22-44-59-00; fax 22-44-67-81; e-mail chinaemb_ci@mfa.gov.cn; Ambassador WEI WENHUA.

Congo, Democratic Republic: Carrefour France-Amérique, RAN Treichville, ave 21, 01 BP 541, Abidjan 01; tel. 21-24-69-06; Ambassador ISABELLE I. NGANGELLI.

Egypt: Immeuble El Nasr, rue du Commerce, 01 BP 2104, Abidjan 01; tel. 20-32-79-25; fax 20-22-30-53; e-mail amegypteci@afnet.net; Ambassador SHERIF YOUSSEF ABBAS SOLIMAN.

Ethiopia: Immeuble Nour Al-Hayat, 01 BP 3712, Abidjan 01; tel. 20-21-33-65; fax 20-21-37-09; e-mail ambethio@gmail.com; Ambassador ABDULAZIZ AHMED ADEM.

France: rue Lecoeur, 17 BP 175, Abidjan 17; tel. 20-20-04-04; fax 20-20-04-47; e-mail scac.abidjan-amba@diplomatie.gouv.fr; internet www.ambafrance-ci.org.

Gabon: Immeuble Les Heveas, blvd Carde, 01 BP 3765, Abidjan 01; tel. 22-44-51-54; fax 22-44-75-05; Ambassador HENRI BEKALÉ-AKWÉ.

Germany: 39 blvd Hassan II, Cocody, 01 BP 1900, Abidjan 01; tel. and fax 22-44-20-41; e-mail d.bo.abj@africaonline.co.ci; internet www.abidjan.diplo.de; Ambassador ROLF ULRICH.

Ghana: Lot 2393, rue J 95, Cocody-les-Deux-Plateaux, 01 BP 1871, Abidjan 01; tel. 20-33-11-24; fax 20-22-33-57; Ambassador KABRAL BLAY-AMIHERE.

Guinea: Immeuble Duplessis, 08 BP 2280, Abidjan 08; tel. 20-22-25-20; fax 20-32-82-45; Ambassador (vacant).

Holy See: Apostolic Nunciature, rue Jacques Aka, 08 BP 1347, Abidjan 08; tel. 22-40-17-70; fax 22-40-17-74; e-mail nuntius@aviso.ci; Apostolic Nuncio Mgr MARIO ROBERTO CASSARI.

India: Cocody Danga Nord, 06 BP 318, Abidjan 06; tel. 22-42-37-69; fax 22-42-66-49; Ambassador AMARENDRA KHATUA.

Israel: Immeuble Nour Al-Hayat, 01 BP 1877, Abidjan 01; tel. 20-21-49-53; fax 20-21-87-04; e-mail info@abidjan.mfa.gov.il; Ambassador MICHAËL ARBEL.

Italy: 16 rue de la Canebière, Cocody, 01 BP 1905, Abidjan 01; tel. 22-44-61-70; fax 22-44-35-87; e-mail ambitali@aviso.ci; internet www.ambabidjan.esteri.it; Ambassador GIOVANNI POLIZZI.

Japan: Immeuble Alpha 2000, ave Chardy, 01 BP 1329, Abidjan 01; tel. 20-21-28-63; fax 20-21-30-51; Ambassador TETSUO SHIOGUCHI.

Korea, Democratic People's Republic: Abidjan; Ambassador RI JAE RIM.

Korea, Republic: Immeuble le Mans, 8e étage, 01 BP 3950, Abidjan 01; tel. 20-32-22-90; fax 20-22-22-74; e-mail ambcoabj@mofat.go.kr; Ambassador KIM JONG-IL.

Lebanon: Immeuble Trade Center, ave Noguès, 01 BP 2227, Abidjan 01; tel. 20-33-28-24; fax 20-32-11-37; Ambassador ALI AJAMI.

Liberia: Immeuble La Symphonie, ave Général de Gaulle, 01 BP 2514, Abidjan 01; tel. 20-22-23-59; fax 22-44-14-75; Ambassador KRONYANH M. WEEFUR.

Libya: Immeuble Shell, 01 BP 5725, Abidjan 01; tel. 20-22-01-27; fax 20-22-01-30; Ambassador FATHI NASHAD.

Mali: 46 blvd Lagunaire, 01 BP 2746, Abidjan 01; tel. 20-32-31-47; fax 20-21-55-14; Ambassador SADA SAMAKÉ.

Mauritania: rue Pierre et Marie Curie, 01 BP 2275, Abidjan 01; tel. 22-41-16-43; fax 22-41-05-77; Ambassador ABDERRAHIM OULD HADRAMI.

Morocco: 24 rue de la Canebière, 01 BP 146, Cocody, Abidjan 01; tel. 22-44-58-73; fax 22-44-60-58; e-mail sifmaabj@aviso.ci; Ambassador HASSAN BENNANI.

Niger: 23 ave Angoulvant, 01 BP 2743, Abidjan 01; tel. 21-26-28-14; fax 21-26-41-88; Ambassador ADAM ABDOULAYE DAN MARADI.

Nigeria: Immeuble Maison du Nigéria, 35 blvd de la République, 01 BP 1906, Abidjan 01; tel. 20-22-30-82; fax 20-21-30-83; e-mail info@nigeriaembassy-ci.org; internet www.nigeriaembassy-ci.org; Ambassador ALBERT O. SOYOMBO.

Norway: Immeuble N'Zarama, blvd Lagunaire, 01 BP 607, Abidjan 01; tel. 20-22-25-34; fax 20-21-91-99; e-mail emb.abidjan@mfa.no; internet www.norvege.ci; Ambassador ODD-EGIL ANDHØY.

Russia: BP 583, Riviera, Abidjan 01; tel. 22-43-09-59; fax 22-43-11-66; e-mail ambrus@globeaccess.net; Ambassador OLEG V. KOVALCHUK.

Saudi Arabia: Plateau, Abidjan; Ambassador (vacant).

Senegal: Immeuble Nabil Choucair, 6 rue du Commerce, 08 BP 2165, Abidjan 08; tel. 20-33-28-76; fax 20-32-50-39; Ambassador MOUSTAPHA SÈNE.

South Africa: Villa Marc André, rue Mgr René Kouassi, Cocody, 08 BP 1806, Abidjan 08; tel. 22-44-59-63; fax 22-44-74-50; e-mail ambafsudpol@aviso.ci; Ambassador G. DUMISANI GWADISO.

Spain: impasse Abla Pokou, Cocody Danga Nord, 08 BP 876, Abidjan 08; tel. 22-44-48-50; fax 22-44-71-22; e-mail embespci@correo.mae.es; Ambassador FRANCISCO ELIAS DE TEJADA LOZANO.

Switzerland: Immeuble Botreau Roussel, 28 ave Delafosse, Plateau, 01 BP 1914, Abidjan 01; tel. 20-21-17-21; fax 20-21-27-70; e-mail vertretung@abi.rep.admin.ch; Ambassador JOHANNES KUNZ.

Tunisia: Immeuble Shell, ave Lamblin, 01 BP 3906, Abidjan 01; tel. 20-22-61-23; fax 20-22-61-24; Ambassador ZINE EL ABIDINE TERRAS.

USA: Cocody Riviera Golf, 01 BP 1712, Abidjan 01; tel. 22-49-40-00; fax 22-49-43-23; e-mail abjpress@state.gov; internet abidjan.usembassy.gov; Ambassador WANDA L. NESBITT.

Judicial System

Since 1964 all civil, criminal, commercial and administrative cases have come under the jurisdiction of the courts of first instance, the assize courts and the Courts of Appeal, with the Supreme Court (referred to in the Constitution of 2000 as the Court of Cassation) as the highest court of appeal.

Supreme Court: rue Gourgas, Cocody, BP V30, Abidjan; tel. 20-22-73-72; fax 20-21-63-04; internet www.gouv.ci/courssupreme.php; comprises three chambers: judicial, administrative and auditing; Pres. TIA KONÉ; Pres. of the Judicial Chamber KAMA YAO; Pres. of the Administrative Chamber GEORGES AMANGOUA.

Courts of Appeal: Abidjan: First Pres. MARIE-FÉLICITÉ ARKHUST HOMA YAO; Bouaké: First Pres. CHRISTIAN ANIBIÉ KAKRÉ ZÉPHIRIN; Daloa: First Pres. GONHI SAHI.

Courts of First Instance: Abidjan: Pres. ANTOINETTE MARSOUIN; Bouaké: Pres. KABLAN AKA EDOUKOU; Daloa: Pres. WOUNE BLEKA; there are a further 25 courts in the principal centres.

High Court of Justice: composed of deputies elected from and by the Assemblée nationale; has jurisdiction to impeach the President or other member of the Government.

Constitutional Council: blvd Carde, BP 4642, Abidjan 01; tel. 20-25-38-50; fax 20-21-21-68; internet www.gouv.ci/conseilconstitutionnel.php; f. 2000 to replace certain functions of the fmr Constitutional Chamber of the Supreme Court; Pres. YANON YAPO GERMAIN; Mems Prof. RENÉ DEGNI SÉGUI, ANDRÉ KOUASSI KOUAKOU, ABRAHAM AKENOU SOUGBRO, MARIE-AGATHE BAROUAN DIOUMINCY LIKAGNÉNÉ, DOMINIQUE RÉGINE SUZANNE THALMAS TAYORO, LOUIS METAN AMANI.

Religion

The Constitution guarantees religious freedom, and this right is generally respected. Religious groups are required to register with the authorities, although no penalties are imposed on a group that fails to register. At the 1998 census it was estimated that about 34% of the population were Christians (mainly Roman Catholics), 27% of the population were Muslims, 15% followed traditional indigenous beliefs, 3% practised other religions, while 21% had no religious affiliation. It is, however, estimated that the proportion of Muslims is in fact significantly higher, as the majority of unregistered foreign workers are Muslims. Muslims are found in greatest numbers in the north of the country, while Christians are found mostly in the southern, central, western and eastern regions. Traditional indigenous beliefs are generally prevalent in rural areas.

ISLAM

Conseil National Islamique (CNI): Mosquée d'Aghien les deux Plateaux, BP 174 Cédex 03, Abidjan 08; tel. and fax 22-42-67-79; internet www.cni-cosim.ci; f. 1993; groups more than 5,000 local communities organized in 13 regional and 78 local organizations; Chair. Imam El Hadj IDRISS KOUDOUSS KONÉ.

Conseil Supérieur Islamique (CSI): 11 BP 71, Abidjan 11; tel. 21-25-24-70; fax 21-24-28-04; f. 1978; Chair. El Hadj MOUSTAPHA KOWEÏT DIABY.

CHRISTIANITY

The Roman Catholic Church

Côte d'Ivoire comprises four archdioceses and 10 dioceses. At 31 December 2005 there were approximately 3.1m. Roman Catholics in the country, comprising about 17.3% of the total population.

CÔTE D'IVOIRE

Bishops' Conference
Conférence Episcopale de la Côte d'Ivoire, BP 713 Cédex 03, Abidjan-Riviera; tel. 22-47-20-00; fax 22-47-60-65.
f. 1973; Pres. Most Rev. LAURENT AKRAN MANDJO (Bishop of Yopougon).

Archbishop of Abidjan: Most Rev. JEAN-PIERRE KUTWA, Archevêché, ave Jean Paul II, 01 BP 1287, Abidjan 01; tel. 20-21-23-08; fax 20-21-40-22.

Archbishop of Bouaké: Most Rev. PAUL-SIMÉON AHOUANAN DJRO, Archevêché, 01 BP 649, Bouaké 01; tel. and fax 31-63-24-59; e-mail archebke@aviso.ci.

Archbishop of Gagnoa: Most Rev. BARTHÉLÉMY DJABLA, Archevêché, BP 527, Gagnoa; tel. and fax 32-77-25-68; e-mail evechegagnoa@africaonline.co.ci.

Archbishop of Korhogo: Most Rev. MARIE-DANIEL DADIET, BP 1581, Yamoussoukro; tel. 36-86-01-18; fax 36-86-08-31; e-mail kamberensis@yahoo.fr.

Protestant Churches

Eglise CMA—Christian and Missionary Alliance: BP 585, Bouaké 01; tel. 31-63-23-12; fax 31-63-54-12; f. 1929; 13 mission stations; Nat. Pres. Rev. CÉLESTIN COFFI.

Eglise du Nazaréen (Church of the Nazarene): 22 BP 623, Abidjan 22; tel. 22-41-07-80; fax 22-41-07-81; e-mail awfcon@compuserve.com; f. 1987; active in evangelism, ministerial training and medical work; Dir JOHN SEAMAN.

Eglise Evangélique des Assemblées de Dieu de Côte d'Ivoire: 04 BP 266, Abidjan 04; tel. 20-37-05-79; fax 20-24-94-65; f. 1960; Pres. JEAN-BAPTISTE NIELBIEN.

Eglise Harriste: Bingerville; f. 1913 by William Wade Harris; affiliated to World Council of Churches 1998; allows polygamous new converts; 100,000 mems, 1,400 preachers, 7,000 apostles; Sec.-Gen. DOGBO JULES.

Eglise Protestante Baptiste Oeuvres et Mission Internationale: 03 BP 1032, Abidjan 03; tel. 23-45-20-18; fax 23-45-56-41; e-mail epbomi@yahoo.com; internet www.epbomi.net; f. 1975; active in evangelism, teaching and social work; medical centre, 6,000 places of worship, 400 missionaries and 193,000 mems; Pres. Rev. Dr YAYE ROBERT DION.

Eglise Méthodiste Unie de Côte d'Ivoire: 41 blvd de la République, 01 BP 1282, Abidjan 01; tel. 20-21-17-97; fax 20-22-52-03; e-mail emuciconf@yahoo.fr; f. 1923; publ. Le Méthodiste (monthly); autonomous since 1985; c. 800,000 mems; Pres. BENJAMIN BONI.

Mission Evangélique de l'Afrique Occidentale (MEAO): BP 822, Bouaflé; tel. and fax 30-68-93-70; e-mail wirci@aviso.ci; f. 1934; 16 missionaries, 5 staff at mission school; Field Dirs HARRY EUVING, PAULINE EUVING; affiliated church: Alliance des Eglises Evangéliques de Côte d'Ivoire (AEECI); 260 churches, 68 full-time pastors; Pres. KOUASSI ALAINGBRÉ PASCAL.

Mission Evangélique Luthérienne en Côte d'Ivoire (MELCI): BP 196, Touba; tel. 33-70-77-11; e-mail melci@aviso.ci; f. 1984; active in evangelism and social work; Dir GJERMUND VISTE.

Union des Eglises Evangéliques du Sud-Ouest de la Côte d'Ivoire and Mission Biblique: 08 BP 20, Abidjan 08; f. 1927; c. 250 places of worship.

WorldVenture: BP 109, Korhogo; tel. 36-86-01-07; fax 36-86-11-50; f. 1947; fmrly Conservative Baptist Foreign Mission Society, subsequently CB International; active in evangelism, medical work, translation, literacy and theological education in the northern area and in Abidjan.

The Press

DAILIES

24 Heures: rue St Jean, duplex 65, Cocody–Val Doyen I, 10 BP 3302, Abidjan 10; tel. 22-41-29-53; fax 22-41-37-82; e-mail infos@24heures.net; internet www.24heuresci.com; f. 2002; Dir-Gen. ABDOULAYE SANGARÉ; Dir of Publication and Editor-in-Chief JOACHIM BEUGRÉ; circ. 21,000 (2005).

Actuel: Cocody-les-Deux-Plateaux, 06 BP 2868, Abidjan 06; tel. 22-42-63-27; fax 22-42-63-32; f. 1996; organ of the FPI; Dir EUGÈNE ALLOU WANYOU; Editor-in-Chief DIABATÉ A. SIDICK.

L'Aurore: 18 BP 418, Abidjan 18; tel. 05-61-65-75; Editor-in-Chief EHOUMAN KASSY.

Le Courrier d'Abidjan: Riviera Bonoumin, 25 BP 1682, Abidjan 25; tel. 22-43-38-22; fax 22-43-30-46; internet www.lecourrierdabidjan.info; f. 2003.

Douze: rue Louis Lumière, Zone 4C, 10 BP 2462, Abidjan 10; tel. 21-25-54-00; fax 21-24-47-27; e-mail douze@afnet.net; publ. by Editions Olympe; f. 1994; sport; Dir MAZÉ SOUMAHORO; Editor-in-Chief FRANÇOIS BINI.

Fraternité Matin: blvd du Général de Gaulle, 01 BP 1807, Abidjan 01; tel. 20-37-06-66; fax 20-37-25-45; e-mail contact@fratmat.net; internet www.fratmat.net; f. 1964; official newspaper; Dir-Gen. HONORAT DÉ YÉDAGNE; Editorial Dir ALFRED DAN MOUSSA; circ. 26,000 (2005).

L'Intelligent d'Abidjan: Villa 12s, Bâtiment Star 4, 19 BP 1534, Abidjan 19; tel. 22-42-55-56; e-mail intelliabidjan@yahoo.fr; internet www.lintelligentdabidjan.org; f. 2003; Dir-Gen. W. ALAFÉ ASSÉ.

L'Inter: 10 BP 2462, Abidjan 10; tel. 21-21-28-00; fax 21-21-28-05; e-mail inter@linter-ci.com; internet www.linter-ci.com; f. 1998; publ. by Editions Olympe; national and international politics and economics; Dir RAYMOND N'CHO NIMBA; Editor-in-Chief CHARLES A. D'ALMÉIDA; circ. 18,000 (2002).

Le JD (Jeune Démocrate): 23 BP 3842, Abidjan 23; tel. 23-51-62-45; fax 23-51-63-75; f. 1999; Dir IGNACE DASSOHIRI; Editor-in-Chief OCTAVE BOYOU.

Le Jour: 26 Cocody-les-Deux-Plateau, 25 BP 1082, Abidjan 25; tel. 20-21-95-78; fax 20-21-95-80; internet www.lejourplus.com; f. 1994; publ. by Editions Le Nere; independent; Dir of Publication KOUAMÉ KOUAKOU; Editor-in-Chief VICKY DELORE; circ. 15,000 (2002).

Le Journal: Abidjan; internet www.lejournalci.com; f. 2003; supports PDCI—RDA; Dir of Publication NAZAIRE BREKA.

Le Libéral: 01 BP 6938, Abidjan 01; tel. and fax 22-52-21-41; e-mail leliberal@aviso.ci; f. 1997; Dir YORO KONÉ; Editor-in-Chief BAKARY NIMAGA; circ. 15,000.

Le National: Angré, Cocody, 16 BP 165, Abidjan 16; tel. 22-52-27-43; fax 22-52-27-42; f. 1999; nationalist; Publr LAURENT TAPÉ KOULOU; Editor-in-Chief (vacant); circ. 20,000 (2002).

Nord-Sud: Abidjan; f. 2005; Dir MEÏTE SINDOU; circ. 18,000 (2005).

Notr'Aurore: Immeuble SICOGI, Bâtiment K, Appartement 124, Deux-Plateaux Aghien, blvd Latrille, Abidjan; tel. 22-42-08-21; fax 22-42-08-24; f. 2002; nationalist; Editor-in-Chief EMMANUEL GRIÉ.

Notre Voie: Cocody-les-Deux-Plateaux, 06 BP 2868, Abidjan 06; tel. 22-42-63-31; fax 22-42-63-32; e-mail gnh@africaonline.co.ci; internet www.notrevoie.com; f. 1978; organ of the FPI; Dir WANYOU EUGÈNE ALLOU; Editor-in-Chief CÉSAR ETOU; circ. 20,000 (2002).

Le Nouveau Réveil: Adjamé Sud 80 Logements, Tours SICOGI, face Frat-Mat, Bâtiment A, 2e étage, porte 6, 01 BP 10684, Abidjan 01; tel. 20-38-42-00; fax 20-38-67-91; e-mail lenouveaureveil@yahoo.fr; internet www.lenouveaureveil.com; f. 2001 to replace weekly Le Réveil-Hebdo; supports PDCI—RDA; Dir of Publication DENIS KAH ZION; Editor-in-Chief EDDY PEHE; circ. 18,000 (2005).

Le Patriote: 23 rue Paul Langevin, Zone 4C, 22 BP 509, Abidjan 22; tel. 21-21-19-45; fax 21-35-11-83; e-mail info@lepatriote.net; internet www.lepatriote.net; organ of the RDR; Editor-in-Chief MOUSSA TOURÉ; circ. 40,000 (2002).

Le Populaire: 19 blvd Angoulvant, résidence Neuilly, Plateau, 01 BP 5496, Abidjan 01; tel. 21-36-34-15; fax 21-36-43-28; Dir RAPHAËL ORE LAKPÉ.

Soir Info: 10 BP 2462, Abidjan 10; tel. 21-21-28-00; fax 21-21-28-06; e-mail soirinfo@soirinfo.com; internet www.soirinfo.com; f. 1994; publ. by Editions Olympe; independent; Dir MAURICE FERRO BI BALI; Editor-in-Chief ZOROMÉ LOSS; circ. 22,000 (2002).

La Voie: face Institut Marie-Thérèse Houphouët-Boigny, 17 BP 656, Abidjan 17; tel. 20-37-68-23; fax 20-37-74-76; organ of the FPI; Dir ABOU DRAHAMANE SANGARÉ; Man. MAURICE LURIGNAN.

SELECTED BI-WEEKLIES AND WEEKLIES

L'Agora: Immeuble Nana Yamoussou, ave 13, rue 38, Treichville, 01 BP 5326, Abidjan 01; tel. 21-34-11-72; f. 1997; weekly; Dir FERNAND DÉDÉ; Editor-in-Chief BAMBA ALEX SOULEYMANE.

Argument: 09 BP 3328, Abidjan 09; tel. 20-37-63-96; f. 1998; weekly; Dir GUY BADIETO LIALY; Editor-in-Chief JEAN-LOUIS PÉHE.

Le Démocrate: Maison du Congrès, ave 2, Treichville, 01 BP 1212, Abidjan 01; tel. 21-24-45-88; fax 21-24-25-61; f. 1991; weekly; organ of the PDCI—RDA; Dir NOËL YAO.

Le Front: Immeuble Mistral, 3e étage, 220 Logements, 11 BP 11 2678, Abidjan 11; tel. 20-38-13-24; fax 20-38-70-83; e-mail quotidienlefront@yahoo.fr; internet www.lefront.com; two a week; Editorial Dir FATOUMATA COULIBALY; Editor KPOKPA BLÉ.

Gbich!: 10 BP 399, Abidjan 10; tel. and fax 21-26-31-94; e-mail gbich@assistweb.net; internet www.gbichonline.com; weekly; satirical; Editor-in-Chief MATHIEU BLEDOU.

Le Nouvel Horizon: 220 Logements, blvd du Général de Gaulle, Adjamé, 17 BP 656, Abidjan 17; tel. 20-37-68-23; f. 1990; weekly; organ of the FPI; Dir ABOU DRAHAMANE SANGARÉ; circ. 15,000.

La Nouvelle Presse: rue des Jardins, Cocody-les-Deux-Plateaux, 01 BP 8534, Abidjan 01; tel. 22-41-04-76; fax 22-41-04-15; f. 1992;

CÔTE D'IVOIRE *Directory*

weekly; publ. by Centre Africain de Presse et d'Edition; current affairs; Editors JUSTIN VIEYRA, JÉRÔME CARLOS; circ. 10,000.

Le Repère: 220 Logements, Adjamé Sud-Tours SICOGI, face Frat-Mat, Bâtiment A, 2e étage P6, 04 BP 1947, Abidjan 04; tel. and fax 20-38-67-91; supports PDCI—RDA; two a week; Dir of Publication DENIS KAH ZION; circ. 10,000 (2004).

Sports Magazine: Yopougon-SOGEFIHA, 01 BP 4030, Abidjan 01; tel. 23-45-14-02; f. 1997; weekly; Dir JOSEPH ABLE.

Téré: 220 Logements, blvd du Général de Gaulle, Adjamé-Liberté, 20 BP 43, Abidjan 20; tel. and fax 20-37-79-42; weekly; organ of the PIT; Dir ANGÈLE GNONSOA.

Top-Visages: rue du Commerce, 23 BP 892, Abidjan 23; tel. 20-33-72-10; fax 20-32-81-05; e-mail contact@topvisages.net; internet www.topvisages.net; weekly; Editor-in-Chief E. TONGA BÉHI; circ. 40,000 (2004).

La Voie du Compatriote: Adjamé St-Michel, 09 BP 2008, Abidjan 09; tel. 20-37-50-13; f. 1998; weekly; Dir SINARI KAL.

SELECTED PERIODICALS

Côte d'Ivoire Magazine: Présidence de la République, 01 BP 1354, Abidjan 01; tel. 20-22-02-22; f. 1998; quarterly; Dir JEAN-NOËL LOUKO.

Juris-Social: Centre National de Documentation Juridique (CNDJ), Villa 381, ilôt 43, face Polyclinique Saint Jacques, blvd Latrille, Cocody-les-Deux-Plateaux, 01 BP 2757, Abidjan 01; tel. 20-22-74-85; fax 20-22-74-86; e-mail cndj@aviso.ci; internet www.cndj.ci; monthly; jurisprudence; CNDJ also publishes quarterly periodical *Juris OHADA*.

La Lettre de l'Afrique de l'Ouest: rue des Jardins, Cocody-les-Deux-Plateaux, 01 BP 8534, Abidjan 01; tel. 22-41-04-76; fax 22-41-04-15; f. 1995; publ. by Centre Africain de Presse et d'Edition; six a year; politics, economics, regional integration; Editors JUSTIN VIEYRA, JÉRÔME CARLOS.

Maisons et Matériaux: 08 BP 2150, Abidjan 08; tel. 22-42-92-17; monthly; Dir THIAM T. DJENEBOU.

Roots-Rock Magazine: Abidjan; tel. 22-42-84-74; f. 1998; monthly; music; Dir DIOMANDÉ DAVID.

RTI-Mag: 08 BP 663, Abidjan 08; tel. 20-33-14-46; fax 20-32-12-06; publ. by Radiodiffusion-Télévision Ivoirienne; listings magazine.

Sentiers: 26 ave Chardy, 01 BP 2432, Abidjan 01; tel. 20-21-95-68; fax 20-21-95-80; e-mail redaction@aviso.ci; Editor-in-Chief DIÉGOU BAILLY.

Stades d'Afrique: blvd du Général de Gaulle, 01 BP 1807, Abidjan 01; tel. 20-37-06-66; fax 20-37-25-45; f. 2000; sports; monthly; Dir-Gen. EMMANUEL KOUASSI KOKORÉ; Editor-in-Chief HÉGAUD OUATTARA.

Le Succès: 21 BP 3748, Abidjan 21; tel. 20-37-71-64; monthly; Dir AKPLA PLAKATOU.

Univers jeunes: 01 BP 3713, Abidjan 01; tel. 20-21-20-00; fax 21-35-35-45; monthly; Editor-in-Chief MOUSSA SY SAVANÉ.

La Voix d'Afrique: rue des Jardins, Cocody-les-Deux-Plateaux, 01 BP 8534, Abidjan 01; tel. 22-41-04-76; fax 22-41-04-15; publ. by Centre Africain de Presse et d'Edition; monthly; Editor-in-Chief GAOUSSOU KAMISSOKO.

NEWS AGENCIES

Agence Ivoirienne de Presse (AIP): ave Chardy, 04 BP 312, Abidjan 04; tel. 20-22-64-13; fax 20-21-35-39; e-mail aip@ci.refer.org; f. 1961; Dir DALLI DEBY.

PRESS ASSOCIATIONS

Association de la Presse Démocratique Ivoirienne (APDI): Abidjan; tel. 20-37-06-66; f. 1994; Chair. JEAN-BAPTISTE AKROU.

Union nationale des journalistes de Côte d'Ivoire (UNJCI): 06 BP 1675, Plateau, Abidjan 06; tel. 20-21-61-07; e-mail prunjci@unjci.org; internet unjci.org; f. 1991; Pres. HONORAT NDJOMOU DE YÉDAGNE.

Publishers

Centre Africain de Presse et d'Edition (CAPE): rue des Jardins, Cocody-les-Deux-Plateaux, 01 BP 8534, Abidjan 01; tel. 22-41-04-76; fax 22-41-04-15; Man. JUSTIN VIEYRA.

Centre d'Edition et de Diffusion Africaines (CEDA): 17 rue des Carrossiers, 04 BP 541, Abidjan 04; tel. 20-24-65-10; fax 21-25-05-67; e-mail infos@ceda-ci.com; internet www.ceda-ci.com; f. 1961; 20% state-owned; general non-fiction, school and children's books, literary fiction; Pres. and Dir-Gen. VENANCE KACOU.

Centre de Publications Evangéliques: 08 BP 900, Abidjan 08; tel. 22-44-48-05; fax 22-44-58-17; e-mail cpe@aviso.ci; internet www.editionscpe.com; f. 1967; evangelical Christian; Dir JULES OUOBA.

Editions Bognini: 06 BP 1254, Abidjan 06; tel. 20-41-16-86; social sciences, literary fiction.

Editions Eburnie: 01 BP 1984, 01 Abidjan; tel. 20-21-64-65; fax 20-21-45-46; e-mail eburnie@aviso.ci; f. 2001; illustrated books for children, social sciences, poetry.

Editions Neter: 01 BP 7370, Abidjan 01; tel. 22-52-52-68; f. 1992; politics, culture, history, literary fiction; Dir RICHARD TA BI SENIN.

Nouvelles Editions Ivoiriennes: 1 blvd de Marseille, 01 BP 1818, Abidjan 01; tel. 21-24-07-66; fax 21-24-24-56; e-mail edition@nei-ci.com; internet www.nei-ci.com; f. 1972; literature, criticism, essays, drama, social sciences, history, in French and English; Dir GUY LAMBIN.

Presses Universitaires et Scolaires d'Afrique (PUSAF—Editions Cissé): 08 BP 177, Abidjan 08; tel. 22-41-12-71; mathematics, economics, medicine.

Université Nationale de Côte d'Ivoire: 01 BP V34, Abidjan 01; tel. 22-44-08-59; f. 1964; academic and general non-fiction and periodicals; Publications Dir GILLES VILASCO.

GOVERNMENT PUBLISHING HOUSE

Imprimerie Nationale: BP V87, Abidjan; tel. 20-21-76-11; fax 20-21-68-68.

Broadcasting and Communications

TELECOMMUNICATIONS

Regulatory Authorities

Agence des Télécommunications de Côte d'Ivoire (ATCI): Immeuble Postel 2001, 4e étage, rue Lecoeur, 18 BP 2203, Abidjan 18; tel. 20-34-43-74; fax 20-34-43-75; e-mail courrier@atci.ci; internet www.atci.ci; f. 1995; Dir-Gen. SYLVANUS KLA.

Conseil des Télécommunications de Côte d'Ivoire: 17 BP 110, Abidjan 17; tel. 20-34-43-04; f. 1995; deals with issues of arbitration.

Service Providers

Atlantique Telecom—Moov (Moov): Immeuble N'Zarama, blvd Lagunaire, 01 BP 10204, Abidjan 01; tel. 20-30-21-19; fax 20-30-21-10; e-mail hfo@atlantiquetelecom.net; internet www.moov.com; f. 2005 as jt venture by Atlantique Télécoms (Côte d'Ivoire) and Elisalat (United Arab Emirates); 70% owned by Etisalat (United Arab Emirates); mobile cellular telecommunications; Dir ABOUBACAR TOURÉ; 700,000 subscribers (Dec. 2006).

Côte d'Ivoire-Télécom (CI-Télécom): Immeuble Postel 2001, rue Lecoeur, 17 BP 275, Abidjan 17; tel. 20-34-40-00; fax 20-21-28-28; internet www.citelecom.ci; f. 1991; 51% owned by France Télécom, 49% state-owned; Pres. YAYA OUATTARA; Man. Dir ALAIN PETIT; 327,000 subscribers (June 2002).

MTN Côte d'Ivoire: Immeuble Loteny, 12 rue Crossons Duplessis, 01 BP 3685, Abidjan 01; tel. 20-31-63-16; fax 20-31-84-50; internet www.mtn.ci; f. 1996 as Loteny Télécom-Télécel; present name adopted 2005; mobile cellular telephone operator in more than 110 urban centres and on principal highway routes; 51% owned by Mobile Telephone Network International (South Africa); Chief Exec. RON ALLARD; 1.63m. subscribers (Dec. 2006).

Orange Côte d'Ivoire: Immeuble Saha, blvd Valéry Giscard d'Estaing, Zone 4C, 11 BP 202, Abidjan 11; tel. 21-23-90-07; fax 21-23-90-11; internet www.orange.ci; f. 1996 as Ivoiris, present name adopted 2002; mobile cellular telephone operator in more than 60 urban centres; 85% owned by France Télécom; Man. Dir BERNARD CLIVET; 1.75m. subscribers (Dec. 2006).

BROADCASTING

Radio

In 1993 the Government permitted the first commercial radio stations to broadcast in Côte d'Ivoire; of the five licences initially granted, four were to foreign stations. Between 1998 and early 2001, a further 52 licences were granted.

Radiodiffusion-Télévision Ivoirienne (RTI): blvd des Martyrs, Cocody, 08 BP883, Abidjan 08; tel. 22-48-61-62; fax 22-44-78-23; e-mail info.rti@rti.ci; internet www.rti.ci; f. 1962; state-owned; two national TV channels, La Première and TV2, and two national radio channels, La Nationale and Fréquence II; Pres. MAURICE BANDAMA; Dir-Gen. AMESSAN BROU; Dir, La Première VICTOR DEBASS KPAN; Dir, TV2 ADÈLE DJEDJE; Dir, Radiodiffusion ELOI OULAÏ.

CÔTE D'IVOIRE

City FM: Immeuble Alpha Cissé, avant la piscine d'Etat, Treichville, 01 BP 7207, Abidjan 01; tel. 21-25-10-28; f. 1999; Pres. and Man. Dir Me ALIOU SIBI.

Radio Espoir: 12 BP 27, Abidjan 12; tel. 21-75-68-02; fax 21-75-68-04; e-mail respoir@aviso.ci; internet www.radioespoir.ci; f. 1990; Roman Catholic; broadcasts in French, local and sub-regional languages; Dir Fr BASILE DIANÉ KOGNAN.

Radio Nostalgie: 01 BP 157, Abidjan 01; tel. 20-21-10-52; fax 20-21-85-53; internet www.nostalgie.ci; f. 1993; Dir-Gen. HERVÉ CORNUEL.

Radio Peleforo Gbon: Route Ferké km 2, BP 841, Korhogo; tel. 21-86-22-62; fax 21-86-20-33.

Radio Soleil: 16 BP 1179, Abidjan 16; tel. 21-99-17-64; fax 21-79-12-48; e-mail ebadouel@irisa.fr.

Côte d'Ivoire also receives broadcasts from the Gabon-based Africa No 1 radio station, from the French-language Africa service of the BBC (United Kingdom), and from Radio France Internationale.

Television

Radiodiffusion-Télévision Ivoirienne (RTI): see Radio section.

Canal Plus Horizons: Abidjan; tel. 20-31-67-67; fax 20-22-72-22; e-mail abonne@canalhorizons.ci; internet www.canalhorizons.com; broadcasts commenced 1994; subsidiary of Canal Plus (France).

Finance

(cap. = capital; res = reserves; dep. = deposits; m. = million; br(s). = branch(es); amounts in francs CFA, unless otherwise indicated)

BANKING

Central Bank

Banque centrale des états de l'Afrique de l'ouest (BCEAO): 01 BP 1769, Abidjan 01; tel. 20-20-84-00; fax 20-22-28-52; internet www.bceao.int; f. 1962; HQ in Dakar, Senegal; bank of issue for the mem. states of the Union économique et monétaire ouest-africaine (UEMOA, comprising Benin, Burkina Faso, Côte d'Ivoire, Guinea-Bissau, Mali, Niger, Senegal and Togo); cap. and res 859,313m., total assets 5,671,675m. (Dec. 2002); Gov. DAMO JUSTIN BARO (acting); Dir in Côte d'Ivoire LANSINA BAKARY; 5 brs in Côte d'Ivoire.

Commercial Banks

Bank of Africa—Côte d'Ivoire (BOA—CI): ave Terrasson de Fougères, angle Rue Gourgas, 01 BP 4132, Abidjan 01; tel. 20-30-34-00; fax 20-30-34-01; e-mail boaci@bkofafrica.com; internet www.bkofafrica.net/cote_d_ivoire.htm; f. 1980; 66.7% owned by Groupe African Financial Holding; cap. and res 4,135m., total assets 81,072m. (Dec. 2003); Dir-Gen. RENÉ FORMEY DE SAINT LOUVENT; 1 br.

Banque Atlantique de Côte d'Ivoire: Immeuble Atlantique, ave Noguès, Plateau, 04 BP 1036, Abidjan 04; tel. 20-31-59-50; fax 20-21-68-52; e-mail baci1@baci.ci; f. 1979; cap. 7,000.0m., total assets 58,830m. (Dec. 2003); Pres. KONE DOSSONGUI; Dir-Gen. JEAN-PIERRE COTI; 3 brs.

Banque de l'Habitat de Côte d'Ivoire (BHCI): 22 ave Joseph Anoma, 01 BP 2325, Abidjan 01; tel. 20-25-39-39; fax 20-22-58-18; e-mail info@bhci.ci; internet www.bhci.ci; f. 1993; cap. and res 1,755m., total assets 16,834m. (Dec. 1999); Chair. DAVID AMUAH; Man. Dir LANCINA COULIBALY; 3 brs.

Banque Internationale pour le Commerce et l'Industrie de la Côte d'Ivoire SA (BICI-CI): ave Franchet d'Espérey, 01 BP 1298, Abidjan 01; tel. 20-20-16-00; fax 20-20-17-00; e-mail michel.lafont@africa.bnpparibas.com; internet www.bicici.org; f. 1962; 67.5% owned by BNP Paribas (France); absorbed BICI Bail de Côte d'Ivoire in 2003 and Compagnie Financière de la Côte d'Ivoire in 2004; cap. and res 38,436.7m., total assets 276,432.1m. (Dec. 2004); Chair. ANGE KOFFY; 35 brs.

Banque Nationale d'Investissement: Immeuble SCIAM, ave Marchand, Plateau, 01 BP 670, Abidjan 01; tel. 20-20-98-00; fax 20-21-35-78; e-mail info@caa.ci.com; cap. and res 28,408m., total assets 253,668m. (Dec. 2003); Pres. and Dir-Gen. VICTOR JÉRÔME NEMBELESSINI-SILUÉ.

Banque Paribas Côte d'Ivoire (Paribas—CI): 17 ave Terrasson de Fougères, 17 BP 09, Abidjan 17; tel. 20-21-86-86; fax 20-21-88-23; f. 1984; 85% owned by BNP Paribas (France); cap. and res 2,938m., total assets 30,697m. (Dec. 1999); Pres. and Dir-Gen. FRANÇOIS DAUGE.

BIAO—Côte d'Ivoire (BIAO—CI): 8–10 ave Joseph Anoma, 01 BP 1274, Abidjan 01; tel. 20-20-07-20; fax 20-20-07-00; e-mail info@biao.co.ci; internet www.biao.co.ci; f. 1980; fmrly Banque Internationale pour l'Afrique de l'Ouest—Côte d'Ivoire; 80% owned by Banque Belgolaise (Belgium), 20% state-owned; cap. 10,000.0m., res 169.9m., dep. 162,074.7m. (Dec. 2003); Pres. SEYDOU ELIMANE DIARRA; 31 brs.

Citibank Côte d'Ivoire: Immeuble Botreau-Roussel, 28 ave Delafosse, 01 BP 3698, Abidjan 01; tel. 20-20-90-00; fax 20-21-76-85; e-mail citibank@odaci.net; total assets US $198.7m. (2003); Dir-Gen. CHARLES KIE.

COFIPA Investment Bank CI: Immeuble Botreau Roussel, ave Delafosse, 04 BP 411, Abidjan 04; tel. 20-30-23-02; fax 20-30-23-01; e-mail dg@cofipa.ci; cap. and res 2,382.5m., total assets 19,171.2m. (Dec. 2002); Pres. BABER TOUNKARA; Dir-Gen. JACKIE VASSEUR.

Compagnie Bancaire de l'Atlantique Côte d'Ivoire (COBACI): Immeuble Atlantique, ave Noguès, 01 BP 522, Abidjan 01; tel. 20-21-28-04; fax 20-21-07-98; e-mail cobaci@africaonline.co.ci; 65% owned by Banque Atlantique–Côte d'Ivoire; cap. 3,002m., res 710m., total assets 38,502m. (Dec. 2003); Pres. DOSSONGUI KONÉ; Dir-Gen. RENÉ MAX DELAFOSSE.

Ecobank Côte d'Ivoire: Immeuble Alliance, 1 ave Terrasson de Fougères, 01 BP 4107, Abidjan 01; tel. 20-21-10-41; fax 20-21-88-16; e-mail ecobankci@ecobank.com; internet www.ecobank.com; f. 1989; 94% owned by Ecobank Transnational Inc (Togo); cap. and res 6,199m., dep. 118,761m. (Dec. 2003); Chair. AKA AOUÉLÉ; 1 br.

Omnifinance: 6e étage, Immeuble Alliance, 17 ave Terrasson de Fougères, 01 BP 6028, Abidjan 01; tel. 20-21-42-08; fax 20-21-42-58; 30% owned by Afriland First Bank (Cameroon); cap. and res 2,400m., total assets 38,322m. (Dec. 2003); Pres. and Dir-Gen. JACOB AMEMA-TEKPO.

Société Générale de Banques en Côte d'Ivoire (SGBCI): 5–7 ave Joseph Anoma, 01 BP 1355, Abidjan 01; tel. 20-20-12-34; fax 20-20-14-92; e-mail ddl.dir@sgbci.net; internet sgbci.groupe.socgen.com; f. 1962; 56.8% owned by Société Générale (France); cap. 15,333m., res 31,822m., total assets 417,424.5m. (Dec. 2003); Pres. TIÉMOKO YADÉ COULIBALY; Dir-Gen. BERNARD LABADENS; 55 brs.

Société Générale de Financement et de Participations en Côte d'Ivoire (SOGEFINANCE): 5–7 ave Joseph Anoma, 01 BP 3904, Abidjan 01; tel. 20-22-55-30; fax 20-32-67-60; f. 1978; 58% owned by SGBCI; cap. and res 2,409m., total assets 5,215m. (Dec. 2003); Pres. JEAN-LOUIS MATTEI; Dir-Gen. MICHEL MIAILLE.

Société Ivoirienne de Banque (SIB): Immeuble Alpha 2000, 34 blvd de la République, 01 BP 1300, Abidjan 01; tel. 20-20-00-00; fax 20-20-01-19; e-mail info@sib.ci; internet www.sib.ci; f. 1962; 51% owned by Calyon Corporate & Investment Bank (France), 49% state-owned; reduction of state holding to 19% proposed; cap. and res 15,733m., total assets 173,809m. (Dec. 2002); Administrator and Dir-Gen. PASCAL FALL; 14 brs.

Standard Chartered Bank Côte d'Ivoire (SCBCI): 23 blvd de la République, face Commissariat du 1er arrondissement, 17 BP 1141, Abidjan 17; tel. 20-30-32-00; fax 20-30-32-01; e-mail mylene.oule@standardchartered.com; internet www.standardchartered.com/ci/index.html; f. 2001; subsidiary of Standard Chartered Bank (United Kingdom); cap. and res 9,218m., total assets 76,289m. (Dec. 2003); Pres. EBENEZER ESSOKA; Dir-Gen. SERGE PHILIPPE BAILLY; 4 brs.

Versus Bank: Immeuble CRAAE-UMOA, blvd Botreau Roussel, angle ave Joseph Anoma, 01 BP 1874, Abidjan 01; tel. 20-25-60-60; fax 20-25-60-99; e-mail infos@versusbank.com; internet www.versusbank.com; f. 2004; Pres. ANDRÉ SIMONE TCHINAH.

Credit Institutions

Afribail—Côte d'Ivoire (Afribail—CI): 8–10 ave Joseph Anoma, 01 BP 1274, Abidjan 01; tel. 20-20-07-20; fax 20-20-07-00; 95% owned by BIAO—CI; cap. and res 334m., total assets 2,651m. (Dec. 2002); Chair. RENÉ AMANY; Pres. and Dir-Gen. ERNEST ALLOU TOGNAN.

Coopérative Ivoirienne d'Epargne et de Crédit Automobile (CIECA): 04 BP 2084, Abidjan 04; tel. 20-22-77-13; fax 20-22-77-35; cap. and res 805m. (Dec. 1998), total assets 1,169m. (Dec. 1999); Dir-Gen. DALLY ZABO.

Société Africaine de Crédit Automobilier (SAFCA): 1 rue des Carrossiers, Zone 3, 04 BP 27, Abidjan 04; tel. 21-21-07-07; fax 21-21-07-00; e-mail safca@aviso.ci; f. 1956; cap. and res 5,681.8m., total assets 22,511.1m. (Dec. 2001); Pres. and Dir-Gen. DIACK DIAWAR.

Société Africaine de Crédit-Bail (SAFBAIL): Immeuble SAFCA, 1 rue des Carrossiers, Zone 3, 04 BP 27, Abidjan 04; tel. 21-24-91-77; fax 21-35-77-90; e-mail safca@aviso.ci; f. 1971; cap. and res 2,922m., total assets 13,414m. (Dec. 1999); Chair. and Man. Dir DIACK DIAWAR.

SOGEFIBAIL—CI: 26 ave Delafosse, 01 BP 1355, Abidjan 01; tel. 20-32-85-15; fax 20-33-14-93; 35% owned by GENEFITEC, 35% by SOGEFINANCE, 25% by SGBCI; cap. and res 2,560.2m., total assets 4,452.3m. (Dec. 2003); Pres. JEAN-LOUIS MATTEI.

Bankers' Association

Association Professionnelle des Banques et Etablissements Financiers de Côte d'Ivoire (APBEFCI): 01 BP 3810, Abidjan 01; tel. 20-21-20-08; affiliated to Conseil National du Patronat Ivoirien (q.v.); Pres. JEAN-PIERRE MEYER.

CÔTE D'IVOIRE   *Directory*

Financial Institution

Caisse Autonome d'Amortissement de Côte d'Ivoire (CAA): Immeuble SCIAM, ave Marchand, 01 BP 670, Abidjan 01; tel. 20-20-98-00; fax 20-21-35-78; e-mail pdgbni@aviso.ci; f. 1959; management of state funds; cap. 10,000m., total assets 308,080m. (Dec. 2000); Chair. ABDOULAYE KONÉ; Man. Dir SÉKOU BAMBA.

STOCK EXCHANGE

Bourse Régionale des Valeurs Mobilières (BRVM): 18 ave Joseph Anoma, 01 BP 3802, Abidjan 01; tel. 20-32-66-85; fax 20-32-66-84; e-mail brvm@brvm.org; internet www.brvm.org; f. 1998 to succeed Bourse des Valeurs d'Abidjan; regional stock exchange serving mem. states of UEMOA; Dir-Gen. JEAN-PAUL GILLET.

INSURANCE

Abidjanaise d'Assurances: Immeuble Woodin Center, ave Noguès, 01 BP 2909, Abidjan 01; tel. 20-22-46-96; fax 20-22-64-81; Dir-Gen. MARC RICHMOND.

African American Insurance Co (AFRAM): Immeuble ex-Monopris, 2 ave Noguès, 01 BP 7124, Abidjan 01; tel. 20-31-30-44; fax 20-32-69-72; Dir-Gen. CHRISTIAN CASEL.

Alliance Africaine d'Assurances (3A): 17 BP 477, Abidjan 17; tel. 20-32-42-52; fax 20-32-54-90; Pres. DAM SARR; Dir-Gen. CORINNE SARR.

AXA Assurances Côte d'Ivoire: ave Delafosse Prolongée, 01 BP 378, Abidjan 01; tel. 20-31-58-98; fax 20-31-88-00; e-mail johnson.boa@AXA-Assurances.ci; f. 1981; fmrly l'Union Africaine—IARD; insurance and reinsurance; Dir-Gen. JACQUES BOUDOU.

AXA Vie Côte d'Ivoire: 9 ave Houdaille, 01 BP 2016, Abidjan 01; tel. 20-22-25-15; fax 20-22-37-60; f. 1985; fmrly Union Africaine Vie; life assurance and capitalization; Chair. JOACHIM RICHMOND; Dir PATRICE DESGRANGES.

Colina: Immeuble Colina, blvd Roume, 01 BP 3832, Abidjan 01; tel. 20-21-65-05; fax 20-22-59-05; e-mail c-dg@colina-sa.com; internet www.colina-sa.com; f. 1980; Chair. MICHEL PHARAON; Dir-Gen. RAYMOND FARHAT.

Compagnie Nationale d'Assurances (CNA): Immeuble Symphonie, 30 ave du Général de Gaulle, 01 BP 1333, Abidjan 01; tel. 20-21-49-19; fax 20-22-49-06; f. 1972; cap. 400m.; insurance and reinsurance; transfer to private ownership pending; Chair. SOUNKALO DJIBO; Man. Dir RICHARD COULIBALY.

Gras Savoye Côte d'Ivoire: Immeuble Trade Center, ave Noguès, 01 BP 5675, Abidjan 01; tel. 20-25-25-00; fax 20-25-25-25; e-mail olivier.dubois@grassavoye.ci; affiliated to Gras Savoye (France); Man. OLIVIER DUBOIS.

Mutuelle Centrale d'Assurances: 15 Immeuble Ebrien, 01 BP 1217, Abidjan 01; tel. 20-21-11-24; fax 20-33-18-37.

Nouvelle Société Africaine d'Assurances (NSIA AGCI): Immeuble Manci, rue A43, 01 BP 1571, Abidjan 01; tel. 20-31-75-00; fax 20-31-98-00; f. 1995; Pres. and Dir-Gen. JEAN KACOU DIAGOU.

NSIA-Vie: Immeuble Zandaman, ave Noguès, 01 BP 4092, Abidjan 01; tel. 20-31-98-00; fax 20-33-25-79; f. 1988; fmrly Assurances Générales de Côte d'Ivoire—Vie (AGCI-Vie); life; Pres. and Dir-Gen. JEAN KACOU DIAGOU.

Société Africaine d'Assurances et de Réassurances en République de Côte d'Ivoire (SAFARRIV): 01 BP 1741, Abidjan 01; tel. 20-21-91-57; fax 20-21-82-72; e-mail groupe.safarriv@safarriv.ci; f. 1975; affilated to AGF Afrique; Pres. TIÉMOKO YADÉ COULIBALY; Man. Dir CHRISTIAN ARRAULT.

Trade and Industry

GOVERNMENT AGENCIES

Autorité pour la Régulation du Café et du Cacao (ARCC): blvd Botreau Roussel, Immeuble CAISTAB, Plateau, 25 BP 1501, Abidjan 25; tel. 22-44-46-15; fax 20-21-29-03; e-mail p.zoungrana@arcc-ci.org; f. 2000; implements regulatory framework for coffee and cocoa trade; Pres. PLACIDE ZOUNGRANA.

Bureau National d'Etudes Techniques et de Développement (BNETD): ancien hôtel 'Le Relais', blvd Hassan II, Cocody, 04 BP 945, Abidjan 04; tel. 22-48-34-00; fax 22-44-56-66; e-mail info@bnetd.ci; f. 1978 as Direction et Contrôle des Grands Travaux; ; management and supervision of major public works projects; Dir-Gen. AHOUA DON-MELLO.

Comité de Privatisation: 6 blvd de l'Indénié, 01 BP 1141, Abidjan 01; tel. 20-22-22-31; fax 20-22-22-35; e-mail cpct@africaonline.co.ci; state privatization authority; Pres. PAUL AGODIO; Dir-Gen. AHOUA DON MELLO.

Compagnie Ivoirienne pour le Développement des Cultures Vivrières (CIDV): Abidjan; tel. 20-21-00-79; f. 1988; production of food crops; Man. Dir BENOÎT N'DRI BROU.

Fonds de Régulation et de Contrôle du Café et du Cacao (FRCC): Abidjan; f. 2002; assists small-scale producers and exporters of coffee and cocoa; administrative bd comprises five representatives of producers, two of exporters, three of banks and insurance cos, two of the state; Pres. ANGELINE KILI; Dir-Gen. KOUAKOU FIRMIN.

Nouvelle PETROCI: Immeuble les Hévéas, 14 blvd Carde, BP V194, Abidjan 01; tel. 20-20-25-00; fax 20-21-68-24; e-mail petrociholding@globeaccess.net; f. 1975 as Société Nationale d'Opérations Pétrolières de la Côte d'Ivoire (PETROCI); restructured 2000 to comprise three companies—Petroci Exploration Production, SA, Petroci Gaz and Petroci Industries Services; all aspects of hydrocarbons devt; Pres. PAUL GUI DIBO; Man. Dir KOFFI ERNEST.

Société pour le Développement Minier de la Côte d'Ivoire (SODEMI): 31 blvd des Martyrs, 01 BP 2816, Abidjan 01; tel. 22-44-29-94; fax 22-44-08-21; e-mail sodemidg@aviso.cg; f. 1962; geological and mineral research; Pres. NICOLAS KOUANDI ANGBA; Man. Dir JEAN-YVES LIKANE.

Société de Développement des Forêts (SODEFOR): blvd François Mitterrand, 01 BP 3770, Abidjan 01; tel. 22-48-30-00; fax 22-44-02-40; e-mail info@sodefor.ci; f. 1966; establishment and management of tree plantations, sustainable management of state forests, marketing of timber products; Man. Dir N'GORAN YAO.

Société pour le Développement des Productions Animales (SODEPRA): 01 BP 1249, Abidjan 01; tel. 20-21-13-10; f. 1970; rearing of livestock; Man. Dir PAUL LAMIZANA.

DEVELOPMENT AGENCIES

Agence Française de Développement (AFD): blvd François Mitterrand, 01 BP 1814, Abidjan 01; tel. 22-40-70-40; fax 22-44-21-78; e-mail afdabidjan@groupe-afd.org; internet www.afd.fr; Country Dir MICHEL GAUTHEY.

Association Française des Volontaires du Progrès (AFVP): 01 BP 2532, Abidjan; tel. 20-22-85-09; fax 20-22-05-96; internet www.afvp.org; f. 1965; Nat. Delegate JEAN-PIERRE JUIF.

Centre de Promotion des Investissements en Côte d'Ivoire (CEPICI): Tour CCIA, 5e étage, BP V152, Abidjan 01; tel. 20-21-40-70; fax 20-21-40-71; e-mail infocepici@bnetd.ci; internet www.cepici.net; f. 1993; investment promotion authority; Dir-Gen. TCHÉTCHÉ N'GUESSAN.

CHAMBERS OF COMMERCE

Chambre d'Agriculture de la Côte d'Ivoire: 11 ave Lamblin, 01 BP 1291, Abidjan 01; tel. 20-32-92-13; fax 20-32-92-20; Sec.-Gen. GAUTHIER N'ZI.

Chambre de Commerce et d'Industrie de Côte d'Ivoire: 6 ave Joseph Anoma, 01 BP 1399, Abidjan 01; tel. 20-33-16-00; fax 20-32-39-42; f. 1992; Pres. JEAN-LOUIS BILLON; Dir-Gen. YAO KOUAME.

TRADE ASSOCIATIONS

Bourse du Café et du Cacao (BCC): 04 BP 2576, Abidjan 04; tel. 20-20-27-20; fax 20-20-28-14; e-mail info@bcc.ci; internet www.bcc.ci; f. 2001 to replace marketing, purchasing and certain other functions of La Nouvelle Caistab (Caisse de Stabilisation et de Soutien des Prix des Productions Agricoles); Pres. LUCIEN TAPÉ DOH; Dir-Gen. TANO KASSI KADIO.

Fédération Ivoirienne des Producteurs de Café et de Cacao (FIPCC): Yamoussoukro; f. 1998; coffee and cocoa growers' asscn; Chair. CISSÉ LOCINÉ; c. 3,000 mems.

Organisation de Commercialisation de l'Ananas et de la Banane (OCAB): Abidjan; pineapple and banana growers' asscn; Exec. Sec. EMMANUEL DOLI.

EMPLOYERS' ORGANIZATIONS

Association Nationale des Producteurs de Café-Cacao de Côte d'Ivoire (ANAPROCI): BP 840, San-Pédro; tel. 34-71-20-98; fax 34-71-14-65; Pres. HENRI KASSI AMOUZOU; Sec.-Gen. THOMAS EYIMIN.

Confédération Générale des Entreprises de Côte d'Ivoire: 01 BP 8666, Abidjan 01; tel. 20-30-08-21; fax 20-22-50-09; e-mail cgeci@cgeci.org; f. 1993 as Conseil National du Patronat Ivoirion; current name adopted 2005; Pres. JEAN DIAGOU KACOU; Dir-Gen. LAKUER OUATTARA; nine affiliated federations, including the following:

Fédération Maritime de Côte d'Ivoire (FEDERMAR): Treichville, ave Christiani, 01 BP 4082, Abidjan 01; tel. 21-22-08-09; fax 21-22-07-90; e-mail issouf.fadika@ci.dti.bollore.com; f. 1958; Pres. ISSOUF FADIKA; Sec.-Gen. VACABA TOURÉ DE MOVALY.

CÔTE D'IVOIRE

Fédération Nationale des Industries et Services de Côte d'Ivoire (FNISCI): 01 BP 1340, Abidjan 01; tel. 20-31-90-70; fax 20-21-53-52; f. 1993; Pres. JOSEPH-DESIRÉ BILEY; Dir-Gen. ADAMA COULIBALY; 180 mems.

Groupement Ivoirien du Bâtiment et des Travaux Publics (GIBTP): 25 rue des Carrossiers, Concession SIDELAF, zone 3, 01 BP 464, Abidjan 01; tel. 21-25-29-46; fax 21-25-29-57; f. 1934 as Syndicat des Entrepreneurs et des Industriels de la Côte d'Ivoire; present name adopted 1997; Pres. KONGO KOUADIO KOUASSI.

Syndicat des Commerçants Importateurs et Exportateurs (SCIMPEX): 01 BP 3792, Abidjan 01; tel. 20-21-54-27; fax 20-32-56-52; Pres. JACQUES ROSSIGNOL; Sec.-Gen. M. KOFFI.

Syndicat Autonome des Producteurs de Café-Cacao de Côte d'Ivoire (SYNAPROCI): Abidjan; f. 2003; Pres. BANNY KOFFI GERMAIN (acting).

Syndicat des Exportateurs et Négociants en Bois de Côte d'Ivoire: Immeuble CCIA, 3e étage, 01 BP 1979, Abidjan 01; tel. 20-21-12-39; fax 20-21-26-42; e-mail unemaf@africaonline.co.ci; f. 1960; Pres. SOULEYMANE COULIBALY.

Syndicat des Producteurs Industriels du Bois (SPIB): Immeuble CCIA, 3e étage, 01 BP 318, Abidjan 01; tel. 20-21-12-39; fax 20-21-26-42; e-mail unemaf@africaonline.co.ci; f. 1943; Pres. WILFRIED BIRKENMAIER.

Union des Entreprises Agricoles et Forestières: Immeuble CCIA, 3e étage, 01 BP 2300, Abidjan 01; tel. 20-21-12-39; fax 20-21-26-42; e-mail unemaf@africaonline.co.ci; f. 1952; Pres. M. YORO BITIZIE.

UTILITIES

Electricity

Compagnie Ivoirienne d'Electricité (CIE): ave Christiani, 01 BP 6932, Abidjan 01; tel. 21-23-33-00; fax 21-24-63-22; e-mail info@cie.ci; internet www.cie.ci; f. 1990; 71% controlled by Société Bouygues group (France); Pres. MARCEL ZADI KESSY; Dir-Gen. MARCEL PELISSOU.

Compagnie Ivoirienne de Production d'Electricité (CIPREL): Tour Sidom, 12e étage, ave Houdaille, 01 BP 4039, Abidjan 01; tel. 20-22-60-97; independent power production; Pres. OLIVIER BOUYGUES.

Gas

Gaz de Côte d'Ivoire (GDCI): 01 BP 1351, Abidjan; tel. 22-44-49-55; f. 1961; transfer to majority private ownership pending; gas distributor; Man. Dir LAMBERT KONAN.

Water

Société de Distribution d'Eau de la Côte d'Ivoire (SODECI): 1 ave Christiani, Treichville, 01 BP 1843, Abidjan 01; tel. 21-23-30-00; fax 21-24-20-33; f. 1959; production, treatment and distribution of drinking water; 46% owned by Groupe Bouygues (France), 51% owned by employees; Chair. MARCEL ZADI KESSY; Man. Dir PIERRE LE TAREAU.

TRADE UNIONS

Dignité: 03 BP 2031, Abidjan 03; tel. 21-37-74-89; fax 20-37-85-00; e-mail dignite@aviso.ci; Sec.-Gen. BASILE MAHAN-GAHE; 10,000 mems (2001).

Fédération des Syndicats Autonomes de la Côte d'Ivoire (FESACI): Abidjan; breakaway group from the Union Générale des Travailleurs de Côte d'Ivoire; Sec.-Gen. MARCEL ETTÉ.

Union Générale des Travailleurs de Côte d'Ivoire (UGTCI): 05 BP 1203, Abidjan 05; tel. and fax 20-24-08-83; e-mail ugtci2005@yahoo.fr; f. 1962; Sec.-Gen. HYACINTHE ADIKO NIAMKEY; 100,000 individual mems; 190 affiliated unions.

Transport

RAILWAYS

The rail network in Côte d'Ivoire totalled 1,316 km in 1999, including 660 km of track from Abidjan to Niangoloko, on the border with Burkina Faso; from there, the railway extends to Kaya, via the Burkinabè capital, Ouagadougou.

SITARAIL—Transport Ferroviaire de Personnel et de Marchandises: Résidence Memanou, blvd Clozel, Plateau, 16 BP 1216, Abidjan 16; tel. 20-20-80-00; fax 20-22-48-47; f. 1995 to operate services on Abidjan–Ouagadougou–Kaya (Burkina Faso) line; Man. Dir PIERRE MARTINEAU.

ROADS

In 2004 there were about 80,000 km of roads, of which some 6,500 km were paved. Some 68,000m. francs CFA was invested in the road network in 1994–98; projects included the upgrading of 3,000 km of roads and 30,000 km of tracks. Tolls were introduced on some roads in the mid-1990s, to assist in funding the maintenance of the network.

Société des Transports Abidjanais (SOTRA): 01 BP 2009, Abidjan 01; tel. 21-24-90-80; fax 21-25-97-21; e-mail sotra@access.net; f. 1960; 60% state-owned; urban transport; Dir-Gen. PHILIPPE ATTEY.

SHIPPING

Côte d'Ivoire has two major ports, Abidjan and San-Pédro, both of which are industrial and commercial establishments with financial autonomy. Abidjan, which handled some 15.0m. metric tons of goods in 2001, is the largest container and trading port in West Africa. Access to the port is via the 2.7-km Vridi Canal. The port at San-Pédro, which handled 1.2m. tons of goods in 1999, remains the main gateway to the south-western region of Côte d'Ivoire. As a result of widespread civil unrest from September 2002, much international freight transport that formerly left or entered the West African region through ports in Côte d'Ivoire was transferred to neighbouring countries.

Port Autonome d'Abidjan (PAA): BP V85, Abidjan; tel. 21-23-80-00; fax 21-23-80-80; e-mail info@paa-ci.org; internet www.paa-ci.org; f. 1992; transferred to private ownership in 1999; Pres. ANGE-FRANÇOIS BARRY-BATTESTI; Man. Dir MARCEL GOSSIO.

Port Autonome de San-Pédro (PASP): BP 339/340, San-Pédro; tel. 34-71-20-00; fax 34-71-27-15; e-mail pasp@pasp.ci; internet sanpedro-portci.com; f. 1971; Man. Dir OGOU ATTEMENE.

AMICI: Km 1, blvd de Marseille, 16 BP 643, Abidjan 16; tel. 21-35-28-25; fax 21-35-28-53; e-mail amici.abj@aviso.ci; f. 1998; 45% owned by Ivorian interests, 25% by Danish interests, 20% by German interests and 10% by French interests.

Compagnie Maritime Africaine—Côte d'Ivoire (COMAF–CI): rond-point du Nouveau Port, 08 BP 867, Abidjan 08; tel. 20-32-40-77; f. 1973; navigation and management of ships; Dir FRANCO BERNARDINI.

SDV—Côte d'Ivoire (SDV–CI): 01 BP 4082, Abidjan 01; tel. 20-20-20-20; fax 20-20-21-20; f. 1943; sea and air transport; storage and warehousing; affiliated to Groupe Bolloré (France); Pres. GILLES CUCHE.

SAGA Côte d'Ivoire: rond-point du Nouveau Port, 01 BP 1727, Abidjan 01; tel. 21-23-23-23; fax 21-24-25-06; f. 1959; merchandise handling, transit and storage; privately owned; Pres. M. GEORGES; Dir-Gen. DAVID CHARRIER.

Société Agence Maritime de l'Ouest Africain—Côte d'Ivoire (SAMOA—CI): rue des Gallions, 01 BP 1611, Abidjan 01; tel. 20-21-29-65; f. 1955; shipping agents; Man. Dir CLAUDE PERDRIAUD.

Société Ivoirienne de Navigation Maritime (SIVOMAR): 5 rue Charpentier, Zone 2B, Treichville, 01 BP 1395, Abidjan 01; tel. 20-21-73-23; fax 20-33-58-53; f. 1977; shipments to ports in Africa, the Mediterranean and the Far East; Dir SIMPLISSE DE MESSE ZINSOU.

Société Ouest-Africaine d'Entreprises Maritimes en Côte d'Ivoire (SOAEM–CI): 01 BP 1727, Abidjan 01; tel. 20-21-59-69; fax 20-32-24-67; f. 1978; merchandise handling, transit and storage; Chair. JACQUES PELTIER; Dir JACQUES COLOMBANI.

SOCOPAO–Côte d'Ivoire: Km 1, blvd de la République, 01 BP 1297, Abidjan 01; tel. 21-24-13-14; fax 21-24-21-30; shipping agents; Shipping Dir OLIVIER RANJARD.

CIVIL AVIATION

There are three international airports: Abidjan–Félix Houphouët-Boigny, Bouaké and Yamoussoukro. In addition, there are 25 domestic and regional airports, including those at Bouna, Korhogo, Man, Odienné and San-Pédro.

Agence Nationale de l'Aviation Civile: 07 BP 148, Abidjan 07; tel. 21-27-74-24; fax 21-27-63-46; civil aviation authority; Dir JEAN KOUASSI ABONOUAN.

Air Inter Ivoire: Aéroport de Port Boüet, 07 BP 62, Abidjan 07; tel. 21-27-84-65; internal flights.

Société Nouvelle Air Ivoire: Immeuble République, pl. de la République, 01 BP 7782, Abidjan 01; tel. 20-25-15-61; fax 20-32-04-90; e-mail info@airivoire.com; internet www.airivoire.com; f. 2000 to replace Air Ivoire (f. 1960); privatized in 2001; 76.42% owned by All Africa Airways, 23.58% state-owned; internal and regional flights.

Tourism

The game reserves, forests, lagoons, coastal resorts, rich ethnic folklore and the lively city of Abidjan are tourist attractions; Côte d'Ivoire also has well-developed facilities for business visitors, including golfing centres. Some 301,000 tourists visited Côte d'Ivoire in 1998; receipts from tourism in that year totalled US $331m. In 2002 receipts from tourism totalled $490m. Tourism has been negatively affected by instability resulting from the *coup d'état* in December 1999, the disputed elections of October 2000, and the widespread civil unrest that commenced in September 2002.

Office Ivoirien du Tourisme et de l'Hôtellerie: Immeuble ex-EECI, pl. de la République, 01 BP 8538, Abidjan 01; tel. 20-25-16-00; fax 20-32-03-88; internet tourismeci.org; f. 1992; Dir Camille Kouassi.

CROATIA

Introductory Survey

Location, Climate, Language, Religion, Flag, Capital

The Republic of Croatia is situated in south-eastern Europe and has a long western coastline on the Adriatic Sea. It is bordered to the north-west by Slovenia, to the north-east by Hungary and to the east by Serbia (the province of Vojvodina). Bosnia and Herzegovina abuts into Croatia, forming a southern border along the Sava river and an eastern border within the Dinaric Alps. The Croatian territory of Dubrovnik, which is situated at the southern tip of the narrowing stretch of Croatia (beyond a short coastal strip of Bosnia and Herzegovina), has a short border with Montenegro. The climate is continental in the hilly interior and Mediterranean on the coast. There is steady rainfall throughout the year, although summer is the wettest season. The average annual rainfall in Zagreb is 890 mm (35 ins). Both the ethnic Croats (who comprised 89.6% of the total population according to the 2001 census) and the Serb minority (4.5%) speak closely related languages of the Southern Slavonic group formerly referred to as variants of Serbo-Croat, but known, since the early 1990s, as Croatian and Serbian, respectively. Croatian is written in the Latin script, while Serbian is more commonly written in the Cyrillic script. There are, in addition, a number of small minority communities in Croatia, notably the Slav Muslim (Bosniak) community (which comprised 0.5% of the total population in 2001). The national flag (proportions 1 by 2) consists of three horizontal stripes, of red, white and dark blue, with the arms of Croatia (a shield of 25 squares, alternately red and white, below a blue crown composed of five shields) fimbriated in red and white and set in the centre of the flag, overlapping all three stripes. The capital is Zagreb.

Recent History

From the 16th century the territory of what is now the Republic of Croatia was divided between the Osmanlı (Ottoman—Turkish) and Habsburg (Austrian) Empires (although Dalmatia and Istria were dominated at different times by Venice and by France, while Ragusa—Dubrovnik—was formerly an independent republic). After the Hungarian revolution of 1848–49, Croatia and Slavonia (the north-eastern region of present-day Croatia) were made Austrian crown-lands. The Habsburg Empire became the Dual Monarchy of Austria-Hungary in 1867, and the territories were restored to the Hungarian Crown in the following year. Croatia gained its autonomy and was formally joined with Slavonia in 1881. However, Hungarian nationalism transformed traditional Croat–Serb rivalries into Southern Slav (Yugoslav) solidarity. Following the collapse of the Austro-Hungarian Empire at the end of the First World War in October 1918, a Kingdom of Serbs, Croats and Slovenes (under the Serbian monarchy) was proclaimed on 4 December. The new Kingdom united Serbia, including Macedonia and Kosovo, with Montenegro and the Habsburg lands (modern Croatia, Slovenia and Vojvodina). The Kingdom was, however, dominated by the Serbs, while the Croats, as the second largest ethnic group, sought a greater share of power. Increasing unrest within the Kingdom culminated in the meeting of a separatist Croat assembly in Zagreb in 1928. King Aleksandar imposed a royal dictatorship in January 1929, formally renaming the country Yugoslavia in October. In 1934 the King was assassinated in France by Croat extremists.

Meanwhile, the Fascist Ustaša (Rebel) movement was gaining support among the discontented Croat peasantry. When German and Italian forces invaded Yugoslavia in 1941, many Croats welcomed the Axis powers' support for the establishment of what was known as the Independent State of Croatia (NDH). This state, which included all of Bosnia and Herzegovina and parts of Serbia as well as much of modern-day Croatia, was proclaimed on 9 April 1941 and was led by the leader of the Ustaša, Ante Pavelić. During the Ustaša regime a vast number of Jews, Serbs, Roma (Gypsies) and political dissidents were murdered in extermination camps. At the same time fierce armed resistance was being waged by the Partisans, who were led by Josip Broz, known as Tito, the Croat-Slovene leader of the Communist Party of Yugoslavia (CPY). By 1943 Tito's forces were able to proclaim a provisional government in a number of areas. The Ustaša state collapsed in 1944, and Croatia was restored to Yugoslavia as one unit of a federal communist republic, which became the Socialist Federal Republic of Yugoslavia (SFRY) in 1963.

During the 1960s there was an increase in nationalism in Croatia. This 'mass movement' (Maspok) was supported by Croatian members of the ruling League of Communists (as the CPY had been renamed), as well as by non-communists. In December 1971 Tito committed himself to opposing the nationalist movement, and the Croatian communist leaders were obliged to resign. Together with others prominent in Maspok, they were arrested, and a purge of the League of Communists of Croatia (LCC) followed. In 1974, however, Tito introduced a new Constitution, which enshrined the federal (almost confederal) and collective nature of the Yugoslav state.

When the power of the LCC (which contained a high proportion of Serbs) began to decline, particularly from 1989, Croatian nationalism re-emerged as a significant force. Dissidents of the 1970s and 1980s were the main beneficiaries. Dr Franjo Tuđman, who had twice been imprisoned for publicly criticizing repression in Croatia, formed the Croatian Democratic Union (CDU) in 1990. This rapidly became the main challenger to the ruling party, which had changed its name to the League of Communists of Croatia—Party of Democratic Reform (LCC—PDR). Tuđman campaigned as a nationalist for multi-party elections to the republican legislature, prompting considerable concern among the Serbs by advocating a 'Greater Croatia' (to include Bosnia).

At the elections to the tricameral republican Sabor (Assembly), which took place on 24 April and 6–7 May 1990, the CDU obtained an absolute majority of seats in each of the three chambers, with 205 out of 351 seats in total. The next largest party was the LCC—PDR, with 73 seats. (Both the CDU and LCC—PDR won further seats in alliance with other parties.) Tuđman was elected President of Croatia, but he attempted to allay Serb fears by offering the vice-presidency of the Sabor to a Serb. However, Serb-dominated areas remained alienated by Tuđman's Croat nationalism. A 'Serb National Council', based at Knin (in the Krajina region of south-western Croatia), was formed in July and organized a referendum on autonomy for the Croatian Serbs. Despite attempts by the Croatian authorities to prohibit the referendum, it took place, amid virtual insurrection in some areas, in late August and early September. In October the 'Serb National Council' announced the results of the referendum, and declared autonomy for the Krajina areas as the 'Serb Autonomous Region—SAR of Krajina'.

Meanwhile, in August 1990 the Socialist Republic of Croatia was renamed the Republic of Croatia. In that month the Sabor voted to dismiss the republican member of the federal State Presidency, Dr Stjepan Suvar, and replace him with Stjepan (Stipe) Mesić, then President of the Government (premier) of Croatia. His appointment was confirmed in October. In December the Sabor enacted a new republican Constitution, which declared Croatia's sovereignty, its authority over its own armed forces and its right to secede from the SFRY. Tensions increased when, in January 1991, the Croatian authorities refused to comply with an order by the federal State Presidency to disarm all paramilitary groups, and subsequently boycotted negotiations on the future of the federation. On 21 February Croatia asserted the primacy of its Constitution and laws over those of the SFRY and declared its conditions for participation in a confederation of sovereign states. Later that month the self-proclaimed SAR of Krajina declared its separation from Croatia and its intention of uniting with Serbia. In April a Croatian National Guard was formed, replacing the Territorial Defence Force. On 19 May some 94% of the voters participating in a referendum (which was largely boycotted by the Serb population) favoured Croatia's becoming a sovereign entity, possibly within a confederal Yugoslavia, while 92% rejected a federal Yugoslavia.

On 25 June 1991 Croatia and Slovenia declared their independence and began the process of dissociation from the SFRY. (Two days later the SAR of Krajina declared its unification with the self-proclaimed Serb 'Community of Municipalities of Bosnian Krajina', based in Banja Luka, in Bosnia and Herzegovina.) During July war effectively began between the Croat and Serb communities in Croatia. In August an SAR of Western Slavonia (in north-eastern Croatia) was declared; the SAR of Slavonia, Baranja and Western Srem (Sirmium) also proclaimed its autonomy later that month. In the same month Tuđman appointed a coalition Government, which was dominated by the CDU. In September the UN placed an embargo on the delivery of all weapons and other military equipment to the territories that formerly comprised the SFRY. In October the Croatian Government refused to extend the three-month moratorium on the process of dissociation from the SFRY that had been agreed during peace negotiations sponsored by the European Community (EC—later European Union, EU, see p. 244) in The Hague, Netherlands, in July. By November the Yugoslav People's Army (JNA), supported by Serbian irregular troops, had secured about one-third of Croatian territory. The main area of conflict was Slavonia, although Serbian and JNA attacks were also concentrated on the port of Zadar, in central Dalmatia. In November, in accordance with the principles formulated at The Hague, the Sabor declared its readiness to enact legislation guaranteeing minority rights, to allay the anxieties of the Serbs. However, there were increasing allegations of atrocities on both sides. The CDU came under pressure from more extreme nationalist elements to make no concessions to the Serbs. One of the most prominent of the nationalist parties was the Croatian Party of Rights (CPR), the armed wing of which, the Croatian Defence Association, was actively involved in the fighting. Meanwhile, in October principally Montenegrin units of the JNA attacked and besieged the coastal city of Dubrovnik; the eastern Slavonian town of Vukovar (where particularly intense fighting had taken place) finally surrendered on 18 November, after the 13th cease-fire agreement negotiated by the EC, which supervised the subsequent civilian evacuation. (At least 260 civilians were massacred by JNA troops during the evacuation.) Both parties indicated readiness to accept a UN peace-keeping force; military action continued, however, while negotiations on the terms for such a force were conducted. The 14th cease-fire agreement, therefore, involved the UN, although it did not bring an end to all the fighting. In mid-December UN Security Council Resolution 724 provided for observers to be sent to the SFRY, in addition to a small team of civilian and military personnel to prepare for a possible peace-keeping force. In the same month a 'Republic of Serb Krajina' (RSK), formed by the union of the three SARs, was proclaimed.

In November 1991 the Supreme Council (a special war cabinet, chaired by Tuđman) ordered all Croats to vacate any federal posts that they held and to place their services at the disposal of the Croatian state. On 5 December Mesić, Yugoslavia's nominal Head of State, resigned, followed by Ante Marković, the federal Prime Minister, on 19 December. On 23 December Germany announced its recognition of Croatia, and on 15 January 1992 the other members of the EC initiated general international recognition of Croatia, which culminated in its accession to the UN in May.

With more than 6,000 dead and 400,000 internally displaced in Croatia, a UN-sponsored, unconditional cease-fire was signed by the Croatian National Guard and the JNA on 2 January 1992. In late February a 14,000-strong UN Protection Force (UNPROFOR) was entrusted with ensuring the withdrawal of the JNA from Croatia and the demilitarization of the three Serb-held enclaves, which were designated UN Protected Areas (UNPAs). In the same month UNPROFOR's mandate in Croatia was extended to cover the so-called 'pink zones' (areas occupied by JNA troops and with majority Serb populations, but outside the official UNPAs).

In mid-May 1992 the JNA began to withdraw from Croatia, in accordance with the UN programme of demilitarization, and the siege of Dubrovnik ended on 28 May. Sporadic shelling continued, however, and UNPROFOR proved unable to prevent the expulsion of more than 1,000 Croats by Serbian forces from Eastern Slavonia. In June Croat forces launched a series of offensives in Serb-held areas, beginning with the shelling of Knin. This development provoked UN Security Council Resolution 762, adopted on 30 June, which required the Croatian Government forces to withdraw to the positions that they had held prior to 21 June and to refrain from entering Serb-controlled areas.

In late July 1992 a military court in Split convicted 19 leading figures from the RSK of threatening the territorial integrity of Croatia. Shortly afterwards, however, as a precondition of their participation in the EC/UN peace conference on the former Yugoslavia, to be held in August, in London, United Kingdom, the leaders of the RSK renounced their claims to independence. In early September the Prime Minister of the Federal Republic of Yugoslavia (FRY, comprising Serbia and Montenegro), Milan Panić, announced Yugoslavia's willingness to recognize Croatia within the borders existing prior to the outbreak of civil war in mid-1991, on the condition that the Serb enclaves be granted special status. During the London peace talks agreement was reached on economic co-operation between representatives of the Croatian Government and of the RSK, and at the end of September Presidents Tuđman of Croatia and Dobrica Ćosić of the FRY agreed to work towards a normalization of relations between their respective countries.

Presidential and legislative elections were held in Croatia on 2 August 1992, under the new Constitution (promulgated in December 1990), which provided for a bicameral legislature comprising a directly elected Zastupnički dom (Chamber of Representatives) and an indirectly elected Županijski dom (Chamber of Counties). Tuđman was re-elected, with 56% of the votes cast, more than twice the proportion obtained by his nearest rival, Dražen Budiša of the Croatian Social Liberal Party (CSLP), while at the legislative elections the ruling CDU obtained a majority, securing 85 of the 138 seats contested in the lower Zastupnički dom. A new Government, under the premiership of Hrvoje Šarinić, was appointed shortly thereafter. In November the Zastupnički dom approved legislation providing for the reorganization of local government areas for electoral purposes, and in January 1993 proportional representation was introduced to replace the former plurality electoral system. Elections to the Županijski dom were held on 7 February. The CDU won 37 of the elective 63 seats, while the CSLP, together with allied parties, obtained 16 seats. (The CPR boycotted the elections.)

Meanwhile, in late January 1993 Croatian troops launched an offensive across the UN peace-keeping lines into Serb-held Krajina, in an effort to gain control of the Maslenica bridge, a vital communications link between northern Croatia and the Dalmatian coast. The Serb forces in Krajina reclaimed weapons that they had earlier surrendered to UNPROFOR, in order to defend themselves. The UN responded by ordering Croatia to withdraw its troops and the Serb forces to return their weapons. On 26 January President Ćosić of Yugoslavia warned the UN that, if UNPROFOR did not intervene, Yugoslavia would dispatch troops to defend the Serbs in Croatia. Two members of UNPROFOR were killed in fighting around the coastal town of Zadar on the following day. The Croats regained control of the Maslenica bridge and Zemunik airport, and by the end of January the peace process in both Croatia and Bosnia and Herzegovina appeared to be in serious jeopardy.

There was extensive political unrest in Croatia throughout 1993. The issues of continuing civil strife in Krajina and of the quest for autonomy in the Istrian peninsula in the north-west of Croatia (see below) proved increasingly problematic for the Government and added to domestic dissatisfaction with the country's desperate economic circumstances and concern regarding Croatian involvement in the conflict in Bosnia and Herzegovina that had commenced in April 1992. In late March Šarinić's Government resigned, following a series of financial scandals and a rapid deterioration in the economic situation. A former executive of the Croatian state petroleum company, Nikica Valentić, was appointed Prime Minister.

At local elections in Istria in early February 1993, the Istrian Democratic Assembly (IDA), a party advocating Istrian autonomy, obtained 72% of the total votes cast. The IDA subsequently proposed that Istria become a transborder region comprising Croatian, Slovenian and Italian areas. The Government, however, strongly opposed any suggestion of Istrian autonomy. In early April a UN-sponsored agreement guaranteed the reconstruction and reopening of the Maslenica bridge, Zemunik airport and the Peruca hydroelectric plant, under UNPROFOR supervision. The Croats reconstructed the bridge themselves, however, and it was duly reopened by Tuđman in July. In the same month Serb troops launched an attack on Croatian forces. In mid-July the UN successfully negotiated the Erdut Agreement between the leaders of Croatia and Serbia, whereby Croat forces were to leave the Maslenica area, which would again be placed under the administration of UNPROFOR. However, the Croats failed to withdraw from Maslenica by the deadline of 31 July and fighting resumed. In August the Croatian Minister of Foreign Affairs, Dr Mate Granić, declared the Erdut Agreement invalid. In September a full-scale mobilization was undertaken among the Serbs of the Eastern Slavonia, Baranja and Western Sirmium. Serb–Croat hostilities extended to Zagreb by mid-September. By this time most of the JNA had withdrawn from Croatia, and some Serb artillery had been placed under UN control, but UNPROFOR forces were not yet in effective control of Croatia's borders.

On 4 October 1993, despite anti-UNPROFOR demonstrations in Croatia, the UN Security Council voted unanimously to extend UNPROFOR's mandate by Resolution 871, which also required the return to Croatian sovereignty of all 'pink zones', the restoration of all communications links between these regions and the remainder of Croatia, and the disarmament of Serb paramilitary groups. The UNPROFOR forces were empowered by the Resolution to act in self-defence. The Croat administration accepted the Resolution, but it was rejected by the assembly of the RSK, which proceeded to order the mobilization of all Serb conscripts in Krajina. Multi-party elections held in the RSK in December were declared illegal by the Constitutional Court of Croatia. In January 1994 Milan Martić, a candidate supported by President Slobodan Milošević of Serbia, was elected 'President' of the RSK.

In mid-January 1994 Croatia and the FRY announced their intention to begin the normalization of relations, including the establishment of representative offices in Zagreb and Belgrade, the Serbian and Yugoslav capital. (A parallel agreement was also signed between representatives of the Croat and Serb communities in Bosnia and Herzegovina.) In the same month the Croatian Government indicated the possibility of direct Croatian intervention in central Bosnia and Herzegovina, prompting the US Permanent Representative to the UN, Madeleine Albright, to threaten the imposition of international sanctions against Croatia. (Croatian army units had from 1992 supported the self-styled breakaway Croat state in western Bosnia and Herzegovina, the 'Croat Community of Herzeg-Bosna'.) In late February President Tuđman approved proposals, advanced by the USA, for a Bosniak (Muslim)-Croat federation within Bosnia and Herzegovina, known as the Federation of Bosnia and Herzegovina, which could, it was declared, ultimately seek formal association with Croatia within a loose confederation. In the RSK, meanwhile, a cease-fire, agreed in December 1993, was extended for a third time, until 31 March 1994. On 30 March a further cease-fire provided for the establishment of a 'buffer' zone, to be monitored by UNPROFOR.

In April 1994 a long-standing public dispute between President Tuđman and Josip Manolić, the President of the Županijski dom and a leading member of the CDU, led to a division in the party. Manolić and other prominent liberals objected to Tuđman's anti-Muslim views and his collusion with Gojko Šušak, the Minister of Defence, who was widely considered responsible for Croatia's actions against the Bosniaks in the Bosnian conflict. Tuđman responded by suspending Manolić from his position within the CDU. In April Manolić, together with Mesić (by this time the President of the Zastupnički dom), left the CDU to form a new party, the Croatian Independent Democrats (CID). The CID, led by Mesić, became the largest opposition party in the Sabor, with 18 deputies. In June the principal opposition parties commenced a boycott of the Sabor, in protest at the appointment of two CDU deputies as Presidents of the parliamentary chambers (Manolić and Mesić having agreed to resign from their posts in mid-May); opposition deputies returned to the Sabor in September.

Meanwhile, the cease-fire in the RSK continued precariously. In September 1994 the UN Security Council renewed the UNPROFOR mandate in Croatia for a further six months. In October a new negotiating forum was established in Zagreb with the aim of resolving the Krajina question; known as the 'Zagreb Group', it comprised two representatives of the EU and the US and Russian ambassadors to Croatia. The group's initial proposal that the RSK be reintegrated into Croatia, but receive extensive autonomy, was rejected by the RSK 'Prime Minister', Borislav Mikelić, in late October. In January 1995 President Tuđman announced that the Government would not renew the UNPROFOR mandate in Croatia upon its expiry at the end of March, claiming that the UN presence had merely reinforced the Serbs' position. In late January the Zagreb Group presented a fresh peace plan. The plan, which emphasized Croatia's territorial integrity, while affording rights to the Serb minority, envisaged the return of one-half of Serb-controlled territory to Croatia, in exchange for extensive regional autonomy for the Krajina Serbs. (The areas to be reintegrated would be demilitarized, and administered by the UN for a minimum of five years.) In February the RSK suspended an economic accord concluded with Croatia in December 1994, following Croatia's decision to terminate UNPROFOR's mandate. However, in March Tuđman reversed his decision to expel UNPROFOR from Croatian territory, two weeks before the UN troops were due to begin their withdrawal. Croatia had agreed to a revised peace-keeping plan, following intensive diplomatic negotiations conducted by the international community (in particular, the USA), as a result of which a compromise UN mandate was to provide for a reduced peace-keeping force (to be known as the UN Confidence Restoration Operation—UNCRO) until October, including several hundred troops to be deployed along Croatia's frontiers with Bosnia and Herzegovina and the FRY (effectively isolating Serb-occupied territory in Croatia from sources of military aid).

In early March 1995, following talks in Zagreb, a formal military alliance was announced between the Croatian 'Herzeg-Bosna' and the (by that time predominantly Bosniak) Bosnian government armies. (A similar agreement establishing a military alliance between the Croatian Serbs and the Bosnian Serbs had been drawn up in February.) UN relief supplies to Serb-held enclaves in Croatia were suspended in March, following the disruption of aid convoys by Croatian Serbs and their rebel Bosniak allies in western Bosnia and Herzegovina. On 13 April Dubrovnik and its airport were attacked by Bosnian Serb artillery. On 1–2 May Croatian government forces regained control of Western Slavonia; large numbers of Serb troops fled the area. Government sources claimed that the attack was necessary in order to restore the Zagreb–Belgrade motorway (which was reopened to civilian traffic on 3 May). The Croatian Serbs retaliated with artillery attacks on Zagreb (where six civilians were killed), Karlovac and Sisak. The international community immediately intensified its efforts to achieve peace in Croatia, and on 3 May, under the mediation of the UN Special Envoy, Yasushi Akashi, the warring parties agreed a cease-fire, according to which Serb artillery was to be surrendered to the UN, in exchange for the safe passage of all Serb civilians and troops from Western Slavonia into Bosnia and Herzegovina. Despite the cease-fire, sporadic fighting continued in the enclave.

In June 1995 Tuđman threatened further offensives to seize Serb-held territories, prompting international criticism. In late July a joint offensive by Croatian government forces and 'Herzeg-Bosna' troops resulted in the seizure of the Serb-held town of Bosansko Grahovo, in western Bosnia and Herzegovina, thereby blocking the principal supply route from Serb-held areas of northern Bosnia and Herzegovina to Serb-held Krajina. On 4 August Croatian government troops launched a massive military operation ('Operation Storm') and rapidly recaptured the Krajina enclave, prompting the largest exodus of refugees since the Yugoslav crisis began in 1991; about 150,000 Croatian Serbs either fled or were forcibly expelled from Krajina and took refuge in Serb-held areas in Bosnia and Herzegovina or in Serbia itself. It was subsequently reported that Serbian troops had been stationed along the border with Croatia (thus strengthening the position of the Serb-held enclave of Eastern Slavonia against possible Croatian attack). In early September the UN announced that some 10,500 peace-keeping troops were to be withdrawn from Croatia, in view of the restoration of government authority over Krajina. On 20 September the Zastupnički dom voted to suspend sections of the law on minorities, which had provided the Krajina Serbs with special rights in areas where they had been a majority; this decision had been preceded two days earlier by a new electoral law reducing the guaranteed representation of the Serb minority in the Croatian legislature from 13 seats to three. The law also provided for 12 seats in the Zastupnički dom to represent some 470,000 Croatian emigrés, thus giving the right to vote to some 291,000 Bosnian Croats (many of whom supported the CDU's associated party in Bosnia and Herzegovina). At the end of September the Croatian Government was reported to have resettled some 100,000 refugees from Bosnia and Herzegovina in Krajina.

During October 1995 fighting continued in parts of Croatia, despite the UN-brokered cease-fire. Heavy clashes were reported between Croatian troops and Serb forces in Eastern Slavonia, and President Tuđman continued to threaten to recapture the enclave by force. On 3 October, however, an 'agreement on basic principles' was signed between Croatian government officials and Serb leaders in Eastern Slavonia, following talks in the Serb-held town of Erdut, conducted under the mediation of the US ambassador to Croatia, Peter Galbraith, and UN negotiator Thorvald Stoltenberg. The 11-point agreement provided for a 'transitional period', during which authority over the enclave would be invested in an interim administration established by the UN, demilitarization of the area and creation of a joint Serb-Croat police force, and the safe return of refugees.

The electoral campaign in advance of the elections to the Zastupnični dom scheduled to take place on 29 October 1995 was marred by widespread allegations of media bias; in early October the state-owned television network banned opposition broadcasts. At the elections the CDU secured about 45% of the votes cast (although the party failed to obtain sufficient votes to achieve the two-thirds' parliamentary majority required to make constitutional amendments). A new Government was appointed in early November, led by the erstwhile Minister of the Economy, Zlatko Matesa.

On 12 November 1995 representatives of the Croatian Government and the Eastern Slavonian Serbs signed an agreement in Erdut on the reintegration of the Eastern Slavonian enclave into Croatia. The signature of this accord followed peace negotiations between Tuđman, Milošević and the President of the Presidency of Bosnia and Herzegovina, Dr Alija Izetbegović, conducted in Dayton, Ohio, USA (where the three leaders signed a comprehensive peace agreement, providing for the division of Bosnia and Herzegovina into two ethnically defined entities—see the chapter on Bosnia and Herzegovina). Under the terms of the accord, Eastern Slavonia was to be placed under the authority of a UN-appointed transitional administration for a period of up to two years prior to its full reintegration into Croatia. The interim administration and UN peace-keeping forces would supervise the demilitarization of the area and the return of refugees and displaced persons. On 15 January 1996, under Resolution 1037, the UN Security Council established the UN Transitional Administration for Eastern Slavonia, Baranja and Western Sirmium (UNTAES), with an initial one-year mandate; UNTAES, comprising some 5,000 troops. A US diplomat, Jacques Paul Klein, was subsequently appointed Transitional Administrator of the region. The UN Security Council also authorized the establishment of a UN Mission of Observers in Prevlaka (UNMOP), comprising 28 military observers, to assume responsibility for monitoring the demilitarization of the Prevlaka peninsula, south-east of Dubrovnik, which was claimed by the FRY, on the grounds of its proximity to a naval base in Montenegro.

In April 1996 the Regional Executive Council of Eastern Slavonia appointed a former RSK 'President' (1992–94), Goran Hadžić, as President of the region. A new Regional Assembly (comprising representatives of Krajina and the five Eastern Slavonian municipalities) and Regional Executive Council were subsequently established. In the same month the Zastupnički dom approved legislation on co-operation between Croatia and the UN International Criminal Tribunal for the Former Yugoslavia (ICTY—based in The Hague), which provided for the transfer of authority to conduct criminal proceedings to the Tribunal and the extradition of the accused.

In May 1996 the Zastupnički dom adopted legislation granting amnesty for crimes committed during the civil conflict in Eastern Slavonia from August 1990 (excepting war crimes), with the aim of encouraging the return of displaced persons to the region. Later in May the demilitarization of Eastern Slavonia commenced; the process was completed within 30 days, as scheduled. In early July an international security force was installed in Eastern Slavonia for the transitional period.

In August 1996, following a meeting between Tuđman and Milošević in Athens, Greece, an agreement was signed, providing for the establishment of full diplomatic relations between Croatia and the FRY; remaining issues of contention, most notably the territorial dispute over Prevlaka, were to be resolved by further negotiations. In October the Council of Europe (see p. 225) agreed to accept Croatia's application for membership, after the Government undertook to ratify the European Convention on Human Rights within one year of admission.

In early April 1997 Serb officials in Eastern Slavonia conducted a referendum (which, however, the Croatian Government and UN officials declared to be illegitimate) regarding the future of the enclave; about 99.5% of the participating electorate voted in favour of Eastern Slavonia remaining a single administrative unit under Serb control after its return to Croatia. In mid-April elections to the Županijski dom and to a number of municipal and regional councils took place. Election monitors from the Organization for Security and Co-operation in Europe (OSCE, see p. 354) declared that the elections had been largely free and fair. The CDU secured 42 of the 63 elective seats in the Županijski dom, while the Croatian Peasants' Party took nine, the CSLP six, the Social Democratic Party of Croatia (SDP, which had been reconstituted from the former LCC–PDR) four, and the IDA two seats. (A further five deputies were to be nominated by Tuđman, of whom two were to be members of the Serb community in Eastern Slavonia.)

During a visit to Eastern Slavonia in early June 1997 Tuđman publicly offered reconciliation to all Serbs who were willing to accept Croatian citizenship, following continued pressure from Madeleine Albright (by this time US Secretary of State), who had met Tuđman in May. On 15 June Tuđman was re-elected as President, obtaining 61.4% of the votes cast; the SDP candidate, Zdravko Tomac, was placed second, with 21.0% of the votes. However, OSCE monitors declared that the election had not been conducted fairly, on the grounds that opposition parties had not been permitted coverage in the state-controlled media. Later in June the Constitutional Court endorsed the results of the election. Tuđman was officially inaugurated for a second term on 5 August. In November the legislature approved constitutional amendments, proposed by Tuđman, which, notably, prohibited the re-establishment of a union of Yugoslav states.

Meanwhile, in July 1997 the Government had announced the initiation of the programme for the return of some 80,000 Croat refugees to Eastern Slavonia. In the same month, despite previous objections from the Croatian Government, the UN Security Council had adopted a resolution extending the mandate of UNTAES (which had already been renewed for an additional six months) until mid-January 1998, owing to UN concern over the continued stability of Eastern Slavonia. (The size of the contingent was reduced from about 5,000 to 2,800.) In mid-January the mandate of UNTAES expired and Eastern Slavonia was officially returned to Croatian authority, precipitating an increase in the number of Serbs leaving the region. In February Tuđman was re-elected Chairman of the CDU. In May the Government announced a programme that relaxed conditions for the return of Serb refugees to Croatia, following pressure from the international community.

In May 1998 Sušak died; Andrija Hebrang (hitherto Minister of Health) was subsequently allocated the defence portfolio. In June Croatia submitted to the UN a proposal for a permanent settlement to the dispute over the Prevlaka peninsula; it was envisaged that a joint Croatian-FRY commission would demarcate the borders between the two countries and that a demilitarized zone would be established for a period of five years. In August Granić and the FRY Minister of Foreign Affairs, meeting in Zagreb, agreed to conduct discussions on the issue of Prevlaka. In October Hebrang resigned from his posts of Minister of Defence and Vice-President of the CDU, as a result of disagreement with Tuđman. Gen. Pavao Miljavac, hitherto Chief of Staff of the army, was subsequently appointed Minister of Defence.

In January 1999 the UN Security Council adopted a resolution on UNMOP, stating that violations of the demilitarized zone in Prevlaka had continued and that negotiations on the normalization of relations between the FRY and Croatia had not resulted in any significant progress. In April Milan Ramljak resigned as Deputy Prime Minister and Minister of Justice. In May, following the first trial of Croats accused of perpetrating human rights violations against Serbs to take place in Croatia, the Zagreb County Court acquitted four defendants of committing war crimes in 1991 and sentenced a further two on lesser charges. In July Croatia submitted an application at the International Court of Justice (ICJ, see p. 20) to institute legal proceedings against the FRY for crimes of genocide allegedly committed by Yugoslav forces in Croatia in 1991–95. In August the Croatian Government complied with a request by the ICTY for the extradition of Vinko Martinović, who had been indicted for crimes committed during the Croat–Muslim conflict in Bosnia and Herzegovina 1993–94. However, the authorities' reluctance to extradite Mladen Naletilić, who had also been indicted for crimes perpetrated during the conflict, prompted severe criticism from the ICTY, while the US Government threatened to impose sanctions against Croatia. Naletilić was finally extradited in March 2000.

In October 1999 Tuđman announced that elections to the Zastupnički dom would take place on 22 December. In November, however, it was announced that Tuđman had undergone emergency medical treatment. He was consequently unable to confirm the election date, and on 26 November the Sabor provisionally transferred the powers of Head of State to the parliamentary Speaker, Vlatko Pavletić. On the following day the mandate of the Zastupnički dom expired, and Pavletić rescheduled the elections to take place on 3 January 2000. An alliance of six opposition parties—the Croatian Peasants' Party (CPP), the Croatian People's Party, the CSLP, the IDA, the Liberal Party and the SDP—known as the Opposition Six, pledged to establish a coalition government in the event that the parties of the coalition won the parliamentary elections. Meanwhile, Tuđman's medical condition deteriorated, and he died on 10 December. Later that month the Government announced that the election for his successor would take place on 24 January 2000.

The elections to the Zastupnički dom on 3 January 2000 were contested by some 55 political associations. A coalition of the SDP and the CSLP (together with two minor parties) secured 47.0% of the votes cast and 71 of the 151 seats, ahead of the CDU, which obtained 30.5% of the votes cast and 45 seats; the alliance of the four other Opposition Six parties, together with the Croatian Social Democrats' Action, won 15.9% of the total votes cast and 25 seats. The Chairman of the SDP, Ivica Račan, was subsequently designated as Prime Minister. Later in January nine candidates emerged to contest the forthcoming presidential election, including the CSLP leader, Dražen Budiša (who was to represent the SDP-CSLP alliance), and the former Yugoslav President Stipe Mesić, who was the joint candidate of the four other principal opposition parties. The CDU elected Mate Granić, hitherto Deputy Prime Minister and Minister of Foreign Affairs, as its presidential candidate, while Vladimir Šeks became acting leader, pending a party congress. In the first round of the election, held on 24 January, Mesić secured 41.1% of the votes cast, while Budiša won 27.7% and Granić 22.5%. Since no candidate received more than 50% of the votes, Mesić and Budiša were to proceed to a second round of voting. On 27 January Pavletić formally appointed Račan to the office of Prime Minister. Račan announced the establishment of a coalition Government, comprising members of the Opposition Six parties. In second round of voting in the presidential election, on 7 February, Mesić secured 56.2% of the votes cast. On 9 February the Sabor adopted a motion expressing confidence in Račan's Government. Following his inauguration as President on 18 February, Mesić pledged to support the return of Serb refugees to Croatia.

In March 2000 the Government established a council for co-operation with the ICTY. In May, however, nationalist groups organized mass demonstrations in protest at the Government's policy of co-operation with the Tribunal. Meanwhile, in early April Granić left the CDU to form a new party, which became known as the Democratic Centre (DC). In May a coalition of the SDP and the Croatian Pensioners' Party won the largest number of seats in the elections to Zagreb City Assembly. In the same month the Zastupnički dom approved constitutional amendments that guaranteed the educational and linguistic rights of minority groups, and representation in the legislature for those groups that constituted more than 8% of the total population. On 25 May Croatia officially joined the 'Partnership for Peace' (PfP, see p. 342) programme of the North Atlantic Treaty Organization (NATO).

In early November 2000 the Zastupnički dom adopted constitutional amendments that reduced the powers of the President and increased those of the legislature (which, henceforth, was to appoint the Government). In March 2001 the Government submitted a proposal to the Zastupnički dom for the abolition of the Županijski dom. Despite the strenuous opposition of the CDU, which held a majority of seats in the upper house, the Zastupnički dom accordingly approved a constitutional amendment converting the Sabor into a unicameral legislature. At local government elections, which took place on 20 May, the SDP-led coalition obtained control of 14 of the 21 County Assemblies. The CDU, secured a majority in only four County Assemblies (compared with 16 in the 1997 elections). In early June the IDA (which had held the European integration portfolio) withdrew from the Government, following differences with the other coalition parties, particularly with regard to the movement's aim to make Italian a second official language in Istria.

In June 2001 the County Court in Rijeka indicted a prominent former rebel Bosniak, Fikret Abdić, for crimes against humanity, including the killing of civilians in a detention camp in 1993. In accordance with a bilateral agreement between the authorities of Croatia and Bosnia and Herzegovina, the trial of Abdić, who had obtained Croatian citizenship in 1995, commenced in the Croatian town of Karlovac in July 2001. (He was sentenced to 20 years' imprisonment in July 2002.) In July 2001, following protracted argument, the Government voted in favour of extraditing two Croat generals suspected of war crimes to the ICTY, in compliance with a secret indictment issued by the Tribunal. Four ministers belonging to the CSLP subsequently resigned in protest at the Government's decision. In mid-July, however, Račan's administration won a motion of confidence in the Sabor, which also approved a statement reaffirming the Government's policy of co-operation with the ICTY. Following the forced resignation of Budiša (who had strongly opposed the extradition) from the leadership of the CSLP, the four representatives of that party rejoined the Government. Later in July one of the indicted suspects, Gen. (retd) Rahim Ademi, surrendered to the ICTY. The other suspect, Gen. (retd) Ante Gotovina, who had been indicted on similar charges, pertaining to having led 'Operation Storm' in 1995, remained at large. (In May 2004 it was announced that Ademi's trial would be transferred to Croatia.)

In late September 2001 Milošević, who had been extradited to the ICTY in June on charges relating to the province of Kosovo (see the chapter on Serbia), was also formally indicted for crimes against humanity and violations of the Geneva Convention; Milošević was held responsible for the killing of large numbers of Croat civilians and the expulsion of some 170,000 non-Serbs from Croatian territory by Serb forces in 1991–92. (Milošević died in March 2006, while on trial at the ICTY.) In early October 2001 a former commander of the Yugoslav navy, together with three further Yugoslav military officers, were indicted by the ICTY for the killing of more than 40 civilians during the bombardment of Dubrovnik in 1991.

In February 2002 Budiša (who had continued to express open antagonism to Račan) was re-elected to the presidency of the CSLP. At the end of the month the CSLP leadership decided to remove the First Deputy Prime Minister, Goran Granić, and a further two CSLP ministers from the Government; it was reported that Budiša questioned their loyalty to the party, owing to their failure to support his apparent opposition to Račan's co-operation with the ICTY. The remaining three CSLP members in the Government subsequently tendered their resignations to demonstrate disagreement with the party leadership. In early March, following lengthy discussions, the coalition parties in the Government reached agreement on a cabinet reorganization. Budiša became First Deputy Prime Minister, while Granić (henceforth an independent) and three of the CSLP representatives were reappointed to the Government. Following a long-standing power struggle with Tuđman's former close associate Ivic Pasalić, Ivo Sanader was re-elected to the leadership of the CDU in April.

In April 2002 the Ministers of Foreign Affairs of Croatia and the FRY signed a protocol on the principles that would be used to confirm the two countries' common border, including, notably, in Prevlaka. In May Martić, the former 'President' of the RSK, who had been indicted in 1996 for war crimes, in particular his alleged responsibility for the bombardment of Zagreb in 1995, surrendered to the ICTY. (His trial commenced in December 2005.) In early July 2002 Budiša finally withdrew the CSLP from the government coalition, after an agreement on joint ownership of the Krško nuclear power installation in Slovenia (see the chapter on Slovenia) was ratified in the Sabor, despite the opposition of 17 of the CSLP's 23 deputies. On 5 July Račan submitted his resignation to Mesić, following the collapse of his administration. Five days later, however, Račan was returned to the office of Prime Minister, after his nomination by Mesić was supported by 84 deputies in the Sabor. On 28 July Račan and the leaders of the other political parties belonging to the ruling coalition reached agreement on a new Council of Ministers, which was approved by the Sabor two days later.

In mid-July 2002 the Presidents of Croatia and the FRY met the members of the collective State Presidency of Bosnia and Herzegovina in Sarajevo (the first trilateral summit meeting since the dissolution of the SFRY). In December the Ministers of Foreign Affairs of Croatia and the FRY reached a provisional accord on Prevlaka, thereby allowing the UN Security Council to end the mandate of UNMOP later that month; under the agreement, the peninsula was to remain demilitarized and joint maritime patrols were to be introduced. In early 2003, in response to continuing international pressure, the Government indicated that it was prepared to demonstrate its full co-operation with the ICTY, and in February Croatia submitted a formal application for membership of the EU. In March a former army commander, Gen. (retd) Mirko Norac (the most senior officer to be convicted by a Croatian court), was sentenced to 12 years' imprisonment for his involvement in the killing of some 50 Croatian Serb civilians in 1991; a further two defendants received terms of 15 years and 10 years, respectively. (In May

2004 the ICTY issued an indictment against Norac on a further five charges relating to an attack by Croatian troops in September 1993. His trial was to be transferred to Croatia). During an official visit to Belgrade in September 2003 (the first to be made by a Croatian Head of State since 1991), Mesić and Svetozar Marović, the Head of State of the State Union of Serbia and Montenegro (which had been reconstituted from the FRY in February 2003), exchanged formal apologies for war crimes perpetrated against the citizens of the two states. In November the former leader of the self-proclaimed SAR of Krajina, Milan Babić, appearing before the ICTY, was charged with war crimes and crimes against humanity, in connection with the 'ethnic cleansing' of Croats from regions under his control in 1991–92. Meanwhile, the Government came under pressure from the ICTY for Gotovina's extradition, which was by now considered a principal precondition for expediting Croatia's accession to the EU.

Legislative elections were conducted on 23 November 2003. The CDU obtained 66 of the 152 elective seats in the Sabor, while the SDP, led by the incumbent Prime Minister, Ivica Račan, won a total of 43 seats, of which 28 were won in coalition with one or two other parties, including the IDA. The CDU negotiated coalition agreements with the CSLP and the DC (which, in coalition, had received three seats) and the CPP (which held 10 seats), and obtained the support of several other deputies, in order to command a narrow parliamentary majority. On 23 December a new, 14-member Government, headed by Sanader and principally comprising CDU members, was approved by 88 votes in the Sabor, and conducted its first session in early January 2004. The administration included former members of the Tuđman administration, notably Hebrang, as Deputy Prime Minister and Minister of Health and Social Welfare; and a former ambassador to the USA, Miomir Žužul, as Minister of Foreign Affairs. The newly elected President of the DC, Vesna Škare Ožbolt, was appointed Minister of Justice.

In March 2004 two retired generals, Ivan Čermak and Mladen Markač, who were charged with crimes relating to the seizure of Krajina by Croatian government forces in 1995, surrendered to the ICTY, following continued international pressure on the Croatian authorities. They subsequently pleaded not guilty before the Tribunal. In April 2004 the European Commission announced that it favoured the opening of accession negotiations with Croatia, subject to the Government's continued compliance with the ICTY. In June, following an EU summit meeting in Brussels, Belgium, Croatia was awarded the official status of candidate country for accession. At the end of June the ICTY imposed a custodial term of 13 years on Babić. The ICTY Prosecutor, Carla Del Ponte, commended the co-operation of the Croatian authorities with the ICTY and indicated that increased numbers of outstanding cases would be transferred to the jurisdiction of courts in Croatia. (Babić committed suicide in detention in March 2006.)

In early January 2005 Žužul, who had been implicated by media reports in corrupt financial practices during the Tuđman regime, announced his resignation (while strongly denying the allegations against him). Although a parliamentary motion expressing 'no confidence' in Žužul had been defeated, opposition parties objected to his leading the forthcoming EU accession negotiations. Meanwhile, the first round of the presidential election, which was contested by 11 candidates, was conducted on 2 January; Mesić, who was supported by an alliance of centre-left parties, led by the SDP, secured 48.9% of the votes cast, narrowly failing to secure a majority. His principal opponent, Jadranka Kosor, a Deputy Prime Minister and the CDU representative, won 20.3% of the votes, and an independent candidate, Boris Mikšić, won 17.8%. At the second round on 16 January Mesić was re-elected to the presidency, receiving 65.9% of the votes cast.

In February 2005, following a meeting with Croatian government leaders, the French and German ministers responsible for European affairs welcomed the progress made by Croatia towards EU integration, but maintained that the accession negotiations, provisionally scheduled to commence on 17 March, remained dependent on the capture and extradition of Gotovina. Meanwhile, in mid-February Sanader announced a government reorganization, after Hebrang tendered his resignation from the Council of Ministers, on grounds of ill health; the new appointments were confirmed by the Sabor on 17 February. Notably, a prominent business executive, Damir Polančec, was nominated to replace Hebrang as Deputy Prime Minister, while the Ministries of Foreign Affairs and of European Integration were merged in reflection of Croatia's aspiration to join the EU, and the incumbent Minister of European Integration, Kolinda Grabar-Kitarović, assumed the combined portfolio. Mesić was inaugurated as President on 18 February. At the end of that month Sanader repeated appeals for Gotovina to surrender to the authorities. In March, following an official report by Del Ponte stating that the Croatian authorities had failed to demonstrate full co-operation with the ICTY, the EU announced the indefinite postponement of accession negotiations. In mid-May elections for local and regional governments were conducted throughout the country; the CDU lost significant support to centre-left coalitions led by the SDP and to the extreme nationalist CPR. On 3 October Croatia was declared eligible to enter into accession negotiations with the EU (which were officially opened on the following day), after Del Ponte, despite reiterating dissatisfaction with government efforts at the end of September, issued an assessment stating that the Government's co-operation with the ICTY had improved. The European Commissioner responsible for Enlargement, Olli Rehn, subsequently urged the authorities to continue progress in meeting membership conditions, particularly in supporting the return of refugees and in improving minority rights.

In early December 2005 Gotovina was apprehended in the Canary Islands, Spain, reportedly as a result of information received by ICTY investigators from the Croatian authorities; his arrest was perceived as removing the main obstacle to the country's NATO and EU membership. On 10 December Gotovina was extradited to the Tribunal, where he pleaded not guilty to seven charges in connection with the killing of 150 Serbs and the forcible expulsion of 150,000 from the Krajina region in August–November 1995. Several thousand nationalist supporters of Gotovina staged demonstrations in Zagreb, and subsequently in Split, to demand the transfer of his trial to Croatian jurisdiction.

In early February 2006 Sanader announced that Škare Ožbolt had been removed from the post of Minister of Justice, amid speculation (which the authorities denied) that her dismissal was related to her having reportedly disclosed to the media details of government financing of the defence of Croatian war crimes suspects at the ICTY. Following her dismissal, the DC withdrew from the Government. In October a parliamentary deputy, Branimir Glavaš, who had been charged with involvement in the killing of Serbs in Slavonia in 1991, surrendered to the Croatian authorities, following the removal of his parliamentary immunity. Glavaš immediately staged a hunger strike in protest at the legal proceedings against him, and in early December the Zagreb County Court ordered that he be released provisionally and his trial postponed. (His trial commenced in Osijek in 2007.)

In January 2007 Račan announced his resignation as Chairman of the SDP on grounds of ill health, and announced his intention to withdraw from political life. (Following his death at the end of April, Zoran Milanović was elected Chairman of the SDP at a party convention in early June.) In June Milan Martić, the former 'President' of the RSK, was sentenced to 35 years' imprisonment at the ICTY on 16 charges of war crimes perpetrated against non-Serbs. In the same month the trial of Norac and Ademi (who had both been transferred to Croatia by the ICTY in November 2005) began at Zagreb County Court. During a visit to Zagreb for a regional energy summit meeting later in June, the Serbian President, Boris Tadić, issued an unprecedented apology to the Croatian people for atrocities committed by Serbs during the war.

On 25 November 2007 elections to the Sabor took place. The CDU secured 66 of the 153 seats, and the SDP obtained 56. Glavaš, of the Croatian Democratic Alliance of Slavonia and Baranja, secured one of the eight seats reserved for representative of national minorities; the party claimed that his parliamentary immunity had been reinstated. In December Sanader received a mandate from Mesić to form a new administration. Later that month the Minister of the Interior, Ivica Kirin, tendered his resignation, after it emerged that he and other senior government officials had participated in a hunting expedition with Mladen Markač (in violation of the conditions for Markač's provisional release from the ICTY, pending his trial); Markač was subsequently returned to The Hague. In early January 2008, following lengthy negotiations, the CDU signed an official coalition agreement with the CPP and CSLP (which, as part of an electoral alliance, had won eight seats in the Sabor), and seven of the eight parties representing ethnic minorities. On 12 January a new Government, comprising representatives of the CDU, the CPP, the CSLP and the Independent Democratic Serb Party (SDSS), and retaining many of the ministers in the previous Government, was approved by 82 deputies in the Sabor. The trial of Gotovina (originally scheduled to take place in May 2007), together with those of Markač and Čermak, commenced at the ICTY in March 2008. In March Deputy Prime Minister Slobodan Uzelac, a member of the SDSS, tendered his resignation in protest at the Croatian Government's decision to recognize Kosovo's declaration of independence on 17 February (see the chapter on Kosovo); however, the SDSS subsequently announced that its representative would remain in the Government.

In early 2007 a longstanding dispute between Croatia and Slovenia over their joint maritime boundary was revived with a diplomatic protest by Slovenia that the Croatian Government had pre-empted a border demarcation by extending concessions for petroleum exploration in the disputed region. (The Slovenian Government had previously threatened to obstruct Croatia's application for EU membership in connection with this dispute—see the chapter on Slovenia.) The Croatian Government demanded that the dispute be referred to international arbitration (a measure that the Slovenian Government strongly opposed). At the beginning of 2008 Croatia implemented legislation enforcing an environmental fishing zone in the Adriatic Sea, which the Government had declared in 2003 with the objective of protecting fishing stocks; Italy and Slovenia opposed the measure, which would result in significant financial damage for their fleets, and the EU repeatedly expressed concern that the legislation would adversely affect Croatia's application for entry. In early January 2008 the Croatian navy seized an Italian trawler, which was fishing in Croatian territorial waters. The EU Commissioner responsible for Enlargement urged the countries affected by the fishing zone to reach a political resolution, while Slovenia (which held the EU presidency) indicated that the issue would impede the negotiation process. In March, following continued pressure from the EU, the Government agreed that implementation of the environmental fishing zone would be postponed until Croatia's entry into the Union; despite divisions within the ruling coalition, the decision was approved in the Sabor.

In February 2007 the ICJ ruled that Serbia (as the successor state to the State Union of Serbia and Montenegro, and the FRY) was not directly responsible for genocide in Bosnia and Herzegovina in 1992–95 (see the chapter on Bosnia and Herzegovina); Croatia's legal representation subsequently proposed that the Government abandon the case submitted to the Court in 1999 against the FRY, in favour of a financial settlement with Montenegro, the military of which had played a leading role in the attack on Dubrovnik in 1991. In October 2007 Croatia secured a non-permanent seat in the UN Security Council, following a vote in the General Assembly. In the same month NATO member states adopted a resolution supporting the accession applications of Croatia (together with Albania and the former Yugoslav republic of Macedonia—FYRM). At a NATO summit meeting, convened in Bucharest, Romania, on 2 April 2008, it was announced that official invitations to begin accession negotiations were to be extended to Croatia and Albania.

Government

According to the 1990 Constitution (amended in March 2001), legislative power is vested in the unicameral Sabor (Assembly), which has between 100 and 160 members and is elected for a four-year term. Executive power is held by the President, who is elected by universal adult suffrage for a period of five years. The Sabor appoints the Prime Minister and (upon the recommendation of the Prime Minister) the ministers. Croatia is divided, for administrative purposes, into 20 counties and the City of Zagreb, 424 municipalities and 123 towns.

Defence

As assessed at November 2007, the estimated total strength of the armed forces was 17,660, comprising an army of 12,300, a navy of 1,700 and an air force of 1,800, and 1,860 general staff. There were, in addition, 3,000 armed military police, and a total of 105,550 reservists. In May 2000 Croatia was admitted to the North Atlantic Treaty Organization's (NATO) 'Partnership for Peace' (see p. 342) programme. Compulsory military service was abolished with effect from the beginning of 2008. The budget for 2007 allocated 4,510m. kuna to defence.

Economic Affairs

In 2006, according to estimates by the World Bank, Croatia's gross national income (GNI), measured at average 2004–06 prices, was US $41,401m., equivalent to $9,330 per head (or $13,680 per head on an international purchasing-power parity basis). During 1996–2006, it was estimated, the population declined at an average annual rate of 0.1%, while gross domestic product (GDP) per head increased, in real terms, by an average of 4.0% per year. Overall GDP increased, in real terms, at an average annual rate of 3.9% in 1996–2006; real GDP increased by 4.8% in 2006.

Agriculture (including hunting, forestry and fishing) contributed 7.1% of GDP in 2006, when it engaged 5.4% of the employed labour force (excluding activities not adequately defined). The principal crops are maize, sugar beet, grapes, wheat and potatoes. The GDP of the agricultural sector increased by 1.3%, in real terms, during 1996–2006; real agricultural GDP increased by 5.8% in 2006.

Industry (including mining, manufacturing, construction and power) contributed 30.3% of GDP in 2006, when it engaged 31.3% of the employed labour force (excluding activities not adequately defined). Industrial GDP increased, in real terms, at an average annual rate of 4.4% during 1996–2006; real GDP in the industrial sector increased by 4.7% in 2006.

The mining sector contributed 5.5% of GDP in 1998, and engaged only 0.6% of the employed labour force in 2006 (excluding activities not adequately defined). Croatia has many exploitable mineral resources, including petroleum, coal and natural gas.

The manufacturing sector contributed 20.4% of GDP in 2006, and engaged 19.9% of the employed labour force (excluding activities not adequately defined). The GDP of the manufacturing sector increased, in real terms, at an average annual rate of 4.3% during 1996–2006; real manufacturing GDP increased by 3.0% in 2006.

Of total electricity production in 2004, some 52.7% was provided by hydroelectric power, 18.6% by natural gas, 16.2% by coal and 12.4% by petroleum. However, the country remains dependent on imported fuel. In 2006 mineral fuels accounted for 15.9% of total imports, according to provisional data.

Services provided 62.6% of GDP in 2006, when the sector engaged 63.3% of the employed labour force (excluding activities not adequately defined). Tourist arrivals numbered 10,385,000 in 2006, compared with 3,805,000 in 1999. The GDP of the services sector increased, in real terms, at an average annual rate of 4.0% in 1996–2006; real GDP in the sector increased by 1.1% in 2006.

In 2006 Croatia recorded a visible trade deficit of US $10,511.0m., while there was a deficit of $3,255.4m. on the current account of the balance of payments. In 2006 the principal source of imports was Italy (supplying 16.7% of total imports, according to provisional figures); other major sources were Germany, Russia, Slovenia, Austria and the People's Republic of China. Italy was also Croatia's principal market for exports (accounting for an estimated 23.1% of the total); other important purchasers were Bosnia and Herzegovina, Germany, Austria and Slovenia. The principal exports in 2006 were machinery and transport equipment, which accounted for an estimated 28.8% of all exports. Other important exports were: mineral fuels and lubricants, basic manufactures, miscellaneous manufactured articles, food and live animals, chemical products and crude materials. The main imports in that year were machinery and transport equipment, which accounted for 32.2% of all imports, according to provisional data. Other significant imports were: basic manufactures, mineral fuels (particularly petroleum and petroleum products), miscellaneous manufactured articles, chemical products, and food and live animals.

Croatia's overall budgetary deficit for 2006 was 4,511m. kuna (equivalent to 1.8% of GDP). The country's total external debt at the end of 2004 amounted to US $30,169m., of which $9,782m. was long-term public debt. In that year the cost of debt-servicing was equivalent to 23.9% of the value of exports of goods and services. Consumer prices increased at an average annual rate of 3.6% in 1996–2006. The average rate of inflation was 3.2% in 2006. The average annual rate of unemployment was 16.6% in 2006, according to official figures.

In February 2003 Croatia made a formal application for membership of the European Union (EU, see p. 244).

The outbreak of conflict in Croatia in the early 1990s resulted in a rapid deterioration of the economy. A new national currency, the kuna, was introduced in May 1994. In October the IMF

CROATIA

extended its first stand-by loan to Croatia, in support of an economic reform programme. The Government subsequently received reconstruction loans from other official creditors. In April 1996 an agreement was reached with the 'London Club' of commercial creditor banks, establishing Croatia's share of the foreign commercial bank debt incurred by the SFRY. Following the election of a coalition Government in early 2000, relations with the USA and with western European Governments improved, resulting in increased financial aid. Following Croatia's application for membership of the EU, it was awarded the official status of candidate country in mid-2004. An EU Stabilization and Association Agreement for Croatia (which laid emphasis on fiscal restraint and the reduction of public-sector wage expenditure) entered into force in February 2005 as a framework for the country's progress towards EU integration, although the opening of accession negotiations was delayed until October (see Recent History). Economic performance remained strong in 2007, with domestic demand underpinned by continued consumption growth. In late 2007 an IMF report recommended that the next Croatian administration focus on reducing the role of the state and restraining expenditure, concomitant with continued structural reforms. The high current-account deficit, estimated to represent some 8.6% of GDP at this time, and increasing level of external debt, at about 85% of GDP, were also particular causes of concern. A new Government, which took office in January 2008, pledged to maintain economic growth, combat inflation (which had risen sharply) and implement the requirements for EU accession. However, EU officials expressed dissatisfaction with the implementation of judicial reforms and anti-corruption measures; following pressure from the Commissioner responsible for Enlargement, the Government rescinded its decision to enforce an environmental fishing zone from the beginning of 2008 (see Recent History), which had presented an obstacle to its objective of receiving an official invitation for entry in that year.

Education

Pre-school education, for children aged from three to six years, is available free of charge. Education is officially compulsory for eight years, between seven and 15 years of age. Primary education, which is provided free, begins at the age of seven and continues for four years. Special education in foreign languages is provided for children of non-Croat ethnic origin, since all national minorities in Croatia have the right to learn their minority language. Secondary education is free (although private schools also exist) and lasts for up to eight years, comprising two cycles of four years each. There are various types of secondary school: grammar, technical and specialized schools and mixed-curriculum schools. In 2002/03 89% of children in the relevant age-group (males 90%; females 89%) were enrolled at primary schools, while the equivalent rate for secondary education was 87% of children in the appropriate age-group (males 86%; females 87%). In 2004/05 a total of 126,322 students were enrolled at 103 institutions of higher education in Croatia, including four universities (in Zagreb, Rijeka, Osijek and Split). Government expenditure on education totalled 7,244.7m. kuna (8.5% of total spending) in 2004.

Public Holidays

2008: 1 January (New Year's Day), 6 January (Epiphany), 24 March (Easter Monday), 1 May (Labour Day), 22 May (Corpus Christi), 22 June (Anti-Fascism Day), 25 June (Statehood Day), 5 August (National Day), 15 August (Assumption), 8 October (Independence Day), 1 November (All Saints' Day), 25–26 December (Christmas).

2009: 1 January (New Year's Day), 6 January (Epiphany), 13 April (Easter Monday), 1 May (Labour Day), 11 June (Corpus Christi), 22 June (Anti-Fascism Day), 25 June (Statehood Day), 5 August (National Day), 15 August (Assumption), 8 October (Independence Day), 1 November (All Saints' Day), 25–26 December (Christmas).

Weights and Measures

The metric system is in force.

Statistical Survey

Source (unless otherwise stated): Central Bureau of Statistics of the Republic of Croatia, 10000 Zagreb, Ilica 3; tel. (1) 4806111; fax (1) 4806148; e-mail stat.info@dzs.hr; internet www.dzs.hr.

Area and Population

AREA, POPULATION AND DENSITY

Area (sq km)	56,594*
Population (census results)	
31 March 1991	4,784,265
31 March 2001†	
Males	2,135,900
Females	2,301,560
Total	4,437,460
Population (official estimates at mid-year)	
2004	4,439,400
2005	4,442,000
2006	4,440,022
Density (per sq km) at mid-2006	78.5

* 21,851 sq miles.
† Data are not directly comparable to those from the 1991 census, owing to a change in the definition used to calculate total population.

POPULATION BY ETHNIC GROUP
(census of 31 March 2001)

	Number ('000)	% of total population
Croat	3,977.2	89.6
Serb	201.6	4.5
Muslim	20.8	0.5
Italian	19.6	0.4
Hungarian	16.6	0.4
Albanian	15.1	0.3
Slovene	13.2	0.3
Czech	10.5	0.2
Roma	9.5	0.2
Others*	153.4	3.5
Total	**4,437.5**	**100.0**

* Including other groups, ethnically non-declared persons and those of unknown ethnicity.

CROATIA

Statistical Survey

ADMINISTRATIVE DIVISIONS
(census of 31 March 2001)

	Area (sq km)	Population	Density (per sq km)
Counties (Županije)			
Bjelovar-Bilogora	2,640	133,084	50.4
Dubrovnik-Neretva	1,781	122,870	69.0
Istria	2,813	206,344	73.4
Karlovac	3,626	141,787	39.1
Koprivnica-Križevci	1,748	124,467	71.2
Krapina-Zagorje	1,229	142,432	115.9
Lika-Senj	5,353	53,677	10.0
Međimurje	729	118,426	162.4
Osijek-Baranja	4,155	330,506	79.5
Požega-Slavonia	1,823	85,831	47.1
Primorje-Gorski kotar	3,588	305,505	85.1
Sisak-Moslavina	4,468	185,387	41.5
Slavonski Brod-Posavina	2,030	176,765	87.1
Split-Dalmatia	4,540	463,676	102.1
Šibenik-Knin	2,984	112,891	37.8
Varaždin	1,262	184,769	146.4
Virovitica-Podravina	2,024	93,389	46.1
Vukovar-Sirmium	2,454	204,768	83.4
Zadar	3,646	162,045	44.4
Zagreb	3,060	309,696	101.2
Capital City			
Zagreb	641	779,145	1,215.5
Total	56,594	4,437,460	78.4

PRINCIPAL TOWNS
(population at 2001 census)

Zagreb (capital)	691,724	Sesvete		44,914
Split	175,140	Varaždin		41,434
Rijeka	143,800	Šibenik		37,060
Osijek	90,411	Sisak		36,785
Zadar	69,556	Velika Gorica		33,339
Slavonski Brod	58,642	Vinkovci		33,239
Pula	58,594	Dubrovnik		30,436
Karlovac	49,082	Vukovar		30,126

Mid-2005 (incl. suburbs, UN estimate): Zagreb 689,000 (Source: UN, *World Urbanization Prospects: The 2005 Revision*).

BIRTHS, MARRIAGES AND DEATHS

	Registered live births Number	Rate (per 1,000)	Registered marriages Number	Rate (per 1,000)	Registered deaths Number	Rate (per 1,000)
2000	43,746	10.0	22,017	5.0	50,246	11.5
2001	40,993	9.2	22,076	5.0	49,552	11.2
2002	40,094	9.0	22,806	5.1	50,569	11.4
2003	39,668	8.9	22,337	5.0	52,575	11.8
2004	40,307	9.1	22,700	5.1	49,756	11.2
2005	42,492	9.6	22,138	5.0	51,790	11.7
2006	41,446	9.3	22,092	5.0	50,378	11.3

Expectation of life (years at birth, WHO estimates): 75.3 (males 71.8; females 78.8) in 2005 (Source: WHO, *World Health Statistics*).

IMMIGRATION AND EMIGRATION

	2004	2005	2006
Immigrants	18,383	14,230	14,978
Emigrants	6,812	6,012	7,692

ECONOMICALLY ACTIVE POPULATION
(annual averages, '000 persons)

	2004	2005	2006
Agriculture, hunting and forestry	84.8	79.1	75.1
Fishing	4.3	4.5	4.5
Mining and quarrying	8.3	8.5	8.8
Manufacturing	288.9	286.7	291.9
Electricity, gas and water supply	27.1	27.3	27.2
Construction	115.0	120.3	130.4
Wholesale and retail trade; repair of motor vehicles, motorcycles and personal and household goods	237.8	240.8	251.2
Hotels and restaurants	80.6	80.7	86.0
Transport, storage and communications	97.2	96.5	98.4
Financial intermediation	31.5	32.9	34.9
Real estate, renting and business activities	84.9	89.5	98.6
Public administration and defence; compulsory social security	107.2	105.1	105.3
Education	89.4	91.9	94.6
Health and social work	85.4	86.9	88.8
Other community, social and personal service activities	54.4	56.9	59.4
Private households with employed persons	10.2	10.6	10.0
Activities not classified	2.6	2.3	2.9
Total employed	1,409.6	1,420.6	1,467.9
Registered unemployed	309.9	308.7	291.6
Total labour force	1,719.5	1,729.3	1,759.5

Health and Welfare

KEY INDICATORS

Total fertility rate (children per woman, 2005)	1.3
Under-5 mortality rate (per 1,000 live births, 2005)	7
HIV/AIDS (% of persons aged 15–49, 2005)	<0.10
Physicians (per 1,000 head, 2003)	2.44
Hospital beds (per 1,000 head, 2005)	5.50
Health expenditure (2004): US $ per head (PPP)	916.8
Health expenditure (2004): % of GDP	7.7
Health expenditure (2004): public (% of total)	81.0
Human Development Index (2005): ranking	47
Human Development Index (2005): value	0.850

For sources and definitions, see explanatory note on p. vi.

Agriculture

PRINCIPAL CROPS
('000 metric tons)

	2004	2005	2006
Wheat	840.0*	601.7	804.6
Barley	180.0*	162.5	215.3
Maize	2,200.0†	2,206.7	1,934.5
Oats	40.0*	49.5	66.6
Potatoes	445.7*	273.4	274.5
Sugar beet	1,200.0*	1,337.8	1,559.7
Dry beans	n.a.	6.0	4.2
Soybeans (Soya beans)	80.0†	119.6	174.2
Sunflower seed	70.0†	78.0	81.6
Rapeseed	26.0†	41.3	20.0
Cabbages	94.0*	51.0	48.8
Tomatoes	54.3*	28.9	29.0
Cucumbers and gherkins	28.2*	11.1	11.1
Green chillies and peppers	37.0*	34.4	46.1
Dry onions	n.a.	25.8	23.8
Garlic*	9.0	9.4	9.4

CROATIA

—continued	2004	2005	2006
Green beans	n.a.	5.4	5.5
Green peas	8.2*	4.0	4.6
Carrots	21.9*	12.6	13.4
Watermelons*	58.7	66.3	66.3
Apples	58.0*	69.7	73.7
Pears	7.6*	6.2	8.9
Peaches and nectarines	8.3*	7.1	6.9
Plums	30.0*	35.9	49.9
Grapes	300.0*	181.0	181.0*
Tobacco (leaves)	10.2*	9.6	9.6*

* FAO estimate(s).
† Unofficial figure.

Aggregate production ('000 metric tons, may include official, semi-official or estimated data): Total cereals 3,247.7 in 2004, 3,026.9 in 2005, 3,028.2 in 2006; Total roots and tubers 445.6 in 2004, 273.4 in 2005, 274.5 in 2006; Total vegetables (incl. melons) 386.3 in 2004, 286.8 in 2005, 297.6 in 2006; Total fruits (excl. melons) 438.8 in 2004, 326.5 in 2005, 382.8 in 2006.

Source: FAO.

LIVESTOCK
('000 head at 31 December)

	2004	2005	2006
Horses	10	9	10
Cattle	466	471	483
Pigs	1,489	1,205	1,488
Sheep	722	796	680
Goats	126	134	103
Chickens	7,492	7,267	7,017
Ducks	226	175	219
Geese	74	68	76
Turkeys	589	431	573

Source: FAO.

LIVESTOCK PRODUCTS
('000 metric tons)

	2004	2005	2006
Cattle meat	31.5	25.0*	25.0†
Sheep meat	2.2	2.8*	2.8†
Pig meat	61.0*	48.5†	48.5†
Chicken meat	38.5*	31.0†	31.0†
Cows' milk	684.4	790.8	848.7
Sheep's milk	8.2	6.7	6.9
Hen eggs	48.1	49.4	50.7
Honey	2.5	2.7	2.2

* Unofficial figures.
† FAO estimate.

Source: FAO.

Forestry

ROUNDWOOD REMOVALS
('000 cubic metres)

	2004	2005	2006
Sawlogs and veneer logs	1,592	1,741	1,795
Pulpwood	514	534	714
Other industrial wood	224	233	304
Fuel wood	936	887	888
Total	3,266	3,395	3,701

Source: FAO.

SAWNWOOD PRODUCTION
('000 cubic metres)

	2004	2005	2006
Coniferous (softwood)	79	84	89
Broadleaved (hardwood)	503	540	580
Total	582	624	669

Source: FAO.

Fishing
(metric tons, live weight)

	2003	2004	2005
Capture	21,836	30,164	34,683
European pilchard (sardine)	12,271	16,357	16,521
European anchovy	3,341	5,044	9,504
Atlantic bluefin tuna	1,139	827	1,021
Cephalopods	351	562	771
Aquaculture	7,605	13,219	13,782
Common carp	1,633	1,575	2,180
Rainbow trout	791	1,075	1,301
European seabass	803	2,300	2,000
Mediterranean mussel	1,900	2,800	2,500
Total catch	29,441	43,383	48,465

Mining
('000 metric tons, unless otherwise indicated)

	2002	2003	2004
Crude petroleum	1,108	1,052	1,005
Natural gas (million cu m)	2,122	2,190	2,201
Bentonite	12.1	13.6	16.0
Ceramic clay	150.0*	188.0*	637.0
Salt (unrefined)	36.9	31.3	23.0
Gypsum (crude)	145.0	166.0	148.0

* Estimate.
Source: US Geological Survey.

Industry

SELECTED PRODUCTS
('000 metric tons, unless otherwise indicated)

	2002	2003	2004
Beer ('000 hectolitres)	3,624	3,679	3,606
Spirits ('000 hectolitres)	151	144	133
Cigarettes (million)	15,047	15,613	14,256
Cotton fabrics and blankets ('000 sq metres)	14,083	12,321	n.a.
Ready-to-wear clothing ('000 sq metres)	19,591	17,710	n.a.
Leather footwear ('000 pairs)	5,135	4,403	n.a.
Motor spirit (petrol)	1,209	1,261	1,226
Gas-diesel oil (distillate fuel oil)	1,640	1,873	1,741
Cement	3,378	3,571	3,514
Tractors (number)	4,524	n.a.	n.a.
Tankers ('000 gross registered tons)	368	471	n.a.
Cargo ships ('000 gross registered tons)	126	83	n.a.
Chairs ('000)	2,051	2,059	n.a.
Electric energy (million kWh)	12,286	12,690	13,295

Source: partly UN, *Industrial Commodity Statistics Yearbook*.

CROATIA

Finance

CURRENCY AND EXCHANGE RATES

Monetary Unit
100 lipa = 1 kuna.

Sterling, Dollar and Euro Equivalents (31 December 2007)
£1 sterling = 9.988 kuna;
US $1 = 4.985 kuna;
€1 = 7.339 kuna;
100 kuna = £10.01 = $20.06 = €13.63.

Average Exchange Rate (kuna per US $)
2005   5.949
2006   5.838
2007   5.365

Note: The Croatian dinar was introduced on 23 December 1991, replacing (and initially at par with) the Yugoslav dinar. On 30 May 1994 the kuna, equivalent to 1,000 dinars, was introduced.

GOVERNMENT FINANCE
(general government operations, cash basis, million kuna)

Summary of Balances

	2004	2005	2006
Revenue	96,427	103,101	112,294
Less Expense	94,287	100,511	107,722
Net cash inflow from operating activities	2,141	2,590	4,572
Less Purchase of non-financial assets	11,360	9,924	10,350
Sales of non-financial assets	865	865	1,267
Cash surplus/deficit	−8,354	−6,470	−4,511

Revenue

	2004	2005	2006
Taxes	56,426	60,521	66,768
Taxes on income, profits and capital gains	12,161	13,397	15,972
Taxes on property	731	764	962
Taxes on goods and services	41,588	44,415	47,895
General taxes on goods and services	30,057	32,447	35,144
Excises	10,625	10,939	11,565
Social contributions	29,478	31,301	33,877
Grants	14	28	200
Other revenue	10,510	11,250	11,448
Total	96,427	103,101	112,294

Expense/Outlays

Expense by economic type	2004	2005	2006
Compensation of employees	25,505	26,680	28,208
Use of goods and services	9,679	10,876	13,302
Interest	4,423	5,103	5,469
Subsidies	5,695	6,000	6,562
Grants	1,009	1,390	1,466
Social benefits	41,022	42,469	44,828
Other expense	6,954	7,993	7,887
Total	94,287	100,511	107,722

Source: IMF, *Government Finance Statistics Yearbook*.

INTERNATIONAL RESERVES
(US $ million at 31 December)

	2004	2005	2006
IMF special drawing rights	0.1	0.3	0.2
Reserve position in IMF	0.2	0.2	0.2
Foreign exchange	8,757.9	8,799.8	11,487.4
Total	8,758.2	8,800.3	11,487.8

Source: IMF, *International Financial Statistics*.

MONEY SUPPLY
(million kuna at 31 December)

	2004	2005	2006
Currency outside banks	10,955.6	12,163.8	14,609.3
Demand deposits at deposit money banks	23,650.3	26,717.5	33,965.1
Total	34,621.0*	38,881.3	48,574.3

* Including other.

Source: IMF, *International Financial Statistics*.

COST OF LIVING
(Consumer Price Index; base: 2000 = 100)

	2004	2005	2006
Food	105.5	110.4	113.1
Fuel and light	122.1	126.9	132.5
Clothing (incl. footwear)	105.0	105.6	108.0
Housing	111.1	115.5	146.6
All items (incl. others)	110.4	114.0	117.7

Source: ILO.

NATIONAL ACCOUNTS
(million kuna at current prices)

Expenditure on the Gross Domestic Product

	2004	2005	2006
Government final consumption expenditure	45,272	47,316	50,442
Private final consumption expenditure	123,123	131,671	140,261
Change in inventories*	5,301	6,699	7,360
Gross fixed capital formation	60,512	65,008	74,792
Total domestic expenditure	234,208	250,694	272,855
Exports of goods and services	102,083	109,080	119,970
Less Imports of goods and services	121,309	128,426	142,234
GDP in purchasers' values	214,983	231,349	250,590
GDP in constant 1997 prices	156,758	163,491	171,277

* Including statistical discrepancy.

Gross Domestic Product by Economic Activity

	2004	2005	2006
Agriculture, hunting, forestry and fishing	13,992	14,650	15,603
Mining and quarrying; manufacturing; electricity, gas and water supply	43,402	47,798	51,420
Construction	12,246	13,036	14,900
Wholesale and retail trade; repair of motor vehicles, motorcycles and personal and household goods	23,178	24,954	26,707
Hotels and restaurants	6,668	7,316	7,954
Transport, storage and communications	18,616	20,100	22,015
Financial intermediation; real estate, renting and business activities	31,862	35,023	39,996
Public administration and defence; compulsory social security; education; health and social work; other community, social and personal services; private households with employed persons	35,843	37,785	40,336
Sub-total	185,807	200,662	218,931
Less Financial intermediation services indirectly measured	6,990	7,945	9,277
Gross value added in basic prices	178,815	192,718	209,653
Taxes, *less* subsidies, on products	36,168	38,631	40,937
GDP in market prices	214,983	231,349	250,590

CROATIA

BALANCE OF PAYMENTS
(US $ million)

	2004	2005	2006
Exports of goods f.o.b.	8,209.9	8,955.2	10,606.2
Imports of goods f.o.b.	−16,560.3	−18,301.3	−21,117.2
Trade balance	−8,350.4	−9,346.1	−10,511.0
Exports of services	9,373.2	9,921.0	10,809.1
Imports of services	−3,565.4	−3,400.3	−3,547.3
Balance on goods and services	−2,542.6	−2,825.4	−3,249.3
Other income received	743.4	746.4	1,014.6
Other income paid	−1,589.6	−1,971.2	−2,404.2
Balance on goods, services and income	−3,388.8	−4,050.2	−4,638.8
Current transfers received	1,974.0	2,027.2	2,053.8
Current transfers paid	−488.2	−551.9	−670.4
Current balance	−1,903.1	−2,574.9	−3,255.4
Capital account (net)	28.5	60.8	−174.1
Direct investment abroad	−346.3	−237.1	−205.8
Direct investment from abroad	1,078.6	1,788.1	3,376.2
Portfolio investment assets	−944.3	−693.7	−487.5
Portfolio investment liabilities	1,235.2	−798.4	−40.0
Other investment assets	−558.7	1,311.1	−936.9
Other investment liabilities	2,661.5	3,392.6	4,758.7
Net errors and omissions	−1,183.1	−1,226.2	−1,307.9
Overall balance	68.2	1,022.3	1,727.2

Source: IMF, *International Financial Statistics*.

External Trade

PRINCIPAL COMMODITIES
(distribution by SITC, US $ million)

Imports c.i.f.	2004	2005	2006*
Food and live animals	1,189.7	1,332.8	1,554.0
Mineral fuels, lubricants, etc.	1,986.9	2,806.1	3,416.0
Petroleum and petroleum products	1,477.2	2,066.0	2,511.0
Chemicals and related products	1,852.0	2,060.9	2,331.1
Basic manufactures	3,259.7	3,533.3	4,193.1
Machinery and transport equipment	5,793.0	6,115.1	6,928.6
Electrical machinery, apparatus etc. (excl. telecommunications and sound equipment)	1,017.5	965.8	1,088.1
Road vehicles and parts†	1,663.0	1,690.6	1,971.4
Other transport equipment and parts†	574.8	585.4	657.5
Miscellaneous manufactured articles	1,972.0	2,144.6	2,492.3
Clothing and accessories (excl. footwear)	378.3	419.5	518.3
Total (incl. others)	16,589.2	18,560.4	21,502.5

Exports f.o.b.	2004	2005	2006*
Food and live animals	505.8	689.2	952.7
Crude materials (inedible) except fuels	448.9	488.1	609.8
Cork and wood	232.6	248.7	285.1
Mineral fuels, lubricants, etc.	908.8	1,218.8	1,567.7
Petroleum and petroleum products	660.9	798.0	994.9
Chemicals and related products	752.2	872.4	951.9
Medicinal and pharmaceutical products	247.5	275.0	281.9
Plastics in primary forms	174.4	222.6	250.3
Basic manufactures	1,189.6	1,290.7	1,545.2
Non-metallic mineral manufactures	266.6	324.8	362.2
Machinery and transport equipment	2,588.1	2,538.2	2,990.4
Electrical machinery, apparatus etc. (excl. telecommunications and sound equipment)	662.4	633.5	710.4
Transport equipment and parts (excl. road vehicles)†	1,089.8	916.1	1,203.9
Miscellaneous manufactured articles	1,425.3	1,462.6	1,544.1
Clothing and accessories (excl. footwear)	630.7	570.4	538.2
Total (incl. others)	8,024.2	8,772.6	10,377.0

* Provisional data.
† Data on parts exclude tyres, engines and electrical parts.

PRINCIPAL TRADING PARTNERS
(US $ million)

Imports c.i.f.	2004	2005	2006*
Austria	1,131.3	1,067.3	1,169.3
Belgium	198.8	203.1	241.0
Bosnia and Herzegovina	348.6	453.2	600.4
China, People's Republic	635.6	873.3	1,146.4
Czech Republic	395.8	434.8	484.8
France	731.9	777.3	849.4
Germany	2,568.9	2,751.3	3,127.1
Hungary	508.7	574.2	650.2
Italy	2,818.9	2,969.5	3,599.4
Japan	280.5	273.7	323.7
Korea, Republic	164.1	182.4	205.0
Netherlands	295.5	373.7	364.8
Russia	1,205.7	1,698.6	2,167.8
Slovenia	1,179.4	1,257.4	1,350.8
Spain	300.2	281.5	343.8
Sweden	249.5	216.2	227.3
Switzerland	201.4	258.8	292.2
United Kingdom	319.6	347.4	406.5
USA	358.3	397.4	367.0
Total (incl. others)	16,589.2	18,560.4	21,502.5

Exports f.o.b.	2004	2005	2006*
Austria	756.6	628.3	626.9
Bosnia and Herzegovina	1,153.8	1,256.1	1,310.5
France	183.8	198.6	212.7
Germany	895.2	936.1	1,071.4
Greece	14.5	114.4	34.3
Hungary	103.2	137.5	171.9
Italy	1,833.8	1,859.8	2,397.0
Liberia	232.5	210.7	107.4
Macedonia, former Yugoslav republic	74.0	81.5	83.3
Malta	62.6	104.6	109.9
Netherlands	76.7	78.5	89.1
Poland	42.3	53.1	108.3
Russia	115.2	112.6	123.6
Serbia and Montenegro	294.0	393.4	516.7
Slovenia	600.8	711.7	851.1
United Kingdom	96.0	124.8	193.0
USA	211.2	305.1	327.2
Total (incl. others)	8,024.2	8,772.6	10,377.0

* Provisional data.

CROATIA   *Statistical Survey*

Transport

RAILWAYS
(traffic)

	2004	2005	2006
Passenger journeys ('000)	36,747	39,842	46,212
Passenger-kilometres (million)	1,213	1,266	1,362
Freight carried ('000 metric tons)	12,234	14,333	15,395
Freight net ton-km (million)	2,493	2,835	3,305

ROAD TRAFFIC
(registered motor vehicles at 31 December)

	2005	2006	2007
Passenger cars	1,382,275	1,435,781	1,479,149
Buses	4,901	4,914	5,033
Registered goods vehicles	153,249	159,147	164,171
Motorcycles and mopeds	128,781	143,486	165,212

* Data at 30 September 2007.

INLAND WATERWAYS
(vessels and traffic)

	2002	2003	2004
Tugs*	37	50	50
Motor barges*	5	6	5
Barges*	132	136	120
Goods unloaded (million metric tons)	1	1	1

* Registered vessels at 31 December.

SHIPPING

Merchant Fleet
(registered at 31 December)

	2004	2005	2006
Number of vessels	272	281	286
Total displacement ('000 grt)	1,016.1	1,135.2	1,157.2

Source: Lloyd's Register-Fairplay, *World Fleet Statistics*.

International Sea-borne Freight Traffic

	2002	2003	2004
Vessels entered (million grt)	33.1	43.1	51.5
Goods loaded ('000 metric tons)	4,597	4,053	4,809
Goods unloaded ('000 metric tons)	6,705	7,364	7,757
Goods in transit ('000 metric tons)	4,443	5,618	7,582

CIVIL AVIATION

	2004	2005	2006
Kilometres flown ('000)	18,106	n.a.	n.a.
Passengers carried ('000)	1,743	2,099	2,079
Passenger-kilometres (million)	1,460	1,989	1,857
Freight carried (metric tons)	5,429	6,088	5,637
Ton-kilometres ('000)	3,582	3,999	3,336

Tourism

FOREIGN TOURIST ARRIVALS BY COUNTRY OF ORIGIN
('000)

	2004	2005	2006
Austria	741	742	790
Bosnia and Herzegovina	163	171	189
Czech Republic	664	616	593
France	393	591	505
Germany	1,580	1,572	1,545
Hungary	403	453	403
Italy	1,232	1,253	1,235
Poland	241	242	276
Slovakia	176	185	218
Slovenia	884	879	913
United Kingdom	208	256	269
USA	98	115	154
Total (incl. others)	7,912	9,995	10,385

Receipts from tourism (US $ million, incl. passenger transport): 6,514 in 2003; 6,945 in 2004; 7,625 in 2005 (Source: World Tourism Organization).

Communications Media

	2001	2002	2003
Radio licences ('000)	1,150	1,163	1,168
Television licences ('000)	1,080	1,092	1,095
Telephone licences ('000)	1,783	1,825	1,853
Mobile cellular telephones ('000 subscribers)*	1,755	2,340	2,553
Personal computers ('000 in use)*	620	760	800
Internet users ('000)*	518	789	1,014
Book production (titles)	3,832	4,296	6,447
Daily newspapers (number)	14	13	12
Non-daily newspapers	251	252	269
Periodicals	2,211	2,255	2,422

* Source: International Telecommunication Union.

2004: Main telephone lines in use 1,887,600; Mobile cellular telephone subscribers 2,807,600; Personal computers 842,000; Internet users 1,375,300; Broadband subscribers 23,000 (Source: International Telecommunication Union).

2005: Main telephone lines in use 1,882,500; Mobile cellular telephone subscribers 3,649,700; Internet users 1,472,400; Broadband subscribers 116,000 (Source: International Telecommunication Union).

2006: Main telephone lines in use 1,832,200; Mobile cellular telephone subscribers 4,469,700; Internet users 1,576,400; Broadband subscribers 251,800 (Source: International Telecommunication Union).

Facsimile machines (number in use): 50,237 in 1997 (Source: UN, *Statistical Yearbook*).

Education

(2006/07 unless otherwise indicated)

	Institutions	Teachers	Students
Pre-primary	1,244	8,079	109,508
Primary schools	2,146	30,450	382,441
Secondary schools	693	22,573	187,977
Higher education	110*	8,764†	136,646*

* 2005/06 data.
† 2004/05 data.

Adult literacy rate (UNESCO estimates): 98.1% (Males 99.3%; Females 97.1%) in 2001 (Source: UNESCO Institute for Statistics).

Directory

The Constitution

The Constitution of the Republic of Croatia was promulgated on 21 December 1990. Croatia issued a declaration of dissociation from the Socialist Federal Republic of Yugoslavia in June 1991, and formal independence was proclaimed on 8 October. Constitutional amendments adopted in November 1997 included a prohibition on the re-establishment of a union of Yugoslav states. The Županijski dom (Chamber of Counties), the upper chamber of the hitherto bicameral legislature, was abolished by a constitutional amendment adopted in March 2001.

The following is a summary of the main provisions of the Constitution:

GENERAL PROVISIONS

The Republic of Croatia is a democratic, constitutional state where power belongs to the people and is exercised directly and through the elected representatives of popular sovereignty.

The Republic is an integral state, while its sovereignty is inalienable, indivisible and non-transferable. State power in the Republic is divided into legislative, executive and judicial power.

All citizens over the age of 18 years have the right to vote and to be candidates for election to public office. The right to vote is realized through direct elections, by secret ballot. Citizens of the Republic living outside its borders have the right to vote in elections for the Sabor (Assembly) and the President of the Republic.

In a state of war or when there is a direct threat to the independence and unity of the Republic, as well as in the case of serious natural disasters, some freedoms and rights that are guaranteed by the Constitution may be restricted. This is decided by the Sabor by a two-thirds' majority of its deputies and, if the Sabor cannot be convened, by the President of the Republic.

BASIC RIGHTS

The following rights are guaranteed and protected in the Republic: the right to life (the death sentence has been abolished), fundamental freedoms and privacy, equality before the law, the right to be presumed innocent until proven guilty and the principle of legality, the right to receive legal aid, the right to freedom of movement and residence, the right to seek asylum, inviolability of the home, freedom and secrecy of correspondence, safety and secrecy of personal data, freedom of thought and expression of opinion, freedom of conscience and religion (all religious communities are equal before the law and are separated from the State), the right of assembly and peaceful association, the right of ownership, entrepreneurship and free trade (monopolies are forbidden), the right to work and freedom of labour, the right to a nationality, the right to strike, and the right to a healthy environment.

Members of all peoples and minorities in the Republic enjoy equal rights. They are guaranteed the freedom to express their nationality, to use their language and alphabet and to enjoy cultural autonomy.

GOVERNMENT

Legislature

Legislative power resides with the unicameral Sabor, which has a minimum of 100 and a maximum of 160 members. The Sabor decides on the adoption and amendment of the Constitution, approves laws, adopts the state budgets, decides on war and peace, decides on the alteration of the borders of the Republic, calls referendums, supervises the work of the Government and other public officials responsible to the Sabor, in accordance with the Constitution and the law, and deals with other matters determined by the Constitution.

Members of the Sabor are elected by universal, direct and secret ballot for a term of four years, and their term is not mandatory. The Sabor may be dissolved, with the approval of the majority of all the deputies. The Sabor has the power to appoint and dismiss the Prime Minister and (upon his recommendation) the ministers.

President of the Republic

The President of the Republic is the Head of State of Croatia. The President represents the country at home and abroad and is responsible for ensuring respect for the Constitution, guaranteeing the existence and unity of the Republic and the regular functioning of state power. The President is elected directly for a term of five years.

The President is the Supreme Commander of the Armed Forces. In the event of war or immediate danger, the President issues decrees having the force of law. The President may convene a meeting of the Government and place on its agenda items that, in his opinion, should be discussed. The President attends the Government's meetings and presides over them.

Ministers

Executive power in the Republic resides with the President, the Prime Minister and the Ministers. The Government of the Republic consists of the Ministers and the Prime Minister. The Government issues decrees, proposes laws and the budget, and implements laws and regulations that have been adopted by the Sabor. In its work, the Government is responsible to the President of the Republic and the Sabor.

JUDICATURE

Judicial power is vested in the courts and is autonomous and independent. The courts issue judgments on the basis of the Constitution and the law. The Supreme Court is the highest court and is responsible for the uniform implementation of laws and equal rights of citizens. Judges and state public prosecutors are appointed and relieved of duty by the State Judicial Council, which is elected by the Sabor for a term of eight years.

The Government

HEAD OF STATE

President of the Republic: STJEPAN MESIĆ (elected 7 February 2000; re-elected 16 January 2005; inaugurated 18 February 2005).

GOVERNMENT
(March 2008)

A coalition comprising representatives of the Croatian Democratic Union (HDZ), the Croatian Peasants' Party (HSS), the Croatian Social Liberal Party (HSLS) and the Independent Democratic Serb Party (SDSS).

Prime Minister: IVO SANADER (HDZ).
Deputy Prime Minister: ĐURĐA ADLEŠIĆ (HSLS).
Deputy Prime Minister: SLOBODAN UZELAC (SDSS).
Deputy Prime Minister, Minister of the Family, Veterans' Affairs and Intergenerational Solidarity: JADRANKA KOSOR (HDZ).
Deputy Prime Minister, Minister of Economy, Labour and Entrepreneurship: DAMIR POLANČEC (HDZ).
Minister of Finance: IVAN ŠUKER (HDZ).
Minister of Defence: BRANKO VUKELIĆ (HDZ).
Minister of Health and Social Welfare: DARKO MILINOVIĆ (HDZ).
Minister of the Interior: BERISLAV RONČEVIĆ (HDZ).
Minister of Foreign Affairs and European Integration: GORDAN JANDROKOVIĆ (HDZ).
Minister of Agriculture, Fisheries and Rural Development: BOŽIDAR PANKRETIĆ (HSS).
Minister of Regional Development, Forestry and Water Management: PETAR ČOBANKOVIĆ (HDZ).
Minister of Maritime Affairs, Transport and Infrastructure: BOŽIDAR KALMETA (HDZ).
Minister of Justice: ANA LOVRIN (HDZ).
Minister of Environmental Protection, Physical Planning and Construction: MARINA MATULOVIĆ-DROPULIĆ (HDZ).
Minister of Science, Education and Sport: DRAGAN PRIMORAC (HDZ).
Minister of Culture: BOŽO BIŠKUPIĆ (HDZ).
Minister of Tourism: DAMIR BAJS (HSS).

MINISTRIES

Office of the President: 10000 Zagreb, Pantovčak 241; tel. (1) 4565191; fax (1) 4565299; e-mail ured@predsjednik.hr; internet www.predsjednik.hr.

Office of the Prime Minister: 10000 Zagreb, trg sv. Marka 2; tel. (1) 4569222; fax (1) 6303023; e-mail premijer@vlada.hr; internet www.vlada.hr.

Ministry of Agriculture, Fisheries and Rural Development: c/o 10000 Zagreb, ul. grada Vukovara 78; tel. (1) 6106111; fax (1) 6109201; e-mail office@mps.hr; internet www.mps.hr.

Ministry of Culture: 10000 Zagreb, Runjaninova 2; tel. (1) 4866666; fax (1) 4866280; internet www.min-kulture.hr.

Ministry of Defence: 10000 Zagreb, trg kralja Petra Krešimira IV 1; tel. (1) 4567111; e-mail infor@morh.hr; internet www.morh.hr.

CROATIA

Ministry of the Economy, Labour and Entrepreneurship: 10000 Zagreb, ul. grada Vukovara 78; tel. (1) 6106111; fax (1) 6109110; e-mail info@mingorp.hr; internet www.mingorp.hr.

Ministry of Environmental Protection, Physical Planning and Construction: 10000 Zagreb, Republike Austrije 20; tel. (1) 3782444; fax (1) 3772822; e-mail kabinet.ministra@zg.tel.hr; internet www.mzopu.hr.

Ministry of the Family, Veterans' Affairs and Intergenerational Solidarity: 10000 Zagreb, Park Stara Trešnjevka 4; tel. (1) 3657800; fax (1) 3657852; e-mail mobms@mobms.hr; internet www.mobms.hr.

Ministry of Finance: 10000 Zagreb, ul. Katančićeva 5; tel. (1) 4591300; fax (1) 4922583; e-mail kabinet@mfin.hr; internet www.mfin.hr.

Ministry of Foreign Affairs and European Integration: 10000 Zagreb, trg Nikole Šubića Zrinskog 7–8; tel. (1) 4569964; fax (1) 4569977; e-mail mvpei@mvpei.hr; internet www.mvpei.hr.

Ministry of Health and Social Welfare: 10000 Zagreb, Ksaver 200A; tel. (1) 4607555; fax (1) 431067; internet www.mzss.hr.

Ministry of the Interior: 10000 Zagreb, ul. grada Vukovara 33; tel. (1) 6122111; fax (1) 6122299; e-mail ministar@mup.hr; internet www.mup.hr.

Ministry of Justice: 10000 Zagreb, ul. Dežmanova 10; tel. (1) 3710666; fax (1) 3710602; e-mail nmikulin@pravosudje.hr; internet www.pravosudje.hr.

Ministry of Maritime Affairs, Transport and Infrastructure: 10000 Zagreb, Prisavlje 14; tel. (1) 6169111; fax (1) 6196519; e-mail minister@mmtpr.hr; internet www.mmtpr.hr.

Minister of Regional Development, Forestry and Water Management: 10000 Zagreb, ul. grada Vukovara 78; tel. (1) 6106600; fax (1) 6109200; e-mail cobankovic@mps.hr; internet www.mps.hr.

Ministry of Science, Education and Sport: 10000 Zagreb, trg Hrvatskih velikana 6; tel. (1) 4569000; fax (1) 4617962; e-mail ured@mzos.hr; internet www.mzos.hr.

Ministry of Tourism: 10000 Zagreb, Prisavlje 14; tel. (1) 6169111; fax (1) 6169181; e-mail damir.bajs@mint.hr; internet www.mint.hr.

President

Presidential Election, First Ballot, 2 January 2005

	Votes	% of votes
Stjepan Mesić*	1,089,398	48.92
Jadranka Kosor (Croatian Democratic Union)	452,218	20.31
Boris Mikšić (Independent)	396,093	17.79
Others	269,095	12.08
Total†	2,227,073	100.00

† Including 20,269 invalid votes (0.91% of the total).

Presidential Election, Second Ballot, 16 January 2005

	Votes	% of votes
Stjepan Mesić*	1,454,451	65.93
Jadranka Kosor (Croatian Democratic Union)	751,692	34.07
Total	2,206,143	100.00

* Candidate of an alliance comprising the Social Democratic Party of Croatia, the Croatian People's Party, the Croatian Peasants' Party, the Istrian Democratic Assembly, the Party of Liberal Democrats (Libra), the Liberal Party, the Primorje and Gorski Kotar Alliance and the Party of Democratic Action of Croatia.

Legislature

Sabor
(Assembly)

10000 Zagreb, trg sv. Marka 6; tel. (1) 4569222; fax (1) 6303018; e-mail sabor@sabor.hr; internet www.sabor.hr.

The unicameral Sabor comprises a minimum of 100 and a maximum of 160 members, who are elected directly for a term of four years. Eight seats are reserved for representatives of minority ethnic groups. Of these, three seats are elected by Serbs, one by Hungarians and one by Italians. One representative is elected by Czechs and Slovaks; one by a constituency comprising Austrians, Bulgarians, Germans, Jews, Poles, Roma, Romanians, Russians, Ruthenians, Turks, Ukrainians and Vlachs; and one by Albanians, Bosniaks, Macedonians, Montenegrins and Slovenes.

President: LUKA BEBIĆ.

General Election, 25 November 2007

Parties	% of votes	Seats
Croatian Democratic Union	36.6	66
Social Democratic Party of Croatia	31.2	56
Croatian Peasants' Party*	6.5	8
Croatian People's Party—Liberal Democrats	6.8	7
Croatian Democratic Alliance of Slavonia and Baranja	1.8	3
Istrian Democratic Assembly	1.5	3
Croatian Pensioners' Party†	4.1	1
Croatian Party of Rights‡	3.5	1
Others	8.0	0
Total	100.0	153|

* In coalition with the Croatian Social Liberal Party, the Primorje-Gorski kotar Alliance, the Democratic Party of Zagorje and the Zagorje Party.
† In alliance with the Democratic Party of Pensioners.
‡ In coalition with the Democratic Centre and Green Party.
| Including eight seats reserved for representatives of national minority groups.

Election Commission

Državno Izborno Povjerenstvo Republike Hrvatske (State Electoral Commission of the Republic of Croatia): 10000 Zagreb, Opatička 8; tel. (1) 4569712; fax (1) 6303509; internet www.izbori.hr; Pres. BRANKO HRVATIN.

Political Organizations

Croatian Bloc—Movement for a Modern Croatia (Hrvatski blok—pokret za modernu Hrvatsku): 10000 Zagreb, ul. Kneza Mislava 11/1; tel. (1) 4617767; fax (1) 4617768; e-mail info@hrvatski-blok.com; internet www.hrvatski-blok.com; f. 2002; Chair. IVIĆ PAŠALIĆ; 13,983 mems (2005).

Croatian Democratic Alliance of Slavonia and Baranja (HDSSB) (Hrvatski demokratski savez Slavonije i Baranje): 31000 Osijek, Ivana Gundulića 5; tel. (31) 250910; fax (31) 250919; e-mail info@hdssb.hr; internet www.hdssb.hr; f. 2006; Pres. VLADIMIR ŠIŠLJAGIĆ.

Croatian Democratic Union (CDU) (Hrvatska demokratska zajednica—HDZ): 10000 Zagreb, trg Žrtava fašizma 4; tel. (1) 4553000; fax (1) 4552600; e-mail hdz@hdz.hr; internet www.hdz.hr; f. 1989; Christian Democrat; Chair. IVO SANADER; 220,000 mems (2005).

Croatian Party of Rights (CPR) (Hrvatska stranka prava—HSP): 10000 Zagreb, Primorska 5; tel. (1) 3778016; fax (1) 3778736; e-mail hsp@hsp.hr; internet www.hsp.hr; f. 1990 as revival of group originally founded in 1861; extreme right-wing nationalist; armed br. was the Croatian Defence Ascn or Hrvatske Obrambene Snage (HOS); Pres. ANTO ĐAPIĆ; 30,979 mems (2006).

Croatian Peasants' Party (CPP) (Hrvatska seljačka stranka—HSS): 10000 Zagreb, ul. Kralja Zvonimira 17; tel. (1) 4553624; fax (1) 4553631; e-mail hss@hss.hr; internet www.hss.hr; f. 1989; Pres. JOSIP FRIŠČIĆ; 43,000 mems (2005).

Croatian Pensioners' Party (HSU) (Hrvatska stranka umirovljenika): 10000 Zagreb, Frankopanska 7/1; tel. (1) 4840058; fax (1) 4815324; e-mail strankahsu@hsu.hr; internet www.hsu.hr; f. 1996; Chair. VLADIMIR JORDAN.

Croatian People's Party—Liberal Democrats (HNS) (Hrvatska narodna stranka—Liberalni demokrati): 10000 Zagreb, Kneza Mislava 8; tel. (1) 4629111; fax (1) 4629110; e-mail hns@hns.hr; internet www.hns.hr; f. 1990; fmrly Croatian People's Party; Pres. VESNA PUSIĆ; 31,500 mems (2006).

Croatian Popular Party (HPS) (Hrvatska pučka stranka): 10000 Zagreb, Ozaljska 93/2; tel. (1) 3633569; fax (1) 3633749; e-mail hps@hps.hr; internet www.hps.hr; f. 1997; Pres. TOMISLAV MERČEP; 23,700 mems (2006).

Croatian Social Liberal Party (CSLP) (Hrvatska socijalno-liberalna stranka—HSLS): 10000 Zagreb, trg N. Š. Zrinskog 17/1; tel. (1) 4810401; fax (1) 4810404; e-mail hsls@hsls.hr; internet www.hsls.hr; f. 1989; merged with the breakaway Liberal Party in Feb. 2006; Pres. ĐURĐA ADLEŠIĆ; 20,000 mems (2005).

Democratic Centre (DC) (Demokratski Centar): 10000 Zagreb, Ilica 48/1; tel. (1) 4831111; fax (1) 4831045; e-mail demokratski-centar@demokratski-centar.hr; internet www.demokratski-centar.hr; f. 2000 by mems of Croatian Democratic Union; pro-European, moderate; Pres. VESNA ŠKARE OŽBOLT; 14,000 mems (2004).

Democratic Party of Pensioners (DSU) (Demokratska Stranka Umirovljenika): 44000 Sisak, Stjepana i Antuna Radića 20; tel. (91) 7631426; f. 2001; Pres. MILIVOJ TIČARIĆ.

Democratic Party of Zagorje (ZDS) (Zagorska demokratska stranka): 49210 Zabok, Matije Gupce 53/1; tel. and fax (49) 222359; e-mail zagorska-demokratska-stranka@kr.htnet.hr; internet www.zds.hr; f. 1997; Pres. STANKO BELINA; 5,500 mems (2002).

Green Party—Green Alternative (Zelena stranka—Zelena alternativa): 52100 Pula, Koparska 58; tel. and fax (52) 501116; e-mail info@zelenisavez.hr; internet www.zelenisavez.hr; f. 2003; Leader JOSIP-ANTON RUPNIK.

Independent Democratic Serb Party (SDSS) (Samostalna demokratska srpska stranka): 32010 Vukovar, Radnički dom 1–3; tel. (32) 423211; fax (32) 424606; e-mail sdss@vk.t-com.hr; internet www.sdss.hr; f. 1995 by Serbs in Eastern Slavonia; liberal, social-democratic; Pres. Dr VOJISLAV STANIMIROVIĆ; 6,000 mems (2004).

Istrian Democratic Assembly (IDS) (Istarski demokratski sabor): 52100 Pula, Splitska 3; tel. (52) 380183; fax (52) 223316; e-mail ids-ddi@pu.htnet.hr; internet www.ids-ddi.com; f. 1990; Pres. IVAN JAKOVČIĆ; 3,900 mems (2006).

Party of Democratic Action of Croatia (SDA) (Stranka demokratske akcije Hrvatske): 10000 Zagreb, Mandaličina 17; tel. (1) 3772212; fax (1) 3771288; e-mail sdah@sdah.hr; internet www.sdah.hr; f. 1990; represents interests of Bosniaks and Muslims; Pres. Prof. ŠEMSO TANKOVIĆ; 4,850 mems (2006).

Primorje-Gorski kotar Alliance (Primorsko Goranski Savez): 51000 Rijeka, Ciottina 19; tel. and fax (51) 335359; e-mail pgs@pgs.hr; internet www.pgs.hr; f. 1990; regionalist; Chair. NIKOLA IVANIŠ; 5,077 mems (2004).

Social Democratic Party of Croatia (SDP) (Socijaldemokratska partija Hrvatske): 10000 Zagreb, Iblerov trg 9; tel. (1) 4552658; fax (1) 4552842; e-mail sdp@sdp.hr; internet www.sdp.hr; f. 1990; fmrly the ruling League of Communists of Croatia (Party of Democratic Reform), renamed as above in 1993; Chair. ZORAN MILANOVIĆ; 25,000 mems (2004).

Zagorje Party (ZS) (Zagorska Stranka): 49210 Zabok, M. Gupca 53; tel. (49) 221224; e-mail info@zagorskastranka.hr; internet www.zagorskastranka.hr; f. 2004; Pres. MILJENKO JERNEIĆ.

Diplomatic Representation

EMBASSIES IN CROATIA

Albania: 10000 Zagreb, Jurišićeva 2A; tel. (1) 4810679; fax (1) 4810682; e-mail ambasada.shqiptare@inet.hr; Ambassador PËLLUMB QAZIMI.

Australia: 10000 Zagreb, Nova Ves 11, 3 Kaptol Centar; tel. (1) 4891200; fax (1) 4891216; e-mail australian.embassy@zg.t-com.hr; internet www.auembassy.hr; Ambassador TRACY REID.

Austria: 10000 Zagreb, Jabukovać 39; tel. (1) 4881050; fax (1) 4834461; e-mail agram.ob@bmaa.gv.at; internet www.bmaa.gv.at; Ambassador HELGA KONRAD.

Belgium: 10000 Zagreb, Pantovčak 125; tel. (1) 4578901; fax (1) 4578903; e-mail ambabel@zg.htnet.hr; Ambassador MARC DE SCHOUTHEETE DE TERVARENT.

Bosnia and Herzegovina: 10000 Zagreb, Josipa Torbara 9; tel. (1) 4683761; fax (1) 4683764; e-mail ambasada-bh-zg@zg.htnet.hr; Ambassador ALEKSANDAR DRAGIČEVIĆ.

Brazil: 10000 Zagreb, trg Nikole Šubića Zrinskog 10/I; tel. (1) 4002250; e-mail brasemb@zg.primatel.hr; Ambassador HAROLDO VALLADAO.

Bulgaria: 10000 Zagreb, Gornje Prekrižje 28; tel. (1) 4646625; fax (1) 4823338; e-mail veleposlanstvo.republike.bugarske@zg.t-com.hr; Ambassador IVAN SIRAKOV.

Canada: 10000 Zagreb, prilaz Đure Deželića 4; tel. (1) 4881200; fax (1) 4881230; e-mail zagreb@dfait-maeci.gc.ca; Ambassador THOMAS MARR.

Chile: 10000 Zagreb, Smičiklasova 23/II; tel. (1) 4611958; fax (1) 4610328; e-mail embajada@echile.hr; internet www.clembassy.hr; Ambassador EMILIO JOSÉ PEDRO RUIZ-TAGLE ORREGO.

China, People's Republic: 10000 Zagreb, Mlinovi 132; tel. (1) 4637011; fax (1) 4637012; e-mail veleposlanstvo.nr.kine1@zg.t-com.hr; Ambassador WU LIANQI.

Czech Republic: 10000 Zagreb, Savska cesta 41; tel. (1) 6177246; fax (1) 6176630; e-mail zagreb@embassy.mzv.cz; internet www.mzv.cz/zagreb; Ambassador KAREL KÜHNL.

Denmark: 10000 Zagreb, trg Nikole Šubića Zrinskog 10; tel. (1) 4924530; fax (1) 4924554; e-mail zagreb@um.dk; Ambassador BERNO KJELDSEN.

Egypt: 10000 Zagreb, Petrova 51B; tel. (1) 2310781; fax (1) 2310619; e-mail veleposlanstvo.egipat@zg.t-com.hr; Chargé d'affaires a.i. EMAN MOHAMED ZAKI MOHARRAM.

Finland: 10000 Zagreb, Miramarska 23; tel. (1) 6312080; fax (1) 6312090; e-mail sanomat.zag@formin.fi; internet www.finland.hr; Ambassador ANN-MARIE NYROOS.

France: 10000 Zagreb, Hebrangova 2; tel. (1) 4893600; fax (1) 4893660; e-mail presse@ambafrance.hr; internet www.ambafrance.hr; Ambassador FRANÇOIS SAINT-PAUL.

Germany: 10000 Zagreb, ul. grada Vukovara 64; tel. (1) 6300100; fax (1) 6155536; e-mail deutsche.botschaft.zagreb@inet.hr; internet www.zagreb.diplo.de; Ambassador HANS JOCHEN PETERS.

Greece: 10000 Zagreb, Opatička 12; tel. (1) 4810444; fax (1) 4810419; e-mail greece-embassy@grembassy.hr; internet www.grembassy.hr; Ambassador OURANIA ARVANITI.

Holy See: 10000 Zagreb, Ksaverska cesta 10 A; tel. (1) 4673996; fax (1) 4673997; e-mail apostolska.nuncijatura.rh@inet.hr; Apostolic Nuncio Most Rev. FRANCISCO-JAVIER LOZANO (Titular Archbishop of Penafiel in Tripolitania).

Hungary: 10000 Zagreb, Pantovčak 255–257A; tel. (1) 4890900; fax (1) 4579301; e-mail mission.zgb@kum.hu; Ambassador PÉTER IMRE GYÖRKÖS.

India: 10000 Zagreb, ul. Boškovićeva 7 A; tel. (1) 4873239; fax (1) 4817907; e-mail ambassador.india@zg.htnet.hr; internet www.indianembassy.hr; Ambassador RAJIVA MISRA.

Iran: 10000 Zagreb, Pantovčak 125C; tel. (1) 4578981; fax (1) 4578987; Ambassador MOHAMMAD HASSAN FADAIFARD.

Israel: 10000 Zagreb, ul. grada Vukovara 271/11; tel. (1) 6169500; fax (1) 6169555; e-mail ambassador@zagreb.mfa.gov.il; Ambassador SHMUEL MEIROM.

Italy: 10000 Zagreb, Medulićeva 22; tel. (1) 4846386; fax (1) 4846384; e-mail amb.zagabria@esteri.it; Ambassador ALESSANDRO PIGNATTI MORANO DI CUSTOZA.

Japan: 10000 Zagreb, Boškovićeva 2; tel. (1) 4870650; fax (1) 4667334; e-mail embassy@jpemb.htnet.hr; Ambassador TETSUHISA SHIRAKAWA.

Korea, Republic: 10000 Zagreb, Novi Goljak 25; tel. (1) 4821282; fax (1) 4821274; Ambassador DAE-HO BYUN.

Libya: 10000 Zagreb, Gornje Prekrižje 51B; tel. (1) 4629250; fax (1) 4629279; e-mail lnb@zg.htnet.hr; Ambassador (vacant).

Macedonia, former Yugoslav republic: 10000 Zagreb, Kralja Zvonimira 6; tel. (1) 4620261; fax (1) 4617369; e-mail veleposlanstvo.republike.makedonije@zg.t-com.hr; Chargé d'affaires a.i. STOJAN RUMENOVSKI.

Malaysia: 10000 Zagreb, Slavujevac 4A; tel. (1) 4834346; fax (1) 4834348; e-mail malzagreb@kln.gov.my; Ambassador AMINAHTUN KARIM SHAHARUDIN.

Montenegro: 10000 Zagreb, trg Nikole Šubića Zrinskog 1/IV; tel. (1) 4573362; fax (1) 4573423; e-mail ambacrnegore@rcg.hr; Ambassador BRANKO LUKOVAC.

Netherlands: 10000 Zagreb, Medvešćak 56; tel. (1) 4642200; fax (1) 4642211; e-mail zag@minbuza.nl; internet www.netherlandsembassy.hr; Ambassador CATHARINA MARIA TROOSTER.

Norway: 10000 Zagreb, Petrinjska 9; tel. (1) 4922829; fax (1) 4922832; e-mail emb.zagreb@mfa.no; internet www.norwegianembassy.hr; Chargé d'affaires a.i. JENS ERIK GRØNDAHL.

Poland: 10000 Zagreb, Krležin Gvozd 3; tel. (1) 4899444; fax (1) 4834577; e-mail ambasada-polska@zg.t-com.hr; Chargé d'affaires a.i. DARIUSZ WIŚNIEWSKI.

Portugal: 10000 Zagreb, trg ban J. Jelačića 5/2; tel. (1) 4882210; fax (1) 4920663; e-mail emb.port.zagreb@zg.htnet.hr; Ambassador LUÍS BARREIROS.

Romania: 10000 Zagreb, Mlinarska 43; tel. (1) 4677550; fax (1) 4677854; e-mail veleposlanstvo.rumunjske@zg.t-com.hr; Ambassador OANA-CRISTINA POPA.

Russia: 10000 Zagreb, Bosanska 44; tel. (1) 3755038; fax (1) 3755040; e-mail veleposlanstvo-ruske-federacije@zg.tel.hr; internet www.croatia.mid.ru; Ambassador MIKHAIL A. KONAROVSKII.

Serbia: 10000 Zagreb, Pantovčak 245; tel. (1) 4579067; fax (1) 4573338; e-mail ambasada@ambasada-srbije.hr; Ambassador (vacant).

Slovakia: 10000 Zagreb, prilaz Đure Deželića 10; tel. (1) 4848941; fax (1) 4848942; e-mail slovak.emb@zg.htnet.hr; Ambassador JÁN BÁNAS.

Slovenia: 10000 Zagreb, Savska cesta 41/II; tel. (1) 6311000; fax (1) 6177236; e-mail vzg@gov.si; Ambassador MILAN OROŽEN ADAMIČ.

Spain: 10000 Zagreb, Tuškanac 21A; tel. (1) 4848950; fax (1) 4848711; e-mail emb.zagreb@mae.es; Ambassador MANUEL SALAZAR PALMA.

Sweden: 10000 Zagreb, Frankopanska 22; tel. (1) 4925100; fax (1) 4925125; e-mail swedish.embassy@zg.tel.hr; Ambassador LARS FRÉDEN.

Switzerland: 10000 Zagreb, Bogovićeva 3; tel. (1) 4810891; fax (1) 4810890; e-mail zag.vertretung@eda.admin.ch; Ambassador ERICH HERMANN PIRCHER.

Turkey: 10000 Zagreb, Masarykova 3/II; tel. (1) 4855200; fax (1) 4855606; e-mail turkishemb@zg.t-com.hr; Chargé d'affaires a.i. GÜL BÜYÜKERSEN ORAL.

Ukraine: 10000 Zagreb, Voćarska 52; tel. (1) 4616296; fax (1) 4633726; e-mail ukremb@zg.t-com.hr; Ambassador MARKIYAN R. LUBKIVSKY.

United Kingdom: 10000 Zagreb, Ivana Lučića 4; tel. (1) 6009100; fax (1) 6009111; e-mail british.embassyzagreb@fco.gov.uk; internet www.britishembassy.gov.uk/croatia; Ambassador Sir JOHN RAMSDEN.

USA: 10010 Zagreb, Thomasa Jeffersona 2; tel. (1) 6612200; fax (1) 6612373; e-mail irc@usembassy.hr; internet www.zagreb.usembassy.gov; Ambassador ROBERT ANTHONY BRADTKE.

Judicial System

The judicial system of Croatia is administered by the Ministry of Justice. The Constitutional Court consists of 11 judges, elected by the Assembly for a period of eight years. The Supreme Court is the highest judicial body in the country, comprising 26 judges, also elected for a period of eight years.

Supreme Court: 10000 Zagreb, trg Nikole Šubića Zrinskog 3; tel. (1) 4810022; fax (1) 4810035; e-mail vsrh@vsrh.hr; internet www.vsrh.hr; Pres. IVICA CRNIĆ.

Constitutional Court: 10000 Zagreb, Marka trg 4; tel. (1) 4550927; fax (1) 4551055; e-mail usud@usud.hr; internet www.usud.hr; Pres. Prof. PETAR KLARIĆ.

State Judicial Council: 10000 Zagreb, trg Nikole Šubića Zrinskog 3; tel. and fax (1) 4811501; Pres. MILAN GUDELJ.

Office of the Public Prosecutor: 10000 Zagreb, Gajeva 30A; tel. (1) 4591888; fax (1) 4591854; e-mail dorh@zg.htnet.hr; Public Prosecutor MLADEN BAJIĆ.

Religion

Most of the population are Christian, the largest denomination being the Roman Catholic Church, of which most ethnic Croats are adherents. The Archbishop of Zagreb is the most senior Roman Catholic prelate in Croatia. The Croatian Old Catholic Church, like other branches of the Old Catholic Church elsewhere in Europe, does not acknowledge the authority of the Vatican or various reforms, including, notably, the doctrine of papal infallibility, agreed at the First Vatican Council of 1869–70. There is a significant Serbian Orthodox minority. According to the 2001 census, 87.8% of the population of Croatia were Roman Catholics, 4.4% were Eastern Orthodox, 1.3% Muslims, and there were small communities of Protestants and Jews.

CHRISTIANITY

The Roman Catholic Church

For ecclesiastical purposes, Croatia comprises four archdioceses (including one, Zadar, directly responsible to the Holy See) and 10 dioceses, including one for Catholics of the Byzantine rite. At 31 December 2005 there were an estimated 3.7m. adherents.

Latin Rite

Bishops' Conference

10000 Zagreb, Kaptol 22; tel. (1) 4811893; fax (1) 4811894; e-mail tanjnistvo@hbk.hr.
f. 1993; Pres. Cardinal JOSIP BOZANIĆ (Archbishop of Zagreb).

Archbishop of Rijeka: Most Rev. IVAN DEVČIĆ, 51000 Rijeka, Slaviše Vajnera Čiče 2; tel. (51) 337999; fax (51) 215287; e-mail kancelarija@ri-nadbiskupija.hr.

Archbishop of Split-Makarska: Most Rev. MARIN BARIŠIĆ, 21000 Split, Poljana kneza Trpimira 7, POB 328; tel. (21) 407501; fax (21) 407530; e-mail marin.barisic@hbk.hr.

Archbishop of Zadar: Most Rev. IVAN PRENDJA, 23000 Zadar, trg Jurja Bijankinija 2; tel. (23) 208650; fax (23) 208640; e-mail nadbiskupija.zadarska@zd.htnet.hr.

Archbishop of Zagreb: Cardinal JOSIP BOZANIĆ, 10001 Zagreb, Kaptol 31; tel. (1) 4894808; fax (1) 4816104; e-mail kancelar@zg-nadbiskupija.hr.

Byzantine Rite

Bishop of Križevci: Most Rev. SLAVOMIR MIKLOVŠ, 10000 Zagreb, Kaptol 20; tel. (1) 4811872; fax (1) 4811873; 21,467 adherents (2004).

Old Catholic Church

Croatian Catholic Church: 10000 Zagreb, ul. Kneza Branimira 11; tel. (1) 4841361; Bishop BERNHARD HEITZ.

Serbian Orthodox Church

Metropolitan of Zagreb and Ljubljana: Bishop JOVAN, Srpska Biskupija, 10000 Zagreb.

The Press

PRINCIPAL DAILIES

Osijek

Glas Slavonije (Voice of Slavonia): 31000 Osijek, Hrvatske Republike 20; tel. (31) 223200; fax (31) 223203; e-mail glas@glas-slavonije.tel.hr; internet www.glas-slavonije.hr; morning; independent; Editor SANJA MARKETIĆ; circ. 25,000.

Pula

Glas Istre (Voice of Istria): 52100 Pula, Riva 10; tel. (52) 591500; fax (52) 211434; internet www.glasistre.hr; morning; Dir ŽELJKO ŽMAK; circ. 20,000.

Rijeka

Novi List (New Paper): 51000 Rijeka, Zvonimirova 20A, POB 130; tel. (51) 32122; fax (51) 213654; internet www.novilist.hr; morning; Editor VELJKO VICEVIĆ; circ. 60,000.

La Voce del Popolo (Voice of the People): 51000 Rijeka, Zvonimirova 20A; tel. (51) 211154; fax (51) 213528; e-mail lavoce@edit.hr; internet www.edit.hr/lavoce; f. 1944; morning; Italian; Editor-in-Chief ERROL SUPERINA; circ. 4,000.

Split

Slobodna Dalmacija (Free Dalmatia): 21000 Split, ul. Hrvatske mornarice 4; tel. (21) 513888; fax (21) 551220; internet www.slobodnadalmacija.com; morning; Editor MLADEN PLESE; circ. 102,000.

Zagreb

Sportske novosti (Sports News): 10000 Zagreb, Slavonska Ave. 4; tel. (1) 341920; fax (1) 341950; morning; Editor DARKO TIRONI; circ. 55,000.

Večernji list (Evening Paper): 10000 Zagreb, Slavonska Ave. 4; tel. (1) 6500600; fax (1) 6500679; e-mail vecernji@vecernji.net.tel.hr; internet www.vecernji-list.hr; evening; Editor RUŽICA CIGLER; circ. 200,000.

Vjesnik (Herald): 10000 Zagreb, Slavonska Ave. 4, POB 104; tel. (1) 6161680; fax (1) 6161650; e-mail vjesnik@vjesnik.hr; internet www.vjesnik.com; morning; Editor IGOR MANDIĆ; circ. 8,000.

PERIODICALS

Arena: 10000 Zagreb, Slavonska Ave. 4; tel. (1) 6162795; fax (1) 6161572; e-mail arena@eph.hr; f. 1957; illustrated weekly; Editor MLADEN GEROVAĆ; circ. 135,000.

Feral Tribune: 21000 Split, Šetalište Bačvice 10; tel. (21) 488949; fax (21) 488941; e-mail info@feral.hr; internet www.feral.hr; f. 1984; weekly; satirical; Editor-in-Chief HENI ERCEG.

Glasnik (Speaker): 10000 Zagreb, trg hrvatskih velikana 4; tel. (1) 453000; fax (1) 453752; fortnightly; Editor ZDRAVKO GAVRAN; circ. 9,000.

Globus: 10000 Zagreb, Slavonska Ave. 4; tel. (1) 6162057; fax (1) 6162058; e-mail globus@eph.hr; internet www.globus.com.hr; f. 1990; political weekly; Editor MIRKO GALIĆ; circ. 110,000.

Gloria: 10000 Zagreb, Slavonska Ave. 2; tel. (1) 6161288; fax (1) 6182042; e-mail gloria@eph.hr; internet www.gloria.com.hr; weekly; Editor DUBRAVKA TOMEKOVIĆ ARALICA; circ. 110,000.

Informator: 10000 Zagreb, Zelinska 3; tel. (1) 6111500; fax (1) 6111446; e-mail informator@informator.hr; internet www

CROATIA

.informator.hr; f. 1952; economic and legal matters; Dir Dr Faruk Redžepagić.

Mila: 10000 Zagreb, Slavonska Ave. 4; tel. (1) 6161982; fax (1) 6162021; e-mail mila@eph.hr; weekly; Editor Zoja Padovan; circ. 110,000.

OK: Croatia: 10000 Zagreb, Slavonska Ave. 4; tel. (1) 6162127; fax (1) 6162125; e-mail ok@eph.hr; f. 1989; illustrated monthly; Editor Neven Kepeski; circ. 55,000.

Privredni vjesnik (Economic Herald): 10000 Zagreb, Kačićeva 9A; tel. (1) 4846661; fax (1) 4846656; e-mail redakcija@privredni-vjesnik.hr; internet www.privredni-vjesnik.hr; f. 1953; weekly; economics, finance; Editor-in-Chief Franjo Žilić; circ. 10,000.

Republika: 10000 Zagreb, trg bana Josipa Jelačića 7; tel. (1) 4816931; fax (1) 4816959; f. 1945; monthly; published by Društvo hrvatskih književnika; literary review; Editor-in-Chief Ante Stamać.

Studio: 10000 Zagreb, Slavonska Ave. 4; tel. (1) 6162085; fax (1) 6162031; e-mail studio@eph.hr; f. 1964; illustrated weekly; Editor Robert Naprta; circ. 45,000.

Vikend (Weekend): 10000 Zagreb, Slavonska Ave. 4; tel. and fax (1) 6162064; 2 a week; Editor Josip Mušnjak; circ. 50,000.

NEWS AGENCIES

HINA News Agency—Hrvatska izvještajna novinska agencija (Croatian Information and News Agency): 10000 Zagreb, trg Marulidev 16; tel. (1) 4808700; fax (1) 4808820; e-mail newsline@hina.hr; internet www.hina.hr; f. 1990; Dir Smiljanka Skugor-Hrnčević.

IKA—Informativna katolička agencija (Catholic Press Agency): 10000 Zagreb, Kaptol 4; tel. (1) 4814951; fax (1) 4814957; e-mail ika-zg@zg.tel.hr; internet www.ika.hr; f. 1993; Man. Editor Anton Šuljić.

Publishers

AGM Publisher: 10000 Zagreb, Mihanovićeva 28; tel. (1) 4856307; fax (1) 4856316; Croatian and foreign literature, arts, economics, science; Gen. Dir Bože Čović.

Algoritam: 10000 Zagreb, Gajeva 12; tel. (1) 4803333; fax (1) 271541; e-mail mm@algoritam.hr; international bestsellers; Pres. Neven Antičević.

August Cesarec: 10000 Zagreb, prilaz Đure Deželića 57; tel. (1) 171071; fax (1) 573695; Croatian and foreign literature.

Ceres: 10000 Zagreb, Tomašićeva 13; tel. (1) 4558501; fax (1) 4550387; e-mail ceres@zg.tel.hr; internet www.ceres.hr; poetry, fiction, and philosophical and scientific writings; Gen. Dir Dragutin Dumančić.

Croatian Academy of Sciences and Arts Publishing Dept (Hrvatska akademija znanosti i umjetnosti, Odjel za izdavačku djelatnost): 10000 Zagreb, Hebrangova 1; tel. (1) 4895173; fax (1) 4895178; e-mail naklada@hazu.hr; internet www.hazu.hr; f. 1861; Sec.-Gen. Slavko Cvetić.

Erasmus Publishing: 10000 Zagreb, Rakušina 4; tel. and fax (1) 433114; Croatian literature; Gen. Dir Srećko Lipovčan.

Europa Press: 10000 Zagreb, Slavonska Ave. 4; tel. (1) 6190011; fax (1) 6190033; Dir Marjan Jurleka.

Golden Marketing-Tehnička Knjiga: 10000 Zagreb, Jurišičeva 10; tel. (1) 4810820; fax (1) 4810821; e-mail gmtk@gmtk.net; f. 1947; academic publisher; Dir Ana Rešetar.

Hena Com: 10000 Zagreb, Horvaćanska 65; tel. and fax (1) 3750206; e-mail hena-com@hena-com.hr; internet www.hena-com.hr; children's books; Gen. Man. Uzeir Husković.

Izvori: 10000 Zagreb, Trnjanska 64; tel. and fax (1) 6112576; e-mail info@izvori.com; internet www.izvori.com; scientific journalism, literature, classics, popular fiction, comic books.

Kršćanska Sadašnjost: 10001 Zagreb, trg Marulićev 14, POB 434; tel. (1) 4828219; fax (1) 4828227; e-mail ks@zg.tel.hr; internet www.ks.hr; theological publications.

M. Krleža Lexicographic Institute (Leksikografski zavod 'Miroslav Krleža'): 10000 Zagreb, Frankopanska 26; tel. (1) 4800333; fax (1) 4800399; f. 1951; encyclopedias, bibliographies and dictionaries; Pres. Tomislav Ladan.

Masmedia: 10000 Zagreb, ul. baruna Trenka 13; tel. (1) 4577400; fax (1) 4577769; e-mail masmedia@zg.tel.hr; business and professional literature; Gen. Dir Stjepan Andrašić.

Matica Hrvatska: 10000 Zagreb, trg Strossmayerov 2; tel. (1) 4878360; fax (1) 4819319; e-mail matica@matica.hr; internet www.matica.hr; f. 1842; arts and science, fiction, popular science, politics, economics, sociology, history; Chair. Prof. Igor Zidić.

Mladost: 10000 Zagreb, Ilica 30; tel. (1) 453222; fax (1) 434878; f. 1947; fiction, science, art, children's books; Gen. Dir Branko Vuković.

Mosta: 10000 Zagreb, Majevička 12A; tel. (1) 325196; fax (1) 327898; popular fiction; Gen. Dir Nladimir Vućur.

Mozaik Knjiga: 10000 Zagreb, Sauska 66; tel. (1) 6178910; fax (1) 6178911; e-mail zdranko.kafol@mozaik-knjiga.hr; internet www.mozaik-knjiga.hr; educational books; Gen. Dir Zdranko Kafol.

Naprijed-Ljevak: 10000 Zagreb, Palmotićeva 30/1; tel. (1) 4804000; fax (1) 4804001; e-mail naklada-ljevak@zg.htnet.hr; internet www.naklada-ljevak.hr; f. 1957; philosophy, psychology, religion, sociology, medicine, dictionaries, children's books, art, politics, economics, tourist guides; Exec. Dir Ivana Ljevak.

Školska Knjiga (Schoolbooks): 10001 Zagreb, Masarykova 28, POB 1039; tel. (1) 4830511; fax (1) 4830510; e-mail skolska@skolskaknjiga.hr; internet www.skolskaknjiga.hr; education, textbooks, art; Dir Dr Dragomir Maderić.

Školske Novine: 10000 Zagreb, Andrije Hebranga 40; tel. (1) 4855720; fax (1) 4855712; education, religion, poetry, textbooks; Gen. Man. Ivan Rodić.

Verbum: 21000 Split, Trumbićeva obala 12; tel. (21) 340260; fax (21) 340270; e-mail naklada@verbum.hr; internet www.verbum.hr; f. 1992; religion, philosophy and humanism; Gen. Man. Miro Radalj.

Znanje (Knowledge): 10000 Zagreb, Mandićeva 2; tel. (1) 3689534; fax (1) 3689531; e-mail znanje@zg.tel.hr; f. 1946; popular science, agriculture, fiction, poetry, essays; Pres. Žarko Šepetavić.

PUBLISHERS' ASSOCIATION

Croatian Publishers' and Booksellers' Asscn (Poslovna Zajednica Izdavača i Knjižara Hrvatske): 10000 Zagreb, Klaićeva 7; fax (1) 171624.

Broadcasting and Communications

TELECOMMUNICATIONS

T-Hrvatski Telekom (T-HT): 10000 Zagreb, Savska cesta 32; tel. (1) 4911000; fax (1) 4911011; e-mail kontakt@t-com.hr; internet www.t.ht.hr; f. 1999; 51% owned by Deutsche Telekom (Germany); Pres. Ivica Mudrinić.

T-Mobile Hrvatska (T-Mobile Croatia): 10000 Zagreb, ul. grada Vukovara 23; tel. (1) 4982000; fax (1) 4982011; e-mail web@t-mobile.hr; internet www.t-mobile.hr; subsidiary of Hravtski Telekom; provides mobile cellular telecommunications services.

VIPnet: 10000 Zagreb, trg Iblerov 10; tel. (1) 4691091; e-mail office@vipnet.hr; internet www.vipnet.hr; wholly owned by Mobilkom Austria; f. 1998; provides mobile cellular telecommunications services.

BROADCASTING

Radio

Croatian Radio: 10000 Zagreb, Dezmanova 6, Dom HRT; tel. (1) 4807199; fax (1) 4807190; internet www.hrt.hr; f. 1926; 3 radio stations; 8 regional stations (Sljeme, Osijek, Pula, Rijeka, Split, Zadar, Dubrovnik and Knin); broadcasts in Croatian, English and Spanish; Dir-Gen. Vanja Sutlić (acting).

Otvoreni Radio: 10010 Zagreb, Cebini 28; tel. (1) 6623700; fax (1) 6623800; e-mail otvoreni@otvoreni.hr; internet www.otvoreni.hr; broadcasts popular music and entertainment programmes nationwide; Dirs Robert Miličević, Daniel Berdais.

Radio 101: Zagreb; internet www.radio101.hr; independent radio station; Editor-in-Chief Zrinka Vrabec-Mojzes.

Radio Baranja: 31300 Beli Manastir, trg Slobode 32/3; e-mail radio-baranja@zg.tel.hr; internet www.radio-baranja.hr; f. 1992; independent; Dir Zlatar Maršić.

Television

Croatian Television (HRT): 10000 Zagreb, Prisavlje 3; tel. (1) 6342634; fax (1) 6343712; e-mail program@hrt.hr; internet www.hrt.hr; f. 1956; 2 channels; Dir-Gen. Vanja Sutlić (acting); Dir Marija Nemčić.

Finance

(cap. = capital; res = reserves; dep. = deposits; m. = million; amounts in kuna; brs = branches)

BANKING

In early 2007 a total of 33 banking institutions were operating in Croatia, of which 16 were under majority foreign ownership. Total bank assets in 2004 amounted to 229,305m. kuna.

Central Bank

Croatian National Bank (Hrvatska Narodna Banka): 10000 Zagreb, trg Hrvatskih velikana 3; tel. (1) 4564555; fax (1) 4550726; e-mail webmaster@hnb.hr; internet www.hnb.hr; in 1991 assumed the responsibilities of a central bank empowered as the republic's bank of issue; cap. 2,500.0m., res 2,552.3m., dep. 39,915.2m. (Dec. 2005); Gov. ŽELJKO ROHATINSKI.

Selected Banks

Croatia Banka d.d. Zagreb: 10000 Zagreb, Kvaternikov trg 9; tel. (1) 2391130; fax (1) 2338141; e-mail intl.division@croatiabanka.hr; internet www.croatiabanka.hr; f. 1989; cap. 204.6m., res –55.3m., dep. 1,133.4m. (Dec. 2006); Pres. of Man. Bd IVAN PURGAR; 23 brs.

Croatian Bank for Reconstruction and Development (Hrvatska Banka za Obnovu i Razvoj—HBOR): 10000 Zagreb, Strossmayerov trg 9; tel. (1) 4591666; fax (1) 4591790; e-mail pmandic@hbor.hr; internet www.hbor.hr; f. 1992; cap. 4,174.7m., res 964.4m., dep. 4,668.8m. (Dec. 2006); name changed in 1995; Pres. IVAN ŠUKER.

Erste & Steiermärkische Bank d.d: 51000 Rijeka, Jadranski trg 3A; tel. (62) 371000; fax (62) 372000; e-mail erstebank@erstebank.hr; internet www.erstebank.hr; f. 2000 by merger of Bjelovarska Banka, Cakoveka Banka and Trgovačka Banka; cap. 1,513.0m., res 751.0m., dep. 31,695.0m. (Dec. 2006); Chair. JOHANNES KINSKY.

Hrvatska Poštanska Banka (Croatian Post Bank): 10000 Zagreb, Jurišićeva 4; tel. (1) 4804400; fax (1) 4810773; internet www.hpb.hr; f. 1991; cap. 584.8m., res 102.8m., dep. 8,651.2m. (Dec. 2006); Chair. JOSIP PROTEGA.

Hypo Alpe-Adria-Bank d.d.: 10000 Zagreb, Slavonska ave 6; tel. (1) 6030000; fax (1) 6035100; e-mail bank.croatia@hypo-alpe-adria.com; internet www.hypo-alpe-adria.hr; f. 1996; cap. 1,994.8m., res 185.5m., dep. 19,809.9m. (Dec. 2006); Chair. RADOJKA OLIĆ.

Istarska Kreditna Banka Umag (Istria Credit Bank Umag): 52470 Umag, Ernesta Miloša 1; tel. (52) 702300; fax (52) 702388; e-mail marketing@ikb.hr; internet www.ikb.hr; f. 1956; commercial and joint-stock bank; cap. 64.9m., res 87.6m., dep. 1,533.2m. (Dec. 2005); Chair. MIRO DODIĆ; 16 brs.

Karlovačka Banka: 47000 Karlovac, Ivana Gorana Kovačića 1; tel. (47) 417501; fax (47) 614206; e-mail karlovacka.banka@kaba.hr; internet www.kaba.hr; f. 1955; cap. 135.0m., res 36.2m., dep. 1,122.8m. (Dec. 2006); Pres. SANDI SOLA.

Međimurska Banka Čakovec (Međimurje Bank Čakovec): 40000 Čakovec, Valenta Morandinija 37; tel. (40) 370500; fax (40) 370620; e-mail info@mb.hr; internet www.mb.hr; f. 1954; cap. 127.9m., res 86.7m., dep. 2,085.4m. (Dec. 2006); Pres. NENAD JEDUD.

OTP Banka Hrvatska d.d.: 23000 Zadar, Domovinskog rata 3; tel. (23) 201500; fax (23) 201859; e-mail info@otpbanka.hr; internet www.otpbanka.hr; f. 1957 as Komunalna Banka Zadar; merged with Dubrovačka Banka Dubrovnik in 2004; acquired by OTP Bank of Hungary and name changed from Nova Banka in 2005; cap. 455.3m., res 259.3m., dep. 8,348.8m. (Dec. 2006); Pres. LÁSZLÓ WOLF; 6 brs.

Podravska Banka d.d.: 48000 Koprivnica, Opatička 1a; tel. (48) 6550; fax (48) 622542; e-mail info@poba.hr; internet www.poba.hr; cap. 168.3m., res 40.7m., dep. 2,106.8m. (Dec. 2006); Pres. JULIO KURUC.

Privredna Banka Zagreb d.d.: 10000 Zagreb, Račkoga 6, POB 1032; tel. (1) 6360000; fax (1) 6360063; e-mail pbz@pbz.hr; internet www.pbz.hr; f. 1966; commercial bank; cap. 1,907.0m., res 4,710.0m., dep. 52,186.0m. (Dec. 2006); Pres. and CEO BOŽO PRKA; 18 brs.

Raiffeisenbank Austria d.d.: 10000 Zagreb, ul. Petrinjska 59; tel. (1) 4566466; fax (1) 4811624; e-mail info@rba.hr; internet www.rba.hr; f. 1994; cap. 2,194.0m., res 472.0m., dep. 29,616.0m. (Dec. 2006); Chair. ZDENKO ADROVIĆ.

Slavonska Banka d.d. Osijek (Slavonian Bank): 31000 Osijek, Kapucinska 29, POB 108; tel. (31) 231231; fax (31) 201039; e-mail info@slavonska-banka.hr; internet www.slavonska-banka.hrslbo.hr; f. 1989; cap. 753.9m., res 286.2m., dep. 7,353.3m. (Dec. 2006); Pres. IVAN MIHALJEVIĆ; 11 brs.

Société Générale-Splitska Banka d.d.: 21000 Split, Boškovića 16; tel. (21) 304304; fax (21) 304034; e-mail info@splitskabanka.hr; internet www.splitskabanka.hr; f. 1966; cap. 491.0m., res 727.0m., dep. 14,550.0m. (Dec. 2006); Pres. JEAN-DIDIER REIGNER.

Štedbanka d.d.: 10000 Zagreb, Slavonska Ave. 3; tel. (1) 6306666; fax (1) 6187015; e-mail stedbanka@stedbanka.hr; internet www.stedbanka.hr; f. 1994; cap. 225.0m., res 31.0m., dep. 711.7m. (Dec. 2006); Pres. ANTE BABIĆ.

Volksbank: 10000 Zagreb, Varšavska 9; tel. (1) 4801300; fax (1) 4801365; e-mail info@volksbank.hr; internet www.volksbank.hr; f. 1997; cap. 292.2m., res 433.6m., dep. 2,790.2m. (Dec. 2006); Chair. TOMASZ TARABA.

Zagrebačka Banka d.d. (Bank of Zagreb): 10000 Zagreb, Paromlinska 2; tel. (1) 6104000; fax (1) 6110533; e-mail zaba@zaba.hr; internet www.zaba.hr; f. 1913; cap. 1,098.0m., res 546.0m., dep. 52,484.0m. (Dec. 2006); Chair. FRANJO LUKOVIĆ; 129 brs.

Bankers' Organization

Croatian Banking Asscn (Hrvatska udruga banaka): 10000 Zagreb, Centar Kaptol, Nova Ves 17; tel. (1) 4860080; fax (1) 4860081; e-mail info@hub.hr; internet www.hub.hr; Man. Dir Dr ZORAN BOHACEK.

Supervisory Authority

Croatian Agency for Supervision of Financial Services (HANFA) (Hrvatska Agencija za Nadzor Financijskih Usluga): 10000 Zagreb, Bogovićeva 1A; tel. (1) 4888740; fax (1) 4811406; e-mail info@hanfa.hr; internet www.hanfa.hr.

STOCK EXCHANGE

Zagreb Stock Exchange (Zagrebačka Burza): 10000 Zagreb, Ksaver 208; tel. (1) 428455; fax (1) 420293; e-mail zeljko.kardum@zse.hr; internet www.zse.hr; f. 1990; Gen. Man. MARINKO PAPUGA.

INSURANCE

In mid-2003 there were 23 licensed insurance companies operating in Croatia; of these, four specialized in life insurance, six in non-life insurance and the remainder covered both life and non-life insurance.

Allianz: 10000 Zagreb, Selska 136–138; tel. (1) 3760367; internet www.allianz.hr/hrv/index.asp; life insurance, annuity, property, motor vehicle and transport insurance, personal accident insurance, health insurance, liability insurance.

Croatia Osiguranje: 10000 Zagreb, Miramarska 22; tel. (1) 6332000; fax (1) 6332020; e-mail informacije@gendir.crosig.hr; internet www.crosig.hr; f. 1884; privatized in 2002, when it accounted for 46% of business in the sector; Pres. HRVOJE VOJKOVIĆ.

Euroherc Osiguranje: 10000 Zagreb, ul. grada Vukovara 282; internet www.euroherc.hr; Pres. RADOSLAV PAVLOVIĆ.

Grawe Hrvatska d.d.: 10000 Zagreb, ul. grada Vukovara 5; tel. (1) 3034000; fax (1) 3034500; e-mail info@grawe.hr; internet www.grawe.hr.

Merkur Osiguranje: 10000 Zagreb, ul. grada Vukovara 237; tel. (1) 6308333; fax (1) 6157130; internet www.merkur.hr.

Triglav Osiguranje d.d.: 10002 Zagreb, ul. Republike Austrije; tel. (1) 3444105; fax (1) 3444173; e-mail iris.urem@triglav-osiguranje.hr; internet www.triglav-osiguranje.hr.

Trade and Industry

GOVERNMENT AGENCIES

Croatian Agency for Small Business: 10000 Zagreb, Prilaz Gjure Deželića 7; tel. (1) 4881000; fax (1) 4881009; e-mail hamag@hamag.hr; internet www.hamag.hr; Pres. of Man. Bd TOMISLAV KOVAČEVIĆ.

Croatian Competition Agency: 10000 Zagreb, Savska cesta 41/VII; tel. (1) 6176448; fax (1) 6176448; e-mail agencija.ztn@aztn.hr; internet www.aztn.hr; Pres. of Competition Council OLGICA SPEVEC.

Croatian Privatization Fund (Hrvatski fond za privatizaciju): 10000 Zagreb, Ivana Lučića 6; tel. (1) 6346111; fax (1) 6115568; e-mail hfp@hfp.hr; internet www.hfp.hr; f. 1994; Pres. DAMIR POLANČEC.

Export and Investment-Promotion Agency (Agencija za promicanje izvoza i ulaganja): 10000 Zagreb, ul. grada Vukovara 78; tel. (1) 6109860; fax (1) 6109868; e-mail igor.maricic@mingosp.hr; Head of Agency IGOR MARIČIĆ.

CHAMBERS OF COMMERCE

Croatian Chamber of Economy (Hrvatska Gospodarska Komora): 10000 Zagreb, trg Rooseveltov 2; tel. (1) 4561555; fax (1) 4828380; e-mail hgk@hgk.hr; internet www.hgk.hr; Pres. NADAN VIDOŠEVIĆ.

Croatian Chamber of Economy—Zagreb Chamber: 10000 Zagreb, Draškovićeva 45, POB 238; tel. (1) 4606777; fax (1)

4606813; e-mail hgkzg@hgk.hr; internet www.zg.hgk.hr; f. 1852; Pres. Dr ZLATAN FRÖHLICH.

Croatian Chamber of Trades and Crafts (Hrvatska obrtnička komora): 10000 Zagreb, Ilica 49/2, POB 166; tel. (1) 4806666; fax (1) 4846610; e-mail hok@hok.hr; internet www.hok.hr; Pres. MATO TOPIĆ.

EMPLOYERS' ASSOCIATION

Croatian Employers Association (Hrvatska udruga poslodavaca—HUP): 10000 Zagreb, Pavla Hatza 12; tel. (1) 4897555; fax (1) 4897556; e-mail hup@hup.hr; internet www.hup.hr; Gen. Dir ŽELJKO IVANČEVIĆ.

UTILITIES

Regulatory Authority

Croatian Energy Regulatory Council (Vijeće za regulaciju energetskih djelatnosti): 10000 Zagreb, Savska 163; tel. (1) 6326260; fax (1) 6326261; e-mail vred@vred.hr; internet www.vred.hr; Pres. Dr MIĆO KLEPO.

Electricity

HEP—Hrvatska Elektroprivreda (Croatian Electricity): 10000 Zagreb, Vukovara 37; tel. (1) 6322111; fax (1) 6170430; e-mail ivan.mravak@hep.hr; internet www.hep.hr; f. 1990; production and distribution of electricity; Dir IVAN MRAVAK.

Gas

Plinacro: 10000 Zagreb, Savska cesta 88A; tel. (1) 6301777; fax (1) 6301787; internet www.plinacro.hr; f. 2001; distribution of natural gas; Chair. MARINA MATULOVIĆ DROPULIĆ.

Water

Hrvatske Vode (Croatian Water): 10000 Zagreb, Vukovara 220; tel. (1) 6307333; fax (1) 6155910; e-mail voda@voda.hr; internet www.voda.hr; f. 1995; state water-management organization; Dir DAVORIN ANDROŠIĆ.

TRADE UNIONS

Independent Trade Unions of Croatia (Nezavisni Hrvatski Sindikati—NHS): 10000 Zagreb; f. 1992; 40,000 mems; Pres. KREŠIMIR SEVER.

Union of Autonomous Trade Unions of Croatia (Savez samosalnih sindikata hrvatske—SSSH): 10000 Zagreb, trg kralja Petra Krešimira IV 2; tel. (1) 4655013; fax (1) 4655040; e-mail international-uatuc@sssh.hr; internet www.sssh.hr; f. 1990; 23 br. unions with 211,000 mems (2007); Pres. ANA KNEŽEVIĆ.

Workers' Trade Union Assen of Croatia (Udruga radničkih sindikata Hrvatske): 10000 Zagreb, Ilića Kralja Držislava 4/1; tel. and fax (1) 4612896; e-mail ursh@inet.hr; internet www.ursh.hr; Pres. BORIS KUNST.

Transport

RAILWAYS

In 2006 there were an estimated 2,726 km of railway lines in Croatia, with direct links to many of the surrounding countries.

Croatian Railways (Hrvatske Željeznice): 10000 Zagreb, Mihanovićeva 12; tel. (1) 4577111; fax (1) 4577730; e-mail hrvatske.zeljeznice@hznet.hr; internet www.hznet.hr; f. 1990; state-owned; public railway transport, construction, modernization and maintenance of railway vehicles; Pres. DAVORIN KOBAK.

ROADS

The Road Fund is responsible for the planning, construction, maintenance and rehabilitation of all inter-urban roads in Croatia. In 2006 there were an estimated 28,788 km of roads in Croatia, of which 1,081 km were motorways. A 75-km motorway linking Dragonje, near the Slovenian border, with Pula in southern Istria was completed in the late 1990s. In June 2000 Croatia and Bosnia and Herzegovina signed a statement on the construction of the Ploče (Dalmatia)–Budapest transport corridor, to link Croatia with Hungary, by way of Bosnia and Herzegovina. The construction of this 'C5' corridor, which commenced in September 2005, was intended to end the isolation of Croatia's southern areas and ensure the optimal use of Ploče's port capacity. A 380-km section of road connecting Zagreb with Split, which was considered to be important for future development of the tourism industry, was completed in mid-2005.

SHIPPING

Following a downturn in traffic during the Balkans conflicts of the 1990s, Croat's shipping trade increased markedly during the first half of the 2000s. The principal ports are located at Rijeka, Sibenek, Split, Ploče, Omišalj, Dubrovnik and Zadar. At the end of 2006 Croatia's merchant fleet had 286 vessels, with a total displacement of 1.2m. grt.

Atlantska Plovidba: 20000 Dubrovnik, od sv. Mihajla 1; tel. (20) 352333; fax (20) 356148; e-mail atlant@atlant.hr; internet www.atlant.hr; f. 1974; Dir ANTE JERKOVIĆ.

Croatia Line: 51000 Rijeka, Riva 18, POB 379; tel. (51) 205111; fax (51) 335811; e-mail erc.hr@croatialine.com; f. 1986; cargo and passenger services; chartering and tramping service; Gen. Man. DARIO VUKIĆ.

Jadrolinija Adriatic Shipping Line: 51000 Rijeka, Riva 16; tel. (51) 666111; fax (51) 213116; e-mail jadrolinija@jadrolinija.hr; internet www.jadrolinija.hr; f. 1872; regular passenger and car-ferry services between Croatian and Italian ports, and along the Adriatic coast of Dalmatia; Pres. SLAVKO LONČAR.

Jadroplov: 21000 Split, Obala kneza Branimira 16; tel. (21) 302666; fax (21) 342198; e-mail jadroplov@jadroplov.com; internet www.jadroplov.com; f. 1984; fleet of 17 vessels and 1,500 containers engaged in linear and tramping service; Gen. Man. NIKŠA GIOVANELLI.

Slobodna Plovidba: 22000 Šibenik, Drage 2; tel. (22) 23755; fax (22) 27860; f. 1976; transport of goods by sea; tourism services; Dir VITOMIR JURAGA.

Tankerska Plovidba: 23000 Zadar, Božidara Petranovića 4; tel. (23) 202202; fax (23) 202375; e-mail info@tankerska.hr; internet www.tankerska.hr; f. 1976; Gen. Dir IVE MUSTAĆ.

CIVIL AVIATION

There are 10 international airports in Croatia.

Croatia Airlines: 10000 Zagreb, Savska cesta 41; tel. (1) 6160066; fax (1) 6176845; e-mail pr@ctn.tel.hr; internet www.croatiaairlines.com; f. 1989 as Zagreb Airlines; name changed 1990; operates domestic and international services; Pres. IVAN MIŠETIĆ.

Tourism

The attractive Adriatic coast and the country's 1,185 islands made Croatia a very popular tourist destination before the early 1990s, when the conflict greatly reduced tourist activity. The industry recovered strongly after 1992. In 2006 the number of foreign tourist arrivals reached some 10.4m., and revenue from tourism (including passenger transport) totalled US $7,625m. in 2005.

Croatian Tourist Board (Hrvatska turistička zajednica): 10000 Zagreb, Ilberov trg 10/4; tel. (1) 4699333; fax (1) 4557827; e-mail info@htz.hr; internet www.croatia.hr; Pres. BOŽIDAR KALMETA.

CUBA

Introductory Survey

Location, Climate, Language, Religion, Flag, Capital

The Republic of Cuba is an archipelago of two main islands, Cuba and the Isla de la Juventud (Isle of Youth), formerly the Isla de Pinos (Isle of Pines), and about 1,600 keys and islets. It lies in the Caribbean Sea, 145 km (90 miles) south of Florida, USA. Other nearby countries are the Bahamas, Mexico, Jamaica and Haiti. The climate is tropical, with the annual rainy season from May to October. The average annual temperature is 25°C (77°F) and hurricanes are frequent. The language spoken is Spanish. Most of the inhabitants are Christians, of whom the great majority are Roman Catholics. The national flag (proportions 1 by 2) has five equal horizontal stripes, of blue, white, blue, white and blue, with a red triangle, enclosing a five-pointed white star, at the hoist. The capital is Havana (La Habana).

Recent History

Cuba was ruled by Spain from the 16th century until 1898, when the island was ceded to the USA following Spain's defeat in the Spanish–American War. Cuba became an independent republic on 20 May 1902, but the USA retained its naval bases on the island and, until 1934, reserved the right to intervene in Cuba's internal affairs. In 1933 an army sergeant, Fulgencio Batista Zaldivar, came to power at the head of a military revolt. Batista ruled the country, directly or indirectly, until 1944, when he retired after serving a four-year term as elected President.

In March 1952, however, Gen. Batista (as he had become) seized power again, deposing President Carlos Prío Socarrás in a bloodless coup. Batista's new regime soon proved to be unpopular and became harshly repressive. In July 1953 a radical opposition group, led by Dr Fidel Castro Ruz, attacked the Moncada army barracks in Santiago de Cuba. Castro was captured, with many of his supporters, but was later released. He went into exile and formed a revolutionary movement which was committed to Batista's overthrow. In December 1956 Castro landed in Cuba with a small group of followers, most of whom were captured or killed. However, 12 survivors, including Castro and the Argentine-born Dr Ernesto ('Che') Guevara, escaped into the hills of the Sierra Maestra, where they formed the nucleus of the guerrilla forces which, after a prolonged struggle, forced Batista to flee from Cuba on 1 January 1959. The Batista regime collapsed, and Castro's forces occupied Havana.

The assumption of power by the victorious rebels was initially met with great popular acclaim. The 1940 Constitution was suspended in January 1959 and replaced by a new 'Fundamental Law'. Executive and legislative power was vested in the Council of Ministers, with Fidel Castro as Prime Minister and his brother Raúl as his deputy and Minister of the Revolutionary Armed Forces. Guevara reportedly ranked third in importance. The new regime ruled by decree but promised to hold elections within 18 months. When it was firmly established, the Castro Government adopted a radical economic programme, including agrarian reform and the nationalization of industrial and commercial enterprises. These drastic reforms, combined with the regime's authoritarian nature, provoked opposition from some sectors of the population, including former supporters of Castro, and many Cubans went into exile.

All US business interests in Cuba were expropriated, without compensation, in October 1960, and the USA severed diplomatic relations in January 1961. A US-sponsored force of anti-Castro Cuban émigrés landed in April 1961 at the Bahía de Cochinos (Bay of Pigs), in southern Cuba, but the invasion was thwarted by Castro's troops. Later in the year, all pro-Government groups were merged to form the Organizaciones Revolucionarias Integradas (ORI). In December 1961 Fidel Castro publicly announced that Cuba had become a communist state, and he proclaimed a 'Marxist-Leninist' programme for the country's future development. In January 1962 Cuba was excluded from active participation in the Organization of American States (OAS). The USA instituted a full economic and political blockade of Cuba. Hostility to the USA was accompanied by increasingly close relations between Cuba and the USSR. In October 1962 the USA revealed the presence of Soviet missiles in Cuba but, after the imposition of a US naval blockade, the weapons were withdrawn. The missile bases, capable of launching nuclear weapons against the USA, were dismantled, thus resolving one of the most serious international crises since the Second World War. In 1964 the OAS imposed diplomatic and commercial sanctions against Cuba.

The ORI was replaced in 1962 by a new Partido Unido de la Revolución Socialista Cubana (PURSC), which was established, under Fidel Castro's leadership, as the country's sole legal party. Guevara resigned his military and government posts in April 1965, subsequently leaving Cuba to pursue revolutionary activities abroad. In October 1965 the PURSC was renamed the Partido Comunista de Cuba (PCC). Although ostracized by most other Latin American countries, the PCC Government maintained and consolidated its internal authority, with little effective opposition. Supported by considerable aid from the USSR, the regime made significant progress in social and economic development, including improvements in education and public health. At the same time, Cuba continued to give active support to left-wing revolutionary movements in Latin America and in many other parts of the world. Guevara was killed in Bolivia, following an unsuccessful guerrilla uprising under his leadership, in October 1967.

In July 1972 Cuba's links with the Eastern bloc were strengthened when the country became a full member of the Council for Mutual Economic Assistance (CMEA—dissolved in 1991), a Moscow-based organization linking the USSR and other communist states. As a result of its admission to the CMEA, Cuba received preferential trade terms and more technical advisers from the USSR and Eastern European countries.

In June 1974 the country's first elections since the revolution were held for municipal offices in Matanzas province. Cuba's first 'socialist' Constitution was submitted to the First Congress of the PCC, held in December 1975, and came into force in February 1976, after being approved by popular referendum. As envisaged by the new Constitution, elections for 169 municipal assemblies were held in October 1976. These assemblies later elected delegates to provincial assemblies and deputies to the Asamblea Nacional del Poder Popular (National Assembly of People's Power), inaugurated in December 1976 as 'the supreme organ of state'. The National Assembly chose the members of a new Council of State, with Fidel Castro as President. The Second Congress of the PCC was held in December 1980, when Fidel Castro and Gen. Raúl Castro (as he had become in 1976) were re-elected First and Second Secretaries, respectively. In December 1981 Fidel Castro was re-elected by the Assembly as President of the Council of State, and Raúl Castro re-elected as First Vice-President.

Cuba continued to be excluded from the activities of the OAS, although the Organization voted in favour of allowing members to normalize their relations with Cuba in 1975. Relations with the USA deteriorated because of Cuban involvement in Angola in 1976 and in Ethiopia in 1977. The relaxation of restrictions on emigration in April 1980 resulted in the departure of more than 125,000 Cubans for Florida, USA. Antagonism continued as Cuba's military and political presence abroad increased, threatening US spheres of influence.

In 1981 Cuba expressed interest in discussing foreign policy with the USA, and declared that the shipment of arms to guerrilla groups in Central America had ceased. High-level talks between the two countries took place in November but US hostility increased. Economic sanctions were strengthened, the major air link was closed, and tourism and investment by US nationals was prohibited in April 1982. Cuba's support of Argentina during the 1982 crisis concerning the Falkland Islands improved relations with the rest of Latin America, and the country's legitimacy was finally acknowledged when it was elected to the chair of the UN General Assembly Committee on Decolonization in September 1982, while continuing to play a leading role in the Non-aligned Movement (despite its firm alliance with the Soviet bloc).

An increase in US military activity in Honduras and the Caribbean region led President Castro to declare a 'state of national alert' in August 1983. The US invasion of Grenada in

October, and the ensuing short-lived confrontation between US forces and Cuban personnel on the island, severely damaged hopes that the two countries might reach an agreement over the problems in Central America, and left Cuba isolated in the Caribbean, following the weakening of its diplomatic and military ties with Suriname in November.

In July 1984 official negotiations were begun with the USA on the issues of immigration and repatriation. In December agreement was reached on the resumption of Cuban immigration to the USA and the repatriation of 2,746 Cuban 'undesirables', who had accompanied other Cuban refugees to the USA in 1980. The repatriation of Cuban 'undesirables' began in February 1985, but, following the inauguration of Radio Martí (a radio station sponsored by the 'Voice of America' radio network, which began to broadcast Western-style news and other programmes to Cuba from Florida), the Cuban Government suspended its immigration accord with the USA. Subsequently, all visits to Cuba by US residents of Cuban origin were banned. The US Government responded by restricting visits to the USA by PCC members and Cuban government officials. In September 1986, as a result of mediation by the Roman Catholic Church, more than 100 political prisoners and their families were permitted to leave Cuba for the USA.

Relations with the USA continued to deteriorate in 1987 when the US Government launched a campaign to direct public attention to violations of human rights in Cuba. The restoration, in October, of the 1984 immigration accord provoked rioting by Cuban exiles detained in US prisons. The accord allowed for the repatriation of 2,500 Cuban 'undesirables' in exchange for a US agreement to allow 23,000 Cubans to enter the USA annually. In 1988 the Government released some 250 political prisoners, and in the following January President Castro pledged to release the remaining 225 political prisoners acknowledged by the regime. In 1989 human rights activists formed a co-ordinating body and increased their operations. The Government responded in August by imprisoning leading activists for up to two years for having published allegedly false information. In September 1991 eight Cuban dissident organizations united to form a single democratic opposition group, the Concertación Democrática Cubana, to campaign for political pluralism and economic reform.

In June 1989 President Castro was confronted by Cuba's most serious political crisis since the 1959 Revolution. It was discovered that a number of senior military personnel were not only involved in smuggling operations in Angola but were also aiding Colombian drugs-traffickers from the infamous Medellín cartel, by enabling them to use Cuban airstrips as refuelling points (en route from Colombia to the USA) in return for bribes. Following court-martial proceedings, Gen. Arnaldo Ochoa Sánchez, who had led the military campaign in Angola, was found guilty of high treason and was executed. Three other officers were also executed. A further purge led to the imposition of harsh sentences on 14 senior officials, including the head of civil aviation and the Ministers of the Interior and of Transport, who had been found guilty of corruption. President Castro insisted that the bureaucracy in Cuba needed to undergo a process of 'purification', but not reform. However, the scandal had clearly undermined the regime's credibility at the international, as well as the domestic, level.

In April 1989 President Gorbachev of the USSR undertook the first official visit to Cuba by a Soviet leader since 1974. The two Heads of State discussed ways in which Cuba's dependence on Soviet aid might be reduced. Although, ostensibly, relations remained good, tensions had arisen, owing to Castro's resistance to Soviet-style reforms. Gorbachev made it clear that, in future, general financial aid would be replaced by assistance for specific projects, thus giving the USSR greater power to influence policy decisions in Cuba. In July President Castro strongly attacked the ideas of *perestroika* and *glasnost*, which he blamed for the 'crisis in socialism'. He pledged to eradicate all market forms of economic activity, despite the fact that Cuba's failure to integrate into the new supply-and-demand system of many Eastern European factories had led to delays in imports and acute shortages.

In October 1990 President Castro announced plans to reduce the PCC's bureaucracy by as much as 50%, including the reassignment of thousands of employees to more productive sectors. In November rationing was extended to all products. Cubans were told to prepare for the possibility of a 'special wartime period' by Raúl Castro, who warned of a possible US military attack if the currently intensified US economic blockade should fail. In spite of the gravity of Cuba's political and economic situation, President Castro was defiant in his rejection of recommendations that, as a condition for the removal of the blockade, Cuba should adopt a market economy and political pluralism.

In September 1991 the USSR announced that it intended to withdraw the majority of its military personnel (some 3,000 troops and advisers) from Cuba. The decision, which was condemned by Cuba as presenting a major threat to its national security, came as the result of US demands that the USSR reduce its aid to Cuba as a precondition to the provision of US aid to the USSR. Cuba's subsequent demands that the USA withdraw its troops from the naval base at Guantánamo were rejected. The Soviet withdrawal was completed in June 1993.

In 1992 President Castro's efforts to quiet internal dissent and bolster the country against the perceived US threat revealed an increasingly militant attitude, as several death sentences were imposed on Cuban dissidents. In the same year the USA began to implement a series of measures strengthening its economic blockade against Cuba. In April US President George Bush issued an executive order barring ships that were engaged in trade with Cuba from entering US ports. In October the Cuban Democracy Act, also known as the 'Torricelli Law', was adopted, making it illegal for foreign subsidiaries of US companies to trade with Cuba. These measures encountered widespread international criticism. In November the UN General Assembly adopted a non-binding resolution demanding the cessation of the trade embargo. The General Assembly continued to adopt similar resolutions on an annual basis.

In July 1992 the National Assembly approved a number of amendments to the Constitution. Under the reforms, President Castro was granted the authority to declare a state of emergency and, in such an event, to assume full control of the armed forces at the head of a National Defence Council. An electoral reform, which had originally been proposed at the Fourth Congress of the PCC in October 1991, was formally adopted, providing for elections to the National Assembly to be conducted by direct vote. The constitutional revisions also included an updating of the business law, legitimizing foreign investment in approved state enterprises and recognizing foreign ownership of property in joint ventures.

On 24 February 1993 elections to the National Assembly and the 14 provincial assemblies were, for the first time, conducted by direct secret ballot. Only candidates nominated by the PCC were permitted to contest the elections. According to official results, 87% of the electorate cast a 'united' ballot (a vote for the entire list of candidates). All 589 deputies of the National Assembly were elected with more than the requisite 50% of the votes. In the following month Fidel Castro and Gen. Raúl Castro were unanimously re-elected by the National Assembly to their respective posts as President and First Vice-President of the Council of State.

In July 1993, with the economic crisis deepening and international reserves exhausted, Castro announced that a 30-year ban on Cuban citizens possessing foreign currency was to be lifted. The measure, which represented a significant departure from the country's centrally planned socialist economy, was intended to attract the large sums of foreign currency (principally US dollars) in circulation on the black market into the economy, and to encourage remittances from Cuban exiles. Restrictions on Cuban exiles travelling to Cuba were also to be relaxed. Concerns that the measures were socially divisive, affording privileges to those receiving currency from relatives abroad, were acknowledged by the Government. In September, in a further move away from traditional economic policy, the Government authorized limited individual private enterprise in a range of 117 occupations. In the same month plans were announced for the introduction of agricultural reforms allowing for the decentralization and reorganization of state farms into 'Units of Basic Co-operative Production', to be managed and financed by the workers themselves.

In April 1994, in a reorganization of the Government, four new ministries were created and a number of state committees and institutes dissolved, reflecting a significant change in the economic management of the country. In early August, however, increasing discontent at deteriorating economic conditions resulted in rioting in the capital, precipitated by a confrontation between police and a large number of Cubans attempting to commandeer a ferry in order to take the vessel to the USA. In a public speech broadcast on the following day Castro indicated that, if the USA failed to halt the promotion of such illegal departures, Cuba would suspend its travel restrictions. The resultant surge of Cubans attempting to reach the USA by sea reached crisis proportions, and the US President, Bill Clinton, was forced to adopt measures to deter them. The automatic refugee status conferred on Cubans under the 1966 Cuban Adjustment Act was revoked, and Cubans were warned that those intercepted by the US Coast Guard would be transported to Guantánamo naval base and would not be allowed entry into the USA. Further measures imposed included the halting of cash remittances from Cuban exiles in the USA. However, these measures failed to stem the flow of Cubans seeking refuge in the USA, and in September 1994 the US and Cuban Governments held bilateral talks to resolve the crisis. As a result of the talks, the USA promised to grant visas allowing for the migration of a minimum of 20,000 Cubans annually. In return, Cuba reintroduced border restrictions. More than 30,000 Cubans were estimated to have left the country during the period when travel restrictions were suspended, although the majority of these were detained by the US authorities and transported to camps in Guantánamo and the Panama Canal Zone. In May 1995 a further immigration accord was signed, bringing to an official end the automatic refugee status that had been revoked in the previous August. The accord also stated that all Cuban refugees intercepted at sea by the USA would thenceforth be repatriated. In addition, the USA agreed to grant visas to the majority of the approximately 20,000 Cuban refugees detained at Guantánamo, although the figure was to be deducted, over a period of four years, from the annual quota of visas granted under the September 1994 accord.

In early 1995 legislative proposals seeking to tighten the US embargo against Cuba were introduced to the US Congress by Senator Jesse Helms and Congressman Dan Burton. The proposals, referred to as the Helms-Burton bill, sought to impose sanctions on countries trading with or investing in Cuba, and threatened to reduce US aid to countries providing Cuba with financial assistance, notably Russia. The proposed law provoked international criticism, and a formal complaint was registered by the European Union (EU, see p. 244), which claimed that the legislation would be in violation of international law and the rules of the World Trade Organization (WTO, see p. 396). The legislation was approved by the House of Representatives in September but was considerably modified by the Senate.

In February 1996 Cuban MiG fighters shot down two US light aircraft piloted by members of the Cuban-American exile group Brothers to the Rescue, killing all four crew members. The action was vigorously condemned by the USA, which rejected Cuban claims that the aircraft had violated Cuban airspace. Further US sanctions were immediately implemented, including the indefinite suspension of charter flights to Cuba. In June the International Civil Aviation Organization confirmed US claims that the aircraft had been shot down over international waters. As a result of the incident, President Clinton reversed his previous opposition to certain controversial elements of the Helms-Burton bill, and in March he signed the legislation, officially entitled the Cuban Liberty and Democratic Solidarity (LIBERTAD) Act, thus making it law. However, Clinton was empowered to issue executive orders, at six-monthly intervals, postponing the implementation of a section of the law, Title III, which allowed US citizens, including naturalized Cuban exiles, to prosecute through US courts any foreign corporation or investor with business dealings involving property that had been expropriated during the Castro regime. Title IV of the Act, which made executives of companies investing in Cuba (and their dependants) liable to exclusion from the USA, was implemented selectively. Approval of the Helms-Burton Act prompted strenuous criticism from Cuba's major trading partners. The EU announced its intention to challenge the extra-territorial provisions of the Act through the WTO, while Mexico and Canada sought to dispute the law under the provisions of the North American Free Trade Agreement. In June Canada initiated a series of legal measures to protect Canadian companies against the Act. Similar legislation was subsequently adopted by Mexico and the EU. In July Clinton imposed a six-month moratorium on Title III of the Act, which had been due to come into force in August. In November, in its annual vote on the US embargo, the UN General Assembly voted for its repeal with the largest majority to date. Notably, the United Kingdom, Germany and the Netherlands, which had all previously abstained on this question, voted in favour of a repeal.

In December 1996 agreement was reached by the members of the EU to make the extent of economic co-operation with Cuba contingent upon progress towards democracy in the country. In that month the Cuban Government adopted legislation to counteract the application of the Helms-Burton Act in an attempt to protect foreign investment in the country. The Government also expressed its readiness to negotiate with the USA regarding the compensation of US citizens with property claims in Cuba. In February 1997 the WTO, at the petition of the EU, established a disputes panel to rule on the legality of the Act's extra-territorial provisions. However, in April the EU and the USA reached an agreement on a resolution of the dispute whereby the USA was to continue deferring the implementation of Title III indefinitely, and the EU was to suspend its petition to the WTO while negotiations continued towards a multilateral accord defining investment principles, with particular emphasis on expropriated foreign assets. In a move widely interpreted as a concession to mounting domestic pressure to end restrictions on exports of food and medicines from the USA to Cuba, in March 1998 it was agreed that shipments of both commodities, via non-governmental organizations (NGOs), were to be permitted. In addition, President Clinton ended the ban on direct flights between the USA and Cuba (imposed in 1996) and on the transfer of cash remittances from the USA to Cuba. However, the Cuban Government was extremely critical of a further outline agreement on extraterritorial legislation drafted by the US Government and the EU in May, which it considered to be highly concessionary on the part of the EU, at the expense of Cuban interests. Under the terms of the agreement, in return for a commitment from President Clinton to seek congressional consensus for a relaxation of the application of the Helms-Burton Act, EU member states would participate in the compilation of a register of former US assets in Cuba (considered to have been illegally expropriated) and would observe firm US recommendations regarding their exclusivity. President Clinton repeatedly exercised his right to postpone the implementation of Title III. His successor, George W. Bush, continued to suspend the implementation of Title III at six-monthly intervals.

On 11 January 1998 elections to the National Assembly (enlarged from 589 to 601 seats) and to the 14 provincial assemblies were conducted. All 601 candidates who contested the legislative ballot were elected. Of the 7.8m. registered voters, 98% participated in the elections. Only 5% of votes cast were blank or spoiled. At the first meeting of the newly constituted National Assembly on 24 February, the new Council of State was announced, confirming Fidel and Raúl Castro, and the five incumbent Vice-Presidents, in their positions for a further five-year term.

In January 1998 Cuba received its first ever papal visit. During the visit Pope John Paul II was critical of the 'unjust and ethically unacceptable' US embargo against Cuba, and urged the reintegration of Cuba into the international community. In response, in late January, the Guatemalan Government announced that diplomatic relations were to be restored with Cuba, prompting a rebuke from the US Department of State. During February, moreover, it was announced that almost 300 Cuban prisoners were to be released, many as a result of a petition for clemency made by the papal delegation. In April, at a meeting of the UN Commission on Human Rights, the annual US-sponsored vote of censure against the Cuban Government for alleged abuses of human rights was defeated for the first time since 1991. Support for the annual UN General Assembly resolution urging an end to the US embargo against Cuba increased once again in October, receiving the support of 157 member nations. Twelve members abstained from the vote, while only two (the USA and Israel) voted against the resolution.

In mid-March 1999 the Provincial Court in Havana sentenced four prominent political dissidents to prison terms of between three and a half and five years' duration. The decision followed the introduction, in February, of uncompromising new legislation to combat increasing criminal activity and to curb subversion and dissent. The incarceration of the dissidents, together with the imposition of death sentences in March on two Salvadorean nationals (see below), drew criticism of Cuba's respect for human rights from the international community in general, and resulted in a significant deterioration in relations with Canada (Cuba's largest trading partner) and Spain in particular.

In March 1999 two Salvadorean nationals were convicted (and subsequently sentenced to death) on terrorism charges relating to a spate of bomb attacks in mid-1997, allegedly organized by the anti-Castro Cuban-American National Foundation (CANF, based in Florida). In December 1999 the US Department of Justice acquitted five Cuban exiles, including a member of the

CANF executive, accused of plotting to assassinate President Castro in Venezuela in 1997. Three Guatemalan nationals, arrested in March 1998, stood trial in November 2001 on charges of terrorist action, allegedly organized and financed by the CANF.

Despite a further easing of restrictions relating to the US embargo in August 1999, and well-publicized visits to Cuba by several prominent US politicians, attempts by the US Government to appease the increasingly influential anti-embargo lobby were largely frustrated by an exchange of legal challenges. In March a US judge ruled that payments owed to the Cuban national telecommunications company, which were currently being withheld by a number of US telecommunications companies by judicial request, could be used to help honour a compensation award of US $187m. against the Cuban authorities, made in the USA in 1997 to benefit relatives of four pilots shot down by the Cuban air force in 1996 (see above). The US Government had made known its objection to the ruling, claiming that the decision amounted to interference in foreign policy. In response, in early June a new lawsuit was brought to the Cuban courts by a number of government-sponsored organizations, which were seeking some $181,100m. in compensation for more than 3,000 deaths and more than 2,000 injuries allegedly inflicted on Cuban nationals since the 1959 Revolution by the 'aggressive' policies of the US Government. (In early 2001 the US Administration authorized the transfer of these payments, to compensate relatives of the four pilots.) In September 1999 a unanimous declaration of the National Assembly condemned the US trade embargo as an act of 'genocide'. In October 2000 legislation was passed by the US Congress easing some aspects of the trade embargo, including the export of food and medicine. However, the Cuban Government declared that the conditions attached to the lifting of the restrictions were such that the legislation would tighten, rather than ease, the US embargo. In response, Cuba imposed a 10% tax on all telephone calls between the two countries and, in December, suspended telephone links with the USA, following the refusal of US telecommunications companies to pay the levy.

In the first six months of 2000 Cuban–US relations were dominated by the case of Elián González. In November 1999 Elián, a five-year-old Cuban boy, was rescued from the Atlantic Ocean off the coast of Florida, the sole survivor of a shipwrecked attempt to reach the USA, in which his mother had died. A dispute resulted between the boy's Miami-based relatives, who attempted to have him granted US citizenship, and his father in Cuba, who wanted his son repatriated. The US Department of Justice granted custody to Elián's father, but his Miami relatives refused to relinquish charge of the boy. In April armed Federal Bureau of Investigation (FBI) agents seized Elián from his Miami relatives and he eventually returned to Cuba in June. In Cuba the case prompted public demonstrations in protest at the USA's 'abduction' of the child.

In November 2000, during a visit to Panama to attend the Ibero-American Summit, an alleged plot to assassinate President Castro was uncovered. Anti-Castro activist Luis Posada Carriles was arrested, along with three others. Posada Carriles had escaped from custody in Venezuela, where he was indicted for the bombing of a Cuban aeroplane near Barbados in 1976, and was also implicated in a series of hotel bombings in Havana in 1997. The Cuban Government's request for Posada Carriles' extradition was subsequently refused. In April 2004 Posada Carriles was sentenced in Panama to an eight-year prison term. However, in August of that year, having been pardoned by the Panamanian President, Posada Carriles fled the country. In April 2005 Posada Carriles filed a request for political asylum in the USA; in the following month he was arrested and detained by the US Department of Homeland Security on the charge of illegal entry into the country via the Mexican border. Both the Cuban and Venezuelan Governments demanded his extradition; the former wanted to try him for the hotel bombings, while the latter wished to retry him for the aeroplane bombing. Castro conceded that extradition to Venezuela would be acceptable—while Venezuela had an extradition treaty with the USA, Cuba did not. However, the US Government refused to co-operate, citing the threat posed to, and lack of evidence against, Posada Carriles, prompting both the Cuban and Venezuelan Governments to accuse the USA of hypocrisy in its 'war on terror'. In April 2007 Posada Carriles was released on bail pending his trial on illegal entry charges, and in the following month those charges were dismissed on the grounds that he should not have been questioned over the bombing charges during his immigration interview. His release from prison prompted protests in Cuba.

In May 2002 former US President Jimmy Carter visited Cuba; he was the most prominent US political figure to have travelled to the country since 1928. In an unprecedented televised address Carter criticized the human rights record of the Cuban Government but stated that he believed that the USA should initiate moves towards the lifting of the trade embargo. However, in a speech given on 20 May, the centenary of Cuban independence from Spain, US President George W. Bush affirmed that the embargo and travel restrictions would remain in place until Cuba installed a government that would respect political and civil rights. Cuban–US relations were further strained when, in the same month, the US Administration added Cuba to the list of states it claimed formed an 'axis of evil' that supported international terrorism. The US Under-Secretary of State for Arms Control and International Security, John Bolton, claimed that Cuba was engaged in limited biological warfare research and development and that it had provided biotechnology that could be used for civilian and military purposes by so-called 'rogue states'. (However, in September 2004 it was reported that Cuba actually possessed only a limited capability to manufacture biological weapons and did not appear to be doing so.) In November 2002 Cuba finally acceded to the Treaty on the Non-Proliferation of Nuclear Weapons—NPT (see p. 109).

Also in May 2002 an 11,000-signature petition—part of a dissident initiative known as the 'Varela Project'—was submitted to the National Assembly; it called for a referendum on basic civil and political liberties. In the following month the Government responded by initiating a drive to mobilize popular support for an amendment to the Constitution, declaring the socialist system to be 'untouchable' and ratifying that 'economic, diplomatic and political relations with any other state can never be negotiated in the face of aggression, threat or pressure from a foreign power'. The National Assembly subsequently voted unanimously to adopt a constitutional amendment declaring socialism in Cuba to be permanent and 'irrevocable'. In July, in an indication that the US legislature was moving towards a softening of its stance on Cuba, the US House of Representatives passed legislation easing both travel and trade restrictions to the country; the legislation was also approved by the Senate, although the Bush Administration stated its intention to veto any legislative provisions that might ease the embargo.

On 19 January 2003 elections took place to the National Assembly (enlarged from 601 to 609 seats) and the 14 provincial legislatures. All the candidates elected were unopposed and voter turn-out was 97.6%. Only 3.9% of ballot papers were spoiled or left blank. Fidel Castro was subsequently re-elected as President for a sixth consecutive term.

Relations with the USA worsened in March 2003 when James Cason, Principal Officer of the US Interests Section in Havana, was accused by the Cuban Government of attempting to incite a counter-revolution, having met with opponents of Fidel Castro during his short time in the country and, allegedly, disseminated anti-Government propaganda. Castro subsequently ordered that all those dissidents who had met with Cason be arrested, and imposed strict travel restrictions on all US diplomatic personnel resident in Cuba. The arrests provoked condemnation from international organizations and human rights groups. In April 75 of the dissidents were found guilty of charges of subversion and treason and sentenced to prison terms of up to 28 years. Meanwhile, bilateral tensions were heightened further by government accusations that the USA was encouraging a spate of aeroplane hijackings by Cubans seeking asylum in the USA, owing to its lenient treatment of Cuban emigrants. In the same month, as the Government continued to adopt a more repressive stance towards the opposition, three men found guilty of hijacking a ferry in an attempt to reach the USA were convicted of terrorism and executed following brief trials. In July, after the EU suspended Cuba's application to join its Cotonou Agreement (see below) in protest at the country's recent human rights record, President Castro announced that his Government would reject any aid offered by the EU and would terminate all political contact with the organization. Meanwhile, the EU imposed diplomatic sanctions on Cuba, stating that it would officially welcome Cuban dissidents into its embassies while restricting contact with the Government.

Although there were indications that the US Congress was softening its stance on the issue, in November 2003 it agreed to maintain the ban on US citizens travelling to Cuba in return for additional federal funding. In December a US governmental commission, the Commission for Assistance to a Free Cuba, headed by US Secretary of State Colin Powell, held its inaugural meeting. The Commission's remit was to plan for the end of the Castro regime and the advent of democracy in Cuba. President Bush also reiterated his commitment to strengthening the US embargo on trade and tourism with the island.

The Government continued to operate in an increasingly repressive manner in 2004. In January the Ministry of Computer Science and Communications announced new regulations prohibiting Cuban citizens from gaining unauthorized access to the internet through the state telephone system. As this was the only form of internet access available to most Cubans, the regulations further enforced state control over access to information on the island. In February the USA intensified its ban on travel to Cuba when President Bush signed an order authorizing the US authorities to inspect any vessel sailing in US waters that did not have official permission to travel to Cuba. In April the UN Commission on Human Rights, at its annual session held in Geneva, Switzerland, passed a motion condemning human rights violations in Cuba and mandating the Commission to send a mission to the country in order that it could report on the situation. In response, the Cuban Government declared that it would not permit any human rights monitors to enter the country.

In May 2004 the USA announced that it would intensify its measures against Cuba, stating that it would place further restrictions on remittances into the country and that US military aircraft would be used to prevent Cuban radio stations from blocking pro-democracy broadcasts. In addition, Cuban Americans resident in the USA were only to be permitted to visit their relatives in Cuba once every three years. In response, President Castro orchestrated a protest march in Havana and restricted the quantity of goods available for purchase in US dollars within Cuba. In October the Government announced that circulation of the US dollar in Cuba would not be permitted from the following month; a commission of 10% would also be imposed from then on when changing US dollars into local currency. In the same month the Minister of Basic Industry, Marcos Javier Portal León, was dismissed, largely owing to his failure to prevent a severe shortfall in the country's power supply following the breakdown of its largest power plant. He was replaced by Yadirá García Vera.

In April 2005 the UN Human Rights Commission narrowly passed a resolution condemning the imprisonment of political dissidents and journalists in Cuba. The resolution called for the renewal of the mandate of a UN envoy to investigate alleged human rights abuses in the country. Minister of Foreign Relations Felipe Ramón Pérez Roque publicly dismissed the resolution as 'illegitimate'. In the following month the Assembly for the Promotion of Civil Society in Cuba—organized by Martha Beatriz Roque, one of the 75 dissidents detained in March 2003 (and released in the following year)—took place in Havana. No attempts were made by the Cuban Government to halt the proceedings. However, Castro denounced all attendees of the gathering as 'counter-revolutionaries'; furthermore, two Polish members of the European Parliament were prohibited from entering Cuba prior to the Assembly, and a German and a Czech parliamentarian were ejected from the island on the eve of the gathering—a move that prompted official complaints from both the Czech and German Governments and drew fierce criticism from numerous other European countries. The Assembly itself went ahead without incident; approximately 200 people attended, including James Cason, then Principal Officer of the US Interests Section in Havana, who brought a videotaped message of support from US President Bush. Those in attendance drafted a list of demands for President Castro, including the immediate release of imprisoned dissidents, economic freedom and the return of a multi-party democracy.

In July 2005, in the largest crackdown on dissidents since March 2003, 26 people were arrested during a protest outside the French embassy in Havana. The demonstrators were opposed to France's decision to normalize relations with Cuba (and the decision to invite Minister of Foreign Relations Pérez Roque to the embassy's Bastille Day celebration). A week earlier, government forces had arrested about 30 dissidents gathering to commemorate the deaths of Cubans attempting to reach the USA by boat in 1994. Although most of those detained were freed after a few hours, many feared the arrests signalled a new determination by the Castro Government to clamp down on dissent. In the same month the US Secretary of State, Condoleezza Rice, appointed Caleb McCarry to be Cuba Transition Co-ordinator, a position created at the behest of a special panel appointed by US President Bush and charged with directing the US Government's actions 'in support of a free Cuba' and hastening the end to President Castro's premiership.

After 'Hurricane Dennis' struck the island in July 2005, killing 16 Cubans and causing damage estimated at US $1,400m., the US Government offered financial aid of $50,000 for emergency supplies; in a state television broadcast President Castro expressed gratitude but refused the offer, insisting that Cuba would not accept any assistance from the USA while the US trade embargo remained in place. However, in the wake of 'Hurricane Wilma', which caused serious flooding in Havana and forced the evacuation of over 250,000 Cubans resident across the west of the island in October, Cuba accepted a US offer of an assessment team from the Office of US Foreign Disaster Assistance. However, in early November the US Department of State withdrew the offer after Castro announced he wanted to discuss regional co-operation with the team. A US donation of $100,000 to NGOs working within Cuba to help those affected by the hurricane would proceed, none the less. The Cuban Government dismissed the aid as a veiled method of funding 'the mercenary groups that the US Government organizes and directs in Cuba'. In September the Cuban Government had offered to send 1,500 doctors, together with medical supplies and field hospitals, to the US city of New Orleans following its destruction by 'Hurricane Katrina' (see chapter on the USA). This offer of aid was rejected by President Bush.

President Castro's health was once again the subject of international speculation in November 2005 when long-running rumours that he was suffering from Parkinson's disease were imbued with a new intensity following a series of reports in the US media. The President quickly dismissed the reports as an attempt to undermine his authority. In the same month Castro, expressing concerns about the direction in which Cuba was heading, launched a campaign against corruption and vice as part of a wide-ranging drive to effect a 'total renewal' of Cuban society. In December journalist Mario Enrique Mayo Hernández, one of the 75 dissidents imprisoned without charge in March 2003, was released on medical grounds; Mayo Hernández was the 15th such detainee to be released. According to the Cuban Commission for Human Rights and National Reconciliation, at June 2006 there were an estimated 316 political dissidents in detention within Cuba, a modest decline from 345 detainees at the beginning of the year. However, the NGO attributed this decrease to a change in the Government's tactics rather than to a softening of its stance on dissidents, arguing that the authorities were now resorting to a more eclectic range of measures, including the intimidation of dissidents in their homes.

In April 2006 the PCC announced a structural reorganization that included the re-establishment of the party Secretariat, which had originally been dissolved in 1991; the 12-member executive body was charged with ensuring adherence to the party line and eradicating insubordination and misconduct. In the same month Juan Carlos Robinson was dismissed from the PCC's Political Bureau (Politburo) amidst allegations of corruption and abuse of power; he was convicted on corruption charges in June and was sentenced to 12 years' imprisonment.

In late July 2006 it was announced that President Castro was temporarily to cede power to his brother, Raúl, on account of ill health, having recently undergone intestinal surgery. Planned celebrations for Castro's 80th birthday in August were postponed until December to allow the President more time to recover from his operation; however, his failure to attend the postponed festivities further fuelled speculation that he was still gravely ill and unlikely to return to power.

Although the majority of Fidel Castro's duties were transferred to his brother, control of several prominent areas was delegated elsewhere, including education, ultimate responsibility for which was afforded to Politburo members José Ramón Machado Ventura and Juan Esteban Lazo Hernández, and the 'energy revolution' (see Economic Affairs), which was henceforth to be presided over by Vice-President Carlos Lage Dávila. Raúl Castro's first significant action as acting Head of State was to dismiss Ignacio González Plana as Minister of Information Technology and Communications in late August 2006, appointing Ramiro Valdés, a former Minister of the Interior, in his stead.

A recurrent theme in Raúl Castro's early public addresses was the need to engage in more open discussion of the seminal challenges facing Cuba. At the National Assembly's end-of-year session in late December 2006, from which Fidel Castro was conspicuously absent, the acting President urged the legislature to strive for greater transparency, encouraging Assembly members publicly to accept responsibility for its failings where appropriate. Earlier in December, in an apparent manifestation of a more pragmatic approach to relations with the USA, Castro expressed his amenability to negotiations in order to resolve the protracted dispute. (The US Administration, however, insisted that diplomatic relations would remain unchanged until Castro's words were corroborated by decisive action, which was to include the legalization of political opposition, the release of political dissidents and sustained efforts to improve human rights within Cuba.) On 26 July 2007, in an influential speech to commemorate the attack on the Moncada barracks in 1953, Castro acknowledged Cuba's severe economic difficulties, including under-production, low wages and high prices, and declared that 'structural and conceptual changes' were necessary to overcome them. There was considerable evidence in the months following Castro's speech that Cubans were embracing his invitation to debate the need for change, and that the Government was encouraging greater public criticism of certain aspects of the regime. Notably, in January 2008 a video was released on the internet depicting university students berating the President of the National Assembly, Ricardo Alarcón, during a meeting, and criticizing discrepancies between salaries and prices, restrictions on individual liberties and the lack of political accountability.

In early December 2007 it was announced that Cuba would subscribe to two of the UN's seven conventions on human rights, as well as allowing the recently constituted UN Human Rights Council (the successor to the Human Rights Commission) to scrutinize the status of human rights in the country. Cuba had previously opposed any monitoring of its affairs by the Commission, accusing it of pro-US bias. The conventions, which were signed by Cuba in February 2008, covered civil and political and social, economic and cultural rights, respectively, including freedom of expression and association and the right to travel. Dissident groups expressed scepticism of the Government's commitment to the accords, while on the day of the announcement participants in a protest in support of human rights were attacked by pro-Government militants. Later in December 2007 Fidel Castro prompted further speculation regarding his political future by stating, as part of a letter read out on state television, that he had a duty not to hold on to power or prevent a younger generation from taking office. Despite continuing uncertainties as to his physical condition, Castro was reselected in the same month to contest a seat in the forthcoming legislative elections, a necessary condition to being re-elected President.

Elections to the National Assembly (enlarged from 609 to 614 seats) were held on 20 January 2008. All of the 614 candidates were elected with the requisite 50% of valid votes. The participation rate was 96.9%, of whom some 4.8% cast blank or spoiled ballots. In mid-February, six days before the new Assembly was scheduled to convene to elect the Council of State, Fidel Castro—who had not appeared in public since delegating power to his brother in July 2006—announced that he would not aspire to nor accept re-election as its President. On 24 February the Assembly unanimously elected Raúl Castro to succeed his brother as President of the Council of State and of the Council of Ministers. Raúl Castro was replaced as First Vice-President by José Ramón Machado Ventura, a senior member of the PCC's Politburo and a veteran of the Revolution; Machado Ventura's election surprised many observers, who had expected a younger member of the Government to accede to the position. The new President appointed Lt-Gen. Julio Casas Regueiro to be his successor as Minister of the Revolutionary Armed Forces. Castro also obtained the Assembly's approval to consult his brother on major issues of state.

Since 1985 Cuba has succeeded in establishing strong ties throughout Latin America and the Caribbean. Full diplomatic relations were restored with Colombia (suspended since 1981) in 1993, with Chile in 1995 and with Guatemala in 1998. Diplomatic relations were also re-established with the Dominican Republic in 1998 and with Honduras in 2002. In August 1998, during President Fidel Castro's first visit to the Dominican Republic, he attended a summit meeting of the Cariforum grouping of CARICOM (see p. 196) states and the Dominican Republic, at which the Statement of Santo Domingo was endorsed, envisaging full Cuban participation in any successor arrangement to the Fourth Lomé Convention co-operation accord between the EU and the African, Caribbean and Pacific countries. Cuba was afforded observer status to the Lomé Convention (which expired in February 2000 and was replaced in June by the Cotonou Agreement, see p. 301) in 1998. In June 2001 Cuba signed an agreement with CARICOM designed to promote trade and co-operation, and the country hosted a CARICOM summit meeting for the first time in the following year. In March 2003 the EU opened a legation office in Havana. The EU initially declared its support for Cuba's application to join the Cotonou Agreement; however, following the Government's imprisonment of a large number of dissidents in the following month, it subsequently downgraded relations with Cuba and indefinitely postponed the country's application to join the Agreement. In January 2005, however, following the release of some of the jailed dissidents, the EU resumed diplomatic relations with Cuba, for a six-month period; this decision was subsequently extended for one-year periods in June 2006 and June 2007. Meanwhile, in November 1998 Cuba became the 12th full member of the Latin American Integration Association (LAIA, see p. 331), having enjoyed observer status since 1986.

Cuba traditionally enjoyed good relations with Mexico (which was the only Latin American country not to suspend diplomatic relations with the Castro regime in 1961). However, in April 2002 bilateral relations were strained when Mexico lent its support to a resolution sponsored by Uruguay condemning Cuba's human rights record at a meeting of the UN Human Rights Commission. In November Cuban-Mexican relations were improved somewhat after Mexico voted in favour of the annual UN resolution condemning the US trade embargo of Cuba. In 2003 efforts further to improve bilateral relations continued; in November Minister of Foreign Relations Pérez Roque met with his Mexican counterpart at the Ibero-American Summit meeting in Bolivia. However, in May 2004 Mexico recalled its ambassador and expelled the Cuban ambassador to Mexico after President Castro criticized Mexican policy towards Cuba. Peru also withdrew its ambassador from Cuba at the same time. Following talks between the ministers of foreign affairs of the two countries, in July the dispute was resolved and diplomatic relations were restored. Meanwhile, diplomatic relations with Argentina, which had been severed in 2001 following Argentina's support of a UN vote condemning Cuba's human rights record, were restored in October 2003. In August 2004 Cuba broke off diplomatic relations with Panama following that country's pardon of four Cuban exiles, including Luis Posada Carriles (see above), suspected of involvement in an attempt to assassinate President Castro in 2000. The two countries agreed in November to restore diplomatic links, following the denunciation of the pardon by Panama's new President, Martín Torrijos; full diplomatic links were restored in August 2005. In late December the President-elect of Bolivia, Juan Evo Morales Aima, met with President Castro in Havana and signed a bilateral co-operation agreement, which came into effect upon Morales' inauguration in January 2006. Under the terms of the agreement, Cuba was to provide technical support and resources for a literacy campaign, as well as the development of sports programmes, in Bolivia.

Relations between Cuba and Venezuela were bolstered considerably subsequent to Lt-Col (retd) Hugo Chávez Frías's accession to the Venezuelan presidency in 1999. Venezuelan aid was crucial in allowing the Cuban economy to recover from its post-Soviet era economic depression and numerous military exchanges have been conducted between the two countries. In December 2004 Presidents Castro and Chávez (whose increasingly close public friendship has served to undermine the US policy of isolation against Cuba) signed the Alternativa Bolivariana para América Latina y El Caribe (ALBA), which was intended as an alternative to the US-supported proposed Free Trade Area of the Americas (FTAA), from which Cuba had been excluded. Under the terms of the deal, Cuba agreed to provide skilled workers, particularly doctors, to Venezuela, in return for oil at preferential rates. Meanwhile, in October 2005 182 new co-operative agreements were signed between Cuba and Venezuela, including deals pertaining to education, health, energy and petroleum. The relationship between the two countries' respective leaders intensified further in the aftermath of Castro's intestinal surgery in mid-2006, with Chávez visiting Castro several times in hospital. Although Raúl Castro was reported not to enjoy such a close relationship with Chávez, after the former took office in February 2008 the Venezuelan President declared that warm relations between the two countries would continue unchanged.

Cuba strengthened its relations with Asia in 2005 and 2006. Several bilateral agreements were signed between Cuba and Viet Nam in 2005, including a memorandum of understanding (MOU) on health care co-operation in September and a co-operation agreement on science, technology and the environment in December. An MOU on marine biodiversity was signed between Cuba and the People's Republic of China in November of that year; furthermore, the commencement in the latter half of 2006 of Sino-Cuban joint oil and gas explorations, following the signing of a bilateral energy accord in early 2005, heightened already sizeable US concerns about the burgeoning relationship between the two communist states.

Government

Under the 1976 Constitution (the first since the 1959 Revolution, amended in July 1992), the supreme organ of state, and the sole legislative authority, is the Asamblea Nacional del Poder Popular (National Assembly of People's Power), with 609 deputies elected for five years by direct vote. The National Assembly elects 31 of its members to form the Council of State, the Assembly's permanent organ. The Council of State is the highest representative of the State, and its President is both Head of State and Head of Government. Executive and administrative authority is vested in the Council of Ministers, appointed by the National Assembly on the proposal of the Head of State. Municipal, regional and provincial assemblies have also been established. The Partido Comunista de Cuba (PCC), the only authorized political party, is 'the leading force of society and the State'. The PCC's highest authority is the Party Congress, which elects a Central Committee (150 members in 2007) and, as of June 2006, a Secretariat (12 members in 2007) to supervise the Party's work. To direct its policy, the Central Committee elects a Politburo.

Defence

Conscription for military service is for a two-year period, and conscripts also work on the land. As assessed at November 2007, according to Western estimates, the armed forces totalled 49,000 (including ready reserves serving 45 days per year to complete active and reserve units): the army numbered 38,000, the navy 3,000 and the air force 8,000. Army reserves were estimated to total 39,000. Paramilitary forces include 20,000 State Security troops, 6,500 border guards, a civil defence force of 50,000 and a Youth Labour Army of 70,000. A local militia organization (Milicias de Tropas Territoriales—MTT), comprised an estimated 1m. men and women in 2007. Expenditure on defence and internal security for 2006 was estimated at US $1,660m. Despite Cuban hostility, the USA maintains a base at Guantánamo Bay, with 456 naval, 136 marine and 311 army personnel in 2007.

Economic Affairs

In 2006 Cuba's gross domestic product (GDP), measured at current prices, was an estimated 56,181m. pesos. During 1991–2000, it was estimated, GDP declined, in real terms, at an average annual rate of 1.4%. During 2001–07, however, GDP increased, in real terms, at an average annual rate of 7.1%. According to official figures, GDP increased by 7.5% in 2007. During 1996–2006 the population increased by an average of 0.3% per year.

Agriculture (including hunting, forestry and fishing) contributed 3.2% of GDP and employed 20.0% of the employed labour force in 2006. The principal cash crop has traditionally been sugar cane, with sugar and its derivatives accounting for 27.4% of export earnings in 2000; however, by 2006 this figure had declined to 8.0%. In 2002, as a result of the damage caused by 'Hurricane Michelle' in the previous year, together with the ongoing poor harvests, the Government closed 70 sugar mills as the industry became increasingly unprofitable; further closures were announced in 2005, with 40% of remaining mills being replaced by food-processing facilities by 2006. In 2005 sugar production was estimated at 2.1m. metric tons, with production the following year falling even further, to just 1.5m. tons. Production in 2007 was expected to remain relatively unchanged, although further downsizing of the industry was expected to be halted owing to buoyant global sugar prices. In 2005 Cuba produced some 26,000 tons of tobacco, although this increased to 29,700 tons in the following year, when 418.1m. cigars were made; in 2007 it produced 427.7m. cigars. Other important crops are rice (an estimated 434,200 tons in 2006), citrus fruits (373,033 tons in 2006), plantains and bananas. Fishing exports in 2006 declined to 63.6m. pesos, from 72.1m. pesos in the previous year. Cuba's principal seafood export markets were Japan, France, Spain, Italy and Canada. In real terms, the GDP of the agricultural sector declined at an average rate of 0.4% per year during 2001–06. Agricultural GDP decreased by 6.0% in 2006, but recovered dramatically in 2007 by 23.4%.

Industry (including mining, manufacturing, construction and power) contributed 19.9% of GDP and employed 18.1% of the employed labour force in 2006. Industrial GDP increased, in real terms, at an average rate of 4.1% per year in 2001–06. Sectoral growth of 11.8% was recorded in 2006.

Mining contributed 1.3% of GDP and employed 0.5% of the employed labour force in 2006. Nickel is the principal mineral export; in 2004 it accounted for approximately 61% of total export earnings. Production totalled an estimated 75.9m. metric tons in that year. In November 2004 Cuba signed several accords with the People's Republic of China, under which it agreed to provide 4,000 tons of nickel derivative to China annually from 2005. Cuba's state nickel company, Cubaniquel, was also to participate in a joint venture with the Chinese company Minmetal to construct the Las Cariocas nickel plant in Moa, which, once complete, would have an annual production capacity of 22,500 tons. Cuba also produces considerable amounts of chromium and copper, some iron and manganese, and there are workable deposits of gold and silver. The GDP of the mining sector increased by an average of 2.2% per year in 2001–06; sectoral GDP increased by 1.9% in 2006.

Manufacturing contributed 11.1% of GDP in 2006. The sector employed 11.0% of the employed labour force in that year. The principal branches of manufacturing were food products, beverages and tobacco, machinery and industrial chemicals. During 2001–06 manufacturing GDP increased, in real terms, at an average annual rate of 0.7%. The sector's GDP increased by 1.9% in 2006.

Energy is derived principally from petroleum and natural gas. In 2006 Cuba produced approximately 2.9m. metric tons of crude petroleum and 1,085.1m. cu m of natural gas. Imports of mineral fuels accounted for 24.2% of the total cost of imports in 2006. In 2004 the country generated 95.3% of its electricity requirement from domestically produced petroleum. Electricity shortages, while not an unusual phenomenon on the island, were particularly severe during the second half of both 2004 and 2005, when power failures, sometimes lasting up to 14 hours, occurred on an almost daily basis. In January 2006 President Fidel Castro launched an 'energy revolution', designed to reduce power shortages. According to *Granma* (the official newspaper of the PCC), in its first 12 months of operation the energy programme had reduced power cuts by 90% compared with 2005; this was reported to have been achieved by means of the commissioning of new generating plants, improved power efficiency and conservation, price increases on electricity supplied to household consumers and new oil and gas discoveries. In November 2001 Venezuela agreed to meet one-third of Cuba's petroleum requirements, on preferential terms, in exchange for medical and sports services; in 2003 Venezuela exported an average of 53,000 barrels per day (b/d) to Cuba. In September 2005 Cuba was one of the signatories of the PetroCaribe accord, under which Caribbean nations were allowed to purchase petroleum from Venezuela at reduced prices. In 1999 Cuba opened up 112,000 sq km of its waters to foreign exploration. Various foreign companies subsequently signed exploration contracts and in mid-2004 the Spanish company Repsol YPF commenced drilling in the area. The discovery of a sizeable petroleum deposit off the coast of Santa Cruz del Norte was a significant boost to hopes for self-sufficiency; production commenced in 2006 and was expected to yield up to 100m. barrels of oil. In addition, it was hoped that exploratory projects in Cuba's offshore basins in the Gulf of Mexico would uncover further deposits. In late 2001 construction of a 25-km petroleum pipeline, to be operated by the state petroleum company, between Matanzas province and Puerto Escondido was completed.

Services accounted for 76.9% of GDP in 2006, while the sector employed 61.8% of the total employed force in the same year. Tourism is one of the country's principal sources of foreign exchange, earning an estimated US $1,920m. in 2005, and development of the sector remains a priority of the Government. In spite of the intensification of measures levied against Cuba by the US Administration from mid-2004, notably the restriction of visits to Cuba by Cubans resident in the USA to just one every three years, tourist arrivals increased to 2.3m. in 2005, from 2.0m. in 2004; however, it fell slightly in 2006, to 2.2m. visitors. In real terms, the GDP of the service sector increased at an average rate of 8.6% per year during 2001–06. The GDP of the services sector increased by 13.8% in 2006.

In 2007 Cuba recorded a trade deficit of 6,355.4m. pesos, and a deficit of 239.7m. pesos on the current account of the balance of payments. In 2006 the principal source of imports was Venezuela

(23.5%). In that year the Netherlands was the principal market for exports, accounting for 28.0% of the total. Other major trading partners were the People's Republic of China, Spain and Canada. The principal imports in 2006 were machinery and transport equipment and mineral fuels, lubricants and related products. The principal exports in that year were crude materials (excluding fuels) and food and live animals. Burgeoning bilateral relations between Cuba and China saw the former importing Chinese goods to the value of 1,569.4m. pesos in 2006, while the value of exports to China also grew in that year, to 245.7m. pesos.

In 2007 Cuba recorded a provisionally estimated budget deficit of 1,912m. pesos. The country's external debt totalled US $16,000m. at the end of 2006, according to media reports. In September 2007 an accord was reached between Cuba and Russia on the restructuring of Cuba's post-Soviet debt to Russia, estimated at $166m.; however, the agreement did not cover Cuba's debt to the USSR, which was put at $26,000m. In November 2004 a deal signed between the Governments of Cuba and the People's Republic of China provided for a 10-year postponement of payments on the debt owed by the former to the latter. According to official figures, 1.8% of the labour force were unemployed in 2007. Although no index of consumer prices is published, official estimates put inflation at 0.3% in 1999.

Cuba is a member of the Latin American Economic System (see p. 413).

As a result of the severe economic decline prompted by the collapse of the USSR, in 1994 the Castro Government introduced a series of adjustment measures intended to reinvigorate the economy. A new investment law, approved in September 1995, opened all sectors of the economy, with the exception of defence, health and education, to foreign participation. Nevertheless, denied access to medium- and long-term loans, Cuba's indebtedness increased substantially in the 1990s as high-interest short-term loans were contracted in order to finance production, most notably in the sugar industry. The intensification of US sanctions also adversely affected the economy, but by the mid-2000s the Cuban economy had recovered from recession, aided by Venezuelan financing and other foreign loan restructuring. In October 2000 the US Congress approved legislation allowing US food and medicine sales to Cuba, dependent on certain conditions. Imports of most Cuban goods remained illegal and other sanctions legislation remained operational, and from 2004 the US embargo was intensified. According to the New York-based US-Cuba Trade and Economic Council, the total value of food exports from the USA to Cuba in 2002–06 was approximately US $1,553m. The Government's imposition of further restrictions upon private enterprises operating in Cuba rendered Cubans ever more dependent on remittances from relatives abroad. The USA continued to enforce its policy of prohibiting US companies from operating in Cuba, although the island's increased production of hydrocarbons (from an average of 16,000 b/d in 1984 to 76,000 b/d in the second half of 2006) raised the possibility that this ban would be ended. According to the Government, GDP growth in 2006 was estimated at 12.5%, although international analysts estimated growth of around 8%–9% for the same period. According to the Government, the economy grew by 7.5% in 2007, driven by the agriculture and services sectors. The widening trade deficit continued to be a problem, nevertheless, while tourism revenues were estimated to have fallen by 10%–12% in 2007.

Education

Education is universal and free at all levels. Education is based on Marxist-Leninist principles and combines study with manual work. Day nurseries are available for all children after their 45th day, and national schools at the pre-primary level are operated by the State for children of five years of age. Primary education, from six to 11 years of age, is compulsory, and secondary education lasts from 12 to 17 years of age, comprising two cycles of three years each. In 2005 primary enrolment included 97.3% of children in the relevant age-group, while secondary enrolment included 87.2% of the population in the appropriate age-group. In 2006/07 there were an estimated 658,134 students in higher education. Workers attending university courses receive a state subsidy to provide for their dependants. Courses at intermediate and higher levels lay an emphasis on technology, agriculture and teacher training. In 2006 budgetary expenditure on education was estimated at 5,377.0m. pesos (16.0% of total spending).

Public Holidays

2008: 1 January (Liberation Day), 2 January (Armed Forces' Victory Day), 1 May (Labour Day), 25–27 July (Anniversary of the 1953 Revolution), 10 October (Wars of Independence Day), 25 December (Christmas Day), 31 December (New Year's Eve).

2009: 1 January (Liberation Day), 2 January (Armed Forces' Victory Day), 1 May (Labour Day), 25–27 July (Anniversary of the 1953 Revolution), 10 October (Wars of Independence Day), 25 December (Christmas Day), 31 December (New Year's Eve).

Weights and Measures

The metric system is in force.

Statistical Survey

Sources (unless otherwise stated): Cámara de Comercio de la República de Cuba, Calle 21, No 661/701, esq. Calle A, Apdo 4237, Vedado, Havana; tel. (7) 830-4436; fax (7) 833-3042; e-mail pdcia@camara.com.cu; internet www.camaracuba.cu; Oficina Nacional de Estadísticas, Calle Paseo 60, entre 3 y 5, Plaza de la Revolución, Vedado, Havana, CP 10400; tel. (7) 830-0053; fax (7) 33-3083; e-mail oneweb@one.gov.cu; internet www.one.cu.

Area and Population

AREA, POPULATION AND DENSITY

Area (sq km)	109,886*
Population (census results)	
11 September 1981	9,723,605
7–16 September 2002	
Males	5,597,233
Females	5,580,510
Total	11,177,743
Population (official estimates at 31 December)	
2005	11,243,836
2006	11,239,043
2007	11,237,154
Density (per sq km) at 31 December 2007	102.3

* 42,427 sq miles.

CUBA

PROVINCES

	Area (sq km)	Population*	Density (per sq km)	Capital (population*)
Camagüey	15,615.0	783,135	50.2	Camagüey (306,830)
Ciego de Avila	6,783.1	421,138	62.1	Ciego de Avila (109,710)
Cienfuegos	4,180.0	402,104	96.2	Cienfuegos (142,553)
Ciudad de la Habana†	721.0	2,155,885	2,990.1	—
Granma	8,375.5	833,503	99.5	Bayamo (146,599)
Guantánamo	6,168.0	511,135	82.9	Guantánamo (208,431)
La Habana†	5,731.6	740,160	129.1	—
Holguín	9,292.8	1,035,883	111.5	Holguín (275,420)
Isla de la Juventud	2,419.3	86,428	35.7	Nueva Gerona (47,002)
Matanzas	11,802.7	684,460	58.0	Matanzas (130,381)
Pinar del Rio	10,904.0	731,191	67.1	Pinar del Rio (137,799)
Sancti Spíritus	6,736.5	464,535	69.0	Sancti Spíritus (98,505)
Santiago de Cuba	6,156.4	1,044,873	169.7	Santiago de Cuba (426,199)
Las Tunas	6,587.8	533,300	81.0	Las Tunas (150,511)
Villa Clara	8,412.4	809,424	96.2	Santa Clara (208,480)
Total	109,886.2	11,237,154	102.3	—

* Estimates at 31 December 2007.
† Ciudad de la Habana is the capital of La Habana province, but also a province in its own right.

PRINCIPAL TOWNS
(estimated population at 31 December 2006)

La Habana (Havana, the capital)	2,168,255	Las Tunas	150,511
Santiago de Cuba	426,199	Bayamo	146,599
Camagüey	306,830	Cienfuegos	142,553
Holguín	275,420	Pinar del Rio	137,799
Santa Clara	208,480	Matanzas	130,381
Guantánamo	208,431	Ciego de Avila	109,710

BIRTHS, MARRIAGES AND DEATHS*

	Registered live births† Number	Rate (per 1,000)	Registered marriages‡ Number	Rate (per 1,000)	Registered deaths Number	Rate (per 1,000)
2000	143,528	12.9	57,001	5.1	76,463	6.9
2001	138,718	12.4	54,345	4.9	79,395	7.1
2002	141,276	12.6	56,876	5.1	73,882	6.6
2003	136,795	12.2	54,739	4.9	78,434	7.0
2004	127,192	11.3	50,878	4.5	81,095	7.2
2005	120,716	10.7	51,831	4.6	84,824	7.5
2006	111,323	9.9	56,377	5.0	80,840	7.2
2007	113,025	10.1	n.a.	n.a.	80,984	7.2

* Data are tabulated by year of registration rather than by year of occurrence.
† Births registered in the National Consumers Register, established on 31 December 1964.
‡ Including consensual unions formalized in response to special legislation.

Expectation of life (years at birth, WHO estimates): 77.2 (males 75.3; females 79.2) in 2005 (Source: WHO, *World Health Statistics*).

EMPLOYMENT
(census of September 2002, persons aged 15 years and over)

	Males	Females	Total
Agriculture, hunting and forestry	765,355	135,825	901,180
Fishing	23,453	4,812	28,265
Mining and quarrying	14,186	3,028	17,214
Manufacturing	381,836	185,607	567,443
Sugar industry	85,592	25,161	110,753
Electricity, gas and water	44,701	15,843	60,544
Construction	186,913	35,113	222,026
Trade and private repairs	215,921	150,432	366,353
Hotels and restaurants	126,159	100,834	226,993
Transport, storage and communications	179,671	61,424	241,095
Financing, insurance, real estate and business services	76,414	63,221	139,635
Public administration and social security	220,067	111,234	331,301
Science and technological innovation	16,489	15,483	31,972
Education	146,175	279,983	426,158
Public health and social welfare	102,484	231,681	334,165
Culture and sport	83,944	57,766	141,710
Other community, social and personal services	92,600	55,903	148,503
Activities not adequately defined	88,333	18,876	107,209
Total employed	2,764,701	1,527,065	4,291,766
Unemployed*	107,286	25,598	132,884
Total labour force	2,871,987	1,552,663	4,424,650

* Including 32,628 persons seeking work for the first time.

2006 ('000 persons aged 15 years and over, official estimates): Agriculture, hunting, forestry and fishing 951.9; Mining and quarrying 22.0; Manufacturing 525.1; Electricity, gas and water 72.7; Construction 242.4; Trade, restaurants and hotels 603.1; Transport, storage and communications 275.3; Financing, insurance, real estate and business services 116.6; Community, social and personal services 1,945.5; Total employed 4,754.6; Unemployed 92.7; Total labour force 4,847.3.

2007 ('000 persons aged 15 years and over, official estimates): Total employed 4,867.7; Unemployed 88.7; Total labour force 4,956.4.

CIVILIAN EMPLOYMENT IN THE STATE SECTOR
('000 persons)

	1998	1999	2000
Agriculture, hunting, forestry and fishing	733.1	714.4	714.2
Mining and quarrying	47.3	20.8	20.8
Manufacturing	458.9	512.7	512.6
Electricity, gas and water	46.0	51.0	51.0
Construction	178.9	167.1	167.8
Trade, restaurants and hotels	355.2	375.2	375.2
Transport, storage and communications	175.2	157.4	157.4
Financing, insurance, real estate and business services	47.6	54.3	54.3
Community, social and personal services	964.5	952.1	951.8
Total	3,006.7	3,005.0	3,005.1

Health and Welfare

KEY INDICATORS

Total fertility rate (children per woman, 2005)	1.6
Under-5 mortality rate (per 1,000 live births, 2005)	7
HIV/AIDS (% of persons aged 15–49, 2005)	0.10
Physicians (per 1,000 head, 2002)	5.91
Hospital beds (per 1,000 head, 2005)	4.90
Health expenditure (2004): US $ per head (PPP)	229.1
Health expenditure (2004): % of GDP	6.3
Health expenditure (2004): public (% of total)	87.6
Access to water (% of persons, 2004)	91
Access to sanitation (% of persons, 2004)	98
Human Development Index (2005): ranking	51
Human Development Index (2005): value	0.838

For sources and definitions, see explanatory note on p. vi.

Agriculture

PRINCIPAL CROPS
('000 metric tons)

	2004	2005	2006
Rice (paddy)	488.9	367.6	434.2
Maize	398.7	362.5	305.4
Potatoes	328.7	313.1	286.2
Sweet potatoes	486.1	450.0	303.0
Cassava (Manioc)	745.6	675.8	450.0
Yautia (Cocoyam)	244.0	225.9	175.0
Sugar cane	23,800.0	11,600.0	11,060.0
Dry beans	132.9	106.2	70.6
Groundnuts (in shell)*	9.7	9.4	9.4
Coconuts	119.3	113.8	103.9
Cabbages	222.5	256.5	172.8
Tomatoes	788.7	802.6	636.0
Pumpkins, squash and gourds	517.2	550.1	446.5
Cucumbers and gherkins	365.5	219.5	155.7
Chillies and peppers, green	91.7	81.8	62.1
Dry onions	145.1	129.4	112.0
Garlic	58.5	51.0	33.6
Watermelons	90.9	79.6	71.9
Cantaloupes and other melons	90.9	93.0*	93.0*
Bananas	454.2	289.0	339.5
Plantains	761.4	484.5	532.2
Oranges	495.0	389.5	178.4
Tangerines, mandarins, clementines and satsumas	59.7	23.0	19.0
Lemons and limes	22.0	8.0	6.1
Grapefruit and pomelos	225.0	134.1	169.6
Guavas, mangoes and mangosteens	334.7	370.3	308.2
Pineapples	45.6	41.1	45.4
Papayas	119.0	91.8	90.3
Coffee (green)†	15.4	12.0	13.5
Tobacco (leaves)	31.7	26.0	29.7

* FAO estimate(s).
† Unofficial figures.

Aggregate production ('000 metric tons, may include official, semi-official or estimated data): Total cereals 889.4 in 2004, 732.2 in 2005, 744.1 in 2006; Total vegetable fibres 11.7 in 2004, 11.7 in 2005, 11.7 in 2006; Total roots and tubers 1,946.4 in 2004, 1,801.8 in 2005, 1,330.2 in 2006; Total vegetables (incl. melons) 4,186.8 in 2004, 3,296.5 in 2005, 2,765.1 in 2006; Total fruits (excl. melons) 2,806.1 in 2004, 2,033.3 in 2005, 1,887.5 in 2006.

Source: FAO.

LIVESTOCK
('000 head, year ending September)

	2004	2005	2006
Cattle	3,942.6	3,703.7	3,737.2
Horses	464.0	469.5	482.8
Asses, mules or hinnies	30.8	30.3	30.1
Pigs	1,593.4	1,626.0	1,760.8
Sheep	2,410.0	2,361.0	2,761.3
Goats	1,046.6	1,039.5	1,170.9
Chickens	25,033	27,440	29,848

Source: FAO.

LIVESTOCK PRODUCTS
('000 metric tons)

	2004	2005	2006
Cattle meat	55.3	59.9	55.7
Pig meat	98.3	96.7	99.9
Chicken meat	35.6	29.5	31.2
Cows' milk	512.7	353.2	415.2
Hen eggs	76.9	90.9	103.0
Honey	6.2	3.9	6.9

Source: FAO.

Forestry

ROUNDWOOD REMOVALS
('000 cubic metres, excl. bark)

	2004	2005	2006
Sawlogs, veneer logs and logs for sleepers*	400	400	400
Other industrial wood	315	361	361
Fuel wood	1,798	1,818	1,584
Total*	2,513	2,579	2,345

* FAO estimates.
Source: FAO.

SAWNWOOD PRODUCTION
('000 cubic metres, incl. railway sleepers)

	2004	2005	2006*
Coniferous (softwood)	114	132	146
Broadleaved (hardwood)	75	88	97
Total	189	220	243

* FAO estimates.
Source: FAO.

Fishing

('000 metric tons, live weight)

	2003	2004	2005
Capture	41.5	37.3	29.7
Blue tilapia	2.7	2.5	1.6
Lane snapper	1.1	0.9	0.7
Caribbean spiny lobster	5.3	7.6	5.8
Aquaculture*	26.9	27.8	22.6
Silver carp	13.1	15.0	12.3
Total catch*	68.6	65.1	52.3

* FAO estimates.
Note: Figures exclude sponges (metric tons): 57 in 2003; 51 in 2004; 42 in 2005.
Source: FAO.

Mining

('000 metric tons, unless otherwise indicated)

	2004	2005	2006
Crude petroleum	3,253.0	2,935.1	2,900.0
Natural gas (million cu metres)	704.2	743.3	1,085.1
Nickel and cobalt (metal content)	75.9	n.a.	n.a.
Crushed stone ('000 cu metres)	2,400	2,436	n.a.

Industry

SELECTED PRODUCTS
('000 metric tons, unless otherwise indicated)

	2005	2006	2007
Crude steel	245.1	257.2	287.2
Grey cement	1,566.9	1,704.7	1,882.5
Corrugated asbestos-cement tiles	4,332.0	5,311.1	5,193.6
Colour television sets ('000)	128.3	157.5	125.4
Fuel oil	859.2	892.2	980.8
Recapped tyres ('000)	32.9	43.9	n.a.
Woven textile fabrics (million sq metres)	25.2	26.8	31.0
Cigarettes ('000 million)	14.0	13.2	13.6
Cigars (million)	404.2	418.1	427.7
Alcoholic beverages (excl. wines, '000 litres)	825.9	859.2	910.5
Beer ('000 hectolitres)	2,254.8	2,298.1	2,427.6
Soft drinks ('000 hectolitres)	3,187.0	3,442.1	3,538.0
Electric energy (million kWh)	15,342.9	16,468.5	17,623.3

Finance

CURRENCY AND EXCHANGE RATES

Monetary Units
100 centavos = 1 Cuban peso.
1 Cuban peso = 1 convertible peso (official rate).

Sterling, Dollar and Euro Equivalents (31 December 2007)
£1 sterling = 1.855 convertible pesos;
US $1 = 0.926 convertible pesos;
€1 = 1.363 convertible pesos;
100 convertible pesos = £53.91 = $108.00 = €73.37.

Note: The foregoing information relates to official exchange rates. For the purposes of foreign trade, the peso was at par with the US dollar during each of the 10 years 1987–96. In addition, a 'convertible peso' was introduced in December 1994. Although officially at par with the Cuban peso, in March 2005 the 'unofficial' exchange rate prevailing in domestic exchange houses was adjusted to 24 pesos per convertible peso.

STATE BUDGET
(million pesos)

Revenue	2004	2005	2006
Tax revenue	13,952.7	17,840.0	23,608.0
Road and sales tax	7,333.8	9,036.0	14,221.0
Taxes on services	762.3	807.5	1,027.0
Taxes on utilities	1,973.9	2,125.6	1,895.0
Taxes on labour	1,293.8	2,962.2	3,075.0
Personal income tax	329.9	325.8	312.0
Other taxes	693.0	805.1	908.0
Social security contributions	1,565.9	1,777.8	2,170.0
Non-tax revenue	5,239.0	7,683.6	8,751.0
Transfers from state enterprises	2,258.0	2,623.6	2,365.0
Other non-tax revenue	2,981.0	5,060.0	6,386.0
Restitution payments	−369.1	−312.5	−465.0
Total	18,821.6	25,211.1	31,895.0

Expenditure	2004	2005	2006
Current expenditure	17,438.9	23,047.1	26,705.0
Education	3,601.0	4,819.0	5,377.0
Public health	2,089.1	3,169.0	3,629.0
Defence and public order	1,316.5	1,650.0	1,923.0
Social security	2,172.4	2,917.0	3,570.0
Administration	631.8	816.0	965.0
Community services	1,059.6	1,346.0	1,473.0
Art and culture	569.8	780.0	895.0
Science and technology	210.7	247.0	299.0
Sport	242.3	367.0	425.0
Social assistance	596.3	996.0	1,214.0
Other activities	1,297.3	1,651.0	2,093.0
Subsidies, etc. to state enterprises	3,652.1	4,288.0	4,842.0
Subsidy for losses	1,197.1	1,249.0	913.0
Subsidy for price differentials	1,452.2	1,346.0	1,425.0
Sugar price compensation fund	394.0	125.0	n.a.
Investment expenditure	2,286.6	3,064.0	5,019.0
Financial operations	515.9	1,046.0	1,900.0
Total	20,241.6	27,156.0	33,624.0

2007 (million pesos, provisional): *Revenue:* Road and sales tax 16,564; Taxes on utilities 2,209; Social security contributions 2,286; Other revenue 9,531; Total (incl. others) 39,528. *Expenditure:* Business activity 5,783; Education 7,162; Public health 6,283; Social Security 3,900; Social assistance 1,203; Administration 1,197; Total (incl. others) 41,440.

INTERNATIONAL RESERVES
(million pesos at 31 December)

	1987	1988
Gold and other precious metals	17.5	19.5
Cash and deposits in foreign banks (convertible currency)	36.5	78.0
Sub-total	54.0	97.5
Deposits in foreign banks (in transferable roubles)	142.5	137.0
Total	196.5	234.5

MONEY SUPPLY
(million pesos)

	2002	2003	2004
Currency in circulation	6,941.2	6,650.5	7,389.8
Savings	6,675.6	6,840.3	7,134.8
Total	13,616.8	13,490.8	14,524.6

NATIONAL ACCOUNTS
(million pesos at current prices)

Composition of Gross National Product

	1998	1999	2000
Compensation of employees	10,328.3	11,146.9	11,965.8
Operating surplus / Consumption of fixed capital	6,631.8	8,570.3	9,538.2
Gross domestic product (GDP) at factor cost	16,960.1	19,717.2	21,504.0
Indirect taxes, less subsidies	6,940.7	5,786.4	6,130.7
GDP in purchasers' values	23,900.8	25,503.6	27,634.7
Less Factor income paid abroad (net)	599.2	514.1	693.0
Gross national product	23,301.6	24,989.5	26,941.7

Source: UN Economic Commission for Latin America and the Caribbean, *Statistical Yearbook*.

CUBA

Statistical Survey

Expenditure on the Gross Domestic Product

	2004	2005	2006
Government final consumption expenditure	16,416.1	17,867.2	20,864.1
Private final consumption expenditure	21,006.9	22,559.5	29,429.9
Increase in stocks	124.6	773.2	300.0
Gross fixed capital formation	3,237.5	3,821.5	5,486.0
Total domestic expenditure	40,785.1	45,021.4	56,080.0
Exports of goods and services	6,120.8	8,962.9	9,850.0
Less Imports of goods and services	5,841.1	7,822.3	9,749.3
GDP in purchasers' values	41,064.8	46,162.0	56,180.7
GDP at constant 1997 prices	35,023.8	39,167.9	44,063.8

Gross Domestic Product by Economic Activity

	2004	2005	2006
Agriculture, hunting, forestry and fishing	2,091.4	1,860.8	1,795.9
Mining and quarrying	565.9	569.5	716.5
Manufacturing	5,262.9	5,393.5	6,153.4
Electricity, gas and water	583.4	559.4	879.8
Construction	2,007.6	2,398.2	3,320.9
Wholesale and retail trade, restaurants and hotels	9,451.7	10,103.8	14,359.8
Transport, storage and communications	3,328.6	3,640.2	4,001.9
Finance, insurance, real estate and business services	2,183.2	2,200.7	2,412.8
Community, social and personal services	15,195.1	18,941.8	21,949.7
Sub total	40,669.8	45,667.9	55,590.7
Import duties	395.0	494.1	590.0
Total	41,064.8	46,162.0	56,180.7

BALANCE OF PAYMENTS
(million pesos)

	1999	2000	2001
Exports of goods	1,456.1	1,676.8	1,661.5
Imports of goods	−4,365.4	−4,876.7	−4,838.3
Trade balance	−2,909.3	−3,117.2	−3,076.2
Services (net)	2,162.7	2,223.0	2,212.8
Balance on goods and services	−746.6	−894.2	−863.4
Other income (net)	−514.1	−622.2	−502.2
Balance on goods, services and income	−1,260.7	−1,516.4	−1,365.6
Current transfers (net)	798.9	740.4	812.9
Current balance	−461.8	−776.0	−552.7
Direct investment (net)	178.2	448.1	38.9
Other long-term capital (net)	31.7	570.3	328.3
Other capital (net)	275.0	−213.0	227.3
Overall balance	23.1	29.4	41.8

2007 (million pesos): Exports of goods 2,904.8; Imports of goods −9,503.2; Goods acquired at seaports and airports 243.0; *Trade balance* −6,355.4; Services (net) 6,456.0; *Balance of goods and services* 100.6; Income (net) −618.0; Current transfers (net) 277.7; *Current balance* −239.7.

External Trade

PRINCIPAL COMMODITIES
('000 pesos)

Imports c.i.f.	2004	2005	2006
Food and live animals	1,033,460	1,314,958	1,259,538
Cereals and cereal preparations	449,056	545,748	492,300
Wheat and meslin (unmilled)	106,166	124,724	111,448
Rice	170,432	246,118	172,432
Mineral fuels, lubricants, etc.	1,310,386	1,945,343	2,283,777
Chemicals and related products	531,910	603,505	660,371
Basic manufactures	678,607	878,309	1,036,415
Iron and steel	109,031	188,242	185,787
Manufactures of metal	153,819	219,247	308,245
Machinery and transport equipment	1,196,264	1,797,105	3,069,611
Power-generating machinery and equipment	100,857	326,026	709,188
General industrial machinery and equipment and machine parts	277,831	324,481	427,057
Total (incl. others)	5,562,032	7,533,283	9,420,154

Exports f.o.b.	2004	2005	2006
Food and live animals	459,746	273,064	322,516
Fish, crustaceans and molluscs and preparations thereof	88,457	72,064	63,600
Fresh, chilled or frozen fish	87,960	70,941	62,670
Fruit and vegetables	78,838	38,687	28,908
Sugar, sugar preparations and honey	280,608	153,460	221,516
Beverages and tobacco	243,597	250,381	263,836
Crude materials (inedible) except fuels	1,110,096	1,038,646	1,396,877
Metalliferous ores and metal scrap	1,106,384	1,035,214	1,391,625
Petroleum, petroleum products and related materials	11,665	n.a.	n.a.
Chemicals and related products	51,667	102,948	184,150
Basic manufactures	112,723	110,524	95,129
Iron and steel	35,975	43,849	43,238
Machinery and transport equipment	51,810	94,670	228,834
Miscellaneous manufactured articles	146,034	104,265	136,412
Total (incl. others)	2,188,002	1,994,618	2,759,393

2007 (million pesos): Total imports 9,650.0; Total exports 3,850.0.

PRINCIPAL TRADING PARTNERS
('000 pesos)

Imports c.i.f.	2004	2005	2006
Algeria	64,001	142,120	227,955
Argentina	116,351	155,201	114,961
Brazil	176,446	312,241	428,802
Canada	254,796	328,056	340,124
Chile	76,989	60,685	56,160
China, People's Republic	583,010	884,965	1,569,376
Colombia	56,394	82,603	56,632
France	149,893	167,670	196,729
Germany	130,084	309,745	615,747
Italy	269,089	290,832	408,889
Japan	158,995	246,211	174,556
Mexico	242,781	267,874	233,916
Netherlands Antilles	77,713	27,879	476
Russia	74,601	136,836	151,976
Spain	633,035	635,698	845,793
Venezuela	1,142,713	1,859,759	2,209,412
Viet Nam	146,103	251,765	189,847
Total (incl. others)	5,562,032	7,533,283	9,420,154

CUBA

Exports f.o.b.	2004	2005	2006
Belgium	20,164	13,186	7,154
Brazil	46,772	39,718	24,758
Canada	486,794	437,941	546,075
China, People's Republic	80,150	104,848	245,744
Dominican Republic	26,408	38,549	29,734
France	36,940	48,878	51,389
Germany	20,419	17,458	21,394
Japan	25,931	12,772	8,376
Mexico	22,455	19,916	39,315
Netherlands	647,062	598,865	773,621
Portugal	28,282	8,003	19,083
Russia	120,825	52,516	136,712
Spain	174,205	160,573	148,685
Switzerland	25,067	13,290	12,497
Venezuela	225,368	240,039	296,187
Total (incl. others)	2,188,002	1,994,618	2,759,393

2007 (million pesos): Total imports 9,650.0; Total exports 3,850.0.

Transport

RAILWAYS

	2004	2005	2006
Passenger-kilometres (million)	1,760	1,514	1,233
Freight ton-kilometres (million)	1,341	1,371	1,463

ROAD TRAFFIC
(motor vehicles in use at 31 December)

	1996	1997
Passenger cars	216,575	172,574
Buses and coaches	28,089	28,861
Lorries and vans	246,105	156,634

Source: International Road Federation, *World Road Statistics*.

SHIPPING
Merchant Fleet
(registered at 31 December)

	2004	2005	2006
Number of vessels	96	68	68
Total displacement ('000 grt)	126	65	65

Source: Lloyd's Register-Fairplay, *World Fleet Statistics*.

International Sea-borne Freight Traffic
('000 metric tons)

	1988	1989	1990
Goods loaded	8,600	8,517	8,092
Goods unloaded	15,500	15,595	15,440

Source: UN, *Monthly Bulletin of Statistics*.

CIVIL AVIATION
(traffic on scheduled services)

	2001	2002	2003
Kilometres flown (million)	19	15	19
Passengers carried ('000)	882	589	664
Passenger-kilometres (million)	3,171	1,887	2,036
Total ton-kilometres (million)	361	223	224

Source: UN, *Statistical Yearbook*.

Tourism

ARRIVALS BY COUNTRY OF RESIDENCE*

	2004	2005	2006
Canada	563,371	602,377	604,263
France	119,868	107,518	103,469
Germany	143,644	124,527	114,292
Italy	178,570	169,317	144,249
Mexico	79,752	89,154	97,984
Spain	146,236	194,103	185,531
United Kingdom	161,189	199,399	211,075
USA	49,856	37,233	36,808
Venezuela	86,258	185,157	83,832
Total (incl. others)	2,048,572	2,319,334	2,220,567

* Figures include same-day visitors (excursionists).

Tourism receipts (US $ million, incl. passenger transport): 1,846 in 2003; 1,915 in 2004; 1,920 in 2005 (Source: World Tourism Organization).

Communications Media

	2004	2005	2006
Telephones ('000 main lines in use)	768.2	856.0	972.9
Mobile cellular telephones ('000 subscribers)	75.8	135.5	152.7
Personal computers ('000 in use)	300	377	n.a.
Internet users ('000)	150.0	190.0	240.0

Radio receivers ('000 in use): 3,900 in 1997.

Television receivers ('000 in use): 2,800 in 2000.

Facsimile machines (number in use): 392 in 1992.

Book production: 1,004 titles published in 2001.

Daily newspapers: 2 in 2004 (average estimated circulation 727,600 copies).

Sources: UNESCO, *Statistical Yearbook*; UN, *Statistical Yearbook*; International Telecommunication Union.

Education
(2006/07)

	Institutions	Teachers	Students
Pre-primary	1,113	9,228	128,928
Primary	9,047	96,301	838,570
Secondary	1,988	100,969	969,421
Tertiary	65	41,425	658,134

Adult literacy rate (UNESCO estimates): 99.8% (males 99.8%; females 99.8%) in 2002 (Source: UNESCO Institute for Statistics).

Directory

The Constitution

Following the assumption of power by the Castro regime, on 1 January 1959, the Constitution was suspended and a Fundamental Law of the Republic was instituted, with effect from 7 February 1959. In February 1976 Cuba's first socialist Constitution came into force after being submitted to the first Congress of the Communist Party of Cuba, in December 1975, and to popular referendum, in February 1976; it was amended in July 1992. The main provisions of the Constitution, as amended, are summarized below.

Note: On 27 July 2002 the Constitution was further amended to enshrine the socialist system as irrevocable and to ratify that economic, diplomatic and political relations with another state cannot be negotiated in the face of aggression, threat or pressure from a foreign power. A clause was also introduced making it impossible to remove these amendments from the Constitution.

POLITICAL, SOCIAL AND ECONOMIC PRINCIPLES

The Republic of Cuba is a socialist, independent, and sovereign state, organized with all and for the sake of all as a unitary and democratic republic for the enjoyment of political freedom, social justice, collective and individual well-being and human solidarity. Sovereignty rests with the people, from whom originates the power of the State. The Communist Party of Cuba is the leading force of society and the State. The State recognizes, respects and guarantees freedom of religion. Religious institutions are separate from the State. The socialist State carries out the will of the working people and guarantees work, medical care, education, food, clothing and housing. The Republic of Cuba bases its relations with other socialist countries on socialist internationalism, friendship, co-operation and mutual assistance. It reaffirms its willingness to integrate with and co-operate with the countries of Latin America and the Caribbean.

The State organizes and directs the economic life of the nation in accordance with a central social and economic development plan. The State directs and controls foreign trade. The State recognizes the right of small farmers to own their lands and other means of production and to sell that land. The State guarantees the right of citizens to ownership of personal property in the form of earnings, savings, place of residence and other possessions and objects which serve to satisfy their material and cultural needs. The State also guarantees the right of inheritance.

Cuban citizenship is acquired by birth or through naturalization.

The State protects the family, motherhood and matrimony.

The State directs and encourages all aspects of education, culture and science.

All citizens have equal rights and are subject to equal duties.

The State guarantees the right to medical care, education, freedom of speech and press, assembly, demonstration, association and privacy. In the socialist society work is the right and duty, and a source of pride for every citizen.

GOVERNMENT

National Assembly of People's Power

The National Assembly of People's Power (Asamblea Nacional del Poder Popular) is the supreme organ of the State and is the only organ with constituent and legislative authority. It is composed of deputies, over the age of 18, elected by free, direct and secret ballot, for a period of five years. All Cuban citizens aged 16 years or more, except those who are mentally incapacitated or who have committed a crime, are eligible to vote. The National Assembly of People's Power holds two ordinary sessions a year and a special session when requested by one-third of the deputies or by the Council of State. More than one-half of the total number of deputies must be present for a session to be held.

All decisions made by the Assembly, except those relating to constitutional reforms, are adopted by a simple majority of votes. The deputies may be recalled by their electors at any time.

The National Assembly of People's Power has the following functions:

- to reform the Constitution;
- to approve, modify and annul laws;
- to supervise all organs of the State and government;
- to decide on the constitutionality of laws and decrees;
- to revoke decree-laws issued by the Council of State and the Council of Ministers;
- to discuss and approve economic and social development plans, the state budget, monetary and credit systems;
- to approve the general outlines of foreign and domestic policy, to ratify and annul international treaties, to declare war and approve peace treaties;
- to approve the administrative division of the country;
- to elect the President, First Vice-President, the Vice-Presidents and other members of the Council of State;
- to elect the President, Vice-President and Secretary of the National Assembly;
- to appoint the members of the Council of Ministers on the proposal of the President of the Council of State;
- to elect the President, Vice-President and other judges of the People's Supreme Court;
- to elect the Attorney-General and the Deputy Attorney-Generals;
- to grant amnesty;
- to call referendums.

The President of the National Assembly presides over sessions of the Assembly, calls ordinary sessions, proposes the draft agenda, signs the Official Gazette, organizes the work of the commissions appointed by the Assembly and attends the meetings of the Council of State.

Council of State

The Council of State is elected from the members of the National Assembly and represents that Assembly in the period between sessions. It comprises a President, one First Vice-President, five Vice-Presidents, one Secretary and 23 other members. Its mandate ends when a new Assembly meets. All decisions are adopted by a simple majority of votes. It is accountable for its actions to the National Assembly.

The Council of State has the following functions:

- to call special sessions of the National Assembly;
- to set the date for the election of a new Assembly;
- to issue decree-laws in the period between the sessions of the National Assembly;
- to decree mobilization in the event of war and to approve peace treaties when the Assembly is in recess;
- to issue instructions to the courts and the Office of the Attorney-General of the Republic;
- to appoint and remove ambassadors of Cuba abroad on the proposal of its President, to grant or refuse recognition to diplomatic representatives of other countries to Cuba;
- to suspend those provisions of the Council of Ministers that are not in accordance with the Constitution;
- to revoke the resolutions of the Executive Committee of the local organs of People's Power which are contrary to the Constitution or laws and decrees formulated by other higher organs.

For all purposes the Council of State is the highest representative of the Cuban state.

Head of State

The President of the Council of State is the Head of State and the Head of Government and has the following powers:

- to represent the State and Government and conduct general policy;
- to convene and preside over the sessions of the Council of State and the Council of Ministers;
- to supervise the ministries and other administrative bodies;
- to propose the members of the Council of Ministers to the National Assembly of People's Power;
- to receive the credentials of the heads of foreign diplomatic missions;
- to sign the decree-laws and other resolutions of the Council of State;
- to exercise the Supreme Command of all armed institutions and determine their general organization;
- to preside over the National Defence Council;
- to declare a state of emergency in the cases outlined in the Constitution.

In the case of absence, illness or death of the President of the Council of State, the First Vice-President assumes the President's duties.

CUBA

The Council of Ministers

The Council of Ministers is the highest-ranking executive and administrative organ. It is composed of the Head of State and Government, as its President, the First Vice-President, the Vice-Presidents, the Ministers, the Secretary and other members determined by law. Its Executive Committee is composed of the President, the First Vice-President, the Vice-Presidents and other members of the Council of Ministers determined by the President.

The Council of Ministers has the following powers:

to conduct political, economic, cultural, scientific, social and defence policy as outlined by the National Assembly;

to approve international treaties;

to propose projects for the general development plan and, if they are approved by the National Assembly, to supervise their implementation;

to conduct foreign policy and trade;

to draw up bills and submit them to the National Assembly;

to draw up the draft state budget;

to conduct general administration, implement laws, issue decrees and supervise defence and national security.

The Council of Ministers is accountable to the National Assembly of People's Power.

LOCAL GOVERNMENT

The country is divided into 14 provinces and 169 municipalities. The provinces are: Pinar del Río, Habana, Ciudad de la Habana, Matanzas, Villa Clara, Cienfuegos, Sancti Spíritus, Ciego de Avila, Camagüey, Las Tunas, Holguín, Granma, Santiago de Cuba and Guantánamo.

Voting for delegates to the municipal assemblies is direct, secret and voluntary. All citizens over 16 years of age are eligible to vote. The number of delegates to each assembly is proportionate to the number of people living in that area. A delegate must obtain more than one-half of the total number of votes cast in the constituency in order to be elected. The Municipal and Provincial Assemblies of People's Power are elected by free, direct and secret ballot. Nominations for Municipal and Provincial Executive Committees of People's Power are submitted to the relevant assembly by a commission presided over by a representative of the Communist Party's leading organ and consisting of representatives of youth, workers', farmers', revolutionary and women's organizations. The President and Secretary of each of the regional and the provincial assemblies are the only full-time members, the other delegates carrying out their functions in addition to their normal employment.

The regular and extraordinary sessions of the local Assemblies of People's Power are public. More than one-half of the total number of members must be present in order for agreements made to be valid. Agreements are adopted by simple majority.

JUDICIARY

Judicial power is exercised by the People's Supreme Court and all other competent tribunals and courts. The People's Supreme Court is the supreme judicial authority and is accountable only to the National Assembly of People's Power. It can propose laws and issue regulations through its Council of Government. Judges are independent but the courts must inform the electorate of their activities at least once a year. Every accused person has the right to a defence and can be tried only by a tribunal.

The Office of the Attorney-General is subordinate only to the National Assembly and the Council of State, and is responsible for ensuring that the law is properly obeyed.

The Constitution may be totally or partially modified only by a two-thirds' majority vote in the National Assembly of People's Power. If the modification is total, or if it concerns the composition and powers of the National Assembly of People's Power or the Council of State, or the rights and duties contained in the Constitution, it also requires a positive vote by referendum.

The Government

Head of State: Gen. RAÚL CASTRO RUZ (took office 24 February 2008).

COUNCIL OF STATE

President: Gen. RAÚL CASTRO RUZ.
First Vice-President: JOSÉ RAMÓN MACHADO VENTURA.
Vice-Presidents: JUAN ALMEIDA BOSQUE, JUAN ESTEBAN LAZO HERNÁNDEZ, Lt-Gen. ABELARDO COLOMÉ IBARRA, Lt-Gen. JULIO CASAS REGUEIRO, CARLOS LAGE DÁVILA.
Secretary: Dr JOSÉ M. MIYAR BARRUECOS.

Members: JOSÉ RAMÓN BALAGUER CABRERA, PEDRO SÁEZ MONTEJO, ROBERTO FERNÁNDEZ RETAMAR, FELIPE RAMÓN PÉREZ ROQUE, Lt-Gen. LEOPOLDO CINTRA FRÍAS, ORLANDO LUGO FONTE, RAMIRO VALDÉS MENÉNDEZ, TANIA LEÓN SILVEIRA, Lt-Gen. ÁLVARO LÓPEZ MIERA, FRANCISCO SOBERÓN VALDÉS, JULIO MARTÍNEZ RAMÍREZ, INÉS MARÍA CHAPMAN WAUGH, IRIS BETANCOURT TÉLLEZ, GUILLERMO GARCÍA FRÍAS, LUIS SATURNINO HERRERA MARTÍNEZ, MARÍA YOLANDA FERRER GÓMEZ, REGLA DAYAMÍ ARMENTEROS MESA, DIGNORA MONTANO PERDOMO, SALVADOR ANTONIO VALDÉS MESA, MARÍA DEL CARMEN CONCEPCIÓN GONZÁLEZ, CARLOS MANUEL VALENCIAGA DÍAZ, JUAN JOSÉ RABILERO FONSECA, SURINA ACOSTA BROOK.

COUNCIL OF MINISTERS
(April 2008)

President: Gen. RAÚL CASTRO RUZ.
Secretary: CARLOS LAGE DÁVILA.
First Vice-President: JOSÉ RAMÓN MACHADO VENTURA.
Vice-Presidents: OSMANY CIENFUEGOS GORRIARÁN, PEDRO MIRET PRIETO, JOSÉ LUIS RODRÍGUEZ GARCÍA, JOSÉ RAMÓN FERNÁNDEZ ALVAREZ, OTTO RIVERO TORRES.
Minister of Agriculture: MARÍA DEL CARMEN PÉREZ HERNÁNDEZ (acting).
Minister of Foreign Trade: RAÚL DE LA NUEZ RAMÍREZ.
Minister of Domestic Trade: MARINO ALBERTO MURILLO JORGE.
Minister of Information Technology and Communications: RAMIRO VALDÉS MENÉNDEZ.
Minister of Construction: FIDEL FERNANDO FIGUEROA DE LA PAZ.
Minister of Culture: ABEL ENRIQUE PRIETO JIMÉNEZ.
Minister of Economy and Planning: JOSÉ LUIS RODRÍGUEZ GARCÍA.
Minister of Education: ENA ELSA VELÁZQUEZ COBIELLA.
Minister of Higher Education: JUAN VELA VALDÉS.
Minister of Finance and Prices: GEORGINA BARREIRO FAJARDO.
Minister of the Revolutionary Armed Forces: Lt-Gen. JULIO CASAS REGUEIRO.
Minister of the Food Industry: ALEJANDRO ROCA IGLESIAS.
Minister of Foreign Investment and Economic Co-operation: MARTA LOMAS MORALES.
Minister of the Sugar Industry: Gen. ULISES ROSALES DEL TORO.
Minister of Light Industry: JOSÉ SILVANO HERNÁNDEZ BERNÁRDEZ.
Minister of the Fishing Industry: ALFREDO LÓPEZ VALDÉS.
Minister of the Iron, Steel and Engineering Industries: FERNANDO ACOSTA SANTANA.
Minister of Basic Industry: YADIRÁ GARCÍA VERA.
Minister of the Interior: Lt-Gen. ABELARDO COLOMÉ IBARRA.
Minister of Justice: MARÍA ESTHER REUS GONZÁLEZ.
Minister of Foreign Relations: FELIPE RAMÓN PÉREZ ROQUE.
Minister of Labour and Social Security: ALFREDO MORALES CARTAYA.
Minister of Public Health: JOSÉ RAMÓN BALAGUER CABRERA.
Minister of Science, Technology and the Environment: FERNANDO MARIO GONZÁLEZ BERMÚDEZ (acting).
Minister of Transportation: JORGE LUIS SIERRA CRUZ.
Minister of Tourism: MANUEL MARRERO CRUZ.
Minister of Auditing and Control: GLADYS MARÍA BEJERANO PORTELA.
Minister, President of the Banco Central de Cuba: FRANCISCO SOBERÓN VALDÉS.
Minister without Portfolio: RICARDO CABRISAS RUIZ.

MINISTRIES

Ministry of Agriculture: Edif. MINAG, Avda Boyeros y Conill, 10600 Havana; tel. (7) 884-5427; fax (7) 881-2837; e-mail gestion@agrinfor.cu.

Ministry of Auditing and Control: Havana; e-mail webmaster@minauditoria.cu; internet www.minauditoria.cu.

Ministry of Basic Industry: Avda Salvador Allende 666, Havana; tel. (7) 70-7711; e-mail webmaster@one.gov.cu; internet www.minbas.cu.

Ministry of Construction: Avda Carlos Manuel de Céspedes y Calle 35, Plaza de la Revolución, Havana; tel. (7) 81-8385; fax (7) 55-5303; e-mail despacho@micons.cu; internet www.micons.cu.

Ministry of Culture: Calle 2, No 258, entre 11 y 13, Plaza de la Revolución, Vedado, CP 10400, Havana; tel. (7) 55-2260; fax (7) 66-2053; e-mail atencion@min.cult.cu; internet www.min.cult.cu.

CUBA

Ministry of Domestic Trade: Calle Habana 258, Havana; tel. (7) 62-5790.

Ministry of Economy and Planning: 20 de Mayo, entre Territorial y Ayestarán, Plaza de la Revolución, Havana; tel. (7) 881-8789; fax (7) 33-3387; e-mail mep@ceniai.inf.cu.

Ministry of Education: Obispo 160, Havana; tel. (7) 61-4888; internet www.rimed.cu.

Ministry of Finance and Prices: Calle Obispo 211, esq. Cuba, Habana Vieja, Havana; tel. (7) 867-1920; fax (7) 33-8050; e-mail bhcifip@mfp.gov.cu; internet www.mfp.cu.

Ministry of the Fishing Industry: Avda 5, entre 246 y 248, No 24606, Barlovento, Playa, Havana; tel. (7) 209-7930; fax (7) 204-9168; e-mail webpesca@telemar.cu; internet www1.cubamar.cu.

Ministry of the Food Industry: Avda 41, No 4455, entre 48 y 50, Playa, Havana; tel. (7) 203-6801; fax (7) 204-0517; e-mail minal@minal.get.cma.net; internet www.minal.cubaindustria.cu.

Ministry of Foreign Investment and Economic Co-operation: Calle 1ra y 18, No 1803, Miramar, Havana; tel. (7) 203-7035; fax (7) 204-3496; e-mail ministro@minvec.cu; internet www.minvec.cu.

Ministry of Foreign Relations: Calzada 360, esq. G, Vedado, Havana; tel. (7) 55-3537; fax (7) 33-3460; e-mail cubaminrex@minrex.gov.cu; internet www.cubaminrex.cu.

Ministry of Foreign Trade: Infanta 16, esq. 23 y Humbolt, Plaza de la Revolución, Vedado, Havana; tel. (7) 55-0393; fax (7) 55-0376; e-mail opinion@mincex.cu; internet www.mincex.cu.

Ministry of Higher Education: Calle 23, No 565, esq. a F, Vedado, Havana; tel. (7) 55-2335; fax (7) 33-4390; e-mail vecino@reduniv.edu.cu; internet www.mes.edu.cu.

Ministry of Information and Communications: Avdas Independencia y 19 de Mayo, Plaza de la Revolución, Havana; tel. (7) 66-8000; e-mail relaciones@mic.cu; internet www.mic.gov.cu.

Ministry of the Interior: Plaza de la Revolución, Havana; tel. (7) 30-1566; fax (7) 33-5261.

Ministry of the Iron, Steel and Engineering Industries: Avda Rancho Boyeros y Calle 100, Havana; tel. (7) 45-3911; e-mail sime@sime.co.cu.

Ministry of Justice: Calle O, No 216, entre 23 y Humboldt, Vedado, Apdo 10400, Havana 4; tel. (7) 32-6319; e-mail minjus@minjus.cu; internet www.minjus.cu.

Ministry of Labour and Social Security: Calle 23, esq. Calles O y P, Vedado, Havana; tel. (7) 55-0071; fax (7) 33-5816; e-mail webmaster@mtss.cu; internet www.mtss.cu.

Ministry of Light Industry: Empedrado 302, Havana; tel. (7) 209-4779; fax (7) 202-6187; e-mail web@ligera.cu; internet www.ligera.cu.

Ministry of Public Health: Calle 23, No 301, Vedado, Havana; tel. (7) 32-2561; e-mail direccion@mspdne.sld.cu; internet www.dne.sld.cu/minsap.

Ministry of the Revolutionary Armed Forces: Plaza de la Revolución, Havana; internet www.cubagob.cu/otras_info/minfar/far/minfar.htm.

Ministry of Science, Technology and the Environment: Industria y San José, Habana Vieja, Havana; tel. (7) 867-0618; fax (7) 33-8654; e-mail citma@ceniai.inf.cu; internet www.cuba.cu/ciencia/citma/.

Ministry of Sugar: Calle 23, No 171, Vedado, Havana; tel. (7) 55-3194; fax (7) 55-3260; e-mail relint@ocentral.minaz.cu.

Ministry of Tourism: Calle 19, No 710, entre Paseo y A, Vedado, Havana; tel. (7) 33-0545; fax (7) 33-4086; e-mail webmaster@cubatravel.cu; internet www.cubatravel.cu.

Ministry of Transportation: Avda Boyeros, esq. Tulipán, Plaza de la Revolución, Havana; tel. (7) 55-5030; e-mail lupe.cic@mitrans.transnet.cu; internet www.cubagob.cu/des_eco/mitrans.

Legislature

ASAMBLEA NACIONAL DEL PODER POPULAR

The National Assembly of People's Power was constituted on 2 December 1976. In July 1992 the National Assembly adopted a constitutional amendment providing for legislative elections by direct vote. Only candidates nominated by the Partido Comunista de Cuba (PCC) were permitted to contest the elections. At elections to the National Assembly conducted on 20 January 2008, all 614 candidates succeeded in obtaining the requisite 50% of valid votes cast. Of the 8.2m. registered voters, 96.89% participated in the elections. Only 4.76% of votes cast were blank or spoiled.

President: RICARDO ALARCÓN DE QUESADA.

Vice-President: JAIME ALBERTO CROMBET HERNÁNDEZ-BAQUERO.

Secretary: MIRIAM BRITO SARROCA.

Political Organizations

Partido Comunista de Cuba (PCC) (Communist Party of Cuba): Havana; e-mail root@epol.cipcc.inf.cu; internet www.pcc.cu; f. 1961 as the Organizaciones Revolucionarias Integradas (ORI) from a fusion of the Partido Socialista Popular (Communist), Fidel Castro's Movimiento 26 de Julio and the Directorio Revolucionario 13 de Marzo; became the Partido Unido de la Revolución Socialista Cubana (PURSC) in 1962; adopted current name in 1965; 150-member Central Committee, Political Bureau, 12-member Secretariat and five Commissions; 706,132 mems (1994); First Sec. Dr FIDEL CASTRO RUZ; Second Sec. Gen. RAÚL CASTRO RUZ.

Political Bureau

Dr FIDEL CASTRO RUZ, Gen. RAÚL CASTRO RUZ, JUAN ALMEIDA BOSQUE, JOSÉ RAMÓN MACHADO VENTURA, JUAN ESTEBAN LAZO HERNÁNDEZ, Lt-Gen. ABELARDO COLOMÉ IBARRA, PEDRO ROSS LEAL, CARLOS LAGE DÁVILA, Maj-Gen. ULISES ROSALES DEL TORO, CONCEPCIÓN CAMPA HUERGO, YADIRA GARCÍA VERA, ABEL ENRIQUE PRIETO JIMÉNEZ, Lt-Gen. JULIO CASAS REGUEIRO, Lt-Gen. LEOPOLDO CINTRA FRÍAS, RICARDO ALARCÓN DE QUESADA, JOSÉ RAMÓN BALAGUER CABRERA, MISAEL ENAMORADO DAGER, Lt-Gen. RAMÓN ESPINOSA MARTÍN, PEDRO SÁEZ MONTEJO, JORGE LUIS SIERRA LÓPEZ, MIGUEL MARIO DÍAZ CANEL BERMÚDEZ.

There are a number of dissident groups operating in Cuba. These include:

Arco Progresista: f. 2003; alliance of social-democratic groups in and outside Cuba; Spokesperson MANUEL CUESTA MORÚA.

Concertación Democrática Cubana (CDC): f. 1991; alliance of 11 dissident orgs campaigning for political pluralism and economic reform; Leader ELIZARDO SÁNCHEZ SANTA CRUZ.

Cuban Democratic Platform: f. 1990; alliance comprising three dissident orgs:

> **Coordinadora Social Demócrata:** Havana; e-mail morm21@yahoo.com; internet www.cosodecu.org; Pres. BYRON MIGUEL.
>
> **Partido Demócrata Cristiano de Cuba (PDC):** 1236 SW 22 Ave, Miami, FL 33135, USA; tel. (305) 644-3395; fax (305) 644-3311; e-mail miyares@pdc-cuba.org; internet www.pdc-cuba.org; f. 1959 as Movimiento Demócrata Cristiano; name changed as above in 1991; Pres. MARCELINO MIYARES SOTOLONGO; Sec.-Gen. JOSÉ VÁZQUEZ.
>
> **Unión Liberal Cubana:** Paseo de la Retama 97, 29600 Marbella, Spain; tel. (91) 4340201; fax (91) 5011342; e-mail cubaliberal@mercuryin.es; internet www.cubaliberal.org; mem. of Liberal International; Founder and Chair. CARLOS ALBERTO MONTANER.

Partido pro-Derechos Humanos: f. 1988 to defend human rights in Cuba; Pres. HIRAM ABI COBAS; Sec.-Gen. TANIA DÍAZ.

Partido Social Revolucionario Democrático de Cuba: POB 351081, Miami, FL 33135, USA; tel. and fax (305) 541-2334; e-mail psrdc@psrdc.org; internet www.psrdc.org; f. 1992; executive committee of 15 members; Pres. JORGE VALLS; Exec. Sec. ROBERTO SIMEON.

Partido Socialdemócrata de Cuba (PSC): Calle 36, No 105, Nuevo Vedado, 10600 Havana; tel. (7) 881-8203; e-mail vroca@pscuba.org; internet pscuba.org; f. 1996; Pres. VLADIMIRO ROCA ANTÚNEZ; Exec. Sec. CARLOS J. MENÉNDEZ CERVERA; Sec.-Gen. ANTONIO SANTIAGO RUIZ.

Partido Solidaridad Democrática (PSD): POB 310063, Miami, FL 33131, USA; tel. (305) 408-2659; e-mail gladyperez@aol.com; internet www.ccsi.com/~ams/psd/psd.htm; Pres. FERNANDO SÁNCHEZ LÓPEZ.

Diplomatic Representation

EMBASSIES IN CUBA

Algeria: Avda 5, No 2802, esq. 28, Miramar, Havana; tel. (7) 204-2835; fax (7) 204-2702; Ambassador AHCENE KERMAN.

Angola: Avda 5, No 1012, entre 10 y 12, Miramar, Havana; tel. (7) 204-2474; fax (7) 204-0487; e-mail embangol@ceniai.inf.cu; Ambassador ANTONIO J. CONDESSE D. CARVAHLO.

Argentina: Calle 36, No 511, entre 5 y 7, Miramar, Havana; tel. (7) 204-2565; fax (7) 204-2140; e-mail ecuba@enet.cu; Chargé d'affaires a.i. PEDRO VON EYKEN.

Austria: C6617 Avda 5a A, esq. 70, Miramar, Havana; tel. (7) 204-2394; fax (7) 204-1235; e-mail havanna-ob@bmeia.gv.at; Ambassador JOHANNES SKRIWAN.

Bahamas: 3006 Avda 5, No 3006, entre 30 y 32, Miramar, Playa, Havana; tel. (7) 206-9700; fax (7) 206-9701; e-mail embahamas@enet.cu; Ambassador CARLTON WRIGHT.

CUBA

Belarus: Calle 5, No 3802, entre 38 y 40, Miramar, Havana; tel. (7) 204-7330; fax (7) 204-7332; e-mail cuba@belembassy.org; Ambassador POLUYAN IGOR IVANOVICH.

Belgium: Calle 8, No 309, entre 3 y 5, Miramar, Havana; tel. (7) 204-2410; fax (7) 204-1318; e-mail havana@diplobel.org; internet www.diplomatie.be/havana; Ambassador CLAUDIA DE MAESSCHALCK.

Belize: Avda 5, No 3608, entre 36 y 36A, Miramar, Havana; tel. (7) 204-3504; fax (7) 204-3506; e-mail belize.embassy@ip.etecsa.cu; Chargé d'affaires a.i. MARGARET JUAN.

Benin: Calle 20, No 119, entre 1 y 3, Miramar, Havana; tel. (7) 204-2179; fax (7) 204-2334; e-mail ambencub@ceniai.inf.cu; Ambassador GRÉGOIRE LAITIAN HOUDÉ.

Bolivia: Calle 26, No 113, entre 1 y 3, Miramar, Havana; tel. (7) 204-2426; fax (7) 204-2127; e-mail emboliviahabana@cubacel.net; Ambassador SAÚL CHÁVEZ OROZCO.

Brazil: Calle Lamparilla, No 2, 4°K, Habana Vieja, Havana; tel. (7) 66-9052; fax (7) 66-2912; e-mail embhavana@brasil.co.cu; Ambassador BERNARDO PERICÁS NETO.

Bulgaria: Calle B, No 252, entre 11 y 13, Vedado, Havana; tel. (7) 33-3125; fax (7) 33-3297; e-mail embulhav@ceniai.inf.cu; Ambassador TCHAVDAR MLADENOV NIKOLOV.

Burkina Faso: Calle 40, No 516, entre 5 y 7, Miramar, Havana; tel. (7) 204-2217; fax (7) 204-1942; e-mail ambfaso@ceniai.inf.cu; Ambassador DANIEL OUEDRAOGO.

Cambodia: Avda 5, No 7001, entre 70 y 72, Miramar, Havana; tel. (7) 204-1496; fax (7) 204-6400; e-mail cambohav@enet.cu; Ambassador PRES MANOLA.

Canada: Calle 30, No 518, esq. 7, Miramar, Havana; tel. (7) 204-2516; fax (7) 204-2044; e-mail havan@international.gc.ca; internet www.dfait-maeci.gc.ca/cuba; Ambassador ALEXANDRA BUGAILISKIS.

Cape Verde: Calle 20, No 2001, esq. 7, Miramar, Havana; tel. (7) 204-2979; fax (7) 204-1072; e-mail embajadora@caboverde.co.cu; Ambassador CRISPINA ALMEIDA GOMES.

Chile: Avda 33, No 1423, entre 14 y 18, Miramar, Havana; tel. (7) 204-1222; fax (7) 204-1694; e-mail embachilecu@echile.cu; internet www.conchile-lahabana.cu; Ambassador JAIME MANUEL TOHA GONZÁLEZ.

China, People's Republic: Calle 13, No 551, entre C y D, Vedado, Havana; tel. (7) 33-3005; fax (7) 33-3092; e-mail chinaemb_cu@mfa.gov.cn; Ambassador ZHAO RONGXIAN.

Colombia: Calle 14, No 515, entre 5 y 7, Miramar, Havana; tel. (7) 204-1246; fax (7) 204-1249; e-mail embacub@cancilleria.gov.co; Ambassador JULIO LONDOÑO PAREDES.

Congo, Republic: Avda 5, No 1003, Miramar, Havana; tel. and fax (7) 204-9055; Ambassador PASCAL ONGEMBY.

Czech Republic: Avda Kohly, No 259, entre 41 y 43, Nuevo Vedado, CP 10600, Havana; tel. (7) 883-3201; fax (7) 883-3596; e-mail havana@embassy.mzv.cz; internet www.czechembassy.org/wwwo/?zu=havana; Chargé d'affaires a.i. VÍT KORSELT.

Dominican Republic: Avda 5, No 9202, entre 92 y 94, Miramar, Havana; tel. (7) 204-8429; fax (7) 204-8431; Ambassador DANIEL GUERRERO TAVERAS.

Ecuador: Avda 5A, No 4407, entre 44 y 46, Miramar, Havana; tel. (7) 204-2034; fax (7) 204-2868; e-mail embecuad@ceniai.inf.cu; Chargé d'affaires a.i. OSCAR GARCÍA ENDARA.

Egypt: Avda 5, No 1801, esq. 18, Miramar, Havana; tel. (7) 204-2441; fax (7) 204-0905; e-mail emegipto@enet.cu; Ambassador ABDEL FATTAH MOUSTAFA EZZ ELDIN.

France: Calle 14, No 312, entre 3 y 5, Miramar, Havana; tel. (7) 201-3131; fax (7) 201-3107; e-mail internet.la-havane-amba@diplomatie.fr; internet www.ambafrance-cu.org; Ambassador FRÉDÉRIC DORÉ.

The Gambia: Calle 24, No 307, entre 3 y 5, Miramar, Havana; tel. (7) 204-5315; fax (7) 204-5316; Ambassador PA-MODOU NJIE.

Germany: Calle 13, No 652, esq. B, Vedado, Havana; tel. (7) 833-2460; e-mail info@havanna.diplo.de; internet www.havanna.diplo.de; Ambassador CLAUDE ROBERT ELLNER.

Ghana: Avda 5, No 1808, esq. 20, Miramar, Havana; tel. (7) 204-2153; fax (7) 204-2317; e-mail eghana@ceniai.inf.cu; internet www.ghanaembassy.cu; Ambassador CECILIA GYAN AMOAH.

Greece: Avda 5, No 7802, esq. 78, Miramar, Havana; tel. (7) 204-2995; fax (7) 204-1784; e-mail gremb@enet.cu; Ambassador ILIAS MALTEZOS.

Guatemala: Calle 16, No 505, entre 3 y 5, Miramar, Havana; tel. (7) 204-3417; fax (7) 204-3200; e-mail embagucu@ceniai.inf.cu; Ambassador HERBERT ESTUARDO MENECES CORONADO.

Guinea: Calle 20, No 504, entre 5 y 7, Miramar, Havana; tel. (7) 204-2003; fax (7) 204-2380; Ambassador HADIATOU SOW.

Guinea-Bissau: Calle 14, No 313, entre 3 y 5, Miramar, Havana; tel. (7) 204-2689; fax (7) 204-2794; Chargé d'affaires a.i. MALAM DJASSI.

Guyana: Calle 18, No 506, entre 5 y 7, Miramar, Havana; tel. (7) 204-2249; fax (7) 204-2867; e-mail embguyana@ip.etecsa.cu; Ambassador Dr TIMOTHY N. CRITCHLOW.

Haiti: Avda 7, No 4402, esq. 44, Miramar, Havana; tel. (7) 204-5421; fax (7) 204-5423; e-mail embhaiti@enet.cu; internet www.embhaiti.cu; Ambassador MARIE CARMELE ANDRINE CONSTANT.

Holy See: Calle 12, No 514, entre 5 y 7, Miramar, Havana (Apostolic Nunciature); tel. (7) 204-2700; fax (7) 204-2257; e-mail csa@pcn.net; Apostolic Nuncio Most Rev. LUIGI BONAZZI (Titular Archbishop of Atella).

Honduras: Edif. Santa Clara, 1°, 123 Centro de Negocios Miramar, 3a Avda, 78 y 80 Calles, Miramar, Havana; tel. (7) 204-5496; fax (7) 204-5497; e-mail embhocu@enet.cu; Ambassador JUAN RAMÓN ELVIR SALGADO.

Hungary: Calle G, No 458, entre 19 y 21, Vedado, Havana; tel. (7) 833-3365; fax (7) 833-3286; e-mail oficina@embajadadehungria.cu; internet www.mfa.gov.hu/kulkepviselet/cu/hu; Ambassador JÁNOS HORVÁT.

India: Calle 21, No 202, esq. K, Vedado, Havana; tel. (7) 833-3777; fax (7) 833-3287; e-mail hoc@indembassyhavana.cu; internet www.indembassyhavana.cu; Ambassador MITRA VASISHT.

Indonesia: Avda 5, No 1607, esq. 18, Miramar, Havana; tel. (7) 204-9618; fax (7) 204-9617; e-mail indonhav@ceniai.inf.cu; internet www.indohav.cu; Chargé d'affaires a.i. YOEL ROHROHMANA.

Iran: Avda 5, No 3002, esq. 30, Miramar, Havana; tel. (7) 204-2675; fax (7) 204-2770; e-mail embairan@ip.etecsa.cu; Ambassador MOSTAFA ALAEI.

Italy: No 5, Avda 402, Calle 4, Miramar, Havana; tel. (7) 204-5615; fax (7) 204-5659; e-mail ambasciata.avana@esteri.it; internet sedi.esteri.it/avana; Ambassador DOMENICO VECCHIONI.

Jamaica: Avda 5, No 3608, entre 36 y 36A, Miramar, Havana; tel. (7) 204-2908; fax (7) 204-2531; e-mail embjmcub@enet.cu; Ambassador ELINOR FELIX-SHERLOCK.

Japan: Centro de Negocios Miramar, Avda 3, No 1, 5°, esq. 80, Miramar, Havana; tel. (7) 204-3355; fax (7) 204-8902; Ambassador AKIRA TAKAMATSU.

Korea, Democratic People's Republic: Calle 17, No 752, Vedado, Havana; tel. (7) 66-2313; fax (7) 33-3073; Ambassador PAK DONG CHUN.

Laos: Avda 5, No 2808, esq. 30, Miramar, Havana; tel. (7) 204-1056; fax (7) 204-9622; e-mail embalao@ip.etecsa.cu; Ambassador PHOUANGKEO LANGSY.

Lebanon: Calle 17A, No 16403, entre 164 y 174, Siboney, Havana; tel. (7) 208-6220; fax (7) 208-6432; e-mail lbcunet@ceniai.inf.cu; Chargé d'affaires a.i. NAMIR NOUREDDINE.

Libya: Avda 7, No 1402, esq. 14, Miramar, Havana; tel. (7) 204-2192; fax (7) 204-2991; e-mail oficinalibia@ip.etecsa.cu; Ambassador SAAD DAHER ZAMUNA.

Malaysia: Avda 5 y 68, No 6612, Miramar, Havana; tel. (7) 204-8883; fax (7) 204-6888; e-mail malhavana@kln.gov.my; Ambassador Dato' MOHAMED KAMAL BIN YAN YAHAYA.

Mali: Calle 36A, No 704, entre 7 y 9, Miramar, Havana; tel. (7) 204-5321; fax (7) 204-5320; e-mail ambamali@ceniai.inf.cu; Ambassador FIDÈLE DIARRA.

Mexico: Calle 12, No 518, entre 7, Playa, Havana; tel. (7) 204-2553; fax (7) 204-2717; e-mail embamex@ip.etecsa.cu; Ambassador GABRIEL JIMÉNEZ REMUS.

Mongolia: Calle 66, No 505, esq. 5, Miramar, Havana; tel. (7) 204-2763; fax (7) 204-0639; e-mail monelch@ceniai.inf.cu; Ambassador GOMBO BYAMBADORJ.

Mozambique: Avda 7, No 2203, entre 22 y 24, Miramar, Havana; tel. (7) 204-2443; fax (7) 204-2232; e-mail embamoc@ceniai.inf.cu; Ambassador AMADEU PAULO SAMUEL DA CONCEICAO.

Namibia: Avda 5, No 4406, entre 44 y 46, Miramar, Havana; tel. (7) 204-1430; fax (7) 204-1431; e-mail embnamib@ceniai.inf.cu; Ambassador CLAUDIA GRACE UUSHONA.

Netherlands: Calle 8, No 307, entre 3 y 5, Miramar, Havana; tel. (7) 204-2511; fax (7) 204-2059; e-mail hav@minbuza.nl; internet cuba.nlambassade.org; Ambassador W. W. WILDEBOER.

Nicaragua: Calle 20, No 709, entre 7 y 9, Miramar, Havana; tel. (7) 204-1025; fax (7) 204-6323; e-mail embajnicc@enet.cu; Ambassador LUIS CABRERA GONZÁLEZ.

Nigeria: Avda 5, No 1401, entre 14 y 16, Miramar, Havana; tel. (7) 204-2898; fax (7) 204-2202; e-mail enigera@ceniai.inf.cu; Chargé d'affaires a.i. OZOEMANA OBIAJULU NWOBU.

Panama: Calle 26, No 109, entre 1 y 3, Miramar, Havana; tel. (7) 204-0858; fax (7) 204-1674; e-mail panembacuba@ip.etecsa.cu; Ambassador LUIS ANTONIO GÓMEZ PÉREZ.

Paraguay: Calle 34, No 503, entre 5 y 7, Miramar, Havana; tel. (7) 204-0884; fax (7) 204-0883; e-mail cgphav@enet.cu; Chargé d'affaires a.i. AUGUSTO OCAMPOS CABALLERO.

Peru: Calle 30, No 107, entre 1 y 3, Miramar, Havana; tel. (7) 204-3570; fax (7) 204-2636; e-mail embaperu@embaperu.cu; Ambassador JUAN GERMÁN KOSTER KOSTER.

Philippines: Avda 5, No 2207, esq. 24, Miramar, Havana; tel. (7) 204-1372; fax (7) 204-2915; e-mail philhavpe@enet.cu; Ambassador GEORGE B. REYES.

Poland: Calle G, No 452, esq. 19, Vedado, Havana; tel. (7) 833-2439; fax (7) 833-2442; e-mail havpolemb@ct.futuro.pl; internet www.embajadapolonia.cu; Chargé d'affaires a.i. DANIEL GROMANN.

Portugal: Avda 7, No 2207, esq. 24, Miramar, Havana; tel. (7) 204-0149; fax (7) 204-2593; e-mail embport@enet.cu; Ambassador MARIO GODINHO DE MATOS.

Qatar: Hotel Nacional, 211, Havana; tel. (7) 33-3564; fax (7) 73-4700; Ambassador ALI BIN SAAD AL-KHARJI.

Romania: Calle 21, No 307, Vedado, Havana; tel. (7) 33-3325; fax (7) 33-3324; e-mail erumania@ceniai.inf.cu; Ambassador CONSTANTIN SIMIRAD.

Russia: Avda 5, No 6402, entre 62 y 66, Miramar, Havana; tel. (7) 204-2686; fax (7) 204-1038; e-mail embrusia@ceniai.inf.cu; Ambassador ANDREI VIKTOROVICH DIMITRIEV.

Saudi Arabia: Avda 5, No 8206, entre 82 y 84, Miramar, Havana; tel. (7) 204-1045; fax (7) 204-6401; e-mail erasdcu@ceniai.inf.cu; Ambassador MUHAMMAD MUSTAFA TLEIMIDI.

Serbia: Calle 42, No 115, entre 1 y 3, Miramar, Havana; tel. (7) 204-2488; fax (7) 204-2982; e-mail embyuhav@ceniai.inf.cu; Ambassador MILENA LUKOVIC JOVANOVIC.

Slovakia: Calle 66, No 521, entre 5B y 7, Miramar, Havana; tel. (7) 204-1884; fax (7) 204-1883; e-mail embeslovaca@enet.cu; Ambassador IVO HLAVACEK.

South Africa: Avda 5, No 4201, esq. 42, Miramar, Havana; tel. (7) 204-9671; fax (7) 204-1101; e-mail rsacuba@ceniai.inf.cu; internet www.sudafrica.cu; Ambassador THENJIWE ETHEL MTINTSO.

Spain: Cárcel No 51, esq. Zulueta, Havana; tel. (7) 866-8025; fax (7) 866-8006; e-mail embespcu@correo.mae.es; Ambassador CARLOS ALONSO ZALDIVAR.

Sri Lanka: Calle 32, No 307, entre 3 y 5, Miramar, Havana; tel. (7) 204-2562; fax (7) 204-2183; e-mail sri.lanka@enet.cu; Ambassador LIYANAGE KIRITHI AMARASOMA SIGERA.

Sweden: Calle 34, No 510, entre 5 y 7, Miramar, Havana; tel. (7) 204-2831; fax (7) 204-1194; e-mail ambassaden.havanna@foreign.ministry.se; internet www.swedenabroad.com/havanna; Ambassador CHRISTER ELM.

Switzerland: Avda 5, No 2005, entre 20 y 22, Miramar, Havana; tel. (7) 204-2611; fax (7) 204-1148; e-mail swissem@enet.cu; internet www.eda.admin.ch/havana; Ambassador BERTRAND LOUIS.

Syria: Avda 5, No 7402, entre 74 y 76, Miramar, Havana; tel. (7) 204-2266; fax (7) 204-2829; e-mail embsiria@ceniai.inf.cu; Ambassador SHAKER KHAYAT.

Turkey: Avda 5, No 3805, entre 36 y 40, Miramar, Havana; tel. (7) 204-1205; fax (7) 204-2899; e-mail turkemb@ip.etecsa.cu; Ambassador KANDRIYE SANIVAR KIZILDELI.

Ukraine: Avda 5, No 4405, entre 44 y 46, Miramar, Havana; tel. (7) 204-2586; fax (7) 204-2341; e-mail cubukrem@ceniai.inf.cu; Ambassador OLEKSANDR GNYEDYH.

United Kingdom: Calle 34, No 702/4, esq. 7 y 17, Miramar, Havana; tel. (7) 204-1771; fax (7) 204-8104; e-mail embrit@ceniai.inf.cu; internet www.britishembassy.gov.uk/cuba; Ambassador JOHN ANTHONY DEW.

USA (Relations severed in 1961): Interests Section: Calzada, entre L y M, Vedado, Havana; tel. (7) 833-3551; fax (7) 833-1084; e-mail irchavana@state.org; internet havana.usinterestsection.gov; Principal Officer MICHAEL E. PARMLY.

Uruguay: Calle 14, No 506, entre 5 y 7, Miramar, Havana; tel. (7) 204-2311; fax (7) 204-2246; e-mail urucub@ceniai.inf.cu; Ambassador JORGE ERNESTO MAZZAROVICH SEVERI.

Venezuela: Avda 1601, No 5, entre 16 y 18, Miramar, Havana; tel. (7) 204-2612; fax (7) 204-2773; e-mail vencuba@enet.cu; Ambassador ALÍ RODRÍGUEZ ARAQUE.

Viet Nam: Avda 5, No 1802, esq. 18, Miramar, Havana; tel. (7) 204-1502; fax (7) 204-1041; e-mail embaviet@ceniai.inf.cu; internet www.vietnamembassy-cuba.org; Ambassador VU CHI CONG.

Yemen: Calle 16, No 503, entre 5 y 7, Miramar, Havana; tel. (7) 204-1506; fax (7) 204-1131; e-mail gamdan-hav@enet.cu; Ambassador AHMED ALI KALAZ.

Zimbabwe: Avda 3, No 1001, esq. a 10, Miramar, Havana; tel. (7) 204-2857; fax (7) 204-2720; e-mail zimhavana@yahoo.com; Ambassador JEVANA BEN MASEKO.

Judicial System

The judicial system comprises the People's Supreme Court, the People's Provincial Courts and the People's Municipal Courts. The People's Supreme Court exercises the highest judicial authority.

Public Prosecutor: JUAN ESCALONA REGUERA.

PEOPLE'S SUPREME COURT

The People's Supreme Court comprises the Plenum, the six Courts of Justice in joint session and the Council of Government. When the Courts of Justice are in joint session they comprise all the professional and lay judges, the Attorney-General and the Minister of Justice. The Council of Government comprises the President and Vice-Presidents of the People's Supreme Court, the Presidents of each Court of Justice and the Attorney-General of the Republic. The Minister of Justice may participate in its meetings.

President: Dr RUBÉN REMIGIO FERRO.

Vice-Presidents: OSVALDO SÁNCHEZ MARTÍN, EMILIA GONZÁLEZ PÉREZ, EDUARDO RODRÍGUEZ GONZÁLEZ.

Criminal Court

President: CARLOS ZARAGOZA PUPO.

Civil and Administrative Court

President: CARLOS M. DÍAZ TENREIRO.

Labour Court

President: Dr ANTONIO RAUDILLO MARTÍN SÁNCHEZ.

Court for State Security

President: PLÁCIDO BATISTA VERANES.

Economic Court

President: NARCISO COBO ROURA.

Military Court

President: Col JUAN MARINO FUENTES CALZADO.

Religion

There is no established Church, and all religions are permitted, though Roman Catholicism predominates. The Afro-Cuban religions of Regla de Ocha (Santería) and Regla Conga (Palo Monte) also have numerous adherents.

CHRISTIANITY

Consejo de Iglesias de Cuba (CIC) (Cuban Council of Churches): Calle 14, No 304, entre 3 y 5, Miramar, Playa, Havana; tel. (7) 33-1792; fax (7) 33-1788; f. 1941; 11 mem. churches; Pres. Rev. Dr RHODE GONZÁLEZ ZORRILLA.

The Roman Catholic Church

Cuba comprises three archdioceses and eight dioceses. At 31 December 2005, according to the Vatican, there were 6,729,714 adherents, representing some 53% of the total population.

Conferencia de Obispos Católicos de Cuba (COCC) (Bishops' Conference)
Calle 26, No 314, entre 3 y 5, Miramar, Apdo 635, 11300 Havana; tel. (7) 29-2298; fax (7) 24-2168; e-mail cocc@iglesiacatolica.cu; internet www.iglesiacubana.org.
f. 1983; Pres. Cardinal JAIME LUCAS ORTEGA Y ALAMINO (Archbishop of San Cristóbal de la Habana).

Archbishop of Camagüey: JUAN GARCÍA RODRÍGUEZ, Calle Luaces, No 55, Apdo 105, 70100 Camagüey; tel. (32) 229-2268; fax (32) 228-7143; e-mail arzcam@cocc.co.cu.

Archbishop of San Cristóbal de la Habana: Cardinal JAIME LUCAS ORTEGA Y ALAMINO, Calle Habana No 152, esq. a Chacón, Apdo 594, 10100 Havana; tel. (7) 862-4000; fax (7) 866-8109; e-mail cocc@brigadoo.com.

Archbishop of Santiago de Cuba: DIONISIO GUILLERMO GARCÍA IBÁÑEZ, Sánchez Hechevarría No 607, Apdo 26, 90100 Santiago de Cuba; tel. (226) 25480; fax (226) 86186.

The Anglican Communion

Anglicans are adherents of the Iglesia Episcopal de Cuba (Episcopal Church of Cuba).

Bishop of Cuba: Rt Rev. MIGUEL TAMAYO ZALDÍVAR, Calle 6, No 273, Vedado, 10400 Havana; tel. (7) 832-1120; fax (7) 334-3293; e-mail episcopal@ip.etecsa.cu; internet www.cuba.anglican.org.

Protestant Churches

Convención Bautista de Cuba Oriental (Baptist Convention of Eastern Cuba): San Jerónimo, No 467, entre Calvario y Carnicería, Santiago de Cuba 90100; tel. (226) 62-3587; e-mail presidentecb@cbcor.co.cu; internet www.cbcorcu.com; f. 1905; Pres. Rev. ENIO LEONCIO NAVARRO CASTELLANOS; Sec. Rev. ALEXI GARCÍA PUEBLA; more than 300 mem. churches.

Iglesia Metodista en Cuba (Methodist Church in Cuba): Calle K, No 502, 25 y 27, Vedado, 10400 Havana; tel. (7) 832-2991; fax (7) 832-0770; e-mail imecu@enet.cu; internet www.imecu.com; autonomous since 1968; 215 churches, 17,000 mems (2005); Bishop RICARDO PEREIRA DÍAZ.

Iglesia Presbiteriana Reformada en Cuba (Presbyterian-Reformed Church in Cuba): Salud 222, entre Lealtad y Campanario, 10200 Havana; tel. (7) 862-1219; fax (7) 866-8819; e-mail presbit@enet.cu; internet www.prccuba.org; f. 1890; 8,000 mems; Moderator Rev. Dr HÉCTOR MÉNDEZ.

Other denominations active in Cuba include the Apostolic Church of Jesus Christ, the Bethel Evangelical Church, the Christian Pentecostal Church, the Church of God, the Church of the Nazarene, the Free Baptist Convention, the Holy Pentecost Church, the Pentecostal Congregational Church and the Salvation Army.

The Press

DAILIES

Granma: Avda Gen. Suárez y Territorial, Plaza de la Revolución, Apdo 6187, CP 10699, Havana; tel. (7) 881-3333; fax (7) 881-9854; e-mail english@granma.cip.cu; internet www.granma.cubaweb.cu; f. 1965, to replace *Hoy* and *Revolución*; official Communist Party organ; Dir-Gen. LÁZARRO BARREDO MEDINA; Editor-in-Chief OSCAR SÁNCHEZ SERRA; circ. 400,000.

Juventud Rebelde: Avda Territorial y Gen. Suárez, Plaza de la Revolución, Apdo 6344, Havana; tel. (7) 882-0155; fax (7) 33-8959; e-mail cida@jrebelde.cip.cu; internet www.jrebelde.cubaweb.cu; f. 1965; organ of the Young Communist League; Dir ROGELIO POLANCO FUENTES; circ. 250,000.

PERIODICALS

Adelante: Avda A, Rpto Jayamá, Camagüey; e-mail cip222@cip.enet.cu; internet www.adelante.cu; f. 1959; Dir ZARITMA CARDOSO MORENO; Dir-Gen. MABEL GUERRA GARCÍA; circ. 42,000.

Ahora: Salida a San Germán y Circunvalación, Holguín; e-mail ahoraweb@ahora.cu; internet www.ahora.cu; f. 1962; Dir RODOBALDO MARTÍNEZ PÉREZ; circ. 50,000.

Alma Mater: Prado 553, esq. Teniente Rey, Habana Vieja, Havana; e-mail almamater@editoraabril.co.cu; internet www.almamater.cu; f. 1922; aimed at a student readership; Dir TAMARA ROSELLÓ.

ANAP: Obispo 527, Apdo 605, Havana; f. 1961; monthly; organ of the Asociación Nacional de Agricultores Pequeños; information for small farmers; Editor RICARDO MACHADO; circ. 90,000.

Bohemia: Avda Independencia y San Pedro, Apdo 6000, Havana; tel. (7) 81-9213; fax (7) 33-5511; e-mail bohemia@bohemia.co.cu; internet www.bohemia.cu; f. 1908; weekly; politics; Dir JOSÉ FERNÁNDEZ VEGA; circ. 100,000.

El Caimán Barbudo: Casa Editora Abril, Prado 553, entre Dragones y Teniente Rey, Vedado, Havana; e-mail caimanbarbudo@editoraabril.co.cu; internet www.caimanbarbudo.cu; f. 1966; monthly; cultural; Dir FIDEL DÍAZ CASTRO; circ. 47,000.

Cinco de Septiembre: Avda 54, No 3516, entre 35 y 37, CP 55100, Cienfuegos; tel. (43) 52-2144; e-mail cip219@cip.enet.cu; internet www.5septiembre.cu; f. 1980; Dir ALINA ROSELL CHONG; circ. 18,000.

Dedeté: Territorial y Gen. Suárez, Plaza de la Revolución, Apdo 6344, Havana; tel. (7) 82-0134; fax (7) 81-8621; e-mail ddt@jrebelde.cip.cu; internet www.dedete.cubaweb.cu; f. 1969; monthly; humorous supplementary publ. of *Juventud Rebelde*; Dir ALEN LAUZÁN; circ. 70,000.

La Demajagua: Amado Estévez, esq. Calle 10, Rpto R. Reyes, Bayamo; tel. (23) 42-4221; e-mail cip225@cip.enet.cu; internet www.lademajagua.co.cu; f. 1977; Dir LUIS CARLOS FRÓMETA AGÜERO; Editor GISLANIA TAMAYO CEDEÑO; circ. 21,000.

El Deporte, Derecho del Pueblo: Vía Blanca y Boyeros, Havana; tel. (7) 40-6838; f. 1968; monthly; sports supplement of *Granma*; Dir MANUEL VAILLANT CARPENTE; circ. 15,000.

El Economista de Cuba: Asociación Nacional de Economistas de Cuba, Calle 22, No 901 esq. a 901, Miramar, Havana; tel. (7) 209-3303; fax (7) 202-3456; e-mail eleconomista@ciber.cuba.com; internet www.eleconomista.cubaweb.cu; monthly; business; Dir-Gen. ROBERTO VERRIER CASTRO; Editor MAGALI GRACÍA MORÉ.

Escambray: Adolfo del Castillo 10, Sancti Spíritus; tel. (41) 23003; e-mail cip220@cip.enet.cu; internet www.escambray.cu; f. 1979 as daily; weekly from 1992; serves Sancti Spíritus province; Dir JUAN ANTONIO BORREGO DÍAZ; circ. 21,000.

Girón: Avda Camilo Cienfuegos No 10505, P. Nuero, Matanzas; e-mail giron@ma.cc.cu; internet www.giron.co.cu; f. 1960; organ of the Communist Party in Matanzas province; Dir CLOVIS ORTEGA CASTAÑEDA; circ. 25,000.

Guerrillero: Colón esq. Delicias y Adela Azcuy, Pinar del Río; e-mail cip216@cip.enet.cu; internet www.guerrillero.co.cu; f. 1969; organ of Communist Party in Pinar del Río province; Dir ERNESTO OSORIO ROQUE; circ. 33,000.

El Habanero: Gen. Suárez y Territorial, Plaza de la Revolución, Apdo 6269, Havana; e-mail internet@habanero.cip.cu; internet www.elhabanero.cubaweb.cu; f. 1987; Dir ANDRÉS HERNÁNDEZ RIVERO; circ. 21,000.

Invasor: Avda de los Deportes s/n, Ciego de Avila; e-mail cip221@cip.enet.cu; internet www.invasor.cu; f. 1979; provincial periodical; Dir MIGDALIA UTRERA PEÑA; Editor ROBERTO CARLOS DELGADO BURGOS; circ. 10,500.

Juventud Técnica: Prado 553, esq. Teniente Rey, Habana Vieja, Havana; tel. (7) 62-4330; e-mail jtecnica@editoraabril.co.cu; internet www.juventudtecnica.cu; f. 1965; every 2 months; scientific-technical; Dir IRAMIS ALONSO PORRO; Editor DANIA RAMOS; circ. 20,000.

Mar y Pesca: San Ignacio 303, entre Amargura y Teniente Rey, Habana Vieja, Havana; tel. (7) 861-5518; fax (7) 861-6280; e-mail mercado@mpesca.telemar.cu; internet www.cubamar.cu/marpesca; f. 1965; quarterly; fishing; Dir MARIO GUILLOT VEGA; circ. 20,000.

Muchacha: Galiano 264, esq. Neptuno, Havana; tel. (7) 861-5919; f. 1980; monthly; young women's magazine; Dir SILVIA MARTÍNEZ; circ. 120,000.

Mujeres: Galiano 264, entre Neptuno y Concordia, 10200 Havana; tel. (7) 861-5919; e-mail mujeres@enet.cu; internet www.mujeres.cubaweb.cu; f. 1961; weekly; women's magazine; Dir-Gen. ISABEL MOYA RICHARD; circ. 270,000.

El Nuevo Fenix: Independencia 52, esq. Honorato del Castillo, Sancti Spíritus; tel. (41) 27902; e-mail plss@ip.etecsa.cu; internet www.fenix.islagrande.cu; f. 1999; Dir YOLANDA BRITO.

Opciones: Territorial esq. Gen. Suárez, Plaza de la Revolucíon, Havana; tel. (7) 881-8934; fax (7) 881-8621; e-mail opciones@jrebelde.cip.cu; internet www.opciones.cubaweb.cu; f. 1994; weekly; finance, commerce and tourism; Dir ROGELIO POLANCO FUENTES.

Palante: Calle 21, No 954, entre 8 y 10, Vedado, Havana; e-mail palante@palan.cipcc.get.cma.net; internet www.palante.co.cu; f. 1961; weekly; humorous; Dir ROSENDO GUTIÉRREZ ROMÁN; circ. 235,000.

Periódico 26: Avda Carlos J. Finlay s/n, Las Tunas; e-mail cip224@cip.enet.cu; internet www.periodico26.cu; f. 2000; provincial periodical; Dir RAMIRO SEGURA GARCÍA.

Pionero: Calle 17, No 354, Havana; tel. (7) 32-4571; e-mail pionero@editoraabril.co.cu; internet www.pionero.cu; f. 1961; weekly; children's magazine; Dir LUCÍA SANZ ARAUJO; circ. 210,000.

Prisma: Calle 21 y Avda G, No 406, Vedado, Havana; tel. (7) 832-3578; e-mail prisma@pubs.prensa-latina.cu; f. 1979; bimonthly; tourism; Man. Dir LUIS MANUEL ARCE; circ. 15,000 (Spanish), 10,000 (English).

Revista Casa: 3 y G, Vedado, 10400 Havana; tel. (7) 838-2706; fax (7) 834-4554; e-mail revista@casa.cult.cu; internet www.casadelasamericas.com; f. 1959; 6 a year; Latin American theatre; Editor MARUJA SANTOS; Dir ROBERTO FERNÁNDEZ RETAMAR.

RIL: O'Reilly 358, Havana; tel. (7) 62-0777; f. 1972; 2 a month; technical; Dir Exec. Council of Publicity Dept, Ministry of Light Industry; Chief Officer MIREYA CRESPO; circ. 8,000.

Sierra Maestra: Avda de Los Desfiles, Santiago de Cuba; tel. (7) 2-2813; e-mail cip226@cip.enet.cu; internet www.sierramaestra.cu; f. 1957; weekly; Dir ARNALDO CLAVEL CARMENATY; circ. 45,000.

Sol de Cuba: Calle 19, No 60, entre M y N, Vedado, Havana 4; tel. (7) 832-9881; f. 1983; every 3 months; Spanish, English and French editions; Gen. Dir ALCIDES GIRO MITJANS; Editorial Dir DORIS VÉLEZ; circ. 200,000.

Somos Jóvenes: Calle 17, No 354, esq. H, Vedado, Havana; tel. (7) 32-4571; e-mail abadell@gmail.com; internet www.somosjovenes.cu; f. 1977; monthly; Dir MARIETTA MANSO MARTÍN; circ. 200,000.

Temas: Calle 23, No 1155, 5º entre 10 y 12, CP 10400, El Vedado, Havana; tel. and fax (7) 55-3010; e-mail temas@iciaic.cu; internet www.temas.cult.cu; f. 1995; quarterly; cultural, political; Editor RAFAEL HERNÁNDEZ.

Trabajadores: Territorial esq. Gen. Suárez, Plaza de la Revolución, Havana; tel. (7) 79-0819; fax (7) 55-5927; e-mail digital@trabaja.cip.cu; internet www.trabajadores.cubaweb.cu; f. 1970; organ of the trade union movt; Dir JORGE LUIS CANELA CIURANA; circ. 150,000.

Tribuna de la Habana: Territorial esq. Gen. Suárez, Plaza de la Revolución, Havana; tel. (7) 881-8021; e-mail redac@tribuna.cip.cu; internet www.tribuna.co.cu; f. 1980; weekly; Dir JESÚS ÁLVAREZ FERRER; circ. 90,000.

Vanguardia: Calle Céspedes 5, esq. Plácido, Santa Clara, Matanzas; e-mail contacto@vanguardia.cip.cu; internet www.vanguardia.co.cu; f. 1962; Dir F. A. CHANG L.; circ. 24,000.

Venceremos: Avda Ernesto Che Guevara, Km 1½, Guantánamo; tel. (7) 32-7398; e-mail cip227@cip.enet.cu; internet www.venceremos.co.cu; f. 1962; economic, political and social publ. for Guantánamo province; Dir ELIZABETH SANTIESTEBAN PÉREZ; circ. 33,500.

Ventiseis: Avda Carlos J. Finley, Las Tunas; f. 1977; Dir JOSÉ INFANTES REYES; circ. 21,000.

Verde Olivo: Avda Independencia y San Pedro, Havana; tel. (7) 79-8373; internet www.cubagob.cu/otras_info/verde_olivo/sumario.htm; f. 1959; monthly; organ of the Revolutionary Armed Forces; Dir ARMANDO DIÉGUEZ SUÁREZ; circ. 100,000.

Victoria: Carretera de la Fe, Km 1½, Plaza de la Revolución, Nueva Gerona, Isla de la Juventud; tel. (46) 32-4210; e-mail periodic@gerona.inf.cu; f. 1967; Dir SERGIO RIVERO CARRASCO; circ. 9,200.

Zunzún: Obispo 527, Apdo 605, Havana; e-mail zunzun@eabril.jovenclub.cu; internet www.zunzun.cu; f. 1990; children's magazine; Dir MARTHA RÍOS.

PRESS ASSOCIATIONS

Unión de Periodistas de Cuba (UPEC): Avda 23, No 452, esq. a I, Vedado, 10400 Havana; tel. (7) 832-4550; fax (7) 33-3079; e-mail vpetica@upec.co.cu; internet www.cubaperiodistas.cu; f. 1963; Pres. TUBAL PÁEZ HERNÁNDEZ.

Unión de Escritores y Artistas de Cuba (UNEAC): Calle 17, No 354, entre G y H, Vedado, Havana; tel. (7) 53-5081; fax (7) 33-3158; e-mail promeven@uneac.co.cu; internet www.uneac.com; Pres. CARLOS MARTÍ; Exec. Vice-Pres. MIGUEL BARNET.

NEWS AGENCIES

Agencia de Información Nacional (AIN): Calle 23, No 358, esq. J, Vedado, Havana; tel. (7) 881-6423; fax (7) 66-2049; e-mail ain@ainch.ain.sld.cu; internet www.ain.cubaweb.cu/patriotas2/principal2.htm; f. 1974; national news agency; Gen. Dir ESTEBAN RAMÍREZ ALONSO.

Prensa Latina (Agencia Informativa Latinoamericana, SA): Calle 23, No 201, esq. N, Vedado, Havana; tel. (7) 55-3496; fax (7) 33-3068; e-mail difusion@prensa-latina.cu; internet www.prensa-latina.cu; f. 1959; Dir PEDRO MARGOLLES VILLANUEVA.

Publishers

Artecubano Ediciones: Calle 3, No 1205, entre 12 y 14, Playa, Havana; tel. (7) 203-8581; fax (7) 204-2744; e-mail cnap@cubarte.cult.cu; Dir RAFAEL ACOSTA DE ARRIBA.

Casa de las Américas: Calle 3 y Avda G, Plaza de la Revolución, Vedado, 10400 Havana; tel. (7) 552-7106; fax (7) 832-7272; e-mail admin@casa.cult.cu; internet www.casadelasamericas.com; f. 1959; Latin American literature and social sciences; Dir ROBERTO FERNÁNDEZ RETAMAR.

Casa Editora Abril: Prado 553, esq. Teniente Rey y Dragones, Habana Vieja, Havana; tel. (7) 862-7871; fax (7) 862-4330; e-mail eabril@jcce.org.cu; f. 1980; attached to the Union of Young Communists; cultural, children's literature; Dir NIURKA DUMÉNICO GARCÍA.

Ediciones Creart: Calle 4, No 205, entre Línea y 11, Plaza de la Revolución, Havana; tel. (7) 832-9691; fax (7) 66-2582; e-mail creart@cubarte.cult.cu; f. 1994; Dir TANIA LICEA JIMÉNEZ.

Ediciones Unión: Calle 17, No 354, entre G y H, Plaza de la Revolución, Vedado, 10400 Havana; tel. (7) 55-3112; fax (7) 33-3158; e-mail editora@uneac.co.cu; f. 1962; publishing arm of the Unión de Escritores y Artistas de Cuba; Cuban literature, art; Dir OLGA MARTA CABRERA.

Editora Política: Belascoaín No 864, esq. Desagüe y Peñalver, Havana; tel. (7) 879-8553; fax (7) 879-5688; e-mail editora@epol.cipcc.get.cma.net; f. 1963; publishing institution of the Communist Party of Cuba; Dir SANTIAGO DÓRQUEZ PÉREZ.

Editorial Academia: Industria y Barcelona, Capitolio Nacional, 4°, Habana Vieja, 10200 Havana; tel. and fax (7) 863-0315; e-mail editorial@gecyt.cu; f. 1962; attached to the Ministry of Science, Technology and the Environment; scientific and technical; Dir CARLOS J. LEYVA PERDOMO.

Editorial Arte y Literatura: Calle O'Reilly, No 4, esq. Tacón, Habana Vieja, Havana; tel. (7) 862-4326; fax (7) 833-8187; e-mail publicaciones@icl.cult.cu; f. 1967; traditional Cuban literature and arts; Dir ELIZABETH DÍAZ GONZÁLEZ.

Editorial Ciencias Médicas: Línea esq. 1, 11°, Plaza de la Revolución, Vedado, 10400 Havana; tel. (7) 832-5338; fax (7) 33-3063; e-mail cnicm@infomed.sld.cu; attached to the Ministry of Public Health; books and magazines specializing in the medical sciences; Dir DAMIANA MARTIN.

Editorial Ciencias Sociales: Calle Paseo del Che 59, Vedado, Havana; tel. (7) 203-3959; fax (7) 33-3441; e-mail cienciasociales@cubaliteraria.com; internet www.ciencias-sociales.org; f. 1967; attached to the Cuban Book Institute; social and political literature, history, philosophy, juridical sciences and economics; Dir ERNESTO ESCOBAR SOTO.

Editorial Científico-Técnica: Calle 14, No 4104, entre 41 y 43, Playa, Havana; tel. (7) 203-6090; fax (7) 833-3441; f. 1967; attached to the Ministry of Culture; technical and scientific literature; Dir JULIO CÉSAR GUANCHE.

Editorial Félix Varela: San Miguel No 1011, entre Mazón y Basarrate, Plaza de la Revolución, Vedado, 10400 Havana; tel. (7) 877-5617; fax (7) 73-5419; e-mail elsa@enpses.co.cu; Dir ELSA RODRÍGUEZ.

Editorial Gente Nueva: Calle 2, No 58, entre 3 y 5, Plaza de la Revolución, Vedado, 10400 Havana; tel. (7) 833-9489; fax (7) 833-8187; e-mail gentenueva@icl.cult.cu; f. 1967; books for children; Dir MIRTA GONZÁLEZ GUTIÉRREZ.

Editorial José Martí: Calzada 259, entre I y J, Apdo 4208, Plaza de la Revolución, Vedado, 10400 Havana; tel. (7) 832-9838; fax (7) 33-3441; e-mail editjmal@icl.cult.cu; f. 1983; attached to the Ministry of Culture; foreign-language publishing; Dir LOURDES GONZÁLEZ.

Editorial Letras Cubanas: Calle O'Reilly, No 4, esq. Tacón, Habana Vieja, 10100 Havana; tel. (7) 862-4378; fax (7) 33-8187; e-mail elc@icl.cult.cu; f. 1977; attached to the Ministry of Culture; general, particularly classic and contemporary Cuban literature and arts; Dir DANIEL GARCÍA SANTOS.

Editorial de la Mujer: Calle Galiano, No 264, esq. Neptuno, Havana; tel. (7) 862-5398; f. 1995; female literature; Dir ISABEL MOYA RICHARD.

Editorial Oriente: Santa Lucía 356, Santiago de Cuba; tel. (226) 22496; fax (226) 42387; e-mail edoriente@cultstgo.cult.cu; f. 1971; publishes works from the Eastern provinces; fiction, history, female literature and studies, art and culture, practical books and books for children; Dir AIDA BAHR.

Editorial Pablo de la Torriente Brau: Calle 11, No 160, entre K y L, Plaza de la Revolución, Vedado, 10400 Havana; tel. (7) 832-7581; e-mail edpablo@eventos.cip.cu; f. 1985; publishing arm of the Unión de Periodistas de Cuba; Dir IRMA DE ARMAS FONSECA.

Editorial Pueblo y Educación: Avda 3A, No 4601, entre 46 y 60, Playa, Havana; tel. (7) 202-1490; fax (7) 204-0844; e-mail epe@ceniai.inf.cu; f. 1971; textbooks and educational publs; publishes Revista Educación (3 a year, circ. 2,200); Dir CATALINA LAJUD HERRERO.

Editorial San Lope: Calle Gonzalo de Quesada, No 121, entre Lico Cruz y Lucas Ortiz, Las Tunas; tel. (31) 48191; fax (31) 47380; e-mail librolt@tunet.cult.cu; f. 1991; attached to the Ministry of Culture; Dir ACIRYS ESPINOSA MARTÍNEZ.

Editorial Si-Mar: Calle 47, No 1210, entre 36 y Lindero, Plaza de la Revolución, Vedado, 10600 Havana; tel. (7) 881-8168; fax (7) 883-6108; e-mail edicion@simar.cu; f. 1994; Dir SARA MOREJÓN JIMÉNEZ.

GOVERNMENT PUBLISHING HOUSES

Instituto Cubano del Libro: Palacio del Segundo Cabo, Calle O'Reilly, No 4, esq. Tacón, Havana; tel. (7) 862-8091; fax (7) 33-8187; e-mail libro@cubarte.cult.cu; f. 1967; printing and publishing org. attached to the Ministry of Culture which combines several publishing houses and has direct links with others; presides over the National Editorial Council (CEN); Pres. IROEL SÁNCHEZ.

Oficina Publicaciones del Consejo de Estado: Calle 17, No 552, esq. D, Plaza de la Revolución, Vedado, 10400 Havana; tel. (7) 832-9149; fax (7) 57-4578; e-mail palvarez@enet.cu; f. 1972; attached to the Council of State; books, pamphlets and other printed media on historical and political matters; Dir PEDRO ALVAREZ TABÍO.

Broadcasting and Communications

TELECOMMUNICATIONS

Empresa de Radiocomunicación y Radiodifusión (RADIO-CUBA): Edif. Western Union, No 406, entre Obispo y Obrapía, Habana Vieja, Havana; tel. (7) 860-3142; fax (7) 33-8301; e-mail radiocuba@radiocuba.cu; internet www.radiocuba.cu; f. 1967; voice, mobile satellite and television radiocommunication services; Dir-Gen. JUAN G. CAIRO MARIN.

Empresa de Telecomunicaciones de Cuba, SA (ETECSA): Avda 5, entre 76 y 78, Edif. Barcelona, Miramar, Havana; tel. (7) 266-6203; fax (7) 860-5144; e-mail atencionclientes_unc@etecsa.cu; internet www.etecsa.cu; f. 1991; 27% owned by Telecom Italia International, SpA; merged with Empresa de Telecomunicaciones Celulares del Caribe, SA (C-Com) and Teléfonos Celulares de Cuba, SA (CUBACEL) in 2003; Exec. Pres. JOSÉ ANTONIO FERNÁNDEZ.

Instituto de Investigación y Desarrollo de las Telecomunicaciones (LACETEL): Avda Independencia, Km 14½, 1° de Mayo, Rancho Boyeros, CP 19210, Havana; tel. (7) 57-9265; fax (7) 649-5828; e-mail webmaster@lacetel.cu; internet www.lacetel.cu; Dir-Gen. ORLANDO PIÑEIRA OLIVA.

Ministerio de la Informática y las Comunicaciones (Dirección General de Telecomunicaciones): Avda Independencia y 19 de Mayo, Plaza de la Revolución, Havana; tel. (7) 81-7654; e-mail infosoc@mic.cu; internet www.mic.gov.cu; Dir CARLOS MARTÍNEZ ALBUERNE.

Telecomunicaciones Móviles, SA (MOVITEL): Avda 47, No 3405, Reparto Kohly, Playa, Havana; tel. (7) 204-8400; fax (7) 204-4264; e-mail movitel@movitel.co.cu; internet www.movitel.co.cu; mobile telecommunications; Dir-Gen. ASELA FERNÁNDEZ LORENZO.

Transbit: Havana; state-owned; Pres. WALDO REBOREDO.

BROADCASTING

Ministerio de la Informática y las Comunicaciones (Dirección de Frecuencias Radioeléctricas): see Ministries.

Instituto Cubano de Radio y Televisión (ICRT): Edif. Radiocentro, Avda 23, No 258, entre L y M, Vedado, Havana 4; tel. (7) 32-1568; fax (7) 33-3107; e-mail icrt@cecm.get.tur.cu; internet www.cubagob.cu/des_soc/icrt/index.htm; f. 1962; Pres. ERNESTO LÓPEZ DOMÍNGUEZ.

Radio y Televisión Comercial: Calle 26, No 301, esq. 21, Vedado, Havana; tel. (7) 66-2719; fax (7) 33-3939; e-mail g.general@rtvc.com.cu; Dir RENÉ DUQUESNE LÓPEZ.

Radio

In 1997 there were five national networks and one international network, 14 provincial radio stations and 31 municipal radio stations, with a total of some 170 transmitters.

Radio Cadena Agramonte: Calle Cisneros, No 310, entre Ignacio Agramonte y General Gómez, Camagüey; tel. (322) 29-5616; e-mail cip240@cip.enet.cu; internet www.cadenagramonte.cu; f. 1957; digital radio; serves Camagüey; Dir ONELIO CASTILLO CORDERÍ.

Radio Enciclopedia: Calle N, No 266, entre 21 y 23, Vedado, 10400 Havana; tel. (7) 55-4587; e-mail enciclop@ceniai.inf.cu; internet www.radioenciclopedia.cu; f. 1962; national network; instrumental music programmes; 24 hours daily; Dir-Gen. EDELSA PALACIOS GORDO.

Radio Habana Cuba: Infanta 105, Apdo 6240, Havana; tel. (7) 877-6628; fax (7) 881-2927; e-mail radiohc@enet.cu; internet www.radiohc.org; f. 1961; shortwave station; broadcasts in Spanish, English, French, Portuguese, Arabic, Esperanto, Quechua, Guaraní and Creole; Dir-Gen. LUIS LÓPEZ.

Radio Musical Nacional (CBMF): Calle N, No 266, entre 21 y 23, Vedado, Havana; tel. (7) 877-5527; e-mail rmusical@ceniai.inf.cu; internet www.cmbfjazz.cu; f. 1948; national network; classical music programmes; 17 hours daily; Dir LUIZ LÓPEZ-QUINTANA.

Radio Progreso: Infanta 105, esq. a 25, 6°, Apdo 3042, Havana; tel. (7) 877-5519; e-mail progreso@ceniai.inf.cu; internet www.radioprogreso.cu; f. 1929; national network; mainly entertainment and music; 24 hours daily; Dir-Gen. LUIS FERNÁNDEZ.

Radio Rebelde: Edif. ICRT, Avda 23, No 258, entre L y M, Vedado, Apdo 6277, Havana; tel. (7) 831-3514; fax (7) 33-4270; e-mail paginaweb@rrebelde.icrt.cu; internet www.radiorebelde.com.cu; f. 1958; merged with Radio Liberación in 1984; national network; 24-hour news and cultural programmes, music and sports; Dir-Gen. GERARDO CALDERÍN GAÍNZA.

Radio Reloj: Edif. Radiocentro, Calle 23, No 258, entre L y M, Plaza de la Revolución, Vedado, Havana; tel. (7) 55-4185; fax (7) 55-4225; e-mail relojmailj@rreloj.icrt.cu; internet www.radioreloj.cu; f. 1947; national network; 24-hour news service; Dir ISIDRO BETANCOURT SILVA.

Radio Taino: Edif. Radiocentro, Calle 23, No 258, entre L y M, Vedado, Havana; tel. (7) 55-4181; fax (7) 55-4490; e-mail pperez@rtaino.icrt.cu; internet www.radiotaino.cubasi.cu; f. 1985; broadcasts in English and Spanish; Dir PEDRO MANUEL PÉREZ ROQUE.

Television

The Cuban Government holds a 19% stake in the regional television channel Telesur (q.v.), which began operations in May 2005 and is based in Caracas, Venezuela.

Instituto Cubano de Radiodifusión (Televisión Nacional): Avda 23, No 258, Vedado, Havana; tel. (7) 55-4059; fax (7) 33-3107; internet www.cubagob.cu/des_soc/icrt/index.htm; f. 1950; broadcasts through four channels; Pres. ERNESTO LÓPEZ DOMÍNGUEZ.

Canal Educativo: Avda 23, No 258, Vedado, Havana; tel. (7) 55-4059; fax (7) 33-3107; f. 2002; broadcasts on channel 13; educational; Dir IVÁN BARRETO.

Cubavisión: Calle M, No 313, Vedado, Havana; e-mail info@cubavision.icrt.cu; internet www.cubavision.cubaweb.cu; broadcasts on channel 6.

Tele Rebelde: Mazón, No 52, Vedado, Havana; tel. (7) 32-3369; broadcasts on channel 2; Vice-Pres. GARY GONZÁLEZ.

CHTV: Habana Libre Hotel, Havana; f. 1990; subsidiary station of Tele Rebelde; Dir ROSA MARÍA FERNÁNDEZ SOFÍA.

Finance

(cap. = capital; res = reserves; dep. = deposits; m. = million; brs = branches)

BANKING

All banks were nationalized in 1960. Legislation establishing the national banking system was approved by the Council of State in 1984. A restructuring of the banking system, initiated in 1995, to accommodate Cuba's transformation to a more market-orientated economy, was proceeding in the mid-2000s. A new central bank, the Banco Central de Cuba (BCC), was created in 1997 to supersede the Banco Nacional de Cuba (BNC). The BCC was to be responsible for issuing currency, proposing and implementing monetary policy and the regulation of financial institutions. The BNC was to continue functioning as a commercial bank and servicing the country's foreign debt. The restructuring of the banking system also allowed for the creation of an investment bank, the Banco de Inversiones, to provide medium- and long-term financing for investment, and the Banco Financiero Internacional, SA, to offer short-term financing. A new agro-industrial and commercial bank was also to be created to provide services for farmers and co-operatives. The new banking system is under the control of Grupo Nueva Banca, which holds a majority share in each institution. In 2002 there were eight commercial banks, 18 non-banking financial institutions, 13 representative offices of foreign banks and four representative offices of non-banking financial institutions operating in Cuba.

Central Bank

Banco Central de Cuba (BCC): Calle Cuba, No 402, Aguiar 411, Habana Vieja, Havana; tel. (7) 866-8003; fax (7) 866-6601; e-mail plascncia@bc.gov.cu; internet www.bc.gov.cu; f. 1997; sole bank of issue; Pres. FRANCISCO SOBERÓN VALDEZ.

Commercial Banks

Banco de Crédito y Comercio (BANDEC): Amargura 158, entre Cuba y Aguiar, Habana Vieja, Havana; tel. (7) 861-4533; fax (7) 866-8968; e-mail ileana@oc.bandec.cu; f. 1997; Pres. ILEANA ESTÉVEZ.

Banco Exterior de Cuba: Calle 23, No 55, esq. P, Vedado, Municipio Plaza, Havana; tel. (7) 55-0795; fax (7) 55-0794; e-mail bec@bec.co.cu; f. 1999; cap. 450m. pesos, res 2.8m. pesos, dep. 65.5m. pesos (Dec. 2002); Pres. JACOBO PEISON WEINER.

Banco Financiero Internacional, SA: Avda 5, No 9009, esq. 92, Miramar, Municipio Playa, Havana; tel. (7) 267-5000; fax (7) 267-5002; e-mail bfi@bfi.com.cu; f. 1984; autonomous; finances Cuba's foreign trade; Pres. ERNESTO MEDINA; Gen. Man. (Int.) NIVALDO PULDÓN.

Banco Internacional de Comercio, SA: 20 de Mayo y Ayestarán, Apdo 6113, 10600 Havana; tel. (7) 883-6038; fax (7) 883-6028; e-mail bicsa@bicsa.colombus.cu; f. 1993; cap. 193.4m. convertible pesos, res 19.7m. convertible pesos, dep. 775.6m. convertible pesos (Dec. 2005); Chair. and Pres. MARCOS DÍAZ.

Banco Metropolitano: Avda 5 y Calle 112, Playa, 11600 Havana; tel. (7) 204-3869; fax (7) 204-9193; e-mail bm@banco-metropolitano.com; internet www.banco-metropolitano.com; f. 1996; offers foreign currency and deposit account facilities; Pres. MANUEL VALE; Dir-Gen. PEDRO DE LA ROSA GONZÁLEZ.

CUBA

Banco Nacional de Cuba (BNC): Aguiar 456, entre Amargura y Lamparilla, Habana Vieja, Havana; tel. (7) 862-8896; fax (7) 866-9390; e-mail bancuba@bnc.cu; f. 1950; reorganized 1997; Chair. DIANA AMELIA FERNÁNDEZ VILA.

Savings Bank

Banco Popular de Ahorro: Calle 16, No 306, entre 3 y 5, Miramar, Playa, Havana; tel. (7) 202-2545; fax (7) 204-1180; internet www.bancopopulardeahorro.com; f. 1983; savings bank; cap. 30m. pesos, dep. 5,363.7m. pesos; Pres. MANUEL VALE MARRERO; Sec. LOURDES PÉREZ SOLER; 520 brs.

Investment Bank

Banco de Inversiones, SA: Avda 5, No 6802 esq. a 68, Miramar, Havana; tel. (7) 204-3374; fax (7) 204-3377; e-mail inversiones@bdi.cu; internet www.bdi.cu; f. 1996; Exec. Pres. RAÚL E. RANGEL.

INSURANCE
State Organizations

Empresa del Seguro Estatal Nacional (ESEN): Calle 5, No 306, entre C y D, Vedado, Havana; tel. (7) 32-2500; fax (7) 33-8717; e-mail esen@esen.com.cu; internet www.esen.com.cu; f. 1978; motor and agricultural insurance; Dir-Gen. RAFAEL J. GONZÁLEZ PÉREZ.

Seguros Internacionales de Cuba, SA (Esicuba): Cuba No 314, entre Obispo y Obrapía, Habana Vieja, Havana; tel. (7) 33-8400; fax (7) 33-8038; e-mail esicuba@esicuba.cu; f. 1963; reorganized 1986; all classes of insurance except life; Pres. RAMÓN MARTÍNEZ CARRERA.

Trade and Industry

GOVERNMENT AGENCIES

Ministry of Foreign Investment and Economic Co-operation: see Ministries.

Free-Trade Zones National Office: Calle 22, No 528, entre 3 y 5, Miramar, Havana; tel. (7) 204-7636; fax (7) 204-7637; created and regulated by the Ministry of Foreign Investment and Economic Co-operation.

Investment Promotion Center (CPI): Calle 30, No 512, entre 5 y 7, Miramar, Playa, Havana; tel. (7) 202-3873; fax (7) 204-2105; e-mail cpinv@minvec.cu; internet www.cpi-minvec.cu; f. 1994; arm of the Ministry of Foreign Investment and Economic Co-operation; Dir ANAIZA RODRÍGUEZ RODRÍGUEZ.

CHAMBER OF COMMERCE

Cámara de Comercio de la República de Cuba: Calle 21, No 661/701, esq. Calle A, Apdo 4237, Vedado, Havana; tel. (7) 830-4436; fax (7) 833-3042; e-mail pdcia@camara.com.cu; internet www.camaracuba.cu; f. 1963; mems include all Cuban foreign trade enterprises and the most important agricultural and industrial enterprises; Pres. BERTHA DELGADO GUANCHE GARCÍA; Sec.-Gen. FRANK ABEL PORTELA.

AGRICULTURAL ORGANIZATION

Asociación Nacional de Agricultores Pequeños (ANAP) (National Association of Small Farmers): Calle I, No 206, entre Linea y 13, Vedado, Havana; tel. (7) 32-4541; fax (7) 33-4244; internet www.pcc.cu/pccweb/anap.php; f. 1961; 200,000 mems; Pres. ORLANDO LUGO FONTE; Vice-Pres. EVELIO PAUSA BELLO.

STATE IMPORT-EXPORT BOARDS

Alimport (Empresa Cubana Importadora de Alimentos): Infanta 16, 3°, Apdo 7006, Havana; tel. (7) 54-2501; fax (7) 33-3151; e-mail precios@alimport.com.cu; f. 1962; controls import of foodstuffs and liquors; CEO PEDRO ALVAREZ BORREGO.

Autoimport (Empresa Central de Abastecimiento y Venta de Equipos de Transporte Ligero): Galiano 213, entre Concordia y Virtudes, Havana; tel. (7) 61-5322; fax (7) 66-6549; e-mail eric@autoimport.com.cu; imports cars, light vehicles, motor cycles and spare parts; Dir JOSÉ ARAÑABURU.

Aviaimport (Empresa Cubana Importadora y Exportadora de Aviación): Calle 182, No 126, entre 1 y 5, Rpto Flores, Playa, Havana; tel. (7) 33-0142; fax (7) 33-6234; e-mail aviaimport@avianet.cu; import and export of aircraft and components; Man. Dir MARCOS LAGO MARTÍNEZ.

Caribex (Empresa Exportadora del Caribe): Aparthotel Las Brisas, Apdo 3C 23, Villa Panamericana, Havana; tel. (7) 95-1121; fax (7) 95-1120; e-mail webpesca@telemar.cu; internet www1.cubamar.cu; export of seafood and marine products; Dir JACINTO FIERRO BAREFOOT.

Directory

Catec (Empresa Cubana Importadora, Exportadora y Comercializadora de Productos de la Ciencia y la Técnica Agropecuaria): Calle 148, No 905, esq. 9, Miramar, Havana; tel. (7) 208-2164; fax (7) 204-6071; e-mail alina@catec.co.cu; exports, imports and markets scientific and technical products relating to the farming and forestry industries; Dir-Gen. OSVALDO CARVEJAL GABELA.

Construimport (Empresa Central de Abastecimiento y Venta de Equipos de Construcción y sus Piezas): Carretera de Varona, Km 1$\frac{1}{2}$, Capdevila, Havana; tel. (7) 45-2567; fax (7) 66-6180; e-mail construimport@colombus.cu; internet www.construimport.cubaindustria.cu; f. 1969; controls the import and export of construction machinery and equipment; Man. Dir JESÚS SERRANO RODRÍGUEZ.

Consumimport (Empresa Cubana Importadora de Artículos de Consumo General): Calle 23, No 55, 9°, Apdo 6427, Vedado, Havana; tel. (8) 36-7717; fax (8) 33-3847; e-mail comer@consumimport.infocex.cu; f. 1962; imports and exports general consumer goods; Dir MERCEDES REY HECHAVARRÍA.

Copextel (Corporación Productora y Exportadora de Tecnología Electrónica): Calle 194 y 7A, Siboney, Havana; tel. (7) 21-8400; fax (7) 33-1414; e-mail copextel@copextel.com.cu; internet www.copextel.com.cu; f. 1985; exports LTEL personal computers and micro-computer software; Dir NORMA M. GARCÍA BRUZÓN.

Coprefil (Empresa Comercial y de Producciones Filatélicas): Avda 49, No 2831, Rpto Kohly, Havana; tel. (7) 204-9668; fax (7) 204-5077; e-mail coprefil@coprefil.cu; imports and exports postage stamps, postcards, calendars, handicrafts, communications equipment, electronics, watches, etc.; Dir NELSON IGLESIAS FERNÁNDEZ.

Cubaelectrónica (Empresa Importadora y Exportadora de Productos de la Electrónica): Calle 22, No 510, entre 5 y 7, Miramar, Havana; tel. (7) 204-0178; fax (7) 204-1233; e-mail mariaisabel@columbus.cu; f. 1986; imports and exports electronic equipment and devices; Pres. MARÍA ISABEL MOREJÓN PÉREZ.

Cubaexport (Empresa Cubana Exportadora de Alimentos y Productos Varios): Calle 23, No 55, entre Infanta y P, 8°, Vedado, Apdo 6719, Havana; tel. (7) 838-0595; fax (7) 833-3587; e-mail cubaexport@cexport.mincex.cu; f. 1965; export of foodstuffs and industrial products; Man. Dir FRANCISCO SANTIAGO PICHARDO.

Cubafrutas (Empresa Cubana Exportadora de Frutas Tropicales): Calle 23, No 55, Apdo 6683, Vedado, Havana; tel. and fax (7) 79-5653; f. 1979; controls export of fruits, vegetables and canned foodstuffs; Dir JORGE AMARO MOREJÓN.

Cubahidráulica (Empresa Central de Equipos Hidráulicos): Carretera Vieja de Guanabacoa y Linea de Ferrocarril, Rpto Mañana, Guanabacoa, Havana; tel. (7) 97-0821; fax (7) 97-1627; e-mail cubahidraulica@enet.cu; internet www.cubahidraulica.com; imports and exports hydraulic and mechanical equipment, parts and accessories; Dir-Gen. JOSÉ MARRERO CARNACHO.

Cubalse (Empresa para Prestación de Servicios al Cuerpo Diplomático): Avda 3 y Final, Miramar, Havana; tel. (7) 204-2284; fax (7) 204-2282; e-mail cubalse@cm.cubalse.cma.net; f. 1974; imports consumer goods for the diplomatic corps and foreign technicians residing in Cuba; exports beverages and tobacco, leather goods and foodstuffs; other operations include real estate, retail trade, restaurants, clubs, automobile business, state-of-the-art equipment and household appliances, construction, investments, wholesale, road transport, freight transit, shipping, publicity, photography and video, financing, legal matters; Pres. REIDAL RONCOURT FONT.

Cubametales (Empresa Cubana Importadora de Metales, Combustibles y Lubricantes): Infanta 16, 4°, Apdo 6917, Vedado, Havana; tel. (7) 70-4225; fax (7) 33-3477; e-mail pedro@cubametal.infocex.cu; controls import of metals (ferrous and non-ferrous), crude petroleum and petroleum products; also engaged in the export of petroleum products and ferrous and non-ferrous scrap; Dir PEDRO PÉREZ RODRÍGUEZ.

Cubaniquel (Empresa Cubana Exportadora de Minerales y Metales): Calle 23, No 55, 8°, Apdo 6128, Havana; tel. (7) 33-5334; fax (7) 33-3332; e-mail bcorrea@moa.minbas.cu; f. 1961; sole exporter of minerals and metals; Man. Dir RICARDO GONZÁLEZ.

Cubatabaco (Empresa Cubana del Tabaco): Calle O'Reilly, No 104, Apdo 6557, Havana; tel. (7) 861-5775; fax (7) 33-8214; e-mail juan@cubatabaco.cu; f. 1962; controls export of leaf tobacco, cigars and cigarettes to France; Dir JUAN MANUEL DÍAZ TENORIO.

Cubatécnica (Empresa de Contratación de Asistencia Técnica): Calle 12, No 513, entre 5 y 7, Miramar, Havana; tel. (7) 202-3270; fax (7) 204-0923; e-mail comercial@cubatecnica.cu; internet www.cubatecnica.cu; f. 1976; controls export and import of technical assistance; Dir FÉLIX GONZÁLEZ NAVERÁN.

Cubatex (Empresa Cubana Importadora de Fibras, Tejidos, Cueros y sus Productos): Calle 23, No 55, Apdo 7115, Vedado, Havana; tel. (7) 70-2531; fax (7) 33-3321; controls import of fibres, textiles, hides and by-products and export of fabric and clothing; Dir LUISA AMPARO SESÍN VIDAL.

Cubazúcar (Empresa Cubana Exportadora de Azúcar y sus Derivados): Calle 23, No 55, 7°, Vedado, Apdo 6647, Havana; tel. (7) 54-2175; fax (7) 33-3482; e-mail producer@cubazucar.com; internet www.cubazucar.com; f. 1962; controls export of sugar, molasses and alcohol; Pres. JOSÉ LÓPEZ SILVERO.

Ecimact (Empresa Comercial de Industrias de Materiales, Construcción y Turismo): Calle 1C, entre 152 y 154, Miramar, Havana; tel. (7) 21-9783; controls import and export of engineering services and plant for industrial construction and tourist complexes; Dir OCTAVIO CASTILLA CANGAS.

Ecimetal (Empresa Importadora y Exportadora de Objetivos Industriales): Calle 23, No 55, esq. Plaza, Vedado, Havana; tel. (7) 55-0548; fax (7) 33-4737; e-mail ecimetal@infocex.cu; f. 1977; controls import and export of plant, equipment and raw materials for all major industrial sectors; Dir CONCEPCIÓN BUENO.

Ediciones Cubanas (Empresa de Comercio Exterior de Publicaciones): Obispo 527, esq. Bernaza, Apdo 47, Havana; tel. (7) 863-1989; fax (7) 33-8943; e-mail edicuba@cubarte.cult.cu; controls import and export of books and periodicals; Dir NANCY MATOS LACOSTA.

Egrem (Estudios de Grabaciones y Ediciones Musicales): Avda 3, No 1008, entre 10 y 12, Miramar, Playa, Havana; tel. (7) 204-1925; fax (7) 204-2519; e-mail relaciones@egrem.cult.cu; f. 1964; controls the import and export of records, tapes, printed music and musical instruments; Dir Gen. JULIO BALLESTER GUZMÁN.

Emexcon (Empresa Importadora y Exportadora de la Construcción): Calle 25, No 2602, esq. a 26, Playa, Havana; tel. (7) 204-2263; fax (7) 204-1862; e-mail enrique@emexcon.com.cu; f. 1978; consulting engineer services, contracting, import and export of building materials and equipment; Dir ENRIQUE MARTÍNEZ DE LA FÉ.

Emiat (Empresa Importadora y Exportadora de Suministros Técnicos): Avda 47, No 2828, entre 28 y 34, Rpto Kohly, Havana; tel. (7) 203-0345; fax (7) 204-9353; e-mail emiat@enet.cu; f. 1983; imports technical materials, equipment and special products; exports furniture, kitchen utensils and accessories; Man. FIDEL GARCÍA HERNÁNDEZ.

Emidict (Empresa Especializada Importadora, Exportadora y Distribuidora para la Ciencia y la Técnica): Calle 16, No 102, esq. Avda 1, Miramar, Playa, 13000 Havana; tel. (7) 203-5316; fax (7) 204-1768; e-mail emidict@ceniai.inf.cu; internet www.emidict.com.cu; f. 1982; controls import and export of scientific and technical products and equipment, live animals; scientific information; Dir-Gen. CARLOS CANALES ENRÍQUEZ.

Energoimport (Empresa Importadora de Objetivos Electro-energéticos): Amenidad No 124, entre Nueva y 20 de Mayo, Municipio Cerro, 10600 Havana; tel. (7) 70-2501; fax (7) 66-6079; e-mail lage@energonet.com.cu; internet www.energonet.com.cu; f. 1977; controls import of equipment for electricity generation; Dir-Gen. RAÚL E. GARCÍA BARREIRO.

Eprob (Empresa de Proyectos para las Industrias de la Básica): Avda 31A, No 1805, entre 18 y 20, Edif. Las Ursulinas, Miramar, Playa, Apdo 12100, Havana; tel. (7) 202-5562; fax (7) 204-2146; f. 1967; exports consulting services and processing of engineering construction projects, consulting services and supplies of complete industrial plants and turn-key projects; Man. Dir GLORIA EXPÓSITO DÍAZ.

Eproyiv (Empresa de Proyectos para Industrias Varias): Calle 33, No 1815, entre 18 y 20, Playa, Havana; tel. (7) 24-2149; e-mail eproyiv@ceniai.inf.cu; f. 1967; consulting services, feasibility studies, devt of basic and detailed engineering models, project management and turn-key projects; Dir MARTA ELENA HERNÁNDEZ DÍAZ.

Esi (Empresa de Suministros Industriales): Calle Aguiar, No 556, entre Teniente Rey y Muralla, Havana; tel. (7) 62-0696; fax (7) 33-8951; f. 1985; imports machinery, equipment and components for industrial plants; Dir-Gen. FRANCISCO DÍAZ CABRERA.

Fecuimport (Empresa Cubana Importadora y Exportadora de Ferrocarriles): Avda 7A, No 6209, entre 62 y 66, Apdo 6003, Miramar, Havana; tel. (7) 203-3764; f. 1968; imports and exports railway equipment; Pres. DOMINGOS HERRERA.

Ferrimport (Empresa Cubana Importadora de Artículos de Ferretería): Calle 23, No 55, 2°, Vedado, Apdo 6258, Havana; tel. (7) 870-6678; fax (7) 879-4417; f. 1965; importers of industrial hardware; Dir-Gen. ALEJANDRO MUSTELIER.

Fondo Cubano de Bienes Culturales: Calle 36, No 4702, esq. Avda 47, Rpto Kohly, Playa, Havana; tel. (7) 204-8005; fax (7) 204-0391; e-mail fcbc@fcbc.cult.cu; f. 1978; controls export of fine handicraft and works of art; Dir-Gen. JOSÉ GONZÁLEZ FERNÁNDEZ-LARREA.

Habanos, SA: Avda 3, No 2006, entre 20 y 22, Miramar, Havana; tel. (7) 204-0510; fax (7) 204-0511; e-mail habanos@habanos.cu; internet www.habanos.com; f. 1994; controls export of leaf and pipe tobacco, cigars and cigarettes to all markets; jt venture with Altadis, SA (Spain).

ICAIC (Instituto Cubano del Arte e Industria Cinematográficos): Calle 23, No 1155, Vedado, Havana 4; tel. (7) 55-3128; fax (7) 33-3032; e-mail animados@animados.icaic.cu; internet www.cubacine.cu/dibujosanimados/index.htm; f. 1959; production, import and export of films and newsreel; Dir CAMILO VIVES PALLÉS.

Imexin (Empresa Importadora y Exportadora de Infraestructura): Avda 5, No 1007, esq. a 12, Miramar, Havana; tel. (7) 204-0658; fax (7) 204-0622; e-mail imexinsa@ceniai.inf.cu; f. 1977; controls import and export of infrastructure; Man. Dir RAÚL BENCE VIJANDE.

Maprinter (Empresa Cubana Importadora y Exportadora de Materias Primas y Productos Intermedios): Edif. MINCEX, Calle 23, No 55, entre P y Infanta, 8°, Plaza de la Revolución, Vedado, Havana; tel. (7) 878-0711; fax (7) 833-3535; e-mail direccion@maprinter.mincex.cu; internet www.maprinter.cu; f. 1962; controls import and export of raw materials and intermediate products; Dir-Gen. ODALYS ALDAMA VALDÉS.

Maquimport (Empresa Cubana Importadora de Maquinarias y Equipos): Calle 23, No 55, 6°, entre P y Infanta, Vedado, Apdo 6052, Havana; tel. (7) 55-0632; fax (7) 66-2217; imports industrial goods and equipment; Dir ROBERTO E. TORRES.

Marpesca (Empresa Cubana Importadora y Exportadora de Buques Mercantes y de Pesca): Conill No 580, esq. Avda 26, Nuevo Vedado, Havana; tel. (7) 881-1846; fax (7) 879-1010; f. 1978; imports and exports ships and port and fishing equipment; Pres. JOSÉ CEREIJO CASAS.

Medicuba (Empresa Cubana Importadora y Exportadora de Productos Médicos): Máximo Gómez 1, esq. Egido, Havana; tel. (7) 62-4061; fax (7) 33-8516; e-mail alfonso@medicuba.sld.cu; enterprise for the export and import of medical and pharmaceutical products; Dir ALFONSO SÁNCHEZ DÍAZ.

Produimport (Empresa Central de Abastecimiento y Venta de Productos Químicos y de la Goma): Calle Consulado 262, entre Animas y Virtudes, Havana; tel. (7) 62-0581; fax (7) 62-9588; f. 1977; imports and exports spare parts for motor vehicles; Dir ARTURO J. CINTRA GÓNGORA.

Propes (Empresa Importadoro y Proveedora de Productos para la Pesca): Calle 22, No 2, esq. Calzada, Vedado, Havana; tel. (7) 830-3770; fax (7) 55-1729; e-mail pesmar@apropes.fishnavy.inf.cu; importer and distributor of a wide variety of equipment and accessories pertaining to the fishing industry; Dir-Gen. PEDRO BLAS ARTEAGA.

Quimimport (Empresa Cubana Importadora y Exportadora de Productos Químicos): Calle 23, No 55, entre Infanta y P, Apdo 6088, Vedado, Havana; tel. (7) 33-3394; fax (7) 33-3190; e-mail global@quimimport.infocex.cu; controls import and export of chemical products; Dir ARMANDO BARRERA MARTÍNEZ.

Suchel (Empresa de Jabonería y Perfumería): Calzada de Buenos Aires 353, esq. a Durege, Apdo 6359, Havana; tel. (7) 649-8008; fax (7) 649-5311; e-mail direccion@suchel.co.cu; f. 1977; imports materials for the detergent, perfumery and cosmetics industry, exports cosmetics, perfumes, hotel amenities and household products; Dir JOSÉ GARCÍA DÍAZ.

Tecnoazúcar (Empresa de Servicios Técnicos e Ingeniería para la Agro-industria Azucarera): Calle 12, No 310, entre 3 y 5, Miramar, Playa, Havana; tel. (7) 29-5441; fax (7) 33-1218; e-mail promocion@tecnoazucar.cu; internet www.tecnoazucar.cubasi.cu; imports machinery and equipment for the sugar industry, provides technical and engineering assistance for the sugar industry; exports sugar-machinery equipment and spare parts; provides engineering and technical assistance services for sugar-cane by-product industry; Dir-Gen. HÉCTOR COMPANIONI ECHEMENDÍA.

Tecnoimport (Empresa Importadora y Exportadora de Productos Técnicos): Edif. La Marina, Avda del Puerto 102, entre Justiz y Obrapía, Habana Vieja, Havana; tel. (7) 861-5552; fax (7) 66-9777; e-mail celeste@ti.gae.com.cu; f. 1968; imports technical products; Dir ADEL IZQUIERDO RODRÍGUEZ.

Tecnotex (Empresa Cubana Exportadora e Importadora de Servicios, Artículos y Productos Técnicos Especializados): Avda 47, No 3419, Playa, Havana; tel. (7) 861-3536; fax (7) 66-6270; e-mail ailede@tecnotex.qae.com.cu; f. 1983; imports specialized technical and radiocommunications equipment, exports outdoor equipment and geodetic networks; Dir RENÉ ROJAS RODRÍGUEZ.

Tractoimport (Empresa Central de Abastecimiento y Venta de Maquinaria Agrícola y sus Piezas de Repuesto): Avda Rancho Boyeros y Calle 100, Apdo 7007, Havana; tel. (7) 45-2166; fax (7) 267-0786; e-mail direccion@tractoimport.co.cu; f. 1962; import of tractors and agricultural equipment; also exports pumps and agricultural implements; Dir-Gen. ABDEL GARCÍA GONZÁLEZ.

Transimport (Empresa Central de Abastecimiento y Venta de Equipos de Transporte Pesados y sus Piezas): Calle 102 y Avda 63, Marianao, Apdo 6665, 11500 Havana; tel. (7) 260-0329; fax (7) 267-9050; e-mail direccion@transimport.co.cu; f. 1968; controls import and export of vehicles and transportation equipment; Dir-Gen. JUAN CARLOS TASSÉ BELLOT.

UTILITIES

Electricity

Unión Nacional Eléctrica (UNE): Havana; public utility; Dir-Gen. Juan Antonio Pruna.

Water

Aguas de la Habana: Fomento y Recreo, Rpto Palatino, Cerro, Havana; e-mail jmtura@ahabana.co.cu; water supplier; Dir-Gen. Jose María Tura Torres.

Instituto Nacional de Recursos Hidraulicos (INRH) (National Water Resources Institute): Calle Humbolt, No 106, esq. a P, Plaza de la Revolución, Vedado, Havana; tel. (7) 836-5571; e-mail webmaster@hidro.cu; internet www.hidro.cu; regulatory body; Pres. René Mesa Villafaña.

TRADE UNIONS

All workers have the right to become members of a national trade union according to their industry and economic branch.

The following industries and labour branches have their own unions: Agriculture, Chemistry and Energetics, Civil Workers of the Revolutionary Armed Forces, Commerce and Gastronomy, Communications, Construction, Culture, Defence, Education and Science, Food, Forestry, Health, Light Industry, Merchant Marine, Mining and Metallurgy, Ports and Fishing, Public Administration, Sugar, Tobacco and Transport.

Central de Trabajadores de Cuba (CTC) (Confederation of Cuban Workers): Palacio de los Trabajadores, San Carlos y Peñalver, Havana; tel. (7) 78-4901; fax (7) 55-5927; e-mail digital@trabaja.cip.cu; internet www.trabajadores.cubaweb.cu; f. 1939; affiliated to WFTU and CPUSTAL; 19 national trade unions affiliated; Gen. Sec. Pedro Ross Leal; 2,767,806 mems (1996).

Transport

The Ministry of Transportation controls all public transport.

RAILWAYS

The total length of railways in 1998 was 14,331 km, of which 9,638 km were used by the sugar industry. The remaining 4,520 km were public service railways operated by Ferrocarriles de Cuba. All railways were nationalized in 1960. In 2001 Cuba signed an agreement with Mexico for the maintenance and repair of rolling stock.

Ferrocarriles de Cuba: Edif. Estación Central, Egido y Arsenal, Havana; tel. (7) 70-1076; fax (7) 33-1489; f. 1960; operates public services; Dir-Gen. Fernando Pérez López; divided as follows:

División Occidente: serves Pinar del Río, Ciudad de la Habana, Havana Province and Matanzas.

División Centro: serves Villa Clara, Cienfuegos and Sancti Spíritus.

División Centro-Este: serves Camagüey, Ciego de Avila and Tunas.

División Oriente: serves Santiago de Cuba, Granma, Guantánamo and Holguín.

División Camilo Cienfuegos: serves part of Havana Province and Matanzas.

ROADS

In 1999 there were an estimated 60,858 km of roads, of which 4,353 km were highways or main roads. The Central Highway runs from Pinar del Río in the west to Santiago, for a length of 1,144 km. In addition to this paved highway, there are a number of secondary and 'farm-to-market' roads. A small proportion of these secondary roads is paved, but many can be used by motor vehicles only during the dry season.

SHIPPING

Cuba's principal ports are Havana (which handles 60% of all cargo), Santiago de Cuba, Cienfuegos, Nuevitas, Matanzas, Antilla, Guayabal and Mariel. Maritime transport has developed rapidly since 1959, and at 31 December 2006 Cuba had a merchant fleet of 68 ships (with a combined total displacement of 64,674 grt). In late 2007 the Government announced expenditure of US $180m. on modernization of the country's ports in 2007–10.

Coral Container Lines, SA: Calle Oficios No 170, 1°, Habana Vieja, Havana; tel. (7) 67-0854; fax (7) 67-0850; e-mail caribe@coral.com.cu; f. 1994; liner services to Europe, Canada, Brazil and Mexico; 11 containers; Chair. and Man. Dir Evelio González González.

Empresa Consignataria Mambisa: San José No 65, entre Prado y Zulueta, Habana Vieja, Havana; tel. (7) 862-2061; fax (7) 33-8111; e-mail mercedes@mambisa.transnet.cu; shipping agent, bunker suppliers; Man. Dir Mercedes Pérez Newhall.

Empresa Cubana de Fletes (Cuflet): Calle Oficios No 170, entre Teniente Rey y Amargura, Apdo 6755, Havana; tel. (7) 61-2604; e-mail antares@antares.transnet.cu; freight agents for Cuban cargo; Man. Dir Carlos Sánchez Perdomo.

Empresa de Navegación Caribe (Navecaribe): Calle San Martín, No 65, 4°, entre Agramonte y Pasco de Martí, Habana Vieja, Havana; tel. (7) 61-8611; fax (7) 33-8564; e-mail enccom@transnet.cu; f. 1966; operates Cuban coastal fleet; Dir Ramón Durán Suárez.

Empresa de Navegación Mambisa: San Ignacio No 104, Apdo 543, Havana; tel. (7) 869-7901; fax (7) 61-0044; operates dry cargo, reefer and bulk carrier vessels; Gen. Man. Gumersindo González Feliú.

Naviera del Caribe (Carimar): Calle Oficios No 170, entre Amargura y Teniente Rey, 3°, Habana Vieja, Havana; tel. (7) 67-0925; fax (7) 204-8627; e-mail ftarrau@coral.com.cu.

Naviera Frigorífica Marítima (Friomar): 5a Avda y 240, Barlovento, Playa, Havana; tel. (7) 209-8171; fax (7) 204-5864; e-mail friocom@fishnavy.inf.cu; specializes in shipping of refrigerated cargo; Dir Jorge Fernández.

Naviera Mar América: 5a Avda y 246, Edif. No 3, 1°, Barlovento, Playa, Havana; tel. (7) 209-8076; fax (7) 204-8889; e-mail nubia@maramerica.fishnavy.inf.eu.

Naviera Petrocost: 5a Avda y 246, Barlovento, Playa, Havana; tel. (7) 209-8067; fax (7) 204-5113; e-mail aleida@petrocost.fishnavy.inf.cu; transports liquid cargo to domestic and international destinations.

Naviera Poseidon: 5a Avda y 246, Edif. No 3, 2°, Barlovento, Playa, Havana; tel. (7) 209-8073; fax (7) 204-8627; e-mail yepe@poseidon.fishnavy.inf.cu.

Nexus Reefer: 5a Avda y 246, Edif. No 7, 1°, Barlovento, Playa, Havana; tel. (7) 204-8205; fax (7) 204-8490; e-mail sandra@antares.fishnavy.inf.cu; merchant reefer ships; Gen. Dir Quirino L. Gutiérrez López.

CIVIL AVIATION

There are a total of 21 civilian airports, with 11 international airports, including Havana, Santiago de Cuba, Camagüey, Varadero and Holguín. Abel Santamaría International Airport opened in Villa Clara in early 2001. In January 2003 the King's Gardens International Airport in Cayo Coco was opened. The airport formed part of a new tourist 'offshore' centre. The international airports were all upgraded and expanded during the 1990s and a third terminal was constructed at the José Martí International Airport in Havana. In 2001 three North American airlines were permitted to commence direct flights from Miami and New York to Havana. A programme of improvements to five of the country's international airports was announced by the Government in late 2007.

Aerocaribbean: Calle 23, No 64, esq. P, Vedado, Havana; tel. (7) 832-7584; fax (7) 336-5016; e-mail reserva@cacsa.avianet.cu; internet www.aero-caribbean.com; f. 1982; international and domestic scheduled and charter services; Chair. Julián Alvarez Infiesta.

Aerogaviota: Avda 47, No 2814, entre 28 y 34, Rpto Kolhy, Havana; tel. (7) 203-0668; fax (7) 204-2621; e-mail vpcom@aerogaviota.avianet.cu; f. 1994; operated by Cuban air force.

Empresa Consolidada Cubana de Aviación (Cubana): Aeropuerto Internacional José Martí, Terminal 1, Avda Rancho Boyeros, Havana; tel. (7) 266-4644; fax (7) 33-4056; e-mail pax@avianet.cu; internet www.cubana.co.cu; f. 1929; international services to North America, Central America, the Caribbean, South America and Europe; internal services from Havana to 14 other cities; Pres. Ricardo Santillán Miranda.

Instituto de Aeronáutica Civil de Cuba (IACC): Calle 23, No 64, Plaza de la Revolución, Vedado, Havana; tel. (7) 33-4949; fax (7) 33-4553; e-mail iacc@avianet.cu; internet www.cubagob.cu/des_eco/iacc/home.htm; f. 1985; Pres. Rogelio Acevedo González.

Tourism

Tourism began to develop after 1977, with the easing of travel restrictions by the USA, and Cuba subsequently attracted European tourists. In 2006 the number of hotel rooms had reached 46,704. In 2005 receipts from tourism totalled an estimated US $1,920m. Tourist arrivals stood at 2,220,567 in 2006, a slight decrease from the 2,319,334 recorded in 2005.

Cubanacán: Calle 23, No 156, entre O y P, Vedado, 10400 Havana; tel. (7) 833-4090; fax (7) 22-8382; e-mail com_electronic@cubanacan.cyt.cu; internet www.cubanacan.cu; f. 1987; Pres. Manuel Vila.

Empresa de Turismo Internacional (Cubatur): Calle F, No 157, entre Calzada y Novena, Vedado, Havana; tel. (7) 835-4155; fax (7) 836-3170; e-mail casamatriz@cubatur.cu; internet www.cubatur.cu; f. 1968.

CYPRUS

Introductory Survey

Location, Climate, Language, Religion, Flag, Capital

The Republic of Cyprus is an island in the eastern Mediterranean Sea, about 100 km south of Turkey. The climate is mild, although snow falls in the mountainous south-west between December and March. Temperatures in Nicosia are generally between 5°C (41°F) and 36°C (97°F). About 75% of the population speak Greek and almost all of the remainder Turkish. The Greek-speaking community is overwhelmingly Christian, and nearly all Greek Cypriots adhere to the Orthodox Church of Cyprus, while most of the Turkish Cypriots are Muslims. The national flag of the Republic of Cyprus (proportions 3 by 5) is white, with a gold map of Cyprus, above two crossed green olive branches, in the centre. The national flag of the 'Turkish Republic of Northern Cyprus' (proportions 2 by 3) has a white field, with a red crescent and star to the left of centre between two narrow horizontal bands of red towards the upper and lower edges. The capital is Nicosia.

Recent History

A guerrilla war against British rule in Cyprus was begun in 1955 by Greek Cypriots seeking unification (*Enosis*) with Greece. Their movement, the National Organization of Cypriot Combatants (EOKA), was led politically by Archbishop Makarios III, the head of the Greek Orthodox Church in Cyprus, and militarily by Gen. George Grivas. Archbishop Makarios was suspected by the British authorities of being involved in EOKA's campaign of violence, and in March 1956 he and three other *Enosis* leaders were deported. After a compromise agreement between the Greek and Turkish communities, a Constitution for an independent Cyprus was finalized in 1959. Makarios returned from exile and was elected the country's first President in December 1959. Cyprus became independent on 16 August 1960, although the United Kingdom retained sovereignty over two military base areas.

A constitutional dispute resulted in the withdrawal of the Turks from the central Government in December 1963, and there was serious intercommunal violence. In March 1964 a UN Peacekeeping Force in Cyprus (UNFICYP, see p. 88) was established to prevent a recurrence of fighting between the Greek and Turkish Cypriot communities. The effective exclusion of the Turks from political power led to the creation of separate administrative, judicial and legislative organs for the Turkish community. Discussions with a view to establishing a more equitable constitutional arrangement began in 1968; these continued intermittently for six years without achieving any agreement, as the Turks favoured some form of federation while the Greeks advocated a unitary state. Each community received military aid from its mother country, and officers of the Greek Army controlled the Greek Cypriot National Guard.

In 1971 Gen. Grivas returned to Cyprus, revived EOKA and began a terrorist campaign for *Enosis*, directed against the Makarios Government and apparently supported by the military regime in Greece. Grivas died in January 1974, and in June Makarios ordered a purge of EOKA sympathizers from the police, National Guard and civil service, accusing the Greek regime of subversion. On 15 July Makarios was deposed in a military coup led by Greek officers of the National Guard, who appointed as President Nikos Sampson, an extremist Greek Cypriot politician and former EOKA militant. Makarios escaped from the island the following day and travelled to the United Kingdom. At the request of Rauf Denktaş, the Turkish Cypriot leader, the Turkish army intervened to protect the Turkish community and to prevent Greece from using its control of the National Guard to take over Cyprus. Turkish troops landed on 20 July and rapidly occupied the northern third of Cyprus, dividing the island along what became the Green Line (also known as the Attila Line), which runs from Morphou through Nicosia to Famagusta. Sampson resigned on 23 July, and Glavkos Klerides, the President of the House of Representatives, became acting Head of State. The military regime in Greece collapsed the same day. In December Makarios returned to Cyprus and resumed the presidency. However, the Turkish Cypriots established a de facto Government in the north, and in February 1975 declared a 'Turkish Federated State of Cyprus' ('TFSC'), with Denktaş as President.

Makarios died in August 1977. He was succeeded as President by Spyros Kyprianou, a former Minister of Foreign Affairs and the President of the House of Representatives since 1976. Following a government reorganization in September 1980, the powerful communist party, the Anorthotiko Komma Ergazomenou Laou (AKEL—Progressive Party of the Working People), withdrew its support from the ruling Dimokratiko Komma (DIKO—Democratic Party), and Kyprianou lost his overall majority in the legislature. At the next general election, held in May 1981, AKEL and the Dimokratikos Synagermos (DISY—Democratic Rally) each won 12 seats in the House. DIKO, however, won only eight seats, so the President remained dependent on the support of AKEL.

In the 'TFSC' a new Council of Ministers was formed in December 1978, under Mustafa Çağatay, a former minister belonging to the Ulusal Bırlık Partisi (UBP—National Unity Party). At elections held in June 1981 President Denktaş was returned to office, but his party, the UBP, lost its legislative majority, and the Government that was subsequently formed by Çağatay was defeated in December. In March 1982 Çağatay formed a coalition Government, comprising the UBP, the Demokratik Halk Partisi (Democratic People's Party) and the Türkiye Bırlık Partisi (Turkish Unity Party).

In September 1980 UN-sponsored intercommunal peace talks were resumed. The constitutional issue remained the main problem: the Turkish Cypriots demanded equal status for the two communities, with equal representation in government and strong links with the mother country, while the Greeks, although accepting the principle of an alternating presidency, favoured a strong central government and objected to any disproportionate representation for the Turkish community, which constituted less than 20% of the population. Discussions on a UN plan involving a federal council, an alternating presidency and the allocation of 70% of the island to the Greek community faltered in February 1982, when the Greek Prime Minister, Andreas Papandreou, proposed the withdrawal of all Greek and Turkish troops and the convening of an international conference rather than the continuation of intercommunal talks. Meanwhile, in April 1981 it was agreed to establish a Committee on Missing Persons in Cyprus, comprising one representative of each community and a representative of the International Committee of the Red Cross (ICRC), to investigate the fate of 1,619 Greek Cypriots and 803 Turkish Cypriots listed as missing since the 1974 invasion. In May 1983 the UN General Assembly voted in favour of the withdrawal of Turkish troops from Cyprus, whereupon Denktaş threatened to boycott any further intercommunal talks and to seek recognition for the 'TFSC' as a sovereign state; simultaneously it was announced that the Turkish lira was to replace the Cyprus pound as legal tender in the 'TFSC'.

On 15 November 1983 the 'TFSC' made a unilateral declaration of independence as the 'Turkish Republic of Northern Cyprus' ('TRNC'), with Denktaş as President. Çağatay subsequently resigned the premiership and as leader of the UBP, and an interim Government was formed in December under Nejat Konuk (Prime Minister of the 'TFSC' during 1976–78 and President of the Legislative Assembly from 1981). Like the 'TFSC', the 'TRNC' was recognized only by Turkey, and the declaration of independence was condemned by the UN Security Council. The 'TRNC' and Turkey established diplomatic relations in April 1984, and the 'TRNC' formally rejected UN proposals for a suspension of its declaration of independence prior to further talks.

During 1984 a 'TRNC' Constituent Assembly drafted a new Constitution, which was approved by 70% of voters at a referendum in May 1985. At a presidential election in the 'TRNC' on 9 June Denktaş was returned to office, with more than 70% of votes cast. A general election followed on 23 June, at which the UBP, led by Dr Derviş Eroğlu, won 24 of the 50 seats in the Legislative Assembly. In July Eroğlu became 'TRNC' Prime Minister, leading a coalition Government comprising the UBP and the Toplumcu Kurtuluş Partisi (TKP—Communal Liberation Party).

In February 1983 Kyprianou was returned to the Greek Cypriot presidency for a second term, taking 56.5% of the votes. In November 1985, following a debate on his leadership, the House of Representatives was dissolved. Legislative elections proceeded in December: Kyprianou's DIKO secured 16 seats in the chamber (which, under a constitutional amendment, had been enlarged to 56 Greek Cypriot deputies), while DISY, which won 19 seats, and AKEL, with 15, failed to reach the two-thirds' majority required to amend the Constitution and thus challenge the President's tenure of power. Kyprianou failed to secure a third presidential term in February 1988; the election was won at a second round of voting by Georghios Vassiliou, an economist who presented himself as an independent but was unofficially supported by AKEL and the Socialistiko Komma Kyprou EDEK (EDEK—EDEK Socialist Party of Cyprus). Vassiliou undertook to restore a multi-party National Council (originally convened by President Makarios) to address the Cyprus issue.

Settlement plans proposed by the UN Secretary-General in July 1985 and in April 1986 were rejected by the Turkish Cypriots and the Greek Cypriots, respectively. Further measures concerning the demilitarization of the island, reportedly proposed by the Greek Cypriot Government, were rejected by Denktaş, who maintained that negotiations on the establishment of a two-zone, federal republic should precede any demilitarization. In March 1988 the new Greek Cypriot President rejected various proposals submitted by Denktaş, via the UN, including a plan to form committees to study the possibilities of intercommunal co-operation. Following a meeting with the revived National Council in June, however, Vassiliou agreed to a proposal by the UN Secretary-General that he and Denktaş should resume intercommunal talks, without pre-conditions, in their capacity as the leaders of two communities. Denktaş also approved the proposal, and a UN-sponsored summit meeting between the Greek and Turkish Cypriot leaders took place in Geneva, Switzerland, in August. Vassiliou and Denktaş subsequently began direct negotiations, under UN auspices, in September. Despite resuming negotiations at the UN in February 1990, these were abandoned in March, chiefly because Denktaş demanded recognition of the right to self-determination for Turkish Cypriots.

In April 1988 Eroğlu resigned as 'TRNC' Prime Minister, following a disagreement between the UBP and its coalition partner (since September 1986), the Yeni Doğuş Partisi (New Dawn Party), which was demanding greater representation in the Government. At the request of Denktaş, Eroğlu formed a new Council of Ministers in May, comprising mainly UBP members but also including independents. In April 1990 Denktaş secured nearly 67% of the votes cast in an early presidential election. Eroğlu retained the office of Prime Minister, after the UBP won 34 of the 50 seats in the 'TRNC' Legislative Assembly at elections in May. (Following by-elections for 12 seats in October 1991, the UBP increased its representation in the Assembly to 45 members.)

In July 1990 the Government of Cyprus formally applied to join the European Community (EC, now European Union—EU, see p. 244). Denktaş condemned the application, on the grounds that the Turkish Cypriots had not been consulted, and stated that the action would prevent the resumption of intercommunal talks. In June 1993, none the less, the European Commission approved the eligibility of Cyprus for EC membership, although it insisted that the application should be linked to progress in the latest UN-sponsored talks concerning the island.

At the May 1991 elections for the Greek Cypriot seats in the House of Representatives, the conservative DISY, in alliance with the Komma Phileleftheron (Liberal Party), received 35.8% of the votes cast, thereby securing 20 of the 56 seats in the legislature. AKEL unexpectedly made the most significant gains, obtaining 30.6% of the votes and 18 seats.

Following unsuccessful attempts to promote the resumption of discussions between Vassiliou and Denktaş by the UN, the EC and the USA during 1990–91, the new UN Secretary-General, Dr Boutros Boutros-Ghali, made the resolution of the Cyprus problem a priority. UN envoys visited Cyprus, Turkey and Greece in February 1992, and in January and March Boutros-Ghali himself held separate meetings in New York, USA, with Vassiliou and Denktaş. However, no progress was achieved on the fundamental differences between the two sides concerning territory and displaced persons. In mid-1992 Boutros-Ghali conducted a second round of talks in New York with Vassiliou and Denktaş, subsequently involving direct discussions between the two leaders. The talks aimed to arrive at a draft settlement based on proposals by Boutros-Ghali and endorsed by UN Security Council Resolution 750, advocating 'uninterrupted negotiations' until a settlement was reached. Discussions centred on UN proposals for the demarcation of Greek Cypriot and Turkish Cypriot areas of administration under a federal structure. However, following a disclosure to the Turkish Cypriot press that the proposed area of Turkish administration was some 25% smaller than the 'TRNC', Denktaş asserted that the UN's territorial proposals were totally unacceptable to the 'TRNC' Government, while political opinion in the Greek Cypriot area was divided. The discussions ended in August, again without having achieved significant progress. A third round of UN-sponsored talks, which commenced in New York in late October, were adjourned in the following month.

At an election to the Greek Cypriot presidency in February 1993 the DISY leader, Glavkos Klerides, narrowly defeated the incumbent Vassiliou at a second round of voting. Vassiliou subsequently formed a new party, the Kinema ton Eleftheron Dimokraton (KED—Movement of Free Democrats). UN-sponsored negotiations were reconvened in New York in May, focusing on the Secretary-General's plan to introduce a series of what were termed 'confidence-building measures', which included the proposed reopening, under UN administration, of the international airport at Nicosia. The talks were abandoned in June, when the Turkish Cypriot negotiators declined to respond to the UN proposals.

In November 1993 Klerides and Andreas Papandreou, who had recently resumed the Greek premiership, agreed at a meeting in Athens that their countries would take joint decisions in negotiations for the settlement of the Cyprus problem. The two leaders also agreed on a common defence doctrine, whereby Greece was to provide Cyprus with a guarantee of air, land and naval protection.

An early general election was held in the 'TRNC' in December 1993, partly in response to increasing disagreement between President Denktaş and Prime Minister Eroğlu over the handling of the UN-sponsored peace talks. The UBP lost its majority in the Legislative Assembly, retaining only 17 of the 50 seats, and at the end of the month a coalition Government was formed by the Demokrat Parti (DP—Democrat Party), which had been supported by Denktaş, and the left-wing Cumhuriyetçi Türk Partisi (CTP—Republican Turkish Party). Together the DP and the CTP won 53.4% of the votes cast and 28 seats. The leader of the DP, Hakkı Atun (hitherto the Speaker of the Assembly), was appointed as Prime Minister of the new administration.

In February 1994, following the confirmation by both authorities of their acceptance, in principle, of the 'confidence-building measures', UN officials undertook 'proximity talks' separately with the Greek and Turkish Cypriot leaders. However, Denktaş considered that the proposals under discussion differed from the intention of the measures originally agreed, and therefore refused to accept the document that was presented to both sides in March. A report issued in May by Boutros-Ghali for consideration by the UN Security Council held the 'TRNC' authorities responsible for the breakdown of the process. In the following month the UN conducted negotiations to reclarify the measures. Denktaş accepted certain proposed amendments, including the withdrawal of Turkish Cypriot troops from the access road to Nicosia international airport, but no substantive progress was made.

In July 1994 the UN Security Council adopted Resolution 939, advocating a new initiative on the part of the Secretary-General to formulate a solution for peace, based on a single nationality, international identity and sovereignty. In response, in the following month the 'TRNC' Legislative Assembly approved measures seeking to co-ordinate future foreign and defence policies with those of Turkey, asserting that no peace solution based on the concept of a federation would be acceptable, and demanding political and sovereign status equal to that of Greek Cyprus.

The issue of Cyprus's bid to accede to the EU had greatly disrupted the progress of negotiations. In June 1994 EU Heads of Government, meeting in Corfu, Greece, confirmed that Cyprus would be included in the next round of expansion of the Union. Denktaş remained adamant that any approach by the Greek Cypriots to the EU would prompt the 'TRNC' to seek further integration with Turkey. In early 1995 US officials commenced discussions with the two sides in an attempt to break the deadlock: while Denktaş insisted that the 'TRNC' would oppose

Cyprus's application for EU membership until a settlement for the island had been reached, the Greek Cypriot Government demanded 'TRNC' acceptance of the application as a pre-condition to pursuing the talks. In March the EU agreed to consider Cyprus's membership application without discrimination based on the progress (or otherwise) of settlement talks. This was ratified in June by a meeting of the EU-Cyprus Association Council, at which it was agreed to commence pre-accession dialogue.

Meanwhile, in February 1995 Hakkı Atun and the 'TRNC' Government resigned, following serious disagreements with Denktaş regarding the redistribution of Greek Cypriot-owned housing and land. However, the UBP failed to negotiate the formation of a new coalition, and in the following month Atun was reappointed Prime Minister. At a presidential election held on 15 April, Denktaş received a mere 40.4% of votes cast in the first poll, only securing a conclusive victory against Eroğlu, with 62.5% of the votes, at a second round on 22 April. Following protracted inter-party negotiations, a new coalition of the DP and the CTP, under Atun's premiership, took office in June.

In August 1995 the 'TRNC' Legislative Assembly adopted legislation concerning compensation for Greek-owned property in the north. In October Özker Özgür resigned as Deputy Prime Minister, reportedly owing to his disapproval of Denktaş's uncompromising attitude regarding the Cyprus issue. In the following month Atun submitted the resignation of his entire Government, after Denktaş rejected a new list of CTP ministers. A new DP-CTP coalition, again under Atun's leadership and with Mehmet Ali Talat (of the CTP) replacing Özgür as Deputy Prime Minister, took office in December.

Elections for the Greek Cypriot seats in the House of Representatives on 26 May 1996 produced little change in the composition of the legislature. DISY retained 20 seats, with 34.5% of the votes cast; AKEL took 19 seats, an increase of one, with 33.0% of the votes, while DIKO secured 10 seats, a loss of one, with 16.4%. Persistent policy differences within the 'TRNC' coalition caused the Government to resign in July, and in August the DP and the UBP signed a coalition agreement whereby UBP leader Eroğlu became Prime Minister of a new administration.

Meanwhile, in April 1996 the UN Security Council endorsed a US initiative (announced in late 1995) to promote a federal-based settlement for Cyprus. In May the United Kingdom appointed Sir David Hannay, a former Permanent Representative to the UN, as its first Special Representative to Cyprus. In June, in advance of a visit to the island by the UN Secretary-General's newly appointed Special Representative in Cyprus, Han Sung-Joo, Boutros-Ghali held discussions, separately, with Denktaş and Klerides, with the intention of generating support for future direct bilateral negotiations. However, international mediation efforts were diminished by a sharp escalation in intercommunal hostilities. In October a UN-mediated military dialogue, involving senior commanders of the Greek and Turkish Cypriot armed forces, was initiated to consider proposals for reducing intercommunal tension. Further mediation efforts were undermined in November by alleged violations of Greek Cypriot airspace by Turkish military aircraft, as well as by Greek Cypriot efforts to prevent tourists from visiting the 'TRNC' and the continued opposition of the 'TRNC' to the Cypriot application to join the EU.

In December 1996 the European Court of Human Rights (ECHR) ruled that Turkey was in breach of the European Convention on Human Rights by denying a woman access to her property as a result of its occupation in the north. The ruling implicated Turkey as fully responsible for activities in the 'TRNC' and for the consequences of the military action in 1974.

In January 1997 an agreement signed by the Greek Cypriot Government and Russia regarding the purchase of an advanced anti-aircraft missile system became the focus of political hostilities between the Greek and Turkish Cypriots, and the cause of considerable international concern. The purchase agreement was condemned by the 'TRNC' as an 'act of aggression', and the potential for conflict over the issue increased when Turkey declared its willingness to use military force to prevent the deployment of the system. Greece in turn reiterated that it would defend Cyprus against any Turkish attack. US mediators sought urgent meetings with the Cypriot leaders, and were assured by the Greek Cypriot Government that deployment would not take place until May 1998 at the earliest and would be dependent upon the progress made in talks. In addition, both sides approved UN-supported measures to reduce tension in the border area, although the Greek Cypriots rejected a US proposal for a ban on all military flights over the island. Later in January 1997 Turkey threatened to establish air and naval bases in the 'TRNC' if Greece continued to promote plans for the establishment of military facilities in the Greek Cypriot zone, and at the end of the month Turkish military vessels arrived in the 'TRNC' port of Famagusta. Turkey and the 'TRNC' also declared their commitment to a joint military concept whereby any attack on the 'TRNC' would be deemed a violation against Turkey.

In June 1997, following proximity talks between Klerides and Denktaş that had begun in March, the Cypriot leaders agreed to take part in direct UN-sponsored negotiations in the USA in July, under the chairmanship of the UN Special Envoy for Cyprus, Dr Diego Córdovez. The discussions took place under the auspices of the new UN Secretary-General, Kofi Annan, and with the participation of Richard Holbrooke, the newly appointed US Special Envoy to Cyprus. Further private direct talks took place in Nicosia at the end of July, when agreement was reached to co-operate in efforts to trace persons missing since the hostilities in 1974. However, a second formal round of UN-sponsored negotiations, convened in Switzerland in August 1997, collapsed without agreement, after Denktaş demanded the suspension of Cyprus's application for EU membership, to which he remained opposed on the grounds that accession negotiations, scheduled to begin in 1998, were to be conducted with the Greek Cypriot Government, ignoring the issue of Turkish Cypriot sovereignty. (The EU had in the previous month formally agreed that Cyprus would be included in the next phase of the organization's enlargement.) An agreement by the 'TRNC' and Turkey, prior to the latest round of UN-sponsored talks, to create a joint committee to co-ordinate the partial integration of the 'TRNC' into Turkey was widely regarded as a response to the EU's decision to negotiate future membership with the Greek Cypriot Government while excluding Turkey from EU expansion. Although negotiations concerning security issues were held under UN auspices in Nicosia in September, US and UN efforts during October and November to promote progress in the talks, including visits to Cyprus by both Holbrooke and Córdovez, achieved little success, partly owing to the imminence of the Greek Cypriot presidential election. Denktaş rejected Holbrooke's attempts to persuade the 'TRNC' to join the Greek Cypriot Government at EU accession talks in 1998, insisting on EU recognition of the 'TRNC' and the simultaneous admission of Turkey to EU membership. Meanwhile, tension remained high, as Turkish fighter aircraft violated Greek Cypriot airspace in October 1997 in retaliation for Greek participation in Greek Cypriot military manoeuvres.

In November 1997 DIKO voted to leave the Greek Cypriot ruling coalition in advance of the presidential election, and the party's five government members resigned their posts. On 15 February 1998, at the second round of voting in the presidential election, Klerides defeated Georghios Iacovou, an independent candidate supported by AKEL and DIKO, securing 50.8% of the votes cast. A new coalition Government, composed of members of DISY, EDEK, the Enomeni Dimokrates (EDI—United Democrats—formed in 1996 by a merger of Vassiliou's KED and the Ananeotiko Dimokratiko Socialistiko Kinema) and independents, was sworn in at the end of the month.

The Greek Cypriot Government began accession talks with the EU in March 1998, and in the following month Cyprus confirmed its application for associate membership of Western European Union (see p. 426). In May Holbrooke visited Cyprus and held discussions with Klerides and Denktaş, with the aim of relaunching formal negotiations. However, no progress was made; Holbrooke cited the principal obstacles as Denktaş's demands for recognition of the 'TRNC' and for the withdrawal of the Cypriot application to join the EU, and the decision of the EU further to delay Turkey's application for membership. In August Denktaş rejected a UN plan for the reunification of Cyprus, proposing instead a confederation of equal status; this was deemed unacceptable by Klerides on the grounds that it would legitimize the status of the 'TRNC'.

In June 1998 a number of Greek military aircraft landed at the Paphos airfield in southern Cyprus for the first time since the airfield's completion in January. Shortly afterwards Turkish military aircraft made reciprocal landings in the 'TRNC'. In July the Greek Cypriot Government condemned the arrival of Turkish military naval vessels and aircraft in the 'TRNC' for the celebrations of the anniversary of the Turkish invasion of the island. During the course of the year Turkish aircraft were accused of violating Greek Cypriot airspace on a number of occasions, and in October Turkish fighter planes allegedly harassed Greek military aircraft that were participating in joint exercises with Greek Cypriot forces. Earlier in the month, however, Denktaş had proposed a non-aggression treaty between the two sides. Joint Turkish-'TRNC' military exercises were held in November.

In December 1998 it was formally announced that the contentious Russian missile system would not be deployed in Cyprus, following diplomatic pressure from Greece, the EU (which threatened to suspend Cypriot accession talks if the deployment proceeded), the USA and the UN. The decision was also influenced by the adoption earlier in the month of two resolutions by the UN Security Council (both of which were dismissed by Denktaş): the first renewed the UNFICYP mandate and appealed for the resumption of negotiations on reunification as a single sovereign state (apparently rejecting the 'TRNC' Government's proposed confederation), and the second expressed concern at the lack of progress towards a political settlement and advocated a phased reduction of military personnel and armaments on the island. The missiles were reportedly deployed in Crete, Greece, in March 1999, following the signature in February of an agreement by the Greek and Greek Cypriot Governments to the effect that Cyprus would own the missiles although they would be under Greek operational control. Klerides's reversal of policy regarding the missiles' deployment provoked intense domestic criticism, and prompted the withdrawal of EDEK (to which party the Minister of Defence belonged) from the Greek Cypriot governing coalition. (In 2000 Kinima Sosialdimokraton EDEK, KISOS—Movement of Social Democrats, was established as a successor movement to EDEK.)

Meanwhile, at legislative elections held in the 'TRNC' on 6 December 1998 the UBP increased its representation to 24 seats (from 16 in 1993), while the DP held only 13 seats. The TKP won seven seats and the CTP the remaining six. At the end of the month a new UBP-TKP Council of Ministers received presidential approval. Eroğlu remained as Prime Minister, and the TKP leader, Mustafa Akıncı, became Minister of State and Deputy Prime Minister.

In June 1999 the UN Security Council, extending the mandate of UNFICYP for a further six months, adopted a resolution urging the Greek and Turkish Cypriot authorities to participate in UN-sponsored negotiations in late 1999 without preconditions or proscribed issues. In December Denktaş and Klerides attended proximity talks in New York under the auspices of the UN, at which Annan acted as a mediator; however, the indirect talks were undermined by a decision taken that month at a summit meeting of EU Heads of State and Government in Helsinki, Finland, that a political settlement for Cyprus was not a precondition to the accession of the Greek Cypriot Government to the EU. This decision was widely acknowledged to be a response to Greece's reversal of its opposition to Turkey's EU membership application, and the summit thus accorded Turkey formal status as a candidate for EU membership. Although Denktaş criticized the EU decision on Cyprus's accession, a second round of UN-mediated proximity talks began in Geneva in January 2000, but again ended without any substantive progress.

A first round of presidential voting in the 'TRNC', conducted on 15 April 2000, was contested by eight candidates. Denktaş won 43.7% of the votes cast, thus failing to secure the majority necessary for outright victory. Denktaş and his closest contender, Eroğlu (who had received 30.1% at the first round), were to have contested a second round of polling, but on 19 April Eroğlu announced his withdrawal from the process and Denktaş was consequently proclaimed President.

In mid-June 2000 the UN Security Council extended the mandate of UNFICYP for a further six months. Resolution 1303 notably excluded any reference to the authority of the 'TRNC', citing only the Government of Cyprus, and at the end of the month the 'TRNC' instituted a number of retaliatory measures against UNFICYP, including measures to impede the movement of UN forces and new tariffs for UN vehicles and for the use of utilities supplied by the north. 'TRNC' and Turkish forces also crossed into the buffer zone and established a checkpoint at a village inhabited by Greek Cypriots.

A third round of proximity talks (mediated by the UN Special Adviser on Cyprus, Alvaro de Soto, and focusing on 'core' issues of territory, constitutional arrangements, property rights and guarantees) took place in Geneva in July–August 2000. Again, there were no direct exchanges between the Greek Cypriot and Turkish Cypriot representatives, and the talks ended without progress. A further round of indirect negotiations began in New York in September. Klerides boycotted the early stages of the talks, in protest at a statement in which Annan had, in the view of the Greek Cypriots, implied that the 'TRNC' was equal in authority to the internationally recognized Cypriot Government; however, the Greek Cypriot leader resumed attendance after receiving assurances that the UN would act in accordance with earlier Security Council resolutions on the Cyprus issue. Nevertheless, the Greek and Turkish Cypriots remained apparently irreconcilable on the issue of a future structure for Cyprus, with the former advocating a reunified, bi-communal federation and the latter a looser confederation based on equal sovereignty. A fifth round of UN-sponsored proximity talks was convened in Geneva in November. After separate meetings with both Klerides and Denktaş, Annan expressed his view that the negotiations had progressed, and both leaders were invited to further discussions in January 2001. Later in November 2000, however, Denktaş stated that he would not return to the talks until such time as the 'TRNC' was accorded international recognition. His decision, taken with the support of the Government of Turkey, apparently reflected anger in the 'TRNC' that the UN Secretary-General had emphasized that any agreement on Cyprus must be based on the premise of a single sovereign entity, and in Turkey that the European Commission had, in a draft partnership agreement published earlier in November, stipulated among preconditions for Turkish admission to the EU Turkey's willingness to promote a settlement for Cyprus based on UN resolutions. De Soto visited Cyprus in December in an effort to foster a resumption of dialogue, but Denktaş reiterated that the 'TRNC' would not take part in any further talks unless its sovereignty was recognized; he warned, furthermore, that in the absence of such recognition UNFICYP would no longer be welcome in the 'TRNC'. In the same month the UN Security Council adopted Resolution 1331, extending the mandate of the force for a further six-month period; the resolution urged the 'TRNC' to revoke the restrictive measures imposed against UNFICYP in June, noting that these had undermined the operational effectiveness of the peace-keeping force.

In February 2001 Denktaş reiterated his determination to eschew further UN proximity talks while the international community continued to regard the Greek Cypriot Government as the legitimate Government for the whole of Cyprus. He also criticized the EU for making a settlement to the Cyprus problem a condition for further progress on Turkey's application for EU membership. The divide between the two communities was further aggravated by an ECHR judgment in May that found Turkey guilty of extensive violations of human rights arising from its 1974 invasion and occupation of Northern Cyprus. Whereas the Greek Cypriot Government welcomed the ruling, Denktaş claimed that it justified his refusal to participate in further talks.

At elections for the Greek Cypriot members of the House of Representatives on 27 May 2001, AKEL secured a narrow victory over DISY, taking 20 seats (with 34.7% of the votes cast), compared with the latter's 19 (34.0%). DIKO held nine seats (14.8%), one fewer than in 1996. In June the AKEL leader, Demetris Christofias, was elected as the new President of the legislature, defeating the DISY leader, Nicos Anastasiades, with support from the DIKO deputies.

The governing coalition of the 'TRNC' collapsed in late May 2001, following disagreement between the UBP and the TKP on the issue of whether to rejoin talks on the future status of the island. In June the UBP and the DP agreed to form a new coalition administration, with Eroğlu continuing as Prime Minister. The DP leader, Salih Coşar, became Minister of State and Deputy Prime Minister in a Government that was expected to be more supportive than its predecessor of President Denktaş's policy on the Cyprus question.

In early December 2001 Presidents Klerides and Denktaş met briefly for the first time in four years; following the meeting, Alvaro de Soto stated that the two leaders had agreed to recommence direct talks on the future of the island in January 2002 'without preconditions'. On 5 December 2001 Klerides became the first Greek Cypriot leader to visit the Turkish Cypriot northern sector since the island's partition, when he travelled to the 'TRNC' to meet with Denktaş. The resumption of contacts was broadly welcomed in the 'TRNC', but Greek Cypriot opposition parties and representatives of Greek Cypriots whose relatives had been 'missing' since the invasion, or who had been forced from their homes in the north, were critical of Klerides's visit. Denktaş made a reciprocal visit to meet with his Greek Cypriot counterpart at the end of December. Formal direct negotiations commenced on 21 January 2002, with a view to reaching agreement by the end of June. The discussions were mediated by de Soto, who indicated that their focus would be a power-sharing arrangement of Greek and Turkish regions within a proposed federal Cyprus. None the less, the political positions of the two parties remained apparently irreconcilable: the 'TRNC' continued to promote a solution based around a confederation of two separate states, while the Greek Cypriots sought a united island with a high degree of communal autonomy. In May, amid growing pessimism regarding the progress of the talks, Annan travelled to Cyprus, where he met separately with Klerides and Denktaş in an unsuccessful attempt to encourage a compromise before the scheduled date.

Talks continued during 2002. In September Annan hosted Klerides and Denktaş in Paris, France, with de Soto in attendance. A further such meeting was held in New York in October, but was disrupted when Denktaş underwent emergency heart surgery while there. On 11 November the UN presented a comprehensive new peace plan (which became known as the 'Annan Plan') to Klerides and Denktaş. The plan envisaged the creation of a common federal state with two equal components, but a single international legal personality. The state would have a joint six-member presidential council, with members holding a 10-month rotating presidency, and a bicameral legislature, comprising a 48-member senate with an equal number of deputies from both sides, and a 48-member proportionally composed chamber of deputies. A common supreme court would have three judges from both sides, and three non-Cypriots. Dispossessed property owners would receive compensation, and the 'TRNC' would return territory to the Greek side, reducing the former's share of the island from 36% to 28.5%. Cyprus would be demilitarized, but Greece and Turkey would each be permitted to station up to 9,999 troops on the island, and UNFICYP would retain its presence. The two leaders initially agreed to use the plan as a basis for future negotiations, but in early December Denktaş rejected a revised version of it.

The progress of EU accession talks meant that the need for a settlement to the Cyprus problem was increasingly urgent. At the EU summit held in Copenhagen, Denmark, in mid-December 2002, Cyprus was formally invited to join the EU in 2004. However, it was reiterated that if no peace agreement was forthcoming, only the Greek part of the island would be admitted. Meanwhile, Greece, which assumed the presidency of the EU in January 2003, had earlier emphasized that it would veto the admission of other EU candidate countries if Cyprus was not admitted at the next round of expansion. Turkey, for its part, had warned in November 2001 that it might annex northern Cyprus if a divided island under a Greek Cypriot government was admitted to the EU.

In the Greek Cypriot presidential election held on 16 February 2003 the DIKO leader, Tassos Papadopoulos (who was also supported by AKEL), was elected outright, with 51.5% of the votes cast. Klerides, who had sought a renewal of his mandate for 16 months, in order to oversee the peace process and Cyprus's accession, won 38.8% of the votes. Papadopoulos appointed a new Government, which for the first time included four AKEL representatives. There were concerns that Papadopoulos's victory would delay the implementation of the UN peace plan, as he was widely believed to favour a less compromising approach towards the Turkish Cypriots than his predecessor. The new President immediately demanded changes to the Annan Plan that would allow all Greek Cypriot refugees to return to the north. Annan extended, to 10 March, a deadline previously set at 28 February for agreement on the island's future, which would thus allow a unified Cyprus to accede to the EU, and Papadopoulos and Denktaş held discussions in The Hague, Netherlands. However, the new deadline passed without agreement: Denktaş denounced the Annan Plan as unacceptable, and refused to continue discussions. The office of the UN Secretary-General's Special Adviser on Cyprus was subsequently closed down. In early April the Greek Cypriot Government rejected an offer by Denktaş to return the eastern town of Varosha, stating that the UN plan should be the principal basis for negotiation.

On 16 April 2003 President Papadopoulos signed Cyprus's Treaty of Accession to the EU in Athens, thereby confirming that Cyprus would join the organization on 1 May 2004. Under the terms of the treaty, only the Greek Cypriot south was to be admitted to the EU in the absence of a settlement on the divided status of the island. Later that month the Turkish Cypriot authorities announced that they would open the 'TRNC' border to the Greek part of the island for the first time in 30 years, allowing Turkish Cypriots to visit that area for one-day trips and permitting Greek Cypriots to visit the north for up to three nights. The Greek Cypriot Government was hesitant in welcoming the move, stating that the opening of the border should not be regarded as a substitute for a settlement in accordance with UN resolutions. Popular approval of the decision in both the north and south of the island was evident, however, and by July more than 900,000 people were reported to have crossed the border. However, the issue of the ownership of properties abandoned as a consequence of the 1974 division of the island remained largely unresolved. In June 2003 the UN Security Council extended the mandate of UNFICYP for a further six months. The Treaty of Accession was unanimously approved by the Greek Cypriot House of Representatives on 14 July and ratified by Papadopoulos on 28 July. In the same month Denktaş again declared that the UN plan for the reunification of Cyprus was unacceptable.

At legislative elections held in the 'TRNC' on 14 December 2003, the pro-EU CTP won the largest share of the votes, with 35.2%, narrowly defeating the ruling UBP, which secured 32.9%. However, parliamentary seats were distributed equally between pro-EU parties and parties that remained opposed to the reunification of Cyprus under the terms of the Annan Plan; thus the election results were inconclusive with regard to the issue of EU accession. On 16 December Eroğlu resigned and Talat was appointed as the new Turkish Cypriot Prime Minister. At the beginning of January 2004 Talat agreed to enter into a coalition with the DP (led by the President's son, Serdar Denktaş), despite differences of opinion between the CTP and the DP over the reunification issue. On 13 January President Denktaş approved a new coalition Government nominated by Talat, comprising six CTP ministers and four DP ministers. Serdar Denktaş was appointed Deputy Prime Minister and Minister of Foreign Affairs in the new administration.

The formation of a new Turkish Cypriot Government gave renewed impetus to the search for a political settlement. In early February 2004, under the aegis of Secretary-General Annan, Denktaş and Papadopoulos attended a further round of discussions in New York. On 13 February agreement was reached for the resumption of bilateral negotiations based on the Annan Plan (providing for a federation of two politically equal states), with a schedule for reaching a settlement prior to the island's accession to the EU on 1 May. In late February Papadopoulos and Denktaş resumed UN-sponsored negotiations in Nicosia, in an effort to finalize the details of a settlement, which was to be submitted for approval by both the Greek and Turkish Cypriot communities at concurrent referendums scheduled for 24 April. However, intensive discussions between the two leaders failed to resolve the remaining issues of disagreement and were relocated to Bürgenstock, Switzerland, in late March (where the Greek and Turkish Prime Ministers also joined the process). Denktaş, who continued to reject the UN plan, refused to continue his participation in the negotiations and was replaced by Talat as head of the Turkish Cypriot delegation. At the end of March Annan presented a finalized version of the peace plan, which was accepted by the 'TRNC' leadership and by the Greek and Turkish Governments; however, Papadopoulos (in a reversal of previous Greek Cypriot government policy) campaigned against this final settlement, which he strongly opposed on the grounds that it provided for the establishment of a recognized Turkish Cypriot state. (The Greek Cypriot Minister of Communications, Kikis Kazamias, resigned in protest at Papadopoulos's stance on the reunification plan.) At the referendums held on 24 April the Annan Plan was endorsed by Turkish Cypriots by 64.9% of votes cast, but rejected by Greek Cypriots by 75.8% of the votes. Consequently, only the Greek Cypriot-administered part of the island was admitted to the EU on 1 May; the *acquis communautaire* was suspended in the 'TRNC', pending a future political settlement. Following appeals by Talat, the EU proposed measures for the resumption of direct trade between the two sides of the island, and consequently for the export of commodities produced in the 'TRNC' to EU member states.

At the end of April 2004 the 'TRNC' coalition Government lost its parliamentary majority, after two DP deputies withdrew their support and resigned from the Legislative Assembly. In May Papadopoulos appointed replacements for Kazamias and Iacovos Keravnos, who had resigned from the post of Greek Cypriot Minister of Finance to become Cyprus's first EU Commissioner. The 'TRNC' relaxed documentation requirements concerning travel to Turkish-administered Cyprus in that month, and ended time restrictions on visits by Greek Cypriots in June. In October the UN Security Council renewed the mandate of UNFICYP until June 2005, but (despite opposition from the Greek Cypriot community) significantly reduced the size of the contingent. On 20 October 2004 Talat tendered his resignation, following the failure of his lengthy efforts to form a new 'TRNC' coalition administration. On the following day Denktaş invited Eroğlu (as leader of UBP, the strongest party in the Legislative Assembly) to nominate a new government; at the end of the month, however, Eroğlu returned the mandate to the President, after being unable to secure sufficient support from other parliamentary parties. In November Denktaş redesignated Talat as Prime Minister, but he again failed to reach a coalition agreement and also returned the mandate later that month. Denktaş subsequently announced that early legislative elections would be conducted in the 'TRNC' on 20 February 2005, while Talat's incumbent Government remained in office in an interim capacity.

The EU's provisional invitation to Turkey, issued on 17 December 2004, to open accession negotiations in October 2005, again focused international attention on the necessity of reaching a political settlement in Cyprus. The Turkish Prime Minister, Reçep Tayyip Erdoğan, accepted a condition to extend Turkey's customs accord with the EU to cover the 10 new member states that had joined the organization in May 2004, including Cyprus; however, Erdoğan insisted that the protocol would not constitute official Turkish recognition of the authorities of Greek Cypriot-administered Cyprus, instead agreeing to a compromise arrangement whereby Turkey made a commitment for future recognition.

At the elections to the 'TRNC' Legislative Assembly on 20 February 2005 Talat's CTP secured 44.5% of votes cast and 24 of the 50 seats in the chamber (a gain of seven seats), while the UBP won 31.6% of the votes (19 seats). The CTP was thus obliged to seek a renewed parliamentary alliance with Serdar Denktaş's anti-reunification DP, which had secured 13.4% of the vote (six seats), to enable Talat to command a parliamentary majority. On 8 March President Denktaş approved a new 'TRNC' coalition Government (the composition of which was effectively unchanged from the previous administration), formed by Talat under a slightly amended power-sharing arrangement. However, Talat had been nominated by the CTP to contest the presidential election on 17 April, and it was expected that in the event that Talat was elected to the presidency, the Secretary-General of the CTP, Ferdi Sabit Soyer, would be designated premier. On 9 March Talat met with the Secretary-General of AKEL, Demetris Christofias, in the first discussions between 'TRNC' and Greek Cypriot leaders since the April 2004 referendums.

Nine candidates contested the 'TRNC' presidential election, held on 17 April 2005: Mehmet Ali Talat was elected outright, with 55.6% of votes cast, while Eroğlu, his closest rival, secured 22.7%. Talat, who pledged his commitment to achieving reunification of Cyprus, was inaugurated on 24 April. He duly nominated Soyer as Prime Minister, and a new CTP-DP coalition Government was approved by the Legislative Assembly on 28 April.

In April 2005 the ECHR issued a significant decision upholding a Greek Cypriot property claim against Turkey and rejecting the contention that the 'TRNC' authorities had provided adequate restitution for such claims by establishing a property commission. The case reflected Greek Cypriot concerns over increasing sales of property in the 'TRNC' involving houses and land owned legally by Greek Cypriots. Following Talat's election, prospects for a resumption of settlement talks were increased in May, when the Greek Cypriot envoy to the UN met officials from the organization in New York. In June, however, Annan reported to the Security Council that conditions were not favourable for a resumption of UN-sponsored talks, although he declared that the situation would be reviewed at a later date. The Greek Cypriot House of Representatives ratified the EU constitutional treaty at the end of June by 30 votes to 19, with one abstention. Meanwhile, in mid-June the UN Security Council renewed the mandate of UNFICYP for a further six months; in mid-December the mission was extended again, to mid-June 2006. In July 2005, pending an EU decision on the opening of accession negotiations in October, the Turkish Government signed the requisite customs protocol with Cyprus and the other nine new EU member states, but appended a declaration reaffirming that the accord did not constitute official recognition of Greek Cyprus. In September EU member states adopted a draft declaration stating that Turkish recognition of Cyprus was necessary to the accession process, but without stipulating a date for this (thereby posing no obstacle to the beginning of accession negotiations).

Following intensive debate between the various member states (see the chapter on Turkey), Turkey's accession negotiations with the EU were officially approved on 3 October.

Eroğlu resigned from the leadership of the UBP in November 2005. (His successor, Hüseyin Özgürgün, was elected in February 2006.) Later in November 2005 'TRNC' officials attempted to dismantle a significant roadblock in central Nicosia, but the Greek Cypriot authorities subsequently withdrew permission for its removal. In December the 'TRNC' Legislative Assembly approved provisions for Greek Cypriots to apply for the restitution of property, which the Government indicated were in accordance with a further ruling against Turkey by the ECHR later that month. Meanwhile, it was reported that the Greek Cypriot Government, as a member of the European Council, had prevented both the implementation of the proposed trade measures and the ratification of associated legislation granting €259m. in financial assistance to the 'TRNC'. The 'TRNC' authorities (insisting that the two issues be addressed as a single plan) protested that the EU had made the disbursement of aid conditional on the fulfilment of several demands by the Greek Cypriot administration, including the restoration of property.

In January 2006 the Turkish Government proposed a resumption of dialogue concerning the reunification of Cyprus, and presented an 'action plan' to the UN Secretary-General, under which Turkish ports and airports would be opened to Cypriot traffic in exchange for the ending of trade restrictions against the 'TRNC'. The Greek Cypriot Government immediately rejected the Turkish proposals, emphasizing that the Turkish authorities were required to open ports and airports to all EU member states by the end of 2006 as a condition to progress in the accession negotiations. The British Government supported the initiative; however, the arrival on the island of the British Secretary of State for Foreign and Commonwealth Affairs, Jack Straw, to discuss the proposals with both authorities prompted Greek Cypriot protests in Nicosia. Straw's mediation efforts ended in failure, after Papadopoulos refused to meet him, criticizing Straw's decision to visit Talat in his presidential office as an implicit recognition of the 'TRNC'. In February the EU finally approved an aid disbursement of €139m. for the 'TRNC', after agreeing to a Greek Cypriot demand that the financial assistance be addressed separately to the proposed trade measures; the Turkish Government (which had insisted that the provisions for direct trade be included) protested strongly at the EU decision.

On 21 May 2006 elections were conducted to the Greek Cypriot House of Representatives, resulting in no major changes to its composition. According to official results released by the Ministry of the Interior, AKEL and DISY both won 18 seats, attracting 31.1% and 30.3% of the votes cast, respectively, while DIKO secured 11 seats, with 17.9% of the ballot. Also securing representation were Kinima Sosialdimokraton EDEK (KISOS—Movement of Social Democrats), with five seats (8.9%), the Evropaiko Komma (Evro.Ko—European Party—which contested an election for the first time), with three seats (5.8%), and the Kinima Oikologoi Perivallontistoi (Cyprus Green Party—Movement of Ecologists and Environmentalists), with one seat (2.0%).

A reorganization of the Greek Cypriot Council of Ministers in June 2006 included the appointment of Yiorgos Lillikas of AKEL (previously responsible for commerce, industry and tourism) as Minister of Foreign Affairs and of an independent, Phivos Klokkaris, as Minister of Defence. Later that month the UN Security Council extended UNFICYP's mandate for another six months; in mid-December the Council again renewed the mission's mandate, until mid-June 2007. In July 2006, following a UN-mediated meeting, Papadopoulos and Talat reached a framework agreement on an initiative—known as 'the 8 July process'—to resolve technical issues between the two communities, with the objective of resuming the formal peace process. At the end of that month Greek and Turkish Cypriot negotiators exchanged lists of issues as a basis for future discussions. (In September Klokkaris tendered his resignation owing to ill health, while the Greek Cypriot Minister of the Interior, Andreas Christou, also resigned in order to contest local government elections in December.)

Following the onset of hostilities between the militant Shi'a organization Hezbollah and Israeli armed forces on 12 July 2006 (see the chapter on Lebanon), Cyprus became the main transit point for refugees fleeing southern Lebanon by sea, and applied to the EU for financial assistance in managing the influx. By 14 August, upon which date a UN-imposed cease-fire agreement entered into effect, some 60,000 civilians (mainly foreign nationals) fleeing the fighting in Lebanon had been evacuated through Cyprus, although most had stayed on the island only briefly. The Greek Cypriot Minister of Finance announced that the cost to the authorities had been equivalent to US $223,000 per day, and the EU pledged some $8.9m. towards meeting the expense. Following an offer by Cyprus to serve as a base for the transportation of international peace-keeping troops and humanitarian aid to Lebanon, the UN announced that it was to establish on the island a headquarters for an expanded Interim Force in Lebanon.

In the 'TRNC', three parliamentary deputies resigned from the UBP and one from the DP in early September 2006, and collectively established a new organization, the Özgürlük ve Reform Partisi (ORP—Freedom and Reform Party). Soyer subsequently dissolved the Government, citing prolonged disagreements within the coalition over a reallocation of ministerial positions and policy regarding the reunification of Cyprus. Having received the necessary mandate, on 13 September Soyer formed a new coalition administration with the ORP, which was approved by Talat on 25 September. The leader of the ORP, Turgay Avcı, became Deputy Prime Minister and Minister of Foreign Affairs, and two other ORP representatives were also included within the administration. On 5 October the new Government secured a motion of confidence in the Legislative Assembly by 28 of the 50 deputies; however, the DP and the UBP, which had boycotted the session and staged a protest outside the parliamentary building, refused to recognize its legitimacy.

In November 2006 the European Commission published a critical report on Turkey's accession progress, in which it issued an ultimatum demanding that the Turkish Government open ports and airports in accordance with the 2005 customs protocol by early December 2006, prior to a meeting of EU foreign ministers. Despite mediation efforts by the Finnish Government, which held the rotating presidency of the EU, Turkey emphasized that it was not prepared to comply with the EU stipulation. In early December, following indications that the continuing impasse would result in the partial suspension of Turkey's accession negotiations, the Turkish Government offered to open one port and one airport to Greek Cyprus, in exchange for the resumption of international flights to the 'TRNC' airport of Ercan and direct trade to the port of Famagusta. The Greek Cypriot Government immediately rejected the proposal and, together with Greece and Austria, continued to demand a total cessation of EU discussions with Turkey. In mid-December EU ministers of foreign affairs agreed to a suspension of negotiations on eight of the 35 policy areas (concerning trade and external relations).

Municipal elections in Greek-administered Cyprus were conducted on 17 December 2006. A candidate of the governing coalition, Eleni Mavou, became the first woman to be elected mayor, securing the mayoralty in Nicosia; the ruling coalition also attained the mayoralty in Limassol. At the end of December, following a meeting between Demetris Christofias and Soyer in the northern part of Nicosia, it was announced that both sides had expressed willingness to enter into further dialogue concerning a resolution for Cyprus. On 22 January 2007 a meeting of EU foreign ministers issued a statement urging immediate action towards the ending of trade restrictions against the 'TRNC', in accordance with the EU's commitment made in 2004. In February Archbishop Chrysostomos of the Greek Orthodox Church of Cyprus and Ahmet Yonluer, head of the 'TRNC' Religious Affairs Directorate, met for the first time since 1974, and discussed methods of fostering dialogue between the two communities with a view to increasing inter-religious tolerance. In the following month the Greek Cypriot Government orchestrated the demolition of a wall that had divided Nicosia into Greek and Turkish sectors for more than four decades and which had come to symbolize the wider divisions and conflict within Cyprus. It remained unclear as to whether the 'TRNC' would respond to calls from the Greek Cypriot Government to remove its troops from the area in a reciprocal gesture of goodwill. However, it was hoped that the dismantling of the barrier would pave the way for an official crossing-point to be established in the heart of the capital (see below). (Since 2004 several crossing-points had been opened elsewhere along the Green Line.)

In July 2007 AKEL announced its decision to withdraw from the governing coalition, thereby enabling party leader Christofias to stand in the presidential election scheduled to take place in early 2008. The four government portfolios relinquished by AKEL—those of foreign affairs, the interior, health, and communications and works—were awarded later that month to Erato Kozakou-Marcoullis, Christos Patsalides, Costas Kadis and Maria Malachtou-Pamballi, respectively, all of whom were independents.

A strategic partnership agreement was signed between Turkish Prime Minister Erdoğan and his British counterpart, Gordon Brown, in October 2007. The accord, which called for closer political, economic, cultural and commercial connections between the 'TRNC' and the United Kingdom, provoked strong criticism from the Greek Cypriot administration, despite assurances from the British ambassador to Cyprus that it in no way reflected a shift in the British Government's policy towards Cyprus.

The Greek Cypriot Government appeared increasingly keen to develop its ties with the Middle East, and in November–December 2007 Minister of Foreign Affairs Kozakou-Marcoullis embarked upon a regional tour, visiting Lebanon, Egypt, Syria and Israel to discuss bilateral relations, regional issues and the Cyprus problem. While in the Egyptian capital, Cairo, she met with Amr Moussa, Secretary-General of the League of Arab States (the Arab League, see p. 332), and signed a memorandum of understanding, which was intended to bolster political and economic relations between Cyprus and the Arab League. In January 2008 Kozakou-Marcoullis visited Jordan and the Palestinian territories; discussions in the former included the planned opening later in the year of a Cypriot embassy in the Jordanian capital, Amman, while talks in the latter focused predominantly on the Middle East peace process.

Meanwhile, the UN Security Council voted unanimously in December 2007 to adopt Resolution 1789, extending the mandate of UNFICYP until 15 June 2008. The Security Council also noted 'with deep concern' the lack of progress made towards satisfying the principles outlined in the 8 July process, and urged both sides 'to engage constructively' with UN mediatory efforts to create a political environment in which full negotiations might be allowed to take place. The 'TRNC' representative to the UN, Kemal Gokeri, criticized the resolution's wording, branding its reference to the 'Government of Cyprus' as 'unacceptable'.

In the first round of presidential elections, held on 17 February 2008, Papadopoulos was unexpectedly eliminated from the running, a result attributed by many to increasing levels of popular frustration at his perceived intractability with regard to the Cyprus problem. Despite emphasizing in the run-up to the polls his intention to revive reunification talks with the 'TRNC', Papadopoulos's hardline stance on Greek Cypriot rights was considered by many to be a significant obstacle to negotiation efforts. The independent Ioannis Kasoulides, a former Minister of Foreign Affairs, garnered 33.51% of the ballot, and Christofias secured 33.29%, relegating Papadopoulos, with 31.79% of the vote, into third place; voter turn-out was 89.6% of the registered electorate. The run-off election between the two highest-polling candidates, held on 24 February, was a relatively close contest, from which Christofias emerged victorious, with 240,604 votes (53.37% of the ballot), compared with 210,195 votes cast in favour of Kasoulides (46.63%); turn-out was again high, at 90.8%. It was strongly hoped that the election of Christofias, who became the EU's first communist head of state, would facilitate the procurement of a swift and lasting resolution to the island's long-running division (and, therefore, prove advantageous to Turkish hopes of EU accession). During his electoral campaign, he expressed a staunch desire to 'reunite the state, the people, the institutions and the economy', and had pledged his firm commitment to the holding of reunification negotiations with the 'TRNC', although at the time of his election Christofias had yet to provide details of how a settlement might be reached. The President of the European Commission, José Manuel Barroso, urged Christofias to commence reunification talks 'without delay'.

Christofias was formally inaugurated as the new Greek Cypriot President on 28 February 2008, and the new Council of Ministers, which retained only one member of the outgoing cabinet, was sworn in on the following day. The allocation of portfolios effectively, though unofficially, restored the tripartite coalition that had governed Greek Cyprus prior to AKEL's withdrawal in July 2007: four ministries were to be headed by AKEL, and two each by DIKO and KISOS, with responsibility for the remaining two being awarded to AKEL-backed independents. Notable appointments included those of Markos Kyprianou (DIKO—hitherto EU Commissioner for Health) as Minister of Foreign Affairs and Charilaos Stavrakis (independent—Chief Executive of the Bank of Cyprus) as Minister of Finance; Neoklis

Sylikiotis (AKEL), who had served as Minister of the Interior for 10 months during Papadopoulos's presidency, was returned to his former post.

In mid-March 2008 it was announced that Christofias was to meet with Talat in Nicosia later that month in order to discuss the resumption of reunification talks. The announcement followed a meeting, held earlier in March, between the two leaders' aides, during which convergence was reported to have been reached on a number of disputed issues, including arrangements for the proposed Green Line crossing-point in the heart of Nicosia. At their discussions in Nicosia on 21 March, Christofias and Talat agreed to: open the Ledra Street crossing as a symbol of reconciliation between their two communities (this occurred on 3 April); establish a number of working groups and technical committees; and devise a precise agenda for UN-sponsored reunification negotiations to take place. A subsequent meeting between Christofias and Talat was scheduled for June.

Government

The 1960 Constitution provided for a system of government in which power would be shared by the Greek and Turkish communities in proportion to their numbers. This Constitution officially remains in force, but since the ending of Turkish participation in the Government in 1963, and particularly since the creation of a separate Turkish area in northern Cyprus in 1974, each community has administered its own affairs, refusing to recognize the authority of the other's Government. The Greek Cypriot administration claims to be the Government of all Cyprus, and (apart from Turkey) is internationally recognized as such, although it has no Turkish participation. The northern area is under the de facto control of the 'Turkish Republic of Northern Cyprus' ('TRNC'—for which a new Constitution was approved by a referendum in May 1985). The 'TRNC' is recognized only by Turkey. The Greek Cypriot President is elected for a term of five years and appoints a Council of Ministers. (Under the 1960 Constitution, the position of Vice-President and three posts in the Council of Ministers were reserved for Turkish Cypriots.) The Greek Cypriot House of Representatives comprises 56 deputies, who are elected for a five-year term (under the Constitution, as amended in 1985, the House of Representatives officially comprised 80 seats, of which 24 were allocated to Turkish Cypriots). The 'TRNC' elects its own 50-member Legislative Assembly for a term of five years and has an independent judicial system. The President of the 'TRNC' is elected for a term of five years and appoints a Prime Minister, who forms a 10-member Council of Ministers.

Defence

The formation of the National Guard was authorized by the House of Representatives in 1964, after the withdrawal of the Turkish members. Men between 18 and 50 years of age are liable to 25 months' conscription. As assessed at November 2007, the National Guard comprised an army of 10,000 regulars (including some 8,700 conscripts), with an estimated 200 seconded Greek Army officers, and 60,000 reserves. A further 950 Greek army personnel were stationed in Cyprus at that time. There is also a Greek Cypriot paramilitary police force of at least 750. In 2007 the defence budget for the Greek Cypriot area was some C£142m.

As assessed at November 2007, the 'TRNC' had an army of an estimated 5,000 regulars and 26,000 reserves. There was also a paramilitary armed police force of about 150. Men between 18 and 50 years of age are liable to 24 months' conscription. The 'TRNC' forces were being supported by an estimated 36,000 Turkish troops. In 2006 the defence expenditure of the 'TRNC' was estimated at YTL 100.0m.

Following a significant reduction in the size of the UN Peace-keeping Force in Cyprus (UNFICYP, see p. 88), as prescribed by a UN Security Council resolution adopted in October 2004, the contingent numbered 923 uniformed personnel (861 troops, 62 police), supported by 145 local and international civilian staff at the end of November 2007. There are British military bases (with personnel numbering 2,960, as assessed at November 2007) at Akrotiri, Episkopi and Dhekelia.

Economic Affairs

In 2004, according to estimates by the World Bank, Cyprus's gross national income (GNI), measured at average 2002–04 prices, was US $13,633m., equivalent to $18,430 per head (or $21,490 per head on an international purchasing-power parity basis). During 1996–2006, it was estimated, the population increased at an average annual rate of 1.5%, while gross domestic product (GDP) per head increased, in real terms, by an average of 2.2% per year in 1996–2004. Overall GDP increased, in real terms, by an annual average of 3.6% in 1996–2004; growth was 3.7% in 2004. In the 'TRNC' GNI was officially estimated at $1,283.7m., or $5,949 per head, in 2003; GNI per head was estimated at $8,095 in 2004. GNI increased, in real terms, at an average annual rate of 4.0% in 1995–2003, while real GDP increased at an average annual rate of 4.8% in 1994–99. GDP declined by 5.4% in 2001, but increased by 6.2% in 2002 and by 10.6% in 2003.

In the Greek Cypriot area, agriculture (including hunting, forestry and fishing) contributed 2.6% of GDP in 2006, according to provisional figures. An estimated 4.3% of the employed labour force were engaged in the sector in 2006. The principal export crops of the area are citrus fruit (which accounted for 9.2% of domestic export earnings in 2003), potatoes (7.3%) and vegetables; grapes are cultivated notably for the wine industry, and barley is the principal cereal crop. In an effort to offset the island's vulnerability to drought, during the 1990s the Greek Cypriot Government granted concessions for the construction and operation of several desalination plants. The GDP of the area's agricultural sector declined by an average of 0.1% per year in 1996–2006; however, agricultural GDP increased by an estimated 3.6% in 2006. In the 'TRNC' the agricultural sector contributed 7.2% of GDP in 2006, according to provisional figures, and engaged 9.3% of the employed labour force in 2004. The principal crops of the 'TRNC' are citrus fruit, vegetables, potatoes, barley and wheat. The 'TRNC' imports water from Turkey in order to address the problem of drought. The GDP of the agricultural sector increased by an average of 3.6% per year in 1995–2006. Agricultural GDP increased by 2.8% in 2005, but declined by 0.1% in 2006.

Industry (comprising mining, manufacturing, construction and power) accounted for 19.1% of GDP in 2006, according to provisional figures, and engaged an estimated 22.6% of the employed labour force in the Greek Cypriot area. Industrial GDP increased by an average of 2.0% per year in 1996–2006; growth in the sector was estimated at 3.0% in 2006. In the 'TRNC' the industrial sector contributed 18.8% of GDP in 2006, according to provisional figures, and engaged 20.5% of the employed labour force in 2004. Industrial GDP in the 'TRNC' increased at an annual average rate of 7.0% in 1995–2006. The GDP of the industrial sector increased by a robust 20.0% in 2006.

In the Greek Cypriot area mining and quarrying, principally the extraction of material for the construction industry, provided only 0.4% of GDP in 2006, according to provisional figures, and engaged about 0.2% of the employed labour force. In 2001 it was announced that 25 foreign oil companies had expressed interest in acquiring exploration rights for potential petroleum and gas deposits in the eastern Mediterranean within Cyprus's economic zone. The GDP of the mining sector increased at an average annual rate of 6.8% in 1996–2006. Mining GDP rose by 2.0% in 2006. In the 'TRNC' mining and quarrying contributed 0.7% of GDP in 2006, according to provisional figures, and engaged 0.1% of the employed labour force in 2004. The GDP of the 'TRNC' mining sector increased by an average of 7.2% per year in 1995–2006. Mining GDP increased by 21.1% in 2006.

In the Greek Cypriot area manufacturing accounted for 8.4% of GDP in 2006, according to provisional figures, and engaged about 10.4% of the employed labour force. The GDP of the manufacturing sector declined by an average of 0.6% per year in 1996–2006, decreasing by an estimated 0.9% in 2005, but increasing by 0.7% in 2006. In the 'TRNC' the manufacturing sector provided 5.2% of GDP in 2006, according to provisional figures, and engaged 10.6% of the employed labour force in 2004. The GDP of the 'TRNC' manufacturing sector increased at an average annual rate of 2.8% in 1995–2006. Manufacturing GDP rose by 5.1% in 2006.

Energy is derived almost entirely from imported petroleum, and mineral fuels comprised 16.1% of total imports (including goods for re-export) in the Greek Cypriot area in 2005. The Greek Cypriot Government is encouraging the development of renewable energy sources, including solar, wind and hydroelectric power. Mineral fuels and lubricants comprised 13.8% of total imports in the 'TRNC' in 2005.

The services sector in the Greek Cypriot area contributed 78.3% of GDP in 2006, according to provisional figures, and engaged 73.1% of the employed labour force. Within the sector, financial and business services provided 26.4% of total GDP in 2006, according to provisional figures, and generated 12.8% of employment. In 2003 there were 29 'offshore' banking units in the Greek Cypriot area, and the number of registered 'offshore' enterprises was estimated to total more than 40,000. The Greek Cypriot authorities have also attempted to enhance the island's status as an entrepôt for shipping and trade throughout the Eastern Mediterranean. Tourist arrivals to the Greek Cypriot area increased by 5.2% in 2005 but declined by 2.8%, to about 2.4m., in 2006. Receipts from tourism in that year amounted to an estimated C£1,045.9m. In the Greek Cypriot zone the GDP of the services sector increased at an average annual rate of 4.4% in 1996–2006; the sector recorded estimated growth of 4.1% in 2006. In the 'TRNC' the services sector contributed 74.0% of GDP in 2006, according to provisional figures, and engaged 70.2% of the employed labour force in 2004. In 2005 a total of 652,779 tourists (488,023 of whom were from Turkey) visited the 'TRNC', and net tourism receipts were estimated at US $328.8m. Services GDP in the 'TRNC' increased by an average of 5.8% per year in 1994–99.

In 2006 the Greek Cypriot area recorded a visible trade deficit of US $5,022.9m. and a deficit of $1,090.6m. on the current account of the balance of payments. In 2006 the principal source of imports to the Greek Cypriot area was Greece (17.3%), followed by Italy, the United Kingdom, Germany and Israel. The United Kingdom was the principal purchaser of Greek Cypriot exports in that year, taking 14.6% of the total; Greece and France were also important markets. The principal exports from the Greek Cypriot zone in 2004 were machinery and transport equipment, food and live animals, chemicals and related products, and miscellaneus manufactured articles. Among the principal imports in that year were machinery and transport equipment, manufactured products, mineral fuels and lubricants, and chemicals and related products. The 'TRNC' recorded a visible trade deficit in 2006 of $1,225.9m., while there was a deficit of $282.0m. on the current account of the balance of payments. In 2005 the principal imports to the 'TRNC' were machinery and transport equipment, basic manufactures, mineral fuels and lubricants, and food and live animals; the principal exports were industrial products, food and live animals, and minerals. Turkey is by far the principal trading partner of the 'TRNC', supplying 65.1% of imports and taking 50.2% of exports in 2005 (although the United Kingdom purchased 20.3% of exports in that year).

In 2007 the Greek Cypriot Government recorded a budget deficit of an estimated C£175.2m., equivalent to 1.1% of GDP. External debt totalled C£1,796.0m. at the end of 1999, of which C£1,142.3m. was medium- and long-term public debt. In that year the cost of debt-servicing was equivalent to 5.8% of the value of exports of goods and services. General government consolidated debt totalled US $5,198.8m. (70.4% of GDP) in 2004. The annual rate of inflation averaged 2.8% in 1996–2006. Consumer prices increased by an average of 2.5% in 2006. The rate of unemployment in the Greek Cypriot area was some 5.3% of the labour force at the end of 2005. A budgetary deficit of 344.2m. new Turkish lira was estimated in the 'TRNC' in 2006. In the 'TRNC' the average increase in prices for the 12 months to December averaged 22.6% in 2000–06; the end-of-year rate of inflation was 19.2% in 2006 and 9.4% in 2007. According to the first ever 'TRNC' labour force survey, conducted in October 2004, the unemployment rate was 9.4%, significantly higher than official estimates.

Following an application by the Greek Cypriot Government in July 1990, the Greek-controlled southern sector of Cyprus officially acceded to the European Union (EU, see p. 244) on 1 May 2004 (see below). The 'TRNC' has guest status at the Economic Co-operation Organization (ECO, see p. 238).

The economy of Cyprus and its future development are inextricably linked to the continuing division of the island, which further intensive efforts by the UN and the EU in early 2004 failed to resolve. As a result of the Greek Cypriots' rejection of the Annan Plan in April, only the Greek Cypriot-administered part of the island joined the EU on 1 May 2004, with the EU's *acquis communautaire* being suspended in the Turkish Cypriot area, pending an eventual resolution of the political dispute. The Turkish Cypriot economy consequently remained heavily dependent on financial aid from Turkey, although, in recognition of the Turkish Cypriots' vote in favour of the Annan Plan for reunification, the EU declared its intention to reduce the wide economic disparities between the northern and southern parts of Cyprus, with the resumption of international trade via Greek-administered Cyprus and pledges of considerable financial assistance. The easing of restrictions on movement across the internal border from April 2003 had brought considerable benefits to the Turkish Cypriot economy, in particular to the tourism sector, prompting large numbers of Greek Cypriots and foreign tourists to travel to the north. The holiday property sector in the 'TRNC', adversely affected by uncertainty over the legal status of property owned by Greek Cypriots prior to the 1974 invasion, was revived following the Greek Cypriot rejection of the Annan Plan. However, the proposed ending of international trade restrictions against the 'TRNC' was not realized, owing to continued opposition from the Greek Cypriot Government, while the associated pledges of EU aid also remained suspended in 2005. Following persistently high levels of inflation in the 'TRNC' (which used the Turkish lira as currency), the new Turkish lira was also introduced there at the beginning of 2005. Meanwhile, the application of fiscal restraint enabled the Greek Cypriot administration to join the EU's exchange rate mechanism in April, leading to a strengthening of the Cyprus pound. In February 2006 the EU finally approved a disbursement of €139m. for economic reconstruction in the 'TRNC', after agreeing to a Greek Cypriot demand that the issue of financial assistance be addressed separately to the proposed trade measures. On 1 January 2008 the Greek Cypriot area officially adopted the euro as its currency, following a generally successful programme of fiscal adjustment. Adoption of the European single currency was expected to bolster the volume of trade between Greek-administered Cyprus and the euro zone, and to lead to large increases in flows of foreign investment. Tourism receipts were also forecast to rise, with a greater number of people from other EU member states predicted to visit the island. There were concerns, however, that consumer prices would rise in the initial months of transition and place an upward pressure on wages. High public sector salaries had previously been identified as a long-term structural issue in need of address, particularly given the comparatively low rates of corporate and income taxation.

Education

In the Greek Cypriot sector elementary education, which is compulsory and available free of charge, is provided in six grades for children between five-and-a-half and 12 years of age. Secondary education is free for all years of study and lasts for six years, with three compulsory years at the Gymnasium being followed by three non-compulsory years at a technical school or a Lyceum. Comprehensive secondary schools were introduced in 1995. There are five options of specialization at the Lyceums: classical, science, economics, commercial/secretarial and foreign languages. According to UNESCO estimates, in 2004/05 total enrolment in primary education included 99.3% of pupils in the relevant age-group, while the comparable ratio for secondary enrolment was 94.1%. Technical and vocational colleges provide higher education for teachers, technicians, engineers, hoteliers and caterers, foresters, nurses and health inspectors. The University of Cyprus was established in September 1992, and there were a further 35 post-secondary institutions in 2005/06 (including two other state universities—the Open University of Cyprus and the Cyprus University of Technology). In that year 20,578 students (including 5,630 foreign pupils) were enrolled in tertiary education in the Greek Cypriot area, while a total of 20,969 students from Greek Cyprus were studying at universities abroad. Public expenditure on education by the central Government in the Greek Cypriot area was estimated at C£499.3m. (equivalent to 6.9% of GDP) in 2004.

Education in the Turkish Cypriot zone is controlled by the 'TRNC'. Pre-primary education is provided by kindergartens for children of five and six years of age. Primary education is free and compulsory: it comprises elementary schools for the 7–11 age-group, and secondary-junior schools for the 12–14 age-group. Secondary education, for the 15–17 age-group, is provided by high schools and vocational schools, including colleges of agriculture, nursing and hotel management; it is free, but not compulsory. In 2005/06 41,865 students were enrolled at higher education establishments in the 'TRNC'. The Eastern Mediterranean University, established at Famagusta in 1986, is the principal tertiary institution, with 15,091 students in 2005/06; there are, in addition, six private universities, a teacher-training college, a technological institute and a private business college.

Public Holidays

2008: 1 January (New Year's Day), 6 January (Epiphany)*, 10 March (Green Monday)*, 20 March (Birth of the Prophet)†,

CYPRUS

25 March (Greek Independence Day)*, 1 April (Anniversary of Cyprus Liberation Struggle), 23 April (National Sovereignty and Children's Day)†, 25–28 April (Easter)*, 1 May (May Day), 19 May (Youth and Sports Day)†, 16 June (Pentecost)*, 20 July (Peace and Freedom Day, anniversary of the Turkish invasion in 1974)†, 1 August (Communal Resistance Day)†, 15 August (Assumption)*, 30 August (Victory Day)†, 1 October (Independence Day)*, 1–3 October (Ramazam Bayram—end of Ramadan)†, 28 October (Greek National Day)*, 29 October (Turkish Republic Day)†, 15 November (TRNC Day)†, 9–12 December (Kurban Bayram—Feast of the Sacrifice)†, 25–26 December (Christmas)*.

2009: 1 January (New Year's Day), 6 January (Epiphany)*, 2 March (Green Monday)*, 9 March (Birth of the Prophet)†, 25 March (Greek Independence Day)*, 1 April (Anniversary of Cyprus Liberation Struggle), 17–20 April (Easter)*, 23 April (National Sovereignty and Children's Day)†, 1 May (May Day), 19 May (Youth and Sports Day)†, 31 May (Pentecost)*, 20 July (Peace and Freedom Day, anniversary of the Turkish invasion in 1974)†, 1 August (Communal Resistance Day)†, 15 August (Assumption)*, 30 August (Victory Day)†, 20–22 September (Ramazam Bayram—end of Ramadan)†, 1 October (Independence Day)*, 28 October (Greek National Day)*, 29 October (Turkish Republic Day)†, 15 November (TRNC Day)†, 27–30 November (Kurban Bayram—Feast of the Sacrifice)†, 25–26 December (Christmas)*.

* Greek and Greek Orthodox.
† Turkish and Turkish Muslim.

Weights and Measures

Although the imperial and the metric systems are understood, Cyprus has a special internal system:

Weights

400 drams = 1 oke = 2.8 lb (1.27 kg).
44 okes = 1 Cyprus kantar.
180 okes = 1 Aleppo kantar.

Capacity

1 liquid oke = 2.25 pints (1.28 litres).
1 Cyprus litre = 5.6 pints (3.18 litres).

Length and Area

1 pic = 2 feet (61 cm).

Area

1 donum = 14,400 sq ft (1,338 sq m).

Statistical Survey

Source (unless otherwise indicated): Department of Statistics and Research, Ministry of Finance, Michalakis Karaolis St, 1444 Nicosia; tel. (2) 309301; fax (2) 661313; e-mail enquiries@cystat.mof.gov.cy; internet www.mof.gov.cy.

Note: Since July 1974 the northern part of Cyprus has been under Turkish occupation. As a result, some of the statistics relating to subsequent periods do not cover the whole island. Some separate figures for the 'TRNC' are also given.

AREA AND POPULATION

Area: 9,251 sq km (3,572 sq miles), incl. Turkish-occupied region; 5,896 sq km (2,276 sq miles), government-controlled area only.

Population: 703,529 (males 345,322, females 358,207), excl. Turkish-occupied region, at census of 1 October 2001 (adjusted figures); 867,600, incl. 88,900 in Turkish-occupied region, at 31 December 2006 (official estimate). Note: Figures for the Turkish-occupied region exclude settlers from Turkey, estimated at 115,000 in 2001.

Density (at 31 December 2006): 93.8 per sq km.

Ethnic Groups (31 December 2001, estimates): Greeks 639,400 (80.6%), Turks 87,600 (11.1%), Others 66,100 (8.3%); Total 793,100.

Principal Districts (population at 31 December 2006, estimates): Lefkosia 307,100; Ammochostos 43,000; Larnaka (Larnaca) 130,100; Lemesos (Limassol) 223,600; Pafos (Paphos) 74,900; Total 867,600 (incl. 88,900 in Turkish-occupied region).

Principal Towns (population at 1 October 2001): Nicosia (capital) 205,633 (excl. Turkish-occupied portion); Limassol 160,733; Larnaca 71,740; Paphos 47,198.

Births, Marriages and Deaths (government-controlled area, 2006): Registered live births 5,127 (birth rate 11.3 per 1,000); Registered marriages 12,617 (incl. 5,252 non-residents of Cyprus); Registered deaths 5,127 (death rate 6.7 per 1,000).

Expectation of Life (years at birth, WHO estimates): 79.3 (males 77.1; females 81.5) in 2005. Source: WHO, *World Health Statistics*.

Employment (government-controlled area, '000 persons aged 15 years and over, excl. armed forces, 2006): Agriculture, hunting, forestry and fishing 15.2; Mining and quarrying 0.7; Manufacturing 37.3; Electricity, gas and water 2.9; Construction 40.0; Trade, restaurants and hotels 87.1; Transport, storage and communications 20.2; Financial intermediation 18.9; Real estate, renting and business activities 26.7; Public administration and defence 29.9; Education 24.8; Health and social work 14.2; Other community, social and personal service activities 21.6; Private households 14.8; Extra-territorial organizations 2.9; Total 357.3. Figures exclude employment on British sovereign bases. Source: ILO.

HEALTH AND WELFARE

Key Indicators

Total Fertility Rate (children per woman, 2005): 1.6.
Under-5 Mortality Rate (per 1,000 live births, 2005): 5.
HIV/AIDS (% of persons aged 15–49, 2001): 0.25.
Physicians (per 1,000 head, 2002): 2.34.
Hospital Beds (per 1,000 head, 2005): 3.4.
Health Expenditure (2004): US $ per head (PPP): 1,128.0.
Health Expenditure (2004): % of GDP: 5.8.
Health Expenditure (2004): public (% of total): 44.3.
Human Development Index (2005): ranking: 28.
Human Development Index (2005): index: 0.903.

For sources and definitions, see explanatory note on p. vi.

AGRICULTURE

Principal Crops (government-controlled area, '000 metric tons, 2006): Wheat 9.9; Barley 58.4; Potatoes 124.8; Olives 23.5; Cabbages 4.5; Tomatoes 34.5; Cucumbers and gherkins 15.6; Dry onions 7.0; Bananas 7.0; Oranges 48.0; Tangerines, mandarins, etc. 41.5; Lemons and limes 18.5; Grapefruit and pomelos 30.0; Apples 10.8; Grapes 52.4; Cantaloupes and other melons 10.0.

Livestock (government-controlled area, '000 head, 2006, FAO estimates): Cattle 57.7; Sheep 272.2; Goats 344.9; Pigs 452.6; Chickens 3,065.0; Asses, mules or hinnies 6.7.

Livestock Products (government-controlled area, '000 metric tons, 2006): Sheep meat 2.7; Goat meat 4.2; Pig meat 52.5; Chicken meat 27.0; Cows' milk 138.4 (official figure); Sheep's milk 16.6 (FAO estimate); Goats' milk 29.5 (FAO estimate); Hen eggs 94.6 (FAO estimate).

Forestry (government-controlled area, '000 cubic metres, 2006): Roundwood removals (excl. bark) 7.4; Sawnwood production (incl. railway sleepers) 3.9.

Fishing (government-controlled area, metric tons, live weight, 2005): Capture 1,916 (FAO estimate—Bogue 214; Picarels 250); Aquaculture 2,333 (European seabass 583; Gilthead seabream 1,465); Total catch 4,249 (FAO estimate).

Source: FAO.

MINING

Selected Products (government-controlled area, '000 metric tons, 2006, provisional figures): Sand and gravel 13,200.0; Gypsum 149.4; Bentonite 98.5; Umber 13.3.

CYPRUS

INDUSTRY

Selected Products (government-controlled area, 2005 unless otherwise indicated): Wine 28.6m. litres; Beer 37.7m. litres; Soft drinks 66.6m. litres; Cigarettes 3,803m. (2001); Footwear 361,095 pairs; Bricks 89.5m.; Floor and wall tiles 320,000 sq m (2004); Cement 84,635 metric tons; Electric energy 39,307 million kWh.

FINANCE

Currency and Exchange Rates: 100 cents = 1 Cyprus pound (Cyprus £). *Sterling, Dollar and Euro Equivalents* (31 December 2007): £1 sterling = 79.69 Cyprus cents; US $1 = 39.78 Cyprus cents; €1 = 58.56 Cyprus cents; Cyprus £10 = £12.55 sterling = $25.14 = €17.08. *Average Exchange Rate* (Cyprus £ per US dollar): 0.4641 in 2005; 0.4589 in 2006; 0.4261 in 2007. Note: The government-controlled area of Cyprus adopted the euro on 1 January 2008, and this became the sole legal tender in these areas from the end of the same month; however, most of the relevant historical data in this survey continues to be presented in terms of Cyprus pounds.

Budget (government-controlled area, Cyprus £ million, 2007): *Revenue:* Taxation 2,959.6 (Direct taxes 1,023.8, Indirect taxes 1,494.3, Social security contributions 441.5); Other current revenue 409.5; Total 3,369.1, excl. grants from abroad (60.0). *Expenditure:* Current expenditure 3,333.1 (Wages and salaries 961.4, Other goods and services 276.4, Social security payments 563.2, Subsidies 50.0, Interest payments 397.7, Pensions and gratuities 209.7, Social pension 31.2, Other current transfers 783.6, Unallocated 60.0); Capital expenditure (investments) 211.2; Total 3,544.3. Source: Budgets and Fiscal Control Directorate, Ministry of Finance, Nicosia.

International Reserves (government-controlled area, US $ million at 31 December 2006): Gold (national valuation) 295.7; IMF special drawing rights 4.1; Reserve position in IMF 21.2; Foreign exchange 5,621.5; Total 5,942.5. Source: IMF, *International Financial Statistics*.

Money Supply (government-controlled area, Cyprus £ million at 31 December 2006): Currency outside banks 607.8; Demand deposits at deposit money banks 1,137.3; Total money (incl. others) 2,014.9. Source: IMF, *International Financial Statistics*.

Cost of Living (government-controlled area, Retail Price Index; base: 2000 = 100): 111.7 in 2004; 114.5 in 2005; 117.4 in 2006. Source: IMF, *International Financial Statistics*.

Gross Domestic Product in Market Prices (government-controlled area, Cyprus £ million at current prices): 7,405.8 in 2004; 7,879.1 in 2005; 8,424.2 in 2006 (provisional figure).

Expenditure on the Gross Domestic Product (government-controlled area, Cyprus £ million at current prices, 2006, provisional figures): Government final consumption expenditure 1,570.0; Private final consumption expenditure 5,433.8; Increase in stocks 20.8; Gross fixed capital formation 1,708.8; *Total domestic expenditure* 8,733.4; Exports of goods and services 4,063.4; *Less* Imports of goods and services 4,372.8; *GDP in market prices* 8,424.2.

Gross Domestic Product by Economic Activity (government-controlled area, Cyprus £ million at current prices, 2006, provisional figures): Agriculture and hunting 180.2; Fishing 16.8; Mining and quarrying 26.6; Manufacturing 632.6; Electricity, gas and water supply 153.7; Construction 629.7; Wholesale and retail trade 947.1; Restaurants and hotels 533.6; Transport, storage and communications 591.8; Financial intermediation 547.1; Real estate, renting and business activities 1,441.8; Public administration and defence 776.0; Education 436.9; Health and social work 289.0; Other community, social and personal services 282.9; Private households with employed persons 59.7; *Sub-total* 7,545.5; Import duties 87.1; Value-added tax 791.6; *GDP in market prices* 8,424.2.

Balance of Payments (government-controlled area, US $ million, 2006): Exports of goods f.o.b. 1,416.6; Imports of goods f.o.b. −6,439.5; *Trade balance* −5,022.9; Exports of services 7,273.5; Imports of services −2,987.1; *Balance on goods and services* −736.5; Other income received 2,174.7; Other income paid −2,738.7; *Balance on goods, services and income* −1,300.5; Current transfers received 836.4; Current transfers paid −626.6; *Current balance* −1,090.6; Capital account (net) 33.7; Direct investment abroad −862.5; Direct investment from abroad 1,527.9; Portfolio investment assets −4,838.6; Portfolio investment liabilities 4,079.6; Financial derivatives assets 1.8; Financial derivatives liabilities 16.3; Other investment assets −5,127.6; Other investment liabilities 7,467.4; Net errors and omissions −181.6; *Overall balance* 1,025.6. Source: IMF, *International Financial Statistics*.

EXTERNAL TRADE

Total Trade (government-controlled area, Cyprus £ million): *Imports c.i.f.:* 2,679.3 in 2004; 2,966.8 in 2005; 3,182.7 in 2006 (provisional figure). *Exports f.o.b. (incl. re-exports):* 548.0 in 2004; 719.2 in 2005; 644.0 in 2006 (provisional figure).

Principal Commodities (government-controlled area, Cyprus £ '000, 2003): *Imports c.i.f.:* Intermediate inputs 726,410; Consumer goods 666,574; Transport equipment 326,800; Fuels and lubricants 226,795; Capital goods 262,928; Total (incl. others) 2,314,248. *Exports f.o.b.:* Agricultural products 76,276 (Citrus fruits 19,018; Potatoes 15,051; Cheese 9,664); Manufactured products 119,850 (Cigarettes 6,839; Cement 9,110; Pharmaceutical products 38,742; Clothing 9,810); Minerals 9,769; Total (incl. others) 205,936. Figures for exports exclude re-exports (Cyprus £ '000): 261,979. Also excluded are domestic exports of stores and bunkers for ships and aircraft (Cyprus £ '000): 8,884. *2004* (US $ million, distribution by SITC): Imports c.i.f.: Food and live animals 516.5; Mineral fuels and lubricants 686.7 (Petroleum and products 665.9); Chemicals and related products 546.7; Basic manufactures 873.9 (Iron and steel 199.1); Machinery and transport equipment 1,896.6 (Passenger cars 649.0); Miscellaneous manufactured articles 955.0 (Clothing and accessories 256.6); Total (incl. others) 5,728.9. Exports f.o.b.: Food and live animals 194.4 (Vegetables and fruit 110.7); Beverages and tobacco 78.5; Mineral fuels and lubricants 83.9 (Petroleum and products 83.9); Chemicals and related products 141.8 (Medicinal and pharmaceutical products 109.6); Machinery and transport equipment 434.5 (Road vehicles 214.1); Miscellaneous manufactured articles 131.8; Total (incl. others) 1,171.5 (Source: UN, *International Trade Statistics Yearbook*).

Principal Trading Partners (government-controlled area, Cyprus £ million, 2006): *Imports c.i.f.:* China, People's Repub. 134.4; France 136.5; Germany 285.9; Greece 559.8; Israel 200.0; Italy 368.5; Japan 78.1; Netherlands 136.5; Russia 26.6; Spain 93.5; Syria 7.6; United Kingdom 288.0; USA 50.9; Total (incl. others) 3,226.9. *Exports f.o.b. (incl. re-exports):* France 48.0; Germany 29.7; Greece 86.1; Japan 7.3; Lebanon 14.9; Netherlands 9.3; Russia 9.7; Syria 9.6; United Arab Emirates 29.7; United Kingdom 95.0; USA 4.8; Total (incl. others) 650.7.

TRANSPORT

Road Traffic (government-controlled area, licensed motor vehicles, 31 December 2006): Private passenger cars 363,383; Taxis and self-drive cars 9,562; Buses and coaches 3,221; Lorries and vans 115,723; Motorcycles 40,359; Total (incl. others) 550,792.

Shipping (government-controlled area, freight traffic, '000 metric tons, 2005): Goods loaded 1,902, Goods unloaded 6,135. *Merchant Fleet:* At 31 December 2006 a total of 971 merchant vessels (combined displacement 19,032,189 grt) were registered in Cyprus (Source: Lloyd's Register-Fairplay, *World Fleet Statistics*).

Civil Aviation (government-controlled area, 2006): Overall passenger traffic 6,642,865; Total freight transported 39,327 metric tons.

TOURISM

Foreign Tourist Arrivals (government-controlled area, '000): 2,349.0 in 2004; 2,470.1 in 2005; 2,400.9 in 2006.

Arrivals by Country of Residence (government-controlled area, 2006): France 37,779; Germany 152,808; Greece 126,768; Ireland 47,463; Israel 34,197; Norway 50,664; Russia 114,763; Sweden 94,028; Switzerland 41,559; United Kingdom 1,360,136; Total (incl. others) 2,400,924.

Tourism Receipts (government-controlled area, Cyprus £ million): 982.3 in 2004; 1,005.7 in 2005; 1,045.9 in 2006.

COMMUNICATIONS MEDIA

Radio Receivers (government-controlled area, 1997): 310,000 in use.

Television Receivers (government-controlled area, 2000): 122,000 in use.

Telephones (main lines in use, 2005): 408,300.

Facsimile Machines (provisional or estimated figure, number in use, 1993): 7,000.

Mobile Cellular Telephones (subscribers, 2006): 777,500.

Personal Computers ('000 in use, 2005): 249.

Internet Users ('000, 2006): 356.6.

Broadband Subscribers ('000, 2006): 49.6.

Book Production (government-controlled area, 1999): 931 titles.

Newspapers (2000): 8 daily (circulation 87,000 copies); 38 non-daily (circulation 200,000 copies).

Periodicals (2000): 50 daily (circulation 372,000 copies).

Sources: mainly UNESCO, *Statistical Yearbook*, UN, *Statistical Yearbook,* and International Telecommunication Union.

EDUCATION

2005/06 (government-controlled area): Pre-primary: 682 institutions, 1,948 teachers, 26,557 pupils; Primary: 365 institutions, 4,348 teachers, 59,401 pupils; Secondary (Gymnasia and Lyceums): 158 institutions, 6,942 teachers, 65, pupils; Tertiary (incl. University of Cyprus): 36 institutions, 1,403 teachers, 20,578 students (of which 5,630 foreign students). Note: 20,969 Cypriot students were studying abroad.

Adult Literacy Rate (UNESCO estimates): 96.8% (males 98.6%; females 95.1%) in 2001. Source: UNESCO Institute for Statistics.

'Turkish Republic of Northern Cyprus'

Sources: Statistics and Research Dept, State Planning Organization, Prime Ministry, Lefkoşa (Nicosia), Mersin 10, Turkey; tel. (22) 83141; fax (22) 85988; e-mail trnc-spo@management.emu.edu.tr; internet www.devplan.org.

AREA AND POPULATION

Area: 3,242 sq km (1,251 sq miles).

Population (at census of 30 April 2006): 256,644 (males 138,568, females 118,076).

Density (at census of 30 April 2006): 79.2 per sq km.

Population by Country of Nationality (self-declaration at census of 30 April 2006): 'TRNC' 135,106; Joint 'TRNC' and other 42,925 (with Turkey 34,370, with United Kingdom 3,854, with Other 4,701); Turkey 70,525; United Kingdom 2,729; Bulgaria 797; Iran 759; Pakistan 475; Moldova 354; Germany 181; Other 2,793; *Total* 256,644.

Districts (population at census of 30 April 2006): Lefkoşa 84,776; Mağusa 63,603; Girne 57,902; Güzelyurt 29,264; İskele 21,099.

Principal Towns (population within the municipal boundary at census of 30 April 2006): Lefkoşa (Nicosia) 49,868 (Turkish-occupied area only); Gazi Mağusa (Famagusta) 35,381; Girne (Kyrenia) 23,839; Güzelyurt 12,391.

Births, Marriages and Deaths (registered, 2001): Live births 2,550 (birth rate 15.0 per 1,000); Marriages 1,090 (marriage rate 5.2 per 1,000); Deaths 781 (death rate 8.0 per 1,000). *2005:* Birth rate 16.0 per 1,000; Death rate 7.0 per 1,000.

Expectation of life (years at birth, 2005): Males 71.0; Females 75.6.

Employment (labour force survey, October 2004): Agriculture, forestry and fishing 6,933; Mining and quarrying 92; Manufacturing 7,925; Construction 6,775; Electricity, gas and water 516; Wholesale and retail trade 11,900; Hotels and restaurants 4,060; Transport, storage and communications 4,497; Financial institutions 2,910; Real estate and renting 3,001; Public administration 11,624; Education 7,574; Health 2,229; Other community services 4,476; *Total employed* 74,511; Total unemployed 7,709; *Total labour force* 82,220.

HEALTH AND WELFARE
Key Indicators

Total Fertility Rate (children per woman, 2005): 1.9.

Under-5 Mortality Rate (per 1,000 live births, 2005): 9.0.

Physicians (per 1,000 head, 2002): 2.0.

Hospital Beds (per 1,000 head, 2004): 5.9.

AGRICULTURE

Principal Crops ('000 metric tons, 2001): Wheat 7.6; Barley 102.1; Potatoes 14.0; Legumes 2.5; Tomatoes 8.3; Onions 1.7; Artichokes 1.2; Watermelons 9.7; Melons 3.0; Cucumbers 2.1; Carobs 2.8; Olives 3.1; Lemons 10.7; Grapefruit 15.8; Oranges 61.6; Tangerines 2.0.

Livestock ('000 head, 2001): Cattle 34.2; Sheep 202.7; Goats 54.8; Chickens 4,238.

Livestock Products ('000 metric tons, unless otherwise indicated, 2001): Sheep's and goats' milk 11.4; Cows' milk 66.5; Sheep meat 3.3; Goat meat 0.8; Cattle meat 2.1; Chicken meat 6.8; Wool 0.2; Eggs (million) 13.4.

Fishing (metric tons, 2001): Total catch 400.

FINANCE

Currency and Exchange Rates: Turkish currency: 100 kuruş = 1 new Turkish lira. *Sterling, Dollar and Euro Equivalents* (31 December 2007): £1 sterling = 2.328 new liras; US $1 = 1.162 new liras; €1 = 1.711 new liras; 100 new Turkish liras = £42.95 = $86.05 = €58.45. Note: A new currency, the new Turkish lira, equivalent to 1,000,000 of the former units, was introduced on 1 January 2005. Figures in this survey have been converted retrospectively to reflect this development. *Average Exchange Rate* (new liras per US dollar): 1.344 in 2005; 1.429 in 2006; 1.303 in 2007.

Budget ('000 new Turkish liras, 2006, provisional figures): *Revenue:* Local revenue 1,166,212.3 (Direct taxes 287,208.5, Indirect taxes 473,417.4, Other income 167,336.7, Fund revenues 238,249.8); Foreign aid 283,403.0; Loans 260,951.2; Total 1,710,566.5. *Expenditure:* Personnel 607,941.1; Other goods and services 90,971.3; Transfers 731,024.1; Investments 215,054.4; Defence 100,000.0; Total 1,744,991.0.

Cost of Living (Retail Price Index at June; base: 1998/99 = 100): 718.8 in 2005; 804.8 in 2006; 913.8 in 2007.

Expenditure on the Gross Domestic Product ('000 new Turkish liras at current prices, 2003, provisional figures): Government final consumption expenditure 482,674; Private final consumption expenditure 1,071,916; Increase in stocks 30,900; Gross fixed capital formation 300,218; *Total domestic expenditure* 1,885,707; Net exports of goods and services –56,763; *GDP in purchasers' values* 1,828,944; *GDP at constant 1977 prices* (million liras) 9,523.6.

Gross Domestic Product by Economic Activity ('000 new Turkish liras, 2006, provisional figures): Agriculture, forestry and fishing 241,457.8; Mining and quarrying 23,763.9; Manufacturing 172,515.0; Electricity and water 163,249.3; Construction 271,053.9; Wholesale and retail trade 420,439.0; Restaurants and hotels 159,931.7; Transport and communications 402,237.4; Finance 239,440.2; Ownership of dwellings 95,803.2; Business and personal services 385,565.9; Government services 772,820.7; *Sub-total* 3,348,278.0; Import duties 371,970.4; *GDP in purchasers' values* 3,720,248.4.

Balance of Payments (US $ million, 2006): Merchandise exports f.o.b. 65.1; Merchandise imports c.i.f. –1,291.0; *Trade balance* –1,225.9; Services and unrequited transfers (net) 943.9; *Current balance* –282.0; Capital movements (net) 180.0; Other short-term capital movements (net) 70.7; Net errors and omissions –11.3; *Overall balance* –42.6.

EXTERNAL TRADE

Principal Commodities (US $ million, 2005): *Imports c.i.f.:* Food and live animals 110.5; Beverages and tobacco 54.4; Mineral fuels, lubricants, etc. 172.8; Basic manufactures 310.1; Machinery and transport equipment 385.8; Miscellaneous manufactured articles 101.1; Total (incl. others) 1,255.5. *Exports f.o.b.:* Food and live animals 24.6; Industrial products 41.1; Minerals 2.4; Total 68.1.

Principal Trading Partners (US $ million, 2005): *Imports c.i.f.:* Turkey 817.4; United Kingdom 101.4; USA 8.3; Total (incl. others) 1,255.5. *Exports f.o.b.:* Turkey 34.2; United Kingdom 13.8; Total (incl. others) 68.1.

TRANSPORT

Road Traffic (registered motor vehicles, 2001): Saloon cars 76,850; Estate cars 9,168; Pick-ups 3,825; Vans 9,131; Buses 2,077; Trucks 1,593; Lorries 6,335; Motorcycles 16,424; Agricultural tractors 6,594; Total (incl. others) 134,454.

Shipping (2001): Freight traffic ('000 metric tons): Goods loaded 247.2, Goods unloaded 898.1; Vessels entered 3,220.

Civil Aviation (2001): Passenger arrivals and departures 691,431; Freight landed and cleared (metric tons) 4,297.

TOURISM

Visitors (2005): 652,779 (including 488,023 Turkish).

Tourism Receipts (US $ million, 2005): 328.8.

COMMUNICATIONS MEDIA

Radio Receivers (2001, provisional): 82,364 in use.

Television Receivers (2001, provisional): 70,960 in use.

Telephones (31 December 2002): 87,745 subscribers.

Mobile Cellular Telephones (31 December 2002): 147,522 subscribers.

EDUCATION

2005/06: *Primary and Pre-primary schools:* 267 institutions, 1,605 teachers, 21,886 pupils; *Secondary Schools:* 30 institutions, 1,214 teachers, 9,956 students; *General High Schools:* 22 institutions, 796 teachers, 6,319 students; *Vocational Schools:* 13 institutions, 462 teachers, 2,265 students; *Universities:* 9 institutions, 35,473 students (of which 10,586 Turkish Cypriots, 28,565 from Turkey, 2,714 from other countries). Note: 1,650 'TRNC' students were studying abroad.

Adult Literacy Rate (at census of 15 December 1996): 93.5%.

Directory

The Constitution

The Constitution, summarized below, entered into force on 16 August 1960, when Cyprus became an independent republic.

THE STATE OF CYPRUS

The State of Cyprus is an independent and sovereign Republic with a presidential regime.

The Greek Community comprises all citizens of the Republic who are of Greek origin and whose mother tongue is Greek or who share the Greek cultural traditions or who are members of the Greek Orthodox Church.

The Turkish Community comprises all citizens of the Republic who are of Turkish origin and whose mother tongue is Turkish or who share the Turkish cultural traditions or who are Muslims.

The official languages of the Republic are Greek and Turkish.

The Republic shall have its own flag of neutral design and colour, chosen jointly by the President and the Vice-President of the Republic.

The Greek and the Turkish Communities shall have the right to celebrate respectively the Greek and the Turkish national holidays.

THE PRESIDENT AND VICE-PRESIDENT

Executive power is vested in the President and the Vice-President, who are members of the Greek and Turkish Communities respectively, and are elected by their respective communities to hold office for five years.

The President of the Republic as Head of the State represents the Republic in all its official functions; signs the credentials of diplomatic envoys and receives the credentials of foreign diplomatic envoys; signs the credentials of delegates for the negotiation of international treaties, conventions or other agreements; signs the letter relating to the transmission of the instruments of ratification of any international treaties, conventions or agreements; confers the honours of the Republic.

The Vice-President of the Republic, as Vice-Head of the State, has the right to be present at all official functions; at the presentation of the credentials of foreign diplomatic envoys; to recommend to the President the conferment of honours on members of the Turkish Community, which recommendation the President shall accept unless there are grave reasons to the contrary.

The election of the President and the Vice-President of the Republic shall be direct, by universal suffrage and secret ballot, and shall, except in the case of a by-election, take place on the same day but separately.

The office of the President and of the Vice-President shall be incompatible with that of a Minister or of a Representative or of a member of a Communal Chamber or of a member of any municipal council including a Mayor or of a member of the armed or security forces of the Republic or with a public or municipal office.

The President and Vice-President of the Republic are invested by the House of Representatives.

The President and the Vice-President of the Republic in order to ensure the executive power shall have a Council of Ministers composed of seven Greek Ministers and three Turkish Ministers. The Ministers shall be designated respectively by the President and the Vice-President of the Republic who shall appoint them by an instrument signed by them both. The President convenes and presides over the meetings of the Council of Ministers, while the Vice-President may ask the President to convene the Council and may take part in the discussions.

The decisions of the Council of Ministers shall be taken by an absolute majority and shall, unless the right of final veto or return is exercised by the President or the Vice-President of the Republic or both, be promulgated immediately by them.

The executive power exercised by the President and the Vice-President of the Republic conjointly consists of:

Determining the design and colour of the flag.

Creation or establishment of honours.

Appointment of the members of the Council of Ministers.

Promulgation by publication of the decisions of the Council of Ministers.

Promulgation by publication of any law or decision passed by the House of Representatives.

Appointments and termination of appointments as in Articles provided.

Institution of compulsory military service.

Reduction or increase of the security forces.

Exercise of the prerogative of mercy in capital cases.

Remission, suspension and commutation of sentences.

Right of references to the Supreme Constitutional Court and publication of Court decisions.

Address of messages to the House of Representatives.

The executive powers which may be exercised separately by the President and Vice-President include: designation and termination of appointment of Greek and Turkish Ministers respectively; the right of final veto on Council decisions and on laws concerning foreign affairs, defence or security; the publication of the communal laws and decisions of the Greek and Turkish Communal Chambers respectively; the right of recourse to the Supreme Constitutional Court; the prerogative of mercy in capital cases; and addressing messages to the House of Representatives.

THE COUNCIL OF MINISTERS

The Council of Ministers shall exercise executive power in all matters, other than those which are within the competence of a Communal Chamber, including the following:

General direction and control of the government of the Republic and the direction of general policy.

Foreign affairs, defence and security.

Co-ordination and supervision of all public services.

Supervision and disposition of property belonging to the Republic.

Consideration of Bills to be introduced to the House of Representatives by a Minister.

Making of any order or regulation for the carrying into effect of any law as provided by such law.

Consideration of the Budget of the Republic to be introduced to the House of Representatives.

THE HOUSE OF REPRESENTATIVES*

The legislative power of the Republic shall be exercised by the House of Representatives in all matters except those expressly reserved to the Communal Chambers.

The number of Representatives shall be 50, subject to alteration by a resolution of the House of Representatives carried by a majority comprising two-thirds of the Representatives elected by the Greek Community and two-thirds of the Representatives elected by the Turkish Community.

Out of the number of Representatives 70% shall be elected by the Greek Community and 30% by the Turkish Community separately from amongst their members respectively, and, in the case of a contested election, by universal suffrage and by direct and secret ballot held on the same day.

The term of office of the House of Representatives shall be for a period of five years.

The President of the House of Representatives shall be a Greek, and shall be elected by the Representatives elected by the Greek Community, and the Vice-President shall be a Turk and shall be elected by the Representatives elected by the Turkish Community.

* Following a constitutional amendment in 1985, the number of seats in the House of Representatives was increased to 80 (of which 56 were allocated to Greek Cypriot deputies and 24 reserved for Turkish Cypriots).

CYPRUS

THE COMMUNAL CHAMBERS

The Greek and the Turkish Communities respectively shall elect from amongst their own members a Communal Chamber.

The Communal Chambers shall, in relation to their respective Community, have competence to exercise legislative power solely with regard to the following:

All religious, educational, cultural and teaching matters.

Personal status; composition and instances of courts dealing with civil disputes relating to personal status and to religious matters.

Imposition of personal taxes and fees on members of their respective Community in order to provide for their respective needs.

THE PUBLIC SERVICE AND THE ARMED FORCES

The public service shall be composed as to 70% of Greeks and as to 30% of Turks.

The Republic shall have an army of 2,000 men, of whom 60% shall be Greeks and 40% shall be Turks.

The security forces of the Republic shall consist of the police and gendarmerie and shall have a contingent of 2,000 men. The forces shall be composed as to 70% of Greeks and as to 30% of Turks.

OTHER PROVISIONS

The following measures have been passed by the House of Representatives since January 1964, when the Turkish members withdrew:

The amalgamation of the High Court and the Supreme Constitutional Court (see Judicial System section).

The abolition of the Greek Communal Chamber and the creation of a Ministry of Education.

The unification of the Municipalities.

The unification of the Police and the Gendarmerie.

The creation of a military force by providing that persons between the ages of 18 and 50 years can be called upon to serve in the National Guard.

The extension of the term of office of the President and the House of Representatives by one year intervals from July 1965 until elections in February 1968 and July 1970 respectively.

New electoral provisions; abolition of separate Greek and Turkish rolls; abolition of post of Vice-President, which was re-established in 1973.

The Government

HEAD OF STATE

President: DEMETRIS CHRISTOFIAS (took office 28 February 2008).

COUNCIL OF MINISTERS
(March 2008)

A coalition Government comprising the Anorthotiko Komma Ergazomenou Laou (AKEL), the Dimokratiko Komma (DIKO), the Kinima Sosialdimokraton EDEK (KISOS) and AKEL-backed independents (Ind.).

Minister of Foreign Affairs: MARKOS KYPRIANOU (DIKO).
Minister of Defence: COSTAS PAPACOSTAS (AKEL).
Minister of Finance: CHARILAOS STAVRAKIS (Ind.).
Minister of the Interior: NEOKLIS SYLIKIOTIS (AKEL).
Minister of Justice and Public Order: KYPROS CHRYSOSTOMIDES (Ind.).
Minister of Commerce, Industry and Tourism: ANTONIS PASCHALIDES (DIKO).
Minister of Education and Culture: ANDREAS DEMETRIOU (Ind.).
Minister of Health: CHRISTOS PATSALIDES (DIKO).
Minister of Labour and Social Insurance: SOTIROULLA CHARALAMBOUS (AKEL).
Minister of Communications and Works: NICOS NICOLAIDES (KISOS).
Minister of Agriculture, Natural Resources and the Environment: MICHALIS POLYNIKI CHARALAMBIDES (KISOS).
Government Spokesman: STEPHANOS STEPHANOU (AKEL).

Note: Under the Constitution of 1960, the position of Vice-President and three posts in the Council of Ministers are reserved for Turkish Cypriots. However, there has been no Turkish participation in the Government since December 1963.

MINISTRIES

Office of the President: Presidential Palace, Demosthenis Severis Ave, 1400 Nicosia; tel. 22867400; fax 22867594; e-mail president@presidency.gov.cy; internet www.cyprus.gov.cy.

Ministry of Agriculture, Natural Resources and the Environment: Loukis Akritas Ave, 1411 Nicosia; tel. 22408307; fax 22781156; e-mail registry@moa.gov.cy; internet www.moa.gov.cy.

Ministry of Commerce, Industry and Tourism: 6 Andreas Araouzos St, 1421 Nicosia; tel. 22867100; fax 22375120; e-mail perm.sec@mcit.gov.cy; internet www.mcit.gov.cy.

Ministry of Communications and Works: 28 Achaion St, Agios Andreas, 1424 Nicosia; tel. 22800288; fax 22776266; e-mail permsec@mcw.gov.cy; internet www.mcw.gov.cy.

Ministry of Defence: 4 Emmanuel Roides Ave, 1432 Nicosia; tel. 22807622; fax 22676182; e-mail defense@mod.gov.cy; internet www.mod.gov.cy.

Ministry of Education and Culture: Kimonos & Thoukydidou, Akropolis, 1434 Nicosia; tel. 22800600; fax 22305974; e-mail registry@moec.gov.cy; internet www.moec.gov.cy.

Ministry of Finance: Cnr Michalakis Karaolis St and Gregoriou Afxentiou St, 1439 Nicosia; tel. 22601192; fax 22602750; e-mail registry@mof.gov.cy; internet www.mof.gov.cy.

Ministry of Foreign Affairs: Presidential Palace Ave, 1447 Nicosia; tel. 22401000; fax 22661881; e-mail minforeign1@mfa.gov.cy; internet www.mfa.gov.cy.

Ministry of Health: Byron Ave, 1448 Nicosia; tel. 22309526; fax 22305803; e-mail ministryofhealth@cytanet.com.cy; internet www.moh.gov.cy.

Ministry of the Interior: Demosthenis Severis Ave, Ex Secretariat Compound, 1453 Nicosia; tel. 22867867; fax 22867778; e-mail cgregoriades@moi.gov.cy; internet www.moi.gov.cy.

Ministry of Justice and Public Order: 125 Athalassa Ave, 1461 Nicosia; tel. 22805955; fax 22518356; e-mail registry@mjpo.gov.cy; internet www.mjpo.gov.cy.

Ministry of Labour and Social Insurance: 7 Byron Ave, 1463 Nicosia; tel. 22401600; fax 22670993; e-mail administration@mlsi.gov.cy; internet www.mlsi.gov.cy.

President and Legislature

PRESIDENT

Presidential Election, First Ballot, 17 February 2008

Candidate	Valid votes	%
Demetris Christofias (AKEL)	150,016	33.29
Ioannis Kasoulides (Ind., with DISY support)	150,996	33.51
Tassos Papadopoulos (DIKO)	143,249	31.79
Marios Matsakis (DIKO)	3,460	0.77
Costas Kyriacou (Ind.)	1,092	0.24
Costas Themistocleous (Ind.)	753	0.17
Andreas Efstratiou (Ind.)	713	0.16
Christodoulos Neophytou (Ind.)	243	0.05
Anastasis Michael (Ind.)	117	0.03
Total	450,639	100.00

Presidential Election, Second Ballot, 24 February 2008

Candidate	Votes	%
Demetris Christofias (AKEL)	240,604	53.37
Ioannis Kasoulides (Ind., with DISY support)	210,195	46.63
Total*	469,143	100.00

*Including 18,344 blank or invalid votes (3.91% of total votes cast).

HOUSE OF REPRESENTATIVES

The House of Representatives originally consisted of 50 members, 35 from the Greek community and 15 from the Turkish community, elected for a term of five years. In January 1964 the Turkish members withdrew and set up the 'Turkish Legislative Assembly of the Turkish Cypriot Administration' (see below). At the 1985 elections the membership of the House was expanded to 80 members, of whom 56 were to be from the Greek community and 24 from the Turkish community (according to the ratio of representation specified in the Constitution).

President: MARIOS KAROYIAN.

CYPRUS

Elections for the Greek Representatives, 21 May 2006

Party	Votes	% of Votes	Seats
AKEL	131,066	31.1	18
DISY	127,776	30.3	18
DIKO	75,458	17.9	11
KISOS	37,533	8.9	5
Evro.Ko	24,196	5.8	3
KOP	8,193	2.0	1
Others	16,865	4.0	—
Total*	421,087	100.0	56

* Excluding 14,724 invalid votes.

Political Organizations

Agonistiko Dimokratiko Kinima (ADIK) (Fighting Democratic Movement): POB 216095, 80 Arch. Makariou III St, Flat 401, 1077 Nicosia; tel. 22765353; fax 22375737; e-mail info@adik.org.cy; internet www.adik.org.cy; f. 1999; centre-right; supports independent and united Cyprus and a settlement based on UN resolutions; Pres. DINOS MICHAELIDES; Gen. Sec. Dr YIANNIS PAPADOPOULOS.

Anorthotiko Komma Ergazomenou Laou (AKEL) (Progressive Party of the Working People): POB 21827, 4 E. Papaioannou St, 1513 Nicosia; tel. 22761121; fax 22761574; e-mail k.e.akel@cytanet.com.cy; internet www.akel.org.cy; f. 1941; successor to the Communist Party of Cyprus (f. 1926); Marxist-Leninist; supports united, sovereign, independent, federal and demilitarized Cyprus; over 14,000 mems; Sec.-Gen. (vacant).

Dimokratiko Komma (DIKO) (Democratic Party): POB 23979, 50 Grivas Dhigenis Ave, 1080 Nicosia; tel. 22873800; fax 22873801; e-mail diko@diko.org.cy; internet www.diko.org.cy; f. 1976; absorbed Enosi Kentrou (Centre Union, f. 1981) in 1989; supports settlement of the Cyprus problem based on UN resolutions; Pres. MARIOS KAROYIAN; Gen. Sec. VASSILIS PALMAS.

Dimokratikos Synagermos (DISY) (Democratic Rally): POB 25305, 25 Pindarou St, 1308 Nicosia; tel. 22883000; fax 22752751; e-mail disy@disy.org.cy; internet www.disy.org.cy; f. 1976; absorbed Democratic National Party (DEK) in 1977, New Democratic Front (NEDIPA) in 1988 and Liberal Party in 1998; advocates the reunification of Cyprus on the basis of a bi-zonal federation; also advocates market economy with restricted state intervention and increased state social role; 40,000 mems; Pres. NIKOS ANASTASIADES; Dir-Gen. GEORGE LIVERAS.

Enomeni Dimokrates (EDI) (United Democrats): POB 23494, 1683 Nicosia; tel. 22663030; fax 22664747; e-mail info@edi.org.cy; internet www.edi.org.cy; f. 1996 by merger of Ananeotiko Dimokratiko Sosialistiko Kinema (ADISOK—Democratic Socialist Reform Movement) and Kinema ton Eleftheron Dimokraton (KED—Movement of Free Democrats); Pres. PRAXOULA ANTONIADOU KYRIAKOU; Gen. Sec. MICHALIS SHIANIS.

Epalxi Anasygrotisis Kentrou (EPALXI) (Political Forum for the Restructuring of the Centre): 1 Lambousa St, 1095 Nicosia; POB 22119, 1517 Nicosia; tel. 22777000; fax 22779939; e-mail info@epalxi.com; internet www.epalxi.com; f. 1998; aims to achieve a wider grouping of all centrist social-democratic movements; supports a settlement to the Cyprus problem based on the principles of the Rule of Law, international law and respect for human rights for all citizens, and the establishment of a democratic federal system of govt.

Evropaiko Komma (Evro.Ko) (European Party): POB 22496, 1522 Nicosia; tel. 22460033; fax 22761144; e-mail evropaiko.komma@cytanet.com.cy; internet www.evropaikokomma.org; f. 2005 by fmr mems of Neoi Orizontes (NEO) and other political orgs; Pres. DEMETRIS SYLLOURIS.

Kinima Oikologoi Perivallontistoi (KOP) (Cyprus Green Party—Movement of Ecologists and Environmentalists): POB 29682, 169 Athalassas Ave, 1722 Nicosia; tel. 22518787; fax 22512710; e-mail greenparty@cytanet.com.cy; internet www.cyprusgreens.org; f. 1996; opposed to any geographical division of the island; Gen. Sec. GEORGE PERDIKES.

Kinima Sosialdimokraton EDEK (KISOS) (Movement of Social Democrats): POB 21064, 40 Byron Ave, 1096 Nicosia; tel. 22670121; fax 22678894; e-mail socialdimokratestypos@cytanet.com.cy; internet www.edek.org.cy; f. 2000 as successor to Socialistico Komma Kyprou (EDEK—Socialist Party of Cyprus, f. 1969); supports independent, non-aligned, unitary, demilitarized Cyprus; Pres. YIANNAKIS OMIROU; Hon. Pres. Dr VASSOS LYSSARIDES.

Kinisi Politikou Eksychronismou (Movement for Political Reforms): 22 Stasikratous St, 1065 Nicosia; tel. 22668894; fax 22668892; f. 1995; supports settlement of the Cyprus problem based on UN resolutions.

Komma Evrodimokratikis Ananeosis (KEA) (Eurodemocratic Renewal Party): 176 Athalassa Ave, Office 402, 2025 Nicosia; tel. 22514551; fax 22513565; e-mail info@eliades-paschalides.com.cy; f. 1998; supports federal settlement to the Cyprus problem based on UN resolutions; Pres. ANTONIS PASCHALIDES.

Diplomatic Representation

EMBASSIES AND HIGH COMMISSIONS IN CYPRUS

Australia: 4 Annis Komninis St, 2nd Floor, 1060 Nicosia; tel. 22753001; fax 22766486; e-mail auscomm@logos.cy.net; internet www.cyprus.embassy.gov.au; High Commr GARTH LESLIE HUNT.

Austria: POB 23961, 34 Demosthenis Severis Ave, 1687 Nicosia; tel. 22410151; fax 22680099; e-mail nicosia-ob@bmeia.gv.at; Ambassador EVA HAGER.

Belgium: 2A Chilonos St, Office 102, 1101 Nicosia; tel. 22449020; fax 22774717; e-mail nicosia@diplobel.be; internet www.diplomatie.be/nicosia; Chargé d'affaires a.i. PIERRE GILLON.

Bulgaria: POB 24029, 13 Konst. Paleologos St, 2406 Engomi, Nicosia; tel. 22672486; fax 22676598; e-mail bulgaria@cytanet.com.cy; Ambassador PETER GEORGIEV VODENSKI.

China, People's Republic: POB 24531, 30 Archimedes St, 2411 Engomi, Nicosia; tel. 22352182; fax 22353530; e-mail eocinc@spidernet.com.cy; internet cy.china-embassy.org; Ambassador ZHAO YALI.

Cuba: POB 28923, 1 Androcleous St, 1060 Nicosia; tel. 22769743; fax 22753820; e-mail embacuba@spidernet.com.cy; Ambassador PABLO RODRIGUEZ VIDAL.

Czech Republic: POB 5202, 48 Arsinois St, 1307 Nicosia; tel. 22421118; fax 22421059; e-mail nicosia@embassy.mzv.cz; internet www.mzv.cz/nicosia; Ambassador JAN BONDY.

Denmark: POB 20995, 7 Dositheou St, Parabldg Block C, 4th Floor, 1071 Nicosia; tel. 22377417; fax 22377472; e-mail nicamb@um.dk; internet www.ambnicosia.um.dk; Ambassador SVEND WAEVER.

Egypt: POB 21752, 14 Ayios Prokopios St, Engomi, 2406 Nicosia; tel. 22449050; fax 22449081; e-mail info@egyptianembassy.org.cy; internet www.egyptianembassy.org.cy; Ambassador AHMAD IBRAHIM RAGHEB.

Finland: POB 21438, Arch. Makarios III Ave 9, 1508 Nicosia; tel. 22458020; fax 22477880; e-mail sanomat.nic@formin.fi; internet www.finland.org.cy; Ambassador RISTO PIIPPONEN.

France: 14–16 Saktouri St, 2nd Floor, Agioi Omologitai, 1080 Nicosia; tel. 22585300; fax 22585335; e-mail ambafrance@cytanet.com.cy; internet www.ambafrancechypre.org; Ambassador NICOLAS GALEY.

Georgia: 26 Eleonon St, Strovolos, 2057 Nicosia; tel. 22357327; fax 22357307; e-mail geoembassy@cytanet.com.cy; Ambassador LASHA ZHVANIA.

Germany: 10 Nikitaras St, Ay. Omoloyitae, 1080 Nicosia; POB 25705, 1311 Nicosia; tel. 22451145; fax 22665694; e-mail info@nikosia.diplo.de; internet www.nikosia.diplo.de; Ambassador Dr ROLF KAISER.

Greece: POB 21799, 8–10 Byron Ave, 1096 Nicosia; tel. 22445111; fax 22680649; e-mail info@greekembassy-cy.org; internet www.greekembassy-cy.org; Ambassador DEMETRIOS RALLIS.

Holy See: POB 21964, Holy Cross Catholic Church, Paphos Gate, 1010 Nicosia (Apostolic Nunciature); tel. 22662132; fax 22660767; e-mail holcross@logos.cy.net; Apostolic Nuncio Most Rev. ANTONIO FRANCO (Titular Archbishop of Gallese—resident in Jerusalem) (designate).

Hungary: 2 Prigkipos Karolou St, Ayios Dhometios, 2373 Nicosia; tel. 22459130; fax 22459134; e-mail huembnic@cytanet.com.cy; Ambassador JANOS KISFALVI.

India: POB 25544, 3 Indira Gandhi St, Engomi, 2413 Nicosia; tel. 22351741; fax 22352062; e-mail hicomind@spidernet.com.cy; internet www.hcinicosia.org.cy; High Commr LAVANYA PRASAD.

Iran: POB 8145, 42 Armenias St, Akropolis, Nicosia; tel. 22314459; fax 22315446; e-mail iranemb@cytanet.com.cy; Ambassador Dr SAYED REZA HADJ-ZARGARBASHI.

Ireland: 7 Aiantas St, Ayios Omoloyites, 1082 Nicosia; POB 23848, 1686 Nicosia; tel. 22818183; fax 22660050; e-mail nicosiaembassy@dfa.ie; Ambassador TOM BRADY.

Israel: POB 25159, 4 Ioanni Grypari St, 1090 Nicosia; tel. 22369500; fax 22666338; e-mail ambassadorsec3@nicosia.mfa.gov.il; internet nicosia.mfa.gov.il; Ambassador AVRAHAM HADDAD.

Italy: POB 27695, 11 25th March St, Engomi, 2408 Nicosia; tel. 22357635; fax 22357616; e-mail ambnico.mail@esteri.it; internet www.ambnicosia.esteri.it; Ambassador LUIGI NAPOLITANO.

CYPRUS

Lebanon: POB 21924, 6 Chiou St, Ayios Dhometios, 1515 Nicosia; tel. 22878282; fax 22878293; Ambassador MICHEL EL-KHOURY.

Libya: POB 22487, 7 Stassinos Ave, 1060 Nicosia; tel. 22460055; fax 22452710; e-mail lapbcy@cytanet.com.cy; Ambassador KHALIFA M. FERGIANI.

Netherlands: POB 23835, 34 Demosthenis Severis Ave, 1080 Nicosia; tel. 22873666; fax 22872399; e-mail nic@minbuza.nl; internet www.nlembassy.org.cy; Ambassador JAN ERIC VAN DEN BERG.

Poland: POB 22743, 12–14 Kennedy Ave, 1087 Nicosia; tel. 22753784; fax 22751981; e-mail secretariat@polamb.org.cy; Ambassador ZBIGNIEW SZYMANSKI.

Portugal: Arch. Makarios III Ave 9, Severis Bldg, 5th Floor, POB 27407, 1645 Nicosia; tel. 22375131; fax 22756456; e-mail portembnic@cytanet.com.cy; Ambassador ANTONIO JORGE JACOB CARVALHO.

Qatar: Nicosia; Ambassador MUBARAK ABD AR-RAHMAN MUBARAK AN-NASSER.

Romania: POB 22210, 27 Pireos St, Strovolos, 2023 Nicosia; tel. 22495333; fax 22517383; e-mail rompol@cytanet.com.cy; Ambassador ANDREEA PASTARNAC.

Russia: POB 21845, Ayios Prokopias St and Archbishop Makarios III Ave, Engomi, 2406 Nicosia; tel. 22774622; fax 22774854; e-mail russia1@cytanet.com.cy; internet www.cyprus.mid.ru; Ambassador ANDREI A. NESTERENKO.

Serbia: 2 Vasilissis Olgas St, Engomi, 1903 Nicosia; tel. 22777511; fax 22775910; e-mail nicosia@scg.org.cy; internet www.serbia.org.cy; Ambassador MIRKO JELIĆ.

Slovakia: POB 21165, 4 Kalamatas St, 2002 Strovolos, Nicosia; tel. 22879681; fax 22311715; e-mail skembassy@cytanet.com.cy; Ambassador ANNA TURENICOVA.

Spain: POB 28349, 32 Strovolos Ave, 2018 Strovolos, Nicosia; tel. 22450410; fax 22491291; e-mail enmora@cytanet.com.cy; Ambassador JOSÉ MANUEL CERVERA DE GÓNGORA.

Sweden: POB 21621, 9 Archbishop Makarios Ave, Severis Bldg, Second Floor, 1065 Nicosia; tel. 22458088; fax 22374522; e-mail ambassaden.nicosia@foreign.ministry.se; internet www.swedenabroad.se/nicosia; Ambassador INGEMAR LINDAHL.

Switzerland: 46 Themistocles Dervis St, Medcon Tower, 1066 Nicosia; POB 20739, 1663 Nicosia; tel. 22466800; fax 22766008; e-mail nic.vertretung@eda.admin.ch; internet www.eda.admin.ch/nicosia; Ambassador MARIANNE ENGLER.

Syria: POB 21891, 24 Nikodimos Mylona St, Ayios Antonios, 1071 Nicosia; tel. 22817333; fax 22756963; e-mail syremb@cytanet.com.cy; Chargé d'affaires NADER NADER.

Ukraine: 10 Andrea Miaouli St, Makedonitissa, Engomi, 2415 Nicosia; tel. 22464380; fax 22464381; e-mail info@ukrembassy.com.cy; internet www.ukrembassy.com.cy; Chargé d'affaires a.i. ANATOLIY MALIUSKA.

United Kingdom: POB 21978, Alexander Pallis St, 1587 Nicosia; tel. 22861100; fax 22861125; e-mail brithc.2@cytanet.com.cy; internet www.britishhighcommission.gov.uk/cyprus; High Commr PETER JOSEPH MILLETT.

USA: Metochiou and Ploutarchou, Engomi, 2407 Nicosia; POB 24536, 1385 Nicosia; tel. 22393939; fax 22780944; e-mail consularnicosia@state.gov; internet cyprus.usembassy.gov; Ambassador RONALD L. SCHLICHER.

Judicial System

Supreme Council of Judicature: Nicosia; The Supreme Council of Judicature is composed of the President and Judges of the Supreme Court. It is responsible for the appointment, promotion, transfer, etc., of the judges exercising civil and criminal jurisdiction in the District Courts, the Assize Courts, the Family Courts, the Military Court, the Rent Control Courts and the Industrial Dispute Court.

SUPREME COURT

Supreme Court

Charalambos Mouskos St, 1404 Nicosia; tel. 22865741; fax 22304500; e-mail chief.reg@sc.judicial.gov.cy; internet www.supremecourt.gov.cy.

The Constitution of 1960 provided for a separate Supreme Constitutional Court and High Court but in 1964, in view of the resignation of their neutral presidents, these were amalgamated to form a single Supreme Court.

The Supreme Court is the final appellate court in the Republic and the final adjudicator in matters of constitutional and administrative law, including recourses on conflict of competence between state organs on questions of the constitutionality of laws, etc. It deals with appeals from Assize Courts, District Courts and other inferior courts as well as from the decisions of its own judges when exercising original jurisdiction in certain matters such as prerogative orders of *habeas corpus, mandamus, certiorari*, etc., and in admiralty cases.

President: CHRISTOS ARTEMIDES.

Judges: PETROS ARTEMIS, IOANNIS CONSTANTINIDES, FRIXOS NICOLAIDES, TAKIS ELIADES, ANDREAS KRAMVIS, RALLIS GAVRIELIDES, DEMETRIOS H. HADJIHAMBIS, EFI PAPADOPOULOU, MICHAEL PHOTIOU, MYRON NICOLATOS, GEORGE EROTOKRITOU, STELIOS NATHANAEL.

Attorney-General: PETROS CLERIDES.

OTHER COURTS

As required by the Constitution, a law was passed in 1960 providing for the establishment, jurisdiction and powers of courts of civil and criminal jurisdiction, i.e. of six District Courts and six Assize Courts. In accordance with the provisions of new legislation, approved in 1991, a permanent Assize Court, with powers of jurisdiction in all districts, was established.

In addition to a single Military Court, there are specialized courts concerned with cases relating to industrial disputes, rent control and family law.

'Turkish Republic of Northern Cyprus'

The Turkish intervention in Cyprus in July 1974 resulted in the establishment of a separate area in northern Cyprus under the control of the Autonomous Turkish Cypriot Administration, with a Council of Ministers and separate judicial, financial, police, military and educational machinery serving the Turkish community.

On 13 February 1975 the Turkish-occupied zone of Cyprus was declared the 'Turkish Federated State of Cyprus', and Rauf Denktaş declared President. At the second joint meeting held by the Executive Council and Legislative Assembly of the Autonomous Turkish Cypriot Administration, it was decided to set up a Constituent Assembly which would prepare a constitution for the 'Turkish Federated State of Cyprus' within 45 days. This Constitution, which was approved by the Turkish Cypriot population in a referendum held on 8 June 1975, was regarded by the Turkish Cypriots as a first step towards a federal republic of Cyprus. The main provisions of the Constitution are summarized below:

The 'Turkish Federated State of Cyprus' is a democratic, secular republic based on the principles of social justice and the rule of law. It shall exercise only those functions that fall outside the powers and functions expressly given to the (proposed) Federal Republic of Cyprus. Necessary amendments shall be made to the Constitution of the 'Turkish Federated State of Cyprus' when the Constitution of the Federal Republic comes into force. The official language is Turkish.

Legislative power is vested in a Legislative Assembly, composed of 40 deputies, elected by universal suffrage for a period of five years. The President is Head of State and is elected by universal suffrage for a period of five years. No person may be elected President for more than two consecutive terms. The Council of Ministers shall be composed of a prime minister and 10 ministers. Judicial power is exercised through independent courts.

Other provisions cover such matters as the rehabilitation of refugees, property rights outside the 'Turkish Federated State', protection of coasts, social insurance, the rights and duties of citizens, etc.

On 15 November 1983 a unilateral declaration of independence brought into being the 'Turkish Republic of Northern Cyprus', which, like the 'Turkish Federated State of Cyprus', was not granted international recognition.

The Constituent Assembly, established after the declaration of independence, prepared a new constitution, which was approved by the Turkish Cypriot electorate on 5 May 1985. The new Constitution is very similar to the old one, but the number of deputies in the Legislative Assembly was increased to 50.

HEAD OF STATE

President of the 'Turkish Republic of Northern Cyprus': MEHMET ALI TALAT (inaugurated 24 April 2005).

COUNCIL OF MINISTERS
(March 2008)

A coalition of the Cumhuriyetçi Türk Partisi (CTP) and the Özgürlük ve Reform Partisi (ORP).

Prime Minister: FERDI SABIT SOYER (CTP).

CYPRUS

Deputy Prime Minister and Minister of Foreign Affairs: TURGAY AVCI (ORP).

Minister of Economy and Tourism: ERDOĞAN ŞANDLIDAĞ (ORP).

Minister of the Interior, Rural Affairs and Housing: ÖZKAN MURAT (CTP).

Minister of Finance: AHMET UZUN (CTP).

Minister of National Education and Culture: CANAN ÖZTOPRAK (CTP).

Minister of Agriculture: ÖNDER SENNAROĞLU (ORP).

Minister of Public Works and Transport: SALIH USAR (CTP).

Minister of the Environment and Natural Resources: MUSTAFA GÖKMEN (ORP).

Minister of Health and Social Welfare: EŞREF VAIZ (CTP).

Minister of Labour and Social Security: SONAY ADEM (CTP).

MINISTRIES

Office of the President: Lefkoşa (Nicosia), Mersin 10, Turkey; tel. 2283444; fax 2272252; e-mail info@kktc-cb.org; internet www.trncpresidency.org.

Prime Minister's Office: Selcuklu Rd, Lefkoşa (Nicosia), Mersin 10, Turkey; tel. 2283141; fax 2277225; e-mail info@kktcbasbakanlik.org; internet www.kktcbasbakanlik.org.

Deputy Prime Minister's Office and Ministry of Foreign Affairs: Selcuklu Rd, Lefkoşa (Nicosia), Mersin 10, Turkey; tel. 2283365; fax 2284847; e-mail bakanlik@trncinfo.org; internet www.trncinfo.org.

Ministry of Agriculture: Salih Mecit Sok. 16, Lefkoşa (Nicosia), Mersin 10, Turkey; tel. 2283735; fax 2286945; e-mail info@kktob.org; internet www.kktob.org.

Ministry of Economy and Tourism: Selçuklu Rd, Lefkoşa (Nicosia), Mersin 10, Turkey; tel. 2289629; fax 2285625; internet www.ekonomiveturizmbakanligi.com.

Ministry of the Environment and Natural Resources: Lefkoşa (Nicosia), Mersin 10, Turkey; tel. 2275032; fax 2283776.

Ministry of Finance: Lefkoşa (Nicosia), Mersin 10, Turkey; tel. 2283116; fax 2278230; e-mail bim@kktcmaliye.com; internet www.kktcmaliye.com.

Ministry of Health and Social Welfare: Lefkoşa (Nicosia), Mersin 10, Turkey; tel. 2277283; fax 2283893; e-mail saglik@kktc.net; internet www.saglikbakanligi.com.

Ministry of the Interior, Rural Affairs and Housing: Lefkoşa (Nicosia), Mersin 10, Turkey; tel. 2283344; fax 2285054.

Ministry of Labour and Social Security: Lefkoşa (Nicosia), Mersin 10, Turkey; tel. 2275032; fax 2283776.

Ministry of National Education and Culture: Lefkoşa (Nicosia), Mersin 10, Turkey; e-mail meb@mebnet.net; internet www.mebnet.net.

Ministry of Public Works and Transport: Lefkoşa (Nicosia), Mersin 10, Turkey; tel. 2283666; fax 2281891.

PRESIDENT

Election, 17 April 2005

Candidates	Votes	%
Mehmet Ali Talat (Cumhuriyetçi Türk Partisi)	55,943	55.80
Dr Derviş Eroğlu (Ulusal Bırlık Partisi)	22,869	22.80
Dr Mustafa Arabacioğlu (Demokrat Parti)	13,302	13.30
Nuri Çevikel (Yeni Partisi)	4,816	4.80
Zeki Besiktepeli (Ind.)	1,728	1.70
Hüseyin Angolemli (Toplumcu Kurtulus Partisi)	1,054	1.10
Arif Salih Kirdag (Ind.)	306	0.30
Ayhan Kaymak (Ind.)	168	0.20
Total	100,186	100.00

LEGISLATIVE ASSEMBLY

Speaker: FATMA EKENOĞLU (CTP).

General Election, 20 February 2005

Party	Votes	% of votes	Seats*
Cumhuriyetçi Türk Partisi	577,444	44.5	25
Ulusal Bırlık Partisi	410,813	31.7	17
Demokrat Parti	174,721	13.5	7
Bariş ve Demokrasi Hareketi	75,747	5.8	1
Others	55,284	4.5	—
Total	1,294,009	100.0	50

* The distribution of seats includes the results of a by-election, which was held on 25 June 2006 to fill two vacant seats. One representative of the Ulusal Bırlık Partisi (UBP) subsequently became an independent deputy. In September three parliamentary deputies resigned from the UBP and one from the Demokrat Parti and collectively established a new organization, the Özgürlük ve Reform Partisi.

ELECTORAL COMMISSION

Yüksek Seçim Kurulu (YSK) (Higher Council of Elections): Lefkoşa (Nicosia), Mersin 10, Turkey; Pres. METIN A. HAKKI.

POLITICAL ORGANIZATIONS

Çözüm ve AB Partisi (CABP) (Solution and European Union Party): 145 Bedreddin Demirel Ave, Lefkoşa (Nicosia), Mersin 10, Turkey; tel. 2280618; fax 2289366; Leader ALI EREL.

Cumhuriyetçi Türk Partisi (CTP) (Republican Turkish Party): 99A Şehit Salahi, Şevket Sok., Lefkoşa (Nicosia), Mersin 10, Turkey; tel. 2273300; fax 2281914; e-mail info@ctp-bg.com; internet www.ctp-bg.com; f. 1970 by mems of the Turkish community in Cyprus; district orgs at Gazi Mağusa (Famagusta), Girne (Kyrenia), Güzelyurt (Morphou) and Lefkoşa (Nicosia); Leader FERDI SABIT SOYER; Gen. Sec. ÖMER KALYONCU.

Demokrat Parti (DP) (Democrat Party): Hasane Ilgaz Sok. 13A, Lefkoşa (Nicosia), Mersin 10, Turkey; tel. 2283795; fax 2287130; e-mail yenidem@kktc.net; internet www.demokratparti.net; f. 1992 by disaffected representatives of the Ulusal Bırlık Partisi; merged with the Yeni Doğuş Partisi (New Dawn Party; f. 1984) and Sosyal Demokrat Partisi (Social Democrat Party) in May 1993; Leader SERDAR DENKTAŞ.

Kıbrıs Adalet Partisi (KAP) (Cyprus Justice Party): 1 Osman Paşa Ave, Köşklüçiftlik, Lefkoşa (Nicosia), Mersin 10, Turkey; tel. 2270274; fax 2289938; Leader OĞUZ KALEIOĞLU.

Kıbrıs Sosyalist Partisi (KSP) (Cyprus Socialist Party): Lefkoşa (Nicosia), Mersin 10, Turkey; e-mail ksp@kibrissosyalistpartisi.org; internet www.kibrissosyalistpartisi.org; Gen. Sec. YUSUF ALKIM.

Milliyetçi Bariş Partisi (MBP) (National Peace Party): Lefkoşa (Nicosia), Mersin 10, Turkey; f. 2003; Leader ERTUĞRUL HASIPOĞLU.

Özgürlük ve Reform Partisi (ORP) (Özgür Parti—Freedom and Reform Party): Lala Mustafa Paşa Sok. 18, Köşklüçiftlik, Lefkoşa (Nicosia), Mersin 10, Turkey; tel. 2290593; fax 2270537; internet www.ozgurparti.com; f. 2006 by breakaway parliamentary deputies; Leader Dr TURGAY AVCI.

Serbest Düşünce Partisi (Free Thought Party): Lefkoşa (Nicosia), Mersin 10, Turkey; f. 2004 by fmr mems of the Demokrat Parti; Chair. SALIH COSAR.

Toplumcu Demokrasi Partisi (TDP) (Communal Democracy Party): 33A Mehmet Akif Cad., Lefkoşa (Nicosia), Mersin 10, Turkey; tel. 2279456; fax 2271172; e-mail info@toplumcudemokrasipartisi.com; internet www.toplumcudemokrasipartisi.com; f. 2007, by merger between the Bariş ve Demokrasi Hareketi (Peace and Democracy Movement) and the Toplumcu Kurtulus Partisi (Communal Liberation Party).

Ulusal Bırlık Partisi (UBP) (National Unity Party): 9 Atatürk Meydanı, Lefkoşa (Nicosia), Mersin 10, Turkey; tel. 2273972; fax 2288732; e-mail ubp@kibris.net; internet www.ubp-kktc.org; f. 1975; right of centre; opposes reunification of Cyprus; Pres. TAHSIN ERTUGRULOĞLU; Sec.-Gen. NAZIM ÇAVUŞOĞLU.

Yeni Partisi (New Party): Lefkoşa (Nikosia), Mersin 10, Turkey; f. 2004; Leader NURI ÇEVIKEL.

Yurtsever Bırlık Hareketi (YBH) (Patriotic Unity Movement): Lefkoşa (Nicosia), Mersin 10, Turkey; tel. 2274917; fax 2288931; e-mail ybh@north-cyprus.net; f. 1989 as New Cyprus Party (YKP); publishes weekly newsletter Yeniçag; Leader REMZI YEKTAOĞLU.

DIPLOMATIC REPRESENTATION

Embassy in the 'TRNC'

Turkey: Bedrettin Demirel Cad., T.C. Lefkoşa Büyükelçisi, Lefkoşa (Nicosia), Mersin 10, Turkey; tel. 2272314; fax 2282209; e-mail tclefkbe@emu.edu.tr; internet www.tclefkosabe.org; Ambassador AYDAN KARAHAN.

Turkey is the only country officially to have recognized the 'Turkish Republic of Northern Cyprus'.

JUDICIAL SYSTEM

Supreme Court: Lefkoşa (Nicosia), Mersin 10, Turkey; tel. 2287535; fax 2285265; e-mail mahkeme@kktc.net; internet www.mahkemeler.net; The highest court in the 'TRNC' is the Supreme Court. The Supreme Court functions as the Constitutional Court, the Court of Appeal and the High Administrative Court. The Supreme Court, sitting as the Constitutional Court, has exclusive jurisdiction to adjudicate finally on all matters prescribed by the Constitution. The Supreme Court, sitting as the Court of Appeal, is the highest appellate court in the 'TRNC' in both civil and criminal cases. It also has original jurisdiction in certain matters of judicial review. The Supreme Court, sitting as the High Administrative Court, has exclusive jurisdiction on matters relating to administrative law.

The Supreme Court is composed of a president and seven judges.

President: METIN HAKKI.

Judges: CELÂL KARABACAK, TANER ERGINEL, NEVVAR NOLAN, MUSTAFA ÖZKÖK, GÖNÜL ERÖNEN, SEYIT A. BENSEN.

Subordinate Courts: Judicial power other than that exercised by the Supreme Court is exercised by the Assize Courts, District Courts and Family Courts.

Supreme Council of Judicature

The Supreme Council of Judicature, composed of the president and judges of the Supreme Court, a member appointed by the President of the 'TRNC', a member appointed by the Legislative Assembly, the Attorney-General and a member elected by the Bar Association, is responsible for the appointment, promotion, transfer and matters relating to the discipline of all judges. The appointments of the president and judges of the Supreme Court are subject to the approval of the President of the 'TRNC'.

Attorney-General: ASKAN ILGEN.

Religion

Greeks form 77% of the population and most of them belong to the Orthodox Church, although there are also adherents of the Armenian Apostolic Church, the Anglican Communion and the Roman Catholic Church (including Maronites). Most Turks (about 18% of the population) are Muslims.

CHRISTIANITY

The Orthodox Church of Cyprus

The Autocephalous Orthodox Church of Cyprus, founded in AD 45, is part of the Eastern Orthodox Church; the Church is independent, and the Archbishop, who is also the Ethnarch (national leader of the Greek community), is elected by representatives of the towns and villages of Cyprus. The Church comprises six dioceses, and in 1995 had an estimated 600,000 members.

Archbishop of Nova Justiniana and all Cyprus: Archbishop CHRYSOSTOMOS II, POB 1130, Archbishop Kyprianos St, Nicosia; tel. 22430696; fax 22432470.

Metropolitan of Paphos: Bishop CHRYSOSTOMOS.

Metropolitan of Kitium: Bishop CHRYSOSTOMOS, POB 40036, 6300 Larnaca; tel. 24652269; fax 24655588; e-mail mlarnaca@logosnet.cy.net.

Metropolitan of Kyrenia: Bishop PAULUS.

Metropolitan of Limassol: Bishop ATHANASIOS.

Metropolitan of Morphou: Bishop NEOPHYTIOS.

The Roman Catholic Church

Latin Rite

The Patriarchate of Jerusalem covers Israel, Jordan and Cyprus. The Patriarch is resident in Jerusalem (see the chapter on Israel).

Vicar Patriarchal for Cyprus: Fr UMBERTO BARATO, Holy Cross Catholic Church, Paphos Gate, POB 21964, 1010 Nicosia; tel. 22662132; fax 22660767; e-mail holcross@logos.cy.net.

Maronite Rite

Most of the Roman Catholics in Cyprus are adherents of the Maronite rite. Prior to June 1988 the Archdiocese of Cyprus included part of Lebanon. At 31 December 2005 the archdiocese contained an estimated 10,000 Maronite Catholics.

Archbishop of Cyprus: Most Rev. BOUTROS GEMAYEL, POB 22249, Maronite Archbishop's House, 8 Ayios Maronas St, Nicosia; tel. 22678877; fax 22668260; e-mail archmar@cytanet.com.cy.

The Anglican Communion

Anglicans in Cyprus are adherents of the Episcopal Church in Jerusalem and the Middle East, officially inaugurated in January 1976. The Church has four dioceses. The diocese of Cyprus and the Gulf includes Cyprus, Iraq and the countries of the Arabian peninsula.

Bishop in Cyprus and the Gulf, President Bishop of the Episcopal Church in Jerusalem and the Middle East: Right Rev. MICHAEL LEWIS, c/o POB 22075, Diocesan Office, 2 Grigoris Afxentiou St, 1516 Nicosia; tel. 22671220; fax 22674553; e-mail cygulf@spidernet.com.cy; internet www.cypgulf.org; Archdeacon in Cyprus Very Rev. STEPHEN COLLIS.

Other Christian Churches

Among other denominations active in Cyprus are the Armenian Apostolic Church and the Greek Evangelical Church.

ISLAM

Most adherents of Islam in Cyprus, of whom the majority reside in the 'TRNC', are Sunni Muslims of the Hanafi sect. In 2006 an estimated 99% of Turkish Cypriots were Muslims, compared with less than 3% of Greek Cypriots. The religious head of the Muslim community in the 'TRNC' is the Grand Mufti.

Grand Mufti of the 'TRNC': Sheikh AS-SAYYID MUHAMMAD NAZIM ADIL AL-QUBRUSI AL-HAQQANI, PK 142, Lefkoşa (Nicosia), Mersin 10, Turkey.

The Press

GREEK CYPRIOT DAILIES

Alithia (Truth): 26A Pindaros and Androklis St, 1060 Nicosia; POB 21695, 1512 Nicosia; tel. 22763040; fax 22763945; e-mail news@alithia-news.com; f. 1952 as a weekly, 1982 as a daily; morning; Greek; right-wing; Man. Dir FRIXOS N. KOULERMOS; Chief Editor PAMBOS CHARALAMBOUS; circ. 11,000.

Cyprus Mail: 24 Vassilios Voulgaroktonos St, 1010 Nicosia; POB 21144, 1502 Nicosia; tel. 22818585; fax 22676385; e-mail mail@cyprus-mail.com; internet www.cyprus-mail.com; f. 1945; morning; English; independent; Man. Dir KYRIACOS IAKOVIDES; Editor KOSTA PAVLOWITCH; circ. 6,000.

Haravgi (Dawn): ETAK Bldg, 6 Ezekia Papaioannou St, 1075 Nicosia; POB 21556, 1510 Nicosia; tel. 22766666; fax 22765154; e-mail haravgi@spidernet.com.cy; internet www.haravgi.com.cy; f. 1956; morning; Greek; organ of AKEL; Dir and Chief Editor ANDROULLA GIOUROV; Publr KYPROS KOURTELLARIS; circ. 10,000.

Machi (Combat): POB 27628, 14A Danaes St, Engomi, 2408 Nicosia; tel. 22356676; fax 22356701; e-mail syntaxi@maxinewspaper.com; internet www.maxinewspaper.com; f. 1960; morning; Greek; right-wing; Gen. Man. MINA SAMPSON; Chief Editor PAMBOS MITIDES; circ. 4,750.

O Phileleftheros (Liberal): Commercial Centre, 1 Diogenous St, 6th–7th Floor, Engomi, 2404 Nicosia; POB 21094, 1501 Nicosia; tel. 22744000; fax 22590122; e-mail mailbox@phileleftheros.com; internet www.phileleftheros.com.cy; f. 1955; morning; Greek; independent, moderate; Exec. Dir MYRTO MARKIDOU-SELIPA; Senior Editor ARISTOS MICHAELIDES; circ. 28,000.

Politis (Citizen): 8 Vassilios Voulgaroktonos St, 1010 Nicosia; POB 22894, 1524 Nicosia; tel. 22861861; fax 22861871; e-mail info@politis-news.com; internet www.politis.com.cy; f. 1999; morning; Greek; independent; Publr YIANNIS PAPADOPOULOS; Chief Editors ANDREAS PARASCHOS, SOTERIS PAROUTIS.

Simerini (Today): POB 21836, 31 Archangelos Ave, Strovolos, 2054 Nicosia; tel. 22580580; fax 22580570; e-mail mail@simerini.com; internet www.simerini.com; f. 1976; morning; Greek; right-wing; supports DISY; Pres. KOSTAS HADJIKOSTIS; Publr PETROS ZACHARIADES; circ. 17,000.

TURKISH CYPRIOT DAILIES

Afrika: Lefkoşa (Nicosia), Mersin 10, Turkey; tel. 2271338; fax 2274585; e-mail avrupa@kktc.net; internet www.afrikagazetesi.com; frmly Avrupa; Turkish; independent; Editor ŞENER LEVENT; circ. 3,000.

Halkın Sesi (Voice of the People): 172 Girne Cad., Lefkoşa (Nicosia), Mersin 10, Turkey; tel. 2273141; fax 2272612; e-mail halkinsesi@north-cyprus.net; internet www.halkinsesi.org; f. 1942; morning; Turkish; independent Turkish nationalist; Editor AKAY CEMAL; circ. 15,000.

Kıbrıs: Dr Fazil Küçük Bul., Yeni Sanayi Bölgesi, Lefkoşa (Nicosia), Mersin 10, Turkey; tel. 2252555; fax 2255176; e-mail info@kibrisgazetesi.com; internet www.kibrisgazetesi.com; Turkish; Editor BAŞARAN DÜZGÜN; circ. 13,000.

CYPRUS

Ortam (Political Conditions): 7 Cengiz Han Sok, Koskluciflik, Lefkoşa (Nicosia), Mersin 10, Turkey; tel. 2274872; fax 2283784; e-mail ortam@north-cyprus.net; internet www.ortamgazetesi.com; f. 1981; Turkish; organ of the TKP; Editor-in-Chief Mehmet Davulcu; circ. 1,250.

Vatan (Homeland): 46 Müftü Ziyai Sok., PK 842, Lefkoşa (Nicosia), Mersin 10, Turkey; tel. 2277557; fax 2277558; e-mail atekman@vatangazetesi.net; internet www.vatangazetesi.com; f. 1991; Turkish; Editor Ali Tekman.

Yeni Düzen (New System): Organize Sanayi Bölgesi, Lefkoşa (Nicosia), Mersin 10, Turkey; tel. 2256658; fax 2253240; e-mail yeniduzen@defne.net; internet www.yeniduzengazetesi.com; Turkish; organ of the CTP; Editor Cenk Mutluyakali; circ. 1,250.

GREEK CYPRIOT WEEKLIES

Athlitiki tis Kyriakis: 53 Demosthenis Severis, 9th Floor, 1080 Nicosia; tel. 22664344; fax 22664543; f. 1996; Greek; athletics; Dir Panayiotis Felloukas; Chief Editor Michalis Papageorgiou; circ. 4,000.

Cyprus Financial Mirror: POB 16077, 2085 Nicosia; tel. 22678666; fax 22678664; e-mail shavasb@financialmirror.com; internet www.financialmirror.com; f. 1993; English (with Greek-language supplement); independent; Dirs Shavasb Bohdjalian, Masis der Parthogh; circ. 4,000.

Cyprus Weekly: POB 24977, Suite 102, Trust House, Gryparis St, 1306 Nicosia; tel. 22666047; fax 22668665; e-mail weekly@spidernet.com.cy; internet www.cyprusweekly.com.cy; f. 1979; English; independent; Publishing Dirs Georges der Parthogh, Alex Efthyvoulos, Andreas Hadjipapas; Chief Editor Martyn Henry; circ. 18,000.

Ergatiki Phoni (Workers' Voice): POB 25018, SEK Bldg, 23 Alkeou St, Engomi, 2018 Nicosia; tel. 22849849; fax 22849850; f. 1947; Greek; organ of SEK trade union; Dir Dimitris Kettenis; Chief Editor Xenis Xenofontos; circ. 10,000.

Ergatiko Vima (Workers' Tribune): POB 21885, 1514 Nicosia; tel. 22866400; fax 22349382; f. 1956; Greek; organ of PEO trade union; Chief Editor Neophitos Papalazarou; circ. 14,000.

Official Gazette: Printing Office of the Republic of Cyprus, Nicosia; tel. 22405811; fax 22303175; e-mail entozzi@gpo.mof.gov.cy; internet www.mof.gov.cy/gpo; f. 1960; Greek; publ. by the Govt of the Republic of Cyprus; circ. 5,000.

Paraskinio (Behind the Scenes): 6 Psichikou St, Strovolos, Nicosia; tel. 22322959; fax 22322940; f. 1987; Greek; Dir and Chief Editor D. Michael; cir. 3,000.

Selides (Pages): POB 21094, 1 Diogenous St, Engomi, 2404 Nicosia; POB 21094, 1501 Nicosia; tel. 22744000; fax 22590516; e-mail mailbox@phileleftheros.com; internet www.phileleftheros.com; f. 1991; Greek; Exec. Dir Myrto Markidou-Selipa; Chief Editor Maria Menikou; circ. 16,500.

Super Flash: POB 23647, 11 Kolokotronis St, Kaimakli, Nicosia; tel. 22316674; fax 22316582; f. 1979; youth magazine; Greek; Dir Demetris Aloneftis; circ. 4,000.

Tharros (Courage): POB 27628, 14A Danaes St, Engomi, Nicosia; tel. 22356676; fax 22354599; e-mail syntaxi@maxinewspaper.com; internet www.maxinewspaper.com; f. 1961; Greek; right-wing; Gen. Man. Angelos Papademetriou; Chief Editor Pambos Mitides; circ. 5,500.

To Periodiko: POB 21836, Dias Bldg, 23 Alkeou St, Strovolos, 1513 Nicosia; tel. 22580680; fax 22662247; f. 1986; Greek; Dir Antis Hadjikostis; Chief Editor Kostis Diogenous; circ. 16,000.

TURKISH CYPRIOT WEEKLIES

Cyprus Today: Dr Fazil Küçük Bul., PK 831, Lefkoşa (Nicosia), Mersin 10, Turkey; tel. 2252555; fax 2252934; e-mail cyprustoday@yahoo.com; f. 1991; English; political, social, cultural and economic; Editor Gill Fraser; circ. 5,000.

Ekonomi (The Economy): 90 Bedrettin Demirel Cad., Lefkoşa (Nicosia), Mersin 10, Turkey; tel. 2283760; fax 2283089; f. 1958; Turkish; publ. by the Turkish Cypriot Chamber of Commerce; Editor-in-Chief Sami Taşarkan; circ. 3,000.

Safak: PK 228, Lefkoşa (Nicosia), Mersin 10, Turkey; tel. 2271472; fax 2287910; f. 1992; Turkish; circ. 1,000.

Yeni Çağ: 28 Ramadan Cad., Lefkoşa (Nicosia), Mersin 10, Turkey; tel. 2274917; fax 2271476; e-mail irtibat@yeniggazetesi.com.tr; internet www.yeniggazetesi.com.tr; f. 1990; Turkish; pro-opposition; Editor Murat Kanatli; circ. 600.

OTHER WEEKLIES

The Blue Beret: POB 21642, HQ UNFICYP, 1590 Nicosia; tel. 22614550; fax 22614461; e-mail unficyp-blue-beret@un.org; internet www.unficyp.org; monthly journal of the UN Peace-keeping Force in Cyprus (UNFICYP); English; f. 1964; circ. 1,500; Editor José Diaz.

Lion: 55 AEC Episkopi, BFPO 53; tel. 25962052; fax 25963181; e-mail lioncy@cytanet.com.cy; distributed to British Sovereign Base Areas, UN Forces and principal Cypriot towns; weekly; includes British Forces Broadcasting Services programme guide; Editor Louise Carrigan; circ. 5,000.

Middle East Economic Survey: Middle East Petroleum and Economic Publications (Cyprus), POB 24940, 31 Evagoras Ave, Evagoras Complex, 1066 Nicosia; tel. 22665431; fax 22671988; e-mail info@mees.com; internet www.mees.com; f. 1957 (in Beirut, Lebanon); weekly review and analysis of petroleum, finance and banking, and political devts; Publr Basim W. Itayim; Editor-in-Chief Gerald Butt.

GREEK CYPRIOT PERIODICALS

Cool: POB 8205, 86 Iphigenias St, 2091 Nicosia; tel. 22378900; fax 22378916; f. 1994; Greek; youth magazine; Chief Editor Prometheas Christophides; circ. 4,000.

Cypria (Cypriot Woman): POB 28506, 56 Kennedy Ave, 11th Floor, Strovolos, 2080 Nicosia; tel. 22494907; fax 22427051; e-mail pogo@spidernet.com.cy; f. 1983; every 2 months; Greek; Owner Maro Karayianni; circ. 7,000.

Cyprus P.C.: POB 24989, 6th Floor, 1 Kyriakou Matsi St, 1306 Nicosia; tel. 22765999; fax 22765909; e-mail pc@infomedia.cy.net; f. 1990; monthly; Greek; computing magazine; Dir Lakis Varnava; circ. 5,000.

Cyprus Time Out: POB 3697, 4 Pygmalionos St, 1010 Nicosia; tel. 22472949; fax 22360668; f. 1978; monthly; English; Dir Ellada Sophocleous; Chief Editor Lyn Haviland; circ. 8,000.

Cyprus Today: c/o Ministry of Education and Culture, 1434 Nicosia; tel. 22800933; fax 22518042; e-mail eioannou@culture.moec.gov.cy; f. 1963; quarterly; English; cultural and information review; publ. and distributed by Press and Information Office; Dir of Cultural Services Dr Eleni Nikita; circ. 15,000.

Cyprus Tourism: POB 51697, Limassol; tel. 25337377; fax 25337374; f. 1989; bi-monthly; Greek and English; tourism and travel; Man. Dir G. Erotokritou; circ. 250,000.

Dimosios Ypallilos (Civil Servant): 3 Demosthenis Severis Ave, 1066 Nicosia; tel. 22844445; fax 22665199; e-mail pasydy@spidernet.com.cy; internet www.pasydy.org; f. 1927; weekly; Greek; publ. by the Cyprus Civil Servants' Trade Union (PASYDY); circ. 14,000.

Enosis (Union): 71 Piraeus & Tombazis, Nicosia; tel. 22756862; fax 22757268; f. 1996; monthly; Greek; satirical; Chief Editor Vasos Ftochopolilos; circ. 2,000.

Eva: 6 Psichikou St, Strovolos, Nicosia; tel. 22322959; fax 22322940; f. 1996; Greek; Dir Dinos Michael; Chief Editors Charis Pontikis, Katia Savvidou; circ. 4,000.

Hermes International: POB 24512, Nicosia; tel. 22570570; fax 22581617; f. 1992; quarterly; English; lifestyle, business, finance, management; Chief Editor John Vickers; circ. 8,500.

I Kypros Simera (Present Day Cyprus): 1 Apellis St, 1456 Nicosia; tel. 22801182; fax 22666123; e-mail alyritsas@pio.moi.gov.cy; f. 1983; fortnightly; Greek; publ. by the Press and Information Office of the Ministry of the Interior; Principal Officers Miltos Miltiadou, Andreas Lyritsas; circ. 3,500.

Nicosia This Month: POB 20365, Flat 303, Kennedy Ave, Nicosia; tel. 22441922; fax 22519743; e-mail info@gnora.com; internet www.gnora.com; f. 1984; monthly; English; Chief Editor Andreas Hadjkyriacos; circ. 4,000.

Omicron: POB 25211, 1 Commercial Centre Diogenous, 2nd Floor, 1307 Nicosia; tel. 22590110; fax 22590410; f. 1996; Greek; Dir Nikos Chr. Pattichis; Chief Editor Stavros Christodoulou; circ. 8,000.

Paediki Chara (Children's Joy): POB 136, 18 Archbishop Makarios III Ave, 1065 Nicosia; tel. 22817585; fax 22817599; e-mail poed@cytanet.com.cy; f. 1962; monthly; for pupils; publ. by the Pancyprian Union of Greek Teachers; Editor Demetris Mikellides; circ. 15,000.

Synergatiko Vima (The Co-operative Tribune): Kosti Palama 5, 1096 Nicosia; tel. 22680757; fax 22660833; e-mail coop.confeder@cytanet.com.cy; f. 1983; monthly; Greek; official organ of the Pancyprian Co-operative Confederation Ltd; circ. 5,000; Sec. Pavlos Theodotou.

Synthesis (Composition): 6 Psichikou St, Strovolos, Nicosia; tel. 22322959; fax 22322940; f. 1988; every 2 months; Greek; interior decorating; Dir Dinos Michael; circ. 6,000.

Tele Ores: POB 28205, 4 Acropoleos St, 1st Floor, 2091 Nicosia; tel. 22513300; fax 22513363; f. 1993; fortnightly; Greek; television guide; Chief Editor Prometheas Christophides; circ. 17,000.

TV Kanali (TV Channel): POB 25603, 5 Aegaleo St, Strovolos, Nicosia; tel. 22353603; fax 22353223; f. 1993; Greek; Dirs A. Stavrides, E. Hadjiefthymiou; Chief Editor Charis Tomazos; circ. 13,000.

TURKISH CYPRIOT PERIODICALS

Güvenlik Kuvvetleri Magazine: Lefkoşa (Nicosia), Mersin 10, Turkey; tel. 2275880; publ. by the Security Forces of the 'TRNC'.

Halkbilimi (Folklore): Hasder, PK 199, Lefkoşa (Nicosia), Mersin 10, Turkey; tel. 2283146; fax 2287798; e-mail hasder@hasder.org; internet www.hasder.org; f. 1986; annual; publ. of Hasder Folk Arts Foundation; academic, folkloric; Turkish, with a short summary in English; Chief Editor KANI KANOL; circ. 750 (2007).

Kıbrıs—Northern Cyprus Monthly: Ministry of Foreign Affairs and Defence, Lefkoşa (Nicosia), Mersin 10, Turkey; tel. 2283365; fax 2284847; e-mail pio@trncpio.org; internet www.trncpio.org; f. 1963; Editor GÖNÜL ATANER.

Kıbrısli Türkün Sesi: 44 Mecidiye St, Lefkoşa (Nicosia), Mersin 10, Turkey; tel. 2278520; fax 2287966; monthly; political; Exec. Dir DOGAN HARMAN; Gen. Co-ordinator CEVDET ALPARSLAN.

Kültür Sanat Dergisi: Girne Cad. 92, Lefkoşa (Nicosia), Mersin 10, Turkey; tel. 2283313; e-mail info@turkishbank.com; internet www.turkishbank.com; Turkish; publ. of Türk Bankası; circ. 1,000.

Kuzey Kıbrıs Kültür Dergisi (North Cyprus Cultural Journal): PK 157, Lefkoşa (Nicosia), Mersin 10, Turkey; tel. 2231298; f. 1987; monthly; Turkish; Chief Editor GÜNSEL DOĞASAL.

NEWS AGENCIES

Cyprus News Agency: POB 23947, 1687 Nicosia; tel. 22556009; fax 22556103; e-mail director@cna.org.cy; internet www.cna.org.cy; f. 1976; Greek, Turkish and English; Dir and Editor-in-Chief GEORGE PENINTAEX (acting); Chair. of Bd COSTAKIS CONSTANTINOU.

Kuzey Kıbrıs Haber Ajansı (Northern Cyprus News Agency): Alirizin Efendi Cad., Vakiflar Işhani, Kat 2, No. 3, Ortaköy, Lefkoşa (Nicosia), Mersin 10, Turkey; tel. 2281922; fax 2281934; f. 1977; Dir-Gen. M. ALI AKPINAR.

TürkAjansı-Kıbrıs (TAK) (Turkish News Agency of Cyprus): POB 355, 30 Mehmet Akif Cad., Lefkoşa (Nicosia), Mersin 10, Turkey; tel. 2282773; fax 2271213; e-mail tak@emu.edu.tr; internet kktc.gov.nc.tr/tak; f. 1973; Dir EMIR HÜSEYN ERSOY.

Publishers

GREEK CYPRIOT PUBLISHERS

Andreou Chr. Publications: POB 22298, 67A Regenis St, 1520 Nicosia; tel. 22666877; fax 22666878; e-mail andreou2@cytanet.com.cy; f. 1979; biography, literature, history, regional interest.

Chrysopolitissa: 27 Al. Papadiamantis St, 2400 Nicosia; tel. 22353929; e-mail rina@spidernet.com.cy; f. 1973; theatre, literature.

Costas Epiphaniou: Ekdoseis Antiprosopies Ltd, POB 2451, 1521 Nicosia; tel. 22750873; fax 22759266; f. 1973; Dir COSTAS EPIPHANIOU.

Anastasios G. Leventis Foundation: 40 Gladstonos St, POB 22543, 1095 Nicosia; tel. 22667706; fax 22675002; e-mail leventcy@zenon.logos.cy.net; internet www.leventisfoundation.org; f. 1980; Dir VASSOS KARAGEORGHIS.

KY KE M: POB 4108, Nicosia; tel. 22450302; fax 22463624; Pres. NIKOS KOUTSOU.

MAM Ltd (The House of Cyprus and Cyprological Publications): POB 21722, 1512 Nicosia; tel. 22753536; fax 22375802; e-mail mam@mam.com.cy; internet www.mam.com.cy; f. 1965.

Nikoklis Publishing House: POB 20300, 2150 Nicosia; tel. 22334918; fax 22330218; history, geography, culture, travel; Man. Dr ANDREAS SOPHOCLEOUS.

Omilos Pnevmatikis Ananeoseos: 1 Omirou St, 2407 Engomi, Nicosia; tel. 22775854; literature.

Pierides Foundation: POB 40025, 6300 Larnaca; tel. 24651345; fax 24657227; e-mail centrart@spidernet.com.cy; internet www.pieridesfoundation.com.cy; f. 1974.

POLTE (Pancyprian Organization of Tertiary Education): c/o Higher Technical Institute, Nicosia; tel. 22305030; fax 22494953; Pres. KOSTAS NEOKLEOUS.

TURKISH CYPRIOT PUBLISHERS

Action Global Communications: 6 Kondilaki St, 1090 Lefkoşa (Nicosia), Mersin 10, Turkey; tel. 22818884; fax 22873634; e-mail office@actionprgroup.com; internet www.actionprgroup.com; f. 1971; affiliate of Weber Shandwick; has 44 offices in the emerging markets; travel, aviation and hospitality; Man. Dir TONY CHRISTODOULOU.

Bırlık Gazetesi: Yediler Sok., Lefkoşa (Nicosia), Mersin 10, Turkey; tel. 2272959; f. 1980; Dir MEHMET AKAR.

Bolan Matbaası: 35 Pençizade Sok., Lefkoşa (Nicosia), Mersin 10, Turkey; tel. 2274802.

Devlet Basımevi (Turkish Cypriot Government Printing House): Şerif Arzik Sok., Lefkoşa (Nicosia), Mersin 10, Turkey; tel. 2272010; Dir S. KÜRŞAD.

Halkın Sesi Ltd: 172 Girne Cad., Lefkoşa (Nicosia), Mersin 10, Turkey; tel. 2273141.

Kema Matbaası: 1 Tabak Hilmi Sok., Lefkoşa (Nicosia), Mersin 10, Turkey; tel. 2272785.

North Cyprus Research and Publishing Centre (CYREP): PK 327, Lefkoşa (Nicosia), Mersin 10, Turkey; tel. 8555179; fax 2272592; e-mail gazioglu@kktc.net; Man. Editor AHMET C. GAZIOĞLU.

K. Rüstem & Bro.: 22–24 Girne Cad., Lefkoşa (Nicosia), Mersin 10, Turkey; tel. 2271418.

Tezel Matbaası: 35 Şinasi Sok., Lefkoşa (Nicosia), Mersin 10, Turkey; tel. 2271022.

Broadcasting and Communications

TELECOMMUNICATIONS

Cyprus Telecommunications Authority (CYTA): POB 24929, Telecommunications St, Strovolos, 1396 Nicosia; tel. 22701000; fax 22494940; e-mail enquiries@cyta.com.cy; internet www.cyta.com.cy; provides, maintains and develops electronic communications networks and provides services—both nationally and internationally—for voice and data applications in fixed and mobile communications; Chair. STAVROS KREMMOS; Dep. CEO PHOTIOS SAVVIDES.

Telekomünikasyon Diaresi Müdürlüğü (Directorate of Telecommunications): Lefkoşa (Nicosia), Mersin 10, Turkey; tel. 2281888; fax 2288666; f. 1963; state-owned; admin. and operation of telecommunications services; Gen. Man. MUSTAFA BERKTUĞ.

BROADCASTING

Radio

British Forces Broadcasting Service, Cyprus: Akrotiri, BFPO 57; tel. 25278518; fax 25278580; e-mail bfbscyprus@bfbs.com; internet www.ssvc.com/bfbs/radio/cyprus; f. 1948; broadcasts daily radio and television services in English; Station Man. ALAN PHILLIPS; Engineering Man. DAVID GILL.

Cyprus Broadcasting Corporation (CyBC): POB 24824, CyBC St, 2120 Nicosia; tel. 22862000; fax 22314050; e-mail rik@cybc.com.cy; internet www.cybc.com.cy; f. 1952; four 24-hour radio channels, two of which are mainly Greek; channel 2 broadcasts programmes in Turkish, English and Armenian; Chair. ANDREAS ALONEFTIS; Dir-Gen. MARIOS MAVRIKIOS.

Logos: Church of Cyprus, POB 27400, 1644 Nicosia; tel. 22355444; fax 22355737; e-mail director@logos.cy.net; Chair. ANDREAS PHILIPPOU; Dir-Gen. CHRISTODOULOS PROTOPAPAS.

Radio Astra: 145 Athalassas Ave, Strovolos, 2024 Nicosia; tel. 22368888; fax 22319262; e-mail astra@cytanet.com.cy; internet www.astra.com.cy; Dir JAKIS HADJIGEORGIOU.

Radio Proto: POB 21836, 31 Archangelos St, Parissinos, 2054 Nicosia; tel. 22580400; fax 22580425; e-mail web@radioproto.com; internet www.radioproto.com; Chair. KOSTAS HADJIKOSTIS; Gen. Man. PAVLOS PAPACHRISTODOULOU.

Bayrak Radio and TV Corpn (BRTK): BRTK Sitesi, Dr Fazıl Kucuk Bul., Lefkoşa (Nicosia), Mersin 10, Turkey; tel. 2255555; fax 2254581; e-mail info@brtk.net; internet www.brtk.net; f. 1963 as Bayrak Radio; in July 1983 it became an independent Turkish Cypriot corpn, partly financed by the Govt; now has five radio stations on air: Radio Bayrak, Bayrak International (international music, 24-hour, and news in English, Greek, Russian, Arabic and German), Bayrak FM (popular music, 24-hour), Bayrak Classic (classical music, 24-hour) and Bayrak Turkish Music (Turkish classical and folk music, 18-hour); Chair. of Bd VASFI CANDAN; Gen. Man. AHMET OKAN; Head of Radio PERAL AĞCATAŞ.

First FM and Interfirst FM: Lefkoşa (Nicosia), Mersin 10, Turkey; f. 1996.

Kıbrıs FM / Kıbrıs TV: Dr Fazil Küçük Blvd, Yeni Sanayi Bolgesi, Lefkoşa (Nicosia), Mersin 10, Turkey; tel. 2252555; fax 2253707; e-mail kibrisibrisgazetesi.com; Dir ERDINCH GUNDUZ.

Radio Emu: Eastern Mediterranean University, Gazi Mağusa (Famagusta), Mersin 10, Turkey; e-mail radioemu@cc.emu.edu.tr; internet www.emu.edu.tr.

Television

Greek Cypriot viewers have access to Greek television channels via satellite. Several Turkish channels are transmitted to the 'TRNC'.

Antenna TV Cyprus (ANT1 Cyprus): POB 20923, 1655 Nicosia; tel. 22200200; fax 22200210; e-mail info@antenna.com.cg; internet www

.ant1.gr/www/en/companies/tv/154855.aspx; f. 1983; Chair. LOUKIS PAPAPHILIPPOU; Man. Dir STELIOS MALEKOS.

British Forces Broadcasting Service, Cyprus: Akrotiri, BFPO 57; tel. 25952009; fax 25278580; e-mail dusty.miller@bfbs.com; f. 1948; broadcasts a daily TV service; Station Man. IAN NOAKES; Engineering Man. ADRIAN ARNOLD.

Cyprus Broadcasting Corporation (CyBC): POB 24824, CyBC St, 2120 Nicosia; tel. 22862000; fax 22314050; e-mail tvweb@cybc.com.cy; internet www.cybc.com.cy; f. 1957; Pik 1 (CyBC 1) one Band III 100/10-kW transmitter on Mount Olympus. Pik 2 (CyBC 2) one Band IV 100/10-kW ERP transmitter on Mount Olympus. ET1 one Band IV 100/10-kW ERP transmitter on Mount Olympus for transmission of the ETI Programme received, via satellite, from Greece. The above three TV channels are also transmitted from 80 transposer stations; Chair. ANDREAS ALONEFTIS; Dir-Gen. MARIOS MAVRIKIOS.

Lumiere TV Ltd: POB 25614, 1311 Nicosia; tel. 22357272; fax 22354638; e-mail administration@ltv.com.cy; internet www.lumieretv.com; f. 1992; encoded signal; Pres. JOSEPH AVRAAMIDES; Man. Dir GEORGE XINARIS.

MEGA TV: POB 27400, 1644 Nicosia; tel. 22477777; fax 22477737; e-mail info@megatv.com.cy; Gen. Man. GEORGE MAMALAKIS.

Sigma Radio TV Ltd: POB 21836, 2054 Nicosia; tel. 22580100; fax 22358646; e-mail andy@sigmatv.com; internet www.sigmatv.com; f. 1995; island-wide coverage; Chair. and Dir KOSTAS HADJICOSTIS; Man. Dir ANDY HADJICOSTIS.

Bayrak Radio and TV Corpn (BRTK): BRTK Sitesi, Dr Fazıl Kucuk Bul., Lefkoşa (Nicosia), Mersin 10, Turkey; tel. 2255555; fax 2254581; e-mail info@brtk.net; internet www.brt.net; f. 1976; in July 1983 it became an independent Turkish Cypriot corpn, partly financed by the Govt; Bayrak TV; transmits programmes in Turkish, Greek and English; Chair. of Bd VASFI CANDAN; Dir-Gen. HÜSEYIN GÜRŞAN; Head of Television TÜLIN URAL.

Gene TV: Bevel Yusuf Cad. 8, Yenişehir, Lefkoşa (Nicosia), Mersin 10, Turkey; tel. 2280790; fax 2276363; Dir ERTAN BIRINCI.

Kanal T: Dr Fazıl Küçük Cad., Foto Filiz Binaları, Göçmenköy, Lefkoşa (Nicosia), Mersin 10, Turkey; tel. 2237678; fax 2234257; Owner ERSIN FATAR.

Finance

(br.(s) = branches; cap. = capital; res = reserves; dep. = deposits; m. = million; amounts in Cyprus pounds, unless otherwise indicated, except for Turkish Cypriot banks)

BANKING

Central Banks

Central Bank of Cyprus: POB 25529, 80 Kennedy Ave, 1076 Nicosia; tel. 22714100; fax 22378153; e-mail cbcinfo@centralbank.gov.cy; internet www.centralbank.gov.cy; f. 1963; became fully independent from govt control in July 2002; cap. 15m., res 19.9m., dep. 2,694.8m. (Dec. 2006); Gov. ATHANASIOS ORPHANIDES.

Central Bank of the 'Turkish Republic of Northern Cyprus': Lefkoşa (Nicosia), Mersin 10, Turkey; tel. 2283216; fax 2285240; e-mail ileti@kktcmb.trnc.net; internet www.kktcmb.trnc.net; f. 1984; Gov. ERDOĞAN KÜÇÜK.

Greek Cypriot Banks

Alpha Bank Cyprus Ltd: POB 21661, 1095 Nicosia; tel. 22888888; fax 22773744; e-mail secretariat@alphabank.com.cy; internet www.alphabank.com.cy; f. 1960 as Lombard Banking (Cyprus) Ltd; name changed to Lombard NatWest Banking Ltd in 1989 and as above in 1998; locally incorporated although foreign-controlled; 100% owned by Alpha Bank, Athens; cap. 69.8m., res 71.9m., dep. 1,794.5m. (Dec. 2006); Chair. SPYROS N. FILARETOS; Man. Dir CONSTANTINOS KOKKINOS; 33 brs.

Bank of Cyprus Public Company Ltd: POB 21472, 51 Stassinos St, Ayia Paraskevi, 2002 Strovolos 140, 1599 Nicosia; tel. 22842100; fax 22378111; e-mail info@cy.bankofcyprus.com; internet www.bankofcyprus.com; f. 1899; reconstituted 1943 by the amalgamation of Bank of Cyprus, Larnaca Bank Ltd and Famagusta Bank Ltd; cap. 276.9m., res 437.8m., dep. 12,794.8m. (Dec. 2006); Chair. ELEFTHERIOS IOANNOU; Vice-Chair. ANDREAS ARTEMIS; 144 brs in Cyprus, 139 brs abroad.

Co-operative Central Bank Ltd: POB 24537, 8 Gregoris Afxentiou St, 1096 Nicosia; tel. 22743000; fax 22673088; e-mail coopbkfd.gm@spidernet.com.cy; internet www.coopbank.com.cy; f. 1937 under the Co-operative Societies Law; banking and credit facilities to mem. societies, importer and distributor of agricultural requisites, insurance agent; cap. 18.6m., res 7.0m., dep. 1,376.2m. (Dec. 2005); Chair. D. STAVROU; CEO, Sec. and Gen. Man. E. CHLORAKIOTIS; 4 brs.

Hellenic Bank Public Company Ltd: 200 cnr Limassol and Athalassa Ave, 2025 Nicosia; tel. 22500000; fax 22500050; e-mail hellenic@hellenicbank.com; internet www.hellenicbank.com; f. 1974; financial services group; cap. 60.5m., res 152.1m., dep. 3,338.1m. (Dec. 2006); Chair. Dr ANDREAS P. PANAYIOTOU; CEO MAKIS KERAVNOS; 82 brs in Cyprus, 25 abroad.

Kommunalkredit International Bank Ltd: POB 56018, Berengaria Bldg, 25 Spyrou Araouzou, 3603 Limassol; tel. 25820350; fax 25820352; e-mail kib@kib.com.cy; internet www.kib.com.cy; f. 2002; 100% owned by Kommunalkredit Austria AG; cap. €244m., total assets €9,000m. (Dec. 2006); Exec. Dirs BERNHARD ACHBERGER, WILLIBALD SCHEBESTA, PATRICK SOETENS.

Marfin Popular Public Company Ltd: POB 22032, Laiki Bank Bldg, 154 Limassol Ave, 1598 Nicosia; tel. 22552000; fax 22811496; e-mail laiki.telebank@laiki.com; internet www.laiki.com; f. 1901 as People's Savings Bank of Limassol; operated under several subsequent names, incl. The Cyprus Popular Bank Public Company Ltd, before adopting present name in Dec. 2006; full commercial banking; cap. 395.2m., res 1,287.8m., dep. 10,117.9m. (Dec. 2006); Chair. KIKIS N. LAZARIDES; CEO ANDREAS VGENOPOULOS; 114 brs in Cyprus, 5 brs abroad.

National Bank of Greece (Cyprus) Ltd: 15 Arch. Makarios III Ave, 1597 Nicosia; tel. 22840000; fax 22840010; e-mail cloizou@nbg.com.cy; f. 1994 by incorporating all local business of the National Bank of Greece SA; full commercial banking; cap. 23m. (Nov. 2000); Chair. TAKIS ARAPOGLOU; Man. Dir M. KOKKINOS; 23 brs.

Universal Bank Public Ltd: 6th Floor, Universal Tower, 85 Dhigenis Akritas Ave, 1070 Nicosia; tel. 22883333; fax 22358702; e-mail unimail@usb.com.cy; internet www.universalbank.com.cy; f. 1925 as Yialousa Savings Ltd (closed 1974, reopened 1990), renamed Universal Savings Bank Ltd 2001, renamed as above 2004; cap. 15.1m., res 13.5m., dep. 230.0m. (Dec. 2006); Chair. SYMEON MATSIS; Gen. Man. Dr SPYROS EPISKOPOU; 15 brs.

Turkish Cypriot Banks

(amounts in new Turkish liras, unless otherwise indicated; note: figures have been converted retrospectively to reflect the introduction on 1 January 2005 of the new unit of currency, equivalent to 1,000,000 of the old Turkish lira)

Akdeniz Garanti Bankası Ltd: PK 149, 2–4 Celaliye Sok., Inönü Meydanı, Lefkoşa (Nicosia), Mersin 10, Turkey; tel. 2286742; fax 2286741; e-mail agbltd@superonline.com; f. 1989 as Mediterranean Guarantee Bank; cap. and res 3.6m., dep. 173.8m. (Dec. 2004); Chair. BENGU SONYA.

Asbank Ltd: 8 Mecidiye Sok., PK 448, Lefkoşa (Nicosia), Mersin 10, Turkey; tel. 2283023; fax 2281244; e-mail info@asbank.com.tr; internet www.asbank.com.tr; f. 1986; cap. 5.1m., res 6.8m., dep. 188.1m. (Dec. 2006); Chair. ALTAY ADADEMIR; Gen. Man. TASTAN M. ALTUNER; 8 brs.

CreditWest Bank Ltd: PK 843, 2 Müftü Ziyai Eefendi Sok., Lefkoşa (Nicosia), Mersin 10, Turkey; tel. 2288222; fax 2283603; e-mail info@creditwestbank.com; internet www.creditwestbank.com; f. 1993 as Kıbrıs Altınbaş Bank Ltd; name changed as above Oct. 2006; cap. US $5.8m., res $9.5m., dep. $163.8m. (Dec. 2006); Chair. SOFU ALTINBAŞ; Gen. Man. ÖZCAN TEKGÜMÜŞ.

First Merchant Bank OSH Ltd: 25 Şerif Arzik Sok., Lefkoşa (Nicosia), Mersin 10, Turkey; tel. 2275373; fax 2275377; e-mail fmb@firstmerchantbank.com; f. 1993; also provides offshore services; cap. US $10.0m., res $10.4m., dep. $9.9m. (Dec. 2004); Chair. and Gen. Man. Dr H. N. YAMAN.

Kıbrıs Continental Bank Ltd: 35–37 Girne Cad., Lefkoşa (Nicosia), Mersin 10, Turkey; tel. 2273220; fax 2286334; e-mail cbank_salim@kktc.net; internet www.kibriscontinentalbank.com; f. 1998; cap. US $4,200m., res $3,600m., dep. $22,000m. (Dec. 2004); Chair. OSMAN KARAISMAILOĞLU; Gen. Man. SERACETTIN BAKTAY.

Kıbrıs Iktisat Bankası Ltd (Cyprus Economy Bank Ltd): 151 Bedreddin Demiral Cad., Lefkoşa (Nicosia), Mersin 10, Turkey; tel. 2285300; fax 2281311; e-mail info@iktisatbank.com; internet www.iktisatbank.com; f. 1990; cap. 14.6m., res 3.0m., dep. 207.3m. (Dec. 2006); Chair., CEO and Gen. Man. METE OZMERTER.

Kıbrıs Türk Kooperatif Merkez Bankası Ltd (Cyprus Turkish Co-operative Central Bank): 49–55 Mahmut Paşa Sok., PK 823, Lefkoşa (Nicosia), Mersin 10, Turkey; tel. 2283207; fax 2276787; e-mail info@koopbank.com; internet www.koopbank.com; f. 1959; cap. 11.6m., res 19.1m., dep. 956.3m. (Dec. 2005); banking and credit facilities to mem. societies and individuals; Chair. DOĞAN ŞAHALI; Gen. Man. NURI ERHAT; 14 brs.

Kıbrıs Vakıflar Bankası Ltd (Cyprus Vakıflar Bank Ltd): PK 212, 66 Atatürk Cad., Yenisehir, Lefkoşa (Nicosia), Mersin 10, Turkey; tel. 2275169; fax 2285872; e-mail kvb@kktc.net; f. 1982; cap. 17m., res 10.0m., dep. 500.4m. (Dec. 2006); Pres. and Chair. OSMAN BAYHANLI; Gen. Man. ALPAY R. ADANIR; 10 brs.

CYPRUS

Limassol Turkish Co-operative Bank Ltd: 10 Orhaneli Sok., Kyrenia, PK 247, Mersin 10, Turkey; tel. 2280333; fax 2281350; e-mail info@limasolbank.com.tr; internet www.limasolbank.com; f. 1939; cap. 7.0m., res 0.6m., dep. 96.7m. (Dec. 2001); Chair. GÜZEL HALIM; Gen. Man. TANER EKDAL.

Türk Bankası Ltd (Turkish Bank Ltd): 92 Girne Cad., PK 242, Lefkoşa (Nicosia), Mersin 10, Turkey; tel. 2283313; fax 2282432; e-mail info@turkishbank.net; internet www.turkishbank.com; f. 1901; cap. 51.2m., res 37.3m., dep. 663.9m. (Dec. 2006); Chair. M. TANJU ÖZYOL; Gen. Man. C. YENAL MUSANNIF; 14 brs.

Universal Bank Ltd: POB 658, 57 Mehmet Akif Ave, Lefkoşa (Nicosia), Mersin 10, Turkey; tel. 2286262; fax 2287826; e-mail univers@kktc.net; internet www.bankunivers.com; f. 1997; cap. 3.9m., res 0.9m., dep. 58.1m. (Dec. 2005); Chair. ILHAN KÖSEOĞLU; Gen. Man. ERCAN ÖZGÜM.

Viyabank Ltd: Ataturk Cad., 16 Muhtar Yusuf Galleria, Lefkoşa (Nicosia), Mersin 10, Turkey; tel. 2288902; fax 2285878; e-mail gm@viyabank.com; internet www.viyabank.com; f. 1998; cap. US $14.0m., res $0.9m., dep. $5.7m. (Dec. 2007); Pres. SALVO TARAGANO; Chair. ERDOĞAN SEVINÇ; 1 br.

Yakin Dogu Bank Ltd (Near East Bank Ltd): POB 47, 1 Girne Cad., Lefkoşa (Nicosia), Mersin 10, Turkey; tel. 2283834; fax 2284180; e-mail ydbank@kktc.net; cap. 7.0m., res 0.4m., dep. 56.9m. (Dec. 2005); Chair. Dr SUAT I. GÜNSEL; Gen. Man. KAMIL NURI ÖZERK.

Yeşilada Bank Ltd: POB 626, 11 Atatürk Ave, Lefkoşa (Nicosia), Mersin 10, Turkey; tel. 2281789; fax 2281962; e-mail info@yesilada-bank.com; internet www.yesilada-bank.com; cap. 8.0m., res −5.1m., dep. 11.7m. (Dec. 2005); Chair. and Pres. ISMET KOTAK; Gen. Man. MUSTAFA UZUN.

Investment Organization

The Cyprus Investment and Securities Corpn Ltd: POB 20597, 1660 Nicosia; tel. 22881700; fax 22338800; e-mail info@cisco.bankofcyprus.com; internet www.cisco-online.com.cy; f. 1982 to promote the devt of capital market; brokerage services, fund management, investment banking; mem. of Bank of Cyprus Group; issued cap. 22m. (2004); Chair. VASSILIS G. ROLOGIS; Gen. Man. ANNA SOFRONIOU.

Development Bank

The Cyprus Development Bank Public Company Ltd: POB 21415, Alpha House, 50 Archbishop Makarios III Ave, 1065 Nicosia; tel. 22846500; fax 22846600; e-mail info@cdb.com.cy; internet www.cyprusdevelopmentbank.com; f. 1963; 88.01% owned by Govt, 11.99% owned by European Investment Bank (Luxembourg); cap. 12.4m., res 11.9m., dep. 142.8m. (Dec. 2006); aims to accelerate the economic devt of Cyprus by providing medium- and long-term loans for productive projects, developing the capital market, encouraging joint ventures and providing technical and managerial advice to productive private enterprises; Chair. ANDREAS MOUSKOS; CEO CHRISTAKIS TAOUSHANIS; 1 br.

'Offshore' (International) Banking Units

In 2003 there were 29 Offshore Banking Units (OBUs) operating in Cyprus.

Agropromstroybank: POB 55297, Maximos Court B, 17 Leontiou St, Limassol; tel. 25384747; fax 25384858; Man. ALEXANDER MOKHONKO.

Allied Bank SAL: POB 54232, 3rd Floor, Flat 31, Lara Court, 276 Archbishop Makarios III Ave, Limassol; tel. 25363759; fax 25372711; Local Man. GEORGES ABI CHAMOUN.

Arab Bank PLC: POB 25700, 1 Santaroza Ave, 1393 Nicosia; tel. 22899100; fax 22760890; e-mail arabbank@spidernet.com.cy; OBU licence granted 1997; Area Exec. TOUFIC J. DAJAN.

Arab Jordan Investment Bank SA: POB 54384, Libra Tower, 23 Olympion St, Limassol; tel. 25351351; fax 25360151; e-mail info@ajib.com; internet www.ajib.com; f. 1978; cap. and dep. US $388m., total assets $410m. (Dec. 1999); Man. ABED ABU DAYEH.

AVTOVAZBANK: POB 52270, 4062 Limassol; tel. 25354594; fax 25362582; e-mail avbkcy@cytanet.com.cy; internet www.avtovazbank.ru; f. 1993; Local Man. SERGEI BONDARENKO.

Banca Română de Comerţ Exterior (Bancorex) SA: POB 22538, Margarita House, 5th Floor, 15 Them. Dervis St, 1309 Nicosia; tel. 22677992; fax 22677945; Local Man. GRIGORE IOAN BUDISAN.

Bank of Beirut and the Arab Countries SAL: POB 56201, Emelle Bldg, 1st Floor, 135 Archbishop Makarios III Ave, Limassol; tel. 25381290; fax 25381584; e-mail bbaccyp@spidernet.com.cy; Man. ELIE TABET.

Banque du Liban et d'Outre-Mer SAL: POB 53243, P. Lordos Centre Roundabout, Byron St, Limassol; tel. 25376433; fax 25376292; Local Man. S. FARAH.

BNP Paribas (Cyprus) Ltd: POB 50058, Kanika Business Centre, 319 28th October St, 3600 Limassol; tel. 25840840; fax 25840698; e-mail cyprus@bnpparibas.com; internet www.cyprus.bnpparibas.com; Man. Dir THIERRY GIGANT.

Banque SBA: 8C Iris House, Kanika Enaerios Complex, John Kennedy St, Limassol; tel. 25588650; fax 25581643; e-mail sba.cyprus@banque-sba.com; internet www.banque-sba.com; br. of Banque SBA (fmrly Société Bancaire Arabe), Paris (France); Local Man. ADNAN NUWAYHED.

Barclays Bank PLC: POB 27320, 88 Dhigenis Akritas Ave, 1644 Nicosia; tel. 22654400; fax 22754233; e-mail barclays@spidernet.com.cy; Cyprus Dir JONATHAN MILLS.

BEMO (Banque Européenne pour le Moyen-Orient SAL): POB 6232, Doma Court, 1st–2nd Floors, 227 Archbishop Makarios III Ave, Limassol; tel. 25583628; fax 25588611; e-mail bemolobu@spidernet.com.cy; Local Man. N. A. HCHAIME.

Byblos Bank SAL: POB 50218, Loucaides Bldg, 1 Archbishop Kyprianou St/St Andrew St, 3602 Limassol; tel. 25341433; fax 25367139; e-mail byblos@spidernet.com.cy; internet www.byblosbank.com.lb; Man. ANTOINE SMAIRA.

Crédit Libanais SAL: POB 53492, Chrysalia Court, 1st Floor, 206 Archbishop Makarios III Ave, 3030 Limassol; tel. 25376444; fax 25376807; e-mail clibhh@cytanet.com.cy; Local Man. HAYAT HARFOUCHE.

Crédit Suisse First Boston (Cyprus) Ltd: POB 57530, 199 Christodolou Hadsipavlou Ave, 3316 Limassol; tel. 25341244; fax 25817424; internet www.credit-suisse.com; f. 1996; OBU status granted 1997; Gen. Man. ANTONIS ROUVAS.

DEPFA Investment Bank Ltd: POB 20909, 10 Diomidous St, 1665 Nicosia; tel. 22396300; fax 22396399; e-mail erol.riza@depfa.com; internet www.depfa.com; OBU licence granted 1998; Chair. and CEO GERHARD BRUCKERMANN.

Emporiki Bank of Greece SA: 1 Iona Nicolaou, POB 27587, Engomi, 2431 Nicosia; tel. 22663686; fax 22663688; e-mail ibu@combank.com.cy; fmrly Commercial Bank of Greece; name changed as above in 2003; Man. K. RIALAS.

Federal Bank of the Middle East Ltd: POB 25566, J&P Bldg, 90 Archbishop Makarios III Ave, 1391 Nicosia; tel. 22888444; fax 22888555; e-mail mail@fbme.com; internet www.fbme.com; f. 1983; cap. US $46.0m., dep. $283.3m. (Dec. 2002); CEO FADI M. SAAB; 2 brs.

First Investment Bank Ltd: POB 16023, cnr of Kennedy Ave & 39 Demofiritos St, 4th Floor, Flat 401, 2085 Nicosia; tel. 22760150; fax 22376560; Gen. Man. ENU NEDELE.

HSBC Bank (Cyprus) Ltd: POB 25718, Para Bldg, Block C, 7 Dositheou St, 1311 Nicosia; tel. 22376116; fax 22376121; internet www.hsbc.com; CEO ANDRI ANTONIADES; 1 br.

Karić Banka: POB 26522, Flat 22, Cronos Court, 66 Archbishop Makarios III Ave, Nicosia; tel. 22374980; fax 22374151; Man. Dir O. ERDELIJANOVIĆ.

Lebanon and Gulf Bank SAL International Banking Unit: POB 40337, Akamia Centre, 3rd Floor, Flat 309, cnr of Gregoriou Afxentiou and Archbishop Makarios III Ave, 6303 Larnaca; tel. 24620500; fax 24620708; e-mail lgbcy@logoscy.net; Local Man. F. SAADE.

Russian Commercial Bank (Cyprus) Ltd: POB 56868, 2 Amathuntos St, 3105 Limassol; tel. 25837300; fax 25342192; e-mail rcb@rcbcy.com; internet www.rcbcy.com; f. 1995; cap. US $10.8m., res $42.5m., dep. $2,272.3m. (Dec. 2006); CEO MICHAEL V. KUZOVLEV.

Société Générale Cyprus Ltd: 20 Ayias Paraskevis, 2002 Nicosia; tel. 22399777; fax 22399700; e-mail customer-info.cyprus@socgen.com; internet www.sgcyprus.com; cap. US $2.0m., res $3.6m., dep. $247.5m. (Dec. 2005); Chair. MAURICE SEHNAOUI; Gen. Man. JEAN-CLAUDE BOLOUX.

STOCK EXCHANGE

Cyprus Stock Exchange: POB 25427, Kampou St, IMC Strovolos, 1309 Nicosia; tel. 22712300; fax 22570308; e-mail info@cse.com.cy; internet www.cse.com.cy; official trading commenced in March 1996; 140 cos listed in Jan. 2008; Chair. GIORGOS KOUFARIS; Gen. Man. NONDAS METAXAS.

INSURANCE

Insurance Companies Control Service: Ministry of Finance, POB 23364, 1682 Nicosia; tel. 22602952; fax 22302938; e-mail insurance@mof.gov.cy; internet www.mof.gov.cy; f. 1969 to control insurance cos, insurance agents, brokers and agents for brokers in Cyprus; Superintendent VICTORIA NATAR.

CYPRUS

Greek Cypriot Insurance Companies

Aegis Insurance Co Ltd: POB 23450, 7 Klimentos St, Ayios Antonios, 1061 Nicosia; tel. 22343644; fax 22343866; Chair. ARISTOS KAISIDES; Principal Officer PANTELAKIS SOUGLIDES.

Aetna Insurance Co Ltd: POB 8909, 19 Stavrou St, 2035 Strovolos; tel. 22510933; fax 22510934; f. 1966; Chair. KONSTANTINOS L. PRODROMOU; Principal Officer KONSTANTINOS TSANGARIS.

Agrostroy Insurance Co Ltd: POB 6624, 89 Kennedy Ave, Office 201, 1077 Nicosia; tel. 22379210; fax 22379212; f. 1996; offshore captive co operating outside Cyprus; Chair. VALERIE V. USHAKOV; Principal Officer IOANNIS ELIA.

Akelius Insurance Ltd: POB 23415, 36 Laodikias St, 1683 Nicosia; tel. 22318883; fax 22318925; e-mail info@akelius.com; internet www.akelius.com; f. 1987; offshore co operating outside Cyprus; Chair. ROGER AKELIOUS; CEO IOANNIS LOIZOU; Principal Officer DEMETRIS SYLLOURIS.

Allied Assurance & Reinsurance Co Ltd: POB 5509, 66 Grivas Dhigenis Ave, 1310 Nicosia; tel. 22672235; fax 22677656; f. 1982; offshore co operating outside Cyprus; Chair. HENRI J. G. CHALHOUB; Principal Officer DEMETRIOS DEMETRIOU.

Alpha Insurance Ltd: POB 26516, cnr Kennedy Ave and Stasinou St, 1640 Nicosia; tel. 22379999; fax 22379097; e-mail customer_service@alphainsurance.com.cy; internet www.alpha-insurance.gr/cyprus; f. 1993; Chair. VASILIOS KARAINDROS; Principal Officer and Sec. EVANGELOS ANASTASIADES.

Antarctic Insurance Co Ltd: POB 613, 199 Archbishop Makarios III Ave, Neokleou Bldg, 3030 Limassol; tel. 25362818; fax 25359262; offshore captive co operating outside Cyprus; Principal Officer ANDREAS NEOKLEOUS.

Apac Ltd: POB 25403, 5 Mourouzi St, Apt 1, 1055 Nicosia; tel. 22343086; fax 22343146; f. 1983; captive offshore co operating outside Cyprus; Chair. KYPROS CHRYSOSTOMIDES; Principal Officer GEORGHIOS POYATZIS.

Asfalistiki Eteria I 'Kentriki' Ltd: POB 25131, Kentriki Tower, 33 Klimentos St, 1061 Nicosia; tel. 22745745; fax 22745746; e-mail kentriki@logosnet.cy.net; internet www.kentriki.com.cy; f. 1985; Chair. ARISTOS CHRYSOSTOMOU; Man. Dir GEORGHIOS GEORGALLIDES.

Aspis Liberty Life Ltd: POB 26070, 1st Floor, 1 Andrea Chaliou St, 2408 Egkomi, 1666 Nicosia; tel. 22869300; fax 22869350; e-mail info@libertylife.com.cy; internet www.libertylife.com.cy; f. 1994 as Liberty Life Insurance Ltd; name changed as above in 2007; mem. of Aspis Pronia Group; Chair. PAULOS PSOMIADES; Man. Dir YIANNOS CHRISTOFI.

Aspis Pronia Insurance Co Ltd: POB 25183, 101 Acropolis Ave, 2012 Strovolos; tel. 22871087; fax 22492402; e-mail aspis@spidernet.com.cy; f. 1996; Chair. P. PSOMIADES; Principal Officer CHRISTAKIS ELEFTHERIOU.

Atlantic Insurance Co Ltd: POB 24579, 37 Prodromou St, 2nd Floor, 1090 Nicosia; tel. 22664052; fax 22661100; e-mail atlantic@spidernet.com.cy; f. 1983; Chair. and Man. Dir ZENIOS PYRISHIS; Principal Officer EMILIOS PYRISHIS.

Axioma Insurance (Cyprus) Ltd: POB 24881, 2 Ionni Klerides St, Demokritos No. 2 Bldg, Flat 83, 1070 Nicosia; tel. 22374197; fax 22374972; offshore co operating outside Cyprus; Principal Officer KONSTANTINOS KYAMIDES.

B & B Marine Insurance Ltd: POB 22545, 46 Gladstonos St, 1095 Nicosia; tel. 22666599; fax 22676476; f. 1996; offshore co operating outside Cyprus; Chair. DMITGRI MOLTCHANOV; Principal Officer GEORGHIOS YIANGOU.

Berytus Marine Insurance Ltd: POB 50132, 284 Archbishop Makarios III Ave, 3105 Limassol; tel. 25369404; fax 25377871; f. 1997; offshore co operating outside Cyprus; Principal Officer CHRIS GEORGHIADES.

Cathay Insurance Co Ltd: POB 54708, 21 Vasili Michailidi, 3727 Limassol; f. 1997; offshore captive co operating outside Cyprus; Principal Officer ARETI CHARIDEMOU.

Commercial General Insurance Ltd: POB 21312, Commercial Union House, 101 Archbishop Makarios III Ave, 1506 Nicosia; tel. 22505000; fax 22376155; e-mail info@cgi.com.cy; internet www.cgi.com.cy; f. 1974; Group Chair. ANDREAS C. ARTEMIS; Group Man. Dir CONSTANTINOS P. DEKATRIS.

Cygnet Insurance Ltd: POB 58482, 56 Grivas Dhigenis Ave, Anna Tower, 4th Floor, Office 42, 3101 Limassol; tel. 25583253; fax 25584514; e-mail tcsl@logos.cy.net; f. 1997; offshore captive co operating outside Cyprus; Principal Officer MARIOS LOUKAIDES.

Cyprialife Ltd: POB 20819, 64 Archbishop Makarios III Ave and 1 Karpenisiou St, 1077 Nicosia; tel. 22887300; fax 22374450; e-mail cyprialife@cytanet.com.cy; f. 1995; Chair. KIKIS LAZARIDES; Principal Officer DIMIS MICHAELIDES.

Direct Insurance Company Ltd: POB 22274, 35–37 Byzantium St, 1585 Nicosia; tel. 22664433; fax 22665139; Chair. STAVROS DAVERONAS.

Emergency Market Insurance Ltd: POB 613, 199 Archbishop Makarios Ave, Neokleous Bldg, 3030 Limassol; tel. 25362818; fax 25359262; f. 1997; offshore captive co operating outside Cyprus; Principal Officer ANDREAS NEOKLEOUS.

Eurolife Ltd: POB 21655, Eurolife House, 4 Evrou, 1511 Nicosia; tel. 22474000; fax 22341090; internet www.eurolife.com.cy; Chair. COSTAS SEVERIS.

Eurosure Insurance Co Ltd: POB 21961, Eurosure Tower, 5 Limassol Ave, 2112 Aglantzia, 1515 Nicosia; tel. 22882500; fax 22882599; e-mail info@eurosure.com; internet www.eurosure.com; Chair. LUKE BENFIELD.

Excelsior General Insurance Co Ltd: POB 6106, 339 Ayiou Andreou St, Andrea Chambers, Of. 303, Limassol; tel. 25427021; fax 25312446; f. 1995; Chair. CLIVE E. K. LEWIS; Principal Officer MARIA HADJIANTONIOU.

General Insurance of Cyprus Ltd: POB 21668, 2–4 Themistoklis Dervis St, 1511 Nicosia; tel. 22848700; fax 22676682; e-mail general@gic.bankofcyprus.com; internet www.gic.com.cy; f. 1951; wholly owned subsidiary of the Bank of Cyprus; Chair. GEORGE GEORGIADES; Gen. Man. STELIOS CHRISTODOULOU.

Geopolis Insurance Ltd: POB 8530, 6 Neoptolemou St, 2045 Strovolos, Nicosia; tel. 22490094; fax 22490494; f. 1993; Chair. MARIOS PROIOS; Principal Officer NIKOS DRYMIOTIS.

Granite Insurance Co Ltd: POB 613, 199 Archbishop Makarios III Ave, Neokleou Bldg, 3030 Limassol; tel. 25362818; fax 25359262; captive offshore co operating outside Cyprus; Chair. and Gen. Man. KOSTAS KOUTSOKOUMNIS; Principal Officer ANDREAS NEOKLEOUS.

Greene Insurances Ltd: POB 132, 4th Floor, Berengaria Bldg, 25 Spyrou Araouzou, 3603 Limassol; tel. 25362424; fax 25363842; f. 1987; Chair. GEORGHIOS CHRISTODOULOU; Principal Officer JOSIF CHRISTOU.

Hermes Insurance Ltd: POB 24828, 1st Floor, Anemomylos Bldg, 8 Michalakis Karaolis St, 1095 Nicosia; tel. 22666999; fax 22667999; e-mail cyprus-credit-insurance@cytanet.com.cy; f. 1980; Chair. and Man. Dir P. G. VOGAZIANOS.

I.G.R. Co Ltd: POB 21343, 20 Vasilissias Friderikis St, El Greco House, Office 104, 1066 Nicosia; tel. 22473688; fax 22455259; f. 1996; offshore co operating outside Cyprus; Principal Officer CHRISTODOULOS VASSILIADES.

Laiki Insurance Co Ltd: POB 25218, 45 Vyzantiou St, Strovolos, 1307 Nicosia; tel. 22887600; fax 22887502; e-mail laikiebank@laiki.com; internet www.laiki.com; f. 1981; Group Chair. SOUD BA'ALAWY; Group CEO ANDREAS VGENOPOULOS.

LCF Reinsurance Co Ltd: POB 60479, Abacus House, 58 Grivas Dhigenis Ave, 8103 Paphos, Nicosia; tel. 22555000; fax 22555001; f. 1984; Chair. ALAIN COPINE; Principal Officer SOPHIA XINARI.

Ledra Insurance Ltd: POB 23942, 66 Griva Dhigenis Ave, 1080 Nicosia; tel. 22743700; fax 22677656; f. 1994; Chair. CONSTANTINOS LOIZIDES; Principal Officer ALECOS PULCHERIOS.

Marketrends Insurance Ltd: 34 Costi Palama, 1096 Nicosia; tel. 22558000; fax 22558100; e-mail markins@cytanet.com.cy; Man. Dir DEMETRIS ALETRARIS.

Medlife Insurance Ltd: POB 21675, City Forum, 5th Floor, 11 Florinis St, 1305 Nicosia; tel. 22675181; fax 22671889; e-mail office@medlife.net; internet www.medlife.net; f. 1995; Chair. Dr WOLFGANG GOSCHNIK.

Minerva Insurance Co Ltd: POB 20866, 8 Epaminondas St, 1684 Nicosia 137; tel. 22445134; fax 22455528; f. 1970; Chair. and Gen. Man. K. KOUTSOKOUMNIS.

Pancyprian Insurance Ltd: POB 21352, Pancyprian Tower, 66 Grivas Dhigenis Ave, 1095 Nicosia; tel. 22743743; fax 22677656; e-mail pancyprian@hellenicbank.com; f. 1993; Chair. PANOS GHALANOS; Gen. Man. PETROS KYRIAKIDES.

Paneuropean Insurance Co Ltd: POB 553, 88 Archbishop Makarios III Ave, 1660 Nicosia; tel. 22377960; fax 22377396; f. 1980; Chair. N. K. SHACOLAS; Gen. Man. POLIS MICHAELIDES.

Philiki Insurance Co Ltd: POB 22274, 35–37 Byzantium St, 2026 Strovolos, Nicosia; tel. 22664433; fax 22665139; f. 1982; Chair. NIKOS SHAKOLAS; Principal Officer DOROS ORPHANIDES.

Progressive Insurance Co Ltd: POB 22111, 44 Kallipoleos St, 1071 Nicosia; tel. 22758585; fax 22754747; e-mail progressive@cytanet.com.cy; Chair. ANDREAS HADJIANDREOU; Principal Officer TAKIS HADJIANDREOU.

Royal Crown Insurance Co Ltd: POB 24690, Royal Crown House, 20 Mnasiadou St, Nicosia 1302; tel. 22885555; fax 22670757; e-mail info@royalcrowninsurance.com; internet www.royalcrowninsurance.com; f. 1992; Chair. and Gen. Man. PHILIOS ZACHARIADES.

CYPRUS   *Directory*

Saviour Insurance Co Ltd: POB 23957, 8 Michalakis Karaolis St, Anemomylos Bldg, Flat 204, 1687 Nicosia; tel. 22675085; fax 22676097; f. 1987; Chair. ROBERT SINCLAIR; Principal Officer KONSTANTINOS KITTIS.

Technolink Insurance Services Ltd: POB 7007, 70 Kennedy Ave, Papavasiliou House, 1076 Nicosia; tel. 22496000; fax 22493000; f. 1996; offshore captive co operating outside Cyprus; Principal Officer GEORGHIOS YIALLOURIDES.

Tercet Insurance Ltd: POB 2545, 46 Gladstonos St, 1095 Nicosia; tel. 22466456; fax 22466476; f. 1994; Chair. ANDREAS STYLIANOU; Principal Officer MARIA PIPINGA.

Triada Insurance Ltd: POB 21675, cnr Themistoklis Dervis & Florinis St, Stadyl Bldg, 6th Floor, 1512 Nicosia; tel. 22675182; fax 22675926; f. 1996; offshore captive co operating outside Cyprus; Principal Officer ANDREAS STYLIANOU.

Trust International Insurance Co (Cyprus) Ltd: POB 54857, 284 Archbishop Makarios III Ave, Fortuna Bldg, 2nd Floor, 4007 Limassol; tel. 25369404; fax 25377871; f. 1992; Chair. GHAZI K. ABU NAHL; Principal Officer CHR. GEORGHIADES.

Universal Life Insurance Company Ltd: POB 21270, Universal Tower, 85 Dhigenis Akritas Ave, 1505 Nicosia; tel. 22882222; fax 22882200; e-mail unilife@unilife.com.cy; internet www.universallife.com.cy; f. 1970; Chair. PHOTOS PHOTIADES; CEO ANDREAS GEORGHIOU.

UPIC Ltd: POB 57237, Nicolaou Pentadromos Centre, 10th Floor, Ayias Zonis St, 3314 Limassol; tel. 25347664; fax 25347081; e-mail upic@spidernet.com.cy; f. 1992; Principal Officer POLAKIS SARRIS.

Veritima Insurance Ltd: POB 956, 2B Orpheus St, Office 104, 1070 Nicosia; tel. 22375646; fax 22375620; f. 1996; offshore captive co operating outside Cyprus; Principal Officer SANDROS DIKEOS.

VTI Insurance Co Ltd: POB 50613, 199 Archbishop Makarios III Ave, Neokleou Bldg, 4004 Limassol; tel. 25362818; fax 25359262; f. 1994; Chair. SOTERIS PITTAS; Principal Officer ANDREAS NEOKLEOUS.

Turkish Cypriot Insurance Companies

Akfinans Sigorta Insurance Ltd: 16 Osman Paşa Cad., Lefkoşa (Nicosia), POB 451, Mersin 10, Turkey; tel. 2284506; fax 2285713; e-mail akfinans@akfinans.com; internet www.akfinans.com; f. 1996; Gen. Man. MEHMET KADER.

Altınbaş Sigorta Ltd: Müftü Ziya Sok. 2, Lefkoşa (Nicosia), Mersin 10, Turkey; tel. 2288222; fax 2276648.

Anadolu Anonim: Memduh Asaf Sokak 8, Lefkoşa (Nicosia), Mersin 10, Turkey; tel. 2279595; fax 2279596; e-mail bolge50@anadolusigorta.co.tr.

Ankara Sigorta: PK 551, Bedrettin Demirel Cad., Lefkoşa (Nicosia), Mersin 10, Turkey; tel. 2285815; fax 2283099.

Başak Sigorta AŞ: Mehmet Akif Cad. 95, Lefkoşa (Nicosia), Mersin 10, Turkey; tel. 2280208; fax 2286160.

Bey Sigorta Ltd: Atatürk Cad. 5, Yenişehir, Lefkoşa (Nicosia), Mersin 10, Turkey; tel. 2288241; fax 2287362.

Gold Insurance Ltd: Salih Mecit Sok. 9, Lefkoşa (Nicosia), Mersin 10, Turkey; tel. 2286500; fax 2286300; e-mail info@gold-insurance.com; internet www.gold-insurance.com; f. 1996; ULKER FAHRI.

Güneş Sigorta AŞ: Vakıflar İş Hanı 1C Girne Cad., Lefkoşa (Nicosia), Mersin 10, Turkey; tel. 2287333; fax 2281585.

Güven Sigorta (Kıbrıs) Sirketi AŞ: Mecidiye Sok. 8, Lefkoşa (Nicosia), Mersin 10, Turkey; tel. 2283023; fax 2281431.

İnan Sigorta TAŞ: Mehmet Akif Cad. 98, Kumsal, Lefkoşa (Nicosia), Mersin 10, Turkey; tel. 2283333; fax 2281976.

İsviçre Sigorta AŞ: Arkom Ltd, PK 693, Lefkoşa (Nicosia), Mersin 10, Turkey; tel. 2282125; fax 2288236; e-mail arkom@kktc.net.

Kıbrıs Sigorta: Osman Paşa Cad., Yağcıoğlu Işhanı 4, Lefkoşa (Nicosia), Mersin 10, Turkey; tel. 2283022; fax 2279277.

Ray Sigorta AŞ: Bedrettin Demirel Cad. Arabacıoğlu Apt. 7, Lefkoşa (Nicosia), Mersin 10, Turkey; tel. 2270380; fax 2270383.

Saray Sigorta: 182 Girne Cad., Lefkoşa (Nicosia), Mersin 10, Turkey; tel. 2272976; fax 2279001.

Şeker Sigorta (Kıbrıs) Ltd: Mahmut Paşa Sok. 14/A, PK 664, Lefkoşa (Nicosia), Mersin 10, Turkey; tel. 2285883; fax 2274074.

Zirve Sigorta Ltd: Gültekin Şengör Sok., Abahorlu Türk Apt. 9, Lefkoşa (Nicosia), Mersin 10, Turkey; tel. 2275633; fax 2283600.

Trade and Industry

GREEK CYPRIOT CHAMBERS OF COMMERCE AND INDUSTRY

Cyprus Chamber of Commerce and Industry: POB 21455, 38 Grivas Dhigenis Ave, 1509 Nicosia; tel. 22889800; fax 22669048; e-mail chamber@ccci.org.cy; internet www.ccci.org.cy; f. 1927; Pres. VASSILIS ROLOGIS; Sec.-Gen. PANAYIOTIS LOIZIDES; 8,000 mems, 120 affiliated trade asscns.

Famagusta Chamber of Commerce and Industry: POB 53124, 339 Ayiou Andreou St, Andrea Chambers Bldg, 2nd Floor, Office No. 201, 3300 Limassol; tel. 25370165; fax 25370291; e-mail chamberf@cytanet.com.cy; internet www.fcci.org.cy; f. 1952; Pres. ANDREAS MATSIS; Sec. and Dir IACOVOS HADJIVARNAVAS; 400 mems and 20 assoc. mems.

Larnaca Chamber of Commerce and Industry: POB 40287, 12 Gregoriou Afxentiou St, Skouros Bldg, Apt 43, 4th Floor, 6302 Larnaca; tel. 24655051; fax 24628281; e-mail lcci@spidernet.com.cy; Pres. ANDREAS LOUROUTZIATIS; Sec. GEORGE PSARAS; 600 mems and 25 assoc. mems.

Limassol Chamber of Commerce and Industry: POB 347, Berengaria Bldg, 25 Spyrou Araouzou, 3603 Limassol; tel. 25662556; fax 25661655; e-mail chamberl@dial.cylink.com.cy; internet www.kypros.com/EVEL/; f. 1962; Pres. DIMITRIS SOLOMONIDES; Sec. and Dir CHRISTOS ANASTASSIADES; 750 mems.

Nicosia Chamber of Commerce and Industry: POB 21455, 38 Grivas Dhigenis Ave, Chamber Bldg, 1509 Nicosia; tel. 22889600; fax 22667433; e-mail reception@ncci.org.cy; internet www.ncci.org.cy; f. 1952; Pres. CHRISTODOULOS ANGASTINIOTIS; Dir SOCRATES HERACLEOUS; 1,520 mems.

Paphos Chamber of Commerce and Industry: POB 82, Tolmi Court, 1st Floor, cnr Athinon Ave and Alexandrou Papayou Ave, 8100 Paphos; tel. 26235115; fax 26244602; e-mail evepafos@cytanet.com.cy; Pres. THEODOROS ARISTODEMOU; Sec. KENDEAS ZAMPIRINIS; 530 mems and 6 assoc. mems.

TURKISH CYPRIOT CHAMBERS OF COMMERCE AND INDUSTRY

Turkish Cypriot Chamber of Commerce: 90 Bedrettin Demirel Cad., PK 718, Lefkoşa (Nicosia), Mersin 10, Turkey; tel. 2283645; fax 2283089; e-mail ktto@ktto.net; internet www.ktto.net; f. 1958; Chair. HASAN KUTLU İNCE; Sec.-Gen. JANEL BURCAN; more than 9,000 mems.

Turkish Cypriot Chamber of Industry: 126 Mehmet Akif Cad., Lefkoşa (Nicosia), Mersin 10, Turkey; tel. 2287889; fax 2284595; e-mail kibso@kibris.net; internet www.kktcsanayiodasi.org; f. 1977; Pres. SALIH TUNAR; Sec.-Gen. MUSTAFA GÜNDÜZ; 400 mems.

GREEK CYPRIOT EMPLOYERS' ORGANIZATION

Cyprus Employers' & Industrialists' Federation: POB 21657, 30 Grivas Dhigenis Ave, 1511 Nicosia; tel. 22665102; fax 22669459; e-mail info@oeb.org.cy; internet www.oeb.org.cy; f. 1960; 53 mem. trade asscns, 400 direct and 3,000 indirect mems; Chair. Dr ANDREAS PITTAS; Dir-Gen. MICHAEL PILIKOS; The largest of the trade asscn mems are: Cyprus Building Contractors' Asscn; Land and Building Developers' Asscn; Asscn of Cyprus Tourist Enterprises; Cyprus Shipping Asscn; Cyprus Footwear Manufacturers' Asscn; Cyprus Metal Industries Asscn; Cyprus Bankers Employers' Asscn; Cyprus Asscn of Business Consultants; Mechanical Contractors Asscn of Cyprus; Union of Solar Energy Industries of Cyprus.

TURKISH CYPRIOT EMPLOYERS' ORGANIZATION

Kıbrıs Türk şverenler Sendikası (Turkish Cypriot Employers' Association): PK 674, Lefkoşa (Nicosia), Mersin 10, Turkey; tel. 2273673; fax 2277479; Chair. HASAN SUNGUR.

GREEK CYPRIOT UTILITIES

Electricity

Electricity Authority of Cyprus (EAC): POB 24506, 1399 Nicosia; tel. 22201000; fax 22201020; e-mail eac@eac.com.cy; internet www.eac.com.cy; generation, transmission and distribution of electric energy in govt-controlled area; also licensed to install and commercially exploit wired telecommunication network; total installed capacity 988 MW in 2006; Chair. CHARILAOS STAVRAKIS; Gen. Man. MOYSIS STAVROU.

Water

Water Development Department: Demosthenis Severis Ave, 1413 Nicosia; tel. 22803390; fax 22675019; e-mail eioannou@wdd.moa.gov.cy; internet www.moa.gov.cy/wdd; f. 1939; owned by Ministry of Agriculture, Natural Resources and the Environment; dam storage capacity 327.5m. cu m; Dir CHRISTODOULOS ARTEMIS.

CYPRUS

TURKISH CYPRIOT UTILITIES
Electricity

Cyprus Turkish Electricity Corpn: Lefkoşa (Nicosia), Mersin 10, Turkey; tel. 2283730; fax 2286945; e-mail info@kibtek.com; internet www.kibtek.com.

TRADE UNIONS
Greek Cypriot Trade Unions

Cyprus Civil Servants' Trade Union (PASYDY): 3 Demosthenis Severis Ave, 1066 Nicosia; tel. 22844300; fax 22668639; e-mail pasydy@spidernet.com.cy; internet www.pasydy.org; f. 1927; regd 1966; restricted to persons in the civil employment of the Govt and public authorities; 6 brs with a total membership of 15,383; Pres. ANDREAS CHRISTODOULOU; Gen. Sec. GLAFKOS HADJIPETROU.

Dimokratiki Ergatiki Omospondia Kyprou (DEOK) (Democratic Labour Federation of Cyprus): POB 21625, 40 Byron Ave, 1511 Nicosia; tel. 22676506; fax 22670494; e-mail deok@cytanet.com.cy; f. 1962; 5 workers' unions with a total membership of 7,316; Gen. Sec. DIOMEDES DIOMEDOUS.

Pankypria Ergatiki Omospondia (PEO) (Pancyprian Federation of Labour): POB 21885, 31–35 Archermos St, Nicosia 1045; tel. 22886400; fax 22349382; e-mail peo@peo.org.cy; internet www.peo.org.cy; f. 1946; regd 1947; previously the Pancyprian Trade Union Cttee (f. 1941, dissolved 1946); 8 unions and 176 brs with a total membership of 75,000; affiliated to the WFTU; Gen. Sec. PAMBIS KYRITSIS.

Pankyprios Omospondia Anexartition Syntechnion (Pancyprian Federation of Independent Trade Unions): 4 B Dayaes St, 2369 Ay. Dhometios; POB 7521, 2430 Nicosia; tel. 22356414; fax 22354216; f. 1956; regd 1957; has no political orientation; 8 unions with a total membership of 798; Gen. Sec. KYRIACOS NATHANAEL.

Synomospondia Ergaton Kyprou (SEK) (Cyprus Workers' Confederation): POB 25018, 11 Strovolos Ave, 2018 Strovolos, 1306 Nicosia; tel. 22849849; fax 22849850; e-mail sek@org.cy.net; f. 1944; regd 1950; 7 federations, 5 labour centres, 47 unions, 12 brs with a total membership of 65,000; affiliated to the ITUC and the European Trade Union Confed.; Gen. Sec. NIKOS MOYSEOS; Deputy Gen. Sec. PETROS THEOPHANOUS.

Union of Cyprus Journalists: POB 23495, Rik Ave 12, 1683 Nicosia; tel. 22446090; fax 22446095; e-mail cyjourun@logosnet.cy.net; internet www.esk.org.cy; f. 1959; Chair. ANDREAS KANNAOUROS.

Turkish Cypriot Trade Unions

Devrimci İşçi Sendikaları Federasyonu (Dev-İş) (Revolutionary Trade Unions' Federation): 6 Serabioğlu Sok., 748 Lefkoşa (Nicosia), Mersin 10, Turkey; tel. 2286462; fax 2286463; e-mail devis@defne.net; f. 1976; 4 unions with a total membership of 1,850 (2002); affiliated to the WFTU; Pres. ALI GULLE; Gen. Sec. MEHMET SEYIS.

Kıbrıs Türk İşçi Sendikaları Federasyonu (TÜRK-SEN) (Turkish Cypriot Trade Union Federation): POB 829, 7–7A Şehit Mehmet R. Hüseyin Sok., Lefkoşa (Nicosia), Mersin 10, Turkey; tel. 2272444; fax 2287831; e-mail turksen@north-cyprus.net; f. 1954; regd 1955; 12 unions with a total membership of 5,250 (1998); affiliated to ITUC, the European Trade Union Confed., the Commonwealth Trade Union Council and the Confed. of Trade Unions of Turkey (Türk-İş); Pres. ARSLAN BIÇAKLI; Gen. Sec. ERKAN BIRER.

Transport

RAILWAYS

There are no railways in Cyprus.

ROADS

In 2004 there were 12,059 km of roads in the government-controlled areas, of which 268 km were motorways; according to the International Road Federation, some 62.2% of the road network was paved in 2002. The Nicosia–Limassol four-lane dual carriageway, which was completed in 1985, was subsequently extended with the completion of the Limassol and Larnaca bypasses. Highways also connect Nicosia and Larnaca, Nicosia and Anthoupolis-Kokkinotrimithia, Larnaca and Kophinou, Aradippo and Dhekelia, Limassol and Paphos, and Dhekelia and Ammochostos (Famagusta). The north and south are now served by separate transport systems, and there are no services linking the two sectors.

SHIPPING

Until 1974 Famagusta, a natural port, was the island's most important harbour, handling about 83% of the country's cargo. Since its capture by the Turkish army in August of that year the port has been officially declared closed to international traffic. However, it continues to serve the Turkish-occupied region.

The main ports that serve the island's maritime trade at present are Larnaca and Limassol, which were constructed in 1973 and 1974, respectively. Both ports have since been expanded and improved. There is also an industrial port at Vassiliko and there are three specialized petroleum terminals, at Larnaca, Dhekelia and Moni. A second container terminal became operational at Limassol in 1995.

In addition to serving local traffic, Limassol and Larnaca ports act as transhipment load centres for the Eastern Mediterranean, North Adriatic and Black Sea markets and as regional warehouse and assembly bases for the Middle East, North Africa and the Persian (Arabian) Gulf. Freight handled at Cypriot ports amounted to 8,036,368 metric tons in 2005.

Both Kyrenia and Karavostassi are under Turkish occupation and have been declared closed to international traffic. Karavostassi used to be the country's major mineral port, dealing with 76% of the total mineral exports. However, since the war minerals have been passed through Vassiliko which is a specified industrial port. A hydrofoil service operates between Kyrenia and Mersin on the Turkish mainland. Car ferries sail from Kyrenia to Taşucu and Mersin, in Turkey.

At 31 December 2006 the Greek Cypriot shipping registry comprised 971 merchant vessels, with an aggregate displacement of 19.0m. grt.

Department of Merchant Shipping: POB 56193, Kylinis St, Mesa Geitonia, 4007 Limassol; tel. 25848100; fax 25848200; e-mail maritimeadmin@dms.mcw.com.cy; internet www.shipping.gov.cy; f. 1977; Dir SERGHIOS SERGHIOU.

Cyprus Ports Authority: POB 22007, 23 Crete St, 1516 Nicosia; tel. 22817200; fax 22765420; e-mail cpa@cpa.gov.cy; internet www.cpa.gov.cy; f. 1973; Chair. CHRYSIS PRENTZAS; Gen. Man. YIANNAKIS KOKKINOS.

Cyprus Shipping Council: POB 56607, City Chambers, 1st Floor, 6 Regas Fereos St, 3309 Limassol; tel. 25360717; fax 25358642; e-mail csc@csc-cy.org; internet www.csc-cy.org; Pres. Capt. DIRK FRY; Gen. Sec. THOMAS A. KAZAKOS.

Greek Cypriot Shipping Companies

Amer Shipping Ltd: POB 27363, 602 Ghinis Bldg, 58–60 Dhigenis Akritas Ave, 1644 Nicosia; tel. 22875188; fax 22751460; e-mail ateam@amershipping.com; internet www.amershipping.com; Man. Dir ANIL DESHPANDE.

C. F. Ahrenkiel Shipmanagement (Cyprus) Ltd: POB 53594, 4th Floor, O & A Tower, 25 Olympion St, 3033 Limassol; tel. 25854000; fax 25854001; Man. Dir VASSOS STAVROU.

Columbia Shipmanagement Ltd: POB 51624, Columbia House, Dodekanissou St, 3507 Limassol; tel. 25843100; fax 25320325; e-mail marketing@csmcy.com; internet www.columbia.com.cy; f. 1978; Chair. HEINRICH SCHOELLER; Man. Dir DIRK FRY.

Hanseatic Shipping Co Ltd: POB 50127, 3601 Limassol; tel. 25846400; fax 25745245; e-mail management@hanseatic.com.cy; internet www.hanseaticshipping.com; f. 1972; CEO ANDREAS J. DROUSSIOTIS; Man. Dir HOLGER PITTELKAU.

Interorient Navigation Co Ltd: POB 51309, 3 Thalia St, 3504 Limassol; tel. 25840300; fax 25575895; e-mail info@interorient.com.cy; internet www.interorient.com; Man. Dir JAN LISSOW.

Louis Cruise Lines: POB 21301, 1506 Nicosia; 20 Amphipoleos St, 2025 Strovolos; tel. 22588168; fax 22442949; e-mail investors@louisgroup.com; internet www.louiscruises.com; Exec. Chair. COSTAKIS LOIZOU; CEO STELIOS KILIARIS.

Marlow Navigation Co Ltd: POB 4077, Marlow Bldg, cnr 28th October St and Sotiris Michaelides St, Limassol; tel. 25348888; fax 25748222; e-mail marlow@marlow.com.cy; Gen. Man. ANDREAS NEOPHYTOU.

Oldendorff Ltd, Reederei 'Nord' Klaus E: POB 56345, Libra Tower, 23 Olympion St, 3306 Limassol; tel. 25841400; fax 25345077; e-mail mail@rnkeo.com.cy; internet www.rnkeo.com; Chair. and Man. Dir CHRISTIANE E. OLDENDORFF; Gen. Man. Capt. KEITH V. OBEYESEKERA.

Seatankers Management Co Ltd: POB 53562, Deana Beach Apartments, Block 1, 4th Floor, Promachon Eleftherias St, 4103 Limassol; tel. 25858300; fax 25323770; e-mail seatank@cytanet.com.cy; Dirs COSTAS PALLARIS, DIMITRIS HANNAS.

Turkish Cypriot Shipping Companies

Armen Shipping Ltd: Altun Tabya Yolu No. 10–11, Gazi Mağusa (Famagusta), Mersin 10, Turkey; tel. 3664086; fax 3665860; e-mail armen@armenshipping.com; Dir VARGIN VARER.

Compass Shipping Ltd: Seagate Court, Gazi Mağusa (Famagusta), Mersin 10, Turkey; tel. 3666393; fax 3666394.

CYPRUS

Ertürk Ltd: Kyrenia (Girne), Mersin 10, Turkey; tel. 8155834; fax 8151808; Dir KEMAL ERTÜRK.

Fergun Maritime Co: Kyrenia (Girne), Mersin 10, Turkey; tel. 8154993; ferries to Turkish ports; Owner FEHIM KÜÇÜK.

Kıbrıs Türk Denizcilik Ltd, Şti (Turkish Cypriot Maritime Co Ltd): 3 Bülent Ecevit Bul., Gazi Mağusa (Famagusta), Mersin 10, Turkey; tel. 3665995; fax 3667840; e-mail cypship@superonline.com.

Medusa Marine Shipping Ltd: Aycan Apt, Gazi Mağusa (Famagusta), Mersin 10, Turkey; tel. 3663945; fax 3667800; Dir ERGÜN TOLAY.

Orion Navigation Ltd: Seagate Court, Gazi Mağusa (Famagusta), Mersin 10, Turkey; tel. 3662643; fax 3664773; e-mail orion@analiz.net; f. 1976; shipping agents; Dir O. LAMA; Shipping Man. L. LAMA.

Tahsin Transtürk ve Oğlu Ltd: 11 Kizilkule Yolu, Gazi Mağusa (Famagusta), Mersin 10, Turkey; tel. 3665409.

CIVIL AVIATION

There is an international airport at Nicosia, which can accommodate all types of aircraft, including jet-engined airliners. It has been closed since 1974, following the Turkish invasion. A new international airport was constructed at Larnaca, from which flights operate to Europe, the USA, the Middle East and the Persian (Arabian) Gulf. Another international airport at Paphos began operations in 1983. A project to expand and modernize Larnaca and Paphos airports commenced in June 2006, and was scheduled for completion by 2009.

Cyprus Airways: POB 21903, 21 Alkeou St, Engomi, 2404 Nicosia; tel. 22663054; fax 22663167; e-mail webcenter@cyprusairways.com; internet www.cyprusairways.com; f. 1947; jointly owned by Cyprus Govt (69.62%) and local interests; wholly owned subsidiaries Cyprair Tours Ltd, Duty Free Shops Ltd and Zenon NDC Ltd; services throughout Europe and the Middle East; restructuring plan announced Oct. 2005; Exec. Chair. KIKIS LAZARIDES.

Eurocypria Airlines (ECA): POB 40970, 97 Artemidos Ave, Artemis Bldg, 6308 Larnaca; tel. 24658005; fax 24658573; e-mail eurocypria@cytanet.com.cy; internet www.eurocypria.com; f. 1991; services to European destinations from Larnaca and Paphos; Chair. Dr LAZAROS S. SAVVIDES; Gen. Man. GEORGE SOUROULLAS.

In 1975 the Turkish authorities opened Ercan (fmrly Tymbou) airport, and a second airport was opened at Geçitkale (Lefkoniko) in 1986. However, only Turkey and Azerbaijan recognize the airports as legitimate points of entry; flights from all other countries involve a preliminary stopover at one of Turkey's airports.

Kıbrıs Türk Hava Yolları (Cyprus Turkish Airlines): Bedrettin Demirel Cad., PK 793, Lefkoşa (Nicosia), Mersin 10, Turkey; tel. 2283901; fax 2274304; e-mail info@kthy.aero; internet www.kthy.net; f. 1974; jointly owned by the Turkish Cypriot Community Assembly Consolidated Improvement Fund and Turkish Airlines Inc; services to Turkey and five European countries; Gen. Man. M. ZEKI ZIYQ.

Tourism

In 2006 an estimated 2.4m. foreign tourists visited the Greek Cypriot area and receipts from tourism amounted to some C£1,045.9m. In 2005 there were 95,648 hotel beds in the Greek Cypriot zone. In 2005 652,779 tourists (488,023 of whom were from Turkey) visited the Turkish Cypriot area, while revenue from tourism amounted to an estimated US $328.8m.

Cyprus Tourism Organisation (CTO): POB 24535, 19 Leoforos Lemesou, Aglantzia, 2112 Nicosia; tel. 22691100; fax 22331644; e-mail cytour@visitcyprus.com; internet www.visitcyprus.com; Chair. PHOTIS PHOTIOU.

North Cyprus Tourism Centre: Ministry of Economy and Tourism, Selçuklu Rd, Lefkoşa (Nicosia), Mersin 10, Turkey; tel. 2289629; fax 2273976; e-mail info@northcyprus.cc; internet www.northycyprus.cc.

THE CZECH REPUBLIC

Introductory Survey

Location, Climate, Language, Religion, Flag, Capital

The Czech Republic lies in central Europe and comprises the Czech Lands of Bohemia and Moravia and part of Silesia. Its neighbours are Poland to the north, Germany to the north-west and west, Austria to the south and Slovakia to the east. The climate is continental, with warm summers and cold winters. The average mean temperature is 9°C (49°F). Czech, a member of the west Slavonic group, is the official language. There is a sizeable Slovak minority and also small Polish, German, Silesian, Roma, Hungarian and other minorities. The major religion is Christianity. The national flag (proportions 2 by 3) has two equal horizontal stripes, of white and red, on which is superimposed a blue triangle (half the length) at the hoist. The capital is Prague (Praha).

Recent History

In October 1918, following the collapse of the Austro-Hungarian Empire at the end of the First World War, the Republic of Czechoslovakia was established. The new state united the Czech Lands of Bohemia and Moravia, which had been incorporated into the Austrian Empire in the 16th and 17th centuries, and Slovakia, which had been under Hungarian rule for almost 1,000 years. After the Nazis came to power in Germany in 1933, there was increased agitation in the Sudetenland (an area in northern Bohemia that was inhabited by about 3m. German-speaking people) for autonomy within, and later secession from, Czechoslovakia. In 1938, to appease German demands, the British, French and Italian Prime Ministers concluded an agreement with the German leader, Adolf Hitler, whereby the Sudetenland was ceded to Germany, and other parts of Czechoslovakia were transferred to Hungary and Poland. The remainder of Czechoslovakia was invaded and occupied by Nazi armed forces in March 1939, and a German protectorate was established in Bohemia and Moravia. In Slovakia, which had been granted self-government in late 1938, a separate state was formed, under the pro-Nazi regime of Jozef Tiso.

After Germany's defeat in the Second World War (1939–45), the pre-1938 frontiers of Czechoslovakia were restored, although a small area in eastern Slovakia was ceded to the USSR in June 1945. Almost all of the German-speaking inhabitants were expelled, and the Sudetenland was settled by Czechs from other parts of Bohemia. In response to Slovakian demands for greater autonomy, a legislature (the Slovenská národná rada—Slovakian National Council) and an executive Board of Commissioners were established in Bratislava, the Slovakian capital. At elections in 1946 the Communist Party of Czechoslovakia (KSČ) emerged as the leading party, winning 38% of the votes cast. The party's leader, Klement Gottwald, became Prime Minister in a coalition Government. After ministers of other parties resigned, communist control became complete on 25 February 1948. A People's Republic was established on 9 June. Gottwald replaced Eduard Beneš as President, a position that he held until his death in 1953. The country aligned itself with the Soviet-led Eastern European bloc, joining the Council for Mutual Economic Assistance (CMEA) and the Warsaw Pact. Government followed a rigid Stalinist pattern, and in the early 1950s there were many political trials. Although these ended under Gottwald's successors, Antonín Zápotocký and, from 1956, Antonín Novotný, there was no relaxation of policy until 1963, when a new Government, with Jozef Lenárt as Prime Minister, was formed. Meanwhile, the country was renamed the Czechoslovak Socialist Republic, under a new Constitution, proclaimed in July 1960.

In January 1968 Alexander Dubček succeeded Novotný as First Secretary of the KSČ, and in March Gen. Ludvík Svoboda succeeded Novotný as President. Oldřich Černík became Prime Minister in April. The new Government envisaged widespread reforms, including the introduction of a federal system of government, a more democratic electoral system, and a greater degree of separation between party and state. In August Warsaw Pact forces (numbering an estimated 600,000) invaded Czechoslovakia, occupying Prague and other major cities. Mass demonstrations in protest at the invasion were held throughout the country, and many people were killed in clashes with occupation troops. The Soviet Government exerted heavy pressure on the Czechoslovak leaders to suppress their reformist policies and in April 1969 Dubček was replaced by a fellow Slovak, Dr Gustáv Husák, as First (subsequently General) Secretary of the KSČ. Under Husák's leadership, there was a severe purge of the KSČ membership and most of Dubček's supporters were removed from the Government. All the reforms of 1968 were duly abandoned, with the exception of the federalization programme. This was implemented in January 1969, when the unitary Czechoslovak state was transformed into a federation, with separate Czech and Slovakian Republics, each having its own legislature and Government. A Federal Government was established as the supreme executive organ of state power, and the legislature was transformed into a bicameral Federální shromáždění (Federal Assembly). The first legislative elections since 1964 were held in November 1971, and 99.8% of the votes cast were in favour of candidates of the National Front (the communist-dominated organization embracing all the legal political parties in Czechoslovakia).

In May 1975 Husák was appointed to the largely ceremonial post of President of Czechoslovakia, retaining his positions of Chairman of the National Front and General Secretary of the KSČ. He held the latter post until December 1987, when he was replaced by Miloš Jakeš, an economist and member of the Presidium of the party's Central Committee. However, Husák remained as President of the Republic.

Although Jakeš affirmed his commitment to the moderate programme of reform initiated by Husák, repressive measures continued against the Roman Catholic Church and dissident groups, such as Charter 77, which had been established in January 1977 by intellectuals and former politicians to campaign for the observance of civil and political rights. Despite continued attempts to suppress the movement, it played a leading role in anti-Government demonstrations, which began in 1988. In February 1989, following one such demonstration, the Czech playwright Václav Havel (a leader of Charter 77), was sentenced to nine months' imprisonment. (He was released in May, following international condemnation.) Anti-Government demonstrations followed in May, August and October.

In November 1989 the protest actions evolved into a process of dramatic, yet largely peaceful, political change, which subsequently became known as the 'velvet revolution'. On 17 November an anti-Government demonstration in Prague, the largest public protest for 20 years, was violently dispersed by the police; large numbers of demonstrators (mainly students) were injured. Large-scale protests continued in Prague and in other towns. Later that month a new opposition group, Civic Forum, was established as an informal alliance, which united several existing opposition and human rights organizations, including Charter 77, and rapidly attracted widespread popular support. Meanwhile, Dubček addressed mass rallies in Bratislava and Prague, expressing his support for the opposition's demands for reform. On 24 November it was announced that Jakeš and the entire membership of the Presidium of the Central Committee had resigned. Karel Urbánek, a member of the Presidium, replaced Jakeš as General Secretary of the party, and a new Presidium was elected. The opposition demands for the ending of censorship and the release of all political prisoners were accepted by the authorities, and at the end of November the articles guaranteeing the KSČ's predominance were deleted from the Constitution.

In early December 1989 the Federal Government was reorganized. However, Civic Forum and its Slovakian counterpart, Public Against Violence (VPN), denounced the new Government, since the majority of its ministers had served in the previous administration, and it included only five non-communists. Ladislav Adamec subsequently resigned as Prime Minister, and was replaced by Marián Čalfa. In the following week a new, interim Federal Government was formed, with a majority of non-communist members, including seven non-party supporters of Civic Forum. Husák resigned from the office of President of the Republic and, at the end of December, was replaced by Havel.

Dubček was elected Chairman of the Federální shromáždění. At an emergency congress of the KSČ, held in December, the position of General Secretary of the Central Committee was abolished. Adamec was appointed to the new post of Chairman of the party.

In April 1990 the Federální shromáždění voted to rename the country the Czech and Slovak Federative Republic (CzSFR). The decision, which followed intense controversy, satisfied Slovakian demands that the new title should reflect the equal status of Slovakia within the federation. On 8–9 June the first democratic legislative elections since 1946 were held in Czechoslovakia. A total of 27 political associations contested representation to the Federální shromáždění and to each republican legislature, with the participation of some 97% of the electorate. In the elections at federal level, the highest proportion of the total votes cast (about 46%) was secured by Civic Forum, in the Czech Lands, and by VPN in Slovakia. The KSČ won a greater proportion of the votes (about 14%) than had been expected, obtaining the second highest representation in the Federální shromáždění. The Christian Democratic Union (a coalition of the Czechoslovak People's Party, the Christian Democratic Party—KDS and the Slovakian-based Christian Democratic Movement—KDH) obtained some 12% of the votes cast. Two parties that had campaigned for regional autonomy or secession secured more than the 5% minimum required for representation in the legislature: the Movement for Autonomous Democracy–Society for Moravia and Silesia (HSD–SMS) and the separatist Slovak National Party (SNS). The newly elected Federální shromáždění was to serve a transitional two-year term, during which time it was to draft new federal and republican constitutions and elect a new President of the Republic. In late June Dubček was re-elected Chairman of the Federální shromáždění. A new Federal Government, announced in that month, comprised 16 members: four from Civic Forum, three from VPN, one from the KDH and eight independents. In early July Havel was re-elected to the post of President.

In the latter half of 1990 there was increasing support in Slovakia for autonomy. A widening division emerged between the more moderate Slovakian movements, such as VPN and the KDH, and a minority of more radical parties, which campaigned for full independence. In early March 1991 Vladimír Mečiar, the Slovakian Prime Minister and a founding member of VPN, announced the formation of a minority faction within VPN (the Movement for a Democratic Slovakia—HZDS), in support of greater autonomy. Meanwhile, disagreement over the direction of post-communist politics and economic management had led to a split within Civic Forum, with conservatives and economic liberals forming the Civic Democratic Party (ODS), led by Václav Klaus. In late March representatives of all political forces in Czechoslovakia reached agreement on the framework of a new federal constitution. Mečiar's policies and aggressive style of leadership were seen by many as detrimental to the future of Czech-Slovakian relations, and in April the Slovenská národná rada voted to remove him from the Slovakian premiership. Following this, the HZDS was established as a separate political group. By late 1991 discussions in the Federální shromáždění on the new constitution had reached an impasse. President Havel repeatedly proposed the holding of a referendum on the possible division of Czechoslovakia into two separate states, as the only democratic means of resolving the issue. The constitutional debate continued in the first half of 1992, with increasing Slovakian support for the loosest possible confederation, comprising two nominally independent states. The majority of Czech politicians, however, were in favour of preserving the existing state structure, and rejected such proposals as impracticable. In March it was agreed that the constitutional talks would be postponed until after the legislative elections due to take place in mid-1992.

The legislative elections of 5–6 June 1992 proved to be decisive in the eventual dismantling of Czechoslovakia, particularly as Mečiar's HZDS emerged as the dominant political force in Slovakia. With about 34% of the total votes cast in Slovakia, the party obtained 57 seats (the second largest representation) in the 300-member Federální shromáždění. The leading party in the Slovakian Government, the KDH (which advocated a continued federation), won only 9% of the votes cast in Slovakia, securing 14 seats in the Federální shromáždění, one seat fewer than the separatist SNS. Václav Klaus's party, the ODS (in coalition with the KDS), won the largest proportion (about 34%) of the total votes cast in the Czech Lands. The ODS was one of only two parties to contest the elections in both republics, and in Slovakia it received 4% of the votes cast. In total, the ODS won 85 seats in the Federální shromáždění, thus becoming the largest party in the legislature. Two other splinter groups of the former Civic Forum, including the Civic Democratic Alliance (ODA), failed to win representation in the Federální shromáždění, as did the Civic Democratic Union (formerly VPN), in Slovakia. The successor organizations to the communist parties of the two republics achieved considerable success: the Left Bloc (which included the Communist Party of Bohemia and Moravia—KSČM) won a total of 34 seats in the Federální shromáždění, while the Slovakian-based Party of the Democratic Left secured 23 seats. The representation of parties in the new republican legislatures did not differ greatly from that of the Federální shromáždění although the ODA and the HSD–SMS succeeded in winning seats in the Česká národní rada (Czech National Council).

Negotiations on the formation of a new federal government, initiated by the ODS and the HZDS, only served to emphasize the two leading parties' fundamental divergence of opinion on the future of the CzSFR. Nevertheless, a transitional Federal Government, dominated by members of the ODS and the HZDS, was appointed in early July 1992. The new Prime Minister was Jan Stráský of the ODS, who had served as a Deputy Prime Minister in the outgoing Czech Government. There was increasing recognition by Czech politicians that the constitutional talks on the future of Czechoslovakia were no longer viable and that a complete separation was preferable to the compromise measures that most Slovakian parties favoured. The principal task of the new Federal Government, it was acknowledged, was to supervise the eventual dissolution of the CzSFR. Meanwhile, in late June the new Slovakian Government was announced, with Mečiar as Prime Minister. All but one of the ministers were members of the HZDS. A new coalition Czech Government, dominated by the ODS and with Klaus as Prime Minister, was appointed in early July. In the same month the Federální shromáždění failed to elect a new president in three rounds of voting. Havel's re-election as President had been blocked by the HZDS and the SNS, and in mid-July he resigned.

The events of June and July 1992 had ensured that the emergence of two independent states was inevitable. On 17 July the Slovenská národná rada approved a (symbolic) declaration of Slovakian sovereignty, and in the following week the Czech and Slovakian Prime Ministers agreed, in principle, to the dissolution of the CzSFR. In the following months extensive negotiations were conducted to determine the modalities of the division, which was to take effect from 1 January 1993. International observers expressed surprise not only that the dissolution of Czechoslovakia should be effected in so short a time, but also that the majority of Czechs and Slovakians (more than 60%, according to the results of public opinion polls) were still opposed to the country's division. Moreover, it appeared that Slovakian leaders were less intent on leaving the federation. Indeed, the failure of the Federální shromáždění, in early October 1992 and again in mid-November, to adopt legislation permitting the dissolution of the CzSFR was the result of opposition by (mainly) HZDS deputies. However, the two republican Prime Ministers, supported by their respective Governments, stressed that the process of partition was irreversible. In late October the Czech and Slovakian Governments ratified a number of accords, including a customs union treaty to abolish trade restrictions between the two republics following their independence. Finally, on 25 November the Federální shromáždění adopted legislation providing for the constitutional disbanding of the federation, having secured the necessary three-fifths' majority by a margin of only three votes. Accordingly, the Federal Government accelerated the process of dividing the country's assets and liabilities as well as its armed forces. In most cases federal property was divided territorially. It was agreed, however, that the two states would continue to share some federal infrastructure and would retain a single currency for the immediate future, although central banks for each state were established. (Two separate currencies were introduced in February 1993.)

On 17 December 1992 a treaty pledging cordial relations and co-operation was signed, followed by the establishment of diplomatic relations between the two republics. At midnight on 31 December all federal structures were dissolved and the Czech Republic and the Slovak Republic came into being. The dissolution of the CzSFR had thus been entirely peaceful. As legal successors to Czechoslovakia, the two republics were quickly recognized by the states that had maintained diplomatic relations with the CzSFR, as well as by those international bodies of which the CzSFR had been a member. Existing treaties and agreements to which the CzSFR had been a party were to be honoured by both republics.

In anticipation of the establishment of the Czech Republic as an independent state, the existing legislature was replaced by a bicameral body, in accordance with the Czech Constitution (adopted in mid-December 1992); the 200-member Česká národní rada was transformed into a Poslanecká sněmovna (Chamber of Deputies—lower house); an upper house, the Senát (Senate), was to be elected at a later date. In late January 1993 the Poslanecká sněmovna elected Havel as the Czech Republic's first President. The composition of the Government remained largely unchanged. It included among its principal objectives the pursuance of the former Federal Government's economic reforms, including its programme of large-scale privatization.

Relations between the Czech Republic and Slovakia were troubled in early 1993 by disagreements over former Czechoslovak assets and property that still remained to be divided. In April 1994 the Poslanecká sněmovna adopted legislation permitting the restitution of property expropriated from Czech Jews during the period of Nazi occupation (1938–45). At local elections in November, the ODS was confirmed as the party with the broadest support (receiving some 31% of the total votes cast). Renewed controversy emerged in 1995 over the so-called 'lustration', or screening, law, which had been adopted by the Czechoslovak Federální shromáždění in October 1991. The law effectively banned former communist functionaries, as well as members of the former state security service and the People's Militia (the KSČ's paramilitary force), from holding senior political, economic and judicial posts. In September 1995 the Poslanecká sněmovna voted to extend until 2000 the legislation on screening (which had been due to expire in late 1996). In the following month Havel rejected the decision, but the Chamber approved it for a second time, and the extension of the law entered into force.

The first general election since the dissolution of the CzSFR took place on 31 May and 1 June 1996. The ODS (which had merged with the KDS in April) won 68 of the 200 seats in the Poslanecká sněmovna (with 29.6% of the total votes cast), while the Czech Social Democratic Party (ČSSD), which had become a major force of the centre-left under the leadership of Miloš Zeman, greatly increased its parliamentary representation, winning 61 seats (26.4%). As a result, the coalition of the ODS, the Christian Democratic Union-Czechoslovak People's Party (KDU-ČSL, which obtained 18 seats) and the ODA (13 seats) lost its overall majority, achieving a total of 99 seats. The KSČM and the Association for the Republic—Republican Party of Czechoslovakia secured 22 and 18 seats, respectively. Despite losing its parliamentary majority, the governing coalition remained intact. The ČSSD refused to join the coalition, but agreed to give tacit support on most issues to a minority government. In early July Klaus formed a new Government; in a major concession to the ČSSD, Zeman was appointed Chairman of the Poslanecká sněmovna. The ruling coalition obtained a majority of the votes in the elections to the 81-seat Senát, held in mid-November, winning 52 seats.

Tension within the ODS and between the ruling coalition parties intensified in October 1997, and Josef Zieleniec resigned from his position as Minister of Foreign Relations and as Deputy Chairman of the ODS. In November allegations of impropriety in the funding of the ODS led to the resignation of the Klaus administration (which denied the accusations), following the withdrawal of the KDU-ČSL and the ODA from the coalition. Josef Tošovský, hitherto Governor of the Czech National Bank, was designated Prime Minister in December, and a new, interim Government, comprising seven non-political ministers, four ODS members, three KDU-ČSL members and three ODA members, was appointed in January 1998. The ODS was divided over its participation in the new administration, and the party's ministers subsequently defected to the Freedom Union (US), a newly established breakaway party, which had 31 seats in the Poslanecká sněmovna by mid-February.

On 20 January 1998 Havel was narrowly re-elected to the presidency. At the end of that month the Government won a vote of confidence in the Poslanecká sněmovna. In April the Czech Republic's proposed membership of the North Atlantic Treaty Organization (NATO, see p. 340) was formally approved by the legislature, after the ČSSD withdrew its demand for a referendum on the issue.

Early elections to the Poslanecká sněmovna were held on 19–20 June 1998. The ČSSD retained its position (held since the earlier defection of the ODS deputies to the US) as the largest party in the Poslanecká sněmovna, winning 74 seats (with 32.3% of the votes cast), while the ODS secured 63 seats (with 27.7% of the votes). The remaining seats were divided between the KSČM (with 24 seats), the KDU-ČSL (20) and the US (19). The rate of voter participation was 74%. Zeman was given the task of attempting to form a government. In July Zeman and Klaus signed an agreement whereby the ODS pledged not to initiate or support a motion expressing 'no confidence' in a minority ČSSD government, in exchange for a number of senior parliamentary posts, including the chairmanship of the Poslanecká sněmovna (to which Klaus was later elected), and a commitment to early constitutional reform. On 17 July Zeman was formally appointed Prime Minister, and a new Council of Ministers was subsequently formed. Elections to renew one-third of the seats in the Senát were held in two rounds in November. The ČSSD won only three of the 27 seats contested, while the ODS secured nine seats, and a four-party informal alliance, comprising the KDU-ČSL, the ODA, the Democratic Union (DEU) and the US, won 13 seats.

In May 1999 a decision by the Council of Ministers to complete the construction of the controversial Temelín nuclear power plant in southern Bohemia, despite a resolution by the European Parliament opposing its completion, provoked international concern and strong criticism from President Havel and environmental groups. In July Ivo Svoboda was dismissed from the post of Minister of Finance. (In May 2002 he was charged with embezzlement during his term in office, and he was sentenced to five years' imprisonment in March 2004.) In September 1999 the Council of Ministers approved a number of proposals for constitutional change, which had been drafted by a joint ČSSD-ODS commission. The amendments aimed to restrict presidential powers, including the right to appoint the Prime Minister and the heads of principal state institutions, and the right to grant amnesty. (The Poslanecká sněmovna approved the changes in January 2000, despite an opposition boycott of the vote.) In November 1999 celebrations commemorating the 10th anniversary of the 'velvet revolution' coincided with a protest against the existing political system, organized by a group of former student leaders who had participated in the events of November 1989. Their appeal had been signed by some 150,000 supporters by early December 1999, when a large rally was staged in Prague.

In late January 2000 the ČSSD and the ODS extended their agreement on bilateral co-operation. In accordance with this agreement, the Council of Ministers was reorganized in March–April. In elections to one-third of seats in the Senát in November, the alliance of the KDU-ČSL, the ODA, the DEU and the US secured 16 seats, thereby increasing its overall representation to 39 seats (although narrowly failing to obtain a majority in the chamber). In early April 2001 Vladimír Špidla, the Deputy Prime Minister and Minister of Labour and Social Affairs, was elected unopposed to the chairmanship of the ČSSD; Zeman had agreed to relinquish the party leadership (although he was to remain Prime Minister pending legislative elections, scheduled to take place in June 2002).

In late 2001 the US and DEU merged to form a single organization. In February 2002 it was announced that the electoral alliance of the KDU-ČSL, ODA and US-DEU had been dissolved, owing to inter-party disagreement; however, the KDU-ČSL and US-DEU subsequently formed a further grouping, known as the Coalition. At elections to the Poslanecká sněmovna on 14–15 June, the ČSSD was the most successful party (with 30.2% of the votes cast). President Havel invited Špidla to commence negotiations to form a government, and on 9 July an agreement establishing a new administration was signed by the leaders of the ČSSD and the Coalition. In mid-July a 17-member coalition Government, headed by Špidla and dominated by the ČSSD, was officially appointed by Havel. In early August the new administration was approved by 101 votes in the Poslanecká sněmovna.

Prior to the expiry of Havel's second term on 2 February 2003, voting took place in both legislative chambers to select a successor. Following several inconclusive rounds of voting in January, Klaus (who had relinquished the chairmanship of the ODS) was finally elected President on 28 February, defeating the candidate of the ruling coalition, Jan Sokol, with 142 of the 281 votes cast in both chambers. Klaus was inaugurated on 7 March. Four days later the Government won a vote of confidence in the Poslanecká sněmovna (which had been requested by the Prime Minister) by one vote. In mid-June the results of a referendum (see below) approved the Czech Republic's proposed accession to the European Union—EU (see p. 244). Klaus, notably, did not urge voters to support accession. In late September the Government narrowly survived a vote of 'no confidence' over its plans for fiscal reform, and the Poslanecká sněmovna subsequently adopted the reform proposals. In the following month the Minister of Finance, Bohuslav Sobotka, was also appointed a Deputy Prime Minister, with responsibility for implementing the public-finance reform programme.

In June 2004 a new political party, the Democratic Union of the Czech Republic, was founded by members of the former DEU. At the end of June Špidla resigned as head of the Government and as leader of the ČSSD, after narrowly surviving a vote of confidence in his leadership of the ČSSD. Of 181 delegates, 103 voted against Špidla; although it fell short of the three-fifths' majority needed to remove him, the result indicated that Špidla had lost the support of the majority of his party. The vote followed a defeat for the ČSSD in the Czech Republic's first elections to the European Parliament earlier in the month (following the country's accession to the EU on 1 May), in which the ČSSD had obtained only two of the 24 seats contested. Špidla's resignation was formally accepted at the beginning of July. Klaus subsequently requested that Stanislav Gross, the acting leader of the ČSSD and hitherto the First Deputy Prime Minister and Minister of the Interior, form a new Government. The new administration, which was formally appointed in August, included six new ministers and again comprised members of the KDU-ČSL and the US-DEU, as well as members of the ČSSD. Later in August it narrowly survived a vote of confidence in the Poslanecká sněmovna, with 101 of the 200 deputies voting in favour of the Government. In October–November an election for one-third of seats in the Senát was conducted; the ČSSD won no seats, while the number of seats held by the opposition ODS increased substantially. In local elections in the same month the ODS won the largest proportion of votes cast (36.4%).

In early 2005 Gross was the subject of allegations of financial impropriety. Nevertheless, he was re-elected as Chairman of the ČSSD in late March. At the end of that month the KDU-ČSL (which demanded Gross's resignation) withdrew from the governing coalition, causing the Government to lose its majority in the Poslanecká sněmovna. After several ministers announced that they no longer considered themselves to be part of the Government, Gross resigned on 25 April. On the same day Klaus appointed the Minister of Regional Development, Jiří Paroubek, the deputy leader of the ČSSD, as Prime Minister. The new Council of Ministers formed by Paroubek, which was substantially the same as the outgoing Government (with the renewed participation of the KDU-ČSL), was confirmed in office on 13 May by a vote of confidence in the Poslanecká sněmovna. In late September Gross resigned as leader of the ČSSD. In January 2006 Klaus appointed Jiří Havel as Deputy Prime Minister, responsible for the Economy, replacing Milan Jahn.

In May 2006 Paroubek was elected Chairman of the ČSSD. Later that month he took legal action for defamation against the Chairman of the ODS, Mirek Topolánek, who had accused him of having connections with organized crime. Legislative elections took place on 2–3 June. The ODS won 81 of the 200 seats in the Poslanecká sněmovna, with 35.4% of the votes cast; the ČSSD secured 74 seats, with 32.3% of the votes, the KSČM obtained 26 seats (12.8%), the KDU-ČSL 13 seats (7.2%) and the Green Party six (6.3%). Some 64% of the electorate participated in the elections. Paroubek accused the ODS of perpetrating malpractice in the electoral campaign by instigating the publication of claims that government members were implicated in organized crime. Topolánek was invited by Klaus to form a new administration and, following negotiations between party leaders, a coalition agreement between the ODS, the KDU-ČSL and the Green Party was signed on 26 June. The ČSSD, however, refused to support Topolánek's proposed coalition government, which, with 100 seats in the Poslanecká sněmovna, had the support of one deputy fewer than the 101 required to hold a majority. A protracted impasse ensued, with six failed attempts to elect a new Chairman of the Poslanecká sněmovna. Finally, on 14 August a member of the ČSSD, Miloslav Vlček, was elected provisionally as Chairman. Two days later Klaus accepted the resignation of Paroubek's Government and officially appointed Topolánek as Prime Minister. However, Topolánek's proposed coalition government again failed to secure support and attempts by the ČSSD to form an alliance with the KDU-ČSL also proved unsuccessful. A minority ODS-led administration was consequently formed by Topolánek and, after approval by Klaus, was installed on 4 September. In early October, however, the Government lost a vote of confidence in the Poslanecká sněmovna, and Topolánek subsequently tendered his resignation. Elections to one-third of the seats in the Senát took place in two rounds on 20–21 October and 27–28 October; the ODS (excluding independent candidates with ODS support) secured 12 seats, the ČSSD six seats and the KDU-ČSL four seats. The ODS was the most successful party in local elections held concurrently with the first round of senatorial polling. In November Klaus redesignated Topolánek as Prime Minister, with a mandate to form a new coalition administration. Following further lengthy negotiations, in late December Topolánek presented a further ODS coalition with the KDU-ČSL and the Green Party, which, however, Klaus refused to accept.

On 9 January 2007 Klaus officially appointed the coalition administration, which comprised eight members of the ODS, five of the KDU-ČSL and four of the Green Party. The new Government was narrowly endorsed by a motion of confidence in the Poslanecká sněmovna on 19 January, receiving 100 votes, after two ČSSD deputies agreed to abstain from voting. Although the stability of the new administration and its ability to implement economic reforms remained uncertain, the imminent prospect of further legislative elections was thereby averted. Jiří Čunek (who had been elected Chairman of the KDU-ČSL in December 2006) received the post of Deputy Prime Minister and Minister of Regional Development, while the leader of the Green Party, Martin Bursík, became Deputy Prime Minister and Minister of the Environment. In June 2007 a motion of 'no confidence' in the Government, initiated by the ČSSD and KSČM, was defeated in the Poslanecká sněmovna. In August Topolánek narrowly succeeded in securing approval in the Poslanecká sněmovna for an extensive programme of fiscal reforms (with 101 votes), although the plan was less stringent than originally proposed. Nevertheless, divisions between the ODS and other parties in the ruling coalition increased, and public dissatisfaction with the Government became more widespread, as a result of the adoption of the reforms and opposition to US plans to establish a military base near Prague (see below). Controversy over Čunek, who was subject to a criminal investigation into his alleged acceptance of a bribe from a real-estate company in 2002, was also perceived to be damaging to the Government; Čunek resigned in early November 2007. In early December a further motion of 'no confidence', initiated by the ČSSD in protest at the introduction of tax increases and medical charges under the reform programme, was again narrowly defeated.

A presidential election was conducted in both legislative chambers on 8–9 February 2008. Klaus, representing the ODS, was opposed by Jan Švejnar, an economics professor with joint US-Czech nationality, who was supported by the ČSSD and other non-government groupings. In three rounds of voting, Klaus, although securing the highest number of votes, failed to receive a sufficient majority to be re-elected to the presidency. The KSČ subsequently nominated a member of the European Parliament, Jana Bobos, to contest a second election, but she withdrew her candidacy. On 15 February a new election took place, again contested by Klaus and Švejnar. After inconclusive first and second rounds, Klaus was narrowly elected in a third round of voting, with 141 votes; Švejnar received 111 votes. On 7 March (on the expiry of his term of office) Klaus was inaugurated for a second term. In early April Čunek, who had been cleared of the charges against him, was reappointed to the Government, assuming his former position as Deputy Prime Minister and Minister of Regional Development.

In August 1997 the Government began to address the issues affecting the Roma population (unofficially estimated at some 300,000), after hundreds of Roma, claiming to have suffered persecution in the Czech Republic, attempted to obtain political asylum in Canada (which subsequently reimposed visa requirements for Czech visitors) and the United Kingdom. The Government established an interministerial commission for Roma community affairs in October and outlined further measures aimed at improving the situation of Roma in the Czech Republic. In early 1998 the Government formed a second commission, headed by Roma, to address issues affecting the Roma population, and a 40-year law restricting their nomadic way of life was revoked. None the less, a large number of Roma continued to seek political asylum abroad. In early 2005 the Government published its first report on Roma since 1997, according to which education among Roma was improving and reported levels of discrimination were decreasing. However, employment opportunities had not increased, with some 70% of Roma unemployed, and living standards were reported to be worsening. In November 2007 the European Court of Human Rights found the Czech Republic to be in breach of the European convention on human rights for educational discrimination against the Roma population; Roma children were often segregated and placed in 'special schools' for children with learning difficulties.

The Czech Republic is a member, with Slovakia, Hungary and Poland, of the Visegrad Group (established, following the collapse of communist rule, to promote economic, defence and other co-operation in the region). Relations with Slovakia were strained in the 1990s, mainly because of disagreements over the division of former federal property. In mid-September 1998, however, following talks between Miloš Zeman and Vladimír Mečiar, the Slovakian Prime Minister, it was announced that a joint Czech-Slovakian committee would meet in an attempt to further discussions on unresolved issues. The success of opposition parties in Slovakian legislative elections held at the end of that month, and the subsequent change of government, led to a further improvement in bilateral relations. Measures providing for dual Czech-Slovakian citizenship became fully effective in October 1999, and in November an agreement on the division of former federal property was signed in Bratislava by Zeman and Mikuláš Dzurinda, Mečiar's successor. The agreement provided for the exchange of shares between the Czech Republic's Komerční banka and Slovakia's Všeobecná úverová banka and the restitution of gold reserves to Slovakia. The gold had been held by the Czech Central Bank as collateral for debts owed by Slovakia to the Czech Republic. These debts had proved to be a major obstacle during negotiations, as they had never been recognized by Slovakia. The Czech Government consequently opted effectively to relieve Slovakia of its debts by buying the Central Bank's claim for a symbolic one koruna, despite the opposition of several Czech politicians. In May 2000 Zeman and Dzurinda signed an agreement that resolved the remaining problems associated with the division of jointly held assets.

Since the end of the Second World War Czech-German relations have been dominated by two issues: the question of compensation for Czech victims of Nazism, and demands for the restitution of property to the Sudeten Germans who were driven from Czechoslovakia in 1945–46. A joint declaration was finally signed by the Czech and German Ministers of Foreign Affairs in December 1996, and by Prime Minister Klaus of the Czech Republic and Federal Chancellor Helmut Kohl of Germany in January 1997. In the declaration, Germany admitted that it was to blame for the Nazi occupation and the partition of Czechoslovakia in 1938–39, while the Czech Republic apologized for the abuses of human rights that were committed during the deportation of ethnic Germans. The declaration did not, however, entitle the expelled Sudeten Germans to make claims for compensation. A Czech-German fund was established in January 1998 to finance joint projects, in particular benefiting victims of the Nazis. Relations were strained somewhat later that year, however, when the nomination of Sudeten Germans to a Czech-German advisory council was rejected by Zeman, who claimed that the nominees had opposed the January 1997 declaration that had provided for the establishment of the council. In February 2002 Zeman and Dzurinda announced that they would not be attending a summit meeting of the Visegrad countries, scheduled to take place on 1 March, following a demand by their Hungarian counterpart, Viktor Orbán, for the abolition of the Beneš Decrees, which had provided for the expulsion of ethnic Germans, as well as Hungarians, from the Sudetenland. In April the Poslanecká sněmovna unanimously approved a resolution stipulating the inviolability of the Beneš Decrees. In July 2005, during a visit to Austria, Prime Minister Jiří Paroubek proposed that Sudeten Germans be permitted to claim compensation, if they could prove that they had opposed Nazism. Although President Klaus vehemently condemned the proposal, Austrian Chancellor Dr Wolfgang Schüssel welcomed Paroubek's conciliatory efforts. In August the Czech Government formally apologized to Sudeten Germans actively opposed to Nazism who had experienced persecution after the Second World War.

The issue of the nuclear power installation at Temelín, in southern Bohemia, has impeded good relations between the Czech Republic and Austria. Despite pressure from the Austrian Government, which suspended imports of Czech electricity, the nuclear power plant commenced production in October 2000. In December the Czech Republic and Austria signed an agreement, whereby the plant was not to operate at commercial capacity until its safety and its environmental impact had been fully evaluated. In August 2001 the European Commission issued a controversial report: the Czech authorities maintained that the report demonstrated the safety of the plant and immediately commenced its reconnection with the national power network; however, Austrian anti-nuclear organizations announced that they were to submit a legal challenge to the resumption of operations at the plant, which was also strongly criticized by the Austrian authorities. Later that year Schüssel threatened to veto the Czech Republic's accession to the EU unless the matter was satisfactorily resolved. Further safety issues were eventually agreed, and in April 2003 the Temelín installation commenced production at full capacity, following the commencement of operations of a second reactor.

The Czech Republic became a member of the Council of Europe (see p. 225) in June 1993. In August the Czech Republic and Russia signed a treaty of friendship and co-operation (replacing the Russian-Czechoslovak treaty of 1992). In March 1994, despite Russia's apparent opposition, the Czech Republic joined NATO's 'Partnership for Peace' programme of military co-operation. In 1996 the Poslanecká sněmovna approved legislation prohibiting the storage of nuclear weapons on Czech territory, except where international treaties are concerned, thereby allowing for full membership of NATO. In July 1997 the Czech Republic, together with Hungary and Poland, was invited to commence membership negotiations. A protocol providing for the accession of the three states to NATO was signed in December, and in March 1999 the Czech Republic, Hungary and Poland became full members of the Alliance. Associate membership of Western European Union (see p. 426) was subsequently granted. In January 2007 Prime Minister Topolánek entered into negotiations with the USA regarding the establishment of a military base in the Czech Republic as part of the proposed US National Missile Defence programme. Domestic opposition to the plans (which were also seemingly opposed by Russia) had resulted in the establishment of a group comprising some 40 Czech and international civic organizations, and protests were staged in Prague under the group's direction at the end of January. In June protests took place in Prague by opponents of the planned military installation, prior to the arrival of US President George W. Bush. At a NATO summit meeting, which took place in Bucharest, Romania, in early April 2008, member states endorsed US plans to position missile defence bases in the Czech Republic and Poland; coinciding with the meeting, the Czech Government announced that it had reached agreement with the USA on establishing a US anti-missile radar station in the region of Brdy, near Prague.

The Czech Republic was one of a number of central and eastern European states invited to commence negotiations in March 1998 on possible entry to the EU. In December 2002, at a summit meeting in Copenhagen, Denmark, the Czech Republic was one of 10 nations formally invited to join the EU in May 2004. A plebiscite on EU membership was held in the Czech Republic on 13–14 June 2003. Of the 55.2% of the electorate who took part in the referendum, 77.3% voted in support of Czech membership of the EU. The Czech Republic became a full member on 1 May 2004. In December 2007 the Czech Republic, together with eight other nations, implemented the EU's Schengen Agreement, enabling its citizens to travel to and from other member states without border restrictions.

Government

Legislative power is held by two chambers, the 200-member Poslanecká sněmovna (Chamber of Deputies) and the 81-member Senát (Senate). Members of the Poslanecká sněmovna and the Senát are elected for terms of four and six years, respectively, by universal adult suffrage. (One-third of the seats in the Senát are renewable every two years.) The President of the Republic (Head of State) is elected for a term of five years by a joint session of the legislature. The President, who is also Commander of the Armed Forces, may be re-elected for a second consecutive term. He appoints the Prime Minister and, on the latter's recommendation, the other members of the Council of Ministers (the highest organ of executive power). For administrative purposes, the Czech Republic is divided into 14 self-governing regions.

Defence

As assessed at November 2007, the total active armed forces numbered 23,092, comprising an army of 16,962 and an air force of 6,130. There were additionally 15,992 civilian Ministry of Defence staff. Paramilitary forces totalled 3,100. A programme of military reorganization was expected to be completed in 2010–12. In November 2004 legislation was approved to abolish compulsory military service. In March 1994 the Czech Republic joined the North Atlantic Treaty Organization's (NATO) 'Partnership for Peace' (see p. 342) programme of military co-operation, and it was formally admitted to the Alliance in March 1999. In January 2007 the Czech Republic and USA entered into negotiations regarding the proposed establishment of a military base in the Czech Republic (to be operated by about 200 US civilian and military personnel) as part of the US National Missile Defence programme. The budget for 2007 allocated 53,900m. koruna to defence.

Economic Affairs

In 2006, according to estimates by the World Bank, the Czech Republic's gross national income (GNI), measured at average 2004–06 prices, was US $129,542m., equivalent to $12,680 per head (or $21,470 per head on an international purchasing-power parity basis). During 1996–2006, it was estimated, the population decreased at an annual average rate of 0.1%, while gross domestic product (GDP) per head increased, in real terms, by an average of 2.9% per year. Overall GDP increased, in real terms, at an average annual rate of 2.8% in 1996–2006. According to official figures, real GDP increased by 6.4% in 2006.

In 2006 agriculture (including hunting, forestry and fishing) contributed 2.7% of GDP and engaged 3.8% of the employed labour force. The principal crops are wheat, sugar beet, barley, rapeseed, potatoes, maize and hops (the Czech Republic is a major beer producer and exporter). According to estimates by the World Bank, the GDP of the agricultural sector increased, in real terms, at an average annual rate of 0.7% in 1996–2006. Agricultural GDP increased by 3.0% in 2005, but declined by 7.3% in 2006.

In 2006 industry (including manufacturing, mining, construction and power) contributed 39.1% of GDP and engaged 40.0% of the employed labour force. According to estimates by the World Bank, the GDP of the industrial sector increased, in real terms, at an average annual rate of 3.1% in 1996–2006. Real industrial GDP increased by 11.5% in 2006.

In 2006 the mining and quarrying sector contributed 1.4% of GDP and engaged an estimated 1.1% of the employed labour force. The principal minerals extracted are coal and lignite. According to the Czech Statistical Office, production in the mining and quarrying sector declined each year in 1995–99, but increased by 6.9% in 2000. Although production also increased in 2002 and 2004, declines were recorded in 2001 and 2003. Sectorial production decreased by 8.7% in 2005, but recovered in the following year, when growth was 13.2%.

In 2006 the manufacturing sector contributed 27.2% of GDP and engaged 28.2% of the employed labour force. According to the World Bank, the GDP of the manufacturing sector increased at an annual average rate of 6%, in real terms, in 1996–2006. Sectoral GDP increased by 14.0% in 2006.

In 2004 coal provided 60.3% of total electricity production and nuclear power 31.4%. Imports of mineral fuels comprised 9.6% of the value of total imports in 2006.

In 2006 the services sector contributed 58.2% of GDP and engaged 56.3% of the employed labour force. Tourism is an important source of revenue, providing receipts of some US $5,580m. in 2005. According to the World Bank, the GDP of the services sector increased, in real terms, at an average annual rate of 2.5% in 1996–2006. Real GDP in the services sector increased by 3.7% in 2006.

In 2006 the Czech Republic recorded a visible trade surplus of US $1,922m., and there was a deficit of $6,052m. on the current account of the balance of payments. In that year the principal source of imports (accounting for 28.3% of the total) was Germany; other major sources were the People's Republic of China, Russia, Poland and Slovakia. Germany was also the principal market for exports (taking 31.7% of the total) in that year; other important purchasers were Slovakia, Poland, France and Austria. The principal exports in 2006 were machinery and transport equipment (accounting for 53.1% of exports), basic manufactures, miscellaneous manufactured articles and chemical products. The principal imports in that year were machinery and transport equipment (accounting for 41.0% of imports), basic manufactures, miscellaneous manufactured articles, chemicals and related products, and mineral fuels.

In 2006 there was a budgetary deficit of 97,580m. koruna (equivalent to 3.0% of GDP). The Czech Republic's total external debt was US $45,561m. at the end of 2004, of which $12,020m. was long-term public debt. In that year the cost of debt-servicing was equivalent to 10.5% of the value of exports of goods and services. The annual rate of inflation averaged 3.9% in 1996–2006. Consumer prices increased by 2.6% in 2006. At the end of September 2007 some 5.2% of the labour force was registered as unemployed, the lowest rate for 10 years.

In late 1995 the Czech Republic became the first post-communist state in Eastern Europe to be admitted to the Organisation for Economic Co-operation and Development (OECD, see p. 347). In May 2004 the country became a full member of the European Union (EU, see p. 244).

The Czech Republic was considered to have successfully undertaken the transition to a market economic system. In 1992–95 the Czech Republic's programme of rapid privatization, price and currency stabilization and the establishment of a new banking system attracted widespread foreign investment, although economic growth decelerated in 1996, and a budgetary deficit was recorded for the first time. In 1999 the economy began to recover, following the relaxation of monetary policies and significant progress in the restructuring of banks and state enterprises. The country subsequently benefited from strong export performance, and from a dramatic increase in foreign direct investment. Growth in GDP was recorded from 2000, although the restructuring process resulted in a rapidly increasing overall fiscal deficit and also contributed to a significant rise in the rate of unemployment. Following the Czech Republic's accession to the EU in May 2004, it was reported that the budgetary deficit, equivalent to 5.6% of GDP in 2003, was the highest of any member state. (The EU stipulated that member countries should record a deficit of less than 3% of GDP in the two years preceding the adoption of the European currency, the euro.) Although in 2006 a budgetary deficit equivalent to 3.0% of GDP was recorded, the 2007 deficit was estimated by the IMF at just above the 3% target level. In August 2007 the Government installed at the beginning of the year with narrow parliamentary support (see above) succeeded in securing approval for a programme of fiscal reforms (which was, however, less stringent than that originally proposed). The measures, which entered into effect at the beginning of 2008, were designed to strengthen the fiscal position through increases in indirect taxes, a reduction in social welfare payments and the introduction of medical charges.

Education

Pre-school education is available for children aged between three and six years. Education is officially compulsory for children aged between six and 15 years, who attend basic school, covering both primary (grades 1–5) and lower secondary (grades 6–9) levels. In 1999/2000 some 90.4% of children in the relevant age-group were enrolled in primary schools. Education continues at upper secondary schools, of which there are three types: gymnasia (providing general education and preparing students mainly for university entry); secondary vocational schools; and secondary technical schools. Students follow three- to four-year courses. In 2004 enrolment in secondary education was equivalent to 96% of children in the relevant age-group. Tertiary education comprises higher professional schools, which offer three-year courses, and universities, at which most courses last from five to six years. In 2005/06 some 295,363 students attended 25 universities. In 2004 total budgetary expenditure on education amounted to 116,359m. koruna.

Public Holidays

2008: 1 January (New Year's Day), 24 March (Easter Monday), 1 May (Labour Day), 8 May (Liberation Day), 5 July (Day of the Apostles SS Cyril and Methodius), 6 July (Anniversary of the Martyrdom of Jan Hus), 28 September (Czech Statehood Day), 28 October (Independence Day), 17 November (Freedom and Democracy Day), 24–25 December (Christmas), 26 December (St Stephen's Day).

2009: 1 January (New Year's Day), 13 April (Easter Monday), 1 May (Labour Day), 8 May (Liberation Day), 5 July (Day of the Apostles SS Cyril and Methodius), 6 July (Anniversary of the Martyrdom of Jan Hus), 28 September (Czech Statehood Day), 28 October (Independence Day), 17 November (Freedom and Democracy Day), 24–25 December (Christmas), 26 December (St Stephen's Day).

Weights and Measures

The metric system is in force.

THE CZECH REPUBLIC

Statistical Survey

Source: mainly Czech Statistical Office, Na padesátém 81, 100 82 Prague 10; tel. 274051111; internet www.czso.cz.

Area and Population

AREA, POPULATION AND DENSITY

Area (sq km)	78,868*
Population (census results)	
3 March 1991	10,302,215
1 March 2001	
Males	4,982,071
Females	5,247,989
Total	10,230,060
Population (official estimates at mid-year)	
2004	10,206,923
2005	10,234,092
2006	10,266,646
Density (per sq km) at mid-2006	130.2

* 30,451 sq miles.

POPULATION BY ETHNIC GROUP
(census of 1 March 2001)

	Number	%
Czech (Bohemian)	9,249,777	90.4
Moravian	380,474	3.7
Slovak	193,190	1.9
Polish	51,968	0.5
German	39,108	0.4
Roma (Gypsy)	11,746	0.1
Silesian	10,878	0.1
Others and unknown	292,919	2.9
Total	10,230,060	100.0

REGIONS
(mid-2006)

	Area (sq km)	Population	Density (per sq km)
Central Bohemia (Středočeský)	11,014	1,166,537	105.9
Highlands (Vysočina)	6,796	511,114	75.2
Hradec Králové (Královéhradecký)	4,758	549,122	115.4
Karlovy Vary (Karlovarský)	3,315	304,573	91.9
Liberec (Liberecký)	3,163	429,803	135.9
Moravia-Silesia (Moravskoslezský)	5,427	1,249,909	230.3
Olomouc (Olomoucký)	5,267	639,423	121.4
Pardubice (Pardubický)	4,519	506,808	112.2
Plzeň (Plzeňský)	7,561	552,898	73.1
Prague City (Praha)	496	1,183,576	2,386.2
South Bohemia (Jihočeský)	10,057	628,831	62.5
South Moravia (Jihomoravský)	7,196	1,130,990	157.2
Ústí nad Labem (Ústecký)	5,335	823,193	154.3
Zlín (Zlínský)	3,964	589,869	148.8
Total	78,868	10,266,646	130.2

PRINCIPAL TOWNS
(population at mid-2006)

Praha (Prague, capital)	1,183,576	Pardubice	88,365
Brno	366,384	Havířov	84,360
Ostrava	309,495	Zlín	78,106
Plzeň (Pilsen)	163,019	Kladno	69,290
Olomouc	100,112	Most	67,727
Liberec	98,396	Karviná	63,253
České Budějovice (Budweis)	94,653	Frýdek-Místek	59,503
Ústí nad Labem	94,638	Opava	59,358
Hradec Králové	94,395		

BIRTHS, MARRIAGES AND DEATHS

	Registered live births		Registered marriages		Registered deaths	
	Number	Rate (per 1,000)	Number	Rate (per 1,000)	Number	Rate (per 1,000)
1999	89,471	8.7	53,523	5.2	109,768	10.7
2000	90,910	8.8	55,321	5.4	109,001	10.6
2001	90,715	8.9	52,374	5.1	107,755	10.5
2002	92,786	9.1	52,732	5.2	108,243	10.6
2003	93,685	9.2	48,943	4.8	111,288	10.9
2004	97,664	9.6	51,447	5.0	107,177	10.5
2005	102,211	10.0	51,829	5.1	107,938	10.5
2006*	105,831	10.0	52,860	5.1	104,441	10.5

* Preliminary.

Expectation of life (years at birth, WHO estimates): 76.1 (males 72.9; females 79.3) in 2005 (Source: WHO, *World Health Statistics*).

IMMIGRATION AND EMIGRATION

	2004	2005	2006
Immigrants	53,453	60,294	68,183
Emigrants	34,818	24,065	33,463

ECONOMICALLY ACTIVE POPULATION
('000 persons aged 15 years and over)

	2004	2005	2006
Agriculture, hunting, forestry and fishing	202	189	182
Mining and quarrying	59	49	55
Manufacturing	1,274	1,296	1,362
Electricity, gas and water	76	77	77
Construction	436	459	436
Wholesale and retail trade, repair of motor vehicles, motorcycles and personal household goods	631	615	614
Hotels and restaurants	175	182	187
Transport, storage and communications	364	360	361
Financial intermediation	94	97	92
Real estate, renting and business activities	282	288	321
Public administration, defence and compulsory social security	323	333	326
Education	279	297	288
Health and social welfare	324	328	330
Other community, social and personal services	184	190	193
Households with employed persons	3	3	3
Extraterritorial organizations	1	1	1
Not classifiable by economic activity	1	2	1
Total employed	4,707	4,764	4,828
Registered unemployed	426	410	371
Total labour force	5,133	5,174	5,199

Source: ILO.

THE CZECH REPUBLIC

Statistical Survey

Health and Welfare

KEY INDICATORS

Total fertility rate (children per woman, 2005)	1.2
Under-5 mortality rate (per 1,000 live births, 2005)	4
HIV/AIDS (% of persons aged 15–49, 2005)	0.1
Physicians (per 1,000 head, 2003)	3.51
Hospital beds (per 1,000 head, 2005)	8.4
Health expenditure (2004): US $ per head (PPP)	1,412.4
Health expenditure (2004): % of GDP	7.3
Health expenditure (2004): public (% of total)	89.2
Human Development Index (2005): ranking	32
Human Development Index (2005): value	0.891

For sources and definitions, see explanatory note on p. vi.

Agriculture

PRINCIPAL CROPS
('000 metric tons)

	2004	2005	2006
Wheat	5,043	4,145	3,506
Barley	2,331	2,195	1,898
Maize	552	703	606
Rye*	313	197	75
Oats	227	151	155
Potatoes	862	1,013	692
Sugar beet	3,579	3,496	3,138
Dry peas	72	79	72
Rapeseed	935	769	880
Cabbages	81	65	68
Tomatoes	22	24	36
Cauliflowers	16	12	9
Cucumbers and gherkins	17	22	37
Dry onions	77	61	45
Carrots and turnips	41	38	34
Apples	281	209	264
Pears	14	11	14
Peaches and nectarines	8	5	20
Plums	37	20	46
Grapes	70	63	58
Hops	6	8	5

* Including mixed crops of wheat and rye.

Aggregate production ('000 metric tons, may include official, semi-official or estimated data): Total cereals 8,792 in 2004, 7,668 in 2005, 6,394 in 2006; Total roots and tubers 862 in 2004, 1,013 in 2005, 692 in 2006; Total vegetables (incl. melons) 333 in 2004, 295 in 2005, 305 in 2006; Total fruits (excl. melons) 526 in 2004, 389 in 2005, 507 in 2006.

LIVESTOCK
('000 head at 1 March)

	2004	2005	2006
Horses	20	21	23
Cattle	1,428	1,397	1,374
Pigs	3,127	2,877	2,840
Sheep	116	140	148
Goats	12	13	14
Chickens	14,116	14,322	14,670
Rabbits and hares*	5	5	5
Turkeys	837	816	456

* FAO estimates.

LIVESTOCK PRODUCTS
('000 metric tons, unless otherwise indicated)

	2004	2005	2006
Cattle meat	97	81	80
Pig meat	426	380	359
Chicken meat	201	213	207
Cows' milk (million litres)	2,680	2,821	2,775
Hen eggs	98	89	87

Forestry

ROUNDWOOD REMOVALS
('000 cubic metres)

	2004	2005	2006
Sawlogs, veneer logs and logs for sleepers	8,428	8,153	9,737
Pulpwood	5,893	5,742	6,206
Other industrial wood	390	390	390
Fuel wood	1,190	1,225	1,345
Total	15,601	15,510	17,678

Fishing*
(metric tons)

	2003	2004	2005
Common carp	20,950	20,458	21,074
Others	3,847	3,454	3,623
Total catch	24,797	23,912	24,697

* Figures refer only to fish caught by the Fishing Association (formerly State Fisheries) and members of the Czech and Moravian Fishing Union.

Mining

('000 metric tons)

	2003	2004	2005
Hard coal	13,382	14,648	12,728
Brown coal and lignite	50,390	48,290	49,125
Crude petroleum	310	299	306
Kaolin	4,155	3,862	3,882

Source: US Geological Survey.

Industry

SELECTED PRODUCTS
('000 metric tons, unless otherwise indicated)

	2003	2004	2005
Wheat flour and meal	761	829	856
Refined sugar	521	557	573
Wine ('000 hectolitres)	740	662	661
Beer ('000 hectolitres)	18,216	18,596	18,885
Cotton yarn (metric tons)	60,550	58,744	52,477
Woven cotton fabrics ('000 metres)	182,286	167,141	128,331
Woollen fabrics ('000 metres)	16,073	16,107	16,913
Woven flax fabrics ('000 metres)	12,071	12,683	9,936
Paper and paperboard	197	190	213
Footwear ('000 pairs)	1,202	1,074	963
Nitrogenous fertilizers*†	251	271	270
Soap	30	26	26
Cement†	3,465	3,709	3,978
Pig-iron†	5,200	5,385	4,600
Crude steel†	6,800	7,033	6,200
Trucks (number)	666	306	229
Electric energy (million kWh)	83,227	84,333	82,578

* Production in terms of nitrogen.
† Source: US Geological Survey.

Motor spirit (petrol) ('000 metric tons): 1,246 in 2001.

Gas-diesel (distillate fuel) oil ('000 metric tons): 2,412 in 2001.

Residual fuel oils ('000 metric tons): 667 in 2001.

Coke ('000 metric tons): 3,537 in 2001.

Motorcycles and mopeds: 13,488 in 2001.

Bicycles: 53,985 in 2001.

THE CZECH REPUBLIC

Finance

CURRENCY AND EXCHANGE RATES

Monetary Units
100 halérů (singular: haléř—heller) = 1 Czech koruna (Czech crown or Kč.).

Sterling, Dollar and Euro Equivalents (31 December 2007)
£1 sterling = 36.217 koruna;
US $1 = 18.078 koruna;
€1 = 26.613 koruna;
1,000 koruna = £27.61 = $55.32 = €37.58.

Average Exchange Rate (koruna per US $)
2005   23.957
2006   22.596
2007   25.700

Note: In February 1993 the Czech Republic introduced its own currency, the Czech koruna, to replace (at par) the Czechoslovak koruna.

STATE BUDGET
(million koruna)

Revenue	2004	2005	2006
Tax revenue	716,682	770,372	801,610
Income tax	180,708	195,048	187,061
Value-added tax	140,383	146,823	153,516
Consumption tax	82,795	103,626	112,561
Social security and employment insurance premiums and contributions	293,318	311,195	333,725
Pension insurance premiums	241,556	256,278	274,833
Non-tax revenue, capital revenue and subsidies received	52,525	96,088	121,450
Total	769,207	866,460	923,060

Expenditure	2004	2005	2006
Non-investment purchases and related expenses	75,842	82,609	92,278
Social security benefits	314,279	326,381	355,113
Pensions	230,907	247,401	272,934
Capital expenditure	66,138	81,989	108,542
Total (incl. others)	862,892	922,798	1,020,640

INTERNATIONAL RESERVES
(US $ million at 31 December)

	2004	2005	2006
Gold (national value)	37	33	39
IMF special drawing rights	5	12	17
Reserve position in IMF	410	181	111
Foreign exchange	27,844	29,138	31,054
Total	28,296	29,364	31,221

Source: IMF, *International Financial Statistics*.

MONEY SUPPLY
('000 million koruna at 31 December)

	2004	2005	2006
Currency outside banks	236.8	263.8	295.3
Demand deposits at deposit money banks	787.2	897.2	1,028.3
Total money (incl. others)	1,026.3	1,162.8	1,325.6

Source: IMF, *International Financial Statistics*.

COST OF LIVING
(Consumer Price Index; base: 1994 = 100)

	2004	2005	2006
Food	109.0	110.3	111.5
Clothing	87.7	83.1	78.1
Fuel and light	123.1	131.0	146.9
Rent	129.8	132.5	135.7
All items (incl. others)	109.7	111.7	114.6

Source: ILO.

NATIONAL ACCOUNTS
('000 million koruna at current prices)

Expenditure on the Gross Domestic Product

	2004	2005	2006
Final consumption expenditure	2,041.9	2,126.9	2,243.5
Households	1,417.7	1,465.7	1,554.4
General government	624.2	661.3	689.1
Gross capital formation	774.4	772.8	873.8
Gross fixed capital formation	727.2	746.1	812.9
Changes in inventories	43.9	23.8	57.9
Net acquisition of valuables	3.3	2.9	3.0
Total domestic expenditure	2,816.3	2,899.7	3,117.3
Exports of goods and services	1,973.4	2,154.7	2,448.2
Less Imports of goods and services	1,972.3	2,059.9	2,345.3
GDP in purchasers' values	2,817.4	2,994.4	3,220.3
GDP at constant 2000 prices	2,476.1	2,636.8	2,805.2

Gross Domestic Product by Economic Activity

	2004	2005	2006
Agriculture, hunting and forestry	82.8	78.2	77.6
Fishing	0.6	0.6	0.5
Mining and quarrying	34.2	38.0	39.8
Manufacturing	678.9	710.1	790.0
Electricity, gas and water	99.6	98.2	108.0
Construction	165.3	181.4	197.5
Wholesale and retail trade	288.8	341.0	356.4
Restaurants and hotels	55.8	55.9	54.5
Transport, storage and communications	272.6	267.4	286.1
Financial intermediation	88.6	86.2	90.7
Real estate, renting and business activities	329.6	371.6	407.7
Public administration and defence; compulsory social security	142.8	155.6	160.9
Education	104.3	110.2	119.5
Health and social work	102.8	108.8	119.3
Other community, social and personal service activities	84.9	82.9	95.8
Private households with employed persons	0.4	0.4	0.4
Sub-total	2,532.3	2,686.3	2,904.8
Taxes on products	319.1	340.8	349.5
Less Subsidies on products	34.1	32.7	34.0
GDP in purchasers' values	2,817.4	2,994.4	3,220.3

THE CZECH REPUBLIC

BALANCE OF PAYMENTS
(US $ million)

	2004	2005	2006
Exports of goods f.o.b.	67,219	77,951	95,119
Imports of goods f.o.b.	−68,265	−76,294	−93,197
Trade balance	−1,046	1,657	1,922
Exports of services	9,699	10,800	11,795
Imports of services	−9,218	−9,954	−11,237
Balance on goods and services	−565	2,503	2,480
Other income received	3,398	4,390	5,381
Other income paid	−9,535	−10,874	−13,585
Balance on goods, services and income	−6,702	−3,981	−5,725
Current transfers received	1,830	3,129	2,783
Current transfers paid	−1,666	−2,291	−3,111
Current balance	−6,538	−3,143	−6,052
Capital account (net)	−595	202	388
Direct investment abroad	−1,037	27	−1,355
Direct investment from abroad	4,978	11,602	6,021
Portfolio investment assets	−2,565	−3,467	−3,004
Portfolio investment liabilities	4,795	79	1,877
Financial derivatives assets	−660	−130	−506
Financial derivatives liabilities	514	18	220
Other investment assets	−1,072	−4,728	−1,686
Other investment liabilities	2,325	2,978	3,506
Net errors and omissions	118	440	684
Overall balance	263	3,879	92

Source: IMF, *International Financial Statistics*.

External Trade

COMMODITY GROUPS
(distribution by SITC, million koruna)

Imports f.o.b.	2004	2005	2006
Food and live animals	72,150	81,648	88,182
Beverages and tobacco	10,668	11,781	13,080
Crude materials (inedible) except fuels	52,916	51,356	57,069
Mineral fuels, lubricants, etc.	122,146	167,614	201,421
Chemicals and related products	194,833	201,476	218,622
Basic manufactures	360,757	374,319	428,208
Machinery and transport equipment	739,946	736,902	859,484
Miscellaneous manufactured articles	190,676	199,979	222,778
Total (incl. others)	1,749,095	1,829,962	2,093,842

Exports f.o.b.	2004	2005	2006
Food and live animals	47,430	61,062	62,388
Beverages and tobacco	8,924	10,609	10,855
Crude materials (inedible) except fuels	47,315	47,193	54,466
Mineral fuels, lubricants, etc.	49,938	57,393	62,520
Chemicals and related products	103,951	118,975	128,970
Basic manufactures	388,540	406,324	447,265
Machinery and transport equipment	876,137	949,152	1,136,357
Miscellaneous manufactured articles	198,492	215,575	235,698
Total (incl. others)	1,722,657	1,868,586	2,141,110

PRINCIPAL TRADING PARTNERS
(million koruna)

Imports f.o.b.	2004	2005	2006
Austria	70,058	73,025	77,390
Belgium	34,341	36,107	41,170
China, People's Republic	90,990	94,102	127,806
France	83,046	83,410	98,866
Germany	554,336	550,495	592,692
Hungary	36,665	39,433	49,608
Italy	92,950	87,567	97,438
Japan	59,463	58,179	63,211
Netherlands	48,534	72,760	81,563
Poland	83,113	91,000	118,325
Russia	70,908	104,598	125,867
Slovakia	93,915	99,802	109,788
Spain	35,269	35,378	39,817
Sweden	19,436	29,998	22,579
Switzerland	26,837	28,040	28,096
United Kingdom	50,733	44,907	54,017
USA	54,464	46,071	48,770
Total (incl. others)	1,749,095	1,829,962	2,093,842

Exports f.o.b.	2004	2005	2006
Austria	103,698	104,668	109,590
Belgium	44,428	49,366	61,359
France	79,493	92,124	118,925
Germany	623,099	628,530	679,597
Hungary	46,763	50,878	63,665
Italy	74,693	78,628	98,976
Netherlands	73,987	68,526	78,559
Poland	90,426	102,341	121,779
Romania	14,138	19,948	26,049
Russia	24,172	33,646	42,509
Slovakia	145,542	161,348	180,046
Spain	38,014	47,680	57,389
Sweden	20,079	28,003	35,244
Switzerland	21,289	23,542	29,531
United Kingdom	81,244	86,464	101,750
USA	38,965	49,749	49,400
Total (incl. others)	1,722,657	1,868,586	2,141,110

Transport

RAILWAYS
(traffic)

	2004	2005	2006*
Passenger-km (million)	6,589	6,667	6,922
Freight net ton-km (million)	15,091	14,866	15,779

* Preliminary.

ROAD TRAFFIC
(motor vehicles in use at 31 December)

	2004	2005	2006
Passenger cars*	3,815,547	3,958,708	4,108,610
Buses and coaches	19,948	20,134	20,331
Commercial vehicles	371,437	415,101	468,282
Trailers	153,828	170,111	189,786
Motorcycles	756,559	794,000	822,703

* Including vans.

INLAND WATERWAYS
(freight carried, '000 metric tons)

	2004	2005	2006*
Imports	299	364	336
Exports	253	546	378
Internal	621	685	419
Total (incl. others)	1,275	1,956	2,023

* Preliminary.

CIVIL AVIATION

	2003	2004	2005
Kilometres flown ('000)	70,522	87,824	96,833*
Passengers carried ('000)	4,584	5,750	6,330
Freight carried (metric tons)	19,852	21,450	19,510*
Passenger-km ('000)	7,096,292	8,815,000	9,735,710
Freight ton-km ('000)	41,563	46,259	44,668*

* Preliminary.

2006 ('000, preliminary): Passengers carried 6,685; Passenger-km 10,228,000.

Tourism

FOREIGN TOURIST ARRIVALS*

Country of origin	2004	2005	2006
Austria	183,871	184,235	175,911
Denmark	127,671	117,738	115,336
France	256,429	257,683	240,280
Germany	1,569,369	1,606,947	1,617,431
Italy	391,192	405,079	399,023
Japan	122,613	153,980	145,804
Netherlands	273,757	295,856	284,499
Poland	253,916	261,576	273,659
Russia	164,036	185,705	239,632
Slovakia	266,917	260,212	281,854
Spain	201,110	224,327	220,050
United Kingdom	650,622	657,110	566,225
USA	292,588	303,641	322,026
Total (incl. others)	6,061,225	6,336,128	6,435,474

*Figures refer to visitors staying for at least one night at registered accommodation facilities.

Tourism receipts (US $ million, incl. passenger transport): 4,069 in 2003; 4,960 in 2004; 5,580 in 2005 (Source: World Tourism Organization).

Communications Media

	2003	2004	2005
Radio transmitters	162	148	150
Television transmitters	217	223	224
Telephones ('000 main lines in public networks)	13,335.0	14,210.2	14,993.2
Mobile cellular telephones ('000 subscribers)	9,708.7	10,782.6	11,775.9
Personal computers ('000 in use)*	2,100	2,200	2,450
Internet users ('000)*	2,395.0	2,576.0	2,758.0
Broadband subscribers ('000)*	34.7	236.0	709.1
Book production (titles)	16,451	15,749	15,350
Daily newspapers (number)	96	108	116
Other periodicals (number)	3,276	3,727	4,283

* Source: International Telecommunication Union.

Internet users ('000): 3,541.3 in 2006 (Source: International Telecommunication Union).

Broadband subscribers ('000): 1,086.6 in 2006 (Source: International Telecommunication Union).

Education

(2005/06)

	Institutions	Teachers	Students
Pre-primary	4,834	22,484	282,183
Basic (primary and lower secondary)	4,474	63,158	916,575
Upper secondary:			
general	354	10,980	144,605
technical	906	18,273	227,418
vocational	731	18,099	205,582
Tertiary:			
higher professional schools	171	1,923	28,792
universities	25	15,016	295,363

Directory

The Constitution

The following is a summary of the main provisions of the Constitution of the Czech Republic, which was adopted on 16 December 1992 and entered into force on 1 January 1993:

GENERAL PROVISIONS

The Czech Republic is a sovereign, unified and democratic law-abiding state, founded on the respect for the rights and freedoms of the individual and citizen. All state power belongs to the people, who exercise this power through the intermediary of legislative, executive and judicial bodies. The fundamental rights and freedoms of the people are under the protection of the judiciary.

The political system is founded on the free and voluntary operation of political parties respecting fundamental democratic principles and rejecting force as a means to assert their interests. Political decisions derive from the will of the majority, expressed through the free ballot. Minorities are protected in decision-making by the majority.

The territory of the Czech Republic encompasses an indivisible whole, whose state border may be changed only by constitutional law. Procedures covering the acquisition and loss of Czech citizenship are determined by law. No one may be deprived of his or her citizenship against his or her will.

GOVERNMENT
Legislative Power

Legislative power in the Czech Republic is vested in two chambers, the Poslanecká sněmovna (Chamber of Deputies) and the Senát (Senate). The Poslanecká sněmovna has 200 members, elected for a term of four years. The Senát has 81 members, elected for a term of six years. Every two years one-third of the senators are elected. Both chambers elect their respective Chairmen and Deputy Chairmen from among their members. Members of both chambers of the legislature are elected on the basis of universal, equal and direct suffrage by secret ballot. All citizens of 18 years and over are eligible to vote.

The legislature enacts the Constitution and laws; approves the state budget and the state final account; and approves the electoral law and international agreements. It elects the President of the Republic (at a joint session of both chambers), supervises the activities of the Government, and decides upon the declaration of war.

President of the Republic

The President of the Republic is Head of State. He or she is elected for a term of five years by a joint session of both chambers of the legislature. The President may not be elected for more than two consecutive terms.

The President appoints, dismisses and accepts the resignation of the Prime Minister and other members of the Government, dismisses the Government and accepts its resignation; convenes sessions of the Poslanecká sněmovna; may dissolve the Poslanecká sněmovna; names the judges of the Constitutional Court, its Chairman and Deputy Chairmen; appoints the Chairman and Deputy Chairmen of the Supreme Court; has the right to return adopted constitutional laws to the legislature; initials laws; and appoints members of the Council of the Czech National Bank. The President also represents the State in external affairs; is the Supreme Commander of the Armed Forces; receives heads of diplomatic missions; calls elections to the Poslanecká sněmovna and to the Senát; and has the right to grant amnesty.

THE CZECH REPUBLIC

Council of Ministers

The Council of Ministers is the highest organ of executive power. It is composed of the Prime Minister, the Deputy Prime Ministers and Ministers. It is answerable to the Poslanecká sněmovna. The President of the Republic appoints the Prime Minister, on whose recommendation he/she appoints the remaining members of the Council of Ministers and entrusts them with directing the ministries or other offices.

JUDICIAL SYSTEM

Judicial power is exercised on behalf of the Republic by independent courts. Judges are independent in the exercise of their function. The judiciary consists of the Supreme Court, the Supreme Administrative Court, high, regional and district courts.

The Constitutional Court is a judicial body protecting constitutionality. It consists of 15 judges appointed for a 10-year term by the President of the Republic with the consent of the Senát.

The Government

HEAD OF STATE

President: Václav Klaus (inaugurated 7 March 2008).

COUNCIL OF MINISTERS
(April 2008)

A coalition of the Civic Democratic Party (ODS), the Christian Democratic Union-Czechoslovak People's Party (KDU-ČSL) and the Green Party.

Prime Minister: Mirek Topolánek (ODS).
Deputy Prime Minister and Minister of Regional Development: Jiří Čunek (KDU-CSL).
Deputy Prime Minister and Minister of Labour and Social Affairs: Petr Nečas (ODS).
Deputy Prime Minister and Minister of the Environment: Martin Bursík (Green Party).
Deputy Prime Minister, responsible for European Affairs: Alexandr Vondra (ODS).
Minister of Foreign Affairs: Karel Schwarzenberg (Green Party).
Minister of Defence: Vlasta Parkanová (KDU-ČSL).
Minister of the Interior: Ivan Langer (ODS).
Minister of Industry and Trade: Martin Říman (ODS).
Minister of Agriculture: Petr Gandalovič (ODS).
Minister of Health Care: Tomáš Julínek (ODS).
Minister of Justice: Jiří Pospíšil (ODS).
Minister of Finance: Miroslav Kalousek (KDU-ČSL).
Minister of Education, Youth and Sport: Ondřej Liška (Green Party).
Minister of Culture: Václav Jehlička (KDU-ČSL).
Minister of Transport: Aleš Řebíček (ODS).
Chairman of the Legislative Council of the Government: Cyril Svoboda (KDU-CSL).
Minister without Portfolio: Džamila Stehlíková (Green Party).

MINISTRIES

Office of the President: Pražský hrad, 119 08 Prague 1; tel. 224371111; fax 224373300; e-mail ladislav.jakl@hrad.cz; internet www.hrad.cz.
Office of the Government: náb. E. Beneše 4, 118 01 Prague 1; tel. 224002111; fax 224003090; e-mail posta@vlada.cz; internet www.vlada.cz.
Ministry of Agriculture: Těšnov 17, 117 05 Prague 1; tel. 22181111; fax 224810478; e-mail info@mze.cz; internet www.mze.cz.
Ministry of Culture: Maltéské nám. 471/1, 118 11 Prague 1; tel. 257085111; fax 224318155; e-mail posta@mkcr.cz; internet www.mkcr.cz.
Ministry of Defence: Tychonova 1, 160 01 Prague 6; tel. 973201111; fax 973200149; e-mail info@army.cz; internet www.army.cz.
Ministry of Education, Youth and Sport: Karmelitská 8, 118 12 Prague 1; tel. 257193111; fax 257193790; e-mail info@msmt.cz; internet www.msmt.cz.
Ministry of the Environment: Vršovická 65, 100 10 Prague 10; tel. 267121111; fax 267310308; e-mail posta@env.cz; internet www.env.cz.
Ministry of Finance: Letenská 15, 118 00 Prague 1; tel. 257041111; fax 257042788; e-mail podatelna@mfcr.cz; internet www.mfcr.cz.
Ministry of Foreign Affairs: Loretánské nám. 5, 118 00 Prague 1; tel. 224181111; fax 224182048; e-mail info@mzv.cz; internet www.mzv.cz.
Ministry of Health Care: Palackého nám. 4, 128 01 Prague 2; tel. 224971111; fax 224972111; e-mail mzcr@mzcr.cz; internet www.mzcr.cz.
Ministry for Industry and Trade: Na Františku 32, Politichýh vězňů 20, 110 15 Prague 1; tel. 224851111; fax 224811089; e-mail mpo@mpo.cz; internet www.mpo.cz.
Ministry of the Interior: Nad štolou 3, 170 34 Prague 7; tel. 974811111; fax 261433552; e-mail posta@mvcr.cz; internet www.mvcr.cz.
Ministry of Justice: Vyšehradská 16, 128 10 Prague 2; tel. 2219977111; fax 224919927; e-mail msp@msp.justice.cz; internet www.justice.cz.
Ministry of Labour and Social Affairs: Na poříčním právu 1, 128 01 Prague 2; tel. 221921111; fax 224918391; e-mail posta@mpsv.cz; internet www.mpsv.cz.
Ministry for Regional Development: Staroměstské nám. 6, 110 15 Prague 1; tel. 224861111; fax 224861333; e-mail public@mmr.cz; internet www.mmr.cz.
Ministry of Transport: nábř. L. Svobody 12, POB 9, 110 15 Prague 1; tel. 972211111; fax 972231184; e-mail posta@mdcr.cz; internet www.mdcr.cz.

Legislature

The Czech Constitution, which was adopted in December 1992, provides for a bicameral legislature as the highest organ of state authority in the Czech Republic (which was established as an independent state on 1 January 1993, following the dissolution of the Czech and Slovak Federative Republic). The lower house, the Poslanecká sněmovna (Chamber of Deputies), retained the structure of the Czech National Council (the former republican legislature). The upper chamber, the Senát (Senate), was first elected in November 1996.

Poslanecká sněmovna
(Chamber of Deputies)

Sněmovní 4, 118 26 Prague 1; tel. 257171111; fax 257534469; e-mail posta@psp.cz; internet www.psp.cz.

Chairman: Miloslav Vlček.

General Election, 2–3 June 2006

Party	Votes	% of votes	Seats
Civic Democratic Party	1,892,475	35.38	81
Czech Social Democratic Party	1,728,827	32.32	74
Communist Party of Bohemia and Moravia	685,328	12.81	26
Christian Democratic Union-Czechoslovak People's Party	386,706	7.22	13
Green Party	336,487	6.29	6
Others	319,153	5.97	—
Total	**5,348,976**	**100.00**	**200**

Senát
(Senate)

Valdštejnské nám. 4, 118 01 Prague 1; tel. 257071111; fax 257534499; e-mail webmaster@senat.cz; internet www.senat.cz.

Chairman: Přemysl Sobotka.

One-third of the 81 seats of the Senát are renewed every two years. Following a partial election, held in two rounds on 20–21 October 2006 and 27–28 October 2006, the strength of the parties was as follows:

Party	Seats
Civic Democratic Party	39
Czech Social Democratic Party	11
Christian Democratic Union-Czechoslovak People's Party	8
Association of Independents-European Democrats	2
Communist Party of Bohemia and Moravia	2
Civic Democratic Alliance	1
Movement of Independents for Harmonious Development of Municipalities and Towns	1
Independents	17
Total	**81**

THE CZECH REPUBLIC

Election Commission

Státní volební komise (SVK) (State Electoral Commission—SEC): U Obecního domu 3, 112 20 Prague 1; tel. 261446231; fax 224221865; e-mail krausova@mvcr.cz; internet www.volby.cz; Chair. Minister of the Interior.

Political Organizations

Association of Independents-European Democrats (SNK-ED) (SNK Evropští demokraté): Malá Štěpánská 7, 120 00 Prague 2; tel. 222517068; fax 222516569; e-mail info@snked.cz; internet www.snked.cz; f. Jan. 2006 by merger of the Association of Independents and the European Democrats; centre-right; aims to combat corruption; Chair. HELMUT DOHNÁLEK.

Christian Democratic Union-Czechoslovak People's Party (KDU-ČSL) (Křestanská a demokratická unie-Československá strana lidová): Palác Charitas, Karlovo nám. 5, 128 01 Prague 2; tel. 226205111; fax 226205100; e-mail info@kdu.cz; internet www.kdu.cz; f. 1992; Chair. JIŘÍ ČUNEK.

Civic Democratic Alliance (ODA) (Občanská demokratická aliance): Štefánikova 21, 150 00 Prague 5; tel. and fax 257327072; e-mail oda@oda.cz; internet www.oda.cz; f. 1991 as a formal political party, following a split in Civic Forum (f. 1989); fmrly an informal group within Civic Forum; conservative; Chair. JIŘINA NOVÁKOVÁ.

Civic Democratic Party (ODS) (Občanská demokratická strana): Jánský vršek 13, 110 00 Prague 1; tel. 234707111; fax 234707101; e-mail hk@ods.cz; internet www.ods.cz; f. 1991 following a split in Civic Forum (f. 1989); merged with Christian Democratic Party in 1996; liberal-conservative; Chair. MIREK TOPOLÁNEK.

Communist Party of Bohemia and Moravia (KSČM) (Komunistická strana Čech a Moravy): Politických vězňů 9, 110 00 Prague 1; tel. 222897111; fax 222897207; e-mail info@kscm.cz; internet www.kscm.cz; f. 1990 as a result of the reorganization of the fmr Communist Party of Czechoslovakia; c. 95,500 mems; Chair. VOJTĚCH FILIP.

Communist Party of Czechoslovakia (KSČ) (Komunistická strana Československá): Milánská 457, 100 00 Prague 10; e-mail ksc@ksc.cz; internet www.ksc.cz; f. 1995 as Party of Czechoslovak Communists; renamed as above 1999; 19,980 mems; Sec.-Gen. ŠTĚPÁN MIROSLAV.

Conservative Party (Konzervativní strana): U Průhonu 6, 170 00 Prague 7; tel. and fax 220808572; e-mail info@konzervativnistrana.cz; internet www.konzervativnistrana.cz; f. 1990 by fmr mems of right-wing faction in ODA; Chair. JAN FOŘT.

Czech Social Democratic Party (ČSSD) (Česká strana sociálně demokratická): Lidový dům, Hybernská 7, 110 00 Prague 1; tel. 296522111; fax 224222190; e-mail info@socdem.cz; internet www.www.cssd.cz; f. 1878; prohibited 1948; re-established 1990; fmrly the Czechoslovak Social Democratic Party; Chair. JIŘÍ PAROUBEK.

Democratic Union of the Czech Republic (DEU-ČR) (Demokratická Unie České Republiky): Všebořická 603, Ústí nad Labem, 400 01; tel. 737261969; fax 472742808; e-mail dorant@pvtnet.cz; internet www.deucr.cz; f. 2004 by mems of the fmr Democratic Union; Chair. JAN DORANT.

Free Democrats—Liberal National Social Party (SD—LSNS) (Svobodní demokraté—Liberální strana národně sociální): Republiky nám. 7, 111 49 Prague 1; tel. 221618554; fax 224223443; e-mail sdlsns@mbox.vol.cz; internet www.ecn.cz/env/volby/sd/home.htm; f. 1995 by merger of Free Democrats (fmrly Civic Movement) and Liberal National Social Party (fmrly Czechoslovak Socialist Party); Chair. JIŘÍ DIENSTBIER.

Freedom Union-Democratic Union (US-DEU) (Unie svobody-Demokratická unie—Unie): Kozí 916/5, 110 00 Prague 1; tel. 257011411; fax 257011439; e-mail info@unie.cz; internet www.unie.cz; Freedom Union founded 1998 following a split in the Civic Democratic Party; merged with Democratic Union in 2001; Chair. JAN ČERNÝ.

Green Party (Strana zelených): Murmanská 13/1246, 100 00 Prague 10; tel. and fax 272737592; e-mail predsednictvo@zeleni.cz; internet www.zeleni.cz; f. 1990; Pres. MARTIN BURSÍK.

Independent Democrats (NEZDEM) (Nezávislí demokraté): Dlouhá 12, Prague 1; tel. 602337712; fax 224818655; e-mail info@nezdem.cz; internet www.nezdem.cz; f. 2005; Chair. Dr VLADIMÍR ŽELEZNÝ.

Movement of Independents for Harmonious Development of Municipalities and Towns (HNHRM) (Hnutí nezávislých za harmonický rozvoj obcí a měst): Studánka 243, 452 47 Varnsdorf 3; f. 1998; Pres. JOSEF HAMBÁLEK.

National Party (Národní strana): Anenský klášter, Anenské nám. 2, POB 604, 111 21 Prague 1; tel. 604206068; e-mail info@narodni-strana.cz; internet www.narodni-strana.cz; right wing; registered in 2002; Chair. PETRA EDELMANNOVÁ.

Diplomatic Representation

EMBASSIES IN THE CZECH REPUBLIC

Afghanistan: Na Kazance 634/7, 171 00 Prague 7; tel. 233544228; fax 233542009; e-mail afg.prague@centrum.cz; Ambassador MOHAMMAD KACEM FAZELLY.

Albania: Pod kaštany 22, 160 00 Prague 6; tel. 233370594; fax 233377232; e-mail alembprg@mbox.vol.cz; Ambassador QAZIM TEPSHI.

Algeria: V tišině 483/10, POB 204, 160 41 Prague 6; tel. 233371142; fax 233371144; e-mail ambalger@mbox.vol.cz; internet www.algerie.cz; Chargé d'affaires a.i. HICHEM KIMOUCHE.

Argentina: Panská 6, 110 00 Prague 1; tel. 224212448; fax 222241246; e-mail embar@iol.cz; Ambassador JUAN EDUARDO FLEMING.

Austria: Viktora Huga 10, 151 15 Prague 5; tel. 257090511; fax 257316045; e-mail austrianembassy@vol.cz; internet www.austria.cz; Ambassador MARGOT KLESTIL-LÖFFLER.

Azerbaijan: Na Míčánce 32, 160 00 Prague 6; tel. 246032422; fax 246032423; TAHIR TAGHIZADE.

Belarus: Sádky 626, 171 00 Prague 7; tel. 233540899; fax 233540925; Chargé d'affaires a.i. VASIL MARKOVICH.

Belgium: Valdštejnská 6, 118 01 Prague 1; tel. 257533524; fax 257533750; e-mail prague@diplobel.org; Ambassador RAF VAN HELLEMONT.

Bosnia and Herzegovina: Opletalova 27, 110 00 Prague 1; tel. 224422510; fax 222210183; e-mail embbh@iol.cz; Ambassador IVAN ORLIĆ.

Brazil: Panská 5, 110 00 Prague 1; tel. 224321910; fax 224312901; e-mail chebrem@mbox.vol.cz; Ambassador LEDA LUCIA MARTINS CAMARGO.

Bulgaria: Krakovská 6, 110 00 Prague 1; tel. 222211258; fax 222211728; e-mail bulvelv@mbox.vol.cz; Ambassador ZDRAVKO POPOV.

Canada: Muchova 6, 160 00 Prague 6; tel. 272101800; fax 272101890; e-mail canada@canada.cz; internet www.canada.cz; Ambassador MICHAEL CALCOTT.

Chile: U Vorlíků 4/623, 160 00 Prague 6; tel. 224315064; fax 224316069; e-mail echilecz@mbox.vol.cz; Ambassador MARCELO ROZAS LÓPEZ.

China, People's Republic: Pelléova 18, 160 00 Prague 6; tel. 224311323; fax 224319888; e-mail chinaemb-cz@mfa.gov.cn; internet www.chinaembassy.cz; Ambassador HUO YUZHEN.

Congo, Democratic Republic: Soukenická 34, 110 00 Prague 1; tel. and fax 222314656; fax 286850898; e-mail ambrdcpraha@hotmail.com; Chargé d'affaires a.i. PIERRE KABEYA MILAMBU.

Costa Rica: Hellichova 458/1, 118 00 Prague 1; tel. 257310582; fax 257310572; e-mail embcr_rc@rree.go.cr; Chargé d'affaires a.i. WILLIAM JOSÉ CALVO CALVO.

Croatia: V Průhledu 9, 162 00 Prague 6; tel. 233340479; fax 233343464; e-mail velrhprag@vol.cz; internet www.cz.mvp.hr; Ambassador MARIJAN RAMUŠĆAK.

Cuba: Sibiřské nám. 1, 160 00 Prague 6; tel. 224311253; fax 233341029; e-mail embacubapraga@embacuba.cz; Chargé d'affaires a.i. BARBARA ELENA MONTALVO ALVAREZ.

Cyprus: Pod Hradbami 9, 160 00 Prague 6; tel. 224316833; fax 224317529; e-mail embassy@kypros.cz; Ambassador ACHILLEAS ANTONIADES.

Denmark: Maltézské nám. 5, POB 25, 118 01 Prague 1; tel. 257531600; fax 257531609; e-mail prgamb@um.dk; internet www.ambprag.um.dk; Chargé d'affaires a.i. MALENE HEDLUND.

Egypt: Pelléova 14, 160 00 Prague 6; tel. 224311506; fax 224311157; e-mail embassyegypt@centrum.cz; Ambassador AMAL MOSTAFA K. MOURAD.

Estonia: Na Kampě 1, 118 00 Prague 1; tel. 257011180; fax 257011181; e-mail embassy.prague@estemb.cz; internet www.estemb.cz; Ambassador MATI VAARMANN.

Finland: Hellichova 1, 118 00 Prague 1; tel. 251177251; fax 251177241; e-mail sanomat.pra@formin.fi; internet www.finland.cz; Ambassador HANNU VEIKKO KYRÖLÄINEN.

France: Velkopřevorské nám. 2, POB 102, 118 000 Prague 1; tel. 251171711; fax 251171720; e-mail ambafrcz@france.cz; internet www.france.cz; Ambassador CHARLES FRIES.

THE CZECH REPUBLIC

Georgia: Na Zátorce 13, 160 00 Prague 6; tel. 233311749; fax 233383291; e-mail prague.emb@mfa.gov.ge; Ambassador VLADIMER CHIPASHVILI.

Germany: Vlašská 19, POB 88, 118 01 Prague 1; tel. 257113111; fax 257534056; e-mail zreg@prag.auswaertiges-amt.de; internet www.deutsche-botschaft.cz; Ambassador HELMUT ELFENKÄMPER.

Ghana: V tišině 4, 160 00 Prague 6; tel. 233377236; fax 233375647; e-mail ghanaemb@mbox.vol.cz; Ambassador VERONICA SHARON BOAKYE KUFUOR.

Greece: Na Ořechovce 19, 162 00 Prague 2; tel. 222250943; fax 222253686; e-mail greekemb@czn.cz; Ambassador VASSILIOS IKOSSI-PENTARCHOS.

Holy See: Voršilská 12, 110 00 Prague 1; tel. 224999811; fax 224999833; e-mail nunciatgc@mbox.vol.cz; Apostolic Nuncio Most Rev. DIEGO CAUSERO (Titular Archbishop of Gradum).

Hungary: Pod Hradbami 17, 160 00 Prague 6; tel. 220317200; fax 233322104; e-mail huembprg@vol.cz; internet www.mfa.gov.hu/kulkepviselet/cz/hu; Ambassador ISTVÁN SZABÓ.

India: Valdštejnská 6, 118 00 Prague 1; tel. 257533490; fax 257533378; e-mail indembprague@bohem-net.cz; internet www.india.cz; Ambassador DINKAR PRAKASH SRIVASTAVA.

Indonesia: Nad Budánkami II/7, 150 21 Prague 5; tel. 257214388; fax 257212105; e-mail informace@indonesian-embassy.cz; internet www.indonesian-embassy.cz; Ambassador SALIM SAID.

Iran: Na Zátorce 18, 160 00 Prague 6; tel. 220570454; fax 233380255; e-mail embircz@volny.cz; Chargé d'affaires a.i. MAJID NILI AHMADABADI.

Iraq: Na Zátorce 10, 160 00 Prague 6; tel. 224326976; fax 224321715; e-mail iraqiembassy@volny.cz; Ambassador DHIA AL-DABBASS.

Ireland: Tržiště 13, 118 00 Prague 1; tel. 257530061; fax 257531387; e-mail pragueembassy@dfa.ie; internet www.embassyofireland.cz; Ambassador DONAL HAMILL.

Israel: Badeniho 2, 170 06 Prague 7; tel. 233325109; fax 233320092; e-mail ambassador-sec@prague.mfa.goo.il; internet prague.mfa.gov.il; Ambassador ARIE ARAZI.

Italy: Nerudova 20, 118 00 Prague 1; tel. 233080111; fax 257531522; e-mail ambasciata.praga@esteri.it; internet www.ambpraga.esteri.it; Ambassador FABIO PIGLIAPOCO.

Japan: Maltézské nám. 6, 118 01 Prague 1; tel. 257533546; fax 257532377; e-mail info@japanembassy.cz; internet www.cz.emb-japan.go.jp; Ambassador HIDEAKI KUMAZAWA.

Kazakhstan: Romaina Rollanda 12, 160 00 Prague 6; tel. 233375642; fax 233371019; e-mail kzembas@bon.cz; internet www.kazembassy.cz; Ambassador ANARBEK KARASHEV.

Korea, Democratic People's Republic: Na Větru 395/18, 162 00 Prague 6; tel. 224320783; fax 224318817; e-mail vel.kldr@seznam.cz; Ambassador PYONG GAP RI.

Korea, Republic: Slavíčkova 5, 160 00 Prague 6; tel. 2234090411; fax 2234090450; Ambassador CHO SEONG-YONG.

Kuwait: Na Zátorce 26, 160 00 Prague 6; tel. 2205707781; fax 220700787; Ambassador ABDULAZIZ ABDULLAH AD-DUAIJ.

Latvia: Hradešínská 3, POB 54, 101 00 Prague 10; tel. 255700881; fax 255700880; e-mail embassy.czech@mfa.gov.lv; internet www.latvia.cz; Ambassador ARGITA DAUDZE.

Lebanon: Lazarská 6, 120 00 Prague 2; tel. 224930495; fax 224934534; e-mail czklebemb@vol.cz; Ambassador JAAD EL-HASSAN.

Lithuania: Pod Klikovkou 1916/2, 150 00 Prague 5; tel. 257210122; fax 257210124; e-mail amb.cz@urm.lt; internet cz.mfa.lt; Ambassador OSVALDAS ČIUKŠYS.

Luxembourg: Tržiště 13, 118 00 Prague 1; tel. 257181800; fax 257532537; e-mail alena.veliskova@mae.etat.lu; internet www.ambalux.cz; Ambassador JEAN FALTZ.

Macedonia, former Yugoslav republic: Balbínova 392/4, 120 00 Prague 2; tel. 222521093; fax 222521108; e-mail prague@mfa.gov.mk; Chargé d'affaires a.i. GOCE KARAJANOV.

Malaysia: Washingtonova 25, 110 00 Prague 1; tel. 234706611; fax 296326192; e-mail mwprague@mwprague.cz; Ambassador SALMAN AHMAD.

Malta: Lázeňská 4, 118 00 Prague 1; tel. 257531874; fax 257530968; e-mail srmr@seznam.cz; Ambassador MARIO QUAGLIOTTI.

Mexico: Nad Kazankou 8, 171 00 Prague 7; tel. 283061530; fax 233550477; e-mail embamex@rep-checa.cz; internet www.rep-checa.cz; Ambassador JOSÉ LUIS BERNAL RODRÍGUEZ.

Moldova: Na Zátorce 12, 160 00 Prague 6; tel. 233323762; fax 233323765; e-mail secretariat@ambasadamoldova.cz; internet www.ambasadamoldova.cz; Ambassador VALERIAN CRISTEA.

Mongolia: Na Marně 5, 160 00 Prague 6; tel. 224311198; fax 224314827; e-mail monemb@bohem-net.cz; internet www.mongolembassy.net; Ambassador ENKHTUR OCHIR.

Morocco: Mickiewiczova 6, 160 00 Prague 6; tel. 233325656; fax 233322634; e-mail sifamapragu@iol.cz; Ambassador MOHAMMED RACHID IDRISSI KAITOUNI.

Netherlands: Gotthardská 6/27, 160 00 Prague 6; tel. 233015200; fax 233015254; e-mail nlgovpra@ti.cz; internet www.netherlandsembassy.cz; Ambassador JAN-LUCAS VAN HOORN.

Norway: Hellichova 1/458, 118 00 Prague 1; tel. 257323737; fax 257326827; e-mail emb.prague@mfa.no; internet www.noramb.cz; Ambassador PETER NICOLAY RAEDER.

Pakistan: Páté Baterie 7/761, 162 00 Prague 6; tel. 233312868; fax 233312885; e-mail parepprague@gmail.com; Ambassador ATHAR MAHMOOD.

Peru: Muchova 9, 160 00 Prague 6; tel. 224316210; fax 224314749; e-mail embaperu.praga@post.cz; Ambassador ALBERTO EFRAÍN SALAS BARAHONA.

Philippines: Senovážné náměstí 8, 110 00 Prague 1; tel. 224216397; fax 224216390; e-mail praguepe@phembassy.cz; Ambassador CARMELITA RODRÍGUEZ SALAS.

Poland: Valdštejnská 8, 118 01 Prague 1; tel. 257530388; fax 257530135; e-mail ambrpczechy@mbox.vol.cz; internet www.prague.polemb.net; Ambassador JAN PASTWA.

Portugal: Pevnostní 9, 160 00 Prague 6; tel. 257311230; fax 257311234; e-mail embport@mbox.vol.cz; internet www.embportugal.cz; Ambassador FERNANDO MANUEL OLIVEIRA DE CASTRO BRANDÃO.

Romania: Nerudova 5, POB 87, 118 01 Prague 1; tel. 257534210; fax 257531017; e-mail embrprg@mbox.vol.cz; internet www.rouemb.cz; Chargé d'affaires a.i. DAN ADRIAN BALANESCU.

Russia: Pod kaštany 1, 160 00 Prague 6; tel. 233374100; fax 233377235; e-mail embrus@tiscali.cz; internet www.czech.mid.ru; Ambassador ALEKSEI L. FEDOTOV.

Saudi Arabia: Na Hřebenkách 70, 150 00 Prague 5; tel. 257316597; fax 257316593; e-mail rse@saudi-embassy.cz; Ambassador Prince MANSOUR BIN KHALID BIN ABDULLAH AL-FARHAN AL-SAUD.

Serbia: Mostecká 15, 118 00 Prague 1; tel. 257532075; fax 257533948; e-mail yuambacz@mbox.vol.cz; Ambassador VLADIMIR VEREŠ.

Slovakia: Pod hradbami 1, 160 00 Prague 6; tel. 233113051; fax 233113054; e-mail skembassy@mfa.sk; Ambassador LADISLAV BALLEK.

Slovenia: Pod hradbami 15, 160 41 Prague 6; tel. 233081211; fax 224314106; e-mail vpr@gov.si; Ambassador FRANK BUT.

South Africa: Ruská 65, POB 133, 100 00 Prague 10; tel. 267311114; fax 267311395; e-mail saprague@nextra.cz; Ambassador NOMSA QHAMKILE DUBE.

Spain: Badeniho 401/4, 170 00 Prague 7; tel. 233097211; fax 233341770; e-mail embpraha@gts.cz; internet www.embajada-esp-praga.cz; Ambassador ANTONIO PEDAUYÉ Y GONZÁLEZ.

Sweden: Úvoz 13-Hradčany, POB 35, 160 12 Prague 6; tel. 220313200; fax 220313240; e-mail ambassaden.prag@foreign.ministry.se; Ambassador CATHERINE VON HEIDENSTAM.

Switzerland: Pevnostní 7/588, POB 84, 162 01 Prague 6; tel. 220400611; fax 224311312; e-mail vertretung@pra.rep.admin.ch; Ambassador JEAN-FRANÇOIS KAMMER.

Syria: Českomalínská 20/7, 160 00 Prague 6; tel. 224310952; fax 224317911; e-mail souria@volny.cz; Ambassador NADRA FAYEZ SAYYAF.

Thailand: Romaina Rollanda 3, 160 00 Prague 6; tel. 220571435; fax 220570049; e-mail thaiemb@volny.cz; internet www.thaiembassy.cz; Ambassador THANARAT THANAPUTTI.

Tunisia: Nad Kostelem 8, 147 00 Prague 4; tel. 244460652; fax 244460825; e-mail atprague@vol.cz; Ambassador RADHOUANE LARIF.

Turkey: Na Ořechovce 69, 162 00 Prague 616; tel. 224311402; fax 224311279; e-mail turkembprague@ms.easynet.cz; Ambassador KORAY TARGAY.

Ukraine: Charlese de Gaulla 29, 160 00 Prague 6; tel. 233342000; fax 233344366; e-mail emb_cz@mfa.gov.ua; internet www.ukrembassy.cz; Ambassador IVAN D. KULEBA.

United Kingdom: Thunovská 14, 118 00 Prague 1; tel. 257402111; fax 257402296; e-mail info@britain.cz; internet www.britain.cz; Ambassador LINDA JOY DUFFIELD.

Uruguay: Muchova 9, 160 00 Prague 6; tel. 224314755; fax 224313780; e-mail urupra@urupra.cz; Ambassador (vacant).

USA: Tržiště 15, 118 01 Prague 1; tel. 257022000; fax 257022809; e-mail webmaster@usembassy.cz; internet www.usembassy.cz; Ambassador RICHARD W. GRABER.

Venezuela: Sněmovní 9, 118 00 Prague 1; tel. 257534253; fax 257534257; e-mail embaven@iol.cz; internet www.embajada-venezuela.cz; Chargé d'affaires a.i. LUIS GERONIMO SOTILLO MENDEZ.

Viet Nam: Plzeňská 214/2578, 150 00 Prague 5; tel. 257211540; fax 257211792; Ambassador VUONG THUA PHONG.
Yemen: Pod hradbami 5, 160 00 Prague 6; tel. 233331568; fax 233332204; e-mail yemenemb@seznam.cz; Ambassador AHMED SALEM AL-JABALI.

Judicial System

The judicial system comprises the Supreme Court, the Supreme Administrative Court, high, regional and district courts. There is also a 15-member Constitutional Court.
Supreme Court (Nejvyšší soud): Buresova 20, 657 37 Brno; tel. 541593111; fax 541213493; e-mail mbox@nsoud.cz; internet www.nsoud.cz; Chair. IVA BROŽOVÁ.
Supreme Administrative Court (Nejvyšší správní soud): Moravské nám. 6, 657 40 Brno; tel. 542532311; fax 542532361; e-mail podatelna@nssoud.cz; internet www.nssoud.cz; Pres. JOSEF BAXA.
Office of the Chief Prosecutor: Jezuitska 4, 660 55 Brno; tel. 542512111; fax 542219621; e-mail posta@nsz.brn.justice.cz; internet portal.justice.cz; Chief Prosecutor RENÁTA VESECKÁ.
Constitutional Court (Ústavní soud): Joštova 8, 660 83 Brno 2; tel. 542162111; fax 542161309; e-mail podani@concourt.cz; internet www.concourt.cz; Chair. PAVEL RYCHETSKÝ.

Religion

According to the results of the March 2001 national census, about 60% of the population profess no religious belief. Among believers, the principal religion is Christianity, and the largest denomination is the Roman Catholic Church.

CHRISTIANITY

Ecumenical Council of Churches in the Czech Republic (Ekumenická rada církví v České republice): Donská 5/370, 101 00 Prague 10; tel. and fax 271742326; e-mail ekumrada@iol.cz; internet www.ecumenicalcouncil.cz; f. 1955; 11 mem. churches; Pres. Bishop PAVEL ČERNÝ; Gen. Sec. JITKA KRAUSOVÁ.

The Roman Catholic Church

Latin Rite

The Czech Republic comprises two archdioceses and six dioceses. There is also an Apostolic Exarchate for Catholics of the Byzantine Rite. According to the results of the March 2001 national census, there were 2,740,780 adherents in the Czech Republic, equivalent to some 27% of the total population. The Roman Catholic Church estimated a total of 3,280,236 adherents in the country at 31 December 2005, equivalent to 32.1% of the total population.
Czech Bishops' Conference: Thákurova 3, 160 00 Prague 6; tel. 223315421; fax 224310144; e-mail cbk2@ktf.cuni.cz; f. 1990; Pres. Most Rev. JAN GRAUBNER (Archbishop of Olomouc).
Archbishop of Olomouc: Most Rev. JAN GRAUBNER, Archibiskupský Ordinát, Biskupské nám. 2, POB 193, 771 01 Olomouc; tel. 587405111; fax 585222244; e-mail arcibol@arcibol.cz; internet www.ado.cz.
Archbishop of Prague: Cardinal Dr MILOSLAV VLK, Hradčanské nám. 56/16, 119 02 Prague 1; tel. 220392123; fax 220515396; e-mail apha@apha.cz; internet www.apha.cz.

Byzantine Rite

Apostolic Exarch in the Czech Republic: Most Rev. Dr LADISLAV HUČKO (Titular Bishop of Orea), Haštalské nám. 4, 110 00 Prague 1; tel. 221778491; fax 222312817; e-mail exarchat@volny.cz; internet www.exarchat.cz; 170,704 adherents (Dec. 2005).

The Eastern Orthodox Church

Orthodox Church in the Czech Lands and Slovakia (Pravoslavná církev v Českých zemích a na Slovensku): Resslova 9A, 120 00 Prague 2; tel. 224920686; fax 224916100; e-mail cilova@pravoslavnacirkev.cz; internet www.pravoslavnacirkev.cz; divided into two eparchies in the Czech Republic: Prague and Olomouc-Brno; and two eparchies in Slovakia: Prešov and Michalovce; Archbishop of Prague, Metropolitan of the Czech Lands and Slovakia His Beatitude Dr KRYŠTOF.

Protestant Churches

Brethren Evangelical Free Church (Církev bratrská): Soukenická 15, 110 00 Prague 1; tel. and fax 22318131; e-mail sekretariat@cb.cz; internet www.cb.cz; f. 1880; 9,368 mems, 62 churches; mem. of the Ecumenical Council of Churches in the Czech Republic and the International Federation of Free Evangelical Churches; Pres. PAVEL ČERNÝ; Sec. KAREL FOJTÍK.
Evangelical Church of Czech Brethren (Českobratrská církev evangelická): Jungmannova 9, 111 21 Prague 1; tel. 224999211; fax 224999219; e-mail srcce@srcce.cz; internet www.srcce.cz; f. 1781; united since 1918; Presbyterian; active in Bohemia, Moravia and Silesia; 102,000 adherents and 261 parishes (2006); Pres. JOEL RUML; Synodal Curator MAHULENA ČEJKOVÁ.
Silesian Evangelical Church of the Augsburg Confession (Slezská církev evangelická a.v.): Na nivách 7, 737 01 Český Těšín; tel. 558731804; fax 558731815; e-mail sceav@sceav.cz; internet www.sceav.cz; Lutheran; 40,000 mems; Bishop VLADISLAV VOLNÝ.
Unity of Brethren of the Czech Republic—Unitas Fratrum (Jednota bratrská v České republice): Kollárova 456, 509 01 Nová Paka; tel. 326736274; internet www.jbcr.info; f. 1457, reorganized 1862; widely known as the 'Moravian Church'; 2,500 mems; 19 parishes; Pres. Rev. JAROSLAV PLEVA.

Other Christian Churches

Apostolic Church in the Czech Republic (Apoštolská církev ČR): V Zídkách 402, 280 02 Kolín; tel. 321720457; fax 321727668; e-mail ustredi.kolin@apostolskacirkev.cz; internet www.apostolskacirkev.cz; f. 1989; 5,634 mems; Bishop RUDOLF BUBIK.
Church of the Seventh-day Adventists—Czech and Slovak Union (Církev adventistů sedmého dne—Česko-Slovenská Unie): Zálesí 50, 142 00 Prague 4; tel. 241471939; fax 244471863; e-mail unie@casd.cz; internet www.casd.cz; f. 1919; 7,744 mems; 138 congregations; Pres. PAVEL ŠIMEK.
Czechoslovak Hussite Church (Církev československá husitská): Wuchterlova 5, 166 26 Prague 6; tel. 220398111; fax 220398123; e-mail external.affairs@ccsh.cz; internet www.ccsh.cz; f. 1920; 99,103 mems (2006); six dioceses, divided into 295 parishes; Chair. Patriarch TOMÁŠ BUTTA.

JUDAISM

Federation of Jewish Communities in the Czech Republic (Federace židovských obcí v ČR): Maiselova 18, 110 00 Prague 1; tel. 224800824; fax 224810912; e-mail sekretariat@fzo.cz; internet www.fzo.cz; 3,000 mems in 10 registered communities; Pres. JIŘÍ DANÍČEK; Chief Rabbi EPHRAIM KAROL SIDON.

The Press

PRINCIPAL DAILIES

There were 116 national and regional daily newspapers published in 2005.

Brno

Brněnský deník—Rovnost (Brno Daily—Equality): Milady Horákové 9, 602 00 Brno; tel. 545558256; fax 545571717; e-mail j.pokorna@rovnost.cz; internet brnensky.denik.cz; f. 1885; fmrly *Rovnost* (Equality); morning; Editor-in-Chief PAVEL MACKŮ; circ. 62,000.

České Budějovice

Českobudějovický deník (České Budějovice Daily): Vrbenská 23, 370 45 České Budějovice; tel. 387411993; fax 387411825; e-mail redakce.ceskobudejovicky@denik.cz; internet ceskobudejovicky.denik.cz; f. 1992; frmly *Českobudějovické Listy* (České Budějovice Paper); morning; Editor-in-Chief HANA SVÍTILOVÁ; circ. 53,000.

Hradec Králové

Hradecký deník (Hradec Králové Daily): Kladská 17, 500 03 Hradec Králové; tel. 495800833; fax 495800889; e-mail jitka.zajickova@denik.cz; internet hradecky.denik.cz; f. 1992; fmrly *Hradecké noviny* (Hradec Králové News); Editor-in-Chief JITKA ZAJÍČKOVÁ; circ. 30,000.

Ostrava

Moravskoslezský deník (Moravia-Silesia Daily): Mlýnská 10, 701 11 Ostrava; tel. 596176311; fax 596176312; e-mail redakce.moravskoslezsky@denik.cz; internet www.msdenik.cz; f. 1991; Editor-in-Chief TOMÁŠ SIŘINA; circ. 130,000.
Svoboda (Freedom): Mlýnská 10, 701 11 Ostrava; tel. 592472311; fax 592472312; f. 1991; morning; Editor-in-Chief JOSEF LYS; circ. 100,000.

Plzeň

Plzeňský deník (Plzeň Daily): Kovářská 4, 304 83 Plzeň; tel. 377168332; fax 377168355; e-mail sekretariat.zapad@denik.cz;

internet www.plzenskydenik.cz; f. 1992; Editor-in-Chief ZUZANA VOLAŘÍKOVÁ; circ. 50,000.

Prague

České noviny/Czech Happenings: Neris s.r.o. Opletalova 5, 110 00 Prague 1; tel. 222098439; fax 222098113; e-mail cn@mail.ctk.cz; internet www.ceskenoviny.cz; f. 1996; online only, in Czech and English; also produces *Finanční noviny* (Financial News) and *Sportovní noviny* (Sport News); Editor-in-Chief KAREL PETRÁK.

Hospodářské noviny (Economic News): Dobrovského 25, 170 55 Prague 7; tel. 233071111; fax 233072005; e-mail data@hn.economia.cz; internet www.ihned.cz; f. 1957; morning; Editor-in-Chief PETR ŠIMŮNEK; circ. 125,000 (2003).

Lidové noviny (People's News): Pobřežní 20/224, 186 21 Prague 8; tel. 267098700; fax 267098799; e-mail internet@lidovky.cz; internet lidovky.zpravy.cz; f. 1893, re-established 1988; morning; Editor-in-Chief PAVEL ŠAFR; circ. 80,000 (2003).

Mladá fronta Dnes (The Youth Front Today): Anděl Media Centrum, Karla Engliše 519/11, 150 00 Prague; tel. 225061111; fax 222062229; e-mail mfdnes@mfdnes.cz; internet www.mfdnes.cz; f. 1990; morning; independent; Editor-in-Chief ROBERT ČÁSENSKÝ; circ. 350,000.

Právo (Right): Slezská 2127/13, 121 50 Prague 2; tel. 221001111; fax 221001361; e-mail redakce@pravo.cz; internet pravo.novinky.cz; f. 1920 as *Rudé právo*; present name adopted 1995; morning; Editor-in-Chief ZDENĚK PORYBNÝ; circ. 250,000.

Šíp (The Arrow): Přátelství 986, 104 00 Prague 10–Uhříněves; tel. 221999305; fax 221999304; e-mail redakce@deniksip.cz; internet www.deniksip.cz; f. 2005 to replace *Večerník Praha* (Evening Prague); popular; Editor-in-Chief MARTIN ŠVEHLÁK; circ. 130,000.

Ústí nad Labem

Ústecký deník (Ústí nad Labem Daily): Klíšská 25, 400 01 Ústí nad Labem; tel. 475246825; fax 475246829; e-mail redakce.ustecky@denik.cz; internet www.usteckydenik.cz; f. 1993; Editor-in-Chief ALENA VOLFOVÁ; circ. 95,000.

PRINCIPAL PERIODICALS

Ateliér (Studio): Na Poříčí 30, 110 00 Prague 1; tel. and fax 221732338; e-mail atelier.art@volny.cz; internet www.atelier-journal.cz; f. 1988; visual arts; fortnightly; Editor-in-Chief BLANKA POLÁKOVÁ.

Auto Tip: Střelničná 1680/8, 182 21 Prague 8; tel. 266193173; fax 266193172; e-mail v.kodym@axelspringer.cz; f. 1990; fortnightly for motorists; Editor-in-Chief VÍTĚZSLAV KODYM; circ. 60,000.

Blesk (Lightning): U průhonu 13, 170 00 Prague 7; tel. 225977616; fax 222714641; e-mail blesk@blesk.cz; internet www.blesk.cz; weekly; popular; Editor-in-Chief JIŘÍ FABIÁN; circ. 300,000.

Českomoravský profit (Bohemia and Moravia Profit): Vinohradská 230, 100 00 Prague 10; tel. 225010366; fax 225010377; e-mail profit@profit.cz; internet www.profit.cz; business, investment; weekly; f. 1991; Editor-in-Chief MARTIN SCHMARCZ.

Czech Business and Trade: V jirchářích 8, 110 00 Prague 1; tel. 221406623; fax 224934383; e-mail journal@ppagency.cz; internet www.ppagency.cz/en/cbt.html; f. 1928; monthly; publ. in English, German, Spanish, Russian and French; Editor-in-Chief Dr PAVLA PODSKALSKÁ; circ. 15,000.

Divadelní noviny (Theatre News): Celetná 7, 110 00 Prague 1; tel. 224809114; fax 222315912; e-mail divadelni.noviny@divadlo.cz; internet www.divadlo.cz/noviny; fortnightly; Editor-in-Chief JAN KOLÁŘ.

Ekonom (Economist): Dobrovského 25, 170 55 Prague 7; tel. 233071301; fax 233072002; e-mail ekonom@economia.cz; internet ekonom.ihned.cz; weekly; Editor-in-Chief ZBYNEK FIALA; circ. 30,000.

Euro: Holečkova 103/31, 150 00 Prague 5; tel. 251026111; fax 257328774; e-mail redakce@euro.cz; internet www.euro.cz; weekly; finance, business, economics; f. 1999; Editor-in-Chief ISTVÁN LÉKÓ.

Instinkt (Instinct): Panská 7, 110 00 Prague 1; tel. 296827110; fax 296827292; e-mail instinkt@instinkt-online.cz; internet www.instinkt-online.cz; fmrly *Mladý svět* (The Young World); illustrated weekly; Editor-in-Chief PETR SKOČDOPOLE.

Katolický týdeník (Catholic Weekly): Londýnská 44, 120 00 Prague 2; tel. 224250395; fax 224257041; e-mail redakce@katolicky-tydenik.cz; internet www.katyd.cz; f. 1989; weekly; Editor-in-Chief ANTONÍN RANDA; circ. 70,000.

Květy (Flowers): Na Florenci 3, 117 14 Prague 1; tel. and fax 224219549; f. 1834; illustrated family weekly; Editor-in-Chief JINDŘICH MAŘAN; circ. 320,000.

PC World: Seydlerova 2451/11, 158 00 Prague 5; tel. 257088111; fax 265208121; e-mail pcworld@idg.cz; internet www.pcworld.cz; monthly; Editor JANA PELIKÁNOVÁ.

Prague Post: Štěpánská 20, 110 00 Prague 1; tel. 296334400; fax 296334450; e-mail office@praguepost.com; internet www.praguepost.com; f. 1991; political, economic and cultural weekly in English; Man. Editor MARK NESSMITH; circ. 15,000.

Reflex: Žerotínova 38, 130 50 Prague 3; tel. 225097111; fax 222582013; e-mail reflex@ringier.cz; internet www.reflex.cz; f. 1990; social, weekly; Editor-in-Chief PETR BÍLEK; circ. 60,000.

Respekt (Respect): Křemencova 10, 110 00 Prague 1; tel. 224930685; fax 224930792; e-mail redakce@respekt.cz; internet www.respekt.cz; f. 1990; political and cultural weekly; Editor-in-Chief MARTIN M. ŠIMEČKA; circ. 25,000.

Romano Hangos/Romský hlas (Romany Voice): Francouzská 84, 602 00 Brno; tel. 545246674; e-mail rhangos@volny.vz; internet www.romanohangos.cz; f. 1999; weekly; in Romany and Czech; Editor-in-Chief KAREL HOLOMEK.

Sondy (Soundings): W. Churchilla 2, 130 00 Prague 3; tel. 224462328; fax 224462313; e-mail sondy@cmkos.cz; internet www.tydenik-sondy.cz; f. 1990; weekly; journal of the Czech (Bohemian)-Moravian Confederation of Trade Unions; Editor-in-Chief JANA KAŠPAROVÁ; circ. 40,000.

100+1 (Sto plus jedna) ZZ–Zahraniční zajímavost (100+1 ZZ–Foreign Interest): Karlovo nám. 5, 120 00 Prague 2; tel. 224914793; fax 224916922; e-mail sto@stoplus.cz; internet stoplusjedna.newtonit.cz; f. 1964; every two weeks; foreign press digest incl. culture, politics, history, sport, health, etc.; Man. Editor MARIE KYSILKOVÁ; circ. 85,000.

Tvar (Form): Na Florenci 3, 110 00 Prague 1; tel. 222828399; fax 222828397; e-mail tvar@ucl.cas.cz; internet www.itvar.cz; every two weeks; literature and literary criticism; Editor-in-Chief LUBOR KASAL.

Týden (The Week): Panská 7, 110 00 Prague 3; tel. 296827110; fax 224239408; internet www.tyden.cz; f. 1994; Editor-in-Chief DALIBOR BALŠINEK; 30,000.

Týdeník Rozhlas (Radio Weekly): Jeseniova 36, 130 00 Prague 3; tel. 222715036; fax 222712616; internet www.radioservis-as.cz/tydenik; f. 1923; Editor-in-Chief MILAN ŠEFL; circ. 170,000.

Vesmír (The Universe): Na Florenci 3, 111 21 Prague 1; tel. 222828393; fax 222828396; e-mail redakce@vesmir.cz; internet www.vesmir.cz; f. 1871; monthly; popular science magazine; Editor IVAN M. HAVEL; circ. 10,500–11,000.

Vlasta: Žitná 18, 120 00 Prague 2; tel. 296162256; f. 1947; weekly; illustrated magazine for women; Editor-in-Chief KATEŘINA ŠMÁLKOVÁ; circ. 380,000.

Zahrádkář (Gardener): Rokycanova 15, 130 00 Prague 3; tel. 222781771; fax 222782711; e-mail zahradkari@vol.cz; internet www.zahradkari.cz/zahradkar/casopis.htm; f. 1969; monthly; organ of the Czech Union of Allotment and Leisure Gardeners (Český zahrádkářský svaz); Editor-in-Chief ANTONÍN DOLEJŠÍ; circ. 200,000.

NEWS AGENCY

Česká tisková kancelář (ČTK) (Czech News Agency): Opletalova 5–7, 111 44 Prague 1; tel. 222098111; fax 224225376; e-mail ctk@mail.ctk.cz; internet www.ctk.cz; f. Nov. 1992, assuming control of all property and activities (in the Czech Lands) of the former Czechoslovak News Agency; news and photo-exchange service with all international and many national news agencies; maintains network of foreign correspondents; Czech and English general and economic news service; publishes daily bulletins in English; Gen. Dir Dr MILAN STIBRAL.

PRESS ASSOCIATION

Syndicate of Journalists of the Czech Republic (Syndikát novinářů České republiky): Senovážné nám. 23, 110 00 Prague 1; tel. 224142455; fax 224142458; e-mail sncr@mbox.vol.cz; internet www.syndikat-novinaru.cz; f. 1877; reorganized 1990; 5,000 mems; Chair. MIROSLAV JELÍNEK.

Publishers

Academia: Legerova 61, 120 00 Prague 2; tel. 224941976; fax 224941982; e-mail academia@academia.cz; internet www.academia.cz; f. 1953; scientific books, periodicals; Dir JITKA ZYKÁNOVÁ (acting).

Akropolis: U Nikolajky 10, 150 00 Prague 5; tel. 251560234; e-mail tomas.akropolis@worldonline.cz; internet www.akropolis.info; f. 1990; Dir JIŘÍ TOMÁŠ.

Albatros: Na Pankraci 30, 140 00 Prague 4; tel. 234633271; fax 234633262; e-mail albatros@bonton.cz; internet www.albatros.cz; f. 1949; literature for children and young people, encyclopedias; Dir MARTIN SLAVÍK.

THE CZECH REPUBLIC

Argo: Milíčova 13, 130 00 Prague 3; tel. 222781601; fax 222780184; e-mail argo@argo.cz; internet www.argo.cz; f. 1992; literature, translations, history, social sciences; Dir MILAN GELNAR.

Atlantis: PS 374, Česká 15, 602 00 Brno; tel. and fax 542213221; e-mail atlantis-brno@volny.cz; internet www.volny.cz/atlantis; f. 1989.

BB Art: Bořivojova 85, 130 00 Prague 3; tel. 222721538; fax 222720525; e-mail bbart@bbart.cz; internet www.bbart.cz.

Beta: Květnového vítězství 332, 149 00 Prague 4; tel. 272910733; fax 271913830; e-mail info@dobrovsky.cz; internet www.dobrovsky.cz; f. 1990.

Brána: Hradešínská 30/1956, 101 00 Prague 10; tel. and fax 271740586; e-mail brana–praha@volny.cz; internet www.brana-knihy.cz.

Brázda: Braunerova 4, 180 00 Prague 8; tel. 284841098; e-mail nakladatelstvi.brazda@sendme.cz; internet www.nakladatelstvi-brazda.wz.cz; specialist and popular literature on agriculture, forestry, animals, hobbies, fishing, nature.

Ekopress: U Líhní 100, 142 01 Prague 4; tel. and fax 244471676; e-mail expedice@ekopress.cz; internet www.ekopress.cz; economics, information technology, languages.

Epocha: Kaprova 12/40, 110 00 Prague 1; tel. 224810352; fax 224810353; internet www.epocha.cz; non-fiction, history, esp. military, biography, fiction; f. 1996.

Fragment: Radiová 1, 102 27 Prague 10; tel. 267008272; fax 267008273; e-mail fragment@fragment.cz; internet www.fragment.cz; children's; f. 1991; Dirs JAN EISLER, PAVEL NÝČ.

Grada Publishing: U Průhonu 22, 170 00 Prague 7; tel. 220386401; fax 220386400; e-mail info@gradapublishing.cz; internet www.gradapublishing.cz; f. 1991; Dir MILAN BRUNÁT.

Host: Radlas 5, 602 00 Brno; tel. 545214468; fax 545214470; e-mail redakce@hostbrno.cz; internet www.hostbrno.cz; f. 1990; fiction, literary criticism and theory.

Ivo Železný: U Libeňského pivovaru 10, 180 00 Prague 8; tel. 284825117; internet www.iz.cz.

Kalich: Jungmannova 9, 101 78 Prague 1; tel. 224947505; fax 224947504; e-mail kalich@evangnet.cz; internet www.kalich.evangnet.cz; f. 1920; principally books of evangelical Christian interest; Dirs MICHAL PLZÁK, MARKÉTA LANGOUÁ.

Karolinum: Ovocný trh 3/5, 116 36 Prague 1; tel. 224491276; fax 224212041; e-mail cupress@cuni.cz; internet cupress.cuni.cz; publishing house of the Charles University in Prague; Dir JAROSLAV JIRSA.

Labyrint (Labyrinth): Jablonecká 715, POB 52, 190 00 Prague 9; tel. and fax 224922422; e-mail labyrint@wo.cz; internet labyrint.net; publishing house and cultural magazine; principally prose, poetry and the arts; also illustrated children's titles; f. 1992; Dir and Editor-in-Chief JOACHIM DVOŘÁK.

Levné knihy: Václavské nám. 38/794 110 00 Prague 1; tel. 283933085; e-mail info@levneknihy.cz; internet www.levneknihy.cz; mainly classic Czech and international fiction at discounted prices; f. 2000.

Libri: Na hutmance 7, 158 00 Prague 5; tel. 251612302; fax 251511013; e-mail libri@libri.cz; internet www.libri.cz; f. 1992; encyclopedias, specialist literature; Dir KAREL ŽALOUDEK.

Melantrich: Václavské nám. 36, 112 12 Prague 1; tel. 222093215; fax 224213176; f. 1919; general, fiction, humanities, newspapers and magazines; Dir MILAN HORSKÝ.

Mladá fronta (The Youth Front): Mezi Vodami 1952/9, 143 00 Prague 4; tel. 225276282; fax 225276278; e-mail prodej@mf.cz; internet www.mf.cz; f. 1945; science fiction and fantasy literature, philosophy, sociology; Editor-in-Chief VLASTIMIL FIALA.

Motto: Spoluprá 4, 140 00 Prague 4; tel. and fax 261225619; e-mail erdakce@motto.cz; internet www.motto.cz.

Nakladatelství Lidové noviny: Jana Masaryka 56, 120 00 Prague 2; tel. 222512079; fax 222514012; e-mail info@nln.cz; internet www.nln.cz; fiction, history, languages, guidebooks, popular science; Dir EVA PLEŠKOVÁ.

Naše vojsko (Our Military): Mašovická 202/8, 142 00 Prague 4; tel. 224313071; fax 224311204; e-mail info@nasevojsko.com; internet nasevojsko.atlasobchod.cz; f. 1945; military history and theory.

Odeon: Nádražní 32, 150 00 Prague 1; tel. 296536111; f. 1953; literature, poetry, fiction (classical and modern), literary theory, art books, reproductions; Dir MILUŠE SLAPNIČKOVÁ.

Olympia: Klimentská 1, 115 88 Prague 1; tel. 233089983; fax 222312137; e-mail olympia@mbox.vol.cz; internet www.iolympia.cz; f. 1954; sports, tourism, encyclopedias, fiction, illustrated books; Dir Dr VLADIMÍR TIKAL.

Panton: Radlická 99, 150 00 Prague 5; f. 1958; publishing house of the Czech Musical Fund; books on music, sheet music, records; Dir KAREL ČERNÝ.

Paseka: Chopinova 4, 120 00 Prague 2; tel. 222710752; fax 222718886; e-mail paseka@paseka.cz; internet www.paseka.cz; f. 1989; Owner LADISLAV HORÁČEK.

Portál: Klapkova 2, 182 00 Prague 8; tel. 283028111; fax 283028112; e-mail naklad@portal.cz; internet www.portal.cz; f. 1992; pedagogy, psychology, social work, dictionaries; Dir JAROSLAV KUCHAŘ; Editor-in-Chief JAROSLAV SCHROTTER.

Práce (Labour): Václavské nám. 17, 112 58 Prague 1; tel. 224009100; fax (2) 2320989; f. 1945; trade-union movement, fiction, general, periodicals; Dir JANA SCHMIDTOVÁ.

Rybka Publishers: V Jirchářích 6, 110 00 Prague 1; tel. 224932263; fax 224932017; e-mail mrybka@mbox.vol.cz; internet www.rybkapub.cz; Dir MICHAL RYBKA.

Sagit: Horní 1, 700 30 Ostrava 3; tel. 596785999; fax 596786000; e-mail sagit@sagit.cz; internet www.sagit.cz; law, accounting, tax.

Scientia: Radimova 37/50, 169 00 Prague 6; tel. 233350199; fax 220513511; e-mail e.kesnerova@scientia.cz; internet www.scientia.cz; f. 1992; pedagogic literature.

Slon Sociologické Nakladatelství: Jilská 1, 110 00 Prague 1; tel. and fax 222220025; e-mail redakce@slon-knihy.cz; internet slon-knihy.cz; f. 1991; sociology; Dir ALENA MILTOVÁ.

SPN pedagogické nakladatelství (SPN Pedagogical Publishing House): Ostrovní 30, 110 00 Prague 1; tel. and fax 224931451; e-mail spn@spn.cz; internet www.spn.cz; f. 1775; fmrly Státní pedagogické nakladatelství (State Pedagogical Publishing House); school and university textbooks, dictionaries, literature; Dir VÁCLAV HOLICKÝ.

Twisted Spoon Press: Preslova 12, POB 21, 150 21 Prague 5; tel. 257 327 488; e-mail info@twistedspoon.com; internet www.twistedspoon.com; English-language translations of a variety of writings from Central and Eastern Europe; f. 1992; Dir HOWARD SIDENBERG.

Vyšehrad: Víta Nejedlého 15, 130 00 Prague 3; tel. and fax 224221703; e-mail info@vysehrad.cz; internet www.ivysehrad.cz; f. 1934; religion, philosophy, history, fiction; Dir PRAVOMIL NOVÁK; Chief Editor MARIE VÁLKOVÁ.

PUBLISHERS' ASSOCIATION

Association of Czech Booksellers and Publishers (Svaz českých knihkupců a nakladatelů): Jana Masaryka 56, 120 00 Prague 2; tel. and fax 224219944; internet www.sckn.cz; f. 1879; Chair. JITKA UHDEOVÁ.

Broadcasting and Communications

TELECOMMUNICATIONS

České Radiokomunikace: U Nákladového nádraží 3144, 4 130 00 Prague 3; tel. 242411111; fax 242417595; e-mail info@cra.cz; internet www.radiokomunikace.cz; f. 1994; privatized 2000; Chair. of Bd and Dir-Gen. MIROSLAV ČUŘÍN.

EuroTel: Vyskočilova 1442/1B, PO Box 70, 140 21 Prague 4; tel. 267011111; fax 267011101; internet www.eurotel.cz; f. 1991; mobile cellular communications; 51.1% owned by Telefónica (Spain), 48.9% owned by Český Telecom; Chief Exec. SALVADOR ANGLADA.

T-Mobile Czech Republic: Tomíčkova 2144/1, 149 00 Prague 4; tel. 603603603; e-mail info@t-mobile.cz; internet www.t-mobile.cz; fmrly RadioMobil; 60.8% owned by C-Mobil, 39.2% by České Radiokomunikace, a.s. (39.2%); f. 1996; Gen. Dir ROLAND MAHLER.

Telefónica O2 Czech Republic (Czech Telecom): Olšanská 5, 130 34 Prague 3; tel. 840114114; fax 266316666; e-mail jindrich.trpisovsky@o2.com; internet www.telecom.cz; f. 1992 as SPT Telecom; renamed 2000 as Český Telecom; present name adopted 2006; monopoly operator of long-distance and international services; 51.1% owned by Telefónica (Spain); Pres. and Chief Exec. JAIME SMITH BASTERRA.

Vodafone Czech Republic: Vinoradská 167, 100 00 Prague 10; internet www.vodafone.cz; f. 2000; Man. Dir KARLA D. STEPHENS.

RADIO

The Czech Republic has a dual state and private broadcasting system, with one publicly owned radio broadcaster, Český rozhlas (Czech Radio), and two private, nation-wide radio broadcasters, Frekvence 1, and Radio Impuls.

Local stations broadcast from Prague, Brno, České Budějovice, Hradec Králové, Ostrava, Plzeň, Ústí nad Labem and other towns. By the end of 2003 74 licences for local terrestrial radio broadcasting had been granted.

Český rozhlas (Czech Radio): Vinohradská 12, 120 99 Prague 2; tel. 221551111; fax 221551342; e-mail info@rozhlas.cz; internet www.rozhlas.cz; broadcasts nation-wide programmes (including ČRo 1

THE CZECH REPUBLIC

Radiožurnál, ČRo 2 Praha, ČRo 3 Vlava) and Radio Praha's programme to foreign countries (CRo 7); Dir-Gen. VÁCLAV KASÍK.

Country Radio: Říčanská 3, 101 00 Prague 10; tel. 25102411; fax 251024224; e-mail info@countryradio.cz; internet www.countryradio.cz; commercial station; Dir RADEK VELECHOVSKÝ.

Evropa 2: Wenzigova 4, 120 00 Prague 2; tel. 257001111; fax 257001807; internet www.evropa2.cz; commercial station; Pres. MICHAEL FLEISCHMANN.

Frekvence 1: Wenzigova 4, 120 00 Prague 2; tel. 257001111; fax 224262412; e-mail info@frekvence1.cz; internet www.frekvence1.cz; commercial station; Pres. MICHAEL FLEISCHMANN.

Radio FM Plus: Zikmunda Wintra 21, 301 01 Plzeň; tel. 377676111; fax 377422221; internet www.fmplus.cz; commercial station; Dir VÁCLAV JEŽEK.

Radio Free Europe/Radio Liberty: Vinohradská 1, 110 00 Prague 1; fax 221123420; internet www.rferl.org; non-profit corpn financed by the federal Govt of the USA; broadcasts c. 1,000 hours weekly in 28 languages to Eastern Europe, Eurasia and the Middle East; Chair. KENNETH Y. TOMLINSON; Dir of Broadcasting JEFF TRIMBLE.

Radio Impuls: Kovářská 15, 190 00 Prague 9; tel. 255700700; fax 255700727; internet www.radioimpuls.cz; f. 1999; Man. Dir JIŘÍ HRABÁK.

TELEVISION

In 2000 there were five main terrestrial television stations: the two state-run channels, ČT1 and ČT2, reached 98% and 71% of the population, respectively, while two private commercial stations, Nova TV and Prima TV, were received by 99% and approximately 50%, respectively. At the end of 2003 there were 13 regional television broadcasters and 16 local television broadcasters.

Česká televize (Czech Television): Kavčí hory, 140 70 Prague 4; tel. 261131111; fax 26927202; internet www.czech-tv.cz; f. 1992; state-owned; two channels (ČT1 and ČT2); studios in Prague, Brno and Ostrava; Dir JIŘÍ JANEČEK.

Nova TV: Kříženeckého nám. 322/5, 152 52 Prague 5; tel. 233100111; e-mail volejte.novu@nova.cz; internet www.nova.cz; f. 1994, through a joint venture with Central European Media Enterprises Ltd (CME—of the USA) as the Czech Republic's first independent commercial station; majority owned by CME; Gen. Dir PETR DVOŘÁK.

Prima TV: Na žertvách 24, 180 00 Prague 8; tel. 266700111; fax 266700201; e-mail informace@iprima.cz; internet www.iprima.cz; f. 1993; CEO MAREK SINGER.

Finance

(cap. = capital; res = reserves; dep. = deposits; m. = million; brs = branches; amounts in Czech koruna)

BANKING

With the establishment of independent Czech and Slovak Republics on 1 January 1993, the State Bank of Czechoslovakia was divided and its functions were transferred to the newly created Czech National Bank and National Bank of Slovakia. The Czech National Bank is independent of the Government.

At 30 November 2004 35 banks were operating in the Czech Republic, nine of which were majority-owned by Czech investors, 17 of which were majority-owned by foreign investors and nine of which were branches of foreign banks.

Central Bank

Czech National Bank (Česká národní banka): Na Příkopě 28, 115 03 Prague 1; tel. 224411111; fax 224412404; e-mail info@cnb.cz; internet www.cnb.cz; f. 1993; bank of issue, the central authority of the Czech Republic in the monetary sphere, legislation and foreign exchange permission; central bank for directing and securing monetary policy, supervision of the financial market; cap. 1,400m., res –118,059m., dep. 554,476m. (Dec. 2005); Gov. ZDENĚK TŮMA; 7 brs.

Commercial Banks

BAWAG Bank CZ: Vitezná 1/126, 150 00 Prague 5; tel. 257006111; fax 257006200; e-mail info@bawag.cz; internet www.bawag.cz; f. 1997 as Interbanka a.s.; acquired by Bank für Arbeit und Wirtschaft Aktiengesellschaft (BAWAG—Austria) in 2004; merged with BAWAG International Bank CZ, a.s. (fmrly Dresdner Bank CZ) in 2005, and name changed as above; cap. 1,708.7m., res 1,684.7m., dep. 28,898.2m. (Dec. 2006); Chair. MARKUS HERMANN.

Česká exportní banka, a.s. (Czech Export Bank): Vodičkova 34, POB 870, 111 21 Prague 1; tel. 222843111; fax 224211266; e-mail ceb@ceb.cz; internet www.ceb.cz; f. 1995; cap. 1,850.0m., res 623.0m., dep. 22,734.0m. (Dec. 2006); Chair. JOSEF TAUBER.

Česká spořitelna, a.s. (Czech Savings Bank): Olbrachtova 1929/62, 140 00 Prague 4; tel. 261071111; fax 261073032; e-mail csas@csas.cz; internet www.csas.cz; f. 1825; 98% holding owned by Erste Bank AG (Austria); total assets 728,393.0m., dep. 636,390.0m. (Dec. 2006); Chair. and CEO JOHN JAMES STACK; 637 brs.

Československá obchodní banka, a.s. (CSOB) (Czechoslovak Commercial Bank): Radlická 333/150, 150 57 Prague 5; tel. 224111111; fax 224225049; e-mail info@csob.cz; internet www.csob.cz; f. 1965; owned by KBC Bank NV (Belgium); commercial and foreign-trade transactions; cap. 5,105m., res 22,349m., dep. 675,033m. (Dec. 2006); Chair. and CEO PAVEL KAVÁNEK; 320 brs.

Citibank, a.s.: Evropská 178, 166 40 Prague 6; tel. 233061111; fax 233061617; internet www.citibank.com/czech; f. 1991; 100%-owned subsidiary of Citibank Overseas Investment Corpn (USA); cap. 2,925.0m., res 3,471.6m., dep. 53,982.6m. (Dec. 2005); Chair. and Man. Dir JAVED KUREISHI.

eBanka, a.s.: Na Příkopě 19, 117 19 Prague 1; tel. 222115222; fax 222115500; e-mail info@ebanka.cz; internet www.ebanka.cz; f. 1997; present name adopted 2001; cap. 1,184.5m., res 1.9m., dep. 18,972.2m. (Dec. 2006); Chair. MARTIN KOLOUCH.

HVB Bank Czech Republic, a.s.: Nám. republiky 3A/2090, 110 00 Prague 1; tel. 221112111; fax 221112132; internet www.hvb.cz; f. 1999; subsidiary of Bayerische Hypo- und Vereinsbank (Germany); cap. 5,125m., res 3,923m., dep. 146,362m. (Dec. 2005); Chair. DAVID GRUND.

J&T Banka, a.s.: Pobřežní 14/297, 186 00 Prague 8; tel. 221710111; fax 221710211; e-mail info@jtbank.cz; internet www.jtbank.cz; f. 1998; cap. 1,513.7m., res 1,081.0m., dep. 19,273.6m. (Dec. 2006); PATRIK TKÁČ.

Komerční banka, a.s.: Na Příkopě 33, POB 839, 114 07 Prague 1; tel. 222432111; fax 224243020; e-mail mojebanka@kb.cz; internet www.kb.cz; f. 1990; 60.4% owned by Société Générale (France); cap. 19,005.0m., res 31,013.0m., dep. 525,084.0m. (Dec. 2006); Chair. and Chief Exec. LAURENT GOUTARD; 381 brs.

Raiffeisenbank, a.s.: Olbrachtova 9/2006, 140 21 Prague 4; tel. 221141111; fax 221142111; e-mail info@rb.cz; internet www.rb.cz; f. 1993; owned by Raiffeisenbank (Austria); cap. 3,614.0m., res 997.4m., dep. 80,893.4m. (Dec. 2006); Chair. LUBOR ŽALMAN.

Volksbank CZ, a.s.: Lazarská 8, 120 00 Prague 2; tel. 221969911; fax 221969951; e-mail mail@volksbank.cz; internet www.volksbank.cz; cap. 819m., res 281m., dep. 17,584m. (Dec. 2005); cap. 1,145m. (May 2007); f. 1993; Chair. JOHANN LURF; 20 brs.

Živnostenská banka, a.s.: Na Příkopě 858/20, POB 421, 113 80 Prague 1; tel. 224121111; fax 224125555; e-mail info@zivnobanka.cz; internet www.zivnobanka.cz; f. 1868; owned by Bank Austria Creditanstalt AG; cap. 1,360m., res 1,788m., dep. 43,062m. (Dec. 2005); Chair. and CEO JIŘÍ KUNERT; 8 brs.

Bankers' Organization

Czech Bankers' Association (Česká bankovní asociace): Vodičkova 30, 110 00 Prague 1; tel. 224422080; fax 224422090; e-mail cba@czech-ba.cz; internet www.czech-ba.cz; f. 1992; Pres. JIŘÍ KUNERT.

STOCK EXCHANGE

Prague Stock Exchange (Burza cenných papírů Praha): Rybná 14, 110 05 Prague 1; tel. 221831111; fax 221833040; e-mail info@pse.cz; internet www.pse.cz; f. 1992; Chair. PETR KOBLIC.

Regulatory Authority

Czech Securities Commission (Komise pro cenné papíry): Washingtonova 7, 111 21 Prague 1; tel. 221096111; fax 221096110; e-mail podatelna@sec.cz; internet www.sec.cz; f. 1998; Chair. PAVEL HOLLMANN.

INSURANCE

There were 40 companies providing insurance services in the Czech Republic in 2004, including seven foreign-owned institutions. Of these, 21 provided non-life insurance, three provided life insurance and 16 provided universal insurance.

Allianz pojišťovna, a.s.: Rubesova 4, 120 00 Prague 2; tel. 224405638; fax 224405560; e-mail klient@allianz.cz; internet www.allianz.cz; f. 1993; owned by Allianz AG (Germany).

Česká pojišťovna a.s. (Czech Insurance Corpn): Na Pankráci 121, 140 21 Prague 4; tel. 224551111; fax 224552200; e-mail klient@cpoj.cz; internet www.cpoj.cz; f. 1827; mem. of financial group PPF Group; issues life, accident, fire, aviation, industrial and marine insurance and all classes of reinsurance; CEO and Chair. of Bd LADISLAV BARTONÍČEK.

ČSOB pojišťovna (ČSOB Insurance): Masarykovo nám. 1458, 532 18 Pardubice; tel. 467007111; fax 467007444; e-mail info@csobpoj.cz; internet www.csobpoj.cz; life insurance, accident insurance, property insurance, vehicle insurance, mandatory insurance, travel insurance, risk insurance; Chair. and Gen. Dir JEROEN VAN LEEUWEN.

Generali pojišťovna a.s. (Generali Insurance): Bělehradská 132, 120 84 Prague 2; tel. 221091111; fax 221091300; internet www.generali.cz; life insurance, accident insurance, health insurance, travel insurance, vehicle insurance, liability insurance, risk insurance; Chair. of Bd and Gen. Dir JAROSLAV MLYNÁŘ.

ING pojišťovna: Nádražní 25, 150 00 Prague 5; tel. 257471111; fax 257473555; e-mail klient@ing.cz; internet www.ing.cz; f. 1992; owned by ING (Netherlands); financial and investment insurance, life and health insurance; Gen. Dir DICK OKHUIJSEN.

Kooperativa pojišťovna (Co-operative Insurance Co): Templová 747, 110 01 Prague 1; tel. 221000111; fax 22322562; e-mail info@koop.cz; internet www.koop.cz; life and non-life insurance; f. 1993; Chair. and Gen. Man. VLADIMÍR MRÁZ.

Uniqa pojišťovna, a.s.: Bělohorská 19, 160 12 Prague 6; tel. 225393111; fax 225393777; e-mail info@uniqa.cz; internet www.uniqa.cz/uniqa_cz; owned by Uniqa Versicherungen AG (Austria).

Trade and Industry

GOVERNMENT AGENCIES

Czech Trade Promotion Agency (Česká agentura na podporu obchodu): Dittrichova 21, POB 76, 128 01 Prague 2; tel. 224907500; fax 224907503; e-mail info@czechtrade.cz; internet www.czechtrade.cz; Gen. Dir IVAN JUKL.

CzechInvest—Investment and Business Development (Agentura pro podporu podnikání a investic): Štěpánská 15, 120 00 Prague 2; tel. 296342500; fax 296342502; e-mail agentura@czechinvest.org; internet www.czechinvest.org; f. 1992; foreign investment agency; incorporates fmr Agency for the Development of Industry (Czech Industry); Dir-Gen. TOMÁŠ HRUDA.

CHAMBER OF COMMERCE

Economic Chamber of the Czech Republic (Hospodářská komora ČR): Freyova 27, 190 00 Prague 9; tel. 296696111; fax 296646221; internet www.komora.cz; f. 1850; has almost 15,000 members (trading corporations, industrial enterprises, banks and private enterprises); Pres. JAROMÍR DRÁBEK.

EMPLOYERS' ORGANIZATIONS

Association of Entrepreneurs of the Czech Republic (Sdružení podnikatelů ČR): Škrétova 6/44, 120 59 Prague 2; tel. and fax 222215373; e-mail spcr1989@volny.cz; internet www.sdruzenispcr.cz; Chair. BEDŘICH DANDA.

Confederation of Industry of the Czech Republic (Svaz průmyslu a dopravy ČR): Mikulandská 7, 113 61 Prague 1; tel. 224934088; fax 224934597; e-mail spcr@spcr.cz; internet www.spcr.cz; f. 1990; Dir-Gen. ZDENĚK LIŠKA; Pres. JAROSLAV MÍL.

UTILITIES

Electricity

České energetické závody Skupina (ČEZ) (Czech Power Co Group): Duhová 2/1444, 140 53 Prague 4; tel. 271131111; fax 271132001; e-mail cez@cez.cz; internet www.cez.cz; f. 1992; production and distributions co; 67.6% owned by National Property Fund; merged with five regional distribution cos in 2003; also operates two nuclear-energy plants at Dukovany and Temelín; Gen. Man. MARTIN ROMAN; 7,600 employees.

Dalkia Česká republika: 28 října 3123/152, 709 74 Ostrava; tel. 596609111; fax 596609300; internet www.dalkia.cz; f. 1992; Chair. of Bd ZDENĚK DUBA; Dir-Gen. FRANÇOIS HABÈGRE.

E.ON Česká republika: Lannova 205/16, 370 49 České Budějovice; tel. 387312682; fax 386359803; e-mail info@eon.cz; internet www.eon.cz; f. 2005; comprises two subsidiary cos: E.ON Energie; and E.ON Distribuce; Chair. MICHAL FEHN.

International Power Opatovice: Pardubice 2, 532 13 Opatovice nad Labem 2; tel. 466843111; fax 466536030; e-mail info@ipplc.cz; internet www.eop.cz; f. 1992; fmrly Opatovice Electricity (Elektrarny Opatovice); present name adopted 2005; generation and distribution co; 100% owned by International Power PLC (United Kingdom); Dir-Gen. FRANTIŠEK HEJČL.

Pražská energetika (Prague Energy Co): Na Hroudě 1492/4, 100 00 Prague 10; tel. 267051111; fax 267310817; internet www.pre.cz; distribution co to Prague city and surrounding area; Chair. and Gen. Man. Ing. DRAHOMÍR RUTA.

Gas

Jihomoravská plynárenská (JmP) (South Moravian Gas Co): Plynárenská 499/1, 657 02 Brno; tel. 545548111; fax 545578571; e-mail jmpas@jmpas.cz; internet www.jmpas.cz; distribution co; Chair. DAN TOK.

RWE-Transgas: Limuzská 12, 100 98 Prague 10; tel. 267971111; fax 267776965; e-mail info@transgas.cz; internet www.rwe-transgas.cz; f. 1971; majority-owned by RWE Energie AG (Germany); import and distribution co; Chair. of Bd and Chief Exec. MARTIN HERRMANN.

Severomoravsjká plynárenská (SmP) (North Moravian Gas Co): Plynární 2748/6, 702 72 Ostrava; tel. 840111115; fax 596113985; e-mail info@smpas.cz; internet www.smpas.cz; f. 1994; distribution co; Chair. of Bd REINHOLD FRANK.

Water

Pražské vodovody a kanalizace (PVK) (Prague Water Supply and Sewerage Co): Pařížská 11, 110 00 Prague 1; tel. 221095111; fax 272172379; e-mail info@pvk.cz; internet www.pvk.cz; f. 1998; owned by Veolia Voda (France); Chair. of Bd PHILIPPE GUITARD.

TRADE UNIONS

Czech (Bohemian)-Moravian Confederation of Trade Unions (Českomoravská konfederace odborových svazů): W. Churchilla nám. 2, 113 59 Prague 3; tel. 224461111; fax 222718994; e-mail cmkos@cmkos.cz; internet www.cmkos.cz; f. 1990; 33 affiliated unions (2007); Pres. MILAN ŠTĚCH.

Affiliated unions include the following:

Czech (Bohemian)-Moravian Trade Union of Workers in Education (Českomoravský odborový svaz školství): W. Churchilla nám. 2, 113 59 Prague 3; tel. 234461111; fax 222722685; e-mail cmos.skolstvi@cmkos.cz; internet www.skolskeodbory.cz; Pres. FRANTIŠEK DOBŠÍK; 80,000 mems.

Trade Union of the Health Service and Social Care of the Czech Republic (Odborový svaz zdravotnictví a sociální péče ČR): Koněvova 54, 130 00 Prague 3; tel. 267204300; fax 222718211; e-mail osz_cr@cmkos.cz; internet osz_cmkos.cz; f. 1990; Pres. JIŘÍ SCHLANGER; 45,000 mems.

Trade Union of Workers in Textile, Clothing and Leather Industry of Bohemia and Moravia (Odborový svaz pracovníků textilního, oděvního a kožedělného průmyslu Čech a Moravy): W. Churchilla nám. 2, 113 59 Prague 3; tel. 222718931; fax 222721372; e-mail ostok@cmkos.cz; internet www.ostok.cz; Pres. MIROSLAVA PALEČKOVÁ; 79,600 mems.

Trade Union of Workers in Woodworking Industry, Forestry and Management of Water Supplies in the Czech Republic (Odborový svaz pracovníků dřevozpracujícího odvětví, lesního a vodního hospodářství v České republice): W. Churchilla nám. 2, 113 59 Prague 3; tel. 234463091; fax 222716373; e-mail dlv.sekretariat@cmkos.cz; internet www.osdlv.cmkos.cz; Pres. RUDOLF KYNCL; 24,000 mems.

UNIOS (Odborový svaz UNIOS): W. Churchilla nám. 2, 113 59 Prague 3; tel. 224463172; fax 224463185; e-mail unios@cmkos.cz; internet unios.cmkos.cz; f. 1994; to succeed Czech-Moravian Trade Union of Workers in Services (f. 1994); Pres. KAREL SLADKOVSKÝ; 38,000 mems.

Transport

RAILWAYS

In 2003 the total length of the Czech railway network was 9,520 km.

České dráhy (Czech Railways): nábř. L. Svobody 1222/12, 110 15 Prague 1; tel. 972211111; fax 222328784; e-mail infoservis@gr.cdrail.cz; internet www.cdrail.cz; f. 1993; Gen. Dir JOSEF BAZALA.

Prague Public Transport Co (Dopravní podnik hl. m. Prahy): Sokolovska 217/42, 190 22 Prague 9; tel. 296192011; e-mail dpp@r.dpp.cz; internet www.dpp.cz; f. 1974; operates public transport services in Prague, including buses, trams, funicular cars, suburban train services and Prague underground railway (55 km and 54 stations operational in 2006); Gen. Dir MILAN HOUFEK.

ROADS

In 2003 there were an estimated 128,067 km of roads in the Czech Republic, including 518 km of motorways and 320 km of expressways. There were 564 km of motorways in 2005.

INLAND WATERWAYS

The total length of navigable waterways in the Czech Republic is 663.6 km. The Elbe (Labe) and its tributary, the Vltava, connect the Czech Republic with the North Sea via the port of Hamburg (Germany). The Oder provides a connection with the Baltic Sea and the port of Szczecin (Poland). The Czech Republic's river ports are Prague-Holešovice, Prague-Radotín, Kolín, Mělník, Ústí nad Labem and Děčín, on the Vltava and Elbe.

ČSPL Děčín: K. Čapka 211/1, 405 91 Děčín; tel. 412561111; fax 412510140; e-mail info@cspl.cz; internet www.cspl.cz; f. 1922; fmrly Czechoslovak Elbe Navigation Co (Československá plavba labská); river transport of goods to Germany, Poland, the Netherlands, Belgium, Luxembourg, France and Switzerland; Chair. of Bd JIŘÍ KRATOCHVIL.

CIVIL AVIATION

There are main civil airports at Prague (Ruzyně), Brno, Karlovy Vary and Ostrava, operated by the Czech Airport Administration.

ČSA—České aerolinie (Czech Airlines): Ruzyně Airport, 160 08 Prague 6; tel. 239007007; fax 224314273; e-mail call.centre@csa.cz; internet www.csa.cz; f. 1923; services to destinations in Europe, the Near, Middle and Far East, North Africa and North America; Pres. and Chair. RADOMÍR LAŠÁK.

Smart Wings: K letišti 1068/30, 160 08 Prague 6; tel. 255700827; internet www.smartwings.net; f. 2005; low-cost airline to various European destinations.

Tourism

The Czech Republic has magnificent scenery, with summer and winter sports facilities. Prague, Kutna Hora, Olomouc, Český Krumlov and Telč are among the best-known of the historic towns, and there are famous castles and cathedrals and numerous resorts, as well as spas with natural mineral springs at Karlovy Vary (Carlsbad) and Mariánské Lázně (Marienbad). In 2006 a total of 6,435,474 tourist arrivals were recorded. In 2005 receipts from tourism totalled US $5.6m., compared with $3.4m. in 2002.

CzechTourism: Vinohradská 46, POB 32, 120 41 Prague 2; tel. 221580111; fax 224247516; e-mail info@czechtourism.cz; internet www.czechtourism.com; f. 1993; Dir ROSTISLAV VONDRUSKA.

DENMARK

Introductory Survey

Location, Climate, Language, Religion, Flag, Capital

The Kingdom of Denmark is situated in northern Europe. It consists of the peninsula of Jutland, the islands of Zealand, Funen, Lolland, Falster and Bornholm, and 401 smaller islands. The country lies between the North Sea, to the west, and the Baltic Sea, to the east. Denmark's only land frontier is with Germany, to the south. Norway lies to the north of Denmark, across the Skagerrak, while Sweden, the most southerly region of which is separated from Zealand by the narrow Øresund strait, lies to the north-east. Outlying territories of Denmark are Greenland and the Faroe Islands, both of which are situated in the North Atlantic Ocean. Denmark is low-lying and the climate is temperate, with mild summers and cold, rainy winters. The language is Danish. Almost all of the inhabitants profess Christianity: the Evangelical Lutheran Church, to which some 83% of the population belong, is the established Church, and there are also small communities of other Protestant groups and of Roman Catholics. The national flag (proportions 28 by 37) displays a white cross on a red background, the upright of the cross being to the left of centre. The capital is Copenhagen (København).

Recent History

In 1945, following the end of German wartime occupation, Denmark recognized the independence of Iceland, which had been declared in the previous year. Home rule was granted to the Faroe Islands in 1948 and to Greenland in 1979. Denmark was a founder member of the North Atlantic Treaty Organization (NATO, see p. 340) in 1949 and of the Nordic Council (see p. 424) in 1952. In January 1973, following a referendum, Denmark entered the European Communities (EC), now European Union (EU, see p. 244).

In 1947 King Frederik IX succeeded to the throne on the death of his father, Christian X. Denmark's Constitution was radically revised in 1953: new provisions allowed for female succession to the throne, abolished the upper house of the Folketing (parliament) and amended the franchise. King Frederik died in January 1972, and his eldest daughter, Margrethe II, became the first queen to rule Denmark for nearly 600 years.

The system of proportional representation, which is embodied in the 1953 Constitution, makes it difficult for a single party to gain a majority in the Folketing. The minority Government of Venstre (Liberals), led by Poul Hartling and formed in 1973, was followed in 1975 by a minority Government of the Socialdemokraterne (Social Democrats) under Anker Jørgensen. Jørgensen led various coalitions and minority Governments until 1982. General elections in 1977, 1979 and 1981 were held against a background of growing unemployment and attempts to tighten control of the economy. In September 1982 divisions within the Cabinet over Jørgensen's economic policy led the Government to resign.

Det Konservative Folkeparti (the Conservative People's Party), which had been absent from Danish coalitions since 1971, formed a centre-right four-party Government—with Venstre, the Centrum-Demokraterne (Centre Democrats) and the Kristeligt Folkeparti (Christian People's Party)—led by Poul Schlüter, who became Denmark's first Conservative Prime Minister since 1894. Holding only 66 of the Folketing's 179 seats, the coalition narrowly avoided defeat over its economic programme in October 1982 and again in September 1983, when larger reductions in public spending were proposed. In December the right-wing Fremskridtspartiet (Progress Party) withdrew its support for further cuts in expenditure, and the Government was defeated. A general election was held in January 1984 and Schlüter's Government remained in office, with its component parties holding a total of 77 seats, and relying on the support of members of Det Radikale Venstre (Social Liberals).

In January 1986 the left-wing parties in the Folketing combined to reject the ratification by Denmark of the Single European Act (which amended the Treaty of Rome—the agreement that founded the EC—so as to establish the EC's single market and allow the EC Council of Ministers to take decisions by a qualified majority vote if unanimity was not achieved). Opponents of ratification, led by the Socialdemokraterne, argued that it would lead to a diminution of Denmark's power to maintain strict environmental controls. In a national referendum in February, however, 56.2% of the votes cast were in favour of ratification of the Act, and the Folketing formally approved it in May.

At a general election held in September 1987 Schlüter's coalition retained 70 seats in the Folketing, while the opposition Socialdemokraterne lost two of their 56 seats. Jørgensen later resigned as leader of the latter party. Several smaller and extremist parties made considerable gains, thus weakening the outgoing coalition, while the main opposition parties were unable to command a working majority. Schlüter eventually formed a new Cabinet comprising representatives of the former governing coalition. However, Det Radikale Venstre had earlier declared that they would not support any administration that depended on the support of the Fremskridtspartiet.

In April 1988 the Folketing adopted an opposition-sponsored resolution requiring the Government to inform visiting warships of the country's ban on nuclear weapons. The British and US Governments were highly critical of the resolution. Schlüter consequently announced an early general election for May 1988, on the issue of Denmark's membership of NATO and defence policy. The election result was, however, inconclusive, and negotiations lasting three weeks were necessary before Schlüter was appointed to seek a basis for viable government. In early June a new minority coalition, comprising members of Det Konservative Folkeparti, Venstre and Det Radikale Venstre, formed a Cabinet under Schlüter. The new Government restored good relations with its NATO allies by adopting a formula that requested all visiting warships to respect Danish law in its territorial waters, while making no specific reference to nuclear weapons.

The Government proposed large reductions in social welfare provision for 1989, and attacked demands by the Fremskridtspartiet for less taxation as unrealistic. The Fremskridtspartiet, however, continued to increase in popularity, and in November 1989 its share of the vote rose significantly in municipal elections, while Det Konservative Folkeparti lost support. The Government, therefore, proposed to reduce the rates of taxation in 1990, despite opposition on the part of the Socialdemokraterne to the accompanying decreases in welfare expenditure. An early general election was organized for December 1990. Although the Socialdemokraterne retained the largest share of the vote (winning 69 seats), Schlüter formed a minority coalition Government, comprising Det Konservative Folkeparti, which had lost five seats in the election, and Venstre, which had gained an additional seven seats. As expected, Det Radikale Venstre, while no longer part of the Government, continued to support the majority of the new coalition Government's policies.

In May 1992 the Folketing voted, by 130 votes to 25, to approve the Treaty on European Union (the Maastricht Treaty), which further expanded the scope of the Treaty of Rome. In a national referendum held in June, however, 50.7% of the votes cast were against ratification of the Treaty. This unexpected result caused consternation among Denmark's European partners, and during the rest of the year discussions took place among representatives of EC countries, who sought to establish a formula that, without necessitating the renegotiation of the Treaty, would allow the Danish Government to conduct a second referendum with some hope of success. In December EC heads of government agreed that Denmark should be allowed exemption from certain provisions of the Treaty, namely the final stage of European Monetary Union (including the adoption of a single currency); participation in a common defence policy; common European citizenship; and co-operation in legal and home affairs. Despite uncertainty as to how far these exemptions were legally binding, the agreement was endorsed by seven of the eight parties represented in the Folketing (the exception being the Fremskridtspartiet), and in a second referendum, held in May 1993, 56.7% of the votes cast were in favour of ratification. In June 1994 the Government announced that it would seek an amendment to the Maastricht

Treaty to ensure that environmental safety took precedence over European free-trade initiatives.

Meanwhile, in January 1993 Schlüter resigned from the premiership after a judicial inquiry disclosed that he had misled the Folketing in April 1989 over a scandal that had its origin in 1987, when the then Minister of Justice, Erik Ninn-Hansen, had illegally ordered civil servants to delay issuing entry visas to the families of Tamil refugees from Sri Lanka. In subsequent negotiations between political parties, Poul Nyrup Rasmussen, the leader of the Socialdemokraterne, obtained sufficient support to form a new government, and in late January 1993 a majority coalition Government took office: it comprised members of the Socialdemokraterne and three small centre parties (Det Radikale Venstre, the Centrum-Demokraterne and the Kristeligt Folkeparti). The new Government gave priority to securing an affirmative vote for the Maastricht Treaty (see above).

In a general election held in September 1994, three months earlier than scheduled, the Socialdemokraterne won a reduced number of seats, although they retained the largest share of the vote. Venstre, led by Uffe Ellemann-Jensen, gained an additional 13 seats, but the Kristeligt Folkeparti, a member of the outgoing coalition, failed to secure representation in the new legislature. None the less, Nyrup Rasmussen was able to form a minority Government with his two remaining coalition partners, Det Radikale Venstre and the Centrum-Demokraterne, and denied that the Government would be dependent for support on the left-wing Socialistisk Folkeparti (SF, Socialist People's Party). In December 1996, however, the Centrum-Demokraterne withdrew from the coalition, following the Government's decision to seek support from left-wing parties in order to achieve parliamentary approval for legislation relating to the 1997 budget.

In February 1998 Nyrup Rasmussen announced that an early general election would be conducted on 11 March, in advance of a referendum on the Amsterdam Treaty on European integration (drafted at a meeting of EU members in the Netherlands in June 1997), which was scheduled to be held in late May. Despite the fact that the Centrum-Demokraterne supported an informal electoral alliance comprising Det Konservative Folkeparti and Venstre in the election, Nyrup Rasmussen's Government was returned to office with a narrow majority in the Folketing: the Socialdemokraterne, together with their coalition partner Det Radikale Venstre and other informal allies, secured a total of 90 seats, compared with 89 seats won by the centre-right opposition. The right-wing Dansk Folkeparti (Danish People's Party), which campaigned for stricter immigration controls, performed strongly in its first general election, winning 13 seats. Following Venstre's defeat in the general election, Ellemann-Jensen resigned as party leader and was replaced by Anders Fogh Rasmussen.

On 28 May 1998 Danish voters narrowly endorsed the ratification of the Amsterdam Treaty. The referendum followed the rejection in April by the Danish Supreme Court of a legal challenge to the constitutional validity of the Maastricht Treaty, which had been brought by a group of private individuals who were opposed to further European integration.

In early November 1999 serious rioting erupted in a district of Copenhagen which housed a high concentration of immigrants. The rioting, which was the most serious to occur in Denmark for six years, was reportedly provoked by an earlier judicial ruling, in accordance with which a man of Turkish origin became the first Danish-born person to receive an expulsion order from the country. (The man, convicted on charges of theft, had failed to apply for the Danish citizenship to which he was entitled.) The court decision was announced just days after the readmittance to the membership of the right-wing Fremskridtspartiet of the party's founder, Mogens Glistrup, who was renowned for his vociferous opposition to immigration; Glistrup's extreme racist sentiments, expressed following the court ruling, led, later in November, to the resignation from the party of all four of its representatives in the Folketing, leaving the Fremskridtspartiet with no parliamentary representation.

On 28 September 2000 the Government held a national referendum regarding adoption of the single European currency, the euro. Approval for the euro had been strong when the referendum was called in May, but had declined throughout the months preceding the vote, despite the support of the Government, the majority of the major political parties, the industrial sector, banks, trade unions, and the media. In the event, 53.1% of the votes cast were opposed to membership of the single currency; the rate of participation was 87.5%. Immediately thereafter the central bank raised interest rates by 0.5% to defend the krone; opposition parties claimed the move was politically motivated in order to vindicate views expressed by supporters of the euro prior to the referendum.

At a general election held on 20 November 2001, four months earlier than scheduled, the Socialdemokraterne won 52 seats in the Folketing, meaning that, for the first time since 1920, it was no longer the party with the largest representation in the legislature. Venstre won 56 seats and, under Fogh Rasmussen, formed a minority coalition Government with Det Konservative Folkeparti, which secured 16 seats. The Dansk Folkeparti performed well, winning 22 seats; the leaders of Venstre stressed, however, that the far-right, anti-immigration party would not exert any influence over government policy. Nevertheless, by the end of November 2001 the Government had announced its intention to remove the legal right of refugees to bring their families to Denmark, to extend the period of residence required to obtain a residence permit from three to seven years, and to deport immediately all immigrants convicted of crimes—all of which was to be financed primarily by a privatization programme and a substantial reduction in development aid. A new Ministry of Refugee, Immigration and Integration Affairs was also created. The proposed legislation came into force, with the support of the Dansk Folkeparti, in July 2002. Following the 2001 general election there was a period of internecine struggle within the Socialdemokraterne, which culminated in Nyrup Rasmussen's resignation as party leader in November 2002 and his replacement by Mogens Lykketoft.

Following the publication of a draft new constitution of the EU in May 2003, which was intended to promote the smooth functioning of the organization following the accession of 10 new member states in May 2004, the Prime Minister announced that Danish citizens would be granted a referendum on its contents. With other smaller members, the Danish Government was concerned to protect the role of less populous EU member states. Of particular concern were plans for a permanent president for the Council of the EU to replace the existing system of a six-month rotating presidency, and the proposal to limit the number of Commissioners in the future, both of which, it was feared, would diminish the role of smaller nations. In late February 2005, following his party's re-election to power (see below), Fogh Rasmussen announced that a national referendum would be held on 27 September on whether to endorse the proposed EU constitution. However, following the rejection of the proposed constitution at referendums in France and the Netherlands in mid-2005, plans for a Danish referendum were postponed indefinitely. In October 2007 an agreement was reached over a new treaty to replace the rejected constitutional treaty during an informal summit of the European Council in Lisbon, Portugal. On 11 December Fogh Rasmussen announced that the new treaty, the Treaty of Lisbon, would be ratified by members of the Folketing; the decision was supported both by the Socialdemokraterne and by Det Radikale Venstre and followed a report published by the Ministry of Justice, in which it was claimed that a referendum was unnecessary. The new treaty, which was expected to be ratified by early 2009, was signed by the heads of state and of government of the 27 EU member states during a summit meeting, held in Lisbon. Meanwhile, in November 2007, following the general election (see below), Fogh Rasmussen confirmed his intention to hold a referendum during the next parliamentary term over the four exemptions from the provisions of the Maastricht Treaty—the adoption of the euro, participation in a common defence policy, common European citizenship and co-operation in legal and home affairs—that had been negotiated in 1992 to secure the ratification of the Treaty.

Despite bitter opposition, the Government, with the support of the Dansk Folkeparti, proposed controversial legislation in June 2004 to replace the 14 county authorities with five new administrative regions and to reduce the number of municipalities from 271 to 98. The new regions were to have responsibility for hospital administration, general urban planning, collective transportation and several social welfare institutions. Most of the remaining policy areas currently handled by counties were to be dealt with by municipal authorities. In October the opposition parties jointly submitted a resolution demanding that the Government reschedule the general election, which was due to be held in 2005, so that it took place prior to the parliamentary vote on the proposed reforms in the first half of 2005. The motion was defeated by 57 votes to 49.

In mid-January 2005, however, Prime Minister Fogh Rasmussen announced that the general election would indeed be held early, on 8 February, citing the forthcoming ballot on the municipal reforms. There followed a brief period of campaigning during which the election was presented as a quasi-presidential contest between Fogh Rasmussen and Lykketoft. In the event, however, both Venstre and the Socialdemokraterne lost support to the other, smaller parties. At the election Venstre won 52 seats, constituting a loss of four seats, compared with the 2001 election, but enough to secure victory as the party with the largest representation in the Folketing; Fogh Rasmussen thus became the first ever Venstre Prime Minister to win a second term, and renewed his party's governing coalition with Det Konservative Folkeparti (which secured 18 seats). The Socialdemokraterne won 47 seats, representing a loss of five seats; Lykketoft subsequently resigned as party leader and was replaced by Helle Thorning-Schmidt. The Dansk Folkeparti increased its representation in the legislature to 24 seats, while Det Radikale Venstre made the largest gain, winning 17 seats. Fogh Rasmussen reorganized his Cabinet later that month, although the most senior positions remained unchanged. The legislation on municipal reform was adopted during the first half of 2005, and entered into force on 1 January 2007.

The newspaper *Jyllands-Posten* provoked considerable anger among Muslim communities by printing 12 caricatures of the Prophet Muhammad at the end of September 2005. Depiction of Muhammad is forbidden by Islamic tradition, but the cartoons in *Jyllands-Posten* were considered particularly offensive. Protests against the publication of the caricatures took place in Denmark and a number of predominantly Muslim countries. Despite receiving death threats against its staff, the editors of the newspaper refused to issue an apology. In October the Prime Minister declined to meet 11 ambassadors from countries opposed to the caricatures' publication, stating that he neither possessed nor desired the power to limit the freedom of the press. Tensions were heightened when a radical Islamist cleric, who had been granted asylum in Denmark, led a delegation to the Middle East in December, in an attempt to widen support for the protests. Included in the documents that he showed to delegates at a meeting of the Organization of the Islamic Conference (OIC) and which provoked further condemnation of the cartoons, were three offensive images that had not been published by the press in Denmark. In late January 2006 Saudi Arabia recalled its ambassador to Denmark and Libya closed its embassy in Copenhagen, citing the Danish Government's failure to intervene in the matter. At the end of the month the editors of *Jyllands-Posten* finally apologized for causing offence (although not for publishing the caricatures). Fogh Rasmussen welcomed the apology, but again defended the freedom of the press; meanwhile, the interior ministers of 17 Arab states issued a statement urging the Danish Government to punish those responsible for the cartoons and their publication. Muslim outrage over the images continued to escalate in February, as they were reprinted by publications in several other European countries. Many Muslims boycotted Danish goods and violent anti-Danish protests took place in several countries, while the Danish embassies in Syria, Lebanon and Iran were attacked. The Iranian Government recalled its ambassador from Copenhagen and announced that it was suspending all trade links with Denmark. (The ambassador returned in April.) In early February the Ministry of Foreign Affairs advised Danes not to travel to Saudi Arabia, Syria or Yemen, and to avoid visiting a further 15 countries unless strictly necessary. Meanwhile, the Prime Minister appeared on an Arabic television station to apologize for offence caused by the caricatures, while defending freedom of expression. On the following day he held a meeting with all foreign ambassadors in Copenhagen in a further attempt to ease tensions. However, protests continued world-wide, and in mid-February the Danish embassies in Indonesia, Iran, Lebanon, Pakistan and Syria were temporarily closed owing to security concerns. By late 2007 tensions over the cartoons appeared to have dissipated. However, in early February 2008 Danish police arrested three men on suspicion of planning to murder one of the artists responsible for the cartoons. On the following day several of Denmark's major daily newspapers, including *Jyllands-Posten*, reprinted the cartoons, citing support for freedom of speech.

As a minority coalition, the Government continued to rely, as it had since 2001, on the parliamentary support of the populist, anti-immigrant Dansk Folkeparti, giving the party significant influence over government policy. In June 2006, however, the Government secured cross-party support for an agreement to reform the welfare system. The reforms aimed to reduce social security expenditure and increase the labour supply to address the fiscal implications of an ageing population.

In May 2007 a prominent member of the Folketing for Det Radikale Venstre, Naser Khader, resigned from that party and announced the formation of a new party, Ny Alliance (New Alliance), which, according to Khader and his two co-founders, Anders Samuelsen (formerly of Det Radikale Venstre) and Gitte Seeberg (previously of Det Konservative Folkeparti), would aim to reduce the influence of the Dansk Folkeparti on government policy. Following a period of internal conflict within Det Radikale Venstre, in June the party leader, Marianne Jelved, resigned. She was replaced by Margrethe Vestager.

In early September 2007 Danish police arrested eight men of Middle Eastern and African origin in Copenhagen on suspicion of plotting imminent bomb attacks within Denmark and of possessing explosive materials. Later that month the Prime Minister effected a minor reorganization of his Government. Karen Jespersen, formerly the Minister of Social Affairs in 1993–2000 under Nyrup Rasmussen, was appointed as Minister of Social Affairs and of Gender Equality, replacing Eva Kjer Hansen, who became Minister for Food, Agriculture and Fisheries. Jakob Axel Nielsen, of Det Konservative Folkeparti, entered the Government as Minister of Transport and Energy. In late October 2007 Fogh Rasmussen announced that legislative elections were to take place in November, some two years before the scheduled end of the parliamentary term, citing forthcoming cross-party negotiations over welfare reform.

At the general election, which took place on 13 November 2007, the two main parties again lost support to smaller rivals. None the less, Venstre remained the strongest party in the Folketing, winning 46 seats (26.3% of the valid votes cast), while its partner in the outgoing coalition Government, Det Konservative Folkeparti, retained its 18 seats in the legislature (10.4%). The Socialdemokraterne lost one seat, winning 45 seats (25.5% of the votes cast). The results of the smaller parties confounded the expectations of many observers. The Dansk Folkeparti increased its representation in the Folketing to 25 seats (13.9% of the votes cast), while the SF made the most significant gains of any party, claiming some 23 seats (13.0%). However, Ny Alliance performed poorly compared with its ratings in opinion polls prior to the election, winning only five seats (2.8%), and was outperformed by Det Radikale Venstre, which nevertheless lost almost half of its seats, taking nine (5.1%).

Following discussions between all of the major parties, on 23 November 2007 Fogh Rasmussen announced the renewal of the minority coalition between Venstre and Det Konservative Folkeparti and effected a cabinet reorganization. Among the most notable changes were the appointment of Venstre's Lars Løkke Rasmussen (hitherto Minister of the Interior and Health) as Minister of Finance, and the creation of a new Ministry of Climate and Energy, under Connie Hedegaard of Det Konservative Folkeparti, previously Minister of the Environment and Nordic Co-operation. The family, gender equality, interior and social affairs portfolios were merged under a new Ministry of Social Welfare, while a separate Ministry of Health and Prevention was also created.

The coalition parties' poor performance at the general election required the Government to continue to rely upon parliamentary support from Dansk Folkeparti. The decision of a member of Det Konservative Folkeparti to leave that party in December 2007 and to remain in the Folketing as an independent increased the Government's reliance on the smaller parties, prompting concerns of perpetual disagreement with regard to the Government's programme, particularly over asylum and immigration. In mid-January 2008 the coalition Government concluded an agreement with the Dansk Folkeparti over a reform of asylum policy that would allow a small number of unsuccessful asylum seekers who had so far been unable to return to their countries of origin to live in private accommodation. Opposition parties, including Ny Alliance, were excluded from the talks and subsequently accused the Government of reneging on a promise to hold cross-party talks after the election. Nevertheless, later that month Khader announced that his party would vote in favour of the proposals, stating that Ny Alliance was a centre-right party and would thus support the governing coalition. This statement prompted Seeberg to resign from the party at the end of that month, citing her opposition to Ny Alliance's implicit co-operation with the Dansk Folkeparti. In early February Khader was forced to announce a temporary 'pause for reflection' within Ny Alliance after another of its parliamentarians left the party to join Venstre, but two weeks later he confirmed that the party intended to continue in its present form.

In May 1999 the Danish Government signed a maritime boundary agreement with representatives of the Faroese and British Governments, thus ending a 30-year dispute over the location of the boundaries of an area covering 42,000 sq km in the North Sea, which was potentially rich in petroleum reserves.

Following the dissolution of the USSR at the end of 1991, Denmark rapidly established diplomatic relations with the former Soviet Baltic states of Estonia, Latvia and Lithuania, and was a founder member of the Council of Baltic Sea States (see p. 224), established in 1992.

The Danish Government contributed a warship, a submarine and 160 troops to the US-led military operation in Iraq to remove the regime of Saddam Hussain in early 2003. Deep public divisions over the Government's support for the invasion were reflected in the Folketing: only 93 members voted to approve the deployment of troops, a motion which was passed only with the support of the Dansk Folkeparti. Following the collapse of Saddam Hussain's regime in April, a 410-strong Danish peace-keeping force was dispatched to Iraq and was stationed near Basra (in southern Iraq) under British command. The Government was also involved in plans for the post-war redevelopment of Iraq. In late April 2004 the Minister of Defence, Svend Aage Jensby, resigned amid allegations made by the opposition that the Danish military authorities had exaggerated the threat posed by Saddam Hussain in an attempt to justify the military action in Iraq; Jensby was replaced by Søren Gade Jensen. The mandate for Danish troops in Iraq was extended for successive periods of six months until January 2006, with the support of the Dansk Folkeparti, the Socialdemokraterne and Det Radikale Venstre. However, the latter two parties insisted that they would not agree to any further extensions beyond that for July agreed in January, urging the Government to prepare a strategy for the withdrawal of Danish troops from Iraq. The Folketing concurrently approved a government proposal to send an additional 200 soldiers to participate in the NATO-led International Security Assistance Force (ISAF) in Afghanistan, bringing the number of Danish troops deployed in that country to some 360.

A government proposal to reduce the number of Danish troops in Iraq by 80 was approved by the Folketing in May 2006; the legislature also voted to extend the mandate of the remaining Danish contingent in Iraq by 12 months. In February 2007 the Prime Minister announced that all Danish troops were to be withdrawn from Iraq by August of that year. However, a replacement contingent of around 50 troops and advisers would undertake an observer mission in that country. (The withdrawal of troops from Iraq was completed as planned on 1 August.) Meanwhile, Fogh Rasmussen suggested that a significant number of those troops withdrawn from Iraq would join the ISAF mission in Afghanistan later in the year, and on 1 June 2007 the Folketing approved a two-stage deployment of Danish troops that increased the size of the Danish contingent in Afghanistan to 420 by August and to 520 by October.

In October 2004 the Minister of Science, Technology and Innovation, Helge Sander, announced that Denmark would attempt to prove that the seabed beneath the North Pole (the Polar Basin) was a natural continuation of Greenland and that Denmark could thus claim legal ownership of any natural resources discovered there. Denmark allocated 150m. kroner for the Polar Basin project, which was being conducted in co-operation with the Governments of the Faroe Islands and Greenland. However, other claimants to the Pole (currently considered international territory) included Canada, Norway, Russia and the USA. In July 2005 the Danish Government made a formal protest to the Canadian ambassador after the Canadian Minister of National Defence landed on Hans Island without first notifying the Danish Government. The sovereignty of the island—an uninhabited, rocky outcrop in the Nares Strait between Canada's Ellesmere Island and north-west Greenland—had been in dispute for more than 30 years, and would affect Denmark's claim for ownership of the North Pole. Two weeks later it was reported that a Danish naval vessel was sailing to Hans Island from the Grønnedal naval base in southern Greenland in order to enforce Danish sovereignty, although the Danish navy stated that the journey was an annual event and had not been prompted by the diplomatic dispute. In September the ministers responsible for foreign affairs of both countries agreed to hold talks on sovereignty and to inform each other of any activities around the island.

Government

Denmark is a constitutional monarchy. Under the 1953 constitutional charter, legislative power is held jointly by the hereditary monarch (who has no personal political power) and the unicameral Folketing (parliament), which has 179 members, including 175 from metropolitan Denmark and two each from the Faroe Islands and Greenland. Members are elected for four years (subject to dissolution) on the basis of proportional representation. Executive power is exercised by the monarch through a Cabinet, which is led by the Prime Minister and is responsible to the Folketing. Following municipal reforms which came into effect on 1 January 2007, Denmark comprises five administrative regions, one city and one borough, all with elected regional councils, and 98 municipalities (see Recent History).

Defence

As assessed at November 2007, Denmark maintained an army of 14,240 (including 6,000 conscripts), a navy of 3,650 (350 conscripts) and an air force of 3,830 (440 conscripts). There was, in addition, a volunteer Home Guard (Hjemmeværnet) numbering some 53,700. Military service is compulsory and lasts for a period of 4–10 months. Denmark abandoned its neutrality after the Second World War and has been a member of the North Atlantic Treaty Organization (NATO, see p. 340) since 1949. In 1992 Denmark assumed observer status in Western European Union (WEU, see p. 426). The defence budget for 2007 was 22,700m. kroner.

Economic Affairs

In 2006, according to estimates by the World Bank, Denmark's gross national income (GNI), measured at average 2004–06 prices, was US $280,677m., equivalent to US $51,700 per head (or $36,460 per head on an international purchasing-power parity basis). During 1996–2006 Denmark's population grew at an average annual rate of 0.3%, while gross domestic product (GDP) per head increased, in real terms, at an average rate of 1.8% per year. Overall GDP increased, in real terms, at an average annual rate of 2.1% in 1996–2006; growth was 3.2% in 2006.

Agriculture (including forestry and fishing) contributed 1.6% of GDP in 2006 and employed 3.0% of the economically active population in 2004. The principal activities are pig-farming and dairy farming; Denmark is a major exporter of pork products, and exports of meat and meat preparations accounted for 5.5% of total export revenue in 2006. Most of Denmark's agricultural production is exported, and the sector accounted for 8.8% of total exports in 2006. The fishing industry accounted for 3.1% of total export earnings in 2006 and engaged 0.1% of the employed labour force in 2004. Agricultural GDP increased, in real terms, at an average annual rate of 1.2% in 1996–2005; the GDP of the sector increased by 1.7% in 2005.

Industry (including mining, manufacturing, construction, power and water) provided 26.0% of GDP in 2006 and employed 23.5% of the working population in 2004. Industrial GDP increased, in real terms, at an average annual rate of 1.0% in 1996–2005; it declined marginally, by just 0.03% in 2004, before increasing by 1.1% in 2005.

Mining provided 3.6% of GDP in 2006 and accounted for only 0.2% of employment in 2004. Denmark has few natural resources, but exploration for petroleum reserves in the Danish sector of the North Sea in the 1970s proved successful. Natural gas has also been extensively exploited. There is a significant reserve of sand in north-western Jutland which could potentially be exploited for rich yields of titanium, zirconium and yttrium. The GDP of the mining sector increased, in real terms, at an average annual rate of 1.0% in 2002–05; the sector's GDP grew by 0.5% in 2005.

Manufacturing contributed 14.6% of GDP in 2006 and employed 16.0% of the working population in 2004. Measured by value of turnover, in 2006 the most important manufacturing industries were food products (accounting for 22.3% of the total), non-electric machinery and equipment (12.5%), electronic components (12.5%), chemicals and pharmaceuticals (10.5%), metal products (8.4%) and computers and electric motors (7.5%). Manufacturing GDP increased, in real terms, at an average annual rate of 0.5% in 1996–2004; it declined by 3.7% in 2003 and 2.6% in 2004.

Energy is derived principally from petroleum and natural gas. Since 1997 Denmark has produced enough energy to satisfy its domestic consumption. In 2005 crude petroleum production amounted to 131m. barrels and total gas output was 9,500m.

DENMARK

Introductory Survey

cu m. In 2006 imports of mineral fuels accounted for 6.6% of the total cost of imports, while exports of mineral fuels contributed 11.6% of total export revenue. In 2004 46.1% of electricity was produced from coal, 24.7% from natural gas and 4.0% from petroleum. The use of renewable sources of energy (including wind power) has been encouraged. In 2006 Denmark derived 15% of its energy from renewable sources (mostly wind-turbines), and planned to increase the share to 30% by 2025.

Services provided 72.4% of GDP in 2006 and engaged 73.2% of the employed population in 2004. Shipping is an important sector in Denmark. In real terms, the combined GDP of the service sectors increased at an average rate of 2.3% per year in 1996–2005; it rose by 3.3% in 2005.

In 2006, according to the IMF, Denmark recorded a visible trade surplus of US $2,906m. and a surplus of $6,696m. on the current account of the balance of payments. Most Danish trade is with the other member states of the European Union (EU, see p. 244), which accounted for 72.5% of imports and 69.3% of exports in 2006. The principal source of imports in 2006 was Germany (contributing 21.5% of the total); other major suppliers were Sweden (14.3%), the Netherlands (6.2%) and the United Kingdom (5.8%). Germany was also the principal market for exports (accounting for 16.8% of the total); other major purchasers included Sweden (14.2%), the United Kingdom (9.0%) and the USA (6.7%). The principal exports in 2006 were machinery and transport equipment (accounting for 27.4% of total export revenue), food and live animals (16.0%), miscellaneous manufactured articles (15.9%) and chemicals and related products (12.7%). The principal imports in 2006 were machinery and transport equipment (accounting for 36.1% of total import costs), basic manufactures (16.7%), miscellaneous manufactured articles (14.7%) and chemicals and related products (10.8%).

In 2006 there was a budget surplus of 60,072m. kroner, equivalent to 4.2% of GDP. Public sector debt was equivalent to 36% of GDP in 2005. The average annual rate of inflation was 2.1% in 1996–2006. Consumer prices increased by 1.7% in 2007. The rate of unemployment was 4.1% in 2006.

Denmark is a member of the EU, the Nordic Council (see p. 424) and the Nordic Council of Ministers (see p. 424).

Denmark is a small open economy, which is highly dependent on trade with other countries. Owing to its reliance on trade, a principal objective of the country's economic policy has been to maintain a stable exchange rate. Denmark did not, however, participate in the EU's programme of Economic and Monetary Union (EMU), although it has maintained a stable rate of exchange with the common European currency, the euro. As a result of the reforms embarked upon in the 1980s, Denmark has enjoyed sustained economic growth, low unemployment and a generous system of social welfare provisions. The reforms created a system known as flexicurity, which emphasizes both flexibility for employers, allowing them to hire or dismiss workers easily while keeping labour costs low, and security for employees, by providing for government-subsidized retraining programmes and generous unemployment benefits. As in many other EU countries in the mid-2000s, Denmark was faced with a serious challenge to the long-term prospects of its economy as a result of demographic changes, resulting in a smaller labour force and a larger elderly population, a combination which would affect the sustainability of public finances. An agreement to reform the welfare system was reached in June 2006, which included the gradual increase in the retirement and early retirement ages to 67 and 62 years respectively and measures to increase the labour supply, including improved job opportunities for older workers, an increase in the participation of immigrants in the work-force and a reduction of restrictions on some foreign workers. However, restrictions on the freedom of movement of workers from the eight Central and Eastern European countries that joined the EU in May 2004 were extended for up to three more years in 2006. The priority of the Government that was re-elected in November 2007 remained the reform of the welfare system and the public services, which led to an expansionary fiscal policy. The other principal consideration of the Government remained widespread labour shortages. The Government introduced measures to increase the supply of labour, with particular emphasis on encouraging students and older workers into employment. Modest reductions in income tax, which were to take effect in 2008–09, were also aimed at stimulating labour supply. A commission to examine further methods to reform and reduce income tax was established in late 2007. The shortage of labour was expected to result in higher wage increases in the short term, which would contribute to the decline in competitiveness of Danish industries. GDP growth, which had been robust in 2004–06, declined slightly in 2007 and was expected to slow further in 2008.

Education

Education is compulsory for nine years between seven and 16 years of age. The State is obliged to offer a pre-school class and a 10th voluntary year. In 2005/06 enrolment at pre-primary level was equivalent to 94% of children in the relevant age-group. State-subsidized private schools are available, but about 90% of pupils attend municipal schools. Primary and lower secondary education begins at seven years of age and lasts for nine (optionally 10) years. This includes at least six years at primary school. Enrolment at primary level included 96% (males 95%; females 96%) of those in the relevant age-group in 2005/06. Secondary education is divided into two cycles of three years, the first beginning at 13 years of age, the second at the age of 16 or 17. Students may transfer to vocational courses at this stage. Total enrolment at secondary level in 2005/06 included 91% of those in the relevant age-group (males 90%; females 92%). There are eight universities and many other institutions of further and higher education. Higher education institutions are categorized either as colleges, which offer mainly vocational courses, or as universities. In addition, the traditional folk high schools offer a wide range of further education opportunities, which do not confer any professional qualification. In 2005/06 enrolment at tertiary level was equivalent to 81% of those in the relevant age-group (males 68%; females 94%). In 2007 general government expenditure on education totalled an estimated 129,949m. kroner, representing 15.1% of total budget spending.

Public Holidays

2008: 1 January (New Year's Day), 20–24 March (Easter), 18 April (General Prayer Day), 1 May (Ascension Day), 12 May (Whit Monday), 5 June (Constitution Day), 24–26 December (Christmas).

2009: 1 January (New Year's Day), 9–13 April (Easter), 8 May (General Prayer Day), 21 May (Ascension Day), 1 June (Whit Monday), 5 June (Constitution Day), 24–26 December (Christmas).

Weights and Measures

The metric system is in force.

Statistical Survey

Source (unless otherwise stated): Danmarks Statistik, Sejrøgade 11, POB 2550, 2100 Copenhagen Ø; tel. 39-17-39-17; fax 39-17-39-99; e-mail dst@dst.dk; internet www.dst.dk.

Note: The figures in this survey relate only to metropolitan Denmark, excluding the Faroe Islands (see p. 1548) and Greenland (see p. 1554), figures for which are dealt with in separate chapters.

Area and Population

AREA, POPULATION AND DENSITY

Area (sq km)	43,098*
Population (census results)	
1 January 1991	5,146,469
1 January 2001	
Males	2,644,319
Females	2,704,893
Total	5,349,212
Population (official estimate at 1 January)	
2006	5,427,459
2007	5,447,084
2008	5,475,791
Density (per sq km) at 1 January 2008	127.1

* 16,640 sq miles.

ADMINISTRATIVE DIVISIONS
(At 1 January 2008)

Region	Area (sq km)	Population	Density (per sq km)
Hovedstaden	2,561.3	1,645,825	642.6
Midtjylland	13,124.3	1,237,041	94.3
Nordjylland	7,933.3	578,839	73.0
Sjælland	7,273.2	819,427	112.7
Syddanmark	12,206.2	1,194,659	97.9
Total	43,098.3	5,475,791	127.1

PRINCIPAL MUNICIPALITIES
(population at 1 January 2007)

København (Copenhagen, the capital)	503,699	Roskilde	81,017
Århus (Aarhus)	296,170	Næstved	80,133
Aalborg	194,149	Horsens	79,020
Odense	186,745	Slagelse	76,949
Esbjerg	114,148	Sønderborg	76,825
Vejle	104,101	Holbæk	68,451
Randers	92,984	Hjørring	67,118
Frederiksborg (Frederiksberg)	92,234	Guldborgsund	63,540
Viborg	91,405	Frederikshavn	62,877
Kolding	87,183	Helsingør	61,012
Silkeborg	86,540	Aabenraa	60,044
Herning	83,598		

BIRTHS, MARRIAGES AND DEATHS

	Registered live births		Registered marriages		Registered deaths	
	Number	Rate (per 1,000)	Number	Rate (per 1,000)	Number	Rate (per 1,000)
2000	67,084	12.6	38,844	7.3	57,998	10.9
2001	65,458	12.2	36,567	6.8	58,355	10.9
2002	64,075	11.9	37,210	6.9	58,610	10.9
2003	64,599	12.0	35,041	6.5	57,574	10.7
2004	64,609	11.9	37,711	7.0	55,806	10.3
2005	64,282	11.9	36,148	6.7	54,962	10.1
2006	64,984	12.0	36,452	6.7	55,477	10.2
2007	64,082	11.8	n.a.	n.a.	55,604	10.2

Expectation of life (years at birth, WHO estimates): 78.0 (males 75.6; females 80.4) in 2005 (Source: WHO, *World Health Statistics*).

ECONOMICALLY ACTIVE POPULATION
(sample surveys, '000 persons aged 15 to 66 years, April–June)

	2004	2005	2006
Agriculture, hunting and forestry	81.2	80.4	79.4
Fishing	3.4	n.a.	n.a.
Mining and quarrying	4.3	n.a.	5.6
Manufacturing	434.5	442.3	427.6
Electricity, gas and water supply	15.9	15.2	16.6
Construction	184.5	192.5	201.2
Wholesale and retail trade; repair of motor vehicles, motorcycles and personal and household goods	406.3	400.8	409.1
Hotels and restaurants	68.9	69.7	76.7
Transport, storage and communications	185.5	175.3	176.1
Financial intermediation	81.3	88.9	93.0
Real estate, renting and business activities	248.0	253.4	275.9
Public administration and defence; compulsory social security	163.8	166.7	168.2
Education	213.0	216.1	211.1
Health and social work	480.6	474.8	486.9
Other community, social and personal service activities	140.5	141.6	150.7
Private households with employed persons	3.2	n.a.	n.a.
Extra-territorial organizations and bodies	1.6	n.a.	n.a.
Activities not adequately defined	3.9	3.7	n.a.
Total employed	2,720.1	2,732.8	2,786.6
Unemployed	162.6	143.3	117.9
Total labour force	2,882.7	2,876.1	2,904.5
Males	1,531.5	1,525.6	1,600.2
Females	1,351.2	1,350.5	1,304.3

Source: ILO.

Health and Welfare

KEY INDICATORS

Total fertility rate (children per woman, 2005)	1.8
Under-5 mortality rate (per 1,000 live births, 2005)	5
HIV/AIDS (% of persons aged 15–49, 2005)	0.2
Physicians (per 1,000 head, 2002)	2.93
Hospital beds (per 1,000 head, 2003)	4.0
Health expenditure (2004): US $ per head (PPP)	2,779.6
Health expenditure (2004): % of GDP	8.6
Health expenditure (2004): public (% of total)	82.3
Human Development Index (2005): ranking	14
Human Development Index (2005): value	0.949

For sources and definitions, see explanatory note on p. vi.

DENMARK

Statistical Survey

Agriculture

PRINCIPAL CROPS
('000 metric tons)

	2004	2005	2006
Wheat	4,758.5	4,887.2	4,801.6
Barley	3,589.1	3,797.2	3,270.3
Rye	146.2	132.0	130.0
Oats	309.9	315.0	274.1
Triticale (wheat-rye hybrid)	159.5	151.6	156.3
Potatoes	1,629.4	1,576.4	1,361.2
Sugar beet	2,828.6	2,762.6	2,314.2
Dry peas	83.3	43.2	26.2
Other pulses	12.7	9.8	6.0
Rapeseed	468.1	342.2	434.7
Cabbages	28.0	27.6	24.6
Lettuce	9.8	10.2	10.2
Tomatoes	20.7	17.6	17.6
Cucumbers and gherkins	18.7	19.0	19.0
Dry onions	53.0	53.0	55.7
Green peas	13.5	14.4	9.1
Carrots	62.8	62.8	69.1
Apples	35.3	35.3	31.8

Aggregate production ('000 metric tons, may include official, semi-official or estimated data): Total cereals 8,963 in 2004, 9,283 in 2005, 8,632 in 2006; Total roots and tubers 1,629 in 2004, 1,576 in 2005, 1,361 in 2006; Total vegetables (incl. melons) 254 in 2004, 253 in 2005, 253 in 2006; Total fruits (excl. melons) 71 in 2004, 73 in 2005, 72 in 2006.

Source: FAO.

LIVESTOCK
(at May)

	2004	2005	2006
Horses	39,209	47,472	52,882
Cattle	1,645,764	1,544,296	1,572,000
Pigs	13,233,235	13,466,283	12,604,000
Sheep	140,950	169,000	206,000
Chickens ('000 head)	16,136	16,901	16,826
Turkeys ('000 head)	149	115	122
Ducks ('000 head)	299	314	295
Geese ('000 head)	14	20	6

LIVESTOCK PRODUCTS
('000 metric tons)

	2004	2005	2006
Cattle meat	150	136	129
Pig meat	1,810	1,793	1,749
Chicken meat	187	183	166
Cows' milk	4,569	4,584	4,627
Butter	47	n.a.	n.a.
Cheese	336	n.a.	n.a.
Hen eggs	83	80	77

Source: FAO.

Forestry

ROUNDWOOD REMOVALS
('000 cu m, excl. bark)

	2004	2005	2006
Sawlogs, veneer logs and logs for sleepers	386	1,006	671
Pulpwood	165	651	500
Other industrial wood	17	25	26
Fuel wood	948	1,281	1,162
Total	**1,516**	**2,963**	**2,358**

Source: FAO.

SAWNWOOD PRODUCTION
('000 cu m, incl. railway sleepers)

	2003	2004	2005*
Coniferous (softwood)	225	175	175
Broadleaved (hardwood)	23	21	21
Total	**248**	**196**	**196**

* FAO estimates.

2006: Figures assumed to be unchanged from 2005 (FAO estimates).

Source: FAO.

Fishing

('000 metric tons, live weight)

	2003	2004	2005
Capture	1,036.2	1,090.0	910.6
Norway pout	23.0	13.6	n.a.
Blue whiting (Poutassou)	88.0	89.5	39.1
Sandeels (Sandlances)	283.2	299.6	157.1
Atlantic herring	114.8	136.8	167.5
European sprat	262.1	274.1	329.8
Blue mussel	92.5	99.5	69.2
Aquaculture	37.8	42.8	39.0
Rainbow trout	35.3	40.5	36.6
Total catch	**1,073.9**	**1,132.7**	**949.6**

Source: FAO.

Mining

('000 metric tons, unless otherwise indicated)

	2003	2004	2005
Crude petroleum (million barrels)	133	135	131
Natural gas (million cu m)*	8,300	9,000	9,500
Limestone (agricultural)	700	700	700
Chalk	1,900	1,950	1,950
Salt	605	610	610
Peat	295	296	298

* Figures refer to gross output; marketable production (estimate, million cu m) was 7,300 in 2003.

Source: US Geological Survey.

DENMARK

Industry

SELECTED PRODUCTS
('000 metric tons, unless otherwise indicated)

	2003	2004	2005
Pig meat:			
Fresh, chilled or frozen	1,216	1,274	1,240
Salted, dried or smoked	127	105	266
Poultry meat and offals	199	192	173
Fish fillets, etc.: fresh, chilled, frozen	65	61	61
Salami, sausages, etc.	85	74	67
Beet and cane sugar (solid)	512	453	509
Beer ('000 hectolitres)	8,352	8,550	n.a.
Flours, meals and pastes of fish	258	302	320
Oil cake and meal	160	249	291
Cigarettes (million)	12,897	13,459	14,867
Cement	2,642	2,946	2,923
Motor spirit (petrol) (million litres)	2,461	2,231	2,526
Gas oils	3,544	3,146	3,253
Motor and fuel oils	1,709	1,857	1,567
Asphalt for road surfaces	2,656	3,706	3,869
Washing powders, softeners, etc.	150	141	134
Refrigerators for household use ('000)	42	35	30

Finance

CURRENCY AND EXCHANGE RATES

Monetary Units
100 øre = 1 Danish krone (plural: kroner).

Sterling, Dollar and Euro Equivalents (31 December 2007)
£1 sterling = 10.168 kroner;
US $1 = 5.075 kroner;
€1 = 7.471 kroner;
100 Danish kroner = £9.83 = $19.70 = €13.38.

Average Exchange Rate (kroner per US $)
2005   5.9969
2006   5.9468
2007   5.4435

GENERAL BUDGET
(million kroner, estimates)

Revenue	2004	2005	2006
Income taxes	435,996	477,782	475,092
Personal income tax	365,992	381,469	402,364
Corporation tax	46,504	59,275	59,010
Real interest tax	23,499	37,038	13,717
Social security contributions	17,090	17,138	17,561
Other labour market contributions	2,895	2,907	3,169
Current taxes on wealth and real property	25,974	26,753	28,529
Taxes on goods and services	235,488	254,747	270,712
VAT	143,277	155,466	167,600
Taxes on specific goods	72,929	76,343	79,404
Stamp duty	6,531	8,577	8,667
Other taxes	133	144	148
Other current revenue	101,550	102,568	100,652
Capital revenue (incl. taxes)	12,158	9,991	9,434
Total	831,284	892,030	905,297

Expenditure	2004	2005	2006
General public services	109,043	105,452	106,188
Defence	23,686	24,015	25,644
Public order and safety	15,008	15,796	16,310
Education	120,223	123,365	124,471
Health	101,832	106,781	114,568
Social protection	337,184	346,345	346,868
Housing and community amenities	9,538	9,233	9,720
Religious, recreational and cultural services	26,135	24,844	25,430
Economic services	53,243	55,829	58,449
Environmental protection	7,534	8,539	8,577
Total	803,427	820,199	836,225

INTERNATIONAL RESERVES
(US $ million at 31 December)*

	2004	2005	2006
Gold (national valuation)	970	1,098	1,360
IMF special drawing rights	45	112	342
Reserve position in IMF	843	309	222
Foreign exchange	38,196	32,510	29,160
Total	40,054	34,029	31,084

* Data referring to holdings of gold and foreign exchange exclude deposits made with the European Monetary Institute.

Source: IMF, *International Financial Statistics*.

MONEY SUPPLY
(billion kroner at 31 December)

	2004	2005	2006
Currency outside banks	43.72	47.27	50.72
Demand deposits at banks	492.54	595.76	648.46
Total money (incl. others)	536.62	643.62	699.46

Source: IMF, *International Financial Statistics*.

COST OF LIVING
(Consumer Price Index; base: 2000 = 100)

	2005	2006	2007
Food and non-alcoholic beverages	107.3	110.2	115.1
Alcoholic beverages and tobacco	98.6	99.4	101.1
Clothing and footwear	101.1	99.1	97.4
Housing, water, electricity, gas and other fuels	114.6	117.9	120.4
Furnishings, household, etc.	108.4	109.4	110.8
Health	107.9	109.0	109.7
Transport	114.7	117.6	119.5
Communications	89.1	87.6	87.6
Recreation and culture	101.5	102.6	102.9
Education	142.0	146.1	152.7
Restaurants and hotels	113.0	115.8	118.8
Miscellaneous goods and services	120.3	122.4	122.9
All items	110.2	112.3	114.2

DENMARK

Statistical Survey

NATIONAL ACCOUNTS

National Income and Product
(million kroner at current prices)

	2004	2005	2006
Compensation of employees	785,579	817,874	863,729
Gross operating surplus and mixed income	458,623	500,597	524,500
Gross domestic income at factor cost	1,244,202	1,318,471	1,388,229
Taxes, *less* subsidies, on production	2,319	−3,109	−2,318
Gross value added	1,246,521	1,315,362	1,385,911
Taxes on products	231,697	250,668	266,226
Less Subsidies on products	18,819	14,063	14,535
GDP in purchasers' values	1,459,399	1,551,967	1,637,603
Factor income from abroad	101,386	152,792	182,244
Less Factor income paid abroad	94,651	139,636	159,577
Gross national income	1,466,134	1,565,122	1,660,271
Current taxes on income, wealth, etc. abroad (net)	2,935	3,562	4,175
Other current transfers to and from abroad (net)	−36,909	−34,530	−35,725
Gross national disposable income	1,432,160	1,534,154	1,628,722

Expenditure on the Gross Domestic Product
('000 million kroner at current prices)

	2004	2005	2006
Government final consumption expenditure	388.5	401.4	418.3
Private final consumption expenditure	708.5	754.1	796.0
Increase in stocks	7.0	6.0	13.1
Gross fixed capital formation	283.5	317.1	362.6
Total domestic expenditure	1,387.5	1,478.6	1,590.0
Exports of goods and services	667.3	757.1	849.4
Less Imports of goods and services	595.4	683.8	801.9
GDP in purchasers' values	1,459.4	1,552.0	1,637.6
GDP at constant 1995 prices	1,217.4	1,254.6	1,294.8

Source: IMF, *International Financial Statistics*.

Gross Domestic Product by Economic Activity
(million kroner at current prices)

	2004	2005	2006
Agriculture, horticulture and forestry	22,484	18,245	20,835
Fishing	1,440	1,569	2,003
Mining and quarrying	36,777	50,987	49,211
Manufacturing	180,460	186,507	201,693
Electricity, gas and water supply	24,603	24,540	26,633
Construction	68,158	73,539	82,574
Wholesale and retail trade, restaurants and hotels	165,240	168,647	173,359
Transport, post and telecommunications	105,893	120,798	124,578
Finance and insurance	67,078	73,913	80,861
Real estate and renting activities	130,675	136,915	144,097
Business services	98,406	102,721	109,144
Public administration and defence; compulsory social security	81,397	82,904	84,986
Education	71,716	74,036	77,029
Health care activities	57,537	59,799	62,042
Social work activities	79,694	81,001	84,044
Other community, social and personal service activities	54,965	59,240	62,821
Gross value added at basic prices	1,246,521	1,315,362	1,385,911
Taxes on products	231,697	250,668	266,226
Less subsidies on products	18,819	14,063	14,535
GDP in purchasers' values	1,459,399	1,551,967	1,637,603

BALANCE OF PAYMENTS
(US $ million)

	2004	2005	2006
Exports of goods f.o.b.	75,050	82,660	90,903
Imports of goods f.o.b.	−65,524	−75,243	−87,997
Trade balance	9,527	7,417	2,906
Exports of services	36,304	43,616	51,749
Imports of services	−33,401	−37,218	−44,953
Balance on goods and services	12,430	13,816	9,703
Other income received	12,784	23,538	28,532
Other income paid	−15,114	−23,476	−27,120
Balance on goods, services and income	10,100	13,878	11,115
Current transfers received	5,120	3,845	3,687
Current transfers paid	−9,279	−7,992	−8,105
Current balance	5,941	9,731	6,696
Capital account (net)	13	307	−42
Direct investment abroad	9,930	−15,018	−7,987
Direct investment from abroad	−8,804	13,050	6,261
Portfolio investment assets	−24,768	−32,796	−24,928
Portfolio investment liabilities	10,055	21,134	9,130
Financial derivatives liabilities	3,206	2,184	2,618
Other investment assets	−9,021	−19,779	−23,994
Other investment liabilities	378	22,476	35,196
Net errors and omissions	11,644	−2,794	−8,872
Overall balance	−1,426	−1,506	−5,922

Source: IMF, *International Financial Statistics*.

External Trade

PRINCIPAL COMMODITIES
(distribution by SITC, million kroner)

Imports c.i.f.	2004	2005	2006
Food and live animals	38,885	41,833	46,234
Crude materials (inedible) except fuels	12,733	12,369	14,913
Mineral fuels, lubricants, etc.	21,519	30,228	33,207
Petroleum, petroleum products, etc.	17,040	24,509	27,686
Chemicals and related products	43,164	42,603	54,718
Medical and pharmaceutical products	12,844	13,978	15,399
Basic manufactures	65,126	72,041	84,382
Machinery and transport equipment	144,280	161,871	182,197
Machinery specialized for particular industries	12,185	13,021	15,554
General industrial machinery, equipment and parts	18,722	20,800	24,443
Office machines and automatic data-processing equipment	19,838	22,289	22,336
Telecommunications and sound equipment	20,219	28,787	28,735
Other electrical machinery, apparatus, etc.	18,977	21,024	27,369
Road vehicles (incl. air-cushion vehicles) and parts*	18,977	21,024	42,452
Miscellaneous manufactured articles	60,119	64,311	74,470
Clothing and accessories (excl. footwear)	18,486	19,939	22,184
Total (incl. others)	400,125	445,797	505,379

DENMARK

Statistical Survey

Exports f.o.b.	2004	2005	2006
Food and live animals	76,344	71,675	87,096
Meat and meat preparations	28,057	27,939	30,107
Fish (not marine mammals), crustaceans, molluscs and aquatic invertebrates	14,735	16,126	17,041
Crude materials (inedible) except fuels	16,986	17,188	21,119
Mineral fuels, lubricants, etc.	39,346	52,524	63,270
Petroleum, petroleum products, etc.	32,848	43,576	50,375
Chemicals and related products	61,406	68,838	68,913
Medicinal and pharmaceutical products	33,640	38,250	39,379
Basic manufactures	45,180	47,786	55,821
Machinery and transport equipment	124,726	140,573	148,970
Power generating machinery and equipment	15,678	20,680	24,140
Machinery specialized for particular industries	15,966	15,986	17,306
General industrial machinery, equipment and parts*	31,537	32,902	35,124
Telecommunications and sound equipment	17,229	24,041	20,643
Other electrical machinery, apparatus, etc.	14,669	15,723	18,965
Miscellaneous manufactured articles	74,673	79,141	86,495
Furniture and parts	16,013	15,908	16,084
Clothing and accessories (excl. footwear)	15,743	17,220	19,851
Total (incl. others)	452,400	501,552	544,628

*Data on parts exclude tyres, engines and electrical parts.

PRINCIPAL TRADING PARTNERS
(million kroner)

Imports c.i.f.	2004	2005	2006
Austria	4,788	5,218	5,680
Belgium	13,857	15,321	16,751
China, People's Republic	16,094	21,707	26,511
Finland	8,672	9,901	11,344
France (incl. Monaco)	18,396	19,164	22,385
Germany	87,041	93,050	108,423
Ireland	4,379	5,207	6,191
Italy	16,292	18,554	19,988
Japan	3,799	4,471	4,489
Korea, Republic	6,395	4,238	4,223
Netherlands	27,030	29,646	31,380
Norway	18,841	20,159	23,371
Poland	7,532	8,836	11,559
Russia	5,560	7,767	8,173
Spain	6,787	9,034	9,743
Sweden	53,956	62,020	72,273
Switzerland	3,991	5,544	6,598
United Kingdom	24,222	26,650	29,331
USA	15,192	11,909	15,188
Total (incl. others)	400,125	445,797	505,379

Exports f.o.b.	2004	2005	2006
Austria	4,109	3,985	4,125
Belgium	7,661	7,518	8,039
China, People's Republic	6,026	6,475	7,011
Finland	12,946	13,888	16,430
France (incl. Monaco)	22,577	26,118	25,342
Germany	79,949	86,223	91,678
Ireland	6,917	7,213	7,553
Italy	15,538	16,778	18,210
Japan	13,730	11,657	11,170
Netherlands	25,161	25,846	26,761
Norway	25,242	26,750	30,975
Poland	7,043	10,199	10,895
Russia	6,032	7,397	9,751
Spain	14,012	13,634	15,970
Sweden	58,026	66,099	77,509
Switzerland	4,853	4,883	4,915
United Kingdom	39,522	44,042	48,817
USA	26,352	33,438	36,486
Total (incl. others)	452,400	501,552	544,628

Transport

RAILWAYS
(traffic)

	2004	2005	2006
Passengers carried ('000)	202,100	207,477	211,073
Passenger-kilometres (million)	6,074	6,136	6,274
Goods carried ('000 tons)	8,167	7,706	7,477
Ton-kilometres (million)	2,169	1,976	1,893

ROAD TRAFFIC
(motor vehicles in use at 1 January)

	2005	2006	2007
Private cars	1,915,821	1,964,682	2,020,013
Vans	388,809	421,203	459,082
Buses, coaches	14,191	14,402	14,552
Lorries	34,317	34,546	35,154
Tractors	13,021	13,774	14,538
Motorcycles and mopeds	162,128	171,917	184,036

SHIPPING

Merchant Fleet
(registered at 31 December)

	2004	2005	2006
Number of vessels	834	832	798
Total displacement ('000 grt)	7,581.9	8,069.8	8,580.4

Source: Lloyd's Register-Fairplay, *World Fleet Statistics*.

Sea-borne Freight Traffic at Danish Ports*
('000 metric tons loaded and unloaded)

	2001	2002	2003
Ålborg	2,581	2,652	2,756
Århus	9,980	9,621	9,983
Copenhagen	6,688	5,996	6,769
Fredericia	15,763	16,585	16,513
Kalundborg	8,530	7,613	8,342
Skaelskør	645	132	445
Others	49,785	51,684	59,146
Total	93,972	94,283	103,954

*Including domestic traffic and ferry traffic.

DENMARK

International Sea-borne Shipping*
(freight traffic, '000 metric tons)

	2002	2003	2004
Goods loaded	24,648	25,411	25,149
Goods unloaded	29,296	33,792	32,074

* Excluding international ferry traffic.

CIVIL AVIATION
(traffic on scheduled services)*

	2001	2002	2003
Kilometres flown (million)	92	81	78
Passengers carried ('000)	6,382	6,322	5,886
Passenger-kilometres (million)	6,952	7,453	7,202
Total ton-kilometres (million)	876	925	885

* Including an apportionment (2/7) of international operations by Scandinavian Airlines System (SAS).

Source: UN, *Statistical Yearbook*.

Tourism

FOREIGN TOURIST ARRIVALS
(at accommodation establishments)

Country of residence	2003	2004	2005
Germany	1,574,028	1,751,172	1,857,014
Netherlands	125,822	227,215	211,973
Norway	526,611	643,273	669,356
Sweden	681,520	854,915	846,014
United Kingdom	118,458	223,951	233,470
USA	66,014	110,464	122,892
Total (incl. others)	3,473,808	4,421,442	4,698,668

Tourism receipts (US $ million, excl. passenger transport): 6,658 in 2003; 7,269 in 2004; 5,690 in 2005.

Source: World Tourism Organization.

Communications Media

	2004	2005	2006
Book production: titles*	14,829	13,227	13,402
Daily newspapers:			
number	32	32	34
average circulation ('000 copies)†	1,352	1,288	1,360
Telephones ('000 main lines in use)	3,491.3	3,348.5	3,098.4
Mobile cellular telephones ('000 subscribers)	5,166.9	5,449.2	5,840.9
Personal computers ('000 in use)	3,543	3,543	n.a.
Internet users ('000)	2,725.0	2,854.0	3,171.2
Broadband subscribers ('000)	1,017.6	1,349.0	1,728.4

* Including pamphlets (4,726 in 2003; 4,659 in 2004; 3,835 in 2005).
† On weekdays.

Television receivers ('000 in use, estimate): 4,600 in 2001.

Facsimile machines ('000 in use): 250 in 1995.

Sources: partly International Telecommunication Union; UN, *Statistical Yearbook*.

Education

(1994/95, unless otherwise indicated)

	Institutions	Teachers	Students*
Pre-primary	4,395	19,200	243,617
Primary	n.a.	33,100	414,103
Secondary:			
general	n.a.	37,000	339,586
vocational	n.a.	13,100	125,366
Higher	n.a.	9,600	233,362

* 2004/05.

2003: *Institutions:* Primary and secondary (general) 2,842; Secondary (vocational) 157; Higher 162. *Students:* Primary and secondary (general) 1,130,206; Secondary (vocational) 172,225; Higher 183,694.

2004: *Institutions:* Primary and secondary (general) 2,846; Secondary (vocational) 150; Higher 166. *Students:* Primary and secondary (general) 780,238; Secondary (vocational) 176,205; Higher 185,291.

2005: *Institutions:* Primary and secondary (general) 2,837; Secondary (vocational) 186; Higher 169. *Students:* Primary and secondary (general) 787,843; Secondary (vocational) 180,514; Higher 184,495.

Directory

The Constitution

The *Grundlov* (constitutional charter), summarized below, was adopted on 5 June 1953.

GOVERNMENT

The form of government is a constitutional monarchy. The legislative authority rests jointly with the Crown and the Folketing (parliament). Executive power is vested in the Crown, and the administration of justice is exercised by the courts. The Monarch can constitutionally 'do no wrong'. She exercises her authority through the Ministers appointed by her. The Ministers are responsible for the government of the country. The Constitution establishes the principle of parliamentarism under which individual Ministers or the whole Cabinet must retire when defeated in the Folketing by a vote of 'no confidence'.

MONARCH

The Monarch acts on behalf of the State in international affairs. Except with the consent of the Folketing, she cannot, however, take any action that increases or reduces the area of the Realm or undertake any obligation, the fulfilment of which requires the co-operation of the Folketing or which is of major importance. Nor can the Monarch, without the consent of the Folketing, terminate any international agreement that has been concluded with the consent of the Folketing.

Apart from defence against armed attack on the Realm or on Danish forces, the Monarch cannot, without the consent of the Folketing, employ military force against any foreign power.

PARLIAMENT

The Folketing is an assembly consisting of not more than 179 members, two of whom are elected in the Faroe Islands and two in Greenland. Danish nationals, having attained 18 years of age, with permanent residence in Denmark, have the franchise and are eligible for election. The members of the Folketing are elected for four years. Election is by a system of proportional representation, with direct and secret ballot on lists in large constituencies. A bill adopted by the Folketing may be submitted to referendum, when such referendum is claimed in writing by not less than one-third of the members of the Folketing and not later than three working days after the adoption. The bill is void if rejected by a majority of the votes cast, representing not less than 30% of all electors.

The Government

HEAD OF STATE

Queen of Denmark: HM Queen MARGRETHE II (succeeded to the throne 14 January 1972).

DENMARK

THE CABINET
(March 2008)

A coalition of Venstre (V—Liberals) and Det Konservative Folkeparti (DKF—Conservative People's Party).

Prime Minister: ANDERS FOGH RASMUSSEN (V).
Deputy Prime Minister and Minister of Economic and Business Affairs: BENDT BENDTSEN (DKF).
Minister of Foreign Affairs: Dr PER STIG MØLLER (DKF).
Minister of Finance: LARS LØKKE RASMUSSEN (V).
Minister of Employment: CLAUS HJORT FREDERIKSEN (V).
Minister of Justice: LENE ESPERSEN (DKF).
Minister of Culture: BRIAN MIKKELSEN (DKF).
Minister of Taxation: KRISTIAN JENSEN (V).
Minister of Education and of Nordic Co-operation: BERTEL HAARDER (V).
Minister of Social Welfare and of Gender Equality: KAREN JESPERSEN (V).
Minister of Science, Technology and Innovation: HELGE SANDER (V).
Minister of Development Co-operation: ULLA TØRNÆS (V).
Minister of Defence: SØREN GADE JENSEN (V).
Minister of Food, Agriculture and Fisheries: EVA KJER HANSEN (V).
Minister of Climate and Energy: CONNIE HEDEGAARD (DKF).
Minister of Transport: CARINA CHRISTENSEN (DKF).
Minister of Health and Prevention: JAKOB AXEL NIELSEN (DKF).
Minister of Refugee, Immigration and Integration Affairs and of Ecclesiastical Affairs: BIRTHE RØNN HORNBECH (V).
Minister of the Environment: TROELS LUND POULSEN (V).

MINISTRIES

Prime Minister's Office: Christiansborg, Prins Jørgens Gård 11, 1218 Copenhagen K; tel. 33-92-33-00; fax 33-11-16-65; e-mail stm@stm.dk; internet www.stm.dk.

Ministry of Climate and Energy: Stormgade 2–6, 1470 Copenhagen K; tel. 33-92-28-00; fax 33-92-28-01; e-mail kemin@kemin.dk; internet www.kemin.dk.

Ministry of Culture: Nybrogade 2, 1203 Copenhagen K; tel. 33-92-33-70; fax 33-91-33-88; e-mail kum@kum.dk; internet www.kum.dk.

Ministry of Defence: Holmens Kanal 42, 1060 Copenhagen K; tel. 33-92-33-20; fax 33-32-06-55; e-mail fmn@fmn.dk; internet forsvaret.dk/fmn.

Ministry of Ecclesiastical Affairs: Frederiksholms Kanal 21, POB 2123, 1015 Copenhagen K; tel. 33-92-33-90; fax 33-92-39-13; e-mail km@km.dk; internet www.km.dk.

Ministry of Economic and Business Affairs: Slotsholmsgade 10–12, 1216 Copenhagen K; tel. 33-92-33-50; fax 33-12-37-78; e-mail oem@oem.dk; internet www.oem.dk.

Ministry of Education: Frederiksholms Kanal 21, 1220 Copenhagen K; tel. 33-92-50-00; fax 33-92-55-67; e-mail uvm@uvm.dk; internet www.uvm.dk.

Ministry of Employment: Ved Stranden 8, 1061 Copenhagen K; tel. 72-20-50-00; fax 33-12-13-78; e-mail bm@bm.dk; internet www.bm.dk.

Ministry of the Environment: Højbro Pl. 4, 1200 Copenhagen K; tel. 72-54-60-00; fax 33-32-22-27; e-mail mim@mim.dk; internet www.mim.dk.

Ministry of Finance: Christiansborg Slotspl. 1, 1218 Copenhagen K; tel. 33-92-33-33; fax 33-32-30-80; e-mail fm@fm.dk; internet www.fm.dk.

Ministry of Food, Agriculture and Fisheries: Slotsholmsgade 12, 1216 Copenhagen K; tel. 33-92-33-01; fax 33-14-50-42; e-mail fvm@fvm.dk; internet www.fvm.dk.

Ministry of Foreign Affairs: Asiatisk Pl. 2, 1448 Copenhagen K; tel. 33-92-00-00; fax 32-54-05-33; e-mail um@um.dk; internet www.um.dk.

Ministry of Health and Prevention: Slotsholmsgade 10–12, 1216 Copenhagen K; tel. 72-26-90-00; fax 72-26-90-01; e-mail sum@sum.dk; internet www.sum.dk.

Ministry of Justice: Slotsholmsgade 10, 1216 Copenhagen K; tel. 72-26-84-00; fax 33-93-35-10; e-mail jm@jm.dk; internet www.jm.dk.

Ministry of Refugee, Immigration and Integration Affairs: Holbergsgade 6, 1057 Copenhagen K; tel. 33-92-33-80; fax 33-11-12-39; e-mail inm@inm.dk; internet www.nyidanmark.dk.

Ministry of Science, Technology and Innovation: Bredgade 43, 1260 Copenhagen K; tel. 33-92-97-00; fax 33-32-35-01; e-mail vtu@vtu.dk; internet videnskabsministeriet.dk.

Ministry of Social Welfare: Holmens Kanal 22, 1060 Copenhagen K; tel. 33-92-93-00; fax 33-93-25-18; e-mail sm@socialministeriet.dk; internet www.social.dk.

Ministry of Taxation: Nicolai Eigtveds Gade 28, 1402 Copenhagen K; tel. 33-92-33-92; fax 33-14-91-05; e-mail skm@skm.dk; internet www.skm.dk.

Ministry of Transport: Frederiksholms Kanal 27, 1220 Copenhagen K; tel. 33-92-33-55; fax 33-12-38-93; e-mail trm@trm.dk; internet www.trm.dk.

Legislature

FOLKETING

Christiansborg, 1240 Copenhagen K; tel. 33-37-55-00; fax 33-32-85-36; e-mail folketinget@folketinget.dk; internet www.folketinget.dk.

President of the Folketing: THOR PEDERSEN.
Secretary-General: JENS VIBJERG.

General Election, 13 November 2007
(metropolitan Denmark only)

Party	Votes	% of votes	Seats
Venstre (Liberals)	908,472	26.26	46
Socialdemokraterne (Social Democrats)	881,037	25.47	45
Dansk Folkeparti (Danish People's Party)	479,532	13.86	25
Socialistisk Folkeparti (Socialist People's Party)	450,975	13.04	23
Det Konservative Folkeparti (Conservative People's Party)	359,404	10.40	18
Det Radikale Venstre (Social Liberals)	177,161	5.12	9
Ny Alliance (New Alliance)	97,295	2.81	5
Enhedslisten—de Rød-Grønne (Red-Green Alliance)	74,982	2.17	4
Kristendemokraterne (Christian Democrats)	30,013	0.87	—
Total (incl. others)	3,459,414	100.00	179*

*Includes two members from the Faroe Islands and two from Greenland.

Political Organizations

Arbejderpartiet Kommunisterne (APK) (Workers' Communist Party): Skibhusvej 100, 5000 Odense C; tel. 66-14-89-83; fax 66-19-19-83; e-mail apk@apk2000.dk; internet www.apk2000.dk; f. 2000; Marxist-Leninist; Chair. DORTE GRENAA.

CentrumDemokraterne (Centre Democrats): Herlev Bygade 40, 1st Floor, 2730 Herlev; tel. 33-12-71-15; fax 33-12-01-15; e-mail landskontoret@centrumdemokraterne.dk; internet www.centrumdemokraterne.dk; f. 1973; opposes extreme ideologies, supports EU and NATO; Chair. ABDERRAHMAN BEN HADDOU.

Danmarks Kommunistiske Parti (Communist Party of Denmark): Frederikssundsvej 64, 2400 Copenhagen NV; tel. 33-91-66-44; fax 33-32-03-72; e-mail dkp@dkp.dk; internet www.dkp.dk; f. 1919; Chair. HENRIK STAMER HEDIN.

Danmarks Nationalsocialistike Bevægelse (DNSB) (Danish National Socialist Movement): Hundige Strandvej 153, POB 32, 2670 Greve; tel. 43-90-98-55; fax 43-90-72-71; internet www.dnsb.info; f. 1983; Leader JONNI HANSEN.

Dansk Folkeparti (Danish People's Party): Christiansborg, 1240 Copenhagen K; tel. 33-37-51-99; fax 33-37-51-91; e-mail df@ft.dk; internet www.danskfolkeparti.dk; f. 1995 by defectors from the Progress Party; right-wing, populist; Leader PIA KJÆRSGAARD.

Enhedslisten—de Rød-Grønne (Red-Green Alliance): Studiestræde 24, 1455 Copenhagen K; tel. 33-93-33-24; fax 33-32-03-72; e-mail landskontoret@enhedslisten.dk; internet www.enhedslisten.dk; f. 1989 by three left-wing parties; membership of individual socialists; 24-mem. collective leadership; 4,525 mems. (Jan. 2008).

Folkebevægelsen mod EU (People's Movement Against the European Union): Tordenskjoldsgade 21, 1055 Copenhagen N; tel. 35-36-37-40; fax 35-82-18-06; e-mail folkebevaegelsen@folkebevaegelsen.dk; internet www.folkebevaegelsen.dk; f. 1972; opposes membership of the EU, in favour of self-determination for Denmark and all European countries; 21-mem. collective leadership; Nat. Sec. POUL GERHARD KRISTIANSEN.

DENMARK

Fremskridtspartiet (Progress Party): Stationsmestervej 11, 9200 Aalborg SV; tel. 70-26-20-27; fax 70-26-23-27; e-mail frp@frp.dk; internet www.frp.dk; f. 1972; right-wing; advocates deportation of Muslims from Denmark, gradual abolition of income tax, disbandment of most of the civil service, and abolition of diplomatic service and about 90% of all legislation; Leader OVE JENSEN.

De Grønne (Green Party): Bispeparken 30, 2nd Floor, 2400 Copenhagen NV; tel. 35-85-48-43; e-mail green@fremtidsmaskinen.dk; internet www.groenne.dk; f. 1983; reformed 1991; Nat. Sec. JEAN THIERRY.

Grønne Demokrater (Green Democrats): c/o Poul Christiansen, Toftegårdsvej 3, 7000 Fredericia; tel. 75-94-16-16; e-mail nr3@regnbuen-fredericia.dk; internet www.groennedemokrater.dk.

JuniBevægelsen (June Movement): Kronprinsensegade 2, 1114 Copenhagen K; tel. 33-93-00-46; fax 33-93-30-67; e-mail jb@j.dk; internet www.j.dk; f. 1992; opposes EU federalism; Leader HANNE DAHL.

Kommunistisk Parti (Communist Party): Ryesgade 3F, 2200 Copenhagen K; tel. 35-35-60-69; e-mail info@kommunister.dk; internet www.kommunister.dk; f. 2006 by merger of Danmarks Kommunistiske Parti/Marxister-Leninister and a breakaway faction of the KPiD; Committee Chairs. JOAN AGOT PEDERSEN, MORTEN RASMUSSEN.

Kommunistisk Parti i Danmark (KPiD): Frederikssundsvej 82, 2400 Copenhagen NV; tel. 38-88-28-33; e-mail kpid@kommunisterne.dk; internet www.kommunisterne.dk; f. 1993; Chair. BETTY FRYDENSBJERG CARLSSON.

Det Konservative Folkeparti (Conservative People's Party): Nyhavn 4, 1051 Copenhagen K; tel. 33-13-41-40; fax 33-93-37-73; e-mail info@konservative.dk; internet www.konservative.dk; f. 1916; advocates free initiative and the maintenance of private property, but recognizes the right of the State to take action to keep the economic and social balance; Leader BENDT BENDTSEN.

Kristendemokraterne (Christian Democrats): Allégade 24A, 2000 Frederiksberg; tel. 33-27-78-10; fax 33-21-31-16; e-mail kd@kd.dk; internet www.kd.dk; f. 1970 as Kristeligt Folkeparti (Christian People's Party); present name adopted 2003; emphasizes the need for political decisions based on Christian ethics; Chair. BODIL KORNBEK.

Ny Alliance (New Alliance): Christiansborg, 1240 Copenhagen K; tel. 29-37-93-14; e-mail nyalliance@nyalliance.dk; internet www.nyalliance.dk; f. 2007 by former members of Det Radikale Venstre and Det Konservative Folkeparti; centrist, advocates liberalization of immigration policy and is pro-EU; Leader NASER KHADER.

Det Radikale Venstre (Social Liberals): Christiansborg, 1240 Copenhagen K; tel. 33-37-47-47; fax 33-13-72-51; e-mail radikale@radikale.dk; internet www.radikale.dk; f. 1905; supports international *détente* and co-operation within regional and world orgs, social reforms without socialism, incomes policy, workers' participation in industry, state intervention in industrial disputes, state control of trusts and monopolies, strengthening private enterprise; Nat. Chair. SØREN BALD; Parliamentary Leader MARGRETHE VESTAGER.

Retsforbundet—Danmarks Retsforbund (Justice Party): Lyngbyvej 42, 2100 Copenhagen Ø; tel. 39-20-44-88; fax 39-20-44-50; e-mail sekretariat@retsforbundet.dk; internet www.retsforbundet.dk; f. 1919; programme is closely allied to Henry George's teachings (single land-value tax, free trade); Chair. FINN BECKER-CHRISTENSEN.

Schleswigsche Partei/Slesvigsk Parti (SP) (Schleswig Party): Vestergade 30, 6200 Åbenrå; tel. 74-62-38-33; fax 74-62-79-39; e-mail sp@bdn.dk; internet www.schleswigsche-partei.dk; f. 1920; represents the German minority in North Schleswig; Chair. GERHARD D. MAMMEN.

Socialdemokraterne (Social Democrats): Danasvej 7, 1910 Frederiksberg C; tel. 72-30-08-00; fax 72-30-08-50; e-mail kirsten@socdem.dk; internet www.socialdemokraterne.dk; f. 1871; finds its chief adherents among workers, employees and public servants; 55,000 mems; Leader HELLE THORNING-SCHMIDT; Party Sec. LARS MIDTIBY.

Socialistisk Arbejderparti (Socialist Workers' Party): Studiestræde 24, 1st Floor, 1455 Copenhagen K; tel. 33-33-79-48; fax 33-33-03-17; e-mail sap@sap-fi.dk; internet www.sap-fi.dk.

Socialistisk Folkeparti (SF) (Socialist People's Party): Christiansborg, 1240 Copenhagen K; tel. 33-37-44-44; fax 33-32-72-48; e-mail sf@sf.dk; internet www.sf.dk; f. 1959; modern socialist party; Chair. VILLY SØVNDAL; Parliamentary Leader OLE SOHN; Sec. TURID LEIRVOLL.

Venstre, Danmarks Liberale Parti (Liberals): Søllerødvej 30, 2840 Holte; tel. 45-80-22-33; fax 45-80-38-30; e-mail venstre@venstre.dk; internet www.venstre.dk; f. 1870; supports free trade, a minimum of state interference, and the adoption, in matters of social expenditure, of a modern general social security system; 61,018 mems (2006); Pres. ANDERS FOGH RASMUSSEN; Sec.-Gen. JENS SKIPPER RASMUSSEN.

Venstresocialisterne (VS) (Left Socialist Party of Denmark): Solidaritetshuset, Griffenfeldsgade 41, 2200 Copenhagen N; tel. and fax 35-35-06-08; e-mail vs@venstresocialisterne.dk; internet www.venstresocialisterne.dk; f. 1968; revolutionary, Marxist, democratic, socialist party.

Diplomatic Representation

EMBASSIES IN DENMARK

Albania: Fredriksholms Kanal 4, 1220 Copenhagen K; tel. 33-91-79-79; fax 33-91-79-69; e-mail embassyofalbania@mail.dk; Ambassador AFËRDITA DALLA.

Algeria: Hellerupvej 66, 2900 Hellerup; tel. 33-11-94-40; fax 33-11-58-50; e-mail ambalda@mail.tele.dk; internet www.algerianembassy.dk; Ambassador LATIFA BENAZZA.

Argentina: Borgergade 16, 4th Floor, 1300 Copenhagen K; tel. 33-15-80-82; fax 33-15-55-74; e-mail edina@mrecic.gov.ar; Ambassador JUAN CARLOS KRECKLER.

Australia: Dampfærgevej 26, 2100 Copenhagen Ø; tel. 70-26-36-76; fax 70-26-36-86; e-mail australianembassydenmark@gmail.com; internet www.denmark.embassy.gov.au; Ambassador SHARYN JANE MINAHAN.

Austria: Sølundsvej 1, 2100 Copenhagen Ø; tel. 39-29-41-41; fax 39-29-20-86; e-mail kopenhagen-ob@bmeia.gv.at; Ambassador Dr ERWIN KUBESCH.

Belgium: Øster Allé 7, 2100 Copenhagen Ø; tel. 35-25-02-00; fax 35-25-02-11; e-mail copenhagen@diplobel.be; internet www.diplomatie.be/copenhagen; Ambassador MARC VAN CRAEN.

Benin: Gamlehave Allé 12, 2920 Charlottenlund; tel. 39-68-10-30; fax 39-68-10-32; e-mail ambabenin@c.dk; internet www.ambabenin.dk; Chargé d'affaires a.i. ZACHARIE RICHARD AKPLOGAN.

Bolivia: Store Kongensgade 81, 2nd Floor, 1264 Copenhagen K; tel. 33-12-49-00; fax 33-12-49-03; e-mail embocopenhagen@mail.dk; Ambassador EUGENIO POMA AÑAGUAYA.

Bosnia and Herzegovina: H. C. Andersens Blvd 48, 2nd Floor, 1553 Copenhagen V; tel. 33-33-80-40; fax 33-33-80-17; e-mail info@embassybh.dk; internet www.embassybh.dk; Ambassador SEAD MASLO.

Brazil: Kastelsvej 19, 3rd and 4th Floors, 2100 Copenhagen Ø; tel. 39-20-64-78; fax 39-27-36-07; e-mail ambassade@brazil.dk; internet www.brazil.dk; Ambassador GEORGES LAMAZIÈRE.

Bulgaria: Gamlehave Allé 7, 2920 Charlottenlund; tel. 39-64-24-84; fax 39-63-49-23; e-mail bg-embassy@mail.tdcadsl.dk; Ambassador IVAN I. DIMITROV.

Burkina Faso: Svanemøllevej 20, 2100 Copenhagen Ø; tel. 39-18-40-22; fax 39-27-18-86; e-mail mail@ambaburkina.dk; internet www.ambaburkina.dk; Ambassador CÉLINE M. YODA.

Canada: Kr. Bernikowsgade 1, 1105 Copenhagen K; tel. 33-48-32-00; fax 33-48-32-20; e-mail copen@international.gc.ca; internet www.canada.dk; Ambassador FREDERICKA GREGORY.

Chile: Kastelsvej 15, 3rd Floor, 2100 Copenhagen Ø; tel. 35-38-58-34; fax 35-38-42-01; e-mail embassy@chiledk.dk; internet www.chiledk.dk; Ambassador RICARDO CONCHA.

China, People's Republic: Øregårds Allé 25, 2900 Hellerup; tel. 39-46-08-89; fax 39-62-54-84; e-mail mail@chinaembassy.dk; internet www.chinaembassy.dk; Ambassador XIE HANGSHENG.

Côte d'Ivoire: Gersonsvej 8, 2900 Hellerup; tel. 39-62-88-22; fax 39-62-01-62; e-mail ambaivoire@mail.tele.dk; internet www.ambacotedivoire.org; Ambassador DJÉROU ROBERT LY.

Croatia: Frederiksgade 19, 1st Floor, 1265 Copenhagen K; tel. 33-91-90-95; fax 33-91-71-31; e-mail croemb.denmark@mvp.hr; Ambassador ALEKSANDAR HEINA.

Cuba: Kastelsvej 19, 3rd Floor, 2100 Copenhagen Ø; tel. and fax 39-40-15-06; e-mail embadin@hotmail.com; internet www.cubaembassy.dk; Ambassador GUILLERMO VÁZQUEZ MORENO.

Cyprus: Borgergade 28, 1st Floor, 1300 Copenhagen K; tel. 33-91-58-88; fax 33-91-58-77; e-mail consulate@cyprus-embassy.dk; Ambassador ANTONIS TOUMAZIS.

Czech Republic: Ryvangs Allé 14–16, 2100 Copenhagen Ø; tel. 39-10-18-10; fax 39-29-09-30; e-mail copenhagen@embassy.mzv.cz; internet www.mfa.cz/copenhagen; Ambassador IVAN JANČÁREK.

Egypt: Kristianiagade 19, 2100 Copenhagen Ø; tel. 35-43-70-70; fax 35-25-32-62; e-mail egyptembassydenmark@yahoo.com; Ambassador AFAF ALI SAYED AL-MAZARIKI.

Estonia: Aurehøjvej 19, 2900 Hellerup; tel. 39-46-30-70; fax 39-46-30-76; e-mail sekretar@estemb.dk; internet www.estemb.dk; Ambassador MEELIKE PALLI.

DENMARK

Finland: Skt Annæ Pl. 24, 1250 Copenhagen K; tel. 33-13-42-14; fax 33-32-47-10; e-mail sanomat.kob@formin.fi; internet www.finlandsambassade.dk; Ambassador EERO KALEVI SALOVAARA.

France: Kongens Nytorv 4, 1050 Copenhagen K; tel. 33-67-01-00; fax 33-93-97-52; e-mail presse@ambafrance-dk.org; internet www.ambafrance-dk.org; Ambassador BÉRENGÈRE QUINCY.

Georgia: Nybrogade 10, 1st Floor, 1203 Copenhagen K; tel. 39-11-00-00; fax 39-11-00-01; e-mail copenhagen.emb@mfa.gov.ge; internet www.denmark.mfa.gov.ge; Ambassador DAVID T. KERESELIDZE.

Germany: Stockholmsgade 57, POB 2712, 2100 Copenhagen Ø; tel. 35-45-99-00; fax 35-26-71-05; e-mail tyskeamba@email.dk; internet www.kopenhagen.diplo.de; Ambassador Dr GERHARD NOURNEY.

Ghana: Egebjerg Allé 13, 2900 Hellerup; tel. 39-62-82-22; fax 39-62-16-52; e-mail ghana@mail.dk; Ambassador MAUREEN ABLA AMEMATEKPOR.

Greece: Hammerensgade 4, 1267 Copenhagen K; tel. 33-11-45-33; fax 33-93-16-46; e-mail greekembcop@post.tele.dk; Ambassador DIMITRIS CONTOUMAS.

Hungary: Strandvejen 170, 2920 Charlottenlund; tel. 39-63-16-88; fax 39-63-00-52; e-mail missioncph@kum.hu; internet www.mfa.gov.hu/kulkepviselet/dk/hu; Ambassador Dr ANDRÁS JÁNOS TÓTH.

Iceland: Strandgade 89, 1401 Copenhagen K; tel. 33-18-10-50; fax 33-18-10-59; e-mail icemb.coph@utn.stjr.is; Ambassador SVAVAR GESTSSON.

India: Vangehusvej 15, 2100 Copenhagen Ø; tel. 39-18-28-88; fax 39-27-02-18; e-mail india@email.dk; internet www.indian-embassy.dk; Ambassador PARTHA SARATHI RAY.

Indonesia: Ørehøj Allé 1, 2900 Hellerup; tel. 39-62-44-22; fax 39-62-44-83; e-mail unitkomkph@kbricph.dk; internet www.kbricph.dk; Ambassador ABDUL RAHMAN SALEH.

Iran: Svanemøllevej 48, 2100 Copenhagen Ø; tel. 39-16-00-03; fax 39-16-00-75; e-mail info@iran-embassy.dk; internet www.iran-embassy.dk; Ambassador MUHAMMAD REZA MORSHEDZADEH.

Iraq: Granhøjen 18, 2900 Hellerup; tel. 39-45-02-70; fax 39-40-69-97; e-mail kbnemb@iraqmofamail.net; Chargé d'affaires a.i. FARIS FATOUHI.

Ireland: Østbanegade 21, 2100 Copenhagen Ø; tel. 35-42-32-33; fax 35-43-18-58; e-mail ireland@mail.dk; Ambassador JOSEPH HAYES.

Israel: Lundevangsvej 4, 2900 Hellerup; tel. 88-15-55-00; fax 88-15-55-55; e-mail reception@copenhagen.mfa.gov.il; internet copenhagen.mfa.gov.il; Ambassador DAVID WALZER.

Italy: Gammel Vartov Vej 7, 2900 Hellerup; tel. 39-62-68-77; fax 39-62-25-99; e-mail info.copenaghen@esteri.it; internet www.ambcopenaghen.esteri.it; Ambassador ANDREA GIUSEPPE MOCHI ONORY DI SALUZZO.

Japan: Pilestræde 61, 1112 Copenhagen K; tel. 33-11-33-44; fax 33-11-33-77; e-mail info@embjapan.dk; internet www.embjapan.dk; Ambassador MASAKI OKADA.

Korea, Republic: Svanemøllevej 104, 2900 Hellerup; tel. 39-46-04-00; fax 39-46-04-22; e-mail korembdk@mofat.go.kr; internet www.mofat.go.kr/denmark; Ambassador MYUNG-SOO LEE.

Latvia: Rosbæksvej 17, 2100 Copenhagen Ø; tel. 39-27-60-00; fax 39-27-61-73; e-mail embassy.denmark@mfa.gov.lv; Ambassador ANDRIS RAZANS.

Lithuania: Bernstorffsvej 214, 2920 Charlottenlund; tel. 39-63-62-07; fax 39-63-65-32; e-mail amb.dk@urm.lt; internet dk.mfa.lt; Ambassador RASA KAIRIENĖ.

Luxembourg: Fridtjof Nansens Pl. 5, 1st Floor, 2100 Copenhagen Ø; tel. 35-26-82-00; fax 35-26-82-08; e-mail copenhague.amb@mae.etat.lu; internet www.luxembourgembassy.dk; Ambassador PIERRE-LOUIS LORENZ.

Macedonia, former Yugoslav republic: Skindergade 28A, 1st Floor, 1159 Copenhagen K; tel. 39-76-69-20; fax 39-76-69-23; e-mail copenhagen@mfa.gov.mk; Chargé d'affaires a.i. SALIM KJERIMI.

Malta: Amaliegade 8B, 2nd Floor, 1256 Copenhagen K; tel. 33-15-30-90; fax 33-15-30-91; e-mail maltaembassy.copenhagen@gov.mt; Ambassador Dr NOEL BUTTIGIEG-SCICLUNA.

Mexico: Bredgade 65, 1st Floor, 1260 Copenhagen K; tel. 39-61-05-00; fax 39-61-05-12; e-mail info@mexican-embassy.dk; internet www.sre.gob.mx/dinamarca; Ambassador MARTHA ELENA FEDERICA BÁRCENA COQUI.

Morocco: Øregårds Allé 19, 2900 Hellerup; tel. 39-62-45-11; fax 39-62-24-49; e-mail sifamaeco@yahoo.fr; Ambassador AÏCHA AL-KABBAJ.

Nepal: Svanemøllervej 92, 2900 Hellerup; tel. 44-44-40-26; fax 44-44-40-27; e-mail embdenmark@gmail.com; Ambassador VIJAYKANT LAL KARNA.

Netherlands: Toldbodgade 33, 1253 Copenhagen K; tel. 33-70-72-00; fax 33-14-03-50; e-mail kop@minbuza.nl; internet www.nlembassy.dk; Ambassador GERARD JOHAN HENDRIK CHRISTIAAN KRAMER.

Nicaragua: Kastelsvej 7, Ground Floor, 2100 Copenhagen Ø; tel. 35-55-48-70; fax 35-55-48-75; e-mail embajada@emb-nicaragua.dk; Ambassador Dr RICARDO JOSÉ ALVARADO NOGUERA.

Norway: Amaliegade 39, 1256 Copenhagen K; tel. 33-14-01-24; fax 33-14-06-24; e-mail emb.copenhagen@mfa.no; internet www.norsk.dk; Ambassador JØRG WILLY BRONEBAKK.

Pakistan: Valeursvej 17, 2900 Hellerup; tel. 39-62-11-88; fax 39-40-10-70; e-mail parepcopenhagen@pakistan-embassy.dk; Ambassador FAWZIA MUFTI ABBAS.

Poland: Richelieus Allé 12, 2900 Hellerup; tel. 39-46-77-00; fax 39-46-77-66; e-mail mail@ambpol.dk; internet www.copenhagen.polemb.net; Ambassador ADAM HALAMSKI.

Portugal: Toldbodgade 31, 1st Floor, 1253 Copenhagen K; tel. 33-13-13-01; fax 33-14-92-14; e-mail embport@get2net.dk; Ambassador JOSÉ BOUZA SERRANO.

Romania: Strandagervej 27, 2900 Hellerup; tel. 39-40-71-77; fax 39-62-78-99; e-mail roemb@mail.tele.dk; internet copenhaga.mae.ro; Ambassador Dr THEODOR PALEOLOGU.

Russia: Kristianiagade 5, 2100 Copenhagen Ø; tel. 35-42-55-85; fax 35-42-37-41; e-mail embrus@mail.dk; internet www.denmark.mid.ru; Ambassador TEIMURAZ O. RAMISHVILI.

Saudi Arabia: Lille Strandvej 27, 2900 Hellerup; tel. 39-62-12-00; fax 39-62-60-09; e-mail embassy@saudiemb.dk; Ambassador ABD AR-RAHMAN SAAD AL-HADLAQ.

Serbia: Svanevænget 36, 2100 Copenhagen Ø; tel. 39-29-77-84; fax 39-29-79-19; e-mail serbianemb@city.dk; Ambassador VIDA OGNJENOVIĆ.

Slovakia: Vesterled 26–28, 2100 Copenhagen Ø; tel. 39-20-99-11; fax 39-20-99-13; e-mail embassy@copenhagen.mfa.sk; Ambassador LUBOMÍR GOLIAN.

Slovenia: Amaliegade 6, 2nd Floor, 1256 Copenhagen K; tel. 33-73-01-20; fax 33-15-06-07; e-mail vkh@gov.si; internet kopenhagen.veleposlanistvo.si; Ambassador RUDOLF GABROVEC.

South Africa: Gammel Vartov Vej 8, POB 128, 2900 Hellerup; tel. 39-18-01-55; fax 39-18-40-06; e-mail sa.embassy@southafrica.dk; internet www.southafrica.dk; Ambassador DOLANA FAITH MSIMANG.

Spain: Kristianiagade 21, 2100 Copenhagen Ø; tel. 35-42-47-00; fax 35-42-47-26; e-mail emb.copenhague@mae.es; internet www.mae.es/embajadas/copenhague; Ambassador MELITÓN CARDONA TORRES.

Sweden: Skt Annæ Pl. 15A, 1250 Copenhagen K; tel. 33-36-03-70; fax 33-36-03-95; e-mail ambassaden.kopenhamn@foreign.ministry.se; internet www.swedenabroad.com/copenhagen; Ambassador LARS GRUNDBERG.

Switzerland: Amaliegade 14, 1256 Copenhagen K; tel. 33-14-17-96; fax 33-33-75-51; e-mail cop.vertretung@eda.admin.ch; internet www.eda.admin.ch/copenhagen; Ambassador ANDRÉ FAIVET.

Thailand: Norgesmindevej 18, 2900 Hellerup; tel. 39-62-50-10; fax 39-62-50-59; e-mail mail@thai-embassy.dk; Ambassador CHOLCHINEEPAN CHIRANOND.

Turkey: Rosbækvej 15, 2100 Copenhagen Ø; tel. 39-20-27-88; fax 39-20-51-66; e-mail turkembassy@internet.dk; internet www.turkishembassy.dk; Ambassador MELIH MEHMET AKAT.

Uganda: Sofievej 15, 2900 Hellerup; tel. 39-62-09-66; fax 39-61-01-48; e-mail info@ugandaembassy.dk; internet www.ugandaembassy.dk; Ambassador JOSEPH TOMUSANGE.

Ukraine: Toldbodgade 37A, 1st Floor, 1253 Copenhagen K; tel. 33-16-16-35; fax 33-16-00-74; e-mail embassy.ua@mail.tele.dk; internet www.ukraine-embassy.dk; Ambassador NATALIIA MYKOLAÏVNA ZARUDNA.

United Kingdom: Kastelsvej 36–40, 2100 Copenhagen Ø; tel. 35-44-52-00; fax 35-44-52-93; e-mail enquiry.copenhagen@fco.gov.uk; internet www.britishembassy.dk; Ambassador DAVID FROST.

USA: Dag Hammarskjölds Allé 24, 2100 Copenhagen Ø; tel. 33-41-71-00; fax 35-43-02-23; e-mail usembassycopenhagen@state.gov; internet www.usembassy.dk; Ambassador JAMES PALMER CAIN.

Venezuela: Toldbodgade 31, 3rd Floor, 1253 Copenhagen K; tel. 33-93-63-11; fax 33-37-76-59; e-mail emvendk@mail.dk; internet www.ve-ambassade.dk; Ambassador VICENTE EMILIO VALLENILLA.

Viet Nam: Bernstorffsvej 30C, 2900 Hellerup; tel. 39-18-39-32; fax 39-18-41-71; e-mail embvndk@hotmail.com; internet www.vietnamemb.dk; Ambassador NGUYEN XUAN HÔNG.

Judicial System

In Denmark the judiciary is independent of the Government. Judges are appointed by the Crown on the recommendation of the Minister of Justice and cannot be dismissed except by judicial sentence.

The ordinary courts are divided into three instances, the Lower Courts, the High Courts and the Supreme Court. There is one Lower Court for each of the 84 judicial districts in the country. These courts must have at least one judge trained in law and they hear all criminal and civil cases. The two High Courts serve Jutland and the islands respectively. They serve as appeal courts for cases from the Lower Courts. Each case must be heard by at least three judges. The Supreme Court, at which at least five judges must sit, is the court of appeal for cases from the High Courts. Usually only one appeal is allowed from either court, but in special instances the Board of Appeal may give leave for a second appeal, to the Supreme Court, from a case that started in a Lower Court. Furthermore, in certain minor cases, appeal from the Lower Courts to the High Courts is allowed only by leave of appeal from the Board of Appeal.

There is a special Maritime and Commercial Court in Copenhagen, consisting of a President and two Vice-Presidents with legal training and a number of commercial and nautical assessors. The Land Registration Court, which was established on 1 January 2007, deals with disputes regarding the registration of titles to land, marriage settlements and mortgage payments. The West High Court serves as the appeal court for cases from the Land Registration Court.

An Ombudsman is appointed by the Folketing after each general election, and is concerned with the quality and legality of the administration of the laws and administrative provisions. Although the Ombudsman holds no formal power to change decisions taken by the administration, he may, on a legal basis, express criticism of acts and decisions of administrative bodies. He is obliged to present an annual report to the Folketing.

Supreme Court

Prins Jørgens Gård 13, 1218 Copenhagen K; tel. 33-63-27-50; fax 33-15-00-10; e-mail post@hoejesteret.dk; internet www.domstol.dk/hojesteret.

President of the Supreme Court: TORBEN MELCHIOR.

Judges: PETER BLOK, JENS PETER CHRISTENSEN, BØRGE DAHL, NIELS GRUBBE, ASBJØRN JENSEN, POUL DAHL JENSEN, LENE PAGTER KRISTENSEN, LARS BAY LARSEN, PEER LORENTZEN, MARIANNE HØJGAARD PEDERSEN, MICHAEL REKLING, VIBEKE RØNNE, THOMAS RØRDAM, JYTTE SCHARLING, JON STOKHOLM, POUL SØGAARD, PER SØRENSEN, POUL SØRENSEN, HENRIK WAABEN, PER WALSØE.

President of the East High Court: BENT CARLSEN.

President of the West High Court: BJARNE CHRISTENSEN.

President of the Maritime and Commercial Court: JENS FEILBERG.

President of the Land Registration Court: SØRUP HANSEN.

Ombudsman: HANS GAMMELTOFT-HANSEN.

Religion

In 2005 some 83.1% of the population belonged to the Evangelical Lutheran Church in Denmark. In 2002 the second largest religion was Islam, constituting approximately 3% of the population (170,000 persons), followed by communities of Roman Catholics (36,000), Jehovah's Witnesses (15,000), Jews (7,000), Baptists (5,500), Pentecostalists (5,000) and the Church of Jesus Christ of Latter-day Saints (Mormons—4,500). The German minority in South Jutland and other non-Danish communities (particularly Scandinavian groups) have their own religious communities.

CHRISTIANITY

National Council of Churches in Denmark (Danske Kirkers Råd): Peter Bangs Vej 1D, 2000 Frederiksberg; tel. 35-43-29-43; fax 38-87-14-93; e-mail dkr@danskekirkersraad.dk; internet www.danskekirkersraad.dk; f. 1939; associate council of the World Council of Churches; 15 mem. churches; Chair. ANDERS GADEGAARD; Gen. Sec. MADS CHRISTOFFERSEN.

The National Church

Evangelical Lutheran Church in Denmark
(Den evangelisk-lutherske Folkekirke i Danmark)

Nørregade 11, 1165 Copenhagen K; tel. 33-47-65-00; fax 33-14-39-69; e-mail folkekirken@folkekirken.dk; internet www.folkekirken.dk.

The established Church of Denmark, supported by the State; no bishop exercises a presiding role, but the Bishop of Copenhagen is responsible for certain co-ordinating roles. The Council on International Relations of the Evangelical Lutheran Church in Denmark (Peter Bangs Vej 1D, 2000 Frederiksberg; e-mail interchurch@interchurch.dk; internet www.interchurch.dk) is responsible for ecumenical relations. Membership in 2005 was 4,498,703 (83.1% of the population).

Bishop of København: ERIK NORMAN SVENDSEN.

Bishop of Helsingør: LISE LOTTE REBEL.
Bishop of Roskilde: JAN LINDHARDT.
Bishop of Lolland-Falster: STEEN SKOVSGAARD.
Bishop of Odense: KRESTEN DREJERGAARD.
Bishop of Ålborg: SØREN LODBERG HVAS.
Bishop of Viborg: KARSTEN NISSEN.
Bishop of Århus: KJELD HOLM.
Bishop of Ribe: ELISABETH DONS CHRISTENSEN.
Bishop of Haderslev: NIELS HENRIK ARENDT.

The Roman Catholic Church

Denmark comprises a single diocese, directly responsible to the Holy See. At 31 December 2005 there were an estimated 36,634 adherents in the country (around 0.7% of the population). The Bishop participates in the Scandinavian Episcopal Conference (based in Sweden).

Bishop of København: CZESLAW KOZON, Katolsk Bispekontor, Bredgade 69A, 1260 Copenhagen K; tel. 33-11-60-80; fax 33-14-60-86; e-mail bispekontor@katolsk.dk; internet www.katolsk.dk.

Other Churches

Apostolic Church in Denmark: Lykkegaardsvej 100, 6000 Kolding; tel. 79-32-16-00; fax 79-32-16-01; e-mail servicecenter@apostolic.dk; internet www.apostolskkirke.dk; Nat. Leader JOHANNES HANSEN.

Baptistkirken i Danmark (Baptist Union of Denmark): Købnerhus, Lærdalsgade 7, 2300 Copenhagen S; tel. 32-59-07-08; fax 32-59-01-33; e-mail info@baptist.dk; internet www.baptistkirken.dk; f. 1839; 5,100 mems; Pres. FINN BASNOV.

Church of England: St Alban's Church, Churchillparken 11, 1263 Copenhagen K; tel. 39-62-77-36; fax 39-62-77-35; e-mail chaplain@st-albans.dk; internet www.st-albans.dk; f. 1728; Chaplain MARK OAKLEY.

Church of Jesus Christ of Latter-day Saints (Mormons): Guldbergsvej 31, 5000 Odense C; tel. 66-11-17-00; fax 99-11-17-25; e-mail noa@noa.dk; f. in Denmark 1850; c. 4,500 mems in 23 congregations; Dir, Public Affairs NIELS-OVE ANDERSEN.

Danish Mission Covenant Church (Det Danske Missionsforbund): Rosenlunden 17, 5000 Odense C; tel. 66-14-83-31; fax 66-14-83-00; e-mail ddm@email.dk; internet www.missionsforbundet.dk; Exec. Dir PALLE BYG.

First Church of Christ, Scientist, Copenhagen: Nyvej 7, 1851 Frederiksberg C; tel. 33-13-08-91; e-mail cs.rr@email.dk; also in Århus; tel. 86-16-22-78.

German Lutheran Church: Skt Petri Church Office, Larslejsstræde 11, 1451 Copenhagen K; tel. 33-13-38-33; fax 33-13-38-35; e-mail kirchenbuero@sankt-petri.dk; internet www.sankt-petri.dk.

Methodist Church: Metodistkirkens Social Arbejde, Rigensgade 21, 1316 Copenhagen K; tel. 33-93-25-96; fax 33-93-65-39; e-mail msac@image.dk; f. 1910; Chair. FINN UTH.

Moravian Brethren: The Moravian Church, 6070 Christiansfeld; f. in Denmark 1773; Pastor JØRGEN BØYTLER; Lindegade 26, 6070 Christiansfeld; tel. 74-56-14-20; fax 74-56-14-21; email boeytler@post7.tele.dk.

Norwegian Seamen's Church: Kong Håkons Kirke, Ved Mønten 9, 2300 Copenhagen S; tel. 32-57-11-03; fax 32-57-40-05; e-mail kobenhavn@sjomannskirken.no; internet www.sjomannskirken.no; f. 1958.

Reformed Church: Reformed Synod of Denmark, Spindlerhus, Jyllandsgade 41, 7000 Fredericia; tel. 75-92-05-51; e-mail s.hofmeister@reformert.dk; internet www.reformert.dk; Moderator Rev. SABINE HOFMEISTER.

Russian Orthodox Church: Alexander Nevski Church, Bredgade 53, 1260 Copenhagen K; tel. 33-13-60-46; fax 33-13-28-85; e-mail ruskirke@ruskirke.dk; internet www.ruskirke.dk; f. 1883; Rector Fr SERGY PLEKHOV.

Seventh-day Adventists: Syvende Dags Adventistkirken, POB 15, Concordiavej 16, 2850 Nærum; tel. 45-58-77-77; fax 45-58-77-78; e-mail adventistkirken@adventist.dk; internet www.adventist.dk; f. 1863; Pres. BJORN OTTESEN; Sec. THOMAS MULLER.

Society of Friends: Danish Quaker Centre, Drejervej 17, 2400 Copenhagen NV; tel. and fax 36-47-00-95; internet www.kvaekerne.dk.

Swedish Lutheran Church: Svenska Gustafskyrkan, Folke Bernadottes Allé, 2100 Copenhagen Ø; tel. 33-15-54-58; fax 33-15-02-94; e-mail info.danmark@skut.org; internet www.skut.org/danmark.

BAHÁ'Í FAITH

Bahá'í: Det Nationale Åndelige Råd, Sofievej 28, 2900 Hellerup; tel. 39-62-35-18; e-mail sekretariat@bahai.dk; internet www.bahai.dk.

DENMARK

ISLAM

The Muslim Community: Nusrat Djahan Mosque (and Ahmadiyya Mission), Eriksminde Allé 2, 2650 Hvidovre; tel. 36-75-35-02; fax 36-75-00-07.

JUDAISM

Jewish Community: Mosaisk Trossamfund, Ny Kongensgade 6, 1472 Copenhagen K; tel. 33-12-88-68; fax 33-12-33-57; e-mail mt@mosaiske.dk; internet www.mosaiske.dk; c. 2,500 mems; Chief Rabbi BENT LEXNER.

The Press

There are more than 220 separate newspapers, including some 32 principal dailies. The average total circulation of daily newspapers in 2005 was 1,288,000 on weekdays.

Most newspapers and magazines are privately owned and published by joint concerns, co-operatives or limited liability companies. The main concentration of papers is held by the Berlingske Group, which owns *Berlingske Tidende*, *B.T.* and *Weekendavisen*, and the provincial *Jydskevestkysten* and *Århus Stiftstidende*.

The largest-selling newspaper in Denmark is *Jyllands-Posten*, published in Viby, a suburb of Århus. Its main competitors are *Politiken* and *Berlingske Tidende*, both published in Copenhagen, but there is no truly national press. Copenhagen accounts for 20% of the national dailies and about one-half of the total circulation. No paper is directly owned by a political party, although all papers show a fairly pronounced political leaning.

PRINCIPAL DAILIES
(circulation figures refer to July–Dec. 2006, unless otherwise indicated)

Aabenraa

Der Nordschleswiger: Skibbroen 4, POB 1041, 6200 Aabenraa; tel. 74-62-38-80; fax 74-62-94-30; e-mail redaktion@nordschleswiger.dk; internet www.nordschleswiger.dk; f. 1946; German; Editor-in-Chief SIEGFRIED MATLOK; circ. 2,329.

Ålborg

Nordjyske Stiftstidende: Langagervej 1, POB 8000, 9220 Ålborg Øst; tel. 99-35-35-35; fax 99-35-33-75; e-mail nordjyske@nordjyske.dk; internet www.nordjyske.dk; f. 1767; adopted present name in 1999, following the merger of six regional dailies; mornings; Liberal independent; Publr and Editor-in-Chief PER LYNGBY; circ. weekdays 62,075, Sundays 72,028.

Århus

Århus Stiftstidende: Banegårdspl. 11, 8000 Århus C; tel. 87-40-10-10; fax 87-40-13-21; e-mail redaktionen@stiften.dk; internet www.stiften.dk; f. 1794; evening and weekend mornings; Liberal independent; Editor-in-Chief ERIK FRODELUND; circ. weekdays 33,543, Sundays 45,379.

Esbjerg

Jydskevestkysten: Banegårdspladsen, 6700 Esbjerg; tel. 75-12-45-00; fax 75-13-62-62; e-mail jydskevestkysten@jv.dk; internet www.jv.dk; f. 1917 as *Vestkysten*; merged with *Jydske Tidende* in 1991 to form present daily; morning; Liberal; Editor-in-Chief METTE BOCK; circ. weekdays 76,550, Sundays 86,693.

Helsingør

Helsingør Dagblad: Klostermosevej 101, 3000 Helsingør; tel. 49-22-21-10; fax 49-22-18-61; e-mail k.roed@hdnet.dk; internet www.hdnet.dk; Editor-in-Chief JOHN BECH; circ. 6,163.

Herlev

Licitationen: Marienlundsvej 46D, POB 537, 2730 Herlev; tel. 70-15-02-22; fax 44-85-89-19; e-mail licitationen@licitationen.dk; internet www.licitationen.dk; news for construction industry; Editor-in-Chief KLAUS TØTTRUP; circ. 5,276.

Herning

Herning Folkeblad: Østergade 25, 7400 Herning; tel. 96-26-37-00; fax 97-22-36-00; e-mail hf@herningfolkeblad.dk; internet www.herningfolkeblad.dk; f. 1869; evening; Liberal; Editor-in-Chief FLEMMING LARSEN; circ. 13,065.

Hillerød

Dagbladet/Frederiksborg Amts Avis: Milnersvej 44–46, 3400 Hillerød; tel. 48-24-41-00; fax 42-25-48-40; internet www.dagbladetonline.dk; f. 1874; morning; Liberal; Editor TORBEN DALBY LARSEN; circ. weekdays 27,578.

Holbæk

Holbæk Amts Venstreblad: Ahlgade 1, 4300 Holbæk; tel. 59-48-02-00; fax 59-44-50-34; e-mail redaktion@venstrebladet.dk; internet www.venstrebladet.dk; f. 1905; evening; Social Liberal; Editor-in-Chief MOGENS FLYVHOLM; circ. 15,218.

Holstebro

Dagbladet Holstebro-Struer: Lægårdvej 86, 7500 Holstebro; tel. 99-12-83-00; fax 97-41-03-20; e-mail holstebro@bergske.dk; internet www.bergske.dk; evening; Liberal independent; Editor-in-Chief PER WESTERGAARD; circ. 11,154.

Horsens

Horsens Folkeblad: Søndergade 47, 8700 Horsens; tel. 76-27-20-00; fax 75-62-02-18; e-mail redaktionen@horsens-folkeblad.dk; internet www.horsens-folkeblad.dk; f. 1866; evening; Liberal; Editor JENS BEBE; circ. 16,363.

Kalundborg

Kalundborg Folkeblad: Skibbrogade 40, 4400 Kalundborg; tel. 88-88-44-00; fax 59-51-02-80; e-mail red.kf@nordvest.dk; internet www.kalundborg-folkeblad.dk; Editor-in-Chief CLAUS SØRENSEN; circ. 7,261.

Kerteminde

Kjerteminde Avis: Ndr. Ringvej 54, 5300 Kerteminde; tel. 65-32-10-04; fax 65-32-39-04; e-mail info@kj-avis.dk; Editor JØRGEN WIND-HANSEN; circ. 1,940.

København
(Copenhagen)

Berlingske Tidende: Pilestræde 34, 1147 Copenhagen K; tel. 33-75-75-75; fax 33-75-20-20; e-mail redaktion@berlingske.dk; internet www.berlingske.dk; f. 1749; morning; Conservative independent; Editor-in-Chief LISBETH KNUDSEN; circ. weekdays 122,933, Sundays 141,579.

Børsen: Møntergade 19, 1140 Copenhagen K; tel. 33-32-01-02; fax 33-12-24-45; e-mail redaktionen@borsen.dk; internet www.borsen.dk; f. 1896; morning; independent; business news; Editor-in-Chief LEIF BECK FALLESEN; circ. 70,503.

B.T.: Kr. Bernikowsgade 6, POB 200, 1006 Copenhagen K; tel. 33-75-75-33; fax 33-75-20-33; e-mail bt@bt.dk; internet www.bt.dk; f. 1916; morning; Conservative independent; Editor-in-Chief KRISTIAN LUND; circ. weekdays 92,735, Sundays 133,353.

Dagbladet Arbejderen: Ryesgade 3F, 1. sal, 2200 Copenhagen N; tel. 35-35-21-93; fax 35-37-20-39; e-mail redaktion@arbejderen.dk; internet www.arbejderen.dk; Editor-in-Chief BIRTHE SØRENSEN.

Dagbladet Information: Store Kongensgade 40C, POB 188, 1006 Copenhagen K; tel. 33-69-60-00; fax 33-69-61-10; e-mail inf-dk@information.dk; internet www.information.dk; f. 1943 (founded underground during occupation and then legally in 1945); morning; independent; Editor-in-Chief PALLE WEIS; circ. 21,045.

Ekstra Bladet: Rådhuspladsen 37, 1785 Copenhagen V; tel. 33-11-13-13; fax 33-14-10-00; e-mail post@ekstrabladet.dk; internet www.eb.dk; f. 1904; evening; Liberal independent; Editor-in-Chief POUL MADSEN; Man. Dir LARS HENRIK MUNCH; circ. weekdays 108,478, Sundays 144,308.

Kristeligt Dagblad: Rosengården 14, 1174 Copenhagen K; tel. 33-48-05-00; fax 33-48-05-01; e-mail kristeligt-dagblad@kristeligt-dagblad.dk; internet www.kristeligt-dagblad.dk; f. 1896; morning; independent; Editor-in-Chief ERIK BJERAGER; circ. 26,145.

Politiken: Politikens Hus, Rådhuspladsen 37, 1785 Copenhagen V; tel. 33-11-85-11; fax 33-15-41-77; e-mail indland@pol.dk; internet www.politiken.dk; f. 1884; morning; Liberal independent; Editor-in-Chief TØGER SEIDENFADEN; circ. weekdays 121,571, Sundays 156,221.

Næstved

Sjællandske: Dania 38, 4700 Næstved; tel. 72-45-11-00; fax 72-45-11-17; e-mail red@sj-medier.dk; internet www.sjællandske.dk; f. 2005 by merger of Næstved Tidende (f. 1866) and Sjællands Tidende (f. 1815); Liberal; Editor SØREN BAUMANN; circ. 22,232.

Nykøbing

Lolland-Falsters Folketidende: Tværgade 14, 4800 Nykøbing F; tel. 54-88-02-00; fax 54-85-02-96; e-mail redaktion@folketidende.dk; internet www.folketidende.dk; f. 1873; evening; Liberal; Editor SØREN KNUDSEN; circ. 21,527.

DENMARK

Morsø Folkeblad: Elsøvej 105, 7900 Nykøbing M; tel. 97-72-10-00; fax 97-72-10-10; e-mail mf@mf.dk; internet www.mf.dk; Editor LEIF KRISTIANSEN; circ. 5,728.

Odense

Fyens Stiftstidende: Banegårdspl., 5100 Odense C; tel. 66-11-11-11; fax 65-93-25-74; e-mail redaktion@fyens.dk; internet www.fyens.dk; f. 1772; morning; independent; Editor-in-Chief EGON TØTTRUP; circ. weekdays 57,970, Sundays 72,472.

Randers

Randers Amtsavis: Nørregade 7, 8900 Randers; tel. 87-12-20-00; fax 87-12-21-21; e-mail e-mail@amtsavisra.dk; f. 1810; evening; independent; Editor-in-Chief OLE C. JØRGENSEN; circ. 11,972.

Ringkøbing

Dagbladet Ringkøbing-Skjern: Sankt Blichersvej 5, POB 146, 6950 Ringkøbing; tel. 99-75-73-00; fax 99-75-74-30; e-mail ringkoebing@bergske.dk; internet www.dagbladetringskjern.dk; evening; Editor FLEMMING HVIDFELDT; circ. 6,455.

Rønne

Bornholms Tidende: Nørregade 11–13, 3700 Rønne; tel. 56-90-30-00; fax 56-90-30-92; e-mail redaktion@bhstid.dk; internet www.bornholmstidende.dk; f. 1866; evening; Liberal; Editor-in-Chief DAN QVITZAU; circ. 12,840.

Silkeborg

Midtjyllands Avis: Papirfabrikken 18, 8600 Silkeborg; tel. 86-82-13-00; fax 86-81-35-77; e-mail silkeborg@midtjyllandsavis.dk; internet www.midtjyllandsavis.dk; f. 1857; daily except Sundays; Editor-in-Chief STEFFEN LANGE; circ. 15,886.

Skive

Skive Folkeblad: Gemsevej 7–9, 7800 Skive; tel. 97-51-34-11; fax 97-51-28-35; e-mail redaktionen@skivefolkeblad.dk; internet www.skivefolkeblad.dk; f. 1880; Social Liberal; Editor OLE DALL; circ. 12,036.

Svendborg

Fyns Amts Avis: Skt Nicolai Gade 3, 5700 Svendborg; tel. 62-21-46-21; fax 62-22-06-10; e-mail post@faa.dk; internet www.fynsamtsavis.dk; f. 1863; Liberal; Editor-in-Chief JØRGEN KREBS; circ. 17,140.

Vejle

Vejle Amts Folkeblad: Bugattivej 8, 7100 Vejle; tel. 75-85-77-88; fax 75-85-72-47; e-mail vaf@vejleamtsfolkeblad.dk; internet www.vejleonline.dk; f. 1865; evening; Liberal; Editor ARNE MARIAGER; circ. 17,400.

Viborg

Viborg Stifts Folkeblad: Vesterbrogade 8, 8800 Viborg; tel. 89-27-63-00; fax 89-27-64-80; e-mail viborg@bergske.dk; internet www.viborg-folkeblad.dk; f. 1877; evening; Liberal Democrat; also published: *Viborg Nyt* (weekly); Editor LARS NORUP; circ. 11,068.

Viby

Jyllands-Posten: Grøndalsvej 3, 8260 Viby J; tel. 87-38-38-38; fax 87-38-31-99; e-mail jp@jp.dk; internet www.jp.dk; f. 1871; independent; Editor-in-Chief CARSTEN JUSTE; circ. weekdays 143,723, Sundays 192,492.

OTHER NEWSPAPERS

Den Blå Avis (East edition): Generatorvej 8D, 2730 Herlev; tel. 44-85-44-44; internet www.dba.dk; 2 a week; circ. 73,000.

Den Blå Avis (West edition): Marselisborg Havnevej 26, POB 180, 8100 Århus C; tel. 87-31-31-31; fax 86-20-20-02; internet www.dba.dk; Thursday; circ. 46,160.

Weekendavisen: Vimmelskaftet 47, 3. sal, 1161 Copenhagen K; tel. 33-75-25-33; fax 33-75-20-50; e-mail bwa@weekendavisen.dk; internet www.weekendavisen.dk; f. 1749; Conservative independent; Friday; Editor-in-Chief ANNE KNUDSEN; circ. 58,678.

POPULAR PERIODICALS

(circulation figures refer to July–Dec. 2006, unless otherwise indicated)

Ældre Sagen: Nørregade 49, 1165 Copenhagen K; tel. 33-96-86-86; fax 33-96-86-87; e-mail aeldresagen@aeldresagen.dk; internet www.aeldresagen.dk; 6 a year; members' magazine for senior citizens; Editor SANNA KJÆR HANSEN; circ. 500,000.

Alt for damerne: Hellerupvej 51, 2900 Hellerup; tel. 39-45-74-00; fax 39-45-74-80; e-mail alt@altfordamerne.dk; internet www.altfordamerne.dk; f. 1946; weekly; women's magazine; Editor-in-Chief HANNE HØIBERG; circ. 80,689.

Anders And & Co: Vognmagergade 11, 1148 Copenhagen K; tel. 70-20-50-35; fax 33-30-57-60; internet www.andeby.dk; weekly; children's magazine; Editor TOMMY MELLE; circ. 62,924.

Basserne: Vognmagergade 11, 1148 Copenhagen K; tel. 33-33-75-35; fax 33-33-75-05; e-mail basserne@tsf.egmont.com; internet www.basserne.dk; fortnightly; children and youth; circ. 14,159.

Billed-Bladet: Otto Mønsteds Gade 3, 1506 Copenhagen V; tel. 36-15-35-00; e-mail bb@billed-bladet.dk; internet www.billed-bladet.dk; f. 1938; weekly; royal family and celebrity pictures; Editor-in-Chief ANNEMETTE KRAKAU; circ. 197,060.

Bo Bedre: Strandboulevarden 130, 2100 Copenhagen Ø; tel. 39-17-20-00; fax 39-29-01-99; e-mail bobedre@bobedre.dk; internet www.bobedre.dk; monthly; homes and gardens; Editor-in-Chief ERIK RIMMER; circ. 86,096.

Familie Journal: Vigerslev Allé 18, 2500 Valby; tel. 36-15-22-22; fax 36-15-22-99; e-mail redaktion@familiejournalen.dk; internet www.familiejournalen.dk; f. 1877; weekly; Editor-in-Chief PETER DALL; circ. 208,284.

Femina: Vigerslev Allé 18, 2500 Valby; tel. 36-15-23-00; fax 36-15-23-99; e-mail redaktionen@femina.dk; internet www.femina.dk; f. 1873; weekly; Editor JUTTA LARSEN; circ. 77,080.

Gør Det Selv: Strandboulevarden 130, 2100 Copenhagen Ø; tel. 39-17-20-00; fax 39-21-09-99; e-mail gds@bp.bonnier.dk; internet www.goerdetselv.dk; f. 1975; every 3 weeks; do-it-yourself; Editor RUNE MICHAELSEN; circ. 39,426.

Helse: Hejrevej 37, 2100 Copenhagen NV; tel. 35-25-05-25; fax 35-26-87-60; e-mail helse@helse.dk; internet www.helse.dk; f. 1955; monthly; social, mental and physiological health; circ. 270,000.

Hendes Verden: Hellerupvej 51, 2900 Hellerup; tel. 39-45-75-50; fax 39-45-75-99; e-mail hv@hendesverden.dk; internet www.hendesverden.dk; f. 1937; weekly; for women; Editor IBEN NIELSEN; circ. 53,066.

Her & Nu: Hellerupvej 51, 2900 Hellerup; tel. 39-45-77-00; fax 39-45-77-17; e-mail herognu@herognu.com; internet www.herognu.com; weekly (Thursday); publ. by Egmont Magasiner A/S; illustrated television and film guide; news about the Royal family and celebrities; Editor MICHAEL RASMUSSEN; circ. 115,909.

Hjemmet (The Home): Hellerupvej 51, 2900 Hellerup; tel. 39-45-76-00; fax 39-45-76-60; e-mail red@hjemmet.dk; internet www.hjemmet.dk; weekly; Editor-in-Chief BJARNE RAVNSTED; circ. 164,601.

I form: Strandboulevarden 130, 2100 Copenhagen Ø; tel. 39-17-20-00; fax 39-17-23-11; e-mail iform@iform.dk; internet www.iform.dk; 17 a year; sport, health, nutrition, sex, psychology; Editor KAREN LYAGER HORVE; circ. 50,055.

Idé-nyt: Gl. Klausdalsbrovej 495, 2730 Herlev; tel. 44-53-40-00; fax 44-92-11-21; e-mail idenyt@idenyt.dk; internet www.idenyt.dk; f. 1973; 10 a year; free magazine (regional editions); homes and gardens; circ. 1,752,848.

Illustreret Videnskab: Strandboulevarden 130, 2100 Copenhagen Ø; tel. 39-17-20-00; fax 39-17-23-12; internet www.illustreretvidenskab.dk; 17 a year; popular science; Editor JENS E. MATTHIESEN; circ. 68,713.

Kig ind: Vigerslev Allé 18, 2500 Valby; tel. 36-15-20-00; internet kigind.jubii.dk; weekly (Thursday); publ. by Aller Press A/S; fashion and celebrity news; circ. 71,633.

Mad og Bolig: Vigerslev Allé 18, 2500 Valby; tel. 36-15-20-00; fax 36-15-27-95; e-mail mb@madogbolig.dk; internet www.madogbolig.dk; f. 1991; 10 a year; gastronomy, wine, interiors and travel; Editor JETTE ØSTERLUND; circ. 40,179.

Månedsmagasinet IN: Vigerslev Allé 18, 2500 Valby; tel. 36-15-20-00; fax 36-15-27-94; e-mail in@in.dk; internet www.in.dk; fashion; Editor-in-Chief CAMILLA LINDEMANN; circ. 41,357.

Motor: Firskovvej 32, POB 500, 2800 Lyngby; tel. 45-27-07-07; fax 45-27-09-93; e-mail motor@fdm.dk; internet www.fdm.dk; f. 1906; monthly; cars and motoring; Editor-in-Chief BO CHRISTIAN KOCH; circ. 237,684.

Samvirke: FDB Samvirke, Fanøgade 15, 2100 Copenhagen Ø; tel. 39-47-00-00; fax 39-47-00-01; e-mail fdb@fdb.dk; f. 1928; consumer monthly; Editor-in-Chief SØREN BERG; circ. 375,000.

Se og Hør: Vigerslev Allé 18, 2500 Valby; tel. 36-15-24-00; fax 36-15-24-99; e-mail redaktionen@seoghoer.dk; internet www.seoghoer.dk; f. 1940; news and TV; Editor HENRIK QVORTRUP; circ. 195,881.

Sofus' Lillebror: Keesing Krydsordsforlaget A/S, Bernhard Bangs Allé 23, 2000 Frederiksberg; tel. 33-33-75-35; fax 33-33-75-05; monthly; children and youth; circ. 44,000.

TIPS-bladet: Kristen Bernikowsgade 4, 3rd Floor, 1105 Copenhagen K; tel. 49-70-89-00; fax 49-70-88-30; e-mail redaktion@tipsbladet

DENMARK

.dk; internet www.tipsbladet.dk; twice weekly; sport; circ. weekday 8,332; weekend 12,570; Editor-in-Chief NIELS FRYDENLUND.

Ud og Se: Frederiksberg Runddel 1, 2000 Frederiksberg; tel. 33-22-20-20; fax 33-22-99-59; e-mail ingo@jungersted.com; internet www.jungersted.com; free travel monthly; publ. by DSB; circ. 208,630.

Ude og Hjemme: Vigerslev Allé 18, 2500 Valby; tel. 36-15-25-25; fax 36-15-25-99; e-mail redaktionen@udeoghjemme.dk; internet www.udeoghjemme.dk; f. 1926; family weekly; Editor JØRN BAUENMAND; circ. 174,874.

Ugebladet Søndag: Otto Mønsteds Gade 3, 1505 Copenhagen V; tel. 36-15-34-00; fax 36-15-34-01; e-mail soendag@soendag.dk; f. 1921; weekly; family magazine; Editor JOHNNY JOHANSEN; circ. 97,376.

Vi Unge: Vi Unge Gruppen, Marielundvej 46D, 2730 Herlev; tel. 44-85-88-00; e-mail redaktionen@viunge.dk; internet www.viunge.dk; for teenage girls; Editor-in-Chief KATRINE MEMBORG; circ. 45,994.

SPECIALIST PERIODICALS

ABF-Nyt: Vester Farimagsgade 1, 8th Floor, Postboks 239, 1501 Copenhagen V; tel. 33-86-28-30; fax 33-86-28-55; e-mail abf@abf-rep.dk; for members of Andelsboligforeningernes Fællesrepræsentation (ABF, Co-operative Housing Association); 4 a year; Editor JAN HANSEN; circ. 60,185.

Aktive Kvinder: Niels Hemmingsensgade 10, 2. sal, 1153 Copenhagen K; tel. 33-13-12-22; fax 33-33-03-28; e-mail mail@aktivekvinder.dk; internet www.aktivekvinder.dk; f. 1920; 4 a year; home management; Editor KIRSTEN WULFF; circ. 25,000.

Aktuel Elektronik: Naverland 35, 2600 Glostrup; tel. 43-24-26-28; fax 43-24-26-26; e-mail rsh@techmedia.dk; internet www.techmedia.dk/blade/AEL.asp; 22 a year; computing and information technology; Editor-in-Chief ROLF SYLVESTER-HVID; circ. 6,502.

Alt om Data: Sejrøgade 7-9, 2100 Copenhagen Ø; tel. 33-74-71-03; fax 33-74-71-91; e-mail redaktion@altomdata.dk; internet www.altomdata.dk; f. 1983; monthly; Editor-in-Chief LARS BENNETZEN; circ. 12,066 (July–Dec. 2006).

Automatik: Algade 10, POB 80, 4500 Nykøbing; tel. 53-41-23-10; engineering; monthly; circ. 39,250.

Bådnyt: Vigerslev Allé, 2500 Valby; tel. 36-15-22-78; fax 36-15-26-96; e-mail knut@baadnyt.dk; internet www.baadnyt.dk; monthly; boats; Editor KNUT IVERSEN; circ. 9,092.

Beboerbladet: Frederiksberg Runddel 1, 2000 Frederiksberg; tel. 33-22-20-20; fax 33-22-99-59; e-mail info@jungersted.com; internet www.jungersted.com; quarterly; for tenants in public housing; circ. 550,917.

Beredskab: Hedelykken 10, 2640 Hedehusene; tel. 35-24-00-00; fax 35-24-00-01; e-mail bf@beredskab.dk; internet www.beredskab.dk; f. 1934; 6 a year; civil protection and preparedness; publ. by the Danish Civil Protection League; circ. 10,783.

Bilsnak: Park Allé 355, 2605 Brøndby; tel. 43-28-82-00; fax 43-63-27-22; e-mail redaktion@bilsnak.dk; internet www.bilsnak.dk; f. 1976; 3 a year; cars; Editor OLE KAUFFELDT; circ. 185,530.

Boligen: Studiestræde 50, 1554 Copenhagen V; tel. 33-76-20-21; fax 33-76-20-01; e-mail bl@bl.dk; internet www.bl.dk; 11 a year; publ. by Boligselskabernes Landsforening; housing asscns, architects; Editor GERT NIELSEN; circ. 32,500.

BygTek: Stationsparken 25, 2600 Glostrup; tel. 45-43-29-00; fax 45-43-13-28; e-mail redaktion@odsgard.dk; internet www.odsgard.dk; monthly; building and construction; Editor-in-Chief PETER ODSGARD; circ. 22,478.

Computerworld: Carl Jacobsens Vej 25, 2500 Valby; tel. 77-30-03-00; fax 77-30-03-01; e-mail redaktionen@computerworld.dk; internet www.computerworld.dk; f. 1981; 2 a week; computing; Editor-in-Chief MIKAEL LINDHOLM; circ. 16,373 (July–Dec. 2006).

Cyklister: Dansk Cyklist Forbund, Rømersgade 5, 1362 Copenhagen K; tel. 33-32-31-21; fax 33-32-76-83; e-mail dcf@dcf.dk; internet www.dcf.dk; f. 1905; 6 a year; organ of Danish Cyclist Federation; Editor LOTTE MALENE RUBY; circ. 14,756 (July–Dec. 2006).

DLG Nyt: Axelborg, Vesterbrogade 4A, 1503 Copenhagen V; tel. 33-69-87-00; fax 33-69-87-28; e-mail info@dlg.dk; internet www.dlg.dk; 11 a year; farming; Editor-in-Chief KRISTIAN HUNDEBØLL.

Effektivt Landbrug: Odensevej 29, 5550 Langeskov; tel. 70-15-12-37; fax 70-15-12-47; e-mail effektivt@effektivtlandbrug.dk; internet www.landbrugnet.dk; 21 a year; farming; Editor BØJE ØSTERLUND; circ. 31,407.

Finans: Applebys Pl. 5, 1411 Copenhagen K; tel. 32-96-46-00; e-mail ys@finansforbundet.dk; internet www.finansforbundet.dk; 11 a year; for employees in the financial sector; Editor-in-Chief YVONNE SCHANTZ; circ. 53,000.

Folkeskolen: Vandkunsten 12, POB 2139, 1015 Copenhagen K; tel. 33-69-64-00; fax 33-69-64-26; e-mail folkeskolen@dlf.org; internet www.folkeskolen.dk; 32 a year; teaching; Editor THORKILD THEJSEN; circ. 87,275.

Directory

Havebladet: Frederikssundsvej 304A, 2700 Brønshøj; tel. 38-28-87-50; fax 32-28-83-50; e-mail info@kolonihave.dk; internet www.kolonihave.dk; 5 a year; publ. by Kolonihaveforbundet for Danmark; gardening; circ. 40,500.

High Fidelity: Blegdamsvej 112A, 2100 Copenhagen Ø; tel. 70-23-70-01; fax 70-23-70-02; e-mail hifired@hifi.dk; internet www.hifi.dk; f. 1967; 8 a year; Editor-in-Chief MICHAEL MADSEN; circ. 25,000.

Hunden: Mediehuset Wiegaarden, 9500 Hobro; tel. 98-51-20-66; fax 98-51-20-06; e-mail hunden-redaktionen@wiegaarden.dk; internet www.dansk-kennel-klub.dk; 10 a year; organ of Dansk Kennel Klub; circ. 30,000.

Ingelise (Alt om Håndarbejde): Ved Søen 1, Jels, 6630 Rødding; tel. 70-11-70-80; fax 73-99-66-22; internet www.ingelise.dk; crafts; Editor-in-Chief INGELISE BJERRE; circ. 40,225 (July–Dec. 2006).

Ingeniøren: POB 373, Skelbækgade 4, 1503 Copenhagen V; tel. 33-26-53-00; fax 33-26-53-01; e-mail ing@ing.dk; internet www.ing.dk; f. 1892; weekly engineers' magazine; Editor-in-Chief ARNE STEINMARK; circ. 66,138 (July–Dec. 2006).

Jaeger: Hojnæsvej 56, 2610 Rødovre; tel. 36-72-42-00; fax 36-72-09-11; e-mail post@jaegerne.dk; internet www.jaegerforbundet.dk; monthly except July; hunting; circ. 78,841.

Jern- og Maskinindustrien: Marielundvej 46E, 2730 Herlev; tel. 70-11-37-00; fax 44-85-89-62; e-mail jm@jernindustri.dk; internet www.jernindustri.dk; 22 a year; iron and metallic industries; Editor-in-Chief HENRIK FOUGT.

Kommunalbladet: Weidekampsgade 8, 0900 Copenhagen; tel. 33-30-43-43; fax 33-30-44-49; e-mail redaktionen@kommunalbladet.dk; internet www.kommunalbladet.dk; 21 a year; municipal administration, civil servants; Editor HENRIK MUNKSGAARD; circ. 70,000.

Komputer for Alle: Strandboulevarden 130, 2100 Copenhagen Ø; tel. 39-10-30-72; e-mail red@komputer.dk; internet www.komputer.dk; 18 a year; publ. by Bonnier Publications A/S; computers; Editor-in-Chief LEIF JONASSON; circ. 42,919 (July–Dec. 2006).

Landsbladet Kvæg: Vester Farimagsgade 6, 1606 Copenhagen V; tel. 33-39-47-00; fax 33-39-47-49; e-mail kvaeg@dlmedier.dk; monthly; for cattle-breeders and dairy-farmers; circ. 8,000.

Lederne: Vermlandsgade 65, 2300 Copenhagen S; tel. 32-83-32-83; fax 32-83-32-84; e-mail lh@lederne.dk; internet www.lederne.dk; 11 a year; for managers; Editor-in-Chief ULLA BECHSGAARD; circ. 86,438 (2005/06).

Metal: Nyropsgade 38, 1602 Copenhagen V; tel. 33-63-20-00; fax 33-63-21-51; e-mail metal@danskmetal.dk; internet www.danskmetal.dk; 9 a year; metal industries; Editor-in-Chief JENS HOLMSGAARD; circ. 143,678.

Spejdersnus: The Danish Guide and Scout Association, Arsenalvej 10, 1436 Copenhagen K; tel. 32-64-00-50; fax 32-64-00-75; e-mail dds@dds.dk; e-mail nyheder@dds.dk; internet www.dds.dk; 7 a year; organ of the Scout Movement; circ. 38,900.

Stat & Kommune Indkøb: POB 162, Glostrup Torv 6, 2600 Glostrup; tel. 43-43-31-21; fax 43-43-15-13; e-mail saki@saki.dk; internet www.saki.dk; monthly; public works and administration; Editor DAN MORRISON.

Sygeplejersken: Skt Annæ Pl. 30, POB 1084, 1008 Copenhagen K; tel. 33-15-15-55; fax 33-93-47-82; e-mail redaktionen@dsr.dk; internet www.tfs.dk; 50 a year; nursing; Editor-in-Chief SIGURD NISSEN-PETERSEN; circ. 74,000.

Tidsskrift for Sukkersyge—Diabetes: Rytterkasernen 1, 5000 Odense C; tel. 66-12-90-06; fax 65-91-49-08; e-mail df@diabetes.dk; internet www.diabetes.dk; f. 1940; 6 a year; diabetes; Dirs FLEMMING KJERSGAARD JOHANSEN, KARIN MULVAD; circ. 62,000.

Ugeskrift for Læger: Trondhjemsgade 9, 2100 Copenhagen Ø; tel. 35-44-85-00; fax 35-44-85-02; e-mail ufl@daol.dk; weekly; medical; Editor-in-Chief TORBEN KITAJ; circ. 22,000.

NEWS AGENCY

Ritzaus Bureau I/S: Store Kongensgade 14, 1264 Copenhagen K; tel. 33-30-00-00; fax 33-30-00-01; e-mail ritzau@ritzau.dk; internet www.ritzau.dk; f. 1866; general, financial and commercial news; owned by all Danish newspapers; Chair., Bd of Dirs ERIK BJERAGER; Gen. Man. and Editor-in-Chief UFFE RIIS SØRENSEN.

PRESS ASSOCIATIONS

Dansk Fagpresse (Association of the Danish Specialized Press): Pressens Hus, Skindergade 7, 1159 Copenhagen K; tel. 33-97-40-00; fax 33-91-26-70; e-mail df@danskfagpresse.dk; internet www.danskfagpresse.dk; Chair. SVEND BIE; Man. Dir CHRISTIAN KIERKEGAARD.

Dansk Magasinpresses Udgiverforening (Danish Magazine Publishers' Association): Hammerensgade 6, 1267 Copenhagen K; tel. 33-11-88-44; fax 33-15-01-86; e-mail dmu-mags@internet.dk;

DENMARK

internet www.dmu-mags.dk; f. 1949; Chair. KJELD LUCAS; Dir FINN SKOVSGAARD.

Danske Dagblades Forening (Danish Newspaper Publishers' Association): Pressens Hus, Skindergade 7, 1159 Copenhagen K; tel. 33-97-40-00; fax 33-14-23-25; e-mail ddf@danskedagblade.dk; internet www.danskedagblade.dk; comprises managers and editors-in-chief of all newspapers; general representative for the Danish press; Chair. JENS BEBE; Man. Dir EBBE DAL.

Publishers

Aarhus Universitetsforlag: Langelandsgade 177, 8200 Aarhus N; tel. 89-42-53-70; fax 89-42-53-80; e-mail unipress@au.dk; internet www.unipress.dk; reference, non-fiction and educational; Man. Dir CLAES HVIDBAK.

Forlaget åløkke A/S: Porskærvej 15, Nim, 8740 Brædstrup; tel. 75-67-11-19; fax 75-67-10-74; e-mail alokke@get2net.dk; internet www.alokke.dk; f. 1977; educational, children's books, audio-visual and other study aids; Man. Dir BERTIL TOFT HANSEN.

Akademisk Forlag A/S (Danish University Press): Pilestrade 52, 3. sal, POB 54, 1002 Copenhagen K; tel. 33-43-40-80; fax 33-43-40-99; e-mail akademisk@akademisk.dk; internet www.akademisk.dk; f. 1962; history, health, linguistics, university textbooks, educational materials; Dir ESBEN ESBENSEN.

Forlaget Amanda: Rathsacksvej 7, 1862 Frederiksberg C; tel. 33-79-00-11; fax 33-27-60-79; e-mail forlag@danskf.dk; internet www.danskfl.dk; art, culture, school books, non-fiction; Editorial Dir CHARLOTTE SVENDSTRUP.

Forlaget Apostrof ApS: Berggreensgade 24, 2100 Copenhagen Ø; tel. 39-20-84-20; fax 39-20-84-53; e-mail apostrof@apostrof.dk; internet www.apostrof.dk; f. 1980; psychotherapy and contemporary psychology, fiction and non-fiction for children; Publrs MIA THESTRUP, OLE THESTRUP.

Arkitektens Forlag: Overgaden ove Vandet 10, 1A, 1415 Copenhagen K; tel. 32-83-69-00; fax 32-83-69-41; e-mail eksp@arkfo.dk; internet www.arkfo.dk; architecture, planning.

Forlaget Artia (Ars Audiendi ApS): Vognmagergade 9, 1120 Copenhagen K; tel. 33-12-28-98; fax 33-14-12-63; fiction, non-fiction, science fiction, music, horror; Publr ERIK LÆSSØE STILLING; Dir PETER SCHANTZ.

Aschehoug Dansk Forlag A/S: Landemærket 8, POB 2179, 1017 Copenhagen K; tel. 33-30-55-22; fax 33-30-58-22; e-mail info@ash.egmont.com; internet www.aschehoug.dk; imprints: Aschehoug (fiction), Aschehoug Fakta (non-fiction, reference, children's books), Sesam (educational, children's books, history); Man. Dir (Aschehoug) ANETTE WAD.

Peter Asschenfeldt's nye Forlag A/S: Ny Adelgade 8–10, 1104 Copenhagen K; tel. 33-37-07-60; fax 33-91-03-04; fiction; Publr PETER ASSCHENFELDT.

Blackwell Munksgaard: Rosenørns Allé 1, 1970 Frederiksberg C; tel. 77-33-33-33; fax 77-33-33-77; e-mail info@mks.blackwellpublishing.com; internet www.blackwellpublishing.com; f. 1917 as Munksgaard International Publishers Ltd; present name adopted 2000; scientific journals on medicine and dentistry; Man. Dir LIZ KUKLA.

Thomas Bloms Forlag ApS: Skovenggaardsvej 8, 9490 Pandrup; tel. 98-24-85-25; fax 98-24-80-60; fiction, non-fiction, children's books, talking books; Publrs CONNIE BLOM, THOMAS BLOM.

Bogans Forlag: Kastaniebakken 8, POB 39, 3540 Lynge; tel. 48-18-80-55; fax 48-18-87-69; e-mail bogan@post.tele.dk; f. 1974; general paperbacks, popular science, non-fiction, humour, health; Publr EVAN BOGAN.

Borgens Forlag A/S: Valbygårdsvej 33, 2500 Valby, Copenhagen; tel. 36-15-36-15; fax 36-15-36-16; e-mail post@borgen.dk; internet www.borgen.dk; f. 1948; fiction, poetry, children's books, humour, general non-fiction; Man. Dir NIELS BORGEN.

Carit Andersens Forlag A/S: Upsalagade 18, 2100 Copenhagen Ø; tel. 35-43-62-22; fax 35-43-51-51; e-mail info@caritandersen.dk; internet www.caritandersen.dk; Publr ERIK ALBRECHTSEN.

Forlaget Carlsen A/S: Krogshøjvej 32, 2880 Bagsværd; tel. 44-44-32-33; fax 44-44-36-33; e-mail carlsen@carlsen.dk; internet www.carlsen.dk; children's books; Man. Dir JESPER HOLM.

Cicero (Chr. Erichsens Forlag A/S): Ørnevej 45, 2400 Copenhagen NV; tel. 33-16-03-08; fax 33-16-03-07; e-mail info@cicero.dk; internet www.cicero.dk; f. 1902; fiction, non-fiction, art, culture; Publrs NIELS GUDBERGSEN, ALIS CASPERSEN.

DA-Forlag/Dansk Arbejdsgiverforening: Vester Voldgade 113, 1552 Copenhagen V; tel. 33-38-93-67; fax 33-91-09-32; e-mail ehj@da.dk; non-fiction and reference.

Directory

Dafolo A/S: Suderbovej 22–24, 9900 Frederikshavn; tel. 96-20-66-66; fax 98-42-97-11; e-mail dafolo@dafolo.dk; internet www.dafolo.dk; educational books; Publr MICHAEL SCHELDE.

Dansk BiblioteksCenter A/S: Tempovej 7–11, 2750 Ballerup; tel. 44-86-77-77; fax 44-86-78-91; e-mail dbc@dbc.dk; internet www.dbc.dk; bibliographic data, information services; Man. Dir MOGENS BRABRAND JENSEN.

Dansk Historisk Håndbogsforlag A/S: Buddingevej 87A, 2800 Lyngby; tel. 45-93-48-00; fax 45-93-47-47; e-mail genos@worldonline.dk; f. 1976; genealogy, heraldry, law, culture and local history, facsimile editions, microfiches produced by subsidiary co; Owners and Man. Dirs RITA JENSEN, HENNING JENSEN.

Dansk Psykologisk Forlag: Kongvejen 155, 2830 Virum; tel. 35-38-16-55; fax 35-38-16-65; e-mail dk-psych@dpf.dk; internet www.dpf.dk; educational books, health, psychology; Man. Dir HENRIK SKOVDAHL.

Det Danske Bibelselskab/Det Kongelige Vajsenhus' Forlag: Frederiksborggade 50, 1360 Copenhagen K; tel. 33-12-78-35; fax 33-93-21-50; e-mail bibelselskabet@bibelselskabet.dk; internet www.bibelselskabet.dk; bibles, religious and liturgical books, children's books; Dir HENRIK NIELSEN.

Christian Ejlers' Forlag ApS: Sølvgade 38/3, 1307 Copenhagen K; tel. 33-12-21-14; fax 33-12-28-84; e-mail liber@ejlers.dk; internet www.ejlers.dk; f. 1967; educational, academic and multi-media; Publr ELISABETH JENSEN.

Forlaget for Faglitteratur A/S: Biens Allé 6, 2300 Copenhagen S; tel. 32-59-79-07; medicine, technology.

Flachs: Øverødvej 98, 2840 Holte; tel. 45-42-48-30; fax 45-42-48-29; e-mail flachs@flachs.dk; internet www.flachs.dk; fiction, non-fiction, reference, educational and children's books; Publrs ALLAN FLACHS, ANETTE FLACHS.

Palle Fogtdal A/S: Østergade 22, 1100 Copenhagen K; tel. 33-15-39-15; fax 33-93-35-05; e-mail pallefogtdal@pallefogtdal.dk; Danish history, photography; Man. Dir PALLE FOGTDAL.

Forum: Købmagergade 62, 4th Floor, 1150 Copenhagen K; tel. 33-41-18-30; fax 33-41-18-31; f. 1940; history, fiction, biographies, quality paperbacks and children's books; Man. Dir TORBEN MADSEN.

Fremad: Købmagergade 62, POB 2252, 1019 Copenhagen K; tel. 33-41-18-10; fax 33-41-18-11; f. 1912; general trade, fiction, non-fiction, juveniles, reference, children's books; Man. Dir NIELS KØLLE.

G.E.C. Gad Forlag A/S: Klosterstræde 9, 1157 Copenhagen K; tel. 77-66-60-00; fax 77-66-60-01; e-mail reception@gads-forlag.dk; internet www.gads-forlag.dk; f. 1855; biographies, history, reference, educational materials; Publ. Dir ULRIK HVILSHØJ.

Gyldendalske Boghandel, Nordisk Forlag A/S: Klareboderne 3, 1001 Copenhagen K; tel. 33-75-55-55; fax 33-75-55-56; e-mail gyldendal@gyldendal.dk; internet www.gyldendal.dk; f. 1770; fiction, non-fiction, reference books, paperbacks, children's books, textbooks; Man. Dir STIG ANDERSEN.

Haase & Søns Forlag A/S: Løvstræde 8, 1152 Copenhagen K; tel. 33-11-78-80; fax 33-11-59-59; e-mail haase@haase.dk; internet www.haase.dk; f. 1877; educational books, audio-visual aids, humour, fiction, non-fiction; imprints: Natur og Harmoni, Rasmus Navers Forlag; Man. Dir MICHAEL HAASE.

Edition Wilhelm Hansen A/S: Bornholmsgade 1, 1266 Copenhagen K; tel. 33-11-78-88; fax 33-14-81-78; e-mail ewh@ewh.dk; internet www.ewh.dk; f. 1857; music books, school and educational books; Man. Dir TINE BIRGER CHRISTENSEN.

Hernovs Forlag: Nørrebakken 25, 2820 Gentofte; tel. 32-96-33-14; fax 32-96-04-46; e-mail admin@hernov.dk; internet www.hernov.dk; f. 1941; fiction, non-fiction, classic literature and children's; Man. Dir ELSE HERNOV.

Holkenfeldt 3: Fuglevadsvej 71, 2800 Lyngby; tel. 45-93-12-21; fax 45-93-82-41; fiction, non-fiction, reference, sport, humour; Publr KAY HOLKENFELDT.

Høst & Søns Forlag: Købmagergade 62, POB 2212, 1018 Copenhagen K; tel. 33-38-28-88; fax 33-38-28-98; e-mail hoest@hoest.dk; internet www.hoest.dk; f. 1836; fiction, crafts and hobbies, languages, books on Denmark, children's books; Man. Dir ERIK C. LINDGREN.

Forlaget Hovedland: Elsdyvej 21, 8270 Højbjerg; tel. 86-27-65-00; fax 86-27-65-37; e-mail mail@hovedland.dk; internet www.hovedland.dk; fiction, non-fiction, environment, sport, health, crafts; Publr STEEN PIPER.

Forlaget Klematis A/S: Østre Skovvej 1, 8240 Risskov; tel. 86-17-54-55; fax 86-17-59-59; fiction, non-fiction, crafts, children's books; Dir CLAUS DALBY.

Forlaget Per Kofod ApS: Strandgade 32A, 3000 Helsingør; tel. 33-32-70-27; fax 33-32-70-78; e-mail info@per-kofod.com; internet www.per-kofod.com; fiction, non-fiction, art and culture; Publr PER KOFOD.

DENMARK

Krak: Virumgaardsvej 21, 2830 Virum; tel. 45-95-65-00; fax 45-95-65-65; e-mail krak@krak.dk; internet www.krak.dk; f. 1770; business information, maps and yearbooks; Dir OVE LETH-SØRENSEN.

Egmont Lademann A/S: Gerdasgade 37, 2500 Valby; tel. 36-15-66-00; fax 36-44-11-62; internet www.lademann.dk; f. 1954; non-fiction, reference.

Lindhardt og Ringhof A/S: Pilestræde 52, 1112 Copenhagen K; tel. 33-69-50-00; fax 33-69-50-01; e-mail lr@lindhardt-og-ringhof.dk; internet www.lindhardt-og-ringhof.dk; general fiction and non-fiction; Dir MORTEN HESSELDAHL.

Forlagsgruppen Lohse: Korskærvej 25, 7000 Fredericia; tel. 75-93-44-55; fax 75-92-42-75; e-mail info@lohse.dk; internet www.lohse.dk; f. 1868; imprints: Korskær, Fokal, Logia, Kolon; religion, children's books, biographies, devotional novels; Dir THORKILD HØJVIG; Editorial Dir THOMAS B. MIKKELSEN.

Forlaget Lotus: Bryggervangen 76, 2100 Copenhagen Ø; tel. 29-61-20-01; e-mail fialotus@post7.tele.dk; internet www.forlagetlotus.dk; management, health, religion, the occult, educational; Publr FINN ANDERSEN.

Magnus Informatik A/S: Palægade 4, 1261 Copenhagen K; tel. 70-20-33-14; fax 33-96-01-01; e-mail magnus@magnus.dk; internet www.magnus.dk; f. 1962; guidebooks, journals, law; Man. Dir MORTEN ARNBERG.

Medicinsk Forlag ApS: Rønnebærvej 20, 4500 Nykøbing Sj; tel. and fax 47-17-65-92; e-mail anni@mediciniskforlag.dk; internet www.medicinskforlag.dk; astrology, medical and scientific books; Man. Dir ANNI LINDELØV.

Modtryk Forlaget: Anholtsgade 4, 8000 Århus C; tel. 87-31-76-00; fax 87-31-76-01; e-mail forlaget@modtryk.dk; internet www.modtryk.dk; f. 1972; children's and school books, fiction, thrillers and non-fiction; Man. Dir ILSE NØRR.

Nyt Nordisk Forlag-Arnold Busck A/S: Købmagergade 49, 1150 Copenhagen K; tel. 33-73-35-75; fax 33-73-35-76; e-mail nnf@nytnordiskforlag.dk; internet www.nytnordiskforlag.dk; f. 1896; textbooks, school books, guidebooks, fiction and non-fiction; Man. Dir OLE A. BUSCK; Dir JESPER T. FENSVIG.

Nyt Teknisk Forlag A/S: Bastbygningen, Ingerslevsgade 44, 1705 Copenhagen V; tel. 63-15-17-00; fax 33-86-23-61; e-mail info@nyttf.dk; internet www.nyttf.dk; f. 1948; owned by Erhvervsskolernes Forlag; technical books, reference, educational, science, popular science; Publr HENRIK LARSEN.

Jørgen Paludans Forlag ApS: 4 Straedet, 3100 Hornbæk; tel. 49-75-15-36; fax 49-75-15-37; language teaching, non-fiction, psychology, history, politics, economics, reference; Man. Dir JØRGEN PALUDAN.

C.A. Reitzels Boghandel og Forlag A/S: Nørregade 20, 1165 Copenhagen K; tel. 33-12-24-00; fax 33-14-02-70; f. 1819; reference books, philosophy, educational and academic books, Hans Christian Andersen, Kierkegaard; Dir SVEND OLUFSEN.

Hans Reitzels Forlag A/S: Østergade 13, POB 1073, 1008 Copenhagen K; tel. 33-38-28-00; fax 33-38-28-08; e-mail hrf@hansreitzel.dk; internet www.hansreitzel.dk; f. 1949; education, philosophy, psychology, sociology; Publ. Dir HANNE SALOMONSEN.

Forlaget Rhodos: Holtegaard, Hørsholmvej 17, 3050 Humelbæk; tel. 32-54-30-20; fax 32-54-30-22; e-mail rhodos@rhodos.dk; internet www.rhodos.dk; f. 1959; university books, art, science, fiction, poetry; Dir RUBEN BLAEDEL.

Samlerens Forlag A/S: POB 2252, Købmagergade 62, 1019 Copenhagen K; tel. 33-41-18-00; fax 33-41-18-01; e-mail torben_madsen@samleren.dk; internet www.samlerens.dk; Danish and foreign fiction, contemporary history and politics, biographies; Man. Dir TORBEN MADSEN.

Scandinavia: Drejervej 11–21, 2400 Copenhagen NV; tel. 35-31-03-30; fax 35-31-03-34; e-mail jvo@scanpublishing.dk; internet www.scanpublishing.dk; f. 1973; children's books, religion, Hans Christian Andersen; Dir JØRGEN VIUM OLESEN.

Det Schønbergske Forlag A/S: Landemærket 5, 1119 Copenhagen K; tel. 33-73-35-85; fax 33-73-35-86; f. 1857; fiction, humour, psychology, biography, children's books, paperbacks, textbooks; Dir JOAKIM WERNER; Editor ARVID HONORÉ.

Spektrum: Købmagergade 62, POB 2252, 1019 Copenhagen K; tel. 33-41-18-30; fax 33-41-18-31; non-fiction, history, biographies, science, psychology, religion, philosophy, arts; Man. Dir OLE KNUDSEN.

Strandbergs Forlag ApS: 475 Vedbæk Strandvej, 2950 Vedbæk; tel. 42-89-47-60; fax 42-89-47-01; cultural history, travel; Publr HANS JØRGEN STRANDBERG.

Strubes Forlag og Boghandel ApS: Dag Hammarskjölds Allé 36, 2100 Copenhagen Ø; tel. 31-42-53-00; fax 31-42-23-98; health, astrology, philosophy, the occult; Man. Dir JONNA STRUBE.

Tiderne Skifter: Læderstræde 5, 1. sal, 1201 Copenhagen K; tel. 33-18-63-90; fax 33-18-63-91; e-mail tiderneskifter@tiderneskifter.dk; internet www.tiderneskifter.dk; fiction, sexual and cultural politics, psychology, science, religion, arts; Man. Dir CLAUS CLAUSEN.

Forlaget Thomson: Nytorv 5, 1450 Copenhagen K; tel. 33-74-07-00; fax 33-93-30-77; textbooks, legal, economic, financial, management, business, accounting; Editorial Dir VIBEKE CHRISTIANSEN.

Unitas Forlag: Peter Bangs Vej 1D, 2000 Frederiksberg; tel. 36-16-64-81; fax 38-11-64-81; e-mail info@unitasforlag.dk; internet www.unitasforlag.dk; religion, fiction, education, children's books; Man. PEDER GUNDERSEN.

Forlaget Vindrose A/S: Valbygaardsvej 33, 2500 Valby; tel. 36-15-36-15; fax 36-15-36-16; f. 1980; general trade, fiction and non-fiction; Man. Dir NIELS BORGEN.

Wisby & Wilkens: Vesterled 45, 8300 Odder; tel. 70-23-46-22; fax 70-23-47-22; e-mail mail@wisby-wilkens.com; internet www.wisby-wilkens.com; f. 1986; children's books, crafts, fiction, health, humour, science, religion; imprint: Mikro (drama, poetry, humour); Publr JACOB WISBY.

PUBLISHERS' ASSOCIATION

Forlæggerforeningen: Skindergade 7, 1159 Copenhagen K; tel. 33-15-66-88; fax 33-15-65-88; e-mail danishpublishers@danishpublishers.dk; internet www.danishpublishers.dk; f. 1837; formerly Den danske Forlæggerforening; 50 mems, 3 associate mems; Chair. PETER MOLLERUP; Man. Dir IB TUNE OLSEN.

Broadcasting and Communications

TELECOMMUNICATIONS

Regulatory Organization

IT- og Telestyrelsen (National IT and Telecom Agency): Holsteinsgade 63, 2100 Copenhagen Ø; tel. 45-35-00-00; fax 45-35-00-10; e-mail itst@itst.dk; internet www.itst.dk; f. 2002 by merger of State Information and Television Agencies; under the Ministry of Science, Technology and Innovation, in charge of administration and regulation of the telecommunications sector as laid down in telecommunications legislation; works on legislation; government centre of expertise in telecommunications; Dir-Gen. JØRGEN ABILD ANDERSEN; Dep. Dirs-Gen. FINN PETERSEN, MARIE MUNK.

Major Service Providers

GN Store Nord A/S: Lautrupbjerg 7, POB 99, 2750 Ballerup; tel. 45-75-00-00; fax 45-75-00-09; e-mail info@gn.com; internet www.gn.com; f. 1969; Pres. and CEO TOON BOUTEN.

Telecom A/S: Telegade 2, 2630 Tåstrup; tel. 42-52-91-11; fax 42-52-93-31; Man. Dir GREGERS MOGENSEN.

TDC A/S: Nørregade 21, 0900 Copenhagen; tel. 70-20-35-10; fax 66-63-73-19; e-mail tdcpresse@tdc.dk; internet www.tdc.dk; f. 1995 as Tele Danmark A/S; present name adopted 2000; fmrly state-owned telecommunications co; transferred to private ownership in 1998; Chair. HENNING DYREMOSE; CEO JENS ALDER.

BROADCASTING

Regulatory Authority

Mediesekretariatet: Vognmagergade 10, 1., 1120 Copenhagen K; tel. 33-18-68-68; fax 33-18-68-69; e-mail radrad@mediesekretariatet.dk; internet www.mediesekretariatet.dk; f. 2001; Dir ERIK NORDAHL SVENDSEN.

Radio

DR RADIO: DR Byen, Emil Holms Kanal 20, 0999 Copenhagen C; tel. 35-20-30-40; fax 35-20-26-44; e-mail drkommunikation@dr.dk; internet www.dr.dk; fmrly Danmarks Radio; independent statutory corpn; Dir-Gen. KENNETH PLUMMER; Dir of Radio LEIF LØNSMANN; operates a foreign service (Radio Denmark), nine regional stations and four national channels

The four national channels are as follows:

Channel 1: broadcasts for 110 hours per week on FM, in Danish (Greenlandic programmes weekly); simulcast on DAB; Head FINN SLUMSTRUP.

Channel 2: a music channel, broadcasts on FM for 45 hours per week nationally, in Danish, as well as regional and special (for foreign workers) programmes; Head STEED FREDERIKSEN.

Channel 3: broadcasts on FM for 24 hours per day, in Danish; primarily a popular music channel, it also broadcasts news in Greenlandic, Faroese and in English; simulcast on DAB; Head JESPER GRUNWALD.

Channel 4: broadcasts on FM for about 97 hours per week; news, entertainment and regional programmes; simulcast on DAB.

DENMARK

Directory

Radio 100FM: Rådhuspladsen 45, 1550 Copenhagen V; tel. 33-37-89-00; fax 33-37-89-67; e-mail info@radio100fm.dk; internet www.radio100fm.dk; f. 2003; owned by Talpa Radio International (Netherlands).

There are also some 250 operators licensed for low-power FM transmissions of local and community radio, etc.

Digital Radio

Digital audio broadcasting (DAB) began in Denmark in 2002, with 10 transmitters in operation covering the main cities of Copenhagen, Århus, Odense and Aalborg. The transmitter network has since expanded to cover 90% of the population. The main DAB operator is DR RADIO, which offers five music channels (DR Soft, DR Rock, DR Boogie Radio, DR Jazz and DR Klassisk), four news channels (DR Nyheder, DR Erhverv, DR Sport and DR Politik) and eight other channels (DR Plus, DR Litteratur, DR Kanon Kamelen, DR Event, DR Gyldne Genhør and simulcasts of Channel 1, Channel 3 and Channel 4).

Television

Canal Digital Danmark: Stationsparken 25, 2600 Glostrup; tel. 70-27-27-75; fax 70-27-27-63; e-mail cma@canaldigital.dk; internet www.canaldigital.dk; f. 1997; wholly owned by Telenor AS (Norway); Dir-Gen. JENS B. ARNESEN.

DR TV: DR Byen, Emil Holms Kanal 20, 0999 Copenhagen C; tel. 35-20-30-40; fax 35-20-26-44; e-mail dr-kommunikation@dr.dk; internet www.dr.dk; operates two services, DR 1 and DR 2; Dir-Gen. KENNETH PLUMMER; Dir of Television and New Media LARS GRARUP.

    DR 1: terrestrial television channel; Controller JØRGEN RAMSKOV.

    DR 2: satellite television channel; Controller TORBEN FRØLICH.

TV 2/DANMARK A/S: Rugaardsvej 25, 5100 Odense C; tel. 65-91-91-91; fax 65-91-33-22; e-mail tv2@tv2.dk; internet www.tv2.dk; began broadcasts in 1988; Denmark's first national commercial and public service TV station; changed to a state share co in 2003; part-privatization pending; Dir-Gen. PER MIKAEL JENSEN; Dir of Programmes PALLE STRØM.

TV 3 Viasat: Wildersgade 8, 1408 Copenhagen K; tel. 35-25-90-00; fax 35-25-90-10; e-mail tv3@viasat.dk; internet www.tv3.dk; reaches 71% of the country via cable and satellite; Man. Dir LARS BO ANDERSEN; Dir of Programmes HENRIK RAVN.

There are some 50 operators licensed for local television transmission.

Broadcasting Association

Forenede Danske Antenneanlæg (FDA) (Danish Cable Television Asscn): Annebergparken 21, POB 151, 4500 Nykøbing Sjælland; tel. 59-96-17-00; fax 59-96-17-17; e-mail fda@fda.dk; internet www.fda.dk; f. 1983; organizes 350 local networks, representing c. 425,000 connected households; Man. Dir SØREN BIRKSØ SØRENSEN.

Finance

(cap. = capital; res = reserves; dep. = deposits; m. = million; brs = branches; amounts in kroner, unless otherwise indicated)

BANKING

The first Danish commercial bank was founded in 1846. In 1975 restrictions on savings banks were lifted, giving commercial and savings banks equal rights and status, and restrictions on the establishment of full branches of foreign banks were removed. In 1988 all remaining restrictions on capital movements were ended. In 2006 there were some 152 banks and savings banks in operation. All banks are under government supervision, and public representation is obligatory on all bank supervisory boards.

Supervisory Authority

Finanstilsynet (Danish Financial Supervisory Authority): Gammel Kongevej 74A, 1850 Frederiksberg C; tel. 33-55-82-82; fax 33-55-82-00; e-mail finanstilsynet@ftnet.dk; internet www.ftnet.dk; agency of the Ministry of Economic and Business Affairs; Man. Dir HENRIK BJERRE-NIELSEN.

Central Bank

Danmarks Nationalbank: Havnegade 5, 1093 Copenhagen K; tel. 33-63-63-63; fax 33-63-71-03; e-mail nationalbanken@nationalbanken.dk; internet www.nationalbanken.dk; f. 1818; self-governing; sole right of issue; conducts monetary policy; administers reserves of foreign exchange; cap. 50m., res 52,077m., dep. 247,226m. (Dec. 2006); Chair. of the Bd of Govs NILS BERNSTEIN; Govs TORBEN NIELSEN, JENS THOMSEN.

Commercial Banks

Alm. Brand Bank: Midtermolen 7, 2100 Copenhagen; tel. 35-47-48-49; fax 35-47-47-35; e-mail bank@almbrand.dk; internet www.almbrand.dk; f. 1988; cap. 351m., dep. 17,297m. (Dec. 2006); Chair. CHRISTIAN N. B. ULRICH; Pres. and CEO HENRIK NORDAM; 25 brs.

Amagerbanken A/S: Amagerbrogade 25, 2300 Copenhagen S; tel. 32-66-66-66; fax 32-54-45-34; e-mail international@amagerbanken.dk; internet www.amagerbanken.dk; f. 1903; cap. 222m., res 90m., dep. 20,471m. (Dec. 2006); Chair. N. E. NIELSEN; CEO and Man. Dir KNUD CHRISTENSEN; 28 brs.

Arbejdernes Landsbank A/S: Panoptikonbygningen, Vesterbrogade 5, 1502 Copenhagen V; tel. 38-48-48-48; fax 38-48-50-52; e-mail info@al-bank.dk; internet www.al-bank.dk; f. 1919; cap. 300m., res 294m., dep. 18,759m. (Dec. 2006); Chair. POUL ERIK SKOV CHRISTENSEN; Gen. Mans EBBE CASTELLA, GERT R. JONASSEN; 60 brs.

Danske Andelskassers Bank A/S: Baneskellet 1, Hammershøj, 8830 Tjele; tel. 87-99-30-00; fax 87-99-30-98; e-mail foreign@dabank.dk; internet www.dabank.dk; f. 1970; cap. 125m., res 148m., dep. 4,774m. (Dec. 2006); Chair. of Supervisory Bd GERT HANSEN; Gen. Mans BENT HOEJGAARD JAKOBSEN, VAGN T. RAVN; 26 brs.

Danske Bank A/S: Holmens Kanal 2–12, 1092 Copenhagen K; tel. 33-44-00-00; fax 70-12-10-80; internet www.danskebank.com; f. 1871 as Danske Landmandsbank; approx. 285,000 shareholders; merged with Copenhagen Handelsbank and Provinsbanken in 1990 to form Den Danske Bank A/S; present name adopted 2000; acquired the insurance group Danica in 1995, the Norwegian Fokus Bank in 1999, Real Denmark in 2000, Bikubanken Girobank A/S in 2001, and Northern Bank and National Irish Bank in 2004; cap. 6,988m., res 88,138m., dep. 2,545,633m. (Dec. 2006); Chair. PETER STRAARUP; 465 brs.

Forstædernes Bank A/S (FB Bank Copenhagen A/S): Kalvebod Brygge 47, 1560 Copenhagen V; tel. 33-52-52-52; fax 33-52-52-53; e-mail finans@forbank.dk; internet www.forbank.dk; f. 1902; cap. 414m., res 133m., dep. 26,497m. (Dec. 2006); subsidiary, Den Fri Bank (f. 1994), provides telephone banking service to individual customers; Chair. HELMER OLSEN; Man. Dir KJELD MOSEBO CHRISTENSEN; 20 brs.

Jyske Bank A/S: Vestergade 8–16, 8600 Silkeborg; tel. 89-22-22-22; fax 89-22-24-90; e-mail jyskebank@jyskebank.dk; internet www.jyskebank.dk; f. 1855; cap. 620m., res 1,916m., dep. 132,060m. (Dec. 2006); Chair. SVEN BUHRKALL; CEO ANDERS DAM; 124 brs.

Nordea Bank Danmark A/S: Strandgade 3, 1401 Copenhagen V; tel. 33-33-33-33; fax 33-33-63-63; internet www.nordea.dk; f. 1990 as Unibank A/S by merger of Andelsbanken, Privatbanken and SDS; in 1999 the bank merged with the insurance co Tryg-Baltica Forsikring A/S, but remained part of the Unidanmark A/S group, which became part of Nordea Group (Finland) in 2000; cap. €2,594m., res –€111m., dep. €148,740m. (Dec. 2006); Pres. and CEO LARS G. NORDSTRÖM; 344 brs.

Nordjyske Bank A/S: Jernbanegade 4–8, POB 701, 9900 Frederikshavn; tel. 99-21-22-23; fax 96-33-50-67; e-mail email@nordjyskebank.dk; internet www.nordjyskebank.dk; f. 1970 as Egnsbank Nord A/S, current name adopted 2002 following merger with Vendsyssel Bank A/S; cap. 80m., res 5m., dep. 5,720m. (Dec. 2004); Chair. HANS JOERGEN KAPTAIN; CEO and Man. Dir JENS OLE JENSEN; 17 brs.

Nørresundby Bank A/S: Torvet 4, 9400 Nørresundby; tel. 98-70-37-00; fax 98-19-18-78; e-mail udland@nrsbank.dk; internet www.noerresundbybank.dk; f. 1898; cap. 46m., res 14m., dep. 7,166m. (Dec. 2006); Chair. KJELD KOLIND JENSEN; Man. Dir and CEO ANDREAS RASMUSSEN; 19 brs.

Nykredit Bank A/S: Kalvebod Brygge 1–3, 1780 Copenhagen V; tel. 33-42-18-00; fax 33-42-18-01; e-mail nykredit-bank@nykredit.dk; internet www.nykredit.dk/bank; f. 1986 as Sankt Annae Bank A/S; present name adopted 1994; cap. 1,400m., res 147m., dep. 87,058m. (Dec. 2006); Chair. HENNING KRUSE PETERSEN; Dirs KIM DUUS, JES KLAUSBY, KARSTEN KNUDSEN.

Ringkjøbing Bank A/S: Torvet 2, 6950 Ringkjøbing; tel. 99-75-32-00; fax 97-32-15-46; e-mail info@riba.dk; internet www.riba.dk; f. 1872; cap. 32m., res 0m., dep. 6,689m. (Dec. 2006); Chair. POUL HJULMAND; Man. Dir PREBEN KNUDSGAARD; 10 brs.

Ringkjøbing Landbobank A/S: Torvet 1, 6950 Ringkøbing; tel. 97-32-11-66; fax 97-32-18-18; e-mail post@landbobanken.dk; internet www.landbobanken.dk; f. 1886; cap. 26m., res 159m., dep. 14,859m. (Dec. 2006); Chair. JENS KJELDSEN; Gen. Mans BENT NAUR KRISTENSEN, JOHN BULL FISKER; 16 brs.

Roskilde Bank A/S: Algade 14, POB 39, 4000 Roskilde; tel. 46-34-84-00; fax 46-34-83-50; e-mail info@roskildebank.dk; internet www.roskildebank.dk; f. 1884; cap. 114m., res 126m., dep. 24,929m. (Dec. 2006); Chair. PETER MÜLLER; Man. NIELS VALENTIN HANSEN; 25 brs.

Sparbank A/S: Adelgade 8, POB 505, 7800 Skive; tel. 96-16-16-16; fax 96-16-14-45; e-mail sp@rbankvest.dk; internet www.sparbank.dk; f. 1857; fmrly Sparbank Vest, present name adopted 2007; cap.

121m., dep. 10,999m. (Dec. 2006); Chair. ALEX NIELSEN; CEO HENNING HÜRDUM; 39 brs.

Sydbank A/S: Peberlyk 4, POB 169, 6200 Åbenrå; tel. 74-36-36-36; fax 74-36-35-49; e-mail info@sydbank.dk; internet www.sydbank.com; f. 1970; cap. 700m., res 396m., dep. 93,060m. (Dec. 2006); Chair. KRESTEN PHILIPSEN; CEO CARSTEN ANDERSEN; 108 brs.

Savings Banks

Fionia Bank A/S: Vestre Stationsvej 7, POB 189, 5100 Odense C; tel. 65-20-40-60; fax 65-91-01-10; e-mail udland@fioniabank.dk; internet www.fioniabank.dk; f. 1974; fmrly Amtssparekassen Fyn A/S, present name adopted 2004; cap. 181m., res 789m., dep. 22,960m. (Dec. 2006); Chair. BO STAERMOSE; Man. Dir FINN B. SORENSEN; 37 brs.

Lån & Spar Bank: Højbro Pl. 9–11, POB 2117, 1014 Copenhagen K; tel. 33-78-20-00; fax 33-78-23-05; e-mail lsb@lsb.dk; internet www.lsb.dk; f. 1880; present name adopted 1990; cap. 271m., res 42m., dep. 7,580m. (Dec. 2006); Chair. TOMMY AGERSKOV THOMSEN; Man. Dir and CEO PETER SCHOU; 14 brs.

Spar Nord Bank: Skelagervej 15, POB 162, 9100 Ålborg; tel. 96-34-40-00; fax 96-34-45-75; e-mail sparnord@sparnord.dk; internet www.sparnordbank.com; f. 1967; cap. 571m., res 578m., dep. 50,941m. (Dec. 2006); CEO LASSE NYBY; Man. Dirs LARS MØLLER, JOHN LUNDSGAARD; 80 brs.

Bankers' Organization

Finansrådet: Finansrådets Hus, Amaliegade 7, 1256 Copenhagen K; tel. 33-70-10-00; fax 33-93-02-60; e-mail mail@finansraadet.dk; internet www.finansraadet.dk; f. 1990; 144 mems; Chair. PETER SCHÜTZE; Man. Dir JØRGEN HORWITZ.

STOCK EXCHANGE

NASDAQ OMX Nordic Exchange Copenhagen: Nikolaj Pl. 6, POB 1040, 1007 Copenhagen K; tel. 33-93-33-66; fax 33-12-86-13; internet www.nasdaqomx.com; f. 2005 by merger of Københavns Fondsbørs and OMX (Sweden); became part of OMX Nordic Exchange with Helsinki (Finland) and Stockholm (Sweden) exchanges in 2006; acquired by NASDAQ Stock Market, Inc (USA) in 2008; Group CEO ROBERT GREIFELD; Group Pres. MAGNUS BÖCKER.

INSURANCE
Principal Companies

Alm. Brand af 1792: Lyngby Hovedgade 4, POB 1792, 2800 Lyngby; tel. 45-96-70-00; fax 45-93-05-46; e-mail almbrand@almbrand.dk; internet www.almbrand.dk; f. 1792; subsidiaries: finance, life, non-life and reinsurance; Chief Gen. Man. BENT KNIE-ANDERSEN.

Codan Forsikring A/S: Codanhus, Gl. Kongevej 60, 1790 Copenhagen V; tel. 33-55-55-55; fax 33-55-21-22; f. 1915 as Forsikringsselskabet Codan A/S; adopted present name 2000; controlled by Royal and Sun Alliance Group Ltd (UK); acquired insurance operations of Hafnia Holdings in 1993; accident, life; CEO JENS ERIK CHRISTENSEN.

Danica Liv I, Livsforsikringsaktieselskab: Parallelvej 17, 2800 Lyngby; tel. 45-23-23-23; fax 45-23-20-20; e-mail servicecentre@danica.dk; internet www.danica.dk; f. 1842 as state insurance co; privatized 1990; pensions, life and non-life.

A/S Det Kjøbenhavnske Reassurance-Compagni (Copenhagen Re): Midtermolen 7, POB 325, 2100 Copenhagen Ø; tel. 35-47-45-45; fax 35-47-72-72; e-mail copre@copre.com; internet www.copre.com; f. 1915; reinsurance.

Købstædernes Forsikring: Grønningen 1, 1270 Copenhagen K; tel. 33-14-37-48; fax 33-32-06-66; e-mail kab@kab.dk; internet www.kab.dk; f. 1761; non-life; Chair. SVEND ERIK CHRISTENSEN; CEO MOGENS N. SKOV.

Kompas Rejseforsikring A/S: Klausdalsbrovej 601, 2750 Ballerup; tel. 44-68-81-00; fax 44-68-84-00; e-mail kompas@kompas.dk; internet www.kompas.dk; travel, health; Man. PER GULDBRANDSEN.

Max Levig & Cos Eft.: Klausdalsbrovej 601, 2750 Ballerup; tel. 44-20-39-60; fax 44-20-66-70; f. 1890; Gen. Man. HUGO ANDERSEN.

PFA Pension: Marina Park, Sundkrogsgade 4, 2100 Copenhagen Ø; tel. 39-17-50-00; fax 39-17-59-50; f. 1917; life; non-life, property; Gen. Mans HENRIK HEIDEBY, A. KÜHLE.

Skandia: Stamholmen 151, 2650 Hvidovre; tel. 70-12-47-47; fax 70-12-47-48; e-mail skandia@skandia.dk; internet www.skandia.dk; f. 1798 as Kgl. Brand A/S; adopted present name 2000; owned by Old Mutual plc (United Kingdom); all branches; Man. Dir CHARSTEN CHRISTENSEN.

Topdanmark Forsikring A/S: Borupvang 4, 2750 Ballerup; tel. 44-68-33-11; fax 44-68-19-06; e-mail topdanmark@topdanmark.dk; internet www.topdanmark.dk; f. 1985; all classes, with subsidiaries; CEO MICHAEL PRAM RASMUSSEN.

Tryg Vesta Group A/S: Klausdalsbrovej 601, 2750 Ballerup; tel. 70-11-20-20; fax 44-20-67-00; e-mail trygvesta@trygvesta.com; internet www.trygvesta.com; f. 1995 by merger of Tryg Forsikring A/S and Baltica Forsikring A/S; CEO STINE BOSSE.

Insurance Association

Forsikring & Pension: Forsikringenshus, Amaliegade 10, 1256 Copenhagen K; tel. 33-43-55-00; fax 33-43-55-01; e-mail fp@forsikringogpension.dk; internet www.forsikringogpension.dk; f. 1918; as Assurandør-Societetet; present name adopted 1999; Man. Dir PER BREMER RASMUSSEN; 200 mems.

Trade and Industry
GOVERNMENT AGENCY

Dansk Industri (Confederation of Danish Industries): H. C. Andersens Blvd 18, 1787 Copenhagen V; tel. 33-77-33-77; fax 33-77-33-00; e-mail di@di.dk; internet www.di.dk; f. 1992; Dir HANS SKOV CHRISTENSEN.

DEVELOPMENT ORGANIZATION

Det Økonomiske Råd (Danish Economic Council): Amaliegade 44, 1256 Copenhagen K; tel. 33-44-58-00; fax 33-32-90-29; e-mail dors@dors.dk; internet www.dors.dk; f. 1962; supervises national economic development and helps to co-ordinate the actions of economic interest groups; 26 members representing both sides of industry, the Government and independent economic experts; Co-Chairs Prof. PETER BIRCH SØRENSEN, Prof. JAN ROSE SKAKSEN, Prof. MICHAEL ROSHOLM, Prof. EIRIK SCHRØDER AMUNDSEN.

CHAMBER OF COMMERCE

Dansk Erhverv (Danish Chamber of Commerce): Børsen, 1217 Copenhagen K; tel. 33-74-60-00; fax 33-74-60-80; e-mail info@danskerhverv.dk; internet www.danskerhverv.dk; f. 1742; Pres. POUL-ERIK PEDERSEN; Man. Dir LARS KROBÆK; approx. 20,000 mem. cos.

INDUSTRIAL AND TRADE ASSOCIATIONS

Dansk Energi: Rosenørns Allé 9, 1970 Frederiksberg C; tel. 35-30-04-00; fax 35-30-04-01; e-mail de@danskenergi.dk; internet www.danskenergi.dk; f. 1923; fmrly Dansk Elvaerkers Forening (Asscn of Danish Energy Cos); promotes the interests of Danish producers and suppliers of electricity; Chair. POUL ARNE NIELSEN; 100 mem. cos.

Landbrugsraadet (Danish Agricultural Council): Axeltorv 3, 1609 Copenhagen V; tel. 33-39-40-00; fax 33-39-41-41; e-mail agriculture@agriculture.dk; internet www.landbrugsraadet.dk; f. 1919; Pres. PETER GAEMELKE; Dir KLAUS BUSTRUP; 41 mems.

Mejeriforeningen (Danish Dairy Board): Frederiks Allé 22, 8000 Århus C; tel. 87-31-20-00; fax 87-31-20-01; e-mail info@mejeri.dk; internet www.mejeri.dk; f. 1912; Chair. BENT JUUL SØRENSEN; Man. Dir MICHAEL STEVNE; 30 mems.

Oliebranchens Fællesrepræsentation (OFR) (Danish Petroleum Industry Asscn): Landemærket 10, 5th Floor, POB 120, 1119 Copenhagen K; tel. 33-45-65-10; fax 33-45-65-11; e-mail ofr@oliebranchen.dk; internet www.oliebranchen.dk; representative org. for petroleum industry; Chair. STEFFEN PEDERSEN; Sec.-Gen. PETER STIGSGAARD.

EMPLOYERS' ORGANIZATIONS

Bryggeriforeningen (Danish Brewers' Asscn): Faxehus, Gamle Carlsberg Vej 16, 2500 Valby; tel. 72-16-24-24; fax 72-16-24-44; e-mail info@bryggeriforeningen.dk; internet www.bryggeriforeningen.dk; f. 1899; Chair. JOERN TOLSTRUP ROHDE; Dir NIELS HALD; 14 mems.

Dansk Arbejdsgiverforening (Confederation of Danish Employers): Vester Voldgade 113, 1790 Copenhagen V; tel. 33-38-90-00; fax 33-12-29-76; e-mail da@da.dk; internet www.da.dk; f. 1896; Chair. JØRGEN VORSHOLT; Dir-Gen. JØRN NEERGAARD LARSEN; 13 mem. orgs.

Dansk Landbrug (Danish Agriculture): Axelborg, Vesterbrogade 4A 4. sal, 1620 Copenhagen V; tel. 33-39-46-00; fax 33-39-46-06; e-mail dl@dansklandbrug.dk; internet www.dansklandbrug.dk; f. 2003; merger of Danske Landboforeninger (f. 1893) and Dansk Familielandbrug (f. 1906); Chair. PETER GAEMELKE; Sec.-Gen. CARL AAGE DAHL; 53,000 mems.

Danske Maritime (Danish Maritime): Amaliegade 33B, 4, 1256 Copenhagen K; tel. 33-13-24-16; fax 33-11-10-96; e-mail mail@danishmaritime.org; internet www.danishmaritime.org; f. 1919;

DENMARK

Directory

fmrly Skibsværftsforeningen (Asscn of Danish Shipbuilders); Man. Dir THORKIL H. CHRISTENSEN.

Håndværksrådet (Danish Federation of Small and Medium-sized Enterprises): Islands Brygge 26, POB 1990, 2300 Copenhagen S; tel. 33-93-20-00; fax 33-32-01-74; e-mail hvr@hvr.dk; internet www.hvr.dk; f. 1879; Chair. POUL ULSØE; Man. PAUL MOLLERUP; 110 asscns with 25,000 mems.

Industriens Arbejdsgivere i København (The Copenhagen Employers' Federation): 1787 Copenhagen V; tel. 33-77-33-77; fax 33-77-33-00; mem. of Dansk Industri (q.v.); Chair. FLEMMING TOMDRUP; Sec. OLE CHRISTENSEN; 413 mems.

Kopenhagen Fur (Danish Fur Breeders' Asscn): Langagervej 60, POB 1479, 2600 Glostrup; tel. 43-26-10-00; fax 43-26-11-26; e-mail mail@kopenhagenfur.com; internet www.kopenhagenfur.com; fmrly Dansk Pelsdyravlerforening; co-operative of 2,300 mems; Dir TORBEN NIELSEN.

Provinsindustriens Arbejdsgiverforening (Federation of Employers in Provincial Industry): 1787 Copenhagen V; tel. 33-77-33-77; fax 33-77-33-00; f. 1895; mem. of Dansk Industri (q.v.); Chair. HANS KIRK; Sec. ANDERS SØNDERGAARD LARSEN.

Sammenslutningen af Landbrugets Arbejdsgiverforeninger (SALA) (Danish Confederation of Employers' Asscns in Agriculture): Vester Farimagsgade 1, 5. sal, POB 367, 1504 Copenhagen V; tel. 33-13-46-55; fax 33-11-89-53; e-mail info@sala.dk; internet www.sala.dk; Dir NILS JUHL ANDREASEN.

UTILITIES

Energistyrelsen (Danish Energy Authority): Amaliegade 44, 1256 Copenhagen K; tel. 33-92-67-00; fax 33-11-47-43; e-mail ens@ens.dk; internet www.ens.dk; f. 1976; govt agency under Ministry of Transport and Energy; Dir IB LARSEN.

Energitilsynet (Danish Energy Regulatory Authority): Nyropsgade 30, 1780 Copenhagen V; tel. 72-26-80-70; fax 33-18-14-27; e-mail et@dera.dk; internet www.energitilsynet.dk; f. 2000; independent authority; regulates prices and access to transmission networks for electricity, gas and heating supply cos; bd mems appointed by Minister of Transport and Energy; Chair. UFFE BUNDGAARD-JØRGENSEN.

Sikkerhedsstyrelsen (Danish Safety Technology Authority): Nørregade 63, 6700 Esbjerg; tel. 33-73-20-00; fax 33-73-20-99; e-mail sik@sik.dk; internet www.sik.dk; f. 1907; fmrly Elektricitetsrådet (Electricity Council); current name adopted 2004; responsible for the legislation, and enforcement thereof, regarding safety of electrical and gas products and installations, ATEX products, toys and general products in Denmark; Chair. ULLA RÖTTGER; Man. Dir SØREN KRØIGAARD.

Electricity

DONG Energy A/S: Kraftværksvej 53, Skærbæk, 7000 Fredericia; tel. 45-99-55-11-11; e-mail dong@dong.dk; internet www.dongenergy.dk; f. 2006 by merger of six energy cos: DONG, Elsam, E2, Nesa, Copenhagen Energy's power activities and Frederiksberg Forsyning; petroleum and natural gas exploration, production, storage and distribution; production and sale of electricity, wind power and geothermal energy; CEO ANDERS ELDRUP.

EnergiMidt A/S: Tietgensvej 2–4, 8600 Silkeborg; tel. 70-15-15-60; fax 87-22-87-11; e-mail info@energimidt.dk; internet www.energimidt.dk; co-operative society; 162,000 customers; energy supplier; Chair. JENS JØRN JUSTESEN; Man. Dir HOLGER BLOK.

Energinet.dk A/S: Tonne Kjærsvej 65, 7000 Fredericia; tel. 70-10-22-44; fax 76-24-51-80; e-mail info@energinet.dk; internet www.energinet.dk; f. 2005 by merger of Eltra, Elkraft System, Elkraft Transmission and Gastra; state-owned; co-ordinates supply of electricity, gas and co-generated heat; subsidiaries: Energinet.dk Gas Storage, Eltransmission.dk A/S, Fibertransmission.dk A/S and Gastransmission.dk A/S; CEO PEDER ØSTERMARK ANDREASEN.

Vattenfall A/S: Støberigade 12-14, 2450 Copenhagen SV; tel. 88-27-50-00; fax 70-25-15-71; e-mail marianne.grydgaard@vattenfall.com; internet www.vattenfall.dk; f. 1996; 100%-owned by Vattenfall AB (Sweden); generation and supply of thermal and wind energy; acquired assets of Elsam and E2 in 2006; Group CEO LARS G. JOSEFSSON.

Gas

Dansk Gasteknisk Forening (Danish Technical Gas Asscn): c/o Dansk Gasteknisk Center a/s, Dr Neergaards Vej 5B, 2970 Hørsholm; tel. 45-16-96-00; fax 45-16-96-01; e-mail dgf@dgc.dk; internet www.gasteknik.dk; f. 1911; promotes the use of gas; Sec. PETER I. HINSTRUP; 680 mems.

DONG Energy: see Electricity.

Hovedstadsregionens Naturgas I/S (HNG): Gladsaxe Ringvej 11, 2860 Søborg; tel. 39-54-70-00; fax 39-67-23-98; e-mail ks@hng.dk; internet www.hng.dk; f. 1979; distribution and sale of gas in Greater Copenhagen region; Chair. NICK HÆKKERUP; Man. Dir. NIELS ERIK ANDERSEN.

Københavns Energi (Copenhagen Energy): Ørestads Blvd 35, 2300 Copenhagen S; tel. 33-95-33-95; fax 33-95-20-20; e-mail ke@ke.dk; internet www.ke.dk; f. 1857 as Københavns Belysningsvæsen; present name adopted 1999; merger with Københavns Vand 2001; supplier of gas, heating and water in Copenhagen and surrounding area; Chair. LARS THERKILDSEN; Man. Dir POUL MORTENSEN.

Naturgas Fyn A/S: Ørbækvej 260, 5220 Odense SØ; tel. 63-15-64-15; fax 66-15-51-27; e-mail ngf@ngf.dk; internet www.ngf.dk; distribution of gas on island of Funen; Chair. LARS ERIK HORNEMANN; Man. Dir RENÉ VOSS.

CO-OPERATIVE

Co-op Danmark A/S (Co-operative of Denmark): Roskildevej 65, 2620 Albertslund; tel. 43-86-43-86; fax 43-86-33-86; e-mail coop@coop.dk; internet www.coop.dk; f. 1896; fmrly Fællesforeningen for Danmarks Brugsforeninger; CEO PER BANK; 1,113,506 mems.

TRADE UNIONS

Landsorganisationen i Danmark (LO) (Danish Confederation of Trade Unions): Islands Brygge 32D, 2300 Copenhagen S; tel. 35-24-60-00; fax 35-24-63-00; e-mail lo@lo.dk; internet www.lo.dk; Pres. HARALD BØRSTING; Vice-Pres. LIZETTE RISGAARD; 1,031 brs.

Comprises 18 affiliated unions with a total membership of 1,299,702 mems (2006):

Blik og Rørarbejderforbundet i Danmark (Danish Union of Plumbers and Allied Workers): Immerkær 42, 2650 Hvidovre; tel. 36-38-36-38; fax 36-38-36-39; e-mail forbundet@blikroer.dk; internet www.blikroer.dk; f. 2002; Chair. MAX MEYER; 8,747 mems (2006).

Dansk Artist Forbund (DAF): Dronningensgade 68, 4th Floor, 1420 Copenhagen K; tel. 33-32-66-77; fax 33-33-73-30; e-mail artisten@artisten.dk; internet www.artisten.dk; f. 1918; Chair. LENA BROSTRØM DIDERIKSEN; 1,440 mems (2006).

Dansk El-Forbund (Electricians' Union): Vodroffsvej 26, 1900 Frederiksberg C; tel. 33-29-70-00; fax 33-29-70-70; e-mail def@def.dk; internet www.def.dk; Pres. JÖRGEN JUUL RASMUSSEN; 29,874 mems (2006).

Dansk Frisør og Kosmetiker Forbund (Danish Hairdressers' and Beauticians' Union): Lersø Park Allé 21, 2100 Copenhagen Ø; tel. 35-83-18-80; fax 35-82-14-62; e-mail info@dfkf.dk; internet www.dfkf.dk; Chair. POUL MONGGAARD; 5,053 mems (2006).

Dansk Funktionærforbund—Serviceforbundet (Danish Federation of Salaried Employees): Upsalagade 20, 2100 Copenhagen Ø; tel. 70-15-04-00; fax 70-15-04-05; e-mail dff-s@dff-s.dk; internet www.dff-s.dk; Pres. KARSTEN HANSEN; 24,370 mems (2006).

Dansk Jernbaneforbund (Railway Workers): Søndermarksvej 16, 2500 Valby; tel. 36-13-25-00; fax 36-13-25-01; e-mail dj@djf.dk; internet www.djf.dk; f. 2002; Chair. ULRIK SALMONSEN; 5,410 mems (2006).

Dansk Metal (Metalworkers): Nyropsgade 38, POB 308, 1780 Copenhagen V; tel. 33-63-20-00; fax 33-63-21-50; e-mail metal@danskmetal.dk; internet www.danskmetal.dk; f. 1888; Pres. THORKILD E. JENSEN; 135,088 mems (2006).

Fag og Arbejde (Trade and Labour—FOA): Staunings Pl. 1–3, POB 11, 1790 Copenhagen V; tel. 46-97-26-26; fax 46-97-23-00; e-mail foa@foa.dk; internet www.foa.dk; f. 2005; merger of Forbundet af Offentligt Ansatte and Pædagogisk Medhjælper Forbund; Chair. DENIS KRISTENSEN; 201,862 mems (2006).

Fagligt Fælles Forbund (United Federation of Danish Workers—3F): Kampmannsgade 4, 1790 Copenhagen V; tel. 70-30-03-00; fax 70-30-03-01; e-mail 3f@3f.dk; internet www.3f.dk; f. 2005; merger of Kvindeligt Arbejderforbund and Specialarbejderforbundet; Chair. POUL ERIK SKOV CHRISTENSEN; 352,451 mems (2006).

Forbundet Trae-Industri-Byg i Danmark (Timber Industry and Construction Workers): Mimersgade 41, 2200 Copenhagen N; tel. 88-18-70-00; fax 88-18-71-10; e-mail tib@tib.dk; internet www.tib.dk; Pres. ARNE JOHANSEN; 67,494 mems (2006).

HK Danmark (Union of Commercial and Clerical Employees in Denmark): Weidekampsgade 8, POB 470, 0900 Copenhagen C; tel. 33-30-43-43; fax 33-30-40-99; e-mail hk@hk.dk; internet www.hk.dk; f. 1900; Chair. JOHN DAHL; 345,968 mems (2006).

Hærens Konstabel- og Korporalforening (Union of Enlisted Privates and Corporals in the Danish Army): Kronprinsensgade 8, 1114 Copenhagen K; tel. 33-93-65-22; fax 33-93-65-23; e-mail hkkf@hkkf.dk; internet www.hkkf.dk; f. 1959; Chair. FLEMMING VINTHER; 4,272 mems (2006).

Malerforbundet i Danmark (Painters): Lersø Parkallé 109, 2100 Copenhagen Ø; tel. 39-16-79-00; fax 39-19-79-10; e-mail maler@maler.dk; internet www.maler.dk; f. 1890; Pres. JØRN ERIK NIELSEN; 13,296 mems (2006).

DENMARK

Nærings- og Nydelsesmiddelarbejder Forbundet NNF (Food, Sugar Confectionery, Chocolate, Dairy Produce and Tobacco Workers): C. F. Richs Vej 103, POB 1479, 2000 Frederiksberg; tel. 38-18-72-72; fax 38-18-72-00; e-mail nnf@nnf.dk; internet www.nnf.dk; f. 1980; Pres. OLE WEHLAST; 40,582 mems (2006).

Socialpædagogernes Landsforbund (National Federation of Social Educators in Denmark): Brolæggerstræde 9, 1211 Copenhagen K; tel. 33-96-28-00; fax 33-96-29-96; e-mail sl@sl.dk; internet www.sl.dk; Pres. KIRSTEN NISSEN; 34,216 mems (2006).

Spillerforeningen: Pilestræde 35, 1st Floor, 1112 Copenhagen K; tel. 33-12-11-28; fax 33-12-56-21; e-mail mail@spillerforeningen.dk; internet www.spillerforeningen.dk; f. 1977; represents footballers in Denmark and Danish footballers abroad; Chair. THOMAS LINDRUP; 685 mems (2006).

Teknisk Landsforbund (Professional Technicians): Nørre Voldgade 12, 1358 Copenhagen K; tel. 33-43-65-00; fax 33-43-66-77; e-mail tl@tl.dk; internet www.tl.dk; f. 1919; Pres. GITA ALICE GRÜNING; 28,894 mems (2006).

Akademikernes Centralorganisation (Danish Confederation of Professional Asscns): Nørre Voldgade 29, POB 2192, 1017 Copenhagen K; tel. 33-69-40-40; fax 33-93-85-40; e-mail ac@ac.dk; internet www.ac.dk; Pres. SINE SUNESEN.

Comprises 10 affiliated unions with a total membership of 254,000 mems (2007), of which the following are the largest:

C3, ledelse og økonomi (Asscn of Danish Business Economists): Søtorvet 5, POB 2043, 1012 Copenhagen K; tel. 33-14-14-46; fax 33-14-11-49; e-mail organisation@c3.dk; internet www.c3.dk; f. 2005 by merger of Yngre Civiløkonomerne, Civiløkonomerne, KARRYERE and CA, økonomernes a-kasse; Dir CARSTEN MADSEN; c. 16,000 mems.

Danmarks Jurist- og Økonomforbund (Asscn of Danish Lawyers and Economists): Gothersgade 133, POB 2126, 1015 Copenhagen K; tel. 33-95-97-00; fax 33-95-99-99; e-mail djoef@djoef.dk; internet www.djoef.dk; Dir MOGENS KRING RASMUSSEN; 48,877 mems (2007).

Dansk Magisterforening (Danish Asscn of Masters and PhDs): Nimbusparken 16, 2000 Frederiksberg; tel. 38-15-66-00; fax 38-15-66-66; e-mail dm@dm.dk; internet www.dm.dk; Dir LENE VENNITS; 35,677 mems (2007).

Forbundet Kommunikation og Sprog (Danish Union of Communication and Language Professionals): Skindergade 45–47, POB 2246, 1019 Copenhagen K; tel. 33-91-98-00; fax 33-91-68-18; e-mail info@kommunikationogsprog.dk; internet www.kommunikationogsprog.dk; fmrly Erhvervssprogligt Forbund (Danish Asscn of Business Language Graduates); Dir JAN ANKLER; 7,504 mems (2007).

Gymnasieskolernes Lærerforening (Danish National Union of Upper Secondary School Teachers): Vesterbrogade 16, 1620 Copenhagen V; tel. 33-29-09-00; fax 33-29-09-01; e-mail gl@gl.org; internet www.gl.org; Dir ENDRE SZÖCS; 11,835 mems (2007).

Ingeniørforeningen i Danmark (Society of Danish Engineers): Ingeniørhuset, Kalvebod Brygge 31–33, 1780 Copenhagen V; tel. 33-18-48-48; fax 33-18-48-99; e-mail ida@ida.dk; internet www.ida.dk; Dir IB OUSTRUP; 62,351 mems (2007).

Lægeforeningen (Danish Medical Asscn): Trondhjemsgade 9, 2100 Copenhagen Ø; tel. 35-44-85-00; fax 35-44-85-05; e-mail dadl@dadl.dk; internet www.laeger.dk; Dir BENTE HYLDAHL FOGH; 23,156 mems (2007).

FTF (Confederation of Professionals in Denmark): Niels Hemmingsens Gade 12, POB 1169, 1010 Copenhagen K; tel. 33-36-88-00; fax 33-36-88-80; e-mail ftf@ftf.dk; internet www.ftf.dk; f. 1952; Chair. BENTE SORGENFREY; 457,122 mems (2006).

Transport

In June 1998 an 18-km combined tunnel-and-bridge road and rail link across the Great Belt, linking the islands of Zealand and Funen, was completed; the project incorporated the world's second longest suspension bridge. A 15.9-km road and rail link across the Øresund Strait, between Copenhagen and Malmö, Sweden, was completed in July 2000. A 22-km underground light railway system in Copenhagen was completed in May 2003.

RAILWAYS

Banedanmark (Rail Net Denmark): Amerika Pl. 15, 2100 Copenhagen Ø; tel. 82-34-00-00; fax 82-34-45-72; e-mail banedanmark@bane.dk; internet www.banedanmark.dk; f. 1997 as Banestyrelsen to assume, from the DSB (see below), responsibility for the maintenance and development of the national rail network; controls 2,349 km of line, of which 602 km are electrified; also manages signalling and train control; CEO ANNE BIRGITTE LUNDHOLT.

DSB (Danish State Railways): Sølvgade 40, 1349 Copenhagen K; tel. 33-14-04-00; fax 33-51-41-20; e-mail dsb@dsb.dk; internet www.dsb.dk; wholly owned by Ministry of Transport and Energy; became an independent public corpn in Jan. 1999; privatization pending; operates passenger services; Chair. MOGENS GRANBORG; CEO SØREN ERIKSEN.

A total of 495 km, mostly branch lines, is run by 15 private companies.

ROADS

At 31 December 2003 Denmark had an estimated 71,847 km of paved roads, including 918 km of motorways, 701 km of national roads and 9,988 km of secondary roads.

SHIPPING

The Port of Copenhagen is the largest port in Denmark and the only one to incorporate a Free Port Zone. The other major ports are Århus, Fredericia, Alborg and Esbjerg, all situated in Jutland. There are petroleum terminals, with adjacent refineries, at Kalundborg, Stigsnæs and Fredericia. Ferry services are provided by Scandlines (see below) and by various private companies.

Farvandsvæsenet (Royal Danish Administration of Navigation and Hydrography): Overgaden oven Vandet 62B, POB 1919, 1023 Copenhagen K; tel. 32-68-95-00; fax 32-57-43-41; e-mail frv@frv.dk; internet www.frv.dk; Dir SVEND ESKILDSEN.

Port Authorities

Århus: Port Authority of Århus, Mindet 2, POB 130, 8100 Århus C; tel. 86-13-32-66; fax 86-12-76-62; e-mail port@aarhus.dk; internet www.aarhushavn.dk; Port Dir BJARNE MATHIESEN.

Associated Danish Ports A/S (ADP): Vesthavnsvej 33, 7000 Fredericia; tel. 79-21-50-00; fax 79-21-50-05; e-mail post@adp-as.dk; internet www.adp-as.dk; has authority for ports of Fredericia and Nyborg; Man. Dir JENS PETER PETERS.

Copenhagen: Copenhagen Malmö Port AB, Containervej 9, POB 900, 2100 Copenhagen Ø; tel. 35-46-11-11; fax 35-46-11-64; e-mail cmport@cmport.com; internet www.cmport.com; f. by merger of ports of Copenhagen and Malmö; Man. Dir LARS KARLSSON; Port Capt. S. ANDERSEN.

Esbjerg: Port of Esbjerg, Hulvejen 1, 6700 Esbjerg; tel. 75-12-41-44; fax 75-13-40-50; e-mail adm@portesbjerg.dk; internet www.portesbjerg.dk; Port Dir OLE INGRISCH; Head of Maritime Dept TORBEN JENSEN.

Frederikshavn: Frederikshavn Havn, Oliepieren 7, POB 129, 9900 Frederikshavn; tel. 96-20-47-00; fax 96-20-47-11; e-mail info@frederikshavnhavn.dk; internet www.frederikshavnhavn.dk; Man.-Dir PREBEN REINHOLT; Harbour Capt. JESPER G. THOMSEN.

Kalundborg: Kalundborg Port Authority, Baltic Pl., POB 54, 4400 Kalundborg; tel. 59-53-44-00; fax 59-53-40-03; e-mail info@portofkalundborg.dk; internet www.portofkalundborg.dk.

Sønderborg: Sønderborg Havn, Nørrebro 1, 6400 Sønderborg; tel. 74-42-27-65; fax 74-43-30-19; e-mail havnen@sonderborg.dk; internet www.sonderborg.dk/havn; Harbour Master LASS ANDERSEN.

Principal Shipping Companies

Corral Line A/S: Havnevej 18, 6320 Egernsund; e-mail info@corralline.com; tel. 74-44-14-35; fax 74-44-14-75; formerly Sønderborg Rederiaktieselskab; 8 livestock carriers of 19,302 grt; shipowners, managers, chartering agents; world-wide; Man. Dir B. CLAUSEN.

Rederiet Otto Danielsen: Kongevejen 272A, 2830 Virum; tel. 45-83-25-55; fax 45-83-17-07; e-mail od@ottodanielsen.com; internet www.ottodanielsen.com; f. 1944; 7 general cargo vessels, totalling 20,793 grt, under foreign flags; general tramp trade, chartering, ship sales; Fleet Man. JØRN STAUREBY.

Dannebrog Rederi A/S: Rungsted Strandvej 113, 2960 Rungsted Kyst; tel. 45-17-77-77; fax 45-17-77-70; e-mail dbrog@dannebrog.com; internet www.dannebrog.com; f. 1883; 3 ro-ro vessels, product chemical tanker services; liner service USA–Europe, US Gulf–Caribbean, Mediterranean–Caribbean; Man. Dir JOHAN WEDELL-WEDELLSBORG.

DFDS A/S: Sundkrogsgade 11, 2100 Copenhagen Ø; tel. 33-42-33-42; fax 33-42-33-41; e-mail dfds@dfds.com; internet www.dfds.com; f. 1866; 5 car/passenger ships and 60 freight vessels; passenger and car ferry services between Denmark, Belgium, Finland, France, Germany, Ireland, Latvia, Lithuania, the Netherlands, Norway, Poland, Sweden and the United Kingdom; Pres. and CEO NIELS SMEDEGAARD.

H. Folmer & Co: Fredericiagade 57, 1310 Copenhagen K; tel. 33-13-25-10; fax 33-13-54-64; e-mail folmer@folmer.dk; internet www.folmer.dk; f. 1955; 14 general cargo vessels of 14,100 grt; world-wide tramping; Man. Owners J. J. FOLMER, UFFE MARTIN JENSEN.

J. Lauritzen A/S: Sankt Annæ Pl. 28, POB 2147, 1291 Copenhagen K; tel. 33-96-80-00; fax 33-96-80-01; e-mail tni@j-l.com; internet www.j-lauritzen.com; f. 1884; operates reefer ships, LPG/C carriers and bulk ships; Pres. and CEO TORBEN JANHOLT.

A. P. Møller—Mærsk A/S: Esplanaden 50, 1098 Copenhagen K; tel. 33-63-33-63; fax 33-63-41-08; e-mail cphinfo@maersk.com; internet www.maersk.com; f. 1904; fleet of 113 container vessels, 19 products tankers, 3 crude petroleum tankers, 5 gas carriers, 10 car carriers, 59 offshore vessels and 22 drilling rigs; further tonnage owned by subsidiary cos in Singapore and the UK; world-wide liner and feeder services under the name of Maersk Line, and world-wide tanker, bulk, offshore and rig services; CEO NILS SMEDEGAARD ANDERSEN.

Dampskibsselskabet Norden A/S: Amaliegade 49, 1256 Copenhagen K; tel. 33-15-04-51; fax 33-15-61-99; e-mail mail@ds-norden.com; internet www.ds-norden.com; f. 1871; operates about 60 tankers and bulk carriers; world-wide tramping; Pres. and CEO CARSTEN MORTENSEN.

Scandlines Danmark A/S: Dampfærgevej 10, 2100 Copenhagen Ø; tel. 33-15-15-15; fax 35-29-02-01; e-mail scandlines@scandlines.dk; internet www.scandlines.dk; f. 1998 by merger of Scandlines A/S and Deutsche Fährgesellschaft Ostsee GmbH (Germany); maintains offices in Germany and Sweden; acquired by Deutsche Seereederei GmbH in 2007; operates 12 ferry routes around Denmark and throughout the Baltic.

A/S Em. Z. Svitzer: Pakhus 48, Sundkaj 9, 2100 Copenhagen Ø; tel. 39-19-39-19; fax 39-19-39-09; e-mail chartering@svitzer.dk; internet www.svitzer.com; f. 1833; wholly owned subsidiary of A. P. Møller—Mærsk Group; 22 tugs and salvage vessels and a barge fleet; salvage, towage and barge services; Gen. Man. KELD BALLE MORTENSEN.

A/S Dampskibsselskabet Torm: Tuborg Havnevej 18, 2900 Hellerup; tel. 39-17-92-00; fax 39-17-93-93; e-mail mail@torm.dk; internet www.torm.dk; f. 1889; 5 LR1 product tankers (401,729 dwt), 5 LR2 product tankers (499,961 dwt), 13 MR product tankers (591,955 dwt), 7 Panamax bulk carriers (493,289 dwt) and 2 Handysize bulk carriers (55,629 dwt) plus 7 further tankers on order (2004); operator of a time-chartered fleet; CEO KLAUS KJÆRULFF.

Shipping Association

Danmarks Rederiforening (Danish Shipowners' Asscn): Amaliegade 33, 1256 Copenhagen K; tel. 33-11-40-88; fax 33-11-62-10; e-mail info@shipowners.dk; internet www.shipowners.dk; f. 1884; 37 mems, representing 8.8m grt (May 2007); Chair. of the Bd TORBEN JANHOLT; Man. Dir PETER BJERREGAARD.

CIVIL AVIATION

The main international airport is Copenhagen Airport, situated about 10 km from the centre of the capital. The following domestic airports have scheduled flights to European and Scandinavian destinations: Ålborg, Århus and Billund in Jutland. Other domestic airports include: Roskilde (30 km south-west of Copenhagen); Esbjerg, Karup, Skrydstrup, Stauning, Sønderborg and Thisted in Jutland; Odense in Funen; and Bornholm Airport on the island of Bornholm.

Statens Luftfartsvæsen (Civil Aviation Administration): Luftfartshuset, Ellebjergvej 50, POB 744, 2450 Copenhagen SV; tel. 36-18-60-00; fax 36-18-60-01; e-mail dcaa@slv.dk; internet www.slv.dk; Dir-Gen. KURT LYKSTOFT LARSEN.

Scandinavian Airlines System (SAS): SAS Huset, Lufthavnsboulevarden 10, POB 150, 2770 Kastrup; tel. 32-32-00-00; fax 32-32-21-49; internet www.sas.dk; f. 1946; the national carrier of Denmark, Norway and Sweden. It is a consortium owned two-sevenths by SAS Danmark A/S, two-sevenths by SAS Norge ASA and three-sevenths by SAS Sverige AB. Each parent org. is a limited co owned 50% by its respective govt and 50% by private shareholders. The SAS group includes the consortium and the subsidiaries in which the consortium has a majority or otherwise controlling interest; the Board consists of two members from each of the parent cos and the chairmanship rotates among the three national chairmen on an annual basis; strategic alliance with Lufthansa (Germany) formed in 1995; Chair. JOHN DUEHOLM; CEO SUSANNE LARSEN.

National Airlines

Cimber Air Denmark: Sønderborg Airport, Lufthavnsvej 2, 6400 Sønderborg; tel. 74-42-22-77; fax 74-42-65-11; e-mail marketing@cimber.dk; internet www.cimber.dk; f. 1950; operates domestic service in co-operation with Lufthansa and SAS; operates charter flights and total route systems for other cos throughout Europe; Pres., CEO JORGEN NIELSEN.

MyTravel Airways A/S: Copenhagen Airport South, Hangar 276, 2791 Dragør; tel. 32-47-72-00; fax 32-45-12-20; e-mail mytravelairways@mytravel.dk; internet www.mytravelairways.dk; f. 2002; flights to major destinations in Europe; Pres. TOM CLAUSEN.

Sterling Airlines A/S: Copenhagen Airport South, 2791 Dragør; tel. 70-33-33-70; fax 70-33-23-23; e-mail dcdq@starair.dk; internet www.sterling.dk; f. 1987; acquired by FL Group (Iceland) in 2006; scheduled and charter flights to over 40 destinations in Europe; Pres. and CEO ALMAR ÖRN HILMARSSON.

SUN-AIR of Scandinavia A/S: Cumulusvej 10, 7190 Billund; tel. 76-50-01-00; fax 75-33-86-18; e-mail info@sunair.dk; internet www.sunair.dk; f. 1978; also maintains offices at Aalborg, Århus, Billund and Thisted Airports; operates charter flights, sells and leases aircraft and operates aircraft maintenance services, operates a franchise of scheduled flights throughout northern Europe in co-operation with British Airways since 1996; Dir NIELS SUNDBERG.

Tourism

In 2005 foreign tourist arrivals in Denmark totalled 4,698,668; in that year receipts from tourism totalled US $5,960m.

VisitDenmark: Islands Brygge 43, 2300 Copenhagen S; tel. 32-88-99-00; fax 32-88-99-01; e-mail contact@visitdenmark.com; internet www.visitdenmark.com; f. 1967; fmrly Danmarks Turistråd (Danish Tourist Board); Dir DORTE KIILERICH.

DANISH EXTERNAL TERRITORIES
THE FAROE ISLANDS

Introductory Survey

Location, Climate, Language, Religion, Flag, Capital
The Faroe Islands are a group of 18 islands (of which 17 are inhabited) in the Atlantic Ocean, between Scotland and Iceland. The main island is Streymoy, where more than one-third of the population resides. The climate is mild in winter and cool in summer, with a mean temperature of 7°C (45°F). Most of the inhabitants profess Christianity: the majority of Faroese belong to the Evangelical Lutheran Church of Denmark. The principal language is Faroese, but Danish is a compulsory subject in all schools. The flag (proportions 16 by 22) displays a red cross, bordered with blue, on a white background, the upright of the cross being to the left of centre. The capital is Tórshavn, which is situated on Streymoy.

History and Government
The Faroe Islands have been under Danish administration since Queen Margrethe I of Denmark inherited Norway in 1380. The islands were occupied by the United Kingdom while Denmark was under German occupation during the Second World War, but they were restored to Danish control immediately after the war. The Home Rule Act of 1948 gave the Faroese control over all their internal affairs. The Faroe Islands did not join the European Community (now European Union—EU, see p. 244) with Denmark in 1973. There is a local parliament (the Løgting—Lagting in Danish), but the Danish Folketing (Parliament), to which the Faroese send two members, is responsible for defence and foreign policy, constitutional matters, and the judicial and monetary systems. The transfer of competency in some areas from Denmark to the Faroe Islands began in 2005 (see below). The Faroes control fishing resources within their fisheries zone, and in September 1992 a long-standing dispute between Denmark and the Faroes was settled when the Danish Government agreed to give the Faroese authorities legislative and administrative power over mineral resources, including those beneath the bed of the sea in the area adjacent to the islands. This agreement removed one of the major obstacles to exploration for hydrocarbons off the Faroe Islands, where geologists consider that prospects for discovering reserves of petroleum and natural gas are favourable. In 1994 the Faroe Islands accordingly awarded a US company a licence to begin exploratory surveys, despite the existence of a long-standing dispute between Denmark and the United Kingdom over the demarcation of the continental shelf west of the Shetland Islands and south-east of the Faroe Islands, which had threatened to delay prospecting. This dispute was resolved in mid-1999, however, when representatives of the Faroese Government (the Landsstýri) signed an agreement with the Danish and British Governments regarding the location of the boundaries of the area concerned. The area, known as the 'golden corner' (formerly the White Zone), was believed to be potentially rich in petroleum reserves. Following the issue by the Faroese Government of a number of licences in mid-August 2000, exploratory drilling commenced in the 'golden corner' in mid-2001 (see Economic Affairs).

The centre-left coalition Government of the Social Democratic Party (SDP), Republicans and the People's Party, formed in 1975, collapsed in 1980 over a plan, opposed by the conservative People's Party, to extend through the winter months a government-owned ferry service linking the islands with Denmark, Norway and Scotland. At a general election, held in November, conservative political groups slightly increased their share of the popular vote. Although there was no material change in the balance of party representation in the Løgting, the Union Party formed a centre-right coalition with the People's Party and the Home Rule Party in January 1981. A general election was held in November 1984, and in December a four-party, centre-left coalition Government was formed under the premiership of Atli Dam, comprising his SDP, the Home Rule Party, the Republican Party and the Christian People's Party combined with the Progressive and Fishing Industry Party (CPP-PFIP).

Elections in 1988 demonstrated a shift to the right in the Faroes, to the benefit of the People's Party. Its one member in the Danish Folketing increased his support in the national elections of September 1987 and May 1988. At a Faroese general election in November 1988 the incumbent Government lost its majority, and the People's Party became the largest party in the Løgting. In January 1989, after 10 weeks of negotiations, a centre-right coalition, comprising the People's Party, the Republican Party, the Home Rule Party and the CPP-PFIP, and led by Jógvan Sundstein (Chairman of the People's Party), was formed. The coalition was committed to economic austerity and support for the fishing industry. In June, however, the CPP-PFIP and the Home Rule Party withdrew their support for the Government. After three weeks a new coalition was formed. Sundstein remained Prime Minister (Løgmaður), and his People's Party was supported by the Republican Party and the Union Party. In October 1990, however, these two parties withdrew their support for the coalition Government. As a result, an early general election was held in November. The SDP obtained the largest share of the vote, winning 10 seats (an increase of three), while the People's Party, which led the outgoing coalition, won seven seats (a loss of one seat).

In January 1991 a coalition between the SDP and the People's Party was formed, under Atli Dam. He was replaced in January 1993 by Marita Petersen (also of the SDP). In April the People's Party withdrew from the coalition, and was replaced by the Republican Party and the Home Rule Party. At a general election, held in July 1994, the Union Party became the largest party in the Løgting, winning eight seats (an increase of two), while the SDP's allocation of seats was reduced from 10 to five. In September a coalition of the Union Party, the SDP, the Home Rule Party and the newly formed Labour Front took office. Edmund Joensen (Chairman of the Union Party) replaced Petersen as Prime Minister. In 1996 the People's Party replaced the SDP in the governing coalition. Joensen remained Prime Minister, while Anfinn Kallsberg of the People's Party succeeded Jóannes Eidesgaard of the SDP as Minister of Finance and Economics. A general election was held on 30 April 1998, at which both the Republican Party and the People's Party each increased their representation to eight seats, while the number of seats secured by the SDP rose from five to seven; the representation of the Union Party was reduced from eight seats to six. In mid-May a coalition Government was formed by members of the People's Party, the Republican Party and the Home Rule Party, with Kallsberg as Prime Minister.

Tensions with the Danish Government in the early 1990s, the nationalistic persuasion of the new Government and the prospect of offshore petroleum discoveries revived Faroese ambitions for political and economic independence. (The Faroese had narrowly favoured independence from Denmark in a referendum in 1946, but the decision had been overturned by the Danish Folketing.) In October 1998 the Løgting adopted a resolution in support of the Government's intention (announced earlier that year) to seek status for the Faroe Islands as a 'sovereign nation' under the Danish monarchy, having a common monetary system with Denmark; it was envisaged by the Faroese Government that sovereignty for the islands would be most appropriately achieved through continued co-operation with Denmark within a new constitutional framework, based on a bilateral treaty between the two countries as equal, independent partners. A commission charged with the development of a proposal for a Faroese constitution was established by the Government in February 1999, and submitted its conclusions to the Løgting in June 2000. The Faroese envisaged retaining the Danish Queen Margrethe II as their Head of State and maintaining the link between their local currency and the Danish krone. The islands would seek to continue to co-operate with Denmark in social affairs, justice, health and air traffic control, and would also maintain present arrangements such as mutual rights of residence, employment and education. The Faroes would also seek to join the North Atlantic Treaty Organization (NATO, see p. 340) and the UN.

Negotiations between the Danish and Faroese administrations concerning the future independence of the Faroe Islands began in March 2000, but swiftly stalled after the Danish Government confirmed that it would not oppose Faroese independence but would terminate annual subsidies (of about 1,000m. kroner) to the Faroes in four years should secession take place, compared with the 15 years envisaged by the Faroese. The Danish Prime Minister, Poul Nyrup Rasmussen, rejected an offer of mediation from the Icelandic premier, Davíð Oddsson. Discussions were resumed later in the year, but finally collapsed in late October, prompting Kallsberg to announce a plan to hold a referendum on independence in 2001. The Faroese had initially envisaged the successful negotiation of a treaty with the Danish Government prior to a referendum. The referendum, which in February was scheduled to be held on 26 May, was to include four issues: the full transfer of authority to the Faroese by 2012; the establishment of an economic fund to guarantee financial security during the transitional period; the gradual elimination of subsidies from Denmark; and the holding of a further referendum establishing the Faroe Islands as an independent state by 2012. The Danish Government reacted strongly to plans for a plebiscite, claiming that Denmark would regard it as a de facto referendum on sovereignty and that a vote in favour of the proposals for independence would result in the halting of Danish aid within four years. The reluctance of the Faroese population to lose Danish subsidies and disagreement within the Faroese coalition Government resulted in the cancellation of the referendum in early March 2001. Shortly afterwards agreement was reached within the Faroese Government on a plan for independence, which was subsequently submitted to the Danish authorities.

At the general election, held on 30 April 2002, the People's Party won seven seats in the Løgting; it subsequently formed a coalition Government with the Republican Party (which had secured eight seats), the Home Rule Party and the Centre Party (one seat apiece); the Union Party secured eight seats in the Løgting, and the SDP won seven seats.

The Minister of Fisheries, Jørgen Niclasen, resigned in January 2003 following revelations of financial improprieties regarding loans he had made to prawn trawlers using public funds; Kallsberg assumed the portfolio.

On 26 June 2003 the Danish Prime Minister, Anders Fogh Rasmussen, made an official visit to the Faroe Islands. During his visit he and Kallsberg signed a bill providing a legal basis for the transfer of competencies from the Danish to the Faroese Governments. The legislation did not in itself transfer any powers (this was to be done subsequently, with a separate resolution required in the Løgting for each power to be transferred), but it did detail those powers that would remain with the Danish Folketing, namely: the Danish Constitution; Danish citizenship; the Danish Supreme Court; currency and monetary policy; and foreign, security and defence policy. As with other bilateral agreements, identical versions of the bill, in both Faroese and Danish, were to pass before the Løgting and the Folketing, respectively.

In December 2003 the Republican Party withdrew from the ruling coalition, causing the collapse of the Government. The crisis was precipitated by the publication of a book that alluded to Kallsberg's past involvement in accounting fraud; he was accused of misappropriating 912,000 kroner between 1977 and 1981. Claiming that the money had subsequently been repaid and that he had not personally gained from the affair, Kallsberg rejected demands by the leader of the Republican Party, Høgni Hoydal, to issue a public apology or to resign. Following the collapse of the Government Kallsberg called an early election.

At the general election, held on 20 January 2004, the Republican Party won eight seats, while the Union Party, the SDP and the People's Party each won seven seats. A new coalition Government was officially formed on 3 February, with Eidesgaard as Prime Minister. Whereas the previous coalition had been composed of only pro-independence parties, the new administration comprised the People's Party, which supported independence, and the Union Party and the SDP, which both favoured continued union with Denmark. The new Government was expected to opt for the compromise arrangement of greater independence from Denmark without severing ties.

In January 2004 Eidesgaard dismissed the Minister of Fisheries, Jóhan Dahl, following allegations that Dahl had evaded a business debt years ago that his late business partner's widow had been obliged to pay. Bjørn Kalsø was appointed to replace Dahl the following day. In March the Government abolished the Ministry of Petroleum, which became the Faroese Petroleum Administration, part of the Ministry of Trade and Industry. In February 2006 the Petroleum Administration was merged with the Faroese Geological Survey to form the Faroese Earth and Energy Directorate.

In March 2004 the Government proposed a resolution recognizing that, despite the Faroes' long-standing policy of neutrality, they were a de facto member of NATO and had been so for some 50 years. Conservative members of the Løgting offered to support the Islands' formal accession to NATO.

In August 2004 the Danish Minister of Foreign Affairs, Per Stig Møller, paid a one-day visit to the Faroes during which he promised the islanders greater influence over Faroese foreign policy issues, and stated that the islands would be given 'full insight' into any issues affecting Faroese defence policy. The Faroe Islands would also be permitted to attend NATO meetings whenever relevant issues were under discussion.

The legislation on the transfer of competencies was enacted on 29 July 2005 (the Faroese National Day). Following its enactment the Faroese Government intended to transfer to its control powers covering civil emergency preparedness, company law, copyright law and industrial property rights, and the established church—all during its current term of office (which was due to last until 2008). Areas that remained to be transferred at a later stage were: the regulation of immigration and border control; criminal law; legislation and administration of the financial sector; health care; the judicial courts (excluding the Danish Supreme Court); the issuing of passports; the police and prosecution service; the prison service; and public pensions. Independently of this process, an additional piece of new legislation was presented to the Løgting and the Folketing to grant the Faroese Government authority to negotiate and conclude agreements under international law with other states and international organizations, and to allow (under certain circumstances) the Faroe Islands to become a member of international organizations in their own right. This bill was passed and enacted concurrently with the transfer of competencies bill. In July 2006 Eidesgaard and Fogh Rasmussen signed an agreement for the Faroese Government to assume ownership of Vágar Airport from Denmark; the Government was also reviewing the option to assume responsibility for civil aviation. In early May 2007 Bárður Nielsen resigned as Minister of Finance and was replaced by fellow Union Party member Magni Laksáfoss. The Danish Minister of Foreign Affairs, Møller, paid a two-day visit to the Faroes in early October, during which he met with members of the Løgting to discuss the Faroese Government's 'Vision 2015' development programme, in addition to future Faroese membership of the EU and the European Free Trade Association (EFTA, see p. 412).

In late November 2007 Jacob Vestergaard resigned as Minister of the Interior, following accusations that he had exceeded his mandate in removing two employees of a transport company from their posts. He was replaced by Heðin Zachariasen of the People's Party. Following the failure of attempts by the Government to negotiate a reduction of the mandatory campaign period from eight to six weeks, which, it argued, would allow the completion of outstanding measures in its programme, Eidesgaard dissolved the Løgting in early December, in advance of a general election, scheduled for mid-January 2008.

The general election duly took place on 19 January 2008; the rate of participation was 89.3%. The Republican Party retained its eight seats in the Løgting, and thus remained the largest party in the legislature, while the Union Party and People's Party each won seven seats (as in 2004). The SDP, however, won just six seats (one fewer than in 2004), prompting speculation over the continuation of Eidesgaard's premiership. Negotiations ensued between the main parties and, on 4 February, a new coalition Government, comprising the SDP, the Republican Party and the Centre Party (which had won three seats at the general election), took office. Eidesgaard remained as Prime Minister, while Høgni Hoydal took the newly created role of Minister of Foreign Affairs. Of the remaining six ministers, three were from the Republican Party, two from the SDP and one from the Centre Party.

In international affairs, the Faroe Islanders attracted opprobrium for their traditional slaughter of pilot whales, an important source of food. After foreign journalists publicized the whaling in 1986, stricter regulations were imposed on whaling operations. In July 1992 the Faroese Government threatened to leave the International Whaling Commission (IWC, see p. 404), following the latter's criticism of whaling methods practised in the Faroe Islands. It was, however, claimed that the Faroese did not have the legal right to withdraw from the Commission independently of Denmark. In September the Faroe Islands, Greenland, Norway and Iceland agreed to establish the North Atlantic Marine Mammal Commission, in protest at what they viewed as the IWC's preoccupation with conservation. The Faroe Islands resumed commercial hunting of the minke whale in 1993 and began trading in whale meat in 2002 after a halt of 14 years. In March 2003 it was reported that the Faroe Islands were to begin importing whale meat from Norway.

In late September 2006 the Government signed an interim agreement with Denmark, Iceland and Norway regarding the demarcation of the continental shelf north of the Faroe Islands. In February 2007 Eidesgaard and the Icelandic Minister of Foreign Affairs, Valgerður Sverrisdóttir, signed a bilateral agreement delimiting the maritime boundary between their respective territories, thereby ending a dispute lasting for three decades regarding overlapping claims to an area of around 3,650 sq km. By mid-2008 the agreement still required the approval of both the Løgting and the Icelandic legislature, the Althingi.

In May 2006 a parliamentary committee on foreign relations recommended that the Prime Minister initiate membership negotiations with the EFTA. Eidesgaard subsequently began visiting the member states of EFTA in order to promote the future membership of the Faroe Islands.

Economic Affairs

In 2003, according to official estimates, gross national income (GNI), was 10,053m. kroner (at current prices), equivalent to 209,774 kroner per head. Between 1973 and 1988, it was estimated, gross national product (GNP) increased, in real terms, at an average rate of 4.5% per year, with real GNP per head rising by 3.3% annually. Between 1989 and 1993, however, real GNP decreased dramatically, at an average rate of 9.4% per year. During 1994–95 real GNP increased by 4.2%. The population declined at an average annual rate of 1.6% in 1989–95, but increased by 0.9% per year in 1995–2007. Gross domestic product (GDP) increased, in real terms, by 9.5% in 2002 and by an estimated 3.6% in 2003.

Agriculture (principally sheep-farming) and fishing contributed 20.5% of GDP in 2000. In 2006 the sector provided 11.6% of employment. Potatoes and other vegetables are the main crops. Only about 6% of the land surface is cultivated.

Fishing is the dominant industry. In 1999 fishing, aquaculture and fish-processing accounted for 25.1% of GDP; the sector employed 18.9% of the labour force in 2006. Fish products accounted for 94.1% of exports in 2006. Most fishing takes place within the 200-nautical-mile (370-km) fisheries zone imposed around the Faroes in 1977. Fish farming, principally of salmon, began in the 1980s. The traditional hunting of pilot whales continues to provide an important source of meat for the Faroese. The Faroe Islands resumed commercial hunting of the minke whale in 1993 and began trading in whale meat in 2002 after a halt of 14 years.

Industry (including mining, manufacturing, construction and power) contributed 19.0% of GDP in 2000. In 2006 the sector provided 22.5% of employment. The dominant sectors are fishing-related industries, such as fish-drying and -freezing, and ship maintenance and repairs.

Mining and quarrying contributed only 0.3% of GDP in 2000 and engaged 0.3% of the employed labour force in 2006. 'Brown coal' (lignite) is mined on Suðuroy. The potential for petroleum production around the islands is believed to be significant. Exploratory drilling commenced in 2001 in an area south-east of the Faroe Islands. In November the US company Amerada Hess announced that it had discovered petroleum in considerable quantities. In January 2002 the Faroes Oil and Gas Company (FOGC—Føroya Kolvetni) became the first Faroese company to be listed on the London Stock Exchange. A second licensing round for offshore drilling took place in 2005 and a third in late 2007. In 2006 the Faroese Petroleum Administration and the Faroese Geological Survey were merged into a new organization, Jarðfeingi (the Faroese Earth and Energy Directorate).

Manufacturing contributed 11.4% of GDP in 2000. The dominant sector is fish-processing, which accounted for 5.7% of GDP in 1999 and engaged 7.5% of the employed labour force in 2006. Technical repairs and shipyards contributed 2.1% of GDP in 1999, while exports of vessels accounted for 2.0% of exports in 2006. A small textile industry exports traditional Faroese woollens.

In 2005 55% of the islands' electricity production was provided by thermal energy, 40% by hydroelectric power and 4% by wind power. In July 2003 Elfelagið SEV, the state electricity company, announced that it was to construct a power station in conjunction with a Scottish firm, Wavegen. The power station was to use tunnels built into cliffs on the shoreline to exploit energy from the sea. Imports of fuels and related products accounted for 18.4% of imports in 2006.

The services sector accounted for 60.6% of GDP in 2000. In 2006 the sector provided 65.9% of employment. In November 2003 an independent Faroese securities market was launched in co-operation with the Icelandic stock market.

In 2006 the Faroe Islands recorded a trade deficit of 614m. kroner, and there was a deficit of 142m. kroner on the current account of the balance of payments. Denmark was the Faroes' principal source of imports (30.1%) in 2006; other major suppliers were Norway (20.2%) Germany (7.6%) and Sweden (6.0%). The United Kingdom was the principal market for exports (26.4%) in that year; other major purchasers were Denmark (12.0%), France (including Monaco—9.9%) and Spain (8.1%). In 2006 the European Union (EU, see p. 244) as a whole took 71.2% of exports and supplied 61.0% of imports. The principal imports in 2006 were intermediate goods (accounting for 94.6% of the total cost of imports), while fish products accounted for 94.1% of total exports in the same year.

Danish subsidies are an important source of income to the islands, and accounted for 14.8% of total government revenue in 2003. In that year, including the central government grant of 848m. kroner as revenue, the Faroese Government recorded a budget surplus of 408m. kroner. In 2004 the net foreign debt was estimated at 2,956m. kroner. The annual average rate of inflation was 2.7% in 1996–06; consumer prices rose by 2.9% in 2007. Unemployment was 1.4% of the labour force in 2007 (compared with 16% in mid-1995).

The Faroe Islands did not join the European Community (now EU) with Denmark in 1973, but did secure favourable terms of trade with Community members and special concessions in Denmark and the United Kingdom. Agreements on free trade were concluded between the Faroe Islands and Iceland, Norway, Sweden, Finland and Austria in 1992–93 and between the Faroe Islands and the EU in January 2004; a new free-trade agreement between the Faroe Islands and Iceland was concluded in September 2005. In 2006 the Faroe Islands decided to initiate negotiations for membership of the European Free Trade Association (EFTA, see p. 412). In international fisheries organizations, where Denmark is represented by the EU, the Kingdom maintains separate membership in respect of the Faroe Islands (and Greenland). The Faroe Islands is also a member of the Nordic Council (see p. 424).

During the 1980s the Faroes' principal source of income, the fishing industry, was expanded with the help of substantial investment and official subsidies, financed by external borrowing. However, depletion of stocks and the resulting decline in catches, together with a fall in export prices, led to a reduction in export earnings and a financial crisis in the early 1990s. The Danish Government attempted to stabilize the economy by restructuring the banking sector and by extending significant loans. Denmark's annual subsidy provides nearly one-third of the Faroes' budget. The discovery of substantial and commercially viable reserves of natural gas and petroleum would enable the Faroese economy to diversify, thereby reducing its overwhelming dependence on Danish subsidies as well as on the fisheries sector. From the end of the 1990s until the mid-2000s the Faroe Islands experienced a period of economic prosperity with high levels of growth and low unemployment. A nation-wide strike in May 2003, together with a sharp decline in fish prices, lower economic activity and tax reductions, contributed to a fall in GDP growth to an estimated 3.6% in 2003, compared with 9.5% in 2002. In 2004–05 this downward trend continued as the fishing catch and aquaculture production declined. However, increases in private consumption and investment in 2006 led to estimated GDP growth of 10.4%. This figure was estimated to have slowed to 4.6% in 2007, largely due to a contraction in production capacity as a result of labour shortages. The economic recovery was partly due to increases in fish prices and revenue from fisheries, although increased petroleum prices raised costs incurred by the fishing fleets.

Education

The education system is similar to that of Denmark, except that Faroese is the language of instruction. Danish is, however, a compulsory subject in all schools. The Faroese Academy was upgraded to the University of the Faroe Islands in 1990.

In 2003 government expenditure on education was 817m. kroner (representing 15.3% of total estimated budgetary spending).

Public Holidays

Public holidays in the Faroe Islands are the same as those for Denmark. In addition, the Faroese also celebrate Flag Day on 25 April and St Olavsøka on 28–29 July each year. Various regional holidays are also observed in May–July.

Statistical Survey

Sources (unless otherwise stated): Statistics Faroe Islands, Traðagøta 39, POB 2068, 165 Argir; tel. 352028; fax 352038; e-mail hagstova@hagstova.fo; internet www.hagstova.fo; Faroese Government Office, Hovedvagtsgade 8, 2, 1103 Copenhagen K; tel. 33-14-08-66; fax 33-93-85-75;; Landsbanki Føroya (Faroese Government Bank), Staravegur 5, POB 229, 110 Tórshavn; tel. 308120; fax 318537; e-mail landsbank@landsbank.fo; internet landsbankin.fo.

AREA AND POPULATION

Area: 1,398.9 sq km (540.1 sq miles).

Population: 48,350 at 1 January 2007 (males 25,135, females 23,215).

Density (1 January 2007): 34.6 per sq km.

Principal Towns (population at 1 January 2007): Tórshavn (capital) 12,393; Klaksvík 4,666; Hoyvík 3,133; Argir 1,907; Fuglafjørður 1,558; Vágur 1,402; Tvøroyri 1,179; Vestmanna 1,234; Miðvágur 1,046.

Births, Marriages and Deaths (2006): Registered live births 661 (birth rate 13.7 per 1,000); Registered marriages 277 (marriage rate 5.7 per 1,000); Registered deaths 416 (death rate 8.6 per 1,000).

Expectation of Life (years at birth, 2005): Males 76.9; Females 81.4.

Immigration and Emigration (2004): *Immigration:* Denmark 1,140; Finland 5; Greenland 30; Iceland 39; Norway 35; Poland 5; Serbia and Montenegro 5; Sweden 4; Thailand 3; United Kingdom 37; USA 8; Total (incl. others) 1,412. *Emigration:* Denmark 1,243; Greenland 20; Finland 1; Iceland 51; Norway 37; Poland 12; Serbia and Montenegro 11; Sweden 14; Thailand 18; United Kingdom 46; USA 16; Total (incl. others) 1,559. *2005:* Immigrants 1,218; Emigrants 1,640. *2006:* Immigrants 1,480; Emigrants 1,558.

Economically Active Population (persons aged 16–74 with at least 7 hours paid work per month, 2006): Agriculture 57; Fishing 2,404; Aquaculture 441; Mining 69; Fish-processing 1,889; Shipyards and machine shops 653; Other production 1,052; Construction 1,850; Energy supply 135; Wholesale and retail trade 3,169; Restaurants and hotels 504; Sea transport 581; Other transport 647; Communication 607; Finance and insurance 936; Business services 757; Household services 238; Public administration and services 8,613; Non-profit organizations 507; Unspecified 151; *Total employed* 25,260; Total unemployed 876; *Total labour force* 26,136 (males 13,833, females 12,303). *2007:* Total unemployed 491.

HEALTH AND WELFARE
Key Indicators
Physicians (per 1,000 head, 2003): 1.7.
Hospital Beds (per 1,000 head, 2006): 5.4.

AGRICULTURE, ETC.
Principal Crop (2006, FAO estimate): Potatoes 1,508 metric tons.
Livestock ('000 head, year ending September 2006, FAO estimates): Cattle 2; Sheep 68.
Livestock Products (metric tons, 2006, FAO estimates): Cattle meat 77; Sheep meat 521.
Fishing ('000 metric tons, live weight, 2005): Capture 565.9 (Atlantic cod 35.8; Haddock 24.7; Saithe (Pollock) 76.0; Blue whiting (Poutassou) 267.4; Capelin 19.8; Atlantic herring 71.9); Aquaculture 23.5 (Atlantic salmon 19.0); *Total catch* 589.3.
Source: FAO.

INDUSTRY
Selected Products ('000 metric tons, 1996): Frozen or chilled fish 123; Salted and processed fish products 15; Aquaculture products 13; Oils, fats and meal of aquatic animals 124; *2006:* Electric energy (million kWh) 259.5; Soft drinks ('000 litres) 1,974; Beer ('000 litres) 2,326.

FINANCE
(Danish currency is in use)
Budget (government budget, million kroner, 2006): *Revenue:* Taxes and duties 3,482; Interest, dividends 156; Transfers from the Danish Government 658; Loan repayments 101; Total (incl. others) 4,088. *Expenditure:* Salaries 1,775; Purchase of goods and services 874; Construction and fixed assets production 238; Transfers to households 1,164; Total (incl. others) 3,946.
Cost of Living (Consumer Price Index at Jan.–March; base: 2001 = 100): All items 103.6 in 2005; 104.5 in 2006; 107.5 in 2007.
Gross Domestic Product (million kroner at current prices, estimates): 9,753 in 2004; 9,991 in 2005; 10,963 in 2006.
National Income and Product (million kroner at current prices, 2006, estimates): Compensation of employees 6,896; Gross operating surplus 2,805; *Gross domestic product (GDP) at factor cost* 9,702; Taxes on products (net) 1,289; Other taxes on production (net) –28; *GDP in market prices* 10,963.
Expenditure on the Gross Domestic Product (million kroner at current prices, 2003): Government final consumption expenditure 2,765; Private final consumption expenditure 5,568; Change in stocks –171; Gross fixed capital formation 2,792; *Total domestic expenditure* 10,954; Exports of goods and services 4,421; *Less* Imports of goods and services 5,672; *GDP in purchasers' values* 9,703.
Gross Domestic Product by Sector (million kroner at current prices, 2006, estimates): Non-financial sector 5,478; Financial sector 491; Public services 2,211; Households 1,896; *Sub-total* 10,076; *Less* Imputed financial services 374; *GDP at factor cost* 9,702; Indirect taxes, less subsidies 1,261; *GDP in purchasers' values* 10,963.
Balance of Payments (million kroner, 2006, estimates): Exports of goods f.o.b. 3,869; Imports of goods c.i.f. –4,483; *Trade balance* –614; Exports of services 593; Imports of services –1,278; *Balance on goods and services* –1,299; Net transfers and income 1,157; *Current balance* –142.

EXTERNAL TRADE
Principal Commodities (million kroner, 2006): *Imports c.i.f.:* Intermediate goods 4,427 (Agriculture and fish breeding 121, Construction industry 454, Other industries 865, Fuel, etc. 862, Machinery and capital equipment 506, Transport equipment, except ships 339, Goods for household consumption 1,280); Salt 9; Fresh fish 20; Frozen fish 23; Fish for reduction 68; Ships and airplanes 132; Total 4,678. *Exports f.o.b.:* Fish products 3,642 (Cod 595;, Haddock 319, Pollock 574, Salmon 374, Trout 99, Blue whiting 171, Herring 123, Atlantic mackerel 69, Prawns 89, Other fish products 1,229); Vessels 76; Other products 151; Total 3,869.
Principal Trading Partners (million kroner, 2006): *Imports c.i.f.:* China, People's Rep. 147; Denmark 1,406; France (incl. Monaco) 123; Germany 354; Italy 91; Finland 41; Netherlands 87; Norway 944; Sweden 283; United Kingdom 196; Spain 37; Total (incl. others) 4,678. *Exports f.o.b.:* Canada 61; China, People's Rep. 78; Denmark 466; France (incl. Monaco) 384; Germany 223; Iceland 105; Italy 99; Japan 129; Norway 456; Russia 115; Spain 315; Sweden 27; United Kingdom 1,021; USA 25; Total (incl. others) 3,869.

TRANSPORT
Road Traffic (registered motor vehicles, 1 January 2007): Private motor cars 19,211 (incl. 101 taxis); Buses 224; Lorries and vans 4,228; Motorcycles 859; Mopeds 1,622.
Shipping: *Merchant Fleet* (31 December 2006): 165 vessels, Total displacement 219,256 grt (Source: Lloyd's Register-Fairplay, *World Fleet Statistics*). International Sea-borne Freight Traffic (1996, '000 metric tons): Goods loaded 223, Goods unloaded 443.

TOURISM
Nationality of Overnight Guests at Guesthouses (2006): Faroe Islands 30,383; Denmark 44,147; Iceland 7,793; Norway 11,423; Sweden 2,249; Finland 1,285; United Kingdom and Ireland 4,842; Germany 3,922; USA and Canada 1,583; Austria and Switzerland 906; Total (incl. others) 116,236.

COMMUNICATIONS MEDIA
Radio Receivers (1997): 26,000 in use (Source: UNESCO, *Statistical Yearbook*).
Television Receivers (1997): 15,000 in use (Source: UNESCO, *Statistical Yearbook*).
Book Production (2006): 142 titles.
Newspapers (2006): 16 titles per week (circulation 50,700).
Telephones ('000 main lines in use, 2006): 23.4.
Facsimile Machines (1993): 1,400 in use. Source: UN, *Statistical Yearbook*.
Mobile Cellular Telephones ('000 subscribers, 2006): 49.5.
Internet Users ('000, 2006): 13.

EDUCATION
Institutions (2000/01): Basic schools 61 (Secondary schools 21); Upper secondary schools 3; Higher preparatory institutions 3.
Teachers (2002/03): 697 (full-time equivalent) in primary and secondary schools.
Students (2002/03, unless otherwise indicated): Pre-primary (1998/99) 59; Primary 5,567; Secondary 2,131; Upper secondary 600; Higher preparatory 165; Business schools 351; Fishery college 31; Social care and healthcare school 60; Technical schools 108; University 154; Total further education (1996/97) 2,166.

Directory

The Government

The legislative body is the Løgting (Lagting in Danish), which consists of 33 members, who are elected for four years on a basis of proportional representation. Following reforms implemented in 2007, the seven electoral constituencies that comprised the Faroe Islands were merged into a single constituency. All Faroese over the age of 18 years have the right to vote. Based on the strength of the parties in the Løgting, a Government, the Landsstýri, is formed. This is the administrative body in certain spheres, chiefly relating to Faroese economic affairs. The Løgmaður (Prime Minister) has to ratify all laws approved by the Løgting. Power is decentralized and there are about 50 local authorities. The Ríkisumboðsmaður, or High Commissioner, represents the Danish Government, and has the right to address the Løgting and to advise on joint affairs. All Danish legislation must be submitted to the Landsstýri before becoming law in the Faroe Islands.

The Danish Folketing (parliament), to which the Faroese send two members, is responsible for defence and foreign policy, constitutional matters and the judicial and monetary systems.

LANDSSTÝRI
(March 2008)

A coalition of the Social Democratic Party (SDP), the Republican Party (RP) and the Centre Party (CP).
Prime Minister (with responsibility for Cabinet Affairs): JÓANNES EIDESGAARD (SDP).
Minister of Foreign Affairs: HØGNI HOYDAL (RP).
Minister of Finance: KARSTEN HANSEN (CP).
Minister of Fisheries and Resources: TÓRBJØRN JACOBSEN (RP).

DANISH EXTERNAL TERRITORIES

Minister of Trade and Industry: Bjørt Samuelsen (RP).
Minister of Justice: Helena Dam á Neystabø (SDP).
Minister of Education, Culture and Research: Kristina Háfoss (RP).
Minister of Health and Social Affairs: Hans Pauli Strøm (SDP).

Government Offices

Ríkisumboðsmaðurin (Danish High Commission): Amtmansbrekkan 6, POB 12, 110 Tórshavn; tel. 351200; fax 310864; e-mail riomfr@fo.stm.dk; internet www.fo.stm.dk; High Commissioner Dan Michael Knudsen.

Løgtingsskrivstovan (Parliament Office): Tinghúsvegur 1–3, POB 208, 110 Tórshavn; tel. 363900; fax 363901; e-mail logting@logting.fo; internet www.logting.fo.

Løgmansskrivstovan (Prime Minister's Office): Tinganes, POB 64, 100 Tórshavn; tel. 351010; fax 351015; e-mail info@tinganes.fo; internet www.tinganes.fo.

Ministry of Education, Culture and Research: Hoyvíksvegur 72, POB 3279, 110 Tórshavn; tel. 355050; fax 355055; e-mail mmr@mmr.fo; internet www.mmr.fo.

Ministry of Finance: Traðagøta 39, POB 2039, 165 Argir; tel. 352020; fax 352025; e-mail fmr@fmr.fo; internet www.fmr.fo.

Ministry of Fisheries and Natural Resources: Heykavegur 6, POB 347, 110 Tórshavn; tel. 353030; fax 353035; e-mail fisk@fisk.fo; internet www.fisk.fo.

Ministry of Health and Social Affairs: Eirargarður 2, 100 Tórshavn; tel. 304050; fax 354045; e-mail ahr@ahr.fo; internet www.ahr.fo.

Ministry of Justice: POB 159, 110 Tórshavn; tel. 358080; fax 358085; e-mail imr@imr.fo; internet www.imr.fo.

Ministry of Trade and Industry: Tinganes, POB 377, 110 Tórshavn; tel. 356060; fax 356065; e-mail vmr@vmr.fo; internet www.vmr.fo.

Representation of the Faroes: North Atlantic House, Strandgade 91, 4th Floor, 1401 Copenhagen K, Denmark; tel. 32-83-37-70; fax 32-83-37-75; e-mail faroes.representation.dk@tinganes.fo; internet www.faroes.dk.

LØGTING

The Løgting has 33 members, elected by universal adult suffrage.
Speaker: Hergeir Nielsen (Republican Party).
Election, 19 January 2008

Party	Votes	% of votes	Seats
Tjóðveldisflokkurin (Republican Party)	7,250	23.30	8
Sambandsflokkurin (Union Party)	6,529	20.99	7
Fólkaflokkurin (People's Party)	6,240	20.06	7
Javnaðarflokkurin (Social Democratic Party)	6,018	19.34	6
Miðflokkurin (Centre Party)	2,610	8.39	3
Sjálvstýrisflokkurin (Home Rule Party)	2,244	7.21	2
Miðnámsflokkurin (Students' Party)	221	0.71	—
Total	31,112	100.00	33

Political Organizations

Fólkaflokkurin (People's Party): Áarvegur 2, POB 242, 100 Tórshavn; tel. 312491; fax 322091; e-mail folkaflokkurin@logting.fo; internet folkaflokkurin.fo; f. 1940; conservative-liberal party, favours free enterprise and wider political and economic autonomy for the Faroes; Chair. Jørgen Niclasen.

Hin Stuttligi Flokkurin (The Funny Party): Frammi við Garðar, 410 Kollafjørður; tel. 421698; f. 2004; seeks to lampoon the political establishment; Leader Johan Dalsgaard.

Javnaðarflokkurin (Social Democratic Party—SDP): Áarvegur, POB 208, 110 Tórshavn; tel. 312493; fax 319397; e-mail javnadarflokkarin@logting.fo; internet www.j.fo; f. 1925; Chair. Jóannes Eidesgaard.

Kristiligi Fólkaflokkurin, Føroya Framburðs- og Fiskivinnuflokkurin (Christian People's Party, Progressive and Fishing Industry Party—CPP-PFIP): à Brekku 5, 700 Klaksvík; tel. 457580; fax 457581; f. 1954; centrist party; Chair. Niels Pauli Danielsen.

Miðflokkurin (Centre Party): Áarvegur 2, POB 3237, 110 Tórshavn; tel. 314988; fax 312206; e-mail midflokkurin@post.olivant.fo; internet www.midflokkurin.fo; f. 1992; Chair. Jenis av Rana.

Sambandsflokkurin (Union Party): Áarvegur 2, POB 208, 110 Tórshavn; tel. 312492; fax 312496; e-mail samband@post.olivant.fo; internet www.samband.fo; f. 1906; favours the maintenance of close relations between the Faroes and the Kingdom of Denmark; conservative in internal affairs; Chair. Kaj Leo Johannesen.

Sjálvstýrisflokkurin (Home Rule Party): POB 141, 600 Saltangará; tel. 312494; fax 512494; e-mail post@sjalvstyrisflokkurin.fo; internet www.sjalvstyri.fo; f. 1906; social-liberal; advocates eventual political independence for the Faroes within the Kingdom of Denmark; Chair. Kári P. Højgaard.

Tjóðveldisflokkurin (Republican Party): Kongagøta 11, POB 143, 100 Tórshavn; tel. 312200; fax 312262; e-mail loysing@post.olivant.fo; internet www.tjodveldi.fo; f. 1948; left-wing party, advocates the secession of the Faroes from Denmark; Chair. Høgni Hoydal.

Religion

CHRISTIANITY

The Faroes Church (Evangelical Lutheran Church of Denmark) regained its diocese in November 1990, and the suffragan bishop became Bishop of the Faroe Islands. The Church had 40,526 members in 2006, accounting for 83.8% of the population. The largest independent group is the Plymouth Brethren. There is also a small Roman Catholic community.

Evangelical Lutheran Church

Føroya Biskupur (Bishop of the Faroe Islands): Føroya Stiftsstjórn, J. Paturssonargøta 20, POB 8, 110 Tórshavn; tel. 311995; fax 315889; e-mail stift@folkakirkjan.fo; internet www.folkakirkjan.fo; Bishop Jógvan Fríðriksson.

BAHÁ'Í FAITH

Bahá'í: Bahá'í Miðstøðin, Hoydalsvegur 19, POB 1095, 110 Tórshavn; tel. 315025; e-mail bahai@bahai.fo; internet www.bahai.fo.

The Press

In 2006 there were two daily newspapers in the Faroe Islands, *Dimmalætting* and *Sosialurin*, with a combined circulation of 16,500.

Dimmalætting: Smyrilsvegur 13, POB 3019, 110 Tórshavn; tel. 541200; fax 541201; e-mail post@dimma.fo; internet www.dimma.fo; f. 1878; 5 a week; Editor Árni Gregersen; circ. 8,500.

FF/FA-Blaðið: Vágsbotnur, POB 58, 110 Tórshavn; tel. 312169; fax 318769; fortnightly; Editor Vilmund Jacobsen; circ. 2,700.

Norðlýsið: Rygsvegur 3, POB 58, 700 Klaksvík; tel. 456285; fax 456498; e-mail nordpres@post.olivant.fo; internet www.nordlysid.fo; f. 1915; weekly; Editor John William Joensen; circ. 6,400.

Oyggjatíðindi: Lýðarsvegur 19, POB 3312, 110 Tórshavn; tel. 314411; fax 316410; e-mail oyggjat@post.olivant.fo; internet www.oyggjatidindi.com; 2 a week; circ. 3,500.

Sosialurin: Vágsbotnur, POB 76, 100 Tórshavn; tel. 341800; fax 341801; e-mail post@sosialurin.fo; internet www.sosialurin.fo; f. 1927; 5 a week; one-third owned by Føroya Tele; Editor Eirikur Lindenskov; circ. 8,000.

Vikublaðið: Yviri við Strond 17, POB 3269, 110 Tórshavn; tel. 321000; fax 321005; e-mail vikublad@vikublad.fo; internet www.vikublad.fo; f. 2001; distributed free of charge; Editor Ernst S. Olsen; circ. 19,300.

Vinnuvutan: Íslandsvegur 22, POB 3202, 110 Tórshavn; tel. 363600; fax 363601; e-mail info@vinnuvitan.fo; internet www.vinnuvitan.fo; f. 2004; weekly; business issues; Editor Óli á Deild Olsen; circ. 2,300.

NEWS AGENCY

Ritzaus Bureau: Gamli Vegur 3; tel. 316366; f. 1980; Man. Randi Mohr.

Publisher

Bókadeild Føroya Lærarafelags: Pedda við Steinsgøta 9, 100 Tórshavn; tel. 317644; fax 319644; e-mail bfl@bfl.fo; internet www.bfl.fo; division of Faroese Teachers Asscn; run on a commercial basis, but receives govt grants; children's books, a children's magazine (*Strok*) and a teachers' magazine (*Skúlablaðið*); Dir Niels Jákup Thomsen; Editors Marna Jacobsen, Turið Kjølbro.

Broadcasting and Communications

TELECOMMUNICATIONS

The Faroese telecommunications industry, formerly a monopoly under Føroya Tele, was opened to competition in the early 2000s.

Post- og Fjarskiftiseftirlitið (Postal and Telecommunications Regulatory Authority): POB 73, Skálatrøð 20, 110 Tórshavn; tel.

356020; fax 356035; e-mail fse@fse.fo; internet www.fse.fo; f. 1997; independent govt agency with regulatory powers; Dir JÓGVAN THOMSEN.

Føroya Tele: POB 27, 110 Tórshavn; tel. 303030; fax 303031; e-mail ft@ft.fo; internet www.tele.fo; f. 1906; owned by Faroese Govt; fixed-line and mobile cellular telecommunications, broadband internet services; Chair. HÁKUN STEINGRÍMSSON; CEO KRISTIAN REINERT DAVIDSEN.

Kall p/f: Óðinshædd 2, 100 Tórshavn; tel. 202020; fax 202021; e-mail kall@kall.fo; internet www.kall.fo; f. 1999; offers PSTN, ADSL and GSM services; CEO BJARNI ASKHAM BJARNASON.

BROADCASTING

Radio

Kringvarp Føroya (Faroese Broadcasting Corpn): Norðari Ringvegur, Postboks 1299, 110 Tórshavn Beinleiðis; tel. 347500; fax 347521; e-mail uf@uf.fo; internet www.uf.fo; f. 2005 by merger of Sjónvarp Føroya (Faroese Television) and Útvarp Føroya (Radio Faroe Islands); Man. JÓGVAN JESPERSEN.

Television

p/f Televarpið: Klingran 1, POB 3128, 110 Tórshavn; tel. 340340; fax 340341; e-mail televarp@televarp.fo; internet www.televarp.fo; f. 2002; digital terrestrial broadcaster; provides 28 channels; subsidiary of Føroya Tele; Man. Dir LAILU HENTZE.

Finance

BANKS

(cap. = capital; res = reserves; dep. = deposits; m. = million; brs = branches; amounts in kroner)

Landsbanki Føroya (Faroese Government Bank): Staravegur 5, POB 229, 110 Tórshavn; tel. 308120; fax 318537; e-mail landsbank@landsbank.fo; internet landsbankin.fo; fiscal administrator for the Faroe Islands, primarily with respect to the national treasury, but also acts as fiscal adviser/administrator for public bodies and agencies; Man. Dir SIGURÐ POULSEN.

Eik Banki P/F: Yviri við Strond 2, POB 34, 110 Tórshavn; tel. 348000; fax 348800; e-mail eik@eik.fo; internet www.eik.fo; f. 1832; cap. 2,074m., res 282m., dep. 12,705m. (Sept. 2007); Chair. FRITHLEIF OLSEN; Chief Man. Dir MARNER JACOBSEN; 16 brs.

Føroya Banki P/F (Faroese Bank): Húsagøta 3, POB 3048, 110 Tórshavn; tel. 311350; fax 315850; e-mail fbk@foroyabanki.fo; internet www.foroyabanki.fo; f. 1994 following merger of Føroya Banki (f. 1906) and Sjóvinnubankin (f. 1932); 99.4% owned by Faroese Govt through Finansieringsfonden af 1992; privatization pending; cap. 200m., res 3m., dep. 5,890m. (Dec. 2006); Chair. JÓHAN PÁLL JOENSEN; CEO JANUS PETERSEN; 18 brs.

Norðoya Sparikassi: Ósávegur 1, POB 149, 700 Klaksvík; tel. 475000; fax 476000; e-mail ns@ns.fo; internet www.ns.fo; savings bank; Man. Dir EYÐFINN REYÐBERG.

Suðuroya Sparikassi P/F: POB 2, 900 Vágur; tel. 359870; fax 359871; e-mail sparsu@sparsu.fo; internet www.sparsu.fo; savings bank; Man. Dir SØREN L. BRUHN.

STOCK EXCHANGE

Virðisbrævamarknaður Føroya P/F (VMF) (Faroese Securities Market): c/o Landsbanki Føroya, Staravegur 5, POB 229, 110 Tórshavn; tel. 308120; fax 318537; internet vmf.fo; f. 2000; lists Faroese securities in co-operation with Kauphöll Íslands (Icelandic stock exchange); Chair. STEFÁN HALLDÓRSSON.

INSURANCE

Føroya Lívstrygging P/F: Kopargøta, POB 206, 110 Tórshavn; tel. 311111; fax 351110; e-mail liv@liv.fo; internet www.liv.fo; f. 1967; reorg. 2000; owned by Faroese Govt; partial privatization pending; life insurance; Man. Dir TUMMAS ELIASEN.

Trygd P/F: Gongin 7, POB 44, 110 Tórshavn; tel. 358100; fax 317211; e-mail trygd@trygd.fo; internet www.trygd.fo; f. 1932; activities suspended 1940–97; owned by Føroya Banki P/F; all types of insurance, both marine and non-marine; Man. Dir JEAN DJURHUUS.

Tryggingarfelagið Føroyar P/F: Kongabrúgvin, POB 329, 110 Tórshavn; tel. 345600; fax 345601; e-mail tf@trygging.fo; internet www.trygging.fo; f. 1998; all types of insurance, both marine and non-marine; Man. GUNNAR Í LIÐA.

Trade and Industry

GOVERNMENT AGENCIES

Jarðfeingi (Faroese Earth and Energy Directorate): Brekkutún 1, POB 3059, 110 Tórshavn; tel. 357000; fax 357001; e-mail jardfeingi@jardfeingi.fo; internet www.jardfeingi.fo; f. 2006 by merger of Oljufyrisitingin (Faroese Petroleum Administration) and Jarðfrøðisavnið (Faroese Geological Survey); responsible for the administration and responsible utilization of all Faroese earth and energy resources, including hydrocarbons; Dir SIGURÐ Í JÁKUPSSTOVU.

Kappingarráðið (Competition Council): Skálatrøð 20, POB 73, 110 Tórshavn; tel. 356040; fax 356055; e-mail terje@kapping.fo; internet www.kapping.fo; f. 1997; consists of a Chairman and three members, appointed by the Minister of Trade and Industry for a four-year term; Chair. JÓGVAN THOMSEN.

INDUSTRIAL AND TRADE ASSOCIATIONS

L/F Føroya Fiskasøla—Faroe Seafood P/F: Vestara Bryggja, POB 68, 110 Tórshavn; tel. 355555; fax 355550; e-mail meinhard@faroe.com; internet www.faroe.com; f. 1948; restructured 1995; joint stock co of fish producers; exports all seafood products; Chair. ÓLI HANSEN; Man. Dir MEINHARD JACOBSEN.

Føroya Reiðarafelag (Faroe Shipowners' Asscn): Gongin 10, POB 361, 110 Tórshavn; tel. 311800; fax 320380; internet www.shipowner-fo.com; f. 1908; Chair. JÁKUP SÓLSTEIN; Dir ÓLAVUR JØKLADAL.

SamVit (Faroe Islands Enterprise): Bryggjubakki 12, POB 259, 110 Tórshavn; tel. 353100; fax 353101; e-mail trade@trade.fo; internet www.trade.fo; f. 2006 by merger of Faroe Islands Trade Council and Faroe Islands Tourist Board; Man. Dir ELIN HEINESEN.

Vinnuhúsið (House of Industry): Smærugøta 9A, POB 1038, 100 Tórshavn; tel. 309900; fax 309901; e-mail industry@industry.fo; internet www.industry.fo; confed. of industrial orgs; 12 branches representing all areas of Faroese industry; Dir MARITA RASMUSSEN.

UTILITIES

Electricity

Elfelagið SEV: POB 319, 110 Tórshavn; tel. 346800; fax 346801; e-mail sev@sev.fo; internet www.sev.fo; owned by Faroese Govt; Dir HÁKUN DJURHUUS.

Gas

AGA Føroyar Sp/f (Føroya Gassøla): Akranesgøta 2, POB 1088, 110 Tórshavn; tel. 315544; fax 311706; e-mail gassola@post.olivant.fo; Dir ANFINN HANSON.

Water

Local councils are responsible for the provision of water.

EMPLOYERS' ORGANIZATION

Føroya Arbeiðsgevarafelag (Faroese Employers' Asscn): Vinnuhúsið, POB 1038, 110 Tórshavn; tel. 311864; fax 317278; e-mail industry@industry.fo; internet www.industry.fo; more than 600 mem. cos; owns and manages House of Industry (see above); organized in 12 sectoral asscns, including Faroe Trade Masters Asscn, Faroe Fish Producers' Asscn, Faroe Fish Farming Asscn, Fed. of Faroes Industries, Faroe Merchant and Shopkeepers Asscn and Faroe Oil Industries Asscn; Chair. JÓHAN PÁLL JOENSEN.

TRADE UNION

Føroya Arbeiðarafelag (Faroese Labour Organization): Tjarnarðeild 5–7, POB 56, 110 Tórshavn; tel. 312101; fax 315374; e-mail fafelag@fafelag.fo; internet www.fafelag.fo; Chair. INGEBORG VINTHER.

Transport

There are about 458 km of roads in the Faroe Islands. A 4.9-km tunnel running under the sea, linking Vágur to Streymoy, was opened in December 2002. A second tunnel, linking Borðoy with Eysturoy, was opened in 2006. Two further tunnels were planned, one linking Sandoy with southern Streymoy, and one joining Eysturoy with Streymoy.

The main harbour is at Tórshavn; the other ports are at Fuglafjørður, Klaksvík, Skálafjørður, Tvøroyri, Vágur and Vestmanna. Between mid-May and mid-September a summer ro-ro ferry service links the Faroe Islands with Iceland, Scotland, the Shetland Islands (United Kingdom), Denmark and Norway.

There is an airport on Vágur.

DANISH EXTERNAL TERRITORIES   *Greenland*

Atlantic Airways P/F: Vágur Airport, 380 Sørvágur; tel. 341000; fax 341001; e-mail info@atlantic.fo; internet www.atlantic.fo; f. 1987; owned by Faroese Govt; privatization pending; scheduled and charter passenger and cargo services to Denmark (Copenhagen, Billund and Aalborg), Greenland, Iceland (Reykjavík), Norway (Stavanger and Oslo) and the United Kingdom (London, the Shetland Islands and Aberdeen); Man. Dir MAGNI ARGE.

Smyril Line: Jonas Broncksgøta 37, POB 370, 110 Tórshavn; tel. 345900; fax 345950; e-mail office@smyril-line.fo; internet www.smyril-line.com; f. 1983; 38% owned by Shetland Development Trust (United Kingdom); ferry services to Denmark, Iceland, Norway and Scotland (United Kingdom); Man. Dir ANDRAS RÓIN.

Tourism

Tourism is the Islands' second largest industry after fishing.
SamVit (Faroe Islands Enterprise): Bryggjubakka 17, POB 118, 100 Tórshavn; tel. 355800; fax 355801; e-mail tourist@tourist.fo; internet www.faroeislands.com; f. 2006 by merger of Faroe Islands Tourist Board and Faroe Islands Trade Council; Dir ELIN HEINESEN.

GREENLAND

Introductory Survey

Location, Climate, Language, Religion, Flag, Capital

Greenland (Kalaallit Nunaat) is the world's largest island, with a total area of 2,166,086 sq km, and lies in the North Atlantic Ocean, east of Canada. Most of the territory is permanently covered by ice, but 410,449 sq km of coastland are habitable. Greenlandic, an Inuit (Eskimo) language, and Danish are the official languages. The majority of the population profess Christianity and belong mainly to the Evangelical Lutheran Church of Denmark. There are also small communities of other Protestant groups and of Roman Catholics. The flag (proportions 2 by 3) consists of two equal horizontal stripes (white above red), on which is superimposed a representation of the rising sun (a disc divided horizontally, red above white) to the left of centre. Nuuk (Godthåb) is the capital.

Recent History

Greenland first came under Danish rule in 1380. In the revision of the Danish Constitution in 1953, Greenland became part of the Kingdom and acquired the representation of two members in the Danish Folketing (Parliament). In October 1972 the Greenlanders voted, by 9,658 to 3,990, against joining the European Community (EC, now European Union—EU, see p. 244) but, as part of Denmark, were bound by the Danish decision to join. Resentment of Danish domination of the economy, education and the professions continued, taking expression when, in 1977, the nationalist Siumut (Forward) movement formed a left-wing party. In 1975 the Minister for Greenland appointed a commission to devise terms for Greenland home rule, and its proposals were approved, by 73.1% to 26.9%, in a referendum among the Greenland electorate in January 1979. Siumut, led by a Lutheran pastor, Jonathan Motzfeldt, secured 13 seats in the 21-member Landsting (the local legislature) at a general election in April, and a five-member Landsstyre (Home Rule Government), with Motzfeldt as Prime Minister, took office in May. From 1979 the island gradually assumed full administration of its internal affairs.

In February 1982 a referendum was held to decide Greenland's continued membership of the EC. This resulted in a 53% majority in favour of withdrawal. Negotiations were begun in May, with the Danish Government acting on Greenland's behalf, and were concluded in March 1984 (with effect from 1 February 1985): Greenland was accorded the status of an overseas territory in association with the Community, with preferential access to EC markets.

At the April 1983 general election to the Landsting (enlarged, by measures adopted in 1982, to between 23 and 26 seats, depending on the proportion of votes cast), Siumut and the conservative Atassut (Solidarity) party won 12 seats each, while the Inuit Ataqatigiit (Inuit Brotherhood—IA) obtained two seats. Siumut once again formed a Government, led by Motzfeldt, dependent on the support of the IA members in the Landsting: this support was withdrawn in March 1984, when the IA members voted against the terms of withdrawal from the EC, and Motzfeldt resigned. In the ensuing general election, held in June, Siumut and Atassut won 11 seats each, while the IA took three seats. Motzfeldt formed a coalition Government, comprising Siumut and the IA.

In March 1987 the coalition Government collapsed, following a dispute between Siumut and the IA over policy towards the modernization of the US radar facility at Thule, which was claimed by the IA to be in breach of the 1972 US-Soviet Anti-Ballistic Missile Treaty. A general election was held in May. Siumut and Atassut retained 11 seats each in the Landsting (which had been enlarged in 1986, to 27 seats—23 of which were to be obtained by election in multi-member constituencies, while four were to be supplementary seats); the IA won four seats, and the remaining seat was secured by the newly formed Issittup Partiia, which was demanding the privatization of the trawler fleet. Motzfeldt eventually formed a new coalition Government with the IA. In May 1988, at elections to the Danish Folketing, Siumut was the most successful party. In June the coalition between Siumut and the IA collapsed, and Motzfeldt formed a new Siumut Government, with support from Atassut. In December 1990, when Atassut withdrew its support for the Siumut administration (following allegations that government ministers had misused public funds), Motzfeldt organized an early general election for March 1991, at which both Siumut and Atassut obtained a reduced share of the vote, while the IA's quota rose. Accordingly, Siumut retained 11 seats in the Landsting, while Atassut's representation decreased to eight seats and the IA's increased to five. A new party, the liberal Akulliit Partiiaat, won two seats, and the remaining place was taken by the Issittup Partiia. Siumut and the IA formed a coalition Government, with the Chairman of Siumut, Lars Emil Johansen, as Prime Minister.

At the general election held in March 1995 Siumut increased its representation in the Landsting (enlarged to 31 seats) to 12 seats, while Atassut won 10 seats and the IA obtained six. A coalition Government was formed between Siumut and Atassut, following the withdrawal from negotiations of the IA, owing to disagreements regarding the question of independence. Johansen retained the premiership, while Daniel Skifte, the leader of Atassut, was appointed Minister of Finance and Housing. In early 1997 Johansen asserted that Greenland could achieve economic independence from Denmark on the basis of its unexploited mineral resources. In September Johansen resigned from the Landsstyre and was replaced as Prime Minister by Motzfeldt.

At the general election held in February 1999 Siumut remained the largest party in the Landsting, winning 11 seats. Atassut obtained eight seats, while the IA won seven seats. On 22 February a coalition Government was formed between Siumut and the IA. Jonathan Motzfeldt retained the premiership, while Josef Motzfeldt, the Chairman of the IA, was appointed Minister of Economy, Trade and Taxation.

In September 2001 Jonathan Motzfeldt was forced to resign as leader of Siumut during the party's annual congress, after he was held responsible for a deficit of 3,000m. kroner on the part of Royal Greenland (the island's main fish and seafood export company); however, he retained the post of Prime Minister. In December the IA withdrew from the coalition Government, accusing Siumut of lacking direction in its policies. Siumut subsequently formed a new coalition Government with Atassut, in which the ministerial posts formerly held by the IA were taken over by members of Atassut.

At the general election held on 3 December 2002 Siumut won 10 seats in the Landsting, compared with eight for the IA and seven for Atassut. Demokraatit (the Democrats—a new party formed in October 2002) won five seats and Katusseqatigiit (Alliance of Independent Candidates) one seat. Later that month Siumut and the IA formed a coalition Government, viewed by many as being strongly pro-independence, under the new Siumut Prime Minister, Hans Enoksen.

The Government was, however, extremely short-lived: the appointment to the most senior post of the civil service of Jens Lybeth, Enoksen's electoral campaign manager and close personal friend, prompted accusations of favouritism. Lybeth then engaged the services of Maannguaq Berthelsen, an Inuit 'healer', to 'chase away evil spirits' from government offices, urging some 600 civil servants to use similar methods to promote harmony between Greenlanders and Danes. In the ensuing furore, Enoksen was obliged to dismiss Lybeth. Josef Motzfeldt, the Deputy Prime Minister and Chairman of the IA, remained dissatisfied with the situation, and approached Demokraatit to discuss ousting Enoksen and forming a new Government. Enoksen, again compelled to act, dissolved the coalition in mid-January 2003 and formed a new Government in coalition with Atassut.

The new Government was dogged by political controversy, most notably the discord between the coalition partners concerning the revision of a commercial fishing agreement with the EU. In early September 2003 the leaders of Siumut called for a formal investigation into allegations that Augusta Salling, the Minister of Finance and Chairperson of Atassut, was involved in an accounting discrepancy amounting to some 97m. kroner. Salling threatened to withdraw Atassut from the coalition unless she received a guarantee that she would not face a motion of 'no confidence' when the Landsting assembled later that month. Siumut was unwilling to give her such a guarantee, and the governing coalition was consequently dissolved on 9 September. Siumut and the IA formed a new coalition Government, with Enoksen as Prime Minister, on 13 September.

In January 2004, following negotiations between Enoksen and the Danish Prime Minister, Anders Fogh Rasmussen, it was announced that the Danish Government and the Landsstyre were to appoint a joint commission in early 2004 to explore ways of granting greater devolution to Greenland, after civil servants had presented their recommendations. Greenland was to remain within the Danish commonwealth, however, and would continue receiving grants from Denmark. In March 2005, following a request by the joint commission to the Danish Ministry of Justice, Greenlanders were granted recognition as a separate people under international law. Whether this required recognition by the UN, and whether it granted Greenlanders sovereign rights, remained unresolved.

In April 2005 the resignation of Jørgen Wæver Johansen, the Minister of Self-governance, Justice and Petroleum, following a series of disagreements with Enoksen, prompted a government reorganization. In June Jens Napâtôk, the Minister of Infrastructure, Housing and the Environment, resigned following revelations that he had used public funds for personal expenses. Tension in the ruling coalition intensified in August, when an audit report showed that Rasmus Frederiksen, the Minister of Fisheries and Hunting, had also misused public funds, prompting his resignation from the Landsstyre. A further four members of the Government could not provide sufficient documentation for their spending. The governing coalition finally collapsed in September, when Siumut and the IA failed to reach an agreement in budget negotiations on Siumut's proposal to introduce a system of child benefit payments financed through a compulsory savings scheme.

Enoksen called an early election, which was held on 15 November 2005. Siumut retained 10 seats in the Landsting, with 30.7% of the votes cast, while Demokraatit increased its representation to seven seats, receiving 22.8%, and the IA also took seven seats, with 22.6%. Atassut secured 19.1% of the votes cast (six seats) and Katusseqatigiit 4.1% (one seat). A turn-out of 74.9% was recorded. After intense negotiations, Siumut, Atassut and the IA formed a coalition Government, with Enoksen as Prime Minister, on 25 November. Jørgen Wæver Johansen returned to the Landsstyre as Minister of Housing, Infrastructure, Minerals and Petroleum.

In late April 2007 the governing coalition collapsed, marking the culmination of an ongoing dispute between the IA and Siumut regarding government policy on the regulation of the prawn fishing industry. On 1 May a new coalition comprising Siumut and Atassut took office. Enoksen remained as Prime Minister and Finn Karlsen of Atassut became Deputy Prime Minister, while regaining his previous role as Minister for Fisheries, Hunting and Agriculture. The appointment of Lars Emil Johansen as Minister of Finance and Foreign Affairs proved controversial, owing to his role as one of Greenland's two representatives in the Danish Folketing and, on 30 May, he resigned from the Government. On 1 July Enoksen effected a government reorganization, in which the Minister for Family Affairs and Justice, Aleqa Hammond of Siumut, was appointed to replace Johansen. The family affairs and justice portfolio was divided and its responsibilities were allocated to other members of the Landsstyre. On 1 January 2008 a minor reshuffle of ministerial responsibilities was effected. Arkalo Abelsen relinquished the environment portfolio, while gaining that of family affairs (and thus became Minister for Family Affairs and Health), and Kim Kielsen took the title of Minister for Infrastructure, the Environment, Minerals and Petroleum.

In January 2008 Enoksen announced that a referendum was to take place in Greenland on 25 November regarding greater autonomy for Greenland and increased control for Greenland over its mineral resources. This followed extended negotiations on the issues by a joint Danish-Greenlandic commission. In the same month Jonathan Motzfeldt was forced to resign as Chairman of the Landsting following an article in a Greenlandic newspaper that revealed allegations of sexual assault made against him by a female employee in 2007. Motzfeldt was, however, to remain as a member of parliament and as chairman of the Danish-Greenlandic commission on future autonomy; he was subsequently replaced as Chairperson of the Landsting by Ruth Heilmann, also of Siumut.

Denmark remains ultimately responsible for Greenland's foreign relations. Greenland does, however, have separate representation on the Nordic Council (see p. 424), and is a member of the Inuit Circumpolar Conference (see p. 413). Denmark, a member of the North Atlantic Treaty Organization (NATO, see p. 340), retains its responsibility for defence. Danish-US military co-operation in Greenland began in 1951, when Denmark signed a defence agreement with the US Government to allow four US bases in Greenland, including the Thule airbase, near the Uummannaq Inuit settlement. Two years after the establishment of the base the indigenous Inuits, whose hunting grounds had been severely diminished by the development of the base, were forcibly resettled further north in Qaanaaq. Under a 1981 agreement on the defence of Greenland, two US radar bases were established on the island, at Thule and at Kangerlussuaq (Søndre Strømfjord). An agreement between the USA and Denmark for the reduction of the size of the bases from 325,000 ha to 160,000 ha took effect from October 1986, and the land thus available was returned to the Inuit. In March 1991 the USA agreed to transfer ownership and control of the base at Kangerlussuaq to the Greenland Government in September 1992, in exchange for the right to use it again in the future. In August 1999 the Danish High Court ordered the Danish Government to pay compensation of 500,000 kroner to Inuits who had been forced to leave their land in 1953 to allow for the expansion of the base at Thule. The Thule tribe appealed against the ruling, demanding 235m. kroner as compensation for lost living space and hunting grounds and arguing that the US-Denmark defence agreement was void under constitutional and international law. The Supreme Court rejected the tribe's appeal in November 2003, ruling that the agreement was still valid and approving the compensation recommended by the High Court.

Jonathan Motzfeldt and the Danish Minister of Foreign Affairs, Mogens Lykketoft, agreed in February 2001 not to adopt an official policy on the proposed US missile defence system, which would involve the upgrading of the early-warning radar station in the Thule base, pending an official request by the USA. Motzfeldt did, however, express personal concern at the plans, and called on the USA to discuss the proposals with its NATO allies. He added that Greenland would not accept the plans if they proved to be in breach of the 1972 Anti-Ballistic Missile Treaty, or if Russia opposed them. Josef Motzfeldt and the opposition parties of the Folketing had expressed strong opposition to the proposals, claiming that they risked provoking another 'arms race'. Public opinion in Greenland was also strongly opposed to the plans; many feared that they would place Greenland at the centre of potential future conflicts.

In January 2001 the newly inaugurated US President, George W. Bush, stated in a letter to the Prime Minister, Jonathan Motzfeldt, that Greenland 'should be open for dialogue' on the future of the Thule base. That the letter was sent directly to Motzfeldt rather than to Copenhagen caused consternation in Denmark, which still controlled Greenland's foreign policy. In September 2002 the USA returned the town of Dundas (also known as Uummannaq in Greenlandic) and its surroundings to Greenland; the USA had incorporated it into the Thule base some 50 years earlier. The US Administration formally submitted a request to upgrade the facilities at the Thule base in December 2002. In May 2003 Enoksen and the Danish Minister of Foreign Affairs, Dr Per Stig Møller, signed a Danish-Greenlandic principle agreement under which Greenland was to gain greater influence in foreign policy relating to the island, in return for its support for the modernization of the Thule base as part of the US missile defence programme. Henceforth Denmark was to consult Greenland on foreign policy matters in which Greenland was directly involved; the Landsstyre was to participate in future negotiations with Denmark on Greenland's foreign policy. Greenland was to be a co-signatory to future international agreements, provided they did not compromise local rights.

In May 2004 Greenland, Denmark and the USA reached an agreement on the upgrading of radar facilities at the Thule base as part of the US missile defence programme. The Landsstyre, the Foreign and Security Policy Committee of the Landsting and the Danish Folketing all approved the agreement unanimously, and it was signed on 6 August by the Deputy Prime Minister, Josef Motzfeldt, the US Secretary of State, Colin Powell, and Per Stig Møller. Under the agreement both Greenland and Denmark were to have representatives at the base, and Greenland's flag was to be flown there alongside those of the USA and Denmark. The USA was required both to consult with Greenland and Denmark on any further developments at the base and henceforth to notify the Landsstyre of any US aircraft landing outside the regular airports in Greenland. Agreements were also concluded on wider co-operation between Greenland and the USA, in areas such as research, energy, the environment and education.

In June 1980 the Danish Government declared an economic zone extending 200 nautical miles (370 km) off the east coast of Greenland. This, however, caused a dispute with Norway over territorial waters, owing to the existence of the small Norwegian island of Jan Mayen, 460 km off the east coast of Greenland. In 1988 Denmark requested the International Court of Justice (ICJ), based in The Hague, Netherlands, to arbitrate on the issue of conflicting economic zones. A delimitation line was established by the ICJ in June 1993. A subsequent accord on maritime delimitation, agreed between the Governments of Norway, Greenland and Iceland in November 1997, established the boundaries of a 1,934-sq km area of Arctic sea that had been excluded from the terms of the 1993 settlement. In January 2002 Greenland and the Faroe Islands renewed an agreement granting the mutual right to fish in each other's waters.

Government

Greenland is part of the Kingdom of Denmark, and the Danish Government, which remains responsible for foreign affairs, defence and justice, is represented by the Rigsombudsmand, or High Commissioner, in Nuuk (Godthåb). Most functions of government are administered by the 'Home Rule Government', the Landsstyre. The formation of this executive is dependent upon support in the local legislature, the Landsting. The Landsting has 31 members elected for a maximum term of four years, on a basis of proportional representation. Greenland also elects two members to the Danish Folketing (Parliament). For administration purposes, Greenland is divided into 18 municipalities, of which the largest is Nuuk. The merger of the 18 municipalities into four larger bodies was ongoing in mid-2008; the reform was due to enter into effect on 1 January 2009.

Defence

The Danish Government, which is responsible for Greenland's defence, co-ordinates military activities through its Greenland Command. The Greenland Command, which also undertakes fisheries control and sea rescues, is based at the Grønnedal naval base, in south-west Greenland. Greenlanders are not liable for military service. As part of the Kingdom of Denmark, Greenland belongs to the North Atlantic Treaty Organization (NATO, see p. 340). The USA operates an airbase, at Pituffik in Thule (see Recent History). In 2006 the Danish Government spent 231m. kroner (37.6% of total central government expenditure on Greenland) on the territory's defence (including the Fisheries Inspectorate).

Economic Affairs

In 2005, according to official figures, Greenland's gross national income (GNI) was 7,506m. kroner, equivalent to 239,000 kroner per head. The population increased at an average annual rate of 0.1% in 1990–2000. The economy enjoyed overall growth during the 1970s and 1980s, but gross domestic product (GDP) declined by 9%, in real terms, in 1990, and continued to decline significantly (owing to depleted fish stocks and the discontinuation of lead and zinc mining) until 1994, when a real growth rate of 5% was recorded. Positive growth has since been maintained, and GDP increased, in real terms, by 2.0% in 2005.

Agriculture (including animal husbandry, fishing and hunting) employed 7.3% of those in paid employment in 2003. Fishing dominates the commercial economy, as well as being important to the traditional way of life. In 2006 the fishing industry accounted for a provisional 88.0% of Greenland's total export revenue. In 2005 216,300 metric tons of fish (excluding aquatic mammals) were landed in Greenland, compared with 147,300 tons in 1991. The traditional occupation of the Greenlanders is seal-hunting (for meat and fur), which remains important in the north. The most feasible agricultural activity in the harsh climate is livestock-rearing, and only sheep-farming has proved to be of any commercial significance. There are also herds of domesticated reindeer. However, owing to the effects of global warming, in the 2000s some farmers began to cultivate barley.

Industry (including mining, manufacturing, construction and public works) employed some 17.5% of those in paid employment in 2003. Mining earned 13.0% of total export revenue in 1990, but in 2003 employed less than 0.1% of the working population. Lead, zinc and some silver were extracted from a mine at Marmorilik in the north-west until its closure in 1990. In February 2008 a Greenlandic company applied to reopen the mine, planning to begin production by the end of the year. Mineral deposits in Greenland also include gold, diamonds and niobium (a metal used in the manufacture of electronic components). In August 2004 NunaMinerals opened the Nalulaq Goldmine at Kirkspirdalen, in southern Greenland, and announced that it had discovered further significant reserves of gold ore at Storoeen, 40 km east of Nuuk. Seismic analyses have indicated that there are significant reserves of petroleum and natural gas beneath the sea off the western coast of Greenland, and petroleum traces have been discovered in rocks in Disko Bay. Licences were granted for petroleum exploration in 2004 and 2007 as global warming facilitated access to deposits through the melting of sheet ice.

Manufacturing is mainly dependent upon the fishing industry and is dominated by processing plants for the shrimp industry. Water power (melt water from the ice-cap and glaciers) is an important potential source of electricity. All mineral fuels are imported. In 2006 crude petroleum accounted for a provisional 21.8% of total imports. Manufacturing employed 7.9% of the working population in 2003.

The services sector employed 75.2% of the working population in 2003; it is dominated by public administration, which alone employed 45.8% of the working population in that year. Tourism is increasingly important but the sector is limited by the short season and high costs.

In 2006 Greenland recorded a trade deficit of 1,036m. kroner. The principal trading partner remains Denmark, although its monopoly on trade ceased in 1950. Denmark supplied 59.8% of imports and received 86.6% of exports in 2006. Trade is still dominated by companies owned by the Landsstyre. The principal exports are fish and fish products (accounting for a provisional 88.0% of total exports in 2006), and the principal imports are machinery and transport equipment (accounting for 22.0% of total imports in 2006), manufactured goods, food and petroleum products.

Greenland is dependent upon large grants from the central Danish Government. In 2005 central government expenditure on Greenland included some 3,069m. kroner in the form of a direct grant to the Landsstyre. Greenland has few debts, and also receives valuable revenue from the European Union (EU, see p. 244), for fishing licences. The 2006 budget recorded a surplus of 383m. kroner. The annual rate of inflation averaged 1.9% in 1995–2007; consumer prices increased by 1.7% in 2007. In 2006 7.3% of the labour force were unemployed.

Greenland, although a part of the Kingdom of Denmark, withdrew from the European Community (now EU) in 1985 (see Recent History). It remains a territory in association with the EU, however, and has preferential access to European markets. The loss of EU development aid has been offset by the annual payment for member countries to retain fishing rights in Greenlandic waters. Greenland, the EU, and Denmark signed a new partnership agreement in June 2006, allowing Greenland to continue to receive its EU subsidy in return for EU control over policies such as scientific research and climate change.

Greenland's economy is dominated by the fishing industry. Migration to the towns and the rejection of a traditional lifestyle by many young people have, however, created new social and economic problems. Dependence on a single commodity leaves the economy vulnerable to the effects of depletion of fish stocks and fluctuating international prices. Any development or progress is possible only with Danish aid, which is already fundamental to Greenlandic finances. A national tourist board was founded in 1992, and concentrated primarily on sustainable tourism projects. In January 2005 the Government announced that (as in Canada) it was to allow tourists to hunt polar bears and keep their pelts as souvenirs. The Government envisaged an annual souvenir quota of 30 polar bear pelts. A similar quota already existed for musk oxen, which was set at 350 animals in early 2005. However, in March 2008 a temporary ban was imposed on the export of polar bear products with effect from 1 April, owing to environmental concerns. After significant economic expansion in the late 1990s, growth slowed in 2000–04, owing to a decline in shrimp prices and high oil prices. Economic conditions improved somewhat in 2005 and 2006, with a rise in shrimp prices.

Education

The educational system is based on that of Denmark, except that the main language of instruction is Greenlandic. Danish is, however, widely used. There is a school in every settlement. In 2001/02 there were 87 municipal primary and lower-secondary schools, with 11,368 pupils and 1,191 teachers (including 380 temporarily employed teachers). In 2003/04 there were 11,344 pupils at primary schools. In 1999/2000 there were three secondary schools with 571 pupils. There is a teacher-training college in Nuuk, and a university centre opened in 1987. In 2006 expenditure on education by the Landsstyre amounted to 1,225m. kroner (representing 21.9% of total budget spending).

Public Holidays

Public holidays are the same as those for Denmark, with the exception of Constitution Day, which is not celebrated in Greenland. In addition, Greenlanders celebrate Mitaartut on 6 January, and Ullortuneq (Greenland's national day—literally: 'the longest day') on 21 June. Various regional holidays are also held to celebrate the return of the sun following the end of the long polar night; the timing of these vary according to latitude.

Statistical Survey

Sources: Statistics Greenland, *Statistical Yearbook;* Greenland Home Rule Government—Denmark Bureau, Pilestræde 52, POB 2151, 1122 Copenhagen K; tel. 33-13-42-24; fax 33-13-49-71; Statistics Greenland, POB 1025, 3900 Nuuk; tel. 345000; fax 322954; e-mail stat@gs.gh.gl; internet www.statgreen.gl.

AREA, POPULATION AND DENSITY

Area: Total 2,166,086 sq km (836,330 sq miles); Ice-free portion 410,449 sq km (158,475 sq miles).

Population: 56,648 (males 30,005, females 26,643) at 1 January 2007 (incl. 50,366 born in Greenland).

Density (1 January 2007, ice-free portion): 0.14 per sq km.

Principal Towns (population at 1 January 2007): Nuuk (Godthåb, the capital) 15,047; Sisimiut 6,140; Ilulissat 4,996; Qaqortoq 3,490; Aasiaat 3,189.

DANISH EXTERNAL TERRITORIES   *Greenland*

Births, Marriages and Deaths (2003): Registered live births 895 (birth rate 15.8 per 1,000); Registered marriages (1999) 253 (marriage rate 4.5 per 1,000); Registered deaths 412 (death rate 7.3 per 1,000). *2005:* Registered live births 887; Registered deaths 466.

Expectation of Life (years at birth, 2003): Males 64.1; Females 69.5.

Immigration and Emigration (2006): Immigrants 2,404 (Persons born in Greenland 890, Persons born outside Greenland 1,514); Emigrants 3,048 (Persons born in Greenland 1,358, Persons born outside Greenland 1,690).

Economically Active Population (persons with annual income exceeding 40,000 kroner, 2003): Animal husbandry, fishing and hunting 1,900; Quarrying 23; Manufacturing 2,058; Energy supply 470; Construction 2,030; Wholesale business 130; Retail trade 2,917; Hotels and restaurants 766; Transportation and tourism 1,576; Post and telecommunications service 384; Financial services, pensions and real estate 492; Other business services 369; Cleaning services 479; Public administration 11,969; Education, social institutions, nurseries etc. 58; Organizations and institutions 213; Entertainment, sport and culture 275; Other services 44; International organizations 5; Activities not classified 786; Total 27,494 (including 550 personnel employed from Danish mainland). *2006:* Total employed 30,058; Total unemployed 2,379; Total labour force 32,437.

HEALTH AND WELFARE
Key Indicators

Physicians (per 1,000 head, 2000): 1.6.

Health Expenditure (2000): million kroner: 792; % of current budgetary expenditure: 18.4.

AGRICULTURE, ETC.

Livestock (2006): Sheep 21,289, Horses 217, Beehives 8, Poultry 140, Cattle 24, Reindeer 2,318.

Livestock Products (metric tons, 2006): Sheep meat 360 (Source: FAO).

Hunting (2000): Fox skins 87, Polar bears 49.

Fishing ('000 metric tons, live weight, 2005, estimates): Greenland halibut 30.0; Lumpfish (Lumpsucker) 8.1; Capelin 16.2; Northern prawn 136.2; Total catch (incl. others) 216.3. The total excludes aquatic mammals, which are recorded by number rather than by weight. In 2004 the number of aquatic mammals caught was: Minke whale 177; Fin whale 13; Humpback whale 5; Long-finned pilot whale 297; Harbour porpoise 2,600; White whale 102; Narwhal 246; Walrus 236; Harp seal 64,442; Harbour seal 580; Ringed seal 68,693; Bearded seal 1,152; Hooded seal 3,273. Source: FAO.

INDUSTRY

Selected Products: Frozen fish 21,700 metric tons (2001); Electric energy 311 million kWh (2002); Dwellings completed 225 (2006). Source: partly UN, *Industrial Commodity Statistics Yearbook.*

FINANCE
(Danish currency is in use)

Central Government Expenditure (by Ministry, million kroner, 2000): *Current:* Finance 2,725 (Grant to Home Rule Government 2,725), Defence (incl. Fisheries Inspection) 268, Justice 165, Environment and Energy 58, Transport 38, Research 7, Prime Minister's Office 8, Labour 3, Agriculture and Fisheries 1, Business and Industry 2, Total 3,274. *Capital:* 0. *Total:* 3,274. *2003:* Grant to Home Rule Government 2,952m. kroner.

Budget (general government, million kroner, 2006): *Revenue:* Gross operating surplus 367; Interest, etc. 328; Taxes on production and imports 658 (Taxes on imports 536); Taxes on income, wealth, etc. 2,754; Transfers 4,069 (from Danish state 3,747); Total (incl. others) 8,299; *Expenditure:* Final consumption expenditure 5,568 (Compensation of employees 3,211); Income transfers 1,765 (Households 1,051); Non-financial capital accumulation 398 (Acquisition of new fixed assets 368); Investment grants and capital transfers 186 (Households 63); Total 7,916.

Cost of Living (Consumer Price Index; at July each year; base: July 1995 = 100): All items 119.3 in 2005; 122.7 in 2006; 124.8 in 2007.

Gross Domestic Product (million kroner at current market prices, provisional): 9,397 in 2003; 9,855 in 2004; 10,210 in 2005.

National Income and Product (million kroner at current prices, 2005, provisional): Compensation of employees 8,275; Gross operating surplus 1,895; *GDP at factor cost* 10,170; Indirect taxes 665; *Less* Subsidies 625; *GDP at market prices* 10,210; Net salary transfers –242; *Gross national income* 9,968; Expenditure of Danish Government 3,662; *Gross disposable national income* 13,630.

EXTERNAL TRADE

Principal Commodities (million kroner, 2006, provisional): *Imports c.i.f.:* Food and live animals 570; Beverages and tobacco 106; Raw materials, inedible 37; Petroleum oils and lubricants 758 (Crude petroleum, etc. 754); Chemicals and chemical products 179; Manufactured goods and products thereof 539 (Non-metallic mineral manufactures 110); Machinery and transport equipment 759 (Road vehicles 118); Manufactured products 488; Total (incl. others) 3,454. *Exports f.o.b.:* Food and live animals 2,040 (Fish and fish products 2,037); Raw materials, inedible 178; Machinery and transport equipment 27; Manufactured products 33; Miscellaneous articles and transactions 102; Total exports (incl. others) 2,418.

Principal Trading Partners (million kroner, 2006, provisional): *Imports c.i.f.:* China, People's Republic 60; Denmark 2,064; Germany 104; Japan 35; Norway 61; Sweden 778; USA 56; Total (incl. others) 3,454. *Exports f.o.b.:* Denmark 2,094; Iceland 38; Germany 25; Spain 168; United Kingdom 46; USA 29.2; Total (incl. others) 2,418.

TRANSPORT

Road Traffic (registered motor vehicles excl. emergency services, 2005): Private cars 2,861; Taxis 203; Buses 64; Lorries 1,467; Motorcycles 15.

Shipping (2000): Number of vessels 162 (passenger ships 7, dry cargo ships 39, fishing vessels 110, others 6); Total displacement 59,938 grt (passenger ships 5,780 grt, dry cargo ships 6,411 grt, fishing vessels 47,046 grt, others 701 grt).

International Sea-borne Freight Traffic ('000 cubic metres, 2003): Goods loaded 357; Goods unloaded 350.

International Transport (passengers conveyed between Greenland, Denmark and Iceland): Ship (1983) 94; Aircraft (2002) 103,562.

TOURISM

Occupancy of Registered Hotel Accommodation (nights, 2006): 245,432 (incl. 101,387 by Danish visitors).

COMMUNICATIONS MEDIA

Radio Receivers (1997): 27,000 in use.

Television Receivers (1997): 22,000 in use.

Telephones ('000 main lines in use, 2006): 25.3.

Facsimile Machines (1992): 1,153 in use.

Mobile Cellular Telephones ('000 subscribers, 2006): 32.2.

Internet Users ('000, 2006): 38.0.

Book Publishing (titles, 2006): 142.

Sources: UNESCO, *Statistical Yearbook,* International Telecommunication Union and UN, *Statistical Yearbook.*

EDUCATION

(municipal primary and lower-secondary schools only, 2001/02)
Institutions: 87.

Teachers: 1,191 (incl. 380 temporarily employed teachers and 202 non-Greenlandic-speaking teachers (2000/01)).

Students: 11,368.

2006/07 (Primary schools only): Teachers 1,216; Students 10,688.

Directory
The Government

Based on the strength of the parties in the legislature, the Landsting, an executive, the Landsstyre, is formed. Since 1979 the Landsstyre has gradually assumed control of the administration of Greenland's internal affairs. Jurisdiction in constitutional matters, foreign affairs and defence remains with the Danish Government, the highest representative of which, in Greenland, is the Rigsombudsmand or High Commissioner. Greenland sends two representatives to the Danish legislature, the Folketing.

LANDSSTYRE
(March 2008)

A coalition of Siumut (S) and Atassut (A).

DANISH EXTERNAL TERRITORIES

Prime Minister: HANS ENOKSEN (S).
Deputy Prime Minister and Minister for Fisheries, Hunting and Agriculture: FINN KARLSEN (A).
Minister of Finance and Foreign Affairs: ALEQA HAMMOND (S).
Minister of Industry, Labour and Vocational Training: SIVERTH K. HEILMANN (A).
Minister for Infrastructure, the Environment, Minerals and Petroleum: KIM KIELSEN (S).
Minister of Culture, Education, Research and the Church: TOMMY MARØ (S).
Minister for Family Affairs and Health: ARKALO ABELSEN (A).

Government Offices

Rigsombudsmanden i Grønland (High Commission of Greenland): Indaleeqqap Aqq. 3, POB 1030, 3900 Nuuk; tel. 321001; fax 324171; e-mail riomgr@gl.stm.dk; internet www.rigsombudsmanden.gl; High Commissioner SØREN HALD MØLLER.

Grønlands Hjemmestyre (Greenland Home Rule Government): POB 1015, 3900 Nuuk; tel. 345000; fax 325002; e-mail govsec@gh.gl; internet www.nanoq.gl.

Representation of Greenland: Strandgade 91, 3rd Floor, POB 2151, 1016 Copenhagen K; tel. 32-83-38-00; fax 32-83-38-01; e-mail journal@ghsdk.dk; internet www.nanoq.gl/Groenlands_Repraesentation_i_Koebenhavn.aspx.

Legislature

The legislative body is the Landsting, with 31 members elected for four years, on a basis of proportional representation. Greenlanders and Danes resident in Greenland for at least six months prior to an election and over the age of 18 years have the right to vote.

LANDSTING

Chairman: RUTH HEILMANN (Siumut).

Election, 15 November 2005

	Votes	% of votes	Seats
Siumut (Forward)	8,861	30.68	10
Demokraatit (Democrats)	6,595	22.83	7
Inuit Ataqatigiit (Inuit Brotherhood)	6,516	22.56	7
Atassut (Solidarity)	5,528	19.14	6
Katusseqatigiit (Alliance of Independent Candidates)	1,169	4.05	1
Total (incl. others)	28,885	100.00	31

Political Organizations

Arnat Partiiat (Women's Party): POB 1723, 3900 Nuuk; f. 1999; feminist party; campaigns for equal representation for women in Parliament.

Atassut (Solidarity): POB 399, 3900 Nuuk; tel. 323366; fax 325840; e-mail atassut@greennet.gl; internet www.atassut.gl; f. 1978 and became political party in 1981; supports close links with Denmark and favours EU membership for Greenland; Chair. FINN KARLSEN.

Demokraatit (Democrats—D): POB 164, 3900 Nuuk; tel. 345000; fax 311084; e-mail demokrat@demokrat.gl; internet www.demokrat.gl; f. 2002; Chair. PER BERTHELSEN.

Inuit Ataqatigiit (Inuit Brotherhood—IA): POB 321, 3900 Nuuk; tel. 323702; fax 323232; e-mail ia@greennet.gl; internet www.ia.gl; f. 1978; socialist party, demanding that Greenland citizenship be restricted to those of Inuit parentage; advocates Greenland's eventual independence from Denmark; Chair. KUUPIK KLEIST.

Kattusseqatigiit (Alliance of Independent Candidates): POB 2331, 3900 Nuuk; tel. 346252; fax 346235; e-mail afr@ilulissat.gl; internet www.kattusseqatigiit.gl; Chair. ANTHON FREDERIKSEN.

Siumut (Forward): POB 357, 3900 Nuuk; tel. 322077; fax 322319; e-mail siumut@greennet.gl; internet www.siumut.gl; f. 1971 and became political party in 1977; aims to promote collective ownership and co-operation, and to develop greater reliance on Greenland's own resources; favours greatest possible autonomy within the Kingdom of Denmark; social democratic party; Chair. HANS ENOKSEN.

Judicial System

The island is divided into 18 court districts and these courts all use lay assessors. For most cases these lower courts are for the first instance and appeal is to the Landsret, the higher court in Nuuk, which is the only one with a professional judge. This court hears the more serious cases in the first instance and appeal in these cases is to the High Court (Østre Landsret) in Copenhagen.

Religion

CHRISTIANITY

The Greenlandic Church, of which most of the population are adherents, forms an independent diocese of the Evangelical Lutheran Church in Denmark and comes under the jurisdiction of the Landsstyre and of the Bishop of Greenland. There are 17 parishes and in 2006 there were 25 ministers serving in Greenland.

Biskoppen over Grønlands Stift (Bishop of Greenland): SOFIE PETERSEN, Evangelical Lutheran Church, POB 90, 3900 Nuuk; tel. 321134; fax 321061; e-mail sop@gh.gl.

There are also small groups of other Protestant churches and of Roman Catholics.

The Press

There are no daily newspapers in Greenland.

Arnanut: Spindlersbakke 10B, POB 150, 3900 Nuuk; tel. 343570; fax 322499; e-mail arnanut@sermitsiaq.gl; internet www.arnanut.gl; f. 2003; quarterly; women's magazine; Editor IRENE JEPPSEN.

Atuagagdliutit/Grønlandsposten: Qullilerfik 2, POB 39, 3900 Nuuk; tel. 321083; fax 325483; e-mail redaktion@ag.gl; internet www.ag.gl; f. 1861; 2 a week; Editor-in-Chief STINE SKIFTE.

Niviarsiaq: POB 357, 3900 Nuuk; tel. 322077; fax 322319; e-mail contact@niviarsiaq.net; organ of Siumut; monthly; Editor MIKAEL PETERSEN.

Sermitsiaq: Spindlersbakke 10B, POB 150, 3900 Nuuk; tel. 343570; fax 322499; e-mail krarup@sermitsiaq.gl; internet www.sermitsiaq.gl; f. 1958; weekly; Editor POUL KRARUP.

Publishers

Atuakkiorfik A/S: Hans Egedesvej 3, POB 840, 3900 Nuuk; tel. 322122; fax 322500; e-mail sale@atuakkiorfik.gl; internet www.atuakkiorfik.gl; f. 1956; general fiction and non-fiction, children's and textbooks, public relations; Man. NUKARAQ EUGENIUS.

Ilinniusiorfik Undervisningsmiddelforlag: H. J. Rinksvej 35, 1st Floor, POB 1610, 3900 Nuuk; tel. 349889; fax 326236; e-mail ilinniusiorfik@ilinniusiorfik.gl; internet www.ilinniusiorfik.gl; owned by Home Rule Govt; textbooks and teaching materials; non-profit-making org.; Man. ABIA ABELSEN.

Broadcasting and Communications

TELECOMMUNICATIONS

TELE Greenland A/S: POB 1002, 3900 Nuuk; tel. 341255; fax 322255; e-mail tele@tele.gl; internet www.tele.gl; f. 1994; owned by Home Rule Govt; also owner of Greenland's postal service; Chair. KAJ EGEDE; Man. Dir BRIAN BUUS PEDERSEN.

BROADCASTING

Radio

Kalaallit Nunaata Radioa (KNR)—Grønlands Radio: Kissarneqqortuunnguaq 15, POB 1007, 3900 Nuuk; tel. 361600; fax 361502; e-mail info@knr.gl; internet www.knr.gl; f. 1958; 5 AM stations, 45 FM stations; bilingual programmes in Greenlandic and Danish, 17 hours a day; Dir LARS LENNERT-SANDGREN.

Avannaata Radioa: POB 223, 3952 Ilulissat; tel. 943633; fax 943618; e-mail avannaata@radio.knr.gl; regional station in north Greenland.

Kujataata Radioa: POB 158, 3920 Qaqortoq; regional station in south Greenland.

Radio—5 OZ 20: SPE BOX 139, 3970 Pituffik; FM/stereo, non-commercial station; broadcasts 21 hours a day; news, music, etc.; Station Man. INGRID KRISTENSEN.

Television

Kalaallit Nunaata Radioa TV: POB 1007, Kissarneqqortuunnguaq 15, 3900 Nuuk; tel. 361600; fax 361502; e-mail info@knr.gl; internet www.knr.gl; broadcasts by VHF transmitter to all of Greenland; commercial; most programmes in Danish; Dir LARS LENNERT-SANDGREN.

Finance

BANK
(cap. = capital; res = reserves; dep. = deposits; m. = million; brs = branches; amounts in kroner)

Bank of Greenland—GrønlandsBANKEN A/S: Imaneq 33, POB 1033, 3900 Nuuk; tel. 347700; fax 347707; e-mail banken@banken.gl; internet www.banken.gl; f. 1967 as Bank of Greenland A/S; present name adopted following merger with Nuna Bank A/S in 1997; cap. 180m., res 401m., dep. 2,928m. (Dec. 2006); Pres. and Gen. Man. SVEND-ERIK DANIELSEN; Gen. Man. JESPER FLENSTED NIELSEN; Chair. BENT H. JAKOBSEN; 5 brs.

Trade and Industry

GOVERNMENT AGENCY

Råstofdirektoratet (Bureau of Minerals and Petroleum): POB 930, Imaneq 29, 3900 Nuuk; tel. 346800; fax 324302; e-mail bmp@gh.gl; internet www.bmp.gl; f. 1998; performs the central administrative co-ordinating and regulatory tasks regarding exploration and production of mineral resources in Greenland; Dep. Min. JØRN SKOV NIELSEN.

GOVERNMENT-OWNED COMPANIES

KNI A/S (Greenland Trade Service): POB 319, J. M. Jensenip Aqq. 2, 3911 Sisimiut; tel. 862444; fax 866263; internet www.pilersuisoq.gl; f. 1992; statutory wholesale and retail trading co, petroleum and fuel supply; Chair. SIMON OLSEN; Man. Dir SØREN LENNERT MORTENSEN.

Pisiffik A/S: POB 1009, 3911 Sisimiut; tel. 862900; fax 864175; e-mail mos@pisiffik.gl; f. 1993; statutory wholesale and retail trading co; co-owned by Dagrofa A/S (Denmark) and Home Rule Govt; Chair. VILLY RASMUSSEN; Man. MICHAEL ØSTERGAARD.

Royal Greenland A/S: POB 1073, 3900 Nuuk; tel. 324422; fax 323349; e-mail info@royalgreenland.com; internet www.royalgreenland.com; f. 1774; trade monopoly ended 1950; Home Rule Govt assumed control 1986; established as share co 1990 (all shares owned by Home Rule Govt); fishing group based in Greenland with subsidiaries in Japan, the United Kingdom, Scandinavia, the USA, Italy, France and Germany; main products are coldwater prawns and halibut; five trawlers; factories in Greenland, China, Denmark, Germany, Norway, and Poland; Chair. PETER GRØNVOLD SAMUELSEN; CEO FLEMMING KNUDSEN.

EMPLOYERS' ASSOCIATION

Grønlands Arbejdsgiveforening (GA) (Greenland Employers' Asscn): Jens Kreutzmannip Aqq. 3, POB 73, 3900 Nuuk; tel. 321500; fax 324340; e-mail ga@ga.gl; internet www.ga.gl; c. 300 mem. orgs; Chair. HENRIK SØRENSEN; Dir HENRIK LETH.

TRADE UNION

Sulinermik Inuussutissarsiuteqartut Kattuffiat (SIK) (Greenland Workers' Union): POB 9, 3900 Nuuk; tel. 29922133; fax 29924939; internet www.randburg.com/gr/workersu.html; f. 1956 as Grønlands Arbejeder Sammenslutning (GAS); Pres. JESS G. BERTHELSEN; Sec. OLE KRISTIAN KLEIST; c. 6,000 mems.

Transport

Owing to the long distances and harsh conditions there are no roads connecting towns in Greenland. Domestic traffic is mainly by aircraft (fixed-wing and helicopter), boat, snowmobile and dog-sled. There are airports or heliports in all towns for domestic flights. The main international airport is located on a former US military base at Kangerlussuaq (Søndre Strømfjord). There are smaller international airports at Narsarsuaq and Kulusuk. In 2007 Air Greenland commenced a weekly direct route to Baltimore, MD (USA), to operate between June and August (commercial flights between Greenland and the USA having hitherto been routed via Denmark or Iceland). Scandinavian Airlines System (SAS) also offers direct flights from Aalborg, Århus and Copenhagen (all Denmark) to Kangerlussuaq airport, which operate during May–September.

The main port is at Nuuk; there are also all-year ports at Paamiut (Frederikshåb), Maniitsoq (Sukkertoppen) and Sisimiut (Holsteinsborg). In addition, there are shipyards at Nuuk, Qaqortoq, Paamiut, Maniitsoq, Sisimiut and Aasiaat. Coastal motor vessels operate passenger services along the west coast from Upernavik to Nanortalik.

SHIPPING COMPANY

Royal Arctic Line A/S: Aqqusinersuaq 52, POB 1580, 3900 Nuuk; tel. 349100; fax 322450; e-mail marketing@ral.dk; internet www.ral.gl; f. 1993; owned by Home Rule Govt; five container vessels of 49,230 grt and one general cargo vessel of 1,171 grt; Chair. MARTHA LABANSEN; Man. Dir JENS ANDERSEN.

AIRLINE

Air Greenland: POB 1012, Nuuk Airport, 3900 Nuuk; tel. 343434; fax 327288; e-mail info@airgreenland.gl; internet www.airgreenland.gl; f. 1960 as Grønlandsfly A/S; air services to the 24 principal centres in Greenland, and to Copenhagen (Denmark); commenced weekly direct service to Baltimore, MD (USA) in 2007, operating during June–August; supply, survey, ice-reconnaissance services and helicopter/fixed-wing charters; owned by Danish Govt, Home Rule Govt and SAS; Chair. JULIA PARS; Man. Dir MICHAEL BINZER.

Tourism

The national tourist board of Greenland, Greenland Tourism, was established in 1992 in order to develop tourism in Greenland, and concentrates primarily on developing sustainable tourism projects. In 2006 245,432 accommodation nights were recorded at registered hotels, including 101,387 by Danish visitors.

Greenland Tourism and Business Council: POB 1615, Hans Egedesvej 29, 3900 Nuuk; tel. 342820; fax 322877; e-mail info@greenland.com; internet www.greenland.com; f. 1992; Chair. BJARNE EKLUND; CEO THOMAS ROSENKRANDS.

DJIBOUTI

Introductory Survey

Location, Climate, Language, Religion, Flag, Capital

The Republic of Djibouti is in the Horn of Africa, at the southern entrance to the Red Sea. It is bounded on the north by Eritrea, on the north, west and south-west by Ethiopia, and on the south-east by Somalia. The land is mainly volcanic desert, and the climate hot and arid. There are two main ethnic groups, the Issa, who are of Somali origin and comprise 50% of the population, and the Afar, who comprise 40% of the population and are of Ethiopian origin. Both groups are Muslims, and they speak related Cushitic languages. The official languages are Arabic and French. The flag has two equal horizontal stripes, of light blue and light green, with a white triangle, enclosing a five-pointed red star, at the hoist. The capital is Djibouti.

Recent History

In 1945 the area now comprising the Republic of Djibouti (then known as French Somaliland) was proclaimed an overseas territory of France, and in 1967 was renamed the French Territory of the Afars and the Issas. The Afar and the Issa have strong connections with Ethiopia and Somalia, respectively. Until the 1960s ethnic divisions were not marked; subsequently, however, internal tensions arose. Demands for independence were led by the Issa community, and, under pressure from the Organization of African Unity (OAU, now the African Union, see p. 164) to grant full independence to the territory, France acted to improve relations between the two communities. Following a referendum in May 1977, the territory became independent on 27 June. Hassan Gouled Aptidon, a senior Issa politician, became the first President of the Republic of Djibouti.

In March 1979 Gouled formed a new political party, the Rassemblement populaire pour le progrès (RPP), which was declared the sole legal party in October 1981. In June 1981 Gouled had been elected to a further six-year term as President. Legislative elections were held in May 1982, when candidates were chosen from a single list approved by the RPP. At the next presidential and legislative elections, held in April 1987, Gouled was re-elected, while RPP-sponsored candidates for all 65 seats in the legislature were elected unopposed.

Until the mid-1980s there was little overt opposition to the RPP regime; however, political tensions began to escalate during 1987, prompting Gouled to reorganize the Government. In April 1989 inter-tribal hostilities erupted in the capital and the Afar town of Tadjourah. Inter-ethnic tensions persisted, and in May 1990 fighting broke out between the Issa and the Gadabursi communities in the capital.

In April 1991 the Front pour la restauration de l'unité et de la démocratie (FRUD) was formed by a merger of three insurgent Afar movements. In November the FRUD launched a full-scale insurrection against the Government and by late November the FRUD controlled many towns and villages in the north of the country. The Government introduced mass conscription and requested military assistance from France (see below) to repel what it described as 'external aggression' by soldiers loyal to the deposed President Mengistu of Ethiopia. The FRUD denied that it constituted a foreign aggressor, claiming that its aim was to secure fair political representation for all ethnic groups in Djibouti.

In early 1992, under pressure from France to accommodate opposition demands for democratic reform, President Gouled appointed a commission to draft a new constitution, which was to restore the multi-party system and provide for free elections. The FRUD stated its willingness to negotiate with Gouled and undertook to observe a cease-fire, subject to satisfactory progress on democratic reforms. Gouled, however, reasserted that the FRUD was controlled by 'foreign interests' and accused France of failing to honour its defence agreement. By late January most of northern Djibouti was under FRUD control, although armed conflict between the FRUD and the Government continued. In June Ahmed Dini, who had been Djibouti's first Prime Minister after independence, assumed the leadership of the FRUD.

President Gouled's constitutional plan, which was announced in April 1992, conceded the principle of political pluralism, but proposed few other changes and retained a strong executive presidency. The plan was rejected by the opposition parties and by the FRUD, although cautiously welcomed by France. A constitutional referendum, which was held in September, was boycotted by all the opposition groups; the Government, however, stated that, with 75.2% of the electorate participating, 96.8% of voters had endorsed the new Constitution. At the 30 September deadline for party registration, only the RPP and the Parti du renouveau démocratique (PRD), an opposition group formed earlier in 1992 under the leadership of Mohamed Djama Elabe, were granted legal status. The application for registration by the opposition Parti national démocratique (PND) was initially rejected, although it was allowed in October. Elections to the Assemblée nationale were held on 18 December, and all 65 seats were won by the RPP. However, turn-out was less than 50%, leading to charges from the PND that the legislature was unrepresentative.

Five candidates stood in Djibouti's first contested presidential election, which was held on 7 May 1993: Gouled, Elabe, Aden Robleh Awalleh (for the PND) and two independents. The election was again notable for a low turn-out (49.9%), but resulted in a clear victory for Gouled, who, according to official results, obtained 60.8% of the valid votes cast.

In March 1994 serious divisions emerged within the FRUD leadership. It was reported that the political bureau, led by Ahmed Dini, had been dissolved and that dissident members had formed an 'executive council', headed by Ougoureh Kifleh Ahmed. This dissident leadership (Ali Mohamed Daoud was subsequently declared President) sought support within the movement for a negotiated political settlement of the conflict. In June Kifleh Ahmed and the Government agreed terms for a cease-fire, and formal negotiations for a peace settlement began in July. Executive bodies of both FRUD factions continued to operate during the latter half of 1994, and parallel national congresses rejected the legitimacy of the opposing faction's leadership. In December an agreement signed by Kifleh Ahmed and the Minister of the Interior, Idris Harbi Farah, provided for a permanent cessation of hostilities, the incorporation of FRUD armed forces into the national force, the recognition of the FRUD as a legal political party, the multi-ethnic composition of a new council of ministers and the reform of electoral procedures prior to the next legislative elections. In accordance with the peace agreement, 300 members of the FRUD armed forces were integrated into the national army in March 1995. However, there was little further implementation of the accord, and there was considerable criticism of the agreement by the radical faction of the FRUD (which, under the leadership of Ahmed Dini, favoured a continuation of military operations and launched a number of small-scale attacks against government targets in late 1995) and other opposition groups. Nevertheless, Ali Mohamed Daoud and Kifleh Ahmed were appointed to posts in the Government in June. In March 1996 the Government granted legal recognition to the FRUD, which became the country's fourth and largest political party. However, Ibrahim Chehem Daoud, a former high-ranking official in the FRUD, who opposed reconciliation with the Government, formed a new group, FRUD-Renaissance.

In early 1996 President Gouled's prolonged hospitalization in France prompted a succession crisis within the RPP, between the President's nephew and principal adviser, Ismael Omar Gelleh, and his private secretary, Ismael Gedi Hared. In March the Minister of Justice and Islamic Affairs, Bahdon Farah, who was opposed to Gelleh, was dismissed from the Council of Ministers, together with Ahmed Bulaleh Barreh, the Minister of Defence. In April Bahdon Farah established a splinter group of the RPP, the Groupe pour la démocratie de la république (RPP—GDR), which included 13 of the 65 members of the Assemblée nationale. The President of the Assemblée subsequently claimed that the RPP—GDR would remain banned while Bahdon Farah continued to hold his position as Secretary-General of the RPP. In May Gouled expelled Gedi Hared from the RPP's executive committee, together with Bahdon Farah and former ministers Barreh and Ali Mahamade Houmed, all of whom opposed Gelleh. In June Gedi Hared formed an opposition alliance, the Coordination de l'opposition djiboutienne, embracing the PND, the Front uni de l'opposition djiboutienne (a coalition of internal opposition groups) and the RPP—GDR. In August Gedi Hared, Bahdon Farah and Barreh were among five people sentenced to six months' imprisonment and the suspension of their civil rights for five years for 'insulting the Head of State'. The detainees were released from prison in January 1997, following a presidential pardon, although their civil rights were not restored. (In early September 2001 it was announced that the Government had proposed an amnesty for the five, under which their civil rights would be restored and that they would be entitled to stand in the legislative elections of January 2003.)

In April 1997 the FRUD faction led by Ali Mohamed Daoud announced its intention to participate in the forthcoming legislative elections and to present joint electoral lists with the RPP. At the legislative elections, held on 19 December, the RPP-FRUD alliance won all the seats in the Assemblée nationale. The rate of voter participation was officially recorded at 63.8%. The PRD and the PND presented candidates in some districts, but neither succeeded in gaining representation. In late December President Gouled formed a new Council of Ministers.

In February 1999 President Gouled confirmed that he would not stand in the forthcoming presidential election; the RPP named Gelleh as its presidential candidate. At the election, held on 9 April, Gelleh won 74.4% of the votes cast, convincingly defeating his sole opponent, Moussa Ahmed Idris, who represented an opposition coalition, the Opposition djiboutienne unifiée (ODU), including the PND, the PRD and the Dini wing of the FRUD. Electoral participation was estimated at 60%. Following his inauguration as President on 7 May, Gelleh reappointed Barkad Gourad Hamadou as Prime Minister, at the head of a new Council of Ministers.

In early February 2000 the Government and the Dini wing of the FRUD signed a peace agreement in Paris, France. The accord provided for an end to hostilities, the reciprocal release of prisoners, the return of military units to positions held before the conflict, freedom of movement for persons and goods, the reintegration of FRUD insurgents into their previous positions of employment, and an amnesty for the rebels. In late March Dini returned to Djibouti from a self-imposed nine-year exile and announced his intention to assist in the implementation of the peace agreement. Meanwhile, earlier that month the RPP had convened its eighth congress, at which Gouled officially announced his retirement from active politics. Gelleh was elected to succeed him as party President.

In early February 2001 Barkad Gourad Hamadou resigned as Prime Minister on the grounds of ill health, after some 22 years in office. Dileita Mohamed Dileita, hitherto ambassador to Ethiopia, was appointed as Hamadou's replacement in March.

In May 2001 it was announced that an agreement bringing an official end to hostilities between the Government and the FRUD had been signed. The Government, for its part, pledged to establish a number of more representative local bodies and to introduce an 'unrestricted multi-party system' by September 2002. In early July 2001 President Gelleh effected a minor reorganization of the Council of Ministers, with moderate FRUD members allocated two portfolios.

On 4 September 2002, to coincide with the 10th anniversary of the approval of the new Constitution, the limit on the number of permitted political parties (previously fixed at four) was lifted. Henceforth, all parties would be recognized, subject to approval by the Ministry of the Interior and Decentralization, and, during the following months, a number of new parties registered with the intention of participating in the forthcoming legislative elections. At the elections, held on 10 January 2003, the Union pour la majorité présidentielle (UMP), a coalition comprising the RPP, the FRUD, the PND and the Parti populaire social démocrate, won 62.7% of the total votes cast; in accordance with the electoral laws, as it had won the majority of votes in each of the five constituencies, the UMP secured all 65 seats in the Assemblée nationale. Therefore, despite receiving 37.3% of votes cast, the opposition coalition, the Union pour l'alternance démocratique (UAD), comprising the Alliance républicaine pour la démocratie (ARD), the PRD (which in November was renamed the Mouvement du renouveau démocratique), the Parti djiboutien pour la démocratie and the Union djiboutienne pour la démocratie et la justice, failed to attain any legislative representation. According to official figures, the rate of voter participation was 48.4%. Later that month Idriss Arnaoud Ali, the deputy Secretary-General of the RPP, was appointed President of the Assemblée nationale; the Council of Ministers remained unaltered.

In late July 2003 the Djibouti Government announced that owing to 'security and economic' reasons all illegal immigrants would be required to leave Djibouti by the end of August. The deadline was subsequently extended until mid-September, by which time more than 80,000 immigrants, predominantly from Ethiopia and Somalia, had voluntarily left the country. The USA, which in August had warned of the possibility of terrorist attacks against Western targets in Djibouti, denied allegations that it had exerted pressure on the Government to expel the illegal immigrants. Following the expiry of the deadline, security forces commenced operations to arrest and expel any remaining immigrants not in possession of identity papers.

At the presidential election held on 8 April 2005 Gelleh, who was unopposed following the withdrawal of the sole challenger, the Parti djiboutien pour le développement President Mohamed Daoud Chehem, was returned for a second term of office. Numerous opposition groups had appealed for a boycott of the election; however, official figures put the rate of voter participation at 78.9% and confirmed that Gelleh had received 100% of the votes cast. Gelleh reorganized the Government in mid-May, most notably appointing Ali Farah Assoweh, hitherto the Secretary-General of the Ministry of Presidential Affairs, as Minister of the Economy, Finance and Planning, in charge of Privatization.

In January 2006 a new labour code entered into force (having been approved by the Council of Ministers in February 2005). Reports subsequently emerged in February–April 2006 that a number of prominent trade union officials had been arrested by the security forces. Many trade union leaders had strongly criticized the revised labour code, which required trade unions to obtain the permission of the Attorney-General, the Labour Inspectorate and the Ministries of the Interior and Decentralization, of Justice, Muslim and Penal Affairs, and of Human Rights and Labour and Vocational Training in order to operate. The Attorney-General was also authorized to dissolve a trade union at the request of one of the above ministries. In late November the death was announced of former President Gouled; a three-day period of national mourning was observed.

In early December 2006 the ARD expressed its dissatisfaction with the lack of democratic reform in Djibouti since the party signed a peace agreement with the Government in 2001. Following its national conference that took place on 1–2 December 2006 the ARD issued a statement which labelled the Government as a destabilizing force in the region and called for a renewed campaign of civil disobedience.

Legislative elections were held on 8 February 2008. The opposition parties had announced their intention to boycott the ballot, and thus the elections were contested solely by candidates from the UMP, which, according to official results, took 94.1% of the total votes cast and secured all 65 seats in the Assemblée nationale. The rate of voter participation was estimated at 72.6%.

Separate treaties of friendship and co-operation were signed in 1981 with Ethiopia, Somalia, Kenya and Sudan, with the aim of resolving regional conflicts. Djibouti's interest in promoting regional co-operation was exemplified by the creation, in February 1985, of the Intergovernmental Authority on Drought and Development (now the Intergovernmental Authority on Development—IGAD, see p. 311), with six (now seven) member states; Djibouti was chosen as the site of its permanent secretariat, and President Gouled became the first Chairman.

Following the overthrow of the Ethiopian President, Mengistu Haile Mariam, in May 1991, Djibouti established good relations with the successor transitional Government in that country. In November 1997 Djibouti granted official recognition to the self-proclaimed 'Republic of Somaliland', which declared independence in 1991. In late 1999 President Gelleh drafted a peace plan aimed at reunifying Somali territory, to which the leaders of 'Somaliland' expressed their vehement opposition. Relations deteriorated further in April 2000 when the 'Somaliland' authorities closed the common border with Djibouti, following an incident in which a Djiboutian delegation was refused permission to leave its aircraft after landing at Hargeisa airport in 'Somaliland'. 'Somaliland' officials claimed that Djibouti was encouraging ethnic violence and had been responsible for a series of bomb attacks in Hargeisa. In response, Djibouti expelled three 'Somaliland' diplomats and closed the 'Somaliland' liaison office in Djibouti town. Furthermore, in May the 'Somaliland' authorities issued a ban on all flights from Djibouti to its territory; the Djibouti Government responded by prohibiting all flights to and from 'Somaliland'. The Djibouti-sponsored Somali national reconciliation conference, chaired by Gelleh, opened in May in Arta, about 40 km south of Djibouti town. The conference was attended by some 900 representatives of Somali clans and political and armed groups, and in August, following three months of extensive negotiations, the newly created Somali Transitional National Assembly elected Abdulkasim Salad Hasan President of Somalia. Relations between Djibouti and 'Somaliland' were further strained in April 2001 after the Djibouti authorities closed the common border and outlawed the transport of all goods and people between the two territories. In October a delegation from 'Somaliland', led by its minister responsible for foreign affairs, held talks with Djibouti officials in an attempt to improve relations; although several bilateral agreements were concluded, the common border remained closed. Following the death of President Mohamed Ibrahim Egal in May 2002, Gelleh moved swiftly to establish cordial relations with the new President of 'Somaliland', Dahir Riyale Kahin.

In December 1995 the Djibouti Government protested to the Eritrean authorities about alleged incursions by Eritrean troops into north-eastern Djibouti. These allegations were vehemently denied by Eritrea. Relations between the two countries were strained in April 1996, when President Gouled rejected a map of Eritrea submitted by the Eritrean Minister of Foreign Affairs, which reportedly included a 20-km strip of territory belonging to Djibouti. In November 1998 Djibouti suspended diplomatic relations with Eritrea, following accusations by that country that it was supporting Ethiopia in the Eritrea–Ethiopia border dispute. Gouled had been actively involved in an OAU committee mediating on the dispute, which earlier in the month had proposed a peace plan that was accepted by Ethiopia, but not by Eritrea. In November 1999 President Gelleh was praised by the Ethiopian President for his efforts in promoting a peace settlement in Somalia and in December the Djibouti and Ethiopian Governments signed a protocol of understanding on military co-operation, with the aim of establishing a further mutual defence pact. In March 2000, following Libyan mediation, Djibouti and Eritrea announced that they had resumed diplomatic relations. In December relations between Djibouti and Ethiopia temporarily deteriorated after plans were announced to increase handling charges at Djibouti port by more than 150%, which the Ethiopian authorities maintained violated a 1999 trade agreement between the two countries. However, in February 2001 the Dubai Port Authority, which had assumed control of Djibouti port in May 2000, agreed to reduce the tariffs, and bilateral relations subsequently improved. Following lengthy negotiations, in mid-November 2006 Djibouti and Ethiopia signed an agreement allowing for goods imported by Ethiopia to be transported via Djibouti port over the following 20 years. However, relations between the two countries deteriorated somewhat in late December owing to Djibouti's alleged support for the Islamist Supreme Somali Islamic Courts' Council organization (see chapter on Somalia).

In September 1994 the office of the UN High Commissioner for Refugees (UNHCR) initiated a programme of voluntary repatriation for Ethiopian refugees in Djibouti. According to UNHCR, some 35,000 Ethiopians returned voluntarily to their homes between early 1995 and April 1996. UNHCR estimated that at 31 December 2005 there were 10,456 refugees in Djibouti; by the end of 2006 the number of refugees was believed to have declined to 7,021, of whom 6,414 were Somali.

Djibouti's stance during the Gulf War of January–February 1991 strengthened its ties with France, and in February the Djibouti and French Governments signed defence treaties, extending military co-operation, although France refused to intervene militarily in the conflict between the Government and the FRUD. The failure of the Government to conclude a peace agreement with the FRUD strained relations with France in 1993–94. Relations improved as a result of the peace accord of December 1994, but tensions remained between the two countries. In April 1998, during a visit to Djibouti by the French Minister of Defence, it was announced that France planned to reduce its military presence in the country from 3,200 troops to 2,600 by 2000. However, in October 1999, the suspension of the troop reduction programme was announced and France confirmed its guarantees of Djibouti's territorial integrity. In July 2002, as part of a restructuring of the French forces in Djibouti, a new French army base was inaugurated, and in May 2003 the French Government agreed to provide Djibouti with €30m. per year of development aid over a 10-year period, of which €5m. would be used to maintain military bases and port facilities. France remained the leading donor of aid to Djibouti in 2004, granting €20m. of public development assistance. In late January 2005 relations between the two countries became strained when Djibouti expelled six French aid workers and closed the Radio France Internationale transmitter in the country. The action was perceived to be in response to France's summoning on 10 January of the Djiboutian chief of security services to appear before an inquiry into the death of Bernard Borrel, a French judge attached to the Djibouti Ministry of Justice, in Djibouti in 1995. (An inquiry conducted by French officials in Djibouti later that year had concluded that Borrel had committed suicide; however, his family had never accepted this verdict.) Relations appeared to have improved by May 2005 when President Gelleh made an official visit to Paris to meet with President Chirac. In mid-January 2006, however, Djibouti requested that the International Court of Justice in The Hague, Netherlands, intervene in the case after French investigators indicated that Borrel could have been assassinated. Relations further deteriorated in early October when French magistrates issued arrest warrants for the head of Djibouti's security services, Hassan Said, and Chief Prosecutor Djama Souleiman Ali on suspicion of deliberately obstructing the investigation into Borrel's death. Djibouti, for its part, reacted angrily and refused to accept the warrants, adding that it no longer retained any confidence in the French judicial system.

The attacks on the World Trade Center in New York and the Pentagon in Washington, DC, on 11 September 2001 resulted in a significant enhancement of Djibouti's strategic importance to the USA and its allies. In early October Djibouti demonstrated its support for the US-led coalition against terrorism by establishing a seven-member Comité national de lutte contre le terrorisme to monitor domestic security conditions. Djibouti agreed to grant access to its port and airfields, and coalition members stated their intention to use Djibouti as a base from where to monitor developments in Somalia, Sudan and other countries in the region. In December a German military delegation discussed the possibility of establishing a base camp for German naval forces participating in the war on terrorism with Djibouti officials, and in January 2002 Djibouti and Germany signed a memorandum of understanding on the status of German military and civilian personnel in Djibouti. The accord granted German military personnel access to Djibouti's port and airfields to conduct surveillance missions in the region, and some 1,200 German naval personnel were subsequently stationed in Djibouti, although this number had been reduced to 320 by early 2005. In December 2002 the US Secretary of Defense, Donald Rumsfeld, visited the 1,500 US troops based off the coast of Djibouti who formed the Combined Joint Task Force-Horn of Africa (CJTF-HOA), which was to monitor ship movements in the Red Sea and along the East African coast. In mid-January 2003 Gelleh and several ministers met US President George W. Bush and other senior US officials during a visit to Washington, DC. According to Gelleh, the USA agreed to provide US $8m. over the following two years for education and health projects in Djibouti and pledged to reopen the office of the US Agency for International Development. In February Djibouti and the USA concluded an agreement that allowed US forces to use Djiboutian military installations, and in May CJTF-HOA moved its headquarters on shore to a base in Djibouti. Throughout 2004 US military presence in Djibouti increased further with the construction of a new port at Doraleh and there were ongoing negotiations between the US Navy and the Emirates National Oil Company regarding the possible relocation of refuelling operations to Djibouti from Yemen. The USA also doubled its budget for training the Djibouti military to $325,000 in 2004. This training included courses in professionalizing officers, management of defence resources and coastal security. In April 2006 a report published by the human rights organization Amnesty International accused Djibouti of collaborating with US authorities in a practice known as 'rendition'. The report alleged that terrorist suspects detained by the US intelligence services had been held in secret prisons in Djibouti and later transferred to countries where torture was tolerated. In early January 2007 Djibouti criticized the USA after US forces based in Djibouti launched a series of air strikes against suspected members of the radical Islamist al-Qa'ida (Base) organization in southern Somalia.

Government

Executive power is vested in the President, who is directly elected by universal adult suffrage for a six-year term. Legislative power is held by the Assemblée nationale, consisting of 65 members elected for five years. The Council of Ministers, presided over by a Prime Minister, is responsible to the President. The Republic comprises five electoral districts.

Defence

Since independence, a large portion of the annual budget has been allocated to military expenditure, and defence absorbed an estimated 13.7% of total government budgetary expenditure in 2000. The total armed forces of Djibouti, in which all services form part of the army, was assessed at 10,950 in November 2007 (including 200 naval and 250 air force personnel, and 1,400 gendarmes), and there was a 2,500-strong national security force. At the same time there were about 2,850 French troops stationed in Djibouti, while the US-led Combined Joint Task Force-Horn of Africa also had its headquarters in the country. In January 2002 Djibouti and Germany signed a memorandum of understanding on the status of German military and civilian personnel in Djibouti, granting German military personnel access to Djibouti's port and airfields to conduct surveillance missions in the region; some 257 German naval personnel were stationed in Djibouti in 2007. The defence budget for 2007 amounted to 2,950m. Djibouti francs.

Economic Affairs

In 2006, according to estimates by the World Bank, Djibouti's gross national income (GNI), measured at average 2004–06 prices, was US $857m., equivalent to $1,060 per head (or $2,540 on an international purchasing-power parity basis). During 1996–2006, it was estimated, the population increased at an average annual rate of 2.6%, owing partly to the influx of refugees from neighbouring Ethiopia and Somalia (although the population was expected to have decreased during 2004–05 following the mass expulsion of foreign migrants), while gross domestic product (GDP) per head decreased, in real terms, by an average of 0.5% per year. Overall GDP increased, in real terms, at an average annual rate of 2.1% during 1996–2006; growth of 4.8% was recorded in 2006.

Agriculture (including hunting, forestry and fishing) provided only 3.6% of GDP in 2006, according to official figures, although some 76.5% of the labour force were engaged in the sector in mid-2005 according to FAO. There is little arable farming, owing to Djibouti's unproductive terrain, and the country is able to produce only about 3% of its total food requirements. More than one-half of the population are pastoral nomads, herding goats, sheep and camels. During 1996–2005, according to the World Bank, the real GDP of the agricultural sector increased at an average annual rate of 2.4%; agricultural GDP increased by 4.6% in 2005.

Industry (comprising manufacturing, construction and utilities) provided 16.8% of GDP in 2006, according to official figures, and engaged 11.0% of the employed labour force in 1991. Industrial activity is mainly limited to a few small-scale enterprises. During 1996–2005, according to the World Bank, industrial GDP increased at an average annual rate of 3.1%; it increased by 6.7% in 2005.

The manufacturing sector contributed 2.8% of GDP in 2006. Almost all consumer goods have to be imported. Manufacturing GDP increased by an average of 1.2% per year in 1996–2005, according to the World Bank. The GDP of the sector increased by 1.5% in 2005.

In 1986 work commenced on a major geothermal exploration project, funded by the World Bank and foreign aid. In that year Saudi Arabia granted Djibouti US $21.4m. for the purchase and installation of three electricity generators, with a combined capacity of 15 MW. Total electricity generating capacity rose from 40 MW to 80 MW in 1988, when the second part of the Boulaos power station became operative. This figure continued to rise during the 1990s, and in 2006 Djibouti produced 306.0m. kWh of electricity. Nevertheless, imported fuels continued to satisfy a large proportion of Djibouti's energy requirements. Imports of petroleum products accounted for 18.5% of the value of total imports in 1999. In December 2004 Djibouti and Ethiopia agreed to connect their power generating facilities in an attempt to increase access to electricity.

Djibouti's economic viability is based on trade through the international port of Djibouti, and on the developing service sector, which accounted for 79.6% of GDP in 2006, according to official figures, and engaged 13.8% of the employed labour force in 1991. In May 2000 the Government and Dubai Ports International (DPI—now Dubai Ports World) signed an agreement providing DPI with a 20-year contract to manage the port of Djibouti. During 1996–2005, according to the World Bank, the GDP of the services sector increased at an average annual rate of 1.8%. Services GDP increased by 2.0% in 2005.

In 2006 Djibouti recorded a visible trade deficit of US $280.5m., and there was a deficit of $99.1m. on the current account of the balance of payments. According to the IMF, the principal sources of imports in 2002 were Ethiopia (11.1%) and France (7.6%). The principal markets for exports in that year were Somalia (57.2%) and Yemen (24.5%). The principal imports in 1999 were food and beverages, machinery and electrical appliances, qat (a narcotic leaf), petroleum products and vehicles and transport equipment. Most exports are unclassified.

Djibouti recorded a budget deficit of 3,130m. Djibouti francs in 2006 (equivalent to 2.3% of GDP). The country's total external debt was US $424.2m. at the end of 2005, of which $389.0m. was long-term public debt. In 2003 the cost of debt-servicing was equivalent to an estimated 14.6% of revenue from exports of goods and services. The annual rate of inflation averaged 2.3% during 1996–2006. Consumer prices increased by an estimated 3.0% in 2006. In 1996 unemployment was estimated to affect some 58% of the labour force.

Djibouti is a member of the Intergovernmental Authority on Development (see p. 311) and numerous other international organizations, including the African Development Bank (see p. 162), the Arab Fund for Economic and Social Development (see p. 174) and the Islamic Development Bank (see p. 329). In 1995 Djibouti became a member of the World Trade Organization (see p. 396).

Djibouti has traditionally relied heavily on foreign assistance and in April 1996 the IMF approved Djibouti's first stand-by credit, equivalent to US $6.7m. In October 1999 the IMF agreed a $26.5m. loan to support the Government's three-year economic reform programme, and an initial payment of $3.8m. was released immediately. However, the payment of the balance was conditional on Djibouti implementing its 1999–2002 programme of economic and financial reform, which included reforms to tax, revenue administration and budget management; the completion of the army demobilization programme; the reform of the civil service; and the publication of a privatization programme for the six principal state-owned enterprises. Although there were continued delays in the army demobilization programme and the reform of the civil service, in November 2001 the IMF disbursed a further $5.0m., and in December 2002, following the completion of the third policy review, the IMF released funds totalling $6.0m. However, attempts by the Djiboutian authorities during 2004 and 2005 to secure further assistance from the IMF proved unsuccessful, largely owing to the significant investment made in the economy by the USA and France. In May 2003 France had agreed to contribute €30m. per year over a 10-year period in order to maintain its military presence in the country, while the USA was to pay Djibouti $31m. for hosting its military base; when combined, these payments would cover more than 80% of the annual wage bill for the civil service. Moreover, in late 2003 the USA also announced that Djibouti would receive aid worth some $90m. during 2004, making Djibouti the largest recipient of US assistance in Africa. The IMF welcomed the reform of Djibouti's labour code, which came into force in late January 2006, as a means for the country to better compete in the international market. However, trade union leaders expressed concerns that their right to organize would be eroded by the new code (see Recent History). Further reforms of the country's commercial and investment codes were also planned, and the arrival in 2006 of two foreign banks expanded the banking sector, which hitherto had been dominated by two French-owned companies. GDP growth of 4.8% in 2006 had been underpinned by private investment in the port, construction and service sectors, concomitant with fiscal expansion due to strong revenues. The IMF forecast that GDP growth would increase in 2008, reaching 5.7% compared with 4.8% in 2007, while consumer prices were estimated to have increased by 3.5% in that year.

Education

The Government has overall responsibility for education. Primary education generally begins at six years of age and lasts for six years. Secondary education, usually starting at the age of 12, lasts for seven years, comprising a first cycle of four years and a second of three years. In 1996 the total enrolment at primary and secondary schools was equivalent to 26% of the school-age population (31% of boys; 22% of girls). In 2004/05 primary enrolment included 33% of pupils in the relevant age-group

DJIBOUTI

Statistical Survey

(36% of boys; 29% of girls), and secondary enrolment was equivalent to 19% of pupils in the relevant age-group (22% of boys; 15% of girls). Budgetary current expenditure on education in 2002 was 3,937m. Djibouti francs, equivalent to 12.8% of total government expenditure. In January 2006 the Pôle Universitaire de Djibouti, which opened in 2000 and had 1,746 students in 2004/05, was replaced by the Université de Djibouti as the sole establishment for higher education.

Public Holidays

2008: 1 January (New Year's Day), 10 January*† (Muharram, Islamic New Year), 20 March* (Mouloud, Birth of the Prophet), 1 May (Workers' Day), 27 June (Independence Day), 1 October* (Id al-Fitr, end of Ramadan), 9 December* (Id al-Adha, Feast of the Sacrifice), 25 December (Christmas Day), 29 December*† (Muharram, Islamic New Year).

2009: 1 January (New Year's Day), 9 March* (Mouloud, Birth of the Prophet), 1 May (Workers' Day), 27 June (Independence Day), 20 September* (Id al-Fitr, end of Ramadan), 27 November* (Id al-Adha, Feast of the Sacrifice), 18 December* (Muharram, Islamic New Year), 25 December (Christmas Day).

* These holidays are dependent on the Islamic lunar calendar and may vary by one or two days from the dates given.

† This festival occurs twice (marking the start of the Islamic years AH 1429 and 1430) within the same Gregorian year.

Weights and Measures

The metric system is in force.

Statistical Survey

Source (unless otherwise stated): Ministère de l'Economie, des Finances et de la Planification, chargé de la Privatisation, Cité Ministérielle, BP 13, Djibouti; tel. 353331; fax 356501; e-mail cabmefpp@intnet.dj; internet www.ministere-finances.dj.

AREA AND POPULATION

Area: 23,200 sq km (8,958 sq miles).

Population: 220,000 (1976 estimate), including Afars 70,000, Issas and other Somalis 80,000, Arabs 12,000, Europeans 15,000, other foreigners 40,000; 519,900 (including refugees and resident foreigners) at 31 December 1990 (official estimate); 833,000 (UN estimate) at mid-2007 (Source: UN, *World Population Prospects: The 2006 Revision*).

Density (mid-2007): 35.9 per sq km.

Principal Towns (estimated population in 1991): Djibouti (capital) 329,337; Ali-Sabieh 16,423; Tadjourah 7,309; Obock 6,476; Dikhil 20,480 (Source: Thomas Brinkhoff, *City Population*, internet www.citypopulation.de. *Mid-2005* (incl. suburbs, UN estimate): Djibouti 555,000 (Source: UN, *World Urbanization Prospects: The 2005 Revision*).

Births, Marriages and Deaths (2000–05, UN estimates): Average annual birth rate 31.4 per 1,000; Average annual death rate 12.0 per 1,000 (Source: UN, *World Population Prospects: The 2006 Revision*). *1999* (capital district only): Births 7,898; Marriages 3,808.

Expectation of Life (years at birth, WHO estimates): 54.5 (males 53.3; females 55.5) in 2005. Source: WHO, *World Health Statistics*.

Economically Active Population (estimates, '000 persons, 1991): Agriculture, etc. 212; Industries 31; Services 39; *Total* 282 (males 167, females 115) (Source: UN Economic Commission for Africa, *African Statistical Yearbook*). *Mid-2005* ('000 persons, estimates): Agriculture, etc. 309; Total labour force 404 (Source: FAO).

HEALTH AND WELFARE

Key Indicators

Total Fertility Rate (children per woman, 2005): 4.8.

Under-5 Mortality Rate (per 1,000 live births, 2005): 133.

HIV/AIDS (% of persons aged 15–49, 2005): 3.10.

Physicians (per 1,000 head, 2004): 0.18.

Hospital Beds (per 1,000 head, 2000): 1.61.

Health Expenditure (2004): US $ per head (PPP): 87.2.

Health Expenditure (2004): % of GDP: 6.3.

Health Expenditure (2004): public (% of total): 69.2.

Access to Water (% of persons, 2004): 73.

Access to Sanitation (% of persons, 2004): 82.

Human Development Index (2005): ranking: 149.

Human Development Index (2005): index: 0.516.

For sources and definitions, see explanatory note on p. vi.

AGRICULTURE, ETC.

Principal Crops ('000 metric tons, 2006, FAO estimates): Tomatoes 1.3; Other vegetables 24.0 (incl. melons); Lemons and limes 1.8; Other fruit 1.6.

Livestock ('000 head, 2006, FAO estimates): Cattle 297; Sheep 466; Goats 512; Asses 9; Camels 69.

Livestock Products ('000 metric tons, 2006, FAO estimates): Cattle meat 6.1; Sheep meat 2.2; Goat meat 2.4; Camel meat 0.7; Cows' milk 8.1; Camels' milk 5.9.

Fishing (metric tons, live weight, 2005, FAO estimates): Groupers 60; Snappers and jobfishes 60; Porgies and seabreams 30; Barracudas 15; Carangids 15; Seerfishes 50; Other tuna-like fishes 15; Total catch (incl. others) 260.

Source: FAO.

INDUSTRY

Electric Energy (million kWh): 266.6 in 2004; 303.0 in 2005; 306.0 in 2006. Source: Banque Centrale de Djibouti, *Rapport Annuel 2006*.

FINANCE

Currency and Exchange Rates: 100 centimes = 1 Djibouti franc. *Sterling, Dollar and Euro Equivalents* (30 November 2007): £1 sterling = 367.24 Djibouti francs; US $1 = 177.72 Djibouti francs; €1 = 262.33 Djibouti francs; 1,000 Djibouti francs = £2.72 = $5.63 = €3.81. *Exchange Rate:* Fixed at US $1 = 177.721 Djibouti francs since February 1973.

Budget (million Djibouti francs, 2006): *Revenue:* Tax revenue 32,553 (Direct taxes 13,190, Indirect taxes 13,250, Registration fees, etc. 6,113); Other revenue (incl. property sales) 10,158; Total 42,711 (excl. official grants 5,277). *Expenditure:* Current expenditure 40,816; Capital expenditure 10,302 (Foreign-financed 5,774); Total 51,118. Source: Banque Centrale de Djibouti, *Rapport Annuel 2006*.

International Reserves (US $ million at 31 December 2006, excl. gold): IMF special drawing rights 0.82; Reserve position in IMF 1.65; Foreign exchange 117.85; Total 120.32. Source: IMF, *International Financial Statistics*.

Money Supply (million Djibouti francs at 31 December 2005): Currency outside banks 13,272; Demand deposits at commercial banks 34,456; Total money 47,728. Source: IMF, *International Financial Statistics*.

Cost of Living (Consumer Price Index; base: 2000 = 100): All items 107.5 in 2004; 111.3 in 2005; 114.6 in 2006. Source: African Development Bank.

Expenditure on the Gross Domestic Product (US $ million at current prices, 2006): Government final consumption expenditure 193.29; Private final consumption expenditure 472.38; Gross capital formation 247.59; *Total domestic expenditure* 913.26; Exports of goods and services 276.48; *Less* Imports of goods and services 428.96; *GDP in purchasers' values* 760.77. Source: African Development Bank.

Gross Domestic Product by Economic Activity (million Djibouti francs at current factor cost, 2006): Agriculture, hunting, forestry and fishing 4,367; Manufacturing (incl. mining) 3,374; Electricity and water 7,006; Construction and public works 9,960; Trade and tourism 23,024; Transport and communications 32,248; Finance and insurance 16,119; Public administration 22,967; Other services 2,266; *GDP at factor cost* 121,331; Indirect taxes, *less* subsidies 15,472; *GDP in purchasers' values* 136,803. Source: Banque Centrale de Djibouti, *Rapport Annuel 2006*.

Balance of Payments (US $ million, 2006): Exports of goods f.o.b. 55.2; Imports of goods f.o.b. –335.7; *Trade balance* –280.5; Exports of services 257.1; Imports of services –95.6; *Balance on goods and* *services* –119.0; Other income received 34.9; Other income paid –11.8; *Balance on goods, services and income* –96.0; Current transfers received 3.7; Current transfers paid –6.8; Current balance –99.1; Capital account (net) 16.8; Direct investment from abroad 108.3; Other investment assets –62.0; Other investment liabilities 18.8; Net errors and omissions –57.8; *Overall balance* –75.0. Source: IMF, *International Financial Statistics*.

EXTERNAL TRADE

Principal Commodities: *Imports c.i.f.* (million Djibouti francs, 1999): Food and beverages 6,796; Qat 3,300; Petroleum products 2,944; Chemical products 1,620; Clothing and footwear 1,251; Metals and metal products 1,355; Machinery and electrical appliances 3,399; Vehicles and transport equipment 2,781; Total (incl. others) 27,131. *Exports f.o.b.* (distribution by SITC, US $ '000, 1992): Food and live animals 3,292 (Rice 726, Coffee and coffee substitutes 1,773); Crude materials (inedible) except fuels 867; Basic manufactures 771; Machinery and transport equipment 1,260 (Road vehicles and parts 585, Other transport equipment 501); Commodities not classified according to kind 9,481; Total (incl. others) 15,919. Source: UN, *International Trade Statistics Yearbook*.

Principal Trading Partners: *Imports c.i.f.* (percentage of total trade, 2002): Ethiopia 11.1; France 7.6; Italy 3.1; Japan 2.5; Netherlands 4.4; Saudi Arabia 15.8; Singapore 2.2; United Kingdom 3.3; Yemen 1.3. *Exports f.o.b.* (percentage of total trade, 2002): Ethiopia 4.4; Somalia 57.2; Yemen 24.5. Source: IMF, *Djibouti: Statistical Appendix* (March 2004).

TRANSPORT

Railways (traffic, 2002): Passengers ('000) 570; Freight ton-km (million) 201. Source: IMF, *Djibouti: Statistical Appendix* (March 2004).

Road Traffic (estimates, motor vehicles in use, 1996): Passenger cars 9,200; Lorries and vans 2,040. Source: International Road Federation, *World Road Statistics*.

Shipping: *Merchant Fleet* (registered at 31 December 2006): 15 vessels (displacement 5,160 grt) (Source: Lloyd's Register-Fairplay, *World Fleet Statistics*). *Freight Traffic* ('000 metric tons, 2006): Goods 3,838; Fuels 1,627 (Source: Banque Centrale de Djibouti, *Rapport Annuel 2006*).

Civil Aviation (international traffic, 2006): *Passengers:* 17,957; *Freight:* 9,987 metric tons. Source: Banque Centrale de Djibouti, *Rapport Annuel 2006*.

TOURISM

Tourist Arrivals ('000): 20 in 1996; 20 in 1997; 20 in 1998.

Receipts from Tourism (US $ million): 6.9 in 2003; 6.8 in 2004; 7.1 in 2005.

Source: World Tourism Organization.

COMMUNICATIONS MEDIA

Newspapers (1995): 1 non-daily (estimated circulation 1,000).

Periodicals (1989): 7 (estimated combined circulation 6,000).

Radio Receivers (1997): 52,000 in use.

Television Receivers (2000): 45,000 in use.

Telephones (2006): 10,800 main lines in use.

Facsimile Machines (1999): 69 in use.

Mobile Cellular Telephones (2006): 44,100 subscribers.

Personal Computers (2005): 21,000 in use.

Internet Users (2006): 11,000.

Sources: mainly UNESCO, *Statistical Yearbook*; UN, *Statistical Yearbook*; International Telecommunication Union.

EDUCATION

Pre-primary (2004/05): 2 schools; 350 pupils; 32 teaching staff.

Primary (2005/06): 82 schools; 46,523 pupils.

Secondary (2005/06): First cycle 17,180 pupils; Second cycle 6,767 pupils.

Higher (2004/05): 1,746 students; 96 teaching staff.

Sources: UNESCO, *Statistical Yearbook*; Ministère de l'éducation nationale et de l'enseignement supérieur; Université de Djibouti.

Adult Literacy Rate (UNESCO estimate): 65.5% in 2003. Source: UN Development Programme, *Human Development Report*.

Directory

The Constitution

A new Constitution was approved by national referendum on 4 September 1992 and entered into force on 15 September.

The Constitution of Djibouti guarantees the basic rights and freedoms of citizens; the functions of the principal organs of state are delineated therein.

The President of the Republic, who is Head of State and Head of Government, is directly elected, by universal adult suffrage, for a period of six years, renewable only once. The President nominates the Prime Minister and, following consultation with the latter, appoints the Council of Ministers. The legislature is the 65-member Assemblée nationale, which is elected, also by direct universal suffrage, for a period of five years.

The 1992 Constitution provided for the establishment of a maximum of four political parties. On 4 September 2002, however, this limit on the number of political parties was revoked.

The Government

HEAD OF STATE

President and Commander-in-Chief of the Armed Forces: ISMAEL OMAR GELLEH (inaugurated 7 May 1999, re-elected 8 April 2005).

COUNCIL OF MINISTERS
(March 2008)

Prime Minister: DILEITA MOHAMED DILEITA.

Minister of Justice, Muslim and Penal Affairs, in charge of Human Rights: MOHAMED BARKAT ABDILLAHI.

Minister of the Interior and Decentralization: YACIN ELMI BOUH.

Minister of Defence: OUGOUREH KIFLEH AHMED.

Minister of Foreign Affairs and International Co-operation: MAHAMOUD ALI YOUSSOUF.

Minister of the Economy, Finance and Planning, in charge of Privatization: ALI FARAH ASSOWEH.

Minister of Trade and Industry: RIFKI ABDULKADER BAMAKHRAMA.

Minister of Agriculture, Livestock and Fishing: ABDULKADER KAMIL MOHAMED.

Minister of Communication and Culture, in charge of Post and Telecommunications, and Government Spokesperson: ALI ABDI FARAH.

Minister of National and Higher Education: ABDI IBRAHIM ABSIEH.

Minister of Employment, Integration and Professional Training: MOUSSA AHMED HASSAN.

Minister of Energy and Natural Resources: MOUSSA BOUH ODOWA.

Minister of Equipment and Transport: ALI HASSAN BAHDON.

Minister of Health: ABDALLAH ABDILLAHI MIGUIL.

Minister of Presidential Affairs and Investment Promotion, in charge of Relations with Parliament: OSMAN AHMED MOUSSA.

Minister of Housing, Urban Planning and the Environment: ELMI OBSIEH WAISS.

Minister of Youth, Sports, Leisure and Tourism: HASNA BARKAT DAOUD.

Minister of the Promotion of Women, Family Well-being and Social Affairs: NIMO BOULHAN HOUSSEIN.

Minister of Muslim Affairs and Endowments: HAMOUD ABDI SOULTAN.

Minister-delegate to the Minister of Foreign Affairs in charge of International Co-operation: AHMED ALI SILAY.

Secretary of State in the Office of the Prime Minister, in charge of National Solidarity: MOHAMED AHMED AWALEH.

MINISTRIES

Office of the President: Djibouti; e-mail sggpr.intnet.dj; internet www.presidence.dj.
Office of the Prime Minister: BP 2086, Djibouti; tel. 351494; fax 355049.
Ministry of Agriculture, Livestock and Fishing: BP 453, Djibouti; tel. 351297.
Ministry of Communication and Culture: BP 32, 1 rue de Moscou, Djibouti; tel. 355672; fax 353957; e-mail mccpt@intnet.dj; internet www.mccpt.dj.
Ministry of Defence: BP 42, Djibouti; tel. 352034.
Ministry of the Economy, Finance and Planning: BP 13, Djibouti; tel. 353331; fax 356501; e-mail sg_mefpp@intnet.dj; internet www.ministere-finances.dj.
Ministry of Employment Integration and Professional training: Djibouti; tel. 351838; fax 357268; e-mail adetip@intnet.dj.
Ministry of Energy and Natural Resources: BP 175, Djibouti; tel. 350340.
Ministry of Equipment and Transport: Palais du Peuple, BP 2501, Djibouti; tel. 350990; fax 355975.
Ministry of Foreign Affairs and International Co-operation: blvd Cheik Osman, BP 1863, Djibouti; tel. 352471; fax 353049.
Ministry of Health: BP 296, Djibouti; tel. 353331; fax 356300.
Ministry of Housing, Urban Planning and the Environment: BP 11, Djibouti; tel. 350006; fax 351618.
Ministry of the Interior and Decentralization: BP 33, Djibouti; tel. 352542; fax 354862; internet www.elec.dj.
Ministry of Justice and Penal Affairs: BP 12, Djibouti; tel. 351506; fax 354012.
Ministry of of Muslim Affairs and Endowments: Djibouti.
Ministry of National and Higher Education: BP 16, Cité Ministérielle, Djibouti; tel. 350997; fax 354234; e-mail education.gov@intnet.dj; internet www.education.gov.dj.
Ministry of Presidential Affairs and Investment Promotion: Djibouti.
Ministry of the Promotion of Women, Family Well-being and Social Affairs: BP 458, Djibouti; tel. and fax 350439; e-mail minfemme@intnet.dj; internet www.ministere-femme.dj.
Ministry of Trade and Industry: BP 1846, Djibouti; tel. 351682.
Ministry of Youth, Sports, Leisure and Tourism: BP 2506, Djibouti; tel. 355886; fax 356830.

President and Legislature

PRESIDENT

At the presidential election held on 8 April 2005 the incumbent Ismael Omar Gelleh of the Rassemblement populaire pour le progrès secured 100% of the valid votes cast. Gelleh was the sole candidate at the election following the withdrawal, in March, from the contest of Mohamed Daoud Chehem, the representative of the Parti djiboutien pour la démocratie.

ASSEMBLÉE NATIONALE

Assemblée Nationale: BP 138, pl. Lagarde, Djibouti; tel. 350172; internet www.assemblee-nationale.dj.
Speaker: IDRISS ARNAOUD ALI.

Elections to the Assemblée nationale were held on 8 February 2008. The 65 seats were contested solely by candidates from the Union pour la majorité présidentielle (UMP) after opposition parties boycotted the ballot. According to official results, the UMP received 103,463 (94.1%) of the 109,999 votes cast; the remaining 6,536 votes were invalid. Voter turn-out was estimated at 72.6%.

Election Commission

Commission électorale nationale indépendante: Djibouti; f. 2002; President ADEN AHMED DOUALEH.

Political Organizations

On 4 September 2002, to coincide with the 10th anniversary of the approval of the Constitution, restrictions on the number of legally permitted political parties (hitherto four) were formally removed.

Union pour l'alternance democratique (UAD): 2 rue de Pékin, Héron, Djibouti; tel. 341822; fax 829999; e-mail realite_djibouti@yahoo.fr; coalition of major opposition parties; Pres. ISMAËL GUEDI HARED.

Alliance républicaine pour le développement (ARD): BP 1488, Marabout, Djibouti; tel. 250919; e-mail realite_djibouti@yahoo.fr; internet www.ard-djibouti.org; f. 2002; Leader AHMAD YOUSSOUF HOUMED; Sec.-Gen. KASSIM ALI DINI.

Mouvement pour le renouveau démocratique et le développement (MRD): BP 3570, ave Nasser, Djibouti; e-mail lerenouveau@mrd-djibouti.org; internet www.mrd-djibouti.org; f. 1992 as the Parti du renouveau démocratique; renamed as above in 2002; Pres. DAHER AHMED FARAH; Sec.-Gen. SOULEIMAN HASSAN FAIDAL.

Parti djiboutien pour le développement (PDD): BP 892, Djibouti; tel. 353243; f. 2002; Pres. MOHAMED DAOUD CHEHEM; Sec.-Gen. ABDILLAHI MOHAMED SALAH.

Union djiboutienne pour la démocratie et la justice (UDJ): Djibouti; Chair. ISMAËL GUEDI HARED.

Union pour la majorité présidentiel (UMP): Djibouti; internet www.ump.dj; coalition of major parties in support of Pres. Gelleh; Pres. DILEITA MOHAMED DILEITA.

Front pour la restauration de l'unité et de la démocratie (FRUD): Djibouti; tel. 250279; f. 1991 by merger of three militant Afar groups; advocates fair representation in govt for all ethnic groups; commenced armed insurgency in Nov. 1991; split into two factions in March 1994; the dissident group, which negotiated a settlement with the Govt, obtained legal recognition in March 1996 and recognizes the following leaders; Pres. ALI MOHAMED DAOUD; Sec.-Gen. OUGOUREH KIFLEH AHMED; a dissident group, FRUD-Renaissance (led by IBRAHIM CHEHEM DAOUD), was formed in 1996.

Parti national démocratique (PND): BP 10204, Djibouti; tel. 342194; f. 1992; Pres. ADEN ROBLEH AWALLEH.

Parti populaire social démocrate (PPSD): BP 434, Route Nelson Mandela, Djibouti; f. 2002; Pres. MOUMIN BAHDON FARAH; Sec.-Gen. HASSAN IDRISS AHMED.

Rassemblement populaire pour le progrès (RPP): Djibouti; e-mail rpp@intnet.dj; internet www.rpp.dj; f. 1979; sole legal party 1981–92; Pres. ISMAEL OMAR GELLEH; Sec.-Gen. IDRISS ARNAOUD ALI.

Union pour la réforme (UPR): Djibouti; f. 2006; Pres. IBRAHIM CHEHEM DAOUD.

The following organizations are proscribed:

Front des forces démocratiques (FFD): Leader OMAR ELMI KHAIREH.

Front de libération de la côte des Somalis (FLCS): f. 1963; Issa-supported; has operated from Somalia; Chair. ABDALLAH WABERI KHALIF; Vice-Chair. OMAR OSMAN RABEH.

Front uni de l'opposition djiboutienne (FUOD): f. 1992; based in Ethiopia; united front of internal opposition groups, incl. some fmr mems of the RPP; Leader MAHDI IBRAHIM A. GOD.

Mouvement de la jeunesse djiboutienne (MJD): Leader ABDOULKARIM ALI AMARKAK.

Mouvement pour l'unité et la démocratie (MUD): advocates political pluralism; Leader MOHAMED MOUSSA ALI 'TOURTOUR'.

Organisation des masses Afar (OMA): f. 1993 by mems of the fmr Mouvement populaire de libération; Chair. AHMED MALCO.

Parti centriste et des reformes démocratiques (PCRD): f. 1993 in Addis Ababa, Ethiopia, by a breakaway faction of the FRUD; seeks official registration as an opposition party; Chair. HASSAN ABDALLAH WATTA.

Parti populaire djiboutien (PPD): f. 1981; mainly Afar-supported; Leader MOUSSA AHMED IDRIS.

Union des démocrates djiboutiens (UDD): affiliated to the FUOD; Chair. MAHDI IBRAHIM AHMED.

Union démocratique pour le progrès (UDP): f. 1992; advocates democratic reforms; Leader FARAH WABERI.

Union des mouvements démocratiques (UMD): f. 1990 by merger of two militant external opposition groups; Pres. MOHAMED ADOYTA.

Diplomatic Representation

EMBASSIES IN DJIBOUTI

China, People's Republic: BP 2021, rue Addis Ababa, Lotissement Heron, Djibouti; tel. 352246; fax 354833; e-mail chinaemb_dj@mfa.gov.cn; Ambassador WANG XIAODU.

Egypt: BP 1989, Djibouti; tel. 351231; fax 356657; e-mail ambegypte2004@gawab.com; Ambassador AHMED ABDEL WAHED ZEIN.

DJIBOUTI

Eritrea: BP 1944, Djibouti; tel. 354961; fax 351831; Ambassador MOHAMED SAÏD MANTAY.

Ethiopia: rue Clochette, BP 230, Djibouti; tel. 350718; fax 354803; e-mail ethemb@intnet.dj; Ambassador SHEMSUDIN AHMED.

France: 45 blvd du Maréchal Foch, BP 2039, Djibouti; tel. 350963; fax 350272; e-mail ambfrdj@intnet.dj; internet www.ambafrance-dj.org; Ambassador DOMINIQUE DECHERF.

Libya: BP 2073, Djibouti; tel. 350202; Ambassador KAMEL AL-HADI ALMARASH.

Oman: Djibouti; tel. 350852; Ambassador SAOUD SALEM HASSAN AL-ANSI.

Qatar: Ambassador HADI NASSER MANSOUR AL-HAJIRI.

Russia: BP 1913, Plateau du Marabout, Djibouti; tel. 350740; fax 355990; e-mail russiaemb@intnet.dj; Ambassador MIKHAIL TSVIGOUN.

Saudi Arabia: BP 1921, Djibouti; tel. 351645; fax 352284; Ambassador ABDULAZIZ MUHAMMAD AL-EIFAN.

Somalia: BP 549, Djibouti; tel. 353521; Ambassador MUSE HIRSI FAHIYE.

Sudan: BP 4259, Djibouti; tel. 356404; fax 356662; Ambassador OSAMA SALAHUDDIN.

United Arab Emirates: Djibouti; Ambassador SAÏD BEN HAMDAM BEN MUHAMMAD AN-NAGHI.

USA: Villa Plateau du Serpent, blvd du Maréchal Joffre, BP 185, Djibouti; tel. 353995; fax 353940; e-mail amembadm@bow.intnet.dj; internet djibouti.usembassy.gov; Ambassador W. STUART SYMINGTON.

Yemen: BP 194, Djibouti; tel. 352975; Ambassador ABDOURAB ALI AS-SALAFI.

Judicial System

The Supreme Court was established in 1979. There is a high court of appeal and a court of first instance in Djibouti; each of the five administrative districts has a 'tribunal coutumier'.

President of the Court of Appeal: KADIDJA ABEBA.

Religion

ISLAM

Almost the entire population are Muslims.

Qadi of Djibouti: MOGUE HASSAN DIRIR, BP 168, Djibouti; tel. 352669.

Haut Conseil Islamique (High Islamic Council): Djibouti; f. 2004; 7 mems; Pres. CHEIKH MOGUEH DIRIR SAMATAR; Sec.-Gen. ALI MOUSSA OKIEH.

CHRISTIANITY

The Roman Catholic Church

Djibouti comprises a single diocese, directly responsible to the Holy See. There were an estimated 7,000 adherents in the country at 31 December 2005.

Bishop of Djibouti: GIORGIO BERTIN, Evêché, blvd de la République, BP 94, Djibouti; tel. and fax 350140; e-mail evechcat@intnet.dj.

The Anglican Communion

Within the Episcopal Church in Jerusalem and the Middle East, Djibouti lies within the jurisdiction of the Bishop in Egypt.

Other Christian Churches

Eglise Protestante: blvd de la République, BP 416, Djibouti; tel. 351820; fax 350706; e-mail eped@intnet.dj; internet membres.lycos.fr/missiondjibouti; f. 1957; Pastor NATHALIE PAQUEREAU.

Greek Orthodox Church: blvd de la République, Djibouti; tel. 351325; c. 350 adherents; Archimandrite STAVROS GEORGANAS.

The Ethiopian Orthodox Church is also active in Djibouti.

The Press

L'Atout: Palais du peuple, Djibouti; twice a year; publ. by the Centre National de la Promotion Culturelle et Artistique.

Carrefour Africain: BP 393, Djibouti; fax 354916; fortnightly; publ. by the Roman Catholic mission; circ. 500.

La Nation de Djibouti: pl. du 27 juin, BP 32, Djibouti; tel. 352201; fax 353937; internet www.lanation.dj; e-mail lanation@intnet.dj; three times a week; Dir ABDOULRASHID IDRISS; circ. 4,300.

Le Progrès: Djibouti; weekly; publ. by the RPP; Publr ALI MOHAMED HUMAD.

Le Renouveau: BP 3570, ave Nasser, Djibouti; tel. 351474; weekly; independent; publ. by the MRD; Editor-in-Chief DAHER AHMED FARAH.

La République: Djibouti; weekly; independent; Editor-in-Chief AMIR ADAWEH.

Revue de l'ISERT: BP 486, Djibouti; tel. 352795; twice a year; publ. by the Institut Supérieur d'Etudes et de Recherches Scientifiques et Techniques (ISERT).

Le Temps: Djibouti; opposition newspaper; Owners MOUSSA AHMED IDRIS, ALI MEIDAL WAIS.

NEWS AGENCY

Agence Djiboutienne d'Information (ADI): 1 rue de Moscou, BP 32, Djibouti; tel. 354013; fax 354037; e-mail adi@intent.dj; internet www.adi.dj; f. 1978.

Broadcasting and Communications

TELECOMMUNICATIONS

Djibouti Télécom: 3 blvd G. Pompidou, BP 2105, Djibouti; tel. 352777; fax 359200; e-mail adjib@intnet.dj; internet www.adjib.dj; f. 1999 to replace Société des Télécommunications Internationales; 100% state-owned; Dir-Gen. ABDIRAHMAN M. HASSAN.

BROADCASTING

Radio and Television

Djibnet: BP 1409, Djibouti; tel. 354288; e-mail webmaster@djibnet.com; internet www.djibnet.com.

Radiodiffusion-Télévision de Djibouti (RTD): BP 97, 1 ave St Laurent du Var, Djibouti; tel. 352294; fax 356502; e-mail rtd@intnet.dj; internet www.rtd.dj; f. 1967; state-controlled; programmes in French, Afar, Somali and Arabic; 17 hours radio and 5 hours television daily; Dir-Gen. (Radio) ABDI ATTEYEH ABDI; Dir-Gen. (Television) MOHAMED DJAMA ADEN.

Telesat Djibouti: Route de l'Aéroport, BP 3760, Djibouti; tel. 353457.

Finance

(cap. = capital; res = reserves; dep. = deposits; m. = million; brs = branches; amounts in Djibouti francs)

BANKING

Central Bank

Banque Centrale de Djibouti: BP 2118, ave St Laurent du Var, Djibouti; tel. 352751; fax 356288; e-mail bndj@intnet.dj; internet www.banque-centrale.dj; f. 1977 as Banque Nationale de Djibouti; present name adopted 2002; bank of issue; cap. and res 6,056m. (Feb. 2005); Gov. DJAMA MAHAMOUD HAID; Gen. Man. AHMED OSMAN.

Commercial Banks

Banque pour le Commerce et l'Industrie—Mer Rouge (BCI—MR): pl. Lagarde, BP 2122, Djibouti; tel. 350857; fax 354260; e-mail djibouti.bddi.bcimr@africa.bnpparibas.com; f. 1977; 51% owned by Banque Nationale de Paris Intercontinentale; cap. 2,092.5m., res 209.3m., dep. 46,389.2m. (Dec. 2004); Pres. JEAN-JACQUES SANTINI; CEO FRANÇOIS DU PEUTY; 6 brs.

Banque Indosuez—Mer Rouge (BIS—MR): 10 pl. Lagarde, BP 88, Djibouti; tel. 353016; fax 351638; e-mail secretariat@bimr-banque.com; f. 1908 as Banque de l'Indochine; present name adopted 1977; owned by Crédit Agricole, France; cap. 1,500.0m., res 526.7m., dep. 43,322.0m. (Dec. 2006); Chair. and CEO LUC BEISO.

Investment Bank of Africa: Djibouti; f. 2000; subsidiary of AFH Holding (Luxembourg); cap. 300m.; CEO ILIA KARAS.

Development Bank

Banque de Développement de Djibouti: angle ave Georges Clemenceau et rue Pierre Curie, BP 520, Djibouti; tel. 353391; fax 355022; f. 1983; 39.2% govt-owned; cap. and res 1,233m., total assets 3,081m. (Dec. 1997); Dir-Gen. ABDOURAHMAN ISMAEL GELLEH.

Banking Association

Association Professionnelle des Banques: c/o Banque pour le Commerce et l'Industrie—Mer Rouge, pl. Lagarde, BP 2122, Djibouti; tel. 350857; fax 354260; Pres. MOHAMED ADEN.

INSURANCE

Les Assureurs de la Mer Rouge et du Golfe Arabe (AMERGA): 8 rue Marchand, BP 2653, Djibouti; tel. 352510; fax 355623; e-mail direction.m@amerga.com; internet www.amerga.com; f. 2000; Dirs THIERRY MARILL, LUC MARILL, ABDOURAHMAN BARKAT ABDILLAHI, MOHAMED ADEN ABOUBAKER.

Ethiopian Insurance Corpn: rue de Marseille, BP 2047, Djibouti; tel. 352306.

GXA Assurances: rue Marchand, BP 200, Djibouti; tel. 353636; fax 353056; e-mail gxa@intnet.dj; Country Man. CHRISTIAN BOUCHER.

Trade and Industry

CHAMBER OF COMMERCE

Chambre de Commerce de Djibouti: BP 84, pl. Lagarde, Djibouti; tel. 351070; fax 350096; e-mail ccd@intnet.dj; f. 1906; 24 mems, 12 assoc. mems; Pres. SAÏD OMAR MOUSSA; First Vice-Pres. ABDOURAHMAN MAHAMOUD BOREH.

TRADE ASSOCIATION

Office National d'Approvisionnement et de Commercialisation (ONAC): BP 79, Djibouti; tel. 350327; fax 356701; Chair. MOHAMED ABDOULKADER.

UTILITIES

Electricity

Electricité de Djibouti (EdD): blvd de la République, BP 175, Djibouti; tel. 352851; fax 354396; e-mail clientele@edd.dj; internet www.edd.dj; Dir-Gen. DJAMA ALI GELLEH.

Water

Office National des Eaux de Djibouti (ONED): blvd de la République, BP 1914, Djibouti; tel. 351159; fax 354423.

Société des Eaux de Tadjourah: c/o Ministry of Trade and Industry, BP 1846, Djibouti; tel. 351682.

TRADE UNIONS

Union Djiboutienne du Travail: rue Pierre Pascal, BP 2767, Djibouti; tel. 823979; fax 355084; e-mail udt_djibouti@yahoo.fr; f. 1992; confed. of 21 trade unions; Chair. HASSAN CHER HARED; Sec.-Gen. ADEN MOHAMED ABDOU.

Union Générale des Travailleurs Djiboutiens (UGTD): Sec.-Gen. ABDO SIKIEH.

Transport

RAILWAYS

Chemin de Fer Djibouti–Ethiopien (CDE): BP 2116, Djibouti; tel. 350280; fax 351256; f. 1909; adopted present name in 1981; jtly owned by govts of Djibouti and Ethiopia; 781 km of track (121 km in Djibouti) linking Djibouti with Addis Ababa; Pres. ISMAIL IBRAHIM HOUMED.

ROADS

In 1996 there were an estimated 2,890 km of roads, comprising 1,090 km of main roads and 1,800 km of regional roads; some 12.6% of the roads were paved. Of the remainder, 1,000 km are serviceable throughout the year, the rest only during the dry season. About one-half of the roads are usable only by heavy vehicles. In 1981 the 40-km Grand Bara road was opened, linking the capital with the south. In 1986 the Djibouti–Tadjoura road, the construction of which was financed by Saudi Arabia, was opened, linking the capital with the north. In 1996 the Islamic Development Bank granted Djibouti a loan of US $3.6m. to finance road construction projects. In May 2004 the European Development Fund approved a $38.4m. road construction project between Djibouti and Addis Ababa, and in October the Kuwait Fund for Arabic Economic Development approved a $20m. loan to build a road between Tadjourah and Obock.

SHIPPING

Djibouti, which was established as a free port in 1981, handled 4,847,200 metric tons of freight in 2004.

Djibouti Maritime Management Investment Company (DMMI): Djibouti; f. 2004 to manage Djibouti's fishing port.

Port Autonome International de Djibouti: BP 2107, Djibouti; tel. 351031; fax 356187; e-mail david.hawker@port.dj; managed by Dubai Ports World, UAE since 2000; Gen. Man. DAVID HAWKER.

Maritime and Transit Services Enterprise: rue de Marseille, BP 680, Djibouti; tel. 353204; fax 354149; e-mail mtsdjib@bowintnet.dj.

Principal Shipping Agents

Almis Shipping Line & Transport Co: BP 85, Djibouti; tel. 356998; fax 356996; Man. Dir MOHAMED NOOR.

Cie Maritime et de Manutention de Djibouti (COMAD): ave des Messageries Maritimes, BP 89, Djibouti; tel. 351028; fax 350466; e-mail hettam@intnet.dj; f. 1990; stevedoring; Man. Dir ALI A. HETTAM.

Global Logistics Services Djibouti: rue Clemenceau, POB 3239, Djibouti; tel. 839000; fax 352283; e-mail gls.djibouti@gls-logistics.tk; shipping, clearing and freight-forwarding agent; Gen. Man. MOHAMED A. ELMI.

Global Shipping Services (GSS): POB 2666, Djibouti; tel. 251302; fax 353395; e-mail gss@intnet.dj; shipping agents; Man. Dir ALI A. HETTAM.

Inchcape Shipping Services & Co (Djibouti) SA: 9–11 rue de Genève, BP 81, Djibouti; tel. 353844; fax 353294; internet www.iss-shipping.com; f. 1942; Dir-Gen. AHMED OSMAN GELLEH.

International Transit Services: POB 1177, Djibouti; tel. 251155; fax 353258; e-mail its02@intnet.dj; Man. Dir ROBLEH MOHAMED.

J. J. Kothari & Co Ltd: rue d'Athens, BP 171, Djibouti; tel. 350219; fax 351778; e-mail kothari@intnet.dj; shipping agents; also ship managers, stevedores, freight forwarders; Dirs S. J. KOTHARI, NALIN KOTHARI.

Société Djiboutienne de Trafic Maritime (SDTM): blvd Cheik Osman, BP 640, Djibouti; tel. 352351; fax 351103.

Société Maritime L. Savon et Ries: blvd Cheik Osman, BP 2125, Djibouti; tel. 352351; fax 351103; e-mail smsr@intnet.dj; Dir FRANÇOIS CAPIOMONT; Gen. Man. JEAN-PHILIPPE DELARUE.

CIVIL AVIATION

The international airport is at Ambouli, 6 km from Djibouti. There are six other airports providing domestic services.

Air Djibouti (Red Sea Airlines): BP 499, rue Marchand, Djibouti; tel. 356723; fax 356734; f. 1971; fmrly govt-owned, transferred to private ownership in 1997; internal flights and services to destinations in Africa, the Middle East and Europe; Chair. SAÀD BEN MOUSSA AL-JANAIBI.

Daallo Airlines: BP 2565, Djibouti; tel. 340672; e-mail daallo@intnet.dj; f. 1992; operates services to Somalia, Saudi Arabia, the United Arab Emirates, France and the Netherlands; Man. Dir MOHAMED IBRAHIM YASSIN.

Djibouti Airlines (Puntavia Airline de Djibouti): BP 2240, pl. Lagarde, Djibouti; tel. 351006; fax 352429; e-mail djibouti-airlines@intnet.dj; internet www.djiboutiairlines.com; f. 1996; scheduled and charter regional and domestic flights; Man. Dir Capt. MOUSSA RAYALEH WABERI.

Tourism

Djibouti offers desert scenery in its interior and watersport facilities on its coast. A casino operates in the capital. There were about 20,000 tourist arrivals in 1998. Receipts from tourism totalled US $7.1m. in 2005

Office National du Tourisme de Djibouti (ONTD): pl. du 27 juin, BP 1938, Djibouti; tel. 353790; fax 356322; e-mail onta@intnet.dj; internet www.office-tourisme.dj; Dir MOHAMED ABDILLAHI WAIS.

DOMINICA

Introductory Survey

Location, Climate, Language, Religion, Flag, Capital

The Commonwealth of Dominica is situated in the Windward Islands group of the West Indies, lying between Guadeloupe, to the north, and Martinique, to the south. The climate is tropical, though tempered by sea winds, which sometimes reach hurricane force, especially from July to September. The average temperature is about 27°C (80°F), with little seasonal variation. Rainfall is heavy, especially in the mountainous areas, where the annual average is 6,350 mm (250 ins), compared with 1,800 mm (70 ins) along the coast. English is the official language, but a local French patois, or Creole, is widely spoken. In parts of the north-east an English dialect, known as Cocoy, is spoken by the descendants of Antiguan settlers. There is a small community of Carib Indians on the east coast. Almost all of the inhabitants profess Christianity, and about 66% are Roman Catholics. The national flag (proportions 1 by 2) has a green field, with equal stripes of yellow, white and black forming an upright cross, on the centre of which is superimposed a red disc containing a parrot surrounded by 10 five-pointed green stars (one for each of the island's parishes). The capital is Roseau.

Recent History

Dominica was first settled by Arawaks and then Caribs. Control of the island was fiercely contested by the Caribs, British and French during the 17th and 18th centuries. The British eventually prevailed and Dominica formed part of the Leeward Islands federation until 1939. In 1940 it was transferred to the Windward Islands and remained attached to that group until the federal arrangement was ended in December 1959. Under a new Constitution, effective from January 1960, Dominica (like each other member of the group) achieved a separate status, with its own Administrator and an enlarged Legislative Council.

At the January 1961 elections to the Legislative Council, the ruling Dominica United People's Party was defeated by the Dominica Labour Party (DLP), formed from the People's National Movement and other groups. Edward LeBlanc, leader of the DLP, became Chief Minister. In March 1967 Dominica became one of the West Indies Associated States, gaining full autonomy in internal affairs, with the United Kingdom retaining responsibility for defence and foreign relations. The House of Assembly replaced the Legislative Council, the Administrator became Governor and the Chief Minister was restyled Premier. At elections to the House in October 1970, LeBlanc was returned to power as Premier.

In July 1974 LeBlanc retired, and was replaced as DLP leader and Premier by Patrick John, formerly Deputy Premier and Minister of Finance. At elections to the enlarged House of Assembly in March 1975 the DLP was returned to power. Following a decision in 1975 by the Associated States to seek independence separately, Dominica became an independent republic within the Commonwealth on 3 November 1978. John became Prime Minister, and Frederick Degazon, formerly Speaker of the House of Assembly, was eventually elected President.

In May 1979 two people were killed by the Defence Force at a demonstration against the Government's attempts to introduce legislation that would restrict the freedom of trade unions and the press. The deaths fuelled increasing popular opposition to the Government, and a pressure group, the Committee for National Salvation (CNS), was formed to campaign for John's resignation. Government opponents organized a general strike which lasted 25 days, with John relinquishing power only after all his cabinet ministers had resigned and President Degazon had gone into hiding abroad (there was a succession of Acting Presidents; Degazon finally resigned in February 1980). Oliver Seraphin, the candidate proposed by the CNS, was elected Prime Minister, and an interim Government was formed to prepare for a general election after six months.

A general election was eventually held in July 1980, when the Dominica Freedom Party (DFP) achieved a convincing victory, winning 17 of the 21 elective seats in the House of Assembly. Eugenia Charles, the party's leader, became the Caribbean's first female Prime Minister. Both John, who contested the election as leader of the DLP, and Seraphin, who stood as leader of the newly formed Democratic Labour Party (DEMLAB), lost their seats. The DLP and DEMLAB had both suffered from major political scandals prior to the election.

Fears for the island's security dominated 1981. In January the Government disarmed the Defence Force (which was officially disbanded in April), following reports that weapons were being traded for marijuana. Against a background of increasing violence and the declaration of a state of emergency, however, there were two coup attempts involving former Defence Force members. John, the former Prime Minister, was also implicated and imprisoned. In June 1982 John and his fellow prisoners were tried and acquitted, but the Government secured a retrial in October 1985. John and the former Deputy Commander of the Defence Force each received a prison sentence of 12 years. In 1986 the former Commander of the Defence Force was hanged for the murder of a police officer during the second coup attempt. The death sentences on five other soldiers were commuted to life imprisonment.

After his release in June 1982, John attempted to form a new left-wing coalition party. By 1985 the DLP, DEMLAB, the United Dominica Labour Party and the Dominica Liberation Movement had united to form a left-wing grouping, known as the Labour Party of Dominica (LPD). The new leader, however, was Michael Douglas, a former Minister of Finance. At a general election in July 1985 the DFP was returned to power, winning 15 of the 21 elective seats in the House of Assembly. The opposition LPD won five seats, with the remaining seat being won by Roosevelt (Rosie) Douglas, the brother of the LPD leader, whose candidature was not officially endorsed by the LPD. Following the election, the LPD began an 18-month boycott of the House, in protest at the Government's decision to curtail live broadcasts of parliamentary proceedings. By July 1987 the DFP's strength in the House had increased to 17 seats, with four seats still being held by the LPD.

Dissatisfaction at continued government austerity measures was offset by the success of the land reform programme. Since independence, the Government had acquired nearly all the large estates, often in an attempt to forestall violence. In 1986 the first of the estates was divided, and tenure granted to the former workers. Despite the success of this programme, the opposition LPD and the Dominica United Workers' Party (UWP—formed in 1988) bitterly denounced many other government policies and criticized Charles's style of leadership. The two opposition parties failed to agree on the formation of an electoral alliance, however, and the DFP was returned for a third term in government at a general election in May 1990. The DFP won a total of 11 seats, the UWP became the official opposition (with six seats) and the LPD won four seats.

A programme, introduced in 1991, granting Dominican citizenship to foreigners in return for a minimum investment of US $35,000 in the country caused considerable controversy. The UWP expressed opposition to the policy, and in 1992 a pressure group, 'Concerned Citizens', organized protests demanding that the programme be modified. In response to such pressure, the Government announced in July that the minimum investment was to be increased substantially, the number of applications was to be limited to 800 and restrictions were to be placed on the investors' right to vote in Dominica. By early 1995 some 615 people (mainly Taiwanese) had been granted citizenship under the scheme, and about US $7.1m. had been invested in the country.

At a general election in June 1995 the DFP's 15-year tenure was finally ended as the UWP secured a narrow victory. The leader of the UWP, Edison James, was subsequently appointed as Prime Minister, and the LPD and DFP leaders agreed to occupy the position of Leader of the Opposition in alternate years, commencing with Brian Alleyne, Eugenia Charles's successor. In July a legal dispute arose concerning the eligibility to serve in the House of Assembly of one of the DFP's members, Charles Savarin, owing to a potential conflict of interests. As a result of the dispute, the position of Leader of the Opposition was transferred to the LPD leader, Rosie Douglas. In April 1996, however, Savarin was elected leader of the DFP following Alleyne's resignation.

In December 1997 the Government's citizenship programme again provoked controversy. It was alleged that, under the scheme, passports were being sold by agents for between US $15,000 and $20,000, and claimed that about 400 people had acquired citizenship in 1997. The opposition LPD accused the Government of undermining the credibility of Dominican citizenship, and in August 1998 Rosie Douglas demanded an inquiry into the programme, following an administrative error that had allowed an Australian, who was sought by investigators in connection with a business collapse, to acquire citizenship. In late 1999 it was announced that the Dominican Government had stopped granting citizenship to Russians, following reports that up to 300 Russians had paid $50,000 each to obtain a Dominican passport. In addition, there were complaints from the US Government that the trade in passports had increased 'suspicions of money-laundering' in Dominica.

A general election was held on 31 January 2000. The UWP suffered a narrow electoral defeat, while the LPD was returned to power after two decades in opposition, winning 10 of the 21 elective seats in the House of Assembly and receiving 43% of total votes cast. The UWP secured nine seats (with 43% of the votes), and the DFP (which contested the election in alliance with the LPD) won two. Douglas was named as Prime Minister and formed a coalition Government with the DFP (which was allocated two ministerial portfolios). On taking office, the new Government immediately suspended the controversial citizenship programme. However, following a review, in April 2000 the Government announced that the programme should be resumed, claiming that changes had been made to ensure that passports would not be granted to those with a criminal record. The programme was relaunched in June 2002, with a fee of US $100,000 for individual applicants.

On 1 October 2000 Prime Minister Douglas died suddenly of a heart attack. Two days later, following a vote in the House of Assembly, Pierre Charles, previously the Minister of Communications and Works, was sworn in as premier. In March 2001 Charles was confirmed as DLP leader at the party's annual conference. In November Charles placed Ambrose George, the Minister of Finance, on two weeks' leave of absence following the arrest on money-laundering charges of a businessman with whom he was travelling in Puerto Rico. Upon his return to government George was stripped of the finance portfolio, which passed to Charles, and given the post of Minister of Industry, Physical Planning and Enterprise Development.

Meanwhile, in December 2000 legislation was approved in the House of Assembly making the crime of money-laundering punishable by up to seven years' imprisonment and a fine of EC $1m. At the same time, the Government introduced stricter regulations governing its 'offshore' banking sector, following Dominica's inclusion on a blacklist published by the Financial Action Task Force earlier in the year. Dominica was removed from the blacklist in October 2002, in light of the progress the Government had made in improving its anti-money-laundering measures. Part of these measures was the approval, in December 2001, of the Exchange of Information Bill, designed to give foreign authorities greater access to information about Dominica's 'offshore' banks.

In July 2002 the Public Service Union (PSU) organized a large-scale demonstration in the capital, Roseau, to protest against controversial tax increases introduced in a budget that was intended to engender economic recovery. In November a DFP deputy, dissatisfied with the Prime Minister's handling of the economic crisis, withdrew his support from the Government, leaving the governing coalition with a majority of one seat. In February 2003 the PSU, objecting to Government proposals to reduce the size of the public sector work-force and to compel workers to take two days of unpaid leave every month, organized a six-day strike. The strike ended after the Government agreed to review its proposal to reduce the public sector wage bill. The industrial action further damaged the position of the embattled Government and possibly jeopardized the granting of a structural adjustment loan from the World Bank. In February 2004 a new government programme, endorsed by the IMF, to reduce public sector salaries by 5% was denounced as 'unconstitutional' by the PSU. However, in November the High Court ruled that the government plans were lawful and the 5% salary reduction remained in place until July 2005.

On 1 October 2003 Nicholas Liverpool succeeded Vernon Shaw as President.

On 6 January 2004 Charles died of a heart attack. The LPD nominated Roosevelt Skerrit, hitherto Minister of Education, Youth and Sports, as his replacement. Skerrit was sworn in as Prime Minister on 8 January after his nomination had been endorsed by the coalition's other member, the DFP. On the same day, Skerrit appointed his first Cabinet; notable appointments included the return of Ambrose George (who had left the Cabinet in 2002), as Minister of Agriculture and the Environment. On 29 February Skerrit was elected leader of the LPD; George was appointed deputy leader.

In spite of the country's economic difficulties, exacerbated by the damage caused by severe earthquakes and landslides in November 2004, at the general election on 5 May 2005 the LPD again won an overall majority of seats (12 of the 21 available from 51.7% of the votes cast) in the House of Assembly. The UWP secured eight seats (and 43.9% of the votes), one fewer than in the previous election; a close ally of the LPD, standing as an independent candidate, won the remaining seat. The junior coalition partner, the DFP, was defeated in the two constituencies in which it competed; however, its leader, Charles Savarin, was appointed as a senator and retained his place in Skerrit's new administration as Minister of Foreign Affairs, Trade, Labour and the Public Service. In December 2005 Earl Williams, a former cabinet minister, was chosen to succeed Edison James as leader of the UWP, and proceeded to replace him as Leader of the Opposition in July 2007 when James resigned from office. In September 2006 former deputy leader of the party, Julius Timothy, defected to the LPD in acceptance of Prime Minister Skerrit's invitation to the Cabinet as Minister for Economic Development and Planning. Skerrit effected a cabinet reorganization in October 2007, in which he assumed responsibility for foreign affairs (from Savarin), and also for finance and social security. Savarin became Minister of Public Utilities, Energy, Ports and the Public Service, and Francine Baron Royer was appointed as Dominica's first female Attorney-General.

In foreign policy, Dominica has close links with France and the USA. France helped in suppressing the coup attempts against the DFP Government in 1981, and Dominica was the first Commonwealth country to benefit from the French aid agency Fonds d'aide et de coopération. In October 2005 Dominica signed an agreement with France to combat illegal immigration, primarily from Haiti and the Dominican Republic. In the same month the USA announced a US $2m. per year aid programme, administered by USAID, to help improve Dominica's international competitiveness. In 2001 Libya granted Dominica, in common with other eastern Caribbean islands, access to a $2,000m. development fund. In February 2005 the Government announced that Libya was paying for the construction of two schools on the island and for 15 scholarships for Dominican students to attend university courses in Libya. In October 2001 Pierre Charles and the Cuban Minister of Foreign Affairs, Felipe Pérez Roque, signed a bilateral accord on tourism; they also agreed to co-operate further in trade and commerce. In September 2005 the Government became one of 13 Caribbean administrations to sign the PetroCaribe accord, under which Dominica would be allowed to purchase petroleum from Venezuela at reduced prices. Owing to insufficient existing petroleum storage and refining capacity on the island, an agreement was signed in mid-2006 between the Government and PDVSA, the state-managed Venezuelan oil company, for the construction of a Fuel Storage and Distribution Plant to assist in dissemination of oil under the PetroCaribe initiative. The facility, with an oil storage capacity of 39,000 barrels, was scheduled for completion in late 2007. In January 2008 Skerrit announced that Dominica would sign a trade agreement, the Bolivarian Alternative for Latin America (Alternativa Bolivariana para América Latina y el Caribe—ALBA), intended to be an alternative to the proposed Free Trade Area of the Americas (FTAA), advanced by the USA.

Following a visit to the Chinese capital, Beijing, on 29 March 2004 Skerrit announced that Dominica would establish diplomatic relations with the People's Republic of China in place of Taiwan. (China agreed to provide an estimated US $111m. in budgetary support, infrastructure grants and education exchanges.) A Chinese embassy was duly opened in Roseau in mid-June. Skerrit was heavily criticized by the opposition over the severing of relations with Taiwan. In January 2005 Skerrit accused the UWP of jeopardizing Dominica's nascent relations with China by accepting campaign funds from Taiwan. In February Edison James announced he was to commence legal action against Skerrit for slander; Skerrit had allegedly accused James of writing to the Chinese embassy requesting that China withdraw its funding for the construction of a new sports stadium before the impending election. Earlier in the year the Chinese embassy in Roseau courted further controversy by condemning the display of Taiwanese flags by UWP supporters and expressed strongly worded dismay at local opposition to the 'one China principle'.

Dominica's perceived attachment to so-called 'chequebook diplomacy' was criticized again in December 2004 when Japan provided funding of some EC $33m. for the construction of a fisheries complex on the island, allegedly in return for supporting the Japanese Government's pro-whaling stance. Dominica was among other OECS member states criticized for voting in favour of the proposed lifting of a 20-year moratorium on commercial whaling—tendered by Japan—during the annual meeting of the International Whaling Commission (IWC) in June 2006. In April 2007 Prime Minister Skerrit made an official visit to Japan, following which he announced that Japanese funding for a further fisheries facility had been secured. Skerrit also stated his intention to renew Dominica's support for the Japanese Government's bid to resume commercial whaling. The President of the Caribbean Conservation Association and former Minister of the Environment in the Dominican Government, Atherton Martin, accused his country of behaving like 'an international prostitute' for agreeing to support Japan at the IWC while accepting financial assistance from the Japanese Government. Following Japan's success at the IWC meeting in Alaska, USA, in May, in securing permission to resume whaling activity, Edison James, cautioned that the decision could adversely affect Dominica's tourist industry, a significant proportion of which came from whale-watching.

Government

Legislative power is vested in the unicameral House of Assembly, comprising 30 members (nine nominated and 21 elected for five years by universal adult suffrage). Executive authority is vested in the President, who is elected by the House, but in most matters the President is guided by the advice of the Cabinet and acts as the constitutional Head of State. He appoints the Prime Minister, who must be able to command a majority in the House, and (on the Prime Minister's recommendation) other ministers. The Cabinet is responsible to the House. The island is divided into 10 administrative divisions, known as parishes, and there is limited local government in Roseau, the capital, and in the Carib Territory.

Defence

The Dominican Defence Force was officially disbanded in 1981. There is a police force of about 300, which includes a coastguard service. The country participates in the US-sponsored Regional Security System.

Economic Affairs

In 2006, according to estimates by the World Bank, Dominica's gross national income (GNI), measured at average 2004–06 prices, was US $287.0m., equivalent to $3,960 per head (or $6,490 per head on an international purchasing-power parity basis). Between 1996 and 2006 the population remained more or less constant, while gross domestic product (GDP) per head increased, in real terms, by an average of 1.5% per year. Overall GDP increased, in real terms, by an average of 1.6% per year in 1996–2006; GDP increased by 4.1% in 2006.

Agriculture (including forestry and fishing) is the principal economic activity, accounting for 16.3% of GDP in 2006. In 2005 the sector engaged 21.1% of the employed labour force, according to FAO estimates. The principal cash crop is bananas. The banana industry, which was already experiencing difficulties (owing to a decline in prices), was adversely affected by a September 1997 ruling of the World Trade Organization (WTO, see p. 396) against Dominica's preferential access to the European (particularly the British) market. In 2002 banana output was estimated to have decreased to 29,000 metric tons (from 33,000 tons in the previous year), remaining at the same level thereafter. In 2006 receipts from banana exports amounted to an estimated US $7.5m. (some 17.6% of total domestic exports). Other important crops include coconuts (which provide copra for export as well as edible oil and soap), mangoes, avocados, papayas, ginger, citrus fruits and, mainly for domestic consumption, vegetables. Non-banana crops have rapidly grown in significance during recent years, from one-half of total crop production before 2000 to nearly four-fifths in 2005. Livestock-rearing and fishing are also practised for local purposes. In December 2004 the construction of a EC $33m., Japanese-funded fisheries complex at Marigot was announced. Numerous other Japanese-funded fisheries projects have been donated to Dominica in recent years. Dominica has extensive timber reserves (more than 40% of the island's total land area is forest and woodland), and international aid agencies are encouraging the development of a balanced timber industry. The GDP of the agricultural sector decreased at an average annual rate of 1.8% in 1996–2004. In real terms, agricultural GDP expanded by 3.5% in 2004, but declined by an estimated 0.4% in 2005, a contraction largely attributed to the decline in banana production owing to adverse weather conditions. Conditions improved in 2006 and agricultural GDP increased by 3.4% as result.

Industry (comprising mining, manufacturing, construction and utilities) provided 21.9% of GDP in 2006, and employed an estimated 22.0% of the employed labour force in 2001. Real industrial GDP increased at an average rate of 0.1% per year during 1996–2004; the sector increased by an estimated 6.4% in 2004. The mining sector contributed only 0.9% of GDP in 2006. There is some quarrying of pumice, and there are extensive reserves of limestone and clay. Pumice is useful to the construction industry, which accounted for 8.5% of GDP in 2006, and employed 9.8% of the employed labour force in 2001. Extensive infrastructure development by the Government has maintained high levels of activity in the construction sector in recent years, although the sector's GDP decreased at an average annual rate of 1.3%, in real terms, during 1996–2004; the sector's GDP expanded by 3.5% in 2005 and by 8.5% in 2006. The Government has also encouraged the manufacturing sector, which is mainly small-scale and dependent upon agriculture, in an attempt to diversify the economy. In 2006 manufacturing contributed 7.2% of GDP and, in 2001, an estimated 10.6% of the employed workforce were engaged in manufacturing, mining and quarrying activities. Real manufacturing GDP decreased at an average rate of 0.6% per year during 1996–2004; the sector expanded by 1.5% in 2005, but declined by 2.0% in 2006. There is a banana-packaging plant, a brewery and factories for the manufacturing and refining of crude and edible vegetable oils and for the production of soap, canned juices and cigarettes. Furniture, paint, cardboard boxes and candles are also significant manufactures.

In 2000 some 70% of Dominica's energy requirements were supplied by hydroelectric power. Investment in a hydroelectric development scheme and in the water supply system has been partially financed by the export of water, from Dominica's extensive reserves, to drier Caribbean islands such as Aruba. A hydroelectric power-station, with a generating capacity of 1.24 MW, began operation at Laudat in 1990. In 2006 Dominica's imports of mineral fuels totalled 15.5% of the cost of total imports, according to preliminary figures. In 1998 a geothermal energy project in Soufrière began producing electricity, following investment of EC $25m. from a US company. The state-owned Dominica Electricity Services (Domlec) was privatized in 1996, with the British Government's overseas private finance institution, the Commonwealth Development Corporation (CDC), buying 72% of the company (in 2004 this share of the company was sold to the US-based WRB enterprises). Construction of a new 20-MW electric power plant, at an estimated cost of $80m., was completed in 2001. New electricity supply legislation, instituted in November 2006, was to establish an independent regulatory commission to oversee the sector and, in a repeal of the Electricity Supply Act (1996), would foreshorten Domlec's monopoly licence by 10 years, effectively liberalizing the market by 2015.

Services engaged an estimated 58.8% of the employed labour force in 2001, and provided 61.9% of GDP in 2006. The combined GDP of the service sectors increased at an average rate of 0.8% per year during 1996–2004; the sector expanded by 3.8% in 2005 and by a further 4.6% in 2006. The tourism industry, which contributed an estimated 8.2% of GDP and 7.7% of employment in 2004, according to the World Travel and Tourism Council, is of increasing importance to the economy, and exploits Dominica's natural history and scenery. Successive governments have placed considerable emphasis on the country's potential as an 'eco-tourism' destination, pursuing a development programme funded by the European Union (EU, see p. 244) and certification from an international sustainable tourism body, Green Globe 21. The majority of tourists are cruise-ship passengers. Arrivals from cruise ships increased dramatically from 6,777 in 1990 to 239,544 in 2000. However, the US Government's 'war on terror' had a negative impact upon the region's tourism trade in 2001 and 2002: cruise-ship passengers fell to 136,859 in the latter year. A recovery began in 2003 (when there were a total of

DOMINICA

177,044 arrivals), which helped to increase total tourism receipts by 14.5% (to EC $141.2m.). In 2004 the number of cruise-ship passengers was reported to have more than doubled, to 383,614, although the optimism this engendered was tempered by the substantially lower figure of 301,511 passengers recorded in 2005. This sector recovered somewhat in 2006 when 379,503 cruise-ship passengers were estimated to have visited Dominica in that year. Tourism receipts for 2006 were estimated at $183.9m. In August 2004 the Government abandoned a long-standing plan to construct a new international airport; supplemented by $9.0m. in infrastructural development assistance from the Venezuelan Government; the earmarked funding was instead diverted towards the redevelopment of the existing Melville Hall Airport, with completion anticipated in early 2008.

In 2006 Dominica recorded an estimated visible trade deficit of EC $281.1m. and a deficit of $200.9m. on the current account of the balance of payments. The principal source of imports in 2004 was the USA, which accounted for 36.7% of total imports, followed by Trinidad and Tobago and the United Kingdom. The principal market for exports in 2004 was Jamaica, with 20.1% of the total. The United Kingdom, which receives a large proportion of Dominica's banana production, was the second largest market, receiving 17.9% of total domestic exports in that year. The principal imports in 2004 were machinery and transport equipment, basic manufactures (such as paper), and food and live animals. The principal exports in the same year were soap and bananas.

In 2005/06, according to preliminary estimates by the IMF, there was an estimated budget surplus of EC $9.7m. At the end of 2005 Dominica's total external debt was US $231.5m., all of which was long-term public debt. The cost of debt-servicing in that year was equivalent to 13.2% of the value of exports of goods and services. The annual rate of inflation averaged 1.6% in 2000–2006; consumer prices increased by an average of 2.4% in 2006. An estimated 10.9% of the labour force were unemployed in 2001.

Dominica is a member of the Organization of American States (see p. 360), the Caribbean Community and Common Market (CARICOM, see p. 196), the Organisation of Eastern Caribbean States (see p. 425), and is a signatory of the Cotonou Agreement, the successor arrangement to the Lomé Conventions between the African, Caribbean and Pacific (ACP) countries and the EU. Dominica is also a member of the Eastern Caribbean Securities Exchange (based in Saint Christopher and Nevis).

The Dominican economy is heavily dependent on the production of bananas, and is thus vulnerable to adverse weather conditions and price fluctuations. Efforts to expand the country's economic base have been impeded by poor infrastructure and, in terms of tourism (despite the Government's success in promoting 'eco-tourism'), a paucity of desirable beaches. Banana exports decreased from the end of the 1990s, owing to drought and a fall in producer prices. Fears of a further contraction of the sector with the end of the EU's preferential import regime, which was replaced by a universal tariff system from 2006, were partly assuaged by burgeoning regional demand and increased production, precipitated by auspicious weather conditions in that year. A significant portion of Dominica's banana crop was destroyed in 2007 by Hurricane Dean, a powerful tropical storm which swept across the island in August of that year. Damage caused by the storm was estimated to total some EC $162m., equivalent to almost 20% of GDP. In early 2008 the IMF allocated approximately EC $9m. in emergency aid while CARICOM assigned a further EC $20m. for the rehabilitation of the agricultural sector and for road building projects. While adverse climatic conditions constrained economic growth in 2007 (which was estimated at 3.2% by the IMF), increased capital expenditures in the public and private sectors stimulated an expansion in construction activities. The Government earmarked a substantial portion of the EC $69.1m. capital outlay to a new housing development programme (launched in January 2007), which aimed to provide affordable housing to Dominicans on low incomes.

Education

Education is free and is provided by both government and denominational schools. There are also a number of schools for the mentally and physically handicapped. Education is compulsory for 10 years between five and 15 years of age. Primary education begins at the age of five and lasts for seven years. In 2004/05 enrolment at primary schools included 87.7% of children in the relevant age-group. Secondary education, beginning at 12 years of age, lasts for five years. Universal secondary education was introduced from September 2005. Enrolment at secondary schools during the academic year 2004/05 included 90.4% of pupils in the relevant age-group. A teacher-training college and nursing school provide further education, and there is also a branch of the University of the West Indies on the island. In 1997 the Government announced plans to invest EC $17.9m., mainly financed by a World Bank loan, in a Basic Education Reform project. In February 2005 the Government announced that funding provided by Libya would pay for the construction of a primary school in Portsmouth and a high school in Goodwill, near Roseau. Estimated budgetary expenditure on schools was $4.1m. in 2001/02 (equivalent to 1.5% of total expenditure).

Public Holidays

2008: 1 January (New Year's Day), 2 January (Merchants' Holiday), 4–5 February (Masquerade, Carnival), 21 March (Good Friday), 24 March (Easter Monday), 1 May (May or Labour Day), 12 May (Whit Monday), 6 August (Emancipation, August Monday), 3 November (Independence Day), 4 November (Community Service Day), 25–26 December (Christmas).

2009: 1 January (New Year's Day), 2 January (Merchants' Holiday), 23–24 February (Masquerade, Carnival), 10 April (Good Friday), 13 April (Easter Monday), 1 May (May or Labour Day), 1 June (Whit Monday), August (Emancipation, August Monday), 3 November (Independence Day), November (Community Service Day), 25–26 December (Christmas).

Weights and Measures

The metric system is replacing the imperial system of weights and measures.

Statistical Survey

Source (unless otherwise stated): Eastern Caribbean Central Bank; internet www.eccb-centralbank.org.

AREA AND POPULATION

Area: 751 sq km (290 sq miles).

Population: 71,727 (males 36,434, females 35,293) at census of 12 May 2001. *2006* (mid-year estimate): 70,964.

Density (mid-2006): 94.5 per sq km.

Population by Ethnic Group (*de jure* population, excl. those resident in institutions, 1981): Negro 67,272; Mixed race 4,433; Amerindian (Carib) 1,111; White 341; Total (incl. others) 73,795 (males 36,754, females 37,041. Source: UN, *Demographic Yearbook*.

Principal Town (population at 1991 census): Roseau (capital) 15,853. *Mid-2003* (UN estimate, incl. suburbs): Roseau 27,401 (Source: UN, *World Urbanization Prospects: The 2003 Revision*).

Births, Marriages and Deaths (registrations, 2002 unless otherwise indicated): Live births 1,081 (birth rate 15.4 per 1,000); Marriages (1998) 336 (marriage rate 4.4 per 1,000); Deaths 594 (death rate 8.4 per 1,000) (Source: UN, *Demographic Yearbook*). *2003:* Crude birth rate 15.0 per 1,000; Crude death rate 7.9 per 1,000.

Expectation of Life (years at birth, WHO estimates): 74.0 (males 72.4; females 75.7) in 2005. Source: WHO, *World Health Statistics*.

Economically Active Population ('000 persons aged 15 years and over, 2001): Agriculture, hunting, forestry and fishing 5.22; Manufacturing (incl. mining and quarrying) 2.10; Utilities 0.41; Construction 2.42; Wholesale and retail trade, restaurants and hotels 5.12; Transport, storage and communication 1.56; Financing, insurance, real estate and business services 1.14; Community, social and personal services 6.77; Activities not adequately defined 0.08; *Total employed* 24.81; Unemployed 3.05; *Total labour force* 27.86 (males 17.03, females 10.83). Source: ILO.

DOMINICA

HEALTH AND WELFARE
Key Indicators

Total Fertility Rate (children per woman, 2005): 1.9.
Under-5 Mortality Rate (per 1,000 live births, 2005): 15.
Physicians (per 1,000 head, 1997): 0.50.
Hospital Beds (per 1,000 head, 2004): 3.9.
Health Expenditure (2004): US $ per head (PPP): 309.3.
Health Expenditure (2004): % of GDP: 5.9.
Health Expenditure (2004): public (% of total): 71.3.
Access to Water (% of persons, 2004): 97.
Access to Sanitation (% of persons, 2004): 84.
Human Development Index (2005): ranking: 71.
Human Development Index (2005): value: 0.798.

For sources and definitions, see explanatory note on p. vi.

AGRICULTURE, ETC.

Principal Crops ('000 metric tons, 2006, FAO estimates): Sweet potatoes 2.0; Cassava 1.0; Yautia (Cocoyam) 4.6; Taro (Dasheen) 11.2; Yams 8.5; Sugar cane 4.4; Coconuts 10.9; Cabbages 0.7; Pumpkins 0.9; Cucumbers 1.5; Carrots 0.5; Bananas 10.3; Plantains 5.8; Oranges 9.3; Lemons and limes 0.7; Grapefruit 19.1; Guavas, mangoes and mangosteens 1.4; Avocados 0.5. *Aggregate Production* ('000 metric tons, may include official, semi-official or estimated data): Fruits (excl. melons) 48.3.
Livestock ('000 head, year ending September 2006, FAO estimates): Cattle 13.4; Pigs 5.0; Sheep 7.6; Goats 9.7; Chickens 190.
Livestock Products ('000 metric tons, 2006, FAO estimates): Cattle meat 0.5; Pig meat 0.4; Chicken meat 0.3; Cows' milk 6.1; Hen eggs 0.2.
Fishing (metric tons, live weight, 2005, FAO estimates): Capture 579 (Skipjack tuna 38; Yellowfin tuna 118; Marlins, sailfishes, etc. 44; Common dolphinfish 53); Aquaculture 0; *Total catch* 579.
Source: FAO.

MINING

Pumice ('000 metric tons, incl. volcanic ash): Estimated production 100 per year in 1988–2004. Source: US Geological Survey.

INDUSTRY

Production (2006, metric tons, unless otherwise indicated, preliminary): Laundry soap 3,605; Toilet soap 4,296; Dental cream 1,376; Liquid disinfectant 1,861; Crude coconut oil 855 (2001); Coconut meal 331 (2001); Electricity 79.2 million kWh (2004). Sources: IMF, *Dominica: Statistical Appendix* (September 2007), and UN, *Industrial Commodity Statistics Yearbook*.

FINANCE

Currency and Exchange Rates: 100 cents = 1 Eastern Caribbean dollar (EC $). *Sterling, US Dollar and Euro Equivalents* (30 November 2007): £1 sterling = EC $5.579; US $1 = EC $2.700; €1 = EC $3.985 EC $100 = £17.92 = US $37.04 = €25.09. *Exchange Rate:* Fixed at US $1 = EC $2.70 since July 1976.
Budget (EC $ million, 2005/06): *Revenue:* Tax revenue 247.9 (Taxes on income and profits 50.5, Taxes on property 7.5, Taxes on domestic goods and services 123.2, Taxes on international trade and transactions 66.6); Other current revenue 21.2; Capital revenue 0.8; Total 269.8, excl. grants received (106.3). *Expenditure:* Current expenditure 244.0 (Wages and salaries 109.6, Goods and services 46.7, Interest payments 34.6, Transfers and subsidies 53.0); Capital expenditure and net lending 77.8; Total 321.8.
International Reserves (US $ million at 31 December 2006): Reserve position in IMF 0.01; Foreign exchange 63.02; Total 63.03. Source: IMF, *International Financial Statistics*.
Money Supply (EC $ million at 31 December 2006): Currency outside banks 45.44; Demand deposits at commercial banks 131.63; Total money (incl. others) 177.26. Source: IMF, *International Financial Statistics*.
Cost of Living (Retail Price Index, base: 2000 = 100): All items 105.4 in 2004; 107.7 in 2005; 110.3 in 2006. Source: IMF, *International Financial Statistics*.
Gross Domestic Product (EC $ million at constant 1990 prices): 539.31 in 2004; 557.50 in 2005; 587.16 in 2006.
Expenditure on the Gross Domestic Product (EC $ million at current prices, 2006): Government final consumption expenditure 161.10; Private final consumption expenditure 611.49; Gross fixed capital formation (incl. increase in stocks) 247.37; *Total domestic expenditure* 1,019.96; Exports of goods and services 377.27; *Less* Imports of goods and services 540.75; *GDP in purchasers' values* 856.48.
Gross Domestic Product by Economic Activity (EC $ million at current prices, 2006): Agriculture, hunting, forestry and fishing 118.39; Mining and quarrying 6.39; Manufacturing 52.58; Electricity and water 38.40; Construction 62.01; Wholesale and retail trade 87.72; Restaurants and hotels 21.63; Transport 63.26; Communications 29.29; Finance and insurance 80.79; Real estate and housing 24.21; Government services 131.36; Other services 12.36; *Sub-total* 728.39; *Less* Financial intermediation services indirectly measured (FISIM) 57.26; *Gross value added in basic prices* 671.13; Taxes, less subsidies, on products 185.34; *GDP in market prices* 856.48.
Balance of Payments (EC $ million, 2006): Goods (net) –281.1; Services (net) 117.7; *Balance on goods and services* –163.5; Other income (net) –83.9; *Balance on goods, services and income* –247.4; Current transfers (net) 46.4; *Current balance* –200.9; Capital transfers 114.7; Direct investment from abroad 88.2; Portfolio investment 0.1; Other investment (net) 34.1; *Overall balance* 36.2.

EXTERNAL TRADE

Principal Commodities (US $ million, 2004): *Imports c.i.f.:* Food and live animals 24.0 (Meat and meat preparations 5.4; Cereals and cereal preparations 4.8); Refined petroleum products 14.6; Animal and vegetable oils 3.9; Chemicals, etc. 16.2; Basic manufactures 24.7 (Paper products 5.7; Metal manufactures 5.9); Machinery and transport equipment 36.6 (Telecommunications and sound equipment 10.6; Road vehicles 8.6); Miscellaneous manufactured articles 17.1; Total (incl. others) 145.1. *Exports f.o.b.:* Food and live animals 14.3 (Vegetables and roots and tubers 1.6; Bananas 8.8); Stone, sand and gravel 2.2; Chemicals, etc. 22.5 (Perfumes, cosmetics, toilet products, etc. 5.7; Soap 12.7; Disinfectants 1.8); Total (incl. others) 41.3. Source: UN, *International Trade Statistics Yearbook*.
Principal Trading Partners (US $ million, 2004): *Imports c.i.f.:* Barbados 5.0; Brazil 1.7; Canada 3.9; China 1.8; Colombia 1.1; France 7.2; Guyana 1.9; Jamaica 1.9; Japan 6.8; Netherlands 2.0; Saint Lucia 4.3; Saint Vincent and the Grenadines 1.6; Trinidad and Tobago 26.3; United Kingdom 9.5; USA 53.2; Venezuela 1.9; Total (incl. others) 145.1. *Exports f.o.b.:* Antigua and Barbuda 4.1; Barbados 1.9; Belize 0.8; France 3.9; Guyana 2.6; Jamaica 8.3; Netherlands Antilles 0.9; Saint Christopher and Nevis 1.2; Saint Lucia 1.6; Saint Vincent and the Grenadines 0.4; Suriname 0.7; Trinidad and Tobago 3.1; United Kingdom 7.4; USA 1.9; Total (incl. others) 41.3. Source: UN, *International Trade Statistics Yearbook*.

TRANSPORT

Road Traffic (motor vehicles licensed in 1994): Private cars 6,491; Taxis 90; Buses 559; Motorcycles 94; Trucks 2,266; Jeeps 461; Tractors 24; Total 9,985. *2000* (motor vehicles in use): Passenger cars 8,700; Commercial vehicles 3,400. Source: partly UN, *Statistical Yearbook*.
Shipping: *Merchant Fleet* (registered at 31 December 2006): 100 vessels (total displacement 614,481 grt) (Source: Lloyd's Register-Fairplay, *World Fleet Statistics*); *International Freight Traffic* ('000 metric tons, estimates, 1993): Goods loaded 103.2; Goods unloaded 181.2.
Civil Aviation (1997): Aircraft arrivals and departures 18,672; Freight loaded 363 metric tons; Freight unloaded 575 metric tons.

TOURISM

Visitor Arrivals: 466,278 (80,087 stop-over visitors, 2,577 excursionists, 383,614 cruise-ship passengers) in 2004; 388,480 (86,319 stop-over visitors, 650 excursionists, 301,511 cruise-ship passengers) in 2005; 472,882 (92,474 stop-over visitors, 905 excursionists, 379,503 cruise-ship passengers) in 2006.
Tourism Receipts (EC $ million): 163.71 in 2004; 153.97 in 2005; 183.91 in 2006.

COMMUNICATIONS MEDIA

Radio Receivers (1997): 46,000 in use.
Television Receivers (1999): 17,000 in use.
Telephones (2004): 21,000 main lines in use.
Facsimile Machines (1996): 396 in use.
Mobile Cellular Telephones (2004): 41,800 subscribers.
Personal Computers (2004): 13,000 in use.
Internet Users (2005): 26,00.
Broadband Subscribers (2004): 3,300.

DOMINICA

Non-daily Newspapers (2004): 3.

Sources: mainly UNESCO, *Statistical Yearbook*, International Telecommunication Union and UN, *Statistical Yearbook*.

EDUCATION

Institutions (1994/95): Pre-primary 72 (1992/93); Primary 64; Secondary 14; Tertiary 2.

Teachers (2004/05 unless otherwise indicated): Pre-primary 153; Primary 519; Secondary 496; Tertiary 34 (1992/93).

Pupils (2004/05 unless otherwise indicated): Pre-primary 1,563 (2002/03); Primary 9,441; General secondary 7,218; Secondary vocational 258; Tertiary 461 (1995/96).

Sources: UNESCO, *Statistical Yearbook*, Institute for Statistics; Caribbean Development Bank, *Social and Economic Indicators*; UN Economic Commission for Latin America and the Caribbean, *Statistical Yearbook*.

Adult Literacy Rate (2004): 88.0%. Source: UN Development Programme, *Human Development Report*.

Directory

The Constitution

The Constitution came into effect at the independence of Dominica on 3 November 1978. Its main provisions are summarized below:

FUNDAMENTAL RIGHTS AND FREEDOMS

The Constitution guarantees the rights of life, liberty, security of the person, the protection of the law and respect for private property. The individual is entitled to freedom of conscience, of expression and assembly and has the right to an existence free from slavery, forced labour and torture. Protection against discrimination on the grounds of sex, race, place of origin, political opinion, colour or creed is assured.

THE PRESIDENT

The President is elected by the House of Assembly for a term of five years. A presidential candidate is nominated jointly by the Prime Minister and the Leader of the Opposition and on their concurrence is declared elected without any vote being taken; in the case of disagreement the choice will be made by secret ballot in the House of Assembly. Candidates must be citizens of Dominica aged at least 40 who have been resident in Dominica for five years prior to their nomination. A President may not hold office for more than two terms.

PARLIAMENT

Parliament consists of the President and the House of Assembly, composed of 21 elected Representatives and nine Senators. According to the wishes of Parliament, the latter may be appointed by the President—five on the advice of the Prime Minister and four on the advice of the Leader of the Opposition—or elected. The life of Parliament is five years.

Parliament has the power to amend the Constitution. Each constituency returns one Representative to the House who is directly elected in accordance with the Constitution. Every citizen over the age of 18 is eligible to vote.

THE EXECUTIVE

Executive authority is vested in the President. The President appoints as Prime Minister the elected member of the House who commands the support of a majority of its elected members, and other ministers on the advice of the Prime Minister. Not more than three ministers may be from among the appointed Senators. The President has the power to remove the Prime Minister from office if a resolution expressing 'no confidence' in the Government is adopted by the House and the Prime Minister does not resign within three days or advise the President to dissolve Parliament.

The Cabinet consists of the Prime Minister, other ministers and the Attorney-General in an ex officio capacity.

The Leader of the Opposition is appointed by the President as that elected member of the House who, in the President's judgement, is best able to command the support of a majority of the elected members who do not support the Government.

The Government

HEAD OF STATE

President: Dr NICHOLAS LIVERPOOL (assumed office 1 October 2003).

CABINET
(March 2008)

Prime Minister and Minister of Finance, Social Security and of Foreign Affairs: ROOSEVELT SKERRIT (LPD—popularly referred to as DLP).

Attorney-General: FRANCINE BARON ROYER.

Minister of Agriculture, Fisheries and Forestry: MATTHEW WALTERS (DLP).

Minister of Carib Affairs: KELLY GRANEAU (DLP).

Minister of Community Development, Culture, Gender Affairs and Information: LORRAINE BANNIS-ROBERTS.

Minister of Economic Development and Urban Renewal: JULIUS TIMOTHY (DLP).

Minister of Education, Human Resource Development, Sports and Youth Affairs: VINCE HENDERSON (DLP).

Minister of Health and the Environment: JOHN FABIEN (DLP).

Minister of Housing, Lands and Communications: REGINALD AUSTRIE (DLP).

Minister of National Security, Immigration and Labour: RAYBURN BLACKMORE.

Minister of Public Utilities, Energy, Ports and the Public Service: Sen. CHARLES SAVARIN (DFP).

Minister of Public Works and Infrastructural Development: AMBROSE GEORGE (DLP).

Minister of Tourism, Legal Affairs and Civil Aviation: IAN DOUGLAS (DLP).

Minister of Trade, Industry, Consumer Affairs and Private Sector Relations with responsibility for CARICOM, OECS and Diaspora Affairs: Sen. Dr COLIN MCINTYRE.

Parliamentary Secretary in the Ministry of Education, Human Resource Development, Sports and Youth Affairs: IAN PINARD (DLP).

Parliamentary Secretary in the Office of the Prime Minister: Sen. PETER ST JEAN.

Parliamentary Secretary in the Ministry of Public Works and Infrastructural Development: URBAN BARON.

MINISTRIES

Office of the President: Morne Bruce, Roseau; tel. 4482054; fax 4498366; e-mail presidentoffice@cwdom.dm.

Office of the Prime Minister: 6th Floor, Financial Centre, Roseau; tel. 2663279; fax 4485200.

All other ministries are at Government Headquarters, Kennedy Ave, Roseau; tel. 4482401.

CARIB TERRITORY

This reserve of the remaining Amerindian population is located on the central east coast of the island. The Caribs enjoy a measure of local government and elect their chief.

Chief: CHARLES WILLIAMS.

Waitukubuli Karifuna Development Committee (WAIKADA): Salybia, Carib Territory; tel. 4457336.

Legislature

HOUSE OF ASSEMBLY

Speaker: ALIX BOYD-KNIGHT.

Clerk: ALEX F. PHILLIP.

Senators: 9.

Elected Members: 21.

DOMINICA

General Election, 5 May 2005

Party	Valid votes cast	%	Seats
Labour Party of Dominica	19,640	51.73	12
Dominica United Workers' Party	16,678	43.93	8
Dominica Freedom Party	1,211	3.19	—
Independents	434	1.14	1
Total	37,963	100.00	21

Election Commission

Electoral Office: Cross St, Roseau; tel. 4482401; fax 4485200; Chair. RITA SERAPHINE.

Political Organizations

Dominica Freedom Party (DFP): 37 Great George St, Roseau; tel. 4482104; fax 4481795; f. 1968; Leader MICHAEL ASTAPHAN; Chair. FELIX WILSON.

Dominica United Workers' Party (UWP): 47 Cork St, Roseau; tel. 4485051; fax 4498448; e-mail workers@cwdom.dm; internet www.unitedworkersparty.com; f. 1988; Leader EARL WILLIAMS; Pres. RON GREEN.

Labour Party of Dominica (LPD): 18 Hanover St, Roseau; tel. 4488511; e-mail dlp@cwdom.dm; f. 1985 as a merger and reunification of left-wing groups, incl. the Dominica Labour Party (DLP; f. 1961); Leader ROOSEVELT SKERRIT; Deputy Leader AMBROSE GEORGE.

People's Democratic Movement (PDM): Roseau; f. 2006; Leader Dr WILLIAM E. (PARA) RIVIERE.

Diplomatic Representation

EMBASSIES IN DOMINICA

China, People's Republic: Ceckhall, Morne Daniel, POB 2247, Roseau; tel. 4490080; fax 4400088; internet dm.chineseembassy.org; Ambassador DENG BOQING.

Venezuela: 20 Bath Rd, 3rd Floor, POB 770, Roseau; tel. 4483348; fax 4486198; e-mail embven@cwdom.dm; Ambassador CARMEN MARTÍNEZ DE GRIJALVA.

Judicial System

Justice is administered by the Eastern Caribbean Supreme Court (based in Saint Lucia), consisting of the Court of Appeal and the High Court. One of the 16 puisne judges of the High Court is resident in Dominica and presides over the Court of Summary Jurisdiction. The District Magistrate Courts deal with summary offences and civil offences involving limited sums of money (specified by law).

Puisne Judge: DAVIDSON BAPTISTE.
Registrar: REGINALD WINSTON.

Religion

Most of the population profess Christianity, but there are some Muslims, Bahá'ís and Jews. The largest denomination is the Roman Catholic Church (with some 66% of the inhabitants in 2005).

CHRISTIANITY

The Roman Catholic Church

Dominica comprises the single diocese of Roseau, suffragan to the archdiocese of Castries (Saint Lucia). At 31 December 2005 there were an estimated 42,174 adherents in the country. The Bishop participates in the Antilles Episcopal Conference (currently based in Port of Spain, Trinidad and Tobago).

Bishop of Roseau: Rt Rev. GABRIEL MALZAIRE, Bishop's House, Turkey Lane, POB 790, Roseau; tel. 4482837; fax 4483404; e-mail bishop@cwdom.dm; internet www.dioceseofroseau.org.

The Anglican Communion

Anglicans in Dominica are adherents of the Church in the Province of the West Indies. The country forms part of the diocese of the North Eastern Caribbean and Aruba. The Bishop is resident in Antigua, and the Archbishop of the Province is the Bishop of the Bahamas and the Turks and Caicos Islands.

Other Christian Churches

Christian Union Church of the West Indies: Dominica Island District, 1 Rose St, Goodwill, POB 28, Roseau; tel. 4482725; e-mail marcusfrancis@hotmail.com; internet www.cccuhq.org; Island District Supt MARCUS FRANCIS.

Other denominations include Methodist, Pentecostal, Baptist, Church of God, Presbyterian, the Assemblies of Brethren, Moravian and Seventh-day Adventist groups, and the Jehovah's Witnesses.

BAHÁ'Í FAITH

National Spiritual Assembly: 79 Victoria St, POB 136, Roseau; tel. 4483881; fax 4488460.

The Press

The Chronicle: Wallhouse, Loubiere, POB 1724, Roseau; tel. 4486661; fax 4480047; e-mail manager@dachronicle.com; internet www.dachronicle.com; f. 1909; Friday; progressive independent; Editor J. ANTHONY WHITE (acting); Gen. Man. J. ANTHONY WHITE; circ. 3,200.

Official Gazette: Government Printery, Roseau; tel. 4482401, ext. 330; weekly; circ. 550.

The Sun: Sun Inc, 50 Independence St, POB 2255, Roseau; tel. 4484744; fax 4484764; e-mail acsun@cwdom.dm; internet www.news-dominica.com; f. 1998; weekly; Editor CHARLES JAMES.

The Times: 15 Kennedy Ave, Roseau; tel. 4403949; fax 4404056; e-mail admin@thetimes.dm; internet www.thetimes.dm; f. 2004; Friday; Editor MATT PELTIER.

The Tropical Star: Canefield, Roseau; tel. 4484634; fax 4485984; e-mail tpl@cwdom.dm; weekly; circ. 3,000; Editor NIGEL LAWRENCE.

Broadcasting and Communications

TELECOMMUNICATIONS

Regulatory Authority

National Telecommunications Regulatory Commission of Dominica (NTRC Dominica): 42-2 Kennedy Ave, POB 649, Roseau; tel. 4400627; fax 4400835; e-mail secretariat@ntrcdm.org; internet www.ectel.int/ntrcdm; f. 2000 as the Dominican subsidiary of the Eastern Caribbean Telecommunications Authority (ECTEL)—established simultaneously in Castries, Saint Lucia, to regulate telecommunications in Dominica, Grenada, Saint Christopher and Nevis, Saint Lucia and Saint Vincent and the Grenadines; Chair. JULIAN JOHNSON.

Major Service Providers

Cable & Wireless Dominica: Hanover St, POB 6, Roseau; tel. 2551000; fax 2551111; e-mail pr@cwdom.dm; internet www.cwdom.dm; CEO COLIN CHARLES JAMES.

Digicel Dominica: Wireless Ventures (Dominica) Ltd, POB 2236, Roseau; tel. 6161500; fax 4403189; e-mail customercare.dominica@digicelgroup.com; internet www.digiceldominica.com; acquired Cingular Wireless' Caribbean operations and licences in 2005; owned by an Irish consortium; Chair. DENIS O'BRIEN; Eastern Caribbean CEO KEVIN WHITE.

BROADCASTING

Radio

Dominica Broadcasting Corporation: Victoria St, POB 148, Roseau; tel. 4483283; fax 4482918; e-mail dbsmanager@dbcradio.net; internet www.dbcradio.net; f. 1971; govt station; daily broadcasts in English; 2 hrs daily in French patois; 10 kW transmitter on the medium wave band; FM service; programmes received throughout Caribbean excluding Jamaica and Guyana; Chair. IAN MUNRO; Programme Dir SHERMAINE GREEN-BROWN.

Kairi FM: 42 Independence St, POB 931, Roseau; tel. 4487331; fax 4487332; e-mail info@kairifm.com; internet www.kairifm.com; f. 1994; CEO FRANKIE (KRAZY TEE) BELLOT.

Voice of Life Radio (ZGBC): Gospel Broadcasting Corpn, Loubiere, POB 205, Roseau; tel. 4487017; fax 4400551; e-mail volradio@

DOMINICA

cwdom.dm; internet www.voiceoflife.com; f. 1975; 24 hrs daily FM; Station Man. CLEMENTINA MUNRO.

Television

There is no national television service, although there is a cable television network serving 95% of the island.

Marpin Telecom and Broadcasting Co Ltd: 5–7 Great Marlborough St, POB 2381, Roseau; tel. 5004107; fax 5002965; e-mail manager@marpin.dm; internet www.marpin.dm; f. 1982, present name adopted in 1996; commercial; cable and internet services; CEO RON ABRAHAM.

Finance

(cap. = capital; res = reserves; dep. = deposits; m. = million; brs = branches; amounts in East Caribbean dollars)

The Eastern Caribbean Central Bank, based in Saint Christopher, is the central issuing and monetary authority for Dominica.

Eastern Caribbean Central Bank—Dominica Office: Financial Centre, 3rd Floor, Kennedy Ave, POB 23, Roseau; tel. 4488001; fax 4488002; e-mail eccbdom@cwdom.dm; internet www.eccb-centralbank.org; Country Dir EDMUND ROBINSON.

BANKS

FirstCaribbean International Bank (Barbados) Ltd: Old Street, POB 4, Roseau; tel. 4482571; fax 4483471; internet www.firstcaribbeanbank.com; f. 2002 following merger of Caribbean operations of Barclays Bank PLC and CIBC; Barclays relinquished its stake to CIBC in June 2006; Exec. Chair. MICHAEL MANSOOR; CEO CHARLES PINK; Country Dir PAUL FRAMPTON.

National Bank of Dominica: 64 Hillsborough St, POB 271, Roseau; tel. 4484401; fax 4483982; e-mail ncbdom@cwdom.dm; internet www.nbdominica.com; f. 1976 as the National Commercial Bank of Dominica; name changed as above after privatization in Dec. 2003; cap. 11.0m., res 14.1m., dep. 474.9m. (June 2006); 49% govt-owned; Chair. NORMAN ROLLE; Man. Dir GREGORY DE GANNES; 6 brs.

DEVELOPMENT BANK

Dominica Agricultural, Industrial and Development (DAID) Bank: cnr Charles Ave and Rawles Lane, Goodwill, POB 215, Roseau; tel. 4482853; fax 4484903; e-mail aidbank@cwdom.dm; internet www.aidbank.com; f. 1971; responsible to Ministry of Finance; planned privatization suspended in 1997; provides finance for the agriculture, tourism, housing, education and manufacturing sectors; total assets 119.8m. (June 2002); Chair. AMBROSE SYLVESTER; Gen. Man. Dr EMALINE HARRIS-CHARLES (acting).

STOCK EXCHANGE

Eastern Caribbean Securities Exchange: based in Basseterre, Saint Christopher and Nevis; tel. (869) 466-7192; fax (869) 465-3798; e-mail info@ecseonline.com; internet www.ecseonline.com; f. 2001; regional securities market designed to facilitate the buying and selling of financial products for the eight member territories—Anguilla, Antigua and Barbuda, Dominica, Grenada, Montserrat, Saint Christopher and Nevis, Saint Lucia and Saint Vincent and the Grenadines; Gen. Man. TREVOR BLAKE; Chair. K. DWIGHT VENNER.

INSURANCE

In 2006 there were 32 insurance companies operating in Dominica. Several British, regional and US companies have agents in Roseau. Local companies include the following:

First Domestic Insurance Co Ltd: 19–21 King George V St, POB 1931, Roseau; tel. 4498202; fax 4485778; e-mail insurance@cwdom.dm; internet www.firstdomestic.dm; f. 1993; Man. Dir and CEO CURTIS TONGE.

Insurance Specialists and Consultants: 19–21 King George V St, POB 20, Roseau; tel. 4487175.

Jeff's Services Ltd: 3 Goodwill Rd, Roseau; tel. 4483501; fax 4488856.

Windward Islands Crop Insurance Co (Wincrop): Vanoulst House, Goodwill, POB 469, Roseau; tel. 4483955; fax 4484197; f. 1987; regional; coverage for weather destruction of, mainly, banana crops; Man. KERWIN FERREIRA; brs in Grenada, Saint Lucia and Saint Vincent.

Trade and Industry

DEVELOPMENT ORGANIZATIONS

Invest Dominica: Valley Rd, POB 293, Roseau; tel. 4482045; fax 4485840; e-mail industry@dominica.dm; internet www.investdominica.dm; f. 1988 as National Development Corpn (NDC) by merger of Industrial Development Corpn (f. 1974) and Tourist Board; NDC disbanded in April 2007 by act of parliament and replaced by two separate entities, Invest Dominica and Discover Dominica (see tourism) from 1 July 2007; promotes local and foreign investment to increase employment, production and exports; Chair. GERRY AIRD; Exec. Dir RHODA LETANG (acting).

National Development Foundation of Dominica: POB 313, Roseau; tel. 4483240; fax 4480225; e-mail ndfd@cwdom.dom; promotes investment of funds and resources from local businesses and foreign agencies to facilitate economic and social devt projects in Dominica; Exec. Dir CHRISTABEL CHARLES.

Organisation of the Eastern Caribbean States Export Development Unit (EDU): Financial Centre, 4th Floor, Kennedy Ave, POB 769, Roseau; tel. 4482240; fax 4485554; e-mail informationcentre@oecs-edu.org; internet www.oecs.org/edu; f. 1997 as Eastern Caribbean States Export Devt and Agricultural Diversification Unit; reformed as above in 2000; OECS regional devt org.; Exec. Dir COLIN BULLY.

INDUSTRIAL AND TRADE ASSOCIATIONS

Dominica Association of Industry and Commerce (DAIC): 14 Church St, POB 85, Roseau; tel. and fax 4491962; e-mail daic@cwdom.dm; internet www.daic.dm; f. 1972 by a merger of the Manufacturers' Asscn and the Chamber of Commerce; represents the business sector, liaises with the Govt, and stimulates commerce and industry; 100 mems; Pres. FRANCIS EMANUEL; CEO ACHILLE CHRIS JOSEPH.

Dominica Banana Producers Ltd (DBPL): Vanoulst House, POB 1620, Roseau; tel. 4482671; fax 4486445; f. 1934 as Dominica Banana Growers' Asscn; restructured 1984 as the Dominica Banana Marketing Corpn; renamed as above in 2003; state-supported, scheduled for privatization; Chair. RICHARD CHARLES; Gen. Man. RAYMOND AUSTRIE.

Dominica Export-Import Agency (DEXIA): Bay Front, POB 173, Roseau; tel. 4482780; fax 4486308; e-mail info@dexia.dm; internet www.dexia.dm; f. 1986; replaced the Dominica Agricultural Marketing Board and the External Trade Bureau; exporter of Dominican agricultural products, trade facilitator and importer of bulk rice and sugar; Gen. Man. GREGOIRE THOMAS.

EMPLOYERS' ORGANIZATION

Dominica Employers' Federation: 14 Church St, POB 1783, Roseau; tel. 4482314; fax 4484474; e-mail def@cwdom.dm; Pres. ACKROYD BIRMINGHAM.

UTILITIES

Regulatory Body

Independent Regulatory Commission: Roseau; f. 2006 to oversee the electricity sector.

Electricity

Dominica Electricity Services Ltd (Domlec): 18 Castle St, POB 1593, Roseau; tel. 2256000; fax 4485397; e-mail support@domleconline.com; internet www.domlec.dm; national electricity service; 72% owned by WRB Enterprises Ltd (USA) since take-over of the Commonwealth Devt Corpn's (United Kingdom) stake in 2004; Chair. ROBERT BLANCHARD, Jr; Man. Dir JOEL HUGGINS.

Water

Dominica Water and Sewerage Co Ltd (DOWASCO): 3 High St, POB 185, Roseau; tel. 4484811; fax 4485813; e-mail dowasco@cwdom.dm; state-owned; Chair. LARRY BARDOUILLE; Gen. Man. JOHN FABIEN.

TRADE UNIONS

Dominica Amalgamated Workers' Union (DAWU): 43 Hillsborough St, POB 137, Roseau; tel. 4482343; fax 4480086; e-mail wawuunion@hotmail.com; f. 1960; Gen. Sec. ELIAS LEAH SHILLINGFORD (acting); 500 mems (1996).

Dominica Association of Teachers: 7 Boyds Ave, POB 341, Roseau; tel. and fax 4488177; e-mail dat@cwdom.dm; internet www.dateachers.4t.com; Pres. CELIA NICHOLAS; Gen. Sec. ISABELLA PRENTICE; 630 mems (1996).

Dominica Public Service Union: cnr Valley Rd and Windsor Lane, POB 182, Roseau; tel. 4482102; fax 4488060; e-mail dcs@cwdom.dm; f. 1940; registered as a trade union in 1960; representing all grades of civil servants, including firemen, prison officers, nurses, teachers and postal workers; Pres. MERVIN ANTHONY; Gen. Sec. THOMAS LETANG; 1,400 mems.

Dominica Trade Union: 70–71 Independence St, Roseau; tel. 4498139; fax 4499060; e-mail domtradun@hotmail.com; f. 1945; Pres. HAROLD SEALEY; Gen. Sec. LEO J. BERNARD NICHOLAS; 400 mems (1995).

National Workers' Union: 102 Independence St, POB 387, Roseau; tel. 4485209; fax 4481934; e-mail icss@cwdom.dm; f. 1977; Pres.-Gen. RAWLINGS F. A. JEMMOTT; Gen. Sec. FRANKLIN FABIEN; 450 mems (1996).

Waterfront and Allied Workers' Union: 43 Hillsborough St, POB 181, Roseau; tel. 4482343; fax 4480086; e-mail wawuunion@hotmail.com; f. 1965; Pres. KERTIST AUGUSTUS; Asst Secs and Treasurers DAVID JEMMOTT, GORDON BAPTISTE; 1,500 mems.

Transport

ROADS

In 1999 there were an estimated 780 km (485 miles) of roads, of which about 50.4% was paved; there were also numerous tracks. A three-year Road Improvement Programme was announced in May 2007—under the 9th European Development (EDF) National Indicative Programme—and was to include an allocation of EC $8m. towards financing the development and maintenance of the country's road network. Plans to construct an important road link between Petite Soufriere and Rosalie under the 9th EDF, at an estimated cost of $12m., were postponed pending the procurement of additional financing.

SHIPPING

A deep-water harbour at Woodbridge Bay serves Roseau, which is the principal port. Several foreign shipping lines call at Roseau, and there is a high-speed ferry service between Martinique and Guadeloupe which calls at Roseau eight times a week. Ships of the Geest Line call at Prince Rupert's Bay, Portsmouth, to collect bananas, and there are also cruise-ship facilities there. There are other specialized berthing facilities on the west coast.

Dominica Port Authority (DPA): POB 243, Roseau; tel. 4484131; fax 4486131; e-mail domport@cwdom.dm; f. 1972; pilotage and cargo handling; Gen. Man. BENOIT BARDOUILLE.

CIVIL AVIATION

Melville Hall Airport, 64 km (40 miles) from Roseau, and Canefield Airport, 5 km (3 miles) from Roseau, are the two airports on the island. A EC $15m. contract to upgrade Melville Hall Airport was signed with a French construction company in August 2004 and the Government redirected funds—which had been partly provided by the European Union, from the previous (Dominica United Worker's Party) administration's plan to build a brand new international airport—for the development. The Government of Venezuela also contributed $9m. towards the expansion. The project was scheduled for completion by mid-2008. A scheme to rebuild the road from Roseau to the airport at a cost of $54m., funded by the French Government, was expected to commence in the same year. The regional airline LIAT (based in Antigua and Barbuda, and in which Dominica is a shareholder) acquired its troubled rival, Caribbean Star Airline (also headquartered in Antigua and Barbuda), in late 2007. The two airlines had separately offered almost identical schedules which, now consolidated, provide daily services and, together with Air Caraibe, connect Dominica with all the islands of the Eastern Caribbean, including the international airports of Puerto Rico, Antigua, Guadeloupe and Martinique.

Tourism

The Government has designated areas of the island as nature reserves, to preserve the beautiful, lush scenery and the rich, natural heritage that constitute Dominica's main tourist attractions. Birdlife is particularly prolific, and includes several rare and endangered species, such as the Imperial parrot. There are also two marine reserves. Tourism is not as developed as it is among Dominica's neighbours, but the country is being promoted as an 'eco-tourism' and cruise destination. There were an estimated 472,882 visitors in 2006 (of whom 379,503 were cruise-ship passengers). Receipts from tourism totalled an estimated EC $183.9m. in 2006.

Discover Dominica Authority: Valley Rd, POB 293, Roseau; tel. 4482045; fax 4485840; e-mail tourism@dominica.dm; internet www.discoverdominica.com; f. 1988 following merger of Tourist Board with Industrial Devt Corpn; CEO and Dir of Tourism STEVE BORNN.

Dominica Hotel and Tourism Association (DHTA): 17 Castle St, POB 384, Roseau; tel. 4403430; fax 4403433; e-mail dhta@cwdom.dm; internet www.dhta.org; Pres. JONATHON VIDAL; 79 mems.

THE DOMINICAN REPUBLIC

Introductory Survey

Location, Climate, Language, Religion, Flag, Capital

The Dominican Republic occupies the eastern part of the island of Hispaniola, which lies between Cuba and Puerto Rico in the Caribbean Sea. The country's only international frontier is with Haiti, to the west. The climate is sub-tropical, with an average annual temperature of 27°C (80°F). In Santo Domingo temperatures are generally between 19°C (66°F) and 31°C (88°F). The west and south-west of the country are arid. Hispaniola lies in the path of tropical cyclones. The official language is Spanish. Almost all of the inhabitants profess Christianity, and some 87% are Roman Catholics. There are small Protestant and Jewish communities. The national flag (proportions 5 by 8) is blue (upper hoist and lower fly) and red (lower hoist and upper fly), quartered by a white cross, with the national coat of arms, showing a quartered shield in the colours of the flag (on which are superimposed national banners, a cross and an open Bible) between scrolls above and below, at the centre of the cross. The capital is Santo Domingo.

Recent History

The Dominican Republic became independent in 1844, although it was occupied by US military forces between 1916 and 1924. General Rafael Leónidas Trujillo Molina overthrew the elected President, Horacio Vázquez, in 1930 and dominated the country until his assassination in May 1961. The dictator ruled personally from 1930 to 1947 and indirectly thereafter. His brother, Héctor Trujillo, was President from 1947 until August 1960, when he was replaced by Dr Joaquín Balaguer Ricardo, hitherto Vice-President. After Rafael Trujillo's death, President Balaguer remained in office, but in December 1961 he permitted moderate opposition groups to participate in a Council of State, which exercised legislative and executive powers. Balaguer resigned in January 1962, when the Council of State became the Provisional Government. A presidential election in December 1962, the country's first free election for 38 years, was won by Dr Juan Bosch Gaviño, the founder and leader of the Partido Revolucionario Dominicano (PRD), who had been in exile since 1930. President Bosch, a left-of-centre democrat, took office in February 1963 but was overthrown in the following September by a military coup. The leaders of the armed forces transferred power to a civilian triumvirate, led by Emilio de los Santos. In April 1965 a revolt by supporters of ex-President Bosch overthrew the triumvirate. Civil war broke out between pro-Bosch forces and military units headed by Gen. Elías Wessin y Wessin, who had played a leading role in the 1963 coup. The violence was eventually suppressed by the intervention of some 23,000 US troops, who were formally incorporated into an Inter-American peace force by the Organization of American States (OAS). The peace force withdrew in September 1965.

Following a period of provisional government under Héctor García Godoy, a presidential election in June 1966 was won by Balaguer, the candidate of the Partido Reformista Social Cristiano (PRSC). The PRSC, founded in 1964, also won a majority of seats in both houses of the new Congreso Nacional (National Congress). A new Constitution was promulgated in November. Despite his association with the Trujillo dictatorship, Balaguer initially proved to be a popular leader, and in May 1970 he was re-elected for a further four years. In February 1973 a state of emergency was declared when guerrilla forces landed on the coast. Captain Francisco Caamaño Deño, the leader of the 1965 revolt, and his followers were killed. Bosch and other opposition figures went into hiding. Bosch later resigned as leader of the PRD (founding the Partido de la Liberación Dominicana—PLD), undermining hopes of a united opposition in the May 1974 elections, when Balaguer was re-elected with a large majority.

In the May 1978 presidential election Balaguer was defeated by the PRD candidate, Silvestre Antonio Guzmán Fernández. This was the first occasion in the country's history when an elected President yielded power to an elected successor. An attempted military coup in favour of Balaguer was prevented by pressure from the US Government. On assuming office in August, President Guzmán undertook to professionalize the armed forces by removing politically ambitious high-ranking officers. In June 1981 he declared his support for Jacobo Majluta Azar, his Vice-President, as his successor, but in November the PRD rejected Majluta's candidacy in favour of Dr Salvador Jorge Blanco, a left-wing senator, who was elected President in May 1982. In the congressional election, held simultaneously, the PRD secured a majority in both the Senado (Senate) and the Cámara de Diputados (Chamber of Deputies). Blanco assumed office in August. Although a member of the Socialist International, he maintained good relations with the USA (on which the country is economically dependent) and declared that he would not resume relations with Cuba.

In February 1985 a series of substantial price increases led to violent clashes between demonstrators and the security forces. Public unrest was exacerbated by the Government's decision in April to accept the IMF's terms for further financial aid. Further violence preceded the presidential and legislative elections of May 1986. The three principal candidates in the presidential election were all former Presidents: Balaguer of the PRSC; Majluta, who, having registered La Estructura, his right-wing faction of the PRD, as a separate political party in July 1985, nevertheless secured the candidacy of the ruling PRD; and Bosch of the PLD. The counting of votes was suspended twice following allegations by Majluta of fraud by the PRSC and by the Junta Central Electoral (JCE—Central Electoral Board). Balaguer was finally declared the winner by a narrow margin. In the simultaneous legislative elections, the PRSC won 21 of the 30 seats in the Senado and 56 of the 120 seats in the Cámara de Diputados.

Upon taking office as President for the fifth time in August 1986, Balaguer initiated an investigation into alleged corrupt practices by members of the outgoing administration. Blanco, the outgoing President, was charged with embezzlement and the illegal purchase of military vehicles. (In August 1991 he was finally convicted of 'abuse of power' and misappropriation of public funds, and sentenced to 20 years' imprisonment. However, in September 1994 legislation granting him amnesty was approved by the Cámara de Diputados.) The financial accounts of the armed forces were examined, and the former Secretary of State for the Armed Forces was subsequently imprisoned. In September 1987 the Cabinet resigned, at the request of the President, to enable him to restructure the Government. Some 35,000 government posts were abolished, in an attempt to reduce public spending, and expenditure was to be redirected to a programme of public works projects, which were expected to create almost 100,000 new jobs. Nevertheless, the civil unrest continued in the remainder of the decade.

With presidential and legislative elections due to take place in May 1990, Balaguer's prospects for re-election were impeded considerably by the continuing deterioration of the economy. The principal contender for the presidency was the PLD candidate, Bosch, who concentrated his election campaign on seeking support from the private sector, promising privatization of state-owned companies. When the initial results indicated a narrow victory for Balaguer, Bosch accused the ruling PRSC and the JCE of fraud, necessitating a recount, supervised by monitors from the OAS. Almost two months after the election, Balaguer was declared the official winner. The PRSC also secured a narrow majority in the Senado. No party won an outright majority in the Cámara de Diputados, although this did not threaten seriously to impede government policies, in view of Balaguer's extensive powers to govern by decree.

In August 1990, in an attempt to reduce inflation, the Government announced a programme of austerity measures, almost doubling the price of petrol and essential foodstuffs. In response the trade unions called a 48-hour general strike and in the ensuing conflict with the security forces some 14 people were killed. The price increases were partially offset by an increase of 30% in the salaries of army personnel and civilian employees in the public sector. The trade unions, however, rejected an identical offer by the private sector and threatened further strike action if their demands for basic food subsidies and considerable wage increases were not satisfied. In September a three-day general strike was organized by the Organizaciones Colectivas Populares (OCP). In the following month another general strike was called by the OCP and the Central General de Trabajadores (CGT), with the stated aim of ousting Balaguer from power. Violent clashes with the security forces in Santo Domingo resulted in four deaths. In August 1991 the Government concluded a stand-by agreement with the IMF, in spite of trade-union and public opposition.

In January 1994 the PLD announced it had formed an alliance with the right-wing Fuerza Nacional Progresista (FNP) in order to contest the forthcoming general election. In the same month Balaguer officially announced his intention to contest the forthcoming presidential election; his nomination received the support of the majority of the PRSC. However, his decision prompted 20 members of the PRSC executive to withdraw from the party in order to support the presidential candidate of the Unidad Democrática (UD), Fernando Alvarez Bogaert, himself a defecting member of the PRSC. The UD subsequently signed an electoral pact with the PRD.

The official results of the presidential and legislative elections of May 1994 were delayed, amid accusations of widespread voting irregularities. Interim results indicated a narrow victory for Balaguer in the presidential contest. However, the PRD claimed that the PRSC, which had effective control of the JCE, had removed the names of some 200,000 PRD supporters from the electoral rolls. A full recount was undertaken. In July an investigative commission confirmed that, as a result of serious irregularities, some 73,000 of the registered electorate had been denied a vote. Despite an atmosphere of growing political instability, Balaguer rejected opposition demands for the formation of a provisional government. Strike action in protest at the electoral irregularities was reported to have seriously affected several regions, including the capital, during that month. On 2 August the JCE announced the final election results, having apparently overlooked the findings of the electoral investigative commission. Balaguer was proclaimed the winner of the presidential election by a margin of less than 1% of the votes cast.

Talks aimed at ending the political crisis caused by the election were held in early August 1994, with the mediation of the OAS and the Roman Catholic Church, and resulted in the signing of the Pact for Democracy. Under the terms of the accord (agreed by all the major parties), a fresh presidential election was to be held in November 1995 and a series of constitutional reforms would be adopted, providing for the prohibition of the re-election of a president to a consecutive term, a new electoral system for the head of state (see below), and the reorganization of the judiciary. Additionally, the legislative and municipal elections were to be held mid-way through the presidential term. As a result of the accord, José Francisco Peña Gómez, the PRD leader, cancelled a series of planned strikes and demonstrations organized by his party. However, at a session of the Congreso Nacional, held on 14 August, the deputies of the PRSC, with the support of those of the PLD, voted to extend Balaguer's mandate from 18 months to two years. The PRD withdrew from the legislature in protest, and Peña Gómez announced that his party would boycott the Congreso and resume strike action. The OAS also criticized the Congreso for violating the terms of the Pact for Democracy. The constitutional amendments that the Pact envisaged were, however, approved by the Congreso. On 16 August Balaguer was inaugurated as President for a seventh term.

In April 1996 the energy shortfall again reached crisis proportions, with power cuts averaging between 14 and 20 hours per day. The crisis prompted renewed demands for the Congreso to expedite legislation enabling the privatization of the state electricity company, Corporación Dominicana de Electricidad (CDE), which, owing largely to inefficiency and corruption, operated at a considerable loss.

The May 1996 presidential election, the first for some 30 years in which Balaguer was not a candidate, was conducted according to a new system, introduced since 1994, whereby a second round of voting would be conducted between the two leading candidates should no candidate secure an absolute majority in the initial ballot. In the first round Peña Gómez won 46% of the votes, while the candidate of the PLD, Leonel Fernández Reyna, obtained 39%. The candidate of the PRSC, Jacinto Peynado (who had received only nominal support from Balaguer), obtained just 15% of the votes. At the second round of the presidential election, conducted on 30 June, Fernández won 51% of the votes to Peña Gómez's 49%. The establishment, earlier in the month, of an electoral alliance between the PLD and PRSC, entitled the Frente Nacional Patriótico, had ensured Fernández the support of the PRSC voters. While the PRSC failed to retain the presidency, Balaguer appeared to have succeeded in retaining considerable influence in the new administration, since the PLD's minority representation in the Congreso meant the party would be dependent on the support of the PRSC to implement planned institutional reforms. However, in early August relations between Fernández and Balaguer deteriorated when the PRSC signed an unexpected agreement with the PRD, which guaranteed the PRSC the presidency of the Senado while the PRD obtained that of the Cámara de Diputados. On 16 August Fernández was inaugurated, and the Cabinet, consisting almost exclusively of PLD members, was sworn in.

In 1997, as part of a campaign to eliminate deep-seated corruption in the country's institutions, Fernández restructured both the police and the judiciary. He also oversaw a restructuring of the Supreme Court, including the appointment of 15 new judges. Responsibility for appointing judges at all other levels of the judicial system was transferred from the Senado to the Supreme Court, principally to avoid appointments being influenced by political considerations. Nevertheless, growing dissatisfaction with the continuing deterioration of public services and Fernández's failure to honour promises made during his election campaign provoked widespread disturbances and strike action throughout the country in 1997 and early 1998, with violent confrontations between demonstrators and the security forces resulting in several deaths. In October, in an effort to defuse the volatile social and political climate, Fernández introduced a recovery plan aimed at overcoming electricity and food shortages. However, in the following month a two-day general strike was organized by an 'umbrella' protest group, the Coordinadora Nacional de Organizaciones Populares (CNOP), in support of demands for pay increases, reductions in the price of fuel and basic foodstuffs and improved public services.

At legislative elections held in May 1998 the PRD won 83 seats in the 149-seat Cámara de Diputados (enlarged from 120 seats), while the PLD obtained 49 seats and the PRSC secured the remaining 17 seats. In the Senado the PRD won 24 seats, while the PLD won four and the PRSC two seats. The number of registered voters who abstained from participating in the poll was, at some 48%, the highest on record. In July 1998 the outgoing Congreso approved controversial legislation granting an amnesty to all public officials accused of corruption since 1978. The new legislature was inaugurated in August 1998. However, the PRD failed to secure the presidency of the Cámara de Diputados when a dissident group of PRD deputies joined forces with the PLD and the PRSC to re-elect the outgoing President of the Chamber, Héctor Rafael Peguero Méndez, to the post. Peguero had been expelled from the PRD in July, after refusing to accept the party's choice of candidate for the position.

Violent protests against electricity and water shortages and declining living standards continued in 1998 and 1999. In May 1999 the privatization of the CDE began.

In the first round of the May 2000 presidential election, Rafael Hipólito Mejía Domínguez, the PRD candidate, received 49.9% of the votes cast, while the PRD candidate, Danilo Medina Sánchez, won 24.9%. Former President Balaguer, standing as the PRSC's candidate for a potential eighth presidential term, won 24.6% of the ballot. Despite Mejía's failure to secure the constitutionally required 50%, a second ballot was not held and the JCE allowed Mejía to declare himself the winner. He was inaugurated as President on 16 August and a new Cabinet was officially appointed. The PRD crusade against the previous PLD administration's alleged corruption proved controversial, creating open hostility between the two parties. In November former President Fernández led a protest, following the arrest of various former senior government officials on corruption charges. Fernández himself was later similarly accused and arrested; however, they were all subsequently released, owing to lack of evidence. With only 73 PRD deputies in the 149-seat lower house (10 of the 83 elected in May 1998 had been expelled from the party), Mejía lacked a parliamentary majority, and was dependent for support on the PRSC.

In early 2001 President Mejía initiated a series of fiscal measures, increasing value-added tax, introducing taxes on luxury goods and obliging larger companies to pay corporation taxes in stages throughout the year. Fuel prices increased following the implementation of a fixed tax, but there was no violent popular response. The Government also introduced a poverty mitigation programme, including training, infrastructural programmes and education, social security, health and housing reforms. The political programme also included decentralization of power and the restructuring of the public sector.

THE DOMINICAN REPUBLIC

There was some opposition to the measures, including a strike by hospital workers in protest at the proposed welfare reforms.

In December 2000 the Senado approved constitutional amendments to extend the presidential term to five years and the congressional term to six years, and to lower the minimum requirement of votes in a presidential election. The legislation was condemned by many politicians and, in order to appease opposition to the bill, Mejía subsequently appointed a Committee on Constitutional Reform to assess the situation. In October 2001 the Committee submitted a constitutional reform bill to the Congreso, the principal provision of which was to reduce the proportion of votes needed to win a presidential election to 45% (or 40% if the leading candidate had at least a 10% majority). The Senado subsequently voted to include in the constitutional amendments a clause permitting the re-election of a President. Mejía opposed the inclusion of this reform, and in December the Supreme Court ruled the proposed legislation to be unconstitutional. However, in January 2002 the Cámara de Diputados approved the formation of a National Constituent Assembly and in July, following re-examination, a bill of amendment permitting presidential re-election received assent from the National Assembly.

Legislative elections were held on 16 May 2002. The PRD secured 73 seats in the Cámara de Diputados, the PLD 41 (a reduction of its representation by eight seats) and the PRSC 36. The PRD also won 29 of 32 seats available in the Senado; however, the failure of the PRD to secure an outright majority in the lower house ensured its continued dependence upon the support of the PRSC for the passage of legislation.

In May 2003 the dissolution of the commercial bank Banco Intercontinental, SA (Baninter), following the exposure of huge losses at the bank owing to fraud, had serious political, as well as economic, implications. The President of Baninter, Ramón Báez Figueroa, allegedly had links to the PLD, thus damaging the reputation of that party as well as the Government. Figueroa and two other bank officials were later arrested on fraud charges. The Government's subsequent decision to guarantee all the deposits held at Baninter, at a cost of approximately US $2,200m., resulted in the onset of an economic crisis so severe that the Government was forced to request IMF assistance; in August a $618m. stand-by arrangement with the IMF was concluded. In October 2007 Figueroa was convicted of fraud and sentenced to 10 years' imprisonment.

In November 2003 a 24-hour general strike took place, during which violent clashes occurred between the security forces and anti-Government protesters in several cities, resulting in the deaths of at least seven people. The strike was organized by the CNOP in protest at governmental mismanagement of the economy and, in particular, the failure to resolve the ongoing, and increasingly severe, power shortages (the partially privatized electricity company, CDE, had been renationalized in that year). In late January 2004 a 48-hour general strike was held, during which at least nine people were killed and many more injured.

At the presidential election held on 16 May 2004, former President Fernández of the PLD defeated the incumbent Mejía by a decisive margin, securing 57% of the votes cast, sufficient to ensure that no second round of voting would be necessary. Mejía, seeking a second presidential term despite previous assurances that he would not, attracted 34% of the ballot, while the PRSC candidate, Rafael Eduardo Estrella Virella, was third placed with 9% of the votes. On taking office in August, President Fernández pledged to alleviate the chronic power shortages in the country. The new Government promised to standardize electricity rates and introduce subsidies for poorer sections of the population, while, at the same time, reducing the theft of electricity. It also pledged to meet 70% of national demand, an increase from 50%. Although power supplies initially improved, following the Government's payment of US $50m. towards the debt owed to electricity suppliers, by 2005 the electricity shortages had returned to pre-election levels. The country's ongoing power crisis also continued to exacerbate the civil unrest across the country: in August protests against the blackouts led to one death.

In July 2005 the Government launched a new anti-crime plan, which assigned an additional 2,000 police officers to patrol duty and an additional 1,000 to the criminal investigations department. The project was supported by a US $125m. loan. At the time of the plan's implementation only 8,000 of the serving 32,000 police officers were on patrol duty; the plan aimed gradually to increase that number to 16,000 in order to combat

Introductory Survey

violent crime more effectively, the reported incidence of which had increased sharply in the previous 12 months.

Legislative and municipal elections were held on 16 May 2006. For the first time in its history, the PLD secured a congressional majority in both legislative chambers, winning 96 seats in the Cámara de Diputados (which had been increased from 150 to 178 seats so as to reflect the population growth since the 2002 elections) and 22 seats in the Senado. The PRD's legislative representation was reduced to 60 seats in the Cámara de Diputados and just six seats in the Senado, while the PRSC won 22 in the former and four in the latter. Following the installation of the new legislature President Fernández announced several changes to the Cabinet, including the appointment of Lt-Gen. Ramón Aquino García as Secretary of State for the Armed Forces, in place of Rear-Adm. José Sigfrido Pared Pérez. In the same month, on his first visit to the Dominican Republic, UN Secretary-General Kofi Annan praised the country's endeavours in reducing poverty and improving education, health and sanitation. Meanwhile, in July, new legislation imposing stricter restrictions on opening times for venues selling alcohol was introduced, in the hope of reducing the rate of crime, particularly within urban areas.

In January 2007 the Technical Secretariat of the Presidency merged with the National Planning Office to form the Secretariat of State for the Economy, Planning and Development; the incumbent Technical Secretary to the Presidency, Juan Temístocles Montás, was appointed to head the Secretariat. President Fernández effected a minor cabinet reshuffle in August: Omar Ramírez Tejada replaced Dr Max Puig as Secretary of State for the Environment and Natural Resources, Víctor Díaz Rúa was appointed Secretary of State for Public Works and Communications in succession to Manuel de Jesús Pérez, and Francisco Javier García was replaced as Secretary of State for Industry and Commerce by Melanio Paredes.

A presidential election was scheduled for 16 May 2008, with a second round of voting to be held on 30 June if no candidate achieved 50% of the vote in the first round. Fernández, who was elected as the PLD's candidate in May 2007 despite the party's previous opposition to the re-election of a President, was expected to secure a second term in office; although the Government's reputation had been affected by a number of corruption allegations, opinion polls conducted in early 2008 suggested that rapid economic growth under Fernández's presidency had contributed to his popularity. The other principal candidates in the election were Miguel Vargas of the PRD and Amable Aristy of the PRSC.

The continuing illegal import of plantation labour into the Dominican Republic from Haiti was a major issue for successive Governments. Following the army coup of September 1991 in Haiti, tens of thousands of Haitians fled to the Dominican Republic. However, few were granted refugee status. In 1994 reports of large-scale smuggling from the Dominican Republic to Haiti, in defiance of UN sanctions against the Haitian military dictatorship, led to the establishment of a UN monitoring mission to observe the enforcement of the embargo until the lifting of UN sanctions (in October 1994). In 1997 the Dominican and Haitian Presidents agreed to put an immediate end to large-scale repatriations and for the repatriation process to be monitored by an international body to ensure the observance of human rights. In June 1998 Fernández became the first Dominican head of state to visit Haiti since 1936. At the meeting the two Presidents reached agreement on the establishment of joint border patrols to combat the traffic of drugs, arms and other contraband across the countries' joint border. In late 1999, following the summary deportation of some 8,000 Haitians, the two Governments signed a protocol limiting the repatriations.

In early 2001, following an increase in tensions in Haiti, military forces deployed on the Dominican–Haitian border also were reinforced in an attempt to prevent both illegal immigration and drugs-trafficking. In late 2002 the USA pledged weapons, technical assistance and joint military exercises in order to help the Dominican armed forces patrol the border area. In early 2004, in response to escalating political instability in Haiti, security in the border area was increased again. Following the overthrow of the Haitian President, Jean-Bertrand Aristide, in February 2004, bilateral relations deteriorated when supporters of Aristide accused the Dominican authorities of having aided the insurgents who had led the rebellion against him. In December 2004 the Senado approved a resolution calling for the 'cleansing and deportation' of illegal Haitian immigrants. Following the murder of a Dominican woman in May 2005, allegedly carried out by two Haitian men, the Dominican army forcibly repatriated thousands of Haitians resident in the Dominican Republic. The army insisted that only illegal immigrants had been targeted, but human rights organizations—including the Inter-American Commission on Human Rights—accused the army of acting indiscriminately, claiming that many Dominicans of Haitian descent and legal immigrants had been deported. In July the Fernández Government again intensified border security measures, in order to reduce the number of illegal immigrants and to close down conduits for drugs-trafficking. In December, in response to the murder of a Dominican businessman, apparently by Haitians, residents in the northern town of Villa Trina set fire to settlements housing Haitian immigrants. Later that month President Fernández made an official visit to Haiti; however, hopes that the visit would ease tensions were quashed when violent demonstrations erupted outside the presidential palace, in protest at the treatment of Haitians in the Dominican Republic. The protests prompted Fernández to curtail his stay in Haiti and led to the withdrawal of most of the Dominican Republic's embassy staff in the Haitian capital, Port-au-Prince. The mass deportations of Haitians resident in the Dominican Republic continued unabated in 2006, with an estimated 15,000–20,000 being forcibly repatriated. Human rights groups were becoming increasingly outspoken about the Dominican mistreatment of illegal immigrants, and in December a US congressional delegation strongly criticized treatment of Haitian workers on Dominican sugar farms, prompting the Dominican Government to respond angrily in the face of what it perceived to be unwarranted intervention in its domestic affairs. In September 2007 a new military border security force, the Cuerpo Especializado de Seguridad Fronteriza (Cesfront), began patrolling the frontier, reportedly repatriating some 10,000 illegal Haitian immigrants in its first two months of operation.

In 2006 President Fernández expended considerable energy in efforts to strengthen relations with the Dominican Republic's Asian allies. In April he hosted an official visit by Taiwanese President Chen Shui-bian, during which the two heads of state discussed a possible bilateral free trade agreement. In June, as part of a 14-day tour of East Asia, Fernández made a reciprocal visit to the Taiwanese capital, Taipei, during which a bilateral trade accord was again the main focus of dialogue, the first round of negotiations for which were subsequently held in Santo Domingo in October. The Taiwanese Government pledged aid to the value of US $50m. over a four-year period to assist with the construction of a national science and industrial technology park in Santo Domingo. The two other destinations in President Fernández's tour were Japan and the Republic of Korea, where he met with the Japanese Prime Minister and the Korean President, respectively. In September the Dominican Government announced that it had established formal diplomatic relations with Viet Nam, following discussions between President Fernández and Vietnamese President Nguyen Minh Triet during the summit meeting of the Non-aligned Movement held earlier that month in Havana, Cuba.

Government

The Dominican Republic comprises 31 provinces, each administered by an appointed governor, and a Distrito Nacional (DN) containing the capital. Under the 1966 Constitution (as amended in 1994), legislative power is exercised by the bicameral Congreso Nacional (National Congress), with a Senado (Senate) of 32 members and a Cámara de Diputados (Chamber of Deputies) comprising 178 members. Members of both houses are elected for four years by universal adult suffrage. Executive power lies with the President, who is also elected by direct popular vote for four years. He is assisted by a Vice-President and a Cabinet comprising Secretaries of State.

Defence

Military service is voluntary and lasts for four years. As assessed at November 2007, the armed forces totalled an estimated 24,500 men: army 15,000, air force 5,500 and navy 4,000. Paramilitary forces numbered 15,000. The defence budget for 2007 was an estimated RD $9,000m.

Economic Affairs

In 2006, according to estimates by the World Bank, the Dominican Republic's gross national income (GNI), measured at average 2004–06 prices, was US $27,359m., equivalent to $2,850 per head (or $8,290 per head on an international purchasing-power parity basis). During 1996–2006, it was estimated, the population increased by an average of 1.7% per year, while gross domestic product (GDP) per head increased, in real terms, by an average of 4.2% per year. Overall GDP increased, in real terms, by an average of 5.9% per year in 1996–2006. According to central bank figures, real GDP increased by 9.3% in 2005 and by 10.7% in 2006.

According to official data, agriculture, including hunting, forestry and fishing, contributed 6.8% of GDP and employed an estimated 14.8% of the employed labour force in 2006. The principal cash crops are sugar cane (sugar and sugar derivatives accounted for an estimated 6.9% of total export earnings in 2006), coffee, cocoa beans and tobacco. Agricultural GDP increased, in real terms, by an average of 3.1% per year during 1996–2006. Real agricultural GDP increased by 8.6% in 2006.

Industry (including mining, manufacturing, construction and power) employed an estimated 21.9% of the economically active population and contributed 31.2% of GDP in 2006. Industrial GDP increased, in real terms, by an average of 4.4% per year during 1996–2006. Real industrial GDP increased by 6.5% in 2006.

Mining contributed 0.5% of GDP, but employed less than an estimated 0.1% of the economically active population, in 2006. The major mineral export is ferro-nickel (providing approximately 36.8% of total export earnings—excluding exports to free trade zones—in 2006). Gold and silver are also exploited, and there are workable deposits of gypsum, limestone and mercury. The slump in world prices forced the ferro-nickel mine at Bonao to close in late 1998. Following an increase in prices in early 2000, the mine was reopened; however, it was closed intermittently in 2001 and 2002, before reopening in 2003. In 2002 the Government reached agreement with Placer Dome of Canada on a 25-year concession to operate the Sulfuros de Pueblo Viejo mine. There were plans to develop other mines throughout the country. Real mining GDP increased by an annual average of 3.2% during 1996–2006. The GDP of the mining sector declined, in real terms, by 0.1% in 2005, but increased by 11.0% in 2006.

Manufacturing contributed 21.4% of GDP and employed an estimated 14.1% of the economically active population in 2006. Important branches of manufacturing included beer, cigarettes and cement. At the end of 2006, according to the Consejo Nacional de Zonas Francas de Exportación (National Free Zones Council), there were 555 companies operating in 56 free trade zones in the Dominican Republic, employing some 148,411 people. This represented a significant decrease on the previous year, when 154,781 people had been employed in the sector. The contraction of the textile-dominated free trade zones was largely attributable to the ending of the World Trade Organization's Agreement on Textiles and Clothing, which governed textile export quotas, in December 2004. The GDP of the manufacturing sector increased, in real terms, at an average rate of 4.5% per year during 1996–2006. Real manufacturing GDP increased by 3.2% in 2006.

Energy is derived principally from petroleum; however, there is no domestic petroleum production. Imports of crude petroleum and related products accounted for an estimated 20.9% of the total cost of imports in 2006. In the early 2000s construction was under way on a variety of energy projects, including: a 300 MW oil-fired power-station and a 300 MW gas-fired power-station, including a liquefied natural gas terminal; a regasification plant and a 500 MW gas-fired power-station; a hydroelectric dam in Altagracia, to supply drinking water and electricity to the province; and four mini-hydroelectric plants, together generating 16 MW. The Monción dam in Santiago Rodríguez, which included a 54 MW hydroelectric plant, was inaugurated in September 2001 and a wind park in Puerto Plata became operational in mid-2002. The Dominican Republic signed, in 2005, the PetroCaribe agreement with Venezuela, under which it would be allowed to purchase petroleum from Venezuela at reduced prices. In July 2006 work commenced on the construction of the 99 MW Palomino hydroelectric plant in San Juan de Maguana, which was expected to be completed by mid-2008. In October delays in the delivery of crude oil from the USA and Venezuela resulted in widespread fuel shortages, which, combined with the intermittent electricity supply (see below), led to a temporary paralysis of transport, trade and industry across much of the country.

The services sector contributed 62.0% of GDP in 2006, and employed an estimated 63.2% of the economically active population in the same year. The tourism sector was the country's primary source of foreign exchange earnings. In 2007 an estimated 4,428,005 tourists visited the Dominican Republic;

receipts from tourism, excluding passenger transport, totalled US $3,508m. in 2005. In January 2007 the Secretariat of State for Tourism announced plans designed to improve the performance of the tourism sector, including the launch of a national airline and the creation of a new national institute for tourism infrastructure. The GDP of the services sector expanded at an average annual rate of 6.3% during 1996–2006. Real services GDP increased by 10.7% in 2006.

In 2006 the Dominican Republic recorded a visible trade deficit of US $4,750.2m., and there was a deficit of $786.1m. on the current account of the balance of payments. In 2005 the principal source of imports was the USA (35.0%); other major suppliers were Canada, Japan and Brazil. In the same year the USA was the principal market for exports (32.3% of the total); other significant purchasers were Haiti and Puerto Rico. The principal exports in 2005 were ferro-nickel and petroleum products; exports from the free trade zones in that year amounted to $4,553.7m. The principal imports in 2006 were petroleum products, petroleum and durable goods.

In 2006 there was an estimated budgetary deficit of RD $1,355.2m. (equivalent to 0.1% of GDP). The Dominican Republic's total external debt at the end of 2005 was estimated at US $7,398m., of which $6,094m. was long term public debt. In that year the cost of debt-servicing was equivalent to 6.9% of total revenue from exports of goods and services. In 1999–2006 the average annual rate of inflation was 15.1%. Consumer prices increased by 4.2% in 2005 and by 7.6% in 2006. An estimated 16.0% of the total labour force was unemployed in October 2006.

The Dominican Republic was granted observer status in the Caribbean Community and Common Market (CARICOM, see p. 196) in 1984. An agreement, originally signed in August 1998, establishing a free trade area between CARICOM countries and the Dominican Republic, came into effect on 1 December 2001. The country was one of the African, Caribbean and Pacific nations covered by the European Union's (EU) Cotonou Agreement (see p. 301), which guaranteed access to EU markets. In September 2005 the Congreso Nacional approved the country's membership of the proposed Dominican Republic-Central American Free Trade Agreement (DR-CAFTA) with the USA. Implementation of the accord took place in March 2007 (see below).

Upon taking office in August 2004, President Fernández stressed that his Government would pursue an economic policy based on securing stability through the reduction of government spending and inflation. In February 2005 the Fernández Government concluded a new stand-by agreement with the IMF worth US $665.2m. In February 2008 the IMF released its eighth and final review of the agreement, which had been extended in February 2007, and issued a final tranche of aid equivalent to US $122.3m. In May 2005 the World Bank approved a new Country Assistance Strategy for the Dominican Republic, which was to provide financial assistance of US $360m., together with technical and advisory services, during 2006–09. Implementation of DR-CAFTA had been scheduled for January 2006, but legislative reforms required for the accord to take effect in the Dominican Republic were not approved until November, resulting in enactment being delayed until the following March. In order to resolve the ongoing power shortages, the Fernández Government in 2004 obtained credit to pay its debts to the various power companies. Nevertheless, the situation worsened throughout 2005 as global petroleum prices rose to unprecedented levels and electricity prices rose by 42%. In January 2006 the Government announced that it would invest US $500m. to cover the deficit of the energy sector in that year and would spend an additional $11m. on the construction of new plants. Despite the IMF's warning that the administration should reduce expenditure on the power sector, in 2007 government subsidies reached US $611m., $200m. higher than the agreed figure. Legislation, approved in July of that year, criminalizing electricity theft (it was estimated that only 58.4% of electricity distributed in the Dominican Republic was paid for) was expected substantially to increase profitability in the sector; however, President Fernández delayed implementation of the law until the end of March 2008, a move the opposition interpreted as an attempt not to lose popularity in advance of the May presidential election. According to the IMF, GDP grew by 8.0% in 2007, and growth of about 4.5% was forecast for 2008.

Education

Education is, where possible, compulsory for children between the ages of six and 14 years. Primary education begins at the age of six and lasts for eight years. Secondary education, starting at 14 years of age, lasts for four years. In 2005 primary enrolment included 87.7% of children in the relevant age-group, while secondary enrolment included 53.0% of children in the relevant age-group (males 47.4%; females 58.8%). In 1997/98 there were 4,001 primary schools, and in 1996/97 there were an estimated 1,737 secondary schools. There are eight universities. In October 2001 the Government announced the investment of US $52m. in the construction and reparation of schools. Budgetary expenditure on education by the Secretariat of State for Education in 2005 was RD $15,650.7m., representing 8.1% of total government spending.

Public Holidays

2008: 1 January (New Year's Day), 6 January (Epiphany), 21 January (Our Lady of Altagracia), 26 January (Birth of Juan Pablo Duarte), 27 February (Independence Day), 21 March (Good Friday), 5 May (for Labour Day), 16 May (Presidential Election), 22 May (Corpus Christi), 16 August (Restoration Day), 24 September (Our Lady of Mercedes), 10 November (for Constitution Day), 25 December (Christmas Day).

2009: 1 January (New Year's Day), 5 January (for Epiphany), 21 January (Our Lady of Altagracia), 26 January (Birth of Juan Pablo Duarte), 27 February (Independence Day), 10 April (Good Friday), 4 May (for Labour Day), 11 June (Corpus Christi), 16 August (Restoration Day), 24 September (Our Lady of Mercedes), 9 November (for Constitution Day), 25 December (Christmas Day).

Weights and Measures

The metric system is officially in force but the imperial system is often used.

Statistical Survey

Sources (unless otherwise stated): Oficina Nacional de Estadística, Edif. de Oficinas Gubernamentales, 9°, Avda México, esq. Leopoldo Navarro, Santo Domingo, DN; tel. 682-7777; fax 685-4424; e-mail info@one.gob.do; internet www.one.gob.do; Banco Central de la República Dominicana, Calle Pedro Henríquez Ureña, esq. Leopoldo Navarro, Apdo 1347, Santo Domingo, DN; tel. 221-9111; fax 686-7488; e-mail info@bancentral.gov.do; internet www.bancentral.gov.do.

Area and Population

AREA, POPULATION AND DENSITY

Area (sq km)	
Land	48,137
Inland water	597
Total	48,734*
Population (census results)	
24 September 1993	7,293,390
18–20 October 2002	
Males	4,297,326
Females	4,265,215
Total	8,562,541
Population (official estimates)†	
2003	8,717,000
2004	8,873,000
2005	9,033,000
Density (per sq km) at 2005	185.4

* 18,816 sq miles.
† Preliminary figures, rounded to nearest 100 persons.

Population (UN estimates at mid-year): 9,615,000 in 2006; 9,760,000 in 2007 (Source: UN, *World Population Prospects: The 2006 Revision*).

PROVINCES

	Area (sq km)	Population (census of Oct. 2002)	Density (per sq km)
Distrito Nacional Region			
Distrito Nacional	104.4	913,540	8,750.4
Santo Domingo	1,296.4	1,817,754	1,402.2
Valdesia Region			
Peravia	997.6	169,865	170.3
San Cristóbal	1,265.8	532,880	421.0
Monte Plata	2,632.1	180,376	68.5
San José de Ocoa	650.2	62,368	95.9
Norcentral Region			
Espaillat	839.0	225,091	268.3
Puerto Plata	1,856.9	312,706	168.4
Santiago	2,839.0	908,250	319.9
Nordeste Region			
Duarte	1,605.4	283,805	176.8
María Trinidad Sánchez	1,271.7	135,727	106.7
Salcedo	440.4	96,356	218.8
Samaná	853.7	91,875	107.6
Enriquillo Region			
Baoruco	1,282.2	91,480	71.3
Barahona	1,739.4	179,239	103.0
Independencia	2,006.4	50,833	25.3
Pedernales	2,074.5	21,207	10.2
Este Region			
El Seibo	1,786.8	89,261	50.0
La Altagracia	2,474.3	182,020	73.6
La Romana	654.0	219,812	336.1
San Pedro de Macorís	1,255.5	301,744	240.3
Hato Mayor	1,329.3	87,631	65.9
El Valle Region			
Azua	2,531.8	208,857	82.5
Elías Piña	1,426.2	63,879	44.8
San Juan	3,569.4	241,105	67.5
Noroeste Region			
Dajabón	1,020.7	62,046	60.8
Monte Cristi	1,924.4	111,014	57.7
Santiago Rodríguez	1,111.1	59,629	53.7
Valverde	823.4	158,293	192.2
Cibao Central Region			
La Vega	2,287.0	385,101	168.4
Sánchez Ramírez	1,196.1	151,179	126.4
Monseñor Nouel	992.4	167,618	168.9
Total	48,137.0*	8,562,541	177.9*

* Land area only.

PRINCIPAL TOWNS
(population at census of October 2002)

Santo Domingo DN (capital)	2,302,759	San Felipe de Puerto Plata	146,882
Santiago de los Caballeros	622,101	Higuey	141,751
San Cristóbal	220,767	Moca	131,733
Concepción de la Vega	220,279	San Juan de la Maguana	129,224
San Pedro de Macorís	217,141	Monseñor Nouel	115,743
La Romana	202,488	Baní	107,926
San Francisco de Macorís	156,267	Bajos de Haina	80,835

Mid-2007 ('000, incl. suburbs, UN estimate): Santo Domingo DN 2,154 (Source: UN, *World Urbanization Prospects: The 2007 Revision*).

BIRTHS AND DEATHS
(annual averages, UN estimates)

	1990–95	1995–2000	2000–05
Birth rate (per 1,000)	28.2	26.7	25.2
Death rate (per 1,000)	6.0	6.0	5.9

Source: UN, *World Population Prospects: The 2006 Revision*.

Marriages: 24,467 in 2002 (2.9 per 1,000); 29,467 in 2003 (3.4 per 1,000); 23,094 in 2004 (2.6 per 1,000) (Source: UN, *Demographic Yearbook*).

Expectation of life (years at birth, WHO estimates): 68.2 (males 65.1; females 71.7) in 2005 (Source: WHO, *World Health Statistics*).

ECONOMICALLY ACTIVE POPULATION
('000 persons aged 10 years and over, official estimates at April 2007)

	Males	Females	Total
Agriculture, hunting, forestry and fishing	486.4	28.4	514.8
Mining and quarrying	3.0	0.0	3.0
Manufacturing	352.8	140.0	492.8
Electricity, gas and water supply	23.3	7.4	30.6
Construction	239.4	6.9	246.3
Wholesale and retail trade	481.4	247.7	729.1
Hotels and restaurants	100.5	116.9	217.4
Transport, storage and communications	229.5	26.4	256.0
Financial intermediation Real estate, renting and business activities	30.4	40.5	71.0
Public administration and defence	105.1	45.0	150.0
Education Health and social work Other community, social and personal service activities	275.8	538.3	814.2
Total employed	2,327.6	1,197.5	3,525.1
Unemployed	237.9	413.8	651.7
Total labour force	2,565.5	1,611.3	4,176.9

THE DOMINICAN REPUBLIC

Health and Welfare

KEY INDICATORS

Total fertility rate (children per woman, 2005)	2.6
Under-5 mortality rate (per 1,000 live births, 2005)	31
HIV/AIDS (% of persons aged 15–49, 2005)	1.1
Physicians (per 1,000 head, 2000)	1.88
Hospital beds (per 1,000 head, 2005)	2.2
Health expenditure (2004): US $ per head (PPP)	377.0
Health expenditure (2004): % of GDP	6.0
Health expenditure (2004): public (% of total)	31.6
Access to water (% of persons, 2004)	95
Access to sanitation (% of persons, 2004)	78
Human Development Index (2005): ranking	79
Human Development Index (2005): value	0.779

For sources and definitions, see explanatory note on p. vi.

Agriculture

PRINCIPAL CROPS
('000 metric tons)

	2004	2005	2006*
Rice (paddy)	576.6	644.9	700.0
Maize	37.7	39.2	31.0
Potatoes	36.8	49.6	49.6
Sweet potatoes	27.6	35.7	35.7
Cassava (Manioc)	90.5	97.5	93.6
Yautia (Cocoyam)	69.3	31.7	31.7
Sugar cane	5,547.2	4,848.1	5,160.0
Dry beans	22.8	22.7	24.3
Coconuts	181.5	107.5	107.5
Oil palm fruit*	154.3	165.0	165.0
Tomatoes	285.8	291.5	291.5
Pumpkins, squash and gourds	32.7	38.9	38.9
Chillies and peppers, green	29.2	28.1	28.1
Dry onions	37.1	49.7	49.7
Garlic	2.0	1.1	1.1
Carrots and turnips*	20.0	23.9	23.9
Cantaloupes and other melons*	57.7	61.0	61.0
Bananas	468.4	547.4	547.4
Plantains	310.9	412.0	412.0
Oranges	80.0	100.8	100.8
Guavas, mangoes and mangosteens*	160.0	170.0	170.0
Avocados	281.8	113.6	113.6
Pineapples	92.6	65.8	65.8
Papayas*	25.3	25.9	25.9
Coffee (green)	38.8	43.5	43.5
Cocoa beans†	47.3	31.4	31.4
Tobacco (leaves)	11.6†	12.0*	12.0

* FAO estimate(s).
† Unofficial figure(s).

Aggregate production ('000 metric tons, may include official, semi-official or estimated data): Total cereals 620.0 in 2004, 633.9 in 2005, 734.0 in 2006; Total roots and tubers 240.6 in 2004, 226.6 in 2005, 226.6 in 2006; Total vegetables (incl. melons) 520.0 in 2004, 545.8 in 2005, 545.5 in 2006; Total fruits (excl. melons) 1,456.2 in 2004, 2,265.8 in 2005, 1,479.7 in 2006.

Source: FAO.

LIVESTOCK
('000 head, year ending September)

	2003	2004	2005
Horses*	343	343	343
Asses and mules*	291	291	291
Cattle	2,160.0*	2,165.0	2,200.0*
Pigs*	577.5	578.0	580.0
Sheep*	122.0	123.0	123.0
Goats*	188.5	189.0	190.0
Poultry*	46,500	47,000	47,500

* FAO estimate(s).

2006: Figures assumed to be unchanged from 2005 (FAO estimates).
Source: FAO.

LIVESTOCK PRODUCTS
('000 metric tons)

	2003	2004	2005*
Cattle meat	69.5	71.5	73.2
Pig meat	63.9	52.2	78.0
Chicken meat	157.0	238.2	296.6
Cows' milk	637.4	661.6	751.7
Hen eggs	67.3	63.6	80.2
Honey	3.2	2.0*	2.0

* FAO estimate(s).
2006: Figures assumed to be unchanged from 2005 (FAO estimates).
Source: FAO.

Forestry

ROUNDWOOD REMOVALS
('000 cubic metres, excl. bark)

	2004*	2005	2006
Sawlogs, veneer logs and logs for sleepers	4	9	11
Other industrial wood	3	3*	3*
Fuel wood	556	556*	878*
Total*	562	568	892

* FAO estimate(s).
Source: FAO.

Fishing

('000 metric tons, live weight)

	2003	2004	2005
Capture	18.1	14.2	11.1
Tilapia	0.7	0.9	0.8
Groupers, seabasses	0.6	0.4	0.4
Common carp	0.4	0.6	0.5
Snappers and jobfishes	1.7	1.0	1.0
King mackerel	0.5	0.2	0.2
Blackfin tuna	0.3	0.1	0.1
Caribbean spiny lobster	0.8	1.0	1.0
Stromboid conchs	1.7	1.2	1.5
Aquaculture	1.9	2.0	1.0
Common carp	0.5	0.5	0.0
Total catch	20.0	16.2	12.1

Source: FAO.

Mining

('000 metric tons)

	2003	2004	2005
Ferro-nickel	69.6	75.8	61.1
Nickel (metal content of laterite ore)	45.3	46.0	45.9*
Gypsum	250.3	459.5	370.1
Rock salt	107.0	—	—

* Estimate.
Source: US Geological Survey.

THE DOMINICAN REPUBLIC

Industry

SELECTED PRODUCTS
('000 metric tons, unless otherwise indicated)

	2003	2004	2005*
Flour and derivatives ('000 quintales†)	2,303.9	2,516.4	2,543.2
Refined sugar	127.7	124.0	139.2
Cement	2,906.7	2,653.6	2,778.7
Beer ('000 hectolitres)	3,552.6	3,546.1	4,540.9
Cigarettes (million)	3,469.2	3,445.9	3,300.3

* Preliminary figures.
† 1 quintale is equivalent to 46 kg.

2004 ('000 barrels, estimates): Motor spirit (petrol) 2,000; Jet fuel 1,900; Distillate fuel oil 2,900; Residual fuel oil 4,600 (Source: US Geological Survey).

Finance

CURRENCY AND EXCHANGE RATES

Monetary Units
100 centavos = 1 Dominican Republic peso (RD $ or peso oro).

Sterling, Dollar and Euro Equivalents (31 December 2007)
£1 sterling = 68.801 pesos;
US $1 = 34.342 pesos;
€1 = 50.555 pesos;
1,000 Dominican Republic pesos = £14.53 = $29.12 = €19.78.

Average Exchange Rate (RD $ per US $)
2005 30.409
2006 33.365
2006 33.262

BUDGET
(RD $ million)

Revenue	2004	2005*	2006*
Tax revenue	117,298.1	148,450.1	177,812.1
Taxes on income and profits	24,373.9	29,569.6	38,981.9
Taxes on goods and services	53,468.3	77,143.0	103,530.1
Taxes on international trade and transactions	37,226.2	37,800.1	26,839.2
Other current revenue	8,944.9	9,134.5	11,013.4
Capital revenue	9,290.1	8,571.8	46,942.3
Total	135,533.1	166,156.4	235,767.8

Expenditure	2004	2005*	2006*
Current expenditure	107,885.8	123,062.4	154,532.1
Wages and salaries	29,813.0	37,898.5	44,269.9
Other services	5,417.3	8,810.6	12,345.1
Materials and supplies	7,824.7	12,442.5	15,487.2
Current transfers	51,084.7	53,916.2	66,426.5
Interest payments	13,711.6	10,794.6	15,778.1
Internal debt	2,868.2	4,244.5	4,636.7
External debt	10,843.4	6,550.0	11,141.4
Capital expenditure	54,715.5	64,955.2	79,880.5
Machines and equipment	2,033.3	3,421.2	2,237.8
Construction of works and agricultural plantations	7,304.7	13,777.3	16,928.7
Capital transfers	17,105.4	21,466.3	17,975.4
Total (incl. others)	162,601.3	188,017.5	234,412.6

* Preliminary figures.

INTERNATIONAL RESERVES
(US $ million at 31 December)

	2004	2005	2006
Gold*	8.0	9.4	11.6
IMF special drawing rights	1.6	0.6	24.5
Foreign exchange	796.7	1,842.6	2,091.2
Total	806.2	1,852.6	2,127.3

* Valued at market-related prices.

Source: IMF, *International Financial Statistics*.

MONEY SUPPLY
(RD $ million at 31 December)

	2004	2005	2006
Currency outside banks	32,548	38,326	43,979
Demand deposits at commercial banks	43,241	54,344	63,439
Total money (incl. others)	76,153	92,926	107,604

Source: IMF, *International Financial Statistics*.

COST OF LIVING
(Consumer Price Index including direct taxes; base: 2000 = 100)

	2004	2005	2006
Food, beverages and tobacco	237.0	233.0	242.8
Clothing	163.5	178.9	193.0
Rent	206.6	226.9	253.7
All items (incl. others)	221.2	230.4	247.9

Source: ILO.

NATIONAL ACCOUNTS

National Income and Product
(RD $ million at current prices)

	2003	2004	2005
GDP in market prices	601,142	914,751	1,055,731
Net primary income from abroad	−42,171	−71,827	−56,893
Gross national income (GNI)	558,971	842,924	998,838
Less Consumption of fixed capital	30,198	46,631	n.a.
Net national income	528,773	796,293	n.a.

Source: IMF, *International Financial Statistics*.

Expenditure on the Gross Domestic Product
(RD $ million at current prices)

	2004	2005	2006
Final consumption expenditure	766,450.5	907,434.9	1,065,812.9
Households / Non-profit institutions serving households	710,022.6	839,097.0	980,528.7
General government	56,427.9	68,337.9	85,284.2
Gross capital formation	135,570.8	168,397.8	218,983.7
Gross fixed capital formation	134,108.7	166,933.4	217,398.8
Changes in inventories / Acquisitions, less disposals, of valuables	1,462.1	1,464.4	1,584.9
Total domestic expenditure	902,021.3	1,075,832.7	1,284,796.6
Exports of goods and services	384,773.0	306,312.1	356,834.8
Less Imports of goods and services	377,757.5	362,142.8	451,829.5
GDP in market prices	909,036.8	1,020,002.0	1,189,801.9
GDP at constant 1991 prices	239,835.9	262,051.3	290,015.2

THE DOMINICAN REPUBLIC

Gross Domestic Product by Economic Activity
(RD $ million at current prices)

	2004	2005	2006
Agriculture, hunting, forestry and fishing	59,257.8	70,092.2	77,702.7
Mining and quarrying	4,083.5	3,642.5	5,955.4
Manufacturing	211,557.1	215,031.4	243,110.8
Local manufacturing	145,152.0	165,635.6	189,814.5
Free trade zones	66,405.1	49,395.8	53,296.3
Electricity and water	22,588.0	23,559.2	28,011.9
Construction	41,297.8	59,227.0	76,995.1
Wholesale and retail trade	70,899.1	86,567.8	104,660.4
Restaurants and hotels	121,422.8	118,265.9	138,489.3
Transport and storage	67,223.0	76,903.1	90,745.7
Communications	22,574.0	23,883.3	30,045.2
Finance, insurance and business activities	37,926.9	39,899.1	53,504.6
Real estate	76,159.1	92,609.5	104,648.7
General government services	25,458.0	33,281.6	40,037.7
Education	22,647.5	27,584.4	31,253.1
Health	19,459.5	22,164.4	24,292.2
Other services	66,595.6	77,717.0	85,566.4
Sub-total	869,149.4	970,428.4	1,135,019.5
Less Financial intermediation services indirectly measured	21,160.2	30,088.1	34,119.9
Gross value added in basic prices	847,989.2	940,340.3	1,100,899.6
Taxes, *less* subsidies	61,047.5	79,661.7	88,902.2
GDP in market prices	909,036.8	1,020,002.0	1,189,801.9

BALANCE OF PAYMENTS
(US $ million)

	2004	2005	2006
Exports of goods f.o.b	5,935.9	6,144.7	6,440.0
Imports of goods f.o.b.	-7,888.0	-9,869.4	-11,190.2
Trade balance	-1,952.1	-3,724.7	-4,750.2
Exports of services	3,503.9	3,913.2	4,223.5
Imports of services	-1,213.2	-1,466.5	-1,557.6
Balance on goods and services	338.6	-1,278.0	-2,084.3
Other income received	336.3	418.0	556.9
Other income paid	-2,155.3	-2,315.0	-2,292.0
Balance on goods, services and income	-1,480.4	-3,175.0	-3,819.4
Current transfers received	2,701.4	2,907.7	3,245.2
Current transfers paid	-173.9	-210.6	-211.9
Current balance	1,047.1	-477.9	-786.1
Direct investment from abroad	909.1	1,023.0	1,183.3
Portfolio investment assets	-7.6	-82.1	-328.3
Portfolio investment liabilities	-16.7	330.9	910.2
Other investment assets	-428.7	235.5	-660.3
Other investment liabilities	-338.6	55.9	451.4
Net errors and omissions	-986.7	-378.7	-499.7
Overall balance	177.8	706.6	270.5

Source: IMF, *International Financial Statistics*.

External Trade

PRINCIPAL COMMODITIES

Imports f.o.b. (US $ million)*	2004	2005	2006†
Consumer goods	2,573.4	3,892.1	4,444.7
Durable goods	381.1	841.4	699.2
Foodstuffs	225.5	281.4	390.1
Petroleum products	1,087.9	1,659.4	1,835.6
Raw materials	1,954.6	2,345.9	2,987.0
Artificial plastic materials	137.9	152.9	197.8
Petroleum and petroleum products	579.6	791.7	952.6
Cast iron and steel	202.8	281.2	391.6
Capital goods	840.1	1,128.3	1,366.1
For transport	74.3	205.9	237.4
For industry	222.3	254.0	259.4
Machinery	225.4	254.0	293.7
Total (incl. others)	5,368.1	7,366.3	8,797.8

* Figures exclude imports into free trade zones.
† Preliminary figures.

Exports f.o.b. (US $ million)*	2004	2005	2006†
Sugar and sugar cane derivatives	94.1	101.1	132.5
Raw cane sugar	74.0	74.3	104.8
Cocoa and cocoa manufactures	55.9	41.6	67.0
Cocoa beans	48.5	33.0	57.8
Tobacco and tobacco manufactures	43.2	18.3	11.4
Ferro-nickel	390.0	380.8	709.9
Other goods	427.9	508.9	617.1
Petroleum products	218.6	321.0	356.3
Total	1,250.7	1,395.2	1,931.2

* Figures exclude exports from free trade zones, which totalled: US $4,685.2m. in 2004; US $4,749.7m. in 2005; US $4,553.7m. in 2006.
† Preliminary figures.

PRINCIPAL TRADING PARTNERS
(US $ '000)

Imports c.i.f.	2003	2004	2005*
Argentina	69,386.6	76,430.2	75,984.0
Brazil	161,355.7	221,715.0	194,162.5
Canada	97,909.6	47,055.1	421,730.0
China, People's Republic	76,593.3	84,514.4	137,897.9
Colombia	122,696.6	143,740.8	85,409.1
Denmark	25,152.0	40,104.9	48,216.1
France	38,367.5	31,944.2	44,813.6
Germany	88,984.5	76,945.1	85,373.0
Italy	45,747.6	36,713.4	60,899.0
Japan	139,419.4	139,153.9	336,412.2
Mexico	104,648.6	112,033.6	152,846.7
Panama	98,929.5	97,536.7	134,797.5
Puerto Rico	57,229.8	59,700.5	66,082.8
Spain	174,136.3	178,995.0	135,024.4
Taiwan	82,456.2	119,273.0	135,180.3
Trinidad and Tobago	59,403.9	64,716.5	24,684.6
USA	1,618,586.1	1,595,297.5	1,420,475.3
Venezuela	89,139.1	82,532.4	37,523.8
Total (incl. others)	3,676,701.2	3,703,256.7	4,055,703.0

THE DOMINICAN REPUBLIC

Exports f.o.b.	2003	2004	2005*
Belgium-Luxembourg	26,898.6	10,355.8	32,914.7
Canada	32,725.4	54,231.0	22,537.3
China, People's Republic	275.9	7,251.4	27,848.4
Cuba	8,836.3	14,017.2	10,156.0
France	12,719.6	12,526.5	8,753.3
Germany	13,370.1	25,588.7	35,404.0
Haiti	111,784.1	64,449.8	122,088.5
Italy	13,757.0	15,970.3	14,258.4
Jamaica	14,347.4	7,515.1	11,540.3
Japan	13,085.2	35,240.9	26,730.6
Korea, Republic	n.a.	84,216.8	71,434.1
Netherlands	34,161.1	88,681.9	67,513.2
Panama	8,557.8	5,191.0	7,491.1
Puerto Rico	115,196.0	78,166.4	105,506.2
Spain	21,530.3	16,013.6	22,260.2
United Kingdom	23,321.5	16,912.6	49,691.0
USA	335,547.4	299,870.3	349,197.2
Total (incl. others)	908,854.2	906,586.9	1,081,600.8

* Preliminary figures.

Transport

ROAD TRAFFIC
(motor vehicles in use)

	2002	2003	2004
Passenger cars ('000)	1,888.3	1,894.6	1,916.0
Commercial vehicles ('000)	415.7	426.9	450.0

Source: UN, *Statistical Yearbook*.

SHIPPING

Merchant Fleet
(registered at 31 December)

	2004	2005	2006
Number of vessels	28	24	24
Total displacement ('000 grt)	13.3	10.2	10.0

Source: Lloyd's Register-Fairplay, *World Fleet Statistics*.

International Sea-borne Freight Traffic
('000 metric tons)

	1996	1997	1998
Goods loaded	112	152	139

Source: UN, *Monthly Bulletin of Statistics*.

CIVIL AVIATION
(traffic on scheduled services)

	1997	1998	1999
Kilometres flown (million)	1	1	0
Passengers carried ('000)	34	34	10
Passengers-km (million)	16	16	5
Total ton-km (million)	1	1	0

Source: UN, *Statistical Yearbook*.

Tourism

ARRIVALS BY NATIONALITY

	2005	2006	2007*
Canada	427,074	509,323	587,370
France	309,529	306,302	287,432
Germany	234,368	226,737	217,279
Italy	133,954	144,115	146,808
Puerto Rico	65,343	85,776	55,547
Spain	255,675	273,517	267,077
United Kingdom†	223,642	243,823	225,349
USA	1,010,012	1,092,317	1,080,066
Total (incl. others)	4,081,295	4,383,765	4,428,005

* Provisional figures.
† Includes arrivals from England and Scotland only.

Tourism receipts (US $ million, excl. passenger transport): 3,128 in 2003; 3,152 in 2004; 3,508 in 2005 (Source: World Tourism Organization).

Communications Media

	2004	2005	2006
Telephones ('000 main lines in use)	936.2	896.3	897.0
Mobile cellular telephones ('000 subscribers)	2,534.1	3,623.3	4,605.7
Internet users ('000)	800	1,500	2,000
Broadband users ('000)	37.3	65.9	66.5

Daily newspapers: 11 in 2004 (average circulation 365,000 copies).

Non-daily newspapers: 8 in 2000 (average circulation 215,000 copies).

Radio receivers ('000 in use): 1,440 in 1997.

Television receivers ('000 in use): 790 in 1998.

Facsimile machines (number in use): 2,300 in 1996.

Sources: UNESCO, *Statistical Yearbook*; UN, *Statistical Yearbook*; International Telecommunication Union.

Education

(2004/05, unless otherwise stated)

	Teachers	Males	Females	Total
Pre-primary	8,924	91,112	88,837	179,949
Primary	53,015	672,292	617,453	1,289,745
Secondary	30,583	372,264	436,088	808,352
General	28,625	356,245	412,106	768,351
Vocational	1,958	16,019	23,982	40,001
Higher*	11,367	113,520	180,045	293,565

* Estimates for 2003/04.

Institutions: Primary 4,001 (1997/98); General secondary 1,737 (1996/97).

Source: UNESCO, mostly Institute for Statistics.

Adult literacy rate (UNESCO estimates): 87.0% (males 86.8%; females 87.2%) in 2002 (Source: UNESCO Institute for Statistics).

Directory

The Constitution

The Constitution of the Dominican Republic was promulgated on 28 November 1966, and amended on 14 August 1994 and 25 July 2002. Its main provisions are summarized below:

The Dominican Republic is a sovereign, free, independent state; no organizations set up by the State can bring about any act which might cause direct or indirect intervention in the internal or foreign affairs of the State or which might threaten the integrity of the State. The Dominican Republic recognizes and applies the norms of general and American international law and is in favour of and will support any initiative towards economic integration for the countries of America. The civil, republican, democratic, representative Government is divided into three independent powers: legislative, executive and judicial.

The territory of the Dominican Republic is as laid down in the Frontier Treaty of 1929 and its Protocol of Revision of 1936.

The life and property of the individual citizen are inviolable; there can be no sentence of death, torture nor any sentence which might cause physical harm to the individual. There is freedom of thought, of conscience, of religion, freedom to publish, freedom of unarmed association, provided that there is no subversion against public order, national security or decency. There is freedom of labour and trade unions; freedom to strike, except in the case of public services, according to the dispositions of the law.

The State will undertake agrarian reform, dedicating the land to useful interests and gradually eliminating the latifundios (large estates). The State will do all in its power to support all aspects of family life. Primary education is compulsory and all education is free. Social security services will be developed. Every Dominican has the duty to give what civil and military service the State may require. Every legally entitled citizen must exercise the right to vote, i.e. all persons over 18 years of age and all who are or have been married even if they are not yet 18.

GOVERNMENT

Legislative power is exercised by Congress which is made up of the Senate and Chamber of Deputies, elected by direct vote. Senators, one for each of the 31 Provinces and one for the Distrito Nacional, are elected for four years; they must be Dominicans in full exercise of their citizen's rights, and at least 25 years of age. Their duties are to elect the President and other members of the Electoral and Accounts Councils, and to approve the nomination of diplomats. Deputies, one for every 50,000 inhabitants or fraction over 25,000 in each Province and the Distrito Nacional, are elected for four years and must fulfil the same conditions for election as Senators.

Decisions of Congress are taken by absolute majority of at least half the members of each house; urgent matters require a two-thirds' majority. Both houses normally meet on 27 February and 16 August each year for sessions of 90 days, which can be extended for a further 60 days.

Executive power is exercised by the President of the Republic, who is elected by direct vote for a four-year term. The President may serve one further consecutive term, and is thereafter not eligible to serve as President or Vice-President. The successful presidential candidate must obtain an overall majority of the votes cast; if necessary, a second round of voting is held 45 days later, with the participation of the two parties that obtained the highest number of votes. The President must be a Dominican citizen by birth or origin, over 30 years of age and in full exercise of citizen's rights. The President must not have engaged in any active military or police service for at least a year prior to election. The President takes office on 16 August following the election. The President of the Republic is Head of the Public Administration and Supreme Chief of the armed forces and police forces. The President's duties include nominating Secretaries and Assistant Secretaries of State and other public officials, promulgating and publishing laws and resolutions of Congress and seeing to their faithful execution, watching over the collection and just investment of national income, nominating, with the approval of the Senate, members of the Diplomatic Corps, receiving foreign Heads of State, presiding at national functions, decreeing a State of Siege or Emergency or any other measures necessary during a public crisis. The President may not leave the country for more than 15 days without authorization from Congress. In the absence of the President, the Vice-President will assume power, or failing him, the President of the Supreme Court of Justice. The legislative and municipal elections are held two years after the presidential elections, mid-way through the presidential term.

LOCAL GOVERNMENT

Government in the Distrito Nacional and the Municipalities is in the hands of local councils, with members elected proportionally to the number of inhabitants, but numbering at least five. Each Province has a civil Governor, designated by the Executive.

JUDICIARY

Judicial power is exercised by the Supreme Court of Justice and the other Tribunals; no judicial official may hold another public office or employment, other than honorary or teaching. The Supreme Court is made up of at least 11 judges, who must be Dominican citizens by birth or origin, at least 35 years old, in full exercise of their citizen's rights, graduates in law and have practised professionally for at least 12 years. The National Judiciary Council appoints the members of the Supreme Court, who in turn appoint judges at all other levels of the judicial system. There are nine Courts of Appeal, a Lands Tribunal and a Court of the First Instance in each judicial district; in each Municipality and in the Distrito Nacional there are also Justices of the Peace.

OTHER PROVISIONS

Elections are directed by the Central Electoral Board. The armed forces are essentially obedient and apolitical, created for the defence of national independence and the maintenance of public order and the Constitution and Laws.

The artistic and historical riches of the country, whoever owns them, are part of the cultural heritage of the country and are under the safe-keeping of the State. Mineral deposits belong to the State. There is freedom to form political parties, provided they conform to the principles laid down in the Constitution. Justice is administered without charge throughout the Republic.

This Constitution can be reformed if the proposal for reform is supported in Congress by one-third of the members of either house or by the Executive. A special session of Congress must be called and any resolutions must have a two-thirds' majority. There can be no reform of the method of government, which must always be civil, republican, democratic and representative.

The Government

HEAD OF STATE

President: LEONEL FERNÁNDEZ REYNA (took office 16 August 2004).
Vice-President: Dr RAFAEL FRANCISCO ALBURQUERQUE DE CASTRO.

CABINET
(March 2008)

Secretary of State for Foreign Affairs: CARLOS MORALES TRONCOSO.

Secretary of State for the Interior and Police: FRANKLIN ALMEYDA.

Secretary of State for the Armed Forces: Lt-Gen. RAMÓN ANTONIO AQUINO GARCÍA.

Secretary of State for Finance: VICENTE BENGOA ALBIZU.

Secretary of State for Education: ALEJANDRINA GERMÁN.

Secretary of State for Agriculture: SALVADOR JIMÉNEZ.

Secretary of State for Public Works and Communications: VÍCTOR JOSÉ DÍAZ RÚA.

Secretary of State for Public Health and Social Welfare: Dr BAUTISTA ROJAS GÓMEZ.

Secretary of State for Industry and Commerce: MELANIO PAREDES.

Secretary of State for Labour: JOSÉ RAMÓN FADUL.

Secretary of State for Tourism: FÉLIX JIMÉNEZ.

Secretary of State for Sport, Physical Education and Recreation: FELIPE JAY PAYANO.

Secretary of State for Culture: JOSÉ RAFAEL LANTIGUA.

Secretary of State for Higher Education, Science and Technology: LIGIA AMADA DE MELO.

Secretary of State for Women: FLAVIA GARCÍA.

Secretary of State for Youth: MANUEL CRESPO.

Secretary of State for the Environment and Natural Resources: OMAR RAMÍREZ TEJADA.

Secretary of State for the Economy, Planning and Development: JUAN TEMÍSTOCLES MONTÁS.

Administrative Secretary to the Presidency: LUIS MANUEL BONETTI.

Secretary of State without Portfolio: Dr MIGUEL MEJÍA.

Secretary of State without Portfolio: EDUARDO SELMAN.

SECRETARIATS OF STATE

Administrative Secretariat of the Presidency: Palacio Nacional, Avda México, esq. Dr Delgado, Santo Domingo, DN; tel. 686-4771; fax 688-2100; internet www.presidencia.gov.do.

Secretariat of State for the Economy, Planning and Development: Palacio Nacional, Avda México, esq. Dr Delgado, Bloque B, 2°, Santo Domingo, DN; tel. 695-8028; fax 695-8432; e-mail informacion@economia.gov.do; internet www.economia.gov.do.

Secretariat of State for Agriculture: Autopista Duarte, Km 6.5, Los Jardines del Norte, Santo Domingo, DN; tel. 547-3888; fax 227-1268; e-mail sec.agric@verizon.net.do; internet www.agricultura.gov.do.

Secretariat of State for the Armed Forces: Plaza de la Independencia, Avda 27 de Febrero, esq. Luperón, Santo Domingo, DN; tel. 530-5149; fax 531-1309; e-mail informaticsefa@verizon.net.do; internet www.secffaa.mil.do.

Secretariat of State for Culture: Centro de Eventos y Exposiciones, Avda George Washington, esq. Presidente Vicini Burgos, Santo Domingo, DN; tel. 221-4141; fax 221-3342; e-mail contacto@cultura.gov.do; internet www.cultura.gov.do.

Secretariat of State for Education: Avda Máximo Gómez 10, esq. Santiago, Santo Domingo, DN; tel. 688-9700; fax 689-8907; e-mail marcastillo@see.gov.do; internet www.see.gov.do.

THE DOMINICAN REPUBLIC

Secretariat of State for the Environment and Natural Resources: Plaza Naco 28, Avda Tiradentes, esq. Fantico Falco, Ensanche Naco, Santo Domingo, DN; tel. 567-4300; fax 683-4774; e-mail contacto@medioambiente.gov.do; internet www.medioambiente.gov.do.

Secretariat of State for Finance: Avda México 45, esq. Leopoldo Navarro, Apdo 1478, Santo Domingo, DN; tel. 687-5131; fax 682-0498; e-mail webmaster@finanzas.gov.do; internet www.finanzas.gov.do.

Secretariat of State for Foreign Affairs: Avda Independencia 752, Santo Domingo, DN; tel. 535-6280; fax 533-5772; e-mail postmaster@serex.gov.do; internet www.serex.gov.do.

Secretariat of State for Higher Education, Science and Technology: Avda Máximo Gómez 31, esq. Pedro Henríquez Ureña, Santo Domingo, DN; tel. 731-1100; fax 535-4694; e-mail info@seescyt.gov.do; internet www.seescyt.gov.do.

Secretariat of State for Industry and Commerce: Edif. de Ofs Gubernamentales, 7°, Avda Francia, esq. Leopoldo Navarro, Santo Domingo, DN; tel. 685-5171; fax 686-1973; e-mail info@seic.gov.do; internet www.seic.gov.do.

Secretariat of State for the Interior and Police: Edif. de Ofs Gubernamentales, 13°, Avda Francia, esq. Leopoldo Navarro, Santo Domingo, DN; tel. 686-6251; fax 689-6599; e-mail info@seip.gov.do; internet www.seip.gov.do.

Secretariat of State for Labour: Centro de los Héroes, Avda Jiménez Moya 9, esq. República de Líbano, Santo Domingo, DN; tel. 535-4404; fax 535-4833; e-mail webmaster@set.gov.do; internet www.set.gov.do.

Secretariat of State for Public Health and Social Welfare: Avda San Cristóbal, esq. Tiradentes, Ensanche La Fe, Santo Domingo, DN; tel. 541-3121; fax 540-6445; e-mail correo@sespas.gov.do; internet www.sespas.gov.do.

Secretariat of State for Public Works and Communications: Avda San Cristóbal, esq. Tiradentes, Ensanche La Fe, Santo Domingo, DN; tel. 565-2811; fax 562-3382; e-mail info@seopc.gov.do; internet www.seopc.gov.do.

Secretariat of State for Sport, Physical Education and Recreation: Avda Ortega y Gasset, Centro Olímpico, Santo Domingo, DN; tel. 565-3325; fax 563-6586; e-mail j.yapor@sedefir.gov.do; internet www.sedefir.gov.do.

Secretariat of State for Tourism: Bloque D, Edif. de Ofs Gubernamentales, Avda México, esq. 30 de Marzo, Apdo 497, Santo Domingo, DN; tel. 221-4660; fax 682-3806; e-mail sectur@codetel.net.do; internet www.godominicanrepublic.com.

Secretariat of State for Women: Bloque D, Edif. de Ofs Gubernamentales, Avda México, esq. 30 de Marzo, Santo Domingo, DN; tel. 685-3755; fax 686-0911; e-mail info@sem.gov.do; internet www.sem.gov.do.

Secretariat of State for Youth: Avda Jiménez Moya 71, esq. Desiderio Arias, Ensanche La Julia, Santo Domingo, DN; tel. 732-7227; fax 535-7227; e-mail informacion@sej.gov.do; internet www.juventud.gov.do.

President and Legislature

PRESIDENT

Election, 16 May 2004

Candidate	% of votes cast
Leonel Fernández Reyna (PLD)	57.11
Rafael Hipólito Mejía Domínguez (PRD)	33.65
Rafael Eduardo Estrella Virella (PRSC)	8.65
Total (incl. others)	100.00

CONGRESO NACIONAL

The Congreso Nacional comprises a Senado and a Cámara de Diputados.

President of the Senado: ANDRÉS BAUTISTA GARCÍA (PRD).

President of the Cámara de Diputados: ALFREDO PACHECO (PRD).

General Election, 16 May 2006

	Seats	
	Senate	Chamber of Deputies
Partido de la Liberación Dominicana (PLD)	22	96
Partido Revolucionario Dominicano (PRD)	6	60
Partido Reformista Social Cristiano (PRSC)	4	22
Total	32	178

Election Commission

Junta Central Electoral (JCE): Avda 27 de Febrero, esq. Gregorio Luperón, Santo Domingo; tel. 539-5419; e-mail Dfernandez@jce.do; internet www.jce.do; govt-appointed body; Pres. Dr JULIO CÉSAR CASTAÑOS GUZMÁN.

Political Organizations

In early 2008 there were 24 political parties recognized by the Junta Central Electoral.

Alianza por la Democracia (APD): Jonás Salk 102, Zona Universitaria, Santo Domingo, DN; tel. 687-0337; fax 687-0360; f. 1992 by breakaway group of the PLD; Pres. MAX PUIG.

Bloque Institucional Socialdemócrata (BIS): Avda Bolívar 24, esq. Uruguay, Ensanche Lugo, Apdo 5413, Santo Domingo, DN; tel. 333-5432; fax 682-3375; e-mail adm@bis.org.do; internet www.bis.org.do; f. 1989 by breakaway group of PRD under Dr José Francisco Peña Gómez; Pres. Dr JOSÉ FRANCISCO PEÑA GUABA; Sec.-Gen. ROLFIS M. BÁEZ CALCAÑO.

Fuerza Nacional Progresista (FNP): Emilio A. Morel 17, Ensanche La Fe, Santo Domingo, DN; tel. 562-1070; right-wing; Leader MARINO VINICIO CASTILLO.

Fuerza de la Revolución: Avda Independencia 258, Apdo 2651, Santo Domingo, DN; e-mail fr@nodo50.ix.apc.org; internet www.fuerzadelarevolucion.org; f. 1996 by merger of the Partido Comunista Dominicano, Movimiento Liberador 12 de Enero, Fuerza de Resistencia y Liberación Popular, Fuerza Revolucionaria 21 de Julio and other revolutionary groups; Marxist-Leninist; Sec.-Gen. FERNANDO PEÑA.

Partido Demócrata Popular: Carmen de Mendoza de Corniel 78, El Millón, Santo Domingo, DN; tel. 701-6035; Pres. RAMÓN NELSON DIDIEZ NADAL.

Partido de la Liberación Dominicana (PLD): Avda Independencia 401, Santo Domingo, DN; tel. 685-3540; fax 687-5569; e-mail pldorg@pld.org.do; internet www.pld.org.do; f. 1973 by breakaway group of PRD; left-wing; Leader LEONEL FERNÁNDEZ REYNA; Sec.-Gen. REINALDO PARED PÉREZ.

Partido Quisqueyano Demócrata Cristiano (PQDC): Avda Bolívar 51, esq. Uruguay, Santo Domingo, DN; tel. 682-5873; fax 689-2881; e-mail pqd@verizon.net.do; f. 1968; right-wing; Pres. ELÍAS WESSIN CHÁVEZ; Sec.-Gen. LORENZO VALDEZ CARRASCO.

Partido Reformista Social Cristiano (PRSC): Avda Tiradentes, esq. San Cristóbal, Ensanche La Fe, Apdo 1332, Santo Domingo, DN; tel. 621-7772; e-mail S.seliman@codetel.net.do; f. 1964; centre-right party; Pres. FEDERICO ANTÚN BATLLE; Sec.-Gen. VÍCTOR GÓMEZ CASANOVA.

Partido Revolucionario Dominicano (PRD): Avda Dr Comandante Enrique Jiménez Moya 14, Bella Vista, Santo Domingo, DN; tel. 687-2193; e-mail prensa_tribunalp.r.d@hotmail.com; internet www.prd.partidos.com; f. 1939; democratic socialist; mem. of Socialist International; Pres. RAMÓN ALBUQUERQUE RAMÍREZ; Sec.-Gen. ORLANDO JORGE MERA.

Partido Revolucionario Independiente (PRI): Avda Bolívar 257, Gazcue, Santo Domingo, DN; tel. 238-5525; e-mail Trajano.S@codetel.net.do; f. 1985 after split by the PRD's right-wing faction; Pres. Dr TRAJANO SANTANA; Sec.-Gen. Dr VÍCTOR R. DÍAZ ALBA.

Partido de los Trabajadores Dominicanos (PTD): Avda Bolívar 101, esq. Dr Báez, Gazcue, Santo Domingo, DN; tel. 685-7705; fax 333-6443; e-mail partido_trab_dom@hotmail.com; f. 1979; Communist; Pres. JOSÉ GONZÁLEZ ESPINOZA; Sec.-Gen. ANTONIO FLORIÁN.

THE DOMINICAN REPUBLIC

Diplomatic Representation

EMBASSIES IN THE DOMINICAN REPUBLIC

Argentina: Avda Máximo Gómez 10, Apdo 1302, Santo Domingo, DN; tel. 682-2977; fax 221-2206; e-mail edomi@mreic.gov.ar; Ambassador JORGE J. A. ROBALLO.

Belize: Carretera La Isabela, Calle Proyecto 3, Arroyo Manzano 1, Santo Domingo, DN; tel. 567-7146; fax 567-7159; e-mail domrep@embelize.org; internet www.embelize.org; Ambassador R. EDUARDO LAMA S.

Brazil: Eduardo Vicioso 64, esq. Avda Winston Churchill, Apdo 1655, Santo Domingo, DN; tel. 532-0868; fax 532-0917; e-mail contacto@embajadadebrasil.org.do; internet www.embajadadebrasil.org.do; Ambassador RONALDO EDGAR DUNLOP.

Canada: Apdo 2054, Santo Domingo, DN; tel. 685-1136; fax 682-2691; e-mail sdmgo@international.gc.ca; internet www.dominicanrepublic.gc.ca; Ambassador PATRICIA FORTIER.

Chile: Avda Anacaona 11, Mirador del Sur, Santo Domingo, DN; tel. 532-7800; fax 530-8310; e-mail embaj.chile@codetel.net.do; Ambassador ERIC CAMPAÑA BARRIOS.

China (Taiwan): Avda Rómulo Betancourt 1360, Secto Bella Vista, Santo Domingo, DN; tel. 532-5461; fax 532-5649; e-mail dom@mofa.gov.tw; internet www.roc-taiwan-do.com; Ambassador TSAI MENG-HUNG.

Colombia: Avda Abraham Lincoln 502, 2°, Santo Domingo, DN; tel. 562-1670; e-mail erdomini@cancilleria.gov.co; Chargé d'affaires a.i. DIANA MERCEDES CARVAJAL TOSCANO.

Costa Rica: Ensanche Serralles, entre Abraham Lincoln y Lope de Vega, Calle Malaquías Gil 11 Altos, Santo Domingo, DN; tel. 683-7209; fax 565-6467; e-mail embarica@codetel.net.do; Ambassador MARTA EUGENIA NÚÑEZ MADRIZ.

Cuba: Francisco Prats Ramírez 808, El Millón, Santo Domingo, DN; tel. 537-2113; fax 537-9820; e-mail embadom@verizon.net.do; internet embacu.cubaminrex.cu/dominicana; Ambassador JUAN DOMINGO ASTIASARÁN CEBALLO.

Ecuador: Rafael Augusto Sánchez 17, Edif. Profesional Saint Michel, Of. 301, Ensanche Naco, Apdo 808, Santo Domingo, DN; tel. 563-8363; fax 563-8153; e-mail mecuador@yahoo.com; Ambassador CARLOS ALONSO MANRIQUE MUÑOZ.

El Salvador: Haim López Penha 32, Santo Domingo, DN; tel. 565-4311; fax 541-7503; e-mail emb.salvador@verizon.net.do; Ambassador ERNESTO FERREIRO RUSCONI.

France: Calle Las Damas 42, Zona Colonial, Santo Domingo, DN; tel. 695-4300; fax 695-4311; e-mail ambafrance@ambafrance-do.org; internet www.ambafrance-do.org; Ambassador CÉCILE POZZO DI BORGO.

Germany: Edif. Torre Piantini, 16°, Calle Gustavo Mejía Ricart 196, esq. Avda Abraham Lincoln, Santo Domingo, DN; tel. 542-8949; fax 542-8955; e-mail info@santo-domingo.diplo.de; internet www.santo-domingo.diplo.de; Ambassador CHRISTIAN GERMANN.

Guatemala: Edif. Corominas Pepín, 9°, Avda 27 de Febrero 233, Santo Domingo, DN; tel. 381-0249; fax 381-0278; e-mail guaterd@codetel_net.do; Ambassador CÉSAR AUGUSTO MÉNDEZ PINELO.

Haiti: Avda Juan Sánchez Ramírez 33, Santo Domingo, DN; tel. 686-5778; fax 686-6096; e-mail amb.haiti@codetel.net.do; Ambassador FRITZ CENEAS.

Holy See: Avda Máximo Gómez 27, Apdo 312, Santo Domingo, DN (Apostolic Nunciature); tel. 682-3773; fax 687-0287; Apostolic Nuncio Most Rev. JÓZEF WESOŁOWSKI (Titular Archbishop of Slebte).

Honduras: Calle Arístides García Mella, esq. Rodríguez Objío, Edif. El Buen Pastor VI, Apt 1B, 1°, Mirador del Sur, Santo Domingo, DN; tel. 482-7992; fax 482-7505; e-mail e.honduras@codetel.net.do; Ambassador NERY MAGALY FÚNES.

Israel: Pedro Henríquez Ureña 80, Santo Domingo, DN; tel. 472-0774; fax 472-1785; e-mail ambassador@santodomingo.mfa.gov.il; internet santodomingo.mfa.gov.il; Ambassador AMOS RADIAN.

Italy: Rodríguez Objío 4, Santo Domingo, DN; tel. 682-0830; fax 682-8296; e-mail ambital@verizon.net.do; internet www.ambsantodomingo.esteri.it; Ambassador ENRICO GUICCIARDI.

Jamaica: Avda Enriquillo 61, Los Cacicazgos, Santo Domingo, DN; tel. 482-7770; fax 482-7773; e-mail emb.jamaica@verizon.net.do; Chargé d'affaires a.i. THOMAS F. ALLAN MARLEY.

Japan: Torre BHD, 8°, Avda Winston Churchill, esq. Luis F. Thomén, Santo Domingo, DN; tel. 567-3365; fax 566-8013; internet www.do.emb-japan.go.jp; Ambassador HARUO OKAMOTO.

Korea, Republic: Avda Sarasota 98, Santo Domingo, DN; tel. 532-4314; fax 532-3807; e-mail embcod@mofat.go.kr; internet dom.mofat.go.kr; Ambassador LIN BYUNG-TAIK.

Mexico: Arzobispo Meriño 265, esq. Las Mercedes, Zona Colonial, Santo Domingo, DN; tel. 687-6444; fax 687-7872; e-mail embamex@codetel.net.do; Ambassador ENRIQUE MANUEL LOAEZA TOVAR.

Netherlands: Max Henríquez Ureña 50, entre Avda Winston Churchill y Abraham Lincoln, Ensanche Piantini, Apdo 855, Santo Domingo, DN; tel. 262-0320; fax 565-4685; e-mail std@minbuza.nl; internet www.holanda.org.do; Chargé d'affaires a.i. N. J. VAN DAM.

Nicaragua: Edif. Metrópolis II, Apto D-O, Calle Eric Ekman, esq. Euclides Morillo, Arroyo Hondo, Santo Domingo, DN; tel. 563-2311; fax 565-7961; e-mail embanic-rd@codetel.net.do; Chargé d'affaires a.i. CORINA GARCÍA DEL SOLAR.

Panama: Benito Monción 255, Gazcue, Santo Domingo, DN; tel. 688-3789; fax 685-3665; e-mail emb.panam@codetel.net.do; Ambassador MIROSLAVA ROSAS DE MOTA.

Peru: Mayreni 31, Urbanización Los Cacicazgos, Santo Domingo, DN; tel. 482-3300; fax 482-3334; e-mail embaperu@verizon.net.do; Ambassador VICENTE ALEJANDRO AZULA DE LA GUERRA.

Spain: Avda Independencia 1205, Apdo 1468, Santo Domingo, DN; tel. 535-6500; fax 535-1595; e-mail embespdo@mail.mae.es; Ambassador MARÍA DE LA ALMUDENA MAZARRASA ALVEAR.

United Kingdom: Edif. Corominas Pepin, 7°, Avda 27 de Febrero 233, Santo Domingo, DN; tel. 472-7111; fax 472-7574; e-mail brit.emb.sadom@codetel.net.do; internet www.britishembassy.gov.uk/dominicanrepublic; Ambassador IAN ALAN WORTHINGTON.

USA: César Nicolás Pensón, esq. Leopoldo Navarro, Santo Domingo, DN; tel. 221-2171; fax 685-6959; e-mail irc@usemb.gov.do; internet www.usemb.gov.do/index.htm; Ambassador P. ROBERT FANNIN.

Uruguay: Torre Ejecutiva Gapo, Local 401, Luis F. Thomen 110, Ensanche Evaristo Morales, Santo Domingo, DN; tel. 227-3475; fax 472-4231; e-mail embur@verizon.net.do; Ambassador DUNCAN BORIS CROCI DE MULA.

Venezuela: Avda Anacoana 7, Mirador del Sur, Santo Domingo, DN; tel. 537-8578; fax 537-8780; e-mail embvenezuela@codetel.net.do; Ambassador FRANCISCO ALBERTO BELISARIO LANDIS.

Judicial System

The Judicial Power resides in the Suprema Corte de Justicia (Supreme Court of Justice), the Cortes de Apelación (Courts of Appeal), the Juzgados de Primera Instancia (Tribunals of the First Instance), the municipal courts and the other judicial authorities provided by law. The Supreme Court is composed of at least 11 judges (16 in January 2007) and the Attorney-General, and exercises disciplinary authority over all the members of the judiciary. The Attorney-General of the Republic is the Chief of Judicial Police and of the Public Ministry, which he represents before the Supreme Court of Justice. The Consejo Nacional de la Magistratura (National Judiciary Council) appoints the members of the Supreme Court, which in turn appoints judges at all other levels of the judicial system.

Corte Suprema

Centro de los Héroes, Calle Juan de Dios Ventura Simó, esq. Enrique Jiménez Moya, Apdo 1485, Santo Domingo, DN; tel. 533-3191; fax 532-2906; e-mail suprema.corte@verizon.net.do; internet www.suprema.gov.do.

President: Dr JORGE SUBERO ISA.

Vice-President and President of First Court: Dr RAFAEL LUCIANO PICHARDO.

Second Vice-President: Dra EGLYS MARGARITA ESMURDOC.

President of Second Court: Dr HUGO ÁLVAREZ VALENCIA.

Justices: Dra MARGARITA A. TAVARES, VÍCTOR JOSÉ CASTELLANOS ESTRELLA, Dr JULIO IBARRA RÍOS, Dr EDGAR HERNÁNDEZ MEJÍA, Dra DULCE M. RODRÍGUEZ DE GORIS, Dra ANA ROSA BERGÉS DREYFOUS, Dr JUAN LUPERÓN VÁSQUEZ, Dr JULIO ANÍBAL SUÁREZ, Dra ENILDA REYES PÉREZ, Dr JOSÉ ENRIQUE HERNÁNDEZ MACHADO, Dr PEDRO ROMERO CONFESOR, Dr DARÍO OCTAVIO FERNÁNDEZ ESPINAL.

Attorney-General: RADHAMEÉS JIMÉNEZ PEÑA.

Religion

The majority of the inhabitants belong to the Roman Catholic Church, but freedom of worship exists for all denominations. The Baptist, Evangelist and Seventh-day Adventist churches and the Jewish faith are also represented.

CHRISTIANITY

The Roman Catholic Church

The Dominican Republic comprises two archdioceses and nine dioceses. At 31 December 2005 adherents represented about 87.0% of the population.

THE DOMINICAN REPUBLIC

Bishops' Conference

Conferencia del Episcopado Dominicano, Apdo 186, Calle Isabel la Católica 55, Santo Domingo, DN; tel. 685-3141; fax 689-9454; internet www.ced.org.do.

f. 1985; Pres. Most Rev. RAMÓN BENITO DE LA ROSA Y CARPIO (Archbishop of Santiago de los Caballeros).

Archbishop of Santiago de los Caballeros: Most Rev. RAMÓN BENITO DE LA ROSA Y CARPIO, Arzobispado, Duvergé 14, Apdo 679, Santiago de los Caballeros; tel. 582-2094; fax 581-3580; e-mail arzobisp.stgo@verizon.net.do.

Archbishop of Santo Domingo: Cardinal NICOLÁS DE JESÚS LÓPEZ RODRÍGUEZ, Arzobispado, Isabel la Católica 55, Apdo 186, Santo Domingo, DN; tel. 685-3141; fax 688-7270; e-mail arzobispado@verizon.net.do.

The Anglican Communion

Anglicans in the Dominican Republic are under the jurisdiction of the Episcopal Church in the USA. The country is classified as a missionary diocese, in Province IX.

Bishop of the Dominican Republic: Rt Rev. JULIO CÉSAR HOLGUÍN KHOURY, Santiago 114, Apdo 764, Santo Domingo, DN; tel. 688-6016; fax 686-6364; e-mail iglepidom@verizon.net.do; internet www.dominicanepiscopalchurch.org.

BAHÁ'Í FAITH

National Spiritual Assembly of the Bahá'ís of the Dominican Republic: Cambronal 152, esq. Beller, Santo Domingo, DN; tel. 687-1726; fax 687-7606; e-mail bahai.rd.aen@verizon.net.do; internet www.bahai.org.do; f. 1961; 402 localities.

The Press

Dirección General de Información, Publicidad y Prensa: Palacio Nacional, Santo Domingo, DN; f. 1983; govt supervisory body; Dir RAFAEL NÚÑEZ.

DAILIES

Santo Domingo

El Caribe: Calle Doctor Defilló 4, Los Prados, Apdo 416, Santo Domingo, DN; tel. 683-8100; fax 544-4003; e-mail redaccion@elcaribe.com.do; internet www.elcaribecdn.com; f. 1948; morning; circ. 32,000; Pres. FÉLIX M. GARCÍA; Dir MANUEL A. QUIROZ.

Diario Libre: Avda Abraham Lincoln, esq. Max Henríquez Ureña, Santo Domingo, DN; internet www.diariolibre.com.

Hoy: Avda San Martín 236, Santo Domingo, DN; tel. 565-5581; fax 567-2424; e-mail webmaster@hoy.com.do; internet www.hoy.com.do; f. 1981; morning; Editor LUIS M. CARDENAS; circ. 40,000.

Listín Diario: Paseo de los Periodistas 52, Ensanche Miraflores, Santo Domingo, DN; tel. 686-6688; fax 686-6595; e-mail listin.redacc@codetel.net.do; internet www.listin.com.do; f. 1889; morning; Dir-Gen. MIGUEL FRANJUL; Editor-in-Chief FABIO CABRAL; circ. 88,050.

La Nación: Calle San Antonio 2, Zona Industrial de Herrera, Santo Domingo, DN; tel. 537-2444; fax 537-4865; e-mail editor.nacion@codetel.net.do; afternoon.

El Nacional: Avda San Martín 236, Santo Domingo, DN; tel. 565-5581; fax 565-4190; e-mail elnacional@codetel.net.do; internet www.elnacional.com.do; f. 1966; evening and Sunday; Dir RADHAMÉS GÓMEZ PEPÍN; circ. 45,000.

El Nuevo Diario: Avda Francia 41, Santo Domingo, DN; tel. 687-7450; fax 687-3205; e-mail redaccionnd@verizon.net.do; internet www.elnuevodiario.com.do; morning; Exec. Dir COSETTE BONNELLY.

El Siglo: Calle San Antón 2, Zona Industrial de Herrera, Apdo 20213, Santo Domingo, DN; tel. 518-4000; fax 518-4035; e-mail elsiglo@elsiglord.com; Editorial Dir OSVALDO SANTANA.

Santiago de los Caballeros

La Información: Carretera Licey, Km 3, Santiago de los Caballeros; tel. 581-1915; fax 581-7770; e-mail e.informacion@codetel.net.do; f. 1915; morning; Dir FERNANDO A. PÉREZ MEMÉN; circ. 15,000.

PERIODICALS AND REVIEWS

Agricultura: Autopista Duarte, Km 6.5, Los Jardines del Norte, Santo Domingo, DN; tel. 547-3888; fax 227-1268; organ of the Secretariat of State for Agriculture; f. 1905; monthly; Dir MIGUEL RODRÍGUEZ, Jr.

Agroconocimiento: Apdo 345-2, Santo Domingo, DN; monthly; agricultural news and technical information; Dir DOMINGO MARTE; circ. 10,000.

¡Ahora!: San Martín 236, Apdo 1402, Santo Domingo, DN; tel. 565-5581; e-mail revistaahora@internet.net.do; internet www.ahora.com.do; f. 1962; weekly; Editor RAFAEL MOLINA MORILLO.

La Campiña: San Martín 236, Apdo 1402, Santo Domingo, DN; f. 1967; Dir Ing. JUAN ULISES GARCÍA B.

Carta Dominicana: Avda Tiradentes 56, Santo Domingo, DN; tel. 566-0119; f. 1974; monthly; economics; Dir JUAN RAMÓN QUIÑONES M.

Deportes: San Martín 236, Apdo 1402, Santo Domingo, DN; f. 1967; sports; fortnightly; Dir L. R. CORDERO; circ. 5,000.

Eva: San Martín 236, Apdo 1402, Santo Domingo, DN; f. 1967; fortnightly; Dir MAGDA FLORENCIO.

Horizontes de América: Santo Domingo, DN; f. 1967; monthly; Dir ARMANDO LEMUS CASTILLO.

Letra Grande, Arte y Literatura: Leonardo da Vinci 13, Mirador del Sur, Avda 27 de Febrero, Santo Domingo, DN; tel. 531-2225; f. 1980; monthly; art and literature; Dir JUAN RAMÓN QUIÑONES M.

Renovación: José Reyes, esq. El Conde, Santo Domingo, DN; fortnightly; Dir OLGA QUISQUEYA VIUDA MARTÍNEZ.

NEWS AGENCIES

La Noticia: Julio Verne 14, Santo Domingo, DN; tel. 535-0815; f. 1973; evening; Pres. JOSÉ A. BREA PEÑA; Dir BOLÍVAR BELLO.

Publishers

SANTO DOMINGO

Arte y Cine, C por A: San Martín 45, Santo Domingo, DN; tel. 682-0342; fax 686-8354.

Editora Alfa y Omega: José Contreras 69, Santo Domingo, DN; tel. 532-5577.

Editora de las Antillas: Santo Domingo, DN; tel. 685-2197.

Editora Dominicana, SA: 23 Oeste, No 3 Luperón, Santo Domingo, DN; tel. 688-0846.

Editora El Caribe, C por A: Calle Doctor Defilló 4, Los Prados, Apdo 416, Santo Domingo, DN; tel. 683-8100; fax 544-4003; e-mail editora@elcaribe.com.do; internet www.elcaribe.com.do; f. 1948; Dir MANUEL QUIROZ.

Editora Hoy, C por A: San Martín, 236, Santo Domingo, DN; tel. 566-1147.

Editora Listín Diario, C por A: Paseo de los Periodistas 52, Ensanche Miraflores, Apdo 1455, Santo Domingo, DN; tel. 686-6688; fax 686-6595; f. 1889; Pres. Dr ROGELIO A. PELLERANO.

Editorama, SA: Calle Eugenio Contreras, No 54, Los Trinitarios, Apdo 2074, Santo Domingo, DN; tel. 596-6669; fax 594-1421; e-mail editorama@verizon.net.do; internet www.editorama.com; f. 1970; Pres. JUAN ANTONIO QUIÑONES MARTE.

Editorial Padilla, C por A: Avda 27 de Febrero, Santo Domingo, DN; tel. 379-1550; fax 379-2631.

Editorial Santo Domingo: Santo Domingo, DN; tel. 532-9431.

Editorial Stella: Avda 19 de Marzo 304, Santo Domingo, DN; tel. 682-2281; fax 687-0835.

Julio D. Postigo e Hijos: Santo Domingo, DN; f. 1949; fiction; Man. J. D. POSTIGO.

Publicaciones Ahora, C por A: Avda San Martín 236, Apdo 1402, Santo Domingo, DN; tel. 565-5580; fax 565-4190; Pres. JULIO CASTAÑO.

Publicaciones América: Santo Domingo, DN; Dir PEDRO BISONÓ.

SANTIAGO DE LOS CABALLEROS

Editora el País, SA: Carrera Sánchez, Km 6½, Santiago de los Caballeros; tel. 532-9511.

Broadcasting and Communications

Instituto Dominicano de las Telecomunicaciones (INDOTEL): Avda Abraham Lincoln, No 962, Edif. Osiris, Santo Domingo, DN; tel. 732-5555; fax 732-3904; e-mail centrodeasistencia@indotel.org.do; internet www.indotel.org.do; f. 1998; Pres. Dr JOSÉ RAFAEL VARGAS.

TELECOMMUNICATIONS

Ericsson República Dominicana: Avda Winston Churchill esq. Víctor Garrido Puello, Edif. Empresarial Hylsa, 2°, Nivel, Santo Domingo, DN; tel. 683-7723; fax 616-0962; f. 2000; mobile cellular telephone network provider; subsidiary of Telefon AB LM Ericsson (Sweden); Country Man. PETER FÄLLLMAN.

Orange Dominicana, SA: Calle Víctor Garrido Puello 23, Edif. Orange, Ensanche Piantini, Santo Domingo, DN; tel. 859-6555;

THE DOMINICAN REPUBLIC

e-mail servicio.cliente@orange.com.do; internet www.orange.com.do; f. 2000; mobile cellular telephone operator, providing GSM network coverage to 89% of the Dominican Republic population; subsidiary of Orange SA (France); Pres. FREDERICK DEBORD.

Tricom Telecomunicaciones de Voz, Data y Video: Avda Lope de Vega 95, Ensanche Naco, Santo Domingo, DN; tel. 476-6000; fax 567-4412; e-mail sc@tricom.com.do; internet www.tricom.net; f. 1992; Pres. and CEO CARL CARLSON; Chair. RICARDO VALDEZ ALBIZU.

Compañía Dominicana de Teléfonos, C por A (Claro—Codetel): Avda John F. Kennedy 54, Apdo 1377, Santo Domingo, DN; tel. 220-1111; fax 543-1301; internet www.codetel.net.do; f. 1930; owned by América Móvil, SA de CV (Mexico); operates mobile services as Claro and fixed-line services as Codetel; Pres. OSCAR PEÑA CHACÓN.

BROADCASTING
Radio

There were some 130 commercial stations in the Dominican Republic. The government-owned broadcasting network, Radio Televisión Dominicana (see Television), operates nine radio stations.

Asociación Dominicana de Radiodifusoras (ADORA): Paul Harris 3, Centro de los Héroes, Santo Domingo, DN; tel. 535-4057; Pres. ROBERTO VARGAS.

Cadena de Noticias (CDN) Radio: Calle Doctor Defilló 4, Los Prados, Apdo 416, Santo Domingo, DN; tel. 683-8100; fax 544-4003; e-mail inforadio@cdn.com.do; internet www.elcaribecdn.com/cdnradio.aspx.

Television

Antena Latina, Canal 7: Calle Gustavo Mejía Ricart 45, Ensanche Naco, Santo Domingo, DN; tel. 412-0707; fax 333-0707; e-mail contacto@antenalatina7.com; internet www.antenalatina7.com; f. 1999; Pres. MIGUEL BONETTI DUBREIL; Editor-in-Chief MIGUEL ANGEL ORDÓÑEZ.

Cadena de Noticias (CDN) Televisión: Calle Doctor Defilló 4, Los Prados, Apdo 416, Santo Domingo, DN; tel. 262-2100; fax 567-2671; e-mail direccion@cdn.com.do; internet www.elcaribecdn.com/cdntv.aspx; broadcasts news on Channel 37.

Color Visión, Canal 9: Emilio A. Morel, esq. Luis Pérez, Ensanche La Fe, Santo Domingo, DN; tel. 566-5876; fax 732-9347; e-mail colorvision@verizon.net.do; internet www.colorvision.com.do; f. 1969; majority-owned by Corporación Dominicana de Radio y Televisión; commercial station; Dir-Gen. MANUEL QUIROZ MIRANDA.

Radio Televisión Dominicana, Canal 4: Dr Tejada Florentino 8, Apdo 869, Santo Domingo, DN; tel. 689-2120; e-mail rm.colombo@codetel.net.do; internet www.rtvd.com; govt station; Channel 4; Dir-Gen. RAMÓN EMILIO COLOMBO; Gen. Man. AGUSTÍN MERCADO.

Teleantillas, Canal 2: Autopista Duarte, Km 7½, Los Prados, Apdo 30404, Santo Domingo, DN; tel. 567-7751; fax 540-4912; e-mail webmaster@tele-antillas.tv; internet www.tele-antillas.tv; f. 1979; Gen. Man. HÉCTOR VALENTÍN BÁEZ.

Telecentro, Canal 13: Avda Pasteur 204, Santo Domingo, DN; tel. 687-9161; fax 542-7582; e-mail webmaster@telecentro.com.do; internet www.telecentro.com.do; Santo Domingo and east region; Pres. JOSÉ MIGUEL BÁEZ FIGUEROA.

Tele-Inde Canal 13: Avda Pasteur 101, Santo Domingo, DN; tel. 687-9161; commercial station; Dir JULIO HAZIM.

Telemicro, Canal 5: San Martín, Avda 27 de Febrero, Santo Domingo, DN; tel. 689-8151; fax 686-6528; e-mail programacion@telemicro.com.do; internet www.telemicro.com.do; f. 1982.

Telesistema, Canal 11: Avda 27 de Febrero 52, esq. Máximo Gómez, Sector Bergel, Santo Domingo, DN; tel. 563-6661; fax 472-1754; e-mail info@telesistema11.tv; internet www.telesistema11.tv; Pres. JOSÉ L. CORREPIO.

Finance
(cap. = capital; res = reserves; dep. = deposits; m. = million; brs = branches; amounts in pesos)

BANKING
Supervisory Body

Superintendencia de Bancos: 52 Avda México, esq. Leopoldo Navarro, Apdo 1326, Santo Domingo, DN; tel. 685-8141; fax 685-0859; e-mail rcamilo@supbanco.gov.do; internet www.supbanco.gov.do; f. 1947; Supt RAFAEL CAMILO ABRÉU.

Central Bank

Banco Central de la República Dominicana: Calle Pedro Henríquez Ureña, esq. Leopoldo Navarro, Apdo 1347, Santo Domingo, DN; tel. 221-9111; fax 687-7488; e-mail info@bancentral.gov.do; internet www.bancentral.gov.do; f. 1947; cap. and res 2,371.4m., dep. 215,453.0m. (Dec. 2006); Gov. HÉCTOR VALDEZ ALBIZU; Man. PEDRO SILVERIO ALVAREZ.

Commercial Banks

Banco BHD, SA: Avda 27 de Febrero, esq. Avda Winston Churchill, Santo Domingo, DN; tel. 243-3232; fax 243-3363; e-mail servicio@bhd.com.do; internet www.bhd.com.do; f. 1972; cap. 2,763.9m., res 872.6m., dep. 40,705.1m. (Dec. 2006); Pres. LUIS EUGENIO MOLINA ACHÉCAR; 35 brs.

Banco Dominicano del Progreso, SA: Avda John F. Kennedy 3, Apdo 1329, Santo Domingo, DN; tel. 563-3233; fax 563-2455; e-mail informacion@progreso.com.do; internet www.progreso.com.do; f. 1974; merged with Banco Metropolitano, SA, and Banco de Desarrollo Dominicano, SA, in 2000; cap. 1,004.4m., res 249.5m., dep. 11,433.5m. (Dec. 2002); Pres. JUAN B. VICINI LLUBERES; 20 brs.

Banco Múltiple Leon, SA: Avda John F. Kennedy, esq. Tiradentes, Apdo 1502, Santo Domingo, DN; tel. 476-2000; fax 473-2050; e-mail info@leon.com.do; internet www.leon.com.do; f. 1981; fmrly Banco Nacional de Crédito, SA; became Bancrédito, SA, in 2002; adopted current name Dec. 2003; cap. 1,516.7m., res 139.7m., dep. 21,723.6m. (Dec. 2006); Pres. and CEO MANUEL PEÑA-MORROS; 56 brs.

Banco Popular Dominicano: Avda John F. Kennedy 20, Torre Popular, Apdo 1441, Santo Domingo, DN; tel. 544-5555; fax 544-5899; e-mail contactenos@bpd.com.do; internet www.bpd.com.do; f. 1963; cap. 7,487.3m., res 1,706.6m., dep. 92,582.5m. (Dec. 2006); Pres., Chair. and Gen. Man. MANUEL ALEJANDRO GRULLÓN; 184 brs.

Banco de Reservas de la República Dominicana (Banreservas): Isabel la Católica 201, Apdo 1353, Santo Domingo, DN; tel. 968-2000; fax 685-0602; e-mail sperdomo@brrd.com; internet www.banreservas.com.do; f. 1941; state-owned; cap. 3,500,000m., res 4,851.0m., dep. 100,449.4m. (Dec. 2006); Pres. VICENTE BENGOA ALBIZU (Secretary of State for Finance); Administrator DANIEL TORIBIO; 112 brs.

Development Banks

Banco Agrícola de la República Dominicana: Avda G. Washington 601, Apdo 1057, Santo Domingo, DN; tel. 535-8088; fax 535-8022; e-mail bagricola@bagricola.gov.do; internet www.bagricola.gov.do; f. 1945; govt agricultural devt bank; Gen. Administrator PAÍNO ABREU COLLADO.

Banco de Desarrollo Ademi, SA: Avda Rafael Augusto Sánchez 33, Plaza Intercaribe, Suite 203, Apdo 2887, Santo Domingo, DN; tel. 732-4411; fax 732-4401; e-mail lauralluberes@ademi.org.do; internet www.ademi.org.do; Pres. MARGARITA DE FERRARI LLUBERES.

Banco de Desarrollo Agropecuario Norcentral, SA: Avda Independencia 801, esq. Avda Máximo Gómez, Santo Domingo, DN; tel. 686-0984; fax 687-0825.

Banco de Desarrollo de Exportación, SA: Fatino Falco, entre Avda Lope de Vega y Tiradentes 201, Santo Domingo, DN; tel. 566-5841; fax 565-1769.

Banco de Desarrollo Industrial, SA: Avda Sarasota 27, esq. La Julia, Santo Domingo, DN; tel. 535-8586; fax 535-6069.

Banco de Desarrollo Intercontinental, SA: Edif. Lilian, 5°, Avda Lope de Vega, esq. Gustavo Mejía Ricart, Santo Domingo, DN; tel. 544-0559; fax 563-6884.

Banco Nacional de la Construcción: Avda Alma Mater, esq. Pedro Henríquez Ureña, Santo Domingo, DN; tel. 685-9776; f. 1977; Gen. Man. LUIS MANUEL PELLERANO.

Banco de la Pequeña Empresa, SA: Avda Bolívar 233, entre Avda Abraham Lincoln y Avda Winston Churchill, Santo Domingo, DN; tel. 534-8383; fax 534-8385.

STOCK EXCHANGE

Bolsa de Valores de la República Dominicana, SA: Edif. Empresarial, 1°, Avda John F. Kennedy 16, Apdo 25144, Santo Domingo, DN; tel. 567-6694; fax 567-6697; e-mail info@bolsard.com; internet www.bolsard.com; Pres. MARINO GINEBRA.

INSURANCE
Supervisory Body

Superintendencia de Seguros: Secretaría de Estado de Finanzas, Avda México 54, esq. Leopoldo Navarro, Santo Domingo, DN; tel. 221-2606; fax 685-5096; e-mail servicio@superseguro.gov.do; f. 1969; Supt CÉSAR CABRERA.

Insurance Companies

American Life and General Insurance Co, C por A: Edif. ALICO, 5°, Avda Abraham Lincoln, Apdo 131, Santo Domingo, DN; tel. 533-7131; fax 535-0362; e-mail caribalico@codetel.net.do; general; Gen. Man. FRANCISCO CABREJA.

THE DOMINICAN REPUBLIC

Directory

Angloamericana de Seguros, SA: Avda Gustavo Mejía Ricard 8, esq. Hermanos Roque Martínez, Ensanche El Millón, Santo Domingo, DN; tel. 682-6073; fax 686-5970; e-mail angloamericana@verizon.net.do; internet www.angloam.com.do; f. 1996; Pres. NELSON HEDI HERNÁNDEZ P.; Vice-Pres. ESTEBAN BETANCES FABRÉ.

Atlántica Insurance, SA: Avda 27 de Febrero 365A, 2°, Apdo 826, Santo Domingo, DN; tel. 565-5591; fax 565-4343; e-mail atlanticains@codetel.net.do; Dir-Gen. Lic. RHINA RAMÍREZ DE PERALTA; Pres. GAMALIER PERALTA.

Bankers Security Life Insurance Society: Calle Gustavo Mejía Ricart 61, Apdo 1123, Santo Domingo, DN; tel. 544-2626; fax 567-9389; e-mail eizquierdo@bpd.com.do; Pres. Lic. ESTELA MA. FIALLO T.

BBVA Seguros: Santo Domingo, DN; f. 2006; bought by Scotiabank in 2007; Pres. MIGUEL JARSUN.

BMI Compañía de Seguros, SA: Avda Tiradentes 14, Edif. Alfonso Comercial, Apdo 916, Ensanche Naco, Santo Domingo, DN; tel. 562-6660; fax 562-6849; e-mail gerencia@bmi.com.do; Exec. Vice-Pres. PEDRO DA CUNHA.

Bonanza Compañía de Seguros, SA: Avda John F. Kennedy, Edif. Bonanza, Santo Domingo, DN; tel. 565-5531; fax 566-1087; e-mail bonanza.dom@codetel.net.do; Pres. Lic. DARIO LAMA.

Británica de Seguros, SA: Max Henríquez Ureña 35, Apdo 3637, Santo Domingo, DN; tel. 542-6863; fax 544-4542; e-mail wharper@codetel.net.do; Pres. JOHN HARPER SALETA.

Centro de Seguros La Popular, C por A: Gustavo Mejía Ricart 61, Apdo 1123, Santo Domingo, DN; tel. 566-1988; fax 567-9389; f. 1965; general except life; Pres. Lic. ROSA FIALLO.

La Colonial, SA: Avda Sarasota 75, Bella Vista, Santo Domingo, DN; tel. 508-8000; fax 508-0608; e-mail info@lacolonial.com.do; internet www.lacolonial.com.do; f. 1971; general; Pres. Dr MIGUEL FERIS IGLESIAS; Exec. Vice-Pres. LUIS EDUARDO GUERRERO ROMÁN.

Compañía de Seguros Palic, SA: Avda Abraham Lincoln, esq. José Amado Soler, Apdo 1132, Santo Domingo, DN; tel. 562-1271; fax 562-1825; e-mail cia.seg.palic2@codetel.net.do; Pres. JOSÉ ANTONIO CARO GINEBRA; Exec. Vice-Pres. MILAGROS DE LOS SANTOS.

Confederación del Canadá Dominicana: Calle Salvador Sturla 17, Ensanche Naco, Santo Domingo, DN; tel. 544-4144; fax 540-4740; e-mail confedom@codetel.net.do; f. 1988; Pres. Lic. MOISES A. FRANCO.

Federal Insurance Company: Edif. La Cumbre, 4°, Avda Tiradentes, esq. Presidente González, Santo Domingo, DN; tel. 567-0181; fax 567-8909; e-mail eizquierdo@bpd.com.do; Pres. LUIS AUGUSTO GINEBRA H.

General de Seguros, SA: Avda Sarasota 55, esq. Pedro A. Bobea, Apdo 2183, Santo Domingo, DN; tel. 535-8888; fax 532-4451; e-mail general.seg@codetel.net.do; f. 1981; general; Pres. Dr FERNANDO A. BALLISTA DÍAZ.

La Mundial de Seguros, SA: Avda Máximo Gómez, No 31, Santo Domingo, DN; tel. 685-2121; fax 682-3269; general except life and financial; Pres. PEDRO D'ACUNHA.

La Peninsular de Seguros, SA: Edif. Corp. Corominas Pepín, 3°, Avda 27 de Febrero 233, Santo Domingo, DN; tel. 472-1166; fax 563-2349; e-mail peninsu@aacr.net; general; Pres. Lic. ERNESTO ROMERO LANDRÓN.

Progreso Compañía de Seguros, SA (PROSEGUROS): Edif. Torre Progreso, 2°, Avda Winston Churchill, esq. Ludovino Fernández, Ensanche Carmelita, Santo Domingo, DN; tel. 541-7182; fax 541-7915; e-mail JuanGa@progreso.com.do; Pres. VICENZO MASTROLILLI; Exec. Vice-Pres. Lic. JUAN GARRIGÓ.

Reaseguradora Hispaniola, SA: Avda Gustavo Mejía Ricart, Edif. 8, 2°, esq. Hermanos Roque Martínez, Ensanche El Millón, Santo Domingo, DN; tel. 548-7171; fax 548-6007; e-mail rehsa@verizon.net.do; Pres. NELSON HEDI HERNÁNDEZ P.

Seguros BanReservas: Avda Jiménez Moya, esq. Calle 4, Centro Technológico Banreservas, Ensanche La Paz, Santo Domingo, DN; tel. 960-7200; fax 960-5148; e-mail smahfoud@segbanreservas.com; internet www.segurosbanreservas.com; Pres. Lic. DANIEL TORIBIO MARMOLEJOS; Exec. Vice-Pres. RAFAEL MEDINA.

Seguros La Isleña, C por A: Edif. Centro Coordinador Empresarial, Avda Núñez de Cáceres, esq. Guarocuya, Santo Domingo, DN; tel. 567-7211; fax 565-1448; Pres. HUÁSCAR RODRÍGUEZ; Exec. Vice-Pres. MARÍA DEL PILAR RODRÍGUEZ.

Seguros Pepín, SA: Edif. Corp. Corominas Pepín, Avda 27 de Febrero 233, Santo Domingo, DN; tel. 472-1006; fax 565-9176; general; Pres. Dr BIENVENIDO COROMINAS PEPÍN.

Seguros Popular: Avda Winston Churchill 1100, Torre Universal América, Apdo 1052, Santo Domingo, DN; tel. 544-7200; fax 544-7999; e-mail escribenos@seguropopular.com.do; internet www.universal.com.do; f. 1964 as La Universal de Seguros; merged with Grupo Asegurador América in 2000; general; Pres. ERNESTO IZQUIERDO.

Seguros San Rafael, C por A: Leopoldo Navarro 61, esq. San Francisco de Macorís, Edif. San Rafael, Apdo 1018, Santo Domingo, DN; tel. 688-2231; fax 686-2628; e-mail sanrafael@codetel.net.do; general; Admin.-Gen. RAMÓN PERALTA.

El Sol de Seguros, SA: Torre Hipotecaria, 2°, Avda Tiradentes 25, Santo Domingo, DN; tel. 562-6504; fax 544-3260; general; Pres. ANTONIO ALMA.

Sudamericana de Seguros, SA: El Conde 105, frente al Parque Colón, Santo Domingo, DN; tel. 685-0141; fax 688-8074; Pres. VINCENZO MASTROLILLI.

Insurance Association

Cámara Dominicana de Aseguradores y Reaseguradores, Inc: Edif. Torre BHD, 5°, Luis F. Thomen, esq. Winston Churchill, Apdo 601, Santo Domingo, DN; tel. 566-0014; fax 566-2600; e-mail cadoar@verizon.net.do; internet www.cadoar.org.do; f. 1972; Pres. Lic. JUAN GARRIGÓ.

Trade and Industry

GOVERNMENT AGENCIES

Comisión Nacional de Energía (CNE): Calle Gustavo Mejía Ricart 73, esq. Agustín Lara, 3°, Ensanche Serralles, Santo Domingo, DN; tel. 732-2000; fax 547-2073; e-mail info@cne.gov.do; internet www.cne.gov.do; f. 2001; responsible for regulation and development of energy sector; Exec. Dir RUBÉN MONTÁS.

Comisión para la Reforma de la Empresa Pública: Edif. Latinoamericana de Seguros, 6°, Gustavo Mejía Ricart 73, esq. Agustín Lara, Ensanche Serrallés, Santo Domingo, DN; tel. 683-3591; fax 683-3888; e-mail crepdom@verizon.net.do; internet www.crepdom.gov.do; commission charged with divestment and restructuring of state enterprises; Pres. FERNANDO ROSA.

Consejo Estatal del Azúcar (CEA) (State Sugar Council): Centro de los Héroes, Apdo 1256/1258, Santo Domingo, DN; tel. 533-1161; fax 533-1305; internet www.cea.gov.do; f. 1966; management of operations contracted to private consortiums in 1999 and 2000; Dir-Gen. Dr ENRIQUE MARTÍNEZ.

Corporación Dominicana de Empresas Estatales (CORDE) (Dominican State Corporation): Avda General Antonio Duvergé, Apdo 1378, Santo Domingo, DN; tel. 533-5171; f. 1966 to administer, direct and develop state enterprises; Dir-Gen. FERNANDO DURÁN.

Instituto de Estabilización de Precios (INESPRE): Plaza Independencia, Avda Luperon, esq. 27 de Febrero, Apdo 86-2, Santo Domingo, DN; tel. 537-0020; fax 531-0198; e-mail inespre.comp@verizon.net.do; f. 1969; price commission; Exec. Dir JOSÉ FRANCISCO PEÑA GUABA.

Instituto Nacional de la Vivienda: Avda Tiredentes, esq. Pedro Henríquez Ureña, Santo Domingo, DN; tel. 732-0600; e-mail invi@codetel.net.do; f. 1962; low-cost housing institute; Dir-Gen. Ing. JUAN ANTONIO VARGAS.

DEVELOPMENT ORGANIZATIONS

Centro para el Desarrollo Agropecuario y Forestal, Inc. (CEDAF): Calle José A. Soler 50, Santo Domingo, DN; tel. 544-0616; fax 544-4727; e-mail cedaf@cedaf.org.do; internet www.cedaf.org.do; f. 1987 to encourage the devt of agriculture, livestock and forestry; fmrly known as Fundación de Desarrollo Agropecuario, Inc. (FDA); Pres. JOSÉ MIGUEL BONETTI; Sec.-Gen. JERRY W. DUPUY.

Consejo Nacional para el Desarrollo Minero: Santo Domingo, DN; f. 2000; encourages the devt of the mining sector; Exec. Dir MIGUEL PENA; Sec.-Gen. PEDRO VÁSQUEZ.

Departamento de Desarrollo y Financiamiento de Proyectos (DEFINPRO): c/o Banco Central de la República Dominicana, Pedro Henríquez Ureña, esq. Leopoldo Navarro, Apdo 1347, Santo Domingo, DN; tel. 221-9111; fax 687-7488; f. 1993; associated with AID, IDB, WB, KFW; encourages economic devt in productive sectors of economy, excluding sugar; authorizes complementary financing to private sector for establishing and developing industrial and agricultural enterprises and free-zone industrial parks; Dir ANGEL NERY CASTILLO PIMENTEL.

Fundación Dominicana de Desarrollo (Dominican Development Foundation): Mercedes No 4, Apdo 857, Santo Domingo, DN; tel. 688-8101; fax 686-0430; e-mail info@fdd.org.do; internet www.fdd.org.do; f. 1962 to mobilize private resources for collaboration in financing small-scale development programmes; 384 mems; Pres. OSVALDO BRUGAL; Exec. Dir Lic. ADA WISCOVITCH CARLO.

Instituto de Desarrollo y Crédito Cooperativo (IDECOOP): Centro de los Héroes, Apdo 1371, Santo Domingo, DN; tel. 533-8131; fax 535-5148; f. 1963 to encourage the devt of co-operatives; Dir JAVIER PEÑA NÚÑEZ.

THE DOMINICAN REPUBLIC *Directory*

CHAMBERS OF COMMERCE

Cámara Americana de Comercio de la República Dominicana: Torre Empresarial, 6°, Avda Sarasota 20, Santo Domingo, DN; tel. 381-0777; fax 381-0286; e-mail amcham@verizon.net.do; internet www.amcham.org.do; Pres. CHRISTOPHER PANIAGUA.

Cámara de Comercio y Producción de Santo Domingo: Arz. Nouel 206, Zona Colonial, Apdo 815, Santo Domingo, DN; tel. 682-2688; fax 685-2228; e-mail ccpsd@camarasantodomingo.org.do; internet www.ccpsd.org.do; f. 1910; 1,500 active mems; Pres. JUAN BANCALARI; Vice-Pres. OSCAR VALIENTE.

There are official Chambers of Commerce in the larger towns.

INDUSTRIAL AND TRADE ASSOCIATIONS

Asociación Dominicana de Hacendados y Agricultores: 265 Avda 27 de Febrero, al lado de Plaza Central, Santo Domingo, DN; tel. 565-0542; fax 565-8696; farming and agricultural org.; Pres. CESARIO CONTRERAS.

Asociación Dominicana de Zonas Francas Inc (ADOZONA): Avda Sarasota 20, 4°, Torre Empresarial AIRD, Apdo 3184, Santo Domingo; tel. 472-0251; fax 472-0256; e-mail info@adozona.org; internet www.adozona.org; f. 1988; Pres. LUIS MANUEL PELLERANO; Exec. Dir JOSÉ MANUEL TORRES.

Asociación de Industrias de la República Dominicana Inc.: Avda Sarasota 20, Torre Empresarial AIRD, 12°, Santo Domingo, DN; tel. 472-0000; fax 472-0303; e-mail aird@verizon.net.do; internet www.aird.org.do; f. 1962; industrial org.; Pres. YANDRA PORTELA VILA.

Centro Dominicano de Promoción de Exportaciones (CEDOPEX): Plaza de la Bandera, Avda 27 de Febrero, Apdo 199-2, Santo Domingo, DN; tel. 530-5505; fax 531-5136; e-mail emartinez@cei-rd.gov.do; internet www.cei-rd.gov.do; promotion of exports and investments; Exec. Dir EDDY MARTÍNEZ MANZUETA.

Consejo Nacional de la Empresa Privada (CONEP): Avda Sarasota 20, Torre Empresarial, 12°, Ensanche La Julia, Santo Domingo, DN; tel. 472-7101; fax 472-7850; e-mail conep@conep.org.do; internet www.conep.org.do; Pres. Lic. ELENA VIYELLA DE PALIZA.

Consejo Nacional de Zonas Francas de Exportación: Leopoldo Navarro 61, Edif. San Rafael, 5°, Apdo 21430, Santo Domingo, DN; tel. 686-8077; fax 686-8079; e-mail e.castillo@cnzfe.gov.do; internet www.cnzfe.gov.do; co-ordinating body for the free trade zones; Exec. Dir LUISA FERNÁNDEZ DURÁN.

Consejo Promotor de Inversiones (Investment Promotion Council): Avda Abraham Lincoln, Edif. Alico, 2°, Santo Domingo, DN; tel. 532-3281; fax 533-7029; Exec. Dir and CEO FREDERIC EMAM ZADÉ.

Corporación de Fomento Industrial (CFI): Avda 27 de Febrero, Plaza La Bandera, Apdo 1452, Santo Domingo, DN; tel. 530-0010; fax 530-1303; e-mail corp.fomento@verizon.net.do; internet www.cfi.gov.do; f. 1962 to promote agro-industrial development; Dir-Gen. JERGES RUBÉN JIMÉNEZ BICHARA.

Dirección General de Minería: Edif. de Ofs Gubernamentales, 10°, Avda México, esq. Leopoldo Navarro, Santo Domingo, DN; tel. 685-8191; fax 686-8327; e-mail direc.mineria@verizon.net.do; internet www.dgm.gov.do; f. 1947; govt mining and hydrocarbon org.; Dir-Gen. OCTAVIO LÓPEZ.

Instituto Agrario Dominicano (IAD): Avda 27 de Febrero, Santo Domingo, DN; tel. 530-8272; e-mail hector.garcia@iad.gov.do; internet www.iad.gov.do; Dir-Gen. Ing. AGRON SALVADOR JIMÉNEZ A.

Instituto de Innovación en Biotecnología e Industria (INDOTEC): Calle Oloff Palme, esq. Núñez de Cáceres, San Gerónimo, Santo Domingo, DN; tel. 566-8121; fax 227-8808; e-mail iibi@verizon.net.do; internet www.iibi.gov.do; fmrly Instituto Dominicano de Tecnología Industrial (INDOTEC); name changed as above in 2005; Pres. FRANCISCO JAVIER GARCÍA; Exec. Dir Dra BERNARDA A. CASTILLO.

Instituto Nacional del Azúcar (INAZUCAR): Avda Jiménez Moya, Apdo 667, Santo Domingo, DN; tel. 532-5571; fax 533-2402; e-mail inst.azucar2@verizon.net.do; internet www.inazucar.gov.do; f. 1965; sugar institute; Exec. Dir FAUSTINO JIMÉNEZ.

EMPLOYERS' ORGANIZATIONS

Confederación Patronal de la República Dominicana (COPARDOM): Torre Empresarial AIRD, Suite 207, Avda Sarasota 20, Santo Domingo, DN; tel. 381-4233; fax 381-4266; e-mail copardom@copardom.org.do; f. 1946; Pres. RADHAMÉS MARTÍNEZ.

Consejo Nacional de Hombres de Empresa Inc.: Edif. Motorámbar, 7°, Avda Abraham Lincoln 1056, Santo Domingo, DN; tel. 562-1666; Pres. JOSÉ MANUEL PALIZA.

Federación Dominicana de Comerciantes: Carretera Sánchez Km 10, Santo Domingo, DN; tel. 533-2666; Pres. IVAN GARCÍA.

UTILITIES

Regulatory Authority

Superintendencia de Electricidad: Edif. CREP, 5°, Avda Gustavo Mejía Ricart 73, esq. Agustín Lara, Ensanche Serrallés, Apdo 1725, Santo Domingo, DN; tel. 683-2500; fax 544-1637; e-mail sielectric@sie.gov.do; internet www.sie.gov.do; f. 2001; Pres. FRANCISCO MÉNDEZ.

Electricity

AES Dominicana: Santo Domingo; f. 1997; subsidiary of AES Corpn, USA; largest private electricity generator in the Dominican Republic; Pres. ANDRES GLUSKI.

Corporación Dominicana de Empresas Eléctricas Estatales (CDEEE): Edif. Principal CDE, Centro de los Héroes, Avda Independencia, esq. Fray C. de Utrera, Santo Domingo, DN; tel. 535-9098; fax 533-7204; e-mail info@cde.gov.do; internet www.cde.gov.do; f. 1955; state electricity co; partially privatized in 1999, renationalized in 2003; Dir-Gen. RAFAEL DE JESÚS PERELLÓ; Exec. Vice-Pres. Ing. RADHAMÉS SEGURA.

Empresa de Generación Hidroeléctrica Dominicana (EGEHID): Avda Independencia Centro los Héroes 256, Santo Domingo, DN; tel. 535-1100; fax 535-7472; internet www.hidroelectrica.gov.do; distributor of hydroelectricity.

Unidad de Electrificación Rural y Suburbana (UERS): Avda José Andrés Aybar Castellanos 136, Ensanche La Esperilla, Santo Domingo, DN; tel. 227-7666; internet www.uers.gov.do; f. 2006; manages supply of electricity to rural areas; Dir-Gen. ANTONIO HERRERA CRUZ.

There are three electricity distribution companies operating in the Dominican Republic. Empresa Distribuidora de Electricidad del Norte (Ede-Norte), responsible for distribution in the north of the country, and Empresa Distribuidora de Electricidad del Sur (Ede-Sur), in the south, are owned by the Government, while Empresa Distribuidora de Electricidad del Este (Ede-Este), in the east, is jointly owned by the Government and AES Dominicana (q.v.), a subsidiary of the US company AES. In November 2004 AES Dominicana divested its 50% stake in Ede-Este, owing to continued problems in the country's power sector. In 2006 the Government began restructuring Ede-Norte and Ede-Sur, prior to privatization.

Gas

AES Andrés: Santo Domingo; internet www.aes.com; f. 2003; subsidiary of AES Corpn, USA; 319 MW gas-fired plant and liquefied natural gas terminal; Pres. ANDRES GLUSKI.

Water

As part of the continuing programme of repair to the country's infrastructure, in 2001 construction began on aqueducts, intended to supply water to the provinces of Bahoruco, Barahona, Duarte, Espaillat, Independencia and Salcedo.

Corporación del Acueducto y Alcantarillado de Santo Domingo: Calle Euclides Morillo 65, Arroyo Hondo, Santo Domingo, DN; tel. 562-3500; fax 541-4121; e-mail info@caasd.gov.do; internet www.caasd.gov.do; f. 1973; Dir MARIANO GERMÁN MEJÍA.

Instituto Nacional de Aguas Potables y Alcantarillado (INAPA): Centro Comercial El Millón, Calle Guarocuya, Apdo 1503, Santo Domingo, DN; tel. 567-1241; fax 567-8972; e-mail info@inapa.gov.do; internet www.inapa.gov.do; Exec. Dir FRANK RODRÍGUEZ.

Instituto Nacional de Recursos Hidráulicos: Avda Jiménez de Moya, Centro de los Héroes, Santo Domingo, DN; tel. 532-3271; fax 532-2321; internet www.indrhi.gov.do; f. 1965; Exec. Dir HÉCTOR RODRÍGUEZ PIMENTEL.

TRADE UNIONS

Central General de Trabajadores (CGT): Juan Erazo 14, Villa Juana, 5°, Santo Domingo, DN; tel. 688-3932; e-mail central.gt@codetel.net.do; f. 1972; 13 sections; Sec.-Gen. RAFAEL ABREU; 65,000 mems.

Central de Trabajadores Independientes (CTI): Juan Erazo 133, Santo Domingo, DN; tel. 688-3932; f. 1978; left-wing; Sec.-Gen. RAFAEL SANTOS.

Central de Trabajadores Mayoritarias (CTM): Tunti Cáceres 222, Santo Domingo, DN; tel. 562-3392; Sec.-Gen. NÉLSIDA MARMOLEJOS.

Confederación Autónoma de Sindicatos Clasistas (CASC) (Autonomous Confederation of Trade Unions): Juan Erazo 14, Villa Juana, 4°, Santo Domingo, DN; tel. 687-8533; fax 689-1439; e-mail cascnacional@codetel.net.do; f. 1962; supports PRSC; Sec.-Gen. GABRIEL DEL RÍO.

Confederación Nacional de Trabajadores Dominicanos (CNTD) (National Confederation of Dominican Workers): Calle José de Jesús Ravelo 56, Villa Juana, 2°, Santo Domingo, DN; tel. 221-2117; fax 221-3217; e-mail cntd@codetel.net.do; f. 1988 by merger; 11 provincial federations totalling 150 unions are affiliated; Sec.-Gen. JACOBO RAMOS; c. 188,000 mems.

Confederación de Trabajadores Unitaria (CTU) (United Workers' Confederation): Edif. de las Centrales Sindicales, 3°, Villa Juana, Juan Erazo 14, Santo Domingo, DN; tel. 221-9443; fax 689-1248; e-mail ctu01@codetel.net.do; f. 1991; Pres. VICTOR RUFINO ALVAREZ.

Transport

RAILWAYS

In April 2001 plans were announced for the construction of a passenger and freight railway from the coastal port of Haina to Santiago, with the possibility of subsequent extension to Puerto Plata and Manzanillo. The Government invested US $50m.–$100m. in 2006 on the installation of an underground railway system in Santo Domingo. Construction of the first line—14 km in length, between Villa Mella and Centro de los Héroes—commenced in late 2005 and was expected to be completed in 2008. Two further lines were being planned, and the completed network was to have a total length of some 60 km.

Dirección General de Tránsito Terrestre: Avda San Cristóbal, Santo Domingo, DN; tel. tel. 565-2811; e-mail e-mail dgtt_dom@hotmail.com; internet www.dgtt.gov.do; f. 1966; operated by Secretary of State for Public Works and Communications; Dir-Gen. Ing. RAFAEL T. CRESPO PÉREZ.

Ferrocarriles Unidos Dominicanos: Santo Domingo, DN; govt-owned; 142 km of track from La Vega to Sánchez and from Guayubín to Pepillo principally used for the transport of exports.

There are also a number of semi-autonomous and private railway companies for the transport of sugar cane, including:

Ferrocarril Central Río Haina: Apdo 1258, Haina; 113 km open.

Ferrocarril de Central Romana: La Romana; 375 km open; Pres. C. MORALES.

ROADS

In 2005 there were an estimated 17,000 km of roads, of which about 6,225 km were paved. There is a direct route from Santo Domingo to Port-au-Prince in Haiti. The Mejía administration undertook an extensive road-building programme from 2000, aiming primarily to reduce traffic congestion in Santo Domingo. In April 2007 a new road, the 'Cruz del Isleño Macao', was inaugurated in the province of La Altagracia. The road, built at a cost of more than RD $174m., was expected to increase tourism in the region.

Dirección General de Carreteras y Caminos Vecinales: Santo Domingo, DN; fax 567-5470; f. 1987; govt supervisory body; Dir-Gen. ELIZABETH PERALTA BRITO.

Autoridad Metropolitana de Transporte (AMET): Avda Expreso V Centenario, esq. Avda San Martín, Santo Domingo, DN; tel. 686-6520; fax 686-3447; e-mail info@amet.gov.do; internet www.amet.gov.do; Dir-Gen. SIGFRIDO FERNÁNDEZ FADUL.

SHIPPING

The Dominican Republic has 14 ports, of which Río Haina is by far the largest, handling about 70% of imports in 2004. Other important ports are Boca Chica, Santo Domingo and San Pedro de Macorís on the south coast, and Puerto Plata in the north. The Caucedo port and transhipment centre, near the Las Americas international airport, opened in 2003 and was destined specifically for use by free trade zone businesses.

A number of foreign shipping companies operate services to the island.

Agencias Navieras B&R, SA: Avda Abraham Lincoln 504, Apdo 1221, Santo Domingo, DN; tel. 562-1661; fax 562-3383; e-mail ops@navierasbr.com; internet www.navierasbr.com; f. 1919; shipping agents and export services; Man. JUAN PERICHE PIDAL.

Armadora Naval Dominicana, SA: Isabel la Católica 165, Apdo 2677, Santo Domingo, DN; tel. 689-6191; Man. Dir Capt. EINAR WETTRE.

Autoridad Portuaria Dominicana: Avda Máximo Gómez, Santo Domingo, DN; tel. 535-8462; Exec. Dir Prof. ARSENIO BORGES.

Frederic Schad, Inc.: José Gabriel García 26, Apdo 941, Santo Domingo, DN; tel. 221-8000; fax 688-7696; e-mail mail@fschad.com; internet www.fschad.com; f. 1922; logistics and shipping agent.

Líneas Marítimas de Santo Domingo, SA: José Gabriel García 8, Apdo 1148, Santo Domingo, DN; tel. 689-9146; fax 685-4654; Pres. C. LLUBERES; Vice-Pres. JUAN T. TAVARES.

CIVIL AVIATION

There are international airports at Santo Domingo, Puerto Plata, Punta Cana, Santiago, La Romana, Samaná and Barahona. A new international airport, Aeropuerto Internacional La Isabela, at El Higuero, near Santo Domingo, was scheduled to become operational in 2004. Construction went ahead, at a cost of over RD $2,000m., without the requisite technical feasibility studies being carried out and despite warnings about the suitability of the chosen site. After a lengthy delay in securing approval from the relevant national and international aviation authorities, the new airport finally commenced operations in mid-2006, replacing the Aeropuerto Internacional de Herrera, which was closed down in February of that year. Another new airport, President Juan Bosch International Airport, in El Catey, in the north of the country, was inaugurated in February 2007. Most main cities have domestic airports.

Dirección General de Aeronáutica Civil: Avda México, esq. Avda 30 de Marzo, Apdo 1180, Santo Domingo, DN; tel. 221-7909; fax 221-6220; e-mail aeronautica.c@verizon.net.do; internet www.dgac.gov.do; f. 1955; govt supervisory body; Dir-Gen. JORGE BOTELLO FERNÁNDEZ.

Aerochago: Aeropuerto Internacional de las Américas, Santo Domingo, DN; tel. 549-0709; fax 549-0708; f. 1973; operates cargo and charter service in Central America and the Caribbean; Gen. Man. PEDRO RODRÍGUEZ.

Aerolíneas Argo: Santo Domingo, DN; f. 1971; cargo and mail services to the USA, Puerto Rico and the US Virgin Islands.

Aerolíneas Dominicanas (Dominair): El Sol 62, Apdo 202, Santiago de los Caballeros; tel. 581-8882; fax 582-5074; f. 1974; owned by Aeropostal (Venezuela); scheduled and charter passenger services.

Aerolíneas Santo Domingo: Edif. J. P., Avda 27 de Febrero 272, esq. Seminario, Santo Domingo, DN; e-mail reservas@airsantodomingo.com.do; f. 1996; operates scheduled and charter internal, regional and international flights; Pres. HENRY W. AZAR.

Aeromar Airlines: Avda Winston Churchill 71, esq. Desiderio Arias, Ensanche La Julia, Santo Domingo, DN; tel. 533-4447; fax 533-4550; e-mail customer_service@aeromarairlines.com; internet www.aeromarairlines.com; cargo and passenger services; Pres. RAYMUNDO POLANCO.

Caribbean Atlantic Airlines (Caribair): Aeropuerto Internacional de Herrera, Santo Domingo, DN; tel. 542-6688; fax 567-7033; e-mail caribair@caribair.com.do; internet www.caribair.com.do; f. 1962; operates scheduled flights to Haiti, and domestic and regional charter flights.

Compañía Dominicana de Aviación C por A: Avda Jiménez Moya, esq. José Contreras, Apdo 1415, Santo Domingo, DN; tel. 532-8511; fax 535-1656; f. 1944; operates on international routes connecting Santo Domingo with the Netherlands Antilles, Aruba, the USA, Haiti and Venezuela; operations suspended 1995, privatization pending; Chair. Dr RODOLFO RINCÓN; CEO MARINA GINEBRA DE BONNELLY.

Tourism

Strenuous efforts were made to improve the tourism infrastructure, with RD $200m. spent on increasing the number of hotel rooms by 50%, road improvements and new developments. In 2001 tourism developments were under way in the south-western province of Pedernales, in Monte Cristi and in Cap Cana. The total number of visitors to the Dominican Republic in 2006 was 4,383,765. In 2004 receipts from tourism, excluding passenger transport, totalled US $3,180m. There were 59,870 hotel rooms in the Dominican Republic in 2005. The Secretariat of State for Tourism announced plans to construct new hotels comprising a further 3,500 rooms before the end of 2006.

Secretaría de Estado de Turismo: Bloque D, Edif. de Ofs Gubernamentales, Avda México, esq. 30 de Marzo, Apdo 497, Santo Domingo, DN; tel. 221-4660; fax 682-3806; e-mail sectur@codetel.net.do; internet www.dominicana.com.do.

Asociación Dominicana de Agencias de Viajes: Calle Padre Billini 263, Apdo 2097, Santo Domingo, DN; tel. 687-8984; Pres. RAMÓN PRIETO.

Consejo de Promoción Turística: Avda México 66, Santo Domingo, DN; tel. 685-9054; fax 685-6752; e-mail cpt@codetel.net.do; Dir EVELYN PAIEWONSKY.

ECUADOR

Introductory Survey

Location, Climate, Language, Religion, Flag, Capital

The Republic of Ecuador lies on the west coast of South America. It is bordered by Colombia to the north, by Peru to the east and south, and by the Pacific Ocean to the west. The Galápagos Islands, about 960 km (600 miles) offshore, form part of Ecuador. The climate is affected by the Andes mountains, and the topography ranges from the tropical rainforest on the coast and in the eastern region to the tropical grasslands of the central valley and the permanent snowfields of the highlands. The official language is Spanish, but Quechua and other indigenous languages are very common. Almost all of the inhabitants profess Christianity, and almost 90% are Roman Catholics. The national flag (proportions 1 by 2) has three horizontal stripes, of yellow (one-half of the depth), blue and red. The state flag has, in addition, the national emblem (an oval cartouche, showing Mount Chimborazo and a steamer on a lake, surmounted by a condor) in the centre. The capital is Quito.

Recent History

Ecuador was ruled by Spain from the 16th century until 1822, when it achieved independence as part of Gran Colombia. In 1830 Ecuador seceded and became a separate republic. A long-standing division between Conservatives (Partido Conservador), whose support is generally strongest in the highlands, and Liberals (Partido Liberal, subsequently Partido Liberal Radical), based in the coastal region, began in the 19th century. Until 1948 Ecuador's political life was characterized by a rapid succession of presidents, dictators and juntas. Between 1830 and 1925 the country was governed by 40 different regimes. From 1925 to 1948 there was even greater instability, with a total of 22 heads of state.

Dr Galo Plaza Lasso, who was elected in 1948 and remained in power until 1952, was the first President since 1924 to complete his term of office. He created a climate of stability and economic progress. Dr José María Velasco Ibarra, who had previously been President in 1934–35 and 1944–47, was elected again in 1952 and held office until 1956. A 61-year-old tradition of Liberal Presidents was broken in 1956, when a Conservative candidate, Dr Camilo Ponce Enríquez, took office. He was succeeded in 1960 by Velasco, who campaigned as a non-party Liberal. In the following year, however, President Velasco was deposed by a coup, and was succeeded by his Vice-President, Dr Carlos Julio Arosemena Monroy. The latter was himself deposed in 1963 by a military junta, led by Capt. (later Rear-Adm.) Ramón Castro Jijón, the Commander-in-Chief of the Navy, who assumed the office of President. In 1966 the High Command of the Armed Forces dismissed the junta and installed Clemente Yerovi Indaburu, a wealthy business executive and a former Minister of Economics, as acting President. Yerovi was forced to resign when the Constituent Assembly, elected in October, proposed a new Constitution which prohibited the intervention of the armed forces in politics. In November he was replaced as provisional President by Dr Otto Arosemena Gómez, who held office until the elections of 1968, when Velasco returned from exile to win the presidency for the fifth time.

In 1970 Velasco, with the support of the army, suspended the Constitution, dissolved the Congreso Nacional (National Congress) and assumed dictatorial powers to confront a financial emergency. In 1972 he was overthrown for the fourth time by a military coup, led by Brig.-Gen. Guillermo Rodríguez Lara, the Commander-in-Chief of the Army, who proclaimed himself Head of State. In 1976 President Rodríguez resigned, and power was assumed by a three-man military junta, led by Vice-Adm. Alfredo Poveda Burbano, the Chief of Staff of the Navy. The new junta announced its intention to lead the country to a truly representative democracy. A national referendum approved a newly drafted Constitution in January 1978 and presidential elections took place in July. No candidate achieved an overall majority, and a second round of voting was held in April 1979, when a new legislature was also elected. Jaime Roldós Aguilera of the Concentración de Fuerzas Populares was elected President and he took office in August, when the Congreso was inaugurated and the new Constitution came into force. Roldós promised social justice and economic development, and guaranteed freedom for the press, but he encountered antagonism from both the conservative sections of the Congreso Nacional and the trade unions. In 1981 Roldós died and was replaced by the Vice-President, Dr Osvaldo Hurtado Larrea. Hurtado encountered opposition from left-wing politicians and trade unions for his efforts to reduce government spending and from right-wing and commercial interests, which feared encroaching state intervention in the private economic sector. In January 1982 the heads of the armed forces resigned and the Minister of Defence was dismissed, when they opposed Hurtado's attempts to settle amicably the border dispute with Peru (see below).

In March 1983 the Government introduced a series of austerity measures, which encountered immediate opposition from the trade unions and private sector employees. Discontent with the Government's performance was reflected in the results of the presidential and congressional elections of January 1984, when the ruling party, Democracia Popular-Unión Demócrata Cristiana (DP-UDC), lost support. At a second round of voting in May León Febres Cordero, leader of the Partido Social Cristiano (PSC) and presidential candidate of the conservative Frente de Reconstrucción Nacional, unexpectedly defeated Dr Rodrigo Borja Cevallos, representing the left-wing Izquierda Democrática (ID).

The dismissal of the Chief of Staff of the Armed Forces, Lt-Gen. Frank Vargas Pazzos, brought about a military crisis in 1986. Vargas and his supporters barricaded themselves inside the Mantas military base until they had forced the resignation of both the Minister of Defence and the army commander, who had been accused by Vargas of embezzlement. Vargas then staged a second rebellion at the military base where he had been detained. Troops loyal to the President made an assault on the base, captured Vargas and arrested his supporters. In January 1987 President Febres Cordero was abducted and, after being held for 11 hours, was released in exchange for Vargas, who was granted an amnesty. In July 58 members of the air force were sentenced to up to 16 years' imprisonment for involvement in the abduction of the President.

In June 1986 President Febres Cordero lost the majority that his coalition of parties had held in the Congreso Nacional. In May 1988 Dr Rodrigo Borja Cevallos (of the ID) won the presidential election, defeating Abdalá Bucaram Ortiz of the Partido Roldosista Ecuatoriano (PRE). Borja took office as President in August, promising to act promptly to address Ecuador's increasing economic problems. However, large demonstrations in protest against the consequent economic austerity measures swiftly followed.

In February 1989 the Government conducted a campaign to confiscate weapons belonging to paramilitary organizations. In March Alfaro Vive ¡Carajo! (AVC), a leading opposition (hitherto guerrilla) group, urged paramilitary forces across the political spectrum to surrender their weapons. The Government agreed to guarantee the civil rights of AVC members and to initiate a national dialogue in return for the group's demobilization. (The AVC demobilized fully by February 1991 and was absorbed by the ID in October.) The guerrilla organization Montoneros Patria Libre dissociated itself from the agreement and pledged to continue violent opposition.

In October 1990 a serious conflict arose between the Government and the legislature when the newly elected President of the Congreso Nacional, Dr Averroes Bucaram, attempted to stage a legislative coup against President Borja. Bucaram initially impeached several ministers, who were subsequently dismissed by the Congreso. The legislature then dismissed the Supreme Court justices and other high-ranking members of the judiciary, and appointed new courts with shortened mandates. Both the Government and the judiciary refused to recognize these actions, on the grounds that the Congreso had exceeded its constitutional powers. Bucaram then announced that the Congreso would initiate impeachment proceedings against Borja himself. However, this move was averted when three opposition deputies transferred their allegiance, so restoring Borja's congressional majority. Bucaram was subsequently dismissed as congressional President.

In May 1990 about 1,000 indigenous Indians marched into Quito to demand official recognition of the land rights and languages of the indigenous population and to win compensation from petroleum companies for environmental damage. In the following month the Confederación Nacional de Indígenas del Ecuador (CONAIE—National Confederation of the Indigenous Population of Ecuador) organized an uprising covering seven Andean provinces. Roads were blockaded, haciendas occupied, and supplies to the cities interrupted. Following the arrest of 30 Indians by the army, the rebels took military hostages. The Government offered to hold conciliatory negotiations with CONAIE, in exchange for the hostages. Discussions between CONAIE and President Borja collapsed in August but were resumed in February 1991, following the seizure by Indian groups in the Oriente of eight oil wells. As a result, the Government promised to consider the Indians' demands for stricter controls on the operations of the petroleum industry, and for financial compensation. In April 1992 several thousand Amazon Indians marched from the Oriente to Quito to demand that their historical rights to their homelands be recognized. In May President Borja agreed to grant legal title to more than 1m. ha of land in the province of Pastaza to the Indians.

At legislative elections in May 1992 the PSC gained the highest number of seats in the enlarged Congreso Nacional. The Partido Unidad Republicano (PUR), formed prior to the elections by the former PSC presidential candidate, Sexto Durán Ballén, in order to contest the presidential election, won the second highest number of seats, and was to govern with its ally, the PC. However, as the two parties' seats did not constitute a majority in the Congreso, support from other centre-right parties, particularly the PSC, was sought. In the second round of the presidential election, Durán defeated Nebot.

In September 1992 the Government's announcement of a programme of economic austerity measures prompted violent demonstrations and several bomb attacks in Quito and Guayaquil and a general strike in May 1993. The 'Modernization Law', a crucial part of the controversial austerity programme (which was to provide for the privatization of some 160 state-owned companies and the reduction in the number of employees in the public sector by 100,000), was approved by the Congreso in August. In November striking teachers organized demonstrations throughout the country, demanding wage increases and reforms in the education system. During the protests two demonstrators were killed and many injured. Furthermore, the Government's decision in January 1994 to increase the price of fuel by more than 70% provoked violent demonstrations throughout the country and a general strike. In the following month the Tribunal of Constitutional Guarantees declared the rise to be unconstitutional, although President Durán refused to recognize the ruling. The unpopularity of Durán's PUR-PC governing alliance was demonstrated at mid-term congressional elections in May, when it won only nine of the 77 seats.

Environmental concerns regarding the exploitation of the Oriente by the petroleum industry continued to be expressed by national and international groups during 1993. In November five Amazon Indian tribes began legal proceedings against the international company Texaco to claim compensation totalling US $1,500m. for its part in polluting the rainforest. (It was estimated that some 17m. barrels of oil had been spilt during the company's 25 years of operations in the region.) In June 1994 the increasingly vociferous indigenous movement organized large-scale demonstrations across the country, in protest at a recently approved Land Development Law. The law, which allowed for the commercialization of Amerindian lands for farming and resource extraction, provoked serious unrest and a general strike, during which a state of emergency was declared and the army mobilized. Seven protesters were killed, and many injured, in clashes with the security forces. The law was subsequently judged to be unconstitutional by the Tribunal of Constitutional Guarantees, although, again, President Durán refused to accept the ruling. In July the law was modified to extend the rights of landowners and those employed to work on the land.

In August 1994 a national referendum on constitutional reform finally took place, on President Durán's initiative, following much disagreement between the Government and the judiciary and opposition parties. All but one of the eight proposed reforms (which included measures to alter the electoral system and the role of the Congreso Nacional, and the establishment of a bicameral legislature) were approved; however, only some 50% of eligible voters participated, of whom some 20% returned void ballot papers.

Protests against the Government's economic programme of austerity measures and privatizations in January 1995 resulted in the deaths of two students in Quito during clashes with riot police. During May–July there was severe disruption as a result of further strikes. In July the country was plunged into a serious political crisis when Vice-President Alberto Dahik admitted giving funds from the state budget to opposition deputies (allegedly for use in local public-works projects) in return for their support for the Government's economic reform programme. Dahik refused to resign, despite the initiation of impeachment proceedings, and rejected the criminal charges against him. In a further development (believed by some observers to be an attempt to obstruct the case against Dahik) the President of the Supreme Court and two other justices were dismissed, provoking widespread concern over executive interference in the judiciary. In September impeachment proceedings began against the new Minister of Finance, Mauricio Pinto, for his role in various alleged financial irregularities. Impeachment proceedings against Dahik began in October, and on 11 October the Vice-President resigned.

In September 1995 troops were dispatched to the Galápagos Islands, following disturbances among the islanders, who were demanding the Government's acceptance of a special law granting increased political and financial autonomy to the islands, in addition to some US $16m. in priority economic aid. Concerned about the potentially disastrous effect of the protests on the country's important tourism industry, the Government quickly withdrew its opposition to the proposed legislation and agreed to establish a specialist commission to draft a new law acceptable to all parties. Moreover, in October petroleum workers resumed strike action in protest at the Government's privatization plans, and in one incident occupied the state oil company, PETROECUADOR, building, taking two cabinet ministers hostage for several hours. The strike, together with a severe drought, which halted production at the Paute hydroelectric plant, resulted in serious energy shortages in late 1995.

A referendum on government proposals for constitutional reform was held in November 1995. All of the proposed changes were rejected in the plebiscite; the result was widely regarded as a reflection of the Government's continued unpopularity. Despite its decisive defeat, the Government announced its intention to pursue its programme of reforms. Widespread strikes and demonstrations by teachers and students in the same month led to the resignation of the Minister of Education. Industrial action among employees in the energy sector continued, and in January 1996 army units were deployed at prominent sites throughout the country in order to prevent further unrest. However, an industrial dispute by transport workers in March resulted in serious disruption in the capital and prompted a series of strikes in other sectors.

A presidential election, held in May 1996, failed to produce an outright winner, thus necessitating a second round of voting for the two leading contenders, Jaime Nebot Saadi of the PSC and Abdalá Bucaram Ortiz of the PRE. An increasingly vocal and politically organized indigenous movement resulted in the strong performance of Freddy Ehlers, the candidate for the newly formed Movimiento Nuevo País—Pachakútik (MNPP), a coalition of Amerindian and labour groups. The MNPP also emerged as a significant new force in the legislature, with a total of eight seats, at a concurrently held legislative election. At the second round of voting in the presidential election in July, Bucaram was the unexpected victor, receiving 55% of total votes. The success of Bucaram was widely interpreted as an expression of disenchantment with established party politics. Following his inauguration in August, Bucaram sought to allay the fears of the business community (prompted by his proposals for costly social reform), stating that existing economic arrangements would be maintained.

A 48-hour general strike began in January 1997, prompted by increases of up to 600% in the price of certain commodities and a climate of considerable dissatisfaction with the President's leadership. Protests intensified in early February and, in response, troops were deployed in the capital. Violent clashes erupted between protesters and security personnel and Bucaram was barricaded inside the presidential palace. On 6 February, at an emergency session, the Congreso Nacional voted to dismiss the President on the grounds of mental incapacity (and thus evade the normal impeachment requirements of a two-thirds' majority). A state of emergency was declared, and the erstwhile Speaker, Fabián Alarcón Rivera, who had assumed the presidency in an acting capacity, urged demonstrators to storm the presidential palace. Bucaram, however, refused to leave office and claimed that he would retain power by force if necessary. The situation was further complicated by the claim of the Vice-President, Rosalia Arteaga, to be the legitimate constitutional successor to Bucaram. Confusion over the correct procedure led to fears of a military coup, despite a declaration of neutrality by the armed forces. Bucaram fled from the presidential palace on 9 February, and on the following day Arteaga was declared interim President. However, by 11 February Arteaga had resigned amid continued constitutional uncertainty, and Alarcón was reinstated as President. Alarcón, who sought political reform and the restoration of economic confidence, announced a reorganization of cabinet portfolios (which included no members of the two largest parties in the Congreso, the PSC and the PRE) and the creation of a commission to investigate allegations of corruption against Bucaram and his administration. In March Bucaram's extradition from Panama (where he had been granted political asylum) was requested in order that he face charges of misappropriating some US $90m. of government funds. In May, in response to Bucaram's declaration that he intended to contest Ecuador's next presidential election, the legislature voted almost unanimously in favour of a motion to impose an indefinite ban on Bucaram's candidacy in any future ballot. (In January 1998 the Supreme Court issued a four-year prison sentence, *in absentia*, to Bucaram for libel and in April 2001 he was indicted on corruption charges.)

At a national referendum in May 1997 the most notable results were that 76% supported the decision to remove Bucaram from office and 68% supported the appointment of Alarcón as interim President. Some 65% of voters also favoured the creation of a national assembly to consider constitutional reform. Alarcón's apparent success in the referendum, however, was undermined by high voter absenteeism (41%) and by the launch, in June, of an official congressional inquiry into allegations that leading drugs-traffickers in the country had contributed to political party funds, and, particularly, to Alarcón's Frente Radical Alfarista.

In January 1998, following persistent pleas from international environmental and scientific organizations for greater protection of the Galápagos Islands, the Congreso Nacional approved a law which aimed to preserve the islands' unique environment more effectively. An element of the law, providing for an extension of the marine reserve around the islands from 15 to 40 nautical miles, attracted intense criticism from powerful fishing interests in the country and was, consequently, vetoed by Alarcón, prompting condemnation by environmentalists and small-scale fishing concerns.

On 10 August 1998, following the conclusion of the discussions of the constituent assembly, a new Constitution came into force. Although it retained the majority of the provisions of the 1979 Constitution, a number of significant reforms were introduced, including the enlargement of the Congreso Nacional from 82 to 121 seats, the abolition of mid-term elections and the completion of a presidential term by the Vice-President in the case of the indefinite absence of the President.

At a presidential election on 31 May 1998 the DP candidate and mayor of Quito, Jamil Mahuad Witt, emerged as the strongest contender. At the second round of voting on 12 July, between Mahuad and his closest rival, Alvaro Noboa Pontón of the PRE, Mahuad narrowly defeated Noboa. Noboa rejected the result, making allegations of widespread voting irregularities, none of which was upheld by the Supreme Electoral Tribunal or the international observers present in the country. Mahuad was sworn in on 10 August and appointed a Cabinet consisting predominantly of independent members. The new President's stated objectives focused on economic recovery following a decrease in world petroleum prices and the infrastructural and sociological damage caused by El Niño (a periodic warming of the tropical Pacific Ocean). In addition, Mahuad proposed a number of social programmes (involving the creation of new jobs and the construction of low-cost homes).

A programme of severe adjustment measures, which included huge rises in the cost of domestic gas and electricity, as well as substantial increases in public transport fares and fuel prices, was introduced in September 1998, prompting the Frente Unitario de Trabajadores (FUT) and CONAIE to organize a general strike in the following month. Subsequent rioting and violent confrontation between demonstrators and security personnel resulted in the deaths of four people. In February 1999 disagreement over economic policy led to the resignation of the Minister of Finance, and severe disruption arising from extensive fuel shortages prompted the resignation of the Minister of Energy and Mines. In the same month the leader of the left-wing Movimiento Popular Democrático, Jaime Hurtado González, was assassinated in Quito. The killing was linked to a right-wing Colombian paramilitary group.

In March 1999 a substantial decrease in the value of the sucre led President Mahuad to declare a week-long bank holiday in an attempt to prevent the withdrawal of deposits and reduce the pressure on the currency. A few days later a 60-day state of emergency was declared by the Government in response to a two-day strike, organized by leaders of the main trade unions and Indian groups. In addition, the Government announced an economic retrenchment programme in an attempt to restore investor confidence and prevent economic collapse. Measures included an increase in fuel prices of up to 160%, a number of tax rises, the partial 'freezing' of bank accounts, and the planned privatization of certain state-owned companies. These prompted a further series of protests and the resignation of the majority of the board of the central bank. The main opposition party, the PSC, similarly refused to endorse the austerity programme, thus compelling the President to compromise with the proposal of less severe economic measures, which were narrowly approved by the Congreso, after which time Mahuad lifted the state of emergency. However, a further rise in prices and the collapse of a major bank (the Banco del Progreso) later in March led to renewed protests.

In April 1999 the Government announced an emergency plan entitled 'Ecuador 2000', which aimed to revive the economy and included a number of requisite measures to gain the support of the IMF. It incorporated numerous social and public works development schemes, tax reforms and moves towards less centralized government. The plan was approved by the IMF, which, it was hoped, would provide an estimated US $400m. in initial financing. However, in July taxi drivers and public transport workers took nation-wide industrial action in protest at increases in fuel prices and at the 'Ecuador 2000' plan. In response, the Government imposed a further state of emergency and called in the military. The state of emergency was lifted in mid-July, after President Mahuad agreed to 'freeze' fuel prices and allow co-operatives and transport companies access to 'frozen' bank deposits. In the following month the Government announced its inability to honour repayments on its foreign debt (which was equivalent to some 90% of gross domestic product). The default led to a restructuring agreement with the IMF at the end of September.

In early January 2000, in an attempt to curb increasing unrest, amid indications that the economic crisis was deteriorating, President Mahuad imposed a state of emergency. However, on 21 January he was forced to flee from the presidential palace following large-scale protests in Quito by thousands of mainly Indian demonstrators, who were supported by sections of the armed forces, over the President's perceived mismanagement of the economic crisis (especially his controversial decision to replace the sucre with the US dollar). A three-man council was established to oversee the country. However, Gen. Carlos Mendoza, the Chief of Staff of the Armed Forces, disbanded the council within 24 hours of its creation, and announced the appointment of former Vice-President Gustavo Noboa Bejerano as President. This move followed talks with US officials, who had warned that foreign aid to Ecuador would be curtailed if power was not restored to the elected Government. The coup was condemned by governments around the world and by international organizations. Noboa, whose appointment as Head of State was endorsed by a large majority in the Congreso Nacional, promised to restore economic stability to the country. However, Indian activists who had supported the short-lived three-member council continued to demonstrate against the assumption of the presidency by Noboa, whom they viewed as ideologically similar to Mahuad. Noboa appointed Pedro Pinto Rubianes as the new Vice-President and formed a new Cabinet, comprising members of the DP, the PSC and the PRE, in February.

In February 2000 four members of the armed forces, who allegedly participated in the events leading up to Mahuad's removal from office, were apprehended on charges of insurrection. It was later announced that as many as 113 army officers were to be charged in connection with the previous month's events. In May the entire military high command was replaced, even though later that month the Congreso approved an amnesty for military officers and civilians arrested in connection with the coup.

Congressional approval for a controversial economic reform programme, which included the adoption of the US dollar as the official currency, as well as fiscal adjustments and an acceleration in the privatization process, was secured in February 2000. CONAIE organized a series of demonstrations in protest at the dollarization policy and to demand a referendum on the dissolution of the Congreso Nacional and the Supreme Court. Palliative measures introduced by the Government, including an increase in the minimum wage, were rejected by trade unions and indigenous organizations. Nevertheless, the process of dollarization formally began in March and in September the US dollar officially became Ecuador's sole currency. The announcement by the Government in May of an IMF-approved economic adjustment package, which included a sharp increase in the price of fuel, provoked further antagonism between the Government and trade unions and indigenous organizations. However, in September CONAIE entered into renewed negotiations with the Government after its calls for mass demonstrations in the previous month had met with only moderate support.

Both the DP and the PSC performed well in municipal and provincial elections held throughout the country in May 2000, suggesting significant popular acceptance of the structural reforms. In August the Government offered to resign in support of the President after the governing coalition lost its majority in the Congreso (divisions within the DP had resulted in several of its members aligning themselves with the centre-left opposition). The coalition's lack of a parliamentary majority endangered the proposed reform (also known as Trole 11) of the labour and petroleum sectors, as well as the privatization process. In late August President Noboa resorted to presidential decree to pass the proposed Trole 11 legislation, prompting CONAIE and trade unions immediately to launch an appeal to the Constitutional Tribunal on the legality of such a move. In January 2001 the Constitutional Tribunal upheld almost one-third of the objections against Trole 11, and, most notably, declared unconstitutional the clause concerning the proposed privatization of state-owned companies.

Popular resentment against the Government erupted in January 2001 after significant increases in fuel prices and transport costs were implemented. Thousands of Indian protesters occupied Quito and roadblocks were erected across the Andean highlands and the Amazon lowlands. In February the Government imposed a national state of emergency, which was lifted only after the Government acceded to the demands for a reduction in fuel prices in return for an end to the protests, which were marred by violence.

In February 2002 indigenous and civic groups in the northeast of the country occupied petroleum refineries, halted construction of a new oil pipeline and blocked major roads, prompting President Noboa to declare a state of emergency in the provinces of Sucumbíos and Orellana. In April, as a concession to the protesters, the Government pledged to direct funds to local infrastructure development.

Presidential and legislative elections were held on 20 October 2002. In the congressional ballot, the PSC won 24 of the 100 contested seats, followed by the ID (15 seats), the PRE (14) and the right-wing Partido Renovador Institucional de Acción Nacional (PRIAN, 10 seats). The presidential election, held concurrently, was notable for a low rate of voter participation (63%) and for the electorate's rejection of candidates presented by traditional parties. None of the 11 candidates obtained sufficient votes to secure the presidency, and a second round of voting was held on 24 November, between Lucio Gutiérrez Borbua (a former colonel who had been imprisoned for participating in the coup against President Mahuad in 2000) and Alvaro Noboa Pontón (a banana magnate and founder of the PRIAN). Gutiérrez, who campaigned on a populist, anti-corruption platform, and whose own party (the Partido Sociedad Patriótica 21 de Enero) was supported by the MNPP, secured the presidency, winning 59% of the votes in the second round of the election, compared with Noboa's 41%.

As President-elect, Gutiérrez made clear his intention to honour Ecuador's debt obligations and continue negotiations with the IMF. Upon taking office in January 2003, he immediately decreed a series of measures including a freeze on public-sector wages, a 35% increase in domestic petroleum prices and a 10% rise in electricity tariffs. In early February, following the IMF's approval of Ecuador's draft budget, the Government announced a new US $500m. package of multilateral loans.

The new lending was conditional upon the implementation of a series of fiscal and administrative reforms, and the allocation of a higher proportion of oil revenues towards the country's estimated $17,000m. foreign debt. In late February, however, the opposition-controlled Congreso vetoed a tax reform law and reallocated intended debt repayments to health and education, in defiance of the President. Nevertheless, in March the IMF approved a $205m. stand-by loan, which was followed by further lending from multilateral creditors.

During 2003 the new Government found it increasingly difficult to gain approval for any of its proposed reforms in the opposition-dominated legislature. Proposed legislation to improve supervision of the financial sector was rejected in May. In the same month teachers began a strike to demand that the Government pay outstanding backdated salaries. The industrial action ended in June after the Government agreed to pay increases in the sector. As a result of the legislative impasse, the governing coalition looked increasingly fragile throughout the year. In June the President of CONAIE, Leonidas Iza, threatened to suspend its alliance with the Gutiérrez administration if the latter did not abandon its plans to increase fuel prices. Workers at PETROECUADOR withdrew their labour in June in protest at the proposed partial privatization of the company. The strike ended after the Government abandoned the production-sharing proposals and pledged to discuss future reform of the sector with trade unions. During July several smaller parties withdrew from the governing coalition, including the left-wing Movimiento Popular Democrático and the Ecuarunari. Then, in early August, MNPP deputies walked out of a legislative vote on social security reform, which prompted President Gutiérrez to effect a cabinet reshuffle, in which all MNPP ministers were replaced. In September President Gutiérrez secured a legislative alliance with the PSC, which resulted in the approval of far-reaching reforms to labour practices within the civil service.

Meanwhile, trade unions and indigenous groups continued to protest at the Government's decision to reduce fuel subsidies, and in November 2003 teaching unions declared an indefinite strike in objection to the level of funding in the sector. On 27 November indigenous groups organized a demonstration in the capital in protest at President Gutiérrez's alleged failure to fulfil electoral pledges of social welfare reform. In the same month the Minister of Tourism, Nelson Herrera, resigned following accusations that he had used a private aeroplane belonging to César Fernández Cevallos, a former governor of Manabí who had been arrested in October on drugs-trafficking charges. Furthermore, the Congreso ordered an investigation into reports that Fernández Cevallos had contributed financially to the electoral campaign of President Gutiérrez. Gutiérrez's attempts to re-establish support for his Government suffered a reversal in early 2004 following a series of cabinet resignations, including those of the agriculture, energy, housing and environment ministers.

On 1 February 2004 an assassination attempt on the CONAIE leader Iza ended the uneasy truce between the Government and indigenous organizations and reignited calls for President Gutiérrez's resignation. However, in mid-February negotiations began between CONAIE and government representatives. In May the Confederación de las Nacionalidades Indígenas de la Amazonia Ecuatoriana (CONFENIAE—The Confederation of Amazonian Indigenous Peoples) withdrew its support for the Gutiérrez administration in favour of the opposition policies of CONAIE, accusing the Government of failing to fulfil its commitments.

Throughout 2004 the Gutiérrez Government was implicated in several corruption scandals. In March the former governor of the province of Manabí, who had been arrested on drugs-trafficking charges in October 2003, confirmed that he had contributed to the President's election campaign. Then, in May, the Minister of Social Welfare, Patricio Acosta, was forced to resign after being implicated in a corruption investigation in the USA. In the same month several oil companies accused the President of involvement in the bribing of officials at a PETROECUADOR subsidiary. Then, on 1 June, the Minister of the Economy and Finance, Mauricio Pozo, resigned as congressional investigation began into his alleged use of social security funds to alleviate the budget deficit.

Dissatisfaction with the administration of President Gutiérrez was evident in the results of local elections in October 2004, when the ruling PSP secured only two of 22 provincial mayoralties. Furthermore, in early November opposition parties, led by the PSC, began congressional proceedings to impeach the President on charges of misuse of public funds during the recent election campaign. However, support for the motion failed after the Government succeeded in assembling a so-called 'new majority' in the Congreso (a pro-Government bloc comprising the PSP, the PRE, the PRIAN, the Movimiento Popular Democrático, the Concentración de Fuerzas Populares, the Partido Socialista–Frente Amplio and independents).

In early December 2004 the Congreso voted to replace 27 of the 31 members of the Supreme Court, in which, President Gutiérrez alleged, the PSC exerted undue influence. Most of the new judges were allied with, or were sympathetic to, the pro-Government parties. The replacement of the Supreme Court judges was condemned by opposition groups, business leaders and foreign governments as unconstitutional. The dismissed judges subsequently established a 'Supreme Court-in-exile' in protest. In late January 2005 President Gutiérrez sought congressional approval for a proposed referendum on the composition of the Supreme Court, the Electoral Court and the Constitutional Court. Gutiérrez's proposal prompted the resignation, in late February, of the Minister of the Interior, Jaime Damerval, who instead favoured the establishment of an electoral council to designate replacements to the Supreme Court. He was replaced by Javier Ledesma. Opposition groups speculated that the purge of the Supreme Court was a preliminary step towards allowing former President Bucaram to end his exile in Panama without facing charges for misuse of public funds. Indeed, in early April Bucaram returned to Ecuador after the new President of the Supreme Court, Guillermo Castro, a staunch ally of Bucaram and a co-founder of the PRE, annulled his 1998 conviction. Castro claimed that Bucaram had been denied due process during his trial. Proceedings were also suspended against former President Noboa and former Vice-President Dahik on the same grounds.

In mid-February 2005 opposition parties organized a march in Quito in protest at the Government's increasingly authoritarian measures. It was estimated that as many as 150,000 people attended the demonstration. Well-supported opposition demonstrations in Quito and elsewhere were held throughout March and April. In response to the increasingly vociferous public protests, on 15 April Gutiérrez announced the dissolution of the Supreme Court. None the less, on 19 April some 30,000 demonstrators surrounded the presidential palace to demand the President's resignation. On the following day the Congreso voted almost unanimously to dismiss Gutiérrez from office for 'abandonment of his post' (Gutiérrez fled to Brazil, where he claimed asylum). Alfredo Palacio Gonzales, hitherto Vice-President, was subsequently appointed head of state, pending a new presidential election.

From 25 April 2005 the new President began to make appointments to a new Cabinet composed largely of independent technocrats, which included, notably, Rafael Correa Delgado as Minister of Economy and Finance. Palacio announced his intention to honour Ecuador's international obligations, although he appealed for greater debt forgiveness from international creditors in order to increase social spending and restore stability to the country. In late April the Congreso voted to dismiss the judges sitting on the Constitutional and Electoral Courts. Following protracted and often heated debate, both in the Congreso and wider society, over the method of selection, in late November new judges were eventually appointed to the Supreme Court by an ostensibly independent selection panel.

During its first 10 months in office, Palacio's Government was extremely unstable, with 34 ministerial changes. Most notably, in September 2005 Mauricio Gándara resigned as Minister of Government and Police following criticism of his response to the occupation, begun the previous month, of petroleum production facilities in the provinces of Sucumbíos and Orellana. Protesters, demanding greater state control over the oil industry and more equitable distribution of its revenues, effectively suspended Ecuador's crude-petroleum exports, leading to a state of emergency being declared in the two provinces and the deployment of troops to quell disorder. The occupations ceased at the end of August after Palacio pledged to revise contracts with foreign energy companies in order to increase the state's share of revenue (from about 20% to 50%) and to allocate more petroleum revenue to social services in the two provinces. Gándara's replacement, Oswaldo Molestina, lasted little more than a month in the post, resigning in mid-October following a disagreement with the President over the draft of a proposed referendum (see below).

Furthermore, in August 2005 Rafael Correa Delgado resigned as Minister of Economy and Finance after disagreeing with the President over plans to borrow US $300m. from Venezuela. On leaving the Cabinet, Correa declared himself unable to implement fully his policies of reallocating petroleum revenues to social projects and of reasserting state control over the petroleum industry. Correa's replacement, Magdalena Borreiro, was largely responsible for Ecuador's successful issue of debt as bonds in December (see Economic Affairs). In spite of this, at the end of that month she was dismissed from office and was, in early January 2006, replaced by Diego Borja.

The Palacio Government's attempts to obtain congressional approval for a proposed referendum on the establishment of a constituent assembly met with increasing opposition in the latter half of 2005. The Congreso had consistently rejected government plans to create a constituent assembly—which would have had powers to dismiss the President, to dissolve the legislature and Supreme Court and to amend the Constitution—in favour of a constitutional assembly, with more limited powers to make constitutional changes. The Supreme Court also unanimously rejected the proposal. A further congressional vote on the matter was held in December, but that too was defeated. On the same day Palacio issued a decree to the Supreme Court to organize the referendum, prompting the Congreso to threaten his impeachment. Facing defeat, a week later the entire Cabinet offered to resign, although most ministers retained their posts. A further vote, on an amended version of the reforms, was defeated by the Congreso in January 2006.

Former President Gutiérrez returned from exile in mid-October 2005. He was immediately arrested on charges of sedition and imprisoned. From prison he declared his intention to stand as the PSP's candidate in the presidential election that was scheduled to be held in October 2006. In March Gutiérrez was freed after the Supreme Court dismissed the charges against him. However, in May an electoral court removed his political rights for two years signifying an end to his attempts to contest the forthcoming presidential election.

Further unrest affected the petroleum sector in 2006. In early March employees at refineries in Napo, Orellana and Sucumbíos began a 48-hour strike over non-payment of their salaries. Their employers, contracting companies hired by PETROECUADOR, claimed, in turn, that they were owed some US $51m. by PETROECUADOR. The striking workers, who also reiterated their demands for greater state control of the industry, occupied oil production facilities, prompting the Government to declare a state of emergency. In the middle of the month CONAIE organized a widely supported nation-wide protest in solidarity with the oil-workers and also to demand a referendum on government plans to negotiate a free trade agreement with the USA. The unrest prompted the resignation of the new Minister of Government and Police, Alfredo Castillo Bujase, who declared himself to be in sympathy with the protesters. Although a survey conducted at this time revealed that only 13% of Ecuadoreans supported the idea of the free trade agreement with the USA, at the end of the month the talks entered their final stage.

Negotiations on the free trade agreement with the USA were suspended in mid-May 2006 following the announcement by the Government that it had revoked the contract of Occidental Petroleum (OP, of the USA) and that it would confiscate its assets in Ecuador. The three oilfields operated by OP were subsequently to be controlled by PETROECUADOR. The Government's action was the result of an alleged breach of contract by OP when it sold a 40% stake in its concession to the Canadian company EnCana. OP announced its intention to seek US $1,000m. in damages by taking the matter to arbitration at the International Center for the Settlement of Investment Disputes in Washington, DC, USA. The foreign trade minister, Jorge Illingworth, resigned following the breakdown of negotiations with the USA; he was replaced, on an interim basis, by the chief negotiator in the free trade agreement talks, Manuel Chiriboga, who later also resigned over the affair. (Joaquín Zevallos subsequently assumed the foreign trade portfolio.) The USA's decision to withdraw from talks with Ecuador was criticized by the Secretary-General of the Organization of American States (OAS, see p. 360), José Miguel Insulza. In mid-June a further state of emergency was declared in order to help PETROECUADOR maintain normal levels of production at the oilfields previously controlled by OP.

On 6 July 2006 President Palacio requested that all cabinet members submit their resignations. Eleven of the 15 ministers were subsequently reappointed to their posts, including Minister of Labour and Employment Galo Chiriboga Zambrano, although Chiriboga was shortly afterwards appointed head of PETROECUADOR. Roberto Illingworth became foreign trade minister, but resigned after one week following pressure from a business lobby group. He was replaced by Tomás Peribonio. Diego Borja was replaced as Minister of Economy and Finance by Armando Rodas Espinel. In August the defence minister, Gen. (retd) Oswaldo Jarrin, resigned and Gen. (retd) Marcelo Delgado Alvea was appointed in his place.

Presidential and legislative elections were held on 15 October 2006. In the first round of the presidential ballot Alvaro Noboa Pontón of the PRIAN, whose electoral pledges included increasing foreign investment and employment, won the largest share of the votes of the 17 candidates, with 26.8%, while his closest rival, former finance minister Rafael Correa Delgado, won 22.8%. Correa, who during his campaign had pledged to dissolve the Congreso and to rewrite the Constitution, as well as to sever Ecuador's ties with the IMF and the World Bank and renegotiate its contracts with foreign oil companies, had been widely expected to win the first round of voting. Of the remaining candidates, Gilmar Gutiérrez of the PSP, brother of the former President, won 17.4%, while León Roldós Aguilera, a former Vice-President supported by the ID (which contested the election in alliance with the social-democratic Red Etica y Democrática—RED), won 14.8%. Noboa and Correa duly proceeded to a second round of voting. In the congressional ballot the PRIAN won the most seats, 27 out of 100, followed by the PSP with 21, the ID/RED with 13 and the PSC with 12. Correa's Alianza País, contesting the elections in alliance with the Partido Socialista—Frente Amplio coalition, failed to win any seats in the Congreso. In mid-October Espinel resigned as Minister of Economy and Finance, citing disagreements with President Palacio. He was replaced by José Jouvin, former Governor of the Central Bank. (Jouvin was dismissed by Palacio at the end of December, but it was agreed that a successor would not be appointed until after the inauguration of the new President.) In the second round of the presidential election, which took place on 26 November, Correa emerged victorious, with 56.7% of the votes, compared with Noboa's 43.3%. Participation in the second round of the ballot was 67.7%. The new President expressed his commitment to investing in Ecuador's social sector and to strengthening the country's ties with its neighbours, at the expense of its proposed free trade agreement with the USA. He declared that his first act after his inauguration would be to promulgate a referendum on the creation of a constituent assembly.

Tension between the newly elected Congreso and the President-elect was apparent in the first week of January 2007, when the new legislature held its first meeting away from the parliament building to avoid protests by Correa's supporters. In the week before his inauguration on 15 January, Correa warned the main parties in the Congreso to apply due process to the filling of key government posts; none the less, the PRIAN expressed its intent to nominate the attorney-general, while the PSP was expected to appoint the head of the national audit office. Later, however, the PRIAN and the PSC failed to agree on who was to fill the position of head of the election commission (Tribunal Supremo Electoral—TSE). On 8 January Ximena Bohórquez, estranged wife of former President Gutiérrez, and Irina Vargas, both of the PSP, were expelled from the Congreso for deviating from the party line by supporting Correa's campaign for a constituent assembly. The other three major opposition parties in the Congreso—the PRIAN, the PSC and the DP—UDC, who with the PSP controlled 62 of the 100 congressional seats—imposed similar discipline on their members. Several days later, however, former President Gutiérrez, the leader of the PSP, announced his party's support for a constituent assembly, for the first time creating a majority of supporters of the initiative within the Congreso.

Following his inauguration President Correa set out his plan for the constituent assembly, which was to be composed of 130 members. The decision on whether to hold a referendum on the new institution rested with the TSE, which comprised seven members from the main parties in the Congreso. However, following a series of protests by Government supporters, culminating in the storming of its offices by a group of demonstrators, the TSE handed responsibility for the decision over to the Congreso. At the end of January 2007 thousands of demonstrators surrounded the Congreso to demand that the deputies approve the referendum; some entered the building, forcing the deputies to evacuate. In mid-February, after a series of nation-wide pro-Government demonstrations, the Congreso finally approved Correa's proposal for a referendum. The plebiscite, which according to opinion polls was supported by around 70% of the electorate, was scheduled for 15 April. It was approved by the TSE at the beginning of March but without the amendment demanded by the Congreso. Four days later the Congreso filed a lawsuit against the referendum with the Constitutional Court, and subsequently voted to remove the President of the TSE, Jorge Acosta, from his post. The TSE immediately retaliated by suspending the rights of the 57 deputies who supported the lawsuit, all from the four opposition parties, for one year; as a result the Congreso, which was now inquorate, was forced to suspend its session. Correa called on his supporters to demonstrate once again in favour of the constituent assembly. In mid-March violent clashes occurred outside the parliament building between the barred deputies and their supporters and the police. On 20 March, however, as hundreds of government supporters gathered outside, 21 alternates of the suspended deputies attended the congressional session, thereby giving it a quorum and ending the two week long impasse. None the less, at the end of March the Congreso was again suspended after a provincial judge issued an injunction reinstating the suspended deputies; he, in turn, was dismissed by the TSE. According to preliminary results of the referendum of 15 April, an overwhelming majority of those voting, some 78.1%, were in favour of the constituent assembly. Voting for the composition of the new body took place on 30 September and resulted in a significant majority (some 70% of total votes and 80 seats) for Correa's Alianza País. The assembly was inaugurated on 29 November and the Congreso went into recess. Proposals produced by the assembly were expected to be presented to the electorate in a referendum in mid-2008 and, if approved, could lead to presidential and congressional elections in late 2008.

In early December 2006 residents of Junín, a remote village in north-western Ecuador, captured 57 employees (34 of whom were ex-military) of the Canadian mining company Ascendant Copper, which, they claimed, had failed to follow Ecuadorean law by consulting the local communities over its activities. The captors demanded that the Government intervene to resolve the dispute. Ascendant Copper's employees, who were subsequently released unharmed, had been armed with revolvers and tear gas and had been involved in clashes with members of the local, largely indigenous population. (Two earlier attempts by foreign companies to open a copper mine in the area had ended in failure, following protests by the region's anti-mining community.) Two weeks later the Government announced that Ascendant Copper had contravened Ecuadorean law and demanded that it cease its activities.

In January 2007 Guadalupe Larriva, Ecuador's first female and civilian defence minister (appointed in the previous month), was killed in a helicopter crash, together with her daughter and five military officers. She was replaced by Lorena Escudero, but persistent criticism and uncertainty surrounding the accident, coupled with controversy over plans to allow the armed forces to vote, led to Escudero's resignation in August. She was replaced by Wellington Sandoval.

Allegations of corruption against the finance minister, Ricardo Patiño, resulted in an investigation by the Attorney-General and the initiation of impeachment proceedings in May 2007. In July Congress approved a non-binding motion of censure against Patiño on the grounds of embezzlement, illicit association and revealing privileged financial information. Later that month he was transferred to the coastal affairs portfolio.

A series of demonstrations took place in early 2007 at oil installations in Ecuador's Oriente by community and indigenous groups demanding a greater share of the profits from foreign companies operating in the region. The protesters succeeded in disrupting production at the facilities and consequently in April Correa granted increased powers to the security forces to suppress further demonstrations around the country's oil installations. The protests continued, however, and in November the interior minister, Gustavo Larrea, and President of PETROECUADOR, Carlos Pareja, were dismissed for failing to prevent further demonstrations, which had resulted in a 20% decrease in the daily output of oil. A state of emergency was subsequently introduced in the province of Orellana in order to safeguard oil production, which was responsible for generating some 35% of government revenue.

Ecuador's oil industry attracted international attention in mid-2007 when the Government announced its intention to seek compensation for leaving its oil reserves in the country's Amazonian region untouched. Several concerns, including the state oil companies of Venezuela, Brazil, Chile and China, had been hoping to secure operating contracts in the area, which includes the Yasuní national park. Correa expressed the view that, in the interests of the environment and the indigenous communities inhabiting the area, his Government would prefer to leave the reserves unexploited. He requested a total of US $350m. per year from the international community as compensation for leaving the oil, which was estimated to increase Ecuador's total oil production by 8%, in the ground.

In early 2007 UNESCO added the Galápagos Islands to its 'in danger' list, stating that the World Heritage Site was seriously threatened by invasive species, growing tourism and associated immigration. Correa signed an emergency decree aimed at tackling the crisis, which included the expulsion of illegal workers from the islands. By June, however, Correa admitted that Ecuador had failed to protect the Galápagos; his statement followed the discovery of the shells of eight endangered Galápagos giant tortoises, killed by poachers. Fears for the fauna of the archipelago were heightened when the bodies of 53 Galápagos sea lions were found beaten to death on Pinta Island in January 2008. These events, together with other similar incidents, led many environmental experts and other observers to question the Government's ability to protect the islands adequately.

In a further development described as environmentally disastrous, Correa legalized the sale of shark fins from sharks caught accidentally by Ecuadorean fishermen. Although fishing for sharks remained illegal, the removal of the ban on selling their fins resulted in a dramatic increase (of more than 1,000 per day, according to some reports) in the number of sharks landed, including many species threatened with extinction. The policy had been intended as a means of alleviating the poverty of many of Ecuador's fishermen, given that shark fins were known to sell for some US $100 each, but was denounced by environmentalists as ecologically damaging with serious negative implications for the entire food chain.

In April 1999 the World Trade Organization (WTO) upheld the complaint, put forward by the USA, Ecuador and four other Latin American countries, that the European Union (EU) unfairly favoured Caribbean banana producers. A two-tier tariff rate quota arrangement was agreed between Ecuadorean government officials and leaders of Caribbean banana-producing countries in November, easing restrictions on Latin American banana exporters and consequently assisting Ecuadorean producers. Furthermore, EU quotas for Latin American producers were to be phased out by 2006 and replaced by a uniform tariff system. However, in January 2005 the Government expressed its strong opposition to the EU's proposed tariff of €230 per metric ton on Latin American banana imports, due to come into effect in January 2006. The WTO ruled against this tariff in August 2005 and in October it further ruled against a revised EU tariff of €187 per ton.

The long-standing border dispute with Peru over the Cordillera del Cóndor erupted into war in January 1981. A cease-fire was declared a few days later under the auspices of the guarantors of the Rio Protocol of 1942 (Argentina, Brazil, Chile and the USA). The Protocol was not recognized by Ecuador, as it awarded the area, which affords access to the Amazon river system, to Peru. In January 1992 discussions on the border dispute were resumed. However, in January 1995 serious fighting broke out between the two sides. Following offers from the OAS and the four guarantor nations of the Rio Protocol, representatives of the two Governments met for negotiations in Rio de Janeiro, Brazil, and a cease-fire agreement was concluded in February. An observer mission, representing the four guarantor nations, was dispatched to the border, to oversee the separation of forces and demilitarization of the border area. Following intensive negotiations, agreement on the delimitation of the demilitarized zone in the disputed area was reached in July, and in October Ecuador finally repealed the state of emergency. A resumption of negotiations in September 1996 resulted in the signing of the Santiago Agreement by both sides in the following month, which was to provide a framework for a definitive solution to the issue. Following further negotiations in early 1998 a number of commissions were established to examine specific aspects of a potential agreement between Ecuador and Peru. On 26 October talks culminated in Brasília in the signing of an accord confirming Peru's claim regarding the delineation of the border, but granting Ecuador navigation and trading rights on the Amazon and its tributaries and the opportunity to establish two trading centres in Peru (although this was not to constitute sovereign access). Both countries confirmed that two ecological parks were to be created along the common border, where military personnel would not be allowed access.

Following the suspected involvement of Colombian paramilitaries in the murder of an Ecuadorean politician in Quito in February 1999 (see above) and reports of the presence of these troops in the country, Ecuador's military presence was strengthened at its border with Colombia. Nevertheless, criminal and military activities attributed to Colombian combatants continued on Ecuadorean territory and the number of Colombian refugees in Ecuador increased steadily. In March 2003 bilateral relations suffered after the new Government of Lucio Gutiérrez ruled out the possibility of formally classifying the Fuerzas Armadas Revolucionarias de Colombia—Ejército del Pueblo (FARC—EP, commonly known as the FARC) as a terrorist organization. In October, however, allegations emerged that members of the Ecuadorean army had supplied a rocket used by the FARC in an attack in the Colombian capital, Bogotá. The Ecuadorean military protested the allegations and deployed some 7,000 troops to patrol the joint border. In November the Ecuadorean Government cancelled plans to allow the USA to construct three logistical centres in the country's northern provinces.

Following the initiation in April 2004 of the so-called 'Plan Patriota' offensive by the Colombian military against the FARC, the Ecuadorean Government again expressed concern at an increase in illegal incursions into its territory by Colombian combatants. In response, Ecuador increased its troop numbers on its border with Colombia. Relations improved in November after the Colombian Government, following protests from Ecuador, agreed temporarily to halt aerial fumigation of coca crops in border areas from January 2006. In that month, at a meeting between the two countries' defence ministers in the Colombian capital, the Ecuadorean Minister of National Defence, Gen. (retd) Oswaldo Jarrín, agreed to strengthen policing of the common border. However, later that month the Government made protests to the Colombian authorities after three helicopters and two aeroplanes of the Colombian armed forces allegedly attacked an Ecuadorean village. In the following month President-elect Correa cancelled a trip to Colombia. Although no official reason was given, it was thought that a contributory factor to tension between the two countries may have been Correa's refusal during his electoral campaign to refer to FARC as a 'terrorist' group; the organization subsequently sent Correa a congratulatory message on his election. A further trip to Bogotá by Correa was cancelled later in the month in protest at the resumption by Colombia of aerial fumigation of coca crops near the Ecuadorean border, which the Government described as a 'hostile act'. Following intervention by the OAS, an agreement was reached whereby Colombia was to notify Ecuador in advance of any plans to spray the border area and the OAS was to conduct a full investigation into the effects of the herbicide glyphosate on the local population. Outgoing Minister of Foreign Affairs Francisco Carrión opposed the deal, expressing his concern that there was no text of the agreement and that it had not been brokered by the UN. In early February 2007 the dispute continued when the new Ecuadorean foreign minister, María Fernanda Espinosa, accused Colombia of having resumed spraying without notification; Colombia claimed, however, that it had never officially suspended the programme, but had rather temporarily ceased activity owing to adverse weather conditions. Later that month President Correa announced the implementation of 'Plan Ecuador', which was intended to counteract the effects of 'Plan Colombia', a US-backed operation by that country to eliminate FARC and their source of funding, the coca crops. As part of 'Plan Ecuador', Correa declared that the 500,000 Colombian refugees residing in Ecuador would be granted formal asylum status. Relations between the two countries deteriorated significantly following a military incursion by Colombian forces into Ecuadorean territory in March 2008, during which a FARC leader, Raúl Reyes, was killed along with 16 other rebels. The Colombian Government claimed that documents seized during the raid proved that Correa was interested in establishing official relations with FARC and that a member of his Government had met Reyes for discussions. (Correa dismissed the claims, countering that his Government's involvement had been solely on humanitarian grounds as part of efforts to secure the release of hostages; his claim was supported by the French ambassador in Quito.) The Ecuadorean Government responded to the incident by expelling Colombia's ambassador in Quito, withdrawing its

ECUADOR

own ambassador from Bogotá and by sending troops to the border.

On 29 June 2006 the heads of PETROECUADOR and PDVSA, the Venezuelan state oil company, and President Palacio signed an agreement under which 65,000 barrels per day of Ecuadorean oil would be refined in Venezuela in return for refined products of an equivalent value. The deal was to last for five years. Following his inauguration President Correa also stressed his commitment to strengthening Ecuador's relations with Venezuela and to regional integration.

In late 2007 President Correa made an official state visit to China to sign an agreement aimed at enhancing bilateral relations, particularly with regard to energy, agriculture, technology and infrastructure.

Government

Executive power is vested in the President, who is directly elected by universal adult suffrage for a four-year term (starting from 15 January of the year following his election). The President is not eligible for re-election. Legislative power is held by the 100-member unicameral Cámara Nacional de Representantes (National Chamber of Representatives), which is also directly elected for a four-year term. Ecuador comprises 21 provinces, composed of 193 cantons, 322 urban parishes and 757 rural parishes. Each province has a Governor, who is appointed by the President.

Defence

Military service, which lasts one year, is selective for men at the age of 20. As assessed in November 2007, Ecuador's armed forces numbered 57,100: army 47,000, navy 6,100 (including 1,500 marines) and air force 4,000. The defence budget in 2007 was estimated to be US $918m.

Economic Affairs

In 2006, according to estimates by the World Bank, Ecuador's gross national income (GNI), measured at average 2004–06 prices, was US $38,113.7m., equivalent to $2,840 per head (or $4,400 per head on an international purchasing-power parity basis). During 1996–2006, it was estimated, the population increased at an average annual rate of 1.5%, while gross domestic product (GDP) per head increased, in real terms, at an average annual rate of 1.7%. Overall GDP increased, in real terms, at an average annual rate of 3.2% in 1996–2006; GDP increased by 4.5% in 2006.

Agriculture (including hunting, forestry and fishing) contributed an estimated 7.0% of GDP in 2006. According to the International Labour Organization, in 2006 some 8.3% of the active labour force were employed in the agricultural sector. Ecuador is the world's leading exporter of bananas, and coffee and cocoa are also important cash crops. The seafood sector, particularly the shrimp industry, was also a significant contributor to the economy. Ecuador's extensive forests yield valuable hardwoods, and the country is a leading producer of balsawood. Exports of cut flowers increased in importance from the mid-1980s, and generated a provisional US $346m. in earnings in 2004 (equivalent to 4.5% of the total value of exports). According to the World Bank, during 1996–2006 agricultural GDP increased at an average annual rate of 4.0%. Sectoral GDP grew by 2.5% in 2006.

Industry (including mining, manufacturing, construction and power) employed 21.8% of the active urban labour force in 2006, and provided an estimated 36.2% of GDP in 2006. According to the World Bank, during 1996–2006 industrial GDP increased at an average annual rate of 2.6%. The sector grew by 2.1% in 2005 and by a further 4.0% in 2006.

Mining contributed an estimated 23.8% of GDP in 2006, although the mining sector employed only 0.4% of the urban labour force in the same year. Petroleum and its derivatives remained the major exports in the early 21st century. According to the US Energy Information Administration (EIA), production averaged 388,000 barrels per day (b/d) in 2006. In January 2007 proven petroleum reserves were estimated at 4,500m. barrels. Earnings from petroleum exports amounted to US $7,544.3m. in 2006, equivalent to 60% of the total value of exports. Natural gas is extracted, but only a small proportion is retained. In January 2006 proven reserves of natural gas were 345,000m. cu ft, according to the EIA. Gold, silver, copper, antimony and zinc are also mined. In real terms, the GDP of the mining sector increased at an average rate of 4.1% per year during 1997–2006. According to provisional figures by the Central Bank, mining GDP increased by 1.1% in 2005, and by 1.0% in 2006.

Introductory Survey

Manufacturing contributed an estimated 9.4% of GDP in 2006 and employed 13.8% of the active labour force in urban areas in the same year. The most important branches of manufacturing were food, beverages and tobacco, textiles, clothing and leather and mineral and basic metallic products. Petroleum refining was also important. During 1996–2006 manufacturing GDP increased at an average annual rate of 2.5%, according to the World Bank. Sectoral GDP increased by 2.5% in 2006.

Energy is derived principally from hydroelectric plants, responsible for 58.9% of total production in 2004, with petroleum accounting for most of the remainder. The country had an estimated installed capacity of 3.3m. MW in 2002, of which about one-half was produced domestically. Most domestic output comes from the Paute hydroelectricity plant. It was hoped that hydroelectricity stations at Mazar, south of Paute, and San Francisco, on the Pastaza river, would be completed by 2008 and 2010, respectively, in order to alleviate the effects of the frequent power shortages, especially in the dry season. The new plant at Mazar was expected to produce a further 190 MW of electricity, while the station at San Francisco would provide a further 212 MW. Imports of mineral fuels and lubricants comprised 7.7% of the value of total imports in 2005.

The services sector contributed an estimated 56.7% of GDP in 2006. Some 69.9% of the active urban labour force were employed in services in the same year. The sector's GDP increased at an average annual rate of 3.5% during 1996–2006, according to World Bank figures. It increased by 5.2% in 2006.

In 2006 Ecuador recorded a visible trade surplus of US $1,729m., and a surplus of $1,503m. on the current account of the balance of payments. In 2006 the principal source of imports was the USA (accounting for 23.4% of the total); that country was also the principal market for exports (53.6%). Other major trading partners were the People's Republic of China, Colombia, Germany, Italy, Japan, the Republic of Korea, Panama and Peru. The principal exports in 2006 were petroleum and petroleum derivatives (59.6%), bananas and plantains (9.6%) and seafood products (10.1%). The principal imports in 2006 were mineral products (21.1%), machinery and apparatus (20.5%) and metal and basic manufactures of metal (9.1%).

In 2006 there was a projected budgetary deficit of about US $28.3m. In that year some 35.3% of government expenditure was financed by revenue from petroleum. Ecuador's total external debt was US $17,129m. at the end of 2005, of which $10,662m. was long-term public debt. In that year the cost of debt-servicing was equivalent to 30.6% of the total value of exports of goods and services. The average annual rate of inflation in 1996–2006 was 25.4%; the rate averaged 3.2% in 2006. The average rate of unemployment in urban areas stood at 7.8% in late 2006.

Ecuador is a member of the Andean Community (see p. 170), the Organization of American States (OAS, see p. 360) and of the Asociación Latinoamericana de Integración (ALADI, see p. 331). In 2007 Ecuador rejoined the Organization of the Petroleum Exporting Countries (OPEC, see p. 373), having previously given up membership in 1992. In 1995 Ecuador joined the World Trade Organization (WTO, see p. 396). In December 2004 Ecuador was one of 12 countries that were signatories to the agreement, signed in Cusco, Peru, creating the South American Community of Nations (Comunidad Sudamericana de Naciones, which was renamed the Union of South American Nations—Unión de Naciones Suramericanas, UNASUR, or, in Portuguese, União das Nações Sul-Americanas—UNASUL, in April 2007), intended to promote greater regional economic integration.

In the mid-1990s Ecuador's proven petroleum reserves almost tripled following discoveries in the Amazon region, and the Government signed contracts with numerous companies for further exploration and drilling. A new pipeline for heavy crudes became operative in September 2004, despite concerted protests from indigenous groups and environmental activists. The economy also benefited in the early 2000s from higher international oil prices. However, further expansion of the petroleum sector was impeded by political turmoil, trade union opposition and a lack of interested investors. Furthermore, Ecuador's limited refining capacity meant it relied on other countries to benefit from its reserves. In May 2006 the Government announced that Venezuela would help to finance construction of a new oil refinery in Ecuador. In the same month the Government seized oil fields from US company Occidental Petroleum; the state received an extra US $563.2m. in oil revenues in that year as a result, although it also led the USA to suspend negotiations towards a free trade agreement with Ecuador. Nevertheless, the new left wing President, Rafael Correa Delgado, who took office in January 2007, signalled that he did not intend to pursue a bilateral agreement with the USA, even after the expiry of the US Andean Trade Promotion and Drug Eradication Act (ATP-DEA). The new administration planned to finance an ambitious social development programme and increase capital expenditure by strengthening state intervention in the oil sector. This culminated in December 2007 when significant revisions were made to the contractual framework enshrined in the 2006 Hydrocarbons Law. Private oil firms operating in Ecuador were, henceforth, required to pay 99% of extraordinary profits, known as 'windfall' profits (defined as profits accrued as a direct result of rising oil prices) to the Government. The additional revenue was then directed into an Oil Stability Fund (Fondo de Estabilización Petrolera) and channelled into budgetary operations (particularly energy subsidies, which accounted for around 25% of revenues annually). The increasing presence of the state in the oil sector decreased the rate of investment in 2007; observers noted that oil production declined in firms subject to partial and full state ownership during 2006–07. The IMF estimated that Ecuador's real GDP increased by 2.7% in 2007, and forecast slower growth of 2.4% for 2008.

Education

Education is compulsory for 10 years, to be undertaken between five and 15 years of age, and all state schools are free. Private schools continue to play a vital role in the educational system. Primary education begins at six years of age and lasts for six years. Secondary education, in general and specialized technical or humanities schools, begins at the age of 12 and lasts for up to six years, comprising two equal cycles of three years each. In 2004 enrolment at primary schools included 97.7% of pupils in the relevant age-group, while the comparable ratio for secondary schools was 52.2%. University courses extend for up to six years, and include programmes for teacher training. Total expenditure on education by the central Government was estimated at 1,957,051m. sucres (equivalent to 3.5% of GNP) in 1996. In many rural areas Quechua and other indigenous Indian languages are used in education.

Public Holidays

2008: 1 January (New Year's Day), 6 January (Epiphany), 4–5 February (Carnival), 20 March (Holy Thursday), 21 March (Good Friday), 22 March (Easter Saturday), 1 May (Labour Day), 22 May (Corpus Christi), 24 May (Battle of Pichincha), 24 July (Birth of Simón Bolívar), 10 August (Independence of Quito), 9 October (Independence of Guayaquil), 12 October (Discovery of America), 2 November (All Souls' Day), 3 November (Independence of Cuenca), 6 December (Foundation of Quito), 25 December (Christmas Day), 31 December (New Year's Eve).

2009: 1 January (New Year's Day), 6 January (Epiphany), 23–24 February (Carnival), 9 April (Holy Thursday), 10 April (Good Friday), 11 April (Easter Saturday), 1 May (Labour Day), 24 May (Battle of Pichincha), 11 June (Corpus Christi), 24 July (Birth of Simón Bolívar), 10 August (Independence of Quito), 9 October (Independence of Guayaquil), 12 October (Discovery of America), 2 November (All Souls' Day), 3 November (Independence of Cuenca), 6 December (Foundation of Quito), 25 December (Christmas Day), 31 December (New Year's Eve).

Weights and Measures

The metric system is in force.

Statistical Survey

Sources (unless otherwise stated): Instituto Nacional de Estadística y Censos, Juan Larrea 534 y Riofrío, Quito; tel. (2) 529-858; e-mail inec1@ecnet.ec; internet www.inec.gov.ec; Banco Central del Ecuador, Avda Amazonas y Atahualpa, Casilla 339, Quito; tel. (2) 257-2522; fax (2) 295-5458; internet www.bce.fin.ec; Ministerio de Industrialización y Competitividad, Avda Eloy Alfaro y Amazonas, Quito; tel. (2) 254-6107; fax (2) 250-3818; e-mail info@micip.gov.ec; internet www.micip.gov.ec.

Area and Population

AREA, POPULATION AND DENSITY

Area (sq km)	272,045*
Population (census results)†	
25 November 1990	9,648,189
25 November 2001	
Males	6,018,353
Females	6,138,255
Total	12,156,608
Population (official projected estimates at mid-year)	
2005	13,215,089
2006	13,408,270
2007	13,605,485
Density (per sq km) at mid-2007	50.0

* 105,037 sq miles.
† Excluding nomadic tribes of indigenous Indians and any adjustment for underenumeration, estimated to have been 6.3% in 1990; the 1990 total was subsequently revised to 9,697,979.

REGIONS AND PROVINCES
(projected population estimates at mid-2007)

	Area (sq km)	Population	Density (per sq km)	Capital
Sierra	63,269	6,111,542	96.6	—
Azuay	8,125	678,746	83.5	Cuenca
Bolívar	3,940	180,293	45.8	Guaranda
Cañar	3,122	226,021	72.4	Azogues
Carchi	3,605	166,116	46.1	Tulcán
Chimborazo	6,072	443,522	73.0	Riobamba
Cotopaxi	6,569	400,411	61.0	Latacunga
Imbabura	4,559	397,704	87.2	Ibarra
Loja	11,027	434,020	39.4	Loja
Pichincha	12,915	2,683,272	207.8	Quito
—continued	Area (sq km)	Population	Density (per sq km)	Capital
Tungurahua	3,335	501,437	150.4	Ambato
Costa	67,646	6,720,798	99.4	—
El Oro	5,850	608,032	103.9	Machala
Esmeraldas	15,239	438,576	28.8	Esmeraldas
Guayas	20,503	3,617,504	176.4	Guayaquil
Los Ríos	7,175	742,241	103.4	Babahoyo
Manabí	18,879	1,314,445	69.6	Portoviejo
Amazónica	130,834	662,948	5.1	—
Morona Santiago	25,690	131,337	5.1	Macas
Napo	11,431	96,029	8.4	Tena
Orellana	22,500	110,782	4.9	Puerto Francisco de Orellana (Coca)
Pastaza	29,774	75,782	2.5	Puyo
Sucumbíos	18,328	163,447	8.9	Nueva Loja
Zamora Chinchipe	23,111	85,571	3.7	Zamora
Insular	8,010	22,678	2.8	—
Archipiélago de Colón (Galápagos)	8,010	22,678	2.8	Puerto Baquerizo (Isla San Cristóbal)
Uncharted areas	2,289	87,519	38.2	—
Total	272,045	13,605,485	50.0	

Note: Two new provinces, Santo Domingo de los Tsáchilas and Santa Elena, were created in late 2007.

Source: partly Stefan Helders, *World Gazetteer*.

ECUADOR

PRINCIPAL TOWNS
(2001 census)

Guayaquil	1,985,379	Ambato		154,095
Quito (capital)	1,399,378	Riobamba		124,807
Cuenca	277,374	Quevedo		120,379
Machala	204,578	Loja		118,532
Santo Domingo de los Colorados	199,827	Milagro		113,440
Manta	183,105	Ibarra		108,535
Portoviejo	171,847	Esmeraldas		95,124

Mid-2007 ('000, incl. suburbs, UN estimates): Guayaquil 2,514; Quito 1,701 (Source: UN, *World Urbanization Prospects: The 2007 Revision*).

BIRTHS, MARRIAGES AND DEATHS
(excluding nomadic Indian tribes)*

	Registered live births†		Registered marriages		Registered deaths	
	Number	Rate (per 1,000)	Number	Rate (per 1,000)	Number	Rate (per 1,000)
1999	305,284	25.2	77,593	n.a.	55,921	4.6
2000	296,149	24.1	74,875	n.a.	56,420	4.6
2001	278,170	22.3	67,741	n.a.	55,214	4.4
2002	275,300	21.7	66,208	n.a.	55,549	4.4
2003	262,004	20.4	65,393	5.1	53,521	4.2
2004	254,362	19.5	63,299	n.a.	54,729	4.2
2005	252,725	19.1	66,612	5.0	56,825	4.3
2006	n.a.	n.a.	74,036	5.5	57,940	4.3

* Registrations incomplete.

† Figures include registrations of large numbers of births occurring in previous years. The number of births registered in the year of occurrence was: 218,108 in 1999, 202,257 in 2000, 192,786 in 2001, 183,792 in 2002; 178,549 in 2003; 168,893 in 2004; 168,324 in 2005 and 185,056 in 2006.

Expectation of life (years at birth, WHO estimates): 72.6 (males 69.9; females 75.4) in 2005 (Source: WHO, *World Health Statistics*).

ECONOMICALLY ACTIVE POPULATION
(ISIC major divisions, urban areas only, '000 persons aged 10 years and over, at November of each year, unless otherwise indicated)

	2004	2005	2006
Agriculture, hunting and forestry	320.8	273.5	285.0
Fishing	37.5	51.1	48.9
Mining and quarrying	16.1	10.7	15.8
Manufacturing	539.0	537.2	555.5
Electricity, gas and water	22.9	18.8	19.4
Construction	248.7	258.7	290.1
Wholesale and retail trade; repair of motor vehicles, motorcycles and personal and household goods	1,096.2	1,099.0	1,151.8
Hotels and restaurants	171.1	190.8	225.4
Transport, storage and communications	264.7	280.1	292.3
Financial intermediation	49.1	51.9	47.9
Real estate, renting and business activities	189.8	199.7	200.7
Public administration and defence; compulsory social security	173.9	168.2	170.3
Education	263.0	258.9	281.0
Health and social work	137.8	132.0	116.0
Other community, social and personal service activities	176.1	158.7	162.9
Private households with employed persons	150.4	201.7	167.7
Extra-territorial organizations and bodies	1.4	0.7	0.9
Total employed	3,858.5	3,891.9	4,031.6
Unemployed	362.1	333.6	341.8
Total labour force	4,220.6	4,225.5	4,373.4
Males	2,449.2	2,471.1	2,559.9
Females	1,771.5	1,754.3	1,813.5

Source: ILO.

Health and Welfare

KEY INDICATORS

Total fertility rate (children per woman, 2005)	2.7
Under-5 mortality rate (per 1,000 live births, 2005)	25
HIV/AIDS (% of persons aged 15–49, 2005)	0.3
Physicians (per 1,000 head, 2000)	1.48
Hospital beds (per 1,000 head, 2003)	1.40
Health expenditure (2004): US $ per head (PPP)	261.4
Health expenditure (2004): % of GDP	5.5
Health expenditure (2004): public (% of total)	40.7
Access to water (% of persons, 2004)	94
Access to sanitation (% of persons, 2004)	89
Human Development Index (2005): ranking	89
Human Development Index (2005): value	0.772

For sources and definitions, see explanatory note on p. vi.

Agriculture

PRINCIPAL CROPS
('000 metric tons)

	2003	2004	2005
Rice (paddy)	1,385	1,778	1,471
Barley	23	22	23
Maize	684	882	895
Potatoes	382	413	339
Cassava (Manioc)	86	89	100
Sugar cane	5,835	6,119	6,834
Dry beans	16	18	23
Soybeans (Soya beans)	109	107	60
Coconuts	21	23	20
Oil palm fruit	1,522*	1,844	1,930
Tomatoes	45	85	72
Onions and shallots (green)	70	77	93
Carrots and turnips	23	28	27
Watermelons	29	30	32
Bananas	6,454	6,132	6,118
Plantains	788	735	708
Oranges	68	125	79
Tangerines, mandarins, clementines and satsumas	18	25	35
Mangoes	89	124	n.a.
Pineapples	67	75	66
Papayas	63	37	43
Coffee (green)	83	87	103
Cocoa beans	88	90	94
Abaca (Manila hemp)	28*	31	n.a.

* FAO estimate.

2006: Most production assumed to be unchanged from 2005 (FAO estimates), apart from: Rice (paddy) 1,365 (FAO estimate); Barley 26 (unofficial figure); Maize 820 (FAO estimate).

Aggregate production ('000 metric tons, may include official, semi-official or estimated data): Total cereals 2,704 in 2004, 2,410 in 2005, 2,233 in 2006; Total roots and tubers 511 in 2004, 453 in 2005, 452 in 2006; Total vegetables (incl. melons) 360 in 2004, 374 in 2005, 374 in 2006; Total fruits (excl. melons) 7,521 in 2004, 7,536 in 2005, 7,536 in 2006.

Source: FAO.

LIVESTOCK
('000 head, year ending September)

	2003	2004	2005
Cattle	4,985	5,083	4,971
Sheep	1,014	1,047	1,053
Pigs	1,410	1,282	1,281
Horses	400	411	411
Goats	141	135	144
Asses, mules or hinnies	306	298	295
Chickens	102,457	103,352	104,217

2006: Figures assumed to be unchanged from 2005 (FAO estimates).

Source: FAO.

ECUADOR

LIVESTOCK PRODUCTS
('000 metric tons)

	2003	2004	2005
Cattle meat	202.6	205.5	206.5
Sheep meat	10.5	10.6	11.4
Pig meat	147.9	157.1	164.6
Goat meat	1.1	1.2	1.2
Chicken meat	207.4	207.7	208.6
Cows' milk	2,386.2	2,456.5	2,537.0
Sheep's milk*	6.2	6.3	6.4
Goats' milk*	2.6	2.6	2.6
Hen eggs	74.0	74.1	75.0
Wool: greasy*	1.3	1.4	1.7

* FAO estimates.

2006: Figures assumed to be unchanged from 2005 (FAO estimates).

Source: FAO.

Forestry

ROUNDWOOD REMOVALS
('000 cubic metres, excluding bark)

	2004	2005*	2006*
Sawlogs, veneer logs and logs for sleepers	298	298	298
Pulpwood*	913	913	913
Fuel wood*	5,427	5,507	5,574
Total	6,638	6,718	6,785

* FAO estimates.

Source: FAO.

SAWNWOOD PRODUCTION
('000 cubic metres, including railway sleepers)

	2002	2003*	2004
Coniferous (softwood)	150	150	95
Broadleaved (hardwood)	600	600	660
Total	750	750	755

* FAO estimates.

2005–06: Figures assumed to be unchanged from 2004 (FAO estimates).

Source: FAO.

Fishing

('000 metric tons, live weight)

	2003	2004	2005
Capture*	397.9	336.8	407.7
Pacific thread herring	6.9	8.6	4.2
Anchoveta (Peruvian anchovy)	33.4	11.3	10.8
Pacific anchoveta	19.5	5.1	8.4
Frigate and bullet tunas	36.3	19.7	5.6
Skipjack tuna	133.1	87.8	143.0
Yellowfin tuna	40.8	44.1	43.6
Bigeye tuna	20.2	26.5	25.0
Chub mackerel	33.3	51.8	113.4
Aquaculture*	74.5	77.3	78.3
Whiteleg shrimp*	55.5	56.3	56.3
Nile tilapia*	19.0	21.0	22.0
Total catch*	472.4	414.1	486.0

* FAO estimates.

Source: FAO.

Mining

('000 barrels, unless otherwise indicated)

	2003	2004	2005*
Crude petroleum	153,539	192,517	194,169
Natural gas (gross, million cu m)	1,287	1,422	1,609
Gold (kilograms)†	4,819	5,158	5,416

* Preliminary.
† Metal content of ore only.

Source: US Geological Survey.

Industry

SELECTED PRODUCTS
('000 barrels, unless otherwise indicated)

	2003	2004	2005
Jet fuels	1,879	2,235	2,500*
Motor spirit (gasoline)	9,338	8,816	6,954*
Distillate fuel oils	11,752	13,397	13,064*
Residual fuel oils	23,622	22,851	21,255*
Liquefied petroleum gas	2,358	2,412	2,259*
Crude steel ('000 metric tons)	80	72	85*
Cement ('000 metric tons)	3,100	3,000	3,000*
Electric energy (million kWh)†	11,556	11,702	n.a.

* Preliminary estimate.
† Source: UN, *Industrial Commodity Statistics Yearbook*.

Source: mostly US Geological Survey.

Finance

CURRENCY AND EXCHANGE RATES

Monetary Units
  United States currency is used: 100 cents = 1 US dollar ($).

Sterling and Euro Equivalents (31 December 2007)
  £1 sterling = US $2.003;
  €1 = US $1.472;
  US $100 = £49.92 = €67.93.

Note: Ecuador's national currency was formerly the sucre. From 13 March 2000 the sucre was replaced by the US dollar, at an exchange rate of $1 = 25,000 sucres. Both currencies were officially in use for a transitional period of 180 days, but from 9 September sucres were withdrawn from circulation and the dollar became the sole legal tender.

BUDGET
(consolidated central government accounts, US $ million)

Revenue	2004	2005	2006*
Petroleum revenue	1,557.9	1,567.3	1,718.6
Non-petroleum revenue	3,620.7	4,484.3	5,176.3
Taxation	3,165.5	3,741.0	4,243.9
Taxes on goods and services	1,921.7	2,195.5	2,485.6
Value-added tax	1,719.6	1,974.9	2,228.2
Taxes on income	701.9	936.6	1,068.0
Import duties	453.7	546.5	618.2
Other non-petroleum revenue	445.3	356.4	452.6
Transfers	9.8	386.9	479.9
Total	5,178.6	6,051.6	6,895.0

* Provisional.

ECUADOR

Expenditure	2004	2005	2006*
Wages and salaries	2,048.8	2,299.0	2,581.4
Purchases of goods and services	363.4	355.2	458.5
Interest payments	813.5	855.2	941.8
Transfers	591.1	722.1	776.0
Other current expenditure	286.5	489.0	584.3
Capital expenditure	1,394.5	1,511.6	1,669.0
Total	5,497.8	6,232.1	7,011.0

* Provisional.

Note: Data exclude adjustment in treasury accounts for expenditure (US $ million): –28.3 in 2006.

INTERNATIONAL RESERVES
(US $ million at 31 December)

	2004	2005	2006
Gold (national valuation)	368.0	433.4	533.9
IMF special drawing rights	56.1	21.8	7.6
Reserve position in IMF	26.6	24.5	25.8
Foreign exchange	986.9	1,667.9	1,456.1
Total	1,437.6	2,147.6	2,023.4

Source: IMF, *International Financial Statistics*.

MONEY SUPPLY
(US $ million at 31 December)

	2004	2005	2006
Currency outside banks	58.1	62.8	66.0
Demand deposits at deposit money banks	2,315.0	2,726.6	3,268.0
Total money (incl. others)*	2,510.0	3,000.3	3,611.1

* Includes private-sector deposits at the Central Bank.
Source: IMF, *International Financial Statistics*.

COST OF LIVING
(Consumer Price Index; base: 2000 = 100)

	2002	2003	2004
Food (incl. alcoholic beverages)	141.7	145.8	146.9
Fuel (excl. light)	203.9	n.a.	n.a.
Clothing	132.5	124.6	115.9
Rent	198.1	n.a.	n.a.
All items (incl. others)	154.9	167.1	171.7

2005: All items (incl. others) 175.5.
2006: All items 181.2.
Source: ILO.

NATIONAL ACCOUNTS
(US $ million at current prices)

Expenditure on the Gross Domestic Product

	2004	2005	2006*
Government final consumption expenditure	3,716.3	4,133.6	4,536.2
Private final consumption expenditure	21,962.5	24,549.9	26,878.6
Changes in stocks	587.0	669.8	623.2
Gross fixed capital formation	7,045.4	8,175.2	8,932.5
Total domestic expenditure	33,311.2	37,528.5	40,970.5
Exports of goods and services	8,982.5	11,480.3	14,192.2
Less Imports of goods and services	9,651.4	11,821.9	13,760.9
GDP in market prices	32,642.2	37,186.9	41,401.8
GDP in constant 2000 prices	19,572.2	20,747.2	21,555.5

* Provisional.

Gross Domestic Product by Economic Activity

	2004	2005	2006*
Agriculture, hunting, forestry and fishing	2,218.6	2,462.8	2,777.5
Petroleum and other mining	5,338.4	7,475.1	9,411.5
Manufacturing (excl. petroleum refining)	2,881.2	3,296.0	3,725.3
Manufacture of petroleum derivatives	–1,357.3	–2,079.0	–2,854.5
Electricity, gas and water	578.5	541.1	554.3
Construction	2,680.1	3,099.7	3,481.6
Wholesale and retail trade	3,999.0	4,402.3	4,827.9
Hotels and restaurants	561.6	602.3	638.7
Transport, storage and communications	3,647.8	4,137.8	4,425.8
Financial intermediation	669.6	895.4	1,086.7
Real estate, renting and business activities	3,821.2	4,305.4	4,810.9
Public administration and defence	1,769.3	1,945.9	2,147.6
Education	2,294.8	2,660.1	3,024.3
Health and social welfare	870.6	986.3	1,081.1
Other community, social and personal service activities	278.6	288.0	294.2
Private households with employed persons	50.2	48.2	59.8
Sub-total	30,302.2	35,067.3	39,492.6
Less Financial intermediation services indirectly measured	–705.1	–783.6	–1,005.4
Gross value added in basic prices	29,597.1	34,283.7	38,487.2
Taxes, less subsidies, on products	3,045.2	2,903.2	2,914.7
GDP in market prices	32,642.2	37,186.9	41,401.8

* Provisional.

BALANCE OF PAYMENTS
(US $ million)

	2004	2005	2006
Exports of goods f.o.b.	7,968	10,427	13,125
Imports of goods f.o.b.	–7,684	–9,695	–11,396
Trade balance	284	732	1,729
Exports of services	1,014	1,012	1,016
Imports of services	–1,968	–2,142	–2,341
Balance on goods and services	–670	–398	404
Other income received	37	86	165
Other income paid	–1,940	–2,029	–2,115
Balance on goods, services and income	–2,572	–2,340	–1,546
Current transfers received	2,049	2,756	3,179
Current transfers paid	–18	–120	–130
Current balance	–542	295	1,503
Capital account (net)	8	13	14
Direct investment from abroad	837	493	271
Portfolio investment assets	–191	–228	–641
Portfolio investment liabilities	—	–2	–743
Other investment assets	–973	–845	–2,044
Other investment liabilities	571	67	1,142
Net errors and omissions	681	477	424
Overall balance	391	269	–74

Source: IMF, *International Financial Statistics*.

ECUADOR

External Trade

PRINCIPAL COMMODITIES
(distribution by SITC, US $ million)

Imports c.i.f.	2004	2005	2006
Manufactured foodstuffs	327.3	380.1	402.4
Mineral products	1,020.3	1,742.1	2,359.2
Chemicals and related products	1,032.0	1,156.5	1,322.2
Plastic, rubber and articles thereof	501.0	600.1	677.2
Wood pulp; cellulose fibres; paper and paperboard	260.0	267.3	311.9
Textile yarn, fabric, etc.	306.2	350.9	373.1
Metals and basic manufactures of metal	661.8	792.5	1,014.9
Machinery and apparatus; electrical parts; sound-recorders or reproducers; television image and sound recorders	1,804.8	2,197.3	2,293.6
Transport goods	822.7	1,154.8	1,408.1
Total (incl. others)	7,554.6	9,549.4	11,201.6

Exports f.o.b.	2004	2005	2006
Bananas and plantains	1,023.6	1,084.4	1,213.0
Cocoa	103.0	118.2	140.0
Natural flowers	354.8	397.9	446.3
Fresh fish, crustaceans and molluscs	420.8	577.3	700.7
Mineral products	3,911.0	5,412.8	6,970.5
Crude petroleum oils, etc.	3,898.5	5,396.8	6,934.0
Chemicals and pharmaceuticals	88.7	77.6	128.9
Manufactured foodstuffs	771.3	949.4	1,062.8
Preparations of fish	393.2	519.8	579.4
Canned fish	362.3	489.6	532.2
Other manufactured goods	863.1	1,204.6	1,610.2
Petroleum derivatives	335.5	473.0	610.3
Metal manufactures	209.0	351.7	582.4
Vehicles and parts thereof	79.0	168.5	342.4
Total (incl. others)	7,752.9	10,100.0	12,658.1

PRINCIPAL TRADING PARTNERS
(US $ million)

Imports c.i.f.	2004	2005	2006
Argentina	219.9	303.0	370.4
Brazil	434.7	621.4	824.0
Chile	378.4	373.3	447.0
China, People's Republic	400.4	563.5	731.1
Colombia	1,234.3	1,345.8	1,456.5
Germany	195.7	219.2	223.3
Italy	90.3	107.0	157.5
Japan	283.9	338.2	429.9
Korea, Republic	170.7	486.8	413.2
Mexico	224.0	288.4	340.4
Netherlands	130.2	148.4	118.3
Panama	359.2	436.4	446.0
Peru	228.9	358.6	326.0
Spain	114.6	130.2	135.9
Taiwan	61.2	140.0	100.9
USA	1,577.3	1,922.3	2,622.6
Venezuela	480.7	413.0	391.9
Total (incl. others)	7,554.6	9,549.1	11,201.6

Exports f.o.b.	2004	2005	2006
Belgium and Luxembourg	75.7	78.1	101.6
Chile	125.8	305.2	552.8
Colombia	334.8	511.0	706.2
Germany	198.2	201.4	222.1
Guatemala	36.2	153.6	195.4
Italy	356.0	386.2	422.2
Korea, Republic	146.9	3.6	6.0
Malaysia	78.9	73.1	122.4
Netherlands	130.3	204.4	200.3
Panama	1,088.9	679.5	337.0
Peru	605.8	876.1	1,036.6
Spain	114.7	217.7	293.9
Russia	272.2	308.7	347.1
USA	3,298.2	5,050.1	6,781.2
Venezuela	126.4	139.8	317.4
Total (incl. others)	7,752.8	10,100.0	12,658.1

Transport

RAILWAYS
(traffic)

	2002	2003	2004
Passenger-km (million)	33	4	2

Source: UN, *Statistical Yearbook*.

ROAD TRAFFIC
(motor vehicles in use at 31 December)

	1999	2000	2001
Passenger cars	532,170	550,448	529,359
Buses and coaches	9,917	9,183	8,962
Lorries and vans	51,686	55,580	54,698
Road tractors	3,630	5,118	5,588
Motorcycles and mopeds	26,641	25,711	22,574

2004: Passenger cars 413,432; Buses and coaches 10,488; Lorries and vans 299,521; Motorcycles and mopeds 40,645.

Source: IRF, *World Road Statistics*.

SHIPPING

Merchant Fleet
(registered at 31 December)

	2004	2005	2006
Number of vessels	206	217	220
Total displacement ('000 grt)	264.6	274.9	280.5

Source: Lloyd's Register-Fairplay, *World Fleet Statistics*.

International Sea-borne Freight Traffic
('000 metric tons)

	1988*	1989*	1990
Goods loaded	8,402	10,020	11,783
Goods unloaded	2,518	2,573	1,958

*Source: UN, *Monthly Bulletin of Statistics*.

ECUADOR

CIVIL AVIATION
(traffic on scheduled services)

	2003	2004	2005
Kilometres flown (million)	9.1	10.8	11.4
Passengers carried ('000)	1,123	n.a.	n.a.
Passenger-km (million)	673.7	788.3	867.1
Total ton-km (million)	4.8	5.0	5.4

Source: UN, *Statistical Yearbook for Latin America and the Caribbean*.

Tourism

FOREIGN VISITOR ARRIVALS*

Country of residence	2003	2004	2005
Argentina	15,395	15,354	16,788
Chile	16,656	17,541	18,149
Colombia	205,353	179,434	164,123
France	13,490	13,336	13,155
Germany	18,598	19,451	20,316
Peru	153,520	191,303	209,743
Spain	20,111	26,669	39,702
United Kingdom	19,554	20,867	21,929
USA	159,851	182,114	188,942
Venezuela	14,084	15,544	16,152
Total (incl. others)	760,776	818,927	860,784

* Figures refer to total arrivals (including same-day visitors), except those of Ecuadorean nationals residing abroad.

Tourism receipts (US $ million, incl. passenger transport): 408 in 2003; 464 in 2004; 488 in 2005.

Source: World Tourism Organization.

Communications Media

	2004	2005	2006
Telephones ('000 main lines in use)	1,612.3	1,701.5	1,753.8
Mobile cellular telephones ('000 subscribers)	3,544.2	6,246.3	8,485.0
Personal computers ('000 in use)	724	616	n.a.
Internet users ('000)	624.6	968.0	1,549.0
Broadband subscribers ('000)	11.6	26.8	n.a.

Radio receivers ('000 in use): 5,040 in 1999.

Facsimile machines: 30,000 in use in 1996.

Daily newspapers: 36 in 2000 (average circulation 1,220,000).

Sources: UNESCO, *Statistical Yearbook*; UN, *Statistical Yearbook*; International Telecommunication Union.

Education

(2003/04 unless otherwise indicated)

	Teachers	Males ('000)	Females ('000)	Total ('000)
Pre-primary	13,285	112.4	108.8	221.2
Primary	86,012	1,014.4	975.3	1,989.7
Secondary:				
general	59,566*	398.5	375.3	773.8
technical/vocational	15,119*	107.1	115.6	222.7
Higher	15,271†	n.a.	n.a.	206.5‡

* Estimate.
† 2000/01 figure.
‡ 1990/91 figure.

Institutions (2002/03): Pre-primary 5,244; Primary 18,203; Secondary 3,486.

Sources: UNESCO Institute for Statistics; Ministerio de Educación y Cultura.

Adult literacy rate (UNESCO estimates): 91.0% (males 92.3%; females 89.7%) in 2001 (Source: UNESCO Institute for Statistics).

Directory

The Constitution

The 1945 Constitution was suspended in June 1970. In January 1978 a referendum was held to choose between two draft Constitutions, prepared by various special constitutional committees. In a 90% poll, 43% voted for a proposed new Constitution and 32.1% voted for a revised version of the 1945 Constitution. The new Constitution came into force on 10 August 1979. In November 1997 a National Constituent Assembly was elected for the purpose of reviewing the Constitution, and a new Constitution, which retained many of the provisions of the 1979 Constitution, came into force on 10 August 1998. The main provisions of the Constitution are summarized below:

CHAMBER OF REPRESENTATIVES

The Constitution of 1998 states that legislative power is exercised by the Chamber of Representatives, which sits for a period of 60 days from 10 August. The Chamber is required to set up four full-time Legislative Commissions to consider draft laws when the House is in recess. Special sessions of the Chamber of Representatives may be called.

Representatives are elected for four years from lists of candidates drawn up by legally recognized parties. Twelve are elected nationally; two from each Province with over 100,000 inhabitants, one from each Province with fewer than 100,000; and one for every 200,000 citizens or fractions of over 150,000. Representatives are eligible for re-election.

In addition to its law-making duties, the Chamber ratifies treaties, elects members of the Supreme and Superior Courts, and (from panels presented by the President) the Comptroller-General, the Attorney-General and the Superintendent of Banks. It is also able to overrule the President's amendment of a bill that it has submitted for Presidential approval. It may reconsider a rejected bill after a year or request a referendum, and may revoke the President's declaration of a state of emergency. The budget is considered in the first instance by the appropriate Legislative Commission and disagreements are resolved in the Chamber.

PRESIDENT

The presidential term is four years (starting from 15 January of the year following his election), and there is no re-election. The President appoints the Cabinet, the Governors of Provinces, diplomatic representatives and certain administrative employees, and is responsible for the direction of international relations. In the event of foreign invasion or internal disturbance, the President may declare a state of emergency and must notify the Chamber, or the Tribunal for Constitutional Guarantees if the Chamber is not in session.

As in other post-war Latin-American Constitutions, particular emphasis is laid on the functions and duties of the State, which is given wide responsibilities with regard to the protection of labour; assisting in the expansion of production; protecting the Indian and peasant communities; and organizing the distribution and development of uncultivated lands, by expropriation where necessary.

Voting is compulsory for every Ecuadorean citizen who is literate and over 18 years of age. An optional vote has been extended to illiterates (under 15% of the population by 1981). The Constitution guarantees liberty of conscience in all its manifestations, and states that the law shall not make any discrimination for religious reasons.

The Government

HEAD OF STATE

President: RAFAEL CORREA DELGADO (took office 15 January 2007).
Vice-President: LENÍN MORENO GARCÉS.

CABINET
(April 2008)

Minister of External Relations, Trade and Integration: María Isabel Salvador.
Minister of the Economy and Finance: Fausto Ortiz de la Cadena.
Minister of Government, Worship, Police and Municipalities: Fernando Bustamante.
Minister of Electricity and Renewable Energy: Alecksey Mosquera.
Minister of National Defence: Dr Javier Ponce Cevallos.
Minister of Urban Development and Housing: María de los Angeles Duarte.
Minister of Education: Raúl Vallejo Corral.
Minister of Public Health: Dr Caroline Chang.
Minister of Agriculture, Livestock, Aquaculture and Fishing: Walter Poveda Ricaurte.
Minister of the Environment: Marcela Aguiñaga.
Minister of Labour and Employment: Antonio Gagliardo.
Minister of Tourism: Verónica Sión.
Minister of Economic and Social Inclusion: Dr Jeanette Sánchez Zurita.
Minister of Industry and Competition: Raúl Sagasti.
Minister of Transport and Public Works: Jorge Marún.
Minister of Sport: Dr Raúl Carrión Fiallos.
Minister of Culture: Antonio Preciado Bedoya.
Minister of Coastal Affairs: Carolina Portalupi (acting).
Minister of Mining and Petroleum: Galo Chiriboga.
Minister of Justice and Human Rights: Dr Charbel Gustavo Jalkh.

Co-ordinating Ministers

Co-ordinating Minister for National and International Security: Dr Gustavo Larrea.
Co-ordinating Minister for Production: Susana Cabeza de Vaca.
Co-ordinating Minister for Economic Policy: Dr Pedro Páez.
Co-ordinating Minister for Social Development: Nathalie Cely.
Co-ordinating Minister for Politics: Ricardo Armando Patiño Aroca.
Co-ordinating Minister for Cultural and Natural Heritage: Doris Solís Carrión.
Co-ordinating Minister for Strategic Sectors: Derlis Palacios Guerrero.

MINISTRIES

Office of the President: Palacio Nacional, García Moreno 1043, Quito; tel. (2) 221-6300; internet www.presidencia.gov.ec.
Office of the Vice-President: Manuel Larrea y Arenas, Edif. Consejo Provincial de Pichincha, 21°, Quito; tel. (2) 250-4953; fax (2) 250-3379.
Ministry of Agriculture, Livestock, Aquaculture and Fishing: Avda Eloy Alfaro y Amazonas, Quito; tel. (2) 250-4433; fax (2) 256-4531; e-mail webmaster@mag.gov.ec; internet www.mag.gov.ec.
Ministry of Coastal Affairs: Edif. Gobierno del Litoral, 5°, Avda Francisco de Orellana y Justino Cornejo 106, Ciudadela Kennedy Norte, Guayaquil; tel. (4) 268-3138; e-mail comunicaciones@minlitoral.gov.ec.
Ministry of Culture: Quito.
Ministry of the Economy and Finance: Avda 10 de Agosto 1661 y Jorge Washington, Quito; tel. (2) 254-4500; fax (2) 253-0703; internet minfinanzas.ec-gov.net.
Ministry of Education: San Salvador E 6-49 y Eloy Alfaro, Quito; tel. (2) 255-5014; e-mail info@mec.gov.ec; internet www.mec.gov.ec.
Ministry of Electricity and Renewable Energy: Juan León Mera y Orellana, 5°, Quito; tel. (2) 255-0041; fax (2) 255-0018; e-mail menergia2@andinanet.net; internet www.menergia.gov.ec.
Ministry of the Environment: Avda Eloy Alfaro y Amazonas, Edif. M.A.G., Quito; tel. (2) 256-3429; fax (2) 250-0041; e-mail mma@ambiente.gov.ec; internet www.ambiente.gov.ec.
Ministry of External Relations, Trade and Integration: Avda 10 de Agosto y Carrión, Quito; tel. (2) 299-3200; fax (2) 256-4873; e-mail webmast@mmrree.gov.ec; internet www.mmrree.gov.ec.
Ministry of Industry and Competition: Avda Eloy Alfaro y Amazonas, Quito; tel. (2) 254-6107; fax (2) 250-3818; e-mail info@micip.gov.ec; internet www.micip.gov.ec.
Ministry of Government, Worship, Police and Municipalities: Espejo y Benalcázar, Quito; tel. (2) 295-5666; fax (2) 295-8360; e-mail informacion@mingobierno.gov.ec; internet www.mingobierno.gov.ec.
Ministry of Justice and Human Rights: Quito.
Ministry of Labour and Employment: Clemente Ponce 255 y Piedrahita, Quito; tel. (2) 256-6148; fax (2) 250-3122; e-mail informacion@mintrab.gov.ec; internet www.mintrab.gov.ec.
Ministry of Mining and Petroleum: Edif. MOP, Avda Orellana 26-220 y Juan León Mera (esq.), Quito; tel. (2) 255-0018; e-mail lbenalcázar@menergia.gov.ec; internet www.menergia.gov.ec.
Ministry of National Defence: Exposición 208, Quito; tel. (2) 221-6150; fax (2) 256-9386; internet www.midena.gov.ec.
Ministry of Public Health: Juan Larrea 444, Quito; tel. (2) 297-2900; fax 256-9786; e-mail despacho@msp.gov.ec; internet www.msp.gov.ec.
Ministry of Economic and Social Inclusion: Robles 850 entre Páez y 9 de Octubre, Quito; tel. (2) 254-4136; e-mail desmbd@uio.satnet.net; internet www.mbs.gov.ec.
Ministry of Sport: Avda Shyris, 42-31 y Tomás de Berlanga, Quito; tel. (2) 227-0262; internet www.senader.gov.ec.
Ministry of Tourism: Avda Eloy Alfaro 32 y Carlos Tobar, Quito; tel. (2) 250-7559; fax (2) 222-9330; e-mail ministra@turismo.gov.ec; internet www.vivecuador.com.
Ministry of Transport and Public Works: Avda Juan León Mera, esq. Orellana, Quito; tel. (2) 256-0290; internet www.mop.gov.ec.
Ministry of Urban Development and Housing: Avda 10 de Agosto 2270 y Corotero, Quito; tel. (2) 223-8060; fax (2) 256-6785; e-mail mdesur2@ec-gov.net; internet www.miduvi.ec-gov.net.
Office for Public Administration: Palacio Nacional, García Moreno 1043, Quito; tel. (2) 251-5990.

President and Legislature

PRESIDENT

Election, 15 October and 26 November 2006

Candidate	% of votes cast in first ballot	% of votes cast in second ballot
Alvaro Fernando Noboa Pontón (PRIAN)	26.83	43.33
Rafael Correa Delgado (Alianza País/PS—FA)	22.84	56.67
Gilmar Gutiérrez (PSP)	17.42	—
León Roldós Aguilera (ID/Red Etica y Democrática)	14.84	—
Cynthia Vitera (PSC)	9.63	—
Others	8.44	—
Total	**100.00**	**100.00**

CONGRESO

Cámara Nacional de Representantes

President: Jorge Cevallos Macías.

Election, 15 October 2006, preliminary results

Political parties	Seats
Partido Renovador Institucional de Acción Nacional (PRIAN)	27
Partido Sociedad Patriótica 21 de Enero (PSP)	21
Izquierda Democrática (ID)/Red Etica y Democrática	13
Partido Social Cristiano (PSC)	12
Movimiento de Unidad Pluriacional Pachakútik Nuevo País (MNPP—Pachakútik)	7
Partido Roldosista Ecuatoriano (PRE)	6
Movimiento Popular Democrático (MPD)	3
Democracia Popular—Unión Demócrata Cristiana (DP—UDC)	2
Others	9
Total	**100**

ECUADOR

Election Commission

Tribunal Supremo Electoral (TSE): 6 de Diciembre y Bosmediano, Quito; tel. (2) 245-7110; internet www.tse.gov.ec; independent; Pres. JORGE ACOSTA CISNEROS.

Political Organizations

Acción Popular Revolucionaria Ecuatoriana (APRE): centrist; Leader Lt-Gen. FRANK VARGAS PAZZOS.

Alianza País: Of. 501, Edif. Torres Whimper, Diego de Almagro 32-27 y Whimper, Quito; tel. (2) 600-0630; fax (2) 600-1029; e-mail info@rafaelcorrea.com; internet www.rafaelcorrea.com; f. 2006; Pres. RAFAEL CORREA DELGADO.

Coalición Nacional Republicana (CNR): Quito; f. 1986; fmrly Coalición Institucionalista Demócrata (CID).

Concentración de Fuerzas Populares (CFP): Quito; f. 1946; Leader GALO VAYAS; Dir Dr AVERROES BUCARAM SAXIDA.

Democracia Popular—Unión Demócrata Cristiana (DP—UDC): Calle Luis Saá 153 y Hermanos Pazmiño, Apdo 17-01-2300, Quito; tel. (2) 254-7654; fax (2) 250-2995; f. 1978; Christian democrat; Leader Lic. ABSALÓN ROCHA.

Frente Radical Alfarista (FRA): Quito; f. 1972; liberal; Leader IVÁN CASTRO PATIÑO.

Izquierda Democrática (ID): Polonia 161, entre Vancouver y Eloy Alfaro, Quito; tel. (2) 256-4436; fax (2) 256-9295; f. 1977; absorbed Fuerzas Armadas Populares Eloy Alfaro—Alfaro Vive ¡Carajo! (AVC) (Eloy Alfaro Popular Armed Forces—Alfaro Lives, Damn It!) in 1991; Nat. Dir GUILLERMO LANDÁZURI.

Movimiento Independiente para una República Auténtica (MIRA): Quito; f. 1996; Leader Dra ROSALIA ARTEAGA SERRANO.

Movimiento Popular Democrático (MPD): e-mail periodicopcion@andinanet.net; internet bloquempd.tripod.com; Stalinist; Dep. Leader STALIN VARGAS MEZA.

Movimiento de Unidad Pluriacional Pachakútik Nuevo País (MNPP—Pachakútik): Calle Lugo 13-04 y Avda Ladrón de Guevara, La Floresta, Quito; e-mail pachakutik@pachakutik.org.ec; internet www.pachakutik.org.ec; political wing of CONAIE (q.v.); represents indigenous, environmental and social groups; Leader FREDDY EHLERS ZURITA; Nat. Dir GILBERTO TALAHUA.

Partido Comunista Marxista-Leninista de Ecuador: e-mail pcmle@bigfoot.com; internet www.pcmle.org/EM/; Sec.-Gen. CAMILO ALMEYDA.

Partido Conservador (PC): Wilsón 578, Quito; tel. (2) 250-5061; f. 1855; incorporated Partido Unidad Republicano in 1995; centre-right; Leader SIXTO DURÁN BALLÉN.

Partido Demócrata (PD): Quito; Leader Dr FRANCISCO HUERTA MONTALVO.

Partido Liberal Radical (PLR): Quito; f. 1895; held office from 1895 to 1944 as the Liberal Party, which subsequently divided into various factions; perpetuates the traditions of the Liberal Party; Leader CARLOS JULIO PLAZA A.

Partido Renovador Institucional de Acción Nacional (PRIAN): Quito; internet www.prian.org.ec; right-wing, populist; Leader ALVARO FERNANDO NOBOA PONTÓN.

Partido Republicano (PR): Quito; Leader GUILLERMO SOTOMAYOR.

Partido Roldosista Ecuatoriano (PRE): Quito; tel. (2) 246-8227; fax (2) 246-8229; e-mail info@viviendolademocracia.org; f. 1982; populist; Dir ABDALÁ BUCARAM ORTIZ.

Partido Social Cristiano (PSC): Carrión 548 y Reina Victoria, Casilla 9454, Quito; tel. (2) 254-4536; fax (2) 256-8562; internet www.psc.org.ec; f. 1951; centre-right party; Pres. PASCUAL DEL CIOPPO ARAGUNDI.

Partido Socialista—Frente Amplio (PS—FA): Avda Gran Colombia 15-201 y Yaguachi, Quito; tel. (2) 222-1764; fax (2) 222-2184; e-mail info@psecuador.org; internet www.psecuador.org; f. 1926; Pres. GUADALUPE LARRIVA GONZÁLEZ.

Partido Sociedad Patriótica 21 de Enero (PSP): Quito; internet www.sociedadpatriotica.com; contested the 2002 elections in alliance with the MNPP; Leader GILMAR GUTIÉRREZ.

Red Etica y Democracia: Quito; e-mail info@redeticaydemocracia.com; internet www.redeticaydemocracia.com.ec; Leader LEÓN ROLDÓS AGUILERA.

Unión Alfarista—FRA: Quito; f. 1998; centrist; Leader CÉSAR VERDUGA VÉLEZ.

OTHER ORGANIZATIONS

Confederación de las Nacionalidades Indígenas de la Amazonia Ecuatoriana (CONFENIAE): Avda 6 de Diciembre 159 y Pazmino, Of. 408, Apdo 17-01-4180, Quito; tel. (2) 543-973; fax (2) 220-325; e-mail confeniae@applicom.com; internet www.unii.net/confeniae; represents indigenous peoples; mem. of CONAIE; Leader LUIS VARGAS.

Confederación de Nacionalidades Indígenas de Ecuador (CONAIE) (National Confederation of the Indigenous Population of Ecuador): Avda Los Granados 2553 y 6 de Diciembre, Quito; tel. (2) 245-2335; e-mail taskyyaku@yahoo.com; internet conaie.org; f. 1986; represents indigenous peoples; MNPP (q.v.) represents CONAIE in the legislature; Pres. LUÍS MACAS; Vice-Pres. SANTIAGO DE LA CRUZ.

Confederación de los Pueblos de Nacionalidad Kichua del Ecuador (Ecuarunari): Edif. El Conquistador, 1°, Julio Matovelle 128, entre Vargas y Pasaje San Luis, Quito; tel. (2) 258-0700; fax (2) 258-0713; e-mail ecuarunari@ecuarunari.org; internet www.ecuarunari.org; f. 1972; indigenous movt; Pres. HUMBERTO CHOLANGO.

Coordinadora de las Organizaciones Indígenas de la Cuenca Amazónica (COICA): Quito; e-mail com@coica.org; internet www.coica.org; f. 1984; founded in Lima, Peru; moved to Quito in 1993; umbrella group of 9 orgs representing indigenous peoples of the Amazon Basin in Bolivia, Brazil, Colombia, Ecuador, French Guiana, Guyana, Suriname and Venezuela; Gen. Co-ordinator JOCELYN ROGER THERESE; Vice-Gen. Co-ordinator LUIS VARGAS CANELOS.

Federación de Pueblos Indígenas, Campesinos y Negros del Ecuador (Fedepicne): Quito; f. 1996 following split from CONAIE; formally recognized in 2003; Pres. LUIS PACHALA.

Frente Popular (FP): umbrella group of labour unions and other populist orgs; Pres. LUIS VILLACÍS.

ARMED GROUPS

Ejército de Liberación Alfarista: f. 2001; extreme left-wing insurrectionist group; formed by fmr mems of disbanded armed groups Alfaro Vive ¡Carajo!, Montoneros Patria Libre and Sol Rojo; Spokesperson SEBASTIÁN SÁNCHEZ.

Grupos de Combatientes Populares (GCP): Cuenca; communist guerrilla grouping; active since 2000.

Izquierda Revolucionaria Armada (IRA): extreme left-wing revolutionary group opposed to international capitalism.

Montoneros Patria Libre (MPL): f. 1986; advocates an end to authoritarianism.

Milicias Revolucionarias del Pueblo (MRP): extreme left-wing grouping opposed to international capitalism.

Partido Maoísta-Comunista 'Puka Inti': Sec.-Gen. RAMIRO CELI.

Diplomatic Representation

EMBASSIES IN ECUADOR

Argentina: Avda Amazonas 477 y Roca, 8°, Quito; tel. (2) 256-2292; fax (2) 256-8177; e-mail embarge2@uio.satnet.net; Ambassador CARLOS PIÑEIRO IÑIGUEZ.

Bolivia: Avda Eloy Alfaro 2432 y Fernando Ayarza, Apdo 17-210003, Quito; tel. (2) 244-4830; fax (2) 224-4833; e-mail embolivia-quito@andinanet.net; Ambassador JUAN XAVIER ZARATE RIVAS.

Brazil: Edif. España, Avda Amazonas 1429 y Colón, 9° y 10°, Apdo 17-01-231, Quito; tel. (2) 256-3142; fax (2) 250-4468; e-mail ebrasil@embajadadelbrasil.org.ec; internet www.embajadadelbrasil.org.ec; Ambassador ANTONINO MARQUES-PORTO.

Canada: Edif. Eurocenter, 3°, Avda Amazonas 4153, Apdo 17-11-6512, Quito; tel. (2) 250-6162; fax (2) 250-3108; e-mail quito@international.gc.ca; internet www.dfait-maeci.gc.ca/ecuador; Ambassador CHRISTIAN LAPOINTE.

Chile: Edif. Xerox, 4°, Juan Pablo Sanz 3617 y Amazonas, Quito; tel. (2) 224-9403; fax (2) 244-4470; e-mail embachileecu@trans-telco.net; Ambassador ENRIQUE KRAUSS.

China, People's Republic: Avda Atahualpa 349 y Amazonas, Quito; tel. (2) 245-8927; fax (2) 244-4364; e-mail embchina@uio.telconet.net; Ambassador LIU YUQIN.

Colombia: Edif. Arista, Avda Colón 1133 y Amazonas, 7°, Apdo 17-07-9164, Quito; tel. (2) 222-8926; e-mail equito@cancilleria.gov.co; internet www.cancilleria.gov.co; Ambassador CARLOS JOSÉ HOLGUÍN MOLINA (expelled March 2008).

Costa Rica: Rumipamba 692 y República, 1°, Apdo 17-03-301, Quito; tel. (2) 225-4945; fax (2) 225-4087; e-mail embajcr@uio.satnet.net; Ambassador LUZ ARGENTINA CALDERÓN GEI.

Cuba: Mercurio 365, entre La Razón y El Vengador, Quito; tel. (2) 245-6936; fax (2) 243-0594; e-mail embajada@ecuecuador.minrex.gov.cu; Ambassador BENIGNO PÉREZ FERNÁNDEZ.

Dominican Republic: Edif. Albatros, Avda de los Shyris 1240 y Portugal, 2°, Apdo 17-01-387-A, Quito; tel. (2) 243-4232; e-mail

ECUADOR

emrepdom@interactive.net.ec; Ambassador Néstor Juan Cerón Suero.

Egypt: Avda Tarqui 4-56 y Avda 6 de Diciembre, Apdo 9355, Quito; tel. (2) 222-5240; fax (2) 256-3521; e-mail embegipto@ecnet.ec; Ambassador Suzanne Mohamed Gamil Noah.

El Salvador: Edif. Gabriela III, 3°, Avda República de El Salvador 733 y Portugal, Quito; tel. (2) 243-3070; fax (2) 224-2829; e-mail embajada@elsalvador.com.ec; internet www.elsalvador.com.ec; Ambassador Rafael Angel Alfaro Pineda.

France: Calle Leonidas Plaza 107 y Avda Patria, CP 536, Quito; tel. (2) 294-3800; fax (2) 294-3809; e-mail francie@andinanet.net; internet www.ambafrance-ecu.org; Ambassador Didier Lopinot.

Germany: Edif. Citiplaza, 13° y 14°, Avda Naciones Unidas y República de El Salvador, Apdo 17-17-536, Quito; tel. (2) 297-0820; fax (2) 297-0815; e-mail alemania@interactive.net.ec; internet www.quito.diplo.de; Ambassador Christian Berger.

Guatemala: Edif. Gabriela III, 3°, Of. 301, Avda República de El Salvador 733 y Portugal, Apdo 17-03-294, Quito; tel. (2) 245-9700; e-mail embecuador@minex.gob.gt; Ambassador Juan León Alvarado.

Holy See: Avda Orellana 692, Apdo 17-07-8980, Quito; tel. (2) 250-5200; fax (2) 256-4810; e-mail nunapec@impsat.net.ec; Apostolic Nunciature; Apostolic Nuncio Most Rev. Guido Giacomo Ottonello (Titular Archbishop of Sasabe).

Honduras: Edif. World Trade Center, Torre A, 5°, Of. 501, Avda 12 de Octubre 1942 y Luis Cordero, Apdo 17-03-4753, Quito; tel. (2) 222-3985; fax (2) 222-0441; e-mail embhquito@yahoo.com; Ambassador Hernán Antonio Bermúdez Aguilar.

Israel: Edif. Plaza 2000, Avda 12 de Octubre y General Francisco Salazar, Apdo 17-21-08, Quito; tel. (2) 223-7474; fax (2) 223-8055; e-mail info@quito.mfa.gov.il; internet quito.mfa.il; Ambassador Daniel Sabban.

Italy: Calle La Isla 111 y Humberto Albornoz, Apdo 17-03-72, Quito; tel. (2) 256-1077; fax (2) 250-2818; e-mail archivio.quito@esteri.it; internet www.ambitalquito.org; Ambassador Giulio Cesare Piccirilli.

Japan: Juan León Mera 130 y Avda Patria, 7°, Quito; tel. (2) 256-1899; fax (2) 250-3670; e-mail japembec@uio.satnet.net; Ambassador Hiroyuki Hiramatsu.

Korea, Republic: Edif. Citiplaza, 8°, Avda Naciones Unidas y Avda de El Salvador, Quito; tel. (2) 297-0625; fax (2) 297-0630; e-mail embajadadecorea@mail.com; Ambassador Kyung Surk Kin.

Mexico: Avda 6 de Diciembre 4843 y Naciones Unidas, Apdo 17-11-6371, Quito; tel. (2) 292-3770; fax (2) 244-8245; e-mail embajadamexico@embamex.org.ec; internet www.sre.gob.mx/ecuador; Ambassador Héctor Romero Barraza.

Netherlands: Edif. World Trade Center, Torre 1, 1°, Avda 12 de Octubre 1942 y Luis Cordero, Apdo 17-03-72, Quito; tel. (2) 222-9229; fax (2) 256-7917; e-mail nlgovqui@embajadadeholanda.com; internet www.embajadadeholanda.com; Ambassador Kornelis Spaans.

Nicaragua: Edif. World Trade Center, Torre A, Avda 12 de Octubre 1942 con Avda Cordero, Quito; tel. (2) 224-4844; fax (2) 245-3413; Ambassador Donald Castillo Rivas (resident in Colombia).

Panama: Edif. ESPRO, 6°, Alpallana 505 y Whimper, Quito; tel. (2) 250-8856; fax (2) 256-5234; e-mail panaembaecuador@hotmail.com; Ambassador Olgalina Rodríguez de Quijada.

Paraguay: Edif. Torre Sol Verde, 8°, Avda 12 de Octubre esq. Salazar, Apdo 17-03-139, Quito; tel. (2) 290-9005; fax (2) 290-9006; e-mail embapar@uio.telconet.net; Ambassador Felipe Mendoza Olovarrieta.

Peru: Avda República de El Salvador 495 e Irlanda, Apdo 17-07-9380, Quito; tel. (2) 246-8410; fax (2) 225-2560; e-mail embaperu-quito@rree.gob.pe; Ambassador Vicente Rojas Escalante.

Russia: Reina Victoria 462 y Ramón Roca, Quito; tel. (2) 256-6361; fax (2) 256-5531; e-mail embrusia@accessinter.net; Ambassador Valentín Bogomázov.

Spain: General Francisco Salazar E12-73 y Toledo (Sector La Floresta), Apdo 17-01-9322, Quito; tel. (2) 322-6296; fax (2) 322-7805; e-mail emb.quito@mae.es; internet www.embajadaespana.com.ec; Ambassador Juan María Alzina de Aguilar.

Switzerland: Edif. Xerox, 2°, Amazonas 3617 y Juan Pablo Sanz, Apdo 17-11-4815, Quito; tel. (2) 243-4949; fax (2) 244-9314; e-mail qui.vertretung@eda.admin.ch; internet www.eda.admin.ch/quito; Ambassador Markus-Alexander Antonietti.

United Kingdom: Edif. Citiplaza, 14°, Avda Naciones Unidas y República de El Salvador, Apdo 17-01-314, Quito; tel. (2) 297-0800; fax (2) 297-0809; e-mail consuio@uio.satnet.net; internet www.britembquito.org.ec; Ambassador Bernard Gerrard Whiteside.

USA: Avda 12 de Octubre 1942 y Patria 120, Quito; tel. (2) 256-2890; fax (2) 250-2052; internet www.usembassy.org.ec; Ambassador Linda L. Jewell.

Uruguay: Edif. Josueth González, 9°, Avda 6 de Diciembre 2816 y Paul Rivet, Apdo 17-12-282, Quito; tel. (2) 256-3762; fax (2) 256-3763; e-mail uruguay@embajada_uruguay.com.ec; Ambassador Gustavo Vanerio Balbela.

Venezuela: Avda Los Cabildos 115, Apdo 17-01-688, Quito; tel. (2) 226-8636; fax (2) 246-6786; e-mail embavenecua@venezuela.org.ec; Ambassador Oscar Navas Tortolero.

Judicial System

SUPREME COURT OF JUSTICE

Corte Suprema de Justicia

Palacio de Justicia, Avda 6 de Diciembre y Piedrahita 332, Quito; tel. (2) 290-0424; fax (2) 290-0425; e-mail dni-cnj@access.net.ec; internet www.justiciaecuador.gov.ec.

f. 1830, reconstituted 2005; Pres. Jaime Velasco Dávila.

The Supreme Court of Justice was dissolved in April 2005 and reconstituted in December. It is composed of 30 Justices, as well as a President. Three Justices sit in each of its 10 chambers, which comprise three penal law courts, one administrative litigation court, one fiscal law court, three civil law courts and two employment law courts.

Justices: Joffre García Jaime, Pilar Sacoto Sacoto, Roberto Gómez Mera, Luis Abarca Galeas, Luis Octavio Cañar Lojano, Clotario Oswaldo Castro Muñoz, Jaime Bolívar Chávez, Guido Garcés, José Hernán Ulloa, Luis Hernán Salgado Pesántes, Marco Antonio Guzmán Carrasco, Jorge Endara Moncayo, José Vicente Troya Jaramillo, Jorge Jaramillo Vega, Hugo Larrea Romero, Héctor Cabrera Suárez, Viterbo Cevallos Alcívar, Mauro Terán Cevallos, Carlos Ramírez Romero, Ramiro Romero Parducci, José Ramón Jiménez Carbo, César Montaño Ortega, Daniel Encalada Alvarado, Rubén Darío Andrade Vallejo, Ana Isabel Abril Olivo, Alfredo Jaramillo Jaramillo, Rubén Bravo Moreno, Teodoro Coello Vásquez, Gastón Alarcón Elizalde, Hernán Peña Toral.

Attorney-General: Dr Xavier Garaicoa Ortiz.

OTHER COURTS

Higher or Divisional Courts: Ambato, Azogues, Babahoyo, Cuenca, Esmeraldas, Guaranda, Guayaquil, Ibarra, Latacunga, Loja, Machala, Portoviejo, Quito, Riobamba and Tulcán; 90 judges.

Provincial Courts: There are 40 Provincial Courts in 15 districts; other courts include 94 Criminal, 219 Civil, 29 dealing with labour disputes and 17 Rent Tribunals.

Special Courts: National Court for Juveniles.

Religion

There is no state religion but nearly 90% of the population are Roman Catholics. There are representatives of various Protestant Churches and of the Jewish faith in Quito and Guayaquil.

CHRISTIANITY

The Roman Catholic Church

Ecuador comprises four archdioceses, 11 dioceses, seven Apostolic Vicariates and one Apostolic Prefecture. At 31 December 2005 there were an estimated 12,091,876 adherents in the country, equivalent to some 88.4% of the population.

Bishops' Conference

Conferencia Episcopal Ecuatoriana, Avda América 1805 y La Gasca, Apdo 17-01-1081, Quito; tel. (2) 255-8913; fax (2) 250-1429; e-mail dicuenca@etapa.com.ec.

f. 1939 statutes approved 1999; Pres. Mgr Néstor Rafael Herrera Heredia.

Archbishop of Cuenca: Vicente Rodrigo Cisneros Durán Navas, Arzobispado, Manuel Vega 8-66 y Calle Bolívar, Apdo 01-01-0046, Cuenca; tel. (7) 847-234; fax (7) 844-436; e-mail dicuenca@etaponline.ne.ec.

Archbishop of Guayaquil: Antonio Arregui Yarza Holguín, Arzobispado, Calle Clemente Ballén 501 y Chimborazo, Apdo 09-01-0254, Guayaquil; tel. (4) 232-2778; fax (4) 232-9695; e-mail marregui@q.ecua.net.ec; internet www.iglesiacatolicaguayaquil.org.

ECUADOR

Archbishop of Portoviejo: José Mario Ruiz Navas, Arzobispado, Avda Universitaria s/n, Entre Alajuela y Ramos y Duarte, Apdo 13-01-0024, Portoviejo; tel. (5) 263-0404; fax (5) 263-4428; e-mail arzobis@ecua.net.ec.

Archbishop of Quito: Raúl Eduardo Vela Chiriboga, Arzobispado, Calle Chile 1140 y Venezuela, Apdo 17-01-00106, Quito; tel. (2) 228-4429; fax (2) 258-0973; e-mail raul.vela@andinanet.net; internet www.arquidiocesisdequito.org.

The Anglican Communion

Anglicans in Ecuador are under the jurisdiction of Province IX of the Episcopal Church in the USA. The country is divided into two dioceses, one of which, Central Ecuador, is a missionary diocese.

Bishop of Littoral Ecuador: Rt Rev. Alfredo Morante, Calle Bogotá 1010, Barrio Centenario, Apdo 5250, Guayaquil; tel. (2) 443-3050; e-mail iedl@gu.pro.ec.

Bishop of Central Ecuador: (vacant), Apdo 17-11-6165, Quito; e-mail ecuacen@uio.satnet.net.

The Baptist Church

Baptist Convention of Ecuador: Casilla 3236, Guayaquil; tel. (4) 238-4865; Pres. Rev. Harolt Sante Mata; Sec. Jorge Moreno Chavarría.

The Methodist Church

United Evangelical Methodist Church: Evangelical United Church, Rumipamba 915, Apdo 17-03-236, Quito; tel. (2) 226-5158; fax (2) 243-9576; 800 mems, 2,000 adherents.

BAHÁ'Í FAITH

National Spiritual Assembly of the Bahá'ís: Apdo 869A, Quito; tel. (2) 256-3484; fax (2) 252-3192; e-mail ecua9nsa@uio.satnet.net; mems resident in 1,121 localities.

The Press

PRINCIPAL DAILIES

Quito

El Comercio: Avda Pedro Vicente Maldonado 11515 y el Tablón, Apdo 17-01-57, Quito; tel. (2) 267-0999; fax (2) 267-0466; e-mail contactenos@elcomercio.com; internet www.elcomercio.com; f. 1906; morning; independent; Proprs Compañía Anónima El Comercio; Pres. Guadalupe Mantilla de Acquaviva; Editor Marco Arauz; circ. 160,000.

La Hora: Panamericana Norte Kilómetro $3\frac{1}{2}$, Quito; tel. (2) 247-3724; fax (2) 247-5086; e-mail lahora@uio.satnet.net; internet www.lahora.com.ec; f. 1982; Nat. Pres. Dr Francisco Vivanco Riofrío; Exec. Pres. Francisco Vivanco Arroyo; Gen. Editor Juana López Sarmiento.

Hoy: Avda Mariscal Sucre N-71345, Apdo 17-07-0969, Quito; tel. (2) 249-0888; fax (2) 249-1881; e-mail hoy@hoy.com.ec; internet www.hoy.com.ec; f. 1982; morning; independent; Man. Jaime Mantilla Anderson; circ. 72,000.

Ultimas Noticias: Avda Pedro Vicente Maldonado 11515 y el Tablón, Apdo 17-01-57, Quito; tel. (2) 267-0999; fax (2) 267-4923; f. 1938; evening; independent; commercial; Proprs Compañía Anónima El Comercio; Dir David Mantilla Cashmore; circ. 60,000.

Guayaquil

Expreso: Avda Carlos Julio Arosemena, Casilla 5890, Guayaquil; tel. (4) 220-1100; fax (4) 220-0291; e-mail webmaster@granasa.com.ec; internet www.diario-expreso.com; f. 1973; morning; independent; Exec. Editor Martín Ulloa; circ. 60,000.

El Extra: Avda Carlos Julio Arosemena, Casilla 5890, Guayaquil; tel. (4) 220-1100; fax (4) 220-0291; e-mail webmaster@granasa.com.ec; internet www.diario-extra.com; f. 1975; morning; Pres. Errol Cartwright Betancourt; Editor Henry Holguín; circ. 200,000.

La Razón: Avda Constitución y las Américas, Guayaquil; tel. (4) 228-0100; fax (4) 228-5110; e-mail cartas@larazonecuador.com; internet www.larazonecuador.com; f. 1965; morning; independent; Propr Roberto Isaías Dassum; Dir Jorge E. Pérez Pesantes; circ. 35,000.

La Segunda: Calle Colón 526 y Boyacá, Casilla 6366, Guayaquil; tel. (4) 232-0635; fax (4) 232-0539; f. 1983; morning; Propr Carlos Mansur; Dir Vicente Adum Antón; circ. 60,000.

El Telégrafo: Avda 10 de Agosto 601 y Boyacá, Casilla 415, Guayaquil; tel. (4) 232-6500; fax (4) 232-3265; e-mail cartas@telegrafo.com.ec; internet www.telegrafo.com.ec; f. 1884; morning; independent; commercial; Proprs El Telégrafo CA; Dir Carlos Navarrete Castillo; circ. 45,000 (weekdays), 55,000 (Sundays).

El Universo: Avda Domingo Comín y Alban, Casilla 09-01-531, Guayaquil; tel. (4) 249-0000; fax (4) 249-1034; e-mail editores@telconet.net; internet www.eluniverso.com; f. 1921; morning; independent; Pres. Nicolás Pérez Lapentti; Dir Carlos Pérez Barriga; circ. 174,000 (weekdays), 290,000 (Sundays).

Cuenca

El Tiempo: Avda Loja y Rodrigo de Triana, Cuenca; tel. (7) 882-551; fax (7) 882-555; e-mail redaccion@eltiempo.com.ec; internet www.eltiempo.com.ec; f. 1965; morning; independent; Dir Dr René Toral Calle; Editor Ricardo Tello Carrión; circ. 35,000.

El Mercurio: Avda las Américas (sector El Arenal); tel. (7) 880-110; fax (7) 817-266; e-mail redaccion@elmercurio.com.ec; Dir Nicanor Merchán Luco.

PERIODICALS

Quito

La Calle: Casilla 2010, Quito; f. 1956; weekly; politics; Dir Carlos Enrique Carrión; circ. 20,000.

Cámara de Comercio de Quito: Avda Amazona y República, Casilla 202, Quito; tel. (2) 244-3787; fax (2) 243-5862; f. 1906; monthly; commerce; Pres. Andrés Pérez Espinosa; Exec. Dir Armando Tomaselli; circ. 10,000.

Carta Económica del Ecuador: Toledo 1448 y Coruña, Apdo 3358, Quito; f. 1969; weekly; economic, financial and business information; Pres. Dr Lincoln Larrea B.; circ. 8,000.

Chasqui: Avda Diego de Almagro 32-133 y Andrade Marín, Apdo 17-01-584, Quito; tel. (2) 254-8011; fax (2) 250-2487; e-mail chasqui@ciespal.net; f. 1997; monthly; media studies; publ. of the Centro Internacional de Estudios Superiores de Comunicación para América Latina; Dir Edgar Jaramillo; Editor Luis Eladio Proaño.

El Colegial: Calle Carlos Ibarra 206, Quito; tel. (2) 221-6541; f. 1974; weekly; publ. of Student Press Asscn; Dir Wilson Almeida Muñoz; circ. 20,000.

Cosas: Edif. Alpallana 2, 3°, Alpallana 289 y Diego Almagro, Quito; tel. (2) 250-8742; fax (2) 250-8747; e-mail redaccion@cosas.com.ec; internet www.cosas.com.ec; women's interest; Editor Crista Rodas; Man. Caridad Vela.

Ecuador Guía Turística: Mejía 438, Of. 43, Quito; f. 1969; fortnightly; tourist information in Spanish and English; Propr Prensa Informativa Turística; Dir Jorge Vaca O.; circ. 30,000.

Gestión: Avda González Suárez 335 y San Ignacio, 2°, Quito; tel. (2) 223-6848; fax (2) 255-9930; e-mail info@dinediciones.com; internet www.gestion.dinediciones.com; f. 1994; monthly; economy and society; Gen. Man. Hernán Altamirano; Editor Juanita Ordóñez; circ 15,000.

Integración: Solano 836, Quito; quarterly; economics of the Andean countries.

Letras del Ecuador: Casa de la Cultura Ecuatoriana, Avda 6 de Diciembre, Casilla 67, Quito; f. 1944; monthly; literature and art; non-political; Dir Dr Teodoro Vanegas Andrade.

El Libertador: Olmedo 931 y García Moreno, Quito; f. 1926; monthly; Pres. Dr Benjamín Terán Varea.

Mensajero: Benalcázar 478, Apdo 17-01-4100, Quito; tel. (2) 221-9555; f. 1884; monthly; religion, culture, economics and politics; Man. Oswaldo Carrera Landázuri; circ. 5,000.

Quince Días: Sociedad Periodística Ecuatoriana, Los Pinos 315, Panamericana Norte Km $5\frac{1}{2}$, Quito; tel. (2) 247-4122; fax (2) 256-6741; fortnightly; news and regional political analysis.

Guayaquil

Análisis Semanal: Elizalde 119, 10°, Apdo 4925, Guayaquil; tel. (4) 232-6590; fax (4) 232-6842; e-mail wspurrier@ecuadoranalysis.com; internet www.ecuadoranalysis.com; weekly; economic and political affairs; Editor Walter Spurrier Baquerizo.

Ecuador Ilustrado: Guayaquil; f. 1924; monthly; literary; illustrated.

El Financiero: Casilla 6666, Guayaquil; tel. (4) 220-5051; e-mail elfinanciero@elfinanciero.com; internet www.elfinanciero.com; weekly; business and economic news; f. 1990; Dir David Pérez MacCollum.

Generación XXI: Aguirre 730 y Boyacá, Guayaquil; tel. (4) 232-7200; fax (4) 232-0499; e-mail webmaster@vistazo.com; internet www.generacion21.com; youth; Gen. Editor Sebastian Melieres.

Revista Estadio: Aguirre 730 y Boyacá, Apdo 1239, Guayaquil; tel. (4) 232-7200; fax (4) 232-0499; e-mail estadio@vistazo.com; internet www.revistaestadio.com; f. 1962; fortnightly; sport; Dir-Gen. Sebastian Melieres; Editor César Torres Tinajero; circ. 40,000.

ECUADOR

Revista Hogar: Aguirre 724 y Boyacá, Apdo 09-01-1239, Guayaquil; tel. (4) 232-7200; f. 1964; monthly; Man. Editor ROSA AMELIA ALVARADO; circ. 42,000.

Vistazo: Aguirre 730 y Boyacá, Casilla 09-01-1239, Guayaquil; tel. (4) 232-7200; fax (4) 232-0499; e-mail vistazo@vistazo.com; internet www.vistazo.com; f. 1957; fortnightly; general; Gen. Editor PATRICIA ESTUPIÑÁN DE BURBANO; circ. 85,000.

Publishers

Artes Gráficas Ltda: Avda 12 de Octubre 1637, Casilla 456A, Quito; Man. MANUEL DEL CASTILLO.

Casa de la Cultura Ecuatoriana: Avdas 6 de Diciembre y Patria; tel. (2) 222-3391; e-mail info@cce.org.ec; Dir JAIME PAREDES.

Centro de Educación Popular: Avda América 3584, Apdo 17-08-8604, Quito; tel. (2) 252-5521; fax (2) 254-2369; e-mail centro@cedep.ec; f. 1978; communications, economics; Dir DIEGO LANDÁZURI.

CEPLAES: Avda 6 de Diciembre 2912 y Alpallana, Apdo 17-11-6127, Quito; tel. (2) 254-8547; fax (2) 256-6207; f. 1978; agriculture, anthropology, education, health, social sciences, women's studies; Exec. Dir ALEXANDRA AYALA.

CIDAP: Hermano Miguel 3-23, Casilla 01-011-943, Cuenca; tel. (7) 282-9451; fax (7) 283-1450; e-mail cidapl@cidap.org.ec; internet www.cidap.org.ec; art, crafts, games, hobbies; Dir CLAUDIO MALO GONZALES.

CIESPAL (Centro Internacional de Estudios Superiores de Comunicación para América Latina): Avda Diego de Almagro 32-133 y Andrade Marín, Apdo 17-01-584, Quito; tel. (2) 254-8011; fax (2) 250-2487; e-mail ejaramillo@ciespal.net; internet www.ciespal.net; f. 1959; communications, technology; Dir EDGAR JARAMILLO.

Corporación Editora Nacional: Roca E9–59 y Tamayo, Apdo 17-12-886, Quito; tel. (2) 255-4358; fax (2) 256-6340; e-mail cen@accessinter.net; f. 1977; archaeology, economics, education, geography, political science, history, law, literature, philosophy, social sciences; Pres. ERNESTO ALBÁN GÓMEZ.

Corporación de Estudios y Publicaciones: Acuna 168 y J. Agama, Casilla 17-21-0086, Quito; tel. (2) 222-1711; fax (2) 222-6256; e-mail cep@accessinter.net; f. 1963; law, public administration.

Cromograf, SA: Coronel 2207, Guayaquil; tel. (4) 234-6400; children's books, paperbacks, art productions.

Ediciones Abya-Yala: Avda 12 de Octubre 1430, Apdo 17-12-719, Quito; tel. (2) 250-6251; fax (2) 250-6267; e-mail editorial@abyayala.org; internet www.abyayala.org; f. 1975; anthropology, environmental studies, languages, education, theology; Pres. Fr JUAN BOTTASSO; Dir-Gen. P. XAVIER HERRÁN.

Ediciones Valladolid: Colón 818 y Santa Elena, Guayaquil; tel. (4) 232-9956; e-mail edival@andinanet.net; internet edival.ecuaemail.com; f. 1996; reference; Owner and Man. CÉSAR VALLADOLID.

Editorial Don Bosco: Vega Muñoz 10-68 y General Torres, Cuenca; tel. (7) 283-1745; fax (7) 284-2722; e-mail edibosco@bosco.org.ec; internet www.lns.com.ec; f. 1920; Gen. Man. P. EDUARDO SANDOVAL; Deputy Man. FANNY FAJARDO Z.

Editorial El Conejo: 6 de Diciembre 2309 y La Niña, Quito; tel. (2) 222-7948; fax (2) 250-1066; e-mail econejo@attglobal.net; internet www.editorialelconejo.com; f. 1979; non-profit publr of educational and literary texts; Dir ABDÓN UBIDIA.

Editorial Edinacho SA: Bartolomé Sánchez Lote 6 y Calle C Lotización Muñoz Carvajal, Carcelén, 5932, Quito; tel. (2) 247-0429; fax (2) 247-0430; e-mail edinacho@ecnet.ec; f. 1985; Man. GERMÁN SEGURA; Editor Dr DALIA MARÍA NOBOA.

Eguez-Pérez en Nombre Colectivo/Abrapalabra Editores: América 5378, Casilla 464A, Quito; tel. and fax (2) 254-4178; f. 1990; drama, education, fiction, literature, science fiction, social sciences; Man. IVAN EGUEZ.

Grupo Bueno Editores, SA: Selva Alegre 5-287 y la Isla, Quito; tel. (2) 320-0200; fax (2) 320-2177; e-mail buenoeditores@yahoo.com; internet www.grupoedibueno.com; f. 1981; Pres. SEGUNDO BUENO QUICHIMBO; Gen. Man. DIANA BUENO MEJÍA.

Libresa SA: Murgeon 364 y Ulloa, Quito; tel. (2) 223-0925; fax (2) 250-2992; e-mail info@libresa.com; internet www.libresa.com; f. 1979; education, literature, philosophy; Pres. FAUSTO COBA ESTRELLA; Man. JAIME PEÑA NOVOA.

Libros Técnicos Litesa Cía Ltda: Avda América 542, Casilla 456A, Quito; tel. (2) 252-8537; Man. MANUEL DEL CASTILLO.

Pontificia Universidad Católica del Ecuador, Centro de Publicaciones: Avda 12 de Octubre 1076 y Carrión, Apdo 17-01-2184, Quito; tel. (2) 252-9250; fax (2) 256-7117; e-mail puce@edu.ec; internet www.puce.edu.ec; f. 1974; literature, natural science, law, anthropology, sociology, politics, economics, theology, philosophy,

history, archaeology, linguistics, languages and business; Rector Dr JOSÉ RIBADENEIRA ESPINOSA; Dir Dr MARCO VINICIO RUEDA.

Trama Ediciones: Edif. Marinoar, planta baja, entre Catalina Aldaz y El Batán, Eloy Alfaro 34-85, Quito; tel. (2) 224-6315; fax (2) 224-6317; e-mail trama@trama.ec; internet www.trama.com.ec; f. 1977; architecture, design, art and tourism; Dir-Gen. ROLANDO MOYA TASQUER.

Universidad Central del Ecuador: Departamento de Publicaciones, Servicio de Almacén Universitario, Ciudad Universitaria, Avda América y Avda Pérez Guerrero, Apdo 3291, Quito; tel. (2) 222-6080; fax (2) 250-1207.

Universidad de Guayaquil: Departamento de Publicaciones, Biblioteca General 'Luis de Tola y Avilés', Apdo 09-01-3834, Guayaquil; tel. (4) 251-6296; f. 1930; general literature, history, philosophy, fiction; Man. Dir LEONOR VILLAO DE SANTANDER.

Broadcasting and Communications

TELECOMMUNICATIONS

Asociación Ecuatoriana de Radiodifusión (AER): Edif. Atlas, 8°, Of. 802, Calle Justino Cornejo con Francisco de Orellana, Guayaquil; tel. and fax (4) 229-1783; ind. asscn; Pres. Ing. ANTONIO GUERRERO ONESSA.

Consejo Nacional de Telecomunicaciones (CONATEL): Avda Diego de Almagro 31-95 y Alpallana, Casilla 17-07-9777, Quito; tel. (2) 294-7800; fax (2) 250-5119; e-mail comunicacion@conatel.gov.ec; internet www.conatel.gov.ec; Pres. JUAN CARLOS AVILÉS.

Secretaría Nacional de Telecomunicaciones: Avda Diego de Almagro 31-95 y Alpallana, Casilla 17-07-9777, Quito; tel. (2) 294-7800; fax (2) 290-1010; e-mail comunicacion@conatel.gov.ec; internet www.conatel.gov.ec/website/senatel/senatel.php; Secretario Nacional de Telecomunicaciones Dr ROQUE HERNÁNDEZ LUNA.

Superintendencia de Telecomunicaciones (SUPTEL): Edif. Olimpo, Avda 9 de Octubre 1645 y Berlín, Casilla 17-21-1797, Quito; tel. (2) 222-2448; fax (2) 256-6688; e-mail supertel@server.supertel.gov.ec; internet www.supertel.gov.ec; Superintendente de Telecomunicaciones (vacant).

Major Service Providers

Alegro PCS (Telecsa, SA): Edif. Vivaldi, Amazonas 3837 y Corea, Quito; tel. and fax (2) 299-0000; e-mail info@alegropcs.com; internet www.alegropcs.com; co-owned by Andinatel and Pacifictel; cellular telephone provider.

Andinatel: Edif. Zeta, Avda Amazonas y Veintimilla, Quito; tel. (2) 256-1004; fax (2) 256-2240; e-mail ventas@andinatel.com; internet www.andinatel.com; scheduled for privatization; Pres. GUILLERMO MOLINA; Exec. Pres. EDISON LEÓN PÉREZ (acting).

AT&T Ecuador: Avda República de El Salvador 34-4211, Of. 2C, Quito; internet www.att.com.

Ecutel (Ecuador Telecom): Edif. Plaza 2000, 2°, Avda Gen. Salazar y 12 de Octubre, Quito; tel. (2) 223-0093; fax (2) 224-0494; e-mail servicios@ecutel.net; internet www.ecutel.net.

Movistar Ecuador: Edif. BellSouth, Avda República y esq. La Pradera, Quito; tel. (2) 222-7700; internet www.movistar.com.ec; f. 1997; name changed from BellSouth Ecuador to above in 2005; owned by Telefónica Móviles, SA (Spain); mobile telephone services.

Pacifictel: Calle Panamá y Roca, Guayaquil; tel. (4) 230-8724; internet www.pacifictel.net; scheduled for privatization; Exec. Pres. (vacant).

Porta: Quito; e-mail callcenter@conecel.com; internet www.porta.net; f. 1993; mobile telecommunications provider; subsidiary of América Móvil group (Mexico).

BROADCASTING

Regulatory Authority

Consejo Nacional de Radiodifusión y Televisión (CONARTEL): Edif. Inglaterra, Amazonas 33275 e Inglaterra, Quito; tel. (2) 226-1000; fax (2) 292-1637; e-mail correo@conartel.gov.ec; internet www.conartel.gov.ec; Pres. Dr JORGE YUNDA MACHADO.

Radio

There are nearly 300 commercial stations, 10 cultural stations and 10 religious stations. The following are among the most important stations:

Radio Católica Nacional: Avda América 1830 y Mercadillo, Casilla 17-03-540, Quito; tel. (2) 254-1557; fax (2) 256-7309; e-mail buenanoticia@radiocatolica.org.ec; internet www.radiocatolica.org.ec; f. 1985; Dir-Gen. Dr RAMIRO ARROYO PONCE.

ECUADOR

Radio Centro: Avda República de El Salvador 836 y Portugal, Quito; tel. (2) 244-8900; fax (2) 250-4575; f. 1977; Pres. EDGAR YÁNEZ VILLALOBOS.

Radio Colón: Avellanas E5-107 y Avda Eloy Alfaro, Casilla 17-07-9927, Quito; tel. 248-4574; fax (2) 248-5666; e-mail escucha@radiocolon.ec; internet www.radiocolon.ec; f. 1934; Pres. Dr GERARDO CASTRO; Dir BERNARDO NUSSBAUM.

Radio CRE Satelital (CORTEL, SA): Edif. El Torreón, 9°, Avda Boyacá 642 y Padre Solano, Apdo 4144, Guayaquil; tel. (4) 256-4290; fax (4) 256-0386; e-mail cre@cre.com.ec; internet www.cre.com.ec; Pres. RAFAEL GUERRERO VALENZUELA.

Radio Latina: Quito; internet www.radiolatina.com.ec; f. 1990; Pres. JUAN CARLOS ISAÍAS.

Radio La Luna: Quito; internet www.radiolaluna.com; Owner PACO VELASCO.

Radio Quito: Avda 10 de Agosto 2441 y Colón, Casilla 17-21-1971, Quito; tel. (2) 250-8301; fax (2) 250-3311; e-mail radioquito@ecuadoradio.ec; internet www.elcomercio.com/radio_quito.html; f. 1940; owned by El Comercio newspaper.

Radio Sonorama (HCAEL): Avda Eloy Alfaro 5400 y Los Granados, Casilla 130B, Quito; tel. (2) 244-8403; fax (2) 244-5858; f. 1975; Pres. SANTIAGO PROAÑO.

Radio Sucre: Joaquín Orrantia y Miguel H. Alcivar (Casa de las Américas Kennedy Norte), Guayaquil; tel. (4) 268-0588; fax (4) 268-0592; e-mail info@radiosucretv.com; internet www.radiosucre.com.ec; f. 1983; Pres. VICENTE ARROBA DITTO; Dir YOTTI DANIEL GUERRA ÁVILA.

La Voz de los Andes (HCJB): Villalengua 884 y Avda 10 de Agosto, Casilla 17-17-691, Quito; tel. (2) 226-6808; fax (2) 226-7263; e-mail tdltorre@hcjb.org.ec; internet www.vozandes.org; f. 1931; operated by World Radio Missionary Fellowship; programmes in 11 languages (including Spanish and English) and 22 Quechua dialects; Evangelical; Int. Dir Radio CURT COLE; Gen. Man. JOHN E. BECK.

Television

Cadena Ecuatoriana de Televisión—TC Televisión Canal 10: Avda de las Américas, frente al Aeropuerto, Casilla 09-01-673, Guayaquil; tel. (4) 239-7664; fax (4) 228-7544; f. 1969; commercial; Pres. ROBERTO ISAÍAS; Gen. Man. JORGE KRONFLE.

Corporación Ecuatoriana de Televisión—Ecuavisa Canal 2: Cerro El Carmen, Casilla 1239, Guayaquil; tel. (4) 230-0150; fax (4) 230-3677; f. 1967; Pres. XAVIER ALVARADO ROCA; Gen. Man. FRANCISCO AROSEMENA ROBLES.

Teleamazonas Cratel, CA: Granda Centeno Oeste 429 y Brasil, Casilla 17-11-04844, Quito; tel. (2) 397-4444; fax (4) 244-1620; e-mail guerrero@teleamazonas.com; internet www.teleamazonas.com; f. 1974; commercial; Gen. Man. SEBASTIÁN CORRAL.

Teleandina Canal 23: Avda de la Prensa 3920 y Fernández Salvador, Quito; tel. (2) 259-9403; fax (2) 259-2600; f. 1991; Pres. HUMBERTO ORTIZ FLORES; Dir PATRICIO AVILES.

Televisión del Pacífico, SA—Gamavisión: Avda Eloy Alfaro 5400 y Río Coca, Quito; tel. (2) 226-2222; fax (2) 226-2284; e-mail gerenciageneral@gamavision.com; internet www.gamavision.com; f. 1978; Pres. and Gen. Man. NICOLÁS VEGA.

Televisora Nacional—Ecuavisa Canal 8: Bosmediano 447 y José Carbo, Bellavista, Quito; tel. (2) 244-6472; fax (2) 244-5488; commercial; f. 1970; Pres. PATRICIO JARAMILLO.

Finance

(cap. = capital; res = reserves; dep. = deposits; m. = million; brs = branches; amounts in US dollars unless otherwise indicated)

SUPERVISORY AUTHORITIES

Junta Monetaria Nacional (National Monetary Board): Quito; tel. (2) 251-4833; fax (2) 257-0258; f. 1927; Pres. JAIME ACOSTA VELASCO.

Superintendencia de Bancos y Seguros: Avda 12 de Octubre 1561 y Madrid, Casilla 17-17-770, Quito; tel. (2) 255-4225; fax (2) 250-6812; e-mail alejo@e-mail.superban.gov.ec; internet www.superban.gov.ec; f. 1927; supervises national banking system, including state and private banks and other financial institutions; Supt Dr ALFREDO VERGARA RECALDE.

BANKING

Central Bank

Banco Central del Ecuador: Avda Amazonas y Atahualpa, Casilla 339, Quito; tel. (2) 257-2522; fax (2) 257-2526; internet www.bce.fin.ec; f. 1927; cap. 2.5m., res 1,616.1m., dep. 2,918.1m. (Dec. 2006); Pres. EDUARDO CABEZAS MOLINA; Gen. Man. MAURICIO PAREJA CANELOS; 2 brs.

Other State Banks

Banco Ecuatoriano de la Vivienda: Avda 10 de Agosto 2270 y Cordero, Casilla 3244, Quito; tel. (2) 252-1311; f. 1962; Pres. Abog. JUAN PABLO MONCAGATTA; Gen. Man. Dr PATRICIO CEVALLOS MORÁN.

Banco del Estado (BDE): Avda Atahualpa 628 y 10 de Agosto, Casilla 17-01-00373, Quito; tel. (2) 225-0800; fax (2) 225-0320; f. 1979; Pres. LEONARDO VICUÑA.

Banco Nacional de Fomento: Ante 107 y 10 de Agosto, Casilla 685, Quito; tel. (2) 294-6500; internet www.bnf.fin.ec; f. 1928; Pres. JUAN BAUTISTA PIANA BRUNO; 70 brs.

Corporación Financiera Nacional (CFN): Avda Juan León Mera 130 y Patria, Casilla 17-21-01924, Quito; tel. (2) 256-4900; fax (2) 222-3823; e-mail mbenitez@q.cfn.fin.ec; internet www.cfn.fin.ec; state-owned bank providing export credits, etc.; f. 1964; Gen. Man. IVAN TOBAR CORDERO.

Commercial Banks

Quito

Banco Amazonas, SA: Avda Amazonas 4430 y Villalengua, Casilla 121, Quito; tel. (2) 226-0400; fax (2) 225-5123; e-mail basacomp@porta.net; internet www.bancoamazonas.com; f. 1976; cap. 9.6m., res 0.4m., dep. 122.6m. (Dec. 2006); affiliated to Banque Paribas; Pres. RAFAEL FERRETTI BENÍTEZ; Vice-Pres. ROBERTO SEMINARIO.

Banco Caja de Crédito Agrícola Ganadero, SA: Avda 6 de Diciembre 225 y Piedrahita, Quito; tel. (2) 252-8521; f. 1949; Man. HUGO GRIJALVA GARZÓN; Pres. NICOLÁS GUILLÉN.

Banco Consolidado del Ecuador: Avda Patria 740 y 9 de Octubre, Casilla 9150, Suc. 7, Quito; tel. (2) 256-0369; fax (2) 256-0719; f. 1981; cap. 2,874m., res 4,338m., dep. 5,545m. sucres (Oct. 1998); Chair. JAIME GILINSKI; Gen. Man. ANTONIO COY; 2 brs.

Banco General Rumiñahui: Avda República 720 y Eloy Alfaro, Quito; tel. (2) 250-9929; fax (2) 256-3786; e-mail bcainstitucional@bgr.com.ec; internet www.bgr.com.ec; total assets 192.0m. (Dec. 2004); Gen. Man. Gen. GUSTAVO HERRERA.

Banco Internacional, SA: Avda Patria E-421 y 9 de Octubre, Casilla 17-01-2114, Quito; tel. (2) 256-5547; fax (2) 256-5758; e-mail cromero@bancointernacional.com.ec; internet www.bancointernacional.com.ec; f. 1973; cap. 8,600m. (Dec. 2000); Pres. JOSÉ ENRIQUE FUSTER CAMPS; Gen. Man. RAÚL GUERRERO ANDRADE; 58 brs.

Banco del Pichincha, CA: Avda Amazonas 4560 y Pereira, Casilla 261, Quito; tel. (2) 298-0980; fax (2) 298-1226; internet www.pichincha.com; f. 1906; cap. 111.0m., res 71.0m., dep. 3,033.2m. (Dec. 2005); 61.82% owned by Exec. Pres. and Chair.; Exec. Pres. and Chair. Dr FIDEL EGAS GRIJALVA; Gen. Man. FERNANDO POZO CRESPO; 218 brs.

Produbanco: Avda Amazonas 3775 y Japón, Casilla 17-03-38-A, Quito; tel. (2) 299-9000; fax (2) 244-7319; internet www.produbanco.com; f. 1978 as Banco de la Producción; name changed as above in 1996; cap. 60m., res 11.38m., dep. 542.36m. (Dec. 2004); part of Grupo Financiero Producción; Pres. ABELARDO PACHANO BERTERO; Dir RODRIGO PAZ DELGADO; 55 brs.

UniBanco: Avda República 500 y Pasaje Carrión, Edif. Pucara, 1°, Quito; tel. (2) 290-7576; fax (2) 222-5000; f. 1964 as Banco de la Producción; name changed as above in 1995; Pres. SALVADOR PEDRERO; Treas. JUAN FERNANDO BERMEO.

Cuenca

Banco del Austro: Sucre y Borrero (esq.), Casilla 01-01-0167, Cuenca; tel. (7) 831-646; fax (7) 832-633; internet www.bancodelaustro.com; f. 1977; total assets 249.8m. (Sept. 2004); Pres. JUAN ELJURI ANTÓN; Gen. Man. PATRICIO ROBAYO IDROVO; 19 brs.

Guayaquil

Banco Bolivariano, CA: Junín 200 y Panamá, Casilla 09-01-10184, Guayaquil; tel. (4) 230-5000; fax (4) 256-6707; e-mail info@bolivariano.com; internet www.bolivariano.com; f. 1978; cap. 50.0m., res 10.3m., dep. 739.9m. (Dec. 2006); 61.2% owned by Tabos Investment, SA; Chair. JOSÉ SALAZAR BARRAGÁN; Pres. and CEO MIGUEL BABRA LEÓN; 53 brs.

Banco del Pacífico: Francisco de P. Ycaza 200, Casilla 09-01-988, Guayaquil; tel. (4) 256-6010; fax (4) 232-8333; e-mail webadmin@pacifico.fin.ec; internet www.bp.fin.ec; f. 2000 by merger of Banco del Pacífico and Banco Continental; cap. 80.0m., res 4.5m., dep. 680.1m. (Dec. 2004); Exec. Pres. FÉLIX HERRERO BACHMEIER; 227 brs.

Banco Industrial y Comercial—Baninco: Pichincha 335 e Illingworth, Casilla 5817, Guayaquil; tel. (4) 232-3488; f. 1965; Pres. Ing. CARLOS MANZUR PERES; Gen. Man. GABRIEL MARTÍNEZ INTRIAGO; 2 brs.

Banco Territorial, SA: Panamá 814 y V. M. Rendón, Casilla 09-01-227, Guayaquil; tel. and fax (4) 256-6695; f. 1886; Pres. ROBERTO GOLDBAUM; Gen. Man. Ing. GUSTAVO HEINERT.

ECUADOR   *Directory*

Loja

Banco de Loja: esq. Bolívar y Rocafuerte, Casilla 11-01-300, Loja; tel. (4) 757-1682; fax (4) 753-3019; internet www.bancodeloja.fin.ec; f. 1968; cap. 10,000m., res 4,207m., dep. 70,900m. sucres (Dec. 1996); Pres. Ing. STEVE BROWN HIDALGO; Man. Ing. LEONARDO BURNEO MULLER.

Machala

Banco de Machala, SA: Avda 9 de Mayo y Rocafuerte, Casilla 711, Machala; tel. (4) 256-6800; fax (4) 292-2744; internet www.bmachala.com; f. 1962; cap. 19.5m., res 3.5m., dep. 238.1m. (Dec. 2006); Pres. Dr ESTEBAN QUIROLA FIGUEROA; Exec. Pres. and Gen. Man. Dr MARIO CANESSA ONETO; 2 brs.

Portoviejo

Banco Comercial de Manabí, SA: Avda 10 de Agosto 600 y 18 de Octubre, Portoviejo; tel. (4) 265-3888; fax (4) 263-5527; f. 1980; Pres. Dr RUBÉN DARÍO MORALES; Gen. Man. ARISTO ANDRADE DÍAZ.

'Multibanco'

Banco de Guayaquil, SA: Plaza Ycaza 105 y Pichincha, Casilla 09-01-1300, Guayaquil; tel. (4) 251-7100; fax (4) 251-4406; e-mail servicios@bankguay.com; internet www.bancoguayaquil.com; f. 1923; absorbed the finance corpn FINANSUR in 1990 to become Ecuador's first 'multibanco', carrying out commercial and financial activities; cap. 145,000m., dep. 3,198,862m. sucres (Dec. 1998); Pres. DANILO CARRERA DROUET; Exec. Pres. GUILLERMO LASSO MENDOZA; 50 brs.

Associations

Asociación de Bancos Privados del Ecuador: Edif. Delta 890, 7°, Avda República de El Salvador y Suecia, Casilla 17-11-6708, Quito; tel. (2) 246-6670; fax (2) 246-6702; e-mail echiribo@asobancos.org.ec; internet www.asobancos.org.ec; f. 1965; 36 mems; Pres. ANGELO CAPUTI; Exec. Pres. CÉSAR ROBALINO GONZAGA.

Asociación de Compañías Financieras del Ecuador (AFIN): Robles 653 y Amazonas, 13°, Of. 1310-11, Casilla 17-07-9156, Quito; tel. (2) 255-0623; fax (2) 256-7912; Pres. Ing. FRANCISCO ORTEGA.

STOCK EXCHANGES

Bolsa de Valores de Guayaquil: 9 de Octubre 110 y Pichincha, Guayaquil; tel. (4) 256-1519; fax (4) 256-1871; e-mail mmurillo@bvg.fin.ec; internet www.mundobvg.com; Pres. RODOLFO KRONFLE AKEL; Dir-Gen. ENRIQUE AROSEMENA BAQUERIZO.

Bolsa de Valores de Quito: Edif. Londres, 8°, Avda Amazonas 21–252 y Carrión, Casilla 17-01-3772, Quito; tel. (2) 222-1333; fax (2) 250-0942; e-mail informacion@bolsadequito.com; internet www.bolsadequito.com; f. 1969; Chair. PATRICIO PEÑA ROMERO; Exec. Pres. MÓNICA VILLAGÓMEZ DE ANDERSON.

INSURANCE

Instituto Ecuatoriano de Seguridad Social: Avda 10 de Agosto y Bogotá, Apdo 2640, Quito; tel. (2) 254-7400; fax (2) 250-4572; internet www.iess.gov.ec; f. 1928; various forms of state insurance provided; directs the Ecuadorean social insurance system; provides social benefits and medical service; Pres. Dr RAÚL ZAPATER HIDALGO.

Principal Companies

Ace Seguros, SA: Edif. Antisana, 4°, Avdas Amazonas 3655 y Juan Pablo Sanz, Quito; tel. (2) 292-0555; fax (2) 244-5817; e-mail serviciocliente@ace-ina.com; internet www.acelatinamerica.com; Exec. Pres. IGNACIO BORJA NOBOA.

AIG Metropolitana Cía de Seguros y Reaseguros, SA: Avda Brasil 293 y Antonio Granda Centeno, 5°, Quito; tel. (2) 292-4425; fax (2) 292-4434; e-mail ask.aiu@aig.com; internet www.aigworldsource.com; part of American International Group, Inc (USA); Exec. Pres. DIANA PINILLA ROJAS.

Alianza Cía de Seguros y Reaseguros, SA: Avdas 12 de Octubre 1795 y Baquerizo Moreno, Apdo 17-17-041, Quito; tel. (2) 256-6143; fax (2) 256-4059; e-mail alianzauio@segurosalianza.com; internet www.segurosalianza.com; f. 1982; Gen. Man. CARLOS ROMERO ROMERO.

Atlas Cía de Seguros, SA: Edif. Torre Atlas, 11°, Kennedy Norte, Justino Cornejo y Avda Luis Orrantia, Guayaquil; tel. (4) 269-0430; fax (4) 228-3099; e-mail seguros@atlas.com.ec; internet www.atlas.com.ec; f. 1984; Pres. MARCO PINO PALACIOS; Gen. Man. MARKUS FREY KELLER.

Bolívar Cía de Seguros del Ecuador, SA: Edif. Las Cámaras, 11° y 12°, Avda Francisco de Orellana, Guayaquil; tel. (2) 268-1777; fax (2) 268-3363; e-mail ssanmiguel@seguros-bolivar.com; internet www.seguros-bolivar.com; f. 1957; Pres. FABIÁN ORTEGA TRUJILLO.

Cía Reaseguradora del Ecuador, SA: Edif. Intercambios, 1°, Junín 105 y Malecón Simón Bolívar, Casilla 09-01-6776, Guayaquil; tel. (4) 256-4461; fax (4) 256-4454; e-mail oespinoz@ecuare.fin.ec; f. 1977; Man. Dir Ing. OMAR ESPINOSA ROMERO.

Cía de Seguros Cóndor, SA: Plaza Ycaza 302, Apdo 09-01-5007, Guayaquil; tel. (4) 256-5300; fax (4) 256-0144; e-mail asalame@bonita.com; internet www.seguroscondor.com; f. 1966; Gen. Man. AUGUSTO SALAME ARZUBIAGA.

Cía de Seguros EcuatorianoSuiza, SA: Avda 9 de Octubre 2101 y Tulcán, Apdo 09-01-0937, Guayaquil; tel. (4) 245-2444; fax (4) 245-2971; e-mail veronica.mackliff@ecuasuiza.com; internet www.ecuasuiza.com; f. 1954; Pres. JOSÉ SALAZAR BARRAGÁN; Gen. Man. LUIS FERNANDO SALAS RUBIO.

Cía Seguros Unidos, SA: Edif. Metrocar, 2°, 10 de Agosto y Avda Mariana de Jesús, Quito; tel. (2) 252-6466; fax (2) 245-0920; internet www.sunidos.fin.ec; Gen. Man. JUAN RIVAS DOMENECH.

Nacional Cía de Seguros, SA: Panamá 809 y Rendón, Guayaquil; tel. (4) 456-0700; fax (4) 456-6327; f. 1940; Gen. Man. BRUNO ORLANDINI.

Panamericana del Ecuador, SA: Calle Portugal E-12-72 y Avda Eloy Alfaro, Quito; tel. (2) 246-8840; fax (2) 246-9650; e-mail larango@panamericana.com.ec; internet www.panamericana.com.ec; f. 1973; Pres. PATRICIO ALVAREZ PLAZA; Gen. Man. LUIS FELIPE ARANGO PARDO.

Seguros Rocafuerte, SA: Edif. Filanbanco, 15°, Plaza Carbo 505 y 9 de Octubre, Apdo 09-04-6491, Guayaquil; tel. (4) 232-6125; fax (4) 232-9353; e-mail segroca@gye.satnet.net; internet www2.tvcable.com.ec; f. 1967; life and medical; Exec. Pres. Ing. NORMAN PICHARDO VAN DER DIJS.

Seguros Sucre, SA: Edif. San Francisco 300, 6°, Pedro Carbo 422 y Avda 9 de Octubre, Apdo 09-01-480, Guayaquil; tel. (4) 256-3399; fax (4) 231-4163; e-mail epena@segurossucre.fin.ec; internet www.bp.fin.ec; f. 1944; Gen. Man. EDUARDO PEÑA TRIVIÑO.

La Unión Cía Nacional de Seguros: Urb. Los Cedros, Km 5 $\frac{1}{2}$, Vía a la Costa, Apdo 09-01-1294, Guayaquil; tel. (4) 285-1500; fax (4) 285-1700; e-mail rgoldbaum@seguroslaunion.com; internet www.seguroslaunion.com; f. 1943; Exec. Pres. ROBERTO GOLDBAUM; Gen. Man. CARLOS EDUARDO ESPINOSA COVELLI.

Trade and Industry

GOVERNMENT AGENCIES

Consejo Nacional de Modernización del Estado (CONAM): Edif. CFN, 10°, Avda Juan León Mera 130 y Patria, Quito; tel. (2) 250-9432; fax (2) 222-8450; e-mail info@conam.gov.ec; internet www.conam.gov.ec; f. 1994; responsible for overseeing privatizations; Pres. CARLOS VEGA.

Consejo Nacional para la Reactivación de la Producción y la Competitividad (CNPC): Edif. Plaza 2000, Torre B, 1°, Esq. Avda 12 de Octubre 24-593 y Francisco Salazar, Quito; tel. (2) 255-4840; e-mail info@cnpc.gov.ec; internet www.cnpc.gov.ec; promotes competitiveness of Ecuadorean businesses; Exec. Dir VERÓNOCA SIÓN DE JOSSE.

Empresa de Comercio Exterior (ECE): Quito; f. 1980 to promote non-traditional exports; state owns 33% share in co; share capital 25m. sucres.

Fondo de Promoción de Exportaciones (FOPEX): Juan León Mera 130 y Patria, Casilla 163, Quito; tel. (2) 256-4900; fax (2) 256-2519; f. 1972; export promotion; Dir ELIANA SANTAMARÍA M.

Fondo de Solidaridad: Avda 6 de Diciembre 25–75 y Colón, Edif. Partenón, Quito; tel. (2) 220-0429; internet www.fondodesolidaridad.gov.ec; f. 1996; govt devt agency; responsibility for overseeing privatization of electricity sector; Pres. JORGE BURBANO.

Instituto Ecuatoriano de Reforma Agraria y Colonización (IERAC): f. 1973 to supervise the Agrarian Reform Law under the auspices and co-ordination of the Ministry of Agriculture and Fisheries; Dir LUIS LUNA GAYBOR.

Superintendencia de Compañías del Ecuador: Roca 660 y Amazonas, Casilla 687, Quito; tel. (2) 254-1606; fax (2) 256-6685; e-mail superintcias@q.supercias.gov.ec; internet www.supercias.gov.ec; f. 1964; responsible for the legal and accounting control of commercial enterprises; Supt GONZALO FABIÁN ALBUJA CHAVES; Sec.-Gen. VÍCTOR CEVALLOS VÁSQUEZ.

DEVELOPMENT ORGANIZATIONS

Centro Nacional de Promoción de la Pequeña Industria y Artesanía (CENAPIA): Quito; agency to develop small-scale industry and handicrafts; Dir EDGAR GUEVARA (acting).

Centro de Reconversión Económica del Azuay, Cañar y Morona Santiago (CREA): Avda México entre Unidad Nacional

ECUADOR
Directory

y las Américas, Casilla 01-01-1953, Cuenca; tel. (7) 281-7500; fax (7) 281-7134; f. 1959; devt org.; Dir Dr JUAN TAMA.

Consejo Nacional de Desarrollo (CONADE): Juan Larrea y Arenas, Quito; fmrly Junta Nacional de Planificación y Coordinación Económica; aims to formulate a general plan of economic and social devt and supervise its execution; also to integrate local plans into the national; Chair. GALO ABRIL OJEDA; Sec. PABLO LUCIO PAREDES.

Fondo de Desarrollo del Sector Rural Marginal (FODERUMA): f. 1978; allots funds to rural devt programmes in poor areas.

Fondo Nacional de Desarrollo (FONADE): f. 1973; national devt fund.

Instituto de Colonización de la Región Amazónica (INCREA): f. 1978; encourages settlement in and economic devt of the Amazon region; Dir Dr DIMAS GUZMÁN.

Instituto Ecuatoriano de Recursos Hidráulicos (INERHI): undertakes irrigation and hydroelectric projects; Man. Ing. EDUARDO GARCÍA GARCÍA.

Organización Comercial Ecuatoriana de Productos Artesanales (OCEPA): Carrión 1236 y Versalles, Casilla 17-01-2948, Quito; tel. (2) 254-1992; fax (2) 256-5961; f. 1964; develops and promotes handicrafts; Gen. Man. MARCELO RODRÍGUEZ.

Programa Nacional del Banano y Frutas Tropicales: Guayaquil; promotes the devt of banana and tropical-fruit cultivation; Dir Ing. JORGE GIL CHANG.

Programa Regional de Desarrollo del Sur del Ecuador (PREDESUR): Pasaje María Eufrasia 100 y Mosquera Narváez, Quito; tel. (2) 254-4415; f. 1972; promotes the devt of the southern area of the country; Dir Ing. LUIS HERNÁN EGUIGUREN CARRIÓN.

CHAMBERS OF COMMERCE AND INDUSTRY

Cámara de Comercio de Ambato: Montalvo 630, Ambato; tel. and fax (3) 284-1906; e-mail camcomam@uio.satnet.net; Pres. PABLO VÁSCONEZ.

Cámara de Comercio de Cuenca: Avda Federico Malo 1-90, 2°, Casilla 4929, Cuenca; tel. (7) 282-7531; fax (7) 283-3891; e-mail cccuenca@etapa.com.ec; internet www.cccuenca.com; f. 1919; 5,329 mems; Pres. JUAN PABLO VINTIMILLA.

Cámara de Comercio Ecuatoriano-Americana (Amcham Quito-Ecuador): Quito; tel. (2) 250-7450; fax (2) 250-4571; e-mail info@ecamcham.com; internet www.ecamcham.com; f. 1974; promotes bilateral trade and investment between Ecuador and the USA; brs in Ambato, Cuenca and Manta; Pres. MAURICIO ROBALINO; Vice-Pres. ALBERTO SANDOVAL.

Cámara de Comercio Ecuatoriano Canadiense (Ecuadorean-Canadian Chamber of Commerce): Quito; internet www.ecucanchamber.org; Exec. Dir PATRICIA BUSTAMANTE; Pres. JANIO SÁNCHEZ.

Cámara de Comercio de Guayaquil: Avda Francisco de Orellana y V. H. Sicouret, Centro Empresarial 'Las Cámaras', 2° y 3°, Guayaquil; tel. (4) 268-2771; fax (4) 268-2766; e-mail info@lacamara.org; internet www.lacamara.org; f. 1889; 31,000 affiliates; Pres. EDUARDO MARURI MIRANDA.

Cámara de Comercio de Machala: Edif. Cámara de Comercio, 2°, Rocafuerte y Buenavista, CP 825, Machala, Cuenca; tel. (7) 293-0640; fax (7) 293-4454; e-mail ccomach@ecua.net.ec; Pres. JOSÉ MENDIETA E.

Cámara de Comercio de Manta: Edif. Banco del Pichincha, 1°, Avda 2, entre Calles 10 y 11, Manta; tel. and fax (5) 262-1306; e-mail cacoma@manta.telconet.net; Pres. MARIANO ZAMBRANO S.

Cámara de Comercio de Quito: Edif. Las Cámaras, 6°, Avda República y Amazonas, 6°, Casilla 17-01-202, Quito; tel. (2) 244-3787; fax (2) 243-5862; e-mail ccq@ccq.org.ec; internet www.ccq.org.ec; f. 1906; 12,000 mems; Pres. BLASCO PEÑAHERRERA SOLAH; Exec. Dir GUIDO TOLEDO ANDRADE.

Cámara de Industrias de Cuenca: Edif. Cámara de Industrias de Cuenca, 12° y 13°, Avda Florencia Astudillo y Alfonso Cordero, Cuenca; tel. (7) 284-5053; fax (7) 284-0107; internet www.industriascuenca.org.ec; f. 1936; Pres. Ing. MARCEJO JARAMILLO CRESPO.

Cámara de Industrias de Guayaquil: Avda Francisco de Orellana y M. Alcívar, Casilla 09-01-4007, Guayaquil; tel. (4) 268-2618; fax (4) 268-2680; e-mail caindgye@cig.org.ec; internet www.cig.ec; f. 1936; Pres. ALBERTO DASSUM A.

Federación Nacional de Cámaras de Comercio del Ecuador: Avda Olmedo 414 y Boyacá, Guayaquil; tel. (4) 232-3130; fax (4) 232-3478; Pres. BLASCO PEÑAHERRERA SOLAH; Exec. Vice-Pres. Dr ROBERTO ILLINGWORTH.

Federación Nacional de Cámaras de Industrias: Avda República y Amazonas, 10°, Casilla 2438, Quito; tel. (2) 245-2994; fax (2) 244-8118; e-mail camara@camindustriales.org.ec; internet www.camindustriales.org.ec; f. 1974; Pres. Ing. GUSTAVO PINTO.

INDUSTRIAL AND TRADE ASSOCIATIONS

Asociación de la Industria Hidrocarburífera del Ecuador (AIHE): Edif. Puerta del Sol, 8°, Avda Amazonas 37-102, Quito; tel. (2) 226-1270; fax (2) 226-1272; e-mail infoil@aihe.org.ec; internet www.aihe.org.ec; f. 1997 as Asociación de Compañías Petroleras de Exploración y Explotación de Hidrocarburos del Ecuador (ASOPEC); name changed as above in 2002; asscn of 24 int. and domestic hydrocarbon cos; Pres. RENÉ ORTIZ.

Centro de Desarrollo Industrial del Ecuador (CENDES): Apdo 2845, Guayaquil; tel. (4) 198-9432; f. 1962; carries out industrial feasibility studies, supplies technical and administrative assistance to industry, promotes new industries, supervises investment programmes; Gen. Man. CLAUDIO CREAMER GUILLÉN.

Corporación de Desarrollo e Investigación Geológico-Minero-Metalúrgica (CODIGEM): Avda 10 de Agosto 5844 y Pereira, Casilla 17-03-23, Quito; tel. (2) 225-4673; fax (2) 225-4674; e-mail prodemi2@prodeminca.org.ec; f. 1991 to direct mining exploration and exploitation; Exec. Pres. Ing. JORGE BARRAGÁN G.

Corporación de Promoción de Exportaciones e Inversiones (CORPEI): Edif. Centro Empresarial Las Cámaras, Avda Francisco de Orellana y Miguel H. Alcívar, 2°, Guayaquil; tel. (4) 268-1550; fax (4) 268-1551; e-mail aissa@corpei.org.ec; internet www.corpei.org.ec; f. 1997 to promote exports and investment; CEO RICARDO E. ESTRADA.

Fondo Nacional de Preinversión (FONAPRE): Jorge Washington 624 y Amazonas, Casilla 17-01-3302, Quito; tel. (2) 256-3261; f. 1973 to undertake feasibility projects before investment; Pres. LUIS PARODÍ VALVERDE; Gen. Man. Ing. EDUARDO MOLINA GRAZZIANI.

EMPLOYERS' ORGANIZATIONS

Asociación de Atuneros: Malecón s/n, Muelle Portuario de Manta 1, Manta; tel. and fax (5) 262-6467; e-mail atunec@manta.ecua.net.ec; asscn of tuna producers; Pres. LUCÍA FERNÁNDEZ DE GENNA.

Asociación de Cafecultores del Cantón Piñas: García Moreno y Abdón Calderón, Quito; coffee growers' asscn.

Asociación de Comerciantes e Industriales: Avda Boyacá 1416, Guayaquil; traders' and industrialists' asscn.

Asociación de Compañías Consultoras del Ecuador: Edif. Delta 890, 4°, República de El Salvador y Suecia, Quito; tel. (2) 246-5048; fax (2) 245-1171; e-mail acce@acce.com.ec; internet www.consultoresecuador.com; asscn of consulting cos; Pres. RODOLFO RENDÓN.

Asociación de Industriales Gráficos de Pichincha: Edif. de las Cámaras, 8°, Amazonas y República, Quito; tel. (2) 292-3141; fax (2) 245-6664; e-mail aigquito@aig.org.ec; internet www.aig.org.ec; asscn of the graphic industry; Pres. ENRIQUE CORTEZ.

Asociación Ecuatoriana de Industriales de la Madera: Edif. de las Cámaras, 7°, República y Amazonas, Quito; tel. (2) 226-0980; fax (2) 243-9560; e-mail secre@aima.org.ec; internet www.aima.org.ec; wood mfrs' asscn; Pres. CÉSAR ALVAREZ.

Asociación de Industriales Textiles del Ecuador (AITE): Edif. Las Cámaras, 8°, Avda República y Amazonas, Casilla 2893, Quito; tel. (2) 229-4434; fax (2) 244-5159; e-mail aite@aite.org.ec; internet www.aite.com.ec; f. 1938; textile mfrs' asscn; 40 mems; Pres. FERNANDO PÉREZ.

Asociación de Productores Bananeros del Ecuador (APROBANA): Guayaquil; banana growers' asscn; Pres. NICOLÁS CASTRO.

Asociación Nacional de Empresarios (ANDE): Edif. España, 6°, Of. 67, Avda Amazonas 25–23 y Colón, Casilla 17-01-3489, Quito; tel. (2) 223-8507; fax (2) 250-9806; e-mail ande@uio.satnet.net; internet www.ande.org.ec; national employers' asscn; Pres. PEDRO VILLAMAR; Vice-Pres. ERNESTO RIBADENEIRA TROYA.

Asociación Nacional de Exportadores de Cacao y Café (ANECAFE): Casilla 4774, Manta; tel. (2) 229-2782; fax (2) 229-2885; e-mail anacafe@uio.satnet.net; cocoa and coffee exporters' asscn.

Asociación Nacional de Exportadores de Camarones: Pres. LUIS VILLACÍS.

Asociación Nacional de Molineros: 6 de Diciembre 3470 e Ignacio Bossano, Quito; tel. (2) 246-5597; fax (2) 246-4754; Exec. Dir RAFAEL CALLEJAS.

Cámara de Agricultura: Casilla 17-21-322, Quito; tel. (2) 223-0195; Pres. ALBERTO ENRÍQUEZ PORTILLA.

Consorcio Ecuatoriano de Exportadores de Cacao y Café: cocoa and coffee exporters' consortium.

Corporación Nacional de Exportadores de Cacao y Café: Guayaquil; cocoa and coffee exporters' corporation.

ECUADOR

Federación Nacional de Cooperativas Cafetaleras del Ecuador (FENACAFE): Jipijapa; tel. (4) 260-0631; e-mail orgcafex@mnb.satnet.net; coffee co-operatives' fed.

Unión Nacional de Periodistas: Joaquín Auxe Iñaquito, Quito; national press assen.

There are several other coffee and cocoa organizations.

STATE HYDROCARBON COMPANY

PETROECUADOR (Empresa Estatal Petróleos del Ecuador): Alpallana E-8-86 y Avda 6 de Diciembre, Casilla 17-11-5007, Quito; tel. (2) 256-3060; fax (2) 250-3571; e-mail rin@petroecuador.com.ec; internet www.petroecuador.com.ec; f. 1989; state petroleum co; Exec. Pres. FERNANDO ZURITA FABRE.

Operaciones Río Napo, SA: Quito; f. 2006 by PETROECUADOR to manage oilfields previously run by Occidental (USA).

UTILITIES

Regulatory Authorities

Ministry of Energy and Mines: see section on The Government (Ministries).

Centro Nacional de Control de Energía (CENACE): Panamericana Sur Km 17.5, Sector Santa Rosa de Cutuglagua, Casilla 17-21-1991, Quito; tel. (2) 299-2030; fax (2) 299-2031; e-mail garguello@cenace.org.ec; f. 1999; co-ordinates and oversees national energy system; Exec. Dir GABRIEL ARGÜELLO RÍOS.

Comisión Ecuatoriana de Energía Atómica: Juan Larrea 15-36 y Riofrío, Casilla 17-01-2517, Quito; tel. (2) 254-5861; fax (2) 256-3336; e-mail comecen1@comecenat.gov.ec; atomic energy commission; Exec. Dir CELIANO ALMEIDA; Head of Information HIPSY CIFUENTES.

Consejo Nacional de Electricidad (CONELEC): Avda Amazonas 33-299 e Inglaterra, Quito; tel. (2) 226-8746; fax (2) 226-8737; e-mail conelec@conelec.gov.ec; internet www.conelec.gov.ec; f. 1999; supervises electricity industry following transfer of assets of the former Instituto Ecuatoriano de Electrificación (INECEL) to the Fondo de Solidaridad; pending privatization as six generating companies, one transmission company and 19 distribution companies; Pres. ALECKSEY MOSQUERS RODRÍGUEZ.

Directorate of Renewable Energy and Energy Efficiency (Ministry of Energy and Mines): J. L. Mera y Orellana, Edif. MOP, 6°, Quito; tel. and fax (2) 255-0018; e-mail jvasconez@menergia.gov.ec; internet www.menergia.gov.ec; f. 1995; research and devt of new and renewable energy sources; Dir Ing. JOSÉ VASCONEZ E.

Directorate-General of Hydrocarbons: Avda 10 de Agosto 321, Quito; supervision of the enforcement of laws regarding the exploration and devt of petroleum.

Electricity

Corporación Eléctrica de Guayaquil, SA: Urb. La Garzota, Sector 3, Manzana 47; tel. (4) 224-8006; fax (4) 224-8040; major producer and distributor of electricity, mostly using oil-fired or diesel generating capacity; partially privatized in 2003.

Empresa Eléctrica Quito, SA (EEQ): Avda 10 de Agosto y Las Casas, Quito; tel. (2) 252-5013; fax (2) 250-3817; e-mail asoeeq@eeq.com.ec; internet www.eeq.com.ec; f. 1894; produces electricity for the region around Quito, mostly from hydroelectric plants; Sec. Gen. JORGE MARTÍNEZ.

Empresa Eléctrica Regional El Oro, SA (EMELORO): Dir Arízaga 1810 y Santa Rosa, esq. Machala, El Oro; tel. (7) 293-0500; e-mail mandrad@emeloro.gov.ec; internet www.emeloro.gov.ec; electricity production and generation in El Oro province; Chair. GONZALO QUINTANA GALVEZ; Exec. Pres. HENRY GALZARA CORREA.

Empresa Eléctrica Regional del Sur, SA (EERSSA): internet www.eerssa.com; f. 1973; electricity production and generation in Loja and Zamora Chinchipe provinces; Man. DANIEL MAHAUAD ORTEGA.

Empresa Eléctrica Riobamba, SA: Veloz 20-12 y Tarqui, Riobamba; tel. (3) 296-1693; fax (3) 296-5257; state-owned utility; Pres. OSWALDO GARCÍA DAVALOS.

Water

Instituto Ecuatoriano de Obras Sanitarias: Toledo 684 y Lérida, Troncal, Quito; tel. (2) 252-2738.

TRADE UNIONS

Frente Unitario de Trabajadores (FUT): f. 1971; left-wing; 300,000 mems; Pres. JAIME ARCINIEGAS AGUIRRE; comprises:

Confederación Ecuatoriana de Organizaciones Clasistas Unitarias de Trabajo (CEDOCUT): Edif. Cedocut 5°, Flores 846 y Manabí, Quito; tel. (2) 295-4551; fax 295-4013; e-mail presidocut@cedocut.org; internet www.cedocut.org; f. 1938; humanist; Pres. MESÍAS TATAMUEZ MORENO; Vice-Pres. WILSON ÁLVAREZ BEDÓN; 1,065 mem. orgs, 86,416 individual mems.

Confederación Ecuatoriana de Organizaciones Sindicales Libres (CEOSL): Avda Tarqui 15-26, 6°, Casilla 17-11-373, Quito; tel. (2) 252-2511; fax (2) 250-0836; e-mail ceosl@hoy.net; internet www.uocra.org/itcilo/vero.htm; f. 1962; Pres. JAIME ARCINIEGAS AGUIRRE; Sec.-Gen. GUILLERMO TOUMA GONZÁLEZ.

Confederación de Trabajadores del Ecuador (CTE) (Confederation of Ecuadorean Workers): 9 de Octubre 26106 y Marieta de Veintimilla, Casilla 17-014166, Quito; tel. (2) 252-0456; fax (2) 252-0445; e-mail presidencia@cte-ecuador.org; internet www.cte-ecuador.org; f. 1944; Pres. SANTIAGO YAGUAL YAGUAL; Vice-Pres. EDGAR SARANGO CORREA.

Central Católica de Obreros: Avda 24 de Mayo 344, Quito; tel. (2) 221-3704; f. 1906; craft and manual workers and intellectuals; Pres. CARLOS E. DÁVILA ZURITA.

A number of trade unions are not affiliated to the above groups. These include the Federación Nacional de Trabajadores Marítimos y Portuarios del Ecuador (FNTMPE—National Federation of Maritime and Port Workers of Ecuador) and both railway trade unions.

Transport

RAILWAYS

All railways are government-controlled. In 2000 the total length of track was 956 km.

Empresa Nacional de Ferrocarriles del Estado (ENFE): Calle Bolívar 443, Casilla 159, Quito; tel. (2) 221-6180; e-mail enfegg@andinanet.net; Gen. Man. SERGIO COELLAR.

There are divisional state railway managements for the following lines: Guayaquil–Quito, Sibambe–Cuenca and Quito–San Lorenzo.

ROADS

There were 43,197 km of roads in 2001, of which 16.7% were paved. The Pan-American Highway runs north from Ambato to Quito and to the Colombian border at Tulcán and south to Cuenca and Loja. Major rebuilding projects were undertaken in late 1998 with finance from several development organizations to restore roads damaged by the effects of El Niño (a periodic warming of the tropical Pacific Ocean).

SHIPPING

The following are Ecuador's principal ports: Guayaquil, Esmeraldas, Manta and Puerto Bolívar.

Acotramar, CA: General Gómez 522 y Coronel Guayaquil, Casilla 4044, Guayaquil; tel. (4) 240-1004; fax (4) 244-4852.

Ecuanave, CA: Junín 415 y Córdova, 4°, Casilla 09-01-30H, Guayaquil; tel. (4) 229-3808; fax (4) 228-9257; e-mail ecuanav@ecua.net.ec; Chair. P. ERNESTO ESCOBAR; Man. Dir A. GUILLERMO SERRANO.

Flota Bananera Ecuatoriana, SA: Edif. Gran Pasaje, 9°, Plaza Ycaza 437, Guayaquil; tel. (4) 230-9333; f. 1967; owned by Govt and private stockholders; Pres. DIEGO SÁNCHEZ; Gen. Man. JORGE BARRIGA.

Flota Mercante Grancolombiana, SA: Guayaquil; tel. (4) 251-2791; f. 1946 with Colombia and Venezuela; on Venezuela's withdrawal, in 1953, Ecuador's 10% interest was increased to 20%; operates services from Colombia and Ecuador to European ports, US Gulf ports and New York, Mexican Atlantic ports and East Canada; offices in Quito, Cuenca, Bahía, Manta and Esmeraldas; Man. Naval Capt. J. ALBERTO SÁNCHEZ.

Flota Petrolera Ecuatoriana (FLOPEC): Edif. FLOPEC, Avda Amazonas 1188 y Cordero, Casilla 535-A, Quito; tel. (2) 255-2100; fax (2) 250-1428; e-mail planificacion@flopec.com.ec; internet www.flopec.com.ec; f. 1972; Gen. Man. Capt. RAÚL SAMANIEGO GRANJA.

Logística Marítima, CA (LOGMAR): Avda Córdova 812 y V. M. Rendón, 1°, Casilla 9622, Guayaquil; tel. (4) 230-7041; Pres. J. COELLOG; Man. IGNACIO RODRÍGUEZ BAQUERIZO.

Naviera del Pacífico, CA (NAPACA): El Oro 101 y La Ría, Casilla 09-01-529, Guayaquil; tel. (4) 234-2055; Pres. LUIS ADOLFO NOBOA NARANJO.

Servicios Oceánicos Internacionales, SA: Avda Domingo Comin y Calle 11, Casilla 79, Guayaquil; Pres. CARLOS VALDANO RAFFO; Man. FERNANDO VALDANO TRUJILLO.

Transfuel, CA: Avda Pedro Menéndez Gilbert s/n, diagonal Hospital Solca, Guayaquil; tel. (4) 229-3808; fax 229-6512; Chair. JORGE JARAMILLO DE LA TORRE, ALFREDO ESCOBAR.

Transportes Navieros Ecuatorianos (Transnave): Edif. Citibank, 4°–7°, Avda 9 de Octubre 416 y Chile, Casilla 4706, Guayaquil; tel. (4) 256-1455; fax (4) 256-6273; transports general cargo within the European South Pacific Magellan Conference, Japan West Coast

ECUADOR

South America Conference and Atlantic and Gulf West Coast South America Conference; Pres. Vice-Adm. YÉZID JARAMILLO SANTOS; Gen. Man. RUBÉN LANDÁZURI ZAMBRANO.

CIVIL AVIATION

There are two international airports: Mariscal Sucre, near Quito, and Simón Bolívar, near Guayaquil. A new airport in Quito was scheduled for completion in 2009, while the new José Joaquín de Olmedo airport in Guayaquil opened in August 2006.

LAN Ecuador, SA: Avda de las Américas s/n, Guayaquil; tel. (4) 269-2850; fax (4) 228-5433; internet www.lanecuador.com; f. 2002; commenced operations in April 2003, following acquisition of assets of Ecuatoriana by LAN Chile; scheduled daily flights between Quito, Guayaquil, Miami and New York; Dir BRUNO ARDITO.

TAME Línea Aérea del Ecuador: Avda Amazonas 1354 y Colón, 6°, Casilla 17-07-8736, Sucursal Almagro, Quito; tel. (2) 250-9375; fax (2) 255-4907; e-mail tamejefv@impsat.net.ec; internet www.tame.com.ec; f. 1962; fmrly Transportes Aéreos Mercantiles Ecuatorianos, SA; removed from military control in 1990, state-owned; domestic scheduled and charter services for passengers and freight; Pres. JORGE CABEZAS; Gen. Man. BOLÍVAR MORA VINTIMILLA.

The following airlines also offer national and regional services: Aerotaxis Ecuatorianos, SA (ATESA); Cía Ecuatoriana de Transportes Aéreos (CEDTA); Ecuastol Servicios Aéreos, SA; Ecuavia Cía Ltda; Aeroturismo Cía Ltda (SAVAC).

Tourism

Tourism has become an increasingly important industry in Ecuador, with 860,784 foreign arrivals (including same-day visitors) in 2005. Of total visitors in that year, some 24% were from Peru, 22% came from the USA and 19% were from Colombia. In 2005 receipts from the tourism industry amounted to US $488m.

Asociación Ecuatoriana de Agencias de Viajes y Turismo (ASECUT): Edif. Banco del Pacífico, 5°, Avda Amazonas 22–94 y Veintimilla, Casilla 9421, Quito; tel. (2) 250-3669; fax (2) 250-0238; e-mail asecut@pi.pro.ec; f. 1953; Pres. ALFONSO SEVILLA.

Federación Hotelera del Ecuador (AHOTEC): América 5378 y Diguja, Quito; tel. (2) 244-3425; fax (2) 245-3942; e-mail ahotec@interactive.net.ec; internet www.hotelesecuador.com.ec; Pres. JOSÉ OCHOA; Exec. Dir DIEGO UTRERAS.

EGYPT

Introductory Survey

Location, Climate, Language, Religion, Flag, Capital

The Arab Republic of Egypt occupies the north-eastern corner of Africa, with an extension across the Gulf of Suez into the Sinai Peninsula, sometimes regarded as lying within Asia. Egypt is bounded to the north by the Mediterranean Sea, to the north-east by Israel, to the east by the Red Sea, to the south by Sudan, and to the west by Libya. The climate is arid, with a maximum annual rainfall of only 200 mm around Alexandria. More than 90% of the country is desert, and some 99% of the population live in the valley and delta of the River Nile. Summer temperatures reach a maximum of 43°C (110°F) and winters are mild, with an average day temperature of about 18°C (65°F). Arabic is the official language. More than 90% of the population are Muslims, mainly of the Sunni sect. The remainder are mostly Christians, principally Copts. The national flag (proportions 2 by 3) has three equal horizontal stripes, of red, white and black; the white stripe has, in the centre, the national emblem (a striped shield superimposed on an eagle, with a cartouche beneath bearing the inscription, in Kufic script, 'Arab Republic of Egypt') in gold. The capital is Cairo (Al-Qahirah).

Recent History

Egypt, a province of Turkey's Ottoman Empire from the 16th century, was occupied by British forces in 1882. The administration was controlled by British officials, although Egypt remained nominally an Ottoman province until 1914, when a British protectorate was declared. The country was granted titular independence on 28 February 1922. Fuad I, the reigning Sultan, became King. He was succeeded in 1936 by his son, King Faruq (Farouk). The Anglo-Egyptian Treaty of 1936 recognized full Egyptian sovereignty, and after the Second World War British forces withdrew from Egypt, except for a military presence in the Suez Canal Zone. When the British mandate in Palestine was ended in 1948, Arab armies intervened to oppose the newly proclaimed State of Israel. A cease-fire was agreed in 1949, leaving Egyptian forces occupying the Gaza Strip.

On 23 July 1952 power was seized by a group of young army officers in a bloodless coup led by Lt-Col (later Col) Gamal Abd an-Nasir (Nasser). Farouk abdicated in favour of his infant son, Ahmad Fuad II, and went into exile. Gen. Muhammad Nagib (Neguib) was appointed Commander-in-Chief of the army and Chairman of the Revolution Command Council (RCC). In September Neguib was appointed Prime Minister and Military Governor, with Nasser as Deputy Prime Minister. In December the 1923 Constitution was abolished, and all political parties were dissolved in January 1953. The monarchy was abolished on 18 June 1953 and Egypt was proclaimed a republic, with Neguib as President and Prime Minister. In April 1954 Neguib was succeeded as Prime Minister by Nasser. In October Egypt and the United Kingdom signed an agreement providing for the withdrawal of all British forces from the Suez Canal by June 1956. President Neguib was relieved of all his remaining posts in November 1954, whereupon Nasser became acting Head of State.

The establishment of military rule was accompanied by wide-ranging reforms, including the redistribution of land, the promotion of industrial development and the expansion of social welfare services. In foreign affairs, the new regime was strongly committed to Arab unity, and Egypt played a prominent part in the Non-aligned Movement. In 1955, having failed to secure Western armaments on satisfactory terms, Egypt accepted military assistance from the USSR.

A new Constitution was approved by a national referendum in June 1956; Nasser was elected President unopposed, and the RCC was dissolved. In July, following the departure of British forces, the US and British Governments withdrew their offers of financial assistance for Egypt's construction of the Aswan High Dam. Nasser responded by announcing the nationalization of the Suez Canal Company, so that revenue from Canal tolls could be used to finance the dam's construction. The takeover of the Canal was a catalyst for Israel's invasion of the Sinai Peninsula on 29 October. British and French forces launched military operations against Egypt two days later. Intense pressure from the UN and the USA resulted in a cease-fire on 6 November and supervision by the UN of the invaders' withdrawal.

Egypt and Syria merged in February 1958 to form the United Arab Republic (UAR), with Nasser as President. The new state strengthened earlier ties with the USSR and other countries of the communist bloc. In September 1961 Syria seceded from the UAR, but Egypt retained this title for a further decade.

In December 1962 Nasser established the Arab Socialist Union (ASU) as the country's only recognized political organization. In May 1967 he secured the withdrawal of the UN Emergency Force from Egyptian territory. Egypt subsequently reoccupied Sharm esh-Sheikh, on the Sinai Peninsula, and closed the Straits of Tiran to Israeli shipping. This precipitated the so-called Six-Day War, or June War, when Israel quickly defeated neighbouring Arab states, including Egypt. The war left Israel in control of the Gaza Strip and a large area of Egyptian territory, including the whole of the Sinai Peninsula. The Suez Canal was blocked, and remained closed until June 1975.

Nasser died suddenly in September 1970, and was succeeded by his Vice-President, Col Anwar Sadat. In September 1971 the UAR was renamed the Arab Republic of Egypt, and a new Constitution took effect. Egypt, Libya and Syria formed a Federation of Arab Republics in 1972, but this proved to be ineffective. In 1976 Egypt terminated its Treaty of Friendship with the USSR. Relations with the USA developed meanwhile, as President Sadat came to rely increasingly on US aid.

In October 1973 Egyptian troops crossed the Suez Canal to recover territory lost to Israel in 1967. After 18 days of fighting a cease-fire was achieved. In 1974–75 the US Secretary of State, Dr Henry Kissinger, negotiated disengagement agreements whereby Israel evacuated territory in Sinai and Israeli and Egyptian forces were separated by a UN-controlled buffer zone. In a dramatic peace-making initiative, opposed by many Arab countries, Sadat visited Israel in 1977 and addressed the Knesset (parliament). The leaders of Syria, Libya, Algeria, Iraq, the People's Democratic Republic of Yemen (PDRY) and the Palestine Liberation Organization (PLO) condemned Egypt, which responded by severing diplomatic relations with the five dissenting countries. In September 1978, following talks held at the US presidential retreat at Camp David, Maryland, Sadat and the Israeli Prime Minister, Menachem Begin, signed two agreements: the first provided for a five-year transitional period during which the inhabitants of the Israeli-occupied West Bank of Jordan and the Gaza Strip would obtain full autonomy and self-government; the second provided for a peace treaty between Egypt and Israel. The latter was signed in March 1979, whereafter Israel made phased withdrawals from the Sinai Peninsula, the last taking place in April 1982. The League of Arab States (the Arab League, see p. 332) expelled Egypt following the signing of the peace treaty, and imposed political and economic sanctions. Nevertheless, Egypt continued to forge relations with Israel, and in February 1980 the two countries exchanged ambassadors for the first time.

In 1974 Sadat began to introduce a more liberal political and economic regime. Political parties (banned since 1953) were allowed to participate in the 1976 elections for the Majlis ash-Sha'ab (People's Assembly), and in July 1978 Sadat formed the National Democratic Party (NDP), with himself as leader. In 1979 the special constitutional status of the ASU was ended. In October 1981 Sadat was assassinated by members of Islamic Jihad, a group of militant fundamentalist Islamists. He was succeeded by Lt-Gen. Muhammad Hosni Mubarak, his Vice-President and a former Commander-in-Chief of the air force. Immediately following Sadat's assassination a national state of emergency was declared. A new electoral law required parties to receive a minimum of 8% of the total vote in order to secure representation in the People's Assembly. This prompted opposition parties to boycott elections to local councils and to the Majlis ash-Shura (Advisory Council). At legislative elections in May 1984 the ruling NDP won 72.9% of the total vote. Of the four other participating parties, only the New Wafd Party (or New Delegation Party), in alliance with the Muslim Brotherhood, achieved representation, with 15.1%.

Meanwhile, a division in the Arab world between a 'moderate' grouping (including Jordan, Iraq and the Gulf states), which viewed the participation of Egypt as indispensable to any diplomatic moves towards solving the problems of the region, and a 'radical' grouping, led by Syria, became increasingly evident. The PLO leader, Yasser Arafat, visited President Mubarak for discussions in December 1983, signifying the end of estrangement between Egypt and the PLO, and in 1984 Jordan resumed diplomatic relations with Egypt. These two developments led to the profound involvement of Egypt in the pursuit of a negotiated settlement of the Palestinian question. In November 1987, at a summit conference in Jordan attended by the majority of Arab leaders, President Hafiz Assad of Syria obstructed proposals to readmit Egypt to the Arab League. However, recognizing Egypt's support for Iraq in the Iran–Iraq War and acknowledging the influence that Egypt could exercise on the problems of the region, the conference approved a resolution placing the establishment of diplomatic links with Egypt at the discretion of member states. Egypt was readmitted to the Arab League in May 1989.

The general election held in April 1987 resulted in a large majority for the ruling NDP. Of the 448 elective seats in the People's Assembly, the NDP won 346, the opposition parties together won 95, and independents seven. An electoral alliance of the Socialist Labour Party (SLP), the Liberal Socialist Party (LSP) and the Muslim Brotherhood won a combined total of 60 seats, of which the Brotherhood took 37 to become the largest single opposition group in the legislature. At a referendum held in October Mubarak was confirmed as President for a second six-year term of office by 97.1% of voters. In March 1988 the national state of emergency was renewed for a further three years.

Following Iraq's invasion and annexation of Kuwait in August 1990, Egypt convened an emergency summit meeting of Arab leaders at which 12 of the 20 Arab League states supported a resolution demanding the withdrawal of Iraqi forces from Kuwait and, in response to Saudi Arabia's request for international assistance to deter potential aggression by Iraq, voted to send an Arab force to the Persian (Arabian) Gulf region. The Egyptian contingent within the multinational force eventually amounted to 35,000 troops. Egypt emerged from the Gulf conflict with its international reputation enhanced, largely as a result of what was regarded as Mubarak's firm leadership of 'moderate' Arab opinion.

Legislative elections in November and December 1990 were boycotted by the principal opposition parties, in protest at the Government's refusal to concede to demands that the elections be removed from the supervision of the Ministry of the Interior and that the state of emergency be repealed. Of the 444 elective seats in the new Assembly, the NDP won 348, the National Progressive Unionist Party (NPUP or Tagammu) six, and independent candidates (the majority of whom were affiliated to the NDP) 83. Voting for the remaining seven seats was suspended. The national state of emergency was renewed for a further three years in June 1991, in view of what the Government stated was the continued threat of internal and external subversion. The legislation was subsequently extended at three-yearly intervals, most recently in 2006 (see below).

President Mubarak was formally proposed for a third term of office in July 1993, and in October his nomination was approved by some 96.3% of the valid votes cast at a national referendum. The opposition parties, none of which had endorsed Mubarak's candidature, demanded reforms including the amendment of the Constitution to allow direct presidential elections, the unrestricted formation of political parties and the introduction of a two-term limit to the presidency.

Legislative elections were held in November–December 1995, at which candidates of the NDP won 316 seats, thus retaining a decisive (albeit reduced) majority in the People's Assembly. The New Wafd Party took six seats, the NPUP five, and the LSP and the Nasserist Party one seat each. Of the 115 independent candidates elected, 99 were reported to have immediately joined or rejoined the NDP. Allegations of electoral malpractices on the part of agents acting for the NDP were widespread. A new Council of Ministers was appointed in January 1996, with Kamal Ahmad al-Ganzouri, hitherto Minister of Planning, appointed Prime Minister (in place of Dr Atif Sidqi, who had held the post since 1986).

In June 1999 Mubarak was formally nominated for a fourth presidential term; his nomination was approved by 93.8% of the valid votes cast in a national referendum held in September. Of the four main legal opposition parties, only the Nasserist Party had refused to endorse Mubarak's candidature. In October Mubarak appointed Dr Atif Muhammad Obeid, previously Minister of the Public Enterprise Sector and responsible for the Government's privatization programme, to succeed al-Ganzouri as Prime Minister.

In June 2000 the Government ordered the closure of the Ibn Khaldoun Center for Social and Development Studies, and the centre's director, Prof. Sa'adeddin Ibrahim (a prominent academic and pro-democracy activist), was arrested on suspicion of collecting funds without prior authority and defaming Egypt through his work. It was alleged that Ibrahim had accepted more than US $220,000 from the European Commission to produce a video documentary on the electoral process in Egypt. In May 2001 Ibrahim was sentenced to seven years' imprisonment with hard labour, having been convicted of receiving unauthorized funding from overseas, embezzlement and forgery; 27 employees of the Ibn Khaldoun Center also received custodial terms ranging from one to five years. The verdicts were criticized by many Western governments and by national and international human rights organizations. Ibrahim was released from detention in February 2002, pending a retrial at the Supreme State Security Court. In July, however, following the conclusion of the second trial, Ibrahim again received a seven-year gaol sentence. The verdict provoked renewed international criticism and the USA subsequently announced that it would suspend new aid, worth $130m., to Egypt. In December the Court of Cassation overturned Ibrahim's sentence and ordered a further retrial, and in March 2003 Ibrahim and his 27 co-defendants were acquitted of all charges.

The Supreme Constitutional Court issued a judgment in July 2000 that the People's Assembly elected in 1995 was illegitimate (as was the Assembly elected in 1990), and that the existing electoral system was invalid since the constitutional requirement that the judiciary have sole responsibility for the supervision of elections had not been adhered to. President Mubarak subsequently convened an extraordinary session of the Assembly, at which amendments to the existing electoral legislation were unanimously approved: these provided for judges to monitor voting at both the main and auxiliary polling stations in the impending general election.

Almost 4,000 candidates contested the 444 elective seats in the People's Assembly at polls conducted in three rounds, each of two stages, beginning on 18 October, 29 October and 8 November 2000. The NDP increased its majority, with candidates of the ruling party taking 353 seats. Independent candidates secured 72 seats, but it was reported that 35 of these had either joined or rejoined the NDP shortly after the elections. The New Wafd Party won seven seats, the NPUP six, the Nasserist Party three and the LSP one seat. Voting for the two seats in one constituency in Alexandria was postponed following the arrest of some 20 Muslim Brotherhood activists. At least 14 people were killed during the polls, while large numbers of Islamists were detained for public order offences.

At partial elections to the Advisory Council in May 2001 74 of the 88 contested seats were won by the NDP, while independent candidates took the remaining 14 seats. In November President Mubarak effected a minor reorganization of the Council of Ministers. Most notably, the Ministry of Economics was abolished and responsibility for most of its functions was devolved to the new Governor of the Central Bank of Egypt.

In February 2002 the worst rail disaster in Egypt's history, in which 373 people were killed after a train travelling from Cairo to Luxor caught fire, precipitated the resignation of the Minister of Transport and of the Chairman of Egyptian National Railways. New ministers of transport, health and civil aviation (responsibility for the last being devolved from the Ministry of Transport) were appointed in March.

At the eighth congress of the NDP held in Cairo in September 2002, Mubarak was re-elected Chairman of the organization, while his second son, Gamal, was elected Secretary-General for Policy, effectively making him the third most senior figure in the party and further fuelling speculation that he was being groomed eventually to succeed his father. The Deputy Prime Minister and Minister of Agriculture and Land Reclamation, Dr Yousef Amin Wali, was replaced as the NPD's Secretary-General by the Minister of Information, Muhammad Safwat esh-Sherif.

During 2003 the NDP appeared to acquiesce to demands for greater political liberalization and continued the modernization process instigated by Gamal Mubarak in the previous year. In June the People's Assembly approved the creation of a National Council for Human Rights as well as the closure of a number of the State Security Courts; the power of judges to sentence offenders to imprisonment with hard labour was also abolished. At the NDP's first annual party conference held in September, President Mubarak announced that all military orders issued under the emergency laws, which had been in place since the assassination of President Sadat in 1981, would be abolished, except those that were 'necessary to maintain public order and security'. However, a committee established by the Prime Minister to review the existing emergency powers recommended that only six of the 13 military orders could be withdrawn. Nevertheless, restrictions and limitations pertaining to the formation of new political parties and the activities of existing political organizations were also to be reviewed, and Gamal Mubarak pledged to take steps to ensure that all Egyptians would receive the fundamental rights of participatory democracy and equality. In November 2003 the President was taken ill during a speech to the People's Assembly, prompting rumours that he would name a Vice-President. However, in January 2004 he publicly denied intensifying speculation that his son was being groomed to fill this position and assume the presidency in the event of his death.

Further partial elections took place to the 264-member Advisory Council in May and June 2004. The NDP won 70 of the 88 seats contested, while 17 of the remaining seats were secured by NDP members who had stood as independents; one seat was taken by the NPUP. A further 44 members of the Council were appointed by the President. In late June esh-Sherif was elected Speaker of the Advisory Council, replacing Dr Mustafa Kamal Helmi. The Minister of Culture, Farouk Abd al-Aziz Hosni, assumed the information portfolio. In early July the death was announced of the Minister of Transport, Hamdy ash-Shayeb. Shortly afterwards Prime Minister Obeid announced the resignation of his entire administration, precipitating a long-anticipated reorganization of the Council of Ministers. Dr Ahmad Mahmoud Muhammad Nazif, a technocrat and the former Minister of Communications and Information Technology, was appointed Prime Minister and charged with forming a new cabinet. In mid-July President Mubarak inaugurated a new 35-member Government, which was also reported to be of a technocratic, reformist nature. Notable changes intended to assist the process of economic reform included the creation of a Ministry of Investment and the merger of the Ministries of Foreign Trade and of Industry and Technological Development. Several appointees in the new Council of Ministers were regarded as having close links with Gamal Mubarak, including Ahmad Aboul Gheit, hitherto Egypt's Permanent Representative to the UN, who became Minister of Foreign Affairs.

In October 2004 a new political party, Al-Ghad (Tomorrow), was approved by the Egyptian authorities after its fourth application. This decision was apparently prompted by criticism from the USA regarding the slow pace of democratic reform in the country, which had seen only two new political parties being licensed since 1977. The party, under the leadership of former New Wafd Party deputy Ayman Abd al-Aziz an-Nour, set out its aims of combating poverty and improving the living conditions of Egypt's citizens. It brought to 18 the number of officially recognized parties. In January 2005 an-Nour was arrested by the Egyptian authorities and charged with having forged signatures required in order to secure his party's registration by the authorities. After being released on bail in March, an-Nour announced that he intended to contest the presidential election scheduled for later that year; he was, however, formally charged with forgery in May. His trial commenced in Cairo in June, but was subsequently postponed until late September, thus permitting the Al-Ghad leader to contest the presidential election (see below). In December an-Nour was given a five-year prison sentence, having been found guilty of the forgery charges; he began an appeal against the sentence in February 2006, citing violations of his rights during detention and serious flaws in the original trial. However, in May the Court of Cassation rejected an-Nour's appeal and upheld the original sentence, a decision that was strongly criticized by the USA, the European Union (EU) and domestic and international human rights organizations. Despite a further appeal against his sentence on medical grounds, in early 2007 an-Nour was deemed by the Egyptian authorities to be in sufficient health to serve his full prison term; the same ruling was issued by a Cairo court in March 2008.

Meanwhile, Egypt's first terrorist attack for seven years occurred in early October 2004, at the height of the Jewish holiday season, when three bombs exploded in the resorts of Taba, Ras Shitan and Nuweiba on the Sinai Peninsula, killing 34 people—many of whom were Israelis—and injuring more than 100. In late October five Egyptians suspected of involvement in the bombings were arrested and the blame for the attacks was placed upon a Palestinian, Ayad Said Salah, who had been living in Egypt and who had died in the explosion in Taba. The Ministry of the Interior announced that Salah had acted to highlight the deteriorating situation in the Gaza Strip. In March 2005 three Egyptians were charged—one *in absentia*—in connection with the bombings, while it was reported that two others suspected of involvement in the attacks had been killed by security forces in the previous month. (See below for details of further convictions in 2006.)

Opposition to Mubarak augmented towards the end of 2004, with the release in October of a statement by more than 650 Egyptian activists, politicians and intellectuals urging a constitutional amendment to prevent the President from standing for another term in office. In December some 1,000 people demonstrated in Cairo against the possibility that Mubarak might seek a fifth presidential term or that his son might succeed him. In February 2005 Mubarak did announce plans for democratic reform in Egypt—specifically, the altering of the Constitution to allow for direct, contested presidential elections. The constitutional amendment was drafted by a parliamentary committee in early May and immediately provoked criticism. Many opposition parties argued that the proposed changes, which stated that a presidential candidate would need the support of at least 65 members of the People's Assembly, would prevent candidates from outside the ruling party from standing for the presidency. Nevertheless, the amendment was overwhelmingly approved by the People's Assembly on 10 May, despite several opposition deputies walking out in protest. (The amendment stipulated that political parties required 5% of parliamentary seats in order to field a presidential candidate.) At the referendum held on 25 May 82.9% of the electorate voted in favour of the changes. Participation was officially recorded at 53.6%; however, opposition figures claimed that actual turn-out was as low as 5%.

Egypt was the target of terrorist attacks perpetrated by Egyptian militants twice in 2005. In early April three foreign tourists were killed in a bomb attack in Cairo, and in late July at least 60 people, some of them foreigners, were killed and around 200 injured following three bomb attacks at hotels in the Red Sea resort of Sharm esh-Sheikh. In October it was announced that a security fence would be erected around the resort in order to prevent further attacks by militants. In August 2007 four Egyptian nationals were sentenced to terms of life imprisonment, having been convicted of involvement in the Cairo bombing of April 2005; a further five defendants were handed down terms of between one and 10 years, and four were acquitted.

Meanwhile, at the first ever multi-candidate presidential election held on 7 September 2005 President Mubarak was re-elected for a fifth consecutive six-year term. Mubarak won 88.6% of the vote, while Ayman an-Nour of Al-Ghad came second, with 7.6%, and No'man Khalil Gomaa of the New Wafd Party secured third place, with 2.9%. Seven other candidates stood in the election, all receiving less than 0.5% of the vote. Turn-out was registered at only 23.0%, attributed in part to the appeal by several opposition parties for a boycott of the poll. The election was marred by opposition protests in Cairo, accusations of a media bias towards Mubarak and controversy surrounding the newly established Presidential Election Commission's decision to ban independent groups from monitoring the ballot. Mubarak was sworn in on 27 September.

Elections to contest the 444 elective seats in the People's Assembly were conducted in three stages on 9 November, 20 November and 1 December 2005 (with run-off elections held on 15 and 26 November and 7 December). Prior to the elections the Muslim Brotherhood announced that it would be presenting a list of 150 members as independent candidates. Unlike in previous polls, where campaigning by Muslim Brotherhood candidates had been banned, the Egyptian authorities now allowed the party to campaign freely. Prior to and during the elections, however, more than 850 members of the Muslim Brotherhood were arrested amid reports of clashes between NDP and Muslim Brotherhood supporters. In total, more than 10 people were killed in rioting during the ballot. Official results issued in mid-December revealed that the NDP had won 311 of the 432 decided seats (with 71.9% of the vote). The most notable gains, however, were made by the Muslim Brotherhood, which increased its representation from 17 seats to 88. Other independent candidates won 24 seats, while the remaining 12 seats were won by the New Wafd Party (six), the NPUP (two) and Al-Ghad (one). Turn-out was low (at only 26.2% of the electorate) and voting had to be postponed for 12 seats in six constituencies owing to violence. On 12 December Mubarak appointed five women and five Coptic Christians to the 10 presidentially appointed seats in the People's Assembly in order to increase their level of parliamentary representation. In late December Mubarak announced that he would retain Nazif as Prime Minister and asked him to form a new government. Observers commented that the new ministerial appointments, which included several businessmen, would accelerate the pace of reform in the country and reinforce the position of Gamal Mubarak, who was named as one of three Deputy Secretary-Generals of the NDP in January 2006.

President Mubarak's decision, in February 2006, to postpone local elections scheduled for April of that year until 2008 attracted criticism both externally, in particular from the USA, and internally from the Muslim Brotherhood. The amended Constitution required independent candidates standing for the presidency to obtain the support of at least 10 local councillors, and Egyptian Islamists claimed that the delay in holding the polls would thus ensure that the NDP retained control over nominations for the presidency. Meanwhile, four senior judges who had persistently criticized government interference in judicial matters and made allegations of vote-rigging in the legislative elections of 2005 were stripped of their immunity and were to face an investigation by a state security court. In April–May 2006 the Government's decision to prosecute two of the judges provoked angry demonstrations in Cairo, which were forcibly dispersed by the security forces; hundreds of protesters were arrested for their roles in the demonstrations, including an estimated 400 members of the Muslim Brotherhood (some of whom were later released).

On 24 April 2006 23 people were killed, and around 150 injured, following three co-ordinated explosions in the Red Sea resort of Dahab; President Mubarak condemned the attacks as 'a wicked terrorist act'. Days later the People's Assembly voted to approve a two-year extension to the national state of emergency, despite earlier indications from Prime Minister Nazif that new anti-terrorism legislation would be implemented in its place.

In January 2006 the New Wafd Party Chairman, No'man Gomaa, was removed from office by a 'reformist' group of party officials, who promised to hold a leadership election shortly thereafter. Gomaa strongly contested his 'unconstitutional' removal from office and later that month filed a lawsuit with the Administrative Court. In April the leadership dispute erupted into a violent disturbance, when Gomaa and a number of his supporters occupied the party headquarters in Cairo; 21 people were injured in the clashes that ensued between the two rival factions. Gomaa and five of his supporters were later arrested by the security forces for their role in the violence. In June Mahmoud Abaza was elected unopposed as party Chairman.

In a minor reorganization of the Council of Ministers effected in August 2006, Mamdouh Mohi ed-Din Mari was appointed as Minister of Justice, replacing Mahmoud Aboul Leil Rashed. The role of Minister of Planning and Local Development was separated into a revised planning portfolio, retained by the incumbent minister, Dr Osman Muhammad Osman (who was also named Minister of State for Economic Development), and the newly created post of Minister of State for Local Development.

Speculation regarding the possible candidacy of Gamal Mubarak to succeed his father as President intensified following the NDP annual conference in September 2006, during which Gamal Mubarak urged Egypt to forge a new vision for the Middle East and announced the resumption of the country's programme to develop peaceful nuclear technology (see Economic Affairs). However, in a speech to mark the official opening of the People's Assembly in November, President Mubarak hinted that he intended to govern for life.

In December 2006 the President put forward proposals for a total of 34 amendments to the Constitution, including a reduction of presidential powers in favour of the People's Assembly and the Council of Ministers, and steps to ease restrictions on political parties' candidates for presidential elections. Opposition figures, however, criticized a number of the proposals, in particular the reversal of earlier legislation providing for full judicial supervision of elections. Instead, an 11-member Higher Election Commission, to be appointed by the Government and chaired by the Minister of Justice, was henceforth to monitor the legislative election process. In addition to substituting a reference in the Constitution to the 'socialist character of the state' with the fact that Egypt's economy was now based on 'market principles', one of the most significant changes was an increase in the powers of the security forces to monitor, detain and imprison citizens suspected of involvement in terrorist activities. Mubarak also proposed a formal ban on the establishment of political parties based on religion, one of a number of changes aimed at curbing the growing influence of the Muslim Brotherhood. Hundreds of the organization's activists were detained by the authorities in late 2006 and early 2007. A national referendum on the constitutional amendments, which—despite a boycott of the proceedings by members and affiliates of the Muslim Brotherhood—were approved by a significant majority of deputies in the People's Assembly in mid-March, took place on 26 March. According to official figures, the 34 constitutional amendments were endorsed by 75.9% of voters, although turn-out was estimated by the Ministry of Justice at only 27.1%. Opposition parties, including the Muslim Brotherhood, immediately contested the outcome of the poll, while independent human rights organizations also expressed their doubts concerning the validity of the result. In early April the Egyptian Organization for Human Rights (EOHR) and five other human rights organizations alleged that the actual turn-out in the referendum had been around 5%, and that numerous instances of electoral fraud had occurred.

Concerns about the extent of freedom of expression in Egypt again came to the fore in the early part of 2007, particularly as increasing numbers of dissidents were using the internet as a means of protesting against the Mubarak regime or the wider establishment. The Government, for example, took a firm stance against criticism of the regime by online diarists. A new liberal political grouping, the Democratic Front Party, was registered by the authorities in May, under the leadership of Dr Osama al-Ghazali Harb, a former member of the NDP and editor-in-chief of the political journal *As-Siyassa ad-Dawliya*, and former cabinet minister Dr Yehia el-Gamal. By mid-2007 the number of legalized political organizations in Egypt had increased to 24.

In late April 2007, meanwhile, 40 senior members of the Muslim Brotherhood were tried—seven of these *in absentia*—on charges of leading an illegal group that participated in terrorist activities. A renewed and widespread crackdown on the activities of the group was reported by officials of the Brotherhood in August, amid reports that the organization was for the first time preparing to establish a political party and to publish full details of its agenda. In the following month the editors of four independent newspapers were given one-year prison sentences and also fined, after they had been found guilty by a court in Cairo of defamation against President Mubarak and his son, Gamal. In early 2008 Muslim Brotherhood leaders protested that further mass arrests of their members represented a concerted campaign by the authorities to prevent them from contesting the local elections scheduled for April (having been postponed from 2006—see above). The organization claimed in late February 2008 that up to 500 activists were in detention, and in early April announced that they would boycott the polls.

Partial elections to select 88 members of the Advisory Council were held on 11 and 18 June 2007; 84 seats were secured by the NDP, three by independents aligned to the NDP and one by the NPUP. The Muslim Brotherhood thus failed to win a seat, despite having fielded candidates who stood as independents. A further 44 members of the Council were appointed by President Mubarak. In early November Mubarak was re-elected unchallenged as leader of the NDP at the party's ninth congress; it was the first time since the President assumed the NDP leadership in 1981 that members had voted by secret ballot. There was renewed speculation concerning the likelihood of Gamal Mubarak succeeding his father as President after it was revealed that the party's Politburo and Secretariat-General had been merged to form a new Supreme Council. Some commentators noted that the change, which resulted in Gamal now belonging to the NDP's governing body (he had not been a member of the Politburo), meant that he now met the constitutional requirement that presidential candidates must either stand as independents or be members of the governing body of a legal political party. However, party officials were swift to deny that this had been the reason for the reform.

In mid-January 2008 the Egyptian Government summoned EU ambassadors to protest against a draft resolution that had been adopted by the European parliament in which Egypt's emergency legislation, police practices (especially the alleged use of torture against detainees) and official treatment of religious minorities were all strongly criticized. The EU also demanded the immediate release from prison of the Al-Ghad leader, Ayman an-Nour (see above).

Since 1992 the Government's attempts to suppress Islamist fundamentalism have dominated the domestic political agenda. During the early 1990s fundamentalist violence increasingly targeted foreign tourists visiting Egypt, as well as foreign investors, and there were frequent confrontations between Islamist militants and the security forces. In May 1993 a report published by the human rights organization Amnesty International alleged that the Egyptian Government was systematically maltreating political detainees, and in November the organization accused the Government of breaching the UN Convention against Torture and Other Cruel, Inhuman or Degrading Treatment or Punishment.

In January 1994 the security forces were reported to have detained some 1,000 suspected fundamentalist activists in response to attacks on their members during that month. In March nine members of the Vanguards of Conquest (a faction of Islamic Jihad) were sentenced to death after having been convicted of conspiring to assassinate the Prime Minister in November 1993. In July 1994 a further five members of the militant group received death sentences for the attempted assassination of the Minister of the Interior in August 1993. Meanwhile, in April 1994 the chief of the anti-terrorist branch of the State Security Investigation Section was assassinated by members of Gama'ah al-Islamiyah (one of Egypt's principal militant Islamist groups), prompting retaliatory security operations.

In early 1995 the Government began to take steps to isolate the more moderate Muslim Brotherhood and to weaken its political influence in the approach to that year's legislative elections. Several leading members of the Brotherhood were arrested, and both President Mubarak and the Minister of the Interior claimed that there was evidence of links between the movement and Islamist extremists. The Government also acted to curb Islamist influence within professional organizations; in February the judiciary was accorded wide powers to intervene in union elections and to prevent Muslim Brotherhood members from standing. In June Mubarak escaped an assassination attempt, apparently carried out by Islamist militants, while he was travelling to a summit meeting of the Organization of African Unity (OAU, now African Union—AU) in Addis Ababa, Ethiopia. Egypt's claim that the gunmen had been aided by Sudanese agents was denied by the Sudanese Government. (In September 1996 three Egyptians were sentenced to death by the Ethiopian Supreme Court for their involvement in the attempted assassination.)

In April 1996 12 prominent members of the Muslim Brotherhood were arrested and charged with attempting to revive the movement's activities and restore its links with extremist groups. Three of those detained were founder members of a new political organization, the Al-Wasat (Centre) Party, which the authorities claimed was serving as a 'front' for Brotherhood activities. The party's founders—who included Muslims, Christians, leftists and Nasserist activists—insisted, however, that they were seeking to create a political group that occupied the middle ground between the State and its fundamentalist Islamist opponents. (Twice in 1998 and again in June 1999 Al-Wasat was denied legal status by the authorities.)

In September 1997 a military court in Haekstep, north of the capital, conducted a military trial on an unprecedented scale of suspected Islamist militants; of 98 defendants convicted, four were sentenced to death and eight to life imprisonment. A few days later nine German tourists were killed as a result of an attack on a tourist bus in Cairo. However, in an apparent attempt to protect the country's vital tourism industry, the Egyptian Government claimed that the attack was an isolated incident unconnected with terrorism. (In May 1998 two men were hanged, having been convicted in October 1997 of the attack.) In November 1997 the massacre near Luxor of 70 people, including 58 foreign tourists, by members of Gama'ah al-Islamiyah severely undermined both the tourism sector and the claims of the Government to have suppressed Islamist violence. Mubarak criticized the security forces' failure to protect tourists, and dismissed the Minister of the Interior. The President ordered a heightened security presence at all tourist sites and placed the Prime Minister at the head of a special committee charged with devising a plan to safeguard the tourism sector. In December a number of Gama'ah al-Islamiyah's exiled leaders claimed that the Luxor massacre had been perpetrated by a 'rogue' element acting without the authorization of the group's central leadership; furthermore, the leaders in exile announced that Gama'ah al-Islamiyah (at least, those members under their specific authority) would no longer target tourists in their conflict with the Government. (In May 1999 security officials in Switzerland alleged that the Saudi Arabian-born militant Islamist Osama bin Laden had financed the Luxor killings.)

New state security measures adopted by the Ministry of the Interior during 1998 included a relaxation of the criteria whereby affiliation to Islamist groups was assumed, and the release of some Islamist prisoners who had renounced connections with illegal organizations. In March Gama'ah al-Islamiyah declared a unilateral cease-fire and announced a new strategy of exerting maximum political pressure on the Government by non-violent means. Although the Government gave no formal acknowledgement of the apparent cease-fire, the process of releasing imprisoned Islamist militants was subsequently accelerated. In April some 1,200 Gama'ah al-Islamiyah detainees were freed (reportedly among them two of the group's leaders who were involved in the assassination of President Sadat in 1981), and a further 1,200 left prison in December. In February 1999 it was reported that three men suspected of involvement in the 1997 Luxor attack had been arrested on the Uruguayan–Brazilian border and were expected to stand trial in Cairo. In the same month proceedings began against 107 alleged members of Islamic Jihad who were charged with conspiring to overthrow the Government. In April 1999 nine of the defendants were sentenced to death; 78 received sentences ranging from one year to life imprisonment, all with hard labour, while 20 were acquitted. In June 20 members of Gama'ah al-Islamiyah were given custodial sentences, having been convicted by a military court of planning a bomb attack on President Mubarak's Alexandria residence in 1996; that death sentences were not imposed was interpreted by the organization's lawyers as a positive response to the recent cease-fire declaration.

The unofficial truce between the Government and Gama'ah al-Islamiyah was apparently jeopardized in September 1999, when security forces in Giza shot dead four alleged members of the organization, including its military commander. In November charges against 20 alleged members of the Muslim Brotherhood, who had been arrested in the previous month, were altered by the military court where they were standing trial from 'belonging' to the Muslim Brotherhood to 'participating in the founding and management' of the organization; any conviction under these charges was likely to result in much harsher sentences. The trial was initially postponed for procedural reasons but resumed in January 2000 (see below).

In January 2000 three days of violent clashes between Muslims and Copts in the southern village of el-Kosheh resulted in the deaths of an estimated 20 Christians and one Muslim. A subsequent inquiry conducted by the EOHR inferred that the primary cause of the violence was the 'economic inequalities' between the relatively prosperous Coptic majority and the poorer Muslim minority. In February 2001 four Muslims were sentenced to custodial terms of up to 10 years for their part in the violence, while a further 92 defendants were acquitted. However, after the Court of Cassation ordered a retrial of all 96 defendants, in February 2003 two men were sentenced to prison terms of 15 years and three-and-a-half years, respectively; the remainder were again acquitted. In June 2004 these sentences were again reviewed, with three men receiving one and two-year prison terms, and the fourth man's 15-year sentence being reduced to 13 years. Once again, the other 92 defendants were acquitted. In April 2006 two Coptic Christians were killed in a series of attacks against Coptic churches in Alexandria. Later in that month violent clashes erupted between groups of Coptic protesters and Muslims in the city, during which several people were wounded and some 67 arrested. Further sectarian violence was reported in Giza in May 2007, having been precipitated by fears among local Muslim residents that a Christian church was to be extended.

In February 2000 senior members of Islamic Jihad publicly urged for the first time the cessation of the organization's armed activities, appealing to militants to concentrate their activities on the liberation of the al-Aqsa Mosque in Jerusalem. In March between 500 and 1,000 Islamists, mostly members of Gama'ah al-Islamiyah or Islamic Jihad, were reportedly released from prison; a further 500 Islamists were freed in July. Yet, despite regular releases of large numbers of militants since 1998, human rights organizations maintained that more than 15,000 remained in Egyptian detention, many of whom were being held without charge under the country's emergency laws. Furthermore, during the approach to the 2000 legislative elections the authorities arrested increasing numbers of Muslim

Brotherhood members, in what was widely acknowledged as an effort to prevent their standing as candidates for the People's Assembly. In November the Higher Military Court in Cairo pronounced guilty verdicts on 15 of those arrested in late 1999 on charges of reviving the Brotherhood, sentencing them to between three and five years' imprisonment; the five other defendants were acquitted.

President Mubarak was swift to condemn the suicide attacks on New York and Washington, DC, USA, of 11 September 2001. Several members of Islamic Jihad were alleged to have assumed significant roles in the suicide attacks, held to have been perpetrated by Osama bin Laden's militant Islamist al-Qa'ida (Base) network. Dr Ayman az-Zawahiri, the leader of Islamic Jihad who was said to be bin Laden's closest associate, was presumed responsible for the organization of the attacks, and another Egyptian, Muhammad Atef, who was reportedly killed by US forces in Afghanistan in November, was, according to US intelligence, believed to have been al-Qa'ida's chief military planner. Furthermore, an Egyptian national was suspected of having piloted one of the hijacked aircraft that hit the World Trade Center in New York. Following the events of 11 September more than 260 suspected Islamists were detained in Egypt, and arrests of Islamists continued on a large scale during 2002. In August 16 members of the Muslim Brotherhood were sentenced to terms of imprisonment ranging from three to five years after being convicted of inciting anti-Government demonstrations. In the following month 51 militants, who had initially been arrested in May 2001, were sentenced to up to 15 years' imprisonment for conspiring to overthrow the Government. In August 2002, meanwhile, a number of imprisoned senior members of Gama'ah al-Islamiyah reiterated their commitment to the cease-fire declared in 1998 and announced, in a series of interviews published in the weekly *Al-Mussawar*, their complete renunciation of violence. Some 900 members of the organization were released from prison in October 2003.

In March 2004 26 people, including three British nationals, were sentenced to prison terms of between one and five years for membership of the illegal militant group Hizb at-Tahrir al-Islami (Islamic Liberation Party), which aims to unite all Muslim countries in a single Islamic state and which had been banned in Egypt since 1974 following an attempted coup. Accusations of torture followed the verdict, and the British defendants claimed that they had been forced into signing confessions. However, the three men were released from prison in February 2006, having served more than two-thirds of their sentences.

The Egyptian authorities instigated the largest crackdown on the activities of the Muslim Brotherhood for many years in May 2004: in a series of raids 54 members of the Muslim Brotherhood were arrested, and shops and publishing houses were closed down. This represented the first campaign against the organization since Muhammad Mahdi Akif had assumed its leadership in January, following the sudden death of the Supreme Guide, Mamoun al-Hodeibi. Protests by Muslim Brotherhood activists increased in early 2005, as they demanded political reforms in advance of the elections scheduled to take place that year. Round-ups of Muslim Brotherhood members thus continued, with hundreds of activists—including four of the group's leaders—being arrested in May. Three days prior to the national referendum in late May (see above), Mahmoud Izzat, the organization's Secretary-General, was arrested during a Muslim Brotherhood demonstration in the capital, where protesters were calling for a boycott of the referendum. Izzat was released in August, and the four other leaders arrested in May were freed in October. (See above for details regarding further measures taken against the Muslim Brotherhood by the authorities during 2006–08.)

In April 2006 the Ministry of the Interior announced that more than 900 members of Gama'ah al-Islamiyah had been released from gaol, including one of the organization's founders, Najeh Ibrahim. In May Egyptian security forces announced that they had killed Nasser Khamis al-Mallahi, the leader of the Tawhid wa al-Jihad (Unification and Holy War) group, which was widely suspected of carrying out the Sinai bombings during 2004–06 (see above). Following a trial that began in March 2006, in November three militants of Tawhid wa al-Jahid were sentenced to death, having been convicted of involvement in the October 2004 bombings in Taba and Ras Shitan, which killed 34 people; of the 10 other defendants, two were imprisoned for life and eight were handed down sentences of between five and 15 years.

Egyptian mediation was prominent in the Middle East peace process throughout the 1990s. The country played an important role in the efforts leading to the convening of the Middle East peace conference in Madrid, Spain, in October 1991, and an Egyptian delegation attended the first, symbolic session of the conference. Egyptian mediators were influential in the secret negotiations between Israel and the PLO that led to the signing of the Declaration of Principles on Palestinian Self-Rule in September 1993, and PLO and Israeli delegations subsequently began to meet regularly in Cairo or Taba to discuss the detailed implementation of the Declaration of Principles. In May 1994 an agreement on Palestinian self-rule in the Gaza Strip and the Jericho area (for full details, see the chapter on Israel) was signed in Cairo by the Israeli Prime Minister, Itzhak Rabin, and the PLO Chairman, Yasser Arafat, at a ceremony presided over by Mubarak. However, despite an official visit to Egypt by President Ezer Weizman in December (the first such visit by an Israeli Head of State), relations between Egypt and Israel began to deteriorate. Egypt hosted summit meetings of Arab leaders in December 1994 and February 1995, prompting censure from the Israeli Government, and further tension arose when Mubarak reiterated his warning that Egypt would not sign the Treaty on the Non-Proliferation of Nuclear Weapons (or Non-Proliferation Treaty—NPT), which was due for renewal in April 1995, unless Israel also agreed to sign it; he urged other states to do likewise. In March 1995 Israel offered to sign the NPT once it had concluded peace treaties with all of the Arab states and with Iran, and to allow Egypt to inspect its research nuclear reactor at Nahal Shorek (but not the nuclear facility at Dimona). Egypt rejected both offers, but adopted a more conciliatory line on the issue. Meanwhile, Egypt's stance with regard to the NPT antagonized the USA, which insisted that the continuation of US aid to Egypt depended on Egypt's signing the Treaty.

Egypt continued its mediatory role in the complex negotiations that eventually led to the signing, in Washington, DC, of the Israeli-Palestinian Interim Agreement on the West Bank and the Gaza Strip in September 1995. In November Mubarak made his first presidential visit to Israel to attend the funeral of the assassinated Israeli Prime Minister, Itzhak Rabin. Egypt also participated in meetings leading to the resumption of peace negotiations between Israel and Syria at the end of 1995. In March 1996, following a series of Palestinian suicide bomb attacks in Israel, Egypt and the USA co-hosted a one-day 'Summit of Peacemakers' in Sharm esh-Sheikh. Egypt's relations with Israel deteriorated again in April, as a consequence of Israeli military operations in Lebanon (q.v.). In June, in response to the apparently rejectionist stance of the new Israeli administration of Binyamin Netanyahu with regard to the exchange of land for peace, Mubarak convened an emergency summit meeting of the Arab League in Cairo—the first such meeting for six years. The summit's final communiqué reaffirmed the Arab states' commitment to peace, but warned that any further rapprochement between them and Israel depended on Israel's returning all the Arab land that it occupied in 1967.

President Mubarak cautiously welcomed the Wye River Memorandum signed by Netanyahu and Arafat in October 1998 (see the chapter on Israel). However, in January 1999 Egypt suspended all contacts with the Israeli Government in protest against its decision to suspend implementation of the agreement. The election, in May, of the leader of the One Israel alliance, Ehud Barak, to the Israeli premiership was generally welcomed in Egypt, but in July the Egyptian Minister of Foreign Affairs emphasized that there could be no normalization of Egyptian–Israeli relations prior to the resumption of comprehensive peace talks. Egyptian mediation was subsequently influential in discussions between Israeli and Palestinian negotiators that led to the signing of the Sharm esh-Sheikh Memorandum by Barak and Arafat in September 1999 (see the chapter on Israel). Both the Israeli and Palestinian leaders made brief visits to Cairo prior to the US-hosted summit at Camp David in July 2000. After the failure of the summit, Mubarak emphasized that he would not pressure Arafat to make concessions regarding the central issue of the status of Jerusalem, and urged all Arab states to unite in support of the Palestinians until they regained all their legitimate rights in accordance with the pertinent UN resolutions.

Following the outbreak in late September 2000 of violent clashes between Palestinians and Israeli security forces in Jerusalem, which swiftly spread throughout the West Bank and Gaza, President Mubarak assumed an important role in attempting to prevent the violence from escalating into a major regional crisis. Most notably, in mid-October, following mediation by UN Secretary-General Kofi Annan, Barak and Arafat agreed to lead delegations to a summit meeting at Sharm esh-Sheikh, brokered by US President Bill Clinton. Two days of intensive negotiations resulted in an agreement on the establishment of a fact-finding committee to investigate the causes of what had become known as the al-Aqsa *intifada* (uprising), but a tentative truce proved unviable. Later that month an emergency meeting of Arab League heads of state was convened in Cairo, at which Arab leaders held Israel solely to blame for the continuing violence. In late November Egypt recalled its ambassador to Tel-Aviv, denouncing Israel's 'escalation of aggression and deliberate use of force against the Palestinian people'. Relations deteriorated further at the end of that month when an Egyptian engineer, Sherif Filali, was charged with having gathered information regarding Egyptian economic and military projects for the Israeli overseas intelligence service, Mossad. In June 2001 Filali was acquitted of the charges by the State Security Court; however, in September Mubarak invoked emergency legislation to reverse the acquittal and ordered a retrial. In March 2002 Filali was convicted of providing information to Israel with the intent of harming Egypt's national interests, and was sentenced to 15 years' imprisonment with hard labour.

Following his election to the Israeli premiership in February 2001, it was alleged that the right-wing Likud leader, Ariel Sharon, had requested that the USA decrease military assistance to Egypt. Mubarak subsequently warned Sharon that he would interpret any such demand as a 'hostile action' and that it would significantly alter Egypt's attitude towards Israel. Nevertheless, at an Arab League summit on the Palestinian situation, held in Jordan in March, Mubarak deflected demands (as he had at the Cairo emergency summit in October 2000) from more radical Arab states that Egypt and Jordan should sever diplomatic relations with Israel entirely. In April 2001 a joint Egyptian-Jordanian peace plan urged an immediate halt to Israeli construction of settlements and a withdrawal of Israeli forces to pre-*intifada* positions. The plan was supported by the new US Administration of President George W. Bush, the EU and the Arab world; however, Mubarak's claim, following a meeting in Cairo in April with the Israeli Deputy Prime Minister and Minister of Foreign Affairs, Shimon Peres, to have secured the agreement of both Israel and the Palestinians to the Egyptian-Jordanian proposal proved premature, and diplomatic progress stalled as violence continued to escalate in subsequent months. At an emergency meeting of Arab League ministers of foreign affairs in Cairo in May, it was agreed to suspend all political contacts with Israel until its attacks on Palestinians were halted; Egypt suspended all non-diplomatic contacts with Israel in April 2002.

In July 2002, following an Israeli air force attack on Gaza City, which resulted in the death of a senior figure from the Palestinian Islamic Resistance Movement (Hamas) and a further 15 civilians, Mubarak denounced the actions of the Israeli military and accused Sharon of deliberately ordering the attacks in order to sabotage Palestinian peace efforts. Although the President strongly welcomed the publication, in April 2003, of the 'roadmap' peace plan drafted by the Quartet group (comprising the UN, the USA, the EU and Russia—see the chapter on Israel), Egyptian efforts to secure a cease-fire by armed Palestinian factions made no further progress, and in May Mubarak informed the visiting US Secretary of State, Colin Powell, that Egypt required evidence that Israel would accept the internationally sponsored roadmap before it would again attempt to broker a cease-fire agreement.

In December 2003 representatives from the leading Palestinian factions attended further talks in Cairo, although attempts to secure a cease-fire proved unsuccessful; a unilateral truce agreed by the groups in June had collapsed in August. The Israeli Deputy Prime Minister and Minister of Foreign Affairs, Silvan Shalom, met with President Mubarak in Geneva, Switzerland, later in December and the following week Egypt's Minister of Foreign Affairs, Ahmad Maher, travelled to Israel for discussions with Sharon and Shalom. The meeting was overshadowed, however, by an attack on Maher, perpetrated by Palestinian extremists, while he was visiting the al-Aqsa Mosque in Jerusalem. The assault, which resulted in Maher being hospitalized, was condemned by both Israeli and Palestinian leaders. Further talks between Mubarak and Shalom were held in Cairo in March 2004; the discussions reportedly focused on security arrangements in the event of an Israeli withdrawal from the Gaza Strip. In April Mubarak travelled to the USA to discuss the roadmap with President Bush; the US President also met with Sharon and endorsed Sharon's proposals for an Israeli 'disengagement' from Gaza, which also involved the consolidation of six Jewish settlements in the West Bank. It was envisaged that Egyptian forces would assume responsibility for border security in Gaza after Israel's unilateral withdrawal, which Sharon maintained would be completed by the end of 2005 (although in the event it was completed by September). In December 2004, after talks held in Jerusalem between the Israeli Minister of Defence, Lt-Gen. Shaul Mofaz, and the Egyptian intelligence chief, Omar Suleiman, it was agreed that 750 Egyptian troops would be stationed on the border with Gaza ahead of the Israeli withdrawal, in a bid to prevent arms from being smuggled into the territory for use by Palestinian militants.

Following the terrorist attacks in the Sinai region in October 2004 (see above), Egypt made clear its wish to send troops into the demilitarized buffer zone along the border with Israel, claiming that a military presence there could prevent further attacks. In early December Egypt released an Israeli businessman who had been convicted of espionage in 1997, in exchange for the release of six Egyptian students from prison in Israel. Later in the month Ahmad Aboul Gheit, Egypt's Minister of Foreign Affairs, and Suleiman visited Israel to confirm the deal and it was announced that Egypt would soon return an ambassador to Tel-Aviv. In mid-December 2004 a new trade deal between Egypt and Israel was signed allowing duty-free export between three newly established 'qualified industrial zones' and the USA, provided that at least 11.7% of the goods were manufactured in Israel. Despite being positively received within many Egyptian business circles, the protocol triggered angry demonstrations in Cairo among those who believed it would give Israel too much economic power over the country. In March 2005 Muhammad Asim Ibrahim, the former Egyptian ambassador to Sudan, assumed the role of ambassador to Israel.

In the months prior to the Israeli withdrawal from the Gaza Strip in August–September 2005 (see the chapter on Israel), Israel and Egypt held official talks regarding the deployment of Egyptian forces along the border with Gaza. On 1 August a deal was reached 'in principle' whereby 750 Egyptian border guards would police the southern border and attempt to prevent arms-smuggling. The deal was approved by the Israeli Cabinet on 28 August and by the Knesset three days later. In late October it was announced that the border with Gaza would be reopened at the Rafah checkpoint to allow key border crossings, and on 26 November some 1,500 Palestinians passed into Egypt. In February 2006, following Hamas's decisive victory in the first Palestinian legislative elections since 1996, leaders of the organization held discussions in Cairo regarding the formation of a new administration. Egypt subsequently began to exert pressure on Hamas to reconsider its position regarding Israel's right to existence, while urging Israel not to impose sanctions on the Hamas-led administration appointed in March 2006.

The election of a new Israeli Government under Prime Minister Ehud Olmert in March 2006 led to renewed Egyptian efforts to revive the Middle East peace process. In early June Mubarak and Olmert held their first summit meeting in Sharm esh-Sheikh, during which Olmert agreed to meet with Palestinian President Mahmud Abbas for talks later in that month. However, in late June, as Israeli armed forces carried out a new campaign in Gaza following the abduction by Palestinian militants of an Israeli soldier (two other soldiers died in the raid), the proposed meeting between Olmert and Abbas was postponed; subsequent Egyptian efforts to negotiate the soldier's release proved unsuccessful and were ongoing in 2007. In July 2006 Mubarak expressed Egypt's solidarity with Lebanon after Israel launched a large-scale offensive against Hezbollah positions in southern Lebanon in response to the kidnapping by Hezbollah militants of two Israeli soldiers and the killing of several others in a cross-border raid, and amid a series of missile attacks on northern Israel (see the chapters on Israel and Lebanon). In late October 3,000 additional Egyptian troops were deployed along the border with Gaza following reports by an Israeli newspaper that Israel was planning an attack in the border area aimed at destroying underground tunnels, which it claimed were being used by militants to smuggle weapons into Gaza.

After the commencement of serious factional fighting between militias of the rival Hamas and Fatah factions in the Gaza Strip following the formation of a Hamas-dominated administration in the West Bank and Gaza in March 2006, Egyptian officials were involved in diplomatic efforts, led principally by Saudi Arabia, to secure a lasting cease-fire between the two sides and establish a Palestinian national unity cabinet. Although a power-sharing administration was formed in mid-March 2007, Hamas militants seized control of Gaza in mid-June, effectively dividing the Palestinian territories into two separate entities (for a more detailed account, see the chapter on the Palestinian Autonomous Areas). The Egyptian authorities admitted in mid-April 2007 that two months previously an Egyptian engineer employed at the country's nuclear energy agency had been detained and charged with espionage on behalf of Mossad; Israel denied the claims. The defendant, Muhammad Sayed Saber Ali, was sentenced to life imprisonment by a state security court in late June, together with two foreign nationals who had been tried *in absentia*. Meanwhile, in the same month President Mubarak hosted a summit meeting of regional leaders, including Olmert, Abbas and King Abdullah of Jordan, in Sharm esh-Sheikh, with a view to restarting Middle East peace negotiations based on the 'land-for-peace' plan proposed by Saudi Arabia in 2002.

Despite initial hopes for an improvement in the regional situation following the international peace conference held in Annapolis, Maryland, USA, in late November 2007, Mubarak was highly critical of Israel's continued expansion of Jewish settlements in the West Bank, which he said would seriously hinder the prospects of a comprehensive peace deal being achieved by the US Administration's intended deadline of the end of 2008. The Israeli Deputy Prime Minister and Minister of Defence, Ehud Barak, ordered virtually a complete blockade on the Gaza Strip in mid-January 2008, in an attempt to counter the growing number of rockets being launched onto Israeli border towns from the Strip by militants of the Hamas group. In late January Palestinian fighters succeeded in breaching the Rafa crossing that divides Gaza from Egypt and hundreds of thousands of Palestinians entered Egypt in search of food, fuel and medical supplies. The crossing had been almost permanently closed since Hamas's takeover of the Strip in June 2007 because the Egyptian Government, as does Israel, refuses to recognize Hamas as the legitimate administration there. Egyptian officials responded by offering their backing to a plan proposed by President Abbas that would allow for the PA, rather than Hamas, to assume control of the Egypt–Gaza border. The breaches in the border were repaired in early February 2008; however, there were reports of exchanges of gunfire between Egyptian security forces and Palestinian gunmen as tensions continued.

Although the USA announced in April 1996 that it would supply advanced military equipment to Egypt, including 21 F-16 fighter aircraft, in acknowledgement of the country's key role in the Middle East peace process, relations between Egypt and the USA have remained tense. In August 1998 Egypt was highly critical of US military air-strikes against targets in Afghanistan and Sudan held by the US authorities to be associated with Osama bin Laden. Tensions were further exacerbated by the air-strikes undertaken against Iraq by US and British forces in December, since Mubarak had consistently urged a diplomatic solution to the issue of weapons inspections (see the chapter on Iraq). Differences persisted as the US Secretary of Defense, William Cohen, visited Cairo and other regional capitals in March 1999 to seek support for a renewed air campaign against Iraq. While in Egypt Cohen agreed to supply Egypt with US $3,200m. of defence equipment, including a further 24 F-16 fighter aircraft. Following a further visit by Cohen, it was announced in April 2000 that the USA would supply short-range missiles in order to modernize Egypt's air-defence system. Meanwhile, Mubarak visited Washington, DC, in June 1999 and the two countries made significant progress on proposals for the resumption of Middle East peace talks, culminating in the signing of the Sharm esh-Sheikh Memorandum in September.

In late 2000 the Egyptian and US leaders co-operated closely in their efforts to mediate in the Middle East crisis (see above). During a visit to the USA in April 2001 President Mubarak met with President George W. Bush for the first time and urged the USA actively to support the Egyptian-Jordanian peace plan (see above). Meanwhile, Bush, who had indicated that Iraq would be his Administration's priority in terms of Middle East policy, expressed his unease at Egypt's lack of support for international sanctions against Saddam Hussain; he also urged Egypt to return its ambassador to Israel. Relations between Egypt and the USA deteriorated in mid-2002 following the imprisonment of Sa'adeddin Ibrahim (see above) and the subsequent announcement by the Bush Administration that it would suspend any additional foreign aid to Egypt in protest at what it considered to be the country's poor treatment of pro-democracy campaigners and human rights organizations. It was emphasized, however, that existing aid programmes would not be affected (the USA provides Egypt with annual assistance worth some $1,700m.). Bilateral relations were further strained in September after David Welch, the US ambassador to Egypt, writing in the daily *Al-Ahram*, criticized a number of Egyptian publications for suggesting that al-Qa'ida had not been responsible for the previous year's attacks on the mainland USA. Welch was subsequently declared *persona non grata* in a widely published open letter signed by a number of prominent Egyptian intellectuals.

As the likelihood of a US-led military campaign to oust the Iraqi regime of Saddam Hussain increased during late 2002, President Mubarak was one of a number of Arab leaders who expressed their concern at the effects of military intervention in Iraq on the Middle East as a whole, as well as its implications for the unity of Iraq. In September Mubarak received the Iraqi Minister of Foreign Affairs and requested that Iraq comply with pertinent UN resolutions and allow UN weapons inspectors to operate freely within the country. However, a series of Arab League meetings in early 2003 served to highlight the deepening divisions over the issue among Arab states. Following the commencement of US-led hostilities against the Iraqi regime in mid-March, there were a number of anti-war demonstrations in Cairo, resulting in the arrest of some 800 protesters. At the end of March Mubarak warned that the conflict would ignite Islamist fanaticism and create '100 new bin Ladens'. None the less, the ousting of Saddam Hussain in early April was met with considerable ambivalence by Egypt.

In April 2004 Mubarak criticized the US Administration for its refusal to condemn the killing by Israeli forces of the newly appointed Hamas leader Abd al-Aziz ar-Rantisi in the Gaza Strip. In January 2006 the USA was reported to have ended negotiations with Egypt concerning a bilateral trade accord, in protest against the imprisonment of the Al-Ghad leader, Ayman an-Nour (see above). However, during a visit to Egypt in February, US Secretary of State Condoleezza Rice denied that the talks had ended and insisted that the delay was unrelated to concerns over the progress of Egyptian domestic reform. After a tour of the Gulf states in March, the Egyptian President issued a stern warning to the US Administration not to take military action against Iran, which was facing increasing pressure from the international community regarding its nuclear programme (see the chapter on Iran). Mubarak warned that such action would provoke retaliatory attacks by insurgent groups within Iraq and by movements such as the Iranian-supported Shi'ite fundamentalist Hezbollah in Lebanon. In May a proposal to reduce US aid to Egypt, in response to the recent stalling on political and economic reform, was defeated in the US House of Representatives; the initiative, none the less, demonstrated the growing frustration on the part of the USA over the issue of reform. In December President Mubarak condemned the execution of former Iraqi President Saddam Hussain, who had been sentenced to death by the Supreme Iraqi Criminal Tribunal in November; Mubarak reiterated an earlier warning that the death of Saddam Hussain would provoke an escalation of sectarian conflict in Iraq. Egypt has hosted a large number of Iraqi refugees since 2003, with UNHCR estimating the number at close to 70,000 in September 2007.

The waning importance of US-Egyptian relations to both countries again became apparent in mid-January 2008, when President Bush visited Egypt only briefly at the end of an eight-day tour of the Middle East intended principally to accelerate the relaunch of the peace process and to secure Arab support in the US Administration's ongoing efforts to persuade Iran to abandon its nuclear programme. The US leadership had been strongly critical of Egypt for its failure to secure its border with the Gaza Strip following the takeover of the territory by Hamas militants in June 2007 and to prevent Palestinian militants from smuggling weapons into Gaza for use in attacks against Israeli targets. In December 2007 the US Congress voted to withhold US $100m. in aid to Egypt until the USA had received assurances that the authorities in Cairo had imposed sufficient measures to bring to an end the cross-border arms-smuggling and had also taken steps to improve the country's human rights record.

In December 2003 President Mubarak held talks with the Iranian President, Dr Sayed Muhammad Khatami, in Geneva, representing the first meeting between the leaders of the two countries since bilateral diplomatic relations were severed following the Islamic Revolution in Iran of 1979. In January 2004 it was reported that they planned to restore diplomatic relations, although Egypt refused officially to confirm this. In December Iran handed over to Egypt Moustafa Hamzah, a leader of Gama'ah al-Islamiyah and the alleged mastermind of a 1995 assassination attempt on President Mubarak, representing a significant step towards improving bilateral relations. After Khatami's successor, President Mahmoud Ahmadinejad, declared in May 2007 that Iran was prepared to resume diplomatic ties with Egypt and to open an embassy in Cairo, senior officials from the respective countries held what were said to have been 'constructive' discussions, which included a visit by the Speaker of the Iranian Majlis (parliament), Gholam-Ali Haddad-Adel, to Cairo at the end of January 2008. Despite the evident thaw in bilateral relations, however, it appeared that the Egyptian leadership was reluctant to proceed with the normalization until Iran first ended what it deemed to be its interference in the internal affairs of several Arab countries, notably Iraq, Lebanon and the Palestinian territories.

Egypt's relations with Libya improved steadily during the 1990s, and Egypt joined the Community of Sahel-Saharan States (CEN-SAD, see p. 411), which was established in Tripoli in 1997. Meanwhile, bilateral links were dominated by the repercussions of the Lockerbie bombing (see the chapter on Libya), with Egypt actively seeking to avert a confrontation between Libya and the USA and its Western allies. Following the suspension of UN sanctions against Libya in April 1999, the national carrier, EgyptAir, resumed regular flights to Tripoli in July 2000; Libyan air services to Egypt resumed later that month.

Egypt has a long-standing border dispute with Sudan concerning the so-called Halaib triangle. Relations deteriorated sharply in mid-1995, after Egypt accused Sudan of complicity in the attempted assassination of President Mubarak in Addis Ababa (see above). Egypt strengthened its control of the Halaib triangle, and subsequently (in contravention of a bilateral agreement concluded in 1978) imposed visa and permit requirements on Sudanese nationals visiting or resident in Egypt. In September 1995 the OAU accused Sudan of direct involvement in the assassination attempt, and in December the organization demanded that Sudan extradite immediately three individuals sought in connection with the attack. (It was reported in mid-1999 that one of the suspects had been extradited to Cairo.) In February 1996 the Sudanese authorities introduced permit requirements for Egyptian nationals resident in Sudan. President Mubarak met with his Sudanese counterpart, Brig. Omar Hassan Ahmad al-Bashir, at the Arab League summit meeting in Cairo in May. In July, however, Egypt accused Sudan of harbouring Egyptian terrorists, contrary to an agreement concluded at the summit meeting. None the less, Egypt opposed the imposition by the UN of more stringent economic sanctions against Sudan (q.v.), on the grounds that they would harm the Sudanese people more than the regime.

Bilateral security talks recommenced in August 1997 after a year-long suspension. In February 1998 river transport resumed between the Egyptian port of Aswan and Wadi Halfa in Sudan, and in April the two countries agreed to establish a joint ministerial committee. Although Sudan considered the presence of Sudanese opposition leaders in Egypt an obstacle to the normalization process, a meeting in Cairo, in May 1999, between representatives of the Sudanese Government and Sudan's former President Gaafar Muhammed Nimeri, to discuss arrangements for his return from exile, represented significant progress on this issue. In December Egypt and Sudan agreed to a full normalization of relations, and resolved to co-operate in addressing their border dispute. The new Egyptian ambassador to Sudan assumed his post in Khartoum in March 2000, and in September a number of bilateral co-operation accords were signed. In January 2004 Mubarak and al-Bashir signed what was termed the 'four freedoms' agreement, which allowed for freedom of movement, residence, work and property ownership between the two countries; the agreement came into effect in September. At further talks in December the two sides agreed to accelerate plans to link their respective road and railway networks. In December 2005 at least 27 Sudanese asylum-seekers were killed, and hundreds arrested, when Egyptian police stormed a demonstration outside an office of the UN High Commissioner for Refugees in Cairo. The migrants had been protesting against conditions in Egypt for up to three months, and were demanding to be resettled in another country. An official Egyptian investigation into the causes of the Sudanese deaths concluded that the asylum-seekers had died as the result of a 'stampede', a ruling that led human rights groups in December 2007 to demand that the Egyptian Government agree to allow an independent inquiry into the incident. During 2006–07 Egyptian officials were involved in mediation efforts to find a regional solution to the conflict in Sudan's Darfur region, and in January 2008 the country deployed 1,200 troops to Darfur as part of a joint AU-UN peace-keeping force.

Meanwhile, in 2004 disputes over the Nile began to escalate as Tanzania confirmed that it intended to build a 170-km pipeline to draw water from Lake Victoria. This decision contravened the Nile Water Agreement drawn up in 1929 between Egypt and the United Kingdom, which states that Egypt has the right to veto any work which might threaten the flow of the river and allows the country to inspect the entire length of the Nile. Talks began in Uganda in March 2004 between the 10 countries that share the Nile's waters, and an agreement was reached in April 2006 whereby a permanent commission was to be established to oversee management, planning and use of the river. In June 2007 the ministers responsible for water affairs in the Nile Basin countries signed a Nile River Basin Co-operative Framework Agreement, which required ratification by the 10 states prior to coming into effect.

Government

Legislative power is held by the unicameral Majlis ash-Sha'ab (People's Assembly), which has 454 members: 10 nominated by the President and 444 directly elected for five years from 222 constituencies. In May 2005 a constitutional amendment was approved by national referendum to introduce a system of direct, contested presidential elections; further changes to the Constitution were adopted in March 2007 (see Recent History). The President, who is Head of State, has executive powers and may appoint one or more Vice-Presidents, a Prime Minister and a Council of Ministers. His term is for six years and he may be elected for subsequent terms. There is also a 210-member advisory body, the Shura Council. The country is divided into 27 governorates.

Defence

As assessed at November 2007, Egypt had total armed forces of 468,500 (army 340,000, air defence command 80,000, navy 18,500, air force 30,000), with 479,000 reserves. There is a selective three-year period of national service. There are active paramilitary forces of an estimated 397,000. Budgeted defence expenditure for 2006/07 was forecast at £E17,403m.

Economic Affairs

In 2006, according to estimates by the World Bank, Egypt's gross national income (GNI), measured at average 2004–06 prices, was US $101,658m., equivalent to $1,350 per head (or $4,690 per head on an international purchasing-power parity basis). During 1996–2006, it was estimated, the population increased at an average annual rate of 1.9%, while gross domestic product (GDP) per head increased, in real terms, by 2.7% per year. Overall GDP increased, in real terms, at an average annual rate of 4.6% in 1996–2006; real GDP increased by 6.8% in 2006.

Agriculture (including forestry and fishing) contributed 14.1% of GDP in 2005/06, and employed an estimated 30.9% of the economically active population in 2005. The principal crops include sugar cane, wheat, maize, rice, and fruit and vegetables (particularly tomatoes). Cotton is the principal cash crop. Exports of food and live animals accounted for 9.2% of total exports in 2004. According to the African Development Bank (ADB), during 1996–2006 agricultural GDP increased at an average annual rate of 5.0%. Agricultural GDP grew by an estimated 3.2% in 2005/06, according to Central Bank of Egypt (CBE) figures.

Industry (including mining, manufacturing, construction and power) provided 38.4% of GDP in 2005/06, and engaged about 21.5% of the employed labour force in 2005. According to the ADB, during 1996–2006 industrial GDP expanded at an average annual rate of 7.1%. Industrial GDP increased by an estimated 10.5% in 2005/06, according to CBE data.

Mining contributed 15.5% of GDP in 2005/06. Egypt's mineral resources include petroleum, natural gas, phosphates, manganese, uranium, coal, iron ore and gold. Although the mining sector employed only 0.2% of the working population in 2005, petroleum and petroleum products accounted for 39.4% of total export earnings in 2004. Petroleum production averaged an estimated 678,000 barrels per day in 2006, and at the end of that year Egypt's oil reserves were estimated to total 3,700m. barrels (sufficient to sustain production at 2006 levels for 15 years). At the end of 2006 Egypt's proven natural gas reserves totalled 1,940,000m. cu m, sustainable for a little over 43 years at constant production levels (totalling 44,800m. cu m in 2006). Until the early part of this century all the natural gas produced was consumed domestically, but the Government began exporting the commodity in 2003. In mid-2003 BP Egypt announced the largest petroleum discovery in the country for 14 years, and there were also major discoveries of natural gas and condensate during 2003–05. Mining GDP increased by 20.8% in 2005/06.

Manufacturing contributed 17.0% of GDP in 2005/06, and engaged some 11.5% of the employed labour force in 2005. Based on the value of output, the main branches of manufacturing are food products, petroleum refining, chemicals, textiles, metals and metal products, and non-metallic mineral manufactures. In 2003 the Government announced major plans to develop the petrochemicals industry. According to the ADB, during 1996–2006 the real GDP of the manufacturing sector increased by an average of 7.3% per year. Manufacturing GDP expanded by 5.8% in 2005/06, according to the CBE.

Energy is derived principally from natural gas (which provided 70.8% of total electricity output in 2004), petroleum (16.2%) and hydroelectric power (12.5%). In 2004 fuel imports accounted for an estimated 8.3% of the value of merchandise imports. In September 2006 the Government announced that the programme to develop peaceful nuclear technology, which had been suspended in the mid-1980s, was to recommence. A project to construct a 1,000 MW nuclear plant on the Mediterranean coast at Dabaa was approved in September 2006, with a scheduled completion date of 2015.

Services contributed 47.5% of GDP in 2005/06, and employed about 47.6% of the working population in 2005. For much of the 1990s the tourism sector was severely undermined by the campaign of violence aimed by militant Islamists at tourist targets, and visitor numbers and tourism revenues declined significantly. A recovery in the sector was subsequently hindered by the regional insecurity arising from the Israeli–Palestinian violence from late 2000, the terrorist attacks against the USA in September 2001 and the US-led intervention in Iraq in early 2003. The effect on the tourism industry of the Sinai bombings in 2004–06, however, appeared to be minimal: it was estimated that the number of visitors to Egypt had increased by some 6% in 2005, and a further increase, of 5.5%, was recorded in 2006. According to the ADB, in 1996–2006 the real GDP of the services sector increased by an average of 5.8% per year. Services GDP increased by an estimated 5.7% in 2005/06, according to CBE figures.

In 2006 Egypt recorded a visible trade deficit of US $8,438m., although there was a surplus of $2,635m. on the current account of the balance of payments. In 2004 the principal source of imports (10.3%) was the USA; other major suppliers were Germany, the People's Republic of China, Italy and Algeria. The principal market for exports was Italy (12.5%), followed by the USA, Spain and the Netherlands. Egypt's principal exports in 2004 were mineral fuels and lubricants, basic manufactures, food and live animals, crude materials and chemicals. The principal imports were machinery and transport equipment, food and live animals, basic manufactures and chemicals.

For the financial year 2006/07 there was a preliminary deficit of just £E257m. in the central government budget (equivalent to only 0.04% of GDP). Egypt's external debt totalled US $34,114m. at the end of 2005, of which $24,892m. was long-term public debt. In that year the cost of servicing the foreign debt was equivalent to 6.8% of the value of exports of goods and services. The annual rate of inflation averaged 5.5% in 1995–2006. Consumer prices increased by an average of 7.6% in 2006. An estimated 9.0% of the total labour force were unemployed at the end of 2006.

Egypt is a member of the Common Market for Eastern and Southern Africa (COMESA, see p. 205), the Council of Arab Economic Unity (see p. 222), the Organization of Arab Petroleum Exporting Countries (OAPEC, see p. 366) and the African Petroleum Producers' Association (see p. 407).

Following an impressive macro-economic performance during much of the 1990s, characterized by strong GDP growth and low inflation, Egypt's economy suffered a series of major reverses from the late 1990s; a serious liquidity crisis, resulting primarily from a depletion in the main sources of hard currency, prompted intervention by the Government and the Central Bank in mid-2000. The Egyptian pound's fixed exchange rate against the US dollar was informally abandoned, and in January 2001, under a series of fiscal reforms, control over the exchange rate was transferred to the Central Bank, which introduced a 'managed peg' system. Nevertheless, in 2001 the pound was devalued on a further three occasions and in January 2003, in anticipation of further economic difficulties resulting from a likely US-led military campaign in Iraq, the Government abandoned the pound's peg to the US dollar and allowed the currency to float freely. The USA agreed to provide US $2,300m. worth of loan guarantees and economic grants to offset the expected economic repercussions of the conflict, namely significantly decreased revenues from tourism and the Suez Canal. Nevertheless, the tourism industry experienced a resurgence in 2003 and sectoral growth continued during 2004–06, despite terrorist attacks by militant Islamist groups in Cairo and on the Sinai Peninsula. In 2006/07 (year to June) a record 9.7m. tourists visited Egypt, and economic growth was impressive, reaching 7.1%. This success was driven by high foreign direct investment ($11,100m. in 2006/07), after fiscal reforms introduced since the Government of Prime Minister Ahmad Nazif was appointed in mid-2004 included the creation of a Ministry of Investment. The non-hydrocarbon sectors also contributed to the economy's strong performance in 2006/07: construction and manufacturing GDP grew by 16.0% and 7.3%, respectively. Exports increased by 35%, while revenues from the Suez Canal totalled a record $4,600m. Meanwhile, oil production remained high in spite of expected decreases, and new discoveries of deposits remained possible. Owing to the consistently high global oil prices, this has led to expectations of increased state petroleum revenues. However, Egypt's recent period of sustained economic growth has only served to highlight the large disparity between the country's rich and poor. Indeed, the economic expansion—while allowing many Egyptians to enter the burgeoning middle class—has resulted in high rates of inflation, which has in turn only widened the divide. In January 2008 Nazif pledged to expand the Government's social security provisions to include 1m. families rather than the current 650,000, and to create more job opportunities for young Egyptians. Official figures suggested that unemployment fell rapidly in 2006/07 (although international observers expressed scepticism), and strong economic growth was anticipated for 2007/08.

Education

Education at all levels is available free of charge, and is officially compulsory for eight years between six and 14 years of age. Primary education, beginning at six years of age, lasts for five years. Secondary education, from 11 years of age, lasts for a further six years, comprising two cycles (the first being preparatory) of three years each. In 2004/05, according to UNESCO estimates, primary enrolment included 93.7% of children in the relevant age-group, while the comparable ratio for secondary enrolment was 82.1%. In 2004/05 there were an estimated 2,594,186 students enrolled at higher education institutions. The Al-Azhar University and its various preparatory and associated institutes provide instruction and training in various disciplines, with emphasis on adherence to Islamic principles and teachings. Budget forecasts for 2006/07 allocated £E27,108m. (some 13.5% of total expenditure) to education.

Public Holidays

2008: 1 January (New Year), 10 January*† (Muharram, Islamic New Year), 20 March* (Mouloud/Yum an-Nabi, Birth of Muhammad), 25 April (Sinai Day), 28 April (Sham an-Nessim, Coptic Easter Monday), 23 July (Revolution Day), 30 July* (Leilat al-Meiraj, Ascension of Muhammad), 1 October* (Id al-Fitr, end of Ramadan), 6 October (Armed Forces Day), 24 October (Popular Resistance Day), 9 December* (Id al-Adha, Feast of the Sacrifice), 23 December (Victory Day), 29 December*† (Muharram, Islamic New Year).

2009: 1 January (New Year), 9 March* (Mouloud/Yum an-Nabi, Birth of Muhammad), 20 April (Sham an-Nessim, Coptic Easter Monday), 25 April (Sinai Day), 23 July (Revolution Day), 19 July* (Leilat al-Meiraj, Ascension of Muhammad), 20 September* (Id al-Fitr, end of Ramadan), 6 October (Armed Forces Day), 24 October (Popular Resistance Day), 27 November* (Id al-Adha, Feast of the Sacrifice), 18 December* (Muharram, Islamic New Year), 23 December (Victory Day).

* These holidays are dependent on the Islamic lunar calendar and may vary by one or two days from the dates given.

† This festival occurs twice (marking the start of the Islamic years AH 1429 and 1430) within the same Gregorian year.

Coptic Christian holidays include: Christmas (7 January), Palm Sunday and Easter Sunday.

Weights and Measures

The metric system is in force, but some Egyptian measurements are still in use.

EGYPT

Statistical Survey

Statistical Survey

Sources (unless otherwise stated): Central Agency for Public Mobilization and Statistics, POB 2086, Cairo (Nasr City); tel. (2) 4020574; fax (2) 4024099; e-mail misr@capmas.gov.eg; internet www.capmas.gov.eg; Research Department, National Bank of Egypt, Cairo.

Area and Population

AREA, POPULATION AND DENSITY

Area (sq km)	1,002,000*
Population (census results)†	
31 December 1996	59,312,914
21 November 2006	
Males	37,101,628
Females	35,479,025
Total	72,580,653
Density (per sq km) at 21 November 2006	72.4

* 386,874 sq miles; inhabited and cultivated territory accounts for 55,039 sq km (21,251 sq miles).

† Excluding Egyptian nationals abroad, totalling an estimated 2,180,000 in 1996 and an estimated 3,901,396 in 2006.

GOVERNORATES
(population at 2006 census)

Governorate	Area (sq km)	Population	Density (per sq km)	Capital
Cairo	214.20	7,786,640	36,352.2	Cairo
Alexandria	2,679.36	4,110,015	1,534.0	Alexandria
Port Said	72.07	570,768	7,919.6	Port Said
Ismailia	1,441.59	942,832	654.0	Ismailia
Suez	17,840.42	510,935	28.6	Suez
Damietta	589.17	1,092,316	1,854.0	Damietta
Dakahlia	3,470.90	4,985,187	1,436.3	El-Mansoura
Sharkia	4,179.55	5,340,058	1,277.7	Zagazig
Kalyoubia	1,001.09	4,237,003	4,232.4	Banha
Kafr esh-Sheikh	3,437.12	2,618,111	761.7	Kafr esh-Sheikh
Gharbia	1,942.21	4,011,921	2,065.6	Tanta
Menoufia	1,532.13	3,270,404	2,134.5	Shebien el-Kom
Behera	10,129.48	4,737,129	467.7	Damanhour
Giza	85,153.56	6,272,571	73.7	Giza
Beni-Suef	1,321.50	2,290,527	1,733.3	Beni-Suef
Fayoum	1,827.10	2,512,792	1,375.3	El-Fayoum
Menia	2,261.70	4,179,309	1,847.9	El-Menia
Asyout	1,553.00	3,441,597	2,216.1	Asyout
Suhag	1,547.20	3,746,377	2,421.4	Suhag
Qena	1,795.60	3,001,494	1,671.6	Qena
Luxor	55.00	451,318	8,205.8	Luxor
Aswan	678.45	1,184,432	1,745.8	Aswan
Red Sea	203,685.00	288,233	1.4	Hurghada
El-Wadi el-Gidid	376,505.00	187,256	0.5	El-Kharga
Matruh	212,112.00	322,341	1.5	Matruh
North Sinai	27,574.00	339,752	12.3	El-Areesh
South Sinai	33,140.00	149,335	4.5	Et-Tour
Total	**997,738.40***	**72,580,653**	**72.4***	—

* The official, rounded national total is 1,002,000 sq km.

PRINCIPAL TOWNS
(population at 1996 census)*

Cairo (Al-Qahirah, the capital)	6,789,479	Zagazig (Az-Zaqaziq)	267,351
Alexandria (Al-Iskandariyah)	3,328,196	El-Fayum (Al-Fayyum)	260,964
Giza (Al-Jizah)	2,221,868	Ismailia (Al-Ismailiyah)	254,477
Shoubra el-Kheima (Shubra al-Khaymah)	870,716	Kafr ed-Dawar (Kafr ad-Dawwar)	231,978
Port Said (Bur Sa'id)	469,533	Aswan	219,017
Suez (As-Suways)	417,610	Damanhour (Damanhur)	212,203
El-Mahalla el-Koubra (Al-Mahallah al-Kubra)	395,402	El-Menia (Al-Minya)	201,360
Tanta	371,010	Beni-Suef (Bani-Suwayf)	172,032
El-Mansoura (Al-Mansurah)	369,621	Qena (Qina)	171,275
Luxor (Al-Uqsor)	360,503	Suhag (Sawhaj)	170,125
Asyout (Asyut)	343,498	Shebien el-Kom (Shibin al-Kawn)	159,909

* Figures refer to provisional population. Revised figures include: Cairo 6,800,992; Alexandria 3,339,076; Port Said 472,335; Suez 417,527.

Mid-2005 ('000, incl. suburbs, UN estimates): Cairo 11,128; Alexandria 3,770 (Source: UN, *World Urbanization Prospects: The 2005 Revision*).

BIRTHS, MARRIAGES AND DEATHS

	Registered live births		Registered marriages		Registered deaths	
	Number	Rate (per 1,000)	Number	Rate (per 1,000)	Number	Rate (per 1,000)
1998	1,687,252	27.5	503,651	8.2	399,772	6.5
1999	1,693,025	27.0	525,412	8.3	401,433	6.4
2000	1,751,854	27.4	592,381	n.a.	404,699	6.3
2001	1,741,308	26.7	457,534	n.a.	404,531	6.2
2002	1,766,589	26.5	510,547	n.a.	424,034	6.4
2003	1,777,418	26.1	537,092	n.a.	440,149	6.5
2004	1,779,500	25.0	550,709	n.a.	440,790	6.2
2005	1,800,972	25.0	522,751	n.a.	450,646	6.3

Source: UN, *Demographic Yearbook*.

Registered marriages (number): 522,887 in 2006.

Expectation of life (years at birth, WHO estimates): 68.0 (males 66.1; females 70.0) in 2005 (Source: WHO, *World Health Statistics*).

ECONOMICALLY ACTIVE POPULATION
(sample surveys, '000 persons aged 15 years and over)

	2003	2004	2005
Agriculture, hunting and forestry	5,250.1	5,820.5	5,814.6
Fishing	161.2	137.7	157.6
Mining and quarrying	32.0	32.0	29.0
Manufacturing	1,976.9	2,085.1	2,229.7
Electricity, gas and water supply	228.7	218.5	245.3
Construction	1,341.0	1,399.5	1,649.8
Wholesale and retail trade; repair of motor vehicles, motorcycles and personal and household goods	2,161.1	2,252.0	2,141.2
Hotels and restaurants	291.3	334.4	366.4
Transport, storage and communications	1,145.3	1,171.4	1,322.7
Financial intermediation	199.9	195.8	169.2
Real estate, renting and business activities	347.2	355.1	400.5
Public administration and defence; compulsory social security	2,025.1	1,926.2	1,849.5
Education	1,969.1	1,845.5	1,908.2

EGYPT

—continued	2003	2004	2005
Health and social work	545.6	503.3	503.3
Other community, social and personal service activities	408.8	404.5	464.8
Private households with employed persons	33.8	34.4	52.6
Extra-territorial organizations and bodies	—	—	2.7
Activities not adequately defined	1.5	1.5	34.3
Total employed	18,118.6	18,717.4	19,341.7
Unemployed	2,240.7	2,153.9	2,450.0
Total labour force	20,359.3	20,871.3	21,791.7
Males	15,838.4	15,879.0	16,787.2
Females	4,520.9	4,992.3	5,004.5

Source: ILO.

2006 (sample survey, '000 persons aged 15 years and over, at 31 December): Total employed 21,229 (males 16,839, females 4,390); Unemployed 2,098 (males 1,075, females 1,023); Total labour force 23,327 (males 17,914, females 5,413).

Health and Welfare

KEY INDICATORS

Total fertility rate (children per woman, 2005)	3.1
Under-5 mortality rate (per 1,000 live births, 2005)	33
HIV/AIDS (% of persons aged 15–49, 2005)	<0.1
Physicians (per 1,000 head, 2003)	0.54
Hospital beds (per 1,000 head, 2005)	2.20
Health expenditure (2004): US $ per head (PPP)	258.3
Health expenditure (2004): % of GDP	6.1
Health expenditure (2004): public (% of total)	38.2
Access to water (% of persons, 2004)	98
Access to sanitation (% of persons, 2004)	70
Human Development Index (2005): ranking	112
Human Development Index (2005): value	0.708

For sources and definitions, see explanatory note on p. vi.

Agriculture

PRINCIPAL CROPS
('000 metric tons)

	2004	2005	2006
Wheat	7,177.9	8,185.0	8,308.0
Rice (paddy)	6,352.4	6,125.3	6,500.0*
Barley	163.1	167.0	167.0*
Maize	6,236.1	7,085.2	6,838.0
Sorghum	863.7	853.0	890.0
Potatoes	2,546.6	2,500.0*	2,500.0
Sweet potatoes	270.6	300.0*	300.0
Taro (Coco yam)	116.7	100.0*	100.0
Sugar cane	16,230.4	16,317.3	16,317.3*
Sugar beet	2,860.5	3,429.5	3,429.5*
Dry broad beans	330.5	281.7	315.0
Groundnuts (in shell)	191.8	199.6	180.0*
Olives	315.2	310.0*	310.0*
Cottonseed	446.3	335.0†	350.0†
Cabbages	541.9	550.0*	550.0*
Artichokes	54.5	70.0*	70.0*
Lettuce and chicory	136.0	140.0	140.0*
Tomatoes	7,640.8	7,600.0*	7,600.0*
Cauliflowers	131.2	130.0*	130.0*
Pumpkins, squash and gourds	678.3	690.0*	690.0
Cucumbers and gherkins	583.1	600.0*	600.0
Aubergines (Eggplants)	1,046.7	1,000.0*	1,000.0*
Chillies and green peppers	467.4	460.0*	460.0*
Dry onions	895.5	1,302.1	1,302.1*
Garlic	187.8	162.1	162.1
Green beans*	215.0	215.0	215.0
Green peas	293.4	290.0*	290.0*
Carrots and turnips	151.9	150.0*	150.0*
Okra	112.4	110.0*	110.0*
Bananas	875.1	880.0*	880.0*
Oranges	1,850.0	1,789.0†	1,789.0*

—continued	2004	2005	2006
Tangerines, mandarins, clementines and satsumas	661.3	665.0*	665.0*
Lemons and limes	338.1	338.0*	338.0*
Apples	546.2	550.0*	550.0*
Peaches and nectarines	360.9	360.0*	360.0*
Strawberries	105.0	100.0*	100.0*
Grapes	1,275.3	1,300.0*	1,300.0*
Watermelons	1,588.5	1,500.0*	1,500.0*
Cantaloupes and other melons	563.0	565.0*	565.0*
Figs	160.1	170.0*	170.0*
Guavas, mangoes and mangosteens	375.5	380.0*	380.0*
Dates	1,166.2	1,170.0*	1,170.0*
Cotton (lint)†	292.0	263.0	263.0

* FAO estimate(s).
† Unofficial figure(s).

Aggregate production ('000 metric tons, may include official, semi-official or estimated data): Total cereals 20,825.2 in 2004, 22,404.9 in 2005, 22,736.4 in 2006; Total roots and tubers 2,937.7 in 2004, 2,903.8 in 2005, 2,903.8 in 2006; Total vegetables (incl. melons) 15,927.2 in 2004, 16,165.5 in 2005, 16,165.5 in 2006; Total fruits (excl. melons) 8,205.8 in 2004, 8,196.0 in 2005, 8,196.0 in 2006.

Source: FAO.

LIVESTOCK
('000 head, year ending September)

	2003	2004	2005
Cattle	4,227	4,369	4,500*
Buffaloes	3,777	3,845	3,920*
Sheep	4,939	5,043	5,150*
Goats	3,811	3,889	3,960*
Pigs*	31	31	30
Horses*	62	62	62
Asses, mules or hinnies*	3,071	3,071	3,071
Camels*	135	135	120
Rabbits*	9,250	9,250	9,250
Chickens*	95,000	95,000	95,000
Ducks*	9,200	9,200	9,200
Geese*	9,100	9,100	9,100
Turkeys*	1,950	1,850	1,850

* FAO estimate(s).

2006: Figures assumed to be unchanged from 2005 (FAO estimates).

Source: FAO.

LIVESTOCK PRODUCTS
('000 metric tons)

	2003	2004	2005
Cattle meat	286.6	325.2	320.0*
Buffalo meat	229.2	268.7	270.0*
Sheep meat	49.6	40.4	42.5*
Goat meat	21.0	16.9	18.0*
Pig meat	1.6	1.5	1.5*
Camel meat*	38.8	40.0	40.0
Rabbit meat*	69.8	74.5	77.3
Chicken meat*	664.2	664.2	664.2
Cows' milk	2,597.6	2,125.9	1,695.0†
Buffaloes' milk	2,549.6	2,226.8	2,300.0*
Sheep's milk*	93.0	93.0	93.0
Goats' milk*	15.1	15.1	15.1
Hen eggs*	240.0	240.0	240.0
Honey	8.4	8.0	8.0*
Wool: greasy*	7.6	7.6	n.a.

* FAO estimate(s).
† Unofficial figure.

2006: Figures assumed to be unchanged from 2005 (FAO estimates).

Source: FAO.

EGYPT

Statistical Survey

Forestry

ROUNDWOOD REMOVALS
('000 cubic metres, excluding bark, FAO estimates)

	2004	2005	2006
Sawlogs, veneer logs and logs for sleepers	134	134	134
Other industrial roundwood	134	134	134
Fuel wood	16,792	16,949	17,059
Total	17,060	17,217	17,327

Source: FAO.

SAWNWOOD PRODUCTION
('000 cubic metres, incl. railway sleepers)

	1998	1999	2000
Total (all broadleaved)	3	4	4

2001–06: Output assumed to be unchanged from 2000 (FAO estimates).
Source: FAO.

Fishing

('000 metric tons, live weight)

	2003	2004	2005
Capture*	430.8	393.5	349.6
Nile tilapia	150.2	140.6	116.5
Mudfish	43.1	26.8	25.8
Other mullets	37.2	35.7	29.6
Aquaculture	445.2	471.5	539.7
Grass carp	88.5	40.4	n.a.
Silver carp	n.a.	75.6	n.a.
Nile tilapia	199.6	199.0	217.0
Flathead grey mullet	135.6	132.7	156.4
Total catch*	876.0	865.0	889.3

* FAO estimates.
Source: FAO.

Mining

('000 metric tons, unless otherwise indicated, year ending 30 June, estimates)

	2003	2004	2005
Crude petroleum ('000 barrels)	221,219	216,956	218,000
Natural gas (million cu m)	30,969	31,000	31,000
Iron ore*	2,237	2,400	2,600
Salt (unrefined)	1,341	1,400	1,400
Phosphate rock	2,183	2,219	2,730
Gypsum (crude)	792	1,000	1,000
Kaolin	260	260	260

* Figures refer to gross weight. The estimated iron content is 50%.
Source: US Geological Survey.

Industry

SELECTED PRODUCTS
('000 metric tons, unless otherwise indicated)

	2001	2002	2003
Cigarettes (million)	61,000	62,018	63,396
Mineral water ('000 hectolitres)	644	947	3,367
Caustic soda	38	42	50
Jet fuels	1,331	1,693	1,469
Kerosene	966	796	918
Distillate fuel oils	6,635	7,702	8,235
Motor spirit (gasoline)	5,613	6,046	6,306
Residual fuel oil (Mazout)	10,589	10,003	10,532
Petroleum bitumen (asphalt)	878	905	890
Cement	26,811	23,000	16,281
Electric energy (million kWh)	76,808	85,946	91,932

2004 ('000 metric tons, unless otherwise indicated): Jet fuels 2,080; Kerosene 507; Distillate fuel oils 7,922; Residual fuel oil 11,273; Petroleum bitumen (asphalt) 876; Cement 28,000; Electrical energy (million kWh) 101,299.

Source: UN, *Industrial Commodity Statistics Yearbook*.

Finance

CURRENCY AND EXCHANGE RATES

Monetary Units
1,000 millièmes = 100 piastres = 5 tallaris = 1 Egyptian pound (£E).

Sterling, Dollar and Euro Equivalents (31 October 2007)
£1 sterling = £E11.411;
US $1 = £E5.503;
€1 = £E7.950;
£E100 = £8.76 sterling = $18.17 = €12.58.

Note: From February 1991 foreign exchange transactions were conducted through only two markets, the primary market and the free market. With effect from 8 October 1991, the primary market was eliminated, and all foreign exchange transactions are effected through the free market. In January 2001 a new exchange rate mechanism was introduced, whereby the value of the Egyptian pound would be allowed to fluctuate within narrow limits: initially, as much as 1% above or below a rate that was set by the Central Bank of Egypt, but would be adjusted periodically in response to market conditions. The trading band was widened to 3% in August, and in January 2003 the Government adopted a floating exchange rate.

Average Exchange Rate (Egyptian pound per US $)
2004 6.196
2005 5.779
2006 5.733

GOVERNMENT FINANCE
(budgetary central government operations, cash basis, £E million, year ending 30 June, preliminary)

Summary of Balances

	2004/05	2005/06	2006/07
Revenue	110,865	151,266	176,320
Less Expense	114,317	165,640	176,577
Net cash inflow from operating activities	–3,452	–14,374	–257
Less Purchases of non-financial assets	23,275	21,212	23,825
Cash surplus/deficit	–26,727	–35,586	–24,082

EGYPT

Revenue

	2004/05	2005/06	2006/07
Taxes	75,760	97,779	113,573
Taxes on income, profits and capital gains	31,571	48,269	57,289
Individuals	9,315	9,381	9,661
Corporations and other enterprises	22,257	38,888	47,627
Taxes on goods and services	31,431	34,699	39,861
Taxes on international trade and transactions	7,745	9,654	10,374
Grants	2,854	2,379	3,548
Other revenue	32,251	51,108	59,199
Total	110,865	151,266	176,320

Expense/Outlays

Expense by economic type	2004/05	2005/06	2006/07
Compensation of employees	41,546	46,719	51,529
Use of goods and services	12,613	14,429	16,021
Subsidies	13,765	54,245	53,961
Other payments	21,692	19,740	20,279
Total (incl. others)	114,317	165,640	176,577

Outlays by function of government	2004/05	2005/06	2006/07
General public services	40,317	44,423	49,091
Defence	14,804	15,933	17,403
Public order and safety	8,901	10,523	11,123
Economic affairs	11,762	11,336	13,333
Environmental protection	493	412	3,553
Housing and community amenities	6,003	5,614	5,916
Health	7,258	9,665	9,873
Recreation, culture and religion	7,306	7,635	8,572
Education	25,818	25,636	27,108
Social protection	14,930	55,673	54,432
Total	137,592	186,851	200,402

Source: IMF, *Government Finance Statistics Yearbook*.

INTERNATIONAL RESERVES
(US $ million at 31 December)

	2004	2005	2006
Gold*	717	779	1,119
IMF special drawing rights	165	101	121
Foreign exchange	14,108	20,508	24,341
Total	14,990	21,388	25,581

* National valuation.

Source: IMF, *International Financial Statistics*.

MONEY SUPPLY
(£E million at 31 December)

	2003	2004	2005
Currency outside banks	52,475	59,795	69,331
Demand deposits at deposit money banks	36,627	43,320	51,806
Total money (incl. others)*	93,520	108,498	125,466

* Of which amounts, foreign currency deposits accounted for £E52,864m. in 2003, £E56,810m. in 2004 and £E40,816m. in 2005.

Source: IMF, *International Financial Statistics*.

COST OF LIVING
(Consumer Price Index; base: 2000 = 100)

	2001	2002	2003
Food, beverages and tobacco	101.1	105.3	112.3
Fuel and light	100.6	100.6	100.6
Clothing and footwear	102.1	104.3	105.9
Rent	100.2	100.7	102.2
All items (incl. others)	102.2	105.0	109.5

All items: 127.4 in 2004; 133.7 in 2005; 143.9 in 2006.

Source: ILO.

NATIONAL ACCOUNTS
(£E million, year ending 30 June)

Expenditure on the Gross Domestic Product
(at current prices)

	2003/04	2004/05	2005/06
Government final consumption expenditure	61,900	68,600	75,900
Private final consumption expenditure	347,800	385,300	441,200
Changes in inventories	2,600	300	—
Gross fixed capital formation	79,600	96,500	115,700
Total domestic expenditure	491,900	550,700	632,800
Exports of goods and services	137,000	163,400	193,200
Less Imports of goods and services	143,600	175,600	208,300
GDP in market prices	485,300	538,500	617,700
GDP at constant 2001/02 prices	407,000	425,200	454,300

Source: IMF, *International Financial Statistics*.

Gross Domestic Product by Economic Activity
(at current factor cost)

	2003/04	2004/05	2005/06
Agriculture, hunting, forestry and fishing	90,935.3	75,291.2	81,766.2
Mining	66,738.8	64,025.9	89,833.9
Manufacturing	234,243.8	89,980.9	98,693.4
Electricity	10,992.5	7,837.5	8,879.9
Water	2,555.9	1,940.6	2,157.9
Construction	45,271.6	20,106.0	23,763.0
Restaurants and hotels	25,073.8	16,712.8	18,797.9
Transport and communications	59,274.8	51,915.3	59,891.8
Suez Canal	16,388.2	20,154.4	23,399.3
Wholesale and retail trade	71,543.8	56,365.7	63,582.7
Financial intermediation	38,617.9	37,883.0	41,295.0
Real estate, renting and business activities	16,776.2	17,579.7	19,055.6
General government services	61,889.2	51,754.6	56,930.1
Education, health and personal services	27,889.0	15,117.8	16,497.5
GDP at factor cost	751,802.6	506,511.0	581,144.9

Source: Central Bank of Egypt.

BALANCE OF PAYMENTS
(US $ million)

	2004	2005	2006
Exports of goods f.o.b.	12,320	16,073	20,546
Imports of goods f.o.b.	−18,895	−23,818	−28,984
Trade balance	−6,576	−7,745	−8,438
Exports of services	14,197	14,643	16,135
Imports of services	−8,020	−10,508	−11,569
Balance on goods and services	−399	−3,611	−3,873
Other income received	572	1,425	2,560
Other income paid	−818	−1,460	−1,822
Balance on goods, services and income	−645	−3,645	−3,134
Current transfers received	4,615	5,831	5,933
Current transfers paid	−48	−82	−163
Current balance	3,922	2,103	2,635
Capital account (net)	n.a.	−40	−36
Direct investment abroad	−159	−92	−148
Direct investment from abroad	1,253	5,376	10,043
Portfolio investment assets	324	−60	−703
Portfolio investment liabilities	−85	3,528	3
Other investment assets	−5,888	−3,246	−9,743
Other investment liabilities	94	85	252
Net errors and omissions	−45	−2,427	634
Overall balance	−584	5,226	2,937

Source: IMF, *International Financial Statistics*.

EGYPT

External Trade

Note: Figures exclude trade in military goods.

PRINCIPAL COMMODITIES
(distribution by SITC, US $ million)*

Imports c.i.f.	2002	2003	2004
Food and live animals	2,971.1	2,316.3	2,280.8
Cereals and cereal preparations	1,428.1	1,153.0	1,104.3
Wheat and meslin (unmilled)	819.2	606.5	727.3
Maize (unmilled)	594.2	528.8	364.7
Crude materials (inedible) except fuels	953.7	758.2	1,154.7
Cork and wood	429.7	373.9	400.7
Simply worked wood and railway sleepers	408.7	363.8	381.6
Mineral fuels, lubricants, etc.	499.0	562.9	1,103.5
Liquefied propane and butane	289.8	362.8	550.1
Chemicals and related products	1,535.7	1,325.9	1,596.3
Medicinal and pharmaceutical products	500.8	361.7	361.9
Basic manufactures	1,872.7	1,554.5	2,097.6
Iron and steel	610.0	415.7	675.8
Machinery and transport equipment	2,505.7	2,066.2	2,529.1
Machinery specialized for particular industries	458.1	389.1	528.3
General industrial machinery, equipment and parts	561.6	459.4	585.8
Electrical machinery, apparatus, etc.	489.3	341.1	437.1
Miscellaneous manufactured articles	575.5	437.8	512.8
Total (incl. others)	12,552.5	10,892.7	13,331.8

Exports f.o.b.	2002	2003	2004
Food and live animals	392.1	487.6	730.7
Cereals and cereal preparations	111.0	158.5	236.0
Rice	106.0	149.9	232.1
Vegetables and fruit	196.5	214.3	353.0
Crude materials (inedible) except fuels	486.5	529.4	730.7
Textile fibres (excl. wool tops) and waste	345.7	386.7	502.5
Cotton	331.1	365.9	482.9
Mineral fuels, lubricants, etc.	1,572.5	2,653.2	3,419.5
Petroleum, petroleum products, etc.	1,507.7	2,485.3	3,115.6
Crude petroleum oils, etc.	316.7	340.9	403.7
Refined petroleum products	1,181.0	2,110.2	2,666.8
Chemicals and related products	304.4	459.3	441.2
Basic manufactures	997.4	1,122.3	1,641.4
Textile yarn, fabrics, etc.	251.2	278.4	273.6
Textile yarn	112.3	129.6	111.0
Iron and steel	235.3	376.0	521.3
Non-ferrous metals	117.2	94.0	131.0
Aluminium and aluminium alloys	115.5	92.3	125.6
Miscellaneous manufactured articles	399.0	331.2	345.3
Clothing and accessories (excl. footwear)	208.2	233.0	237.4
Total (incl. others)	4,691.6	6,160.8	7,912.8

* Totals include trade in free zones, not classifiable by commodity. The total value of imports in free zones was (US $ million): 1,237.4 in 2002; 1,529.7 in 2003; 1,466.1 in 2004. The total value of exports in free zones was (US $ million): 433.5 in 2002; 384.9 in 2003; 454.7 in 2004.

Source: UN, *International Trade Statistics Yearbook*.

PRINCIPAL TRADING PARTNERS*

Imports c.i.f.	2002	2003	2004
Algeria	207.7	312.6	534.6
Argentina	305.2	335.5	324.7
Australia	483.8	208.2	358.6
Belgium	123.5	110.7	150.5
Brazil	366.1	369.8	417.4
China, People's Republic	562.6	535.5	675.3
France (incl. Monaco)	541.6	448.6	422.8
Germany	828.2	715.8	876.5
India	367.1	146.5	213.4
Italy	632.7	537.8	646.6
Japan	334.8	270.6	347.4
Korea, Republic	210.0	191.3	250.9
Malaysia	130.9	72.8	262.1
Netherlands	222.9	178.9	216.5
Romania	108.7	102.9	144.5
Russia	430.4	373.6	374.3
Saudi Arabia	345.9	252.8	509.7
Spain	155.7	127.5	143.0
Sweden	148.8	131.1	152.8
Switzerland-Liechtenstein	186.3	145.8	164.8
Turkey	223.7	170.9	253.2
Ukraine	242.8	218.1	449.7
United Kingdom	312.5	262.4	319.4
USA	1,691.9	1,272.9	1,366.6
Total (incl. others)	12,552.5	10,892.7	13,331.8

Exports f.o.b.	2002	2003	2004
Belgium	50.6	94.6	135.7
China, People's Republic	222.4	100.1	124.7
France (incl. Monaco)	117.9	166.5	163.9
Germany	96.1	120.6	141.9
Greece	79.4	138.3	115.1
India	413.6	465.0	387.4
Iraq	67.3	52.0	54.0
Israel	45.9	13.0	10.7
Italy	501.6	757.7	987.0
Japan	71.2	98.0	58.0
Jordan	97.1	96.7	159.9
Korea, Republic	48.9	96.4	189.4
Lebanon	74.0	104.7	303.0
Libya	70.1	109.4	71.8
Netherlands	201.4	228.0	402.1
Saudi Arabia	134.2	185.3	233.0
Singapore	60.9	50.7	135.5
Spain	152.9	287.9	435.3
Syria	60.7	74.1	199.7
Turkey	78.2	142.3	241.3
United Arab Emirates	79.1	116.0	126.9
United Kingdom	79.1	146.9	151.2
USA	388.5	520.9	589.2
Total (incl. others)†	4,691.6	6,160.7	7,912.8

* Imports by country of consignment, exports by country of destination. Totals include trade in free zones, not classifiable by country.
† Including bunkers and ships' stores (US $ million): 459.5 in 2002; 566.7 in 2003; 772.5 in 2004.

Source: UN, *International Trade Statistics Yearbook*.

Transport

RAILWAYS
(traffic, year ending 30 June)

	2001/02	2002/03	2003/04
Passenger-km (million)	39,083	46,185	52,682
Net ton-km (million)	4,188	4,104	4,663

Source: UN, *Statistical Yearbook*.

EGYPT

ROAD TRAFFIC
(licensed motor vehicles in use at 31 December)

	1995*	1996	1997
Passenger cars	1,280,000	1,099,583	1,154,753
Buses and coaches	36,630	39,781	43,740
Lorries and vans	387,000	489,542	510,766
Motorcycles and mopeds	397,000	427,864	439,756

* Estimates from IRF, *World Road Statistics*.

2002: Passenger cars ('000): 1,847.0; Commercial vehicles ('000): 650.0 (Source: UN, *Statistical Yearbook*).

SHIPPING
Merchant Fleet
(registered at 31 December)

	2004	2005	2006
Number of vessels	341	344	348
Displacement ('000 grt)	1,143.2	1,128.7	1,141.7

Source: Lloyd's Register-Fairplay, *World Fleet Statistics*.

International sea-borne freight traffic ('000 metric tons, incl. ships' stores, 2004, figures are rounded): Goods loaded 12,700; Goods unloaded 28,500 (Source: UN, *Monthly Bulletin of Statistics*).

SUEZ CANAL TRAFFIC

	1998	1999	2000
Transits (number)	13,472	13,490	14,141
Displacement ('000 net tons)	386,069	384,994	438,962
Northbound goods traffic ('000 metric tons)	160,346	153,582	209,446
Southbound goods traffic ('000 metric tons)	118,107	153,088	158,535
Net tonnage of tankers ('000)	89,976	67,872	105,237

Source: Suez Canal Authority, *Yearly Report*.

CIVIL AVIATION
(traffic on scheduled services)

	2001	2002	2003
Kilometres flown (million)	59	59	58
Passengers carried ('000)	2,981	3,141	2,916
Passenger-km (million)	8,241	8,357	7,517
Total ton-km (million)	991	1,009	921

Source: UN, *Statistical Yearbook*.

Tourism

ARRIVALS BY NATIONALITY
('000)

	2003	2004	2005
France	310.8	465.2	495.2
Germany	693.4	993.2	979.6
Israel	310.0	389.9	256.3
Italy	795.9	1,010.4	823.2
Libya	305.4	344.5	376.4
Netherlands	131.5	188.5	205.9
Palestine	187.8	172.2	217.4
Russia	497.5	785.4	777.7
Saudi Arabia	269.1	309.6	361.1
United Kingdom	357.2	546.9	838.0
USA	125.8	169.7	195.8
Total (incl. others)	6,044.2	8,103.6	8,607.8

Tourism receipts (US $ million, incl. passenger transport): 4,704 in 2003; 6,328 in 2004; 7,206 in 2005.

Source: World Tourism Organization.

Communications Media

	2004	2005	2006
Telephones ('000 main lines in use)	9,464.1	10,396.1	10,807.7
Mobile cellular telephones ('000 subscribers)	7,643.1	13,629.6	18,001.1
Personal computers ('000 in use)	2,300	2,800	n.a.
Internet users ('000)	3,900	5,100	6,000
Broadband subscribers ('000)	28.9	90.1	205.5

1997: Radio receivers ('000 in use) 20,500.

1998: Book production 1,410 titles.

1999: Daily newspapers 16 (average circulation 2,080,000 copies); Other periodicals 45 (average circulation 1,371,000 copies); Facsimile machines ('000 in use) 34.2.

2000: Television receivers ('000 in use) 12,000.

Sources: UNESCO, *Statistical Yearbook*; International Telecommunication Union.

Education

(2004/05, unless otherwise indicated, estimates)

	Schools	Teachers	Students
Pre-primary	3,172*	22,897	515,656
Primary	15,533†	373,104	9,563,627
Preparatory	7,544†	193,469*	4,345,356†
Secondary:			
general	1,595†	322,040‡	5,933,065
technical	1,826†	165,669‡	2,244,255
Higher	356*	80,658‡	2,594,186

* 1998/99 figure.
† 1999/2000 figure.
‡ 2003/04 figure.

Sources: UNESCO Institute for Statistics; Ministry of Education.

Al-Azhar (1999/2000, provisional figures): Primary: 2,631 schools; 707,633 students. Preparatory: 1,805 schools; 316,108 students. Secondary: 1,081 schools; 269,469 students.

Adult literacy rate (UNESCO estimates): 71.4% (males 83.0%; females 59.4%) in 2005 (Source: UNESCO Institute for Statistics).

Directory

A new telephone numbering system was being introduced throughout Egypt from March 2007; the conversion was expected to be completed by the end of 2008. Consequently, many of the telephone numbers listed in the Directory were subject to change.

The Constitution

A new Constitution for the Arab Republic of Egypt was approved by referendum on 11 September 1971. Amendments to the Constitution were endorsed by the People's Assembly on 30 April 1980, 10 May 2005 and 19 March 2007, and subsequently approved at national referendums. The main provisions of the 1971 Constitution, as amended, are summarized below:

THE STATE

The Arab Republic of Egypt is a democratic state based on citizenship. The Egyptian people are part of the Arab nation and work for the realization of its comprehensive unity.

Islam is the religion of the state and Arabic its official language. Principles of Islamic law (*Shari'a*) are the principal source of legislation.

Sovereignty is for the people alone and they are the source of authority.

The political system of the Arab Republic of Egypt is a multiparty system, within the framework of the basic elements and principles of the Egyptian society as stipulated in the Constitution. Political parties are regulated by law.

Citizens have the right to establish political parties according to the law and no political activity shall be exercised nor political parties established on a religious referential authority, on a religious basis or on discrimination on grounds of gender or origin.

THE FUNDAMENTAL ELEMENTS OF SOCIETY

Social solidarity is the basis of Egyptian society, and the family is its nucleus.

The State ensures the equality of men and women in both political and social rights in line with the provisions of Muslim legislation.

Work is a right, an honour and a duty which the State guarantees together with the services of social and health insurance, pensions for incapacity and unemployment.

The economic basis of the Republic is a democratic system based on market principles.

Ownership is of three kinds: public, co-operative and private. The public sector assumes the main responsibility for the regulation and growth of the national economy under the development plan.

Property is subject to the people's control.

Private ownership is safeguarded and may not be sequestrated except in cases specified in law nor expropriated except for the general good against fair legal compensation. The right of inheritance is guaranteed in it.

Nationalization shall only be allowed for considerations of public interest in accordance with the law and against compensation.

Agricultural holding may be limited by law.

The State follows a comprehensive central planning and compulsory planning approach based on quinquennial socio-economic and cultural development plans whereby the society's resources are mobilized and put to the best use.

The public sector assumes the leading role in the development of the national economy. The State provides absolute protection of this sector as well as the property of co-operative societies and trade unions against all attempts to tamper with them.

PUBLIC LIBERTIES, RIGHTS AND DUTIES

All citizens are equal before the law. They have equal public rights and duties without discrimination on grounds of race, ethnic origin, language, religion or creed. Personal liberty is a natural right and no one may be arrested, searched, imprisoned or restricted in any way without a court order.

Houses have sanctity, and shall not be placed under surveillance or searched without a court order with reasons given for such action.

The law safeguards the sanctities of the private lives of all citizens; so have all postal, telegraphic, telephonic and other means of communication which may not therefore be confiscated, or perused except by a court order giving the reasons, and only for a specified period.

Public rights and freedoms are also inviolate and all calls for atheism and anything that reflects adversely on divine religions are prohibited.

The freedom of opinion, the Press, printing and publications and all information media are safeguarded.

Press censorship is forbidden, so are warnings, suspensions or cancellations through administrative channels. Under exceptional circumstances, as in cases of emergency or in wartime, censorship may be imposed on information media for a definite period. A Supreme Press Council safeguards the freedom of the press, checks government censorship and looks after the interests of journalists.

Egyptians have the right to permanent or provisional emigration and no Egyptian may be deported or prevented from returning to the country.

Citizens have the right to private meetings in peace provided they bear no arms. Egyptians also have the right to form societies that have no secret activities. Public meetings are also allowed within the limits of the law.

SOVEREIGNTY OF THE LAW

All acts of crime should be specified together with the penalties for the acts.

Recourse to justice is a right of all citizens. Those who are financially unable will be assured of means to defend their rights.

Except in cases of *flagrante delicto* no person may be arrested or their freedom restricted unless an order authorizing arrest has been given by the competent judge or the public prosecution in accordance with the provisions of law.

SYSTEM OF GOVERNMENT

The President, who must be of Egyptian parentage and at least 40 years old, is elected by direct popular vote under the supervision of an independent Presidential Election Commission. His term is for six years and he may be re-elected for 'other terms'. He may take emergency measures in the interests of the State but these measures must be approved by referendum within 60 days.

The People's Assembly, elected for five years, is the legislative body and approves general policy, the budget and the development plan. It shall have 'not less than 350' elected members, at least one-half of whom shall be workers or farmers, and the President may appoint up to 10 additional members. In exceptional circumstances the Assembly, by a two-thirds' vote, may authorize the President to rule by decree for a specified period but these decrees must be approved by the Assembly at its next meeting. The law governing the composition of the People's Assembly was amended in May 1979 (see People's Assembly, below).

The Assembly may pass a vote of no confidence in a Deputy Prime Minister, a Minister or a Deputy Minister, provided three days' notice of the vote is given, and the Minister must then resign. In the case of the Prime Minister, the Assembly may 'prescribe' his responsibility and submit a report to the President: if the President disagrees with the report but the Assembly persists, then the matter is put to a referendum: if the people support the President the Assembly is dissolved; if they support the Assembly the President must accept the resignation of the Government. The President may not dissolve the Assembly except in case of necessity prematurely. Should the Assembly be dissolved over a certain matter, the new Assembly may not be dissolved over the same matter. A decree by the President dissolving the Assembly must include a call for new elections to be held within 60 days.

Executive Authority is vested in the President, who may appoint one or more Vice-Presidents and appoints all Ministers. He may also dismiss the Vice-Presidents and Ministers. The President has 'the right to refer to the people in connection with important matters related to the country's higher interests.' The Government is described as 'the supreme executive and administrative organ of the state'. Its members, whether full Ministers or Deputy Ministers, must be at least 35 years old. Further sections define the roles of Local Government, Specialized National Councils, the Judiciary, the Higher Constitutional Court, the Socialist Prosecutor-General, the Armed Forces and National Defence Council and the Police.

In accordance with the 1980 constitutional amendments, the President appointed a Consultative Council to preserve the principles of the revolutions of 23 July 1952 and 15 May 1971.

The State shall seek to safeguard public security to counter the dangers of terrorism. The law shall, under the supervision of the judiciary, regulate special provisions related to evidence and investigation procedures required to counter such dangers. The President may refer any terrorist crime to any judiciary body stipulated in the Constitution or the law.

POLITICAL PARTIES

In accordance with the 1980 constitutional amendments, the political system depends on multiple political parties. In June 1977 the People's Assembly had adopted a new law on political parties, which, subject to certain conditions, permitted the formation of political parties for the first time since 1953. The law was passed in accordance with Article Five of the Constitution, which describes the political system as 'a multi-party one' with four main parties: 'the ruling National Democratic Party, the Socialist Workers (the official opposition), the Liberal Socialists and the Unionist Progressive'.

The Government

HEAD OF STATE

President: Muhammad Hosni Mubarak (confirmed as President by referendum, 13 October 1981, after assassination of President Anwar Sadat; re-elected and confirmed by referendum 5 October 1987, 4 October 1993 and 26 September 1999; re-elected by direct popular vote 7 September 2005).

COUNCIL OF MINISTERS
(March 2008)

Prime Minister: Dr Ahmad Mahmoud Muhammad Nazif.

Minister of Agriculture and Land Reclamation: Amin Ahmad Abaza.

Minister of Defence and Military Production: Field Marshal Muhammad Hussain Tantawi.

Minister of Foreign Affairs: Ahmad Aboul Gheit.

Minister of Justice: Mamdouh Mohi ed-Din Mari.

Minister of the Interior: Maj.-Gen. Habib Ibrahim el-Adli.

Minister of Information: Anas el-Fiki.

Minister of Culture: Farouk Abd al-Aziz Hosni.

Minister of Education: Dr Yousri Saber Hussein el-Gamal.

Minister of Investment: Dr Mahmoud Mohi ed-Din.

Minister of Trade and Industry: Eng. Rashid Muhammad Rashid.

Minister of Tourism: Zohair Garanah.

Minister of Housing, Utilities and Urban Communities: Eng. Ahmad Amin al-Maghrabi.

Minister of Manpower and Emigration: Aisha Abd al-Hadi Abd al-Ghani.

Minister of Awqaf (Islamic Endowments): Dr Mahmoud Hamdi Zakzouk.

Minister of Economic Development: Dr Osman Muhammad Osman.

Minister of Health and Population: Dr Hatem Mostafa el-Gabaly.

Minister of Higher Education and Scientific Research: Dr Hany Mahfouz Helal.

Minister of Water Resources and Irrigation: Dr Mahmoud Abu Zeid.

Minister of Social Solidarity: Dr Ali es-Sayed el-Moselhi.

Minister of International Co-operation: Faiza Muhammad Aboulnaga.

Minister of Electricity and Energy: Dr Hassan Ahmad Younes.

Minister of Transport: Eng. Muhammad Loutfi Mansour.

Minister of Finance: Dr Yousuf Boutros-Ghali.

Minister of Communications and Information Technology: Dr Tareq Muhammad Kamel.

Minister of Petroleum: Eng. Amin Samih Samir Fahmy.

Minister of Civil Aviation: Gen. Ahmad Muhammad Shafiq Zaki.

Minister of State for Legal and Parliamentary Councils: Dr Mufid Mahmoud Shehab.

Minister of State for Administrative Development: Dr Ahmad Mahmoud Darwish.

Minister of State for Local Development: Muhammad Abd as-Salam al-Mahgoub.

Minister of State for Environmental Affairs: Eng. Maged George Elias Ghattas.

Minister of State for Military Production: Dr Sayed Abdouh Moustafa Meshaal.

MINISTRIES

Office of the Prime Minister: 2 Sharia Majlis ash-Sha'ab, Cairo; tel. (2) 27935000; fax (2) 27958048; e-mail questions@cabinet.gov.eg; internet www.cabinet.gov.eg.

Ministry of Agriculture and Land Reclamation: 5 Sharia Shooting Club, Cairo (Dokki); tel. (2) 7615967; fax (2) 7614263; e-mail drfadia@hotmail.com; internet www.agri.gov.eg.

Ministry of Awqaf (Islamic Endowments): Sharia Sabri Abu Alam, Bab el-Louk, Cairo; tel. (2) 3926163; fax (2) 3928602; e-mail mawkaf@idsc1.gov.eg.

Ministry of Civil Aviation: Sharia Matar, Cairo; tel. (2) 2671074; fax (2) 2679470; e-mail info@civilaviation.gov.eg; internet www.civilaviation.gov.eg.

Ministry of Communications and Information Technology: Smart Village, km 28, Sharia Cairo–Alexandria, Cairo; tel. (2) 5341300; e-mail webmaster@mcit.gov.eg; internet www.mcit.gov.eg.

Ministry of Culture: 2 Sharia Shagaret ed-Dor, Cairo (Zamalek); tel. (2) 7486957; fax (2) 3461417; e-mail mculture@idsc.gov.eg.

Ministry of Defence and Military Production: Sharia 23 July, Kobri el-Kobba, Cairo; tel. (2) 4032159; fax (2) 2916227; e-mail mod@idsc.gov.eg.

Ministry of Economic Development: Sharia Salah Salem, Cairo (Nasr City); tel. (2) 4014526; fax (2) 4014627; e-mail contact_mop@hotmail.co.uk; internet www.mop.gov.eg.

Ministry of Education: 12 Sharia el-Falaky, Cairo; tel. (2) 7959939; fax (2) 7942700; e-mail info@mail.emoe.org; internet www.emoe.org.

Ministry of Electricity and Energy: POB 222, 8 Sharia Ramses, Abbassia Sq., Cairo (Nasr City); tel. (2) 4017845; fax (2) 2616302; e-mail moee_info@hotmail.com; internet www.moee.gov.eg.

Ministry of Finance: Ministry of Finance Towers, Cairo (Nasr City); tel. (2) 3428886; fax (2) 6861861; e-mail finance@mof.gov.eg; internet www.mof.gov.eg.

Ministry of Foreign Affairs: Corniche en-Nil, Cairo (Maspiro); tel. (2) 5746871; fax (2) 5747839; e-mail info@mfa.gov.eg; internet www.mfa.gov.eg.

Ministry of Health and Population: Sharia Majlis ash-Sha'ab, Lazoughli Sq., Cairo; tel. (2) 7941507; fax (2) 7953966; e-mail webmaster@mohp.gov.eg; internet www.mohp.gov.eg.

Ministry of Higher Education and Scientific Research: 101 Sharia Qasr el-Eini, Cairo; tel. (2) 7953437; fax (2) 7941005; e-mail info@egy-mhe.gov.eg; internet www.egy-mhe.gov.eg.

Ministry of Housing, Utilities and Urban Communities: 1 Sharia Ismail Abaza, Qasr el-Eini, Cairo; tel. (2) 7921440; fax (2) 7921423; e-mail mhuuc@idsc1.gov.eg; internet www.housing-utility.gov.eg.

Ministry of Information: Radio and TV Bldg, Corniche en-Nil, Cairo (Maspiro); tel. (2) 5748984; fax (2) 5748981; e-mail rtu@idsc.gov.eg; internet www.minfo.gov.eg.

Ministry of the Interior: Sharia Sheikh Rihan, Bab el-Louk, Cairo; tel. (2) 7948308; fax (2) 7945529; e-mail moi1@idsc.gov.eg.

Ministry of International Co-operation: 8 Sharia Adly, Cairo; tel. (2) 3901801; internet www.mic.gov.eg.

Ministry of Investment: POB 11562, 3 Sharia Salah Salem, Cairo (Nasr City); tel. (2) 24055653; fax (2) 24055635; e-mail contact-moi@investment.gov.eg; internet www.investment.gov.eg.

Ministry of Justice: Justice and Finance Bldg, Sharia Majlis ash-Sha'ab, Lazoughli Sq., Cairo; tel. (2) 7922263; fax (2) 7958103; e-mail mojeb@idsc.gov.eg.

Ministry of Manpower and Emigration: 3 Sharia Yousuf Abbas, Cairo (Nasr City); tel. (2) 4042910; e-mail manpower@mome.gov.eg; internet www.mome.gov.eg.

Ministry of Military Production: 5 Sharia Ismail Abaza, Qasr el-Eini, Cairo; tel. (2) 7921589; fax (2) 7948739; e-mail fac009@iscc.gov.eg.

Ministry of Petroleum: 1 Sharia Ahmad ez-Zomor, Cairo (Nasr City); tel. (2) 6706401; fax (2) 6706419; e-mail contactus@petroleum.gov.eg; internet www.petroleum.gov.eg.

Ministry of State for Administrative Development: POB 11763, 3 Sharia Salah Salem, Cairo (Nasr City); tel. (2) 4025739; fax (2) 2628003; e-mail info@ad.gov.eg; internet www.ad.gov.eg.

Ministry of State for Environmental Affairs: 30 Sharia Misr Helwan ez-Zirai, Maadi, Cairo; tel. (2) 25256452; fax (2) 25256490; e-mail eeaa@eeaa.gov.eg; internet www.eeaa.gov.eg.

Ministry of State for Legal and Parliamentary Councils: Sharia Majlis ash-Sha'ab, Qasr el-Eini, Cairo; tel. (2) 7926335; fax (2) 7642721; e-mail parli@idsc.gov.eg.

Ministry of Tourism: Misr Travel Tower, 32 Sharia Emtidad Ramses, Abbassia Sq., Cairo; tel. (2) 6828435; fax (2) 6859463; e-mail mot@idsc.gov.eg; internet www.egypt.travel.

Ministry of Trade and Industry: 2 Sharia Latin America, Cairo (Garden City); tel. (2) 7921167; fax (2) 7955025; e-mail mfti@mfti.gov.eg; internet www.mfti.gov.eg.

Ministry of Transport: 105 Sharia Qasr el-Eini, Cairo; tel. (2) 7955566; fax (2) 7955564; e-mail garb@idsc.gov.eg.

EGYPT

Ministry of Water Resources and Irrigation: Sharia Gamal Abd an-Nasser, Corniche en-Nil, Imbaba, Cairo; tel. (2) 5449440; fax (2) 5449410; e-mail minister@mwri.gov.eg; internet www.mwri.gov.eg.

President and Legislature

PRESIDENT

Presidential Election, 7 September 2005

Candidates	Votes	%
Muhammad Hosni Mubarak	6,316,784	88.57
Ayman Abd al-Aziz an-Nour	540,405	7.58
No'man Khalil Gomaa	208,891	2.93
Dr Osama Abd ash-Shafi Shaltout	29,857	0.42
Wahid Fakhry al-Uqsuri	11,881	0.17
Ibrahim Muhammad Abd al-Moneim Turk	5,831	0.08
Mamdouh Kenawy	5,481	0.08
Ahmad as-Sabahi	4,393	0.06
Fawzi Khalil Ghazal	4,222	0.06
Dr Rifaat al-Agroudy	4,106	0.06
Total*	**7,131,851**	**100.00**

* Excluding 173,685 invalid votes (2.4% of total votes cast).

LEGISLATURE

Majlis ash-Sha'ab
(People's Assembly)

There are 222 constituencies, which each elect two deputies to the Assembly. Ten deputies are appointed by the President, giving a total of 454 seats.

Speaker: Dr AHMAD FATHI SURUR.
Deputy Speakers: ZEINAB RADWAN, ABD AL-AZIZ MOUSTAFA.
Elections, 9 and 20 November and 1 December 2005

	Seats
National Democratic Party	311
Independents: Muslim Brotherhood	88
Independents: others*	24
New Wafd Party	6
National Progressive Unionist Party	2
Al-Ghad (Tomorrow) Party	1
Total†	**432‡**

* Of the 24 seats won by independents, two went to representatives of the non-licensed Karama party and one to a representative of the United National Front for Change.
† There are, in addition, 10 deputies appointed by the President.
‡ The results for 12 seats in six constituencies were to be contested at a later date owing to violence during polling or allegations of voting irregularities.

Majlis ash-Shura
(Advisory Council)

In September 1980 elections were held for a 210-member **Shura (Advisory) Council**, which replaced the former Central Committee of the Arab Socialist Union: 140 members were elected and the remaining 70 appointed by the President. The opposition parties boycotted elections to the Council in October 1983 and October 1986, in protest against the 8% electoral threshold. In June 1989 elections to 153 of the Council's 210 seats were contested by opposition parties (the 'Islamic Alliance', consisting of the Muslim Brotherhood, the LSP and the SLP). However, all of the seats in which voting produced a result (143) were won by the NDP. NDP candidates secured 88 of the 90 seats on the Council to which mid-term elections were held in June 1995. The remaining two elective seats were gained by independent candidates. On 21 June new appointments were made to 47 vacant, non-elective seats. Most opposition parties chose not to contest partial elections to the Council held in June 1998. The NDP won 85 of the 88 contested seats, and independent candidates three. In partial elections held in May 2001 the NDP won 74 of the 88 contested seats, while independents won the remaining 14 seats. Further partial elections took place to the 264-member Council between 23 May and 19 June 2004, with the NDP winning 70 of the 88 seats contested and 17 of the remaining seats being taken by NDP members who had stood as independents; one seat was won by the National Progressive Unionist Party (Tagammu). A further 44 members of the Council were appointed by the President, so that one-half of its membership had been renewed or replaced. Partial elections to select 88 members of the Council were held on 11 and 18 June 2007. The NDP secured 84 of the seats; of the remaining four, three were won by NDP-aligned independents and one by the NPUP.

Despite having fielded candidates who stood as independents, the Muslim Brotherhood failed to secure a single seat. A further 44 presidential appointees were also announced at this time.

Speaker: MUHAMMAD SAFWAT ESH-SHERIF.
Deputy Speakers: ABDERRAHMAN FARAG MOHSEN, MUHAMMAD MORSI.

Election Commissions

Higher Election Commission: Cairo; regulates legislative elections; comprises 11 mems, chaired by the Minister of Justice; Chair. MAHDOUH MOHI ED-DIN MARI.

Presidential Election Commission: 3rd Floor, 117 Abd al-Aziz Fahmy St, Cairo (Heliopolis); f. 2005; independent; comprises 10 mems, presided over by the Chief Justice of the Supreme Constitutional Court and four other ex officio mems of the judiciary; of the remaining five mems (who are independent, public figures), three are appointed by the People's Assembly and two by the Advisory Council; Chair. Hon. MAHER SAYED IBRAHIM ABD AL-WAHID.

Political Organizations

By mid-2007 there were 24 registered political organizations in Egypt; the principal parties are listed below.

Arab Democratic Nasserist Party: Cairo; f. 1992; advocates maintaining the principles of the 1952 Revolution, achieving a strong national economy and protecting human rights; Chair. DIAA ED-DIN DAOUD.

Democratic Front Party (Hizb al-Gabha ad-Dimuqrati): e-mail info@democraticfront.org; internet www.democraticfront.org; f. 2007 by fmr mems of the National Democratic Party; seeks to promote liberal democracy, the rule of law and a civil society; Founder and Chair. Dr YEHIA EL-GAMAL; Founder and Vice-Chair. Dr OSAMA AL-GHAZALI HARB.

Democratic People's Party (Hizb ash-Shaab ad-Dimuqrati): f. 1992; Chair. ANWAR AFIFI.

Democratic Unionist Party (Hizb al-Ittihad ad-Dimuqrati): Cairo; f. 1990; advocates unity between Egypt and Sudan, the separation of politics and religion, economic devt and improved public services; Pres. IBRAHIM MUHAMMAD ABD AL-MONEIM TURK.

Egypt Arab Socialist Party (Hizb Misr al-Arabi al-Ishtiraki): f. 1976; seeks to maintain principles of the 1952 Revolution and to preserve Egypt's Islamic identity; Leader WAHID FAKHRY AL-UQSURI.

Egyptian Green Party (Hizb al-Khudr al-Misri): 9 Sharia at-Tahrir, Cairo (Dokki); tel. and fax (2) 33364748; e-mail awadenator@gmail.com; internet www.egyptiangreens.com; f. 1990; Pres. ABD AL-MONEIM EL-ASAR (acting); Gen. Sec. MUHAMMAD AWAD.

Free Social Constitutional Party: f. 2004; seeks introduction of further political, social and economic reforms; Chair. MAMDOUH QENAWI.

Al-Ghad (Tomorrow) Party: Cairo; e-mail info@elghad.org; internet www.elghad.org; f. 2004; aims to combat poverty and to improve the living conditions of Egypt's citizens; Founder AYMAN ABD AL-AZIZ AN-NOUR; Chair. IHAB EL-KHOLI.

Liberal Socialist Party (LSP) (Al-Ahrar): Cairo; f. 1976; advocates expansion of 'open door' economic policy and greater freedom for private enterprise and the press; Chair. MUHAMMAD FARID ZAKARIA, (vacant).

Misr el-Fatah (Young Egypt Party): f. 1990; pursues a socialist, nationalist and reformist agenda; Chair. ABD AL-HAKIM ABD AL-MAJID KHALIL.

National Accord Party (Hizb al-Wifaq al-Qawmi): f. 2000; Arab nationalist; Chair. Dr RIFAAT AL-AGROUDY.

National Democratic Party (NDP): Cairo; e-mail org_admin@ndp.org.eg; internet www.ndp.org.eg; f. 1978; govt party established by Anwar Sadat; absorbed Arab Socialist Party; Leader MUHAMMAD HOSNI MUBARAK; Sec.-Gen. MUHAMMAD SAFWAT ESH-SHERIF.

National Progressive Unionist Party (Hizb at-Tagammu' al-Watani at-Taqadomi al-Wahdawi—Tagammu): 1 Sharia Karim ed-Dawlah, Cairo; tel. (2) 5791628; fax (2) 5784867; internet www.al-ahaly.com; f. 1976; left-wing; seeks to defend the principles of the 1952 Revolution; Founder KHALED MOHI ED-DIN; Chair. Dr MUHAMMAD RIFA'AT ES-SAID; 160,000 mems.

New Wafd Party (New Delegation Party): POB 357, 1 Boulos Hanna St, Cairo (Dokki); tel. (2) 3383111; fax (2) 3359135; e-mail contact@alwafd.org; internet www.alwafd.org; f. 1919 as Wafd Party; banned 1952; re-formed as New Wafd Party Feb. 1978; disbanded June 1978; re-formed 1983; seeks further political, economic and social reforms, greater democracy, the abolition of emergency legislation and improvements to the health and education sectors; Chair. MAHMOUD ABAZA.

Social Justice Party: Cairo; f. 1993; advocates equal rights for all citizens and national unity; Chair. Dr MUHAMMAD ABD AL-AAL HASSAN.

Socialist Labour Party (SLP): 12 Sharia Awali el-Ahd, Cairo; f. 1978; official opposition party; pro-Islamist; seeks establishment of economic system based on *Shari'a* (Islamic) law, unity between Egypt, Sudan and Libya, and the liberation of occupied Palestinian territory; Leader IBRAHIM SHUKRI.

Solidarity Party (Hizb at-Takaful): f. 1995; advocates imposition of 'solidarity' tax on the rich in order to provide for the needs of the poor; Chair. Dr OSAMA ABD ASH-SHAFI SHALTOUT.

Ummah (People's) Party (Hizb al-Umma): f. 1983; social democratic party; Leader AHMAD AS-SABAHI KHALIL.

The following organizations are proscribed by the Government:

Egyptian Islamic Jihad (al-Jihad—Holy Struggle): f. late 1970s as Islamic Jihad; militant Islamist grouping established following the imposition of a ban on the Muslim Brotherhood; reported to have merged its activities with those of the al-Qa'ida (Base) network of Osama bin Laden in the late 1990s; seeks to overthrow the Egyptian Govt and replace it with an Islamic state; since late 1990s has also adopted anti-Western ideology; Leader Dr AYMAN AZ-ZAWAHIRI.

Gama'ah al-Islamiyah (Islamic Group): militant Islamist group founded following the imposition of a ban on the Muslim Brotherhood; seeks to overthrow the Egyptian Govt and replace it with an Islamic state; declared a cease-fire in March 1999, although subsequent reports stated that some leaders of the group had rescinded their support for a truce; Spiritual Leader Sheikh OMAR ABD AR-RAHMAN; Chair. of the Shura Council MOUSTAFA HAMZAH; Mil. Cmmdr ALA ABD AR-RAQIL.

Muslim Brotherhood (Al-Ikhwan al-Muslimun): internet www.ikhwanonline.com; f. 1928, with the aim of establishing an Islamic society; banned in 1954; moderate; advocates the adoption of *Shari'a* law as the sole basis of the Egyptian legal system; Supreme Guide MUHAMMAD MAHDI AKIF; Sec.-Gen. MAHMOUD IZZAT.

Vanguards of Conquest (Tala'at al-Fatah): militant Islamist grouping; breakaway group from Islamic Jihad; Leader YASSER TAWFIQ AS-SIRRI.

Diplomatic Representation

EMBASSIES IN EGYPT

Afghanistan: 59 Sharia el-Orouba, Cairo (Heliopolis); tel. (2) 4177236; fax (2) 4177238; e-mail afghan_emb_cairo@hotmail.com; Ambassador Dr M. RAHIM SHERZOY.

Albania: Ground Floor, 27 Sharia Gezira al-Wissta, Cairo (Zamalek); tel. (2) 7361815; fax (2) 7356966; e-mail embassy.cairo@mfa.gov.al; Chargé d'affaires a.i. ELIR HOXHA.

Algeria: 14 Sharia Bresil, Cairo (Zamalek); tel. (2) 3418527; fax (2) 3414158; Ambassador ABD AL-QADER HAGGAR.

Angola: 12 Midan Fouad Mohi ed-Din, Mohandessin, Cairo; tel. (2) 3377602; fax (2) 708683; Ambassador PEDRO HENDRICK VAAL NETO.

Argentina: 1st Floor, 8 Es-Saleh Ayoub St, Cairo (Zamalek); tel. (2) 27351501; fax (2) 27364355; e-mail argemb@idsc.gov.eg; Ambassador LUIS ENRIQUE CAPPAGLI.

Armenia: 20 Sharia Muhammad Mazhar, Cairo (Zamalek); tel. (2) 7374157; fax (2) 7374158; e-mail hovakimyan_liana@yahoo.com; internet www.armembegypt.com; Ambassador Dr ROUBEN KARAPETIAN.

Australia: 11th Floor, World Trade Centre, Corniche en-Nil, Cairo 11111 (Boulac); tel. (2) 5750444; fax (2) 5781638; e-mail cairo.austremb@dfat.gov.au; internet www.egypt.embassy.gov.au; Ambassador Dr ROBERT BOWKER.

Austria: 5th Floor, Riyadh Tower, 5 Sharia Wissa Wassef, cnr of Sharia en-Nil, Cairo 11111 (Giza); tel. (2) 5702975; fax (2) 5702979; e-mail kairo-ob@bmaa.gv.at; internet www.austriaegypt.org; Ambassador Dr KURT SPALLINGER.

Azerbaijan: Villa 16/24, Rd 10, Maadi Sarayat, Cairo; tel. (2) 23583790; fax (2) 23583725; e-mail azsefqahira@link.net; internet www.azembassy.org.eg; Ambassador FAIG BAGIROV.

Bahrain: 15 Sharia Bresil, Cairo (Zamalek); tel. (2) 3407996; fax (2) 3416609; Ambassador KHALIL IBRAHIM ATH-THAWADI.

Bangladesh: POB 136, 20 Sharia Gezeret El Arab, Mohandessin, Cairo; tel. (2) 33462003; fax (2) 33462008; e-mail bdoot@link.net; Ambassador NASIM FIRDAUS.

Belarus: 26 Sharia Gaber Ibn Hayan, Cairo (Dokki); tel. and fax (2) 7499171; e-mail egypt@belembassy.org; Ambassador SERGEI MIKHNEVICH.

Belgium: POB 37, 20 Sharia Kamal esh-Shennawi, Cairo 11511 (Garden City); tel. (2) 7947494; fax (2) 7943147; e-mail cairo@diplobel.org; internet www.diplomatie.be/cairo; Ambassador DANIEL LEROY.

Bolivia: 21 New Ramses Centre, Sharia B. Oman, Cairo 11794 (Dokki); tel. (2) 7624362; fax (2) 7624360; e-mail embolivia_cairo@yahoo.com; Chargé d'affaires a.i. RAÚL PALZA ZEBALLOS.

Bosnia and Herzegovina: 42 Sharia as-Sawra, Cairo (Dokki); tel. (2) 7499191; fax (2) 7499190; e-mail ambbih@link.net; Ambassador RADOMIR KOSIĆ.

Brazil: 1125 Corniche en-Nil Ave, Cairo 11561 (Maspiro); tel. (2) 5773013; fax (2) 5774860; e-mail brasemb@soficom.com.eg; internet www.brazilembcairo.org; Ambassador ELIM SATURNINO FERREIRA DUTRA.

Brunei: 24 Sharia Hassan Assem, Cairo (Zamalek); tel. (2) 7380097; fax (2) 7366375; e-mail ebdic@intouch.com; Ambassador Haji MUHARRAM BIN Haji PIAH.

Bulgaria: 6 Sharia el-Malek el-Ajdal, Cairo (Zamalek); tel. (2) 3413025; fax (2) 3413826; e-mail mka@link.com.eg; Ambassador ALEXANDAR OLSHEVSKI.

Burkina Faso: POB 306, Ramses Centre, 22 Sharia Wadi en-Nil, Mohandessin, Cairo 11794; tel. (2) 3808965; fax (2) 3806974; Ambassador SOPHIE SOW.

Burundi: 22 Sharia en-Nakhil, Madinet ed-Dobbat, Cairo (Dokki); tel. (2) 3373078; fax (2) 3378431; Ambassador GERVAIS NDIKUMAGNEGE.

Cambodia: 2 Sharia Tahawia, Cairo (Giza); tel. (2) 3489966; Ambassador IN SOPHEAP.

Cameroon: POB 2061, 15 Sharia Muhammad Sedki Soliman, Mohandessin, Cairo; tel. (2) 3441101; fax (2) 3459208; Ambassador MOUCHILI NJI MFOUAYO ISMAILA.

Canada: POB 1667, 26 Kamel esh-Shenawy, Cairo (Garden City); tel. (2) 7943110; fax (2) 7963548; e-mail cairo@dfait-maeci.gc.ca; internet www.dfait-maeci.gc.ca/cairo/menu-en.asp; Ambassador PHILIP MACKINNON.

Central African Republic: 41 Sharia Mahmoud Azmy, Mohandessin, Cairo (Dokki); tel. (2) 3446873; Ambassador HENRY KOBA.

Chad: POB 1869, 12 Midan ar-Refaï, Cairo 11511 (Dokki); tel. (2) 3373379; fax (2) 3373232; Ambassador OUSMAN KALIBOU BELLA.

Chile: El-Asmak Bldg, 1 Sharia Saleh Ayoub, Cairo (Zamalek); tel. (2) 7358711; fax (2) 7353716; e-mail embchile@link.net; Ambassador SAMUEL FERNÁNDEZ ILLAMES.

China, People's Republic: 14 Sharia Bahgat Ali, Cairo (Zamalek); tel. (2) 7361219; fax (2) 7359459; e-mail webmaster_eg@mfa.gov.cn; internet eg.china-embassy.org/eng; Ambassador WU SIKE.

Colombia: 6 Sharia Gueriza, Cairo (Zamalek); tel. (2) 3414203; fax (2) 3407429; e-mail colombemb@idsc.gov.eg; Ambassador JAIME GIRÓN DUARTE.

Congo, Democratic Republic: 5 Sharia Mansour Muhammad, Cairo (Zamalek); tel. (2) 3403662; fax (2) 3404342; Ambassador KAMIMBAYA WA DJONDO.

Côte d'Ivoire: 9 ave Shehab, rue Ibrahim Soliman, Mohandessin, Cairo; tel. (2) 3034373; fax (2) 3050148; e-mail acieg@ambaci-egypte.org; internet www.ambaci-egypte.org; Ambassador N'GUESSAN MARCEL KONAN.

Croatia: 3 Sharia Abou el-Feda, Cairo (Zamalek); tel. (2) 7383155; fax (2) 7355812; e-mail croemb.cairo@mvpei.hr; internet eg.mfa.hr; Ambassador DRAŽEN MARGETA.

Cuba: Apartment 1, 13th Floor, 10 Sharia Kamel Muhammad, Cairo (Zamalek); tel. (2) 7360651; fax (2) 7360656; e-mail cubaemb@link.net; Ambassador ANGEL DALMAU FERNÁNDEZ.

Cyprus: 17 Sharia Omar Tosson, Ahmed Orabi, Mohandessin, Cairo; tel. (2) 3455967; fax (2) 3455969; Ambassador PHAEDON ANASTASIOU.

Czech Republic: 1st Floor, 4 Sharia Dokki, Cairo 12511 (Giza); tel. (2) 37485531; fax (2) 37485892; e-mail cairo@embassy.mzv.cz; internet www.mfa.cz/cairo; Ambassador MILOSLAV STAŠEK.

Denmark: 12 Sharia Hassan Sabri, Cairo 11211 (Zamalek); tel. (2) 7396500; fax (2) 7396588; e-mail caiamb@um.dk; internet www.ambkairo.um.dk; Ambassador TORBEN BRYLLE.

Djibouti: 11 Sharia el-Gazaer, Aswan Sq., Cairo (Agouza); tel. (2) 3456546; fax (2) 3456549; Ambassador Sheikh MOUSSA MOHAMED AHMED.

Ecuador: Suez Canal Bldg, 4 Sharia Ibn Kasir, Cairo (Giza); tel. (2) 3496782; fax (2) 3609327; e-mail ecuademb@idsc.gov.eg; Ambassador FRANKLIN BAHAMONDE.

Eritrea: 6 Sharia el-Fallah, Mohandessin, Cairo; tel. (2) 3033503; fax (2) 3030516; e-mail eritembe@yahoo.com; Ambassador MAHMOUD OMAR CHIRUM.

Ethiopia: Mesaha Sq., Villa 11, Cairo (Dokki); tel. (2) 3353693; fax (2) 3353699; e-mail ethio@ethioembassy.org.eg; Ambassador IBRAHIM IDRIS.

Finland: 13th Floor, 3 Sharia Abou el-Feda, Cairo 11511 (Zamalek); tel. (2) 7363722; fax (2) 7371376; e-mail sanomat.kai@formin.fi; internet www.finland.org.eg; Ambassador HANNU HALINEN.

France: POB 1777, 29 Sharia Charles de Gaulle, Cairo (Giza); tel. (2) 5703916; fax (2) 5718498; e-mail questions@ambafrance-eg.org; internet www.ambafrance-eg.org; Ambassador PHILIPPE COSTE.

Gabon: 17 Sharia Mecca el-Moukarama, Cairo (Dokki); tel. (2) 3379699; Ambassador JOSEPH MAMBOUNGOU.

Georgia: 28 Sharia Sad el-Aali, Cairo (Dokki); tel. (2) 3359024; fax (2) 3366129; e-mail geoembeg@link.com.eg; Ambassador GIORGI JANJGHAVA.

Germany: 8B Sharia Berlin (off Sharia Hassan Sabri), Cairo (Zamalek); tel. (2) 27282000; fax (2) 27282159; e-mail germemb@tedata.net.eg; internet www.cairo.diplo.de; Ambassador BERND ERBEL.

Ghana: 1 Sharia 26 July, Cairo (Zamalek); tel. (2) 3444455; fax (2) 3032292; Ambassador AKILAJA O. AKIWUMI.

Greece: 18 Sharia Aicha at-Taimouria, Cairo 11451 (Garden City); tel. (2) 7950443; fax (2) 7963903; e-mail grembcai@internetgypt.com; Ambassador PANAYOTIS VLASSOPOULOS.

Guatemala: 5th Floor, 17 Sharia Port Said, Maadi, Cairo; tel. (2) 3802914; fax (2) 3802915; e-mail embegipto@minex.gob.gt; Ambassador FLORIDALMA FRANCO PAIZ.

Guinea: 46 Sharia Muhammad Mazhar, Cairo (Zamalek); tel. (2) 7358109; fax (2) 7361446; Ambassador El Hadj OUSMANE CAMARA.

Guinea-Bissau: 37 Sharia Lebanon, Madinet el-Mohandessin, Cairo (Dokki).

Holy See: Apostolic Nunciature, Safarat al-Vatican, 5 Sharia Muhammad Mazhar, Cairo (Zamalek); tel. (2) 7352250; fax (2) 7356152; e-mail nunteg@yahoo.com; Apostolic Nuncio Most Rev. MICHAEL LOUIS FITZGERALD (Titular Archbishop of Nepte).

Honduras: 21 Sharia Aicha at-Taimouria, Cairo (Garden City); tel. (2) 3409510; fax (2) 3413835.

Hungary: 29 Sharia Muhammad Mazhar, Cairo (Zamalek); tel. (2) 7358659; fax (2) 7358648; e-mail huembcai@soficom.com.eg; Ambassador LÁSZLÓ KÁDÁR.

India: 5 Sharia Aziz Abaza, Cairo (Zamalek); tel. (2) 3927702; e-mail infoemb@indembcairo.com; internet www.indembcairo.com; Ambassador ACHAMKULANGARE GOPINATHAN.

Indonesia: POB 1661, 13 Sharia Aicha at-Taimouria, Cairo (Garden City); tel. (2) 7947200; fax (2) 7962495; e-mail pwkcairo@access.com.eg; Ambassador Dr BACHTIAR ALY.

Iraq: Cairo; tel. (2) 7358087; fax (2) 7366956; e-mail caiemb@iraqmofamail.net; Ambassador SAFIA TALEB AS-SOUHAIL.

Ireland: POB 2681, 3 Sharia Abou el-Feda, Cairo (Zamalek); tel. (2) 7358264; fax (2) 7362863; e-mail irishemb@rite.com; Ambassador GERRY CORR.

Israel: 6 Sharia Ibn el-Malek, Cairo (Giza); tel. (2) 33321500; fax (2) 33321555; e-mail info@cairo.mfa.gov.il; Ambassador SHALOM COHEN.

Italy: 15 Sharia Abd ar-Rahman Fahmi, Cairo (Garden City); tel. (2) 7943194; fax (2) 7940657; e-mail ambasciata.cairo@esteri.it; internet www.ambilcairo.esteri.it; Ambassador ANTONIO BADINI.

Japan: 9th Floor, Cairo Centre Bldg, 2 Sharia Abd al-Kader Hamza; tel. (2) 7953962; fax (2) 7963540; e-mail center@embjapan.org.eg; internet www.eg.emb-japan.go.jp; Ambassador KAORU ISHIKAWA.

Jordan: 6 Sharia Juhaini, Cairo; tel. (2) 7499912; fax (2) 7601027; e-mail jocairo2@ie-eg.com; Ambassador OMAR RIFAI.

Kazakhstan: 9 Wahib Doss St, Maadi, Cairo; tel. and fax (2) 3809804; fax (2) 3586546; e-mail kazaemb@link.net; Ambassador BAGDAD K. AMREYEV.

Kenya: POB 362, 7 Sharia el-Mohandes Galal, Cairo (Dokki); tel. (2) 3453628; fax (2) 3443400; Ambassador BISHAR ABDIRAHMAN HUSSEIN.

Korea, Democratic People's Republic: 6 Sharia as-Saleh Ayoub, Cairo (Zamalek); tel. (2) 3408219; fax (2) 3414615; Ambassador JANG MYONG SON.

Korea, Republic: 3 Sharia Boulos Hanna, Cairo (Dokki); tel. (2) 3611234; fax (2) 3611238; Ambassador CHOI SEUNG-HOH.

Kuwait: 12 Sharia Nabil el-Wakkad, Cairo (Dokki); tel. (2) 3602661; fax (2) 3602657; Ambassador AHMAD KHALID AL-KALIB.

Lebanon: 22 Sharia Mansour Muhammad, Cairo (Zamalek); tel. (2) 7382823; fax (2) 7382818; Ambassador KHALED ZIADEH.

Lesotho: 10 Sharia Bahr al-Ghazal, Sahafeyeen, Cairo; tel. (2) 3447025; fax (2) 3025495.

Liberia: 11 Sharia Bresil, Cairo (Zamalek); tel. (2) 3419864; fax (2) 3473074; Ambassador Dr BRAHIMA D. KABA.

Libya: 7 Sharia as-Saleh Ayoub, Cairo (Zamalek); tel. (2) 3401864; Ambassador SALEH AD-DROUFI.

Lithuania: 47 Sharia Ahmed Heshmat, Cairo (Zamalek); tel. (2) 7364329; fax (2) 7364326; e-mail amb.eg@urm.lt; Ambassador GINUTIS DAINIUS VOVERIS.

Malaysia: 21 El Aanab, Mohandessin, Cairo (Giza); tel. (2) 7610013; fax (2) 7610216; e-mail mwcairo2@soficom.com.eg; Ambassador Datuk ZAINAL ABIDIN ABDUL KADIR.

Mali: POB 844, 3 Sharia al-Kansar, Cairo (Dokki); tel. and fax (2) 3371841; e-mail mali.eg@ie.eg.com; Ambassador MAMADOU KABA.

Malta: 1 Sharia es-Saleh Ayoub, Cairo (Zamalek); tel. (2) 7362368; fax (2) 7362371; e-mail maltaembassy.cairo@gov.mt; Ambassador GIOVANNI MICELI.

Mauritania: 114 Mohi ed-Din, Abou-el Ezz, Mohandessin, Cairo; tel. (2) 3490671; fax (2) 3489060; Ambassador MUHAMMAD LEMINE OULD.

Mauritius: 156 Sharia es-Sudan, Mohandessin, Cairo; tel. (2) 7618102; fax (2) 7618101; e-mail embamaur@thewayout.net; Ambassador R. SOOBADAR.

Mexico: 5th Floor, Apartment 502–503, 17 Sharia Port Said, 11431 Cairo (Maadi); tel. (2) 3580256; fax (2) 3591887; e-mail mexemb@idsc.gov.eg; internet www.sre.gob.mx/egipto; Ambassador JAIME NUALART.

Mongolia: 3 Midan en-Nasr, Cairo (Dokki); tel. (2) 3460670; Ambassador D. BAYARKHÜÜ.

Morocco: 10 Sharia Salah ed-Din, Cairo (Zamalek); tel. (2) 7364718; fax (2) 7361937; e-mail morocemb@link.net; Ambassador MUHAMMAD FARAG AD-DOKALI.

Mozambique: 9th Floor, 3 Sharia Abu el-Feda, Cairo (Zamalek); tel. (2) 3320647; fax (2) 3320383; e-mail emozcai@intouch.com; Ambassador DANIEL EDUARDO MONDLANE.

Myanmar: 24 Sharia Muhammad Mazhar, Cairo (Zamalek); tel. (2) 3404176; fax (2) 3416793; Ambassador U AUNG GYI.

Nepal: 9 Sharia Tiba, Madinet el-Kobah, Cairo (Dokki); tel. (2) 3603426; fax (2) 704447; Ambassador RAMBHAKTA P. B. THAKUR.

Netherlands: 18 Sharia Hassan Sabri, Cairo (Zamalek); tel. (2) 7395500; fax (2) 7365249; e-mail kai-ca@minbuza.nl; internet www.mfa.nl/cai-en/homepage; Ambassador TJEERD DE ZWAAN.

New Zealand: 8th Floor, North Tower, Nile City Bldg, Sharia Corniche en-Nil, Cairo (Boulac); tel. (2) 4619178; fax (2) 4619181; Ambassador RENE WILSON.

Niger: 101 Sharia Pyramids, Cairo (Giza); tel. (2) 3865607; Ambassador MOULOUD AL-HOUSSEINI.

Nigeria: 13 Sharia Gabalaya, Cairo (Zamalek); tel. (2) 3406042; fax (2) 3403907; Ambassador MOHAMMED GHALI OMAR.

Norway: 8 Sharia el-Gezirah, Cairo (Zamalek); tel. (2) 7353340; fax (2) 7370709; e-mail emb.cairo@mfa.no; internet www.norway-egypt.org; Ambassador LASSE SIGURD SEIM.

Oman: 52 Sharia el-Higaz, Mohandessin, Cairo; tel. (2) 3036011; fax (2) 3036464; Ambassador ABDULLAH BIN HAMED AL-BUSAIDI.

Pakistan: 8 Sharia es-Salouli, Cairo (Dokki); tel. (2) 37487806; fax (2) 37480310; e-mail parepcairo@hotmail.com; Ambassador ARIF AYUB.

Panama: POB 62, 4A Sharia Ibn Zanki, Cairo 11211 (Zamalek); tel. (2) 3400784; fax (2) 3411092; Chargé d'affaires a.i. ROY FRANCISCO LUNA GONZÁLEZ.

Peru: 8 Sharia Kamel esh-Shenawi, Cairo (Garden City); tel. (2) 3562973; fax (2) 3557985; Ambassador MANUEL VERAMENDI I. SERRA.

Philippines: Villa 28, Sharia 200, Cairo (Degla Maadi); tel. (2) 25213062; fax (2) 25213048; e-mail cairope@dfa.gov.ph; Ambassador PETRONILA P. GARCIA.

Poland: 5 Sharia el-Aziz Osman, Cairo (Zamalek); tel. (2) 7367456; fax (2) 7355427; e-mail secretary@kair.polemb.net; internet www.kair.polemb.net; Ambassador JAN NATKAŃSKI.

Portugal: 1 Sharia es-Saleh Ayoub, Cairo (Zamalek); tel. (2) 7350779; fax (2) 7350790; e-mail embpcai@link.net; Ambassador FERNANDO RAMOS MACHADO.

Qatar: 10 Sharia ath-Thamar, Midan an-Nasr, Madinet al-Mohandessin, Cairo; tel. (2) 7604693; fax (2) 7603618; e-mail cairo@mofa.gov.qa; Ambassador MUHAMMAD BIN HAMAD AL-KHALIFA.

Romania: 6 El-Kamel Muhammad, Cairo (Zamalek); tel. (2) 27360107; fax (2) 27360851; e-mail roembegy@link.net; Ambassador GHEORGHE DUMITRU.

Russia: 95 Sharia Giza, Cairo (Giza); tel. (2) 3489353; fax (2) 3609074; Ambassador MIKHAIL BOGDANOV.

Rwanda: 23 Sharia Babel, Mohandessin, Cairo (Dokki); tel. (2) 3350532; fax (2) 3351479; Ambassador CÉLESTIN KABANDA.

San Marino: 5 Sharia Ramez, Mohandessin, Cairo; tel. (2) 3602718; Ambassador GIACOMO MARIA UGOLINI.

Saudi Arabia: 2 Sharia Ahmad Nessim, Cairo (Giza); tel. (2) 3490775; Ambassador HISHAM MOHI ED-DIN AN-NAZIR.

EGYPT

Senegal: 46 Sharia Abd al-Moneim Riad, Mohandessin, Cairo (Dokki); tel. (2) 3460946; fax (2) 3461039; e-mail mamadousow@hotmail.com; Ambassador MAMADOU SOW.

Serbia: 33 Sharia Mansour Muhammad, Cairo (Zamalek); tel. (2) 7354061; fax (2) 7353913; e-mail yugoemb_kairo@yahoo.com; Ambassador DEJAN VASILJEVIĆ.

Sierra Leone: *Interests served by Saudi Arabia.*

Singapore: 40 Sharia Babel, Cairo 11511 (Dokki); tel. (2) 37490468; fax (2) 37480562; e-mail singemb_cai@sgmfa.gov.sg; internet www.mfa.gov.sg/cairo; Ambassador WONG KWOK PUN.

Slovakia: 3 Sharia Adel Hussein Rostom, Dokki, Cairo (Giza); tel. (2) 33358240; fax (2) 33355810; e-mail zukahira@tedata.net.eg; Ambassador PETER ZSOLDOS.

Slovenia: 6th Floor, 21 Sharia Soliman Abaza, Mohandessin, Cairo; tel. (2) 7491771; fax (2) 7497141; e-mail vka@gov.si; Ambassador BORUT MAHNIČ.

Somalia: 27 Sharia es-Somal, Cairo (Dokki), Giza; tel. (2) 3374577; Ambassador ABDALLA HASSAN MAHMOUD.

South Africa: 6th Floor, 55 Rd 18, Maadi, Cairo; tel. (2) 23594365; fax (2) 3595015; e-mail saembcai@tedata.net.eg; internet saembassyinegypt.com; Ambassador SONTO KUDJOE.

Spain: 41 Sharia Ismail Muhammad, Cairo (Zamalek); tel. (2) 7356462; fax (2) 7352132; e-mail spainemb@startnet.com.eg; Ambassador ANTONIO LÓPEZ MARTÍNEZ.

Sri Lanka: POB 1157, 8 Sharia Sri Lanka, Cairo (Zamalek); tel. (2) 7350047; fax (2) 7367138; e-mail slembare@menanet.net; internet www.lankaemb-egypt.com; Ambassador W. HETTIARACHCHI.

Sudan: 4 Sharia el-Ibrahimi, Cairo (Garden City); tel. (2) 3545043; fax (2) 3542693; Ambassador MUHAMMAD HASSAN AL-HAJ.

Sweden: POB 131, 13 Sharia Muhammad Mazhar, Cairo (Zamalek); tel. (2) 7289200; fax (2) 7354357; e-mail ambassaden.kairo@foreign.ministry.se; internet www.embassyofsweden.org; Ambassador STIG ELVEMAR.

Switzerland: POB 633, 10 Sharia Abd al-Khalek Sarwat, Cairo; tel. (2) 5758284; fax (2) 5745236; e-mail vertretung@cai.rep.admin.ch; internet www.eda.admin.ch/cairo; Ambassador CHARLES-EDOUARD HELD.

Syria: 18 Sharia Abd ar-Rehim Sabry, POB 435, Cairo (Dokki); tel. (2) 3358806; fax (2) 3377020; Ambassador YOUSUF AL-AHMAD.

Tanzania: 10 Anas Ibn Malek Street Mohandessin, Cairo; tel. (2) 3374286; fax (2) 3374155; Ambassador MUHAMMAD A. FOUM.

Thailand: 9 Tiba St, Cairo (Dokki); tel. (2) 37603553; fax (2) 37605076; e-mail royalthai@link.net; internet www.thaiembassy.org/cairo; Ambassador NOPPADON THEPPITAK.

Tunisia: 26 Sharia el-Jazirah, Cairo (Zamalek); tel. (2) 3418962; Ambassador ASH-SHAZLI AN-NAFATI.

Turkey: 25 Sharia Felaki, Cairo (Bab el-Louk); tel. (2) 7963318; fax (2) 7958110; Ambassador ŞAFAK GÖKTÜRK.

Uganda: 66 Rd 10, Maadi, Cairo; tel. (2) 3802514; fax (2) 3802504; e-mail ugembco@link.net; Ambassador IBRAHIM MUKIIBI.

Ukraine: 50 Sharia 83, Maadi, Cairo; tel. (2) 3786871; fax (2) 3786873; e-mail emb_eg@mfa.gov.ua; Ambassador YEVHEN MYKYTENKO.

United Arab Emirates: 4 Sharia Ibn Sina, Cairo (Giza); tel. (2) 3609721; e-mail uaeembassyca@online.com.eg; Ambassador AHMAD AZ-ZA'ABI.

United Kingdom: 7 Sharia Ahmad Ragheb, Cairo (Garden City); tel. (2) 7940852; fax (2) 7940859; e-mail info@britishembassy.org.eg; internet www.britishembassy.org.eg; Ambassador DOMINIC ASQUITH.

USA: 8 Sharia Kamal ed-Din Salah, Cairo (Garden City); tel. (2) 7973300; fax (2) 7973200; e-mail consularcairo@state.gov; internet cairo.usembassy.gov; Ambassador FRANCIS JOSEPH RICCIARDONE.

Uruguay: 6 Sharia Lotfallah, Cairo (Zamalek); tel. (2) 7353589; fax (2) 7368123; e-mail urugemb@idsc.gov.eg; Ambassador CÉSAR WALTER FERRER BURLE.

Uzbekistan: 18 Sad el-Aali St, Cairo (Dokki); tel. (2) 3361723; fax (2) 3361722; Ambassador SOLIH R. INOGAMOV.

Venezuela: POB 1217, 15A Sharia Mansour Muhammad, Cairo (Zamalek); tel. (2) 7363517; fax (2) 7367373; e-mail eov@idsc.gov.eg; Ambassador VICTOR R. CARAZO.

Viet Nam: 8 Sharia Madina El Monawara, Cairo (Dokki); tel. (2) 7617309; fax (2) 3368612; e-mail vinaemb@intouch.com; Ambassador DUONG HUYNH LAP.

Yemen: 28 Sharia Amean ar-Rafai, Cairo (Dokki); tel. (2) 3614224; fax (2) 3604815; Ambassador ABD AL-WALI ABD AL-WALITH.

Zambia: 6 Abd ar-Rahman Hussein, Mohandessin, Cairo (Dokki); tel. (2) 7610282; fax (2) 7610833; Ambassador CECIL ALMOS HOLMES.

Zimbabwe: 40 Sharia Ghaza, Mohandessin, Cairo; tel. (2) 3030404; fax (2) 3059741; e-mail zimcairo@thewayout.net; Ambassador AARON MABOYI-NCUBE.

Judicial System

The Courts of Law in Egypt are principally divided into two juridical court systems: Courts of General Jurisdiction and Administrative Courts. Since 1969 the Supreme Constitutional Court has been at the top of the Egyptian judicial structure.

THE SUPREME CONSTITUTIONAL COURT

The Supreme Constitutional Court is the highest court in Egypt. It has specific jurisdiction over: (i) judicial review of the constitutionality of laws and regulations; (ii) resolution of positive and negative jurisdictional conflicts and determination of the competent court between the different juridical court systems, e.g. Courts of General Jurisdiction and Administrative Courts, as well as other bodies exercising judicial competence; (iii) determination of disputes over the enforcement of two final but contradictory judgments rendered by two courts each belonging to a different juridical court system; (iv) rendering binding interpretation of laws or decree laws in the event of a dispute in the application of said laws or decree laws, always provided that such a dispute is of a gravity requiring conformity of interpretation under the Constitution.

President: Hon. MAHER SAYED IBRAHIM ABD AL-WAHID.

COURTS OF GENERAL JURISDICTION

The Courts of General Jurisdiction in Egypt are effectively divided into four categories, as follows: (i) the Court of Cassation; (ii) the Courts of Appeal; (iii) the Tribunals of First Instance; (iv) the District Tribunals; each of the above courts is divided into Civil and Criminal Chambers.

Court of Cassation

The Court of Cassation is the highest court of general jurisdiction in Egypt. Its sessions are held in Cairo. Final judgments rendered by Courts of Appeal in criminal and civil litigation may be petitioned to the Court of Cassation by the Defendant or the Public Prosecutor in criminal litigation and by any of the parties in interest in civil litigation on grounds of defective application or interpretation of the law as stated in the challenged judgment, on grounds of irregularity of form or procedure, or violation of due process, and on grounds of defective reasoning of judgment rendered. The Court of Cassation is composed of the President, 41 Vice-Presidents and 92 Justices.

President and Chairman of the Supreme Judicial Council: Hon. MOQBAL SHAKER.

Courts of Appeal: Each Court of Appeal has geographical jurisdiction over one or more of the governorates of Egypt, and is divided into Criminal and Civil Chambers. The Criminal Chambers try felonies, and the Civil Chambers hear appeals filed against such judgment rendered by the Tribunals of First Instance where the law so stipulates. Each Chamber is composed of three Superior Judges. Each Court of Appeal is composed of President, and sufficient numbers of Vice-Presidents and Superior Judges.

Tribunals of First Instance: In each governorate there are one or more Tribunals of First Instance, each of which is divided into several Chambers for criminal and civil litigations. Each Chamber is composed of: (a) a presiding judge, and (b) two sitting judges. A Tribunal of First Instance hears, as an Appellate Court, certain litigations as provided under the law.

District Tribunals: Each is a one-judge ancillary Chamber of a Tribunal of First Instance, having jurisdiction over minor civil and criminal litigations in smaller districts within the jurisdiction of such Tribunal of First Instance.

PUBLIC PROSECUTION

Public prosecution is headed by the Prosecutor-General, assisted by a number of deputies, and a sufficient number of chief prosecutors, prosecutors and assistant prosecutors. Public prosecution is represented at all levels of the Courts of General Jurisdiction in all criminal litigations and also in certain civil litigations as required by the law. Public prosecution controls and supervises enforcement of criminal law judgments.

Prosecutor-General: ABD AL-MAGID MAHMOUD ABD AL-MAGID.

ADMINISTRATIVE COURTS SYSTEM (CONSEIL D'ETAT)

The Administrative Courts have jurisdiction over litigations involving the State or any of its governmental agencies. The Administrative Courts system is divided into two courts: the Administrative Courts and the Judicial Administrative Courts, at the top of which is the High Administrative Court. The Administrative Prosecutor investigates administrative crimes committed by government officials and civil servants.

President of Conseil d'Etat: Hon. SAMIR ABD AL-HALIM AHMAD AL-BADAWY.

THE STATE COUNCIL

The State Council is an independent judicial body which has the authority to make decisions in administrative disputes and disciplinary cases within the judicial system.

Chairman: Hon. ES-SAYED MUHAMMAD NOHAL.

THE SUPREME JUDICIAL COUNCIL

The Supreme Judicial Council was reinstituted in 1984, having been abolished in 1969. It exists to guarantee the independence of the judicial system from outside interference and is consulted with regard to draft laws organizing the affairs of the judicial bodies.

Religion

According to the 1986 census, some 94% of Egyptians are Muslims (and almost all of these follow Sunni tenets). According to government figures published in the same year, there are about 2m. Copts (a figure contested by Coptic sources, whose estimates range between 6m. and 7m.), forming the largest religious minority, and about 1m. members of other Christian groups. There is also a small Jewish minority.

ISLAM

There is a Higher Council for the Islamic Call, on which sit: the Grand Sheikh of al-Azhar (Chair.); the Minister of Awqaf (Islamic Endowments); the President and Vice-President of Al-Azhar University; the Grand Mufti of Egypt; and the Secretary-General of the Higher Council for Islamic Affairs.

Grand Sheikh of Al-Azhar: Sheikh MUHAMMAD SAYED ATTIYAH TANTAWI.

Grand Mufti of Egypt: Sheikh ALI GOMAA.

CHRISTIANITY

Orthodox Churches

Armenian Apostolic Orthodox Church: POB 48, 179 Sharia Ramses, Faggalah, Cairo; tel. (2) 25901385; fax (2) 25906671; Prelate Bishop ASHOT MNATSAKANIAN; 7,000 mems.

Coptic Orthodox Church: St Mark Cathedral, POB 9035, Anba Ruess, 222 Sharia Ramses, Abbassia, Cairo; tel. (2) 2857889; fax (2) 2825683; e-mail coptpope@tecmina.com; internet www.copticpope.org; f. AD 61; Patriarch Pope SHENOUDA III; c.13m. followers in Egypt, Sudan, other African countries, the USA, Canada, Australia, Europe and the Middle East.

Greek Orthodox Patriarchate: POB 2006, Alexandria; tel. (3) 4868595; fax (3) 4875684; e-mail patriarchate@greekorthodox-alexandria.org; internet www.greekorthodox-alexandria.org; f. AD 43; Pope and Patriarch of Alexandria and All Africa THEODOROS II; 3m. mems.

The Roman Catholic Church

Armenian Rite

The Armenian Catholic diocese of Alexandria, with an estimated 6,000 adherents at 31 December 2005, is suffragan to the Patriarchate of Cilicia. The Patriarch is resident in Beirut, Lebanon.

Bishop of Alexandria: Rt Rev. KRIKOR-OKOSDINOS COUSSA, Patriarcat Arménien Catholique, 36 Sharia Muhammad Sabri Abou Alam, 11121 Cairo; tel. (2) 3938429; fax (2) 3932025; e-mail pacal@tedata.net.eg.

Chaldean Rite

The Chaldean Catholic diocese of Cairo had an estimated 500 adherents at 31 December 2005.

Bishop of Cairo: Rt Rev. YOUSSEF IBRAHIM SARRAF, Evêché Chaldéen, Basilique-Sanctuaire Notre Dame de Fatima, 141 Sharia Nouzha, 11316 Cairo (Heliopolis); tel. and fax (2) 6355718; e-mail fatimasarraf@yahoo.com.

Coptic Rite

Egypt comprises the Coptic Catholic Patriarchate of Alexandria and five dioceses. At 31 December 2005 there were an estimated 161,327 adherents in the country.

Patriarch of Alexandria: Archbishop ANTONIOS NAGUIB, Patriarcat Copte Catholique, POB 69, 34 Sharia Ibn Sandar, Koubbeh Bridge, 11712 Cairo; tel. (2) 2571740; fax (2) 4545766; e-mail p_coptocattolico@yahoo.it.

Latin Rite

Egypt comprises the Apostolic Vicariate of Alexandria (incorporating Heliopolis and Port Said), containing an estimated 33,700 adherents at 31 December 2005.

Vicar Apostolic: Rt Rev. GIUSEPPE BAUSARDO (Titular Bishop of Ida in Mauretania), 10 Sharia Sidi el-Metwalli, Alexandria; tel. (3) 4876065; fax (3) 4878169; e-mail latinvic@link.net.

Maronite Rite

The Maronite diocese of Cairo had an estimated 5,430 adherents at 31 December 2005.

Bishop of Cairo: Rt Rev. FRANÇOIS EID, Evêché Maronite, 15 Sharia Hamdi, Daher, 11271 Cairo; tel. and fax (2) 5939610; e-mail feid43@yahoo.com.

Melkite Rite

His Beatitude Grégoire III Laham (resident in Damascus, Syria) is the Greek-Melkite Patriarch of Antioch and all the East, of Alexandria and of Jerusalem.

Patriarchal Exarchate of Egypt and Sudan: Greek Melkite Catholic Patriarchate, 16 Sharia Daher, 11271 Cairo; tel. (2) 5905790; fax (2) 5935398; e-mail grecmelkitecath_egy@hotmail.com; 6,500 adherents (31 December 2005); General Patriarchal Vicar for Egypt and Sudan Most Rev. Archbishop (JOSEPH) JULES ZEREY (Titular Archbishop of Damietta).

Syrian Rite

The Syrian Catholic diocese of Cairo had an estimated 1,637 adherents at 31 December 2005.

Bishop of Cairo: Rt Rev. CLÉMENT-JOSEPH HANNOUCHE, Evêché Syrien Catholique, 46 Sharia Daher, 11271 Cairo; tel. (2) 5901234; fax (2) 5923932.

The Anglican Communion

The Anglican diocese of Egypt, suspended in 1958, was revived in 1974 and became part of the Episcopal Church in Jerusalem and the Middle East, formally inaugurated in January 1976. The Province has four dioceses: Jerusalem, Egypt, Cyprus and the Gulf, and Iran, and its President is the Bishop in Egypt. The Bishop in Egypt has jurisdiction also over the Anglican chaplaincies in Algeria, Djibouti, Eritrea, Ethiopia, Libya, Somalia and Tunisia.

Bishop in Egypt: Rt Rev. Dr MOUNEER HANNA ANIS, Diocesan Office, POB 87, 5 Sharia Michel Lutfalla, 11211 Cairo (Zamalek); tel. (2) 7380829; fax (2) 7358941; e-mail diocese@link.net; internet www.geocities.com/dioceseofegypt.

Other Christian Churches

Coptic Evangelical Organization for Social Services: POB 162, 11811 El Panorama, Cairo; tel. (2) 26221425; fax (2) 26221434; e-mail gm@ceoss.org.eg; internet www.ceoss.org.eg; Chair. Dr MERVAT AKHNOUKH ABSAKHROUN; Dir-Gen. Dr NABIL SAMUEL ABADIR.

Other denominations active in Egypt include the Coptic Evangelical Church (Synod of the Nile) and the Union of the Armenian Evangelical Churches in the Near East.

JUDAISM

The 1986 census recorded 794 Jews in Egypt, and there were reported to be fewer than 100 by the mid-2000s.

Jewish Community: Main Synagogue, Shaar Hashamayim 17, Adly St, Cairo; tel. (2) 4824613; fax (2) 7369639; e-mail bassatine@yahoo.com; f. 19th century; Pres. CARMEN WEINSTEIN.

The Press

Despite a fairly high illiteracy rate in Egypt, the country's press is well developed. Cairo is one of the region's largest publishing centres.

All newspapers and magazines are supervised, according to law, by the Supreme Press Council. The four major publishing houses of Al-Ahram Establishment, Dar al-Hilal, Dar Akhbar el-Yom and At-Tahrir Printing and Publishing House operate as separate entities and compete with each other commercially.

The most authoritative daily newspaper is the very long-established *Al-Ahram*.

DAILIES

Alexandria

Bareed ach-Charikat (Companies' Post): POB 813, Alexandria; f. 1952; evening; Arabic; commerce, finance, insurance and marine affairs; Editor S. BENEDUCCI; circ. 15,000.

EGYPT
Directory

Al-Ittihad al-Misri (Egyptian Unity): 13 Sharia Sidi Abd ar-Razzak, Alexandria; f. 1871; evening; Arabic; Propr ANWAR MAHER FARAG; Dir HASSAN MAHER FARAG.

Le Journal d'Alexandrie: 1 Sharia Rolo, Alexandria; evening; French; Editor CHARLES ARCACHE.

La Réforme: 8 Passage Sherif, Alexandria; French.

As-Safeer (The Ambassador): 4 Sharia as-Sahafa, Alexandria; f. 1924; evening; Arabic; Editor MUSTAFA SHARAF.

Tachydromos-Egyptos: 4 Sharia Zangarol, Alexandria; tel. (3) 35650; f. 1879; morning; Greek; liberal; Publr PENNY KOUTSOUMIS; Editor DINOS KOUTSOUMIS; circ. 2,000.

Cairo

Al-Ahram (The Pyramids): Sharia al-Galaa, Cairo 11511; tel. (2) 5801600; fax (2) 5786023; e-mail ahramdaily@ahram.org.eg; internet www.ahram.org.eg; f. 1875; morning, incl. Sun.; Arabic; international edn publ. in London, United Kingdom; North American edition published in New York, USA; Chair. MURSI ATALLAH; Chief Editor OSAMA SARAYA; circ. 900,000 (weekdays), 1.1m. (Fri.).

Al-Ahram al-Misaa' (The Evening Al-Ahram): Sharia al-Galaa, Cairo 11511; f. 1990; evening; Arabic; Editor-in-Chief MURSI ATALLAH.

Al-Ahrar: 58 Manshyet as-Sadr, Kobry al-Kobba, Cairo; tel. (2) 4823046; fax (2) 4823027; f. 1977; organ of Liberal Socialist Party; Editor-in-Chief SALAH QABADAYA.

Al-Akhbar (The News): Dar Akhbar al-Yawm, 6 Sharia as-Sahafa, Cairo; tel. (2) 5782600; fax (2) 5782530; e-mail akhbarelyom@akhbarelyom.org; internet www.elakhbar.org.eg; f. 1952; Arabic; Chair. MUHAMMAD MAHDI FADLI; Editor-in-Chief MUHAMMAD BARAKAT; circ. 780,000.

Arev: 3 Sharia Sulayman Halabi, Cairo; tel. (2) 25754703; e-mail arev@intouch.com; f. 1915; evening; Armenian; official organ of the Armenian Liberal Democratic Party; Editor ASSBED ARTINIAN.

Daily News Egypt: 37 Amman St, Cairo (Dokki); tel. (2) 33352561; fax (2) 33352562; e-mail editor@thedailynewsegypt.com; internet www.thedailynewsegypt.com; f. 2005 as Daily Star Egypt; renamed as above in 2007; English; independent; publ. by Egyptian Media Services; Editor RANIA AL-MALKY.

The Egyptian Gazette: 111–115 Sharia Ramses, Cairo; tel. (2) 5783333; fax (2) 5784646; e-mail ask@egyptiangazette.net.eg; internet www.egyptiangazette.net.eg; f. 1880; morning; English; Chair. MUHAMMAD ABD AL-HADEED; Editor-in-Chief RAMADAN A. KADER; circ. 90,000.

Al-Gomhouriya (The Republic): 24 Sharia Zakaria Ahmad, Cairo; tel. (2) 5781515; fax (2) 5781717; e-mail eltahrir@eltahrir.net; internet www.algomhuria.net.eg; f. 1953; morning; Arabic; mainly economic affairs; Chair. MUHAMMAD ABU HADID; Editor-in-Chief MUHAMMAD ALI IBRAHIM; circ. 900,000.

Al-Masry al-Youm: Cairo; e-mail admin@almasry-alyoum.com; internet www.almasry-alyoum.com; f. 2003; Arabic; independent, privately owned; Editor-in-Chief MAGDY AL-GALAD; circ. 100,000.

Al-Misaa' (The Evening): 24 Sharia Zakaria Ahmad, Cairo; tel. (2) 5781010; fax (2) 5784747; e-mail eltahrir@eltahrir.net; internet www.almessa.net.eg; f. 1956; evening; Arabic; political, social and sport; Editor-in-Chief MUHAMMAD FOUDAH; Man. Dir ABD AL-HAMROSE; circ. 450,000.

Phos: 14 Sharia Zakaria Ahmad, Cairo; f. 1896; morning; Greek; Editor S. PATERAS; Man. BASILE A. PATERAS; circ. 20,000.

Le Progrès Egyptien: 24 Sharia Zakaria Ahmad, Cairo; tel. (2) 5783333; fax (2) 5781110; e-mail ask@progres.net.eg; internet www.progres.net.eg; f. 1893; morning incl. Sun.; French; Chair. ABU AL-HADID; Editor-in-Chief AHMED AL-BARDISSI; circ. 60,000.

Al-Wafd: 1 Sharia Boulos Hanna, Cairo (Dokki); tel. (2) 3482079; fax (2) 3602007; e-mail contact@alwafd.org; internet www.alwafd.org; f. 1984; organ of the New Wafd Party; Editor-in-Chief ANWAR EL-HAWARI; circ. 360,000.

PERIODICALS

Alexandria

Al-Ahad al-Gedid (New Sunday): 88 Sharia Said M. Koraim, Alexandria; tel. (3) 807874; f. 1936; weekly; Editor-in-Chief and Publr GALAL M. KORAITEM; circ. 60,000.

Alexandria Medical Journal: 4 Sharia G. Carducci, Alexandria; tel. (3) 4829001; fax (3) 4833076; f. 1922; quarterly; English, French and Arabic; publ. by Alexandria Medical Asscn; Editor Prof. TOUSSOUN ABOUL AZM.

Amitié Internationale: 59 ave el-Hourriya, Alexandria; tel. (3) 23639; f. 1957; quarterly; Arabic and French; publ. by Asscn Egyptienne d'Amitié Internationale; Editor Dr ZAKI BADAOUI.

L'Annuaire des Sociétés Egyptiennes par Actions: 23 Midan Tahrir, Alexandria; f. 1930; annually in Dec.; French; Propr ELIE I. POLITI; Editor OMAR ES-SAYED MOURSI.

Egyptian Cotton Gazette: POB 1772, 12 Muhammad Talaat Nooman St, Ramel Station, Alexandria; tel. (3) 4806971; fax (3) 4873002; e-mail info@alcotexa.org; internet www.alcotexa.org; f. 1947; 2 a year; English; organ of the Alexandria Cotton Exporters' Asscn; Chief Editor GALAL AR-REFAI.

Informateur des Assurances: 1 Sharia Sinan, Alexandria; f. 1936; monthly; French; Propr ELIE I. POLITI; Editor SIMON A. BARANIS.

Sina 'at en-Nassig (L'Industrie Textile): 5 rue de l'Archevêché, Alexandria; monthly; Arabic and French; Editor PHILIPPE COLAS.

Voce d'Italia: 90 Sharia Farahde, Alexandria; fortnightly; Italian; Editor R. AVELLINO.

Cairo

Al-Ahali (The People): Sharia Kareem ad-Dawli, Tala'at Harb Sq., Cairo; tel. (2) 7786583; fax (2) 3900412; f. 1978; weekly; publ. by the National Progressive Unionist Party; Chair. LOTFI WAKID; Editor-in-Chief ABD AL-BAKOURY.

Al-Ahram al-Arabi: Sharia al-Galaa, Cairo 11511; tel. (2) 5786100; e-mail arabi@ahram.org.eg; internet arabi.ahram.org.eg; f. 1997; weekly (Sat.); Arabic; political, social and economic affairs; Chair. MURSI ATALLAH; Editor-in-Chief OSAMA SARAYA.

Al-Ahram Hebdo: POB 1057, Sharia al-Galaa, Cairo 11511; tel. (2) 7703100; fax (2) 7703314; e-mail hebdo@ahram.org.eg; internet hebdo.ahram.org.eg; f. 1993; weekly (Wed.); French; publ. by Al-Ahram Establishment; Chair. MURSI ATALLAH; Editor-in-Chief MUHAMMAD SALMAWI.

Al-Ahram al-Iqtisadi (The Economic Al-Ahram): Sharia al-Galaa, Cairo 11511; tel. (2) 25786100; fax (2) 25786833; e-mail ik@ahram.org.eg; internet ik.ahram.org.eg; Arabic; weekly (Mon.); economic and political affairs; publ. by Al-Ahram Establishment; Chair. MURSI ATALLAH; Chief Editor ISSAM RIFA'AT; circ. 85,362.

Al-Ahram Weekly (The Pyramids): Al-Ahram Bldg, Sharia al-Galaa, Cairo 11511; tel. (2) 5786100; fax (2) 5786833; e-mail weeklymail@ahram.org.eg; internet weekly.ahram.org.eg; f. 1989; English; weekly; publ. by Al-Ahram Establishment; Chair. MURSI ATALLAH; Editor-in-Chief ASSEM EL-KERSH; circ. 150,000.

Akhbar al-Adab: 6 Sharia as-Sahafa, Cairo; tel. (2) 5795620; fax (2) 5782510; e-mail akhbarelyom@akhbarelyom.org; internet www.akhbarelyom.org.eg/adab; f. 1993; literature and arts for young people; Editor-in-Chief GAMAL AL-GHITANI.

Akhbar al-Hawadith: 6 Sharia as-Sahafa, Cairo; tel. (2) 5782600; fax (2) 5782510; e-mail akhbarelyom@akhbarelyom.org; internet www.akhbarelyom.org.eg/hawadeth; f. 1993; weekly; crime reports; Editor-in-Chief MUHAMMAD BARAKAT.

Akhbar an-Nogoom: 6 Sharia as-Sahafa, Cairo; tel. (2) 5782600; fax (2) 5782510; e-mail akhbarelyom@akhbarelyom.org; internet www.akhbarelyom.org.eg/nogoom; f. 1991; weekly; theatre and film news; Editor-in-Chief AMAL OSMAN.

Akhbar ar-Riadah: 6 Sharia as-Sahafa, Cairo; tel. (2) 5782600; fax (2) 5782510; e-mail akhbarelyom@akhbarelyom.org; internet www.akhbarelyom.org.eg/riada; f. 1990; weekly; sport; Editor-in-Chief IBRAHIM HEGAZY.

Akhbar as-Sayarat: 6 Sharia as-Sahafa, Cairo; e-mail akhbarelyom@akhbarelyom.org; internet www.akhbarelyom.org.eg/sayarat; f. 1998; car magazine; Editor-in-Chief SOLIMAN QENAWI.

Akhbar el-Yom (Daily News): 6 Sharia as-Sahafa, Cairo; tel. (2) 5782600; fax (2) 5782520; e-mail akhbarelyom@akhbarelyom.org; internet elakhbar.org.eg; f. 1944; weekly (Sat.); Arabic; Chair. MUHAMMAD MAHDI FADLI; Editor-in-Chief MOMTAZ AL-QUT; circ. 1,184,611.

Akher Sa'a (Last Hour): Dar Akhbar el-Yom, Sharia as-Sahafa, Cairo; tel. (2) 5782600; fax (2) 5782530; e-mail akhbarelyom@akhbarelyom.org; internet www.akhbarelyom.org.eg/akhersaa; f. 1934; weekly (Sun.); Arabic; independent; consumer and news magazine; Editor-in-Chief MAHMOUD SALAH; circ. 150,000.

Aqidaty (My Faith): 24–26 Sharia Zakaria Ahmad, Cairo; tel. (2) 5783333; fax (2) 5781110; e-mail eltahrir@eltahrir.net; internet www.aqidati.com; weekly; Arabic; Islamic newspaper; Editor-in-Chief ABD AR-RAOUF ES-SAYED; circ. 300,000.

Al-Arabi an-Nasseri: Cairo; tel. (2) 7961018; fax (2) 7953127; e-mail contact_us@al-araby.com; internet www.al-araby.com; f. 1993; weekly; publ. by the Nasserist Party; Editor-in-Chief MAHMOUD EL-MARAGHI.

Al-Azhar: Idarat al-Azhar, Sharia al-Azhar, Cairo; e-mail info@alazhar.org; internet www.alazhar.org; f. 1931; Islamic monthly; Arabic; supervised by the Egyptian Council for Islamic Research of Al-Azhar University; Dir MUHAMMAD FARID WAGDI.

Al-Bitrul (Petroleum): Cairo; monthly; publ. by the Egyptian General Petroleum Corpn.

Computerworld Middle East: World Publishing Ltd (Egypt), 41A Masaken al-Fursan Bldg, Sharia Kamal Hassan Ali, Cairo 11361; tel. (2) 3460601; fax (2) 3470118; monthly; English; specialist computer information.

Contemporary Thought: University of Cairo, Cairo; quarterly; Editor Dr Z. N. MAHMOUD.

Ad-Da'wa (The Call): Cairo; monthly; Arabic; organ of the Muslim Brotherhood.

Ad-Doctor: 8 Sharia Hoda Sharawi, Cairo; f. 1947; monthly; Arabic; Editor Dr AHMAD M. KAMAL; circ. 30,000.

Droit al-Haqq: Itihad al-Mohameen al-Arab, 13 Sharia Itihad, Cairo; 3 a year; publ. by the Arab Lawyers' Union.

Echos: 1–5 Sharia Mahmoud Bassiouni, Cairo; f. 1947; weekly; French; Dir and Propr GEORGES QRFALI.

Egypt Today: 3A Sharia 199, IBA Media Bldg, Degla, Maadi, Cairo; tel. (2) 7555000; fax (2) 7555050; e-mail editor@egypttoday.com; internet www.egypttoday.com; f. 1979; monthly; English; current affairs; Editor-in-Chief Dr MURSI SAAD ED-DIN; circ. 11,500–14,500.

The Egyptian Mail: 24–26 Sharia Zakaria Ahmad, Cairo; internet www.algomhuria.net.eg/egyptian_mail/m1/; weekly; Sat. edn of The Egyptian Gazette; English; Editor-in-Chief ALI IBRAHIM; circ. 40,000.

El-Elm Magazine (Sciences): 24 Sharia Zakaria Ahmad, Cairo; tel. (2) 5781010; fax (2) 5784747; e-mail ask@elm.net.eg; internet www.elm.net.eg; f. 1976; monthly; Arabic; publ. with the Academy of Scientific Research in Egypt; circ. 70,000.

Al-Fusoul (The Seasons): 17 Sharia Sherif Pasha, Cairo; monthly; Arabic; Propr and Chief Editor SAMIR MUHAMMAD ZAKI ABD AL-KADER.

Al-Garidat at-Tigariyat al-Misriya (The Egyptian Business Paper): 25 Sharia Nubar Pasha, Cairo; f. 1921; weekly; Arabic; circ. 7,000.

Hawa'a (Eve): Dar al-Hilal, 16 Sharia Muhammad Ezz el-Arab, Cairo 11511; tel. (2) 3625450; fax (2) 3625469; f. 1892; weekly (Sat.); Arabic; women's magazine; Chief Editor EKBAL BARAKA; circ. 210,502.

Al-Hilal Magazine: Dar al-Hilal, 16 Sharia Muhammad Ezz el-Arab, Cairo 11511; tel. (2) 3625450; fax (2) 3625469; f. 1895; monthly; Arabic; literary; Editor MAIDI AS-SAYID AD-DAQAQ.

Horreyati: 24 Sharia Zakaria Ahmad, Cairo; tel. (2) 5781010; fax (2) 5784747; e-mail eltahrir@eltahrir.net; internet www.horreyati.net.eg; f. 1990; weekly; social, cultural and sport; Editor-in-Chief MUHAMMAD NOUR ED-DIN; circ. 250,000.

Industrial Egypt: POB 251, 26A Sharia Sherif Pasha, Cairo; tel. (2) 3928317; fax (2) 3928075; f. 1924; quarterly bulletin and year book of the Federation of Egyptian Industries in English and Arabic; Editor ALI FAHMY.

L'Informateur Financier et Commercial: 24 Sharia Sulayman Pasha, Cairo; f. 1929; weekly; Dir HENRI POLITI; circ. 15,000.

Al-Iza'a wat-Television (Radio and Television): 16 Sharia Muhammad Ezz el-Arab, Cairo 11511; tel. (2) 3643314; fax (2) 3543030; f. 1935; weekly; Arabic; Man. Editor MAHMOUD ALI; circ. 80,000.

El-Keraza (The Sermon): St Mark Cathedral, POB 9035, Anba Ruess, 222 Sharia Ramses, Abbassia, Cairo; e-mail coptpope@tecmina.com; internet www.copticpope.org; weekly newspaper of the Coptic Orthodox Church; Arabic and English; Editor-in-Chief Pope SHENOUDA III.

Al-Kawakeb (The Stars): Dar al-Hilal, 16 Sharia Muhammad Ezz el-Arab, Cairo 11511; tel. (2) 3625450; fax (2) 3625469; f. 1952; weekly; Arabic; film magazine; Editor-in-Chief FAWZI MUHAMMAD IBRAHIM; circ. 86,381.

Kitab al-Hilal: Dar al-Hilal, 16 Sharia Muhammad Ezz el-Arab, Cairo 11511; tel. (2) 3625450; fax (2) 3625469; monthly; Founders EMILE, SHOUKRI ZEIDAN; Editor MAIDI AS-SAYID AD-DAQAQ.

Al-Kora wal-Malaeb (Football and Playgrounds): 24 Sharia Zakaria Ahmad, Cairo; tel. (2) 5783333; fax (2) 5784747; f. 1976; weekly; Arabic; sport; circ. 150,000.

Al-Liwa' al-Islami (Islamic Standard): 11 Sharia Sherif Pasha, Cairo; f. 1982; weekly; Arabic; govt paper to promote official view of Islamic revivalism; Propr AHMAD HAMZA; Editor MUHAMMAD ALI SHETA; circ. 30,000.

Magallat al-Mohandessin (The Engineer's Magazine): 28 Sharia Ramses, Cairo; f. 1945; publ. by The Engineers' Syndicate; 10 a year; Arabic and English; Editor and Sec. MAHMOUD SAMI ABD AL-KAWI.

Al-Magallat az-Zira'ia (The Agricultural Magazine): Cairo; monthly; agriculture; circ. 30,000.

Medical Journal of Cairo University: Qasr el-Eini Hospital, Sharia Qasr el-Eini, Cairo; tel. and fax (2) 3655768; f. 1933; Qasr el-Eini Clinical Society; quarterly; English; Editor-in-Chief MADIHA KHATTAB.

MEN Economic Weekly: Middle East News Agency, 4 Sharia Hoda Sharawi, Cairo; tel. (2) 3933000; fax (2) 3935055.

The Middle East Observer: 41 Sharia Sherif, Cairo; tel. and fax (2) 3939732; e-mail meo@soficom.eg; internet www.middleeastobserver.com; f. 1954; weekly; English; specializes in economics of Middle East and African markets; also publishes supplements on law, foreign trade and tenders; agent for IMF, UN and IDRC publications, distributor of World Bank publications; Man. Owner AHMAD FODA; Chief Editor HESHAM A. RAOUF; circ. 20,000.

Middle East Times Egypt: 2 Sharia el-Malek el-Afdal, Cairo (Zamalek); tel. (2) 3419930; fax (2) 3413725; e-mail met@ritsec1.com.eg; f. 1983; weekly; English; Man. Editor ROD CRAIG; circ. 6,000.

Al-Mussawar: Dar al-Hilal, 16 Sharia Muhammad Ezz el-Arab, Cairo 11511; tel. (2) 3625450; fax (2) 3625469; f. 1924; weekly; Arabic; news; Chair. and Editor-in-Chief ABD AL-KADER SHUHAYIB; circ. 130,423.

Nesf ad-Donia: Sharia al-Galaa, Cairo 11511; tel. (2) 5786100; internet www.ahram.org.eg; f. 1990; weekly; Arabic; women's magazine; publ. by Al-Ahram Establishment; Editor-in-Chief SANAA AL-BESI.

October: Dar al-Maaref, 1119 Sharia Corniche en-Nil, Cairo; tel. (2) 5777077; fax (2) 5744999; internet www.octobermag.com; f. 1976; weekly; Arabic; Chair. and Editor-in-Chief ISMAIL MUNTASSIR; circ. 140,500.

Al-Omal (The Workers): 90 Sharia al-Galaa, Cairo; weekly; Arabic; publ. by the Egyptian Trade Union Federation; Chief Editor AHMAD HARAK.

PC World Middle East: World Publishing Ltd (Egypt), 41A Masaken al-Fursan Bldg, Sharia Kamal Hassan Ali, Cairo 11361; tel. (2) 34606; fax (2) 3470118; monthly; computers.

Le Progrès Dimanche: 24 Sharia al-Galaa, Cairo; tel. (2) 5781010; fax (2) 5784747; weekly; French; Sun. edition of Le Progrès Egyptien; Editor-in-Chief KHALED ANWAR BAKIR; circ. 35,000.

Rose al-Yousuf: 89A Sharia Qasr el-Eini, Cairo; tel. (2) 7923514; fax (2) 7925540; internet www.rosaonline.net; f. 1925; weekly; Arabic; political; circulates throughout all Arab countries; Editor-in-Chief ABDULLAH KAMAL ES-SAYED; circ. 35,000.

As-Sabah (The Morning): 4 Sharia Muhammad Said Pasha, Cairo; f. 1922; weekly (Thurs.); Arabic; Editor RAOUF TAWFIK.

Sabah al-Kheir (Good Morning): 89A Sharia Qasr el-Eini, Cairo; tel. (2) 3540888; fax (2) 3556413; f. 1956; weekly (Thurs.); Arabic; light entertainment; Chief Editor RAOUF TAWFIK; circ. 70,000.

Ash-Shaab (The People): 313 Sharia Port Said, Sayeda Zeinab, Cairo; tel. (2) 3909716; fax (2) 3900283; e-mail elshaab@idsc.gov.eg; f. 1979; bi-weekly (Tues. and Fri.); organ of Socialist Labour Party; pro-Islamist; Editor-in-Chief MAGDI AHMAD HUSSEIN; circ. 130,000.

Shashati (My Screen): 24 Sharia Zakaria Ahmad, Cairo; tel. (2) 5781010; fax (2) 5784747; e-mail eltahrir@eltahrir.net; internet www.shashati.net.eg; weekly; art, culture, fashion and television news.

As-Siyassa ad-Dawliya: Al-Ahram Bldg, 12th Floor, Sharia al-Galaa, Cairo 11511; tel. (2) 25786249; fax (2) 25792899; e-mail siyassa@ahram.org.eg; internet www.siyassa.org.eg; f. 1965; quarterly; politics and foreign affairs; publ. by Al-Ahram Establishment; Editor-in-Chief Dr OSAMA AL-GHAZALI HARB; Man. Editor KAREN ABOUL KHEIR.

Tabibak al-Khass (Family Doctor): Dar al-Hilal, 16 Sharia Muhammad Ezz el-Arab, Cairo; tel. (2) 3625473; fax (2) 3625442; monthly; Arabic.

At-Tahrir (Liberation): 5 Sharia Naguib, Rihani, Cairo; e-mail eltahrir@eltahrir.net; internet www.eltahrir.net; weekly; Arabic; Editor MUHAMMAD ALI IBRAHIM.

At-Taqaddum (Progress): c/o 1 Sharia Jarim ed-Dawlah, Cairo; f. 1978; weekly; organ of National Progressive Unionist Party.

Tchehreh Nema: 14 Sharia Hassan el-Akbar (Abdine), Cairo; f. 1904; Iranian; monthly; political, literary and general; Editor MANUCHEHR TCHEHREH NEMA MOADEB ZADEH.

Watani (My Country): 27 Sharia Abd al-Khalek Sarwat, Cairo; tel. (2) 3927201; fax (2) 3935946; e-mail watani@watani.com.eg; internet www.wataninet.com; f. 1958; weekly (Sun.); Arabic and English, with French supplement; independent newspaper addressing Egyptians in general and the Christian Copts in particular; Editor-in-Chief YOUSSEF SIDHOM; circ. 60,000–100,000.

Al-Watani al-Youm: Cairo; tel. (2) 3024163; fax (2) 3047328; e-mail alwatanyalyoum@ndp.org.eg; internet www.ndp.org.eg/alwatanyalyoum; f. 2006; weekly; organ of the National Democratic Party; Editor-in-Chief MUHAMMAD HASSAN EL-ALFY.

Yulio (July): July Press and Publishing House, Cairo; f. 1986; weekly; Nasserist; Editor ABDULLAH IMAM; also a monthly cultural magazine; Editor MAHMOUD AL-MARAGHI.

EGYPT
Directory

NEWS AGENCY

Middle East News Agency (MENA): POB 1165, 17 Sharia Hoda Sharawi, Cairo; tel. (2) 3933000; fax (2) 3935055; e-mail newsroom@mena.org.eg; internet www.mena.org.eg; f. 1955; regular service in Arabic, English and French; Chair. and Editor-in-Chief ABDULLAH HASSAN ABD AL-FATTAH.

PRESS ASSOCIATIONS

Egyptian Press Syndicate: Cairo; Chair. MAKRAM MUHAMMAD AHMED.

Foreign Press Association: Room 2037, Marriott Hotel, Cairo; tel. (2) 3419957.

Publishers

The General Egyptian Book Organization: POB 235, Sharia Corniche en-Nil, Cairo (Boulac) 11221; tel. (2) 25775109; fax (2) 25754213; e-mail info@egyptianbook.org.eg; internet www.egyptianbook.org.eg; f. 1961; editing, publishing and distribution; organizer of Cairo International Book Fair; affiliated to the Ministry of Culture; Chair. Dr NASSER AL-ANSARY; Gen. Dir AHMAD SALAH ZAKI.

ALEXANDRIA

Dar al-Matbo al-Gadidah: 5 Sharia St Mark, Alexandria; tel. (3) 4825508; fax (3) 4833819; agriculture, information sciences and social sciences.

Egyptian Printing and Publishing House: Ahmad es-Sayed Marouf, 59 Safia Zaghoul, Alexandria; f. 1947.

Maison Egyptienne d'Editions: Ahmad es-Sayed Marouf, Sharia Adib, Alexandria; f. 1950.

Maktab al-Misri al-Hadith li-t-Tiba wan-Nashr: 7 Sharia Noubar, Alexandria; also at 2 Sharia Sherif, Cairo; Man. AHMAD YEHIA.

CAIRO

Al-Ahram Establishment: Al-Ahram Bldg, 6 Sharia al-Galaa, Cairo 11511; tel. (2) 5786100; fax (2) 5786023; e-mail ahram@ahram.org.eg; internet www.ahram.org.eg; f. 1875; publ. newspapers, magazines and books, incl. Al-Ahram; Chair. and Chief Editor SALAH EL-GHAMRI; Dep. Chair. and Gen. Man. ALI GHONEIM.

American University in Cairo Press: 113 Sharia Qasr el-Eini, POB 2511, Cairo 11511; tel. (2) 7976926; fax (2) 7941440; e-mail aucpress@aucegypt.edu; internet www.aucpress.com; political history, economics, Egyptology and Arabic literature in English translation; Dir MARK LINZ.

Boustany's Publishing House: 4 Sharia Aly Tawfik Shousha, Cairo (Nasr City) 11371; tel. and fax (2) 2623085; e-mail boustany@link.net; internet www.boustanys.com; f. 1900; fiction, poetry, history, biography, philosophy, language, literature, politics, religion, archaeology and Egyptology; Chief Exec. FADWA BOUSTANY.

Cairo University Press: Al-Giza, Cairo; tel. (2) 7279584; fax (2) 7277288.

Dar Akhbar el-Yom: 6 Sharia as-Sahafa, Cairo; tel. (2) 5748100; fax (2) 5748895; e-mail akhbarelyom@akhbarelyom.org; internet www.akhbarelyom.org; f. 1944; publ. Al-Akhbar (daily), Akhbar el-Yom (weekly) and colour magazine, Akher Sa'a (weekly); Chair. MUHAMMAD MAHDI FADLI.

Dar al-Farouk: 12 Sharia Dokki, Sixth Floor, Cairo (Giza); tel. (2) 37622830; fax (2) 33380474; e-mail support@darelfarouk.com.eg; internet www.darelfarouk.com.eg; wide range of books incl. educational, history, science and business; Chair. FAROUK M. AL-AMARY; Gen. Man Dr KHALED F. AL-AMARY.

Dar al-Gomhouriya: 24 Sharia Zakaria Ahmad, Cairo; tel. (2) 5781010; fax (2) 5784747; affiliate of At-Tahrir Printing and Publishing House; publications include the dailies Al-Gomhouriya, Al-Misaa', The Egyptian Gazette and Le Progrès Egyptien; Pres. MUHAMMAD ABOUL HADID.

Dar al-Hilal: 16 Sharia Muhammad Ezz el-Arab, Cairo 11511; tel. (2) 3625450; fax (2) 3625469; f. 1892; publ. Al-Hilal, Riwayat al-Hilal, Kitab al-Hilal, Tabibak al-Khass (monthlies); Al-Mussawar, Al-Kawakeb, Hawa'a, Samir (weeklies); Chief Exec. ABD AL-KADER SHUHAYIB.

Dar al-Kitab al-Masri: POB 156, 33 Sharia Qasr en-Nil, Cairo 11511; tel. (2) 3922168; fax (2) 3924657; e-mail info@daralkitabalmasri.com; internet www.daralkitabalmasri.com; f. 1929; publishing, printing and distribution; publrs of books on Islam and history, as well as dictionaries, encyclopaedias, textbooks, children's and general interest books; Pres. and Man. Dir Dr HASSAN EZ-ZEIN.

Dar al-Maaref: 1119 Sharia Corniche en-Nil, Cairo; tel. (2) 25777077; fax (2) 25744999; e-mail maaref@idselgov.eg; internet www.octobermag.com; f. 1890; publishing, printing and distribution of wide variety of books in Arabic and other languages; publrs of October magazine; Chair. ISMAIL MUNTASSIR.

Dar an-Nashr (formerly Les Editions Universitaires d'Egypte): POB 1347, 41 Sharia Sherif, Cairo 11511; tel. (2) 3934606; fax (2) 3921997; f. 1947; university textbooks, academic works and encyclopaedia.

Dar ash-Shorouk (Egyptian Publishers Association): 8 Sibaweh Al Masri, Cairo (Nasr City) 11371; tel. (2) 24023399; fax (2) 24037567; e-mail dar@shorouk.com; internet www.shorouk.com; f. 1968; publishing, printing and distribution; publrs of books on current affairs, history, Islamic studies, literature, art and children's books; Chair. IBRAHIM EL-MOALLEM.

Dar ath-Thaqafa: 32 Sharia Sabry Abou Alam, Cairo; tel. (2) 4646361; fax (2) 4610291; e-mail info@daralthaqafa.com; internet www.daralthaqafa.com; f. 1968; Pres. KHALED MAHMOUD GABER.

Editions le Progrès: 6 Sharia Sherif Pasha, Cairo; Propr WADI SHOUKRI.

Egyptian Co for Printing and Publishing: 40 Sharia Noubar, Cairo; tel. (2) 21310; Chair. MUHAMMAD MAHMOUD HAMED.

Elias Modern Publishing House: 1 Sharia Kenisset Ar-Rum El-Kathulik, Daher, Cairo 11271; tel. (2) 25903756; fax (2) 25880091; e-mail info@eliaspublishing.com; internet www.eliaspublishing.com; f. 1913; publishing, printing and distribution; publ. dictionaries, children's books and books on linguistics, poetry and arts; Chair. NADIM ELIAS; Man. Dir LAURA KFOURY.

Al-Khira Press: 8 Sharia Soliman el-Halabi, Cairo; tel. and fax (2) 5744809; Owner ABD AL-MEGUID MUHAMMAD.

Librairie La Renaissance d'Egypte (Hassan Muhammad & Sons): POB 2172, 9 Sharia Adly, Cairo; f. 1930; religion, history, geography, medicine, architecture, economics, politics, law, philosophy, psychology, children's books, atlases and dictionaries; Man. HASSAN MUHAMMAD.

Maktabet Misr: POB 16, 3 Sharia Kamal Sidki, Cairo; tel. (2) 5898553; fax (2) 7870051; e-mail info@misrbookshop.com; f. 1932; publ. wide variety of fiction, biographies and textbooks for schools and universities; Man. AMIR SAID GOUDA ES-SAHHAR.

Nahdet Misr Group: An-Nahda Tower, 21 Sharia Ahmad Orabi, Sphinx Sq., Mohandessin, Cairo (Giza); tel. (2) 33464903; fax (2) 33462576; e-mail publishing@nahdetmisr.com; internet www.nahdetmisr.com; f. 1938; fiction, children's literature and educational books; also publ. magazines incl. Mickey (weekly); Chair. MUHAMMAD AHMAD IBRAHIM.

National Centre for Educational Research and Development: 12 Sharia Waked, el-Borg el-Faddy, POB 836, Cairo; tel. (2) 3930981; f. 1956; fmrly Documentation and Research Centre for Education (Ministry of Education); bibliographies, directories, information and education bulletins; Dir Prof. ABD EL-FATTAH GALAL.

National Library Press (Dar al-Kutub): POB 11638, 8 Sharia as-Sabtteya, Cairo; tel. (2) 5750886; fax (2) 5765634; e-mail info@darelkotob.org; bibliographic works; Pres. and Dir-Gen. SAMIR GHARIB.

At-Tahrir Printing and Publishing House: 24 Sharia Zakaria Ahmad, Cairo; tel. (2) 5781222; fax (2) 2784747; e-mail eltahrir@eltahrir.net; internet www.eltahrir.net; f. 1953; affiliated with the Shura (Advisory) Council; Pres. and Chair. of Bd MUHAMMAD ABOUL HADID.

Broadcasting and Communications

TELECOMMUNICATIONS

Regulatory Authority

National Telecom Regulatory Authority (NTRA): Smart Village, Bldg No. 4, km 28, Sharia Cairo–Alexandria, Cairo; tel. (2) 35344000; fax (2) 35344155; e-mail info@tra.gov.eg; internet www.ntra.gov.eg; f. 2000; Chair. Dr TAREQ MUHAMMAD KAMEL; Exec. Pres. Dr AMR BADAWI.

Principal Operators

Telecom Egypt: POB 2271, Sharia Ramses, Cairo 11511; tel. (2) 5793444; fax (2) 5744244; e-mail telecomegypt@telecomegypt.com.eg; internet www.telecomegypt.com.eg; f. 1957; provider of fixed-line telephone services; Chair. AKIL HAMED BESHIR.

Egyptian Company for Mobile Services (MobiNil): The World Trade Center, 1191 Corniche en-Nil, Boulaq, Cairo; tel. (2) 5747000; fax (2) 5747111; e-mail customercare@mobinil.com; internet www.mobinil.com; began operation of the existing state-controlled mobile telecommunications network in 1998; owned by France Telecom and Orascom Telecom; 13.7m. subscribers (Sept. 2007); Chair. NAGHIB SAWARIS; Pres. and CEO ISKANDER N. (ALEX) SHALABY.

Etisalat Misr: POB 4, B124, Smart Village, Cairo–Alexandria Desert Road, Cairo; tel. (2) 35346333; internet www.etisalat.com.eg; f. 2007 as Egypt's third mobile telephone service provider; subsidiary of Etisalat (United Arab Emirates); Chair. GAMAL ES-SADAT; CEO SALEH EL-ABDOULI.

Orascom Telecom: 2005A Nile City Towers, South Tower, Corniche en-Nil, Ramlet Beaulac, 11221 Cairo; tel. (2) 4615050; fax (2) 4615054; e-mail info@orascom.com; internet www.orascomtelecom.com; Chair. and CEO NAGUIB SAWARIS.

Vodafone Egypt: 7A Corniche en-Nil, Maadi, 11431 Cairo; tel. (2) 5292000; e-mail public.relations@vodafone.com; internet www.vodafone.com.eg; f. 1998 by the MisrFone consortium; mobile telephone service provider; majority-owned by Vodafone International (UK); 12.2m. subscribers (Sept. 2007); Chair. IAN GRAY; CEO RICHARD DALY.

BROADCASTING

Radio

Egyptian Radio and Television Union (ERTU): POB 11511, Cairo 1186; tel. (2) 5787120; fax (2) 746989; e-mail info@ertu.org; internet www.ertu.org; f. 1928; home service radio programmes in Arabic, English and French; foreign services in Arabic, English, French, German, Spanish, Portuguese, Italian, Swahili, Hausa, Urdu, Indonesian, Pashtu, Farsi, Turkish, Somali, Uzbek, Albanian, Afar, Amharic; Pres. AHMAD ANIS.

Middle East Radio: Société Egyptienne de Publicité, 24–26 Sharia Zakaria Ahmad, Cairo; tel. (2) 5781010; fax (2) 5784747.

Television

Egypt has two direct television broadcast satellites. The second satellite, Nilesat 102, was launched in August 2000.

Egyptian Radio and Television Union (ERTU): see Radio.

Dream TV: Cairo; f. 2001; privately owned satellite television station; broadcasts on Dream 1 and Dream 2 networks, providing sports, music and entertainment programmes; Chair. Dr AHMAD BAHGAT.

El-Mehwar TV: Cairo; e-mail ElMehwar@ElMehwar.tv; internet www.elmehwar.tv; f. 2001; privately owned; entertainment and current affairs programmes; Founder Dr HASSAN RATEB.

Finance

(cap. = capital; res = reserves; dep. = deposits; m. = million; brs = branches; amounts in Egyptian pounds unless otherwise stated)

BANKING

Central Bank

Central Bank of Egypt (CBE): 31 Sharia Qasr en-Nil, Cairo; tel. (2) 3931514; fax (2) 3926361; e-mail info@cbe.org.eg; internet www.cbe.org.eg; f. 1961; controls Egypt's monetary policy and supervises the banking and insurance sectors; cap. 1,000m., res 1,331.1m., dep. 187,029.7m. (June 2005); Gov. and Chair. Dr FAROUK ABD EL-BAKY EL-OKDAH; Dep. Govs TAREK HASSAN ALI AMER, TAREK FATHI KANDIL; 3 brs.

Commercial and Specialized Banks

Alexandria Commercial and Maritime Bank, SAE: POB 2376, 85 ave el-Hourriya, Alexandria 21519; tel. (3) 3921237; fax (3) 3913706; e-mail foreign@acmb.com.eg; internet www.acmb.com.eg; f. 1981; Union National Bank (United Arab Emirates) has 94.8% interest and others 5.2%; cap. 112.1m., res 59.2m., dep. 2,039.4m. (Dec. 2006); Chair. Sheikh NAHAYAN MUBARAK AN-NAHAYAN; Man. Dir MUHAMMAD NASSER ABDEEN; 9 brs.

Bank of Alexandria: 49 Sharia Qasr en-Nil, Cairo; tel. (2) 3913822; fax (2) 3910481; e-mail foreign@alexbank.com; internet www.alexbank.com; f. 1957; 80% stake acquired by Gruppo Sanpaolo IMI (Italy) in Oct. 2006; cap. 800m., res 870.3m., dep. 27,643.3m. (June 2006); Chair. MAHMOUD SAYED ABD AL-LATIF; 196 brs.

Banque du Caire, SAE: POB 9022, Banque du Caire Tower, 6 Sharia Dr Moustafa Abu Zahra, Nasr City, Cairo 11371; tel. (2) 2647400; fax (2) 403725; e-mail intl.division@bdc.com.eg; internet www.bdc.com.eg; f. 1952; state-owned; privatization pending; cap. 1,600.0m., res 1,300.8m., dep. 40,721.9m. (June 2006); Chair. MUHAMMAD KAMAL ED-DIN BARAKAT; Gen. Man. GAMIL YASSA; 216 brs in Egypt, 5 abroad.

Banque Misr, SAE: 151 Sharia Muhammad Farid, Cairo; tel. (2) 3912711; fax (2) 3919779; e-mail staff@banquemisr.com.eg; internet www.banquemisr.com.eg; f. 1920; merger with Misr Exterior Bank in 2004; privatization pending; cap. 1,800m., res 1,676.9m., dep. 101,952.8m. (June 2006); Chair. MUHAMMAD KAMAL AD-DIN BARAKAT; Gen. Man. AMR MUHAMMAD EL-MAHDAY YOUSUF; 438 brs.

Commercial International Bank (Egypt), SAE: POB 2430, Nile Tower Bldg, 21–23 Sharia Charles de Gaulle, Cairo (Giza); tel. (2) 5703043; fax (2) 5703086; e-mail info@cibeg.com; internet www.cibeg.com; f. 1975 as Chase National Bank (Egypt), SAE; adopted present name 1987; National Bank of Egypt has 19.91% interest, Bankers Trust Co (USA) 18.76%, International Finance Corpn 5%; cap. 1,950m., res 575.1m., dep. 32,812.8m. (Dec. 2006); Exec. Chair. and Man. Dir HISHAM EZZ AL-ARAB; 112 brs.

Egyptian Arab Land Bank: 78 Sharia Gameat ad-Dowal al-Arabia, Mohandessin, 12311 Cairo; tel. (2) 3368074; fax 3389218; e-mail foreign@eal-bank.com; internet www.eal-bank.com; f. 1880; state-owned; Chair. MUHAMMAD FATHY ES-SEBAI; 23 brs in Egypt, 15 abroad.

Export Development Bank of Egypt (EDBE): 108 Mohi ed-Din Abou al-Ezz, Cairo 12311 (Dokki); tel. (2) 7619006; fax (2) 3385938; e-mail info@edbebank.com; internet www.edbebank.com; f. 1983 to replace National Import-Export Bank; cap. 600.0m., res 206.62m., dep. 5,142.1m. (June 2006); Chair. HISHAM AHMAD HASSAN; Vice-Chair. OLA ABD AL-AZIZ GADALLAH; 10 brs.

HSBC Bank Egypt, SAE: POB 126, Abou el-Feda Bldg, 3 Sharia Abou el-Feda, Cairo (Zamalek); tel. (2) 7359186; fax (2) 7364010; e-mail hsbcegypt@hsbc.com; internet www.egypt.hsbc.com; f. 1982 as Hong Kong Egyptian Bank; changed name to Egyptian British Bank in 1994; changed name to above in 2001; the Hongkong and Shanghai Banking Corpn has a 94.5% shareholding, other interests 5.5%; cap. 1,072.5m., res 239.8m., dep. 15,399.2m. (Dec. 2006); Chair. and Man. Dir ABD AS-SALAM EL-ANWAR; 24 brs.

National Bank for Development (NBD): POB 647, 5 Sharia el-Borsa el-Gedida, Cairo 11511; tel. (2) 3928849; fax (2) 3905681; e-mail nbd@internetegypt.com; internet www.nbdegypt.com; f. 1980; 16 affiliated National Banks for Development merged with NBD in 1992; 51% share bought by Abu Dhabi Islamic Bank in 2007; cap. 281.9m., res 34.6m., dep. 8,241.3m. (Dec. 2006); Chair. and Man. Dir AL ISMAIL SHAKER; 68 brs.

National Bank of Egypt: POB 11611, National Bank of Egypt Tower, 1187 Corniche en-Nil, Cairo; tel. (2) 5749101; fax (2) 5762672; e-mail nbe@nbe.com.eg; internet www.nbe.com.eg; f. 1898; merger with Mohandes Bank and Bank of Commerce and Development in 2005; privatization pending; handles all commercial banking operations; cap. 2,250.0m., res 4,303.2m., dep. 160,727.9m. (June 2006); Chair. HUSSEIN ABD AL-AZIZ HUSSEIN; 401 brs.

Principal Bank for Development and Agricultural Credit (PBDAC): 110 Sharia Qasr el-Eini, 11623 Cairo; tel. (2) 27951229; fax (2) 27948337; e-mail pbdac@pbdac.com.eg; internet www.pbdac.com.eg; f. 1976 to succeed former credit orgs; state-owned; cap. 1,500.0m., res 299.7m., dep. 14,156.4m. (June 2006); Chair. ALI ISMAEL SHAKER; 167 brs.

Société Arabe Internationale de Banque (SAIB): POB 124, 56 Sharia Gamet ed-Dowal al-Arabia, Mohandessin, Cairo (Giza); tel. (2) 7499464; fax (2) 3603497; f. 1976; Arab International Bank has a 46.0% share, other interests 54.0%; cap. US $120.0m., res $25.5m., dep. $663.5m. (Dec. 2006); Chair. Dr HASSAN ABBAS ZAKI; Man. Dir HASSAN ABD AL-MEGUID; 7 brs.

The United Bank (UBE): Cairo Center, 106 Sharia Qasr el-Eini, Cairo; tel. (2) 7920146; fax (2) 7920153; e-mail info@ube.net; internet www.theubeg.com; f. 1981 as Dakahlia National Bank for Development, renamed United Bank of Egypt 1997; current name adopted in 2006, when merged with Nile Bank and Islamic International Bank for Investment and Development; Chair. and Man. Dir MUHAMMAD ASHMAWY; 37 brs.

Social Bank

Nasser Social Bank: POB 2552, 35 Sharia Qasr en-Nil, Cairo; tel. (2) 3924484; fax (2) 3921930; f. 1971; state-owned; interest-free savings and investment bank for social and economic activities, participating in social insurance, specializing in financing co-operatives, craftsmen and social institutions; cap. 20m.; Chair. NASSIF TAHOON.

Multinational Banks

Arab African International Bank: 5 Midan as-Saray al-Koubra, POB 60, Majlis esh-Sha'ab, Cairo 11516 (Garden City); tel. (2) 7945094; fax (2) 7958493; internet www.aaibank.com; f. 1964 as Arab African Bank; renamed 1978; acquired Misr-America International Bank in 2005; cap. US $100.0m., res $106.8m., dep. $4,543.0m. (Dec. 2006); commercial investments and retail banking; shareholders are Central Bank of Egypt, Kuwait Investment Authority (49.37% each); and individuals and Arab institutions; Chair. MAHMOUD A. AN-NOURI; Vice-Chair. and Man. Dir HASSAN E. ABDALLA; 27 brs in Egypt, 3 abroad.

EGYPT

Arab International Bank: POB 1563, 35 Sharia Abd al-Khalek Sarwat, Cairo; tel. (2) 3918794; fax (2) 3916233; f. 1971 as Egyptian International Bank for Foreign Trade and Investment; renamed 1974; cap. US $300.0m., res $174.5m., dep. $3,296.7m. (June 2006); offshore bank; aims to promote trade and investment in shareholders' countries and other Arab countries; owned by Egypt, Libya, UAE, Oman, Qatar and private Arab shareholders; Chair. Dr ATIF MUHAMMAD OBEID; Man. Dir HANAFY HUSSEIN; 7 brs.

Commercial Foreign Venture Banks

Ahli United Bank: POB 1159, 9th Floor, World Trade Center, 1191 Corniche en-Nil; tel. (2) 25801200; fax (2) 25757052; e-mail info@deltabank-egypt.com; internet www.ahliunited.com; f. 1978 as Delta International Bank; name changed as above in 2007; Ahli United Bank BSC (Bahrain) owns 35.3%; cap. 500m., res 169.8m., dep. 2,914,331m. (Dec. 2006); Chair. FAHAD AR-RAJAAN; 18 brs.

Bank Audi SAE: 104 Corniche en-Nil, Cairo.; tel. (2) 33362516; fax (2) 37483818; e-mail contactus.egypt@banqueaudi.com; internet www.banqueaudi.com/egypt/egypt.html; f. 1978 as Cairo Far East Bank SAE; name changed as above in 2006, when acquired by Bank Audi SAL (Lebanon); cap. 570.8m., dep. 5,073.6m. (Dec. 2006); Chair. MONA FAHMY YASSINE; Man. Dir AHMAD G. HAMDI; 16 brs.

Barclays Bank Egypt, SAE: POB 110, 12 Midan esh-Sheikh Yousuf, Cairo (Garden City); tel. (2) 3662600; fax (2) 3662810; f. 1975 as Cairo Barclays Int. Bank; renamed Banque du Caire Barclays International in 1983 and Cairo Barclays Bank in 1999; name changed as above in 2004; wholly owned by Barclays Bank; acquired 40% stake held by Banque du Caire in 2004; cap. 362.0m., res 9.0m., dep. 4,977.5m. (Dec. 2004); Man. Dir KHALID EL-GIBALY; 8 brs.

Blom Bank Egypt: POB 144, 54 Sharia Lebanon, Mohandessin, Cairo; tel. (2) 3039825; fax (2) 3039804; e-mail mrbfr@ie-eg.com; internet www.blombankegypt.com; f. 1977 as Misr Romanian Bank, name changed as above 2006; Blom Bank SAL (Lebanon) has 99.7% stake; cap. 500.0m., res 57.8m., dep. 3,210.0m. (Dec. 2005); Chair. SAAD AZHARI; CEO and Man. Dir ALAA ED-DIN SAMAHA; 11 brs.

BNP Paribas Egypt: POB 2441, 3 Latin America St, Cairo (Garden City); tel. (2) 7948323; fax (2) 7942218; e-mail customersupport@africa.bnpparibas.com; internet www.egypt.bnpparibas.net; f. 1977 as Banque du Caire et de Paris SAE, name changed to BNP Paribas Le Caire in 2001 and as above in 2006; BNP Paribas (France) has 95.2% interest and Banque du Caire 4.8%; cap. 500.0m., res –34.0m., dep. 8,962.9m. (Dec. 2006); Chair. JEAN THOMAZEAU; Man. Dir PHILIPPE JOANNIER; 8 brs.

Crédit Agricole Egypt, SAE: POB 1825, 4/6 Hassan Sabri St, Cairo 11511 (Zamalek); tel. (2) 7382661; fax (2) 7380450; internet www.eab-online.com; f. 2006 by merger of Calyon Bank Egypt (Egyptian affiliate of Crédit Agricole Group—France) and Egyptian American Bank; owned by Crédit Agricole Groupe, Mansour and Maghrabi Investment and Development, and Egyptian investors; cap. 1,148.0m., res 238.7m., dep. 13,841.7m. (Dec. 2006); Chair. YASSIN MANSOUR; Man. Dir ADRIAN PHARES; 44 brs.

Egyptian Gulf Bank: POB 56, El-Orman Plaza Bldg, 8–10 Sharia Ahmad Nessim, Cairo (Giza); tel. (2) 3368359; fax (2) 3490002; e-mail h.r.egb@mst1.mist.com.eg; internet www.egbbank.com.eg; f. 1981; Misr Insurance Co has 24.9% interest; cap. 537.2m., res 28.2m., dep. 3,820.8m. (Dec. 2006); Chair. KHALDOUN BAKRY BARAKAT; CEO and Man. Dir OMAR A. ALSEESI; 10 brs.

Egyptian-Saudi Finance Bank: POB 455, 60 Sharia Mohy ad-Din Abu al-Ezz, Cairo (Dokki); tel. (2) 7481777; fax (2) 7611436; e-mail centeral@esf-bank.com; internet www.esf-bank.com; f. 1980 as Pyramids Bank; Al-Baraka Banking Group (Bahrain) has 73.7% interest; cap. 500.0m., res 23.1m., dep. 6,557.5m. (Dec. 2006); Chair. Sheikh SALEH ABDULLAH KAMEL; Man. Dir ASHRAF AHMAD MOUSTAFA EL-GHAMRAWY; 14 brs.

Faisal Islamic Bank of Egypt, SAE: POB 2446, 149 Sharia et-Tahrir, Galaa Sq., Cairo (Dokki); tel. (2) 37621285; fax (2) 37621281; e-mail foreigndept@faisalbank.com.eg; internet www.faisalbank.com.eg; f. 1979; all banking operations conducted according to Islamic principles; cap. 528.1m., res 60.0m., dep. 17,674.7m. (Dec. 2006); Chair. Prince MUHAMMAD AL-FAISAL AS-SAOUD; Gov. ABD AL-HAMID ABU MOUSSA; 20 brs.

Piraeus Bank—Egypt: POB 92, 4th Floor, Evergreen Bldg, 10 Sharia Talaat Harb, Majlis ash-Sha'ab, Cairo; tel. (2) 5764644; fax (2) 5799862; internet www.ecb.com.eg; f. Jan. 2006, following the acquisition of Egyptian Commercial Bank by the Piraeus Bank Group (Greece) in June 2005; cap. 500m., res 23.5m., dep. 4,971.4m. (Dec. 2006); Chair. and CEO MUHAMMAD GAMAL MOHARAM; 40 brs.

Suez Canal Bank, SAE: POB 2620, 7 Abd el-Kader Hamza St, Cairo (Garden City); tel. (2) 7940737; fax (2) 7944996; e-mail info@scbank.com.eg; f. 1978; cap. 500.0m., res 1,052.6m., dep. 10,702.9m. (Dec. 2006); Chair. and Man. Dir HISHAN RAMEZ ABD AL-HAFEZ; 26 brs.

Al-Watany Bank of Egypt: POB 63, 13 Sharia Semar, Dr Fouad Mohi ed-Din Sq., Gameat ed-Dewal al-Arabia, Mohandessin, Cairo 12655; tel. (2) 3362764; fax (2) 3362763; internet www.alwatany.net; f. 1980; National Bank of Kuwait bought 51% stake in 2007; cap. 750.0m., res 224.2m., dep. 8,691.7m. (Dec. 2006); Chair. SHEIKHA KHALED EL-BAHR; Man. Dir Dr YASSER ISMAIL HASSAN; 20 brs.

Non-Commercial Banks

Arab Banking Corporation—Egypt: 1 Sharia es-Saleh Ayoub, Cairo (Zamalek); tel. (2) 7362684; fax (2) 7363643; e-mail abcegypt@arabbanking.com.eg; internet www.arabbanking.com.eg; f. 1982 as Egypt Arab African Bank; acquired by Arab Banking Corpn (Bahrain) in 1999; Arab Banking Corpn has 93% interest, other interests 7%; cap. 500.0m., res 37.8m., dep. 1,870.0m. (Dec. 2006); commercial and investment bank; Chair. GHAZI ABD AL-JAWAD; Man. Dir and CEO ISSAM EL-WAKIL; 12 brs.

Arab Investment Bank: POB 826, Cairo Sky Center Bldg, 8 Sharia Abd al-Khalek Sarwat, Cairo; tel. (2) 5768097; fax (2) 5770329; e-mail arinbank@mst1.mist.com.eg; internet arab-investment-bank.egypt.com/index.asp; f. 1978 as Union Arab Bank for Development and Investment; Egyptian/Syrian/Libyan jt venture; cap. 85.8m., res 7.0m., dep. 2,266.8m. (Dec. 2006); Chair. Prof. Dr MUHAMMAD AHMAD AR-RAZAZ; Man. Dir OMAR A. ALSEESI; 13 brs.

EFG-Hermes: 59 Sharia et-Tahrir, Cairo 12311 (Dokki); tel. (2) 3383626; fax (2) 3383616; e-mail corporate@efg-hermes.com; internet www.efg-hermes.com; f. 1984; offices in Cairo, Alexandria and Mansoura; cap. 405.4m., res 109.0m., dep. 1,166.6m. (Dec. 2005); Chair. and CEO YASSER EL-MALLAWANY.

Housing and Development Bank, SAE: POB 234, 12 Syria St, Mohandessin, Cairo (Giza); tel. (2) 37492013; fax (2) 37600712; e-mail hdbank@hdb-egy.com; internet www.hdb-egy.com; f. 1979; cap. 500m., res 101.7m., dep. 4,898.2m. (Dec. 2006); Chair. and Man. Dir FATHY ES-SEBAIE MANSOUR; 40 brs.

Industrial Development Bank of Egypt: 110 Sharia al-Galaa, Cairo 11511; tel. (2) 25772468; fax (2) 25751227; e-mail exoffice@idbe-egypt.com; internet www.idbe-egypt.com; f. 1947 as Industrial Bank; re-established as above in 1976; cap. 500.0m., res 6.1m., dep. 1,513.5m. (June 2006); Chair. SHAHIN SERAGELDIN; 13 brs.

Misr Iran Development Bank: POB 219, Nile Tower Bldg, 21 Charles de Gaulle Ave, Cairo 12612 (Giza); tel. (2) 5727311; fax (2) 5701185; e-mail midb@mst1.mist.com.eg; internet www.midb.com.eg; f. 1975; Iran Foreign Investment Co has 40.14% interest, Bank of Alexandria and Misr Insurance Co each have 29.93% interest; cap. 502.2m., res 160.8m., dep. 4,921.8m. (Dec. 2006); Chair. and Man. Dir ISMAIL HASSAN MUHAMMAD; Gen. Man. HAMDY HASSAN MOUSSA HASSAN; 11 brs.

National Société Générale Bank, SAE: POB 2664, 5 Sharia Champollion, 11111 Cairo; tel. (2) 7707000; fax (2) 7707799; e-mail info@nsgb.com.eg; internet www.nsgb.com.eg; f. 1978; Société Générale (France) has 78.38% interest, other interests 21.62%; merger with Misr International Bank SAE in 2006; cap. 2,028.0m., res 395.5m., dep. 34,278.4m. (Dec. 2006); Chair. and Man. Dir MUHAMMAD OSMAN ED-DIB; Vice-Chair. and Man. Dir GUY POUPET; 102 brs.

STOCK EXCHANGES

Capital Market Authority: POB 618, 20 Sharia Emad ed-Din, Cairo 11111; tel. (2) 5779696; fax (2) 5755339; e-mail cmaegypt@cma.gov.eg; internet www.cma.gov.eg; f. 1979; Chair. Dr AHMAD SAAD ABD AL-LATIF; Dep. Chair. ALAA ELDIN MUHAMMAD AMER FARGHALI.

Cairo and Alexandria Stock Exchanges (CASE): 4A Sharia esh-Sherifein, Cairo; 11 Sharia Talaat Harb, Menshia, Alexandria; tel. (2) 23921447; fax (2) 23924214; tel. (3) 4843600; fax (3) 4843604; e-mail webmaster@egyptse.com; internet www.egyptse.com; f. 1883; Chair. MAGED SHAWKY.

INSURANCE

Al-Ahly Insurance: Cairo; state-owned; scheduled for privatization.

Allianz Egypt: POB 266, Saridar Bldg, 92 Sharia et-Tahrir, Cairo (Dokki); tel. (2) 37605445; fax (2) 37605446; e-mail info@allianz.com.eg; internet www.allianz.com.eg; f. 1976 as Arab International Insurance Co; Allianz AG (Germany) purchased 80% stake in 2000; name changed as above in 2004; general and life insurance; Exec. Chair. JOHN METCALF; Chair. and Man. Dir JEAN-CLAUDE GUÉRIN.

Al-Chark Insurance Co: 15 Sharia Qasr en-Nil, Cairo; tel. (2) 5746172; fax (2) 5756974; e-mail info@alchark.com; internet www.alchark.com; f. 1931; scheduled for privatization; general and life; Chair. HAMMAM MUHAMMAD HAMMAM BADR.

Egyptian Reinsurance Co, SAE: POB 950, 7 Sharia Abd al-Latif Boltia, Cairo (Garden City); tel. (2) 27918300; fax (2) 27957041; e-mail egyptre@egyptre.com; internet www.egyptre.com; f. 1957;

scheduled for privatization; Chair. and CEO GAMAL HAMZA; COO SAMIA HEEDA.

Al-Iktisad esh-Shabee, SAE: 11 Sharia Emad ed-Din, Cairo; f. 1948; Man. Dir and Gen. Man. W. KHAYAT.

Misr Insurance Co: POB 261, 44A Sharia Dokki, Cairo (Dokki); tel. (2) 3355350; fax (2) 3370428; e-mail micfin@frcu.eun.eg; internet www.misrins.com; f. 1934; all classes of insurance and reinsurance; scheduled for privatization; Chair. Dr MOAWAD HASSAN HASSANEIN EL-HABASHI.

Mohandes Insurance Co: POB 62, 3 El-Mesaha Sq., Cairo (Dokki); tel. (2) 3352162; fax (2) 3352697; e-mail mohandes@mist1.mist.com.eg; f. 1980; privately owned; insurance and reinsurance; Chair. and Man. Dir SAMIR MOUSTAFA METWALLI.

Al-Mottahida: POB 804, 9 Sharia Sulayman Pasha, Cairo; f. 1957.

National Insurance Co of Egypt, SAE: POB 592, 41 Sharia Qasr en-Nil, Cairo; tel. (2) 3910731; fax (2) 3933051; internet www.ahlya.com; f. 1900; cap. 100m.; scheduled for privatization; Chair. MUHAMMAD ABUL-YAZEED.

Provident Association of Egypt, SAE: POB 390, 9 Sharia Sherif Pasha, Alexandria; f. 1936; Man. Dir G. C. VORLOOU.

Trade and Industry

GOVERNMENT AGENCY

Egyptian Geological Survey and Mining Authority (EGSMA): 3 Sharia Salah Salem, Abbassia, 11517 Cairo; tel. (2) 6828013; fax (2) 4820128; e-mail info@egsma.gov.eg; internet www.egsma.gov.eg; f. 1896; state supervisory authority concerned with geological mapping, mineral exploration and other mining activities; Chair. HUSSEIN HAMOUDA.

DEVELOPMENT ORGANIZATION

General Authority for Investment and Free Zones (GAFI): Sharia Salah Salem, Nasr City, Cairo 11562; tel. (2) 24055452; fax (2) 22633751; e-mail investorservices@gafinet.org; internet www.gafinet.org; Chair. ASSEM MUHAMMAD FAHMY RAGAB.

CHAMBERS OF COMMERCE

Federation of Chambers of Commerce (FEDCOC): 4 el-Falaki Sq., Cairo; tel. (2) 7951164; e-mail fedcoc@menanet.net; f. 1955; Pres. KHALED ABOU ISMAIL.

Alexandria

Alexandria Chamber of Commerce: 31 Sharia el-Ghorfa Altogariya, Alexandria; tel. (3) 809339; fax (2) 808993; f. 1922; Pres. MOUSTAFA YACOUT EN-NAGGAR.

Cairo

American Chamber of Commerce in Egypt: 33 Sharia Sulayman Abaza, Cairo (Dokki); tel. 3381050; fax (2) 3381060; e-mail info@amcham.org.eg; internet www.amcham.org.eg; f. 1981; Pres. Dr TAHER HELMY; Exec. Dir HISHAM A. FAHMY.

Cairo Chamber of Commerce: 4 el-Falaki Sq., Cairo; tel. (2) 3558261; fax (2) 3563603; f. 1913; Pres. MAHMOUD EL-ARABY; Sec.-Gen. MOSTAFA ZAKI TAHA.

In addition, there are 20 local chambers of commerce.

EMPLOYERS' ORGANIZATION

Federation of Egyptian Industries: 1195 Corniche en-Nil, Ramlet Boulal, Cairo; and 65 Gamal Abd an-Nasir Ave, Alexandria; tel. (2) 5796950; fax (2) 5796953 (Cairo); tel. and fax (3) 4916721 (Alexandria); e-mail info@fei.org.eg; internet www.fei.org.eg; f. 1922; Chair. GALAL ABD AL-MAKSOOD EZ-ZORBA.

PETROLEUM AND GAS

Arab Petroleum Pipelines Co (SUMED): POB 158, Es-Saray, 431 El-Geish Ave, Louran, Alexandria; tel. (3) 5835152; fax (3) 5831295; internet www.sumed.org; f. 1974; EPGC has 50% interest, Saudi Arabian Oil Co 15%, International Petroleum Investment Co (United Arab Emirates) 15%, Kuwait Real Estate Investment Consortium 14.22%, Qatar Petroleum 5%, other Kuwaiti companies 0.78%; Suez–Mediterranean crude oil transportation pipeline (capacity: 117m. metric tons per year) and petroleum terminal operators; Chair. and Man. Dir Eng. HAZEM AMIN HAMMAD.

Belayim Petroleum Co (PETROBEL): POB 7074, Sharia el-Mokhayam, Cairo (Nasr City); tel. (2) 2621738; fax (2) 2609792; f. 1977; capital equally shared between EGPC and International Egyptian Oil Co, which is a subsidiary of ENI of Italy; petroleum and gas exploration, drilling and production; Chair. and Man. Dir MEDHAT ES-SAYED.

Egyptian General Petroleum Corpn (EGPC): POB 2130, 4th Sector, Sharia Palestine, New Maadi, Cairo; tel. (2) 7065358; fax (2) 7028813; e-mail info@egpc.com.eg; internet www.egpc.com.eg; state supervisory authority generally concerned with the planning of policies relating to petroleum activities in Egypt with the object of securing the devt of the petroleum industry and ensuring its effective administration; Chair. MOUSTAFA SHAARAWI; Dep. Chair. HASAB EN-NABI ASAL.

General Petroleum Co (GPC): POB 743, 8 Sharia Dr Moustafa Abou Zahra, Cairo (Nasr City); tel. (2) 4030975; fax (2) 4037602; f. 1957; wholly owned subsidiary of EGPC; operates mainly in Eastern Desert; Chair. HUSSEIN KAMAL.

Egyptian Natural Gas Holding Co (EGAS): POB 8064, 85c Sharia Nasr, 11371 Cairo (Nasr City); tel. (2) 4055845; fax (2) 4055876; e-mail egas@egas.com.eg; internet www.egas.com.eg; f. 2001 as part of a restructuring of the natural gas sector; Chair. Eng. MAHMOUD LATIF.

GASCO: Ring Rd, Exit 12, Sharia et-Tesien, 5th Settlement, Cairo; tel. (2) 6171510; fax (2) 6171514; e-mail info@gasco.com.eg; internet www.gasco.com.eg; f. 1997; Chair. and Man. Dir Eng. ISMAIL KARARA.

Gulf of Suez Petroleum Co (GUPCO): POB 2400, 4th Sector, Sharia Palestine, New Maadi, Cairo 11511; tel. (2) 3520985; fax (2) 3531286; f. 1965; partnership between EGPC and BP Egypt (UK/USA); developed the el-Morgan oilfield in the Gulf of Suez, also holds other exploration concessions in the Gulf of Suez and the Western Desert; Chair. REFAAT KHAFAGA; Man. Dir L. D. MCVAY.

Western Desert Petroleum Co (WEPCO): POB 412, Borg eth-Thagr Bldg, Sharia Safia Zagloul, Alexandria; tel. (3) 4928710; fax (3) 4934016; f. 1967 as partnership between EGPC (50% interest) and Phillips Petroleum (35%) and later Hispanoil (15%); developed Alamein, Yidma and Umbarka fields in the Western Desert and later Abu Qir offshore gasfield in 1978 followed by NAF gas field in 1987; Chair. Eng. MUHAMMAD MOHI ED-DIN BAHGAT.

UTILITIES

Electricity

In 1998 seven new electricity generation and distribution companies were created, under the direct ownership of the Egyptian Electricity Authority (EEA). In 2000 the EEA was restructured into a holding company (the Egyptian Electricity Holding Co—see below) controlling five generation and seven distribution companies. A specialized grid company was to manage electricity transmission. The Government commenced partial privatizations of the generation and distribution companies in 2001–02, while retaining control of the hydroelectric generation and grid management companies. There were nine electricity distribution companies in 2004. In 2006 the Ministry of Electricity and Energy announced a five-year plan to add 7,800 MW to the national grid by 2012.

Egyptian Electricity Holding Co: Sharia Ramses, Cairo (Nasr City); tel. (2) 4030681; fax (2) 4029828; e-mail Mawad@moee.gov.eg; internet www.egelec.com; fmrly the Egyptian Electricity Authority, renamed as above in 2000; Chair. MUHAMMAD MUHAMMAD AWAD.

Alexandria Electricity Distribution: 9 Sharia Sidi el-Metwally, Alexandria; tel. (3) 3911967; fax (3) 3933223; Chair. Eng. MAHMOUD HASSAN ASHOOR.

East Delta Electricity Production Co (EDEPC): Sharia Shebein el-Koam, Ismailia; tel. (6) 4365146; e-mail mhassan@moee.gov.eg; internet www.edepc1.com; Chair. MUHAMMAD MAHMOUD ALI HASSAN.

North Cairo Electricity Distribution: Cairo; tel. (2) 6707730; fax (2) 2878635; e-mail ncedc_eg@yahoo.com; Gen. Man. LOFTY EL-MOSHTLY.

Upper Egypt Electricity Production Co: El Kurimat, Atfih, Giza; tel. (2) 8410862; fax (2) 8410765; e-mail a.diab@ueepc.com; internet www.ueepc.com.

Gas

Egypt Gas: Corniche en-Nil, Warak-Imbaba, Cairo; tel. and fax (2) 5408882; e-mail cairo@egyptgas.com.eg; internet www.egyptgas.com.eg; f. 1983; Chair. and Man. Dir NABIL HASHEM.

Water

National Association for Potable Water and Sanitary Drainage (NOPWASD): 6th Floor, Mogamma Bldg, et-Tahrir Sq., Cairo; tel. (2) 3557664; fax (2) 3562869; f. 1981; water and sewerage authority; Chair. MUHAMMAD KHALED MOUSTAFA.

TRADE UNIONS

Egyptian Trade Union Federation (ETUF): 90 Sharia al-Galaa, Cairo; tel. (2) 5740362; fax (2) 5753427; f. 1957; 23 affiliated unions; 5m. mems; affiliated to the International Confederation of Arab

Trade Unions and to the Organization of African Trade Union Unity; Pres. MUHAMMAD ES-SAYED RASHID; Gen. Sec. MUHAMMAD ES-SAYED MORSI.

General Trade Union of Air Transport: G2, Osman Ibn Affoun, Sofin Sq., Cairo; tel. (2) 2413165; fax (2) 6336149; 11,000 mems; Pres. Eng. CHEHATA MUHAMMAD CHEHATA; Gen. Sec. MUHAMMAD HUSSEIN.

General Trade Union of Banks and Insurance: 2 Sharia el-Kady el-Fadel, Cairo; 56,000 mems; Pres. MAHMOUD MUHAMMAD DABBOUR; Gen. Sec. ABDOU HASSAN MUHAMMAD ALI.

General Trade Union of Building and Wood Workers: 9 Sharia Emad ed-Din, Cairo; tel. (2) 5913486; fax (2) 5915849; e-mail gtubww@hotmail.com; 500,000 mems; Pres. SAYED TAHA HASSAN; Gen. Sec. MUHAMMAD BAHAA.

General Trade Union of Chemical Workers: 90 Sharia al-Galaa, Cairo; fax (2) 5750490; 120,000 mems; Pres. IBRAHIM EL-AZHARY; Gen. Sec. GAAFER ABD AL-MONEM.

General Trade Union of Commerce: 54D Sharia el-Gomhouriya, Alfy Borg, Cairo; tel. (2) 5903159; fax (2) 5914144; f. 1903; 120,000 mems; Pres. FOUAD TOMA; Gen. Sec. SAMIR A. SHAFI.

General Trade Union of Food Industries: 3 Sharia Housni, Hadaek el-Koba, Cairo; 111,000 mems; Pres. SAAD M. AHMAD; Gen. Sec. ADLY TANOUS IBRAHIM.

General Trade Union of Health Services: 22 Sharia esh-Sheikh Qamar, es-Sakakiny, Cairo; 56,000 mems; Pres. IBRAHIM ABOU EL-MUTI IBRAHIM; Gen. Sec. AHMAD ABD AL-LATIF SALEM.

General Trade Union of Hotels and Tourism Workers: POB 606, 90 Sharia al-Galaa, Cairo; tel. and fax (2) 773901; 70,000 mems; Pres. MUHAMMAD HILAL ESH-SHARKAWI.

General Trade Union of Maritime Transport: 36 Sharia Sharif, Cairo; 46,000 mems; Pres. THABET MUHAMMAD ES-SEFARI; Gen. Sec. MUHAMMAD RAMADAN ABOU TOR.

General Trade Union of Military Production: 90 Sharia al-Galaa, Cairo; 64,000 mems; Pres. MOUSTAFA MUHAMMAD MOUNGI; Gen. Sec. FEKRY IMAM.

General Trade Union of Mine Workers: 5 Sharia Ali Sharawi, Hadaek el-Koba, Cairo; 14,000 mems; Pres. ABBAS MAHMOUD IBRAHIM; Gen. Sec. AMIN HASSAN AMER.

General Trade Union of Petroleum Workers: 5 Sharia Ali Sharawi, Hadaek el-Koba, Cairo; tel. (2) 4820091; fax (2) 4834551; 60,000 mems; Pres. FAUZI ABD AL-BARI; Gen. Sec. AMIR ABD ES-SALAM.

General Trade Union of Postal Workers: 90 Sharia al-Galaa, Cairo; 80,000 mems; Pres. HASSAN MUHAMMAD EID; Gen. Sec. SALEM MAHMOUD SALEM.

General Trade Union of Press, Printing and Information: 90 Sharia al-Galaa, Cairo; tel. (2) 740324; 55,000 mems; Pres. MUHAMMAD ALI EL-FIKKI; Gen. Sec. AHMAD AD-DESSOUKI.

General Trade Union of Public and Administrative Workers: 2 Sharia Muhammad Haggag, Midan et-Tahrir, Cairo; tel. (2) 5742134; fax (2) 5752044; e-mail mostommmostafa@hotmail.com; 250,000 mems; Pres. Dr AHMAD ABDELZAHER; Gen. Sec. MUKHTAR HAMOUDA.

General Trade Union of Public Utilities Workers: POB 194, 6 Sharia Ramses, Cairo; tel. (2) 5799614; fax (2) 5799616; e-mail rostommostafa@hotmail.com; f. 1956; 290,000 mems; Pres. MUHAMMAD ES-SAYED MORSI ALY; Gen. Sec. USAMA GAMAL ABD AS-SAMIEE.

General Trade Union of Railway Workers: POB 84 (el-Faggalah), 15 Sharia Emad ed-Din, Cairo; tel. (2) 5930305; fax (2) 5917776; 90,000 mems; Pres. SABER AHMAD HUSSAIN; Gen. Sec. YASSIN SOLIMAN.

General Trade Union of Road Transport: 90 Sharia al-Galaa, Cairo; tel. (2) 2552955; fax (2) 25754919; 245,000 mems; Pres. RADWAN MASEKH AS-SAYED; Gen. Sec. AHMAD WAGIEH.

General Trade Union of Telecommunications Workers: POB 651, Cairo; 60,000 mems; Pres. KHAIRI HACHEM; Sec.-Gen. IBRAHIM SALEH.

General Trade Union of Textile Workers: 327 Sharia Shoubra, Cairo; 244,000 mems; Pres. ALI MUHAMMAD DOUFDAA; Gen. Sec. HASSAN TOULBA MARZOUK.

General Trade Union of Workers in Agriculture and Irrigation: 31 Sharia Mansour, Cairo (Bab el-Louk); tel. (2) 3541419; 150,000 mems; Pres. MUKHTAR ABD AL-HAMID; Gen. Sec. FATHI A. KURTAM.

General Trade Union of Workers in Engineering, Metal and Electrical Industries: 90 Sharia al-Galaa, Cairo; tel. (2) 742519; 160,000 mems; Pres. SAID GOMAA; Gen. Sec. MUHAMMAD FARES.

Union of Egyptian Medical Professionals: 6 Sharia Hadika, Cairo (Garden City); tel. (2) 3561098; Pres. Dr HAMDI MAHMOUD AS-SAYYED.

Transport

RAILWAYS

The area of the Nile Delta is well served by railways. Lines also run from Cairo southward along the Nile to Aswan, and westward along the coast to Salloum. As part of an integrated transport strategy being developed by the Government in 2007, Egypt's railway network was scheduled to be upgraded and expanded. Proposed new lines included one connecting Cairo to 10th of Ramadan City and another linking Alexandria to Borg al-Arab.

Egyptian National Railways: Station Bldg, Midan Ramses, Cairo 11794; tel. (2) 5751000; fax (2) 5740000; f. 1852; length 8,600 km; 42 km electrified; a 346-km line to carry phosphate and iron ore from the Bahariya mines, in the Western Desert, to the Helwan iron and steel works in south Cairo, was opened in 1973, and the Qena–Safaga line (length 223 km) came into operation in 1989; Chair. (vacant).

Alexandria Passenger Transport Authority: POB 466, Aflaton, esh-Shatby, Alexandria 21111; tel. (3) 5975223; fax (3) 5971187; e-mail apta@link.net; internet www.alexapta.org; f. 1860; controls City Tramways (28 km), Ramleh Electric Railway (16 km), suburban buses and minibuses (1,688 km); 119 tram cars, 519 suburban buses and minibuses; 362 suburban buses and minibuses from private sector; Chair. and Tech. Dir Eng. SHERINE KASSEM.

Cairo Metro: National Authority for Tunnels, POB 466, Ramses Bldg, Midan Ramses, Cairo 11794; tel. (2) 5742968; fax (2) 5742950; tel. infoc@nat.org.eg; internet www.nat.org.eg; construction of the first electrified, 1,435-mm gauge underground transport system in Africa and the Middle East began in Cairo in 1982. Line 1 has a total of 35 stations (5 underground), connects el-Marg el Gedida with Helwan and is 44 km long with a 4.7-km tunnel beneath central Cairo; Line 2 links Shoubra el-Kheima with Giza, at el-Monib station, totalling 21.6 km (13 km in tunnel), and with 20 stations (12 underground), two of which interconnect with Line 1; the first section of Line 3, which will connect Imbaba and Mohandesin with Cairo International Airport and will total 34.2 km (30.3 km in tunnel) with 29 stations (27 underground), was due to open in 2010; Chair. Eng. SAÂD HASSAN SHEHATA.

Cairo Transport Authority: Sharia Ramses, el-Gabal el-Ahmar, Cairo (Nasr City); tel. (2) 6845712; fax (2) 8654858; owned by the Govenorate of Cairo; length 78 km (electrified); gauge 1,000 mm; operates 16 tram routes and 24 km of light railway; 720 cars; Chair. NABIL EL-MAZNEY.

Lower Egypt Railway: El-Mansoura; f. 1898; length 160 km; gauge 1,000 mm; 20 diesel railcars.

ROADS

The estimated total length of the road network in 2004 was 45,500 km. There are good metalled main roads as follows: Cairo–Alexandria (desert road); Cairo–Banha–Tanta–Damanhour–Alexandria; Cairo–Suez (desert road); Cairo–Ismailia–Port Said or Suez; Cairo–Fayoum (desert road). The Ahmad Hamdi road tunnel (1.64 km) beneath the Suez Canal was opened in 1980. A 320-km macadamized road linking Mersa Matruh, on the Mediterranean coast, with the oasis town of Siwa was completed in 1986. A second bridge over the Suez Canal was completed in 2001.

General Authority for Roads, Bridges and Land Transport—Ministry of Transport: 105 Sharia Qasr el-Eini, Cairo; tel. (2) 7957429; fax (2) 7950591; e-mail garblt@garblt.com; Chair. Eng. ADEL MUHAMMAD YOUSUF.

SHIPPING

Egypt's principal ports are Alexandria, Port Said and Suez. A port constructed at a cost of £E315m., and designed to handle up to 16m. metric tons of grain, fruit and other merchandise per year (22% of the country's projected imports by 2000) in its first stage of development, was opened at Damietta in 1986. The second stage was to increase handling capacity to 25m. tons per year. In 2002 the Ministry of Transport announced proposals to open up the ports to private management, while keeping the infrastructure under state ownership. The modernization of the quays at Alexandria port and two new container terminals at Dakahlia port were completed during the first half of 2007.

Alexandria Port Authority: 106 Sharia el-Hourriya, Alexandria 26514; tel. (3) 4874321; fax (3) 4869714; e-mail support@apa.gov.eg; internet www.apa.gov.eg; f. 1966; Chair. Rear-Adm. TAWFIK ABU GENDIA; Vice-Chair. Rear-Adm. MOHSEN MUHAMMAD ALI.

Major Shipping Companies

Alexandria Shipping and Navigation Co: POB 812, 557 ave el-Hourriya, Alexandria; tel. (3) 62923; services between Egypt, Europe, the USA, Red Sea and Mediterranean; 5 vessels; Chair. Eng. MAHMOUD ISMAIL; Man. Dir ABD AL-AZIZ QADRI.

Arab Maritime Petroleum Transport Co (AMPTC): POB 143, 9th Floor, Nile Tower Bldg, 21 Sharia Giza, 12211 Giza; tel. (2) 5701311; fax (2) 3378080; e-mail amptc.cairo@amptc.net; internet www.amptc.net; 11 vessels; Gen. Man. SULAYMAN AL-BASSAM.

Egyptian Navigation Co: POB 82, 2 Sharia en-Nasr, Alexandria 21511; tel. (3) 4800050; fax (3) 4871345; e-mail enc@dataxprs.com.eg; internet www.enc.com.eg; f. 1930; owners and operators of Egypt's mercantile marine; international trade transportation; 12 vessels; Chair. and Man. Dir AMR GAMAL ED-DIN ROUSHDY.

International Maritime Services Co: 20 Sharia Salah Salem, Alexandria; tel. (3) 4840817; fax (3) 4869177; e-mail agency@imsalex.com; internet www.imsalex.com; Chair. Capt. MONTASSER ES-SOKKARY.

Memnon Tours Co: POB 2533, 49 Sharia Nobar, Cairo (Bab el-Louk); tel. (2) 7956353; fax (2) 7956557; e-mail info@memnontours.com; internet www.memnontours.com; 7 vessels; Chair. ADEL SALOUMA.

Misr Petroleum Co: POB 228, Misr Petroleum House, 6 Sharia Orabi, Cairo; tel. (2) 5755000; fax (2) 5745436; internet www.misrpetroleum.com; 8 vessels; Chair. Eng. SALAH ED-DIN HASSAN.

National Navigation Co: 4 Sharia Ehegaz, Cairo (Heliopolis); tel. (2) 4525575; fax (2) 4526171; e-mail nnc@nnc.egnet.net; internet www.nnc.egnet.net; 11 vessels; Chair. and Man. Dir MUHAMMAD SHAWKI YOUNIS.

Pan-Arab Shipping Co: POB 39, 404 ave el-Hourriya, Rushdi, Alexandria; tel. (3) 5468835; fax (3) 5469533; f. 1974; Arab League Co; 5 vessels; Chair. Adm. MUHAMMAD SHERIF ES-SADEK; Gen. Man. Capt. MAMDOUH EL-GUINDY.

As-Salam Shipping & Trading Establishment: Apartment 203, 24 Sharia Ahmad Talceer, Cairo (Heliopolis); tel. (2) 908535; fax (2) 4175390; 6 vessels.

Samatour Shipping Co: As-Salam Bldg, 4 Sharia Naguib er-Rihani, Rami Station, Alexandria; tel. (3) 4822028; fax (3) 4832003; 5 vessels; Chair. SALEM A. SALEM.

Sayed Nasr Navigation Lines: 5 Sharia Dr Ahmad Amin, Cairo (Heliopolis); tel. (2) 2457643; fax (2) 2457736; 6 vessels.

Société Coopérative des Pétroles: Coopérative Bldg, 94 Sharia Qasr el-Eini, Cairo; tel. (2) 7360623; fax (2) 7956404; Chair. Dr TAMER ABU BAKR; Gen. Dir OSAMA IBRAHIM.

THE SUEZ CANAL

In 2005 a total of 18,176 vessels, with a net displacement of 671m. tons, used the Suez Canal, linking the Mediterranean and Red Seas.

Length of canal 190 km; maximum permissible draught: 17.68 m (58 ft); breadth of canal at water level and breadth between buoys defining the navigable channel at −11 m: 365 m and 225 m, respectively, in the northern section and 305 m and 205 m in the southern section.

Suez Canal Authority (Hay'at Canal as-Suways): Irshad Bldg, Ismailia; Cairo Office: 6 Sharia Lazoughli, Cairo (Garden City); tel. (64) 9100000; fax (64) 914784; e-mail scanalb@idsc.net.eg; f. 1956; Chair. Adm. AHMAD ALI FADEL.

Suez Canal Container Handling Co: Cairo; f. 2000, with 30-year concession to operate the East Port Said container terminal.

CIVIL AVIATION

There are more than 20 civil airports in Egypt. The main international airports are at Heliopolis (23 km from the centre of Cairo) and Alexandria (7 km from the city centre). An international airport was opened at Nuzhah in 1983. The Ministry of Transport announced the restructuring and modernization of the civil aviation sector in early 2001. In that year airports were under construction at el-Alamein, west of Alexandria (opened in 2005), and at Asyout; however, plans for the construction of a new airport in west Cairo were suspended in late 2001. The existing Cairo International Airport was to be expanded, with a third terminal (scheduled to open by mid-2008) and a new runway, while the expansion of Sharm esh-Sheikh airport was also undertaken. Further expansion plans were announced in late 2003, including the construction of a new international airport at Borg al-Arab and the expansion of airports at Luxor and Hurghada.

In 2000 19.5m. passengers and 188,783 metric tons of cargo passed through Egypt's airports.

EgyptAir: Administration Complex, Cairo International Airport, Cairo (Heliopolis); tel. (2) 2674700; fax (2) 2663773; e-mail callcenter@egyptair.com; internet www.egyptair.com.eg; f. 1932 as Misr Airwork; known as United Arab Airlines 1960–71; operates internal services in Egypt and external services throughout the Middle East, Far East, Africa, Europe and the USA; Chair. and CEO SHERIF SAAD ED-DIN GALAL.

Egyptian Civil Aviation Authority: ECAA Complex, Sharia Airport, Cairo 11776; tel. (2) 2677610; fax (2) 2470351; e-mail egoca@idsc.gov.eg; f. 2000; Chair. Dr IBRAHIM MUHAMMAD MUTAWALLI AD-DUMEIRI.

Egyptian Holding Co for Airports and Air Traffic: Cairo; f. 2001; responsible for management and development of all Egyptian airports; Pres. ABD AL-FATTAH KATTU.

   Cairo Airport Authority (CAA): Cairo International Airport, Cairo (Heliopolis); tel. (2) 2474245; fax (2) 2432522; under management of Egyptian Holding Co since 2003.

   Egyptian Airports Co: Cairo; f. 2001; responsible for new airport projects; Pres. NAGI SAMUEL.

Tourism

Tourism is currently Egypt's second largest source of revenue, generating US $7,206m. (including passenger transport) in 2005. Traditionally the industry has attracted tourists to the country's pyramids and monuments. However, recently the industry has diversified: the Red Sea coastline has 1,000 km of beaches, along which several developments (benefiting from new international airports such as that at Taba) are under construction and where scuba diving is a popular pursuit. In 2001 the Biblioteca Alexandrina opened in Alexandria. The tourism industry was adversely affected in the mid-1990s by the campaign of violence by militant Islamists; although some recovery in tourist numbers was recorded by the end of the decade, the sector was again affected by the crisis in Israeli–Palestinian relations from late 2000, the repercussions of the suicide attacks on the USA in September 2001 and the US-led intervention in Iraq in early 2003. Nevertheless, 8.1m. tourists visited Egypt in 2004 (compared with 5.2m. in 2002) and, despite further terrorist attacks in the Sinai region during 2004–06, it appeared by 2006 that these had had a limited effect on the tourism industry. Tourist arrivals in 2005 increased to 8.6m., and it was reported that a record 9.7m. tourists had visited the country in 2006/07 (year to June).

Ministry of Tourism: Misr Travel Tower, 32 Sharia Emtidad Ramses, Abbassia Sq., Cairo; tel. (2) 6828435; fax (2) 6859463; e-mail mot@idsc.gov.eg; internet www.egypt.travel; f. 1965; brs at Alexandria, Port Said, Suez, Luxor and Aswan; Minister of Tourism ZOHAIR GARANAH.

Egyptian General Authority for the Promotion of Tourism: Misr Travel Tower, Abbassia Sq., Cairo; tel. (2) 2853576; fax (2) 2854363; e-mail contact@touregypt.net; internet www.touregypt.net; Chair. ADEL ABD AL-AZIZ.

Egyptian General Co for Tourism and Hotels (EGOTH): 4 Sharia Latin America, 11519 Cairo (Garden City); tel. (2) 7946026; fax (2) 7953328; e-mail info@egoth.com.eg; internet www.egoth.com.eg; f. 1961; affiliated to the holding co for Tourism and Cinema; Chair. and Man. Dir NABIL SELIM.

EL SALVADOR

Introductory Survey

Location, Climate, Language, Religion, Flag, Capital

The Republic of El Salvador lies on the Pacific coast of Central America. It is bounded by Guatemala to the west and by Honduras to the north and east. The climate varies from tropical on the coastal plain to temperate in the uplands. The language is Spanish. About 74% of the population are Roman Catholics, and other Christian churches are represented. The civil flag (proportions 2 by 3) consists of three equal horizontal stripes, of blue, over white, over blue. The state flag differs by the addition, in the centre of the white stripe, of the national coat of arms. The capital is San Salvador.

Recent History

El Salvador was ruled by Spain until 1821, and became independent in 1839. Since then the country's history has been one of frequent coups and outbursts of political violence. General Maximiliano Hernández Martínez became President in 1931, and ruthlessly suppressed a peasant uprising, with an alleged 30,000 killings (including that of Farabundo Martí, the leader of the rebel peasants), in 1932. President Hernández was deposed in 1944, and the next elected President, Gen. Salvador Castañeda Castro, was overthrown in 1948. His successor as President, Lt-Col Oscar Osorio (1950–56), relinquished power to Lt-Col José María Lemus, who was deposed by a bloodless coup in 1960. He was replaced by a military junta, which was itself supplanted by another junta in January 1961. Under this Junta, the conservative Partido de Conciliación Nacional (PCN) was established and won all 54 seats in elections to the Asamblea Legislativa (Legislative Assembly) in December. A member of the Junta, Lt-Col Julio Adalberto Rivera, was elected unopposed to the presidency in 1962. He was succeeded by the PCN candidate, Gen. Fidel Sánchez Hernández, in 1967.

In the 1972 presidential election Col Arturo Armando Molina Barraza, candidate of the ruling PCN, was elected. His rival, José Napoleón Duarte, the leader of the left-wing coalition party, Unión Nacional de Oposición, staged an abortive coup in March, and Col Molina took office in July, despite allegations of massive electoral fraud. Similar allegations were made during the 1977 presidential election, after which the PCN candidate, Gen. Carlos Humberto Romero Mena, took office.

Reports of violations of human rights by the Government were widespread in 1979. The polarization of left and right after 1972 was characterized by an increase in guerrilla activity. In October 1979 President Romero was overthrown and replaced by a Junta of civilians and army officers. The Junta, which promised to install a democratic system and to organize elections, declared a political amnesty and invited participation from the guerrilla groups, but violence continued between government troops and guerrilla forces, and elections were postponed. In January 1980 an ultimatum from progressive members of the Government resulted in the formation of a new Government, a coalition of military officers and the Partido Demócrata Cristiano (PDC). In March the country moved closer to full-scale civil war following the assassination of the Roman Catholic Archbishop of San Salvador, Oscar Romero, an outspoken supporter of human rights.

In December 1980 José Napoleón Duarte, the 1972 presidential candidate and a member of the Junta, was sworn in as President. In January 1981 the guerrillas launched their 'final offensive' and, after initial gains, the opposition front, Frente Democrático Revolucionario—FDR (allied with the guerrilla front, the Frente Farabundo Martí para la Liberación Nacional—FMLN), proposed negotiations with the USA. The US authorities referred them to the Salvadorean Government, which refused to recognize the FDR while it was linked with the guerrillas. The USA affirmed its support for the Duarte Government and provided civilian and military aid. During 1981 the guerrilla forces unified and strengthened their control over the north and east of the country. Attacks on economic targets continued, while the army retaliated by acting indiscriminately against the local population in guerrilla-controlled areas. By December there were an estimated 300,000 Salvadorean refugees, many of whom had fled to neighbouring countries.

At elections to a National Constituent Assembly, conducted in March 1982, the PDC failed to win an absolute majority against the five right-wing parties, which, together having obtained 60% of the total votes, formed a Government of National Unity. Major Roberto D'Aubuisson Arrieta, leader of the extreme right-wing Alianza Republicana Nacionalista (ARENA), became President of the National Constituent Assembly. In April a politically independent banker, Dr Alvaro Magaña Borja, was elected interim President, after pressure from the armed forces. However, the Assembly voted to award itself considerable power over the President. Military leaders then demanded that five ministerial posts be given to members of the PDC, fearing that, otherwise, US military aid would be withdrawn. A presidential election was scheduled for 1983, and a new constitution was to be drafted. During 1982 about 1,600 Salvadorean troops were trained in the USA, and US military advisers were reported to be actively participating in the conflict.

The presidential election was postponed until March 1984, as a result of disagreement in the National Constituent Assembly over the new Constitution, which finally became effective in December 1983. The issue of agrarian reform caused a serious dispute between D'Aubuisson's ARENA party and the PDC, and provoked a campaign by right-wing 'death squads' against trade unionists and peasant leaders. (In 1980 the governing Junta had nationalized some 60% of the country's prime arable land as part of a three-phase agrarian reform initiative, which envisaged the eventual redesignation of 90% of El Salvador's farmland. However, subsequent phases of the expropriation and reallocation programme had been suspended in March 1981 and May 1982, prompting US Government threats to withdraw financial and military assistance.) In December 1983 ARENA secured the support of the Assembly for the reactivation of a severely compromised reform programme, which provided for a maximum permissible landholding of 245 ha (rather than 100 ha as originally envisaged). This represented an important victory for the ARENA party, which had been isolated in the Assembly following the collapse of its alliance with the PCN in February.

Following a period of intense activity by 'death squads' in late 1983, when the weekly total of murders exceeded 200, the US Government urged the removal of several high-level officials, military officers and political figures who were linked to the murders. The failure of the US-trained 'rapid reaction' battalions and frequent reports of army atrocities undermined both public confidence in the Government and US President Ronald Reagan's efforts to secure further US aid for El Salvador. In February 1984, following a number of strategic territorial advances, the FDR-FMLN proposed the formation of a broadly based provisional government, as part of a peace plan without preconditions. The plan was rejected by the Government. The guerrillas refused to participate in the presidential election, conducted in March 1984, and attempted to prevent voting in various provinces. As no candidate emerged with a clear majority, a second round of voting was held in May, when José Napoleón Duarte, the candidate of the PDC, defeated Maj. D'Aubuisson, the ARENA candidate.

Following his inauguration in June 1984, President Duarte instituted a purge of the armed forces and the reorganization of the police force, including the disbanding of the notorious Treasury Police. Both the FDR-FMLN and the President expressed their willingness to commence peace negotiations. Following pressure from the Roman Catholic Church and trade unions, the Government opened discussions with guerrilla leaders in Chalatenango in October. A second round of negotiations, held in November, ended amid accusations of intransigence from both sides.

At legislative and municipal elections in March 1985 the PDC won a convincing victory over the ARENA-PCN electoral alliance, thereby securing a clear majority in the new Asamblea. The PDC's victory, coupled with internal divisions within the right-wing grouping, precipitated a decline in the popularity and influence of the alliance, which culminated in the resignation of D'Aubuisson in September.

Despite a perceived decline in political violence and abuses of human rights in 1985–86, the failure of the Government and the rebels to agree an agenda for renewed negotiations during this period prompted speculation that a military solution would be sought to end the civil war. Such speculation was supported by reports of the armed forces' growing domination of the conflict and by the success of the army's 'Unidos para reconstruir' campaign, a social and economic programme, launched in July 1986, to recover areas that had been devastated by the protracted fighting.

In March 1987 guerrillas carried out a successful attack on the army garrison at El Paraíso, which enabled them to take the military initiative in the civil war. Later in the year, however, the Salvadorean Government's participation in a peace plan for Central America, which was signed on 7 August in Guatemala City, encouraged hopes that a peaceful solution could be found to the conflict. Discussions between the Government and the FDR-FMLN were eventually held in October, when agreement was reached on the formation of two committees to study the possibility of a cease-fire and an amnesty.

Despite the inauguration, in September 1987, of a National Reconciliation Commission, appointed by the President in August, and the Government's proclamation, in November, of a unilateral cease-fire, no long-term cessation of hostilities was maintained by either side. The political situation deteriorated further in late 1987, following President Duarte's public denunciation of Roberto D'Aubuisson's complicity in the murder of Archbishop Romero in 1980. Furthermore, in 1988 there were increasing reports of the resurgence of 'death squads', and it was suggested that abuses of human rights were rapidly returning to the level reached at the beginning of the internal conflict.

In February 1988 the FMLN launched a campaign of bombings and transport disruptions, in order to undermine preparations for the forthcoming legislative and municipal elections. At the elections, in March, ARENA secured control of more than 200 municipalities, including San Salvador, hitherto held for more than 20 years by the PDC. The party also regained an overall majority in the Asamblea.

By the end of 1988 it was estimated that as many as 70,000 Salvadoreans had died in the course of the civil war, while the US Administration had provided some US $3,000m. in aid to the Government. Moreover, by early 1989 many areas appeared to be without government, following the resignations of some 75 mayors and nine judges, purportedly because of death threats by the FMLN. In late January, however, radical new peace proposals were announced by the FMLN, which, for the first time, expressed its willingness to participate in the electoral process. The FMLN proposed that the presidential election be postponed from March to September, and offered a 60-day cease-fire (30 days on each side of a September election date). However, negotiations about this proposal failed to produce agreement. The FMLN advocated a boycott of the election, to be held on 19 March, and intensified its campaign of violence. The ballot resulted in victory for the ARENA candidate, Alfredo Cristiani Burkard. The level of abstention was estimated at almost 50%. Cristiani took office on 1 June 1989.

In August 1989 the Heads of State of five Central American countries signed an agreement in Tela, Honduras. The accord included an appeal to the FMLN to abandon its military campaign and to 'initiate dialogue' with the Salvadorean Government. In November, in accordance with the Tela agreement, the UN Security Council authorized the creation of the UN Observer Group for Central America (ONUCA), a multinational military force, to monitor developments in the region. In the same month the FMLN launched a military offensive, and throughout the month the fiercest fighting for nine years took place. The Government declared a state of siege, and stability was further undermined when, on 16 November, gunmen murdered the head of a San Salvador Jesuit university and five other Jesuit priests. On 12 January 1990, however, the FMLN announced that it would accept an offer made by the Salvadorean Government whereby the UN Secretary-General, Javier Pérez de Cuéllar, was to arrange the reopening of peace talks. In March President Cristiani announced that he was willing to offer a comprehensive amnesty, territorial concessions and the opportunity to participate fully in political processes to members of the FMLN, as part of a broad-based peace proposal. Later in the year, however, hopes for the successful negotiation of a peaceful settlement were frustrated by the failure of the two sides to reach a consensus, at a series of UN-sponsored discussions, on the crucial issue of the future role, structure and accountability of the armed forces.

By the end of September 1990 all hopes for a cease-fire had been abandoned. A renewed FMLN offensive was undertaken by the newly proclaimed National Army for Democracy (the establishment of which marked the reorganization of the FMLN's previous divisions into a more conventional army structure) in several departments in November. The conflict was considered to have entered into a new phase when, in the same month, a government aircraft was shot down by guerrilla forces armed with surface-to-air missiles supplied by Nicaraguan military personnel.

Negotiations between the Government and the FMLN continued throughout 1991, interspersed with violent exchanges between the guerrillas and the security forces. On 10 March elections to the Asamblea (enlarged from 60 to 84 seats) and to 262 municipalities were conducted. While guerrilla forces refrained from disrupting the proceedings (the FMLN announced a three-day cease-fire), it was reported that many voters were intimidated by an escalation in military operations, and more than 50% of the electorate failed to cast a vote. The final results revealed that ARENA had lost its majority in the Asamblea, but continued to command considerable support, with 39 seats. The party also retained significant support in the local elections, with victories in 175 of the 262 municipalities.

In late March 1991 a new initiative for the negotiation of a peace settlement was presented by the FMLN in Managua, Nicaragua, following a meeting between foreign affairs ministers from Central America and the European Community (EC, now European Union—EU, see p. 244). This new proposal dispensed with previous stipulations put forward by the guerrillas that military and constitutional reforms should be effected prior to any cease-fire, and suggested that concessions on both sides could be adopted simultaneously. The constitutional requirement that amendments to the Constitution be ratified by two successive legislative assemblies lent impetus to negotiations in April, the current Asamblea being scheduled to dissolve at the end of the month. Despite the attempts of uncompromising right-wing members of the Asamblea to sabotage the proceedings, a last-minute agreement on human rights (including the creation of a three-member 'truth commission', to be appointed by the UN Secretary-General) and on judicial and electoral reform was reached by the Government and the FMLN, and was swiftly approved by the Asamblea, prior to its dissolution. The working structure of a cease-fire and the detailed reform and purge of the armed forces were set aside for negotiation at a later date.

In May 1991 the UN Security Council voted to create an observer mission to El Salvador (ONUSAL), to be charged with the verification of accords reached between the Government and the FMLN. Initially the mission was to be resident in six regional centres for a 12-month period, and was expected to participate in any future cease-fire and peaceful reintegration programme. The creation of ONUSAL was denounced by right-wing groups within El Salvador as unwarranted interference and as an insult to national sovereignty.

In August 1991 both sides attended a round of discussions in New York, USA, where a new framework for peace was agreed. A National Commission for the Consolidation of Peace (COPAZ) was to be created (comprising representatives of both sides, as well as of all major political parties), which would supervise the enforcement of guarantees for the political integration of the guerrillas. The FMLN also secured guaranteed territorial rights for peasants settled in guerrilla-controlled areas, and the participation of former FMLN members in a National Civilian Police (Policía Nacional Civil—PNC), which was to be under the control of a new Ministry of the Interior and Public Security. At the same time, the Asamblea approved constitutional reforms, whereby the Central Electoral Commission would be replaced by a Supreme Electoral Tribunal, composed of five magistrates (one from each of the five most successful parties at the previous presidential election), to be elected by the Asamblea.

In December 1991, following renewed discussions between the Government and the guerrilla leaders, a new peace initiative was announced. Under the terms of the agreement, a formal cease-fire was to be implemented on 1 February 1992, under the supervision of some 1,000 UN personnel. The FMLN was to begin a process of disarmament, to be implemented in five stages (simultaneous with the dissolution of the notorious, military-controlled, 17,000-strong rapid deployment battalions), leading to full disarmament by 31 October. The success of the cease-fire agreement was expected to be dependent upon the adequate implementation, by the Government, of previously agreed reforms to the judiciary, the electoral system, guarantees of territorial rights, human rights, and guerrilla participation in civil defence, and of newly agreed reforms whereby the armed forces would be purged of those most responsible for abuses of human rights during the previous 12 years, and would be reduced in size by almost one-half, over a 22-month period.

On 16 January 1992, at Chapultepec Castle in Mexico City, the formal peace accord was ratified and was witnessed by the new UN Secretary-General, Boutros Boutros-Ghali, the US Secretary of State, James Baker, Heads of State from Central America, South America and Europe, representatives of El Salvador's military high command and all 84 members of the Asamblea. On 1 February some 30,000 Salvadoreans gathered in San Salvador to celebrate the first day of the cease-fire and to attend the formal installation of COPAZ.

Although mutual allegations of failure to comply with the terms of the peace accord persisted during 1992, prompting the temporary withdrawal, in May, of the FMLN from COPAZ, and resulting in further UN mediation and the negotiation of a revised timetable for disarmament, the cease-fire was carefully observed by both sides. In San Salvador on 15 December (declared National Reconciliation Day), at a ceremony attended by President Cristiani, FMLN leaders, the UN Secretary-General and Central American Heads of State and government representatives, the conflict was formally concluded, the terms of the December 1991 agreement having been fulfilled to the satisfaction of both sides. On the same day the FMLN was officially registered and recognized as a legitimate political party.

In November 1992, in accordance with the terms of the December 1991 peace accord, the Comisión de la Verdad (Truth Commission) announced the names of more than 200 military personnel alleged to have participated in abuses of human rights during the civil war. By early 1993, however, despite the urgences of the UN Secretary-General, the reluctance of the Government to comply with the conditions of the peace accord, relating to the removal from the armed forces of those personnel (particularly officers) identified by the Commission, threatened the further successful implementation of the process of pacification, and prompted the FMLN to delay the demobilization of its forces and the destruction of its remaining arsenals. The situation was exacerbated in March by the publication of the Commission's report, which attributed responsibility for the vast majority of the war's 75,000 fatalities to the counter-insurgency measures of the armed forces, including the systematic eradication, by the security forces, of civilians thought to harbour left-wing sympathies. Some 400 murders were attributed to the FMLN. Forty military personnel, identified by name as those responsible for various human rights atrocities, included the late ARENA founder Roberto D'Aubuisson Arrieta, who was identified as the authority behind the organization of 'death squads' in the early 1980s, and the murder of Archbishop Oscar Romero; also identified was the Minister of Defence and Public Security, Gen. René Emilio Ponce, his deputy, Gen. Orlando Zepeda, and the former air force chief, Gen. Juan Rafael Bustillo, who were believed to have ordered the murder of six prominent Jesuits in 1989. (In September 1991 Col Guillermo Benavides and an army lieutenant were found guilty of murder and sentenced to a maximum of 30 years' imprisonment; the seven other men charged were acquitted on the grounds that they were simply following orders. In September 2004 air force Captain Alvaro Rafael Saravia was found guilty of planning and facilitating the murder of Archbishop Romero in a civil case brought in a US court. He was ordered, in absentia, to pay US $2.5m. in compensation and $7.5m. in punitive damages.) The report recommended that the judiciary should be reorganized, and that all individuals identified by the report should be permanently excluded from all institutions of national defence and public security, and should be barred from holding public office for a period of 10 years.

While the conclusions of the report were welcomed by the FMLN, representatives of the Government and the armed forces challenged the legal validity of the document, despite the insistence of UN officials that the recommendations of the report were mandatory under the terms of the peace accord. However, later in March 1993, the strength of ARENA's representation in the Asamblea overcame opposition from the PDC, the Convergencia Democrática (CD, a left-wing alliance comprising two of the leading groups within the FDR-FMLN and the Partido Social Demócrata) and the Movimiento Nacional Revolucionario (MNR), and secured the approval of an amnesty law to extend to all political crimes committed before 1992, prompting widespread public outrage, which was compounded, in the following month, by the release of the two prisoners sentenced for the murder of the six Jesuits. In June the Government compromised to some extent, by announcing the compulsory retirement of several veteran military officers, including Gen. Ponce, although their immunity from prosecution was guaranteed.

The findings of the Truth Commission—together with the disclosure of information following the declassification by the US Administration, in November 1993, of hitherto confidential documents relating to the Administrations of former US Presidents Ronald Reagan and George Bush, Sr—suggested that detailed knowledge of abuses of human rights was suppressed by US officials in order to continue to secure congressional funding for the Government in El Salvador in the 1980s. Evidence also emerged that US military training had been provided, in at least one instance, for a civilian group in El Salvador operating as a 'death squad'.

Meanwhile, in June 1993 the FMLN had agreed to comply with an ultimatum issued by the UN, that the location and destruction of all remaining arms caches in El Salvador and neighbouring countries should be swiftly implemented. In December, bowing to pressure from the UN, President Cristiani inaugurated a four-member commission of investigation (the Joint Group for the Investigation of Illegal Armed Groups), to examine allegations of political motivation behind an escalation in violent attacks against members of the FMLN in late 1993. The conclusions of the commission claimed that officials from numerous government departments, together with current and former members of the security forces, were continuing to participate in organized crime and in politically motivated acts of violence.

Voting to elect a new president, vice-president, legislature, 262 mayors and 20 members of the Central American parliament took place on 20 March 1994. ARENA's presidential candidate, Armando Calderón Sol, failed to secure the clear majority needed for outright victory in the first poll, and was forced to contest a second round of voting against the second placed candidate, Rubén Zamora Rivas, the joint CD-FMLN-MNR nominee, on 24 April, which Calderón Sol won. ARENA candidates also achieved considerable success in the legislative elections and in the municipal poll. FMLN candidates were also considered to have performed well in the party's first electoral contest, winning 21 seats in the Asamblea and a number of rural municipalities. Calderón Sol was inaugurated on 1 June and a new Cabinet was installed.

Meanwhile, serious divisions emerged within the FMLN during 1994, and in December two constituent parties, the Resistencia Nacional (RN) and the Expresión Renovadora del Pueblo (ERP—formerly the Fuerzas Armadas de la Resistencia Nacional and the Ejército Revolucionario Popular guerrilla groups, respectively) announced their withdrawal from the FMLN, owing to a divergence of political interests. In March 1995 the Secretary-General of the ERP, Joaquín Villalobos (who had been highly critical of the predominance of political extremism), announced the formation of a new centre-left political force, the Partido Demócrata (PD), comprising the ERP, the RN, the MNR and a dissident faction of the PDC. The new party demonstrated an immediate willingness to co-operate with the country's most prominent political forces.

In September 1994 and January 1995, in protest at the Government's failure to honour the terms of the 1992 peace accord with regard to financial compensation and other benefits for demobilized military personnel, retired soldiers occupied the Asamblea and took a number of deputies hostage. On both occasions the occupation was ended swiftly and peacefully following the Government's agreement to enter into direct negotiations with the former soldiers. Nevertheless, demonstrations by army veterans during March and November were forcibly curtailed by the security forces, prompting concern that such incidents might provoke a renewed escalation of armed conflict.

In May 1994 the UN Security Council voted to extend the ONUSAL mandate for a further six months in order to supervise the full implementation of the outstanding provisions of the peace agreement. Of particular concern were delays in the reform of the judiciary, the initiation of the land reform programme and the full integration and activation of the PNC. In September the UN Secretary-General appealed to the Government and to the international community for increased financial commitment to the peace process. In the same month, in the context of increasing levels of crime and social unrest, the

ONUSAL mandate was further extended, pending the effective habilitation of the PNC; a further extension, until the end of April 1995, was approved by the UN Security Council in November. A small contingent of UN observers, MINUSAL, was mandated to remain in El Salvador until April 1996, the revised deadline for the fulfilment of the outstanding terms of the peace accord. By this date, however, full implementation of those terms of the accord relating to land allocation for refugees and former combatants, and to the reform of the judiciary and the electoral code, had yet to be achieved. A reduced MINUSAL contingent was further mandated to oversee Government efforts to fulfil the outstanding terms of the agreement, and the mission was formally terminated on 31 December 1996.

The results of the congressional and municipal elections of 16 March 1997 demonstrated a significant increase in support for the FMLN, particularly in the capital, where the party won seven of the 16 contested seats and secured the mayoralty. The results of the legislative poll revealed a considerable erosion of ARENA's predominance in the Asamblea, with the party securing 29 seats, just one more than the FMLN.

The presidential election of 7 March 1999 was won by Francisco Flores Pérez, the candidate of ARENA, who obtained 52% of the votes in the first round. Despite contesting the election in alliance with the Unión Social Cristiana, the candidate of the FMLN, Facundo Guardado, received only 29% of the ballot. Voter participation was the lowest recorded in the country's history, with less than 40% of the registered electorate choosing to vote. Flores was inaugurated on 1 June. However, the Government was embarrassed by allegations that foreign funds, donated for disaster relief following the impact of 'Hurricane Mitch' in November 1998, had been diverted by ARENA to former paramilitaries in an attempt to buy votes for Flores in the presidential election. Dissatisfaction with the ARENA Government was demonstrated in the results of the legislative elections of 12 March 2000, in which the FMLN became the largest single party in the Asamblea, winning 31 of the 84 seats, while ARENA secured 29 seats. Voter turn-out was only 33%.

In early 2001 more than 1,100 people were killed, some 4,000 people were injured, and a further 1.5m. people were left homeless by two earthquakes. Reconstruction costs were estimated at US $1,900m., representing around 14% of gross domestic product (GDP). In March the Inter-American Development Bank (IDB, see p. 308) pledged $1,278.5m. in aid. In September the US immigration authorities granted Temporary Protected Status valid for one year (subsequently renewed until March 2009) to Salvadorean illegal immigrants residing in the USA and released those held in custody.

During 2001 internal divisions deepened between the more orthodox and the reformist elements of the FMLN, culminating in October in the expulsion of the reformist FMLN leader, Facundo Guardado. In November Salvador Sánchez Cerén, from the party's orthodox wing, was elected leader. Following Sánchez's election, in January 2002 six reformist FMLN deputies left the party, thus reducing the FMLN's legislative representation to 25 seats. ARENA became the largest parliamentary bloc, with 29 seats. In April the six FMLN dissidents joined with Guardado to form a new party, the Movimiento Renovador.

In June 2002 two former army generals and defence ministers, Gen. (retd) Carlos Eugenio Vides Casanova and Gen. (retd) José Guillermo García, were convicted by a US court of 'crimes against humanity'. The case was brought by three Salvadorean civilians who had been tortured by troops under the generals' commands during the civil war.

In a general election held on 16 March 2003 the FMLN retained its 31 seats in the Asamblea Legislativa. ARENA performed less well than expected, securing 27 seats, two fewer than in the last legislature. The PCN increased its number of seats from 14 to 16, while the PDC retained its five seats. Support for ARENA also faltered in the concurrently held local elections, with the ruling party retaining control of 109 of the country's 262 municipalities (from 126). Following the elections, President Flores announced an initiative, named 'Mano Dura' (Iron Fist), to combat the rising violent crime in the country, particularly that attributed to street gangs, or *maras*. The initiative included provision for the restructuring of the PNC and a revision of the penal code.

A presidential election was held on 21 March 2004. In spite of the party's poor electoral performance in the previous year, the ARENA candidate, businessman Elías Antonio (Tony) Saca, secured an overwhelming victory, obtaining 57.7% of the votes cast. Schafik Jorge Handal, the former guerrilla who was the nominee of the FMLN, attracted some 35.7% of the ballot, while Héctor Silva Argüello, representing a coalition of the PDC and the Centro Democrático Unido, and the PCN candidate, José Rafael Machuca Zelaya, secured 3.9% and 2.7% of the votes cast, respectively. The voter turn-out was much improved, at 66.2%. Saca was inaugurated as President on 1 June and a new Cabinet, largely comprising ARENA members, was installed. The new Government's stated priorities were to reduce violent crime and to increase employment through development of the tourism industry and promotion of foreign investment, particularly in the free zones. To this end, President Saca created a Ministry of Tourism, headed by Luis Cardenal, and announced plans to liberalize the sugar and pharmaceutical sectors.

Upon taking office President Saca undertook to reduce gang-related crime. An initiative, known as 'Súper Mano Dura' (Super Iron Fist), launched in September 2004, gained widespread support. The initiative was an extension of President Flores's 'Mano Dura' campaign, which the Supreme Court had ruled unconstitutional. The new campaign included proposals to appoint prosecutors dedicated to bringing charges against members of the *maras*, or street gangs and to rehabilite gang members. The Government's new initiative also included proposals to reduce crime and violence within prisons, such as the segregation of gang members (in mid-August some 31 inmates had died as a result of fighting between gang members in the La Esperanza prison). In addition, it was suggested that army barracks be used to relieve overcrowding in the country's gaols, which in 2004 contained 12,000 inmates, twice the intended capacity. (Nevertheless, in early January 2007 a further 21 inmates died during a riot in the Apanteos prison.)

As a result of the 'Súper Mano Dura' initiative, by mid-2005 an estimated 9,000 gang members had been arrested, of whom some 4,000 remained imprisoned. However, the murder rate continued to increase. In May Saca introduced extensive house-to-house searches with the stated aims of confiscating illegal firearms and drugs and arresting known murderers. The preventive searches were widely criticized by opposition deputies, civil rights groups, lawyers and members of the judiciary as a breach of the Constitution and an echo of methods employed during the civil war. In July Saca announced the creation of a new task force, the Fuerza de Tarea Conjunta (comprising police officers, 1,100 police academy cadets and 1,000 army reservists) intended to reinforce police presence in the five departments with the highest rates of violent crime. However, according to police figures, the murder rate increased by 3.4% to 3,906 killings in 2006.

In the legislative elections of 12 March 2006 the FMLN increased its parliamentary representation to 32 seats. ARENA still held the largest number of seats, 34, while the PCN secured 10 seats and the PDC won six seats. The Frente Democrático Revolucionario (FDR), a party founded in June 2005 by dissident FMLN deputies, won just two seats. This gave the right-wing parties a working majority in the Asamblea, although the FMLN regained its power to veto proposals that required a two-thirds' majority, which it had lost in 2005 owing to defections. The FMLN also won the politically important mayoralty of San Salvador.

Domestic security remained a priority for the Government throughout 2006. In June Minister of Internal Affairs René Mario Figueroa proposed a new strategy to address the persistent problem of violent crime, in particular the low conviction rate of suspects. The so-called 'Plan Maestro de Seguridad' (Security Master Plan) was designed to increase the judicial conviction rate by improving the quality of evidence submitted by the police to public prosecutors. A significant element of the initiative was to consider gangs as manifestations of organized crime. Then, in July, the Government overcame opposition from the FMLN to secure legislative approval of reforms to restrict the legal possession of firearms. In November President Saca announced that the Fuerza de Tarea Conjunta and the PNC were each to be strengthened by an additional 2,000 recruits. The President further proposed to focus resources on impounding illegal weapons in the 20 most violent municipalities, following the reported success of a similar experiment to control firearms in the town of San Martín. In early February 2007 the Government announced a joint initiative with the US Department of State to combat the *maras*: the US Federal Bureau of Intelligence (FBI) was to assist with the establishment of a Transnational Anti-Gang unit to identify and prosecute gang members. Official figures released in late 2007 showed that the number of murders committed in the first nine months of that year had fallen by 10% compared to the same period in 2006, providing some evidence that the Government's initiatives against violent crime had proved effective.

Meanwhile, in early July 2006 a demonstration against the rising costs of electricity and public transport deteriorated into violence outside the University of El Salvador, resulting in the deaths of two police officers. The public transport sector attracted further attention in September when services were disrupted as a result of industrial action by employees. Some 300 buses were withdrawn from service between San Salvador and the eastern city of San Miguel in protest at the murder of public transport workers (an estimated 80 deaths had been reported by September of that year) and the extortion of money from transport companies, offences that were attributed, in large part, to gang members.

In January 2007 President Saca subdivided the internal affairs portfolio to create a new Ministry of Public Security and Justice. Figueroa assumed responsibility for the new portfolio and he was succeeded as Minister of Internal Affairs (with the reduced remit of immigration and natural disasters) by hitherto deputy minister Silvia Aguilar, who was in turn replaced by Juan Miguel Bolaños Torres. Moreover, Jorge Isidro Nieto Menéndez was appointed Minister of Public Works following the resignation, owing to health reasons, of David Gutiérrez Miranda. There were further public protests in July against government plans to 'decentralize' the supply of drinking water by transferring control to local authorities (criticized by opposition groups as a form of privatization), during which 12 demonstrators were arrested under recently introduced anti-terrorism legislation. In September, in response to the incident, the Asamblea Legislativa approved a reform of the penal code that increased prison sentences for those convicted of acts of public disorder, including obstructing roads and invading buildings. In late December Gen. Jorge Alberto Molina Contreras, hitherto Chief of Staff of the Armed Forces, was appointed Minister of National Defence in succession to Gen. Otto Romero Orellana. Shortly afterwards, in mid-January 2008, Francisco Laínez Rivas resigned as Minister of Foreign Affairs in order to seek nomination as ARENA's candidate for the presidential elections scheduled for March 2009, and was replaced by Marisol Argueta de Barillas. Meanwhile, in October 2007 the FMLN named Mauricio Funes, a well-known journalist from the moderate wing of the party, as its presidential candidate. In a primary election held in March 2008 the ARENA candidacy was secured by Rodrigo Avila, a former Director-General of the PNC.

In an attempt to resolve a territorial dispute between El Salvador and Honduras over three islands in the Gulf of Fonseca and a small area of land on the joint border, President Duarte and President Azcona of Honduras submitted the dispute to the International Court of Justice (ICJ) for arbitration in December 1986. In September 1992 both countries accepted the ruling of the ICJ, which awarded one-third of the disputed mainland and two of the three disputed islands to El Salvador. Following prolonged negotiations, the two parties signed a convention in January 1998 specifying the rights and obligations of those affected, including the right to choose between Honduran and Salvadorean citizenship. In July 2001 El Salvador and Honduras signed a development plan for the border area between the two countries. In April 2006 the long-standing dispute was ended when the Presidents of both countries met to formally ratify the demarcation of the border. At the same time, as a sign of improved bilateral co-operation, the two heads of state announced plans to revive a joint project to construct a 704 MW hydroelectric plant on the Lempa River.

Government

Executive power is held by the President, assisted by the Vice-President and the Cabinet. The President is elected for a five-year term by universal adult suffrage. Legislative power is vested in the Asamblea Legislativa (Legislative Assembly), with 84 members elected by universal adult suffrage for a three-year term.

Defence

Military service is by compulsory selective conscription of men between 18 and 30 years of age for one year. As assessed at November 2007, the armed forces totalled 15,660, of whom an estimated 13,850 (including 4,000 conscripts) were in the army, 860 were in the navy and 950 (including some 200 conscripts) were in the air force. There were in addition some 9,900 joint reserves. The police force, the Policía Nacional Civil, created in 1991, numbered around 12,000 personnel in 2005 and was to increase to 16,000. Defence expenditure for 2007 was budgeted at 974m. colones.

Economic Affairs

In 2006, according to estimates by the World Bank, El Salvador's gross national income (GNI), measured at average 2004–06 prices, was US $17,782m., equivalent to $2,540 per head (or $5,340 per head on an international purchasing-power parity basis). In 1996–2006 the population increased at an average annual rate of 1.9%, while gross domestic product (GDP) per head increased, in real terms, by an average of 0.9% per year. Overall GDP increased, in real terms, at an average annual rate of 2.8% in 1996–2006. GDP grew by 3.8% in 2006.

Agriculture (including hunting, forestry and fishing) contributed an estimated 10.5% of GDP and employed some 18.9% of the employed labour force in 2006. The principal cash crops are coffee and sugar cane. Maize, beans, rice and millet are the major subsistence crops. Following the earthquakes that struck the country in early 2001, the Inter-American Development Bank (IDB) pledged some US $1,278.5m. in emergency assistance, of which $132.6m. was intended for rehabilitation and development of agriculture; a further $101.0m. was made available for redevelopment of the coffee industry, which had been particularly badly affected. In October 2002 the Government announced that it would loan some $192m. to the coffee industry over the next three years. In 2006 coffee output stood at 85,350 metric tons, compared with 87,963 tons in the previous year. Coffee's share of export earnings continued to decrease: in 2000 coffee accounted for 22.4% of export earnings, excluding *maquila* zones, but this had fallen to 9.9% in 2006. El Salvador's fishing catch was relatively small; however, in mid-2003 a Spanish firm, Grupo Calvo, opened a tuna-processing plant at Punta Gorda, which aimed to export 25,000 metric tons of tuna per year. In 2004 the fishing catch increased by 22.2%, to 44,600 tons, before decreasing slightly to 43,300 tons in 2006. During 1996–2006 agricultural GDP increased at an average annual rate of 1.7%. The sector's GDP increased by an estimated 7.5% in 2006.

Industry (including mining, manufacturing, construction and power) contributed an estimated 28.2% of GDP and engaged 36.6.2% of the employed labour force in 2006. During 1996–2006 industrial GDP increased at an average annual rate of 3.5%. The sector's GDP increased by 3.5% in 2006.

El Salvador has no significant mineral resources, and the mining sector employed less than 0.1% of the economically active population and contributed only 0.4% of GDP in 2006. Small quantities of gold, silver, sea-salt and limestone are mined or quarried. During 1996–2006 the GDP of the mining sector increased at an average rate of 1.7% and rose by an estimated 4.8% in 2006.

Manufacturing contributed an estimated 21.5% of GDP and employed 15.8% of the active labour force in 2006. The most important branches of manufacturing (excluding the *maquila* industry) were food products, chemical products, petroleum products, textiles, apparel (excluding footwear) and beverages. During 1996–2006 manufacturing GDP increased at an average annual rate of 3.7%. The sector's GDP increased by 3.2% in 2006. There is a thriving *maquila* sector, which in 2004 generated more than one-half (an estimated 55%) of the country's total exports. In 1995–2000 *maquila* exports increased at an average annual rate of 20%. However, as a consequence of the natural disasters in El Salvador, the faltering US economy and competition from the People's Republic of China, growth decreased substantially after 2000. The sector directly employed an estimated 88,500 people in 2005. The implementation of the Dominican Republic-Central American Free Trade Agreement (DR-CAFTA) with the USA in March 2006 was expected to engender growth in the *maquila* sector.

Energy is derived principally from imported fuel. Imports of mineral products accounted for an estimated 14.3% of the cost of merchandise imports in 2005. In 2005 El Salvador derived over two-fifths (an estimated 42.1%) of its electricity from petroleum, compared with just 6.8% in 1990. An estimated further 36.4% of total electricity production in 2005 was contributed by hydroelectric installations. In 2001 construction began on an electricity interconnection between El Salvador and Honduras, part of a planned Central American regional power network.

The services sector contributed an estimated 61.3% of GDP and employed 58.2% of the economically active population in 2006. The GDP of the services sector increased by an average of 2.9% per year in 1996–2006. The sector grew by 3.8% in 2006. Receipts from tourism grew substantially in the early 21st century, rising from US $235m. in 2001 to $862m. in 2006.

In 2006 El Salvador recorded a visible trade deficit of US $3,689.3m., while there was a deficit of $854.9m. on the current account of the balance of payments. Following the earthquakes in 2001, remittances from workers abroad increased, with payments from the USA alone totalling some US $1,935m. in that year. Remittances in 2007 totalled $3,695.3m. In 2006 almost one-third of total imports (an estimated 48.0%, including imports into *maquila* zones) was provided by the USA; other major suppliers were Guatemala, Costa Rica and Honduras. The USA was also the principal market for exports (taking an estimated 57.1% of exports, including exports from the *maquila* sector, in 2006); other significant purchasers were Guatemala, Honduras and Costa Rica. In 2006 the main exports were food and live animals (particularly coffee), textiles and chemicals and related products. In the same year the principal imports were chemicals and related products, minerals and foodstuffs.

In 2005 there was an estimated budgetary deficit of US $111m., equivalent to some 0.7% of GDP. El Salvador's external debt totalled US $7,088m. at the end of 2005, of which $5,513m. was long-term public debt. In that year the cost of debt-servicing was $649m., equivalent to 8.6% of exports of goods and services. The average annual rate of inflation was 2.8% in 1998–2005; consumer prices rose by 4.9% in 2006, according to the Central Bank. Some 6.6% of the labour force were unemployed in 2006.

In March 2001 a free trade agreement with Mexico was implemented. In May the Central American countries, including El Salvador, reached the basis of a deal with Mexico, the 'Plan Puebla–Panamá', to integrate the region through joint transport, industry and tourism projects. The Plan made little progress, although in April 2007 there were plans to reinvigorate negotiations on the project. Negotiations towards a further Central American free trade agreement, which became known as DR-CAFTA, were concluded between El Salvador, Costa Rica, Guatemala, Honduras, Nicaragua and the USA in December 2003 (the Dominican Republic joined the initiative in the following year). DR-CAFTA entailed the gradual elimination of tariffs on most industrial and agricultural products over the next 10 and 20 years, respectively. The Agreement was ratified by the legislature in December 2004 and came into effect in March 2006.

El Salvador is a member of the Central American Common Market (CACM, see p. 201), which aims to increase trade within the region and to encourage monetary and industrial co-operation.

Considerable progress in reducing financial imbalances and in addressing the problem of widespread poverty was achieved from the mid-1990s, although the country still remained overly reliant on remittances for spending. In 2007 funds from Salvadoreans working abroad were equivalent to an estimated 18% of GDP. While remittances proved a valuable means by which to stimulate domestic expenditure, there remained concerns that large inflows of US dollars were increasing dependency on the US market. Remittances from this source were expected to decrease dramatically in 2008, following a contraction in the US construction industry, which provided employment for a large proportion of Salvadorean workers. In January 2001 the US dollar was formally introduced as an official currency, alongside the colón, to which it was anchored at a fixed rate of exchange. Although dollarization provided much needed stability in the banking system, it also heightened the Salvadorean economy's vulnerability to changes in US monetary policy. The continued depreciation of the US dollar was likely to increase the price of imports in 2008, however, it was hoped that a simultaneous rise in export revenues would alleviate pressure on the current account deficit. Furthermore, the implementation of the DR-CAFTA agreement and the approval of new free trade agreements with Colombia and Taiwan was expected to bolster the external sector in 2008. Real GDP increased by 4.2% in 2007, according to IMF estimates, while consumer prices rose by 4.4%.

Education

There are two national universities and more than 30 private universities. Education is provided free of charge in state schools, and there are also numerous private schools. Pre-primary education, beginning at four years of age and lasting for three years, and primary education, beginning at seven years of age and lasting for nine years, are officially compulsory. In 2004/05 enrolment at primary schools was equivalent to 92.7% of children in the relevant age-group. Secondary education begins at the age of 16 and lasts for two years for an academic diploma or three years for a vocational one. In 2003 enrolment in secondary education was equivalent to 49.0% of students in the relevant age-group. Budgetary expenditure on education by the central Government in 2006 totalled US $510.7m., equivalent to 15.3% of total expenditure.

Public Holidays

2008: 1 January (New Year's Day), 20–23 March (Easter), 1 May (Labour Day), 4–6 August* (El Salvador del Mundo Festival), 15 September (Independence Day), 12 October (Discovery of America), 2 November (All Souls' Day), 25 December (Christmas Day), 31 December (New Year's Eve).

2009: 1 January (New Year's Day), 9–12 April (Easter), 1 May (Labour Day), 4–6 August* (El Salvador del Mundo Festival), 15 September (Independence Day), 12 October (Discovery of America), 2 November (All Souls' Day), 25 December (Christmas Day), 31 December (New Year's Eve).

* 1–6 August in San Salvador.

Weights and Measures

The metric system is officially in force. Some old Spanish measures are also used, including:
    25 libras = 1 arroba;
    4 arrobas = 1 quintal (46 kg);
    1 manzana = 0.699 ha.

Statistical Survey

Sources (unless otherwise stated): Banco Central de Reserva de El Salvador, Alameda Juan Pablo II y 17 Avda Norte, Apdo 01-106, San Salvador; tel. 2271-0011; fax 2271-4575; internet www.bcr.gob.sv; Dirección General de Estadística y Censos, Edif. Centro de Gobierno, Alameda Juan Pablo II y Calle Guadalupe, San Salvador; tel. 2286-4260; fax 2286-2505; internet www.digestyc.gob.sv.

Area and Population

AREA, POPULATION AND DENSITY

Area (sq km)	
Land	20,721
Inland water	320
Total	21,041*
Population (census results)†	
28 June 1971	3,554,648
27 September 1992	
Males	2,485,613
Females	2,632,986
Total	5,118,599
Population (official estimates at mid-year)	
2005	6,874,926
2006	6,990,658
2007	7,104,999
Density (per sq km) at mid-2007	337.7

* 8,124 sq miles.
† Excluding adjustments for underenumeration.

DEPARTMENTS
(official population estimates, 2007)

	Area (sq km)	Population	Density (per sq km)
Ahuachapán	1,239.6	369,496	298.1
Santa Ana	2,023.2	630,903	311.8
Sonsonate	1,225.8	530,988	433.2
Chalatenango	2,016.6	204,740	101.5
La Libertad	1,652.9	823,511	498.2
San Salvador	886.2	2,266,387	2,557.4
Cuscatlán	756.2	216,446	286.2
La Paz	1,223.6	328,666	268.6
Cabañas	1,103.5	158,395	143.5
San Vicente	1,184.0	174,928	147.7
Usulután	2,130.4	352,063	165.3
San Miguel	2,077.1	558,942	269.1
Morazán	1,447.4	181,285	125.2
La Unión	2,074.3	308,249	148.6
Total	21,040.8	7,104,999	337.7

PRINCIPAL TOWNS
(official population estimates, 2007)*

San Salvador (capital)	513,869	Nueva San Salvador	202,935
Soyapango	301,885	Ciudad Delgado	176,873
Apopa	223,652	Ilopango	162,370
Mejicanos	213,779	San Martín	150,008

* Figures refer to municipios, which may each contain rural areas as well as an urban centre.

BIRTHS, MARRIAGES AND DEATHS

	Registered live births Number	Rate (per 1,000)	Registered marriages Number	Rate (per 1,000)	Registered deaths Number	Rate (per 1,000)
1999	153,636	25.0	34,306	5.6	28,056	4.6
2000	150,176	23.9	28,231	4.5	28,154	4.5
2001	138,354	21.6	29,216	4.6	29,559	4.6
2002	129,363	19.9	26,077	4.0	27,458	4.2
2003	124,476	18.7	25,071	3.8	29,377	4.4
2004	119,710	17.7	25,240	3.7	30,058	4.4
2005	112,769	16.4	24,475	3.6	30,933	4.5
2006	107,111	15.3	24,500	3.5	31,453	4.5

Expectation of life (years at birth, WHO estimates): 71.5 (males 68.5; females 74.3) in 2005 (Source: WHO, *World Health Statistics*).

ECONOMICALLY ACTIVE POPULATION
(ISIC major divisions, '000 persons aged 10 years and over)

	2004	2005	2006
Agriculture, hunting, forestry and fishing	483.1	518.0	506.6
Mining and quarrying	1.8	2.5	2.2
Manufacturing	423.4	418.9	423.4
Electricity, gas and water	10.3	7.3	10.3
Construction	162.8	146.8	181.3
Trade, restaurants and hotels	739.5	764.9	803.1
Transport, storage and communication	125.8	120.9	120.4
Financing, insurance, real estate and business services	103.1	122.8	114.9
Public administration, defence and social security	98.4	100.3	105.9
Education	87.0	97.2	93.8
Other community, social and personal services	171.7	180.0	189.5
Private households with employed persons	118.7	111.5	134.5
Other activities not adequately defined	0.8	—	—
Total employed	2,526.4	2,591.1	2,685.9
Unemployed	183.9	201.6	188.7
Total labour force	2,710.2	2,792.6	2,874.6

Health and Welfare

KEY INDICATORS

Total fertility rate (children per woman, 2005)	2.8
Under-5 mortality rate (per 1,000 live births, 2005)	27
HIV/AIDS (% of persons aged 15–49, 2004)	0.9
Physicians (per 1,000 head, 2002)	1.24
Hospital beds (per 1,000 head, 2005)	0.9
Health expenditure (2004): US $ per head (PPP)	375
Health expenditure (2004): % of GDP	7.9
Health expenditure (2004): public (% of total)	44.4
Access to water (% of persons, 2004)	84
Access to sanitation (% of persons, 2004)	62
Human Development Index (2005): ranking	103
Human Development Index (2005): value	0.735

For sources and definitions, see explanatory note on p. vi.

Agriculture

PRINCIPAL CROPS
('000 metric tons)

	2004	2005	2006
Rice (paddy)	26.5	26.0	30.5
Maize	648.0	727.6	741.7
Sorghum	147.6	141.4	165.0
Yautia (Cocoyam)*	50.6	49.7	52.0
Sugar cane	4,920.8	4,404.9	5,280.4
Dry beans	84.3	65.1	90.5
Coconuts	112.0	54.1	57.0
Watermelons	52.3	68.9	86.8
Bananas*	65.8	66.2	66.2
Plantains	75.7	78.0	82.7
Oranges	38.8	56.3	59.7
Coffee (green)	83.1	88.6	85.4

* FAO estimates.
Source: FAO.

LIVESTOCK
('000 head, year ending September)

	2004	2005	2006
Horses*	96	n.a.	96
Asses, mules or hinnies*	27	27	27
Cattle	1,259	1,257	1,319
Pigs	355	356	436
Sheep*	5	n.a.	5
Goats*	11	n.a.	11
Chickens	13,209	13,437	13,706

* FAO estimates.
Source: FAO.

LIVESTOCK PRODUCTS
('000 metric tons)

	2004	2005	2006
Cattle meat	26.5	27.0	30.6
Pig meat	7.9	10.8	14.2
Chicken meat	92.1	98.6	101.4
Cows' milk	399.8	447.6	492.5
Hen eggs, in shell	67.4	67.4	68.8

Source: FAO.

Forestry

ROUNDWOOD REMOVALS
('000 cubic metres, excl. bark, FAO estimates)

	2004	2005	2006
Sawlogs, veneer logs and logs for sleepers	682	682	682
Fuel wood	4,173	4,199	4,204
Total	4,855	4,881	4,886

Source: FAO.

SAWNWOOD PRODUCTION
('000 cubic metres, incl. railway sleepers, FAO estimates)

	2003	2004	2005
Total (all broadleaved, hardwood)	68.0	16.3	16.3

2006: Figures assumed to be unchanged from 2005 (FAO estimates).
Source: FAO.

Fishing

('000 metric tons, live weight)

	2003	2004	2005
Capture	35.4	42.4	41.1
Nile tilapia	1.2	0.9	1.1
Other freshwater fishes	1.0	0.9	0.4
Croakers and drums	0.8	0.5	0.6
Skipjack tuna	4.5	6.9	4.7
Yellowfin tuna	6.6	12.9	6.7
Bigeye tuna	1.1	1.0	0.8
Sharks, rays, skates, etc.	1.0	0.9	1.2
Other marine fishes	3.3	3.1	4.6
Pacific seabobs	1.1	0.8	0.5
Marine molluscs	0.6	2.9	0.1
Aquaculture	1.1	2.2	2.2
Total catch	36.5	44.6	43.3

Source: FAO.

Mining

(metric tons, unless otherwise specified)

	2003	2004	2005*
Gypsum	5,600*	5,600*	5,600
Limestone ('000 metric tons)	1,194	1,161	1,150
Salt (marine)	31,366	31,400*	31,400

* Estimate(s).
Source: US Geological Survey.

Industry

SELECTED PRODUCTS
('000 metric tons, unless otherwise indicated)

	2002	2003	2004
Raw sugar	465	530	n.a.
Motor gasoline (petrol)	127	135	143
Kerosene	15	19	22
Distillate fuel oil	151	195	199
Residual fuel oil	526	485	543
Liquefied petroleum gas (refined)	14	12	14
Cement*	1,318	1,390	1,256
Electric energy (million kWh)	4,100	4,128	4,564

* Source: US Geological Survey.
Source: mostly UN, *Industrial Commodity Statistics Yearbook*.

Finance

CURRENCY AND EXCHANGE RATES

Monetary Units
100 centavos = 1 Salvadorean colón.

Sterling, Dollar and Euro Equivalents (31 December 2007)
£1 sterling = 17.529 colones;
US $1 = 8.750 colones;
€1 = 12.881 colones;
100 Salvadorean colones = £5.70 = $11.43 = €7.76.

Note: The foregoing information refers to the principal exchange rate, applicable to official receipts and payments, imports of petroleum and exports of coffee. In addition, there is a market exchange rate, applicable to other transactions. The principal rate was maintained at 8.755 colones per US dollar from May 1995 to December 2000. However, in January 2001, with the introduction of legislation making the US dollar legal tender, the rate was adjusted to $1 = 8.750 colones. Both currencies were to be accepted for a transitional period.

EL SALVADOR

CENTRAL GOVERNMENT BUDGET
(US $ million)

Revenue*	2004	2005†	2006†
Current revenue	2,048	2,259	2,648
Tax revenue	1,820	2,132	2,488
Taxes on earnings	634	668	n.a.
Import duties	177	181	n.a.
Value-added tax	952	95	n.a.
Non-tax revenue	228	1,104	n.a.
Capital revenue	1	0	0
Total	2,049	2,258	2,648

Expenditure‡	2004	2005†	2006†
Current expenditure	1,925	2,057	2,285
Remunerations	745	765	836
Goods and services	356	410	391
Interest payments	320	371	447
Transfers	504	511	612
To other government bodies	321	319	350
To the private sector	183	193	262
Capital expenditure	371	438	494
Gross investment	223	239	256
Total	2,295	2,495	2,779

* Excluding grants received (US $ million): 47 in 2004; 49 in 2005; 36 in 2006.
† Preliminary figures.
‡ Excluding lending minus repayments (US $ million): –22 in 2004; –11 in 2005; –16 in 2006.

INTERNATIONAL RESERVES
(US $ million at 31 December)

	2004	2005	2006
Gold (national valuation)	138.9	110.2	84.0
IMF special drawing rights	38.8	35.7	37.6
Foreign exchange	1,715.2	1,687.1	1,777.3
Total	1,892.9	1,833.0	1,898.9

Source: IMF, *International Financial Statistics*.

MONEY SUPPLY
(US $ million at 31 December)

	2004	2005	2006
Currency outside banks	35.4	34.2	33.7
Demand deposits at deposit money banks	1,167.0	1,257.2	1,453.8
Total money (incl. others)	1,252.6	1,351.3	1,562.7

Source: IMF, *International Financial Statistics*.

COST OF LIVING
(Consumer Price Index; base: 2000 = 100)

	2004	2005	2006
Food and non-alcoholic beverages	188.6	197.6	208.0
Rent, water, electricity, gas and other fuels	189.8	198.0	206.4
Clothing	109.2	109.8	111.1
Health	203.3	211.9	222.5
Transport	134.4	145.3	157.5
All items (incl. others)	180.2	187.9	197.1

NATIONAL ACCOUNTS
(US $ million at current prices)

Expenditure on the Gross Domestic Product

	2004	2005*	2006*
Final consumption expenditure	15,963.4	17,574.4	19,315.9
Households	14,438.9	15,942.4	17,315.9
General government	1,524.5	1,632.0	1,782.2
Gross capital formation	2,559.7	2,683.1	3,008.3
Gross fixed capital formation	2,473.8	2,610.0	3,008.3
Changes in inventories	85.9	73.1	—
Total domestic expenditure	18,523.1	20,257.5	22,324.2
Exports of goods and services	4,397.1	4,572.7	5,070.3
Less Imports of goods and services	7,121.9	7,714.8	8,740.9
GDP in purchasers' values	15,798.3	17,115.4	18,653.6
GDP at constant 1990 prices	8,157.7	8,419.7	8,772.0

* Preliminary.

Gross Domestic Product by Economic Activity

	2004	2005*	2006*
Agriculture, hunting, forestry and fishing	1,400.9	1,657.6	1,874.8
Mining and quarrying	56.5	59.2	64.4
Manufacturing	3,495.8	3,609.5	3,844.7
Construction	657.8	710.7	778.8
Electricity, gas and water	280.2	301.9	349.2
Transport, storage and communications	1,450.0	1,555.8	1,726.2
Wholesale and retail trade, restaurants and hotels	3,127.1	3,411.6	3,702.0
Finance and insurance	707.4	769.4	836.3
Real estate and business services	659.3	712.7	766.2
Owner-occupied dwellings	1,189.5	1,273.2	1,322.0
Community, social, domestic and personal services	1,212.5	1,260.0	1,358.4
Government services	1,044.4	1,110.7	1,229.4
Sub-total	15,281.4	16,432.3	17,852.4
Import duties and value-added tax	1,119.6	1,286.7	1,498.6
Less Imputed bank service charge	602.7	648.6	697.5
GDP in purchasers' values	15,798.3	17,070.2	18,653.6

* Preliminary.

BALANCE OF PAYMENTS
(US $ million)

	2004	2005	2006
Exports of goods f.o.b.	3,339.2	3,428.8	3,567.3
Imports of goods f.o.b.	–5,999.5	–6,533.6	–7,256.6
Trade balance	–2,660.3	–3,104.8	–3,689.3
Exports of services	1,089.6	1,127.9	1,503.0
Imports of services	–1,154.1	–1,210.3	–1,484.3
Balance on goods and services	–2,724.8	–3,187.2	–3,670.6
Other income received	143.7	182.7	237.9
Other income paid	–601.6	–754.1	–757.0
Balance on goods, services and income	–3,182.7	–3,758.6	–4,189.7
Current transfers received	2,615.1	2,919.1	3,396.6
Current transfers paid	–60.1	–71.4	–61.8
Current balance	–627.7	–910.9	–854.9
Capital account (net)	100.3	93.6	96.2
Direct investment abroad	2.8	–217.3	50.2
Direct investment from abroad	363.3	605.5	203.6
Portfolio investment assets	–124.8	93.6	69.6
Portfolio investment liabilities	181.9	86.4	715.1
Other investment assets	–159.8	–168.1	66.7
Other investment liabilities	–140.4	410.5	–87.6
Net errors and omissions	352.0	–52.1	–187.3
Overall balance	–52.5	–58.9	71.6

Source: IMF, *International Financial Statistics*.

EL SALVADOR

External Trade

PRINCIPAL COMMODITIES
(US $ million)

Imports c.i.f.*	2004	2005†	2006†
Live animals and animal products; vegetables, crops and related products, primary	422.1	471.8	526.9
Food, beverages and tobacco manufactures	368.4	427.3	616.0
Mineral products	720.4	962.3	1,113.0
Crude petroleum oils	225.8	288.9	375.2
Refined petroleum oils	206.2	243.8	286.1
Chemicals and related products	602.3	685.3	730.4
Therapeutic and preventative medicines	183.9	204.8	208.1
Plastics, artificial resins and articles thereof	305.0	366.9	399.1
Wood pulp, paper, paperboard and articles thereof	238.9	260.5	357.4
Metals and articles thereof	378.4	378.5	506.2
Cast iron and steel	202.9	188.1	256.0
Mechanical machinery and apparatus	389.4	421.3	519.5
Electrical machinery and appliances	383.1	403.2	576.9
Radio and television transmitters and receivers, and parts thereof	169.9	143.1	220.2
Transport equipment	393.0	343.9	350.1
Total (excl. others)	4,870.7	5,431.4	6,424.0

* Excluding imports into *maquila* zones (US $ million): 1,458.2 in 2004; 1,402.9 in 2005 (preliminary); 1,203.8 in 2006 (preliminary).
† Preliminary figures.

Exports f.o.b.*	2004	2005†	2006†
Live animals and animal products, primary	34.5	40.2	39.5
Vegetables, crops and related products, primary	167.7	202.8	237.1
Coffee, including roasted and decaffeinated	123.4	163.6	188.7
Food, beverages and tobacco manufactures	278.5	368.3	534.1
Unrefined sugar	37.3	66.6	71.7
Manufactured cereal products, toasted or inflated	45.0	47.6	54.0
Mineral products	71.3	58.0	98.8
Chemical products	159.2	170.4	195.6
Therapeutic and preventative medicines	70.4	78.9	92.5
Plastics, rubber and articles thereof	86.6	108.0	121.8
Wood pulp, paper, paperboard and articles thereof	128.8	142.5	158.5
Paper and cardboard packaging	47.3	50.8	52.9
Textiles and articles thereof	130.2	116.8	121.7
Metals and articles thereof	166.3	187.8	208.3
Iron and steel products, laminated	59.4	64.9	58.6
Other iron and steel products	47.9	57.3	66.1
Electrical machinery and appliances	72.3	77.3	74.4
Total (incl. others)	1,381.5	1,572.0	1,911.2

* Excluding exports from *maquila* zones (US $ million): 1,923.1 in 2004; 1,814.5 in 2005 (preliminary); 1,602.0 in 2006 (preliminary).
† Preliminary figures.

PRINCIPAL TRADING PARTNERS
(US $ million)

Imports c.i.f.*	2004	2005†	2006†
Brazil	168.4	261.0	301.4
Canada	46.5	53.2	60.8
Colombia	58.2	60.8	83.7
Costa Rica	174.5	180.5	219.2
Ecuador	94.7	115.5	155.6
France	66.9	81.2	47.0
Germany	92.7	117.0	124.6
Guatemala	506.0	554.7	611.2
Honduras	153.6	153.4	173.7
Italy	36.2	38.2	69.4
Japan	134.1	125.2	152.6
Mexico	374.2	530.7	590.0
Netherlands Antilles	62.7	90.4	62.0
Nicaragua	111.5	126.2	150.0
Panama	146.3	164.7	206.9
Spain	104.7	71.2	83.9
Taiwan	47.6	71.3	76.1
USA	2,969.7	2,929.4	3,085.8
Venezuela	244.6	223.5	135.1
Total (incl. others)	4,870.8	5,431.4	6,424.0

* Including imports into *maquila* zones (mostly from USA) (US $ million): 1,458.2 in 2004; 1,402.9 in 2005 (preliminary); 1,203.8 in 2006 (preliminary).
† Preliminary figures.

Exports f.o.b.*	2004	2005†	2006†
Costa Rica	100.4	109.0	121.1
Dominican Republic	25.2	37.8	49.2
Germany	34.2	44.6	59.9
Guatemala	386.8	409.4	455.0
Honduras	205.5	251.7	282.2
Mexico	35.8	40.0	41.6
Nicaragua	128.6	143.4	169.0
Panama	46.1	50.6	63.1
Spain	37.7	62.7	59.3
USA	2,166.2	2,054.5	2,005.8
Total (incl. others)	3,304.6	3,386.5	3,513.3

* Including exports from *maquila* zones (mostly to USA) (US $ million): 1,923.1 in 2004; 1,814.5 in 2005 (preliminary); 1,602.0 in 2006 (preliminary).
† Preliminary figures.

Transport

RAILWAYS
(traffic)

	1999	2000
Number of passengers ('000)	543.3	687.3
Passenger-kilometres (million)	8.4	10.7
Freight ('000 metric tons)	188.6	136.2
Freight ton-kilometres (million)	19.4	13.1

Source: Ferrocarriles Nacionales de El Salvador.

ROAD TRAFFIC
(motor vehicles in use at 31 December)

	1998	1999	2000
Passenger cars	187,440	197,374	207,259
Buses and coaches	34,784	36,204	37,554
Lorries and vans	166,065	177,741	189,812
Motorcycles and mopeds	32,271	35,021	37,139

Source: Servicio de Tránsito Centroamericano (SERTRACEN).

EL SALVADOR

SHIPPING

Merchant Fleet
(registered at 31 December)

	2004	2005	2006
Number of vessels	14	14	14
Total displacement ('000 grt)	5.6	6.6	6.6

Source: Lloyd's Register-Fairplay, *World Fleet Statistics*.

CIVIL AVIATION
(traffic on scheduled services)

	2001	2002	2003
Kilometres flown (million)	26	26	34
Passengers carried ('000)	1,692	1,804	2,182
Passenger-km (million)	2,907	3,300	3,616
Total ton-km (million)	308	309	336

Source: UN, *Statistical Yearbook*.

Tourism

TOURIST ARRIVALS BY COUNTRY OF ORIGIN
(excluding Salvadorean nationals residing abroad)

	2004	2005	2006
Canada	14,804	16,462	20,901
Costa Rica	29,405	34,744	33,056
Germany	4,810	4,624	3,997
Guatemala	326,437	392,235	509,624
Honduras	128,319	203,243	245,784
Mexico	22,973	25,069	23,106
Nicaragua	141,627	166,306	121,483
Panama	9,073	10,320	9,871
Spain	9,271	9,311	8,428
USA	225,910	236,936	225,040
Total (incl. others)	966,416	1,154,386	1,257,952

Receipts from tourism (US $ million): 425 in 2004; 644 in 2005; 862 in 2006.

Sources: Instituto Salvadoreño de Turismo.

Communications Media

	2004	2005	2006
Telephones ('000 main lines in use)	887.8	971.5	1,036.8
Mobile cellular telephones ('000 subscribers)	1,832.6	2,411.8	3,851.6
Internet users ('000)	588	637	n.a.
Broadband subscribers ('000)	29.3	42.3	n.a.

Radio receivers ('000 in use): 2,940 in 1999.
Television receivers ('000 in use): 1,260 in 2000.
Daily newspapers: 5 in 2004 (circulation 250,000).
Non-daily newspapers: 6 in 1996 (circulation 52,000).
Book production: 663 in 1998.
Personal computers ('000 in use): 350 in 2005.

Sources: UNESCO, *Statistical Yearbook*, International Telecommunication Union.

Education

(2004/05, unless otherwise indicated)

		Students ('000)		
	Teachers	Males	Females	Total
Pre-primary	8,866	106.1	106.4	212.5
Primary	35,315	541.9	503.6	1,045.5
Secondary	21,083	262.1	262.1	524.2
Tertiary	8,070	55.4	67.0	122.4

Institutions (2001/02): Pre-primary 4,838; Primary 5,414; Secondary 757; Tertiary 43.

Sources: Ministry of Education and UNESCO Institute for Statistics.

Adult literacy rate (UNESCO estimates): 80.6% (males 82.1%; females 79.2%) in 2004 (Source: UNESCO Institute for Statistics).

Directory

The Constitution

The Constitution of the Republic of El Salvador came into effect on 20 December 1983.

The Constitution provides for a republican, democratic and representative form of government, composed of three Powers—Legislative, Executive, and Judicial—which are to operate independently. Voting is a right and duty of all citizens over 18 years of age. Presidential and congressional elections may not be held simultaneously.

The Constitution binds the country, as part of the Central American Nation, to favour the total or partial reconstruction of the Republic of Central America. Integration in a unitary, federal or confederal form, provided that democratic and republican principles are respected and that basic rights of individuals are fully guaranteed, is subject to popular approval.

LEGISLATIVE ASSEMBLY

Legislative power is vested in a single chamber, the Asamblea Legislativa, whose members are elected every three years and are eligible for re-election. The Asamblea's term of office begins on 1 May. The Asamblea's duties include the choosing of the President and Vice-President of the Republic from the two citizens who shall have gained the largest number of votes for each of these offices, if no candidate obtains an absolute majority in the election. It also selects the members of the Supreme and subsidiary courts; of the Elections Council; and the Accounts Court of the Republic. It determines taxes; ratifies treaties concluded by the Executive with other States and international organizations; sanctions the Budget; regulates the monetary system of the country; determines the conditions under which foreign currencies may circulate; and suspends and reimposes constitutional guarantees. The right to initiate legislation may be exercised by the Asamblea (as well as by the President, through the Cabinet, and by the Supreme Court). The Asamblea may override, with a two-thirds' majority, the President's objections to a Bill which it has sent for presidential approval.

PRESIDENT

The President is elected for five years, the term beginning and expiring on 1 June. The principle of alternation in the presidential office is established in the Constitution, which states the action to be taken should this principle be violated. The Executive is responsible for the preparation of the Budget and its presentation to the Asamblea; the direction of foreign affairs; the organization of the armed and security forces; and the convening of extraordinary sessions of the Asamblea. In the event of the President's death, resignation, removal or other cause, the Vice-President takes office for the rest of the presidential term; and, in case of necessity, the Vice-President may be replaced by one of the two Designates elected by the Asamblea.

JUDICIARY

Judicial power is exercised by the Supreme Court and by other competent tribunals. The Magistrates of the Supreme Court are elected by the Legislature, their number to be determined by law. The Supreme Court alone is competent to decide whether laws, decrees and regulations are constitutional or not.

EL SALVADOR   *Directory*

The Government

HEAD OF STATE

President: ELÍAS ANTONIO (TONY) SACA (assumed office 1 June 2004).
Vice-President: ANA VILMA DE ESCOBAR.

CABINET
(March 2008)

Minister of Finance: WILLIAM JACOBO HÁNDAL HÁNDAL.
Minister of Foreign Affairs: MARISOL ARGUETA DE BARILLAS.
Minister of Internal Affairs: JUAN MIGUEL BOLAÑOS TORRES.
Minister of Public Security and Justice: RENÉ MARIO FIGUEROA FIGUEROA.
Minister of the Economy: YOLANDA MAYORA DE GAVIDIA.
Minister of Education: DARLYN MEZA.
Minister of National Defence: Gen. JORGE ALBERTO MOLINA CONTRERAS.
Minister of Labour and Social Security: JOSÉ ROBERTO ESPINAL ESCOBAR.
Minister of Public Health and Social Welfare: Dr JOSÉ GUILLERMO MAZA BRIZUELA.
Minister of Agriculture and Livestock: MARIO SALAVERRÍA NOLASCO.
Minister of Public Works: JORGE ISIDRO NIETO MENÉNDEZ.
Minister of the Environment and Natural Resources: CARLOS JOSÉ GUERRERO.
Minister of Tourism: JOSÉ RUBÉN ROCHI PARKER.

MINISTRIES

Ministry for the Presidency: Avda Cuba, Calle Darío González 806, Barrio San Jacinto, San Salvador; tel. 2248-9000; fax 2248-9370; e-mail casapres@casapres.gob.sv; internet www.casapres.gob.sv.

Ministry of Agriculture and Livestock: Final 1a, Avda Norte y Avda Manuel Gallardo, Santa Tecla; tel. 2241-1700; fax 2229-9271; e-mail info@mag.gob.sv; internet www.mag.gob.sv.

Ministry of the Economy: Edif. C1–C2, Centro de Gobierno, Alameda Juan Pablo II y Calle Guadalupe, San Salvador; tel. 2231-5600; fax 2221-5446; e-mail webmaster@minec.gob.sv; internet www.minec.gob.sv.

Ministry of Education: Edif. A, Centro de Gobierno, Alameda Juan Pablo II y Calle Guadalupe, San Salvador; tel. 2281-0044; fax 2281-0077; e-mail educacion@mined.gob.sv; internet www.mined.gob.sv.

Ministry of the Environment and Natural Resources: Edif. MARN, Calle y Col. Las Mercedes, Carretera a Santa Tecla, Km 5.5, San Salvador; tel. 2223-0444; fax 2260-3115; e-mail info@marn.gob.sv; internet www.marn.gob.sv.

Ministry of Finance: Blvd Los Héroes 1231, San Salvador; tel. 2244-3000; fax 2244-6408; e-mail webmaster@mh.gob.sv; internet www.mh.gob.sv.

Ministry of Foreign Affairs: Calle El Pedregal, Blvd Cancillería, Ciudad Merliot, Antiguo Cuscatlán; tel. 2231-1000; fax 2243-9656; e-mail webmaster@rree.gob.sv; internet www.rree.gob.sv.

Ministry of Internal Affairs: Centro de Gobierno, Edif. B-1, Alameda Juan Pablo II y Avda Norte 17, San Salvador; tel. 2233-7000; fax 2233-7018; e-mail DT@gobernacion.gob.sv; internet www.gobernacion.gob.sv.

Ministry of Labour and Social Security: Centro de Gobierno, Edifs 2 y 3, Alameda Juan Pablo II y 17 Avda. Norte, San Salvador; tel. 2209-3700; fax 2209-3756; e-mail informacion@mtps.gob.sv; internet www.mtps.gob.sv.

Ministry of National Defence: Alameda Dr Manuel E. Araújo, Km 5, Carretera a Santa Tecla, San Salvador; tel. 2250-0100; e-mail fuerzaarmada@faes.gob.sv; internet www.fuerzaarmada.gob.sv.

Ministry of Public Health and Social Welfare: Calle Arce 827, San Salvador; tel. 2221-0966; fax 2221-0991; e-mail webmaster@mspas.gob.sv; internet www.mspas.gob.sv.

Ministry of Public Security and Justice: San Salvador.

Ministry of Public Works: Plantel la Lechuza, Carretera a Santa Tecla Km 5.5, San Salvador; tel. 2528-3000; fax 2279-3723; e-mail moptvdu@mop.gob.sv; internet www.mop.gob.sv.

Ministry of Tourism: Edif. Carbonel 1, Alameda Dr Manuel Enrique Araujo y Pasaje Carbonel, Col. Roma, San Salvador; tel. 2243-7835; fax 2223-6120; e-mail info@corsatur.gob.sv; internet www.elsalvadorturismo.gob.sv/miniturismo.htm.

President and Legislature

PRESIDENT

Election, 21 March 2004

Candidates	Votes	% of votes
Elías Antonio (Tony) Saca (ARENA)	1,314,436	57.71
Schafik Jorge Handal (FMLN)	812,519	35.68
Héctor Silva Argüello (PDC/CDU)	88,737	3.90
José Rafael Machuca Zelaya (PCN)	61,781	2.71
Total	**2,277,473**	**100.00**

ASAMBLEA LEGISLATIVA

President: RUBÉN ORELLANA MENDOZA.
General Election, 12 March 2006

Party	Votes	% of total	Seats
Alianza Republicana Nacionalista (ARENA)	620,117	39.40	34
Frente Farabundo Martí para la Liberación Nacional (FMLN)	624,635	39.69	32
Partido de Conciliación Nacional (PCN)	172,341	10.95	10
Partido Demócrata Cristiano (PDC)	106,509	6.77	6
Cambio Democrático-Frente Democrático Revolucionario (CD-FDR)	48,661	3.09	2
Other parties	1,516	0.10	—
Total	**1,573,779**	**100.00**	**84**

Election Commission

Tribunal Supremo Electoral (TSE): 15a Calle Poniente 4223, Col. Escalón, San Salvador; tel. 2263-4641; fax 2263-4678; e-mail info@tse.gob.sv; internet www.tse.gob.sv; f. 1992; Pres. WALTER ARAUJO.

Political Organizations

Alianza Republicana Nacionalista (ARENA): Prolongación Calle Arce 2423, entre 45 y 47 Avda Norte, San Salvador; tel. 2260-4400; fax 2260-5918; internet www.arena.com.sv; f. 1981; right-wing; Pres. ELÍAS ANTONIO (TONY) SACA; Exec. Dir MIGUEL TOMÁS LÓPEZ.

Cambio Democrático (CD): Casa 197, Calle Héctor Silva, Col. Médica, San Salvador; tel. 2225-5978; fax 2281-9635; e-mail hdada@asamblea.gob.sv; f. 1987 as Convergencia Democrática (CD); changed name to Centro Democrático Unido (CDU) in 2000; changed name as above in 2005; contested 2006 legislative election in alliance with the Frente Democrático Revolucionario (q.v.); Sec.-Gen. HÉCTOR DADA HIREZI; Dep. Sec. JUAN JOSÉ MARTEL.

Frente Democrático Revolucionario (FDR): Avda Sierra Nevada 926, Col. Miramonte, San Salvador; tel. 2237-8844; fax 2260-1547; e-mail info@fdr.org.sv; internet www.fdr.org.sv; f. 2005; left-wing, reformist; breakaway faction of FMLN; contested 2006 legislative election in alliance with Cambio Democrático (q.v.); Co-ordinator Gen. JULIO HERNÁNDEZ.

Frente Farabundo Martí para la Liberación Nacional (FMLN): 29 Calle Poniente 1316, Col. Layco, San Salvador; tel. 2226-5236; e-mail fmlncp@integra.com.sv; internet www.fmln.org.sv; f. 1980 as the FDR (Frente Democrático Revolucionario—FMLN) as a left-wing opposition front to the PDC-military coalition Government; the FDR was the political wing and the FMLN was the guerrilla front; military operations were co-ordinated by the Dirección Revolucionaria Unida (DRU); achieved legal recognition 1992; comprised various factions, including Communist (Leader SALVADOR SÁNCHEZ CERÉN), Renewalist (Leader OSCAR ORTIZ) and Terceristas (Leader GERSON MARTÍNEZ); Co-ordinator-Gen. MEDARDO GONZÁLEZ.

Partido de Conciliación Nacional (PCN): 15 Avda Norte y 3a Calle Poniente 244, San Salvador; tel. 2221-3752; fax 2281-9272; e-mail czepeda@asamblea.gob.sv; internet www.pcn.com.sv; f. 1961; right-wing; Sec.-Gen. CIRO CRUZ ZEPEDA.

Partido Demócrata Cristiano (PDC): Centro de Gobierno, Alameda Juan Pablo II y 11 Avda Norte bis 507, San Salvador; tel. 2281-5498; fax 7998-1526; e-mail pdcsal@navegante.com.sv; internet www.pdc.org.sv; f. 1960; 150,000 mems; anti-imperialist, advocates

EL SALVADOR

self-determination and Latin American integration; Sec.-Gen. RODOLFO ANTONIO PARKER SOTO.

Partido Nacional Liberal (PNL): 5a Calle Poniente y 3a Avda Norte 226, San Salvador; tel. 2222-6511; Leader OSCAR SILDER CHÁVEZ HERNÁNDEZ.

Diplomatic Representation

EMBASSIES IN EL SALVADOR

Argentina: Calle La Sierra 3-I-B, Col. Escalón, San Salvador; tel. 2263-3638; fax 2263-3687; e-mail esalv@mrecic.gov.ar; Ambassador RUBÉN NÉSTOR PATTO.

Belize: Calle el Bosque Norte y Calle Lomas de Candelaria 1, Bloque P, Col. Jardines de la Cima, 1a Etapa, San Salvador; tel. 2248-1423; fax 2273-6244; e-mail embassyofbelizeinelsal@yahoo.com; Ambassador DARWIN GABOUREL.

Brazil: Blvd de Hipódromo 132, Col. San Benito, San Salvador; tel. 2298-1993; fax 2279-3934; e-mail brasemb@es.com.sv; Ambassador EDUARDO PRISCO PARAISO RAMOS.

Canada: Centro Financiero Gigante, Torre A, Lobby 2, Alameda Roosevelt y 65 Avda Sur, Col. Escalón, San Salvador; tel. 2279-4655; fax 2279-0765; e-mail ssal@dfait-maeci.gc.ca; internet www.dfait-maeci.gc.ca/elsalvador; Ambassador STÉPHANIE ALLARD-GOMEZ.

Chile: Pasaje Bellavista 121, 9a Calle Poniente, Col. Escalón, San Salvador; tel. 2263-4285; fax 2263-4308; e-mail conchile@conchileelsalvador.com.sv; internet www.conchileelsalvador.com.sv; Ambassador MANUEL MATTA ARAGAY.

China (Taiwan): Avda La Capilla 716, Col. San Benito, Apdo 956, San Salvador; tel. 2263-1330; fax 2263-1329; e-mail sinoemb3@intercom.com.sv; Ambassador CARLOS S. C. LIAO.

Colombia: Calle El Mirador 5120, Col. Escalón, San Salvador; tel. 2263-1936; fax 2263-1942; e-mail elsalvador@minrelext.gov.co; Ambassador FABIO TORRIJOS QUINTERO.

Costa Rica: 85 Avda Sur y Calle Cuscatlán 4415, Col. Escalón, San Salvador; tel. 2264-3863; fax 2264-3866; e-mail embajada@embajadacostarica.org.sv; internet www.embajadacostarica.org.sv; Ambassador INGRID HERRMANN ESCRIBANO.

Dominican Republic: Edif. Colinas 1°, Blvd El Hipódromo 253, Zona Rosa, Col. San Benito, San Salvador; tel. 2223-4036; fax 2223-3109; e-mail endosal@saltel.net; Ambassador ROBERTO VICTORIA.

Ecuador: Pasaje Los Pinos 241, entre 77 y 79 Avda Norte, San Salvador; tel. and fax 2263-5258; e-mail ecuador@integra.com.sv; Ambassador Dr GALO LARENAS SERRANO.

France: 1 Calle Poniente 3718, Col. Escalón, Apdo 474, San Salvador; tel. 2279-4016; fax 2298-1536; e-mail ambafrance@es.com.sv; internet www.embafrancia.com.sv; Ambassador FRANCIS ROUDIÈRE.

Germany: 7a Calle Poniente 3972, esq. 77a Avda Norte, Col. Escalón, Apdo 693, San Salvador; tel. 2247-0000; fax 2247-0099; e-mail info@san-salvador.diplo.de; internet www.san-salvador.diplo.de; Ambassador JÜRGEN STEINKRÜGER.

Guatemala: 15 Avda Norte 135, San Salvador; tel. 2271-2225; fax 2221-3019; e-mail embelsalvador@minex.gob.gt; Ambassador Dr JOSÉ LUIS CHEA URRUELA.

Holy See: 87 Avda Norte y 7a Calle Poniente, Col. Escalón, Apdo 01-95, San Salvador (Apostolic Nunciature); tel. 2263-2931; fax 2263-3010; e-mail nunels@telesal.net; Apostolic Nuncio Most Rev. LUIGI PEZZUTO (Titular Archbishop of Torre di Proconsolare).

Honduras: 89 Avda Norte 561, entre 7 y 9 Calle Poniente, Col. Escalón, San Salvador; tel. 2263-2808; fax 2263-2296; Ambassador JOSÉ SALOMÓN FARJADO BUESO.

Israel: Centro Financiero Gigante, Torre B, 11°, Alameda Roosevelt y Avda Sur 63, San Salvador; tel. 2211-3434; fax 2211-3443; e-mail info@sansalvador.mfa.gov.il; internet sansalvador.mfa.gov.il; Ambassador MATTANYA COHEN.

Italy: Calle la Reforma 158, Col. San Benito, Apdo 0199, San Salvador; tel. 2223-4806; fax 2298-3050; e-mail ambasciatore.sansalvador@esteri.it; internet www.ambsansalvador.esteri.it; Ambassador CATERINA BERTOLINI.

Japan: World Trade Center, Torre 1, 6°, 89 Avda Norte y Calle El Mirador, Col. Escalón, Apdo 115, San Salvador; tel. 2224-4740; fax 2298-6685; internet www.sv.emb-japan.go.jp; Ambassador SHISEI KAKU.

Korea, Republic: 5a Calle Poniente 3970, entre 75 y 77 Avda Norte, Col. Escalón, San Salvador; tel. 2263-9145; fax 2263-0783; e-mail embcorea@mofat.go.kr; Ambassador OH DAE-SUNG.

Mexico: Calle Circunvalación y Pasaje 12, Col. San Benito, Apdo 432, San Salvador; tel. 2243-3190; fax 2243-0437; e-mail embamex@intercom.com.sv; internet portal.sre.gob.mx/elsalvador; Ambassador BERENICE RENDÓN TALAVERA.

Nicaragua: Calle El Mirador y 93 Avda Norte 4814, Col. Escalón, San Salvador; tel. 2263-8770; fax 2263-2292; e-mail embanic@integra.com.sv; Ambassador GILDA MARÍA BOLT GONZÁLEZ.

Panama: 203 Edif. Gran Plaza, Blvd El Hipódromo, Col. San Benito, San Salvador; tel. 2245-5410; fax 2245-5205; e-mail embpan@telesat.net; Ambassador LUIS ENRIQUE TORRES HERRERA.

Peru: Avda Masferrer Norte 17P, Cumbres de la Escalafón, Col. Escalón, San Salvador; tel. 2275-5566; fax 2259-8082; e-mail embperu@telesal.net; Ambassador LUIS JUAN CHUQUIHUARA CHIL.

Spain: Calle La Reforma 164 bis, Col. San Benito, San Salvador; tel. 2257-5700; fax 2298-0402; e-mail embespsv@correo.mae.es; internet www.mae.es/embajadas/sansalvador; Ambassador JOSÉ JAVIER GÓMEZ-LLERA Y GARCÍA-NAVA.

USA: Blvd Santa Elena Sur, Antiguo Cuscatlán, San Salvador; tel. 2278-4444; fax 2278-1815; internet www.usinfo.org.sv; Ambassador CHARLES L. GLAZER.

Uruguay: Edif. Gran Plaza 405, Blvd del Hipódromo, Col. San Benito, San Salvador; tel. 2279-1627; fax 2279-1626; Ambassador JULIO CÉSAR BENÍTEZ SÁENZ.

Venezuela: 7a Calle Poniente, entre 75 y 77 Avda Norte, Col. Escalón, San Salvador; tel. 2263-3977; fax 2211-0027; e-mail embajadadevenezuela@telesal.net; Chargé d'affaires a.i. WALDIMIR RUIZ TIRADO.

Judicial System

Supreme Court of Justice

Frente a Plaza José Simeón Cañas, Centro de Gobierno, San Salvador; tel. 2271-8888; fax 2271-3767; internet www.csj.gob.sv.

f. 1824; composed of 15 Magistrates, one of whom is its President; the Court is divided into four chambers: Constitutional Law, Civil Law, Criminal Law and Litigation; Pres. AGUSTÍN GARCÍA CALDERÓN.

Courts of First Instance: 201 courts throughout the country.

Courts of Appeal: 26 chambers composed of two Magistrates.

Courts of Peace: 322 courts throughout the country.

Procurator-General: MARCOS GREGORIO SÁNCHEZ TREJO.

Procurator-General for the Defence of Human Rights: OSCAR HUMBERTO LUNA.

Religion

Roman Catholicism is the dominant religion, but other denominations are also permitted. In 2003 21.2% of the population belonged to Protestant churches. The Baptist Church, Seventh-day Adventists, Jehovah's Witnesses, and the Church of Jesus Christ of Latter-day Saints (Mormons) are represented.

CHRISTIANITY

The Roman Catholic Church

El Salvador comprises one archdiocese and seven dioceses. At 31 December 2005, according to the Vatican, Roman Catholics represented some 75.1% of the total population.

Bishops' Conference

Conferencia Episcopal de El Salvador, 15 Avda Norte 1420, Col. Layco, Apdo 1310, San Salvador; tel. 2225-8997; fax 2226-5330; e-mail cedes.casa@telesal.net; internet www.iglesia.org.sv.

f. 1974; Pres. Most Rev. FERNANDO SÁENZ LACALLE (Archbishop of San Salvador).

Archbishop of San Salvador: Most Rev. FERNANDO SÁENZ LACALLE, Arzobispado, Avda Dr Emilio Alvarez y Avda Dr Max Bloch, Col. Médica, Apdo 2253, San Salvador; tel. 2226-6066; fax 2226-4979; e-mail arzfsl@vip.telesal.net.

The Anglican Communion

El Salvador comprises one of the five dioceses of the Iglesia Anglicana de la Región Central de América. The Iglesia Anglicana has some 5,000 members.

Bishop of El Salvador: Rt Rev. MARTÍN DE JESÚS BARAHONA PASCACIO, 47 Avda Sur, 723 Col. Flor Blanca, Apdo 01-274, San Salvador; tel. 2223-2252; fax 2223-7952; e-mail martinba@gbm.net; internet www.cristosal.org.

The Baptist Church

Baptist Association of El Salvador: Avda Sierra Nevada 922, Col. Miramonte, Apdo 347, San Salvador; tel. 2226-6287; e-mail

EL SALVADOR   Directory

asociacionbautistaabes@hotmail.com; internet www.ublaonline.org/paises/elsalvador.htm; f. 1933; Pres. MANUEL ENRIQUE RIVAS; 4,427 mems.

Other Churches

Sínodo Luterano Salvadoreño (Salvadorean Lutheran Synod): Final 49 Avda Sur, Calle Paralela al Bulevar de los Próceres, San Salvador; tel. 2225-2843; fax 2248-3451; e-mail comunicaciones@sinodoluterano.org.sv; Pres. Bishop MEDARDO E. GÓMEZ SOTO; 12,000 mems.

The Press

DAILY NEWSPAPERS

San Miguel

Diario de Oriente: Avda Gerardo Barrios 406, San Miguel; internet www.elsalvador.com/diarios/oriente; Editor ROBERTO VALENCIA.

San Salvador

Co Latino: 23a Avda Sur 225, Apdo 96, San Salvador; tel. 2271-0671; fax 2271-0971; e-mail info@diariocolatino.com; internet www.diariocolatino.com; f. 1890; evening; Editor FRANCISCO ELÍAS VALENCIA SORIANO; circ. 15,000.

El Diario de Hoy: 11 Calle Oriente 271, Apdo 495, San Salvador; tel. 2271-0100; fax 2271-2040; e-mail redaccion@elsalvador.com; internet www.elsalvador.com; f. 1936; morning; independent; Dir ENRIQUE ALTAMIRANO MADRIZ; circ. 115,000.

Diario Oficial: 4a Calle Poniente y 15a, Avda Sur 829, San Salvador; tel. 2555-7821; fax 2222-4936; e-mail diariooficial@imprentanacional.gob.sv; internet www.imprentanacional.gob.sv/diariooficial.htm; f. 1875; govt publ; Dir LUIS ERNESTO FLORES L.; circ. 1,000.

El Mundo: 15 Calle Poniente y 7a Avda Norte 521, San Salvador; tel. 2234-8000; fax 2222-1490; e-mail mercadeo@elmundo.com.sv; internet www.elmundo.com.sv; f. 1967; morning; Exec. Dir ONNO WUELFERS; circ. 40,215.

La Prensa Gráfica: 3a Calle Poniente 130, San Salvador; tel. 2271-1010; fax 2271-4242; e-mail lpg@gbm.net; internet www.laprensagrafica.com; f. 1915; general information; conservative, independent; Editor RODOLFO DUTRIZ; circ. 97,312 (weekdays), 115,564 (Sundays).

Santa Ana

Diario de Occidente: 1a Avda Sur 3, Santa Ana; tel. 2441-2931; internet www.elsalvador.com/diarios/occidente; f. 1910; circ. 6,000.

PERIODICALS

Cultura: Concultura, Ministerio de Educación, 17 Avda Sur 430, San Salvador; tel. 2222-0665; fax 2271-1071; internet www.concultura.gob.sv; quarterly; educational; Pres. FEDERICO HERNÁNDEZ AGUILAR; Dir JOSÉ HERNÁN ARTEAGA HUEZO.

Ella Magazine: Final blvd Santa Elena, frente a embajada de EUA, Antiguo Cuscatlán, La Libertad; tel. 2241-2000; e-mail ella@laprensa.com.sv; internet www.laprensagrafica.com; publ. by La Prensa Gráfica.

Motor Magazine: Final blvd Santa Elena, frente a embajada de EUA, Antiguo Cuscatlán, La Libertad; tel. 2241-2000; e-mail motor@laprensa.com.sv; internet www.laprensagrafica.com; publ. by La Prensa Gráfica; Editor ROBERTO FLORES PINTO.

Proceso: Universidad Centroamericana, Blvd Los Próceres, Apdo 01-168, San Salvador; tel. 2210-6600; fax 2210-6655; e-mail cidai@cidai.uca.edu.sv; f. 1980; weekly newsletter, published by the Documentation and Information Centre of the Universidad Centroamericana José Simeón Cañas; Dir LUIS ARMANDO GONZÁLEZ.

Revista Judicial: Centro de Gobierno, San Salvador; tel. 2222-4522; organ of the Supreme Court of Justice; Dir Dr MANUEL ARRIETA GALLEGOS.

PRESS ASSOCIATION

Asociación de Periodistas de El Salvador (Press Association of El Salvador): Edif. Casa del Periodista, Paseo Gen. Escalón 4130, San Salvador; tel. 2263-5335; e-mail info@apes.org.sv; internet www.apes.org.sv; Pres. SERAFIN VALENCIA.

Publishers

Centro de Paz (CEPAZ): Col. Libertad, Avda Washington 405, San Salvador; tel. and fax 2226-2117; social history.

Clásicos Roxsil, SA de CV: 4a Avda Sur 2–3, Nueva San Salvador; tel. 2228-1832; fax 2228-1212; e-mail roxanabe@navegante.com.sv; f. 1976; textbooks, literature; Dir ROSA VICTORIA SERRANO DE LÓPEZ; Editorial Dir ROXANA BEATRIZ LOPEZ.

Distribuidora de Textos Escolares (D'TEXE): Edif. C, Paseo y Condominio Miralvalle, San Salvador; tel. 2274-2031; f. 1985; educational; Dir JORGE A. LÓPEZ HIDALGO.

Dirección de Publicaciones e Impresos: Concultura, 17a Avda Sur 430, San Salvador; tel. 2271-1886; fax 2271-1071; e-mail publicaciones.direccion@concultura.gob.sv; internet www.dpi.gob.sv; f. 1953; literary and general; Dir MIGUEL ANGEL RIVERA LARIOS.

Ediciones Thau: Carretera a Santa Tecla, Km 8.5, Antiguo Cuscatlán; tel. 2263-2149; fax 2263-2172; e-mail descobarg@ujmd.edu.sv; Dir DAVID ESCOBAR GALINDO.

Editorial Delgado: Universidad 'Dr José Matías Delgado', Km 8.5, Carretera Panamericana, Antiguo Cuscatlán; tel. 2278-1011; e-mail jalas@ujmd.edu.sv; internet www.ujmd.edu.sv; f. 1984; Dir Dr DAVID ESCOBAR GALINDO.

UCA Editores: Apdo 01-575, San Salvador; tel. 2273-4400; fax 2273-3556; e-mail distpubli@ued.uca.edu.sv; internet www.uca.edu.sv; f. 1975; social science, religion, economy, literature and textbooks; Dir RODOLFO CARDENAL.

PUBLISHERS' ASSOCIATION

Cámara Salvadoreña del Libro: Col. Flor Blanca, 47 Avda Norte y 1a Calle Poniente, Apdo 3384, San Salvador; tel. 2275-0231; fax 2261-2231; e-mail camsalibro@integra.com.sv; f. 1974; Pres. ANA MOLINA DE FAUVET; Exec. Dir AMÉRICA DE DOMÍNGUEZ.

Broadcasting and Communications

TELECOMMUNICATIONS

Regulatory Authority

Superintendencia General de Electricidad y Telecomunicaciones (SIGET): 16a Calle Poniente y 37 Avda Sur 2001, Col. Flor Blanca, San Salvador; tel. 2257-4438; fax 2257-4498; e-mail fernado.arguello@siget.gob.sv; internet www.siget.gob.sv; f. 1996; Supt FERNANDO ARGÜELLO TÉLLEZ.

Major Service Providers

Digicel: Local 27, 2°, Centro Comercial Plazamundo, San Salvador; tel. 2277-5366; fax 2277-8966; internet www.digicel.com.sv; provider of mobile telecommunications; owned by Digicel (USA).

Telecom El Salvador: Edif. Palic, 40°, Alameda Manuel E. Araujo y Calle Nueva 1, San Salvador; tel. 7800-8155; internet www.telecom.com.sv; terrestrial telecommunications network, fmrly part of Administración Nacional de Telecomunicaciones (Antel), which was divested in 1998; changed name from CTE Antel Telecom in 1999; acquired by América Móvil, SA de CV (Mexico) in 2003; Chair. PATRICK SLIM DOMIT.

Telefónica El Salvador: San Salvador; e-mail telefonica.empresas@telefonicamail.com.sv; internet www.telefonica.com.sv; manages sale of telecommunications frequencies; fmrly Internacional de Telecomunicaciones (Intel), which was divested in 1998; controlling interest owned by Telefónica, SA (Spain); Pres. CÉSAR ALIERTA.

    Telefónica Movistar: Torre Telefónica (Torre B de Centro Financiero Gigante), Alameda Roosevelt y 63 Avda Sur, Col. Escalón, San Salvador; tel. 2257-4000; internet www.telefonica.com.sv/movistar; provider of mobile telecommunications; 92% owned by Telefónica Móviles, SA (Spain), part of Telefónica, SA; Pres. ANTONIO VIANA-BAPTISTA; CEO JUAN ANTONIO ABELLÁN RÍOS.

Telemóvil: Centro Financiero, Gigante Torre D, 9°, Avda Roosevelt, San Salvador; tel. 2246-9977; fax 2246-9999; e-mail servicioalcliente@tigo.com.sv; internet www.telemovil.com; provider of mobile telecommunications and internet services; subsidiary of Millicom International Cellular (Luxembourg).

RADIO

Asociación Salvadoreña de Radiodifusores (ASDER): Bloco 6, No 33, Residencial San Luis, Avda Izalco, San Salvador; tel. 2222-0872; fax 2274-6870; e-mail asder@ejje.com; internet www.asder.com.sv; f. 1965; Pres. Dr JOSÉ LUIS SACA MELÉNDEZ.

Radio Nacional de El Salvador: Dirección General de Medios, Calle Monserrat, Plantel Ex-IVU, San Salvador; e-mail radio.elsalvador@gobernacion.gob.sv; internet www.radioelsalvador.com.sv; f. 1926; non-commercial cultural station; Dir-Gen. JAIME VILANOVA.

There are 64 commercial radio stations.

EL SALVADOR

TELEVISION

Canal 2, SA: Carretera a Nueva San Salvador, Apdo 720, San Salvador; tel. 2223-6744; e-mail canal2@tcs246.com; internet www.teledos.com; commercial; Pres. BORIS ESERSKI; Gen. Man. SALVADOR I. GADALA MARÍA.

Canal 4, SA: Carretera a Nueva San Salvador, Apdo 720, San Salvador; tel. 2224-4555; owned by Telecorporación Salvadoreña (TCS); commercial; Pres. BORIS ESERSKI; Man. RONALD CALVO.

Canal 6, SA: Km 6, Carretera Panamericana a Santa Tecla, San Salvador; tel. 2209-5068; fax 2209-2033; e-mail director@elnoticiero.com.sv; internet www.elnoticiero.com.sv; f. 1972; owned by Telecorporación Salvadoreña (TCS); commercial; Exec. Dir JUAN CARLOS ESERSKI; Man. Dr PEDRO LEONEL MORENO MONGE.

Canal 8 (Agape TV): 1511 Calle Gerardo Barrios, Col. Cucumacuyán, San Salvador; tel. 2281-2828; fax 2271-3414; e-mail info@agapetv8.com; internet www.agapetv8.com; Catholic, family channel; Pres. FLAVIÁN MUCCI.

Canal 12: Urb. Santa Elena 12, Antiguo Cuscatlán, San Salvador; tel. 2278-0622; fax 2278-0722; internet www.canal12.com.sv; f. 1984; Dir ALEJANDRO GONZÁLEZ.

Canal 15: 4a Avda Sur y 5a Calle Oriente 301, San Miguel; tel. and fax 2661-3298; f. 1994; Pres. OSCAR ANTONIO SAFIE; Gen. Man. JOAQUÍN APARICIO.

Canal 19: Final Calle Los Abetos 1, Col. San Francisco, San Salvador; e-mail serviciosmegavision@salnet.net; internet www.canal19tv.com.sv; owned by Grupo Megavisión; children's channel; Pres. OSCAR ANTONIO SAFIE; Gen. Man. MARIO CAÑAS.

Canal 21: 1a Calle Poniente entre 85 y 87 Avda Norte, Apdo 2789, San Salvador; tel. 2283-2121; fax 2283-2132; e-mail serviciosmegavision@salnet.net; internet www.canal21tv.com.sv; f. 1993; owned by Grupo Megavisión; Pres. OSCAR ANTONIO SAFIE; Dir HUGO ESCOBAR.

Fundación Canal 25: Final Calle Libertad 100, Ciudad Merliot, Nueva San Salvador; tel. 2248-2525; fax 2278-8526; e-mail jmira@enlace.org; internet www.enlace.org; f. 1997; commercial; Gen. Man. JORGE MIRA.

Tecnovisión Canal 33: Calle Arce 1120, San Salvador; tel. 2275-8888; e-mail jgomez@utec.edu.sv; internet www.utec.edu.sv; owned by the Universidad Tecnológica de El Salvador; Pres. MAURICIO LOUCEL.

Finance

(cap. = capital; p.u. = paid up; res = reserves; dep. = deposits; m. = million; brs = branches; amounts in colones unless otherwise stated)

BANKING

Supervisory Bodies

Superintendencia del Sistema Financiero: 7a Avda Norte 240, Apdo 2942, San Salvador; tel. 2281-2444; fax 2281-1621; internet www.ssf.gob.sv; Pres. LUIS ARMANDO MONTENEGRO.

Superintendencia de Valores: Antiguo Edif. BCR, 1a Calle Poniente y 7a Avda Norte, San Salvador; tel. 2281-8900; fax 2221-3404; e-mail superval@superval.gob.sv; internet www.superval.gob.sv; Pres. and Supt ROGELIO JUAN TOBAR GARCÍA.

Central Bank

Banco Central de Reserva de El Salvador: Alameda Juan Pablo II y 17 Avda Norte, Apdo 01-106, San Salvador; tel. 2281-8000; fax 2281-8011; e-mail comunicaciones@bcr.gob.sv; internet www.bcr.gob.sv; f. 1934; nationalized Dec. 1961; entered monetary integration process 1 Jan. 2001; cap. US $115.0m., res $76.2m., dep. $1,433.2m. (Dec. 2006); Pres. LUZ MARÍA SERPAS DE PORTILLO; Vice-Pres. MARTA EVELYN DE RIVERA.

Commercial and Mortgage Banks

Banco Agrícola: Blvd Constitución 100, San Salvador; tel. 2267-5787; fax 2267-5775; e-mail info@bancoagricola.com; internet www.bancoagricola.com; f. 1955; merged with Banco Desarrollo in July 2000; acquired Banco Capital in Nov. 2001; cap. US $200.0m., res $155.8m., dep. $2,707.8m. (Dec. 2006); Pres. RODOLFO ROBERTO SCHILDKNECHT; 8 brs.

Banco Cuscatlán de El Salvador, SA: Edif. Pirámide Cuscatlán, Km 10, Carretera a Santa Tecla, Apdo 626, San Salvador; tel. 2212-2000; fax 2228-5700; e-mail info@bancocuscatlan.com; internet www.bancocuscatlan.com; f. 1972; privately owned; cap. US $135.0m., res $123.8m., dep. $1,966.5m. (Dec. 2006); Pres. JOSÉ MAURICIO SAMAYOA RIVAS; 31 brs.

Directory

Banco Hipotecario de El Salvador: Pasaje Senda Florida Sur, Col. Escalón, Apdo 999, San Salvador; tel. 2250-7101; fax 2250-7039; internet www.bancohipotecario.com.sv; f. 1935; cap. US $14.5m., res $14.2m., dep. $238.1m. (Dec. 2005); Pres. JOSÉ ROBERTO NAVARRO ESCOBAR; 12 brs.

Banco Promérica: 71 Avda Sur y Paseo Gen. Escalón 3669, Col. Escalón, San Salvador; tel. 2243-3344; fax 2245-2979; e-mail baprosal@promerica.com.sv; internet www.promerica.com.sv; f. 1996; privately owned; Chair. RAMIRO ORTIZ GURDÍAN; Exec. Pres. EDUARDO A. QUEVEDO MORENO.

Banco Uno, SA: Paseo Gen. Escalón y 69 Avda Sur 3563, Col. Escalón, San Salvador; tel. 2245-0055; fax 2245-0080; internet www.bancouno.com.sv; cap. US $11.4m., res $9.9m., dep. $150.6m. (Dec. 2002); Pres. ALBINO ROMÁN.

Financiera Calpiá: Paseo Gen. Escalón 5438, San Salvador; tel. 2264-1194; fax 2264-1647; e-mail financiera@calpia.com.sv; Pres. PEDRO DALMAU GORRITA.

HSBC El Salvador: Edif. Centro Financiero, Avda Manuel E. Araujo y Avda Olímpica 3550, Apdo 0673, San Salvador; tel. 2298-4444; fax 2298-0102; e-mail info@bancosal.com; internet www.bancosal.com; f. 1885 as Banco Salvadoreño, SA; adopted current name 2007; cap. US $90m., res $113.1m., dep. $1,559.8m. (Dec. 2006); Pres. and Chair. JOSÉ MAURICIO FELIPE SAMAYOA RIVAS; Exec. Dir GERARDO JOSÉ SIMÁN SIRI; 74 brs.

Public Institutions

Banco de Fomento Agropecuario: Km 10.5, Carretera al Puerto de la Libertad, Nueva San Salvador; tel. 2228-5188; fax 2228-5199; f. 1973; state-owned; cap. 14.9m., res 4.2m., dep. 137.2m. (Dec. 2006); Pres. JOSÉ GUILLERMO FUNES ARAUJO; Gen. Man. ROBERTO DE JESÚS SOLORZANO CASTRO; 27 brs.

Banco Multisectorial de Inversiones: Edif. Century Plaza, Alameda Manuel Enrique Araujo, San Salvador; tel. 2267-0000; fax 2267-0011; e-mail bmigada@bmi.gob.sv; internet www.bmi.gob.sv; f. 1994; Pres. Dr NICOLA ANGELUCCI SILVA.

Federación de Cajas de Crédito (FEDECREDITO): 25 Avda Norte y 23 Calle Poniente, San Salvador; tel. 2209-9696; fax 2226-7161; internet www.fedecredito.com.sv; f. 1943; Pres. MACARIO ARMANDO ROSALES ROSA.

Fondo Social Para la Vivienda: Calle Rubén Darío, entre 15 y 17 Avda Sur, San Salvador; tel. 2271-2774; e-mail comunicaciones@fsv.gob.sv; internet www.fsv.gob.sv; Pres. Lic. ENRIQUE OÑATE.

Banking Association

Asociación Bancaria Salvadoreña (ABANSA): Alameda Roosevelt 2511, entre 47 y 49 Avda Sur, San Salvador; tel. 2298-6938; fax 2223-1079; internet www.abansa.org.sv; Pres. JOSÉ GUSTAVO BELISMELIS VIDES.

STOCK EXCHANGE

Mercado de Valores de El Salvador, SA de CV (Bolsa de Valores): Urb. Jardines de la Hacienda, Blvd Merliot y Avda Las Carretas, Antiguo Cuscatlán, La Libertad, San Salvador; tel. 2212-6400; fax 2278-4377; e-mail info@bves.com.sv; internet www.bves.com.sv; f. 1992; Pres. ROLANDO DUARTE SCHLAGETER.

INSURANCE

AIG Unión y Desarrollo, SA: Calle Loma Linda 265, Col. San Benito, Apdo 92, San Salvador; tel. 2250-3200; fax 2250-3201; e-mail aig.elsalvador@aig.com; internet www.aigelsalvador.com; f. 1998; following merger of Unión y Desarrollo, SA and AIG; Exec. Dir RAMÓN ÁVILA QUEHL; Gen. Man. PEDRO ARTANA.

Aseguradora Agrícola Comercial, SA: Alameda Roosevelt 3104, Apdo 1855, San Salvador; tel. 2260-3344; fax 2260-5592; e-mail informacion@acsasal.com.sv; internet www.acsasal.com.sv; f. 1973; Pres. LUIS ALFREDO ESCALANTE SOL; Gen. Man. LUIS ALFONSO FIGUEROA.

Aseguradora Popular, SA: Paseo Gen. Escalón 5338, Col. Escalón, San Salvador; tel. 2263-0700; fax 2263-1246; e-mail aseposapresi@telesal.net; f. 1975; Pres. Dr CARLOS ARMANDO LAHÚD; Gen. Man. HERIBERTO PÉREZ AGUIRRE.

Aseguradora Suiza Salvadoreña, SA (ASESUISA): Alameda Dr Manuel Enrique Araujo, Plaza Suiza, Apdo 1490, San Salvador; tel. 2209-5000; fax 2209-5001; e-mail info@asesuisa.com; internet www.asesuisa.com; f. 1969; acquired in 2001 by Inversiones Financieras Banco Agrícola (Panama); Pres. MAURICIO MEYER COHEN; Gen. Man. RICARDO COHEN.

La Central de Seguros y Fianzas, SA: Avda Olímpica 3333, Apdo 01-255, San Salvador; tel. 2279-3544; fax 2223-7647; e-mail hroque@lacentral.com.sv; internet www.lacentral.com.sv; f. 1983; Pres. EDUARDO ENRIQUE CHACÓN BORJA; Man. HECTOR ROQUE RUBALLO.

EL SALVADOR

Compañía General de Seguros, SA: Calle Loma Linda 223, Col. San Benito, Apdo 1004, San Salvador; tel. 2279-3777; fax 2223-0719; e-mail cogeseg@cgs.com.sv; internet www.cgs.com.sv; f. 1955; Pres. José Gustavo Belismelis Vides; Gen. Man. Dr Pedro Geoffroy.

Internacional de Seguros, SA (Interseguros): Centro Financiero Banco Salvadoreño, 5°, Avda Olímpica 3550, Col. Escalón, San Salvador; tel. 2238-0202; fax 2238-5727; e-mail interseguros@interseguros.com.sv; internet www.interseguros.com.sv; f. 1958; merged with Seguros Universales in 2004; Pres. Dr Enrique García Prieto; Gen. Man. Alejandro Cabrera Rivas.

Mapfre La Centro Americana, SA: Alameda Roosevelt 3107, Apdo 527, San Salvador; tel. 2257-6666; fax 2223-2687; e-mail lacentro@lacentro.com; internet www.lacentro.com; f. 1915; Pres. Antonio Penedo Casmartiño; Gen. Man. Gilmar Navarrete.

Seguros e Inversiones, SA (SISA): 10.5 km Carretera Panamericana, Santa Tecla; tel. 2229-8888; fax 2229-8187; internet www.sisa.com.sv; f. 1962; Pres. Alfredo Félix Cristiani Burkard; Exec. Dir José Eduardo Montenegro.

Association

Asociación Salvadoreña de Empresas de Seguros (ASES): Condominio Plaza Suiza L-A17, San Benito, San Salvador; tel. 2298-0209; fax 2298-0212; e-mail asesgeneral@ases.com.sv; internet www.ases.com.sv; Pres. Eduardo Montenegro Palomo; Exec. Dir Raúl Betancourt Menéndez.

Trade and Industry

GOVERNMENT AGENCIES AND DEVELOPMENT ORGANIZATIONS

Consejo Nacional de Ciencia y Tecnología (CONACYT): Col. Médica, Avda Dr Emilio Alvarez, Pasaje Dr Guillermo Rodríguez Pacas 51, San Salvador; tel. 2226-2800; fax 2225-6255; e-mail ulisest@conacyt.gob.sv; internet www.conacyt.gob.sv; f. 1992; formulation and guidance of national policy on science and technology; Exec. Dir Carlos Roberto Ochoa Córdoba.

Corporación de Exportadores de El Salvador (COEXPORT): Edif. 'A', No 23, Condominios del Mediterráneo, Col. Jardines de Guadalupe, San Salvador; tel. 2243-1328; fax 2243-3159; e-mail info@coexport.com; internet www.coexport.com; f. 1973 to promote Salvadorean exports; Pres. Vilma de Calderón; Exec. Dir Silvia M. Cuéllar Sicilia.

Corporación Salvadoreña de Inversiones (CORSAIN): 1a Calle Poniente, entre 43 y 45 Avda Norte, San Salvador; tel. 2224-4242; fax 2224-6877; e-mail audisjus@cortedecuentas.gob.sv; Pres. Gino Rolando Bettaglio Rivas.

Fondo Social para la Vivienda (FSV): Calle Rubén Darío y 17 Avda Sur 455, San Salvador; tel. 2271-1662; fax 2271-2910; e-mail comunicaciones@fsv.gob.sv; internet www.fsv.gob.sv; f. 1973; provides loans to workers for house purchases; Pres. Enrique Oñate Muyshondt; Gen. Man. Francisco Antonio Guevara.

Instituto Salvadoreño de Transformación Agraria (ISTA): Final Col. Las Mercedes, Km 5.5, Carretera a Santa Tecla, San Salvador; tel. 2224-6000; fax 2224-0259; e-mail informacion@ista.gob.sv; internet www.ista.gob.sv; f. 1976 to promote rural devt; empowered to buy inefficiently cultivated land; Pres. Miguel Tomás López.

CHAMBER OF COMMERCE

Cámara de Comercio e Industria de El Salvador: 9a Avda Norte y 5a Calle Poniente, Apdo 1640, San Salvador; tel. 2244-2000; fax 2271-4461; e-mail camara@camarasal.com; internet www.camarasal.com; f. 1915; 2,000 mems; Pres. Elena María de Alfaro; Exec. Dir Max Orellano Solís; brs in San Miguel, Santa Ana and Sonsonate.

INDUSTRIAL AND TRADE ASSOCIATIONS

Asociación Azúcarera de El Salvador: 103 Avda Norte y Calle Arturo Ambrogi 145, Col. Escalón, San Salvador; tel. 2263-0378; fax 2263-0361; e-mail asosugar@sal.gbm.net; internet www.asociacionazucarera.com; national sugar asscn, fmrly Instituto Nacional del Azúcar; Pres. Dr Francisco Armando; Vice-Pres. Tomás Regalado Dueñas.

Asociación Cafetalera de El Salvador (ACES): 67 Avda Norte 116, Col. Escalón, San Salvador; tel. 2223-3024; fax 2223-7471; e-mail ascafes@telesal.net; f. 1930; coffee growers' asscn; Pres. José Roberto Inclán Robredo; Exec. Dir Amir Salvador Alabí.

Asociación de Ganaderos de El Salvador: 1a Avda Norte 1332, San Salvador; tel. 2225-7208; f. 1932; livestock breeders' asscn; Pres. Javier Reyes.

Asociación Salvadoreña de Beneficiadores y Exportadores de Café (ABECAFE): 87a Avda Norte 720, Col. Escalón, San Salvador; tel. 2263-2834; fax 2263-2833; e-mail abecafe@telesal.net; coffee producers' and exporters' asscn; Pres. Carlos Borgonovo.

Asociación Salvadoreña de Industriales: Calles Roma y Liverpool, Col. Roma, Apdo 48, San Salvador; tel. 2279-2488; fax 2279-1880; e-mail asi@asi.com.sv; internet www.asi.com.sv; f. 1958; 400 mems; manufacturers' asscn; Pres. Napoleón Guerrero Berrios; Exec. Dir Lic. Jorge Arriaza.

Cámara Agropecuaria y Agroindustrial de El Salvador (CAMAGRO): Calle El Lirio 19, Col. Maquilishuat, San Salvador; tel. 2264-4622; fax 2236-9448; e-mail contactenos@camagro.com; internet www.camagro.com; Dir Ricardo Esmahan d'Aubuisson.

Consejo Salvadoreño del Café (CSC) (Salvadorean Coffee Council): 75 Avda Norte y 7a Calle Poniente 3876, Col. Escalón, San Salvador; tel. 2267-6600; fax 2263-3998; e-mail csc@consejocafe.org.sv; internet www.salvadorancoffees.com; f. 1989 as successor to the Instituto Nacional del Café; formulates policy and oversees the coffee industry; Exec. Dir Ricardo Espitia.

Cooperativa Algodonera Salvadoreña, Ltda (COPAL): 49 Avda Norte 161, San Salvador; tel. 2298-9330; fax 2298-9331; f. 1940; 185 mems; cotton growers' asscn; Pres. Luiz Méndez Novoa.

Unión de Cooperativas de Cafetaleras de RL (UCAFES): Avda Río Lempa, Calle Adriático 44, Jardines de Guadalupe, San Salvador; tel. 2243-2238; fax 2298-1504; union of coffee-growing co-operatives; Pres. Federico Barilla.

EMPLOYERS' ORGANIZATION

There are several business associations, the most important of which is the Asociación Nacional de Empresa Privada.

Asociación Nacional de Empresa Privada (ANEP) (National Private Enterprise Association): 1a Calle Poniente y 71a Avda Norte 204, Col. Escalón, Apdo 1204, San Salvador; tel. 2224-1236; fax 2223-8932; e-mail communicaciones.anep@telesal.net; internet www.anep.org.sv; national private enterprise asscn; Pres. Federico Colorado; Exec. Dir Raúl Melara Morán.

UTILITIES

Electricity

Comisión Ejecutiva Hidroeléctrica del Río Lempa (CEL): 9a Calle Poniente 950, San Salvador; tel. 2211-6000; fax 2222-9359; e-mail naguilar@cel.gob.sv; internet www.cel.gob.sv; f. 1948; hydro-electric electricity generation; Pres. Nicolás Antonio Salume Babún.

Superintendencia General de Electricidad y Telecomunicaciones (SIGET): Col. Flor Blanca, 16a Calle Poniente 2001, San Salvador; tel. 2257-4438; fax 2257-4498; e-mail fernando.arguello@siget.gob.sv; internet www.siget.gob.sv; f. 1996; Supt Fernando Argüello Téllez.

Electricity Companies

In order to increase competition, the electricity-trading market was opened up in October 2000.

AES Aurora: e-mail consultas@aes.com; internet www.aeselsalvador.com; Pres. Carlos Alfredo Marozzi; operates four distribution cos in El Salvador:

CLESA: 23 Avda Sur y 5a Calle Oriente, Barrio San Rafael, Santa Ana; tel. 2447-6000; fax 2447-6155; f. 1982.

Compañía de Alumbrado Electric (CAESS): Calle El Bambú, Col. San Antonio, Ayutuxtepeque, San Salvador; tel. 2207-2011; fax 2232-5012.

Distribuidora Eléctrica de Usulután (DEUSEM): Usulután; f. 1957.

EEO: Final 8a, Calle Poniente, Calle a Ciudad Pacífico, Plantel Jalacatal, San Miguel.

Distribuidora de Electricidad del Sur (DELSUR): 117 Avda Las Acacias, Col. San Benito, San Salvador; tel. 2233-5400; fax 2243-8662; e-mail comunicaciones@delsur.com.sv; internet www.delsur.com.sv; Pres. Iván Díaz; Gen. Man. Alexis Butto.

La Geo: San Salvador; tel. 2211-6700; fax 2211-6746; e-mail comunicaciones@lageo.com.sv; internet www.lageo.com.sv; f. 1999; jt venture between state and ENEL Latin America; operates Ahuachapan and Berlin geothermal fields; Gen. Man. José Antonio Rodríguez.

Water

Administración Nacional de Acueductos y Alcantarillados (ANDA): Edif. ANDA, Final Avda Don Bosco, Col. Libertad, San Salvador; tel. 2225-3534; fax 2225-3152; internet www.anda.gob.sv;

EL SALVADOR

f. 1961; maintenance of water supply and sewerage systems; Pres. CÉSAR DANIEL FUNES; Gen. Man. FRINEÉ CASTILLO DE ZALDAÑA.

TRADE UNIONS

Central de Trabajadores Democráticos (CTD) (Democratic Workers' Confederation): 1a Avda Norte y 19 Calle Poniente 12, San Salvador; tel. and fax 2235-8043; e-mail comuctd@netcomsa.com; Sec.-Gen. AMADEO GARCÍA ESPINOZA.

Central de Trabajadores Salvadoreños (CTS) (Salvadorean Workers' Confederation): 224A Pasaje Espínola, Col. Manzano, San Jacinto, San Salvador; tel. 2270-5246; fax 2270-1703; f. 1966; Christian Democratic; Pres. FÉLIX BLANCO; 35,000 mems.

Confederación General de Sindicatos (CGS) (General Confederation of Unions): Edif. Kury, 3a Calle Oriente 226, San Salvador; tel. and fax 2222-3527; f. 1958; admitted to ITUC/ORIT; Sec.-Gen. JOSÉ ISRAEL HUIZA CISNEROS; 27,000 mems.

Confederación General del Trabajo (CGT) (General Confederation of Workers): 141 Avda B, Calle 2, Col. El Roble, San Salvador; tel. and fax 2222-6109; f. 1983; 20 affiliated unions; Sec.-Gen. JOSÉ RENÉ PÉREZ; 85,000 mems.

Confederación Sindical de Trabajadores de El Salvador (CSTS) (Salvadorean Workers' Union Federation): Blvd Universitario 2226, Col. San José, San Salvador; e-mail csts-es@navegante.com.sv; conglomerate of independent left-wing trade unions; Sec.-Gen. NEFTALÍ COLOCHO.

Confederación Unitaria de Trabajadores Salvadoreños (CUTS) (United Salvadorean Workers' Federation): 141 Avda A, Col. San José, San Salvador; tel. and fax 2225-3756; e-mail proyectocuts@salnet.net; left-wing.

Federación Nacional Sindical de Trabajadores Salvadoreños (FENASTRAS) (Salvadorean Workers' National Union Federation): 10a Avda Norte 120, San Salvador; f. 1975; left-wing; 35,000 mems in 16 affiliates; Sec.-Gen. JUAN JOSÉ HUEZO.

Unidad Nacional de Trabajadores Salvadoreños (UNTS) (National Unity of Salvadorean Workers): Centro de Gobierno El Salvador, Calle 27 Poniente 432, Col. Layco, Apdo 2479, San Salvador; tel. 2225-7811; fax 2225-0558; f. 1986; largest trade union conglomerate; Leader MARCO TULIO LIMA.

Unión Comunal Salvadoreña (UCS) (Salvadorean Communal Union): 2a Calle Oriente y Avda Melvyn Jones, Santa Tecla, San Salvador; tel. 2228-2023; fax 2229-1111; peasants' asscn; 100,000 mems; Gen. Sec. GUILLERMO BLANCO.

Some unions, such as those of the taxi drivers and bus owners, are affiliated to the Federación Nacional de Empresas Pequeñas Salvadoreñas—Fenapes, the association of small businesses.

Transport

Comisión Ejecutiva Portuaria Autónoma (CEPA): Edif. Torre Roble, Blvd de Los Héroes, Apdo 2667, San Salvador; tel. 2224-1133; fax 2224-0907; internet www.cepa.gob.sv; f. 1952; operates and administers the ports of Acajutla (on Pacific coast) and Cutuco (on Gulf of Fonseca) and the El Salvador International Airport, as well as Ferrocarriles Nacionales de El Salvador; Pres. ALBINO ROMÁN ORTIZ.

RAILWAYS

In 2005 there were 554.8 km of railway track in the country. The main track linked San Salvador with the ports of Acajutla and Cutuco (also known as La Unión) and with Santa Ana. The Salvadorean section of the International Railways of Central America ran from Anguiatú on the El Salvador–Guatemala border to the Pacific ports of Acajutla and Cutuco and connected San Salvador with Guatemala City and the Guatemalan Atlantic ports of Puerto Barrios and Santo Tomás de Castilla. Operation of the railway network was suspended in 2005, owing to the high cost of maintenance.

Ferrocarriles Nacionales de El Salvador (FENADESAL): Avda Peralta 903, Apdo 2292, San Salvador; tel. 2271-5632; fax 2271-5650; internet www.fenadesal.gob.sv; 555 km of track; in 1975 Ferrocarril de El Salvador and the Salvadorean section of International Railways of Central America were merged and are administered by the Railroad Division of CEPA (q.v.); Gen. Man. SALVADOR SANABRIA.

ROADS

The country's highway system is well integrated with its railway services. There were some 10,886 km of roads in 2000, including the Pan-American Highway (306 km). Following the earthquakes of early 2001, the Inter-American Development Bank pledged some US $106.0m. to the transport sector for the restoration and reconstruction of roads and bridges.

Fondo de Conservación Vial (FOVIAL): Carretera a La Libertad km 10.5, Antiguo Cuscatlán, San Salvador; tel. 2228-8425; internet www.fovial.com; f. 2000; responsible for maintaining the road network; Pres. JORGE ISIDRO NIETO MENÉNDEZ (Minister of Public Works); Exec. Dir MARTÍN MORALES.

SHIPPING

The port of Acajutla is administered by CEPA (see above). Services are also provided by foreign lines. The port of Cutuco (La Unión) has been inactive since 1996; however, an expanded port was under construction in 2007.

CIVIL AVIATION

The El Salvador International Airport is located 40 km (25 miles) from San Salvador in Comalapa. An expansion of the airport was completed in 1998, with a second expansion phase of hotel and commercial space to be completed early in the 21st century. The former international airport at Ilopango is used for military and private civilian aircraft; there are an additional 88 private airports, four with permanent-surface runways.

Continental Airlines: Edif. Torre Roble, 9°, Blvd de los Héroes, San Salvador; tel. 2260-3263; fax 2260-3331; e-mail amolina@coair.com; internet www.continental.com.

Delta Airlines: World Trade Center, 3°, Local 304, 89 Avda Norte, Calle El Mirador, Col. Escalón, San Salvador; tel. 2264-2483; fax 2264-5300; e-mail cristina.minervini@delta.com; internet www.delta.com.

TACA International Airlines: Local 21, Centro Comercial Galerías, Paseo Gen. Escalón y 71 Avda Norte, San Salvador; tel. 2339-9155; fax 2223-3757; internet www.taca.com; f. 1939; passenger and cargo services to Central America and the USA; Pres. FEDERICO BLOCH; Gen. Man. BEN BALDANZA.

United Airlines: Local 14, Centro Comercial Galerías, Paseo Gen. Escalón, San Salvador; tel. 2279-3900; fax 2298-5539; e-mail patricia.mejia@ual.com; internet www.unitedelsalvador.com; f. 1910; Pres. and CEO GLENN F. TILTON.

Tourism

El Salvador was one of the centres of the ancient Mayan civilization, and the ruined temples and cities are of great interest. The volcanoes and lakes of the uplands provide magnificent scenery, while there are fine beaches along the Pacific coast. The civil war, from 1979 to 1992, severely affected the tourism industry. Following the earthquakes of early 2001, the Inter-American Development Bank pledged some US $3.6m. to the tourism and historical and cultural heritage sectors, for the reconstruction and renovation of recreational centres and the development of culture and heritage. The sector recovered thereafter and in 2006 tourism receipts stood at $862m. In the same year the number of tourist arrivals was 1,257,952, while the number of rooms available in 2005 stood at 5,757.

Asociación Salvadoreña de Hoteles: 123 Pasaje 1, Avda Olímpica, Col. Escalón, San Salvador; tel. 2298-3629; fax 2298-3628; e-mail asocdehoteles@navegante.com.sv; f. 1996; Pres. CARLOS ALBERTO DELGADO Z.; Sec. BELLYNI SIGUENZA.

Buró de Convenciones de El Salvador: Edif. Olimpic Plaza, 73 Avda Sur 28, 2°, San Salvador; tel. 2224-0819; fax 2223-4912; internet www.convencioneselsalvador.com.sv; f. 1973; assists in organization of national and international events; Pres. ALFREDO MORALES; Exec. Dir ADRIANA DE GALE.

Cámara Salvadoreña de Turismo (CASATUR): 123 Pasaje 1, Avda Olímpica, Col. Escalón, San Salvador; tel. 2279-2156; fax 2223-9775; e-mail info@casatur.com; internet www.casatur.com; f. 1978; non-profit org. concerned with promotion of tourism in El Salvador; Pres. CARLOS ALBERTO DELGADO; Exec. Dir ENA LÓPEZ PORTILLO.

Corporación Salvadoreña de Turismo (CORSATUR): Edif. y Pasaje Carbonel 1, Alameda Doctor Manuel Enrique Araujo, Col. Roma, San Salvador; tel. 2241-3200; fax 2223-6120; e-mail info@corsatur.gob.sv; internet www.elsalvador.travel; f. 1997; Asst Gen. Man. DENISSE CAMPOS.

Feria Internacional de El Salvador (FIES): Avda La Revolución 222, Col. San Benito, Apdo 493, San Salvador; tel. 2243-0244; fax 2243-3161; e-mail feria@fies.gob.sv; internet www.fies.gob.sv; f. 1965; Pres. BENJAMÍN TRABANINO LLOBELL.

Instituto Salvadoreño de Turismo (ISTU) (National Tourism Institute): Calle Rubén Darío 619, San Salvador; tel. 2222-5727; fax 2222-1208; e-mail informacion@istu.gob.sv; internet www.istu.gob.sv; f. 1950; Pres. MANUEL AVILÉS; Man. Dir ARTURO HILERMANN.

EQUATORIAL GUINEA

Introductory Survey

Location, Climate, Language, Religion, Flag, Capital

The Republic of Equatorial Guinea consists of the islands of Bioko (formerly Fernando Póo and subsequently renamed Macías Nguema Biyogo under the regime of President Macías), Corisco, Great Elobey, Little Elobey and Annobón (previously known also as Pagalu), and the mainland region of Río Muni (previously known also as Mbini) on the west coast of Africa. Cameroon lies to the north and Gabon to the east and south of Río Muni, while Bioko lies off shore from Cameroon and Nigeria. The small island of Annobón lies far to the south, beyond the islands of São Tomé and Príncipe. The climate is hot and humid, with average temperatures higher than 26°C (80°F). The official languages are Spanish and French. In Río Muni the Fang language is spoken, as well as those of coastal tribes such as the Combe, Balemke and Bujeba. Bubi is the indigenous language on Bioko, although Fang is also widely used, and Ibo is spoken by the resident Nigerian population. An estimated 90% of the population are adherents of the Roman Catholic Church, although traditional forms of worship are also followed. The national flag (proportions 2 by 3) has three equal horizontal stripes, of green, white and red, with a blue triangle at the hoist and the national coat of arms (a silver shield, containing a tree, with six yellow stars above and a scroll beneath) in the centre of the white stripe. The capital is Malabo (formerly Santa Isabel).

Recent History

Portugal ceded the territory to Spain in 1778. The mainland region and the islands were periodically united for administrative purposes. In July 1959 Spanish Guinea, as the combined territory was known, was divided into two provinces: Río Muni, on the African mainland, and Fernando Póo (now Bioko), with other nearby islands. From 1960 the two provinces were represented in the Spanish legislature. In December 1963 they were merged again, to form Equatorial Guinea, with a limited measure of self-government.

After 190 years of Spanish rule, independence was declared on 12 October 1968. Francisco Macías Nguema, Equatorial Guinea's first President, formed a coalition Government from all the parties represented in the new National Assembly. In February 1970 Macías outlawed all existing political parties and formed the Partido Unico Nacional (PUN), which later became the Partido Unico Nacional de los Trabajadores (PUNT). Macías appointed himself Life President in July 1972. A new Constitution, giving absolute powers to the President was adopted in July 1973.

In August 1979 President Macías was overthrown in a coup led by his nephew, Lt-Col (later Gen.) Teodoro Obiang Nguema Mbasogo, hitherto the Deputy Minister of Defence. (Obiang Nguema subsequently ceased to use his forename.) Macías was found guilty of treason, genocide, embezzlement and violation of human rights, and was executed in September. The Spanish Government, which admitted prior knowledge of the coup, was the first to recognize the new regime, and remained a major supplier of financial and technical aid. In August 1982 Obiang Nguema was reappointed President for a further seven years, and later that month a new Constitution, which provided for an eventual return to civilian government, was approved by 95% of voters in a referendum.

The imposition, from 1979 to 1991, of a ban on organized political activity within Equatorial Guinea, and persistent allegations against the Obiang Nguema regime of human rights abuses and corruption, resulted in the development of a substantial opposition-in-exile. During the 1980s Obiang Nguema's rule was threatened on a number of occasions. A series of attempted coups were reported and in January 1986 the President reinforced his control by assuming the post of Minister of Defence. In August 1987 Obiang Nguema announced the establishment of a 'governmental party', the Partido Democrático de Guinea Ecuatorial (PDGE), while continuing to reject demands for the legalization of opposition parties. At legislative elections held in July 1988, 99.2% of voters endorsed a single list of candidates who had been nominated by the President.

In June 1989, at the first presidential election to be held since independence, Obiang Nguema, the sole candidate, reportedly received the support of more than 99% of the electorate. Opposition groupings criticized the conduct of the election and declared the result invalid. Following his success, the President appealed to dissidents to return to Equatorial Guinea and declared an amnesty for political prisoners. However, Obiang Nguema reiterated his opposition to the establishment of a multi-party system, and in December 1990 it was reported that about 30 advocates of the introduction of a plural political system had been imprisoned.

A new Constitution, containing provisions for a multi-party political system, was approved by an overwhelming majority of voters at a national referendum in November 1991. However, opposition movements rejected the Constitution, owing to the inclusion of clauses exempting the President from any judicial procedures arising from his tenure of office and prohibiting citizens who had not been continuously resident in Equatorial Guinea for 10 years from standing as election candidates, while requiring all political parties to submit a large deposit (which could not be provided by funds from abroad) as a condition of registration. In January 1992 a transitional Government (comprising only members of the PDGE) was formed, and a general amnesty was extended to all political exiles. The UN published a report in January that criticized the human rights record of the Equato-Guinean authorities and some of the provisions incorporated in the new Constitution. Throughout 1992 the security forces continued to arrest members of opposition parties.

Multi-party legislative elections held in November 1993 were boycotted by most of the parties in the Plataforma de Oposición Conjunta—an alliance of opposition parties formed in September 1992—in protest at Obiang Nguema's refusal to review contentious clauses of the electoral law promulgated in January 1993 or to permit impartial international observers to inspect the electoral register. The UN declined a request by the Equato-Guinean authorities to monitor the elections, contending that correct electoral procedures were evidently being infringed. Representatives of the Organization of African Unity (OAU—now the African Union—AU, see p. 164) were present and estimated that 50% of the electorate participated. The PDGE won 68 of the 80 seats in the House of Representatives, while, of the six opposition parties that presented candidates, the Convención Socialdemocrática Popular obtained six seats, the Unión Democrática y Social de Guinea Ecuatorial (UDS) won five seats and the Convención Liberal Democrática (CLD) secured one. Widespread electoral irregularities were alleged to have occurred and, prior to the elections, opposition politicians were reportedly subjected to intimidation by the security forces. In December Silvestre Siale Bileka, hitherto Prime Minister of the interim Government, was appointed Prime Minister of the new administration, which included no opposition representatives.

In April 1994 Severo Moto Nsa, the founding leader of one of the most influential exiled opposition parties, the Partido del Progreso de Guinea Ecuatorial (PPGE), based in Spain, returned to Equatorial Guinea. In June, in response to pressure from international aid donors, the Government agreed to amend the controversial electoral law and to conduct a preliminary electoral census prior to local elections. In September, however, the authorities began to compile a full population census, instead of preparing for the local elections, which had been scheduled for November. The census was boycotted by opposition parties, and many people were arrested in ensuing clashes with the security forces. The local elections were postponed.

In early 1995 the Constitution and electoral law were amended to reduce from 10 to five the minimum number of years required for candidates to have been resident in Equatorial Guinea. In February several leading members of the PPGE, including Moto Nsa, were arrested for allegedly plotting to overthrow Obiang Nguema; in April they were found guilty by a military court and sentenced to terms of imprisonment. (Moto Nsa received a sentence of 28 years.) The convictions and sentences were widely condemned by foreign Governments and in August Obiang

Nguema unexpectedly pardoned all the convicted PPGE members.

Local elections were staged, on a multi-party basis, in September 1995. According to the official results, the ruling PDGE won an overall victory, securing a majority of the votes cast in two-thirds of local administrations. Allegations by the opposition (which claimed to have obtained 62% of the votes) that serious electoral malpractice had occurred were supported by the Spanish ambassador to Equatorial Guinea. A monitoring team of international observers agreed that some electoral irregularities had taken place.

At a presidential election held in February 1996 Obiang Nguema was returned to office, reportedly securing more than 90% of the votes cast. However, influential opposition leaders boycotted the contest, in protest at alleged electoral irregularities and official intimidation. In March Obiang Nguema appointed a new Prime Minister, Angel Serafin Seriche Dougan (hitherto a Deputy Minister); an enlarged Council of Ministers was announced in April. Representatives of opposition parties had declined a presidential invitation to participate in the new administration.

In May 1997 Moto Nsa was arrested by the Angolan authorities with a consignment of arms, which were reportedly intended for use in a planned coup. Following his release in June, Moto Nsa was granted refuge in Spain. Meanwhile, the PPGE was banned; the party subsequently divided into two factions, one of which was led by Moto Nsa. In August Moto Nsa and 11 others were convicted *in absentia* of treason; Moto Nsa was sentenced to 101 years' imprisonment. In September the Government protested strongly to Spain for granting political asylum to Moto Nsa. Shortly afterwards French was declared the second official national language. In February 1998 the House of Representatives approved a new electoral law, which banned political coalitions.

In January 1998 armed protesters launched three successive attacks against military targets on Bioko, killing four soldiers and three civilians. The terrorist action was alleged to have been perpetrated by members of the secessionist Movimiento para la Autodeterminación de la Isla de Bioko (MAIB), which was founded in 1993 by ethnic Bubis (the original inhabitants of the island, who, following independence, had become outnumbered by the mainland Fang). Subsequently hundreds of Bubis and resident Nigerians were arrested; many were reportedly also severely tortured. In May 1998 some 116 detainees were tried by a military court in connection with the January attacks, on charges including terrorism and treason. Fifteen of the defendants were found guilty of the most serious charges and sentenced to death; however, in response to international pressure the death sentences were commuted to sentences of life imprisonment in September.

During early 1999 six unregistered opposition parties exiled in Spain, including the MAIB and Moto Nsa's faction of the PPGE, formed a new alliance, the Coordinadora de la Oposición Conjunta. Equatorial Guinea's second multi-party legislative elections took place in early March, amid allegations of electoral malpractice and of the systematic intimidation of opposition candidates by the security forces. The elections were contested by 13 parties, and some 99% of the electorate was estimated to have voted. According to the official results, the ruling PDGE obtained more than 90% of the votes, increasing its representation from 68 to 75 of the 80 seats in the House of Representatives. Two opposition parties, the Unión Popular (UP) and the Convergencia para la Democracia Social (CPDS), secured four seats and one seat, respectively. Both parties, however, refused to participate in the new administration, in protest at alleged violations of the electoral law. The UP, the CPDS and five other opposition organizations campaigned, without success, to have the election results annulled. Following the election, Seriche Dougan was reappointed to the premiership, and in late July a new Council of Ministers was announced.

The new administration dismissed hundreds of civil servants, including a number of high-ranking officials, during its first three months in office, as part of efforts to eradicate corruption. Furthermore, in January 2000 a number of judicial officials, including the President of the Supreme Tribunal and the President of the Constitutional Court, were dismissed. Former Prime Minister Silvestre Siale Bileka was appointed to the presidency of the Supreme Tribunal. Nevertheless, in March the new Special Representative for Equatorial Guinea at the UN Human Rights Commission condemned the Equato-Guinean authorities for systematic and serious human rights violations.

The Special Representative further stated that, despite some minor advances, real democracy did not exist in the country and accused the Government of refusing to authorize the formation of human rights non-governmental organizations. Following intense lobbying by several African countries, the mandate of the Special Representative was terminated in April 2002. However in December a new UN Human Rights Rapporteur arrived in Equatorial Guinea, with a mandate to investigate claims of human rights violations.

In late February 2001 Seriche Dougan announced the resignation of his Government, in response to further pressure from the President and the legislature. Cándido Muatetema Rivas, formerly Deputy Secretary-General of the PDGE, was subsequently appointed as Prime Minister and formed a new Council of Ministers. Five members of the opposition were appointed to the new Government, including Jeremías Ondo Ngomo, the President of the UP, as Minister-delegate for Communications and Transport. In July Obiang Nguema was nominated as the PDGE candidate for the 2003 presidential election. In the same month the President made overtures to exiled political groups, urging them to legalize their political movements in Equatorial Guinea.

In May and June 2002 some 144 members of opposition parties were tried on charges relating to an alleged plot to oust Obiang Nguema, following their arrest in March. In June 68 of the defendants received sentences of up to 20 years' imprisonment; those convicted included the Secretary-General of the CPDS, Plácido Micó Abogo, and Felipe Ondo Obiang, the Chairman of the Fuerza Demócrata Republicana (FDR).

In early November 2002 President Obiang Nguema announced that the presidential election would be brought forward to 15 December (from February 2003). A National Electoral Council was created, although international bodies were unwilling to monitor voting in view of the apparent weakness of the country's electoral institutions. Nevertheless, several leading members of both the exiled and resident opposition—including Celestino Bonifacio Bacale of the CPDS and Tomás Mecheba Fernández of the Partido Socialista de Guinea Ecuatorial—declared their intention to contest the election. Alfonso Nsué Mokuy of the CLD also agreed to participate in the election, as did the Deputy Minister of Public Works, Housing and Urban Affairs, Carmelo Modú Acusé Bindang (the President of the UDS), and the Deputy Minister of Communications and Transport, Ondo Ngomo (of the UP).

On 15 December 2002, with voting already under way, Bacale and other opposition candidates announced their withdrawal from the election, alleging widespread irregularities in voting procedures. Their claims related to the apparent lack of secrecy in voting, the insufficient number of ballot papers for opposition candidates and voter intimidation. According to the official results, Obiang Nguema was re-elected to the presidency, with 97.1% of the votes cast. The conduct of the election was condemned by the European Union (EU, see p. 244). Despite the newly re-elected President's call for the opposition leaders to join the PDGE in a government of national unity, 'radical' opposition parties continued to refuse to participate in Obiang Nguema's administration. In February 2003 a new Government was formed, again headed by Prime Minister Rivas. Meanwhile, the CPDS continued to demand the release of all opposition members imprisoned in June 2002, including Micó Abogo. Micó Abogo was granted a conditional presidential pardon in August 2003, and was released along with some 17 other political opponents of the regime sentenced in the previous year. However, the Government denied claims that Ondo Obiang had died in custody, stating that he had been transferred to another prison on the mainland. Also in August, Moto Nsa and the leaders of two other Equato-Guinean opposition parties announced the formation of a government-in-exile in Madrid, Spain.

In mid-March 2004 the Government announced that a group of 15 suspected mercenaries had been arrested on suspicion of planning a *coup d'état*, which President Obiang Nguema subsequently claimed had been funded by multinational companies and organized by Moto Nsa with the collusion of the Spanish Government. Following the death in custody of one of the accused, in November the remaining 14 defendants were found guilty of involvement in the coup attempt and received lengthy custodial sentences. Although Moto Nsa denied any involvement in the affair, he was sentenced *in absentia* by the court in Malabo to 63 years' imprisonment, while Nick du Toit, a former South African special forces officer alleged to have been the operational leader of the group in Equatorial Guinea, was sentenced to 34 years' imprisonment. Human rights organizations condemned the trial for grave abuses of procedure. Simon Mann, a South African-based British security consultant and the alleged leader of the coup plot, had been convicted in September of attempting illegally to procure weapons and was sentenced to seven years' imprisonment (subsequently reduced to four) in Zimbabwe, where he was arrested. At the completion of that sentence in 2007, the Equato-Guinean authorities sought to extradite Mann in order to undergo further legal proceedings. That request was granted by a judge in Zimbabwe in May and in early February 2008 Mann was transported to custody in Equatorial Guinea. Meanwhile, in August 2004 Sir Mark Thatcher (a businessman and son of the former British Prime Minister Baroness Thatcher) had been arrested in Cape Town, South Africa, on suspicion of having provided financial support for the alleged coup attempt. Thatcher initially denied any involvement in the affair; however, in January 2005 he admitted contravening South African anti-mercenary legislation and was fined R3m. (more than US $500,000) and given a four-year suspended sentence. In September 2005, following investigations into another alleged coup plot in October 2004, 23 members of the armed forces were convicted of treason and handed down lengthy gaol sentences. A further six senior members of the armed forces were sentenced to terms of imprisonment in the following month. Human rights groups claimed that confessions had been extracted under torture from those convicted.

Meanwhile, legislative and municipal elections were held concurrently on 25 April 2004. The PDGE won 68 of the 100 seats in an expanded House of Representatives, while a coalition of eight parties allied to Obiang Nguema, styled the 'democratic opposition', secured a further 30 seats. International observers and the CPDS, which took the remaining two seats, denounced the results as fraudulent. The PDGE and its allies also won 237 of the 244 council seats in the country's 30 municipalities. The rate of participation by eligible voters was estimated at 97%. In mid-June Prime Minister Rivas announced the resignation of his Government and Obiang Nguema subsequently appointed a new PDGE-dominated Council of Ministers, headed by Miguel Abia Biteo Boricó, hitherto Minister of State for Parliamentary Relations and Judicial Affairs.

In May 2004 the authorities claimed to have averted another attempt to overthrow the Government (originating in Gabon) and linked it to an opposition politician exiled in the USA since the 1970s. Five people were killed and five more captured by Equato-Guinean security forces following an attack on a military garrison on the island of Corisco. In response to this suspected coup attempt there followed several arrests in Bata and Libreville, Gabon, of persons linked to the PPGE.

On 10 August 2006 the Government resigned, following accusations of corruption and ineptitude from President Obiang Nguema. None the less, many previous members of the Council of Ministers were reappointed to the new administration, including the President's son, Teodoro (Teodorín) Nguema Obiang Mangue, as Minister of Agriculture and Forestry. Ricardo Mangué Obama Nfubea succeeded Miguel Abia Biteo Borico as Prime Minister; it was notable that the new incumbent was the first premier of Fang ethnicity to hold the office since independence.

Equatorial Guinea enjoyed exceptionally high revenues from petroleum exports from the late 1990s; allegations emerged, however, that members of the Obiang Nguema regime were accruing private profits from national petroleum exports. In May 2003 controversy arose when the US-based Riggs Bank acknowledged that some US $500m. had been paid into an account to which President Obiang Nguema was the sole signatory; international petroleum companies were alleged to be the source of the funds, which were 'frozen' by the US Senate in July 2004 pending further investigations. In January 2005 Riggs Bank admitted criminal liability in assisting Obiang Nguema in improper financial transactions. It was subsequently estimated that the funds totalled $700m., all of which was released by the US Senate, reportedly after appeals by the Obiang Nguema Government that the money was required to combat a cholera epidemic in the country. However, upon their release the funds were allegedly transferred to accounts in foreign countries. Meanwhile, in February 2004 Obiang Nguema issued a decree providing for the creation of a National Commission for Personal Ethics, which would oblige all public employees to declare their assets. However, in July a US Senate report concluded that to secure contracts and co-operation petroleum companies made substantial payments to government officials, their families or entities owned by them. In late January 2005 the Equato-Guinean authorities announced the discovery of chronic and systematic fraud in several government ministries. Controversy arose in November 2006, following reports that the President's son Teodorín had purchased a property for $35m. in the USA (in addition to two luxury homes in South Africa, with regard to which he was embroiled already in legal proceedings).

While Spain (the former colonial power) has traditionally been a major trading partner and aid donor, Equatorial Guinea's entry in 1983 into the Customs and Economic Union of Central Africa (replaced in 1999 by the Communauté économique et monétaire de l'Afrique centrale, see p. 307) represented a significant move towards a greater integration with neighbouring francophone countries. In 1985 Equatorial Guinea joined the Franc Zone (see p. 306), with financial assistance from France. Obiang Nguema has regularly attended Franco-African summit meetings. In 1989 the Spanish Government agreed to cancel one-third of Equatorial Guinea's public debt to Spain and in 1991 cancelled a further one-third of the bilateral debt. From mid-1993, however, Equato-Guinean-Spanish relations deteriorated, and in January 1994 the Spanish Government withdrew one-half of its aid to Equatorial Guinea in retaliation for the expulsion in December 1993 of a Spanish diplomat whom the Equato-Guinean authorities had accused of interfering in the country's internal affairs. In September 1997 the Obiang Nguema administration protested strongly to the Spanish Government over Spain's offer of political asylum to the opposition leader Severo Moto Nsa (see above). On several occasions in 1998 the Equato-Guinean Government accused Spain of attempting to destabilize Equatorial Guinea by providing funds to opposition organizations. However, in October 1999 the Spanish Government agreed to resume full assistance to its former colony, and during a visit to Madrid in March 2001 Obiang Nguema held talks with Spanish Prime Minister José María Aznar, who agreed to normalize relations with Equatorial Guinea in the economic field. In 2003 relations improved further following Spain's support for Equatorial Guinea's territorial claims to the island of Mbagne (Mbañé, Mbanie, see below), and the Spanish Ministers of Health and Consumer Affairs and of Foreign Affairs visited Malabo in November. In February 2004 the two Governments signed a new two-year agreement on development co-operation, worth some €34m. In April the Spanish Government cancelled 50% of Equatorial Guinea's debt, estimated at some €70m. Relations were strained, however, following accusations made in September by Boricó that the previous Spanish administration of José María Aznar had actively colluded with the alleged coup attempt directed by Moto Nsa uncovered earlier in March (see above) and that the incumbent Spanish Government, led by Prime Minister José Luis Rodríguez Zapatero, had withheld information regarding this alleged collusion. The Zapatero administration denied the claims.

In late February 2005 Obiang Nguema held talks in Bata with the Spanish Minister of Foreign Affairs and Co-operation, Miguel Angel Moratinos Cuyaubé, during which both parties expressed their desire to maintain cordial relations and high levels of co-operation between the two countries. Although Moratinos reassured Obiang Nguema that the Spanish Government would act forcefully to prevent any preparations being made in Spanish territory to destabilize or overthrow the Obiang Nguema administration, he reiterated that the extradition of Moto Nsa was a judicial matter, in which the Spanish Government would not intervene. However, in December the Spanish Government announced that Moto Nsa's asylum was to be revoked in the light of evidence that Moto Nsa's had conspired to overthrow the Obiang Nguema regime. Moto Nsa announced his intention to return to Equatorial Guinea to demand the immediate holding of fair elections. Meanwhile, in June Moto Nsa had participated in a demonstration by exiled opposition groups at the Equato-Guinean embassy in Spain, which resulted in damage to embassy property (leading to the embassy's closure) and minor injuries to some of its staff. The Spanish and Equato-Guinean Governments condemned the demonstrators' actions. In November 2006 President Obiang Nguema paid his first state visit to Spain since 1990 (in order to open the country's new embassy).

In November 1999 Equatorial Guinea, Angola, Cameroon, the Republic of the Congo, Gabon, Nigeria and São Tomé and Príncipe established an international committee to demarcate maritime borders in the Gulf of Guinea. The development of petroleum reserves in the region during the 1990s had revived long-standing frontier disputes. In September 2000 Equatorial Guinea and Nigeria formally resolved their maritime border dispute, reaching an agreement (signed in December 2001) on the demarcation of the border, which was expected to encourage further petroleum exploration and development in that area. In August 2007 it was announced that the Nigerian naval forces had agreed to co-operate in patrolling the Gulf of Guinea.

In March 2003 relations between Equatorial Guinea and Gabon were strained following the occupation of the small island of Mbagne (Mbañé, Mbanie) by a contingent of Gabonese troops. Both countries had long claimed ownership of Mbagne and two smaller islands, which lie in potentially oil-rich waters in Corisco Bay, north of the Gabonese capital, Libreville, and south-west of the Equato-Guinean mainland. In June Equatorial Guinea rejected a Gabonese proposal to share any petroleum revenues from the island, and discussions between the two sides ended without agreement in December. However, in January 2004 Equatorial Guinea and Gabon issued a joint communiqué, accepting the appointment of a UN mediator in the dispute. In July a provisional agreement was reached to explore jointly for petroleum in the disputed territories. At a meeting in Libreville in January 2005 the Presidents of both countries expressed optimism that an amicable agreement would soon be finalized. However, in late 2006 negotiations were suspended indefinitely, potentially to be pursued at the International Court of Justice (see p. 20). In September 2007 the Equato-Guinean authorities sought the support of French President Nicolas Sarkozy in resolving the dispute over Mbagne.

Government

In November 1991 a new Constitution was approved in a referendum, providing for the introduction of multi-party democracy. Executive power is vested in the President, whose seven-year term of office is renewable indefinitely. The President is immune from prosecution for offences committed before, during or after his tenure of the post. Legislative power is held by a 100-member House of Representatives, which serves for a term of five years. Both the President and the House of Representatives are directly elected by universal adult suffrage. The President appoints a Council of Ministers, headed by a Prime Minister, from among the members of the House of Representatives.

Defence

As assessed at November 2007, there were 1,100 men in the army, 120 in the navy and 100 in the air force. There was also a paramilitary force, trained by French military personnel. Military service is voluntary. The estimated defence budget for 2005 was 3,800m. francs CFA. Spain has provided military advisers and training since 1979, and military aid has also been received from the USA.

Economic Affairs

In 2006, according to estimates by the World Bank, Equatorial Guinea's gross national income (GNI), measured at average 2004–06 prices, was US $4,246m., equivalent to $8,250 per head (or $10,150 per head on an international purchasing-power parity basis). During 1996–2006, it was estimated, the population increased at an average annual rate of 2.4%, while gross domestic product (GDP) per head increased, in real terms, by an average of 22.5% per year in 1996–2006. Overall GDP increased, in real terms, at an average annual rate of 57.6% in 1996–2006. Real GDP increased by 6.9% in 2005, but it declined by 4.9% in 2006.

Agriculture (including hunting, forestry and fishing) contributed an estimated 2.7% of GDP in 2006 (compared with 51.6% of GDP in 1995), according to World Bank figures. The sector employed an estimated 68.1% of the labour force in mid-2005, according to FAO estimates. The principal cash crop is cocoa, which, according to the Banque de France, provided an estimated 0.2% of total export earnings in 2003. The Government is encouraging the production of bananas, spices (vanilla, black pepper and coriander) and medicinal plants for export. The main subsistence crops are cassava and sweet potatoes. Exploitation of the country's vast, but rapidly diminishing, forest resources (principally of okoumé and akoga timber) provided an estimated 1.8% (or 31,100m. francs CFA) of export revenue in 2003, according to the Banque de France. Almost all industrial fishing activity is practised by foreign fleets, notably by those of countries of the European Union. During 2000–06, according to the World Bank, the real GDP of the agricultural sector declined at an average annual rate of 1.8%. However, agricultural GDP increased by 2.1% in 2005, and by 3.0% in 2006.

According to the World Bank, industry (including mining, manufacturing, construction and power) contributed an estimated 94.3% of GDP in 2006 (compared with 29.7% of GDP in 1995). During 2000–2006, according to the World Bank, industrial GDP increased at an average annual rate of 21.1%. However, industrial GDP declined by 5.9% in 2006.

Extractive activities were minimal during the 1980s, and the mining sector employed less than 0.2% of the working population in 1983. However, the development of onshore and offshore reserves of petroleum and of offshore deposits of natural gas led to unprecedented economic growth during the 1990s. Exports of petroleum commenced in 1992 and provided an estimated 92.0% of total export earnings in 2003, according to the Banque de France. The petroleum sector contributed an estimated 93.6% of GDP in 2005 (compared with 18.2% of GDP in 1995). Petroleum production increased from 56,601 barrels per day (b/d) in 1997 to an estimated 385,970 b/d in 2006, according to the US Energy Information Administration (EIA). Proven reserves of petroleum were some 1,100m. barrels in January 2007. Natural gas extraction also increased rapidly from the 1990s. Proven reserves at the country's largest gas field, Alba, were some 1,300,000m. cu ft in early 2006, while in early 2008 it was estimated that the country contained probable reserves of around 4,000,000m. cu ft. The existence of deposits of gold, uranium, iron ore, titanium, tantalum and manganese has also been confirmed. During 1997–2002 the GDP of the petroleum sector increased at an average annual rate of 32.9%, according to the IMF; growth in 2002 was 21.4%.

The manufacturing sector contributed only 8.6% of GDP in 2006, according to the World Bank. Wood-processing constitutes the main commercial manufacturing activity. During 2000–06 manufacturing GDP increased at an average annual rate of 59.2%; growth in 2006 was 8.9%.

An estimated total of 30m. kWh of electric energy was generated in 2005. According to the EIA, in 2004 Equatorial Guinea had 15.4 MW of proven installed capacity and 5 MW–30 MW of estimated additional capacity. There was about 4 MW of oil-fired thermal capacity and 1 MW of hydroelectric capacity on the mainland. Bioko was supplied by one hydroelectric plant (on the Riaba river) with an estimated capacity of 3.6 MW and two thermal plants, including the 10.4-MW Punta Europa gas-fired plant located at the northern end of the island. Also in that year, there was a further 4 MW–6 MW of generation capacity at the AMPCO complex on Bioko. Imports of fuel products comprised 8.6% of the value of total imports in 2003.

The services sector contributed an estimated 3.0% of GDP in 2006. The dominant services are trade, restaurants and hotels, and government services. During 2000–06, according to the World Bank, the GDP of the services sector increased at an average annual rate of 16.3%. It grew by 9.5% in 2006.

In 2005 there was a visible trade surplus of 5,219,100m. francs CFA, while the deficit on the current account of the balance of payments was 897,600m. francs CFA. In 2002 the Federal Republic of Yugoslavia (now Serbia) was the principal source of imports (29.1%), while the USA was the principal destination of exports (28.3%). Other major trading partners were Spain, the People's Republic of China, the United Kingdom and France. In 2002 petroleum and timber constituted the principal sources of export revenue, while in 1990 the principal imports were ships and boats, petroleum and related products and food and live animals.

In 2005 a budget surplus of 832,294m. francs CFA was provisionally estimated (equivalent to 23.4% of GDP). Equatorial Guinea's external debt was US $290.9m. at the end of 2004, of which $244.4m. was long-term public debt. The rate of inflation averaged 6.8% per year in 2000–05. The annual average rate of inflation was 4.8% in 2005.

Equatorial Guinea is a member of the Central African organs of the Franc Zone (see p. 307), including the Communauté économique et monétaire de l'Afrique centrale (CEMAC, see p. 307).

Equatorial Guinea suffered a severe economic decline under the Macías regime. The Obiang Nguema administration has achieved some success in rehabilitating and diversifying the primary sector, although the significance of the country's traditional industries has declined substantially since the commencement of petroleum exports in 1992, and production of that commodity led to exceptional economic growth from the late 1990s. Economic relations with the USA have strengthened in recent years as a result of major investments in the development of Equato-Guinean oilfields by US energy companies and in late

2005 Obiang Nguema signed an agreement to co-operate on hydrocarbon development with the People's Republic of China. Equatorial Guinea was expected to benefit from the competition between the USA and China for stakes in the hydrocarbons sector, while there were also proposals to establish a new Joint Development Zone between Equatorial Guinea and Gabon in the disputed Corisco Bay, a region rich in petroleum and gas reserves. In 2004 rapid expansion of the hydrocarbon industry led to spectacular GDP growth of 34%. Although the economy was estimated to have contracted by some 5% in 2006, analysts expected a recovery in 2007, with growth of 21.5% projected. This was attributed to increased revenues from the profitable petroleum and timber sectors, with the former benefiting from improvements in production processes and the rising price of the commodity. The Government announced in late 2007 that it intended to invest US $12,260m. over the next five years in programmes designed to help diversify the economy and in public infrastructure development, including, *inter alia*, the construction of hospitals, motorways, a new airport and a new hydroelectric power plant. Despite these positive trends, however, in January 2006 the UN Development Programme announced that more than 70% of Equato-Guineans subsisted in poverty on less than $2 per day. The absence of any visible improvement in living standards among the general population since the early 1990s has been variously attributed to corruption, the disadvantageous terms of many contracts negotiated by the state petroleum company, and reduced international aid. There also remained concerns that the country's petroleum revenues would be squandered as a result of senior level graft; a Transparency International report in 2007 ranked Equatorial Guinea as the 10th most corrupt country in the world.

Education

Education is officially compulsory and free for five years between the ages of six and 11 years. Primary education starts at six years of age and normally lasts for five years. Secondary education, beginning at the age of 12, spans a seven-year period, comprising a first cycle of four years and a second cycle of three years. According to UNESCO estimates, in 2001/02 total enrolment at primary schools included 85% of children in the relevant age-group (males 92%; females 78%), while secondary enrolment in 2000/01 included 24% of children in the relevant age-group (males 30%; females 18%). In 1999/2000 there were 1,003 pupils in higher education. Since 1979, assistance in the development of the educational system has been provided by Spain. Two higher education centres, at Bata and Malabo, are administered by the Spanish Universidad Nacional de Educación a Distancia. The French Government also provides considerable financial assistance. There is also a university, founded in 1995, at Malabo. In September 2002 a new National Plan for Education was ratified. The initiative aimed to improve basic literacy and introduce education on health-related topics. In 1993 budgetary expenditure on education by the central Government amounted to an estimated 9.3% of total expenditure.

Public Holidays

2008: 1 January (New Year's Day), 21–24 March (Easter), 1 May (Labour Day), 25 May (AU Day), 12 October (Independence Day), 10 December (Human Rights Day), 25 December (Christmas).

2009: 1 January (New Year's Day), 10–13 April (Easter), 1 May (Labour Day), 25 May (AU Day), 12 October (Independence Day), 10 December (Human Rights Day), 25 December (Christmas).

Weights and Measures

The metric system is in force.

Statistical Survey

Source (unless otherwise stated): Dirección Técnica de Estadística, Secretaría de Estado para el Plan de Desarrollo Económico, Malabo.

AREA AND POPULATION

Area: 28,051 sq km (10,831 sq miles): Río Muni 26,017 sq km, Bioko 2,017 sq km, Annobón 17 sq km.

Population: 300,000 (Río Muni 240,804, Bioko 57,190, Annobón 2,006), comprising 144,268 males and 155,732 females, at census of 4–17 July 1983 (Source: Ministerio de Asuntos Exteriores, Madrid); 406,151 at census of 4 July 1994 (provisional). *Mid-2007* (UN estimate): 507,000 (Source: UN, *World Population Prospects: The 2006 Revision*).

Density (mid-2007): 18.1 per sq km.

Provinces (population, census of July 1983): Kié-Ntem 70,202; Litoral 66,370; Centro-Sur 52,393; Wele-Nzas 51,839; Bioko Norte 46,221; Bioko Sur 10,969; Annobón 2,006.

Principal Towns (population at 1983 census): Bata 24,100; Malabo (capital) 15,253. *Mid-2007* (incl. suburbs, UN estimate): Malabo 96,000 (Source: UN, *World Urbanization Prospects: The 2007 Revision*).

Births and Deaths (UN estimates, annual averages): Birth rate 39.8 per 1,000 in 2000–05; Death rate 16.4 per 1,000 in 2000–05. Source: UN, *World Population Prospects: The 2006 Revision*.

Expectation of Life (years at birth, WHO estimates): 46.2 (males 45.3; females 47.1) in 2005. Source: WHO, *World Health Statistics*.

Economically Active Population (persons aged 6 years and over, 1983 census): Agriculture, hunting, forestry and fishing 59,390; Mining and quarrying 126; Manufacturing 1,490; Electricity, gas and water 224; Construction 1,929; Trade, restaurants and hotels 3,059; Transport, storage and communications 1,752; Financing, insurance, real estate and business services 409; Community, social and personal services 8,377; Activities not adequately defined 984; *Total employed* 77,740 (males 47,893, females 29,847); Unemployed 24,825 (males 18,040, females 6,785); *Total labour force* 102,565 (males 65,933, females 36,632). Note: Figures are based on unadjusted census data, indicating a total population of 261,779. The adjusted total is 300,000 (Source: ILO, *Yearbook of Labour Statistics*). *Mid-2005* ('000 persons, official estimates): Agriculture, etc. 139; Total labour force 204 (Source: FAO).

HEALTH AND WELFARE

Key Indicators

Total Fertility Rate (children per woman, 2005): 5.9.

Under-5 Mortality Rate (per 1,000 live births, 2005): 205.

HIV/AIDS (% of persons aged 15–49, 2005): 3.2.

Physicians (per 1,000 head, 2004): 0.3.

Hospital Beds (per 1,000 head, 2005): 2.2.

Health Expenditure (2004): US $ per head (PPP): 223.2.

Health Expenditure (2004): % of GDP: 1.6.

Health Expenditure (2004): public (% of total): 77.1.

Access to Water (% of persons, 2004): 43.

Access to Sanitation (% of persons, 2004): 53.

Human Development Index (2005): ranking: 127.

Human Development Index (2005): value: 0.642.

For sources and definitions, see explanatory note on p. vi.

AGRICULTURE, ETC.

Principal Crops ('000 metric tons, 2005, FAO estimates unless otherwise indicated): Sweet potatoes 37; Cassava 44; Coconuts 5; Oil palm fruit 33; Bananas 21; Plantains 33; Cocoa beans 3 (unofficial figure); Green coffee 4 (unofficial figure). Note: data for individual crops were not available for 2006. *Aggregate Production* ('000 metric tons, may include official, semi-official or estimated data, 2006): Total roots and tubers 105; Total fruits (excl. melons) 54.

Livestock ('000 head, year ending September 2005, FAO estimates): Cattle 5; Pigs 6; Sheep 38; Goats 9. Note: Data for 2006 were not available.

Forestry (2006, FAO estimates): Roundwood removals ('000 cubic metres): Fuel wood 447 (assumed to be unchanged since 1983); Sawlogs, veneer logs and logs for sleepers 419; Total 866.

EQUATORIAL GUINEA

Fishing (metric tons, live weight, 2005, FAO estimates): Freshwater fishes 1,000; Clupeoids 1,900; Sharks, rays, skates, etc. 100; Total catch (incl. others) 3,500.
Source: FAO.

MINING

Production (2006): Crude petroleum 145 million barrels; Natural gas 2,000 million cubic metres. Source: US Geological Survey.

INDUSTRY

Palm Oil ('000 metric tons): 4.5 in 1999; 4.5 in 2000–05 (FAO estimates). Source: FAO.

Veneer Sheets ('000 cubic metres, FAO estimates): 9.3 in 1997; 15.0 in 1998–2006. Source: FAO.

Electric Energy (million kWh, estimates): 26 in 2002; 26 in 2003; 27 in 2004. Source: UN, *Industrial Commodity Statistics Yearbook*.

FINANCE

Currency and Exchange Rates: 100 centimes = 1 franc de la Coopération financière en Afrique centrale (CFA). *Sterling, Dollar and Euro Equivalents* (31 December 2007): £1 sterling = 892.702 francs CFA; US $1 = 445.593 francs CFA; €1 = 655.957 francs CFA; 10,000 francs CFA = £11.20 = $22.44 = €15.24. *Average Exchange Rate* (francs CFA per US dollar): 527.468 in 2005; 522.890 in 2006; 479.267 in 2007. *Note:* An exchange rate of 1 French franc = 50 francs CFA, established in 1948, remained in force until January 1994, when the CFA franc was devalued by 50%, with the exchange rate adjusted to 1 French franc = 100 francs CFA. This relationship to French currency remained in effect with the introduction of the euro on 1 January 1999. From that date, accordingly, a fixed exchange rate of €1 = 655.957 francs CFA has been in operation.

Budget (million francs CFA, 2005): *Revenue:* Petroleum sector 1,440,885; Non-oil revenue 87,940; Total revenue 1,528,825 (excl. grants 1,417). *Expenditure:* Current expenditure 158,958 (Interest payments 2,134); Capital expenditure 446,003 (Foreign-financed 1,417); Total expenditure 604,961 (excl. net lending and other 92,987). Source: IMF, *Republic of Equatorial Guinea: Selected Issues and Statistical Appendix* (June 2006).

International Reserves (US $ million at 31 December 2006, excl. gold): IMF special drawing rights 0.66; Foreign exchange 3,066.08; Total 3,066.74. Source: IMF, *International Financial Statistics*.

Money Supply ('000 million francs CFA at 31 December 2006): Currency outside deposit money banks 68.21; Demand deposits at deposit money banks 192.10; *Total money* (incl. others) 261.01. Source: IMF, *International Financial Statistics*.

Cost of Living (Consumer Price Index; base: 2000 = 100): 126.2 in 2003; 132.7 in 2004; 139.1 in 2005 (estimate). Source: IMF, *Republic of Equatorial Guinea: Selected Issues and Statistical Appendix* (June 2006).

Expenditure on the Gross Domestic Product ('000 million francs CFA at factor cost, 2005, estimates): Government final consumption expenditure 111.0; Private final consumption expenditure 270.6; Gross fixed capital formation 1,188.4; *Total domestic expenditure* 1,570.0; Exports of goods and non-factor services 3,791.5; *Less* Imports of goods and services 1,803.9; *GDP at factor cost* 3,557.8. Source: IMF, *Republic of Equatorial Guinea: Selected Issues and Statistical Appendix* (June 2006).

Gross Domestic Product by Economic Activity ('000 million francs CFA, 2005, estimates): Agriculture, hunting, forestry and fishing 74.3; Petroleum sector 3,299.5; Industry (incl. manufacturing, electricity and construction) 61.1; Services (incl. trade, transport and communications; finance and housing, government services and other services) 90.3; *Sub-total* 3,525.2; Import duties and subsidies 32.6; *GDP at market prices* 3,557.8. Source: IMF, *Republic of Equatorial Guinea: Selected Issues and Statistical Appendix* (June 2006).

Balance of Payments ('000 million francs CFA, 2005, preliminary figures): Exports of goods f.o.b. 7,124.6; Imports of goods c.i.f. −1,905.6; *Trade balance* 5,219.1; Exports of services 71.2; Imports of non-factor services −1,517.9; Net other income −4,603.4; *Balance on goods, services and income* −831.0; Private transfers (net) −86.7; Official transfers (net) 20.1; *Current balance* −897.6; Direct foreign investment 1,564.8; Medium- and long-term capital (net) −23.8; Short-term capital (net) 684.3; Errors and omissions 72.4; *Overall balance* 1,400.0. Source: IMF, *Republic of Equatorial Guinea: Selected Issues and Statistical Appendix* (June 2006).

EXTERNAL TRADE

Principal Commodities (distribution by SITC, US $ '000, 1990): *Imports c.i.f.:* Food and live animals 4,340; Beverages and tobacco 3,198 (Alcoholic beverages 2,393); Crude materials (inedible) except fuels 2,589 (Crude fertilizers and crude minerals 2,102); Petroleum and petroleum products 4,738; Chemicals and related products 2,378; Basic manufactures 3,931; Machinery and transport equipment 35,880 (Road vehicles and parts 3,764, Ships, boats and floating structures 24,715); Miscellaneous manufactured articles 2,725; Total (incl. others) 61,601. *Exports f.o.b.:* Food and live animals 6,742 (Cocoa 6,372); Beverages and tobacco 3,217 (Tobacco and tobacco manufactures 2,321); Crude materials (inedible) except fuels 20,017 (Sawlogs and veneer logs 12,839, Textile fibres and waste 7,078); Machinery and transport equipment 24,574 (Ships, boats and floating structures 23,852); Total (incl. others) 61,705. Source: UN, *International Trade Statistics Yearbook*. *2002* ('000 million francs CFA): Imports c.i.f. 768.9; Exports 1,547.0 (Petroleum 1,468.0; Timber 67.2). Source: IMF, *Equatorial Guinea: Selected Issues and Statistical Appendix* (December 2003).

Principal Trading Partners ('000 million francs CFA, 2002; figures are approximate): *Imports c.i.f.:* France 80; Italy 36; Netherlands 37; United Kingdom 122; USA 114; Yugoslavia, Fed. Repub. 224; Total (incl. others) 769. *Exports f.o.b.:* Cameroon 76; China, People's Repub. 269; Germany 22; Italy 40; Spain 391; USA 438; Total (incl. others) 1,547. Source: IMF, *Equatorial Guinea: Selected Issues and Statistical Appendix* (December 2003).

TRANSPORT

Road Traffic (estimates, motor vehicles in use at 31 December 1996): Passenger cars 1,520; Lorries and vans 540. Source: IRF, *World Road Statistics* **1997:** Passenger cars 1,173.

Shipping: *Merchant Fleet* (at 31 December 2006): Vessels 40; Total displacement 29,391 grt (Source: Lloyd's Register-Fairplay, *World Fleet Statistics*). *International Sea-borne Freight Traffic* ('000 metric tons, 1990): Goods loaded 110; Goods unloaded 64 (Source: UN, *Monthly Bulletin of Statistics*).

Civil Aviation (traffic on scheduled services, 1998): Passengers carried ('000) 21; Passenger-km (million) 4. Source: UN, *Statistical Yearbook*.

COMMUNICATIONS MEDIA

Radio Receivers (1997): 180,000 in use.

Television Receivers (1997): 4,000 in use.

Newspaper (1996): 1 daily (estimated circulation 2,000).

Book Production (1998): 17 titles.

Telephones (2005): 10,000 main lines in use.

Facsimile Machines (1998): 65 in use.

Mobile Cellular Telephones (2005): 96,900 subscribers.

Personal Computers (2005): 7,000 in use.

Internet Users (2006): 8,000.

Broadband Subscribers (2005): 200.

Sources: UNESCO, *Statistical Yearbook*; UN, *Statistical Yearbook*; International Telecommunication Union.

EDUCATION

Pre-primary (2002/03): Schools 180*; Teachers 600; Students 22,604.

Primary (2004/05): Schools 483*; Teachers 2,307†; Students 75,809.

Secondary (2001/02, estimates): Teachers 894‡; Students 21,173.

Higher (1999/2000): Teachers 206†; Students 1,003.

* 1998 figure.
† 2002/03 figure, estimate.
‡ 1999/2000 figure.
Source: UNESCO Institute for Statistics.

Adult Literacy Rate: 87.0% (males 93.4%; females 80.5%) in 2000. Source: UNESCO Institute for Statistics.

Directory

The Constitution

The present Constitution was approved by a national referendum on 16 November 1991 and amended in January 1995. It provided for the introduction of a plural political system and for the establishment of a legislative House of Representatives (Cámara de Representantes del Pueblo). The term of office of the President is seven years, renewable on an indefinite number of occasions. The President is immune from prosecution for offences committed before, during or after his tenure of the post. The Cámara de Representantes serves for a term of five years. Both the President and the Cámara de Representantes are directly elected by universal adult suffrage. The President appoints a Council of Ministers, headed by a Prime Minister.

The Government

HEAD OF STATE

President and Supreme Commander of the Armed Forces: Brig.-Gen. (retd) (TEODORO) OBIANG NGUEMA MBASOGO (assumed office 25 August 1979; elected President 25 June 1989; re-elected 25 February 1996 and 15 December 2002).

COUNCIL OF MINISTERS
(February 2008)

All ministers are affiliated to the Partido Democrático de Guinea Ecuatorial (PDGE), except where otherwise indicated.

Prime Minister and Head of Government: RICARDO MANGUÉ OBAMA NFUBEA.
First Deputy Prime Minister: ANICETO EBIACA MUETE.
Second Deputy Prime Minister: DEMETRIO ELO NDONG NSEFUMU.
Minister at the Presidency of the Republic in Charge of Political and Administrative Affairs: CARMELO MODÚ AKUSE BINDANG (UDS).
Minister at the Presidency of the Republic in Charge of Information, Culture and Tourism: ALFONSO NSUE MOKUY (CLD).
Minister at the Presidency of the Republic in Charge of Missions: ALEJANDRO EVUNA OWONO ASANGONO.
Minister in Charge of Relations with Parliament and Legal Affairs of the Government: ANGEL MISI MIBUY.
Minister at the Prime Minister's Office in charge of Sub-regional Integration: BALTASAR ENGONGA EJO.
Minister of External Relations, International Co-operation and Francophone Affairs: PASTOR MICHA ONDO BILE.
Minister of Justice, Religion and Penitentiary Institutions: MAURICIO BOKUNG ASUMU.
Minister of the Interior and Local Corporations: CLEMENTE ENGONGA NGUEMA ONGUENE.
Minister of National Defence: ANTONIO NDONG NGUEMA MIKWE.
Minister of National Security: MANUEL NGUEMA MBA.
Minister of Transport, Technology, Post and Telecommunications: ENRIQUE MERCADER COSTA.
Minister of Infrastructure and Urban Development: MIGUEL NSUE MICHA.
Minister of the Economy, Trade and Business Development: JAIME ELA NDONG.
Minister of Planning, Economic Development and Public Investment: JOSÉ ELA OYANA.
Minister of Finance and the Budget: MARCELINO OWONO EDU.
Minister of Mines, Industry and Energy: ATANASIO ELA NTOUGOU NSA.
Minister of Education, Science and Sports: CRISTOBAL MEÑANA ELA.
Minister of Health and Social Welfare: ANTONIO MARTIN NDONG NCHUCHUMA.
Minister of Labour and Social Security: EVANGELINA OYO EBULE.
Minister of Social Affairs and Women's Advancement: EULALIA ENVO BELA.
Minister of Agriculture and Forestry: TEODORO (TEODORÍN) NGUEMA OBIANG MANGUE.
Minister of Fisheries and the Environment: VICENTE RODRÍGUEZ SIOSA.
Minister of Information, Culture and Tourism, Government Spokesperson: SANTIAGO NSOBEYA EFUMAN NCHAMA.
Minister of Public Service and Administrative Planning: VICENTE EYATE TOMI.

In addition, there are 18 Deputy Ministers and 13 Secretaries of State.

MINISTRIES

Ministry of Agriculture and Forestry: Apdo 504, Malabo.
Ministry of the Economy, Trade and Business Development: BP 404, Malabo; tel. (09) 31-05; fax (09) 20-43.
Ministry of External Relations, International Co-operation and Francophone Affairs: Malabo; tel. (09) 32-20; fax (09) 31-32.
Ministry of Finance and the Budget: Malabo; internet www.ceiba-guinea-ecuatorial.org/guineees/indexbienv1.htm.
Ministry of the Interior and Local Corporations: Malabo; fax (09) 26-83.
Ministry of Justice, Religion and Penitentiary Institutions: Malabo; fax (09) 21-15.
Ministry of Mines, Industry and Energy: Calle 12 de Octubre s/n, Malabo; tel. (09) 35-67; fax (09) 33-53; e-mail d.shaw@ecqc.com; internet www.equatorialoil.com.
Ministry of National Defence: Malabo; tel. (09) 27-94.
Ministry of National Security: Malabo; tel. (09) 34-69.
Ministry of Social Affairs and Women's Advancement: Malabo; tel. (09) 34-69.
Ministry of Transport, Technology, Post and Telecommunications: Malabo; internet www.ceiba-guinea-ecuatorial.org/guineees/transport.htm.

President and Legislature

PRESIDENT

Gen. (Teodoro) Obiang Nguema Mbasogo was re-elected to the presidency unopposed on 15 December 2002, securing 97.1% of votes cast, following the withdrawal of all other candidates.

CÁMARA DE REPRESENTANTES DEL PUEBLO
(House of Representatives)

Speaker: Dr SALOMÓN NGUEMA OWONO.
General Election, 25 April 2004

Party	Seats
Partido Democrático de Guinea Ecuatorial (PDGE)	68
Democratic opposition*	30
Convergencia para la Democracia Social (CPDS)	2
Total	100

*A coalition of eight parties allied to President Obiang Nguema, including the Convención Socialdemocrática Popular (CSDP), the Partido de la Convergencia Social Democráta (PCSD) and the Unión Popular (UP).

Election Commission

Constitutional Court: Malabo; Pres. FRANCISCO NGOMO MBENGONO.

Political Organizations

Alianza Democrática Progresista (ADP): Pres. FRANCISCO MBÁ OLÚ BAHAMONDE.
Alianza Nacional para la Restauración Democrática de Guinea Ecuatorial (ANRD): 95 Ruperto Chapi, 28100 Madrid, Spain; tel. (91) 623-88-64; f. 1974; Sec.-Gen. LUIS ONDO AYANG.
Alianza Popular de Guinea Ecuatorial (APGE): pro-Govt party; Pres. CARMELO MBA; Vice-Pres. TOMÁS BUEICHEKÚ.
Convención Liberal Democrática (CLD): Pres. ALFONSO NSUE MOKUY.
Convención Socialdemocrática Popular (CSDP): Leader SECUNDINO OYONO.
Convergencia para la Democracia Social (CPDS): Calle Tres de Agosto, Apdo 72, 2°, 1 Malabo; tel. (09) 20-13; e-mail cpds@intnet.gq;

internet www.cpds-gq.org; Pres. SANTIAGO OBAMA NDONG; Sec.-Gen. PLÁCIDO MICÓ ABOGO.

Demócratas por el Cambio (DECAM): coalition based in Madrid, Spain; e-mail press@guinea-ecuatorial.org; internet www.guinea-ecuatorial.org; f. 2005; 16 mem. orgs; Gen. Co-ordinator JUSTO BOLEKIA BOLEKÁ.

Foro-Democracia Guinea Ecuatorial (FDGE).

Fuerza Demócrata Republicana (FDR): f. 1995; opposition grouping based in Spain; Leader GERMÁN TOMO.

Movimiento para la Autodeterminación de la Isla de Bioko (MAIB): e-mail info@maib.org; internet www.maib.org; f. 1993 by Bubi interests seeking independence of Bioko; clandestine; Gen. Co-ordinator WEJA CHICAMPO (arrested on 4 March 2004, released and took up exile in Spain in June 2006); Spokesman Dr ENRIQUE BONEKE.

Movimiento Nacional de Liberación de Guinea Ecuatoriana (MONALIGE): POB 1484, Brooklyn, New York 11202-1484, USA; e-mail monalige@equatorialguinea-monalige.com; internet www.equatorialguinea-monalige.com; clandestine opposition party based in USA; Pres. Dr ADOLFO OBIANG BIKO.

Partido de la Convergencia Social Demócrata (PCSD): Pres. BUENAVENTURA MESUY.

Partido Democrático de Guinea Ecuatorial (PDGE): Malabo; f. 1987; sole legal party 1987–92; Chair. Gen. (TEODORO) OBIANG NGUEMA MBASOGO; Sec.-Gen. FILIBERTO NTUTUMU NGUEMA NCHAMA.

Partido para el Desarrollo (PPD): based in Spain; f. 2001; Pres. ELOY ELO MVE MBENGOMO.

Partido del Progreso de Guinea Ecuatorial (PPGE): Madrid, Spain; e-mail ppge@telepolis.com; internet www.guinea-ecuatorial.org; f. 1983; Christian Democrat faction led by SEVERO MOTO NSA.

Partido de Reconstrucción y Bienestar Social (PRBS): Pres. FLORENTINO ECOMO NSOGO.

Partido Social Demócrata (PSD): Pres. BENJAMÍN BALINGA.

Partido Socialista de Guinea Ecuatorial (PSGE): Sec.-Gen. TOMÁS MECHEBA FERNÁNDEZ-GALILEA.

Resistencia Nacional de Guinea Ecuatorial (RENAGE): Apdo de Correos 40, 28930 Móstoles, Madrid, Spain; f. 2000; alliance of seven opposition groups; Leader DANIEL M. OYONO.

Unión para la Democracia y el Desarrollo Social (UDDS): f. 1990; Sec.-Gen. ANTONIO SIBACHA BUEICHEKU.

Unión Democrática Independiente (UDI): Leader DANIEL M. OYONO.

Unión Democrática Nacional (UDEMA): Pres. JOSÉ MECHEBA.

Unión Democrática y Social de Guinea Ecuatorial (UDS): Pres. CARMELO MODÚ ACUSÉ BINDANG.

Unión Popular (UP): f. 1992; conservative; Pres. JEREMÍAS ONDO NGOMO.

Unión Popular—Progresista (UP—Progresista): Leader PEDRO EKONG.

Unión para la Reconciliación y el Progreso (URP).

Diplomatic Representation

EMBASSIES IN EQUATORIAL GUINEA

Angola: Malabo; Ambassador EMILIO JOSÉ DO CARVALHO.

Cameroon: 37 Calle Rey Boncoro, Apdo 292, Malabo; tel. and fax (09) 22-63; Ambassador JOHN NCHOTU AKUM.

China, People's Republic: Carretera del Aeropuerto, Apdo 44, Malabo; tel. (09) 35-05; fax (09) 23-81; e-mail chinaemb_gq@mfa.gov.cn; Ambassador YAN XIAOMIN.

France: Carretera del Aeropuerto, Apdo 326, Malabo; tel. (09) 20-05; fax (09) 23-05; e-mail chancellerie.malabo-amba@diplomatie.gouv.fr; internet www.ambafrance-gq.org; Ambassador HENRI DENIAUD.

Gabon: Calle de Argelia, Apdo 18, Malabo; Ambassador JEAN-BAPTISTE MBATCHI.

Guinea: Malabo.

Korea, Democratic People's Republic: Malabo; tel. (09) 20-47; Ambassador (vacant).

Morocco: Avda Enrique, Apdo 329, Malabo; tel. (09) 26-50; fax (09) 26-55; Chargé d'affaires a.i. ELHASSAN DAHMAN.

Nigeria: 4 Paseo de los Cocoteros, Apdo 78, Malabo; tel. and fax (09) 33-85; Chargé d'affaires a.i. A. ONAH.

Russia: Malabo; Ambassador LEV A. VAKHRAMEYEV.

South Africa: Parque de las Avenidas de Africa s/n, POB 5, Malabo; tel. (09) 77-37; fax (09) 27-46; e-mail malabo@foreign.gov.za; Ambassador MOKGETHI MONAISA (resident in Gabon).

Spain: Parque de las Avenidas de Africa s/n, Malabo; tel. (09) 20-20; fax (09) 26-11; e-mail embespgq@correo.mae.es; Ambassador CARLOS ROBLES FRAGA.

USA: K-3, Carretera de Aeropuerto, Malabo; tel. (09) 88-95; fax (09) 88-94; e-mail usembassymalabo@yahoo.com; internet malabo.usembassy.gov; Ambassador DONALD C. JOHNSON.

Judicial System

The Supreme Court of Justice and the Constitutional Court sit in Malabo. The Supreme Court has four chambers (Civil and Social, Penal, Administrative and Common) and consists of a President and 12 magistrates, from whom the President of each chamber is selected. There are Territorial High Courts in Malabo and Bata, which also sit as courts of appeal. Courts of first instance sit in Malabo and Bata, and may be convened in the other provincial capitals. Local courts may be convened when necessary.

President of the Supreme Court of Justice: SERGIO ESONO ABESO TOMO.

Attorney-General: JOSÉ OLO OBONO.

Religion

More than 90% of the population are adherents of the Roman Catholic Church. Traditional forms of worship are also followed.

CHRISTIANITY

The Roman Catholic Church

Equatorial Guinea comprises one archdiocese and two dioceses. An estimated 93.3% of the population were adherents at 31 December 2005.

Bishops' Conference

Arzobispado, Apdo 106, Malabo; tel. (09) 29-09; fax (09) 21-76; e-mail arzobispadomalabo@hotmail.com.

f. 1984; Pres. Most Rev. ILDEFONSO OBAMA OBONO (Archbishop of Malabo).

Archbishop of Malabo: Most Rev. ILDEFONSO OBAMA OBONO, Arzobispado, Apdo 106, Malabo; tel. (09) 29-09; fax (09) 21-76; e-mail arzobispadomalabo@hotmail.com.

Protestant Church

Iglesia Reformada Evangélica de Guinea Ecuatorial (Evangelical Reformed Church of Equatorial Guinea): Apdo 195, Malabo; f. 1960; c. 8,000 mems.

The Press

Ebano: Malabo; f. 1940; weekly; govt-controlled.

El árbol del centro: Apdo 180, Malabo; tel. (09) 21-86; fax (09) 32-75; Spanish; cultural review; 6 a year; publ. by Centro Cultural Español de Malabo; Dir GLORIA NISTAL.

Hoja Parroquial: Malabo; weekly.

La Gaceta: Malabo; f. 1996; bi-weekly.

La Verdad: Talleres Gráficos de Convergencia para la Democracia Social, Calle Tres de Agosto 72, Apdo 441, Malabo; publ. by the Convergencia para la Democracia Social; 5 annually; Editor PLÁCIDO MICÓ ABOGO.

Poto-poto: Bata; f. 1940; weekly; govt-controlled.

Voz del Pueblo: Malabo; publ. by the Partido Democrático de Guinea Ecuatorial.

PRESS ASSOCIATION

Asociación para la Libertad de Prensa y de Expresión en Guinea Ecuatorial (ASOLPEGE Libre): Calle Isla Cabrera 3, 5°, 46026 Valencia, Spain; tel. (660) 930629; e-mail asopge_ngo@hotmail.com; f. 1997; name changed as above following relocation to Spain in 2003; Pres. PEDRO NOLASCO NDONG OBAMA.

Publisher

Centro Cultural Español de Malabo: Apdo 180, Malabo; tel. (09) 21-86; fax (09) 27-22; e-mail ccem@orange.gq; Spanish support withdrawn 2002.

EQUATORIAL GUINEA

Broadcasting and Communications

TELECOMMUNICATIONS

Dirección General de Correos y de Telecomunicaciones: Malabo; tel. (09) 28-57; fax (09) 25-15; Man. Dir M. DAUCHAT.

Guinea Ecuatorial de Telecomunicaciones, SA (GETESA): Calle Rey Boncoro 27, Apdo 494, Malabo; tel. (09) 28-15; fax (09) 33-13; e-mail contact@getesa.gq; internet www.getesa.gq; f. 1987; 60% state-owned, 40% owned by France Telecom; Man. FRANCISCO NVE NSOGO.

RADIO

Radio Africa and Radio East Africa: Apdo 851, Malabo; e-mail pabcomain@aol.com; commercial station; owned by Pan American Broadcasting; music and religious programmes in English.

Radio Nacional de Guinea Ecuatorial: Apdo 749, Barrio Comandachina, Bata; Apdo 195, 90 Avda 30 de Agosto, Malabo; tel. (08) 25-92; fax (08) 20-93; tel. (09) 22-60; fax (09) 20-97; govt-controlled; commercial station; programmes in Spanish, French and vernacular languages; Dir (Bata) SEBASTIÁN ELÓ ASEKO; Dir (Malabo) JUAN EYENE OPKUA NGUEMA.

Radio Santa Isabel: Malabo; Spanish and French programmes.

Radio Televisión Asonga: Bata; private.

TELEVISION

Televisión Nacional: Malabo; broadcasts in Spanish and French; Dir ANTONIO NKULU OYE.

Finance

(cap. = capital; res = reserves; dep. = deposits; m. = million; brs = branches; amounts in francs CFA)

BANKING

Central Bank

Banque des Etats de l'Afrique Centrale (BEAC): Apdo 501, Malabo; tel. (09) 20-10; fax (09) 20-06; e-mail beacmal@beac.int; HQ in Yaoundé, Cameroon; agency also in Bata; f. 1973; bank of issue for mem. states of the Communauté économique et monétaire de l'Afrique centrale (CEMAC, fmrly Union douanière et économique de l'Afrique centrale), comprising Cameroon, the Central African Repub., Chad, the Repub. of the Congo, Equatorial Guinea and Gabon; cap. 45,000m., res 176,661m., total assets 2,144,626m. (Nov. 2003); Gov. JEAN-FÉLIX MAMALEPOT; Dir in Equatorial Guinea FRANCISCO GARCÍA BERNICO; 2 brs in Equatorial Guinea.

Commercial Banks

Banco Nacional de Guinea Ecuatorial (BANGE): Bata; f. 2005.

BGFIBANK Guinea Ecuatorial: Calle de Bata s/n, Apdo 749, Malabo; tel. (09) 63-52; fax (09) 63-73; e-mail agence_malabo@bgfi.com; internet www.bgfi.com/htm/en/bgfibank/branch-malabo.html; 55% owned by BGFIBANK, 35% owned by private shareholders, 10% state-owned; incorporated June 2001; cap. 25,065m., total assets 270,877m. (Dec. 2004); Chair. PATRICE OTHA; Gen. Man. HENRI-CLAUDE OYIMA.

Caisse Commune d'Epargne et d'Investissement Guinea Ecuatorial (CCEI-GE): Calle del Presidente Nasser, Apdo 428, Malabo; tel. (09) 22-03; fax (09) 33-11; e-mail geccei@hotmail.com; 51% owned by Afriland First Bank (Cameroon); f. 1995; cap. and res 5,172m., total assets 81,191m. (Dec. 2003); Pres. BÁLTASAR ENGONGA EDJO'O; Dir-Gen. JOSEPH CÉLESTIN TINDJOU DJAMENI.

Commercial Bank Guinea Ecuatorial (CBGE): Carretera de Luba, Apdo 189, Malabo; e-mail cbgebank@cbc-bank.com; internet www.cbc-bank.com; f. 2003; cap. 1,500m. (Jan. 2003).

Société Générale des Banques GE (SGBGE): Calle Argelia 6, Apdo 686, Malabo; tel. (09) 33-37; fax (09) 33-66; e-mail jmjgarcia@yahoo.fr; internet groupe.socgen.com/bhfm/sgbge/home_f.htm; f. 1986; present name adopted 1998; 32.44% owned by Société Générale SA (France), 31.78% state-owned, 11.45% owned by Société Générale de Banques au Cameroun, 10.97% owned by local investors; cap. and res 2,780m., total assets 48,624m. (Dec. 2001); Chair. MARCELINO OWONO EDU; Man. Dir CHRISTIAN DELMAS; brs in Bata and Malabo.

Development Banks

Banco de Fomento y Desarrollo (BFD): Malabo; f. 1998; 30% state-owned; cap. 50m.

Banque de Développement des Etats de l'Afrique Centrale: see Franc ZoneFinancial Institution

Directory

Caja Autónoma de Amortización de la Deuda Pública: Ministry of the Economy, Trade and Business Devt, Apdo 404, Malabo; tel. (09) 31-05; fax (09) 20-43; management of state funds; Dir-Gen. RAFAEL TUN.

INSURANCE

Equatorial Guinean Insurance Company, SA (EGICO): Avda de la Libertad, Malabo; state-owned.

Trade and Industry

GOVERNMENT AGENCIES

Cámaras Oficiales Agrícolas de Guinea: Bioko and Bata; purchase of cocoa and coffee from indigenous planters, who are partially grouped in co-operatives.

Empresa General de Industria y Comercio (EGISCA): Malabo; f. 1986; parastatal body jtly operated with the French Société pour l'Organisation, l'Aménagement et le Développement des Industries Alimentaires et Agricoles (SOMDIA); import-export agency.

Oficina para la Cooperación con Guinea Ecuatorial (OCGE): Malabo; f. 1981; administers bilateral aid from Spain.

DEVELOPMENT ORGANIZATIONS

Agencia Española de Cooperación Internacional para el Desarrollo (AECID): Parque de las Avenidas de Africa, Malabo; tel. (09) 16-21; fax (09) 29-32; internet www.aecid.es.

Asociación Bienestar Familiar de Guinea Ecuatorial: BP 984, Malabo; tel. and fax (09) 33-13; e-mail abifage1@hotmail.com; family welfare org.

Asociación Hijos de Lommbe (A Vonna va Lommbe): Malabo; e-mail avvl@bisa.com; internet www.bisala.com/avvl.html; f. 2000; agricultural devt org.

Camasa: Finca Sampaka, Km 7 Camino a Luba, Malabo; tel. (09) 86-92; e-mail casamallo@hotmail.com; internet www.camasa.net; f. 1906; agricultural devt on Bioko island; operates projects for the cultivation and export of cocoa, pineapple, coffee, vanilla, nutmeg, peppers and tropical flowers.

Centro de Estudios e Iniciativas para el Desarrollo de Guinea Ecuatorial (CEIDIGE): Malabo; e-mail ceidbata@intnet.gq; internet www.eurosur.org/CEIDGE/portada.html; umbrella group of devt NGOs; Pres. JOSÉ ANTONIO NSANG ANDEME.

Family Care Guinea Ecuatorial (FGCE): Malabo; f. 2000; health and education devt; Dir LAUREN TAYLOR STEVENSON.

Instituto Nacional de Promoción Agropecuaria (INPAGE): Malabo; govt agricultural devt agency; reorg. 2000.

Sociedad Anónima de Desarrollo del Comercio (SOADECO-Guinée): Malabo; f. 1986; parastatal body jtly operated with the French Société pour l'Organisation, l'Aménagement et le Développement des Industries Alimentaires et Agricoles (SOMDIA); devt of commerce.

CHAMBERS OF COMMERCE

Cámara de Comercio, Agrícola y Forestal de Malabo: Avda de la Independencia, Apdo 51, Malabo; tel. (09) 23-43; fax (09) 44-62; Dir ENRIQUE MERCADER COASTA.

Cámara Oficial de Comercio de Bioko: Avda de la Independencia 43, Apdo 51, Malabo; tel. and fax (09) 45-76; e-mail camara@orange.gq; Pres. VIDAL CHONI BECOBA.

INDUSTRIAL AND TRADE ASSOCIATIONS

Guinea Ecuatorial de Petróleo (GEPetrol): Calle Acacio Mane 39, BP 965, Malabo; tel. (09) 67-69; fax (09) 66-92; e-mail bonifacio.monsuy@ge-petrol.com; internet www.equatorialoil.com/pages/GEPetrol%20page.htm; f. 2001; state-owned petroleum company; National Dir CÁNDIDO NSUE OKOMO.

INPROCAO: Malabo; production, marketing and distribution of cocoa.

Sociedad Nacional de Gas de Guinea Ecuatorial (SONAGAS, G.E.): Malabo; f. 2005; oversees gas exploration and devt; Dir-Gen. JUAN ANTONIO NDONG.

Total Ecuatoguineana de Gestión (GE—Total): Malabo; f. 1984; 50% state-owned, 50% by Total (France); petroleum marketing and distribution.

Unión General de Empresas Privadas de la República de Guinea Ecuatorial (UGEPRIGE): Apdo 138, Malabo; tel. (27) 83-26; fax (09) 05-59.

Utilities

Electricity

ENERGE: Malabo; state-owned electricity board.

Sociedad de Electricidad de Guinea Ecuatorial (SEGESA): Carretera de Luba, Apdo 139, Malabo; tel. (09) 34-66; fax (09) 33-29; e-mail segesa@internet.gq; state-owned electricity distributor; Man. Dir BENITO ONDO.

TRADE UNIONS

A law permitting the establishment of trade unions was introduced in 1992.

Transport

RAILWAYS

There are no railways in Equatorial Guinea.

ROADS

In 1999 there were an estimated 2,880 km of roads and tracks.

Bioko: a semi-circular tarred road serves the northern part of the island from Malabo down to Batete in the west and from Malabo to Bacake Grande in the east, with a feeder road from Luba to Moka and Bahía de la Concepción.

Río Muni: a tarred road links Bata with the town of Mbini (Río Benito) in the west; another road, partly tarred, links Bata with the frontier post of Ebebiyín in the east and then continues into Gabon; other earth roads join Acurenam, Mongomo and Anisok.

SHIPPING

The main ports are Bata (general cargo and most of the country's export timber), Malabo (general), Luba (bananas, timber and petroleum), Mbini and Cogo (timber).

CIVIL AVIATION

There are two international airports, at Malabo (Santa Isabel Airport) and Bata. The national carrier, EGA—Ecuato Guineana de Aviación (which has been in liquidation since 1990), continues to provide limited regional and domestic services, as well as a weekly service to Madrid, Spain. Scheduled services between Malabo and Madrid are operated by Iberia and Líneas Aéreas de España. Direct flights to Paris, France, London, United Kingdom, and Zürich, Switzerland, are also available. SONAGESA, jointly operated by GEPetrol and SONAIR of Angola, offers direct connections between Malabo and Houston, TX, USA.

Air Consul: Apdo 77, Malabo; tel. and fax (09) 32-91; e-mail airconsul@intnet.gq; Man. FERNANDEZ ARMESTO.

EGA—Ecuato Guineana de Aviación: Apdo 665, Malabo; tel. (09) 23-25; fax (09) 33-13; internet www.ecuatoguineana.com/ega/ega.htm; regional and domestic passenger and cargo services; Pres. MELCHOR ESONO EDJO.

Swissair Guinée Equatoriale: Malabo; tel. (09) 18-81; fax (09) 18-80; two flights weekly between Malabo and Zürich, Switzerland; Man. M. HOFFSTETTER.

Tourism

Tourism remains undeveloped. Future interest in this sector would be likely to focus on the unspoilt beaches of Río Muni and Bioko's scenic mountain terrain.

ERITREA

Introductory Survey

Location, Climate, Language, Religion, Flag, Capital

The State of Eritrea, which has a coastline on the Red Sea extending for almost 1,000 km, is bounded to the north-west by Sudan, to the south and west by Ethiopia, and to the south-east by Djibouti. Its territory includes the Dahlak islands, a low-lying coralline archipelago off shore from Massawa. Rainfall is less than 500 mm per year in lowland areas, increasing to 1,000 mm in the highlands. The temperature gradient is similarly steep: average annual temperatures range from 17°C (63°F) in the highlands to 30°C (86°F) in Massawa. The Danakil depression in the south-east, which is more than 130 m below sea-level in places, experiences some of the highest temperatures recorded, frequently exceeding 50°C (122°F). The major language groups in Eritrea are Afar, Bilien, Hedareb, Kunama, Nara, Rashaida, Saho, Tigre and Tigrinya. English is rapidly becoming the language of business and is the medium of instruction at secondary schools and at university. Arabic is also widely spoken. The population is fairly evenly divided between Tigrinya-speaking Christians (mainly Orthodox), the traditional inhabitants of the highlands, and the Muslim communities of the western lowlands, northern highlands and east coast; there are also systems of traditional belief adhered to by a small number of the population. The national flag (proportions 1 by 2) consists of a red triangle with its base corresponding to the hoist and its apex at the centre of the fly, in which is situated, towards the hoist, an upright gold olive branch with six clusters of three leaves each, framed by a wreath of two gold olive branches; the remainder of the field is green at the top and light blue at the base. The capital is Asmara.

Recent History

The Treaty of Ucciali, which was signed in 1889 between Italy and Ethiopia, gave the Italian Government control over what is today the State of Eritrea. Italian exploitation of the colony continued until the defeat of the Axis powers by the Allied forces in East Africa during the Second World War. The Eritrean national identity, which was established during the Italian colonial period, was further subjugated under British administration during 1941–52. As the Allied powers and the UN discussed the future of the former Italian colony, Ethiopian territorial claims helped to foment a more militant nationalism among the Eritrean population. In 1952 a federation was formed between Eritrea and Ethiopia; however, the absence of adequate provisions for the creation of federal structures allowed Ethiopia to reduce Eritrea's status to that of an Ethiopian province by 1962.

Resistance to the Ethiopian annexation was first organized in the late 1950s, and in 1961 the Eritrean Liberation Front (ELF) launched an armed struggle. In the mid-1970s a reformist group broke away from the ELF and formed the Popular Liberation Forces (renamed the Eritrean People's Liberation Front, EPLF, in 1977), and the military confrontation with the Ethiopian Government began in earnest. A major consequence of the split between the two groups was the civil war of 1972–74. After two phases of desertion from the ELF to the EPLF, firstly in 1977–78 and secondly in 1985 (following a second civil war), the ELF was left without a coherent military apparatus.

Following the 1974 revolution in Ethiopia and the assumption of power by Mengistu Haile Mariam in 1977, thousands of new recruits joined the EPLF, and the armed struggle transformed into full-scale warfare. The numerically and materially superior Ethiopian forces achieved significant victories over the EPLF, which, following defeat in the highlands, was forced to retreat to its stronghold in the north of Eritrea. The EPLF launched counter-attacks throughout the late 1980s and slowly drove back the Ethiopian forces on all fronts. By 1989 the EPLF had gained control of the north and the west of the country, and in late 1989 the EPLF captured Massawa port, severing a major supply-route to the Ethiopian forces, who were by now besieged in Asmara. In May 1991 units of the EPLF entered Asmara, after the Ethiopian troops had fled, and immediately established an interim administration.

Following the liberation of Asmara by the EPLF, and of Addis Ababa, Ethiopia, by the Ethiopian People's Revolutionary Democratic Front (EPRDF), a conference was convened in London, United Kingdom, in August 1991. Both the USA and the Ethiopian delegation accepted the EPLF administration as the legitimate provisional Government of Eritrea, and the EPLF agreed to hold a referendum on independence in 1993. The provisional Government, which was to administer Eritrea during the two years prior to the referendum, drew most of its members from the EPLF. The Government struggled to rehabilitate and develop Eritrea's war-torn economy and infrastructure, and to feed a population largely dependent on food aid. The agricultural sector had been severely disrupted by the war, and urban economic activity was almost non-existent.

At the UN-supervised referendum held in April 1993, 99.8% of Eritreans who voted endorsed national independence. The anniversary of the liberation of Asmara, 24 May, was proclaimed Independence Day, and on 28 May Eritrea formally attained international recognition. In June Eritrea was admitted to the Organization of African Unity (OAU, now the African Union—AU, see p. 164). Following Eritrea's accession to independence, a four-year transitional period was declared, during which preparations were to proceed for establishing a constitutional and pluralist political system. At the apex of the transitional Government were three state institutions: the Consultative Council (the executive authority formed from the ministers, provincial administrators and heads of government authorities and commissions); the National Assembly (the legislative authority formed from the Central Committee of the EPLF, together with 30 members from the Provincial Assemblies and 30 individuals selected by the Central Committee); and the judiciary. One of the National Assembly's first acts was the election as Head of State of Issaias Afewerki, the Secretary-General of the EPLF, by a margin of 99 votes to five.

In February 1994 the EPLF transformed itself into a political party, the People's Front for Democracy and Justice (PFDJ). An 18-member Executive Committee and a 75-member Central Committee were elected; President Afewerki was elected Chairman of the latter. In March the National Assembly adopted a series of resolutions whereby the former executive body, the Consultative Council, was formally superseded by a State Council. Other measures adopted included the creation of a 50-member Constitutional Commission and the establishment of a committee charged with the reorganization of the country's administrative divisions. It was decided that the National Assembly would henceforth comprise the 75 members of the PFDJ Central Committee and 75 directly elected members. However, no mechanism was announced for their election. All but eight of the 50 members of the Constitutional Commission were government appointees, and there was no provision for any opposition participation in the interim system.

A draft constitution was discussed at international conventions held by the Constitutional Commission in July 1994 and January 1995. In May the National Assembly approved proposals to create six administrative regions to replace the 10 regional divisions that had been in place since colonial rule. In November the Assembly approved new names for the regions and finalized details of their exact boundaries and sub-divisions.

In early 1997 the Government established a Constituent Assembly, comprising 527 members (150 from the National Assembly, with the remainder selected from representatives of Eritreans residing abroad or elected by regional assemblies), to discuss and ratify the draft constitution. On 23 May the Constituent Assembly adopted the Constitution, authorizing 'conditional' political pluralism and instituting a presidential regime, with a President elected for a maximum of two five-year terms. The President, as Head of State, would appoint a Prime Minister and judges of the Supreme Court; his or her mandate could be revoked should two-thirds of the members of the National Assembly so demand. The Constituent Assembly was disbanded, and a Transitional National Assembly (consisting of the 75 members of the PFDJ Central Committee, 60 members of the Constituent Assembly and 15 representatives of Eritreans residing abroad) was empowered to act as the legislature until the holding of elections to a new National Assembly.

It was initially announced that Eritrea's first post-independence elections, which were scheduled to have been held in 1998, but were postponed indefinitely following the outbreak of hostilities with Ethiopia (see below), would take place in December 2001. However, during 2001 the likelihood of elections taking place in that year diminished, as President Afewerki assumed an increasingly authoritarian position. In February he dismissed the Minister of Local Government, Mahmoud Ahmed Sherifo and dissolved the electoral commission, which Sherifo had been appointed to head. In June Afewerki replaced the Ministers of Trade and Industry and of Maritime Resources. They were among a group of 15 senior PFDJ officials, including 11 former government ministers, who, in May, had signed a letter publicly accusing Afewerki of working in an 'illegal and unconstitutional manner'. In August the Chief Justice of the Supreme Court was dismissed after he openly expressed his disapproval of Afewerki's continued interference in court operations. In mid-September six of the G-15, as the signatories of the letter criticizing Afewerki had become known, were arrested, and the Government announced the 'temporary suspension' of the independent press. A few days later a further five members of the G-15 were detained.

Although no formal postponement of the legislative elections was announced, the failure of the National Assembly to convene to ratify legislation on the electoral system and on political pluralism by December 2001 made further delay inevitable. In late January 2002 the National Assembly ratified the electoral law, but failed to set an election date. Meanwhile, dissident members of the ruling PFDJ, including several members of the G-15, announced the formation, in exile, of a new political party, the Eritrean People's Liberation Front—Democratic Party (EPLF—DP).

During 2004 several parties took steps to form a viable opposition movement to the PFDJ. In February, following talks in Germany, the EPLF—DP announced that it would reform as the Eritrean Democratic Party (EDP), under the continued leadership of Mesfin Hagos. In May numerous former members of the ELF and the PFDJ combined to establish the Eritrean Popular Movement (EPM). In August two new coalitions were formed; the first united the EPM and four smaller parties under the umbrella of the Eritrean National Alliance (ENA), while the second brought the EDP, the ELF and the Eritrean Liberation Front—Revolutionary Council together. In late December representatives of these two alliances met in Khartoum, Sudan, for talks with the Ethiopian Prime Minister, Meles Zenawi, and the Sudanese President, Omar Hassan Ahmad al-Bashir, aimed at settling issues surrounding the border conflict with Ethiopia (see below). In January 2005 Hiruy Tedla Bairu was elected leader of the ENA and an opposition conference was scheduled for later that month.

In August 2005 the Minister of Foreign Affairs, Ali Sayyid Abdullah, died and Muhammad Omar was appointed to succeed him on an interim basis. In April 2007 President Afewerki appointed Osman Salih Muhammad, hitherto Minister of Education, as Minister of Foreign Affairs. The education portfolio was assumed by the Administrator of Maakel Province, Semere Rusom.

Hopes that national legislative elections would finally take place were raised in 2004 as elections to the regional assemblies were held in May with some 92% of registered voters casting their ballots. The Electoral Commission praised the high level of participation and overall fairness of the election process and indicated that the success of these elections paved the way for free national elections in the future. However, by early 2008 no date had been set for the holding of elections.

Relations between the transitional Government and Sudan, which had supported the EPLF during the war, deteriorated in December 1993, following an incursion by members of an Islamist group, the Eritrean Islamic Jihad (EIJ), into Eritrea from Sudan, during which all the members of the group, and an Eritrean army commander, were killed. In response, President Afewerki stressed the links between the EIJ and the Sudanese National Islamic Front, led by Dr Hassan at-Turabi, implying that the latter had prior knowledge of the incursion. However, following a swift denial by the Sudanese Government that it would interfere in the affairs of neighbouring states, Afewerki reaffirmed his support for the Sudanese authorities and his commitment to improving bilateral relations.

Relations between Eritrea and Sudan worsened in November 1994, when the Eritrean authorities accused Sudan of training 400 terrorists since August. Sudan accused Eritrea of training some 3,000 Sudanese rebels in camps within Eritrea. In December Eritrea severed diplomatic relations with Sudan. Further destabilization was provoked in early 1995 by attacks and infiltration in Gash-Barka Province by the EIJ. The Eritrean authorities subsequently claimed to have identified six training camps on the Sudanese side of the border and also alleged that large numbers of Eritrean refugees in Sudan had been arrested by Sudanese security forces. Sudan responded by proposing Eritrea's suspension from the Intergovernmental Authority on Drought and Development (IGADD, now the Intergovernmental Authority on Development—IGAD, see p. 311), which had been attempting to mediate in Sudan's civil war. The Sudanese Government protested strongly against Eritrea's growing support for the Sudanese opposition grouping, the National Democratic Alliance (NDA), which held a number of conferences in Asmara in the mid-1990s.

In early 1999 Sudan took steps to resolve its differences with Ethiopia, thus increasing the tension between Eritrea and Sudan. In April, however, Sudan indicated its willingness also to improve relations with Eritrea, and in May a reconciliatory agreement was signed in Qatar, which, *inter alia*, restored diplomatic relations between the two countries. Following the renewed outbreak of hostilities between Eritrea and Ethiopia in May (see below), some 94,000 Eritreans crossed the border into Sudan. After the cessation of fighting in June, many Eritrean refugees were repatriated with the assistance of the UN High Commissioner for Refugees (UNHCR), and by January 2002 some 36,500 Eritreans had returned home. In January 2003 refugee status was withdrawn from more than 320,000 Eritreans in Sudan, although UNHCR maintained that its repatriation programme would continue until all those registered had been returned home. In July 2001 Eritrea and Sudan signed an agreement on border security, which aimed to eradicate smuggling and illegal infiltration, as well as ensure the safe passage of people and goods across the common border. In October 2002 relations between the two countries again deteriorated after the Sudanese Government claimed that Eritrean forces had assisted the NDA's capture of Hanashkoreb in eastern Sudan. Although Eritrea strenuously denied any involvement in the incident, Sudan closed the common border with immediate effect. Following a meeting with the Yemeni President, Ali Abdullah Saleh, and Meles in December 2003, al-Bashir accused Eritrea of arming and training rebels in the Darfur region of Sudan and maintained that Eritrea was a destabilizing force in the region. Eritrea refuted the allegations. In early March 2004 two explosions in Tesseney, close to the Sudanese border, resulted in the deaths of at least three people and seven others were killed in an explosion in Barentu in late May. The Eritrean authorities accused Sudanese groups of carrying out the attacks; however, Sudan strongly denied any involvement and stated that the explosions had been the work of Eritrean opposition forces. In June 2005 Eritrea was accused by Sudan of providing military assistance to the rebel Eastern Front, which had launched attacks on government forces in eastern Sudan, while Eritrea denounced alleged Sudanese human rights abuses in Darfur. However, in mid-October Muhammad Omar met with his Sudanese counterpart, Dr Lam Akol, in Khartoum, where they agreed to work towards restoring cordial relations between the two countries. Relations further improved in 2006, following two separate rounds of peace talks in Asmara between the Sudanese Government and the Eastern Front during June—July. Meanwhile, in mid-June President Afewerki met al-Bashir in Khartoum, and later that month the two countries agreed to restore diplomatic relations to ambassadorial level. However, in September al-Bashir accused Eritrea of interference in the Darfur region and urged Eritrea to expel the leaders of the National Redemption Front, which had launched attacks on Sudanese Government forces in Darfur, from its territory. Nevertheless, al-Bashir and the Eastern Front leadership returned to Asmara in mid-October to sign a peace agreement (see chapter on Sudan). In early November the common border between Eritrea and Sudan was officially re-opened.

In November 1995 there were reports that Eritrean troops had attempted to land on the Red Sea island of Greater Hanish, one of three islands (the others being Lesser Hanish and Zuqar) claimed by both Eritrea and Yemen. The disputed islands had been used by Eritrea (with apparent Yemeni approval) during its struggle for independence from Ethiopia. Yemen had subsequently resumed its claims to the islands, because of both their strategic importance (located close to a principal shipping lane) and the possible existence of exploitable petroleum reserves in their surrounding waters. Following fighting in mid-December, Eritrean forces succeeded in occupying Greater Hanish. In May 1996 Eritrea and Yemen signed an arbitration accord in Paris, France, whereby the two sides agreed to submit the dispute to an international tribunal. In October 1998 the tribunal ruled that Yemen had sovereignty over Greater and Lesser Hanish, and all islands to their north-west, while Eritrea had sovereignty over the Mohabaka islands. The court recommended that the fishing traditions around the islands be maintained, thereby granting access to the Hanish islands to Eritrean and Yemeni fishermen. Both countries accepted the ruling, and shortly afterwards agreed to establish a joint committee to strengthen bilateral co-operation.

In September 1993 the first meeting of the Ethiopian-Eritrean joint ministerial commission was held in Asmara, during which agreement was reached on measures to allow the free movement of nationals between each country, and on co-operation regarding foreign affairs and economic policy. Meetings held between President Afewerki and the Ethiopian President, Meles Zenawi, in December underlined the good relations prevailing between the two Governments.

However, relations deteriorated in late 1997 following Eritrea's adoption of a new currency (the nakfa) to replace the Ethiopian birr and the subsequent disruption of cross-border trade. In May 1998 fighting erupted between Eritrean and Ethiopian troops in the border region after both countries accused the other of having invaded their territory. Hostilities escalated in June around Badme, Zalambessa and Assab, resulting in numerous casualties for both sides. A peace plan devised by the USA and Rwanda in early June was unsuccessful, although later that month Eritrea and Ethiopia agreed to an aerial cease-fire, following US and Italian mediation. In August the proposals of an OAU mediation committee, which convened in Ouagadougou, Burkina Faso, were rejected by Eritrea. In November President Afewerki and Prime Minister Meles of Ethiopia were present at different sessions of a special meeting of the OAU mediation committee in Ouagadougou, which was also attended by the Heads of State of Burkina Faso, Zimbabwe and Djibouti. The committee's peace proposals were accepted by Ethiopia, but rejected by Eritrea. That country, moreover, demanded that Djibouti withdraw from the committee, accusing it of providing assistance to Ethiopia in the conflict. Other international mediation attempts in late 1998 failed to resolve the dispute, and in February 1999 the aerial cease-fire was broken and fighting resumed in the border region. In April both sides claimed that they were now prepared to accept and implement the OAU peace proposals, and at the OAU summit held in Algiers, Algeria, in July they confirmed their commitment to the OAU's Framework Agreement. Afewerki announced that Eritrean troops would be withdrawn from all territory captured from Ethiopia since 6 May 1998. Under the agreement, Ethiopia was also required to withdraw from all Eritrean territory captured since 6 February 1999, which, in effect, would see both sides return to their positions before the war. After requesting clarification of technical arrangements to end the war, Ethiopia informed the OAU in September that it had rejected the peace agreement, owing to inconsistencies contained therein. Eritrea accused Ethiopia of deliberately stalling proceedings, while secretly preparing for a fresh offensive.

Throughout late 1999 and early 2000 there were reports of numerous clashes between Eritrean and Ethiopian troops, and both countries continued to promote and assist opposition groups hostile to their foe. In late April 2000 delegations from both countries agreed to attend OAU-sponsored talks in Algiers, although they refused to meet directly. The talks collapsed and in mid-May hostilities between the two countries resumed; Ethiopia launched a major offensive near Badme and Zalambessa and succeeded in repulsing the Eritrean forces. The UN Security Council subsequently unanimously approved the imposition of a 12-month arms embargo on Eritrea and Ethiopia. By late May Ethiopian forces had seized Zalambessa and Eritrean troops were withdrawn from the disputed areas, although Afewerki maintained that this was merely a 'gesture of goodwill' designed to revive the peace talks, which resumed in Algiers on 29 May. Two days later Meles stated that the war was over and that his troops had withdrawn from most of the territory it had captured from Eritrea. Following negotiations in early June both sides expressed their readiness, in principle, to accept the OAU's cease-fire agreement, and on 18 June the Ethiopian and Eritrean Ministers of Foreign Affairs signed an agreement, which provided for an immediate cease-fire and the deployment of a UN peace-keeping force in a 25-km temporary security zone (TSZ) inside Eritrea until the issue of the demarcation of the border had been settled. It was estimated that some 100,000 people had been killed and up to 1.5m. Eritreans displaced since 1998. Indirect negotiations regarding the technical issues of the peace accord, involving representatives from both countries, took place in Washington, DC, USA, in early July 2000 and continued in Algiers in October. Meanwhile, in September the UN Security Council approved the deployment of the UN Mission in Ethiopia and Eritrea (UNMEE), a 4,200-strong peace-keeping force, which was placed under the command of the Special Representative of the UN Secretary-General, Legwaila Joseph Legwaila. On 12 December Eritrea and Ethiopia signed an agreement in Algiers, which formally ended the conflict between the two countries. The agreement provided for a permanent cessation of all hostilities, the immediate return of all prisoners of war, the demarcation of the common border by an independent commission and the establishment of a Claims Commission to assess the issues of compensation and reparations. Furthermore, both countries pledged to co-operate with an independent investigation, which aimed to determine the origins of the conflict.

By late January 2001 the UNMEE force had been fully deployed and on 18 April, after all troops had been withdrawn from the border area, UNMEE declared the establishment of the TSZ, marking the formal separation of the Eritrean and Ethiopian forces. In late June UNMEE presented the final map of the TSZ to Eritrea and Ethiopia, although it emphasized that it would not influence the work of the neutral boundary commission charged with determining the border between the two countries. Despite this announcement, the Ethiopian Government expressed its dissatisfaction with the map. At the eighth meeting of the Military Co-ordination Commission (MCC) in August both countries reiterated their objections to the current boundaries of the TSZ. In mid-September UNMEE's mandate was extended for a further six months, although Legwaila acknowledged that the mission faced an extremely difficult task in achieving lasting peace, as the two countries remained 'polarized', and also admitted that neither country had fully adhered to the terms of the cease-fire agreement. In mid-December the two countries began presenting their cases for border demarcation to the five-member Boundary Commission at the International Court of Justice (see p. 20) in The Hague, Netherlands. In mid-March 2002 UNMEE's mandate was extended until mid-September.

The Boundary Commission delivered its findings in April 2002; however, the Commission did not identify on which side of the boundary line Badme lay, stating that it was awaiting delineation on the ground, which was expected to take up to one year. In the absence of any decision by the Boundary Commission, both countries claimed to have been awarded Badme. In May Ethiopia formally requested 'interpretation, correction and consultation' of the Boundary Commission's report, but this was rejected by the Commission in late June. In March 2003 the Boundary Commission categorically ruled Badme to be Eritrean territory. Meles subsequently complained that the decision was 'wrong and unjust' and vowed to continue to contest the ruling. The demarcation of the border was delayed until October; both the MCC and the UN expressed their frustration at the slow progress being made. The Security Council stated that Ethiopia had committed itself under the 2000 Algiers agreement to accept the Boundary Commission's decision as 'final and binding' and urged it to accept and implement the ruling. Both Legwaila and the Chairman of the Boundary Commission, Elihu Lauterpacht, were critical of Ethiopia's lack of compliance with its obligations under the terms of the peace accord, and the ongoing impasse was further compounded by the Commission's announcement in late October that border demarcation had been delayed indefinitely. Ethiopia maintained that it had agreed to allow demarcation to take place in the eastern sector of the border region, but that it refused to accept the ruling in other areas and had expressed grave concerns about the competency of the Boundary Commission. Eritrea continued, however, to insist that the ruling be fully implemented.

UN concerns over the lack of progress on the part of both Eritrea and Ethiopia in implementing the border ruling continued during 2004. In March UNMEE's mandate was extended by a further six months. In April Legwaila highlighted the difficulties faced by UN peace-keepers in the region owing to continuing travel restrictions placed upon them by the Eritrean authorities, who closed the road from Asmara to Barentu to all UNMEE vehicles for over a month. Following accusations by Eritrean officials in May of serious malpractice on the part of the UN forces, Legwaila issued an ultimatum to Eritrea that it should either co-operate with the UN peace-keeping forces or ask its troops to leave. In September UNMEE's mandate was extended until March 2005 and it was announced that the peace-keeping mission would be reduced with 550 Kenyan troops stationed on the eastern part of the border being replaced by helicopter patrols by the end of January. Meanwhile, in November 2004 Ethiopia stated that it had, in principle, accepted the Boundary Commission's ruling of April 2002 and was prepared to re-enter into talks with Eritrea regarding the demarcation of the border. However, Eritrea dismissed this announcement as little more than a further attempt by Ethiopia to stall the process.

Relations deteriorated further in early 2005 as the UN Security Council and the European Union (EU, see p. 244) expressed concern over troop redeployments on both sides of the border. UNMEE's mandate was extended by six months in March and the Security Council appealed to both countries to reduce troop numbers to December 2004 levels. In September 2005 UNMEE's mandate was again extended until March 2006. In October 2005 Ethiopia reaffirmed its acceptance of the Boundary Commission's ruling, and signalled its willingness to recommence talks with Eritrea. Despite protests from Legwaila and the UN Secretary-General, Kofi Annan, later that month Eritrea imposed restrictions upon the movements of UN vehicles, including a ban upon all UNMEE helicopter flights on its side of the border. In late November the UN Security Council unanimously adopted Resolution 1640, which demanded an end to all restrictions on UNMEE activities and the full implementation of the Boundary Commission's ruling, while also evoking the possibility of sanctions against Eritrea and Ethiopia, should the two countries not comply. In December Eritrea requested that all UNMEE peace-keepers and staff from Canada, Russia, the USA and EU member states leave the country. Some 180 UN staff were subsequently moved into Ethiopia, along with peace-keeping troops, within the 10-day deadline set by Eritrean officials. Later that month the Claims Commission, based in The Hague, ruled that Eritrea was 'liable to compensate Ethiopia' for an attack in May 1998, ruling that, under the UN Charter, Eritrea had not itself come under attack first, invalidating its claim of self-defence and violating international law. Eritrea subsequently accepted the decision.

In early March 2006 representatives of Eritrea and Ethiopia attended a Boundary Commission meeting in London aimed at resolving the border dispute, during which an agreement was reached to hold further discussions in April. Those talks were, however, subsequently postponed until late May. Meanwhile, in late March Legwaila ended his term as Special Representative to the UN Secretary-General and expressed his disappointment at the continued impasse in the peace process. On 31 May the UN Security Council adopted Resolution 1681, which extended UNMEE's mandate for four months, while reducing the number of military personnel by 1,000 to 2,300. The Security Council called upon Eritrea to lift all restrictions placed upon UNMEE activities; however, the request was later rejected by the Eritrean authorities. In late September UNMEE's mandate was extended until 31 January 2007.

In mid-October 2006 UN officials urged Eritrea to withdraw 1,500 of its troops and 14 armoured vehicles from the TSZ, whom the Eritrean Government claimed were harvesting crops from state-run farms in the area. In mid-November both countries declined to attend a meeting of the Boundary Commission in The Hague to discuss border demarcation and subsequently rejected its recommendations. Following the meeting, the Boundary Commission issued a statement, which expressed frustration at both countries' refusal to co-operate with the Commission and insisted that, should no agreement be in place by November 2007, the Commission would unilaterally begin the physical demarcation of the border. Ethiopia later condemned the decision as 'illegal'. In late 2006 relations further deteriorated following accusations that Eritrea had actively supported Islamist fighters in Somalia, who previously had called for a 'holy war' against Ethiopian troops stationed in that country, in an attempt to extend the border conflict (see chapter on Somalia). The Eritrean Government denied any involvement, but warned Ethiopia that Somalia would become a 'quagmire' for its armed forces should conflict erupt. In late December it was reported that a significant number of Eritreans had been captured or killed by Ethiopian troops while fighting alongside Islamist forces in Somalia, a claim that was strongly denied by the Eritrean authorities. On 31 January 2007 the UN Security Council approved Resolution 1741, which extended UNMEE's mandate by six months, while further reducing the size of the mission, to 1,700 military personnel. UNMEE's mandate was subsequently further extended until the end of July 2008.

With Eritrea and Ethiopia continuing to dispute the demarcation of the common border, concerns that conflict could resume were heightened in September 2007 when both Governments deployed troops to the border region. In a letter to his Eritrean counterpart, the Ethiopian Minister of Foreign Affairs, Seyoum Mesfin, stated that the Ethiopian Government considered Eritrea to be in material breach of the Algiers agreement as its troops had occupied the TSZ and had restricted the movement of the UNMEE force. In November Eritrea accused Ethiopia of planning an invasion, although these allegations were strongly denied by the Ethiopian authorities. Both parties again insisted that they were committed to a peaceful resolution of the border dispute; however, neither side complied with the Boundary Commission's request of November 2006 physically to demarcate the border by the end of November 2007. In early December, prior to announcing its own dissolution, the Commission stated that the boundary that it had determined in November 2006 represented the official border between the two countries.

As a result of restrictions imposed by Eritrea, in early February 2008 UNMEE began preparations to withdraw its peace-keepers from that country and to relocate them across the border into Ethiopia. In previous months the UN had repeatedly urged the Eritrean Government to lift restrictions on the delivery of fuel supplies; however, these requests were not met and in mid-February UN personnel were forced to leave the area. It was subsequently reported that a number of peace-keepers had been prevented from leaving Eritrea and the UN Security Council expressed its concern at the 'impediments and logistical constraints' placed upon the force.

According to estimates by the Internal Displacement Monitoring Centre, in 2006 there remained some 40,000–45,000 internally displaced persons in Eritrea. In an effort to promote 'self-sufficiency', in September 2005 the Eritrean Government imposed severe restrictions on the distribution of food aid, and reduced from 1.3m. to 72,000 the number of people entitled to receive free food. The move was widely criticized, especially by the UN, and prompted fears of acute food shortages among one-third of the population who were estimated to be dependent on humanitarian assistance.

Government

In May 1991 the Eritrean People's Liberation Front (EPLF, restyled as the People's Front for Democracy and Justice—PFDJ—in February 1994) established a provisional Government to administer Eritrea, pending the holding of a national referendum on the issue of independence. The EPLF did not invite other organizations to participate, although it promised that free elections would be held following the referendum. The referendum was held in April 1993, and Eritrea was proclaimed an independent state in the following month. A transitional Government was established, at the apex of which were three state institutions: the Consultative Council (the executive authority formed from the ministers, provincial administrators, and heads of government authorities and commissions); the National Assembly (the legislative authority comprising the Central Committee of the EPLF, 30 additional members from the Provincial Assemblies and 30 individuals selected by the Central Committee); and the judiciary. In March 1994 the Consultative Council was superseded by a State Council. At independence a four-year transitional period was declared, during which preparations were to proceed for the establishment of a constitutional and pluralist political system. Meanwhile, in March 1994 the National Assembly voted to alter its composition: it would thenceforth comprise the 75 members of the PFDJ Central Committee and 75 directly elected members. In May 1997, following the adoption of the Constitution, the Constituent Assembly empowered a Transitional National Assembly (comprising the 75 members of the PFDJ Central Committee, 60 members of the former Constituent Assembly, and 15 representatives of Eritreans residing abroad) to act as the legislature until elections were held for a new National Assembly.

Defence

Eritrea's armed forces increased rapidly during the 1999–2000 border conflict with Ethiopia and, as assessed at November 2007,

ERITREA

despite the cessation of hostilities in June 2000, were estimated to number 201,750, including an army of about 200,000, a navy of 1,400 and an air force of about 350. In July 2000 the UN Security Council adopted a resolution (No. 1312) establishing the UN Mission in Ethiopia and Eritrea (UNMEE), which was to supervise the cease-fire and the implementation of a peace agreement. At the end of November 2007 UNMEE numbered 1,464 troops, 212 military observers, as well as 147 international civilians and 202 local civilians; UNMEE had a total authorized strength of 4,200 troops (including 230 military observers). In February 2008 UNMEE commenced its withdrawal from Eritrea after that country refused to restore fuel supplies to the peace-keeping force. National service is compulsory for all Eritrean citizens between 18 and 40 years of age (with certain exceptions), for a 16-month period, including four months of military training. Budgeted expenditure on defence (including the demobilization of ex-combatants) in 2005 was estimated at 1,000m. nakfa.

Economic Affairs

In 2006, according to estimates by the World Bank, Eritrea's gross national income (GNI), measured at average 2004–06 prices, was US $889m., equivalent to $200 per head (or $1,090 per head on an international purchasing-power parity basis). During 1996–2006, it was estimated, the population increased at an average annual rate of 3.7%, while gross domestic product (GDP) per head decreased, in real terms, by an average of 2.4% per year during 1996–2006. Overall GDP increased, in real terms, at an average annual rate of 1.2% in 1996–2006; growth in 2005 was 0.5%, but GDP contracted by 1.0% in 2006.

By far the most important sector of the economy is agriculture, which sustains 90% of the population. In 2006 agriculture (including forestry and fishing) accounted for an estimated 17.5% of GDP; the sector employed an estimated 76.0% of the economically active population in mid-2005, according to FAO. Most sedentary agriculture is practised in the highlands, where rainfall is sufficient to cultivate the main crops: sorghum, teff (an indigenous grain), sesame seed, potatoes, millet and barley. As a result of serious environmental degradation (caused directly and indirectly by the war of independence), water scarcity and unreliable rainfall, projects have been undertaken to build water reservoirs and small dams, while badly eroded hillsides have been terraced and new trees planted in order to prevent soil erosion. Fishing activity is on a very small scale—the total catch reached just 4,027 tons in 2005—although, according to the UN, sustainable yields of as much as 70,000 tons per year may be possible. In real terms, the GDP of the agricultural sector increased at an average annual rate of 0.1% in 1996–2006. Agricultural GDP increased by 5.2% in 2006.

In 2006 industrial production (comprising mining, manufacturing, construction and utilities) accounted for an estimated 23.0% of GDP. Some 5.0% of the labour force were employed in the industrial sector in 1990. Industrial GDP increased, in real terms, at an average annual rate of 2.9% in 1996–2004. Industrial GDP increased by 1.9% in 2003, but declined by 0.4% in 2004.

Eritrea's mineral resources are believed to be of significant potential value, although in 2002 mining and quarrying accounted for less than 0.1% of GDP. Of particular importance, in view of Eritrea's acute energy shortage, is the possibility of large reserves of petroleum and natural gas beneath the Red Sea. An exploration agreement, with CMS Oil and Gas of the USA, was signed in 2001 following the end of the conflict with Ethiopia. Other mineral resources include potash, zinc, magnesium, copper, iron ore, marble and gold. New legislation on mining, adopted in 1995, declared all mineral resources to be state assets, but recognized an extensive role for private investors in their exploitation. In September 2004, following the discovery in August of high-grade gold and copper in Western Eritrea, the Eritrean authorities prohibited all mining exploration by foreign companies while it reassessed its mining legislation. The ban was lifted in January 2005 with the Government announcing the possibility of increasing its option to buy into projects from the current maximum of 20% to 30%.

The manufacturing sector provided an estimated 8.7% of GDP in 2006. Until mid-1997 imported petroleum was processed at the Assab refinery, whose entire output of petroleum products was delivered to Ethiopia. The authorities announced that they would import refined petroleum for the immediate future. In late 2004 the Government suspended the sale of petrol to the public following fuel rationing precipitated by the rising cost of petroleum on world markets. The GDP of the sector increased, in real terms, at an average annual rate of 4.1% in 1996–2004; manufacturing GDP increased by 1.9% in 2004.

Most electric energy is provided by four thermal power stations, largely dependent on imported fuel. Imports of fuel and energy comprised an estimated 8.9% of the total cost of imports in 2000. However, electricity is provided to only 10% of the population, the remainder relying on fuel wood and animal products. In mid-1999 the discovery of geothermal potential at the Alid volcanic centre raised hopes that Eritrea's energy problems could be alleviated.

The services sector contributed an estimated 59.5% of GDP in 2006. The dominant services are trade, public administration and transport. The GDP of the services sector increased, in real terms, at an average annual rate of 1.6% in 1996–2004. Services GDP increased by 1.4% in 2004.

In 2006, according to the African Development Bank, Eritrea recorded a trade deficit of US $481.8m., and there was a deficit of $24.2m. on the current account of the balance of payments. In 2003 the principal sources of non-petroleum imports were the USA (accounting for an estimated 15.9% of the total), the United Arab Emirates and Italy. Exports in that year were mostly to Sudan (19.7%, compared with 83.8% in 2002) and Italy. Eritrea's principal exports in 2003 were food and live animals (36.4% of the total), crude materials and basic manufactures. The main non-petroleum imports in that year were food and live animals (40.5% of the total), machinery and transport equipment and basic manufactures.

In 2002 it was estimated that Eritrea's budget deficit reached 2,728.5m. nakfa, equivalent to 30.2% of GDP. Eritrea's external debt at the end of 2005 totalled US $735.5m., of which $723.0m. was long-term public debt. In 2003 the cost of debt-servicing represented 14.1% of the value of exports of goods and services. The annual rate of inflation averaged 14.3% in 1996–2006. Consumer prices increased by an estimated average of 14.2% in 2006. In 2003 unemployment and underemployment were estimated to affect as many as 50% of the labour force.

In 1993 Eritrea was admitted to the group of African, Caribbean and Pacific (ACP) countries party to the Lomé Convention; in September 2001 Eritrea ratified the Cotonou Agreement (see p. 301), the successor of the Lomé Convention. Eritrea became a member of the IMF in 1994.

Since independence the Eritrean Government has experienced severe difficulties and many of its initial economic aims have not been realised. In November 1997 the introduction of the nakfa as the national currency (Eritrea had retained the Ethiopian birr as its monetary unit since independence), initially at par with the birr, led to the outbreak of hostilities with Ethiopia. Cross-border trade was adversely affected and in May 1998 Ethiopia re-routed its maritime commerce via Djibouti. Trade with Ethiopia, which previously accounted for two-thirds of Eritrean exports, virtually ceased, and Eritrea was estimated to have spent at least US $1m. per day on the war. This expenditure, coupled with the failure of successive harvests, increased Eritrea's already considerable reliance on donations from aid organizations, and the need to feed, clothe and shelter the vast numbers of people displaced during the war has placed a further strain on government finances. The mining sector has expanded in recent years following the discovery of large mineral deposits around Bisha and Asmara. It was hoped that the development of that sector would, in the long term, reduce the dependence upon remittances from abroad, which are estimated to amount to $400m. per year, and in particular on the agricultural sector, which remains susceptible to drought and poor harvests. The gold mine at Bisha was expected to commence production in 2010 and it was estimated that proceeds from the export of gold could provide up to 40% of government revenue in the future. In late 2007 the Government granted licenses to a number of Chinese firms for the exploration of gold and other minerals. This reflected an effort by the Eritrean authorities to improve relations with the People's Republic of China; imports from that county had increased dramatically in 2006. Economic ties have also been sought with Arab nations, particularly Libya, Saudi Arabia, the United Arab Emirates and Qatar. Nevertheless, GDP growth of just 1.3% was projected in 2008 and serious challenges remained. It was estimated that some 400,000 people, mainly youths, were engaged in military service, thus depriving the country of a large section of its workforce, and the potential resumption of hostilities with Ethiopia threatened further to adversely affect the country's economic prospects. Furthermore, in 2007 Eritrea's total external debt totalled some $700m. (equivalent to 65% of GDP) and relations with donor

ERITREA

institutions were increasingly strained as a result of the Government's authoritarian policies.

Education

Education is provided free of charge in government schools and at the University of Asmara. There are also some fee-paying private schools. Education is officially compulsory for children between seven and 13 years of age. Primary education begins at the age of seven and lasts for five years. Secondary education, beginning at 12 years of age, lasts for up to six years, comprising a first cycle of two years and a second of four years. According to UNESCO estimates, in 2003/04 primary enrolment included 48% of children in the relevant age-group (boys 52%; girls 44%), while the comparable ratio for secondary enrolment was only 24% (boys 28%; girls 19%). Total government expenditure on education and training in 2002 was an estimated 467.2m. nakfa (7.6% of total spending). In 2004/05 there were an estimated 5,500 students enrolled on bachelor degree courses at the University of Asmara. The University of Asmara was officially closed in September 2006. Higher education would henceforth be provided by six newly-established technical institutes, each associated with a relevant Government ministry. The institutes provide education in the fields of science, technology, business and economics, social sciences, agriculture and marine training.

Public Holidays

2008: 1 January (New Year's Day), 6 January (Epiphany), 24 May (Independence Day), 20 June (Martyrs' Day), 1 September (anniversary of the start of the armed struggle), 1 October* (Id al-Fitr, end of Ramadan), 9 December* (Id al-Adha/Arafat), 25 December (Christmas).

2009: 1 January (New Year's Day), 6 January (Epiphany), 24 May (Independence Day), 20 June (Martyrs' Day), 1 September (anniversary of the start of the armed struggle), 20 September* (Id al-Fitr, end of Ramadan), 27 November* (Id al-Adha/Arafat), 25 December (Christmas).

* These holidays are dependent on the Islamic lunar calendar and may vary by one or two days from the dates given.

Weights and Measures

The metric system is in force.

Statistical Survey

Source (unless otherwise stated): Ministry of Trade and Industry, POB 1844, Asmara; tel. (1) 118386; fax (1) 110586.

Area and Population

AREA, POPULATION AND DENSITY*

Area (sq km)	121,144†
Population (census results)	
9 May 1984	
Males	1,374,452
Females	1,373,852
Total	2,748,304
Population (UN estimates at mid-year)‡	
2005	4,527,000
2006	4,692,000
2007	4,851,000
Density (per sq km) at mid-2007	40.0

* Including the Assab district.
† 46,774 sq miles.
‡ Source: UN, *World Population Prospects: The 2006 Revision*.

PRINCIPAL TOWNS
(estimated population at January 2008)

Asmara (capital)	1,146,822		Keren	71,749
Assab	88,983		Mitsiwa (Massawa)	45,975

Source: Stefan Helders, *World Gazetteer* (internet www.world-gazetteer.com).

BIRTHS AND DEATHS
(averages per year, UN estimates)

	1990–95	1995–2000	2000–05
Birth rate (per 1,000)	40.2	39.6	40.5
Death rate (per 1,000)	14.3	11.8	10.6

Source: UN, *World Population Prospects: The 2006 Revision*.

Expectation of life (years at birth, WHO estimates): 60.9 (males 58.8; females 62.7) in 2005 (Source: WHO, *World Health Statistics*).

Health and Welfare

KEY INDICATORS

Total fertility rate (children per woman, 2005)	5.3
Under-5 mortality rate (per 1,000 live births, 2004)	78
HIV/AIDS (% of persons aged 15–49, 2005)	2.40
Physicians (per 1,000 head, 2004)	0.05
Health expenditure (2004): US $ per head (PPP)	27.4
Health expenditure (2004): % of GDP	4.5
Health expenditure (2004): public (% of total)	39.2
Access to water (% of persons, 2004)	60
Access to sanitation (% of persons, 2004)	9
Human Development Index (2005): ranking	157
Human Development Index (2005): value	0.483

For sources and definitions, see explanatory note on p. vi.

ERITREA

Agriculture

PRINCIPAL CROPS
('000 metric tons)

	2003	2004	2005
Wheat	3.4	5.1	0.7
Barley	8.6	11.1	9.3
Maize	4.5	3.2	2.5
Millet	11.7	8.0	17.4
Sorghum	64.1	44.6	114.3
Potatoes	10.9	16.0	17.5
Other roots and tubers*	85.0	85.0	85.0
Dry beans	0.3	0.6	0.2
Dry broad beans*	1.8	1.8	1.8
Dry peas	1.4	0.1	0.1
Chick-peas	0.1	3.5	3.5*
Lentils	0.1	0.1	0.2
Vetches*	4.5	4.5	4.5
Other pulses*	27.0	25.0	25.0
Groundnuts (in shell)	1.2*	0.8	2.5
Sesame seed	7.0	5.0	18.5
Linseed	0.1*	0.1	0.0
Vegetables*	23.0	23.0	23.0
Fruits*	2.0	2.0	2.0

* FAO estimate(s).

2006 ('000 metric tons): Dry beans 0.5; Potatoes 15.5. Note: Data for most individual crops were not available for 2006.

Aggregate production ('000 metric tons, may include official, semi-official or estimated data): Total cereals 79.6 in 2004, 151.7 in 2005, 151.7 in 2006; Total roots and tubers 101.0 in 2004, 102.5 in 2005, 100.5 in 2006; Total vegetables (incl. melons) 23.0 in 2004, 23.0 in 2005, 23.0 in 2006; Total fruits (excl. melons) 2.3 in 2004, 2.3 in 2005, 2.3 in 2006.

Source: FAO.

LIVESTOCK
('000 head, year ending September, FAO estimates)

	2003	2004	2005
Cattle	1,927	1,930	1,950
Sheep	2,100	2,100	2,100
Goats	1,700	1,700	1,700
Camels	75	75	75
Chickens	1,370	1,370	1,370

Note: Data for 2006 were not available.
Source: FAO.

LIVESTOCK PRODUCTS
('000 metric tons, FAO estimates)

	2003	2004	2005
Cattle meat	16.7	16.7	16.7
Sheep meat	6.7	6.7	5.6
Goat meat	5.8	5.8	5.8
Chicken meat	2.3	2.3	2.1
Camels' milk	5.1	5.1	5.1
Cows' milk	39.2	39.2	39.2
Goats' milk	8.5	8.5	8.5
Sheep's milk	3.9	3.9	3.9
Hen eggs	2.0	2.0	2.0
Wool: greasy	0.8	0.8	0.8

Note: Data for 2006 were not available.
Source: FAO.

Fishing

(metric tons, live weight of capture)

	2003	2004	2005
Lizardfishes	1,688	3,886	2,364
Sea catfishes	207	217	57
Threadfin breams	525	819	615
Snappers and jobfishes	227	102	27
Barracudas	1,845	411	208
Carangids	343	301	120
Queenfishes	387	212	38
Penaeus shrimps	451	413	235
Total catch (incl. others)	6,689	7,404	4,027

Source: FAO.

Mining

('000 metric tons, unless otherwise indicated, estimates)

	2003	2004	2005
Gold (kilograms)	9	33	25
Marble ('000 sq m)	1,777.8	780.3	36.0
Limestone	3	3	3
Salt	5	3	6

Source: US Geological Survey.

Industry

SELECTED PRODUCTS
('000 metric tons, unless otherwise indicated)

	2003	2004	2005
Cement	45	45	45
Basalt	111.7	499.3	184.0
Gravel	340.1	169.3	219.8
Coral	70*	95.1	91.3
Electric energy (million kWh)	276	283	n.a.

* Estimate.

Sources: US Geological Survey; UN, *Industrial Commodity Statistics Yearbook*.

Finance

CURRENCY AND EXCHANGE RATES

Monetary Units
100 cents = 1 nakfa.

Sterling, Dollar and Euro Equivalents (31 December 2007)
£1 sterling = 30.802 nakfa;
US $1 = 15.375 nakfa;
€1 = 22.634 nakfa;
1,000 nakfa = £32.47 = $65.04 = €44.18.

Note: Following its secession from Ethiopia in May 1993, Eritrea retained the Ethiopian currency, the birr. An exchange rate of US $1 = 5.000 birr was introduced in October 1992 and remained in force until April 1994, when it was adjusted to $1 = 5.130 birr. Further adjustments were made subsequently. In addition to the official exchange rate, the Bank of Eritrea applied a marginal auction rate (determined at fortnightly auctions of foreign exchange, conducted by the National Bank of Ethiopia) to aid-funded imports and to most transactions in services. A more depreciated preferential rate applied to remittances of foreign exchange by Eritreans abroad, to proceeds from exports and to most payments for imports. On 1 April 1997 Eritrea unified the official and preferential exchange rates at $1 = 7.20 birr (which had been the preferential rate since January 1996). In November 1997 the Government introduced a separate national currency, the nakfa, replacing (and initially at par with) the Ethiopian birr. The exchange rate in relation to the US dollar was initially set at the prevailing unified rate, but from 1 May 1998 a mechanism to provide a market-related exchange rate was established.

Average Exchange Rate (nakfa per US $)
2005 15.3679
2006 15.3750
2007 15.3750

ERITREA

BUDGET
(million nakfa)

Revenue*	2000	2001†	2002‡
Tax revenue	982.7	1,278.8	1,538.2
Direct taxes	473.5	572.9	552.8
Taxes on personal income	122.7	136.9	159.6
Taxes on business profits	299.9	387.5	337.2
Rehabilitation tax	10.4	2.9	1.8
Domestic sales tax (incl. stamp duties)	238.1	297.0	368.3
Import duties and taxes	271.0	409.0	617.1
Port fees and charges	59.4	103.3	148.5
Other current revenue	743.4	429.4	575.6
Extraordinary revenue	322.9	174.9	29.2
Total	**2,108.3**	**1,986.4**	**2,291.4**

Expenditure	2000	2001†	2002‡
Current expenditure	4,333.8	4,160.4	4,147.2
General services	2,722.2	2,444.7	2,619.5
Internal affairs	25.9	36.4	46.9
Regional administration	328.8	326.7	164.8
Foreign affairs	102.7	103.6	179.1
Defence§	2,220.3	1,883.6	2,104.4
Economic services	55.7	64.6	71.1
Agriculture and natural resources	32.9	34.3	37.5
Mining and energy	2.9	3.1	3.4
Construction and urban development	7.8	9.2	13.7
Transport and communications	5.6	5.7	6.7
Social services	361.8	345.6	394.8
Education and training	163.8	182.0	182.9
Health	99.3	97.6	110.8
Demobilization of ex-combatants	—	6.9	7.8
Capital expenditure	1,064.9	2,005.0	1,991.1
General services	117.4	241.2	227.8
Economic development	581.4	1,359.0	955.6
Agriculture and natural resources	116.2	164.7	131.3
Trade, industry and tourism	1.2	4.7	5.8
Construction, transport and communications	262.7	551.2	378.4
Social development	366.1	404.8	807.7
Education	262.2	231.2	284.3
Health	85.9	143.2	478.2
Total	**5,398.7**	**6,165.4**	**6,138.3**

* Excluding grants received (million nakfa): 1,204.8 in 2000 (current 1,165.5, capital 39.3); 1,375.6 (preliminary) in 2001 (current 913.6, capital 462.0); 1,118.4 (estimate) in 2002 (current 510.0, capital 608.4).
† Preliminary figures.
‡ Estimates.
§ Including some demobilization costs.
Source: IMF, *Eritrea: Selected Issues and Statistical Appendix* (June 2003).

INTERNATIONAL RESERVES
(US $ million at 31 December)

	1999	2000	2001
Gold (national valuation)	19.7	10.4	10.5
Reserve position in IMF	0.0	0.0	0.0
Foreign exchange	34.2	25.5	39.7
Total	**53.9**	**35.9**	**50.3**

Foreign exchange: 30.3 in 2002; 24.7 in 2003; 34.7 in 2004; 27.9 in 2005; 25.3 in 2006.
Gold (national valuation): 44.3 in 2002; 46.2 in 2003; 56.5 in 2004; 51.8 in 2005; 47.3 in 2006.
Source: IMF, *International Financial Statistics*.

MONEY SUPPLY
(million nakfa at 31 December)

	2004	2005	2006
Currency outside banks	3,253	3,654	3,515
Demand deposits at banks	4,491	5,414	6,056
Total money (incl. others)	**7,799**	**9,102**	**9,636**

Source: IMF, *International Financial Statistics*.

COST OF LIVING
(Consumer Price Index at December; base: 2000 = 100)

	2004	2005	2006
All items	196.2	225.6	257.7

Source: African Development Bank.

NATIONAL ACCOUNTS

Expenditure on the Gross Domestic Product
(US $ million)

	2004	2005	2006
Final consumption expenditure	1,462.92	1,298.41	1,467.93
Gross capital formation	201.36	185.74	218.29
Total domestic expenditure	**1,664.28**	**1,484.15**	**1,686.22**
Exports of goods and services	95.24	63.69	74.13
Less Imports of goods and services	831.50	585.64	675.86
GDP in market prices	**928.01**	**962.20**	**1,084.49**
GDP at factor cost at constant 2000 prices	**671.39**	**703.62**	**714.17**

Source: African Development Bank.

Gross Domestic Product by Economic Activity
(million nakfa at current prices)

	2000	2001*	2002*
Agriculture, forestry and fishing	871.1	1,279.2	941.3
Mining and quarrying	5.8	2.8	3.3
Manufacturing†	644.2	772.6	939.1
Electricity and water	68.4	80.8	100.8
Construction	607.8	746.3	954.0
Wholesale and retail trade	1,136.2	1,369.5	1,672.6
Transport and communications	727.8	877.0	1,071.3
Financial services	189.2	228.0	278.5
Dwellings and domestic services	121.9	143.5	169.5
Public administration and services	1,037.7	1,197.7	1,387.6
Other services	362.7	436.6	528.0
GDP at factor cost	**5,772.8**	**7,134.0**	**8,045.8**
Indirect taxes, *less* subsidies	427.7	637.0	985.4
GDP in purchasers' values	**6,200.5**	**7,771.0**	**9,031.2**

* Preliminary figures.
† Including handicrafts and small-scale industry.
Source: IMF, *Eritrea: Selected Issues and Statistical Appendix* (June 2003).

2005 (million nafka at current prices): Agriculture, hunting, forestry, fishing 1,959; Mining, manufacturing and utilities 1,649 (Manufacturing 1,477); Construction 1,511; Wholesale, retail trade, restaurants and hotels 2,669; Transport, storage and communications 1,678; Other activities 3,804; Sub-total 13,270. Source: UN Statistics Division, National Accounts Main Aggregates Database.

ERITREA

BALANCE OF PAYMENTS
(US $ million)

	2000	2001*	2002†
Exports of goods f.o.b.	36.7	19.9	51.8
Imports of goods c.i.f.	−470.3	−536.7	−533.4
Trade balance	−433.5	−516.7	−481.7
Exports of services	60.7	127.5	132.6
Imports of services	−28.3	−33.4	−30.3
Balance on goods and services	−401.1	−422.6	−379.4
Other income (net)	−1.4	−4.6	−6.1
Balance on goods, services and income	−402.5	−427.2	−385.5
Private unrequited transfers (net)	195.7	175.0	205.6
Official unrequited transfers (net)	102.4	120.8	80.3
Current balance	−104.5	−131.4	−99.6
Capital account (net)	—	7.3	3.6
Financial account	98.7	94.8	64.6
Short-term capital (net)	−14.7	18.7	15.9
Net errors and omissions	−9.5	36.5	−7.6
Overall balance	−15.2	7.2	−39.0

* Preliminary figures.
† Estimates.

Source: IMF, *Eritrea: Selected Issues and Statistical Appendix* (June 2003).

2006 (US $ million): Exports of goods 11.45; Imports of goods −493.22; Trade balance −481.76; Net service and factor income −49.85; Net current transfers 507.42; Current account balance −24.19 (Source: African Development Bank).

External Trade

PRINCIPAL COMMODITIES
(distribution by SITC, US $ '000)

Imports c.i.f. (excl. petroleum)	2001	2002	2003
Food and live animals	110.9	153.0	175.2
Animal and vegetable oils, fats and waxes	13.6	7.4	19.3
Chemicals and related products	45.5	36.4	26.2
Basic manufactures	101.5	115.6	63.3
Machinery and transport equipment	107.4	155.9	97.2
Miscellaneous manufactured articles	34.0	46.9	40.7
Total (incl. others)	422.9	537.9	432.8

Exports f.o.b.	2001	2002	2003
Food and live animals	8.8	37.7	2.4
Crude materials (inedible) except fuels	3.0	6.0	2.1
Chemicals and related products	0.7	0.6	0.1
Basic manufactures	5.6	4.8	1.1
Miscellaneous manufactured articles	0.5	1.5	0.7
Total (incl. others)	19.0	51.8	6.6

Source: UN, *International Trade Statistics Yearbook*.

PRINCIPAL TRADING PARTNERS
(US $ million)

Imports c.i.f.	2001	2002	2003
Belgium	11.9	13.7	8.6
Germany	11.8	16.4	6.7
Italy	79.0	70.4	50.1
Netherlands	13.9	17.4	10.4
Saudi Arabia	70.0	70.0	45.4
United Arab Emirates	64.6	90.7	52.9
United Kingdom	9.6	10.0	11.7
USA	20.4	38.5	68.9
Total (incl. others)	422.9	537.9	432.8

Exports f.o.b.	2001	2002	2003
Djibouti	—	0.8	—
Germany	0.7	0.5	0.1
India	3.2	0.5	0.5
Italy	2.1	1.8	0.8
Netherlands	0.4	0.3	0.7
Saudi Arabia	0.3	0.1	—
Sudan	9.7	43.4	1.3
Total (incl. others)	19.0	51.8	6.6

Source: UN, *International Trade Statistics Yearbook*.

Transport

ROAD TRAFFIC
(motor vehicles in use)

	1996	1997	1998
Number of registered vehicles	27,013	31,276	35,942

SHIPPING

Merchant Fleet
(registered at 31 December)

	2004	2005	2006
Number of vessels	12	11	15
Displacement (grt)	21,092	20,755	21,455

Source: Lloyd's Register-Fairplay, *World Fleet Statistics*.

CIVIL AVIATION

	1996	1997	1998
Passengers ('000)	168.1	173.8	105.2

Tourism

ARRIVALS BY COUNTRY OF ORIGIN

	2003	2004	2005
Germany	1,252	1,005	1,045
India	2,580	2,420	2,985
Italy	2,334	3,476	3,246
Japan	103	1,063	1,018
Kenya	695	1,481	796
Sudan	717	992	664
United Kingdom	1,106	1,079	888
USA	1,745	1,611	1,611
Total (incl. others)	80,029	87,298	83,307

Tourism receipts (US $ million, incl. passenger transport): 74 in 2003; 73 in 2004; 66 in 2005.

Source: World Tourism Organization.

ERITREA

Communications Media

	2004	2005	2006
Telephones ('000 main lines in use)	39.3	37.7	37.5
Mobile cellular telephones ('000 subscribers)	20	40.4	62.0
Personal computers ('000 in use)	15	35	n.a.
Internet users ('000)	50.0	80.0	100.0

2000: Television receivers ('000 in use) 100; Facsimile machines 1,771 in use.

Radio receivers ('000 in use): 345 in 1997.

Book production (1993): 106 titles (including 23 pamphlets) and 420,000 copies (including 60,000 pamphlets). Figures for books, excluding pamphlets, refer only to school textbooks (64 titles; 323,000 copies) and government publications (19 titles; 37,000 copies).

Sources: mainly UNESCO, *Statistical Yearbook*; International Telecommunication Union.

Education

(2004/05, unless otherwise indicated)

	Institutions*	Teachers	Pupils
Pre-primary	95	829	31,244
Primary	695	7,642	377,512
Secondary: General	44	4,058	215,080
Secondary: Teacher-training	2	47*	922*
Secondary: Vocational	n.a.	168	1,864
University and equivalent level	n.a.	429†	4,612†

* 2001/02 figure(s).
† 2003/04 figure.

Sources: UNESCO; Ministry of Education, Asmara.

Adult literacy rate (UNESCO estimates): 56.7% (males 68.2%; females 45.6%) in 2003 (Source: UN Development Programme, *Human Development Report*).

Directory

The Constitution

On 23 May 1997 the Constituent Assembly unanimously adopted the Eritrean Constitution. A presidential regime was instituted, with the President to be elected for a maximum of two five-year terms. The President, as Head of State, has extensive powers and appoints, with the approval of the National Assembly (the legislature), the ministers, the commissioners, the Auditor-General, the President of the central bank and the judges of the Supreme Court. The President's mandate can be revoked if two-thirds of the members of the National Assembly so demand. 'Conditional' political pluralism is authorized. Pending the election of a new National Assembly, legislative power was to be held by a Transitional National Assembly, comprising the 75 members of the People's Front for Democracy and Justice (PFDJ) Central Committee, 60 members of the former Constituent Assembly and 15 representatives of Eritreans residing abroad.

The Government

HEAD OF STATE

President: ISSAIAS AFEWERKI (assumed power May 1991; elected President by the National Assembly 8 June 1993).

CABINET
(February 2008)

President: ISSAIAS AFEWERKI.
Minister of Defence: Gen. SEBHAT EPHREM.
Minister of Justice: FAWZIA HASHIM.
Minister of Foreign Affairs: OSMAN SALIH MUHAMMAD.
Minister of Information: ALI ABDU.
Minister of Finance: BERHANE ABREHE.
Minister of Trade and Industry: Dr GIORGIS TEKLEMIKAEL.
Minister of Agriculture: AREFAINE BERHE.
Minister of Labour and Human Welfare: ASKALU MENKERIOS.
Minister of Marine Resources: AHMED HAJI ALI.
Minister of Construction: ABRAHA ASFAHA.
Minister of Energy and Mines: TESFAI GEBRESELASSIE.
Minister of Education: SEMERE RUSOM.
Minister of Health: Dr SALIH MEKKI.
Minister of Transport and Communications: WOLDEMIKAEL ABRAHA.
Minister of Tourism: AMNA NUR HUSSEIN.
Minister of Land, Water and the Environment: WOLDEMICHAEL GEBREMARIAM.
Minister of Local Government: NAIZGHI KIFLU.

MINISTRIES AND COMMISSIONS

Office of the President: POB 257, Asmara; tel. (1) 122132; fax (1) 125123.

Ministry of Agriculture: POB 1048, Asmara; tel. (1) 181499; fax (1) 181415.

Ministry of Construction: POB 841, Asmara; tel. (1) 114588; fax (1) 120661.

Ministry of Defence: POB 629, Asmara; tel. (1) 165952; fax (1) 124990.

Ministry of Education: POB 5610, Asmara; tel. (1) 113044; fax (1) 113866; internet www.erimoe.gov.er.

Ministry of Energy and Mines: POB 5285, Asmara; tel. (1) 116872; fax (1) 127652.

Ministry of Finance: POB 896, Asmara; tel. (1) 118131; fax (1) 127947.

Ministry of Fisheries: POB 923, Asmara; tel. (1) 120400; fax (1) 122185; e-mail mofisha@eol.com.er.

Ministry of Foreign Affairs: POB 190, Asmara; tel. (1) 127838; fax (1) 123788; e-mail tesfai@wg.eol.

Ministry of Health: POB 212, Asmara; tel. (1) 117549; fax (1) 112899.

Ministry of Information: POB 872, Asmara; tel. (1) 120478; fax (1) 126747; internet www.shabait.com.

Ministry of Justice: POB 241, Asmara; tel. (1) 127739; fax (1) 126422.

Ministry of Labour and Human Welfare: POB 5252, Asmara; tel. (1) 181846; fax (1) 181760; e-mail mlhw@eol.com.er.

Ministry of Land, Water and the Environment: POB 976, Asmara; tel. (1) 118021; fax (1) 123285.

Ministry of Local Government: POB 225, Asmara; tel. (1) 114254; fax (1) 120014.

Ministry of Tourism: POB 1010, Asmara; tel. (1) 126997; fax (1) 126949; e-mail eritrea_tourism@cts.com.er; internet www.shaebia.org/mot.html.

Ministry of Trade and Industry: POB 1844, Asmara; tel. (1) 118386; fax (1) 120586.

Ministry of Transport and Communications: POB 1840, Asmara; tel. (1) 114222; fax (1) 127048; e-mail motc.rez@eol.com.er.

Eritrean Relief and Refugee Commission: POB 1098, Asmara; tel. (1) 182222; fax (1) 182970; e-mail john@errec.er.punchdown.org.

Land and Housing Commission: POB 348, Asmara; tel. (1) 117400.

Provincial Administrators

There are six administrative regions in Eritrea, each with regional, sub-regional and village administrations.

Anseba Province: SALMA HASSAN.
Debub Province: MUSTAFA NUR HUSSEIN.
Debubawi Keyih Bahri Province: TSEGEREDA WOLDEGERGIS.
Gash-Barka Province: KAHSAI GEBREHIWOT.
Maakel Province: SEMERE RUSOM.
Semenawi Keyih Bahri Province: ABDALLA MUSA.

Legislature

NATIONAL ASSEMBLY

In accordance with transitional arrangements formulated in Decree No. 37 of May 1993, the National Assembly consists of the Central Committee of the People's Front for Democracy and Justice (PFDJ) and 60 other members: 30 from the Provincial Assemblies and an additional 30 members, including a minimum of 10 women, to be nominated by the PFDJ Central Committee. The legislative body 'outlines the internal and external policies of the government, regulates their implementation, approves the budget and elects a president for the country'. The National Assembly is to hold regular sessions every six months under the chairmanship of the President. In his role as Head of the Government and Commander-in-Chief of the Army, the President nominates individuals to head the various government departments. These nominations are ratified by the legislative body. In March 1994 the National Assembly voted to alter its composition: it would henceforth comprise the 75 members of the Central Committee of the PFDJ and 75 directly elected members. In May 1997, following the adoption of the Constitution, the Constituent Assembly empowered a Transitional National Assembly (comprising the 75 members of the PFDJ, 60 members of the former Constituent Assembly and 15 representatives of Eritreans residing abroad) to act as the legislature until elections were held for a new National Assembly.

Chairman of the Transitional National Assembly: ISSAIAS AFEWERKI.

Election Commission

Electoral Commission: Asmara; f. 2002; 5 mems appointed by the President; Commissioner RAMADAN MOHAMMED NUR.

Political Organizations

Afar Federal Alliance: e-mail afa_f@hotmail.com; f. 2003.
Democratic Movement for the Liberation of Eritrean Kunama: Postfach 620 124, 50694, Köln, Germany; e-mail kcs@baden-kunama.com; internet www.baden-kunama.com; based in Germany; represents the Kunama minority ethnic group.
Eritrean Democratic Party (EDP): e-mail info@selfi-democracy.com; internet www.selfi-democracy.com; f. 2001 as the Eritrean People's Liberation Front—Democratic Party (EPLF—DP); breakaway group from the PFDJ; name changed to above in 2004; Chair. MESFIN HAGOS.
Eritrean Islamic Jihad (EIJ): radical opposition group; in Aug. 1993 split into a mil. wing and a political wing.
Eritrean Islamic Party for Justice and Development (EIPJD) (Al-Hizb Al-Islami Al-Eritree Liladalah Wetenmiya): internet www.alkhalas.org; f. 1988 as Eritrean Islamic Jihad Movement; changed name to al-Khalas in 1998; political wing of EIJ; Leader KHALIL MUHAMMAD AMER.
Eritrean Liberation Front (ELF): f. 1958; commenced armed struggle against Ethiopia in 1961; subsequently split into numerous factions (see below); mainly Muslim support; opposes the PFDJ; principal factions:

Eritrean Liberation Front—Central Command (ELF—CC): f. 1982; Chair. ABDALLAH IDRISS.
Eritrean Liberation Front—National Council (ELF—NC): Leader Dr BEYENE KIDANE.
Eritrean Liberation Front—Revolutionary Council (ELF—RC): Chair. AHMED WOLDEYESUS AMMAR.

Eritrean Democratic Alliance (EDA): internet www.erit-alliance.com; f. 1999 as the Alliance of Eritrean National Forces, became Eritrean National Alliance in 2002, adopted present name in 2004; broad alliance of 16 parties opposed to PFDJ regime; Chair. BERHANE YEMANE 'HANJEMA'; Sec.-Gen. HUSAYN KHALIFA.
Eritrean People's Democratic Front (EPDF): e-mail main-office@sagem-eritra.org; internet www.democrasia.org; f. 2004 by merger of People's Democratic Front for the Liberation of Eritrea and a faction of ERDF; Leader TEWOLDE GEBRESELASSIE.
Eritrean Popular Movement (EPM): f. 2004; Leader ABDALLAH ADEM.
Eritrean Revolutionary Democratic Front (ERDF): e-mail webmaster@eritreana.com; internet www.eritreana.com; f. 1997 following merger of Democratic Movement for the Liberation of Eritrea and a faction of People's Democratic Front for the Liberation of Eritrea; Leader BERHANE YEMANE 'HANJEMA'.
Gash Setit Organization: Leader ISMAIL NADA.

Movement for Democratic Change: Leader Dr TESFAI BRINJI.
People's Front for Democracy and Justice (PFDJ): POB 1081, Asmara; tel. (1) 121399; fax (1) 120848; e-mail webmaster@shaebia.org; internet www.shaebia.org; f. 1970 as the Eritrean Popular Liberation Forces, following a split in the Eritrean Liberation Front; renamed the Eritrean People's Liberation Front in 1977; adopted present name in Feb. 1994; Christian and Muslim support; in May 1991 took control of Eritrea and formed provisional Govt; formed transitional Govt in May 1993; Chair. ISSAIAS AFEWERKI; Sec.-Gen. ALAMIN MOHAMED SAID.
Red Sea Afar Democratic Organization: Afar opposition group; Sec.-Gen. IBRAHIM HAROUN.

Diplomatic Representation

EMBASSIES IN ERITREA

China, People's Republic: 16 Ogaden St, POB 204, Asmara; tel. and fax (1) 185271; e-mail chemb@eol.com.er; Ambassador SHU ZHAN.
Djibouti: POB 5589, Asmara; tel. (1) 354961; fax (1) 351831; Ambassador AHMAD ISSA.
Egypt: 5 Dej Afworki St, POB 5570, Asmara; tel. and fax (1) 123294; Ambassador IBRAHIM KHALIL ABDALLAH.
France: POB 209, Asmara; tel. (1) 126599; fax (1) 123298; Ambassador PIERRE COULONT.
Germany: SABA Building, 8th Floor, Warsay St, POB 4974, Asmara; tel. (1) 186670; fax (1) 186900; e-mail info@asmara.diplo.de; internet www.asmara.diplo.de; Ambassador ALEXANDER BECKMANN.
Iran: Asmara; Ambassador REZA AMERI.
Israel: 32 Abo St, POB 5600, Asmara; tel. (1) 188521; fax (1) 188550; e-mail info@asmara.mfa.gov.il; Ambassador MENAHEM KANAFI.
Italy: POB 220, 11 171–1 St, Asmara; tel. (1) 120160; fax (1) 121115; e-mail ambasciata.asmara@esteri.it; internet www.ambasmara.esteri.it; Ambassador GAETANO MARTINEZ TAGLIAVIA.
Libya: Asmara.
Netherlands: 16 Bihat Street, POB 5860, Asmara; tel. (1) 127628; fax (1) 127591; e-mail asm@minibuza.nl; internet www.mfa.nl/asm; Ambassador NELLEKE LINSSEN.
Norway: 11 173–1 St, POB 5801, Asmara; tel. (1) 122138; fax (1) 122180; internet www.norway.gov.er; Chargé d'affaires a.i. ARMAN AARDAL.
Russia: 21 Zobel St, POB 5667, Asmara; tel. (1) 127162; fax (1) 127164; e-mail rusemb@eol.com.er; Ambassador ALEXANDER OBLOV.
Saudi Arabia: POB 5599, Asmara; tel. (1) 120171; fax (1) 121027; Ambassador NASSER AR-RASHEIDAN.
South Africa: Intercontinental Hotel, Rm 101, Asmara; tel. (1) 150400; fax (1) 151940; e-mail saemb@eol.com.er.
Sudan: Asmara; tel. (1) 202072; fax (1) 200760; e-mail sudanemb@eol.com.er; Ambassador MOHAMED AL-HASSAN.
United Kingdom: 66–68 Mariam Ghimbi St, POB 5584, Asmara; tel. (1) 120145; fax (1) 120104; e-mail asmara.enquiries@fco.gov.uk; Ambassador NICHOLAS ASTBURY.
USA: POB 211, 179 Ala St, Asmara; tel. (1) 120004; fax (1) 127584; e-mail usembassyasmara@state.gov; internet asmara.usembassy.gov; Ambassador RONALD K. MCMULLEN.
Yemen: POB 5566, Asmara; tel. (1) 114434; fax (1) 117921; Ambassador Dr AKRAM ABD AL-MARIK AL-QABRI.

Judicial System

The judicial system operates on the basis of transitional laws which incorporate pre-independence laws of the Eritrean People's Liberation Front, revised Ethiopian laws, customary laws and post-independence enacted laws. The independence of the judiciary in the discharge of its functions is unequivocally stated in Decree No. 37, which defines the powers and duties of the Government. It is subject only to the law and to no other authority. The court structure is composed of first instance sub-zonal courts, appellate and first instance zonal courts, appellate and first instance high courts, a panel of high court judges, presided over by the President of the High Court, and a Supreme Court presided over by the Chief Justice, as a court of last resort. The judges of the Supreme Court are appointed by the President of the State, subject to confirmation by the National Assembly.

Supreme Court: Asmara.
High Court: POB 241, Asmara; tel. (1) 127739; fax (1) 201828; e-mail prshict@eol.com.er.

Religion

Eritrea is almost equally divided between Muslims and Christians. Most Christians are adherents of the Orthodox Church, although there are Protestant and Roman Catholic communities. A small number of the population follow traditional beliefs.

CHRISTIANITY

The Eritrean Orthodox Church

In September 1993 the separation of the Eritrean Orthodox Church from the Ethiopian Orthodox Church was agreed by the respective church leaderships. The Eritrean Orthodox Church announced that it was to create a diocese of each of the country's then 10 provinces. The first five bishops of the Eritrean Orthodox Church were consecrated in Cairo, Egypt, in September 1994. In May 1998 Eritrea's first Patriarch (Abune) was consecrated in Alexandria, Egypt. In January 2006 Eritrea's third Patriarch, Abune Antonios I (who had been under house arrest since August 2005), was deposed by the Holy Synod.

Patriarch (Abune): DIOSKOROS.

The Roman Catholic Church

At 31 December 2005 there were an estimated 156,397 adherents in the country, comprising just 3.0% of the total population.

Bishop of Asmara: Rt Rev. ABBA MENGHISTEAB TESFAMARIAM, 19 Gonder St, POB 244, Asmara; tel. (1) 120206; fax (1) 126519; e-mail kimehret@gemel.com.er.

Bishop of Barentu: Rt Rev. THOMAS OSMAN, POB 9, Barentu; tel. and fax (1) 127283.

Bishop of Keren: Rt Rev. KIDANE YEBIO, POB 460, Keren; tel. (1) 401907; fax (1) 401604; e-mail cek@gemel.com.er.

The Anglican Communion

Within the Episcopal Church in Jerusalem and the Middle East, Eritrea lies within the jurisdiction of the Bishop in Egypt.

Leader: ASFAHA MAHARY.

ISLAM

Eritrea's main Muslim communities are concentrated in the western lowlands, the northern highlands and the eastern coastal region.

Leader: Sheikh AL-AMIN OSMAN AL-AMIN.

The Press

There is no independent press in Eritrea.

Business Perspective: POB 856, Asmara; tel. (1) 121589; fax (1) 120138; monthly; Tigrinya, Arabic and English; publ. by Eritrean National Chamber of Commerce; Editor MOHAMMED-SFAF HAMMED.

Chamber News: POB 856, Asmara; tel. (1) 120045; fax (1) 120138; monthly; Tigrinya, Arabic and English; publ. by Asmara Chamber of Commerce.

Eritrea Profile: POB 247, Asmara; tel. (1) 114114; fax (1) 127749; e-mail eritreaprofile@yahoo.com; internet www.shabait.com; f. 1994; twice-weekly; English; publ. by the Ministry of Information; Editor-in-Chief IDRIS AWAD AL-KARIM (acting).

Hadas Eritra (New Eritrea): Asmara; f. 1991; six times a week; English, Tigrinya and Arabic; govt publ.; Editor PAULOS NETABAY ABRAHAM; circ. 49,200.

Newsletter: POB 856, Asmara; tel. (1) 121589; fax (1) 120138; e-mail encc@aol.com.er; monthly; Tigrinya, Arabic and English; publ. by Eritrean National Chamber of Commerce; Editor MOHAMMED-SFAF HAMMED.

Broadcasting and Communications

Ministry of Transport and Communications (Communications Department): POB 4918, Asmara; tel. (1) 115847; fax (1) 126966; e-mail motc.rez@eol.com.er; Dir-Gen. ESTIFANOS AFEWERKI.

TELECOMMUNICATIONS

Eritrea Telecommunication Services Corpn (EriTel): 11 Semaetat St, POB 234, Asmara; tel. (1) 124655; fax (1) 120938; e-mail eritel@tse.com.er; internet www.tse.com.er; f. 1991; operates fixed-line and mobile cellular networks; Gen. Man. TESFASELASSIE BERHANE.

TFanus: 46 Daniel Comboni Street, POB 724, Asmara; tel. (1) 202590; fax (1) 126457; internet www.tfanus.com.er; f. 1996; internet service provider.

BROADCASTING

Radio

Voice of the Broad Masses of Eritrea (Dimtsi Hafash): POB 242, Asmara; tel. (1) 120426; fax (1) 126747; govt-controlled; programmes in Arabic, Tigrinya, Tigre, Saho, Oromo, Amharic, Afar, Bilien, Nara, Hedareb and Kunama; Dir-Gen. TESFAI KELETA; Technical Dir BERHANE GEREZGIHER.

Voice of Liberty: Asmara; e-mail VoL@selfi-democracy.com; internet selfi-democracy.com; radio programme of the EDP; broadcasts for one hour twice a week.

Television

ERI-TV: Asmara; tel. (1) 116033; f. 1992; govt station providing educational, tech. and information service; broadcasting began in 1993; programming in Arabic, English, Tigre and Tigrinya; broadcasts for eight hours daily; Dir-Gen. ALI ABDU.

Finance

(cap. = capital; res = reserves; dep. = deposits; m. = million; brs = branches; amounts in nakfa)

In November 1997 Eritrea adopted the nakfa as its unit of currency, replacing the Ethiopian birr, which had been Eritrea's monetary unit since independence.

BANKING

Central Bank

Bank of Eritrea: POB 849, 21 Victory Ave, Asmara; tel. (1) 123036; fax (1) 123162; e-mail kibreabw@boe.gov.er; f. 1993; bank of issue; Gov. TEKIE BEYENE.

Other Banks

Commercial Bank of Eritrea: POB 219, 208 Liberty Ave, Asmara; tel. (1) 121844; fax (1) 124887; e-mail gm.cber@gemel.com.er; f. 1991; cap. 400.0m., res 344.5m., dep. 13,791.6m. (Dec. 2004); Chair. BERHANE ABREHE; Gen. Man. YAMANE TESFAI; 15 brs.

Eritrean Development and Investment Bank: POB 1266, 29 Bedho St, Asmara; tel. (1) 126777; fax (1) 201976; e-mail edib@gemel.com.er; f. 1996; cap. 45m., total assets 194.2m. (Dec. 2003); provides medium- to long-term credit; Chair. HABTEAB TESFATSION; Gen. Man. Dr GOITOM W. MARIAM; 4 brs.

Housing and Commerce Bank of Eritrea: POB 235, Bahti Meskerem Sq., Asmara; tel. (1) 120350; fax (1) 202209; internet www.shaebia.org/new-hcb.html; e-mail hcb@gemel.com.er; f. 1994; cap. 33m., total assets 1,824.7m. (Dec. 1999); finances residential and commercial construction projects and commercial loans; Chair. HAGOS GHEBREHIWET; Gen. Man. BERHANE GHEBREHIWET; 10 brs.

INSURANCE

National Insurance Corporation of Eritrea Share Co (NICE): NICE Bldg, 171 Bidho Ave, POB 881, Asmara; tel. (1) 123000; fax (1) 123240; e-mail nice@nic-eritrea.com.er; internet www.nice-eritrea.com; f. 1992; partially privatized in 2004; 60% govt-owned; general and life; Gen. Man. ZERU WOLDEMICHAEL.

Trade and Industry

CHAMBER OF COMMERCE

Eritrean National Chamber of Commerce: POB 856, Asmara; tel. (1) 121589; fax (1) 120138; e-mail encc@gemel.com.er.

TRADE ASSOCIATION

Red Sea Trading Corporation: 29/31 Ras Alula St, POB 332, Asmara; tel. (1) 127846; fax (1) 124353; f. 1983; import and export services; operated by the PFDJ; Gen. Man. KUBROM DAFLA.

UTILITIES

Electricity

Eritrean Electricity Authority (EEA): POB 911, Asmara; fax (1) 121468; e-mail eeahrg@eol.com.er.

Water

Dept of Water Resources: POB 1488, Asmara; tel. (1) 119636; fax (1) 124625; e-mail wrdmlwe@eol.com.er; f. 1992.

ERITREA

Transport

Eritrea's transport infrastructure was severely damaged during the three decades of war prior to independence. International creditors have since provided loans for the repair and reconstruction of the road network and for the improvement of port facilities.

RAILWAYS

The 306-km railway connection between Agordat, Asmara and the port of Massawa was severely damaged during the war of independence and ceased operation in 1975. However, in 1999 an 81-km section of the Asmara–Massawa line (between Massawa and Embatkala) became operational, and in 2001 a further 18-km section, connecting Embatkala and Ghinda, was added. In February 2003 the reconstruction of the entire Asmara–Massawa line was completed.

Eritrean Railway: POB 6081, Asmara; tel. (1) 123365; fax (1) 201785; Co-ordinator, Railways Rehabilitation Project AMANUEL GEBRESELLASIE.

ROADS

In 1999 there were an estimated 4,010 km of roads in Eritrea, of which some 874 km were paved. Roads that are paved require considerable repair, as do many of the bridges across seasonal water courses destroyed in the war. The programme to rehabilitate the road between Asmara and the port of Massawa was completed in 2000.

SHIPPING

Eritrea has two major seaports: Massawa, which sustained heavy war damage in 1990, and Assab, which has principally served Addis Ababa, in Ethiopia. Under an accord signed between the Ethiopian and Eritrean Governments in 1993, the two countries agreed to share the facilities of both ports. Since independence, activity in Massawa has increased substantially; however, activity at Assab declined following the outbreak of hostilities with Ethiopia in May 1998. In 1998 a total of 463 vessels docked at Massawa, handling 1.2m. metric tons of goods; 322 vessels docked at Assab, which handled 1.0m. tons of goods. At 31 December 2006 Eritrea's registered merchant fleet numbered 15 vessels, with a total displacement of 21,455 grt.

Dept of Maritime Transport: POB 679, Asmara; tel. (1) 121317; fax (1) 121316; e-mail motc.rez@eol.com.er; Dir-Gen. ALEM TZEHAIE.

Port and Maritime Transport Authority: POB 851, Asmara; tel. (1) 111399; fax (1) 113647; Dir WELDE MIKAEL ABRAHAM.

BC Marine Services: 189 Warsay St, POB 5638, Asmara; tel. (1) 202672; fax (1) 12747; e-mail info@bc-marine.com; internet www.bc-marine.com; f. 2000; services include marine consultancy, marine survey and ship management; brs in Assab and Massawa; Dir Capt. NAOD GEBREAMLAK HAILE.

Cargo Inspection Survey Services: St No. 171-5-171, POB 906, Asmara; tel. (1) 120369; fax (1) 121767; e-mail gellatly@eol.com.er.

Eritrean Shipping Lines: 80 Semaetat Ave, POB 1110, Asmara; tel. (1) 120359; fax (1) 120331; f. 1992; provides shipping services in Red Sea and Persian (Arabian) Gulf areas and owns and operates four cargo ships; Gen. Man. TEWELDE KELATI.

Maritime Ship Services Enterprise: POB 99, Massawa; tel. (1) 552729; fax (1) 552483; e-mail ersasmsw@tse.co.er; shipping agents.

CIVIL AVIATION

The international airport is at Asmara.

Civil Aviation Department: POB 252, Asmara; tel. (1) 124335; fax (1) 124334; e-mail motc.rez@eol.com.er; handles freight and passenger traffic for eight scheduled carriers which use Asmara airport; Dir-Gen. PAULOS KAHSAY.

Eri-Air: Asmara; f. 2001; weekly charter flights to Italy; Man. Dirs TEWOLDE TESFAMARIAM, HAILEMARIAM GEBRECHRISTOS.

Eritrean Airlines: 89 Harnet Ave, POB 222, Asmara; tel. (1) 125500; fax (1) 125465; e-mail customer-rel@eritreanairlines.com.er; internet www.flyeritrea.com; CEO KUBROM DAFLA.

Tourism

The Ministry of Tourism is overseeing the development of this sector, although its advance since independence has been inhibited by the country's war-damaged transport infrastructure, and by subsequent conflicts with Ethiopia and other regional tensions. Eritrea possesses many areas of scenic and scientific interest, including the Dahlak Islands (a coralline archipelago rich in marine life), offshore from Massawa, and the massive escarpment rising up from the coastal plain and supporting a unique ecosystem. In 2005 83,307 tourists visited Eritrea. Tourist receipts in that year amounted to US $66m. Since May 2006 it has been necessary for foreign nationals to obtain a permit 10 days in advance in order to travel outside of the capital.

Eritrean Tourism Service Corporation: Asmara; operates govt-owned hotels.

ESTONIA

Introductory Survey

Location, Climate, Language, Religion, Flag, Capital

The Republic of Estonia is situated in north-eastern Europe. The country is bordered to the south by Latvia, and to the east by Russia. Estonia's northern coastline is on the Gulf of Finland and its territory includes more than 1,520 islands, mainly off its western coastline in the Gulf of Rīga and the Baltic Sea. The largest of the islands are Saaremaa and Hiiumaa, in the Gulf of Rīga. The climate is influenced by Estonia's position between the Eurasian land mass and the Baltic Sea and the North Atlantic Ocean. The mean January temperature in Tallinn is −0.6°C (30.9°F); in July the mean temperature is 17.1°C (62.8°F). Average annual precipitation is 568 mm. The official language is Estonian, which is a member of the Baltic-Finnic group of the Finno-Ugric languages; it is closely related to Finnish. Many of the Russian residents, who comprise over 25% of the total population, do not speak Estonian. Most of the population profess Christianity and, by tradition, Estonians belong to the Evangelical Lutheran Church. Smaller Protestant sects and the Eastern Orthodox Church are also represented. The national flag (proportions 7 by 11) consists of three equal horizontal stripes, of blue, black and white. The capital is Tallinn.

Recent History

The Russian annexation of Estonia, formerly under Swedish rule, was formalized in 1721. During the latter half of the 19th century, as the powers of the dominant Baltic German nobility declined, Estonians experienced a national cultural revival, which culminated in political demands for autonomy during the 1905 Russian Revolution, and for full independence after the beginning of the First World War. On 30 March 1917 the Provisional Government in Petrograd (St Petersburg), which had taken power after the abdication of Tsar Nicholas II in February, approved autonomy for Estonia. A Maapäev (Provisional Council) was elected as the country's representative body. However, in October the Bolsheviks staged a coup in Tallinn, and declared the Estonian Soviet Executive Committee as the sole Government of Estonia. As German forces advanced towards Estonia in early 1918, the Bolshevik troops were forced to leave. The major Estonian political parties united to form the Estonian Salvation Committee, and on 24 February an independent Republic of Estonia was proclaimed. A Provisional Government, headed by Konstantin Päts, was formed, but Germany refused to recognize Estonia's independence, and the country was occupied by German troops until the end of the First World War. Following the capitulation of Germany in November, the Provisional Government assumed power. After a period of armed conflict between Soviet and Estonian troops, the Republic of Estonia and Soviet Russia signed the Treaty of Tartu on 2 February 1920, under the terms of which the Soviet Government recognized Estonia's independence and renounced any rights to its territory. Estonian independence was recognized by the major Western powers in January 1921, and Estonia was admitted to the League of Nations.

Independence lasted until 1940. During most of this time the country had a liberal-democratic political system, in which the Riigikogu (State Assembly) was the dominant political force. Significant social, cultural and economic advances were made in the 1920s, including radical land reform. However, the decline in trade with Russia and the economic depression of the 1930s, combined with the political problems of a divided parliament, caused public dissatisfaction. In March 1934 Prime Minister Päts seized power in a bloodless coup and introduced a period of authoritarian rule. The Riigikogu and political parties were disbanded, but in 1938 a new Constitution was adopted, which provided for a presidential system of government, with a bicameral legislature. In April 1938 Päts was elected President.

In August 1939 the USSR and Germany signed a non-aggression treaty (the Nazi-Soviet or Molotov-Ribbentrop Pact). The 'Secret Protocols' to the treaty provided for the occupation of Estonia (along with various other territories) by the USSR. In September Estonia was forced to sign an agreement that permitted the USSR to base Soviet troops there. In June 1940 the Government, in accordance with a Soviet ultimatum, resigned, and a new administration was appointed by the Soviet authorities, with Johannes Vares-Barbarus as Prime Minister. In July elections were held, in which only candidates approved by the Soviet authorities were permitted to participate. On 21 July the Estonian Soviet Socialist Republic was proclaimed by the new legislature, and on 6 August the republic was formally incorporated into the USSR. Soviet rule in Estonia lasted less than one year. In that short period, however, Soviet policy resulted in mass deportations of Estonians, the expropriation of property and severe restrictions on cultural life.

German forces entered Estonia in July 1941 and remained in occupation until September 1944. Thereafter, following a short-lived attempt to reinstate Estonian independence, Soviet troops occupied the whole of the country, and the process of 'sovietization' was resumed. By the end of 1949 most Estonian farmers had been forced to join collective farms. Heavy industry was expanded, with investment concentrated on electricity generation and the chemicals sector. Structural change in the economy was accompanied by increased political repression, with deportations of Estonians continuing until the death of Stalin (Iosif V. Dzhugashvili) in 1953. The most overt form of opposition to Soviet rule was provided by the 'forest brethren' (*metsavennad*), a guerrilla movement, which continued to conduct armed operations against Soviet personnel and institutions until the mid-1950s. In the late 1960s, as in other Soviet republics, more traditional forms of dissent appeared, concentrating on cultural issues, provoked by the increasing domination of the republic by immigrant Russians and other Slavs.

During the late 1970s and the 1980s the issues of 'russification' and environmental degradation became subjects of intense debate in Estonia. The policy of *glasnost* (openness), introduced by the Soviet leader, Mikhail Gorbachev, in 1986, allowed such discussion to spread beyond dissident groups. In August 1987 a demonstration attended by some 2,000 people commemorated the anniversary of the signing of the Nazi-Soviet Pact, and an Estonian Group for the Publication of the Molotov-Ribbentrop Pact (MRP-AEG) was subsequently formed. During 1988 the Nazi-Soviet Pact was duly published, and the MRP-AEG reformed as the Estonian National Independence Party (ENIP), proclaiming the restoration of Estonian independence as its political objective. Another opposition group, the Estonian Popular Front (EPF), was formally constituted at its first congress in October, and included many members of the ruling Communist Party of Estonia (CPE). The EPF was more cautious than the ENIP, advocating the transformation of the USSR into a confederal system; the CPE was forced to adapt its policies to retain a measure of public support. On 16 November the Estonian Supreme Soviet (Supreme Council—legislature) adopted a declaration of sovereignty, which included the right to annul all-Union (USSR) legislation. The Presidium of the USSR Supreme Soviet declared the sovereignty legislation unconstitutional, but the Estonian Supreme Soviet affirmed its decision in December.

The adoption of Estonian as the state language was accepted by the Supreme Soviet in January 1989, and the tricolour of independent Estonia was reinstated as the official flag. Despite the successes of the opposition, differing political tactics were employed by the radical ENIP and the EPF. The ENIP refused to nominate candidates for elections to the all-Union Congress of People's Deputies in March. Instead, the ENIP leadership announced plans for the registration by citizens' committees of all citizens of the 1918–40 Republic of Estonia and their descendants. Voters on an electoral register, thus compiled, would elect an Eesti Kongress (Congress of Estonia) as the legal successor to the pre-1940 Estonian legislature. The EPF, however, participated in the elections to the Congress of People's Deputies and won 27 of the 36 contested seats. Five seats were won by the International Movement (Intermovement), a political group composed predominantly of ethnic Russians, which was established in July 1988 to oppose the growing influence of the Estonian opposition movements in the republic. In October 1989 delegates at the second congress of the EPF voted to adopt the restoration of Estonian independence as official policy. In

November the Estonian Supreme Soviet voted to annul the 1940 decision of its predecessor to enter the USSR, declaring that the decision had been reached under coercion from Soviet armed forces.

On 2 February 1990 a mass rally was held to commemorate the anniversary of the 1920 Treaty of Tartu. Deputies attending the rally later met to approve a declaration urging the USSR Supreme Soviet to begin negotiations on restoring Estonia's independence. On 22 February 1990 the Estonian Supreme Soviet approved the declaration, and on the following day it voted to abolish the constitutional guarantee of power enjoyed by the CPE. This formal decision permitted largely free elections to take place to the Estonian Supreme Soviet in March. The EPF won 43 of the 105 seats, and 35 were won by the Association for a Free Estonia and other pro-independence groups. The remainder were won by members of the Intermovement. Candidates belonging to the CPE, which was represented in all these groups, won 55 seats. At the first session of the new legislature, Arnold Rüütel, previously Chairman of the Presidium of the Supreme Soviet, was elected to the new post of Chairman of the Supreme Soviet, in which was vested those state powers that had been the preserve of the First Secretary of the CPE. On 30 March the Supreme Soviet adopted a declaration that proclaimed the beginning of a transitional period towards independence and denied the validity of Soviet power in the republic.

In late February and early March 1990 some 580,000 people (excluding those who had migrated to Estonia after the Soviet occupation of 1940 and their descendants) took part in elections to the rival parliament to the Supreme Soviet, the Eesti Kongress. The Congress convened on 11–12 March 1990 and declared itself the constitutional representative of the Estonian people. The participants adopted resolutions demanding the restoration of Estonian independence and the withdrawal of Soviet troops from Estonia.

In April 1990 the Supreme Soviet elected Edgar Savisaar, a leader of the EPF, as Prime Minister, and on 8 May it voted to restore the first five articles of the 1938 Constitution, which described Estonia's independent status. The formal name of pre-1940 Estonia, the Republic of Estonia, was also restored, as were the state emblems, flag and anthem. Although formal economic sanctions were not imposed on Estonia (as was the case with Lithuania), relations with the Soviet authorities were severely strained. In mid-May President Gorbachev annulled the republic's declaration of independence, declaring that it violated the USSR Constitution. The Estonian leadership's request for negotiations on the status of the republic was refused by Gorbachev, who insisted that the independence declaration be rescinded before negotiations could begin. There was also opposition within the republic, mostly from ethnic Russians affiliated to the Intermovement.

When troops of the USSR's Ministry of the Interior attempted military intervention in the other Baltic republics (Latvia and Lithuania) in January 1991, the Estonian leadership anticipated similar confrontation. Barricades and makeshift defences were erected, but no military action was taken. However, events in Latvia and Lithuania intensified popular distrust of Estonian involvement in a new union, which was being negotiated by other Soviet republics. Consequently, Estonia refused to participate in a referendum on the future of the USSR, which took place in nine of the republics in March. The Estonian authorities had conducted a poll on the issue of independence earlier in the same month. According to the official results, 82.9% of the registered electorate took part, of whom 77.8% voted in favour of Estonian independence.

When the conservative communist 'State Committee for the State of Emergency' announced that it had seized power in the USSR on 19 August 1991, Estonia, together with the other Baltic republics, expected military intervention to overthrow the pro-independence Governments. Gen. Fyodor Kuzmin, the Soviet commander of the Baltic military district, informed Rüütel that he was taking full control of Estonia. Military vehicles entered Tallinn on 20 August, and troops occupied the city's television station. However, the military command did not prevent a session of the Estonian Supreme Council from convening on the same day. Deputies adopted a resolution declaring the full and immediate independence of Estonia, thus ending the transitional period that had begun in March 1990. After it became evident, on 22 August 1991, that the Soviet coup had collapsed, the Government began to take measures against persons who had supported the coup. The anti-Government movements, the Intermovement and the Communist Party of the Soviet Union were banned in Estonia.

As the Estonian Government moved to assert its authority over former Soviet institutions, other countries quickly began to recognize its independence. On 6 September 1991 the recently formed USSR State Council finally recognized the re-establishment of Estonian independence. Later in the month Estonia, together with the other Baltic states, was admitted to the UN, as well as to the Conference on Security and Co-operation in Europe (CSCE), later the Organization for Security and Co-operation in Europe (OSCE, see p. 354). During the remainder of 1991 Estonia established diplomatic relations with most major states and was offered membership of leading international organizations. In internal politics there was hope for a cessation of conflict between the Eesti Kongress and the Supreme Council, with the establishment of a Constitutional Assembly, composed of equal numbers of delegates from each body, which was to draft a new constitution.

In January 1992, following a series of disputes with the Supreme Council, Savisaar resigned as Prime Minister and was replaced by the erstwhile Minister of Transport, Tiit Vähi. A new Council of Ministers, which included seven ministers from the previous Government, was approved by the Supreme Council at the end of the month.

The draft Constitution that had been prepared by the Constitutional Assembly was approved by some 91% of the electorate in a referendum held in late June 1992. Under the recently adopted Citizenship Law, only citizens of pre-1940 Estonia and their descendants, or those who had successfully applied for citizenship, were entitled to vote. This ruling drew strong criticism from Russian leaders, concerned that the rights of the large Russian minority in Estonia, most of whom had not been granted citizenship and were thus disenfranchised, were being violated. The new Constitution, which entered into force in early July 1992, provided for a parliamentary system of government, with a strong presidency. An election to the new legislature, the Riigikogu, was to be held in September, concurrently with a direct presidential election (although subsequent presidents would be elected by the Riigikogu).

Legislative and presidential elections were duly held on 20 September 1992, with the participation of some 67% of the electorate. The country's Russian and other ethnic minorities, who represented 42% of the total population at that time, were again barred from voting (with the exception of those whose applications for citizenship had been granted). The elections to the 101-seat Riigikogu were contested by some 40 parties and movements, largely grouped into eight coalitions. The nationalist Pro Patria alliance emerged with the largest number of seats (29). The Secure Home alliance, which comprised some former communists, obtained 17 seats. The centrist Popular Front alliance (led by the EPF) won 15 seats. The Moderates electoral alliance obtained 12 seats and the ENIP won 10 seats. None of the four candidates in the presidential election won an overall majority of the votes. The Riigikogu was thus required to choose from the two most successful candidates: Rüütel, now a leading member of the Secure Home alliance, and Lennart Meri, a former Minister of Foreign Affairs, who was supported by Pro Patria. In early October the Pro Patria-dominated Riigikogu elected Meri as Estonia's President.

A new coalition Government, with a large representation of Pro Patria members, as well as members of the Moderates and the ENIP, was announced in mid-October 1992. Earlier in the month Mart Laar, the leader of Pro Patria, had been chosen as Prime Minister. Laar indicated that the principal objectives of his administration would be to negotiate the withdrawal of all Russian troops remaining in Estonia, as well as to accelerate the country's privatization programme. In late November four of the five constituent parties of the Pro Patria alliance united to form the National Pro Patria Party (NPPP), with Laar as its Chairman.

In November 1993 Laar survived a vote of 'no confidence' in the Riigikogu. Also in November, the EPF was disbanded. In January 1994 Laar reshuffled four principal portfolios in the Council of Ministers. In May–June four members of the Council of Ministers resigned. Defections from the Pro Patria faction within the Riigikogu resulted in Laar's supporters retaining control of only 19 seats in the legislature by September. Following the revelation in that month that Laar had secretly contravened an agreement with the IMF, a vote of 'no confidence' in the Prime Minister was endorsed by the Riigikogu. In October Andres Tarand, hitherto Minister of the Environment, was appointed to replace Laar. A new Council of Ministers, which included representatives of Pro Patria, the Moderates, the ENIP and liberal and right-wing parties, was announced in the following month.

The results of the legislative elections, held on 5 March 1993, reflected widespread popular dissatisfaction with the parties of the governing coalition. The largest number of seats in the Riigikogu (41 of the total of 101) was won by an alliance of the centrist Estonian Coalition Party (ECP, led by Vähi) and the Rural Union (in which Rüütel was a prominent figure). A coalition of the newly established Estonian Reform Party (ERP, led by Siim Kallas, the President of the Bank of Estonia) and liberal groups obtained 19 seats, followed by Savisaar's Estonian Centre Party (16). The NPPP (in coalition with the ENIP) won only eight seats, while the Moderates alliance obtained six seats. The 'Estonia is Our Home' alliance (which represented the Russian-speaking minority) won six seats; this development was broadly welcomed as a potentially stabilizing factor. The participation rate was almost 70%.

Vähi was confirmed as Prime Minister by the legislature in early April 1995, and the new Government—a coalition of the ECP/Rural Union and the Estonian Centre Party—was appointed later in the month. The Government survived only until early October, when it was revealed that Savisaar, the Minister of the Interior, had made clandestine recordings of conversations that he had held with other politicians concerning the formation of a new coalition government. The Estonian Centre Party subsequently refused to accept his dismissal by Vähi. As a result of the effective collapse of the coalition, Vähi and the remaining members of the Council of Ministers tendered their resignations. In mid-October President Meri reappointed Vähi as Prime Minister, and a coalition Government, comprising members of the ECP/Rural Union and the ERP, was formed in late October. In December the NPPP and the ENIP, which had campaigned jointly for the legislative elections in March, merged to form the Pro Patria Union (PPU).

A presidential election was held in the Riigikogu on 26 August 1996, contested by the incumbent, Meri, and Rüütel, now of the Estonian Country People's Party. Following two further inconclusive rounds of voting, a larger electoral college, comprising the 101 deputies of the legislature and 273 representatives of local government (as provided for by the Constitution), was convened on 20 September. As none of the five candidates contesting the election secured an overall majority of the votes, a further round of voting was held to choose between the leading candidates, Meri and Rüütel. The election was won by Meri, with 52% of the votes cast, and in October he was duly sworn in as President for a second term.

In October 1996 local government elections were held, in which the ERP gained control of the Tallinn city government. In November the ECP concluded a co-operation agreement with the Estonian Centre Party, which had held no representation in the Government since October 1995. Disagreements among the coalition partners led to the collapse of the Tallinn city leadership, and Savisaar was appointed as the new Chairman of the city government, replacing the newly elected ERP candidate. The ERP threatened to leave the Government unless the co-operation agreement with the Estonian Centre Party was cancelled, and in late November 1996 six ministers, including Kallas (hitherto the Minister for Foreign Affairs) resigned, causing the collapse of the ruling coalition. Following the failure of negotiations between the ECP, the Estonian Centre Party and the Development Party, a minority Government, comprising the ECP, the Rural Union and independent members, was appointed in December. In early 1997 a series of allegations of abuse of office was made against Vähi. Although a legislative motion of 'no confidence', presented by the leaders of four opposition parties, was defeated by a narrow margin, Vähi tendered his resignation in February. Mart Siimann, the leader of the ECP parliamentary faction, was appointed Prime Minister, and was asked to form a new Government. In March a new minority Government, which comprised a coalition of the ECP, the Rural Union and independent members, was appointed. In September Vähi announced his resignation from the ECP and his retirement from political life. His position as Chairman of the ECP was assumed by Siimann.

At legislative elections, held on 7 March 1999, the Estonian Centre Party won 28 of the 101 seats available; the ERP and the PPU each secured 18 seats, the Moderates (in alliance with the People's Party) 17, the Estonian Country People's Party seven, and the United People's Party of Estonia six. Just 57.4% of the electorate participated. Although the Estonian Centre Party obtained the largest number of seats, it was unable to form a majority coalition. A centre-right coalition Government was thus formed by the ERP, the PPU and the Moderates, with each party receiving five ministerial posts; Laar, by that time leader of the PPU, was appointed Prime Minister (the post he had held in 1992–94).

In May 1999 it was announced that some 300,000 non-citizens permanently resident in Estonia (principally comprising ethnic Russians) were to be allowed to participate in local elections to be held in October. At the local elections, the governing ERP-PPU-Moderates alliance obtained control of 13 of Estonia's 15 county governments, and, in alliance with representatives of the Russian population, of Tallinn City Council, where Jüri Mõis was appointed Mayor of Tallinn, after resigning as Minister of the Interior. In November the Moderates' Party and the People's Party merged to form the People's Party Moderates. In June 2000 a new party, the Estonian People's Union (EPU), was formed by the merger of the Estonian Rural People's Party, the Rural Union and the Pensioners' and Families' Party. In April 2001 a vote of 'no confidence', brought against Prime Minister Laar, was narrowly defeated. Mõis resigned in May, after being threatened with a fifth confidence vote. A member of the PPU, Tõnis Palts, was elected as his successor.

Inconclusive rounds of voting in the presidential election took place in the Riigikogu on 27–28 August 2001. The terms of the Constitution prevented the incumbent, Meri, from standing for a third term of office, and the first round of the election was contested by Tarand of the People's Party Moderates and Peeter Kreitzberg of the opposition Estonian Centre Party. Tarand was replaced as the candidate of the ruling coalition by Peeter Tulviste of the PPU in the second and third rounds of voting, but neither candidate emerged as the victor. An electoral college, composed of the 101 parliamentary deputies and 266 representatives of local government, was therefore convened on 21 September. Toomas Savi of the governing ERP (members of which had, hitherto, abstained from voting), and Rüütel, now the Honorary Chairman of the opposition EPU, participated at this stage, progressing to a second round, as the candidates with the greatest number of votes. Rüütel eventually emerged as the victor in the 'run-off' election, in which he secured 186 votes. He was sworn in as President on 8 October. The protracted electoral process had led to renewed demands for electoral reform, and some Estonians expressed concern at the election of a former communist official as President.

In late September 2001 Mikhel Pärnoja tendered his resignation as Minister of Economic Affairs. In early December the ERP announced that it was to leave the Tallinn city Government. It subsequently signed a coalition agreement with the Estonian Centre Party, in what was widely regarded as an attempt to distance itself from the increasingly unpopular national Government of which it remained a part. Palts was forced to resign as Mayor, when a censure motion, brought by members of the Estonian Centre Party, was passed by a significant majority. His PPU left the city Government, and Savisaar was elected as Mayor of Tallinn in mid-December. These developments prompted Prime Minister Laar's Government to resign on 8 January 2002.

In mid-January 2002 the Estonian Centre Party and the ERP signed an agreement on the formation of an interim, coalition government, despite their contrasting political ideals; eight ministers were to be appointed from the Estonian Centre Party and six from the ERP. The parties of the coalition held fewer than one-half of the seats in the Riigikogu and, therefore, required the support of the EPU. On 22 January Kallas of the ERP was approved as Prime Minister, despite failing to obtain the support of his former government allies, the PPU and the People's Party Moderates.

In July 2002, following a ruling by the Supreme Court prohibiting the formation of electoral blocs, the Riigikogu voted to permit their existence until 2005, in order to avoid a delay in holding the forthcoming local elections. The elections duly took place in October 2002. Parties represented in the national Government won the majority of the votes cast. In November 2002 Savisaar was re-elected as Mayor of Tallinn. Meanwhile, in response to their parties' poor performance, in late October Toomas Hendrik Ilves resigned as Chairman of the People's Party Moderates, and Laar resigned the chairmanship of the PPU. In February 2003 the Riigikogu approved an extension of the terms of local councils, from three years to four, in the first amendment to be made to the Constitution since its adoption. In early February the Minister of the Interior, Ain Seppik of the

Estonian Centre Party, resigned, following severe criticism of his actions as a judge at the Supreme Court during the Soviet era.

Eleven parties participated in the parliamentary elections held on 2 March 2003, in which the Estonian Centre Party received 25.4% of the votes cast and 28 seats in the 101-member Riigikogu. The right-wing Union for the Republic Res Publica (founded in 2001) obtained 24.6% and 28 seats, and the ERP took 17.7% and 19 seats; the Estonian People's Union, the PPU and the People's Party Moderates also secured more than the 5% of the votes required to achieve representation in the Riigikogu. The level of participation by the electorate was 58.2%. Although the Estonian Centre Party secured the largest number of votes cast, Union for the Republic Res Publica instead invited the ERP, the Estonian People's Union and the PPU to join it in a four-member coalition. However, the ERP and the Estonian People's Union objected to the inclusion of the PPU, and on 27 March agreement was reached on the formation of a three-party government. After Savisaar declined the President's offer to form a government, on 2 April Juhan Parts, the leader of Union for the Republic Res Publica and a former chief auditor at the Bank of Estonia, was nominated as Prime Minister. The new coalition Government, approved on 9 April, consisted of five members of that party, five members of the ERP and four representatives of the Estonian People's Union. In mid-September the Minister of Finance, Palts, resigned, after an investigation was initiated into allegations of tax evasion dating from before his appointment to the Council of Ministers; Taavi Veskimagi was appointed in his place.

In February 2004 a congress of the People's Party Moderates voted formally to change the party's name to the Estonian Social Democratic Party (ESDP). Following Estonia's accession to the European Union (EU, see p. 244) in May (see below), in the following month the country took part in its first elections to the European Parliament. In October Savisaar resigned as Mayor of Tallinn, as the result of a vote of 'no confidence' by the city council. He was replaced by Palts. In November Margus Hanson resigned as Minister of Defence, following the theft from his home of classified documents (his immunity from prosecution was removed in March 2005, and he became the subject of a criminal investigation into the matter). Also in November 2004 Andrus Ansip, the new Minister of the Economy and Communications (following the resignation of Meelis Atonen in September), was elected Chairman of the ERP, replacing Kallas, who had been appointed as the country's representative to the European Commission. In December the Estonian Centre Party apparently sought to increase its support among the ethnic Russian population of Estonia, controversially signing a co-operation agreement with the *de facto* ruling party of Russia, United Russia. As a consequence, a number of Estonian Centre Party members who supported closer co-operation and integration with the EU left the party; by the end of January 2005 the party's faction in the Riigikogu had diminished from 28 to 19 members.

In February 2005 the Minister of Foreign Affairs, Kristiina Ojuland, was dismissed from office, after a security audit revealed the disappearance of 91 classified documents. Ojuland and the ERP contested her dismissal; the ensuing crisis led to tensions within the governing coalition, although the ERP ultimately accepted the appointment of Rein Lang as her successor. Nevertheless, on 21 March the Riigikogu passed a motion of 'no confidence' in Minister of Justice Ken-Marti Vaher, and three days later Parts announced the resignation of his Government. On 31 March the Estonian Centre Party, the ERP and the Estonian People's Party agreed to form a coalition, and Ansip was nominated to lead a new government, which was sworn into office on 13 April. Municipal elections took place on 16 October (in which, for the first time, voting was permitted by way of the internet). The Estonian Centre Party won 25.5% of the votes cast nation-wide, followed by the ERP, the Estonian People's Union and the PPU; the Union for the Republic Res Publica won just 8.5% of the ballot, compared with 15.2% in 2002. In Tallinn, the Estonian Centre Party won some 41% of the votes cast, but the party's Chairman, Savisaar, ultimately opted to retain his post as Minister of Economic Affairs and Communications, rather than be reappointed mayor; in mid-November Juri Ratas of the Estonian Centre Party was elected Mayor of Tallinn.

In mid-August 2006 the Estonian Centre Party and the Estonian People's Union signed an agreement pledging their support for the candidacy of Rüütel in the forthcoming presidential election, scheduled to take place in the legislature later that month. However, in the following week the two parties announced that they were to boycott the ballot after Rüütel announced that he would seek re-election only if the vote was decided by the electoral college system. In the initial ballot, held on 28 August 2006, former Speaker of the Riigikogu Ene Ergma, the sole candidate, attracted 65 votes, narrowly failing to secure the required two-thirds' majority (68 votes). Two further rounds of voting proved similarly inconclusive, with the former foreign minister, Ilves (on both occasions the lone contender), securing 64 votes in each round. Responsibility for electing the President thus passed to the electoral college, which duly convened on 23 September and voted for Ilves over Rüütel by a margin of 174 to 162; Ilves was inaugurated on 9 October. Later that month Minister of the Environment Villu Reiljan tendered his resignation, amid widespread allegations that he had been involved in corrupt property deals. Also in October the PPU and the Union for the Republic Res Publica formally merged to form the Union of Pro Patria and Res Publica. (Following a lengthy dispute over its leadership, it had been agreed that Tõnis Lukas, hitherto Chairman of the PPU, and Taavi Veskimägi, hitherto Chairman of the Union for the Republic Res Publica, would co-chair the new party.)

In early December 2006 President Ilves announced that legislative elections were to be held on 4 March 2007. Following the successful trial of electronic voting in municipal elections in 2005, all registered voters were entitled to cast their votes by way of the internet, although only a relatively small number did so. According to official results, the ERP was the most successful party at the elections, obtaining 31 seats and 27.8% of the votes cast, narrowly followed by the Estonian Centre Party, with 29 seats and 26.1% of the votes. The Union of Pro Patria and Res Publica obtained 19 seats and 17.9% of the votes, the ESDP 10 seats and 10.6% of the votes, and the Estonian Greens and the Estonian People's Union each obtained six seats and 7.1% of the votes. As in 2003, the Estonian Centre Party, despite its strong performance in the polls, was excluded from the new Government. In late March 2007 the ERP, the Union of Pro Patria and Res Publica, and the ESDP announced that they had agreed to form a centre-right coalition, which would command 60 of the 101 seats in the Riigikogu. A new Government, again under the premiership of Ansip, and comprising six members of the ERP, five of the Union of Pro Patria and Res Publica, and three of the ESDP, was installed on 4 April. Urmas Paet of the ERP was retained as Minister of Foreign Affairs; Jüri Pihl of the ESDP was awarded the interior portfolio, while Jaak Aaviksoo of the Union of Pro Patria and Res Publica assumed responsibility for defence.

Since the restoration of Estonian independence in 1991, the republic's relations with its eastern neighbour, Russia, have been strained by a number of issues, most notably the presence of former Soviet troops and the rights of the large Russian minority in Estonia (equivalent to 25.7% of the population in January 2005, according to official figures, with a significantly higher proportion being recorded in Tallinn). Under the Citizenship Law of 1992 (a modified version of that adopted in 1938), non-ethnic Estonians who settled in the republic after its annexation by the USSR in 1940, and their descendants, were obliged to apply for naturalization. Many of the requirements for naturalization—including an examination in the Estonian language—were criticized by the Russian Government as being excessively stringent, and discriminatory against the Russian-speaking minority. A new citizenship law, adopted in January 1995, gave non-citizens until 12 July to apply for residence and work permits, by which time almost 330,000 people (more than 80% of the total) had submitted applications. The deadline was extended until 30 November 1996, and by October of that year some 110,000 people had taken Russian citizenship, while continuing to reside in Estonia. In May 1997 the Ministry of the Interior announced that Soviet passports were no longer valid in Estonia. In December 1998 the Riigikogu approved legislation requiring elected officials to demonstrate sufficient command of Estonian to participate in the basic bureaucratic procedures of office. The legislation became effective in May 1999, and on 1 July a further amendment to the Language Law, pertaining to those employed in the services sector, came into force. In April 2000, following a statement by the OSCE High Commissioner on National Minorities that the language legislation contradicted international standards on freedom of expression, the law was amended, to make knowledge of Estonian compulsory only where it was deemed necessary for the sake of public interest (for example, in areas such as public health and security). In November 2001 the requirement that electoral candidates be able to speak Estonian was abolished, although legislation adopted in the same month made Estonian the official language of parliament.

With the dissolution of the USSR in 1991, several thousand former Soviet troops remained stationed (under Russian command) on Estonian territory. Their withdrawal commenced in 1992, but the Russian leadership increasingly linked the progress of the troop withdrawals with the question of the citizenship, and other rights, of the Russian-speaking minority in Estonia. In July 1994 a bilateral agreement was reached, awarding civil and social guarantees to all Russian military pensioners in Estonia. The withdrawal of former Soviet troops was completed on 29 August.

A further cause of tension in Estonian-Russian relations concerned Estonia's demand for the return of some 2,000 sq km (770 sq miles) of territory that had been ceded to Russia in 1944. In June 1994 Russian President Boris Yeltsin ordered the unilateral demarcation of Russia's border with Estonia according to the post-1944 boundary, although no agreement with Estonia had been concluded. During 1995 Estonia abandoned its demand for the return of the disputed territories. Instead, the Estonian Government appealed only for minor amendments to be made to the existing line of demarcation, in order to improve border security; more importantly, it insisted that Russia recognize the Treaty of Tartu of 1920 (in which Russia recognized Estonia's independence) as the basis of future relations between the two countries. However, the Russian Government maintained that the Treaty had lost its legal force, having been superseded by the declaration on bilateral relations signed by Russia and Estonia in 1991. In November 1996 the Estonian authorities announced that they were prepared to omit references to the Treaty of Tartu from the border agreement, and declared that it would be signed by Estonia and Russia at a summit of the OSCE in December. However, the Russian Government continued to refuse to sign the agreement.

Relations between Estonia and Russia remained strained, and in September 2000 Estonia decreed that from 2001 a full visa regime would come into effect between the two countries (as part of Estonia's preparations for EU membership), despite Russian misgivings. Further tensions arose in December 2003, when the Riigikogu approved amendments to legislation on foreign nationals, which prevented Russian military pensioners from obtaining permanent residency in Estonia. The Russian Government warned that any abrogation of the bilateral agreement of July 1994 would be likely severely to damage Estonian-Russian relations. President Rüütel refused an invitation from President Putin to attend celebrations in Moscow, the Russian and former Soviet capital, on 9 May 2005, commemorating the 60th anniversary of the end of the Second World War in Europe, on the grounds that, for Estonia, it marked the beginning of almost 50 years of Soviet occupation; the Lithuanian President also refused the invitation. (An agreement signed between Russia and Germany in September, on the construction of a North European Gas Pipeline, which was to carry natural gas from Russia to Germany under the Baltic Sea, bypassing the Baltic countries, also threatened adversely to affect relations.) Meanwhile, on 18 May the Ministers of Foreign Affairs of Estonia and Russia signed a border agreement. The treaty was ratified by the Riigikogu two days later, but the addition of a preamble making reference to the Soviet occupation of Estonia prompted Russia to revoke the agreement and demand renewed negotiations.

Hopes that bilateral relations might improve increased in June 2006 when the Russian ambassador to Estonia offered his country's condolences to Estonians on the anniversary of the Soviet mass deportations in 1941. However, in mid-February 2007 the approval of legislation by the Riigikogu providing for the relocation of a Soviet war monument in Tallinn, together with draft legislation proposing a ban on politically motivated public displays of Soviet and Nazi symbols in Estonia, provoked intense indignation from the Russian Government. Russian Minister of Foreign Affairs Sergei Lavrov described the anticipated relocation of the monument as 'blasphemous', on the grounds that Soviet soldiers were buried beneath the monument, while Estonian President Ilves denounced the Riigikogu's approval of the legislation and assured the Russian authorities that he would veto the new law. When the monument was dismantled, in late April, pending its relocation, several days of rioting ensued in Tallinn, as a result of which at least one person was killed and several hundred injured; at least 800 people were arrested. The Russian authorities submitted a formal protest to the Estonian ambassador in Moscow, while the Russian state-sponsored youth organization Nashi (Our Own) blockaded the Estonian embassy. In May Russia's state railway monopoly announced the suspension of deliveries of petroleum products to Estonia, purportedly on the grounds that it planned to carry out maintenance of the rail link to Estonia. The Estonian Minister of Foreign Affairs also claimed that elements in the Russian administration were responsible for a series of 'cyber-attacks' against the internet sites of Estonian government ministries, agencies and companies. In June President Ilves made an official visit to the USA, during which US President George W. Bush endorsed the Estonian Government's proposal for the establishment of a North Atlantic Treaty Organization (NATO, see p. 340) 'cyber-defence' research centre in Tallinn, with US participation. In July the remains of eight Soviet soldiers previously under the monument were reburied in Tallinn in an official ceremony (which the Russian ambassador to Estonia refused to attend). In January 2008 the trial of four protesters accused of instigating unrest in April 2007 commenced in Tallinn. Also in January 2008 an ethnic Russian student resident in Estonia received a fine of 17,500 kroons for a cyber-attack against the ERP internet site. In March the Estonian authorities announced that defence force commanders of eight countries (Estonia, Latvia, Lithuania, Italy, Germany, Spain, Slovakia and the USA) were to sign a co-operation agreement for the establishment of the 'cyber-defence' centre in May.

Estonia pursues close relations with its Baltic neighbours, Latvia and Lithuania. In late 1991 the three states established a consultative interparliamentary body, the Baltic Assembly, with the aim of developing political and economic co-operation. The Baltic Assembly has maintained close links with the Nordic Council, and Estonia is also a member of the Council of Baltic Sea States (see p. 224), established in March 1992. In January 2007 the Baltic states agreed to establish a joint NATO Response Force by 2010.

In November 2006 US President George W. Bush made the inaugural visit to Estonia by a US Head of State, accompanied by US Secretary of State Condoleezza Rice. During his stay, President Bush met with President Ilves and Prime Minister Ansip, as well as numerous other prominent politicians and businessmen. In a joint press conference given by Ilves and Bush, the US President thanked Ilves for the Estonian Government's support in the US-led 'war on terror' and expressed his appreciation for Estonian co-operation 'in the name of common aims and values'.

An important focus of Estonia's foreign policy was the attainment of full membership of the EU. In July 1995 Estonia became an associate member, and in December it officially applied for full membership; formal accession negotiations began on 31 March 1998. In October 2002 the European Commission approved a report, which identified 10 countries, including Estonia, as ready to join the EU on 1 May 2004. A national referendum was held on 14 September 2003, in which voters were asked whether they supported Estonia's proposed accession to the EU in 2004 and the adoption of legislation amending the country's Constitution; 66.8% of votes cast by 64.1% of the electorate were in favour of Estonia's accession, which duly took effect on 1 May 2004. In June Estonia was one of three new EU member states (alongside Lithuania and Slovenia) to be admitted to the exchange rate mechanism (ERM 2) as a precursor to adopting the common European currency, the euro; the Estonian Government subsequently announced that it intended to adopt the euro by 1 January 2007. However, in April 2006 the Government acknowledged that it would not be in a position to meet this deadline, predominantly owing to high inflation caused by sharp increases to international petroleum prices since 2004. In early 2008, following indications by EU analysts, the Central Bank of Estonia announced that the euro was unlikely to be adopted before 2012, owing to continuing high rates of inflation. In May 2006 Estonia became the 15th country to ratify the draft European constitutional treaty, following its approval by 73 members of the Riigikogu. Meanwhile, in March 1994 Estonia joined NATO's 'Partnership for Peace' programme of military co-operation. In November 2002, at a NATO summit meeting held in Prague, Czech Republic, Estonia was one of seven countries to be invited formally to accede to the Alliance in 2004. Estonia became a full member of NATO on 29 March 2004. Estonia is also a member of the Council of Europe (see p. 225). In December 2007 Estonia, together with eight other nations, implemented the EU's Schengen Agreement, enabling its citizens to travel to and from other member states without border controls.

ESTONIA

Government

Legislative authority resides with the Riigikogu (State Assembly), which has 101 members, elected by universal adult suffrage for a four-year term. The Riigikogu elects the President (Head of State) for a term of five years. The President is also Supreme Commander of Estonia's armed forces. Executive power is held by the Council of Ministers, which is headed by the Prime Minister, who is nominated by the President. For administrative purposes, Estonia is divided into 15 counties (*maakonds*), which in turn are subdivided into cities, rural municipalities and towns.

Defence

Before regaining independence in 1991, Estonia had no armed forces separate from those of the USSR. Following the establishment of its own Ministry of Defence in April 1992, Estonia began to form a national army. As assessed at November 2007, its total armed forces numbered 4,100, comprising an army of 3,600 (including conscripts), a navy of 300, and an air force of 200. There was also a reserve militia of 16,000. There is a paramilitary border guard numbering 2,600 troops, under the command of the Ministry of the Interior. The duration of military service was reduced from 12 to eight months in 2000, and a plan for the reform of the armed forces was approved. In February 1994 Estonia joined the North Atlantic Treaty Organization's (NATO) 'Partnership for Peace' (see p. 342) programme of military co-operation. In November 2002 Estonia was invited to join NATO, and it became a full member on 29 March 2004. The budget for 2007 allocated 4,250m. kroons to defence.

Economic Affairs

In 2006, according to World Bank estimates, Estonia's gross national income (GNI), measured at average 2004–06 prices, was US $15,307m., equivalent to $11,410 per head (or $17,540 per head on an international purchasing-power parity basis). During 1996–2006, it was estimated, the population declined at an average annual rate of 0.5%, while gross domestic product (GDP) per head increased, in real terms, by an average of 8.2% per year. Overall GDP increased, in real terms, at an average annual rate of 7.6% during 1996–2006. Real GDP increased by 11.4% in 2006 and by 7.1% in 2007.

Agriculture (including hunting, forestry and fishing) contributed 3.1% of GDP in 2006, when the sector provided 5.0% of employment. Animal husbandry is the main activity in the agricultural sector. Some 27.4% of Estonia's land is cultivable. The principal crops are grains, potatoes, and fruit and vegetables. Forestry products are also important. During 1996–2006 agricultural GDP declined, in real terms, at an average annual rate of 0.9%. The GDP of the sector increased by 1.0% in 2006.

Industry (including mining and quarrying, manufacturing, construction and power) contributed 28.4% of GDP in 2006, when the sector provided 33.5% of employment. The sector is dominated by machine-building, electronics and electrical engineering. During 1996–2006 industrial GDP increased, in real terms, at an average annual rate of 9.1%. Industrial GDP increased by 12.2% in 2006.

Mining and quarrying contributed 1.0% of GDP in 2006, when it provided 0.8% of employment. Estonia's principal mineral resource is oil-shale, and there are also deposits of peat and phosphorite ore. There are total estimated reserves of oil-shale of some 4,000 metric tons. However, annual extraction of oil-shale had declined to some 14m. tons by 2006, compared with some 31m. tons in 1980. Phosphorite ore is processed to produce phosphates for use in agriculture, but development of the industry has been accompanied by increasing environmental problems. In 1995–2006 mining and quarrying GDP increased, in real terms, at an average annual rate of 5.7%. According to official figures, the GDP of the mining and quarrying sector increased by 7.3% in 2006.

In 2006 the manufacturing sector accounted for 16.5% of GDP and engaged 21.1% of the employed labour force. The sector is based on products of food- and beverage-processing (especially dairy products), textiles and clothing, fertilizers and other chemical products, and wood and timber products (particularly furniture). In 1996–2006 the GDP of the manufacturing sector increased, in real terms, at an average annual rate of 10.8%. Real manufacturing GDP increased by 12.8% in 2006.

The country relies on oil-shale for over 90% of its energy requirements. The construction of Estlink, an under-sea electrical cable connecting the electricity networks of Estonia and Finland, commenced operations in December 2006. In 2006 imports of mineral fuels accounted for 15.9% of total imports.

The services sector accounted for 68.5% of GDP in 2006, and engaged 61.5% of the employed population. During 1996–2006 the GDP of the services sector increased, in real terms, by an annual average of 8.1%. The GDP of the sector increased by 11.1% in 2006.

In 2006 Estonia recorded a visible trade deficit of US $2,738.5m., while there was a deficit of $2,445.8m. on the current account of the balance of payments. After 1991 trade with the West, particularly the Nordic countries, increased considerably. In 2006 Finland was Estonia's principal trading partner, accounting for 18.4% of imports and 18.2% of exports. Other important sources of imports were Russia, Germany, Sweden and Lithuania. Sweden, Latvia, Russia and the USA were important purchasers of exports. In 2006 the principal exports were machinery and electrical goods (24.6% of total export revenue), mineral products (16.0%), wood and wood products, base metals, miscellaneous manufactured articles, vehicles and textiles. The principal imports in that year were machinery and electrical goods (25.5% of the total), vehicles, base metals, mineral products, chemical products and textiles.

In 2006 a budgetary surplus of 12,788m. kroons was recorded, equivalent to 6.2% of GDP. Estonia's external debt totalled US $11,255m. at the end of 2005, of which $435m. was long-term public debt. In the same year the cost of debt-servicing was equivalent to 13.7% of the value of exports of goods and services. During 2000–06 the annual rate of inflation averaged 3.7%. Consumer prices increased by 4.5% in 2006 and by 6.6% in 2007. In 2007 4.7% of the labour force were officially registered as unemployed.

Estonia acceded to the European Union (EU, see p. 244) in May 2004.

Even before it regained independence in mid-1991, Estonia had begun a transition to a market economy. However, despite Estonia's relative prosperity during the Soviet period, the collapse of the USSR and its internal economic system resulted in serious economic difficulties. The annual rate of inflation reached 1,076% in 1992. The introduction in June of a new currency, the kroon, fixed to the German Deutsche Mark (and later the common European currency, the euro), enhanced international financial confidence in the country. Following a programme of radical monetary reform, the average annual rate of inflation was reduced to 89% in 1993. Estonia's final stand-by arrangement with the IMF expired in 2001. Meanwhile, the country became a popular location for high-technology firms, particularly those from Nordic or Scandinavian countries, to establish outsourced operations, as a result of Estonia's well-educated, multilingual work-force as well as the relatively low rates of wages and corporate taxation. In 2003 the Government adopted a programme for the phased diminution of the rate of personal income tax, from 26% in 2003 to 20% in 2007. After joining the EU in May 2004, Estonia was one of three new EU member states to qualify for membership of the exchange rate mechanism (ERM 2) in June. However, despite hopes that Estonia would be among the first of the new EU member states to accede to the euro zone, a subsequent increase in the rate of annual consumer-price inflation, to well in excess of the maximum rate of 3% permitted for euro adoption, had the effect of delaying the country's eventual adoption of the currency. At 2008 Estonia's accession to the euro zone was expected to occur no earlier than 2012. Growth in 2007 slowed markedly, with growth in the manufacturing and retail sectors, in particular, being lower than had been anticipated.

Education

Compulsory education begins at the age of seven and lasts for nine years: primary school (Grades 1–6) and lower secondary (Grades 7–9). Students may then attend either general secondary school (Grades 10–12) or vocational school. In 2005/06 there were 39 higher-education institutions, including the University of Tartu (founded in 1632) and Tallinn University, with a total of 67,760 students enrolled. The language of instruction at all levels is predominantly Estonian, although there is some teaching available in Russian and English. In 2004/05 some 23% of students at primary and secondary schools received tuition in Russian. In 2004 enrolment at primary schools was equivalent to 100% of the corresponding age group, while enrolment in secondary education was equivalent to 98% of the relevant age-group (males 97%; females 99%). In 2003 enrolment in tertiary education was equivalent to 63.5% of those aged 19 and 38.6% of those aged 19–25. Government outlays on educa-

ESTONIA

tion amounted to 10,484m. kroons in 2005 (17.9% of total expenditure in that year).

Public Holidays

2008: 1 January (New Year's Day), 24 February (Independence Day), 21 March (Good Friday), 1 May (Spring Day), 23 June (Victory Day, anniversary of the Battle of Võnnu in 1919), 24 June (Midsummer Day, Jaanipäev), 20 August (Restoration of Independence Day), 25–26 December (Protestant and Catholic Christmas).

2009: 1 January (New Year's Day), 24 February (Independence Day), 10 April (Good Friday), 1 May (Spring Day), 23 June (Victory Day, anniversary of the Battle of Võnnu in 1919), 24 June (Midsummer Day, Jaanipäev), 20 August (Restoration of Independence Day), 25–26 December (Protestant and Catholic Christmas).

Weights and Measures

The metric system is in force.

Statistical Survey

Source (unless otherwise stated): Statistical Office of Estonia (Statiskaamet), Endla 15, Tallinn 0100; tel. 625-9202; fax 625-9370; e-mail stat@stat.ee; internet www.stat.ee.

Area and Population

AREA, POPULATION AND DENSITY

Area (sq km)	45,227*
Population (census results)†	
12 January 1989	1,565,662
31 March 2000	
Males	631,851
Females	738,201
Total	1,370,052
Population (official estimates at 1 January)†	
2006	1,344,684
2007	1,342,409
2008	1,340,602
Density (per sq km) at 1 January 2008	29.6

* 17,462 sq miles.
† Figures refer to permanent inhabitants. The *de facto* total was 1,572,916 at the 1989 census and 1,356,931 at the 2000 census.

POPULATION BY ETHNIC GROUP
(1 January 2007)

	Number	% of total population
Estonian	921,062	68.6
Russian	344,280	25.6
Ukrainian	28,158	2.1
Belarusian	16,133	1.2
Finnish	11,035	0.8
Others	21,741	1.6
Total	**1,342,409**	**100.0**

POPULATION BY COUNTY
(official estimates, 1 January 2007)

County	Area (sq km)*	Population	Density (per sq km)	County town (with population)
Harju	4,333	522,147	120.5	Tallinn (396,852)
Hiiu	1,023	10,168	9.9	Kärdla (3,695)
Ida-Viru	3,364	171,748	51.1	Jõhvi (11,375)
Järva	2,623	36,328	13.8	Paide (9,759)
Jõgeva	2,604	37,108	14.2	Jõgeva (6,326)
Lääne	2,383	27,713	11.6	Haapsalu (11,741)
Lääne-Viru	3,465	67,560	19.5	Rakvere (16,665)
Pärnu	4,807	88,727	18.5	Pärnu (44,074)
Põlva	2,165	31,387	14.5	Põlva (6,515)
Rapla	2,980	36,743	12.3	Rapla (5,742)†
Saare	2,922	34,978	12.0	Kuressaare (14,948)
Tartu	2,993	149,001	49.8	Tartu (101,965)
Valga	2,044	34,455	16.9	Valga (13,862)
Viljandi	3,423	56,075	16.4	Viljandi (20,190)
Võru	2,305	38,271	16.6	Võru (14,522)
Total	**43,432**	**1,342,409**	**30.9**	

* Excluding that part of Lake Peipsi which belongs to Estonia, and the area of Lake Võrtsjärv.
† Estimated population at 1 January 2002 (Rapla is a city without municipal status, and is included in Rapla rural municipality).

PRINCIPAL TOWNS
(estimated population, excluding suburbs, at 1 January 2007)

Tallinn (capital)	396,852	Kohtla-Järve	45,399
Tartu	101,965	Pärnu	44,074
Narva	66,712		

BIRTHS, MARRIAGES AND DEATHS*

	Registered live births		Registered marriages		Registered deaths	
	Number	Rate (per 1,000)	Number	Rate (per 1,000)	Number	Rate (per 1,000)
1999	12,425	9.0	5,590	4.1	18,447	13.4
2000	13,067	9.5	5,485	4.0	18,403	13.4
2001	12,632	9.3	5,647	4.1	18,516	13.6
2002	13,001	9.6	5,853	4.3	18,355	13.5
2003	13,036	9.6	5,699	4.2	18,152	13.4
2004	13,992	10.4	6,009	4.4	17,685	13.1
2005	14,350	10.7	n.a.	n.a.	17,316	12.9
2006	14,877	11.1	n.a.	n.a.	17,316	12.9

* Revised figures, based on the results of the 1989 and 2000 population censuses.

Expectation of life (years at birth, WHO estimates): 72.9 (males 67.3; females 78.2) in 2005 (Source: WHO, *World Health Statistics*).

ESTONIA

EMPLOYMENT
(annual averages, '000 persons aged 15–74 years)

	2004	2005	2006
Agriculture, hunting and forestry	31.4	29.4	29.9
Fishing	3.6	2.8	2.2
Mining and quarrying	8.0	5.9	5.2
Manufacturing	140.9	139.5	136.4
Electricity, gas and water supply	12.0	12.5	12.4
Construction	46.8	48.7	62.8
Wholesale and retail trade	80.0	80.6	88.7
Hotels and restaurants	16.2	22.1	22.3
Transport, storage and communications	51.5	54.6	61.5
Financial intermediation	7.9	6.9	7.3
Real estate, renting and business activities	39.4	46.4	48.1
Public administration and defence; compulsory social security	36.9	37.2	39.0
Education	54.5	54.9	58.5
Health and social work	37.5	35.0	37.5
Activities not adequately defined	28.8	31.1	34.3
Total employed	**595.5**	**607.4**	**646.3**

Unemployed (annual averages, '000 persons aged 15–74): 63.5 in 2004; 52.2 in 2005; 41.0 in 2006.

Health and Welfare

KEY INDICATORS

Total fertility rate (children per woman, 2005)	1.4
Under-5 mortality rate (per 1,000 live births, 2005)	7
HIV/AIDS (% of persons aged 15–49, 2005)	1.3
Physicians (per 1,000 head, 2000)	4.48
Hospital beds (per 1,000 head, 2004)	5.8
Health expenditure (2004): US $ per head (PPP)	751.5
Health expenditure (2004): % of GDP	5.3
Health expenditure (2004): public (% of total)	76.0
Human Development Index (2005): ranking	44
Human Development Index (2005): value	0.860

For sources and definitions, see explanatory note on p. vi.

Agriculture

PRINCIPAL CROPS
('000 metric tons)

	2004	2005	2006
Wheat	196.6	263.4	219.6
Barley	293.5	366.7	302.7
Rye	18.1	20.4	17.8
Oats	72.7	84.2	63.6
Triticale (wheat-rye hybrid)	16.0	15.0	5.4
Potatoes	166.5	209.8	152.6
Dry peas	3.2	5.7	5.5
Rapeseed	68.6	83.1	84.6
Cabbages and other brassicas	16.6	17.8	17.1
Cucumbers and gherkins	6.7	9.9	3.7
Carrots and turnips	14.6	15.6	10.9
Apples	2.2	10.7	10.7

Aggregate production ('000 metric tons, may include official, semi-official or estimated data): Total cereals 608.1 in 2004, 760.1 in 2005, 619.3 in 2006; Total roots and tubers 173.2 in 2004, 212.9 in 2005, 154.6 in 2006; Total vegetables (incl. melons) 54.5 in 2004, 63.5 in 2005, 40.5 in 2006; Total fruits (excl. melons) 8.1 in 2004, 16.8 in 2005, 16.8 in 2006.

Source: FAO.

LIVESTOCK
('000 head, year ending September)

	2004	2005	2006
Cattle	257	250	250
Pigs	345	340	347
Sheep	31	38	50
Chickens	1,929	2,161*	1,854
Rabbits*	43	40	40

* FAO estimates.

Source: FAO.

LIVESTOCK PRODUCTS
('000 metric tons, unless otherwise indicated)

	2004	2005	2006
Cattle meat	14.8	13.2	14.5
Pig meat	38.4	38.1	35.1
Chicken meat	14.8	13.7	12.8
Cows' milk	651.9	670.0	689.7
Butter	22.6	27.8	n.a.
Cheese	6.4	5.9	n.a.
Hen eggs	14.4	13.1	11.2
Honey (metric tons)	555	638	638*

* FAO estimate.

Source: mostly FAO.

Forestry

ROUNDWOOD REMOVALS
('000 cubic metres, excl. bark)

	2004	2005	2006
Sawlogs, veneer logs and logs for sleepers	3,300	2,770	2,920
Pulpwood	1,500	1,280	1,350
Other industrial wood	700	400	430
Fuel wood	1,300	1,050	1,100
Total	**6,800**	**5,500**	**5,800**

Source: FAO.

SAWNWOOD PRODUCTION
('000 cubic metres, incl. railway sleepers)

	2004	2005	2006
Coniferous (softwood)	1,889	1,909	1,910
Broadleaved (hardwood)	140	153	120
Total	**2,029**	**2,063**	**2,030**

Source: FAO.

Fishing

('000 metric tons, live weight)

	2003	2004	2005
Capture	80.2	88.6	99.6
Atlantic herring	27.4	27.4	22.1
European sprat	29.4	37.3	55.3
Northern prawn	13.0	13.6	12.4
Aquaculture	0.4	0.3	0.6
Total catch	**80.6**	**88.9**	**100.1**

Source: FAO.

ESTONIA

Mining

('000 metric tons)

	2004	2005	2006
Oil-shale	14,000	14,600	14,000
Peat	767	1,034	1,207

Industry

SELECTED PRODUCTS
('000 metric tons, unless otherwise indicated)

	2004	2005	2006
Distilled spirits ('000 hectolitres)	187.9	167.9	183.1
Wine ('000 hectolitres)	60.7	88.8	77.4
Beer ('000 hectolitres)	1,202.8	1,342.5	1,431.1
Soft drinks ('000 hectolitres)	828.5	1,090.3	1,318.1
Woven cotton fabric ('000 sq metres)	106,569	83,523	58,815
Carpets ('000 sq metres)	1,997	2,111	2,335
Footwear ('000 pairs)	1,919	1,702	1,658
Plywood ('000 cubic metres)	45.5	71.0	n.a.
Particle board ('000 cubic metres)	217.6	230.6	248.7
Fibreboard (million sq metres)	20.4	22.4	21.5
Chemical wood pulp	68.6	67.1	69.0
Paper	69.6	69.6	67.4
Nitrogenous fertilizers*	61.0	92.9	98.2
Building bricks (million)	24.4	26.0	31.0
Cement	614.6	726.0	848.9
Electric energy (million kWh)	10,304	10,205	9,731

* In terms of nitrogen (N).

Finance

CURRENCY AND EXCHANGE RATES

Monetary Units
100 cents = 1 kroon.

Sterling, Dollar and Euro Equivalents (31 December 2007)
£1 sterling = 21.313 kroons;
US $1 = 10.638 kroons;
€1 = 15.660 kroons;
1,000 kroons = £46.92 = $94.00 = €63.85.

Average Exchange Rate (kroons per US $)
2005   12.584
2006   12.466
2007   11.434

Note: In June 1992 the kroon replaced the rouble of the former USSR in Estonia, initially at a rate of one kroon per 10 roubles.

GOVERNMENT FINANCE
(general government transactions, non-cash basis, million kroons)*

Summary of Balances

	2004	2005	2006
Revenue	53,756	62,013	75,792
Less Expense	48,736	55,209	63,004
Net operating balance	5,020	6,804	12,788
Less Net acquisition of non-financial assets	2,341	3,443	5,408
Net lending/borrowing	2,678	3,360	7,381

Revenue

	2004	2005	2006
Tax revenue	30,299	35,081	42,359
Taxes on goods and services	12,275	15,918	19,902
Taxes on income, profits and capital gains	12,037	12,232	14,803
Taxes on property	475	506	517
Social security contributions	15,824	18,114	21,356
Total (incl. others)	53,756	62,013	75,792

Expense/Outlays

Expense by economic type†	2004	2005	2006
Compensation of employees	14,674	16,307	18,274
Use of goods and services	10,636	11,646	13,505
Consumption of fixed capital	2,257	2,527	2,966
Interest	304	304	329
Subsidies	1,356	1,740	2,075
Social benefits	17,051	19,155	22,001
Total (incl. others)	48,736	55,209	63,004

Outlays by function of government	2004	2005
General public services	4,028	4,607
Defence	2,193	2,373
Public order and safety	3,396	3,891
Economic affairs	5,840	7,009
Environment protection	996	1,530
Housing and community amenities	405	283
Health	5,963	6,958
Recreation, culture and religion	3,241	4,305
Education	9,581	10,484
Social protection	15,435	17,212
Total	51,077	58,652

* Figures represent a consolidation of the operations of the Government, comprising all central and local government accounts.
† Including net acquisition of non-financial assets.

Source: IMF, *Government Finance Statistics Yearbook*.

INTERNATIONAL RESERVES
(US $ million at 31 December)

	2004	2005	2006
Gold (national valuation)	3.61	4.24	5.23
IMF special drawing rights	0.08	0.08	0.09
Reserve position in IMF	0.01	0.01	0.01
Foreign exchange	1,788.13	1,943.12	2,781.14
Total	1,791.83	1,947.45	2,786.47

* National valuation.

Source: IMF, *International Financial Statistics*.

MONEY SUPPLY
(million kroons at 31 December)

	2004	2005	2006
Currency outside banks	7,714.2	8,747.1	10,067.7
Demand deposits at banks	28,388.2	39,841.7	51,702.8
Total money (incl. others)	36,177.5	48,673.4	61,861.3

Source: IMF, *International Financial Statistics*.

COST OF LIVING
(Consumer Price Index; base: 2000 = 100)

	2004	2005	2006
Food (incl. beverages)	114.2	118.3	124.2
Fuel and light	138.5	150.4	163.4
Clothing (incl. footwear)	109.1	111.1	114.0
Rent	120.0	125.8	154.1
All items (incl. others)	114.4	119.0	124.3

Source: ILO.

ESTONIA

NATIONAL ACCOUNTS
(million kroons at current prices)

Expenditure on the Gross Domestic Product

	2004	2005	2006
Final consumption expenditure	109,518.2	123,778.4	145,857.9
Households	80,459.7	91,387.3	109,203.2
Non-profit institutions serving households	2,029.7	2,448.4	2,780.1
General government	27,028.8	29,942.7	33,874.6
Gross capital formation	52,452.1	59,828.1	79,156.2
Gross fixed capital formation	47,090.6	53,742.6	70,569.4
Changes in inventories / Acquisitions, less disposals, of valuables	5,361.5	6,085.5	8,586.8
Total domestic expenditure	161,970.4	183,606.4	225,014.1
Exports of goods and services	111,209.4	138,556.8	164,418.5
Less Imports of goods and services	123,222.4	149,564.6	187,830.3
Statistical discrepancy	−34.3	2,793.5	5,459.1
GDP in market prices	149,923.1	175,392.0	207,061.4
GDP at constant 2000 prices	128,921.6	142,013.2	157,901.2

Gross Domestic Product by Economic Activity

	2004	2005	2006
Agriculture, hunting and forestry	5,064.8	5,233.5	5,270.3
Fishing	272.4	347.9	326.2
Mining and quarrying	1,383.8	1,520.4	1,737.2
Manufacturing	22,904.1	26,440.2	29,988.3
Electricity, gas and water supply	4,597.1	5,559.9	6,398.5
Construction	7,605.0	10,415.0	13,461.3
Wholesale and retail trade; repair of motor vehicles, motorcycles and personal and household goods	20,586.8	24,049.5	28,407.4
Hotels and restaurants	2,168.0	2,563.4	3,145.8
Transport, storage and communications	16,899.1	18,595.8	22,179.1
Financial intermediation	5,110.5	5,585.4	6,649.8
Real estate, renting and business activities	24,708.8	28,952.1	35,524.2
Public administration and defence; compulsory social security	7,486.8	8,158.5	9,200.0
Education	6,269.2	7,010.0	7,789.3
Health and social work	3,971.0	4,812.2	5,539.5
Other community, social and personal service activities	4,548.9	5,336.2	6,094.4
Gross value added in basic prices	133,576.6	154,580.1	181,711.4
Taxes on products / *Less* Subsidies on products	16,346.5	20,811.9	25,350.0
GDP in market prices	149,923.1	175,392.0	207,061.4

BALANCE OF PAYMENTS
(US $ million)

	2004	2005	2006
Exports of goods f.o.b.	5,982.7	7,783.0	9,635.1
Imports of goods f.o.b.	−8,002.1	−9,627.8	−12,373.6
Trade balance	−2,019.3	−1,844.8	−2,738.5
Exports of services	2,830.1	3,155.9	3,492.8
Imports of services	−1,755.8	−2,156.0	−2,459.7
Balance on goods and services	−945.1	−844.8	−1,705.4
Other income received	436.0	669.3	978.9
Other income paid	−1,072.9	−1,369.2	−1,730.0
Balance on goods, services and income	−1,582.0	−1,544.8	−2,456.5
Current transfers received	424.3	497.4	474.1
Current transfers paid	−299.9	−397.6	−463.4
Current balance	−1,457.6	−1,444.9	−2,445.8
Capital account (net)	93.2	139.8	411.9

—continued	2004	2005	2006
Direct investment abroad	−268.2	−608.9	−1,038.6
Direct investment from abroad	971.8	2,996.8	1,599.7
Portfolio investment assets	−380.6	−871.6	−1,230.3
Portfolio investment liabilities	1,114.3	−1,360.3	43.4
Financial derivatives assets	−2.9	1.3	−14.6
Financial derivatives liabilities	2.6	−8.8	21.1
Other investment assets	−901.2	−886.9	124.4
Other investment liabilities	1,086.0	2,440.6	3,226.9
Net errors and omissions	13.8	−11.4	−77.6
Overall balance	271.2	385.5	620.4

Source: IMF, *International Financial Statistics*.

External Trade

PRINCIPAL COMMODITIES
(distribution by HS, million kroons)

Imports c.i.f.	2004	2005	2006
Prepared foodstuffs; beverages, spirits and vinegar; tobacco and manufactured substitutes	5,051.5	6,016.6	6,661.3
Mineral products	7,244.2	11,841.0	26,964.5
Mineral fuels, mineral oils and products of their distillation; bituminous substances, etc.	6,989.9	11,493.3	26,568.9
Products of chemical or allied industries	7,316.8	8,719.3	10,806.3
Plastics, rubber and articles thereof	5,011.5	6,235.1	7,809.8
Plastics and articles thereof	4,066.2	5,094.9	6,349.0
Pulp of wood or of other fibrous cellulosic material; waste and scrap of paper or paperboard	2,416.3	2,659.1	3,288.5
Paper-making material; paper and paperboard and articles thereof	2,083.5	2,297.6	2,911.2
Textiles and textile articles	7,101.0	7,475.8	8,545.8
Base metals and articles of base metal	11,534.4	13,202.1	15,885.9
Iron and steel	5,153.4	5,753.8	6,435.3
Articles of iron and steel	3,312.0	3,963.5	4,758.1
Machinery and mechanical appliances; electrical equipment; sound and television apparatus	30,251.1	39,901.0	42,738.3
Nuclear reactors, boilers, machinery and mechanical appliances; parts thereof	10,901.3	13,075.3	16,136.2
Electrical machinery equipment and parts; sound and television apparatus parts and accessories	19,349.8	26,825.7	26,602.1
Vehicles, aircraft, vessels and associated transport equipment	12,528.6	13,242.2	20,201.3
Railway or tramway locomotives, rolling-stock and parts thereof	1,808.4	416.0	613.6
Vehicles other than railway or tramway rolling-stock, and parts and accessories	10,325.0	12,473.2	18,687.8
Total (incl. others)	104,881.3	128,365.3	167,399.7

ESTONIA

Statistical Survey

Exports f.o.b.	2004	2005	2006
Live animals and animal products	2,586.8	2,882.8	3,323.5
Prepared foodstuffs; beverages, spirits and vinegar; tobacco and manufactured substitutes	2,366.6	2,759.8	3,604.0
Cocoa and cocoa preparations	58.5	62.9	128.5
Mineral products	3,388.8	7,314.7	19,423.0
Mineral fuels, mineral oils and products of their distillation	3,165.7	7,041.1	19,073.3
Products of chemical or allied industries	3,490.1	4,169.0	4,926.1
Plastics, rubber and articles thereof	1,853.2	2,709.4	3,428.4
Wood and articles thereof; wood charcoal	9,681.1	10,769.5	11,059.7
Pulp of wood or of other fibrous cellulosic material; waste and scrap of paper or paperboard	1,520.0	1,931.4	2,865.7
Paper-making material; paper and paperboard and articles thereof	1,137.5	1,256.5	1,775.1
Textiles and textile articles	6,667.8	6,985.9	6,402.4
Non-knitted clothing and accessories	2,721.0	3,020.5	2,747.1
Base metals and articles of base metal	6,405.8	8,800.0	11,101.3
Iron and steel	2,902.4	4,215.3	5,341.8
Articles of iron or steel	2,020.2	2,874.3	3,164.2
Machinery and mechanical appliances; electrical equipment; sound and television apparatus	20,313.1	27,270.5	29,743.1
Nuclear reactors, boilers, machinery and mechanical appliances; parts thereof	3,100.0	4,945.1	6,383.7
Electrical machinery equipment and parts; sound and television apparatus parts and accessories	17,213.1	22,325.4	23,359.5
Vehicles, aircraft, vessels and associated transport equipment	4,535.0	6,544.0	8,147.9
Miscellaneous manufactured articles	6,927.3	7,832.5	8,787.4
Furniture; bedding, mattresses, cushions, etc.; lamps and lighting fittings; prefabricated buildings	6,284.5	7,026.8	7,832.9
Total (incl. others)	74,614.3	96,747.3	121,017.6

PRINCIPAL TRADING PARTNERS
(million kroons)

Imports c.i.f.	2004	2005	2006
Belarus	1,277.3	1,623.7	2,281.1
Belgium	1,952.7	2,372.4	3,032.2
China, People's Repub.	2,000.9	2,676.8	3,431.4
Czech Republic	1,077.5	1,099.1	1,609.4
Denmark	2,789.2	3,107.4	3,929.1
Finland	23,164.5	25,336.9	30,800.0
France	2,047.0	2,562.4	3,082.8
Germany	13,443.2	17,860.3	20,597.3
Hungary	1,503.9	1,382.3	1,561.8
Italy	2,529.2	3,272.8	4,288.2
Japan	1,440.0	2,502.6	1,734.2
Latvia	4,861.8	6,006.1	9,687.6
Lithuania	5,612.2	7,678.5	10,761.3
Netherlands	3,780.1	4,397.7	5,732.8
Norway	816.3	989.2	1,048.7
Poland	3,445.3	4,727.4	6,313.0
Russia	9,660.4	11,810.6	21,704.8
Sweden	10,184.2	11,366.9	15,354.9
Ukraine	1,414.5	1,156.6	1,298.1
United Kingdom	2,330.3	3,023.9	3,382.4
USA	1,242.9	1,847.4	1,919.1
Total (incl. others)	104,881.3	128,435.5	167,399.7

Exports f.o.b.	2004	2005	2006
Belgium	858.6	1,252.9	1,255.5
Denmark	2,466.1	3,138.0	3,114.0
Finland	17,167.2	25,477.8	22,081.4
France	1,118.2	1,151.8	1,567.1
Germany	6,190.7	6,000.2	6,108.0
Hungary	2,723.4	2,178.6	2,168.2
Italy	667.7	789.7	901.1
Latvia	5,981.5	8,541.7	10,970.1
Lithuania	3,306.9	4,473.6	5,804.8
Netherlands	2,241.9	2,378.3	2,752.7
Norway	2,429.7	2,788.4	3,177.9
Poland	781.4	1,122.1	1,439.6
Russia	4,178.4	6,284.0	9,470.5
Sweden	11,410.2	12,725.7	14,787.5
Ukraine	1,257.0	1,156.6	1,847.9
United Kingdom	2,786.4	3,393.6	3,095.2
USA	2,376.1	2,992.7	7,996.9
Total (incl. others)	74,614.3	96,747.3	121,017.6

Transport

RAILWAYS
(traffic)

	2004	2005	2006
Passengers carried ('000)	5,272	5,138	5,301
Passenger-kilometres (million)	192.5	247.0	256.0
Freight carried ('000 metric tons)	72,257	69,894	61,502
Freight ton-kilometres (million)	10,648.4	10,629.4	10,504.3

ROAD TRAFFIC
('000 motor vehicles in use at 31 December)

	2004	2005	2006
Passenger cars	471.2	493.8	554.0
Buses and coaches	5.3	5.2	5.3
Lorries and vans	85.7	86.2	92.9
Motorcycles	9.1	10.2	12.6

SHIPPING
Merchant Fleet
(registered at 31 December)

	2004	2005	2006
Number of vessels	149	134	138
Total displacement ('000 grt)	334.9	292.5	416.7

Source: Lloyd's Register-Fairplay, *World Fleet Statistics*.

International Sea-borne Freight Traffic
('000 metric tons)

	2004	2005	2006
Goods loaded	41,966	42,179	43,506
Goods unloaded	4,402	4,563	6,313

ESTONIA

CIVIL AVIATION
(traffic on scheduled services)

	2004	2005	2006
Passengers carried ('000)	969.9	1,516.2	1,464.8
Passenger-km (million)	725.5	1,105.9	1,133.0
Freight carried ('000 tons)	4.7	5.8	5.2
Total ton-km (million)	3.3	3.7	2.8

Tourism

FOREIGN TOURIST ARRIVALS BY COUNTRY OF ORIGIN*

	2003	2004	2005
Finland	706,473	843,871	799,139
Germany	68,151	85,643	109,346
Latvia	29,230	40,956	51,558
Russia	37,320	42,348	53,427
Sweden	66,751	89,042	108,234
United Kingdom and Ireland	30,151	38,903	62,926
Total (incl. others)	1,112,746	1,374,414	1,453,418

* Figures refer to arrivals at registered accommodation establishments.

Tourism receipts (US $ million, excl. passenger transport): 671 in 2003; 887 in 2004; 948 in 2005 (Source: World Tourism Organization).

Communications Media

	2004	2005	2006
Telephones ('000 main lines in use)	444	442	542
Mobile cellular telephones ('000 subscribers)	1,256	1,445	1,659
Personal computers ('000 in use)	620	650	n.a.
Internet users ('000)	670	690	760
Broadband subscribers ('000)	139	179	228
Book production: titles	3,994	4,060	4,040
Book production: copies (million)	5.8	6.0	7.3
Daily newspapers: number	13	15	16
Non-daily newspapers: number	120	123	127
Other periodicals: number	1,171	1,190	1,158
Other periodicals: average annual circulation ('000 copies)	23,500	25,300	28,600

1996: Radio receivers in use 221,000.

2001: Television receivers in use 900,000.

Sources: partly UN, *Statistical Yearbook*, and International Telecommunication Union.

Education
(2004/05 unless otherwise indicated)

	Institutions	Teachers	Students
Pre-primary	600	7,480*	52,900
Primary	323	7,702†	85,000
General secondary	234	12,259†	99,000
Special	46	n.a.	5,545
Vocational and professional	68	1,177†	29,915‡
Universities, etc.	37	6,842§	67,760‡

* Source: UNESCO.
† Figures refer to estimates for 2001/02 (Source: UNESCO).
‡ Including students enrolled in evening and correspondence courses.
§ Figure refers to teaching staff in tertiary institutions in 2004/05 (Source: UNESCO).

Adult literacy rate (estimates based on census data): 99.8% (males 99.8%; females 99.8%) in 2000 (Source: UNESCO Institute for Statistics).

Directory

The Constitution

A new Constitution, based on that of 1938, was adopted by a referendum held on 28 June 1992. It took effect on 3 July. The following is a summary of its main provisions.

FUNDAMENTAL RIGHTS, LIBERTIES AND DUTIES

Every child with one parent who is an Estonian citizen has the right, by birth, to Estonian citizenship. Anyone who, as a minor, lost his or her Estonian citizenship has the right to have his or her citizenship restored. The rights, liberties and duties of all persons, as listed in the Constitution, are equal for Estonian citizens as well as for citizens of foreign states and stateless persons who are present in Estonia.

All persons are equal before the law. No one may be discriminated against on the basis of nationality, race, colour, sex, language, origin, creed, political or other persuasions. Everyone has the right to the protection of the state and the law. Guaranteeing rights and liberties is the responsibility of the legislative, executive and judicial powers, as well as of local government. Everyone has the right to appeal to a court of law if his or her rights or liberties have been violated.

The state organizes vocational education and assists in finding work for persons seeking employment. Working conditions are under state supervision. Employers and employees may freely join unions and associations. Estonian citizens have the right to engage in commercial activities and to form profit-making associations. The property rights of everyone are inviolable. All persons legally present in Estonia have the right to freedom of movement and choice of abode. Everyone has the right to leave Estonia.

Everyone has the right to health care and to education. Education is compulsory for school-age children. Everyone has the right to instruction in Estonian.

The official language of state and local government authorities is Estonian. In localities where the language of the majority of the population is other than Estonian, local government authorities may use the language of the majority of the permanent residents of that locality for internal communication.

THE PEOPLE

The people exercise their supreme power through citizens who have the right to vote by: i) electing the Riigikogu (State Assembly or legislature); ii) participating in referendums. The right to vote belongs to every Estonian citizen who has attained the age of 18 years.

THE RIIGIKOGU

Legislative power rests with the Riigikogu. It comprises 101 members, elected every four years in free elections on the principle of proportionality. Every citizen entitled to vote who has attained 21 years of age may stand as a candidate for the Riigikogu.

The Riigikogu adopts laws and resolutions; decides on the holding of referendums; elects the President of the Republic; ratifies or rejects foreign treaties; approves the candidate for Prime Minister to form the Council of Ministers; adopts the national budget and approves the report on its execution; may declare a state of emergency, or, on the proposal of the President, declare a state of war, order mobilization and demobilization.

The Riigikogu elects from among its members a Chairman (Speaker) and two Deputy Chairmen to direct its work.

ESTONIA

THE PRESIDENT

The President of the Republic is the Head of State of Estonia. The President represents Estonia in international relations; appoints and recalls, on the proposal of the Government, diplomatic representatives of Estonia and accepts letters of credence of diplomatic representatives accredited to Estonia; declares regular (and early) elections to the Riigikogu; initiates amendments to the Constitution; nominates the candidate for the post of Prime Minister; and is the Supreme Commander of Estonia's armed forces.

The President is elected by secret ballot of the Riigikogu for a term of five years. No person may be elected to the office for more than two consecutive terms. Any Estonian citizen by birth, who is at least 40 years of age, may stand as a candidate for President.

Should the President not be elected after three rounds of voting, the Speaker of the Riigikogu convenes, within one month, an Electoral Body to elect the President.

THE GOVERNMENT

Executive power is held by the Government of the Republic (Council of Ministers). The Government implements national, domestic and foreign policies; directs and co-ordinates the work of government institutions; organizes the implementation of legislation, the resolutions of the Riigikogu, and the edicts of the President; submits draft legislation to the Riigikogu, as well as foreign treaties; prepares a draft of the national budget and presents it to the Riigikogu; administers the implementation of the national budget; and organizes relations with foreign states.

The Government comprises the Prime Minister and Ministers. The President of the Republic nominates a candidate for Prime Minister, who is charged with forming a new government.

JUDICIAL SYSTEM

Justice is administered solely by the courts. They are independent in their work and administer justice in accordance with the Constitution and laws. The court system is composed of rural and city, as well as administrative, courts (first level); district courts (second level); and the Supreme Court of the Republic of Estonia (the highest court in the land).

The Government

HEAD OF STATE

President: TOOMAS HENDRIK ILVES (elected by vote of the Riigikogu 23 September 2006; inaugurated 9 October 2006).

COUNCIL OF MINISTERS
(March 2008)

A coalition of the Estonian Reform Party (ERP), the Union of Pro Patria and Res Publica, and the Estonian Social Democratic Party (ESDP).

Prime Minister: ANDRUS ANSIP (ERP).
Minister of the Interior: JÜRI PIHL (ESDP).
Minister of Foreign Affairs: URMAS PAET (ERP).
Minister of Justice: REIN LANG (ERP).
Minister of Economic Affairs and Communications: JUHAN PARTS (Union of Pro Patria and Res Publica).
Minister of Finance: IVARI PADAR (ESDP).
Minister of the Environment: JAANUS TAMKIVI (ERP).
Minister of Culture: LAINE JÄNES (ERP).
Minister of Education and Research: TÕNIS LUKAS (Union of Pro Patria and Res Publica).
Minister of Agriculture: HELIR-VALDOR SEEDER (Union of Pro Patria and Res Publica).
Minister of Social Affairs: MARET MARIPUU (ERP).
Minister of Defence: JAAK AAVIKSOO (Union of Pro Patria and Res Publica).
Minister of Population and Ethnic Affairs: URVE PALO (ESDP).
Minister of Regional Affairs: SIIM-VALMAR KIISLER (Union of Pro Patria and Res Publica).

MINISTRIES

Office of the President: A. Weizenbergi 39, Tallinn 15050; tel. 631-6202; fax 631-6250; internet www.president.ee.
Office of the Prime Minister: Stenbocki maja, Rahukohtu 3, Tallinn 15161; tel. 693-5555; fax 693-5554; e-mail valitsus@rk.ee; internet www.peaminister.ee.
Ministry of Agriculture: Lai 39/41, Tallinn 15056; tel. 625-6101; fax 625-6200; e-mail pm@agri.ee; internet www.agri.ee.
Ministry of Culture: Suur Karja 23, Tallinn 15076; tel. 628-2222; fax 628-2200; e-mail min@kul.ee; internet www.kul.ee.
Ministry of Defence: Sakala 1, Tallinn 15094; tel. 717-0022; fax 717-0001; e-mail info@kmin.ee; internet www.mod.gov.ee.
Ministry of Economic Affairs and Communications: Harju 11, Tallinn 15072; tel. 625-6342; fax 631-3660; e-mail info@mkm.ee; internet www.mkm.ee.
Ministry of Education and Research: Munga 18, Tartu 50088; tel. 735-0222; fax 735-0250; e-mail hm@hm.ee; internet www.hm.ee.
Ministry of the Environment: Narva mnt 7A, Tallinn 15172; tel. 626-2802; fax 626-2801; e-mail min@envir.ee; internet www.envir.ee.
Ministry of Finance: Suur-Ameerika 1, Tallinn 15006; tel. 611-3558; fax 696-6810; e-mail info@fin.ee; internet www.fin.ee.
Ministry of Foreign Affairs: Islandi Väljak 1, Tallinn 15049; tel. 637-7000; fax 637-7099; e-mail vminfo@vm.ee; internet www.vm.ee.
Ministry of the Interior: Pikk 61, Tallinn 15065; tel. 612-5007; fax 612-5087; e-mail info@siseministeerium.ee; internet www.siseministeerium.ee.
Ministry of Justice: Tõnismägi 5A, Tallinn 15191; tel. 620-8100; fax 620-8109; e-mail info@just.ee; internet www.just.ee.
Ministry of Social Affairs: Gonsiori 29, Tallinn 15027; tel. 626-9301; fax 699-2209; e-mail info@sm.ee; internet www.sm.ee.

Legislature

Riigikogu
(State Assembly)

Lossi plats 1A, Tallinn 15165; tel. 631-6331; fax 631-6334; e-mail riigikogu@riigikogu.ee; internet www.riigikogu.ee.

Speaker: TOOMAS VAREK.

General Election, 4 March 2007

Parties	Votes	%	Seats
Estonian Reform Party	153,044	27.82	31
Estonian Centre Party	143,518	26.08	29
Union of Pro Patria and Res Publica	98,347	17.87	19
Estonian Social Democratic Party	58,363	10.61	10
Estonian Greens	39,279	7.14	6
Estonian People's Union	39,215	7.13	6
Others	18,447	3.35	—
Total	550,213	100.00	101

Election Commission

Estonian National Electoral Committee (Vabariigi Valimiskomisjon): Lossi plats 1A, Tallinn 15181; tel. 631-6540; fax 631-6541; e-mail val@riigikogu.ee; internet www.vvk.ee; Chair. HEIKI SIBUL.

Political Organizations

Constitution Party (Konstitutsioonierakond): Estonia pst. 7, Tallinn 10143; tel. 645-5335; fax 645-5336; e-mail eurp@hot.ee; internet www.kpartei.ee; f. 1994; represents the Russian-speaking minority in Estonia; fmrly Estonian United People's Party; Chair. SERGEI JURGENS; 1,615 mems.

Estonian Centre Party (Eesti Keskerakond): Toom-Rüütli 3/5, Tallinn 10130; tel. 627-3460; fax 627-3461; e-mail keskerakond@keskerakond.ee; internet www.keskerakond.ee; f. 1991; absorbed the Estonian Green Party in 1998 and the Estonian Pensioners' Party in 2005; Chair. EDGAR SAVISAAR; Gen. Sec. KADRI MUST; 9,000 mems.

Estonian Christian Democrats (Eesti Kristlikud Demokraadid): Narva mnt. 51, Tallinn 10151; tel. 626-1430; fax 626-1431; e-mail ekd@ekd.ee; internet www.ekd.ee; f. 1998; fmrly Estonian Christian People's Party; present name adopted April 2006; Chair. ALDO VINKEL.

Estonian Greens (Erakond Eestimaa Rohelised): Toom-Rüütli 10–3, Tallinn 10130; tel. and fax 584-3883; e-mail info@erakond.ee; internet roheline.erakond.ee; f. 2006; Co-Chair. MAREK STRANDBERG, MIKK SARV, VALDUR LAHTVEE.

Estonian People's Union (EPU) (Eestimaa Rahvaliit): Pärnu mnt. 30–6, Tallinn 10141; tel. 644-8578; fax 648-5053; e-mail erl@

ESTONIA

erl.ee; internet www.erl.ee; f. 2000 by merger of the Estonian Pensioners' and Families' Party and the Estonian Rural People's Union; merged with the New Estonia Party in Jan. 2003; right-wing; Hon. Chair. ARNOLD RÜÜTEL; Chair. VILLU REILJAN; 9,000 mems (2005).

Estonian Reform Party (ERP) (Eesti Reformierakond): Tõnismagi 9, Tallinn 10119; tel. 680-8080; fax 680-8081; e-mail info@reform.ee; internet www.reform.ee; f. 1994; liberal; Chair. ANDRUS ANSIP; 5,000 mems.

Estonian Social Democratic Party (ESDP) (Sotsiaaldemokraatlik Erakond): Ahtri 10A, Tallinn 10151; tel. 611-6040; fax 611-6050; e-mail kantselei@sotsdem.ee; internet www.sotsdem.ee; f. 1999 as the People's Party Moderates, by merger of the People's Party and the Moderates' Party; name changed in 2004; Chair. IVARI PADAR; Sec.-Gen. RANDEL LÄNTS; 3,200 mems.

Republican Party (Vabariiklik Partei): Kuperjanovi 56-5, Tartu 50409; tel. 521-4512; e-mail leping.vp@mail.ee; internet www.vabariiklikpartei.ee; f. 1999; Chair. KRISTJAN-OLARI LEPING.

Union of Pro Patria and Res Publica (IRL) (Isamaa ja Res Publica Liit): Wismari 11, Tallinn 10136; tel. 669-1070; fax 669-1071; e-mail info@irl.ee; internet www.isamaajarespublicaliit.ee; f. 2006 by merger of the Pro Patria Union (f. 1995) and the Union for the Republic Res Publica (f. 2001); centre-right; 8,500 mems; Chair. MART LAAR.

Diplomatic Representation

EMBASSIES IN ESTONIA

Austria: Vambola 6, Tallinn 10114; tel. 627-8740; fax 631-4365; e-mail tallinn-ob@bmeia.gv.at; Ambassador Dr ANGELIKA SAUPE-BERCHTHOLD.

Belgium: Rataskaevu 2, Tallinn 10123; tel. 627-4100; fax 627-4101; e-mail tallinn@diplobel.be; internet www.diplomatie.be/tallinn; Ambassador PIERRE DUBUISSON.

China, People's Republic: Narva mnt. 98, Tallinn 15009; tel. 601-5830; fax 601-5833; e-mail chinaemb@online.ee; internet www.chinaembassy.ee; Ambassador XIE JUNPING.

Czech Republic: Lahe 4, Tallinn 10150; tel. 627-4400; fax 631-4716; e-mail tallinn@embassy.mzv.cz; internet www.mfa.cz/tallinn; Ambassador MILOŠ LEXA.

Denmark: Wismari 5, Tallinn 15047; tel. 630-6400; fax 630-6421; e-mail tllamb@um.dk; internet www.ambtallinn.um.dk; Ambassador KIRSTEN GEELAN.

Finland: Kohtu 4, Tallinn 15180; tel. 610-3200; fax 610-3281; e-mail sanomat.tal@formin.fi; internet www.finland.ee; Ambassador JAAKKO KALELA.

France: Toom-Kuninga 20, Tallinn 15185; tel. 631-1492; fax 631-1385; e-mail france@datanet-ee.org; internet www.ambafrance-ee.org; Ambassador DANIEL LABROSSE.

Georgia: Koidu 70/7, Tallinn 10129; tel. and fax 698-8590; e-mail embassy.georgia@mail.ee; Chargé d'affaires ZURAB MARSHANIA.

Germany: Toom-Kuninga 11, Tallinn 15048; tel. 627-5300; fax 627-5304; e-mail tallinn@germany.ee; internet www.tallinn.diplo.de; Ambassador JULIUS BOBINGER.

Greece: Pärnu mnt. 12, Tallinn 10148; tel. 640-3560; fax 640-3561; e-mail grembest@yahoo.com; Ambassador CHRISTOS KARAPANOS.

Hungary: Narva mnt. 122, Tallinn 15025; tel. 605-1880; fax 605-4088; e-mail mission.tal@kum.hu; internet www.mfa.gov.hu/kulkepviselet/ee/ee; Ambassador JÓZSEF VIG.

Ireland: Demini Bldg, Viru 1/Vene 2, Tallinn 10123; tel. 681-1888; fax 681-1889; e-mail tallinnembassy@dfa.ie; Ambassador NOEL KILKENNY.

Italy: Vene 2, Tallinn 10123; tel. 627-6160; fax 631-1370; e-mail ambasciata.tallinn@esteri.it; internet www.ambtallinn.esteri.it; Ambassador FABRIZIO PIAGGESI.

Japan: Harju 6, Tallinn 15069; tel. 631-0531; fax 631-0533; e-mail jaapansk@online.ee; internet www.japemb.ee; Chargé d'affaires a.i. TOSHIKO SHIMIZU.

Latvia: Tõnismägi 10, Tallinn 10119; tel. 627-7850; fax 625-7855; e-mail embassy.estonia@mfa.gov.lv; Ambassador INESE SEGLIŅA.

Lithuania: Uus 15, Tallinn 15070; tel. 616-4990; fax 641-2013; e-mail amb.ee@urm.lt; internet www.ee.mfa.lt; Ambassador JUOZAS BERNATONIS.

Netherlands: Rahukohtu 4-I, Tallin 10130; tel. 680-5500; fax 680-5501; e-mail info@netherlandsembassy.ee; internet www.netherlandsembassy.ee; Ambassador HENK VAN DER ZWAN.

Norway: Harju 6, Tallinn 15054; tel. 627-1000; fax 627-1001; e-mail emb.tallinn@mfa.no; internet www.norra.ee; Ambassador STEIN VEGARD HAGEN.

Poland: Suur-Karja 1, Tallinn 10140; tel. 627-8206; fax 644-5221; e-mail poola.info@mail.ee; internet www.tallinn.polemb.net; Ambassador TOMASZ CHŁOŃ.

Portugal: Kohtu 10, Tallinn 10130; tel. 611-7468; fax 611-7467; e-mail emb.portugal.tallin@gmail.com; Ambassador ANA PAULA BAPTISTA GRADE ZACARIAS.

Russia: Pikk 19, Tallinn 10133; tel. 646-4175; fax 646-4178; e-mail vensaat@online.ee; internet www.rusemb.ee; Ambassador NIKOLAI N. USPENSKII.

Spain: Liivalaia 13/15, 6th Floor, Tallinn 10118; tel. 667-6651; fax 631-3767; e-mail emb.tallinn@mae.es; internet www.mae.es/embajadas/tallin; Ambassador EDUARDO IBÁNES LÓPEZ-DÓRIGA.

Sweden: Pikk 28, Tallinn 15055; tel. 640-5600; fax 640-5695; e-mail swedemb@neti.ee; internet www.sweden.ee; Ambassador DAG HARTELIUS.

Turkey: Narva mnt. 30, Tallinn 10152; tel. 627-2880; fax 627-2885; e-mail tallinn@turkishembassy.ee; Ambassador FATMA SULE SOYSAL.

Ukraine: Lahe 6, Tallinn 15170; tel. 601-5815; fax 601-5816; e-mail embukr@eol.ee; internet www.hot.ee/ukrembassy; Ambassador PAVLO O. KIRYAKOV.

United Kingdom: Wismari 6, Tallinn 10136; tel. 667-4700; fax 667-4755; e-mail information@britishembassy.ee; internet www.britishembassy.ee; Ambassador PETER CARTER.

USA: Kentmanni 20, Tallinn 15099; tel. 668-8100; fax 668-8134; e-mail usasaatkond@state.gov; internet www.usemb.ee; Ambassador STANLEY DAVIS (DAVE) PHILLIPS.

Judicial System

Supreme Court
(Riigikohus)

Lossi 17, Tartu 50093; tel. 730-9002; fax 730-9003; e-mail info@riigikohus.ee; internet www.nc.ee.

Chief Justice and Chairman of the Constitutional Review Chamber: MÄRT RASK.

Chairman of the Civil Chamber: ANTS KULL.

Chairman of the Criminal Chamber: HANNES KIRIS.

Chairman of the Administrative Law Chamber: TÕNU ANTON.

Office of the Chancellor of Justice (Õiguskantsleri Kantselei): Kohtu 8, Tallinn 15193; tel. 693-8404; fax 693-8401; e-mail info@oiguskantsler.ee; internet www.oiguskantsler.ee; f. 1993; reviews general application of legislative and executive powers and of local governments for conformity with the Constitution, supervises activities of state agencies in guaranteeing constitutional rights and freedoms; Chancellor of Justice ALLAR JÕKS.

Public Prosecutor's Office (Riigiprokuratuur): Wismari 7, Tallinn 15188; tel. 613-9400; fax 613-9402; e-mail info@prokuratuur.ee; internet www.prokuratuur.ee; State Prosecutor-Gen. NORMAN AAS.

Religion

CHRISTIANITY
Protestant Churches

Estonian Conference of Seventh-day Adventists (Seitsmenda Päeva Adventistide Kogudus Eesti Liit): Lille 18, Tartu 51010; tel. and fax 734-3211; e-mail office@advent.ee; internet www.advent.ee; f. 1917; Pres. TÕNU JUGAR.

Estonian Evangelical Lutheran Church (Eesti Evangeelne Luterlike Kirik): Kiriku plats 3, Tallinn 10130; tel. 627-7350; fax 627-7352; e-mail konsistoorium@eelk.ee; internet www.eelk.ee; Archbishop Most Rev. ANDRES PÕDER.

Union of Free Evangelical Christian and Baptist Churches of Estonia (Eesti Evangeeliumi Kristlaste ja Baptistide Koguduste Liit): Koskla 2/9, Tallinn 10615; tel. 670-0698; fax 650-6008; e-mail eekbl@ekklesia.ee; internet www.ekklesia.ee; f. 1884; Pres. JOOSEP TAMMO.

United Methodist Church in Estonia (Eesti Metodisti Kirik): EMK Kirikuvalitsus, Narva mnt. 51, Tallinn 10152; tel. 668-8477; fax 668-8498; e-mail keskus@metodistikirik.ee; internet www.metodistikirik.ee; f. 1907; forms part of the Northern European Area of the United Methodist Church; Superintendent TAAVI HOLLMAN.

The Eastern Orthodox Church

Between 1923 and 1940 the Estonian Apostolic Orthodox Church (EAOC) was under the jurisdiction of the Ecumenical Patriarchate of Constantinople (based in Istanbul, Turkey). Following the Soviet occupation of Estonia in 1940, the EAOC was banned and its

ESTONIA

churches and communities were placed under the jurisdiction of the Moscow Patriarchate. The leaders of the EAOC went into exile in Stockholm, Sweden. After the restoration of Estonian independence, in 1993 Estonia recognized the EAOC as the legal successor of the Orthodox Church in operation before the Second World War, and in February 1996 the Ecumenical Patriarchate restored the EAOC to its jurisdiction. The Estonian Orthodox Church of the Moscow Patriarchate was officially registered in April 2002.

Estonian Apostolic Orthodox Church (Eesti Apostlik Õigeusu Kirik): Wismari 32, Tallinn 10136; tel. 660-0780; fax 660-0782; e-mail eaok@eaok.ee; internet www.eoc.ee; Metropolitan of Tallinn and All Estonia STEPHANOS; 60 congregations.

Estonian Orthodox Church (Moscow Patriarchate) (Moskva Patriarhaadi Eesti Õigeusu Kirik/Estonskaya Pravoslavnaya Tserkov Moskovskogo Patriarkhata): Pikk 64/4, Tallinn 10133; tel. 641-1301; fax 641-1302; e-mail mpeok@hot.ee; internet www.orthodox.ee; Metropolitan of Tallinn and All Estonia KORNELIUS; 32 congregations.

The Roman Catholic Church

At 31 December 2005 there were an estimated 5,745 Roman Catholic adherents (of both the Latin and Byzantine rites) in Estonia.

Office of the Apostolic Administrator: Jaan Poska 47, Tallinn 10150; tel. 601-3079; fax 601-3190; e-mail admapost@online.ee; Apostolic Administrator Most Rev. PHILIPPE JEAN-CHARLES JOURDAN (Titular Bishop of Pertusa).

ISLAM

Estonian Islamic Congregation: Sütiste 52–76, Tallinn 13420; tel. 652-2403; f. 1928; Chair. of Bd TIMUR SEIFULLEN.

JUDAISM

In the early 2000s there were an estimated 3,000 Jews resident in Estonia, principally in Tallinn.

Jewish Community of Estonia (Eesti Juudi Kogukond/Yevreiskaya Obshchina Estonii): Karu 16, Tallinn; POB 3576, Tallinn 10507; tel. and fax 662-3034; e-mail community@jewish.ee; internet www.jewish.ee; Chair. ILYA SUNDELEVICH.

The Press

In 2006 there were 16 officially registered daily newspapers and 127 non-daily newspapers published in Estonia. In that year 1,158 periodicals were published.

PRINCIPAL NEWSPAPERS

In Estonian except where otherwise stated.

Äripäev (Business Daily): Pärnu mnt. 105, Tallinn 19094; tel. 667-0222; fax 667-0165; e-mail aripaev@aripaev.ee; internet www.aripaev.ee; f. 1989; five days a week; business and finance; Editor-in-Chief IGOR RÕTOV; circ. 17,200.

Den za Dnem (Day After Day): Pärnu mnt. 130, Tallinn 11313; tel. 678-8288; fax 678-8290; e-mail toimetus@dzd.ee; internet www.vestidd.ee; f. 1991; weekly; in Russian; circ. 18,500.

Eesti Ekspress (Estonian Express): Narva mnt. 11E, Tallinn 10151; tel. 669-8030; fax 669-8154; e-mail ekspress@ekspress.ee; internet www.ekspress.ee; f. 1989; weekly; owned by Ekspress Grupp; Editor-in-Chief HANS H. LUIK; circ. 49,300.

Eesti Kirik (Estonian Church): Ülikooli, Tartu 51003; tel. 743-1437; fax 743-3243; internet www.eestikirik.ee; f. 1923; weekly; organ of the Estonian Evangelical Lutheran Church; Editor-in-Chief SIRJE SEMM; circ. 2,100.

Eesti Päevaleht (Estonian Daily): Pärnu mnt. 67A, POB 433, Tallinn 10151; tel. 680-4400; fax 680-4401; e-mail mail@epl.ee; internet www.epl.ee; f. 1905; daily; 50% owned by Ekspress Grupp; Editor-in-Chief LEA LARIN; circ. 37,000.

Maaleht (Country News): Toompuiestee 16, Tallinn 10137; tel. 661-3300; fax 661-3344; e-mail ml@maaleht.ee; internet www.maaleht.ee; f. 1987; weekly; problems and aspects of politics, culture, agriculture and country life; Editor-in-Chief PEETER ERNITS; circ. 42,000.

Meie Meel (Our Mind): POB 104, Tallinn 0090; fax 646-1625; e-mail meiemeel@zzz.ee; f. 1991; weekly; youth paper; Editor-in-Chief MARE VETEMAA; circ. 20,700.

Molodezh Estonii (Youth of Estonia): Narva mnt. 13A, Tallinn 10502; tel. 623-0150; fax 623-0156; e-mail moles@moles.ee; internet www.moles.ee; f. 1991; in Russian; Editor-in-Chief ILYA NIKOFOROV.

Postimees (Postman): Maakri 23A, Tallinn 10145; tel. 666-2302; fax 666-2301; e-mail online@postimees.ee; internet www.postimees.ee; f. 1857; daily; Editor-in-Chief URMAS KLAAS; circ. 60,200.

Sirp: POB 388, Tallinn 10503; tel. 640-5770; fax 640-5771; e-mail sirp@sirp.ee; internet www.sirp.ee; f. 1940; weekly; the arts; Editor-in-Chief MIHKEL MUTT; circ. 3,500.

SL Õhtuleht (Evening Gazette): Narva mnt. 13, POB 106, Tallinn 10151; tel. 614-4000; fax 614-4001; e-mail leht@sloleht.ee; internet www.sloleht.ee; f. 2000; daily; 50% owned by Ekspress Grupp; Editor-in-Chief VÄINO KOORBERG; circ. 67,200.

Vesti dnya (News of the Day): Madala 16, Tallinn 10315; tel. 602-6861; tel. 665-1111; e-mail editor@vesti.ee; internet www.vesti.ee; five days a week; in Russian; also *Vesti nedeli* (News of the Week), Fridays; Chief Editor ALEKSANDR CHAPLYGIN; circ. 6,100.

PRINCIPAL PERIODICALS

Akadeemia: Ülikooli 21, Tartu 51007; tel. 742-3050; fax 744-1975; e-mail akadeemia@akad.ee; internet www.akad.ee; f. 1989; monthly; journal of the Union of Writers; Editor-in-Chief TOOMAS KIHO; circ. 2,260.

Eesti Arst (Estonian Physician): Pepleri 32, Tartu 51010; tel. and fax 742-7825; e-mail eestiarst@eestiarst.ee; internet www.eestiarst.ee; f. 1922; monthly; Editor-in-Chief VÄINO SINISALU; circ. 4,000.

Eesti Loodus (Estonian Nature): Veski 4, POB 110, Tartu 50002; tel. 742-1186; fax 742-1143; e-mail toimetus@el.loodus.ee; internet www.loodusajakiri.ee/eesti_loodus; f. 1933; monthly; popular science; illustrated; Editor-in-Chief TOOMAS KUKK; circ. 5,200.

Eesti Naine (Estonian Woman): Maakri 23A, Tallinn 10145; tel. 666-2233; fax 666-2557; e-mail katrin.streimann@kirjastus.ee; internet www.eestinaine.ee; f. 1924; monthly; Editor-in-Chief KATRIN STREIMANN; circ. 24,000.

Hea Laps (Good Kid): Harju 1, Tallinn 10146; tel. 631-4428; e-mail hea.laps@mail.ee; internet kommikas.kalev.ee/healaps; monthly; for children; Editor-in-Chief LEELO TUNGAL.

Horisont (Horizon): Narva mnt. 5, Tallinn 10117; tel. 661-6163; fax 641-8033; e-mail horisont@horisont.ee; f. 1967; 6 a year; popular science; Editor-in-Chief INDREK ROHTMETS; circ. 3,000.

Keel ja Kirjandus (Language and Literature): Roosikrantsi 6, Tallinn 10119; tel. 644-9228; fax 644-1800; e-mail kk@eki.ee; internet www.eki.ee/keeljakirjandus; f. 1958; monthly; publ. by Academy of Sciences and Union of Writers; Editor-in-Chief MART MERI; circ. 900.

Kodukiri (Your Home): Maakri 23A, Tallinn 10145; tel. 666-2550; fax 666-2558; e-mail velve.saar@kirjastus.ee; internet www.kodukiri.ee; f. 1992; monthly; Editor-in-Chief KATRIN KUUSEMÄE; circ. 50,000.

Looming (Creation): Harju 1, Tallinn 10146; tel. 627-6425; e-mail looming@hot.ee; f. 1923; journal of the Union of Writers; fiction, poetry, literary criticism; Editor-in-Chief UDO UIBO; circ. 1,800.

Loomingu Raamatukogu (Library of Creativity): Harju 1, Tallinn 10146; tel. 627-6425; e-mail lr@looming.ee; f. 1957; publ. by the Union of Writers of Estonia; poetry, fiction and non-fiction by Estonian and foreign authors; Editor-in-Chief TOOMAS HAUG; circ. 1,400.

Maakodu (Country Home): Toompuiestee 16, Tallinn 10137; tel. 660-5306; fax 662-2292; e-mail meelim@maaleht.ee; internet www.maaleht.ee/?page=maakodu; f. 1989; monthly; Editor-in-Chief MEELI MÜÜRIPEAL; circ. 12,000.

Oil Shale: Kohtu 6, Tallinn 10130; tel. 646-7512; fax 646-6026; e-mail aili@kirj.ee; internet www.kirj.ee/oilshale; f. 1984; quarterly; geology, chemistry, mining, oil-shale industry; Editor-in-Chief ANTO RAUKAS; circ. 350.

Põllumajandus (Agriculture): Lai 39, Tallinn 10133; tel. 641-1161; f. 1932; monthly; Editor-in-Chief ARVO SIRENDI; circ. 1,000.

Teater, Muusika, Kino (Theatre, Music, Cinema): Voorimehe 9, Tallinn 10146; tel. and fax 646-4742; internet www.temuki.ee; f. 1982; monthly; Editor-in-Chief MADIS KOLK; circ. 1,500.

Vikerkaar (Rainbow): Voorimehe 9, Tallinn 10146; tel. 646-4059; e-mail vikerkaar@teleport.ee; internet www.vikerkaar.ee; f. 1986; monthly; fiction, poetry, critical works; Editor-in-Chief MÄRT VÄLJATAGA; circ. 1,500.

NEWS AGENCY

BNS (Baltic News Service): Pärnu mnt. 105, Tallinn 15043; tel. 610-8800; fax 610-8811; e-mail bns@bns.ee; internet www.bns.ee; f. 1990; daily news bulletins in English, Estonian, Latvian, Lithuanian and Russian; Chief Exec. GEORGE SHABAD.

PRESS ORGANIZATIONS

Estonian Journalists' Union (Eesti Ajakirjanike Liit): Gonsiori 21/409, Tallinn 10147; tel. and fax 646-3699; e-mail eal@eal.ee; internet www.eal.ee; f. 1919; Dir MERIKE VIILUP.

Estonian Newspaper Association (Eesti Ajalehtede Liit): Pärnu mnt. 67A, Tallinn 10134; tel. 646-1005; fax 631-1210; e-mail eall@eall

.ee; internet www.eall.ee; f. 1990; 41 mem. newspapers; Chair. AAVO KOKK.

Estonian Press Council (Avaliku Sõna Nõukogu): Gonsiori 21, Tallinn 15020; tel. and fax 646-3699; e-mail asn@asn.org.ee; internet www.asn.org.ee; f. 1997; non-governmental org.; Chair. Prof. EPP LAUK.

Publishers

Eesti Raamat (Estonian Book): Laki 26, Tallinn 12915; tel. and fax 658-7889; e-mail georg.grynberg@mail.ee; internet www.eestiraamat.ee; f. 1940; fiction for children and adults; Dir ANNE-ASTRI KASK.

Estonian Academy Publishers (EAP): Kohtu 6, Tallinn 10130; tel. 645-4504; fax 646-6026; e-mail niine@kirj.ee; internet www.kirj.ee; f. 1994; publishes journals incl. *Proceedings of the Estonian Academy of Sciences*, *Linguistica Uralica*, etc.; Dir ÜLO NIINE.

Estonian Encyclopedia Publishers (Eesti Entsüklopeediakirjastus): Narva mnt. 4, Tallinn 10117; tel. 699-9620; fax 699-9621; e-mail ene@ene.ee; internet www.ene.ee; f. 1991; reference works in Estonian and Russian; Man. Dir HARDO AASMÄE.

Huma: Vene 14, Tallinn 10123; tel. and fax 644-0955; e-mail info@huma.ee; internet www.huma.ee; f. 1990; fiction, non-fiction, children's books, art, calendars; Dir LIIVI KESKPAIK.

Ilmamaa: Vanemuise 19, Tartu 51014; tel. 742-7290; fax 742-7320; internet www.ilmamaa.ee; f. 1992; general fiction, philosophy, cultural history; Dir MART JAGOMÄGI.

Ilo Publishing House: Madara 14, Tallinn 10612; tel. 661-0550; fax 661-0556; e-mail ilo@ilo.ee; internet www.ilo.ee; f. 1990; dictionaries, reference books, textbooks, history, management, psychology, law and children's books; Dir JAAK KAARMA.

Koolibri: Pärnu mnt. 10, Tallinn 10148; tel. 651-5300; fax 651-5301; e-mail koolibri@koolibri.ee; internet www.koolibri.ee; f. 1991; textbooks, dictionaries, children's books; Man. Dir KALLE KALJURAND.

Kunst (Fine Art): Lai 34, Tallinn 10133; POB 105, Tallinn 10502; tel. 641-1766; fax 641-1762; e-mail kunst.myyk@mail.ee; f. 1957; fine arts, fiction, tourism, history, biographies; Dir SIRJE HELME.

Logos: Narma mnt. 51, Tallinn 10152; e-mail logos@logos.ee; internet www.logos.ee; f. 1991; Christian; Chair. TIINA NÕLVAK.

Monokkel: POB 311, Tallinn 10503; tel. 501-6307; fax 656-9176; e-mail monokkel@hot.ee; internet www.hot.ee/monokkel; f. 1988; history, fiction; Dir ANTS ÕÕBIK.

Õllu: Harju 1, Tallinn 10146; tel. 652-2038; fiction; Chair. of Bd HEINO KIIK.

Tartu University Press: Tiigi 78, Tartu 50410; tel. 737-5961; fax 737-5944; e-mail tyk@psych.ut.ee; internet www.tyk.ee; f. 1958; science, textbooks, etc.; Dir VAIKO TIGANE.

Tiritamm: Laki 26, Tallinn 12915; tel. and fax 656-3570; e-mail tiritamm@tiritamm.ee; internet www.eestikirjastused.com/tiritamm; f. 1991; children's books; Dir SIRJE SAIMRE.

Valgus: Tulika 19, Tallinn 10613; tel. 650-5025; fax 650-5104; e-mail info@kirjastusvalgus.ee; internet www.kirjastusvalgus.ee; f. 1965; scientific literature, resource materials and textbooks; Editor-in-Chief EVA KOLLI.

Varrak: Pärnu mnt. 67A, Tallinn 10134; tel. 646-1116; e-mail varrak@varrak.ee; internet www.varrak.ee; f. 1991; history, philosophy and sociology, literary fiction, science fiction, popular fiction and children's literature; Man. Dir PRIIT MAIDE.

PUBLISHERS' ASSOCIATION

Estonian Publishers' Association (Eesti Kirjastuste Liit): Roosikrantsi 6/207, Tallinn 10119; tel. 644-9866; fax 641-1443; internet www.estbook.com; f. 1991; Dir-Gen. KRISTIINA RAID.

Broadcasting and Communications

TELECOMMUNICATIONS

Service Providers

Eesti Telekom AS (Estonian Telecom Ltd): Roosikrantsi 2, Tallinn 10119; tel. 631-1212; fax 631-1224; e-mail mailbox@telekom.ee; internet www.telekom.ee; f. 1992 as Eesti Telefon (subsequently a subsidiary, renamed Elion in 2003); privatized in 1999; subsidiaries include Eesti Mobiltelefon AS (EMT) and Elion Enterprises (q.v.); Chair. and Chief Exec. JAAN MÄNNIK.

Elion Enterprises: Endla 16, Tallinn 15033; tel. 639-7213; fax 639-7341; e-mail info@elion.ee; internet www.elion.ee; wholly owned subsidiary of Eesti Telekom AS; telecommunications and IT provider; Chair. and CEO VALDUR LAID.

Elisa Eesti: Vilmsi 47, POB 289, 10126 Tallinn; tel. 681-1963; fax 681-1961; e-mail info@elisa.ee; internet www.elisa.ee; mobile cellular telecommunications.

EMT: Valge 16, Tallinn 19095; tel. 639-7130; fax 639-7132; e-mail info@emt.ee; internet www.emt.ee; f. 1991; wholly owned subsidiary of Eesti Telekom; CEO VALDO KALM.

Tele2 Eesti: Jõe 2A, 10151 Tallinn; tel. 686-6866; fax 686-6877; e-mail tele2@tele2.ee; internet www.tele2.ee; mobile cellular telecommunications.

BROADCASTING

Supervisory Authority

Broadcasting Council: Gonsiori 21, Tallinn 15020; tel. 611-4305; fax 611-4457; e-mail rhn@er.ee; mems appointed by Riigikogu (State Assembly).

Radio

In 2005 there were 27 private radio broadcasters operating in Estonia (one with an international broadcasting licence, 16 with regional licences and 11 with local licences), in addition to the public broadcaster, Eesti Rahvusringhääling, which was formed in 2007 by the merger of the public television and radio broadcasters.

Eesti Rahvusringhääling (ERR) (Estonian Public Broadcasting): Gonsiori 21, Tallinn 15029; tel. 628-4100; fax 628-4155; e-mail err@err.ee; internet www.err.ee; f. 2007 by merger of Eesti Televisioon and Eesti Raadio; radio broadcasts comprise five domestic channels (three in Estonian, one in Russian and one in English, French and German) and an external service in English; television broadcasts comprise one channel with programmes in Estonian and Russian; Chair. and Dir-Gen. MARGUS ALLIKMAA.

Raadio Elmar: Õpetaja 9A, Tartu 51003; tel. 742-7520; fax 774-2044; e-mail elmar@elmar.ee; internet www.elmar.ee; one of six radio stations owned by Trio Grupp; Dir JAAN HABICHT.

Raadio Kuku: Narva mnt. 63, Tallinn 20606; tel. 630-7660; fax 601-5759; e-mail kuku@kuku.ee; internet www.kuku.ee; Chair. of Bd REIN LANG.

Raadio Sky Plus: Pärnu mnt. 139c, Tallinn 11317; tel. 678-8777; fax 678-8710; e-mail sky@sky.ee; internet www.skyplus.fm; owned by Sky Media; Chief Exec. ILMAR KOMPUS.

Raadio Uuno: Veerenni 58A, Tallinn 11314; tel. 630-7080; fax 630-7085; e-mail uuno@uuno.ee; internet www.uuno.ee; Chair. REIN LANG.

Star FM: Peterburi tee 81, Tallinn 11415; tel. 622-0288; fax 622-0294; e-mail info@starfm.ee; internet www.starfm.ee; Chair. SVEN NUTMANN.

Tartu Pereraadio (Tartu Family Radio): Annemõisa 8, Tartu 50718; tel. and fax 748-8458; e-mail tartu@pereraadio.ee; internet www.pereraadio.ee; f. 1994; Christian; Pres. JOEL LUHAMETS.

Television

There are three national commercial television stations and one public broadcaster in Estonia. In addition, five cable television licences have been issued.

Eesti Rahvusringhääling (ERR) (Estonian Public Broadcasting): Gonsiori 21, Tallinn 15029; tel. 628-4100; fax 628-4155; e-mail err@err.ee; internet www.err.ee; f. 2007 by merger of Eesti Televisioon and Eesti Raadio; radio broadcasts comprise five domestic channels (three in Estonian, one in Russian and one in English, French and German) and an external service in English; television broadcasts comprise one channel with programmes in Estonian and Russian; Chair. and Dir-Gen. MARGUS ALLIKMAA.

Kanal 2 (Channel 2): Maakri 23A, Tallinn 10145; tel. 666-2450; fax 666-2451; e-mail info@kanal2.ee; internet www.kanal2.ee; f. 1993; commercial; Chair. HANS ERIK MATRE.

TV3: Peterburgi tee 81, Tallinn 11415; tel. 622-0200; fax 622-0201; e-mail tv3@tv3.ee; internet www.tv3.ee; f. 1996; owned by Modern Times Group (Sweden); Exec. Dir TOOMAS VARA.

Broadcasting Association

Association of Estonian Broadcasters (AEB) (Eesti Ringhäälingute Liit): Ülemiste tee 3A, Tallinn 11415; tel. and fax 633-3235; e-mail erl@online.ee; internet www.ringhliit.ee; f. 1992; 16 mems; Man. Dir URMAS LOIT.

ESTONIA

Finance

(cap. = capital; res = reserves; dep. = deposits; m. = million; brs = branches; amounts in kroons)

BANKING

Central Bank

Bank of Estonia (Eesti Pank): Estonia pst. 13, Tallinn 15095; tel. 668-0719; fax 668-0836; e-mail info@epbe.ee; internet www.bankofestonia.info; f. 1919; closed 1940; re-established 1990; bank of issue; cap. 600m., res 3,201.8m., dep. 17,553.7m. (Dec. 2006); Pres. Andres Lipstok.

Commercial Banks

Estonian Credit Bank (Eesti Krediidipank): Narva mnt. 4, Tallinn 15014; tel. 669-0900; fax 661-6037; e-mail info@krediidipank.ee; internet www.krediidipank.ee; f. 1992; 59.82% owned by Latvijas Biznesa banka (Latvia); cap. 143.0m., res 19.2m., dep. 3,149.1m. (Dec. 2006); Pres. Alexei Sytnikov; Chair. of Bd Andrus Kluge; 12 brs.

AS Hansapank: Liivalaia 8, Tallinn 15040; tel. 631-0310; fax 631-0410; e-mail hansa@hansa.ee; internet www.hansa.ee; f. 1991; merged with Estonian Savings Bank (Eesti Hoiupank) in 1998; 59.7% owned by FöreningsSparbanken AB (Sweden); cap. €202.8m., res €72.2m., dep. €16,081.2m. (Dec. 2006); Chair. of Council Jan Liden; Chair. of Bd Erkki Raasuke; 96 brs.

AS Sampo Pank (Sampo Bank): Narva mnt. 11, Tallinn 15015; tel. 630-2100; fax 630-2200; e-mail info@sampopank.ee; internet www.sampopank.ee; f. 1992; present name adopted 2000; wholly owned by Sampo Bank plc (Finland); cap. 898.0m., res 40.0m., dep. 20,345.0m. (Dec. 2006); Chair. of Management Bd Aivar Rehe; 13 brs.

SEB Eesti Ühispank (SEB Estonian Union Bank): Tornimäe 2, Tallinn 15010; tel. 665-5100; fax 665-5102; e-mail postkast@seb.ee; internet www.seb.ee; f. 1992 by the merger of 10 small banks; 100% owned by Scandinaviska Enskilda Banken (SEB—Sweden); cap. 665.6m., res 4,029.2m., dep. 60,546.3m. (Dec. 2006); Pres. Ahti Asmann; Chair. Bo Magnusson; 90 brs.

Tallinn Business Bank (Tallinna Äripank): Vana-Viru 7, Tallinn 10111; tel. 668-8000; fax 668-8001; e-mail info@tbb.ee; internet www.tbb.ee; f. 1991; cap. 229.8m., res 23.1m., dep. 426.0m. (Dec. 2006); Chair. of Bd Valerii Haritonov.

Banking Association

Estonian Banking Association (Eesti Pangaliit): Ahtri 12, Tallinn 10151; tel. 611-6567; fax 611-6568; e-mail pangaliit@pangaliit.ee; internet www.pangaliit.ee; f. 1992; Chair. Vahur Kraft; Man. Dir Katrin Talihärm.

STOCK EXCHANGE

Tallinn Stock Exchange (Tallinna Börs): Tartu mnt. 2, Tallinn 10145; tel. 640-8800; fax 640-8801; e-mail tallinn@omxgroup.com; internet www.omxgroup.com/balticmarket; f. 1995; 61.6% owned by the OMX group (Sweden); Chair. Andrus Alber.

INSURANCE

At the end of 2003 there were five insurance organizations providing life insurance, and eight providing non-life insurance, operating in Estonia. The following were among the principal companies operating at that time.

Estonian Insurance Association (Eesti Kindlustusseltside Liit): Mustamäe tee 44, Tallinn 10621; tel. 667-1800; fax 667-1801; e-mail info@eksl.ee; internet www.eksl.ee; f. 1993; Chair. Indrek Holst.

Insurance Companies

ERGO: Lauteri 5, Tallinn 10114; tel. 610-6500; fax 610-6501; e-mail info@ergo.com; internet www.ergo-kindlustus.ee; provides non-life insurance (as ERGO Kindlustus) and life insurance (ERGO Elukindlustus); Chair. of Bd Olga Reznik.

Hansa Elukindlustus (Hansa Life Insurance): Liivalaia 12, Tallinn 15036; tel. 613-1120; fax 613-1130; e-mail hek@hansa.ee; internet www.hansa.ee; wholly owned by Hansapank; fmrly Hansapanga Elukindlustuse; present name adopted 2004; life insurance; Chair. of Council Priit Põldoja.

If Eesti Kindlustus (If Estonia Insurance): Pronksi 19, Tallinn 10124; tel. 667-1099; fax 667-1016; e-mail info@if.ee; internet www.if.ee; f. 1999; non-life; Chief Exec. Olavi Laido.

QBE Kindlustuse Eesti: Liivalaia 13/15, Tallinn 10118; tel. 667-1400; fax 667-1401; e-mail info@qbe-estonia.com; internet www.qbeeurope.com/estonia; owned by QBE International (Australia); fmrly Nordea Kindlustus Eesti; present name adopted 2004.

Directory

Salva Kindlustuse (Salva Insurance): Pärnu mnt. 16, Tallinn 10141; tel. 680-0500; fax 680-0501; e-mail salva@salva.ee; internet www.salva.ee; non-life insurance.

Seesam: Vambola 6, Tallinn 10114; tel. 628-1801; fax 631-2109; e-mail seesam@seesam.ee; internet www.seesam.ee; wholly owned by Keskinäinen Henkivakuutusosakeyhtiö Suomi (Suomi Mutual Life Assurance Co—Finland); provides life insurance (as Seesam Elukindlustuse) and non-life insurance (Seesam Rahvusvaheline Kindlustuse); Chair. of Management Bd Ivo Kuldmäe.

Ühispanga Elukindlustus (Union Bank Life Insurance): Tornimäe 2, Tallinn 15010; tel. 665-6840; fax 665-6847; e-mail info@seb.ee; internet www.seb.ee; f. 1998; wholly owned by SEB Eesti Ühispank; life insurance; Chair. of Council Ain Hanschmidt.

Trade and Industry

GOVERNMENT AGENCIES

Consumer Protection Board (Tarbijakaitseametist): Kiriku 4, Tallinn 15071; tel. 620-1700; fax 620-1701; e-mail info@consumer.ee; internet www.tka.riik.ee; f. 1994; Dir-Gen. Helle Aruniit.

Enterprise Estonia (Ettevõtluse Arendamise Sihtasutus): Liivalaia 13/15, Tallinn 10118; tel. 627-9700; fax 627-9427; e-mail eas@eas.ee; internet www.eas.ee; Chair. Tea Varrak.

Estonian Centre for Standardization (Eesti Standardikeskus) (EVS): Aru 10, Tallinn 10317; tel. 605-5050; fax 605-5070; e-mail info@evs.ee; internet www.evs.ee; f. 1999; Man. Dir Priit Kikas.

Estonian Competition Authority (Kohkurentsiamet): Auna 6, Tallinn 10317; tel. 667-2400; fax 667-2401; e-mail info@konkurentsiamet.ee; internet www.konkurentsiamet.ee; f. 2008 as one of two successor bodies to the Estonian Competition Board, Estonian National Communications Board, Estonian Railway Inspectorate, Estonian Energy Market Inspectorate and Technical Inspectorate; supervises competition, and has specific powers in the sectors of fuel and energy, and electronic and postal communications; Dir-Gen. Märt Ots.

Estonian Investment Agency: Roosikrantsi 11, Tallinn 10119; tel. 627-9420; fax 627-9427; e-mail invest@eas.ee; internet www.investinestonia.com; Dir Andrus Viirg.

Estonian Technical Surveillance Authority (Tehnilise Järelevalve Amet): Sõle 23A, 10614 Tallinn; tel. 667-2000; fax 667-2001; e-mail info@tja.ee; internet www.tja.ee; f. 2008 as one of two successor bodies to Estonian Competition Board, Estonian National Communications Board, Estonian Railway Inspectorate, Estonian Energy Market Inspectorate and Technical Inspectorate; coordinates management of the use of radio frequencies (incl. broadcasting), manages numbering plan for telecommunications services, various responsibilities in the field of telecommunications and other forms of communications, incl. railways; Dir-Gen. Raigo Uukkivi.

CHAMBERS OF COMMERCE

Estonian Chamber of Agriculture and Commerce (Eesti Põllumajandus-Kaubanduskoda): Vilmsi 53G, Tallinn 10147; tel. 600-9349; fax 600-9350; e-mail info@epkk.ee; internet www.epkk.ee; Chair. Alar Oppar.

Estonian Chamber of Commerce and Industry (ECCI) (Eesti Kaubandus-Tööstuskoda): Toom-Kooli 17, Tallinn 10130; tel. 646-0244; fax 646-0245; e-mail koda@koda.ee; internet www.koda.ee; f. 1925; brs in Tartu, Jõhvi, Pärnu and Kuressaare; Pres. Toomas Luman.

INDUSTRIAL AND TRADE ASSOCIATIONS

Asscn of Construction Material Producers of Estonia (Eesti Ehitusmaterjalide Tootjate Liit—EETL): Kiriku 6, Tallinn 10130; tel. 648-1918; fax 648-9062; e-mail eetl@hot.ee; internet www.hot.ee/eetl; Dir Enno Rabane.

Asscn of Estonian Food Industry (Eesti Toiduainetööstuse Liit): Saku 15/105, Tallinn 11314; tel. 648-4978; fax 631-2718; e-mail info@toiduliit.ee; internet www.toiduliit.ee; f. 1993; Man. Dir Sirje Potisepp.

Central Union of Estonian Farmers (Eestimaa Põllumeeste Keskliit): J. Vilmsi 53G, Tallinn 10147; tel. and fax 600-8616; e-mail info@eptk.ee; internet www.eptk.ee; Chair. of Bd Kalev Kreegipuu.

Estonian Asscn of Fisheries (Eesti Kalaliit): Pärnu mnt 139E, Tallinn 11317; tel. and fax 654-9302; e-mail kalaliit@online.ee; internet www.kalaliit.ee; f. 1995; Chair. Jaan Jalakas; Man. Dir Valdur Noormägi.

Estonian Asscn of Information Technology and Telecommunications (Eesti Infotehnoloogia ja Telekommunikatsiooni Liit):

Endla 3, Tallinn 10122; tel. 630-7430; fax 631-1323; e-mail info@itl.ee; internet www.itl.ee; f. 2000; 36 mems; Chief Exec. JÜRI JÕEMA.

Estonian Asscn of Small and Medium-sized Enterprises (EVEA) (Eesti Väike-Ja Keskmiste Ettevõtjate Assotsiatsioon): Pronksi 3, Tallinn 10124; tel. 640-3935; fax 631-2451; e-mail evea@evea.ee; internet www.evea.ee; f. 1988; Pres. RIIVO SINIJÄRV; Man. Dir MARGIT KALLASTE.

Estonian Forest Industries Asscn (Eesti Metsatööstuse Liit—EMTL): Viljandi mnt. 18A, Tallinn 11216; tel. 656-7643; fax 656-7644; e-mail info@emtl.ee; internet www.emtl.ee; f. 1996; Man. Dir ANDRES TALIJÄRV.

Estonian Meat Asscn (Eesti Lihaliit): Lai 39/41, Tallinn 10133; tel. 641-1179; fax 641-1035; e-mail lihaliit@hot.ee; f. 1989; Chair. of Bd AIGAR PINDMAA; Man. Dir PEETER GRIGORJEV.

Estonian Oil Asscn (Eesti Õliühing): Kiriku 6, Tallinn 10130; tel. 620-1930; fax 620-1935; f. 1993; Chair. RAIVO VARE.

Estonian Trade Council (Eesti Väliskaubanduse Liit): Liimi 1, Tallinn 10621; tel. 659-7015; fax 656-3923; e-mail etc@etc.ee; internet www.etc.ee; f. 1991; non-profit non-govt org.; promotes export trade; Chair. of Bd TAMBET MADE.

Estonian Furniture Industry Federation (Eesti Mööblitootjate Liit): Pärnu mnt. 158B, Tallinn 11317; tel. 655-8525; fax 655-8524; e-mail info@furnitureindustry.ee; internet www.furnitureindustry.ee; Chair. JUHO TOOMIK; Man. Dir AIN TATS.

Federation of the Estonian Chemical Industry (Eesti Keemiatööstuse Liit): Peterburi tee 46, Tallinn 11415; tel. and fax 613-9775; e-mail info@keemia.ee; internet www.keemia.ee; f. 1991; Man. Dir HALLAR MEYBAUM.

Federation of the Estonian Engineering Industry (Eesti Masinatööstuse Liit—EML): Mustamäe tee 4, Tallinn 10621; tel. 611-5893; fax 656-6640; e-mail emliit@emliit.ee; internet www.emliit.ee; f. 1991; represents over 100 metalworking, machine-building, electrotechnics and electronics enterprises; Chair. of Bd JÜRI RIIVES.

Union of Estonian Automobile Enterprises (Eesti Autoettevõtete Liit): Magasini 31, Tallinn 10138; tel. 641-2511; fax 641-2523; e-mail al@autoettevoteliit.ee; internet www.autoettevoteliit.ee; f. 1990; Dir VILLEM TORI.

Union of Estonian Paper Manufacturers (Eesti Paberitööstuse Liit): Tööstuse 19, Kohila 79801; tel. 483-3564; fax 483-2132; e-mail kohilapv@netexpress.ee; Chair. of Bd HENNO PAVELSON.

EMPLOYERS' ORGANIZATION

Estonian Employers' Confederation (Eesti Tööandjate Kesliit): Kiriku 6, Tallinn 10130; tel. 699-9301; fax 699-9310; e-mail ettk@ettk.ee; internet www.ettk.ee; f. 1991 as Confederation of Estonian Industry; Chair. of Bd MEELIS VIRKEBAU; Man. Dir TIIT LAJA.

UTILITIES

Electricity

Under terms agreed with the European Union, Estonia was permitted to postpone the liberalization of its electricity market until 2013, in order to allow the requisite investment to be made in the oil-shale power plants that generate most of the country's electricity supply.

Eesti Energia was involved in the Estlink project, which connected the electricity networks of Estonia and Finland by means of a submarine transmission cable. Operations commenced in January 2007.

Eesti Energia (Estonian Energy Co): Laki 24, Tallinn 12915; tel. 715-2222; fax 715-2200; e-mail info@energia.ee; internet www.energia.ee; f. 1939; producer, transmitter and distributor of thermal and electric energy; manufacture of electric motors; electrical engineering; Chair. SANDOR LIIVE; 8,000 employees.

Gas

Eesti Gaas (Estonian Gas Co): Liivalaia 9, Tallinn 10118; tel. 630-3003; fax 631-3884; e-mail info@gaas.ee; internet www.gaas.ee; f. 1993; purchases and distributes natural gas; constructs pipelines; calibrates gas meters; Chair. AARNE SAAR; 255 employees.

Water

Tallinna Vesi (Tallinn Water Co): Ädala 10, Tallinn 10614; tel. 626-2200; fax 626-2300; e-mail tvesi@tvesi.ee; internet www.tallinnavesi.ee; f. 1997; supply and treatment of water; collection and treatment of waste water; 50.4% owned by United Utilities Tallinna (a subsidiary of United Utilities International, United Kingdom), 49.6% by Tallinn City Government; Chair. and Chief Exec. BOB GALLIENE; Dir-Gen. ENNO PERE; 359 employees.

TRADE UNIONS

Asscn of Estonian Energy Workers' Trade Unions (Eesti Energeetikatöötajate Ametiühingute Liit—EEAÜL): Gonsiori 3A, Tallinn 10117; tel. 715-5522; fax 715-5528; e-mail enn.luuk@energia.ee; internet www.energeetik.ee; Pres. ENN LUUK.

Confederation of Estonian Employee Unions (Teenistujate Ametiliitude Keskorganisatsioon—TALO): Gonsiori 21, Tallinn 10147; tel. 641-9800; e-mail talo@online.ee; internet www.talo.ee; f. 1992; comprises 13 mem. unions from the broadcasting, cultural, customs, education, engineering, journalism, radiology and scientific sectors; Chair. AGO TUULING.

Confederation of Estonian Trade Unions (Eesti Ametiühingute Keskliit—EAKL): Pärnu mnt. 41A, Tallinn 10119; tel. 641-2800; fax 641-2802; e-mail eakl@eakl.ee; internet www.eakl.ee; f. 1990; 26 branch and professional trade union mems; Chair. KADI PARNITS; estimated 95,000 individual mems.

Estonian Communication Workers' Trade Union (Eesti Sidetöötajate Ametiühingute Liit—ESAL): Masti 2/5, Tallinn 11911; tel. 601-1606; fax 601-1124; e-mail esal@esal.org.ee; internet www.esal.org.ee; Chair. ÕIE VÄLJAS.

Estonian Light Industry Workers' Trade Union (Eesti Kergetööstustöötajate Ametiühingute Liit): Reimani 5/4, Tallinn 10124; tel. and fax 643-1640; mem. of Confederation of Estonian Trade Unions; Chair. EVI JAAGURA.

Estonian Transportation and Roadworkers' Union (Eesti Transpordi-ja Teetöötajate Ametiühing—ETTA): Kalju 7/1, Tallinn 10414; tel. 641-3131; fax 641-3129; e-mail etta@etta.ee; internet www.etta.ee; mem. of the Confederation of Estonian Trade Unions; Chair. PEEP PETERSON.

Transport

RAILWAYS

In 2003 there were 967 km of railway track in use, of which 131 km were electrified. Main lines link Tallinn with Narva and St Petersburg (Russia), Tartu and Pskov (Russia). Passenger services, except for the suburban services around Tallinn, are relatively limited, however. A project known as Rail Baltica, which aimed to construct a fast railway line linking Tallinn with Rīga (Latvia), Vilnius (Lithuania), Warsaw (Poland) and Berlin (Germany), was under development.

Edelaraudtee: Kaare 25, Türi 72213; tel. 385-7123; fax 385-7121; e-mail info@edel.ee; internet www.edel.ee; f. 1997; owned by GB Railways (United Kingdom); operates intercity passenger services on the routes: Tallinn–Tartu; Tallinn–Narva; Tartu–Varga; Tallinn–Vijandi–Pärnu; and Tartu–Orava; Dir KALVI PUKKA.

Eesti Raudtee (Estonian Railways): Pikk 36, Tallinn 15073; tel. 615-8610; fax 615-8710; e-mail raudtee@evr.ee; internet www.evr.ee; f. 1918; privatized in 2001; re-nationalization completed in 2007; rail infrastructure operator and freight carrier; Chair. of Management Bd KAIDO SIMMERMANN; Chair of Supervisory Bd TÕNIS HAAVEL; 2,300 employees (2007).

Elektriraudtee (Electric Railways): Vabaduse pst. 176, Tallinn 10917; tel. 673-7400; fax 673-7440; e-mail info@elektriraudtee.ee; internet www.elektriraudtee.ee; f. 1998; suburban passenger services in Tallinn region.

ROADS

In 2006 Estonia had a total road network of 56,850 km, of which 1,601 km were main roads, 12,438 km were secondary roads, 2,385 km were basic roads and 37,209 km were local roads. In 2006 21% of the total road network was asphalted.

Estonian Road Administration (Maanteeamet): Pärnu mnt. 463A, Tallinn 10916; tel. 611-9300; fax 611-9360; e-mail estroad@mnt.ee; internet www.mnt.ee; f. 1990; govt org.; five regional road offices and one regional road administration; Gen. Dir RIHO SÕRMUS.

INLAND WATERWAYS

In 2006 there were 320 km of navigable inland waterways.

SHIPPING

Tallinn is the main port for freight transportation. There are regular passenger services between Tallinn and Helsinki, Finland. A service between Tallinn and Stockholm, Sweden, was inaugurated in 1991. In 2006 a deep-sea port for cruise ships (owned by the Port of Tallinn) was opened on the island of Saaremaa. At December 2006 the merchant fleet comprised 138 vessels, totalling 416,666 grt.

Estonian Maritime Administration (EMA) (Veeteede Amet): Valge 4, Tallinn 11413; tel. 620-5500; fax 620-5506; e-mail eva@vta.ee; internet www.vta.ee; f. 1990; govt org.; administers and implements state maritime safety policies, ship-control, pilot, lighthouse and hydrography services; Gen. Dir ANDRUS MAIDE; 375 employees.

Principal Shipping Companies

Eesti Merelaevandus (ESCO) (Estonian Shipping Co): Sadama 4, Tallinn 15096; tel. 640-9500; fax 640-9595; e-mail online@eml.ee; internet www.eml.ee; f. 1940; owned by Tschudi Shipping Co (Norway); liner services, ship chartering and cargo shipping; Man. Dir TOM STAGE PETERSEN; 500 employees.

Saaremaa Laevakompanii (Saaremaa Shipping Co): Kohtu 1, Kuressaare 93812; tel. 452-4350; fax 452-4350; e-mail slk@laevakompanii.ee; internet www.laevakompanii.ee; f. 1992; passenger and cargo services between mainland Estonia and Saaremaa, Hiiumaa and Vormsi islands; Dir-Gen. TÕNIS RIHVK.

Tallink Grupp: Tartu mnt 13, Tallinn 10145; tel. 640-9800; fax 640-9810; e-mail info@tallink.ee; internet www.tallink.ee; f. 1989 as a joint-venture Estonian-Finnish co; in 1996–2002 known as Hansatee Grupp, reverted to previous name in 2002; passenger and cargo transport; operates high-speed ferries between Tallinn and Helsinki, Finland; also operates routes to St Petersburg, Russia, and Stockholm, Sweden; Chair. of Management Bd ENN PANT.

Shipowners' Association

Estonian Shipowners' Association (Eesti Laevaomanike Liit): Luise 1A, Tallinn 10142; tel. and fax 646-0109; e-mail reederid@hot.ee; Pres. Capt. TOIVO NINNAS.

Port Authority

Port of Tallinn (Tallinna Sadam): Sadama 25, Tallinn 15051; tel. 631-8555; fax 631-8166; e-mail ts@ts.ee; internet www.ts.ee; f. 1991; the Port of Tallinn consists of five constituent harbours: Old City, Muuga, Paljassaare, Paldiski South and Saaremaa; Chair. of Bd AIN KALJURAND; Harbour Master E. HUNT; 550 employees (2007).

Port of Sillamäe (Sillamäe Sadam—Silport): Suur-Karja 5, Tallinn 10140; tel. 640-5271; fax 640-5279; e-mail silport@silport.ee; internet www.silport.ee; operations commenced Oct. 2005; deep-sea port; navigable all-year; railway facilities; free-trade zone; four terminals; privately owned; Chair. VITALY IVANOV.

CIVIL AVIATION

There are direct regular passenger air services linking the international airport at Tallinn with several countries in northern, central and western Europe.

Civil Aviation Administration (Lennuamat): Rävala pst. 8, Tallinn 10143; tel. 610-3500; fax 610-3501; e-mail ecaa@ecaa.ee; internet www.ecaa.ee; f. 1990; Dir-Gen. KOIT KASKEL.

Avies: Lennujaama 2, Tallinn 11101; tel. 605-8022; fax 621-2951; e-mail info@avies.ee; internet www.avies.ee; f. 1991; domestic passenger services between Tallinn and Saaremaa and Hiiumaa islands, international scheduled and charter passenger and cargo services; Man. Dir VLADIMIR PISARKOV.

Estonian Air: Lennujaama 13, Tallinn 11101; tel. 640-1160; fax 640-1161; e-mail info@estonian-air.ee; internet www.estonian-air.com; f. 1991; passenger and cargo flights to destinations across Europe; Pres. BØRGE THORNBECH.

Tourism

Estonia has a wide range of attractions for tourists, including the historic towns of Tallinn and Tartu, extensive nature reserves and coastal resorts. In 2006 the first deep-sea port for cruise ships was opened on Estonia's biggest island, Saaremaa. In 2005 there were 1,453,418 foreign visitors to Estonia (measured by arrivals at registered accommodation establishments). In 2005 receipts from tourism totalled US $948m.

Estonian Tourist Board (Turismiarenduskeskus): Liivalaia 13/15, Tallinn 10118; tel. 627-9770; fax 627-9777; e-mail info@visitestonia.com; internet www.visitestonia.com; f. 1990; Dir TARMO MUTSO.

ETHIOPIA

Introductory Survey

Location, Climate, Language, Religion, Flag, Capital

The Federal Democratic Republic of Ethiopia is a land-locked country in eastern Africa; it has a long frontier with Somalia near the Horn of Africa. Sudan lies to the west, Eritrea to the north, Djibouti to the north-east and Kenya to the south. The climate is mainly temperate because of the high plateau terrain, with an average annual temperature of 13°C (55°F), abundant rainfall in some years and low humidity. The lower country and valley gorges are very hot and subject to recurrent drought. The official language is Amharic, but many other local languages are also spoken. English is widely used in official and commercial circles. The Ethiopian Orthodox (Tewahido) Church, an ancient Christian sect, has a wide following in the north and on the southern plateau. In much of the south and east the inhabitants include Muslims and followers of animist beliefs. The national flag (proportions 1 by 2) has three equal horizontal stripes, of green, yellow and red, superimposed in the centre of which is a blue disk bearing a yellow pentagram, resembling a star, with single yellow rays extending outwards from the inner angles of the star. The capital is Addis Ababa.

Recent History

In September 1974 Emperor Haile Selassie was deposed by the armed forces and his imperial regime was replaced by the Provisional Military Administrative Council (PMAC), known popularly as the Dergue (Committee), led by Brig.-Gen. Teferi Benti. In December Ethiopia was declared a socialist state; however, a radical programme of social and economic reforms led to widespread unrest, and in February 1977 Lt-Col Mengistu Haile Mariam executed Teferi and his closest associates, and replaced him as Chairman of the PMAC and as Head of State.

During 1977–78, in an attempt to end opposition to the regime, the Government imprisoned or killed thousands of its opponents. Political power was consolidated in a Commission for Organizing the Party of the Working People of Ethiopia (COPWE), largely dominated by military personnel. In September 1984, at the COPWE's third congress, the Workers' Party of Ethiopia (WPE) was formally inaugurated. Mengistu was unanimously elected Secretary-General of the party, which modelled itself on the Communist Party of the Soviet Union. In February 1987, at a referendum, some 81% of the electorate endorsed a new Constitution and in June national elections were held to an 835-seat legislature, the National Shengo (Assembly). In September, at the inaugural meeting of the new legislature, the PMAC was abolished, and the People's Democratic Republic of Ethiopia was declared. The National Shengo unanimously elected Mengistu as President of the Republic, and a 24-member Council of State was also elected, to act as the Shengo's permanent organ.

Numerous groups, encouraged by the confusion resulting from the 1974 revolution, launched armed insurgencies against the Government. Of these, the most effective were based in the Ogaden, Eritrea and Tigrai regions. Somalia laid claim to the Ogaden, which is populated mainly by ethnic Somalis. Somali troops supported incursions by forces of the Western Somali Liberation Front, and in 1977 the Somalis made major advances in the Ogaden. In 1978, however, they were forced to retreat, and by the end of 1980 Ethiopian forces had gained control of virtually the whole of the Ogaden region.

The former Italian colony of Eritrea was merged with Ethiopia, in a federal arrangement, in September 1952, and annexed to Ethiopia as a province in November 1962. A secessionist movement, the Eritrean Liberation Front (ELF), was founded in Egypt in 1958. The ELF eventually split into several rival factions, the largest of which was the Eritrean People's Liberation Front (EPLF). In 1978 government troops re-established control in much of Eritrea, and the EPLF retreated to the northern town of Nakfa. In 1982 an offensive by government troops failed to capture Nakfa, and in 1984 the EPLF made several successful counter-attacks. In mid-1986 government forces abandoned the north-east coast to the rebels.

An insurgent movement also emerged in Tigrai province in the late 1970s. The Tigrai People's Liberation Front (TPLF) was armed and trained by the EPLF, but relations between the two groups deteriorated sharply in the mid-1980s. The TPLF was weakened by conflict with other anti-Government groups, and in 1985 and 1986 government forces had considerable success against the TPLF.

In September 1987 the newly elected National Shengo announced that five areas, including Eritrea and Tigrai, were to become 'autonomous regions' under the new Constitution. Eritrea was granted a considerable degree of self-government, but both the EPLF and the TPLF rejected the proposals. In March 1988 EPLF forces captured the town of Afabet; the TPLF took advantage of the movement of government forces to Eritrea and overran all the garrisons in north-western and north-eastern Tigrai. In early 1989, following major defeats in north-west Tigrai, government forces abandoned virtually the whole region to the TPLF.

Following the capture of Massawa port by the EPLF in February 1990 (presenting a direct threat to the continued survival of the Ethiopian army in Eritrea), President Mengistu was obliged to make a number of concessions. In March Ethiopian socialism was virtually abandoned, when the WPE was renamed the Ethiopian Democratic Unity Party, and membership was opened to non-Marxists. Mengistu began introducing elements of a market economy and dismantling many of the economic structures that had been established after the 1974 revolution.

By late April 1991, troops of the Ethiopian People's Revolutionary Democratic Front (EPRDF)—an alliance of the TPLF and the Ethiopian People's Democratic Movement (EPDM)—had captured Ambo, a town 130 km west of Addis Ababa, while EPLF forces were 50 km north of Assab, Ethiopia's principal port. On 21 May, faced with the prospect of the imminent defeat of his army, Mengistu fled the country. On 28 May, following the failure of negotiations in the United Kingdom, and with the public support of the USA, units of the EPRDF entered Addis Ababa. They encountered little resistance, and the EPRDF established an interim Government, pending the convening of a multi-party conference in July, which was to elect a transitional government. Meanwhile, the EPLF had gained control of the Eritrean capital, Asmara, and announced the establishment of a provisional Government to administer Eritrea until the holding of a referendum, within two years, on the issue of independence.

In July 1991 a national conference adopted amendments to a national charter, presented by the EPRDF, and elected an 87-member Council of Representatives, which was to govern for a transitional period of two years, after which free national elections were to be held. The national charter provided guarantees for freedom of association and expression, and for self-determination for Ethiopia's various ethnic groups. The EPLF was not officially represented at the conference, but came to an agreement with the EPRDF, whereby the EPRDF accepted the formation of the EPLF's provisional Government of Eritrea and the determination by referendum of the future of the region. In late July the Council of Representatives established a commission to draft a new constitution and elected Meles Zenawi, the leader of the EPRDF (and of the TPLF), as Chairman of the Council, a position that made him President of the transitional Government and Head of State; in August it appointed a Council of Ministers.

In November 1992 the provisional Government of Eritrea announced that a UN-supervised referendum on the area's status would be held in April 1993. The Sudanese Government expressed its readiness to assist the Eritrean Referendum Commission in conducting a plebiscite among some 250,000 Eritrean refugees still residing in Sudan. The referendum revealed overwhelming support for Eritrean independence, which was duly proclaimed on 24 May 1993.

Elections to a Constituent Assembly were conducted in Ethiopia in June 1994, in which the EPRDF won 484 of the 547 seats. The Constituent Assembly was inaugurated in October to debate a draft Constitution, which it ratified in December. The new Constitution provided for the establishment of a federal government and the division of the country (renamed the Federal

Democratic Republic of Ethiopia) into nine states and two chartered cities. It provided for regional autonomy, including the right of secession. A new legislature, the Federal Parliamentary Assembly, was to be established, comprising two chambers: the House of People's Representatives (consisting of no more than 550 directly elected members) and the House of the Federation (composed of 117 deputies, elected by the new state assemblies).

The EPRDF and its allies won an overwhelming victory in elections to the House of People's Representatives and state assemblies in May 1995. Most opposition parties boycotted the poll. International observers accepted that the elections were conducted in a largely free and fair manner.

On 21 August 1995 legislative power was transferred from the transitional Council of Representatives to the Federal Parliamentary Assembly. On 22 August the transitional administration was terminated, and the country's new Constitution and designation as the Federal Democratic Republic of Ethiopia were formally instituted. Later that day Dr Negasso Gidada, the EPRDF nominee, and a member of the Oromo People's Democratic Organization (OPDO, which was in alliance with the EPRDF), was elected President of the Federal Republic. A new Prime Minister, Meles Zenawi, was elected from among the members of the House of People's Representatives; Meles nominated a 17-member Council of Ministers, which was duly approved by the Federal Parliamentary Assembly.

During late 1995 and early 1996 the Meles administration was criticized for its harsh treatment of opposition activists. In June 1996 Dr Taye Wolde Semayat, the Secretary-General of the Ethiopian Teachers' Association, was arrested with several associates and accused of leading a clandestine political organization (the Ethiopian National Patriotic Front—ENPF), which had allegedly been responsible for several terrorist acts. The arrests were strongly criticized by human rights groups, which claimed that the detainees were guilty only of expressing discontent at certain government policies. Meanwhile, the Somali-based al-Ittihad al-Islam (Islamic Union Party—which sought independence for Ethiopia's Ogaden province) claimed responsibility for bomb explosions at hotels in Addis Ababa and Dire Dawa in early 1996, and for the attempted assassination in July of the Minister of Transport and Communications. Government forces launched numerous reprisal attacks on al-Ittihad bases in Somalia during 1996–98, resulting in the deaths of several hundred al-Ittihad members.

Meanwhile, the trial of 69 former government officials, including ex-President Mengistu, opened in Addis Ababa in December 1994, although proceedings were adjourned on numerous occasions. The defendants, 23 of whom were being tried *in absentia* (including Mengistu, who was in exile in Zimbabwe) and five of whom had died while awaiting trial, were accused of crimes against humanity and of genocide, perpetrated during 1974–91. In February 1997 the office of the Special Prosecutor announced that an additional 5,198 people would be indicted for war crimes and genocide, of whom nearly 3,000 would be tried *in absentia*. In November 1999 South Africa refused a request from the Ethiopian Government to extradite Mengistu, after it emerged that he was receiving medical treatment in that country. In March 2001 Mengistu was granted permanent residence in Zimbabwe, thus removing any possibility of his extradition. In April the Ethiopian High Court found 37 people (13 *in absentia*) guilty of crimes against humanity and genocide; they were sentenced to up to 20 years' 'rigorous' imprisonment. In December 2006 Mengistu, along with 71 others, was found guilty of genocide, and in January 2007 he was sentenced *in absentia* to life imprisonment. However, the Zimbabwean Government reaffirmed its refusal to extradite Mengistu.

Elections to the House of People's Representatives and the House of the Federation were held concurrently on 14 May 2000, except in the Somali regional state, where voting was postponed until 31 August, owing to severe drought. Voting was also repeated in several constituencies after accusations of irregularities were upheld by the National Electoral Board (NEB). According to results published by the NEB in September, the OPDO won the largest number of seats in the House of People's Representatives, taking 178 of the 546 available. The OPDO's major partners in the EPRDF coalition, the Amhara National Democratic Movement (ANDM—as the EPDM had been renamed in 1994) and the TPLF, gained 134 and 38 seats, respectively. A number of smaller groups in the EPRDF won a further 19 seats. The EPRDF thus comfortably retained a large majority in the lower chamber. In mid-October the new legislature was sworn in, and Meles was re-elected as Prime Minister.

During 2001 the Meles administration suffered a number of internal set-backs. In May Ethiopia's Head of Security and Intelligence, Kinfe Gebremedhin, a staunch supporter of the Prime Minister, was assassinated in Addis Ababa. In late June President Gidada was dismissed from the executive committee of the OPDO, after it was alleged that he had refused to accept the party's programme of reform and was providing support to dissidents opposed to Meles. Gidada, in turn, accused the Government of embarking on a campaign of propaganda against him. Gidada was also expelled from the EPRDF; however, he remained insistent that he would complete his presidential term, which was scheduled to end in October. In August relations between the Prime Minister and the President were further strained by Gidada's criticism of the appointment of the army Chief-of-Staff, Abedula Gemeda, to the leadership of the OPDO. Nevertheless, by mid-September it appeared that Meles had succeeded in re-establishing control over the TPLF, and therefore the EPRDF, following his re-election as Chairman of the party. On 8 October 2001 Lt Girma Wolde Giorgis was elected by the legislature to replace Gidada as President of Ethiopia. Later that month Prime Minister Meles effected a major reorganization of the Council of Ministers.

During 2003 a number of new political parties and coalition organizations were formed with the intention of challenging the ruling EPRDF at the legislative elections scheduled for mid-2005. Meles also intended to reorganize the EPRDF, in order to transform it into a national, non-ethnic party, of which the TPLF, the ANDM and the OPDO would form regional branches. The most significant of the new groupings were the United Ethiopian Democratic Party, which was created by the merger of the Ethiopian Democratic Unity Party and the Ethiopian Democratic Party, and the United Ethiopian Democratic Forces (UEDF), under the leadership of Dr Beyene Petros.

In January 2004 Petros requested that Meles review and reform the electoral law and begin negotiations, with the aim of legalizing all opposition parties. In May several thousand supporters of four opposition parties gathered in Addis Ababa to protest against the lack of a neutral election board to oversee the legislative elections, which were scheduled to be contested on 15 May 2005, and to voice their concerns about the situation in the Gambela region (see below). In November the ruling EPRDF held its first ever meeting with opposition groups and announced its intention to review existing electoral legislation. However, despite unveiling a number of amendments to the electoral law in January 2005, which included granting opposition groups access to state-controlled media and the provision for opposition parties to call meetings and organize demonstrations, the Government did not adhere to earlier pledges to alter the composition of the NEB.

The legislative elections were held, as scheduled, on 15 May 2005, although voting in the Somali regional state was postponed until 21 August. Provisional results for the House of People's Representatives, published by the NEB in late May, awarded the EPRDF 302 seats, the Coalition for Unity and Democracy (CUD) 122 and the UEDF 57; the rate of voter participation was recorded at more than 90%. The results in some 300 constituencies were, however, disputed by both the EPRDF and opposition parties amid allegations of electoral fraud, while concerns over voting irregularities were also raised by observers from the European Union (EU, see p. 244). The NEB agreed to undertake investigations in 143 of the contested constituencies and the release of the official results, scheduled for 8 June, was postponed. In early June violence erupted in Addis Ababa as police attempted to disperse large numbers of students protesting against the provisional results of the poll; according to reports, at least 36 people were killed and over 100 were injured. (The protests took place despite the introduction of a ban on political demonstrations shortly after the elections.) More than 3,000 people were detained following the elections and the Chairman of the CUD, Hailu Shawel, and his deputy were temporarily placed under house arrest. Later in June the EU brokered an agreement between the EPRDF and the CUD and the UEDF, according to which both sides pledged to accept the findings of the NEB's investigations. The NEB announced the official results of the legislative elections in early September, including results from the Somali regional state and from 31 constituencies where voting had been reheld, according to which the EPRDF took 327 seats, the CUD 109 seats and the UEDF 52 seats. A number of smaller parties secured the remaining seats. Despite agreeing to accept the NEB's decision, the CUD renewed its allegations of electoral fraud and in early October some 100 CUD deputies boycotted the opening of the House of People's Representatives.

On 11 October 2005 the House of People's Representatives approved the composition of Prime Minister Meles' Council of Ministers, which included several new appointees. Nevertheless, Addiso Leggese was reappointed Deputy Prime Minister and Minister of Agriculture and Rural Development, while the key portfolios of finance and economic development, trade and industry and foreign affairs remained unchanged.

In November 2005 there were further violent clashes in Addis Ababa between police and demonstrators protesting against alleged voting irregularities in the legislative elections. It was reported that some 46 people were killed and around 150 people were injured during the confrontations. Shawel and a number of senior members of the CUD were among some 130 people arrested later in November and who were subsequently charged with treason and attempted genocide. Proceedings against those accused, 25 of whom were being tried *in absentia*, commenced in the Federal High Court in February 2006. In March charges against 18 defendants were dropped. In June 2007 38 of the defendants were found guilty of violating the Constitution and 30 of those convicted were sentenced to life imprisonment, with the remainder handed lesser terms; however, in July all 38 were pardoned and freed from prison.

Meanwhile, in January 2006 the British Government announced that it was to suspend indefinitely its direct budgetary support to Ethiopia, owing to concerns over the political situation in the country. In May a new opposition coalition, the Alliance for Freedom and Democracy (AFD), was formed by the CUD and four rebel factions: the Ethiopian People's Patriotic Front; the Ogaden National Liberation Front (ONLF); the Oromo Liberation Front (OLF) and the Sidama Liberation Front. The AFD, which was supported by the UEDF, was to demand a conference to resolve the country's political problems. In the same month inter-ethnic clashes occurred between the Borena and the Gudgi communities in the south of the country, leaving between 100 and 150 people dead and several thousand homeless. In June the Ministry of Defence announced that more than 100 rebels had been killed by its troops in the Amhara region and claimed that the anti-government forces had entered the country from Eritrea.

In mid-2006 heavy rains caused severe floods in the south and east of the country, particularly in the Omo Valley region; over 600 people died and some 200,000 were in need of emergency relief. Renewed flooding affected almost 300,000 people in the Ogaden region in late October. In August Meles announced that thousands of troops had been deployed against ONLF rebels, who were allegedly receiving support from Eritrea and Somali Islamists, in the Ogaden region. The ONLF leader responded by declaring that the organization was prepared to enter into talks with the Ethiopian Government and denied claims that his forces had been responsible for the killing of civilians. In the same month it was reported that around 150 members of the Ethiopian army had defected to Eritrea, including a senior commander who intended to join the OLF; two other key military figures allegedly followed in mid-September.

In October 2006 it emerged that an official inquiry into the violent dispersal of demonstrations after the May 2005 elections had been suppressed by the Government; 193 protesters were said to have been killed by Ethiopian security forces. Also in October 2006 two EU officials were arrested on the Kenyan border while attempting to smuggle two Ethiopians out of the country and were subsequently expelled. The EU condemned the action. In early March 2007 five members of staff of the British embassy in Addis Ababa, including one French citizen, were kidnapped in the Afar region near the Eritrean border during a sightseeing tour, but were released unharmed 12 days later. However, eight Ethiopians abducted at the same time were detained by their captors, who appeared to be a rebel group based in the Afar desert.

From December 2003 clashes between the Anuak and Nuer communities over disputed land in the Gambela region of the country escalated. The increase in violence was precipitated by the killing of eight officials from the office of the UN High Commissioner for Refugees (UNHCR) and the Federal Agency for Refugee and Returnee Affairs, reportedly committed by the Anuak, who had been angered by the proposed construction on their land of a camp to house Nuer refugees. The Anuak community was the target of a number of revenge attacks, which resulted in the death of some 100 people (although opposition sources indicated that the actual casualty figures were much higher), and it was alleged that the Government had actively encouraged reprisals against the Anuak community. As the violence escalated some 15,000 Anuak, including the President of the region Okelo Akuai, sought refuge in Sudan. In late January 2004 some 200 people were killed after Anuak militants attacked a gold mine where many new settlers to the region were working. In March the Government released a statement apologizing for its inadequate response towards the escalating violence in the Gambela region, and pledged to bring the perpetrators to justice. By mid-2004 the situation had calmed significantly and about 8,000 of those who had fled in January had returned to Gambela. In December UNHCR resumed operations in the region. An attack on a bus en route from Addis Ababa to Gambella in June 2006, in which at least 14 people died, was blamed on Anuak rebels.

Attempts by the Government to reduce the country's reliance on foreign food aid intensified in March 2004 when Prime Minister Meles announced proposals to relocate up to 2m. people from the dry highlands to more fertile areas along the border with Sudan. However, the three-year plan was criticized by several international aid agencies that warned that the land set aside for the relocation was notorious for diseases, such as malaria, and lacked the necessary infrastructure to host those being resettled. Indeed, in June the UN was forced to intervene and provide emergency assistance for some 250,000 people who had been relocated, while UNICEF provided medication and mosquito nets to combat the spread of malaria. In January 2006 UNICEF estimated that some 10m. Ethiopians would require food aid that year.

Relations with Somalia have been problematic since the Ogaden War of 1977–78. However, in April 1988 Ethiopia and Somalia agreed to re-establish diplomatic relations, to withdraw troops from their common border and to exchange prisoners of war. The transitional Government of Ethiopia declared a policy of non-interference in the affairs of neighbouring states and adopted a neutral stance in Somalia's civil conflict. In November 2000 the President of Somalia, Abdulkassim Salad Hasan, visited Ethiopia for the first time since his election in August. This followed a visit to Ethiopia by the President of the self-proclaimed 'Republic of Somaliland' earlier that month. During his visit Hasan held talks with senior Ethiopian officials, but, although relations between the two countries were reported to have improved as a result of the discussions, the Ethiopian authorities continued to refuse to recognize officially the Hasan administration and urged it to reach agreements with its opponents. In January 2001 relations between the countries deteriorated after the Somali Prime Minister accused Ethiopia of continuing to assist the Somali-based Rahawin Resistance Army (RRA), which had taken control of a number of towns in southwest Somalia, and maintained that Ethiopia was behind an assassination attempt on the Speaker of Somalia's transitional legislature. The accusations were strenuously denied by the Ethiopian authorities, which stated that no Ethiopian troops were in Somali territory. Later in the year Ethiopia agreed to mediate between the Somali Transitional National Government (TNG) and the Somali Reconciliation and Restoration Council, which had been established in Ethiopia in March to rival the TNG. Relations between Somalia and Ethiopia were further strained by Meles' claim that a number of al-Ittihad members were represented in the Somali TNG; the accusation was, however, forcefully denied by Hasan. Relations between Ethiopia and Somalia improved in early 2005 and Ethiopia signalled its support for the new Somali President, Col Abdullahi Yussuf Ahmed, following his election in January. In March Meles, along with a number of other regional leaders, offered to send peacekeeping troops to Somalia. In January 2006 President Abdullahi Yussuf met with Meles in Addis Ababa for talks on improving bilateral co-operation between the two countries. In June, however, an Islamist group, the Union of Islamic Courts, took control of Mogadishu from a group of secular faction leaders (the TNG having relocated to the southern town of Baidoa earlier in the year), and later conquered much of southern Somalia. The group subsequently restructured and restyled itself the Somali Supreme Islamic Courts Council (SSICC). Its moderate Chairman, Sheikh Sharif Sheikh Ahmed, became chairman of its executive committee, while Sheikh Hassan Dahir Aweys, the former deputy leader of al-Ittihad, was appointed head of the legislative council. Sheikh Ahmed accused Ethiopia of sending 300 troops into Somalia in support of the TNG, but this was denied by the Ethiopian Government, which claimed that it was merely reinforcing its border against possible attack. Meles later declared Sheikh Aweys, alleged by the USA to have links to terrorist organizations, to be a threat to Ethiopia. Sheikh Aweys responded by calling for talks on the 'occupied' Ogaden region. In August, however, there were further reports that Ethiopian troops had entered Somalia and were moving towards Baidoa, a fact which was denied by the TNG and by Meles' Government. Somalia's Islamists subsequently declared a 'holy war' on Ethiopia. In October Meles admitted the presence of military trainers in Baidoa and described his country as being 'technically at war' with its neighbour and prepared for conflict. In late November it was reported that an Ethiopian military convoy had been ambushed by Islamist fighters near Baidoa; the following month supporters of the SSICC headed for Tiyeglow, a town near the Ethiopian border, with the intention of isolating the TNG in Baidoa. In mid-December the SSICC issued a deadline for Ethiopian troops to leave Somalia within one week or face a major attack; the following week, amid reports of heavy fighting between Ethiopian troops and Islamist militias near Baidoa, Sheikh Aweys urged all Somalis to join the 'war' against Ethiopia. At the end of the month Meles admitted for the first time to active military involvement by his country in Somalia, claiming that his troops were defending Ethiopia's sovereignty against what he termed terrorists and anti-Ethiopian elements. The following day Ethiopian fighter jets attacked two airports in Somalia. Ethiopia was supported in its actions by the African Union (AU, see p. 164), which conceded that the presence of Islamist militias so close to its borders might be perceived as a threat. The UN estimated that at the end of 2006 at least 8,000 Ethiopian troops were deployed in Somalia. Although some troops left Somalia in January 2007, it was unclear how many would return to Ethiopia before the proposed 8,000-strong AU peace-keeping force had been deployed in their place. In late June Meles pledged to withdraw Ethiopian forces from Somalia upon the arrival of sufficient peace-keeping troops; however, the pervading instability in Somalia continued to prevent the deployment of any such mission and Ethiopian troops remained in Somalia in early 2008.

Following the military coup in Sudan in April 1985, full diplomatic relations were restored between Ethiopia and Sudan. Relations between the two countries were strained in the late 1980s, however, by the influx into Ethiopia of thousands of Sudanese refugees, fleeing from famine and civil war in southern Sudan. The vast majority of an estimated 380,000 refugees were reported to have returned to Sudan by early 1991, as a result of the civil war in Ethiopia. The change of government in Ethiopia in May 1991 led to a considerable improvement in relations, and in October President Meles and Sudan's leader, Lt-Gen. al-Bashir, signed an agreement on friendship and co-operation. In September 1995 the Ethiopian administration adopted a number of sanctions against Sudan, including the suspension of air flights between the two countries and a reduction in Sudanese diplomatic representation in Ethiopia, after the Sudanese authorities refused to extradite three men allegedly involved in an assassination attempt on President Mubarak of Egypt in Addis Ababa in June. Relations between the two countries subsequently improved, and in October 1998 Ethiopia reportedly resumed air flights to Sudan. The Ethiopian authorities were also reported to have closed the Sudan People's Liberation Army offices in western Ethiopia, while Sudan closed the OLF base in Khartoum. In November 1999 Prime Minister Meles received al-Bashir in Addis Ababa, where they announced their intent to form closer economic ties between the two countries. In November 2004 the two countries finalized the demarcation of their common border on paper and requested financial assistance from international organizations in order to demarcate the border on the ground.

In November 1991 the leaders of Ethiopia and Kenya signed a co-operation agreement, although in October 1992 it was reported that the Kenyan Government was secretly giving asylum to Ethiopian dissidents. In April 1997 the two countries agreed to strengthen border controls following an attack by Ethiopian tribesmen in Kenya's frontier region. Additional security measures were agreed in late 1998, following an incursion by Ethiopian tribesmen into Kenya. In March 1999 Kenyan security forces exchanged fire with Ethiopian troops pursuing OLF rebels across the border. Kenya accused Ethiopia of violating international law, and relations between the two countries became further strained after Ethiopian soldiers attacked villages along the border. Bilateral relations deteriorated yet further during late 2000 and early 2001 after it was reported that some 50 Kenyans had been killed by Ethiopian militia forces. In January 2001 representatives from both countries met in Nairobi, Kenya, and agreed to take steps aimed at ending disputes along the common border. However, both countries' military and security forces continued activities in the border area; in June 2004 the Kenyan authorities arrested significant numbers of OLF combatants and during early 2005 Ethiopian troops were heavily criticized for repeated incursions into northern Kenya.

Ethiopia and the newly independent Eritrea signed a treaty of co-operation during a visit by the Eritrean President, Issaias Afewerki, to Addis Ababa in July 1993. The agreement included provisions on the joint utilization of resources and co-operation in the energy, transport, defence and education sectors. A further agreement, signed in late 1994, provided for the free movement of goods between the two countries without payment of customs dues.

In late 1997 relations with Eritrea deteriorated, following that country's adoption of a new currency (to replace the Ethiopian birr) and the subsequent disruption of cross-border trade. Fighting between Ethiopian and Eritrean troops erupted in early May 1998, with both countries accusing the other of having invaded their territory. In mid-June the USA and Italy successfully mediated an aerial cease-fire, but a resolution passed by the UN Security Council later that month, demanding that Ethiopia and Eritrea cease hostilities forthwith, was ignored. In an attempt to end the dispute, the Organization of African Unity (OAU), now the AU, established a mediation committee in June, which presented its report to the Ethiopian and Eritrean Ministers of Foreign Affairs at a meeting in Ouagadougou, Burkina Faso, in August; however, its proposals were rejected by Eritrea, necessitating the convening of a special meeting of the mediation committee in Ouagadougou in November. Ethiopia welcomed the committee's proposals, which stressed the need to demilitarize and demarcate the disputed region, but Eritrea rejected the plans.

In February 1999, after two weeks of intense fighting, Ethiopia recaptured the disputed town of Badme, and the Eritrean Government announced that it had accepted the OAU peace plan that it had rejected in late 1998. However, Ethiopia appeared eager to maximize its opportunity to secure access to the coast, ignoring appeals by the UN Security Council for an immediate cease-fire. Fighting erupted again in March 1999, as the two sides continued to blame each other for obstructing the OAU's peace efforts.

In July 1999 the deadlock between Ethiopia and Eritrea appeared to have been broken at the OAU summit meeting in Algiers, Algeria, when the two warring countries confirmed their commitment to the OAU peace proposals, under which both sides would withdraw from all territory captured since the outbreak of the conflict, thus effectively returning them to their pre-war frontiers. In August Eritrea formally accepted the latest OAU peace plan; however, in the following month Ethiopia announced that it had rejected the proposals, as the technical arrangements did not guarantee a return to the *status quo ante*. In April 2000 it was announced that some 8m. people in Ethiopia were in danger of starvation, and both the Ethiopian and Eritrean Governments were strongly criticized by aid agencies for continuing to spend vast amounts on funding their war efforts, while millions of their citizens endured severe food shortages.

In mid-May 2000 Ethiopian troops launched a major offensive near the disputed towns of Badme and Zalambessa, repelling the Eritrean forces. An announcement by the UN Security Council that it would impose sanctions and an embargo on the sale of all military supplies to the two countries, if fighting did not cease within three days, provoked violent protests outside the British and US embassies in Addis Ababa. However, hostilities continued, and on 18 May the UN Security Council unanimously approved the imposition of a 12-month arms embargo on Ethiopia and Eritrea. Shortly afterwards Zalambessa fell to the Ethiopian forces, and on 25 May the Eritrean Government announced the withdrawal of its troops from all disputed areas. On 31 May Prime Minister Meles stated that Ethiopia had no territorial claims over Eritrea and that the war between the two countries was over; nevertheless, sporadic fighting continued to take place. In early June both sides expressed their willingness, in principle, to accept the OAU's peace proposals and on 18 June the Ethiopian and Eritrean Ministers of Foreign Affairs signed an agreement, which provided for an immediate cease-fire and the establishment of a 25-km temporary security zone (TSZ) on the Eritrean side of the common border until the issue of the final demarcation of the border had been settled. It was estimated that as many as 120,000 people had been killed since the beginning of the conflict in 1998, and that more than 350,000 Ethiopians had been internally displaced. Indirect negotiations involving representatives from both countries, at which the technical issues of the peace agreement were to be discussed, commenced in Washington, DC, USA, in early July and continued in Algiers in October. Meanwhile, in mid-September the UN Security Council approved the deployment of a 4,200-strong UN Mission in Ethiopia and Eritrea (UNMEE).

In December 2000 Ethiopia and Eritrea signed an agreement in Algiers, which formally brought an end to the conflict. The agreement provided for a permanent cessation of all hostilities, the return of all prisoners of war, the demarcation of the common border by an independent commission, and the establishment of a Claims Commission to assess the issues of compensation and reparations. Furthermore, both countries pledged to co-operate with an independent investigation into the origins of the conflict. By late January 2001 the UNMEE force had arrived in the region, and, in compliance with the provisions for the establishment of a TSZ along the Ethiopia–Eritrea border, Ethiopian troops commenced their withdrawal from the territory they had captured from Eritrea. In March UNMEE's mandate was extended until September. Despite Eritrea's dissatisfaction at the southern boundary of the prospective TSZ, on 16 April it was announced that the withdrawal of its forces was complete. In mid-May the arms embargo imposed on the two countries by the UN in May 2000 was lifted. In late June 2001 UNMEE presented the final map of the TSZ to Ethiopia and Eritrea, although it emphasized that it would not influence the work of the neutral Boundary Commission charged with determining the border between the two countries. Despite this announcement, the Ethiopian Government expressed its dissatisfaction with the map, and at the eighth Military Co-ordination Committee (MCC) meeting in August both countries again stated their objections to the current boundaries of the TSZ. In mid-September UNMEE's mandate was extended for a further six months, although the head of the mission, Legwaila Joseph Legwaila, acknowledged that UNMEE faced an extremely difficult task in achieving lasting peace.

In mid-December 2001 Ethiopia and Eritrea began presenting their cases for border demarcation to the five-member Boundary Commission at the International Court of Justice (see p. 20) in The Hague, Netherlands. In mid-March 2002 UNMEE's mandate was extended until mid-September. The Boundary Commission delivered its findings in April. Both Ethiopia and Eritrea had committed themselves in advance to the acceptance of the report, which was carefully balanced, thus allowing both sides to claim success. However, the Commission did not identify on which side of the boundary line Badme lay, stating that it was awaiting delineation on the ground, which was expected to take up to one year, as extensive demining was required prior to placing boundary markers. In the absence of any decision, both countries immediately claimed to have been awarded Badme. Ethiopia formally requested 'interpretation, correction and consultation' of the Boundary Commission's report in May; this was rejected in late June.

In early March 2003 the Boundary Commission reported to the UN Security Council that Ethiopia's requests for changes to the border ruling, in order to 'take better account of human and physical geography', threatened to undermine the peace process as a whole. Despite Ethiopia's claims that it had been promised that demarcations could be refined, later in March the Boundary Commission categorically ruled Badme to be Eritrean territory, thus rejecting Ethiopia's territorial claim over the town. Meles subsequently complained that the decision was 'wrong and unjust' and vowed to continue to contest the ruling.

The demarcation of the border, which had originally been scheduled to take place in May 2003, was postponed until July, and then further delayed until October. In a letter to the UN Security Council in October, Prime Minister Meles requested the establishment of a new body to resolve the crisis and again denounced the Boundary Commission's ruling as 'unacceptable'. However, the Security Council stated that Ethiopia had, under the 2000 Algiers accord, committed itself to accept the Boundary Commission's decision as 'final and binding' and urged it to accept and implement the border ruling. The Chairman of the Boundary Commission, Elihu Lauterpacht, and Legwaila criticized Ethiopia's lack of compliance with its obligations under the terms of the peace agreement and the ongoing impasse was further compounded by the Boundary Commission's announcement in late October that the demarcation of the border had been delayed indefinitely.

The process suffered a further reverse in mid-November 2003, when Eritrea withdrew its ambassador to the AU and accused the organization of neglecting its responsibilities over the dispute with Ethiopia. In December Lloyd Axworthy, a former Canadian Minister of Foreign Affairs, was appointed as the UN's special envoy to the region, tasked with resolving the stalled peace process between Ethiopia and Eritrea. While Ethiopia welcomed the appointment and pledged to work closely with Axworthy, the Eritrean Government expressed its opposition to the appointment, as it feared that it would result in amendments to the Boundary Commission's ruling.

In 2004 UNMEE's mandate was extended by a further six months in March and again in September. In November Ethiopia indicated that it would co-operate with UNMEE when Meles announced a five-point plan aimed at resolving the disputed border issue and declared that Ethiopia had, in principle, accepted the Boundary Commission's ruling. Meles' statement was dismissed by the Eritrean authorities as an attempt by Ethiopia to further stall the process. In mid-December the UN withdrew some 550 Kenyan troops from the TSZ in an attempt to reduce the costs of its military presence in the area.

Ethiopia and Eritrea continued to increase troop numbers in the border area in 2005, raising fears of a return to conflict. However, Ethiopia sought to reassure the international community that troop movements and the construction of trenches on its side of the TSZ were for defensive purposes only. UNMEE's mandate was extended for six months in March and again in September. In October Prime Minister Meles reiterated Ethiopia's position regarding the Boundary Commission's ruling, and its willingness to re-establish talks with Eritrea. In November the UN Security Council adopted Resolution 1640, which demanded full acceptance by Ethiopia of the Boundary Commission's ruling regarding border demarcation, that Eritrea lift restrictions on UNMEE operations, and that troop numbers on both sides of the border be reduced with immediate effect. The two countries were warned that economic sanctions would be imposed should they not comply. Later that month Ethiopian troops entered the TSZ for a period of five days, in breach of the 2000 Algiers accord.

In early March 2006 a Boundary Commission meeting took place in London, United Kingdom. Agreement was reached between Ethiopia and Eritrea to hold further talks the following month, although these were subsequently postponed. On 31 May the UN Security Council adopted Resolution 1681, which extended UNMEE's mandate for a further four months but reduced the number of military personnel in the region by 1,000 to 2,300. A further appeal was issued to the Eritrean authorities to lift all restrictions on UNMEE activities but this was rejected. In September UNMEE's mandate was extended until 31 January 2007. In mid-November both countries failed to attend a meeting of the Boundary Commission in The Hague and rejected its proposals; the Commission, in response, issued a statement expressing frustration with the two countries' lack of co-operation and informing them that in the event of no agreement having been reached by November 2007 it would begin the physical demarcation of the border itself. Ethiopia's relations with Eritrea came under further strain in December, owing to its military support of pro-Government forces in Somalia, who were struggling to reclaim territory from Islamist militias. Reports that Eritreans were fighting alongside the Islamist forces were strongly denied by the Eritrean Government. On 31 January 2007 the UN Security Council's Resolution 1741 extended UNMEE'S mandate by six months and further reduced its personnel, to 1,700. UNMEE's mandate was again extended by six months in July, and on 30 January 2008 it was prolonged until the end of July 2008.

Concerns that conflict between Ethiopia and Eritrea could resume were heightened in September 2007 when both Governments deployed troops to the border region. In a letter to his Eritrean counterpart, the Ethiopian Minister of Foreign Affairs Seyoum Mesfin indicated that his Government was considering withdrawing from the Algiers agreement and stated that the Ethiopian Government considered Eritrea to be in material breach of the Algiers agreement as its troops had occupied the TSZ and had restricted the movement of the UNMEE force. In November Ethiopia strongly denied allegations of a planned invasion into Eritrean territory. Both parties again insisted that they were committed to a peaceful resolution of the border dispute; however, neither side complied with the Boundary

Commission's request of November 2006 physically to demarcate the border by the end of November 2007. In early December, prior to announcing its own dissolution, the Commission stated that the boundary that it had determined in November 2006 represented the official border between the two countries.

Eritrean-imposed restrictions on the movements of UN peace-keeping personnel and the delivery of fuel hampered efforts led the UN to announce in early February 2008 that it was beginning preparations to withdraw its peace-keepers from that country and to relocate them across the border into Ethiopia. In previous months the UN had repeatedly urged the Eritrean Government to lift restrictions on the delivery of fuel supplies; however, these requests were not met and in mid-February UN personnel were forced to leave the area. It was subsequently reported that a number of peace-keepers had been prevented from leaving Eritrea and the UN Security Council expressed it concern at the 'impediments and logistical constraints' placed upon the force.

In 1984 some 13,000 Falashas, a Jewish group in Ethiopia, reached Sudan, from where they were flown to Israel in a secret airlift. In May 1991 Israel evacuated a further 14,000 Falashas from Addis Ababa; some 10,000 Falashmura (Ethiopian Christians whose forefathers had converted from Judaism) were subsequently granted Israeli citizenship on humanitarian grounds. In March 1999 Israel pledged to examine the possibility of bringing the estimated 19,000 Jews remaining in Ethiopia to Israel, and in April 2000 the Israeli Minister of the Interior visited Ethiopia to investigate the claims of some 26,000 Ethiopians who maintained that they belonged to the Falashmura community and were thus eligible to settle in Israel under Israeli law. In February 2003 the Israeli Government ruled that the Falashmura had been forced to convert to Christianity to avoid religious persecution and that they had the right to settle in Israel. In January 2005 Israel announced that it would accelerate the emigration process and that the remaining 20,000 Ethiopian Falashas and Falashmura would arrive in Israel by 2007.

In recent years the People's Republic of China has developed closer ties with Ethiopia and has made significant economic investment in the country. However, in late April 2007 members of the ONLF killed more than 70 people, including nine Chinese oil workers, in an attack on a petroleum installation in the Somali region; seven Chinese citizens were kidnapped, although they were released unharmed five days later.

Government

In August 1995 the Council of Representatives, a body established in 1991 to govern the country during the transitional period after the overthrow of the Mengistu regime, formally transferred power to a newly elected legislature, the Federal Parliamentary Assembly. Under the provisions of a new Constitution, adopted in December 1994, the country became a federation, consisting of nine states and two chartered cities, the capital, Addis Ababa, and Dire Dawa. The states have their own parliamentary assemblies, which also elect representatives to the House of the Federation, the upper chamber of the Federal Parliamentary Assembly. The lower chamber, the House of People's Representatives, consists of no more than 550 directly elected deputies. The Federal Parliamentary Assembly elects a President as Head of State. However, the President fulfils mainly ceremonial functions, executive power being the preserve of the Prime Minister. The Prime Minister, who is elected by the House of People's Representatives, appoints the Council of Ministers (subject to approval by the legislature), and acts as Commander-in-Chief of the armed forces.

Defence

In December 1991 Ethiopia's transitional Government announced that a 'national defence army', based on already active EPRDF troops, would constitute Ethiopia's armed forces during the transitional period. In October 1993 the Minister of Defence announced that preparations were under way to create a 'multi-ethnic defence force', comprising members of all the different ethnic groups in Ethiopia. Extensive demobilization of former members of the TPLF has since taken place. In September 1996 the Government sold its naval assets. Owing to the war with Eritrea during 1999–2000, there was a large increase in the size of the armed forces and in defence expenditure. As assessed at November 2007, Ethiopia's active armed forces numbered an estimated 138,000, comprising an army of about 135,000 and an air force of some 3,000. The defence budget for 2007 was estimated at 3,000m. birr. In July 2000 the UN Security Council adopted a resolution (No. 1312) establishing the UN Mission in Ethiopia and Eritrea (UNMEE), which was to supervise the cease-fire and the implementation of a peace agreement between the two countries. At the end of November 2007 UNMEE numbered 1,464 troops, 212 military observers, as well as 147 international civilians and 202 local civilians; UNMEE had a total authorized strength of 4,200 troops (including 230 military observers).

Economic Affairs

In 2006, according to estimates by the World Bank, Ethiopia's gross national income (GNI), measured at average 2004–06 prices, was US $12,874m., equivalent to $180 per head (or $1,190 per head on an international purchasing-power parity basis): one of the lowest recorded levels of GNI per head for any country in the world. During 1996–2006, it was estimated, the population increased at an average annual rate of 2.2%, while gross domestic product (GDP) per head increased, in real terms, by an average of 2.4% per year. Overall GDP increased, in real terms, at an average annual rate of 4.8% during 1996–2006; it increased by 9.0% in 2006.

Agriculture (including forestry and fishing) contributed 48.1% of GDP in 2006, according to the World Bank, while the sector employed 80.2% of the labour force in March 2005. The principal cash crop is coffee (which accounted for 35.4% of export earnings in 2003). The principal subsistence crops are cereals (teff, maize, sorghum, wheat and barley) and sugar cane. During 1996–2006 agricultural GDP increased at an average annual rate of 3.3%. Agricultural GDP increased by 11.2% in 2006. In early 2006 the Ethiopian Government imposed a ban on the export of teff, maize, sorghum and wheat in an effort to bring prices of those commodities under control following sharp rises.

Industry (including mining, manufacturing, construction and power) employed 6.6% of the labour force in March 2005, and provided 12.6% of GDP in 2006. During 1996–2006 industrial GDP increased by an average of 6.2% per year. It rose by 7.4% in 2006.

Mining contributed only an estimated 0.5% of GDP (at constant 1999/2000 factor cost) in 2004/05, and employed less than 0.3% of the labour force in March 2005. Ethiopia has reserves of petroleum, although these have not been exploited, and there are also deposits of copper and potash. Gold, tantalite, soda ash, kaolin, dimension stones, precious metals and gemstones, salt, and industrial and construction materials are mined. In April 2000 a US company discovered large petroleum deposits in the west of the country, and in June 2003 the Ethiopian Government granted an one-year exploration licence to Petronas of Malaysia. The licence was renewed in early 2004 to allow exploration over a larger area. During 2000/01–2004/05 mining GDP increased by an estimated average of 3.9% per year; growth in 2004/05 was an estimated 7.9%.

Manufacturing employed only 4.9% of the labour force in March 2005, and contributed 4.7% of GDP in 2006. During 1996–2006 manufacturing GDP increased at an average annual rate of 4.6%. It increased by 8.1% in 2006.

In years of normal rainfall, energy is derived principally from Ethiopia's massive hydroelectric power resources. In 2005/06 98.6% of Ethiopia's electricity was produced by hydroelectric power schemes. Imports of mineral fuels accounted for 11.9% of the cost of total imports in 2003. In late 1995 the Government announced plans to develop geothermal energy sources at 15 sites in various regions of the country. Ethiopia's electricity generating capacity had reached 790 MW by 2006.

Services, which consisted mainly of wholesale and retail trade, public administration and defence, and transport and communications, employed 13.1% of the labour force in March 2005, and contributed 39.3% of GDP in 2006. The combined GDP of the service sectors increased, in real terms, at an average rate of 5.9% per year during 1996–2006. It rose by 8.5% in 2006.

In 2006 Ethiopia recorded a visible trade deficit of US $3,080.9m., and there was a deficit of $1,785.9m. on the current account of the balance of payments. In 2003 the principal source of imports (14.3%) was the USA; other major suppliers were the People's Republic of China, Italy, Japan, India and the United Kingdom. The principal market for exports in that year were Djibouti (19.4%), Germany, Japan, Saudi Arabia, Italy, and Somalia. The principal exports in 2003 were coffee, crude materials and leather and leather products. The principal imports in that year were machinery and transport equipment, food and live animals, basic manufactures, mineral fuels and related products, and chemicals and related products.

ETHIOPIA

In the fiscal year 2004/05 it was estimated that Ethiopia's budgetary deficit reached 4,519m. birr. Ethiopia is the principal African recipient of concessionary funding, and one of the largest recipients of European Union (EU) aid. At the end of 2005 Ethiopia's total external debt was US $6,259m., of which $5,897m. was long-term public debt. In that year the cost of debt-servicing was equivalent to an estimated 4.1% of total earnings from the export of goods and services. The annual rate of inflation averaged 3.6% in 1996–2006, according to the IMF. Consumer prices increased by 12.3% in 2006. In March 2005, 1,653,700 people were registered as unemployed, representing 5.0% of the total labour force.

Ethiopia is a member of the African Development Bank (see p. 162) and the Common Market for Eastern and Southern Africa (see p. 205). In July 2001 Ethiopia ratified the Cotonou Agreement (see p. 301), the successor of the Lomé Convention of the EU. Ethiopia submitted a request for accession to the World Trade Organisation (see p. 396) in January 2003.

Ethiopia remains one of the poorest countries in the world, and the country's economy continues to suffer from the effects of recurrent, catastrophic drought, which severely disrupts agricultural production. The scarcity of land and the lack of agricultural development have resulted in massive environmental degradation and, in turn, widespread poverty and famine. The Ethiopian economy is also heavily dependent on assistance and grants from abroad, particularly in times of drought. A number of donors suspended aid during the war with Eritrea; however, following the cessation of fighting in mid-2000 (see above), the World Bank agreed to resume development assistance. Despite successful harvests in recent years and strong GDP growth in both 2004 and 2005, by 2006 some 10m. people were believed to require food aid. In early 2005, as part of its highly ambitious goal of achieving food self-sufficiency by 2007, the Government launched a project which aimed to improve agricultural and economic infrastructure. Plans were also announced, in conjunction with the World Bank, to upgrade the country's road network in order to enable swifter distribution of emergency food assistance, and major investment agreements were concluded with India and the People's Republic of China in 2007, the latter providing the Ethiopian Electric Power Corpn with 1,400m. birr to extend high voltage power lines across the country. Nevertheless, further major structural reforms were necessary if economic growth was to continue, while increasing concern was also expressed that the country's rapid population growth would negate recent positive economic trends. Furthermore, political uncertainty, in particular with regard to ongoing instability in Ethiopia's relations with both Eritrea and Somalia, was likely to have a negative effect on the Ethiopian economy. Meanwhile, coffee continues to account for more than 60% of export revenues and an improvement in recent harvests—the Government also projected an 8% increase for the forthcoming growing season—contributed significantly to further high levels of GDP growth. An increase of 10.5% was estimated in 2007, while growth in 2008 was forecast at 9.6%.

Education

Education in Ethiopia is available free of charge up to grade 10, and, after a rapid growth in numbers of schools, it became compulsory between the ages of seven and 13 years. Since 1976 most primary and secondary schools have been controlled by local peasant associations and urban dwellers' associations. In 1994 Ethiopia adopted a new Education and Training Policy and Strategy, which restructured the education system and aimed to improve the quality of education. Primary education begins at seven years of age and lasts for eight years. Secondary education, beginning at 15 years of age, lasts for a further four years, comprising two cycles of two years each, the second of which provides preparatory education for entry to the tertiary level. A system of vocational and technical education also exists parallel to the preparatory programme. According to UNESCO estimates, in 2004/05 total enrolment at primary schools included 56% of children in the appropriate age-group (58% of boys; 55% of girls); in that year enrolment at secondary schools included 28% of children in the relevant age-group (34% of boys; 22% of girls). There are 21 institutions of higher education in Ethiopia, including six universities (in Addis Ababa, Bahir Dar, Alemanya, Jimma, Awassa and Makele). A total of 91,655 students were enrolled in higher education in 2004/05, according to government statistics. The 2004/05 budget allocated an estimated 10.9% (2,956m. birr) of total expenditure to education.

Public Holidays

2008: 7 January* (Christmas), 19 January* (Epiphany), 2 March (Battle of Adowa), 20 March† (Mouloud, Birth of the Prophet), 25 April* (Good Friday), 28 April* (Easter Monday), 1 May (May Day), 5 May (Patriots' Victory Day), 28 May (Downfall of the Dergue), 11 September (New Year's Day), 27 September* (Feast of the True Cross), 1 October† (Id al-Fitr, end of Ramadan), 9 December† (Id al-Adha/Arafat).

2009: 7 January* (Christmas), 19 January* (Epiphany), 2 March (Battle of Adowa), 9 March† (Mouloud, Birth of the Prophet), 17 April* (Good Friday), 20 April* (Easter Monday), 1 May (May Day), 5 May (Patriots' Victory Day), 28 May (Downfall of the Dergue), 11 September (New Year's Day), 20 September† (Id al-Fitr, end of Ramadan), 27 September* (Feast of the True Cross), 27 November† (Id al-Adha/Arafat).

* Coptic holidays.

† These holidays are dependent on the Islamic lunar calendar and may vary by one or two days from the dates given.

Note: Ethiopia uses its own solar calendar; the Ethiopian year 2000 began on 12 September 2007.

Weights and Measures

The metric system is officially in use. There are also many local weights and measures.

ETHIOPIA

Statistical Survey

Source (unless otherwise stated): Central Statistical Authority, POB 1143, Addis Ababa; tel. (1) 553010; fax (1) 550334; internet www.csa.gov.et.

Note: Unless otherwise indicated, figures in this Survey refer to the territory of Ethiopia after the secession of Eritrea in May 1993.

Area and Population

AREA, POPULATION AND DENSITY

Area (sq km)	1,133,380*
Population (census results)	
9 May 1984†	39,868,501
11 October 1994	
Males	26,910,698
Females	26,566,567
Total	53,477,265
Population (official estimates at mid-year)	
2005	73,908,000
2006	75,067,000
2007	77,127,000
Density (per sq km) at mid-2007	68.1

* 437,600 sq miles.
† Including an estimate for areas not covered by the census.

ADMINISTRATIVE DIVISIONS
(estimated population at mid-2007)

	Males	Females	Total
Regional States			
1 Tigrai	2,193	2,256	4,449
2 Afar	787	631	1,418
3 Amhara	9,805	9,819	19,624
4 Oromia	13,626	13,678	27,304
5 Somali	2,384	2,060	4,444
6 Benishangul/Gumuz	322	318	640
7 Southern Nations, Nationalities and Peoples	7,619	7,702	15,321
8 Gambela	129	124	253
9 Harari	104	99	203
Chartered Cities			
1 Dire Dawa	206	206	412
2 Addis Ababa	1,469	1,590	3,059
Total	38,644	38,483	77,127

PRINCIPAL TOWNS
(official estimates at mid-2007)

Addis Ababa (capital)	3,059,000	Mekele	177,090
Dire Dawa	293,173	Bahir Dar	175,185
Nazret	239,525	Jimma	166,592
Gondar	204,001	Debre Zeit	137,413
Dessie	177,116	Awasa	131,300

BIRTHS AND DEATHS
(annual averages, UN estimates)

	1990–95	1995–2000	2000–05
Birth rate (per 1,000)	46.9	44.1	40.7
Death rate (per 1,000)	17.2	15.8	14.4

Source: UN, *World Population Prospects: The 2006 Revision*.

Expectation of life (years at birth, WHO estimates): 51.5 (males 49.8; females 53.4) in 2005 (Source: WHO, *World Health Statistics*).

ECONOMICALLY ACTIVE POPULATION
('000 persons aged 10 years and over, March 2005)*

	Males	Females	Total
Agriculture, hunting, forestry and fishing	14,209.4	10,998.8	25,208.2
Mining and quarrying	51.4	30.6	82.1
Manufacturing	444.0	1,085.3	1,529.4
Electricity, gas and water	25.2	7.7	32.9
Construction	349.9	95.7	445.6
Wholesale and retail trade; repair of motor vehicles, motorcycles and personal and household goods	652.2	984.9	1,637.1
Hotels and restaurants	96.8	672.3	769.1
Transport, storage and communications	132.0	14.5	146.4
Financial intermediation	21.6	16.3	37.9
Real estate, renting and business services	36.1	16.2	52.3
Public administration and defence; compulsory social security	242.0	125.9	367.9
Education	178.2	104.5	282.7
Social work	45.6	32.5	78.1
Community, social and personal services	303.5	135.2	438.7
Households with employed persons	23.1	225.5	248.6
Extra-territorial organizations and bodies	42.7	25.1	67.9
Not classifiable by economic activity	6.5	3.8	10.3
Total employed	16,860.3	14,574.8	31,435.1
Unemployed	427.9	1,225.8	1,653.7
Total labour force	17,288.2	15,800.6	33,088.8

* Excluding armed forces.
Source: ILO.

Health and Welfare

KEY INDICATORS

Total fertility rate (children per woman, 2005)	5.7
Under-5 mortality rate (per 1,000 live births, 2005)	164
HIV/AIDS (% of persons aged 15–49, 2003)	4.40
Physicians (per 1,000 head, 2003)	0.03
Hospital beds (per 1,000 head, 1990)	0.24
Health expenditure (2004): US $ per head (PPP)	21.1
Health expenditure (2004): % of GDP	5.3
Health expenditure (2004): public (% of total)	51.5
Access to water (% of persons, 2004)	22
Access to sanitation (% of persons, 2004)	13
Human Development Index (2005): ranking	169
Human Development Index (2005): value	0.406

For sources and definitions, see explanatory note on p. vi.

ETHIOPIA
Statistical Survey

Agriculture

PRINCIPAL CROPS
('000 metric tons)

	2004	2005	2006
Wheat	2,177	2,307	2,779
Barley	1,376	1,398	1,410
Maize	2,906	3,912	4,030
Oats	58	57	58
Millet (Dagusa)	313	397	500
Sorghum	1,718	2,200	2,313
Potatoes	510	450	450
Sweet potatoes	452	409	409
Yams	193	172	172
Sugar cane	2,454	n.a.	2,600*
Dry beans	175.5	176.0*	176.0*
Dry broad beans	552	516	599
Dry peas	230	197	209
Chick-peas	163	217	125
Lentils	55	63	65
Vetches	125	147	71
Soybeans (Soya beans)	835	3,812	5,812
Groundnuts (in shell)	29.1	34.2	34.5
Castor beans*	15	15	15
Rapeseed	29.3	24.4	25.8
Safflower seed	7	6	6*
Sesame seed	115.4	148.9	160.0
Cottonseed†	43	40	43
Cotton (lint)†	20	23	22
Linseed	151.9	125.9	128.0
Cabbages*	164	174	174
Tomatoes	36	35	35*
Green onions and shallots*	20	20	20
Dry onions	230	176	176*
Garlic*	79	86	86
Bananas	182	211	211*
Oranges	17	16*	16*
Mangoes*	174	182	182
Avocados*	82.3	83.4	83.4
Papayas*	246.9	259.2	259.2
Coffee (green)	156.2	171.6	260.0†

* FAO estimate(s).
† Unofficial figure(s).

Aggregate production ('000 metric tons, may include official, semi-official or estimated data): Total cereals 10,700 in 2004, 13,369 in 2005, 13,394 in 2006; Total roots and tubers 5,664 in 2004, 5,721 in 2005, 5,721 in 2006; Total vegetables (incl. melons) 1,060 in 2004, 1,029 in 2005, 1,029 in 2006; Total fruits (excl. melons) 884 in 2004, 934 in 2005, 934 in 2006.

Source: FAO.

LIVESTOCK
('000 head, year ending September)

	2004	2005	2006
Cattle	38,749	40,390	43,125
Sheep	18,075	20,734	23,633
Goats	14,851	16,364	18,560
Asses and mules	4,248	4,630	4,824
Horses	1,518	1,569	1,655
Camels	n.a.	n.a.	232*
Pigs*	28	29	29
Poultry	35,656	32,222	34,199

* FAO estimate(s).
Source: FAO.

LIVESTOCK PRODUCTS
('000 metric tons, FAO estimates)

	2004	2005	2006
Cattle meat	331.5	336.0	350.2
Sheep meat	55.1	56.6	68.9
Goat meat	28.7	28.7	48.6
Pig meat	1.6	1.7	1.7
Chicken meat	47.1	52.0	53.4
Game meat	75	77	77
Cows' milk	1,500	1,500	1,575
Goats' milk	17.3	17.3	17.3
Sheep's milk	41.5	42.5	42.5
Hen eggs	36.6	36.6	36.6
Honey	39.7	41.2	41.2
Wool: greasy	12	12	12

Source: FAO.

Forestry

ROUNDWOOD REMOVALS
('000 cubic metres, excl. bark, FAO estimates)

	2004	2005	2006
Sawlogs, veneer logs and logs for sleepers	4	4	4
Pulpwood	7	7	7
Other industrial wood	2,917	2,917	2,917
Fuel wood	93,029	94,481	95,703
Total	95,957	97,409	98,631

Source: FAO.

SAWNWOOD PRODUCTION
('000 cubic metres, incl. railway sleepers)

	2001	2002	2003
Coniferous (softwood)	25*	1	0
Broadleaved (hardwood)	35*	13	17
Total	60	14	17

* FAO estimate.
2004–06: Figures assumed to be unchanged from 2003 (FAO estimates).
Source: FAO.

Fishing

(metric tons, live weight of capture)

	2003	2004	2005
Rhinofishes	668	100	267
Other cyprinids	394	415	427
Tilapias	4,653	5,590	3,604
North African catfish	2,662	2,532	2,366
Nile perch	168	919	2,260
Total catch (incl. others)	10,113	10,451	9,797

Source: FAO.

Mining

('000 metric tons, unless otherwise indicated, year ending 7 July, estimates)

	2002/03	2003/04	2004/05
Gold (kilograms)	3,875	3,443	3,900
Limestone	2,290	2,380	2,800
Gypsum and anhydrite	48	51	52
Pumice	219	271	320

Source: US Geological Survey.

ETHIOPIA

Industry

SELECTED PRODUCTS
('000 metric tons, year ending 7 July, unless otherwise indicated)

	2000/01	2001/02	2002/03
Wheat flour	165	143	137*
Macaroni and pasta	26	23	30*
Raw sugar	251	248*	268*
Wine ('000 hectolitres)	25	27*	32*
Beer ('000 hectolitres)	1,605	1,812*	2,123*
Mineral waters ('000 hectolitres)	395	395*	433*
Soft drinks ('000 hectolitres)	677	995	845*
Cigarettes (million)	1,904	1,511*	1,511*
Cotton yarn	5.7	7.7*	5.5*
Woven cotton fabrics ('000 sq m)	45,000	45,000*	41,000*
Nylon fabrics ('000 sq m)	1,300	1,000*	1,400*
Footwear (including rubber, '000 pairs)	n.a.	6,677	7,138
Soap	14.8	19.2*	11.6*
Tyres ('000)*	209	198	191
Clay building bricks ('000)*	20	22	21
Quicklime*	11	8	11
Cement*	819	919	890

* Year ending 31 December of later year.
Source: UN, *Industrial Commodity Statistics Yearbook*.

Cement (hydraulic, '000 metric tons, year ending 7 July): 1,130.1 in 2003; 1,315.9 in 2004; 1,568.0 in 2005 (estimate) (Source: US Geological Survey).

Beer of millet ('000 metric tons): 220.7 in 2001; 208.0 in 2002; 244.1 in 2003 (Source: FAO).

Beer of barley ('000 metric tons): 388.2 in 2001; 411.7 in 2002; 322.0 in 2003 (Source: FAO).

Finance

CURRENCY AND EXCHANGE RATES

Monetary Units
100 cents = 1 birr.

Sterling, Dollar and Euro Equivalents (31 December 2007)
£1 sterling = 18.433 birr;
US $1 = 9.201 birr;
€1 = 13.544 birr;
100 birr = £5.43 = $10.87 = €7.38.

Average Exchange Rate (birr per US $)
2005   8.666
2006   8.699
2007   8.949

GENERAL BUDGET
(rounded figures, million birr, year ending 7 July)

Revenue	2002/03	2003/04	2004/05
Taxation	8,244	10,907	12,265
Taxes on income and profits	2,878	2,832	3,569
Personal income	833	948	1,132
Business profits	1,639	1,303	1,714
Domestic indirect taxes	1,668	2,200	2,589
Import duties	3,564	5,276	5,746
Export duties	1	0	0
Other revenue	2,906	3,011	3,202
Reimbursements and property sales	204	185	193
Sales of goods and services	190	376	873
Total*	11,149	13,917	15,467

Expenditure	2002/03	2003/04	2004/05
Current expenditure	13,527	11,961	13,036
General services	4,679	5,048	5,767
Economic services	1,223	1,356	1,468
Social services	3,183	3,253	3,775
Interest and charges	1,219	1,080	1,011
External assistance (grants)†	2,890	699	721
Capital expenditure	6,313	8,271	11,515
Economic development	3,342	4,773	7,766
Social development	1,331	2,233	3,310
General services and compensation	444	1,265	455
External assistance (grants)†	1,196	1,047	1,513
Total	19,840	20,232	24,551

* Excluding grants received from abroad (million birr): 4,533 in 2002/03; 4,001 in 2003/04; 4,565 in 2004/05.
† Imputed value of goods and services provided, mainly aid in kind.

Source: IMF, *Federal Democratic Republic of Ethiopia: Selected Issues and Statistical Appendix* (May 2006).

INTERNATIONAL RESERVES
(US $ million at 31 December, excluding gold)

	2004	2005	2006
IMF special drawing rights	0.5	0.2	0.1
Reserve position in IMF	11.2	10.3	11.0
Foreign exchange	1,485.1	1,111.0	821.6
Total	1,496.8	1,121.5	832.7

Source: IMF, *International Financial Statistics*.

MONEY SUPPLY
(million birr, at 31 December)

	2004	2005	2006
Currency outside banks	8,274.5	9,623.3	11,606.4
Demand deposits at commercial banks	13,933.1	16,132.1	20,207.0
Total money (incl. others)	22,312.0	25,980.7	32,056.2

Source: IMF, *International Financial Statistics*.

COST OF LIVING
(Consumer Price Index; base: 2000 = 100)

	2004	2005	2006
All items	113.4	126.6	143.8

Source: IMF, *International Financial Statistics*.

NATIONAL ACCOUNTS

Expenditure on the Gross Domestic Product
(million birr at current prices; year ending 7 July)

	2002/03	2003/04	2004/05
Government final consumption expenditure	10,904	11,739	13,766
Private final consumption expenditure	52,096	68,745	79,466
Statistical discrepancy	−1	0	0
Gross capital formation	15,502	17,827	25,402
Total domestic expenditure	78,501	98,311	118,634
Exports of goods and services	9,779	12,913	15,826
Less Imports of goods and services	20,136	27,333	37,784
GDP in purchasers' values	68,144	83,892	96,676

Source: IMF, *Federal Democratic Republic of Ethiopia: Selected Issues and Statistical Appendix* (May 2006).

2006 (US $ million): General government final consumption expenditure 1,644.50; Household final consumption expenditure 11,352.29; Gross capital formation 2,626.00; Exports of goods and services 2,008.02; *Less* Imports of goods and services 4,336.84; GDP at current market prices 13,293.97 (Source: African Development Bank).

ETHIOPIA

Gross Domestic Product by Economic Activity
(at constant 1999/2000 factor cost; year ending 7 July)

	2001/02	2002/03	2004/05
Agriculture, hunting, forestry and fishing	27,361	32,100	35,948
Mining and quarrying	350	378	408
Manufacturing	3,561	3,752	3,939
Electricity and water	1,577	1,688	1,789
Construction	3,176	3,437	3,729
Trade and related services	7,694	8,194	8,686
Hotels and restaurants	1,348	1,436	1,522
Transport and communications	3,470	3,713	3,973
Finance and insurance	1,301	1,377	1,466
Real estate and renting	4,815	5,012	5,213
Public administration and defence	3,268	3,333	3,433
Education	1,966	2,182	2,422
Health	734	793	857
Domestic and other services	1,310	1,375	1,444
Private households with employed persons	191	198	206
Statistical discrepancy	−468	−496	−528
Total	**61,654**	**68,472**	**74,506**

Source: IMF, *Federal Democratic Republic of Ethiopia: Selected Issues and Statistical Appendix* (May 2006).

BALANCE OF PAYMENTS
(US $ million)

	2004	2005	2006
Exports of goods f.o.b.	678.3	917.3	1,024.7
Imports of goods f.o.b.	−2,768.5	−3,700.9	−4,105.6
Trade balance	**−2,090.2**	**−2,783.5**	**−3,080.9**
Exports of services	1,005.5	1,012.1	1,174.0
Imports of services	−958.3	−1,193.8	−1,170.7
Balance on goods and services	**−2,043.0**	**−2,965.2**	**−3,077.6**
Other income received	31.7	43.4	55.8
Other income paid	−60.3	−48.0	−37.8
Balance on goods, services and income	**−2,071.6**	**−2,969.8**	**−3,059.7**
Current transfers received	1,420.6	1,426.0	1,297.2
Current transfers paid	−16.8	−23.9	−23.4
Current balance	**−667.8**	**−1,567.8**	**−1,785.9**
Direct investment from abroad	—	265.1	545.3
Other investment assets	−261.8	302.2	73.3
Investment liabilities	335.0	191.2	357.7
Net errors and omissions	−354.1	486.3	1,161.3
Overall balance	**−948.8**	**−322.9**	**351.7**

Source: IMF, *International Financial Statistics*.

External Trade

PRINCIPAL COMMODITIES
(distribution by SITC, US $ '000)

Imports c.i.f.	2001	2002	2003
Food and live animals	218.9	151.8	499.6
Cereals and cereal preparations	197.9	133.6	458.1
Unmilled wheat and meslin	136.4	107.1	362.8
Unmilled durum wheat	47.6	52.8	188.7
Mineral fuels, lubricants, etc.	316.3	197.0	320.7
Refined petroleum products	315.8	196.2	320.2
Chemicals and related products	210.6	207.0	239.7
Manufactured fertilizers	44.6	66.1	26.1
Basic manufactures	346.6	298.9	463.2
Textile yarn, fabrics, etc.	71.2	65.7	90.6
Iron and steel	104.2	100.6	172.9
Universals, plates and sheets	47.6	40.5	61.3
Machinery and transport equipment	503.9	514.3	822.1

Imports c.i.f.—continued	2001	2002	2003
Machinery specialized for particular industries	75.0	77.6	115.3
General industrial machinery equipment and parts	60.3	48.7	76.1
Telecommunications, sound recording and reproducing equipment	45.2	47.4	102.0
Electrical machinery, apparatus, etc.*	67.2	65.9	133.1
Road vehicles and parts†	169.3	191.7	255.3
Passenger motor cars (excl. buses)	53.5	69.4	79.2
Lorries and special purposes motor vehicles	73.2	75.4	87.9
Motor vehicles for goods transport, etc.	66.3	72.3	83.7
Miscellaneous manufactured articles	138.0	170.0	213.6
Total (incl. others)	1,810.9	1,593.5	2,685.9

* Excluding telecommunications and sound equipment.
† Excluding tyres, engines and electrical parts.

Exports f.o.b.	2001	2002	2003
Food and live animals	203.1	244.2	255.3
Unmilled cereals	18.1	12.0	11.3
Vegetables and fruit	29.6	41.5	27.1
Beans, peas and other leguminous vegetables, dried and shelled	20.8	30.5	18.5
Raw sugar beet and cane, solid	0.9	20.4	15.6
Coffee, not roasted, coffee husks and skins	145.1	159.8	181.4
Crude materials (inedible) except fuels	140.7	107.3	197.3
Raw hides and skins (excl. furs)	27.9	8.7	2.3
Oil seeds and oleaginous fruit	37.7	40.0	61.1
Sesame seeds	24.5	31.3	47.9
Miscellaneous manufactured articles	50.4	57.1	50.6
Leather	46.7	53.4	43.1
Sheep and lamb skin leather	26.5	29.0	28.5
Commodities and transactions not elsewhere specified	4.5	3.5	0.0
Non-monetary gold, unwrought or semi-manufactured	4.5	3.5	0.0
Total (incl. others)	402.6	414.9	512.7

Source: UN, *International Trade Statistics Yearbook*.

Exports (million birr, 2004): Coffee, tea, mate and spices 1,649.1; Oil seeds and oleaginous fruits, miscellaneous grains, seeds and fruit; industrial or medicinal plants; straw and fodder 530.6; Vegetable plaiting materials; vegetable products not elsewhere specified or included 948.1; Sugars and sugar confectionery 134.0; Raw hides and skins (excluding fur) and leather 389.6; Cotton 160.1; Total 4,470.9.

PRINCIPAL TRADING PARTNERS
(US $ million)

Imports c.i.f.	2001	2002	2003
Belgium	37.9	40.9	28.4
China, People's Republic	134.8	144.8	313.7
Denmark	21.0	10.3	19.6
Djibouti	48.9	60.3	26.8
Egypt	17.8	19.4	29.9
France (incl. Monaco)	58.2	25.9	74.3
Germany	87.0	83.6	89.0
India	91.1	93.5	175.5
Indonesia	28.2	26.0	41.3
Italy	135.2	140.5	245.9
Japan	78.5	113.0	195.8
Kenya	15.1	17.4	23.1
Korea, Republic	42.8	21.5	43.5
Kuwait	1.0	0.3	128.3
Malaysia	12.1	7.3	29.2

ETHIOPIA

Imports c.i.f.—continued	2001	2002	2003
Netherlands	41.8	38.9	60.4
Russia	8.8	15.7	30.0
Saudi Arabia	201.1	111.0	131.3
Sweden	38.4	30.1	32.7
Turkey	22.8	35.1	62.2
United Arab Emirates	112.1	114.3	40.5
United Kingdom	61.7	73.0	150.5
USA	167.5	126.5	384.4
Yemen	132.4	7.9	5.8
Total (incl. others)	1,811.0	1,593.5	2,685.9

Exports f.o.b.	2001	2002	2003
Belgium	7.3	12.4	14.5
China, People's Republic	4.5	7.4	5.0
Djibouti	71.4	54.3	99.4
Egypt	2.6	4.9	2.2
France (incl. Monaco)	11.6	11.1	8.5
Germany	23.1	49.5	57.6
Greece	2.9	4.8	3.7
Iceland	11.8	2.3	0.3
India	17.4	11.0	7.4
Indonesia	3.4	2.4	1.4
Israel	14.0	15.1	14.4
Italy	42.6	41.0	31.7
Japan	37.2	37.3	43.7
Netherlands	4.6	4.2	5.7
Pakistan	2.1	13.8	1.3
Saudi Arabia	37.8	28.1	35.4
Somalia	13.4	9.6	28.9
Switzerland-Liechtenstein	8.3	10.2	16.1
Turkey	0.2	5.6	10.9
United Arab Emirates	6.4	8.1	10.8
United Kingdom	15.8	17.3	15.6
USA	19.6	16.7	22.7
Yemen	8.0	7.6	16.1
Total (incl. others)	402.6	414.9	512.7

Source: UN, *International Trade Statistics Yearbook*.

Transport

RAILWAYS
(traffic, year ending 7 July)*

	2002/03	2003/04	2004/05
Addis Ababa–Djibouti:			
Passenger-km (million)	253	40	34
Freight (million net ton-km)	—	81	56

* Including traffic on the section of the Djibouti–Addis Ababa line which runs through the Republic of Djibouti. Data pertaining to freight include service traffic.

ROAD TRAFFIC
(motor vehicles in use, year ending 7 July)

	2000	2001	2002
Passenger cars	59,048	59,737	67,614
Buses and coaches	9,334	11,387	18,067
Lorries and vans	34,355	43,375	34,102
Motorcycles and mopeds	n.a.	2,198	2,575
Road tractors	6,809	1,275	1,396
Total	109,546	117,972	123,754

Source: IRF, *World Road Statistics*.

SHIPPING
Merchant Fleet
(registered at 31 December)

	2004	2005	2006
Number of vessels	8	8	9
Displacement (grt)	79,441	79,441	99,912

Source: Lloyd's Register-Fairplay, *World Fleet Statistics*.

International Sea-borne Shipping
(freight traffic, '000 metric tons, year ending 7 July)

	1996/97	1997/98	1998/99
Goods loaded	242	201	313
Goods unloaded	777	1,155	947

Source: former Ministry of Transport and Communications, Addis Ababa.

CIVIL AVIATION
(traffic on scheduled services)

	2002	2003	2004
Passenger-km (million)	3,300	3,600	4,400
Total ton-km ('000)	83,500	93,500	117,100

Source: UN, *Monthly Bulletin of Statistics*.

Tourism

TOURIST ARRIVALS BY COUNTRY OF ORIGIN

	2003	2004	2005
Canada	4,434	5,169	8,396
Djibouti	21,708	14,627	4,179
France	5,482	4,501	5,899
Germany	5,719	6,256	6,731
India	3,602	4,641	7,125
Italy	6,348	7,696	7,983
Japan	1,622	1,658	1,708
Kenya	7,072	7,217	9,277
Netherlands	3,044	3,227	4,387
Saudi Arabia	6,283	9,778	5,382
Sudan	3,769	3,787	5,343
United Kingdom	8,978	10,627	11,254
USA	22,496	28,112	32,282
Yemen	2,651	2,975	3,102
Total (incl. others)*	179,910	184,079	227,398

* Including Ethiopian nationals residing abroad.

Receipts from tourism (US $ million, incl. passenger transport): 336 in 2003; 458 in 2004; 533 in 2005.

Source: World Tourism Organization.

ETHIOPIA

Communications Media

	2004	2005	2006
Telephones ('000 main lines in use)	484.4	610.3	725.0
Mobile cellular telephones ('000 subscribers)	155.5	410.6	866.7
Personal computers ('000 in use)	225	113	n.a.
Internet users ('000)	113	164	164
Broadband subscribers ('000)	0.1	0.2	0.3

Book production: 444 titles in 1999.

Non-daily newspapers: 78 in 1998 (average combined circulation 402,000).

Daily newspapers: 2 in 1998 (average circulation 23,000 copies).

Radio receivers ('000 in use): 11,340 in 2000.

Television receivers ('000 in use): 1,260 in 2000.

Facsimile machines (number in use): 3,594 in 2000.

Sources: UNESCO, *Statistical Yearbook*; UN, *Statistical Yearbook*; International Telecommunication Union.

Education

(1999/2000 unless otherwise indicated)

	Institutions	Teachers	Students
Pre-primary	834	4,584*	153,280*
Primary	11,490	110,945*	8,019,287*
Secondary: general	410	77,775*	4,382,571*
Secondary: teacher training	12	294	4,813
Secondary: skill development centres	25	367	2,474
Secondary: technical and vocational	25	4,957*	106,336*
University level	6	4,803†	172,111†
Other higher: Government	11	578	18,412
Non-government	4	140	8,376

* 2004/05 figure.
† 2003/04 figure.

Sources: Ministry of Education, Addis Ababa; UNESCO Institute for Statistics.

Adult literacy rate (UNESCO estimates): 35.9% (males 50.0%; females 22.8%) in 2004 (Source: UNESCO Institute for Statistics).

Directory

The Constitution

The Constitution of the Federal Democratic Republic of Ethiopia was adopted by the transitional Government on 8 December 1994. The following is a summary of the main provisions of the Constitution, which came into force on 22 August 1995.

GENERAL PROVISIONS

The Constitution establishes a federal and democratic state structure and all sovereign power resides in the nations, nationalities and peoples of Ethiopia. The Constitution is the supreme law of the land. Human rights and freedoms, emanating from the nature of mankind, are inviolable and inalienable. State and religion are separate and there shall be no state religion. The State shall not interfere in religious matters and vice versa. All Ethiopian languages shall enjoy equal state recognition; Amharic shall be the working language of the Federal Government.

FUNDAMENTAL RIGHTS AND FREEDOMS

All persons are equal before the law and are guaranteed equal and effective protection, without discrimination on grounds of race, nation, nationality, or other social origin, colour, sex, language, religion, political or other opinion, property, birth or other status. Everyone has the right to freedom of thought, conscience and religion and the freedom, either individually or in community with others, and in public or private, to manifest his religion or belief in worship, observance, practice and teaching. Every person has the inviolable and inalienable right to life, privacy, and the security of person and liberty.

DEMOCRATIC RIGHTS

Every Ethiopian national, without discrimination based on colour, race, nation, nationality, sex, language, religion, political or other opinion, or other status, has the following rights: on the attainment of 18 years of age, to vote in accordance with the law; to be elected to any office at any level of government; to freely express oneself without interference; to hold opinions without interference; to engage in economic activity and to pursue a livelihood anywhere within the national territory; to choose his or her means of livelihood, occupation and profession; and to own private property.

Every nation, nationality and people in Ethiopia has the following rights: an unconditional right to self-determination, including the right to secession; the right to speak, to write and to develop its own language; the right to express, to develop and to promote its culture, and to preserve its history; the right to a full measure of self-government which includes the right to establish institutions of government in the territory that it inhabits. Women shall, in the enjoyment of rights and protections provided for by this Constitution, have equal rights with men.

STATE STRUCTURE

The Federal Democratic Republic of Ethiopia shall have a parliamentarian form of government. The Federal Democratic Republic shall comprise nine States. Addis Ababa shall be the capital city of the Federal State.

STRUCTURE AND DIVISION OF POWERS

The Federal Democratic Republic of Ethiopia comprises the Federal Government and the member States. The Federal Government and the States shall have legislative, executive and judicial powers. The House of People's Representatives is the highest authority of the Federal Government. The House is responsible to the people. The State Council is the highest organ of state authority. It is responsible to the people of the State. State government shall be established at state and other administrative levels deemed necessary. Adequate power shall be granted to the lowest units of government to enable the people to participate directly in the administration of such units. The State Council has legislative power on matters falling under state jurisdiction. Consistent with the provisions of this Constitution, the Council has the power to draft, adopt and amend the state constitution. The state administration constitutes the highest organ of executive power. State judicial power is vested in its courts. The States shall respect the powers of the Federal Government. The Federal Government shall likewise respect the powers of the States. The Federal Government may, when necessary, delegate to the States powers and functions granted to it by the Constitution.

THE FEDERAL HOUSES

There shall be two Federal Houses: the House of People's Representatives and the House of the Federation.

Members of the House of People's Representatives shall be elected by the people for a term of five years on the basis of universal suffrage and by direct, free and fair elections held by secret ballot. Members of the House, on the basis of population and special representation of minority nationalities and peoples, shall not exceed 550; of these, minority nationalities and peoples shall have at least 20 seats. The House of People's Representatives shall have legislative power in all matters assigned by this Constitution to federal jurisdiction. The political party or coalition of political parties that has the greatest number of seats in the House of People's Representatives shall form and lead the Executive. Elections for a new House shall be concluded one month prior to the expiry of the House's term.

The House of the Federation is composed of representatives of nations, nationalities and peoples. Each nation, nationality and people shall be represented in the House of the Federation by at least one member. Each nation or nationality shall be represented by one additional representative for each one million of its population. Members of the House of the Federation shall be elected by the State Councils. The State Councils may themselves elect representatives to the House of the Federation, or they may hold elections to have the representatives elected by the people directly. The House of the

Federation shall hold at least two sessions annually. The term of mandate of the House of the Federation shall be five years. No one may be a member of the House of People's Representatives and of the House of the Federation simultaneously.

PRESIDENT OF THE REPUBLIC

The President of the Federal Democratic Republic of Ethiopia is the Head of State. The House of People's Representatives shall nominate the candidate for President. The nominee shall be elected President if a joint session of the House of People's Representatives and the House of the Federation approves his candidacy by a two-thirds' majority vote. The term of office of the President shall be six years. No person shall be elected President for more than two terms. The President's duties include the opening of the Federal Houses; appointing ambassadors and other envoys to represent the country abroad; granting, upon recommendation by the Prime Minister and in accordance with law, high military titles; and granting pardons.

THE EXECUTIVE

The highest executive powers of the Federal Government are vested in the Prime Minister and in the Council of Ministers. The Prime Minister and the Council of Ministers are responsible to the House of People's Representatives. In the exercise of state functions, members of the Council of Ministers are collectively responsible for all decisions they make as a body. Unless otherwise provided in this Constitution, the term of office of the Prime Minister is the duration of the mandate of the House of People's Representatives. The Prime Minister is the Chief Executive, the Chairman of the Council of Ministers, and the Commander-in-Chief of the national armed forces. The Prime Minister shall submit for approval to the House of People's Representatives nominees for ministerial posts from among members of the two Houses or from among persons who are not members of either House and possess the required qualifications. The Council of Ministers is responsible to the Prime Minister and, in all its decisions, is responsible to the House of People's Representatives. The Council of Ministers ensures the implementation of laws and decisions adopted by the House of People's Representatives.

STRUCTURE AND POWERS OF THE COURTS

Supreme Federal judicial authority is vested in the Federal Supreme Court. The House of People's Representatives may, by a two-thirds' majority vote, establish nation-wide, or in some parts of the country only, the Federal High Court and First-Instance Courts it deems necessary. Unless decided in this manner, the jurisdictions of the Federal High Court and of the First-Instance Courts are hereby delegated to the state courts. States shall establish State Supreme, High and First-Instance Courts. Judicial powers, both at federal and state levels, are vested in the courts. Courts of any level shall be free from any interference or influence of any governmental body, government official or from any other source. Judges shall exercise their functions in full independence and shall be directed solely by the law. The Federal Supreme Court shall have the highest and final judicial power over federal matters. State Supreme Courts shall have the highest and final judicial power over state matters. They shall also exercise the jurisdiction of the Federal High Court.

MISCELLANEOUS PROVISIONS

The Council of Ministers of the Federal Government shall have the power to decree a state of emergency in the event of an external invasion, a breakdown of law and order that endangers the constitutional order and cannot be controlled by the regular law enforcement agencies and personnel, a natural disaster or an epidemic. State executives can decree a state-wide state of emergency should a natural disaster or an epidemic occur.

A National Election Board independent of any influence shall be established, to conduct free and fair elections in federal and state constituencies in an impartial manner.

The Government

HEAD OF STATE

President: Lt GIRMA WOLDE GIORGIS (took office 8 October 2001; re-elected by vote of the House of People's Representatives 9 October 2007).

COUNCIL OF MINISTERS
(February 2008)

Prime Minister: MELES ZENAWI.
Deputy Prime Minister and Minister of Agriculture and Rural Development: ADDISO LEGGESE.
Minister and Economic Adviser to the Prime Minister: NEWAYEKRISTOS GEBRAB.
Minister and Public Organization and Participation Adviser to the Prime Minister: ABAY TSEHAYE.
Minister and Public Relations Adviser to the Prime Minister: BEREKET SIMON.
Minister and Special Adviser to the Prime Minister: Dr FASIL NAHOM.
Minister and National Security Affairs Adviser: MULUGETA ALEMSEGED.
Minister and Adviser to the Deputy Prime Minister: Prof. MESFIN ABEBE.
Minister of Foreign Affairs: SEYOUM MESFIN.
Minister of Health: Dr TEWEDROS ADHANOM.
Minister of Capacity Building: TEFERA WALWA.
Minister of Defence: KUMA DEMEKESA.
Minister of Energy and Mines: ALEMAYEHU TEGENU.
Minister of Finance and Economic Development: SUFYAN AHMED.
Minister of Information: BERHAN HAILU.
Minister of Education: Dr SINTAYEHU WOLDEMIKAEL.
Minister of Federal Affairs: SIRAJ FEGETA.
Minister of Trade and Industry: GIRMA BIRU.
Minister of Justice: ASSEFA KESSITO.
Minister of Transport and Communications: JUNEDI SADO.
Minister of Cabinet Affairs: BIRHANU ADELO.
Minister of Labour and Social Affairs: HASAN ABDELLA.
Minister of Water Resources: ASEFAW DINGAM.
Minister of Revenues: MELUKA FENTA.
Minister of Youth and Sports: ASTER MAMO.
Minister of Women's Affairs: HIRUT DILEBO.
Minister of Culture and Tourism: MAHMUD DIRIR.

MINISTRIES

Office of the President: POB 1031, Addis Ababa; tel. (11) 1551000; fax (11) 1552030.
Office of the Prime Minister: POB 1013, Addis Ababa; tel. (11) 1552044; fax (11) 1552020.
Ministry of Agriculture and Rural Development: POB 62347, Addis Ababa; tel. (11) 5538134; fax (11) 5530776.
Ministry of Capacity Building: Addis Ababa; tel. (11) 1552800; fax (11) 1553338.
Ministry of Culture and Tourism: POB 2183, Addis Ababa; tel. (11) 5512310; fax (11) 5512889; e-mail info@tourismethiopia.org; internet www.tourismethiopia.org.
Ministry of Defence: POB 1373, Addis Ababa; tel. (11) 5511777; fax (11) 5516053.
Ministry of Education: POB 1367, Addis Ababa; tel. (11) 1553133; fax (11) 1550877.
Ministry of Energy and Mines: POB 486, Addis Ababa; tel. (11) 5153689; fax (11) 5517874.
Ministry of Federal Affairs: POB 1031, Addis Ababa; tel. (11) 5512766; fax (11) 1552030.
Ministry of Finance and Economic Development: POB 1037, Addis Ababa; tel. (11) 1552800; fax (11) 1550118; internet www.mofaed.org.
Ministry of Foreign Affairs: POB 393, Addis Ababa; tel. (11) 5517345; fax (11) 5514300; e-mail mfa.addis@telecom.net.et; internet www.mfa.gov.et.
Ministry of Health: POB 1234, Addis Ababa; tel. (11) 5517011; fax (11) 5519366.
Ministry of Information: Addis Ababa; tel. (11) 1551100; fax (11) 1569678; internet www.moinfo.gov.et.
Ministry of Infrastructure: POB 1238, Addis Ababa; tel. (11) 5516166; fax (11) 5515665; e-mail publicrelation@moi.gov.et; internet www.moi.gov.et.
Ministry of Justice: POB 1370, Addis Ababa; tel. (11) 512288; fax (11) 517775; internet www.mojet.gov.et.
Ministry of Labour and Social Affairs: POB 2056, Addis Ababa; tel. (11) 5517080; fax (11) 5518396.
Ministry of Revenue: POB 2559, Addis Ababa; tel. (11) 4667466; fax (11) 4662628; internet www.mor.gov.et.
Ministry of Trade and Industry: POB 704, Addis Ababa; tel. (11) 5518025; fax (11) 5514288.
Ministry of Water Resources: POB 5744, Addis Ababa; tel. (11) 6611111; fax (11) 6611700.

ETHIOPIA

Ministry of Women's Affairs: Addis Ababa.
Ministry of Works and Urban Development: POB 1238, Addis Ababa; tel. (11) 5518292; fax (11) 527969.
Ministry of Youth and Sports: POB 1364, Addis Ababa; tel. (11) 5517020.

Regional Governments

Ethiopia comprises nine regional governments, one chartered city (Addis Ababa) and one Administrative Council (Dire Dawa), which are vested with authority for self-administration. The executive bodies are respectively headed by Presidents (regional states) and Chairmen (Addis Ababa and Dire Dawa).

PRESIDENTS
(February 2008)

Tigrai: TSEGAYE BERHE.
Afar: ESMAEL ALISERO.
Amhara: AYALEW GOBEZE.
Oromia: Gen. ABEDULA GEMEDA.
Somali: ABDULAHI HASAN MOHAMMED.
Benishangul/Gumuz: YAREGAL AYSHESHIM.
Southern Nations, Nationalities and Peoples: SHIFERAW SHIGUTTE.
Gambela: UMED UBONG.
Harari: MURAD ABDULHADIN.

CHAIRMEN
(February 2008)

Dire Dawa: ABDULAZIZ MOHAMMED.
Addis Ababa: BERHANU DERESSA.

Legislature

FEDERAL PARLIAMENTARY ASSEMBLY

The legislature comprises an upper house, the House of the Federation (Yefedereshn Mekir Bet), with 108 seats (members are selected by state assemblies and are drawn one each from 22 minority nationalities and one from each professional sector of the remaining nationalities, and serve for a period of five years), and a lower house of no more than 550 directly elected members, the House of People's Representatives (Yehizbtewekayoch Mekir Bet), who are also elected for a five-year term.

Speaker of the House of the Federation: DEGIFE BULA.
Deputy Speaker of the House of the Federation: MOHAMMED SIREE.

Yehizbtewekayoch Mekir Bet
(House of People's Representatives)

Speaker: TESHOME TOGA.
Deputy Speaker: SHITAYE MINALE.
General Election, 15 May 2005*

Party	Seats
Ethiopian People's Revolutionary Democratic Front (EPRDF)	327
Coalition for Unity and Democracy (CUD)	109
United Ethiopian Democratic Forces (UEDF)	52
Oromo Federalist Democratic Movement (OFDM)	11
Somali People's Democratic Party (SPDP)	24
Benishangul Gumuz People's Democratic Unity Front (BGPDUF)	8
Afar National Democratic Party (ANDP)	8
Gambela People's Democratic Movement (GPDM)	3
Sheko-Majenger People's Democratic Unity Organization (SMPDUO)	1
Harari National League (HNL)	1
Argoba National Democratic Organization (ANDO)	1
Independent	1
Total	**546**

* Owing to alleged electoral irregularities at some polling stations, voting was repeated in 31 constituencies on 21 August, when a by-election for a further seat was also conducted. Voting for 24 seats in the Somali Regional State additionally took place on that date.

Election Commission

National Electoral Board of Ethiopia (NEBE): POB 40812, Addis Ababa; tel. (1) 514911; fax (1) 514929; internet www.electionsethiopia.org; f. 1993; independent board of seven politically non-affiliated mems appointed, on the Prime Minister's recommendation, by the House of People's Representatives; Chair. KEMAL BEDRI KELO.

Political Organizations

Afar People's Democratic Organization (APDO): fmrly Afar Liberation Front (ALF); based in fmr Hararge and Wollo Admin. Regions; Leader ISMAIL ALI SIRRO.

Coalition of Ethiopian Democratic Forces (COEDF): f. 1991 in the USA by the Ethiopian People's Revolutionary Party—EPRP (the dominant member), together with a faction of the Ethiopian Democratic Union (EDU) and the Ethiopian Socialist Movement (MEISON); opposes the EPRDF; Chair. MERSHA YOSEPH.

Coalition for Unity and Democracy (CUD): 8605 Cameron St, Suite M-0, Silver Spring, MD 20910, USA; tel. (202) 541-9507; fax (202) 541-1090; e-mail kinijitinfo@kinijit.org; internet www.kinijit.org; f. 2004 as a coalition of four parties opposed to the EPRDF; the All Ethiopia Unity Party, the Ethiopian Democratic League, the Ethiopian Democratic Unity Party and the Rainbow Ethiopia: Movement for Democracy and Justice merged in late 2005 to form a single party; Pres. HAILU SHAWEL; Vice-Pres. BIRTUKAN MIDEKSA.

Ethiopian National Democratic Party (ENDP): f. 1994 by merger of five pro-Govt orgs with mems in the Council of Representatives; comprises: the Ethiopian Democratic Organization, the Ethiopian Democratic Organization Coalition (EDC), the Gurage People's Democratic Front (GPDF), the Kembata People's Congress (KPC), and the Wolaita People's Democratic Front (WPDF); Chair. FEKADU GEDAMU.

Ethiopian People's Revolutionary Democratic Front (EPRDF): Addis Ababa; f. 1989 by the TPLF as an alliance of insurgent groups seeking regional autonomy and engaged in armed struggle against the EDUP Govt; Chair. MELES ZENAWI; Vice-Chair. ADDISO LEGGESE; in May 1991, with other orgs, formed transitional Govt.

Amhara National Democratic Movement (ANDM): based in Tigrai; represents interests of the Amhara people; fmrly the Ethiopian People's Democratic Movement (EPDM); adopted present name in 1994; Chair. ADDISO LEGGESE.

Oromo People's Democratic Organization (OPDO): f. 1990 by the TPLF to promote its cause in Oromo areas; based among the Oromo people in the Shoa region; Leader Gen. ABEDULA GEMEDA.

Tigrai People's Liberation Front (TPLF): f. 1975; the dominant org. within the EPRDF; Chair. MELES ZENAWI; Vice-Chair. SEYOUM MESFIN.

Gambela People's Democratic Front (GPDF): pro-Govt group based in the Gambela region; Chair. AKILO NIGILIO.

Ogaden National Liberation Front (ONLF): e-mail foreign@onlf.org; internet www.onlf.org; f. 1984; seeks self-determination for the Ogaden region; Chair. MOHAMED OMAR OSMAN.

Oromo Federalist Democratic Movement (OFDM): Chair. BULCHA DEMEKSA.

Oromo Liberation Front (OLF): POB 73247, Washington, DC 20056, USA; tel. (202) 462-5477; fax (202) 332-7011; e-mail olfinfodesk@earthlink.net; internet www.oromoliberationfront.org; f. 1973; seeks self-determination for the Oromo people; participated in the Ethiopian transitional Govt until June 1992; Chair. DAWUD IBSA AYANA; Vice-Chair. ABDULFATTAH A. MOUSSA BIYYO.

Sheko-Majenger People's Democratic Unity Organization (SMPDUO).

Sidama Liberation Front (SLF): e-mail info@sidamaliberation-front.org; internet www.sidamaliberation-front.org; campaigns for self-determination for Sidama people.

Somali Abo Liberation Front (SALF): operates in fmr Bale Admin. Region; has received Somali military assistance; Sec.-Gen. MASURAD SHU'ABI IBRAHIM.

Somali People's Democratic Party: f. 1998 by merger of Ogaden National Liberation Front (ONLF) and the Ethiopian Somali Democratic League (ESDL—an alliance comprising the Somali Democratic Union Party, the Issa and Gurgura Liberation Front, the Gurgura Independence Front, the Eastern Gabooye Democratic Organization, the Eastern Ethiopian Somali League, the Horyal Democratic Front, the Social Alliance Democratic Organization, the Somali Abo Democratic Union, the Shekhash People's Democratic Movement, the Ethiopian Somalis' Democratic Movement and the

ETHIOPIA

Per Barreh Party); Chair. MOHAMOUD DIRIR GHEDDI; Sec.-Gen. SULTAN IBRAHIM.

Southern Ethiopian People's Democratic Front (SEPDF): f. 1992; as an alliance of 10 ethnically based political groups from the south of the country; was represented in the transitional Council of Representatives, although five of the participating groups were expelled from the Council in April 1993.

United Ethiopian Democratic Forces (UEDF): POB 73246, Washington, DC 20056-3246, USA; e-mail UEDFHIBRET@yahoo.com; internet www.hebret.com; f. 2003; USA-based org.; Chair. FASIKA BELETE.

   Afar Revolutionary Democratic Unity Front (ARDUF): f. 1993.

   All Amhara Unity Party (AAUP).

   All Ethiopian Socialist Movement (MEISON): f. 1968.

   Ethiopian Social Democratic Federal Party (ESDFP): f. 1993 as the Council of Alternative Forces for Peace and Democracy in Ethiopia; adopted present form in November 2004; opposes the EPRDF; Chair. Dr BEYENE PETROS.

   Ethiopian Medhin Democratic Party (MEDHIN): internet www.medhin.org; US-based org.; Chair. Prof. SEYOUM GELAYE.

   Ethiopian National United Front (ENUF): POB 2206, Washington, DC 20013-2206, USA; tel. (202) 785-1618; e-mail info@enufforethiopia.net; internet www.enufforethiopia.net; f. 2001; USA-based org.; Chair. BEKELE MOLLA.

   Ethiopian People's Federal Democratic Unity Party (HibreHizb): Vice-Sec. Lt AYALSEW DESSIE.

   Ethiopian People's Revolutionary Party (EPRP): e-mail espic@aol.com; internet www.eprp.com; f. 1972; Leader MERSHA YOSEPH.

   Oromo National Congress (ONC): Addis Ababa; tel. (1) 512104; Chair. Dr MERERE GUDINA.

   Southern Ethiopian People's Democratic Coalition (SEPDC): opposition alliance; Chair. Dr BEYENE PETROS.

   Tigraian Alliance for National Democracy (TAND): Leader MEKONNEN ZELLELEW.

United Ethiopian Democratic Party (UEDP): POB 101458, Addis Ababa; tel. (11) 5508727; fax (11) 5508730; e-mail uedpmedhinpr@gmail.com; internet www.uedpmedhin.org; f. 2003 by the merger of Ethiopian Democratic Unity Party and the Ethiopian Democratic Party; Sec.-Gen. Dr ADMASSU GEBREYEHU.

United Oromo Liberation Forces (UOLF): f. 2000 in Asmara, Eritrea, as a common Oromo Front seeking to overthrow the Ethiopian Govt; Sec.-Gen. GALASA DILBO; alliance comprises:

   Islamic Front for the Liberation of Oromia: Leader ABDELKARIM IBRAHIM HAMID.

   Oromo Liberation Council (OLC).

   Oromo Liberation Front (OLF): see above.

   Oromo People's Liberation Front (OPLF).

   Oromo People's Liberation Organization (OPLO).

   United Oromo People's Liberation Front (UOPLF).

Unity of Ethiopians for Democratic Change (UEDC): f. 2007; as replacement for the Alliance for Freedom and Democracy; coalition of political parties and rebel groups opposed to the Govt.

   Benishangul People's Movement (BPM): rebel group operating in western Ethiopia.

   Ethiopian People's Patriotic Front (EPPF): e-mail info@eppf.net; internet www.eppf.net; armed anti-Govt group operating mainly in north-western Ethiopia.

   Southern Ethiopia People's Front for Justice and Equality (SEPFJE): armed anti-Govt group operating in southern Ethiopia.

   Tigrai People's Democratic Movement (TPDM): f. 1979; rebel group operating in northern Tigrai region of Ethiopia.

Western Somali Liberation Front (WSLF): POB 978, Mogadishu, Somalia; f. 1975; aims to unite the Ogaden region with Somalia; maintains guerrilla forces of c. 3,000 men; has received support from regular Somali forces; Sec.-Gen. ISSA SHAYKH ABDI NASIR ADAN.

The following parties have parliamentary representation: **Afar National Democratic Party (ANDP); Argoba National Democratic Organization (ANDO); Benishangul Gumuz People's Democratic Unity Front (BGPDUF); Gambela People's Democratic Movement (GPDM); Harari National League (HNL); Somali People's Democratic Party (SPDP).**

Diplomatic Representation

EMBASSIES IN ETHIOPIA

Algeria: Woreda 23, Kebele 13, House No. 1819, POB 5740, Addis Ababa; tel. (11) 3719666; fax (11) 3719669; Ambassador NOUREDDINE AOUAM.

Angola: Woreda 18, Kebele 26, House No. 6, POB 2962, Addis Ababa; tel. (11) 5510085; fax (11) 5514922; Ambassador MANUEL DOMINGOS AUGUSTO.

Austria: POB 1219, Addis Ababa; tel. (11) 3712144; fax (11) 3712140; e-mail addis-abeba-ob@bmeia.gv.at; internet www.aussenministerium.at/addisabeba; Ambassador RUDOLF AGSTNER.

Belgium: Comoros St, Kebele 8, POB 1239, Addis Ababa; tel. (11) 6611813; fax (11) 6613646; e-mail addisababa@diplobel.org; internet www.diplomatie.be/addisababa; Ambassador GUNTHER SLEEUWAGEN.

Benin: Addis Ababa; Ambassador EDOUARD AHO-GELLE.

Botswana: POB 22282, Addis Ababa; tel. (11) 715422; fax (11) 714099; Ambassador ZIBANE JOHN NTAKHWANA.

Brazil: Bole Sub-City, Kebele 2, House No. 2830, POB 2458, Addis Ababa; tel. (11) 6620401; fax (11) 6620412; e-mail embradisadm@ethionet.et; Ambassador RENATO XAVIER.

Bulgaria: Haile Gabreselassie Rd, Woreda 17, Kebele 13, POB 987, Addis Ababa; tel. (11) 6610032; fax (11) 6613373; e-mail bulemba@ethionet.et; Chargé d'affaires a.i. EMIL TRIFONOV.

Burkina Faso: Kebele 19, House No. 281, POB 19685, Addis Ababa; tel. (11) 6615863; fax (11) 6625857; e-mail ambfet@telecom.net.et; Ambassador BRUNO ZIDOUEMBA.

Burundi: POB 3641, Addis Ababa; tel. (11) 4651300; e-mail burundi.emb@telecom.net.et; Ambassador PHILIPPE NTAHONKURIYE.

Cameroon: Bole Rd, Woreda 18, Kebele 26, House No. 168, POB 1026, Addis Ababa; tel. (11) 5504488; fax (11) 5518434; Ambassador JEAN-HILAIRE MBÉA MBÉA.

Canada: Nefas Silk Lafto Kifle Ketema 3, Kebele 4, House No. 122, POB 1130, Addis Ababa; tel. (11) 3713022; fax (11) 3713033; e-mail addis@international.gc.ca; internet www.dfait-maeci.gc.ca/africa/ethiopia-contact-en.asp; Ambassador YVES BOULANGER.

Cape Verde: Kebele 3, House No. 107, POB 200093, Addis Ababa; tel. (11) 6635466; Chargé d'affaires a.i. CUSTODIA LIMA.

Chad: Bole Rd, Woreda 17, Kebele 20, House No. 2583, POB 5119, Addis Ababa; tel. (11) 6613819; fax (11) 6612050; Ambassador MAITINE DJOUMBE.

China, People's Republic: Jimma Rd, Woreda 24, Kebele 13, House No. 792, POB 5643, Addis Ababa; tel. (11) 3711960; fax (11) 3712457; e-mail chinaemb_et@mfa.gov.cn; internet et.china-embassy.org; Ambassador LIN LIN.

Congo, Democratic Republic: Makanisa Rd, Woreda 23, Kebele 13, House No. 1779, POB 2723, Addis Ababa; tel. (11) 3710111; fax (11) 3713485; Ambassador GÉRARD MAPANGO KEMISHANGA.

Congo, Republic: Woreda 3, Kebele 51, House No. 378, POB 5639, Addis Ababa; tel. (11) 5514188; fax (11) 5514331; Ambassador RAYMOND SERGE BALE.

Côte d'Ivoire: Woreda 23, Kebele 13, House No. 1308, POB 3668, Addis Ababa; tel. (11) 3711213; fax (11) 3712178; Ambassador MDALO GBOUAGBRE.

Cuba: Woreda 17, Kebele 19, House No. 197, POB 5623, Addis Ababa; tel. (11) 620459; fax (11) 620460; e-mail embacuba@ethiopia.cubaminrex.cu; Ambassador RICARDO GARCÍA DÍAZ.

Czech Republic: Kebele 15, House No. 29, POB 3108, Addis Ababa; tel. (11) 5516132; fax (11) 5513471; e-mail addisabeba@embassy.mzv.cz; internet www.mzv.cz/addisababa; Ambassador ZDENĚK DOBIÁŠ.

Denmark: c/o Embassy of Norway, Nefas Silk Lafto Kifle Ketema, Kebele 3, House No. 1019, POB 12955, Addis Ababa; tel. (11) 3711377; fax (11) 3711399; e-mail addambdk@ethionet.et; internet www.ambaddisababa.um.dk; Ambassador PERNILLE DAHLER KARDEL.

Djibouti: POB 1022, Addis Ababa; tel. (11) 6613200; fax (11) 6612786; Ambassador ISMAÏL GOULAL BOUDINE.

Egypt: POB 1611, Addis Ababa; tel. (11) 1226422; fax (11) 1226432; Ambassador SHAMEL NASSER.

Equatorial Guinea: Bole Rd, Woreda 17, Kebele 23, House No. 162, POB 246, Addis Ababa; tel. (11) 6626278; Ambassador (vacant).

Eritrea: POB 2571, Addis Ababa; tel. (11) 5512844; fax (11) 5514911; Chargé d'affaires a.i. SAHIH OMER.

Finland: Mauritania St, Kebele 12, House No. 1431, POB 1017, Addis Ababa; tel. (11) 3205920; fax (11) 3205923; e-mail sanomat.add@formin.fi; Ambassador KIRSTI AARNIO.

ETHIOPIA

France: Kabana, POB 1464, Addis Ababa; tel. (11) 1236022; fax (11) 1236029; e-mail scacamb@ethionet.et; internet www.ambafrance-ethiopie.org; Ambassador STÉPHANE GOMPERTZ.

Gabon: Woreda 17, Kebele 18, House No. 1026, POB 1256, Addis Ababa; tel. (11) 6611075; fax (11) 6613700; Ambassador EMMANUEL ISSOZE-NGONDET.

The Gambia: Kebele 3, House No. 79, POB 60083, Addis Ababa; tel. (11) 6624647; fax (11) 6627895; e-mail gambia@ethionet.et; Ambassador Dr OMAR A. TOURAY.

Germany: Yeka Kifle Ketema, Kebele 6, POB 660, Addis Ababa; tel. (11) 1235139; fax (11) 1235152; e-mail germemb@ethionet.et; internet www.addis-abeba.diplo.de; Ambassador Dr CLAAS DIETER KNOOP.

Ghana: Jimma Rd, Woreda 24, Kebele 13, House No. 108, POB 3173, Addis Ababa; tel. (11) 3711402; fax (11) 3712511; Ambassador JOHN EVONLAH AGGREY.

Greece: off Debre Zeit Rd, POB 1168, Addis Ababa; tel. (11) 4654911; fax (11) 4654883; internet www.telecom.net.et/~greekemb; Ambassador DIONISIOS KOUNTOUREAS.

Guinea: Debre Zeit Rd, Woreda 18, Kebele 14, House No. 58, POB 1190, Addis Ababa; tel. (11) 4651308; fax (11) 4651250; Ambassador SEKOU CAMARA.

Holy See: POB 588, Addis Ababa (Apostolic Nunciature); tel. (11) 3712100; fax (11) 3711499; Apostolic Nuncio Most Rev. MOLINER INGLÉS RAMIRO (Titular Archbishop of Sarda).

India: Kabena, POB 528, Addis Ababa; tel. (11) 1552100; fax (11) 1552521; Ambassador GURJIT SINGH.

Indonesia: Mekanisa Rd, POB 1004, Addis Ababa; tel. (11) 3712104; fax (11) 3710873; e-mail indoeth@hotmail.com; Ambassador DEDDY SUDARMAN.

Iran: 317–318 Jimma Rd, POB 1144, Addis Ababa; tel. (11) 3710037; fax (11) 3712299; internet www.iranembassy-addis.net; Ambassador ABABA KIUMARS FOTOUHI QIYAM.

Ireland: Sierra Leone St, Kebele 6, House No. 21, POB 9585, Addis Ababa; tel. (11) 4665050; fax (11) 4665020; e-mail ireland.emb@ethionet.et; Chargé d'affaires a.i. DON SEXTON.

Israel: Woreda 16, Kebele 22, House No. 283, POB 1266, Addis Ababa; tel. (11) 6460999; fax (11) 64619619; e-mail embassy@addisababa.mfa.gov.il; internet addisababa.mfa.gov.il; Ambassador YAACOV AMITAI.

Italy: Villa Italia, POB 1105, Addis Ababa; tel. (11) 1235717; fax (11) 1235689; e-mail ambasciata.addisabeba@esteri.it; Ambassador RAFFAELE DE LUTIO.

Japan: Woreda 18, Kebele 7, House No. 653, POB 5650, Addis Ababa; tel. (11) 5511088; fax (11) 5511350; e-mail japan-embassy@telecom.net.et; Ambassador KINICHI KOMANO.

Kenya: Woreda 16, Kebele 1, POB 3301, Addis Ababa; tel. (11) 610033; fax (11) 611433; Ambassador FRANKLIN ESIPILA.

Korea, Democratic People's Republic: Woreda 20, Kebele 40, House No. 892, POB 2378, Addis Ababa; tel. (11) 6182828; Ambassador O UL ROK.

Korea, Republic: Jimma Rd, Old Airport Area, POB 2047, Addis Ababa; tel. (11) 4655230; e-mail skorea.emb@telecom.net.et; Ambassador JHUNG BYUNG KUCK.

Kuwait: Woreda 17, Kebele 20, House No. 128, POB 19898, Addis Ababa; tel. (11) 6615411; fax (11) 6612621; Ambassador FAISAL MUTLAQ AL-ADWAHI.

Lesotho: Asmara Rd, Woreda 17, Kebele 16, House No. 157, POB 7483, Addis Ababa; tel. (11) 6614368; fax (11) 6612837; Ambassador MOTLATSI RAMAFOLE.

Liberia: Roosevelt St, Woreda 21, Kebele 4, House No. 237, POB 3116, Addis Ababa; tel. (11) 5513655; Ambassador Dr EDWARD GBOLOCO HOWARD CLINTON.

Libya: Ras Tessema Sefer, Woreda 3, Kebele 53, House No. 585, POB 5728, Addis Ababa; tel. (11) 5511077; fax (11) 5511383; Ambassador ALI ABDALLA AWIDAN.

Madagascar: Woreda 17, Kebele 19, House No. 629, POB 60004, Addis Ababa; tel. (11) 612555; fax (11) 610127; e-mail emb.mad@telecom.net.et; Ambassador JEAN PIERRE RAKOTOARIVONY.

Malawi: Bole Rd, Woreda 23, Kebele 13, House No. 1021, POB 2316, Addis Ababa; tel. (11) 3711280; fax (11) 3719742; e-mail malemb@telecom.net.et; Ambassador JAMES DONALD KALILAGNWE.

Mali: Kebele 03, House No. 418, Addis Ababa; tel. (11) 168990; fax (11) 162838; e-mail keitamoone@maliembassy-addis.org; internet www.maliembassy-addis.org; Ambassador AL-MAAMOUN BABA LAMINE KEÏTA.

Mauritania: Lidete Kifle Ketema, Kebele 2, House No. 431 A, POB 200015, Addis Ababa; tel. (11) 3729165; fax (11) 3729166; Ambassador MOHAMED ABDELLAHI OULD BABANA.

Mauritius: Kebele 03, House No. 750, POB 200222, Kifle Ketema, Addis Ababa; tel. (1) 6615997; fax (1) 6614704; e-mail mmaddis@ethionet.et; Ambassador TAYE WAN CHAT KWONG.

Morocco: 210 Bole Rd, POB 60033, Addis Ababa; tel. (11) 5508440; fax (11) 5511828; e-mail morocco.emb@ethionet.et; Ambassador ABDELJEBBAR BRAHIME.

Mozambique: Woreda 17, Kebele 23, House No. 2116, POB 5671, Addis Ababa; tel. (11) 3712905; fax (11) 3710021; e-mail embamoc-add@telecom.net.et; Ambassador MANUEL TOMÁS LUBISSE.

Namibia: Woreda 17, Kebele 19, House No. 2, POB 1443, Addis Ababa; tel. (11) 6611966; fax (11) 6612677; Ambassador GEORGE LISWANISO.

Netherlands: Woreda 24, Kebele 13, House No. 1, POB 1241, Addis Ababa; tel. (11) 3711100; fax (11) 3711577; e-mail add@minbuza.nl; internet www.netherlandsembassyethiopia.org; Ambassador ALPHONS HENNEKENS.

Niger: Woreda 9, Kebele 23, POB 5791, Addis Ababa; tel. (11) 4651305; fax (11) 4651296; Ambassador DIAMBALLA MAIMOUNA.

Nigeria: POB 1019, Addis Ababa; tel. (11) 1550644; Chargé d'affaires a.i. CHIGOZIE OBI-NNADOZIE.

Norway: POB 8383, Addis Ababa; tel. (11) 3710799; fax (11) 3711255; e-mail emb.addisababa@mfa.no; internet www.norway.org.et; Ambassador JENS-PETTER KJEMPRUD.

Poland: Bole Sub-City, Kebele 3, House No. 2111, POB 27207, Addis Ababa; tel. (11) 6185401; fax (11) 6610000; e-mail polemb@ethionet.et; internet www.addisabeba.polemb.net; Chargé d'affaires a.i. DANUTA BOLIMOWSKA.

Portugal: Sheraton Addis, Taitu Street, POB 6002, Addis Ababa; tel. (11) 171717; fax (11) 173403; e-mail embportadis@hotmail.com; Ambassador Dr VERA MARIA FERNANDES.

Romania: Houses 9–10, Bole Kifle Ketema, Kebele 03, POB 2478, Addis Ababa; tel. (11) 6610156; fax (11) 6611191; e-mail roembaddis@ethionet.et; Chargé d'affaires a.i. GABRIEL BRANZARU.

Russia: POB 1500, Addis Ababa; tel. (11) 6612060; fax (11) 6613795; e-mail russemb@ethionet.et; Ambassador MIKHAIL Y. AFANASIEV.

Rwanda: Africa House, Woreda 17, Kebele 20, POB 5618, Addis Ababa; tel. (11) 6610300; fax (11) 6610411; Ambassador NYILINKINDI GASPARD.

Senegal: Africa Ave, POB 2581, Addis Ababa; tel. (11) 6611376; fax (11) 6610020; e-mail ambassene-addis@ethionet.et; Ambassador AMADOU KÉBÉ.

Serbia: POB 1341, Addis Ababa; tel. (11) 5517804; fax (11) 5514192; e-mail serbembaddis@ethionet.et; Ambassador IVAN ZIVKOVIĆ.

Sierra Leone: POB 5619, Addis Ababa; tel. (11) 3710033; fax (11) 3711911; Ambassador IBRAHIM M. KAMARA.

Somalia: Bole Kifle Ketema, Kebele 20, House No. 588, POB 1643, Addis Ababa; tel. (11) 6180673; fax (11) 6180680; Ambassador ABDIKARIM FARAH.

South Africa: POB 1091, Addis Ababa; tel. (11) 3713034; fax (11) 3711330; e-mail sa.embassy.addis@telecom.net.et; Ambassador CHRIS PEPANI.

Spain: Entoto Ave, POB 2312, Addis Ababa; tel. (11) 1222544; fax (11) 1222541; e-mail emb.addisabeba@mae.es; Ambassador MARÍA DEL CARMEN DE LA PEÑA CORCUERA.

Sudan: Kirkos, Kebele, POB 1110, Addis Ababa; tel. (11) 5516477; fax (11) 5519989; e-mail sudan.embassy@telecom.net.et; Ambassador ABU ZAID AL-HASSAN.

Sweden: Ras Tessema Sefer, Woreda 3, Kebele 53, House No. 891, POB 1142, Addis Ababa; tel. (11) 5511255; fax (11) 5514558; e-mail ambassaden.addis-abeba@foreign.ministry.se; internet www.swedenabroad.com/addisabeba; Ambassador STAFFAN TILLANDER.

Switzerland: Jimma Rd, Old Airport Area, POB 1106, Addis Ababa; tel. (11) 3711107; fax (11) 3712177; e-mail add.vertretung@eda.admin.ch; Ambassador PETER REINHARDT.

Tanzania: POB 1077, Addis Ababa; tel. (11) 5511063; fax (11) 5517358; Ambassador MSUYA W. MANGACHI.

Togo: Addis Ababa; Ambassador TILIOUFEI KOFFI ESAW.

Tunisia: Wereda 17, Kebele 19, Bole Rd, POB 100069, Addis Ababa; tel. (11) 6612063; fax (11) 6614568; Ambassador MUHAMMAD ADEL SMAOUI.

Turkey: POB 1506, Addis Ababa; tel. (11) 6613161; fax (11) 6611688; e-mail turk.emb@ethionet.et; Ambassador ALI RIZA COLAK.

Uganda: Kirkos Kifle Ketema, Kebele 35, House No. 31, POB 5644, Addis Ababa; tel. (11) 5513088; fax (11) 5514355; Ambassador EDITH GRACE SSEMPALA.

Ukraine: Woreda 17, Kebele 3, House No. 2116, POB 2358, Addis Ababa; tel. (11) 6611698; fax (11) 6621288; e-mail emb_et@mfa.gov.ua; Ambassador VLADYSLAV DEMYANENKO.

ETHIOPIA   *Directory*

United Kingdom: POB 858, Addis Ababa; tel. (11) 6612354; fax (11) 6610588; e-mail britishembassy.addisababa@fco.gov.uk; internet www.britishembassy.gov.uk/ethiopia; Ambassador NORMAN LING.

USA: Entoto St, POB 1014, Addis Ababa; tel. (11) 5174000; fax (11) 5174001; e-mail pasaddis@state.gov; internet addisababa.usembassy.gov; Ambassador DONALD Y. YAMAMOTO.

Venezuela: Bole Kifle Ketama, Kebele 21, House No. 314–16, POB 1909, Addis Ababa; tel. (11) 6460601; fax (11) 5154162; Ambassador LUIS MARIANO JOUBERTT MATA.

Yemen: POB 664, Addis Ababa; Ambassador Dr AMIN MUHAMMAD AL-YOUSFI.

Zambia: POB 1909, Addis Ababa; tel. (11) 3711302; fax (11) 3711566; Ambassador LAZAROUS KAPAMBWE.

Zimbabwe: POB 5624, Addis Ababa; tel. (11) 6613877; fax (11) 6613476; e-mail zimbabwe.embassy@telecom.net.et; Ambassador Dr ANDREW HAMA MTETWA.

Judicial System

The 1994 Constitution stipulates the establishment of an independent judiciary in Ethiopia. Judicial powers are vested in the courts, both at federal and state level. The supreme federal judicial authority is the Federal Supreme Court. This court has the highest and final power of jurisdiction over federal matters. The federal states of the Federal Democratic Republic of Ethiopia can establish Supreme, High and First-Instance Courts. The Supreme Courts of the federal States have the highest and the final power of jurisdiction over state matters. They also exercise the jurisdiction of the Federal High Court. According to the Constitution, courts of any level are free from any interference or influence from government bodies, government officials or any other source. In addition, judges exercise their duties independently and are directed solely by the law.

Federal Supreme Court: Addis Ababa; tel. (11) 5448425; comprises civil, criminal and military sections; its jurisdiction extends to the supervision of all judicial proceedings throughout the country; the Supreme Court is also empowered to review cases upon which final rulings have been made by the courts (including the Supreme Court) where judicial errors have occurred; Pres. KEMAL BEDRI.

Federal High Court: POB 3483, Addis Ababa; tel. (11) 2751911; fax (11) 2755399; e-mail fedhc@telecom.net.et; hears appeals from the state courts; has original jurisdiction; Pres. ADIL AHMED.

Awraja Courts: regional courts composed of three judges, criminal and civil.

Warada Courts: sub-regional; one judge sits alone with very limited jurisdiction, criminal only.

Religion

About 45% of the population are Muslims and about 40% belong to the Ethiopian Orthodox (Tewahido) Church. There are also significant Evangelical Protestant and Roman Catholic communities. The Pentecostal Church and the Society of International Missionaries carry out mission work in Ethiopia. There are also Hindu and Sikh religious institutions. It has been estimated that 5%–15% of the population follow animist rites and beliefs.

CHRISTIANITY

Ethiopian Orthodox (Tewahido) Church

The Ethiopian Orthodox (Tewahido) Church is one of the five oriental orthodox churches. It was founded in AD 328, and in 1989 had more than 22m. members, 20,000 parishes and 290,000 clergy. The Supreme Body is the Holy Synod and the National Council, under the chairmanship of the Patriarch (Abune). The Church comprises 25 archdioceses and dioceses (including those in Jerusalem, Sudan, Djibouti and the Western Hemisphere). There are 32 Archbishops and Bishops. The Church administers 1,139 schools and 12 relief and rehabilitation centres throughout Ethiopia.

Patriarchate Head Office: POB 1283, Addis Ababa; tel. (11) 1116507; Patriarch (Abune) Archbishop PAULOS; Gen. Sec. L. M. DEMTSE GEBRE MEDHIN.

The Roman Catholic Church

At 31 December 2005 Ethiopia contained an estimated 66,464 adherents of the Alexandrian-Ethiopian Rite and 516,262 adherents of the Latin Rite.

Bishops' Conference: Ethiopian and Eritrean Episcopal Conference, POB 2454, Addis Ababa; tel. (11) 1550300; fax (11) 1553113; e-mail ecs@ethionet.et; internet www.ecs.org.et; f. 1966; Pres. Most Rev. BERHANEYESUS DEMEREW SOURAPHIEL (Metropolitan Archbishop of Addis Ababa).

Alexandrian-Ethiopian Rite

Adherents are served by one archdiocese (Addis Ababa) and two dioceses (Adigrat and Emdeber).

Archbishop of Addis Ababa: Most Rev. BERHANEYESUS DEMEREW SOURAPHIEL, Catholic Archbishop's House, POB 21903, Addis Ababa; tel. (11) 1111667; fax (11) 1551348; e-mail ecs@telecom.net.et.

Latin Rite

Adherents are served by the five Apostolic Vicariates of Awasa, Harar, Meki, Nekemte and Soddo-Hosanna, and by the Apostolic Prefectures of Gambela and Jimma-Bonga.

Other Christian Churches

The Anglican Communion: Within the Episcopal Church in Jerusalem and the Middle East, the Bishop in Egypt has jurisdiction over seven African countries, including Ethiopia.

Armenian Orthodox Church: St George's Armenian Church, POB 116, Addis Ababa; f. 1923; Deacon VARTKES NALBANDIAN.

Ethiopian Evangelical Church (Mekane Yesus): POB 2087, Addis Ababa; tel. (11) 5533293; fax (11) 5534148; e-mail amanuelandmeli@gmail.com; internet www.eecmy.org; Pres. Rev. ITEFFA GOBENA; f. 1959; affiliated to Lutheran World Fed., All Africa Confed. of Churches and World Council of Churches; c. 4.67m. mems (2006).

Greek Orthodox Church: POB 571, Addis Ababa; tel. and fax (11) 1226459; Metropolitan of Axum Most Rev. PETROS YIAKOUMELOS.

Seventh-day Adventist Church: POB 145, Addis Ababa; tel. (11) 5511319; e-mail info@ecd.adventist.org; internet www.ecd.adventist.org; f. 1907; Pres. TINSAE TOLESSA; 130,000 mems.

ISLAM

Leader: Haji MOHAMMED AHMAD.

JUDAISM

A phased emigration to Israel of about 27,000 Falashas (Ethiopian Jews) took place during 1984–91. In February 2003 the Israeli Government ruled that the Falashmura (Ethiopian Christians whose forefathers had converted from Judaism) had been forced to convert to Christianity to avoid religious persecution and that they had the right to settle in Israel. In January 2004 Ethiopia and Israel agreed to allow the Falashmura to be flown to Israel; some 17,000 Falashmura and a further 3,000 Falashas were expected to arrive in Israel by 2007.

The Press

DAILIES

Addis Zemen: POB 30145, Addis Ababa; f. 1941; Amharic; publ. by the Ministry of Information; circ. 40,000.

The Daily Monitor: POB 22588, Addis Ababa; tel. (11) 1560788; e-mail themonitor@telecom.net.et; f. 1993; English; Editor-in-Chief NAMRUD BERHANE TSAHAY; circ. 6,000.

Ethiopian Herald: POB 30701, Addis Ababa; tel. (11) 5156690; f. 1943; English; publ. by the Ministry of Information; Editor-in-Chief TSEGIE GEBRE-AMLAK; circ. 37,000.

PERIODICALS

Abyotawit Ethiopia: POB 2549, Addis Ababa; fortnightly; Amharic.

Addis Tribune: Tambek International, POB 2395, Addis Ababa; tel. (11) 6615228; fax (11) 6615227; e-mail tambek@telecom.net.et; internet www.addistribune.com; f. 1992; weekly; English; Editor-in-Chief YOHANNES RUPHAEL; circ. 6,000.

Addis Zimit: POB 2395, Addis Ababa; tel. (11) 1118613; fax (11) 1552110; f. 1993; weekly; Amharic; Editor-in-Chief (vacant); circ. 8,000.

Al-Alem: POB 30232, Addis Ababa; tel. (11) 5158046; fax (11) 5516819; f. 1941; weekly; Arabic; publ. by the Ministry of Information; Editor-in-Chief TELSOM AHMED; circ. 2,500.

Asqual: Editor-in-Chief DAWIT FASSIL.

Berisa: POB 30232, Addis Ababa; f. 1976; weekly; Oromogna; publ. by the Ministry of Information; Editor BULO SIBA; circ. 3,500.

Beza: Addis Ababa; weekly; Editor-in-Chief YARED KEMFE.

Birhan Family Magazine: Addis Ababa; monthly; women's magazine.

Birritu: National Bank of Ethiopia, POB 5550, Addis Ababa; tel. (11) 5530040; fax (11) 5514588; e-mail birritu@ethionet.et; internet www.nbe.gov.et; f. 1982; quarterly; Amharic and English; banking,

ETHIOPIA

insurance and macroeconomic news; circ. 2,500; Editor-in-Chief SEMENEH ADGE; Editor MULUGETA AYALEW.

Capital: POB 95, Addis Ababa; tel. (11) 5531759; fax (11) 5533323; e-mail syscom@telecom.net.et; internet www.capitalethiopia.com; f. 1998; weekly; Sunday; publ. by the Ministry of Trade and Industry; business and economics; Editor-in-Chief BEHAILU DESALEGN.

Ethiopian Reporter: Woreda 19, Kebele 56, House No. 221, POB 7023, Addis Ababa; tel. and fax (11) 4421517; e-mail mcc@telecom.net.et; internet www.ethiopianreporter.com; weekly; English and Amharic.

Ethiopis Review: Editor-in-Chief TESFERA ASMARE.

Mabruk: Addis Ababa; weekly; Editor-in-Chief TESAHALENNE MENGESHA.

Maebel: Addis Ababa; weekly; Amharic; Editor-in-Chief ABERA WOGI.

Menilik: Editor-in-Chief ZELALEM GEBRE.

Meskerem: Addis Ababa; quarterly; theoretical politics; circ. 100,000.

Negarit Gazeta: POB 1031, Addis Ababa; irregularly; Amharic and English; official gazette.

Nigdina Limat: POB 2458, Addis Ababa; tel. (11) 5513882; fax (11) 5511479; e-mail aachamber1@telecom.net.et; monthly; Amharic; publ. by the Addis Ababa (Ethiopia) Chamber of Commerce; circ. 6,000.

Press Digest: POB 12719, Addis Ababa; tel. (11) 5504200; fax (11) 5513523; e-mail phoenix.universal@telecom.net.et; f. 1993; weekly.

Satenaw: Editor-in-Chief TAMRAT SERBESA.

Tequami: Addis Ababa; weekly; Editor-in-Chief SAMSON SEYUM.

Tinsae (Resurrection): Addis Ababa; tel. (1) 116507; Amharic and English; publ. by the Ethiopian Orthodox Church.

Tobia Magazine: POB 22373, Addis Ababa; tel. (11) 1556177; fax (11) 1552654; monthly; Amharic; Man. GOSHU MOGES; circ. 30,000.

Tobia Newspaper: POB 22373, Addis Ababa; tel. (11) 1556177; fax (11) 1552654; e-mail akpac@telecom.net.et; weekly; Amharic; Man. GOSHU MOGES; circ. 25,000.

Tomar: Benishangul; weekly; Amharic; Editor-in-Chief BEFEKADU MOREDA.

Wetaderna Alamaw: POB 1901, Addis Ababa; fortnightly; Amharic.

Yezareitu Ethiopia (Ethiopia Today): POB 30232, Addis Ababa; weekly; Amharic and English; publ. by the Ministry of Information; Editor-in-Chief IMIRU WORKU; circ. 30,000.

NEWS AGENCY

Ethiopian News Agency (ENA): Patriot St, POB 530, Addis Ababa; tel. (11) 1550011; fax (11) 1551609; e-mail feedback@ena.gov.et; internet www.ena.gov.et; f. 1942; Chair NETSANET ASFAW.

PRESS ASSOCIATIONS

Ethiopian Free Press Journalists' Association (EFJA): POB 31317, Addis Ababa; tel. and fax (11) 1555021; e-mail efja@telecom.net.et; f. 1993; granted legal recognition in 2000; activities suspended in late 2003; Pres. KIFLE MULAT.

Ethiopian Journalists' Association: POB 30288, Addis Ababa; tel. (11) 1117852; fax (11) 5513365; Pres. KEFALE MAMMO.

Publishers

Addis Ababa University Press: POB 1176, Addis Ababa; tel. (11) 1119148; fax (11) 1550655; f. 1968; educational and reference works in English, general books in English and Amharic; Editor MESSELECH HABTE.

Berhanena Selam Printing Enterprise: POB 980, Addis Ababa; tel. (11) 1553233; fax (11) 1553939; f. 1921; fmrly Govt Printing Press; publishes and prints newspapers, periodicals, books, security prints and other miscellaneous commercial prints; Gen. Man. MULUWORK G. HIWOT.

Educational Materials Production and Distribution Enterprise (EMPDE): POB 5549, Addis Ababa; tel. (11) 6463555; fax (11) 6461295; f. 1999; textbook publishers.

Ethiopia Book Centre: POB 1024, Addis Ababa; tel. (11) 1123336; f. 1977; privately owned; publr, importer, wholesaler and retailer of educational books.

Kuraz Publishing Agency: POB 30933, Addis Ababa; tel. (11) 1551688; state-owned.

Mega Publishing: POB 423, Addis Ababa; tel. (11) 1571714; fax (11) 1571715; general publishers.

Broadcasting and Communications

TELECOMMUNICATIONS

Ethiopian Telecommunication Agency (ETA): Bekelobet, Tegene Bldg, Kirkos District, Kebele 02/03, House No. 542, POB 9991, Addis Ababa; tel. (11) 4668282; fax (11) 4655763; e-mail tele.agency@ethionet.et; internet www.eta.gov.et; aims to promote the devt of high quality, efficient, reliable and affordable telecommunication services in Ethiopia; Dir-Gen. ESHETU ALEMU.

Ethiopian Telecommunications Corpn (ETC): POB 1047, Addis Ababa; tel. (11) 5510500; fax (11) 5515777; e-mail etc-hq@ethionet.et; internet www.ethionet.et; f. 1894; CEO AMARE AMSALU; Chair. DEBRE TSION GEBRE MICHAEL; CEO AMARE AMSALU.

BROADCASTING

Radio

Radio Ethiopia: POB 654, Addis Ababa; tel. (11) 1551011; internet www.angelfire.com/biz/radioethiopia; f. 1941; Amharic, English, French, Arabic, Afar, Oromifa, Tigre, Tigrinya and Somali; Gen. Man. KASA MILOKO.

Radio Torch: POB 30702, Addis Ababa; f. 1994; Amharic; operated by the EPRDF; Gen. Man. MULUGETA GESEE.

Radio Voice of One Free Ethiopia: broadcasts twice a week; Amharic; opposes current Govts of Ethiopia and Eritrea.

Voice of the Revolution of Tigrai: POB 450, Mekele; tel. (34) 4410545; fax (34) 4405485; e-mail vort@telecom.net.et; f. 1985; Tigrinya and Afargna; broadcasts 57 hours per week; supports Tigrai People's Liberation Front.

Television

Ethiopian Television (ETV): POB 5544, Addis Ababa; tel. (11) 5155326; fax (11) 5512685; e-mail etv2@ethionet.et; f. 1964; semi-autonomous station; accepts commercial advertising; programmes transmitted from Addis Ababa to 26 regional stations; Chair. BEREKET SIMON; Gen. Man. SELOME TADDESSE.

Finance

(cap. = capital; res = reserves; dep. = deposits; m. = million; br(s). = branch(es); amounts in birr)

BANKING

Central Bank

National Bank of Ethiopia: POB 5550, Addis Ababa; tel. (11) 5517430; fax (11) 5514588; e-mail beknbe@yahoo.com; internet www.nbe.gov.et; f. 1964; bank of issue; cap. 50.0m., res 2,356.4m., dep. 12,138.4m. (June 2002); Gov. TEKLEWOLD ATNAFU; Vice-Gov. ALEMSEGED ASSEFA; 1 br.

Other Banks

Awash International Bank SC: Africa Ave, POB 12638, Addis Ababa; tel. (11) 6614482; fax (11) 6614477; e-mail awash.bank@telecom.net.et; internet www.awash-bank.com; f. 1994; cap. 110.1m., res 20.4m., dep. 1,042.9m. (Dec. 2002); Chair. and Pres. HAMBISSA WAKWAYA; 32 brs.

Bank of Abyssinia: POB 12947, Addis Ababa; tel. (11) 5530663; fax (11) 5510409; e-mail abyssinia@ethionet.et; internet www.bankofabyssinia.com; f. 1905; closed 1935 and reopened 1996; commercial banking services; cap. 264.7m., res 71.4m., dep. 2,176.9m., total assets 3,014.1m. (June 2006); Chair. ASSELEFECH MULUGETA; 29 brs.

Commercial Bank of Ethiopia: Unity Sq., POB 255, Addis Ababa; tel. (11) 5511271; fax (11) 5514522; e-mail cbemrk@ethionet.et; internet www.combanketh.com; f. 1943; reorg. 1996; state-owned; cap. 619.7m., res 606.5m., dep. 19,514.9m. (June 2003); Chair. MEKONNEM MANYAZEWAL; Pres. GEZAHEGN YILMA DANTEW; 175 brs.

Construction and Business Bank: Higher 21, Kebele 04, POB 3480, Addis Ababa; tel. (11) 5512300; fax (11) 5515103; e-mail cbbsics@ethionet.et; internet www.cbb.com.et; f. 1975 as Housing and Savings Bank; provides credit for construction projects and a range of commercial banking services; state-owned; cap. and res 80.8m., total assets 1,019.1m. (June 2003); Chair. TADESSE HAILE; Gen. Man. ADDISU HABBA; 20 brs.

Dashen Bank: Garad Bldg, Debre Zeit Rd, POB 12752, Addis Ababa; tel. (11) 4661380; fax (11) 4653037; e-mail dashen.bank@ethionet.et; internet www.dashenbanksc.com; f. 1995; share company; cap. 484m., dep. 4,900m. (June 2007); Pres. LULSEGED TEFERI; Chair. TEKLU HAILE; 44 brs.

Development Bank of Ethiopia: Zosip Broz Tito St, POB 1900, Addis Ababa; tel. (11) 5511188; fax (11) 5511606; provides devt finance for industry and agriculture, technical advice and assistance in project evaluation; state-owned; cap. and res 418.8m., total assets 3,163.2m. (June 2002); Chair. ABI W. MESKEL; Gen. Man. WONDWOSSEN TESHOME; 32 brs.

NIB International Bank SC: Africa Avenue, Dembel City Centre, POB 2439, Addis Ababa; tel. (11) 5503288; fax (11) 5504349; internet www.addischamber.com/nibbank.htm; f. 1999; cap. 285.0m., res 44.7m., dep. 1451.8m. (June 2006); Chair. LEMMA H. GIORGISS; Pres. AMERGA KASSA; 27 brs.

United Bank: Mekwor Plaza Bldg, Debe Zeit Rd, POB 19963, Addis Ababa; tel. (11) 4655222; fax (11) 4655243; e-mail hibretbank@telecom.net.et; f. 1998; commercial banking services; cap. and res 96m., dep. 532.7m. (June 2004); Chair. EYESSUS W. ZAFU; Pres. ADMASSU TECHANE; 14 brs.

Wegagen Bank: POB 1018, Addis Ababa; tel. (11) 5532800; fax (11) 5523521; e-mail wagagen@ethionet.et; internet www.wegagenbank.com.et; f. 1997; commercial banking services; cap. 95.4m., total assets 1,660m. (Feb. 2004); Chair. WONDWOSSON KEBEDE; CEO KIDANE NIKODIMOS; 23 brs.

Bankers' Association

Ethiopian Bankers' Association: Addis Ababa; f. 2001; Pres. LEIKUN BERHANU.

INSURANCE

Africa Insurance Co: POB 12941, Addis Ababa; tel. (11) 6637716; fax (11) 6638253; e-mail africains@ethionet.et; internet www.africainsurance.com.et; f. 1994; Gen. Man. KITOS JIRANIE.

Awash Insurance Co: POB 12637, Addis Ababa; tel. (11) 6614420; fax (11) 6614419; Gen. Man. TSEGAYE KEMAS.

Ethiopian Insurance Corpn: POB 2545, Addis Ababa; tel. (11) 5512400; fax (11) 5517499; e-mail eic.mdxvs@ethionet.et; internet www.eic.com.et; f. 1976; life, property and legal liabilities insurance cover; Man. Dir TEWODROS TILAHUN.

Global Insurance SC: POB 180112, Addis Abba; tel. (11) 1567400; fax (11) 1566200; e-mail globalinsu@ethionet.et; f. 1997; cap. 16.8m.; Man. Dir AHMED IBRAHIM; 8 brs; 86 employees.

National Insurance Co of Ethiopia: POB 12645, Addis Ababa; tel. (11) 4661129; fax (11) 4650660; e-mail nice@telecom.net.et; Man. Dir and CEO HABTEMATIAM SHUMGIZAW.

Nile Insurance Co: POB 12836, Addis Ababa; tel. (11) 5537709; fax (11) 5514592; e-mail nileinsu@mail.telecom.net.et; f. 1995; Gen. Man. MAHTSENTU FELEKE.

Nyala Insurance SC: Mickey Leland St, POB 12753, Addis Ababa; tel. (11) 6626667; fax (11) 6626706; e-mail nisco@telecom.net.et; internet www.nyalainsurance.com; Man. Dir NAHU-SENAYE ARAYA.

United Insurance Co SC: POB 1156, Addis Ababa; tel. (11) 5515656; fax (11) 5513258; e-mail united.insurance@telecom.net.et; Chair. GETAMESSAY DEGEFU; Man. Dir IYESUSWORK ZAFU.

Trade and Industry

CHAMBERS OF COMMERCE

Ethiopian Chamber of Commerce and Sectorial Associations: Mexico Sq., POB 517, Addis Ababa; tel. (11) 5514005; fax (11) 5517699; e-mail ethchamb@ethionet.et; internet www.ethiopianchamber.com; f. 1947; regional chambers in 11 localities; Pres. GETACHEW AYENEW; Sec.-Gen. YOSEIF TESFAYE.

Addis Ababa Chamber of Commerce: POB 2458, Addis Ababa; tel. (11) 5513882; fax (11) 5511479; e-mail AAchamber1@telecom.net.et; internet www.addischamber.com; Chair. BERHANE MEWA; Sec.-Gen. SEMUNESH DEMETROS.

INDUSTRIAL AND TRADE ASSOCIATIONS

Ethiopian Beverages Corpn: POB 1285, Addis Ababa; tel. (11) 6186185; Gen. Man. MENNA TEWAHEDE.

Ethiopian Cement Corpn: POB 5782, Addis Ababa; tel. (11) 1552222; fax (11) 1551572; Gen. Man. REDI GEMAL.

Ethiopian Chemical Corpn: POB 5747, Addis Ababa; tel. (11) 6184305; Gen. Man. ASNAKE SAHLU.

Ethiopian Coffee Export Enterprise: POB 2591, Addis Ababa; tel. (11) 5515330; fax (11) 5510762; f. 1977; Chair. SUFIAN AHMED; Gen. Man. DERGA GURMESSA.

Ethiopian Food Corpn: Addis Ababa; tel. (11) 5518522; fax (11) 5513173; f. 1975; produces and distributes food items, including edible oil, ghee substitute, pasta, bread, maize, wheat flour, etc.; Gen. Man. BEKELE HAILE.

Ethiopian Fruit and Vegetable Marketing Enterprise: POB 2374, Addis Ababa; tel. (11) 5519192; fax (11) 5516483; f. 1980; sole wholesale domestic distributor and exporter of fresh and processed fruit and vegetables, and floricultural products; Gen. Man. KAKNU PEWONDE.

Ethiopian Grain Trade Enterprise: POB 3321, Addis Ababa; tel. (11) 4652436; fax (11) 4652792; e-mail egte@ethionet.et; Gen. Man. BERHANE HAILU.

Ethiopian Handicrafts and Small-Scale Industries Development Agency: Addis Ababa; tel. (11) 5157366; f. 1977.

Ethiopian Horticulture Producers and Exporters Association (EHPEA): Haile Selassie Ave, opp. WARYT Bldg, Gelila Bldg, 2nd Floor; POB 22241, Addis Ababa; tel. (11) 6636751; fax (11) 6636753; e-mail ehpea@ethionet.et; internet www.ehpea.org.et; f. 2002; 66 mems; Pres. TSEGAYE ABEBE.

Ethiopian Import and Export Corpn (ETIMEX): Addis Ababa; tel. (11) 5511112; fax (11) 5515411; f. 1975; state trading corpn under the supervision of the Ministry of Trade and Industry; import of building materials, foodstuffs, stationery and office equipment, textiles, clothing, chemicals, general merchandise, capital goods; Gen. Man. ASCHENAKI G. HIWOT.

Ethiopian Oil Seeds and Pulses Export Corpn: POB 5719, Addis Ababa; tel. (11) 1550597; fax (11) 1553299; f. 1975; Gen. Man. ABDOURUHMAN MOHAMMED.

Ethiopia Peasants' Association (EPA): f. 1978 to promote improved agricultural techniques, home industries, education, public health and self-reliance; comprises 30,000 peasant asscns with c. 7m. mems; Chair. (vacant).

Ethiopian Petroleum Enterprise: POB 3375, Addis Ababa; tel. and fax (11) 5512938; f. 1976; Gen. Man. YIGZAW MEKONNEN.

Ethiopian Pharmaceuticals and Medical Supplies Corpn (EPHARMECOR): POB 21904, Addis Ababa; tel. (11) 2134577; fax (11) 2752555; f. 1976; manufacture, import, export and distribution of pharmaceuticals, chemicals, dressings, surgical and dental instruments, hospital and laboratory supplies; Gen. Man. GIRMA BEPASSO.

Ethiopian Sugar Corpn: POB 133, Addis Ababa; tel. (11) 5519700; fax (11) 5513488; Gen. Man. ABATE LEMENGH.

Green Star Food Co LLC: POB 5579, Addis Ababa; tel. (11) 5526588; fax (11) 5526599; e-mail greenstar@telecom.net.et; f. 1984; fmrly the Ethiopian Livestock and Meat Corpn; production and marketing of canned and frozen foods; Gen. Man. DAWIT BEKELE.

National Leather and Shoe Corpn: POB 2516, Addis Ababa; tel. (11) 5514075; fax (11) 5513525; f. 1975; produces and sells semi-processed hides and skins, finished leather, leather goods and footwear; Gen. Man. GIRMA W. AREGAI.

National Textiles Corpn: POB 2446, Addis Ababa; tel. (11) 5157316; fax (11) 5511955; f. 1975; production of yarn, fabrics, knitwear, blankets, bags, etc.; Gen. Man. FIKRE HUGIANE.

Natural Gum Processing and Marketing Enterprise: POB 62322, Addis Ababa; tel. (11) 5527082; fax (11) 5518110; e-mail natgum@ethionet.et; internet www.naturalgum.ebigchina.com; f. 1976; state-owned; Gen. Man. TEKLEHAIMANOT NIGATU BEYENE.

UTILITIES

Electricity

Ethiopian Electric Power Corpn (EEPCO): De Gaulle Sq., POB 1233, Addis Ababa; tel. (11) 1560042; fax (11) 1550822; e-mail eelpa@telecom.net.et; internet www.eepco.gov.et; Chair. HAILEMELEKOT TEKLE GIORGIS; Gen. Man. MIHRET DEBEBE.

Water

Addis Ababa Water and Sewerage Authority: POB 1505; Addis Ababa; tel. (11) 6623902; fax (11) 6623924; e-mail aawsa.ha@ethionet.et; f. 1971; Gen. Man. H. GIORGIS GETACHEW ESHETE.

Water Resources Development Authority: POB 1045, Addis Ababa; tel. (11) 6612999; fax (11) 6611245; Gen. Man. GETACHEW GIZAW.

TRADE UNION

Confederation of Ethiopian Trade Unions (CETU): POB 3653, Addis Ababa; tel. (11) 5155473; fax (11) 5514532; e-mail cetu@telecom.net.et; f. 1975; comprises nine industrial unions and 22 regional unions with a total membership of 320,000 (1987); President KASAHUN FULLO.

Transport

RAILWAYS

Chemin de Fer Djibouti-Ethiopien (CDE): POB 1051, Addis Ababa; tel. (11) 5517250; fax (11) 5513533; f. 1909; adopted present

ETHIOPIA   *Directory*

name in 1981; jtly owned by Govts of Ethiopia and Djibouti; 781 km of track (660 km in Ethiopia), linking Addis Ababa with Djibouti; Pres. ISMAIL IBRAHIM HOUMED.

ROADS

In 2004 the total road network comprised an estimated 36,469 km of primary, secondary and feeder roads, of which 6,980 km were paved, the remainder being gravel roads. In addition, there are some 30,000 km of unclassified tracks and trails. A highway links Addis Ababa with Nairobi in Kenya, forming part of the Trans-East Africa Highway. In mid-2003 work commenced on the second phase of the Road Sector Development Programme, which aimed to upgrade 80% and 63% of paved and gravel roads, respectively, to an acceptable condition by 2007.

Comet Transport SC: POB 2402, Addis Ababa; tel. (11) 4403963; fax (11) 4426024; e-mail cometrans@telecom.net.et; f. 1994; Gen. Man. FELEKE YIMER.

Ethiopian Freight Transport Corpn: POB 2538, Addis Ababa; tel. (11) 5515211; fax (11) 5519740; restructured into five autonomous enterprises in 1994.

Ethiopian Road Transport Authority: POB 2504, Addis Ababa; tel. (11) 5510244; fax (11) 5510715; e-mail kasahun_khmariam@yahoo.com; enforces road transport regulations, promotes road safety, registers vehicles and issues driving licences; Gen. Man. KASAHUN H. MARIAM.

Ethiopian Roads Authority: POB 1770, Addis Ababa; tel. (11) 5517170; fax (11) 5514866; e-mail era2@ethionet.et; internet www.era.gov.et; f. 1951; construction and maintenance of roads, bridges and airports; Dir-Gen. ZAID WOLDE GEBREAL.

Public Transport Corpn: POB 5780, Addis Ababa; tel. (11) 5153117; fax (11) 5510720; f. 1977; urban bus services in Addis Ababa and Jimma, and services between towns; restructured into three autonomous enterprises in 1994 and scheduled for privatization; Man. Dir AHMED NURU.

SHIPPING

The formerly Ethiopian-controlled ports of Massawa and Assab now lie within the boundaries of the State of Eritrea (q.v.). Although an agreement exists between the two Governments allowing Ethiopian access to the two ports, which can handle more than 1m. metric tons of merchandise annually, in mid-1998 Ethiopia ceased using the ports, owing to the outbreak of hostilities. Ethiopia's maritime trade currently passes through Djibouti (in the Republic of Djibouti), and also through the Kenyan port of Mombasa. An agreement was also signed in July 2003 to allow Ethiopia to use Port Sudan (in Sudan). At 31 December 2006 Ethiopia's registered merchant fleet numbered nine vessels, with a total displacement of 99,912 grt.

Ethiopian Shipping Lines Corpn: POB 2572, Addis Ababa; tel. (11) 5518280; fax (11) 5519525; e-mail esl@telecom.net.et; internet www.ethiopianshippinglines.com.et; f. 1964; serves Red Sea, Europe, Mediterranean, Gulf and Far East with its own fleet and chartered vessels; Chair. GETACHEW BELAY; Gen. Man. AMBACHEW ABRAHA.

Marine Transport Authority: Ministry of Infrastructure, POB 1238, Addis Ababa; tel. (11) 5158227; fax (11) 5515665; f. 1993; regulates maritime transport services; Dept Head ASKAL W. GEORGIS.

Maritime and Transit Services Enterprise: POB 1186, Addis Ababa; tel. (11) 5517564; fax (11) 5518197; e-mail mtse@telecom.net.et; internet www.telecom.net/~mtse; f. 1979; services include stevedoring, storehandling, bagging, forwarding and trucking; Chair. GETACHEW GEBRE; Gen. Man. AHMED YASSIN.

CIVIL AVIATION

Ethiopia has two international airports (at Addis Ababa and Dire Dawa) and around 40 airfields. Bole International Airport in the capital handles 95% of international air traffic and 85% of domestic flights. A programme to modernize the airport, at an estimated cost of 819m. birr (US $130m.), was undertaken during 1997–2001. Construction of airports at Axum, Lalibela and Gondar was completed in April 2000.

Ethiopian Airlines: Bole International Airport, POB 1755, Addis Ababa; tel. (11) 6612222; fax (11) 6611474; e-mail publicrelations@ethiopianairlines.com; internet www.flyethiopian.com; f. 1945; operates regular domestic services and flights to 47 international destinations in Africa, Europe, Middle East, Asia and the USA; Chair. SEYOUM MESFIN; CEO GIRMA WAKE.

Ethiopian Civil Aviation Authority: POB 978, Addis Ababa; tel. (11) 6650252; fax (11) 6650269; e-mail civil.aviation@ethionet.et; regulatory authority; provides air navigational facilities; Dir-Gen. MESFIN FIKRU.

Tourism

Ethiopia's tourist attractions include the early Christian monuments and churches, the ancient capitals of Gondar and Axum, the Blue Nile (or Tississat) Falls and the National Parks of the Simien and Bale Mountains. Tourist arrivals in 2005 totalled 227,398. In that year receipts from tourism (including passenger transport) amounted to US $533m.

Ministry of Culture and Tourism: POB 2183, Addis Ababa; tel. (11) 5512310; fax (11) 5512889; e-mail info@tourismethiopia.org; internet www.tourismethiopia.org.

FIJI

Introductory Survey

Location, Climate, Language, Religion, Flag, Capital

The Republic of Fiji comprises more than 300 islands, of which 100 are inhabited, situated about 1,930 km (1,200 miles) south of the equator in the Pacific Ocean. The four main islands are Viti Levu (on which almost 70% of the country's population lives), Vanua Levu, Taveuni and Kadavu. The climate is tropical, with temperatures ranging from 16°C to 32°C (60°F–90°F). Rainfall is heavy on the windward side. Fijian and Hindi are the principal languages but English is also widely spoken. In 1996 about 58% of the population were Christians (mainly Methodists), 34% Hindus and 7% Muslims. The national flag (proportions 1 by 2) is light blue, with the United Kingdom flag as a canton in the upper hoist. In the fly is the main part of Fiji's national coat of arms: a white field quartered by a red upright cross, the quarters containing sugar canes, a coconut palm, a stem of bananas and a dove bearing an olive branch; in chief is a red panel with a yellow crowned lion holding a white cocoa pod. The capital is Suva, on Viti Levu.

Recent History

The first Europeans to settle on the islands were sandalwood traders, missionaries and shipwrecked sailors, and in October 1874 Fiji was proclaimed a British possession. In September 1966 the British Government introduced a new Constitution for Fiji. It provided for a ministerial form of government, an almost wholly elected Legislative Council and the introduction of universal adult suffrage. Rather than using a common roll of voters, however, the Constitution introduced an electoral system that combined communal (Fijian and Indian) rolls with cross-voting. In September 1967 the Executive Council became the Council of Ministers, with Ratu Kamisese Mara, leader of the multiracial (but predominantly Fijian) Alliance Party (AP), as Fiji's first Chief Minister. Following a constitutional conference in April–May 1970, Fiji achieved independence, within the Commonwealth, on 10 October 1970. The Legislative Council was renamed the House of Representatives, and a second parliamentary chamber, the nominated Senate, was established. The British-appointed Governor became Fiji's first Governor-General, while Ratu Sir Kamisese Mara (as he had become in 1969) took office as Prime Minister.

Fiji was, however, troubled by racial tensions. Although the descendants of indentured Indian workers who were brought to Fiji in the late 19th century had grown to outnumber the native inhabitants, they were discriminated against in political representation and land ownership rights. A new electoral system was adopted in 1970 to ensure a racial balance in the legislature.

At the general election held in March and April 1977 the National Federation Party (NFP), traditionally supported by the Indian population, won 26 of the 52 seats in the House of Representatives, but was unable to form a government and subsequently split into two factions. The AP governed in a caretaker capacity until the holding of a further general election in September, when it was returned with its largest-ever majority. While the two main parties professed multiracial ideas, the Fijian Nationalist Party campaigned in support of its 'Fiji for the Fijians' programme in order to foster nationalist sentiment.

In 1980 Ratu Sir Kamisese Mara's suggestion that a Government of National Unity be formed was overshadowed by renewed political disagreement between the AP and the NFP (whose two factions had drawn closer together again) over land ownership. Fijians owned 83% of the land and were strongly defending their traditional rights, while the Indian population was pressing for greater security of land tenure. The general election held in July 1982 was also dominated by racial issues. The AP retained power after winning 28 seats, but its majority had been reduced from 20 to four. The NFP won 22 seats and the Western United Front (WUF), which professed a multiracial outlook, took the remaining two seats.

A meeting of union leaders in May 1985 represented the beginning of discussions that culminated in the founding of the Fiji Labour Party (FLP), officially inaugurated in Suva in July. Sponsored by the Fiji Trades Union Congress (FTUC), and under the presidency of Dr Timoci Bavadra, the new party was formed with the aim of presenting a more effective parliamentary opposition, and declared the provision of free education and a national medical scheme to be among its priorities. The FLP hoped to work through farmers' organizations to win votes among rural electorates, which traditionally supported the NFP. During 1985–86 disagreements between the Government and the FTUC over economic policies became increasingly acrimonious, leading to an outbreak of labour unrest and the withdrawal, in June 1986, of government recognition of the FTUC as the unions' representative organization.

At a general election in April 1987 a coalition of the FLP and NFP won 28 seats (19 of which were secured by ethnic Indian candidates) in the House of Representatives, thus defeating the ruling AP, which won only 24 seats. The new Government, led by Bavadra, was therefore the first in Fijian history to contain a majority of ministers of Indian, rather than Melanesian, origin, although Bavadra himself was of Melanesian descent. On 14 May, however, the Government was overthrown by a military coup, led by Lt-Col (later Maj.-Gen.) Sitiveni Rabuka. The Governor-General, Ratu Sir Penaia Ganilau, responded by declaring a state of emergency and appointed a 19-member advisory council, including Bavadra and Rabuka. However, Bavadra refused to participate in the council, denouncing it as unconstitutional and biased in its composition.

Widespread racial violence followed the coup, and there were several public demands for Bavadra's reinstatement as Prime Minister. In July 1987 the Great Council of Fijian Chiefs, comprising the country's 70 hereditary Melanesian leaders, approved plans for constitutional reform. In September negotiations began, on the initiative of Ganilau, between delegations led by the two former Prime Ministers, Bavadra and Mara, to resolve the political crisis. On 22 September it was announced that the two factions had agreed to form an interim bipartisan Government.

On 25 September 1987, however, before the new plan could be implemented, Rabuka staged a second coup and announced his intention to declare Fiji a republic. Despite Ganilau's refusal to recognize the seizure of power, Rabuka revoked the Constitution on 1 October and proclaimed himself Head of State, thus deposing the Queen. Ganilau conceded defeat and resigned as Governor-General. At a meeting in Canada, Commonwealth Heads of Government formally declared that Fiji's membership of the Commonwealth had lapsed. An interim Cabinet, comprising mainly ethnic Fijians, was installed by Rabuka. In late October Rabuka announced that he would resign as Head of State as soon as he had appointed a new President of the Republic. Several cases of violations of human rights by the Fijian army were reported, as the regime assumed powers of detention without trial and suspended all political activity.

On 6 December 1987 Rabuka resigned as Head of State. Although he had previously refused to accept the post, Ganilau, the former Governor-General, became the first President of the Fijian Republic. Mara was reappointed Prime Minister, and Rabuka became Minister of Home Affairs. A new interim Cabinet was announced on 9 December, containing 11 members of Rabuka's administration, but no member of Bavadra's deposed Government.

In February 1988 Rotuma (the only Polynesian island in the country), which lies to the north-west of Vanua Levu, declared itself politically independent of Fiji, whose newly acquired republican status it refused to recognize. Fijian troops were dispatched to the island, however, and soon quelled the dissent.

A new draft Constitution was approved by the interim Government in September 1988. The proposed Constitution was rejected, however, by a multiracial constitutional committee, which considered unnecessary the specific reservation of the principal offices of state for ethnic Fijians. In September 1989 the committee published a revised draft, which was still, however, condemned by Bavadra and the FLP-NFP coalition. In November Bavadra died and was replaced as leader of the FLP-NFP coalition by his widow, Adi Kuini Bavadra.

In January 1990 Rabuka resigned from the Cabinet and returned to his military duties. Mara agreed to remain as Prime

Minister until the restoration of constitutional government. In June the Great Council of Chiefs approved the draft Constitution. At the same time, the Great Council of Chiefs stated its intention to form a new party, the Soqosoqo ni Vakavulewa ni Taukei (SVT) or Fijian Political Party, to advocate the cause of ethnic Fijians. The new Constitution was finally promulgated on 25 July by President Ganilau, and was immediately condemned by the FLP-NFP coalition, which announced that it would boycott any elections held in accordance with the Constitution's provisions. Angered by the fact that a legislative majority was guaranteed to ethnic Fijians (who were reserved 37 of the 70 elective seats, compared with 27 Indian seats), and that the Great Council of Chiefs was to nominate ethnic Fijians to 24 of the 34 seats in the Senate and to appoint the President of the Republic, the opposition organized anti-Constitution demonstrations. The new Constitution was similarly condemned for its racial bias by India, New Zealand and Australia at the UN General Assembly, meeting in New York in October. In May 1991 the Commonwealth stated that Fiji would not be readmitted to the organization until it changed its Constitution.

In July 1991 Rabuka resigned as Commander of the Armed Forces in order to rejoin the Cabinet as Deputy Prime Minister and Minister of Home Affairs, although towards the end of 1991 he relinquished the post in order to assume the leadership of the SVT.

Disagreements between the Government and the FTUC re-emerged at the beginning of 1991. In February a strike by more than 900 members of the Fijian Miners' Union over union recognition, pay and poor working conditions led to the dismissal of some 400 of the workers. In May the Government announced a series of reforms to the labour laws, including the abolition of the minimum wage, restrictions on strike action and derecognition of unions that did not represent at least two-thirds of the workforce. A significant political development announced by the Government in late 1992 was the official recognition of the FTUC (withheld since 1986) as the sole representative of workers in Fiji.

At legislative elections in May 1992 the SVT secured 30 of the 37 seats reserved for ethnic Fijians, while the NFP won 14 and the FLP 13 of the seats reserved for Indian representatives. Following the election, the FLP agreed to participate in Parliament and to support Rabuka in his campaign for the premiership, in return for a guarantee from the SVT of a full review of the Constitution and of trade union and land laws. Rabuka was, therefore, appointed Prime Minister and formed a coalition Government (consisting of 14 members of the SVT and five others).

Remarks made by the Prime Minister in an Australian television interview in October 1992, expressing his implicit support for the repatriation of Fijian Indians, attracted controversy and prompted renewed fears that any reform of the Constitution would be merely superficial. Nevertheless, in December Rabuka formally invited the opposition leaders, Jai Ram Reddy of the NFP and Mahendra Chaudhry of the FLP (formerly the National Secretary of the FTUC), to form a Government of National Unity. The move was largely welcomed, but Indian politicians expressed reluctance to take part in a government whose political control remained fundamentally vested with ethnic Fijians. Rabuka was criticized equally by nationalist extremists of the Taukei Solidarity Movement, who accused him of conceding too much political power to Fijian Indians. Following the appointment of a new Cabinet in June, all 13 of the FLP legislative members began an indefinite boycott of Parliament, in protest at Rabuka's failure to implement the reforms which he had agreed to carry out in return for their support for his election to the premiership in June 1992.

In December 1993 President Ganilau died, following a long illness, and was replaced by Ratu Sir Kamisese Mara, who took office on 18 January 1994 (and was re-elected on 18 January 1999).

At legislative elections held in February 1994 the SVT increased the number of its seats in the House of Representatives to 31, while the Fijian Association Party (FAP, established in January by former members of the SVT) secured only five seats, of a total of 37 reserved for ethnic Fijians. Of the 27 seats reserved for ethnic Indian representatives, 20 were secured by the NFP. The SVT subsequently formed a governing coalition with the General Voters' Party (GVP, which represented the interests of the General Electors—i.e. the minority Chinese and European communities and people from elsewhere in the Pacific region resident in Fiji) and an independent member, under the premiership of Rabuka, who announced the formation of a new Cabinet composed entirely of ethnic Fijians. In response to international concern regarding the continued existence of Fiji's racially biased Constitution, Rabuka announced in June that a Constitutional Review Commission had been established, which, it was hoped, would have completed a review of the Constitution by 1997.

In January 1995 the Government announced that it was to recommend that Parliament vote to repeal the Sunday observance law (imposed after the coups of 1987), which prohibited work, organized entertainment and sport on that day. It was believed that the law had become increasingly unpopular, particularly among the Indian community. However, the announcement aroused intense opposition from nationalist politicians and Methodist church leaders, who organized demonstrations in three cities, attended by more than 12,000 people. In February 1995, however, the House of Representatives voted in favour of removing the regulations. The Senate narrowly rejected the proposal, thus effectively delaying the implementation of any changes. The Sunday observance law was finally repealed in November.

The issue of independence for the island of Rotuma was revived in September 1995 with the return of the King of Rotuma from exile in New Zealand. King Gagaj Sa Lagfatmaro, who had fled to New Zealand following death threats made against him during the military coups of 1987, appeared before the Constitutional Review Commission to petition for the island's independence within the Commonwealth, reiterating his view that Rotuma remained a British colony rather than a part of Fiji.

In September 1995 the Government decided to transfer all state land (comprising some 10% of Fiji's total land area), hitherto administered by the Government Lands Department, to the Native Land Trust Board. The decision was to allow the allocation of land to indigenous Fijians on the basis of native custom. However, concern among the Fijian Indian population increased following reports in early 1996 that many would not be able to renew their land leases (most of which were due to expire between 1997 and 2024) under the Agricultural Landlords and Tenants Act (ALTA). The reports were strongly denied by the Government, despite statements by several Fijian land-owning clans that Indians' leases would not be renewed. Moreover, a recently formed sugar-cane growers' association solely for ethnic Fijians, the Taukei Cane Growers' Association, announced its intention to campaign for ethnic Fijian control of the sugar industry, largely by refusing to renew land leases to ethnic Indians (who held some 85% of sugar farm leases). Concern was expressed that mounting tensions between landowners and tenants could lead to violence, and that the situation was affecting investor confidence. By the end of 2000 almost 2,000 land leases had expired, leaving many tenant farmers and their families homeless. Some 70 farmers, who had expressed a wish not to be resettled, received rehabilitation grants of $F28,000 in December 2000, although the authorities were criticized for their apparent slowness in processing the applications. In January 2001 the administration of native land leases was transferred from ALTA to the Native Lands Trust Act (NLTA), prompting fears of increased bias in favour of ethnic Fijian landowners and further instability in the sugar industry. A further 1,500 leases expired during 2001.

Meanwhile, racial tension intensified in October 1995, following the publication of the SVT's submission to the Constitutional Review Commission. In its report the party detailed plans to abandon the present multiracial form of government, recommending instead the adoption of an electoral system based on racial representation, in which each ethnic group would select its own representatives. The expression of numerous extreme anti-Indian sentiments in the document was widely condemned (by both ethnic Fijians and ethnic Indians) as offensive.

A rift within the GVP in early 1996, which resulted in two of the four GVP members of the House of Representatives withdrawing their support for the Government, prompted Rabuka to seek alternative coalition partners from among the opposition, in an attempt to establish a more secure majority. However, the Prime Minister was unsuccessful in persuading parliamentary members of the FAP (which had strongly criticized the SVT's submission to the Constitutional Review Commission the previous year) to join the Government. The administration's troubles during 1996 contributed to the defeat of the SVT in virtually every municipality at local elections which took place in September.

Existing divisions within the Government were further exacerbated by the presentation to the House of Representatives, in September 1996, of the Constitutional Review Commission's report. The report included recommendations to enlarge the House of Representatives to 75 seats, with 25 seats reserved on a racial basis (12 for ethnic Fijians, 10 for Fijian Indians, two for General Electors and one for Rotuma Islanders), and also proposed that the size of the Senate should be reduced from 34 to 32 members (and the number of nominated ethnic Fijian senators be reduced from 24 to 15). It was also proposed that the Prime Minister should be a Fijian of any race, while the President should continue to be an indigenous Fijian. Rabuka and Mara both endorsed the findings of the report, while several nationalist parties, including the Vanua Independent Party, the Fijian Nationalist United Front Party (FNUFP) and the Taukei Solidarity Movement, expressed extreme opposition to the proposals, and formed a coalition in an attempt to further their influence within Parliament. In addition, a number of SVT members of the House of Representatives aligned themselves with the nationalists, and in early 1997 were reported to be responsible for a series of political manoeuvres within the Cabinet, aimed at undermining Rabuka's position. The parliamentary committee reviewing the report agreed on a majority of the 700 recommendations, but proposed that the House of Representatives be enlarged to only 71 seats, with 46 seats reserved on a racial basis (23 for ethnic Fijians, 19 for Indians, three for General Electors and one for Rotuma Islanders) and 25 seats open to all races. The committee's modified proposals were presented in May to the Great Council of Chiefs, which officially endorsed the recommendations in early June. The Constitution Amendment Bill was approved unanimously by the House of Representatives and the Senate in the following month. Rabuka was anxious to reassure extremist nationalist Fijians, who had vociferously opposed the reforms throughout the debate, that their interests would be protected under the amended Constitution (which was not due to take effect until July 1998) and that indigenous Fijians would continue to play a pre-eminent role in the government of the country.

Despite opposition from both the FLP and the nationalist parties, Fiji was readmitted to the Commonwealth at a meeting of member states in October 1997. In the same month Rabuka was granted an audience with Queen Elizabeth II in London, at which he formally apologized for the military coups of 1987. Events in early 1998 were dominated by political reaction to the imminent promulgation of the new Constitution. An extremist nationalist group of former SVT supporters, including senior church, military and police officials, were rumoured to be planning to overthrow Rabuka's Government. Meanwhile, it was reported that opponents of the Constitution were discussing the establishment of several new political parties. The new Constitution, none the less, came into effect on 27 July 1998.

A dispute between tribal landowners and the Government over compensation payments for land flooded by the Monosavu hydroelectric power station erupted into violence in July 1998. Landowners, who had been demanding compensation worth some $30m. since the plant was constructed in 1983, seized control of the station (which supplies 90% of Fiji's electricity) and carried out a series of arson attacks on Fiji Electricity Authority property. In October 1998 the Government agreed to pay the landowners compensation totalling some $A12m., although many involved in the dispute rejected the offer and announced their intention of pursuing a legal claim against the Government. In October 2005 the dispute finally ended when landowners were paid a total of some $A40m. in compensation for the use of their land by the Fiji Electricity Authority. The award represented the largest compensation claim ever achieved by landowners in Fiji.

The prospect of legislative elections, to be held in early May 1999, prompted reports of political manoeuvring as parties sought to increase their influence by forming alliances. In addition, a number of changes in the country's political organizations occurred in late 1998. Following the death of Josefata Kamikamica, Adi Kuini Vuikaba Speed (widow of former Prime Minister Bavadra) was elected leader of the FAP. Meanwhile, the GVP and the General Electors' Party merged to form the United General Party (UGP) under the leadership of the Minister for Tourism, Transport and Civil Aviation, David Pickering, and Rabuka was re-elected leader of the SVT (despite the party being required to amend its constitution in order for this to be possible). A new party, the Veitokani ni Lewenivanua Vakarisito (VLV, Christian Democratic Alliance), formed by several senior church and military leaders and former members of the nationalist Taukei Solidarity Movement, was widely criticized for its extremist stance and refusal to accept the newly formed, multiracial Constitution.

At legislative elections held on 8–15 May 1999, the first to be held under the new Constitution, Rabuka's coalition Government was defeated by Mahendra Chaudhry, leader of the Indian-dominated FLP, who thus became Fiji's first ethnic Indian Prime Minister. Chaudhry's broad-based Government (a coalition of the FLP, FAP, VLV and the Party of National Unity—PANU) initially seemed threatened by the reluctance of FAP members to serve under an Indian Prime Minister. The leaders were persuaded to remain in the coalition in the interests of national unity, after the intervention of President Mara. Political stability after the elections was further marred by demands for Chaudhry's resignation by the Fijian Nationalist Vanua Takolavo Party (NVTLP), and by a number of arson attacks, allegedly linked to the former ruling SVT (although these allegations were denied by Rabuka). Following the SVT's decisive defeat in the elections, Rabuka resigned as party leader; he was replaced by Ratu Inoke Kubuabola, the former Minister for Communications, Works and Energy. Rabuka was later appointed the first independent Chairman of the newly autonomous Great Council of Chiefs. The NVTLP was widely suspected to have been responsible for three bomb explosions in Suva in August 1999. In the same month a parliamentary vote of no confidence against Prime Minister Chaudhry was overwhelmingly defeated. In the latter half of 1999 there were persistent demands by various nationalist groups (including the SVT) that Chaudhry be replaced by a leader of indigenous Fijian descent, and a number of demonstrations were organized, expressing disillusionment with the Government. In October the opposition coalition was successful in gaining control of a majority of councils in local elections, while the FLP won control of four municipal councils (having previously been in charge of none).

The Government's decision to disband the Fiji Intelligence Service from December 1999 was criticized by the opposition as 'foolish' and racially motivated. An announcement by the Chief Justice in December of a project to amend a number of laws that did not comply with the terms of the new Constitution, together with reports that the Government was planning to withdraw state funds previously provided to assist indigenous Fijian business interests, prompted further accusations of racism on the part of the Government against ethnic Fijians. Consequently, the SVT and the VLV held talks to discuss ways of consolidating the ethnic Fijian political base. Proposed legislation, which would alter the distribution of power between the President and the Prime Minister, attracted further criticism from the opposition, and in February 2000 a faction of the FAP announced its withdrawal from the governing coalition, citing dissatisfaction with Chaudhry's leadership. Of greater significance, however, was the announcement in April that the extremist nationalist Taukei Movement (which had been inactive for several years) had been revived with the sole intention of removing the Prime Minister from office. The group subsequently publicized a campaign of demonstrations and civil disobedience, prompting the army to issue a statement distancing itself from any anti-Government agitation and pledging loyalty to Chaudhry. The campaign attracted considerable public support, however, and culminated in a march through Suva by some 5,000 people in early May.

On 19 May 2000 a group of armed men, led by businessman George Speight, invaded the parliament building and ousted the Government, taking hostage Chaudhry and 30 other members of the governing coalition. President Mara condemned the coup and declared a state of emergency as Speight's supporters rampaged through the streets of Suva, looting and setting fire to Indian businesses. Speight declared that he had reclaimed Fiji for indigenous Fijians and had dissolved the Constitution. Moreover, he threatened to kill the hostages if the military intervened. On 22 May Mara formally invited Rabuka, in his role as chairman of the Great Council of Chiefs, to seek a resolution of the crisis. In the following days the Great Council of Chiefs convened to discuss the situation and proposed the replacement of Chaudhry's Government with an interim administration, an amnesty for Speight and the rebels, and the amendment of the Constitution. Speight rejected the proposals, demanding that Mara also be removed from office. Meanwhile, violent clashes erupted at the headquarters of Fiji Television when the rebels stormed the building following the broadcast of an interview with an opponent of the coup. A police officer was shot dead, television equipment was destroyed and the station's employees were taken hostage. On 29 May Mara resigned and the Commander of the Armed Forces, Frank (Voreqe) Bainimarama, announced the imposition of martial law and a curfew to restore calm and stability to the country. In an expression of his apparent reluctance to assume control, Bainimarama gave Mara a whale's tooth, a traditional Fijian symbol of regret.

Negotiations between the newly installed Military Executive Council and the Great Council of Chiefs continued throughout June 2000. Regular patrols by the security forces curbed rioting in Suva, although outbreaks of violence in rural areas (mostly in the form of attacks on Indian Fijians, the looting and burning of Indian-owned farms and the occupation of several tourist resorts) were reported. On 25 June the four female hostages were released from the parliament building. The Military Executive Council announced its intention to appoint an interim government without consulting Speight and demanded that the rebel leader release the remaining hostages.

An interim administration of 19 indigenous Fijians led by Laisenia Qarase (the former managing director of the Merchant Bank of Fiji) was sworn in on 4 July 2000. Minutes after the ceremony a gun battle erupted outside the parliament building in which four civilians and one rebel were injured; the rebel subsequently died. Speight announced that he would not recognize the interim authority, and most of Fiji's mainstream political parties similarly denounced it, although the Methodist Church declared its support for the body. On 12 July a further nine hostages were released and on the following day the remaining 18, including Chaudhry, were liberated. In accordance with Speight's wishes, Ratu Josefa Iloilovatu Uluivuda (or Josefa Iloilo), hitherto the First Vice-President, was then installed as President. In the same month Chandrika Prasad, a farmer, brought a legal challenge to the abrogation of the 1997 Constitution in the High Court of Fiji. Chaudhry launched an international campaign to reinstate both the Constitution and the coalition government.

Incidents of civil unrest (including the occupation of the hydroelectric dam at Monosavu and of the army barracks on Vanua Levu) continued throughout July 2000 as Speight sought to manipulate existing grievances, particularly disputes over land ownership, in order to mobilize additional support. On 29 July, however, Speight was finally arrested, along with dozens of his supporters, for breaking the terms of his amnesty by refusing to relinquish weapons. Armed rebels responded violently to the arrest, and in Labasa Indian Fijians were rounded up and detained in army barracks by supporters of Speight. In early August more than 300 rebels appeared in court on a variety of firearms and public order offences. Speight was similarly charged with several minor offences. On 11 August Speight and 14 of his supporters were formally charged with treason. During September Speight made several applications for bail, all of which were refused. Meanwhile, the suspended police commissioner, Isikia Savua, revealed that police were conducting an investigation into a commercial deal involving the Fijian mahogany trade, which, it was believed, might have precipitated the coup; Speight had been chairman of both Fiji Pine Corporation and Fiji Hardwood Corporation before being dismissed in 1999. This view was reiterated by the deposed Prime Minister on an overseas tour during October 2000, when Chaudhry expressed his commitment to the restoration of democracy and constitutional rule and stated his belief that the coup had been motivated by commercial vested interests rather than by concern over indigenous rights.

In early November 2000 about 40 soldiers staged a mutiny at army headquarters in Suva. Troops loyal to Bainimarama, who narrowly escaped capture, retook the barracks following an eight-hour assault in which five rebels and four loyal soldiers were killed. It was later revealed that a number of the rebel soldiers had been involved in the coup in May and speculation spread that the mutiny had been another attempted coup. The chairman of the Great Council of Chiefs, Sitiveni Rabuka, denied allegations by New Zealand's Minister of Foreign Affairs and Trade, Phil Goff, that he had been involved in the mutiny. In November 2002 Capt. Shane Stevens was sentenced to life imprisonment after he was found guilty of leading the mutiny two years earlier. Fourteen other soldiers received lesser sentences for their part in the uprising. Bainimarama criticized the majority of the sentences for being too lenient.

Later in November 2000 the High Court ruled that the existing Constitution remained valid and that the elected Parliament, ousted in the coup, remained Fiji's legitimate governing authority. Laisenia Qarase responded by lodging an appeal against the ruling and by declaring that the interim authority, of which he was leader, would continue as the country's national government until new elections could be organized and a new constitution drafted within 18 months.

In mid-December 2000 Chaudhry's campaign to re-establish his Government suffered a significant set-back when the ministers of foreign affairs of Australia and New Zealand announced that they were abandoning their appeal for its reinstatement, although they would continue to support a return to the 1997 Constitution. However, within Fiji, supporters of a return to democracy formed the Fiji First Movement, which aimed to consolidate opposition to the post-coup regime. The group organized a series of protests across the country in late 2000 and early 2001.

In February 2001 an international panel of judges at the Court of Appeal began the hearing against the November 2000 ruling, which found the abrogation of the 1997 Constitution to be illegal. In its final judgment the court ruled that the 1997 Constitution remained the supreme law of Fiji, that the interim civilian government could not prove that it had the support of a majority of Fijian people and was therefore illegal, and that, following Mara's resignation, the office of President remained vacant. The ruling was welcomed by many countries in the region, including Australia and New Zealand, and appeared to be accepted by the interim authority, which announced that it would organize elections as soon as possible. However, on 14 March 2001 Iloilo informed Chaudhry by letter that he had been dismissed as Prime Minister, claiming that by advising Iloilo to dissolve the authority in preparation for elections he had accepted that he no longer had the mandate of Parliament. Chaudhry rejected the decision as unconstitutional and unlawful. Ratu Tevita Momoedonu was appointed Prime Minister on the same day. On the following day, however, Iloilo dismissed Momoedonu, on the advice of the Great Council of Chiefs, and reinstated Laisenia Qarase as head of the interim authority. It was announced that a general election would be held in August–September 2001, and would be conducted under the preferential voting system, similar to that of Australia, as used in Fiji's 1999 election.

There followed a period of factionalism and fragmentation among Fiji's political parties. George Speight had already been appointed President of the new Matanitu Vanua (MV—Conservative Alliance Party), despite facing the charge of treason for his part in the 2000 coup. In May 2001 Qarase formed the Soqosoqo Duavata ni Lewenivanua (SDL—Fiji United Party), a new contender for the indigenous Melanesian vote, thus rivalling the established SVT. Another indigenous party, the Bai Kei Viti, was launched in June. Tupeni Baba, former Deputy Prime Minister in Chaudhry's Government, left the FLP and formed the New Labour United Party (NLUP). The election took place between 25 August and 1 September. Qarase's SDL was victorious, but failed to obtain an overall majority. The SDL secured 31 seats in the House of Representatives (increasing to 32 of the 71 seats after a by-election on 25 September). The FLP won 27 seats, the MV six seats and the NLUP two seats. International monitors were satisfied that the election had been contested fairly.

Following the election, however, by refusing to allow the FLP any representation in his new Cabinet, Qarase was accused of contravening a provision of the Constitution whereby a party winning more than 10% of the seats in the House of Representatives was entitled to a ministerial post. Two members of George Speight's MV were included in the Cabinet. Qarase claimed that Mahendra Chaudhry had not accepted that the Government should be based fundamentally on nationalist Fijian principles. In October 2001, when members of the House of Representatives were sworn in, Chaudhry refused to accept the position of Leader of the Opposition, a title that consequently fell to Prem Singh, leader of the NFP. In December Parliament approved the Social Justice Bill, a programme of affirmative action favouring Fijians and Rotumans in education, land rights and business-funding policies.

The Prime Minister defended himself against demands for his resignation in January 2002 following allegations that he had contravened the Electoral Act by pledging some $F25m. of funds from the Ministry of Agriculture to pro-indigenous Fijian businesses during the 2001 election campaign. In February 2002, furthermore, an appeal court ruled that the Prime Minister had violated the Constitution by failing to incorporate any member of the opposition FLP in his Cabinet. Qarase had previously declared that he would resign if the legal challenge against him were to be successful. (The newly appointed Chief Justice, Daniel Fatiaki, was himself under scrutiny in mid-2002—the Chief Justice being appointed on the advice of the Prime Minister and the Leader of the Opposition, and being responsible for assembling the Supreme Court.) In September the High Court ruled that Prem Singh, the NFP leader, was not entitled to retain his parliamentary seat (the validity of certain votes cast at the 2001 election having been questioned). The disputed seat was therefore allocated to a member of the FLP. Also in September, in advance of a ruling by the Supreme Court on the issue of the inclusion of the FLP in the Cabinet, the Prime Minister effected a ministerial reorganization, assuming personal responsibility for a number of additional portfolios. In April 2003 the Commander of the Armed Forces, Cdre Frank Bainimarama, intervened in the ongoing dispute, stating that if the judicial ruling went against Qarase then he should resign. Meanwhile, rumours circulated that a further coup might be attempted if the Government were ordered to include FLP members in the Cabinet. The Supreme Court finally delivered its ruling on 18 July, finding in favour of Chaudhry and declaring that, in order to uphold the Constitution, Qarase should form a new cabinet including eight members of the FLP. Qarase responded by proposing to retain his current 22-member Cabinet and to add 14 FLP members. Both the opposition and the SVT leader, Sitiveni Rabuka, criticized the proposal, which would result in more than one-half of all members of the House of Representatives serving as government ministers, and would give Fiji the largest cabinet in the world, in proportion to its population. Chaudhry expressed dissatisfaction with the suggestion, claiming that the positions offered to his party were too junior. However, Qarase remained defiant, his intransigence resulting in several more weeks of political impasse. At the end of August Qarase formally nominated a Cabinet which included 14 FLP members (although Chaudhry was not among those named). The opposition, however, continued to resist the proposal, claiming that they should be consulted over the composition of the Cabinet. The ransacking of the FLP office in Lautoka at the beginning of September, in which records and property were destroyed, was believed by many observers to be an act of intimidation against the party.

Meanwhile, in June 2002 the Prime Minister and the FLP leader co-operated briefly in addressing the issue of expiring land leases that were threatening Fiji's sugar industry. A committee, comprising members of both the SDL and FLP, was established to try to negotiate land leases that would satisfy both Indian Fijian tenants and their predominantly ethnic Fijian landowners. Most of the 30-year leases drawn up under the ALTA (see above) were expiring, and both tenants and the FLP were opposed to its replacement by the NLTA, which they saw as disproportionately favouring landowners. Two parliamentary bills had been approved by the Senate in April, reducing the land under state control to around 1% of the total and increasing the amount under the Native Land Trust Board to over 90%. During 2003 more than 1,100 tenants on Vanua Levu were evicted following the expiry of their land leases.

In August 2002, however, the FLP abandoned a second round of land lease discussions and announced that it would boycott most of the proceedings in the current session of Parliament. Chaudhry accused the Government of attempting to accelerate the passage of six bills through Parliament without regard for the mandatory 30 days' notice of a bill being tabled. The Prime Minister protested that this would compel the Government to accept the decision of the Great Council of Chiefs regarding the leases. Tensions between the ruling SDL and the FLP and, furthermore, between indigenous Fijians and Indian Fijians had been further exacerbated by anti-Indian comments made by the Minister for Women, Social Welfare and Land Resettlement, Asenaca Caucau, which the Prime Minister had not denounced. In September Qarase effected a reorganization of cabinet portfolios in which he assumed direct responsibility for the reform of the sugar industry and restated his commitment to resolve the long-standing issue of land leases. By late 2005 more than 3,500 farmers had received a total of $F26m. in assistance under ALTA, which was intended to help with diversification projects, resettlement and, in some cases, the acquisition of new leases.

The trial of George Speight and his accomplices on charges of treason opened in May 2001. (Speight was refused bail to enable him to occupy the seat that he won in the legislative election later in the year.) All the accused pleaded guilty to their involvement in the coup of May 2000, and at the conclusion of the trial in February 2002 Speight received the death sentence. Within hours of the verdict, however, President Iloilo signed a decree commuting the sentence to life imprisonment. Prison sentences of between 18 months and three years were imposed on 10 of Speight's accomplices, the charges of treason having been replaced by lesser charges of abduction. The trial of two other defendants on charges of treason began in July and, after being suspended as a result of technical problems, resumed in November, following the rejection of protests from the defendants that they were protected by an Immunity Decree promulgated by Bainimarama. Both were found guilty in March 2003, when a further 23 people were arrested on charges relating to the coup. In April 2004 an additional 61 soldiers were charged with various crimes connected with their involvement in the coup. Moreover, in the following month Vice-President Ratu Jope Seniloli was charged with having attempted to oust President Mara during the coup, in addition to the existing charges against him. Also in May George Speight made a further court appearance on charges of hostage-taking during the 2000 coup. The leader of the FLP, Mahendra Chaudhry, and a member of Parliament, Ganesh Chand, were claiming US $3.6m. in compensation for the 56 days they were held hostage in the government buildings by Speight and his accomplices. In July 2004 21 soldiers (the second such group) were found guilty of mutiny for their role in the plot to assassinate Bainimarama and to liberate George Speight. Moreover, in November paramount chief Ratu Inoke Takiveikata was sentenced to life imprisonment after being found guilty on several charges relating to the mutiny. (In June 2007, following claims about the impartiality of the presiding judge, a retrial of Takiveikata was ordered.) Meanwhile, in August 2004 Seniloli was found guilty of treason and sentenced to four years' imprisonment. His appeal against the conviction was rejected in November; however, he was unexpectedly released from prison later that month on medical grounds, which were widely disputed. Upon his release Seniloli resigned as Vice-President at the insistence of the military.

In June 2003, during a public reconciliation ceremony, the High Chief of a district of Vanua Levu publicly apologized for his involvement in the coup and announced a ban, in his locality, on words that differentiate ethnic Fijians from their Indian Fijian neighbours. Almost one year later the Great Council of Chiefs issued a historic public apology to all Indian Fijians for injustices committed against them during the coups of 1987 and 2000. Moreover, when, in July 2004, Adi Litia Cakobau (a senator appointed by the Great Council of Chiefs) proposed a motion in the upper house to outlaw the use of the terms Indian Fijian and Indo-Fijian, claiming that they were insulting to ethnic Fijians, the Great Council expressed outrage at her position.

Fears that Fiji was becoming a haven for criminal organizations proved well-founded in June 2004 when illegal drugs and the chemicals associated with their production, valued at an estimated US $500m., were discovered during a raid by Fijian police on three warehouses near the capital, Suva. The warehouses were believed to be the largest laboratory producing the illegal drug methamphetamine in the southern hemisphere. Seven people were arrested during the raid, of whom six were Chinese. In the same month the Pacific Transnational Crime Centre opened in Suva in response to an increase in crime in the region, in particular the activities of criminal networks from outside the Pacific region, which were believed to be establishing operations in the Pacific islands. In late 2005 officials estimated that some 7,000 illegal Asian immigrants had entered Fiji during the previous two years and noted that a corresponding increase in prostitution, illegal gambling, 'money laundering' and illegal fishing had been reported. Concern was expressed that an increase in official bribery had resulted in many immigrants gaining entry to the country with falsified documents. In October 2005 Fiji's appearance, for the first time, on Transparency International's global corruption index (on which the international organization ranked the country as the 55th most corrupt nation in the world) appeared to give credence to these concerns.

In mid-December 2004 (following the resignation of Ratu Jope Seniloli—see above) the Great Council of Chiefs approved President Iloilo's proposal of Ratu Joni Madraiwiwi as the country's next Vice-President. Madraiwiwi took up the post in January 2005. In March 2006 Iloilo was reappointed as President by the Great Council of Chiefs for a further five-year term, despite speculation in late 2005 that he had been considering retiring at the end of his current term. Vice-President Madraiwiwi was also reappointed.

Bainimarama was publicly criticized in April 2005 by the Minister for Home Affairs, Josefa Vosanibola, and told to refrain from making public comments without prior consultation with the Government. The denouncement followed Bainimarama's condemnation of the early release from prison of the former Minister for Lands, Naiqama Lalabalavu, along with a senator who had been convicted on coup-related charges; they had served just 10 days of their sentence. Bainimarama claimed that their release undermined the judiciary and that there could be no reconciliation in Fiji unless the Government recognized that the coup in 2000 and its aftermath had been wrong and needed to be addressed seriously. He also stated that he refused to be silenced by the Government and would continue to speak on issues of national importance.

In May 2005 the Government announced plans for a Reconciliation, Tolerance and Unity Bill, which would allow the review of convictions relating to involvement in the 2000 coup and the pardoning of prisoners. The proposals, however, provoked considerable opposition, particularly from the FLP and from Hindu organizations, and an opinion poll conducted in June suggested that a majority of Fijians did not support the bill. Meanwhile, the repercussions of the 2000 coup continued to feature prominently in the domestic affairs of Fiji, with the Minister for Transport, Simione Kaitani, and four other individuals appearing in court on coup-related charges in May 2005. In the following month nine soldiers convicted for their role in the army mutiny in Labasa during the coup were released from prison.

In January 2006 Bainimarama rejected allegations that he was undermining the stability of the country and preparing to oust the Government in a coup, despite continuing to criticize Qarase's administration as 'ideologically racist'. He reiterated his view that Qarase was determined to promote the goals of the 2000 coup for 'the benefit of the few'. In the following month Bainimarama issued a statement declaring that he would prevent the Reconciliation, Tolerance and Unity Bill (see above) from becoming law. Meanwhile, the reappointment in March 2006, by the Great Council of Chiefs, of Iloilo and Madraiwiwi as President and Vice-President respectively was welcomed by opposition leader Mahendra Chaudhry and by the military as contributing to national stability. Reports in the Fijian press suggested that a delegation of chiefs, supported by the Government, had attempted to persuade Iloilo to relinquish the presidency in favour of an overtly Fijian nationalist candidate.

In late March 2006 Parliament was dissolved in preparation for legislative elections, which took place on 6–13 May. Although 25 political parties contested the election, only three of these won seats in the House of Representatives. The ruling SDL, which had joined forces with a number of smaller, conservative-leaning parties, secured 36 seats, while the FLP won a total of 31 and the United People's Party (UPP—formerly the UGP—representing General Electors) won two seats. The two successful independent candidates agreed to support the SDL, thus increasing the party's representation in the legislature to 38 seats. Concerns over the conduct of the election were raised by several groups following the poll. The FLP and UPP both claimed that many potential voters had been omitted from electoral rolls, while in other constituencies, thousands of excess voting forms had been printed. It was also reported that election officials had rejected 120 ballot boxes for being incorrectly labelled, leading to speculation that the poll had been manipulated by the Government. Keith Knight, chair of the Commonwealth observer group, stated that observers were broadly satisfied with the electoral process, although he regretted the omission of some voters from the register and criticized the electoral system itself for being 'cumbersome and complicated'.

On 18 May 2006 Laisenia Qarase was sworn in for a second term of office. Following his reappointment, the Prime Minister offered seven of the 17 cabinet positions to the FLP, as required by the Constitution, although he restated his opposition to multiparty coalition government and hoped that Chaudhry would not accept the proposal. Chaudhry argued that his party was entitled to more seats and questioned the portfolios offered. The FLP was subsequently assigned nine positions in a 24-member Cabinet. Chaudhry himself declined to accept a cabinet role, choosing to remain as opposition leader, despite his party now forming part of the coalition Government.

Existing tensions between the Government and the military were not improved by Bainimarama's repeated accusations of racism and corruption in Qarase's administration during late 2006. In October Bainimarama issued an ultimatum demanding the resignation of the Government if it failed to reject the Reconciliation, Tolerance and Unity Bill within three weeks. Amid growing fears of a coup, Australian officials intervened to refuse the military access to a consignment of ammunition landed at the port of Suva. In an effort to remove the threat of a coup, the Government attempted to replace Bainimarama while he was visiting peace-keeping troops in the Middle East. Their chosen replacement, however, declined to accept the role and expressed support for Bainimarama. Relations between the Government and the military continued to deteriorate, and on 30 November Bainimarama issued a further ultimatum giving Qarase 24 hours to comply with a list of demands or face intervention. These demands included the removal of all members of the Government who had supported or benefited from the armed coup of 2000 and the suspension of three controversial pieces of legislation (the Reconciliation, Tolerance and Unity Bill, providing amnesties for those convicted of involvement in the 2000 coup, the Qoliqoli Bill, giving ethnic Fijians control of fishing rights and development of the coast, and the Indigenous Claims Tribunal Bill). In a public address on Fijian television Qarase agreed to suspend the legislation condemned by Bainimarama as furthering the racist agenda of the Government. During November 2006 Australia acted to station three warships off the Fijian coast in order to facilitate the evacuation of its nationals should this become necessary.

On 5 December 2006 soldiers took up positions outside the Prime Minister's official residence, seized key installations and set up road blocks around Suva. Bainimarama met President Iloilo, who authorized the dissolution of Parliament and the establishment of an interim administration. In a statement Bainimarama declared that he had assumed executive control of the country, appointing Dr Jona Senilagakali as interim Prime Minister and urging all cabinet ministers to resign within a month. The coup was immediately condemned by New Zealand, the United Kingdom and Australia; Qarase's request for military intervention was refused by Australia, but various sanctions against the country were announced. A state of emergency was subsequently declared. The suspension of Fiji's membership of the Commonwealth was announced on 9 December. Despite widespread international condemnation there was considerable support for the coup within Fiji. Organizations representing Indian Fijians expressed support for Bainimarama, as did the Fiji Human Rights Commission, which had questioned the legitimacy of Qarase's Government.

On 4 January 2007 Bainimarama returned executive power to President Iloilo and on the following day, upon the resignation of Senilagakali, Bainimarama was sworn in as interim Prime Minister. Bainimarama's appointment was swiftly approved by the Great Council of Chiefs. An interim government was subsequently sworn in; appointments included that of Mahendra Chaudhry as Minister for Finance, National Planning, Public Enterprise and the Sugar Industry, Ratu Epeli Nailatikau as Minister for Foreign Affairs and External Trade, and Aiyaz Sayed-Khaiyum as Attorney-General and Minister for Justice, Electoral Reform and Anti-Corruption. Also notable was the selection of Jone Navakamocea, a member of the previous Qarase administration, as Minister for Local Government, Urban Development and Public Utilities. Meanwhile, the Chief Justice of the Supreme Court, Daniel Fatiaki, was suspended pending an evaluation of the judiciary (Fatiaki, who faced several allegations, was scheduled to appear before a tribunal in February 2008). In mid-January 2007, amid reports of intimidation on the part of the military in the aftermath of the coup, President Iloilo issued a decree granting immunity to Bainimarama, Senilagakali and members of the military and police force in the event of disciplinary action or prosecution. In February Bainimarama announced plans to hold elections in 2010, following an assessment of electoral procedures and the completion of a census. This proposal appeared to have been revised in April 2007, when it was reported that the Fijian Government had agreed to the holding of legislative elections within two years, during discussions in Belgium with officials of the European Union (EU) on the issue of the release of development aid, suspended as a result of the coup.

In April 2007 the Great Council of Chiefs rejected Ratu Epeli Nailatikau, Minister for Foreign Affairs and External Trade, as a nominee for the post of Vice-President. The Council was suspended, and the Minister for Fijian Affairs, Heritage, Provincial Development and Multi-Ethnic Affairs, Ratu Epeli Ganilau, announced a review of its procedures. In July Ganilau clarified that the Council itself was not to be terminated, but that matters relating to membership were being assessed. Although the interim Government apparently rescinded the suspension in August, it was later reported that the composition of the Council had been altered. At the end of May Bainimarama declared an end to the state of emergency, and in August he confirmed the scheduling of elections for 13 March 2009, although this date was dependent upon the successful conclusion of pre-election processes. In September 2007 a state of emergency was temporarily reimposed in response to the arrival in Suva of Laisenia Qarase, whose presence was regarded by the Government as a potential threat to stability; the order was rescinded in the following month. In early November some 16 arrests were made after plans for an apparent counter-coup, allegedly to include the assassination of Bainimarama, were reported to have been discovered. Several alleged conspirators, including a former Senator and an intelligence official, were subsequently indicted on charges such as treason and inciting mutiny. A reorganization of the interim Cabinet was announced in January 2008, in which Bainimarama relinquished the home affairs and immigration portfolios, but assumed responsibility for others, including provincial development and indigenous and multi-ethnic affairs. Minor changes were made to the portfolios of leading cabinet members such as Aiyaz Sayed-Khaiyum and Mahendra Chaudhry, while Ratu Epeli Nailatikau remained Minister for Foreign Affairs, with additional responsibility for international co-operation and civil aviation. Meanwhile, Bainimarama took charge of the 'People's Charter for Change', a directive proposed earlier in the year that established new regulations for government procedures. Bainimarama reportedly promoted the Charter, which included anti-racism measures, as a pre-condition for the holding of elections.

In November 1989 the Fijian Government had expelled the Indian ambassador to Fiji for allegedly interfering in Fiji's internal affairs, and the status of the Indian embassy was downgraded to that of a consulate. Relations between Fiji and India deteriorated following the coup of May 1987, when many ethnic Indians emigrated. In January 1989 statistical information, released by the interim Government, indicated that the islands' ethnic Fijians were in a majority for the first time since 1946. Following the adoption of significant constitutional reforms in 1997 diplomatic relations improved considerably, and in October the Indian Government invited Fiji to open a High Commission in New Delhi. In February 1999 India lifted its trade embargo against Fiji (which had been in force for 10 years), and in May India reopened its High Commission in Suva. However, Fiji's relations with the international community suffered a major reversal following the coup of May 2000, which was condemned by the UN, the Commonwealth, the United Kingdom, Australia, New Zealand and several other nations in the region. In June Fiji was partially suspended from the Commonwealth (having been readmitted in October 1997 following its expulsion after the coups of 1987) and a delegation of ministers of foreign affairs from the organization visited the islands to demand the reinstatement of the 1997 Constitution. Australia, New Zealand and the Commonwealth withheld formal recognition of Qarase's Government when Parliament opened in October 2001, but in December the Commonwealth Ministerial Action Group recommended that Fiji be readmitted to meetings of the Commonwealth. In November 2002 Qarase's Government confirmed its intention to reopen the Fijian High Commission in India, claiming that it was needed to cater for the new business and diplomatic links being fostered by the administration. (The mission was reopened in April 2004.) It was reported that Indian business concerns had expressed interest in reviving Fiji's kava industry and that Indian film companies were interested in using Fiji as a location for filming. Sanctions imposed by the EU remained in place until early 2002. In late 2003 the EU announced the resumption of development aid to Fiji (suspended since 2000). The EU suspended non-humanitarian aid after the coup of December 2006.

Relations with France, meanwhile, were severely strained from 1995 by that country's decision to resume nuclear testing in the Pacific region. In January 2002 the French Government removed its sanctions against Fiji, following the islands' democratic election of the previous year.

In May 2005 Fiji received an unscheduled visit from the President of Taiwan, who was making a tour of his Pacific allies. President Chen Shui-bian's visit provoked considerable surprise, as Fiji had never recognized Taiwan but rather maintained diplomatic relations with the People's Republic of China, and led some commentators to speculate that Taiwan was seeking to further its influence in the region. During a five-day official visit to mainland China in the following month, however, Fiji's Prime Minister stressed his Government's continued support for a 'One China' policy. In April 2006 Premier Wen Jiabao of the People's Republic of China made an official visit to Fiji in order to promote greater co-operation between the two countries. During the visit Premier Wen delivered a speech at the opening ceremony of the inaugural meeting of the First Ministerial Conference of the China-Pacific Island Countries Economic Development and Cooperation Forum.

Fiji's relations with various members of the international community were adversely affected by the 2006 coup. In June 2007 New Zealand's high commissioner to Fiji was expelled because of alleged interference in the country's internal affairs. The decision prompted the New Zealand Prime Minister, Helen Clark, to announce plans for an expansion of existing sanctions against Fiji. The interim Government was also subject to international pressure with regard to the schedule for forthcoming elections, with several countries advising against significant delays. In March 2007 the Pacific Islands Forum (see p. 380) Foreign Ministers convened to consider the conclusions of an 'eminent persons' group', which had travelled to Fiji to assess the situation. In addition to its criticism of alleged breaches of human rights after the coup, the group had decided that a swift return to democracy was desirable; as a consequence, the Pacific Islands Forum stressed the need for a revised timetable for elections. A joint working group subsequently outlined the necessary phases of the pre-election process.

Government

Prior to the coup of December 2006, Fiji had a parliamentary form of government with a bicameral legislature, comprising the elected 71-seat House of Representatives and the appointed Senate, with 32 members. The Constitution, which remained in place following the coup of 2006, states that 46 seats in the House are reserved on a racial basis (23 for ethnic Fijians, 19 for Indians, three for other races—General Electors—and one for Rotuma Islanders) and 25 seats are open to all races. The Senate is appointed by the President of the Republic, 14 members on the advice of the Great Council of Chiefs (a 52-member traditional body comprising every hereditary chief (Ratu) of a Fijian clan), nine on the advice of the Prime Minister, eight on the advice of the Leader of the Opposition and one on the advice of the Rotuma Island Council.

Defence

The Fiji Military Forces consist of men in the regular army, the Naval Squadron, the conservation corps and the territorials. The conservation corps was created in 1975 to make use of unemployed labour in construction work. As the country is a member of the Commonwealth, Fijians are entitled to serve in the British armed forces and in 2006 about 2,000 Fijian soldiers were serving in Iraq with the British army, while a further 500 were working as mercenaries in the region. As assessed at November 2007, the total armed forces in Fiji numbered 3,500 men: 3,200 in the army and 300 in the navy. Budgetary expenditure on defence in 2007 was estimated at US $51m.

Economic Affairs

In 2006, according to estimates by the World Bank, Fiji's gross national income (GNI), measured at average 2004–06 prices, was US $2,815m., equivalent to $3,300 per head (or $6,200 on an international purchasing-power parity basis). During 1996–2006, it was estimated, the population increased at an average annual rate of 0.9%, while gross domestic product (GDP) per head increased, in real terms, by an annual average of 1.2%. Overall GDP rose by an annual average of 2.0% over the same period. According to the Reserve Bank of Fiji, GDP increased by 3.6% in 2006. GDP was estimated by the Asian Development Bank (ADB) to have contracted by 3.9% in 2007.

In 2006 agriculture (including forestry and fishing) contributed an estimated 12.5% of GDP. In 2005, according to FAO, the sector engaged 37.6% of the economically active population. The principal cash crop is sugar cane, which normally accounts for about 80% of total agricultural production and 30% of the country's GDP. Production of sugar cane was estimated to have reached almost 3.0m. metric tons in 2006. In that year sugar and molasses together accounted for 19.5% of total export earnings. Output of sugar declined in 2007, and the entire agricultural sector was disrupted by a cyclone in January 2008. Other important export crops are coconuts and ginger, while the most significant subsistence crop is paddy rice, production of which was estimated at 15,200 metric tons in 2006. Honey production was becoming an increasingly significant activity in the mid-2000s. The most important livestock products are beef and poultry meat. Fiji has extensive timber reserves. Wood and wood products accounted for 3.2% of exports in 2006, when they were worth $F38.8m. Fishing is an important activity, and in 2006 fish products earned some $F97.9m. in export revenue (8.1% of total export receipts). During 1996–2006 agricultural GDP declined at an estimated average annual rate of 0.7%. Compared with the previous year, the sector's GDP was estimated to have decreased by 0.6% in 2006. According to the ADB, the agricultural sector contracted by 2.0% in 2007.

Industry (including mining, manufacturing, construction and utilities) engaged 15.0% of the economically active population in 2000, and provided an estimated 21.6% of GDP in 2006. The GDP of the industrial sector was estimated to have increased at an average rate of 2.5% per year during 1996–2006. The industrial sector's GDP was estimated to have increased by 6.0% in 2006, compared with the previous year. In 2007, however, according to the ADB, industrial GDP decreased by 5.8%.

Mining contributed an estimated 0.5% of GDP in 2006. The sector engaged only 0.6% of the economically active population in 2000. Production of gold declined to 1,403 kg in 2006, and in December of that year, owing to lack of profitability, the country's main gold mine ceased operations, resulting in the loss of 1,800 jobs. Export revenue, meanwhile, decreased from $F59.3m., equivalent to 5.0% of total export earnings, in 2005 to $F43.1m. in 2006. Silver and copper are also mined. During 1996–2006 the mining sector's GDP declined at an average rate of 11.1% per year. In 2006 the GDP of the mining sector declined by 49.7%.

Manufacturing contributed an estimated 13.3% of GDP in 2006 and engaged 8.1% of paid employees in 2000. The sector's GDP increased at an estimated average annual rate of 2.9% during 1996–2006. Compared with the previous year, manufacturing GDP increased by an estimated 7.7% in 2006. The most important branch of the sector is food-processing, in particular sugar, molasses and coconut oil. The bottling of mineral water for export became increasingly important from the early 2000s, with production more than doubling between 2001 and 2005, and by 2004 exports of bottled water contributed 4.5% of total export earnings. The loss of preferential access to the US market for Fijian garments at the beginning of 2005 substantially reduced export receipts from this source. The contribution of garments to export earnings decreased from 18.9% of total revenue in 2004 to 7.9% in 2006.

Energy is derived principally from hydroelectric power, which provided some 90% of Fiji's electricity in the late 1990s. Imports of mineral fuels represented 28.8% of the total cost of imports in 2005. In March 2006, in an effort to promote environmental conservation, it was announced that the Fiji Electricity Authority was to receive a 50-year lease for land upon which to develop a new wind farm, as part of a plan for the country to become completely reliant on renewable energy sources by 2011.

The services sector engaged 36.7% of the economically active population in 2000 and contributed an estimated 65.9% of GDP in 2006. During 1996–2006 the sector's GDP rose by an average annual rate of 2.6%. Compared with the previous year, the GDP of the services sector increased by an estimated 5.0% in 2006. The ADB estimated that the services sector contracted by 4.5% in 2007. Although intermittently affected by political unrest, tourism is usually Fiji's largest source of foreign exchange. Visitor arrivals decreased to 522,025 in 2006, when revenue reached $F741.7m., and the number of tourists was reported to have declined further in 2007. Most visitors are from Australia, New Zealand, the USA and the United Kingdom.

Fiji consistently records a trade deficit, which reached $F1,607.9m. in 2006, when the country also recorded a deficit of $F1,238.1m. on the current account of the balance of payments. The principal sources of imports in 2006 were Singapore (34.4%), Australia (22.4%) and New Zealand (15.9%). Other important suppliers were the People's Republic of China and Japan. The principal markets for exports were Australia (17.0%), the United Kingdom (15.1%) and the USA (13.4%). Other important markets include New Zealand and Japan. The principal imports in 2006 were mineral products (33.4% of total costs in that year), along with machinery and transport equipment. Fiji's principal domestic exports were sugar, garments, gold and fish. Fiji also re-exports mineral fuels (including bunkers for ships and aircraft).

The budget deficit (excluding grants) was estimated at $F207.3m. in 2005. A budget deficit equivalent to 2.0% of GDP was projected for 2008. In 2007/08 aid from Australia was projected at $A28.7m, while aid from New Zealand in the same year was budgeted at $NZ6.0m. Fiji's outstanding external debt totalled an estimated US $241m. at the end of 2007. In that year the cost of debt-servicing was equivalent to 3.0% of the revenue from goods and services. The average annual rate of inflation was 2.9% in 1996–2006. The inflation rate reached 4.8% in 2007, according to the ADB. An estimated 6.4% of the total labour force were unemployed at mid-2006. Since 1987 Fiji has suffered a very high rate of emigration, particularly of skilled and professional personnel, including many from the health and education sectors. A consequence of this was an increase in remittances from Fijians working overseas, which were estimated to total US $350m. in 2006 (compared with only US $29m. in 1999). In 2007, however, a substantial reduction in this source of income was reported, partly owing to the decrease in the number of Fijian security personnel employed in the Middle East.

Fiji is a member of the UN Economic and Social Commission for Asia and the Pacific (ESCAP, see p. 35), the Pacific Islands Forum (see p. 380), the Pacific Community (see p. 377), the Colombo Plan (see p. 411) and the International Sugar Organization (see p. 409). Fiji is also a signatory of the South Pacific Regional Trade and Economic Co-operation Agreement—SPARTECA (see p. 381) and the Lomé Conventions and successor Cotonou Agreement (see p. 301) with the European Union (EU). In 1996 Fiji was admitted to the Melanesian Spearhead Group, which among other benefits provides for free trade among members. Fiji is also a member of the Asian Development Bank (ADB, see p. 182).

The removal of the elected Government in the military coup of December 2006 had a serious impact on Fiji's economy. In early 2007 more than 1,000 jobs in the tourism sector were reported to have been lost, and by May of that year hotel occupancy rates were estimated to have decreased to only 30%–35%. The tourist industry was further affected by the cyclone of January 2008. Although some elements of the previous administration's Strategic Development Plan 2007–2011 were to be retained by the Government that seized power in December 2006, the incoming administration decided not to implement an increase in the rate of value added tax (VAT—a major source of government revenue) from 12.5% to 15.0%, which had been announced in November 2006. In the hope of raising Fiji's exports, therefore, the new Government identified areas such as forestry, marine products and mineral water, along with information and communications technology, as priority sectors. However, a serious dispute with the USA arose in early 2008 when the Fijian authorities halted the export of a substantial consignment of mineral water, bottled in the islands for the US-owned company Fiji Water. The Fijian Government claimed that the US subsidiary was using the practice of transfer pricing to export the increasingly popular product to the USA at an artificially low cost, thereby depriving Fiji of revenue from excise duties. The country's foreign-exchange reserves strengthened in 2007 to reach US $618m., sufficient to cover 4.3 months of imports. Rising international prices for essential commodities such as crude petroleum and wheat contributed to substantial increases in consumer prices in early 2008. Following the contraction of 2007, the Government anticipated GDP growth of 2.2% in 2008.

Education

Education in Fiji is compulsory at primary level. The Government planned to extend the duration of compulsory free education in 2002. Primary education begins at six years of age, lasts for eight years and is provided free of charge. Secondary education, beginning at the age of 14, lasts for a further three years. State subsidies are available for secondary and tertiary education in cases of hardship. In 2004 enrolment at primary schools reached 96.2% of pupils in the relevant age-group, while enrolment in secondary schools stood at 82.6% of pupils. In 2005 there were 719 primary schools (with a total enrolment of 141,809 pupils), 162 secondary schools (with an enrolment of 68,521 pupils), and 63 vocational and technical institutions (with 2,115 enrolled students). In the same year Fiji had four teacher-training colleges; a total of 713 students were enrolled. In 2004 16,444 students were enrolled at the University of the South Pacific, which is based in Fiji. A privately funded university opened in Fiji in early 2005 with a total enrolment of 127 students. The institution aimed to increase its enrolment to some 1,000 students in the following year. In late 2005 it was announced that 5,284 new primary-level teaching posts and 3,024 new secondary teaching posts were to be created in 2006. The additional positions were required in response to the establishment of new schools and the introduction of new teaching programmes. Budgetary expenditure on education by the central Government in 2007 was projected at $F195.0m.; the sector was thus to receive the largest allocation of government funds in that year.

FIJI

Public Holidays

2008: 1 January (New Year's Day), 10 March (National Youth and Commonwealth Day), 20 March* (Birth of the Prophet Muhammad), 21–24 March (Easter), 30 May (Ratu Sir Lala Sukuna Day), 16 June (Queen's Official Birthday), 10 October (Fiji Day), 28 October (Diwali), 25–26 December (Christmas).

2009 (provisional): 1 January (New Year's Day), March (National Youth and Commonwealth Day), 20 March* (Birth of the Prophet Muhammad), 10–13 April (Easter), 25 May (Ratu Sir Lala Sukuna Day), 15 June (Queen's Official Birthday), 10 October (Fiji Day), 18 October (Diwali), 25–26 December (Christmas).

* This Islamic holiday is dependent on the lunar calendar and may vary by one or two days from the dates given.

Weights and Measures

The metric system is in force.

Statistical Survey

Sources (unless otherwise stated): Bureau of Statistics, POB 2221, Government Bldgs, Suva; tel. 315144; fax 303656; internet www.statsfiji.gov.fj; Reserve Bank of Fiji, POB 1220, Suva; tel. 313611; fax 301688; e-mail rbf@reservebank.gov.fj; internet www.reservebank.gov.fj.

AREA AND POPULATION

Area (incl. the Rotuma group): 18,376 sq km (7,095 sq miles). Land area of 18,333 sq km (7,078 sq miles) consists mainly of the islands of Viti Levu (10,429 sq km—4,027 sq miles) and Vanua Levu (5,556 sq km—2,145 sq miles).

Population: 775,077 (males 393,931, females 381,146) at census of 25 August 1996; 827,900 (preliminary result) at census of 16 September 2007.

Density (at 2007 census): 45.1 per sq km.

Principal Towns (population at 2007 census, preliminary results): Suva (capital) 75,225; Lautoka 44,143; Lami 10,474; Nadi 11,871; Labasa 7,550; Ba 6,775.

Ethnic Groups (2007 census, preliminary results): Fijians 473,983; Indians 311,591; Rotuman 10,137; Others 32,189; Total 827,900.

Births, Marriages and Deaths (registrations, 2003): Live births 17,701 (birth rate 21.2 per 1,000); Marriages 7,440 (marriage rate 8.9 per 1,000); Deaths 5,068 (death rate 6.1 per 1,000).

Expectation of Life (years at birth, WHO estimates): 68.9 (males 66.2; females 71.9) in 2005. Source: WHO, *World Health Statistics*.

Economically Active Population (persons aged 15 years and over, 1986 census): Agriculture, hunting, forestry and fishing 106,305; Mining and quarrying 1,345; Manufacturing 18,106; Electricity, gas and water 2,154; Construction 11,786; Trade, restaurants and hotels 26,010; Transport, storage and communications 13,151; Financing, insurance, real estate and business services 6,016; Community, social and personal services 36,619; Activities not adequately defined 1,479; *Total employed* 222,971 (males 179,595, females 43,376); Unemployed 18,189 (males 10,334, females 7,855); *Total labour force* 241,160 (males 189,929, females 51,231). *1999* (provisional): Total labour force 330,800 (Unemployed 25,100). *2000* (provisional): Total labour force 341,700 (Unemployed 41,700). *Mid-2005* (estimates in '000): Agriculture, etc. 135; Total labour force 359 (Source: FAO). *Mid-2005:* Total labour force 351,433 (Unemployed 20,507).

HEALTH AND WELFARE
Key Indicators

Total Fertility Rate (children per woman, 2005): 2.8.

Under-5 Mortality Rate (per 1,000 live births, 2005): 18.

HIV/AIDS (% of persons aged 15–49, 2005): 0.1.

Physicians (per 1,000 head, 1999): 0.34.

Health Expenditure (2004): US $ per head (PPP): 284.

Health Expenditure (2004): % of GDP: 4.6.

Health Expenditure (2004): public (% of total): 62.3.

Access to Sanitation (% of persons, 2004): 72.

Human Development Index (2005): ranking: 92.

Human Development Index (2005): value: 0.762.

For sources and definitions, see explanatory note on p. vi.

AGRICULTURE, ETC.

Principal Crops ('000 metric tons, 2006, FAO estimates): Sugar cane 3,000; Coconuts 140.1; Copra 11.3; Rice (paddy) 15.2; Cassava 40.7; Sweet potatoes 7.8; Yams 5.5; Taro 38.0; Aubergines (Egg-plants) 4.3; Bananas 5.7; Pineapples 3.7; Ginger 3.7.

Livestock ('000 head, year ending September 2006, FAO estimates): Cattle 310; Pigs 140; Sheep 5; Goats 260; Horses 44; Chickens 4,250; Ducks 75; Turkeys 65.

Livestock Products (metric tons, 2006, FAO estimates): Poultry meat 12,285; Cattle meat 8,360; Goat meat 1,170; Pig meat 4,129; Hen eggs 3,791; Cows' milk 57,000; Honey 118.

Forestry ('000 cubic metres, 2006, FAO estimates): *Roundwood Removals* (excl. bark): Sawlogs and veneer logs 256; Pulpwood 210; Other industrial wood 6; Fuel wood 37 (FAO estimate); Total 509. *Sawnwood Production* (incl. sleepers): 125.

Fishing ('000 metric tons, live weight, 2005): Capture 41.4* (Albacore 8.9; Yellowfin tuna 2.0; Emperors (scavengers) 1.0*; Other marine fishes 23.8*; Crustaceans 1.1*; Molluscs 2.7*; Corals 1.0*); Aquaculture 0.2*; *Total catch* 41.6*.
* FAO estimate.

Source: FAO.

MINING

Production (kg, 2006): Gold 1,403; Silver 494.

INDUSTRY

Production (metric tons, 2006, unless otherwise indicated): Sugar 307,000; Molasses 142,000 (1997); Coconut oil 8,349; Flour 67,661; Soap 6,140; Cement 143,000; Paint ('000 litres) 3,637; Beer ('000 litres) 22,000; Soft drinks ('000 litres) 168,081; Cigarettes 519; Matches ('000 gross boxes) 144; Electric energy (million kWh) 840; Ice cream ('000 litres) 3,238; Toilet paper ('000 rolls) 26,771.

FINANCE

Currency and Exchange Rates: 100 cents = 1 Fiji dollar ($F). Sterling, US Dollar and Euro Equivalents (31 October 2007): £1 sterling = $F3.1862; US $1 = $F1.5366; €1 = $F2.2199; $F100 = £31.39 = US $65.08 = €45.05. Average Exchange Rate ($F per US $): 1.7331 in 2004; 1.6911 in 2005; 1.7313 in 2006.

General Budget ($F million, 2002): *Revenue:* Current revenue 957.7 (Taxes 789.7, Non-taxes 168.0); Capital revenue 80.5; Total 1,038.2, excl. grants (0.5). *Expenditure:* General public services 149.5; Defence 56.2; Education 168.4; Health 82.0; Social security and welfare 3.4; Housing and community amenities 7.5; Economic services 104.5 (Agriculture 6.5; Industry 31.4; Electricity, gas and water 11.3; Transport and communications 24.5); Other purposes 680.2; Total 1,251.7 (Current 1,013.0, Capital 238.6), excl. net lending (9.4). *2005:* Total revenue 1,227.2 (Current 1,226.7, Capital 0.5); Total expenditure 1,434.5 (Current 1,197.6, Capital 237.0). Source: Asian Development Bank, *Key Indicators of Developing Asian and Pacific Countries*.

International Reserves (US $ million at 31 December 2005): Gold (valued at market-related prices) 0.43; IMF special drawing rights 7.99; Reserve position in IMF 21.89; Foreign exchange 284.87; *Total* 315.18. Source: IMF, *International Financial Statistics*.

Money Supply ($F million at 31 December 2006): Currency outside banks 294.2; Demand deposits at commercial banks 830.4; *Total money* 1,124.7. Source: IMF, *International Financial Statistics*.

Cost of Living (Consumer Price Index; base: 1993 = 100): All items: 134.6 in 2004; 137.7 in 2005; 141.2 in 2006.

Expenditure on the Gross Domestic Product ($F million at current prices, 2005): Government final consumption expenditure 768.7; Private final consumption expenditure 2,398.4; Increase in stocks 34.9; Gross fixed capital formation 929.1; *Total domestic expenditure* 4,131.1; Exports of goods and services 2,788.8; *Less* Imports of goods

FIJI   *Directory*

and services 3,678.2; Statistical discrepancy 1,827.7; *GDP in purchasers' values* 5,069.4.

Gross Domestic Product by Economic Activity ($F million at current prices, 2006, preliminary): Agriculture, forestry and fishing 615.7; Mining and quarrying 24.1; Manufacturing 656.1; Electricity, gas and water 122.3; Construction 265.4; Wholesale and retail trade 926.9; Transport and communications 729.8; Finance, real estate, etc. 670.7; Community, social and personal services 926.7; *Sub-total* 4,937.5; *Less* Imputed bank service charges 289.8; *GDP at factor cost* 4,647.7; Indirect taxes, less subsidies 835.6; *GDP in purchasers' values* 5,483.3.

Balance of Payments ($F million, 2006): Exports of goods f.o.b. 1,231.5; Imports of goods f.o.b. –2,839.4; *Trade balance* –1,607.9; Exports of services 1,339.5; Imports of services –939.2; Other income received 111.9; Other income paid –321.2; *Balance on goods, services and income* –1,416.9; Current transfers received 371.6; Current transfers paid –192.8; *Current balance* –1,238.1.

EXTERNAL TRADE

Principal Commodities ($F million, 2006): *Imports c.i.f.* (distribution by HSC): Animals and animal products 135.6; Vegetable products 153.9; Prepared foodstuffs 124.8; Mineral products 1,043.5; Chemical products 167.8; Plastics and rubber 144.6; Textiles and textile articles 156.6; Base metals and articles thereof 188.8; Machinery, mechanical appliances and electrical equipment 465.7; Transportation equipment 227.0; Total (incl. others) 3,124.3. *Exports f.o.b.*: Animals and animal products 120.3; Vegetable products 54.9; Prepared foodstuffs 398.5; Mineral products 296.7; Wood and wood products 38.8; Textiles and textile articles 114.4; Pearls, precious or semi-precious stones and metals 50.9; Total (incl. others) 1,201.6.

Principal Trading Partners ($F million, 2006, provisional): *Imports c.i.f.*: Australia 698.5; China, People's Republic 112.8; France 25.9; Germany 37.9; Hong Kong 52.9; India 58.8; Indonesia 34.7; Japan 111.5; Malaysia 52.6; New Zealand 496.3; Singapore 1,074.6; Thailand 74.8; USA 90.8; Total (incl. others) 3,124.3. *Exports*: Australia 203.9; Japan 63.0; New Zealand 68.7; Samoa 24.9; Tonga 20.3; United Kingdom 180.9; USA 161.6; Total (incl. others) 1,201.6.

TRANSPORT

Road Traffic (motor vehicles registered at 31 December 2006): Private cars 80,491; Goods vehicles 41,298; Buses 2,175; Taxis 4,831; Rental vehicles 6,251; Motorcycles 4,884; Tractors 5,815; Total (incl. others) 152,556.

Shipping: *Merchant Fleet* (registered at 31 December 2006): Vessels 60; Total displacement ('000 grt) 31.8 (Source: Lloyd's Register-Fairplay, *World Fleet Statistics*). *International Freight Traffic* ('000 metric tons, 1990): Goods loaded 568; Goods unloaded 625 (Source: UN, *Monthly Bulletin of Statistics*).

Civil Aviation (traffic on scheduled services, 2003): Kilometres flown 21 million; Passengers carried 766,000; Passenger-kilometres 2,233 million; Total ton-kilometres 298 million. Source: UN, *Statistical Yearbook*.

TOURISM

Foreign Visitors by Country of Residence (excluding cruise-ship passengers, 2006, provisional): Australia 181,099; Canada 14,029; Japan 29,951; New Zealand 95,757; Pacific Islands 35,955; United Kingdom 63,562; USA 74,449; Total (incl. others) 522,025.

Tourism Receipts ($F million): 717.6 in 2004; 733.2 in 2005; 741.7 in 2006.

COMMUNICATIONS MEDIA

Radio Receivers (1999): 545,000 in use*.

Television Receivers (2000): 92,000 in use†.

Telephones (2005): 112,500 main lines in use†.

Facsimile Machines (1999): 2,815 in use†.

Mobile Cellular Telephones (2005): 205,000 subscribers†.

Personal Computers (2005): 44,000 in use†.

Internet Users (2006): 80,000†.

Broadband Subscribers (2005): 7,000†.

Book Production (1980): 110 titles (84 books, 26 pamphlets); 273,000 copies (229,000 books, 44,000 pamphlets).

Daily Newspapers (2001): 3 (estimated combined circulation 49,124)‡.

Non-daily Newspapers (provisional, 1988): 7 (combined circulation 99,000)*.

* Source: UNESCO, *Statistical Yearbook*.
† Source: International Telecommunication Union.
‡ Source: Audit Bureau of Circulations, Australia.

EDUCATION

Pre-Primary (2002 unless otherwise indicated): 451 schools (2003); 264 teachers; 7,076 pupils.

Primary (at 30 June 2005): 719 schools; 5,006 teachers; 141,089 pupils.

General Secondary (at 30 June 2005): 162 schools; 4,141 teachers; 68,521 pupils.

Vocational and Technical (at 30 June 2005, unless otherwise indicated): 63 institutions; 1,024 teachers (including special schools—2000); 2,115 students.

Teacher Training (at 30 June 2005, unless otherwise indicated): 4 institutions; 97 teachers (2000); 713 students.

Medical (1989): 2 institutions; 493 students.

University (2004): 1 institution; 289 teachers; 16,444 students.

Adult Literacy Rate (UNESCO estimates, 1995–99): 92.9% (males 94.5%, females 91.4%). Source: UN Development Programme, *Human Development Report*.

Directory

The Constitution

On 1 March 2001 President Iloilo reinstated the 1997 Constitution, after the Great Council of Chiefs (Bose Levu Vakaturaga—a traditional body, with some 70 members, consisting of every hereditary chief or Ratu of each Fijian clan) had approved the draft. The Constitution Amendment Bill that was approved in July 1997 included provisions to ensure a multi-racial Cabinet. Following the removal of the country's elected Government in a coup in December 2006, it was declared that the 1997 Constitution was to remain in place. The following is a summary of the main provisions:

The Constitution, which declares Fiji to be a sovereign, democratic republic, guarantees fundamental human rights, a universal, secret and equal suffrage and equality before the law for all Fijian citizens. Citizenship may be acquired by birth, descent, registration or naturalization and is assured for all those who were Fijian citizens before 6 October 1987. Parliament may make provision for the deprivation or renunciation of a person's citizenship. Ethnic Fijians, and the Polynesian inhabitants of Rotuma, receive special constitutional consideration. The Judicial and Legal Services Commission, the Public Service Commission and the Police Service Commission are established as supervisory bodies.

THE GREAT COUNCIL OF CHIEFS

The Great Council of Chiefs (Bose Levu Vakaturaga) derives its authority from the status of its members and their chiefly lineage. The Great Council appoints the President of the Republic and selects 14 nominees for appointment to the Senate, the upper chamber of the Parliament.

The Great Council became fully independent of the Government in mid-1999.

THE EXECUTIVE

Executive authority is vested in the President of the Republic, who is appointed by the Great Council of Chiefs, for a five-year term, to be constitutional Head of State and Commander-in-Chief of the armed forces. The Presidential Council advises the President on matters of national importance. The President, and Parliament, can be empowered to introduce any necessary measures in an emergency or in response to acts of subversion which threaten Fiji.

In most cases the President is guided by the Cabinet, which conducts the government of the Republic. The Cabinet is led by the Prime Minister, who is a Fijian of any ethnic origin and is appointed by the President from among the members of Parliament, on the basis of support in the legislature. The Prime Minister selects

FIJI

the other members of the Cabinet (the Attorney-General, the minister responsible for defence and security and any other ministers) from either the House of Representatives or the Senate on a multi-party and multiracial basis. The Cabinet is responsible to Parliament.

THE LEGISLATURE

Legislative power is vested in the Parliament, which comprises the President, the appointed upper house or Senate and an elected House of Representatives. The maximum duration of a parliament is five years.

The Senate has 32 members, appointed by the President of the Republic for the term of the Parliament. A total of 14 senators are nominated by the Great Council of Chiefs, nine are appointed on the advice of the Prime Minister, eight on the advice of the Leader of the Opposition, and one on the advice of the Rotuma Island Council. The Senate is a house of review, with some powers to initiate legislation, but with limited influence on financial measures. The Senate is important in the protection of ethnic Fijian interests, and its consent is essential to any attempt to amend, alter or repeal any provisions affecting ethnic Fijians, their customs, land or tradition.

The House of Representatives has 71 elected members, who themselves elect their presiding officials and the Speaker from outside the membership of the House, and the Deputy Speaker from among their number (excluding ministers). Voting is communal, with universal suffrage for all citizens of the Republic aged over 21 years. Seats are reserved on a racial basis: 23 for ethnic Fijians, 19 for Indians, three for other races (General Electors), one for Rotuma Islanders and 25 open seats. Elections must be held at least every five years and are to be administered by an independent Supervisor of Elections. An independent Boundaries Commission determines constituency boundaries.

THE JUDICIARY

The judiciary is independent and comprises the High Court, the Fiji Court of Appeal and the Supreme Court. The High Court and the Supreme Court are the final arbiters of the Constitution. The establishment of Fijian courts is provided for, and decisions of the Native Lands Commission (relating to ethnic Fijian customs, traditions and usage, and on disputes over the headship of any part of the Fijian people, with the customary right to occupy and use any native lands) are declared to be final and without appeal.

The Government

HEAD OF STATE

President: Ratu JOSEFA ILOILOVATU ULUIVUDA (appointed 12 July 2000 by an interim authority established following the coup of 19 May 2000; reappointed 8 March 2006; removed from office following the coup of 5 December 2006 and temporarily replaced; reappointed 4 January 2007).

INTERIM CABINET
(April 2008)

Prime Minister, Minister for Public Service, People's Charter for Change, Information, Provincial Development, and Indigenous and Multi-Ethnic Affairs: Cdre FRANK (VOREQE) BAINIMARAMA.

Attorney-General and Minister for Justice, Electoral Reform, Public Enterprises and Anti-Corruption: AIYAZ SAYED-KHAIYUM.

Minister for Finance, National Planning, Sugar Industry and Public Utilities: MAHENDRA CHAUDHRY.

Minister for Foreign Affairs, International Co-operation and Civil Aviation: Ratu EPELI NAILATIKAU.

Minister for Health, Women and Social Welfare: JIKO LUVENI.

Minister for Education, National Heritage, Culture and Arts, Youth and Sports: FILIPE BOLE.

Minister for Labour, Industrial Relations, Employment, Local Government, Urban Development and Housing: LEKH RAM VAYESHNOI.

Minister for Works and Transport: TIMOCI LESI NATUVA.

Minister for Industry, Tourism, Trade and Communication: TOM RICKETTS.

Minister for Lands, Mineral Resources and Environment: NETANI SUKANAIVALU.

Minister for Primary Industries: JOKETANI COKANASIGA.

Minister for Defence, National Security and Immigration: Ratu EPELI GANILAU.

MINISTRIES

Office of the President: Government House, Berkley Cres., Government Bldgs, POB 2513, Suva; tel. 3314244; fax 3301645; internet www.fiji.gov.fj/publish/president.shtml.

Office of the Prime Minister: Government Bldgs, POB 2353, Suva; tel. 3211201; fax 3306034; e-mail pmsoffice@connect.com.fj; internet www.fiji.gov.fj/publish/prime_minister.shtml.

Office of the Attorney-General: Government Bldgs, Victoria Parade, POB 2213, Suva; tel. 3309866; fax 3305421; internet www.ag.gov.fj.

Ministry of Defence, National Security and Immigration: Government Bldgs, POB 2349, Suva; tel. 3211401; fax 3300346; e-mail infohomaff@govnet.gov.fj.

Ministry of Education: Marela House, Thurston St, PMB, Suva; tel. 3314477; fax 3303511; internet www.education.gov.fj.

Ministry of Finance and National Planning: Government Bldgs, POB 2212, Suva; tel. 3307011; fax 3300834; e-mail psfinance@govnet.gov.fj; internet www.mfnp.gov.fj.

Ministry of Foreign Affairs, International Co-operation and Civil Aviation: Government Bldgs, POB 2220, Suva; tel. 3309631; fax 3301741; e-mail info@foreignaffairs.gov.fj; internet www.foreignaffairs.gov.fj.

Ministry of Health, Women and Social Welfare: Government Bldgs, POB 2223, Suva; tel. 3306177; fax 3306163; e-mail info@health.gov.fj; internet www.health.org.fj.

Ministry of Industry, Tourism, Trade and Communication: Government Bldgs, POB 2118, Suva; tel. 3305411; fax 3302617.

Ministry of Information: POB 2225, Government Bldgs, Suva; tel. 3302102; fax 3305139; e-mail info@fiji.gov.fj; internet www.info.gov.fj.

Ministry of Justice: Government Bldgs, Victoria Parade, POB 2213, Suva; tel. 3309866; fax 3302404.

Ministry of Labour and Industrial Relations: Government Bldgs, POB 2216, Suva; tel. 3309155; fax 3304701; e-mail callcentre@labour.gov.fj; internet www.labour.gov.fj.

Ministry of Lands, Mineral Resources and Environment: Government Bldgs, Suva; tel. 3211329; fax 3302730; internet www.lands.gov.fj.

Ministry of Local Government and Urban Development: Government Bldgs, POB 2131, Suva; tel. 3304364; fax 3303515; e-mail msovaki@govnet.gov.fj.

Ministry of Primary Industries: POB 2218, Government Bldgs, Suva; tel. 3301611; fax 3301595.

Ministry of Public Enterprises and Public Sector Reform: Government Bldgs, POB 2278, Suva; tel. 3315577; fax 3315035; internet www.publicenterprises.gov.fj.

Ministry of Works and Transport: Government Bldgs, POB 2493, Suva; tel. 3384111; fax 3383198.

Ministry of Youth and Sports: Government Bldgs, POB 2448, Suva; tel. 3315960; fax 3305348; e-mail vikash.nand@govnet.gov.fj; internet www.youth.gov.fj.

Legislature

Note: Parliament was dissolved on 6 December 2006, following the military coup of the previous day.

PARLIAMENT

Senate

The Senate is also known as the House of Review. The upper chamber comprises 32 appointed members (see The Constitution).

House of Representatives

The lower chamber comprises 71 elected members: 23 representing ethnic Fijians, 19 representing ethnic Indians, three representing other races (General Electors), one for Rotuma Islanders and 25 seats open to all races.

Speaker: Ratu EPELI NAILATIKAU.

FIJI

General Election, 6–13 May 2006

	Communal Seats			Open Seats	Total Seats
	Fijian	Indian	Other*		
Fiji United Party (SDL)	23	—	—	13	36
Fiji Labour Party (FLP)	—	19	—	12	31
United People's Party	—	—	2	—	2
Independents	—	—	2	—	2
Total	23	19	4	25	71

* One Rotuman and three General Electors' seats.

Election Commission

Fiji Electoral Commission: Government Bldgs, POB 2389, Suva; tel. 3300046; fax 3300180; e-mail info@elections.gov.fj; internet www.elections.gov.fj; Chair. MOHAMMED KAMAL-UD-DEAN SAHU KHAN.

Political Organizations

Fiji Indian Liberal Party: Rakiraki; f. 1991; represents the interests of the Indian community, particularly sugar-cane farmers and students; Sec. SWANI KUMAR.

Fiji Labour Party (FLP): POB 2162, Government Bldgs, Suva; tel. 3305811; fax 3305317; e-mail flp@connect.com.fj; internet www.flp.org.fj; f. 1985; Pres. JOKAPECI KOROI; Sec.-Gen. MAHENDRA PAL CHAUDHRY.

Fijian Association Party (FAP): Suva; f. 1995 by merger of Fijian Association (a breakaway faction of the SVT) and the multiracial All Nationals Congress; Leader Adi KUINI SPEED; Pres. Ratu INOKE SERU.

Fijian Nationalist United Front Party (FNUFP): POB 1336, Suva; tel. 3362317; f. 1992 to replace Fijian Nationalist Party; seeks additional parliamentary representation for persons of Fijian ethnic origin, the introduction of other pro-Fijian reforms and the repatriation of ethnic Indians; Leader SAKEASI BAKEWA BUTADROKA.

Janata Party: Suva; f. 1995 by former mems of NFP and FLP.

National Alliance Party of Fiji: POB 2315, Suva; internet www.alliancefiji.com; f. 2005; Pres. Ratu EPELI GAVIDI GANILAU.

National Federation Party (NFP): POB 13534, Suva; tel. 3305811; fax 3305317; f. 1960 by merger of the Federation Party, which was multiracial but mainly Indian, and the National Democratic Party; Leader ATTAR SINGH; Pres. JOGINDRA SINGH.

Nationalist Vanua Takolavo Party (NVTLP): Suva; Leader ILIESA DUVULOCO; Pres. VILIAME SAVU.

Party of National Unity (PANU): Ba; f. 1998 to lobby for increased representation for the province of Ba; merged with Bai Kei Viti and People's National Party (Leader MELI BOGILEKA) in March 2006; Leader Tui Ba Ratu SAIRUSI NAGAGAVOKA.

Soqosoqo Duavata ni Lewenivanua (SDL) (Fiji United Party): c/o House of Representatives, Suva; f. 2001; Leader LAISENIA QARASE; Pres. Ratu KALOKALO LOKI.

Soqosoqo ni Vakavulewa ni Taukei (SVT) (Fijian Political Party): Suva; f. 1990 by Great Council of Chiefs; supports constitutional dominance of ethnic Fijians but accepts multiracialism; Pres. Ratu SITIVENI RABUKA; Gen. Sec. EMA DRUAVESI.

United People's Party (UPP): Suva; f. 1998 by the merger of the General Electors' Party and the General Voters' Party (fmrly the General Electors' Association, one of the three wings of the Alliance Party—AP, the ruling party 1970–87; fmrly United General Party; name changed to above in 2004 to be more multiracial in scope; represents the interests of the minority Chinese and European communities and people from other Pacific Islands resident in Fiji, all of whom are classed as General Electors under the 1998 Constitution; Pres. MICK BEDDOES (acting); Vice-Pres. MARGARET ROUNDS.

Vanua Independent Party: Leader ILIESA TUVALOVO; Sec. URAIA TUISOVISOVI.

In mid-2005 the Soqosoqo Duavata ni Lewenivanua and the Soqosoqo ni Vakavulewa ni Taukei, along with four minor parties, announced their intention to contest the next legislative election as a united body. Prior to the election of May 2006, the Fiji Labour Party, the United People's Party and the Party of National Unity declared their intention to campaign jointly under the name of the People's Coalition Party. Other parties that contested the 2006 election included the Coalition of Independent Nations, the Party of Truth, the Justice and Freedom Party and the Social Liberal Multicultural Party.

Supporters of secession are concentrated in Rotuma.

Diplomatic Representation

EMBASSIES AND HIGH COMMISSIONS IN FIJI

Australia: 37 Princes Rd, POB 214, Suva; tel. 3382211; fax 3382065; e-mail public-affairs-suva@dfat.gov.au; internet www.fiji.embassy.gov.au; High Commissioner JAMES BATLY.

China, People's Republic: 147 Queen Elizabeth Dr., PMB, Nasese, Suva; tel. 3300215; fax 3300950; e-mail chinaemb_fj@mfa.gov.cn; internet fj.china-embassy.org/chn; Ambassador CAI JINBIAO.

France: Dominion House, 7th Floor, Thomson St, Suva; tel. 3312233; fax 3301894; internet www.ambafrance-fj.org; Ambassador JEAN-FRANÇOIS BOUFFANDEAU.

India: POB 471, Suva; tel. 3301125; fax 3301032; e-mail hicomindsuva@is.com.fj; High Commissioner ISHWAR SINGH CHAUHAN.

Japan: Dominion House, 2nd Floor, POB 13045, Suva; tel. 3304633; fax 3302984; e-mail eojfiji@is.com.fj; internet www.fj.emb-japan.go.jp; Ambassador MASASHI NAMEKAWA.

Korea, Republic: Vanua House, 8th Floor, PMB, Suva; tel. 3300977; fax 3303410; e-mail korembfj@mofat.go.kr; Ambassador BONG JOO KIM.

Malaysia: Pacific House, 5th Floor, POB 356, Suva; tel. 3312166; fax 3303350; e-mail mwsuva@connect.com.fj; High Commissioner NAFISAH MOHAMED.

Marshall Islands: 41 Borron Rd, Government Bldgs, POB 2038, Suva; tel. 3387899; fax 3387115; Ambassador MACK KAMINAGA.

Micronesia, Federated States: 37 Loftus St, POB 15493, Suva; tel. 304566; fax 3304081; e-mail fsmsuva@sopacsun.sopac.org.fj; Ambassador SAMSON PRETRICK.

Nauru: Ratu Sukuna House, 7th Floor, Government Bldgs, POB 2420, Suva; tel. 3313566; fax 3302861; High Commissioner KENNAN RANIBOK ADEANG.

New Zealand: Reserve Bank of Fiji Bldg, 10th Floor, Pratt St, POB 1378, Suva; tel. 3311422; fax 3300842; e-mail nzhc@connect.com.fj; High Commissioner CAROLINE MCDONALD (acting).

Papua New Guinea: Credit Corporation House, 3rd Floor, Government Bldgs, POB 2447, Suva; tel. 3304244; fax 3300178; e-mail kundufj@is.com.fj; High Commissioner PETER EAFEARE.

Tuvalu: 16 Gorrie St, POB 14449, Suva; tel. 3301355; fax 3308479; High Commissioner TINE LEUELU.

United Kingdom: Victoria House, 47 Gladstone Rd, POB 1355, Suva; tel. 3229100; fax 3229132; e-mail publicdiplomacysuva@fco.gov.uk; internet www.britishhighcommission.gov.uk/fiji; High Commissioner ROGER SYKES.

USA: 31 Loftus St, POB 218, Suva; tel. 3314466; fax 3308685; e-mail usembsuva@connect.com.fj; internet suva.usembassy.gov; Ambassador LARRY MILES DINGER.

Judicial System

Justice is administered by the Supreme Court, the Fiji Court of Appeal, the High Court and the Magistrates' Courts. The Supreme Court of Fiji is the superior court of record presided over by the Chief Justice. The 1990 Constitution provided for the establishment of Fijian customary courts and declared as final decisions of the Native Lands Commission in cases involving Fijian custom, etc.

Supreme Court

Suva; tel. 3211524; fax 3300674.

Chief Justice: ANTHONY GATES (acting).

President of the Fiji Court of Appeal: (vacant).

Director of Public Prosecutions: JOSAIA NAIGULEVU.

Solicitor-General: CHRISTOPHER PRYDE.

Religion

CHRISTIANITY

Most ethnic Fijians are Christians. Methodists are the largest Christian group, followed by Roman Catholics. In the census of 1996 about 58% of the population were Christian (mainly Methodists, who comprised 36.2% of the total population).

Fiji Council of Churches: Government Bldgs, POB 2300, Suva; tel. and fax (1) 3313798; fax (1) 3313798; e-mail fijichurches@connect.com.fj; f. 1964; nine mem. churches; Pres. Rev. APIMELEKI QILIHO; Gen. Sec. Rev. ISIRELI LEDUA KACIMAIWAI.

The Anglican Communion

In April 1990 Polynesia, formerly a missionary diocese of the Church of the Province of New Zealand, became a full and integral diocese. The diocese of Polynesia is based in Fiji but also includes Wallis and Futuna, Tuvalu, Kiribati, French Polynesia, Cook Islands, Tonga, Samoa and Tokelau. There were an estimated 6,325 adherents in 1996.

Bishop of Polynesia: Rt Rev. JABEZ LESLIE BRYCE, Bishop's Office, 8 Desvoeux Rd, Suva; tel. 3304716; fax 3302687; e-mail episcopus@connect.com.fj.

The Roman Catholic Church

Fiji comprises a single archdiocese. At 31 December 2005 there were an estimated 93,148 adherents in the country.

Bishops' Conference: Episcopal Conference of the Pacific Secretariat (CEPAC), 14 Williamson Rd, POB 289, Suva; tel. 3300340; fax 3303143; e-mail cepac@connect.com.fj; f. 1968; 17 mems; Pres. Most Rev. APURON ANTHONY SABLAN (Archbishop of Agaña, Guam); Sec.-Gen. Fr ROGER MCCARRICK.

Archbishop of Suva: Most Rev. PETERO MATACA, Archdiocesan Office, Nicolas House, 35 Pratt St, POB 109, Suva; tel. 3301955; fax 3301565; e-mail peteromataco@connect.com.fj.

Other Christian Churches

Methodist Church in Fiji & Rotuma (Lotu Wesele e Viti): Epworth Arcade, Nina St, POB 357, Suva; tel. 3311477; fax 3303771; f. 1835; autonomous since 1964; 214,982 mems (2006); Gen. Sec. Rev. A. TUGANE; Pres. Rev. LAISIASA RATABACACA.

Other denominations active in the country include the Assembly of God (with c. 7,000 mems), the Baptist Mission, the Congregational Christian Church and the Presbyterian Church.

HINDUISM

Most of the Indian community are Hindus. According to the census of 1996, some 34% of the population were Hindus.

ISLAM

In 1996 some 7% of the population were Muslim. There are several Islamic organizations:

Fiji Muslim League: POB 3990, Samabula, Suva; tel. 3384566; fax 3370204; e-mail fijimuslim@connect.com.fj; f. 1926; Nat. Pres. HAFIZUD DEAN KHAN; Gen. Sec. MOHAMMAD TAABISH AKBAR; 26 brs and 3 subsidiary orgs.

SIKHISM

Sikh Association of Fiji: Suva; Pres. HARKEWAL SINGH.

BAHÁ'Í FAITH

National Spiritual Assembly: National Office, POB 639, Suva; tel. 3387574; fax 3387772; e-mail nsafijiskm@suva.is.com.fj; mems resident in 490 localities; national headquarters for consultancy and co-ordination.

The Press

NEWSPAPERS AND PERIODICALS

Coconut Telegraph: POB 249, Savusavu, Vanua Levu; f. 1975; monthly; serves rural communities; Editor LEMA LOW.

Fiji Calling: POB 12095, Suva; tel. 3305916; fax 3301930; publ. by Associated Media Ltd; every 6 months; English; Publr YASHWANT GAUNDER.

Fiji Cane Grower: POB 12095, Suva; tel. 3305916; fax 3305256.

Fiji Daily Post: 19 Ackland St, Viria East Industrial Subdivision, Vatuwaqa, Suva; tel. 3275176; fax 3275179; e-mail info@fijidailypost.com; internet www.fijidailypost.com; f. 1987 as *Fiji Post*, daily from 1989; English; 100% govt-owned since Sept. 2003; Chair. MALAKAI NAIYAGA; Editor-in-Chief ROBERT WOLFGRAMM.

Fiji Magic: POB 12095, Suva; tel. 3305916; fax 3302852; e-mail fijimagic@fijilive.com; internet www.fijilive.com/fijimagic; publ. by Associated Media Ltd; monthly; English; Publr YASHWANT GAUNDER; circ. 15,000.

Fiji Republic Gazette: Printing Dept, POB 98, Suva; tel. 3385999; fax 3370203; f. 1874; weekly; English.

Fiji Sun: 12 Amra St, Walubay, Suva; tel. 3307555; fax 3311455; e-mail leonec@fijisun.com.fj; internet www.sun.com.fj; re-established 1999; daily; Editor LEONE CABENATABUA; Publr (vacant).

Fiji Times: 20 Gordon St, POB 1167, Suva; tel. 3304111; fax 3301521; internet www.fijitimes.com; f. 1869; publ. by Fiji Times Ltd; daily; English; Man. Dir TONY YIANNI; Editor NETANI RIKA; circ. 34,000.

Fiji Trade Review: The Rubine Group, POB 12511, Suva; tel. 3313944; monthly; English; Publr GEORGE RUBINE; Editor MABEL HOWARD.

Islands Business: 46 Gordon St, POB 12718, Suva; tel. 3303108; fax 3301423; e-mail editor@ibi.com.fj; internet www.islandsbusiness.com; regional monthly news and business magazine featuring the Fiji Islands Business supplement; English; Editor-in-Chief LAISA TAGA; circ. 8,500.

Na Tui: 422 Fletcher Rd, POB 2071, Government Bldgs, Suva; f. 1988; weekly; Fijian; Publr TANIELA BOLEA; Editor SAMISONI BOLATAGICI; circ. 7,000.

Nai Lalakai: 20 Gordon St, POB 1167, Suva; tel. 3304111; fax 3301521; e-mail fijitimes@is.com.fj; f. 1962; publ. by Fiji Times Ltd; weekly; Fijian; Editor SAMISONI KAKAIVALU; circ. 18,000.

Pacific Business: POB 12095, Suva; tel. 3305916; fax 3301930; publ. by Associated Media Ltd; monthly; English; Publr YASHWANT GAUNDER.

Pacific Telecom: POB 12095, Suva; tel. 3300591; fax 3302852; e-mail review@is.com.fj; publ. by Associated Media Ltd; monthly; English; Publr YASHWANT GAUNDER.

PACNEWS: Pacific Islands News Association, 46 Gordon St, PMB, Suva; tel. 3303623; fax 3317055; e-mail pina@connect.com.fj; internet www.pinanius.com; daily news service for the Pacific region; Editor MAKERETA KOMAI.

Pactrainer: PMB, Suva; tel. 3303623; fax 3303943; e-mail pina@is.com.fj; monthly; newsletter of Pacific Journalism Development Centre; Editor PETER LOMAS.

The Review: POB 12095, Suva; tel. 3305916; fax 3301930; e-mail review@is.com.fj; publ. by Associated Media Ltd; monthly; English; Publr YASHWANT GAUNDER.

Sartaj: John Beater Enterprises Ltd, Raiwaqa, POB 5141, Suva; f. 1988; weekly; Hindi; Editor S. DASO; circ. 15,000.

Shanti Dut: 20 Gordon St, POB 1167, Suva; f. 1935; publ. by Fiji Times Ltd; weekly; Hindi; Editor NILAM KUMAR; circ. 12,000.

Top Shot: Suva; f. 1995; golf magazine; monthly.

Volasiga: 10–16 Toorak Rd, POB 2071, Suva; f. 1988; weekly; Fijian; publ. by Fiji Daily Post; Gen. Man. ANURA BANDARA (acting); Editor SAMISONI BOLATAGICI.

The Weekender: 2 Denison Rd, POB 15652, Suva; tel. 3315477; fax 3305346; publ. by Media Resources Ltd; weekly; English; Publr JOSEFATA NATA.

PRESS ASSOCIATIONS

Fiji Islands Media Association: c/o Vasiti Ivaqa, POB 12718, Suva; tel. 3303108; fax 3301423; national press asscn; operates Fiji Press Club and Fiji Journalism Training Institute; Sec. NINA RATULELE.

Pacific Islands News Association: 46 Gordon St, PMB, Suva; tel. 3303623; fax 3317055; e-mail pina@connect.com.fj; internet www.pinanius.com; f. 1991; regional press asscn; defends freedom of information and expression, promotes professional co-operation, provides training and education; Pres. JOSEPH EALEDONA; Vice-Pres. JONAS CULLWICK.

Publishers

Fiji Times Ltd: POB 1167, Suva; tel. 3304111; fax 3301521; e-mail timesnews@fijitimes.com.fj; f. 1869; Propr News Corpn Ltd; largest newspaper publr; also publrs of books and magazines; Man. Dir TONY YIANNI.

Lotu Pasifika Productions: POB 2401, Suva; tel. 3301314; fax 3301183; f. 1973; cookery, education, poetry, religion; Gen. Man. SERU L. VEREBALAVU.

University of the South Pacific: University Media Centre, POB 1168, Suva; tel. 3313900; fax 3301305; e-mail austin_l@usp.ac.fj; f. 1986; education, natural history, regional interests.

GOVERNMENT PUBLISHING HOUSE

Printing and Stationery Department: POB 98, Suva; tel. 3385999; fax 3370203.

Broadcasting and Communications

TELECOMMUNICATIONS

Fiji International Telecommunicatons Ltd (FINTEL): 158 Victoria Parade, POB 59, Suva; tel. 3312933; fax 3305606; e-mail stuilakepa@fintelfiji.com; internet www.fintelfiji.com; 51% govt-owned; 49% owned by C & W plc; CEO SAKARAIA TUILAKEPA.

Telecom Fiji Ltd: PMB, Suva; tel. 3304019; e-mail taito.tabaleka@tfl.com.fj; internet www.telecomfiji.com.fj; Chair. FELIX ANTHONY; CEO TAITO TABALEKA (acting).

Vodafone Fiji Ltd: PMB, Suva; tel. 3312000; fax 3312007; e-mail aslam.khan@vodafone.com.; internet www.vodafone.com.fj; 51% owned by Telecom Fiji, 49% by Vodafone International Holdings BV; GSM operator; Man. Dir ASLAM KHAN.

In mid-2007 some 15 companies applied for mobile phone operators' licences.

BROADCASTING
Radio

Fiji Broadcasting Corporation Ltd—FBCL (Radio Fiji): 69 Gladstone Rd, POB 334, Suva; tel. 3314333; fax 3301643; internet www.radiofiji.com.fj; f. 1954; statutory body; jointly funded by govt grant and advertising revenue; Radio Fiji 1 broadcasts nationally on AM in English and Fijian; Radio Fiji 2 broadcasts nationally on AM in English and Hindi; Radio Fiji Gold broadcasts nationally on AM and FM in English; 104 FM and Radio Rajdhani 98 FM, mainly with musical programmes, broadcast in English and Hindi respectively, but are received only on Viti Levu; Bula FM, musical programmes, broadcasts in Fijian, received only on Viti Levu; Chair. DANIEL WHIPPY; CEO (vacant).

Communications Fiji Ltd: 231 Waimanu Rd, PMB, Suva; tel. 3314766; fax 3303748; e-mail cfl@fm96.com.fj; f. 1985; operates three commercial stations; FM 96, f. 1985, broadcasts 24 hours per day, on FM, in English; Navtarang, f. 1989, broadcasts 24 hours per day, on FM, in Hindi; Viti FM, f. 1996, broadcasts 24 hours per day, on FM, in Fijian; Man. Dir WILLIAM PARKINSON; Gen. Man. IAN JACKSON.

Radio Light/Radio Naya Jiwan: 15 Tower St, Government Bldgs, POB 2525, Suva; tel. and fax 3319956; fax 3319956; e-mail radiolight@connect.com.fj; internet www.radiolight.org; f. 1990; non-profit religious organization; broadcasts in English (Radio Light FM 106, FM 93.6) and Hindi (Radio Naya Jiwan FM 94.8) and Fijian (Nai Talai FM 103.4); Station Man. and Programmes Dir DOUGLAS ROSE.

Radio Pasifik: POB 1168, University of the South Pacific, Suva; tel. 3231000; fax 3312591; e-mail tagi_sh@usp.ac.fj; f. 1996; educational, non-profit community radio station; broadcasts in English, Fijian, French, Bislama, Tongan, Hindi and other Pacific island languages; Station Man. SHIRLEY TAGI.

Television

Film and Television Unit (FTU): c/o Department of Information, Government Bldgs, Suva; video library; production unit established by Govt and Hanns Seidel Foundation (Germany); a weekly news magazine and local documentary programmes.

Fiji Television Ltd: 20 Gorrie St, POB 2442, Government Bldgs, Suva; tel. 3305100; fax 3305077; e-mail info@fijitv.com.fj; internet www.fijitv.com.fj; f. 1994; operates two services, Fiji 1, a free channel, and Sky Fiji, a three-channel subscription service; Chair. OLOTA ROKOVUNISEI; Group CEO MESAKE NAWARI.

In 1990 two television stations were constructed at Suva and Monsavu, with aid from the People's Republic of China. A permanent television station became operational in July 1994. In 2006 it was announced that the 14% of Fiji Television Ltd held by the Government was to be sold.

Finance
BANKING
(cap. = capital; res = reserves; dep. = deposits; m. = million; brs = branches; amounts in Fiji dollars)

Central Bank

Reserve Bank of Fiji: 1 Pratt St, PMB, Suva; tel. 3313611; fax 3301688; e-mail info@rbf.gov.fj; internet www.reservebank.gov.fj; f. 1984 to replace Central Monetary Authority of Fiji (f. 1973); bank of issue; administers Insurance Act; cap. 2.0m., res 57.6m., dep. 200.7m. (Dec. 2005); Chair. and Gov. SAVENACA NARUBE.

Commercial Bank

Colonial National Bank: 3 Central St, POB 1166, Suva; tel. 3214532; fax 3303217; internet www.colonial.com.fj; f. 1974 as National Bank of Fiji; 51% acquired from Fiji Govt by Colonial Ltd in 1999; owned by Commonwealth Bank of Australia; cap. 15.0m., res 0.3m. (June 2003), dep. 317.2m. (June 2004); Pres. and Chair. MALAKAI NAIYAGA; Gen. Man. MIKE UPPERTON; 15 brs; 45 agencies.

Development Bank

Fiji Development Bank: 360 Victoria Parade, POB 104, Suva; tel. 3314866; fax 3314886; e-mail info@fijidevelopmentbank.com; internet www.fijidevelopmentbank.com; f. 1967; finances the development of natural resources, agriculture, transportation and other industries and enterprises; statutory body; applied for a commercial banking licence in Nov. 2004; cap. 56.1m., res 8.9m. (2005); Chair. TAITO WARADI; 9 brs.

Merchant Banks

Merchant Finance and Investment Company Ltd: 91 Gordon St, POB 14213, Suva; tel. 3314955; fax 3300026; e-mail merchantfi@connect.com.fj; internet www.mfl.com.fj; f. 1986; fmrly Merchant Bank of Fiji Ltd; owned by Fijian Holdings Ltd (80%), South Pacific Trustees (20%); Man. Dir S. WELEILAKEBA; 3 brs.

National MBf Finance (Fiji) Ltd: Burns Philp Bldg, 2nd Floor, POB 13525, Suva; tel. 302232; fax 3305915; e-mail mbf@is.com.fj; f. 1991; Chief Operating Officer SIEK KART; 4 brs.

STOCK EXCHANGE

South Pacific Stock Exchange: Level 2, Plaza One, Provident Plaza, 33 Ellery St, POB 11689, Suva; tel. 3304130; fax 3304145; e-mail info@spse.com.fj; internet www.spse.com.fj; fmrly Suva Stock Exchange; name changed as above in 2000; Chair. BRENDAN HARRISON (acting); Man. MESAKE NAWARI.

INSURANCE

Colonial Health Care: 3 Central St, Private Mail Bag, Suva; tel. 3314400; fax 3308955; internet www.colonial.com.fj/health; Fijian co; fmrly Blue Shield (Pacific) Ltd; assumed present name in 1990 after acquisition by Colonial Fiji Life Ltd; CEO and Pres. WILLIAM G. FRANEY.

Colonial Mutual Life Assurance Society Ltd: Colonial Bldg, PMB, Suva; tel. 314400; fax 3303448; f. 1876; inc in Australia; life; Gen. Man. SIMON SWANSON.

Dominion Insurance Ltd: 231 Waimanu Rd, POB 14468, Suva; tel. 3311055; fax 3303475; e-mail enquiries@dominioninsurance.com.fj; internet www.dominioninsurance.com.fj; general insurance; Chair. HARI PUNJA; Exec. Dir GARY S. CALLAGHAN.

Fiji Reinsurance Corpn Ltd: RBF Bldg, POB 12704, Suva; tel. 3313471; fax 3305679; 20% govt-owned; reinsurance; Chair. Ratu JONE Y. KUBUABOLA; Man. PETER MARIO.

New India Assurance Co Ltd: Harifam Centre, POB 71, Suva; tel. 3313488; fax 3302679; e-mail newindiasuva@connect.com.fj; internet www.niafiji.com; Chief Man. G. RAJAKUMAR.

QBE Insurance (Fiji) Ltd: Queensland Insurance Center, Victoria Parade, POB 101, Suva; tel. 3315455; fax 3300285; e-mail info.fiji@qbe.com; internet www.qbe.com/asiapacific; owned by Australian interests; fmrly known as Queensland Insurance (Fiji) Ltd, name changed as above 2004; Gen. Man. JOHN HUNT.

Tower Insurance Fiji Ltd: Tower House, Thomson St, GPOB 950, Suva; tel. 3315955; fax 3301376; internet www.towerinsurance.com.fj; owned by New Zealand interests; Gen. Man. PAUL ABSELL.

Trade and Industry
GOVERNMENT AGENCIES

Fiji Islands Trade and Investment Bureau: Civic House, 6th Floor, POB 2303, Victoria Parade, Suva; tel. 3315988; fax 3301783; e-mail info@ftib.org.fj; internet www.ftib.org.fj; f. 1980, restyled 1988, to promote and stimulate foreign and local economic development investment; Chair. FRANCIS B. NARAYAN; CEO JESONI VITUSAGAVULU.

Training and Productivity Authority of Fiji (TPAF): Beaumont Rd, POB 6890, Nasinu; tel. 3392000; fax 3340184; e-mail gen-enq@fntc.ac.fj; internet www.tpaf.ac.fj; fmrly Fiji National Training Council; present name assumed in 2002; Dir-Gen. JONE USAMATE.

DEVELOPMENT ORGANIZATIONS

Fiji Development Company Ltd: POB 161, FNPF Place, 350 Victoria Parade, Suva; tel. 3304611; fax 3304171; e-mail hfc@is.com.fj; f. 1960; subsidiary of the Commonwealth Development Corpn; Man. F. KHAN.

Fiji-USA Business Council: c/o FTIB, Victoria Parade, POB 2303, Suva; e-mail info@fijiusa.biz; internet www.fijiusa.biz; f. 1998 to develop and expand trade links between the two countries; Pres. RAMENDRA NARAYAN.

Fijian Development Fund Board: POB 122, Suva; tel. 3312601; fax 3302585; f. 1951; funds derived from payments of $F20 per metric ton from the sales of copra by indigenous Fijians; deposits receive interest at 2.5%; funds used only for Fijian development schemes; CEO VINCENT TOVATA.

Land Development Authority: POB 5442, Raiwaqa; tel. 33384900; fax 33384058; f. 1961 to co-ordinate development plans for land and marine resources; Chair. JONETANI GALUINADI.

CHAMBERS OF COMMERCE

Ba Chamber of Commerce: POB 99, Ba; tel. 6670134; fax 6670132; Pres. DIJENDRA SINGH.

Labasa Chamber of Commerce: POB 992, Labasa; tel. 8811467; fax 8813009; Pres. JAIWANT KRISHNA.

Lautoka Chamber of Commerce and Industry: POB 366, Lautoka; tel. 6661834; fax 6662379; e-mail vaghco@connect.com.fj; Pres. NATWARLAL VAGH.

Levuka Chamber of Commerce: POB 85, Levuka; tel. 3440248; fax 3440252; Pres. ISHRAR ALI.

Nadi Chamber of Commerce: POB 2735, Nadi; tel. 6701704; fax 6702314; e-mail arunkumar@is.com.fj; Pres. VENKAT RAMANI AIYER.

Nausori Chamber of Commerce: POB 228, Nausori; tel. 3478235; fax 3400134; Pres. ROBERT RAJ KUMAR.

Sigatoka Chamber of Commerce: POB 882, Sigatoka; tel. 6500064; fax 6520006; Pres. NATWAR SINGH.

Suva Chamber of Commerce and Industry: 37 Viria Rd, Vatuwaqa Industrial Estate, POB 337, Suva; tel. 3380975; fax 3380854; e-mail secretariat@suvachamber.org; internet www.suvachamber.org; f. 1902; Pres. Dr NUR BANO ALI; 150 mems.

Tavua-Vatukoula Chamber of Commerce: POB 698, Tavua; tel. 6680390; fax 6680390; Pres. SOHAN SINGH.

INDUSTRIAL AND TRADE ASSOCIATIONS

Fiji Kava Council: POB 17724, Suva; tel. 3386576; fax 3371844; Chair. Ratu JOSATEKI NAWALOWALO.

Fiji National Petroleum Co Ltd: Suva; f. 1991; govt-owned, distributor of petroleum products.

Fiji Sugar Corporation Ltd: Western House, 3rd Floor, Cnr of Bila and Vidilo St, PMB, Lautoka; tel. 6662655; fax 6664685; nationalized 1974; buyer of sugar cane and raw sugar mfrs; Chair. BHOO PRASAD GAUTAM; CEO ABDUL SHAMSHER (acting).

Fiji Sugar Marketing Co Ltd: Dominion House, 5th Floor, Thomson St, POB 1402, Suva; tel. 3311588; fax 3300607; Man. Dir JOHN MAY.

Mining and Quarrying Council: 42 Gorrie St, Suva; tel. 33313188; fax 3302183; e-mail employer@is.com.fj; Chief Exec. K. A. J. ROBERTS.

National Trading Corporation Ltd: POB 13673, Suva; tel. 3315211; fax 3315584; f. 1992; a govt-owned body set up to develop markets for agricultural and marine produce locally and overseas; processes and markets fresh fruit, vegetables and ginger products; CEO APIAMA CEGUMALINA.

Native Lands Trust Board: GPOB 116, Suva; tel. 3312733; fax 3312014; e-mail info@nltb.com.fj; internet www.nltb.com.fj; manages holdings of ethnic Fijian landowners; Gen. Man. and CEO KALIVATI BAKANI.

Pacific Fishing Co: Marks St, Suva; tel. 3304405; fish-canning; govt-owned.

Sugar Cane Growers' Council: Canegrowers' Bldg, 3rd Floor, 75 Drasa Ave, Lautoka; tel. 6650466; fax 6650624; e-mail canegrower@is.com.fj; f. 1985; aims to develop the sugar industry and protect the interests of registered growers; CEO JAI GAWANDER; Gen. Man. BALA DASS; Chair. VIJENDRA AUTAR.

Sugar Commission of Fiji: POB 5993, Lautoka; tel. 6664866; fax 6664051; e-mail scof@is.com.fj; Chair. GERALD BARRACK.

Sustainable Forest Industries LTD (SFI): POB 1119, Nabua, Suva; tel. 3384999; fax 3370029; e-mail info@fijimahogany.com; internet www.fijimahogany.com; Man. Dir CHRISTOPHER DONLON.

EMPLOYERS' ORGANIZATIONS

Fiji Employers' Federation: 42 Gorrie St, GPOB 575, Suva; tel. 3313188; fax 3302183; e-mail employer@fef.com.fj; internet www.fef.com.fj; f. 1960; represents 518 major employers with approx. 78,000 employees; Pres. DIXON SEETO (acting); CEO KENNETH A. J. ROBERTS.

Fiji Manufacturers' Association: POB 1308, Suva; tel. and fax 3318811; e-mail fma@connect.com.fj; internet fijimanufacturers.org; f. 1971; CEO DESMOND WHITESIDE; 68 mems.

Local Inter-Island Shipowners' Association: POB 152, Suva; fax 3303389; e-mail consortship@connect.com.fj; Pres. DURGA PRASAD; Sec. LEO B. SMITH.

Textile, Clothing and Footwear Council: POB 10015, Nabua; tel. 3384777; fax 3370446; Pres. RAMESH SOLANKI.

UTILITIES

Electricity

Fiji Electricity Authority (FEA): PMB, Suva; tel. 3311133; fax 3311882; e-mail ceo@fea.com.fj; internet www.fea.com.fj; f. 1966; govt-owned; responsible for the generation, transmission and distribution of electricity throughout Fiji; CEO ROKOSERU NABALARUA.

Water

Department of Water and Sewerage: Government Bldgs, POB 2212, Suva; Dir RAM SUMER SHANDIL.

TRADE UNIONS

Fiji Trades Union Congress (FTUC): 32 Des Voeux Rd, POB 1418, Suva; tel. 3315377; fax 3300306; e-mail ftucl@is.com.fj; f. 1952; affiliated to ITUC; 35 affiliated unions; more than 42,000 mems; Pres. DANIEL URAI MANUFOLAU; Gen. Sec. FELIX ANTHONY.

Principal affiliated unions:

Association of USP Staff (AUSPS): POB U49, Suva; tel. 3232754; fax 3301305; e-mail ausps@usp.ac.fj; f. 1977; Pres. Dr MAHENDRA REDDY; Sec. Dr EBEHARD WEBER.

Federated Airline Staff Association: Nadi Airport, POB 9259, Nadi; tel. 6722877; fax 6720068; e-mail fasa@ats.com.fj; Gen. Sec. VILIKESA NAULUMATUA.

Fiji Aviation Workers' Association: FTUC Complex, 32 Des Voeux Rd, POB 5351, Raiwaqa; tel. 3303184; fax 3311805; Pres. VALENTINE SIMPSON; Gen. Sec. ATTAR SINGH.

Fiji Bank and Finance Sector Employees' Union: 101 Gordon St, POB 853, Suva; tel. 3301827; fax 3301956; e-mail fbeu@connect.com.fj; internet www.fbfseu.org.fj; Nat. Sec. PRAMOD K. RAE.

Fiji Electricity and Allied Workers' Union: POB 1390, Lautoka; tel. 6666353; e-mail feawu@connect.com.fj; Pres. LEONE SAKETA; Sec. J. A. PAUL.

Fiji Garment, Textile and Allied Workers' Union: c/o FTUC, Raiwaqa; f. 1992.

Fiji Nursing Association: POB 1364, Suva; tel. 3305855; e-mail fna@connect.com.fj; Gen. Sec. KUINI LUTUA.

Fiji Public Service Association: 298 Waimanu Rd, POB 1405, Suva; tel. 3311922; fax 3301099; e-mail fpsags@connect.com.fj; f. 1943; 4,000 mems; Pres. REIJIELI NAVUMA; Gen. Sec. RAJESHWAR SINGH.

Fiji Sugar and General Workers' Union: 84 Naviti St, POB 330, Lautoka; tel. 6660746; fax 664888; 25,000 mems; Pres. SHIU LINGAM; Gen. Sec. FELIX ANTHONY.

Fiji Teachers' Union: 1–3 Berry Rd, Government Bldgs, POB 2203, Suva; tel. 3314099; fax 3305962; e-mail ftu@connect.com.fj; f. 1930; 4,300 mems; Pres. BALRAM; Gen. Sec. AGNI DEO SINGH.

Fijian Teachers' Association: POB 14464, Suva; tel. 3315099; fax 3304978; e-mail fta@connect.com.fj; Pres. TEVITA KOROI; Gen. Sec. MAIKA NAMUDU.

Insurance Officers' Association: POB 71, Suva; tel. 3313488; Pres. JAGDISH KHATRI; Sec. DAVID LEE.

Mineworkers' Union of Fiji: POB 876, Tavua; f. 1986; Pres. HENNESY PETERS; Sec. KAVEKINI NAVUSO.

National Farmers' Union: POB 522, Labasa; tel. 8811838; 10,000 mems (sugar-cane farmers); Pres. DEWAN CHAND; Gen. Sec. M. P. CHAUDHRY; CEO MOHAMMED LATIF SUBEDAR.

National Union of Factory and Commercial Workers: POB 989, Suva; tel. 3311155; 3,800 mems; Pres. CAMA TUILEVEUKA; Gen. Sec. JAMES R. RAMAN.

National Union of Hospitality, Catering and Tourism Industries Employees: Nadi Airport, POB 9426, Nadi; tel. 6700906; fax 6700181; e-mail nuhctie@connect.com.fj; Pres. LIVIANA QORO; Sec. DANIEL URAI (acting).

Public Employees' Union: POB 781, Suva; tel. 3304501; 6,752 mems; Pres. SEMI TIKOICINA; Gen. Sec. FILIMONE BANUVE.

Transport and Oil Workers' Union: POB 903, Suva; tel. 3302534; f. 1988; following merger of Oil and Allied Workers' Union and Transport Workers' Union; Pres. J. BOLA; Sec. MICHAEL COLUMBUS.

There are several independent trade unions, including Fiji Registered Ports Workers' Union (f. 1947; Pres. JIOJI TAHOLOSALE).

Transport

RAILWAYS

Fiji Sugar Corporation Railway: Rarawai Mill, POB 155, Ba; tel. 6674044; fax 670505; for use in cane-harvesting season, May–Dec; 595 km of permanent track and 225 km of temporary track (gauge of 600 mm), serving cane-growing areas at Ba, Lautoka and Penang on Viti Levu and Labasa on Vanua Levu; Gen. Man. ADURU KUVA.

ROADS

At the end of 1996 there were some 3,440 km of roads in Fiji, of which 49.2% were paved. A 500-km highway circles the main island of Viti Levu.

SHIPPING

There are ports of call at Suva, Lautoka, Levuka and Savusavu. The main port, Suva, handles more than 800 ships a year, including large passenger liners. Lautoka handles more than 300 vessels and liners and Levuka, the former capital of Fiji, mainly handles commercial fishing vessels. In 1996 a feasibility study into the possible establishment of a free port at Suva was commissioned. In May 1997 the Government approved 14 new ports of entry in the northern, western and central eastern districts of Fiji.

Maritime and Ports Authority of Fiji (MPAF): Administration Bldg, Princes Wharf, POB 780, Suva; tel. 3312700; fax 3300064; corporatized in 1998; Chair. DANIEL ELISHA; Port Master Capt. GEORGE MACOMBER.

Ports Terminals Ltd: POB S13, Suva; tel. 3304725; fax 3304769; e-mail herbert@suv.ptl.com.fj; internet www.fijiports.com.fj/ptl.html; f. 1998; stevedoring, pilotage, storage and warehousing; CEO H. HAZELMAN; Port Man. E. KURUSIGA.

Consort Shipping Line Ltd: Muaiwalu Complex, Rona St, Walubay, POB 152, Suva; tel. 3313344; fax 3303389; CEO HECTOR SMITH; Man. Dir JUSTIN SMIT.

Fiji Maritime Services Ltd: c/o Fiji Ports Workers and Seafarers Union, 36 Edinburgh Drive, Suva; f. 1989 by PAF and the Ports Workers' Union; services between Lautoka and Vanua Levu ports.

Inter-Ports Shipping Corpn Ltd: 25 Eliza St, Walu Bay; POB 152, Suva; tel. 3313638; f. 1984; Man. Dir JUSTIN SMITH.

Pacific Agencies (Fiji) Ltd: Level 2, Gohil Complex, Toorak Rd, Suva; tel. 3315444; fax 3301127; e-mail info@pacshipfiji.com.fj; internet www.pacificagenciesfiji.com; f. 2000 after merger of Burns Philp and Forum Shipping; shipping agents, customs agents and international forwarding agents, crew handling; Sales/Marketing Man. ALFAAZ MALLAM.

Transcargo Express Fiji Ltd: POB 936, Suva; f. 1974; Man. Dir LEO B. SMITH.

Wong's Shipping Co Ltd: Suite 647, Epworth House, Nina St, POB 1269, Suva; tel. 3311867.

CIVIL AVIATION

There is an international airport at Nadi (about 210 km from Suva), a smaller international airport at Nausori (Suva) and 15 other airfields. Nadi is an important transit airport in the Pacific and in 1990 direct flights to Japan also began.

Airports Fiji Ltd: Nadi International Airport, Nadi; tel. 6725777; fax 6725161; e-mail info@afl.com.fj; internet www.airportsfiji.com; f. 1999; owns and operates 15 public airports in Fiji, incl. two int. airports—Nadi International Airport and Nausori Airport; Chair. VILIAME LEQA; CEO Ratu SAKIUSA TUISOLIA.

Air Fiji Ltd: 219 Victoria Parade, POB 1259, Suva; tel. 3314666; fax 3300771; e-mail airfiji@connect.com.fj; internet www.airfiji.com.fj; operates 65 scheduled services daily to 15 domestic destinations; daily service to Tonga and Tuvalu and direct flights to Auckland and Sydney commenced in 1999; charter operations, aerial photography and surveillance also conducted; Chair. DOUG HAZARD; CEO SIALENI VUETAKI.

Air Pacific Ltd: Air Pacific Centre, POB 9266, Nadi International Airport, Nadi; tel. 6720777; fax 6720512; e-mail service@airpacific.com.fj; internet www.airpacific.com; f. 1951 as Fiji Airways, name changed in 1971; domestic and international services from Nausori Airport (serving Suva) to Nadi and international services to Tonga, Solomon Islands, Cook Islands, Vanuatu, Samoa, Japan, Australia, New Zealand and the USA; Kirimati Island (Kiribati) added to the Nadi-Honolulu (Hawaii) route in Oct. 2005; 51% govt-owned, 46.05% owned by Qantas (Australia); Chair. GERALD BARRACK; Man. Dir and CEO JOHN CAMPBELL.

Fijian Airways International: POB 10138, Nadi International Airport, Nadi; tel. 6724702; fax 6724654; f. 1997; service to London via Singapore and Mumbai (India) planned; Chair. NEIL UNDERHILL; CEO ALAN LINDREA.

Pacific Sun: POB 9270, Nadi International Airport, Nadi; tel. 6723555; e-mail enquiries@pacificsun.com.fj; internet www.pacificsun.com.fj; f. 1980; wholly owned subsidiary of Air Pacific Ltd; acquired Sun Air 2007; scheduled flights to domestic and regional destinations; Gen. Man. MANOA KAMIKAMICA.

Vanua Air Charters: Labasa; f. 1993; provides domestic charter and freight services; Propr CHARAN SINGH.

Tourism

Scenery, climate, fishing and diving attract visitors to Fiji, where tourism is an important industry. However, the sector was severely affected by the coup of December 2006. The number of total foreign tourist arrivals decreased from 545,168 in 2006 to an estimated 539,255 in 2007. In 2006 some 34.7% of visitors (excluding cruise-ship passengers) came from Australia, 18.3% from New Zealand, 14.3% from the USA and 12.2% from the United Kingdom. A total of 9,070 hotel rooms were available in 2006. Receipts from tourism totalled an estimated $F741.7m. in 2006.

Fiji Islands Hotels and Tourism Association (FIHTA): 42 Gorrie St, GPOB 13560, Suva; tel. 3302980; fax 3300331; e-mail info@fihta.com.fj; internet www.fihta.com.fj; fmrly Fiji Hotel Association; name changed as above in 2005; 90 active mems, over 300 assoc. mems; Pres. DIXON SEETO; Chief Exec. MEREANI KOROVAVALA.

Fiji Islands Visitors' Bureau: Suite 107, Colonial Plaza, Namaka, POB 9217, Nadi; tel. 6722433; fax 6720141; e-mail infodesk@fijifvb.gov.fj; internet www.bulafiji.com; f. 1923; Chair. PATRICK WONG; Chief Exec. (vacant); Dir of Tourism BANUVE KAUMAITOTOYA.

FINLAND

Introductory Survey

Location, Climate, Language, Religion, Flag, Capital

The Republic of Finland lies in northern Europe, bordered to the far north by Norway and to the north-west by Sweden. Russia adjoins the whole of the eastern frontier. Finland's western and southern shores are washed by the Baltic Sea. The climate varies sharply, with warm summers and cold winters. The mean annual temperature is 5°C (41°F) in Helsinki and −0.4°C (31°F) in the far north. There are two official languages: more than 93% of the population speak Finnish and 6% speak Swedish. There is a small Sámi (Lapp) population in the north. Almost all of the inhabitants profess Christianity, and about 82% belong to the Evangelical Lutheran Church. The national flag (proportions 11 by 18) displays an azure blue cross (the upright to the left of centre) on a white background. The state flag has, at the centre of the cross, the national coat of arms (a yellow-edged red shield containing a golden lion and nine white roses). The capital is Helsinki.

Recent History

Finland formed part of the Kingdom of Sweden until 1809, when it became an autonomous Grand Duchy under the Russian Empire. During the Russian revolution of 1917 the territory proclaimed its independence. Following a brief civil war, a democratic Constitution was adopted in 1919. The Soviet regime that came to power in Russia attempted to regain control of Finland but acknowledged the country's independence in 1920.

Demands by the USSR for military bases in Finland and for the cession of part of the Karelian isthmus, in south-eastern Finland, were rejected by the Finnish Government in November 1939. As a result, the USSR attacked Finland, and the two countries fought the 'Winter War', a fiercely contested conflict lasting 15 weeks, before Finnish forces were defeated. Following its surrender, Finland ceded an area of 41,880 sq km (16,170 sq miles) to the USSR in March 1940. In the hope of recovering the lost territory, Finland joined Nazi Germany in attacking the USSR in 1941. However, a separate armistice between Finland and the USSR was concluded in 1944.

In accordance with a peace treaty signed in February 1947, Finland agreed to the transfer of about 12% of its pre-war territory (including the Karelian isthmus and the Petsamo area on the Arctic coast) to the USSR, and to the payment of reparations, which totalled about US $570m. when completed in 1952. Meanwhile, in April 1948 Finland and the USSR signed the Finno-Soviet Treaty of Friendship, Co-operation and Mutual Assistance (the YYA treaty), which was extended for periods of 20 years in 1955, 1970 and again in 1983. A major requirement of the treaty was that Finland repel any attack made on the USSR by Germany, or its allies, through Finnish territory. (The treaty was replaced by a non-military agreement in 1992, see below.)

Since independence in 1917, the politics of Finland have been characterized by coalition governments (including numerous minority coalitions) and the development of consensus between parties. The Suomen Sosialidemokraattinen Puolue (SDP, Finnish Social Democratic Party) and the Suomen Keskusta (Kesk, Finnish Centre Party) have usually been the dominant participants in government. The conservative opposition gained significant support at a general election in March 1979, following several years of economic crises. A new centre-left coalition Government was formed in May, however, by Dr Mauno Koivisto, a Social Democratic economist and former Prime Minister. This four-party Government, comprising Kesk, the SDP, the Svenska Folkpartiet (SFP, Swedish People's Party) and the Suomen Kansan Demokraattinen Liitto (SKDL, Finnish People's Democratic League—an electoral alliance, which included the communists), continued to pursue deflationary economic policies.

Dr Urho Kekkonen, who had been President since 1956, resigned in October 1981. Koivisto was elected President in January 1982. He was succeeded as head of the coalition by a former Prime Minister, Kalevi Sorsa, a Social Democrat. Towards the end of 1982 the SKDL refused to support austerity measures or an increase in defence spending. This led to the reformation of the coalition in December, without the SKDL, until the general election of March 1983.

At this election the SDP won 57 of the 200 seats in the Parliament (Eduskunta), compared with 52 in the 1979 election, while the conservative opposition Kansallinen Kokoomus (Kok, National Coalition Party) lost three seats. In May Sorsa formed another centre-left coalition, comprising the SDP, the SFP, Kesk and the Suomen Maaseudun Puolue (SMP, Finnish Rural Party).

At a general election held in March 1987, the combined non-socialist parties gained a majority in the Eduskunta for the first time since the election of 1945. Although the SDP remained the largest single party, with 56 seats, the system of modified proportional representation enabled Kok to gain an additional nine seats, winning a total of 53, while increasing its share of the votes cast by only 1%. President Koivisto eventually invited Harri Holkeri, a former Chairman of Kok, to form a coalition Government comprising Kok, the SDP, the SFP and the SMP, thus avoiding a polarization of the political parties within the Eduskunta. Holkeri became the first conservative Prime Minister since 1946.

In February 1988 Koivisto retained office after the first presidential election by direct popular vote (in accordance with constitutional changes adopted in the previous year), following his campaign for a reduction in presidential power. He did not win the required absolute majority, however, and an electoral college was convened. Koivisto was re-elected after an endorsement by Holkeri, who had also contested the presidency and who had received the third highest number of direct votes (behind Paavo Väyrynen, the leader of Kesk).

At a general election held in March 1991, Kesk obtained 55 seats, the SDP gained 48 seats, and Kok 40. In April a coalition Government, comprising Kesk, Kok, the SFP and the Suomen Kristillinen Liitto (SKL, Finnish Christian Union), took office. The new coalition constituted the country's first wholly non-socialist Government for 25 years. The Chairman of Kesk, Esko Aho, was appointed Prime Minister. In March 1993 Koivisto announced that he would not contest the forthcoming presidential election. In the first stage of the election, which took place in January 1994, the two most successful candidates were Martti Ahtisaari (the SDP candidate and a senior UN official), with 25.9% of the votes cast, and Elisabeth Rehn (the SFP candidate and Minister of Defence), with 22.0%, both of whom were firm supporters of Finland's application for membership of the European Union (EU, see p. 244), as the European Community (EC) had been restyled in late 1993. In accordance with constitutional changes adopted since the previous election (stipulating that, if no candidate gained more than 50% of the votes cast, the electorate should choose between the two candidates with the most votes), a second stage of the election took place in February 1994. Ahtisaari secured victory, with 53.9% of the votes cast, and took office in March.

At a general election held in March 1995, the SDP obtained 63 seats in the Eduskunta, Kesk secured 44 seats, Kok 39, and the Vasemmistoliitto (Left Alliance—formed in 1990 by a merger of the communist parties and the SKDL) 22. A new coalition Government was formed in April, comprising the SDP, Kok, the SFP, the Vasemmistoliitto and the Vihreä Liitto (VL, Green League). Paavo Lipponen, the leader of the SDP, replaced Aho as Prime Minister, and Sauli Niinistö, the Chairman of Kok, became Deputy Prime Minister.

Following a general election held in March 1999, the SDP remained the largest party in the Eduskunta, with 51 seats. Kesk won 48 seats and Kok 46 in an election that was characterized by a low rate of voter participation, at 68.3%. In April the five parties of the outgoing Government agreed to form a new coalition. Lipponen remained Prime Minister, while Niinistö was reappointed as Minister of Finance.

A presidential election was held in January and February 2000, at which Ahtisaari did not seek re-election, following his failure to secure the nomination of the SDP. In mid-January seven candidates contested the first round of the ballot, which was won by Tarja Halonen (the SDP candidate and Minister of

Foreign Affairs), who received 40% of the votes cast; the second largest share of the vote (34.4%) was obtained by Aho. Having won a second round of voting on 6 February (with 51.6% of the votes cast), Halonen took office as the first female President of Finland on 1 March.

A new Constitution entered into force on 1 March 2000, under the provisions of which the executive power of the President was significantly reduced while the real authority of the Eduskunta was increased, with the power of decision-making being divided more equally between the Eduskunta, the Cabinet (Valtioneuvosto) and the President. According to the 1919 Constitution, the President had appointed the Prime Minister and the other ministers; however, under the new Constitution, the Eduskunta elected the Prime Minister (who was then officially appointed by the President) and the other government ministers were appointed by the President on the basis of nominations by the Prime Minister. In addition, according to new constitutional provisions, the President was to co-operate more closely with the Cabinet on issues of foreign policy.

Following his defeat in the presidential election, Aho took leave from domestic politics for one year from August 2000 to lecture at Harvard University in the USA. Anneli Jäätteenmäki, a former Minister of Justice, was elected to replace Aho as Chairman of Kesk during his sabbatical. The two principal parties in the coalition (the SDP and Kok) suffered losses at municipal elections held on 22 October, while Kesk secured the largest gains, winning 23.8% of the votes cast to become the largest municipal party. Voter participation in the local elections was only 55.8% of the electorate (compared with 61.3% in 1996). Popular support for Jäätteenmäki's leadership of Kesk prompted Aho's resignation in mid-2002 and the election of Jäätteenmäki as Chairperson.

In November 2000 the stability of the coalition Government was threatened by a controversial proposal by a Finnish electricity company to build a fifth nuclear reactor in Finland, the first such proposal in Western Europe since the mid-1980s. In January 2002 the construction of the new reactor was approved by the Cabinet, despite the opposition of seven ministers, led by the Chairman of the VL and Minister of Health and Social Services, Osmo Soininvaara. The Eduskunta approved the proposal in May, by 107 votes to 92, prompting the resignation of the VL from the coalition Government; the coalition retained a majority in the Eduskunta, however, with 130 seats. It was originally envisaged that the reactor would become operational in early 2009. However, following delays in construction, in December 2007 the company behind the project estimated that the reactor would not commence operations until mid-2011. Meanwhile, after the centre-right coalition Government that took office in April 2007 indicated that it would consider the expansion of the nuclear sector under its energy policy, preliminary plans for the construction of additional reactors were submitted by three energy companies.

In November 2002 the Government survived, by 106 votes to 64, a motion of 'no confidence' over its role in the seriously unprofitable investments of the partly state-owned telecommunications company Sonera. In October a government inquiry into the affair had exonerated the Prime Minister and the Cabinet from any responsibility for a corporate error that had left the company heavily indebted.

A general election was held on 16 March 2003; 69.7% of the electorate participated in the poll. Kesk won the largest representation in the new Eduskunta, securing 55 seats, while the SDP won 53 seats (an increase of two compared with the last election). Although the SDP made gains, the three other members of the former governing coalition lost seats, with Kok suffering the worst reverse, with the loss of six seats (winning 40 seats). The Eduskunta met at the end of March and named Jäätteenmäki as its Speaker. Under the new Constitution, the party with the largest representation was to lead negotiations regarding the formation of a coalition government. Accordingly, in early April Kesk formed a coalition Government with the SDP and the SFP (which had obtained eight seats), with Jäätteenmäki as Prime Minister (her role as Speaker of the Eduskunta was assumed by Lipponen). Jäätteenmäki was the country's first female Prime Minister, and, with her appointment, Finland became the only country in Europe with women simultaneously holding the posts of Prime Minister and President.

Jäätteenmäki's premiership was, however, extremely short-lived. On 18 June 2003, just 63 days after her inauguration, she resigned following allegations that she had improperly used classified foreign ministry information to discredit outgoing Prime Minister Lipponen and secure victory for Kesk in the general election. The leaked documents, one of which recorded exchanges between Lipponen and the US President, George W. Bush, in December 2002, were reportedly used by Jäätteenmäki to portray Lipponen as being overly supportive of US policy regarding Iraq; the majority of Finns were opposed to the US-led military action launched in Iraq in March 2003 to remove the regime of Saddam Hussain. Jäätteenmäki's subsequent claims made to the Eduskunta that the documents were unsolicited were contradicted by Martti Manninen, the presidential aide responsible for divulging their contents. The Deputy Chairman of Kesk, Matti Vanhanen, who had been assigned the post of Minister of Defence in the new Government, was appointed to replace Jäätteenmäki as Prime Minister. Jäätteenmäki, while continuing to reject allegations of any wrongdoing on her part, also stood down from her position as Chairperson of Kesk; Vanhanen was elected to replace her at a special party convention held on 4 October. In December Jäätteenmäki was charged with inciting or assisting Manninen publicly to divulge official secrets. Jäätteenmäki and Manninen (who was charged with violating official secrecy) stood trial in March 2004; Jäätteenmäki was acquitted but Manninen was found guilty and fined 80 days' salary.

In August 2004 Prime Minister Vanhanen confirmed that as the Treaty establishing a Constitution for Europe commanded widespread popular support in Finland a referendum would not be necessary. The constitutional treaty, which aimed to facilitate the smooth functioning of the EU following its enlargement in May 2004, had been signed by the EU Heads of State or of Government in October 2004, but remained subject to ratification by a vote in the national legislature or by referendum in each of the 25 member states. The Eduskunta had been expected to ratify the constitutional treaty in late 2005 or early 2006, but the Finnish parliamentary vote was postponed indefinitely following the rejection of the treaty at public referendums in France and the Netherlands in mid-2005. However, in December 2006, at the end of Finland's presidency of the EU (see below), the Eduskunta approved the ratification of the constitutional treaty by 125 votes to 39, bringing to 16 the number of countries that had ratified the treaty. None the less, as ratification by all member states was required, the constitutional treaty was subsequently abandoned and an Intergovernmental Conference was convened to draft a replacement. The resulting Treaty of Lisbon amending the Treaty on European Union and the Treaty establishing the European Community, which retained many of the provisions of the constitutional treaty (although it amended existing treaties rather than replacing them), was signed in December 2007 by the EU heads of state or of government. It was hoped that the ratification process would be completed by the end of 2008.

A central topic of political discourse in 2004 was Finland's defence policy. The debate was partly prompted by the establishment of EU rapid reaction forces (see below), but was also focused on the compilation of the latest government security and defence policy report. The report confirmed that Finland's defence would continue to be based on the maintenance and development of a credible defence capability as a militarily neutral and non-aligned country, but also retained as a 'possibility' the option of a future application for membership of the North Atlantic Treaty Organization (NATO, see p. 340). The opposition Kok criticized the report, which was submitted to the Eduskunta in late 2004, arguing that the EU's intensifying co-operation on defence, notably the security guarantees contained in the constitutional treaty, meant that Finland was effectively militarily aligned, and demanded an unprecedented parliamentary vote to confirm that Finland could no longer be considered a non-aligned country. The Government defeated the motion by a comfortable margin in December, with the Eduskunta voting to remain non-aligned. The timetable of Finland's accession to the Ottawa Convention, prohibiting anti-personnel landmines, was also agreed in December; Finland would sign the convention in 2012 and destroy its landmines by 2016. However, Finland's plan to replace its landmines with cluster bombs proved controversial in early 2007, following an international conference held in February in Oslo, Norway, during which Finland and 45 other countries agreed to commence talks on a treaty to prohibit cluster bombs. President Halonen and the Finnish Chief of Defence, Adm. Juhani Kaskeala, insisted that the weapons Finland intended to purchase conformed to internationally agreed standards and, thus, their acquisition would not contradict the Oslo agreement.

The Government announced its decision in late 2004 to contribute to two battle groups as part of the EU rapid reaction force; the first with Sweden and Norway as partners (although Norway was not a member of the EU), which Estonia and Ireland also subsequently joined, and the second with Germany and the Netherlands. Participation in the battle groups, which were ready to be deployed to international crisis areas from 2007, raised the issue of the potential reform of the Finnish Peace-keeping Act to permit Finnish contributions to military operations authorized by the EU alone, rather than the present requirement for authorization by the UN or the Organization for Security and Co-operation in Europe (see p. 354).

Lipponen resigned as leader of the SDP at a party conference in June 2005; Eero Heinäluoma, hitherto General Secretary of the party, was elected to succeed him. In September, as part of a government reorganization, Heinäluoma entered the Cabinet as Deputy Prime Minister and Minister of Finance, replacing Antii Kalliomäki, who was appointed Minister of Education.

A presidential election was held on 15 and 29 January 2006. Nine candidates contested the first round of voting, at which the incumbent, Halonen, received the largest share of the votes cast, with 46.3%, followed by Niinistö, representing Kok, who secured 24.1%, and Prime Minister Vanhanen, the Kesk candidate, with 18.6%. Halonen narrowly defeated Niinistö in a second round of voting, in which 77.2% of the electorate participated, with 51.8% of the votes cast. It was thought that her re-election made further progress towards Finland joining NATO unlikely during her second six-year term.

At the general election, held on 18 March 2007, Kesk narrowly retained its position as the largest party in the Eduskunta, securing 51 seats, with 23.1% of the votes cast. The largest gains were made by Kok, which won 50 seats (an increase of 10 seats compared with the last election), with 22.3% of the votes cast. By contrast, the SDP suffered a significant loss, taking only 45 seats (a loss of eight seats compared with 2003), with 21.4% of the votes cast. The election was characterized by the lowest rate of voter participation recorded since 1939, at just 67.9%. As leader of the largest party in the new Eduskunta, Vanhanen led talks over the formation of a new coalition government. In mid-April 2007 Kesk, Kok, the SFP and the VL reached an agreement on the formation of a new, centre-right coalition, under which Kesk and Kok would each hold eight ministerial portfolios and the SFP and the VL two apiece. On 19 April President Halonen officially appointed the new Cabinet, in which Vanhanen remained as Prime Minister. For Kok, the most notable appointments were Jyrki Katainen as Deputy Prime Minister and Minister of Finance and Ilkka Kanerva as Minister for Foreign Affairs. The leader of the SFP, Stefan Wallin, remained in the Government, assuming a new role as Minister of Culture and Sport, while the Chairperson of the VL, Tarja Cronberg, became Minister of Labour. The new administration, which identified reducing taxes and increasing the employment rate as priorities, was the largest ever Finnish Cabinet and also the first in which female members outnumbered their male counterparts. (The new Government comprised a total of 20 ministers, 12 of whom were women.) Niinistö was elected as the new Speaker of the Eduskunta in late April.

The Government was forced to make concessions to health care workers in the public sector in November 2007, after more than 12,000 nurses threatened to resign over a pay dispute. The Eduskunta had earlier adopted legislation that would have allowed municipal authorities to compel nurses who resigned to work in emergencies. Wage increases of 22%–28% over four years were finally agreed, compared with an initial offer of 12% and the 24% rise over two years demanded by the nurses' trade union. Also in November, following a shooting incident at a secondary school in Jokela, in southern Finland, in which a student killed eight people, the Government announced the withdrawal of its objections to proposed new EU legislation that would impose stricter conditions on the acquisition and use of firearms by children under the age of 18.

Minor changes to the Cabinet took effect from January 2008. A new Ministry of Employment and the Economy was established to replace the Ministry of Trade and Industry and the Ministry of Labour. Mauri Pekkarinen, hitherto Minister of Trade and Industry, was appointed as Minister of Economic Affairs, while Cronberg became Minister of Employment within the new ministry. In April 2008 Kanerva was forced to resign as Minister of Foreign Affairs, following revelations in the media that he had sent more than 200 text messages to an erotic dancer on his state-financed mobile cellular telephone. He was succeeded by Alexander Stubb, also of Kok, who had hitherto served as a member of the European Parliament.

Finland has traditionally maintained a neutral stance in foreign affairs. It joined the UN and the Nordic Council (see p. 424) in 1955, but became a full member of the European Free Trade Association (EFTA, see p. 412) only in 1986. In 1989 Finland joined the Council of Europe (see p. 225). A free trade agreement between Finland and the EC took effect in 1974. In March 1992 the Finnish Government formally applied to join the EC. In a referendum on the question of Finland's accession to membership of the EU, which was held on 16 October 1994, 56.9% of the votes cast were in favour of membership, and in November the treaty of accession was ratified after protracted debate in the Eduskunta. Opponents of EU membership highlighted the benefits of Finland's traditional policy of neutrality, particularly with regard to Russian national security considerations. The Government declared, however, that Finland's neutral stance would not be compromised either by joining the EU or by its stated intention to participate in NATO's 'Partnership for Peace' programme, and announced that it would not seek full membership of NATO or Western European Union (WEU, see p. 426). Finland left EFTA and joined the EU, as scheduled, on 1 January 1995. Finland has proved its commitment to European integration, joining Economic and Monetary Union (EMU), which commenced on 1 January 1999. In 2004 Finland announced its participation (330 troops) in two EU battle groups, forming part of the EU's rapid reaction force, which were ready for international deployment to crisis areas from 2007. In late 2006 NATO invited non-member states involved in the 'Partnership for Peace' programme, such as Finland and Sweden, to take part in operations of NATO's rapid reaction force, the NATO Response Force (NRF). The Finnish Government subsequently agreed to the participation of its troops in NRF training exercises, but emphasized that the deployment of soldiers in actual operations would be decided separately on a case-by-case basis.

In July 1999 Finland assumed the presidency of the EU for the first time. During its six-month incumbency the Government had intended to promote economic and cultural links in the so-called 'Northern Dimension'—the Nordic countries, the Baltic states and Russia. In the event, this agenda was superseded by the conflict over the Serbian region of Kosovo and Metohija in Yugoslavia, which led to Western military intervention from March. Finland contributes some 400 troops to the Kosovo Force (KFOR), an international NATO-led force responsible for establishing and maintaining security in Kosovo since 1999, and continues its commitment to peace-keeping in Bosnia and Herzegovina by contributing troops to the EU Force (EUFOR) in that country, known as EUFOR-Althea, which assumed responsibility for operations there in December 2004. Finland assumed the EU presidency for a second time in July 2006 and was immediately praised for its diplomacy, negotiating a common EU stance regarding the conflict in Lebanon between Israeli armed forces and the Shi'ite militant group Hezbollah. Relations between the EU and Russia, energy security and EU enlargement had been considered the most pressing issues during the Finnish presidency. However, by the end of its incumbency in December no major progress had been made regarding Russia, and talks on the proposed accession of Turkey to the EU appeared to have reached an impasse. In late 2007 Finland pledged to contribute troops to a EUFOR mission in eastern Chad and north-eastern Central African Republic, where more than 200,000 refugees from the Darfur region of western Sudan had sought refuge from violence in their own country. The force was to begin deployment in February 2008.

Following the terrorist attacks of 11 September 2001 in the USA, Finland did not participate in the US-led retaliatory military action against the Taliban regime in Afghanistan. Finnish military personnel did, however, take part in the subsequent peace-keeping operation in Afghanistan as part of a wider UN-authorized multinational body (the International Security Assistance Force—ISAF) including NATO forces. NATO assumed formal control of the ISAF in August 2003. In February 2006 the Finnish contribution to the ISAF was increased from around 90 troops to 100, most of whom were to be redeployed from the capital of Afghanistan, Kabul, to the north of the country. Finland was opposed to military action against the regime of Saddam Hussain in Iraq in early 2003 without a UN Security Council resolution, but indicated that it would be prepared to take part in military action under UN auspices and in possible humanitarian and peace-keeping operations. In the event, Finland pledged US $5.1m. for reconstruction in Iraq but did not send any troops.

The pursuance of friendly relations with the USSR, and latterly Russia, has generally been regarded as a priority in Finnish foreign affairs. In October 1989 Mikhail Gorbachev became the first Soviet Head of State to visit Finland since 1975, and recognized Finland's neutral status. The 1948 Finno-Soviet Treaty of Friendship, Co-operation and Mutual Assistance, which bound Finland to a military defence alliance with the USSR and prevented the country from joining any international organization (including the EC) whose members posed a military threat to the USSR, was replaced in January 1992 by a 10-year agreement, signed by Finland and Russia, which involved no military commitment. The agreement was to be automatically renewed for five-year periods unless annulled by either signatory. The new treaty also included undertakings by the two countries not to use force against each other and to respect the inviolability of their common border and each other's territorial integrity. Generally amicable Finno-Russian relations continued in the mid-2000s, with President Halonen and the Russian President, Vladimir Putin, meeting on a number of occasions.

During 2005 Finland hosted a series of peace negotiations between the Indonesian Government and separatist rebels from the Indonesian province of Aceh. Mediated by former President Ahtisaari, the talks led to the signature of a peace agreement in August of that year. Representatives of groups involved in the conflict in Iraq held discussions in Helsinki in September 2007. Facilitated by a conflict prevention organization founded by Ahtisaari, the talks resulted in an agreement on a set of principles for negotiations aimed at achieving national reconciliation.

A joint Finnish-Norwegian survey of the two countries' border in Arctic Lapland concluded in January 2002 that the Inarijoki River, the deepest point of which is taken to mark the border, had changed its course. Consequently, an unnamed island in the middle of the river, which had previously been Norwegian, was found to be part of Finland. Norway accordingly transferred the island to Finland.

Government

Finland has a republican Constitution, under the provisions of which executive power is divided between the Eduskunta (Parliament), the Valtioneuvosto (Cabinet) and the President. The unicameral Eduskunta has 200 members, elected by universal adult suffrage for four years on the basis of proportional representation. The President is elected for six years by direct popular vote. Legislative power is exercised by the Eduskunta. The Eduskunta elects the Prime Minister, who is then appointed by the President. The other government ministers are appointed by the President on the basis of nominations by the Prime Minister. Finland is divided into 452 municipalities, which are guaranteed self-government and are entitled to levy taxes. The province of Ahvenanmaa (the Aland Islands) has rights of legislation in internal affairs.

Defence

As assessed at November 2007, the armed forces of Finland numbered 29,300 (of whom 19,200 were conscripts serving up to 12 months), comprising an army of 20,500 (15,600 conscripts), an air force of 4,700 (1,600 conscripts) and a navy of 4,100 (2,000 conscripts). There were also some 237,000 reserves and a 3,100-strong frontier guard (under the Ministry of the Interior). The proposed defence budget for 2007 was 2,220m. euros (equivalent to 5.5% of total proposed budgetary expenditure). In November 2004 the European Union (EU, see p. 244) ministers responsible for defence agreed to create 13 'battlegroups' (each numbering about 1,500 men), which could be deployed at short notice to crisis areas around the world. The EU battlegroups, two of which were to be ready for deployment at any one time, following a rotational schedule, reached full operational capacity from 1 January 2007. Finland was committed to two battlegroups; the Nordic battle group, which was led by Sweden with contributions from Norway, Estonia and Ireland, and a second battlegroup with Germany and the Netherlands.

Economic Affairs

In 2006, according to estimates by the World Bank, Finland's gross national income (GNI), measured at average 2004–06 prices, was US $213,626m., equivalent to $40,650 per head (or $35,150 per head on an international purchasing-power parity basis). During 1996–2006, it was estimated, the population increased at an average annual rate of 0.3%, while gross domestic product (GDP) per head increased, in real terms, by an average of 3.4% per year. Overall GDP increased, in real terms, at an average annual rate of 3.6% in 1996–2006; growth was 5.5% in 2006.

Agriculture (including hunting, forestry and fishing) contributed an estimated 2.5% of GDP in 2006 and employed 5.0% of the working population in that year. Forestry is the most important branch of the sector, with products of the wood and paper industries providing 20.2% of export earnings in 2004. Animal husbandry is the predominant form of farming. The major crops are barley, oats and sugar beet. During 1996–2006 agricultural GDP increased, in real terms, by an average of 1.2% per year; agricultural GDP declined by 1.0% in 2006.

Industry (including mining, manufacturing, construction and power) provided 32.3% of GDP in 2006 and employed 25.8% of the working population in that year. Industrial GDP increased, in real terms, by an average of 5.2% per year during 1996–2006; industrial GDP increased by 8.7% in 2006.

Mining and quarrying contributed 0.3% of GDP in 2006 and employed 0.2% of the working population in that year. The GDP of the mining sector increased, in real terms, at an average rate of 2.0% per year during 1996–2006; mining GDP increased by 14.6% in 2006. Gold is the major mineral export, and zinc ore, copper ore and lead ore are also mined in small quantities.

Manufacturing provided 23.6% of GDP in 2006 and employed 17.9% of the working population in that year. The most important branches of manufacturing measured by value of output in 2006 were electrical and optical equipment, including the electronics industry (particularly mobile telephones), metal products, non-electrical machinery and equipment and pulp, paper and paper products. The GDP of the manufacturing sector increased, in real terms, at an average rate of 5.6% per year during 1996–2006; the sector's GDP increased by 9.5% in 2006.

Of total energy generated in 2004, 26.5% was derived from nuclear energy, 27.5% from coal, 17.6% from hydroelectric power and 14.9% from natural gas. In early 2008 there were four nuclear reactors in operation. Construction of a fifth nuclear plant, a 1,600-MW nuclear reactor in Olkiluoto in south-west Finland, was scheduled for completion in 2011. Imports of mineral fuels comprised 15.4% of the total cost of imports in 2006.

Services provided 65.1% of GDP in 2006 and engaged 69.2% of the employed labour force in that year. In real terms, the combined GDP of the services sector increased at an average rate of 3.6% per year during 1996–2006; growth in the sector's GDP was 3.8% in 2006.

In 2006 Finland recorded a visible trade surplus of US $11,553m., and there was a surplus of $12,348m. on the current account of the balance of payments. In 2006 the principal source of imports was Russia (providing 14.1% of total imports); other major sources were Germany (13.9%) and Sweden (9.8%). Germany was the principal market for exports in the same year (accounting for 11.3% of total exports); other major purchasers were Sweden (10.5%), Russia (10.1%), the USA (6.5%) and the United Kingdom (6.5%). The European Union (EU, see p. 244) accounted for 54.3% of exports and 53.2% of imports in 2006. The principal exports in that year were machinery and transport equipment (mainly electronic products, notably mobile telephones), basic manufactures (mainly paper and paperboard), chemicals and related products and crude materials. The principal imports were machinery and transport equipment, basic manufactures, mineral fuels and lubricants and chemicals and related products.

In 2006 there was a budgetary surplus of €1,747m., equivalent to 1.0% of GDP. In 2006, according to preliminary official figures, Finland's general government gross public debt was equivalent to 39.1% of GDP. The average annual rate of inflation was 1.5% during 1996–2006. Consumer prices increased by 1.8% in 2006. The rate of unemployment declined from 16.6% in 1994 to 7.7% in 2006. Unemployment stood at 6.0% in December 2007.

Finland is a member of the Nordic Council (see p. 424) and the Organisation for Economic Co-operation and Development (OECD, see p. 347). In January 1995 it left the European Free Trade Association (see p. 412) and joined the EU. Finland participated in Economic and Monetary Union (EMU), introducing the single European currency, the euro, in January 1999.

Following a sharp recession at the beginning of the 1990s, Finland's economy has consistently achieved higher growth rates than the European average. As a result of reforms undertaken in the 1990s, Finland has become one of the most competitive countries in the world. This competitiveness stems from

FINLAND

providing a favourable environment for large international companies, with skilled employees, high levels of labour productivity and transparent and predictable economic policy. Finland hopes to maintain this position by investing heavily in research and development (on which it spent 3.5% of GDP in 2005, second only to Sweden) and education. However, Finland's dependence on the narrow base of the high technology industry, particularly its reliance on telecommunications, notably the largest company in the economy, Nokia, leaves the Finnish economy exposed to global fluctuations in this sector. The significant forestry sector is also vulnerable to external market forces. The success of the Finnish economy was threatened in the longer term by the demographic pressures of a rapidly ageing population, in conjunction with generous welfare benefits. The Ministry of Finance estimated that the old-age dependency ratio (i.e. the number of people over the age of 65 as a percentage of the population aged 15–64) would increase from 24% in 2005 to 45% by 2030. The Government introduced a pension reform programme in 2005, which was expected to encourage older workers to remain in the labour force and to lower the cost of pensions by reducing pension entitlements. The new Government, which took office in April 2007, remained committed to previous economic policy, but placed an increased emphasis on job creation through expansion and tax reduction. Whereas Finland had previously experienced high unemployment levels, by the mid-2000s unemployment had declined significantly and shortages of labour were beginning to manifest themselves in certain sectors. Plans to increase the employment rate focused on the reform of regulation and increasing the participation of older and young workers in the labour force, as well as taking advantage of immigrant workers, whose unemployment rate remained three times greater than that of Finnish nationals. The new Government's programme included tax reductions of €2,200m., comprising income tax cuts and reductions in value-added tax and inheritance tax, funded by continuing budgetary surpluses. The economy continued to expand rapidly in 2007, with real GDP growth estimated at 4.4% and continued trade and current account surpluses. Growth was expected to moderate during 2008 but to remain above the EU average.

Education

Compulsory education was introduced in 1921. By the 1977/78 school year, the whole country had transferred to a new comprehensive education system. Tuition is free and the core curriculum is the same for all students. Compulsory attendance lasts for nine years, and is divided into a six-year lower stage, beginning at the age of seven, and a three-year upper stage (or lower secondary stage), beginning at the age of 13. After comprehensive school, the pupil may continue his or her studies, either at a general upper secondary school, or a vocational upper secondary school. The upper secondary school curriculum is designed for three years but may be completed in two or four years. Courses leading to basic vocational qualifications take three years to complete. The matriculation examination taken at the end of three years of general upper secondary school gives eligibility for higher education, as do three-year vocational diplomas. In 2005 enrolment at pre-primary level included 59% of children in the relevant age-group (59% for both boys and girls). Enrolment at primary schools in that year included 99% of those in the relevant age-group (98% of boys; 99% of girls), while the comparable ratio for secondary enrolment was 95% (95% of boys; 96% of girls). Higher education is provided by 20 universities and 31 polytechnics. In 2005 enrolment at tertiary level was equivalent to 92% of those in the relevant age-group. Of total proposed budgetary expenditure by the central Government in 2008, €6,889m. (equivalent to 15.3% of total proposed expenditure) was allocated to the Ministry of Education.

Public Holidays

2008: 1 January (New Year's Day), 6 January (Epiphany), 21 March (Good Friday), 24 March (Easter Monday), 1 May (May Day and Ascension Day), 11 May (Whitsun), 21 June (Midsummer Day), 1 November (All Saints' Day), 6 December (Independence Day), 24–26 December (Christmas).

2009: 1 January (New Year's Day), 6 January (Epiphany), 10 April (Good Friday), 13 April (Easter Monday), 1 May (May Day), 21 May (Ascension Day), 31 May (Whitsun), 20 June (Midsummer Day), 31 October (All Saints' Day), 6 December (Independence Day), 24–26 December (Christmas).

Weights and Measures

The metric system is in force.

Statistical Survey

Source (unless otherwise specified): Statistics Finland, 00022 Helsinki; tel. (9) 17342220; fax (9) 17342279; e-mail kirjasto@tilastokeskus.fi; internet www.tilastokeskus.fi.

Note: Figures in this survey include data for the autonomous Åland Islands.

Area and Population

AREA, POPULATION AND DENSITY

Area (sq km)	
Land	304,473
Inland water	33,672
Total	338,145*
Population (census results)	
31 December 1995	5,116,826
31 December 2000	
Males	2,529,341
Females	2,651,774
Total	5,181,115
Population (official estimate at 31 December)	
2005	5,255,580
2006	5,276,955
2007	5,299,728
Density (per sq km) at 31 December 2007	15.7†

* 130,559 sq miles.
† Land area only.

REGIONS
(estimated population at 31 December 2006)

	Land area (sq km)*	Population	Density (per sq km)*
Uusimaa (Nyland)	6,366	1,373,600	215.8
Itä-Uusimaa (Östra Nyland)	2,747	93,853	34.2
Varsinais-Suomi (Egentliga Finland)	10,624	457,789	43.1
Satakunta	7,928	229,360	28.9
Kanta-Häme (Egentliga Tavastland)	5,204	169,952	32.7
Pirkanmaa (Birkaland)	12,633	472,181	37.4
Päijät-Häme (Päijänne-Tavastland)	5,133	199,235	38.8
Kymenlaakso (Kymmenedalen)	5,106	184,241	36.1
Etelä-Karjala (Södra Karelen)	5,618	135,255	24.1
Etelä-Savo (Södra Savolax)	14,137	159,492	11.3
Pohjois-Savo (Norra Savolax)	16,808	249,498	14.8

FINLAND

—continued

	Land area (sq km)*	Population	Density (per sq km)*
Pohjois-Karjala (Norra Karelen)	17,782	167,519	9.4
Keski-Suomi (Mellersta Finland)	16,582	269,636	16.3
Etelä-Pohjanmaa (Södra Österbotten)	13,458	193,585	14.4
Pohjanmaa (Österbotten)	7,676	174,211	22.7
Keski-Pohjanmaa (Mellersta Österbotten)	5,284	70,672	13.4
Pohjois-Pohjanmaa (Norra Österbotten)	35,290	380,668	10.8
Kainuu (Kajanaland)	21,567	84,350	3.9
Lappi (Lappland)	93,004	184,935	2.0
Ahvenanmaa (Åland)	1,527	26,923	17.6
Total	304,473	5,276,955	17.3

* Excluding inland waters, totalling 33,672 sq km.

PRINCIPAL TOWNS
(estimated population at 31 December 2006)*

Helsinki (Helsingfors) (capital)	564,521	Kuopio		90,960
Espoo (Esbo)	235,019	Jyväskylä		84,739
Tampere (Tammerfors)	206,368	Pori (Björneborg)		76,185
		Lappeenranta (Villmanstrand)		59,118
Vantaa (Vanda)	189,711			
Turku (Åbo)	175,354	Joensuu		57,797
Oulu (Uleåborg)	130,178	Vaasa (Vasa)		57,622
Lahti	98,766	Kotka		54,607

* According to the regional division of 1 January 2007.

BIRTHS, MARRIAGES AND DEATHS

	Registered live births* Number	Rate (per 1,000)	Registered marriages† Number	Rate (per 1,000)	Registered deaths* Number	Rate (per 1,000)
1999	57,574	11.1	24,271	4.7	49,345	9.6
2000	56,742	11.0	26,150	5.1	49,339	9.5
2001	56,189	10.8	24,830	4.8	48,550	9.4
2002	55,555	10.7	26,969	5.2	49,418	9.5
2003	56,630	10.9	25,815	5.0	48,996	9.4
2004	57,758	11.0	29,342	5.6	47,600	9.1
2005	57,745	11.0	29,283	5.6	47,928	9.1
2006	58,840	11.2	28,236	5.4	48,065	9.1

* Including Finnish nationals temporarily outside the country.
† Data relate only to marriages in which the bride was domiciled in Finland.

Expectation of life (years at birth, WHO estimates): 79.1 (males 75.7; females 82.4) in 2005 (Source: WHO, *World Health Statistics*).

ECONOMICALLY ACTIVE POPULATION
(annual averages, '000 persons aged 15 to 74 years)

	2004	2005	2006
Agriculture, forestry and fishing	122	121	123
Mining and quarrying	6	6	6
Manufacturing	432	433	437
Electricity, gas and water	16	16	16
Construction	157	165	171
Wholesale and retail trade; repair of motor vehicles, and household goods	300	307	313
Hotels and restaurants	75	76	76
Transport, storage and communications	172	170	173
Financial intermediation and insurance	38	38	39
Real estate and business activities	245	254	269
Public administration and defence; compulsory social security	173	172	171
Education	161	161	163
Health and social work	347	354	357
Other community, social and personal service activities	116	118	119
Household service activities	7	8	8
Total employed	2,365	2,398	2,441
Unemployed	229	220	204
Total labour force	2,594	2,618	2,645

Health and Welfare

KEY INDICATORS

Total fertility rate (children per woman, 2005)	1.7
Under-5 mortality rate (per 1,000 live births, 2005)	4
HIV/AIDS (% of persons aged 15–49, 2005)	0.1
Physicians (per 1,000 head, 2004)	3.1
Hospital beds (per 1,000 head, 2005)	7.0
Health expenditure (2004): US $ per head (PPP)	2,202.5
Health expenditure (2004): % of GDP	7.4
Health expenditure (2004): public (% of total)	77.2
Human Development Index (2005): ranking	11
Human Development Index (2005): value	0.952

For sources and definitions, see explanatory note on p. vi.

Agriculture

PRINCIPAL CROPS
('000 metric tons; farms with arable land of 1 hectare or more)

	2004	2005	2006
Wheat	782.3	801.3	684.1
Barley	1,724.7	2,102.9	1,972.1
Rye	62.4	32.4	50.9
Oats	1,002.4	1,073.3	1,028.8
Mixed grain	44.2	47.8	51.4
Potatoes	619.4	742.7	575.7
Rapeseed	74.8	105.6	148.2
Sugar beet	1,063.5	1,183.3	952.0
Cucumbers and gherkins	44.1	44.4	42.8
Carrots	56.9	67.0	57.2

Aggregate production ('000 metric tons, may include official, semi-official or estimated data): Total cereals 3,619 in 2004, 4,059 in 2005, 3,790 in 2006; Total roots and tubers 619 in 2004, 742 in 2005, 576 in 2006; Total vegetables (incl. melons) 237 in 2004, 251 in 2005, 237 in 2006; Total fruits (excl. melons) 15 in 2004, 17 in 2005, 16 in 2006.

Source: FAO.

FINLAND

LIVESTOCK
('000 head at 1 May; farms with arable land of 1 hectare or more)

	2004	2005	2006
Horses*	61	64	66
Cattle	969	959	949
Sheep	109	90	117
Reindeer	201	n.a.	n.a.
Pigs†	1,365	1,401	1,436
Poultry	6,108	5,967	5,859

* Including horses not on farms.
† Including piggeries of dairies.

Source: FAO.

LIVESTOCK PRODUCTS
('000 metric tons)

	2004	2005	2006
Cattle meat	93.3	86.7	87.2
Pig meat	198.5	203.6	208.3
Chicken meat	87.0	86.9	98.0
Cows' milk*	2,449.0	2,433.2	2,413.0
Hen eggs	57.9	58.2	56.7

* Millions of litres.

Source: FAO.

Forestry

ROUNDWOOD REMOVALS
('000 cu m, excl. bark)

	2004	2005	2006
Sawlogs, veneer logs and logs for sleepers	24,256.9	22,443.7	21,883.6
Pulpwood	25,024.0	24,672.3	23,637.7
Fuel wood	5,117.4	5,134.2	5,290.3
Total	54,398.3	52,250.2	50,811.6

Source: FAO.

SAWNWOOD PRODUCTION
('000 cu m, incl. railway sleepers)

	2004	2005	2006
Coniferous (softwood)	13,460.0	12,190.0	12,145.0
Broadleaved (hardwood)	84.1	79.1	81.9
Total	13,544.1	12,269.1	12,226.9

Source: FAO.

Fishing
('000 metric tons, live weight)

	2003	2004	2005
Capture	122.0	135.4	131.7
Roaches	5.4	4.9	5.0
Northern pike	10.1	10.2	10.2
European perch	13.1	13.0	13.1
Vendace	5.3	4.6	4.6
Atlantic herring	64.0	71.1	67.0
European sprat	9.0	16.6	17.9
Aquaculture	12.6	12.8	14.4
Rainbow trout	12.2	12.3	13.7
Total catch	134.5	148.2	146.1

Note: Figures exclude aquatic mammals, recorded by number rather than by weight. The catch of grey seals was 127 in 2003; 135 in 2004; 294 in 2005.

Source: FAO.

Mining
('000 metric tons, unless otherwise indicated)

	2003	2004	2005
Copper ore*	14.9	15.5	15.6†
Nickel ore (metric tons)*	39.4	44.5	40.9
Zinc ore*	70.7	69.3	72.5
Chromium ore†‡	549	580	571
Cobalt (metric tons)§	4,574	5,246	6,158
Mercury (metric tons)†	25	24	15
Silver (metric tons)§	31.1	37.4	24.8
Gold (kilograms)§	5,409	6,222	3,747
Platinum (kilograms)§	461	705	678
Phosphate rock (incl. apatite, metric tons)‖	799	838	823
Peat: for fuel	8,415	8,159	7,696
Peat: for horticulture	929	905	778

* Figures refer to the metal content of ores.
† Estimated production.
‡ Figures refer to the gross weight of chromite. The estimated chromic oxide content (in '000 metric tons) was: 205 in 2002; 206 in 2003; 208 in 2004.
§ Figures refer to production of metal and (for cobalt) powder and salts.
‖ Figures refer to gross weight. The phosphorus oxide content (in metric tons) was: 290 in 2003; 306 in 2004; 300 in 2005.

Source: US Geological Survey.

Industry

SELECTED PRODUCTS
('000 metric tons, unless otherwise indicated)

	2002	2003	2004*
Cellulose	7,503	7,446	7,852
Newsprint	1,190	1,238	1,217
Other paper, boards and cardboards	11,362	12,113	13,218
Plywoods and veneers ('000 cubic metres)	1,135	1,168	1,388
Cement	1,198	1,493	1,270
Pig iron and ferro-alloys	2,829	3,091	3,037
Electricity (net, million kWh)	71,617	80,377	91,975
Sugar	161	202	193
Rolled steel products (metric tons)	3,975	4,090	4,157
Cigarettes (million)	4,130	3,946	n.a.

* Preliminary data.

Finance

CURRENCY AND EXCHANGE RATES

Monetary Units
100 cent = 1 euro (€).

Sterling and Dollar Equivalents (31 December 2007)
£1 sterling = 1.3609 euros;
US $1 = 0.6793 euros;
€10 = £7.35 = $14.72.

Average Exchange Rate (euros per US $)
2005   0.8041
2006   0.7971
2007   0.7306

Note: The national currency was formerly the markka (Finnmark). From the introduction of the euro, with Finnish participation, on 1 January 1999, a fixed exchange rate of €1 = 5.94573 markkaa was in operation. Euro notes and coins were introduced on 1 January 2002. The euro and local currency circulated alongside each other until 28 February, after which the euro became the sole legal tender.

FINLAND

BUDGET
(€ million)*

Revenue	2004	2005†	2006‡
Taxes and other levies	31,191	31,065	33,099
Taxes on income and property	12,941	12,596	12,808
Taxes on turnover	11,143	11,559	13,061
Excise duties	4,612	4,597	4,636
Other taxes	2,465	2,289	2,484
Other levies	30	24	110
Miscellaneous revenues	5,966	4,569	4,482
Sub-total	37,156	35,634	37,581
Interest on investments and profits received	1,197	929	1,025
Loans receivable	172	1,292	846
Total	38,525	37,855	39,452

Expenditure	2004	2005†	2006‡
President of the Republic	9	9	11
Parliament	94	97	104
Council of State	49	49	73
Ministry of Foreign Affairs	778	826	895
Ministry of Justice	671	662	693
Ministry of the Interior	1,425	1,507	1,546
Ministry of Defence	2,131	2,149	2,274
Ministry of Finance	5,113	5,553	5,788
Ministry of Education	5,970	6,197	6,457
Ministry of Agriculture and Forestry	2,645	2,725	2,700
Ministry of Transport and Communications	1,889	1,774	1,723
Ministry of Trade and Industry	941	976	972
Ministry of Social Affairs and Health	9,363	10,028	11,263
Ministry of Labour	2,183	2,164	1,965
Ministry of the Environment	680	691	752
Public debt	2,381	2,447	2,238
Total	36,320	37,855	39,452

* Figures refer to the General Budget only, excluding the operations of the Social Insurance Institution and of other social security funds with their own budgets.
† Projections.
‡ Proposals.

INTERNATIONAL RESERVES
(US $ million at 31 December)

	2004	2005	2006
Gold (Eurosystem valuation)	692.0	810.5	1,004.4
IMF special drawing rights	165.7	161.9	193.2
Reserve position in IMF	630.5	283.4	166.5
Foreign exchange	11,522.0	10,143.1	6,134.6
Total	13,010.2	11,398.9	7,498.7

Source: IMF, *International Financial Statistics*.

MONEY SUPPLY
(€ million at 31 December)

	2004	2005	2006
Currency in circulation*	8,643	9,738	10,817
Demand deposits at banking institutions	46,158	49,368	51,499

* Amount put into circulation by Bank of Finland (€ million): 4,796 in 2004; 5,812 in 2005; 6,885 in 2006.

Source: IMF, *International Financial Statistics*.

COST OF LIVING
(Consumer Price Index; base: 2000 = 100)

	2004	2005	2006
Food and non-alcoholic beverages	108.9	109.2	110.9
Alcoholic beverages and tobacco	93.5	91.8	93.1
Clothing and footwear	100.0	99.4	97.4
Housing, water, electricity, gas and other fuels	106.2	109.2	113.9
Furniture, household equipment	105.0	105.6	106.2
Health	113.0	115.2	115.9
Transport	103.0	105.7	108.0
Communication	88.9	78.8	74.5
Recreation and culture	108.3	108.0	108.2
Education	119.2	123.9	126.7
Restaurants and hotels	108.8	110.8	113.1
Miscellaneous goods and services	108.1	109.1	112.9
All items	105.3	106.2	108.1

NATIONAL ACCOUNTS
(€ million at current prices)

National Income and Product

	2004	2005	2006
Compensation of employees	73,301	77,171	80,684
Operating surplus	38,270	36,862	41,167
Domestic factor incomes	111,571	114,033	121,851
Consumption of fixed capital	22,303	23,784	25,017
Gross domestic product at factor cost	133,874	137,817	146,868
Indirect taxes	21,287	22,140	23,150
Less Subsidies	2,816	2,795	2,956
GDP in purchasers' values	152,345	157,162	167,062
Factor income received from abroad *Less* Factor income paid abroad	937	628	865
Gross national product	153,282	157,790	167,927
Less Consumption of fixed capital	22,303	23,784	25,017
National income in market prices	130,979	134,006	142,910

Expenditure on the Gross Domestic Product

	2004	2005	2006
Government final consumption expenditure	33,314	34,809	36,266
Private final consumption expenditure	78,137	81,212	85,903
Changes in inventories	840	2,568	2,414
Gross fixed capital formation	27,772	29,780	31,987
Total domestic expenditure	140,063	148,369	156,570
Exports of goods and services	60,859	65,730	74,404
Less Imports of goods and services	48,577	56,953	65,683
Statistical discrepancy	—	16	1,771
GDP in purchasers' values	152,345	157,162	167,062
GDP at constant 2000 prices	145,672	149,923	157,428

FINLAND

Gross Domestic Product by Economic Activity

	2004	2005	2006
Agriculture, hunting, forestry and fishing	4,041	3,978	3,673
Mining and quarrying	376	370	463
Manufacturing	31,122	31,445	34,226
Electricity, gas and water	3,099	2,918	3,366
Construction	7,198	8,053	8,818
Wholesale and retail trade; repair of motor vehicles, motorcycles, and personal and household goods	14,016	14,611	15,236
Hotels and restaurants	1,946	2,030	2,151
Transport, storage and communication	14,320	14,135	14,917
Financial intermediation and insurance	3,397	3,083	3,624
Real estate and business activities	23,960	25,207	26,703
Public administration and defence; compulsory social security	6,530	6,794	6,927
Education	6,502	6,776	7,050
Health and social work	11,222	11,915	12,469
Other community, social and personal services	4,784	4,944	5,177
Household service activities	108	122	121
Sub-total	132,621	136,381	144,921
Taxes, less subsidies, on products	19,724	20,781	22,141
GDP in purchasers' values	152,345	157,162	167,062

BALANCE OF PAYMENTS
(US $ million)

	2004	2005	2006
Exports of goods f.o.b.	61,139	65,451	77,431
Imports of goods f.o.b.	–48,369	–55,888	–65,878
Trade balance	12,770	9,563	11,553
Exports of services	15,169	17,005	16,942
Imports of services	–12,284	–15,202	–14,809
Balance on goods and services	15,655	11,367	13,686
Other income received	13,128	14,445	16,158
Other income paid	–12,881	–14,464	–15,901
Balance on goods, services and income	15,903	11,347	13,943
Current transfers received	2,040	1,895	2,005
Current transfers paid	–3,118	–3,475	–3,600
Current balance	14,825	9,767	12,348
Capital account (net)	188	336	191
Direct investment abroad	1,146	–4,669	–64
Direct investment from abroad	3,038	4,556	3,717
Portfolio investment assets	–24,504	–17,614	–35,177
Portfolio investment liabilities	13,110	10,485	19,092
Financial derivatives liabilities	523	2,168	202
Other investment assets	–11,851	–1,306	–16,451
Other investment liabilities	9,230	1,540	13,540
Net errors and omissions	–4,890	–5,443	–1,719
Overall balance	814	–180	–4,321

Source: IMF, *International Financial Statistics*.

External Trade

PRINCIPAL COMMODITIES
(€ million)

Imports c.i.f.	2004	2005	2006
Food and live animals	1,796.7	1,920.2	2,087.2
Beverages and tobacco	372.0	413.8	439.2
Crude materials (inedible) except fuels	3,387.2	3,686.2	5,298.2
Mineral fuels, lubricants, etc.	4,943.3	6,435.2	8,438.1
Animal and vegetable oils and fats	49.6	46.9	48.6
Chemicals and related products	4,756.8	5,314.9	5,915.2
Basic manufactures	5,169.0	5,463.4	6,535.3
Machinery and transport equipment	14,891.0	18,313.3	20,086.7
Miscellaneous manufactured articles	3,976.6	4,355.9	4,804.2
Total (incl. others)	40,269.6	46,769.1	54,889.2

Exports f.o.b.	2004	2005	2006
Food and live animals	815.1	846.1	949.3
Beverages and tobacco	87.9	94.3	111.6
Crude materials (inedible) except fuels	3,179.4	2,994.5	3,694.6
Mineral fuels, lubricants, etc.	2,070.7	2,282.0	3,192.2
Animal and vegetable oils and fats	57.8	57.7	71.6
Chemicals and related products	3,679.5	3,996.2	4,552.4
Basic manufactures	16,330.3	15,731.6	19,212.4
Machinery and transport equipment	19,442.0	23,063.8	25,768.9
Miscellaneous manufactured articles	2,744.0	2,913.7	3,030.5
Total (incl. others)	48,789.6	52,394.5	61,395.5

PRINCIPAL TRADING PARTNERS
(€ million)*

Imports c.i.f.	2004	2005	2006
Belgium	942.8	1,025.9	1,191.6
China, People's Republic	1,959.6	2,818.8	4,127.5
Denmark	1,401.2	1,465.2	1,721.2
Estonia	1,002.8	1,474.1	1,265.7
France	1,863.6	1,677.7	1,794.4
Germany	5,923.9	6,947.4	7,603.4
Italy	1,447.4	1,659.4	1,832.0
Japan	1,499.6	1,538.9	1,583.8
Netherlands	1,684.3	1,869.7	2,430.7
Norway	1,000.2	1,044.7	1,707.0
Russia	5,317.7	6,547.1	7,754.4
Sweden	4,394.9	4,924.2	5,378.8
United Kingdom	1,828.5	2,086.6	2,600.4
USA	1,868.7	1,957.9	2,074.7
Total (incl. others)	40,269.6	46,769.1	54,889.2

Exports f.o.b.	2004	2005	2006
Belgium	1,288.7	1,222.4	1,408.5
China, People's Republic	1,962.3	1,552.9	1,971.4
Denmark	1,081.1	1,242.2	1,304.8
Estonia	1,363.8	1,354.6	1,791.2
France	1,728.4	1,796.7	2,042.6
Germany	5,224.9	5,566.7	6,933.6
Italy	1,461.8	1,616.6	1,946.4
Netherlands	2,488.6	2,530.7	3,152.8
Norway	1,480.4	1,322.4	1,597.6
Russia	4,351.7	5,743.0	6,215.1
Spain	1,293.5	1,286.8	1,527.6
Sweden	5,349.8	5,638.6	6,431.9
United Kingdom	3,451.0	3,518.2	4,000.8
USA	3,122.1	3,057.5	4,011.2
Total (incl. others)	48,789.6	52,394.5	61,395.5

* Imports by country of production; exports by country of consumption.

FINLAND

Transport

RAILWAYS
(traffic)

	2004	2005	2006
Passengers ('000 journeys)	60,134	63,493	64,987
Passenger-km (million)	3,400	3,500	3,600
Freight carried ('000 metric tons)	42,663	40,722	43,560
Freight ton-km (million)	10,100	9,700	11,100

ROAD TRAFFIC
(registered motor vehicles at 31 December)

	2004	2005	2006
Passenger cars	2,346,726	2,430,345	2,505,543
Buses and coaches	10,716	n.a.	n.a.
Lorries and vans	355,182	363,644	376,092
Motorcycles	142,703	156,487	172,283
Snowmobiles*	100,961	103,776	106,562

* Excluding Åland Islands.

SHIPPING

Merchant Fleet
(registered at 31 December)

	2004	2005	2006
Number of vessels	277	283	282
Total displacement ('000 grt)	1,428.9	1,475.2	1,442.6

Source: Lloyd's Register-Fairplay, *World Fleet Statistics*.

International Sea-borne Freight Traffic

	2004	2005	2006
Number of vessels entered	33,181	32,877	32,371
Goods ('000 metric tons):			
loaded	42,740	39,870	44,607
unloaded	53,170	49,770	54,545

CANAL TRAFFIC

	2004	2005	2006
Vessels in transit	35,915	35,590	39,709
Goods carried ('000 metric tons)	2,368	2,228	2,115

CIVIL AVIATION
(traffic on scheduled services, '000)

	2002	2003	2004
Kilometres flown	116,000	123,000	172,000
Passenger-kilometres	13,396,000	14,008,000	17,194,000
Cargo ton-kilometres	221,036	258,161	331,767

Tourism

FOREIGN TOURIST ARRIVALS
(overnight stays at accommodation establishments)

Country of residence	2004	2005	2006*
Estonia	128,246	157,521	195,550
France	217,631	230,976	236,896
Germany	543,114	542,984	541,641
Italy	162,101	146,311	163,540
Netherlands	212,244	200,972	197,363
Norway	205,087	191,533	206,241
Russia	447,210	499,307	673,120
Sweden	608,765	597,641	606,714
United Kingdom	410,310	421,466	477,428
USA	210,949	208,695	207,565
Total (incl. others)	4,383,198	4,498,635	5,036,202

* Preliminary data.

Tourism receipts (US $ million, incl. passenger transport): 2,677 in 2003; 2,976 in 2004; 3,055 in 2005 (Source: World Tourism Organization).

Communications Media

	2004	2005	2006
Newspapers:			
number	204	205	n.a.
total circulation ('000 copies)	3,228	3,209	n.a.
Other periodicals: number	3,553	3,462	n.a.
Book production: titles	12,977	13,667	n.a.
Telephones ('000 main lines in use)*	2,368.0	2,120.0	1,920
Mobile cellular telephones ('000 subscribers)*	4,988	5,270	5,670
Internet users ('000 aged 15 years and over)*	2,680.0	2,800.0	2,925.4
Broadband subscribers ('000)*	800.0	1,174.2	1,428.0

* Source: International Telecommunication Union.

Personal computers ('000 in use, estimate): 2,515 in 2005 (Source: International Telecommunication Union).

Radio receivers ('000 in use): 7,700 in 1997 (Source: UNESCO, *Statistical Yearbook*).

Television receivers ('000 in use): 3,580 in 2000 (Source: International Telecommunication Union).

Facsimile machines ('000 in use): 198 in 1997 (Source: UN, *Statistical Yearbook*).

Education

(2004)

	Institutions	Teachers†	Students
Comprehensive schools*	3,720	44,313	602,300
Senior secondary schools	436	7,295	127,200
Vocational and professional institutions	302	14,058	199,500
Polytechnics	31	6,034	143,200
Universities	20	7,755	174,000

* Comprising six-year primary stage and three-year lower secondary stage.
† 2003 figures.

2005: *Students:* Comprehensive schools 586,381; Senior secondary schools 118,111; Vocational and professional institutions 243,398; Polytechnics 132,783; Universities 176,061.

Directory

The Constitution

The Constitution of Finland entered into force on 1 March 2000, amending the Constitution of July 1919. Its main provisions are summarized below:

FUNDAMENTAL PROVISIONS

Finland is a sovereign republic. The powers of the State are vested in the people, who are represented by the Eduskunta (Parliament). Legislative power is exercised by the Eduskunta, which also decides on state finances; governmental power is held by the President of the Republic and the Cabinet; and judicial power is exercised by independent courts of law. The basic rights and liberties of the individual are guaranteed in the Constitution.

PARLIAMENT

The unicameral Eduskunta comprises 200 representatives, who are elected for a term of four years by a direct, proportional and secret vote. For the parliamentary elections the country is divided, on the basis of the number of Finnish citizens, into at least 12 and at most 18 constituencies. In addition, the Åland Islands form their own constituency for the election of one representative. Registered political parties, and groups of persons who have the right to vote, are entitled to nominate candidates in parliamentary elections. The President of the Republic, in response to a proposal by the Prime Minister, may order that extraordinary parliamentary elections be held. The Eduskunta elects from among its members a Speaker and two Deputy Speakers for each parliamentary session. The proposal for the enactment of legislation is initiated in the Eduskunta either by the Government or through a motion submitted by a representative.

PRESIDENT

The President of the Republic is elected by a direct vote for a term of six years (with the same person restricted to a maximum of two consecutive terms in office). The President will be a native-born Finnish citizen who is entitled to vote. The candidate who receives more than one-half of the votes cast in the election will be elected President. If none of the candidates receives a majority of the votes cast, a further election will be held between the two candidates who have received the most votes. The right to nominate a candidate in the presidential election is held by any registered political party from which at least one representative was elected to the Eduskunta in the most recent elections, as well as by any group of 20,000 persons who have the right to vote. The President of the Republic makes decisions on the basis of proposals submitted by the Cabinet. The foreign policy of Finland is directed by the President of the Republic in co-operation with the Cabinet.

CABINET

The Cabinet comprises the Prime Minister and the necessary number of ministers. The Eduskunta elects the Prime Minister, who is thereafter appointed to the office by the President of the Republic. The President appoints the other ministers on the basis of nominations made by the Prime Minister.

JUDICIARY

The Supreme Court, the Courts of Appeal and the District Courts are the general courts of law. The Supreme Administrative Court and the regional Administrative Courts are the general courts of administrative law. Justice in civil, commercial and criminal matters in the final instance is administered by the Supreme Court, while justice in administrative matters in the final instance is administered by the Supreme Administrative Court. The High Court of Impeachment deals with charges brought against a member of the Government, the Chancellor of Justice, the Parliamentary Ombudsman or a member of the supreme courts for unlawful conduct in office. Tenured judges are appointed by the President of the Republic.

ADMINISTRATION AND SELF-GOVERNMENT

In addition to the Government, the civil administration of the State may consist of agencies, institutions and other bodies. The Åland Islands are guaranteed self-government. Finland is divided into municipalities, which are guaranteed self-government, and are entitled to levy tax. In their native region the Sámi have linguistic and cultural autonomy.

The Government

HEAD OF STATE

President: TARJA HALONEN (took office 1 March 2000; re-elected 29 January 2006).

CABINET
(Valtioneuvosto)
(April 2008)

A coalition of Suomen Keskusta (Finnish Centre Party—Kesk), Kansallinen Kokoomus (National Coalition Party—Kok), Vihreä Liitto (Green League—VL), and the Svenska Folkpartiet (Swedish People's Party—SFP).

Prime Minister: MATTI VANHANEN (Kesk).

Deputy Prime Minister and Minister of Finance: JYRKI KATAINEN (Kok).

Minister of Foreign Affairs: ALEXANDER STUBB (Kok).

Minister of Foreign Trade and Development: PAAVO VÄYRYNEN (Kesk).

Minister of Justice: TUIJA BRAX (VL).

Minister of the Interior: ANNE HOLMLUND (Kok).

Minister of Migration and European Affairs: ASTRID THORS (SFP).

Minister of Public Administration and Local Government: MARI KIVINIEMI (Kesk).

Minister of Defence: JYRI HÄKÄMIES (Kok).

Minister of Education: SARI SARKOMAA (Kok).

Minister of Culture and Sport: STEFAN WALLIN (SFP).

Minister of Agriculture and Forestry: SIRKKA-LIISA ANTTILA (Kesk).

Minister of Transport: ANU VEHVILÄINEN (Kesk).

Minister of Communications: SUVI LINDÉN (Kok).

Minister of Economic Affairs: MAURI PEKKARINEN (Kesk).

Minister of Employment: TARJA CRONBERG (VL).

Minister of Social Affairs and Health: LIISA HYSSÄLÄ (Kesk).

Minister of Health and Social Services: PAULA RISIKKO (Kok).

Minister of the Environment: KIMMO TIILIKAINEN (Kesk).

Minister of Housing: JAN VAPAAVUORI (Kok).

MINISTRIES

Office of the President: Mariankatu 2, 00170 Helsinki; tel. (9) 661133; fax (9) 638247; e-mail kirjaamo@tpk.fi; internet www.president.fi.

Prime Minister's Office: Snellmaninkatu 1A, 00170 Helsinki; POB 23, 00023 Government; tel. (9) 16001; fax (9) 16022165; e-mail registry@vnk.fi; internet www.vnk.fi.

Ministry of Agriculture and Forestry: Hallituskatu 3A, 00170 Helsinki; POB 30, 00023 Government; tel. (9) 16001; fax (9) 16054202; e-mail tiedotus@mmm.fi; internet www.mmm.fi.

Ministry of Defence: Eteläinen Makasiinikatu 8, POB 31, 00131 Helsinki; tel. (9) 16001; fax (9) 653254; e-mail tiedotus@defmin.fi; internet www.defmin.fi.

Ministry of Education: Meritullinkatu 10, 00171 Helsinki; POB 29, 00023 Government; tel. (9) 16004; fax (9) 1359335; e-mail opmkirjaamo@minedu.fi; internet www.minedu.fi.

Ministry of Employment and the Economy: Aleksanterinkatu 4, 00170 Helsinki; POB 32, 00023 Government; tel. (9) 16063546; fax (9) 16062160; e-mail kirjaamo@tem.fi; internet www.tem.fi.

Ministry of the Environment: Kasarmikatu 25, 00131 Helsinki; POB 35, 00023 Government; tel. (20) 490100; fax (9) 16039320; e-mail kirjaamo.ym@ymparisto.fi; internet www.ymparisto.fi.

Ministry of Finance: Snellmaninkatu 1A, Helsinki; POB 28, 00023 Government; tel. (9) 16001; fax (9) 16033123; e-mail valtiovarainministerio@vm.fi; internet www.vm.fi.

Ministry of Foreign Affairs: Merikasarmi, Laivastokatu 22, POB 176, 00161 Helsinki; tel. (9) 16005; fax (9) 629840; e-mail kirjaamo.um@formin.fi; internet formin.finland.fi.

Ministry of the Interior: Kirkkokatu 12, 00170 Helsinki; POB 26, 00023 Government; tel. (9) 16001; fax (9) 16044635; e-mail sm.kirjaamo@intermin.fi; internet www.intermin.fi.

Ministry of Justice: Eteläesplanadi 10, Helsinki; POB 25, 00023 Government; tel. (9) 16003; fax (9) 16067730; e-mail oikeusministerio@om.fi; internet www.om.fi.

FINLAND

Ministry of Social Affairs and Health: Meritullinkatu 8, 00170 Helsinki; POB 33, 00023 Government; tel. (9) 16001; fax (9) 16074126; e-mail kirjaamo.stm@stm.fi; internet www.stm.fi.

Ministry of Transport and Communications: Eteläesplanadi 16–18, 00131 Helsinki; POB 31, 00023 Government; tel. (9) 16002; fax (9) 16028596; e-mail kirjaamo@mintc.fi; internet www.mintc.fi.

President and Legislature

PRESIDENT

Presidential Election, 15 and 29 January 2006

	First round votes (%)	Second round votes (%)
Tarja Halonen (SDP)	46.3	51.8
Sauli Niinistö (Kok)	24.1	48.2
Matti Vanhanen (Kesk)	18.6	—
Heidi Hautala (VL)	3.5	—
Timo Soini (PS)	3.4	—
Johan Kallis (KD)	2.0	—
Rolf Lax (SFP)	1.6	—
Arto Lahti (Independent)	0.4	—
Total	**100.0**	**100.0**

PARLIAMENT

Suomen Eduskunta

Mannerheimintie 30, 00102 Helsinki; tel. (9) 4321; fax (9) 4322274; e-mail eduskunta@eduskunta.fi; internet www.eduskunta.fi.
Speaker: SAULI NIINISTÖ (Kok).
Secretary-General: SEPPO TIITINEN.

General Election, 18 March 2007

Party	Votes	% of votes	Seats
Suomen Keskusta (Kesk—Finnish Centre Party)	640,428	23.1	51
Kansallinen Kokoomus (Kok—National Coalition Party)	616,841	22.3	50
Suomen Sosialidemokraattinen Puolue (SDP—Finnish Social Democratic Party)	594,194	21.4	45
Vasemmistoliitto (V—Left Alliance)	244,296	8.8	17
Vihreä Liitto (VL—Green League)	234,429	8.5	15
Svenska Folkpartiet (SFP—Swedish People's Party)	126,520	4.6	9
Suomen Kristillisdemokraatit (KD—Finnish Christian Democrats)	134,790	4.9	7
Perussuomalaiset/Sannfinländarna (PS—True Finns)	112,256	4.1	5
Others	67,482	2.4	1*
Total	**2,771,236**	**100.00**	**200**

*Including a representative of the Åland Islands.

Election Commission

Election Unit: Eteläesplanadi 10, 00130 Helsinki; POB 25, 00023 Government; tel. (9) 16067572; fax (9) 16067750; e-mail terttu.belgasem@om.fi; internet www.vaalit.fi; dept of the Ministry of Justice; Dir ARTO JÄÄSKELÄINEN.

Political Organizations

In early 2008 there were 12 registered political parties in Finland.

Kansallinen Kokoomus (Kok) (National Coalition Party): Pohjoinen Rautatiekatu 21B, 00100 Helsinki; tel. (20) 7488488; fax (20) 7488505; e-mail jori.arvonen@kokoomus.fi; internet www.kokoomus.fi; f. 1918; moderate conservative political ideology; Chair. JYRKI KATAINEN; Sec.-Gen. TARU TUJANEN; Chair. Parliamentary Group PEKKA RAVI; 50,000 mems.

Perussuomalaiset—Sannfinländarna (PS) (True Finns): Mannerheimintie 40B 56, 00100 Helsinki; tel. (9) 0207430800; fax (9) 0207430801; e-mail peruss@perussuomalaiset.fi; internet www.perussuomalaiset.fi; f. 1995 by mems of defunct Suomen Maaseudun Puolue (Finnish Rural Party); Chair. TIMO SOINI; Sec.-Gen. OSSI SANDVIK; Chair. Parliamentary Group RAIMO VISTBACKA.

Rauhan Ja Sosialismin Puolesta, Kommunistinen Työväenpuolue (For Peace and Socialism, Communist Workers' Party): POB 93, 01301 Vantaa; tel. (9) 8571022; fax (9) 8573097; e-mail ktp@ktpkom.fi; internet www.ktpkom.fi; f. 2004; Leader HANNU HARJU.

Suomen Keskusta (Kesk) (Finnish Centre Party): Apollonkatu 11A, 00100 Helsinki; tel. (9) 75144200; fax (9) 75144240; e-mail puoluetoimisto@keskusta.fi; internet www.keskusta.fi; f. 1906; radical centre party founded to promote the interests of the rural population, now reformist movement favouring individual enterprise, equality and decentralization; Chair. MATTI VANHANEN; Sec.-Gen. JARMO KORHONEN; Chair. Parliamentary Group TIMO KALLI; over 200,000 mems.

Suomen Kommunistinen Puolue (SKP) (Communist Party of Finland): Haapaniemenkatu 7–9B, 9th Floor, 00530 Helsinki; tel. (9) 77438150; fax (9) 77438160; e-mail skp@skp.fi; internet www.skp.fi; f. 1918; incorporated into Vasemmistoliitto (Left Alliance) in 1990; refounded 1997 following disputes in the latter party; Chair. YRJÖ HAKANEN; Sec.-Gen. ARTO VIITANIEMI; over 3,000 mems.

Suomen Kristillisdemokraatit (KD) (Finnish Christian Democrats): Karjalankatu 2C, 7th Floor, 00520 Helsinki; tel. (9) 34882200; fax (9) 34882228; e-mail kd@kd.fi; internet www.kd.fi; f. 1958 as Suomen Kristillinen Liitto; present name adopted 2001; Chair. PÄIVI RÄSÄNEN; Sec.-Gen. SARI ESSAYAH; Chair. Parliamentary Group BJARNE KALLIS; 12,000 mems.

Suomen Senioripuolue (Finnish Senior Citizens' Party): POB 96, 33501 Tampere; tel. (40) 7755788; e-mail vaalitoimisto@senioripuolue.fi; internet www.senioripuolue.fi; f. 2004; Chair. ESKO A. REPO; Sec.-Gen. URMAS MIKKONEN.

Suomen Sosialidemokraattinen Puolue (SDP) (Finnish Social Democratic Party): Saariniemenkatu 6, 00530 Helsinki; tel. (9) 478988; fax (9) 712752; e-mail palaute@sdp.fi; internet www.sdp.fi; f. 1899; constitutional socialist programme; mainly supported by the urban working and middle classes; Chair. EERO HEINÄLUOMA; Gen. Sec. MAARIT FELDT-RANTA; Chair., Parliamentary Group TARJA FILATOV; 56,000 mems.

Suomen Työväenpuolue (Finnish Workers' Party): POB 700, 00101 Helsinki; tel. (40) 7641163; e-mail tyovaenpuolue@suomi24.fi; internet www.tyovaenpuolue.org; f. 1999; Chair. JUHANI TANSKI; Sec.-Gen. HEIKKI MÄNNIKKÖ.

Svenska Folkpartiet (SFP) (Swedish People's Party): POB 430, Simonkatu 8A, 00101 Helsinki; tel. (9) 693070; fax (9) 6931968; e-mail info@sfp.fi; internet www.sfp.fi; f. 1906; liberal party representing the interests of the Swedish-speaking minority; Chair. STEFAN WALLIN; Sec.-Gen. ULLA ACHRÉN; Chair. Parliamentary Group ULLA-MAJ WIDEROOS; 35,700 mems.

Vasemmistoliitto (V) (Left Alliance): Viherniemenkatu 5, 2nd Floor, 00530 Helsinki; tel. (9) 77474209; fax (9) 77474200; e-mail vas@vasemmistoliitto.fi; internet www.vasemmistoliitto.fi; f. 1990 by merger of the Finnish People's Democratic League (f. 1944), the Communist Party of Finland (f. 1918), the Democratic League of Finnish Women, and left-wing groups; Chair. MARTTI KORHONEN; Sec.-Gen. SIRPA PUHAKKA; Chair. Parliamentary Group ANNIKA LAPINTIE; 10,000 mems.

Vihreä Liitto (VL) (Green League): Fredrikinkatu 33A, 3rd Floor, 00120 Helsinki; tel. (9) 58604160; fax (9) 58604161; e-mail vihreat@vihreat.fi; internet www.vihreat.fi; f. 1988; Chair. TARJA CRONBERG; Sec.-Gen. PANU LATURI; Chair. Parliamentary Group ANNI SINNEMÄKI; c. 3,000 mems.

Diplomatic Representation

EMBASSIES IN FINLAND

Argentina: Bulevardi 5A 11, 00120 Helsinki; tel. (9) 42428700; fax (9) 42428701; e-mail embassy@embargentina.fi; internet www.embargentina.fi; Ambassador LILA SUBIRÁN DE VIANA.

Austria: Unioninkatu 22, 00130 Helsinki; tel. (9) 6818600; fax (9) 665084; e-mail helsinki-ob@bmeia.gv.at; Ambassador Dr LORENZ GRAF.

Belgium: Kalliolinnantie 5, 00140 Helsinki; tel. (9) 170412; fax (9) 628842; e-mail helsinki@diplobel.be; internet www.diplomatie.be/helsinki; Ambassador GUIDO COURTOIS.

Brazil: Itäinen puistotie 4B 1, 00140 Helsinki; tel. (9) 6841500; fax (9) 650084; e-mail brasemb.helsinki@kolumbus.fi; internet www.brazil.fi; Ambassador LUIZ SÉRGIO GAMA FIGUEIRA.

Bulgaria: Kuusisaarentie 2B, 00340 Helsinki; tel. (9) 4584055; fax (9) 4584550; e-mail bulembfi@yahoo.com; internet www.mfa.bg/helsinki; Ambassador Dr PLAMEN LUBOMIROV BONCHEV.

FINLAND
Directory

Canada: Pohjoisesplanadi 25B, 00100 Helsinki; tel. (9) 228530; fax (9) 601060; e-mail hsnki@international.gc.ca; internet www.canada.fi; Ambassador SCOTT FRASER.

Chile: Erottajankatu 11, 00130 Helsinki; tel. (9) 6126780; fax (9) 61267825; e-mail info@embachile.fi; internet www.embachile.fi; Ambassador CARLOS PARRA MERINO.

China, People's Republic: Vanha Kelkkamäki 9–11, 00570 Helsinki; tel. (9) 22890110; fax (9) 22890168; e-mail chinaemb_fi@mfa.gov.cn; internet www.chinaembassy-fi.org; Ambassador MA KEQING.

Croatia: Kruunuvuorenkatu 5, 00160 Helsinki; tel. (9) 6222232; fax (9) 6222221; e-mail croemb.helsinki@mvpei.hr; Ambassador Dr DAMIR KUŠEN.

Cuba: Frederikinkatu 61, 3rd Floor, 00100 Helsinki; tel. (9) 6802022; fax (9) 643163; e-mail cuba@cuba.fi; internet emba.cubaminrex.cu/finlandia; Ambassador SERGIO GONZÁLEZ GONZÁLEZ.

Cyprus: Bulevardi 5A 19, 00120 Helsinki; tel. (9) 6962820; fax (9) 677428; e-mail mail@cyprusembassy.fi; internet www.cyprusembassy.fi; Ambassador THALIA PETRIDES.

Czech Republic: Armfeltintie 14, 00150 Helsinki; tel. (9) 6120880; fax (9) 630655; e-mail helsinki@embassy.mzv.cz; internet www.mfa.cz/helsinki; Ambassador VLADIMÍR KOTZY.

Denmark: Keskuskatu 1A, POB 1042, 00100 Helsinki; tel. (9) 6841050; fax (9) 68410540; e-mail helamb@um.dk; internet www.ambhelsingfors.um.dk; Ambassador NIELS KAAS DYRLUND.

Egypt: Itäinen puistotie 2, POB 183, 00140 Helsinki; tel. (9) 4777470; fax (9) 47774721; e-mail secretaryofembassy@hotmail.com; Ambassador MAASOUM MOSTAFA MARZOUK.

Estonia: Itäinen puistotie 10, 00140 Helsinki; tel. (9) 6220260; fax (9) 62202610; e-mail helen.naarits@estemb.fi; internet www.estemb.fi; Ambassador MERLE PAJULA.

France: Itäinen puistotie 13, 00140 Helsinki; tel. (9) 618780; fax (9) 61878342; e-mail ambassade@france.fi; internet www.france.fi; Ambassador GÉRARD CROS.

Germany: POB 5, 00331 Helsinki; Krogiuksentie 4B, 00340 Helsinki; tel. (9) 458580; fax (9) 45858258; e-mail info@deutschland.fi; internet www.helsinki.diplo.de; Ambassador WILFRIED GROLIG.

Greece: Maneesikatu 2A 4, 00170 Helsinki; tel. (9) 6229790; fax (9) 2781200; e-mail info@greekembassy.fi; internet www.greekembassy.fi; Ambassador DIMITRIOS-MICHAIL LOUNDRAS.

Hungary: Kuusisaarenkuja 6, 00340 Helsinki; tel. (9) 484144; fax (9) 480497; e-mail office@unkari.fi; internet www.mfa.gov.hu/emb/helsinki; Ambassador Dr ANDRÁS HAJDU.

Iceland: Pohjoisesplanadi 27C, 00100 Helsinki; tel. (9) 6122460; fax (9) 61224620; e-mail icemb.helsinki@utn.stjr.is; internet www.iceland.org/fi; Ambassador HANNES HEIMISSON.

India: Satamakatu 2A 8, 00160 Helsinki; tel. (9) 2289910; fax (9) 6221208; e-mail indianembassy@indianembassy.fi; internet www.indianembassy.fi; Ambassador PRADEEP SINGH.

Indonesia: Kuusisaarentie 3, 00340 Helsinki; tel. (9) 4470370; fax (9) 4582882; e-mail info@indonesian-embassy.fi; internet www.indonesian-embassy.fi; Ambassador IRIS INDIRA MURTI.

Iran: Kulosaarentie 9, 00570 Helsinki; tel. (9) 6869240; fax (9) 68692410; e-mail embassy@iran.fi; internet www.iran.fi; Ambassador Dr REZA NAZARAHARI.

Iraq: Lars Sonckin tie 2, 00570 Helsinki; tel. (9) 6818870; fax (9) 6848977; e-mail hlsemb@iraqmofamail.net; Ambassador MEBJIL JASIM MUHAMMAD AS-SAMRRAI.

Ireland: Erottajankatu 7A, 00130 Helsinki; tel. (9) 646006; fax (9) 646022; e-mail helsinki@dfa.ie; Ambassador PHILIP MCDONAGH.

Israel: Yrjönkatu 36A, 00100 Helsinki; tel. (9) 6812020; fax (9) 1356959; e-mail info@helsinki.mfa.gov.il; internet helsinki.mfa.gov.il; Ambassador AVI GRANOT.

Italy: Itäinen puistotie 4, 00140 Helsinki; tel. (9) 6811280; fax (9) 6987829; e-mail ambasciata.helsinki@esteri.it; internet www.ambhelsinki.esteri.it; Ambassador ELISABETTA KELESCIAN.

Japan: Unioninkatu 20–22, 00130 Helsinki; tel. (9) 6860200; fax (9) 633012; e-mail inquiry.fi@jpnembassy.fi; internet www.fi.emb-japan.go.jp; Ambassador HITOSHI HONDA.

Korea, Republic: Fabianinkatu 8A, 00130 Helsinki; tel. (9) 2515000; fax (9) 25150055; e-mail korembfi@mofat.go.kr; internet fin.mofat.go.kr; Ambassador PARK HEUNG-SHIN.

Latvia: Armfeltintie 10, 00150 Helsinki; tel. (9) 4764720; fax (9) 47647288; e-mail embassy.finland@mfa.gov.lv; internet www.mfa.gov.lv/fi/helsinki; Ambassador Dr EINARS SEMANIS.

Lithuania: Rauhankatu 13A, 00170 Helsinki; tel. (9) 6844880; fax (9) 68448820; e-mail amb.fi@urm.lt; internet fi.mfa.lt; Ambassador HALINA KOBECKAITĖ.

Malaysia: Aleksanterinkatu 17, 00100 Helsinki; tel. (9) 69697142; fax (9) 69697144; e-mail malhsinki@kln.gov.my; internet www.kln.gov.my/perwakilan/helsinki; Ambassador SYED SULTAN IDRIS.

Mexico: Simonkatu 12A, 7th Floor, 00100 Helsinki; tel. (9) 5860430; fax (9) 6949411; e-mail mexican.embassy@welho.com; Ambassador (vacant).

Morocco: Runeberginkatu 4C, 00100 Helsinki; tel. (9) 6122480; fax (9) 635160; e-mail embassy.of.morocco@co.inet.fi; Chargé d'affaires a.i. TAYEB RAOUF.

Netherlands: Erottajankatu 19B, 00130 Helsinki; tel. (9) 228920; fax (9) 22892228; e-mail hel@minbuza.nl; internet www.netherlands.fi; Ambassador ROBERT J. H. ENGELS.

Norway: Rehbinderintie 17, 00150 Helsinki; tel. (9) 6860180; fax (9) 657807; e-mail emb.helsinki@mfa.no; internet www.norja.fi; Ambassador LEIDULV NAMTVEDT.

Peru: Annankatu 31–33C 44, 00100 Helsinki; tel. (9) 7599400; fax (9) 75994040; e-mail embassy.peru@peruemb.inet.fi; Ambassador MANUEL PICASSO BOTTO.

Poland: Armas Lindgrenintie 21, 00570 Helsinki; tel. (9) 618280; fax (9) 6847477; e-mail amb.poland@helsinki.inet.fi; internet www.helsinki.polemb.net; Ambassador JOANNA HOFMAN.

Portugal: Itäinen puistotie 11B, 00140 Helsinki; tel. (9) 68243713; fax (9) 663550; e-mail emb.port@portugal.fi; Ambassador JOÃO MANUEL DA CRUZ DA SILVA LEITÃO.

Romania: Stenbäckinkatu 24, 00250 Helsinki; tel. (9) 2414414; fax (9) 2413272; e-mail romamb@clinet.fi; internet helsinki.mae.ro; Ambassador LUCIAN FĂTU.

Russia: Tehtaankatu 1B, 00140 Helsinki; tel. (9) 661876; fax (9) 661006; e-mail rusembassy@co.inet.fi; internet www.rusembassy.fi; Ambassador ALEKSANDR YU. RUMYANTSEV.

Serbia: Kulosaarentie 36, 00570 Helsinki; tel. (9) 6848522; fax (9) 6848783; e-mail info.ambascghki@kolumbus.fi; internet www.kolumbus.fi/info.ambasghki; Ambassador VERA MAVRIĆ.

Slovakia: Annankatu 25, 00100 Helsinki; tel. (9) 68117810; fax (9) 68117820; e-mail skemb.hels@sci.fi; internet www.helsinki.mfa.sk; Ambassador VIERA STUPÁKOVÁ.

Slovenia: Eteläesplanadi 24A, 00130 Helsinki; POB 9, 00101 Helsinki; tel. (9) 2289940; fax (9) 6944775; e-mail vhe@mzz-dkp.gov.si; Chargé d'affaires a.i. JADRAN HOČEVAR.

South Africa: Rahapajankatu 1A 5, 3rd Floor, 00160 Helsinki; tel. (9) 68603100; fax (9) 68603160; e-mail saembfin@welho.com; internet www.southafricanembassy.fi; Ambassador BUKELWA GILBERTA HANS.

Spain: Kalliolinnantie 6, 00140 Helsinki; tel. (9) 6877080; fax (9) 660110; e-mail emb.helsinki@mae.es; internet www.mae.es/embajadas/helsinki/es/home; Ambassador RICARDO ZALCAÍN JORGE.

Sweden: POB 329, 00171 Helsinki; Pohjoisesplanadi 7B, 00170 Helsinki; tel. (9) 6877660; fax (9) 655285; e-mail ambassad.helsingfors@foreign.ministry.se; internet www.sverige.fi; Ambassador EVA WALDER-BRUNDIN.

Switzerland: Uudenmaankatu 16A, 00120 Helsinki; tel. (9) 6229500; fax (9) 6229500; e-mail hel.vertretung@eda.admin.ch; internet www.eda.admin.ch/helsinki; Ambassador JOSEF BUCHER.

Thailand: Eteläesplanadi 22C, 3rd Floor, 00130 Helsinki; tel. (9) 6122640; fax (9) 61226466; e-mail info@thaiembassy.fi; internet www.thaiembassy.fi; Ambassador APICHART CHINWANNO (resident in Sweden).

Tunisia: Liisankatu 14B 31, 00170 Helsinki; tel. (9) 6803960; fax (9) 68039610; e-mail at.helsinki@kolumbus.fi; Chargé d'affaires a.i. TAREK BEN SALEM.

Turkey: Puistokatu 1B A 3, 00140 Helsinki; tel. (9) 6811030; fax (9) 655011; e-mail turkish.embassy@welho.com; internet www.turkinsuurlahetysto.fi; Ambassador REHA KESKINTEPE.

Ukraine: Vähäniityntie 9, 00570 Helsinki; tel. (9) 2289000; fax (9) 2289001; e-mail embassy@ukraine.fi; internet www.ukraine.fi; Ambassador OLEKSANDR MAIDANNYK.

United Kingdom: Itäinen puistotie 17, 00140 Helsinki; tel. (9) 22865100; fax (9) 22865262; e-mail info.helsinki@fco.gov.uk; internet www.britishembassy.fi; Ambassador Dr VALERIE CATON.

USA: Itäinen puistotie 14, 00140 Helsinki; tel. (9) 616250; fax (9) 6165135; e-mail webmaster@usembassy.fi; internet finland.usembassy.gov; Ambassador MARILYN WARE.

Venezuela: Bulevardi 1A 62, 00100 Helsinki; tel. (9) 641522; fax (9) 640971; e-mail embavenefin@embavene.fi; internet www.embavene.fi; Chargé d'affaires a.i. ERNESTO NAVAZIO MOSSUCCA.

Viet Nam: Aleksanterinkatu 15A, 5th Floor, 00100 Helsinki; tel. (9) 5626302; fax (9) 6229900; e-mail vietnamfinland@gmail.com; internet www.vietnamembassy-finland.org; Ambassador TRAN NGOC AN.

FINLAND

Judicial System

The administration of justice is independent of the Government and judges can be removed only by judicial sentence. The compulsory retirement age for judges is 67.

SUPREME COURT

Korkein oikeus/Högsta domstolen
Pohjoisesplanadi 3, POB 301, 00171 Helsinki; tel. (10) 3640000; fax (10) 3640154; e-mail korkein.oikeus@om.fi; internet www.kko.fi.
Consists of a President and at least 15 Justices appointed by the President of the Republic. Final court of appeal in civil and criminal cases, supervises judges and executive authorities.
President: PAULIINE KOSKELO.
Justices: GUSTAF MÖLLER, MIKKO TULOKAS, LAURI LEHTIMAJA, KATI HIDÉN, EEVA VUORI, KARI KITUNEN, GUSTAV BYGGLIN, LIISA MANSIKKAMÄKI, PERTTI VÄLIMÄKI, PASI AARNIO, JUHA HÄYHÄ, HANNU RAJALAHTI, ILKKA RAUTIO, TIMO ESKO, SOILE POUTIANEN, MARJUT JOKELA, JUKKA SIPPO.

SUPREME ADMINISTRATIVE COURT

Korkein hallinto-oikeus/Högsta förvaltningsdomstolen
Unioninkatu 16, POB 180, 00131 Helsinki; tel. (10) 3640200; fax (10) 3640382; e-mail korkein.hallinto-oikeus@om.fi; internet www.kho.fi.
Consists of a President and 20 Justices appointed by the President of the Republic. Highest tribunal for appeals in administrative cases.
President: PEKKA HALLBERG.
Justices: AHTI RIHTO, OLOF OLSSON, ESA AALTO, PIRKKO IGNATIUS, RAIMO ANTTILA, PEKKA VIHERVUORI, MARJATTA KAJÁN, HEIKKI KANNINEN, KARI KUUSINIEMI, NIILO JÄÄSKINEN, ILKKA PERE, AHTI VAPAAVUORI, IRMA TELIVUO, JUKKA MATTILA, MATTI PELLONPÄÄ, TUULA PYNNÄ, ANNE E. NIEMI, MATTI HALÉN, SAKARI VANHALA, EILA ROTHER.

COURTS OF APPEAL

There are Courts of Appeal at Turku, Vaasa, Kuopio, Helsinki, Kouvola, and Rovaniemi, consisting of a President and an appropriate number of members.

ADMINISTRATIVE COURTS

There are eight Administrative Courts, which hear the appeals of private individuals and corporate bodies against the authorities in tax cases, municipal cases, construction cases, social welfare and health-care cases and other administrative cases. In certain of these, the appeal must be preceded by a complaint to a separate lower appellate body. The State and municipal authorities also have a right of appeal in certain cases.

DISTRICT COURTS

Courts of first instance for almost all suits. Appeals lie to the Court of Appeal, and then to the Supreme Court. The composition of the District Court is determined by the type of case to be heard. Civil cases and 'ordinary' criminal cases can be considered by one judge. Other criminal cases and family law cases are heard by a judge and a panel of three lay judges (jurors). Other civil cases are heard by three legally-qualified judges. There are 66 District Courts.

SPECIAL COURTS

In addition there are a number of special courts with more restricted jurisdictions. These are: the High Court of Impeachment, the Insurance Court, the Labour Court and the Market Court. There is no constitutional court in Finland, but the Constitutional Committee of Parliament has been entrusted with the process of verifying the compatibility of new legislation with the Constitution.

CHANCELLOR OF JUSTICE

The Oikeuskansleri is responsible for ensuring that authorities and officials comply with the law. He is the chief public prosecutor, and acts as counsel for the Government.
Chancellor of Justice: JAAKKO JONKKA.
Chancellor of Justice's Office: Snellmaninkatu 1A, Helsinki; POB 20, 00023 Government; tel. (9) 16001; fax (9) 16023975; e-mail kirjaamo@okv.fi; internet www.okv.fi.

PARLIAMENTARY OMBUDSMAN

The Eduskunnan Oikeusasiamies is the Finnish Ombudsman appointed by the Eduskunta to supervise the observance of the law.
Parliamentary Ombudsman: RIITTA-LEENA PAUNIO.
Office of the Parliamentary Ombudsman: Arkadiankatu 3, 00102 Helsinki; tel. (9) 4321; fax (9) 4322268; e-mail ombudsman@eduskunta.fi; internet www.oikeusasiamies.fi.

In addition to the Chancellor of Justice and the Parliamentary Ombudsman, there are also specialized authorities that have similar duties in more limited fields. These include the Consumer Ombudsman, the Ombudsman for Equality, the Data Protection Ombudsman, the Ombudsman for Aliens and the Bankruptcy Ombudsman.

Religion

In 2007 81.7% of the population were members of the Evangelical Lutheran Church and around 1% belonged to the Orthodox Church. Some 15% of the population profess no religious affiliation.

CHRISTIANITY

Suomen ekumeeninen neuvosto/Ekumeniska rådet i Finland (Finnish Ecumenical Council): Katajanokankatu 7A, POB 185, 00161 Helsinki; tel. (9) 1802369; fax (9) 174313; e-mail heikki.huttunen@ekumenia.fi; internet www.ekumenia.fi; f. 1917; 11 mem. churches; Pres. Archbishop Dr JUKKA PAARMA; Gen. Sec. Rev. HEIKKI HUTTUNEN.

National Churches

Suomen evankelis-luterilainen kirkko (Evangelical Lutheran Church of Finland): Council for International Relations, Satamakatu 11, POB 185, 00161 Helsinki; tel. (9) 18021; fax (9) 1802350; internet evl.fi; 81.7% of the population were adherents in 2007; Leader Archbishop Dr JUKKA PAARMA.

Suomen Ortodoksinen Kirkko (Orthodox Church of Finland): Karjalankatu 1, 70110 Kuopio; tel. (206) 100230; fax (206) 100231; e-mail info@ort.fi; internet www.ort.fi; 60,000 mems; Leader Archbishop LEO of Karelia and All Finland.

The Roman Catholic Church

Finland comprises the single diocese of Helsinki, directly responsible to the Holy See. At 31 December 2005 there were 9,067 adherents in the country (around 0.2% of the population). The Bishop participates in the Scandinavian Episcopal Conference (based in Sweden).
Bishop of Helsinki: JÓZEF WRÓBEL, Rehbinderintie 21, 00150 Helsinki; tel. (9) 6877160; fax (9) 639820; e-mail curia@catholic.fi; internet www.catholic.fi.

Other Churches

Finlands svenska baptistsamfund (Finland Swedish Baptist Union): Rådhusgatan 44, 5th Floor, POB 54, 65101 Vasa; tel. (6) 3464500; fax (6) 3464510; e-mail fsb@baptist.fi; internet www.baptist.fi; f. 1856; publishes *Missionsstandaret* (12 a year); 1,253 mems; Gen. Sec. NILS ERIK VIKSTRÖM.

Finlands svenska metodistkyrka (United Methodist Church in Finland—Swedish-speaking): Mannerheimgt. 17, 06100 Borgå; e-mail kyrkostyrelsen@metodistkyrkan.fi; internet www.metodistkyrkan.fi; f. 1881; 1,000 mems; District Superintendents Rev. FREDRIK WEGELIUS, Rev. TOM HELLSTEN.

Jehovan Todistajat (Jehovah's Witnesses): Puutarhatie 60, 01300 Vantaa; tel. (9) 825885; fax (9) 82588285; internet www.watchtower.org; 19,630 mems.

Myöhempien Aikojen Pyhien Jeesuksen Kristuksen Kirkko (Church of Jesus Christ of Latter-day Saints—Mormon): Neitsytpolku 3A, 00140 Helsinki; tel. (9) 6962750; fax (9) 69627510; e-mail 2015803@ldschurch.org; internet www.mormonit.fi; 4,504 mems; Mission Pres. PHILLIP ESTES.

Suomen Adventtikirkko (Seventh-day Adventist Church in Finland): POB 94, 33101 Tampere; tel. (3) 3611111; fax (3) 3600454; e-mail advent@sdafin.org; internet www.adventtikirkko.fi; f. 1894; 5,469 mems; Pres. ATTE HELMINEN; Sec. ANNE LESKINEN.

Suomen Baptistiyhdyskunta (Baptists—Finnish-speaking): Kissanmaankatu 19, 33530 Tampere; tel. (30) 3138100; e-mail porttis@hotmail.com; internet www.baptisti.fi; 692 mems; Pres. JARI PORTAANKORVA.

Suomen Vapaakirkko (Evangelical Free Church of Finland): POB 198, 13101 Hämeenlinna; tel. (3) 6445150; fax (3) 6122153; e-mail svk@svk.fi; internet www.svk.fi; f. 1923; 14,300 mems; Pres. Rev. OLAVI RINTALA.

Svenska Kyrkan i Finland (Church of Sweden in Finland): Minervagatan 6, 00100 Helsinki; tel. (9) 443831; fax (9) 4546059; e-mail forsamlingen@olauspetri.inet.fi; f. 1919; 1,300 mems; Rector Dr JARL JERGMAR.

Suomen Metodistikirkko (United Methodist Church—Finnish-speaking): Punavuorenkatu 2, 00120 Helsinki; tel. (9) 628798; fax (9) 6224558; e-mail suomen@metodistikirkko.fi; internet www.metodistikirkko.fi; 782 mems; District Superintendent Rev. TIMO VIRTANEN.

FINLAND

Directory

The Anglican Church and the Salvation Army are also active in the country.

BAHÁ'Í FAITH

Suomen Bahá'í-yhteisö (Bahá'í Community of Finland): POB 423, 00101 Helsinki; tel. (9) 790875; fax (9) 790058; e-mail info@bahai.fi; internet www.bahai.fi; f. 1953; 600 mems.

JUDAISM

Helsingin Juutalainen Seurakunta (Jewish Community of Helsinki): Synagogue and Community Centre, Malminkatu 26, 00100 Helsinki; tel. (9) 5860310; fax (9) 6948916; e-mail srk@jchelsinki.fi; internet www.jchelsinki.fi; 1,200 mems; Pres. RONY SMOLAR; Exec. Dir DAN KANTOR.

ISLAM

Between 1990 and 2000 the number of Muslims increased from 1,000 to approximately 20,000. There are around 20 registered mosques or religious communities.

Suomen Islamilainen Yhdyskunta (Islamic Community of Finland): POB 87, 00101 Helsinki; tel. (9) 2782551; fax (9) 6121156; e-mail yhdyskunta@rabita.fi; internet www.rabita.fi.

The Press

In 2006 there were 53 daily and 151 non-daily newspapers in Finland; the total circulation for all types of newspaper was some 3.2m. A number of dailies are printed in Swedish. The most popular daily papers are *Helsingin Sanomat, Ilta-Sanomat, Aamulehti* and *Iltalehti*.

PRINCIPAL DAILIES

Espoo

Hevosurheilu: Tulkinkuja 3, 02650 Espoo; tel. (20) 7605300; fax (20) 7605390; e-mail hevosurheilu@hevosurheilulehti.fi; internet www.hippos.fi/hippos/hevosurheilu_lehti; independent; Editor-in-Chief JORMA KEMILÄINEN; circ. 26,274.

Helsinki

Helsingin Sanomat: Töölönlahdenkatu 2, POB 77, 00089 Sanomat; tel. (9) 1221; fax (9) 1222366; e-mail janne.virkkunen@sanomat.fi; internet www.hs.fi; f. 1889; independent; Publr SEPPO KIEVARI; Senior Editor-in-Chief JANNE VIRKKUNEN; circ. 417,548 weekdays, 476,211 weekend.

Hufvudstadsbladet: Mannerheimvägen 18, POB 217, 00101 Helsinki; tel. (9) 12531; fax (9) 642930; e-mail nyheter@hbl.fi; internet www.hbl.fi; f. 1864; Swedish language; independent; Editor-in-Chief MAX ARHIPPAINEN; circ. 50,845 weekdays, 52,781 weekend.

Iltalehti: Aleksanterinkatu 9, 00100 Helsinki; tel. (10) 665100; fax (9) 177313; e-mail il.toimitus@iltalehti.fi; internet www.iltalehti.fi; f. 1981; afternoon; independent; Man. Dir and Editor-in-Chief KARI KIVELÄ; circ. 133,007 weekdays, 166,240 weekend.

Ilta-Sanomat: POB 45, 00089 Sanomat; tel. (9) 1221; fax (9) 1223419; e-mail iltasanomat@sanoma.fi; internet www.iltsanomat.fi; f. 1932; afternoon; independent; Man. Dir PEKKA HARJU; Editor-in-Chief ANTTI-PEKKA PIETILÄ; circ. 186,462 weekdays.

Kansan Uutiset: POB 64, 00501 Helsinki; tel. (9) 759601; fax (9) 75960319; e-mail ku@kansanuutiset.fi; internet www.kansanuutiset.fi; f. 1957; organ of the Left Alliance; Editor-in-chief JANNE MÄKINEN; circ. 8,013.

Kauppalehti (The Commercial Daily): POB 189, 00101 Helsinki; tel. (9) 50781; fax (9) 5078419; internet www.kauppalehti.fi; f. 1898; morning; Man. Dir JUHA BLOHSTER; Editor-in-Chief HANNU LEINONEN; circ. 81,377.

Maaseudun Tulevaisuus: Simonkatu 6, POB 440, 00100 Helsinki; tel. (9) 204132100; fax (9) 6944766; internet www.maaseuduntulevaisuus.fi; f. 1916; independent; Man. Dir HEIKKI LAURINEN; Editor-in-Chief LAURI KONTRO; circ. 83,604.

Uutispäivä Demari: Haapaniemenkatu 7–9B, POB 338, 00531 Helsinki; tel. (9) 701041; fax (9) 7010567; e-mail toimitus@demari.fi; internet www.demari.fi; f. 1895; chief organ of the Social Democratic Party; Man. Dir HEIKKI NYKANEN; Editor-in-Chief JUHA PELTONEN; circ. 17,677.

Hämeenlinna

Hämeen Sanomat: Vanajantie 7, POB 530, 13111 Hämeenlinna; tel. (3) 61511; fax (3) 6151410; e-mail toimitus@hameensanomat.fi; internet www.hameensanomat.fi; f. 1879; independent; Man. Dir MATTI VIHERVUORI; Editor-in-Chief OLLI-PEKKA BEHM; circ. 29,860.

Joensuu

Karjalainen: Kosti Aaltosentie 9, POB 99, 80141 Joensuu; tel. (13) 2551; fax (13) 2552363; e-mail toimitus@karjalainen.fi; internet www.karjalainen.fi; f. 1874; independent; Man. Dir RAIMO PUUSTINEN; Editor PEKKA SITARI; circ. 47,351.

Jyväskylä

Keskisuomalainen: Aholaidantie 3, POB 159, 40101 Jyväskylä; tel. (14) 622000; fax (14) 622272; e-mail tietopalvelu@keskisuomalainen.fi; internet www.keskisuomalainen.fi; f. 1871; Man. Dir ERKKI PORANEN; Editor ERKKI LAATIKAINEN; circ. 74,840.

Kajaani

Kainuun Sanomat: Viestitie 2, POB 150, 87101 Kajaani; tel. (8) 61661; fax (8) 6166307; e-mail toimitus@kainuunsanomat.fi; internet www.kainuunsanomat.fi; f. 1918; independent; Man. Dir JUHA RUOTSALAINEN; Editor-in-Chief MATTI PIIRAINEN; circ. 22,322.

Kemi

Pohjolan Sanomat: Sairaalakatu 2, 94100 Kemi; tel. (16) 2911; fax (16) 291300; e-mail ps.toimitus@pohjolansanomat.fi; internet www.pohjolansanomat.fi; f. 1915; Man. Dir MARTTI NIKKANEN; Editor-in-Chief HEIKKI LÄÄKKÖLÄ; circ. 22,161.

Kokkola

Keskipohjanmaa: Kosila, POB 45, 67101 Kokkola; tel. (6) 8272000; fax (6) 8220208; e-mail toimitus@kpk.fi; internet www.keskipohjanmaa.net; f. 1917; independent; Man. Dir EINO LAUKKA; Editor-in-chief LASSI JAAKKOLA; circ. 27,907.

Kotka

Kymen Sanomat: POB 27, 48101 Kotka; tel. (5) 210015; fax (5) 21005206; e-mail uutiset@kymensanomat.fi; internet www.kymensanomat.fi; f. 1902; independent; Man. Dir ANTTI MÄKELÄ; Editor MARKKU ESPO; circ. 25,367.

Kouvola

Kouvolan Sanomat: POB 40, 45101 Kouvola; tel. (5) 280014; fax (5) 28004206; e-mail toimitus@kouvolansanomat.fi; internet www.kouvolansanomat.fi; f. 1909; independent; Man. Dir JUHA OKSANEN; Editor-in-Chief VILLE POHJONEN; circ. 28,827.

Kuopio

Savon Sanomat: POB 68, 70101 Kuopio; tel. (17) 303111; fax (17) 303347; e-mail lukijansanomat@iwn.fi; internet www.savonsanomat.fi; f. 1907; independent; Man. Dir HEIKKI AURASMAA; Editor-in-Chief JARI TOURUNEN; circ. 64,471.

Lahti

Etelä-Suomen Sanomat: Aleksanterinkatu 10, POB 80, 15101 Lahti; tel. (3) 75751; fax (3) 7575466; internet www.ess.fi; f. 1900; independent; Man. Dir JUKKA OTTELA; Editor-in-Chief HEIKKI HAKALA; circ. 60,889.

Lappeenranta

Etelä-Saimaa: POB 3, 53501 Lappeenranta; tel. (5) 538815; fax (5) 53883205; internet www.esaimaa.fi; f. 1885; independent; Man. Dir ANTERO JUNTTILA; Editor PEKKA LAKKA; circ. 32,690.

Mikkeli

Länsi-Savo: POB 6, 50101 Mikkeli; tel. (15) 3501; fax (15) 350337; e-mail toimitus@lansi-savo.fi; internet www.lansi-savo.fi; independent; Man. Dir JUKKA TIKKA; Editor-in-Chief KARI JUUTILAINEN; circ. 25,538.

Oulu

Kaleva: POB 170, 90401 Oulu; tel. (8) 5377111; fax (8) 5377195; e-mail kaleva@kaleva.fi; internet www.kaleva.fi; f. 1899; independent; Man. Dir TAISTO RISKI; Editor-in-Chief RISTO UIMONEN; circ. 82,037.

Pori

Satakunnan Kansa: Valtakatu 12, POB 58, 28100 Pori; tel. (2) 6228111; fax (2) 6228392; e-mail sk.toimitus@satakunnankansa.fi; internet www.satakunnankansa.fi; f. 1873; independent; Man. Dir TUOMO SAARINEN; Editor-in-Chief JOUKO JOKINEN; circ. 55,217.

FINLAND

Rauma

Länsi-Suomi: Susivuorentie 2, POB 5, 26100 Rauma; tel. (2) 83361; fax (2) 8240959; internet www.lansi-suomi.fi; f. 1905; independent; Editor-in-Chief MIKKO HANKALA; circ. 16,712.

Rovaniemi

Lapin Kansa: Veitikantie 2–8, 96100 Rovaniemi; tel. (16) 320011; fax (16) 3200345; e-mail lktoimitus@lapinkansa.fi; internet www.lapinkansa.fi; f. 1928; independent; Man. Dir JUHA RUOTSALAINEN; Editor-in-Chief HEIKKI TUOMI-NIKULA; circ. 34,658.

Salo

Salon Seudun Sanomat: Örninkatu 14, POB 117, 24101 Salo; tel. (2) 77021; fax (2) 7702300; internet www.sss.fi; independent; Man. Dir KIRSTI KIRJONEN; Editor-in-Chief JARMO VÄHÄSILTA; circ. 22,154.

Savonlinna

Itä-Savo: POB 101, 57101 Savonlinna; tel. (15) 3503400; fax (15) 3503403; internet www.ita-savo.fi; Editor KYÖSTI PIENIMÄKI; circ. 18,143.

Seinäjoki

Ilkka: POB 60, 60101 Seinäjoki; tel. (6) 4186555; fax (6) 4186500; e-mail ilkka.toimitus@ilkka.fi; internet www.ilkka.fi; f. 1906; independent; Man. Dir MATTI KORKIATUPA; Editor-in-Chief KARI HOKKANEN; circ. 55,277.

Tampere

Aamulehti: POB 327, 33101 Tampere; tel. (10) 665111; fax (10) 6653140; internet www.aamulehti.fi; f. 1881; Editor MATTI APUNEN; circ. 137,551 weekdays, 142,695 weekend.

Turku

Turun Sanomat: POB 95, 20101 Turku; tel. (2) 2693311; fax (2) 2693274; e-mail ts.toimitus@ts-group.fi; internet www.turunsanomat.fi; f. 1904; independent; Man. Dir KEIJO KETONEN; Editors-in-Chief ARI VALJAKKA, RAIMO VAHTERA, AIMO MASSINEN; circ. 109,988 weekdays, 126,972 weekend.

Tuusula

Keski-Uusimaa: POB 52, 04301 Tuusula; tel. (9) 273000; fax (9) 27300205; e-mail toimitus@keskiuusimaa.fi; internet www.keskiuusimaa.fi; independent; Man. Dir JORMA HÄMÄLÄINEN; Editor-in-Chief EERO LEHTINEN; circ. 20,796.

Vaasa

Pohjalainen: Hietasaarenkatu 19, POB 37, 65101 Vaasa; tel. (6) 3249111; fax (6) 3249355; e-mail kari.mantila@pohjalainen.fi; internet www.pohjalainen.fi; f. 1903; independent; Man. Dir MATTI KORKIATUPA; Editor MARKU MANTILA; circ. 29,565.

Vasabladet: Sandögatan 6, POB 52, 65101 Vaasa; tel. (6) 3260211; fax (6) 3129003; e-mail tips@vasabladet.fi; internet www.vasabladet.fi; f. 1856; Swedish language; Liberal independent; Man. Dir HANS BOIJE; Editor-in-Chief DENNIS RUNDT; circ. 24,435.

PRINCIPAL PERIODICALS

7 päivää: POB 124, 00151 Helsinki; tel. (9) 177777; fax (9) 177477; e-mail asiakaspalvelu@seiska.fi; internet www.seiska.fi; f. 1992; weekly; television and radio; Editor-in-chief EEVA-HELENA JOKITAIPALE; circ. 127,810.

Ahjo: POB 107, 00531 Helsinki; tel. (20) 774001; fax (20) 7741240; e-mail ahjo@metalliliitto.fi; internet www.metalliliitto.fi; fortnightly; for metal industry employees; Editor-in-Chief HEIKKI PISKONEN; circ. 173,000.

Aku Ankka (Donald Duck): POB 40, 00040 Helsinki; tel. (9) 1201; fax (9) 1205569; e-mail asiakaspalvelu@sanomamagazines.fi; internet www.akuankka.fi; f. 1951; weekly; children's; Editor-in-Chief MARKKU KIVEKÄS; circ. 283,334.

Apu: Hitsaajankatu 10, 00081 Helsinki; tel. (9) 75961; fax (9) 781911; e-mail matti.saari@apu.fi; internet www.apu.fi; f. 1933; weekly; family journal; Editor-in-Chief MATTI SAARI; circ. 254,696.

Avotakka: Risto Rytintie 33, 00081 A-lehdet, Helsinki; tel. (9) 75961; fax (9) 75983110; e-mail avotakka@a-lehdet.fi; internet www.avotakka.fi; f. 1967; monthly; interior decorating; Editor-in-Chief SOILI UKKOLA; circ. 102,162.

Diabetes: Kirjoniementie 15, 33680 Tampere; tel. (3) 2860111; fax (3) 3600462; e-mail lehdet@diabetes.fi; internet www.diabetes.fi; f. 1949; 10 a year; health; circ. 61,802.

Eeva: Hitsaajankatu 7/7, 00081 A-lehdet, Helsinki; tel. (9) 75961; fax (9) 786858; e-mail eeva@a-lehdet.fi; internet www.eeva.fi; f. 1933; monthly; women's; Editor-in-Chief LIISA JÄPPINEN; circ. 99,678.

Erä: Esterinportti 1, 00015 Kuvalehdet, Helsinki; tel. (9) 15661; fax (9) 15666210; e-mail era@kuvalehdet.fi; internet www.eralehti.fi; monthly; sport, fishing and outdoor leisure; Editor SEPPO SUURONEN; circ. 52,088.

ET-lehti: POB 100, 00040 Helsinki; tel. (9) 1201; fax (9) 1205428; e-mail kaisa.larmela@helsinkimedia.fi; internet www.et-lehti.fi; monthly; over-50s magazine; Editor-in-Chief KAISA LARMELA; circ. 250,000.

Gloria: POB 100, 00040 Helsinki; tel. (9) 1201; fax (9) 1205427; e-mail gloria@sanomamagazines.fi; internet www.gloria.fi; monthly; women's; Editor-in-Chief RIITTA LINDEGREN; circ. 64,000.

Hymy: Maistraatinportti 1, 00015 Kuvalehdet, Helsinki; tel. (9) 156665; fax (9) 1566511; e-mail esko.tulusto@kuvalehdet.fi; internet www.hymy.fi; monthly; family journal; Editor ESKO TULUSTO; circ. 94,527.

Hyvä Terveys: POB 100, 00040 Sanoma Magazines; tel. (9) 1201; fax (9) 1205456; e-mail hyva.terveys@sanomamagazines.fi; internet www.hyvaterveys.fi; 13 a year; health; Editor-in-Chief MAIJA TOPPILA; circ. 136,584.

IT-Invaliditys: Mannerheimintie 107, 00280 Helsinki; tel. (9) 613191; fax (9) 1461443; e-mail fmd@invalidiliitto.fi; internet www.invalidiliitto.fi/portal/verkkolehti; 12 a year; for handicapped people; Editor-in-Chief SINIKKA RANTALA; circ. 44,207.

Kaksplus: Maistraatinportti 1, 00015 Kuvalehdet, Helsinki; tel. (9) 1566591; fax (9) 1566550; e-mail kaksplus@kuvalehdet.fi; internet www.kaksplus.fi; f. 1969; monthly; for families with young children; Editor-in-Chief EMMA KOIVULA; circ. 38,641.

Katso: Hitsaajankatu 7/5, 00081 A-lehdet, Helsinki; tel. (9) 75961; fax (9) 7583102; e-mail asiakaspalvelu@katso.fi; internet www.katso.fi; f. 1960; weekly; TV, radio, film and video; Editor-in-Chief MARKKU VEIJALAINEN; circ. 70,388.

Kauneus ja terveys: Risto Rytin tie 33, Helsinki; tel. (9) 75961; fax (9) 75983106; e-mail kt@a-lehdet.fi; internet www.kauneusjaterveys.f; monthly; health and beauty; Editor TITTA KIURU; circ. 61,647.

Kirkko ja kaupunki: POB 279, 00181 Helsinki; tel. (9) 0207542000; fax (9) 0207542347; internet www.kirkkojakaupunki.fi; weekly; church and community; Editor-in-Chief SEPPO SIMOLA; circ. 207,382.

Kodin Kuvalehti: POB 100, 00040 Helsinki; tel. (9) 1201; fax (9) 1205468; e-mail kodin.kuvalehti@sanomamagazines.fi; internet www.kodinkuvalehti.fi; fortnightly; family magazine; Editor LEENA KARO; circ. 180,068.

Kotilääkäri: Maistraatinportti 1, 00015 Kuvalehdet, Helsinki; tel. (9) 15661; fax (9) 1566507; e-mail kotilaakari@kuvalehdet.fi; internet www.kotilaakari.fi; f. 1889; monthly; health and beauty; Editor-in-Chief KATJA VALLA; circ. 64,769.

Kotiliesi: Maistraatinportti 1, 00015 Kuvalehdet, Helsinki; tel. (9) 156665; fax (9) 1566511; internet www.kotiliesi.fi; f. 1922; fortnightly; women's; Editor-in-Chief ELINA SIMONEN-HYVÄRINEN; circ. 200,474.

Kotivinkki: Kalevankatu 56, 00180 Helsinki; tel. (9) 773951; fax (9) 77395399; e-mail ritva.kaarakainen@forma.fi; internet www.kotivinkki.fi; monthly; women's; Editor-in-Chief ANNELI MYLLER; circ. 207,550.

Me Naiset: POB 100, 00040 Helsinki; Lapinmäentie 1, 00350 Helsinki; tel. (9) 1201; fax (9) 1205414; e-mail menaiset@sanomamagazines.fi; internet www.menaiset.fi; f. 1952; weekly; women's; Editor RIITTA POLLARI; circ. 115,000.

Metsälehti: Soidinkuja 4, 00700 Helsinki; tel. (9) 1562333; fax (9) 1562335; e-mail paavo.seppanen@metsalehti.fi; internet www.metsalehti.fi; f. 1933; fortnightly; forestry; Editor PAAVO SEPPÄNEN; circ. 37,606.

MikroPC: Annankatu 34–36B, POB 920, 00101 Helsinki; tel. (20) 44240; e-mail kimmo.seppala@talentum.fi; internet mikropc.net; 20 a year; computers; Editor-in-Chief KIMMO SEPPÄLÄ; circ. 29,212.

Partio: Töölönkatu 55, 00250 Helsinki; tel. (9) 88651100; fax (9) 88651199; e-mail info@partio.fi; internet www.partio.fi; six a year; the Scout movement; Editor SAHI LIISA; circ. 57,188.

Pellervo: POB 77, 00101 Helsinki; tel. (9) 4767501; fax (9) 6948845; e-mail finncoop@pellervo.fi; internet www.pellervo.fi; f. 1899; monthly; agricultural and co-operative, home and country life journal; organ of the Confederation of Finnish Co-operatives; Editor-in-Chief KAISU RÄSÄNEN; circ. 32,000.

PerusSuomalainen: Mannerheimintie 40B 56, 00100 Helsinki; tel. (9) 4540411; fax (9) 4540466; e-mail peruss@perussuomalaiset.fi; internet www.perussuomalaiset.fi; f. 1996; 12 a year; organ of the Perussuomalaiset/Sannfinländarna rp (PS—True Finns); Editor ROLF (FRED) SORMO; circ. 100,000.

FINLAND   *Directory*

Pirkka: POB 410, 00811 Helsinki; tel. (9) 42427330; internet www.pirkka.fi; 10 a year; Swedish; Editor-in-Chief MINNA JÄRVENPÄÄ; circ. 1,383,482.

Reserviläinen: Döbelninkatu 2, 00260 Helsinki; tel. (9) 40562018; fax (9) 40562096; e-mail toimitus@reservilainen.fi; internet www.reservilainen.fi; nine a year; military; Editor KARI VAINIO; circ. 60,000.

Sähköviesti/Elbladet: POB 1427, 00101 Helsinki; tel. (9) 53052700; fax (9) 53052801; e-mail ari.vesa@energia.fi; f. 1939; quarterly; publ. by Finnish Electricity Asscn; Editor-in-Chief ARI J. VESA; circ. 101,575.

Seura: Maistraatinportti 1, 00240 Helsinki; tel. (9) 15661; fax (9) 1496472; f. 1934; weekly; family journal; Editor-in-Chief JOUNI FLINKKILÄ; circ. 268,553.

STTK—lehti: POB 248, 00171 Helsinki; tel. (9) 131521; fax (9) 652367; e-mail marja-liisa.rajakangas@sttk.fi; eight a year; organ of Finnish Confederation of Salaried Employees; Editor-in-Chief MARJA-LIISA RAJAKANGAS; circ. 40,000.

Suomen Kuvalehti: Maistraatinportti 1, 00015 Kuvalehdet; tel. (9) 15661; fax (9) 144076; e-mail suomen.kuvalehti@kuvalehdet.fi; internet www.suomenkuvalehti.fi; f. 1916; weekly; illustrated news; Editor-in-Chief TAPANI RUOKANEN; circ. 100,967.

Suosikki: Maistraatinportti 1, 00015 Yhtyneet Kuvalehdet; tel. (9) 1566553; fax (9) 144595; e-mail suosikki@kuvalehdet.fi; internet www.suosikki.fi; f. 1961; owned by Yhtyneet Kuvalehdet Oy; monthly; youth magazine, music, films, fashion; Editor-in-Chief KATJA STÅHL; circ. 46,334.

Suuri Käsityölehti: POB 100, 00040 Helsinki; tel. (9) 1201; fax (9) 1205352; e-mail suuri.kasityolehti@sanomamagazines.fi; internet www.suurikasityo.fi; f. 1974; monthly; needlework, knitting and dress-making magazine; Editor PAULA HIETARANTA; circ. 126,858.

Talouselämä: Annankatu 34–36B, POB 920, 00101 Helsinki; tel. (9) 2044240; fax (9) 204424108; e-mail te@talentum.fi; internet www.talouselama.fi; f. 1938; 43 a year; economy, business; Man. Dir JUHA BLOMSTER; Editor-in-Chief PEKKA SEPPÄNEN; circ. 78,343.

Tekniikan Maailma: Esterinportti 1, 00240 Helsinki; tel. (9) 15661; fax (9) 15666313; e-mail tekniikan.maailma@kuvalehdet.fi; internet www.tekniikanmaailma.fi; f. 1953; 22 a year; motoring, technology, aviation, photography; Editor-in-Chief MARTTI J. MERILINNA; circ. 148,840.

Trendi: Ruoholahdenkatu 21, 00180 Helsinki; tel. (9) 773951; fax (9) 77395321; internet www.trendi.fi; 10 a year; women's lifestyle; circ. 62,063.

Tuulilasi: 00081 A-lehdet; tel. (9) 75961; fax (9) 75983103; e-mail tuulilasi@a-lehdet.fi; internet www.tuulilasi.fi; f. 1963; 16 a year; motoring; Editor-in-Chief LAURI LARMELA; circ. 87,001.

Työ Terveys Turvallisuus: Topeliuksenkatu 41A, 00250 Helsinki; tel. (30) 4741; fax (30) 4742478; f. 1971; 12 a year; occupational safety and health; Editor-in-Chief MATTI TAPIAINEN; circ. 72,525.

Valitut Palat: POB 46, 00441 Helsinki; tel. (9) 503441; fax (9) 5034499; internet www.valitutpalat.fi; monthly; Finnish Reader's Digest; Editor-in-Chief ILKKA VIRTANEN; circ. 224,654.

Voi hyvin: Risto Rytin tie 33, 00081 A-lehdet, Helsinki; tel. (9) 75961; fax (9) 75983109; e-mail voihyvin@a-lehdet.fi; internet www.voihyvin.fi; f. 1986; eight a year; health, wellbeing; Editor JAANA-MIRJAM MUSTAVUORI; circ. 47,000.

Yhteishyvä: Fleminginkatu 34, POB 171, 00511 Helsinki; tel. (9) 1882621; fax (9) 1882626; e-mail kirsi.ervola@sok.fi; internet www.yhteishyva.fi; f. 1905; monthly; free to members of co-operative group; Editor-in-Chief KIRSI ERVOLA; circ. 848,000.

NEWS AGENCY

Oy Suomen Tietotoimisto (STT): Albertinkatu 33, POB 550, 00101 Helsinki; tel. (9) 695811; fax (9) 69581335; e-mail toimitus@stt.fi; internet www.stt.fi; f. 1887; nine provincial branches; independent national agency distributing domestic and international news in Finnish and Swedish; CEO and Editor-in-Chief MIKA PETTERSSON.

PRESS ASSOCIATIONS

Aikakauslehtien Liitto (Periodical Publishers' Association): Lönnrotinkatu 11, 00120 Helsinki; tel. (9) 22877280; fax (9) 603478; internet www.aikakauslehdet.fi; f. 1946; aims to further the interests of publishers of magazines and periodicals, to encourage co-operation between publishers, and to improve standards; Man. Dir MATTI AHTOMIES.

Suomen Journalistiliitto—Finlands Journalistförbund r.y. (Union of Journalists): Hietalahdenkatu 2B 22, POB 252, 00180 Helsinki; tel. (9) 6122330; fax (9) 605396; e-mail info@journalistiliitto.fi; internet www.journalistiliitto.fi; f. 1921; 13,500 mems; Pres. ARTO NIEMINEN; Sec.-Gen. EILA HYPPÖNEN.

Sanomalehtien Liitto—Tidningarnas Förbund (Finnish Newspapers Association): Lönnrotinkatu 11, 00120 Helsinki; tel. (9) 22877300; fax (9) 607989; e-mail info@sanomalehdet.fi; internet www.sanomalehdet.fi; f. 1908; represents newspapers' interests; 200 mem. newspapers; Dir KRISTIINA MARKKULA.

Publishers

Art House Oy: Bulevardi 19C, 00120 Helsinki; tel. (9) 6932727; fax (9) 6949028; e-mail myynti@arthouse.fi; internet www.arthouse.fi; f. 1975; Finnish and foreign fiction, non-fiction, popular science, horror, fantasy, science fiction, detective fiction; Publr PAAVO HAAVIKKO.

Gummerus Kustannus Oy: Arkadiankatu 23B, POB 749, 00101 Helsinki; tel. (10) 6836200; fax (9) 58430200; e-mail publisher@gummerus.fi; internet www.gummerus.fi; f. 1872; fiction, non-fiction, reference, dictionaries, languages; Man. Dir ILKKA KYLMÄLÄ.

Karisto Oy: Paroistentie 2, POB 102, 13101 Hämeenlinna; tel. (3) 63151; fax (3) 6161565; e-mail kustannusliike; internet www.karisto.fi; f. 1900; non-fiction and fiction, printing; Man. Dir SIMO MOISIO.

Kirjapaja: Hietalahdenranta 13, POB 279, 00181 Helsinki; tel. (20) 7542000; fax (20) 7542341; e-mail mira.pitkanen@kirjapaja.fi; internet www.kirjapaja.fi; f. 1942; Christian literature, general fiction, non-fiction, reference, juvenile; Man. Dir MIRA PITKÄNEN.

Kustannus-Mäkelä Oy: POB 14, 03601 Karkkila; tel. (9) 2257995; fax (9) 2257660; e-mail makela@kustannusmakela.fi; internet www.kustannusmakela.fi; f. 1971; juvenile, fiction; Man. Dir ORVO MÄKELÄ.

Oy Like Kustannus Ltd: Meritullinkatu 21, 00170 Helsinki; tel. (9) 1351385; fax (9) 1351372; e-mail likekustannus@dlc.fi; f. 1987; film literature, fiction, non-fiction, comics; Man. Dir HANNU PALOVIITA.

Otava Publishing Co Ltd: Uudenmaankatu 10, 00120 Helsinki; tel. (9) 19961; fax (9) 643136; e-mail otava@otava.fi; internet www.otava.fi; f. 1890; part of Otava-United Magazines Group Ltd; non-fiction, fiction, children's and textbooks; Man. Dir ANTTI REENPÄÄ.

Schildts Förlags Ab: Georgsgatan 18, 00120 Helsinki; tel. (9) 8870400; fax (9) 8043257; e-mail schildts@schildts.fi; internet www.schildts.fi; f. 1913; subjects mainly in Swedish; Man. Dir JOHAN JOHNSON.

Söderström & Co Förlags Ab: Georgsgatan 29A, 00100 Helsinki; tel. (9) 68418620; fax (9) 68418621; e-mail soderstrom@soderstrom.fi; internet www.soderstrom.fi; f. 1891; all subjects in Swedish only; Man. Dir MARIANNE BARGUM.

Suomalaisen Kirjallisuuden Seura, SKS (Finnish Literature Society): POB 259, 00171 Helsinki; tel. (20) 1131231; fax (9) 13123220; e-mail books@finlit.fi; internet www.finlit.fi; f. 1831; Finnish and other Finno-Ugric languages, Finnish literature, literary scholarship, folklore, comparative ethnology and history; Publishing Dir PÄIVI VALLISAARI.

Tammi Publishers: Korkeavuorenkatu 37E, 00130 Helsinki; tel. (9) 6937621; fax (9) 69376278; e-mail tammi@tammi.fi; internet www.tammi.fi; f. 1943; fiction, general, non-fiction, children's, juvenile, textbooks, educational materials, audio books; owned by Bonnier AB; Pres. ANNE VALSTA.

Weilin & Göös Oy: Kappelitie 8, POB 123, 02201 Espoo; tel. (9) 43771; fax (9) 4377270; e-mail weegee@wg.fi; internet www.wg.fi; f. 1872; non-fiction, encyclopaedias.

Werner Söderström Corpn (WSOY): POB 222, Bulevardi 12, 00121 Helsinki; tel. (9) 61681; fax (9) 61683560; internet www.wsoy.fi; f. 1878; fiction and non-fiction, science, juvenile, textbooks, reference, comics, the printing industry; Pres. VELIPEKKA ELONEN.

PUBLISHERS' ASSOCIATION

Suomen Kustannusyhdistys (Finnish Book Publishers' Association): POB 177, 00121 Helsinki; tel. (9) 22877258; fax (9) 6121226; e-mail sirkku.palomaki@skyry.net; internet www.skyry.net; f. 1858; Pres. VELI-PEKKA ELONEN; Dir SAKARI LAIHO; 100 mems.

Broadcasting and Communications

REGULATORY AUTHORITY

Finnish Communications Regulatory Authority (FICORA): Itämerenkatu 3A, POB 313, 00181 Helsinki; tel. (9) 69661; fax (9) 6966410; e-mail info@ficora.fi; internet www.ficora.fi; affiliated to Ministry of Transport and Communications; CEO RAUNI HAGMAN.

TELECOMMUNICATIONS

DNA Ltd: Ansatie 6A B, POB 41, 01741 Vantaa; tel. (44) 0440; internet www.dnaoy.fi; f. 2007; offers mobile communications

FINLAND

Directory

services through DNA Finland Ltd and fixed-network broadband and television services through DNA Services Ltd; Chair. Siivola Risto; CEO Jan-Erik Frostdahl.

Elisa Corpn: Ratavartijankatu 5, Helsinki; POB 1, 00061 Elisa; tel. (10) 26000; fax (10) 26060; internet www.elisa.com; Pres. and CEO Veli-Matti Mattila.

Finnet International Ltd: Sinebrychoffinkatu 11, POB 949, 00101 Helsinki; tel. (9) 315315; fax (9) 605531; e-mail etunimi.sukunimi@finnet.fi; internet www.finnet.fi.

Nokia Oyj: Keilalahdentie 2–4, 02150 Espoo; POB 226, 00045 Nokia Group; tel. 718008000; fax 718038226; internet www.nokia.com; Pres. and CEO Olli-Pekka Kallasvuo.

Telecon Ltd: POB 55, 02231 Espoo; tel. (9) 8042900; fax (9) 8042901; e-mail info@telecon.fi; internet www.telecon.fi; Man. Dir Jouko Jokinen.

TeliaSonera Finland Oyj: Teollisuuskatu 15, Helsinki; POB 220, 00051 Sonera; tel. (20) 401; fax (20) 4069100; e-mail yritysasiakaspalvelu@sonera.com; internet www.teliasonera.fi; f. 2002 by merger of Telia AB (Sweden) and Sonera Ltd; Pres. and CEO Juho Lipsanen.

BROADCASTING

Radio

The first commercial radio stations were introduced in 1985 and stations proliferated rapidly to reach 59 by 1990. The global economic recession of the early 1990s led to the collapse of many commercial stations. However, the industry began to recover in the late 1990s, notably with the launch of the first national commercial radio station, Radio Nova, in May 1997. In 1999 RAB Finland was established to promote and develop the Finnish private radio industry by providing extensive information services free of charge to media planners, buyers and advertisers.

In May 1999 the first part of the national Digital Audio Broadcast (DAB) network was launched by Yleisradio (Finnish Broadcasting Company—YLE) with 10 transmitters (rising to 11 in 2001), covering 2m. people (approximately 40% of the population). The Finnish DAB transmitter network was closed down in 2005; YLE continued its digital transmissions through the Digital Video Broadcasting (DVB) television network.

Yleisradio Oy (YLE) (Finnish Broadcasting Company): POB 90, 00024 Yleisradio; tel. (9) 14801; fax (9) 14803215; e-mail fbc@yle.fi; internet www.yle.fi/fbc; f. 1926; 99.9% state-owned, with management appointed by the Administrative Council; Dir-Gen. Mikael Jungner; Dir of Radio and Deputy Dir-Gen. Seppo Härkönen; Dir of Television Olli-Pekka Heinonen; Dir of Swedish-language Radio and Television Programmes Annika Nyberg Frankenhauser.

YLE R1 (Radio Ylen Ykkönen): 24-hour arts and culture in Finnish; Dir Antti Pajamo.

YLE R2 (Ylex): POB 17, 00024 Helsinki; tel. (9) 14801; fax (9) 1482650; e-mail minna.peltomaki@yle.fi; internet www.yle.fi/ylex; f. 2003; 24-hour popular culture for young people in Finnish; Dir Minna Peltomaki.

YLE R3 (Radio Suomi): 24-hour news, current affairs, sport, regional programmes in Finnish; Dir Raimo Vanninen.

YLE R4 (Radio Extrem): Swedish-language channel for young people; Dir Richard Nordgren.

YLE R5 (Radio Vega): news, current affairs, art, culture and regional programmes in Swedish; Dir Peik Henrichson.

YLE Radio Finland: POB 78, 00024 Yleisradio; tel. (9) 14804320; fax (9) 14801169; e-mail rfinland@yle.fi; internet www.yle.fi/rfinland; broadcasts in Finnish, Swedish, English, German, French, Russian and Classical Latin; Head of International Radio Juhani Niinisto.

YLE Sámi Radio: 99870 Inari; tel. (16) 671261; fax (16) 671265; internet www.yle.fi/samiradio; Sámi-language network covering northern Lapland.

Classic Radio: Lintulahdenkatu 10, 00500 Helsinki; tel. (9) 6126911; fax (9) 61269130; internet www.classicradio.fi.

Digita Oy: POB 135, 00521 Helsinki; tel. (20) 411711; fax (20) 4117234; e-mail pauli.heikkila@digita.fi; internet www.digita.fi; f. 1999; operates the radio and television broadcasting network covering the whole of Finland; 36 main broadcasting stations and 101 substations; Man. Dir Pauli Heikkilä.

Groove FM: Lintulahdenkatu 10, 00500 Helsinki; tel. (9) 6126911; fax (9) 61269130; e-mail tom.bussman@mediasalesfinland.fi; internet www.groovefm.fi.

Iskelmä: Tallberginkatu 1c, 00180 Helsinki; tel. (9) 680960; fax (9) 68096521; e-mail erkka.jaakkola@sbs.fi; internet www.iskelma.fi.

NRJ: Kiviaidankatu 2i, 00210 Helsinki; tel. (9) 681900; fax (9) 68190102; e-mail marko.lintussari@nrj.fi; internet www.nrj.fi; Man. Dir Antti Pakkala.

Radio Nova: Ilmalankatu 2c, 00241 Helsinki; tel. (9) 88488700; fax (9) 88488720; e-mail leena.rotko@radionova.fi; internet www.radionova.fi; largest commercial radio station; 74% owned by Alma Media; Marketing Dir Päivi Nurmesniemi.

Radio SuomiPOP: Lintulahdenkatu 10, 00500 Helsinki; tel. (9) 6126911; fax (9) 61269130; e-mail tom.bussman@mediasalesfinland.fi; internet www.radiosuomipop.fi.

Sport FM: Areenakuja 1, 00240 Helsinki; tel. (9) 2041997; fax (9) 2041994; e-mail tapio.karimies@sport.fm.

The Voice: Tallberginkatu 1c, 00180 Helsinki; tel. (20) 7474000; e-mail info@sbs.fi; internet www.voice.fi.

RAB Finland Oy: Lönnrotinkatu 11a, 00121 Helsinki; tel. (9) 22877341; fax (9) 648221; e-mail info@rabfinland.fi; internet www.rabfinland.fi; f. 1999; promotes Finnish private radio industry by providing extensive information services free of charge; Man. Dir Leo Rantanen.

Television

Digital Video Broadcasting (DVB) began in Finland in 2001. Analogue transmission networks were closed down from 1 September 2007.

Yleisradio (YLE): (see above) operates five national channels: TV 1, TV 2, YLE FST (in Swedish), YLE Extra (a specialized channel for events, live broadcasts, etc.) and YLE Teema (a specialized channel for culture, education and science)

YLE/TV 1: POB 97, 00024 Yleisradio; tel. (9) 14801; fax (9) 14803424; internet www.yle.fi/tv1; f. 1957; programmes in Finnish; Head of Programming Riitta Jalonen.

YLE/TV 2: POB 196, 33101 Tampere; tel. (3) 3456111; fax (3) 3456892; internet www.yle.fi/tv2; f. 1964; programmes in Finnish and Swedish; Dir Päivi Kärkkäinen.

Canal Digital Finland Oy: POB 866, 33101 Tampere; tel. (20) 7699000; fax (20) 7699006; e-mail asiakaspalvelu@canaldigital.fi; internet www.canaldigital.fi.

MTV Finland: 00033 MTV3; 00240 Helsinki; tel. (9) 15001; fax (9) 1500707; e-mail palaute@mtv3.fi; internet www.mtv3.fi; f. 1957; independent nation-wide commercial television company comprising six channels: MTV3 and Subtv, as well as four subscription channels (MTV3 MAX, MTV3 Fakta, Subtv Junior and Subtv Leffa); became part of Alma Media Corpn in 1998; acquired by Bonnier (Sweden) in 2005; Pres. and CEO Pekka Karhuvaara.

SW Television Oy (Channel Four Finland): POB 350, 00151 Helsinki; tel. (9) 45451; fax (9) 4545400; e-mail juha-pekka.louhelainen@nelonen.fi; internet www.nelonen.fi; f. 1997; fmrly Oy Ruutunelonen Ab; independent commercial television co; 95.27% owned by Swelcom Oy; Pres. Juha-Pekka Louhelainen.

Finance

The Bank of Finland is the country's central bank and the centre of Finland's monetary and banking system. It functions 'under guarantee and supervision of the Eduskunta (Parliament) and the Bank supervisors delegated by the Eduskunta'.

At the end of 2006 there were a total of 338 banks operating in Finland.

BANKING

(cap. = capital; res = reserves; dep. = deposits; m. = million; brs = branches; amounts in euros)

Supervisory Authority

Financial Supervision Authority: Snellmaninkatu 1, POB 159, 00101 Helsinki; tel. (9) 18351; fax (9) 1835328; e-mail rahoitustarkastus@bof.fi; internet www.rata.bof.fi; f. 1993; maintains confidence in the financial markets by supervising the markets and the bodies working within them. It functions administratively in connection with the Bank of Finland, but operates as an independent decision-making body; Chair. Matti Louekoski; Dir-Gen. Anneli Tuominen.

Central Bank

Suomen Pankki/Finlands Bank (Bank of Finland): Snellmaninaukio, POB 160, 00101 Helsinki; tel. (10) 83111; fax (9) 174872; e-mail info@bof.fi; internet www.bof.fi; f. 1811; Bank of Issue under the guarantee and supervision of the Eduskunta; cap. €841m., res €689m., dep. €4,047m. (Dec. 2005); Gov. Erkki Liikanen; 4 brs.

Commercial Banks

Nordea Bank Finland PLC (Nordea Pankki Suomi Oyj): Aleksanterinkatu 36b, 00100 Helsinki; tel. (9) 1651; fax (9) 16554500;

FINLAND

internet www.nordea.fi; cap. €1,072m., res €4,055m., dep. €145,340m. (Dec. 2005); CEO Lars G. Nordström; 416 brs.

Sampo Bank PLC: Unioninkatu 22, Helsinki, 00075 Sampo; tel. (10) 51515; fax (10) 5160051; e-mail hannu.vuola@sampopankki.fi; internet www.sampopankki.fi; owned by Den Danske Bank, Denmark; cap. €106m., res €650m., dep. €18,047m. (Dec. 2005); CEO Ilkka Hallavo; 63 brs.

Co-operative Banks

Association of Finnish Local Co-operative Banks: Yliopistonkatu 7, 00101 Helsinki; tel. (9) 6811700; fax (9) 68117070; internet www.paikallisosuuspankit.fi; f. 1997; central organization of local co-operative banking group, which comprises 42 local co-operatives; cap. €200m., dep. €1,600m., total assets €2,062m. (Dec. 2000); 140 brs.

OKO Bank: Teollisuuskatu 1B, POB 308, 00101 Helsinki; tel. (10) 252011; fax (10) 2522002; internet www.okobank.com; f. 1902; cap. €423m., res €792m., dep. €16,707m. (Dec. 2005); part of OP Bank Group; Chair. Reijo Karhinen; Pres. and CEO Erkki Mikael Silvennoinen; 677 brs.

Savings Bank

Aktia Sparbank Abp (Aktia Savings Bank PLC): Mannerheimintie 14, 00100 Helsinki; tel. (10) 2475000; fax (10) 2476356; e-mail aktia@aktia.fi; internet www.aktia.fi; f. 1852 as Helsingfors Sparbank; current name adopted 1997; cap. €71m., res €82m., dep. €3,498m. (Dec. 2005); Chair. Kaj-Gustaf Bergh; Man. Dir Jussi Laitinen; 83 brs.

Mortgage Banks

OP-Asuntoluottopankki (OP Mortgage Bank): POB 308, 00101 Helsinki; tel. (9) 4041; fax (9) 4042620; f. 2000; part of OKO Bank Group; Man. Dir Lauri Iloniemi.

Sampo Asuntoluottopankki (Sampo Housing Loan PLC): Unioninkatu 22, 00075 Sampo; tel. (10) 5135789; fax (10) 5134616; f. 2000; fmrly Suomen Asuntoluottopankki, renamed as above 2005; part of Sampo Group; cap. €6m., total assets €25m. (Dec. 2000).

Investment Bank

Nordiska Investeringsbanken (Nordic Investment Bank): Fabianinkatu 34, POB 249, 00171 Helsinki; tel. (10) 618001; fax (10) 6180725; e-mail info@nib.int; internet www.nib.int; f. 1975; owned by Govts of Denmark, Estonia, Finland, Iceland, Latvia, Lithuania, Norway and Sweden; all member countries are represented in the bd of dirs by their ministers of finance and the economy; cap. €419m., res €1,435m., dep. €14,242m. (Dec. 2006); Pres. and CEO Johnny Åkerholm.

Banking Associations

Finanssialan Keskusliitto r.y. (Federation of Finnish Financial Services): Bulevardi 28, 00120 Helsinki; tel. (20) 7934200; fax (20) 7934202; e-mail fk@fkl.fi; internet www.fkl.fi; f. 2007 by merger of the Finnish Bankers' Association, the Federation of Finnish Insurance Companies, the Employers' Association of Finnish Financial Institutions and the Finnish Finance Houses' Association; Chair. Markku Pohjola; Man. Dir Satu Huber.

Säästöpankkiliitto (Finnish Savings Banks Association): Linnoitustie 9, POB 68, 02601 Espoo; tel. (9) 548051; fax (20) 6029108; internet www.savings-banks.fi; f. 1906; 40 mems; Chair. Jussi Hakala; Man. Dir Markku Ruutu; 256 brs.

Suomen Hypoteekkiyhdistys (Mortgage Society of Finland): Yrjönkatu 9, POB 509, 00101 Helsinki; tel. (9) 228361; fax (9) 647443; e-mail hypo@hypo.fi; internet www.hypo.fi; f. 1860; cap. €36m., total assets €336m. (Dec. 2000); Pres. Matti Inha.

STOCK EXCHANGE

NASDAQ OMX Nordic Exchange Helsinki: Fabianinkatu 14, POB 361, 00131 Helsinki; tel. (9) 616671; fax (9) 61667368; internet www.nasdaqomx.com; f. 1912 as Helsingin Pörssi; merged with OMX AB (Sweden) in 2003; became part of OMX Nordic Exchange with Copenhagen (Denmark), Reykjavík (Iceland) and Stockholm (Sweden) exchanges in 2006; acquired by NASDAQ Stock Market, Inc (USA) in 2008; Group CEO Robert Greifeld; Group Pres. Magnus Böcker.

INSURANCE

In January 2006 there were 65 insurance companies operating in Finland, 21 of which were branches of foreign insurance companies.

A-Vakuutus Oy (A-Vakuutus Mutual Insurance Co): Lapinmäentie 1, 00350 Helsinki; tel. (10) 253000; fax (10) 2532908; e-mail a-vakuutus@a-vakuutus.fi; internet www.a-vakuutus.fi; non-life; Man. Dir Helena Walldén.

Aurum Life Insurance Co. Ltd: POB 308, 00101 Helsinki; tel. (9) 4042528; fax (9) 4043501; Man. Dir Jukka Ruuskanen.

Eurooppalainen Insurance Co Ltd: Lapinmäentie 1, 00013 Pohjola; tel. (10) 55911; fax (10) 5592205; non-life; Man. Dir Jouni Aaltonen.

Garantia Insurance Co Ltd: Salomonkatu 17A, POB 600, 00101 Helsinki; tel. (20) 7479800; fax (20) 7479801; internet www.garantia.fi; non-life; Pres. and CEO Mikael Englund.

If Vahinkovakuutusyhtiö Oy (If P & C Insurance Ltd): Vattuniemenkuja 8A, 00035 Helsinki; tel. 1051512; fax 105145232; internet www.if.fi; subsidiary of Sampo Group; property and casualty.

Keskinäinen Eläkevakuutusyhtiö Ilmarinen (Ilmarinen Mutual Pension Insurance Co): Porkkalankatu 1, 00018 Ilmarinen; tel. (10) 28411; fax (10) 2843445; e-mail info@ilmarinen.fi; internet www.ilmarinen.fi; f. 1961; statutory employment pensions; CEO Harri Sailas.

Keskinäinen Eläkevakuutusyhtiö Tapiola (Tapiola Mutual Pension Insurance Co): 02010 Tapiola; tel. (9) 4531; fax (9) 4532146; internet www.tapiola.fi; Pres. Asmo Kalpala; Man. Dir Olli-Pekka Laine.

Keskinäinen Henkivakuutusosakeyhtiö Suomi (Suomi Mutual Life Assurance Co): Aleksanterinkatu 15B, POB 1068, 00101 Helsinki; tel. (10) 2530066; fax (10) 2527806; e-mail hvpalvelukeskus@suomi-yhtio.fi; internet www.suomi-yhtio.fi; Pres. and CEO Markku Vesterinen.

Keskinäinen Henkivakuutusyhtiö Tapiola (Tapiola Mutual Life Assurance Co): 02010 Tapiola; tel. (9) 4531; fax (9) 4532146; internet www.tapiola.fi; Pres. Asmo Kalpala; Man. Dir Juha-Pekka Halmeenmaki.

Keskinäinen työeläkevakuutusyhtiö Varma (Varma Mutual Pension Insurance Co): POB 1, 00098 Varma; tel. (10) 51513; fax (10) 5144752; e-mail info@varma.fi; internet www.varma.fi; fmrly Varma-Sampo; Man. Dir Matti Vuoria.

Keskinäinen Vakuutusyhtiö Fennia (Fennia Mutual Insurance Co): Asemamiehenkatu 3, 00520 Helsinki; tel. (10) 5031; fax (10) 5035300; internet www.fennia.fi; non-life; Man. Dir Antii Kuljukka.

Keskinäinen Vakuutusyhtiö Kaleva (Kaleva Mutual Insurance Co): Bulevardi 56, 00101 Helsinki; tel. (10) 515225; fax (10) 5167501; internet www.sampo.fi; Man. Dir Matti Rantanen.

Keskinäinen Vakuutusyhtiö Tapiola (Tapiola General Mutual Insurance Co): 02010 Tapiola; tel. (9) 4531; fax (9) 4532146; internet www.tapiola.fi; non-life; Pres. Asmo Kalpala; Man. Dir Juha Seppänen.

Lähivakuutus Keskinäinen Yhtiö (Local Insurance Mutual Co): Lintuvaarantie 2, POB 50, 02601 Espoo; tel. (9) 511011; fax (9) 51101335; e-mail myynti@lahivakuutus.fi; internet www.lahivakuutus.fi; non-life; Man. Dir Harri Kainulainen.

Nordea Life Assurance Finland: Aleksis Kiven Katu 9, 00020 Helsinki; tel. (9) 16527601; fax (9) 8594622; internet www.nordea.fi/selekta; Man. Dir Jukka Venäläinen.

Palonvara Mutual Insurance Co: Saimaankatu 20, 15140 Lahti; tel. (20) 5226960; fax (20) 5226961; e-mail palvelu@palonvara.fi; internet www.palonvara.fi; f. 1912; non-life; Man. Dir Jukka Hertti.

Pankavara Insurance Co Ltd: Kanavaranta 1, POB 309, 00101 Helsinki; tel. (20) 46131; fax (20) 4621447; e-mail jukka.kahkonen@storaenso.com; f. 1943; non-life; Man. Dir Jukka Kähkönen.

Pohjantähti Keskinäinen Vakuutusyhtiö (Pohjantähti Mutual Insurance Co): Keinusaarentie 2, POB 164, 13101 Hämeenlinna; tel. (3) 62671; fax (3) 6169303; e-mail palvelu@pohjantahti.fi; internet www.pohjantahti.fi; f. 1895; non-life; Man. Dir Petri Suni.

Spruce Insurance Ltd: POB 330, 00101 Helsinki; tel. 108611; fax 108621197; e-mail jaana.dromberg@kemira.com; f. 1948; non-life; owned by Kemira Oyj; Man. Dir Jaana Dromberg.

Vahinkovakuutusosakeyhtiö Pohjola (Pohjola Non-Life Insurance Co Ltd): Lapinmäentie 1, 00013 Pohjola; tel. (10) 253000; fax (10) 5592205; internet www.pohjola.fi; non-life; Chair. Mikael Silvennoinen; Pres. Tomi Yli-Kyyny.

Veritas Eläkevakuutus (Veritas Pension Insurance Co Ltd): Olavintie 2, POB 133, 20101 Turku; tel. (10) 55010; fax (10) 5501690; e-mail info@veritas.fi; internet www.veritas.fi; Pres. Matti Ruohonen.

Insurance Associations

Federation of Accident Insurance Institutions: Bulevardi 28, POB 275, 00121 Helsinki; tel. (9) 680401; fax (9) 68040389; internet www.tvl.fi; f. 1920; publishes *Tapaturmavakuutuslehti* 4 times a year (circ. 3,300); Man. Dir Tapani Miettinen.

Finnish Motor Insurers' Centre: Bulevardi 28, 00120 Helsinki; tel. (9) 680401; fax (9) 68040391; e-mail lvk@vakes.fi; internet www.vakes.fi/lvk; f. 1938; Man. Dir Ulla Niku-Koskinen.

FINLAND   *Directory*

Finnish Pension Alliance TELA: Lastenkodinkuja 1, 00180 Helsinki; tel. (10) 6806700; fax (10) 6806706; e-mail tela@tela.fi; internet www.tela.fi; f. 1964; Man. Dir ESA SWANLJUNG.

Nordic Nuclear Insurers: Kalevenkatu 18A, 00100 Helsinki; tel. (9) 6803410; fax (9) 68034115; internet www.atompool.com; Man. Dir PETER GRANQVIST.

Trade and Industry

GOVERNMENT AGENCIES

Finpro: Porkkalankatu 1, POB 358, 00181 Helsinki; tel. (20) 46951; fax (20) 4695200; e-mail info@finpro.fi; internet www.finpro.fi; f. 1919 as Finnish Foreign Trade Association; Chair., Supervisory Bd JOHANNA IKÄHEIMO; Chair., Bd of Dirs JUHA RANTANEN; Pres. and CEO JORMA TURUNEN.

Invest in Finland Bureau: Kaivokatu 8, 00100 Helsinki; tel. (10) 7730300; fax (10) 7730301; e-mail info@investinfinland.fi; internet www.investinfinland.fi; Chair., Bd of Dirs TARMO KORPELA; CEO TUOMO AIRAKSINEN.

DEVELOPMENT ORGANIZATION

Altia Group: Salmisaarenranta 7, POB 350, 00101 Helsinki; tel. (9) 13311; fax (9) 1333361; e-mail viestinta@altiagroup.com; internet www.altiagroup.com; f. 1932; development, manufacture, import, export, wholesale and marketing of alcoholic beverages; state-owned; Pres. and CEO ANTTI PANKAKOSKI.

CHAMBERS OF COMMERCE

Helsingin Seudun Kauppakamari (Helsinki Region Chamber of Commerce): Kalevankatu 12, 00100 Helsinki; tel. (9) 228601; fax (9) 22860228; e-mail kauppakamari@helsinki.chamber.fi; internet www.helsinki.chamber.fi; f. 1917; Man. Dir HEIKKI J. PERÄLÄ; 4,100 mems.

Keskuskauppakamari (Central Chamber of Commerce of Finland): Aleksanterinkatu 17, POB 1000, 00101 Helsinki; tel. (9) 696969; fax (9) 650303; internet www.chamber.fi; f. 1918; Gen. Man. KARI JALAS; represents 19 regional chambers of commerce.

INDUSTRIAL AND TRADE ASSOCIATIONS

Kalatalouden Keskusliitto (Federation of Finnish Fisheries Associations): Malmin kauppatie 26, 00700 Helsinki; tel. (9) 6844590; fax (9) 68445959; e-mail kalastus@ahven.net; internet www.ahven.net; f. 1891; Sec. M. MYLLYLÄ; 616,000 mems.

Kauko-Telko Oy: Kutojantie 4, POB 40, 02630 Espoo; tel. (9) 5211; fax (9) 5216641; e-mail mikko.teittinen@telkogroup.com; internet www.telkogroup.com; f. 1947; export, import and international trade; Pres. MIKKO TEITTINEN.

Kesko Oyj (Retailers' Wholesale Co): Satamakatu 3, 00016 Helsinki; tel. (10) 5311; fax (9) 657465; internet www.kesko.fi; f. 1941; retailer-owned wholesale corporation, trading in foodstuffs, textiles, shoes, consumer goods, hardware, agricultural and builders' supplies, and machinery; Pres. and CEO MATTI HALMESMÄKI.

Maa- ja metsataloustuottajain Keskusliitto MTK r.y. (Central Union of Agricultural Producers and Forest Owners): Simonkatu 6, POB 510, 00100 Helsinki; tel. (20) 4131; fax (20) 4132409; e-mail michael.hornborg@mtk.fi; internet www.mtk.fi; f. 1917; Pres. MICHAEL HORNBORG; Sec.-Gen. PIRKKO HAIKKALA; 164,000 mems.

Metsäteollisuus r.y. (Finnish Forest Industries' Federation): Snellmaninkatu 13, POB 336, 00171 Helsinki; tel. (9) 13261; fax (9) 1324445; e-mail anne.brunila@forestindustries.fi; internet www.forestindustries.fi; f. 1918; Man. Dir ANNE BRUNILA; mems: 120 cos in the forestry industry and sales or trade asscns.

Sähköenergialiitto r.y. (Finnish Electricity Association): POB 100, 00101 Helsinki; tel. (40) 8448317; internet www.sener.fi; f. 1926; 80 mems; development of technical, economic and administrative functions of electricity, business and networks; research and advice on electrical applications; publishes consumer magazine *Sähköviesti/Elbladet*; Man. JORMA VÄKIPARTA.

Suomalaisen Työn Liitto (Association for Finnish Work): Mikonkatu 17, POB 429, 00101 Helsinki; tel. (9) 6962430; fax (9) 69624333; e-mail stl@avainlippu.fi; internet www.avainlippu.fi; f. 1978; public relations for Finnish products and for Finnish work; Chair. of Council MAURI PEKKARINEN; Chair., Bd of Dirs PEKKA SAIRANEN; Man. Dir LARS COLLIN; c. 1,200 mems.

Suomen Betonitieto (Finnish Concrete Industry Asscn): Unioninkatu 14, POB 11, 00131 Helsinki; tel. (9) 6962360; fax (9) 1299291; internet www.betoni.com; f. 1929; Chair. HANNU MARTIKAINEN; Man. Dir OLLI HÄMÄLÄINEN; 51 mems.

Suomen Kaupan Liitto (Federation of Finnish Commerce): Eteläranta 10, 00130 Helsinki; POB 340, 00131 Helsinki; tel. (9) 172850; fax (9) 17285120; e-mail tiedotus@suomenkauppa.fi; internet www.suomenkauppa.fi; f. 2005 by merger of the Federation of Finnish Commerce and Trade and the Commercial Employers' Association; Man. Dir JUHANI PEKKALA; 36 mem. asscns with more than 10,000 firms.

Svenska lantbruksproducenternas centralförbund (Central Union of Swedish-speaking Agricultural Producers): Fredriksgatan 61A, 00100 Helsinki; tel. (9) 5860460; fax (9) 6941358; internet www.slc.fi; f. 1945; Chair. H. FALCK; 15,000 mems.

Teknisen Kaupan Liitto (Association of Finnish Technical Traders): Sarkiniementie 3, 00210 Helsinki; tel. (9) 6824130; fax (9) 68241310; e-mail tekninen.kauppa@tkl.fi; internet www.tkl.fi; f. 1918; organization of the main importers dealing in steel and metals, machines and equipment, heavy chemicals and raw materials; Chair. HEIMO AHO; Man. Dir KLAUS KATARA; 225 mems.

EMPLOYERS' ORGANIZATIONS

Autoliikenteen Työnantajaliitto r.y. (Employers' Federation of Road Transport): Nuijamiestentie 7A, 00400 Helsinki; tel. (9) 47899480; fax (9) 5883995; internet www.alt.fi; Chair. ANTTI NORRLIN; Man. Dir HANNU PARVELA; c. 1,000 mems.

Elinkeinoelämän Keskusliitto (EK) (Confederation of Finnish Industries): Eteläranta 10, POB 30, 00131 Helsinki; tel. (9) 68681; fax (9) 68682812; e-mail tt@tt.fi; internet www.tt.fi; f. 1907; aims to promote co-operation between cos and mem. organizations and to protect the interests of mems in employment issues; 30 asscns consisting of about 5,600 enterprises with 500,000 employees; Chair. ANTTI HERLIN; Dir-Gen. LEIF FAGERNÄS.

Elintarviketeollisuusliitto r.y. (Finnish Food and Drink Industries' Federation): Pasilankatu 2, 00240 Helsinki; tel. (9) 148871; fax (9) 14887201; e-mail info@etl.fi; internet www.etl.fi; Chair. BERTEL PAULIG; Dir-Gen. HEIKKI JUUTINEN.

Kemianteollisuus (KT) r.y. (Chemical Industry Federation): Eteläranta 10, POB 4, 00131 Helsinki; tel. (9) 172841; fax (9) 630225; internet www.chemind.fi; Chair. RISTO RINNE; Man. Dir HANNU VORNAMO.

Kenkä- ja Nahkateollisuus r.y. (Association of Finnish Shoe and Leather Industries): Eteläranta 10, 00130 Helsinki; tel. (9) 172841; fax (9) 179588; e-mail sari.vannela@ryhma.ttliitot.fi; Chair. OLAVI VILJANMAA; Exec. Dir SARI VANNELA.

Kumiteollisuus r.y. (Rubber Manufacturers' Association): Eteläranta 10, 00130 Helsinki; tel. (9) 172841; fax (9) 630225; e-mail tuula.rantalaiho@kumi.ttliitot.fi; internet www.kumiteollisuus.fi; Chair. KIM GRAN; Man. Dir TUULA RANTALAIHO.

Lääketeollisuus r.y. (Pharma Industry Finland—PIF): Eteläranta 10, POB 109, 00131 Helsinki; tel. (9) 61504900; fax (9) 61504940; e-mail pif@pif.fi; internet www.pif.fi; Chair. LASSE SAVONEN; Dir-Gen. SUVI-ANNE SIIMES.

Muoviteollisuus r.y. (Finnish Plastics Industries Federation): Eteläranta 10, 00130 Helsinki; tel. (9) 172841; fax (9) 171164; internet www.plastics.fi; Chair. KARI KALLONEN; Man. Dir KARI TEPPOLA.

Palvelualojen Toimialaliitto r.y. (Association of Support Service Industries): Eteläranta 10, 00130 Helsinki; tel. (9) 172841; fax (9) 176877; internet www.palvelualojentoimialaliitto.com; Chair. HENRIK ARLE; Man. Dir PETER FORSSTRÖM.

Puusepänteollisuuden Liitto r.y. (Association of the Finnish Furniture and Joinery Industries): Snellmaninkatu 13, POB 336, 00171 Helsinki; tel. (9) 1324457; fax (9) 1324447; e-mail jukka.nevala@forestindustries.fi; internet www.puusepanteollisuus.fi; f. 1917; Chair. PEKKA SAIRANEN; Man. Dir JUKKA NEVALA; 80 mem. cos.

Rakennusteollisuus RT r.y. (Confederation of Finnish Construction Industries): Unioninkatu 14 VI, 00130 Helsinki; tel. (9) 12991; fax (9) 628264; e-mail rt@rakennusteollisuus.fi; internet www.rakennusteollisuus.fi; f. 2001; Chair. TARMO PIPATTI; Man. Dir TERHO SALO.

Rannikko- ja Sisävesiliikenteen Työnantajaliitto (RASILA) r.y. (Coastal and Inland Waterway Employers' Association): Satamakatu 4A, 00160 Helsinki; tel. (9) 62267312; fax (9) 669251; Chair. STEFAN HÅKANS; Man. Dir HENRIK LÖNNQVIST.

Satamaoperaattorit r.y. (Finnish Port Operators' Asscn): Köydenpunojankatu 8, POB 268, 00180 Helsinki; tel. (9) 68595310; fax (9) 68595353; internet www.satamaoperaattorit.fi; f. 1906; fmrly Suomen Lastauttajain Liitto (SLL) r.y; Chair. ESA HAAVISTO; Man. Dir JOUKO SANTALA.

Suomen Kiinteistöliitto r.y. (Finnish Real-Estate Federation): Annankatu 24, 00100 Helsinki; tel. (9) 166761; fax (9) 16676400; internet www.kiinteistoliitto.fi; f. 1907; Chair. JUHANI RUSKEEPÄÄ; Man. Dir HARRI HILTUNEN.

Suomen Varustamoyhdistys r.y. (Finnish Shipowners' Association): see under Shipping.

Suunnittelu- ja konsulttitoimistojen liitto (SKOL) r.y. (Finnish Association of Consulting Firms—SKOL): Tapiolan Keskustorni, Tapiontori 1, 02100 Espoo; tel. (20) 5955100; fax (20) 5955111; e-mail skolry@skolry.fi; internet www.skolry.fi; f. 1951; Chair. HEIKKI HORNBORG; Man. Dir TIMO MYLLYS; 255 mems.

Teknokemian Yhdistys r.y. (Finnish Cosmetic, Toiletry and Detergent Association): Eteläranta 10, 00130 Helsinki; tel. (9) 172841; fax (9) 666561; e-mail sari.karjomaa@teknokem.fi; internet www.teknokem.fi; Chair. KIRSI-MARJA KOSKELO; Dir SARI KARJOMAA.

Teknologiateollisuus r.y. (Technology Industries of Finland): Eteläranta 10, POB 10, 00131 Helsinki; tel. (9) 19231; fax (9) 624462; internet www.techind.fi; f. 1903 as Metalliteollisuuden Keskusliitto r.y.; Chair. MATTI ALAHUHTA; Man. Dir MARTTI MÄENPÄÄ.

Tieto- ja tekniikka-alojen työnantajaliitto TIKLI r.y. (Asscn of Electrical and Telecommunications Employers): Yrjönkatu 13A, 00120 Helsinki; tel. (20) 5955000; fax (20) 5955001; e-mail info@tikli.fi; internet www.tikli.fi; fmrly Sähkö- ja telealan työnantajaliitto r.y; Chair. TUOMO RÖNKKÖ; Dir-Gen. HARRI HIETALA; 200 mems.

Toimistoteknisen Kaupan Yhdistys (TTK) r.y. (Finnish Association of Office Technology Traders): Lars Sonckin kaari 12, 02600 Espoo; tel. and fax (9) 761175; e-mail ttk@tkl.fi; internet www.ttkry.com; Chair. PER-OLOF ASTEDT; Man. Dir TURE TÄHTINEN.

Tupakkateollisuusliitto r.y. (Finnish Tobacco Industries' Federation): POB 115, 00241 Helsinki; tel. (9) 644373; fax (9) 14887201; e-mail asta.morsky@etl.fi; Chair. KARI HEIKKILA.

Työnantajain Yleinen Ryhmä r.y. (Finnish Employers' General Group): Eteläranta 10, 00130 Helsinki; tel. (9) 172841; fax (9) 179588; e-mail sari.vannela@ryhma.ttliitot.fi; Chair. MARKKU JOKINEN; Exec. Dir SARI VANNELA.

Viestintätyönantajat VTA (Media Employers' Association): Lönnrotinkatu 11A, 00120 Helsinki; tel. (9) 22877200; fax (9) 603527; Chair. KEIJO KETONEN; Dir JOHANNA VARIS.

Yleinen Teollisuusliitto r.y. (General Industry Association): Eteläranta 10, POB 325, 00131 Helsinki; tel. (9) 6220410; fax (9) 176135; internet www.ytl.fi; Chair. MARKKU TALONEN; Man. Dir MARKKU KÄPPI.

Kultaseppien Työnantajaliitto r.y. (Employers' Association of Goldsmiths): Eteläranta 10, 00130 Helsinki; tel. (9) 172841; fax (9) 179588; e-mail sari.vannela@ryhma.ttliitot.fi; Chair. ILKKA RUOHOLA; Exec. Dir SARI VANNELA.

Palvelutyönantajat r.y. (Employers' Confederation of Service Industries): Eteläranta 10, 00130 Helsinki; tel. (9) 172831; fax (9) 655588; internet www.palveluyonantajat.fi; f. 1945; 13 mem. asscns consisting of about 8,900 enterprises with 362,200 employees; Man. Dir ARTO OJALA.

Suomen Tiiliteollisuusliitto r.y. (Finnish Brick Industry Association): POB 381, 00131 Helsinki; tel. (9) 12991; fax (9) 1299214; e-mail juha.luhanka@rakennusteollisuus.fi; Chair. LARS-ERIK NYSTRÖM.

UTILITIES

Electricity

Fortum Oyj: Keilaniementie 1, 02150 Espoo; POB 1, 00048 Fortum; tel. (10) 4511; fax (10) 4524777; internet www.fortum.fi; f. 1998 following merger of the Imatran Voima Group and the Neste Group; 51.5% state-owned; generation, distribution and sale of electricity and heat, as well as the operation and maintenance of power plants; listed on the Helsinki exchange in Dec. 1998; Exec. Chair. PETER FAGERNÄS; Pres. and CEO MIKAEL LILIUS.

Kemijoki Oy: Valtakatu 9–11, POB 8131, 96101 Rovaniemi; tel. (16) 7401; fax (16) 7402325; e-mail info@kemijoki.fi; internet www.kemijoki.fi; f. 1954; electric power; 66.99% state-owned; Chair. of Supervisory Bd KALERVO NURMIMÄKI; Chair. of Bd of Management TAPIO KUULA; 344 employees.

Pohjolan Voima Oy (PVO): Töölönkatu 4, POB 40, 00101 Helsinki; tel. (9) 693061; fax (9) 69306335; e-mail info@pvo.fi; internet www.pohjolanvoima.fi; Pres. and CEO TIMO RAJALA.

Regional electricity providers operate, of which the largest is Helsingin Energia.

Helsingin Energia (Helsinki Energy): Kampinkuja 2, 00090 Helen; tel. (9) 6171; fax (9) 6172360; e-mail helsingin.energia@helen.fi; internet www.helsinginenergia.fi; f. 1909; municipal undertaking; generates and distributes electrical power and district heating; distributes natural gas; Man. Dir SEPPO RUOHONEN.

Gas

Gasum Oy: Miestentie 1, POB 21, 02151 Espoo; tel. (20) 4471; fax (20) 4478639; e-mail minna.ojala@gasum.fi; internet www.gasum.fi; f. 1994; 31% owned by Fortum, 25% owned by OAO Gazprom (Russia), 24% state-owned and 20% owned by E.ON Ruhrgas International AG (Germany); imports and sells natural gas, owns and operates natural gas transmission system; operates three subsidiaries, Gasum Energiapalvelut Oy, Gasum Paikallisjakelu Oy and Kaasupörssi Oy; Pres. and CEO ANTERO JÄNNES.

Water

Helsingin Vesi (Helsinki Water): Iimalankuja 2A, 00240 Helsinki; POB 1100, 00099 Helsinki; tel. (9) 3101681; fax (9) 31033001; e-mail helsingin.vesi@hel.fi; internet www.helsinginvesi.fi; responsible for water supply and sewerage of the greater Helsinki area; Man. Dir JUKKA PIEKKARI.

CO-OPERATIVES

Pellervo (Confederation of Finnish Co-operatives): Simonkatu 6, POB 77, 00101 Helsinki; tel. (9) 4767501; fax (9) 6948845; e-mail toimisto@pellervo.fi; internet www.pellervo.fi; f. 1899; central organization of co-operatives; Man. Dir VEIKKO HÄMÄLÄINEN; 400 mem. societies (incl. 11 central co-operative societies).

Munakunta (Co-operative Egg Producers' Association): POB 6, 20761 Piispanristi; tel. (2) 214420; fax (2) 2144222; e-mail jan.lahde@munakunta.fi; internet www.kultamuna.fi; f. 1921; Man. Dir JAN LÄHDE; 500 mems.

Suomen Osuuskauppojen Keskusliitto (SOKL) r.y. (Finnish Co-operative Union): POB 171, 00511 Helsinki; tel. (9) 1882222; fax (9) 1882580; f. 1908; Chair. JUKKA HUISKONEN; Man. Dir TAAVI HEIKKILÄ; 44 mems.

Valio Ltd (Finnish Co-operative Dairies' Association): POB 10, 00039 Valio; tel. 10381121; fax 103812323; internet www.valio.com; f. 1905; production and marketing of dairy products; Pres. and CEO PEKKA LAAKSONEN.

TRADE UNIONS

AKAVA (Confederation of Unions for Academic Professionals): Rautatieläisenkatu 6, 00520 Helsinki; tel. (20) 7489400; fax (9) 142595; internet www.akava.fi; f. 1950; 32 affiliates, incl. asscns of doctors, engineers, social workers and teachers; total membership 485,500; Pres. MATTI VILJANEN.

Suomen Ammattiliittojen Keskusjärjestö (SAK) r.y. (Central Organization of Finnish Trade Unions): Siltasaarenkatu 3A, POB 157, 00531 Helsinki; tel. (9) 77211; fax (9) 7721447; e-mail sak@sak.fi; internet www.sak.fi; f. 1907; 21 affiliated unions comprising 1m. mems; Pres. LAURI IHALAINEN.

Principal affiliated unions:

Auto- ja Kuljetusalan Työntekijäliitto (AKT) r.y. (Transport Workers): John Stenbergin ranta 6, POB 313, 00531 Helsinki; tel. (9) 613110; fax (9) 739287; e-mail minna.viitamaki@akt.fi; internet www.akt.fi; f. 1948; Pres. TIMO RÄTY; Sec JUHANI SALMELA; 50,505 mems.

Julkisten ja Hyvinvointialojen Liitto r.y. (JHL) (Public and Welfare Sectors): POB 101 Sörnäisten rantatie 23, 00531 Helsinki; tel. (10) 77031; fax (10) 7703330; e-mail merja.launis@jhl.fi; internet www.jhl.fi; f. 2006 by merger of six unions; Pres. TUIJA LINNA-PIRINEN; 225,000 mems.

Kemianliitto-Kemifacket r.y. (Chemical Workers): Siltasaarenkatu 2, POB 324, 00531 Helsinki; tel. (9) 773971; fax (9) 7538511; internet www.kemianliitto.fi; f. 1993; Pres. TIMO VALLITTU; Sec. SEPPO WIKSTRÖM; 47,616 mems.

Metallityöväen Liitto r.y. (Metalworkers): Hakaniemenranta 1, POB 107, 00531 Helsinki; tel. (20) 774001; fax (20) 7741220; e-mail metalli.posti@metalliliitto.fi; internet www.metalliliitto.fi; f. 1899; Pres. ERKKI VUORENMAA; Sec. MATTI MÄKELÄ; 165,500 mems.

Palvelualojen ammattiliitto PAM r.y. (Service Union United): Paasivuorenkatu 4–6, POB 54, 00531 Helsinki; tel. (20) 774002; fax (20) 7742039; e-mail pam@pam.fi; internet www.pam.fi; f. 1987 as Liikealan ammattiliitto r.y.; present name adopted 2000; Pres. ANN SELIN; Vice-Pres ANSSI VUORIO, KAARLO JULKUNEN; 207,000 mems.

Paperiliitto r.y. (Paperworkers): Paasivuorenkatu 4–6A, POB 326, 00531 Helsinki; tel. (9) 70891; fax (9) 7012279; e-mail info@paperiliitto.fi; internet www.paperiliitto.fi; f. 1906; Pres. JOUKO AHONEN; Gen. Sec. PETRI VANHALA; 47,040 mems.

Posti- ja logistiikka-alan unioni (PAU) r.y. (Post and Logistics): John Stenbergin ranta 6, 00530 Helsinki; tel. (9) 613116; fax (9) 61311750; e-mail pau@pau.fi; internet www.pau.fi; Pres. ESA VILKUNA; 32,000 mems.

FINLAND

Puu- ja erityisalojen Liitto r.y. (Wood and Allied Workers): Haapaniemenkatu 7–9B, POB 318, 00531 Helsinki; tel. (9) 615161; fax (9) 7532506; e-mail puuliitto@puuliitto.fi; internet www.puuliitto.fi; f. 1993 by merger of two unions; Pres. KALEVI VANHALA; 45,586 mems.

Rakennusliitto r.y. (Construction Workers): Siltasaarenkatu 4, POB 307, 00531 Helsinki; tel. (20) 774003; fax (20) 7743062; e-mail info@rakennusliitto.fi; internet www.rakennusliitto.fi; f. 1924; Pres. MATTI HARJUNIEMI; 84,000 mems.

Rautatieläisten Liitto r.y. (RAUTL) (Railwaymen): Hakaniemenranta 1, POB 205, 00531 Helsinki; tel. (9) 774941; fax (9) 7015941; e-mail mauri.lunden@rautl.fi; internet www.rautl.fi; f. 1906; Pres. MAURI LUNDEN; 14,458 mems.

Sähköalojen ammattiliitto r.y. (Electrical Workers): Aleksanterinkatu 15, POB 747, 33101 Tampere; tel. (3) 2520111; fax (3) 2520210; e-mail lauri.lyly@sahkoliitto.fi; internet www.sahkoliitto.fi; f. 1955; Pres. MARTTI ALAKOSKI; 32,000 mems.

Suomen Elintarviketyöläisten Liitto (SEL) r.y. (Food Workers): Siltasaarenkatu 6, POB 213, 00531 Helsinki; tel. (20) 774004; fax (20) 7740604; internet www.selry.fi; f. 1905; Pres. VELI-MATTI KUNTONEN; 39,000 mems.

Suomen Merimies-Unioni SM-U r.y. (Seamen): John Stenbergin ranta 6, 00530 Helsinki; tel. (9) 6152020; fax (9) 61520227; e-mail pekka.teravainen@smury.fi; internet www.smury.fi; f. 1916; Pres. SIMO ZITTING; Sec. PEKKA TERÄVÄINEN; 11,000 mems.

Viestintäalan ammattiliitto r.y. (Media Union): Siltasaarenkatu 4, POB 303, 00531 Helsinki; tel. (9) 616581; fax (9) 61658333; e-mail pertti.raitoharju@viestintaliitto.fi; internet www.viestintaliitto.fi; f. 1894; Pres. PERTTI RAITOHARJU; Sec. IRENE HÄMÄLÄINEN; 24,000 mems.

STTK (Finnish Confederation of Salaried Employees): Mikonkatu 8A, 6th floor, POB 421, 00101 Helsinki; tel. (9) 131521; fax (9) 652367; e-mail mikko.maenpaa@sttk.fi; internet www.sttk.fi; Pres. MIKKO MÄENPÄÄ.

There are 19 affiliated trade unions, including the following:

Ammattiliitto SUORA r.y. (Suomen Rahoitus- ja Erityisalojen ammattiliitto—Financial Sector Union): Ratamestarinkatu 12, 00520 Helsinki; tel. (9) 229141; fax (9) 22914301; e-mail simo.leivo@ammattiliittosuora.fi; internet www.ammattiliittosuora.fi; f. 1931; Pres. TARJA LANKILA; Sec.-Gen. SIMO LEIVO; 37,000 mems.

Erityisalojen Toimihenkilöliitto ERTO r.y. (Special Service and Clerical Employees): Asemamiehenkatu 4, 00520 Helsinki; tel. (20) 1130200; fax (20) 1130201; e-mail info.erto@erto.fi; internet www.erto.fi; f. 1968; Pres. TAPIO HUTTULA; 30,000 mems.

Julkis—ja yksityisalojen toimihenkilöliitto r.y. (JYTY) (Federation of Public- and Private-Sector Employees): Asemamiehenkatu 4, 00520 Helsinki; tel. (9) 1551; fax (9) 1552333; e-mail merja.ailus@jytyliitto.fi; internet www.jytyliitto.fi; f. 1918 as Kunnallisvirkamiesliitto r.y. (KVL); present name adopted 2005; Pres. MERJA AILUS; 68,000 mems and 300 mem. asscns.

Palkansaajajärjestö Pardia r.y. (Confederation of State Employees' Unions): Ratamestarinkatu 11, 00520 Helsinki; tel. (75) 3247500; fax (75) 3247575; e-mail toimisto@pardia.fi; internet www.pardia.fi; 23 mem. unions comprising 67,800 mems; Pres. ANTTI PALOLA.

Suomen lähi- ja perushoitajaliitto SuPer r.y. (Practical Nurses): Ratamestarinkatu 12, 00520 Helsinki; tel. (9) 2727910; fax (9) 27279120; e-mail juhani.palomaki@superliitto.fi; internet www.superliitto.fi; f. 1948; Pres. JUHANI PALOMÄKI; 68,000 mems.

Tehy (Union of Health and Social-Care Professionals): Asemamiehenkatu 4, 00520 Helsinki; POB 10, 00060 Tehy; tel. (9) 54227000; fax (9) 61500278; e-mail tehy.international@tehy.fi; internet www.tehi.fi; f. 1982; Pres. JAANA LAITINEN-PESOLA; 124,000 mems.

Toimihenkilöunioni (TU) (Union of Salaried Employees): Selkämerenkuja 1A, POB 183, 00181 Helsinki; tel. (9) 172731; fax (9) 17273330; e-mail petteri.ojanen@toimihenkilounioni.fi; internet www.toimihenkilounioni.fi; Pres. ANTTI RINNE; 120,000 mems.

Vakuutusväen Liitto r.y. (Insurance Employees): Asemamiehenkatu 2, 00520 Helsinki; tel. (9) 85672400; fax (9) 85672401; e-mail sirpa.spoljaric@jttpalvelut.fi; internet www.vvl.fi; f. 1945; Pres. SIRPA KOMONEN; Gen. Sec. SIRPA SPOLJARIC; 11,000 mems.

Transport

RAILWAYS

Finland had 5,794 km of railways in 2007, of which 3,047 km were electrified, providing internal services and connections with Sweden and Russia. As part of an initiative to upgrade the existing rail network, a high-speed rail link was planned between Helsinki and St Petersburg, Russia; it was expected to be operational in 2010. An underground railway service has been provided by Helsinki City Transport since 1982.

Ratahallintokeskus (RHK) (Finnish Rail Administration): POB 185, 00101 Helsinki; tel. (20) 7515111; fax (20) 7515100; e-mail info@rhk.fi; internet www.rhk.fi; f. 1995; civil service department under the Ministry of Transport and Communications; owns the rail network, together with its equipment, structures and land holdings; wide gauge (1,524 mm); responsible for management, maintenance and development of railways; Chief Dir OSSI NIEMIMUUKKO.

Karhula Railway: Ratakatu 8, 48600 Karhula; tel. (5) 298221; fax (5) 298225; f. 1937; goods transport; operates 10 km of railway (1,524 mm gauge); Man. PERTTI HONKALA.

VR Group: Vilhonkatu 13, POB 488, 00101 Helsinki; tel. (307) 10; fax (307) 21500; internet www.vr.fi; began operating 1862; joint-stock co since 1995; operates 5,784 km of railways; Pres. and CEO HENRI KUITUNEN; Chief Financial Officer VEIKKO VAIKKINEN.

ROADS

Finland had 78,189 km of highways at 1 January 2007, of which 13,264 km were main roads (including 700 km of motorway), 13,519 regional roads and 51,407 other roads. Some 65% of the road network was paved in that year.

Destia: Kumpulantie 11, POB 73, 00521 Helsinki; tel. (20) 44411; fax (20) 4442297; e-mail miia.apukka@destia.fi; internet www.destia.fi; f. 2008 to assume activities of fmr Tieliikelaitos (Finnish Road Enterprise); state-owned enterprise; provides transport infrastructure and transport environment services; Man. Dir HEIKKI KOIVISTO.

Tiehallinto (Finnish Road Administration): POB 33, 00521 Helsinki; tel. (20) 42211; fax (20) 4222202; e-mail info@tiehallinto.fi; internet www.tiehallinto.fi; f. 1799; government agency; divided into central administration and nine road districts; manages the public road network, including bridges and ferries; organizes bids for road construction and maintenance; Dir-Gen. JUKKA HIRVELÄ.

INLAND WATERWAYS

Lakes cover 33,672 sq km. The inland waterway system comprises 7,842 km of buoyed-out channels, 40 open canals and 37 lock canals. The total length of canals is 116 km. In 2006 cargo vessel traffic on inland waterways (including on the Saimaa Canal) amounted to 2.4m. metric tons, timber floating amounted to 0.9m. tons and passenger traffic to 479,709 passengers.

In 1968 the southern part of the Saimaa Canal, which was leased to Finland by the USSR for 50 years, was opened for vessels.

SHIPPING

The chief port of export is Kotka. Reclamation of land was carried out to build a second container port in Kotka. It opened in 2001 and has the capacity to handle 500,000 20-ft equivalent units (TEUs) of cargo per year. The main port of import is Helsinki, which has three specialized harbours. The West Harbour handles most of the container traffic, the North Harbour cargo ferry traffic and the South Harbour passenger traffic. Other important international ports are Turku (Åbo), Rauma and Hamina.

Port Authority Association

Suomen Satamaliitto (Finnish Port Association): Toinen Linja 14, 00530 Helsinki; tel. (9) 7711; fax (9) 7530474; e-mail info@finnports.com; internet www.finnports.com; f. 1923; 29 mems; Man. Dir MATTI AURA.

Port Authorities

Hamina: Satamantie 4, POB 14, 49401 Hamina; tel. (5) 2255400; fax (5) 22554101; e-mail office@portofhamina.fi; internet www.portofhamina.fi; Man. Dir SEPPO HERRALA; Harbour Master JOUNI PUKKI.

Helsinki: Port of Helsinki, Olympiaranta 3, POB 800, 00099 Helsinki; tel. (9) 3101621; fax (9) 31033802; e-mail port.helsinki@hel.fi; internet www.portofhelsinki.fi; Man. Dir HEIKKI NISSINEN; Harbour Master JUKKA KALLIO.

Kotka: Port of Kotka Ltd, Laivurinkatu 7, POB 196, 48100 Kotka; tel. (5) 2344280; fax (5) 2181375; e-mail office@portofkotka.fi; internet www.portofkotka.fi; Man. Dir KIMMO NASKI.

Rauma: Port of Rauma, Hakunintie 19, 26100 Rauma; tel. (2) 8344712; fax (2) 8226369; e-mail harbour.office@portorauma.com; internet www.portorauma.com; Dir HANNU ASUMALAHTI; Harbour Master and Port Security Officer MARI KALLINEN.

Turku: Turku Port Authority, Linnankatu 90, 20100 Turku; tel. (2) 2674111; fax (2) 2674125; e-mail kari.riutta@turku.fi; internet www.port.turku.fi; Man. Dir CHRISTIAN RAMBERG; Harbour Master KARI RIUTTA.

FINLAND

Shipowners' Association

Suomen Varustamoyhdistys r.y. (Finnish Shipowners' Association): Satamakatu 4, POB 155, 00161 Helsinki; tel. (9) 6226730; fax (9) 669251; e-mail office@varustamoyhdistys.fi; internet www.varustamoyhdistys.fi; f. 1932; Chair. RISTO NÄSI; Man. Dir MIKA NYKÄNEN; 8 mems.

Principal Companies

ESL Shipping Oy: Lautatarhankatu 8B, 00580 Helsinki; tel. (9) 75951; fax (9) 787315; e-mail operations@eslshipping.fi; internet www.eslshipping.fi; world-wide tramp services; wholly-owned subsidiary of Aspo Oyj; Pres. MARKUS KARJALAINEN.

Finnlines PLC: Porkkalainkatu 20A, POB 197, 00181 Helsinki; tel. (10) 34350; fax (10) 3435200; e-mail info.fi@finnlines.com; internet www.finnlines.fi; f. 1949; liner and contract services between Finland and other European countries; overland and inland services combined with direct sea links; Pres. and CEO CHRISTER ANTSON; 85 cargo ferries.

Alfons Håkans Oy Ab: Linnankatu 36C, 20100 Turku; tel. (2) 515500; fax (2) 2515873; e-mail office.turku@alfonshakans.fi; internet www.alfonshakans.fi; Man. Dir and Chair. STEFAN HÅKANS; 32 tugs and four barges.

Rettig Oy Ab Bore: Linnankatu 33B, POB 144, 20100 Turku; tel. (2) 5125500; fax (2) 2502087; e-mail info@bore.eu; internet www.bore.eu; f. 1897; acquired Bror Husell Chartering Ab in 2005 and Rederi Ab Engship in 2006; Man. Dir THOMAS FRANCK; 18 cargo ships, three car carriers and one bulk vessel.

RG Line Oy Ab: Vaskiluodon Satama, 65170 Vaasa; tel. (20) 7716810; fax (20) 7716820; e-mail info@rgline.com; internet www.rgline.com; operates ferry services across the Gulf of Bothnia from Vaasa to Umeå.

Tallink Silja Oy: Keilaranta 9, POB 43, 02151 Espoo; tel. (9) 18041; fax (9) 1804402; internet www.tallinksilja.com; f. 2006 by merger of Tallink Finland Oy and Silja Oy; part of the AS Tallink Group; passenger and cargo services in the Baltic; CEO KEIJO MEHTONEN; 12 vessels.

CIVIL AVIATION

An international airport is situated at Helsinki-Vantaa, 19 km from Helsinki. International and domestic services also operate to and from airports at Ivalo, Joensuu, Jyväskylä, Kajaani, Kemi-Tornio, Kruunupyy, Kuopio, Lappeenranta, Mariehamn, Oulu, Pori, Rovaniemi, Savonlinna, Tampere-Pirkkala, Turku, Vaasa and Varkaus. Domestic services are available at airports at Enontekiö, Kittilä, Kuusamo and Mikkeli.

Ilmailuhallinto (Civil Aviation Authority): Ilmailutie 9A, POB 186, 01531 Vantaa; tel. (9) 425011; fax (9) 42502898; e-mail information@fcaa.fi; internet www.civilaviationauthority.fi; f. 2006; independent regulatory body operating under the Ministry of Transport and Communications; Dir-Gen. KIM SALONEN.

Ilmailulaitos Finavia (Civil Aviation Administration): POB 50, 01531 Vantaa; tel. (9) 82771; fax (9) 82772099; e-mail info@finavia.fi; internet www.finavia.fi; state-owned commercial enterprise; provides air navigation services and maintains state-owned airports; CEO SAMULI HAAPASALO.

Principal Airlines

Blue1: POB 168, 01531 Vantaa; tel. (20) 585600; e-mail tom.christides@blue1.fi; internet www.blue1.fi; f. 1988 as Air Botnia; name changed in 2004; domestic and international services; member of SAS Group since 1998; Pres. and CEO STEFAN WENTJÄRVI.

Finnair Oyj: Tietotie 11A, POB 15, 01053 Vantaa; tel. (9) 81881; fax (9) 8184979; internet www.finnair.com; f. 1923; 58.4% state-owned; 16 domestic services, 38 European services and 9 international services (to Asia and North America); Pres. and CEO JUKKA HIENONEN.

Tourism

Europe's largest inland water system, vast forests, magnificent scenery and the possibility of holiday seclusion are Finland's main attractions. Most visitors come from Sweden, Germany, Russia, the United Kingdom, the Netherlands and Norway. Foreign tourist arrivals at registered accommodation establishments totalled 2,083,487 in 2004; in that year receipts from tourism (including passenger traffic) amounted to US $2,867m. Overnight stays by foreign tourists at registered accommodation establishments totalled 5,036,202 in 2006, according to preliminary figures, compared with 4,383,198 in 2004.

Matkailun edistämiskeskus (Finnish Tourist Board): Töölönkatu 11, POB 625, 00101 Helsinki; tel. (10) 6058000; fax (10) 6058333; e-mail mek@mek.fi; internet www.mek.fi; f. 1973; Chair. ERKKI VIRTANEN; Dir JAAKKO LEHTONEN.

FINNISH EXTERNAL TERRITORY
THE ÅLAND ISLANDS

Introductory Survey

Location, Language, Religion, Flag, Capital

The Åland Islands are a group of 6,554 islands (of which some 60 are inhabited) in the Gulf of Bothnia, between Finland and Sweden. About 93% of the inhabitants are Swedish-speaking, and Swedish is the official language; the remaining 5% are Finnish-speaking. The majority profess Christianity, and 88.5% belong to the Evangelical Lutheran Church of Finland. The flag displays a red cross, bordered with yellow, on a blue background, the upright of the cross being to the left of centre. The capital is Mariehamn, which is situated on Åland, the largest island in the group.

History and Government

For geographical and economic reasons, the Åland Islands were traditionally associated closely with Sweden. In 1809, when Sweden was forced to cede Finland to Russia, the islands were incorporated into the Finnish Grand Duchy. However, following Finland's declaration of independence from the Russian Empire in 1917, the Ålanders demanded the right to self-determination and sought to be reunited with Sweden. Their demands were supported by the Swedish Government and people. In 1920 Finland granted the islands autonomy but refused to acknowledge their secession, and in 1921 the Åland question was referred to the League of Nations. In June the League granted Finland sovereignty over the islands, while directing that certain conditions pertaining to national identity be included in the autonomy legislation offered by Finland and that the islands should be a neutral and non-fortified region. Elections were held in accordance with the new legislation, and the new provincial parliament (Landsting) held its first plenary session on 9 June 1922. The revised Autonomy Act of 1951 provided for independent rights of legislation in internal affairs and for autonomous control over the islands' economy. This Act could not be amended or repealed by the Finnish Eduskunta (Parliament) without the consent of the Åland Landsting.

In 1988 constitutional reform introduced the principle of a majority parliamentary government, to be formed by the Lantrådskandidat, the member of the Landsting nominated to conduct negotiations between the parties. These negotiations may yield two alternative outcomes: either the nominee will submit a proposal to create a new government or the nominee will fail to reach agreement on a new government (in which case renewed negotiations will ensue). The first formal parliamentary government and opposition were duly established. The governing coalition consisted of the three largest parties that had been elected to the Landsting in October 1987 (the Centre Party, the Liberals and the Moderates), which together held 22 seats in the 30-member legislature.

At a general election held in October 1991 the Centre Party increased its share of the seats in the Landsting to 10, while the Liberal Party secured seven seats, and the Moderates and Social Democrats won six and four seats respectively. The parties forming the new coalition Government included the Centre and Moderate Parties, while the Liberal Party was replaced by the Social Democratic Party.

A revised Autonomy Act, providing Åland with a greater degree of autonomous control, was adopted in 1991 and took effect on 1 January 1993. The rules regarding legislative authority were modernized, and the right of the Åland legislature (henceforth known as the Lagting) to enact laws was extended. Åland was given greater discretion with respect to its budget, and the revised Act also introduced changes in matters such as right of domicile, land-ownership regulations and administrative authority. The Autonomy Act contains a provision that, in any treaty which Finland may conclude with a foreign state and to which Åland is a party, the Lagting must consent to the statute implementing the treaty in order for the provision to enter into force in Åland. A referendum on the issue of Åland's proposed accession to membership of the European Union (EU, see p. 244) in 1995 was held in November 1994, immediately after similar referendums in Finland and Sweden had shown a majority in favour of membership. (A small majority of Åland citizens had supported Finland's membership.) Despite low participation in the referendum, 73.7% of the votes cast supported membership and Åland duly joined the EU, together with Finland and Sweden, on 1 January 1995. Under the terms of the treaty of accession, Åland was accorded special exemption from tax union with the EU in order to stimulate the ferry and tourism industries. (In 1998 two of Europe's largest ferry operators, Silja and Viking—both Finnish, re-routed their major services via Åland in order to continue to conduct duty-free sales, which were later abolished within the rest of the EU.)

A general election was held in October 1995. The Centre Party secured nine seats and the Liberal Party won eight, while the Moderates and Social Democrats maintained the representation that they had achieved in the previous parliament. The new coalition Government was composed of members of the Centre and Moderate Parties and one independent.

At a general election held in October 1999 the Centre Party and the Liberal Party each won nine seats. The Moderate Party, meanwhile, secured only four seats, compared with six at the previous election, while the Social Democrats maintained their level of representation, with three seats. Independents grouped together in the Obunden Samling won four seats. A coalition Government was formed comprising the Centre Party, the Moderate Party and the Independents. In March 2001, following a 'no-confidence' motion in the Lagting, the Chairman (Lantråd) of the Government, Roger Nordlund of the Centre Party, dissolved the coalition and formed a new administration comprising members of the Centre Party and the Liberal Party.

A general election was held on 19 October 2003, at which the Centre Party and the Liberal Party each won seven seats. The two parties formed a new Government in coalition with the Social Democrats (who had secured six seats) and the Moderate Party (with four seats), under Nordlund. The other parties represented in the Lagting obtained just six seats between them.

In August 2004 the Finnish Government agreed new, more stringent regulations securing the islands' demilitarized status, following reports that this had been violated by troop movements over the past two decades.

In January 2005, following a motion of 'no confidence' in the Lagting, the governing coalition was dissolved and Nordlund formed a new administration comprising members of the Centre Party, the Social Democrats and the Moderate Party.

The opposition Liberal Party became the largest party in the Lagting as a result of a general election held on 21 October 2007, winning 10 seats, with 32.6% of the votes cast. The Centre Party secured eight seats, while the Independents took four and the representation of the Moderate Party and the Social Democrats declined to three seats each. A turn-out of 67.8% was recorded. The Liberal Party and the Centre Party subsequently formed a coalition Government, under Viveka Eriksson, the Liberal leader.

Economic Affairs

In 2004 the gross domestic product (GDP) of the Åland Islands, measured at current prices, was €963m. In 2004 4.9% of the working population were employed in agriculture (including hunting, forestry and fishing), which contributed 2.6% of GDP in 2004. Forests covered 58% of the islands in 2005, and only 9.0% of the total land area was arable. The principal crops are cereals, sugar beet, potatoes and fruit. Dairy-farming and sheep-rearing are also important.

Industry (including mining, manufacturing, construction and power) provided 12.5% of GDP in 2004, and employed 16.2% of the working population in that year. Manufacturing contributed 6.9% of GDP in 2004 and engaged 8.3% of the working population in the same year.

Since 1960 the economy of the islands has expanded and diversified. Fishing has declined as a source of income, and shipping (particularly the operation of ferry services between Finland and Sweden), trade and tourism have become the dominant economic sectors. In 2004 services accounted for 84.9% of GDP and engaged 76.0% of the employed labour force. The transport sector, including shipping, employed 17.4% in 2004, and, together with storage and communications, contributed 33.2% of GDP in that year. The political autonomy of the islands and their strategic location between Sweden and Finland have contributed to expanding banking and trade sectors; financial services engaged 8.8% of the employed labour force in 2004, while trade and hotels employed 13.5%. Tourist arrivals totalled 2,165,428 in 2006. In May 2006 the European Court of Justice ruled that the continued sale of snus (Swedish chewing tobacco) in the Åland Islands breached EU regulations on tobacco products. Trade in snus, particularly on ferries registered in the Islands, had been worth several million euros annually. New legislation adopted by the Lagting in January 2007 with the aim of complying with the Court's judgment was deemed insufficient by the European Commission, as it only prohibited snus (rather than oral tobacco in general) from entering the market, and did not apply to the sale of snus on vessels registered in the Åland Islands once they had left Finnish territorial waters. The case was referred to the Court

FINNISH EXTERNAL TERRITORY The Åland Islands

for a second time in October. Sweden had been granted an exemption from the ban on the sale of oral tobacco.

The Finnish State collects taxes, duties and fees from the Åland Islands, which receives 0.45% of total Finnish government income in return. If the taxes raised in the Åland Islands exceed 0.5% of corresponding Finnish tax revenues, the islands receive the excess amount in the form of a tax redemption. A tax redemption of €11.84m. was paid to the islands in 2003 relating to the fiscal year 2001. Consumer prices increased at an average annual rate of 1.3% in 2000–06; prices rose by 1.8% in 2007. The unemployment rate stood at 2.5% in 2006, compared with 5.2% in 1996. Finland participated in Economic and Monetary Union (EMU), introducing the single European currency, the euro, in January 1999. The Finnish currency, the markka, was used by the islands until the end of 2001. Euro notes and coins were introduced on 1 January 2002, and, as in Finland as a whole, the common European currency, the euro, became the sole legal tender from 1 March 2002.

Education

The education system is similar to that of Finland, except that Swedish is the language of instruction and Finnish an optional subject. The Government allocated €48.7m. to education in 2006, equivalent to 17.0% of total expenditure.

Statistical Survey

Source: Statistics Åland, POB 1187, 22111 Mariehamn; tel. (18) 25490; fax (18) 19495; e-mail info@asub.ax; internet www.asub.ax.

AREA AND POPULATION

Area: 13,517 sq km (5,219 sq miles), of which 1,527 sq km (589 sq miles) is land and 11,990 sq km (4,629 sq miles) is water.

Population (31 December 2006): 26,923 (males 13,353, females 13,571).

Density (land area only, 31 December 2006): 17.6 per sq km.

Principal Towns (31 December 2006): Mariehamn (capital) 10,824; Godby 852; Storby 479; Prästgården 424; Ödkarby 320; Söderby 309.

Births, Marriages and Deaths (2006): Registered live births 295 (birth rate 11.0 per 1,000); Marriages 116 (marriage rate 4.3 per 1,000); Deaths 257 (death rate 9.6 per 1,000).

Expectation of Life (years at birth, 2005): 80.0 (males 78.8; females 81.1).

Immigration and Emigration (2005): Immigrants 844 (Finland 295; Sweden 408); Emigrants 639 (Finland 238; Sweden 360).

Employment (2004): Agriculture, fishing and aquaculture 647; Industry 1,207; Construction 919; Trade and hotels 1,764; Transport 2,285; Financial services 1,152; Public services 4,760; Activities not classified 380; Total employed 13,114. *2007:* Total unemployed 334.

HEALTH AND WELFARE

Physicians (2003): 59.
Hospital Beds (2006): 138.

AGRICULTURE, ETC.

Agricultural Production (metric tons, 2006, unless otherwise stated): Milk ('000 litres) 14,093; Beef 532; Pork 13; Mutton 57; Poultry 1,497 (2002); Eggs 236; Wheat 3,727; Rye 537; Triticale (wheat-rye hybrid) 81 (2003); Barley and oats 2,717; Peas 1; Turnip rape 40; Sugar beet 35,620; Potatoes 17,969; Onions 7,662; Cucumbers 167; Leeks 109; Chinese cabbage and lettuce 1,472; Apples 1,882; Strawberries ('000 litres) 14; Tomatoes 123; Parsley ('000 bunches) 208; Dill ('000 bunches) 199; Celery 27; Carrots 95.

Livestock (2004): Cattle 7,347; Pigs 995; Hens 13,185; Sheep 7,382; Horses 225.

Forestry Production (cu m, roundwood, 2006): Logs 62,349; Pulp 108,912.

Fishing (metric tons, live weight, 2006): Capture 2,433 (Baltic herring and sprat 1,484; Whitefish 91; Perch 156; Pike-perch 33; Pike 38); Aquaculture 4,151; *Total catch* 6,584.

INDUSTRY

Selected Indicators (2006): Electric energy 20m. kWh (incl. 17m. kWh from wind power); Dwellings completed 189.

FINANCE

Currency: Finnish currency was used until the end of 2001. Euro notes and coins were introduced on 1 January 2002, and the euro became the sole legal tender from 1 March. For details of exchange rates, see the chapter on Finland.

Budget (€ '000, 2006): Revenue 292,533; Expenditure 285,870.

Cost of Living (Consumer Price Index; base: 2000 = 100): All items 106.0 in 2005; 107.9 in 2006; 109.8 in 2007.

Expenditure on the Gross Domestic Product (€ million at current prices, 2004): Wages and salaries 383; Employers' contribution to social security 103; Operating surplus 257; Fixed capital depreciation 140; *Total domestic expenditure* 883; Indirect taxes 117; *Less* Subsidies 38; *GDP in market prices* 963.

Gross Domestic Product by Economic Activity (€ million at current prices, 2004): Agriculture, hunting, forestry and fishing 23; Manufacturing 61; Construction 49; Trade, restaurants and hotels 81; Transport, storage and communications 293; Financing, insurance, real estate and business services 180; Government services 184; Unallocated banking services –25; Other community, social and personal services 25; Non-profit institutions 12; *GDP at factor cost* 883; Indirect taxes 117; *Less* Subsidies 38; *GDP in purchasers' values* 963.

EXTERNAL TRADE

2006 (€ '000): Imports 144,973 (Live animals and products thereof 19,752; Pulp and paper 23,735; Machinery, equipment and appliances 24,886); Exports 56,807 (Articles of plastics and rubber 15,821; Wood and cork and products thereof 7,220). Note: Figures exclude trade with mainland Finland.

TRANSPORT

Road Traffic (registered motor vehicles, 31 December 2006): Private motor cars 16,256; Vans 3,220; Lorries 540; Buses 42; Motorcycles 995; Tractors 3,469.

Shipping (2006): *Merchant Fleet:* 59 vessels; Total displacement 956,604 grt. Note: Figures include 20 vessels registered under flags other than Åland or Finland, total displacement 555,673 grt. *Traffic:* 9,650 vessels entered; 2,165,428 passenger arrivals (incl. ferry services).

Civil Aviation (traffic, Mariehamn airport, 2006): Passengers 64,043; Freight 150 metric tons; Post 260 metric tons.

TOURISM

Tourist Arrivals (2006): 235,087.

EDUCATION

Primary and Secondary Schools (2006 unless otherwise indicated): Institutions 25 (Comprehensive schools 25, of which 8 also offer upper-stage education, Upper-stage only 1); Pupils 3,003 (Comprehensive schools 1,998, Upper-stage schools 1,049). *2007:* 2,947 pupils (boys 1,511, girls 1,436).

Pupils Enrolled in Post-Comprehensive Education (2006): Preparatory study programme 513 (males 221, females 292); Vocational 713 (males 368, females 345); Other 51 (males 23, females 28); Åland Polytechnic 359 (males 224, females 135).

Directory

GOVERNMENT AND LEGISLATURE

The legislative body is the Lagting, comprising 30 members, elected every four years on a basis of proportional representation. All Ålanders over the age of 18 years, possessing Åland regional citizenship, have the right to vote and to seek election. An Executive Council (Landskapsregeringen), consisting of five to seven members, is elected by the Lagting, and its Chairman (Lantråd) is the highest-ranking politician in Åland after the Speaker (Talman) of the Lagting. The President has the right to veto Lagting decisions only when the Lagting exceeds its legislative competence, or when there is a threat to the security of the country. The Governor of Åland represents the Government of Finland and is appointed by the Finnish President (with the agreement of the Speaker of the Åland legislature).

Governor: PETER LINDBÄCK.

FINNISH EXTERNAL TERRITORY

Landskapsregeringen
(Executive Council)

Självstyrelsegården, POB 1060, 22111 Mariehamn; e-mail marina.sundstrom@regeringen.ax; internet www.regeringen.ax.

The governing coalition comprises members of the Liberal Party and the Centre Party. Its composition in March 2008 was as follows:

Chairman (Lantråd): VIVEKA ERIKSSON (Liberal Party).
Deputy Chairman (Vicelantråd): BRITT LUNDBERG (Centre Party).
Members: KATRIN SJÖGREN (Liberal Party), JAN-ERIK MATTSSON (Centre Party), ROGER ERIKSSON (Liberal Party), RUNAR KARLSSON (Centre Party), MATS PERÄMAA (Liberal Party).

Lagting
(Parliament)

Speaker (Talman): ROGER NORDLUND (Centre Party).

Election, 21 October 2007

	Votes	% of votes	Seats
Liberalerna på Åland (Liberal Party)	4,176	32.56	10
Åländsk Center (Centre Party)	3,107	24.23	8
Obunden Samling (Independents)	1,573	12.27	4
Ålands Socialdemokrater (Social Democrats)	1,513	11.80	3
Frisinnad Samverkan (Moderate Party)	1,233	9.61	3
Ålands Framtid (Åland's Future)	1,070	8.34	2
HUT-gruppen (HUT-Group)	153	1.19	0
Total	12,825	100.00	30

POLITICAL ORGANIZATIONS

Unless otherwise indicated, the address of each of the following organizations is: Ålands Lagting, POB 69, 22101 Mariehamn; tel. (18) 25000; fax (18) 13302.

Åländsk Center (Centre Party): tel. (18) 25360; fax (18) 16630; e-mail centern@lagtinget.ax; internet www.centern.ax; Chair. VERONICA THÖRNROOS.

Ålands Framstegsgrupp (Progress Group): e-mail ronald.boman@lagtinget.ax; internet www.afg.ax; Chair. and Leader RONALD BOMAN.

Ålands Framtid (Åland's Future): tel. (18) 25366; e-mail info@alandsframtid.nu; internet www.alandsframtid.nu; f. 2003; separatist; Leader ANDERS ERIKSSON; Sec. BIRGITTA BERGMAN-JANSSON.

Ålands Socialdemokrater (Social Democrats): Ekonomiegatan 1, Mariehamn; tel. (18) 25461; e-mail socialdemokraterna@lagtinget.ax; internet www.socialdemokraterna.ax; Chair. BARBRO SUNDBACK; Sec. ANDREW HAGMARK-COOPER.

Frisinnad Samverkan (Moderate Party): tel. (18) 25357; e-mail fs@lagtinget.ax; internet www.fs.ax; Chair. JOHAN EHN; Sec. LILIAN HOLMBERG.

Liberalerna på Åland (Liberal Party): tel. (18) 25362; fax (18) 16075; e-mail liberalerna@lagtinget.ax; internet www.liberalerna.ax; Chair. VIVEKA ERIKSSON; Parliamentary Leader GUNNAR JANSSON; Gen. Sec. CHRISTINA JOHANSSON-GAMMALS.

Obunden Samling (Independents): tel. (18) 25368; e-mail obundna@lagtinget.ax; internet www.obs.ax; f. 1987; Chair. GUN-MARI LINDHOLM; Leader DANNE SUNDMAN.

RELIGION

The majority of the islands' population are Christian. At 31 December 2006 there were 23,820 adherents of the Evangelical Lutheran Church of Finland, accounting for 88.5% of the population. There were also small numbers of Jehovah's Witnesses (49), Roman Catholics (39), Greek Orthodox Christians (24) and Adventists (12); 58 people practised other religions.

THE PRESS

Ålandstidningen: POB 50, Strandgatan 16, 22101 Mariehamn; tel. (18) 26026; fax (18) 15755; e-mail niklas.lampi@alandstidningen.ax; internet www.tidningen.ax; 6 a week; f. 1891; Editor-in-Chief NIKLAS LAMPI; circ. 10,355 (2007).

Nya Åland: POB 21, Uppgårdsvägen 6, 22100 Mariehamn; tel. (18) 23444; fax (18) 23449; e-mail redaktion@nyan.ax; internet www.nyan.ax; f. 1981; 5 a week; Man. Dir STEFAN NORRGRANN; Editor-in-Chief NINA FELLMAN; circ. 7,256 (2005).

BROADCASTING AND COMMUNICATIONS
Telecommunications

Ålands Mobiltelefon Ab: e-mail info@gsm.ax; internet www.gsm.ax; f. 1989; licensed to operate both GSM- and UMTS-networks on the islands.

Ålands Telefonandelslag: POB 22, 22411 Godby; tel. (18) 41053; fax (18) 41299; e-mail godby@altel.ax; internet www.altel.ax; f. 1910.

Mariehamns Telefon Ab: Ålandsvägen 52, POB 1228, 22111 Mariehamn; tel. (18) 27044; fax (18) 15900; e-mail telefon@mtel.ax; internet www.mtel.ax; f. 1892; Dir STIG SELANDER.

Radio and Television

Ålands Radio och TV Ab: Ålandsvägen 24, POB 140, 22101 Mariehamn; tel. (18) 26060; fax (18) 26520; e-mail info@radiotv.ax; internet www.radiotv.ax; f. 1996; broadcasts radio programmes in Swedish, 115.5 hours a week; operates three analogue and five digital television channels; Man. Dir PIA ROTHBERG-OLOFSSON; Editor-in-Chief ASTRID OLHAGEN.

Steel FM: Strandgränd 2, 22100 Mariehamn; tel. (18) 16200; fax (18) 22079; e-mail mail@steelfm.net; internet www.steelfm.net; commercial radio broadcaster.

TV Åland: Styrmansgatan 2 A, 22100 Mariehamn; tel. (18) 14035; fax (18) 14037; e-mail redaktion@tv.ax; internet www.tv.ax; f. 1984; television producer and broadcaster; broadcasts by cable to 75% of islands.

FINANCE
Banks
(cap. = capital; res = reserves; dep. = deposits; m. = million; amounts in euros; brs = branches)

Ålandsbanken Abp (Bank of Åland): Nygatan 2, POB 3, 22101 Mariehamn; tel. (204) 29011; fax (204) 29228; e-mail info@alandsbanken.fi; internet www.alandsbanken.fi; f. 1919 as Ålands Aktiebank; name changed to Bank of Åland Ltd 1980, changed as above in 1998; merged with Ålands Hypoteksbank Ab in November 1995; cap. 22m., res 60m., dep. 1,666m. (Dec. 2003); Man. Dir PETER GRÖNLUND; 28 brs.

Andelsbanken för Åland: Köpmansgatan 2, POB 34, 22101 Mariehamn; tel. (18) 26000; e-mail andelsbanken.for.aland@op.fi; co-operative; mem. of OKO Bank; Dirs HÅKAN CLEMES, ROLAND KARLSSON.

Lappo Andelsbank: 22840 Lappo; tel. (18) 56621; fax (18) 56699; Dir TORSTEN NORDBERG.

Nordea Bank Finland PLC is also represented.

Insurance

Alandia Group: Ålandsvägen 31, POB 121, 22101 Mariehamn; tel. (18) 29000; fax (18) 13290; e-mail mhamn@alandia.com; internet www.alandia.com; f. 1938; life, non-life and marine; comprises three subsidiaries; Gen. Man. LEIF NORDLUND.

Ålands Ömsesidiga Försäkringsbolag (Åland Mutual Insurance Co): Köpmansgatan 6, POB 64, 22101 Mariehamn; tel. (18) 27600; fax (18) 27610; e-mail info@omsen.ax; internet www.omsen.ax; f. 1866; property; Man. Dir GÖRAN LINDHOLM.

Cabanco Insurance Co Ltd: Köpmansgatan 6, POB 64, 22101 Mariehamn; tel. (18) 27690; fax (18) 27699; Man. Dir BO-STURE SJÖLUND.

Hamnia Reinsurance Co Ltd: Köpmansgatan 6, POB 64, 22101 Mariehamn; tel. (18) 27690; fax (18) 27699; Man. Dir BO-STURE SJÖLUND.

TRADE AND INDUSTRY
Chamber of Commerce

Ålands Handelskammare: Torggatan 5, 22100 Mariehamn; tel. (18) 29029; fax (18) 21129; e-mail info@chamber.ax; internet www.chamber.ax; f. 1945; Chair. EDGAR VIKSTRÖM; Man. Dir DANIEL DAHLÉN.

Trade Association

Ålands Företagareförening (Åland Business Asscn): Skarpansvägen 17, 22100 Mariehamn; tel. (18) 23277; fax (18) 23288; e-mail ombudsman@foretagare.ax; internet www.foretagare.ax; f. 1957; c. 190 mem. cos; Chair. DICK JANSSON; Sec. JONNY MATTSSON.

Employers' Organizations

Ålands Arbetsgivareförening (Åland Employers' Asscn): Torggatan 5, 22100 Mariehamn; tel. (18) 29474; fax (18) 21129; f. 1969; Chair. KJELL CLEMES.

FINNISH EXTERNAL TERRITORY

Ålands Fiskodlarförening (Åland Fish Farmers' Asscn): Tingsvägen 3, 22710 Föglö; tel. (18) 17834; fax (18) 17833; e-mail info@fiskodlarna.aland.fi; internet www.fiskodlarna.aland.fi; Chair. MARCUS ERIKSSON; Sec. ANDREAS ENQUIST.

Ålands köpmannaförening (Åland Businessmen's Asscn): Ålandsvägen 34, 22100 Mariehamn; tel. (18) 13650; fax (18) 16519; e-mail kopmannaforeningen@aland.net; f. 1927; Chair. TOM FORSBOM; Sec. STEFAN BLOMQVIST.

Ålands producentförbund (Åland Agricultural Producers' Asscn): Ålands Landsbygdscentrum, 22150 Jomala; tel. (18) 329640; fax (18) 329631; e-mail henry.lindstrom@landsbygd.aland.fi; f. 1946; Chair. ANDERS ENGLUND; Man. Dir HENRY LINDSTROM.

Fraktfartygsföreningen r.f. (Cargo Ship Asscn): Norragatan 7A, 22100 Mariehamn; tel. (18) 23662; fax (18) 23644; e-mail small.ton@aland.net; internet www.fraktfartygsforeningen.fi; f. 1987 as Utrikesfartens Småtonnageförening; present name adopted 2000; Man. Dir OLOF WIDÉN.

Utilities

Electricity

Ålands Elandelslag: Godbyvägen 193, 22100 Mariehamn; tel. (18) 39250; fax (18) 31562; e-mail info@el.ax; internet www.el.ax; distribution; Man. Dir JAN WENNSTRÖM.

Kraftnät Åland: Elverksgatan 10, POB 71, 22101 Mariehamn; tel. (18) 5395; fax (18) 539250; e-mail info@kraftnat.ax; internet www.kraftnat.ax; production; Man. Dir JAN KAHLROTH.

Ålands Vindenergi Andelslag: Hamngatan 8, 22100 Mariehamn; tel. (18) 12065; fax (18) 12090; e-mail info@alandsvindenergi.ax; internet www.alandsvindenergi.ax; operates the 16 wind-power farms on the Åland islands, 9 of which it owns; produces roughly 7% of energy consumed on the islands; Man. Dir HENRIK LINDQVIST.

Water

Ålands Vatten Ab: Vattenverksvägen 34, 22150 Jomala; tel. (18) 32860; fax (18) 31471; e-mail alandsvatten@vatten.ax; internet www.vatten.ax; f. 1970; supplies water to 70% of population; Man. Dir CHRISTIAN NORDAS.

VA-verket: Elverksgatan 1, 22100 Mariehamn; tel. (18) 5310; fax (18) 531507; e-mail jouni.huhtala@mariehamn.aland.fi; internet www.mariehamn.aland.fi/tekniska_verken/va/; Dir JOUNI HUHTALA.

Trade Unions

AKAVA-Åland (Professional Asscn): Storagatan 14, 22100 Mariehamn; tel. (18) 16348; fax (18) 12125; e-mail akava-a@aland.net; Chair. PEKKA ERÄMETSÄ; Gen. Sec. MARIA HAGMAN.

Fackorgan för offentliga arbetsområden på Åland (FOA-Å) (Joint Organization of Civil Servants and Workers (VTY) in Åland): Norragatan 7A 1, 22100 Mariehamn; tel. (18) 16976; e-mail info@foa.inet.fi; Chair. ULLA ANDERSSON; Gen. Sec. ULLA BRITT DAHL.

FFC-facken på Åland: POB 108, 22101 Mariehamn; tel. (18) 16207; fax (18) 17207; internet www.facket.ax; Chair. PER-ÅKE ASPBÄCK; Gen. Sec. HENRIK LAGERBERG.

Tjänstemannaorganisationerna på Åland, TCÅ r.f. (Union of Salaried Employees in Åland): Strandgatan 23, 22100 Mariehamn; tel. (18) 16210; e-mail tca@aland.net; Chair. YVONNE APSHOLM; Dir TUULA MATTSSON.

TRANSPORT

The islands are linked to the Swedish and Finnish mainlands by ferry services and by air services from Mariehamn airport.

Ålandstrafiken: Strandgatan 25, 22100 Mariehamn; tel. (18) 525100; fax (18) 17815; e-mail info@alandstrafiken.ax; internet www.alandstrafiken.ax; operates buses on the islands and ferry services between the islands.

Roads

In 2006 there was a road network of 914.4 km, of which 738.9 km were paved. There is also a bicycle route network, covering some 356.5 km in 2006.

The Åland Islands

Shipping

Ferry services operate from the Åland Islands to Sweden and the Finnish mainland and a new service to Estonia was introduced in 2004.

Ålands Redarförening r.f. (Åland Shipowners' Association): Hamngatan 8, 22100 Mariehamn; tel. (18) 13430; fax (18) 22520; e-mail info@alship.aland.fi; internet www.alship.aland.fi; f. 1934; Chair. BJÖRN BLOMQVIST; Man. Dir HANS AHLSTRÖM; seven mems.

Principal Companies

Birka Line Abp: Östra Esplanadgatan 7, POB 175, 22101 Mariehamn; tel. (18) 27027; fax (18) 27343; e-mail info@birkaline.com; internet www.birkaline.com; f. 1971; shipping service; Man. Dir ANDERS INGVES.

Birka Cargo Ab Ltd: Storagatan 11, POB 175, 22101 Mariehamn; tel. (18) 27320; fax (18) 23223; e-mail info@birkacargo.com; internet www.birkacargo.com; f. 1990 as United Shipping Ltd Ab; 7 ro-ro vessels; Man. Dir STEFAN AXBERG.

Lundqvist Rederierna: Norra Esplanadgatan 9B, 22100 Mariehamn; tel. (18) 26050; fax (18) 26428; e-mail info@lundqvist.aland.fi; internet www.lundqvist.aland.fi; f. 1927; tanker and ro-ro services; Pres. BEN LUNDQVIST; total tonnage c. 820,000 dwt.

Rederiaktiebolaget Eckerö (Eckerö Linjen): Torggatan 2, POB 158, 22101 Mariehamn; tel. (18) 28000; fax (18) 12011; e-mail info@eckerolinjen.fi; internet www.eckerolinjen.fi; f. 1960; operates ferry routes between the Åland Islands and Sweden, and between Finland and Estonia; Man. Dir BJÖRN BLOMGVIST.

Rederi Ab Lillgaard: Skarpansvägen 29B, POB 136, 22101 Mariehamn; tel. (18) 13120; fax (18) 17220; e-mail info@lillgaard.aland.fi; internet www.lillgaard.aland.fi; f. 1966; operates services from the Åland Islands to the Finnish mainland and Sweden; Man. Dir ANDERS NORDLUND.

Rederiaktiebolaget Gustaf Erikson: Norra Esplanadgatan 4B, POB 49, 22101 Mariehamn; tel. (18) 27070; fax (18) 12670; e-mail gustaf.erikson@geson.aland.fi; f. 1913; manages dry cargo and refrigerated vessels; Man. Dir GUN ERIKSON-HJERLING.

Viking Line Abp: Norragatan 4, POB 166, 22101 Mariehamn; tel. (18) 27000; fax (18) 16944; e-mail nn@vikingline.fi; internet www.vikingline.fi; f. 1963; operates cruise and ferry services between Finland and Sweden and throughout the Baltic Sea; 7 car/passenger vessels; total tonnage 212,474 grt; Chair. BEN LUNDQVIST; Man. Dir and Chief Exec. NILS-ERIK EKLUND.

Civil Aviation

The islands' airport is at Mariehamn. In 2006 the airport handled 64,043 passengers, 150 metric tons of freight and 260 tons of post. It is served by Finnair and AirÅland Ab.

AirÅland Ab: Mariehamns flygplats, Flygfältsvägen 67, 22120 Mariehamn; tel. (18) 23710; fax (18) 23730; e-mail info@airaland.com; internet www.airaland.com; f. 2005; routes from Mariehamn to Helsinki and Stockholm; Man. Dir ANDERS ALM.

TOURISM

The Åland archipelago has numerous bays, inlets, islands and open stretches of water, and is an area of great natural beauty. Cycling, canoeing, kayaking and hiking attract tourists to the islands. Most visitors are from the Nordic countries, particularly from mainland Finland and Sweden. In 2006 tourist arrivals totalled 2,165,428.

Ålands Turist Förbund (Åland Tourism Board): Storagatan 8, 22100 Mariehamn; tel. (18) 24000; fax (18) 24265; e-mail info@visitaland.com; internet www.visitaland.com; f. 1989; Man. Dir ANNICA JANSSON.

Ålands Turist och Konferens Ab: Hotell Arkipelag, Strandgatan 31, 22100 Mariehamn; tel. (18) 15349; fax (18) 21077; e-mail info@turist-konferens.aland.fi; internet www.turist-konferens.aland.fi; Man. Dir HENRIK NORDSTRÖM.

FRANCE

Introductory Survey

Location, Climate, Language, Religion, Flag, Capital

The French Republic is situated in western Europe. It is bounded to the north by the English Channel (la Manche), to the east by Belgium, Luxembourg, Germany, Switzerland and Italy, to the south by the Mediterranean Sea, Andorra and Spain, and to the west by the Atlantic Ocean. The island of Corsica is part of metropolitan France, while 12 overseas possessions (French Guiana, Guadeloupe, Martinique, Réunion, French Polynesia, Mayotte, Saint-Barthélemy, Saint-Martin, Saint Pierre and Miquelon, the Wallis and Futuna Islands, the French Southern and Antarctic Territories and New Caledonia) also form an integral part of the Republic. The climate is temperate throughout most of the country, but in the south it is of the Mediterranean type, with warm summers and mild winters. The principal language is French, which has numerous regional dialects, and small minorities speak Breton and Basque. A majority of French citizens profess Christianity, and about 77% of the population are adherents of the Roman Catholic Church. Other Christian denominations are represented, and there are also Muslim and Jewish communities. The national flag (proportions 2 by 3) has three equal vertical stripes, of blue, white and red. The capital is Paris.

Recent History

In September 1939, following Nazi Germany's invasion of Poland, France and the United Kingdom declared war on Germany, thus entering the Second World War. In June 1940 France was forced to sign an armistice, following a swift invasion and occupation of French territory by German forces. After the liberation of France from German occupation in 1944, a provisional Government took office under Gen. Charles de Gaulle, leader of the 'Free French' forces during the wartime resistance. The war in Europe ended in May 1945, when German forces surrendered at Reims. In 1946, following a referendum, the Fourth Republic was established and de Gaulle announced his intention to retire from public life.

France had 26 different Governments from 1946 until the Fourth Republic came to an end in 1958 with an insurrection in Algeria (then an overseas department) and the threat of civil war. In May 1958 the President, René Coty, invited Gen. de Gaulle to form a government. In June the Assemblée nationale (legislature) invested de Gaulle as Prime Minister, with the power to rule by decree for six months. A new Constitution, approved by referendum in September, was promulgated in October; thus the Fifth Republic came into being, with de Gaulle taking office as President in January 1959. The new system provided for a strong presidency, the authority of which would be strengthened by national referendums and a stable executive.

France was a founder member of the European Community (EC, now European Union—EU, see p. 244) and of the North Atlantic Treaty Organization (NATO, see p. 340).

The early years of the Fifth Republic were overshadowed by the Algerian crisis. De Gaulle granted Algeria independence in 1962, withdrew troops and repatriated French settlers. In May 1968 students and workers joined in a revolt against the Government's authoritarian education and information policies, low wage rates and lack of social reform. For a time the republic appeared threatened, but the student movement collapsed and the general strike was settled by large wage rises. In April 1969 President de Gaulle resigned following his defeat in a referendum on regional reform.

Georges Pompidou, who had been Prime Minister from 1962–68, was elected President in June 1969. The Gaullist government coalition was returned at a general election in March 1973. Pompidou died in April 1974. In the presidential election held in May, Valéry Giscard d'Estaing, formerly leader of the centre-right Républicains Indépendants (RI), narrowly defeated François Mitterrand, the First Secretary of the Parti Socialiste (PS). A coalition Government was formed from members of the RI, the Gaullist Union des Démocrates pour la République (UDR) and the centrist parties. In August 1976 Jacques Chirac resigned as Prime Minister and subsequently undertook to transform the UDR into a new party, the Rassemblement pour la République (RPR). In February 1978 the governing non-Gaullist parties formed the Union pour la Démocratie Française (UDF) to compete against RPR candidates in the Assemblée nationale elections held in March, when the governing coalition retained a working majority.

In the April/May 1981 presidential election Mitterrand defeated Giscard d'Estaing. At elections for a new Assemblée, held in June, the PS and associated groups, principally the Mouvement des Radicaux de Gauche (MRG), won an overall majority of seats, following which four members of the Parti Communiste Français (PCF) were appointed to the Council of Ministers. The new Government introduced a programme of social and labour reforms, including the transfer of several major industrial enterprises and financial institutions to state control.

Legislative elections took place in March 1986, using a party-list based system of proportional representation for the first time. Although the PS remained the largest single party in the new Assemblée nationale, the centre-right parties, led by an RPR-UDF alliance, commanded a majority of seats. The PCF suffered a severe decline in support, while the far-right Front National (FN) won legislative representation for the first time. A period of political 'cohabitation' ensued as Mitterrand invited the RPR leader, Chirac, to form a new Council of Ministers.

In April 1986 Chirac introduced legislation that allowed his Government to legislate by decree on economic and social issues and on the proposed reversion to a voting system comprising single-member constituencies for legislative elections. However, Mitterrand insisted on exercising the presidential right to withhold approval of decrees that reversed the previous Government's social reforms. In July Chirac thus resorted to the 'guillotine' procedure (setting a time-limit for consideration of legislative proposals) to gain parliamentary consent for legislation providing for the transfer to the private sector of 65 state-owned companies, which, since it had been approved by the predominantly right-wing Sénat (Senate) and the Constitutional Council, the President was legally bound to approve.

Mitterrand was re-elected as President in May 1988, defeating Chirac. A general election took place in June, with a reintroduced single-seat majority voting system. An alliance of the PS and the MRG secured 276 seats, whilst an alliance of the RPR, the UDF and other right-wing candidates won 272. The PCF won 27 seats, and the FN one (compared with 35 in the previous legislature). Michel Rocard of the PS, who had been appointed as Prime Minister following the presidential election, regained that role. Rocard resigned in May 1991 and was succeeded by Edith Cresson, France's first female Prime Minister, who had resigned eight months previously from her post as Minister of European Affairs. In April 1992 Mitterrand appointed Pierre Bérégovoy, hitherto the Minister of State for the Economy, Finance and the Budget, to replace Cresson as Prime Minister. In June the Assemblée nationale approved constitutional changes allowing the ratification of the Treaty on European Union (the Maastricht Treaty), subject to approval by referendum. In the referendum, held in September, 51.1% of voters supported the treaty's ratification.

At elections to the Assemblée nationale, held in March 1993, the RPR won 247 of the 577 seats, the UDF 213 and the PS 54. Chirac had made it known that he was not available for the post of Prime Minister as he intended to concentrate on his candidacy in the 1995 presidential election. Mitterrand therefore asked another RPR member, Edouard Balladur, a former Minister of Finance, to form a government.

In the first round of voting in the presidential election, on 23 April 1995, Lionel Jospin, the candidate of the PS, obtained 23% of the votes, while Chirac and Balladur, both representing the RPR, took 21% and 19%, respectively. Jean-Marie Le Pen, the leader of the FN, won 15%. In the second round, on 7 May, Chirac (with 53% of the votes) defeated Jospin. Balladur resigned as Prime Minister, and Chirac appointed Alain Juppé (Minister of Foreign Affairs in the previous Government) as his successor. Juppé formed an administration in which the principal portfolios were evenly shared between the RPR and the UDF.

In October Juppé was elected President of the RPR, while Jospin was elected First Secretary of the PS.

In April 1997 Chirac announced that legislative elections would take place in May–June, some 11 months earlier than required. In the first round of voting, held on 25 May, the PS secured 23.5% of total votes cast, the RPR 15.7%, the FN 14.9% and the UDF 14.2%. Following the second round of voting, held on 1 June, the PS secured 241 seats, the RPR 134, the UDF 108 and the PCF 38. Despite its strong performance in the first round, the FN won only one seat. The unexpected victory of the PS, which began a further period of 'cohabitation', was widely attributed to dissatisfaction with Juppé's administration and the imposition of economic austerity measures necessitated under the terms of Economic and Monetary Union (EMU, see p. 288) within the EU. Jospin became Prime Minister, and formed a 'plural left' coalition.

At a by-election in May 1998 the FN lost its only seat in the Assemblée nationale. Meanwhile, in April a court banned Le Pen from holding or seeking public office for two years (reduced to one year on appeal) and gave him a three-month suspended prison sentence after finding him guilty of physical assault on a PS candidate in the 1997 general election. The selection of a potential replacement for Le Pen, necessitated by the ban, to lead the FN list of candidates in the following year's elections to the European Parliament (of which the FN leader was a member), resulted in a major dispute within the party and the creation of two rival factions. Deepening divisions between supporters of Le Pen and those of Bruno Mégret, the party's second-in-command, led to the expulsion of Mégret and six other senior party officials. In January 1999 Mégret launched his own party, which subsequently became known as the Mouvement National Républicain (MNR), and which appeared to follow harsher anti-immigrant policies than the FN. In October 2000 Le Pen was expelled from his seat in the European Parliament, following the rejection of his final appeal against his 1998 conviction in the European Court of Human Rights. However, in January 2001 Le Pen appealed against his exclusion from the European Parliament at the Court of First Instance of the European Communities; pending the result of this appeal Le Pen was permitted to resume his responsibilities in the Parliament. In April 2003 the Court upheld the ban, and Le Pen's period of suspension formally began in May.

In March 1999 a Paris public prosecutor upheld a ruling of the Constitutional Council that the President of the Republic enjoyed immunity from prosecution for all crimes, other than high treason, for the duration of his presidential term. This decision, which was confirmed by an appeal court ruling in January 2000, followed the disclosure of documentation purporting to show that Chirac had been aware of the existence of at least 300 fictitious employees, reputedly including RPR members or supporters, on the payroll of the Paris city council during his tenure as mayor.

At elections to the European Parliament held in June 1999, the RPR, in alliance with Démocratie Libérale (DL, formerly the Parti Républicain), gained only 12.8% of the votes cast, less than the PS, which won 22.0%, and a breakaway Gaullist group, opposed to the terms of the Maastricht Treaty, the Rassemblement pour la France (RPF), led by Charles Pasqua, which secured 13.1%. In December Michèle Alliot-Marie was elected President of the RPR.

In March 2000 Jospin carried out the first major reorganization of the Council of Ministers since taking office. Laurent Fabius, a former Prime Minister, returned to senior office as Minister of the Economy, Finance and Industry and Jack Lang, a former Minister of Culture, became Minister of National Education. In August 2000 the Minister of the Interior, Jean-Pierre Chevènement, the leader and sole minister of the Mouvement des Citoyens (MDC), resigned in protest at government policy towards Corsica (see below). Daniel Vaillant of the PS was appointed in his place. A further ministerial reshuffle was implemented in October.

Evidence of Chirac's apparent knowledge and tolerance of corrupt practice within government increased in September 2000, when a transcript of a video cassette made by Jean-Claude Méry, a former RPR official who had been imprisoned on charges of embezzlement in the mid-1990s, was published posthumously in Le Monde. In the recording Méry stated that Chirac had personally ordered him to arrange for funds of the Paris city council to be diverted to political parties. In December 2000 Michel Roussin, who had been Chirac's principal private secretary from 1989–93, was arrested, while the former unofficial treasurer for the RPR was remanded for questioning. Their testimony, which was leaked to the press, included details of the systematic levying of an illegal commission on public works contracts awarded by the Paris administration. The RPR, the PS and the Parti Républicain were all reportedly implicated in this scheme.

Throughout 2000 the tensions caused by a prolonged period of 'cohabitation' prompted moves towards constitutional change. In June the Assemblée nationale approved a reduction in the presidential term from seven to five years, in order to bring it into line with the life of a parliament. Amid concerns that the Sénat might not support the bill by the two-thirds' majority required for a constitutional change to be approved, Chirac called for a referendum, to be held on 24 September. The referendum attracted only a 30.6% participation rate, the lowest in any constitutional referendum held in metropolitan France. Of those who voted, 73.2% were in favour of the change, which would take effect from the 2002 presidential election. In May 2001, following a series of votes in the two legislative chambers, the Constitutional Council approved a proposal to hold the presidential election in advance of the parliamentary elections due in May 2002; it was felt that this arrangement would be more likely to prevent a further period of 'cohabitation'. Meanwhile, following inconclusive municipal and cantonal elections in March 2001, several ministers resigned from the mayorships that they had won in these elections and two Secretaries of State resigned from their government positions, following Jospin's insistence that henceforth members of the Government would not be permitted simultaneously to hold more than one elected position. In April officials from the RPR, the UDF (which had reconstituted itself as a unified party in 1998), and DL, although not including the senior leadership of the two latter parties, announced their intention to form a unified centre-right platform, which subsequently became known as the Union en Mouvement (UEM), prior to the legislative elections of 2002.

In April 2001 Chirac refused to attend court to give evidence pertaining to the reputedly illegal use of funds in the Paris city council. At the end of the month the investigating judge in the case, Eric Halphen, announced the existence of consistent evidence implicating Chirac, but stated that the doctrine of presidential immunity prevented Chirac from being brought to trial. Although Jospin and the hierarchy of the PS opposed bringing Chirac to trial, the socialist deputy Arnaud Montebourg launched a campaign to bring the case against Chirac to the High Court of Justice, the only court constitutionally able to bring charges against the President.

In June 2001 new revelations concerning Chirac's alleged involvement in financial malpractice emerged, including the first allegations that Chirac had personally benefited from malpractice; the President was alleged to have spent up to 2.4m. francs (a figure subsequently increased to 3.1m. francs) of state 'secret funds'—issued annually by the Office of the Prime Minister for the security services, to pay bonuses to staff, and as a contingency fund—on airline tickets and luxury hotel bills for himself and his family in 1992–95, although suspicions were voiced that the finance for these holidays might have originated from the alleged illicit commission payments made by building firms to the Paris city council. In mid-June 2001 the Assemblée nationale approved a bill, supported by the PS, that proposed removing judicial immunity from the President for acts committed outside his official role; however, the bill was regarded as having a purely symbolic function, as it was unlikely to gain the support of the Sénat or the President. In a television interview broadcast on 14 July, Chirac declared himself innocent of all charges made against him, and confirmed that he would not participate in any court case. At the end of the month a parliamentary committee agreed to a demand by magistrates to see the statements of personal financial wealth made by Chirac between 1988 and 1995; these statements made no reference to the large sums of money with which Chirac had purchased the holidays. Additional revelations concerning Chirac's reputed malpractice as the treasurer of a charity in the late 1970s also emerged at this time.

In August 2001 Jospin announced changes to a law that shortened the maximum working week from 39 to 35 hours, which had been regarded as central to the Government's policy of creating some 700,000 new jobs. The amendments permitted companies with up to 20 employees legally to institute a longer working week, apparently in response to protests by employers at the restrictions engendered by the law. Previous concessions had already been made, after the implementation of the first stage of the legislation was met with widespread protests in February 2000.

In September 2001 the Appeal Court dismissed Halphen as the leading investigator into the case regarding the illicit transfer of funds from building contractors to political parties at the Paris city council; Halphen was ruled to have exceeded his powers by calling the President as a witness, and by introducing certain items of evidence, including the video cassette of Méry. Although the case could be tried again, under a different judge, this decision effectively ruled out any development in the case so long as Chirac remained President. In mid-October 2001 the Court of Cassation confirmed the Constitutional Council's ruling that an incumbent President could not be prosecuted, additionally ruling that a head of state could not undergo formal investigation while in power, even for offences allegedly committed prior to taking office. The Council also suspended the statute of limitations, as a consequence of which Montebourg ended his campaign to bring Chirac to trial.

The first round of the presidential election, held on 21 April 2002, was contested by an unprecedented 16 candidates. Prior to the first round, Chirac and Jospin had been widely expected to progress to a second round. However, partly as a result of the wide choice of candidates, a relatively low rate of participation (only 69.2% of the electorate cast valid votes), and a campaign focus on issues related to 'insecurity' and law and order, Jospin polled only 16.2% of the valid votes cast, while Chirac won 19.9% and Le Pen 16.9%. The splintering of the governmental 'plural left' coalition proved detrimental for Jospin and the PS, as four of the coalition partners presented individual candidates for the presidency, together securing 16.3% of votes cast. Moreover, three Trotskyite candidates together polled some 10.4% of the votes cast. The unexpected qualification of Le Pen for the second-round poll precipitated widespread demonstrations and the majority of the defeated candidates rallied around Chirac as a candidate who represented 'republican values', although Chirac's first-round vote, in both percentage and actual terms, had been the lowest of any outgoing President of the Fifth Republic. In the second round, on 5 May, the turn-out increased slightly—75.4% of the electorate cast valid votes. Although Le Pen's share of the vote rose marginally, Chirac's victory, with 82.2% of the valid votes cast, was widely interpreted as a resounding defeat for the far right. On 6 May Chirac appointed Jean-Pierre Raffarin, of DL, and latterly President of Poitou-Charentes regional council, as Prime Minister. On 7 May Raffarin appointed an interim Government; among the principal appointments were Nicolas Sarkozy as Minister of the Interior, Interior Security and Local Freedoms, Alliot-Marie as Minister of Defence and Dominique de Villepin as Minister of Foreign Affairs. In the period between the presidential election and the elections to the Assemblée nationale, Chirac was instrumental in the organization of a new centre-right electoral alliance to replace the RPR, and to build on the informal alliances forged within the UEM; this alliance was initially titled the Union pour la Majorité Présidentielle (UMP), and was provisionally led by Juppé.

At the legislative elections held on 9 and 16 June 2002 the UMP, which incorporated the greater part of the RPR and DL, and significant elements of the UDF, succeeded in becoming the largest grouping in the new Assemblée, with 355 of the 577 seats, whilst a further 43 representatives of other parties of the centre-right and right were elected, thus ensuring a clear working majority for the pro-presidential grouping. Of the 176 seats awarded to parties of the broad left, the PS was the most successful, with 140 deputies. The FN won 11.3% of votes cast in the first round of polling, but did not receive any seats. The new Government appointed shortly afterwards retained substantially the same members as the previous interim administration and cited law and order, a programme of decentralization, and further privatizations among its principal concerns. Concern about the degree of support for the far right in France, which had heightened following Le Pen's progression to the second round of the presidential election, intensified further, following an attempt, on 14 July, to assassinate President Chirac during a procession in Paris; it subsequently emerged that the assailant, Maxime Brunerie, was a member of a small neo-fascist grouping, Unité Radicale, and had, moreover, contested a municipal election as a candidate of the MNR in 2001. Unité Radicale was formally proscribed in August, and Brunerie was subsequently interned in a psychiatric hospital. (Brunerie was brought to trial in late 2004, and sentenced in December to 10 years' imprisonment.)

In the aftermath of the legislative elections, the UMP consolidated its position, formally constituting itself as the Union pour un Mouvement Populaire in November 2002, absorbing the RPR and DL, in addition to factions of the UDF and the RPF; Juppé was elected as President of the party. In December a UMP group (with an absolute majority of 166 of 321 seats) was formed in the Sénat. Meanwhile, the future ideological direction of the PS became a subject of intense debate within the party; none the less, François Hollande, the First Secretary of the party since 1997, was re-elected to that position, with a clear majority of votes, in May 2003.

Further concerns at the extent of corrupt practices in public life, meanwhile, were raised during the trial in late 2003 of Juppé and 26 other defendants on charges that the Paris city council and private companies had illegally paid staff of the RPR during Juppé's tenure as Secretary-General of the party (in 1988–95) and as Deputy Mayor of Paris (1983–95). In January 2004 Juppé was found guilty and given an 18 months' suspended prison sentence; 13 other business executives also received suspended prison sentences in the case. Juppé was also banned from holding public office for a period of 10 years, but was permitted to remain in office as Mayor of Bordeaux, and as a parliamentary deputy, pending an appeal. Although the constitutional immunity from prosecution and investigation of the President of the Republic prevented any inquiry into Chirac's behaviour, the judges ruled that Juppé had been directly subordinate to Chirac in his capacity as President of the RPR. (Moreover, Chirac was the Mayor of Paris for the entire duration of Juppé's service as the Deputy Mayor.) Following Juppé's conviction, several leading figures in the UMP (of which he remained the President) rallied to his support; notably, Chirac praised what he described as Juppé's honesty, humanity and competence. Chirac also ordered that a judicial investigation be launched into an alleged campaign of intimidation against the judges in the case. In February François Léotard, Minister of National Defence in 1993–95, was found guilty of the illicit transfer of funds to the former Parti Républicain (which, as DL, had now been subsumed into the UMP), and given a 10 months' suspended jail sentence.

In mid-March 2003 the two houses of Parliament, meeting in congress, approved several constitutional changes relating to the implementation of the European arrest warrant and to the proposed decentralization programme, which provided for the eventual possibility of territorial units receiving varying degrees of autonomy and powers (to be decided in each case by law), for the institution of deliberative assemblies and for the holding of local referendums in such territories. Moreover, the amendments permitted the introduction of legislation pertaining to decentralization on a temporary, or experimental, basis. Notably, the first article of the Constitution was amended to assert that the organization of the Republic was decentralized. However, attempts to implement policies that utilized the new constitutional provisions initially proved unsuccessful—in July, in the first instance of the holding of a local referendum under these provisions, voters in Corsica rejected proposals to reorganize the administration of the island (see below), and in December voters in the overseas departments of Guadeloupe (see p. 1832) and Martinique (see p. 1840) rejected proposals to restructure and simplify their territorial administration. In concurrent referendums held in Saint-Barthélemy and Saint-Martin, however, the electorate voted in favour of seceding from Guadeloupe to assume the status of Overseas Collectivities (Collectivités d'outre-mer). (The administrative process was completed in February 2007, when it was approved by the Constitutional Council.) In January 2004 the Assemblée nationale approved an organic law and an ordinary law, the combined effect of which was to grant autonomous status to French Polynesia (see p. 1854); this legislation was finally approved, with minor amendments, in February, by the Constitutional Council.

In July 2003 several reforms to senatorial elections were approved by Parliament; henceforth, senators were to be elected for a term of six years (instead of nine), and one-half (rather than one-third) of the seats were to be renewable every three years. Moreover, with effect from 2010, the number of senators was to be increased from 321 to 346, and the minimum age for eligible candidates to the Sénat was to be reduced from 35 to 30 years.

A major topic of political debate in 2003 and early 2004 concerned the wearing of the *foulard* or other types of veil by female Muslim schoolchildren and students during classes at state educational establishments. Although a 1989 ruling of the Council of State declared that the wearing of religious symbols in state schools did not violate the principle of the secularity of the State, formalized in 1905, so long as they were deemed to be of a 'non-ostentatious' nature, the ruling had subsequently been used to exclude a number of Muslim students from educational establishments. In December 2003 a presidential commission recommended the introduction of legislation explicitly forbidding the wearing of the veil and other conspicuous religious symbols, including Jewish skullcaps and large Christian crosses, in state-run schools and colleges; Chirac expressed support for such a measure, and legislation to that end came into effect in September 2004. More than 600 students initially defied the ban, but, following mediation with their families, this was reduced to 72. By late January 2005 48 Muslim schoolgirls had been expelled for violating the new law by wearing Islamic headscarves, although it was reported that there was almost universal observance of the ban at the start of the new academic year in September.

Widespread public discontent with the Government was reflected in the results of regional and cantonal elections, held in two rounds on 21 and 28 March 2004, following which the parties of the centre-right lost control of 13 regions to parties of the left and centre-left, which thereby controlled all of the regions of metropolitan France excluding Alsace and Corsica. In response to these results, Raffarin tendered his resignation as Prime Minister on 30 March, but was immediately reappointed to that position by President Chirac. The formation of a new Government was announced on 31 March, when several of the principal members of the former administration changed roles. Sarkozy was appointed as Minister of State, Minister of the Economy, Finance and Industry, and was replaced as Minister of the Interior, Internal Security and Local Freedoms by de Villepin. Michel Barnier, hitherto EU Commissioner for Regional Policy and Institutional Reform, returned to government office as Minister of Foreign Affairs. However, in the European parliamentary elections held on 13 June, the UMP suffered another serious defeat, obtaining only 16.6% of votes cast, whereas the PS received 28.9%.

The UMP's electoral performance did not improve at the partial, indirect elections to the Sénat held on 26 September 2004. The PS and its allies made considerable gains, achieving a net increase of 14 seats, while the UMP lost its outright majority in the chamber, with a net loss of six seats. However, the centre-right parties together retained control of the Sénat. Raffarin, whose decision to contest the senatorial elections was widely attributed to the insecurity of his premiership, was duly elected to the Sénat but was unable to assume his seat while he remained in the Government. The first stage of the reforms to the senatorial elections approved in July 2003 took effect at this poll, when the number of senators was increased from 321 to 331.

During 2004 concern was expressed by Chirac and others at the rising number of anti-Jewish and anti-Muslim attacks, attributed largely to extremist Islamist groups and the far right, respectively. The Government announced the establishment of security monitoring committees in each department with the aim of preventing anti-semitic attacks. A report commissioned by the Government was published in October warning that an increase in racism and anti-semitism in France posed a threat to the democratic system. Recorded racist and anti-semitic offences increased by 82% in 2004 compared with 2003, to 1,513, of which 361 were described as violent. In December 2004 new initiatives were introduced to promote the integration of the Muslim population in France. The aim was to combat growing fundamentalism among young Muslims through the encouragement of a moderate 'French Islam'. (Although no official statistics on religious allegiance or ethnicity are published, in the mid-2000s it was generally believed that up to 10% of the population of metropolitan France were Muslims or of North or sub-Saharan African extraction.) The measures, announced by de Villepin, included funding for the building of mosques and courses on French law, customs and language for Islamic religious leaders (*imams*). Meanwhile, the reduction of economic inequality along ethnic lines in French society was a central aim of the Plan for Social Cohesion presented in 2004 by Jean-Louis Borloo, Minister of Employment, Labour and Social Cohesion.

In July 2004 Juppé resigned as President of the UMP, in anticipation of the findings of an appeal against his conviction earlier in the year. In its verdict in December, the appeal court upheld the conviction but reduced the length of the ban on holding public office from 10 years to one (following the verdict Juppé also resigned as Mayor of Bordeaux). Meanwhile, in November Sarkozy was elected President of the UMP. There was widespread speculation that Sarkozy intended to use the leadership of the ruling party as a platform from which to launch his candidature in the presidential election due in 2007. Following the insistence of President Chirac that the head of the UMP would not be permitted simultaneously to hold ministerial office, Sarkozy resigned as Minister of the Economy, Finance and Industry.

In December 2004 Raffarin announced legislative proposals intended to relax further the regulations controlling the 35-hour working week, notably including a proposed increase in the annual quota of supplementary working hours. Left-wing parties denounced the proposals, as did trade unions, which organized large-scale demonstrations across France on 5 February 2005 in protest against the reforms. Nevertheless, the proposals were adopted by the Assemblée nationale in March 2005. Meanwhile, in February the Government announced that the rate of unemployment had increased to the politically significant level of 10% of the population for the first time since February 2000. Serious divisions were evident within the Council of Ministers between de Villepin, a close ally of Chirac, and Raffarin, following comments made by de Villepin during a national broadcast that were perceived as undermining the position of the Prime Minister. Raffarin suffered a further blow to his authority when, on 16 May 2005, around one-half of the working population flouted the abolition of the traditional Whit Monday public holiday. (The holiday had been replaced in August 2004 by a Day of Solidarity, on which workers would attend work for no pay in order to provide additional support for the elderly and the disabled.)

On 29 May 2005 a national referendum took place on the ratification of the Treaty establishing a Constitution for Europe. Following an intense campaign, in which Chirac and leading members of the UMP and the PS had demonstrated their support for the EU constitutional treaty, 54.9% of those voting rejected its ratification. A total of 69.7% of the electorate participated in the referendum. Raffarin subsequently resigned as Prime Minister. He was succeeded by de Villepin, while Sarkozy returned to the Government as Minister of State, Minister of the Interior and Land Management. At a time when Chirac was seeking to win back the support of the electorate, his choice of premier surprised many observers, not least because de Villepin had never held elected office. The new Prime Minister pledged to restore public confidence in the Government within 100 days of assuming office. Major changes also occurred within the PS following the vote. The PS had been divided over the issue, with one faction, led by Hollande, supporting the proposed constitution and another, led by Fabius, opposing it. Official party policy had been established by an internal referendum in December 2004, in which 58% of the votes cast were in favour of ratification. Following the referendum, Fabius and five fellow campaigners against the constitutional treaty were dismissed from the party's executive committee (although Fabius was reinstated in November 2005).

In his first major speech to Parliament, in early June 2005, de Villepin set out his programme of labour reforms, foremost among which was a programme intended to address youth unemployment (see below). In addition to labour reforms, the Government announced that it was to tighten immigration controls by introducing quotas for immigrants with professional skills and accelerating the expulsion of illegal entrants. De Villepin's administration was also to pursue a programme of privatization, including the sale of a 15% stake in Electricité de France (EdF—which was achieved in November). The new Government had already raised €3,400m. from the sale of shares in France Télécom and sold a 22% stake in Gaz de France in July.

In August 2005 it was announced that municipal and cantonal elections, and elections to the Sénat, originally scheduled for 2007, would take place in March and September 2008, respectively, in order to avoid five polls being held in one year (elections to the presidency and to the Assemblée nationale were also due in 2007). In a speech to commemorate his administration's first 100 days in power, and encouraged by the first decrease in the rate of unemployment for four years, de Villepin announced several further economic measures, including the shielding from foreign ownership of 10 strategic industrial sectors (among them defence, nuclear power, computer systems and biotechnology), which prompted concern from the European Commission and accusations of protectionism from his opponents. Despite the decline in unemployment, in early October a nation-wide day of protest was organized by the trade unions against the Government's economic initiatives (in particular the introduction of more flexible labour contracts and the privatization of state enterprises).

Following the rejection by French voters of the EU constitutional treaty, and the unexpected defeat in July 2005 of France's bid to stage the 2012 Olympic Games in Paris, Chirac's popularity suffered a major setback. In October a former aide of Chirac during his tenure as Mayor of Paris, Michel Roussin, was found guilty of corruption in connection with the illegal funding of political parties by construction companies seeking to secure contracts from Paris city council. Roussin, who had been on trial since March, along with 46 other politicians and business executives, including Guy Drut, Minister of Youth and Sports in 1995–97, was given a four-year suspended sentence and fined €50,000. Drut received a 15-month suspended sentence and was also fined €50,000; he was subsequently provisionally suspended from membership of the International Olympic Committee (IOC). In May 2006 Chirac attracted criticism for his decision to pardon Drut, who subsequently resumed membership of the IOC.

On 27 October 2005 violence broke out in Clichy-sous-Bois, a suburb of Paris largely populated by immigrant communities and suffering from high unemployment and poor social housing, following the death of two youths and the injury of a third, in an electricity substation. The youths had allegedly been fleeing a police identity check. Rioting erupted in the area on the following night, subsequently spreading to several neighbouring suburbs in the department of Seine-Saint-Denis, to the north-east of Paris. De Villepin appealed for calm, and at the end of the month Sarkozy, whom civil rights groups had criticized in September for his proposed strict new anti-terrorism legislation, promised the families of the two youths (both of whom were of African extraction) a full investigation into the circumstances surrounding their deaths. However, Sarkozy's uncompromising stance towards the rioters, notably his language, which some condemned as inflammatory in tone, provoked sharp criticism from some commentators and politicians, even within the Government. By early November some 300 towns and cities across France were experiencing unrest, mainly led by young males of North or sub-Saharan African origin, while some 9,500 riot police had been deployed in an attempt to bring the violence under control.

On 6 November 2005, in his first public announcement since the outbreak of unrest, Chirac declared that restoring public order was an 'absolute priority'. On the following day, as the violence claimed its first (and only) victim, de Villepin announced a series of enhanced security measures, including the right of regional préfets to impose curfews. The Prime Minister also set out a programme aimed at improving education, employment and housing in deprived suburban areas. After 11 nights of riots, as many as 1,200 people had been taken into custody. For the first time incidents in provincial cities had become more numerous than those within and around the capital. On 8 November de Villepin announced a state of emergency, invoking a law created in 1955 to quell unrest in Algeria during that country's war of independence, which granted préfets additional powers to issue house-arrest warrants and restrict public gatherings. Initially imposed for a period of 12 days, the state of emergency was extended by Parliament for a further three months on 18 November. (It was eventually lifted on 4 January 2006.) Meanwhile, Sarkozy announced that all convicted rioters who were not of French nationality would be deported, including those holding residence permits (at the time amounting to around 120 of the 1,800 arrested since the start of the riots).

While citing the restoration of law and order as its priority, the administration continued to promote measures to increase the standard of living in impoverished suburban areas; in a national address in mid-November 2005, as the violence subsided, Chirac referred to a 'profound malaise' in French society and announced a scheme to train 50,000 young people in such areas by 2007. By the time of his address nearly 300 schools and public buildings had been burned and 4,770 people had been arrested. In late November 2005 de Villepin proposed amendments to immigration legislation intended to make it more difficult for foreigners to gain entry to France by marrying French nationals and for immigrants to bring in family members. At the beginning of December the Prime Minister launched a national campaign against discrimination, with measures including the imposition of fines on businesses found to have practised discrimination and incentives for companies to locate in deprived areas and to employ young people. In late December the Government's controversial anti-terrorism bill was passed by the Assemblée nationale; the legislation included harsher sentences for convicted terrorists and the state-funded installation of closed-circuit television cameras in sensitive locations.

The PS was widely thought to have failed to capitalize on the social unrest of late 2005, while Sarkozy and de Villepin had both ultimately gained in popularity as a result of their handling of the crisis. These two remained rivals for the UMP candidacy in the presidential election, but Sarkozy's position was considerably strengthened when UMP leaders voted in early December to amend the party's statutes, enabling rank-and-file members to elect their presidential candidate. In mid-January 2006 Sarkozy effectively launched his electoral campaign with a rousing speech in which he called for a more accountable presidency directly responsible for implementing government policy, and a break with France's traditional model of high spending and generous welfare protection.

In March 2006 new youth employment legislation, which had been devised by de Villepin and was due to take effect from early April, provoked a series of mass demonstrations and strike action in Paris and other cities across the country. Under the legislation, which was intended to encourage job creation, a new 'contrat première embauche' (first employment contract—CPE) was to be introduced for those aged under 26. The CPE would allow employers in small companies to dismiss workers more easily during their first two years of employment (following which time standard conditions of employment, which place strict conditions over the dismissal of employees, would apply). In mid-March riot police used tear gas to evacuate some 200 protesting students who were occupying a university building in Paris, and days later at least 250,000 people, principally university students, participated in demonstrations in around 80 cities and towns, with violence erupting at several rallies. Further nation-wide marches organized by trade unions later that month were attended by 500,000 people, according to police, although the unions claimed that 1.5m. protesters had participated. Despite continued public resistance to the new legislation, de Villepin initially refused to accede to demands for its withdrawal, although he did suggest that he would consider a reduction of the period within which employees could more easily be dismissed from two years to one year. However, following further large-scale protests, in mid-April Chirac announced that the CPE would be withdrawn; later that month Parliament duly approved amendments to the legislation, abolishing the CPE and instead instituting a system of state funding for small companies that employed certain categories of young people.

De Villepin's popularity suffered a further reverse in May 2006, following allegations of his involvement in a scandal that had originated in July 2004, when a French magistrate received documents that purported to reveal that a number of senior politicians, including Sarkozy, held secret offshore accounts with a Luxembourg bank, Clearstream, in which illegal payments allegedly relating to the 1991 sale of eight French naval vessels to Taiwan had been deposited. A subsequent investigation proved that the documents had been falsified. However, in late April 2006 a former senior intelligence officer, Philippe Rondot, testified that de Villepin had asked him to conduct an investigation into the allegations before they were known publicly. (In a later interview with Le Figaro, however, Rondot denied that he had been asked specifically to investigate Sarkozy.) In mid-May de Villepin admitted that he had been made aware of the allegations in January 2004 and had ordered the intelligence services to investigate, but denied any wrongdoing. Later in May 2006 magistrates investigating the source of the falsified documents interviewed Sarkozy, whose supporters claimed that de Villepin had ordered the 2004 investigation in an attempt to discredit his rival and called for him to resign as Prime Minister. As the scandal threatened to precipitate the collapse of the Government, it was revealed that Alliot-Marie had ordered a separate investigation into Clearstream, although she insisted that this related solely to allegations made against Ministry of Defence personnel. In mid-May 2006 de Villepin comfortably survived a vote of confidence in the Assemblée nationale, which had been proposed by the PS and supported by the UDF. Nevertheless, the investigation into Clearstream continued in late 2006: in December de Villepin was questioned by magistrates as a witness. De Villepin's defeat over the CPE, his controversial opposition to the proposed merger of Gaz de France with the Suez energy group (see Economic Affairs) and the continuing investigation into Clearstream adversely affected his chances of winning the candidacy of the UMP for the 2007 presidential election and highlighted divisions within the party.

In January 2007 members of the UMP elected Sarkozy unopposed as the party's candidate for the presidency, although only 69% of party members cast a vote. Despite his endorsement by members of the UMP, de Villepin and Chirac declined publicly to declare their support for Sarkozy, whose programme promised a break with the policies of Chirac and combined an agenda of liberal economic reforms and protectionism with authoritarian policies on immigration and law and order. In early March Chirac, as expected, announced that he would retire from politics after the presidential election, but did not endorse Sarkozy's candidacy until two weeks later. On 26 March Sarkozy resigned from the Government, along with the Minister of Health and Social Protection, Xavier Bertrand, who was to manage Sarkozy's electoral campaign. Some opponents had criticized Sarkozy for reneging on an earlier promise to resign from the Government by the end of 2006, not least because the Ministry of the Interior and Land Management was responsible for the conduct of elections in France.

By mid-2006, meanwhile, the President of the Poitou-Charentes Regional Council and partner of Hollande, Ségolène Royal, had emerged as the leading contender for the presidential candidacy of the PS. Opinion polls at that time indicated that the level of support for Royal was equal to that for Sarkozy. In June Royal's criticism of some previously entrenched PS policies, including the 35-hour working week, and her apparent authoritarian stance on law and order caused left-wing rivals to portray her views as similar to those of Sarkozy. Despite her clear advantage in opinion polls, her eventual success was uncertain, with a number of senior PS politicians—including Jospin—expected to enter the contest. In late September Royal and Dominique Strauss-Kahn (Minister of the Economy, Finance and Industry in 1997–99) officially declared their candidacies for the contest (joining Fabius, who had done so in January). Jospin, however, had announced the previous day that he did not intend to contest the ballot. Following a series of debates between the three declared contenders, the PS held a congress in Paris in late November, at which party members elected Royal as their presidential candidate, with 60.6% of the votes cast, compared with 20.8% for Strauss-Kahn and 18.5% for Fabius. In February the PS published a document containing 100 proposals, which many observers regarded as an attempt to appeal to the left wing of the party; the proposals included an increased minimum wage, greater provision of social housing and the merger of EdF and Gaz de France under state ownership. However, during early 2007 Royal suffered a decline in public support, in favour of the UDF candidate, François Bayrou, who presented a centrist programme in an attempt to attract votes from supporters of both the PS and the UMP.

The first round of the presidential election, held on 22 April 2007, was contested by 12 candidates. Sarkozy and Royal progressed to the second round of voting, winning 31.2% and 25.9% of the valid votes cast, respectively. Bayrou won 18.6% of the vote, while Le Pen suffered a significant decline in support compared with 2002, winning only 10.4%. The rate of participation in the election was high, at 83.8% of eligible voters. At the second round of the election, held on 6 May, Sarkozy was elected to succeed Chirac as President, securing 53.1% of the valid votes cast.

Sarkozy formally acceded to the presidency on 16 May 2007, and on the following day the composition of a new Council of Ministers was announced. François Fillon, a close adviser of the President, who had been Minister of National Education, Higher Education and Research in 2004–05, was appointed Prime Minister, while Juppé returned to government office as Minister of State, Minister of Ecology and Sustainable Development. Honouring his campaign pledges to reduce expenditure on public services and address the gender imbalance in French government, Sarkozy significantly reduced the number of cabinet positions to 15, of which seven were allocated to women. The new Council of Ministers also included prominent figures from across the political divide, in an attempt to accord the Government greater political legitimacy in its implementation of radical reforms. Bernard Kouchner, a member of Royal's presidential campaign team, a former minister under Jospin and co-founder of the charity Médecins sans Frontières, was appointed Minister of Foreign and European Affairs, while Hervé Morin, a member of Bayrou's UDF, was allocated the defence portfolio. Among other notable appointments were those of Borloo as Minister of the Economy, Finance and Employment, Alliot-Marie as Minister of the Interior, the Overseas Possessions and Territorial Collectivities and Rachida Dati as Minister of Justice, the first member of an ethnic minority to hold a senior ministerial position in France.

At elections to the Assemblée nationale, held on 10 and 17 June 2007, the UMP remained the largest party in the legislature, but with a reduced majority, winning 313 of 577 seats. The PS, which was in disarray following the loss of the presidential election and the defection of Kouchner, confounded many observers by improving upon a poor performance in the first round of voting, taking a total of 186 seats. Prior to the elections the UDF was restyled the Mouvement Démocrate (MoDem) by its leader, Bayrou, in order to oppose the UMP, while former members of the UDF allied to the President formed a new party, the Nouveau Centre. In the event the Nouveau Centre won 22 seats, while Bayrou's MoDem won just three seats. Following the election Fillon announced the resignation of the Council of Ministers, in response to the relatively disappointing performance of the UMP. Sarkozy reappointed Fillon as Prime Minister and effected a government reorganization. Borloo assumed the role vacated by Juppé, who failed to win re-election to the Assemblée, and Borloo was, in turn, replaced as Minister of the Economy, Finance and Employment by Christine Lagarde (hitherto Minister of Agriculture and Fisheries). Barnier returned to government office, replacing Lagarde in her previous role. The policy of inclusion toward the left was renewed, with the appointment as Ministers-Delegate of a number of figures previously associated with the PS.

Investigations into allegations of wrongdoing on the part of members of the previous administration continued. In July 2007 Chirac (having lost his right to immunity from prosecution following the end of his presidency) was questioned by magistrates over his alleged involvement in the payment of wages to RPR supporters under false pretences during his tenure as Mayor of Paris, while later that month de Villepin was placed under formal investigation by magistrates leading inquiries into the Clearstream affair. In late November Chirac was himself placed under formal investigation with regard to a separate inquiry into financial irregularities during his mayoralty of the capital; he denied any wrongdoing.

In August 2007 Parliament approved government proposals regarding greater autonomy for universities, increased penalties for serial criminal offenders, restrictions on industrial action in the public transport sector and reductions in the level of taxation, all of which had been promised by Sarkozy during the presidential election campaign. However, some observers and supporters of the UMP criticized the Government, accusing it of reneging on promises to reduce by one-half the number of civil servants employed by the state and to introduce measures to decrease the budget deficit. In September the Prime Minister announced the abolition of long-standing agreements over favourable pension rights for public sector workers, prompting criticism from trade union leaders, who organized a 'day of action' in protest at the plans in October. Later that month six trade unions representing railway workers announced that indefinite industrial action in protest at the reforms was to begin in November; unions representing workers in the energy sector subsequently announced their intention to hold a concurrent strike. A nation-wide strike duly commenced on 13 November and continued for a further nine days, while a separate, unrelated strike by teachers, postal workers and other public sector employees took place on 20 November. Talks between trade union leaders and the Government continued, and on 22 November trade union members voted to end the strike: the vote was widely regarded as a victory for Sarkozy. However, opponents of the Government suggested that concessions given by the Government during the negotiations would, in fact, negate the short-term effect on the economy of removing the special pension rights.

In October 2007 new legislation increasing restrictions on immigration was approved by Parliament, despite opposition from the PS, the MoDem and a minority of UMP parliamentarians. The legislation provided for the evaluation of individual immigrants' knowledge of French language and culture, compulsory courses for parents of children who had entered the country as immigrants and the compilation of population statistics based on ethnicity. Opposition to the legislation, however, focused on the provision for voluntary DNA testing of immigrants from non-EU countries who were suspected of falsely claiming to have a relative resident in France. The measure provoked an angry response from the Minister-Delegate for Urban Policy, Fadela Amara, and prompted the PS to refer the proposed legislation to the Constitutional Council (Conseil Constitutionnel). In mid-November the Constitutional Council approved the provision on DNA testing, but declared the compilation of population statistics by ethnicity to be unconstitutional. Later that month three days of rioting occurred in the suburbs of Paris, in response to the death of two Muslim youths on motorcycles in a collision with a police vehicle. Sarkozy condemned the violence of the rioters, which resulted in serious injuries for several police officers, and the Government ordered an inquiry into the disputed deaths of the youths.

In December 2007 the trial of the FN leader, Le Pen, commenced in Paris. He had been charged with conspiring to justify war crimes and denial of crimes against humanity, following comments he had made regarding the occupation of France by German forces in 1940–44 during an interview in a far-right periodical in 2005. In February 2008 he was convicted on both charges and received a three-month suspended prison sentence and a fine of €10,000.

During late 2007 President Sarkozy was the subject of intense criticism as media coverage of his presidency focused increasingly upon his private affairs. In October 2007 it was announced that Sarkozy was to separate from his wife. Sarkozy's prominence in the media increased further in December, when it was revealed that he was in a relationship with a singer and former fashion model, Carla Bruni, whom he married in February 2008. Opinion polls suggested that Sarkozy had suffered a significant decline in popularity among the electorate by early 2008, partly as a result of the perception that he had invited the frequent media coverage of his relationship with Bruni, thus ending a tradition of discretion in the French media regarding the private lives of politicians. Disaffection with Sarkozy may have contributed to the UMP's poor performance at municipal elections on 9 and 16 March; the PS won the largest share of the votes cast and gained control of several large city administrations from the UMP, including Toulouse and Strasbourg. Following the elections a limited cabinet reshuffle took place, principally involving changes of personnel in the less senior ministerial positions and minor changes of attribution in the more senior posts.

Demands for the independence of Corsica increased markedly during the 1960s and 1970s, with particular discontent being expressed at the resettlement there of French citizens displaced from Algeria following its independence in 1962. In 1972 the status of Corsica was upgraded to that of a province, administered by a centrally appointed préfet. (It had hitherto formed an administrative department within the province of Provence-Alpes-Côte d'Azur.) The assassination of two gendarmes at Aléria, in eastern Corsica, in August 1975, marked a significant escalation in the campaign for Corsican independence; from 1976 the clandestine Fronte di Liberazione Naziunale di a Corsica (FLNC) was regarded as the leading pro-independence organization. Also in 1976 the Government, led by the Prime Minister, Chirac, subdivided the province of Corsica into two departments, Corse-du-Sud and Haute-Corse. However, demands for greater autonomy or independence persisted, with intermittent bombing campaigns conducted by separatists both in Corsica and in continental France. As a result of decentralization legislation of 1982, the status of Corsica was elevated to that of a 'collectivité territoriale' (territorial collectivity), with its own directly elected 61-seat assembly, and an administration with augmented executive powers. In April 1991 the Assemblée nationale adopted legislation that granted greater autonomy to Corsica; a seven-member executive council was to be formed, chosen from a 51-member Assemblée de Corse, which would be elected in 1992. In early February 1998, in the most serious act of violence committed by separatist militants to date, the Préfet of Corsica, Claude Erignac, was assassinated. The killing was condemned by the FLNC. In June 2003 the trial of eight suspected accomplices in the assassination of Erignac commenced in Paris, although the primary suspect, Yvan Colonna, remained in hiding. In July all eight received custodial sentences; two of the accused received life sentences, and two others, Jean Castela and Vincent Andriuzzi, who were accused of orchestrating the murder, were sentenced to 30 years' imprisonment. (Castela and Andriuzzi subsequently appealed against their convictions, and were acquitted in February 2006.) Meanwhile, in July 2003 Colonna was captured in southern Corsica and arrested; he was transferred to Paris later in the month, and placed under judicial investigation on suspicion of murder and association with a terrorist organization, although he denied having killed Erignac. The trial of Colonna commenced in November 2007. In mid-December he was convicted of murder and sentenced to life imprisonment; he subsequently announced that he would appeal against the decision.

An arson attack on a bar in the regional capital, Ajaccio, in April 1999 led to the arrest and dismissal of the Préfet, Bernard Bonnet, and the disbandment of the security unit that had been established after the murder of Erignac. Bonnet's arrest was made in response to allegations that the head of the unit, Henri Mazères, had ordered the attack on the bar; Bonnet, Mazères and an aide, Gerard Pardini, received custodial sentences in January 2002 for ordering the arson attacks, although Bonnet denied any involvement and announced that he would appeal. (Bonnet's sentence was upheld at the appeal, which concluded in Bastia in January 2003.)

Meanwhile, negotiations, supported by the Prime Minister, Jospin, that involved the Government and representatives of Corsica commenced in Paris in December 1999. Four groups of Corsican militants called an unconditional cease-fire, and pledged to disarm should their aims, including the recognition of the Corsican people as a nation, and the granting of official status to the Corsican language on the island, be achieved. The peace process resulted in agreement on a number of proposals known as the Matignon Accords. In July 2000 the proposals were approved in the Assemblée de Corse by an overwhelming majority. Under the proposals, subject to the maintenance of peace on Corsica, and the approval of the Assemblée nationale, a referendum would be held on eventual revisions to the Constitution in 2004, prior to the introduction of a single political and administrative body for the island with formal, but limited, legislative powers, replacing the two existing administrative departments. The proposals also provided for instruction in the Corsican language to take place in all primary schools. The proposals provoked the resignation of the Minister of the Interior, Chevènement, while President Chirac and other leading figures in the RPR also expressed their opposition to this proposed act of decentralization. Although most dissident groups maintained a cease-fire following the signature of the Accords, increasing concern was expressed at the prevalence of organized crime in Corsica, while sporadic, low-level attacks by dissident groups continued. On 22 May 2001 the Assemblée nationale approved a more moderate version of the bill to amend the status of Corsica, with a view to presenting a text that would be acceptable to the Constitutional Council; consequently, Corsican language instruction at primary schools was to be optional, rather than compulsory, and the French Parliament would be required to pass enabling legislation before local legislation approved by the Assemblée de Corse could take effect. Corsican separatists expressed disapproval of the amendments. By September the process envisaged by the Accords appeared to be stalling; the moderate nationalist leader, Jean-Guy Talamoni, who had been involved in negotiating the Accords, announced that the moderate separatist Corsica Nazione had decided, by an almost unanimous vote of its militants and representatives, to withdraw from the provisions of the Accords. The final bill on greater autonomy, which had been subject to further amendments, had, none the less, received the approval of both legislative houses by mid-December. The Gaullist parties, which generally opposed the legislation, announced that they would bring the bill before the Constitutional Council. In January 2002 the Constitutional Council ruled that the section of the bill that permitted the Assemblée de Corse to amend national legislation on the island was illegitimate, although the section of the law that permitted the optional use of Corsican language in primary schools was approved.

Following the defeat of Jospin in the first round of the presidential election in April 2002, and a statement by Chirac to the effect that Corsican aspirations for greater autonomy were insignificant, nationalists on the island announced their withdrawal from the Matignon process. In early May the FLNC-Union des Combatants (FLNC-UDC—as the main faction of the organization was now known) announced that it was to resume its dissident campaign, although the group stated its preference for a negotiated settlement. In June the new centre-right Government unexpectedly announced that it was to seek several amendments to the Constitution that would permit the eventual decentralization of a number of powers, and that, moreover, Corsica would be one region which could be expected to be affected by these measures. In July Sarkozy visited Corsica, where he spoke to the Assemblée de Corse and announced their efforts to relaunch a dialogue with nationalists. Following the generally positive reception of these efforts, Raffarin also travelled to the island. However, amid scepticism regarding the Government's intentions, the number of small-scale bomb attacks on the island increased sharply in 2002, to reach the highest annual total recorded (in excess of 220) since 1997. In February 2003 the Assemblée de Corse voted in favour of a proposal, supported by Sarkozy, whereby the two administrative departments in Corsica were to be replaced by a single collectivité, subject to the approval of these measures by a referendum to be held in Corsica. Following the approval, on 17 March, by the Assemblée nationale of various constitutional changes that permitted, *inter alia*, local referendums, it was announced that such a plebiscite was to be held in July on the future administrative structure of the island. Although several separatist groups, including the FLNC-UDC, Corsica Nazione, and the political wing of the FLNC-UDC, Indipendenza, announced their support for the proposals, other more radical groups expressed concern that plans to devolve limited legislative and additional tax-raising powers to the new collectivité, which had been included in the Matignon Accords, had not been revived. At the referendum, held on 6 July, the proposal was defeated, with 51.0% of the votes against the restructuring. A relatively high turn-out of 60.5% was recorded.

Following the defeat of the Government's proposals for restructuring the administration of Corsica, there was an escalation of violence by Corsican separatist groups, both in Corsica and in continental France; in late July 2003 two bombs exploded in Nice, injuring 16 people. The FLNC-UDC, which had announced that it was to end its cease-fire earlier in the month, claimed responsibility for these attacks and for a series of bombings in Corsica; a more militant separatist faction, known as the FLNC des anonymes, also ended its cease-fire and announced its merger with the FLNC-UDC. Moreover, in mid-July deputies of Corsica Nazione announced that they were to suspend participation in the Assemblée de Corse, in protest against the verdict of the trial of the eight accomplices in the murder of Erignac. Corsica Nazione also announced that it was to appeal to the Council of State against the result of the referendum, citing instances of alleged electoral fraud. In mid-September the nationalist deputies resumed their duties at the Assemblée de Corse, and in mid-October the Council of State ruled that, despite having found evidence of some irregularities, the result of the referendum was valid. In late September Sarkozy made his 10th visit as Minister of the Interior, Interior Security and Local Freedoms to Corsica, when he announced that any reopening of the question of constitutional reform with regard to the island was likely to prove counter-productive, and instead announced that measures to combat widespread violence, terrorism and organized crime on Corsica would now be a priority of the Government. However, the incidence of bombings and other attacks accelerated in 2004, despite the FLNC-UDC's reiteration in May of its commitment to the unconditional cease-fire. From January to July there were more than 90 bombings and other attacks recorded, with one-third of these attacks on North African Muslims, most of which were claimed by the Clandestini Corsi group. In October 2006 the 12 members of Clandestini Corsi received prison sentences of between six months and seven years for their role in seven attacks against North African Muslims during January-July 2004. A militant group opposed to the FLNC-UDC cease-fire, the Armata di u Populu Corsu (Corsican People's Army—APC), which claimed responsibility for a number of attacks in Corsica in July and August 2006, also claimed responsibility for a bomb attack in Bordeaux in mainland France in October and issued a warning in November that attacks would escalate if demands for the transfer of Corsican nationalist prisoners from mainland France to the island were not met. (De Villepin had announced in June the construction of a new prison in Corsica to accommodate such prisoners and Clandestini Corsi had declared an unconditional cease-fire in September in order to facilitate their transfer.)

In March 2005 the trial began in Paris of Charles Pieri, a key figure in the FLNC-UDC, which consequently called off its cease-fire. Pieri and more than 20 of his associates were accused of extortion, misappropriation of funds, financing terrorism and associating with criminals for a terrorist enterprise. A bomb attack outside a government building in Ajaccio, in which five people were injured, coincided with the first day of the trial. Pieri was sentenced to 10 years' imprisonment in May. (His appeal against his sentence was overturned in December.) In June, while Unione Naziunale (a coalition of separatist parties, including Corsica Nazione) expressed its desire to reopen dialogue and to seek a compromise with its opponents, the FLNC-UDC announced its responsibility for 21 recent attacks. In late September some 30 members of the Syndicat des Travailleurs Corses (Union of Corsican Workers) in Marseille commandeered a ferry belonging to the Société Nationale Maritime Corse-Méditerranée (SNCM) to protest at that company's proposed privatization. On the following day the sailors were arrested by a helicopter-borne specialist anti-terrorism unit. The scale of the police operation gave rise to violent demonstrations in Bastia and Ajaccio, and the closure of ports in both towns and of the airport in Ajaccio. The blockade was temporarily lifted for two days in early October, to allow some 7,000 stranded tourists to leave the island, but industrial action continued until mid-October, when a negotiated settlement was reached, under which 25% of SNCM would be retained by the Government and a 9% share would be allocated to SNCM employees, with the combined stake amounting to a blocking minority. Militant activity in Corsica continued throughout 2006, with the FLNC-UDC claiming responsibility in January, and again in October, for a series of attacks, primarily targeting public services and holiday homes. In early August a previously unknown group, Clandestini Ribelli, claimed responsibility for an armed attack on a government building in Ajaccio; in a letter published by a local newspaper following the attack, the group warned of further attacks against both French interests and elected officials in Corsica. Later that month an alleged member of Clandestini Ribelli, Jean-Baptiste Andreani, was arrested in connection with the attack and was transferred to Paris, where he was placed under judicial investigation.

In January 2007 a separatist militant, Ange-Marie Tiberi (who was later revealed to be a member of the FLNC-UDC), was killed in Ajaccio when an explosive device he was carrying detonated before reaching its intended target. On 2 May the trial began in Paris of 17 members of FLNC des anonymes, who were accused of perpetrating a series of bombings in Corsica during 2001–02. However, charges against two of those accused were subsequently withdrawn. At the end of May 13 of the remaining defendants were convicted and received sentences of between one and 11 years' imprisonment, while the apparent leader of FLNC des Anonymes, Antoine Marchini, was sentenced to 12 years' imprisonment for his role in the attacks; the remaining defendant was acquitted. In December militants carried out a series of bombings on the island, following the conviction of Colonna (see above) and the arrest of 13 members of Corsica Nazione suspected of involvement in bomb attacks carried out in 2006–07.

The political situation in Corsica remained tense in early 2008. In January around 500 protesters occupied the Assemblée de Corse in Ajaccio after a demonstration led by nationalist groups and trade unions. During the occupation offices within the Assemblée building were set on fire. Later that month five people were arrested in connection with the arson attack on the Assemblée and placed under judicial investigation. The initial judicial hearing at a court in Ajaccio was marked by violent clashes between separatist protesters and police in the regional capital and in Bastia.

In June 1995 Chirac announced that France was to end a moratorium on nuclear testing imposed by Mitterrand in 1992. Six tests were subsequently conducted in French Polynesia, in the Pacific Ocean. The announcement caused widespread outrage in the international community.

In November 1998, following a lengthy campaign for the independence of the Pacific overseas territory of New Caledonia (see p. 1883) by indigenous Melanesian (Kanak) separatists, a referendum on self-determination was held in the territory. At the referendum a gradual transfer of powers to local institutions was approved, and the Republican Constitution was amended accordingly. Further enabling legislation was approved by Parliament in February 1999, and certain powers were transferred to local institutions in 2000. Notably, the constitutional amendments approved in March 2003 that sought to permit other communities eventually to gain increased autonomy were not to apply to New Caledonia.

France granted independence to most of its former colonies after the Second World War. In Indo-China, after prolonged fighting, Laos, Cambodia and Viet Nam became fully independent in 1954. In Africa most of the French colonies in the West and Equatorial regions attained independence in 1960, but, with the notable exception of Guinea, retained their close economic and political ties with France, particularly within the framework of the Franc Zone (see p. 306). From the second half of the 1990s France has been active in promoting the establishment of regional peace-keeping forces in Africa.

In the early 1990s French troops were dispatched to Rwanda to train forces of the Rwandan Government and to supply military equipment, following the outbreak of armed conflict between the Government and the opposition Front patriotique rwandais (FPR, or Inkotanyi). In April 1994 French troops re-entered Rwanda to establish a 'safe humanitarian zone' for refugees fleeing the civil war. Although France declared its presence to be restricted to a transitional period prior to the arrival of UN peace-keeping forces, the FPR accused France of using the operation secretly to transport alleged war criminals out of the country. Evidence emerged in early 1998 that appeared to support allegations that France had sold arms to Rwanda during the massacres in 1994 (after the imposition of a UN embargo on the delivery of military equipment to any party in the conflict). However, a commission of inquiry, subsequently established to investigate the affair, effectively exonerated France, but blamed the international community, and particularly the USA, for failing to provide adequate support for UN forces in the country. The Rwandan Government rejected these findings. Relations between the two countries further deteriorated in late 2006, following the decision in November by a French magistrate to issue arrest warrants for nine senior Rwandan military and government officials on suspicion of involvement in the killing in 1994 of the former Rwandan President, Juvénal Habyarimana. The magistrate also alleged that the Rwandan President, Paul Kagame, had ordered the missile attack in which Habyarimana was killed; however, under French law, as a head of state, Kagame was immune from prosecution. The Rwandan Government denied the allegations, and accused France of attempting to undermine and, ultimately, overthrow it. Rwanda subsequently severed all relations with France: the French ambassador in Kigali was ordered to leave the country within 24 hours and all French aid projects in the country were required to cease operations within 72 hours. In January 2008 the French Minister of Foreign and European Affairs, Kouchner, visited the Rwandan capital for talks with Kagame in an attempt to improve relations between the two countries (although full diplomatic relations had yet to be restored by March 2008).

From late 2002 more than 3,000 French troops were dispatched to Côte d'Ivoire to assist the 550 French troops already based there, initially to protect French citizens resident in the country from civil unrest that erupted in September, and subsequently to monitor a cease-fire, agreed in mid-October, between Ivorian government troops and rebel forces in the north of the country; the troops were subsequently granted authority to enforce the cease-fire, and also that signed with other rebel groups in the west. Following the recommencement of military operations by Ivorian government forces against the rebel-controlled north in November 2004, nine French troops were killed during an air strike on 6 November. The French military, acting on the direct orders of President Chirac, responded by disabling the Ivorian air force on the ground. France's perceived intervention in the conflict provoked riots and protests in the principal city, Abidjan, and elsewhere, and numerous attacks occurred against French civilians and targets. French troops entered Abidjan to secure the international airport and protect French and other foreign citizens, airlifting an estimated 9,000 people out of the city. (The French Government subsequently admitted that its forces had killed some 20 Ivorian civilians during clashes with rioters; the Ivorian authorities claimed the number was significantly higher.) Some 600 troops were subsequently flown in to reinforce the French military presence in Côte d'Ivoire, while diplomatic relations between the two countries remained tense. France was instrumental in drafting a series of arms embargoes imposed on Côte d'Ivoire by the UN in late 2004 and early 2005, which, *inter alia*, granted French and UN troops the power to search vehicles and containers at borders and ports.

In February 2008 President Sarkozy travelled to several countries in Africa for a series of state visits. Sarkozy used the visits to signal his intention to transform relations between France and its allies in Africa. During an address to members of the South African National Assembly on 28 February, Sarkozy announced that France was to renegotiate its bilateral defence agreements with African countries, including those in which French troops were present.

In September 1994, following the killing of five officials at the French embassy in Algiers, Algeria, the French Government initiated an extensive security operation, the results of which included the detention and subsequent expulsion from France of a number of alleged Islamist activists. In December members of the French security forces killed four Islamist militants on board an Air France aircraft, which had been hijacked in Algiers and flown to Marseille. The following day four Roman Catholic priests, three of them French citizens, were killed in Algeria, in apparent reprisal. Eight people were killed in the second half of 1995 in a series of bombings in France, for which the Algerian Groupe islamique armé (GIA) was widely believed to be responsible. In 1998 36 militant Islamists received custodial sentences in France for providing logistical support to the GIA, and in late 1999 a further 24 militants were found guilty of involvement in the bombing campaign. Meanwhile, in December 1996 four people were killed and up to 100 injured in an explosion, which was attributed to Islamist militants, on a commuter train in Paris. In that month the GIA warned that it would continue its campaign of violence in France, unless the French Government undertook to sever ties with the Algerian Government. However, ongoing diplomatic contacts resulted in the reopening of a number of French consulates in Algeria, and in the state visit of the Algerian President, Abdelaziz Bouteflika, to Paris in May 2000, and a reciprocal visit by the French Minister of Foreign Affairs, Hubert Védrine, to Algiers in February 2001. Chirac visited Algeria in December 2001, and following a further improvement in relations between the two countries, the Algerian Prime Minister, Ali Benflis, visited Paris in January 2003. Moreover, in March Chirac became the first French President to participate in an official state visit to Algeria since 1962, and Chirac and Bouteflika signed a declaration providing for increased economic and cultural co-operation between the countries. Despite the complex historical relationship between France and Algeria, and ongoing unrest in that country, Chirac's visit was reportedly widely welcomed in Algeria, in particular as a consequence of Chirac's opposition to US-led military action in Iraq that commenced in that month. In April 2004 Chirac became the first foreign Head of State to visit Algeria following Bouteflika's re-election as President, and during a visit in July by the Minister of Foreign Affairs, Barnier, it was announced that a treaty of friendship between the two states would be concluded in 2005 (although no such treaty had been signed by March 2008). President Bouteflika was present at a ceremony in August 2004 commemorating the 60th anniversary of the Provence landings during the Second World War, which had been orchestrated from Algiers and involved the participation of numerous Algerians. In December 2005 an Algerian man, Rachid Ramda, was extradited to France from the United Kingdom and placed under judicial investigation, accused of perpetrating the 1995 bomb attacks in Paris. In July 2007 Sarkozy visited Algeria for the first time since becoming President in May. During the visit, Sarkozy reiterated his opposition to the proposed treaty of friendship, stating his preference for active co-operation between the two countries. Sarkozy returned to Algeria on 3 December for an official state visit, during which he signed several bilateral agreements with Bouteflika, most notably regarding the development of civil nuclear technology in Algeria. Meanwhile, the trial of Rachid Ramda commenced at a court in Paris in early October. At the end of that month Ramda was convicted both of murder and attempted murder, in relation to the 1995 bombings, and was sentenced to life imprisonment.

France's relations with the USA have frequently been characterized by a desire to establish French independence of action, particularly with regard to military concerns and international relations. In 1966 de Gaulle ordered the withdrawal of France from the integrated military structure of NATO. Although France's eventual re-entry into the integrated military command of the alliance was announced in 1995, the measure has been delayed by the French insistence that NATO troops in southern Europe be under the command of a European officer; moreover, France was to retain control of its nuclear forces. France was a participant, alongside the USA and the United Kingdom, in maintaining a 'no-fly' zone in southern Iraq following the conclusion of the Persian (Arabian) Gulf war in 1991, but withdrew from these duties in December 1998 and criticized aerial raids on Iraq by US and British forces in February 2001. In that month France also announced that it was opposed to the continuation of UN sanctions against Iraq implemented in connection with that country's alleged possession of weapons of mass destruction. In June France recommended to the UN Security Council that foreign investment be permitted in the Iraqi petroleum industry, but, none the less, declared its full support for the 'smart sanctions' proposed by the USA and the United Kingdom at this time. In the aftermath of the attacks in New York and Washington, DC, attributed to the militant Islamist al-Qa'ida (Base) organization, on 11 September 2001, France offered full military and logistical support to the USA, including the dispatch to Afghanistan of marines, engineers and members of the Special Forces, in its campaign against al-Qa'ida. However, France remained a prominent critic of several aspects of the foreign policy of the Administration of the US President, George W. Bush. Although France supported the UN Security Council Resolution 1441 (presented by the USA and the United Kingdom) in November 2002, which demanded the expedited admittance of UN weapons inspectors to Iraq, the French Minister of Foreign Affairs, de Villepin, maintained opposition to any UN Security Council resolution that would authorize any automatic resort to force against Iraq. Moreover, as Spain, the USA and the United Kingdom sought to gain support for a further UN Security Council resolution regarding Iraq's non-compliance with the requirements of Resolution 1441, in March 2003, President Chirac reiterated that France would, at that stage, veto any resolution that would have the effect of legitimizing military action against that country, and was a prominent opponent of the US-led military action that commenced later that month. However, following the conclusion of large-scale hostilities in Iraq, France gave full support to UN Security Council Resolution 1483, approved in late May, which recognized the Coalition Provisional Authority as the legal occupying power in Iraq. The election of Sarkozy as President in May 2007 precipitated a significant improvement in relations between France and the USA. Sarkozy held his first meeting with President Bush in Maine, USA, in August, at which he expressed his intention to establish closer relations between the two countries. In early November Sarkozy returned to the USA for a two-day visit, during which he addressed the US Congress and indicated that France would eventually rejoin NATO's integrated military command, following further progress on a European defence capability.

One of the priorities of French foreign policy under the presidency of Sarkozy was to secure an increased role for France in the Middle East. In August 2007 Kouchner visited Iraq, thus becoming the first French minister responsible for foreign affairs to do so since 2003. Later that month Sarkozy used his first major speech on foreign policy to reiterate his opposition to Iran's nuclear enrichment programme, which many governments in developed countries feared was intended to facilitate the development of an Iranian nuclear force. In December 2007 Sarkozy announced that France was to suspend diplomatic relations with Syria, accusing the Syrian Government of obstructing international efforts to achieve a consensus regarding the appointment of a new President in Lebanon, while also demanding Syria's co-operation regarding the formation of an international tribunal to investigate the assassination, in 2005, of the former Lebanese Prime Minister, Rafik Hariri. However, Syria reacted unfavourably to Sarkozy's intervention and suspended all co-operation with France over Lebanon. During a visit to the Persian (Arabian) Gulf area in January 2008, Sarkozy announced that France was to establish a permanent military base in Abu Dhabi, the United Arab Emirates (UAE), which was scheduled to be operational by 2009. The President also signed an agreement with the UAE, under which France was to assist the development of a programme to produce nuclear energy in that country.

Initiatives by President Sarkozy to establish closer diplomatic and economic relations with Libya provoked widespread criticism. In July 2007 Sarkozy travelled to Libya for an official state visit, during which he signed an agreement on defence co-operation and a memorandum of understanding over the development of civil nuclear technology in Libya. The visit followed a separate trip to Libya by the President's then wife, Cécilia Sarkozy, who had held discussions with the Libyan leader, Col Muammar al-Qaddafi, in an attempt to secure the release from prison of five Bulgarian nationals and a Palestinian who had been sentenced to death for deliberately infecting more than 400 Libyan children with blood containing HIV. (The veracity of the charges was strongly disputed by, among others, Bulgaria, the European Union and the USA.) Qaddafi subsequently released the six prisoners. A state visit to France in December by Qaddafi provoked criticism both from opposition figures and from some politicians aligned with the Government, notably the French Minister-Delegate for Foreign Affairs and Human Rights, Rama Yade. The critics of the visit condemned the human rights record of Qaddafi's regime; the PS and a number of UMP parliamentarians refused to attend a meeting between Qaddafi and members of the Assemblée nationale. Qaddafi and Sarkozy signed several agreements during the visit, including, most controversially, contracts for the sale of military equipment to Libya and a further agreement on nuclear energy.

In May 1992 France and Germany announced that they would establish a joint defence force of 50,000 troops, the 'Eurocorps', which was intended to provide a basis for a European army under the aegis of Western European Union (WEU, see p. 426), and which became operational in November 1995. Belgium, Spain and Luxembourg also agreed to participate in the force. In January 1993 an agreement was signed between NATO and the French and German Governments, establishing formal links between the corps and NATO's military structure. In late 2000 it was announced that France would contribute 12,000 troops, of a total of more than 60,000 that would form a European rapid reaction force, to participate in peace-keeping missions from 2003. Proposals for a new autonomous European military command headquarters near Brussels, with the capacity to plan and execute European operations autonomously, were put forward by Belgium, France, Germany and Luxembourg, following a meeting in Brussels at the end of April 2003. The proposal was opposed by several EU states, notably the United Kingdom, which feared that NATO would be undermined. A compromise was reached in December, under which a small cell of planning staff would be created, situated in NATO's military headquarters in Belgium, which would only be used if NATO declined involvement and national European headquarters needed support. Under a new European plan devised to compensate for the inadequacies of the rapid reaction force, which, although theoretically declared ready for action in May 2003, in practice was adversely affected by shortfalls in equipment, a series of EU 'battlegroups' were established for deployment to crisis areas by 2007. France was the sole contributor to one battlegroup and also participated in two others, one with Belgium and one with Germany, Belgium and Luxembourg.

Following the election of Sarkozy as President in May 2007, relations between France and Germany deteriorated. The German Government expressed its opposition to several of Sarkozy's initiatives on foreign affairs, notably the negotiation of accords on nuclear energy with Libya (see above) and French plans to form a so-called Mediterranean Union, comprising the six EU member states that border the Mediterranean (Cyprus, France, Italy, Malta, Portugal and Spain) and certain littoral Middle Eastern and North African states. Germany feared that the organization would undermine the ongoing Euro-Mediterranean Partnership (the Barcelona Process—a framework launched in 1995 for co-operation between all EU member states and 10 other Mediterranean states.) However, in early March 2008, following negotiations between French and German representatives, Sarkozy and the German Chancellor, Angela Merkel, announced that an agreement had been reached, under which all EU member states would be involved in the formation of the new union, which was restyled the Union for the Mediterranean, and which was due to be inaugurated during a summit meeting in Paris on 13–14 July 2008, two weeks after France was due to assume the Presidency of the Council of the European Union. The Union would also include the 10 Mediterranean partners in the Barcelona Process, including Turkey, which agreed in March to participate, following reassurances from France that the Union would not, as originally envisaged, function as an alternative to Turkey's membership of the EU. (Sarkozy's election campaign platform had included a pledge to oppose Turkey's membership of the EU.)

Government

Under the 1958 Constitution, legislative power is held by the bicameral Parliament (Parliament), comprising a Sénat (Senate) and an Assemblée nationale (National Assembly). The Sénat currently has 331 members (304 for metropolitan France, 15 for the overseas possessions, and 12 for French nationals abroad). Election is by a system of proportional representation in those constituencies represented by four or more senators. A law approved by Parliament in July 2003 introduced a number of reforms to senatorial elections; henceforth, senators were to be elected for a term of six years, with one-half of the seats renewable every three years (compared with a term of nine years and one-third of the seats renewable every three years previously). With effect from 2010, the number of senators was to be increased to 346, and the minimum age for eligible candidates to the Sénat was to be reduced from 35 to 30 years. (The first stage of reform, whereby the number of senators increased from 321 to 331, took place at the partial senatorial elections held in September 2004.) The Assemblée nationale has 577 members, with 555 for metropolitan France and 22 for the overseas possessions.

Members of the Assemblée are elected by universal adult suffrage, under a single-member constituency system of direct election, using a second ballot if the first ballot failed to produce an absolute majority for any one candidate. The term of the Assemblée is five years, subject to dissolution. Executive power is held by the President. Since 1962 the President had been directly elected by popular vote (using two ballots if necessary) for seven years, although a constitutional amendment passed in October 2000 shortened the term of office to five years. The President appoints a Council of Ministers, headed by the Prime Minister, which administers the country and is responsible to Parliament. Under constitutional amendments and legislation instituted in 1998–2000, political parties are penalized financially if they do not ensure parity of men and women in candidatures for elections.

Metropolitan France comprises 22 administrative regions containing 96 departments. Under the decentralization law of March 1982, administrative and financial power in metropolitan France was transferred from the Préfets, who became Commissaires de la République, to locally elected departmental assemblies (Conseils généraux) and regional assemblies (Conseils régionaux). Corsica has its own directly elected legislative assembly (the Assemblée de Corse). The 12 overseas possessions comprise four Overseas Regions and Departments (régions et départements d'outre mer—French Guiana, Guadeloupe, Martinique and Réunion); six Overseas Collectivities (collectivités d'outre mer—French Polynesia, Mayotte, Saint-Barthélemy, Saint-Martin, Saint Pierre and Miquelon and the Wallis and Futuna Islands); and two other territories (the French Southern and Antarctic Territories, and New Caledonia—which has a unique status as a collectivité *sui generis*); all of which are integral parts of the French Republic.

Defence

French military policy is decided by the Supreme Defence Council. Military service was compulsory, and lasted for a period of 10 months, until November 2001, when proposals to create fully professional armed forces, which were submitted to the Assemblée nationale in 1996, took effect. As assessed at November 2007, the total active armed forces numbered 254,895, including an army of 133,500, a navy of 43,995, an air force of 63,600, central service staff numbering 5,200 and a medical corps of 8,600. In addition, there was a paramilitary gendarmerie of 199,148 and 44,465 civilian staff (army 28,500, navy 10,265 and air force 5,700). Total reserves stood at 25,350 (army 11,350; navy 6,000; air force 8,000); there were also 40,000 paramilitary reservists. Defence expenditure was budgeted at €36,200m. in 2007. Although a member of the North Atlantic Treaty Organization (NATO), France withdrew from its integrated military organization in 1966, and possesses its own nuclear weapons. In 1995 it was announced that France was to rejoin NATO's defence committee, and in 1996 President Chirac declared France's intention to rejoin NATO's integrated military command; this was reiterated by Nicolas Sarkozy, following his election as President in May 2007. By early 2008, however, there had been no firm indication as to when this latter move was likely to occur. In November 2004 the European Union (EU, see p. 244) ministers responsible for defence agreed to create 13 'battle-groups' (each numbering about 1,500 men), which could be deployed at short notice to crisis areas around the world. The EU battlegroups, two of which were to be ready for deployment at any one time, following a rotational schedule, reached full operational capacity from 1 January 2007. France was the sole contributor to one battlegroup and also participated in two others, one with Belgium and one with Germany, Belgium and Luxembourg.

Economic Affairs

In 2006, according to estimates by the World Bank, France's gross national income (GNI), measured at average 2004–06 prices, was US $2,297,748m., equivalent to $36,550 per head (or $33,740 on an international purchasing-power parity basis). During 1996–2006, it was estimated, the population increased by an average of 0.5% per year, while gross domestic product (GDP) per head increased, in real terms, by an average of 1.7% per year. Overall GDP increased, in real terms, at an average rate of 2.2% per year in 1996–2006. Real GDP increased by 2.0% in 2006.

Agriculture (including forestry and fishing) contributed 2.5% of GDP, measured in constant 2000 prices, and engaged 3.7% of the economically active population in 2006. The principal crops are wheat, sugar beet, maize and barley. Livestock, dairy products and wine are also important. In July 2005 France was fined €20m. by the European Court of Justice for flouting European Union (EU) fisheries regulations and subjected to a recurring fine of €57.8m. every six months until it complied with EU policy on conserving fish stocks. Agricultural GDP decreased, in real terms, by an average of 0.2% per year in 1996–2005; it declined by 1.9% in 2006, according to official figures.

Industry (including mining, manufacturing, construction and power) provided 22.6% of GDP, measured in constant 2000 prices, and employed 22.6% of the working population in 2006. Industrial GDP increased, in real terms, by an average of 2.1% per year during 1996–2005; according to official figures, it increased by 1.9% in 2006.

Mining and quarrying contributed 0.2% of GDP in 2001, and employed 0.3% of the working population in 1994. Petroleum and natural gas are extracted and metallic minerals, including iron ore, copper and zinc, are mined. The production of coal, an industry which used to dominate the sector, finished in April 2004 with the closure of France's last operating coal mine, at Creutzwald in Lorraine.

Manufacturing provided 13.9% of GDP in 2006, measured in constant 2000 prices, and employed 15.0% of the working population in the same year. According to the World Bank, manufacturing GDP increased, in real terms, at an average annual rate of 1.7% in 1999–2005; growth in 2005 was 1.9%.

France has only limited fossil fuel resources, and in the early 2000s was the world's largest producer of nuclear power per head of population. In 2004 nuclear power provided 79.0% of total electricity production and hydroelectric power 10.5%. In October 2004 Electricité de France (EdF) announced that construction of a new nuclear power station in Normandy would commence in 2007 at a projected cost of €3,000m. In 2006 France had 58 nuclear power stations, many of which would need to be replaced in around 2020. Imports of energy products comprised 15.0% of the value of total merchandise imports in 2006; in the early 2000s the major sources of petroleum imported to France were Saudi Arabia and Norway. In June 2005 it was announced that Cadarache in southern France would be the site for a trial reactor for the International Thermonuclear Experimental Reactor (ITER) project, a nuclear fusion experiment in which the EU was participating, together with the People's Republic of China, Japan, the Republic of Korea, Russia and the USA. The trial reactor was anticipated to begin operating in around 2016 for at least 20 years, with the aim of generating 500 MW of energy. In September 2007 agreement was reached on the terms of a merger of the private energy firm, Suez with the largely state-owned gas company, Gaz de France. The merger, which would create the third biggest utility provider in the world, was expected to be completed by June 2008.

Services accounted for 74.8% of GDP, measured in constant 2000 prices, and employed 73.8% of the working population in 2006. In the late 1990s and early 2000s France was consistently the country with the largest number of tourist visitors in the world; there were an estimated 76,001,000 tourist arrivals in 2005, and tourism receipts in that year totalled US $42,167m., according to the World Tourism Organization. The combined GDP of all service sectors increased, in real terms, at an average rate of 2.4% per year in 1996–2005; it increased by 1.9% in 2006, according to official figures.

In 2006 France recorded a trade deficit of US $37,690m. and there was a deficit of $28,310m. on the current account of the balance of payments. In 2006 the principal source of imports (providing 16.2% of the total) was Germany; other major sources were Italy (8.5%), Belgium (8.4%), Spain (6.9%), the United Kingdom (6.1%) and the USA (6.0%). Germany was also the principal market for exports in that year (accounting for 14.5% of the total); other major trading partners were Spain (9.9%), Italy (9.1%), the United Kingdom (8.5%) Belgium (7.4%) and the USA (6.9%). The EU as a whole provided 59.6% of imports in 2002 and took 62.0% of exports. The principal exports and imports in 2006 were intermediate goods, capital goods, consumer goods and motor vehicles.

The budget deficit for 2006 was equivalent to 2.4% of GDP. In 2004 gross state debt was €1,067,000m., equivalent to 64.7% of GDP. The average annual rate of inflation in 1996–2006 was 1.5%. Consumer prices increased by 2.6% in 2007. According to Eurostat, the rate of unemployment was 8.5% in January 2008.

France is a member of the EU (see p. 244), and participated in the introduction of the European single currency, the euro, on 1 January 1999. It is a member of the Organisation for Economic

Co-operation and Development (see p. 347), and presides over the Franc Zone (see p. 306).

The French economy exhibited strong growth in the late 1990s, which slowed in the early 2000s, but remained slightly higher than the euro area average. However, France was unable to benefit fully from global expansion and a cyclical recovery in Europe in 2005–06 because of weak growth in employment and productivity, resulting in a decline in GDP per head compared with the best-performing countries. France's problems included a fiscal deficit of more than 2.5% of GDP in 2006, public debt exceeding 64% of GDP, an ageing population and inflexible labour and product markets. A new labour contract adopted in 2005 applied only to small enterprises, thus failing adequately to address the effective division of the labour market into a two-tiered system of well-remunerated, highly protected, permanent jobs and poorly paid, fixed-term and temporary jobs. This situation had particularly detrimental effects on the employment prospects of the young, with youth unemployment at 21.5% at the end of 2006, compared with total unemployment of 8.6%. However, unemployment declined steadily from 2006 to early 2008. Successive privatizations in the early 2000s, including the sale of energy utilities and motorway operators, contributed to the reduction of France's fiscal deficit, which had exceeded the limit of 3.0% of national GDP permitted under the EU's Stability and Growth Pact in 2002–04, but was brought below the permitted level, at 2.7%, in 2005. Nicolas Sarkozy was elected to the presidency in May 2007, following campaign pledges to implement radical reforms of the labour laws, taxation and pension and welfare provision in order to restore the economic competitiveness of France. However, opponents subsequently criticized the President for the slow pace of reforms. Tax reforms introduced in July included tax-free status for hours worked in excess of the statutory 35-hour week, as well as other reductions in personal taxation. However, the resulting improvements to real household income were eroded by rising food and energy prices, which, in conjunction with the effects of the banking crisis in the USA, adversely affected the expected increase in consumer confidence. Conversely the resulting loss of tax revenue, with no compensatory reductions in public expenditure, led to an increase in the budget deficit to 2.7% of GDP in 2007, compared with 2.4% in 2006. The increased fiscal deficit threatened the likelihood of France achieving a balanced budget by Sarkozy's new target of 2012, which was already two years later than the eurozone deadline of 2010. GDP growth was expected to slow in 2008, as a result of the slowing of the global economy and the likely effect of the euro's appreciation on export growth.

Education

Administrative responsibility for education in France, from primary to higher levels, rests with 27 educational districts (académies). Education is compulsory and free for children aged six to 16 years. Enrolment at schools in 2005/06 included 99% of children (males 98%; females 99%) in the relevant age-group for primary education and 99% (males 98%; females 100%) for secondary education. Primary education begins at six years of age and lasts for five years. At the age of 11 all pupils enter the first cycle of the Enseignement secondaire, with a four-year general course at a junior comprehensive school (collège). At the age of 15 they may then proceed to the second cycle at a lycée, choosing a course leading to the baccalauréat examination after three years or a course leading to vocational qualifications after two or three years, with commercial, administrative or industrial options. Alongside the collèges and lycées, technical education is provided in the lycées professionnels and the lycées techniques. In 2006/07 16.8% of children attended France's 8,872 private schools, most of which are administered by the Roman Catholic Church.

Controversial legislation approved by the Assemblée nationale in March 2005 abolished, from the start of the academic year in 2006, the popular *travaux personnels encadrés*, autonomous research projects carried out across different subjects, and introduced the *tronc commun*, a minimum core curriculum that excluded artistic subjects.

The minimum qualification for entry to university is the baccalauréat and anyone possessing that qualification is entitled to receive university education. Following the implementation in April 2002 of reforms designed to simplify the degree system, there are three levels of university education. The first degree, the *licence*, is obtained after three years of study. The *master recherche* and *master professionnel* are obtained after five years of study; the *master recherche* is required for progress to the *doctorat*, while the *master professionnel* provides vocational education. The *doctorat* requires eight years' study and the submission of a thesis. Universities are complemented by the prestigious Grandes Ecoles, entry to which is by competitive examination; these institutions have traditionally supplied France's administrative élite. In July 2007 the Assemblée nationale voted to approve a government bill that aimed to give universities greater budgetary control and autonomy in the recruitment of personnel. The reforms were due to enter into effect within a period of five years. Enrolment at tertiary level in 2005/06 was equivalent to 56% of students (males 49%; females 63%) in the relevant age-group. Expenditure on education by all levels of government in 2006 totalled €121,400m. (6.8% of GDP).

Public Holidays

2008: 1 January (New Year's Day), 24 March (Easter Monday), 1 May (Labour Day and Ascension Day), 8 May (Liberation Day), 12 May (Whit Monday), 14 July (National Day, Fall of the Bastille), 15 August (Assumption), 1 November (All Saints' Day), 11 November (Armistice Day), 25 December (Christmas Day).

2009: 1 January (New Year's Day), 13 April (Easter Monday), 1 May (Labour Day), 8 May (Liberation Day), 21 May (Ascension Day), 31 May (Whit Monday), 14 July (National Day, Fall of the Bastille), 15 August (Assumption), 1 November (All Saints' Day), 11 November (Armistice Day), 25 December (Christmas Day).

Weights and Measures

The metric system is in force.

FRANCE

Statistical Survey

Unless otherwise indicated, figures in this survey refer to metropolitan France, excluding the Overseas Possessions

Source (unless otherwise stated): Institut national de la statistique et des études économiques, 18 blvd Adolphe Pinard, 75675 Paris Cedex 14; tel. 1-45-17-50-50; internet www.insee.fr.

Area and Population

AREA, POPULATION AND DENSITY

Area (sq km)	543,965*
Population (census results, *de jure*)†	
5 March 1990	56,615,155
8 March 1999‡	
Males	28,419,419
Females	30,101,269
Total	58,520,688
Population (official estimates at 1 January)	
2006	61,166,822
2007	61,538,322
2008§	61,875,822
Density (per sq km) at 1 January 2008§	113.7

* 210,026 sq miles.
† Excluding professional soldiers and military personnel outside the country with no personal residence in France.
‡ Data are provisional. The revised total is 58,518,395. Figures include double counting.
§ Provisional.

NATIONALITY OF THE POPULATION
(numbers resident in France at 1999 census, revised figures)

Country of citizenship	Population	%
France	55,257,502	94.42
Portugal	553,663	0.95
Morocco	504,096	0.86
Algeria	477,482	0.82
Turkey	208,049	0.36
Italy	201,670	0.34
Spain	161,762	0.28
Tunisia	154,356	0.26
Germany	78,381	0.31
Belgium	66,666	0.11
Yugoslavia*	50,543	0.09
Poland	33,758	0.06
Others	772,760	1.32
Total	**58,520,688**	**100.00**

* The successor states of the former Socialist Federal Republic of Yugoslavia, comprising Bosnia and Herzegovina, Croatia, the former Yugoslav republic of Macedonia, Slovenia and the Federal Republic of Yugoslavia (now Montenegro and Serbia).

REGIONS
(estimated population at 1 January 2006, rounded figures)

	Area (sq km)	Population ('000)	Density (per sq km)	Principal city
Alsace	8,280.2	1,817	219.4	Strasbourg
Aquitaine	41,308.4	3,099	75.0	Bordeaux
Auvergne	26,012.9	1,334	51.3	Clermont-Ferrand
Basse-Normandie	17,589.3	1,449	82.4	Caen
Bourgogne (Burgundy)	31,582.0	1,624	51.4	Dijon
Bretagne (Brittany)	27,207.9	3,081	113.2	Rennes
Centre	39,150.9	2,505	64.0	Orléans
Champagne–Ardenne	25,605.8	1,339	52.3	Châlons-en-Champagne
Corse (Corsica)	8,679.8	279	32.1	Ajaccio
Franche-Comté	16,202.3	1,146	70.7	Besançon
Haute-Normandie	12,317.4	1,811	147.0	Rouen
Ile-de-France	12,012.3	11,491	956.6	Paris
Languedoc-Roussillon	27,375.8	2,520	92.1	Montpellier
Limousin	16,942.3	725	42.8	Limoges
Lorraine	23,547.4	2,339	99.3	Nancy
Midi-Pyrénées	45,347.9	2,755	60.8	Toulouse
Nord-Pas-de-Calais	12,414.1	4,043	325.7	Lille
Pays de la Loire	32,081.8	3,426	106.8	Nantes
Picardie (Picardy)	19,399.5	1,886	97.2	Amiens
Poitou-Charentes	25,809.5	1,713	66.4	Poitiers
Provence-Alpes-Côte d'Azur	31,399.6	4,781	152.3	Marseille
Rhône-Alpes	43,698.2	6,005	137.4	Lyon
Total	**543,965.4**	**61,167**	**112.4**	—

PRINCIPAL TOWNS*
(population at 1999 census, revised figures)

Paris (capital)	2,125,246	Brest	149,634
Marseille (Marseilles)	798,430	Le Mans	146,105
Lyon (Lyons)	445,452	Clermont-Ferrand	137,140
Toulouse	390,350	Amiens	135,501
Nice	342,738	Aix-en-Provence	134,222
Nantes	270,251	Limoges	133,968
Strasbourg	264,115	Nîmes	133,424
Montpellier	225,392	Tours	132,820
Bordeaux	215,363	Villeurbanne	124,215
Rennes	206,229	Metz	123,776
Le Havre	190,905	Besançon	117,733
Reims (Rheims)	187,206	Caen	113,987
Lille	184,493	Orléans	113,126
Saint-Etienne	180,210	Mulhouse	110,359
Toulon	160,639	Rouen	106,592
Grenoble	153,317	Boulogne-Billancourt	106,367
Angers	151,279	Perpignan	105,115
Dijon	149,867	Nancy	103,605

* Figures refer to the population of communes (municipalities).

BIRTHS, MARRIAGES AND DEATHS*

	Registered live births		Registered marriages		Registered deaths	
	Number	Rate (per 1,000)	Number	Rate (per 1,000)	Number	Rate (per 1,000)
2000	774,782	13.1	297,922	5.0	530,864	9.0
2001	770,945	13.0	288,255	4.9	531,073	8.9
2002	761,630	12.7	279,087	4.7	535,144	9.0
2003	761,464	12.7	275,963	4.6	552,339	9.2
2004	767,816	12.7	271,598	4.5	509,429	8.4
2005	774,355	12.7	276,303	4.5	527,533	8.7
2006	796,896	13.0	267,260	4.4	516,416	8.4
2007†	783,500	12.7	260,000	4.2	516,000	8.4

* Including data for national armed forces outside the country.
† Provisional figures rounded to nearest 100.

Expectation of life (years at birth, WHO estimates): 80.4 (males 76.8; females 83.9) in 2005 (Source: WHO, *World Health Statistics*).

FRANCE

ECONOMICALLY ACTIVE POPULATION
(annual averages, '000 persons aged 15 years and over)

	2004	2005	2006
Agriculture, forestry and fishing	993	950	929
Food products, beverages and tobacco	678	678	611
Consumer goods industries	702	691	668
Automobile industry	327	333	303
Equipment goods industries	818	820	839
Intermediate goods industries	1,445	1,390	1,347
Energy	249	234	271
Construction	1,590	1,597	1,632
Commerce	3,315	3,292	3,320
Transportation	1,095	1,076	1,045
Financial activities	674	734	794
Real estate and renting activities	313	347	357
Business services	3,141	3,215	3,281
Domestic and personal services	2,142	2,127	2,193
Education, health and social work	4,625	4,702	4,828
General government and non-profit institutions serving households	2,601	2,663	2,725
Not classifiable by economic activity	77	71	31
Total employed	24,784	24,921	25,174
Unemployed	2,734	2,717	n.a.
Total labour force	27,518	27,637	n.a.
Males	14,809	14,824	n.a.
Females	12,709	12,814	n.a.

Health and Welfare

KEY INDICATORS

Total fertility rate (children per woman, 2005)	1.9
Under-5 mortality rate (per 1,000 live births, 2005)	5
HIV/AIDS (% of persons aged 15–49, 2005)	0.4
Physicians (per 1,000 head, 2004)	3.37
Hospital beds (per 1,000 head, 2004)	7.5
Health expenditure (2004): US $ per head (PPP)	3,040.1
Health expenditure (2004): % of GDP	10.5
Health expenditure (2004): public (% of total)	78.4
Human Development Index (2005): ranking	10
Human Development Index (2005): value	0.952

For sources and definitions, see explanatory note on p. vi.

Agriculture

PRINCIPAL CROPS
('000 metric tons)

	2004	2005	2006
Wheat	39,692.9	36,885.5	35,366.8
Rice (paddy)	115.1	102.3	94.8
Barley	11,031.5	10,313.4	10,412.4
Maize	16,372.0	13,687.7	12,901.8
Rye	170.8	147.3	122.0
Oats	606.0	505.2	464.2
Sorghum (excl. sorghum for forage and silage)	256.6	263.5	306.5
Buckwheat	143.9	124.2	87.0
Triticale (wheat-rye hybrid)	1,833.6	1,809.4	1,697.4
Potatoes	7,255.4	6,604.6	6,354.3
Sugar beet	30,788.3	31,149.6	29,878.8
Broad beans (dry)	364.5	372.2	290.5
Peas (dry)	1,680.8	1,331.3	1,009.6
Soybeans (Soya beans)	147.1	142.5	123.0
Sunflower seed	1,457.2	1,510.5	1,439.7
Rapeseed	3,993.5	4,532.9	4,144.5
Linseed	54.6	59.2	43.2
Cabbages and other brassicas	241.8	201.2	189.2
Artichokes	59.6	50.1	53.5
Lettuce and chicory	472.2	469.0	470.3
Spinach	110.7	117.4	114.1
Tomatoes	848.5	790.3	740.1
Cauliflowers and broccoli	418.8	375.5	362.1

—continued

	2004	2005	2006
Pumpkins, squash and gourds	178.4	167.0	173.8
Cucumbers and gherkins	135.9	134.6	128.6
Onions and shallots (green)	49.5	46.6	45.4
Onions (dry)	445.9	347.7	321.3
Leeks and other alliacious vegetables	186.5	182.9	178.6
Beans (green)	100.4	55.4	50.8
Peas (green)	364.6	359.6	353.9
String beans	364.6	359.6	353.9
Carrots and turnips	672.6	727.0	692.8
Maize (green)	521.5	496.2	464.3
Mushrooms and truffles	165.5	138.5	115.8
Chicory roots	181.2	133.4	41.0
Melons (excl. watermelons)	291.4	297.0	293.8
Apples	2,203.7	1,856.7	1,705.5
Pears	252.3	221.1	220.2
Apricots	166.1	177.0	179.6
Sweet cherries	61.7	66.1	64.7
Peaches and nectarines	396.7	399.9	400.9
Plums and sloes	229.5	209.8	230.4
Strawberries	53.5	57.6	57.2
Grapes	7,564.9	6,790.2	6,692.6
Kiwi fruit	77.8	76.6	76.2
Tobacco (leaves)	25.6	22.9	18.9

Aggregate production ('000 metric tons, may include official, semi-official or estimated data): Total cereals 70,522.6 in 2004, 64,232.3 in 2005, 61,812.7 in 2006; Total roots and tubers 7,255.4 in 2004, 6,838.1 in 2005, 6,618.9 in 2006; Total vegetables (incl. melons) 6,418.0 in 2004, 6,037.8 in 2005, 5,752.3 in 2006; Total fruits (excl. melons) 11,064.4 in 2004, 9,906.6 in 2005, 9,681.7 in 2006.

Source: FAO.

LIVESTOCK
('000 head, year ending 30 September)

	2004	2005	2006
Cattle	19,320	19,310	19,418
Pigs	15,004	14,951	14,840
Sheep	9,151	9,097	8,908
Goats	1,240	1,225	1,228
Horses	344	426	423
Asses and mules or hinnies	32*	32	32
Chickens	197,168	186,548	173,660
Ducks	22,870	22,671	22,939
Turkeys	33,648	28,533	28,332

* Unofficial figure.
Source: FAO.

LIVESTOCK PRODUCTS
('000 metric tons)

	2004	2005	2006
Cattle meat	1,565.5	1,516.9	1,473.1
Sheep meat	102.3	99.5	99.5
Pig meat	2,292.6	2,018.1	2,010.8
Chicken meat	1,106.0*	920.5	819.4
Duck meat	238.1	233.8	233.4
Turkey meat	624.4	549.6	501.1
Cows' milk	24,449.3	24,885.4	24,194.7
Sheep's milk	266.8	263.5	262.8
Goats' milk	552.3	565.1	583.2
Honey†	15.5	15.5	15.5
Hen eggs	1,040.2	n.a.	850.0
Wool: greasy†	22	22	22

* Unofficial figure.
† FAO estimates.
Source: FAO.

FRANCE

Forestry

ROUNDWOOD REMOVALS
('000 cubic metres, excluding bark)

	2004	2005	2006
Sawlogs, veneer logs and logs for sleepers	19,867	18,056	19,300
Pulpwood	10,978	9,806	10,400
Other industrial wood	444	391	440
Fuel wood	2,358	34,918	35,500
Total	33,647	63,171	65,640

Source: FAO.

SAWNWOOD PRODUCTION
('000 cubic metres, including railway sleepers)

	2004	2005	2006
Coniferous (softwood)	7,717	7,748	8,000
Broadleaved (hardwood)	2,057	1,967	1,950
Total	9,774	9,715	9,950

Source: FAO.

Fishing

('000 metric tons, live weight)

	2003	2004	2005
Capture*	638.8	594.4	562.6
Saithe (Pollock)	23.3	17.8	16.8
Atlantic herring	33.7	36.6	41.0
European pilchard (Sardine)	35.3	31.5	37.7
Skipjack tuna	58.8	59.9	58.0
Yellowfin tuna	95.7	87.5	79.9
Atlantic mackerel	28.3	24.3	19.2
Blue whiting (Poutassou)	16.1	19.5	7.2
Angler (Monk)	21.3	21.4	20.8
Aquaculture	239.8	260.7	258.4
Rainbow trout	39.4	35.3	32.4
Pacific cupped oyster	114.6	116.7	118.1
Blue mussel	48.5	67.8	66.3
Total catch*	878.6	855.1	821.0

* FAO estimates.

Note: Figures exclude aquatic plants ('000 metric tons, all capture): 69.9 in 2003; 64.7 in 2004; 76.6 in 2005. Figures also exclude coral (metric tons): 4.5 in 2003; 4.2 in 2004; 11.0 in 2005; and sponges (metric tons, FAO estimates): 1.2 in 2003; 1.0 in 2004; 0.8 in 2005. Also excluded are aquatic mammals, recorded by number rather than by weight. The number of common dolphins caught was: 62 in 2003; 94 in 2004; 70 in 2005.

Source: FAO.

Mining

('000 metric tons, unless otherwise indicated)

	2003	2004*	2005*
Hard coal	1,730	160	—
Brown coal (incl. lignite)	9	—	—
Crude petroleum ('000 barrels)	9,150	8,550	7,775
Natural gas (marketed production, million cu metres)	1,520	1,330	1,400
Silver (kilograms)*†	500	500	500
Gold (kilograms)†	1,470	1,312	—
Kaolin and kaolinitic clay‡	323	316	316
Fluorspar‡	89	90	90
Barite (Barytes)‖	81	81	81
Salt	6,673	6,910	6,730
Gypsum and anhydrite (crude)*	3,500	3,500	3,500
Pozzolan and lapilli*	400	400	400
Mica*	10	10	10
Talc (crude)	346	336	340

* Estimate(s).
† Figures refer to the metal content of ores and concentrates.
‡ Figures refer to marketable production.
‖ Figures refer to barium sulphite (BaSO$_3$) content.

Source: US Geological Survey.

Industry

SELECTED PRODUCTS
('000 metric tons, unless otherwise indicated)

	2001	2002	2003
Margarine	113	100	75
Wheat flour	6,225	4,419	4,380
Raw sugar*	3,962	5,104	4,276
Wine ('000 hectolitres)	55,382	52,020	47,491
Beer of barley*	1,572	1,535	1,544
Cigarettes (million)	41,787	39,600	36,900
Cotton yarn (pure)	86.6	78.7	76.8
Woven cotton fabrics (million sq metres)	548	486	448
Wool yarn (pure)	6.5	5.5	5.1
Woven woollen fabrics (metric tons)	3,168	2,868	2,349
Mechanical and semi-chemical wood pulp	1,522	1,498	1,528
Chemical wood pulp	1,699	1,678	1,707
Newsprint	2,066	1,988	2,138
Other printing and writing paper	6,590	6,668	6,680
Other paper and paperboard (incl. household, but excl. cigarette paper)	5,297	5,481	5,530
Synthetic rubber	667.0	685.2	730.0
Rubber tyres ('000)†	63,790	58,560	63,206
Sulphuric acid	2,051	1,930	1,624
Caustic soda (Sodium hydroxide)	1,782	1,829	1,910
Liquefied petroleum gas ('000 barrels)‡	31,682§	26,901	33,617
Motor gasoline (petrol—'000 barrels)‡	135,488	128,115	143,263
Jet fuels and kerosene ('000 barrels)‡	47,815	41,428	41,356
Distillate fuel oil ('000 barrels)‡	258,822	245,645	261,340
Residual fuel oil ('000 barrels)‡	69,679	66,357	70,847
Coke-oven coke	5,091	4,552	4,601
Cement (excl. clinker)	20,652	20,244	20,544
Pig-iron	12,870	13,224	12,744
Crude steel	19,343	20,258	19,758
Aluminium (unwrought—primary)‡	462	463	445
Lead (unwrought)‡	241.6	195.2	97.7
Zinc (incl. slab and secondary)‡	343.8	338.9	268.4
Radio receivers ('000)	3,508	3,357	3,498
Television receivers ('000)	4,977	5,375	5,657
Merchant ships launched ('000 gross reg. tons)	330	426	480
Passenger motor cars ('000)‖	3,182	3,498	3,704
Lorries and vans ('000)‖	760.8	791.9	780.6
Electric energy (incl. Monaco, million kWh)	548,704	559,186	566,949

* Source: FAO. Data refer to production during crop year ending 30 September.
† Rubber tyres for passenger motor vehicles and similar.
‡ Source: US Geological Survey.
§ Estimate.
‖ Including manufactured components, to be assembled in other territories.

2000 (metric tons): Artificial or synthetic fibres 66,036; Woven fabrics of artificial or synthetic fibres 111,936; Fertilizers 3,710,000.

Source (unless otherwise indicated): UN, *Industrial Commodity Statistics Yearbook*.

2004 ('000 barrels, unless otherwise indicated): Wheat flour ('000 metric tons) 4,348; Wine ('000 hectolitres) 59,107 (Source:FAO); Beer of barley ('000 metric tons) 1,472 (Source: FAO); Coke oven coke ('000 metric tons) 4,616; Liquefied petroleum gas 32,000; Motor gasoline (petrol) 140,000; Kerosene and jet fuel 42,000; Distillate fuel oil 250,000; Residual fuel oil 72,594; Aluminium (unwrought—primary, '000 metric tons) 451; Lead (unwrought, '000 metric tons) 105.6; Zinc (incl. slab and secondary, '000 metric tons) 267.5; Electric energy (million kWh) 572,241. (Source: mostly US Geological Survey).

2005 ('000 barrels, unless otherwise indicated): Wine ('000 hectolitres) 53,414 (Source: FAO); Beer of barley ('000 metric tons) 1,413 (Source: FAO); Liquefied petroleum gas 32,000; Motor gasoline (petrol) 140,000; Kerosene and jet fuel 42,000; Distillate fuel oil 250,000; Residual fuel oil 72,600; Aluminium (unwrought—primary, '000 metric tons) 442; Lead (unwrought, '000 metric tons) 105.5; Zinc (incl. slab and secondary, '000 metric tons) 210.0. (Source: mostly US Geological Survey).

FRANCE

Finance

CURRENCY AND EXCHANGE RATES

Monetary Units
100 cent = 1 euro (€).

Sterling and Dollar Equivalents (31 December 2007)
£1 sterling = 1.3609 euros;
US $1 = 0.6793 euros;
€10 = £7.35 = $14.72.

Average Exchange Rate (euros per US $)
2005   0.8041
2006   0.7971
2007   0.7306

Note: The national currency was formerly the French franc. From the introduction of the euro, with French participation, on 1 January 1999, a fixed exchange rate of €1 = 6.5596 French francs was in operation. Euro notes and coins were introduced on 1 January 2002. The euro and local currency circulated alongside each other until 17 February, after which the euro became the sole legal tender.

GOVERNMENT FINANCE
(general government transactions, non-cash basis, € million)

Summary of Balances

	2004	2005	2006
Revenue	822.86	870.51	910.52
Less Expense	869.76	904.76	939.30
Net operating balance	–46.90	–34.26	–28.79
Less Net acquisition of non-financial assets	13.31	17.00	17.38
Net lending/borrowing	–60.22	–51.26	–46.16

Revenue

	2004	2005	2006
Taxes	444.08	467.47	492.91
Taxes on income, profits and capital gains	169.66	178.68	194.36
Individuals	124.42	133.04	142.48
Taxes on goods and services	185.48	191.84	198.67
Social contributions	299.21	312.32	328.06
Grants	1.37	1.38	1.43
Other revenue	78.20	89.33	88.12
Total	822.86	870.51	910.52

Expense/Outlays

Expense by economic type	2004	2005	2006
Compensation of employees	220.73	227.80	234.72
Use of goods and services	85.83	89.86	94.05
Consumption of fixed capital	40.38	42.55	45.35
Interest	46.08	46.00	46.39
Subsidies	24.71	24.36	26.63
Grants	16.11	n.a.	n.a.
Social benefits	385.26	402.53	420.12
Other expenses	50.66	n.a.	n.a.
Total	869.76	904.76	939.30

Outlays by function of government*	2004	2005	2006
General public services	121.48	123.61	n.a.
Public debt transactions	46.08	46.00	46.39
Defence	32.26	32.90	n.a.
Public order and safety	22.28	23.85	n.a.
Economic affairs	49.28	49.68	n.a.
Environmental protection	13.57	14.00	n.a.
Housing and community amenities	29.79	31.28	n.a.
Health	121.47	125.58	n.a.
Recreation, culture and religion	23.76	25.48	n.a.
Education	102.28	105.61	n.a.
Social protection	366.93	387.71	n.a.
Statistical discrepancy	–0.04	2.07	n.a.
Total	883.08	921.77	956.68

* Including net acquisition of non-financial assets.

Source: IMF, *Government Finance Statistics Yearbook*.

INTERNATIONAL RESERVES
(US $ million at 31 December)

	2004	2005	2006
Gold*	42,039	46,607	55,588
IMF special drawing rights	875	878	948
Reserve position in IMF	5,363	2,878	1,417
Foreign exchange	29,077	23,996	40,287
Total	77,353	74,360	98,240

* Valued at market-related prices.

Source: IMF, *International Financial Statistics*.

MONEY SUPPLY
(€ million at 31 December)

	2004	2005	2006
Currency issued*	97,834	110,171	122,336
Demand deposits at banking institutions	364,054	404,132	431,589

* Currency put into circulation by the Banque de France totalled €47,679m. in 2004, €52,844m. in 2005 and €59,289m. in 2006.

Source: IMF, *International Financial Statistics*.

COST OF LIVING
(Consumer Price Index, December of each year; base: January 1998 = 100)

	2005	2006	2007
Food (incl. non-alcoholic beverages)	114.7	116.8	120.6
Alcoholic beverages and tobacco	143.5	144.3	150.2
Clothing and footwear	104.3	105.0	105.7
Housing, water, gas, electricity, etc.	118.4	123.0	128.3
Furniture and household items	108.3	109.6	110.9
Health care and pharmaceuticals	103.6	103.9	104.1
Transport	119.2	121.0	128.4
Post and telecommunications	87.3	86.3	84.6
Leisure and culture (goods and services)	97.7	95.8	94.5
Education	117.4	120.5	123.8
Hotels, cafés and restaurants	119.4	122.3	125.8
All items (incl. others)	113.0	114.7	117.7

NATIONAL ACCOUNTS

National Income and Product
(€ '000 million at current prices)

	2004	2005	2006
Compensation of employees	866.7	896.3	930.7
Gross operating surplus	458.3	472.4	497.4
Gross mixed income	111.6	113.1	119.4
Gross domestic product (GDP) at factor cost	1,436.6	1,481.8	1,547.5
Taxes on production and imports	257.9	270.0	280.5
Less Subsidies	34.3	33.8	36.1
GDP in market prices	1,660.2	1,717.9	1,792.0
Primary income received from abroad	103.2	118.0	154.1
Less Factor income paid abroad	90.1	104.5	140.3
Gross national income (GNI)	1,673.3	1,731.5	1,805.8
Current transfers from abroad	13.0	13.6	14.3
Less Current transfers paid abroad	37.7	40.3	41.0
Gross national disposable income	1,648.8	1,704.7	1,779.2

FRANCE

Statistical Survey

Expenditure on the Gross Domestic Product
(€ '000 million at current prices)

	2004	2005	2006
Final consumption expenditure	1,333.8	1,386.0	1,440.2
Households	917.7	955.0	993.2
Non-profit institutions serving households	22.3	22.7	23.3
General government	393.8	408.3	423.7
Gross capital formation	324.8	347.7	377.5
Gross fixed capital formation	320.4	340.7	366.4
Changes in inventories	3.6	6.1	10.3
Acquisitions, *less* disposals, of valuables	0.8	0.9	0.8
Total domestic expenditure	1,658.6	1,733.7	1,817.7
Exports of goods and services	426.8	447.3	481.2
Less Imports of goods and services	425.1	462.9	507.0
GDP in market prices	1,660.2	1,717.9	1,792.0
GDP at constant 2000 prices	1,536.3	1,562.6	1,593.7

Gross Domestic Product by Economic Activity
(€ '000 million at constant 2000 prices)

	2004	2005	2006
Agriculture, forestry and fishing	38.1	35.9	35.2
Industry (incl. energy)	242.2	245.0	249.1
Food products, beverages and tobacco	27.9	28.1	28.8
Consumer goods industries	37.3	38.0	38.6
Automobile industry	16.3	16.7	15.1
Equipment goods industries	48.1	49.2	52.2
Intermediate goods industries	81.5	81.8	82.6
Energy	31.0	31.0	31.8
Construction	68.5	70.8	72.8
Mainly market services	741.3	757.1	774.5
Trade	140.6	142.9	144.5
Transportation	56.5	57.4	58.8
Financial activities	71.9	74.1	75.3
Real estate and renting activities	174.0	177.3	182.3
Business services	225.1	230.6	238.2
Domestic and personal services	73.6	75.4	75.8
Mainly non-market services	283.7	286.5	289.3
Education, health, social work	178.5	179.5	180.6
General government and non-profit institutions serving households	105.2	106.9	108.7
Gross value added at basic prices	1,374.5	1,396.7	1,422.5
Taxes, less subsidies, on products*	161.8	321.2	369.5
GDP in market prices	1,536.3	1,717.9	1,792.0

* Obtained as residual.

Note: Totals may not be equal to the sum of components, owing to rounding.

BALANCE OF PAYMENTS
(US $ '000 million)*

	2004	2005	2006
Exports of goods f.o.b.	421.11	439.90	483.11
Imports of goods f.o.b.	−425.95	−468.39	−520.81
Trade balance	−4.85	−28.49	−37.69
Exports of services	112.71	118.76	118.48
Imports of services	−98.38	−105.58	−108.00
Balance on goods and services	9.48	−15.31	−27.21
Other income received	119.72	144.85	186.16
Other income paid	−97.08	−121.76	−159.71
Balance on goods, services and income	32.12	7.77	−0.76
Current transfers received	25.44	25.44	26.96
Current transfers paid	−47.14	−52.74	−54.51
Current balance	10.42	−19.52	−28.31

—continued	2004	2005	2006
Capital account (net)	1.81	0.66	−0.26
Direct investment abroad	−56.90	−119.36	−116.41
Direct investment from abroad	32.83	81.13	81.05
Portfolio investment assets	−232.48	−242.17	−338.59
Portfolio investment liabilities	166.34	224.86	265.85
Financial derivatives liabilities	6.21	6.36	4.14
Other investment assets	−116.16	−276.89	−167.65
Other investment liabilities	193.90	306.01	359.72
Net errors and omissions	−1.87	29.87	−47.74
Overall balance	4.11	−9.05	11.78

* Figures refer to transactions of metropolitan France, French Guiana, Guadeloupe, Martinique, Réunion and Monaco with the rest of the world.

Source: IMF, *International Financial Statistics*.

External Trade

(Note: Figures refer to the trade of metropolitan France, French Guiana, Guadeloupe, Martinique, Réunion and Monaco with the rest of the world, excluding trade in war materials, goods exported under the offshore procurement programme, war reparations and restitutions and the export of sea products direct from the high seas. The figures include trade in second-hand ships and aircraft, and the supply of stores and bunkers for foreign ships and aircraft.)

PRINCIPAL COMMODITIES
(distribution by NES, € million, excluding military supplies)

Imports	2004	2005	2006
Agriculture, forestry and fishing products	32,016	32,894	34,516
Manufactures of food products, beverages and tobacco	23,337	24,027	25,473
Consumer goods	59,400	63,025	66,516
Clothing articles and leather products	16,731	17,591	18,389
Pharmaceutical products, perfumes, soap and cleaning preparations	17,814	18,725	19,592
Household goods and equipment	22,657	24,403	26,301
Motor vehicles	41,073	43,216	45,125
Motor vehicles, bodies and trailers	28,655	30,395	31,898
Parts and accessories for motor vehicles	12,418	12,821	13,228
Capital goods	73,442	79,001	87,629
Ships and boats, aircraft, locomotives and rolling stock and motorcycles	14,254	16,002	18,019
Aircraft and spacecraft	11,157	12,499	14,162
Metal products, machinery and equipment	28,223	29,664	31,730
Electric and electronic equipment	30,965	33,335	37,879
Office machines and computers	14,549	14,530	14,988
Intermediate goods	108,630	115,294	126,717
Chemicals, rubber, plastic and related products	39,259	42,806	45,519
Basic organic chemicals	14,342	16,700	17,634
Basic metals and fabricated metal products	26,641	28,348	35,418
Iron and steel	11,868	12,389	14,610
Electric and electronic components	16,398	17,027	17,505
Energy products	39,099	53,588	63,723
Coal, crude petroleum, gas and uranium; coke, refined petroleum products and nuclear fuel	38,400	53,282	63,178
Crude petroleum and natural gas	26,435	35,739	43,183
Refined petroleum products	9,037	14,083	16,411
Total (incl. others)	355,331	388,596	425,807

FRANCE

Statistical Survey

Exports	2004	2005	2006
Agriculture, forestry and fishing products	39,872	40,523	43,200
Beverages	9,565	9,744	10,909
Consumer goods	51,606	54,546	58,338
Pharmaceutical products, perfumes, soap and cleaning preparations	26,989	28,736	31,036
Pharmaceuticals, medicinal chemicals and botanical products	18,214	19,462	21,087
Household goods and equipment	13,271	13,810	14,510
Motor vehicles	53,421	52,080	50,875
Motor vehicles, bodies and trailers	39,251	38,059	35,663
Parts and accessories for motor vehicles	14,170	14,022	15,212
Capital goods	76,335	81,044	93,506
Ships and boats, aircraft, locomotives and rolling stock and motorcycles	23,734	26,132	31,131
Aircraft and spacecraft	20,917	23,162	27,543
Metal products, machinery and equipment	28,394	30,244	33,604
Electric and electronic equipment	24,207	24,669	28,771
Intermediate goods	103,046	107,600	119,637
Chemicals, rubber, plastic and related products	39,572	41,673	45,636
Basic organic chemicals	15,553	16,955	18,755
Basic metals and fabricated metal products	25,026	27,113	33,025
Iron and steel	12,994	14,057	16,451
Electric and electronic components	18,023	18,684	20,091
Energy products	10,519	15,329	17,339
Coal, crude petroleum, gas and uranium; coke, refined petroleum products and nuclear fuel	7,532	11,827	14,228
Total (incl. others)	336,234	352,584	384,572

Source: former Ministry of the Economy, Finance and Industry, Paris.

PRINCIPAL TRADING PARTNERS
(€ million, excluding military supplies)

Imports	2004	2005	2006
Belgium	26,012	31,518	35,585
China, People's Republic	16,649	21,108	24,262
Germany	61,776	66,962	69,109
Ireland	6,525	7,259	6,386
Italy	32,057	33,977	36,341
Japan	10,807	10,467	10,334
Netherlands	15,903	16,281	17,557
Norway	6,926	6,439	6,802
Poland	3,168	4,010	5,033
Russia	7,360	8,131	10,043
Spain	26,358	27,574	29,178
Sweden	4,588	4,889	5,220
Switzerland	7,999	8,808	9,479
United Kingdom	23,046	22,816	26,033
USA	22,624	22,827	25,497
Total (incl. others)	355,331	388,596	425,807

Exports	2004	2005	2006
Algeria	4,235	4,671	4,033
Austria	3,551	3,440	3,688
Belgium	25,972	26,779	28,643
China, People's Republic	5,285	5,803	8,083
Germany	50,626	51,345	55,828
Greece	3,526	3,133	3,293
Italy	31,426	32,465	35,086
Japan	5,352	5,416	5,704
Netherlands	13,377	14,518	15,875
Poland	4,314	4,729	6,978

Exports—*continued*	2004	2005	2006
Portugal	4,466	4,721	4,885
Russia	3,151	3,368	4,726
Singapore	2,702	3,031	3,468
Spain	33,788	35,966	37,945
Sweden	4,607	4,427	5,033
Switzerland	10,251	10,213	10,424
Turkey	4,236	4,662	5,208
United Kingdom	31,641	31,481	32,763
USA	23,099	24,998	26,412
Total (incl. others)	336,234	352,584	384,572

Source: former Ministry of the Economy, Finance and Industry, Paris.

Transport

RAILWAYS
(traffic)

	2004	2005	2006
Paying passengers ('000 journeys)	944,000	976,000	1,013,000
Passenger-km (million)	74,350	76,480	n.a.
Freight carried ('000 metric tons)	121,980	107,530	108,330
Freight ton-km (million)*	46,350	40,700	n.a.

* Including passengers' baggage.

Source: Société Nationale des Chemins de fer Français, Paris.

ROAD TRAFFIC
('000 motor vehicles in use at 31 December)

	2002	2003	2004
Passenger cars	29,160	29,560	29,900
Lorries and vans	5,903	5,986	6,057
Buses and coaches	81	82	82

Source: International Road Federation, *World Road Statistics*.

INLAND WATERWAYS

	2003	2004	2005
Freight carried ('000 metric tons)	54,661	57,994	59,510
Freight ton-km (million)	6,890	7,316	7,856

Source: Voies navigables de France.

SHIPPING

Merchant Fleet
(registered at 31 December)

	2004	2005	2006
Number of vessels	700	713	713
Total displacement ('000 grt)	1,375.3	1,293.3	1,279.3

Source: Lloyd's Register-Fairplay, *World Fleet Statistics*.

Sea-borne Freight Traffic
('000 metric tons)

	2001	2002	2003
Goods loaded (excl. stores)	101,600	102,900	109,800
Goods unloaded (excl. fish)	239,900	242,300	247,200

Source: former Ministry of Transport, Public Works, Tourism and the Marine, Paris.

CIVIL AVIATION
(revenue traffic on scheduled services)*

	2002	2003	2004
Passengers carried ('000)	57,263	54,860	59,565
Passenger-km (million)	131,373	130,563	151,696
Total ton-km (million)	4,473	4,699	5,463

* Including data for airlines based in French overseas possessions.

Source: Direction Générale de l'Aviation Civile.

FRANCE

Tourism

FOREIGN TOURIST ARRIVALS BY COUNTRY OF ORIGIN
('000, estimates)

	2003	2004	2005
Belgium and Luxembourg	8,614	8,771	8,745
Germany	14,047	13,728	13,204
Italy	7,511	7,400	7,200
Netherlands	12,486	12,387	11,639
Scandinavian states	1,518	1,468	1,542
Spain	2,861	3,009	3,171
Switzerland	3,002	3,079	3,007
United Kingdom and Ireland	14,845	14,648	14,558
USA	2,447	2,621	2,769
Total (incl. others)	75,048	75,121	76,001

Receipts from tourism (US $ million, excl. passenger transport): 36,617 in 2003; 40,693 in 2004; 42,167 in 2005.

Source: World Tourism Organization.

Communications Media

	2004	2005	2006
Telephones ('000 main lines in use)	33,703	33,707	33,897
Mobile cellular telephones ('000 subscribers)	44,544	48,088	51,662
Personal computers ('000 in use)	29,410	35,000	n.a.
Internet users ('000)	23,732	26,154	30,100
Broadband subscribers ('000)	6,561	9,471	12,699

Television receivers ('000 in use): 37,500 in 2001.

Radio receivers ('000 in use): 55,300 in 1997.

Facsimile machines ('000 in use): 2,800 in 1997.

Book production: 51,837 titles in 2000.

Daily newspapers (2005): 103 titles (total average circulation 9,973m.).

Non-daily newspapers (1999, excl. newspapers published on Sundays only): 245 titles (total average circulation 2,236,000 copies).

Other periodicals (1993): 2,683 titles (circulation 120,018,000 copies in 1991).

Sources: UN, *Statistical Yearbook*; UNESCO Institute for Statistics, International Telecommunication Union.

Education

(2004/05, public and private, metropolitan France, French Guiana, Guadeloupe, Martinique and Réunion)

	Students ('000)		
	Males	Females	Total
Pre-primary	1,335.7	1,273.8	2,609.5
Primary	2,011.2	1,913.4	3,924.6
Integration and adaptation schooling	30.9	20.5	51.4
Secondary:			
Lower	1,626.2	1,568.1	3,194.3
Upper—Professional	389.0	324.8	713.8
Upper—General/Technical	681.0	834.6	1,515.5
Higher	n.a.	n.a.	2,268.4

Source: Ministry of National Education, Higher Education and Research, Paris.

Students ('000, 2006/07): Pre-primary 2,578.4; Primary 4,016.9; Integration and adaptation schooling 48.7; Secondary (Lower) 3,100.6; Secondary (Upper—Professional) 719.7; Secondary (Upper—General/Technical) 1,491.2; Higher 2,254.4.

Institutions (2004/05, public and private, metropolitan France, French Guiana, Guadeloupe, Martinique and Réunion): Pre-primary 17,887, Primary and Integration and adaptation schooling 38,741, Secondary (Lower) 6,988, Secondary (Upper—Professional) 1,702, Secondary (Upper—General/Technical) 2,614, Higher (Universities, incl. University Institutes of Technology and Schools of Engineering attached to universities) 265, Higher (Other) 4,099.

Teachers (2004/05, public and private, metropolitan France, French Guiana, Guadeloupe, Martinique and Réunion, excl. trainee teachers): Pre-primary, Primary and Integration and adaptation schooling 364,315, Secondary (Lower) 237,277, Secondary (Upper) 250,367, Higher 87,724.

Directory

The Constitution

The Constitution of the Fifth Republic was adopted by referendum on 28 September 1958, promulgated on 6 October 1958 and subsequently amended as indicated below.

PREAMBLE

The French people hereby solemnly proclaims its attachment to the Rights of Man and to the principles of national sovereignty as defined by the Declaration of 1789, confirmed and complemented by the Preamble of the Constitution of 1946.

By virtue of these principles and that of the free determination of peoples, the Republic hereby offers to the Overseas Territories that express the desire to adhere to them, new institutions based on the common ideal of liberty, equality and fraternity and conceived with a view to their democratic evolution.

Article 1. (As amended by legislation of 4 August 1995 and 17 March 2003.) France shall be a Republic, indivisible, secular, democratic and social. It shall ensure the equality of all citizens before the law, without distinction of origin, race or religion. It shall respect all beliefs. Its organization shall be decentralized.

I. ON SOVEREIGNTY

Article 2. (As amended by legislation of 25 June 1992.) The language of the Republic shall be French.

The national emblem shall be the tricolour flag, blue, white and red.

The national anthem shall be the 'Marseillaise'.

The motto of the Republic shall be 'Liberty, Equality, Fraternity'.

Its principle shall be government of the people, by the people, and for the people.

Article 3. (As amended by legislation of 8 July 1999.) National sovereignty belongs to the people, who shall exercise this sovereignty through their representatives and through the referendum.

No section of the people, nor any individual, may arrogate to themselves or himself the exercise thereof.

Suffrage may be direct or indirect under the conditions stipulated by the Constitution. It shall always be universal, equal and secret.

All French citizens of both sexes who have reached their majority and who enjoy civil and political rights may vote under the conditions to be determined by law.

The law shall promote equal access by women and men to elective offices and positions.

Article 4. (As amended by legislation of 8 July 1999.) Political parties and groups are instrumental in the exercise of suffrage. They may form and carry on their activities freely. They must respect the principles of national sovereignty and of democracy. They shall contribute to the implementation of the principle set out in the last paragraph of Article 3 as provided by the law.

II. THE PRESIDENT OF THE REPUBLIC

Article 5. (As amended by legislation of 4 August 1995.) The President of the Republic shall see that the Constitution is respected. He shall ensure, by his arbitration, the regular functioning of the governmental authorities, as well as the continuity of the State.

He shall be the guarantor of national independence, of the integrity of the territory, and of respect for treaties.

Article 6. (As amended by legislation of 6 November 1962 and 2 October 2000.) The President of the Republic shall be elected for five years by direct universal suffrage. The method of implementation of the present Article shall be determined by an organic law.

Article 7. (As amended by legislation of 6 November 1962, 18 June 1976 and 17 March 2003.) The President of the Republic shall be elected by an absolute majority of the votes cast. If such a majority is not obtained at the first ballot, a second ballot shall take place 14 days later. Those who may stand for the second ballot shall be only the two candidates who, after the possible withdrawal of candidates with more votes, have gained the largest number of votes on the first ballot.

Voting shall begin at the summons of the Government. The election of the new President of the Republic shall take place not less than 20 days and not more than 35 days before the expiry of the powers of the President in office. In the event that the Presidency of the Republic has been vacated for any reason whatsoever, or impeded in its functioning as officially declared by the Constitutional Council, after the matter has been referred to it by the Government and which shall give its ruling by an absolute majority of its members, the functions of the President of the Republic, with the exception of those covered by Articles 11 and 12 hereunder, shall be temporarily exercised by the President of the Sénat (Senate) or, if the latter is in his turn unable to exercise his functions, by the Government.

In the case of vacancy or when the impediment is declared to be permanent by the Constitutional Council, the voting for the election of the new President shall take place, except in case of *force majeure* officially noted by the Constitutional Council, not less than 20 days and not more than 35 days after the beginning of the vacancy or of the declaration of the final nature of the impediment.

If, in the seven days preceding the latest date for the lodging of candidatures, one of the persons who, at least 30 days prior to that date, publicly announced his decision to be a candidate dies or is impeded, the Constitutional Council may decide to postpone the election.

If, before the first ballot, one of the candidates dies or is impeded, the Constitutional Council orders the postponement of the election.

In the event of the death or impediment, before any candidates have withdrawn, of one of the two candidates who received the greatest number of votes in the first ballot, the Constitutional Council shall declare that the electoral procedure must be repeated in full; the same shall apply in the event of the death or impediment of one of the two candidates standing for the second ballot.

All cases shall be referred to the Constitutional Council under the conditions laid down in paragraph 2 of Article 61 below, or under those determined for the presentation of candidates by the organic law provided for in Article 6 above.

The Constitutional Council may extend the periods stipulated in paragraphs 3 and 5 above provided that polling shall not take place more than 35 days after the date of the decision of the Constitutional Council. If the implementation of the provisions of this paragraph results in the postponement of the election beyond the expiry of the powers of the President in office, the latter shall remain in office until his successor is proclaimed.

Articles 49 and 50 and Article 89 of the Constitution may not be put into application during the vacancy of the Presidency of the Republic or during the periods between the declaration of the final nature of the impediment of the President of the Republic and the election of his successor.

Article 8. The President of the Republic shall appoint the Prime Minister. He shall terminate the functions of the Prime Minister when the latter presents the resignation of the Government.

At the suggestion of the Prime Minister, he shall appoint the other members of the Government and shall terminate their functions.

Article 9. The President of the Republic shall preside over the Council of Ministers.

Article 10. The President of the Republic shall promulgate laws within 15 days following the transmission to the Government of the finally adopted law.

He may, before the expiry of this time limit, ask Parliament for a reconsideration of the law or of certain of its Articles. This reconsideration may not be refused.

Article 11. (As amended by legislation of 4 August 1995.) The President of the Republic, on the proposal of the government during [Parliamentary] sessions, or on joint motion of the two Assemblies published in the *Journal Officiel*, may submit to a referendum any bill dealing with the organization of the governmental authorities, with reforms related to the economic or social policy of the nation and to the public services contributing thereto or providing for authorization to ratify a treaty that, without being contrary to the Constitution, might affect the functioning of the institutions.

Where the referendum is held in response to a proposal by the Government, the latter shall make a statement before each Assembly, which shall be followed by a debate.

Where the referendum decides in favour of the government bill, the President of the Republic shall promulgate the law within 15 days following the proclamation of the results of the vote.

Article 12. (As amended by legislation of 4 August 1995.) The President of the Republic may, after consultation with the Prime Minister and the Presidents of the Assemblies, declare the dissolution of the Assemblée nationale (National Assembly).

A general election shall take place 20 days at the least and 40 days at the most after the dissolution.

The Assemblée nationale shall convene by right on the second Thursday following its election. If this meeting takes place between the period provided for the ordinary session, a session shall, by right, be opened for a 15-day period.

There may be no further dissolution within a year following this election.

Article 13. (As amended by legislation of 17 March 2003.) The President of the Republic shall sign the ordinances and decrees decided upon in the Council of Ministers.

He shall make appointments to the civil and military posts of the State.

Councillors of State, the Grand Chancellor of the Legion of Honour, Ambassadors and Envoys Extraordinary, Master Councillors of the Audit Court, prefects, representatives of the State in the Overseas communities governed by Article 74 and in New Caledonia, general officers, rectors of academies [regional divisions of the public educational system] and directors of central administrations shall be appointed in meetings of the Council of Ministers.

An organic law shall determine the other posts to be filled by decision of the Council of Ministers, as well as the conditions under which the power of the President of the Republic to make appointments to office may be delegated by him to be exercised in his name.

Article 14. The President of the Republic shall accredit Ambassadors and Envoys Extraordinary to foreign powers; foreign Ambassadors and Envoys Extraordinary shall be accredited to him.

Article 15. The President of the Republic shall be commander of the armed forces. He shall preside over the higher councils and committees of national defence.

Article 16. When the institutions of the Republic, the independence of the nation, the integrity of its territory or the fulfilment of its international commitments are threatened in a grave and immediate manner and the regular functioning of the constitutional governmental authorities is interrupted, the President of the Republic shall take the measures required by these circumstances, after official consultation with the Prime Minister and the Presidents of the Assemblies, and the Constitutional Council.

He shall inform the nation of these measures in a message.

These measures must be prompted by the desire to ensure to the constitutional governmental authorities, in the shortest possible time, the means of accomplishing their mission. The Constitutional Council shall be consulted with regard to such measures.

Parliament shall meet by right.

The Assemblée nationale may not be dissolved during the exercise of exceptional powers.

Article 17. The President of the Republic shall have the right of pardon.

Article 18. The President of the Republic shall communicate with the two Assemblies of Parliament by means of messages, which he shall cause to be read, and which shall not be the occasion for any debate.

Between sessions, the Parliament shall be convened especially to this end.

Article 19. Official decisions of the President of the Republic, other than those provided for under Articles 8 (first paragraph), 11, 12, 16, 18, 54, 56 and 61, shall be counter-signed by the Prime Minister and, where applicable, by the appropriate ministers.

III. THE GOVERNMENT

Article 20. The Government shall determine and conduct the policy of the nation.

It shall have at its disposal the administration and the armed forces.

It shall be responsible to the Parliament under the conditions and according to the procedures stipulated in Articles 49 and 50.

Article 21. The Prime Minister shall direct the operation of the Government. He shall be responsible for national defence. He shall ensure the execution of the laws. Subject to the provisions of Article 13, he shall have regulatory powers and shall make appointments to civil and military posts.

He may delegate certain of his powers to the ministers.

He shall replace, should the occasion arise, the President of the Republic as the Chairman of the councils and committees provided for under Article 15.

He may, in exceptional instances, replace him as the chairman of a meeting of the Council of Ministers by virtue of an explicit delegation and for a specific agenda.

Article 22. The official decisions of the Prime Minister shall be counter-signed, when circumstances so require, by the ministers responsible for their execution.

Article 23. The functions of Members of the Government shall be incompatible with the exercise of any parliamentary mandate, with the holding of any office, at the national level, in business, professional or labour organizations, and with any public employment or professional activity.

An organic law shall determine the conditions under which the holders of such mandates, functions or employments shall be replaced.

The replacement of the members of Parliament shall take place in accordance with the provisions of Article 25.

IV. THE PARLIAMENT

Article 24. The Parliament shall comprise the Assemblée nationale and the Sénat.

The deputies to the Assemblée nationale shall be elected by direct suffrage.

The Sénat shall be elected by indirect suffrage. It shall ensure the representation of the territorial communities of the Republic. French nationals living outside France shall be represented in the Sénat.

Article 25. An organic law shall determine the term for which each Assembly is elected, the number of its members, their emoluments, the conditions of eligibility, and the offices incompatible with membership of the Assemblies.

It shall likewise determine the conditions under which, in the case of a vacancy in either Assembly, persons shall be elected to replace the deputy or senator whose seat has been vacated until the holding of new complete or partial elections to the Assembly concerned.

Article 26. (As amended by legislation of 4 August 1995.) No Member of Parliament may be prosecuted, subjected to inquiry, arrested, detained or tried as a result of the opinions expressed or votes cast by him in the exercise of his functions.

No Member of Parliament shall be subjected, in regard to any criminal or correctional matter, to arrest or any other custodial or semi-custodial measures other than with the authorization of the Assembly of which he is a member. Such authorization shall not be required in the case of a serious crime or other major offence committed *in flagrante delicto* or a final conviction.

The detention, subjection to custodial or semi-custodial measures, or prosecution of a Member of Parliament shall be suspended for the duration of the session if the Assembly of which he is a member so requires.

The Assembly concerned shall convene as of right for additional sittings in order to permit the preceding paragraph to be applied should circumstances so require.

Article 27. Any compulsory vote shall be null and void.

The right to vote of the members of Parliament shall be personal.

An organic law may, under exceptional circumstances, authorize the delegation of a vote. In this case, no member may be delegated more than one vote.

Article 28. (As amended by legislation of 4 August 1995.) Parliament shall convene by right in one ordinary session a year, which shall start on the first working day of October and shall end on the last working day of June.

The number of days for which each Assembly may sit during the ordinary session shall not exceed 120. The sitting weeks shall be determined by each Assembly.

The Prime Minister, after consulting the President of the Assembly concerned, or the majority of the members of each Assembly may decide to meet for additional sitting days.

The days and hours of sittings shall be determined by the rules of procedure of each Assembly.

Article 29. Parliament shall convene in extraordinary session at the request of the Prime Minister or of the majority of the members comprising the Assemblée nationale, to consider a specific agenda.

When an extraordinary session is held at the request of the members of the Assemblée nationale, the closure decree shall take effect as soon as the Parliament has exhausted the agenda for which it was called, and at the latest 12 days from the date of its meeting.

Only the Prime Minister may ask for a new session before the end of the month following the closure decree.

Article 30. Apart from cases in which Parliament meets by right, extraordinary sessions shall be opened and closed by decree of the President of the Republic.

Article 31. The members of the Government shall have access to the two Assemblies. They shall be heard when they so request.

They may call for the assistance of Commissioners of the Government.

Article 32. The President of the Assemblée nationale shall be elected for the duration of the legislature. The President of the Sénat shall be elected after each partial re-election [of the Sénat].

Article 33. The meetings of the two Assemblies shall be public. An *in extenso* report of the debates shall be published in the *Journal Officiel.*

Each Assembly may sit in secret committee at the request of the Prime Minister or of one-tenth of its members.

V. ON RELATIONS BETWEEN PARLIAMENT AND THE GOVERNMENT

Article 34. (As amended by legislation of 22 February 1996, 28 March 2003 and 1 March 2005.) Laws shall be voted by Parliament.

Legislation shall establish the regulations concerning:

Civil rights and the fundamental guarantees granted to the citizens for the exercise of their public liberties; the obligations imposed by the national defence upon the person and property of citizens;

Nationality, status and legal capacity of persons; marriage contracts, inheritance and gifts;

Determination of crimes and misdemeanours as well as the penalties imposed therefor; criminal procedure; amnesty; the creation of new juridical systems and the status of magistrates;

The basis, the rate and the methods of collecting taxes of all types; the issue of currency.

Legislation likewise shall determine the regulations concerning:

The electoral system of the Parliamentary Assemblies and the local assemblies;

The establishment of categories of public institutions;

The fundamental guarantees granted to civil and military personnel employed by the State;

The nationalization of enterprises and the transfers of the property of enterprises from the public to the private sector.

Legislation shall determine the fundamental principles of:

The general organization of national defence;

The free administration of territorial communities, of their competencies and their resources;

Education;

The protection of the environment;

Property rights, civil and commercial obligations;

Legislation pertaining to employment unions and social security.

The financial laws shall determine the financial resources and obligations of the State under the conditions and with the reservations to be provided for by an organic law.

Social security finance bills shall determine the general conditions for the financial balance of social security and, taking account of their revenue forecasts, shall determine expenditure targets in the manner and under the reserves provided for by an organic law.

Laws pertaining to national planning shall determine the objectives of the economic and social action of the State.

The provisions of the present Article may be detailed and supplemented by an organic law.

Article 35. Parliament shall authorize the declaration of war.

Article 36. Martial law shall be decreed in a meeting of the Council of Ministers.

Its extension beyond 12 days may be authorized only by Parliament.

Article 37. Matters other than those that fall within the domain of law shall be of a regulatory character.

Legislative texts concerning these matters may be modified by decrees issued after consultation with the Council of State. Those legislative texts which shall be adopted after the entry into force of the present Constitution shall be modified by decree only if the Constitutional Council has stated that they have a regulatory character as defined in the preceding paragraph.

Article 37–1. (Appended by legislation of 28 March 2003). Law and regulations may include, for a limited duration and object, dispositions of an experimental character.

Article 38. The Government may, in order to carry out its programme, ask Parliament for authorization to take through ordinances, during a limited period, measures that are normally within the domain of law.

The ordinances shall be enacted in meetings of Ministers after consultation with the Council of State. They shall come into force upon their publication but shall become null and void if the bill for their ratification is not submitted to Parliament before the date set by the enabling act.

At the expiry of the time limit referred to in the first paragraph of the present Article, the ordinances may be modified only by the law in respect of those matters which are within the legislative domain.

Article 39. (As amended by legislation of 22 February 1996 and 28 March 2003.) The Prime Minister and the Members of Parliament alike shall have the right to initiate legislation.

Government bills shall be discussed in the Council of Ministers after consultation with the Council of State and shall be filed with the secretariat of one of the two Assemblies. Finance bills and social security finance bills shall be submitted first to the Assemblée nationale. Without prejudice to the first paragraph of Article 44, bills principally concerning the organization of territorial communities, and bills related to the representative authorities of French nationals living outside France shall be submitted first to the Sénat.

Article 40. Private members' bills and amendments shall be inadmissible when their adoption would have as a consequence either a diminution of public financial resources or an increase in public expenditure.

Article 41. If it shall appear in the course of the legislative procedure that a bill or amendment is not within the domain of law or is contrary to a delegation granted by virtue of Article 38, the Government may declare it inadmissible.

In case of disagreement between the Government and the President of the Assembly concerned, the Constitutional Council, upon the request of one or the other, shall rule within eight days.

Article 42. The discussion of bills shall pertain, in the first Assembly to which they have been referred, to the text presented by the Government.

An Assembly given a text adopted by the other Assembly shall deliberate on the text that is transmitted to it.

Article 43. Government and private members' bills shall, at the request of the Government or of the Assembly concerned, be sent for study to committees especially designated for this purpose.

Government and private members' bills for which such a request has not been made shall be sent to one of the permanent committees, the number of which is limited to six in each Assembly.

Article 44. Members of Parliament and of the Government have the right of amendment.

After the opening of the debate, the Government may oppose the examination of any amendment which has not previously been submitted to committee.

If the Government so requests, the Assembly concerned shall decide, by a single vote, on all or part of the text under discussion, retaining only the amendments proposed or accepted by the Government.

Article 45. Every government or private member's bill shall be considered successively in the two Assemblies of Parliament with a view to the adoption of an identical text.

When, as a result of disagreement between the two Assemblies, it has been impossible to adopt a Government or private member's bill after two readings by each Assembly, or, if the Government has declared the matter urgent, after a single reading by each of them, the Prime Minister shall have the right to convene a joint committee composed of an equal number from both Assemblies charged with the task of proposing a text on the matters still under discussion.

The text elaborated by the joint committee may be submitted by the Government for approval of the two Assemblies. No amendment shall be admissible except by agreement of the Government.

If the joint committee does not succeed in adopting a common text, or if this text is not adopted under the conditions set forth in the preceding paragraph, the Government may, after a new reading by each Assembly, ask the Assemblée nationale to rule definitively. In this case, the Assemblée nationale may reconsider either the text elaborated by the joint committee, or the last text voted by it, modified when circumstances so require by one or several of the amendments adopted by the Sénat.

Article 46. The laws that the Constitution characterizes as organic shall be adopted and amended under the following conditions:

A Government or private member's bill shall be submitted to the deliberation and to the vote of the first Assembly notified only at the expiration of a period of 15 days following its introduction;

The procedure of Article 45 shall be applicable. Nevertheless, lacking an agreement between the two Assemblies, the text may be adopted by the Assemblée nationale on final reading only by an absolute majority of its members;

The organic laws relative to the Sénat must be adopted in identical terms by the two Assemblies;

The organic laws may be promulgated only after a declaration by the Constitutional Council on their constitutionality.

Article 47. The Parliament shall pass finance bills under the conditions to be stipulated by an organic law.

Should the Assemblée nationale fail to reach a decision on first reading within 40 days after a bill has been filed, the Government shall refer it to the Sénat, which must rule within 15 days. The procedure set forth in Article 45 shall then be followed.

Should Parliament fail to reach a decision within 70 days, the provisions of the bill may be enforced by ordinance.

Should the finance bill establishing the resources and expenditures of a fiscal year not be filed in time for it to be promulgated before the beginning of that fiscal year, the Government shall urgently request Parliament for authorization to collect taxes and shall make available by decree the funds needed to meet the Government commitments already voted.

The time limits stipulated in the present Article shall be suspended when the Parliament is not in session.

The Audit Court shall assist Parliament and the Government in supervising the implementation of the finance laws.

Article 47–1. (Appended by legislation of 22 February 1996.) Parliament shall pass social security finance bills in the manner provided for by an organic law.

Should the Assemblée nationale fail to reach a decision on first reading within 20 days following the introduction of a bill, the Government shall refer the bill to the Sénat, which must rule within 15 days. The procedure set out in Article 45 shall then apply.

Should Parliament fail to reach a decision within 50 days, the provisions of the bill may be implemented by ordinance.

The time limits set by this Article shall be suspended when Parliament is not in session and, as regards each assembly, during the weeks when it has decided not to sit in accordance with the second paragraph of Article 28.

The Audit Court shall assist Parliament and the Government in monitoring the implementation of social security finance Acts.

Article 48. (As amended by legislation of 4 August 1995.) Without prejudice to the application of the last three paragraphs of Article 28, the discussion of the bills tabled or agreed upon by the Government shall have priority on the agenda of the Assemblies in the order determined by the Government.

At least one meeting a week shall be reserved, by priority, for questions asked by Members of Parliament and for answers by the Government.

One meeting a month shall be reserved, by priority, for the agenda determined by each Assembly.

Article 49. (As amended by legislation of 4 August 1995.) The Prime Minister, after deliberation by the Council of Ministers, shall make the Government responsible, before the Assemblée nationale, for its programme or, should the occasion arise, for a declaration of general policy.

The Assemblée nationale may challenge the responsibility of the Government by a motion of censure. Such a motion is admissible only if it is signed by at least one-tenth of the members of the Assemblée nationale. The vote may not take place before 48 hours after the motion has been filed. Only the votes that are favourable to a motion of censure shall be counted; the motion of censure may be adopted only by a majority of the members comprising the Assembly. Except as provided for in the following paragraph, a Deputy shall not sign more than three motions of censure during a single ordinary session and more than one during a single extraordinary session.

The Prime Minister may, after deliberation by the Council of Ministers, make the Government responsible before the Assemblée nationale for the adoption of a bill. In this case, the text shall be considered as adopted unless a motion of censure, filed during the 24 hours that follow, is carried under the conditions provided for in the preceding paragraph.

The Prime Minister shall have the right to request the Sénat for approval of a declaration of general policy.

Article 50. When the Assemblée nationale adopts a motion of censure, or when it disapproves the programme or a declaration of general policy of the Government, the Prime Minister must submit the resignation of the Government to the President of the Republic.

Article 51. (As amended by legislation of 4 August 1995.) The closure of the ordinary or of extraordinary sessions shall by right be delayed, should the occasion arise, in order to permit the application of Article 49. Additional sittings shall by right be held for the same purpose.

VI. ON TREATIES AND INTERNATIONAL AGREEMENTS

Article 52. (As amended by legislation of 4 August 1995.) The President of the Republic shall negotiate and ratify treaties.

He shall be informed of all negotiations leading to the conclusion of an international agreement not subject to ratification.

Article 53. Peace treaties, commercial treaties, treaties or agreements relative to international organization, those that commit the finances of the State, those that modify provisions of a legislative nature, those relative to the status of persons, those that call for the cession, exchange or addition of territory may be ratified or approved only by a law.

They shall enter into effect only after having been ratified or approved.

No cession, no exchange, or addition of territory shall be valid without the consent of the populations concerned.

Article 53–1. (Appended by legislation of 25 November 1993.) The Republic may conclude, with European states that are bound by commitments identical with its own in the matter of asylum and the protection of human rights and fundamental liberties, agreements determining their respective competence in regard to the consideration of requests for asylum submitted to them.

However, even if the request does not fall within their competence under the terms of these agreements, the authorities of the Republic shall remain empowered to grant asylum to any foreigner who is persecuted for actions in pursuit of liberty or who seeks protection by France for some other reason.

Article 53–2. (Appended by legislation of 8 July 1999.) The Republic may recognize the jurisdiction of the International Criminal Court as provided for by the treaty signed on 18 July 1998.

Article 54. (As amended by legislation of 25 June 1992.) If the Constitutional Council, the matter having been referred to it by the President of the Republic, by the Prime Minister, by the President of one or the other Assembly, or by any 60 Deputies or 60 Senators, shall declare that an international commitment contains a clause contrary to the Constitution, the authorization to ratify or approve the commitment in question may be given only after amendment of the Constitution.

Article 55. Treaties or agreements duly ratified or approved shall, upon their publication, have an authority superior to that of laws, subject, for each agreement or treaty, to its application by the other party.

VII. THE CONSTITUTIONAL COUNCIL

Article 56. The Constitutional Council shall consist of nine members, whose mandates shall last nine years and shall not be renewable. One-third of the membership of the Constitutional Council shall be renewed every three years. Three of its members shall be appointed by the President of the Republic, three by the President of the Assemblée nationale and three by the President of the Sénat.

In addition to the nine members provided for above, former Presidents of the Republic shall be members ex officio for life of the Constitutional Council.

The President shall be appointed by the President of the Republic. He shall have the deciding vote in case of a tie.

Article 57. The office of member of the Constitutional Council shall be incompatible with that of minister or Member of Parliament. Other incompatibilities shall be determined by an organic law.

Article 58. The Constitutional Council shall ensure the regularity of the election of the President of the Republic.

It shall examine complaints and shall announce the results of the vote.

Article 59. The Constitutional Council shall rule, in the case of disagreement, on the regularity of the election of deputies and senators.

Article 60. (As amended by legislation of 28 March 2003 and 1 March 2005.) The Constitutional Council shall ensure the regularity of the referendum procedure, as provided for in Articles 11 and 89, and in Title XV. It shall announce the results thereof.

Article 61. (As amended by legislation of 29 October 1974.) Organic laws, before their promulgation, and regulations of the Parliamentary Assemblies, before they come into application, must be submitted to the Constitutional Council, which shall rule on their constitutionality.

To the same end, laws may be submitted to the Constitutional Council, before their promulgation, by the President of the Republic, the Prime Minister, the President of the Assemblée nationale, the President of the Sénat, or any 60 deputies or 60 senators.

In the cases provided for by the two preceding paragraphs, the Constitutional Council must make its ruling within one month. Nevertheless, at the request of the Government, in case of urgency, this period shall be reduced to eight days.

In these same cases, referral to the Constitutional Council shall suspend the time limit for promulgation.

Article 62. A provision declared unconstitutional may not be promulgated or implemented.

The decisions of the Constitutional Council may not be appealed to any jurisdiction whatsoever. They shall be binding on the governmental authorities and on all administrative and juridical authorities.

Article 63. An organic law shall determine the rules of organization and functioning of the Constitutional Council, the procedure to be followed before it, and in particular of the periods of time allowed for laying disputes before it.

VIII. ON JUDICIAL AUTHORITY

Article 64. The President of the Republic shall be the guarantor of the independence of the judicial authority.

He shall be assisted by the High Council of the Judiciary.

An organic law shall determine the status of the judiciary.

Judges may not be removed from office.

Article 65. (As amended by legislation of 27 July 1993.) The High Council of the Judiciary shall be presided over by the President of the Republic. The Minister of Justice shall be its Vice-President ex officio and may preside in place of the President of the Republic.

The High Council of the Judiciary shall consist of two sections, one with competence for judges, the other for public prosecutors.

The section with competence for judges shall include, in addition to the President of the Republic and the Minister of Justice, five judges and one public prosecutor, one senior member of the Council of State appointed by the Council of State, and three prominent citizens who are neither members of Parliament nor the judiciary, appointed, respectively, by the President of the Republic, the President of the Assemblée nationale and the President of the Sénat.

The section with jurisdiction for public prosecutors shall include, in addition to the President of the Republic and the Minister of Justice, five public prosecutors and one judge, the senior member of the Council of State and the three prominent citizens referred to in the preceding paragraph.

The section of the High Council of the Judiciary with jurisdiction for judges shall make nominations for the appointment of judges in the Court of Cassation, for the First Presidents of the courts of appeal and the presidents of the tribunaux de grande instance. Other judges shall be appointed with its assent.

It shall serve as the disciplinary council for judges. When acting in that capacity, it shall be presided over by the First President of the Court of Cassation.

The section of the High Council of the Judiciary with jurisdiction for public prosecutors shall give its opinion on the appointment of public prosecutors, with the exception of posts to be filled in the Council of Ministers. It shall give its opinion on disciplinary penalties with regard to public prosecutors. When acting in that capacity, it shall be presided over by the Chief Public Prosecutor at the Court of Cassation.

An organic law shall determine the manner in which this Article is to be implemented.

Article 66. No one may be arbitrarily detained.

The judicial authority, guardian of individual liberty, shall ensure the respect of this principle under the conditions stipulated by law.

Article 66–1. (Appended by legislation of 23 February 2007.) No one may be sentenced to death.

IX. THE HIGH COURT

Article 67. (As amended by legislation of 23 February 2007.) The President of the Republic may not be held accountable for actions performed in the exercise of his office, in accordance with the provisions of Articles 53–2 and 68.

During his term of office, no juridical or administrative authority in France may order the President of the Republic to act as a witness, nor may subject him to investigation. All time limits regarding the prescription or debarment of such cases shall be suspended.

Judicial proceedings or investigations against the President of the Republic may only commence one month after the expiry of his term of office.

Article 68. (As amended by legislation of 27 July 1993 and 23 February 2007.) The President of the Republic may not be removed from office except in the case of actions which are manifestly incompatible with the exercise of his mandate. Any motion to remove him from office must be voted on by Parliament, in the form of the High Court.

Any motion to convene the High Court approved by one of the two Assemblies shall be referred immediately to the other, which must rule within 15 days.

The High Court shall be presided over by the President of the Assemblée nationale, and must rule on the removal from office of the President of the Republic by secret ballot within one month. The decision of the High Court shall be effected immediately.

The provisions of this Article shall be implemented only after approval by a majority of two-thirds of the members of the Assembly that first proposed the motion or of the High Court. No vote may be delegated. Only votes that are favourable to the motion to convene the High Court or to remove the President of the Republic from office shall be counted.

An organic law shall determine the manner in which this Article is to be implemented.

X. ON THE CRIMINAL LIABILITY OF MEMBERS OF GOVERNMENT
(Title and section appended by legislation of 27 July 1993)

Article 68–1. The members of the Government shall be criminally liable for actions performed in the exercise of their office and rated as crimes or misdemeanours at the time they were committed.

They shall be tried by the Court of Justice of the Republic.

The Court of Justice of the Republic shall be bound by such definition of serious crimes and other major offences and such determination of penalties as are laid down by the law.

Article 68–2. The Court of Justice of the Republic shall consist of 15 members: 12 Members of Parliament, elected in equal number from among their ranks by the Assemblée nationale and the Sénat after each general or partial election to these Assemblies, and three judges of the Court of Cassation, one of whom shall preside over the Court of Justice of the Republic.

Any person claiming to be a victim of a crime or misdemeanour committed by a member of the Government in the exercise of his duties may lodge a complaint with a commission of requests.

This commission shall order either the closure of the case or that it be forwarded to the chief public prosecutor at the Court of Cassation for referral to the Court of Justice of the Republic.

The Chief Public Prosecutor at the Court of Cassation may also make a reference ex officio to the Court of Justice of the Republic with the assent of the commission of requests.

An organic law shall determine the manner in which this Article is to be implemented.

Article 68–3. (Appended by legislation of 4 August 1995.) The provisions of this title shall apply to acts committed before its entry into force (on 27 July 1993).

XI. THE ECONOMIC AND SOCIAL COUNCIL

Article 69. The Economic and Social Council, at the referral of the Government, shall give its opinion on the Government bills, draft ordinances and decrees, as well as on the private members' bills submitted to it.

A member of the Economic and Social Council may be designated by the Council to present, before the Parliamentary Assemblies, the opinion of the Council on the Government or private members' bills that have been submitted to it.

Article 70. (As amended by legislation of 4 August 1995.) The Economic and Social Council may likewise be consulted by the Government on any problem of an economic or social character. Any plan, or any bill dealing with a plan, of an economic or social character shall be submitted to it for advice.

Article 71. The composition of the Economic and Social Council and its rules of procedure shall be determined by an organic law.

XII. ON TERRITORIAL COMMUNITIES

Article 72. (As amended by legislation of 28 March 2003.) The territorial communities of the Republic shall be the communes, the departments, regions, communities granted a particular status and overseas communities regulated by Article 74. Any other territorial community shall be created by law, if need be, at the place of one or more of the communities mentioned in this paragraph.

The territorial communities shall serve the purpose of taking decisions for the entirety of competencies which may be best made at their level of jurisdiction.

In conditions provided for by law, these communities shall administer themselves freely by means of elected councils and dispose of a regulatory power for the exercise of their competencies.

In conditions provided for by organic law, and provided that the essential conditions exist for the exercise of a public liberty or a constitutionally guaranteed right, territorial communities or groupings thereof may, depending on the case, as provided for by law or regulations, exercise, in an experimental manner and for a limited object and duration, legislative or regulatory dispositions which govern the exercise of their competencies.

No territorial community may exercise any tutelage over any other. However, when the exercise of a competency necessitates the participation of several territorial units, the law may authorize one of the communities, or one grouping thereof, to organize the modalities of their common action.

In the territorial communities of the Republic, the representative of the State, representative of each member of the Government, shall be responsible for national interests, administrative control and the respect of the law.

Article 72–1. (Appended by legislation of 28 March 2003.) Law shall determine the conditions under which voters of each territorial community may, by exercising the right of petition, demand the inclusion in the agenda of the Deliberative Assembly of that community a question relating to its competencies.

In conditions provided for by organic law, projects of deliberation or of an act relating to the competency of a territorial community may, at the initiative of that community, be submitted, by means of a referendum, to the decision of the voters of that same community.

When the creation of a territorial community granted with a particular status or the modification of the organization thereof is envisaged, the law may approve the consultation of voters registered in the communities concerned. The modification of the boundaries of territorial communities may also follow from the consultation of voters in conditions provided for by law.

Article 72–2. (Appended by legislation of 17 March 2003.) Territorial communities shall benefit from resources which they may dispose of freely in conditions determined by law.

They may receive all or part of the product of taxation of every kind. The law may authorize them to set the basis and levels of taxation within limits determined by law.

The fiscal receipts and other resources belonging to the territorial communities shall represent, for each category of community, a determining share of the sum of their resources. Organic law shall determine the conditions under which this rule is implemented.

Any transfer of competencies between the State and territorial communities shall be accompanied by the attribution of equivalent resources to those which were dedicated to their exercise. Any creation or extension of competencies which necessitates an increase in expenditure by territorial communities shall be accompanied by resources determined by law.

The law shall provide for mechanisms of adjustment intended to promote equality between territorial communities.

Article 72–3. (Appended by legislation of 28 March 2003.) The Republic recognizes, among the French people, the overseas populations, under a common ideal of liberty, equality and fraternity.

Guadeloupe, French Guiana, Martinique, Réunion, Mayotte, Saint Pierre and Miquelon, Wallis and Futuna and French Polynesia shall be governed by Article 73 with regard to Overseas Departments and Regions, and for the territorial communities created by the application of the last paragraph of Article 73, and by Article 74 with regard to other communities.

The status of New Caledonia shall be governed by Title XIII.

The law shall determine the legislative regime and the particular organization of the French Southern and Antarctic Territories.

Article 72–4. (Appended by legislation of 28 March 2003.) No change, for part or the whole of any of the communities referred to in the second paragraph of Article 72–3, from one to the other of the regimes provided for in Articles 73 and 74, may take place without the prior consent having been obtained of the voters of the community, or of that part of the community concerned, in conditions determined by the following paragraph. Any such change of regime shall be determined by organic law.

The President of the Republic, on the proposal of the Government during [Parliamentary] sessions, or on joint motion of the two Assemblies published in the *Journal Officiel*, may decide to consult the voters of a territorial community located overseas on a matter related to its organization, its competencies or its legislative regime. When this consultation relates to a proposed change as provided for in the previous paragraph and is organized in response to the request of the Government, the President shall make a declaration to that end before each Assembly, which shall be followed by a debate.

Article 73. (As amended by legislation of 28 March 2003.) In the overseas departments and regions, laws and regulations shall be fully applicable. They may be subject to adaptations which take account of the particular characteristics and constraints of these communities.

These adaptations may be decided by the communities with regard to subjects in which they exercise competency and should they be so authorized by the law.

By special dispensation referred to in the first paragraph, and in order to take account of their specific qualities, the communities governed by the present Article may be authorized by law to themselves determine the rules applicable on their territory, in a limited number of subjects which fall under the domain of the law.

These rules may not concern nationality, civic rights, guarantees of public liberties, the state and the capacity of persons, the organization of justice, penal law, the penal procedure, foreign policy, defence, security and public order, money, credit and exchange, or electoral law. This list may be clarified and completed by an organic law.

The dispositions provided for in the previous two paragraphs shall not be applicable to either the Department or the Region of Réunion.

The authorizations provided for in the second and third paragraphs shall be decided, at the request of the community concerned, under conditions and reserves provided for in an organic law. They may not be applied should the essential conditions for the exercise of a public liberty or of a constitutionally guaranteed right be brought into question.

The creation by law of a community in replacement of an overseas department or region, or the institution of a single Deliberative Assembly for these two communities shall not occur without the prior consent, received in the form provided for in the second paragraph of Article 72–4, of the voters registered in the totality of those communities.

Article 74. (As amended by legislation of 25 June 1992 and 28 March 2003.) The overseas communities governed by the present Article shall have a status which takes account of their proper interests within the Republic.

This status shall be defined by an organic law, adopted after the advice of the Deliberative Assembly, which shall determine:

the conditions under which the laws and regulations shall be applicable in that community;

the competencies of that community; excepting those already so exercised, the transfer of competencies from the State shall not include those subjects enumerated in the fourth paragraph of Article 73, clarified and completed, if need be, by an organic law;

the rules of the organization and functioning of institutions of the community, and the electoral regime of its Deliberative Assembly;

the conditions under which the institutions of that community shall be consulted upon projects and propositions of law and projects of edict or of decree including dispositions particular to that community, as well as regarding the ratification or approval of international engagements concluded within subjects relating to its competency.

Organic law may also determine, for those communities granted autonomy, the conditions under which:

the Council of State shall exercise judicial control specific to certain categories of acts of the Deliberative Assembly intervening in the scope of activities exercised by the assembly within the domain of the law;

the Deliberative Assembly may modify a law promulgated prior to the entry into force of the status of the community, when the Constitutional Council, referred by the authorities of the community, has stated that the law has intervened in the domain of the competency of this community;

measures justified by local necessities may be taken by the community in favour of its population, with regard to the access to employment, the right of establishment for the exercise of a professional activity or for the protection of property;

the community may participate, under the control of the State, in the exercise of the competencies it maintains, with respect to guarantees accorded to the entirety of the national territory for the exercise of public liberties.

Article 74–1. (Appended by legislation of 28 March 2003.) In those overseas communities to which Article 74 applies and in New Caledonia, the Government may, within those areas which remain within the competence of the State, extend by the means of edicts, with any necessary adaptations, the dispositions of a legislative nature in force in metropolitan France, except where the law shall expressly preclude, for the dispositions concerned, the recourse to this procedure.

Any such edicts shall be taken to the Council of Ministers following the advice of the Deliberative Assemblies concerned and of the Council of State. They enter into force from the time of their publication. They become null and void should they not be ratified by Parliament within a period of eighteen months following publication.

Article 75. Citizens of the Republic who do not have ordinary civil status, the only status referred to in Article 34, may keep their personal status as long as they have not renounced it.

XIII. TRANSITIONAL PROVISIONS RELATING TO NEW CALEDONIA
(Section appended by legislation of 20 July 1998)

Article 76. The population of New Caledonia is called upon to vote by 31 December 1998 on the provisions of the agreement signed at Nouméa on 5 May 1998, and published in the *Journal Officiel* of the French Republic on 27 May 1998.

Persons satisfying the requirements laid down in Article 2 of Act No. 88-1028 of 9 November 1988 shall be eligible to take part in the vote.

The measures required to organize the ballot shall be taken by decree adopted after consultation with the Council of State and discussion in the Council of Ministers.

Article 77. (As amended by legislation of 23 February 2007.) After approval of the agreement by the vote provided for in Article 76, the organic law adopted after consultation with the Deliberative Assembly of New Caledonia shall determine, in order to ensure the development of New Caledonia in accordance with the guidelines set out in that agreement and as required for its implementation:

the competencies of the State which are to be transferred definitively to the institutions of New Caledonia, at what time and in what manner such transfers are to be made, and how the costs incurred thereby are to be apportioned;

the rules for the organization and operation of the institutions of New Caledonia, including the circumstances in which certain categories of act adopted by the Deliberative Assembly of New Caledonia may be referred to the Constitutional Council for review before publication;

the rules concerning citizenship, the electoral system, employment, and ordinary civil status;

the circumstances and the time limits within which the population concerned in New Caledonia is to vote on the attainment of full sovereignty.

Any other measures required to give effect to the agreement referred to in Article 76 shall be determined by law.

(Paragraph appended by legislation of 23 February 2007.) The list designating the names of those persons eligible to vote in the poll referred to in the agreement mentioned in Article 76 and in Act No. 99-209 of 19 March 1999 applies to the poll mentioned in Article 76, and contains names of persons ineligible to vote in elections to the Deliberative Assembly of New Caledonia and its provinces.

[A former Article 76, permitting Overseas Territories to retain their former status within the Republic and a section 'On the Community' (Articles 77–87), providing for a community of autonomous states of common citizenship, were repealed by legislation of 4 August 1995.]

XIV. ON AGREEMENTS OF ASSOCIATION

Article 88. The Republic may make agreements with States that wish to associate themselves with it in order to develop their own civilizations.

XV. ON THE EUROPEAN COMMUNITIES AND THE EUROPEAN UNION
(Section appended by legislation of 27 July 1993)

Article 88–1. (Amended by legislation of 1 March 2005 and 4 February 2008.) The Republic shall participate in the European Communities and in the European Union constituted by States that have freely chosen, by virtue of the treaties that established them, to exercise some of their powers in common.

It may participate in the European Union under the conditions envisaged by the treaty modifying the Treaty on European Union and the treaty establishing the European Communities, signed in Lisbon, Portugal, on 13 December 2007.

Article 88–2. (Amended by legislation of 25 January 1999 and 25 March 2003.) Subject to reciprocity and in accordance with the terms of the Treaty on European Union signed on 7 February 1992, France agrees to the transfer of competencies necessary for the establishment of European economic and monetary union.

Subject to the same reservation and in accordance with the terms of the Treaty establishing the European Community, as amended by the treaty signed on 2 October 1997, the transfer of competencies necessary for the determination of rules concerning freedom of movement for persons and related areas may be agreed.

The law shall determine the rules relative to the European mandate of arrest with regard to acts taken on the basis of the Treaty on European Union.

Article 88–3. Subject to reciprocity and in accordance with the terms of the Treaty on European Union signed on 7 February 1992, the right to vote and stand as a candidate in municipal elections shall be granted only to citizens of the Union residing in France. Such citizens shall neither exercise the office of mayor or deputy mayor nor participate in the designation of Sénat electors or in the election of Senators. An organic law adopted in identical terms by the two Assemblies shall determine the manner of implementation of this Article.

Article 88–4. (Amended by legislation of 25 January 1999.) The Government shall present to the Assemblée nationale and the Sénat any proposals for or drafts of acts of the European Communities or the European Union containing provisions of a legislative nature as soon as they have been transmitted to the Council of the European Union. It may also present to them other proposals or drafts of acts or any document emanating from a European Union institution.

In the manner laid down by the rules of procedure of each Assembly, resolutions may be adopted, even if Parliament is not in session, on the drafts, proposals or documents referred to in the preceding paragraph.

Article 88–5. (Appended by legislation of 1 March 2005.) Any bill authorizing the ratification of a treaty concerning the accession of a State to the European Union or the European Communities shall be submitted to a referendum by the President of the Republic.

XVI. ON AMENDMENT

Article 89. The initiative for amending the Constitution shall belong both to the President of the Republic on the proposal of the Prime Minister and to the Members of Parliament.

The Government or private member's bill for amendment must be adopted by the two Assemblies in identical terms. The amendment shall become definitive after approval by a referendum.

Nevertheless, the proposed amendment shall not be submitted to a referendum when the President of the Republic decides to submit it to Parliament convened in Congress; in this case, the proposed amendment shall be approved only if it is accepted by a three-fifths majority

FRANCE

of the votes cast. The Secretariat of the Congress shall be that of the Assemblée nationale.

No amendment procedure may be undertaken or followed if it is prejudicial to the integrity of the territory.

The republican form of government shall not be the object of an amendment.

ELECTORAL LAW, JULY 1986

The 577 Deputies of the Assemblée nationale are to be directly elected under the former single-member constituency system (in force before the implementation of a system of proportional representation imposed by the electoral law of 1985). Participating parties can nominate only one candidate and designate a reserve candidate, who can serve as a replacement if the elected Deputy is appointed a Minister or a member of the Constitutional Council, or is sent on a government assignment scheduled to last more than six months, or dies. A candidate must receive an absolute majority and at least one-quarter of registered votes in order to be elected to the Assemblée nationale. If these conditions are not fulfilled, a second ballot will be held a week later, for voters to choose between all candidates receiving 12.5% of the total votes on the first ballot. The candidate who receives a simple majority of votes on the second ballot will then be elected. Candidates polling less than 5% of the votes will lose their deposit.

The Government

HEAD OF STATE

President: NICOLAS SARKOZY (took office 16 May 2007).

COUNCIL OF MINISTERS
(March 2008)

Prime Minister: FRANÇOIS FILLON.
Minister of State, Minister of Ecology, Energy, Sustainable Development and Planning: JEAN-LOUIS BORLOO.
Minister of the Interior, the Overseas Possessions and Territorial Collectivities: MICHÈLE ALLIOT-MARIE.
Minister of Foreign and European Affairs: BERNARD KOUCHNER.
Minister of the Economy, Industry and Employment: CHRISTINE LAGARDE.
Minister of Immigration, Integration, National Identity and Shared Development: BRICE HORTEFEUX.
Keeper of the Seals, Minister of Justice: RACHIDA DATI.
Minister of Agriculture and Fisheries: MICHEL BARNIER.
Minister of Labour, Social Relations, the Family and Solidarity: XAVIER BERTRAND.
Minister of National Education: XAVIER DARCOS.
Minister of Higher Education and Research: VALÉRIE PÉCRESSE.
Minister of Defence: HERVÉ MORIN.
Minister of Health, Youth, Sport and Associations: ROSELYNE BACHELOT-NARQUIN.
Minister of Housing and Urban Affairs: CHRISTINE BOUTIN.
Minister of Culture and Communication: CHRISTINE ALBANEL.
Minister of the Budget, Public Finances and the Civil Service: ERIC WOERTH.
Minister-Delegate for Relations with Parliament: ROGER KAROUTCHI.
Minister-Delegate for Forward Planning, Assessment of Public Policies and Development of the Digital Economy: ERIC BESSON.
Minister-Delegate for Transport: DOMINIQUE BUSSEREAU.
Minister-Delegate for Ecology: NATHALIE KOSCIUSKO-MORIZET.
Minister-Delegate for Development in the Region of Paris: CHRISTIAN BLANC.
Minister-Delegate for Planning: HUBERT FALCO.
Minister-Delegate for the Overseas Possessions: YVES JÉGO.
Minister-Delegate for the Interior and Territorial Collectivities: ALAIN MARLEIX.
Minister-Delegate for European Affairs: JEAN-PIERRE JOUYET.
Minister-Delegate for Co-operation and the French-speaking World: ALAIN JOYANDET.
Minister-Delegate for Foreign Affairs and Human Rights: RAMA YADE.
Minister-Delegate for Business, Crafts, Small and Medium-Sized Enterprises, Tourism and Services: HERVÉ NOVELLI.
Minister-Delegate for Employment: LAURENT WAUQUIEZ.
Minister-Delegate for Industry and Consumers, Spokesman for the Government: LUC CHATEL.
Minister-Delegate for External Trade: ANNE-MARIE IDRAC.
Minister-Delegate for Social Cohesion: VALÉRIE LÉTARD.
Minister-Delegate for the Family: NADINE MORANO.
Minister-Delegate for Defence and Veterans: JEAN-MARIE BOCKEL.
Minister-Delegate for Youth, Sport and Associations: BERNARD LAPORTE.
Minister-Delegate for Urban Policy: FADELA AMARA.
Minister-Delegate for the Civil Service: ANDRÉ SANTINI.
High Commissioner for Action against Poverty: MARTIN HIRSCH.

MINISTRIES

Office of the President: Palais de l'Elysée, 55–57 rue du Faubourg Saint Honoré, 75008 Paris; tel. 1-42-92-81-00; fax 1-47-42-24-65; internet www.elysee.fr.

Office of the Prime Minister: Hôtel de Matignon, 57 rue de Varenne, 75007 Paris; tel. 1-42-75-80-00; fax 1-42-75-78-31; e-mail premier-ministre@premier-ministre.gouv.fr; internet www.premier-ministre.gouv.fr.

Ministry of Agriculture and Fisheries: 8 rue de Varenne, 75349 Paris Cedex 07; tel. 1-49-55-49-55; fax 1-49-55-40-39; e-mail infodoc@agriculture.gouv.fr; internet www.agriculture.gouv.fr.

Ministry of the Budget, Public Finances and the Civil Service: 139 rue de Bercy, 75572 Paris Cedex 12; tel. 1-40-04-04-04; fax 1-43-43-75-97; internet www.budget.gouv.fr.

Ministry of Culture and Communication: 3 rue de Valois, 75001 Paris; tel. 1-40-15-80-00; fax 1-40-15-81-72; e-mail point.culture@culture.fr; internet www.culture.gouv.fr.

Ministry of Defence: 14 rue Saint Dominique, 75007 Paris; tel. 1-42-19-30-11; fax 1-47-05-40-91; e-mail courrier-ministre@sdbc.defense.gouv.fr; internet www.defense.gouv.fr.

Ministry of Ecology, Energy, Sustainable Development and Planning: 20 ave de Ségur, 75302 Paris 07; tel. 1-42-19-20-21; e-mail ministre@ecologie.gouv.fr; internet www.developpementdurable.gouv.fr.

Ministry of the Economy, Industry and Employment: 139 rue de Bercy, 75572 Paris Cedex 12; tel. 1-40-04-04-04; fax 1-43-43-75-97; internet www.minefe.gouv.fr.

Ministry of Foreign and European Affairs: 37 quai d'Orsay, 75351 Paris Cedex 07; tel. 1-43-17-53-53; fax 1-43-17-52-03; internet www.diplomatie.gouv.fr.

Ministry of Health, Youth, Sport and Associations: 8 ave de Ségur, 75700 Paris; tel. 1-40-56-60-00; internet www.sante.gouv.fr.

Ministry of Higher Education and Research: 1 rue Descartes, 75231 Paris Cedex 05; tel. 1-55-55-90-90; e-mail secretariat-communication@recherche.gouv.fr; internet www.enseignementsup-recherche.gouv.fr.

Ministry of Housing and Urban Affairs: 72 rue de Varenne, 75700 Paris; tel. 1-42-75-80-00; e-mail infologement.dguhc@equipement.gouv.fr; internet www.logement.gouv.fr.

Ministry of Immigration, Integration, National Identity and Shared Development: 101 rue de Grenelle, 75700 Paris; tel. 1-77-72-61-00; internet www.premier-ministre.gouv.fr/iminidco.

Ministry of the Interior, the Overseas Possessions and Territorial Collectivities: place Beauvau, 75008 Paris; tel. 1-40-07-60-60; fax 1-43-59-89-50; e-mail sirp@interieur.gouv.fr; internet www.interieur.gouv.fr.

Ministry of Justice: 13 place Vendôme, 75042 Paris Cedex 01; tel. 1-44-77-60-60; fax 1-44-77-60-00; e-mail cyberjustice@justice.gouv.fr; internet www.justice.gouv.fr.

Ministry of Labour, Social Relations, the Family and Solidarity: 127 rue de Grenelle, 75007 Paris; tel. 1-44-38-38-38; fax 1-44-38-20-20; internet www.travail.gouv.fr.

Ministry of National Education: 110 rue de Grenelle, 75357 Paris Cedex 07; tel. 1-55-55-10-10; fax 1-45-51-53-63; e-mail info-desco@education.gouv.fr; internet www.education.gouv.fr.

FRANCE

President and Legislature

PRESIDENT

Presidential Election, First Ballot, 22 April 2007

Candidates	Votes	% of votes
Nicolas Sarkozy (Union pour un Mouvement Populaire)	11,448,663	31.18
Ségolène Royal (Parti Socialiste)	9,500,112	25.87
François Bayrou (Union pour la Démocratie Française)	6,820,119	18.57
Jean-Marie Le Pen (Front National)	3,834,530	10.44
Olivier Besancenot (Ligue Communiste Révolutionnaire)	1,498,581	4.08
Philippe De Villiers (Mouvement pour la France)	818,407	2.23
Marie-George Buffet (Parti Communiste Français)	707,268	1.93
Dominique Voynet (Les Verts)	576,666	1.57
Arlette Laguiller (Lutte Ouvrière)	487,857	1.33
José Bové (Alternative à Gauche 2007)	483,008	1.32
Frédéric Nihous (Chasse Pêche Nature Traditions)	420,645	1.15
Gérard Schivardi ('Candidat de maires')	123,540	0.34
Total	**36,719,396**	**100.00**

Presidential Election, Second Ballot, 6 May 2007

Candidate	Votes	% of votes
Nicolas Sarkozy (Union pour un Mouvement Populaire)	18,983,138	53.06
Ségolène Royal (Parti Socialiste)	16,790,440	46.94
Total	**35,773,578**	**100.00**

PARLIAMENT
(Parlement)

Assemblée nationale
(National Assembly)

126 rue de l'Université, 75355 Paris Cedex 07; tel. 1-40-63-60-00; fax 1-45-55-75-23; e-mail infos@assemblee-nationale.fr; internet www.assemblee-nationale.fr.

President: BERNARD ACCOYER (UMP).

General Election, 10 June and 17 June 2007

Party	% of votes cast in first ballot	% of votes cast in second ballot*	Seats
Union pour un Mouvement Populaire (UMP)	33.30	47.26	313
Parti Socialiste (PS)	24.11	35.26	186
Le Nouveau Centre	4.85	3.92	22†
Parti Communiste Français (PCF)	4.82	3.26	15
Parti Radical de Gauche (PRG)	1.54	2.15	7
Les Verts	4.51	3.19	4
Mouvement Démocrate (MoDem)	0.41	—	3†
Rassemblement pour la France (RPF)	0.37	0.29	3
Mouvement pour la France (MPF)	0.80	—	1
Front National (FN)	11.34	1.85	—
Pôle Républicain (PR)	1.19	0.06	—
Chasse Pêche Nature Traditions (CPNT)	1.67	—	—
Ligue Communiste Révolutionnaire (LCR)	1.27	—	—
Lutte Ouvrière (LO)	1.20	—	—
Mouvement National Républicain (MNR)	1.09	—	—
Various right-wing candidates‡	3.65	1.29	9
Various left-wing candidates	1.09	1.27	15
Regionalist candidates	0.26	0.14	1
Various ecologist candidates§	1.17	—	—
Various far-left candidates‖	0.32	—	—
Various far-right candidates¶	0.24	—	—
Others[1]	0.77	0.06	1
Total	**100.00**	**100.00**	**577**

*Held where no candidate had won the requisite overall majority in the first ballot, between candidates who had received at least 12.5% of the votes in that round. The total number of valid votes cast was 25,246,045 in the first round, and 21,221,026 in the second round.
† In May 2007 the Union pour la Démocratie Française (UDF) was restyled as the Mouvement Démocrate (MoDem) by the party leader, François Bayrou, to oppose the UMP party of the President, Nicolas Sarkozy. The UDF was formally reconstituted as the MoDem in November. The Nouveau Centre was formed in May 2007 by elements of the UDF allied to the President.
‡ Including, notably, candidates of the Droite Libérale Chrétienne and the Centre National des Indépendants et Paysans.
§ Including, notably, candidates of Génération Ecologie-Les Bleus and the Mouvement Ecologiste Indépendant.
‖ Including, notably, candidates of the Parti des Travailleurs, Les Motivé-e-s and Les Alternatifs.
¶ Including, notably, candidates of the Parti National Républicain, La France aux Français and the Parti Nationaliste Français.
[1] Including, notably, candidates of the Rassemblement des Contribuables Français, the Parti de la Loi Naturelle and the Union pour la Semaine de Quatre Jours.

Sénat
(Senate)

15 rue de Vaugirard, 75291 Paris Cedex 06; tel. 1-42-34-20-00; fax 1-42-34-26-77; e-mail communication@senat.fr; internet www.senat.fr.

President: CHRISTIAN PONCELET (UMP).

Prior to mid-2003 members of the Sénat were indirectly elected for a term of nine years, with one-third of the seats renewable every three years. A law approved by Parliament in July 2003 introduced a number of reforms to senatorial elections; henceforth, senators were to be elected for a term of six years, with one-half of the seats renewable every three years, and seats were to be allocated through a combination of majority voting and proportional representation. In addition, the minimum age for eligible candidates to the Sénat was reduced from 35 to 30 years. With effect from September 2008, the number of senators was to be increased to 343 and again from 2011, to 348.

A partial election to the Sénat took place on 26 September 2004. Following this election, the number of seats in the Sénat was increased from 321 to 331: 304 for metropolitan France; 15 for the overseas departments and territories; and 12 for French nationals abroad. A partial election took place on 26 August 2007 to fill two vacant seats. The strength of the parties at 4 March 2008 was as follows:

Grouping	Seats
Groupe Union pour un Mouvement Populaire	159
Groupe Socialiste	96
Groupe de l'Union Centriste	30
Groupe Communiste Républicain et Citoyen	23
Groupe du Rassemblement Démocratique et Social Européen	16
Non-attached	6
Total	**330***

*One seat was vacant owing to the death of the President of the Groupe du Rassemblement Démocratique et Social Européen, Jacques Pelletier, on 3 September 2007.

Territorial Collectivity of Corsica

In 1992 Corsica officially assumed the status of a territorial collectivity (collectivité territoriale), in accordance with legislation approved by Parliament in the previous year, gaining a degree of political and administrative autonomy. The island of Corsica is generally considered as one of the 26 régions of Metropolitan France.

The 51-member Assemblée de Corse was constituted following elections held in March 1992. Members of the Assemblée are elected by universal suffrage for a term of six years, according to a system of proportional representation. Three additional seats are allocated to the list receiving the largest number of votes. The nine-member Executive Council (Conseil Exécutif) is elected by the Assemblée from among the members of the largest parliamentary group.

President of the Executive Council (Conseil Exécutif): ANGE SANTINI (UMP—Rassembler pour la Corse).

Members: STÉPHANIE GRIMALDI, ANTOINE SINDALI, JÉRÔME POLVERINI, ANTOINE GIORGI, JEAN-CLAUDE BONACCORSI, SIMONE GUERINI, MARIE-ANGE SUSINI, JEAN-PIERRE LECCIA.

President of the Assemblée de Corse: CAMILLE DE ROCCA SERRA (UMP—Rassembler pour la Corse).

FRANCE   *Directory*

Assemblée de Corse: 22 cours Grandval, 20187 Ajaccio Cedex 1; tel. 4-95-51-65-64; fax 4-95-51-65-66; e-mail contact@corse.fr; internet www.corse.fr; f. 1982.

Election, 21 and 28 March 2004

	Seats
Rassembler pour la Corse	15
La Corse dans la République	9
Unione Naziunale	8
La Corse en Marche	7
Rassembler à Gauche pour une Corse Citoyenne	4
Union Territoriale	4
Ensemble Changeons d'Epoque	4
Total	**51**

Political Organizations

Les Alternatifs: 40 rue de Malte, 75011 Paris; tel. 1-43-57-44-80; fax 1-43-57-64-50; e-mail contact@alternatifs.org; internet www.alternatifs.org; f. 1997; socialist, ecologist, feminist.

Chasse Pêche Nature Traditions (CPNT): BP 87546, 64075 Pau Cedex; tel. 5-59-14-71-71; fax 5-59-14-71-72; e-mail cpnt@cpnt.asso.fr; internet www.cpnt.asso.fr; f. 1989 as Chasse-Pêche-Traditions; emphasizes defence of rural traditions and the sovereignty of the State within Europe; Pres. FRÉDÉRIC NIHOUS; Sec-Gen. EDDIE PUYJALON.

Front National (FN): 4 rue Vauguyon, 92210 Saint-Cloud; tel. 1-41-12-10-00; fax 1-41-12-10-86; e-mail contact@frontnational.com; internet www.frontnational.com; f. 1972; extreme right-wing nationalist; Pres. JEAN-MARIE LE PEN; Sec.-Gen. LOUIS ALIOT.

Génération Ecologie: 19 blvd Pereire, 75017 Paris; tel. 9-52-47-48-40; fax 9-57-47-48-40; e-mail webge@hotmail.fr; internet www.generation-ecologie.com; f. 1991; ecologist; Pres. FRANCE GAMERRE.

Ligue Communiste Révolutionnaire (LCR): 2 rue Richard Lenoir, 93100 Montreuil; tel. 1-48-70-42-30; fax 1-48-59-39-59; e-mail contactlcr@lcr-rouge.org; internet www.lcr-rouge.org; f. 1974; Trotskyist; 3,000 mems; Principal Speakers OLIVIER BESANCENOT, ROSELINE VACHETTA, ALAIN KRIVINE.

Lutte Ouvrière (LO): BP 233, 75865 Paris Cedex 18; tel. 1-48-10-86-20; fax 1-48-10-86-26; e-mail contact@lutte-ouvriere.org; internet www.lutte-ouvriere.org; f. 1968; Trotskyist; Leaders ARLETTE LAGUILLER, FRANÇOIS DUBURG, GEORGES KALDY, ROBERT BARCIA HARDY.

MARS-Gauche Républicaine: 4 allée Nungesser et Coli, 94550 Chevilly-Larue; e-mail contact@mars-gr.org; internet www.mars-gr.org; f. 2007 by merger of Mouvement pour une alternative républicaine et sociale and Gauche Républicaine (both f. 2003); left-wing, anti-liberal; predecessor parties campaigned against the Constitution for Europe; Pres. ERIC COQUEREL; Sec.-Gen. PIERRE CARASSUS.

Mouvement Démocrate (MoDem): 133 bis rue de l'Université, 75007 Paris; tel. 1-53-59-20-00; fax 1-53-59-20-59; internet www.mouvementdemocrate.fr; f. 1978 as the Union pour la Démocratie Française (UDF) to unite for electoral purposes non-Gaullist 'majority' candidates; reconstituted as a unified party in 1998; reconstituted in November 2007 to oppose the UMP; elements of the UDF allied to the President, Nicolas Sarkozy, left the party and formed the Nouveau Centre in May 2007; Pres. FRANÇOIS BAYROU.

Mouvement Ecologiste Indépendant (MEI): 26 rue Nicolaï, 75012 Paris; tel. 3-84-47-48-80; e-mail jacques.lancon@orange.fr; internet www.mei-fr.org; f. 1994; ecologist; 1,000 mems; Pres. ANTOINE WAECHTER; Nat. Sec. JACQUES LANÇON.

Mouvement National Républicain (MNR): 15 rue de Cronstadt, 75015 Paris; tel. 1-56-56-64-34; fax 1-56-56-52-47; e-mail presse@m-n-r.net; internet www.m-n-r.net; f. 1999 by breakaway faction of FN; extreme right-wing nationalist; Pres. BRUNO MÉGRET; Sec.-Gen. NICOLAS BAY.

Mouvement pour la France (MPF): 91 rue du Cherche Midi, 75006 Paris; tel. 1-53-63-53-00; fax 1-73-00-10-51; e-mail communication@pourlafrance.fr; internet www.pourlafrance.fr; f. 1994; far-right, nationalist; Pres. PHILIPPE DE VILLIERS; Sec.-Gen. GUILLAUME PELTIER.

Mouvement Républicain et Citoyen (MRC): 9 rue du Faubourg Poissonière, 75009 Paris; tel. 1-44-83-83-00; fax 1-44-83-83-10; e-mail contact@mrc-france.org; internet www.mrc-france.org; f. 2002 as Pôle Républicain on the basis of the Mouvement des Citoyens; present name adopted 2003; socialist; sceptical of increased European integration or devolution of powers from the nation-state; Hon. Pres. JEAN-PIERRE CHEVÈNEMENT; First Sec. GEORGES SARRE.

Le Nouveau Centre: 84 rue de Grenelle, 75007 Paris; tel. 1-44-39-28-00; fax 1-44-39-28-09; e-mail contact@le-nouveaucentre.org; internet www.le-nouveaucentre.org; f. 2007 by members of the UDF allied to the President, Nicolas Sarkozy, and his UMP party; Pres. HERVÉ MORIN; Parliamentary Leader FRANÇOIS SAUVADET.

Parti Communiste Français (PCF): 2 place du Colonel Fabien, 75019 Paris; tel. 1-40-40-12-12; fax 1-40-40-13-56; e-mail pcf@pcf.fr; internet www.pcf.fr; subscribed to the common programme of the United Left (with the Parti Socialiste) until 1977; advocates independent foreign policy; Nat. Sec MARIE-GEORGE BUFFET.

Parti Radical de Gauche (PRG): 13 rue Duroc, 75007 Paris; tel. 1-45-66-67-68; fax 1-45-66-47-93; e-mail eboyer@prg.com.fr; internet www.planeteradicale.org; f. 1972 as the Mouvement des Radicaux de Gauche; left-wing; Pres. JEAN-MICHEL BAYLET; Sec.-Gen. ELISABETH BOYER.

Parti Socialiste (PS): 10 rue de Solférino, 75333 Paris Cedex 07; tel. 1-45-56-77-00; fax 1-47-05-15-78; e-mail infops@parti-socialiste.fr; internet www.parti-socialiste.fr; f. 1971; First Sec. FRANÇOIS HOLLANDE; 280,000 mems (Nov. 2006).

Rassemblement pour l'Indépendance et la Souveraineté de la France (RIF): BP 10014, 75362 Paris Cedex 08; tel. 1-34-75-19-05; fax 5-56-06-98-52; e-mail secretariat.rif@tele2.fr; internet www.r-i-f.org; f. 2003; nationalist, opposed to the transfer of powers from nation states to the European Union; Pres. JEAN-PAUL BLED; Sec.-Gen. ALAIN BOURNAZEL.

Union pour un Mouvement Populaire (UMP): 55 rue La Boétie, 75384 Paris Cedex 08; tel. 1-40-76-60-00; e-mail webmaster@u-m-p.org; internet www.u-m-p.org; f. 2002; founded as Union pour la Majorité Presidentielle by members of the former Rassemblement pour la République and Démocratie Liberale parties, in conjunction with elements of the UDF, now MoDem (q.v.); centre-right grouping formed to ensure that President Jacques Chirac had a majority grouping in the Assemblée nationale; 317,771 mems. (Jan. 2007); Sec.-Gen. PATRICK DEVEDJIAN; First Vice-Pres. JEAN-PIERRE RAFFARIN.

Associated organizations include:

Centre National des Indépendants et Paysans (CNI): 6 rue Quentin Bauchart, 75008 Paris; tel. 1-47-23-47-00; fax 1-47-23-47-03; e-mail contact@cni.asso.fr; internet www.cnip.asso.fr; f. 1949; right-wing; Pres. ANNICK DU ROSCOAT; Sec.-Gen. BERNARD BEAUDET.

La Gauche Moderne: 10 rue des Haudriettes, 75003 Paris; e-mail webmaster@lagauchemoderne.org; internet www.lagauchemoderne.org; moderate, left-wing; f. 2007 to support President Nicolas Sarkozy and his UMP party; Pres. JEAN-MARIE BOCKEL.

Parti Radical: 1 place de Valois, 75001 Paris; tel. 1-42-61-02-02; fax 1-42-61-02-04; e-mail contact@partiradical.net; internet www.partiradical.net; f. 1901; democratic socialist; fmrly affiliated to UDF, associate mem. of UMP since Nov. 2002; Pres. JEAN-LOUIS BORLOO; Sec.-Gen. LAURENT HÉNART.

Unione Naziunale: Assemblée de Corse, 22 cours Grandval, BP 215, 20187 Ajaccio Cedex 01; tel. 4-95-51-64-85; fax 4-95-50-08-22; e-mail unione.naziunale-ctc@wanadoo.fr; f. 2004 to contest elections to the Assemblée de Corse; coalition of separatist parties, including Corsica Nazione (f. 1992); Leader JEAN-GUY TALAMONI.

Les Verts: 247 rue du Faubourg Saint-Martin, 75010 Paris; tel. 1-53-19-53-19; fax 1-53-19-03-93; e-mail verts@lesverts.fr; internet www.lesverts.fr; f. 1984; ecologist; 9,100 mems (Nov. 2006); Nat. Sec. CÉCILE DUFLOT.

Diplomatic Representation

EMBASSIES IN FRANCE

Afghanistan: 32 ave Raphaël, 75016 Paris; tel. 1-45-25-05-29; fax 1-45-24-60-68; e-mail ambafghane@wanadoo.fr; internet www.ambafghane-paris.com; Ambassador Dr ASSAD OMER.

Albania: 57 ave Marceau, 75116 Paris; tel. 1-47-23-31-00; fax 1-47-23-59-85; e-mail ambassade.paris@mfa.gov.al; Chargé d'affaires a.i. YLLJET ALIÇKA.

Algeria: 50 rue de Lisbonne, 75008 Paris; tel. 1-53-93-20-20; fax 1-42-25-10-25; e-mail chancellerie@amb-algerie.fr; internet www.amb-algerie.fr; Ambassador MISSOUM SBIH.

Andorra: 51 bis rue de Boulainvilliers, 75016 Paris; tel. 1-40-06-03-30; fax 1-40-06-03-64; e-mail ambaixada@andorra.ad; internet www.amb-andorre.fr; Ambassador VICENÇ MATEU ZAMORA.

Angola: 19 ave Foch, 75116 Paris; tel. 1-45-01-58-20; fax 1-45-00-33-71; e-mail barreira.ramiromanuel_@libertysurf.fr; Ambassador VICTOR MANUEL RITA DA FONSECA LIMA.

FRANCE

Antigua and Barbuda: 43 ave de Friedland, 75008 Paris; tel. 1-53-96-93-96; fax 1-53-75-15-69; e-mail carl.roberts@antigua-barbuda.com; Ambassador Dr CARL ROBERTS (resident in London, United Kingdom).

Argentina: 6 rue Cimarosa, 75116 Paris; tel. 1-44-05-27-00; fax 1-45-53-46-33; e-mail efranpol@noos.fr; internet www.ambassadeargentine.net; Ambassador ERIC CALCAGNO Y MAILLMANN.

Armenia: 9 rue Viète, 75017 Paris; tel. 1-42-12-98-00; fax 1-42-12-98-03; e-mail ambarmen@wanadoo.fr; Ambassador EDVARD NALBANDIAN.

Australia: 4 rue Jean Rey, 75724 Paris Cedex 15; tel. 1-40-59-33-00; fax 1-40-59-33-10; e-mail info.paris@dfat.gov.au; internet www.france.embassy.gov.au; Ambassador DAVID A. RITCHIE.

Austria: 6 rue Fabert, 75007 Paris; tel. 1-40-63-30-63; fax 1-45-55-63-65; e-mail paris-ob@bmeia.gv.at; internet www.amb-autriche.fr; Ambassador HUBERT HEISS.

Azerbaijan: 78 ave d'Iéna, 75016 Paris; tel. 1-44-18-60-20; fax 1-44-18-60-25; e-mail ambazer@wanadoo.fr; Ambassador TARIK ISMAÏL OGLOU ALIYEV.

Bahrain: 3 bis place des Etats-Unis, 75116 Paris; tel. 1-47-23-48-68; fax 1-47-20-55-75; e-mail ambassade@ambahrein-france.com; internet www.ambahrein-france.com; Ambassador Dr HASHIM HASSAN AL-BASH.

Bangladesh: 39 rue Erlanger, 75016 Paris; tel. 1-46-51-90-33; fax 1-46-51-90-35; e-mail bangembpar@yahoo.com; Ambassador RUHUL AMIN.

Belarus: 38 blvd Suchet, 75016 Paris; tel. 1-44-14-69-79; fax 1-44-14-69-70; e-mail france@belembassy.org; internet www.france.belembassy.org; Ambassador VIKTAR SHYKH.

Belgium: 9 rue de Tilsitt, 75840 Paris Cedex 17; tel. 1-44-09-39-39; fax 1-47-54-07-64; e-mail paris@diplobel.org; internet www.diplomatie.be/paris; Ambassador PIERRE-DOMINIQUE SCHMIDT.

Benin: 87 ave Victor Hugo, 75116 Paris; tel. 1-45-00-98-82; fax 1-45-01-82-02; e-mail ambassade@ambassade-benin.org; internet www.ambassade-benin.org; Ambassador EDGAR YVES MONNOU.

Bolivia: 12 ave Président Kennedy, 75016 Paris; tel. 1-42-24-93-44; fax 1-45-25-86-23; e-mail ambassade@amb-bolivie.fr; internet www.amb-bolivie.fr; Ambassador LUZMILA CARPIO SANGÜEZA.

Bosnia and Herzegovina: 174 rue de Courcelles, 75017 Paris; tel. 1-42-67-34-22; fax 1-40-53-85-22; e-mail amb.pariz@mvp.gov.ba; Ambassador ŽELJANA ZOVKO.

Brazil: 34 cours Albert 1er, 75008 Paris; tel. 1-45-61-63-00; fax 1-42-89-03-45; e-mail imprensa@bresil.org; internet www.bresil.org; Ambassador JOSÉ MAURICIO BUSTANI.

Brunei: 7 rue de Presbourg, 75116 Paris; tel. 1-53-64-67-60; fax 1-53-64-67-83; e-mail ambassade.brunei@wanadoo.fr; Ambassador Dato' Paduka ZAINIDI HAJI SIDUP.

Bulgaria: 1 ave Rapp, 75007 Paris; tel. 1-45-51-85-90; fax 1-45-51-18-68; e-mail bulgamb@wanadoo.fr; internet www.amb-bulgarie.fr; Ambassador IRINA BOKOVA.

Burkina Faso: 159 blvd Haussmann, 75008 Paris; tel. 1-43-59-90-63; fax 1-42-56-50-07; e-mail amba.burkina.faso@wanadoo.fr; internet www.ambaburkinafrance.org; Chargé d'affaires a.i. PIABIÉ FIRMIN GRÉGOIRE N'DO.

Burundi: 10–12 rue de l'Orme, 75019 Paris; tel. 1-45-20-60-61; fax 1-45-20-02-54; e-mail ambabu.paris@wanadoo.fr; Ambassador ILDEPHONSE NKERAMIHIGO.

Cambodia: 4 rue Adolphe Yvon, 75116 Paris; tel. 1-45-03-47-20; fax 1-45-03-47-40; e-mail ambcambodgeparis@mangoosta.fr; internet www.ambcambodgeparis.info; Ambassador UCH KIMAN.

Cameroon: 21 quai Alphonse Le Gallo, 92100 Boulogne-Billancourt; tel. 1-47-43-98-33; fax 1-46-51-24-52; Ambassador LEJEUNE MBELLA MBELLA.

Canada: 35 ave Montaigne, 75008 Paris; tel. 1-44-43-29-00; fax 1-44-43-29-99; e-mail paris_webmaster@international.gc.ca; internet www.amb-canada.fr; Ambassador MARC LORTIE.

Cape Verde: 3 rue de Rigny, 75008 Paris; tel. 1-42-12-73-50; fax 1-40-53-04-36; e-mail ambassade-cap-vert@wanadoo.fr; internet perso.orange.fr/ambassade-cap-vert; Ambassador JOSÉ ARMADO DUARTE.

Central African Republic: 30 rue des Perchamps, 75116 Paris; tel. 1-45-25-39-74; fax 1-45-27-48-11; e-mail accueil@amb-rcaparis.org; internet www.amb-rcaparis.org; Ambassador JEAN WILLIBIRO SAKO.

Chad: 65 rue des Belles Feuilles, 75116 Paris; tel. 1-45-53-36-75; fax 1-45-53-16-09; e-mail ambassadedutchad@wanadoo.fr; Ambassador HISSÈNE BRAHIM TAHA.

Chile: 2 ave de la Motte-Picquet, 75007 Paris; tel. 1-44-18-59-60; fax 1-44-18-59-61; e-mail echile@amb-chili.fr; internet www.amb-chili.fr; Ambassador MARÍA PILAR ARMANET.

China, People's Republic: 11 ave George V, 75008 Paris; tel. 1-49-52-19-50; fax 1-47-20-24-22; e-mail chinaemb_fr@mfa.gov.cn; internet www.amb-chine.fr; Ambassador KONG QUAN.

Colombia: 22 rue de l'Elysée, 75008 Paris; tel. 1-42-65-46-08; fax 1-42-66-18-60; e-mail eparis@minrelext.gov.co; internet www.embcolfrancia.com; Ambassador FERNANDO CEPEDA ULLOA.

Comoros: 20 rue Marbeau, 75116 Paris; tel. 1-40-67-90-54; fax 1-40-67-72-96; Ambassador SOULAIMANA MOHAMED AHMED.

Congo, Democratic Republic: 32 cours Albert 1er, 75008 Paris; tel. 1-42-25-57-50; fax 1-45-62-16-52; e-mail contact@ambardcparis.com; internet www.ambardcparis.com; Chargé d'affaires a.i. JEAN BUESSO SAMBA.

Congo, Republic: 37 bis rue Paul Valéry, 75116 Paris; tel. 1-45-00-60-57; fax 1-40-67-17-33; e-mail ambacongo_france@yahoo.fr; internet www.ambacongo.org; Ambassador HENRI LOPES.

Costa Rica: 78 ave Emile Zola, 75015 Paris; tel. 1-45-78-96-96; fax 1-45-78-99-66; e-mail embcr@wanadoo.fr; Ambassador ROXANA PINTO LÓPEZ.

Côte d'Ivoire: 102 ave Raymond Poincaré, 75116 Paris; tel. 1-53-64-62-62; fax 1-45-00-47-97; e-mail bureco-fr@cotedivoire.com; Ambassador HYACINTHE MARCEL KOUASSI.

Croatia: 39 ave Georges Mandel, 75116 Paris; tel. 1-53-70-02-80; fax 1-53-70-02-90; e-mail redaction@amb-croatie.fr; internet www.amb-croatie.fr; Ambassador MIRKO GALIČ.

Cuba: 16 rue de Presles, 75015 Paris; tel. 1-45-67-55-35; fax 1-45-66-80-92; e-mail embacu@ambacuba.fr; Ambassador ROGELIO PLACIDO SÁNCHEZ LEVIS.

Cyprus: 23 rue Galilée, 75116 Paris; tel. 1-47-20-86-28; fax 1-40-70-13-44; e-mail paris@mfa.gov.cy; Ambassador PERICLES NEARKOU.

Czech Republic: 15 ave Charles Floquet, 75007 Paris; tel. 1-40-65-13-00; fax 1-40-65-13-13; e-mail paris@embassy.mzv.cz; internet www.mzv.cz/paris; Ambassador PAVEL FISCHER.

Denmark: 77 ave Marceau, 75116 Paris; tel. 1-44-31-21-21; fax 1-44-31-21-88; e-mail paramb@um.dk; internet www.ambparis.um.dk; Ambassador NIELS EGELUND.

Djibouti: 26 rue Emile Ménier, 75116 Paris; tel. 1-47-27-49-22; fax 1-45-53-50-53; e-mail ambassadeur@ambdjibouti.org; Ambassador RACHAD FARAH.

Dominican Republic: 45 rue de Courcelles, 75008 Paris; tel. 1-53-63-95-95; fax 1-45-63-35-63; e-mail embajadom@wanadoo.fr; internet www.amba-dominicaine-paris.com; Ambassador GUILLERMO PIÑA-CONTRERAS ZELLER.

Ecuador: 34 ave de Messine, 75008 Paris; tel. 1-45-61-10-21; fax 1-42-56-06-64; e-mail embajadaenfrancia@ambassade-equateur.fr; internet www.ambassade-equateur.fr; Ambassador MARCO ERAZO BOLAÑOS.

Egypt: 56 ave d'Iéna, 75116 Paris; tel. 1-53-67-88-30; fax 1-47-23-06-43; e-mail ambassadedegypteaparis@hotmail.com; internet www.ambassade-egypte.com; Ambassador NASSER KAMEL.

El Salvador: 12 rue Galilée, 75116 Paris; tel. 1-47-20-42-02; fax 1-40-70-01-95; e-mail embparis@wanadoo.fr; Ambassador JOAQUÍN RODEZNO MUNGUIA.

Equatorial Guinea: 29 blvd de Courcelles, 75008 Paris; tel. 1-45-61-98-20; fax 1-45-61-98-25; e-mail embarege_paris@hotmail.com; Ambassador EDUARDO NDONG ELO NZANG.

Eritrea: 1 rue de Staël, 75015 Paris; tel. 1-43-06-15-56; fax 1-43-06-07-51; Ambassador AHMED HASSAN DEHLI.

Estonia: 17 rue de la Baume, 75008 Paris; tel. 1-56-62-22-00; fax 1-49-52-05-65; e-mail estonie@mfa.ee; internet www.est-emb.fr; Ambassador MARGUS RAVA.

Ethiopia: 35 ave Charles Floquet, 75007 Paris; tel. 1-47-83-83-95; fax 1-43-06-52-14; e-mail embeth@free.fr; Ambassador TADELECH HAÏLE-MIKAEL.

Finland: 1 place de Finlande, 75007 Paris; tel. 1-44-18-19-20; fax 1-45-55-51-57; e-mail sanomat.par@formin.fi; internet www.amb-finlande.fr; Ambassador CHARLES MURTO.

Gabon: 26 bis ave Raphaël, 75016 Paris; tel. 1-72-70-01-50; fax 1-72-81-05-89; e-mail hditsougou@caramail.com; Ambassador JEAN-MARIE ADZÉ.

The Gambia: 117 rue St Lazare, 75008 Paris; tel. 1-72-74-82-61; fax 1-53-04-05-99; e-mail ambgambia_france117@hotmail.com; Chargé d'affaires a.i. MOSES BENJAMIN JALLOW.

Georgia: 104 ave Raymond Poincaré, 75116 Paris; tel. 1-45-02-16-16; fax 1-45-02-16-01; e-mail ambassade.georgie@mfa.gov.ge; internet www.france.mfa.gov.ge; Ambassador MAMUKA KUDAVA.

Germany: 13–15 ave Franklin D. Roosevelt, 75008 Paris; tel. 1-53-83-45-00; fax 1-43-59-74-18; e-mail ambassade@amb-allemagne.fr; internet www.amb-allemagne.fr; Ambassador Dr PETER AMMON.

FRANCE

Ghana: 8 Villa Saïd, 75116 Paris; tel. 1-45-00-09-50; fax 1-45-00-81-95; e-mail ambghanaparis@yahoo.fr; Ambassador Prof. ALBERT OWUSU-SARPONG.

Greece: 17 rue Auguste Vacquerie, 75116 Paris; tel. 1-47-23-72-28; fax 1-47-23-73-85; e-mail gremb.par@mfa.gr; internet www.amb-grece.fr; Ambassador DIMITRIOS PARASKEVOPOULOS.

Guatemala: 2 rue Villebois-Marueil, 75017 Paris; tel. 1-42-27-78-63; fax 1-47-54-02-06; e-mail embaguatefrancia@wanadoo.fr; internet www.ambassadeduguatemala.com; Ambassador ANAISABEL PRERA FLORES.

Guinea: 51 rue de la Faisanderie, 75116 Paris; tel. 1-47-04-81-48; fax 1-47-04-57-65; e-mail accueil@ambaguinee-paris.org; internet www.ambaguinee-paris.org; Ambassador KEITA MAKALÉ CAMARA.

Guinea-Bissau: 94 rue Saint Lazare, 75009 Paris; tel. 1-48-74-36-39; fax 1-48-78-36-39; e-mail ambaguineebxo@wanadoo.fr; Ambassador JOÃO SOARES DA GAMA.

Haiti: 10 rue Théodule Ribot, BP 275, 75017 Paris; tel. 1-47-63-47-78; fax 1-42-27-02-05; e-mail ambhaitiparis@noos.fr; Ambassador LIONEL ETIENNE.

Holy See: 10 ave du Président Wilson, 75116 Paris (Apostolic Nunciature); tel. 1-53-23-01-50; fax 1-47-23-65-44; e-mail noncapfr@wanadoo.fr; Apostolic Nuncio Most Rev. FORTUNATO BALDELLI (Titular Archbishop of Mevania).

Honduras: 8 rue Crevaux, 75116 Paris; tel. 1-47-55-86-45; fax 1-47-55-86-48; e-mail ambassade.honduras@yahoo.com; Ambassador MAX VELÁSQUEZ DIAZ.

Hungary: 7 sq. Vergennes, 75015 Paris; tel. 1-56-36-07-54; fax 1-56-36-02-68; e-mail mission.par@kum.hu; internet www.mfa.gov.hu/emb/paris; Ambassador LÁSZLÓ NIKICSER.

Iceland: 8 ave Kléber, 75116 Paris; tel. 1-44-17-32-85; fax 1-40-67-99-96; e-mail icemb.paris@utn.stjr.is; internet www.iceland.org/fr; Ambassador TÓMAS INGI OLRICH.

India: 15 rue Alfred Dehodencq, 75016 Paris; tel. 1-40-50-70-70; fax 1-40-50-09-96; e-mail eiparis.admin@wanadoo.fr; internet www.amb-inde.fr; Ambassador RANJAN MATHAI.

Indonesia: 47–49 rue Cortambert, 75016 Paris; tel. 1-45-03-07-60; fax 1-45-04-50-32; e-mail kasubpen@amb-indonesie.fr; internet www.amb-indonesie.fr; Ambassador ARIZAL EFFENDI.

Iran: 4 ave d'Iéna, 75116 Paris; tel. 1-40-69-79-00; fax 1-40-70-01-57; e-mail contact@amb-iran.fr; internet www.amb-iran.fr; Ambassador Dr ALI AHANI.

Iraq: 53 rue de la Faisanderie, 75016 Paris; tel. 1-45-53-33-70; fax 1-45-53-33-80; e-mail paremb@iraqmofamail.net; Ambassador MOUAFAK MEHDI ABOUD HAMOUD.

Ireland: 12 ave Foch, 75116 Paris; tel. 1-44-17-67-00; fax 1-44-17-67-60; e-mail paris@dfa.ie; internet www.embassyofirelandparis.com; Ambassador ANNE ANDERSON.

Israel: 3 rue Rabelais, 75008 Paris; tel. 1-40-76-55-00; fax 1-40-76-55-55; e-mail information@paris.mfa.gov.il; internet paris.mfa.gov.il; Ambassador DANIEL SHEK.

Italy: 51 rue de Varenne, 75343 Paris Cedex 07; tel. 1-49-54-03-00; fax 1-45-54-04-10; e-mail ambasciata.parigi@esteri.it; internet www.ambparigi.esteri.it; Ambassador LUDOVICO ORTONA.

Japan: 7 ave Hoche, 75008 Paris; tel. 1-48-88-62-00; fax 1-42-27-50-81; e-mail info-fr@amb-japon.fr; internet www.fr.emb-japan.go.jp; Ambassador YUTAKA IIMURA.

Jordan: 80 blvd Maurice Barrès, 92200 Neuilly-sur-Seine; tel. 1-55-62-00-00; fax 1-55-62-00-06; e-mail amjo.paris@wanadoo.fr; Ambassador DINA KAWAR.

Kazakhstan: 59 rue Pierre Charron, 75008 Paris; tel. 1-45-61-52-00; fax 1-45-61-52-01; e-mail info@amb-kazakhstan.fr; internet www.amb-kazakhstan.fr; Ambassador AMANZHOL ZHANKULIEV.

Kenya: 3 rue Freycinet, 75116 Paris; tel. 1-56-62-25-25; fax 1-47-20-44-41; e-mail paris@amb-kenya.fr; internet www.kenyaembassyparis.org; Ambassador RAYCHELLE AWUOR OMAMO.

Korea, Republic: 125 rue de Grenelle, 75007 Paris; tel. 1-47-53-01-01; fax 1-47-53-00-41; e-mail koremb-fr@mofat.go.kr; internet www.amb-coreesud.fr; Ambassador CHO IL-HWAN.

Kuwait: 25 rue Chateaubriand, 75008 Paris; tel. 1-47-23-54-25; fax 1-47-20-33-59; Ambassador ALI SULAIMAN AS-SAEID.

Laos: 74 ave Raymond Poincaré, 75116 Paris; tel. 1-45-53-02-98; fax 1-47-57-27-89; e-mail ambalaoparis@wanadoo.fr; internet www.laoparis.com; Ambassador SOUTSAKHONE PATHAMMAVONG.

Latvia: 6 villa Saïd, 75116 Paris; tel. 1-53-64-58-10; fax 1-53-64-58-19; e-mail embassy.france@mfa.gov.lv; internet www.am.gov.lv/paris; Ambassador JĀNIS KĀRKLIŅŠ.

Lebanon: 3 villa Copernic, 75116 Paris; tel. 1-40-67-75-75; fax 1-40-67-16-42; e-mail na@ambliban.fr; internet www.ambassadeliban.fr; Ambassador BOUTROS ASSAKER.

Liberia: 12 place du Général Catroux, 75017 Paris; tel. 1-47-63-58-55; fax 1-42-12-76-14; e-mail libem.paris@wanadoo.fr; Ambassador DUDLEY MCKINLEY THOMAS.

Libya: 2 rue Charles Lamoureux, 75116 Paris; tel. 1-47-04-71-60; fax 1-47-55-96-25; Sec. of the People's Bureau Dr MUHAMMAD AL-HARARI.

Lithuania: 22 blvd de Courcelles, 75017 Paris; tel. 1-40-54-50-50; fax 1-40-54-50-75; e-mail chancellerie@amb-lituanie.fr; internet fr.mfa.lt; Ambassador GIEDRIUS ČEKUOLIS.

Luxembourg: 33 ave Rapp, 75007 Paris; tel. 1-45-55-13-37; fax 1-45-51-72-29; e-mail paris.amb@mae.etat.lu; internet www.ambassade-luxembourg.fr; Ambassador GEORGES SANTER.

Macedonia, former Yugoslav republic: 5 rue de la Faisanderie, 75116 Paris; tel. 1-45-77-10-50; fax 1-45-77-14-84; e-mail paris@mfa.gov.mk; Ambassador JON IVANOVSKI.

Madagascar: 4 ave Raphaël, 75016 Paris; tel. 1-45-04-62-11; fax 1-45-03-58-70; e-mail accueil@ambassade-madagascar.fr; internet www.ambassade-madagascar.fr; Ambassador JEAN-PIERRE RAZAFY-ANDRIAMIHAINGO.

Malaysia: 2 bis rue Bénouville, 75116 Paris; tel. 1-45-53-11-85; fax 1-47-27-34-60; e-mail malparis@kln.gov.my; Ambassador Dato' S. THANARAJASINGAM.

Mali: 89 rue du Cherche-Midi, 75263 Paris Cedex 06; tel. 1-45-48-58-43; fax 1-45-48-55-34; e-mail ambamali.paris@wanadoo.fr; Ambassador MOHAMED SALIA SOKONA.

Malta: 92 ave des Champs Elysées, 75008 Paris; tel. 1-56-59-75-90; fax 1-45-62-00-36; e-mail maltaembassy.paris@gov.mt; Ambassador Dr VICKY-ANN CREMONA.

Mauritania: 5 rue de Montévidéo, 75116 Paris; tel. 1-45-04-88-54; fax 1-40-72-82-96; e-mail ambassade.mauritanie@wanadoo.fr; Ambassador MATT MINT MOHAMED EL-MOKHTAR OULD EWNENE.

Mauritius: 127 rue de Tocqueville, 75017 Paris; tel. 1-42-27-30-19; fax 1-40-53-02-91; e-mail ambassade.maurice@online.fr; Ambassador Dr MOHAMMAD HOUSSEIN ISMAËL DILMAHOMED.

Mexico: 9 rue de Longchamp, 75116 Paris; tel. 1-53-70-27-70; fax 1-47-55-65-29; e-mail embfrancia@sre.gob.mx; internet www.sre.gob.mx/francia; Ambassador CARLOS DE ICAZA GONZÁLEZ.

Moldova: 1 rue de Sfax, 75116 Paris; tel. 1-40-67-11-20; fax 1-40-67-11-23; e-mail ambassade.moldavie@wanadoo.fr; internet www.ambassade-moldavie.com; Ambassador VICTORIA IFTODI.

Monaco: 22 blvd Suchet, 75116 Paris; tel. 1-45-04-74-54; fax 1-45-04-45-16; e-mail ambassade.en.france@gouv.mc; Ambassador JACQUES BOISSON.

Mongolia: 5 ave Robert Schuman, 92100 Boulogne-Billancourt; tel. 1-46-05-28-12; fax 1-46-05-30-16; e-mail ambassademongolie@yahoo.fr; internet www.ambassademongolie.fr; Ambassador RADNAABAZAR ALTANGEREL.

Montenegro: 216 blvd Saint-Germain, 75007 Paris; tel. 1-53-63-80-30; fax 1-42-22-83-90; e-mail ambasadacg@orange.fr; Ambassador MILICA PEJANOVIĆ-ĐURIŠIĆ.

Morocco: 5 rue Le Tasse, 75016 Paris; tel. 1-45-20-69-35; fax 1-45-20-22-58; e-mail info@amb-maroc.fr; internet www.amb-maroc.fr; Ambassador FATHALLAH SIJILMASSI.

Mozambique: 82 rue Laugier, 75017 Paris; tel. 1-47-64-91-32; fax 1-44-15-90-13; e-mail embamoc.franca@minec.gov.mz; Ambassador ANA NEMBA UAENE.

Myanmar: 60 rue de Courcelles, 75008 Paris; tel. 1-56-88-15-90; fax 1-45-62-13-30; e-mail me-paris@wanadoo.fr; Ambassador U SAW HLA MIN.

Namibia: 80 ave Foch, 75016 Paris; tel. 1-44-17-32-65; fax 1-44-17-32-73; e-mail namparis@club-internet.fr; Ambassador PANDULENI-KAINO SHINGENGE.

Nepal: 45 bis rue des Acacias, 75017 Paris; tel. 1-46-22-48-67; fax 1-42-27-08-65; e-mail ambassadedunepal@noos.fr; internet www.nepalembassy.org; Ambassador (vacant).

Netherlands: 7–9 rue Eblé, 75007 Paris; tel. 1-40-62-33-00; fax 1-40-62-34-56; e-mail ambassade@amb-pays-bas.fr; internet www.amb-pays-bas.fr; Ambassador HUGO HANS SIBLESZ.

New Zealand: 7 ter rue Léonard de Vinci, 75116 Paris; tel. 1-45-01-43-43; fax 1-45-01-43-44; e-mail nzembassy.paris@fr.oleane.com; internet www.nzembassy.com/france; Ambassador SARAH DENNIS.

Niger: 154 rue de Longchamp, 75116 Paris; tel. 1-45-04-80-60; fax 1-45-04-79-73; e-mail ambassadeniger@wanadoo.fr; internet www.ambassadeniger.org; Ambassador ADAMOU SEYDOU.

Nigeria: 173 ave Victor Hugo, 75116 Paris; tel. 1-47-04-68-65; fax 1-47-04-47-54; e-mail embassy@nigeriafrance.com; internet www.nigeriafrance.com; Ambassador GODFREY BAYOUR PREWARE.

Norway: 28 rue Bayard, 4e étage, 75008 Paris; tel. 1-53-67-04-00; fax 1-53-67-04-40; e-mail emb.paris@mfa.no; internet www.norvege.no; Ambassador BJØRN SKOGMO.

FRANCE

Oman: 50 ave d'Iéna, 75116 Paris; tel. 1-47-23-01-63; fax 1-47-23-77-10; Ambassador Jaifer Salim as-Said.

Pakistan: 18 rue Lord Byron, 75008 Paris; tel. 1-45-62-23-32; fax 1-45-62-89-15; e-mail pakemb_paris@gmail.com; Ambassador Asma Anisa.

Panama: 145 ave de Suffren, 75015 Paris; tel. 1-45-66-42-44; fax 1-45-67-99-43; e-mail panaemba.francia@wanadoo.fr; Ambassador Omar Jaén Suárez.

Paraguay: 1 rue St Dominique, 75007 Paris; tel. 1-42-22-85-05; fax 1-42-22-83-57; e-mail paraguay.ambassade@wanadoo.fr; internet www.mre.gov.py/embaparfrancia; Ambassador Luis Fernando Avalos Giménez.

Peru: 50 ave Kléber, 75116 Paris; tel. 1-53-70-42-00; fax 1-47-04-32-55; e-mail perou.ambassade@amb-perou.fr; internet www.amb-perou.fr; Ambassador Harry Belevan-McBride.

Philippines: 4 Hameau de Boulainvilliers, 75016 Paris; tel. 1-44-14-57-00; fax 1-46-47-56-00; e-mail ambaphilparis@wanadoo.fr; Ambassador José Abeto Zaide.

Poland: 1–3 rue de Talleyrand, 75343 Paris Cedex 07; tel. 1-43-17-34-05; fax 1-43-17-35-07; e-mail info@ambassade.pologne.net; internet www.paris.polemb.net; Ambassador Tomasz Orłowski.

Portugal: 3 rue de Noisiel, 75116 Paris; tel. 1-47-27-35-29; fax 1-44-05-94-02; e-mail mailto@embaixada-portugal-fr.org; internet www.embaixada-portugal-fr.org; Ambassador António Victor Martins Monteiro.

Qatar: 1 rue de Tilsitt, 75008 Paris; tel. 1-45-51-90-71; fax 1-45-51-77-07; e-mail paris@mofa.gov.qa; internet www.qatarambassade.com; Ambassador Muhammad Jaham Abd al-Aziz al-Kuwari.

Romania: 5 rue de l'Exposition, 75007 Paris; tel. 1-47-05-10-46; fax 1-45-56-97-47; e-mail secretariat@amb-roumanie.fr; internet paris.mae.ro; Ambassador Teodor Baconschi.

Russia: 40–50 blvd Lannes, 75116 Paris; tel. 1-45-04-05-50; fax 1-45-04-17-65; e-mail ambrus@orange.fr; internet www.france.mid.ru; Ambassador Aleksandr A. Avdeyev.

Rwanda: 12 rue Jadin, 75017 Paris; tel. 1-42-27-36-31; fax 1-42-27-74-69; e-mail ambaparis@minaffet.gov.rw; Ambassador Emmanuel Ndagijimana (recalled Nov. 2006).

San Marino: 22 rue d'Artois, 75008 Paris; tel. and fax 1-47-23-04-75; e-mail saint-marin@wanadoo.fr; Ambassador Mario de Benedetti.

Saudi Arabia: 5 ave Hoche, 75008 Paris; tel. 1-56-79-40-00; fax 1-56-79-40-01; e-mail amb.arabiesaoudite@gmail.com; Ambassador Dr Muhammad bin Ismail al-Ashekh.

Senegal: 14 ave Robert Schuman, 75007 Paris; tel. 1-47-05-39-45; fax 1-45-56-04-30; e-mail repsen@wanadoo.fr; internet www.ambassenparis.com; Ambassador Doudou Diop Salla.

Serbia: 54 rue Léonard de Vinci, 75116 Paris; tel. 1-40-72-24-17; fax 1-40-72-24-11; e-mail ambasadapariz@wanadoo.fr; internet www.amb-serbie.fr; Ambassador Predrag Simić.

Seychelles: 51 ave Mozart, 75016 Paris; tel. 1-42-30-57-47; fax 1-42-30-57-40; e-mail ambsey@aol.com; Ambassador Claude Morel.

Singapore: 12 sq. de l'ave Foch, 75116 Paris; tel. 1-45-00-33-61; fax 1-45-00-61-79; e-mail singemb_par@sgmfa.gov.sg; internet www.mfa.gov.sg/paris; Ambassador Burhan Gafoor.

Slovakia: 125 rue du Ranelagh, 75016 Paris; tel. 1-44-14-56-00; fax 1-42-88-76-53; e-mail paris@amb-slovaquie.fr; internet www.amb-slovaquie.fr; Ambassador Ján Kuderjavý.

Slovenia: 28 rue Bois-le-Vent, 75116 Paris; tel. 1-44-96-50-71; fax 1-45-24-67-05; e-mail vpa@gov.si; Ambassador Janez Šumrada.

Somalia: 26 rue Dumont d'Urville, 75116 Paris; tel. 1-45-00-88-98; Ambassador Said Hajgi Mohamoud Farah.

South Africa: 59 quai d'Orsay, 75343 Paris Cedex 07; tel. 1-53-59-23-23; fax 1-53-59-23-68; e-mail info@afriquesud.net; internet www.afriquesud.net; Ambassador Nomasonto Mary Sibanda-Thusi.

Spain: 22 ave Marceau, 75008 Paris; tel. 1-44-43-18-00; fax 1-47-23-59-55; e-mail emb.paris@mae.es; internet www.maec.es/subwebs/embajadas/paris; Ambassador Francisco Villar y Ortiz de Urbina.

Sri Lanka: 16 rue Spontini, 75016 Paris; tel. 1-55-73-31-31; fax 1-55-73-18-49; e-mail sl.france@wanadoo.fr; Ambassador Chitranganee Wagiswara.

Sudan: 11 rue Alfred Dehodencq, 75016 Paris; tel. 1-42-25-55-71; fax 1-54-63-66-73; e-mail ambassade-du-soudan@wanadoo.fr; internet www.ambassade-du-soudan.org; Ambassador Ahmed Hamid al-Faki.

Sweden: 17 rue Barbet-de-Jouy, 75007 Paris; tel. 1-44-18-88-00; fax 1-44-18-88-40; e-mail info@amb-suede.fr; internet www.swedenabroad.com/paris; Ambassador Gunnar Lund.

Switzerland: 142 rue de Grenelle, 75007 Paris; tel. 1-49-55-67-00; fax 1-49-55-67-67; e-mail par.vertretung@eda.admin.ch; internet www.eda.admin.ch/paris; Ambassador Ulrich Lehner.

Syria: 20 rue Vaneau, 75007 Paris; tel. 1-40-62-61-00; fax 1-47-05-92-73; e-mail ambassade-syrie@wanadoo.fr; internet www.amb-syr.fr; Chargé d'affaires a.i. Shaghaf Kayali.

Tanzania: 13 ave Raymond Poincaré, 75116 Paris; tel. 1-53-70-63-66; fax 1-47-55-05-46; e-mail ambtanzanie@wanadoo.fr; internet www.amb-tanzanie.fr; Ambassador Hassan Omar Gumbo Kibelloh.

Thailand: 8 rue Greuze, 75116 Paris; tel. 1-56-26-50-50; fax 1-56-26-04-45; e-mail thaipar@wanadoo.fr; Ambassador Thana Duangratana.

Togo: 8 rue Alfred Roll, 75017 Paris; tel. 1-43-80-12-13; fax 1-43-80-06-05; e-mail france@ambassadetogo.org; internet www.ambassadetogo.org; Ambassador Tchao Soto Bere.

Tunisia: 25 rue Barbet-de-Jouy, 75007 Paris; tel. 1-45-55-95-98; fax 1-45-56-02-64; e-mail atn.paris@wanadoo.fr; internet www.amb-tunisie.fr; Ambassador Raouf Najjar.

Turkey: 16 ave de Lamballe, 75016 Paris; tel. 1-53-92-71-12; fax 1-45-20-41-91; e-mail paris.be@mfa.gov.tr; Ambassador Osman Korutürk.

Turkmenistan: 13 rue Picot, 75116 Paris; tel. 1-47-55-05-36; fax 1-47-55-05-68; e-mail turkmenamb@free.fr; Ambassador Tchary G. Niyazov.

Uganda: 13 ave Raymond Poincaré, 75116 Paris; tel. 1-56-90-12-20; fax 1-45-05-21-22; e-mail uganda.embassy@club-internet.fr; Ambassador Elizabeth Paula Napeyok.

Ukraine: 21 ave de Saxe, 75007 Paris; tel. 1-43-06-07-37; fax 1-43-06-02-94; e-mail ambassade-ukraine@wanadoo.fr; internet www.mfa.gov.ua/france; Ambassador Kostiatyn V. Tymochenko.

United Arab Emirates: 2 blvd de la Tour Maubourg, 75007 Paris; tel. 1-44-34-02-00; fax 1-47-55-61-04; e-mail ambassade.emirats@wanadoo.fr; internet www.amb-emirats.fr; Ambassador Saif Sultan Mubarak al-Aryani.

United Kingdom: 35 rue du Faubourg St Honoré, 75383 Paris Cedex 08; tel. 1-44-51-31-00; fax 1-44-51-32-34; e-mail public.paris@fco.gov.uk; internet www.amb-grandebretagne.fr; Ambassador Sir Peter Westmacott.

USA: 2 ave Gabriel, 75382 Paris Cedex 08; tel. 1-43-12-22-22; fax 1-42-66-97-83; internet france.usembassy.gov; Ambassador Craig Roberts Stapleton.

Uruguay: 15 rue Le Sueur, 75116 Paris; tel. 1-45-00-81-37; fax 1-45-01-25-17; e-mail amburuguay.urugalia@fr.oleane.com; internet www.amb-uruguay-france.com; Ambassador Héctor Gros Espiell.

Uzbekistan: 22 rue d'Aguesseau, 75008 Paris; tel. 1-53-30-03-53; fax 1-53-30-03-54; e-mail contact@ouzbekistan.fr; internet www.ouzbekistan.fr; Ambassador Ravshanbek O. Olimov.

Venezuela: 11 rue Copernic, 75116 Paris; tel. 1-45-53-29-98; fax 1-47-55-64-56; e-mail info@amb-venezuela.fr; internet www.embavenez-paris.com; Ambassador Jesús Arnaldo Pérez.

Viet Nam: 62–66 rue Boileau, 75016 Paris; tel. 1-44-14-64-00; fax 1-45-24-39-48; e-mail vnparis@club-internet.fr; Ambassador Nguyên Dinh Bin.

Yemen: 25 rue Georges Bizet, 75116 Paris; tel. 1-53-23-87-87; fax 1-47-23-69-41; e-mail ambyemenparis@easynet.fr; Ambassador Amir Salim al-Eidrous.

Zambia: 18 ave de Tourville, 75007 Paris; tel. 1-56-88-12-70; fax 1-56-88-03-50; e-mail zambianspars@wanadoo.fr; Ambassador Ian Sikazwe.

Zimbabwe: 18 ave de Tourville, 75007 Paris; tel. 1-56-88-16-00; fax 1-56-88-16-09; e-mail zimparisweb@wanadoo.fr; Ambassador David Hamadziripi.

Judicial System

The Judiciary is independent of the Government. Judges of the Court of Cassation and the First President of the Court of Appeal are appointed by the executive from nominations of the High Council of the Judiciary.

Subordinate cases are heard by Tribunaux d'instance, of which there are 476, and more serious cases by Tribunaux de grande instance, of which there are 181. Parallel to these Tribunals are the Tribunaux de commerce, for commercial cases, composed of judges elected by traders and manufacturers among themselves. These do not exist in every district. Where there is no Tribunal de commerce, commercial disputes are judged by Tribunaux de grande instance.

The Conseils de Prud'hommes (Boards of Arbitration) consist of an equal number of workers or employees and employers ruling on the differences that arise over Contracts of Work.

The Tribunaux correctionnnels (Correctional Courts) for criminal cases correspond to the Tribunaux de grande instance for civil cases. They pronounce on all graver offences (délits), including those

FRANCE
Directory

involving imprisonment. Offences committed by juveniles of under 18 years go before specialized tribunals.

From all these Tribunals appeal lies to the Cours d'appel (Courts of Appeal).

The Cours d'assises (Courts of Assize) have no regular sittings, but are called when necessary to try every important case, such as murder. They are presided over by judges who are members of the Cours d'appel, and are composed of elected judges (jury). Their decision is final, except where shown to be wrong in law, and then recourse is had to the Cour de cassation (Court of Cassation). The Cour de cassation is not a supreme court of appeal but a higher authority for the proper application of the law. Its duty is to see that judgments are not contrary either to the letter or the spirit of the law; any judgment annulled by the Court involves the trying of the case anew by a court of the same category as that which made the original decision.

A programme of extensive reforms in the judicial system, which aimed to reduce political control of the Judiciary and to increase citizens' rights, was introduced in stages between 1997 and 2001. A notable innovation introduced by these reforms was the introduction of the convention that a person accused of a crime is presumed innocent unless otherwise proven.

In early 2008 the Government announced its intention significantly to reduce the number of judicial districts, from 1,190 to 862. The reform was to commence on 31 December 2008, with the closure of 63 conseils des prud'hommes nation-wide. From 1 January 2009 a further 55 tribunaux de commerce were scheduled to close, while on 31 December 178 cours d'instance were to close. The reforms were due to be completed on 31 December 2011, following the closure of 23 cours de grande instance.

Cour de Cassation
5 quai de l'Horloge, 75055 Paris RP; tel. 1-44-32-50-50; fax 1-44-32-78-29; e-mail webmstre@courdecassation.fr; internet www.courdecassation.fr.

First President: VINCENT LAMANDA.

Presidents of Chambers: PIERRE BARGUE (1ère Chambre civile), JEAN-LOUIS GILLET (2ème Chambre civile), JEAN-FRANÇOIS WEBER (3ème Chambre civile), CLAIRE FAVRE (Chambre commerciale, financière et économique), EVELYNE COLLOMP (Chambre sociale), BRUNO COTTE (Chambre criminelle).

There are 88 Counsellors and 65 Junior Counsellors.

Solicitor-General: JEAN-LOUIS NADAL.

There is one First Attorney-General and 32 Attorneys-General.

Chief Clerk of the Court: CLAIRE COLLET.

President of the Council of Advocates at the Cour de Cassation: BRUNO POTIER DE LA VARDE.

Cour d'Appel de Paris
34 quai des Orfèvres, 75055 Paris Cedex 01; tel. 1-44-32-52-52; internet www.ca-paris.justice.fr.

First President: JEAN-CLAUDE MAGENDIE.

There are also 61 Presidents of Chambers.

Solicitor-General: LAURENT LE MESLE.

There are also 124 Counsellors, 22 Attorneys-General and 36 Deputies.

Tribunal de Grande Instance de Paris
4 blvd du Palais, 75055 Paris RP; tel. 1-44-32-51-51; fax 1-43-29-12-55; internet www.tgi-paris.justice.fr.

President: JACQUES DEGRANDI.

Solicitor of the Republic of Paris: JEAN-CLAUDE MARIN.

Tribunal de Commerce de Paris
1 quai de Corse, 75181 Paris Cedex 04; tel. 1-44-32-83-83; fax 1-40-46-07-28; e-mail sandrine.lanfrey@greffe-tc-paris.fr; internet www.tc-paris.com.

President: PERRETTE REY.

Tribunaux Administratifs
Certain cases arising between civil servants (when on duty) and the Government, or between any citizen and the Government are judged by special administrative courts.

The Tribunaux administratifs, of which there are 29 in metropolitan France and nine in the overseas possessions, are situated in the capital of each area; the Conseil d'Etat (see below) has its seat in Paris.

Tribunal des Conflits
Decides whether cases shall be submitted to the ordinary or administrative courts.

President: The Keeper of the Seals, Minister of Justice.

Vice-President: MARIE-FRANCE MAZARS.

There are also three Counsellors of the Cour de cassation and four Counsellors of State.

Cour des Comptes
13 rue Cambon, 75100 Paris Cedex 01; tel. 1-42-98-95-00; fax 1-42-60-01-59; e-mail contact@ccomptes.fr; internet www.ccomptes.fr.

An administrative tribunal (Audit Court) competent to judge the correctness of public accounts. It is the arbiter of common law of all public accounts laid before it. The judgments of the Court may be annulled by the Conseil d'Etat.

First President: PHILIPPE SÉGUIN.

Presidents of Chambers: CHRISTIAN BABUSIAUX, JEAN HERNANDEZ, JEAN PICQ, ALAIN PICHON, MARIE-THÉRÈSE CORNETTE, ROLANDE RUELLAN, CHRISTIAN DESCHEEMAEKER, CLAIRE BAZY-MALAURIE.

Solicitor-General: JEAN-FRANÇOIS BÉNARD.

Chambres Régionales et Territoriales des Comptes
In 1983 jurisdiction over the accounts of local administrations (Régions, Départements and Communes) and public institutions (hospitals, council housing, etc.) was transferred from the Cour des comptes to local Chambres régionales. Chambres territoriales were subsequently created in New Caledonia (in 1988), French Polynesia (in 1990), and Mayotte, Saint-Barthélémy, Saint-Martin and Saint Pierre and Miquelon (in 2007). The 32 courts (26 chambre régionales and 6 chambres territoriales) are autonomous but under the jurisdiction of the State. Appeals may be brought before the Cour des comptes.

Conseil d'Etat
Place du Palais-Royal, 75100 Paris 01 SP; tel. 1-40-20-80-00; fax 1-40-20-80-08; e-mail webmestre@conseil-etat.fr; internet www.conseil-etat.fr.

The Conseil d'Etat (Council of State) is the consultative organ of the Government and the supreme administrative court. It gives opinions to the Government in the legislative and administrative domain (interior, finance, public works and social sections) and has three functions in administrative jurisdiction: to judge in the first and last resort such cases as appeals against excess of power laid against official decrees or individuals; to judge appeals against judgments made by Tribunaux administratifs, Cours administratives d'appel and resolutions of courts of litigation; and to annul decisions made by various specialized administrative authorities that adjudicate without appeal, such as the Cour des comptes.

President: The Prime Minister.

Vice-President: JEAN-MARC SAUVÉ.

Presidents of Sections: MARIE-DOMINIQUE HAGELSTEEN, JEAN-MICHEL BELORGEY, YANNICK MOREAU, PIERRE-FRANÇOIS RACINE, BERNARD STIRN, YVES ROBINEAU.

General Secretary: CHRISTOPHE DEVYS.

Conseil Constitutionnel
2 rue de Montpensier, 75001 Paris; tel. 1-40-15-30-00; fax 1-40-20-93-27; e-mail relations-exterieures@conseil-constitutionnel.fr; internet www.conseil-constitutionnel.fr.

President: JEAN-LOUIS DEBRÉ.

Members: VALÉRY GISCARD D'ESTAING (ex officio), JACQUES CHIRAC (ex officio), OLIVIER DUTHEILLET DE LAMOTHE, DOMINIQUE SCHNAPPER, PIERRE JOXE, PIERRE STEINMETZ, JACQUELINE DE GUILLENCHMIDT, JEAN-LOUIS PEZANT, RENAUD DENOIX DE SAINT-MARC, GUY CANIVET.

Religion

CHRISTIANITY

Conseil d'Eglises Chrétiennes en France: 58 ave de Breteuil, 75007 Paris; tel. 1-72-36-69-60; fax 1-73-72-96-67; e-mail conseil.eglises.chretienne@cef.fr; f. 1987; ecumenical organization comprising representatives from all Christian denominations to express opinions on social issues; 21 mems; Pres. Pastor CLAUDE BATY, Most Rev. JEAN-PIERRE RICARD, Most Rev. EMMANUEL ADAMAKIS; Secs Pastor GILL DAUDÉ, Fr MICHEL MALLÈVRE, Archbishop ARSENIOS KARDAMAKIS.

The Roman Catholic Church
For ecclesiastical purposes, France comprises nine Apostolic Regions, together forming 22 archdioceses (of which one, Strasbourg, is directly responsible to the Holy See), 70 dioceses (including one, Metz, directly responsible to the Holy See) and one Territorial Prelature. The Archbishop of Paris is also the Ordinary for Catholics of Oriental Rites. At 31 December 2005 an estimated 76.5% of the population were adherents of the Roman Catholic Church.

FRANCE

Bishops' Conference

Conférence des Evêques de France, 58 ave de Breteuil, 75007 Paris; tel. 1-72-36-68-41; fax 1-73-72-97-22; e-mail cef@cef.fr; internet www.cef.fr; Pres. Cardinal ANDRÉ VINGT-TROIS (Archbishop of Paris); Sec.-Gen. Fr ANTOINE HÉROUARD.

Archbishop of Lyon and Primate of Gaul: Cardinal PHILIPPE BARBARIN, Archevêché, 1 place de Fourvière, 69321 Lyon Cedex 05; tel. 4-72-38-80-90; fax 4-78-36-06-00; e-mail dioceselyon@wanadoo.fr; internet catholique-lyon.cef.fr.

Archbishop of Aix et Arles: Most Rev. CLAUDE FEIDT.

Archbishop of Albi: Most Rev. PIERRE-MARIE CARRÉ.

Archbishop of Auch: Most Rev. MAURICE GARDÈS.

Archbishop of Avignon: Most Rev. JEAN-PIERRE CATTENOZ.

Archbishop of Besançon: Most Rev. ANDRÉ JEAN RENÉ LACRAMPE.

Archbishop of Bordeaux: Cardinal JEAN-PIERRE RICARD.

Archbishop of Bourges: Most Rev. ARMAND MAILLARD.

Archbishop of Cambrai: Most Rev. FRANÇOIS GARNIER.

Archbishop of Chambéry: (vacant).

Archbishop of Clermont: Most Rev. HIPPOLYTE SIMON.

Archbishop of Dijon: Most Rev. ROLAND MINNERATH.

Archbishop of Marseille: Most Rev. GEORGES PAUL PONTIER.

Archbishop of Montpellier: Most Rev. GUY THOMAZEAU.

Archbishop of Paris: Cardinal ANDRÉ VINGT-TROIS.

Archbishop of Poitiers: Most Rev. ALBERT ROUET.

Archbishop of Reims: Most Rev. THIERRY JORDAN.

Archbishop of Rennes: Most Rev. PIERRE D'ORNELLAS.

Archbishop of Rouen: Most Rev. JEAN-CHARLES DESCUBES.

Archbishop of Sens-Auxerre: Most Rev. YVES PATENÔTRE.

Archbishop of Strasbourg: Most Rev. JEAN-PIERRE GRALLET.

Archbishop of Toulouse: Most Rev. ROBERT JEAN-LOUIS LE GALL.

Archbishop of Tours: Most Rev. BERNARD-NICOLAS JEAN-MARIE AUBERTIN.

Protestant Churches

There are some 950,000 Protestants in France.

Eglise méthodiste: 3 rue Paul Verlaine, 30100 Alès; tel. 4-66-86-20-72; the total Methodist community was estimated at 1,000 mems in 2001.

Fédération protestante de France: 47 rue de Clichy, 75311 Paris Cedex 09; tel. 1-44-53-47-00; fax 1-48-74-66-31; e-mail fpf@protestants.org; internet www.protestants.org; f. 1905; Pres. Pastor CLAUDE BATY; Gen. Sec. Pastor PIERRE-ANDRÉ SCHAECHTELIN.

The Federation includes:

Armée du Salut (Foundation and Congregation): 60 rue des Frères Flavien, 75976 Paris Cedex 20; tel. 1-43-62-25-95; fax 1-43-62-25-98; e-mail info@armeedusalut.fr; internet www.armeedusalut.fr; f. 1881; Pres. Lt-Col ALAIN DUCHÊNE.

Communauté protestante évangélique de Vannes: 18 blvd Edouard Herriot, 56000 Vannes; tel. 2-97-47-16-75; fax 2-97-42-44-93; e-mail communauteprotestante.vannes@wanadoo.fr; Pres. Pastor MARK PLUNIER.

Eglise évangélique luthérienne de France: 16 rue Chauchat, 75009 Paris; tel. 1-44-79-04-73; fax 1-44-79-05-81; e-mail usynparis@aol.com; internet www.eelf.org; 40,000 mems; f. 1872; Pres. Pastor JOËL DAUTHEVILLE; Sec. JEANNIE FAVRE.

Eglise protestante de la Confession d'Augsbourg d'Alsace et de Lorraine: 1B quai St Thomas, BP 80022, 67081 Strasbourg Cedex; tel. 3-8825-90-05; fax 3-88-25-90-99; e-mail epal-media@epal.fr; internet www.epal.fr; 210,000 mems; member of Union des Eglises Protestantes d'Alsace et de Lorraine; Pres. Prof. JEAN-FRANÇOIS COLLANGE.

Eglise protestante évangélique: 30 Quéreux de la Laiterie, 17300 Rochefort.

Eglise protestante réformée d'Alsace et de Lorraine: 1B quai St Thomas, BP 80022, 67081 Strasbourg Cedex; tel. 3-88-25-90-10; fax 3-88-25-90-99; e-mail epral@epal.fr; internet www.epal.fr; member of Union des Eglises Protestantes d'Alsace et de Lorraine; 33,000 mems; Pres. Pastor GEOFFROY GOETZ.

Eglise réformée de France: 47 rue de Clichy, 75311 Paris Cedex 09; tel. 1-48-74-90-92; fax 1-42-81-52-40; internet www.eglise-reformee-fr.org; 350,000 mems; Pres. Nat. Council Pastor MARCEL MANOËL; Gen. Sec. Pastor BERTRAND DE CAZENOVE.

Fédération des Eglises évangéliques baptistes de France: 47 rue de Clichy, 75311 Paris Cedex 09; tel. 1-53-20-15-40; fax 1-53-20-15-41; e-mail secretariat@feebf.com; internet www.feebf.com; 6,000 mems; f. 1910; Pres. Pastor CHRISTIAN DE LA ROQUE; Gen. Sec. Pastor ETIENNE LHERMENAULT.

Mission évangélique tzigane de France: 'Les Petites Brosses', 45500 Neuvoy; tel. 2-38-67-03-18; 100,000 mems; f. 1946; Pres. Pastor GEORGES MEYER; Sec. MARIO HOLDENBAUM.

Mission populaire évangélique de France: 47 rue de Clichy, 75009 Paris Cedex 09; tel. 1-48-74-98-58; fax 1-48-78-52-37; e-mail mpefr@wanadoo.fr; internet www.missionpopulaire.org; 4,000 mems; f. 1871; Pres. Pastor BERTRAND VERGNIOL.

Union des Eglises évangéliques libres de France: 12 rue Claude-Perrault, 31500 Toulouse; tel. 5-61-26-06-18; internet www.ueel.org; 2,500 mems; Pres. Pastor PIERRE LACOSTE; Sec. RAYMOND CHAMARD.

Union Nationale des Eglises réformées évangéliques indépendantes de France: 74 rue Henri Revoil, 30900 Nîmes; tel. 4-66-23-95-05; e-mail unerei@wanadoo.fr; internet erei.free.fr; f. 1938; 12,000 mems; Pres. ANTOINE SCHLUCHTER; Sec.-Gen. GÉRARD FINES.

Scots Kirk Paris (Church of Scotland): 17 rue Bayard, 75008 Paris; tel. and fax 1-48-78-47-94; e-mail info@scotskirkparis.com; internet www.scotskirkparis.com; Minister Rev. ALLAN MILLER.

The Orthodox Church

There are about 200,000 Orthodox believers in France, of whom 100,000 are Russian Orthodox and 50,000 Greek Orthodox. There are 85 parishes and eight monasteries.

Administration of Russian Orthodox Churches in Western Europe (Jurisdiction of the Ecumenical Patriarchate): Cathédrale St Alexandre-Nevski, 12 rue Daru, 75008 Paris; tel. and fax 1-46-22-38-91; e-mail administration.diocesaine@exarchat.eu; internet www.exarchat.eu; Pres. Most Rev. GABRIEL (Archbishop of Russian Orthodox Churches in Western Europe and Exarch of the Ecumenical Patriarch).

Assembly of the Orthodox Churches of France (Greek Orthodox Church): Cathédrale St Stéphane, 7 rue Georges Bizet, 75116 Paris; tel. 1-47-20-82-35; fax 1-47-20-83-15; e-mail eglise.orthodoxe.grecque@wanadoo.fr; f. 1997; Metropolitan of France Most Rev. EMMANUEL (ADAMAKIS).

Russian Orthodox Church (Moscow Patriarchate): Métochie des Trois Docteurs à Paris, 75015 Paris; tel. 1-48-28-99-90; fax 1-48-28-74-54; e-mail korsoun@free.fr; internet e.korsoun.free.fr; the diocese of Chersonesus covers France, Portugal, Spain and Switzerland; Archbishop of Chersonesus INNOCENT (VASILIYEV).

The Anglican Communion

Within the Church of England, France forms part of the diocese of Gibraltar in Europe. The Bishop is resident in London (United Kingdom).

Archdeacon of France: Ven. KENNETH LETTS, Presbytère Anglican, 11 rue de la Buffa, 06000 Nice; tel. 4-93-87-19-83; fax 4-93-82-25-09; e-mail anglican@free.fr.

Other Christian Denominations

Société Religieuse des Amis (Quakers, Assemblée de France)/Centre Quaker International: 114 rue de Vaugirard, 75006 Paris; tel. 1-45-48-74-23; e-mail quaker.paris@tiscali.fr; internet quaker.chez-alice.fr; f. 1920; 10 meetings nation-wide; Clerks JEANNE-HENRIETTE LOUIS, AXEL JENSEN.

ISLAM

In numerical terms, Islam is the second most important religion in France; in 2006 there were about 5m. adherents, of whom some 35% resided in the Ile-de-France region. In early 2002 there were an estimated 1,500 Islamic places of worship in France.

Conseil français du culte musulman: Paris; f. 2003 to represent Islamic interests to the public authorities; Pres. Dr DALIL BOUBAKEUR; Vice-Pres FOUAD ALAOUI; Sec.-Gen. HAYDAR DEMIRYUREK.

Fédération Nationale des Musulmans de France (FNMF): Paris; f. 1985; 20 asscns; Pres. MOHAMED BECHARI.

Institut Musulman de la Grande Mosquée de Paris: 2 bis place du Puits de l'Ermite, 75005 Paris; tel. 1-45-35-97-33; fax 1-45-35-16-23; e-mail rectorat@mosquee-de-paris.net; internet www.mosquee-de-paris.net; f. 1926; cultural, diplomatic, social, judicial and religious sections; research and information and commercial annexes; Rector Dr DALIL BOUBAKEUR.

Ligue nationale des Musulmans de France: BP 39, 91103 Corbeil-Essones Cedex; tel. 8-92-68-18-30; e-mail inscription@lnmf.net; internet www.lnmf.net.

JUDAISM

There are about 650,000 Jews in France.

Conseil représentatif des institutions juives de France (CRIF): 39 rue Broca, 75005 Paris; tel. 1-42-17-11-11; fax 1-42-17-

FRANCE   *Directory*

11-50; e-mail infocrif@crif.org; internet www.crif.org; 63 asscns; Pres. RICHARD PRASQUIER.

Consistoire Central—Union des Communautés Juives de France: 19 rue Saint Georges, 75009 Paris; tel. 1-49-70-88-00; fax 1-42-81-03-66; e-mail consis@wanadoo.fr; f. 1808; 230 asscns; Chief Rabbi of France JOSEPH SITRUK; Pres. JEAN KAHN; Dir-Gen. FRÉDÉRIC ATTALI.

Consistoire Israélite de Paris: 17 rue Saint Georges, 75009 Paris; tel. 1-40-82-76-76; internet www.consistoire.org; f. 1808; 40,000 mems; Pres. MOÏSE COHEN; Chief Rabbi of Paris DAVID MESSAS; Chief Rabbi of the Consistoire Israélite de Paris ALAIN GOLDMANN.

Fonds social juif unifié (FSJU): Espace Rachi, 39 rue Broca, 75005 Paris; tel. 1-42-17-10-47; fax 1-42-17-10-45; e-mail info@fsju.org; internet www.fsju.org; f. 1950; unites the principal organizations supporting Jewish cultural, educational and social activity in France, and seeks to establish closer links between French Jewry and Israel; Pres. DAVID DE ROTHSCHILD; Dir DAVID SAADA.

BAHÁ'Í FAITH

Centre National Bahá'í: 45 rue Pergolèse, 75116 Paris; tel. 1-45-00-90-26; e-mail info@bahai.fr; internet www.bahai-fr.org.

The Press

Most major daily newspapers are owned by individual publishers or by the powerful groups that have developed round either a company or a single personality. The major groups are as follows:

Amaury Group: 25 ave Michelet, 93408 Saint Ouen Cedex; tel. 1-40-10-30-30; fax 1-40-11-15-26; owns *Le Parisien*, *Aujourd'hui en France*, the sports daily *L'Equipe*, the bi-weekly magazine *France Football*, the weekly *L'Equipe Magazine*, and the monthly *Vélo Magazine*; Man. Dir MARIE-ODILE AMAURY.

Bayard Presse: 3–5 rue Bayard, 75393 Paris Cedex 08; tel. 1-44-35-60-60; fax 1-44-35-61-61; e-mail communication@bayard-presse.com; internet www.bayardpresse.fr; f. 1873; Roman Catholic press group; owns 143 publs world-wide, incl. the national daily *La Croix*, the magazines *Pèlerin*, *Panorama*, *Notre Temps* and several specialized religious publications; Pres. BRUNO FRAPPAT.

Lagardère Active Média: 121 ave de Malakoff, 75216 Paris Cedex 16; tel. 1-40-69-16-00; fax 1-40-69-18-54; e-mail vblondeau@hfp.fr; internet www.lagardere.com; f. 2006 by merger of Hachette Filipacchi Médias (f. 1999) and Lagardère Active; controls magazines in France incl. *Paris-Match*, *L'Echo des Savanes*, *Pariscope*, *Jeune et Jolie*, *Photo*, *France-Dimanche*, *Elle*, *Télé 7 Jours* and holds stake in 10 regional daily newspapers; owns 260 magazines world-wide; Pres. DIDIER QUILLOT; Editorial Dir CHRISTIAN DE VILLENEUVE.

Mondadori France: 43 rue du Colonel Pierre-Avia, 75015 Paris; tel. 1-46-48-48-48; e-mail contact@mondadori.fr; internet www.mondadori.fr; fmrly Editions Mondiales, and subsequently Emap France; present name adopted 2006; owned by Arnoldo Mondadori Editore, SpA (Italy); controls more than 40 magazines in France, incl. *Nous Deux*, *FHM*, *Science et Vie*, *Télé-Star*, *Top Santé*, *Télépoche*, *Auto Plus* and also specialized magazines; Man. Dir ERNESTO MAURI.

Socpresse: 12 rue de Presbourg, 75116 Paris; one of the largest of the provincial daily press groups; fmrly Hersant Group; owned by Groupe Dassault; owns 20 dailies, numerous weeklies, fortnightlies and periodicals; publishes *Le Figaro*; acquired Groupe Express-Expansion in 2003; Pres. and Dir-Gen. SERGE DASSAULT.

DAILY NEWSPAPERS (PARIS)

La Croix: 3–5 rue Bayard, 75393 Paris Cedex 08; tel. 1-44-35-60-60; fax 1-44-35-60-01; e-mail lecteurs.lacroix@bayard-presse.com; internet www.la-croix.com; f. 1883; Roman Catholic; Dir BRUNO FRAPPAT; circ. in France 95,546 (2006).

Les Echos: 16 rue du Quatre Septembre, 75112 Paris Cedex 02; tel. 1-49-53-65-65; fax 1-45-61-48-92; e-mail redassist@lesechos.fr; internet www.lesechos.fr; f. 1908; acquired by Groupe LVMH in 2007; economic and financial; Dir-Gen. and Dir of Publication NICOLAS BEYTOUT; circ. in France 116,762 (2006).

L'Equipe: 4 rue Rouget-de-l'Isle, 92130 Issy-les-Moulineaux Cedex; tel. 1-40-93-20-20; fax 1-40-93-20-08; e-mail courrierdeslecteurs@lequipe.presse.fr; internet www.lequipe.fr; f. 1946; sport; owned by Groupe Amaury; Chair. LOUIS GILLET; Editorial Dir CLAUDE DROUSSENT; circ. in France 350,528 (2006).

Le Figaro: 14 blvd Haussmann, 75009 Paris; tel. 1-42-21-62-00; fax 1-42-21-64-05; e-mail contact@lefigaro.fr; internet www.lefigaro.fr; f. 1828; morning; news and literary; magazine on Saturdays; three weekly supplements; Pres. SERGE DASSAULT; Dir-Gen. FRANCIS MOREL; Editorial Dir NICOLAS BEYTOUT; circ. in France 322,497 (2006).

France-Soir: 4 rue Léon-Jost, 75017 Paris; tel. 1-56-21-00-00; internet www.francesoir.fr; f. 1941 as *Défense de la France*; present title adopted 1944; Editorial Dir FRANÇOIS MATTEI; circ. in France 27,519 (2006).

L'Humanité: 32 rue Jean Jaurès, 93528 Saint-Denis Cedex; tel. 1-49-22-72-72; fax 1-49-22-74-00; internet www.humanite.presse.fr; f. 1904; communist; morning; Pres. PATRICK LE HYARIC; Editorial Dir PIERRE LAURENT; circ. 51,708 (2006).

International Herald Tribune: 6 bis rue des Graviers, 92521 Neuilly-sur-Seine Cedex; tel. 1-41-43-93-00; fax 1-41-43-93-38; e-mail iht@iht.com; internet www.iht.com; f. 1887; present name adopted 1966; owned by The New York Times Co (USA); English language; Publr MICHAEL GOLDEN; Exec. Editor MICHAEL ORESKES; world-wide circ. 242,073 (2006).

Le Journal Officiel de la République Française: 26 rue Desaix, 75727 Paris Cedex 15; tel. 1-40-58-75-00; fax 1-45-79-17-84; e-mail info@journal-officiel.gouv.fr; internet www.legifrance.gouv.fr; f. 1870; official journal of the Government; publishes laws, decrees, parliamentary proceedings, and economic bulletins; Dir PIERRE-RENÉ LEMAS.

Libération: 11 rue Béranger, 75154 Paris Cedex 03; tel. 1-42-76-17-89; fax 1-42-72-94-93; internet www.liberation.com; f. 1973; 37.8% owned by Edouard de Rothschild; Pres. and Editorial Dir LAURENT JOFFRIN; Dir-Gen. DENIS PIERRARD; circ. in France 127,687 (2006).

Metro: 35 rue Greneta, 75002 Paris; tel. 1-55-34-45-00; fax 1-55-34-45-03; e-mail courrier@publications-metro.fr; internet www.metrofrance.com; f. 2002; distributed free of charge in Paris, Marseille, Lyon, Toulouse, Lille, Bordeaux, Nice, Nantes, Rennes, Strasbourg and Cannes; Propr Metro International (Sweden); Dir-Gen. VALÉRIE DECAMP; Editor FRANÇOIS BOURBOULON; circ. 636,660 (2006).

Le Monde: 80 blvd Auguste Blanqui, 75707 Paris Cedex 13; tel. 1-42-17-20-00; fax 1-42-17-21-21; e-mail lemonde@lemonde.fr; internet www.lemonde.fr; f. 1944; independent; Chair. of Supervisory Bd LOUIS SCHWEITZER; Pres. and Dir of Publication ERIC FOTTORINO; Editorial Dir ALAIN FRACHON; circ. in France 312,265 (2006).

Paris-Turf: Société des Editions France Libre, Bâtiment 270, 45 ave Victor Hugo, 60279 Aubervilliers; e-mail info@paris-turf.com; internet www.paris-turf.com; horse-racing; Editorial Dir FRANÇOIS HALLOPÉ; circ. 74,438 (2006).

Le Parisien: 25 ave Michelet, 93405 Saint-Ouen Cedex; tel. 1-40-10-30-30; fax 1-40-10-35-16; e-mail courriers@leparisien.com; internet www.leparisien.fr; f. 1944; morning; sold in Paris area and surrounding départements; Dir-Gen. JEAN HORNAIN; Editorial Dir VINCENT REIGNER; circ. in France (incl. *Aujourd'hui en France*) 507,679 (2006).

   Aujourd'hui en France: f. 1994; national version of *Le Parisien*; Editorial Dir VINCENT REIGNER.

Le Quotidien du Médecin: 21 rue Camille Desmoulins, 92789 Issy-les-Moulineaux Cedex; tel. 1-73-28-12-70; fax 1-73-28-13-85; e-mail redaction@quotimed.com; internet www.quotimed.com; medical journal; Pres. and Dir-Gen. Dr GÉRARD KOUCHNER; Editorial Dir RICHARD LISCIA; circ. 82,000.

La Tribune: 51 rue Vivienne, 75095 Paris Cedex 02; tel. 1-44-82-16-16; fax 1-44-82-17-92; e-mail directiondelaredaction@latribune.fr; internet www.latribune.fr; economic and financial; Pres., Dir of Publication ALAIN METTERNICH; Editorial Dir FRANÇOIS-XAVIER PIETRI; circ. in France 76,200 (2006).

20 Minutes: 50–52 blvd Hausmann, 75427 Paris Cedex 09; tel. 1-53-26-65-65; fax 1-53-26-65-68; e-mail redac-chef@20minutes.fr; internet www.20minutes.fr; f. 2002; distributed free of charge; Propr Schibsted (Norway); Pres. PIERRE-JEAN BOZO; circ. (2006) 427,062 (Paris), 739,301 (total France).

SUNDAY NEWSPAPERS (PARIS)

Le Journal du Dimanche: 121 ave de Malakoff, 75216 Paris Cedex 16; tel. 1-40-69-16-00; fax 1-40-69-18-54; internet www.lejdd.fr; owned by Groupe Lagardère; Editorial Dir JACQUES ESPÉRANDIEU; circ. 259,315 (2006).

Le Parisien Dimanche: 25 ave Michelet, 93405 Saint Ouen Cedex; tel. 1-40-10-30-30; fax 1-40-10-35-16; e-mail infoat@leparisien.fr; internet www.leparisien.fr; circ. 199,784 (2006).

PRINCIPAL PROVINCIAL DAILY NEWSPAPERS

Amiens

Le Courrier Picard: 29 rue de la République, BP 1021, 80010 Amiens Cedex 01; tel. 3-22-82-60-00; fax 3-22-82-60-12; e-mail courrier@courrier-picard.fr; internet www.courrier-picard.fr; f. 1944; Chair./Man. DOMINIQUE FONTAINE; Editor-in-Chief FRANÇOIS PERRIER; circ. 65,346 (2006).

FRANCE *Directory*

Angers

Le Courrier de l'Ouest: 4 blvd Albert Blanchoin, BP 728, 49007 Angers Cedex 01; tel. 2-41-68-86-88; fax 2-41-44-31-43; f. 1944; acquired in 2005 by Ouest-France group; Pres. and Man. Dir CHRISTIAN COUSTAL; Editor-in-Chief JACQUES BOSSEAU; circ. 98,139 (2006).

Angoulême

La Charente Libre: 16903 Angoulême Cedex 09; tel. 5-45-94-16-00; fax 5-45-94-16-19; e-mail charente@charentelibre.fr; internet www.charentelibre.com; Pres. JEAN-CLAUDE BONNAUD; Editorial Dir JACQUES GUYON; Editor-in-Chief JEAN-LOUIS HERVOIS; circ. 38,345 (2006).

Auxerre

L'Yonne Républicaine: 8–12 ave Jean Moulin, 89000 Auxerre; tel. 3-86-49-52-00; fax 3-86-46-52-35; e-mail direction@lyonne-republicaine.fr; internet www.lyonne-republicaine.fr; f. 1944; Pres. and Dir-Gen. JOËL LOUBERT; Editor-in-Chief PHILIPPE NOIREAUX; circ. 37,130 (2006).

Bordeaux

Sud-Ouest: 1 place Jacques Lemoine, 33094 Bordeaux Cedex; tel. 5-56-00-33-33; fax 5-56-00-32-17; e-mail contact@sudouest.com; internet www.sudouest.com; f. 1944; independent; Pres. and Dir of Publication JEAN-CLAUDE BONNAUD; Editor-in-Chief PATRICK VENRIES; circ. 311,373 (2006).

Bourges

Le Berry Républicain: 1–3 place Berry, 18023 Bourges Cedex; tel. 2-48-27-63-63; fax 2-48-48-17-19; e-mail redaction.berry@centrefrance.com; internet www.leberry.fr; Editor-in-Chief BERNARD STEPHAN; circ. 30,012 (2006).

Chalon-sur-Saône

Le Journal de Saône-et-Loire: 9 rue des Tonneliers, BP 134, 71100 Chalon-sur-Saône; tel. 3-85-44-68-68; fax 3-85-93-02-96; e-mail infos@lejsl.com; internet www.lejsl.com; f. 1826; Dir FRANÇOIS PRETET; circ. 62,020 (2006).

Chartres

L'Echo Républicain: 21 rue Vincent Chevard, 28000 Chartres; internet www.lechorepublicain.fr; f. 1929; Pres. and Dir-Gen. RICHARD METZGER; Editor-in-Chief HUGUES DE LESTAPIS; circ. 28,600 (2006).

Clermont-Ferrand

La Montagne: 28 rue Morel Ladeuil, BP 83, 63000 Clermont-Ferrand Cedex 01; tel. 4-73-17-17-17; fax 4-73-17-18-19; e-mail lamontagne@centrefrance.com; internet www.centrefrance.com; f. 1919; independent; Pres. and Dir-Gen. JEAN-PIERRE CAILLARD; Editorial Dir PIERRE GIRONDE; circ. 192,924 (2006).

Dijon

Le Bien Public-Les Dépêches: 7 blvd du Chanoîne Kir, BP 550, 21015 Dijon Cedex; tel. 3-80-42-42-23; fax 3-80-42-42-10; e-mail bienpublic@lebienpublic.fr; internet www.bienpublic.com; f. 1850 as Le Bien Public; merged with Les Dépêches in 2001; Pres. FRANÇOIS PRETET; Editor-in-Chief JEAN-LOUIS PIERRE; circ. 49,700 (2006).

Epinal

La Liberté de l'Est: 40 quai des Bons Enfants, 88026 Epinal Cedex 07; tel. 3-29-82-98-00; fax 3-29-82-99-29; e-mail contact@lalibertedelest.fr; internet www.lalibertedelest.fr; f. 1945; Chair./Man. Dir ALAIN GARROUY; Editor-in-Chief GÉRARD NOËL; circ. 26,609 (2006).

Grenoble

Le Dauphiné Libéré: Isles des Cordées, 38913 Veurey-Voroize Cedex; tel. 4-76-88-71-00; fax 4-76-88-70-96; e-mail redaction@ledauphine.com; internet www.ledauphine.com; f. 1945; Pres., Dir-Gen. and Editor-in-Chief HENRI-PIERRE GUILBERT; circ. 241,295 (2006).

Lille

La Voix du Nord: 8 place du Général de Gaulle, BP 549, 59023 Lille Cedex; tel. 3-20-78-40-40; fax 3-20-78-42-44; e-mail webvdn@lavoixdunord.fr; internet www.lavoixdunord.fr; f. 1944; Dir-Gen. JACQUES HARDOIN; Editor-in-Chief JEAN-MICHEL BRETONNIER; circ. 288,140 (2006).

Limoges

L'Echo du Centre: 29 rue Claude-Henri Gorceix, 87022 Limoges Cedex 09; tel. 5-55-04-49-99; fax 5-55-04-49-78; f. 1943; five edns; communist; Man. Dir CHRISTIAN AUDOUIN; Editor-in-Chief BERNARD CUNY.

Le Populaire du Centre: 7 rue du Général Catroux, BP 541, 87011 Limoges Cedex; tel. 5-55-58-59-00; fax 5-55-58-59-77; e-mail lepopulaire@centrefrance.com; internet www.lepopulaire.fr; f. 1905; Chair. MARCEL TOURLONIAS; Dir FRANÇOIS GILARDI; circ. 44,319 (2006).

Lyon

Le Progrès: 93 ave du Progrès, 69682 Chassieu; tel. 4-72-22-23-23; fax 4-78-90-52-40; internet www.leprogres.fr; f. 1859; Dir of Publication GÉRARD COLIN; circ. 223,309 (2006).

Tribune de Lyon: 4 place Le Viste, 69002 Lyon; tel. 4-72-69-15-15; fax 4-72-44-92-04; e-mail redaction@tribunedelyonhebdo.fr; internet www.tribunedelyonhebdo.fr; f. 2005; daily; Dir of Publication FRANÇOIS SAPY; circ. 10,000 (2005).

Le Mans

Le Maine Libre: 28–30 place de l'Eperon, BP 299, 72013 Le Mans Cedex 2; tel. 2-43-83-72-72; fax 2-43-28-28-19; e-mail redaction@maine-libre.com; acquired in 2005 by the Ouest-France group; Pres. and Dir-Gen. GÉRARD CHOL; Editor-in-Chief RAYMOND MAUDET; circ. 46,117 (2006).

Marseille

La Marseillaise: 19 cours d'Estienne d'Orves, BP 1862, 13222 Marseille Cedex 01; tel. 4-91-57-75-00; fax 4-91-57-75-25; internet www.journal-lamarseillaise.com; f. 1944; Communist; Man. Dir PAUL BIAGGINI; Editor-in-Chief CHRISTIAN DIGNE.

MarseillePlus: 248 ave Roger-Salengro, 13015 Marseille; tel. 4-91-84-00-00; fax 4-91-84-80-07; e-mail redaction@marseilleplus.com; internet www.marseilleplus.com; f. 2002; Mon.–Fri. mornings; distributed free of charge; circ. 59,660 (2006).

La Provence: 248 ave Roger-Salengro, 13015 Marseille; tel. 4-91-84-45-45; fax 4-91-84-49-95; e-mail contact@laprovence.com; internet www.laprovence.com; f. 1996 by merger of Le Provençal with Le Méridional; Dir of Publication STÉPHANE DUHAMEL; Editorial Dir GILLES DAUXERRE; circ. 153,250 (2006).

Metz

Le Républicain Lorrain: 3 ave des Deux Fontaines, 57140 Woippy; tel. 3-87-34-17-89; fax 3-87-34-17-90; e-mail pm.pernet@republicain-lorrain.fr; internet www.republicain-lorrain.fr; f. 1919; independent; Dir-Gen. and Dir of Publication PIERRE WICKER; Editor-in-Chief JACQUES VIRON; circ. 143,407 (2006).

Montpellier

Midi Libre: Mas de Grille, 34923 Montpellier Cedex 09; tel. 4-67-07-67-07; fax 4-67-07-68-13; internet www.midilibre.com; f. 1944; Pres. and Dir of Publication ALAIN PLOMBAT; Editorial Dir ROGER ANTECH; circ. 148,061 (2006).

Montpellier Plus: 6 rue Maguelone, 34000 Montpellier; tel. 4-99-74-34-38; internet www.montpellierplus.com; f. 2005 by *Midi Libre*; daily; distributed free of charge; circ. 23,423 (2006).

Morlaix

Le Télégramme: 7 voie d'accès au Port, BP 243, 29672 Morlaix; tel. 2-98-62-11-33; fax 2-98-63-45-45; e-mail telegramme@bretagne-online.com; internet www.letelegramme.fr; f. 1944; fmrly *Le Télégramme de Brest et de l'Ouest*; Pres. and Man. Dir EDOUARD COUDURIER; Editor-in-Chief MARCEL QUIVIGER; circ. 199,346 (2006).

Mulhouse

L'Alsace: 18 rue de Thann, 68945 Mulhouse Cedex 09; tel. 3-89-32-70-00; fax 3-89-32-11-26; e-mail redaction@alsapresse.com; internet www.alsapresse.com; f. 1944; Chair. JEAN-DOMINIQUE PRETET; Editor-in-Chief JEAN-MARIE HAEFFELLE; circ. 100,381 (2006).

Nancy

L'Est Républicain: rue Théophraste-Renaudot, Nancy Houdemont, 54185 Heillecourt Cedex; tel. 3-83-59-80-54; fax 3-83-59-80-13; e-mail secretariat.general@estrepublicain.fr; internet www.estrepublicain.fr; f. 1889; Pres. and Dir-Gen. GÉRARD LIGNAC; Editor-in-Chief PIERRE TARIBO; circ. 189,685 (2006).

FRANCE — Directory

Nantes

Presse Océan: 5 rue Santeuil, BP 22418, 44024 Nantes Cedex 01; tel. 2-40-44-24-00; fax 2-40-44-24-59; f. 1944; acquired in 2005 by the Ouest-France group; Chair. CHRISTIAN COUSTAL; Editor-in-Chief JEAN-PIERRE CHAMPIAT; circ. 44,576 (2006).

Nevers

Le Journal du Centre: 3 rue du Chemin de Fer, BP 106, 58001 Nevers; tel. 3-86-71-45-00; fax 3-86-71-45-20; e-mail redaction.jdc@centrefrance.com; internet www.lejdc.fr; f. 1943; Dir of Publication MICHEL HABOUZIT; Editor-in-Chief JEAN-YVES VIF; circ. 29,884 (2006).

Nice

Nice-Matin: 214 route de Grenoble, BP 4, 06290 Nice Cedex 03; tel. 4-93-18-28-38; fax 4-93-83-93-97; internet www.nicematin.fr; f. 1945; Pres. and Dir-Gen. JEAN-PAUL LOUVEAU; Editor-in-Chief DOMINIQUE DABIN; circ. 115,445 (2006).

Orléans

La République du Centre: 31 rue de la République, 45000 Orléans; tel. 2-38-78-79-80; fax 2-38-78-79-79; e-mail dleger@larep.com; internet www.larep.com; f. 1944; Pres. and Dir-Gen. JACQUES CAMUS; Editor-in-Chief DENIS LEGER; circ. 52,829 (2006).

Perpignan

L'Indépendant: 'Le Mas de la Garrigue', 2 ave Alfred Sauvy, 66605 Rivesaltes Cedex; tel. 4-68-64-88-88; fax 4-68-64-88-38; internet www.lindependant.com; f. 1846; daily; also *Indépendant-Dimanche* (Sunday); Dir-Gen. ANDRÉ LAURENS; Editorial Dir MICHEL BADRIGNANS; circ. 64,304 (2006).

Reims

L'Union: 5 rue de Talleyrand, 51083 Reims Cedex; tel. 3-26-50-50-50; fax 3-26-50-51-69; e-mail dirgen@journal-lunion.fr; internet www.lunion.presse.fr; f. 1944; Chair. DANIEL HUTIER; Editor-in-Chief THIERRY DE CABARRUS; circ. 111,870 (2006).

Rennes

Ouest-France: 10 rue du Breil, 35051 Rennes Cedex 09; tel. 2-99-32-60-00; fax 2-99-32-60-25; internet www.ouest-france.fr; f. 1944; publ. by non-profit-making Association pour le soutien des principes de la démocratie humaniste; 40 local editions (weekdays), 9 editions (Sundays); the largest circulation of any daily newspaper in France; Chair./Man. Dir FRANÇOIS RÉGIS HUTIN; Editor-in-Chief JEAN-LUC EVIN; circ. Mon.–Fri. 761,065; Sunday 312,652 (2006).

Roubaix

Nord-Eclair: 42 rue du Général Sarrail, 59052 Roubaix Cedex 1; tel. 3-20-25-02-50; fax 3-20-25-62-98; e-mail contact@nordeclair.fr; internet www.nordeclair.fr; f. 1944; Pres. JACQUES HARDOIN; Dir-Gen. and Editorial Dir JEAN-RENÉ LORE; circ. 29,921 (2006).

Rouen

Paris-Normandie: 19 place du Général de Gaulle, BP 563, 76187 Rouen Cedex; tel. 2-35-14-56-56; fax 2-35-14-56-15; e-mail redaction.web@paris-normandie.fr; internet www.paris-normandie.com; f. 1944; Pres. and Dir-Gen. PHILIPPE HERSANT; Editor-in-Chief GILLES DAUXERRE; circ. 67,776 (2006).

Strasbourg

Les Dernières Nouvelles d'Alsace: 17–21 rue de la Nuée Bleue, BP 406/R1, 67077 Strasbourg Cedex; tel. 3-88-21-55-00; fax 3-88-21-56-41; e-mail dnasug@sdv.fr; internet www.dna.fr; f. 1877; non-party; Dir-Gen. OLIVIER METZGER; Editor-in-Chief DOMINIQUE JUNG; circ. 182,623 (2006).

Toulon

Var Matin: 214 route de Grenoble, BP 4, 06290 Nice Cedex 3; tel. 4-94-06-91-91; fax 4-94-63-49-98; internet www.varmatin.com; f. 1975; Pres. and Dir-Gen. MICHEL COMBOUL; Editor-in-Chief DOMINIQUE DABIN; circ. 73,539 (2006).

Toulouse

La Dépêche du Midi: ave Jean Baylet, 31095 Toulouse Cedex; tel. 5-62-11-33-00; fax 5-61-44-74-74; internet www.ladepeche.com; f. 1870; Dir-Gen EVELYNE-JEAN BAYLET; Editor-in-Chief JEAN-CHRISTOPHE GIESBERT; circ. 192,075 (2006).

Tours

La Nouvelle République du Centre-Ouest: 232 ave de Grammont, 37048 Tours Cedex 1; tel. 2-47-31-70-00; fax 2-47-31-70-70; e-mail nr.redactionenchef@nrco.fr; internet www.lanouvellerepublique.fr; f. 1944; non-party; Pres. OLIVIER SAINT-CRICQ; Editor-in-Chief PASCAL ARNAUD; circ. 219,060 (2006).

Troyes

L'Est-Eclair: 71 ave du Maréchal Leclerc, 10120 St André les Vergers; tel. 3-25-71-75-75; fax 3-25-79-58-54; e-mail redaction@lest-eclair.fr; f. 1945; Dir FRANÇOIS LE SACHÉ; circ. 27,154 (2006).

SELECTED PERIODICALS

(average net circulation figures for the period July 2006–June 2007, unless otherwise stated)

Current Affairs and Politics

Annales—Histoire, Sciences sociales: 54 blvd Raspail, 75006 Paris; tel. 1-49-54-23-77; fax 1-49-54-26-88; e-mail antoine.lilti@ehess.fr; internet www.editions.ehess.fr/revues/annales-histoire-sciences-sociales; f. 1929; every 2 months; Dir ANTOINE LILTI.

Armées d'Aujourd'hui: Délégation à l'Information et à la Communication de la Défense, BP 33, 00445 Armées; tel. 1-56-77-23-03; fax 1-56-77-23-04; e-mail journalistes@dicod.defense.gouv.fr; 10 a year; military and technical; produced by the Délégation à l'Information et à la Communication de la Défense; Editor-in-Chief Commdt YANN RICHERME; circ. 100,000.

Le Canard Enchaîné: 173 rue Saint Honoré, 75051 Paris Cedex 01; tel. 1-42-60-31-36; fax 1-42-27-97-87; e-mail redaction@lecanardenchaine.fr; internet www.canardenchaine.com; f. 1915; weekly; satirical; Dir MICHEL GAILLARD; Editors-in-Chief CLAUDE ANGELI, ERIK EMPTAZ; circ. 340,090 (2005).

Charlie Hebdo: 44 rue de Turbigo, 75003 Paris; tel. 1-44-61-96-10; fax 1-44-61-96-11; e-mail redaction@charliehebdo.fr; f. 1992 (as revival of 1969–81 publication); left-wing, satirical; Editor and Dir of Publication PHILIPPE VAL.

Commentaire: 116 rue du Bac, 75007 Paris; tel. 1-45-49-37-82; fax 1-45-44-32-18; e-mail infos@commentaire.fr; internet www.commentaire.fr; f. 1978; quarterly; Dir JEAN-CLAUDE CASANOVA.

Courrier International: 8 rue Jean-Antoine de Baïf, 75212 Paris Cedex 13; tel. 1-46-46-16-00; fax 1-46-46-16-01; e-mail communication@courrierinternational.com; internet www.courrierinternational.com; f. 1990; weekly; current affairs and political; Pres. and Editorial Dir PHILIPPE THUREAU-DANGIN; circ. 187,315.

Défense Nationale: Ecole Militaire, BP 86-07, 75325 Paris Cedex 07; tel. 1-44-42-38-23; fax 1-44-42-31-89; e-mail redac@defnat.com; internet www.defnat.fr; f. 1939; 11 a year; publ. by Cttee for Study of National Defence; military, economic, political and scientific problems; Dir Gen. CHRISTIAN QUESNOT; Editor Adm. GEORGES GIRARD.

L'Express: 29 rue de Châteaudun, 75308 Paris Cedex 09; tel. 1-75-55-10-00; fax 1-75-55-12-05; e-mail courrier@lexpress.fr; internet www.lexpress.fr; f. 1953; weekly, Thursday; Editorial Dir CHRISTOPHE BARBIER; circ. 440,125.

L'Humanité Dimanche (HD): 32 rue Jean Jaurès, 93528 Saint-Denis Cedex; tel. 1-49-22-72-72; fax 1-49-22-74-00; internet www.humanite.presse.fr; f. 2006 to replace *L'Humanité Hebdo*; current affairs; Sundays; Editor MARTINE BULARD.

Marianne: 32 rue René Boulanger, 75484 Paris Cedex 10; tel. 1-53-72-29-00; fax 1-53-72-29-72; e-mail s.marty@journal-marianne.com; internet www.marianne2.fr; f. 1997; weekly, Saturday; current affairs; Dir MAURICE SZAFRAN; Editorial Dir LAURENT NEUMANN; circ. 273,178.

Le Monde Diplomatique: 1 ave Stephen Pichon, 75013 Paris Cedex; tel. 1-53-94-96-01; fax 1-53-94-96-26; e-mail secretariat@monde-diplomatique.fr; internet www.monde-diplomatique.fr; f. 1954; monthly; international affairs; Pres. and Editorial Dir IGNACIO RAMONET; circ. 126,522.

Le Nouvel Observateur: 10–12 place de la Bourse, 75002 Paris; tel. 1-44-88-34-34; e-mail direction@nouvelobs.com; internet hebdo.nouvelobs.com; f. 1964; weekly, Thursday; left-wing political and literary; Chair. DENIS OLIVENNES; Dir JEAN DANIEL; circ. 453,419.

Paris-Match: 151 rue Anatole-France, 92598 Levallois-Perret Cedex; tel. 1-41-34-72-46; fax 1-41-34-79-59; e-mail parismatch@hfp.fr; internet www.parismatch.com; f. 1949; weekly, Thursday; magazine of French and world affairs; Editorial Dir OLIVIER ROYANT; Editor-in-Chief GILLES MARTIN-CHAUFFIER; circ. 632,791.

Passages: 10 rue Clément, 75006 Paris; tel. 1-43-25-23-57; fax 1-43-25-63-65; e-mail passages@club-internet.fr; internet www.passages-forum.fr; f. 1987; quarterly; multidisciplinary discussions of geostrategic issues, seeking to present major contemporary events in an ethical and historical perspective; Dir EMILE H. MALET.

Le Peuple: 263 rue de Paris, Case 432, 93514 Montreuil Cedex; tel. 1-48-18-83-05; fax 1-48-59-28-31; e-mail lepeuplecgt@free.fr; internet www.lepeuple-cgt.com; f. 1921; fortnightly; official organ of the Confédération Générale du Travail (trade union confederation); Dir DANIEL PRADA; Editor-in-Chief FRANÇOISE DUCHESNE.

Le Point: 74 ave du Maine, 75014 Paris; tel. 1-44-10-10-10; fax 1-44-10-12-19; e-mail support@lepoint.fr; internet www.lepoint.fr; f. 1972; weekly, Thursday; politics and current affairs; Pres. and Dir-Gen. FRANZ-OLIVIER GIESBERT; Editor-in-Chief MICHEL COLOMÈS; circ. 405,702.

Politique Internationale: 11 rue du Bois de Boulogne, 75116 Paris; tel. 1-45-00-15-26; fax 1-45-00-16-87; internet www.politiqueinternationale.com; f. 1978; quarterly; Dir-Gen. PATRICK WAJSMAN; Editor-in-Chief ANNE LE FUR.

Regards: 120 rue Lafayette, 75010 Paris; tel. 1-47-70-01-90; fax 1-47-70-17-49; e-mail regards@regards.fr; internet www.regards.fr; monthly; communist; politics, current affairs, culture; Dir of Publication CATHERINE TRICOT; Editor-in-Chief RÉMI DOUAT.

Revue des Deux Mondes: 97 rue de Lille, 75007 Paris; tel. 1-47-53-61-94; fax 1-47-53-61-99; e-mail contact@revuedesdeuxmondes.fr; internet www.revuedesdeuxmondes.fr; f. 1829; 10 a year; current affairs; Pres. MARC LADREIT DE LACHARRIÈRE; Editor-in-Chief MICHEL CREPU.

Rivarol: 1 rue d'Hauteville, 75010 Paris; tel. 1-53-34-97-97; fax 1-53-34-97-98; e-mail contact@rivarol.com; internet www.rivarol.com; f. 1951; weekly; conservative; political, literary and satirical; Dir and Editor-in-Chief CAMILLE-MARIE GALIC.

Technikart: Passage du Cheval-Blanc, 2 rue de la Roquette, 75011 Paris; tel. 1-43-14-33-44; e-mail rturcat@technikart.com; internet www.technikart.com; monthly; cultural review; Editor-in-Chief RAPHAËL TURCAT; circ. 38,500.

La Vie: 8 rue Jean-Antoine-de-Baïf, 75212 Paris Cedex 13; tel. 1-48-88-46-00; fax 1-48-88-46-01; e-mail vie.forum@mp.com; internet www.lavie.presse.fr; f. 1945; acquired by Le Monde SA in 2003; weekly; general, Christian; Dir of Publication JACQUES GIRAUD; circ. 156,698.

VSD: 15 rue Galvani, 75809 Paris Cedex 17; tel. 1-56-99-47-00; fax 1-56-99-51-28; e-mail lecteurs@vsd.fr; internet www.vsd.fr; f. 1977; weekly, Wednesday; current affairs, leisure; Dir of Publication PHILIPPE LABI; Editor-in-Chief MARC DOLISI; circ. 206,297.

The Arts

L'Architecture d'Aujourd'hui: 6 rue Lhomond, 75005 Paris; tel. 1-44-32-18-69; e-mail sowa@jmplace.com; f. 1930; 6 a year; publ. by Editions J.-M. Place; Editor-in-Chief AXEL SOWA; circ. 3,714.

Art et Décoration: 16–18 rue de l'Amiral Mouchez, 75686 Paris Cedex 14; tel. 1-45-65-48-48; e-mail info@art-decoration.fr; internet www.art-decoration.fr; f. 1897; 8 a year; Dir JEAN MASSIN; Editor-in-Chief DANIEL SOUBEYRAND.

Beaux Arts Magazine: 86–88 rue Thiers, 92100 Boulogne-Billancourt; tel. 1-41-41-55-60; fax 1-41-41-98-35; e-mail courrier@beauxartsmagazine.com; internet www.beauxartsmagazine.com; monthly; review of art, architecture, cinema, design; Dir of Publication THIERRY TAITTINGER; Editor-in-Chief FABRICE BOUSTEAU; circ. 52,365.

Critique: 7 rue Bernard Palissy, 75006 Paris; tel. 1-44-39-39-20; fax 1-45-44-82-36; e-mail critique@wanadoo.fr; f. 1946; nine a year; general review of French and foreign literature, philosophy, art, social sciences and history; Dir PHILIPPE ROGER.

Diapason: 33 rue du Colonel Pierre Avia, 75754 Paris Cedex 15; tel. 1-46-62-20-00; fax 1-46-62-25-33; f. 1956; monthly; classical music; Pres. and Dir-Gen. CLAUDE POMMEREAU; Editor-in-Chief YVES PETIT DE VOIZE; circ. 31,050.

Esprit: 212 rue Saint Martin, 75003 Paris; tel. 1-48-04-92-90; fax 1-48-04-50-53; e-mail redaction@esprit.presse.fr; internet www.esprit.presse.fr; f. 1932; 10 a year; philosophy, history, sociology; Dir OLIVIER MONGIN; Editor-in-Chief MARC-OLIVIER PADIS.

Les Inrockuptibles: 24 rue Saint Sabin, 75011 Paris; tel. 1-42-44-16-16; fax 1-42-44-16-00; e-mail christian.fevret@inrocks.com; internet www.lesinrocks.com; f. 1986; weekly, Tuesday; music, cinema, literature and television; Editorial Dir CHRISTIAN FEVRET; circ. 37,822.

Lire: 29 rue de Châteaudun, 75308 Paris Cedex 09; tel. 1-75-55-10-00; fax 1-75-55-17-04; e-mail redaction@lire.fr; internet www.lire.fr; f. 1975; monthly; literary review; Editorial Dir FRANÇOIS BUSNEL; circ. 76,635.

Livres de France: 35 rue Grégoire-de-Tours, 75006 Paris; tel. 1-44-41-28-00; fax 1-43-29-77-85; f. 1979; 11 a year; Dir JEAN-MARIE DOUBLET.

Livres-Hebdo: 35 rue Grégoire-de-Tours, 75006 Paris; tel. 1-44-41-28-00; fax 1-43-29-77-85; internet www.livreshebdo.fr; f. 1979; weekly; book publishing; Editor-in-Chief CHRISTINE FERRAND.

Le Magazine Littéraire: 74 ave du Maine, 75014 Paris; tel. 1-44-10-10-10; fax 1-44-10-13-94; e-mail courrier@magazine-litteraire.com; internet www.magazine-litteraire.com; f. 1966; monthly; literature; Editorial Dir JEAN-LOUIS HUE; circ. 31,676.

Le Matricule des Anges: BP 20225, 34004 Montpellier Cedex 1; tel. and fax 4-67-92-29-33; e-mail lmda@lmda.net; internet www.lmda.net; f. 1992; monthly; literary criticism; Pres. and Editor-in-Chief PHILIPPE SAVARY.

Le Monde de l'Education: 46 rue du Fer à Moulin, 75005 Paris; tel. 1-44-08-79-11; fax 1-44-08-79-12; e-mail lemonde.education@lemonde.fr; internet www.lemonde.fr/mde; f. 1974; monthly; education; Editor-in-Chief BRIGITTE PERUCCA; circ. 43,156.

La Quinzaine Littéraire: 135 rue Saint-Martin, 75194 Paris Cedex 04; tel. 1-48-87-75-87; fax 1-48-87-13-01; e-mail selis@wanadoo.fr; internet www.quinzaine-litteraire.net; f. 1966; fortnightly; Dir MAURICE NADEAU; Editor-in-Chief ERIC PHALIPPOU; circ. 20,000.

Rock & Folk: 6 rue Olof Palme, 92587 Clichy Cedex; tel. 1-41-40-32-32; internet www.rocknfolk.com; f. 1966; monthly; music; Editor-in-Chief PHILIPPE MANŒUVRE; circ. 36,981.

Les Temps Modernes: 26 rue de Condé, 75006 Paris; tel. 1-43-29-08-47; fax 1-40-51-83-38; f. 1945 by J.-P. Sartre; six a year; literary review; publ. by Gallimard; Dir CLAUDE LANZMANN.

Economic and Financial

Capital: 15 rue Galvani, 75809 Paris Cedex 17; tel. 1-44-15-30-00; e-mail finance@capital.fr; internet www.capital.fr; f. 1991; monthly; business, finance; Editor-in-Chief FRANÇOIS GENTHIAL; circ. 380,503.

Challenges: 33 rue Vivienne, 75002 Paris; tel. 1-58-65-03-03; e-mail pf@challenges.fr; internet www.challenges.fr; weekly; economics and politics; Editor-in-Chief PATRICK FIOLE; circ. 257,614.

L'Expansion: 29 rue de Châteaudun, 75308 Paris Cedex 09; tel. 1-75-55-10-00; fax 1-75-55-17-02; internet www.lexpansion.com; f. 1967; monthly; economics and business; Editorial Dir ALAIN LOUYOT; circ. 159,690.

Marchés Tropicaux et Méditerannéens: 5 rue de Charonne, 75011 Paris; tel. 1-53-63-10-80; fax 1-45-48-75-32; e-mail info@marches-tropicaux.com; internet www.marches-tropicaux.fr; f. 1945; weekly; analysis and information on Africa and the Mediterranean region; Dir of Publication MICHEL MYSZKOWSKI; Editor-in-Chief LUCAS PATRIAT.

Mieux Vivre Votre Argent: 29 rue de Châteaudun, 75308 Paris Cedex 09; tel. 1-75-55-10-00; fax 1-75-55-11-40; e-mail jpviallon@mieuxvivre.fr; internet www.votreargent.fr; monthly; f. 1918; investment, economics; Editorial Dir JEAN-ANTOINE BOUCHEZ; Editor-in-Chief JEAN-FRANÇOIS FILLIATRE; circ. 252,455.

Le Monde-Initiatives: 1–3 ave Stephen Pichon, 75013 Paris; tel. 1-53-94-96-60; fax 1-53-94-96-80; e-mail initiatives@lemonde.fr; f. 2002; monthly; Dir ALAIN LEBAUBE; circ. 50,000 (2002).

Le Nouvel Economiste: 5 passage Piver, 75011 Paris; tel. 1-58-30-64-64; fax 1-58-30-64-65; e-mail patrick.arnoux@nouveleconomiste.fr; internet www.nouveleconomiste.fr; f. 1976; weekly, Thursday; Pres. and Editorial Dir HENRI J. NIJDAM; circ. 20,929.

L'Usine Nouvelle: 12–14 rue Médéric, 75815 Paris Cedex 17; tel. 1-56-79-41-00; fax 1-56-79-42-34; internet www.usinenouvelle.com; f. 1945; weekly, Thursday; technical and industrial journal; Dir PAUL WAGNER; Editor-in-Chief PIERRE-OLIVIER ROUAUD; circ. 36,827.

Valeurs Actuelles: 3–5 rue Saint Georges, 75009 Paris; tel. 1-40-54-11-00; fax 1-40-54-12-85; internet www.valeursactuelles.com; f. 1966; weekly; politics, economics, international affairs; Dir-Gen. GUILLAUME ROQUETTE; circ. 83,694.

La Vie Financière: 14 rue Chapon, 75003 Paris; tel. 1-53-01-70-70; fax 1-53-01-71-13; e-mail jlchampetier@laviefinanciere.com; internet www.laviefinanciere.com; f. 1945; weekly; economics and finance; Editorial Dir GÉRARD BLANDIN; circ. 84,956.

History and Geography

Annales de Géographie: 21 rue de Montparnasse, 75006 Paris; fax 1-44-39-51-10; e-mail infos@armand-colin.com; f. 1891; every 2 months.

Cahiers de Civilisation Médiévale: 24 rue de la Chaine, 86022 Poitiers; tel. 5-49-45-45-63; fax 5-49-45-45-73; e-mail martin.aurell@univ-poitiers.fr; internet www.mshs.univ-poitiers.fr/cescm; f. 1958; quarterly; pluri-disciplinary medieval studies, concentrating on the 10th–12th centuries; Dir MARTIN AURELL; circ. 1,500 (2002).

GEO: 43–45 ave de Clichy, 75850 Paris Cedex 17; tel. 1-56-99-60-83; e-mail kmontemont@prisma-presse.com; internet www.geomagazine.com; f. 1979; monthly; architecture, culture, people, photo-journalism, travel; Editorial Dir JEAN MARTY; circ. 300,123.

FRANCE

La Géographie: 184 blvd Saint Germain, 75006 Paris; tel. 1-45-48-54-62; fax 1-42-22-40-93; e-mail socgeo@socgeo.org; internet www.socgeo.org; f. 1821; quarterly of the Société de Géographie; Chair. Prof. JEAN BASTIÉ.

L'Histoire: 74 ave du Maine, 75014 Paris; tel. 1-44-10-10-10; fax 1-44-10-54-47; e-mail courrier@histoire.presse.fr; internet www.histoire.presse.fr; f. 1978; monthly; Dir-Gen. STÉPHANE KHÉMIS; Editor-in-Chief VALÉRIE HANNIN; circ. 64,444.

Historia: 74 ave du Maine, 75014 Paris; tel. 1-44-10-12-90; fax 1-44-10-12-94; e-mail pczete@tallandier.fr; internet www.historia.presse.fr; f. 1909; monthly; Dir PATRICIA BARBIZET.

National Geographic France: 43–45 ave de Clichy, 75850 Paris Cedex 17; tel. 1-56-99-60-96; e-mail nationalgeographic@ngm-f.com; internet www.nationalgeographic.fr; f. 1999; monthly; geography, people, science, travel; Dir DENIS BERRIAT; Editor-in-Chief FRANÇOIS MAROT; circ. 154,048.

Revue d'Histoire Diplomatique: 13 rue Soufflot, 75005 Paris; tel. 1-43-54-05-97; fax 1-46-34-07-60; f. 1887; quarterly; Dirs MAURICE VAISSE, GEORGES-HENRI SOUTOU.

Revue Historique: 56 rue Jacob, 75006 Paris; e-mail revue.historique@puf.com; f. 1876; quarterly; Dirs CLAUDE GAUVARD, JEAN-FRANÇOIS SIRINELLI.

Revue de Synthèse: Centre International de Synthèse, 45 rue d'Ulm, 75005 Paris; tel. 1-44-32-26-55; fax 1-44-32-22-56; e-mail revuedesynthese@ens.fr; internet www.revue-de-synthese.eu; f. 1900; four a year; history, philosophy, social sciences; Dir and Editor-in-Chief ERIC BRIAN.

Home, Fashion and General

Closer: 43 rue du Colonel Pierre Avia, 75015 Paris; tel. 1-41-86-18-08; internet www.closermag.fr; f. 2005; weekly; celebrity news, TV, radio, films; Editor-in-Chief LAURENCE PIEAU; circ. 420,437.

Cosmopolitan: 10 blvd des Frères Voisin, 92792 Issy-les-Moulineaux Cedex 9; tel. 1-41-46-88-88; fax 1-41-48-84-93; internet www.cosmopolitan.fr; f. 1973; monthly; Editor-in-Chief SYLVIE OVERNOY; circ. 346,105.

Elle: 149–151 rue Anatole France, 92300 Levallois-Perret; tel. 1-41-34-66-75; fax 1-41-34-67-97; e-mail ellemagazine@hfp.fr; internet www.elle.fr; f. 1945; monthly; Dir-Gen. ANNE-MARIE COUDERC; Editor-in-Chief VALÉRIE TORANIAN; circ. 334,770.

Femme Actuelle: 73–75 rue La Condamine, 75854 Paris Cedex 17; tel. 1-44-90-67-50; fax 1-44-90-67-14; e-mail femactu@prisma-presse.com; internet www.femmeactuelle.fr; f. 1984; weekly, Monday; Editorial Dir MARYSE BONNET; circ. 1,058,469.

Ici-Paris: 149–151 rue Anatole France, 92300 Levallois-Perret; tel. 1-41-34-60-00; fax 1-41-34-89-34; f. 1945; weekly; celebrity gossip, news; publ. by Lagadère Active; Editors-in-Chief GIANNI LORENZON, JOËL LAFFAY; circ. 358,331 (2007).

Le Journal de la Maison: 124 rue Danton, 92598 Levallois-Perret; tel. 1-41-10-13-55; fax 1-41-10-13-01; e-mail ccorvaisier@hfp.fr; monthly; home; Editor-in-Chief CAROLINE CORVAISIER; circ. 185,560.

Marie-Claire: 10 blvd des Frères Voisin, 92792 Issy-les-Moulineaux Cedex 9; tel. 1-41-46-88-88; fax 1-41-46-86-86; e-mail mcredac@gmc.tm.fr; internet www.groupemarieclaire.com; f. 1954; monthly; Editor-in-Chief TINA KIEFFER; circ. 419,033.

Marie-France: 10 blvd des Frères Voisin, 92792 Issy-Les-Moulineaux; e-mail mfredac@gmc.tm.fr; f. 1944; monthly; Editorial Dir YSEULT WILLIAMS; circ. 187,300.

Modes et Travaux: 1 rue du Colonel Pierre Avia, 75015 Paris; tel. 1-46-48-48-48; fax 1-46-48-19-53; f. 1919; monthly; publ. by Mondadori France; Editor PATRICIA WAGNER; circ. 385,793.

Notre Temps: 3–5 rue Bayard, 75393 Paris Cedex 08; tel. 1-44-35-60-60; fax 1-44-35-60-31; e-mail redaction@notretemps.com; internet www.notretemps.com; f. 1968; monthly; for retired people; Editor-in-Chief SYLVIE ODY; circ. 886,322.

Nous Deux: 1 rue du Colonel Pierre Avia, 75015 Paris; tel. 1-46-48-43-40; fax 1-41-86-84-02; e-mail contact@mondadori.fr; f. 1947; weekly; Editor MARION MINUIT; circ. 313,742.

Parents: 10 rue Thierry-le-Luron, 92592 Levallois-Perret Cedex; tel. 1-41-34-61-88; fax 1-41-34-70-79; internet www.parents.fr; monthly; magazine for parents; Editorial Dir CATHERINE LELIÈVRE; circ. 309,896.

Pleine Vie: 1 rue du Colonel Pierre Avia, 75015 Paris; tel. 1-41-33-10-31; e-mail jeanne.thiriet@mondadori.fr; f. 1997; monthly; intended for women aged 50 and over; Editor JEANNE THIRIET; circ. 912,918.

Point de Vue: 23 rue du Châteaudun, 75308 Paris Cedex 09; tel. 1-75-55-17-00; e-mail info@pointdevue.fr; internet www.pointdevue.fr; f. 1945; weekly, Wednesday; general illustrated; publ. by Roularta Media; Editorial Dir COLOMBE PRINGLE; circ. 199,181.

Prima: 6 rue Daru, 75379 Paris Cedex 08; tel. 1-44-15-30-00; internet www.prima.fr; f. 1982; monthly; intended for women of 40 years and over; also Prima Maison and Prima Cuisine Gourmande; Editor-in-Chief ARMELLE OGER; circ. 535,984.

Psychologies Magazine: 29 rue de Lisbonne, 75008 Paris; tel. 1-44-95-89-19; fax 1-44-95-01-11; internet www.psychologies.com; monthly; Dir-Gen. ARNAUD DE SAINT SIMON; Editorial Dir HÉLÈNE MATHIEU; circ. 332,096.

Public: 149 rue Anatole France, 92534 Levallois-Perret Cedex; tel. 1-41-34-92-37; fax 1-41-34-90-98; internet www.public.fr; f. 2003; weekly, Monday; celebrity news, TV, radio, films; Editorial Dir NICOLAS PIGASSE; circ. 390,069.

Questions de Femmes: 117 rue de la Tour, 75116 Paris; tel. 1-45-03-80-00; fax 1-45-03-80-23; e-mail fazire@groupe-ayache.com; internet www.questionsdefemmes.com; f. 1996; monthly; Editor-in-Chief FABIENNE AZIRE.

Santé Magazine: 22 rue Letellier, 75015 Paris; tel. 1-43-23-16-60; e-mail direction@santemagazine.fr; internet www.santemagazine.fr; f. 1976; monthly; health; Editor-in-Chief VALÉRIE GIRONE; circ. 244,776.

Top Santé: 1 rue du Colonel Pierre Avia, 75015 Paris; tel. 1-46-48-43-66; e-mail cathy.vichery@mondadori.fr; internet www.topsante.com; f. 1990; monthly; health; Editor SOPHIE DELAUGÈRE; circ. 319,294.

Vivre Plus: 3–5 rue Bayard, 75393 Paris Cedex 08; tel. 1-44-35-60-60; fax 1-44-35-60-37; f. 2004 as Côté Femme; restyled as above 2006; weekly; aimed at women aged 40 years and above; Editor-in-Chief ODILE AMBLARD.

Voici: 6 rue Daru, 75379 Paris Cedex 08; tel. 8-92-68-11-55; e-mail voici@prisma-presse.com; internet www.voici.fr; f. 1987; weekly, Monday; celebrity news, TV, radio, films; Editor-in-Chief LOÏC SELLIN; circ. 462,182.

Vogue Paris: 56A rue du Faubourg Saint Honoré, 75008 Paris; tel. 1-53-43-60-00; fax 1-53-43-61-61; e-mail magazine@vogueparis.com; internet www.vogueparis.com; monthly; Publr XAVIER ROMATET; Editor-in-Chief CARINE ROITFELD; circ. 96,479.

Leisure Interests and Sport

Cahiers du Cinéma: 9 passage de la Boule-Blanche, 75012 Paris; tel. 1-53-44-75-75; fax 1-43-43-95-04; e-mail teraha.cducinema@lemonde.fr; f. 1951; monthly; film reviews; Editorial Dir JEAN-MICHEL FRODON; Editor-in-Chief EMMANUEL BURDEAU; circ. 20,733.

Le Chasseur Français: 48 rue Guynemer, 92865 Issy-les-Moulineaux Cedex 9; tel. 1-41-33-22-01; fax 1-41-33-22-90; internet www.lechasseurfrancais.com; f. 1885; monthly; hunting, shooting, fishing; Editor-in-Chief PHILIPPE COLL; circ. 453,315.

France-Football: 4 rue Rouget de Lisle, 92793 Issy-les-Moulineaux Cedex 9; tel. 1-40-93-20-20; fax 1-40-93-20-17; internet www.francefootball.fr; f. 1947; twice weekly; owned by Amaury Group; Editorial Dir DENIS CHAUMIER; circ. 170,198 (Tues.), 113,431 (Fri.).

Pariscope: 149 ave Anatole France, 92534 Levallois-Perret Cedex; tel. 1-41-34-73-47; fax 1-41-34-78-30; f. 1965; listings and reviews of events in Paris and Ile-de-France; weekly; Dir-Gen. OLIVIER CHAPUIS; Editorial Dir PASCALE DACBERT-LEMAIRE; circ. 83,158.

Photo: 149 rue Anatole France, 92300 Levallois-Perret; tel. 1-41-34-73-27; fax 1-41-34-71-52; e-mail photo@hfp.fr; internet www.photo.fr; f. 1967; monthly; specialist photography magazine; Editorial Dir ERIC COLMET-DAÂGE; circ. 22,840.

Positif: 38 rue Milton, 75009 Paris; tel. 1-43-26-17-80; fax 1-43-26-29-77; e-mail posed@wanadoo.fr; internet www.revue-positif.net; f. 1952; monthly; film reviews; publ. by Editions Scope.

Première: 149–151 rue Anatole France, 92534 Levallois-Perret Cedex; tel. 1-41-34-60-00; internet www.premiere.fr; monthly; film reviews; Editor-in-Chief SOPHIE GRASSIN; circ. 149,036.

Télé 7 Jours: 149–151 rue Anatole France, 92534 Levallois-Perret Cedex; tel. 1-41-34-67-66; fax 1-41-34-79-70; e-mail courriert7j@hfp.fr; internet www.tele7.fr; weekly; television; Editorial Dir THIERRY MOREAU; circ. 1,600,931.

Télé Poche: 150 rue Gallieni, 92644 Boulogne-Billancourt Cedex; tel. 1-41-33-50-02; fax 1-41-33-57-48; e-mail pierreyves.simon@emapfrance.com; internet www.telepoche.fr; f. 1966; weekly; publ. by Mondadori France; television; Pres. and Dir-Gen. ARNAUD ROY DE PUYFONTAINE; Editor-in-Chief ERIC PAVON; circ. 656,857.

Télérama: 8 rue Jean-Antoine de Baïf, Paris 75212 Cedex 13; tel. 1-48-88-48-88; fax 1-47-64-02-04; internet www.telerama.fr; f. 1972; weekly, Wednesday; radio, TV, film, literature and music; Dir BRUNO PATINO; circ. 637,358.

Télé Z: 10 ave de Messine, 75008 Paris; tel. 1-53-83-93-40; fax 1-53-89-97-71; internet www.telez.fr; weekly; television; Dir LAURENT D'EPENOUX; circ. 1,750,750.

FRANCE

Vélo Magazine: 4 rue Rouget de Lisle, 92793 Issy-les-Moulineaux; tel. 1-40-93-20-20; fax 1-40-93-20-09; e-mail redac@velomagazine.fr; internet www.velomagazine.fr; monthly; cycling; Editor-in-Chief GILLES COMTE; circ. 46,757.

Voiles et Voiliers: 21 rue du Faubourg Saint-Antoine, 75550 Paris Cedex 11; tel. 1-44-87-87-87; fax 1-44-87-87-79; internet www.voilesetvoiliers.com; monthly; sailing and nautical sports; Dir CHARLES DE FRÉMINVILLE; circ. 52,539.

Religion and Philosophy

Actualité Juive: 14 rue Raymonde Salez, 93260 Les Lilas; tel. 1-43-60-20-20; fax 1-43-60-20-21; e-mail a-j-presse@actuj.com; internet www.actuj.net; weekly; Dir SERGE BENATTAR; circ. 17,000 (2004).

Etudes: 14 rue d'Assas, 75006 Paris; tel. 1-44-39-48-48; fax 1-44-39-48-17; e-mail etudes@free.fr; internet www.revue-etudes.com; f. 1856; monthly; general interest; Editor-in-Chief PIERRE DE CHARENTENAY.

France Catholique: 60 rue de Fontenay, 92350 Le Plessis-Robinson; tel. 1-46-30-37-38; fax 1-46-30-04-64; e-mail france-catholique@wanadoo.fr; internet www.france-catholique.fr; weekly; Dir FRÉDÉRIC AIMARD; Editor-in-Chief GÉRARD LECLERC; circ. 16,000 (2004).

Le Monde des Religions: 8 rue Jean-Antoine de Baïf, 75212 Paris Cedex 13; tel. 1-48-88-46-00; fax 1-42-27-04-19; e-mail le.monde.des.religions@mp.com.fr; internet www.le-monde-des-religions.fr; f. 2003 to replace *Actualité des Religions*; six a year; Editorial Dir FRÉDÉRIC LENOIR; circ. 51,271.

Pèlerin: 3–5 rue Bayard, 75008 Paris; tel. 1-44-35-60-60; fax 1-44-35-60-21; e-mail rene.poujol@bayard-presse.com; internet www.pelerin.info; f. 1873; weekly; Dir BRUNO FRAPPAT; Editor-in-Chief RENÉ POUJOL.

Prier: 8 rue Jean-Antoine de Baïf, 75212 Paris Cedex 13; tel. 1-48-88-46-00; fax 1-42-27-29-03; e-mail p.pueyo@mp.com.fr; internet www.prier.presse.fr; f. 1978; monthly; review of modern prayer and contemplation; Editor ERIC VINSON.

Réforme: 53–55 ave du Maine, 75014 Paris; tel. 1-43-20-32-67; fax 1-43-21-42-86; e-mail reforme@reforme.net; internet www.reforme.net; f. 1945; weekly; considers current affairs from a Protestant Christian perspective; Dir JEAN-LUC NOUTON; Editor-in-Chief NATHALIE DE SENNVILLE-LEENHARDT; circ. 6,000 (2003).

Revue des Sciences Philosophiques et Théologiques: Le Saulchoir, 43 bis rue de la Glacière, 75013 Paris; tel. 1-44-08-71-99; internet www.rspt.org; f. 1907; quarterly; Dir GILLES BERCEVILLE.

Silence: Ecologie, Alternatives, Non-violence: 9 rue Dumenge, 69317 Lyon Cedex 04; tel. 4-78-39-55-33; fax 4-78-28-85-12; internet www.revuesilence.net; f. 1982; monthly.

Témoignage Chrétien: 49 rue du Faubourg Poissonnière, 75009 Paris; tel. 1-44-83-82-82; fax 1-44-83-82-88; e-mail lecteurs@temoignagechretien.fr; internet www.temoignagechretien.fr; f. 1941; weekly; Christianity and politics; Pres. and Dir of Publication JACQUES MAILLOT; Editorial Dir EMMANUEL LEMIEUX.

La Voix Protestante: 14 rue de Trévise, 75009 Paris; tel. 1-47-70-23-53; fax 1-48-01-09-13; e-mail direction@lavoixprotestante.org; internet www.erf-rp.org; monthly review of Protestant churches in Paris and Eastern regions; Dir DANIEL CASSOU.

Science and Technology

Action Auto-Moto: 149 rue Anatole France, 92534 Levallois-Perret Cedex; tel. 1-41-34-95-25; fax 1-41-34-95-26; internet www.auto-moto.com; monthly; cars; Dir BRUNO LESOUËF; Editorial Dir JEAN SAVARY; circ. 284,713.

Air et Cosmos: 1 bis ave de la République, 75011 Paris; tel. 1-49-29-30-00; fax 1-49-29-32-01; e-mail air-cosmos@air-cosmos.com; internet www.aerospacemedia.com; f. 1963; weekly; aerospace; Dir-Gen. and Editorial Dir ROBERT MONTEUX; Editor-in-Chief JEAN-PIERRE CASAMAYOU; circ. 19,532.

Annales de Chimie—Science des Matériaux: Lavoisier SAS, 14 rue de Provigny, 94236 Cachan Cedex; tel. 1-47-40-67-00; fax 1-47-40-67-02; e-mail acsm@lavoisier.fr; internet acsm.revuesonline.com; f. 1789; six a year; chemistry and material science.

L'Argus de l'Automobile: 1 place Boieldieu, 75082 Paris Cedex 02; tel. 1-53-29-11-00; fax 1-49-27-09-50; internet www.argusauto.com; f. 1927; motoring weekly; Dir ALEXANDRINE BRETON DES LOŸS; circ. 61,364.

Astérisque: Société Mathématique de France, Institut Henri Poincaré, 11 rue Pierre et Marie Curie, 75231 Paris Cedex 05; tel. 1-44-27-67-99; fax 1-40-46-90-96; e-mail revues@smf.ens.fr; internet smf.emath.fr/Publications/Asterisque; f. 1973; 7–9 a year; mathematics; Editor-in-Chief YVES ANDRÉ; Sec. NATHALIE CHRISTIAËN.

L'Astronomie: 3 rue Beethoven, 75016 Paris; tel. 1-42-24-13-74; fax 1-42-30-75-57; e-mail ste.astro.france@wanadoo.fr; internet www.astrosurf.com/saf; f. 1887; monthly; publ. by Société Astronomique de France; Editor-in-Chief MARIE-CLAUDE PASKOFF.

Auto Plus: 33 rue du Colonel Pierre Avia, 75015 Paris; tel. 1-41-33-50-00; fax 1-41-33-57-06; e-mail olivier.bernis@mondadori.fr; internet www.autoplus.fr; fortnightly; cars; Editor-in-Chief OLIVIER BERNIS; circ. 312,925.

Biochimie: Centre universitaire des Saints Pères, 45 rue des Saints Pères, 75270 Paris Cedex 06; tel. 1-40-20-04-12; fax 1-40-20-04-22; e-mail redaction.biochemie@ibpc.fr; internet www.elsevier.com/locate/biochi; f. 1914; monthly; biochemistry; Editor-in-Chief R. MONIER.

Electronique Pratique: 3 blvd Ney, 75018 Paris; tel. 1-44-65-80-80; fax 1-44-65-80-90; e-mail contact@electroniquepratique.com; internet www.electroniquepratique.com; monthly; electronics; Dir PATRICK VERCHER; Editor-in-Chief BERNARD DUVAL.

Industries et Technologies: 12–14 rue Médéric, 75017 Paris; tel. 1-56-79-41-00; fax 1-56-79-45-27; e-mail p.wagner@industries-technologies.com; internet www.industries-technologies.com; f. 1958 as Industries et Techniques; present name adopted 2002; monthly; Editorial Dir PAUL WAGNER.

Ingénieurs de l'Automobile: Editions VB, 15 rue du 19 Janvier, 92380 Garches; tel. 1-47-01-44-74; fax 1-47-01-48-25; e-mail didier.rose@lcda.fr; internet www.lcda.fr/ingenieurs.php; f. 1927; 6 a year; technical automobile review, in French and English; Editor-in-Chief DIDIER ROSE; circ. 9,000 (2007).

Matériaux et Techniques: EDP Sciences, 17 ave du Hoggar, Parc d'Activités de Courtaboeuf, BP 112, 91944 Les Ulis Cedex A; tel. 1-42-78-52-20; fax 1-42-74-40-48; e-mail edps@edpsciences.org; internet www.mattech-journal.org; f. 1913; 6 a year; review of engineering research and progress on industrial materials; publ. by EDP Sciences; Editor-in-Chief RENÉ GRAS.

Le Monde Informatique: IDG Communications France, 5 rue Chantecoq, 92808 Puteaux Cedex; tel. 1-41-97-61-61; fax 1-49-04-79-04; e-mail redac_weblmi@it-news-info.com; internet www.lemondeinformatique.fr; f. 1981; weekly; information science; Editor-in-Chief OLIVIER RAFAL; circ. 29,236.

Le Moniteur des Travaux Publics et du Bâtiment: 17 rue d'Uzès, 75108 Paris Cedex 02; tel. 1-40-13-31-89; fax 1-40-41-94-95; e-mail redac@groupemoniteur.fr; internet www.lemoniteur-expert.com; f. 1903; weekly; construction; Chair. JACQUES GUY; Editor-in-Chief BERTRAND FABRÉ; circ. 51,169.

Psychologie Française: c/o Nicole Dubois, Département de Psychologie, Université Nancy II, BP 3397, 54015 Nancy Cedex; e-mail nicole.dubois@univ-nancy2.fr; internet france.elsevier.com/html/detrevue.cfm?code=PSFR; f. 1956; quarterly; review of the Société Française de Psychologie, publ. by Elsevier France; Editor NICOLE DUBOIS.

La Recherche: 74 ave du Maine, 75014 Paris; tel. 1-40-47-44-00; fax 1-40-47-44-02; e-mail courrier@larecherche.fr; internet www.larecherche.fr; monthly; review of the Société d'éditions scientifiques; Dir STÉPHANE KHÉMIS; Editor-in-Chief ALINE RICHARD; circ. 50,819.

Science et Vie: 1 rue du Colonel Pierre Avia, 75015 Paris; tel. 1-46-48-48-48; fax 1-46-48-48-67; e-mail svmens@mondadori.fr; internet www.science-et-vie.com; f. 1913; monthly; Editorial Dir MATTHIEU VILLIERS; circ. 277,156.

Sciences et Avenir: 12 pl. de la Bourse, 75002 Paris; tel. 1-44-88-34-34; e-mail redaction@sciences-et-avenir.com; internet sciencesetavenirmensuel.nouvelobs.com; monthly; Editor-in-Chief DOMINIQUE LEGLU; circ. 272,481.

NEWS AGENCIES

Agence France-Presse (AFP): 13 place de la Bourse, 75002 Paris; tel. 1-40-41-46-46; fax 1-40-41-73-99; e-mail contact@afp.com; internet www.afp.fr; f. 1944; 24-hour service of world political, financial, sporting news, and photographs; 165 agencies and 2,000 correspondents world-wide; Pres. and Dir-Gen. PIERRE LOUETTE; Editor-in-Chief ERIC WISHART.

Agence Parisienne de Presse: 18 rue Saint Fiacre, 75002 Paris; tel. 1-42-36-95-59; fax 1-42-33-83-24; f. 1949; Man. Dir MICHEL BURTON.

Infomedia M.C.: 8 rue de la Michodière, 75002 Paris; tel. 1-47-42-14-33; fax 1-47-42-14-39; f. 1988; economic and financial news; Dir FRANÇOIS COUDURIER.

PRESS ASSOCIATIONS

Comité de Liaison de la Presse: Paris; tel. 1-53-20-90-56; liaison organization for press, radio and cinema.

Fédération Française des Agences de Presse (FFAP): Paris; tel. 1-42-93-42-57; fax 1-42-93-15-32; e-mail info@agencesdepresse.fr; internet www.ffap.fr; comprises five syndicates (news, photographs, television, general information and multimedia) with a total membership of 109 agencies; Pres. ARNAUD HAMELIN; Dir JACQUES MORANDAT.

FRANCE   *Directory*

Fédération Nationale de la Presse Française (FNPF): 13 rue La Fayette, 75009 Paris; tel. 1-53-20-90-50; fax 1-53-20-90-51; e-mail fnpf@portail-presse.com; internet www.portail-presse.com; f. 1944; mems: Syndicat de la Presse Quotidienne Nationale, Syndicat Professionnel de la Presse, Magazine et d'Opinion, Syndicat de la Presse Quotidienne Régionale, Syndicat de la Presse Quotidienne Départementale, Fédération de la Presse Périodique Régionale, Fédération Nationale de la Presse d'Information Spécialisée; Pres. MICHEL COMBOUL.

Fédération Nationale de la Presse d'Information Spécialisée: 37 rue de Rome, 75008 Paris; tel. 1-44-90-43-60; fax 1-44-90-43-72; e-mail contact@fnps.fr; internet www.fnps.fr; comprises Syndicat National de la Presse Agricole et Rurale (SNPAR), Syndicat National de la Presse Médicale et des Professions de Santé (SNPM), Syndicat de la Presse Culturelle et Scientifique (SPCS), Syndicat de la Presse Economique, Juridique et Politique (SPEJP), Syndicat de la Presse Professionnelle (SP—PRO), Syndicat de la Presse Magazine et Spécialisée (SPMS) and Syndicat de la Presse Sociale (SPS), representing some 1,350 specialized or professional publications; CEO JEAN-MICHEL HUAN.

Fédération de la Presse Périodique Régionale: 72 rue d'Hauteville, 75010 Paris; tel. 1-45-23-98-00; fax 1-45-23-98-01; e-mail sphr@sphr.fr; internet www.sphr.fr; f. 1970; present name adopted 1992; mems: Syndicat de la Presse Hebdomadaire Régionale, Syndicat National des Publications Régionales, Syndicat de la Presse Judiciaire de Province, Syndicat National de la Presse Judiciaire; represents 250 regional periodical publications; Pres. BERNARD BIENVENU; Sec.-Gen. WILLIAMS CAPTIER.

Syndicat de la Presse Quotidienne Régionale: 17 place des Etats-Unis, 75116 Paris; tel. 1-40-73-80-20; fax 1-47-20-48-94; internet www.spqr.fr; f. 1986; regional dailies; Pres. MICHEL COMBOUL; Dir-Gen. BRUNO HOCQUART DE TURTOT.

PRESS INSTITUTE

Institut Français de Presse: 92 rue Blaise Desgoffe, 75006 Paris; tel. 1-44-41-57-93; fax 1-53-63-53-28; e-mail ifp@u-paris2.fr; f. 1951; studies and teaches all aspects of communication and the media; maintains research and documentation centre; open to research workers, students, journalists; Dir JOSIANE JOUËT.

Publishers

Actes Sud: Le Méjan, place Nina-Berberova, BP 38, 13633 Arles; tel. 4-90-49-86-91; fax 4-90-96-95-25; e-mail contact@actes-sud.fr; internet www.actes-sud.fr; f. 1978; French and translated literature, music, theatre, studies of Arabic and Islamic civilizations; Pres. FRANÇOISE NYSSEN; Editorial Dir BERTRAND PY.

Editions Albin Michel: 22 rue Huyghens, 75014 Paris Cedex 14; tel. 1-42-79-10-00; fax 1-43-27-21-58; e-mail virginie.caminade@albin-michel.fr; internet www.albin-michel.fr; f. 1901; general, fiction, history, classics; Pres. FRANCIS ESMÉNARD; Man. Dir RICHARD DUCOUSSET.

Armand Colin Editeur: 21 rue du Montparnasse, 75283 Paris Cedex 06; tel. 1-44-39-54-47; fax 1-44-39-51-10; e-mail infos@armand-colin.com; internet www.armand-colin.com; f. 1870; imprint of Hachette Livre; literature, history, human and social sciences, university textbooks; Dir-Gen. GUILLAUME DERVIEUX.

Assouline: 26–28 rue Danielle Casanova, 75002 Paris; tel. 1-42-60-33-84; e-mail contact@assouline.com; internet www.assouline.com; f. 1994; art, fashion, design, lifestyle; Dir PROSPER ASSOULINE.

Editions de l'Atelier/Editions Ouvrières: 12 ave Soeur Rosalie, 75013 Paris; tel. 1-44-08-95-15; fax 1-44-08-95-00; e-mail editions.atelier@wanadoo.fr; f. 1929; religious, educational, political and social, including labour movement; Dir-Gen. BERNARD STEPHAN.

Editions Aubier: 13 quai Conti, 75006 Paris; tel. 1-40-51-31-00; fax 1-43-29-71-04; internet editions.flammarion.com/editeurs/?aubier; f. 1925; psychoanalysis, literature, philosophy, history and sociology; Man. Dir M. AUBIER-GABAIL.

Editions Balland: 33 rue Saint André des Arts, 75006 Paris; tel. 1-43-25-74-40; fax 1-46-33-56-21; e-mail balland@club-internet.fr; internet www.balland.fr; f. 1967; literature, non-fiction; Chair. and Man. Dir DENIS BOURGEOIS.

Bayard Editions—Centurion: 3–5 rue Bayard, 75393 Paris Cedex 08; tel. 1-44-35-60-60; fax 1-44-35-61-61; e-mail communication@bayardpresse.com; internet www.bayardpresse.com; f. 1870; children's books, religion, human sciences; Pres. ALAIN CORDIER; Man. Dir PATRICK ZAGO.

Beauchesne Editeur: 7 Cité du Cardinal Lemoine, 75005 Paris; tel. 1-53-10-08-18; fax 1-53-10-85-19; e-mail beauchesne2@wanadoo.fr; internet www.editions-beauchesne.com; f. 1850; scripture, religion and theology, philosophy, religious history, politics, encyclopaedias; Man. Dir JEAN-ETIENNE MITTELMANN.

Editions Belfond: 12 ave d'Italie, 75627 Paris Cedex 13; tel. 1-44-16-05-00; fax 1-44-16-05-06; internet www.belfond.fr; f. 1963; fiction, poetry, documents, history, arts; Chair. JÉRÔME TALAMON; Man. Dir FABIENNE DELMOTE.

Berger-Levrault: 3 rue Ferrus, 75014 Paris; tel. 1-40-64-42-32; fax 1-40-64-42-30; e-mail ble@berger-levrault.fr; internet www.berger-levrault.fr; f. 1676; fine arts, health, social and economic sciences, law; Pres. and Dir-Gen. ALAIN SOURISSEAU; Man. Dirs PIERRE-MARIE LEHUCHER, FRANÇOIS POTIER.

Bordas: 89 blvd Blanqui, 75013 Paris; tel. 1-72-36-40-00; fax 1-72-36-40-10; e-mail cjacqueson@bordas.tm.fr; internet www.editions-bordas.com; f. 1946; imprint of Editis; encyclopaedias, dictionaries, history, geography, arts, children's and educational; Pres. OLIVIER QUERENET DE BREVILLE.

Editions Bornemann: 62 rue Blanche, 75009 Paris; tel. 1-42-82-08-16; fax 1-48-74-14-88; f. 1829; art, fiction, sports, nature, easy reading; Chair. and Man. Dir PIERRE C. LAHAYE.

Buchet-Chastel: 7 rue des Canettes, 75006 Paris; tel. 1-44-32-05-60; fax 1-44-32-05-61; e-mail buchet_chastel@buchet_chastel.fr; f. 1929; literature, music, crafts, religion, practical guides; Chair. VERA MICHALSKI; Gen. Man. FRANÇOISE DILLEMANN.

Editions Calmann-Lévy: 31 rue de Fleurus, 75006 Paris; tel. 1-49-54-36-02; e-mail editions@calmann-levy.fr; internet www; f. 1836; French and foreign literature, history, social sciences, economics, sport, leisure; Chair. JEAN-ETIENNE COHEN-SEAT.

Editions Casterman: 36 rue du Chemin Vert, 75011 Paris; tel. 1-55-28-12-00; fax 1-55-28-12-60; e-mail info@casterman.com; internet www.casterman.com; f. 1857; juvenile, comics, fiction, education, leisure, art; Chair. and Man. Dir SIMON CASTERMAN.

Editions du Cerf: 29 blvd de La Tour Maubourg, 75340 Paris Cedex 07; tel. 1-44-18-12-12; fax 1-45-56-04-27; internet www.editionsducerf.fr; f. 1929; religion, social science; Chair. MICHEL BON; Editorial Dir NICOLAS-JEAN SED; Man. Dir ERIC DE CLERMONT-TONNERRE.

Editions Champ Vallon: rue Gérin, 01420 Seyssel; tel. 4-50-56-15-51; fax 4-50-56-15-64; e-mail info@champ-vallon.com; internet www.champ-vallon.com; f. 1980; social sciences, literary history, literary criticism; Dirs MYRIAM MONTEIRO-BRAZ, PATRICK BEAUNE.

Editions Chiron: 10 rue Léon-Foucault, 78184 Saint-Quentin-en-Yvelines; tel. 1-30-14-19-30; fax 1-30-14-19-46; e-mail info@editionschiron.com; internet www.editionschiron.com; f. 1907; sport, education, fitness, health, dance, games; Dir MARINUS VISSER.

Editions Climats: 470 chemin des Pins, 34170 Castelnau-le Lez; tel. 4-99-58-30-91; fax 4-99-58-30-92; e-mail contact@editions-climats.com; internet www.editions-climats.com; f. 1988; literature, arts, political science; Dir ALAIN MARTIN.

Editions Dalloz: 31–35 rue Froidevaux, 75685 Paris Cedex 14; tel. 1-40-64-54-54; fax 1-40-64-54-97; e-mail ventes@dalloz.fr; internet www.dalloz.fr; f. 1824; law, philosophy, political science, business and economics; imprint of Hachette Livre; Pres. and Dir-Gen. CHARLES VALLÉE.

Dargaud: 15–27 rue Moussorgski, 75895 Paris Cedex 18; tel. 1-53-26-32-32; fax 1-53-26-32-00; e-mail contact@dargaud.fr; internet www.dargaud.fr; f. 1943; juvenile, cartoons, comics, video, graphic novels; Chair. and Man. Dir CLAUDE DE SAINT-VINCENT.

De Boccard, Edition-Diffusion: 11 rue de Médicis, 75006 Paris; tel. 1-43-26-00-37; fax 1-43-54-85-83; e-mail deboccard@deboccard.com; internet www.deboccard.com; f. 1866; history, archaeology, religion, orientalism, medievalism; Man. Dir DOMINIQUE CHAULET.

La Découverte: 9 bis rue Abel Hovelacque, 75013 Paris; tel. 1-44-08-84-00; fax 1-44-08-84-39; e-mail ladecouverte@editionsladecouverte.com; internet www.editionsladecouverte.fr; f. 1959; imprint of Editis; economic, social and political science, literature, history; Man. Dir FRANÇOIS GÈZE.

Editions Denoël: 9 rue du Cherche-Midi, 75278 Paris Cedex 06; tel. 1-44-39-73-73; fax 1-44-39-73-90; internet www.gallimard.fr/catalog/html/grp/denoel.htm; f. 1930; imprint of Editions Gallimard; general literature, science fiction, crime, history; Dir-Gen. OLIVIER RUBINSTEIN.

Desclée De Brouwer (DDB): 76 bis rue des Saints Pères, 75007 Paris; tel. 1-45-49-61-92; fax 1-42-22-61-41; e-mail direction@descleedebrouwer.com; internet www.descleedebrouwer.com; f. 1877; religion, philosophy, arts, human sciences; Dir MARC LEBOUCHER.

Diderot Editeur: Paris; tel. 1-48-04-91-45; f. 1995; science, fine arts, history of art and culture.

La Documentation Française: 29 quai Voltaire, 75344 Paris Cedex 07; tel. 1-40-15-70-00; fax 1-40-15-72-30; e-mail depcom@ladocumentationfrancaise.fr; internet www.ladocumentationfrancaise.fr; f. 1945; government pubs; politics, law, economics, culture, science; Man. Dir OLIVIER CAZENAVE.

Dunod: 5 rue Laromiguière, 75005 Paris Cedex; tel. 1-40-46-35-00; fax 1-40-46-49-95; e-mail infos@dunod.com; internet www.dunod.com; f. 1800; science, computer science, electronics, economics, accountancy, management, psychology and humanities; imprint of Hachette Livre; Dir-Gen. NATHALIE DE BAUDRY D'ASSON.

Edilarge Editions Ouest-France: 13 rue du Breil, 35063 Rennes Cedex; tel. 2-99-32-58-27; fax 2-99-32-58-30; internet www.edilarge.com; history, guides; subsidiary of Ouest-France group; fmrly Editions Ouest-France; Chair. FRANCOIS-XAVIER HUTIN; Dir-Gen. SERVANE BIGUAIS.

Edisud: 3120 Route d'Avignon, 13090 Aix-en-Provence; tel. 4-42-21-61-44; fax 4-42-21-56-20; e-mail info@edisud.com; internet www.edisud.com; f. 1971; Dir CHARLY-YVES CHAUDOREILLE.

Editis: 31 rue du Colisée, 75383 Paris Cedex 08; tel. 1-53-53-30-00; fax 1-53-53-37-37; e-mail benoit.liva@vupublishing.net; internet www.editis.com; f. 1835 as Havas; renamed Vivendi Universal Publishing 2001, then VUP-Investima 10 in 2003; present name adopted Oct. 2003; wholly owned subsidiary of Wendel Investissement since Sept. 2004; education, literature, reference; imprints include Bordas, La Découverte, Editions First, Fleuve Noir, Editions Nathan, Editions Robert Laffont, Le Robert; Dir of Publishing ALAIN KOUCK.

Eyrolles: 61 blvd Saint Germain, 75005 Paris; tel. 1-44-41-11-11; fax 1-44-41-11-44; e-mail librairie@eyrolles.com; internet www.eyrolles.com; f. 1918; science, computing, technology, electronics, management, law; Man. Dir JEAN-PIERRE TISSIER.

Fayard: 75 rue des Saints Pères, 75278 Paris Cedex 06; tel. 1-45-49-82-00; fax 1-42-22-40-17; e-mail rights@editions-fayard.fr; internet www.editions-fayard.fr; f. 1857; literature, biography, history, religion, essays, music; Pres. and Dir-Gen. CLAUDE DURAND.

Editions des Femmes Antoinette Fouque: 6 rue de Mézières, 75006 Paris; tel. 1-42-22-60-74; fax 1-42-22-62-73; e-mail info@desfemmes.fr; internet www.desfemmes.fr; f. 1973; mainly women authors; fiction, essays, art, history, politics, psychoanalysis, talking books; Dir ANTOINETTE FOUQUE.

Editions First: 27 rue Cassette, 75006 Paris; tel. 1-45-49-60-00; fax 1-45-49-60-01; e-mail firstinfo@efirst.com; internet www.efirst.com; f. 1992; imprint of Editis; general non-fiction; Pres. VINCENT BARBARE.

Editions Flammarion: 87 quai Panhard et Levassor, 75647 Paris Cedex 13; tel. 1-40-51-31-00; fax 1-43-29-21-48; internet www.flammarion.com; f. 1875; general literature, art, human sciences, sport, children's books, medicine; Chair. TERESA CREMISI.

Editions Fleurus: 15–27 rue Moussorgski, 75895 Paris Cedex 18; tel. 1-53-26-33-35; fax 1-53-26-33-36; e-mail m.daigne@fleurus-mame.fr; f. 1944; arts, education, leisure; Chair. VINCENT MONTAGNE; Man. Dir PIERRE-MARIE DUMONT; also Fleurus Idées, Fleurus Enfants, Fleurus Jeunesse, Mame, Tardy, Critérion, Desclée, Droguet et Ardant.

Fleuve Noir: 12 ave d'Italie, 75627 Paris Cedex 13; tel. 1-44-16-05-00; fax 1-44-16-05-07; e-mail deborah.druba@universpoche.com; imprint of Editis; crime, fantasy and science fiction; Chair. JEAN-CLAUDE DUBOST; Editorial Dir DÉBORAH DRUBA.

Editions Foucher: 31 rue du Fleurus, 75278 Paris Cedex 06; tel. 1-49-54-35-35; fax 1-49-54-35-00; e-mail cfages@editions-foucher.fr; internet www.editions-foucher.fr; f. 1936; science, economics, law, medicine textbooks; Chair. and Man. Dir BERNARD FOULON.

Editions Gallimard: 5 rue Sébastien-Bottin, 75328 Paris Cedex 7; tel. 1-49-54-42-00; fax 1-45-44-94-03; e-mail pub@gallimard.fr; internet www.gallimard.fr; f. 1911; general fiction, literature, history, poetry, children's, philosophy; Dir ANTOINE GALLIMARD; Editorial Dir TERESA CREMISI.

Editions Grasset et Fasquelle: 61 rue des Saints Pères, 75006 Paris; tel. 1-44-39-22-00; fax 1-42-22-64-18; e-mail afarges@grasset.fr; internet www.grasset.fr; f. 1907; contemporary literature, criticism, general fiction and children's books; Pres. OLIVIER NORA.

Librairie Gründ: 60 rue Mazarine, 75006 Paris; tel. 1-43-29-87-40; fax 1-43-29-49-86; internet www.grund.fr; f. 1880; art, natural history, children's books, guides; Chair. ALAIN GRÜND.

Hachette Livre: 43 quai de Grenelle, 75905 Paris Cedex 15; tel. 1-43-92-30-00; fax 1-43-92-30-30; internet www.hachette.com; f. 1826; fifth largest publisher in profit terms world-wide in 2004; group comprises over 40 publishing houses in France and abroad, particularly in the UK and Spain; Pres. and Dir-Gen. ARNAUD NOURRY.

L'Harmattan Edition: 7 rue de l'Ecole Polytechnique, 75005 Paris; tel. 1-40-46-79-20; fax 1-43-25-82-03; e-mail harmat@worldnet.fr; internet www.editions-harmattan.fr; f. 1975; politics, human sciences, developing countries; Dir DENIS PRYEN.

Editions Hatier: 8 rue d'Assas, 75278 Paris Cedex 06; tel. 1-49-54-49-54; fax 1-49-54-49-00-45; e-mail mnmalapert@editions-hatier.fr; internet www.editions-hatier.fr; f. 1880; children's books, fiction, history, science, nature guides; Chair. BERNARD FOULON.

Hermann: 6 rue de la Sorbonne, 75005 Paris; tel. 1-45-57-45-40; fax 1-40-60-12-93; e-mail hermann.sa@wanadoo.fr; internet www.editions-hermann.fr; f. 1876; sciences and art, humanities; Editorial Dir ARTHUR COHEN.

Editions Ibolya Virag: 21 rue du Grand Prieuré, 75001 Paris; tel. and fax 1-43-38-56-05; fax 1-43-38-43-14; e-mail iboya_virag@hotmail.com; f. 1996; fiction, history, Central and Eastern Europe, Russia and Central Asia; Dir IBOLYA VIRAG.

J'ai Lu: 84 rue de Grenelle, 75007 Paris; tel. 1-44-39-34-70; fax 1-45-44-65-52; e-mail ajasmin@jailu.com; internet www.jailu.com; f. 1958; fiction, paperbacks; subsidiary of Flammarion; Chair. CHARLES-HENRI FLAMMARION; Man. Dir BERTRAND LOBRY.

Editions Julliard: 24 ave Marceau, 75008 Paris; tel. 1-53-67-14-00; fax 1-53-67-14-14; internet www.laffont.fr/julliard/index.htm; f. 1931; general literature, biography, essays; imprint of Editions Robert Laffont/Editis.

Editions du JurisClasseur: 141 rue de Javel, 75747 Paris Cedex 15; tel. 1-45-58-93-76; fax 1-45-58-94-00; e-mail editorial@juris-classeur.com; internet www.juris-classeur.com; member of Groupe Lexis-Nexis (ReedElsevier); imprints include Litec and Légisoft; law, economics, taxation; Dirs ANJER HOLL, MARIELLE BERNARD.

Karthala Editions: 22–24 blvd Arago, 75013 Paris; tel. 1-43-31-15-59; fax 1-45-35-27-05; e-mail karthala@wanadoo.fr; internet www.karthala.com; politics, history, geography, anthropolgy, religious studies, Christianity, Islam, the Arabic-speaking world; CEO ROBERT AGENEAU.

Jeanne Laffitte: 25 Cours d'Estienne d'Orves, BP 1903, 13225 Marseille Cedex 01; tel. 4-91-59-80-49; fax 4-91-54-76-33; e-mail librairie@jeanne-laffitte.com; internet www.jeanne-laffitte.com; f. 1972; art, geography, culture, medicine, history; Chair. and Man. Dir JEANNE LAFFITTE.

Editions Robert Laffont: 24 ave Marceau, 75381 Paris Cedex 08; tel. 1-53-67-14-00; fax 1-53-67-14-14; e-mail bvernet@robert.laffont.fr; internet www.laffont.fr; f. 1941; literature, history, translations; imprint of Editis; Dirs LEONELLO BRANDOLINI, NICOLE LATTES.

Larousse: 21 rue du Montparnasse, 75283 Paris Cedex 06; tel. 1-44-39-44-00; fax 1-44-39-43-43; internet www.larousse.net; f. 1852; general, specializing in dictionaries, illustrated books on scientific subjects, encyclopaedias, classics; imprint of Hachette Livre; Pres. and Dir-Gen. PHILIPPE MERLET.

Editions J.-C. Lattès: 17 rue Jacob, 75006 Paris; tel. 1-44-41-74-00; fax 1-43-25-30-47; e-mail mpageix@editions-jclattes.fr; internet www.editions-jclattes.fr; f. 1968; imprint of Hachette Livre; general fiction and non-fiction, biography; Man. Dir ISABELLE LAFFONT.

Letouzey et Ané: 87 blvd Raspail, 75006 Paris; tel. 1-45-48-80-14; fax 1-45-49-03-43; e-mail letouzey@free.fr; internet www.letouzey.com; f. 1885; theology, religion, archaeology, history, ecclesiastical encyclopaedias and dictionaries, biography; Man. Dir FLORENCE LETOUZEY.

LGDJ—Montchrestien: 31 rue Falguière, 75741 Paris Cedex 15; e-mail info@eja.fr; internet www.lgdj.fr; tel. 1-56-54-16-00; fax 1-56-54-16-49; f. 1836; law and economy; Chair. LIONEL GUÉRIN; Dir VINCENT MARTY.

Le Livre de Poche: 31 rue de Fleurus, 75006 Paris; tel. 1-49-54-37-00; fax 1-49-54-37-01; internet www.livredepoche.com; f. 1953; general literature, dictionaries, encyclopaedias; Gen.-Man. CÉCILE BOYER-RUNGE.

Editions Magnard: 20 rue Berbier-du-Mets, 75647 Paris Cedex 13; tel. 1-44-08-85-85; fax 1-44-08-49-79; e-mail contact@magnard.fr; internet www.magnard.fr; f. 1933; children's and educational books; subsidiary of Editions Albin Michel; Man. Dir JEAN-MANUEL BOURGOIS.

Masson Editeur: 120 blvd Saint Germain, 75006 Paris; tel. 1-40-46-60-00; fax 1-40-46-60-01; e-mail infos@masson.fr; internet www.masson.fr; f. 1804; medicine and science, books and periodicals; publrs for various academies and societies; subsidiary of Medimedia; Pres. GÉRARD KOUCHNER.

Mercure de France: 26 rue de Condé, 75006 Paris; tel. 1-55-42-61-90; fax 1-43-54-49-91; internet www.mercuredefrance.fr; f. 1893; general fiction, history, biography, sociology; Pres. and Man. Dir ISABELLE GALLIMARD; Editor NICOLAS BREHAL.

Editions de Minuit: 7 rue Bernard Palissy, 75006 Paris; tel. 1-44-39-39-20; fax 1-45-44-82-36; e-mail contact@lesedtionsdeminuit.fr; internet www.leseditionsdeminuit.fr; f. 1945; general literature; Man. Dir IRÈNE LINDON.

Editions Nathan: 9 rue Méchain, 75014 Paris; tel. 1-45-87-50-00; fax 1-47-07-57-57; internet www.nathan.fr; f. 1881; educational books for all levels; Chair. BERTRAND EVENO; Man. Dir JEAN-PAUL BAUDOIN.

Editions Payot-Rivages: 106 blvd Saint Germain, 75006 Paris; tel. 1-44-41-39-90; fax 1-44-41-39-69; e-mail payotrivages@wanadoo

.com; f. 1917; literature, human sciences, philosophy; Chair. and Dir JEAN-FRANÇOIS LAMUNIÈRE.

A. et J. Picard: 82 rue Bonaparte, 75006 Paris; tel. 1-43-26-96-73; fax 1-43-26-42-64; e-mail livres@librairie-picard.com; internet www.abebooks.com/home/libpicard; f. 1869; archaeology, architecture, history of art, history, pre-history, auxiliary sciences, linguistics, musicological works, antiquarian books; Chair. and Man. Dir CHANTAL PASINI-PICARD.

Editions Plon: 76 rue Bonaparte, 75284 Paris Cedex 06; tel. 1-44-41-35-00; fax 1-44-41-35-01; e-mail stephane.billerey@editions-plon.com; internet www.plon.fr; f. 1884; imprint of Editis; fiction, history, anthropology, human sciences, biography; Chair. OLIVIER ORBAN.

Editions P.O.L.: 33 rue Saint André des Arts, 75006 Paris; tel. 1-43-54-21-20; fax 1-43-54-11-31; e-mail pol@pol-editeur.fr; internet www.pol-editeur.fr; literature; arts; Dir-Gen. PAUL OTCHAKOVSKI-LAURENS.

Presses de la Cité: 12 ave d'Italie, 75625 Paris Cedex 13; tel. 1-44-16-05-00; internet www.pressesdelacite.com; f. 1944; fiction and factual literature for general audience; Dir JEAN ARCACHE.

Presses de Sciences Po: 117 blvd Saint-Germain, 75006 Paris; tel. 1-45-49-83-64; fax 1-45-49-83-34; e-mail info.presses@sciences-po.fr; internet www.sciences-po.fr/edition; f. 1975; history, politics, linguistics, economics, sociology; Dir MARIE-GENEVIÈVE VANDESANDE.

Presses Universitaires de France: 6 ave Reille, 75014 Paris; tel. 1-58-10-31-00; fax 1-58-10-31-80; e-mail info-ventes@puf.com; internet www.puf.com; f. 1921; philosophy, psychology, psychoanalysis, psychiatry, education, sociology, theology, history, geography, economics, law, linguistics, literature, science; Chair. MICHEL PRIGENT.

Presses Universitaires de Grenoble: Saint Martin-d'Héres, 38040 Grenoble Cedex 09; tel. 4-76-82-56-51; fax 4-76-82-78-35; e-mail pug@pug.fr; internet www.pug.fr; f. 1972; psychology, law, economics, management, history, statistics, literature, medicine, science, politics; Man. Dir BERNARD WIRBEL.

Presses Universitaires de Nancy: 42–44 ave de la Libération, BP 3347, 54014 Nancy Cedex; tel. 3-83-96-84-30; fax 3-83-96-84-39; e-mail pun@univ-nancy2.fr; internet www.univ-nancy2.fr/PUN; f. 1976; literature, history, law, social sciences, politics; Administrator EDWIGE HELMER.

Editions Privat: 10 rue des Arts, BP 38028, 31080 Toulouse Cedex 06; tel. 5-61-33-77-00; fax 5-34-31-64-44; e-mail info@editions-privat.com; f. 1839; regional, national and international history, heritage, health; Dir XAVIER PATIER.

Le Serpent à Plumes: 20 rue des Petits Champs, 75002 Paris; tel. 1-55-35-95-85; fax 1-42-61-17-46; e-mail contact@serpentaplumes.com; internet www.serpentaplumes.com; f. 1993; acquired by Editions du Rocher in 2004; world literature; Dir PIERRE ASTIER.

Editions du Seuil: 27 rue Jacob, 75261 Paris Cedex 06; tel. 1-40-46-50-50; fax 1-40-46-43-00; e-mail contact@seuil.com; internet www.seuil.com; f. 1936; acquired by La Martinière in 2003; modern literature, fiction, illustrated books, non-fiction; Pres. and Dir-Gen. DENIS JEAMBAR.

Editions du Signe: 1 rue Alfred Kastler, BP 94, Eckbolsheim, 67038 Strasbourg Cedex 02; tel. 3-88-78-91-91; fax 3-88-78-91-99; e-mail info@editionsdusigne.fr; internet www.editionsdusigne.fr; f. 1987; Christianity; Chair. and Man. Dir CHRISTIAN RIEHL.

Editions Stock: 31 rue de Fleurus, 75006 Paris; tel. 1-49-54-36-55; fax 1-49-54-36-62; e-mail hamalric@editions-stock.fr; internet www.editions-stock.fr; f. 1710; literature, translations, biography, human sciences, guides; Chair. and Editorial. Dir JEAN-MARC ROBERTS; Dir-Gen. HELENE AMALRIC.

Succès du Livre: 60 rue St André des Arts, 75006 Paris; tel. 1-43-29-82-82; fax 1-43-29-60-75; f. 1987; fiction, biography; Chair. JACQUES DOMAS.

Editions de la Table Ronde: 7 rue Corneille, 75006 Paris; tel. 1-43-26-03-95; fax 1-44-07-09-30; f. 1944; fiction, essays, religion, travel, theatre, youth; Pres. DENIS TILLINAC.

Editions Tallandier: 18 rue Dauphine, 75006 Paris; tel. 1-40-46-43-88; fax 1-40-46-43-98; e-mail atalland@st2.tallandier.fr; internet www.tallandier.com; f. 1865; history, reference; Dir HENRI BOVET.

Editions Tawhid: 8 rue Notre Dame, 69003 Lyon; tel. 4-72-74-18-69; e-mail vpc@islam-france.com; internet www.islam-france.com; Islamic interest; Dir TARIQ RAMADAN.

Editions Vigot: 23 rue de l'Ecole de Médecine, 75006 Paris; tel. 1-43-29-54-50; fax 1-46-34-05-89; f. 1890; medicine, pharmacology, nature, veterinary science, sport, fitness, tourism, cookery; Chair. CHRISTIAN VIGOT; Man. Dir DANIEL VIGOT.

Librairie Philosophique J. Vrin: 6 place de la Sorbonne, 75005 Paris; tel. 1-43-54-03-47; fax 1-43-54-48-18; e-mail contact@vrin.fr; internet www.vrin.fr; f. 1911; university textbooks, philosophy, education, science, law, religion; Chair. and Man. Dir A. PAULHAC-VRIN.

Librairie Vuibert: 20 rue Berbier-du-Mets, 75647 Paris Cedex 13; tel. 1-44-08-49-00; fax 1-44-08-49-39; e-mail laurence.brunel@vuibert.fr; internet www.vuibert.com; f. 1877; school and university textbooks, psychology, law; subsidiary of Editions Albin Michel.

XO Editions: 33 ave du Maine, BP 142, 75755 Paris Cedex 15; tel. 1-56-80-26-80; fax 1-56-80-26-72; e-mail xoeditions@xoeditions.com; internet www.xoeditions.com; f. 2000; general fiction, biography, current affairs, politics; Dir BERNARD FIXOT.

PUBLISHERS' AND BOOKSELLERS' ASSOCIATIONS

Cercle de la Librairie (Syndicat des Industries et Commerces du Livre): 35 rue Grégoire de Tours, 75006 Paris Cedex; tel. 1-44-41-28-00; fax 1-44-41-28-40; f. 1847; a syndicate of the book trade, grouping the principal asscns of publishers, booksellers and printers; Chair. DENIS MOLLAT; Man. Dir JEAN-MARIE DOUBLET.

Chambre Syndicale des Editeurs de Musique de France: 5 rue du Helder, 75009 Paris; tel. 1-53-24-80-20; fax 1-53-24-80-29; e-mail cemf@bmg.com; f. 1873; music publishers' asscn; Chair. PIERRE HENRY.

Chambre Syndicale de l'Edition Musicale (CSDEM): 62 rue Blanche, 75009 Paris; tel. 1-48-74-09-29; fax 1-42-81-19-87; e-mail csdem@club-internet.fr; internet www.csdem.org; f. 1978 by merger; music publishers.

Fédération Française Syndicale de la Librairie: 24 place de la République, 14100 Lisieux; tel. 2-31-62-16-87; fax 2-31-63-97-37; f. 1892; booksellers' asscn; Chair. COLETTE HEDOU.

Syndicat National de l'Edition: 115 blvd Saint-Germain, 75006 Paris; tel. 1-44-41-40-50; fax 1-44-41-40-77; internet www.sne.fr; f. 1892; publishers' asscn; 550 mems; Chair. SERGE EYROLLES.

Syndicat National de la Librairie Ancienne et Moderne: 4 rue Gît-le-Cœur, 75006 Paris; tel. 1-43-29-46-38; fax 1-43-25-41-63; e-mail slam-livre@wanadoo.fr; internet www.slam-livre.fr; f. 1914; booksellers' asscn; 220 mems; Pres. ALAIN MARCHISET.

Broadcasting and Communications

TELECOMMUNICATIONS
Regulatory Authorities

Agence Nationale des Fréquences (ANFR): 78 ave du Général de Gaulle, BP 400, 94704 Maisons-Alfort Cedex; tel. 1-45-18-72-72; fax 1-45-18-72-00; e-mail parmentier@anfr.fr; internet www.anfr.fr; Pres. ARNAUD MIQUEL; Dir-Gen. FRANÇOIS RANCY.

Autorité de Régulation des Communications Electroniques et des Postes (ARCEP): 7 sq. Max Hymans, 75730 Paris Cedex 15; tel. 1-40-47-70-00; fax 1-40-47-70-70; e-mail courrier@arcep.fr; internet www.arcep.fr; f. 2005; fmrly Autorité de Régulation des Télécommunications; Pres. PAUL CHAMPSAUR; Dir-Gen. PHILIPPE DISTLER.

Major Service Providers

Bouygues Télécom: Arcs de Seine, 20 quai du Point du Jour, 92640 Boulogne-Billancourt; tel. 1-39-26-75-00; internet www.bouygtel.com; f. 1994; mobile cellular telecommunications; Pres. and Dir-Gen. PHILIPPE MONTAGNER.

France Télécom: 6 place d'Alleray, 75505 Paris Cedex 15; tel. 1-44-44-22-22; fax 1-44-44-80-34; e-mail infos.groupe@orange-ftgroup.com; internet www.francetelecom.com; 33.1% state-owned, following privatization in 2004; acquired Orange (UK) in 2000; Chair. and Chief Exec. DIDIER LOMBARD.

  OrangeFrance: 6 place d'Alleray, 75505 Paris Cedex 15; tel. 1-55-22-22-22; fax 1-55-22-25-50; internet www.orange.fr; f. 1992 as Itineris; present name adopted 2001; mobile cellular telecommunications and internet access; 19.2m. subscribers (Dec. 2002); Pres. and Dir-Gen. SANJIV AHUJA.

Neuf Cegetel: 40–42 quai du Point du Jour, 92659 Boulogne-Billancourt Cedex; tel. 1-70-18-60-00; fax 1-70-18-66-00; internet www.groupeneufcegetel.fr; f. 2005 by merger of Cegetel and Neuf Telecom; 28% owned by SFR, 28% by Louis Dreyfus Telecommunications, 44% by Neuf Telecom's existing shareholders; fixed-line operator providing consumer internet access, corporate services and wholesale services; c. 4m. subscribers (June 2007); Pres. and Dir-Gen. JACQUES VEYRAT; CEO MICHEL PAULIN.

Numericable: 26 rue d'Oradour-sur-Glane, 75737 Paris Cedex 15; tel. 1-55-92-46-00; fax 1-55-92-46-90; e-mail communication@ncnumericable.com; internet www.numericable.fr; f. 2006 by merger of NC Numéricâble (f. 1997) and Noos (f. 1986); fixed-line operator, consumer internet access, cable television; Pres. and Dir Gen. PHILIPPE BESNIER.

SFR: 1 place Carpeaux, Tour Séquoia, 92915 Paris La Défense Cedex; tel. 8-05-77-66-66; internet www.sfr.fr; f. 1993; mobile

FRANCE

Directory

cellular telecommunications; 56% owned by Vivendi SA, 44% by Vodafone Group PLC (United Kingdom); 17.9m. subscribers (2006); Pres. and Dir-Gen. FRANK ESSER; Dir-Gen. PIERRE TROTOT.

BROADCASTING

Conseil Supérieur de l'Audiovisuel (CSA): Tour Mirabeau, 39–43 quai André Citroën, 75739 Paris Cedex 15; tel. 1-40-58-38-00; fax 1-45-79-00-06; internet www.csa.fr; f. 1989 as replacement for the Commission Nationale de la Communication et des Libertés (CNCL); supervises all French broadcasting; awards licences to private radio (including digital radio) and television stations, allocates frequencies, appoints heads of state-owned radio and television cos, monitors programme standards; consists of nine members, appointed for six years: three nominated by the Pres. of the Republic; three by the Pres. of the Assemblée nationale; and three by the Pres. of the Sénat; Pres. MICHEL BOYON; Gen. Man. OLIVIER JAPIOT.

Institut National de l'Audiovisuel: 4 ave de l'Europe, 94366 Bry-sur-Marne Cedex; tel. 1-49-83-26-74; fax 1-49-83-23-89; e-mail dtixiergallix@ina.fr; internet www.ina.fr; f. 1975; research and professional training in the field of broadcasting; radio and TV archives, TV production; Publ. *Les Nouveaux Dossiers de l'Audiovisuel;* (6 a year); Pres. and Dir-Gen. EMMANUEL HOOG.

Télédiffusion de France (TDF): 10 rue d'Oradour-sur-Glane, 75732 Paris Cedex 15; e-mail e-tdf@tdf.fr; internet www.tdf.fr; f. 1975; partly privatized 1987; restructured in 2007; comprises three sections: TDF France, TDF Multimedia and TDF International; responsible for broadcasting programmes produced by the production companies, for the organization and maintenance of the networks, for study and research into radio and television equipment; broadcasts digital terrestrial television; Pres. and Dir-Gen. MICHEL COMBES.

Radio

State-controlled Radio

Public radio services are provided by three entities: Radio France for the domestic audience; Réseau France Outre-Mer for the French overseas departments and territories; and Radio France Internationale for foreign countries (and those of foreign origin in France). Radio France began the digital broadcasting of certain of its channels in early 2000.

Société Nationale de Radiodiffusion (Radio France): 116 ave du Président Kennedy, 75786 Paris Cedex 16; tel. 1-56-40-29-07; fax 1-42-30-14-88; internet www.radio-france.fr; f. 1975; planning and production of radio programmes; provides five national services, 47 local stations and two European services; Chair. JEAN-PAUL CLUZEL; Man. Dir CLAUDE NOREK.

France Bleu: tel. 1-56-40-37-86; internet www.francebleu.com; f. 1980, restructured 2000; network of domestic services; for older people; Dir MICHEL MEYER.

France Culture: tel. 1-56-40-27-91; internet franceculture.com; domestic, nation-wide service; Dir DAVID KESSLER.

France Culture Europe: European service, broadcast by TDF1/TDF2 satellite; cultural and information; Dir LAURE ADLER.

France-Info: tel. 1-56-40-20-43; internet www.france-info.com; domestic, nation-wide service; continuous news and information; f. 1987; Dir PATRICK ROGER.

France Inter: tel. 1-56-40-37-57; internet www.franceinter.com; domestic, nation-wide service; general programmes, for entertainment and information; Dir FRÉDÉRIC SCHLESINGER.

France Musiques: tel. 1-56-40-36-12; internet www.francemusiques.com; domestic, nation-wide service; Dir THIERRY BEAUVERT.

France Vivace: internet www.francevivace.com; broadcast by TDF1/TDF2 satellite; classical music; Dir FRANÇOIS HUDRY.

Le Mouv': tel. 5-62-30-70-16; internet www.lemouv.fr; domestic, nation-wide service; music and general interest for people aged 18–35; f. 1997; Dir STÉPHANE RAMEZI.

Réseau FIP: tel. 1-56-40-16-15; internet www.radiofrance.fr/chaines/fip/radio; f. 1971; comprises nine local stations; continuous music; Dir DOMINIQUE PENSEC.

Radio France Internationale (RFI): 116 ave du Président Kennedy, BP 9516, 75786 Paris Cedex 16; tel. 1-56-40-12-12; fax 1-56-40-47-59; internet www.rfi.fr; f. 1975; broadcasts on MW and FM transmitters, mainly to Africa, Eastern Europe, North America, the Caribbean, South-East Asia and the Middle East, in French; also broadcasts in 19 other languages: Albanian, Arabic, Bulgarian, Cambodian, Créole, Croatian, English, Farsi, German, Laotian, Mandarin, Polish, Portuguese, Romanian, Russian, Serbian, Spanish, Turkish, Vietnamese; Pres. and Dir-Gen. ANTOINE SCHWARZ.

Réseau France Outre-mer (RFO): 35–37 rue Danton, 92240 Malakoff; tel. 1-55-22-71-00; fax 1-55-22-74-76; e-mail rfo@rfo.fr; internet www.rfo.fr; f. 1983; frmly FR3 DOM-TOM; controls broadcasting in the French overseas territories; 10 local stations providing two radio networks, two television channels, the latter broadcasting material from various state and private channels as well as local programmes, and one satellite television channel; Pres. ANDRÉ-MICHEL BESSE.

Independent Radio

BFM: 12 rue d'Oradour sur Glane, 75015 Paris; tel. 1-71-19-11-81; fax 1-71-19-11-80; e-mail nrepa@radiobfm.com; internet www.radiobfm.com; f. 1992; broadcasts on cable and 14 FM frequencies; politics, economics; Pres. ALAIN WEILL.

Chérie FM: 22 rue Boileau, 75203 Paris Cedex 16; tel. 1-40-71-40-00; e-mail vgrandclaude@nrj.fr; internet www.cheriefm.fr; broadcasts popular music and entertainment programming on FM nationwide; mem. of Groupe NRJ; Dir MARC SCALIA.

Europe 1: 121 ave de Malakoff, 75116 Paris; tel. 1-53-35-72-60; e-mail courrier@europe1.fr; internet www.europe1.fr; owned by Groupe Lagardère, which also owns Europe 2 (for younger listeners) and RFM; broadcasting on long wave and 99 FM frequencies; Pres. JEAN-PIERRE ELKABBACH; Dirs-Gen. JÉRÔME DORVILLE, MARC TRONCHOT.

Nostalgie: 22 rue Boileau, 75203 Paris Cedex 16; tel. 1-40-71-40-00; e-mail vgrandclaude@nrj.fr; internet www.nostalgie.fr; mem. of Groupe NRJ; broadcasts popular music and entertainment programming on FM nation-wide; Dir STÉPHANE BOSC.

NRJ: 22 rue Boileau, 75203 Paris Cedex 16; tel. 1-40-71-40-00; e-mail vgrandclaude@nrj.fr; internet www.nrj.fr; broadcasts contemporary popular music and entertainment programming on FM nation-wide; Pres., Exec. Cttee MARC PALLAIN; Dir-Gen. JEAN-PIERRE TRELAT.

Radio Classique: 12 bis place Henri Bergson, 75008 Paris; tel. 1-40-08-50-00; fax 1-40-08-50-80; internet www.radioclassique.fr; f. 1983; classical music; Dir-Gen. FRÉDÉRIC OLIVENNES.

Radio Monte-Carlo (RMC): 12 rue d'Oradour sur Glane, 75015 Paris; tel. 1-71-19-11-91; fax 1-71-19-11-90; internet www.rmcinfo.fr; broadcasting on long wave and 148 FM frequencies; information, talk and sports programmes; Pres. ALAIN WEILL.

RTL: 22 rue Bayard, 75008 Paris; tel. 1-40-70-40-70; fax 1-40-70-42-72; e-mail relation.auditeur@rtl.fr; internet www.rtl.fr; broadcasting on long wave and 150 FM frequencies; Chair. and Man. Dir AXEL DUROUX.

Skyrock: 37 bis rue Grenéta, 75002 Paris; tel. 1-44-88-82-00; fax 1-44-88-89-57; internet www.skyrock.com; f. 1986; contemporary rap and hip-hop music; Pres. and Dir-Gen. PIERRE BELLANGER.

Television

State-controlled Television

France Télévisions: 7 esplanade Henri-de-France, 75907 Paris; tel. 1-56-22-60-00; fax 1-47-20-24-54; internet www.francetelevisions.fr; f. 1992; supervisory authority for the national public television networks (France 2, France 3 and France 5: see below); Pres. PATRICK DE CAROLIS; Sec.-Gen. FRANÇOIS GUILBEAU.

France 2: 7 esplanade Henri-de-France, 75907 Paris Cedex 15; tel. 1-56-22-42-42; e-mail contact@france2.fr; internet www.france2.fr; f. 1975; general programmes for a nation-wide audience; Dir-Gen. PHILIPPE BAUDILLON.

France 3 (F3): 7 esplanade Henri-de-France, 75907 Paris Cedex 15; tel. 1-56-22-30-30; internet www.france3.fr; f. 1975 as France Régions 3 (FR3); general programmes for a nation-wide audience (with a larger proportion of cultural and educational programmes than F2), and regional programmes transmitted from 13 regional stations; Dir-Gen. GENEVIÈVE GIARD.

France 4: 7 esplanade Henri-de-France, 75907 Paris Cedex 15; tel. 1-56-22-68-68; fax 1-56-22-68-69; e-mail valerie.dissaux@france4.tv; internet www.france4.tv; f. 2005; 89% owned by France Télévisions, 11% by Arte; digital TV station; creative and cultural programming; Dir-Gen. HAYET ZEGGAR.

France 5 (F5): 10 rue Horace Vernet, 92785 Issy-les-Moulineaux Cedex 09; tel. 1-56-22-93-93; e-mail telespectateurs@france5.fr; internet www.france5.fr; f. 1994 as La Cinquième; present name adopted 2002; educational programmes and documentaries; Dir-Gen. CLAUDE-YVES ROBIN.

France 24: 5 rue des Nations Unies, 92130 Issy-les-Moulineaux; tel. 1-73-01-24-24; fax 1-73-01-24-56; e-mail webdesk@france24.com; internet www.france24.com; f. 2006; jointly owned by TF1 and France Télévisions; cable, satellite and internet broadcasts; 24-hour news broadcasts in Arabic, English and French; aims to present international news from a French perspective; Pres. ALAIN DE POUZILHAC; Dirs-Gen. JEAN-YVES BONSERGENT, GÉRARD SAINT-PAUL.

ARTE France: 8 rue Marceau, 92785 Issy-les-Moulineaux Cedex 09; tel. 1-55-00-77-77; fax 1-55-00-77-00; internet www.arte-tv.com; f. 1992 to replace La Sept; arts, cultural programmes, in French and German; Pres. JÉRÔME CLÉMENT; Dir-Gen. JEAN ROZAT.

FRANCE   *Directory*

TV5 Monde: 131 ave de Wagram, 75017 Paris; tel. 1-44-18-55-55; internet www.tv5.org; f. 1984; broadcasts French-language programmes via satellite and cable to 203 countries world-wide; 47.38% owned by France Télévisions, 12.50% by ARTE France; Pres. and Dir-Gen. FRANÇOIS BONNEMAIN; Dir of Programmes LAURENT JACOBELLI.

Television programmes for France's overseas departments and territories are provided by Réseau France Outre-mer (see under Radio).

Independent Television

Canal Plus: 1 place du Spectacle, 92863 Issy-Les-Moulineaux Cedex 9; tel. 1-71-35-35-35; fax 1-44-25-12-34; e-mail contact_web@cplus.fr; internet www.cplus.fr; f. 1984; 80% owned by Vivendi, 20% by Groupe Lagadère; coded programmes financed by audience subscription; uncoded programmes financed by advertising sold by Canal Plus; specializes in drama (including films) and sport; launched a 'pay-per-view' service for sports events in 1996; produces 21 theme channels in six countries; Pres. and Dir-Gen. BERTRAND MÉHEUT.

demain.tv: 1 rue Patry, 92220 Bagneux; tel. 1-45-36-89-00; fax 1-45-36-89-01; internet www.demain.fr; e-mail contact@demain.fr; f. 1997; information about employment for job-seekers; Dir-Gen. YACINE SABEG.

Direct8: Tour Bolloré, 31-32 quai de Dion-Bouton, 92811 Puteaux; tel. 1-46-96-31-00; fax 1-46-96-40-94; e-mail emissions@direct8.net; internet www.direct8.fr; f. 2005; free-to-air digital television channel; owned by Bolloré Média; Dir-Gen. JEAN-CHRISTOPHE THIERY.

Gulli: 12 rue d'Oradour-sur-Glane, 75015 Paris; tel. 1-56-36-55-55; fax 1-56-36-55-59; e-mail tachaine@gullitv.fr; internet www.gullitv.fr; f. 2005; free-to-air digital television channel for children; Pres. and Dir-Gen. EMMANUELLE GUILBART.

i>TELE: 6 allée de la 2ème DB, 75015 Paris; tel. 1-53-91-51-00; fax 1-53-91-51-45; e-mail redaction.itv@canal-plus.com; internet www.itele.fr; f. 1999; free-to-air digital television channel; 24-hr news broadcasts; part of Groupe Canal Plus; Pres. and Dir-Gen. VALÉRIE LECASBLE.

LCI (La Chaîne Info): 54 ave de la Voie Lactée, 92656 Boulogne-Billancourt Cedex; tel. 1-41-41-37-37; e-mail comm-lci@lci.fr; internet www.lci.fr; f. 1994; news, information; Pres. PATRICK LE LAY; Dir-Gen. JEAN-CLAUDE DASSIER.

M6: 89 ave Charles de Gaulle, 92575 Neuilly-sur-Seine Cedex; tel. 1-41-92-66-66; fax 1-41-92-66-10; e-mail pholl@m6.fr; internet www.m6.fr; f. 1986 as TV6; re-formed as M6 1987; 46% owned by RTL Group; subsidiaries include W9 (a free-to-air digital television channel); specializes in drama, music and magazines; Chair. of Bd JEAN DRUCKER; CEO NICOLAS DE TAVERNOST.

NT1: 132 ave du Président Wilson, 93213 La Plaine-Saint-Denis; tel. 1-49-22-20-01; e-mail 1-49-22-20-71; internet www.nt1.tv; free-to-air digital television channel; owned by AB Groupe; Pres. ORLA NOONAN.

Télévision Française 1 (TF1): 1 quai du Point du Jour, 92656 Boulogne-Billancourt Cedex; tel. 1-41-41-12-34; fax 1-41-41-28-40; internet www.tf1.fr; f. 1975 as a state-owned channel, privatized 1987; 42.9% owned by Bouygues SA; general programmes; Pres. PATRICK LE LAY; Dir-Gen. NONCE PAOLINI.

Finance

(cap. = capital; res = reserves; dep. = deposits; m. = million; brs = branches; amounts in euros)

BANKING

Central Bank

Banque de France: 31 rue Croix des Petits Champs, 75001 Paris; tel. 1-42-92-42-92; fax 1-42-92-45-00; e-mail infos@banque-france.fr; internet www.banque-france.fr; f. 1800; nationalized 1946; became independent 1994; acts as banker to the Treasury, issues bank notes, controls credit and money supply and administers France's gold and currency assets; in 1993 the National Assembly approved legislation to make the Banque de France an independent central bank, with a General Council to supervise activities and appoint the principal officials, and a nine-member monetary policy committee, independent of government control, to be in charge of French monetary policy; a member of the European System of Central Banks since June 1998; cap. and res 26,281m., dep. 46,649m., total assets 232,162m. (Dec. 2006); Gov. CHRISTIAN NOYER; 130 brs.

State Savings Bank

Caisse des dépôts et consignations: 56 rue de Lille, 75356 Paris Cedex 07; tel. 1-58-50-00-00; fax 1-58-50-02-46; internet www.caissedesdepots.fr; f. 1816; manages state savings system, holds widespread investments in industrial cos; res 15,532m., dep. 75,749m., total assets 200,393m. (Dec. 2006); Pres. and Dir-Gen FRANCIS MAYER; 1 br.

Other Savings Banks

Banque Postale: 44 blvd de Vaugirard, 75757 Paris Cedex 15; tel. 1-55-44-00-00; internet www.labanquepostale.fr; f. 2006; subsidiary of national postal service, La Poste; Chair. PATRICK WERNER; 17,000 brs.

Caisse d'Epargne et de Prévoyance Ile-de-France Paris: BP 9401, 19 rue du Louvre, 75021 Paris Cedex 01; tel. 1-40-41-30-31; fax 1-42-33-45-18; internet www.caisse-epargne.fr; f. 1818; cap. 333.3m., res 914.8m., dep. 25,213.9m. (Dec. 2004); Pres. NICOLE MOREAU; Chair. BERNARD COMOLET; 301 brs.

Caisse Interfédérale de Crédit Mutuel (Groupe Arkéa): 32 rue Mirabeau, 29480 Le Relecq-Kerhoun; tel. 2-98-00-22-22; fax 2-98-30-52-10; internet www.arkea.com; f. 2001; co-operative and mutual savings bank; cap. 810.1m., res 1,689.8m., dep. 34,826.5m. (Dec. 2006); Chair. GEORGES COUDRAY; Gen. Man. JACQUES KERGOAT.

Caisse Nationale des Caisses d'Epargne et de Prévoyance (CNCEP): 50 ave Pierre Mendès, 75201 Paris Cedex 13; tel. 1-58-40-41-42; fax 1-58-40-48-00; internet www.groupe.caisse-epargne.com; f. 1999 by merger; 65% owned by Caisses d'Epargne, 35% by Caisse des Dépots et Consignations; cap. 3,955m., res 12,245m., dep. 469,030m. (Dec. 2006); Chair., Supervisory Bd JACQUES MOUTON; Chair., Management Bd CHARLES MILHAUD.

Commercial Banks

Banca Intesa (France): 23 rue Linois, 75725 Paris Cedex 15; tel. 1-45-23-72-22; fax 1-45-23-70-90; e-mail hoff@bcif.fr; internet www.bcif.fr; f. 1918 as Banca Commerciale Italiana (France); present name adopted 2003; 99.99% owned by Intesa Sanpaolo SpA (Italy); cap. 160.3m., res 34.9m., dep. 788.5m. (Dec. 2006); Chair. ALBERTO VALDEMBRI; Dir-Gen. EUGENIO GUICCIARDI.

Banque AGF: Tour AGF Neptune, 20 place de Seine, La Défense, 92400 Courbevoie; tel. 1-53-24-48-48; fax 1-53-24-48-41; e-mail serviceclient@banqueagf.fr; internet www.banqueagf.fr; f. 2000; affiliated to Group Allianz; cap. 202.0m. (Dec. 2001); Pres. GÉRAUD BRAC DE LA PERRIÈRE; Dir-Gen. DIDIER ETARD.

Banque BIA: 67 ave Franklin D. Roosevelt, 75008 Paris; tel. 1-53-76-62-62; fax 1-42-89-09-59; e-mail contact@bia-paris.fr; internet www.bia-paris.fr; f. 1975 as Banque Intercontinentale Arabe; present name adopted 2006; 50% owned by Banque Extérieure d'Algérie, 50% by Libyan Arab Foreign Bank; cap. 158.1m., res 7.0m., dep. 495.5m. (Dec. 2006); Chair. MUHAMMAD LOUKAL.

Banque de Bretagne: 18 quai Duguay-Trouin, 35084 Rennes Cedex; tel. 2-99-01-75-75; fax 2-99-01-75-00; internet www.bdbretagne.com; f. 1909; 100% owned by BNP Paribas; cap. 52.9m., res 14.0m., dep. 2,143.3m. (Dec. 2005); Pres. JEAN-CLAUDE LALLEMENT; 70 brs.

Banque BSD-CIN: 33 ave le Corbusier, BP 567, 59800 Lille; tel. 3-20-12-64-64; fax 3-20-12-64-05; internet www.cic.fr/bsd-cin; f. 2006 by merger of Banque Scalbert-Dupont (f. 1977) and Crédit Industriel de Normandie (f. 1932); 100% owned by Crédit Industriel et Commercial; Chair. GÉRARD ROMEDEMME; Gen. Man. STELLI PRÉ-MAOR.

Banque CIAL—Crédit Industriel d'Alsace et de Lorraine (CIC Banque CIAL): 31 rue Jean Wenger-Valentin, 67000 Strasbourg; tel. 3-88-37-61-23; fax 3-88-37-71-81; internet www.banquecial.fr; f. 1919; 99.99% owned by Crédit Industriel et Commercial; cap. 25m., dep. 14,600m., total assets 25,405m. (Dec. 2006); Chair. PHILIPPE VIDAL; Gen. Man. PIERRE JACHEZ; 171 brs.

Banque CIO-BRO: BP 84001, 2 ave Jean-Claude Bonduelle, 44040 Nantes Cedex 1; tel. 2-40-12-91-91; fax 2-40-12-93-80; e-mail cio-international@cio.cic.fr; internet www.cic.fr/cio-bro; f. 2006 by merger of Crédit Industriel de l'Ouest (f. 1957) and Banque Régionale de l'Ouest (f. 1913); 100% owned by Crédit Industriel et Commercial; Chair. MICHEL MICHENKO; Man. Dir JEAN-PIERRE BICHON.

Banque Commerciale pour le Marché de l'Entreprise (BCME): allée Louis Lichou, 29480 Le Relecq-Kerhuon Cedex; tel. 2-98-34-68-80; fax 2-98-30-52-10; e-mail contacts@bcme.fr; internet www.bcme.fr; f. 1985; present name adopted 2000; cap. 120.0m., res 36.4m., dep. 2,771.8m. (Dec. 2006); Chair. MARCEL GARNIER; Pres., Executive Bd GILBERT RICHARD; Gen. Man. JACK PERRIEN.

Banque de l'Economie du Commerce et de la Monétique: 34 rue du Wacken, 67913 Strasbourg Cedex 9; tel. 3-88-14-74-74; fax 3-88-14-75-10; e-mail becm@becm.creditmutuel.fr; internet www.becm.fr; f. 1992 as Banque de l'Economie–Crédit Mutuel; cap. 378.3m., dep. 1,546.7m., total assets 8,320.4m. (Dec. 2006); Chief Exec. RENÉ DANGEL; 37 brs.

Banque Espírito Santo et de la Vénétie: 45 ave Georges Mandel, 75116 Paris; tel. 1-44-34-48-00; fax 1-44-34-48-48; e-mail besv@besv.fr; internet www.besv.fr; f. 1945; present name adopted 1998; absorbed Via Banque in 2002; 42% owned by Espírito Santo

Financial Group SA (Luxembourg); cap. 52.2m., res 23.2m., dep. 1,074.0m. (Dec. 2006); Chair. CHRISTIAN MÉNARD.

Banque Fédérative du Crédit Mutuel: 34 rue du Wacken, 67000 Strasbourg; tel. 3-88-14-88-14; fax 3-88-14-67-00; internet www.bfcm.creditmutuel.fr; f. 1895; cap.1,302m., res 5,414m., dep. 264,890m. (Dec. 2006); Pres. and Chair. ETIENNE PFLIMLIN; Dir-Gen. MICHEL LUCAS; 16 brs.

Banque Nationale de Paris Intercontinentale: 12 rue Chauchat, 75009 Paris; tel. 1-40-14-22-11; fax 1-40-14-69-34; internet www.bnpgroup.com; f. 1940; present name adopted 1972; 100% owned by BNP Paribas; cap. 30.5m., res. 8.7m., dep. 577.9m. (Dec. 2004); Chair. and Dir-Gen. JEAN-JACQUES SANTINI.

Banque Neuflize OBC: 3 ave Hoche, 75008 Paris; tel. 1-56-21-70-00; fax 1-56-21-84-60; internet www.neuflizeobc.fr; f. 1966 as De Neuflize, Schlumberger, Mallet & Cie; acquired clients of fmr Banque OBC—Odier Bungener Courvoisier and adopted present name 2006; 100% owned by ABN AMRO France; private banking; cap. 197.2m., res 5.2m., dep. 2,017.2m. (Dec. 2005); Chair., Supervisory Bd JAN KOOPMAN; Pres. and Chair., Man. Bd PIERRE FLEURIOT; 12 brs.

Banque Palatine: 52 ave Hoche, 75008 Paris Cedex 08; tel. 1-47-54-40-22; fax 1-47-54-47-91; e-mail info@palatine.fr; internet www.palatine.fr; fmrly Banque Sanpaolo; present name adopted 2005; 60% owned by Caisse Nationale des Caisses d'Epargne et de Prévoyance, 40% owned by Intesa Sanpaolo SpA (Italy); cap. 402.6m., res 57.2m., dep. 6,903.0m. (Dec. 2006); Chair. NICOLAS MERINDOL; Pres. DANIEL KARYOTIS; Gen. Man. PIERRE-EDOUARD DE COURCELLES; 60 brs.

BNP Paribas: 16 blvd des Italiens, 75009 Paris; tel. 1-40-14-45-46; fax 1-40-14-69-40; internet www.bnpparibas.com; f. 2000 by merger of Banque Nationale de Paris and Paribas; cap. 9,701m., res 25,165m., dep. 1,063,454m. (Dec. 2005); Pres. MICHEL PÉBEREAU; CEO BAUDOUIN PROT.

Calyon Corporate and Investment Bank (Calyon): 9 quai Paul Doumer, 92920 Paris La Défense Cedex; tel. 1-41-89-00-00; fax 1-41-89-15-22; internet www.calyon.com; f. 1975 as Banque Indosuez, subsequently Crédit Agricole Indosuez; present name adopted 2004; 100% owned by Crédit Agricole; merchant and offshore banking; cap. 7,686m., res 2,939m., dep. 528,934m. (Dec. 2006); Pres. JEAN LAURENT; Chief Exec. EDOUARD ESPARBÈS; 13 brs in France, 44 outside France.

Cetelem: 14 bis blvd de l'Hôpital, 75221 Paris Cedex 05; tel. 1-55-43-55-43; fax 1-55-43-55-30; e-mail frederic.tardy@cetelem.fr; internet www.cetelem.fr; f. 1953; owned by BNP Paribas; cap. 848.8m., res 1,423.3m., dep. 32,906.8m. (Dec. 2006); Chair. and CEO FRANÇOIS VILLEROY DE GALHAU.

Compagnie Financière Edmond de Rothschild Banque: 47 rue du Faubourg St Honoré, 75401 Paris Cedex 08; tel. 1-40-17-25-25; fax 1-40-17-24-02; internet www.lcf-rothschild.fr; f. 1971; present name adopted 1986; dep. 1,175.5m., total assets 2,880.9m. (2006); Chair., Exec. Bd MICHEL CICUREL; Gen. Man. GUY GRYMBERG.

Crédit Foncier de France: 19 rue des Capucines, 75001 Paris Cedex 01; tel. 1-42-44-80-00; fax 1-42-44-86-99; e-mail communication@creditfoncier.fr; internet www.creditfoncier.fr; f. 1852; 100% owned by Caisses d'Epargne et de Prévoyance; mortgage banking; cap. 804.7m., res 1,267.9m., dep. 85,655.9m. (Dec. 2006); Chair, Bd. of Dirs FRANÇOIS DROUIN; Chief Exec. FRANÇOIS BLANCARD; 202 brs.

Crédit Industriel et Commercial (CIC): 6 ave de Provence, 75452 Paris Cedex 09; tel. 1-45-96-96-96; fax 1-45-96-96-66; internet www.cic-banques.fr; f. 1990 by merger; present name adopted 2000; 70.81% owned by Banque Fédérative du Crédit Mutuel; cap. 567m., res 5,621m., dep. 189,931m. (Dec. 2006); Chair., Supervisory Bd ETIENNE PFIMLIN; Chair., Management Bd MICHEL LUCAS.

Crédit du Nord: 59 blvd Haussmann, 75008 Paris; tel. 1-40-22-40-22; fax 3-20-57-74-05; internet www.credit-du-nord.fr; f. 1974 by merger; 80% owned by Société Générale; cap. 740.3m., res 394.7m., dep. 20,261.0m. (Dec. 2006); Pres. ALAIN PY; 675 brs.

Fortis Banque France: 29–30 quai de Dion Bouton, 92800 Puteaux; tel. 1-55-67-89-00; e-mail courrier@fortis.com; internet www.fortisbanque.fr; f. 1920 as Banque Parisienne de Crédit au Commerce et à l'Industrie; present name adopted 2000; 99.94% owned by Fortis Bank (Belgium); cap. 35.2m., res 200.2m., dep. 4,688.1m. (Dec. 2005); Pres. and Chair. of Bd MAXIME JADOT; 99 brs.

HSBC France: 103 ave des Champs-Elysées, 75419 Paris Cedex 08; tel. 1-40-70-70-40; fax 1-40-70-70-09; e-mail contact@hsbc.fr; internet www.hsbc.fr; 99.99% owned by HSBC Bank PLC (United Kingdom); f. 2005 by merger of CCF (fmrly Crédit Commercial de France) with three other banks; cap. 378.4m., res 2,910.0m., dep. 85,065.4m. (Dec. 2006); Pres. and CEO CHARLES-HENRI FILIPPI; 223 brs in France.

HSBC Hervet: 184 ave Frédéric et Irène Joliot Curie, 92729 Nanterre Cedex; tel. 1-57-66-52-56; fax 1-57-66-54-16; e-mail marketing@banque-hervet.fr; internet www.hsbc-hervet.fr; f. 1830; 97.9% owned by HSBC France; present name adopted 2005; Chair. of Bd and Pres. FRANÇOIS MORLAT; CEO JACQUES-EMMANUEL BLANCHET; 86 brs.

HSBC Private Bank France: 117 ave des Champs-Elysées, 75386 Paris Cedex 08; tel. 1-49-52-20-00; fax 1-49-52-20-99; internet www.hsbcprivatebankfrance.com; f. 2003 by merger of HSBC Republic Bank France; 100% owned by HSBC Holdings plc; Chief Exec. CHRISTOPHE DE BACKER.

HSBC UBP: 184 ave Frédéric et Irène Joliot Curie, 92729 Nanterre Cedex; tel. 1-57-66-60-00; fax 1-57-66-67-17; internet www.hsbc.fr; f. 1935 as Union de Banques à Paris; present name adopted 2005; 99.5% owned by HSBC France; Chair. and Pres. JACQUES-EMMANUEL BLANCHET.

LCL—Le Crédit Lyonnais: 19 blvd des Italiens, 75002 Paris; tel. 1-42-95-70-00; fax 1-42-68-37-19; internet www.lcl.com; f. 1863 as Crédit Lyonnais; present name adopted 2005; privatized 1999; acquired by Crédit Agricole in June 2003; cap. 1,864m., res 2,263m., dep. 72,567m. (Dec. 2006); Chair.of Bd GEORGES PAUGET; Chief Exec. CHRISTIAN DUVILLET; 1,950 brs.

Lyonnaise de Banque: 8 rue de la République, 69001 Lyon; tel. 4-78-92-02-12; fax 4-78-92-03-00; e-mail ddi@lb.cicomore.fr; internet www.cic.fr/lb; f. 1865; 100% owned by Crédit Industriel et Commercial; cap. 228.3m., res 279.6m., dep. 15,297.7m. (Dec. 2005); Chair. and Chief Exec. RÉMY WEBER; 368 brs.

Natixis: 45 rue Saint Dominique, 75007 Paris Cedex 02; tel. 1-58-32-30-00; internet www.natixis.com; f. 1999 as Natexis Banques Populaires; present name adopted 2006; 34.4% owned by Banque Fédérale des Banques Populaires, 34.4% by Caisse Nationale des Caisses d'Epargne et de Prévoyance; cap. 14,394m., res 2,140m., dep. 380,372m. (Dec. 2006); Exec. Chair. PHILIPPE DUPONT; CEO DOMINIQUE FERRERO.

Société Bordelaise: Cité mondiale, 20 quai des Chartrons, 33058 Bordeaux; tel. 5-57-85-55-00; fax 5-57-85-55-08; internet www.cic.fr/sb; f. 1880; 100% owned by Crédit Industriel et Commercial; cap. 129.1m., res 40.2m., dep. 2,909.2m. (Dec. 2004); Chair. and Dir-Gen. JEAN-JACQUES TAMBURINI; 161 brs.

Société Générale: Tour Société Générale, 17 cours Valmy, 92972 Paris La Défense; tel. 1-42-14-20-00; fax 1-53-43-87-69; internet www.socgen.com; f. 1864; cap. 577m., res 23,256m., dep. 803,449m. (Dec. 2006); Chair. DANIEL BOUTON; 2,000 brs in France.

Société Marseillaise de Crédit (SMC): 75 rue Paradis, 13006 Marseille; tel. 4-91-13-33-33; fax 4-91-13-33-16; e-mail infos@smc.fr; internet www.smc.fr; f. 1865; owned by Compagnie Financière Ile du Rhône; cap. 16.0m., res 104.6m., dep. 2,672.5m. (Dec. 2003); Chair. and Chief Exec. EMMANUEL BARTHÉLÉMY; Gen. Man. and Pres. OLIVIER DELAPORTE; 154 brs.

Société Nancéienne Varin-Bernier (CIC Banque SNVB): 4 place André Maginot, 54074 Nancy; tel. 3-83-34-50-00; fax 3-83-34-50-99; e-mail snvbinter@snvb.cic.fr; internet www.snvb.fr; f. 1881; 100% owned by Crédit Industriel et Commercial; cap. 60.0m., res 222.8m., dep. 7,688.8m. (Dec. 2005); Chair. PHILIPPE VIDAL; Gen. Man. LUC DYMARSKI; 148 brs.

Union de Banques Arabes et Françaises (UBAF): 190 ave Charles de Gaulle, 92523 Neuilly-sur-Seine; tel. 1-46-40-61-01; fax 1-47-38-13-88; e-mail ubaf_paris@ubaf.fr; internet www.ubaf.fr; f. 1970; 47.32% owned by Calyon, 52.68% by Arab interests; commercial, Islamic and merchant banking; cap. 249.1m., res 3.7m., dep. 1,799.2m. (Dec. 2006); Chair., Supervisory Bd FAROUK EL-OKDAH; Chair., Management Bd PATRICK LEGAIT.

VTB Bank (France) SA (BCEN—Eurobank): 79–81 blvd Haussmann, 75382 Paris Cedex 08; tel. 1-40-06-43-21; fax 1-40-06-48-48; internet www.vtb.fr; f. 1921 as Comptoir Parisien de Banque et de Change; changed name to Banque Commerciale pour l'Europe du Nord in 1972; present name adopted 2006; 86.98% owned by VTB Bank Europe PLC (United Kingdom); cap. 185.3m., res —84.4m., dep. 615.2m. (Dec. 2006); Chair., Supervisory Council IGOR ZAVYALOV; Chair., Executive Bd LIUBOV MOKHNACHEVA.

Co-operative Banks

Banque Populaire d'Alsace: 4 quai Kléber, 67000 Strasbourg; tel. 3-88-62-77-11; fax 3-88-62-70-35; internet www.alsace.banquepopulaire.fr; f. 2003 by merger of Banque Populaire de la Région Economique de Strasbourg and Banque Populaire du Haut Rhin; cap. 150.9m., res 139.5m., dep. 4,446.0m. (Dec. 2005); Pres. THIERRY CAHN; Dir-Gen. DOMINIQUE DIDON; 96 brs.

Banque Populaire Bourgogne Franche-Comté: 14 blvd de la Trémouille, BP 310, 21008 Dijon Cedex; tel. 8-20-33-75-00; fax 8-20-20-36-20; internet www.bpbfc.banquepopulaire.fr; f. 2002 by merger of Banque Populaire de Bourgogne and Banque Populaire de Franche-Comté, du Mâconnais et de l'Ain; cap. 272.7m., res 536.7m., dep. 7,361.7m. (Dec. 2006); Pres. JEAN-PHILIPPE GIRARD; Dir-Gen. BERNARD JEANNIN; 151 brs.

FRANCE
Directory

Banque Populaire Côte d'Azur (BPCA): BP 241, 457 promenade des Anglais, 06024 Nice; tel. 4-93-21-52-00; fax 4-93-21-54-45; e-mail contact@cotedazur.banquepopulaire.fr; internet www.cotedazur.banquepopulaire.fr; f. 1986; present name adopted 2002; cap. 71.0m., res 77.3m., dep. 3,654.0m. (Dec. 2005); Pres. BERNARD FLEURY; Gen. Man. JEAN-FRANÇOIS COMAS; 90 brs.

Banque Populaire Loire et Lyonnais: 141 rue Garibaldi, BP 3152, 69003 Lyon; tel. 4-89-95-55-55; fax 4-78-71-03-99; e-mail contact@bp2l.banquepopulaire.fr; internet www.loirelyonnais.banquepopulaire.fr; f. 2000 by merger of Banque Populaire de Lyon and Banque Populaire de la Loire; cap. 151.3m., res 145.3m., dep. 3,713.6m. (Dec. 2005); Chair. HERVÉ GENTY; Gen.-Man. OLIVIER DE MARIGNAN.

Banque Populaire du Massif Central: BP 53, 18 blvd Jean Moulin, 63002 Clermont-Ferrand; tel. 4-73-23-46-23; fax 4-73-23-47-99; internet www.massifcentral.banquepopulaire.fr; f. 1920; cap. 94.5m., res 100.6m., dep. 2,357.7m. (Dec. 2005); Gen. Man. CHRISTIAN DU PAYRAT.

Banque Populaire Rives de Paris: 55 ave de France, 75204 Paris Cedex 13; tel. 1-40-92-61-00; fax 1-46-57-61-53; internet www.rivesparis.banquepopulaire.fr; f. 2004 by merger of BICS-Banque Populaire and Banque Populaire Nord de Paris; cap. 398.0m., res 558.3m., dep. 9,736.7m. (Dec. 2006); Chair. MARC JARDIN; Gen. Man. JEAN CRITON.

Banque Populaire du Sud-Ouest: 10 quai des Queyries, 33072 Bordeaux Cedex; tel. 5-56-01-86-86; fax 5-56-48-99-39; internet www.sudouest.banquepopulaire.fr; f. 1920; cap. 79.4m., res 103.0m., dep. 2,862.0m. (Dec. 2005); Chair. FRANÇOIS DE LA GIRODAY; Gen. Man. FRANCIS THIBAUD.

BRED Banque Populaire: 18 quai de la Rapée, 75604 Paris Cedex 12; tel. 1-48-98-60-00; fax 1-40-04-71-57; e-mail webmaster@bred.fr; internet www.bred.fr; f. 1919; present name adopted 1994; cap. 257.1m., res 593.5m., dep. 22,133.4m. (Dec. 2005); Chair. STEVE GENTILI; Gen. Man. and Chief Exec. JEAN MICHEL LATY; 244 brs (including 52 in the French Overseas Departments).

Caisse Centrale du Crédit Mutuel: 88–90 rue Cardinet, 75847 Paris Cedex 17; tel. 1-44-01-10-10; fax 1-44-01-12-30; internet www.creditmutuel.com; f. 1963; central organization of 12 autonomous banks (Caisses Fédérales); cap. 113.9m., res 149.9m., dep. 7,723.6m. (Dec. 2006); Chair. ETIENNE PFLIMLIN; Gen. Man. THIERRY BRICHANT.

Compagnie Financière du Crédit Mutuel (CFCM): 32 rue Mirabeau, 29480 Le Relecq-Kerhuon; tel. 2-98-00-22-22; fax 2-98-00-49-10; e-mail pierrette.jouanique@cfcm.fr; internet www.cfcm.fr; f. 1960; present name adopted 2001; 100% owned by Caisse Interfederale de Credit Mutuel; cap. 715.0m., res 529.2m., dep. 17,191.1m. (Dec. 2006); Chair. CHRISTIAN TOUZALIN; Exec. Man. Dir HUMBERT DE FRESNOYE; 300 brs.

Crédit Agricole: 91–93 blvd Pasteur, 75015 Paris; tel. 1-43-23-52-02; fax 1-43-23-20-28; internet www.credit-agricole.fr; f. 1920; central institution for co-operative banking group comprising 39 Caisses Regionales and a central bank (CNCA); emphasis on agribusiness; cap. 17,006m., res 13,152m., dep. 949,491m. (Dec. 2006); Pres. RENÉ CARRON; Chief Exec. GEORGES PAUGET; 9,130 brs.

Crédit Coopératif: BP 211, Parc de la Défense, 33 rue des Trois Fontanot, 92002 Nanterre; tel. 1-47-24-85-00; fax 1-47-24-89-25; e-mail din@coopanet.com; internet www.credit-cooperatif.coop; f. 1893; present name adopted 2001; merged with Caisse Centrale de Crédit Coopératif in 2003; cap. 219.0m., res 152.7m., dep. 7,204.8m. (Dec. 2005); Chair., Pres. and Gen. Man. JEAN-CLAUDE DETILLEUX.

Investment Banks

Caisse Centrale de Réescompte (CCR): 44 rue Washington, 75008 Paris; tel. 1-49-53-20-00; fax 1-42-25-60-48; internet www.groupe-ccr.com; f. 1938; cap. 108.2m., res 63.1m., dep. 3,665.0m. (Dec. 2006); owned by UBS AG (Switzerland); Chair., Supervisory Bd GABRIEL HERRERA; Chair., Management Bd DANIEL TERMINET.

Dresdner Bank Gestions France: 108 blvd de la Madeleine, Paris Premier, 75008 Paris; tel. 1-70-36-85-00; fax 1-42-93-03-30; e-mail webmaster-paris@dresdner-bank.de; f. 1979; fmrly Dresdner Kleinwort Benson (Marchés); present name adopted 2001; Chair. ALEXIS PILLET-WILL; Man. KONSTANTIN VON SCHWEINITZ.

Supervisory Body

Association Française des Etablissements de Crédit et des Entreprises d'Investissement (AFECEI): 36 rue Taitbout, 75009 Paris; tel. 1-48-01-88-88; fax 1-48-24-13-31; internet www.afecei.asso.fr; f. 1984; advises Govt on monetary and credit policy and supervises the banking system; 14 mems; Pres. DANIEL BOUTON; Dir-Gen. ARIANE OBOLENSKY.

Banking Association

Fédération Bancaire Française: 18 rue La Fayette, 75440 Paris Cedex 09; tel. 1-48-00-52-52; fax 1-42-46-76-40; e-mail fbf@fbf.fr; internet www.fbf.fr; f. 1941; 500 mems; Pres. CHARLES MILLAUD; Dir-Gen. ARIANE OBOLENSKY.

STOCK EXCHANGE

Euronext Paris: 39 rue Cambon, 75001 Paris; tel. 1-49-27-10-00; fax 1-49-27-11-71; e-mail info@euronext.com; internet www.euronext.fr; formed in 2000 by merger of Amsterdam, Paris and Brussels exchanges, and joined in 2002 by the Lisbon stock exchange and the London futures exchange Liffe; merged with New York Stock Exchange in 2007 to form NYSE Euronext; Chair. and CEO JEAN-FRANÇOIS THÉODORE.

Stock Exchange Associations

Autorité des Marchés Financiers (AMF): 17 place de la Bourse, 75082 Paris Cedex 2; tel. 1-53-45-60-00; fax 1-53-45-61-00; e-mail centrededoc@amf-france.org; internet www.amf-france.org; f. 2003 by merger of Commission des Opérations de Bourse and Conseil des Marchés Financiers; 360 mems (2005); Pres. MICHEL PRADA; Sec.-Gen. GÉRARD RAMEIX.

Fédération Française des Clubs d'Investissement (FFCI): 39 rue Cambon, 75001 Paris; tel. 1-42-60-12-47; fax 1-42-60-10-14; e-mail info@clubinvestissement.com; internet www.clubinvestissement.com; f. 1968; fmrly Fédération Nationale des Associations de Clubs d'Investissement (FNACI); represents investment clubs in matters concerning public and political institutions; Pres. DOMINIQUE LEBLANC; Sec.-Gen. ALDO SICURANI.

INSURANCE

Assurances du Crédit Mutuel IARD, SA: BP 373 R 10, 34 rue du Wacken, 67010 Strasbourg Cedex; tel. 3-88-14-90-90; fax 3-88-14-90-01; internet www.creditmutuel.fr; Pres. MICHEL LUCAS; Dir ALAIN SCHMITTER.

Assurances Générales de France (AGF): 87 rue de Richelieu, 75002 Paris Cedex 02; tel. 1-44-86-20-00; fax 1-44-86-27-90; internet www.agf.fr; f. 1968 by merger; affiliated to Groupe Allianz (Germany); insurance and reinsurance; Pres. JEAN-PHILIPPE THIERRY; Dirs-Gen. LAURENT MIGNON, FRANÇOIS THOMAZEAU, LOUIS DE MONTFERRAND, JEAN-FRANÇOIS LEQUOY.

Aviva: 52 rue de la Victoire, 75009 Paris; e-mail veronique_eriaud@aviva.fr; internet www.aviva.fr; f. 1998 as CGU France by merger to incorporate fmr Abeille Assurances; present name adopted 2002; affiliated to CGNU Group (United Kingdom); Pres. BRUNO ROSTAIN.

AXA Assurances IARD: 21 rue de Châteaudun, 75441 Paris Cedex 09; tel. 1-53-21-16-00; fax 1-53-21-17-96; internet www.axa.com; Chair. of Supervisory Bd JACQUES DE CHATEAUVIEUX; Chair. of Management Bd HENRI DE CASTRIES.

Caisse Centrale des Assurances Mutuelles Agricoles: 8 rue d'Astorg, 75383 Paris Cedex 08; tel. 1-44-56-77-77; fax 1-44-56-79-46; internet www.groupama.com; affiliated to Groupama; Dir STÉPHANE GIN.

Caisse Nationale de Prévoyance-Assurances (CNP): 4 place Raoul Dautry, 75716 Paris Cedex 15; tel. 1-42-18-88-88; fax 1-42-34-70-14; internet www.cnp.fr; general insurance; Pres GILLES BENOIST, EDMOND ALPHANDERY.

Cardif: 4 rue des Frères Caudron, 92858 Rueil-Malmaison Cedex; tel. 1-41-42-83-00; fax 1-41-42-84-17; internet www.cardif.fr; general insurance; Pres. PAUL VILLEMAGNE; Dir-Gen. ERIC LOMBARD.

Ecureuil Vie: 5 rue Masseran, 75007 Paris; tel. 1-58-40-64-00; fax 1-58-40-64-01; life insurance; Pres. PIERRE CARLI; Dir GÉRARD LUNEL.

ERISA: Immeuble Ile de France, 4 place de la Pyramide, 92800 Paris La Défense; tel. 1-41-02-40-40; fax 1-41-02-49-84; life insurance; affiliated to HSBC France; Pres. PATRICK POLLET; Dir JOËLLE DURIEUX.

La Fédération Continentale: 11 blvd Haussmann, 75009 Paris; tel. 1-55-32-74-00; fax 1-55-32-74-01; e-mail webmastre@federation-continentale.fr; internet www.federation-continentale.fr; f. 1961; life insurance; member of Groupe Generali (Italy); Pres. HENRI MOULARD; Dir-Gen. DANIEL COLLIGNON.

Garantie Mutuelle des Fonctionnaires: 76 rue de Prony, 75857 Paris Cedex 17; tel. 1-47-54-10-10; fax 1-47-54-18-97; internet www.gmf.fr; f. 1934; Pres. YVES CAZAUX; Dir CHRISTIAN SASTRE.

Generali France Assurances: 5 rue de Londres, 75456 Paris Cedex 09; tel. 1-55-32-40-00; fax 1-55-32-40-05; e-mail webmaster@agence.generali.fr; internet www.assurances.generali.fr; Pres. CLAUDE TENDIL; Dir ERIC LE GENTIL.

GPA Assurances—Groupe Generali: 7 blvd Haussmann, 75447 Paris Cedex 09; tel. 1-58-34-15-15; fax 1-58-34-10-90; internet www.gpa.fr; Pres. CLAUDE TENDIL; Dir-Gen. JEAN-YVES HERMENIER.

FRANCE   *Directory*

Groupama Vie: 5 rue du Centre, 93199 Noisy Le Grand Cedex; tel. 1-49-31-31-31; fax 1-49-31-31-98; e-mail webmaster@groupama.fr; internet www.groupama.com; life insurance; Dir PIERRE BEAUMIN.

Groupe des Assurances Nationales (GAN): 8–10 rue d'Astorg, Paris 75008; tel. 1-42-47-50-00; fax 1-42-47-67-66; e-mail gan.rimbault.philippe@wanadoo.fr; internet www.gan.fr; f. 1820, fire; f. 1830, life; f. 1865, accident; affiliated to Groupama; Pres. JEAN-FRANÇOIS LEMOUX; Dir HENRI GUS.

La Mondiale: 32 ave Emile Zola, Mons en Baroeul, 59896 Lille Cedex 9; tel. 3-20-67-37-00; fax 3-20-47-70-90; internet www.lamondiale.com; f. 1905; life insurance; Pres. JEAN-LOUIS DE MOURGUES; Dir-Gen. ANDRÉ RENAUDIN.

Mutuelles du Mans Assurances (MMA): 10 blvd Alexandre Oyon, 72030 Le Mans Cedex 09; tel. 2-43-41-72-72; fax 2-43-41-72-26; internet www.mma.fr; f. 1828; life and general insurance; comprises three companies: MMA-IARD, DAS and MMA-VIE; Pres. and Dir-Gen. JEAN-CLAUDE SEYS; Dir-Gen. JACQUES LENORMAND.

Predica: 50 rue de la Procession, 75724 Paris Cedex 15; tel. 1-43-23-58-00; fax 1-43-23-03-47; internet www.ca-predica.fr; affiliated to Crédit Agricole; general insurance; Pres. GUY CHATEAU; Dir-Gen. JEAN-YVES HOCHER.

Previposte: BP 7162, 4 place Raoul Dautry, 75716 Paris Cedex 15; tel. 1-42-18-81-37; fax 1-42-18-94-94; life insurance; Pres. GÉRARD MÉNÉROUD; Dir MARTINE FRIANT.

Socapi: 42 rue des Mathurins, 75008 Paris; tel. 1-44-71-52-00; fax 1-40-17-02-33; internet www.socapi.fr; f. 1985; 100% owned by Groupe des Assurances du Crédit Mutuel; life insurance; Pres. ALAIN SCHMITTER.

Suravenir: BP 103, 232 rue Général Paulet, 29802 Brest Cedex 09; tel. 2-98-34-65-00; fax 2-98-34-65-11; e-mail relations-client@suravenir.fr; internet www.suravenir.fr; f. 1984; general insurance; Pres., Bd MARCEL BARON; Pres., Management LOUIS ECHELARD.

Union des Assurances Fédérales (UAF): 27 ave Claude Vellefaux, 75499 Paris Cedex 10; tel. 1-40-03-10-00; fax 1-40-18-36-93; internet www.uafdirect.fr; life insurance; affiliated to LCL—Le Crédit Lyonnais; Chair. and CEO JEAN-PIERRE WIEDMER.

Insurance Associations

Chambre Syndicale des Courtiers d'Assurances (CSCA): 91 rue Saint Lazare, 75009 Paris; tel. 1-48-74-19-12; fax 1-42-82-91-10; e-mail csca@csca.fr; internet www.csca.fr; f. 2006; c. 1,000 mems; Chair. MONIQUE LECLERC, ROBERT LEBLANC.

Fédération Française des Courtiers d'Assurances et de Réassurances (FCA): 91 rue Saint Lazare, 75009 Paris; tel. 1-48-74-19-12; fax 1-42-82-91-10; e-mail ffca@wanadoo.fr; internet www.csca.fr; f. 1991; Chair. ROBERT LEBLANC; c. 700 mems.

Syndicat Français des Assureurs-Conseils: 14 rue de la Grange Batelière, 75009 Paris; tel. 1-55-33-51-51; fax 1-48-00-93-01; e-mail sfac2@wanadoo.fr; internet www.sfac-assurance.fr; Pres. MONIQUE LECLERC.

Fédération des Agents Généraux d'Assurances (AGEA): 104 rue Jouffroy d'Abbans, 75847 Paris Cedex 17; tel. 1-44-01-18-00; fax 1-43-18-72-60; e-mail regis.devaux@agea.fr; internet www.agea.fr; Pres. GUY BAQUÉ.

Fédération Française des Sociétés d'Assurances (FFSA): 26 blvd Haussmann, 75009 Paris; tel. 1-42-47-90-00; fax 1-42-47-93-11; internet www.ffsa.fr; f. 1937; Chair. GÉRARD DE LA MARTINIÈRE; Sec.-Gen. GILLES WOLKOWITSCH.

Trade and Industry

GOVERNMENT AGENCIES

Agence Française pour les Investissements Internationaux (AFII) (Invest In France Agency—IFA): 77 blvd Saint-Jacques, 75680 Paris Cedex 14; tel. 1-44-87-17-17; fax 1-40-74-73-29; e-mail info@afii.fr; internet www.afii.fr; f. 2001; promotes and assists foreign investment in France; Pres. PHILIPPE FAVRE.

Conseil du Commerce de France: 14 rue de Castiglione, 75001 Paris; tel. 1-40-15-03-03; fax 1-40-15-97-22; Pres. BAUDOUIN MONNOYEUR.

UBIFRANCE—l'Agence Française pour le développement international des entreprises: 10 ave d'Iéna, 75116 Paris; tel. 1-40-73-30-00; fax 1-40-73-39-79; e-mail Claire.rocheteau@ubifrance.fr; internet www.ubifrance.fr; f. 2004 by merger of the Centre Français du Commerce Extérieur and the association UBIFrance; Minister-delegate for External Trade ANNE MARIE IDRAC.

DEVELOPMENT ORGANIZATIONS

Agence pour la Création d'Entreprises (APCE): 14 rue Delambre, 75682 Paris Cedex 14; tel. 1-42-18-58-58; fax 1-42-18-58-00; e-mail info@apce.com; internet www.apce.com; Pres. RENÉ RICOL.

Groupe IDI: 18 ave Matignon, 75008 Paris; tel. 1-55-27-80-00; fax 1-40-17-04-44; f. 1970 as Institut de Développement Industriel; provides venture capital, takes equity shares in small and medium-sized businesses; Chair. CHRISTIAN LANGLOIS MEURINNE; CEO F. MARMISSOLLE.

CHAMBERS OF COMMERCE

There are Chambers of Commerce in all the larger towns for all the more important commodities produced or manufactured.

Assemblée des Chambres Françaises de Commerce et d'Industrie: 45 ave d'Iéna, 75116 Paris; tel. 1-40-69-37-00; e-mail contactsweb@acfci.cci.fr; internet www.acfci.cci.fr; f. 1964; unites 154 local and 21 regional chambers of commerce and industry; Pres. JEAN-FRANÇOIS BERNARDIN.

Chambre de Commerce et d'Industrie de Paris: 27 ave de Friedland, 75382 Paris Cedex 08; tel. 1-55-65-55-65; fax 1-55-65-78-68; e-mail michel.franck@ccip.fr; internet www.ccip.fr; f. 1803; 307,000 mems in Paris and surrounding regions (Hauts de Seine, Seine-Saint-Denis and Val de Marne); Pres. MICHEL FRANCK.

INDUSTRIAL AND TRADE ASSOCIATIONS

Armateurs de France: 47 rue de Monceau, 75008 Paris; tel. 1-53-89-52-52; fax 1-53-89-52-53; e-mail info@armateursdefrance.org; internet www.armateursdefrance.org; f. 1903; fmrly Comité Central des Armateurs de France; shipping; Pres. PATRICK DECAVELE; Delegate-Gen. ANNE BARTHE; 110 mems.

Assemblée Permanente des Chambres d'Agriculture (APCA): 9 ave George V, 75008 Paris; tel. 1-53-57-10-10; fax 1-53-57-10-05; e-mail accueil@apca.chambagri.fr; internet paris.apca.chambagri.fr; f. 1929; Pres. LUC GUYAU; Dir-Gen. ROLAND BAUD.

Association Nationale des Industries Alimentaires (ANIA): 155 blvd Haussmann, 75008 Paris; tel. 1-53-83-86-00; fax 1-45-61-96-64; e-mail infos@ania.net; internet www.ania.net; f. 1971; food produce; Pres. VICTOR SCHERRER.

Chambre Syndicale de l'Ameublement, Négoce de Paris et de l'Ile de France: 15 rue de la Cerisaie, 75004 Paris; tel. 1-42-72-13-79; fax 1-42-72-02-36; e-mail info@meubleparis.net; internet www.meubleparis.net; f. 1860; furnishing; Chair. NICOLE PHILIBERT; 350 mems.

Chambre Syndicale des Céramistes et Ateliers d'Art de France: 4 passage Roux, 75017 Paris; tel. 1-44-01-08-30; fax 1-44-01-08-35; e-mail info@ateliersdart.com; internet www.ateliersdart.com; f. 1886; craft and design trades; Chair. VICTOR DESCHANG.

Chambre Syndicale des Chantiers Navals: 47 rue de Monceau, 75008 Paris; tel. 1-53-89-52-01; fax 1-53-89-52-15; e-mail cscn@club-internet.fr; internet www.cscn.fr; shipbuilding; Chair. JEAN-MARIE POIMBOEUF; Gen. Man. FABRICE THEOBALD.

Comité des Constructeurs Français d'Automobiles: 2 rue de Presbourg, 75008 Paris; tel. 1-49-52-51-00; fax 1-47-23-74-73; internet www.ccfa.fr; f. 1909; motor manufacturing; Chair. XAVIER FELS; 8 mems.

Comité National des Pêches Maritimes et des Elevages Marins (CNPMEM): 134 ave de Malakoff, 75116 Paris; tel. 1-72-71-18-00; fax 1-72-71-18-50; e-mail cnpmem@comite-peches.fr; internet www.comite-peches.fr; marine fisheries.

Comité Professionnel du Pétrole: 212 ave Paul Doumer, 92508 Rueil-Malmaison Cedex; tel. 1-47-16-94-60; fax 1-47-08-10-57; e-mail webmestre@cpdp.org; internet www.cpdp.org; f. 1950; petroleum industry; 80 mems; Pres. JACQUES CHAUMAS.

Commissariat à l'Energie Atomique (CEA) (Atomic Energy Commission): 31–33 rue de la Fédération, 75752 Paris Cedex 15; tel. 1-40-56-10-00; fax 1-40-56-29-70; e-mail dcom@aramis.cea.fr; internet www.cea.fr; f. 1945; promotes the uses of nuclear energy in science, industry and national defence; involved in research on nuclear materials; reactor development; fundamental research; innovation and transfer of technologies; military applications; biotechnologies; robotics; electronics; new materials; radiological protection and nuclear safety; Gen. Administrator PASCAL COLOMBANI; High Commissioner RENÉ PELLAT.

Confédération des Industries Céramiques de France: 114 rue La Boétie, 75008 Paris; tel. 1-58-18-30-40; fax 1-42-66-09-00; e-mail cicf@ceramique.org; f. 1937; ceramic industry; Chair. JACQUES RUSSEIL; Man. Dir FRANÇOIS DE LA TOUR; 85 mems, 5 affiliates.

Les Entreprises du Medicament (LEEM): 88 rue de la Faisanderie, 75782 Paris Cedex 16; tel. 1-45-03-88-70; fax 1-45-03-39-25; e-mail daei@leem.org; internet www.leem.org; fmrly Syndicat National de l'Industrie Pharmaceutique; pharmaceuticals; Chair. CHRISTIAN LAJOUX.

Fédération des Chambres Syndicales de l'Industrie du Verre: 114 rue la Boétie, 75008 Paris; tel. 1-42-65-60-02; fax 1-42-66-23-88; e-mail contact@fedeverre.fr; internet www.fedeverre.fr; f. 1874; glass industry; Pres. MICHEL GARDES.

Fédération des Chambres Syndicales des Minerais, Minéraux Industriels et Métaux non-Ferreux (FEDEM): 17 rue Hamelin, 75016 Paris; tel. 1-40-76-44-0; e-mail contact@fedem.fr; internet www.fedem.fr; f. 1945; minerals and non-ferrous metals; Chair. YVES RAMBAUD; Delegate-Gen. CLAIRE DE LANGERON; 16 affiliated syndicates.

Fédération des Exportateurs des Vins et Spiritueux de France: 95 rue de Monceau, 75008 Paris; tel. 1-45-22-75-73; fax 1-45-22-94-16; e-mail contact@fevs.com; f. 1921; exporters of wines and spirits; Pres. PATRICK RICARD; Delegate-Gen. LOUIS RÉGIS AFFRE; 450 mems.

Fédération Française de l'Acier: 5 rue Luigi Cherubini, 93212 La Plaine Saint-Denis Cedex; tel. 1-71-92-20-00; fax 1-71-92-25-00; e-mail svp.clients@ffa.fr; internet www.ffa.fr; f. 1945; steel-making; Pres. PHILIPPE DARMAYAN; Vice-Pres. BERNARD ROGY.

Fédération Française du Bâtiment: 33 ave Kléber, 75784 Paris Cedex 16; tel. 1-40-69-51-00; fax 1-45-53-58-77; e-mail ffbbox@ffb.fr; internet www.ffbatiment.fr; f. 1906; building trade; Pres. CHRISTIAN BAFFY; 50,000 mems.

Fédération Française des Industries Lainière et Cotonnière (FFILC): BP 121, 37–39 rue de Neuilly, 92113 Clichy Cedex; tel. 1-47-56-30-40; fax 1-47-37-06-20; e-mail uitcotonlaine@textile.fr; internet www.textile.fr; f. 1902; manufacturing of wool, cotton and associated textiles; Pres. CAMILLE AMALRIC; 400 mems.

Fédération Française du Négoce de Bois (FFNB): 215 bis blvd St Germain, 75007 Paris; tel. 1-45-48-28-44; fax 1-45-48-42-89; e-mail contact@bois-mat.com; internet www.bois-mat.com; timber trade; Pres. GÉRAUD SPIRE; Dir-Gen. LAURENT MARTIN-SAINT-LÉON.

Fédération Française de la Tannerie-Mégisserie: 122 rue de Provence, 75008 Paris; tel. 1-45-22-96-45; fax 1-42-93-37-44; e-mail fftm@leatherfrance.com; internet www.leatherfrance.com; f. 1885; leather industry; 100 mems.

Fédération de l'Imprimerie et de la Communication Graphique: 68 blvd Saint Marcel, 75005 Paris; tel. 1-44-08-64-46; fax 1-43-36-09-51; e-mail pressecom@ficg.fr; printing, communication and design; Pres. JACQUES CHIRAT.

Fédération des Industries Electriques, Electroniques et de Communication (FIEEC): 11–17 rue Hameline, 75783 Paris Cedex 16; tel. 1-45-05-70-70; fax 1-45-53-03-93; e-mail comm@fieec.fr; internet www.fieec.fr; f. 1925; electrical and electronics industries; Chair. HENRI STARCK; Delegate-Gen. JEAN-CLAUDE KARPELÈS; c. 1,000 mems.

Fédération des Industries Mécaniques: 39–41 rue Louis Blanc, 92400 Courbevoie; tel. 1-47-17-60-27; fax 1-47-17-64-37; e-mail ppoisson@fimeca.com; internet www.fim.net; f. 1840; mechanical and metal-working; Pres. YVON JACOB; Dir-Gen. CLAUDE CHARRIER.

Fédération des Industries Nautiques: Port de Javel Haut, 75015 Paris; tel. 1-44-37-04-00; fax 1-45-77-21-88; e-mail info@fin.fr; internet www.fin.fr; f. 1964; pleasure-boating; Pres. ANNETTE ROUX; Man. Dir TIBOR SILLINGER; 750 mems (2005).

Fédération des Industries de la Parfumerie (France): 33 Champs Elysées, 75008 Paris; tel. 1-56-69-67-89; fax 1-56-69-67-90; makers of perfume, cosmetics and toiletries; Pres. ALAIN GRANGÉ CABANE.

Fédération Nationale du Bois: 6 rue François 1er, 75008 Paris; tel. 1-56-69-52-00; fax 1-56-69-52-09; e-mail infos@fnbois.com; internet www.fnbois.com; f. 1884; timber and wood products; Chair. LAURENT DENORMANDIE; 1,850 mems.

Fédération Nationale des Chambres Syndicales des Horlogers, Bijoutiers, Joailliers et Orfèvres (HBJO): 249 rue Saint Martin, 75003 Paris; tel. 1-44-54-34-00; fax 1-44-54-34-07; e-mail fedhbjo@wanadoo.fr; internet www.fedehbjo.com; jewellery, watch- and clock-making; Pres. GÉRARD ATLAN; 1,200 mems.

Fédération Nationale de l'Industrie Hôtelière (FNIH): 22 rue d'Anjou, 75008 Paris; tel. 1-44-94-19-94; fax 1-42-65-16-21; e-mail fnih@imagenet.fr; Chair. ANDRÉ DAGUIN.

Fédération Nationale de l'Industrie Laitière: 42 rue de Châteaudun, 75314 Paris Cedex 09; tel. 1-49-70-72-85; fax 1-42-80-63-94; e-mail fnil@atla.asso.fr; internet www.maison-du-lait.com; f. 1946; dairy products; Pres. OLIVIER PICOT.

Fédération Nationale des Industries Électrométallurgiques, Éléctrochimiques et Connexes: 30 ave de Messine, 75008 Paris; tel. 1-45-61-06-63; fax 1-45-63-61-54; Chair. JACQUES GANI.

Fédération Nationale de la Musique: 62 rue Blanche, 75009 Paris; tel. 1-48-74-09-29; fax 1-42-81-19-87; f. 1964; includes Chambre Syndicale de la Facture Instrumentale, Syndicat National de l'Edition Phonographique and other groups; musical instruments, publications and recordings; Chair. PIERRE HENRY; Sec.-Gen. FRANÇOIS WELLEBROUCK.

Les Fondeurs de France: 45 rue Louis Blanc, 92038 Paris La Défense Cedex; tel. 1-43-34-76-30; fax 1-43-34-76-31; e-mail contact@fondeursdefrance.org; internet www.fondeursdefrance.org; f. 1897; metal casting; Pres. ANDRÉ ROBERT-DEHAULT; Dir-Gen. OLIVIER DUCRU; 300 mems.

Groupe Intersyndical de l'Industrie Nucléaire (GIIN): 92038 Paris La Défense Cedex; tel. 1-47-17-62-78; fax 1-47-17-68-91; e-mail contact@giin.fr; internet www.giin.fr; f. 1959; aims to promote the interests of the French nuclear industry; 200 member firms.

Groupement des Industries Françaises Aéronautiques et Spatiales (GIFAS): 8 rue Galilée, 75116 Paris; tel. 1-44-43-17-00; fax 1-40-70-57-36; e-mail infogifas@gifas.asso.fr; internet www.gifas.asso.fr; aerospace industry; Pres. CHARLES EDELSTENNE.

Syndicat Général des Cuirs et Peaux: 18 blvd Montmartre, 75009 Paris; tel. 1-45-08-08-54; fax 1-40-39-97-31; e-mail cuirsetpeaux@wanadoo.fr; internet www.sgcp.net; f. 1977; present name adopted 1996; untreated leather and hides; Chair. DANIEL BELLIARD; 22 mems.

Syndicat Général des Fabricants d'Huile et de Tourteaux de France: 118 ave Achille Peretti, 92200 Neuilly-sur-Seine; tel. 1-46-37-22-06; fax 1-46-37-15-60; f. 1928; edible oils; Pres. HENRI RIEUX; Sec.-Gen. JEAN-CLAUDE BARSACQ.

Syndicat National des Industries de la Communication Graphique et de l'Imprimerie Françaises (SICOGIF): 48 blvd des Batignolles, 75017 Paris; tel. 1-40-08-18-18; fax 1-40-08-00-24; e-mail info@sicogif.com; internet www.sicogif.com; f. 1991; printers' asscn; 310 mems; Chair. JEAN-RAOUL ROSAY; Sec.-Gen. PHILIPPE QUEINEC.

Union des Armateurs à la Pêche de France: 59 rue des Mathurins, 75008 Paris; tel. 1-42-66-32-60; fax 1-47-42-91-12; e-mail uapf75@wanadoo.fr; f. 1945; fishing vessels; Chair. PATRICE LEDUC; Delegate-Gen. MICHEL DION.

Union des Fabricants de Porcelaine de Limoges: 7 bis rue du Général Cérez, 87000 Limoges; tel. 5-55-77-29-18; fax 5-55-77-36-81; e-mail ufpl@porcelainelimoges.org; porcelain manufacturing; Chair. BERTRAND RAYNAUD; Sec.-Gen. MARIE-THÉRÈSE PASQUET.

Union des Industries Chimiques (UIC): Le Diamant A, 14 rue de la République, 92909 Paris La Défense Cedex 10; tel. 1-46-53-11-00; fax 1-46-96-00-59; e-mail uicgeneral@uic.fr; internet www.uic.fr; f. 1860; chemical industry; Pres. M. DEVIC; 25 affiliated unions.

Union des Industries Métallurgiques et Minières (UIMM): 56 ave de Wagram, 75017 Paris; tel. 1-40-54-20-20; fax 1-47-66-22-74; e-mail uimm@uimm.fr; internet www.uimm.fr; metallurgy and mining; Chair. DANIEL DEWAVRIN; 223 mems.

Union des Industries Papetières pour les Affaires Sociales (UNIPAS): 154 blvd Haussmann, 75008 Paris; tel. 1-53-89-25-25; fax 1-53-89-25-26; e-mail contact@unipas.org; internet www.unipas.org; f. 1864; paper, cardboard and cellulose; Chair. JEAN-PIERRE QUÉRÉ; Sec.-Gen. BRIGITTE MILLART.

Union des Industries Textiles: BP 121, 37–39 rue de Neuilly, 92113 Clichy Cedex; tel. 1-47-56-31-00; fax 1-47-30-25-28; e-mail thierry_noblot@textile.fr; internet www.textile.fr; f. 1901; Chair. GUILLAUME SARKOZY; 2,500 mems.

Union professionnelle artisanale (UPA): 53 rue Ampère, 75017 Paris; tel. 1-47-63-31-31; fax 1-47-63-31-10; e-mail upa@upa.fr; internet www.upa.fr; f. 1975; unites crafts and other manual workers in three trade bodies and more than 100 regional organizations; Chair. PIERRE MARTIN.

EMPLOYERS' ORGANIZATIONS

Association Française des Entreprises Privées (AGREF): Paris; represents the interests of 81 of the largest enterprises in France; Chair. BERTRAND COLLOMB.

Centre des Jeunes Dirigeants d'Entreprise (CJD): 19 ave Georges V, 75008 Paris; tel. 1-53-23-92-50; fax 1-40-70-15-66; e-mail cjd@cjd.net; internet www.cjd.net; f. 1938; asscn for young entrepreneurs (under 45 years of age); Pres. FRANÇOISE COURELLE; 2,400 mems (2004).

Confédération Générale des Petites et Moyennes Entreprises (CGPME): 10 terrasse Bellini, 92806 Puteaux Cedex; tel. 1-47-62-73-73; fax 1-47-73-08-86; e-mail contact@cgpme.org; internet www.cgpme.org; small and medium-sized cos; Chair. JEAN-FRANÇOIS ROUBAUD; 1,600,000 mems (2001).

Les Entrepreneurs et Dirigeants Chrétiens (Les EDC): 24 rue Hamelin, 75116 Paris; tel. 1-45-53-09-01; fax 1-47-27-43-32; e-mail lesedc@lesedc.org; internet www.lesedc.org; fmrly Centre Français du Patronat Chrétien; asscn of Christian employers; Nat. Pres. PIERRE DESCHAMPS.

Entreprise et Progrès: 11 rue Anatole de la Forge, 75017 Paris; tel. 1-45-74-52-62; fax 1-45-74-52-63; e-mail progres@noos.fr; internet www.entreprise-progres.net; f. 1970; represents 110 enterprises; Pres. Paul Dubrule; Sec.-Gen. Odile Delort-Maixandeau.

Entreprises de Taille Humaine Indépendantes et de Croissance (ETHIC): 6 Villa Thoréton, 75015 Paris; tel. 1-56-82-20-75; fax 1-56-82-20-37; e-mail l.michon@ethic.fr; internet www.ethic.fr; f. 1976; represents small enterprises and promotes ethical values in business; Pres. Sophie de Menthon.

Mouvement des Entreprises de France (MEDEF): 55 ave Bosquet, 75330 Paris Cedex 07; tel. 1-53-59-19-19; fax 1-45-51-20-44; internet www.medef.fr; f. 1998 to replace Conseil National du Patronat Français; employers' asscn grouping 700,000 cos from all sectors of activity in 85 professional feds and 152 regional orgs; Pres. Laurence Parisot; Dir-Gen. Jacques Creyssel.

UTILITIES

Electricity

Alcatel: 54 rue La Boétie, 75008 Paris; tel. 1-40-76-10-10; fax 1-40-76-14-00; internet www.alcatel.com; f. 1898; telecommunications and business systems, broadband access, terrestrial and submarine optical networks; 60,000 employees; Chair. and CEO Serge Tchuruk; Pres. Philippe Germond.

Charbonnages de France (CdF): 100 ave Albert 1er, BP 220, 92503 Rueil-Malmaison Cedex; tel. 1-47-52-35-00; fax 1-47-51-30-75; e-mail cdf.com@groupecharbonnages.fr; internet www.groupecharbonnages.fr; f. 1946; responsible for coal mining, sales and research in metropolitan France; there are also engineering and electricity divisions; 9,957 employees; Pres. and Dir-Gen. Philippe de Ladoucette.

Electricité de France (EdF): 22–30 ave de Wagram, 75382 Paris Cedex 8; tel. 1-40-42-79-40; fax 1-40-42-22-22; e-mail masteredf@edfgdf.fr; internet www.edf.fr; established under the Electricity and Gas Industry Nationalization Act of 1946; responsible for generating and supplying electricity for distribution to consumers in metropolitan France; 15.0% of the company was sold to the private sector in November 2005; 156,000 employees (2004); Chair. and CEO Pierre Gadonneix.

Gas

Gaz de France: 23 rue Philibert Delorme, 75840 Paris Cedex 17; tel. 1-47-54-24-35; fax 1-47-54-74-42; internet www.gdf.fr; established under the Electricity and Gas Industry Nationalization Act of 1946; responsible for distribution of gas in metropolitan France; partially privatized in 2005; merger with Suez ongoing in April 2008; natural gas reserves: 77,184m. cu m, natural gas production: 4,600m. cu m (2003); 38,100 employees (2003); Chair. and CEO Jean-François Cirelli.

Water

Générale des Eaux: 38 ave Kléber, 75799 Paris Cedex 16; tel. 1-71-75-00-00; fax 1-71-75-03-05; e-mail anne.froger@generale-des-eaux.net; internet www.generale-des-eaux.com; f. 1853; subsidiary of Veolia Water; provides water and other environmental services, as well as telecommunications and construction; Pres. and Dir-Gen. Henri Proglio.

Lyonnaise des Eaux: 1 rue d'Astorg, 75008 Paris; internet www.lyonnaise-des-eaux.fr; f. 1858; fmrly Suez-Lyonnaise des Eaux; present name adopted 2001; subsidiary of Groupe Suez, the merger of which with Gaz de France was approved in 2006; Pres. and CEO Gérard Mestrallet.

TRADE UNIONS

There are three major trade union organizations:

Confédération Française Démocratique du Travail (CFDT): 4 blvd de la Villette, 75955 Paris Cedex 19; tel. 1-42-03-80-00; fax 1-53-72-85-71; e-mail confederation@cfdt.fr; internet www.cfdt.fr; f. 1919 as Confédération Française des Travailleurs Chrétiens—CFTC; present title and constitution adopted 1964; moderate; co-ordinates 1,500 trade unions, 95 departmental and overseas unions, 3 confederal unions and 17 affiliated professional federations, all of which are autonomous. There are also 22 regional orgs; 803,635 mems; affiliated to European Trade Union Confederation and to ITUC; Sec.-Gen. François Chérèque.

Affiliated federations:

CFDT-Agroalimentaire (FGA-CFDT): 47–49 ave Simon Bolivar, 75950 Paris Cedex 19; tel. 1-56-41-50-50; fax 1-56-41-50-30; e-mail fga@cfdt.fr; internet www.fga-cfdt.fr; f. 1980; Sec.-Gen. Hervé Garnier; 56,500 mems (2004).

CFDT-Banques et Sociétés Financières: 47–49 ave Simon Bolivar, 75950 Paris Cedex 19; tel. 1-56-41-54-50; fax 1-56-41-54-51; e-mail federation@cfdt-banques.fr; internet www.cfdt-banques.fr; Sec.-Gen. Jean-Claude Branchereau.

CFDT-Cadres (Managers and Professionals): 47–49 ave Simon Bolivar, 75950 Paris Cedex 19; tel. 1-56-41-55-00; fax 1-56-41-55-01; e-mail contact@cadres.cfdt.fr; internet www.cadres-plus.net; Sec.-Gen. François Fayol.

CFDT-Chimie-Energie (FCE-CFDT): 47–49 ave Simon Bolivar, 75950 Paris Cedex 19; tel. 1-56-41-53-00; fax 1-56-41-53-01; e-mail fce@fce.cfdt.fr; internet www.fce.cfdt.fr; f. 1946; Sec.-Gen. Patrick Pierron; 62,000 mems.

CFDT-Communication, Conseil, Culture (F3C) (Communications, Advisory and Cultural Federation): 47–49 ave Simon Bolivar, 75950 Paris Cedex 19; tel. 1-56-41-54-00; fax 1-56-41-54-01; e-mail f3c@cfdt.fr; internet www.f3c-cfdt.fr; f. 2005; Sec.-Gen. Hervé Morland.

CFDT-Construction-Bois (FNCB-CFDT) (Builders, Wood-workers, Architects, Town-planners): 47–49 ave Simon Bolivar, 75950 Paris Cedex 19; tel. 1-56-41-55-60; fax 1-56-41-55-61; e-mail fncb@cfdt.fr; internet www.cfdt-construction-bois.fr; f. 1934; Sec.-Gen. Joseph Murgia.

CFDT-Education Nationale (SGEN-CFDT) (National Education): 47–49 ave Simon Bolivar, 75950 Paris Cedex 19; tel. 1-56-41-51-00; fax 1-56-41-51-11; e-mail fede@sgen-cfdt.org; internet www.sgen-cfdt.org; f. 1937; Sec.-Gen. Thierry Cadart.

CFDT-Etablissements et Arsenaux de l'Etat: 2–8 rue Gaston Rébuffat, 75940 Paris Cedex 19; tel. 1-56-41-56-80; fax 1-56-41-56-89; e-mail feae@cfdt.fr; Sec.-Gen. Jacques Lepinard.

CFDT-Finances et Affaires Economiques (Finance): 2–8 rue Gaston Rébuffat, 75940 Paris Cedex 19; tel. 1-56-41-55-55; fax 1-56-41-55-59; e-mail finances@cfdt.fr; f. 1936; civil servants and workers within government financial departments; Sec.-Gen. Philippe Leclezio.

CFDT-Fonctionnaires et Assimilés (UFFA) (Civil Servants): 47–49 ave Simon Bolivar, 75950 Paris Cedex 19; tel. 1-56-41-54-40; fax 1-56-41-54-44; e-mail uffa@cfdt.fr; f. 1932; Sec.-Gen. Eric Fritsch.

CFDT-Formation et Enseignement Privés (Independent education): 47–49 ave Simon Bolivar, 75950 Paris Cedex 19; tel. 1-56-41-54-70; fax 1-56-41-54-71; e-mail contact@fep-cfdt.fr; internet www.fep-cfdt.fr; Sec.-Gen. Xavier Nau.

CFDT-Interco (Local Government Workers): 47–49 ave Simon Bolivar, 75950 Paris Cedex 19; tel. 1-56-41-52-52; fax 1-56-41-52-51; e-mail interco@cfdt.fr; internet www.interco-cfdt.fr; Sec.-Gen. Alexis Guénégo.

CFDT-Métallurgie et Mines (Miners, Machinery and Metal Workers): 47–49 ave Simon Bolivar, 75950 Paris Cedex 19; tel. 1-56-41-50-70; fax 1-56-41-50-96; e-mail fgmm@cfdt.fr; internet www.fgmm.cfdt.fr; Sec.-Gen. Dominique Gillier.

CFDT-Protection Sociale, Travail, Emploi (Social Security): 2–8 rue Gaston Rébuffat, 75940 Paris Cedex 19; tel. 1-56-41-51-50; fax 1-56-41-51-51; e-mail pste@cfdt.fr; internet www.pste-cfdt.org; Sec.-Gen. Martial Garcia.

CFDT-Retraités (UCR) (Retired People): 47–49 ave Simon Bolivar, 75950 Paris Cedex 19; tel. 1-56-41-55-20; fax 1-56-41-55-21; e-mail union-retraites@cfdt.fr; Sec.-Gen. Jacques Sense.

CFDT-Services (Trade, Insurance, Legal, Property and other Service Sector Professions): Tour Essor, 14 rue Scandicci, 93508 Pantin Cedex; tel. 1-48-10-65-90; fax 1-48-10-65-95; e-mail services@cfdt.fr; internet www.cfdt-services.fr; Sec.-Gen. Didier Brulé.

CFDT-Services de Santé et Services Sociaux (Health and Social Workers): 47–49 ave Simon Bolivar, 75950 Paris Cedex 19; tel. 1-56-41-52-00; fax 1-42-02-48-08; e-mail santesociaux@cfdt.fr; internet www.fed-cfdt-sante-sociaux.org; Sec.-Gen. Yolande Briand.

CFDT-Transports-Equipement (Transport, Public Works and Housing—FGTE): 47–49 ave Simon Bolivar, 75950 Paris Cedex 19; tel. 1-56-41-56-03; fax 1-42-02-49-96; e-mail lecoq@fgte-cfdt.org; internet www.fgte.org; f. 1977; Sec.-Gen. Joël Lecoq.

Confédération Générale du Travail (CGT): 263 rue de Paris, 93516 Montreuil Cedex; tel. 1-48-18-80-00; fax 1-481-8-84-60; e-mail info@cgt.fr; internet www.cgt.fr; f. 1895; National Congress is held every three years; Sec.-Gen. Bernard Thibault; 700,000 mems.

Affiliated federations:

CGT-Agro-Alimentaire et Forestière (FNAF) (Food Producers): 263 rue de Paris, Case 428, 93514 Montreuil Cedex; tel. 1-48-18-83-27; fax 1-48-51-57-49; e-mail fnaf@fnaf-cgt.com; Sec.-Gen. Freddy Huck.

CGT-Banques et Assurance (Banking and Insurance): 263 rue de Paris, Case 537, 93515 Montreuil Cedex; tel. 1-48-18-83-40; fax 1-49-88-16-36; e-mail fspba@cgt.fr; internet www.nfs.ras.eu.org; Sec.-Gen. Philippe Bourgale.

CGT-Bois Ameublement Connexes (Woodworkers): 263 rue de Paris, Case 414, 93514 Montreuil Cedex; tel. 1-48-18-81-61; fax 1-48-51-59-91; e-mail cgt.bois1@wanadoo.fr; Sec.-Gen. Henri Sanchez.

CGT-Cheminots (Railway Workers): 263 rue de Paris, Case 546, 93515 Montreuil Cedex; tel. 1-49-88-61-00; fax 1-48-57-95-65; e-mail coord@cheminotcgt.fr; internet www.cheminotcgt.fr; Sec.-Gen. DIDIER LE RESTE.

CGT-Commerce: 263 rue de Paris, Case 425, 93514 Montreuil Cedex; tel. 1-48-18-83-11; fax 1-48-18-83-19; e-mail fd.commerce.services@cgt.fr; internet www.commerce.cgt.fr; Sec.-Gen. MICHÈLE CHAY.

CGT-Construction (Building): 263 rue de Paris, Case 413, 93514 Montreuil Cedex; tel. 1-48-18-81-60; fax 1-48-59-10-37; e-mail construction@cgt.fr; internet www.construction.cgt.fr; Sec.-Gen. ERIC AUBIN.

CGT-Equipement et Environnement (Capital Works and Environment): 263 rue de Paris, Case 543, 93515 Montreuil Cedex; tel. 1-48-18-82-81; fax 1-48-51-62-50; e-mail equipement@cgt.fr; internet www.equipement.cgt.fr; Sec.-Gen. JEAN-MARIE RECH.

CGT-Education Recherche Culture (CGT-FERC): 263 rue de Paris, Case 544, 93515 Montreuil Cedex; tel. 1-48-18-82-44; fax 1-49-88-07-43; e-mail ferc@cgt.fr; internet www.ferc.cgt.fr; Sec.-Gen. RICHARD BERAUD.

CGT-Finances: 263 rue de Paris, Case 540, 93515 Montreuil Cedex; tel. 1-48-18-82-21; fax 1-48-18-82-52; e-mail finances@cgt.fr; internet www.finances.cgt.fr; Sec.-Gen. CHRISTOPHE DELECOURT.

CGT-Fonctionnaires (CGT-UGFF) (Civil Servants): 263 rue de Paris, Case 542, 93514 Montreuil Cedex; tel. 1-48-18-82-31; fax 1-48-18-82-11; e-mail ugff@cgt.fr; internet www.ugff.cgt.fr; groups National Education, Finance, Technical and Administrative, Civil Servants, Police, etc.; comprises some 70 national unions and six professional federations; Sec.-Gen. BERNARD LHUBERT.

CGT-Industries Chimiques (Chemical Industries): 263 rue de Paris, Case 429, 93514 Montreuil Cedex; tel. 1-48-18-80-36; fax 1-48-18-80-35; e-mail fnic@cgt.fr; internet www.fnic.cgt.fr; Sec.-Gen. JEAN-MICHEL PETIT.

CGT-Industries du Livre, du Papier et de la Communication (FILPAC) (Printing, Paper Products and Media): 263 rue de Paris, Case 426, 93514 Montreuil Cedex; tel. 1-48-18-80-24; fax 1-48-51-99-07; e-mail filpac@filpac-cgt.fr; internet www.filpac-cgt.fr; Sec.-Gen. MICHEL MULLER.

CGT-Ingénieurs, Cadres et Techniciens (CGT-UGICT) (Engineers, Managerial Staff and Technicians): 263 rue de Paris, Case 408, 93514 Montreuil Cedex; tel. 1-48-18-81-25; fax 1-48-51-64-57; e-mail ugict@cgt.fr; internet www.ugict.cgt.fr; f. 1963; Sec.-Gen. MARIE-JO KOTLICKI.

CGT-Intérimaires (Temporary Workers): 263 rue de Paris, Case 460, 93514 Montreuil Cedex; tel. 1-48-18-84-16; fax 1-48-18-82-59; e-mail contact@interim.cgt.fr; internet www.interim.cgt.fr; Pres. LE NOUAIL MARLIÈRE.

CGT-Journalistes: 263 rue de Paris, Case 570, 93514 Montreuil Cedex; tel. 1-48-18-81-78; fax 1-48-51-58-08; e-mail snj@cgt.fr; Sec.-Gen. MICHEL DIARD.

CGT-Marine Marchande (Merchant Marine): Cercle Franklin, 119 cours de la République, 76000 Le Havre; tel. 2-35-25-04-81; fax 2-35-24-23-77; e-mail off-march@cgt.fr; Sec.-Gen. CHARLES NARELLI.

CGT-Maritimes (Seamen): 263 rue de Paris, Case 420, 93514 Montreuil Cedex; tel. 1-48-18-81-76; fax 1-48-51-59-21; e-mail fnsm-cgt@wanadoo.fr; Sec.-Gen. ALAIN MERLET.

CGT-Métallurgie (FTM) (Metalworkers): 263 rue de Paris, Case 433, 93514 Montreuil Cedex; tel. 1-48-18-21-21; fax 1-48-59-80-66; e-mail metaux@cgt.fr; internet www.ftm-cgt.fr; f. 1891; Sec.-Gen. DANIEL SANCHEZ.

CGT-Mines-Energie (FNME-CGT): 263 rue de Paris, 93516 Montreuil Cedex; tel. 1-56-93-26-50; fax 1-56-93-27-20; e-mail fnme@fnme-cgt.fr; internet www.fnme-cgt.fr; Sec.-Gen. FRÉDÉRIC IMBRECHT.

CGT-Organismes Sociaux (Social Services): 263 rue de Paris, Case 536, 93515 Montreuil Cedex; tel. 1-48-18-83-56; fax 1-48-59-24-75; e-mail fede@orgasociaux.cgt.fr; internet www.orgasociaux.cgt.fr; Sec.-Gen. PHILIPPE HOURCADE.

CGT-Pénitentiaires (Prison Workers): 263 rue de Paris, Case 542, 93514 Montreuil Cedex; tel. 1-48-18-82-42; fax 1-48-18-82-50; e-mail ugsp-cgt2@wanadoo.fr; internet www.ugsp-cgt.org; Sec.-Gen. CÉLINE VERZELETTI.

CGT-Police: 263 rue de Paris, Case 550, 93514 Montreuil Cedex; tel. 1-48-51-51-83; fax 1-48-51-14-43; e-mail cgtpolice@cgt.fr; internet www.police.cgt.fr; f. 1906; Sec.-Gen. MICHEL GASTALDI.

CGT-Ports et Docks: 263 rue de Paris, Case 424, 93514 Montreuil Cedex; tel. 1-48-18-82-96; fax 1-48-18-82-94; e-mail portsetdocks-cgt@wanadoo.fr; Sec.-Gen. DANIEL LEFÈVRE.

CGT-Postes et Télécommunications (CGT-FAPT): 263 rue de Paris, Case 545, 93515 Montreuil Cedex; tel. 1-48-18-84-00; fax 1-48-59-25-22; e-mail fede@cgt-ptt.fr; internet cgtptt.free.fr; Sec.-Gen. ALAIN GAUTHERON.

CGT-Professionnels de la Vente (Sales Workers): Bourse du Travail, 3 rue du Château d'eau, 75010 Paris; tel. 1-42-39-02-99; fax 1-42-39-09-11; e-mail fede.proventecgt@libertysurf.fr; Sec.-Gen. ALAIN SERRE.

CGT-Santé, Action Sociale (Health and Social Services): 263 rue de Montreuil, Case 538, 93514 Montreuil Cedex; tel. 1-48-18-20-99; fax 1-48-18-29-80; e-mail santeas@cgt.fr; internet www.cgt.fr/santeas; f. 1907; Sec.-Gen. NADINE PRIGENT.

CGT-Services Publics (Community Services): 263 rue de Paris, Case 547, 93514 Montreuil Cedex; tel. 1-48-18-83-74; fax 1-48-51-98-20; e-mail fdsp@cgt.fr; internet www.spterritoriaux.cgt.fr; Sec.-Gen. MAÏTÉ LASSALLE.

CGT-Sociétés d'études (Research, Service-sector Workers, Translators, Accountants, Notaries): 263 rue de Paris, Case 421, 93514 Montreuil Cedex; tel. 1-48-18-84-34; fax 1-48-18-84-86; e-mail fsetud@cgt.fr; internet www.soc-etudes.cgt.fr; f. 1980; Pres. NOËL LECHAT.

CGT-Spectacle, Audiovisuel et Action Culturelle (Theatre, Media and Culture): 14–16 rue des Lilas, 75019 Paris; tel. 1-48-03-87-60; fax 1-42-40-90-20; e-mail cgtspectacle@fnsac-cgt.com; internet www.fnsac-cgt.com; Sec.-Gen. JEAN VOIRIN.

CGT-Tabac et Allumettes (Tobacco and Matches): 263 rue de Paris, Case 422, 93514 Montreuil Cedex; tel. 1-48-18-84-19; fax 1-48-51-54-53; e-mail tabacs.allumettes@cgt.fr; Sec.-Gen. FRÉDÉRIQUE BARTLETT.

CGT-Textiles, Habillement, Cuir (Textiles): 263 rue de Paris, Case 415, 93514 Montreuil Cedex; tel. 1-48-18-82-98; fax 1-48-18-83-01; e-mail thc@cgt.fr; internet www.thc-cgt-textile.fr; Sec.-Gen. MAURAD RABHI.

CGT-Transports: 263 rue de Paris, Case 423, 93514 Montreuil Cedex; tel. 1-48-18-80-82; fax 1-48-18-82-54; e-mail transports@cgt.fr; internet www.transports.cgt.fr; Sec.-Gen. PAUL FOURIER.

CGT-Travailleurs de l'Etat (State Employees): 263 rue de Paris, Case 541, 93515 Montreuil Cedex; tel. 1-48-18-86-86; fax 1-48-18-86-87; e-mail trav-etat@cgt.fr; internet www.fnte.cgt.fr; Sec.-Gen. JEAN-LOUIS NAUDET.

CGT-Verre-Céramique (Glassworkers, Ceramics): 263 rue de Paris, Case 417, 93514 Montreuil Cedex; tel. 1-48-18-80-13; fax 1-48-18-80-11; e-mail ver-ceram@cgt.fr; internet www.verreceram-cgt.fr; Sec.-Gen. MOHAMMED OUSSEDIK.

Force Ouvrière (FO): 141 ave du Maine, 75680 Paris Cedex 14; tel. 1-40-52-82-00; fax 1-40-52-82-02; internet www.force-ouvriere.fr; f. 1948 by breakaway from the more left-wing CGT; mem. of ITUC and of the European Trade Union Confederation; Sec.-Gen. JEAN-CLAUDE MAILLY; c. 1m. mems.

Affiliated federations:

Fédération Générale Force Ouvrière (FGFO) (Building, Public Works, Wood, Ceramics, Paper, Cardboard and Building Materials): 170 ave Parmentier, 75010 Paris; tel. 1-42-01-30-00; fax 1-42-39-50-44; e-mail franckserra@wanadoo.fr; internet www.federationgeneralefo.com; Sec.-Gen. FRANCK SERRA.

FO-Action Sociale: 7 passage Tenaille, 75680 Paris Cedex 14; tel. 1-40-52-85-80; fax 1-40-52-85-79; e-mail fnasforceouvriere@wanadoo.fr; Sec.-Gen. MICHEL PAULINI.

FO-Administration Générale de l'Etat: 46 rue des Petites Ecuries, 75010 Paris; tel. 1-42-46-40-19; fax 1-42-46-19-57; e-mail fagefo@wanadoo.fr; internet www.fage-fo.com; f. 1948; Sec.-Gen. JEAN-CLAUDE LE BOURSICAUD.

FO-Agriculture, Alimentation et Tabacs (Agriculture, Food and Tobacco): 7 passage Tenaille, 75680 Paris Cedex 14; tel. 1-40-52-85-10; fax 1-40-52-85-12; e-mail rafael.nedzynski@fgta-fo.org; internet www.fgtafo.fr; Sec.-Gen. RAFAËL NEDZYNSKI.

FO-Cadres et Ingénieurs (UCI) (Managers, Engineers): 2 rue de la Michodière, 75002 Paris; tel. 1-47-42-39-69; fax 1-47-42-03-53; e-mail focadres@force-ouvriere.fr; internet www.uci-fo.com; Sec.-Gen. ERIC PERES.

FO-Cheminots (Railway Workers): 61 rue de la Chapelle, 75018 Paris; tel. 1-55-26-94-00; fax 1-55-26-94-01; e-mail federation@fo-cheminots.com; internet www.fo-cheminots.com; f. 1948; Sec.-Gen. ERIC FALEMPIN.

FO-Coiffure, Esthétique, Parfumerie (Hairdressers, Beauticians and Perfumery): 131 rue Damrémont, 75018 Paris; tel. 1-53-01-61-13; fax 1-53-01-61-45; e-mail fcoiffure@force-ouvriere.fr; Sec.-Gen. GUY MARIN.

FO-Communications (Post and Telecommunications): 60 rue Vergniaud, 75640 Paris Cedex 13; tel. 1-40-78-31-50; fax 1-40-78-30-58; e-mail federation@fo-com.com; internet www.fo-com.com; f. 1947; Sec.-Gen. JACQUES LEMERCIER.

FO-Cuirs, Textiles, Habillement (Leather, Textiles and Clothing): 7 passage Tenaille, 75680 Paris Cedex 14; tel. 1-40-52-83-00; fax 1-40-52-82-99; e-mail fvanderosieren@force-ouvriere.fr; Sec.-Gen. FRANCIS VAN DE ROSIEREN.

FO-Défense, Industries de l'Armement et Secteurs Assimilés (Defence and Arms Manufacture): 46 rue des Petites Ecuries, 75010 Paris; tel. 1-42-46-00-05; fax 1-45-23-12-89; e-mail fediasa@force-ouvriere.fr; internet www.fodefense.com; Sec.-Gen. CHARLES SISTACH.

FO-Employés et Cadres (Office Workers and Private Sector Managerial Staff): 28 rue des Petits Hôtels, 75010 Paris; tel. 1-48-01-91-91; fax 1-48-01-91-92; e-mail fecfo@force-ouvriere.fr; internet www.fecfo.fr; Sec.-Gen. SERGE LEGAGNOA.

FO-Energie et Mines (Energy and Mines): 60 rue Vergniaud, 75640 Paris Cedex 13; tel. 1-44-16-86-20; fax 1-44-16-86-32; e-mail federation@fnem-fo.fr; internet www.fnem-fo.fr; Sec.-Gen. MAX ROYER.

FO-Enseignement, Culture et Formation Professionnelle (Teaching): 6–8 rue Gaston-Lauriau, 93513 Montreuil Cedex; tel. 1-56-93-22-22; fax 1-56-93-22-20; e-mail fnecfpfo@fr.oleane.com; internet fo-fnecfp.fr; Sec.-Gen. FRANÇOIS CHAINTRON.

FO-Equipements, Environnement, Transports et Services (Transport and Public Works): 46 rue des Petites Ecuries, 75010 Paris; tel. 1-44-83-86-20; fax 1-48-24-38-32; e-mail fetsfo@force-ouvriere.fr; internet www.fets-fo.fr; f. 1932; Sec.-Gen. JEAN HEDOU.

FO-Fédéchimie (Chemical Industries): 60 rue Vergniaud, 75640 Paris Cedex 13; tel. 1-45-80-14-90; fax 1-45-80-08-03; e-mail fochimie@force-ouvriere.fr; internet www.fedechimie-cgtfo.com; f. 1948; Sec.-Gen. HERVÉ QUILLET.

FO-Finances: 46 rue des Petites Ecuries, 75010 Paris; tel. 1-42-46-75-20; fax 1-47-70-23-92; e-mail fo.finances@wanadoo.fr; internet www.financesfo.fr; Sec.-Gen. MICHEL MONTEIL.

FO-Fonctionnaires (Civil Servants): 46 rue des Petites Ecuries, 75010 Paris; tel. 1-44-83-69-55; fax 1-42-46-97-80; e-mail fofonctionnaires@force-ouvriere.fr; internet www.fo-fonctionnaires.fr; Sec.-Gen. GÉRARD NOGUÈS.

FO-Livre (Printing Trades): 7 passage Tenaille, 75680 Paris Cedex 14; tel. 1-40-52-85-00; fax 1-40-52-85-01; e-mail psacquepee@force-ouvriere.fr; Sec.-Gen. PATRICE SACQUÉPÉE.

FO-Métaux (Metals): 9 rue Baudouin, 75013 Paris; tel. 1-53-94-54-00; fax 1-45-83-78-87; e-mail contact@fo-metaux.fr; internet www.fo-metaux.com; Sec.-Gen. FRÉDÉRIC HOMEZ.

FO-Mineurs, Miniers et Similaires (Mine Workers): 7 passage Tenaille, 75014 Paris; tel. 1-40-52-85-50; fax 1-40-52-85-48; e-mail fo.mineurs@wanadoo.fr; Sec.-Gen. JEAN-PIERRE DAMM.

FO-Pharmacie, Officine-Industrie VM, Droguerie-Répartition, Laboratoire d'Analyse (Pharmacists, Druggists and Analytical Laboratories): 7 passage Tenaille, 75680 Paris Cedex 14; tel. 1-40-52-85-60; fax 1-40-52-85-61; e-mail fopharma@wanadoo.fr; internet www.fo-pharmacie.com; Sec.-Gen. GILBERT LEBRUMENT.

FO-Police: 146–148 rue Picpus, 75012 Paris; tel. 1-53-46-11-00; fax 1-44-68-07-41; e-mail xbeugnet@force-ouvriere.fr; f. 1948; Sec.-Gen. NICOLAS COMTE.

FO-Services des Départements et Régions (Local and Regional Government): 46 rue des Petites Ecuries, 75010 Paris; tel. 1-42-46-50-52; fax 1-47-70-26-06; e-mail msimonnin@force-ouvriere.fr; f. 1984; Sec.-Gen. MICHÈLE SIMONNIN.

FO-Services Publics et de Santé (Health and Public Services): 153–155 rue de Rome, 75017 Paris; tel. 1-44-01-06-00; fax 1-42-27-21-40; e-mail fosps@force-ouvriere.fr; internet www.fo-publics-sante.org; f. 1947; Sec.-Gen. JEAN-MARIE BELLOT.

FO-Spectacles, Audiovisuel, Presse, Multimedia (FASAPFO) (Theatre, Broadcasting, Press, Multimedia): 2 rue de la Michodière, 75002 Paris; tel. 1-47-42-35-86; fax 1-47-42-39-45; e-mail fasap-fo@wanadoo.fr; Sec.-Gen. FRANÇOISE CHAZAUD.

FO-Transports et Logistique: 7 passage Tenaille, 75680 Paris Cedex 14; tel. 1-40-52-85-65; fax 1-40-52-85-09; e-mail federation@fo-transports.com; Gen. Sec. GÉRARD APRUZZESE.

Other federations:

Confédération Française de l'Encadrement (CFE—CGC): 59–63 rue du Rocher, 75008 Paris; tel. 1-55-30-12-12; fax 1-55-30-13-13; e-mail presse@cfecgc.fr; internet www.cfecgc.fr; f. 1944; organizes managerial staff, professional staff and technicians; co-ordinates unions in every industry and sector; Nat. Pres. BERNARD VAN CRAEYNEST; Sec.-Gen. GÉRARD LABRUNE; 160,000 mems (2006).

Confédération Française des Travailleurs Chrétiens (CFTC): 13 rue des Ecluses Saint Martin, 75483 Paris Cedex 10; tel. 1-44-52-49-00; fax 1-44-52-49-18; e-mail eurint@cftc.fr; internet www.cftc.fr; f. 1919; present form in 1964 after majority CFTC became CFDT (see above); mem. European Trade Union Confederation, World Confederation of Labour; Chair. JACQUES VOISIN; Gen. Sec. JACKY DINTINGER; 132,000 mems.

Fédération Nationale des Syndicats Autonomes de l'Enseignement Supérieur et de la Recherche: 48 rue Vitruve, 75020 Paris; tel. 1-46-59-01-01; fax 1-46-59-01-23; higher education and research; Pres. JEAN-LOUIS CHARLET; Sec.-Gen. MICHEL GAY.

Fédération Nationale des Syndicats d'Exploitants Agricoles (FNSEA) (National Federation of Farmers' Unions): 11 rue de la Baume, 75008 Paris; tel. 1-53-83-47-47; fax 1-53-83-48-48; e-mail fnsea@fnsea.fr; internet www.fnsea.fr; f. 1946; comprises 92 departmental federations and 32,000 local unions; Chair. JEAN-MICHEL LEMÉTAYER; Dir-Gen. PATRICK FERRÈRE; 600,000 mems.

Fédération Syndicale Unitaire (FSU): 3–5 rue de Metz, 75010 Paris; tel. 1-44-79-90-30; fax 1-48-01-02-52; e-mail fsu.nationale@fsu.fr; internet www.fsu.fr; f. 1993; federation of civil service and education workers' unions; Sec.-Gen. GÉRARD ASCHIERI; 180,000 mems (2004).

Syndicat National Unitaire des Instituteurs Professeurs d'écoles et PEGC (SNUipp): 128 blvd Blanqui, 75013 Paris; tel. 1-44-08-69-30; fax 1-44-08-69-40; internet www.snuipp.fr; f. 1993; primary-school teachers; Sec-Gen. GILLES MOINDROT.

UNSA Education: 87 bis ave Georges Gosnat, 94853 Ivry-sur-Seine Cedex; tel. 1-56-20-29-50; fax 1-56-20-29-89; e-mail national@unsa-education.org; internet www.unsa-education.org; f. 1948; federation of teachers' unions; comprises 24 mem. unions; fmrly Fédération de l'Education Nationale; Sec.-Gen. PATRICK GONTHIER.

Transport

RAILWAYS

Most of the French railways are controlled by the Société Nationale des Chemins de fer Français (SNCF), established in 1937, and the Réseau Ferré de France (f. 1997) manages track and infrastructure. The SNCF is divided into 22 régions (areas). In 2007 the SNCF operated 30,990 km of track, of which 14,462 km were electrified. High-speed services (trains à grande vitesse—TGV) operate between Paris and various other destinations: Lyon (TGV Sud-Est), extending to Marseille or Nîmes (TGV Méditerranée), Bordeaux or Nantes (TGV Atlantique), and Lille (TGV Nord Europe). The TGV network covered 1,540 km of track in 2007. A further TGV line, linking Paris with Strasbourg and destinations in Germany, Luxembourg and Switzerland (TGV Est Européen), opened on 10 June 2007. The Parisian transport system is controlled by a separate authority, the Régie Autonome des Transports Parisiens (RATP). A number of small railways in the provinces are run by independent organizations.

Réseau Ferré de France (RFF): 92 ave de France, 75648 Paris Cedex 13; tel. 1-53-94-30-00; fax 1-53-94-38-00; internet www.rff.fr; f. 1997 to assume ownership and financial control of national rail infrastructure; state-owned; Pres. HUBERT DE MESNIL; Dir-Gen. JEAN-MARC DELION.

Société Nationale des Chemins de fer Français (SNCF): 34 rue du Commandant Mouchotte, 75699 Paris Cedex 14; tel. 1-53-25-60-00; fax 1-53-25-61-08; e-mail webcom@sncf.fr; internet www.sncf.fr; f. 1937; Pres. GUILLAUME PÉPY.

Channel Tunnel (Le Tunnel sous la Manche)

Groupe Eurotunnel: BP 69, Coquelles Cedex; tel. 3-21-00-65-43; internet www.eurotunnel.com; Anglo-French consortium contracted to design, finance and construct the Channel Tunnel under a concession granted for a period up to 2052 (later extended to 2086); receives finance exclusively from the private sector, including international commercial banks; the Channel Tunnel was formally opened in May 1994; operates a series of road vehicle 'shuttle' trains and passenger and freight trains through the Channel Tunnel; Chair. and Chief Exec. JACQUES GOUNON.

ROADS

At 31 December 2004 there were 10,490 km of motorways (autoroutes). There were also 25,730 km of national roads (routes nationales), 365,000 km of secondary roads and 550,000 km of major local roads.

Fédération Nationale des Transports Routiers (FNTR): 6 rue Ampère, 75017 Paris; tel. 1-44-29-04-29; fax 1-44-29-04-01; e-mail contact@fntr.fr; internet www.fntr.fr; f. 1933; road transport; Co-Chair. FRANÇOIS BRANCHE, PATRICK VERMOT-DESROCHES; 12,500 mem. cos.

METROPOLITAN TRANSPORT

Régie Autonome des Transports Parisiens (RATP): 54 quai de la Rapée, 75599 Paris Cedex 12; tel. 1-58-78-20-20; fax 1-58-78-31-70;

FRANCE

Directory

internet www.ratp.fr; f. 1949; state-owned; operates the Paris underground (comprising 16 lines totalling 200 km, and 381 stations), RER suburban railways (totalling 115 km in 2007), 3 suburban tram lines, and 345 bus routes; Pres. and Dir-Gen. PIERRE MONGIN.

Five provincial cities also have underground railway systems: Marseille, Lyon, Lille, Rennes and Toulouse. Tram networks have been constructed in several provincial cities since the 1980s.

INLAND WATERWAYS

At 20 February 2007 there were 8,501 km of navigable waterways, of which 1,621 km were accessible to craft of 3,000 metric tons.

Voies navigables de France: 175 rue Ludovic Boutleux, BP 820, 62408 Béthune Cedex; tel. 3-21-63-24-42; e-mail direction-generale@vnf.fr; internet www.vnf.fr; f. 1991; management and development of France's inland waterways; responsible for 3,800 km of navigable canals and 2,900 km of navigable rivers; Pres. FRANÇOIS BORDRY; Dir-Gen. GUY JANIN.

SHIPPING

The six major ports, Marseille, Le Havre, Dunkerque, Nantes-Saint-Nazaire, Rouen and Bordeaux, are operated by autonomous authorities, although the state retains supervisory powers.

Conseil National des Communautés Portuaires: Paris; tel. 1-40-81-86-11; f. 1987; central independent consultative and co-ordinating body for ports and port authorities; more than 50 mems, including 10 trade union mems; Pres. JACQUES DUPUY-DAUBY; Sec.-Gen. M. DE ROCQUIGNY DU FAYEL.

Direction du Transport Maritime, des Ports et du Littoral (DTMPL): 22 rue Monge, 75005 Paris; tel. 1-40-81-72-10; f. 1997; Govt body responsible for the economic development of port and civil maritime activities and the protection of the coast; Dir DIDIER SIMMONET.

Port Autonome Atlantique—Nantes-Saint Nazaire: Nantes; tel. 2-40-44-20-26; fax 2-40-44-21-81; e-mail ser.com@nantes.port .fr; internet www.nantes.port.fr; f. 1966; Pres. MICHEL QUIMBERT; Dir-Gen. FRANÇOIS MARENDET.

Port Autonome de Bordeaux: 3 pl. Gabriel, 33075 Bordeaux; tel. 5-56-90-58-00; fax 5-56-90-58-80; e-mail postoffice@bordeaux-port .fr; internet www.bordeaux-port.fr; Pres. MICHEL SAMMARCELLI; Dir-Gen. PHILIPPE DEISS.

Port Autonome de Dunkerque: terre-plein Guillain, 59386 Dunkerque Cedex 01; tel. 3-28-28-78-78; fax 3-28-28-78-77; e-mail info@portdedunkerque.fr; internet www.portdedunkerque.fr; Pres. JO DAIRIN; Dir-Gen. JEAN-CLAUDE TERRIER.

Port Autonome de Marseille: 23 pl. de la Joliette, BP 1965, 13226 Marseille Cedex 02; tel. 4-91-39-40-00; fax 4-91-39-57-00; e-mail pam@marseille-port.fr; internet www.marseille-port.fr; Pres. CHRISTIAN GARIN; Dir-Gen. ERIC BRASSART.

Port Autonome du Havre: BP 1413, 76067 Le Havre Cedex; tel. 2-32-74-74-00; fax 2-32-74-74-29; e-mail pahmail@havre-port.fr; internet www.havre-port.fr; Chair. JEAN-PIERRE LECOMTE; Dir-Gen. JEAN-MARC LACAVE.

Port Autonome de Rouen: 34 blvd de Boisguilbert, BP 4075, 76022 Rouen Cedex 03; tel. 2-35-52-54-56; fax 2-35-52-54-13; e-mail dg@rouen.port.fr; internet www.rouen.port.fr; Pres. GHISLAIN DE BOISSIEU; Dir-Gen. MARTINE BONNY.

Port de Calais: pl. de l'Europe, 62226 Calais Cedex; tel. 3-21-96-31-20; fax 3-21-34-08-92; e-mail ccic@calais.cci.fr; internet www .calais-port.com; Pres. HENRI RAVISSE.

Principal Shipping Companies

Note: Not all the vessels belonging to the companies listed below are registered under the French flag.

Brittany Ferries: Port du Bloscon, BP 72, 29688 Roscoff Cedex; tel. 2-98-29-28-00; fax 2-98-29-27-00; e-mail compay@brittany-ferries.fr; internet www.brittany-ferries.fr; f. 1972 as Bretagne-Angleterre-Irlande (BAI); transport between France, Ireland, Spain and the United Kingdom; Chair. ALEXIS GOURVENNEC; Man. Dir MICHEL MARAVAL.

Broström Tankers, SAS: 52 ave des Champs-Elysées, 75008 Paris; tel. 1-42-99-66-66; fax 1-42-99-66-20; e-mail brotank.paris@brostrom .fr; internet www.brostroms.se; subsidiary of Broström AB (Sweden); fmrly Van Ommeren Tankers; oil product and chemical coastal tankers and tramping.

Compagnie Maritime Marfret: 13 quai de la Joliette, 13002 Marseille; tel. 4-91-56-91-00; fax 4-91-56-91-01; e-mail mfmedsea@marfret.fr; internet www.marfret.fr; freight services to the Mediterranean, South America, the Caribbean, Canada and northern Europe; Dir-Gen. BERNARD VIDIL.

Consortium Européen de Transports Maritimes (CETRAMAR): 87 ave de la Grande Armée, 75782 Paris Cedex 16; tel. 1-40-66-11-11; fax 1-45-00-77-35; Chair. PHILIPPE POIRIER D'ANGÉ D'ORSAY; Man. Dir ANDRÉ MAIRE; displacement 564,291 grt.

Corsica Ferries: 5 bis rue Chanoine Leschi, 20296 Bastia; tel. 4-95-32-95-95; fax 4-95-32-14-71; internet www.corsicaferries.com; affiliated to Groupe Lota Maritime; passenger and freight ferry services between Corsica, Sardinia, mainland France, and mainland Italy; Pres. PASCAL LOTA.

Esso France: 2 rue des Martinets, 92569 Rueil-Malmaison Cedex; tel. 1-47-10-60-00; fax 1-47-10-60-44; internet www.esso.com/eaff/essofrance; f. 1952; merged with Mobil Oil Française in 2003; Chair. and Man. Dir PATRICK HEINZLE.

Groupe CMA—CGM: Marseille; tel. 4-91-39-30-00; fax 4-91-39-30-95; e-mail webmaster@cma-cgm.com; internet www.cma-cgm.com; f. 1996 by merger of Compagnie Générale Maritime and Compagnie Maritime d'Affrètement; freight services to USA, Canada, the Caribbean, Central and South America, the Mediterranean, the Middle East, the Far East, India, Australia, New Zealand, Indonesia, East Africa and other Pacific and Indian Ocean areas; 25 ships owned; Chair. JACQUES R. SAADÉ; Dir-Gens FARID T. SALEM, ALAIN WILS; displacement 1,900,000 grt (2001).

Louis Dreyfus Armateurs (LDA): 87 ave de la Grande Armée, 75782 Paris Cedex 16; tel. 1-40-66-11-11; fax 1-45-00-23-97; e-mail gehannep@lda.fr; internet www.lda.fr; gas and bulk carriers; Pres. PHILIPPE LOUIS-DREYFUS; Chief Exec. P. GEHANNE.

Navale Française SA: 8 blvd Victor Hugo, 34000 Montpellier; tel. 4-67-58-82-12; fax 4-67-92-98-34; Chair. MARC CHEVALLIER.

SeaFrance: Nouveau Terminal Car Ferry, 62100 Calais; tel. 8-03-04-40-45; e-mail presse@seafrance.net; internet www.seafrance.fr; wholly owned subsidiary of Société Nationale des Chemins de Fer Français; f. 1996 to replace Société Nouvelle d'Armement Transmanche (SNAT); vehicle and passenger services between France and the United Kingdom, Ireland and the Channel Islands; Man. Dir EUDES RIBLIER.

Société d'Armement et de Transport (Socatra): 9 allées de Tourny, 33000 Bordeaux; tel. 5-56-00-00-56; fax 5-56-48-51-23; e-mail direction@socatra.com; internet www.socatra.com; f. 1977; Chair. F. BOZZONI; Man. Dir M. DUBOURG.

Société Européenne de Transport Maritime: 9 allées de Tourny, 33000 Bordeaux; tel. 5-56-00-00-56; fax 5-56-48-51-23; Man. Dirs GILLES BOUTHILLIER, FERNAND BOZZONI; displacement 53,261 grt.

Société Nationale Maritime Corse-Méditerranée (SNCM): 61 blvd des Dames, BP 1963, 13226 Marseille Cedex 02; tel. 4-91-56-32-00; fax 4-91-56-34-94; e-mail info@sncm.fr; internet www.sncm.fr; passenger and roll on/roll off ferry services between France and Corsica, Sardinia, North Africa; also subsidiary Corsica Maritima; 25% state-owned, managed by Veolia Transport (owners of a 28% share) from 2006; Chair. PIERRE VIEU; displacement 141,454 grt.

Société Navale Caennaise: Caen; tel. 2-31-72-54-00; fax 2-31-78-04-94; e-mail veluma@mail.cpod.fr; internet perso.normandnet.fr/navale; f. 1901; cargo services to Europe and West Africa; Chair. and Man. Dir A. LABAT; displacement 59,680 grt.

Société Services et Transports: route du Hoc Gonfreville-L'Orcher, 76700 Harfleur; tel. 2-35-24-72-00; fax 2-35-53-36-25; petroleum and gas transport, passenger transport; Chair. YVES ROUSIER; Man. Dir JACQUES CHARVET; displacement 118,274 grt.

CIVIL AVIATION

The principal international airports are at Orly and Roissy-Charles de Gaulle (Paris), Bordeaux, Lille, Lyon, Marseille, Nice, Strasbourg and Toulouse.

Aéroports de Paris: 291 blvd de Raspail, 75675 Paris Cedex 14; tel. 1-43-35-70-00; fax 1-43-35-72-00; e-mail webmaster@adp.fr; internet www.adp.fr; majority state-controlled authority in charge of Paris airports at Orly and Roissy-Charles de Gaulle, 11 other airports for light aircraft, including Le Bourget, and a heliport at Issy-les-Moulineaux; Pres. PIERRE GRAFF; Man. Dir FRANÇOIS RUBICHON.

Airlines

Air France: 45 rue de Paris, 95747 Roissy Cedex; tel. 1-41-56-78-00; fax 1-41-56-70-29; internet www.airfrance.net; f. 1933; 18.6% state-owned; merged with KLM (Netherlands) in 2004; internal, international, European and inter-continental services; 240 destinations in 105 countries world-wide; Chair. JEAN-CYRIL SPINETTA.

Brit Air: Aéroport, CS 27925-29679 Morlaix; tel. 2-98-63-63-63; fax 2-98-62-77-66; internet www.britair.com; f. 1973; domestic and European flights; 99% owned by Air France; Pres. and Dir-Gen. MARC LAMIDEY.

Corsairfly: 2 ave Charles Lindbergh, 94636 Rungis Cedex; tel. 1-49-79-49-59; fax 1-49-79-49-95; internet www.corsairfly.com; f. 1981; scheduled flights between metropolitan France and Italy, Madagascar, Morocco, Kenya, and the French overseas possessions, and chartered flights to other medium- and long-range destinations; owned by TUI AG Group (Germany); Pres. PIERRE CHESNEAU; Man. Dir HERVÉ PIERRET.

Hex'Air: Aéroport Le Puy, 43320 Loudes; tel. 4-71-08-62-28; fax 4-71-08-04-10; e-mail contact@hexair.com; internet www.hexair.com; f. 1991; domestic services; Pres. Dir-Gen. ALEXANDRE ROUCHON.

Régional—Compagnie Aérienne Européenne: Aéroport Nantes Atlantique, 44345 Bouguenais Cedex; tel. 2-40-13-53-00; fax 2-40-13-53-08; e-mail contact@regional.com; internet www.regional.com; f. 2001 by merger of Flandre Air, Proteus and Regional Airlines; operates European and domestic flights; subsidiary of Air France; Pres. and Dir-Gen. JEAN-YVES GROSSE.

XL Airways France: Bâtiment Mars, Continental Sq. II, 3 place de Berlin, 13760 Tremblay; tel. 1-48-15-90-00; internet www.xlairways.fr; f. 1995 as Star Airlines; acquired by XL Leisure Group (United Kingdom) in 2006; charter and scheduled flights between France and Cuba, the Dominican Republic, Egypt, Finland, Greece, Italy, the Maldives, Mauritius, Mexico, Morocco and Senegal; Dir-Gen. LAURENT MAGNIN.

Airline Associations

Fédération Nationale de l'Aviation Marchande (FNAM): 28 rue de Châteaudun, 75009 Paris; tel. 1-45-26-23-24; fax 1-45-26-23-95; e-mail info@fnam.fr; internet www.fnam.fr; f. 1991; Delegate-Gen. JEAN-PIERRE LE GOFF.

Chambre Syndicale du Transport Aérien (CSTA): 28 rue de Châteaudun, 75009 Paris; tel. 1-45-26-23-24; fax 1-45-26-23-95; e-mail info@fnam.fr; internet www.fnam.fr/syndicats/csta.asp; f. 1947; represents French airlines at national level; Pres. LIONEL GUERIN.

Tourism

France is the world's principal tourist destination. Paris is famous for its boulevards, historic buildings, theatres, art treasures, fashion houses, restaurants and night clubs. The Mediterranean and Atlantic coasts and the French Alps are the most popular tourist resorts. Among other attractions are the many ancient towns, the châteaux of the Loire, the fishing villages of Brittany and Normandy, and spas and places of pilgrimage, such as Vichy and Lourdes. The theme park, Disneyland Resort Paris, also attracts large numbers of tourists. There were 76.0m. tourist arrivals in 2005; tourism receipts in that year totalled US $42,167m. Most visitors are from the United Kingdom, Germany, the Netherlands, Belgium and Italy.

Direction du Tourisme: 23 place de Catalogne, 75685 Paris Cedex 14; tel. 1-70-39-93-00; internet www.tourisme.gouv.fr; Dir MICHEL CHAMPON.

Maison de la France: 23 place de Catalogne, 75685 Paris Cedex 14; tel. 1-42-96-70-00; fax 1-42-96-70-11; internet www.franceguide.com; f. 1987; Pres. ALAIN JACQUIER; Dir-Gen. THIERRY BAUDIER.

There are Regional Tourism Committees in the 23 regions. There are more than 3,600 Offices de Tourisme and Syndicats d'Initiative (tourist offices operated by the local authorities) throughout France.

FRENCH OVERSEAS POSSESSIONS

Ministry of the Interior, the Overseas Possessions and Territorial Collectivities: 27 rue Oudinot, 75007 Paris, France; tel. 1-53-69-20-00; internet www.outre-mer.gouv.fr.
Minister of the Interior, the Overseas Possessions and Territorial Collectivities: MICHÈLE ALLIOT-MARIE.
The national flag of France, proportions two by three, with three equal vertical stripes, of blue, white and red, is used in the Overseas Possessions.

French Overseas Regions and Departments

As amended in March 2003, the Constitution defines French Guiana, Guadeloupe, Martinique and Réunion as being simultaneously Overseas Regions (régions d'outre-mer) and Overseas Departments (départements d'outre-mer) within the French Republic. National legislation is fully applicable, although, other than in the areas of justice, the police, the armed forces and public freedoms, some provision is made for local adaptation within the framework of the law.

FRENCH GUIANA

Introductory Survey

Location, Climate, Language, Religion, Capital
French Guiana (Guyane) lies on the north coast of South America, with Suriname to the west and Brazil to the south and east. The climate is humid, with a season of heavy rains from April to July and another short rainy season in December and January. Average temperature at sea-level is 27°C (85°F), with little seasonal variation. French is the official language, but a Creole patois is also spoken. The majority of the population belongs to the Roman Catholic Church, although other Christian churches are represented. The capital is Cayenne.

Recent History
French occupation commenced in the early 17th century. After brief periods of Dutch, English and Portuguese rule, the territory was finally confirmed as French in 1817. The colony steadily declined, after a short period of prosperity in the 1850s as a result of the discovery of gold in the basin of the Approuague river. French Guiana, including the notorious Devil's Island, was used as a penal colony and as a place of exile for convicts and political prisoners before the practice was halted in 1937. The colony became a Department of France in 1946.

French Guiana's reputation as an area of political and economic stagnation was dispelled by the growth of pro-independence sentiments, and the use of violence by a small minority, compounded by tensions between the Guyanais and large numbers of immigrant workers. In 1974 French Guiana was granted regional status, as part of France's governmental reorganization, thus acquiring greater economic autonomy. In that year, none the less, demonstrations against unemployment, the worsening economic situation and French government policy with regard to the Department led to the detention of leading trade unionists and pro-independence politicians. Further industrial and political unrest in the late 1970s prompted the Parti Socialiste Guyanais (PSG), then the strongest political organization, to demand greater autonomy for the Department. In 1980 there were several bomb attacks against 'colonialist' targets by an extremist group, Fo nou Libéré la Guyane. Reforms introduced by the French Socialist Government in 1982–83 devolved some power over local affairs to the new Conseil régional (Regional Council). In the February 1983 election to the Conseil régional the left-wing parties gained a majority of votes, but not of seats, and the balance of power was held by the separatist Union des Travailleurs Guyanais (UTG), the political wing of which became the Parti National Populaire Guyanais (PNPG) in November 1985. At the election to the Conseil général (General Council) held in March 1985, the PSG and left-wing independents secured 13 seats out of a total of 19.

For the general election to the Assemblée nationale (National Assembly) in March 1986, French Guiana's representation was increased from one to two deputies. The PSG increased its strength on the Conseil régional following a simultaneous election to that body, and Georges Othily of the PSG was re-elected President of the Conseil. Left-wing parties won a majority of seats at the election to the Conseil général in 1988. In September 1989 Othily was elected to take French Guiana's seat in the French Sénat (Senate). Othily had recently been expelled from the PSG for having worked too closely with the opposition parties. However, he attracted support from those who regarded the party's domination of French Guiana as corrupt, and his victory over the incumbent senator, a PSG member, was believed to reflect the level of dissatisfaction within the party. In December Othily formed his own party, the Forces Démocratiques Guyanaises (FDG), which included other dissident members of the PSG.

In March 1992 elections were held to both the Conseil général and the Conseil régional. The PSG dominated in both ballots: party leader Elie Castor retained the presidency of the Conseil général while the PSG Secretary-General, Antoine Karam, was elected as President of the Conseil régional. In a referendum in September, 67% of voters in French Guiana approved ratification of the Treaty on European Union (see p. 244), although a high abstention rate was recorded.

At the March 1993 elections to the Assemblée nationale Léon Bertrand of the Gaullist Rassemblement pour la République (RPR) was re-elected, along with Christiane Taubira-Delannon, the founder of the independent left-wing Walwari movement and an outspoken critic of existing policies for the management of French Guiana's natural resources.

The PSG's representation in the Conseil général fell following the March 1994 cantonal elections; none the less, one of its members, Stéphan Phinéra-Horth, was subsequently elected President of the Conseil (Elie Castor having left the party). Taubira-Delannon, defeated by Karam, failed to secure election, although another member of the Walwari movement did enter the Conseil. In June Taubira-Delannon was elected to the European Parliament as a representative of the Energie Radicale grouping, which secured the greatest percentage of the votes (36%) in the Department, ahead of the government list and a combined list of the parties of the left of the four Overseas Departments.

Beginning in late October 1996 a boycott of classes by secondary-school pupils, who were demanding improved conditions of study, escalated in the following month into a crisis that was regarded as exemplifying wider social tensions between the Department and metropolitan France. The refusal of the Prefect, Pierre Dartout, to receive schools' representatives prompted protests in Cayenne, which swiftly degenerated into rioting and looting, apparently as the protesters were joined by disaffected youths from deprived areas. Considerable material damage was caused to government and commercial property during two nights of violence. The central Government dispatched anti-riot police to assist the local security forces, and it was announced that the Secretary of State for Overseas Departments and Territories, Jean-Jacques de Peretti, and the Minister of National Education, François Bayrou, would visit French Guiana. However, the conviction, shortly afterwards, of several people implicated in the rioting provoked further protests and clashes with security forces, and a one-day general strike in Cayenne, organized by the UTG, resulted in the closure of most businesses and government departments. The extent of the security forces' actions in suppressing the demonstrations was criticized, while the competence of the Department's administrators in their approach to the crisis was the focus of considerable scrutiny. Local officials, meanwhile, denounced the role in the violence not only of unemployed youths but also of separatist groups, alleging that the latter were seeking to exploit the crisis for their own ends. Bayrou and de Peretti subsequently arrived in Cayenne to meet those involved in the crisis. Local administrators and schools' representatives had already reached agreement on the students' material demands, but, to considerable local acclaim, the ministers announced the establishment of separate Academies for French Guiana, Guadeloupe and Martinique, effective from the beginning of 1997. The creation was also announced of additional primary educational facilities, and a programme was declared to improve academic standards in secondary schools. In all, the measures were to cost the French Government more than 500m. francs.

In April 1997 violent incidents followed the arrest of five pro-independence activists suspected of setting fire to the home of the public prosecutor during the disturbances of November 1996. Five others, including leading members of the UTG and the PNPG, were subsequently detained in connection with the arson incident. The transfer of all 10 detainees to Martinique prompted further violent protests in Cayenne: police reinforcements were dispatched by the central Government to help suppress the violence. In July one of the detainees, Jean-Victor Castor, a prominent member of the UTG and the pro-independence Mouvement de la Décolonisation et d'Emancipation Sociale (MDES), who had been released the previous month, was rearrested and accused of assaulting a policeman during the April riots. Following the announcement, in August, that Castor was to remain in custody, some 200 demonstrators clashed with riot police in Cayenne. Castor was released shortly afterwards, and in September a further four separatists, who had been held on remand since April, were also freed.

In late May and early June 1997 Léon Bertrand and Christiane Taubira-Delannon were both re-elected to the Assemblée nationale in elections that were marked by a high rate of abstention. Candidates from pro-independence parties notably gained increased support, winning slightly more than 10% of the votes cast in both constituencies.

Elections to the Conseil régional and the Conseil général were held in March 1998. The PSG's representation in the former declined to 11 seats, with other left-wing candidates securing a further 11 seats (including two won by Walwari). Antoine Karam was re-elected to the presidency of the Conseil régional. The PSG also lost seats in the Conseil général, retaining only five of the 19 seats, while other left-wing candidates took a further five, and independent candidates won seven seats. André Lecante, an independent left-wing councillor, was elected as the body's President, defeating the incumbent, Phinéra-Horth. In late September 1998 Georges Othily was re-elected to the Sénat.

In January 1999 representatives of 10 separatist organizations from French Guiana, Guadeloupe and Martinique, including the MDES and the PNPG, signed a joint declaration denouncing 'French colonialism', in which they stated their intention to campaign for the reinstatement of the three Caribbean Overseas Departments on a UN list of territories to be decolonized. At a congress held in February, members of the Conseil régional and the Conseil général proposed the replacement of the two Conseils with a single body. In October, however, the Prime Minister, Lionel Jospin, precluded from future legislation any merger of the Conseil régional and Conseil général. Following a series of meetings held in late 1999, in December the Presidents of the regional councils of French Guiana, Guadeloupe and Martinique signed a joint declaration in Basse-Terre, Guadeloupe, affirming their intention to propose, to the President and the Government, a legislative amendment aimed at creating a new status of overseas region. However, in February 2000 the Secretary of State for Overseas Departments and Territories, Jean-Jack Queyranne, dismissed the declaration as unconstitutional and exceeding the mandate of politicians responsible. In March, during a visit to the Department by Queyranne, rioting broke out following his refusal to meet a delegation of separatist organizations. Later that month the Conseil régional overwhelmingly rejected reforms proposed by Queyranne in February, which included the creation of a Congrès (Congress) in French Guiana, as well as the extension of the Departments' powers in areas such as regional co-operation. Nevertheless, the proposals were approved by the Assemblée nationale in November, and in December they were ratified by the Constitutional Council.

In November 2000 several people were injured following riots in Cayenne. The demonstrations followed a march, organized by the UTG, demanding greater autonomy for French Guiana, as well as immediate negotiations with the new Secretary of State for Overseas Departments and Territories, Christian Paul. Protesters claimed they had been excluded from talks on French Guiana's status (Paul had invited leaders of various political parties in French Guiana to attend a meeting to be held in France in December, but the offer was rejected by MDES activists, who demanded the meeting be held in Cayenne). Nevertheless, discussions were held in mid-December in Paris at which Paul, various senior politicians from French Guiana and representatives from the PSG, the RPR, Walwari, and the FDG were present. In early January 2001, following further consultations, it was agreed that a document detailing proposals for increased autonomy for French Guiana was to be drawn up by local officials and was to be presented to the French Government for approval. Following a meeting of members of both Conseils in June, a series of proposals on greater autonomy, to be presented to the French Government, was agreed upon. These included: the division of the territory into four districts; the creation of a Territorial Collectivity (collectivité territoriale), governed by a 41-member Assembly elected for a five-year term; and the establishment of an independent executive council. Furthermore, the proposals included a request that the territory be given control over legislative and administrative affairs, as well as legislative authority on matters concerning French Guiana alone. In November the French Government announced itself to be in favour of the suggested constitutional developments; in March 2003 a constitutional amendment conferred the status of Overseas Region (région d'outre-mer) on French Guiana. Referendums held in December in Guadeloupe and Martinique on the question of legislative reform prompted renewed demands by pro-independence campaigners for a referendum to address the issue of greater autonomy for French Guiana. Meanwhile, in mid-2001 the French President, Jacques Chirac, rejected a joint request by French Guiana, Guadeloupe and Martinique that they be permitted to join, as associate members, the Association of Caribbean States (see p. 411).

At elections to the presidency of the Conseil général conducted in March 2001, the left-wing independent candidate Joseph Ho-Ten-You defeated André Lecante. At the legislative elections held in June 2002, Taubira-Delannon was re-elected to the Assemblée nationale with 65% of the vote, and Bertrand with 64%; about two-thirds of registered voters abstained. In July Ange Mancini was appointed Prefect, replacing Henri Masse.

In September 2001 Christian Paul announced the establishment of a number of measures designed to improve security in the Department. Plans included a 20% increase in the police force, the creation of a small 'peace corps' and a continuous police presence in the town of Maripasoula and its surrounding region, following concerns over the security of gold prospectors in the area. In the same month the gendarmerie, in co-operation with the national police, launched 'Operation Anaconda' in the south of the Department, aimed at stopping the illegal gold trade. Unlicensed gold-mining operations were a chief cause of illegal immigration, and a focus for other criminal activities, such as drugs-smuggling and gun-running. They also caused extensive environmental damage, destroying natural habitats, polluting watercourses and spreading disease. 'Operation Anaconda' remained ongoing in early 2008. It was reported that some 6,000 illegal immigrants had been expelled in 2005. In 2006 the number of expulsions rose by more than 50% to 9,711; however, the deportees included a substantial proportion (59%) of recidivists. Official estimates put the total number of illegal immigrants in French Guiana at between 30,000 and 35,000, the majority from Brazil and Suriname. At that time there were some 41,903 registered foreigners living in French Guiana, many attracted by the relative affluence of the Department, where wages were reported to be between four and 10 times as much as in other countries in the region.

In elections to the Conseil régional held in March 2004 the PSG won 17 of the council's 31 seats with 37.7% of the votes cast, while a joint list presented by the FDG and Walwari, and the Union pour un Mouvement Populaire (UMP), each won seven seats, with 31.2% and 31.1% of the ballot, respectively. Antoine Karam was duly re-elected as President of the Conseil régional. In late May 2005 a national referendum was held on ratification of the European Union constitutional treaty: in the Department 60.1% of participating voters were in favour of adopting the treaty; however, voter turn-out was low, at just 23.1%. The treaty was ultimately rejected by a majority of voters in metropolitan France.

In early January 2006 a strike by dockers over working conditions, introduced the previous November, paralysed the port at Dégrad-des-Cannes for 12 days, causing a backlog of more than 200 shipping containers. An agreement was eventually reached with local employers' organizations, but the strike was expected to have had a serious impact on the local economy, particularly on smaller companies and those dependent on primary materials. It was the fourth such strike since January 2005.

In early December 2006 a week of industrial action by employees in the electricity sector led to long periods without power across the Department. The strike was in protest at proposed plans by the state-owned Electricité de France (EdF) to remodel its operations, which employees feared would result in at least a degree of privatization. On 7 December some 200 protesters attended a demonstration in Cayenne to signal their opposition to the blackouts. The industrial action was suspended following an agreement by EdF to schedule negotiations in Paris with trade unions, including the UTG.

At the first round of the national presidential election, held on 22 April 2007, the UMP candidate, Nicolas Sarkozy, won 41.4% of the votes cast in the Department, ahead of Ségolène Royal of the PS, who attracted 32.5% of ballot. At the second round, held on 6 May, Sarkozy secured the presidency, winning 53.1% of the votes cast in the Department. Meanwhile, at elections to the Assemblée nationale, held on 10 and 17 June, Taubira-Delannon, representing Walwari, was re-elected with 63.4% of the votes cast, while the PSG candidate Chantal Berthelot was elected with 52.9% of the ballot.

Government

France is represented in French Guiana by an appointed Prefect. There are two councils with local powers: the Conseil général, with 19 members, and the Conseil régional, with 31 members. Both are elected by universal adult suffrage for a period of six years. French Guiana elects two representatives to the Assemblée nationale in Paris, and sends one elected representative to the Sénat. French Guiana is also represented at the European Parliament.

Defence

As assessed at November 2007, France maintained a military force of 1,300 in French Guiana. There was also a gendarmerie of about 700 personnel.

Economic Affairs

In 2003 French Guiana's gross domestic product (GDP), measured at current prices, was US $1,551m., equivalent to $8,300 per head. Between 1990 and 2001, according to UN estimates, GDP increased, in real terms, at an average rate of 3.1% per year; growth in 2001 was 1.6%. Between the censuses of 1990 and 1999, according to provisional figures, the population increased at an average annual rate of 3.5%. According to official figures, in 2005 French Guiana's GDP was €1,729m., equivalent to €10,550 per head.

Agriculture (including fishing) engaged an estimated 2.1% of the economically active population in 2005. In 2003 the sector contributed 4.6% of GDP. In 2006 agricultural products accounted for some 16.5% of total export earnings, at €41.3m. The dominant activities are fisheries and forestry, although the contribution of the latter to export earnings has declined in recent years. In 2003 exports of shrimps accounted for 11.7% of export earnings; in 2005 shrimp production was recorded at 2,965 metric tons. In October 2005 the Compagnie Française de Pêche Nouvelle went into liquidation, in the face of competition from shrimp producers in Latin America and Asia and rising fuel prices. The principal crops for local consumption are cassava, vegetables and rice, and sugar cane is grown for making rum; rum production in 2006 was 3,175 hl. Livestock rearing was also largely for subsistence. In 2006 Guianese abattoirs produced an estimated 1,908 tons of meat, mostly pork, poultry and beef. Rice, pineapples and citrus fruit are cultivated for export. According to UN estimates, agricultural GDP decreased at an average annual rate of 0.8% in 1990–98; in 1998 agricultural GDP increased by an estimated 0.3%.

Industry, including construction and agrarian and food industries, contributed an estimated 20.3% to GDP in 2003, while in 2005 it engaged 13.7% of the employed labour force. The mining sector is dominated by the extraction of gold, which involves small-scale alluvial operations as well as larger local and multinational mining concerns. The first new concession in 70 years was awarded to Cambior in 2004 for a 25-year period. Estimated figures indicated that in 2005 1,955 kg of gold were mined, a decrease from the reported 2,564 kg in the previous year. Gold accounted for some 49.9% of export earnings in 2004. According to provisional figures, in 2005 exports of gold were worth €42,336m., a decrease on a peak of €95,308m. generated in 2002. Crushed rock for the construction industry is the only other mineral extracted in significant quantities, although exploratory drilling of known diamond deposits began in 1995. Deposits of bauxite, columbo-tantalite and kaolin are also present. There is little manufacturing activity, except for the processing of fisheries products (mainly shrimp-freezing) and the distillation of rum. In 1990–98 industrial GDP (excluding construction) increased at an average annual rate of 7.8%. The construction sector expanded at an average of 2.0% per year in the same period.

French Guiana was heavily dependent on imported fuels for the generation of energy prior to the flooding of the Petit-Saut hydro-electric dam, on the River Sinnamary, in 1994. Together with existing generating plants, the 116-MW dam was expected to satisfy the territory's electrical energy requirements for about 30 years. Imports of fuels and combustibles accounted for 12.3% of total imports in 2006.

The services sector engaged an estimated 84.2% of the employed labour force in 2005 and, according to official sources, contributed 75.2% of GDP in 2003. The European Space Agency's (ESA's) satellite-launching centre at Kourou has provided a considerable stimulus to the economy, most notably the construction sector (which engaged an estimated 5.8% of the employed labour force in 2005). The space centre was estimated to contribute approximately one-quarter of French Guiana's GDP and approximately one-half of its tax revenues. In 2007 there were 12 rocket launches. The tourism sector expanded in the last two decades of the 20th century, although its potential is limited by the lack of infrastructure away from the coast. In 2002 some 65,000 visitor arrivals were recorded, while receipts from tourism increased from an estimated US $42m. to $45m. in that year. In early 2003 the French Minister of the Overseas Possessions announced plans to stimulate the economies of French Guiana, Guadeloupe and Martinique that included the introduction of tax incentives for the hotel sector. In 2003 it was estimated that tourism contributed 3% of GDP.

In 2006 the principal source of imports was metropolitan France (which supplied 39.3% of total imports); the Department's other major suppliers were Trinidad and Tobago (11.9%), Germany and Martinique. Metropolitan France was also the principal market for exports in that year (55.4%); other important purchasers were Switzerland (16.1%), Italy and Germany. The principal imports in 2006 were products of agriculture and food industries, car industry products and fuels and combustibles; the principal exports were metals and metal products, car industry products, and products of agriculture and food industries. In 2006 French Guiana recorded an estimated trade deficit of €643.7m.

According to the 2006 regional budget, expenditure totalled €106.7m., while revenue was €110.7m. The departmental budget for 2006 put revenue at €263.8m., while expenditure was €234.1m. The annual rate of inflation averaged 1.3% in 1996–2006; the average rate of inflation in 2006 was 2.0%, an increase from 1.7% in the previous year. Unemployment in 2005 was estimated at 22.8% of the total labour force. However, there is a shortage of skilled labour, offset partly by immigration. In 2006 the number of unemployed fell to 11,983, compared with 13,292 in the previous year.

As an integral part of France, French Guiana is a member of the European Union (EU, see p. 244).

Economic development in French Guiana has been hindered by the Department's location, poor infrastructure away from the coast and lack of a skilled indigenous labour force, although there is considerable potential for further growth in the fishing, forestry and tourism (notably 'eco-tourism') sectors. A particular concern was the high rate of unemployment. French Guiana's geographical characteristics—large parts of the territory are accessible only by river—have resulted in difficulties in regulating key areas of the economy, such as gold-mining and forestry. Considerable concern has been expressed regarding the ecological consequences of such a lack of controls; moreover, the flooding of a large area of forest (some 340 sq km), as part of the Petit-Saut barrage project, prompted disquiet among environmental groups, as did uncertainty regarding the ecological implications of the satellite-launching programme at Kourou. The budget deficit represents a significant obstacle to growth, while high demand for imported consumer goods (much of which is generated by relatively well-remunerated civil servants, who constitute about two-thirds of the working population) undermines progress in reducing the trade deficit. In mid-July 2005 the Governments of France and Brazil signed an agreement to build a bridge across the Oiapoque, which, it was hoped, would stimulate trade and tourism between Brazil and French Guiana. Meanwhile, in early 2008 the French President, Nicolas Sarkozy, announced a plan to limit the operations of illegal gold prospectors, many of whom cross the southern border from Brazil.

Education

Education is modelled on the French system and is compulsory for children between six and 16 years of age. Primary education begins at six years of age and lasts for five years. Secondary education, beginning at 11 years of age, lasts for up to seven years, comprising a first cycle of four years and a second of three years. Education at state schools is provided free of charge. In 2005/06 there were 42 pre-primary schools, 105 primary schools and 40 secondary schools. In the same period there were 37,501 students in pre-primary and primary education, while in secondary education there were 26,337 (including 3,833 students in vocational education). Some 93% of students were educated in the state sector. Higher education in law, administration and French language and literature is provided by a branch of the Université des Antilles et de la Guyane in Cayenne, and an affiliated technical institute opened at Kourou in 1988 (IUT Kourou); in 2004/05 some 1,371 students were enrolled at the university in French Guiana (the university as a whole had some 11,746 enrolled students at that time). There is also a teacher-training college (IUFM) and an agricultural college. Total government expenditure on education amounted to 851m. French francs in 1993. The French Government announced its decision to increase expenditure in the education sector in 2000–06, including €71m. on the construction of new school buildings.

Public Holidays

2008: 1 January (New Year's Day), 4–5 February (Lenten Carnival), 6 February (Ash Wednesday), 24 March (Easter Monday), 1 May (Labour Day and Ascension Day), 8 May (Victory Day), 12 May (Whit Monday), 10 June (Abolition of Slavery), 14 July (National Day), 15 August (Assumption Day), 1 November (All Saints' Day), 11 November (Armistice Day), 25 December (Christmas Day).

2009: 1 January (New Year's Day), 24–25 February (Lenten Carnival), 27 February (Ash Wednesday), 13 April (Easter Monday), 1 May (Labour Day), 8 May (Victory Day), 21 May (Ascension Day), 1 June (Whit Monday), 10 June (Abolition of Slavery), 14 July (National

FRENCH OVERSEAS POSSESSIONS   *French Guiana*

Day), 15 August (Assumption Day), 1 November (All Saints' Day), 11 November (Armistice Day), 25 December (Christmas Day).

Weights and Measures
The metric system is in force.

Statistical Survey

Sources (unless otherwise indicated): Institut National de la Statistique et des Etudes Economiques (INSEE), Service Régional de Guyane, ave Pasteur, BP 6017, 97306 Cayenne Cédex; tel. 5-94-29-73-00; fax 5-94-29-73-01; internet www.insee.fr/fr/insee_regions/guyane; Chambre de Commerce et d'Industrie de la Guyane (CCIG), Hôtel Consulaire, pl. de l'Esplanade, BP 49, 97321 Cayenne Cédex; tel. 5-94-29-96-00; fax 5-94-29-96-34; internet www.guyane.cci.fr.

AREA AND POPULATION

Area: 83,534 sq km (32,253 sq miles).

Population: 114,808 (males 59,799; females 55,009) at census of 15 March 1990; 157,213 at census of 8 March 1999. *1 January 2007* (estimate): 208,964.

Density (at 1 January 2007, estimate): 2.5 per sq km.

Population by Nationality (1999): Brazilian 7,171; French 110,214; Guyanese 2,37; Haitian 14,143; Surinamese 17,654; Total (incl. others) 156,790.

Principal Towns (population at 1999 census): Cayenne (capital) 50,594; Saint-Laurent-du-Maroni 19,211; Kourou 19,107; Matoury 18,032; Rémire-Montjoly 15,555; Mana 5,445; Macouria 5,050; Maripasoula 3,710. *Mid-2005* (UN estimate, incl. suburbs): Cayenne 59,000 (Source: UN, *World Urbanization Prospects: The 2005 Revision*).

Births, Marriages and Deaths (2006 unless otherwise indicated): Registered live births 6,276 (birth rate 30.5 per 1,000); Registered marriages 596 (2005, marriage rate 3.0 per 1,000); Registered deaths 705 (death rate 3.5 per 1,000).

Expectation of Life (years at birth): 75.9 (males 72.6; females 79.9) in 2007. Source: Pan American Health Organization.

Economically Active Population (persons aged 15 years and over, 1999): Agriculture, forestry and fishing 2,888; Construction 3,256; Industry 3,524; Trade 4,573; Transport 1,616; Education, health and social services 8,990; Public administration 10,337; Other services 8,259; Total employed 43,443 (males 25,703; females 17,740). *2005* (estimates at 31 December): Agriculture 948; Industry 3,599; Construction 2,596; Trade 3,902; Services 34,052; Total employed 45,097; Unemployed 13,292; Total labour force 58,389. Note: Figures for employment exclude 5,929 unsalaried workers. *31 December 2006:* Unemployed 11,983.

HEALTH AND WELFARE
Key Indicators

Total Fertility Rate (children per woman, 2007): 3.3.
Under-5 Mortality Rate (per 1,000 live births, 2006): 15.5.
Physicians (per 1,000 head, c. 2001): 1.4.
Hospital Beds (per 1,000 head, 2005): 3.0.
Access to Water (% of persons, 2004): 84.
Access to Sanitation (% of persons, 2004): 78.
Source: mostly Pan American Health Organization.

For other sources and definitions, see explanatory note on p. vi.

AGRICULTURE, ETC.

Principal Crops ('000 metric tons, 2006, FAO estimates): Rice (paddy) 17.8 (official figure); Cassava 5.6; Sugar cane 5.4; Cabbages 6.6; Tomatoes 5.1; Cucumbers and gherkins 3.8; Green beans 3.3; Bananas 5.8; Plantains 3.4. *Aggregate Production* ('000 metric tons, may include official, semi-official or estimated data): Total vegetables (incl. melons) 26.3; Total fruits (excl. melons) 17.6.

Livestock ('000 head, 2006, FAO estimates): Cattle 9.2; Pigs 10.5; Sheep 2.6.

Livestock Products (metric tons, 2006, FAO estimates): Cattle meat 320; Pig meat 1,100; Chicken meat 4410; Cows' milk 270; Hen eggs 460.

Forestry ('000 cubic metres, 2006, FAO estimates): *Roundwood Removals* (excl. bark): Sawlogs, veneer logs and logs for sleepers 57.0; Other industrial wood 9.0; Fuel wood 105.4; Total 171.4. *Sawnwood Production* (incl. railway sleepers): Total 15.

Fishing (metric tons, live weight, 2005): Capture 5,265 (Marine fishes 2,300—FAO estimate, Shrimps 2,965); Aquaculture 37; *Total catch* 5,302.

Source: FAO.

MINING

Production ('000 metric tons unless otherwise indicated, 2005, estimates): Cement 62,000; Gold (metal content of ore, kilograms, reported figure) 1,955; Sand 1,500. Source: US Geological Survey.

INDUSTRY

Production: Rum 3,175 hl in 2006; Electric energy 714 million kWh in 2005 (Source: l'Institut d'Emission des Départements d'Outre-Mer, *Rapport Annuel 2006*).

FINANCE

Currency and Exchange Rates: 100 cent = 1 euro (€). *Sterling and Dollar Equivalents* (31 December 2007): £1 sterling = €1.3609; US $1 = €0.6793; €10 = £7.35 = $14.72. *Average Exchange Rate* (euros per US dollar): 0.804 in 2005; 0.797 in 2006; 0.731 in 2007. Note: The national currency was formerly the French franc. From the introduction of the euro, with French participation, on 1 January 1999, a fixed exchange rate of €1 = 6.55957 French francs was in operation. Euro notes and coins were introduced on 1 January 2002. The euro and French currency circulated alongside each other until 17 February, after which the euro became the sole legal tender. Some of the figures in this Survey are still in terms of francs.

Budgets (excl. debt rescheduling, € million, 2006): *Regional Government:* Current revenue 65.9 (Taxes 50.5); Capital revenue 44.9; Total 110.7. Current expenditure 50.1; Capital expenditure 56.6; Total 106.7. *Departmental Government:* Revenue 263.8; Expenditure 234.1. Source: Département des Etudes et des Statistiques Locales.

Money Supply (million French francs at 31 December 1996): Currency outside banks 3,000; Demand deposits at banks 1,621; Total money 4,621.

Cost of Living (Consumer Price Index; base: 2000 = 100): 106.4 in 2004; 108.2 in 2005; 110.4 in 2006. Source: ILO.

Gross Domestic Product (US $ million at constant 1990 prices): 1,668 in 2001; 1,695 in 2002; 1,722 in 2003. Source: UN, *Statistical Yearbook*.

Expenditure on the Gross Domestic Product (€ million at current prices, 2003): Total final consumption expenditure 2,293 (General government and non-profit institutions serving households 1,154, Households 1,139); Changes in inventories –29; Gross fixed capital formation 493; *Total domestic expenditure* 2,757; Exports of goods and services 727; *Less* Imports of goods and services 1,276; *GDP in purchasers' values* 2,207.

Gross Domestic Product by Economic Activity (€ million at current prices, 2003): Agriculture, hunting, forestry and fishing 95; Food industries 39; Manufacturing 180; Energy 40; Construction 163; Services 1,564 (Restaurants and hotels 42, Transport –85, Commerce 223, Other market services 560; Non-market services 824); *Sub-total* 2,081; Financial intermediation services indirectly measured –42; Import duties, less subsidies 169; *GDP in purchasers' values* 2,207.

EXTERNAL TRADE

Principal Commodities (€ million, 2006): *Imports c.i.f.:* Products of agriculture and food industries 144; Pharmaceutical products 51; Home equipment 47; Car industry products 101; Mechanical equipment 73; Electronic equipment 63; Fuels and combustibles 93; Total (incl. others) 756. *Exports f.o.b.:* Products of agriculture and food industries 12.9; Boats, planes, trains, and motorcycles 1.8; Car industry products 19.7; Mechanical equipment 6.3; Electronic equipment 11.1; Metals and products thereof 54.4; Total (incl. others) 112.3.

Principal Trading Partners (€ million, 2006): *Imports c.i.f.:* France (metropolitan) 297; Germany 18; Italy 14; Japan 16; Martinique 18; Netherlands 18; Spain 8; Trinidad and Tobago 90; USA 9; Total (incl. others) 756. *Exports f.o.b.:* Australia 2; Belgium 2; France (metropolitan) 62; Germany 7; Guadeloupe 3; Italy 8; Martinique 4; Portugal 2; Suriname 4; Switzerland 18; Total (incl. others) 112.

TRANSPORT

Road Traffic ('000 motor vehicles in use, 2001): Passenger cars 32.9; Commercial vehicles 11.9 (Source: UN, *Statistical Yearbook*). *2002:* 50,000 motor vehicles in use.

FRENCH OVERSEAS POSSESSIONS
French Guiana

International Sea-borne Shipping (traffic, 2005 unless otherwise indicated): International vessels entered 115; Goods loaded 25,103 metric tons; Goods unloaded 472,567 metric tons (Source: CCIG); Passengers carried 275,300 (1998).

Civil Aviation: Freight carried (incl. post) 6,252 metric tons (2005); Passengers carried 374,394 (2006).

TOURISM

Tourist Arrivals by Country (2002, rounded figures): France 40,950; Guadeloupe 5,200; Martinique 9,750; Total (incl. others) 65,000.

Receipts from Tourism (US $ million, incl. passenger transport): 42 in 2001; 45 in 2002.

Source: World Tourism Organization.

COMMUNICATIONS MEDIA

Radio Receivers ('000 in use): 104 in 1997.
Television Receivers ('000 in use): 37 in 1998.
Telephones ('000 main lines in use): 51.0 in 2001.
Facsimile Machines (number in use): 185 in 1990.
Mobile Cellular Telephones ('000 subscribers): 98.0 in 2004.
Personal Computers ('000 in use): 33 in 2004.
Internet Users ('000): 38.0 in 2004.
Daily Newspaper: 1 in 1996 (average circulation 2,000 copies).

Sources: UNESCO, *Statistical Yearbook*; UN, *Statistical Yearbook*; International Telecommunication Union.

EDUCATION

Pre-primary (2005/06): 42 institutions; 12,985 students (12,135 state, 850 private).

Primary (2005/06): 105 institutions (97 state, 8 private); 23,972 students (22,370 state, 1,602 private).

Specialized Pre-primary and Primary (2005/06): 544 students (534 state, 10 private).

Secondary (2005/06): 40 institutions (35 state, 5 private); 26,337 students (24,588 state, 1,749 private). Source: Rectorat de la Guyane *Enquête 19 (1st degré)* and *Enquête 19 (2nd degré)*.

Higher (2004/05): 2,333 students. Source: Ministère de l'Education Nationale, de l'Enseignement Supérieur, de la Recherche et de la Technologie.

Teachers (2004/05): *Primary:* 2,270 teachers (2,160 state, 110 private); *Secondary:* 2,129 teachers (1,982 state, 147 private); *Higher:* 63 teachers. Source: Ministère de l'Education Nationale, *Repères et références statistiques—édition 2005*.

Adult Literacy Rate: 83.0% (males 83.6%; females 82.3%) in 1998. Source: Pan American Health Organization.

Directory

The Government
(March 2008)

Prefect: JEAN-PIERRE LAFLAQUIÈRE, Préfecture, rue Fiedmont, BP 7008, 97307 Cayenne Cédex; tel. 5-94-39-45-00; fax 5-94-30-02-77; e-mail courrier@guyane.pref.gouv.fr; internet www.guyane.pref.gouv.fr.

President of the General Council: PIERRE DÉSERT, Hôtel du Département, pl. Léopold Héder, BP 5021, 97305 Cayenne Cédex; tel. 5-94-29-55-00; fax 5-94-29-55-25; e-mail pdesert@cg973.fr; internet www.cg973.fr.

President of the Economic and Social Committee: ROGER-MICHEL LOUPEC, Cité Administrative Régionale, 4179 route de Montabo, Carrefour de Suzini, BP 7025, 97307 Cayenne Cédex; tel. 5-94-28-96-01; fax 5-94-30-73-65; e-mail cesr@cr-guyane.fr.

President of the Culture, Education and Environment Committee: JEAN-PIERRE BACOT, 66 ave du Général de Gaulle, 97300 Cayenne; tel. 5-94-25-66-84; fax 5-94-37-94-24; e-mail ccee@cr-guyane.fr; internet www.cr-guyane.fr.

Deputies to the French National Assembly: CHRISTIANE TAUBIRA-DELANNON (Walwari), CHANTAL BERTHELOT (PSG).

Representative to the French Senate: GEORGES OTHILY (Rassemblement Démocratique et Social Européen).

Conseil Régional
Cité Administrative Régionale, 4179 route de Montabo, Carrefour de Suzini, BP 7025, 97307 Cayenne Cédex; tel. 5-94-29-20-20; fax 5-94-31-95-22; e-mail cabcrg@cr-guyane.fr; internet www.cr-guyane.fr.

President: ANTOINE KARAM (PSG).

Elections, 21 and 28 March 2004

	Seats
Parti Socialiste Guyanais	17
Forces Démocratiques Guyanaises-Walwari	7
Union pour un Mouvement Populaire	7
Total	**31**

Political Organizations

Forces Démocratiques Guyanaises (FDG): 41 rue du 14 Juillet, BP 403, 97300 Cayenne; tel. 5-94-28-96-79; fax 5-94-30-80-66; e-mail g.othily@senat.fr; f. 1989 by a split in the PSG; Pres. GEORGES OTHILY.

Mouvement de Décolonisation et d'Emancipation Sociale (MDES): 21 rue Maissin, 97300 Cayenne; tel. 5-94-30-55-97; fax 5-94-30-97-73; e-mail mdes.parti@wanadoo.org; internet www.mdes.org; f. 1991; pro-independence; Sec.-Gen. MAURICE PINDARD.

Parti Socialiste (PS): 7 rue de l'Adjudant Pindard, 97334 Cayenne Cédex; tel. 5-94-37-81-33; fax 5-94-37-81-56; departmental br. of the metropolitan party; Leader LÉON JEAN BAPTISTE EDOUARD; Sec. PAUL DEBRIETTE.

Parti Socialiste Guyanais (PSG): 1 Cité Césaire, 97300 Cayenne; tel. 5-94-28-11-44; f. 1956; left-wing; Sec.-Gen. ANTOINE KARAM.

Union pour un Mouvement Populaire (UMP): 42 rue du Docteur Barrat, 97300 Cayenne; tel. 5-94-28-80-74; fax 5-94-28-80-75; e-mail fabiencovis@ump973.org; internet www.u-m-p.org; f. 2002 as Union pour la Majorité Presidentielle by mems of the fmr Rassemblement pour la République and Union pour la Démocratie Française; centre-right; departmental br. of the metropolitan party; Pres., Departmental Cttee GEORGES MICHEL PHINERA HORTH.

Les Verts Guyane: 64 rue Madame Payé, 97300 Cayenne; tel. 5-94-40-97-27; e-mail tamanoir.guyane@wanadoo.fr; internet guyane.lesverts.fr; ecologist; departmental br. of the metropolitan party; Leader BRIGITTE WYNGAARDE.

Walwari: 69 bis ave de la Liberté, 97338 Cayenne Cédex; tel. 5-94-30-07-73; fax 5-94-31-84-95; internet www.walwari.com; f. 1993; left-wing; Leader CHRISTIANE TAUBIRA-DELANONON; Sec.-Gen. JEAN-MARIE TAUBIRA.

Judicial System

Courts of Appeal: see Judicial System, Martinique.

Tribunal de Grande Instance: Palais de Justice, 9 ave du Général de Gaulle, 97300 Cayenne; Pres. DOMINIQUE PANNETIER; Procurators-Gen. CLAIRE LANET, YVES-ARMAND FRASSATI (acting).

Religion

CHRISTIANITY

The Roman Catholic Church

French Guiana comprises the single diocese of Cayenne, suffragan to the archdiocese of Fort-de-France, Martinique. At 31 December 2005 there were an estimated 150,000 adherents in French Guiana, representing some 75% of the total population. French Guiana participates in the Antilles Episcopal Conference, currently based in Port of Spain, Trinidad and Tobago.

Bishop of Cayenne: Rt Rev. EMMANUEL M. P. L. LAFONT, Evêché, 24 rue Madame Payé, BP 378, 97328 Cayenne Cédex; tel. 5-94-28-98-48; fax 5-94-30-20-33; e-mail eveque.cayenne.catho@free.fr; internet diocese.cayenne.free.fr.

The Anglican Communion

Within the Church in the Province of the West Indies, French Guiana forms part of the diocese of Guyana. The Bishop is resident in Georgetown, Guyana. There were fewer than 100 adherents at mid-2000.

Other Churches

At mid-2000 there were an estimated 7,000 Protestants and 7,200 adherents professing other forms of Christianity.

Assembly of God: 1051 route de Raban, 97300 Cayenne; tel. 5-94-35-23-04; fax 5-94-35-23-05; e-mail jacques.rhino@wanadoo.fr; internet www.addguyane.fr; Pres. JACQUES RHINO; c. 500 mems.

FRENCH OVERSEAS POSSESSIONS   *French Guiana*

Church of Jesus Christ of Latter-day Saints (Mormons): Route de la Rocade, 97305 Cayenne; Br. Pres. FRANÇOIS PRATIQUE; c. 250 mems.

Seventh-day Adventist Church: Mission Adventiste de la Guyane, 39 rue Schoëlcher, BP 169, 97324 Cayenne Cédex; tel. 5-94-25-64-26; fax 5-94-37-93-02; e-mail mission.adventiste@wanadoo.fr; f. 1949; Pres. and Chair. NORBERT KANCEL; 2,164 mems.

The Jehovah's Witnesses are also represented.

The Press

France-Guyane: 17 rue Lallouette, 97300 Cayenne; tel. 5-94-29-70-00; fax 5-94-29-70-02; e-mail france.guyane@media-antilles.fr; daily; Publishing Dir FRÉDÉRIC AURAND; Local Dir MARC AUBURTIN; Editor PIERRE GIRARD; circ. 9,000.

Oka.Mag': 11 rue Abel Azor, Cité Manil, 97310 Kourou; tel. 5-94-22-01-41; e-mail oka.mag@wanadoo.fr; internet www.solidarite-guyane.org/okamag.htm; f. 2001; 6 a year; Amerindian interest; circ. 15,000.

La Presse de Guyane: pl. Léopold Héder, 97300 Cayenne; tel. 5-94-29-55-55; fax 5-94-29-55-54; e-mail communication@cg973.fr; publ. by the Conseil général; Editor-in-Chief TCHISSÉKA LOBELT; 5 a week.

La Semaine Guyanaise: 6 ave Pasteur, 97300 Cayenne; tel. 5-94-31-09-83; fax 5-94-31-95-20; e-mail semaine.guyanaise@nplus.gf; weekly; Dir ALAIN CHAUMET.

Ròt Kozé: 21 rue Maissin, 97300 Cayenne; tel. 5-94-30-55-97; fax 5-94-30-97-73; e-mail webmaster@mdes.org; internet www.mdes.org; f. 1990; left-wing organ of the MDES party; monthly; Dir MAURICE PINDARD.

NEWS AGENCIES

Agence France Presse (AFP): 17 résidence Saint-Antoine, chemin Saint-Antoine, 97300 Cayenne; tel. and fax 5-94-39-09-42; e-mail rozga@yahoo.com; Correspondent ALEXANDRE ROZGA.

Foreign Bureau

Reuters (United Kingdom): impasse du 8 Mai 1945, 97300 Cayenne; tel. 5-94-30-44-26; fax 5-94-31-93-24; Correspondent ALEXANDER MILES.

Publishers

Editions Amazone: 2 Centre Commerciale Montjoly, 97354 Montjoly; tel. 6-94-23-18-78; fax 5-94-30-45-00; Dir LÉO MIRA.

Editions Anne C.: 8 Lot Mapaou, route de Baduel, 97300 Cayenne; BP 212, 97325 Cayenne; tel. and fax 5-94-35-20-10; e-mail canne@nplus.gf; internet perso.orange.fr/redris/html/livres.htm; f. 1998; French-Créole children's and youth literature; Dir NICOLE PARFAIT.

Ibis Rouge Editions: chemin de la Levée, 97351 Matoury; tel. 5-94-35-95-66; fax 5-94-35-95-68; e-mail contact@ibisrouge.fr; internet www.ibisrouge.fr; f. 1995; general literature, French-Creole, and academic; Gen. Man. JEAN-LOUIS MALHERBE; agencies in Guadeloupe and Martinique.

PUBLISHERS' ASSOCIATION

Promolivres Guyane: BP 96, 97394 Rémire-Montjoly Cédex; tel. 5-94-29-55-56; fax 5-94-38-52-82; e-mail promolivreguyane@wanadoo.fr; f. 1996; asscn mems incl. editors, book-sellers, journalists and librarians; promotes French Guianese literature; Pres. TCHISSÉKA LOBELT.

Broadcasting and Communications

TELECOMMUNICATIONS

Digicel Antilles Françaises Guyane: see Martinique—Telecommunications.

France Telecom: 76 ave Voltaire, BP 8080, 97300 Cayenne; tel. 5-94-39-91-15; fax 5-94-39-91-00; e-mail eline.miranda@francetelecom.com.

ONLY: 112 ave du Général de Gaulle, 97300 Cayenne; tel. 5-94-28-71-15; fax 5-94-23-93-59; e-mail communication@outremer-telecom.fr; internet www.outremer-telecom.fr; f. 1998 as Outremer Telecom Guyane; subsidiary of Outremer Telecom, France; present name adopted following merger of Volubis, ONLY and OOL in 2006; telecommunications provider; Group CEO JEAN-MICHEL HEGESIPPE.

Orange Caraïbe: see Guadeloupe—Telecommunications.

BROADCASTING

Réseau France Outre-mer (RFO): ave le Grand Boulevard, Z.A.D. Moulin à Vent, 97354 Rémire-Montjoly; tel. 5-94-25-67-00; fax 5-94-25-67-64; internet www.guyane.rfo.fr; acquired by Groupe France Télévisions in 2004; fmrly Société Nationale de Radio-Télévision Française d'Outre-mer, present name adopted 1998; Radio-Guyane Inter accounts for 46.6% of listeners (2003); Télé Guyane/RFO1 and RFO (Tempo) account for 52.3% and 7.5% of viewers, respectively (2003); Gen. Man. FRANÇOIS GUILBEAU; Regional Dir MARTINE SAUVAGE.

Radio

KFM: 6 rue François Arago, 97300 Cayenne; tel. 5-94-31-30-38; fax 5-94-37-84-20; internet www.kfmguyane.com; f. 1993 as Radio Kikiwi; present name adopted 2003.

NRJ Guyane: 2 blvd de la République, 97300 Cayenne; tel. 5-94-39-54-88; fax 5-94-39-54-79; e-mail wladimir@nrjguyane.com; internet www.nrjguyane.com; f. 2006; commercial radio station; Mans WLADIMIR MANGACHOFF, MARC HO-A-CHUCK.

Radio Joie de Vivre: 39 rue Schoëlcher, 97324 Cayenne Cédex; POB 169, 97300 Cayenne; tel. 5-94-31-29-00; fax 5-94-29-47-26; f. 1993; operated by the Seventh-day Adventist church; Gen. Man. ESAÏE AUGUSTE.

Radio Littoméga (RLM): 24 blvd Malouet, BP 108, 97320 Saint-Laurent-du-Maroni; tel. 5-94-34-22-09; e-mail antenne@rlm100.com; internet www.rlm100.com; f. 1994; Dir ARIELLE BERTRAND; Man. ALAIN ACOUCKIA.

Radio Mig: 100 ave du Général de Gaulle, 97300 Cayenne; tel. 5-94-30-77-67; fax 5-94-31-86-81; f. 1995; Créole; affiliated to the MDES party and UTG; Man. YVES ICARE.

Radio Mosaïque: 11 rue Sainte-Catherine, cité Brutus, 97300 Cayenne; tel. 5-94-30-94-76; e-mail guyanes@free.fr; commercial radio station; Man. BÉRIL BELVU.

Radio Ouassailles: rue Maurice Mongeot, 97360 Mana; tel. 5-94-34-80-96; fax 5-94-34-13-89; e-mail radio.ouassailles@wanadoo.fr; f. 1994; French and Créole; Man. RÉMY AUBERT.

Radio Saint-Gabriel: 23 rue Lallouette, BP 372, 97328 Cayenne; tel. 5-94-31-10-28; e-mail radiosaintgabriel@wanadoo.fr; f. 2001; Roman Catholic; Man. ROMAINE ASSARD.

Radio Toucan Fréquence International (TFI): 1 pl. du Vidé, BP 68, 97300 Kourou; tel. 5-94-32-96-11; fax 5-94-39-71-61; e-mail direction@tfifm.com; internet www.tfifm.com; f. 1983; part of Groupe I-Medias Antilles-Guyane; commercial radio station; Dir YVAN DUCOUDRAY-SAINT-PRIX; Man. JEAN-MARC DE CRENY.

Radio UDL (Union Défense des Libertés): ave Félix Eboué, 97323 Saint-Laurent-du-Maroni; tel. 5-94-34-27-90; e-mail redaction973@gmail.com; f. 1982; Man. FLORE LITHAW.

Radio Vinyle Club: 7 pl. Gaston Monnerville, 97310 Kourou; tel. 5-94-22-02-58; fax 5-94-22-38-69; f. 2001; Man. ARNAUT CHARLE.

Radio Voix dans le Désert: 5 route de Raban, chemin du Château d'Eau, 97300 Cayenne; tel. 5-94-31-27-22; fax ; 5-90-37-90-06; f. 1993; operated by the Assembly of God church; Pres. EDDY LAUTRIC; Man. YVON RAMASSANY.

Other radio stations include: Média Tropique FM; Nostalgie Guyane; Ouest FM; Radio 2000; Radio Bonne Nouvelle Guyane; Radio Gabrielle; Radio JAM; Radio Loisirs Guyane; Radio Merci Seigneur; Radio Pagani; Radio Tour l'Isle; Radio Tout'Moun; Radyo ITG; RFM 90; and Sky FM.

Television

Antenne Créole Guyane: 31 ave Louis Pasteur, 97300 Cayenne; tel. 5-94-28-82-88; fax 5-94-29-13-08; e-mail acg@acg.gf; internet www.acg.gf; f. 1994; sole local private TV station; gen. interest with focus on music and sports; produces 30% of own programmes; received by 95% of the population, accounting for 25% of viewers (2003); Pres. MARC HO-A-CHUCK; Gen. Man. WLADIMIR MANGACHOFF.

Canal+ Guyane: 14 Lotissement Marengo, Z.I. de Collery, 97300 Cayenne; tel. 5-94-29-54-55; fax 5-94-30-53-35; f. 1994; subsidiary of Groupe Canal+, France; satellite TV station.

Finance

(cap. = capital; res = reserves; dep. = deposits; m. = million; brs = branches; amounts in French francs)

BANKING

Central Bank

Institut d'Emission des Départements d'Outre-mer (IEDOM): 8 rue Christophe Colomb, BP 6016, 97306 Cayenne Cédex; tel. 5-94-29-36-50; fax 5-94-30-02-76; internet www.iedom.fr; f. 1959; Dir MAX REMBLIN.

Commercial Banks

Banque Française Commerciale Antilles-Guyane (BFC Antilles-Guyane): 8 pl. des Palmistes, BP 111, 97345 Cayenne; tel. 5-94-

29-11-11; fax 5-94-30-13-12; e-mail service-client@bfc-ag.com; internet www.bfc-ag.com; f. 1985; Regional Dir PHILIPPE BISSAINTE.

BNP Paribas Guyane SA: 2 pl. Victor Schoëlcher, BP 35, 97300 Cayenne; tel. 5-94-39-63-00; fax 5-94-30-23-08; e-mail bnpg@bnpparibas.com; internet www.bnpparibas.com; f. 1964 following purchase of BNP Guyane (f. 1855); name changed July 2000; 94% owned by BNP Paribas SA, 3% by BNP Paribas Martinique and 3% by BNP Paribas Guadeloupe; cap. 71.7m., res 100.0m., dep. 2,007m. (Dec. 1994); Dir and CEO MICHEL BELLOT; Gen. Sec. DENIS RUBRICE; 2 brs.

BRED-Banque Populaire (BRED-BP): 5 ave du Général de Gaulle, 97300 Cayenne; tel. 5-94-25-56-80; fax 5-94-31-98-40; Pres. STÈVE GENTILI; 3 brs.

Crédit Agricole: see Martinique—Finance.

Development Bank

Société Financière pour le Développement Economique de la Guyane (SOFIDEG): PK 3, 700 route de Baduel, BP 860, 97339 Cayenne Cédex; tel. 5-94-29-94-29; fax 5-94-30-60-44; f. 1982; bought from the Agence Française de Développement (AFD—q.v.) by BRED-BP in 2003; Dir FRANÇOIS CHEVILLOTTE.

Insurance

AGF Vie & AGF IARD France: Centre Commercial Katoury, BP 933, 97341, Cayenne Cédex; tel. 5-94-28-67-27; fax 5-94-30-99-49; e-mail eagfguyane@wanadoo.fr; internet www.agf.fr; life and short-term insurance.

Groupama Antilles Guyane: see Martinique—Insurance.

Trade and Industry

GOVERNMENT AGENCIES

Direction de l'Agriculture et de la Forêt (DAF): Parc Rebard, BP 5002, 97305 Cayenne Cédex; tel. 5-94-29-63-74; fax 5-94-29-63-63; e-mail daf.guyane@agriculture.gouv.fr; internet daf.guyane.agriculture.gouv.fr.

Direction Régionale et Départementale des Affaires Maritimes (DRAM): 2 bis rue Mentel, BP 6008, 97306 Cayenne Cédex; tel. 5-94-29-36-15; fax 5-94-29-36-16; e-mail stephane.gatto@equipement.gouv.fr; responsible for shipping, fishing and other maritime issues at a nat. and community level.

Direction Régionale de l'Industrie, de la Recherche et de l'Environnement (DRIRE): Pointe Buzaré, BP 7001, 97307 Cayenne; tel. 5-94-29-75-30; fax 5-94-29-07-34; e-mail drire-antilles-guyane@industrie.gouv.fr; internet www.ggm.drire.gouv.fr; active in industry, business services, transport, public works, tourism and distribution; Regional Dir PHILIPPE COMBE.

DEVELOPMENT ORGANIZATIONS

Agence de l'Environnement et de la Maîtrise de l'Energie (ADEME): 28 ave Léopold Heder, Cayenne Cédex; tel. 5-94-31-73-60; fax 5-94-30-76-69; e-mail ademe.guyane@ademe.fr; internet www.ademe.fr.

Agence pour la Création et le Développement des Entreprises en Guyane (ACREDEG): 1 pl. Schoëlcher, BP 325, 97325 Cayenne Cédex; tel. 5-94-25-66-66; fax 5-94-25-43-19; e-mail acredeg@nplus.gf; internet www.acredeg.gf; f. 1998; Pres. JEAN CLAUDE SIMONEAU; Dir RAYMOND CHARPENTIER-TITY.

Agence Française de Développement (AFD): Lotissement les Héliconias, route de Baduel, BP 1122, 97345 Cayenne Cédex; tel. 5-94-29-90-90; fax 5-94-30-63-32; internet www.afd.fr; fmrly Caisse Française de Développement; Man. GENEVIÈVE JAVALOYES.

Fédération des Organisations Amérindiennes de Guyane (FOAG): Centre des Cultures, rue Capt. Charles Claude, 97319 Awala Yalirnapo; tel. 6-94-42-27-76; fax 5-94-33-50-06; e-mail foag@nplus.gf; f. 1993; civil liberties org. representing the rights of the indigenous peoples of French Guiana; Sec.-Gen. Chief JEAN AUBÉRIC CHARLES.

CHAMBERS OF COMMERCE

Chambre d'Agriculture: 8 ave du Général de Gaulle, BP 544, 97333 Cayenne Cédex; tel. 5-94-29-61-95; fax 5-94-31-00-01; e-mail chambre.agriculture.973@wanadoo.fr; Pres. PATRICK LABRANCHE; Dir DANIEL BEREAU.

Chambre de Commerce et d'Industrie de la Guyane (CCIG): Hôtel Consulaire, pl. de l'Esplanade, BP 49, 97300 Cayenne Cédex; tel. 5-94-29-96-00; fax 5-94-29-96-34; e-mail contact@guyane.cci.fr; internet www.guyane.cci.fr; Pres. JEAN-PAUL LE PELLETIER.

Chambre de Métiers: Jardin Botanique, blvd de la République, BP 176, 97324 Cayenne Cédex; tel. 5-94-25-24-70; fax 5-94-30-54-22; e-mail m.toulemonde@cm-guyane.fr; internet www.cm-guyane.fr; Pres. SYLVAIN LEMKI; Sec.-Gen. JOCELYN HO-A-CHUCK.

Jeune Chambre Economique de Cayenne: 1 Cité A. Horth, route de Montabo, BP 1094, Cayenne; tel. 5-94-31-62-99; fax 5-94-31-76-13; internet www.jcecayenne.org; f. 1960; Pres. JEAN-FRANÇOIS EKANDE.

EMPLOYERS' ORGANIZATIONS

Coopérative des Céréales et Oléagineux de Guyane (COCEROG): PK 24, chemin départemental 8, Sarcelles, 97360 Mana; tel. 5-94-34-20-82; fax 5-94-34-02-08.

Groupement Régional des Agriculteurs de Guyane (GRAGE): PK 15 route nationale 1, Domaine de Soula, 97355 Macouria; tel. 5-94-38-71-26; e-mail grage@wanadoo.fr; internet www.grage.gf; affiliated to the Confédération Paysanne; Pres. ALBÉRIC BENTH.

MEDEF Guyane: 27A Résidence Gustave Stanislas, Source de Baduel, BP 820, 97338 Cayenne Cédex; tel. 5-94-31-17-71; fax 5-94-30-32-13; e-mail updg@nplus.gf; f. 2005; fmrly Union des Entreprises de Guyane; Pres. ADRIEN AUBIN.

Ordre des Pharmaciens du Département Guyane: ave Hector Berlioz, 97310 Kourou; tel. 5-94-32-17-62; fax 5-94-32-17-66; e-mail delegation_guyane@ordre.pharmacien.fr; internet www.ordre.pharmacien.fr; Pres LILIANE POGNON, EJULIBERTE PAUILLAC MAM LAM FOUCK.

Syndicat des Exploitants Forestiers et Scieurs de Guyane (SEFSG): Macouria; tel. 5-94-35-26-66; fax 5-94-35-29-92; f. 1987; represents timber processors; Man. M. POMIES.

Syndicat des Transformateurs du Bois de Guyane (STBG): Menuiserie Cabassou, PK 4.5, route de Cabassou, 97354 Remire-Montjoly; tel. 5-94-31-34-49; fax 5-94-35-10-51; f. 2002; represents artisans using wood; Pres. YVES ELISE; Sec. FRANÇOIS AUGER.

UTILITIES

Electricity

Electricité de France Guyane (EdF): blvd Jubelin, BP 6002, 97306 Cayenne; tel. 5-94-39-64-00; fax 5-94-30-10-81; electricity producer; Gen. Man. MARC GIRARD.

Water

Veolia Eau—Guyanaise des Eaux: 2738 route de Montabo, BP 5027, 97306 Cayenne; tel. 5-94-30-32-32; fax 5-94-30-59-60; internet www.veoliaenvironnement.com; CEO HENRI PROGLIO; Gen. Man. JACQUES FOURNET.

TRADE UNIONS

Centrale Démocratique des Travailleurs de la Guyane (CDTG): 99–100 Cité Césaire, BP 383, 97328 Cayenne Cédex; tel. 5-94-31-02-32; fax 5-94-31-81-05; e-mail sg.cdtg@wanadoo.fr; affiliated to the Confédération Française Démocratique du Travail; Sec.-Gen. JEAN-MARC BOURETTE.

Affiliated unions incl.:

SGEN-CFDT: 99–100 Cité Césaire, BP 383, 97328 Cayenne Cédex; tel. 5-94-31-02-32; fax 5-94-35-71-17; e-mail sgen.cfdt.fr; affiliated to the Fédération des Syndicats Généraux de l'Education Nationale et de la Recherche; represents teaching staff.

Fédération Syndicale Unitaire Guyane (FSU): Mont Lucas, Bât G, No C37, 97300 Cayenne; tel. 5-94-30-05-69; fax 5-94-38-36-58; e-mail fsu973@fsu.fr; f. 1993; departmental br. of the Fédération Syndicale Unitaire; represents public sector employees in teaching, research and training, and also agriculture, justice, youth and sports, and culture; Sec. ALAIN BRAVO.

Union Départementale Confédération Française des Travailleurs Chrétiens Guyane (UD CFTC): BP 763, 97337 Cayenne Cédex; tel. 5-94-30-14-85; fax 5-94-35-77-30; e-mail lydie.leneveu@wanadoo.fr.

Union Départementale Force Ouvrière de Guyane (FO): 25 Cité Mirza, rue des Acajous, 97300 Cayenne; tel. and fax 5-94-31-62-55; Sec.-Gen. CHRISTIAN DESFLOTS.

Union Régionale Guyane: 52 rue François Arago, BP 807, 97300 Cayenne; tel. 5-94-21-67-61; fax 5-94-30-89-70.

Union des Travailleurs Guyanais (UTG): 40 ave Digue Ronjon, BP 265, 97326 Cayenne Cédex; tel. 5-94-31-26-42; fax 5-94-30-82-46; e-mail utg1@wanadoo.fr; internet www.utg-guyane.com; Sec.-Gen. ALBERT DARNAL.

UNSA Education Guyane: 46 rue Vermont Polycarpe, BP 341, 97327 Cayenne Cédex; tel. and fax 5-94-30-89-70; Sec.-Gen. MARTINE NIVOIX.

Transport

RAILWAYS
There are no railways in French Guiana.

ROADS
In 2004 there were 1,300 km (808 miles) of roads in French Guiana, of which 397 km were main roads. Much of the network is concentrated along the coast, although proposals for a major new road into the interior of the Department were under consideration.

SHIPPING
Dégrad-des-Cannes, on the estuary of the river Mahury, is the principal port, handling 80% of maritime traffic in 1989. There are other ports at Le Larivot, Saint-Laurent-du-Maroni and Kourou. Saint-Laurent is used primarily for the export of timber, and Le Larivot for fishing vessels. There are river ports on the Oiapoque and on the Approuague. There is a ferry service across the Maroni river between Saint-Laurent and Albina, Suriname. The rivers provide the best means of access to the interior, although numerous rapids prevent navigation by large vessels.

Compagnie Guyanaise de Transport Maritime (CGTM): 26 Avenue de la Liberte, 97300 Cayenne; Man. DENIS BLOUIN.

SOMARIG (Société Maritime et Industrielle de la Guyane): Z. I. de Dégrad-des-Cannes, Rémire, BP 81, 97322 Cayenne Cédex; tel. 5-94-35-42-00; fax 5-94-35-53-44; e-mail cay.hrouchon@cma-cgm.com; internet www.cma-cgm.com; f. 1960; owned by Groupe CMA—GGM (France); Deputy Man. Dir HERVÉ ROUCHON.

CIVIL AVIATION
Rochambeau International Airport, situated 17.5 km (11 miles) from Cayenne, is equipped to handle the largest jet aircraft. There are also airports at Maripasoula, Saul and Saint Georges. Access to remote inland areas is frequently by helicopter.

Air Guyane: Aéroport de Rochambeau, 97300 Matoury; tel. 5-94-35-03-07; fax 5-94-30-54-37; e-mail resa@airguyane.com; internet www.airguyane.com; f. 1980; 46% owned by Guyane Aéro Invest, 20% owned by Sodetraguy; operates domestic services; Pres. CHRISTIAN MARCHAND.

Tourism

The main attractions are the natural beauty of the tropical scenery and the Amerindian villages of the interior. In 2005 there were 27 hotels with some 1,184 rooms. In the same year some 85,000 tourist arrivals were recorded. Receipts from tourism increased from an estimated US $42m. in 2001 to $45m. in 2002.

Comité du Tourisme de la Guyane: 12 rue Lallouette, BP 801, 97338 Cayenne Cédex; tel. 5-94-29-65-00; fax 5-94-29-65-01; e-mail ectginfo@tourisme-guyane.com; internet www.tourisme-guyane.com; Pres. JEAN-ELIE PANELLE; Dir VALÉRIE ROBINEL.

Délégation Régionale au Tourisme, au Commerce et à l'Artisanat pour la Guyane: 9 rue Louis Blanc, BP 7008, 97307 Cayenne Cédex; tel. 5-94-28-92-90; fax 5-94-31-01-04; e-mail drtca973wanadoo.fr; Delegate DIDIER BIRONNEAU.

L'Ensemble Culturel Régional (ENCRE): 82 ave du Général de Gaulle, BP 6007, 97306 Cayenne Cédex; tel. 5-94-28-94-00; fax 5-94-28-94-04; f. 2004 by merger of Ecole Nationale de Musique et de Danse and Office Culturel de la Région Guyane; fmrly Asscn Régionale de Développement Culturel; Pres. ANTOINE KARAM.

Fédération des Offices de Tourisme et Syndicats d'Initiative de la Guyane: 12 rue Lallouette, 97300 Cayenne; tel. 5-94-30-96-29; fax 5-94-31-23-41; e-mail frguyane@fnotsi.net; Pres. ARMAND HILDAIRE.

GUADELOUPE

Introductory Survey

Location, Climate, Language, Religion, Capital
Guadeloupe is the most northerly of the Windward Islands group in the West Indies. Dominica lies to the south, and Antigua and Montserrat to the north-west. Guadeloupe is formed by two large islands, Grande-Terre and Basse-Terre, separated by a narrow sea channel (but linked by a bridge), with a smaller island, Marie-Galante, to the south-east, and another, La Désirade, to the east. The climate is tropical, with an average temperature of 26°C (79°F), and a more humid and wet season between June and November. French is the official language, but a Creole patois is widely spoken. The majority of the population profess Christianity, and belong to the Roman Catholic Church. The capital is the town of Basse-Terre; the other main town and the principal commercial centre is Pointe-à-Pitre, on Grande-Terre.

Recent History
Guadeloupe was first occupied by the French in 1635, and has remained French territory, apart from a number of brief occupations by the British in the 18th and early 19th centuries. It gained departmental status in 1946.

The deterioration of the economy and an increase in unemployment provoked industrial and political unrest during the 1960s and 1970s, including outbreaks of serious rioting in 1967. Pro-independence parties (which had rarely won more than 5% of the total vote at elections in Guadeloupe) resorted, in some cases, to violence as a means of expressing their opposition to the economic and political dominance of white, pro-French landowners and government officials. In 1980 and 1981 there was a series of bomb attacks on hotels, government offices and other targets by a group called the Groupe de Libération Armée, and in 1983 and 1984 there were further bombings by a group styling itself the Alliance Révolutionnaire Caraïbe (ARC). The Government responded by outlawing the ARC and reinforcing the military and police presence throughout Guadeloupe. (The ARC merged with the Mouvement Populaire pour une Guadeloupe Indépendante—MPGI—in 1984.) Further sporadic acts of violence continued in 1985–87, and in January 1988 responsibility for bomb explosions in various parts of the territory was claimed by a previously unknown pro-independence group, the Organisation Révolutionnaire Armée.

In 1974 Guadeloupe was granted the status of a Region, and an indirectly elected Conseil régional (Regional Council) was formed. In direct elections to a new Conseil régional in February 1983, held as a result of the recent decentralization reforms, the centre-right coalition succeeded in gaining a majority of the seats and control of the administration. In January 1984 Lucette Michaux-Chevry, the President of the Conseil général (General Council), formed a new conservative centre party, Le Parti de la Guadeloupe, which remained in alliance with the right-wing Rassemblement pour la République (RPR). However, at the election for the Conseil général held in March 1985, the left-wing combination of the Parti Socialiste (PS) and the Parti Communiste Guadeloupéen (PCG) gained a majority of seats on the enlarged Conseil, and the PS leader, Dominique Larifla, was elected its President. In July demonstrations and a general strike, organized by pro-separatist activists in order to obtain the release of a leading member of the MPGI, quickly intensified into civil disorder and rioting in the main commercial centre, Pointe-à-Pitre.

For the March 1986 general election to the Assemblée nationale (National Assembly), Guadeloupe's representation was increased from three to four deputies. Ernest Moutoussamy and Frédéric Jalton, respectively the incumbent PCG and PS members of the Assemblée, were re-elected; the two remaining seats were won by RPR candidates (Michaux-Chevry and Henri Beaujean). In the concurrent elections for the 41 seats on the Conseil régional, the two left-wing parties together won a majority of seats. As a result, José Moustache of the RPR was replaced as President of the Conseil by Félix Proto of the PS. At an election to the Assemblée nationale in June, Larifla (for the PS) defeated Beaujean, while the three other deputies to the Assemblée retained their seats. In September–October the left-wing parties won 26 of the 42 seats at the election to the Conseil général, and Larifla was re-elected President of the Conseil.

In April 1989 the separatist Union Populaire pour la Libération de la Guadeloupe (UPLG) organized protests in Port Louis to demand the release of 'political prisoners', which led to violent clashes with the police. A number of activists of the now disbanded ARC (including its leader, Luc Reinette) staged a hunger strike while awaiting trial in Paris, accused in connection with politically motivated offences in the Overseas Departments. In the following month the Comité Guadeloupéen de Soutien aux Prisonniers Politiques united 11 organizations in demonstrations against the Government. Demands included the release of the prisoners held in France, a rejection of the Single European Act and the granting of a series of social measures. In June the Assemblée nationale approved legislation granting an amnesty for crimes that had taken place before July 1988, and that were intended to undermine the authority of the French Republic in the Overseas Departments. The agreement of those seeking greater independence in Guadeloupe to work within the democratic framework had gained parliamentary support for the amnesty. However, when the freed activists returned to Guadeloupe in July 1989, they urged increased confrontation with the authorities in order to achieve autonomous rule. In March 1990 the UPLG declared that it would henceforth participate in elections, and would seek associated status (rather than full independence) for Guadeloupe.

In March 1992 concurrent elections were held to the Conseil général and the Conseil régional. Larifla was re-elected as President of the former, despite his refusal to contest as part of the local official PS list of candidates and his leadership of a group of 'dissident' PS members. (The division was not recognized at national level.) In the election to the Conseil régional the official PS list (headed by Jalton) secured nine seats and the dissident PS members seven. Former members of the PCG, who had formed a new organization, the Parti Progressiste Démocratique Guadeloupéen (PPDG), won five seats. The RPR, the centre-right Union pour la Démocratie Française (UDF) and other right-wing candidates formed an electoral alliance, Objectif Guadeloupe, to contest the elections, together securing 15 of the 41 seats in the Conseil régional. Jalton's refusal to reach an agreement with the 'dissident' PS members prompted Larifla's list to support the presidential candidacy of Michaux-Chevry. Thus, despite an overall left-wing majority in the Conseil régional, the right-wing Michaux-Chevry was elected as President. In December 1992, however, the French Conseil d'état declared the election to the Conseil régional invalid, owing to the failure of Larifla's list to pay a deposit on each seat prior to the registration of its candidates. Other heads of lists were subsequently found to have submitted incomplete documents to the election commission, and (although malpractice was discounted) the electoral code necessitated that they be declared ineligible for election to the Conseil régional for one year. Fresh elections took place in January 1994, at which Objectif Guadeloupe took 22 seats, while the PS and 'dissident' PS retained a total of only 10 seats.

In a referendum on 20 September 1992 68% of voters in Guadeloupe endorsed ratification of the Treaty on European Union (see p. 244), although a high abstention rate was recorded.

The persistence of divisions between the socialists was evident at the March 1993 election to the Assemblée nationale. Michaux-Chevry of the RPR was re-elected, as were Moutoussamy (for the PPDG) and Jalton (representing the anti-Larifla faction of the PS). Larifla, meanwhile, was defeated by Edouard Chammougon, a candidate of the independent right, who was elected despite his implication in several corruption scandals (see below). Michaux-Chevry was appointed to the position of Minister-Delegate, with responsibility for human rights and humanitarian action, in Edouard Balladur's centre-right coalition Government. The left retained control of the Conseil général following cantonal elections in March 1994. Larifla was subsequently re-elected President of the Conseil.

Meanwhile, local political affairs were dominated by scandals involving prominent public figures. Twice during 1993 the Antilles-Guyane Chambre régionale des comptes—the body responsible for overseeing public finances in the region—rejected budget figures submitted by Guadeloupe's Conseil régional, deeming that the Conseil's deficit projections were severely underestimated. In January 1994 an administrative tribunal in Basse-Terre ruled that Michaux-Chevry had been unjustified in dismissing (following the first rejection of the budget) the Conseil régional's director of finances, who had submitted departmental accounts, as required by law, to the Chambre régionale des comptes; this judgment was upheld at an appeal in Paris in April 1995. In January 1993 Chammougon, the Mayor of Baie-Mahault, was sentenced to three years' imprisonment, fined and deprived of his civic and civil rights for 10 years, following his conviction on corruption charges dating as far back as 1980. He remained at liberty pending an appeal and the prison sentence was suspended in November; the deprivation of rights was reduced to five years in 1994. In September 1993 Chammougon was further implicated in charges of 'passive corruption' and the abuse and misappropriation of public funds. In November 1994 the French Constitutional Council revoked Chammougon's membership of the Assemblée nationale.

At municipal elections in June 1995, Michaux-Chevry became mayor of Basse-Terre, defeating the incumbent PPDG candidate. Michaux-Chevry and Larifla were elected to the French Sénat (Senate) in September; Philippe Chaulet of the RPR was subsequently elected to take Michaux-Chevry's seat in the Assemblée nationale.

The RPR performed strongly in the election to the Conseil régional in March 1998; Michaux-Chevry was re-elected President of the Conseil. The composition of the Conseil général remained largely unchanged following concurrent cantonal elections, although the RPR doubled its representation; Marcellin Lubeth, of the PPDG, was elected to the presidency, defeating Larifla.

Social and industrial unrest intensified in Guadeloupe in October 1999, prior to a two-day visit by Prime Minister Lionel Jospin. Demonstrations escalated into rioting in Pointe-à-Pitre, following the sentencing of Armand Toto—a leading member of the Union Générale des Travailleurs de la Guadeloupe (UGTG)—to four months' imprisonment for assaulting two policemen and threatening to kill another while occupying the premises of a motor vehicle company in support of a dismissed worker. Moreover, banana producers demonstrated around the port of Basse-Terre, demanding the disbursement of 100m. French francs, and additional assistance for the restructuring of their businesses, as compensation for a significant decline in banana prices on the European market. However, calls issued by several trade union and political organizations for a 48-hour general strike during Jospin's visit were largely ignored, and the Prime Minister announced an emergency plan for the banana sector.

The institutional future of the Overseas Departments provoked much discussion in 1999 and 2000. Following a series of meetings, in December 1999 the Presidents of the Conseils régionaux of French Guiana, Guadeloupe and Martinique signed a joint declaration in Basse-Terre, affirming their intention to propose, to the President and the Government, a legislative amendment, possibly constitutional, aimed at creating a new status of overseas region. The declaration, however, was dismissed by the Secretary of State for Overseas Departments and Territories, Jean-Jack Queyranne, in February 2000 as unconstitutional and exceeding the mandate of politicians responsible. Amended proposals regarding the institutional evolution of Guadeloupe were approved by the Assemblée nationale in November, and in December they were ratified by the Constitutional Council.

In municipal elections held in March 2001 Michaux-Chevry was re-elected mayor of Basse-Terre, despite corruption charges against her. Following her election, Michaux-Chevry relinquished the post to Pierre Martin, in order to comply with regulations that no official may hold more than two elected posts simultaneously (she already held the positions of Senator and President of the Conseil régional). Henri Bangou of the PPDG was also re-elected to the mayoralty of Pointe-à-Pitre. In the concurrently held election to the presidency of the Conseil général, Jacques Gillot of Guadeloupe Unie, Socialisme et Réalité (GUSR) defeated Marcellin Lubeth of the PPDG.

In early June 2001 riots occurred in Pointe-à-Pitre in which a number of people were injured. The riots were in protest at the arrest of the leader of the UGTG, Michel Madassamy, who had been charged in late May with vandalizing a number of shops that had remained open on the day of the anniversary of the abolition of slavery in Guadeloupe, in defiance of the UGTG's recommendations. A period of severe drought, necessitating the rationing of water supplies, served to exacerbate the deteriorating social situation on the island in 2001.

Following a meeting of members of the Conseil régional and the Conseil général in late June 2001, a series of administrative restructuring proposals, to be presented to the French Government, was agreed upon. These included: the division of the territory into four districts; the creation of a Territorial Collectivity (collectivité territoriale), governed by a 41-member Assembly elected for a five-year term; and the establishment of an independent executive council. Furthermore, the proposals included a request that the territory be given control over legislative and administrative affairs, as well as legislative authority on matters concerning Guadeloupe alone. In March 2003 the French parliament approved constitutional changes that, *inter alia*, allowed for local referendums to be held on proposals for greater decentralization in overseas possessions. Under the changes, the Department of Guadeloupe was also designated an Overseas Region (région d'outre-mer). In the referendum, held on 7 December, some 73% of participating voters rejected legislative reforms that envisaged the replacement of the Conseil général and the Conseil régional with a single assembly. The proposals had received the support of both councils, but it was widely feared that restructuring would lead to autonomy for the Department and the consequent loss of central government funding. However, at the referendums concurrently held in the dependencies of Saint-Barthélemy and in the northern part of Saint-Martin, a clear majority of voters in each commune (95.5% and 76.2%, respectively) were in favour of seceding from Guadeloupe to form separate Overseas Collectivities (collectivités d'outre-mer—q.v.). The reorganization was subsequently approved by the French Sénat on 6 February 2007 and by the Assemblée nationale the following day. Two weeks later, on 21 February, Saint-Barthélemy and the French part of Saint-Martin were formally designated Overseas Collectivities. Following elections to their respective Conseils territoriaux (Territorial Councils), held in early July 2007, the two Overseas Collectivities acceded to administrative independence. Each Overseas Collectivity was to elect one representative to the French Sénat (in 2008) and one deputy to the Assemblée nationale (in 2012); in the interim they were to continue to be represented by Guadeloupean parliamentarians.

In mid-2001 the French President, Jacques Chirac, rejected a joint request by French Guiana, Guadeloupe and Martinique that they be permitted to join, as associate members, the Association of Caribbean States. In June 2002 all four incumbent deputies were defeated in an election to the Assemblée nationale; they were replaced by Gabrielle Louis-Carabin and Joël Beaugendre, both representing the Union pour la Majorité Présidentielle (UMP), a right-wing alliance that included the Objectif Guadeloupe, Eric Jalton, also of a right-wing coalition, and Victorin Lurel of the PS. The RPR subsequently merged into the successor party to the UMP, Union pour un Mouvement Populaire (also known as the UMP). In August Dominique Vian replaced Jean-François Carenco as Prefect; she was succeeded in mid-2004 by Paul Girot de Langlade.

At an election to the Conseil régional in March 2004 the UMP alliance, led by Michaux-Chevry, was resoundingly defeated, obtaining only 12 of the 41 seats, compared with the 29 seats won by the Guadeloupe pour Tous list, a coalition comprising the PS, the PPDG, the GUSR and other left-wing candidates. Victorin Lurel of the PS subsequently became President of the Conseil régional.

In early October 2004 the arrest of the trade union leader Michel Madassamy led to a deterioration in the social situation. Madassamy was accused of vandalizing two petrol tankers during the blockade of a service station in Point-à-Pitre in November 2003. In early March 2004 he was found guilty and sentenced to 10 months' imprisonment. Following a failed appeal process, Madassamy was taken into custody early in October. The UGTG challenged the legality of the arrest, and in conjunction with other unions, urged workers to strike in support of Madassamy's release; Madassamy himself began a hunger strike. While there was no call for a general strike, areas affected included the port, the airport, local shops and service stations. Several hundred protesters took to the streets in Point-à-Pitre in late October, leading to a number of arrests. Madassamy was granted conditional release in early November pending a further hearing in early January 2005 when the judge ruled that he should serve a further eight months in prison.

In late May 2005 a national referendum was held on ratification of the European Union constitutional treaty: some 58.6% of participating voters in the Department were in favour of adopting the treaty; however, only 22% of the electorate exercised their right to vote. The treaty was ultimately rejected by a majority of voters in metropolitan France.

In early December 2006 industrial action by employees in the electricity sector led to several days of blackouts, the cancellation of a number of flights and the closure of businesses. The strike action was in protest at plans to remodel operations at state-owned utility Electricité de France Guadeloupe (EDF), which employees feared would entail a degree of privatization. However, the industrial action was suspended after three days following an agreement by EDF to schedule negotiations in Paris with trade unions, including the Confédération Générale du Travail de la Guadeloupe.

At the first round of the national presidential election, held on 22 April 2007, Nicolas Sarkozy of the UMP won 42.6% of votes cast in Guadeloupe, ahead of PS candidate Ségolène Royal, who attracted 38.3% of the vote. At the second round, held on 6 May, Sarkozy emerged victorious, winning 49.2% of the vote in the Department. At elections to the Assemblée nationale, held on 10 and 17 June, Gabrielle Louis-Carabin of the UMP, Victorin Lurel of the PS and Eric Jalton of the PCG were re-elected, while Jeanny Marc-Matthiasin of the GUSR was also successful.

Government

France is represented in Guadeloupe by an appointed prefect. There are two councils with local powers: the 42-member Conseil général (General Council) and the 41-member Conseil régional (Regional Council). Both are elected by universal adult suffrage for a period of up to six years. Guadeloupe elects four deputies to the Assemblée nationale in Paris, and sends three indirectly elected representatives to the Sénat. The Department is also represented at the European Parliament.

Defence

As assessed at November 2007, France maintained a military force of 1,250 and a gendarmerie in the Antilles, with headquarters in Fort-de-France (Martinique).

Economic Affairs

In 2001, according to UN estimates, Guadeloupe's gross domestic product (GDP), measured at current prices, was US $4,460m., equivalent to $10,323 per head. During 1990–2001 GDP increased, in real terms, at an average annual rate of 2.2%; growth in 2001 was 4.6%. Between the censuses of 1990 and 1999, according to provisional figures, the population increased at an average annual rate of 1.0%. In 2004 Guadeloupe's GDP, measured at current prices, was €6,964m., equivalent to €15,910 per head.

Agriculture, hunting, forestry and fishing contributed an estimated 3.0% of GDP in 2004 and engaged an estimated 2.3% of the employed population in 2005. In 2006 agricultural produce (including that related to agrarian production and food industries) accounted for 56.2% of exports. The principal cash crops are bananas and sugar cane. Yams, sweet potatoes and plantains are the chief subsistence crops. Fishing, mostly at an artisanal level, fulfils about two-thirds of domestic requirements, and there is some shrimp-farming. According to UN estimates, agricultural GDP decreased at an average annual rate of 0.3% in 1990–98; the sector increased by 4.1% in 1998.

The industrial sector (including mining, manufacturing, construction, power and food industries) contributed an estimated 13.7% of GDP in 2004 and engaged an estimated 13.2% of the employed population in 2005. Construction contributed 7.8% of GDP in 2004 and engaged an estimated 6.1% of the working population in 2005. The main manufacturing activity is food processing, particularly sugar production, rum distillation, and flour-milling. The sugar industry declined in the 1990s, owing to deteriorating equipment and a reduction in the area planted with sugar cane (from 20,000 ha in 1980 to 9,600 ha in 1999), although there was some recovery in the early 2000s (to 11,500 ha by 2005). Industrial GDP (excluding construction) increased at an average annual rate of 5.2% in 1990–98. Construction expanded at an average rate of 2.2% per year in the same period.

Of some 700,000 tons of petroleum imported annually, about one-third is used for the production of electricity. Efforts are currently being concentrated on the use of renewable energy resources—notably solar, geothermal and wind power—for energy production; there is also thought to be considerable potential for the use of bagasse (a by-product of sugar cane) as a means of generating energy in Guadeloupe. The 64 MW power plant at Le Moule produces some 400m. kWh of electricity annually—almost one-third of Guadeloupe's requirements—using a mixture of coal (75%) and bagasse (25%). Imports of fuels and combustibles accounted for 15.5% of total expenditure on imports in 2006. In 2004 Guadeloupe's total electricity consumption was 1,498m. kWh.

The services sector engaged an estimated 84.6% of the employed population in 2005 and provided an estimated 83.2% of GDP in 2004. Tourism is the Department's principal source of income, and there is significant potential for the further development of the sector, particularly 'eco-tourism'. In 2005 tourist arrivals totalled some 371,985, and in 2001 receipts from tourism amounted to €238m. In 2005 92.4% of arrivals came from metropolitan France or dependent territories.

In 2006 Guadeloupe recorded a trade deficit of some €2,145.9m. The value of exports in that year was €163.9m., less than one-10th of the total value of imports, which were worth €2,309.8m. In 2006 the principal source of imports (54.8%) was metropolitan France, which was also the principal market for exports (54.9%). The USA, Germany, and Trinidad and Tobago are also important trading partners. In the first six months of 2007 trade with the People's Republic of China increased by 43.1%, compared with the same period in the previous year. The principal exports in 2003 were sugar, bananas, boats and rum. The principal imports were machinery and transport equipment (mainly road vehicles), food and live animals, miscellaneous manufactured articles, basic manufactures and chemicals.

Guadeloupe's budget surplus was estimated by the metropolitan authorities to amount to some €92m. in 2005. The departmental budget for 2006 was balanced, with expenditure and revenue of €562.8m. There was an estimated surplus of €48.7m. on the regional budget in 2005. The annual rate of inflation averaged 1.7% in 1996–2006. In 2006 the annual inflation rate was 2.0%. Some 29.7% of the labour force were unemployed in 2005.

As an integral part of France, Guadeloupe belongs to the European Union (EU, see p. 244).

Economic growth in Guadeloupe has been restricted by certain inherent problems: its location; the fact that the domestic market is too narrow to stimulate the expansion of the manufacturing base; the lack of primary materials; and the inflated labour and service costs compared with those of neighbouring countries. Guadeloupe's banana sector was adversely affected by declining prices on the European market from the late 1990s, while the end of the EU's quota system from 2006 was expected to lead to a further contraction in the sector. The sugar industry was also adversely affected by modernization; under reforms introduced in 2006, the sector was entitled to a share of aid worth some €90m. as compensation for price reductions and the cost of restructuring. Industrial action by port workers and in the tourism sector contributed to contractions in those industries in the mid-2000s. Nevertheless, Tourism was estimated to have expanded by some US $1,600m. in 2006. While the sector contributed around 15.5% to GDP in 2007, this contribution was forecast to rise to 17.1% by 2016. GDP expanded by an estimated 5.2% in 2006.

Education

The education system is similar to that of metropolitan France (see chapter on French Guiana). In 2002/03 there were 136 pre-primary and 220 primary schools. In 2000/01 secondary education was provided at 35 institutions. In 2005/06 there were 60,683 students in pre-primary and primary education, while in secondary education there were 53,654 students, of whom some 90% attended state schools. There were also two teacher-training institutes, and colleges of agriculture, fisheries, hotel management, nursing, midwifery and child care. A branch of the Université Antilles-Guyane, at Pointe-à-

FRENCH OVERSEAS POSSESSIONS   *Guadeloupe*

Pitre, has faculties of law, economics, sciences, medicine and Caribbean studies. In 2004/05 there was a total of 8,483 students in higher education. Total government expenditure on education amounted to 2,842m. French francs in 1993.

Public Holidays
2008: 1 January (New Year's Day), 4–5 February (Lenten Carnival), 21–24 March (Easter), 1 May (Labour Day and Ascension Day), 8 May (Victory Day), 12 May (Whit Monday), 27 May (Abolition of Slavery), 14 July (National Day), 15 August (Assumption), 1 November (All Saints' Day), 11 November (Armistice Day), 25 December (Christmas Day).
2009: 1 January (New Year's Day), 23–24 February (Lenten Carnival), 10–13 April (Easter), 1 May (Labour Day), 8 May (Victory Day), 21 May (Ascension Day), 27 May (Abolition of Slavery), 1 June (Whit Monday), 14 July (National Day), 15 August (Assumption), 1 November (All Saints' Day), 11 November (Armistice Day), 25 December (Christmas Day).

Weights and Measures
The metric system is in force.

Statistical Survey

Sources (unless otherwise indicated): Institut National de la Statistique et des Etudes Economiques (INSEE), Service Régional de la Guadeloupe, ave Paul Lacavé, BP 96, 97102 Basse-Terre; tel. 5-90-99-02-50; internet www.insee.fr/fr/insee_regions/guadeloupe; Service de Presse et d'Information, Ministère des Départements et Territoires d'Outre-mer, 27 rue Oudinot, 75700 Paris 07 SP, France; tel. 1-53-69-20-00; fax 1-43-06-60-30; internet www.outre-mer.gouv.fr.

AREA AND POPULATION

(Note: In July 2007 Saint-Barthélemy and Saint-Martin seceded from Guadeloupe to become Overseas Collectivities.)
Area (prior to July 2007—see note above): 1,705 sq km (658.3 sq miles), incl. dependencies (La Désirade, Les Saintes, Marie-Galante, Saint-Barthélemy, Saint-Martin).
Population: 327,002 (males 160,112, females 166,890) at census of 9 March 1982; 387,034 (males 189,187, females 197,847) at census of 15 March 1990; 422,496 (males ..., females ...) at census of 8 March 1999. *1 January 2007* (provisional estimate): 451,000.
Density (1 January 2007, provisional estimate): 264.5 per sq km.
Principal Towns (population at 1999 census): Les Abymes 63,054; Saint-Martin 29,078; Le Gosier 25,360; Baie-Mahault 23,389; Pointe-à-Pitre 20,948; Le Moule 20,827; Petit Bourg 20,528; Sainte Anne 20,410; Basse-Terre (capital) 12,410.
Births, Marriages and Deaths (2005 unless otherwise indicated, provisional figures): Registered live births 7,551 (birth rate 16.0 per 1,000); Registered marriages 1,771 (2004); Registered deaths 3,000 (death rate 6.0 per 1,000). *2007:* Birth rate 14.8 per 1,000; Death rate 6.4 per 1,000. Source: partly Pan American Health Organization.
Expectation of Life (years at birth): 79.2 (males 76.0; females 82.2) in 2007. Source: Pan American Health Organization.
Economically Active Population (persons aged 15 years and over, 1990 census): Agriculture, hunting, forestry and fishing 8,391; Industry and energy 9,630; Construction and public works 13,967; Trade 15,020; Transport and telecommunications 6,950; Financial services 2,802; Other marketable services 26,533; Non-marketable services 34,223; *Total employed* 117,516 (males 68,258, females 49,258); Unemployed 54,926 (males 25,691, females 29,235); *Total labour force* 172,442 (males 93,949, females 78,493). 2005 (estimates at 31 December): Agriculture 2,614; Industry 8,122; Construction 7,055; Trade 17,018; Services 80,480; Total 115,289; Unemployed 48,720; Total labour force 164,009. Note: Figures for employment exclude 20,137 non-salaried workers. *2006:* Unemployed 47,706.

HEALTH AND WELFARE
Key Indicators

Total Fertility Rate (children per woman, 2007): 2.1.
Under-5 Mortality Rate (per 1,000 live births, 2006): 9.0.
Physicians (per 1,000 head, c. 2001): 1.4.
Hospital Beds (per 1,000 head, 2004): 6.1.
Access to Water (% of persons, 2004): 98.
Access to Sanitation (% of persons, 2004): 64.

Source: mostly Pan American Health Organization.
For other sources and definitions, see explanatory note on p. vi.

AGRICULTURE, ETC.

Principal Crops ('000 metric tons, 2006, FAO estimates): Sweet potatoes 3.7; Sugar cane 800.0; Cabbages 2.1; Lettuce and chicory 3.3; Tomatoes 2.8; Cucumbers and gherkins 4.0; Bananas 54.5; Plantains 8.8. *Aggregate Production* ('000 metric tons, may include official, semi-official or estimated data): Total roots and tubers 13.9; Total vegetables (incl. melons) 43.2; Total fruits (excl. melons) 76.2.
Livestock ('000 head, year ending September 2006, FAO estimates): Cattle 73.5; Pigs 30.
Livestock Products ('000 metric tons, 2006, FAO estimates): Cattle meat 3.4; Pig meat 0.9; Chicken meat 1.3; Hen eggs 1.7.
Forestry ('000 cubic metres, 2006, FAO estimates): *Roundwood Removals* (excl. bark): Sawlogs, veneer logs and logs for sleepers 0.3; Fuel wood 31.8; Total 32.1. *Sawnwood Production* (incl. railway sleepers): Total 1.0.
Fishing (metric tons, live weight, 2005, FAO estimates): Capture 10,100 (Common dolphinfish 700; Other mackerel-like fishes 1,600; Marine fishes 7,100; Stromboid conchs 550); Aquaculture 31; *Total catch* 10,131.

Source: FAO.

MINING

Production ('000 metric tons, 2002, estimates): Cement 230; Pumice 210; Salt 49. Source: US Geological Survey.

INDUSTRY

Production: Sugar 73,700 metric tons in 2006; Rum 57,447 hl in 2005; Electric energy 1,603 million kWh in 2006. Source: Institut d'Emission des Départements d'Outre-mer, *Rapport Annuel 2006*.

FINANCE

Currency and Exchange Rates: The French franc was used until the end of February 2002. Euro notes and coins were introduced on 1 January 2002, and the euro became the sole legal tender from 18 February. Some of the figures in this Survey are still in terms of francs. For details of exchange rates, see French Guiana.
Budget: *French Government* (€ million, 2005): Revenue 1,132; Expenditure 1,040. *Regional Budget* (€ million, 2006): Current revenue 239.8 (Taxes 161.1, Other current revenue 78.6); Capital revenues 74.0; Total 313.9. Current expenditure 130.9; Capital expenditure 161.7; Total 292.6 (Source: Département des Etudes et des Statistiques Locales). *Departmental Budget* (excl. debt rescheduling, € million, 2006): Revenue 562.8; Expenditure 562.8 (Source: Département des Etudes et des Statistiques Locales).
Money Supply (million French francs at 31 December 1996): Currency outside banks 1,148; Demand deposits at banks 6,187; Total money 7,335.
Cost of Living (Consumer Price Index; base: 2000 = 100): 108.6 in 2004; 112.1 in 2005; 114.3 in 2006. Source: ILO.
Gross Domestic Product (US $ million at constant 1990 prices): 3,543 in 2001; 3,707 in 2002; 3,844 in 2003. Source: UN, *Statistical Yearbook*.
Expenditure on the Gross Domestic Product (€ million at current prices, 2004): Total final consumption expenditure 6,917 (General government and non-profit institutions serving households 2,560, Households 4,357); Changes in inventories –58; Gross fixed capital formation 1,584; *Total domestic expenditure* 8,443; Exports of goods and services 473; *Less* Imports of goods and services 1,952; *GDP in purchasers' values* 6,964.
Gross Domestic Product by Economic Activity (€ million at current prices, 2004): Agriculture, hunting, forestry and fishing 201; Food industries 91; Other manufacturing 234; Energy 38; Construction 543; Services 5,485 (Restaurants and hotels 248, Transport 235, Commerce 944, Other market services 1,969, Non-market services 2,089); *Sub-total* 6,592; Financial intermediation services indirectly measured (FISIM) –270; Import duties, less subsidies 643; *GDP in purchasers' values* 6,964.

EXTERNAL TRADE

Principal Commodities (€ million, 2006): *Imports c.i.f.:* Products of agriculture and food industries 366.4; Pharmaceutical products 185.5; Home equipment 148.4; Car industry products 285.4; Mechanical equipment 155.9; Electronic equipment 150.8; Fuels and combustibles 358.8; Total (incl. others) 2,309.8. *Exports f.o.b.:* Products of agriculture and food industries 62.8; Boats, planes, trains, and motorcycles 12.2; Electronic equipment 15.1; Metals and metallic products 6.3; Total (incl. others) 163.9.

Principal Trading Partners (€ million, 2006): *Imports c.i.f.:* Aruba 61; China, People's Repub. 64; France (metropolitan) 1,266; Germany 76; Italy 63; Martinique 161; Spain 51; Trinidad and Tobago 72; USA 56; Total (incl. others) 2,309.8. *Exports f.o.b.:* Belgium-Luxembourg 0.6; France (metropolitan) 90.0; French Guiana 4.8; Italy 1.7; Martinique 50.4; United Kingdom 0.7; USA 2.0; Total (incl. others) 163.9.

TRANSPORT

Road Traffic ('000 motor vehicles in use, 2002): Passenger cars 117.7; Commercial vehicles 31.4. Source: UN, *Statistical Yearbook*.

Shipping: *Merchant Fleet* (vessels registered, '000 grt at 31 December 1992): Total displacement 6 (Source: Lloyd's Register-Fairplay, *World Fleet Statistics*). *International Sea-borne Traffic* (1995, unless otherwise indicated): Freight vessels entered 1,257; Freight vessels departed 1,253; Gross freight handled 2,973,169 metric tons; Containers handled 154,263 TEUs; Passengers carried 924,446 (2004).

Civil Aviation (2004): Freight carried 15,738 metric tons; Passengers carried 1,866,739.

TOURISM

Tourist Arrivals by Country (2000): Canada 10,431; France 440,779; Italy 15,670; Switzerland 9,766; USA 92,474; Total (incl. others) 623,134. *2003:* France 386,737; Total (incl. others) 438,819. *2004:* France 406,204; Total (incl. others) 455,981. *2005:* France 343,755; Total (incl. others) 371,985.

Receipts from Tourism (US $ million, incl. passenger transport): 466 in 1998; 375 in 1999; 418 in 2000.

Source: partly World Tourism Organization.

COMMUNICATIONS MEDIA

Radio Receivers ('000 in use): 113 in 1997.

Television Receivers ('000 in use): 118 in 1997.

Telephones ('000 main lines in use): 210.0 in 2001.

Facsimile Machines (number in use): 3,400 in 1996.

Mobile Cellular Telephones ('000 subscribers): 314.7 in 2004.

Personal Computers ('000 in use): 90 in 2004.

Internet Users ('000): 79.0 in 2004.

Daily Newspaper: 1 (estimate) in 1996 (estimated average circulation 35,000 copies).

Sources: UNESCO, *Statistical Yearbook*; UN, *Statistical Yearbook*; International Telecommunication Union.

EDUCATION

Pre-primary (2005/06): 22,130 students (20,108 state, 2,022 private).

Primary (2005/06): 37,300 students (33,402 state, 3,898 private).

Specialized Pre-primary and Primary (2005/06): 1,253 students (1,041 state, 212 private).

Secondary (2005/06): 53,654 students (48,487 state, 5,167 private).

Higher (2004/05): 8,483 students. Source: Ministère de l'Education Nationale, de la Recherche et de la Technologie.

Teachers (2004/05): *Primary:* 3,384 (3,140 state, 244 private); *Secondary:* 4,696 (4,255 state, 441 private); *Higher:* 203. Source: Ministère de l'Education Nationale, *Repères et références statistiques—édition 2005*.

Institutions (2002/03): 136 pre-primary; 220 primary. Source: Ministère de l'Education Nationale, de l'Enseignement Supérieur et de la Recherche, *Repères et références statistiques sur les enseignements, la formation et la recherche 2003*.

Adult Literacy Rate: 90.1% (males 89.7%; females 90.5%) in 1998. Source: Pan American Health Organization.

Directory

The Government

(March 2008)

Prefect: JEAN-JACQUES BROT, Préfecture, Palais d'Orléans, rue Lardenoy, 97109 Basse-Terre Cédex; tel. 5-90-99-39-00; fax 5-90-81-58-32; internet www.guadeloupe.pref.gouv.fr.

President of the General Council: Dr JACQUES GILLOT (GUSR), Hôtel du Département, blvd Félix Eboué, 97109 Basse-Terre; tel. 5-90-99-77-77; fax 5-90-99-76-00; e-mail info@cg971.fr; internet www.cg971.fr.

President of the Economic and Social Committee: JOCELYN JALTON, rue Peynier, 97100 Basse-Terre; tel. 5-90-41-05-25; fax 5-90-41-05-23; e-mail cr-cesr-guadeloupe@wanadoo.fr; internet www.cr-guadeloupe.fr.

President of the Culture, Education and Environment Committee: ALAIN BUFFON, rue Peynier, 97100 Basse-Terre; tel. 5-90-41-05-15; fax 5-90-41-05-23; e-mail cr-cesr-guadeloupe@wanadoo.fr; internet www.cr-guadeloupe.fr.

Deputies to the French National Assembly: ERIC JALTON (PCG), GABRIELLE LOUIS-CARABIN (UMP), JEANNY MARC-MATTHIASIN (GUSR), VICTORIN LUREL (PS).

Representatives to the French Senate: Dr JACQUES GILLOT (Groupe Socialiste), DANIEL MARSIN (Rassemblement Démocratique et Social Européen), LUCETTE MICHAUX-CHEVRY (UMP).

Conseil Régional
ave Paul Lacavé, Petit-Paris, 97109 Basse-Terre; tel. 5-90-80-40-40; fax 5-90-81-34-19; internet www.cr-guadeloupe.fr.

President: VICTORIN LUREL (PS).

Elections, 21 and 28 March 2004

	Seats
Guadeloupe pour Tous*	29
Action Guadeloupe pour l'Initiative et le Rassemblement (AGIR)†	12
Total	41

Seven other lists contested the elections: NOFWAP; Combat Ouvrier; Alternative Citoyenne; Union pour une Guadeloupe Responsable; Lé Verts Sé Nou Tout; Le Renouveau Guadeloupéen; and Priorité à l'Education et à l'Environnement

* Comprising the PS, PPDG, GUSR and other left-wing candidates.
† Comprising the UMP, other right-wing candidates and socialist dissidents.

Political Organizations

Combat Ouvrier: BP 213, 97156 Point-à-Pitre Cédex; tel. 5-90-26-23-58; e-mail redaction@combat-ouvrier.net; Trotskyist; associated with national party Lutte Ouvrière; mem. of the Internationalist Communist Union; Leaders JEAN-MARIE NOMERTIN, GÉRARD SÉNÉ.

Guadeloupe Unie, Socialisme et Réalité (GUSR): Pointe-à-Pitre; e-mail d.larifla@senat.fr; 'dissident' faction of the Parti Socialiste; Pres. DOMINIQUE LARIFLA.

Konvwa pou Liberasyon Nasyon Gwadloup (KLNG): Pointe-à-Pitre; f. 1997; pro-independence; Leader LUC REINETTE.

Parti Communiste Guadeloupéen (PCG): 119 rue Vatable, 97110 Pointe-à-Pitre; tel. 5-90-88-23-07; f. 1944; Sec.-Gen. CHRISTIAN CÉLESTE.

Parti Socialiste (PS): 8 Résidence Légitimus, blvd Légitimus, 97110 Pointe-à-Pitre; tel. and fax 5-90-21-65-72; e-mail fede971@parti-socialiste.fr; internet www.parti-socialiste.fr; divided into two factions to contest the March 1992 and March 1993 elections; Jt First Secs MARLÈNE MELISSE, FAVROT DAVRAIN.

Union pour un Mouvement Populaire (UMP): Les Portes de Saint Martin Bellevue, 97150 Saint Martin; tel. and fax 5-90-87-50-01; fax 5-90-87-75-72; e-mail gabriellelouiscarabin@ump971.org; internet www.u-m-p.org; f. 2002; centre-right; local br. of the metropolitan party; Pres., Departmental Cttee GABRIELLE LOUIS CARABIN.

Les Verts Guadeloupe: 32 rue Alsace-Lorraine, 97110 Pointe-à-Pitre; tel. 5-90-35-41-90; fax 5-90-25-02-62; internet www.guadeloupe.lesverts.fr; ecologist; departmental br. of the metropolitan party; Regional spokespersons HARRY DURIMEL, MARIE LINE PIRBAKAS.

Other political organizations participating in the 2004 elections included Mouvement pour la Démocratie et le Développement

FRENCH OVERSEAS POSSESSIONS

Guadeloupe

(MDDP), Union Populaire pour la Libération de la Guadeloupe (UPLG), Mouvman Gwadloupéyen (MG), Parti Progressiste Démocratique Guadeloupéen (PPDG), Renouveau Socialiste; and the coalitions Priorité à l'Education et à l'Environnement and Union pour une Guadeloupe Responsable.

Judicial System

Cour d'Appel: Palais de Justice, 4 blvd Félix Eboué, 97100 Basse-Terre; tel. 5-90-80-63-36; fax 5-90-80-63-39; First Pres. Dominique Gaschard; Procurator-Gen. Christine Penichon.

There are two Tribunaux de Grande Instance and four Tribunaux d'Instance.

Religion

The majority of the population belong to the Roman Catholic Church.

CHRISTIANITY

The Roman Catholic Church

Guadeloupe comprises the single diocese of Basse-Terre, suffragan to the archdiocese of Fort-de-France, Martinique. At 31 December 2004 there were an estimated 400,000 adherents, representing some 84% of the total population. The Bishop participates in the Antilles Episcopal Conference, based in Port of Spain, Trinidad and Tobago.

Bishop of Basse-Terre: Rt Rev. Ernest Mesmin Lucien Cabo, Evêché, pl. Saint-François, BP 369, 97100 Basse-Terre Cédex; tel. 5-90-81-36-69; fax 5-90-81-98-23; e-mail eveche@catholique-guadeloupe.info.

OTHER CHURCHES

Seventh-day Adventist Church: Eglise Adventiste de la Guadeloupe, BP 19, 97151 Pointe-à-Pitre Cédex; tel. 5-90-82-79-76; fax 5-90-83-44-24; e-mail adventiste.federation@wanadoo.fr; internet www.adventiste-gpe.org; f. 1931; Pres. Alain Angerville; Sec. Daniel Loussala; 11,957 members (2007).

Other denominations active in Guadeloupe include the Baptist Church and Jehovah's Witnesses.

The Press

France Antilles: 1 rue Hincelin, BP 658, 97159 Pointe-à-Pitre; tel. 5-90-90-25-25; fax 5-90-91-78-31; f. 1964; subsidiary of Groupe France Antilles; daily; Chair. Philippe Hersant; Man. Dir Frédéric Aurand; circ. 50,000.

Match: 33 rue Peynier, 97110 Pointe-à-Pitre; tel. 5-90-82-18-68; fax 5-90-82-01-87; fortnightly; Dir Marie Antonia Jabbour; circ. 6,000.

Nouvelles Etincelles: 119 rue Vatable, 97110 Pointe-à-Pitre; tel. 5-90-91-12-77; fax 5-90-83-69-90; f. 1944 as l'Etincelle, organ of the Parti Communiste Guadeloupéen (q.v.); present name adopted 2005; weekly; Editor-in-Chief Danik Zandronis; circ. 5,000.

Sept Mag Communication: Immeuble Curaçao, voie Verte, 97122 Baie-Mahault; weekly; Dir Jacques Canneval; circ. 30,000.

Terre de Guadeloupe: Immeuble Pluriel, 3 rue Ferdinand Forest, 97122 Baie-Mahault; tel. 5-90-25-20-20; fax 5-90-38-29-61; f. 2003; publ. by Groupe Maximini; monthly; local and environmental issues; CEO Jean-Yves Frixon; Publ. Dir Thierry Elfgang; circ. 60,000; also publ. *Maximini News* (f. 2005, daily, circ. 3,500).

TV Magazine Guadeloupe: 1 rue Paul Lacavé, BP 658, 97169 Pointe-à-Pitre; tel. 5-90-90-25-25; weekly.

Publishers

Editions Caret (Centre Antillais de Recherche et d'Edition de Textes): BP 165, 97190 Le Gosier; tel. and fax 5-90-84-82-29; e-mail caret@wanadoo.fr; French-Creole language, culture and fiction; Dir Jacqueline Picard.

Editions Jasor: 46 rue Schoëlcher, 97110 Pointe-à-Pitre; tel. 5-90-91-18-48; fax 5-90-21-07-01; e-mail editionsjasor@orange.fr; French-Creole culture, biography and language, and youth fiction; Dir Régine Jasor.

PLB Editions: route de Mathurin, 97190 Gosier; tel. 5-90-89-91-17; fax 5-90-89-91-05; e-mail plbeditions@wanadoo.fr; internet www.plbeditions.com; f. 1997; regional natural history and French-Creole youth fiction; Dirs Chantal Mattet, Thierry Petit le Brun.

Broadcasting and Communications

TELECOMMUNICATIONS

Digicel Antilles Françaises Guyane: see Martinique—Telecommunications.

ONLY: SCI, Brand, voie Verte, Z. I. de Jarry, 97122 Baie-Mahault; e-mail communication@outremer-telecom.fr; internet www.outremer-telecom.fr; f. 1998 as Outremer Telecom Guadeloupe; present name adopted following merger of Volubis, ONLY and OOL in 2006; subsidiary of Outremer Telecom, France; telecommunications provider; CEO Jean-Michel Hegesippe.

Orange Caraïbe: ZAC de Moudong, Sud Voie No 3, 97122 Baie-Mahault; internet www.orangecaraibe.com; f. 1996; subsidiary of Orange France; mobile cellular telephone operator; network coverage incl. Martinique and French Guiana; Gen. Man. Jean-Philippe Gay.

BROADCASTING

Réseau France Outre-mer (RFO): Destrellan, BP 180, 97122 Baie-Mahault Cédex; tel. 5-90-60-96-96; fax 5-90-60-96-82; e-mail rfo@rfo.fr; internet guadeloupe.rfo.fr; f. 1964; acquired by Groupe France Télévisions in 2004; fmrly Société Nationale de Radio-Télévision Française d'Outre-mer, present name adopted in 1998; radio and TV; Gen. Man. François Guilbeau; Regional Dir Jean Philippe Pascal.

Radio

Europe 2 Fréquence Alizée: l'Houezel, 97190 Le Gosier; tel. 5-90-84-88-86; fax 5-90-84-88-83; e-mail charlotte.combastet@lagardere-active.com; internet www.europe2.fr; f. 1987; subsidiary of Lagardère Active Publicité; commercial music station.

Kilti FM: Impasse Augustin Fresnel, Immeuble 590, Z. I. de Jarry, 97122 Baie-Mahault; tel. 5-90-32-52-61; fax 5-90-25-66-03; e-mail kiltifm@wanadoo.fr; internet www.kiltifm.com; f. 2006; French and Creole.

NRJ Guadeloupe: 2 blvd de la Marne, 97200 Fort-de-France; tel. 5-96-63-63-63; fax 5-96-73-73-15; e-mail webmaster@nrjantilles.com; internet www.nrjantilles.com; Dir Franck Férandier-Sicard; Dir Jean-Christophe Martinez.

Radio Caraïbes International (RCI Guadeloupe): Carrefour Grand Camp, BP 40, 97151 Point-à-Pitre Cédex; tel. 5-90-83-96-96; fax 5-90-83-96-97; internet www.rci.gp; f. 1962; Dir Frank Ferandier-Sicard; Man. Thierry Fundéré; Editor-in-Chief Rodolphe Beppo.

Radio Contact: 40 bis, rue Lamartine, 97110 Point-à-Pitre; tel. 5-96-82-25-41; fax 5-96-91-56-77; internet www.radio-contact.net; operated by l'Asscn Citoyenne de Sauvegarde et de Défense des Intérêts des Guadeloupéens; Dir Octavie Losio; Man. Henri Yoyotte.

Radio Gayak Media Delkaribe: BP 535, 97135 Pointe-à-Pitre Cédex; tel. 6-90-55-85-15; fax 5-90-83-12-30; e-mail gaston971@yahoo.fr; operated by the l'Asscn Guadeloupéenne de Défense et de Valorisation du Patrimoine Historique, Culturel et de l'Environnement; French and Creole; Dir Jean Adélaïde; Man. Danik Ibrahim Zandwonis.

Radio Haute Tension: route de Petit Marquisat, Routhiers, 97130 Capesterre Belle Eau; tel. 5-90-99-08-12; e-mail hautetension2@wanadoo.fr; internet www.radiohautetension.fr; f. 1986; Dir Huguette Hubert; Man. Ruddy Cornelie.

Radio Inter S'Cool (RIS): Lycée Ducharmoy, 97120 Saint-Claude; tel. and fax 5-90-80-38-40; e-mail ris.amme@wanadoo.fr; internet www.radiointerscool.net; educational and school-focused programmes; French and Creole; Pres. Jaques Jovien.

Radio Mornalo 106.2: Immeuble Vivies, rue Thomas Edyson, Z. I. Jarry, 97122 Baie-Mahault; tel. 5-90-32-58-42; fax 5-90-26-02-97; e-mail direction@eurekacaraibes.com; internet www.radio106-2fm.com; f. 2003; commercial radio station; French and Creole; Dir Jean-Marc de Creny.

Radio Tanbou: résidence Espace, 97110 Point-à-Pitre; tel. 5-90-21-66-45; fax 5-90-21-66-48; e-mail kontak@radyotanbou.com; internet www.radyotanbou.com; French and Creole; operated by the l'Asscn pour le Développement de l'Information et de la Culture Guadeloupéenne.

Zouk Radio: Immeuble Général Bricolage, Petit Pérou, 97139 Les Abymes; tel. 5-90-89-25-80; fax 5-90-89-26-22; internet www.zoukradio.fr; commercial music station; French and Creole.

Other radio stations include: Média Tropical Guadeloupe; Radio Actif; Radio Arago; Radio Basses Internationale; Radio Bélo; Radio Climax; Radio Cosmique One; Radio Côte sous le Vent; Radio Eclair; Radio Horizon; Radio Karata; Radio Madras; Radio Massabielle;

Radio Saint-Martin; Radio Saphir; Radio Sofaïa Altitude; Radio Souffle de Vie; Radio Tonic; and Radio Vie Meilleure.

Television

Antilles Télévision (ATV): see Martinique—Television.

Archipel 4: 21 rue Peynier, 97110 Pointe-à-Pitre; tel. 5-93-21-05-20; f. 2002; Chair. JEAN-CLAUDE THOMASEAU.

Canal Plus Antilles: Immeuble Canal Media, Moudong Centre Jarry, 97122 Baie-Mahault; tel. 5-90-32-37-55; fax 5-90-32-37-60; e-mail mrichol@canalantilles.gp; f. 1993; subsidiary of Groupe Canal Plus, France; satellite TV station; Chair DOMINIQUE FAGOT.

Canal 10: Z. I. de Jarry; tel. 5-90-26-73-03; fax 5-90-26-61-25; f. 1990; focus on social, economic and cultural issues in Guadeloupe; produces 100% of its programmes; Man. MICHEL RODRIGUEZ.

Eclair TV (ETV): Basse-Terre Télévision, Pintade, 97100 Basse-Terre; tel. 5-90-60-15-30; fax 5-90-60-15-33; e-mail eclairfm.com@orange.fr; f. 1998; community station local to Basse-Terre; Pres. MARIO-CONSTANT MORADEL.

La Une Guadeloupe (L'A1): 20 rue Henri Becquerel, Z. I. de Jarry, 97122 Baie-Mahault; tel. 5-90-38-06-06; fax 5-90-38-06-07; f. 1998; fmrly TCI; gen. interest; purchases 65% of programmes from TF1, France (2003); Pres. JOSÉ GADDARKHAN.

Finance

(cap. = capital; res = reserves; dep. = deposits; m. = million; brs = branches; amounts in euros unless otherwise indicated)

BANKING

Central Bank

Institut d'Emission des Départments d'Outre-mer (IEDOM): blvd Légitimus, BP 196, 97155 Pointe-à-Pitre Cédex; tel. 5-90-93-74-00; fax 5-90-93-74-25; internet www.iedom.fr; Dir FRANCIS ROCHE TOUSSAINT.

Commercial Banks

Banque des Antilles Françaises: pl. de la Victoire, BP 696, 97110 Pointe-à-Pitre Cédex; tel. 5-90-26-80-07; fax 5-90-26-74-48; internet www.bdaf.gp; f. 1967 by merger of Banque de la Martinique and Banque de la Guadeloupe; subsidiary of Financière Océor, France; cap. 12.2m., res −1.9m., dep. 695.3m. (Dec. 2005); Pres. and Chair. CHRISTIAN CAMUS; Gen. Man. JEAN-MARC VARGEL; 19 brs.

Banque Française Commerciale Antilles-Guyane (BFC Antilles-Guyane): Immeuble BFC AG, Grand Camp-La Rocade, BP 13, 97151 Pointe-à-Pitre Cédex; tel. 5-90-21-56-70; fax 5-90-21-56-80; e-mail f.aujoulat@bfc-ag.com; internet www.bfc-ag.com; f. 1976 as br. of Banque Française Commerciale, SA, separated 1984; total assets 594.6m. (2003); Chair. PIERRE DE BELLEFON; Gen. Man. JEAN MARGUIER.

BNP Paribas Guadeloupe: pl. de la Rénovation, BP 161, 97155 Pointe-à-Pitre; tel. 5-90-90-58-58; fax 5-90-90-04-07; internet www.bnpparibas.com; f. 1941; subsidiary of BNP Paribas, France; CEO JEAN-PIERRE BAJON-ARNAL; Gen. Sec. RAMÓN HERNÁNDEZ; 12 brs.

BRED Banque Populaire (BRED-BP): Immeuble Simcar, blvd Marquisat de Houelbourg, Z. I. Jarry, 97122 Baie-Mahault; tel. 5-90-89-67-00; internet www.bred.banquepopulaire.fr; cap. 242m. (Oct. 2005); Regional Man. THIERRY MOREAU.

Caisse d'Epargne de la Guadeloupe: 20 Lotissement Plazza II, Grand Camp-La Rocade, 97142 Abymes, BP 22, 97151 Pointe-à-Pitre Cédex; tel. 5-90-93-12-12; fax 5-90-93-12-13; Pres. DANIEL NUCCIO.

Crédit Agricole de la Guadeloupe: Petit Pérou, 97176 Abymes Cédex; tel. 5-90-90-65-65; fax 5-90-90-65-89; e-mail catelnet@cr900.credit-agricole.fr; internet www.ca-guadeloupe.fr; total assets 1,228.1m. (Dec. 2003); Pres. CHRISTIAN FLÉREAU; Gen. Man. ROGER WUNSCHEL; 30 brs.

Crédit Maritime de la Guadeloupe: 36 rue Achille René-Boisneuf, BP 292, 97175 Pointe-à-Pitre; tel. 5-90-89-52-42; fax 5-90-83-46-37; e-mail pointe-a-pitre-agence-cmm@creditmaritime.com; internet www.creditmaritime-outremer.com; Dir GÉRARD CADIC; 4 agencies.

Société Générale de Banque aux Antilles (SGBA): I30 rue Frébault, BP 55, 97152 Pointe-à-Pitre; tel. 5-90-25-49-77; fax 5-90-25-49-78; e-mail sgba@wanadoo.fr; internet www.sgba.fr; f. 1979; cap. 18.6m., res −9.6m., dep. 265.1m. (Dec. 2005); Chair. JEAN-LOUIS MATTEI; Gen. Man. JEAN-MAURICE BEAUX; 5 brs in Guadeloupe, 3 brs in Martinique.

Development Banks

Banque de Développement de Petites et Moyennes Entreprises (BDPME): c/o AFD, blvd Légitimus, BP 160, 97159 Pointe-à-Pitre Cédex; tel. 5-90-89-65-58; fax 5-90-21-04-55; Rep. MUGUETTE DAIJARDIN.

Société de Crédit pour le Développement de Guadeloupe (SODEGA): Carrefour Raizet Baimbridge, BP 54, 97152 Pointe-à-Pitre; tel. 5-90-82-65-00; fax 5-90-90-17-91; e-mail crédit@sodega.fr; internet www.sodega.fr; f. 1970; bought from the Agence Française de Développement (q.v.) by BRED Banque Populaire (q.v.) in 2003.

INSURANCE

Some 30 of the principal European insurance companies are represented in Pointe-à-Pitre, and another six companies have offices in Basse-Terre.

AGF Vie France: Immeuble AGF, ZAC Houelbourg-Jarry, BP 2458, 97085 Jarry; tel. 5-90-41-13-14; fax 5-90-41-96-91; e-mail guavie1@agfgua.com; life insurance.

Capma & Capmi: blvd Légitimus, (face à Air France), 97110 Pointe-à-Pitre; tel. 5-90-83-27-12; fax 5-90-91-19-40.

GAN Guadeloupe: 59–61 rue A. R. Boisneuf, BP152, 97171 Pointe-à-Pitre Cédex; tel. 5-90-89-32-00; fax 5-90-04-43; subsidiary of Groupama, France.

Trade and Industry

GOVERNMENT AGENCIES

Direction de l'Agriculture et de la Forêt (DAF): Jardin Botanique, 97100 Basse-Terre; tel. 5-90-99-09-09; fax 5-90-99-09-10; e-mail daf971@agriculture.gouv.fr; internet www.guadeloupe.pref.gouv.fr/daf971; Man. GILBERT GRIVAULT.

Direction Régionale des Affaires Maritimes (DRAM): 1 quai Layrle, BP 473, 97164 Pointe-à-Pitre; tel. 5-90-82-03-13; fax 5-90-90-07-33; responsible for shipping, fishing and other maritime issues at a national and community level.

Direction Régionale du Commerce Extérieur Antilles-Guyane (DRCE): see Martinique—Trade and Industry.

Direction Régionale de l'Industrie, de la Recherche et de l'Environnement (DRIRE): 552 rue de la Chapelle, Z. I. Jarry, 97122 Baie-Mahault; tel. 5-90-38-03-47; fax 5-90-38-03-50; active in industry, business services, transport, public works, tourism and distribution; Departmental Co-ordinator MICHEL MASSON.

DEVELOPMENT ORGANIZATIONS

Agence de l'Environnement et de la Maîtrise de l'Energie (ADEME): Immeuble Café Center, rue Ferdinand Forest, Z. I. Jarry, 97122 Baie-Mahault; tel. 5-90-26-78-05; fax 5-90-26-87-15; e-mail ademe.guadeloupe@ademe.fr; internet www.ademe.fr; developing energy and waste management; Man. GUY SIMONNOT.

Agence pour la Promotion des Investissements en Guadeloupe (APRIGA): 12 Convenance's Center, Lieu-dit Convenance, 97122 Baie-Mahault; tel. 5-90-94-45-40; fax 5-90-95-86-47; e-mail apriga@apriga.com; internet www.apriga.com; f. 1979; as Agence pour la Promotion de l'Industrie de la Guadeloupe; Pres. LYLIANE PIQUION SALOME.

Agence Française de Développement (AFD): blvd Légitimus, BP 160, 97154 Pointe-à-Pitre Cédex; tel. 5-90-89-65-65; fax 5-90-83-03-73; internet www.afd.fr; fmrly Caisse Française de Développement; Man. YVES MALPEL.

CHAMBERS OF COMMERCE

Chambre d'Agriculture de la Guadeloupe: Espace régional Agricole, Convenance BP 35, 97122 Baie-Mahault; tel. 5-90-25-17-17; fax 5-90-26-07-22; e-mail cda_direction@guadeloupe.chambagri.fr; Pres. MAURICE RAMASSAMY.

Chambre de Commerce et d'Industrie de Basse-Terre: 6 rue Victor Hugues, 97100 Basse-Terre; tel. 5-90-99-44-44; fax 5-90-81-21-17; e-mail cci-basse-terre@wanadoo.fr; internet www.basseterre.cci.fr; f. 1832; Pres. GÉRARD THÉOBALD; 32 mems.

Chambre de Commerce et d'Industrie de Pointe-à-Pitre: Hôtel Consulaire, rue Félix Eboué, 97159 Pointe-à-Pitre Cédex; tel. 5-90-93-76-00; fax 5-90-90-21-87; e-mail contact@pointe-a-pitre.cci.fr; internet www.pointe-a-pitre.cci.fr; Pres. COLETTE KOURY; Dir-Gen. JACQUES GARRETA; 34 full mems and 17 assoc. mems.

Chambre de Métiers de la Guadeloupe: route Choisy, BP 61, 97120 Saint-Claude; tel. 5-90-80-23-33; fax 5-90-80-08-93; e-mail sgr@cmguadeloupe.org; internet www.cmguadeloupe.org; Pres. JOËL LOBEAU; 11,630 mems (2005).

Jeune Chambre Economique de Basse-Terre: BP 316, 97100 Basse-Terre; tel. 5-90-81-13-73; e-mail jce.bt@laposte.net; Pres. FABIENNE BOA.

Jeune Chambre Economique de Pointe-à-Pitre: BP 505, 97168 Pointe-à-Pitre Cedex; tel. 5-90-89-01-30; fax 5-90-91-72-98; e-mail jcepap2006@wanadoo.fr; internet www.jcepap.fr; Pres. DELPHINE TINVAL.

FRENCH OVERSEAS POSSESSIONS   *Guadeloupe*

EMPLOYERS' ORGANIZATIONS

Association des Moyennes et Petites Industries (AMPI): Z.I. Jarry, BP 2325, 97187 Jarry Cédex; tel. 5-90-25-06-28; fax 5-90-25-06-29; e-mail mpi.guadeloupe@wanadoo.fr; internet www.mpi-guadeloupe.com; f. 1974; Pres. Patrick Doquin; Gen. Sec Jean Joachim; 116 mem. cos.

Interprofession Guadeloupéenne pour la Canne à Sucre (IGUACANNE): Espace Régional Agricole de Convenance, 97122 Baie-Mahault; f. 2005; represents sugar cane growers, sugar producers and professional bodies; Pres. Victor Nanette.

Ordre des pharmaciens du département Guadeloupe: Rocade Forum de Grand Camp, Bâtiment A, No 1, 97142 Pointe-à-Pitre; tel. 5-90-21-66-05; fax 5-90-21-66-07; Pres. Claudie Espiand.

Syndicat des Producteurs-Exportateurs de Sucre et de Rhum de la Guadeloupe et Dépendances: Z. I. Jarry, 97122 Baie-Mahault; BP 2015, 97191 Pointe-à-Pitre; tel. 5-90-23-53-15; fax 5-90-23-52-34; f. 1937; Pres. Ivan de Dieuleveult; 4 mems.

Union des Entreprises-Mouvement des Entreprises de France (UDE-MEDEF): Immeuble SCI BTB, voie Principale de Jarry, Baie-Mahault; tel. 5-90-26-83-58; fax 5-90-26-83-67; e-mail ude.medef@medef-guadeloupe.com; Pres. Christian Vivies.

UTILITIES

Electricity

Electricité de France Guadeloupe (EdF): BP 85, 97153 Pointe-à-Pitre; tel. 5-90-82-40-34; fax 5-90-83-30-02; e-mail marie-therese.fournier@edfgdf.fr; internet guadeloupe.edf.fr; electricity producer; Man. Jean-Michel Lebeau.

Water

Veolia Water—Compagnie Générale des Eaux Guadeloupe: Centre de la Guadeloupe, 7 Morne Vergain, BP 17, 97139 Abymes, Pointe-à-Pitre; tel. 5-90-89-76-76; fax 5-90-91-39-10; internet www.veoliaeau.com; fmrly SOGEA.

TRADE UNIONS

Centrale des Travailleurs Unis de la Guadeloupe (CTU): Logement Test 14, Bergevin, 97110 Pointe-à-Pitre; BP 120, 97153 Pointe-à-Pitre Cédex; tel. 5-90-28-96-36; fax 5-90-28-81-16; e-mail ctu.gpe@wanadoo.fr; internet www.ctu-guadeloupe.fr; f. 1999 by merger of the FASU-G and Centrale Syndicale des Travailleurs de la Guadeloupe; represents public and private sector workers; collegial directorate of 11 Secs-Gen; 3,500 mems.

Confédération Générale du Travail de la Guadeloupe (CGTG): 4 Cité Artisanale de Bergevin, BP 779, 97110 Pointe-à-Pitre Cédex; tel. 5-90-82-34-61; fax 5-90-91-04-00; f. 1961; Sec.-Gen. Jean-Marie Nomertin; 5,000 mems.

Fédération Départementale des Syndicats d'Exploitants de la Guadeloupe (FDSEA): Chambre d'Agriculture, Rond-Point de Destrellan, 97122 Baie-Mahault; tel. 5-90-26-06-47; fax 5-90-26-48-82; e-mail fdsea5@wanadoo.fr; affiliated to the Fédération Nationale des Syndicats d'Exploitants; Pres. Firmin Lodin Nelson.

Fédération Syndicale Unitaire Guadeloupe (FSU): 2108 Immeuble Cap. Moede, 97142 Grand Camp; tel. 5-90-90-10-21; fax 5-90-90-29-42; e-mail fsu971@fsu.fr; f. 1993; departmental br. of the Fédération Syndicale Unitaire; represents public sector employees in teaching, research and training, and also agriculture, justice, youth and sports, and culture; Sec. José Severien.

SGEN-CFDT: Maison Test 14, BP 676, Bergevin, 97169 Pointe-à-Pitre; tel. 5-90-83-16-50; fax 5-90-91-78-02; e-mail guadeloupe@sgen.cfdt.fr; affiliated to the Fédération des Syndicats Généraux de l'Education Nationale et de la Recherche; represents teaching staff.

Union Départementale de la Confédération Française des Travailleurs Chrétiens (UD CFTC): 29 rue Victor Hugo, BP 245, 97159 Pointe-à-Pitre Cédex; tel. 5-90-82-04-01; f. 1937; Sec.-Gen. Albert Sarkis; 3,500 mems.

Union Départementale des Syndicats Force Ouvrière: 59 rue Lamartine, BP 687, 97110 Pointe-à-Pitre; tel. 5-90-82-86-83; fax 5-90-82-16-12; e-mail udfoguadeloupe@force-ouvriere.fr; Gen. Sec. Max Evariste; 1,500 mems.

Union Générale des Travailleurs de la Guadeloupe (UGTG): rue Paul Lacavé, 97110 Pointe-à-Pitre; tel. 5-90-83-10-07; fax 5-90-89-08-70; e-mail ugtg@ugtg.org; internet www.ugtg.org; f. 1973; confederation of pro-independence trade unions incl. Union des Agents de la Sécurité Sociale (UNASS), l'Union des Employés du Commerce (UEC), Union des Travailleurs de l'Etat et du Département (UTED), l'Union des Travailleurs des Collectivités (UTC), l'Union des Travailleurs de l'Hôtellerie, du Tourisme et de la Restauration (UTHTR), l'Union des Travailleurs des Produits Pétroliers (UTPP), l'Union des Travailleurs de la Santé (UTS), and l'Union des Travailleurs des Télécommunications (UTT); Gen. Sec. Raymond Gauthierot; 4,000 mems.

Union des Moyennes et Petites Entreprises de Guadeloupe (UMPEG): 17 Immeuble Patio, Grand Camp, 97142 Abymes, Pointe-à-Pitre; tel. 5-90-91-79-31; fax 5-90-93-09-18.

Union Régionale Guadeloupe: Immeuble Jabol, 5ème étage, rue de l'Assainissement, 97110 Pointe-à-Pitre; tel. 5-90-91-01-15; fax 5-90-83-08-64; e-mail m.alidor@aol.fr; internet www.unsa.org; mem. of l'Union Nationale des Syndicats Autonomes (UNSA).

UNSA Education Guadeloupe: Immeuble Jabol, 5ème étage, rue de l'Assainissement, 97110 Point-à-Pitre; tel. 5-90-91-01-15; fax 5-90-83-08-64; e-mail pelage.girard@wanadoo.fr; Sec.-Gen. Girard Pelage.

Transport

RAILWAYS

There are no railways in Guadeloupe.

ROADS

In 1990 there were 2,069 km (1,286 miles) of roads in Guadeloupe, of which 323 km were Routes Nationales.

SHIPPING

The Port Autonome de la Guadeloupe comprises five sites. The two principal seaports are at Pointe-à-Pitre, which offers both cargo-handling and passenger facilities, and the container terminal at Jarry (Baie-Mahault); the smaller port of Basse-Terre caters to freight and inter-island passenger traffic. There is also a sugar terminal at Folle-Anse (Saint-Louis); and a marina at Bas-du-Fort with 1,000 berths for pleasure craft.

Port Autonome de la Guadeloupe: Gare Maritime, BP 485, 97165 Pointe-à-Pitre Cédex; tel. 5-90-21-39-00; fax 5-90-21-39-69; e-mail v-tarer@port-guadeloupe.com; internet www.port-guadeloupe.com; port authority; Pres. Gil Thémine; Gen. Man. Christian Broutin.

Compagnie Générale Portuaire: Marina Bas-du-Fort, 97110 Pointe-à-Pitre; tel. 5-90-93-66-20; fax 5-90-90-81-53; e-mail marina@marina-pap.com; internet www.caribbean-marinas.com; port authority; Man. Philippe Chevallier; Harbour Master Tony Breslau; 1,000 berths for non-commercial traffic.

Compagnie Générale Maritime Antilles-Guyane: 30 blvd de la Pointe, Z. I. Jarry, BP 92, 97122 Baie-Mahault; tel. 5-90-25-57-00; fax 5-90-26-74-62; e-mail ptp.dhouzard@cma-cgm.com; subsidiary of CMA-CGM, France; shipping agents, stevedoring; Gen. Man. Dominique Houzard.

Société Guadeloupéenne de Consignation et Manutention (SGCM): 8 rue de la Chapelle, BP 2360, 97001 Jarry Cédex; tel. 5-90-38-05-55; fax 5-90-26-95-39; e-mail gerard.petrelluzzi@sgcm.fr; internet www.sgcm.gp; f. 1994; shipping agents, stevedoring; also operates Navimar Cruises inter-island tour co; Chair. Bernard Aubery; Gen. Man. Gerard Petrelluzzi; 17 berths.

Société de Transport Maritimes Brudey Frères: 78 centre St John Perse, 97110 Pointe-à-Pitre; tel. 5-90-91-60-87; fax 5-90-93-00-79; e-mail brudey.freres@wanadoo.fr; internet www.brudey-freres.fr; f. 1983; inter-island ferry service; Dir Denis Brudey; 6 vessels; c. 400,000 passengers per year.

Transcaraïbes S.A.: BP 2453, 97085 Pointe-à-Pitre; tel. 5-90-26-63-27; fax 5-90-26-67-49; e-mail transcaraibes.gpe@wanadoo.fr; internet www.transcaraibes-sa.com; f. 1976; shipping agents, stevedoring; office in Martinique; Gen. Man. Pascal Pedrosa.

CIVIL AVIATION

Raizet International Airport is situated 3 km (2 miles) from Pointe-à-Pitre and is equipped to handle jet-engined aircraft. There are smaller airports on the islands of Marie-Galante, La Désirade and Saint-Barthélémy.

Air Caraïbes (CAT): ZAC de Dothemare, 97139 Abymes; tel. 5-90-82-47-41; fax 5-90-82-47-49; e-mail vmalialin@aircaraibes.com; internet www.aircaraibes.com; f. 2000 following merger of Air St Martin, Air St Barts, Air Guadeloupe and Air Martinique; owned by Groupe Dubreuil; operates daily inter-island, regional and international services within the Caribbean, and flights to Brazil, French Guiana and Paris; CEO Serge Tsygalnitzky; 16 aircraft; 800,000 passengers (2006).

Air Caraïbes Atlantique: Aéroport, 97232 Le Lamentin; f. 2003; subsidiary of Air Caraïbes; services between Pointe-à-Pitre, Fort-de-France (Martinique) and Paris; Pres. François Hersen.

Tourism

Guadeloupe is a popular tourist destination, especially for visitors from metropolitan France (who account for some 89% of tourists) and the USA. The main attractions are the beaches, the mountainous scenery and the unspoilt beauty of the island dependencies. In 2004 some 455,981 tourists visited Guadeloupe. Receipts from tourism totalled €238m. in 2002. In 2005 there were 93 hotels, with some 6,632 rooms.

Comité du Tourisme: 5 sq. de la Banque, BP 555, 97166 Pointe-à-Pitre Cédex; tel. 5-90-82-09-30; fax 5-90-83-89-22; e-mail info@lesilesdeguadeloupe.com; internet www.lesilesdeguadeloupe.com; Pres. JOSETTE BOREL-LINCERTIN; Dir-Gen. THIERRY GARGAR.

Délégation Régionale au Tourisme: 5 rue Victor Hugues, 97100 Basse-Terre; tel. 5-90-81-10-44; fax 5-90-81-94-82; e-mail drtourisme.guadeloupe@wanadoo.fr; Dir JEAN FRANÇOIS DESBROCHES.

Syndicat d'Initiative de Pointe-à-Pitre: Centre Commercial de la Marina, 97110 Pointe-à-Pitre; tel. 5-90-90-70-02; fax 5-90-90-74-70; internet www.sivap.gp; Pres. DENYS FORTUNE.

MARTINIQUE

Introductory Survey

Location, Climate, Language, Religion, Capital

Martinique is one of the Windward Islands in the West Indies, with Dominica to the north and Saint Lucia to the south. The island is dominated by the volcanic peak of Mont Pelée. The climate is tropical, but tempered by easterly and north-easterly breezes. The more humid and wet season runs from July to November, and the average temperature is 26°C (79°F). French is the official language, but a Creole patois is widely spoken. The majority of the population professes Christianity and belongs to the Roman Catholic Church. The capital is Fort-de-France.

Recent History

Martinique has been a French possession since 1635. The prosperity of the island was based on the sugar industry, which was devastated by the volcanic eruption of Mont Pelée in 1902. Martinique became a Department of France in 1946, when the Governor was replaced by a Prefect, and an elected Conseil général (General Council) was created.

During the 1950s there was a growth of nationalist feeling, as expressed by Aimé Césaire's Parti Progressiste Martiniquais (PPM) and the Parti Communiste Martiniquais (PCM). However, economic power remained concentrated in the hands of the *békés* (descendants of white colonial settlers), who owned most of the agricultural land and controlled the lucrative import-export market. This provided little incentive for innovation or self-sufficiency, and fostered resentment against lingering colonial attitudes.

In 1974 Martinique, together with Guadeloupe and French Guiana, was given regional status as part of France's governmental reorganization. An indirectly elected Conseil régional (Regional Council) was created, with some control over the local economy. In 1982 and 1983 the socialist Government of President François Mitterrand, which had pledged itself to decentralizing power in favour of the Overseas Departments, made further concessions towards autonomy by giving the local councils greater control over taxation, local police and the economy. At the first direct elections to the new Conseil régional, held in February 1983, left-wing parties (the PPM, the PCM and the Fédération Socialiste de la Martinique—FSM) won a majority of seats. This success, and the election of Aimé Césaire as President of the Conseil régional, strengthened his influence against the pro-independence elements in his own party. (Full independence for Martinique attracted support from only a small minority of the population; the majority sought reforms that would bring greater autonomy, while retaining French control.) The Mouvement Indépendantiste Martiniquais (MIM), the most vocal of the separatist parties, fared badly in the elections, obtaining less than 3% of the total vote. At an election to the enlarged Conseil général, held in March 1985, the left-wing parties increased their representation, but the centre-right coalition of the Union pour la Démocratie Française (UDF) and the Rassemblement pour la République (RPR) maintained their control of the administration.

For the general election to the Assemblée nationale (National Assembly) in March 1986, Martinique's representation was increased from three to four deputies. Césaire and a member of the FSM were elected from a unified list of left-wing candidates, while the RPR and the UDF (which had also presented a joint list) each won one seat. In the concurrent election to the Conseil régional the left-wing parties (including the PPM, the FSM and the PCM) won 21 of the 41 seats, and the RPR and the UDF together won the remaining seats. Césaire retained the presidency of the Council until 1988, when he relinquished the post to Camille Darsières (the Secretary-General of the PPM). In September 1986 indirect elections were held for Martinique's two seats in the Sénat. As in the March elections, the left-wing parties united, and, as a consequence, Martinique acquired a left-wing senator for the first time since 1958, a PPM member, while the other successful candidate belonged to the UDF.

Following the recent trend in Martinique, the incumbent, François Mitterrand of the Parti Socialiste (PS), won a decisive majority of the island's votes at the 1988 French presidential election. Left-wing candidates secured all four seats at elections to the Assemblée nationale in June. Furthermore, the parties of the left achieved a majority at elections to the Conseil général later that year. Emile Maurice of the RPR was, none the less, elected President of the Conseil général for a seventh term.

In June 1990 the results of the 1986 election to the Conseil régional were annulled because of a technicality, and another election was held in October. Pro-independence candidates secured nine seats (of which seven were won by the MIM). The PPM, the FSM and the PCM again formed a joint electoral list, but won only 14 seats, and consequently lost their absolute majority on the Conseil régional; Camille Darsières was, however, re-elected to the presidency of the Conseil régional.

At an election to the Conseil général in March 1992, left-wing parties secured 26 seats and right-wing organizations 19. Claude Lise, a PPM deputy to the Assemblée nationale, was elected President of the Conseil général. In concurrent elections to the Conseil régional the RPR and the UDF, contesting the election as the Union pour la France (UPF), won 16 seats, the MIM (which contested the election under the title Patriotes Martiniquais) and the PPM secured nine seats each, and the PCM (under the title Pour une Martinique au Travail) and the FSM (as the Nouvelle Génération Socialiste) won four and three seats, respectively. Emile Capgras of the PCM was elected President of the Conseil régional.

In September 1992 72% of voters in Martinique approved ratification of the Treaty on European Union (see p. 244), although the abstention rate was high. In November of that year banana-growers in Guadeloupe and Martinique suspended economic activity in their respective Departments by obstructing access to ports and airports and blocking roads, in protest at the threatened loss of special advantages under the Single European Act. Order was restored after four days, however, following assurances that subsidies would be maintained and that certain products, such as bananas (one of Martinique's principal exports), would be protected under the proposals.

At the March 1993 elections to the Assemblée nationale there was a marked swing in favour of the parties of the right: André Lesueur and Pierre Petit of the RPR were elected, as was a third right-wing candidate, Anicet Turinay of the UPF. Césaire did not seek re-election, and was replaced at the Assemblée nationale by Camille Darsières. In September 1995 Lise was elected to the Sénat, while the incumbent PPM representative, Rodolphe Désiré, was returned to office.

At elections to the Assemblée nationale in May and June 1997, Turinay and Petit, representing the RPR, were re-elected, together with Darsières of the PPM. Alfred Marie-Jeanne, the First Secretary and a founding member of the MIM, was elected in a constituency hitherto held by the RPR. At elections to the Conseil régional in March 1998, the left retained its majority, while the pro-independence MIM performed well. Marie-Jeanne was elected President of the Conseil régional. In a concurrent election to the Conseil général the left again increased its majority; Lise was re-elected to the presidency of the Conseil général.

A two-month strike by workers in the banana sector, which had severely disrupted economic activity around the port of Fort-de-France, was ended in January 1999, when a pay agreement was reached. The social climate deteriorated further in May, as two companies were affected by strike action. Workers at the Toyota motor company were demanding substantial pay increases and a reduction in working hours, while employees of the Roger Albert distribution group were protesting against the dismissal of two colleagues. In early October tension escalated as trade unions took sympathetic action, blocking access to the main industrial and commercial zones around the capital for two days. Subsequent negotiations between the local authorities and a trade union delegation resulted in an agreement to hold talks on the resolution of the two conflicts. The dispute at Roger Albert was concluded shortly afterwards, following the intervention of Marie-Jeanne, but, despite mediation efforts, industrial action at Toyota continued. In mid-October trade unions organized a week-long blockade of the port of Fort-de-France in protest against proposed redundancies at Toyota. Later that month, prior to a two-day visit to Martinique by Prime

Minister Jospin, banana producers occupied the headquarters of the French naval forces for several days, demanding the disbursement of exceptional aid to compensate for the adverse effect on their industry of a dramatic decline in prices on the European market. Marie-Jeanne, who was opposed to the limited nature of the Government's plans for institutional reform, refused to participate in the events organized for Jospin's stay. The Prime Minister announced an emergency plan for the banana sector and agreed, in principle, to a proposal for greater autonomy for the local authorities in conducting relations with neighbouring countries and territories. In November, following two weeks of direct negotiations between trade union representatives and the management of Toyota, a protocol was signed, marking the end of the five-month dispute; a pay increase was awarded and dismissal proceedings against 12 employees were annulled.

Following a series of meetings, in December 1999 the Presidents of the Conseils régionaux of French Guiana, Guadeloupe and Martinique signed a joint declaration in Basse-Terre, Guadeloupe, affirming their intention to propose, to the Government, a legislative amendment aimed at creating a new status of overseas region, despite an earlier statement by Jospin indicating that the Government did not envisage a change in status for the Departments. Modified proposals regarding the institutional future and socio-economic development of the Departments were approved by the Assemblée nationale and in December were ratified by the Constitutional Council. Following a meeting of members of the Conseil régional and the Conseil général in late June 2001, a series of proposals on greater autonomy, to be presented to the French Government, was agreed upon. These included: the division of the territory into four districts; the creation of a Territorial Collectivity (collectivité territoriale), governed by a 41-member Assembly elected for a five-year term; and the establishment of an independent executive council. Furthermore, the proposals included a request that the territory be given control over legislative and administrative affairs, as well as legislative authority on matters concerning Martinique alone. In November the French Government announced itself to be in favour of the suggested constitutional developments, and in March 2003 the two houses of the French parliament approved constitutional changes that, *inter alia*, allowed for local referendums to be held on proposals for greater decentralization in overseas possessions. The status of Overseas Region (région d'outre-mer) was also conferred on Martinique. In the referendum, held on 7 December, some 51% of participating voters rejected legislative reforms that envisaged the replacement of the Conseil général and the Conseil régional with a single assembly.

In municipal elections held in March 2001 the PPM retained control of the majority of municipalities (including Fort-de-France, where Césaire, retiring as mayor after 55 years, was succeeded by a fellow PPM member, Sérge Letchimy, who defeated Marie-Jeanne, President of the Conseil régional). In the concurrently held election to the Conseil général, Lise was re-elected President. In mid-2001 the French President, Jacques Chirac, rejected a joint request by French Guiana, Guadeloupe and Martinique that they be permitted to join, as associate members, the Association of Caribbean States. At elections to the Assemblée nationale in June 2002, Marie-Jeanne was re-elected, while Turinay lost his seat to Louis-Joseph Manscour of the PS, and Darsières lost his to Pierre-Jean Samot of the left-wing Bâtir le Pays Martinique; Alfred Almont, representing the right-wing alliance of the Union pour la Majorité Présidentielle (UMP) and the RPR, secured the remaining seat. The RPR subsequently merged into the successor party to the UMP, the Union pour un Mouvement Populaire (also known as the UMP). In March 2003 the French Conseil constitutionnel ordered Samot to resign for having received campaign funds for the 2002 election from his party, which was not officially registered at the time. As a result, a by-election was held in May 2003, which was won by Philippe Edmond-Mariette, also of Bâtir le Pays Martinique.

At an election to the Conseil régional in March 2004 the Patriotes Martiniquais, a pro-independence alliance, comprising the MIM and the Conseil National des Comités Populaires and the Alliance pour le Pays Martinique (which was absorbed by the two larger groupings after the first round of voting), won an overwhelming majority, obtaining 28 of the 41 council seats. A joint list comprising the PPM and other left-wing candidates obtained nine seats, while the right-wing Forces Martiniquaises de Progrès secured the remaining four seats.

In late May 2005 a national referendum was held on ratification of the European Union constitutional treaty: 69.0% of voters in the Department were in favour of adopting the treaty, although the turn-out of the electorate was only 28.4%. The treaty was ultimately rejected by a majority of voters in metropolitan France. In early December it was reported that more than 1,000 protesters took part in demonstrations in Fort-de-France against a law that proposed changing the school syllabus to reflect the 'positive' role of French colonialism. The law had been quietly approved in the previous February, and attempts by left-wing representatives in the Assemblée nationale to repeal it had been defeated in late November. The Minister of the Interior, Nicolas Sarkozy, who was known to support the law, was forced to cancel a planned visit to Martinique and Guadeloupe. President Chirac announced later that month that the law was under review and in January 2006 the relevant article of law was removed in accordance with a ruling by the Conseil constitutionnel that it lay outside the competence of the legislature.

In the first round of the national presidential election, held on 22 April 2007, Ségolène Royal of the PS won 48.5% of votes cast on the island, ahead of Sarkozy, the UMP candidate, who attracted 33.8% of the ballot. At the second round, held on 6 May, Royal won 60.5% of the vote in the Department. However, nationally, Sarkozy emerged victorious, securing 53.1% of votes overall. At elections to the Assemblée nationale, held on 10 and 17 June, Marie-Jeanne, Manscour and Almont were all re-elected, while Serge Letchimy of the PPM was also successful. In July Ange Mancini replaced Yves Dassonville as Prefect.

Government

France is represented in Martinique by an appointed prefect. There are two councils with local powers: the 45-member Conseil général (General Council) and the 41-member Conseil régional (Regional Council). Both are elected by universal adult suffrage for a period of up to six years. Martinique elects four deputies to the Assemblée nationale in Paris, and sends two indirectly elected representatives to the Sénat. The Department is also represented at the European Parliament.

Defence

As assessed at November 2007, France maintained a military force of 1,250 and a gendarmerie in the Antilles, with headquarters in Fort-de-France.

Economic Affairs

In 2004 Martinique's gross domestic product (GDP), measured at current prices, was estimated at €6,800m., equivalent to US $17,329 per head. During 1990–2001, according to UN estimates, GDP increased, in real terms, at an average rate of 1.5% per year; growth in 2001 was 2.1%. Between the censuses of 1990 and 1999, according to provisional figures, the population increased at an average annual rate of 0.7%.

Agriculture, hunting, forestry and fishing contributed 2.7% of GDP in 2004, and according to preliminary figures engaged an estimated 5.0% of the active labour force in 2005. The principal cash crops are bananas (which accounted for some 25% of export earnings in 2005), sugar cane (primarily for the production of rum), limes, melons and pineapples. The cultivation of cut flowers is also of some significance. Roots and tubers and vegetables are grown for local consumption. Agricultural production increased at an average rate of 1.3% per year during 1990–98; the sector declined by 0.2% in 1999.

According to preliminary figures, the industrial sector (including construction and public works) engaged 13.3% of the employed population in 2005 and contributed 14.2% of GDP in 2004. The most important manufacturing activities are petroleum refining (exports of fuels and combustibles accounted for 60.5% of the value of total exports in 2006) and the production of agricultural products (14.1% of exports in 2006), the production of rum being of particular significance. Martiniquais rum was accorded the designation of Appellation d'origine contrôlée (AOC) in 1996 (the first AOC to be designated outside metropolitan France). Other areas of activity include metals, cement, chemicals, plastics, wood, printing and textiles. Energy is derived principally from mineral fuels. In 2006 imports of fuels and combustibles (including crude petroleum destined for the island's refinery) accounted for 22.0% of the value of total imports.

The services sector engaged a provisional 81.8% of the employed population in 2005 and provided 83.1% of GDP in 2004. Tourism is a major activity on the island and one of the most important sources of foreign exchange: in 2006 earnings from the tourism industry totalled an estimated €242.5m.; some 78.6% of visitors were from metropolitan France in that year.

In 2006 Martinique recorded a trade deficit of €2,015m., with export earnings worth only approximately 19.5% of the total value of imports. Metropolitan France was the principal source of imports (55.6%) in 2006; Guadeloupe was the principal market for exports (32.9%) in that year. French Guiana, member countries of the European Union (EU, see p. 244) and the USA were also significant trading partners. The principal exports were fuels and combustibles, agricultural products and food industries. The principal imports included fuels and combustibles, food industry products and car industry products.

In 2006 a deficit of €9.1m. was recorded on the regional budget, expenditure amounted to €256.9m. while receipts totalled €266.0m. A balanced departmental budget of €617.3m. was estimated for the same year. The annual rate of inflation averaged 1.7% in 1996–2006; consumer prices increased by 2.4% in 2006. Some 24.7% of the labour force was unemployed in 2005.

FRENCH OVERSEAS POSSESSIONS
Martinique

Martinique's economic development has created a society that combines a relatively high standard of living with a weak economic base in agricultural and industrial production, as well as a chronic trade deficit. Levels of unemployment and emigration are high, although the rate of growth of both these factors has slowed since the mid-1980s. The linking of wage levels to those of metropolitan France, despite the island's lower level of productivity, has increased labour costs and restricted development. In the late 1990s the value of banana exports declined owing to a significant fall in prices on the European market, while the end of the EU's preferential banana import regime from 2006 also threatened Martinique's banana-growing sector. In 2004, in conjunction with Guadeloupe, Martinique received €110m. in EU aid as compensation for the low market price of bananas. In 2003 the French Minister of Overseas Departments announced plans to stimulate the economies of Martinique, Guadeloupe and French Guiana that included the introduction of tax incentives for the hotel sector. Meanwhile, in late 2007 an earthquake in Martinique caused the collapse of buildings and left around one-third of the country without electricity.

Education

The educational system is similar to that of metropolitan France (see chapter on French Guiana). In 2005/06 there were 49,209 pupils in pre-primary and primary education, while in secondary education there were 47,683 students, of whom some 92% attended state schools. Higher education in law, French language and literature, human sciences, economics, medicine and Creole studies is provided in Martinique by a branch of the Université Antilles-Guyane. The university as a whole had 11,746 enrolled students in 2004/05; during 2003/04 some 5,344 students were enrolled at the university in Martinique. There are also two teacher-training institutes, and colleges of agriculture, fisheries, hotel management, nursing, midwifery and child care. Departmental expenditure on education and culture was estimated at €44.1m. in 2006.

Public Holidays

2008: 1 January (New Year's Day), 21–24 March (Easter), 1 May (Labour Day and Ascension Day), 8 May (Victory Day), 12 May (Whit Monday), 22 May (Abolition of Slavery), 14 July (National Day), 15 August (Assumption), 1 November (All Saints' Day), 11 November (Armistice Day), 25 December (Christmas Day).

2009: 1 January (New Year's Day), 10–13 April (Easter), 1 May (Labour Day), 8 May (Victory Day), 21 May (Ascension Day), 22 May (Abolition of Slavery), 1 June (Whit Monday), 14 July (National Day), 15 August (Assumption), 1 November (All Saints' Day), 11 November (Armistice Day), 25 December (Christmas Day).

Weights and Measures
The metric system is in force.

Statistical Survey

Sources (unless otherwise indicated): Institut National de la Statistique et des Etudes Economiques (INSEE), Service Régional de Martinique, Centre Administratif Delgrès, blvd de la Pointe des Sables, Hauts de Dillon, BP 641, 97262 Fort-de-France Cédex; tel. 5-96-60-73-73; fax 5-96-60-73-50; e-mail antilles-guyane@insee.fr; internet www.insee.fr/fr/insee_regions/martinique; Ministère des Départements et Territoires d'Outre-mer, 27 rue Oudinot, 75700 Paris 07 SP; tel. 1-53-69-20-00; fax 1-43-06-60-30; internet www.outre-mer.gouv.fr.

AREA AND POPULATION

Area: 1,100 sq km (424.7 sq miles).

Population: 359,579 (males 173,878, females 185,701) at census of 15 March 1990; 381,427 at census of 8 March 1999. *1 January 2007* (provisional estimate): 401,000.

Density (1 January 2007, provisional estimate): 364.5 per sq km.

Principal Towns (at 1999 census): Fort-de-France (capital) 94,049; Le Lamentin 35,460; Le Robert 21,240; Schoelcher 20,845; Sainte-Marie 20,098; Le François 18,559; Saint-Joseph 15,785; Ducos 15,240. *Mid-2007* (UN estimate, incl. suburbs): Fort-de-France 93,000 (Source: UN, *World Urbanization Prospects: The 2007 Revision*).

Births, Marriages and Deaths (2006 unless otherwise indicated): Registered births 5,370 (birth rate 13.4 per 1,000); Registered marriages 1,425 (2004); Registered deaths 2,610 (death rate 6.5 per 1,000).

Expectation of Life (years at birth): 79.5 (males 76.5; females 82.3) in 2007. Source: Pan American Health Organization.

Economically Active Population (persons aged 15 years and over, 1998): Agriculture and fishing 7,650; Industry 7,103; Construction and public works 10,405; Trade 16,196; Transport 4,383; Financial services and real estate 3,354; Business services 8,376; Public services 14,179; Education 14,991; Health and social security 10,676; Administrative services 18,742; *Total employed* 116,055 (males 62,198, females 53,857); Unemployed 48,537 (males 22,628, females 25,909); *Total labour force* 164,592 (males 84,826, females 79,766). *2005* (provisional figures at 31 December): Agriculture 5,683; Construction 6,328; Other industry 8,873; Trade 14,265; Other services 79,466; *Total employed* (incl. others) 114,615; Unemployed 37,539; *Total labour force* 152,154. Note: Figures for employment exclude 10,876 non-salaried workers. *2006:* Unemployed 35,365.

HEALTH AND WELFARE
Key Indicators

Total Fertility Rate (children per woman, 2007): 1.9.
Under-5 Mortality Rate (per 1,000 live births, 2006): 8.4.
Physicians (per 1,000 head, c. 2001): 19.7.
Hospital Beds (per 1,000 head, 2004): 4.2.

Source: mostly Pan American Health Organization.

For definitions and other sources, see explanatory note on p. vi.

AGRICULTURE, ETC.

Principal Crops ('000 metric tons, 2006, FAO estimates): Yams 7.0; Sugar cane 211; Lettuce and chicory 6.8; Tomatoes 7.7; Cucumbers and gherkins 3.8; Bananas 300.0; Plantains 18.0; Pineapples 16.2. *Aggregate Production* ('000 metric tons, may include official, semi-official or estimated data): Total vegetables (incl. melons) 32.9; Total fruits (excl. melons) 335.6.

Livestock ('000 head, year ending September 2006, FAO estimates): Cattle 25; Sheep 18; Pigs 20; Goats 13.5.

Livestock Products ('000 metric tons, 2006, FAO estimates): Cattle meat 1.8; Pig meat 1.5; Chicken meat 1.0; Cows' milk 2.2; Hen eggs 1.5.

Forestry ('000 cubic metres, 2006, FAO estimates): *Roundwood Removals* (excl. bark): Sawlogs, veneer logs and logs for sleepers 2; Fuel wood 25; Total 27. *Sawnwood Production* (incl. railway sleepers): 1.0.

Fishing (metric tons, live weight, 2005): Capture 5,500—FAO estimate (Clupeoids 3,500; Common dolphinfish 200—FAO estimate; Other marine fishes 1,000—FAO estimate; Caribbean spiny lobster 150; Clams, etc. 600); Aquaculture 92; *Total catch* 5,592—FAO estimate.

Source: FAO.

MINING

Production ('000 metric tons, 2002, estimates): Cement 220; Pumice 130; Salt 200. Source: US Geological Survey.

INDUSTRY

Production ('000 metric tons, 2004, unless otherwise indicated): Motor spirit (petrol) 163; Kerosene 142; Gas-diesel (distillate fuel) oils 178; Residual fuel oils 310; Liquefied petroleum gas 27 (estimate); Electric energy (million kWh) 1,553 (Source: mostly UN, *Industrial Commodity Statistics Yearbook*). *2006:* Raw sugar 4.1; Rum (hl) 74.8.

FINANCE

Currency and Exchange Rates: The French franc was used until the end of 2001. Euro notes and coins were introduced on 1 January 2002, and the euro became the sole legal tender from 18 February. Some of the figures in this Survey are still in terms of francs. For details of exchange rates, see French Guiana.

Budget: *French Government* (million French francs, 1998): Revenue 4,757; Expenditure 8,309. *Regional Budget* (€ million, 2006): Current revenue 219.6 (Taxes 149.4, Other current revenue 70.2); Capital revenue 37.3; Total 256.9. Current expenditure 135.8; Capital expenditure 130.2; Total 266.0. *Departmental Budget* (forecasts, million French francs, 2001): Tax revenue 836.9 (Departmental taxes 332.0, Fuel tax 295.0, Transfer taxes, etc. 58.0, Motor vehicle tax 68.0, Fiscal subsidy 53.0); Other current revenue 886.6 (Refunds of social assistance 65.0, Operational allowance 315.0, Decentralization allowance 477.0); Capital revenue 499.5 (EU development funds 71.0, Capital allowances 59.0, Other receipts 101.4, Borrowing 270.0); Total 2,223.0. Current expenditure 1,482.2 (Finance service 57.1, Permanent staff 394.7, General administration 65.1, Other indirect services 69.0, Administrative services 108.4, Public health

49.9, Social assistance 503.6, Support costs of minimum wage 99.8, Economic services 114.7); Capital expenditure 740.8 (Road system 139.5, Networks 47.9, Education and culture 111.5, Other departmental programmes 101.6, Other public bodies 83.7, Other programmes 96.3, Non-programme expenditure 162.3); Total 2,223.0. *2006* (€ million, excl. debt rescheduling): Total revenue 617.3; Total expenditure 617.3 (Source: Département des Etudes et des Statistiques Locales).

Money Supply (million French francs at 31 December 1998): Currency outside banks 924; Demand deposits at banks 6,330; Total money 7,254.

Cost of Living (Consumer Price Index; base: 2000 = 100): 108.6 in 2004; 111.2 in 2005; 113.9 in 2006. Source: ILO.

Gross Domestic Product (US $ million at constant 1990 prices): 4,105 in 2001; 4,192 in 2002; 4,281 in 2003 (Source: UN, *Statistical Yearbook*).

Expenditure on the Gross Domestic Product (€ million at current prices, 2004): Total final consumption expenditure 6,921 (General government and non-profit institutions serving households 2,625, Households 4,297); Changes in inventories −52; Gross fixed capital formation 1,416; *Total domestic expenditure* 8,285; Exports of goods and services 627; *Less* Imports of goods and services 2,111; *GDP in purchasers' values* 6,800.

Gross Domestic Product by Economic Activity (€ million at current prices, 2004): Agriculture, hunting, forestry and fishing 174; Food industries 128; Other manufacturing 244; Energy 146; Construction 399; Services 5,370 (Restaurants and hotels 210, Transport 218, Commerce 872, Other market services 1,962, Non-market services 2,108); *Sub-total* 6,461; Financial intermediation services indirectly measured (FISIM) −263; Import duties, less subsidies 602; *GDP in purchasers' values* 6,800.

EXTERNAL TRADE

Principal Commodities (€ million, 2006): *Imports c.i.f.*: Products of food industries 369; Pharmaceutical products 181; Home equipment 139; Car industry products 293; Mechanical equipment 152; Electronic equipment 164; Fuels and combustibles 550; Total (incl. others) 2,504. *Exports f.o.b.*: Products of agriculture, fishing and forestry 69; Products of food industries 64; Mechanical equipment 10; Fuels and combustibles 296; Total (incl. others) 489.

Principal Trading Partners (€ million, 2006): *Imports c.i.f.*: Aruba 35; Belgium-Luxembourg 57; France (metropolitan) 1,393; Germany 66; Guadeloupe 50; Italy 85; Japan 34; Netherlands 62; Spain 38; Trinidad and Tobago 43; United Kingdom 382; USA 46; Total (incl. others) 2,504; *Exports f.o.b.*: Antigua 7; France (metropolitan) 107; French Guiana 18; Guadeloupe 161; Haiti 2; Netherlands Antilles 2; Nigeria 18; São Tomé and Príncipe 10; Saint Lucia 62; Spain 4; United Kingdom 2; USA 82; Total (incl. others) 489.

TRANSPORT

Road Traffic ('000 motor vehicles in use, 1995): Passenger cars 95.0; Commercial vehicles 21.5. Source: UN, *Statistical Yearbook*.

Shipping: *Merchant Fleet* (vessels registered '000 grt at 31 December, 1992): 1 (Source: Lloyd's Register of Shipping). *International Sea-borne Traffic* (2006, provisional figures): Goods loaded 950,000 metric tons (petroleum products 359,000 metric tons); Goods unloaded 2,302,000 metric tons (petroleum products 1,109,000 metric tons).

Civil Aviation (2006): Freight (incl. post) carried 13,492 metric tons; Passengers carried 1,644,145.

TOURISM

Tourist Arrivals by Country (excl. same-day visitors and cruise-ship arrivals, 2003): France 357,726; Guadeloupe 40,668; French Guiana 10,619; Total (incl. others) 453,159. *2006:* (excl. same-day visitors and cruise-ship arrivals) Total 503,474 (France 395,512).

Receipts from Tourism (€ million, incl. passenger transport): 234.4 in 2004; 226.5 in 2005; 242.5 in 2006.

COMMUNICATIONS MEDIA

Radio Receivers ('000 in use): 82 in 1997.

Television Receivers ('000 in use): 62 in 1999.

Telephones ('000 main lines in use): 172.0 in 2001.

Facsimile Machines (number in use): 5,200 in 1997.

Mobile Cellular Telephones ('000 subscribers): 295.4 in 2004.

Personal Computers ('000 in use): 82 in 2004.

Internet Users ('000): 107.0 in 2004.

Daily Newspaper: 1 (estimate) in 1996 (estimated average circulation 30,000 copies).

Sources: UNESCO, *Statistical Yearbook*; UN, *Statistical Yearbook*; International Telecommunication Union.

EDUCATION

Pre-primary (2005/06): 18,912 students (17,926 state, 986 private).

Primary (2005/06): 29,859 students (27,722 state, 2,137 private).

Specialized Pre-primary and Primary (2005/06): 438 students.

Secondary (2005/06): 47,683 students (43,809 state, 3,874 private).

Higher (2004/05, unless otherwise indicated): 8,234 students. Source: Ministère de l'Education Nationale, de la Recherche et de la Technologie. *Université Antilles-Guyane (Campus de Schoelcher)*: 5,344 students in 2003/04 (Source: Préfecture de Martinique, *Livret d'accueil des services de l'Etat en Martinique*).

Teachers (2004/05): *Primary:* 3,031 teachers (2,787 state, 244 private); *Secondary:* 4,553 teachers (4,177 state, 376 private); *Higher:* 186 teachers. Source: Ministère de l'Education Nationale, *Repères et références statistiques—édition 2005*.

Institutions (2003/04): 258 primary schools; 41 lower secondary schools; 22 state upper secondary schools; 24 private institutions. Source: Préfecture de Martinique, *Livret d'accueil des services de l'Etat en Martinique*.

Adult Literacy Rate: 98.0% (males 97.6%; females 98.3%) in 2005. Source: Pan American Health Organization.

Directory

The Government

(March 2008)

Prefect: Ange Mancini, Préfecture, 82 rue Victor Sévère, BP 647–648, 97262 Fort-de-France Cédex; tel. 5-96-39-36-00; fax 5-96-71-40-29; e-mail contact.prefecture@martinique.pref.gouv.fr; internet www.martinique.pref.gouv.fr.

President of the General Council: Claude Lise (PPM), Conseil général de la Martinique, blvd Chevalier Sainte-Marthe, 97200 Fort-de-France Cédex; tel. 5-96-55-26-00; fax 5-96-73-59-32; internet www.cg972.fr.

President of the Economic and Social Committee: Michel Crispin, Hôtel de la Région, ave Gaston Deferre, Plateau Roy Cluny, BP 601, 97200 Fort-de-France; tel. 5-96-59-64-43; fax 5-96-59-64-43.

President of the Culture, Education and Environment Committee: Claude Petit, Hôtel de la Région, ave Gaston Deferre, Plateau Roy Cluny, BP 601, 97200 Fort-de-France; e-mail ccee@cr-martinique.fr.

Deputies to the French National Assembly: Louis-Joseph Manscour (PS), Alfred Almont (UMP), Serge Letchimy (PPM), Alfred Marie-Jeanne (MIM).

Representatives to the French Senate: Serge Larcher (Rassemblement Démocratique et Social Européen), Claude Lise (PS).

Conseil Régional

Hôtel de Région, rue Gaston Defferre, BP 601, 97200 Fort-de-France Cédex; tel. 5-96-59-63-00; fax 5-96-72-68-10; e-mail service.communication@cr-martinique.fr; internet www.cr-martinique.fr.

President: Alfred Marie-Jeanne (MIM).

Elections, 21 and 28 March 2004

	Seats
Groupe des Patriotes—MIM CNCP*	28
Convergences Martiniquaises Union de la Gauche†	9
Forces Martiniquaises de Progrès	4
Total	41

* A joint list comprising the Mouvement Indépendantiste Martiniquais, the Conseil National des Comités Populaires and the Alliance pour le Pays Martinique.
† A joint list comprising the Parti Progressiste Martiniquais and other left-wing candidates.

Political Organizations

Bâtir le Pays Martinique: Fort-de-France; f. 1998; left-wing; split from the Parti Communiste Martiniquais; Leader Pierre-Jean Samot; Nat. Sec. David Zobda.

Combat Ouvrier: BP 821, 97258 Fort-de-France Cédex; e-mail redaction@combat-ouvrier.net; internet www.combat-ouvrier.net; Trostskyist; mem. of the Communist Internationalist Union; Leader GHISLAINE JOACHIM-ARNAUD.

Conseil National des Comités Populaires (CNCP): 8 rue Pierre et Marie Curie, Terres Sainville, 97200 Fort-de-France; e-mail robert .sae@wanadoo.fr; f. 1983; pro-independence party affiliated to the Union Général des Travailleurs de Martinique; contested the 2004 regional elections in alliance with the MIM; Leader ROBERT SAÉ.

Fédération Socialiste de la Martinique (FSM): 52 rue du Capitaine Pierre-Rose, 97200 Fort-de-France; tel. 5-96-60-14-88; e-mail fede972@parti-socialiste.fr; internet www.parti-socialiste.fr; local br. of the Parti Socialiste (PS); Sec.-Gen. JEAN CRUSOL.

Forces Martiniquaises de Progrès: 12 rue Ernest Deproge, 97200 Fort-de-France; tel. 5-96-71-83-26; fax 5-96-63-36-19; e-mail miguel .laventure@fmp-regionales.org; internet www.ac2i.com/sites/fmp; f. 1998 to replace the local br. of the Union pour la Démocratie Française; Pres. MIGUEL LAVENTURE.

Mouvement des Démocrates et Écologistes pour une Martinique Souveraine (MODEMAS): Fort-de-France; f. 1992; left-wing, pro-independence; Pres. GARCIN MALSA.

Mouvement Indépendantiste Martiniquais (MIM): Fort-de-France; internet www.mim-mk.org; f. 1978; pro-independence party; First Sec. ALFRED MARIE-JEANNE.

Mouvement Populaire Franciscain: angle des rues Couturier et Holo, 97240 Le François; tel. 5-96-54-20-40; e-mail direction@pont-abel.fr; internet mpf972.site.voila.fr/textesfond_1.html; left-wing; Leader MAURICE ANTISTE.

Osons Oser: Fort-de-France; f. 1998; right-wing; affiliated with the metropolitan Union pour un Mouvement Populaire (UMP); Pres. PIERRE PETIT.

Parti Communiste Martiniquais (PCM): Fort-de-France; Sec.-Gen. GEORGES ERICHOT.

Parti Progressiste Martiniquais (PPM): Quartier Trénelle, 97200 Fort-de-France; tel. 5-96-71-86-83; internet www .ppm-martinique.net; f. 1957; left-wing; Leader SERGE LETCHIMY; Sec.-Gen. PIERRE SUÉDILE.

Rassemblement Démocratique pour la Martinique (RDM): Résidence Pichevin 2, Bâtiment Hildevert, Les Hauts du Port, 97200 Fort-de-France; tel. 5-96-71-89-97; internet www.rdm972.fr; f. 2006; Sec.-Gen. CLAUDE LISE.

Union pour un Mouvement Populaire (UMP): angle des rues de la République et Vincent Allègre, 97212 Saint Joseph; tel. 5-96-57-96-68; fax 5-96-57-32-68; e-mail yanmonplaisir@ump972.org; internet www.u-m-p.org; centre-right; local br. of the metropolitan party; Pres., Departmental Cttee YAN MONPLAISIR.

Les Verts Martinique: Lot D, 54 rue Madinina, Cluny, 97200 Fort-de-France; tel. 5-96-73-07-45; fax 5-96-71-58-21; ecologist; departmental br. of the metropolitan party; Leader LOUIS-LÉONCE LECURIEUX-LAFFERONNAY.

Judicial System

Cour d'Appel de Fort-de-France: Ave St John Perse, Morne Tartenson, BP 634, 97262 Fort-de-France Cédex; tel. 5-96-70-62-62; fax 5-96-63-52-13; e-mail ca-fort-de-france@justice.fr; highest court of appeal for Martinique and French Guiana; First Pres. HERVÉ EXPERT; Procurator-Gen. JEAN-MICHEL DURAND; Chief Clerk BENOÎT BOULET-GERCOURT.

There are two Tribunaux de Grande Instance, at Fort-de-France and Cayenne (French Guiana), and three Tribunaux d'Instance (two in Fort-de-France and one in Cayenne).

Religion

The majority of the population belong to the Roman Catholic Church.

CHRISTIANITY

The Roman Catholic Church

Martinique comprises the single archdiocese of Fort-de-France, with an estimated 312,000 adherents (some 80% of the total population) at 31 December 2005. The Archbishop participates in the Antilles Episcopal Conference, based in Port of Spain, Trinidad and Tobago.

Archbishop of Fort-de-France and Saint-Pierre: Most Rev. GILBERT MARIE MICHEL MÉRANVILLE, Archevêché, 5–7 rue du Révérend Père Pinchon, BP 586, 97207 Fort-de-France Cédex; tel. 5-96-63-70-70; fax 5-96-63-75-21; e-mail archeveche-martinique@wanadoo.fr.

Other Churches

Among the denominations active in Martinique are the Assembly of God, the Evangelical Church of the Nazarene and the Seventh-day Adventist Church.

The Press

Antilla: 60 Jambette Beauséjour, 97200 Fort-de-France; tel. 5-96-75-48-68; fax 5-96-75-58-46; e-mail antilla@wanadoo.fr; weekly; Dir ALFRED FORTUNE.

Combat Ouvrier: BP 213, 97156 Pointe-à-Pitre Cédex; e-mail redaction@combat-ouvrier.org; internet www.combat-ouvrier.org; f. 1971; fortnightly; communist; Dir FRANÇOIS ANAÏS.

France Antilles: pl. Stalingrad, 97200 Fort-de-France; tel. 5-96-59-08-83; fax 5-96-60-29-96; f. 1964; subsidiary of Groupe France Antilles; daily; Dir HENRI MERLE; circ. 30,000 (Martinique edn).

Journal APAL: 8 rue Pierre et Marie Curie, Terres Sainville, 97200 Fort-de-France; tel. 5-96-63-75-23; fax 5-96-70-30-82; e-mail journ .apal@netcaraibes.com; internet www.m-apal.com; f. 1983; monthly; organ of the Conseil Nat. des Comités Populaires (q.v.) and the Union Général des Travailleurs de Martinique (q.v.); Dir ROBERT SAÉ.

Justice: rue André Aliker, 97200 Fort-de-France; tel. 5-96-71-86-83; fax 5-96-63-13-20; e-mail ed.justice@wanadoo.fr; f. 1920; weekly; organ of the Parti Communiste Martinique (q.v.); Dir FERNAND PAPAYA; circ. 8,000.

Le NAIF-Magazine: Résidence K, Pointe des Nègres, route Phare, 97200 Fort-de-France; tel. 5-96-61-62-55; weekly; publ. by CIC; Owner CAMILLE CHAUVET.

Le Progressiste: c/o Parti Progressiste Martiniquais, Quartier Trénelle, 97200 Fort-de-France; tel. 5-96-72-68-56; fax 5-96-71-88-01; weekly; organ of the PPM; Dir PAUL GABOURG; circ. 13,000.

TV Magazine: Immeuble Gouyer, Z. I. Californie, BP 1064, 97200 Fort-de-France; tel. 5-96-42-51-28; fax 5-96-42-98-94; e-mail tv .mag@media-antilles.fr; f. 1989; weekly.

Publishers

Editions Desormeaux: Z. I. la Jambette, 97232 Fort-de-France; tel. 5-96-50-30-30; fax 5-96-50-30-70; e-mail info@editions-desomeaux .com; internet www.editions-desormeaux.com; French-Creole history, language, culture, culinaria, natural history, academic and fiction.

Editions Exbrayat: 5 rue des Oisillons, route de Balata, 97234 Fort-de-France; tel. 5-96-64-60-58; fax 5-96-64-70-42; e-mail editions .exbrayat@exbrayat.com; internet www.exbrayat.com; regional art, history, natural history, culinaria, maps and general fiction; 2 brs in Guadeloupe; Commercial Dir PAQUITA EXBRAYAT-SANCHEZ.

Editions Lafontaine: Bâtiment 12, Maniba, 97222 Case Pilote; tel. and fax 5-96-78-87-98; e-mail info@editions-lafontaine.com; internet www.editions-lafontaine.com; f. 1994; Creole, French and English literature, general fiction, culture, history, youth and educational; Dir JEANNINE 'JALA' LAFONTAINE.

Broadcasting and Communications

TELECOMMUNICATIONS

Digicel Antilles Françaises Guyane: Oasis, Quartier Bois Rouge, 97224 Ducos; tel. 8-10-63-56-35; fax 5-96-42-09-01; e-mail contact@digicelgroup.fr; internet www.digicel.fr; f. 2000 as Bouygues Telecom Caraïbe; acquired from Bouygues Telecom, France, in 2006; mobile cellular telephone operator; network coverage incl. Guadeloupe and French Guiana; Group Chair. DENIS O'BRIEN; Gen. Man. (French West Indies) GHADA GEBARA.

ONLY: Z. I. la Jambette, BP 280, 97285 Lamentin Cédex 2; e-mail communication@outremer-telecom.fr; internet www .outremer-telecom.fr; f. 1998 as Outremer Telecom Martinique; present name adopted following merger of Volubis, ONLY and OOL in 2006; telecommunications provider; subsidiary of Outremer Telecom, France; CEO JEAN-MICHEL HEGESIPPE.

Orange Caraïbe: see Guadeloupe—Telecommunications.

BROADCASTING

Réseau France Outre-mer (RFO): La Clairière, BP 662, 97263 Fort-de-France; tel. 5-96-59-52-00; fax 5-96-63-29-88; internet www .rfo.fr; acquired by Groupe France Télévisions in 2004; fmrly Société Nationale de Radio-Télévision Française d'Outre-mer, present name adopted in 1998; Gen. Man. FRANÇOIS GUILBEAU; Regional Dir LILIANE FRANCIL.

FRENCH OVERSEAS POSSESSIONS   *Martinique*

Radio

Radio Asé Pléré Annou Lité (Radio APAL) (Radio Pèp-la): 8 rue Pierre et Marie Curie, Terres Sainville, 97200 Fort-de-France; tel. 5-96-63-75-23; fax 5-96-70-30-82; e-mail radio.apal@netcaraibes.com; internet www.m-apal.com; f. 1989; affiliated to the Conseil Nat. des Comités Populaires (q.v.) and the Union Général des Travailleurs de Martinique (q.v.); French and Creole; Dir MICHEL NE'DAN; Station Man. JEAN-CLAUDE LOUIS-SYDNEY.

Radio Banlieue Relax (RBR): 107 ave Léona Gabriel, Cité Dillon, 97200 Fort-de-France; tel. 5-96-60-00-90; fax 5-96-73-06-53; e-mail island-night@wanadoo.fr; internet www.rbrfm.com; f. 1981; regional social and cultural programmes; Pres. FRANCIS CLÉORON.

Radio Canal Antilles (RCA): plateau Fofo, 97233 Schoelcher; tel. 5-96-61-74-19; fax 5-96-61-23-58; internet blogantilles.skyblog.com; f. 1980; fmrly Radio 105; regional social and cultural programmes; Radio France Internationale relay; Pres. SERGE POGNON.

Radio Caraïbes International (RCI Martinique): 2 blvd de la Marne, 97200 Fort-de-France Cédex; tel. 5-96-63-98-70; fax 5-96-63-26-59; internet www.rci.fm; commercial radio station; Dir JOSÉ ANELKA; Station Man. VINCENT CHRÉTIEN; Editor-in-Chief JEAN-PHILIPPE LUDON.

Radio Fréquence Atlantique (RFA): 10 rue du Docteur Laveran, 97232 Le Lamentin; tel. 5-96-42-35-51; fax 5-96-51-04-26; operated by Société Martiniquaise de Communication.

Radio Merci Seigneur: 16 rue Pierre et Marie Curie, 97200 Fort-de-France; tel. 5-96-60-44-34; fax 5-96-63-79-73; Evangelical religious programming; Man. JUDES LARCHER.

Other radio stations include: Chérie FM (formerly Campêche FM); Difé Radio; Fun Radio (formerly Maxxi FM); Radio 22; Radio Actif Martinique; Radio Alizés; Radio Archipel; Radio Espérance; Radio Espoir; Radio Inter Tropicale; Radio Solidarité Rurale—La Voix des Mornes; and West Indies Radio.

Television

Antilles Télévision (ATV): 28 ave des Arawacks, Chateauboeuf, 97200 Fort-de-France; tel. 5-96-75-44-44; fax 5-96-75-55-65; internet www.antillestelevision.com; f. 1993; general interest; accounts for 22% of viewers; also broadcasts to French Guiana and Guadeloupe; Chair. JEAN-MAX ELIZÉ; Gen. Man. DANIEL ROBIN; Editor-in-Chief KARL SIVATTE.

Canal Plus Antilles: see Guadeloupe—Television.

Kanal Martinique Télévision (KMT) (Kanal Matinik Télévision): voie 7, Renéville, 97200 Fort-de-France; tel. 5-96-63-64-85; f. 2004; operated by l'Asscn pour le Développement des Techniques Modernes de Communication; Pres. ROLAND LAOUCHEZ.

Finance

(cap. = capital; res = reserves; dep. = deposits; m. = million; brs = branches; amounts in French francs)

BANKING

Central Bank

Institut d'Emission des Départements d'Outre-mer (IEDOM): 1 blvd du Général de Gaulle, BP 512, 97206 Fort-de-France Cédex; tel. 5-96-59-44-00; fax 5-96-59-44-04; e-mail agence@iedom-martinique.fr; internet www.iedom.fr; Dir CHARLES APANON.

Commercial Banks

Banque des Antilles Françaises: see Guadeloupe—Finance.

BNP Paribas Martinique: 72 ave des Caraïbes, BP 588, 97200 Fort-de-France; tel. 5-96-59-46-00; fax 5-96-63-71-42; internet martinique.bnpparibas.net; f. 1941; subsidiary of BNP Paribas, France; 12 brs.

BRED Banque Populaire: Z. I. la Jambette, 97232 Le Lamentin; tel. 5-96-57-75-63; internet www.bred.banquepopulaire.fr; cap. 242m. (Oct. 2005); Regional Man. BRUNO DUVAL; brs in Martinique and French Guiana.

Crédit Agricole: rue Case Nègre, pl. d'Armes, 97232 Le Lamentin Cédex 2; tel. 5-96-66-59-39; fax 5-96-66-59-67; internet www.ca-martinique.fr; f. 1950; total assets 1,263m. (Dec. 2004); Pres. GUY RANLIN; Gen. Man. PASCAL DURIEUX; 30 brs in Martinique and French Guiana.

Société Générale de Banque aux Antilles (SGBA): see Guadeloupe—Finance.

INSURANCE

AGF Vie France: ZAC de l'Etang Z'Abricots, Bâtiment C, 97200 Fort-de-France; tel. 5-96-50-55-61; fax 5-96-50-55-71; life insurance.

Capma & Capmi: La Galleria, Acajou, 97232 Le Lamentin; tel. 5-96-50-49-48; fax 5-96-50-92-38; internet www.capmacapmi.com.

Caraïbe Assurances: 11 rue Victor Hugo, BP 210, 97202 Fort-de-France; tel. 5-96-63-92-29; fax 5-96-63-19-79; subsidiary of Gruppo Generali, Italy.

Groupama Antilles Guyane: 10 Lotissement Bardinet Dillon, BP 559, 97242 Fort-de-France Cédex; tel. 5-96-75-33-33; internet www.groupama.fr; f. 1978; Chair. JEAN JARNAC; Man. Dir DIDIER PEIGNER; 6 brs in Martinique, 7 brs in Guadeloupe, 3 brs in French Guiana.

GAN Antilles Martinique: 30 blvd du Général de Gaulle, BP 421, 97204 Fort-de-France Cédex; tel. 5-96-71-30-07; fax 5-96-63-33-56; subsidiary of Groupama Antilles Guyane; Rep. GILLES CANO.

Groupement Français d'Assurances Caraïbes (GFA Caraïbes): 46–48 rue Ernest Desproges, 97205 Fort-de-France; tel. 5-96-59-04-04; fax 5-96-73-19-72; e-mail contact@gfa-caraibes.fr; internet www.gfa-caraibes.fr; subsidiary of Gruppo Generali, Italy; Chair. JEAN-CLAUDE WULLENS; Man. Dir SERGE CANTIRAN.

Trade and Industry

GOVERNMENT AGENCIES

Direction Régionale du Commerce Extérieur Antilles-Guyane (DRCE): CWTC, Z. I. de Jarry, 97122 Baie-Mahault; tel. 5-96-39-49-90; fax 5-96-60-08-14; e-mail drceantilles@missioneco.org; internet www.missioneco.org/antilles-guyane; Regional Man. THIERRY LALOUX.

Direction Régionale de l'Industrie, de la Recherche et de l'Environnement (DRIRE): see French Guiana—Trade and Industry.

Direction de la Santé et du Développement Social (DSDS): Centre d'Affaires AGORA, ZAC de l'Etang Z'abricots, Pointe des Grives, BP 658, 97263, Fort-de-France Cédex; tel. 5-96-39-42-98; fax 5-96-60-60-12; e-mail dsds972-secretariat-direction@sante.gouv.fr; internet martinique.sante.gouv.fr; Dir CHRISTIAN URSULET.

DEVELOPMENT ORGANIZATIONS

Agence Française de Développement (AFD): ZAC Bouillé, blvd du Général de Gaulle, BP 804, 97244 Fort-de-France Cédex; tel. 5-96-59-44-73; fax 5-96-59-44-88; e-mail afdfortdefrance@groupe-afd.org; internet www.afd.fr; fmrly Caisse Française de Développement; Man. JEAN-YVES CLAVEL.

Secrétariat Général pour les Affaires Régionales (SGAR)—Bureau de la Coopération Régionale: Préfecture, 97262 Fort-de-France; e-mail jean-charles.barrus@martinique.pref.gouv.fr; tel. 5-96-39-49-78; fax 5-96-39-49-59; successor to the Direction de l'Action Economique Régionale (DAER); research, documentation, and technical and administrative advice on investment in industry and commerce; Chief JEAN-CHARLES BARRUS.

CHAMBERS OF COMMERCE

Chambre d'Agriculture: pl. d'Armes, BP 312, 97286 Le Lamentin; tel. 5-96-51-75-75; fax 5-96-51-93-42; e-mail chambagr@ais.mq; internet paris.apca.chambagri.fr; Pres. LOUIS-DANIEL BERTOME; Dir NICAIRE MONROSE.

Chambre de Commerce et d'Industrie de la Martinique: 50 rue Ernest Desproge, BP 478, 97241 Fort-de-France Cédex; tel. 5-96-55-28-00; fax 5-96-60-66-68; e-mail ccim.doi@martinique.cci.fr; internet www.martinique.cci.fr; f. 1907; Pres. CLAUDE POMPIÈRE; Sec. JOSEPH DE JAHAM.

Chambre des Métiers de la Martinique: 2 rue du Temple, Morne Tartenson, BP 1194, 97200 Fort-de-France; tel. 5-96-71-32-22; fax 5-96-70-47-30; e-mail cmm972@wanadoo.fr; internet www.cm-fortdefrance.fr; f. 1970; Sec.-Gen. JOSEPH THOME; 8,000 mems.

EMPLOYERS' ORGANIZATIONS

Banalliance: Centre d'Affaires le Baobab, rue Léon Gontran Damas, 97232 Le Lamentin; tel. 5-96-57-42-42; fax 5-96-57-35-18; f. 1996; Pres. DANIEL DISERT; 220 mems.

Banamart: Quartier Bois Rouge, 97224 Ducos; tel. 5-96-42-43-44; fax 5-96-51-47-70; internet www.banamart.com; f. 2005 by merger of SICABAM and GIPAM; represents banana producers.

Compagnie Bananière de la Martinique (COBAMAR): Immeuble les Palétuviers Z. I. Lézarde, 97232 Le Lamentin; tel. 5-96-30-00-50; fax 5-96-57-14-03; internet www.cobamar.fr; f. 1993; Pres. MARCEL FABRE; 200 mems.

Ordre des Médecins de la Martinique: 80 rue de la République, 97200 Fort-de-France; tel. 5-96-63-27-01; fax 5-96-60-58-00; e-mail martinique@972.medecin.fr; Pres. Dr RENÉ LEGENDRI.

Ordre des Pharmaciens de la Martinique: BP 587, 97207 Fort-de-France Cédex; tel. 5-96-52-23-67; fax 5-96-52-20-92; e-mail delegation_martinique@ordre.pharmacien.fr; Pres. JEAN BIGON.

FRENCH OVERSEAS POSSESSIONS

UTILITIES

Electricity

Electricité de France Martinique (EDF): Pointe des Carrières, BP 573, 97242 Fort-de-France Cédex 01; tel. 5-96-59-20-00; fax 5-96-60-29-76; e-mail edf-services-martinique@edfgdf.fr; internet www.edf.fr/martinique; f. 1975; electricity supplier; successor to Société de Production et de Distribution d'Electricité de la Martinique (SPDEM); Dir ANDRÉ KIENER; 174,753 customers (2006).

Water

Veolia Water-Société Martiniquaise des Eaux (SME): pl. d'Armes, BP 213, 97284 Le Lamentin Cédex 02; tel. 5-96-51-80-51; fax 5-96-51-80-55; internet www.martiniquaisedeseaux.com; f. 1977 as Société Martiniquaise des Eaux.

TRADE UNIONS

Centrale Démocratique Martiniquaise du Travail (CDMT): Maison des Syndicats, Jardin Desclieux, 97200 Fort-de-France; tel. 5-96-70-19-86; fax 5-96-71-32-25; Sec.-Gen. NICOLE ELANA.

Confédération Générale du Travail de la Martinique (CGTM): Maison des Syndicats, Jardin Desclieux, 97200 Fort-de-France; tel. 5-96-60-45-21; f. 1961; affiliated to World Fed. of Trade Unions; Sec.-Gen. GHISLAINE JOACHIM-ARNAUD.

Fédération Départementale des Syndicats d'Exploitants Agricoles de la Martinique (FDSEA): Immeuble Chambre d'Agriculture, pl. d'Armes, 97232 Le Lamentin; tel. 5-96-51-61-46; fax 5-96-57-05-43; e-mail fdsea.martinique@wanadoo.fr; affiliated to the Fédération Nationale des Syndicats d'Exploitants Agricoles; Pres. LOUIS-DANIEL BERTOME.

Fédération Syndicale Unitaire Martinique (FSU): route des Réligieuses, Bât B, Cité Bon Air, 97200 Fort-de-France; tel. 5-96-63-63-27; fax 5-96-71-89-43; e-mail fsu972@fsu.fr; f. 1993; departmental br. of the Fédération Syndicale Unitaire; represents public sector employees in teaching, research and training, and also agriculture, justice, youth and sports, and culture; Sec. SERGE BACLET.

Union Départementale Confédération Française des Travailleurs Chrétiens Martinique (UD CFTC): Maison des Syndicats, Jardins Desclieux, 97200 Fort-de-France; tel. 5-96-60-95-10; fax 5-96-60-39-10; e-mail cftc972@wanadoo.fr; internet www.cftc.fr.

Union Départementale Force Ouvrière Martinique (UD-FO): rue Bouillé, BP 1114, 97248 Fort-de-France Cédex; tel. 5-96-70-07-04; fax 5-96-70-18-20; e-mail udfomartinique@wanadoo.fr; affiliated to the Int. Trade Union Confederation; Sec.-Gen. ERIC BELLEMARE.

Union Général des Travailleurs de Martinique (UGTM): 8 rue Pierre et Marie Curie, Terres Sainville, 97200 Fort-de-France; f. 1999; Pres. LÉON BERTIDE; Sec.-Gen. PATRICK DORÉ.

Union Régionale Martinique: Maison de Syndicats, Jardin Desclieux, Salles 5–7, 97200 Fort-de-France; tel. 5-96-70-16-80; internet www.unsa.org.

UNSA Education Martinique (SE-UNSA): Maison des Syndicats, Salles 6–7, Jardin Desclieux, 97200 Fort-de-France; tel. 5-96-72-64-74; fax 5-96-70-16-80; Sec.-Gen. MICHEL CRISPIN.

Transport

RAILWAYS

There are no railways in Martinique.

ROADS

There were 2,077 km (1,291 miles) of roads in 1998, of which 261 km were motorways and first-class roads.

SHIPPING

Direction des Concessions Services Portuaires: quai de l'Hydro Base, BP 782, 97244 Fort-de-France Cédex; tel. 5-96-59-00-00; fax 5-96-71-35-73; e-mail port@martinique.cci.fr; port services management; Dir FRANTZ THODIARD; Operations Man. VICTOR EUSTACHE.

Direction Régionale des Affaires Maritimes (DRAM): blvd Chevalier de Sainte-Marthe, BP 620, 97261 Fort-de-France Cédex; tel. 5-96-71-90-05; fax 5-96-63-67-30.

CMA-CGM CGM Antilles-Guyane: ave François Mitterrand, BP 574, 97242 Fort-de-France Cédex; tel. 5-96-55-32-00; fax 5-96-63-08-87; e-mail fdf.rjoseph-alexandre@cma-cgm.com; internet www.cma-cgm.com; subsidiary of CMA-CGM, France; also represents other passenger and freight lines; Man. Dir JEAN-CHARLES CREN.

Horn Line: 15 blvd François Reboult, 97200 Fort-de-France; tel. 5-96-71-27-74; fax 5-96-71-27-83; e-mail horn.antilles.fdf@wanadoo.fr; internet www.hornline.com; Dir FRÉDÉRIC DURAND.

CIVIL AVIATION

Fort-de-France–Le Lamentin international airport is located at Le Lamentin, 12 km from Fort-de-France and is equipped to handle jet-engined aircraft.

Direction des Services Aéroportuaires: BP 279, 97285 Le Lamentin; tel. 5-96-42-16-00; fax 5-96-42-18-77; e-mail thodiard@martinique.cci.fr; Dir FRANTZ THODIARD.

Air Caraïbes: see Guadeloupe—Transport.

Tourism

Martinique's tourist attractions are its beaches and coastal scenery, its mountainous interior, and the historic towns of Fort-de-France and Saint-Pierre. In 2005 there were 97 hotels, with some 4,676 rooms. In that year the number of tourists who stayed on the island totalled 484,127. Receipts from tourism increased from an estimated US $247m. in 2003 to $291m. in 2004.

Comité Martiniquais du Tourisme: Immeuble Beaupré, Pointe de Jaham, 97233 Schoelcher; tel. 5-96-61-61-77; fax 5-96-61-22-72; internet www.welcome2martinique.com; Pres. MADELEINE DE GRANDMAISON.

Délégation Régionale au Tourisme: 41 rue Gabriel Périé, 97200 Fort-de-France; tel. 5-96-63-18-61; fax 5-96-73-00-96; internet www.martinique.pref.gouv.fr/pages/delegation.html; Dir PHILIPPE CAYOT.

Fédération Martiniquaise des Offices de Tourisme et Syndicats d'Initiative (FMOTSI): Maison du Tourisme Vert, 9 blvd du Général de Gaulle, BP 491, 97207 Fort-de-France Cédex; tel. 5-96-63-18-54; fax 5-96-70-17-61; internet perso.orange.fr/fmotsi/sommaire.htm; f. 1984; Pres. VICTOR GRANDIN.

RÉUNION

Introductory Survey

Location, Climate, Language, Religion, Capital

Réunion is an island in the Indian Ocean, lying about 800 km (500 miles) east of Madagascar. The climate varies greatly according to altitude: at sea-level it is tropical, with average temperatures between 20°C (68°F) and 28°C (82°F), but in the uplands it is much cooler, with average temperatures between 8°C (46°F) and 19°C (66°F). Rainfall is abundant, averaging 4,714 mm annually in the uplands, and 686 mm at sea-level. The population is of mixed origin, including people of European, African, Indian and Chinese descent. The official language is French. A large majority of the population are Christians belonging to the Roman Catholic Church. The capital is Saint-Denis.

Recent History

Réunion was first occupied by France in 1642, and was ruled as a colony until 1946, when it received full departmental status. In 1974 it became an Overseas Department (Départment d'outre mer) with the status of a region.

In 1978 the Organization of African Unity (OAU, now the African Union, see p. 164) adopted a report recommending measures to hasten the independence of the island, and condemned its occupation by a 'colonial power'. However, this view seemed to have little popular support in Réunion. Although the left-wing political parties on the island advocated increased autonomy (amounting to virtual self-government), few people were in favour of complete independence.

Revised legislation on decentralization in the Overseas Departments was approved by the French Assemblée nationale (National Assembly) in December 1982. Elections to the Conseil régional (Regional Council) took place in Réunion in February 1983, when left-wing candidates won 50.8% of the votes cast.

In elections to the Assemblée nationale in March 1986, Réunion's representation was increased from three to five deputies. The Parti Communiste Réunionnais (PCR) won two seats, while the Union pour la Démocratie Française (UDF), the Rassemblement pour la République (RPR) and a newly formed right-wing party, France-Réunion-Avenir (FRA), each secured one seat. In concurrent elections to the Conseil régional, an alliance between the RPR and the UDF obtained 18 of the 45 seats, while the PCR secured 13 and the FRA eight. The leader of the FRA, Pierre Lagourgue, was elected as President of the Conseil régional.

In the second round of the French presidential election in May 1988, François Mitterrand, the incumbent President and a candidate of the Parti Socialiste (PS), received 60.3% of the votes cast in Réunion, while Jacques Chirac, the RPR Prime Minister, obtained 39.7%. At elections to the Assemblée nationale in June, the PCR won two of the seats allocated to Réunion, while the UDF and the RPR (which contested the elections jointly as the Union du Rassemblement du Centre—URC), and the FRA each won one seat. (The RPR and FRA deputies later became independents, although they maintained strong links with the island's right-wing groups.) Relations between the PCR and the PS subsequently deteriorated, following mutual recriminations concerning their failure to co-operate in the general election.

In the elections for the newly enlarged 44-member Conseil général (General Council) in September and October 1988, the PCR and the PS won nine and four seats respectively, while left-wing independent candidates obtained two seats. The UDF secured six seats and right-wing independent candidates 19, but the RPR, which had previously held 11 seats, won only four. Later in October, Eric Boyer, a right-wing independent candidate, was elected as President of the Conseil général.

In September 1990 several right-wing and centrist movements, including the UDF and the RPR, established an informal alliance, known as the Union pour la France (UPF), to contest the regional elections in 1992.

Meanwhile, in March 1990 violent protests took place in support of an unauthorized television service, Télé Free-DOM, following a decision by the French national broadcasting commission, the Conseil supérieur de l'audiovisuel (CSA), to award a broadcasting permit to a rival company. In February 1991 the seizure by the CSA of Télé Free-DOM's broadcasting transmitters prompted renewed demonstrations in Saint-Denis. Some 11 people were killed in ensuing riots, and the French Government dispatched police reinforcements to restore order. In March a commission of enquiry attributed the riots in February to the inflammatory nature of television programmes that had been broadcast by Télé Free-DOM in the weeks preceding the disturbances, and cited the station's director, Dr Camille Sudre, as responsible. However, the commission refuted allegations by right-wing and centrist politicians that the PCR had orchestrated the violence.

Sudre presented a list of independent candidates (known as Free-DOM) to contest the elections to the Conseil régional, which took place in March 1991; Free-DOM secured 17 seats, while the UPF obtained 14 seats, the PCR nine seats and the PS five seats. In concurrent elections to the Conseil général (newly enlarged to 47 seats), right-wing independent candidates won 20 seats, although the number of PCR deputies increased to 12, and the number of PS deputies to six; Boyer retained the presidency of the Conseil. Following the elections, the Free-DOM list of candidates formed an alliance with the PCR, thereby obtaining a narrow majority of 26 of the 45 seats in the Conseil régional. Under the terms of the agreement, Sudre was to assume the presidency of the Conseil régional. Sudre was accordingly elected as President of the Conseil régional by a majority of 27 votes, with the support of members of the PCR. The PS subsequently appealed against the results of the regional elections on the grounds of media bias; Sudre's privately owned radio station, Radio Free-DOM, had campaigned on his behalf prior to the elections. Following his election to the presidency of the Conseil régional, Sudre announced that Télé Free-DOM was shortly to resume broadcasting. The CSA indicated, however, that it would continue to regard transmissions by Télé Free-DOM as illegal, and liable to judicial proceedings. Jean-Paul Virapoullé, a deputy to the Assemblée nationale, subsequently proposed the adoption of legislation that would legalize Télé Free-DOM and would provide for the establishment of an independent media sector on Réunion. In April Télé Free-DOM's transmitters were returned, and at the end of May a full broadcasting service was resumed (without the permission of the CSA).

In June 1992 a delegation from the Conseil régional met President Mitterrand to submit proposals for economic reforms, in accordance with the aim of establishing parity between Réunion and metropolitan France. In early July, however, the French Government announced increases in social security benefits that were substantially less than had been expected, resulting in widespread discontent on the island. In September the PCR demanded that the electorate refuse to participate in the forthcoming French referendum on ratification of the Treaty on European Union (see p. 244), in protest at the alleged failure of the French Government to recognize the requirements of the Overseas Departments. At the referendum, which took place later that month, the ratification of the Treaty was approved by the voters of Réunion, although only 26.3% of the registered electorate voted.

In March 1993 Sudre announced that he was to contest Virapoullé's seat on behalf of the Free-DOM–PCR alliance in the forthcoming elections to the Assemblée nationale. However, at the elections, which took place later that month, Sudre was defeated by Virapoullé in the second round of voting, while another incumbent right-wing deputy, André Thien Ah Koon (who contested the elections on behalf of the UPF), also retained his seat. The PCR, the PS and the RPR each secured one of the remaining seats.

In May 1993 the French Conseil d'état declared the results of the regional elections in March 1992 to be invalid, and prohibited Sudre from engaging in political activity for a year, on the grounds that programmes broadcast by Radio Free-DOM prior to the elections constituted political propaganda. Sudre subsequently nominated his wife, Margie, to assume his candidacy in further elections to the Conseil régional. In the elections, which took place in June 1993, the Free-DOM list of candidates, headed by Margie Sudre, secured 12 seats, while the UDF obtained 10 seats, the RPR eight seats, the PCR nine seats and the PS six seats. Margie Sudre was subsequently elected as President of the Conseil régional, with the support of the nine PCR deputies and three dissident members of the PS, obtaining a total of 24 votes.

In April 1993 a number of prominent business executives were arrested in connection with the acquisition of contracts by fraudulent means; several senior politicians, including Boyer and Pierre Vergès (the mayor of Le Port and son of Paul Vergès), were also implicated in malpractice, following the investigation into their activities. Both Boyer and Pierre Vergès subsequently fled in order to evade arrest. In August Boyer, who had surrendered to the security forces, was formally charged with corruption and placed in detention. In March 1994 he was found guilty of corruption and imprisoned.

At elections to the Conseil général, which took place in March 1994, the PCR retained 12 seats, while the number of PS deputies increased to 12. The number of seats held by the RPR and UDF declined to five and 11 respectively. The RPR and UDF subsequently attempted to negotiate an alliance with the PCR; however, the PCR and PS established a coalition (despite the long-standing differences between the two parties), thereby securing the support of 24 of the 47 seats in the Conseil général. In April a member of the PS, Christophe Payet, was elected President of the Conseil général; the right-wing parties (which had held the presidency of the Conseil général for more than 40 years) boycotted the poll. The PS and PCR signed an agreement whereby the two parties were to control the administration of the Conseil général jointly, and indicated that centrist deputies might be allowed to join the alliance.

In the second round of the French presidential election, which took place in May 1995, the socialist candidate, Lionel Jospin, secured 56% of votes cast on Réunion, while Jacques Chirac, the official candidate of the RPR, won 44% of the votes (although Chirac obtained the highest number of votes overall). Following Chirac's election to the French presidency, Margie Sudre was nominated Minister of State with responsibility for Francophone Affairs, prompting concern among right-wing organizations on Réunion.

In August 1995 Pierre Vergès was sentenced *in absentia* to a custodial term of 18 months; an appeal was rejected in July 1996. In November 1995 Boyer lost an appeal against his 1994 conviction and was expelled from the French Sénat (Senate).

With effect from the beginning of 1996 the social security systems of the Overseas Departments were aligned with those of metropolitan France. In February Alain Juppé, the French Prime Minister, invited representatives from the Overseas Departments to Paris to participate in discussions on social equality and development. The main issue uniting the political representatives from Réunion was the need to align the salaries of civil servants on the island with those in metropolitan France. Several trade unionists declared themselves willing to enter into negotiations, on condition that only new recruits would be affected. Paul Vergès, joint candidate of the PCR and the PS, was elected to the Sénat in April, securing 51.9% of the votes cast. In the by-election to replace Paul Vergès, which took place in September, Claude Hoarau, the PCR candidate, was elected as a deputy to the Assemblée nationale with 56.0% of the votes cast. A new majority alliance between Free-DOM, the RPR and the UDF was subsequently formed in the Conseil régional, with the re-election of its 19-member permanent commission in October.

In October 1996 the trial of a number of politicians and business executives, who had been arrested in 1993–94 on charges of corruption, took place, after three years of investigations. Jacques de Châteauvieux, the Chairman of Groupe Sucreries de Bourbon, was found guilty of bribery, and was imprisoned, while two senior executives from the French enterprise Compagnie Générale des Eaux were given suspended sentences. Some 20 others were also found guilty of corruption. Pierre Vergès surrendered to the authorities in December and appeared before a magistrate in Saint-Pierre, where he was subsequently detained; in February 1997 he was released by the Court of Appeal.

Four left-wing candidates were successful in elections to the Assemblée nationale held in May and June 1997. Claude Hoarau (PCR) retained his seat and was joined by Huguette Bello and Elie

Hoarau, also both from the PCR, and Michel Tamaya (PS), while Thien Ah Koon, representing the RPR-UDF coalition, was re-elected.

In February 1998 the PCR (led by Paul Vergès), the PS and several right-wing mayors presented a joint list of candidates, known as the Rassemblement, to contest forthcoming elections. In the elections to the Conseil régional, which took place on 15 March, the Rassemblement secured 19 seats, while the UDF obtained nine seats and the RPR eight, with various left-wing candidates representing Free-DOM winning five. Vergès was elected President of the Conseil régional on 23 March, with the support of the deputies belonging to the Rassemblement and Free-DOM groups. In concurrent elections to an expanded 49-member Conseil général, right-wing candidates (including those on the Rassemblement's list) secured 27 seats, while left-wing candidates obtained 22 seats, with the PCR and the PS each winning 10 seats. At the end of the month Jean-Luc Poudroux, of the UDF, was elected President of the Conseil général, owing to the support of two left-wing deputies.

At municipal elections, held in March 2001, the left-wing parties experienced significant losses. Notably, the PS mayor of Saint-Denis, Michel Tamaya, was defeated by the RPR candidate, René-Paul Victoria. The losses were widely interpreted as a general rejection of Jospin's proposals to create a second department on the island. At elections to the Conseil général, held concurrently, the right-wing parties also made substantial gains, obtaining 38 of the 49 seats; the UDF retained its majority, and Poudroux was re-elected as President. In July Elie Hoarau was obliged to resign from the Assemblée nationale, following his conviction on charges of electoral fraud, as a result of which he received a one-year prison sentence and was barred from holding public office for a period of three years.

In the first round of the presidential election, which was held on 21 April 2002, Jospin secured 39.0% of the valid votes cast in the Department (although he was eliminated nationally), followed by Chirac, who received 37.1%. In the second round, on 5 May, Chirac overwhelmingly defeated the candidate of the extreme right-wing Front National, Jean-Marie Le Pen, with 91.9% of the vote. At elections to the Assemblée nationale in June, Thien Ah Koon, allied to the new Union pour la Majorité Présidentielle (UMP, which had recently been formed by the merger of the RPR, the Démocratie Libérale and elements of the UDF), and Bello were re-elected. Tamaya lost his seat to Victoria of the UMP, Claude Hourau lost to Bertho Audifax of the UMP, while Elie Hourau, who was declared ineligible to stand for re-election, was replaced by Christophe Payet of the PS. (In November the UMP was renamed the Union pour un Mouvement Populaire.)

In elections to the Conseil régional, which took place on 21 and 28 March 2004, the Alliance, a joint list of candidates led by the PCR, secured 27 seats. The UMP won 11 seats, and an alliance of the PS and Les Verts Réunion obtained seven seats. Following concurrent elections to the Conseil général, to renew 25 of the 49 seats, right-wing candidates held 30 seats, while left-wing candidates held 19. On 1 April Nassimah Dindar of the UMP was elected to succeed Poudroux as President of the Conseil général. Paul Vergès was re-elected as President of the Conseil régional on the following day. In February 2005 Gélite Hoarau replaced Paul Vergès as the PCR's representative to the Sénat.

In late May 2005 a national referendum on ratification of the proposed constitutional treaty of the European Union was held: 59.9% of Réunion's electorate joined with a majority of French voters in rejecting the treaty; voter turn-out on the island was around 53%.

In early 2006 an outbreak of chikungunya, a debilitating mosquito-borne virus, reached epidemic proportions. Chikungunya was first reported on the island in April 2005; by February 2006 some 157,000 people were believed to have been infected with the virus and it had been linked to the deaths of 77 people. Paul Vergès accused the French Government of mismanagement and of failing to react with sufficient speed to the crisis, while there were also concerns that the insecticides being used to eradicate the mosquitoes were potentially harmful to humans. In February 300 French soldiers were sent to Réunion to assist some 500 troops already deployed on the island. Meanwhile, hotels reported that future reservations were significantly reduced compared with the previous year and estimated a loss of some €15m. to the island's tourism industry. During a visit to Réunion later that month the French Prime Minister, Dominique de Villepin, encouraged tourists to continue to visit the island. He also announced financial assistance amounting to €76m., of which some €60m. was allocated as compensation to local businesses. The remaining €16m. would be spent on disease prevention including €9m. towards research; at that time there was no known cure for chikungunya and experts believed that it would be five years before a vaccine would be available.

In the first round of the French presidential election, held on 22 April 2007, Ségolène Royal of the PS secured 46.2% of the votes cast in Réunion, while Nicolas Sarkozy of the UMP received 25.1%. Both therefore proceeded to the second round of voting on 6 May in which Sarkozy claimed victory at national level; however, voting on Réunion again went in favour of Royal, who received 63.6% of the island vote. At legislative elections in June Victoria and Bello both retained their seats in the Assemblée nationale, but Audifax lost his seat to Jean-Claude Fruteau of the PS. Didier Robert of the UMP defeated Paul Vergès, while Patrick Lebreton of the PS was also elected.

In January 1986 France was admitted to the Indian Ocean Commission (IOC, see p. 412), owing to its sovereignty over Réunion. Réunion was given the right to host ministerial meetings of the IOC, but would not be allowed to occupy the presidency, owing to its status as a non-sovereign state.

Government

France is represented in Réunion by an appointed Prefect. There are two councils with local powers: the 49-member Conseil général and the 45-member Conseil régional. Both are elected for up to six years by direct universal suffrage. Réunion sends five directly elected deputies to the Assemblée nationale in Paris and three indirectly elected representatives to the Sénat. The Department is also represented at the European Parliament.

Defence

Réunion is the headquarters of French military forces in the Indian Ocean and French Southern and Antarctic Territories. As assessed at November 2007, there were 1,000 French troops stationed on Réunion and Mayotte, including a gendarmerie.

Economic Affairs

Réunion's gross national income (GNI) in 1995 was estimated at 29,200m. French francs, equivalent to about 44,300 francs per head. During 1990–97, according to World Bank estimates, Réunion's population increased at an average annual rate of 1.7%. In 2001, according to the UN, Réunion's gross domestic product (GDP), measured at current prices, was US $6,744m., equivalent to $9,188 per head. GDP increased, in real terms, at an average annual rate of 2.9% in 1990–2001; growth in 2001 was 2.4%. According to official estimates, in 2005 Réunion's GDP was €11,990m., equivalent to €15,350 per head.

Agriculture (including hunting, forestry and fishing) contributed 1.6% of GDP in 2004, and engaged 1.5% of the working population in 2005. The principal cash crops are sugar cane (sugar accounted for 41.0% of export earnings in 2006), maize, tobacco, vanilla, and geraniums and vetiver root, which are cultivated for the production of essential oils. Fishing and livestock production are also important to the economy. According to the UN, agricultural GDP increased at an average annual rate of 3.9% during 1990–2000; growth in 2001 was 3.1%.

Industry (including mining, manufacturing, construction and power) contributed 13.7% of GDP in 2004, and employed 6.4% of the working population in 2005. The principal branch of manufacturing is food-processing, particularly the production of sugar and rum. Other significant sectors include the fabrication of construction materials, mechanics, printing, metalwork, textiles and garments, and electronics. According to the UN, industrial GDP (excluding construction) increased at an average annual rate of 4.3% during 1990–99; growth in 2001 was 3.7%.

There are no mineral resources on the island. Energy is derived principally from thermal and hydroelectric power. Power plants at Bois-Rouge and Le Gol produce around 45% of the island's total energy requirements; almost one-third of the electricity generated is produced using bagasse, a by-product of sugar cane. Imports of products of cokeries, petroleum refineries and nuclear industries comprised 10.2% of the value of total imports in 2006.

Services (including transport, communications, trade and finance) contributed 84.6% of GDP in 2004, and employed 74.3% of the working population in 2005. The public sector accounts for more than two-thirds of employment in the services sector. Tourism is also significant; in 2004 430,000 tourists visited Réunion, and tourism revenue totalled €314.4m. However, the following year the number of tourists fell to 409,000 and tourism revenue was €308.8m. In early 2006 hotels reported that reservations had fallen by 60% compared with the previous year owing to an epidemic of the chikungunya virus (see Recent History, above) and the number of tourist arrivals declined to 278,800; receipts in that year totalled just €224.8m.

In 2006 Réunion recorded a trade deficit of €3,673.7m. The principal source of imports in 2006 (excluding trade with metropolitan France for which figures were not available) was Singapore, providing 8.6% of the total. The principal market for exports in that year (excluding metropolitan France), were Mayotte (7.9%), Japan (5.3%) and Madagascar (5.2%). The principal exports in 2006 were sugar and capital equipment. The principal imports in that year were prepared foodstuffs, road motor vehicles and parts, and chemical products.

In 1998 there was an estimated state budgetary deficit of 8,048.9m. French francs. The departmental budget for 2006 amounted to €1,272.0m.; some 35.5% of revenue was to be provided by the State. The annual rate of inflation averaged 1.9% in 1998–2006; consumer prices increased by 2.5% in 2006. An estimated 28.9% of the labour force were unemployed in December 2005.

FRENCH OVERSEAS POSSESSIONS   *Réunion*

Réunion is represented by France in the Indian Ocean Commission (IOC, see p. 412). As an integral part of France, Réunion belongs to the European Union (see p. 244).

Réunion has a relatively developed economy, but is dependent on financial aid from France. The economy has traditionally been based on agriculture, and is therefore vulnerable to poor climatic conditions. From the 1990s the production of sugar cane (which dominates that sector) was adversely affected by increasing urbanization, which resulted in a decline in agricultural land. Favourable economic progress has been largely sustained largely by tourism and economists have identified Réunion's need to expand external trade, particularly with fellow IOC members, if the island's economy is to continue to prosper. It was hoped that a decision to allow Réunion to negotiate co-operation agreements with regional states from 2004 would enhance its trading position. The tourism sector experienced a reverse in 2006, however, with visitor numbers and revenue vastly reduced, owing to the epidemic of the chikungunya virus on the island (see Recent History). Furthermore, Réunion's rate of unemployment remained the highest of all the French Departments in 2005, with youth unemployment of particular concern.

Education

Education is modelled on the French system, and is compulsory for 10 years between the ages of six and 16 years. Primary education begins at six years of age and lasts for five years. Secondary education, which begins at 11 years of age, lasts for up to seven years, comprising a first cycle of four years and a second of three years. In the academic year 2005/06 there were 45,853 pupils enrolled at pre-primary schools, 76,007 at primary schools, and 102,613 at secondary schools. There is a university, with several faculties, providing higher education in law, economics, politics, and French language and literature, and a teacher-training college. In 2005/06 10,562 students were enrolled at the university.

Public Holidays

2008: 1 January (New Year's Day), 24 March (Easter Monday), 1 May (Labour Day), 8 May (Liberation Day), 1 May (Ascension Day), 12 May (Whit Monday), 14 July (National Day, Fall of the Bastille), 15 August (Assumption), 1 November (All Saints' Day), 11 November (Armistice Day), 20 December (Abolition of Slavery Day), 25 December (Christmas Day).

2009: 1 January (New Year's Day), 13 April (Easter Monday), 1 May (Labour Day), 8 May (Liberation Day), 21 May (Ascension Day), 1 June (Whit Monday), 14 July (National Day, Fall of the Bastille), 15 August (Assumption), 1 November (All Saints' Day), 11 November (Armistice Day), 20 December (Abolition of Slavery Day), 25 December (Christmas Day).

Weights and Measures

The metric system is in use.

Statistical Survey

Source (unless otherwise indicated): Institut National de la Statistique et des Etudes Economiques, Service Régional de la Réunion, 15 rue de l'Ecole, 97490 Sainte-Clotilde; tel. 48-81-00; fax 41-09-81; internet www.insee.fr/fr/insee_regions/reunion.

AREA AND POPULATION

Area: 2,507 sq km (968 sq miles).

Population: 597,828 (males 294,256, females 303,572) at census of 15 March 1990; 706,180 (males 347,076, females 359,104) at census of 8 March 1999. *1 January 2006* (official estimate): 783,951.

Density (1 January 2006, official estimate): 312.7 per sq km.

Principal Towns (population at census of March 1999): Saint-Denis (capital) 131,649; Saint-Paul 87,712; Saint-Pierre 69,009; Le Tampon 60,311; Saint-Louis 43,491; Saint-André 43,150. *Mid-2007* (incl. suburbs, UN estimate): Saint-Denis 143,000 (Source: UN, *World Urbanization Prospects: The 2007 Revision*).

Births, Marriages and Deaths (2005): Registered live births 14,610 (birth rate 18.7 per 1,000); Registered marriages 3,030 (marriage rate 3.9 per 1,000); Registered deaths 4,255 (death rate 5.5 per 1,000). *2006:* Registered live births 14,495 (birth rate 18.5 per 1,000); Registered deaths 4,323.

Expectation of Life (years at birth, 2005, provisional figures): 76.1 (males 72.3; females 80.1).

Economically Active Population (persons aged 15 years and over, 1999 census): Agriculture, hunting, forestry and fishing 9,562; Mining, manufacturing, electricity, gas and water 13,424; Construction 11,003; Wholesale and retail trade 24,658; Transport, storage and communications 5,494; Financing, insurance and real estate 4,851; Business services 11,225; Public administration 39,052; Education 23,325; Health and social work 17,376; Other services 13,707; *Total employed* 173,677 (males 100,634, females 73,043); Unemployed 124,203 (males 63,519, females 60,684); *Total labour force* 297,880 (males 164,153, females 133,727). Figures exclude 967 persons on compulsory military service (males 945, females 22). *2005* (salaried workers at 31 December, preliminary): Agriculture 3,189; Industry (incl. energy) 13,692; Construction 14,176; Trade 25,992; Transport 6,745; Financial activities and real estate 5,687; Private services 17,445; Business services 16,185; Health and welfare 16,747; Education 23,731; Public administration 45,649; Total salaried 189,238; Total non-salaried 23,637; Total employed 212,875; Unemployed 86,417; Total labour force 299,292.

HEALTH AND WELFARE

Key Indicators

Total Fertility Rate (children per woman, 2004): 2.5.

Physicians (per 1,000 head, 2007): 1.6.

Hospital Beds (per 1,000 head, 2000): 3.7.

For definitions, see explanatory note on p. vi.

AGRICULTURE, ETC.

Principal Crops ('000 metric tons, 2006, FAO estimates): Maize 11.7; Potatoes 3.7; Sugar cane 2,000; Cabbages 5; Lettuce 2.3; Tomatoes 4; Cauliflower 5.3; Pumpkins, squash and gourds 2.7; Eggplants 3.2; Onions and shallots (green) 5.0; Beans (green) 2.5; Carrots 4.6; Bananas 12.5; Tangerines, mandarins, clementines and satsumas 6.7; Mangoes 4.8; Pineapples 10.5.

Livestock ('000 head, 2006, FAO estimates): Cattle 36.2; Pigs 77.1; Sheep 1.0; Goats 36.1; Chickens 13,500.

Livestock Products ('000 metric tons, 2006, FAO estimates): Cattle meat 1.8; Pig meat 12.0; Chicken meat 14.0; Rabbit meat 2.1; Cow's milk 23.6; Hen eggs 5.9.

Forestry ('000 cubic metres, 1991): *Roundwood Removals:* Sawlogs, veneer logs and logs for sleepers 4.2; Other industrial wood 0.9 (FAO estimate); Fuel wood 31.0 (FAO estimate); Total 36.1. *Sawnwood Production:* 2.2. *1992–2006:* Annual production assumed to be unchanged from 1991 (FAO estimates).

Fishing (metric tons, live weight, 2005, FAO estimates): Capture 4,596 (Albacore 768; Yellowfin tuna 935; Swordfish 1,205; Common dolphinfish 77; Carangids 143; Octopuses, etc. 260); Aquaculture 161; *Total catch* 4,757.

Source: FAO.

INDUSTRY

Selected Products (metric tons, 2006 unless otherwise indicated): Sugar 205,067 (provisional figure); Oil of geranium 2 (provisional figure); Oil of vetiver root 0.4 (2002); Rum (hl) 78,929 (2005); Electric energy (million kWh) 2,365.

FINANCE

Currency and Exchange Rates: The French franc was used until the end of February 2002. Euro notes and coins were introduced on 1 January 2002, and the euro became the sole legal tender from 18 February. Some of the figures in this Survey are still in terms of francs. For details of exchange rates, see Mayotte.

Budget (€ million, 2006): *Regional Budget:* Revenue 761 (Taxes 238, Transfers received 269, Loans 254); Expenditure 761 (Current expenditure 227, Capital 534). *Departmental Budget:* Revenue 1,272.0 (State endowments 451.6, Direct and indirect taxes 640.8, Loans 110, Other subsidies (Europe and other bodies) 41.3, Other revenues and receipts 28.4); Expenditure 1,272.0 (Social welfare 713.0, General services 226.9, Development 98.9, Teaching 77.7, Networks and infrastructure 7.9, Security 49.0, Planning and environment 12.3, Culture, societies, youth and sports 13.2, Traffic 73.1). Source: Conseil général, *Le Budget du Département*.

Money Supply (million francs at 31 December 1996): Currency outside banks 4,050; Demand deposits at banks 7,469; Total money 11,519.

Cost of Living (Consumer Price Index for urban areas, average of monthly figures; base: 2000 = 100): All items 108.1 in 2004; 110.4 in 2005; 113.2 in 2006. Source: ILO.

Expenditure on the Gross Domestic Product (€ million at current prices, 2004): Private final consumption expenditure 7,293; Government final consumption expenditure (incl. non-profit institutions serving households) 4,753; Changes in inventories –81; Gross fixed capital formation 2,166; *Total domestic expenditure* 14,131; Exports

FRENCH OVERSEAS POSSESSIONS   *Réunion*

of goods and services 646; *Less* Imports of goods and services 3,543; *GDP in market prices* 11,234.

Gross Domestic Product by Economic Activity (€ million at current prices, 2004): Agriculture, forestry and fishing 172; Mining, manufacturing, electricity, gas and water 737; Construction 722; Wholesale and retail trade 1,036; Transport and communications 664; Finance and insurance 566; Public administration 1,320; Education, health and social work 2,572; Other services (incl. hotels and restaurants) 2,836; *Sub-total* 10,625; *Less* Financial intermediation services indirectly measured 371; *Gross value added at basic prices* 10,254; Taxes on products, *less* subsidies on products 980; *GDP in market prices* 11,234.

EXTERNAL TRADE

Principal Commodities (€ million, 2006): *Imports:* Prepared foodstuffs 552.8; Road motor vehicles and parts 481.1; Chemical products 437.0; Products of cokeries, petroleum refineries and nuclear industries 400.0; Machinery and mechanical appliances 344.7; Furniture and products from miscellaneous industries 145.8; Radio, television and communications equipment 152.7; Articles of clothing and furs 136.1; Metal products 146.1; Metallurgical products 138.6; Total (incl. others) 3,911.7. *Exports:* Prepared foodstuffs 161.7 (Sugar 97.6); Capital goods 33.0; Intermediate goods 17.9; Road motor vehicles and parts 11.9; Consumer goods 8.5; Crops and livestock products (unprocessed) 4.8; Total (incl. others) 238.0.

Principal Trading Partners (€ million, 2006): *Imports:* Belgium 88.4; China, People's Republic 154.8; Germany 147.6; Italy 126.6; Singapore 337.4; South Africa 79.8; Spain 75.1; Total (incl. others) 3,911.7. *Exports f.o.b.:* China, People's Republic 4.3; Italy 6.7; Japan 12.7; Madagascar 12.3; Mauritius 7.1; Mayotte 18.9; USA 5.1; Total (incl. others) 238.0. Note: Although trade with metropolitan France represented a significant proportion of Réunion's external trade, figures for imports from and exports to France were not available.

TRANSPORT

Road Traffic (1 January 2005): Motor vehicles in use 338,500.

Shipping: *Merchant Fleet* (total displacement at 31 December 1992): 21,000 grt (Source: UN, *Statistical Yearbook*); *Traffic 2006:* Passenger arrivals 12,368; Passenger departures 13,609; Vessels entered 714; Freight unloaded 3,478,100 metric tons; Freight loaded 469,400 metric tons; Containers unloaded 100,894 TEUs; Containers loaded 99,943 TEUs.

Civil Aviation (2006): Passenger arrivals 695,582; Passenger departures 699,779; Freight unloaded 20,664 metric tons; Freight loaded 7,753 metric tons.

TOURISM

Tourist Arrivals ('000): 430 in 2004; 409 in 2005; 279 in 2006.

Arrivals by Country of Residence (2006): France (metropolitan) 209,500; Other EU 10,500; Mauritius 20,100; Total (incl. others) 278,800.

Tourism Receipts (€ million): 314.4 in 2004; 308.8 in 2005; 224.8 in 2006.

COMMUNICATIONS MEDIA

Radio Receivers ('000 in use, 1997): 173 in use. Source: UNESCO, *Statistical Yearbook*.

Television Receivers ('000 in use, 1998): 130 in use. Source: UNESCO, *Statistical Yearbook*.

Telephones ('000 main lines in use, 2004, estimate): 300. Source: International Telecommunication Union.

Facsimile Machines (number in use, 1996): 9,164. Source: UN, *Statistical Yearbook*.

Mobile Cellular Telephones ('000 subscribers, 2005, estimate): 579.2. Source: International Telecommunication Union.

Personal Computers ('000 in use, 2004): 279. Source: International Telecommunication Union.

Internet Users ('000, 2004): 200. Source: International Telecommunication Union.

Book Production (1992): 69 titles (50 books; 19 pamphlets). Source: UNESCO, *Statistical Yearbook*.

Daily Newspapers (1996): 3 (estimated average circulation 55,000 copies). Source: UNESCO, *Statistical Yearbook*.

Non-daily Newspapers (1988, estimate): 4 (average circulation 20,000 copies). Source: UNESCO, *Statistical Yearbook*.

EDUCATION

Pre-primary and Primary (2006/07 unless otherwise indicated): Schools 532 (pre-primary 174, primary 358 in 2003/04); public sector pupils 113,047 (pre-primary 42,097, primary 70,950); private pupils 8,907 (pre-primary 3,174, primary 5,733).

Secondary (2006/07): Schools 121 (112 public sector, 9 private) (2005/06); pupils 102,218 (public sector 96,171, private 6,047).

University (2006/07): Institution 1; students 10,162.

Other Higher (2006/07): Students 4,988.

Teaching Staff (31 December 2006): Pre-primary and primary 6,516; Secondary 8,965; University 457; Other higher 476.

Directory

The Government
(February 2008)

Prefect: PIERRE-HENRY MACCIONI, Préfecture, pl. du Barachois, 97405 Saint-Denis Cédex; tel. 262-40-77-77; fax 262-41-73-74; e-mail courrier@reunion.pref.gouv.fr; internet www.reunion.pref.gouv.fr.

President of the General Council: NASSIMAH DINDAR (UMP), Hôtel du Département, 2 rue de la Source, 97400 Saint-Denis Cédex; tel. 262-90-30-30; fax 262-90-39-99; internet www.cg974.fr.

Deputies to the French National Assembly: HUGUETTE BELLO (PCR), JEAN-CLAUDE FRUTEAU (PS), PATRICK LEBRETON (PS), DIDIER ROBERT (UMP), RENÉ-PAUL VICTORIA (UMP).

Representatives to the French Senate: GÉLITA HOARAU (PCR), ANNE-MARIE PAYET (Union Centriste), JEAN-PAUL VIRAPOULLÉ (UMP).

GOVERNMENT OFFICES

Direction des Actions de Solidarité et d'Intégration (DASI): ave de la Victoire, 97488 Saint-Denis Cédex; tel. 262-90-31-90; fax 262-90-39-94.

Direction de l'Aménagement et du Développement Territorial: ave de la Victoire, 97488 Saint-Denis Cédex; tel. 262-90-86-86; fax 262-90-86-70.

Direction des Déplacements et de la Voirie (DDV): 6 allée Moreau, 97490 Sainte-Clotilde; tel. 262-90-04-44; fax 262-90-37-77.

Direction du Développement Rural, de l'Agriculture et de la Forêt (DDRAF): ave de la Victoire, 97488 Saint-Denis Cédex; tel. 262-90-35-24; fax 262-90-39-89.

Direction de l'Eau: 1A rue Charles Gounaud, 97488 Saint-Denis Cédex; tel. 262-90-04-44; fax 262-21-73-19.

Direction de l'Environnement et de l'Energie (DEE): 16 rue Jean Chatel, 97400 Saint-Denis Cédex; tel. 262-90-24-00; fax 262-90-24-19.

Direction des Finances: ave de la Victoire, 97488 Saint-Denis Cédex; tel. 262-90-39-39; fax 262-90-39-92.

Direction Générale des Services (DGS): 2 rue de la Source, 97488 Saint-Denis Cédex; tel. 262-90-30-92; fax 262-90-30-68.

Direction de l'Informatique (DI): 19 route de la Digue, 97488 Saint-Denis Cédex; tel. 262-90-32-90; fax 262-90-32-99.

Direction de la Logistique (DL): 2 rue de la Source, 97488 Saint-Denis Cédex; tel. 262-90-31-38; fax 262-90-39-91.

Direction du Patrimoine (DP): 6 bis rue Rontaunay, 97488 Saint-Denis Cédex; tel. 262-90-86-86; fax 262-90-86-90.

Direction de la Promotion Culturelle et Sportive (DPCS): 18 rue de Paris, 97488 Saint-Denis Cédex; tel. 262-94-87-00; fax 262-94-87-26.

Direction des Ressources Humaines (DRH): 2 rue de la Source, 97488 Saint-Denis Cédex; tel. 262-90-30-45; fax 262-90-30-10.

Direction de la Vie Educative: ave de la Victoire, 97488 Saint-Denis Cédex; tel. 262-90-32-32; fax 262-90-39-98.

Conseil Régional

Hôtel de Région Pierre Lagourgue, ave René Cassin, Moufia BP 7190, 97719 Saint-Denis, Cédex 9; tel. 262-48-70-00; fax 262-48-70-71; e-mail region.reunion@cr-reunion.fr; internet www.regionreunion.com.

President: PAUL VERGÈS (PCR).

FRENCH OVERSEAS POSSESSIONS   *Réunion*

Election, 21 and 28 March 2004

Party	Seats
Alliance*	27
UMP	11
PS-Les Verts Réunion	7
Total	**45**

* An alliance of seven political parties and movements, dominated by the PCR, and also including Free-DOM.

Political Organizations

Front National (FN)—Fédération de la Réunion (FN): Saint-Denis; tel. 262-51-38-97; e-mail fatna@frontnational.com; internet www.frontnational.com; f. 1972; extreme right-wing; Sec. (vacant).

Mouvement pour l'Indépendance de la Réunion (MIR): f. 1981 to succeed the fmr Mouvement pour la Libération de la Réunion; grouping of parties favouring autonomy; Leader ANSELME PAYET.

Mouvement National Républicain (MNR)—Fédération de la Réunion: tel. 262-22-34-69; Sec. RÉMI BERTIN.

Parti Communiste Réunionnais (PCR): Saint-Denis; f. 1959; Pres. PAUL VERGÈS; Sec.-Gen. ELIE HOARAU.

  Mouvement pour l'Egalité, la Démocratie, le Développement et la Nature: affiliated to the PCR; advocates political unity; Leader RENÉ PAYET.

Parti Radical de Gauche (PRG)—Fédération de la Réunion: 18 rue des Demoiselles, Hermitage les Bains, 97434 Saint-Gilles-les-Bains; tel. 262-33-94-73; internet www.prg93.org; f. 1977; fmrly Mouvement des Radicaux de Gauche; advocates full independence and an economy separate from, but assisted by, France; Pres. RÉMY MASSAIN.

Parti Socialiste (PS)—Fédération de la Réunion (PS): 18 ave Stanislas Gimard, 97490 Saint-Denis; tel. 262-97-46-42; fax 262-28-53-03; e-mail fede974@parti-socialiste.fr; internet www.parti-socialiste.fr; left-wing; Sec. MICHEL VERGOZ.

Union pour la Démocratie Française (UDF): Saint-Denis; internet www.udf.org; f. 1978; centrist.

Union pour un Mouvement Populaire (UMP)—Fédération de la Réunion: 6 bis blvd Vauban, BP 11, 97461 Saint-Denis Cédex; tel. 262-20-21-18; fax 262-41-73-55; f. 2002; centre-right; local branch of the metropolitan party; Departmental Sec. JEAN-LUC POUDROUX.

Les Verts Réunion: 8 rue des Salanganes, Plateau-Caillou, 97460 Saint Paul; tel. 262-55-73-52; fax 262-25-03-03; e-mail sr-verts-reunion@laposte.net; internet www.lesvertsreunion.com; ecologist; Regional Sec. JEAN ERPELDINGER.

Judicial System

Cour d'Appel: Palais de Justice, 166 rue Juliette Dodu, 97488 Saint-Denis; tel. 262-40-58-58; fax 262-20-16-37; Pres. JEAN-PAUL SEBILEAU.

There are two Tribunaux de Grande Instance, one Tribunal d'Instance, two Tribunaux pour Enfants and two Conseils de Prud'hommes.

Religion

A substantial majority of the population are adherents of the Roman Catholic Church. There is a small Muslim community.

CHRISTIANITY

The Roman Catholic Church

Réunion comprises a single diocese, directly responsible to the Holy See. At 31 December 2005 there were an estimated 620,000 adherents, equivalent to some 80.0% of the population.

Bishop of Saint-Denis de la Réunion: Mgr GILBERT AUBRY, Evêché, 36 rue de Paris, BP 55, 97461 Saint-Denis Cédex; tel. 262-94-85-70; fax 262-94-85-73; e-mail eveche.lareunion@wanadoo.fr; internet www.diocese-reunion.org.

The Press

DAILIES

Journal de l'Ile de la Réunion: Centre d'affaires Gamma Cadjee, 62 blvd du Chaudron, BP 40019-97491, Sainte-Clotilde Cédex; tel. 262-48-66-00; fax 262-48-66-50; f. 1956; Dir JACQUES TILLIER; circ. 35,000.

Quotidien de la Réunion et de l'Océan Indien: BP 303, 97712 Saint-Denis Cédex 9; tel. 262-92-15-15; fax 262-28-43-60; f. 1976; Dir MAXIMIN CHANE KI CHUNE; circ. 38,900.

PERIODICALS

AGRI-MAG Réunion: Chambre d'Agriculture, 24 rue de la Source, BP 134, 97463 Saint-Denis Cédex; tel. 262-94-25-94; fax 262-21-06-17; e-mail chambagri.cda-97@wanadoo.fr; f. 2001; monthly; Dir GUY DERAND; Chief Editor HERVÉ CAILLEAUX; circ. 8,000.

Al-Islam: Centre Islamique de la Réunion, BP 437, 97459 Saint-Pierre Cédex; tel. 262-25-45-43; fax 262-35-58-23; e-mail centre-islamique-reunion@wanadoo.fr; internet www.centre-islamique.com; f. 1975; 4 a year; Dir SAÏD INGAR.

L'Eco Austral: Technopole de la Réunion 2, rue Emile Hugot, BP 10003, 97801 Saint-Denis Cédex 9; tel. 262-41-51-41; fax 262-41-31-14; internet www.ecoaustral.com; f. 1993; monthly; regional economic issues; Editor ALAIN FOULON; circ. 50,000.

L'Economie de la Réunion: c/o INSEE, Parc Technologique, 10 rue Demarne, BP 13, 97408 Saint-Denis Messag Cédex 9; tel. 262-48-89-21; fax 262-48-89-89; e-mail insee-contact@insee.fr; internet www.insee.fr/reunion; 4 a year; Dir JEAN GAILLARD; Editor-in-Chief COLLETTE BERTHIER.

L'Eglise à la Réunion: 18 rue Montreuil, 97469 Saint-Denis; tel. 262-41-56-90; fax 262-40-92-17; e-mail eglise-reunion@wanadoo.fr; monthly; Dir ELIE CADET.

Lutte Ouvrière—Ile de la Réunion: BP 184, 97470 Saint-Benoît; fax 262-48-00-98; e-mail contact@lutte-ouvriere-ile-de-la-reunion.org; internet www.lutte-ouvriere-ile-de-la-reunion.org; monthly; Communist; digital.

Le Mémento Industriel et Commercial Réunionnais: 80 rue Pasteur, BP 397, 97468 Saint-Denis; tel. 262-21-94-12; fax 262-41-10-85; e-mail memento@memento.fr; internet www.memento.fr; f. 1970; monthly; Dir CATHERINE LOUAPRE-POTTIER; Editor-in-Chief GEORGES-GUILLAUME LOUAPRE-POTTIER; circ. 20,000.

Témoignages: 6 rue du Général Emile Rolland, BP 1016, 97828 Le Port Cédex; tel. 262-55-21-21; e-mail temoignages@wanadoo.fr; internet www.temoignages.re; f. 1944; affiliated to the PCR; daily; Dir JEAN-MARCEL COURTEAUD; Editor-in-Chief ALAIN ILAN CHOJNOW; circ. 6,000.

Visu: 97712 Saint-Denis Cédex 9; tel. 262-90-20-60; fax 262-90-20-61; weekly; Editor-in-Chief GUY LEBLOND; circ. 53,000.

NEWS AGENCY

Imaz Press Réunion: 12 rue MacAuliffe, 97400 Saint-Denis; tel. 262-20-05-65; fax 262-20-05-49; e-mail ipr@ipreunion.com; internet www.ipreunion.com; f. 2000; photojournalism and news agency; Dir RICHARD BOUHET.

Broadcasting and Communications

TELECOMMUNICATIONS

Orange Réunion: 35 blvd du Chaudron, BP 7431, 97743 Saint-Denis, Cédex 9; tel. 262-20-69-56; fax 262-20-67-79; f. 2000; subsidiary of Orange France; mobile cellular telephone operator.

Outremer Telecom Réunion: 12 rue Henri Cornu, Parc Technologique, 97490 Saint Clotilde; tel. 262-20-023-00; fax 262-97-53-99; internet www.orange.re; telecommunications provider.

Société Réunionnaise du Radiotéléphone (SRR): 21 rue Pierre Aubert, 97490 Sainte Clotide; BP 17, 97408 Saint-Denis, Messag Cédex 9; tel. 262-48-19-70; fax 262-48-19-80; internet www.srr.fr; f. 1995; subsidiary of SFR Cegetel, France; mobile cellular telephone operator; CEO JEAN-PIERRE HAGGAÏ; 431,719 subscribers in Réunion, 46,341 in Mayotte (as Mayotte Télécom Mobile) in 2003.

BROADCASTING

Réseau France Outre-mer (RFO): 1 rue Jean Chatel, 97716 Saint-Denis Cédex; tel. 262-40-67-67; fax 262-21-64-84; internet www.rfo.fr; acquired by Groupe France Télévisions in 2004; fmrly Société Nationale de Radio-Télévision Française d'Outre-mer, present name adopted in 1998; radio and television relay services in French; broadcasts two television channels (Télé-Réunion and Tempo) and three radio channels (Radio-Réunion, France-Inter and France-Culture); Gen. Man. FRANÇOIS GUILBEAU; Regional Dir GÉRALD PRUFER.

Radio

In 2005 there were 46 licensed private radio stations. These included:

Cherie FM Réunion: 3 rue de Kerveguen, 97400 Sainte-Clotilde; tel. 262-97-32-00; fax 262-97-32-32; Editor-in-Chief LEA BERTHAULT.

NRJ Réunion: 3 rue de Kerveguen, 97490 Sainte-Clotilde; tel. 262-97-32-00; fax 262-97-32-32; e-mail acceuil@nrjreunion.com; commercial radio station; Station Man. SYLVAIN PEGUILLAN.

Radio Festival: 3 rue de Kerveguen, 97490 Sainte-Clotilde; tel. 262-97-32-00; fax 262-97-32-32; e-mail redaction@radiofestival.fr; f. 1995; commercial radio station; Pres. MARIO LECHAT; Editor-in-Chief PIERROT DUPUY.

Radio Free-DOM: BP 666, 97473 Saint-Denis Cédex; tel. 262-41-51-51; fax 262-21-68-64; e-mail freedom@freedom.fr; internet www.freedom.fr; f. 1981; commercial radio station; Dir Dr CAMILLE SUDRE.

Television

Antenne Réunion: BP 80001, 97801 Saint-Denis Cédex 9; tel. 262-48-28-28; fax 262-48-28-26; e-mail direction@antennereunion.fr; internet www.antennereunion.fr; f. 1991; broadcasts 10 hours daily; Dir CHRISTOPHE DUCASSE.

Canal Réunion: 6 rue René Demarne, 97490 Sainte-Clotilde; tel. 262-97-98-99; fax 262-97-98-90; e-mail contact@canalreunion.net; internet www.canalreunion.com; subscription television channel; broadcasts a minimum of 19 hours daily; Chair. DOMINIQUE FAGOT; Dir JEAN-BERNARD MOURIER.

TV-4: 8 chemin Fontbrune, 97400 Saint-Denis; tel. 262-52-73-73; broadcasts 19 hours daily.

TV Sud: 10 rue Aristide Briand, 97430 Le Tampon; tel. 262-57-42-42; commenced broadcasting in 1993; broadcasts 4 hours daily.

Other privately owned television services include TVB, TVE, RTV, Télé-Réunion and TV-Run.

Finance

(cap. = capital; res = reserves; dep. = deposits; m. = million; brs = branches)

BANKING

Central Bank

Institut d'Emission des Départements d'Outre-mer: 4 rue de la Compagnie, 97487 Saint-Denis Cédex; tel. 262-90-71-00; fax 262-21-41-32; Dir GUY DEBUYS.

Commercial Banks

Banque Française Commerciale Océan Indien (BFCOI): 60 rue Alexis de Villeneuve, BP 323, 97468 Saint-Denis Cédex; tel. 262-40-55-55; fax 262-20-09-07; Chair. PHILIPPE BRAULT; Dir PHILIPPE LAVIT D'HAUTEFORT; 8 brs.

Banque Nationale de Paris Intercontinentale: 67 rue Juliette Dodu, BP 113, 97463 Saint-Denis; tel. 262-40-30-02; fax 262-41-39-09; internet www.bnpgroup.com; f. 1927; 100% owned by BNP Paribas; Chair. MICHEL PEBEREAU; Man. Dir DANIEL DELANIS; 16 brs.

Banque de la Réunion (BR), SA: 27 rue Jean Chatel, 97711 Saint-Denis Cédex; tel. 262-40-01-23; fax 262-40-00-61; e-mail br@banquedelareunion.fr; internet www.banquedelareunion.fr; f. 1853; subsidiary of Financière Océor; cap. €50.0m., res €52.0m., dep. €1,120.7m. (Dec. 2001); Chair. JEAN-CLAUDE CLARAC; Gen. Man. JEAN-LOUIS FILIPPI; 20 brs.

BRED-Banque Populaire: 33 rue Victor MacAuliffe, 97461 Saint-Denis; tel. 262-90-15-60; fax 262-90-15-99.

Crédit Agricole de la Réunion: Les Camélias, Cité des Lauriers, BP 84, 97462 Saint-Denis Cédex; tel. 262-40-81-81; fax 262-40-81-40; internet www.credit-agricole.fr; f. 1949; total assets €2,564m. (Dec. 2004); Chair. CHRISTIAN DE LA GIRODAY; Gen. Man. PIERRE MARTIN.

Development Bank

Banque Populaire Fédérale de Développement: 33 rue Victor MacAuliffe, 97400 Saint-Denis; tel. 262-21-18-11; Dir OLIVIER DEVISME; 3 brs.

Société Financière pour le Développement Economique de la Réunion (SOFIDER): 3 rue Labourdonnais, BP 867, 97477 Saint-Denis Cédex; tel. 262-40-32-32; fax 262-40-32-00; part of the Agence Française de Développpment; Dir-Gen. CLAUDE PÉRIOU.

INSURANCE

More than 20 major European insurance companies are represented in Saint-Denis.

AGF Vie La Réunion: 185 ave du Général de Gaulle, BP 797, 97476 Saint-Denis Cédex; tel. 262-94-72-23; fax 262-94-72-26; e-mail agfoi-vie@agfoi.com.

Capma & Capmi: 18 rue de la Cie des Indes, 97499 Saint-Denis; tel. 262-21-10-56; fax 262-20-32-67.

Groupama Océan Indien et Pacifique: 13 rue Fénelon, BP 626, 97473 Saint-Denis Cédex; tel. 262-26-12-61; fax 262-41-50-79; Chair. DIDIER FOUCQUE; Gen. Man. MAURICE FAURE (acting).

Trade and Industry

GOVERNMENT AGENCIES

Agence de Gestion des Initiatives Locales en Matière Européenne (AGILE)—Cellule Europe Réunion: 3 rue Felix Guyon, 97400 Saint-Denis; tel. 262-90-10-80; fax 262-21-90-72; e-mail celleurope@agile-reunion.org; internet www.agile-reunion.org; responsible for local application of EU structural funds; Dir SERGE JOSEPH.

Conseil Economique et Social de la Réunion (CESR): 10 rue du Béarn, BP 7191, 97719 Saint-Denis Messag Cédex; tel. 262-97-96-30; fax 262-97-96-31; e-mail cesr-reunion@cesr-reunion.fr; internet www.cesr-reunion.fr; f. 1984; Pres. JEAN-RAYMOND MONDON; Dir DIDIER LAMOTTE.

Direction Départementale de la Jeunesse, des Sports et de la Vie Associative de la Réunion (DDJS): 14 allée des Saphirs, 97487 Saint-Denis Cédex; tel. 262-20-96-40; fax 262-20-96-41; e-mail dd974@jeunesse-sports.gouv.fr; internet www.ddjs-reunion.jeunesse-sports.gouv.fr; Departmental Dir DANIEL BOILLEY.

Direction Régionale des Affaires Culturelles de la Réunion (DRAC): 23 rue Labourdonnais, BP 224, 97464 Saint-Denis Cédex; tel. 262-21-91-71; fax 262-41-61-93; e-mail drac-la.reunion@culture.gouv.fr; internet www.reunion.pref.gouv.fr; f. 1992; responsible to the French Ministry of Culture; Regional Dir LOUIS POULHÈS.

Direction Régionale des Affaires Sanitaires et Sociales de la Réunion (DRASS): 2 bis ave Georges Brassens, BP 9, 97408 Saint-Denis Messag Cédex 9; tel. 262-93-94-95; fax 262-93-95-95; internet www.reunion.pref.gouv.fr/drass.

Direction Régionale du Commerce Extérieur (DRCE): MRST, 100 route de la Rivière des Pluies, 97491 Sainte-Clotilde Cédex; tel. 262-92-24-70; fax 262-92-24-76; e-mail reunion@missioneco.org; internet www.missioneco.org/reunion; Dir PHILIPPE GENIER.

Direction Régionale de l'Environnement (DIREN): 12 allée de la Forêt, Parc de la Providence, 97400 Saint-Denis; tel. 262-94-78-11; fax 262-94-72-55; e-mail estelle.loiseau@reunion.ecologie.gouv.fr; internet www.reunion.ecologie.gouv.fr.

Direction Régionale de l'Industrie, de la Recherche et de l'Environnement: 130 rue Léopold Rambaud, 97491 Sainte Clotilde Cédex; tel. 262-92-41-10; fax 262-29-37-31; internet www.reunion.drire.gouv.fr; Reg. Dir JEAN-CHARLES ARDIN; Sec.-Gen. JACQUELINE LECHEVIN.

DEVELOPMENT ORGANIZATIONS

Agence Française de Développement (AFD): 44 rue Jean Cocteau, BP 2013, 97488 Saint-Denis Cédex; tel. 262-90-00-90; fax 262-21-74-58; e-mail afdstdenis@re.groupe-afd.org; Dir PASCAL PACAUT.

Association pour le Développement Industriel de la Réunion: 8 rue Philibert, BP 327, 97466 Saint-Denis Cédex; tel. 262-94-43-00; fax 262-94-43-09; e-mail adir@adir.info; internet www.adir.info; f. 1975; Pres. MAURICE CERISOLA; Sec.-Gen. FRANÇOISE DELMONT DE PALMAS; 190 mems.

Chambre d'Agriculture de la Réunion: 24 rue de la Source, BP 134, 97463 Saint-Denis Cédex; tel. 262-94-25-94; fax 262-21-06-17; e-mail chambagri.cda-97@wanadoo.fr; Pres. GUY DERAND; Gen. Man. ALAIN TARDY.

Direction de l'Action Economique: Secrétariat Général pour les Affaires Economiques, ave de la Victoire, 97405 Saint-Denis; tel. 262-40-77-10; fax 262-40-77-01.

Jeune Chambre Economique de Saint-Denis de la Réunion: 25 rue de Paris, BP 1151, 97483 Saint-Denis; f. 1963; Chair. JEAN-CHRISTOPHE DUVAL; 30 mems.

Société de Développement Economique de la Réunion (SODERE): 26 rue Labourdonnais, 97469 Saint-Denis; tel. 262-20-01-68; fax 262-20-05-07; f. 1964; Chair. RAYMOND VIVET; Man. Dir ALBERT TRIMAILLE.

CHAMBERS OF COMMERCE

Chambre de Commerce et d'Industrie de la Réunion (CCIR): 15 route de la Balance, 97410 Saint-Pierre; tel. 262-96-96-96; fax 262-94-22-90; internet www.reunion.cci.fr; f. 1830; Pres. ERIC MAGAMOOTOO; Sec. DANIEL MOREAU.

Chambre de Métiers et de l'Artisanat: 42 rue Jean Cocteau, BP 261, 97465 Saint-Denis Cédex; tel. 262-21-04-35; fax 262-21-68-33; e-mail cdm@cm-reunion.fr; internet cm-reunion.fr; f. 1968; Pres. GIRAUD PAYET; Sec. BÉATRICE BADIN; 14 mem. orgs.

EMPLOYERS' ASSOCIATIONS

Conseil de l'Ordre des Pharmaciens: 1 bis rue Sainte Anne, Immeuble le Concorde, Appt. 26, 1er étage, 97400 Saint-Denis; tel. 262-41-85-51; fax 262-21-94-86; Pres. CHRISTIANE VAN DE WALLE.

Coopérative Agricole des Huiles Essentielles de Bourbon (CAHEB): 83 rue de Kerveguen, 97430 Le Tampon; BP 43, 97831 Le Tampon; tel. 262-27-02-27; fax 262-27-35-54; e-mail caheb@geranium-bourbon.com; f. 1963; represents producers of essential oils; Pres. ALAIN DAMBREVILLE; Sec.-Gen. LAURENT JANCI.

Mouvement des Entreprises de France Réunion (MEDEF): 14 rampes Ozoux, BP 354, 97467 Saint-Denis; tel. 262-20-01-30; fax 262-41-68-56; e-mail medef.reunion@wanadoo.fr; Pres. FRANÇOIS CAILLÉ.

Ordre National de Médecins: 2 Résidence Halley, Bât. A, 4 rue Camille-Vergoz, 97400 Saint-Denis; tel. 262-20-11-58; fax 262-21-08-02; e-mail reunion@974.medecin.fr; internet www.odmreunion.net; Pres. Dr YVAN TCHENG.

Syndicat des Fabricants de Sucre de la Réunion: 23 rue Raymond Vergès, Quartier Français, 97441 Sainte-Suzanne; tel. 262-72-18-00; fax 261-72-18-01; e-mail ft@sfsnuu.com; Chair. FLORENT THIBAULT.

Syndicat des Producteurs de Rhum de la Réunion: chemin Frédéline, BP 354, 97453 Saint-Pierre Cédex; tel. 262-25-84-27; fax 262-35-60-92; Chair. OLIVIER THIEBLIN.

Union Réunionnaise des Coopératives Agricoles (URCOOPA): Z. I. Cambaie, BP 90, 97411 Saint-Paul; f. 1982; represents farmers; comprises Coop Avirons (f. 1967), Société Coopérative Agricole Nord-Est (CANE), SICA Lait (f. 1961), and CPPR; Pres. KARL TECHER.

TRADE UNIONS

CFE-CGC de la Réunion: 1 Rampes Ozoux, Résidence de la Rivière, Appt 2A, BP 873, 97477 Saint-Denis Cédex; tel. 262-90-11-95; fax 262-90-11-99; e-mail union@cfecgcreunion.com; internet www.cfecgcreunion.com; departmental br. of the Confédération Française de l'Encadrement-Confédération Générale des Cadres; represents engineers, teaching, managerial and professional staff and technicians; Pres. ALAIN IGLICKI; Sec.-Gen. DANIEL THIAW-WING-KAI.

Confédération Générale du Travail de la Réunion (CGTR): 144 rue du Général de Gaulle, BP 1132, 97482 Saint-Denis Cédex; Sec.-Gen. GEORGES MARIE LEPINAY.

Fédération Départementale des Syndicats d'Exploitants Agricoles de la Réunion (FDSEA): 105 rue Amiral Lacaze, Terre Sainte, 97410 Saint-Pierre; tel. 262-96-33-53; fax 262-96-33-90; e-mail fdsea-reunion@wanadoo.fr; affiliated to the Fédération Nationale des Syndicats d'Exploitants; Sec.-Gen. JEAN-BERNARD HOARAU.

Fedération Réunionnaise du Bâtiment et des Travaux Publics: BP 108, 97462 Saint-Denis Cédex; tel. 262-41-70-87; fax 262-21-55-07; Pres. J. M. LE BOURVELLEC.

Fédération Syndicale Unitaire Réunion (FSU): 4 rue de la Cure, BP 279, 97494 Sainte-Clotilde Cédex; tel. 262-86-29-46; fax 262-22-35-28; e-mail fsu974@fsu.fr; internet sd974.fsu.fr; f. 1993; departmental br. of the Fédération Syndicale Unitaire; represents public sector employees in sectors incl. teaching, research, and training, and also agriculture, justice, youth and sports, and culture; Sec. CHRISTIAN PICARD.

Union Départementale Confédération Française des Travailleurs Chrétiens (UD CFTC): Résidence Pointe des Jardins, 1 rue de l'Atillerie, 97400 Saint-Denis; tel. 262-41-22-85; fax 262-41-26-85; e-mail usctr@wanadoo.fr.

Union Départementale Force Ouvrière de la Réunion (FO): 81 rue Labourdonnais, BP 853, 97477 Saint-Denis Cédex; tel. 262-21-31-35; fax 262-41-33-23; e-mail eric.marguerite@laposte.net; Sec.-Gen. ERIC MARGUERITE.

Union Interprofessionnelle de la Réunion (UIR-CFDT): 58 rue Fénelon, 97400 Saint-Denis; tel. 262-90-27-67; fax 262-21-03-22; e-mail uir.cfdt@wanadoo.fr; affiliated to the Confédération Française Démocratique du Travail; Regional Sec. AXEL ZETTOR.

Affiliated unions incl.:

FEP-CFDT Réunion: 58 rue Fénélon, 97400 Saint-Denis; tel. 262-90-27-67; fax 262-21-03-22; e-mail jpmarchau@uir-cfdt.org; affiliated to the Fédération Formation et Enseignement Privés; represents private-sector teaching staff.

SGEN-CFDT: 58 rue Fénélon, 97400 Saint-Denis; tel. 262-90-27-72; fax 262-21-03-22; e-mail sgen.reunion@wanadoo.fr; internet www.sgen-cfdt-reunion.org; affiliated to the Fédération des Syndicats Généraux de l'Education Nationale et de la Recherche; represents teaching staff; Sec.-Gen. JEAN-LOUIS BELHOTE.

Union Régionale UNSA-Education: BP 169, 97464 Saint-Denis Cédex; tel. 262-20-02-25; fax 262-21-58-65; e-mail hjrmtg@wanadoo.fr; represents teaching staff; Sec.-Gen. JEAN-RAYMOND MONDON.

Transport

ROADS

A route nationale circles the island, generally following the coast and linking the main towns. Another route nationale crosses the island from south-west to north-east linking Saint-Pierre and Saint-Benoît. In 1994 there were 370 km of routes nationales, 754 km of departmental roads and 1,630 km of other roads; 1,300 km of the roads were bituminized. In 2005 discussions were ongoing regarding a proposed 'tram-train' network that would link Saint-Benoît to Saint-Joseph via Saint-Denis. However, the proposals continued to face opposition from ministers who favoured a new bus service and investment in the road network.

Société d'Economie Mixte des Transports, Tourisme, Equipements et Loisirs (SEMITTEL): 24 chemin Benoite-Boulard, 97410 Saint-Pierre; tel. 262-55-40-60; fax 262-55-49-56; e-mail semittel@semittel.fr; f. 1984; bus service operator; Pres. MARRIE PERIANAYAGOM.

Société des Transports Départementaux de la Réunion (SOTRADER): 2 allée Bonnier, 97400 Saint-Denis; tel. 262-94-89-40; fax 262-94-89-50; f. 1995; bus service operator; Gen. Man. ANNIE PHILIPPET FOUCHARD.

SHIPPING

In 1986 work was completed on the expansion of the Port de la Pointe des Galets, which was divided into the former port in the west and a new port in the east (the port Ouest and the port Est), known together as Port Réunion. In 2006 some 3.5m. metric tons of freight were unloaded and 469,400 tons loaded at the two ports. The Chambre de Commerce et d'Industrie de la Réunion also manages three yachting marinas.

Port Authority (Concession Portuaire): rue Evariste de Parny, BP 18, 97821 Le Port Cédex; tel. 262-42-90-00; fax 262-42-47-90; internet www.reunion.port.fr; Dir BRUNO DAVIDSEN.

CMACGM Réunion: 85 rue Jules Verne, Z.I. no 2, BP 2007, 97822 Le Port Cédex; tel. 262-55-10-10; fax 262-43-23-04; e-mail lar.genmbox@cma-cgm.com; internet www.cmacgm.com; f. 1996 by merger of Cie Générale Maritime and Cie Maritime d'Affrêtement; shipping agents; Man. Dir VALÉRIE SEVENO.

Coopérative Ouvrière Réunionaise (COR): 1 voie de Liaison Portuaire, BP 119, 97823 Le Port Cédex; tel. 262-43-05-14; fax 262-43-09-44; e-mail la.cor@wanadoo.fr; stevedoring; Pres. JAQUES VIRIN.

Mediterranean Shipping Co France, S.A. (MSC).

Réunion Ships Agency (RSA): 7 rue Ambroise Croizat, BP 186, 97825 Le Port Cédex; tel. 262-43-33-33; fax 262-42-03-10; e-mail rsa@indoceanic.com; internet www.indoceanic.com; f. 1975; subsidiary of Indoceanic Services; Man. Dir HAROLD JOSÉ THOMSON.

Société d'Acconage et de Manutention de la Réunionnaise (SAMR): 3 ave Théodore Drouhet, Z.A.C. 2000, BP 40, 97821 Le Port Cédex; tel. 262-55-17-55; fax 262-55-17-62; stevedoring; Pres. DOMINIQUE LAFONT; Man. MICHEL ANTONELLI.

Société de Manutention et de Consignation Maritime (SOMACOM): 1 rue Evariste de Parny, BP 2007, 97420 Le Port; tel. 262-42-60-00; fax 262-42-60-10; stevedoring and shipping agents; Gen. Man. DANIEL RIGAT.

Société Réunionnaise de Services Maritimes (SRSM): 3 ave Théodore Drouhet, Z.A.C. 2000, BP 2006, 97822 Le Port Cédex; tel. 262-55-17-55; fax 262-55-17-62; e-mail n.hoarau@dri-reunion.com; freight only; Man. MICHEL ANTONELLI.

CIVIL AVIATION

Réunion's international airport, Roland Garros-Gillot, is situated 8 km from Saint-Denis. A programme to develop the airport was completed in 1994, and in 1997 work commenced on the extension of its terminal, at a cost of some 175m. French francs. The Pierrefonds airfield, 5 km from Saint-Pierre, commenced operating as an international airport in December 1998 following its development at an estimated cost of nearly 50m. French francs. Air France, Corsair and Air Austral operate international services.

Air Austral: 4 rue de Nice, 97400 Saint-Denis; tel. 262-90-90-91; fax 262-29-28-95; e-mail reservation@air-austral.com; internet www.airaustral.com; f. 1975; subsidiary of Air France; Dir-Gen. GÉRARD ETHEVE.

Tourism

Réunion's attractions include spectacular scenery and a pleasant climate. In January 2003 the island had some 2,910 hotel rooms. In 2006 some 279,000 tourists visited Réunion. Receipts from tourism in that year were US $224.8m.

Comité du Tourisme de la Réunion (CTR): pl. du 20 décembre 1848, BP 615, 97472 Saint-Denis Cédex; tel. 262-21-00-41; fax 262-21-00-21; e-mail ctr@la-reunion-tourisme.com; internet www.la-reunion-tourisme.com; Pres. JOCELYNE LAURET.

Délégation Régionale au Commerce, à l'Artisanat et au Tourisme: Préfecture de la Réunion, 97400 Saint-Denis; tel. 262-40-77-58; fax 262-50-77-15; Dir PHILIPPE JEAN LEGLISE.

Office du Tourisme Intercommunal du Nord: 27 rue Amiral Lacaze, 97400 Saint-Denis; tel. 262-41-83-00; fax 262-21-37-76; e-mail otinord@wanadoo.fr; Pres. JEAN-MARIE DUPUIS.

FRENCH OVERSEAS POSSESSIONS

French Overseas Collectivities

As amended in March 2003, the Constitution defines French Polynesia, Mayotte, Saint Pierre and Miquelon, and the Wallis and Futuna Islands as having the status of Overseas Collectivities (collectivités d'outre-mer) within the French Republic. Under an organic law of February 2007, Saint-Barthélemy and Saint-Martin were, additionally, each accorded the status of Overseas Collectivity. The territories within this category have a greater degree of independence than do the Overseas Departments and Territories, with the particular status of each being defined by an individual organic law. Local assemblies may establish internal legislation. An organic law of February 2004 accords to French Polynesia the unique designation of Overseas Country (pays d'outre-mer), while it retains the legal status of an Overseas Collectivity.

FRENCH POLYNESIA

Introductory Survey

Location, Climate, Language, Religion, Flag, Capital

French Polynesia comprises several scattered groups of islands in the South Pacific Ocean, lying about two-thirds of the way between the Panama Canal and New Zealand. Its nearest neighbours are the Cook Islands, to the west, and the Line Islands (part of Kiribati), to the north-west. French Polynesia consists of the following island groups: the Windward Islands (Iles du Vent—including the islands of Tahiti and Moorea) and the Leeward Islands (Iles Sous le Vent—located about 160 km north-west of Tahiti) which, together, constitute the Society Archipelago; the Tuamotu Archipelago, which comprises some 80 atolls scattered east of the Society Archipelago in a line stretching north-west to south-east for about 1,500 km; the Gambier Islands, located 1,600 km south-east of Tahiti; the Austral Islands, lying 640 km south of Tahiti; and the Marquesas Archipelago, which lies 1,450 km north-east of Tahiti. There are 35 islands and 83 atolls in all, of which 76 are populated. The average monthly temperature throughout the year varies between 20°C (68°F) and 29°C (84°F), and most rainfall occurs between November and April, the average annual precipitation being 1,625 mm (64 ins). The official languages are French and Tahitian. Seven Polynesian languages and their dialects are spoken by the indigenous population. The principal religion is Christianity; about 55% of the population is Protestant and some 34% Roman Catholic. The official flag is the French tricolour. Subordinate to this, the French Polynesian flag (proportions 2 by 3), comprises three horizontal stripes, of red, white (half the depth) and red, with, in the centre, the arms of French Polynesia, consisting of a representation in red of a native canoe, bearing a platform supporting five stylized persons, on a circular background (five wavy horizontal dark blue bands, surmounted by 10 golden sunrays). The capital is Papeete, on the island of Tahiti.

Recent History

Tahiti, the largest of the Society Islands, was declared a French protectorate in 1842, and became a colony in 1880. The other island groups were annexed during the last 20 years of the 19th century. The islands were governed from France under a decree of 1885 until 1946, when French Polynesia became an Overseas Territory, administered by a Governor in Papeete. A Territorial Assembly and a Council of Government were established to advise the Governor.

Between May 1975 and May 1982 a majority in the Territorial Assembly sought independence for French Polynesia. Following pressure by Francis Sanford, leader of the largest autonomist party in the Assembly, a new Constitution for the Territory was negotiated with the French Government and approved by a newly elected Assembly in 1977. Under the provisions of the new statute, France retained responsibility for foreign affairs, defence, monetary matters and justice, but the powers of the territorial Council of Government were increased, especially in the field of commerce. The French Governor was replaced by a High Commissioner, who was to preside over the Council of Government and was head of the administration, but had no vote. The Council's elected Vice-President, responsible for domestic affairs, was granted greater powers. An Economic, Social and Cultural Council, responsible for all development matters, was also created, and French Polynesia's economic zone was extended to 200 nautical miles (370 km) from the islands' coastline.

Following elections to the Territorial Assembly in May 1982, the Gaullist Tahoera'a Huiraatira (People's Rally), led by Gaston Flosse, which secured 13 of the 30 seats, formed successive ruling coalitions, first with the Ai'a Api (New Land) party and in September with the Pupu Here Ai'a Te Nunaa Ia Ora party. Seeking self-government, especially in economic matters, elected representatives of the Assembly held discussions with the French Government in Paris in 1983, and in September 1984 a new statute was approved by the French Assemblée nationale (National Assembly). This allowed the territorial Government greater powers, mainly in the sphere of commerce and development; the Council of Government was replaced by a Council of Ministers, whose President was to be elected from among the members of the Territorial Assembly. Flosse became the first President of the Council of Ministers.

At elections held in March 1986 the Tahoera'a Huiraatira gained the first outright majority to be achieved in the Territory, winning 24 of the 41 seats in the Territorial Assembly. Leaders of opposition parties subsequently expressed dissatisfaction with the election result, claiming that the Tahoera'a Huiraatira victory had been secured only as a result of the allocation of a disproportionately large number of seats in the Territorial Assembly to one of the five constituencies. The constituency at the centre of the dispute comprised the Mangareva and Tuamotu islands, where the two French army bases at Hao and Mururoa constituted a powerful body of support for Flosse and the Tahoera'a Huiraatira, which, in spite of winning a majority of seats, had obtained a minority of individual votes in the election. At concurrent elections for French Polynesia's two seats in the Assemblée nationale in Paris, Flosse and Alexandre Léontieff, the candidates of the Rassemblement pour la République (RPR—to which the Tahoera'a Huiraatira was affiliated, latterly the Union pour un Mouvement Populaire), were elected, Flosse subsequently ceding his seat to Edouard Fritch. Later in March the French Prime Minister, Jacques Chirac, appointed Flosse to a post in the French Council of Ministers, assigning him the portfolio of Secretary of State for South Pacific Affairs.

In April 1986 Flosse was re-elected President of the Council of Ministers. However, he faced severe criticism from leaders of the opposition for his allegedly inefficient and extravagant use of public funds, and was accused, in particular, of corrupt electoral practice. Flosse resigned as President in February 1987, and was replaced by Jacques Teuira.

In December 1987, amid growing discontent over his policies, Teuira and the entire Council of Ministers resigned and were replaced by a coalition of opposition parties and the Te Tiaraama party (a breakaway faction of the Tahoera'a Huiraatira) under the presidency of Alexandre Léontieff. The Léontieff Government survived several challenges in the Territorial Assembly to its continuation in office during 1988–89. Amendments to the Polynesian Constitution, which were approved by the French legislature and enacted by July 1990, augmented the powers of the President of the Council of Ministers and increased the competence of the Territorial Assembly. The major purpose of these amendments was to clarify the areas of responsibility of the State, the Territory and the judiciary, which was considered particularly necessary following various disputes about the impending single market of the European Community (EC—now European Union—EU, see p. 244). In June 1989, in protest, 90% of the electorate refused to vote in the elections to the European Parliament.

At territorial elections in March 1991 the Tahoera'a Huiraatira won 18 of the 41 seats. Flosse then formed a coalition with the Ai'a Api, thereby securing a majority of 23 seats in the Territorial Assembly. Emile Vernaudon, leader of the Ai'a Api, was elected President of the Assembly and Flosse was elected President of the Council of Ministers. In September Flosse announced the end of the coalition between his party and the Ai'a Api, accusing Vernaudon of disloyalty, and signed a new alliance with the Pupu Here Ai'a Te Nunaa Ia Ora, led by Jean Juventin.

In April 1992 Flosse was found guilty of fraud (relating to an illegal sale of government land to a member of his family) and there were widespread demands for his resignation. In November Juventin and Léontieff were charged with 'passive' corruption, relating to the construction of a golf course by a Japanese company. In the following month the French Court of Appeal upheld the judgment against Flosse, who received a six-month, suspended prison sentence. The case provoked a demonstration by more than 3,000 people in January 1993, demanding the resignation of Flosse and Juventin. In September 1994 Flosse succeeded in having the conviction rescinded, on a procedural issue, in a second court of appeal. In October 1997, however, Léontieff was found guilty of accepting substantial bribes in order to facilitate a business venture and was sentenced to three years in prison (half of which was to be suspended). In May 1998 Léontieff was sentenced to a further three years' imprisonment (two of which were to be suspended) for corruption.

French presidential elections took place in April–May 1995. During the second round of voting in the Territory, the socialist candidate, Lionel Jospin, received 39% of the total votes, while the RPR candidate, Jacques Chirac, won 61%. (Chirac was elected to the presidency with 52.6% of votes cast throughout the republic.)

In November 1995 the Territorial Assembly adopted a draft statute of autonomy, which proposed the extension of the Territory's powers to areas such as fishing, mining and shipping rights, international transport and communications, broadcasting and the offshore economic zone. France, however, would retain full responsibility for defence, justice and security in the islands. Advocates of independence for French Polynesia criticized the statute for promising only relatively cosmetic changes, while failing to increase the democratic rights of the islanders. The statute was approved by the French Assemblée nationale in December and came into force in April 1996.

At territorial elections held on 13 May 1996 the Tahoera'a Huiraatira achieved an outright majority, although the principal pro-independence party, Tavini Huiraatira/Front de Libération de la Polynésie (FLP), made considerable gains throughout the Territory (largely owing to increased popular hostility towards France since the resumption of nuclear-weapons tests at Mururoa Atoll—see below). The Tahoera'a Huiraatira secured 22 of the 41 seats in the Territorial Assembly, with 38.7% of total votes cast, while Tavini Huiraatira won 10 seats, with 24.8% of votes. Other anti-independence parties won a total of eight seats and an additional pro-independence grouping secured one seat. Flosse defeated the pro-independence leader, Oscar Temaru, by 28 votes to 11 to remain as President of the Council of Ministers later in the month, and Justin Arapari was elected President of the Territorial Assembly. Allegations of voting irregularities led to legal challenges, which annulled the results in 11 constituencies. Following by-elections in May 1998 for the 11 seats, the Tahoera'a Huiraatira increased its representation by one seat. Tavini Huiraatira again claimed that the elections had not been fairly conducted.

At elections for French Polynesia's two seats in the French Assemblée nationale in May 1997 Michel Buillard and Emile Vernaudon, both supporters of the RPR, were elected with 52% and 59% of total votes cast, respectively. However, Oscar Temaru was a strong contender for the western constituency seat, securing 42% of the votes. Flosse was re-elected as the Territory's representative to the French Sénat (Senate) in September 1998.

In March 1999 proposals to increase French Polynesia's autonomy, as part of constitutional reforms, were announced in Paris. These proposals followed an initial agreement between the Territory and the French Government in late 1998, on the future of French Polynesia. In October 1999 the French Sénat adopted a constitutional amendment, approved by the Assemblée nationale in June, granting French Polynesia a greater degree of autonomy. French Polynesia was to be designated as an Overseas Country (pays d'outre-mer), and a new Polynesian citizenship was to be created. Although France was to retain control over areas such as foreign affairs, defence, justice and electoral laws, French Polynesia would have the power to negotiate with other Pacific countries and sign its own international treaties. The constitutional amendment was presented to a joint session of the French Sénat and Assemblée nationale for final ratification in late January 2000, although no decision on the matter was taken.

In November 1999 Flosse was found guilty of corruption, on charges of accepting more than 2.7m. French francs in bribes from the owner of an illegal casino, allegedly to help fund his party. Flosse was sentenced to a two-year suspended prison term, a large fine, and a one-year ban on seeking office. Demonstrations, organized by the pro-independence FLP, took place in Tahiti, in protest at Flosse's refusal to resign from his post as President of the Council of Ministers. In October 2000 Flosse lodged an appeal with the High Court, which reversed the ruling in May 2001. In November 2002 the Court of Appeal in Paris announced that Flosse should be pardoned.

In December 2000 some 2,000 workers went on strike in Papeete, protesting against low wages, and demanding that their pay be raised to a level commensurate with the prosperous state of the French Polynesian economy. In that month provision was made for the number of seats in the Territorial Assembly to be increased from 41 to 49, in an attempt to reflect demographic changes more accurately. At the elections, held on 6 May 2001, the Tahoera'a Huiraatira won 28 seats, securing a fifth successive term in office. The pro-independence Tavini Huiraatira took 13 seats. Flosse was subsequently re-elected President of the Council of Ministers, and a government reorganization ensued.

In January 2002 representatives of state and local government met to review the first five years of the Restructuring Fund, an agreement implemented in 1996 to further the economic autonomy of Polynesia and to regulate financial subsidies to the Territory following the cessation of nuclear testing (see Economic Affairs, below). The President and Prime Minister of France took part in further such meetings in June and July. It was agreed that funding would be extended for 10 years after 2006. The French delegation supported the proposal for a new autonomy statute to grant more powers of self-government to French Polynesia. In June 2002 elections for the Territory's two seats in the Assemblée nationale were won by the Tahoera'a Huiraatira candidates Michel Buillard and Béatrice Vernaudon.

In December 2002 the French Sénat approved a bill providing for a constitutional amendment that would allow French Polynesia (along with Wallis and Futuna) to be designated as an Overseas Country; in Paris both houses of the legislature ratified the amendments to the Constitution in March 2003. In July the Territorial Assembly and the Government ratified the amendments. Meanwhile, in May 2003 it was announced that French Polynesia (together with New Caledonia) would be allocated one additional seat in the French Sénat, probably effective from 2007. Also in May 2003, a strike by 400 doctors, protesting against changes in the social security system, had lasted for several weeks. The union of medical professionals hoped to draw renewed attention to these concerns during President Chirac's visit to French Polynesia in July (see below).

The final text of the autonomy statute was approved by the Assemblée nationale in January 2004, and, with minor amendments, by the Constitutional Council in mid-February. In March, when President Chirac signed the requisite decree, French Polynesia was formally designated as an Overseas Country of France, henceforth being permitted to 'govern itself freely and democratically'. French Polynesia was thus granted greater authority over matters such as labour law, civil aviation and regional relations, with France retaining control of law and order, defence and money supply. In April 2004 the local legislature was dissolved, in preparation for the holding of an election to a new 57-member Assembly in May.

At elections for the newly expanded French Polynesia Assembly held on 23 May 2004, the Tahoera'a Huiraatira, led by Gaston Flosse, won 28 of the 57 seats. An opposition coalition, the Union pour la démocratie (UPD), comprising the pro-independence Tavini Huiraatira and various minor parties, secured 27 seats and the remaining two seats were taken by opposition parties favouring autonomy. The Tahoera'a Huiraatira thus lost its overall majority in the Assembly for the first time in 20 years. Flosse disputed the results, claiming that there had been irregularities in the electoral process, in particular in the Windward Islands, the largest of the constituencies. In June the new legislature elected Antony Géros of Tavini Huiraatira as President of the Assembly. Oscar Temaru, leader of Tavini Huiraatira, was elected President of the Council of Ministers and announced the composition of a streamlined 10-member cabinet two days later.

In early September divisions over the 2004 appropriation bill brought the legislative process to a standstill. Three members of the Assembly resigned from the UPD coalition, two of them to sit as independents, with the third joining the opposition Tahoera'a Huiraatira. In early October separate motions of no confidence were filed against the Government by the Tahoera'a Huiraatira and the newly formed Te' Avei'a (Te Ara) party, made up of six former members of the ruling UPD coalition and the Tahoera'a Huiraatira. In early October Oscar Temaru twice appealed to the French Government to dissolve the Assembly and to hold new elections. On 16 October some 22,000 people took part in the largest demonstration ever witnessed in French Polynesia, demanding the dissolution of the Assembly. However, the French Minister for Overseas Territories, Brigitte Girardin, refused to accept that such demands were justified because French Polynesia's institutions were continuing to function normally. The motions of no confidence were endorsed by 29 of the 57 legislators—the members of the UPD refusing to vote—thus requiring the Assembly to choose a new President of the Council of Ministers. The 23 Tahoera'a Huiraatira and six Te' Avei'a members elected Gaston Flosse as President on 20 October. However, the UPD members boycotted the vote and refused to recognize Flosse's authority. Temaru and his ministers refused to vacate the presidential building (several hundred pro-Temaru supporters were reported to be continuing their occupation of government buildings in early 2005) and Flosse's newly appointed 17-member Council of Ministers—largely drawn from his previous administration, including former Vice-President Edouard Fritch—was forced to work at the adjacent Economic, Social and Cultural Council buildings.

The validity of Oscar Temaru's removal and the subsequent vote to elect Gaston Flosse as President of the Council of Ministers were both upheld by the French Conseil d'état (State Council). Under the new autonomy statute (see above) the Assembly could vote to dissolve itself if it received a petition from 10% of the electorate, then roughly equivalent to 15,000 people; by 19 November 2004 the UPD claimed to have collected 42,890 signatures, representing some 28% of the electorate. Both Temaru and Flosse sent delegations to Paris, to make representations to the French Government, led respectively by Nicole Bouteau (leader of the No Oe e Te Nunaa party) and Edouard

Fritch. Temaru claimed that an audit of the accounts of the previous Flosse administration (1999–2004), begun in September, had been stopped. The French State Council began investigations into the conduct of the May legislative election and in mid-November declared the results in the Windward Islands null and void, thus requiring the holding of by-elections within three months. The decision also meant that the 37 legislators affected automatically lost their seats, among them Flosse, Temaru and the President of the Assembly, Antony Géros, who was replaced by Hiro Tefaarere. At the end of November leading representatives from all parties were summoned to Paris for discussions, which included Flosse, Temaru, Nicole Bouteau, Philip Schyle (of the Fe'tia Api party) and Jacky Briant (of the Heuira-Greens party). Despite an initial agreement in principle to hold a fresh legislative election, the talks broke down in early December. In mid-December the French State Council validated Gaston Flosse's appointment as President.

In early January 2005 it was announced that by-elections would be held in the Windward Islands constituency on 13 February. Nicole Bouteau and Philip Schyle announced that their parties would be standing on a joint platform (the Alliance pour une Démocratie Nouvelle—ADN) offering a 'third way'. Gaston Flosse's Tahoera'a Huiraatira won 10 of the 37 seats, having secured 40.0% of the votes. The seven-party UPD coalition, led by Oscar Temaru, won 25 seats, receiving 46.9% of the votes. The newly formed ADN took the constituency's remaining two seats. Overall, therefore, the Tahoera'a Huiraatira and the UPD now held 27 seats each in the Assembly. The ADN held three seats but refused to co-operate with either the Tahoera'a Huiraatira or the UPD, as a result of which neither of the two groupings was able to form a majority. Temaru brought a motion of no confidence against President Flosse, which was endorsed by 30 of the 57 members. The Assembly had 14 days within which to elect a new President of the Council of Ministers, while Flosse and his Government remained in office in an interim capacity. Temaru announced that he would be standing again for the presidency, while the Tahoera'a Huiraatira put forward Gaston Tong Sang, the serving Minister for Small and Medium-sized Enterprises, Industry, Trade and Energy. The first attempt to elect a President was abandoned, following a boycott by the members of the Tahoera'a Huiraatira, with the result that the required quorum of three-fifths could not be reached. At a second attempt, on 4 March, Temaru was returned as President by 29 votes to 26. There were two blank ballots cast, believed to have been those of Nicole Bouteau and Philip Schyle. Within four days Temaru announced the composition of his new 17-member Council of Ministers, which included Louis Frébault as Minister for Outer Islands Development, the portfolio he had held under the recent Flosse administration. Jacqui Drollet was reappointed as Vice-President. In mid-April Antony Géros was returned as President of the Assembly by 28 votes to 57.

During March and April 2005 fuel supplies were interrupted by a blockade of the port by members of the Groupement d'Interventions de la Polynésie (GIP) protesting at a government review of the 1,300-member organization. The GIP had been established by President Gaston Flosse in 1998, being originally intended to provide relief assistance to areas throughout the region affected by natural disasters; latterly, the organization had diversified into other areas including security, cleaning services and logistics. However, because of its close ties with Flosse, the GIP had developed the reputation of a 'private militia'. Temaru reportedly accused Flosse of trying to destabilize the Government through the GIP, and the police were investigating reports of an 'intelligence unit' within the GIP structure. A further three-day blockade ensued in early August 2005 over the future of some 300 temporary GIP jobs. Later that month plans were announced to restructure the organization, dividing it into two separate bodies, for land and sea operations, with a renewed focus on disaster relief. The land work-force was to be reduced by one-quarter but the employees affected would be guaranteed jobs in other government services, at a cost of some US $6.5m. The new body was to be named To'a Arai ('vigilante force'); the GIP was officially dissolved in mid-January 2006.

In late May 2005 French Polynesia voted on the issue of the European Constitution; however, although 72.9% of voters were in favour of adopting the Constitution, only 27.2% of the electorate voted: the Constitution was ultimately rejected by France. In mid-July the former Secretary-General of the Tahoera'a Huiraatira and minister under Flosse, Jean-Christophe Bouissou, left the party to form the Rautahi party. He was joined in September by two more former ministers, Temauri Foster and Emma Algan: as a result, the Tahoera'a Huiraatira held 23 seats in the Assembly and the UPD 29 seats. In mid-September Temaru reorganized the cabinet portfolios, creating the new post of Minister for Industry, Small and Medium Businesses and Mining; Hiroiti Tefaarere became the 18th member of the Government. Meanwhile, Anne Boquet replaced Michel Mathieu as French High Commissioner, and Emmanuel Porlier was subsequently appointed as French Polynesia's permanent representative to the EU in Brussels. In early November the Government presented an economic reform programme that included a proposed increase in the minimum wage; however, the programme envisaged raising the necessary revenue through a 'solidarity' tax on personal income. Public protest culminated in a four-day general strike and demonstrations in Papeete at the end of that month. The Temaru Government was forced to seek alternative sources of revenue, principally by increasing the duty on alcohol and tobacco. In early December two more members of the Tahoera'a Huiraatira left the party, to sit as independent members of the Assembly, reducing the party's standing to 21 seats, compared with the 29 seats held by the UPD.

In early January 2006 Emile Vanfasse resigned from the Council of Ministers; his duties were divided between Vice-President Jacqui Drollet (who assumed responsibility for the portfolios of economy, finance, budget and tax) and Temaru (who became responsible for civil aviation). In early February Temaru signed a new agreement with Anne Boquet, on behalf of the French Government, regarding the proportion of the economic development grant (dotation générale de développement économique—DGDE—see Economic Affairs) that could be used towards the Government's operating costs: from 50% in 2005 the proportion would be reduced to 35% in 2006, to 30% in 2007 and to 20% from 2008. In mid-December 2005 the Assembly had approved a resolution to adopt a budget for 2006 that envisaged expenditure of 137,800m. francs CFP. The Tahoera'a Huiraatira lodged eight complaints with the French Conseil d'etat against the introduction of new taxes, which included the levies on alcohol and tobacco. It was also reported that the budget had been calculated on the basis that up to 45% of the DGDE would be allocated to operating costs. In mid-January 2006 Boquet referred the matter to the Audit Office, which ruled that the budget was 'imbalanced' by some 2,000m. francs CFP and gave the Temaru Government 30 days in which to present a revised budget or face the possibility of state intervention. A revised budget was approved by the court in mid-March. In late January the Minister for Post and Telecommunications and Sports, Emile Vernaudon, was convicted of having used public property for personal benefit while serving as Mayor of Mahina between 1992 and 1999; he received a one-year suspended prison sentence and was fined US $30,000, but was not disqualified from public office.

In late March 2006 the Minister for Industry and Small and Medium Businesses, Hiro Tefaarere, resigned from the Council of Ministers, citing his frustration with the repeated disputes among the different factions within the UPD; he was replaced by Louis Frébault, hitherto Minister for Outer Islands Development. A wider reallocation of portfolios followed the resignation of Emile Vernaudon as Minister for Post and Telecommunications and Sports, in mid-April, in protest at the increasingly pro-independence stance being adopted by Temaru. Among the principal changes were the replacement of Vernaudon by Michel Yip. Teina Mareeura filled the vacant portfolio of outer islands development. The serving Minister for Youth, Culture and Heritage, Tauhiti Nena, was reappointed to the portfolio of family and women's issues, in place of Valentina Cross, also adding childhood to her list of responsibilities; Léon Lichtlé took the modified portfolio of sports and crafts from Natacha Taurua (a member of Vernaudon's Ai'a Api party). Meanwhile, Temaru ceded some of his responsibilities to Temauri Foster, who became Minister for Decentralization and Development of the Municipalities, and to Domingo Dauphin, who was allocated the newly created post of Minister for Inter-island Civil Aviation and Maritime Transport. In part, the changes were seen as an attempt by Temaru to reinforce his position in the French Polynesian Assembly: earlier that month one of his closest allies, Antony Géros, had been replaced as President of the Assembly by Philip Schyle, of the Fe'tia Api party, who had secured 29 of the 57 members' votes.

In June 2006 a criminal court in Tahiti found former President Gaston Flosse guilty of corruption in relation to his son's purchase of a hotel. Flosse was given a three-month suspended prison sentence, but was not disqualified from his positions as member of the French Polynesian Assembly and representative to the Sénat in Paris. In October members of the O Oe To Oe Rima trade union protesting at rises in the cost of living, along with former employees of the recently dissolved GIP who were demanding compensation, erected road blockades in Papeete. After two weeks of disruption, hundreds of protesters gained access to the presidential palace and other government buildings, demanding that Oscar Temaru, who was attending a Pacific Islands Forum meeting in Fiji, return to Papeete for negotiations. Security forces were deployed to eject the protesters and restore stability. In the following month Pia Hiro, the Minister for Health, resigned and was replaced by Charles Tetaria. Also in November, reports emerged of dissent within the ruling coalition; in December the French Polynesian Assembly approved a motion of no confidence submitted by the opposition against the Government, resulting in President Temaru's removal from office. In late December 31 of the 57 members of the legislature voted in favour of installing Gaston Tong Sang, member of the Tahoera'a Huiraatira party and Mayor of Bora Bora, as President.

At the beginning of January 2007 Tong Sang appointed his cabinet, providing positions for former ministers of the Temaru Government, the most notable of which was the inclusion of Temauri Foster as Vice-President and Minister for Development of the Municipalities.

Tong Sang took the foreign affairs portfolio, while Teva Rohfritch became Minister for Economy, Employment, Energy, Vocational Training, Trade and Industry; Armelle Merceron was appointed Minister for Finance and Civil Service. In mid-January a vote on a no-confidence motion submitted to the legislature by the opposition failed to garner enough support to oust the new Government. Meanwhile, President Tong Sang paid an official visit to France in what was widely regarded as an attempt to improve relations with the French Government following the relatively tense period of Temaru's presidency. In February hundreds of supporters of the opposition took to the streets of Papeete to demand the holding of new elections. In March the former Minister for Post and Telecommunications and Sports, Emile Vernaudon, was convicted of corruption and therefore barred from public office. He was given a suspended 18-month prison sentence (in December he was arrested on further charges). In April Edouard Fritch, the former Vice-President of French Polynesia, was elected President of the Assembly, receiving only one vote more than his rival, Antony Géros. In the same month the formation of the Te Niu Hau Manahune (Principle of Democracy) party was announced. At its inaugural convention the party elected Teina Maraera, the Mayor of Rangiroa, as President, stated its aim of establishing a federal system for French Polynesian archipelagos and declared its support for the candidate of the Union pour un Mouvement Populaire (UMP), Nicolas Sarkozy, in the forthcoming French presidential election. At the second round of this election in May approximately 52% of French Polynesian voters chose Sarkozy, while 48% voted for the Parti Socialiste candidate, Ségolène Royal (a slightly narrower margin than in metropolitan France). In June, at French legislative elections, the two Tahoera'a Huiraatira candidates were elected as deputies to the Assemblée nationale: Buillard, an incumbent deputy, defeated Temaru to regain one of the Territory's seats, while Bruno Sandras was newly elected to the second seat. Temaru was convicted of 'racial discrimination' in July, having used a derogatory term to describe non-Tahitians.

In August 2007 an Air Moorea aircraft flying from Moorea to Tahiti crashed into the sea. Fourteen bodies were recovered, and it appeared that there were no survivors; the 19 passengers reportedly included government and European Commission officials. President Tong Sang subsequently announced a mourning period of two days, and a judicial inquiry into the accident was instigated.

Meanwhile, political instability within French Polynesia continued to pose a threat in 2007. Gaston Tong Sang's Government managed to withstand a second unsuccessful motion of no confidence submitted by the opposition in June, but in July it suffered a serious set-back with the withdrawal of the Tahoera'a Huiraatira, Tong Sang's own party, from the majority grouping in the Assembly. The decision signalled a major shift in local politics, which had perhaps been foreshadowed by the intensification of criticism of Tong Sang by the Tahoera'a Huiraatira President, Gaston Flosse. Five members of the Tahoera'a Huiraatira resigned from the Council of Ministers (although one of the five, Minister for Land, Planning and Urban Development Luc Faatau, subsequently rescinded his resignation). Flosse later admitted that negotiations were taking place between the Tahoera'a Huiraatira and Temaru's Tavini Huiraatira, an unexpected revelation in view of the traditional rivalry between the parties and their divergent stances on independence. However, it appeared that the two parties had a common goal: the removal of the Tong Sang Government. In early August Tong Sang effected a reorganization of the Council of Ministers, allocating some of the newly vacant portfolios to incumbent ministers and assuming personal responsibility, among other duties, for finance and economy. The precarious situation had already prompted the French Government to announce plans for political reform, and Christian Estrosi, the French Minister-Delegate for the Overseas Possessions, urged politicians to 'act responsibly'. Later in August Estrosi held talks with Tong Sang, Flosse, Temaru and other politicians in an attempt to resolve the continuing instability, amid speculation that an early election was under consideration. Soon afterwards, however, a third no-confidence motion was submitted by the Temaru-led opposition against Tong Sang. Despite Tong Sang's offer of further portfolios for the Tahoera'a Huiraatira (a significant point of contention between Tong Sang and Flosse), 35 Assembly members—including some from the Tahoera'a Huiraatira—voted in support of the motion, thus removing Tong Sang from office. The French Conseil d'Etat (Council of State) subsequently ruled that, should the Assembly's selection of a new president require a second round of voting, a relative majority, rather than an absolute majority, would be sufficient. On 13 September Oscar Temaru was elected President, having received 26 votes to defeat the two other candidates, Edouard Fritch and Gaston Tong Sang, in the first round, and 27 votes to secure the presidency in the second round, in which Fritch garnered 17 votes. A new Council of Ministers was duly announced, in which Temaru assumed responsibility for international relations and other portfolios, while Antony Géros was appointed Vice-President and Minister of Finance, Housing and Land Issues.

At a parliamentary session later in September 2007, Temaru stated that a 'pact' had been negotiated between the two major political parties (taken to mean Tavini Huiraatira and the Tahoera'a Huiraatira), thus ensuring a clear majority in the Assembly, which, it was hoped, would lead to greater political stability. Temaru appeared reluctant to accept the French Government's plans for reform without due consideration and a genuine dialogue, and claimed that proposals for an early election were no longer necessary; a majority in the Assembly later voted against the plans. In October Temaru attended discussions in France with the newly elected French President, Nicolas Sarkozy, while reform legislation was being prepared for submission to the French Assemblée nationale. Temaru, who was reportedly not entirely satisfied with the schedule, nevertheless 'respected' Sarkozy's decision to call early elections (the dates of the first and second stages of voting were later confirmed as 27 January 2008 and 10 February, respectively). In mid-November 2007 the reform bill was approved by the French Sénat; eventually to take the form of organic law, among its provisions were the introduction of two election rounds, the reduction of the term of the Assembly and the setting of a maximum of 15 appointees to the Council of Ministers. Meanwhile, following his defeat, Tong Sang announced the creation of the O Porinetia To Tatou Ai'a (Polynesia, Our Homeland) party, which elected him as its President in December. Flosse was re-elected President of the Tahoera'a Huiraatira, while Fritch was named 'President-Delegate', a new position which was expected to ensure his eventual succession to the most senior position in the party.

Prior to the first round of voting, Temaru announced that his political alliance, the Union for Democracy (UPLD), was to sue Estrosi for alleged attempts to influence voters in French Polynesia. According to provisional results of the first round of elections, held on 27 January 2008, the To Tatou Ai'a coalition, of which Tong Sang's O Porinetia To Tatou Ai'a was a leading member, had secured more votes in important constituencies than the UPLD and Tahoera'a Huiraatira. Shortly after the first round, the Minister of Small and Medium Businesses and Industry, Gilles Tefaatau, resigned, having been convicted on a charge of conflict of interest. Tefaatau's departure resulted in the resignations of the entire Council of Ministers, but their reinstatement was announced on the following day, along with the allocation of Tefaatau's portfolio to the Minister of Perliculture, Michel Yip. At the second round of elections on 10 February, To Tatou Ai'a was confirmed as the coalition with the largest representation in the legislature, winning a total of 27 seats, while the UPLD secured 20 and Tahoera'a Huiraatira only 10. Owing to the lack of an overall majority, discussions on the establishment of a coalition ensued, and the election of Edouard Fritch of the Tahoera'a Huiraatira as President of the Assembly suggested that the two pro-autonomy parties had reached an agreement. Days later, the Assembly conducted a vote to select the next President of French Polynesia. Gaston Flosse unexpectedly declared his candidacy and was able to defeat Tong Sang after Temaru, the third candidate, withdrew, and Flosse gained the support of members of the UPLD. A new parliamentary alliance, between the Tahoera'a Huiraatira and the UPLD, had been established: the Union pour le Développement, la Stabilité et la Paix (Union for Development, Stability and Peace—UDSP). The development provoked criticism from the metropolitan UMP, which announced that its affiliation with Flosse was to be terminated. A new cabinet, incorporating several ministers of the previous Temaru Government, was appointed in late February; it included Fritch in the position of Vice-President and Minister for Vocational Training, Labour, Social Dialogue and Municipalities Development. Temaru was elected Assembly President, after Fritch's resignation left a vacancy.

However, the installation of a new Government did not bring about political stability. In April 2008 the establishment of Te Mana o Te May Motu, a new parliamentary grouping said to be allied with To Tatou Ai'a, was announced. Later that month, a no-confidence motion submitted by Tong Sang against the Flosse Government garnered 29 out of 57 votes in the Assembly, resulting in Flosse's removal from office; two members of Flosse's coalition group had reportedly defected to Te Mana o Te May Motu. Tong Sang was elected President, and he subsequently appointed a Council of Ministers comprising coalition partners and one member of the Tahoera'a Huiraatira; among the appointees were Jules Ienfa as Vice-President and Minister for Health, Prevention and Urban Planning and Georges Puchon as Minister for Finance and Budget. Tong Sang himself assumed responsibility for the international relations portfolio.

In July 1962 the French Government transferred its nuclear-testing facilities to Mururoa and Fangataufa atolls, in the Tuamotu Archipelago, establishing the Centre d'Expérimentation du Pacifique (CEP). The first nuclear device was tested at Fangataufa four years later in July 1966. In July 1985 the *Rainbow Warrior*, the flagship of the anti-nuclear environmentalist group, Greenpeace, which was to have led a protest flotilla to Mururoa, was sunk in Auckland Harbour, New Zealand, in an explosion that killed one crew member. Two agents of the French secret service, the Direction Générale de Sécurité Extérieure (DGSE), were subsequently convicted of manslaughter and imprisoned in New Zealand, and relations between France and New Zealand were seriously affected by the resultant dispute, especially regarding the treatment of the two agents (see the chapter on New Zealand for further details). In May 1991, during a visit to New Zealand, the French Prime Minister, Michel Rocard, formally apologized for the bombing of the *Rainbow Warrior*; however, in July tension between France and the region was exacerbated by the French Government's decision to award a medal for 'distinguished service' to one of the agents convicted for his role in the bombing. According to official reports, between 1966 and 1974 France conducted 46 atmospheric tests in the Territory, and 147 underground tests between 1975 and 1991.

In April 1992 the French Government announced that nuclear tests would be suspended until the end of the year. Although the decision was welcomed throughout the South Pacific, concern was expressed in French Polynesia over the economic implications of the suspension, because of the Territory's dependence on income received from hosting the nuclear-testing programme. Similarly, it was feared that unemployment resulting from the ban would have a serious impact on the economy. A delegation of political leaders subsequently travelled to Paris to express its concerns, and in January 1993 accepted assistance worth 7,000m. francs CFP in compensation for lost revenue and in aid for development projects.

Shortly after his election in May 1995, President Jacques Chirac announced that France would resume nuclear testing, with a programme of eight tests between September 1995 and May 1996. The decision provoked almost universal outrage in the international community, and was condemned for its apparent disregard for regional opinion, as well as for undermining the considerable progress made by Western nations towards a worldwide ban on nuclear testing. Scientists also expressed concern at the announcement; some believed that further explosions at Mururoa could lead to the collapse of the atoll, which had been weakened considerably. Large-scale demonstrations and protest marches throughout the region were accompanied by boycotts of French products and the suspension of several trade and defence co-operation agreements. Opposition to the French Government intensified in July 1995, when French commandos violently seized *Rainbow Warrior II*, the flagship of Greenpeace, and its crew, which had been protesting peacefully near the test site. Chirac continued to defy mounting pressure from within the EU, from Japan and Russia, as well as from Australia, New Zealand and the South Pacific region, to reverse the decision to carry out the tests.

French Polynesia became the focus of world attention when the first test took place in September 1995. The action attracted further statements of condemnation from Governments around the world, and provoked major demonstrations in many countries. In Tahiti hitherto peaceful protests soon developed into full-scale riots, as several thousand demonstrators rampaged through the capital, demanding an end to French rule. Meanwhile, violent clashes with police, and the burning of dozens of buildings in Papeete during the riots, left much of the capital in ruins. In defiance of world opinion, a further five tests were carried out, the sixth and final one being conducted in January 1996. In early 1996 the French Government confirmed reports by a team of independent scientists that radioactive isotopes had leaked into the waters surrounding the atoll, but denied that they represented a threat to the environment. However, following the election of a new socialist administration in France in mid-1997, the French Minister of the Environment demanded in August 1998 that the matter be investigated further, stating that she had not been reassured by the initial reports. Work to dismantle facilities at the test site began in 1997 and was completed in July 1998. Some 1,800 French military personnel were still based at the CEP site in 1998.

In September 1998 the trial of more than 60 people charged with offences relating to the riots and protests of September 1995 began in Papeete. Hiro Tefaare, a pro-independence member of the Territorial Assembly and former police officer, was found guilty of instigating the riots and was sentenced to three years' imprisonment (of which 18 months were to be suspended). Furthermore, in September 1999 the French Government was ordered by the Administrative Tribunal to pay 204m. francs CFP in compensation for failing to maintain law and order.

In early 1999 a study by the French Independent Research and Information Commission reported that there was serious radioactive leakage into underground water, lagoons and the ocean at Mururoa and Fangataufa atolls. These claims were dismissed by a New Zealand scientist who had taken part in an earlier study by the International Atomic Energy Agency (IAEA), which had concluded that radiation levels were nearly undetectable. In May a French government official admitted that fractures had been found in the coral cone at the Mururoa and Fangataufa nuclear testing sites. The reports, by Greenpeace, that the atoll was in danger of collapsing had always been previously denied by France. However, France's claim that no serious long-term damage had been done was contested by Greenpeace, which also suggested the need for an urgent independent study of the test sites. In January 2000, in what was considered to be a significant development, the commander of the French armed forces in French Polynesia admitted that there were significant cracks in the coral reef surrounding Mururoa, and that these might lead to the occurrence of a tsunami.

In July 2003 some 2,000 islanders, led by Oscar Temaru, demonstrated in favour of self-determination during an official visit by President Chirac to Papeete. Chirac attempted to assure islanders that the nuclear tests had created no danger to health and pledged that France would assume responsibility should any evidence to the contrary emerge. At the beginning of Chirac's visit, some 200 members of an association of those formerly employed at Mururoa and Fangataufa—Moruroa e Tatou—staged a demonstration to demand that France recognize the existence of a connection between nuclear testing and the subsequent health of those involved, as Australia and the USA had done. Following his election as President of the Council of Ministers, in May 2004 (see above), Temaru agreed to establish a body to investigate the impact of the French nuclear programme on the health of the population and on the environment. He also expressed his support for the Nuclear Veterans' Association, which was seeking compensation from the French Government: according to the group around 30% of some 15,000 former nuclear workers were either suffering—or had died—from cancers or related diseases. In late September a pre-trial investigation began in France in relation to a case filed in November 2003 by the French Nuclear Veterans' Association and Moruroa e Tatou against an unidentified defendant.

In mid-May 2005 the Centre for Documentation and Research on Peace and Conflicts, based in France, published declassified secret reports from 1966 on nuclear testing in the Gambier Islands. The documents suggested that the French military had deliberately suppressed information about the extent of contamination from radioactive fall-out. In mid-July 2005 the Assembly voted to create a commission of inquiry into the nuclear tests. (An attempt by the Tahoera'a Huiraatira to have the commission suspended was dismissed by the Court of Administrative Law in late August.) In October the commission visited Mangareva, Tureia and Hao with officials from the French Commission for Independent Research and Information on Radioactivity (CRIIRAD), which presented its own findings to President Chirac later that month. The commission's report was delivered at the end of January 2006. It found that, contrary to the information given to the public, each of the 46 atmospheric tests between 1966 and 1974 had caused radioactive fall-out on the islands around the test sites; and furthermore, that the military had failed to predict how weather conditions would affect dispersion of the fall-out.

In early February 2006, during a visit to French Polynesia, Marcel Jurien de la Gravière, a special envoy from the French Ministry of Defence, acknowledged that some data had not been released but denied that any information had been deliberately concealed. Both the local Assembly and the Ministry of Defence continued to study the report throughout February. In mid-March a new nuclear veterans' association, Tamarii Moruroa, was established, urging that an independent inquiry be conducted by the IAEA. The association sought to distinguish itself from Moruroa e Tatou by acknowledging the positive role that the tests had played in advancing medical science in particular. Tamarii Moruroa disagreed with the claim that the whole population had been exposed to contamination, believing the stance to be politically motivated. In July the Temaru Government commemorated the 40th anniversary of the first French nuclear test with the unveiling of a memorial for the alleged victims of tests by France, and other countries, in the Pacific. In the following month it emerged that a study conducted by the French Institute of Health and Medical Research had linked a 'small but clear' rise in cases of thyroid cancer in French Polynesia to the nuclear tests. During a visit to Papeete in October 2006 de la Gravière admitted that some of the tests might have affected the health of inhabitants of a number of islands. Medical examinations were to be offered to those thought most likely to be at risk.

Government

French Polynesia was designated as an Overseas Country (pays d'outre-mer) within the French Republic in 2004. Its status is that of an Overseas Collectivity (collectivité d'outre-mer). The French Government is represented in French Polynesia by its High Commissioner, and controls various important spheres of government, including defence, foreign diplomacy and justice. A local Assembly, with 57 members (increased from 49 at the May 2004 election), is elected for a five-year term by universal adult suffrage. The Assembly may elect a President of an executive body, the Council of Ministers, who in turn submits a list of up to 15 members of the Assembly to serve as ministers, for approval by the Assembly.

In addition, French Polynesia elects two Deputies to the French Assemblée nationale (National Assembly) in Paris and one representative to the French Sénat (Senate), all chosen on the basis of universal adult suffrage. (In 2003 it was announced that French Polynesia would be allocated one additional seat in the Sénat, probably effective from 2008.) French Polynesia is also represented at the European Parliament.

Defence

France tested nuclear weapons at Mururoa and Fangataufa atolls, in the Tuamotu Archipelago, between 1966 and 1996 (see Recent History). As assessed at November 2007, France maintained a force of 1,510 military personnel in French Polynesia.

Economic Affairs

In 2000, according to World Bank estimates, French Polynesia's gross national income (GNI), measured at average 1998–2000 prices, was US $3,795m., equivalent to $16,150 per head (or $24,680 per head on an international purchasing-power parity basis). During 1996–2006, it was estimated, the population rose at an average annual rate of 1.7%, while gross domestic product (GDP) per head increased, in real terms, by an average of 1.4% during 1995–2000. According to the UN Economic and Social Commission for Asia and the Pacific (ESCAP), GDP per head increased at an average annual rate of 1.7% in 2000–05. Overall GDP increased at an annual average of 3.3% in 1995–2000 and by the same percentage in 2000–05. In comparison with the previous year, GDP was estimated to have expanded by 3.3% in 2006, to reach $4,492m.

Agriculture, forestry and fishing contributed only 3% of GDP in 2004. The sector engaged 4.1% of the employed labour force at December 2006. Coconuts are the principal cash crop, and in 2006 the estimated harvest was 75,833 metric tons. The quantity of copra exported increased from 5,365.6 metric tons in 2004 to 5,703.1 tons in 2005; however, the value of copra exports decreased from 297.6m. francs CFP to 291.9m. Monoï oil is produced by macerating tiaré flowers in coconut oil, and in 2005 238.2 metric tons of the commodity were exported. Vegetables, fruit (including pineapples, citrus fruit and noni fruit), vanilla and coffee are also cultivated. In 2005 vanilla exports reached 9.7 metric tons, and export revenue totalled 201.6m. francs CFP. Most commercial fishing, principally for tuna, is conducted, under licence, by Japanese and Korean fleets. The total fish catch in 2005 was 12,219 tons. In addition, production by the aquaculture sector, mainly shrimps, reached 67 tons. Another important activity is the production of cultured black pearls. The quantity of cultured pearls totalled 8,450 kg in 2005, when export earnings reached 12,345.9m. francs CFP (compared with 20,173.2m. in 2000). Revenue from pearl exports continued to decrease in 2007, owing to oversupply and a decline in quality. According to ESCAP figures, the GDP of the agricultural sector expanded by 2.0% in 1995–2000 but contracted by 0.2% in 2000–05. Compared with the previous year, agricultural GDP was estimated to have increased by 4.9% in 2006.

Industry (comprising mining, manufacturing, construction and utilities) provided 15% of GDP in 2004. At December 2006 16.6% of the salaried labour force were engaged in the industrial sector. According to ESCAP, industrial GDP increased by 4.7% in 1995–2000 and by 2.6% in 2000–05. Compared with the previous year, the GDP of the industrial sector was estimated to have expanded by 4.0% in 2006. There is a small manufacturing sector, which is heavily dependent on agriculture. Coconut oil and copra are produced, as are beer, dairy products and vanilla essence. Important deposits of phosphates and cobalt were discovered during the 1980s.

Mining and manufacturing provided 11% of GDP in 2001 and engaged 7.1% of the employed labour force at December 2006. Construction is an important industrial activity, contributing 6% of GDP in 2001 and engaging 8.8% of the employed labour force at December 2006.

Hydrocarbon fuels are the main source of energy in French Polynesia, with the Papeete thermal power station providing about three-quarters of the electricity produced. According to the World Bank, fuels accounted for 7.9% of the total value of merchandise imports in 2004. Hydroelectric power dams, with the capacity to generate the electricity requirements of 36% of Tahiti's population, have been constructed. Solar energy is also increasingly important, especially on the less-populated islands. Electricity production totalled 533.5m. kWh in 2006. Output rose to 607.1m. kWh in 2005.

The services sector provided 82% of GDP in 2004 and engaged 79.3% of the salaried labour force at December 2006. The GDP of the services sector expanded by 2.5% in 1995–2000 and by 2.9% in 2000–05, according to ESCAP. Compared with the previous year, the sector's GDP was estimated to have increased by 3.9% in 2006. Tourism is a major source of revenue. In 2007 an estimated 218,241 tourists visited French Polynesia, compared with 221,549 in the previous year. In 2006 32.3% of visitor arrivals were from the USA, 19.1% from France and 9.9% from Japan. Receipts from tourism in 2006 totalled an estimated US $520m. Revenue from the sector was reported to have declined by 20% in 2007.

In 2006, according to the Institut d'Émission d'Outre-Mer (IEOM—the French overseas reserve bank), French Polynesia recorded a visible trade deficit of 134,632m. francs CFP. On the current account of the balance of payments there was a surplus of 3,594m. francs CFP, compared with a surplus of 854m. in the previous year. In 2006, according to provisional figures, the total cost of imports (excluding military transactions) reached 155,423m. francs CFP, while the value of exports totalled 18,651m. francs CFP. In the same year the principal sources of imports were France (which provided 31.0% of total imports), Singapore (12.5%), and the USA (10.4%). The principal markets for exports in that year were Hong Kong (accounting for 32.1% of the total), Japan (27.8%) and France (13.2%). The principal imports included road vehicles (10.1%), and machinery and mechanical appliances (19.9%); the principal exports were cultured pearls, precious and semi-precious stones and related items (providing some 67.4% of total export revenue).

The current budgetary deficit reached 19,187m. francs CFP in 2006. In 2005 state expenditure by France in French Polynesia totalled 148,618m. francs CFP, 15.0% of which was on the military budget. Direct assistance to French Polynesia from France totalled the equivalent of US $1,870m. in 2006, representing a 7% increase in comparison with the previous year.

The annual rate of inflation averaged 1.3% during 1996–2006. According to an official source, the consumer price index rose by 2.4% in 2006. A high unemployment rate (recorded at 13.2% of the labour force in 1996) has been exacerbated by the predominance of young people in the population (in 1996 some 43% of the population were under the age of 20 years).

French Polynesia forms part of the Franc Zone (see p. 306), and is an associate member of the UN Economic and Social Commission for Asia and the Pacific (ESCAP, see p. 35). Although France is also a member of the organization, French Polynesia has membership in its own right of the Pacific Community (see p. 377), which is based in New Caledonia and provides technical advice, training and assistance in economic, cultural and social development to the region. In October 2006 French Polynesia became an associate member of the Pacific Islands Forum (see p. 380).

From the 1960s the traditional agriculture-based economy of French Polynesia was greatly distorted by the presence of large numbers of French military and civilian personnel in connection with the CEP (see Recent History). This situation not only stimulated employment and economic growth in the construction industry and services (notably the building of hotels and other tourism-related activities) at the expense of agriculture, but also encouraged migration from the outer islands to Tahiti. In October 2003 the economic reconversion funds (fonds pour la reconversion de l'économie de la Polynésie française—FREPF) were replaced by an annual economic development grant (DGDE) from metropolitan France, amounting to almost €151m., to compensate for the loss of fiscal and tax revenue resulting from the closure of the CEP; this was to be paid in perpetuity. In mid-2003 the Assemblée nationale in Paris approved the Overseas Territories Development Bill, which would provide support for economic and social development in French Polynesia (together with New Caledonia and Wallis and Futuna) by attracting foreign investment. Discussions began in December 2004 on the replacement of the franc CFP with the euro. In January 2006 the local Assembly voted to adopt a resolution to introduce the euro in French Polynesia. The eventual introduction of the new currency, however, would depend upon French Polynesia, New Caledonia and Wallis and Futuna all reaching a consensus. In 2007 local business leaders expressed their concerns regarding the continued political instability in French Polynesia (see Recent History). These concerns increased in October when a leading international credit ratings agency cited political instability and social unrest as factors in its negative assessment, for the third consecutive year, of French Polynesia. Tourist numbers declined in 2007, and the deceleration of the economy of the USA, the leading source of visitors to French Polynesia, was expected further to depress the islands' tourism industry in 2008. The situation was exacerbated by the continued weakness of the US dollar (which in late 2007 was reported to have reached its lowest point against the Pacific franc for 27 years) and by the rising competition from other tourist destinations.

Education

Education is compulsory for eight years between six and 14 years of age. It is free of charge for day pupils in government schools. Primary education, lasting six years, is financed by the French Polynesian budget, while secondary and technical education are supported by state funds. In 2001/02 there were 54 kindergartens, with 15,136 children enrolled, and 173 primary schools, with 28,988 pupils. Secondary education is provided by both church and government schools. In 2001/02 there were 29,466 pupils at general secondary schools, including some 3,032 pupils enrolled at vocational institutions. The French University of the Pacific was established in French Polynesia in 1987. In 1999 it was divided into two separate branches, of which the University of French Polynesia is now based in Papeete. In 1995 the Papeete branch had 50 teachers and, in 2003/04, some 2,343 students. Total government expenditure on education in French Polynesia was 40,300m. francs CFP in 1999. In 2004 French state spending on education, higher education and research totalled 50,500m. francs CFP.

FRENCH OVERSEAS POSSESSIONS — French Polynesia

Public Holidays

2008: 1 January (New Year's Day), 5 March (Arrival of the Gospel), 21–24 March (Easter), 1 May (Ascension Day, Labour Day), 8 May (Liberation Day), 12 May (Whit Monday), 29 June (Internal Autonomy Day), 14 July (Fall of the Bastille), 15 August (Assumption), 1 November (All Saints' Day), 11 November (Armistice Day), 25 December (Christmas Day).

2009: 1 January (New Year's Day), 5 March (Arrival of the Gospel), 10–13 April (Easter), 1 May (Labour Day), 8 May (Liberation Day), 21 May (Ascension Day), 1 June (Whit Monday), 29 June (Internal Autonomy Day), 14 July (Fall of the Bastille), 15 August (Assumption), 1 November (All Saints' Day), 11 November (Armistice Day), 25 December (Christmas Day).

Weights and Measures

The metric system is in force.

Statistical Survey

Source (unless otherwise indicated): Institut Statistique de la Polynésie Française, Immeuble Uupa, 1er étage, rue Edouard Ahne, BP 395, 98713 Papeete; tel. 473434; fax 427252; e-mail ispf@ispf.pf; internet www.ispf.pf.

AREA AND POPULATION

Area: Total 4,167 sq km (1,609 sq miles); Land area 3,521 sq km (1,359 sq miles).

Population: 245,516 at census of 7 November 2002; 259,596 at census of 20 August 2007.

Population by Island Group (2007 census): Society Archipelago 227,807 (Windward Islands 194,623, Leeward Islands 33,184); Marquesas Archipelago 8,632; Austral Islands 6,310; Tuamotu-Gambier Islands 16,847.

Density (land area only, 2007 census): 73.7 per sq km.

Ethnic Groups (census of 15 October 1983): Polynesian 114,280; 'Demis' 23,625 (Polynesian-European 15,851, Polynesian-Chinese 6,356, Polynesian-Other races 1,418); European 19,320; Chinese 7,424; European-Chinese 494; Others 1,610; Total 166,753. *1988 Census* ('000 persons): Polynesians and 'Demis' 156.3; Others 32.5.

Principal Towns (population at 2007 census): Faa'a 29,851; Papeete (capital) 26,017; Punaauía 25,441; Moorea-Maiao 16,490; Pirae 14,475; Mahina 14,369; Paea 12,084; Taiarapu-Est 11,549; Papara 10,615.

Births, Marriages and Deaths (2006, provisional figures): Registered live births 4,591 (birth rate 17.8 per 1,000); Marriages 1,124 (marriage rate 4.4 per 1,000); Registered deaths 1,145 (death rate 4.4 per 1,000).

Expectation of Life (years at birth, 2006): 74.9 (Males 73.0; Females 76.9).

Economically Active Population (persons aged 14 years and over, 1996 census): Agriculture, hunting, forestry and fishing 10,888; Mining and manufacturing 6,424; Electricity, gas and water 459; Construction 4,777; Trade, restaurants and hotels 9,357; Transport, storage and communications 3,788; Financial services 1,482; Real estate 383; Business services 3,710; Private services 9,033; Education, health and social welfare 10,771; Public administration 13,475; *Total employed* 74,547 (males 46,141, females 28,406); Persons on compulsory military service 1,049 (all males); Unemployed 11,525 (males 6,255, females 5,270); *Total labour force* 87,121 (males 53,445, females 33,676). *2006* (salaried workers at 31 December): Agriculture, hunting, forestry and fishing 2,808; Mining 156; Manufacturing 4,645; Electricity, gas and water 537; Construction 5,961; Trade and repairs 10,250; Hotels and restaurants 7,328; Transport and communications 6,509; Financial services 1,601; Real estate, renting and business services 4,706; Education 615; Health and social action 3,354; Public administration 15,070; Other community and personal service activities 3,134; Persons employed by households 1,366; Total employed 68,040 (males 38,942, females 29,098).

HEALTH AND WELFARE
Key Indicators

Total Fertility Rate (children per woman, 2006): 2.2.

Physicians (per 1,000 head, 2001): 1.8.

For definitions, see explanatory note on p. vi.

AGRICULTURE, ETC.

Principal Crops (metric tons, 2006, FAO estimates): Cassava 4,300; Other roots and tubers 6,100; Sugar cane 3,000; Vegetables and melons 7,200; Pineapples 2,697; Coconuts 75,833; Vanilla 50; Coffee (green) 16.

Livestock (year ending September 2006, FAO estimates): Cattle 12,000; Horses 2,200; Pigs 27,000; Goats 16,500; Sheep 440; Chickens 200,000; Ducks 32,000.

Livestock Products (metric tons, 2006, FAO estimates): Cattle meat 130; Pig meat 1,100; Goat meat 75; Chicken meat 736; Cows' milk 1,350; Hen eggs 1,960; Other poultry eggs 82; Honey 41.

Fishing (metric tons, live weight, 2005): Capture 12,152 (Skipjack tuna 1,123; Albacore 2,524; Yellowfin tuna 1,389; Bigeye tuna 397; Blue marlin 444; Wahoo 606; Common dolphinfish 456; Other marine fishes 2,953); Aquaculture 67; Total catch 12,219. Note: Figures exclude pearl oyster shells: 2,886.

Source: FAO.

INDUSTRY

Selected Products (metric tons unless otherwise indicated): Copra 8,000 (FAO estimate, 2005); Coconut oil 4,300 (FAO estimate, 2005); Oilcake 3,283 (FAO estimate, 2002); Electric energy (Tahiti only) 533.9m. kWh (2006). Source: partly FAO.

FINANCE

Currency and Exchange Rates: 100 centimes = 1 franc de la Communauté française du Pacifique (franc CFP or Pacific franc). *Sterling, Dollar and Euro Equivalents* (31 December 2007): £1 sterling = 162.400 francs CFP; US $1 = 81.062 francs CFP; €1 = 119.332 francs CFP; 1,000 francs CFP = £6.16 = $12.34 = €8.38. *Average Exchange Rate* (francs CFP per US $): 95.95 in 2005; 95.12 in 2006; 87.18 in 2007. Note: Until 31 December 1998 the value of the franc CFP was fixed at 5.5 French centimes (1 French franc = 18.1818 francs CFP). Since the introduction of the euro, on 1 January 1999, an official exchange rate of 1,000 francs CFP = €8.38 (€1 = 119.332 francs CFP) has been in operation. Accordingly, the value of the franc CFP has been adjusted to 5.4969 French centimes (1 French franc = 18.1920 francs CFP), representing a 'devaluation' of 0.056%.

Territorial Budget (million francs CFP, 2006): *Revenue:* 140,928 (Current 117,417, Capital 23,511). *Expenditure:* 131,779 (Current expenditure 98,230, Capital 33,549).

French State Expenditure (million francs CFP, 1996): Civil budget 61,706 (Current 56,564, Capital 5,142); Military budget 46,119 (Current 37,160, Capital 8,959); Pensions 10,458; Total (incl. others) 123,774 (Current 109,060, Capital 14,714). *2003* (million francs CFP): 144,800 (incl. military budget 29,125). *2004* (million francs CFP): 150,453 (incl. military budget 25,055). *2005* (million francs CFP): 148,618 (incl. military budget 22,315).

Money Supply (million francs CFP at 31 December 2006): Currency in circulation 12,821; Demand deposits 141,923; Total money 154,744. Source: Institut d'Emission d'Outre-Mer.

Cost of Living (Consumer Price Index, annual averages; base: 2000 = 100): All items 105.8 in 2005; 108.7 in 2006; 110.9 in 2007. Source: UN, *Monthly Bulletin of Statistics*.

Gross Domestic Product (US $ million at constant 1990 prices): 4,203 in 2004; 4,347 in 2005; 4,492 in 2006. Source: UN Statistics Division, National Accounts Main Aggregates Database.

Expenditure on the Gross Domestic Product (million francs CFP at current prices, 1993): Government final consumption expenditure 126,127; Private final consumption expenditure 202,563; Increase in stocks –536; Gross fixed capital formation 53,494; *Total domestic expenditure* 381,648; Exports of goods and services 34,523; *Less* Imports of goods and services 86,905; *GDP in purchasers' values* 329,266. Source: UN, *National Accounts Statistics*.

Gross Domestic Product by Economic Activity (million francs CFP at current prices, 1997): Agriculture, forestry and fishing 15,534; Manufacturing 26,360; Electricity, gas and water 12,221; Construction 20,104; Trade 81,854; Transport and telecommunications 27,832; Other private services 96,714; Government services 97,238; Domestic services 646; *GDP in purchasers' values* 378,503. Note: Manufacturing of energy-generating products is included in electricity, gas and water. Source: UN, *National Accounts Statistics*. *2004* (percentage distribution of GDP): Agriculture, forestry and fishing 3; Industry 15; Trade 17; Transport and telecommunications 9; Other market services 29; Other non-market services 27; Total 100.

Balance of Payments (million francs CFP, 2006): Exports of goods 18,736; Imports of goods –153,367; *Trade balance* –134,632; Exports of services 104,817; Imports of services –68,273; *Balance on goods and services* –98,089; Other income (net) 54,508; *Balance on goods,* services and income –43,581; Current transfers (net) 47,174; *Current balance* 3,594; Capital account (net) –31; Direct investment (net) 1,944; Portfolio investment assets 54,951; Portfolio investment liabilities –54,553; Other investment assets 318,629; Other investment liabilities –321,980; Overall balance 2,555. Source: Institut d'Emission d'Outre-Mer.

EXTERNAL TRADE

Principal Commodities (million francs CFP, 2006, excl. military transactions, provisional): *Imports c.i.f.:* Live animals and animal products 6,487.5 (Meat and edible meat offal 6,431.7); Prepared foodstuffs; beverages, spirits and vinegar; tobacco and manufactured substitutes 28,285.4; Mineral products 19,982.2 (Mineral fuels, mineral oils and products of their distillation; bituminous substances; mineral waxes 19,979.7); Products of chemical or allied industries 13,445.6 (Pharmaceutical products 6,519.0); Plastics, rubber and articles thereof 5,243.5; Paper-making materials; paper and paperboard and articles thereof 4,735.9; Textiles and textile articles 5,368.4; Base metals and articles thereof 9,170.0; Machinery and mechanical appliances; electrical equipment; sound and television apparatus 30,919.3 (Nuclear reactors, boilers, machinery, mechanical appliances and parts 15,246.5; Electrical machinery, equipment, etc. 11,296.0); Vehicles, aircraft, vessels and associated transport equipment 20,186.3 (Aircraft and aeronautical craft 2,885.0; Sea or river vessels 747.4; Road vehicles, parts and accessories 15,773.9); Miscellaneous manufactured articles 6,100.0; Total (incl. others) 155,423.0. *Exports f.o.b.:* Fish and crustaceans, molluscs and other aquatic invertebrates 415.7; Prepared foodstuffs; beverages, spirits and vinegar; tobacco and manufactured substitutes 2,171.9 (Preparations of vegetables, fruit, nuts or other parts of plants 1,173.4); Natural or cultured pearls, precious or semi-precious stones, precious metals and articles thereof; imitation jewellery; coin 12,579.1; Vehicles, aircraft, vessels and associated transport equipment 2,233.5 (Aircraft, spacecraft and parts 1,536.1); Total (incl. others) 18,651.4.

Principal Trading Partners (million francs CFP, 2006, excl. military transactions, provisional): *Imports:* Australia 4,938.3; Belgium 2,590.1; China, People's Republic 10,382.3; France 48,124.1; Germany 5,375.6; Indonesia 1,795.2; Italy 4,479.1; Japan 4,115.7; Korea, Republic of 3,077.7; Netherlands 1,709.0; New Zealand 10,300.8; Singapore 19,451.0; Spain 2,221.5; Thailand 5,008.3; United Kingdom 2,265.9; USA 16,162.7; Total (incl. others) 155,423.0. *Exports:* Australia 194.2; Belgium 193.4; Canada 229.7; China, People's Republic, 368.2; France 2,461.8; Germany 298.9; Hong Kong 5,994.1; Japan 5,178.6; New Caledonia 377.9; New Zealand 366.5; USA 2,260.4; Total (incl. others) 18,651.4.

TRANSPORT

Road Traffic (1987): Total vehicles registered 54,979; *1996 Census:* Private cars 47,300.

Shipping (2003 unless otherwise indicated): *International Traffic:* Passengers carried 27,852; Freight handled (2004) 1,068,246 metric tons (Goods unloaded 1,037,645 metric tons; Goods loaded 30,601 metric tons). *Domestic Traffic:* Passengers carried 1,407,092; Freight handled 688,940 metric tons. *2005:* Goods unloaded 1,020,662 metric tons; Goods loaded 33,792 metric tons.

Civil Aviation (2006): *International Traffic:* Passengers carried 677,817; Freight handled 13,827 metric tons. *Domestic Traffic:* Passengers carried 855,550; Freight handled 3,558 metric tons (Source: Service d'Etat de l'Aviation Civile en Polynésie Française).

TOURISM

Visitors (excl. cruise passengers and excursionists): 211,893 in 2004; 208,045 in 2005; 221,549 in 2006.

Tourist Arrivals by Country of Residence (2006): Australia 11,426; Canada 6,731; France 42,397; Italy 13,697; Japan 21,986; New Zealand 8,537; Spain 5,202; United Kingdom 7,090; USA 71,621; Total (incl. others) 221,549. Source: Ministère du Tourisme.

Tourism Receipts (US $ million, incl. passenger transport): 359 in 1997; 354 in 1998; 394 in 1999 (Source: World Tourism Organization). *2005:* Receipts from tourism (including passenger transport) US $779 million.

COMMUNICATIONS MEDIA

Radio Receivers (1997): 128,000 in use*.
Television Receivers (2000): 44,000 in use†.
Telephones (2006): 53,600 main lines in use†.
Facsimile Machines (1998): 3,000 in use†.
Mobile Cellular Telephones (subscribers, estimate, 2006): 152,000†.

Personal Computers (number in use, 2005): 28,000†.
Internet Users (2006): 65,000†.
Broadband Subscribers (2006): 18,200†.
Daily Newspapers (2000): 2.

* Source: UNESCO, *Statistical Yearbook*.
† Source: International Telecommunication Union.

EDUCATION

Pre-primary (2006/07 unless otherwise indicated): 40 schools; 408 teachers (1996/97); 15,249 pupils.

Primary (incl. special schools and young adolescents' centres, 2006/07 unless otherwise indicated): 196 schools; 2,811 teachers (1996/97); 26,939 pupils.

Secondary (2006/07 unless otherwise indicated): 99 schools (first and second cycles, incl. special and vocational schools); 2,035 teachers (general secondary only, 1998/99); 19,205 pupils in first cycle (incl. special schools); 13,988 pupils in second cycle (incl. vocational).

Tertiary (2006/07 unless otherwise indicated): 50 teachers (1999); 681 students.

Directory

The Constitution

The constitutional system in French Polynesia was established under the aegis of the Constitution of the Fifth French Republic and specific laws of 1977, 1984 and 1990. The French Polynesia Statute 1984, the so-called 'internal autonomy statute', underwent amendment in a law of July 1990. A further extension of the Territory's powers under the statute was approved by the French Assemblée nationale (National Assembly) in Paris in December 1995. In January 2000 a constitutional amendment granting French Polynesia a greater degree of autonomy was presented to a joint session of the French Sénat (Senate) and Assemblée nationale for final ratification. In March 2003 both the Assemblée nationale and Sénat ratified amendments to the Constitution providing for French Polynesia (along with Wallis and Futuna) to become an Overseas Country (pays d'outre-mer). In July the Territorial Assembly and the Government of French Polynesia ratified the amendments. The approval of the French Conseil d'état (State Council), the French Government and the Constitutional Council duly followed, and in March 2004 French Polynesia became known as an Overseas Country.

Although French Polynesia is designated as an Overseas Country of the French Republic, of which it remains an integral part, its official status is that of an Overseas Collectivity (collectivité d'outremer). The High Commissioner, appointed by the French Government, exercises the prerogatives of the State in matters relating to defence, foreign relations, the maintenance of law and order, communications and citizenship. The head of the local executive and the official who represents French Polynesia is the President of the Government, who is elected by the local Assembly from among its own members. The President appoints and dismisses the Council of Ministers and has competence in international relations as they affect French Polynesia and its exclusive economic zone, and is in control of foreign investments and immigration. The local Assembly, which has financial autonomy in budgetary affairs and legislative authority within French Polynesia, is elected for a term of up to five years on the basis of universal adult suffrage. Following the elections of May 2004, it comprised 57 members: 37 elected by the people of the Windward Islands (Iles du Vent—Society Islands), eight by the Leeward Islands (Iles Sous le Vent—Society Islands), three by the Gambier Islands-East Tuamotu Archipelago, three by the West Tuamotu Archipelago, three by the Austral Islands and three by the Marquesas Islands. The Assembly elects a Permanent Commission from among its members, and itself meets for two ordinary sessions each year and upon the demand of the majority party, the President or the High Commissioner. Local government is conducted by the municipalities. There is an Economic, Social and Cultural Council (composed of representatives of professional groups, trade unions and other organizations and agencies that participate in the economic, social and cultural activities of French Polynesia), an Audit Office and a judicial system, which includes a Court of the First Instance, a Court of Appeal and an Administrative Court. The Overseas Country, as a part of the French Republic, also elects two deputies to the Assemblée nationale and one member of the Sénat, and may be represented in the European Parliament.

FRENCH OVERSEAS POSSESSIONS — French Polynesia

The Government
(April 2008)

High Commissioner: ANNE BOQUET (took office 5 September 2005).
Secretary-General: JACQUES WITKOWSKI.

COUNCIL OF MINISTERS

President, in charge of International Relations and Relations with the French State and the European Union: GASTON TONG SANG.
Vice-President and Minister for Health, Prevention and Urban Planning: JULES IENFA.
Minister of Agriculture, Livestock and Forestry: HAAMOETINI LAGARDE.
Minister for Culture, Crafts, Heritage and the Promotion of Polynesian Languages: JOSEPH KAIHA.
Minister for Economy, Employment, Labour, Vocational Training, Energy and Mining: GUY LEJEUNE.
Minister for Education, Research and Land Transport: TEARII ALPHA.
Minister for Environment and Land Matters: LIONEL TEIHOTU.
Minister for Finance and Budget, in charge of the Development of the Digital Economy: GEORGES PUCHON.
Minister for Fisheries and Sea and Fish Farming: TEMAURI FOSTER.
Minister for Housing, Solidarity, Welfare and Family and Women's Affairs: ARMELLE MERCERON.
Minister for Industry, Small and Medium Enterprises and Trades: MAIRAI SUN.
Minister for Outer Islands Development: OTIME TEURA.
Minister for Pearl Farming and Inter-Island Transport: TEVA HUIOTU-HAPAITAHAA.
Minister for Public Works, Ports and Airports: MOEHAU TERIITAHI.
Minister for Youth and Sports: CLARENTZ VERNAUDON.

GOVERNMENT OFFICES

Office of the High Commissioner of the Republic: Haut-Commissariat de la République en Polynésie Française, BP 115, 98713 Papeete; tel. 468686; fax 468689; e-mail courrier@polynesie-francaise.pref.gouv.fr; internet www.polynesie-francaise.pref.gouv.fr.
Office of the President of the Government: BP 2551, 98713 Papeete; tel. 472121; fax 472210; internet www.presidence.pf.
Government of French Polynesia: BP 2551, Papeete; 28 blvd Saint-Germain, 75005 Paris, France; tel. 472000; fax 419781; tel. 426510; fax 426409.
Economic, Social and Cultural Council (CESC): Immeuble Te Raumaire, ave Bruat, BP 1657, 98713 Papeete; tel. 416500; fax 419242; e-mail cesc@cesc.gov.pf; internet www.cesc.pf; f. 1977 as the Economic and Social Council; present name adopted in 1990; Pres. RAYMONDE RAOULX; Sec.-Gen KATIA TESTARD.
Ministry of Agriculture: route de l'Hippodrome, face à l'Ecole Normale, Pirae, BP 2551, 98713 Papeete; tel. 504455; fax 504460; internet www.agriculture.gov.pf.
Ministry of Education and Higher Education: BP 2551, 98713 Papeete; tel. 472440; fax 855777; internet www.education.gov.pf.
Ministry of the Family, Childhood and Women's Affairs: Immeuble Papineau, 5ème étage, rue Tepano Jaussen, BP 2551, Papeete; tel. 478360; fax 478366; e-mail secretariat.mfc@famille.min.gov.pf; internet www.famille.gov.pf.
Ministry of Health: BP 2551, 98713 Papeete; tel. 460098; fax 433942; internet www.sante.gov.pf.
Ministry of Housing: Immeuble Tefenua, 5ème étage, rue Dumont d'Urville, BP 2551, 98713 Papeete; tel. 549575; fax 454343; internet www.logement.gov.pf.
Ministry of Inter-island Sea and Air Transport: Immeuble Moehau, ave du Prince Hinoi, BP 2551, 98713 Papeete; tel. 502540; fax 502541; internet www.transports-interinsulaires.gov.pf.
Ministry of Postal Services and Telecommunications and the Pearl Farming Industry: Fare Ute, rond-point de la Base Marine, BP 2551, 98713 Papeete; tel. 504200; fax 504201; e-mail contact@postes.min.gov.pf; internet www.postes.gov.pf.
Ministry of Public Works, Energy and Mining, Town Planning, Land Transport, Ports and Airports: Bâtiment Administratif A2, 5ème étage, rue du Commandant Destremeau, BP 2551, 98713 Papeete; tel. 468019; fax 483792; internet www.equipement.gov.pf.
Ministry of the Sea, Fishing, Aquaculture and Research: ave Pouvanaa a Oopa, BP 2551, 98713 Papeete; tel. 472295; fax 4772294; e-mail secretariat.mer@presidence.pf; internet www.mer.gov.pf.
Ministry of Solidarity and Social Exclusion: Immeuble Papineau, 5ème étage, rue Tepano Jaussen, BP 2551, 98713 Papeete; tel. 478330; fax 478331; e-mail secretariat@solidarite.min.gov.pf; internet www.solidarite.gov.pf.
Ministry of Sports and Handicrafts: Immeuble CGMP, rue du Général de Gaulle, BP 2551, 98713 Papeete; tel. 548740; fax 427973; e-mail secretariat@artisanat.min.gov.pf; internet www.artisanat.gov.pf.
Ministry of Sustainable Development: Immeuble Papineau, 6ème étage, rue Tepano Jaussen, BP 2551, 98713 Papeete; tel. 478383; fax 478302; e-mail secretariat.mdd@environment.min.gov.pf; internet www.environnement.gov.pf.
Ministry of Tourism, Economy and Finance, Budget and Communication: ave Pouvanaa a Oopa, BP 2551, 98713 Papeete; tel. 484000; fax 484014; internet www.tourisme.gov.pf.
Ministry of Work, Employment, Professional Training and Civil Service: BP 2551, Papeete; tel. 507120; fax 507129.
Ministry of Youth and Culture: rue Jeanne d'Arc, BP 2551, 98713 Papeete; tel. 501077; fax 531616; internet www.culture.gov.pf.

Legislature

ASSEMBLÉE

President: OSCAR TEMARU.
Assembly: Assemblée de la Polynésie Française, pl. Tarahoi, BP 28, 98713 Papeete; tel. 416100; fax 416149; e-mail seances@assemblee.pf; internet www.assemblee.pf.

Election (second round), 10 February 2008*

Party	Seats
To Tatou Ai'a†	27
Union pour la Démocratie (UPLD)‡	20
Tahoera'a Huiraatira	10
Total	57

* Unofficial results. Three of the 57 seats were determined at the first round of voting, held on 27 January 2008, when the requisite absolute majority was secured.
† Coalition led by O Porinetia To Tatou Ai'a.
‡ Coalition led by Tavini Huiraatira.

PARLEMENT

Deputies to the French Assemblée Nationale: MICHEL BUILLARD (Tahoera'a Huiraatira/Union pour un Mouvement Populaire—UMP), BRUNO SANDRAS (Tahoera'a Huiraatira/UMP).
Representative to the French Sénat: GASTON FLOSSE (Tahoera'a Huiraatira/Union pour un Mouvement Populaire—UMP).

Political Organizations

Ai'a Api (New Land): BP 11185, 98709 Mahina, Tahiti; tel. 504596; fax 504598; e-mail courrier@aiaapi.pf; internet www.aiaapi.pf; f. 1982 after split in Te E'a Api; Leader ÉMILE VERNAUDON.
Fe'tia Api (New Star): c/o Assemblée de la Polynésie Française, BP 140 512, Arue; tel. 416131; fax 416136; f. 1996; part of the Alliance pour une Démocratie Nouvelle coalition; Leader PHILIP SCHYLE.
Heiura-Les Verts Polynésiens: BP 44, Bora Bora; tel. and fax 677174; e-mail heiura@mail.pf; internet www.heiura-lesverts.pf; ecologist; Sec.-Gen. JACKY BRYANT.
Ia Mana Te Nunaa (Power to the People): rue du Commandant Destrémau, BP 1223, Papeete; tel. 426699; f. 1976; advocates 'socialist independence'; Sec.-Gen. JACQUI DROLLET.
No Oe E Te Nunaa (This Country is Yours): Immeuble Fara, rue Nansouty, BP 40205, Fare Tony, 98713 Papeete; tel. 423718; e-mail contact@noetn.com; internet www.noetn.com; favours autonomy; part of the Alliance pour une Démocratie Nouvelle coalition; Leader NICOLE MOEA BOUTEAU; Sec.-Gen. ROSALIE TIRIANA ZAVAN.
O Porinetia To Tatou Ai'a (Polynesia, Our Homeland): 41 rue Colette, BP 4601, 98713 Papeete; tel. 584848; fax 504888; e-mail contact@oporinetia.pf; internet www.oporinetia.pf; f. 2007; est. by fmr members of the Tahoera'a Huiraatira party; leading mem. of To Tatou Ai'a coalition; Pres. GASTON TONG SANG.
Pupu Here Ai'a Te Nunaa Ia Ora: BP 3195, Papeete; tel. 420766; f. 1965; advocates autonomy.
Rautahi (Rally for French Polynesia): BP 60 013, Faa'a Centre; tel. 762000; e-mail rautahi-rpf@mail.pf; internet www.rautahi-be.org;

f. 2005; est. by fmr mems of Tahoera'a Huiraatira; Pres. JEAN-CHRISTOPHE BOUISSOU.

Taatiraa No Te Hau: BP 2916, Papeete; tel. 437494; fax 422546; f. 1977; Pres. ROBERT TANSEAU.

Tahoera'a Huiraatira (People's Rally): rue du Commandant Destremeau, BP 471, Papeete; tel. 429898; fax 450004; e-mail courrier@tahoeraahuiraatira.pf; internet tahoeraahuiraatira.pf; f. 1977; fmrly l'Union Tahitienne; supports links with France, with internal autonomy; affiliated to the metropolitan Union pour un Mouvement Populaire (UMP); Pres. GASTON FLOSSE; Pres.-Delegate EDOUARD FRITCH; Sec.-Gen. BRUNO SANDRAS.

Tapura Amui No Te Faatereraa Manahune-Tuhaa Pae: c/o Assemblée de la Polynésie Française, BP 140 512, Arue; represents the Austral Islands; Leader CHANTAL FLORES.

Tavini Huiraatira No Te Ao Ma'ohi/Front de Libération de la Polynésie (Polynesian People's Servant): c/o Assemblée de la Polynésie Française, BP 140 512, Arue; tel. 733865; e-mail contact@tiamaraa.com; internet www.tiamaraa.com; f. 1977; leading mem. of Union pour la Démocratie (Union for Democracy—UPLD) coalition; independence movement; anti-nuclear; Leader OSCAR TEMARU.

Te' Avei'a (Te Ara): ; e-mail mail@teaveia.pf; internet www.teaveia.pf; f. 2004 by fmr mems of Fe'tia Api and Tavini Huiraatira; Pres. ANTONIO PEREZ.

Te Henua Enana Kotoa: Papeete; Leader LOUIS TAATA.

Te Hono E Tau I Te Honaui (Link Between Generations): Papeete; f. 2002; Leader STANLEY CROSS.

Te Niu Hau Manahune (Principle of Democracy): Rangiroa; f. 2007; Leader TEINA MARAEURA; Sec.-Gen. HINANO TEANOTOGA.

Judicial System

Audit Office: Chambre Territoriale des Comptes, rue Edouard Ahnne, BP 331, 98713 Papeete; tel. 509710; fax 509719; e-mail ctc.pf@mail.pf; Pres. JACQUES BASSET; Clerk of the Court VINCENT BUTERI.

Court of Administrative Law: Tribunal Administratif, ave Bruat, BP 4522, Papeete; tel. 509025; fax 451724; e-mail tadelapolynesiefrancaise@mail.pf; Pres. ALFRED POUPET; Cllrs MARIE-CHRISTINE LUBRANO, HÉLÈNE ROULAND, DANIÈLE GONNOT, LUC CAMPOY; Clerk of the Court DONA GERMAIN.

Court of Appeal: Cour d'Appel de Papeete, 42 ave Puvanaa a Oopa, BP 101, 98713 Papeete; tel. 415500; fax 424416; e-mail sec.pp.ca-papeete@justice.fr; internet www.ca-papeete.justice.fr; Pres. OLIVIER AIMOT; Attorney-Gen. FRANÇOIS DEBY; Clerk of the Court DENISE BIANCONI.

Court of the First Instance: Tribunal de Première Instance de Papeete, ave Bruat BP 101, Papeete; tel. 415543; fax 454012; Pres. GUY RIPOLL; Procurator JEAN BIANCONI; Clerk of the Court KARL LEQUEUX.

Religion

About 54% of the population are Protestants and 38% are Roman Catholics.

CHRISTIANITY

Protestant Church

At mid-2000 there were an estimated 110,000 Protestants.

Maohi Protestant Church: BP 113, Papeete; tel. 460600; fax 419357; e-mail eepf@mail.pf; f. 1884; autonomous since 1963; fmrly l'Eglise Evangélique en Polynésie Française (Etaretia Evaneria I Porinetia Farani); Pres. of Council Rev. TAAROANUI MARAEA; c. 95,000 mems.

The Roman Catholic Church

French Polynesia comprises the archdiocese of Papeete and the suffragan diocese of Taiohae o Tefenuaenata (based in Nuku Hiva, Marquesas Is). At 31 December 2005 there were an estimated 98,060 adherents in French Polynesia. The Archbishop and the Bishop participate in the Episcopal Conference of the Pacific, based in Fiji.

Archbishop of Papeete: HUBERT COPPENRATH, Archevêché, BP 94, Vallée de la Mission, 98713 Papeete; tel. 502351; fax 424032; e-mail catholic@mail.pf.

Other Churches

Other denominations active in French Polynesia include the Assemblies of God, Church of Jesus Christ of Latter-day Saints (Mormon), Sanito and Seventh-day Adventist missions. At mid-2000 there were an estimated 30,000 adherents to other forms of Christianity.

The Press

La Dépêche de Tahiti: Pont de la Fautaua, BP 50, Papeete; tel. 464343; fax 464350; e-mail journalistes@ladepeche.pf; f. 1964; acquired by Groupe France Antilles in 1988; daily; French; Gen. Man. CHRISTOPHE RUET; Editor-in-Chief THIERRY DURIGNEUX; circ. 20,500.

Fenua'Orama: BP 629, 98713 Papeete; tel. 475293; fax 475297; e-mail fenuaorama@france-antilles.pf; publ. by Groupe France Antilles; monthly; women's lifestyle; Editor-in-Chief DANIEL PARDON; circ. 12,000.

L'Hebdo Maohi: BP 42389, Fare Tony, Papeete; tel. and fax 4581827; e-mail journal@hebdo.pf; internet www.hebdo.pf; weekly; Man. and Publ. Dir TERII PAQUIER; circ. 3,000.

Journal Officiel de la Polynésie Française: c/o Imprimerie Officielle, 43 rue des Poilus Tahitiens, BP 117, 98713 Papeete; tel. 500580; fax 425261; e-mail imprimerie.officielle@imprimerie.gov.pf; f. 2004 as *Compte Rendu Intégral des Débats de l'Assemblée de la Polynésie Française*; irregular; publ. by the Imprimerie Officielle; Dir CLAUDINO LAURENT; circ. 100.

Les Nouvelles de Tahiti: Immeuble Sarateva, Carrefour de la Fautaua, BP 629, Papeete; tel. 475200; fax 475209; e-mail redac@lesnouvelles.pf; f. 1957; daily; French; Gen. Man. CHRISTOPHE RUET; Editor-in-Chief MURIEL PONTAROLLO; circ. 6,500.

Le Semeur Tahitien: BP 94, 98713 Papeete; tel. 502350; e-mail catholic@mail.pf; f. 1909; 22 a year; French; publ. by the Roman Catholic Church.

Tahiti Beach Press: BP 887, 98713 Papeete; tel. 426850; fax 423356; e-mail tahitibeachpres@mail.pf; internet www.tahitibeachpress.com; f. 1980; monthly; English; Publr G. WARTI; circ. 10,000.

Tahiti Pacifique Magazine: BP 368, Maharepa, Moorea; tel. 562894; fax 563007; e-mail tahitipm@mail.pf; internet tahiti-pacifique.com; monthly; French; Dir and Editor ALEX W. DU PREL; circ. 6,200.

Ve'a Katorika: BP 94, 98713 Papeete; e-mail catholic@mail.pf; f. 1909; monthly; publ. by the Roman Catholic Church.

Ve'a Porotetani: BP 113, Papeete; tel. 460623; fax 419357; e-mail eepf@mail.pf; f. 1921; monthly; French and Tahitian; publ. by the Maohi Protestant Church; Dir TAARII MARAEA; Editor-in-Chief EVA RAAPOTO; circ. 5,000.

Other publications include *Le To'ere*, weekly; *Conso + Info Plus*, *Tahiti Business*, and *Ve'a Ora Magazine*, monthly; and *Dixit* and *Fenua Economie*, annually.

NEWS AGENCIES

Agence France-Presse (AFP): BP 629, Papeete; tel. 508100; fax 508109.

Tahitipresse (Agence Tahitienne de Presse—ATP): Quartier de la Mission, Bâtiment TNTV rez-de-chaussée, BP 4635, 98713 Papeete; tel. 548787; fax 838382; e-mail agence@tahitipresse.pf; internet www.tahitipresse.pf; f. 2001; bilingual French and English news service providing pictures and printed news reports; Chair. TEVA QUESNOT; Dir LOUIS BRESSON.

Publishers

Editions Haere Po No Tahiti: BP 1958, Papeete 98713; tel. 582636; fax 582333; e-mail haerepotahiti@mail.pf; f. 1981; travel, history, linguistics, literature, culture, anthropology, religion, land tenure and local interest.

Au Vent des Iles: BP 5670, 98716 Pirae; tel. 509595; fax 509597; e-mail mail@auventdesiles.pf; internet www.auventdesiles.pf; f. 1992; South Pacific interest, fiction and trade; Gen. Man. CHRISTIAN ROBERT.

GOVERNMENT PRINTER

Imprimerie Officielle: 43 rue des Poilus Tahitiens, BP 117, 98713 Papeete; tel. 500580; fax 425261; e-mail imprimerie.officielle@imprimerie.gov.pf; f. 1843; printers, publrs; Dir CLAUDINO LAURENT.

Broadcasting and Communications

TELECOMMUNICATIONS

France Câbles et Radio (FCR): Télécommunications Extérieures de la Polynésie Française, BP 99, Papeete; tel. 415400; fax 437553; announced withdrawal from French Polynesia March 2007.

Office des Postes et Télécommunications: Hôtel des Postes, 8 rue de la Reine Pomare IV, 98714 Papeete; tel. 414242; fax 436767;

e-mail contact@opt.pf; internet www.opt.pf; Chair. JEAN-PAUL BARRAL; Dir-Gen. LYDIA NOUVEAU.

Tahiti Nui Telecommunications (TNT): Immeuble Aorai, 3ème étage, rue Edouard Ahnne, BP 550, 98713 Papeete; tel. 415400; fax 4303495; e-mail admin.tnt@tahitinui-telecom.com; f. 2001; owned by OPT; telecommunications provider; Chair. JEAN-CLAUDE TERIIEROOITERAI; Gen. Man. GÉRARD COLAS.

Regulatory Authority

Service des Postes et Telecommunications: BP 5019, 98716 Pirae; tel. 501776; fax 532801; internet www.spt.pf.

BROADCASTING
Radio

RFO Polynésie: 410 rue Dumont d'Urville, BP 60125, Pamatai, 98702 Faa'a; tel. 861616; fax 861611; e-mail rfopfr@mail.pf; internet polynesie.rfo.fr; f. 1934; public service radio and television station operated by Réseau France Outre-Mer (RFO), Paris; daily programmes in French and Tahitian; Regional Man. MICHEL KOPS; Communications Man. JEAN-RAYMOND BODIN.

Private Stations

Since 2004 some 17 stations have been licensed. There are currently around 25 commercial radio stations in French Polynesia.

NRJ Tahiti: BP 50, 98718 Papeete; tel. and fax 421042; fax 464346; affiliated to NRJ France; French; entertainment; broadcasts 14 hrs daily; Station Man. NADINE RICHARDSON.

Radio Bleue (Tahiti FM): BP 11055, PK 10, Mahina; tel. 480098; fax 480825; e-mail redaction@radiobleue.pf; internet www.radiobleue.pf; French; affiliated to the political party Ai'a Api; Editor-in-Chief JEAN-PAUL SERRES.

Radio One: Fare Ute, BP 3601, 98713 Papeete; tel. 434100; fax 423406; e-mail infos@radio1.pf; French; relays Europe 1 news bulletins from Paris; Editor-in-Chief FLORENCE BORDJ.

Radio (Te Reo O) Tefana (La Voix de Tefana): BP 6295, 98702 Faa'a; tel. 819797; fax 825493; e-mail tereo@mail.pf; f. 1987; French and Tahitian; affiliated to the Tavini Huiraatira party; Pres. OSCAR TEMARU; Dir and Station Man. TERIIMATEATA MANA; Editor-in-Chief MICAËL TAPUTU.

Radio Te Vevo O Te Tiaturiraa: 51 rue Dumont d'Urville, BP 1817, 98713 Papeete; tel. 412341; fax 412322; e-mail contacts@mail.pf; religious; affiliated with the Assemblies of God church; Treas. THIERRY ALBERT.

Other radio stations include Pacific FM, Radio Fara, Radio la Voix de l'Espérance (LVDL), Radio Ma'ohi-RTL, Radio Maria No Te Hau, Radio Paofai, Radio Te Vevo No Papara, Star FM and Tiare FM.

Television

RFO Polynésie: see Radio.

TNS (Tahiti Nui Satellite): 8 rue de la Reine Pomare IV, 98714 Papeete; tel. 414370; fax 432707; e-mail tns@opt.pf; internet www.tns.pf; f. 2000; 100% owned by the Office des Postes et Télécommunications; news and entertainment; relays 25 television channels and 6 radio channels, in French, Tahitian and English, incl. TNTV; also relays ABC Asia Pacific Television, Australia, and Canal Plus, France; Man. VETEA TROUCHE-BONNO; over 10,000 subscribers.

TNTV (Tahiti Nui Television): Quartier Mission, BP 348, 98713 Papeete; tel. 473615; fax 532721; e-mail redaction@tntv.pf; internet www.tntv.pf; f. 2000; broadcasts in French and Tahitian 19 hours daily; Chair. CHANTAL GALENON; Editor-in-Chief TIARE NUI PAHUIRI.

Finance

(cap. = capital; res = reserves; dep. = deposits; m. = million; brs = branches; amounts in francs CFP)

BANKING
Commercial Banks

Banque de Polynésie SA: 355 blvd Pomare, BP 530, 98713 Papeete; tel. 466666; fax 466664; e-mail bdp@sg-bdp.pf; internet www.sg-bdp.pf; f. 1973; 80% owned by Société Générale, France; cap. 1,380.0m., res 4,395.4m., dep. 123,148.2m. (Dec. 2006); Chair. JEAN-LOUIS MATTEI; Gen. Man. JEAN-PIERRE DUFOUR; 14 brs.

Banque de Tahiti SA: 38 rue François Cardella, BP 1602, 98713 Papeete; tel. 417000; fax 423376; e-mail contact@bt.pf; internet www.banque-tahiti.pf; f. 1969; owned by Financière Océor (95.4%); merged with Banque Paribas de Polynésie, Aug. 1998; cap. 1,565.3m., res 4,431.8m., dep. 140,999.1m. (Dec. 2005); Chair., Pres. and Gen. Man. DANIEL NUCCIO; Exec. Vice-Pres. and Gen. Sec. STÉPHANE DENIS; 18 brs.

Banque SOCREDO—Société de Crédit et de Développement de l'Océanie: 115 rue Dumont d'Urville, BP 130, 98713 Papeete; tel. 415123; fax 415283; e-mail socres@bank-socredo.pf; internet www.websoc.pf; internet www.socredo.pf; f. 1959; public body; in partnership with the French cos BNP Paribas, Cardif Assurance and Crédit Agricole, which provide technical assistance; cap. 22,000.0m., res 3,926.8m., dep. 188,806.9m. (Dec. 2006); Chair. CLAUDE PERIOU; Gen. Man. JAMES ESTALL; 26 brs.

Insurance

AGF Vie & AGF IART Polynésie Française: Immeuble Sienne, rue Dumont d'Urville, BP 4452, 98713 Papeete; tel. 549100; fax 549101; e-mail gestion-vie@agf.pf; life and general non-life insurance.

GAN Pacifique: 9 ave Bruat, BP 339, 98713 Papeete; tel. 503150; fax 431918; subsidiary of Groupama, France; general non-life insurance; Chair. JEAN-FRANÇOIS LEMOUX; Gen. Man. DIDIER COURIER.

Poe-ma Insurances: Marina Fare Ute, BP 4652, 98713 Papeete; tel. 502650; fax 450097; e-mail info@poema.pf; internet www.papeeteonline.com/sites/poema; f. 1991; general non-life insurance; Man. Dir VINCENT GEORGE.

Trade and Industry

GOVERNMENT AGENCIES

Délégation pour la Promotion des Investissements (DPI): Immeuble Lejeune, 82 rue du Général de Gaulle, BP 504, 98713 Papeete; tel. 543254; fax 543255; e-mail invest@tahiti-invest.com; internet www.tahiti-invest.com; Dir HINANO DEXTER.

Etablissement Public des Grands Travaux (EGT): 51 rue du Commandant Destremeau, BP 9030, Motu Uta, 98715 Papeete; tel. 508100; fax 508102; e-mail contact@egt.pf; internet www.egt.pf; responsible for public works; Pres. JONAS TAHUAITU; Dir ERIC NOBLE-DEMAY.

Service de l'Artisanat Traditionnel (ART): Ancien Immeuble Royal Confort, 2ème étage, Fare Ute, BP 4451, 98713 Papeete; tel. 545400; fax 532321; Dir WILLIAM ELLACOTT.

Service de l'Emploi, de la Formation et de la Insertion Professionnelles (SEFI): Immeuble Papineau, rue Tepano Jaussen, 2ème étage, BP 540, 98713 Papeete; tel. 461212; fax 450280; internet www.sefi.pf; Dir PAUL NATIER.

Service du Commerce Extérieur: 53 rue Nansouty, Immeuble Teissier au 1er étage, BP 20727, 98713 Papeete; tel. 506464; fax 436420; e-mail commerceexterieur@economie.gov.pf; internet www.tahiti-export.pf; Dir WILLIAM VANIZETTE.

Service du Développement de l'Industrie et des Métiers (SDIM): BP 9055, Motu Uta, 98715 Papeete; tel. 502880; fax 412645; e-mail secretariat.sdim@industrie.gov.pf; internet www.sdim.pf; f. 1988; industry and small-business devt administration; Dir DENIS GRELLIER.

Société de Financement du Développement de la Polynésie Française (SOFIDEP): Centre Paofai, Bâtiment BC, 1er étage, blvd Pomare, BP 345, 98713 Papeete; tel. 509330; fax 509333; e-mail sem.sofidep@mail.pf; Dir LOUIS SAVOIE.

DEVELOPMENT ORGANIZATIONS

Agence Française de Développement (AFD): Immeuble Hokule'a, 2 rue Cook Paofai, BP 578, 98713 Papeete; tel. 544600; fax 544601; e-mail afdpapeete@pf.groupe-afd.org; internet www.afd.fr; public body; devt finance institute; Dir LAURENT FONTAINE.

Moruroa e Tatou (Moruroa et Nous): 403 blvd Pomare, BP 5456, 98716 Pirae, Papeete; tel. 430905; e-mail contact@moruroaetatou.org; internet www.moruroaetatou.org; f. 2001; represents former employees of the Centre d'Expérimentation du Pacifique (CEP) and their families; Pres. ROLAND POUIRA OLDHAM; c. 4,300 mems.

SODEP (Société pour le Développement et l'Expansion du Pacifique): BP 4441, Papeete; tel. 429449; f. 1961; by consortium of banks and private interests; regional devt and finance co.

CHAMBERS OF COMMERCE

Chambre de Commerce, d'Industrie, des Services et des Métiers de Polynésie Française (CCISM): 41 rue du Docteur Cassiau, BP 118, 98713 Papeete; tel. 472700; fax 540701; e-mail info@cci.pf; internet www.ccism.pf; f. 1880; Pres. JULES CHANGUES; Gen. Man. ABNER GILLOUX; 34 mems.

Chambre d'Agriculture et de la Pêche Lagonaire: route de l'Hippodrome, BP 5383, Pirae; tel. 425393; fax 438754; e-mail courrier@vanille.pf; f. 1886; Pres. HENRI TAURAA; Sec.-Gen. JACQUES ROOMATAAROA; 10 mems.

Jeune Chambre Economique de Tahiti: BP 20669, Papeete; tel. 810114; fax 702703; e-mail contact@jcitahiti.com; internet www.jcitahiti.com; Pres. MICHEL CERDINI.

EMPLOYERS' ORGANIZATIONS

Confédération Générale des Petites et Moyennes Entreprises de Polynésie Française Te Rima Rohi (CGPME): BP 1733, 98713 Papeete; tel. 426333; fax 835608; e-mail courrier@cgpme.pf; internet www.cgpme.pf; Pres. CHRISTOPHE PLÉE; c. 1,000 mems.

Affiliated organizations include:

Chambre Syndicale des Fleuristes de Polynésie Française: e-mail tahitifleurs@mail.pf; Pres. ALAIN MENARD.

Syndicat de l'Imprimerie, la Presse et la Communication (SIPCOM): BP 625, 98713 Papeete; tel. 424311; fax 422598; e-mail tsn@mail.pf; Pres. TEVA SYLVAIN.

Syndicat des Restaurants, Bars et Snacks Bars de Polynésie Française (SRBSBPF): Le Mandarin, BP 302, 98713 Papeete; tel. 503350; fax 421632; e-mail charl.beaumont@mail.pf; Pres. CHARLES BEAUMONT.

Syndicat Polynésien des Entreprises et Prestataires de Service (SPEPS): e-mail cgpnisarl@mail.pf; Pres. GILLES PASCAL.

Union Polynésienne de l'Hôtellerie (UPHO): 76 rue Wallis, BP 1733 Motu Uta, Papeete; tel. 426333; fax 429553; e-mail upho@tahitinui.net; Pres. CHRISTOPHE BEAUMONT.

Union Polynésienne des Professions Libérales (UPPL): BP 4554, Papeete; e-mail gibeaux.tahiti@mail.pf; Pres. CHARLIE GIBEAUX.

Conseil des Entreprises de Polynésie Française (CEPF): Immeuble Farnham, rue Clappier, BP 972, 98713 Papeete; tel. 541040; fax 423237; e-mail cepf@cepf.pf; internet www.cepf.pf; f. 1983; fmrly Conseil des Employeurs; affiliated to Mouvement des Entreprises de France (MEDEF); comprises 14 professional and interprofessional orgs, representing 492 cos; Pres. JACQUES BILLON-TYRARD; Sec.-Gen. JEAN-CLAUDE LECUELLE.

Affiliated organizations include:

Association des Transporteurs Aériens Locaux de Polynésie Française (ATAL): BP 314, 98713 Papeete; tel. 864004; fax 864009; Pres. MARCEL GALENON.

Association Tahitienne des Professionnels de l'Audiovisuelle: Papeete.

Chambre Syndicale des Commissionnaires en Douane, Agents de Fret et Déménageurs de Polynésie Française: BP 972, 98713 Papeete; tel. 541040; fax 423237; e-mail cscdafd@cepf.pf; Pres. ANTONIA BAMBRIDGE.

Chambre Syndicale des Entrepreneurs du Bâtiment et des Travaux Publics (CSEBTP): BP 2218, 98713 Papeete; tel. 541040; fax 423237; e-mail csebtp@cepf.pf; Pres. PASCAL MOUSSET.

Comité de Polynésie de l'Association Française des Banques: Papeete; tel. 426603; fax 26605; Pres. ERIC POMMIER.

Fédération Générale du Commerce: BP 1607, 98713 Papeete; tel. 541040; fax 422359; e-mail fgc@mail.pf; internet www.fgc.pf; Pres. GILLES YAU; Sec. PATRICIA LO MONACO.

Organisation Professionnelle du Conseil de l'Intérim et de la Formation: Papeete.

Syndicat des Agences Maritimes au Long Cours: BP 274, 98713 Papeete; tel. 428972; fax 432184; Pres. MAEVA SIU.

Syndicat des Employeurs du Secteur de l'Assurance (SESA): BP 358, 98713 Papeete; tel. 506262; fax 506263; Pres. ALAIN LEBRIS.

Syndicat des Industriels de Polynésie Française (SIPOF): Immeuble Farnham, BP 3521, 98713 Papeete; tel. 541040; fax 423237; e-mail sipof@cepf.pf; internet www.sipof.pf; f. 1974; represents workers in industry, engineering, manufacturing and printing; Pres. JIMMY WONG; Sec. STÉPHANE PEREZ; 2,400 mems in 65 cos.

Syndicat Professionnel des Concessionnaires Automobiles: BP 916, 98713 Papeete; tel. 454545; fax 431260; Pres. PAUL YEO CHICHONG.

Union des Industriels de la Manutention Portuaire (UNIM): BP 570, 98713 Papeete; tel. 545700; fax 426262; Pres. JULES CHANGUES.

Groupement Interprofessionnel du Monoï de Tahiti (GIMT): BP 14 165, Arue, Tahiti; tel. 414851; fax 431849; internet www.monoidetahiti.pf; f. 1992; asscn of monoï manufacturers.

UTILITIES

Electricity

Electricité de Tahiti (EDT): route de Puurai, BP 8021, Faa'a-Puurai; tel. 867704; fax 834439; e-mail edt@edt.pf; internet www.edt.pf; subsidiary of Groupe Suez, France; Pres. JOËL ALLAIN; Gen. Man. CHRISTIAN LEKIEFFRE; c. 60,000 customers (2005).

Water

Société Polynésienne des Eaux et Assainissements: BP 20795, 98713 Papeete, Tahiti; fax 421548; e-mail spea@spea.pf.

TRADE UNIONS

Under French Polynesian legislation, to be officially recognized trade unions must receive the vote of at least 5% of the workforce at professional elections.

Chambre Syndicale des Métiers du Génie Civil et des Travaux Publics (CSMGCTP): BP 51120, 98716 Pirae; tel. 502100; fax 436922; Pres. DANIEL PALACZ.

Confédération des Syndicats des Travailleurs de Polynésie/Force Ouvrière (CSTP/FO): Immeuble Farnham, 1er étage, BP 1201, 98713 Papeete; tel. 426049; fax 450635; e-mail pfrebault@cstp-fo.pf; Pres. COCO TERAIEFA CHANG; Sec.-Gen. PATRICK GALENON.

Confédération des Syndicats Indépendants de la Polynésie Française (CSIP): Immeuble Allegret, 1er étage, ave du Prince Hinoï, BP 468, 98713 Papeete; tel. 532274; fax 532275; Sec.-Gen. CYRIL LE GAYIC.

Confédération Syndicale A Tia I Mua (CFDT): Fare Ia Ora, Mamao, BP 4523, Papeete; tel. 544010; fax 450245; e-mail atiaimua@ifrance.com; affiliated to the Confédération Française Démocratique du Travail; Gen. Sec. JEAN-MARIE YAN TU.

Conseil Fédéral des Syndicats Libres de Polynésie O Oe To Oe Rima: Immeuble Brown, 1er étage, BP 52866, 98716 Pirae; tel. 483445; fax 483445; Gen. Sec. RONALD TEROROTUA.

Union Fédérale des Syndicats Autonomes/Confédération OTAHI (OTAHI UFSA): ancien Immeuble SETIL, 1er étage, ave du Prince Hinoï, BP 148, 98713 Papeete; tel. 450654; fax 451327; Sec.-Gen. LUCIE TIFFENAT.

Transport

ROADS

French Polynesia has 792 km of roads, of which about one-third are bitumen-surfaced and two-thirds stone-surfaced.

Service des Transports Terrestres: 93 avenue Pomare V, Fariipiti, BP 4586, 98713 Papeete; tel. 502060; fax 436021; e-mail sce.transp.terrestres@polynesie.gov.pf; internet www.transports-terrestres.pf; f. 1988; Dir ROLAND TSU.

SHIPPING

The principal port is at Papeete, on Tahiti.

Port Authority: Port Autonome de Papeete, BP 9164, Motu Uta, 98715 Papeete; tel. 505454; fax 421950; e-mail portppt@portppt.pf; internet www.portdepapeete.pf; Harbour Master MARCEL PELLETIER; Port Dir YVES DE MONTGOLFIER.

Agence Maritime Internationale de Tahiti: BP 274, 98713 Papeete; tel. 428972; fax 432184; e-mail amitahiti@mail.pf; f. 1978; services from Asia, the USA, Australia, New Zealand and Europe; Gen. Man. MAEVA SIU.

CMA CGM Papeete: 2 rue Wallis, BP 96, Papeete; tel. 545252; fax 436806; e-mail ppt.genmbox@cma-cgm.com; fmrly CGM Tour du Monde SA; shipowners and agents; international freight services; Gen. Man. JOEL LE JULIEN.

Compagnie Polynésienne de Transport Maritime: BP 220, 98713 Papeete; tel. 426242; fax 434889; e-mail reservations@aranui.com; internet www.aranui.com; shipping co; CEO JEAN WONG; Gen. Man. PHILIPPE WONG.

EURL Transport Maritime des Tuamotu Ouest: BP 1816, 98713 Papeete; tel. 422553; fax 422557; inter-island passenger service; Dir SIMÉON RICHMOND.

SA Compagnie Française Maritime de Tahiti: Immeuble Importex, No. 45, Fare Ute, POB 368, 98713 Papeete; tel. 426393; fax 420617; e-mail taporo@mail.pf; Pres. and Man. MORTON GARBUTT.

SARL Société de Transport Insulaire Maritime (STIM): BP 635, 98713 Papeete; tel. 549954; fax 452444; Dir ROLAND PAQUIER.

Société de Navigation des Australes: BP 1890, Papeete; tel. 509609; fax 420609; e-mail snathp@mail.pf; inter-island passenger service; Dir HERVÉ DANTON.

CIVIL AVIATION

There is one international airport, Faa'a airport, 6 km from Papeete, on Tahiti, and there are 46 smaller airports and aerodromes throughout French Polynesia. Since October 2004 the Government has commissioned studies into the possible siting of a new international airport on Tubai in the Austral Islands, or in the Marquesas at either Nuku Hiva or Hiva Oa. International services are operated by

FRENCH OVERSEAS POSSESSIONS

Air France, Air Tahiti Nui, Air New Zealand, LAN-Chile, Hawaiian Airlines (USA) and Air Calédonie International.

Service d'Etat de l'Aviation Civile: BP 6404, 98702, Faa'a, Papeete; tel. 861000; fax 861009; e-mail webmaster@seac.pf; internet www.seac.pf; Dir GUY YEUNG.

Société d'Equipement de Tahiti et ses Iles (SETIL): BP 177, 98713 Papeete; tel. 866060; fax 837391; e-mail setil.aeroports@tahiti-aeroport.pf; internet www.tahiti-aeroport.pf; f. 1966; 50% govt-owned; management and devt of airports at Faa'a, Bora Bora, Huahine, Raiatea, Rangiroa and Moorea; Gen. Man. GUY BESNARD.

Air Moorea: BP 6019, 98702 Faa'a; tel. 864100; fax 864269; e-mail freddy.chanseau@airmoorea.pf; internet www.airmoorea.com; f. 1968; operates internal services between Tahiti and Moorea Island and domestic charter flights; Pres. MARCEL GALENON; CEO FREDDY CHANSEAU.

Air Tahiti: BP 314, 98713 Papeete; tel. 864012; fax 864069; e-mail direction.generale@airtahiti.pf; internet www.airtahiti.aero; f. 1953; Air Polynésie 1970–87; operates domestic services to 46 islands; Chair. CHRISTIAN VERNAUDON; Gen. Man. MARCEL GALENON.

Air Tahiti Nui: Immeuble Dexter, Pont de l'Est, BP 1673, 98713 Papeete; tel. 460303; fax 460290; e-mail fly@airtahitinui.pf; internet www.airtahitinui.com; f. 1996; commenced operations 1998; scheduled services to the USA, France, Japan, New Zealand and Australia; Chair. JEFFREY SALMON; Gen. Delegate Man. YVES WAUTHY.

Tourism

Tourism is an important and developed industry in French Polynesia, particularly on Tahiti. Some 221,549 people visited the country in 2006: 32.3% of arrivals were from the USA, 19.1% from France and 9.9% from Japan. Arrivals were estimated to have decreased to 218,241 in 2007. The number of hotels increased from 44 in 2001 to 49 in 2005, while the number of available rooms decreased from 4,418 to 3,326 during the same period. In 2006 earnings from tourism were an estimated US $520m.

GIE Tahiti Tourisme: Fare Manihini, blvd Pomare, BP 65, 98713 Papeete; tel. 505700; fax 436619; e-mail info@tahiti-tourisme.pf; internet www.tahiti-tourisme.pf; f. 1966 as autonomous public body; transformed into private corpn in 1993; relaunched Dec. 2005 following merger between GIE Tahiti Tourisme and Tahiti Manava Visitors' Bureau; Chair. JACQUES TEHEIURA; CEO DANY PANERO.

Service du Tourisme (STO): Paofai Bldg (Entry D), blvd Pomare, Papeete; tel. 476200; fax 476202; e-mail sto@tourisme.gov.pf; govt dept; manages Special Fund for Tourist Development; Dir MEREHAU MAIRAI.

MAYOTTE

Introductory Survey

Location, Climate, Language, Religion, Capital

Mayotte forms part of the Comoros archipelago, which lies between the island of Madagascar and the east coast of the African mainland. The territory comprises a main island, Mayotte (Mahoré), and a number of smaller islands. The climate is tropical, with temperatures averaging between 24°C and 27°C (75°F to 81°F) throughout the year. The official language is French but Shimaore (Maorese) and Shibushi are also spoken. Islam is the main religion. The capital is Dzaoudzi, which is connected to the island of Pamandzi by a causeway.

Recent History

Since the Comoros unilaterally declared independence in July 1975, Mayotte has been administered separately by France. The independent Comoran state claims sovereignty of Mayotte, and officially represents it in international organizations, including the UN. In December 1976 France introduced the special status of Collectivité territoriale for the island. Following a coup in the Comoros in May 1978, Mayotte rejected the new Government's proposal that it should rejoin the other islands under a federal system, and reaffirmed its intention of remaining linked to France. In December 1979 the Assemblée nationale approved legislation that extended Mayotte's special status for another five years, during which the islanders were to be consulted. In October 1984, however, the Assemblée nationale further prolonged Mayotte's status, and the referendum on the island's future was postponed indefinitely. The UN General Assembly has adopted a number of resolutions in support of the sovereignty of the Comoros over the island. Until 1999 the main political party on Mayotte, the Mouvement Populaire Mahorais (MPM), demanded full departmental status for the island (as held by Réunion), but France was reluctant to grant this in view of Mayotte's lack of development. Following public consultation in 2000, in July 2001 Mayotte was declared a Collectivité départementale.

Meanwhile, at the general election to the Assemblée nationale in March 1986, Henry Jean-Baptiste, a member of the Centre des Démocrates Sociaux (CDS), which was affiliated to the Union pour la Démocratie Française (UDF), was elected as deputy for Mayotte. Relations between the MPM and the French Government rapidly deteriorated after the Franco-African summit in November 1987, when the French Prime Minister, Jacques Chirac, expressed reservations concerning the elevation of Mayotte to the status of an Overseas Department (despite his announcement, in early 1986, that he shared the MPM's aim to upgrade Mayotte's status).

In the second round of the French presidential election, which took place in May 1988, François Mitterrand, the incumbent President and the candidate of the Parti Socialiste (PS), received 50.3% of the votes cast on Mayotte, defeating Chirac, the candidate of the Rassemblement pour la République (RPR). At elections to the Assemblée nationale, which took place in June, Jean-Baptiste retained his seat. (Later that month, he joined the newly formed centrist group in the Assemblée nationale, the Union du Centre—UDC.) In elections to the Conseil général in September and October, the MPM retained the majority of seats.

In 1989–90 concern about the number of Comoran immigrants seeking employment on the island resulted in an increase in racial tension. A paramilitary organization, known as Caiman, was subsequently formed in support of the expulsion of illegal immigrants, but was refused legal recognition by the authorities. In June 1992 increasing resentment resulted in further attacks against Comoran immigrants resident in Mayotte. In early September representatives of the MPM met the French Prime Minister, Pierre Bérégovoy, to request the reintroduction of entry visas to restrict immigration from the Comoros. Later that month the MPM organized a boycott of Mayotte's participation in the French referendum on the Treaty on European Union (see p. 244), in support of the provision of entry visas.

At elections to the Assemblée nationale, which took place in March 1993, Jean-Baptiste was returned, securing 53.4% of votes cast, while the Secretary-General of the RPR, Mansour Kamardine, received 44.3% of the votes.

Elections to the Conseil général (which was enlarged from 17 to 19 members) took place in March 1994: the MPM retained 12 seats, while the RPR secured four seats, and independent candidates three seats. During an official visit to Mayotte in November, the French Prime Minister, Edouard Balladur, announced the reintroduction of entry visas as a requirement for Comoran nationals, and the adoption of a number of security measures, in an effort to reduce illegal immigration to the island. In January 1995 the Comoran Government suspended transport links between Mayotte and the Comoros in response to the measure. In the first round of the French presidential election in April, Balladur received the highest number of votes on Mayotte (although Chirac subsequently won the election).

In elections to the French Senate (Sénat) in September 1995, the incumbent MPM representative, Marcel Henry, was returned by a large majority. During a visit to Mayotte in October, the French Secretary of State for Overseas Departments and Territories pledged that a referendum on the future status of the island would be conducted by 1999. In October 1996 he confirmed that two commissions, based in Paris and Mayotte, were preparing a consultation document, which would be presented in late 1997, and announced that the resulting referendum would take place before the end of the decade.

Partial elections to fill nine seats in the Conseil général were held in March 1997; the MPM secured three seats (losing two that it had previously held), the RPR won three seats, the local PS one seat, and independent right-wing candidates two seats. In elections to the Assemblée nationale Jean-Baptiste, representing the alliance of the UDF and the Force Démocrate (FD, formerly the CDS), defeated Kamardine, securing 51.7% of votes cast in the second round of voting, which took place in June.

In July 1997 the relative prosperity of Mayotte was believed to have prompted separatist movements on the Comoran islands of Nzwani and Mwali to demand the restoration of French rule, and subsequently to declare their independence in August. Illegal immigration from the Comoros continued to prove a major concern for the authorities on Mayotte; during January–February 1997 some 6,000

Comorans were expelled from the island, with many more agreeing to leave voluntarily.

Meanwhile, uncertainty remained over the future status of Mayotte. In April 1998 one of the commissions charged with examining the issue submitted its report, which concluded that the present status of Collectivité territoriale was no longer appropriate, but did not advocate an alternative. In May the MPM declared its support for an adapted form of departmental administration, and urged the French authorities to decide on a date for a referendum. In July Pierre Bayle succeeded Philippe Boisadam as Prefect. In May 1999 Bamana made an appeal that the inhabitants of Mayotte be allowed to organize their own vote on their future, and later that month Jean-Baptiste introduced draft legislation to the Assemblée nationale, which proposed the holding of a referendum regarding the island's future before the end of 1999. In August, following negotiations between the French Secretary of State for Overseas Departments and Territories, Jean-Jack Queyranne, and island representatives, Mayotte members of the RPR and the PS and Bamana (the leader of the MPM) signed a draft document providing for the transformation of Mayotte into a Collectivité départementale, if approved at a referendum. However, both Henry and Jean-Baptiste rejected the document. The two politicians subsequently announced their departure from the MPM and formed a new political party entitled the Mouvement Départementaliste Mahorais (MDM), while reiterating their demands that Mayotte be granted full overseas departmental status.

Following the approval of Mayotte's proposed new status by the Conseil général (by 14 votes to five) and the municipal councils, an accord to this effect was signed by Queyranne and political representatives of Mayotte on 27 January 2000. On 2 July a referendum was held, in which the population of Mayotte voted overwhelmingly in favour of the January accord, granting Mayotte the status of Collectivité départementale for a period of 10 years. In November the commission established to define the terms of Mayotte's new status published a report, which envisaged the transfer of executive power from the Prefect to the Conseil général by 2004, the dissolution of the position of Prefect by 2007 and the concession of greater powers to the local Government, notably in the area of regional co-operation.

At elections to the Conseil général, held in March 2001, no party established a majority. The MPM experienced significant losses, with only four of its candidates being elected, while the RPR won five seats, the Mouvement des Citoyens (MDC) two, the MDM one, the PS one, and various right-wing independent candidates six seats. Bamana was re-elected as President of the Conseil général. The French Parliament approved Mayotte's status as a Collectivité départementale in July 2001. In September Philippe de Mester succeeded Bayle as Prefect.

In the first round of the French presidential election, which was held on 21 April 2002, Chirac received the highest number of votes on Mayotte, winning 43.0% of the valid votes cast; the second round, held on 5 May, was also won resoundingly by Chirac, who secured 88.3% of votes cast on the island, defeating the candidate of the extreme right-wing Front National, Jean-Marie Le Pen. At elections to the Assemblée nationale, held in June, Jean-Baptiste did not stand. Kamardine, representing the recently formed Union pour la Majorité Présidentielle (UMP, which incorporated the RPR, the Démocratie Libérale and significant elements of the UDF), defeated the MDM-UDF candidate, Siadi Vita. Jean-Jacques Brot replaced de Mester as Prefect in July. In November the UMP was renamed the Union pour un Mouvement Populaire.

At elections to the Conseil général in March 2004, the UMP won eight seats in alliance with the MPM, which secured one seat, while the MDM and the MDC, also in alliance, obtained five and two seats, respectively; independent candidates were elected to the remaining three seats. With the election of Saïd Omar Oili, an independent, as President of the Conseil général on 2 April, executive power was transferred from the Prefect to the Conseil. In January 2005 Jean-Paul Kihl replaced Jean-Jacques Brot as Prefect. In late May a national referendum on ratification of the European Union constitutional treaty was held: 86.5% of Mayotte's electorate voted in favour of adopting the treaty; however, it was ultimately rejected by a majority of French voters. In late November more than 500 trade union members protested in Mamoudzou as part of a general strike for greater social equality with metropolitan France. There was a further two-day strike in mid-December involving some 200 union members.

In early October 2005 it was reported that around 3,000 people participated in a protest march in Mamoudzou against illegal immigration. In early November a French parliamentary commission—which included Kamardine—was convened to report on the state of illegal immigration in Mayotte. The commission's first report, which was published in mid-February 2006, found that there were between 45,000 and 60,000 illegal immigrants living in Mayotte, of whom 90% were Comoran. (According to the census of 2002 the official French population numbered 160,265.) The number of births on the island had risen by more than 50% over a 10-year period, reaching 7,676 in 2004, of which some two-thirds were to women lacking official documentation. The report also detailed that between 10,000 and 15,000 immigrants were employed in the unofficial economy with the complicity of the Mahoris populace. The report proposed closer co-operation with the Comoran authorities. Recommendations to stem the flow of immigrants included, *inter alia*, the introduction of biometric identity cards in Mayotte and the Comoros; the construction of a maternity clinic on the Comoran island of Nzwani; and increasing the number of border police. The French Ministry of the Interior targeted the expulsion of 12,000 illegal immigrants from Mayotte in 2006; the number expelled in 2005 was more than 4,500. A boat service was to be re-established between Mayotte and Nzwani to assist with the deportation process. According to the Observatoire de l'Emigration Clandestine Anjouanaise, based in Mayotte, some 200 people die each year attempting illegally to enter Mayotte.

In February 2007 Vincent Bouvier replaced Kihl as Prefect and, although that position was scheduled to be abolished in 2007, in January 2008 Bouvier remained in the post.

Nicolas Sarkozy of the UMP secured 30.5% of the votes cast on Mayotte in the first round of the French presidential election, held on 22 April 2007. However, in the second round, which took place on 6 May, Ségolène Royal of the PS won 60.0% of the votes cast, although Sarkozy was elected to the presidency. At elections to the Assemblée nationale, held on 10 and 17 June, Kamardine was defeated by Abdoulatifou Aly, who was affiliated to the Mouvement Démocrate (MoDem), which had been formed following the presidential election by François Bayrou, the leader of the UDF, to oppose Sarkozy's UMP.

(For further details of the recent history of the island, see the chapter on the Comoros.)

Government

The French Government is represented in Mayotte by an appointed Prefect. There is a Conseil général, with 19 members, elected by universal adult suffrage. Mayotte elects one deputy to the Assemblée nationale, and one representative to the Sénat. Mayotte is also represented at the European Parliament. Under the terms of its status as a Collectivité départementale, which was approved by the French Parliament in July 2001, executive power in Mayotte was transferred from the Prefect to the Conseil général in April 2004; the position of Prefect was scheduled to be dissolved by 2007, although by early 2008 this had yet to be implemented.

Defence

As assessed at November 2007, there were 1,000 French troops stationed in Mayotte and Réunion.

Economic Affairs

Mayotte's gross domestic product (GDP) per head in 2001 was €3,960, according to official figures. Between the censuses of 2002 and 2007 the population of Mayotte increased at an average annual rate of 3.1%.

The economy is based mainly on agriculture. In 2002 10.2% of the employed labour force were engaged in this sector. The principal export crops are ylang ylang (an ingredient of perfume) and vanilla. Mayotte imports large quantities of foodstuffs, which comprised 20.4% of the value of total imports in 2005. In 2003 it was estimated that some 44% of the population was dependent on *gratte* (subsistence) farming. Cassava, maize and pigeon peas are cultivated for domestic consumption; while rice is widely eaten there is little domestic production. More than 90% of farms grow bananas, often mixed with coconuts (grown for their milk and oil, both of which are used in cooking); together banana and coconut plantations occupy some 45% of agricultural land (approximately 20,000 ha in total, some 55% of the surface area of Mayotte). Mangoes are also widespread, and around one-third of mango trees grow wild. Livestock-rearing (of cattle, goats—for meat—and chickens) and fishing are also important activities. Aquaculture was first introduced in 1998 and in 2005 there were five producers catering mainly to the export market.

Industry (which is dominated by the construction sector) engaged 23.0% of the employed population in 2002. There are no mineral resources on the island. Imports of mineral products comprised 14.8% of the value of total imports in 2005 and base metals and metal products comprised 7.0%.

Services engaged 66.8% of the employed population in 2002. The annual number of tourist arrivals (excluding cruise-ship passengers) totalled 31,136 in 2006; receipts from tourism in that year amounted to €16.3m.

In 2006 Mayotte recorded a trade deficit of €284.6m. The principal export in 2005 was ylang ylang; exports of fish were also significant. No export sales of vanilla were made in 2005 owing to global oversupply. The principal imports in that year were foodstuffs, mineral products, machinery and appliances, transport equipment, chemical products and base metals and metal products. The principal source of imports in 2003 was France (55.1%). France was also the principal market for exports (taking 61.4% of exports in that year);

the other significant purchaser was the Comoros (25.0%). Both countries remained the most important export markets in 2005.

In 2005 Mayotte's total budgetary revenue was €269.4, while total expenditure was €252.0m. A budget amounting to €320m. was proposed for 2006. Mayotte recorded deflation of 0.5% in the year to December 2005. Some 30% of the labour force was unemployed in 2003.

Mayotte suffers from a persistently high trade deficit, owing to its reliance on imports, and is largely dependent on French aid. Total French state expenditure in 2005 was €324.3m. From the late 1980s the French Government granted substantial aid to finance a number of construction projects, in an attempt to encourage the development of tourism on the island. Mayotte's remote location, however, continued to prove an impediment to the development of the tourist sector. A five-year Development Plan (1986–91) included measures to improve infrastructure and to increase investment in public works; the Plan was subsequently extended to the end of 1993. In 1995 Mayotte received credit from France to finance further investment in infrastructure, particularly in the road network. As Mayotte's labour force has continued to increase (mostly owing to a high birth rate and the continued arrival of immigrants—see Recent History, above), youth unemployment has caused particular concern. In 1997 37.8% of the unemployed population were under 25 years of age. However, local farmers expressed concern in late 2005 following renewed efforts to bring illegal immigration under control. Many were reliant on 'unofficial' labourers to carry out manual work that local Mahoris refused to accept; the lack of fruit-pickers was already driving up the price of bananas. There were also shortages of fish on the local market as fishermen from Nzwani were no longer allowed to unload their cargo in Mayotte. There were calls for the situation of illegal immigrant workers to be regularized. Meanwhile, development of transport infrastructure remains a priority and projects included the expansion and modernization of the airport at Pamandzi, the construction of a second quay at the port of Longoni and work to improve rural roads.

Education

Education is compulsory for children aged six to 15 years, and comprises five years' primary and five years' secondary schooling. In 2005 there were 113 primary schools on the island. In the same year there were 24 secondary schools, comprising 16 collèges (junior comprehensives) and 8 vocational and technical lycées. Some 10,651 pre-primary school pupils, 31,164 primary school pupils and 14,569 secondary school pupils were enrolled during the same period. A further 6,298 students were enrolled at vocational and technical institutions. There were 2,169 primary school teachers and 1,419 secondary school teachers.

Public Holidays

The principal holidays of metropolitan France are observed.

Statistical Survey

Source (unless otherwise indicated): Institut National de la Statistique et des Etudes Economiques de Mayotte; Z.I. Kawéni, BP 1362, 97600 Mamoudzou; tel. 269-61-36-35; fax 269-61-39-56; e-mail antenne-mayotte@insee.fr; internet www.insee.fr/mayotte.

AREA AND POPULATION

Area: 374 sq km (144 sq miles).

Population: 160,265 at census of 30 July 2002; 186,452 at census of 31 July 2007.

Density (at 2007 census): 498.5 per sq km.

Population by Country of Origin (2002, before adjustment for double counting): Mayotte 103,705; France 6,323; Comoros 45,057; Madagascar-Mauritius-Seychelles 4,601; Total (incl. others) 160,301.

Principal Towns (population of communes at 2007 census): Mamoudzou 53,022; Koungou 19,831; Dzaoudzi (capital) 15,339; Dembeni 10,141.

Births and Deaths (2004): Registered live births 7,452 (birth rate 39.0 per 1,000); Registered deaths 513 (death rate 3.0 per 1,000).

Expectation of Life (years at birth): 74.5 (males 72.0; females 76.0) in 2004.

Economically Active Population (persons aged 15 years and over, census of 30 July 2002): Agriculture and fishing 3,229; Electricity, gas and water 519; Industry 1,105; Construction 5,614; Wholesale and retail trade 5,435; Transport and telecommunications 2,007; Other marketable services 852; Finance and insurance 145; Other non-marketable services 12,608; *Total employed* 31,514 (males 22,182, females 9,332); Unemployed 13,044 (males 5,179, females 7,865); *Total labour force* 44,558 (males 27,361, females 17,197). *December 2005:* Unemployed 12,920.

HEALTH AND WELFARE
Key Indicators

Total Fertility Rate (children per woman, 2004): 4.5.

Physicians (per 1,000 head, 1997): 0.4.

Hospital Beds (per 1,000 head, 1997): 1.4.

For definitions see explanatory note on p. vi.

AGRICULTURE, ETC.

Livestock (2003): Cattle 17,235; Goats 22,811; Chickens 80,565.

Fishing (metric tons, live weight, 2005): Capture 2,214 (Skipjack tuna 472; Yellowfin tuna 302; Tuna-like fishes 274); Aquaculture 164; *Total catch* 2,378. Source: FAO.

INDUSTRY

Electric Energy (million kWh, net production): 139 in 2004.

FINANCE

Currency and Exchange Rates: 100 cent = 1 euro. *Sterling and Dollar Equivalents* (31 December 2007): £1 sterling = €1.3609; US $1 = €0.6793; €100 = £73.48 = US $147.21. *Average Exchange Rate* (euros per US dollar): 0.8041 in 2005; 0.7971 in 2006; 0.7306 in 2007. The French franc was used until the end of February 2002. Euro notes and coins were introduced on 1 January 2002, and the euro became the sole legal tender from 18 February. Some of the figures in this Survey are still in terms of French francs.

Budget of the Collectivity (€ million, 2005): Total revenue 269.4; Total expenditure 252.0.

French State Expenditure (€ million, 2005): Direct expenditure 249.7; Indirect expenditure 73.6; Total expenditure 324.3.

Money Supply (million French francs at 31 December 1997): Currency outside banks 789; Demand deposits 266; Total money 1,055.

Cost of Living (Consumer Price Index for December; base: December 2006 = 100): 96.9 in 2004; 96.4 in 2005; 105.0 in 2007.

Expenditure on the Gross Domestic Product (€ million, 2001, provisional estimates): Government final consumption expenditure 288; Private final consumption expenditure 357; Gross fixed capital formation 151; *Total domestic expenditure* 796; Exports of goods and services 11; *Less* Imports of goods and services 183; *GDP in purchasers' values* 624. Note: Recorded accounts are not available; figures represent the findings of the working group (Comptes Economiques Rapides sur l'Outre-Mer—CEROM) set up to find a methodology to produce reliable GDP estimates.

EXTERNAL TRADE

Principal Commodities (€ million, 2005): *Imports c.i.f.:* Foodstuffs 55.9; Mineral products 40.5; Chemical products 19.5; Plastic materials and rubber 8.2; Base metals and metal products 19.2; Machinery and appliances 36.4; Transport equipment 30.7; Total (incl. others) 274.3. *Exports f.o.b.* (incl. re-exported goods): Foodstuffs 1.0; Chemical products 0.8 (Ylang-ylang 0.5); Plastic materials and rubber 0.8; Base metals and metal products 0.2; Machinery and appliances 1.2; Transport equipment 1.4; Total (incl. others) 5.2. *2006:* Total imports 290.4; Total exports 5.8.

Principal Trading Partners (€ million, 2005): *Imports:* Brazil 7.8; China, People's Republic 11.6; France 135.1; South Africa 7.9; Thailand 7.7; Total (incl. others) 274.3. *Exports:* France 2.2; Comoros 1.9; Réunion 0.8; Total (incl. others) 5.2.

TRANSPORT

Road Traffic (1998): Motor vehicles in use 8,213.

Shipping (2006 unless otherwise indicated): *Maritime Traffic* Vessel movements 530 (2005); Goods unloaded 390,954 metric tons; Goods loaded 66,278 metric tons; Passengers 23,437 (arrivals 7,697, departures 15,740). *Barges* (2002): Passengers 11,845; Light vehicles 532. *Cruise Ships* (2005): Vessel movements 36; Passengers 6,857.

Civil Aviation (2006 unless otherwise indicated): *Passengers Carried:* 209,770, (arrivals 99,024, departures 110,746); *Freight Carried:* 1,312 metric tons; *Post Carried* (2005): 308 metric tons.

TOURISM

Foreign Tourist Arrivals (excluding cruise-ship passengers): 32,191 in 2004; 38,763 in 2005; 31,136 in 2006.

FRENCH OVERSEAS POSSESSIONS   *Mayotte*

Foreign Tourist Arrivals by Country of Residence (2005): France (metropolitan) 11,074; Réunion 22,803; Total (incl. others) 38,763.

Tourism Receipts (€ million): 13.7 in 2004; 14.5 in 2005; 16.3 in 2006.

COMMUNICATIONS MEDIA

Telephones ('000 main lines in use, 2005, estimate): 10.0.

Mobile Cellular Telephones ('000 subscribers, 2005, estimate): 48.1.

Internet Users ('000, 2000): 1.8.

Source: International Telecommunication Union.

EDUCATION

Pre-primary (2005): 67 schools; 10,651 pupils.

Primary (2005): 113 schools; 31,164 pupils.

General Secondary (2005): 16 schools; 14,569 pupils.

Vocational and Technical (2005): 8 institutions; 6,298 students.

Students Studying in France or Réunion (2005): Secondary 2,293; Higher 2,345; Total 4,638.

Teaching Staff (2005): Primary 2,169; Secondary 1,419.

Directory

The Constitution

Mayotte has an elected General Council (Conseil général), comprising 19 members, which assists the Prefect in the administration of the island. Under the status of Collectivité départementale, which was adopted by the French Parliament in July 2001, executive power was transferred from the Prefect to the President of the Conseil général in April 2004, and the position of Prefect was to be dissolved by 2007, although by early 2008 this had yet to be implemented.

The Government
(January 2008)

Prefect: VINCENT BOUVIER.

Secretary-General: CHRISTOPHE PEYREL.

Deputy to the French National Assembly: ABDOULATIFOU ALY (MoDem).

Representatives to the French Senate: ADRIEN GIRAUD (MDM, Union Centriste), SOIBAHADDINE IBRAHIM RAMADANI (UMP).

Economic and Social Adviser: ANZIZA MOUSTOIFA.

GOVERNMENT DEPARTMENTS

Office of the Prefect: BP 676, Kawéni, 97600 Mamoudzou; tel. 269-63-50-00; fax 269-60-18-89; internet www.mayotte.pref.gouv.fr.

Department of Agriculture and Forestry: 15 rue Mariazé, BP 103, 97600 Mamoudzou; tel. 269-61-12-13; fax 269-61-10-31; e-mail daf976@agriculture.gouv.fr.

Department of Education: BP 76, 97600 Mamoudzou; tel. 269-61-10-24; fax 269-61-09-87; e-mail vice-rectorat@ac-mayotte.fr; internet www.ac-mayotte.fr.

Department of Health and Social Security: rue de l'Hôpital, BP 104, 97600 Mamoudzou; tel. 269-61-12-25; fax 269-60-19-56.

Department of Public Works: rue Mariazé, BP 109, 97600 Mamoudzou; tel. 269-61-12-54; fax 269-60-92-85; e-mail de-mayotte@equipement.gouv.fr.

Department of Work, Employment and Training: pl. Mariazé, BP 174, 97600 Mamoudzou; tel. 269-61-16-57; fax 269-61-03-37.

Department of Youth and Sports: rue Mariazé, BP 94, 97600 Mamoudzou; tel. 269-61-10-87; fax 269-61-01-26.

Conseil général
108 rue de l'Hôpital, BP 101, 97600 Mamoudzou; tel. 269-61-12-33; fax 269-61-10-18.

The Conseil général comprises 19 members. At elections held on 21 and 28 March 2004, the Union pour un Mouvement Populaire (UMP) won eight seats in alliance with the Mouvement Populaire Mahorais (MPM), which secured one seat, while the Mouvement Départementaliste Mahorais (MDM) and the Mouvement des Citoyens (MDC), also in alliance, obtained five and two seats, respectively; independent candidates were elected to the remaining three seats.

President: SAÏD OMAR ALI (Independent).

Political Organizations

Fédération de Mayotte de l'Union pour un Mouvement Populaire (UMP): route nationale, Immeuble 'Jardin Créole', 97600 Mamoudzou; tel. 269-61-64-64; fax 269-60-87-89; e-mail ahamed.attoumani@wanadoo.fr; centre-right; local branch of the metropolitan party; Sec.-Gen. MANSOUR KAMARDINE; Departmental Sec. AHAMED ATTOUMANI.

Fédération du Front National: route nationale 1, M'tsahara, 97630 M'tzamboro; BP 1331, 97600 Mamoudzou Cédex; tel. and fax 269-60-50-24; e-mail fatna@frontnational.com; Regional Sec. HUGUETTE FATNA.

Fédération du Mouvement National Républicain (MNR) de Mayotte: 15 rue des Réfugiers, 97615 Pamandzi; tel. and fax 269-60-33-21; Departmental Sec. ABDOU MIHIDJAY.

Mouvement de la Gauche Ecologiste de Mayotte: 33 ave des Jardins, Localité de Pamandzi, 97600 Pamandzi; tel. and fax 269-61-09-70; internet www.lesverts.fr; fmrly Les Verts Mayotte; affiliated to Mouvement de la Gauche Réunionnaise; Gen. Sec. AHAMADA SALIME.

Mouvement Départementaliste Mahorais (MDM): 97610 Dzaoudzi; f. 1999 by fmr mems of the MPM; seeks full overseas departmental status for Mayotte; Pres. ZOUBERT ADINANI.

Mouvement des Citoyens (MDC): Chirongui; Leader ALI HALIFA.

Mouvement Populaire Mahorais (MPM): 97610 Dzaoudzi; seeks departmental status for Mayotte; Leader YOUNOUSSA BAMANA.

Parti Socialiste (PS): Dzaoudzi; local branch of the metropolitan party; Fed. Sec. AHMADA FAHARDINE.

Judicial System

Palais de Justice: Immeuble Espace, BP 106 (Kawéni), 97600 Mamoudzou; tel. 269-61-11-15; fax 269-61-19-63.

Tribunal Supérieur d'Appel
16 rue de l'Hôpital, BP 106, 97600 Mamoudzou; tel. 269-61-11-15; fax 269-61-19-63; Pres. JEAN-BAPTISTE FLORI; Prosecutor JEAN-LOUIS BEC.

Procureur de la République: JEAN-LOUIS BEC.

Tribunal de Première Instance: Pres. ALAIN CHATEAUNEUF.

Religion

Muslims comprise about 98% of the population. Most of the remainder are Christians, mainly Roman Catholics.

CHRISTIANITY

The Roman Catholic Church

Mayotte is within the jurisdiction of the Apostolic Administrator of the Comoros.

Office of the Apostolic Administrator: BP 1012, 97600 Mamoudzou; tel. and fax 269-61-11-53.

The Press

Flash Infos Mayotte: BP 60, 97600 Mamoudzou; tel. 269-61-54-45; fax 269-61-54-47; e-mail flash-infos@wanadoo.fr; internet www.mayottehebdo.com; f. 1999; owned by Somapresse; daily e-mail bulletin; Dir LAURENT CANAVATE.

Le Mahorais: 15 Lot. Bamcolo, Majicavo, 97600 Mamoudzou; tel. 269-61-66-75; fax 269-61-66-72; weekly; French; Publ. Dir SAMUEL BOSHER; Editor-in-Chief CHLOÉ REMONDIÈRE.

Le Mawana: BP 252, Z.I. Kawéni, 97600 Mamoudzou; tel. 269-61-73-84; internet www.lemawana.fr; f. 2005; weekly; French; Publ. Dir MADI ABDOU N'TRO.

Mayotte Hebdo: BP 60, 97600 Mamoudzou; tel. 269-61-20-04; fax 269-60-35-90; e-mail mayotte.hebdo@wanadoo.fr; internet www.mayottehebdo.com; f. 2000; weekly; French; incl. the economic supplement *Mayotte Eco* and cultural supplement *Tounda* (weekly); Dir LAURENT CANAVATE; circ. 2,000.

Zan'Goma: Impasse du Jardin Fleuri, Cavani, 97600 Mamoudzou; f. 2005; monthly; French; Publ. Dir MONCEF MOUHOUDHOIRE.

Broadcasting and Communications

TELECOMMUNICATIONS

France Télécom Mayotte: Résidence Allamanda, rue de la Grande Traversée, 97600 Mamoudzou; tel. 269-61-00-14; fax 269-61-19-02; e-mail richard.roques@francetelecom.com.

Mayotte Télécom Mobile: mobile cellular telephone operator; local operation of Société Réunionnaise du Radiotéléphone based in Réunion.

RADIO AND TELEVISION

Réseau France Outre-mer (RFO): 1 rue du Jardin, BP 103, 97615 Pamandzi; tel. 269-60-10-17; fax 269-60-16-06; e-mail annick.henry@rfo.fr; internet www.rfo.fr; f. 1977; acquired by Groupe France Télévisions in 2004; fmrly Société Nationale de Radio-Télévision Française d'Outre-mer; radio broadcasts in French and more than 70% in Mahorian; television transmissions began in 1986; a satellite service was launched in 2000; Gen. Man. FRANÇOIS GUILBEAU; Regional Dir JEAN-FRANÇOIS MOENNAN.

Finance

(br(s). = branch(es))

BANKS

Issuing Authority

Institut d'Emission d'Outre-mer: ave de la Préfecture, BP 500, 97600 Mamoudzou; tel. 269-61-05-05; fax 269-61-05-02; Dir MAX REMBLIN.

Commercial Banks

Banque Française Commerciale Océan Indien: pl. du Marché, BP 222, 97600 Mamoudzou; tel. 269-61-10-91; fax 269-61-17-40; e-mail mayotte@bfcoi.com; internet www.bfcoi.com; f. 1976; jtly owned by Société Générale and Mauritius Commercial Bank Ltd; Pres. GÉRALD LACAZE; Dir-Gen. JEAN-MARIE D'ESPAGNAC; br. at Dzaoudzi.

Banque de la Réunion: 30 pl. Mariage, 97600 Mamoudzou; tel. 269-61-20-30; fax 269-61-20-28; 3 brs.

BRED Banque Populaire: Centre d'Affaires Mayotte, pl. Mariage, Z.I. 3, 97600 Mamoudzou; tel. 269-90-71-60; fax 269-90-29-57.

INSURANCE

AGF: pl. Mariage, BP 184, 97600 Mamoudzou; tel. 269-61-44-33; fax 269-61-14-89; e-mail jl.henry@wanadoo.fr; Gen. Man. JEAN-LUC HENRY.

Groupama: BP 665, Z.I. Nel, Lot 7, 97600 Mamoudzou; tel. 269-62-59-92; fax 269-60-76-08.

Prudence Créole: Immeuble Sana, rue du Commerce, BP 480, 97600 Mamoudzou; tel. 269-61-11-10; fax 269-61-11-21; e-mail prudencecreolemayotte@wanadoo.fr; 87% owned by Groupe Générali; 2 brs.

Vectra Paic Océan Indien: BP 65, 55 champs des Ylangs, 97680 Combani; tel. 269-62-44-54; fax 269-62-46-97; e-mail cfonteneau@wanadoo.fr.

Trade and Industry

DEVELOPMENT ORGANIZATION

Agence Française de Développement (AFD): ave de la Préfecture, BP 500, 97600 Mamoudzou; tel. 269-61-05-05; fax 269-61-05-02; internet www.afd.fr; Dir JEAN-FRANÇOIS HOARAU.

EMPLOYERS' ORGANIZATIONS

Mouvement des Entreprises de France Mayotte (MEDEF): Z.I. Kawéni, Immeuble GMOI, BP 570, 97600 Mamoudzou; tel. 269-61-44-22; fax 269-61-46-10; e-mail contact@medef-mayotte.com; internet www.medef-mayotte.com; Pres. SERGE CASTEL.

Ordre National des Médecins: BP 675 Kawéni, 97600 Mamoudzou; tel. 269-61-02-47; fax 269-61-36-61.

UTILITIES

Electricity

Electricité de Mayotte (EDM): BP 333, Z.I. Kawéni, 97600 Kawéni; tel. 269-61-44-44; fax 269-60-10-92; e-mail edm.mayotte@wanadoo.fr; f. 1997; subsidiary of SAUR.

Water

Syndicat des Eaux: BP 289, 97600 Mamoudzou; tel. 269-62-11-11; fax 269-62-10-31.

TRADE UNIONS

Confédération Inter-Syndicale de Mayotte (CISMA-CFDT): 18 rue Mahabou, BP 1038, 97600 Mamoudzou; tel. 269-61-12-38; fax 269-61-36-16; f. 1993; affiliated to the Confédération Française Démocratique du Travail; Gen. Sec. SAÏD BOINALI.

Affiliated unions incl.:

ScDEN-CGT: BP 793 Kawéni, 97600 Mamoudzou; tel. and fax 269-61-10-97; e-mail scdencgt.mayotte@free.fr; internet cgtprofsmayotte.free.fr; affiliated to the Confédération Générale du Travail; represents teaching staff; Sec.-Gen. NOEL JEGOU.

SGEN-CFDT: c/o CISMA, 18 rue Mahabou, BP 1038, 97600 Mamoudzou; tel. 269-61-12-38; fax 269-61-18-09; e-mail mayotte@sgen.cfdt.fr; internet etranger.sgen-cfdt.org/mayotte/sgenmayo.htm; affiliated to the Fédération des Syndicats Généraux de l'Education Nationale et de la Recherche; represents teaching staff; Sec.-Gen. FRANÇOISE HOLZAPFEL.

Fédération Départementale des Syndicats d'Exploitants Agricoles de Mayotte (FDSEAM): 150 rue Mbalamanga-Mtsapéré, 97600 Mamoudzou; tel. and fax 269-61-34-83; e-mail fdsea.mayotte@wanadoo.fr; affiliated to la Fédération Nationale des Syndicats d'Exploitants; Pres. AMBODY ALI; Dir MOUHTAR RACHIDE.

SNES Mayotte (SNES-FSU): 12 Résidence Bellecombe, 110 Lotissement Les Trois Vallées, Majicavo, 97600 Mamoudzou; tel. 269-62-50-58; fax 269-62-53-39; e-mail mayotte@snes.edu; internet www.mayotte.snes.edu; affiliated to le Syndicat National des Enseignements de Second Degré; represents teaching staff in secondary education; Sec. FRÉDÉRIC LOUVIER.

Union Départementale Force Ouvrière de Mayotte (FO): 20, rue Mahabou, BP 1109, 97600 Mamoudzou; tel. 269-61-18-39; fax 269-61-22-45; e-mail el.hadi@wanadoo.fr; Sec. Gen. EL HADI SOUMAILA.

Transport

ROADS

In 1998 the road network totalled approximately 230 km, of which 90 km were main roads.

SHIPPING

Coastal shipping is provided by locally owned small craft. There is a deep-water port at Longoni. Construction of a second quay at Longoni was proposed under the 2006 budget.

Service des Affaires Maritimes Mayotte: BP 37, 97615 Pamandzi; tel. 269-60-31-38; fax 269-60-31-39; e-mail sam-mayotte@equipement.gouv.fr; Head of Service MATTHIEU LE GUERN.

Service des Transports Maritimes (STM): BP 186, 97610 Dzaoudzi; tel. 269-60-10-69; fax 269-60-80-25; internet www.mayotte-stm.com; Dir MICHEL KERAMBRUN; 8 vessels.

CIVIL AVIATION

There is an airport at Dzaoudzi, serving daily commercial flights to the Comoros; four-times weekly flights to Réunion; twice-weekly services to Madagascar; and weekly services to Kenya and Mozambique. In January 2004 plans were approved for the construction a new runway to allow the commencement of direct flights to Paris, France. The proposed establishment of Air Mayotte International was abandoned in September 2004. Expansion and modernization of the airport at Pamandzi was envisaged under the 2006 budget.

Air Austral: pl. Mariage, BP 1429, 97600 Mamoudzou; tel. 269-60-90-90; fax 269-61-61-94; e-mail mayotte@air-austral.com; internet www.air-austral.com; Pres. GÉRARD ETHÈVE.

Tourism

Tropical scenery provides the main tourist attraction. Excluding cruise-ship passengers, Mayotte received 31,136 visitors in 2006; tourism receipts totalled €16.3m. in that year. In 2002 there were nine hotels with some 350 rooms.

Comité du Tourisme de Mayotte: rue de la Pompe, BP 1169, 97600 Mamoudzou; tel. 269-61-09-09; fax 269-61-03-46; e-mail contact@mayotte-tourisme.com; internet www.mayotte-tourisme.com; Dir GEORGE MECS.

SAINT-BARTHÉLEMY

Saint-Barthélemy is one of the Leeward Islands in the Lesser Antilles. The volcanic island lies in the Caribbean Sea, 230 km north-west of Guadeloupe and 20 km south-east of Saint-Martin. St-Barthélemy occupies only 21 sq km, but has green-clad volcanic hillsides, as well as white beaches and surrounding reefs and islets. The climate is tropical, moderated by the sea, with an annual average temperature of 27.5°C (81°F) and a more humid and wet season between May and November. The island normally receives about 1,100 mm (43 ins) of rain annually. Saint-Barthélemy has a permanent population of little more than 5,000, which is predominantly white, inhabited by people of Breton, Norman and Poitevin descent. There are fewer descendants of the Swedish, who ruled Saint-Barthélemy for almost one century (until a referendum in 1878). French is the official language, but English and two Creole patois are widely spoken. A Norman dialect of French is also still sometimes in use. The majority of the population profess Christianity, and belong to the Roman Catholic Church. The principal town is Gustavia, its main port, in the south-west.

On 7 December 2003 the Guadeloupean dependency of Saint-Barthélemy participated in a Department-wide referendum on Guadeloupe's future constitutional relationship with France. Although the proposal to streamline administrative and political processes was defeated, an overwhelming majority of those participating in Saint-Barthélemy, 95.5%, voted in favour of secession from Guadeloupe to form a separate Overseas Collectivity (Collectivité d'outre-mer). The reorganization was subsequently approved by the French Sénat on 6 February 2007 and by the Assemblée nationale the following day. Two weeks later, on 21 February, the island was formally designated an Overseas Collectivity.

Legislative elections to form a 19-member legislative assembly, to be known as the Conseil territorial (Territorial Council), were held in July 2007. At the first round of elections, held on 1 July, the Saint-Barth d'abord/Union pour un Mouvement Populaire (Saint-Barth d'abord/UMP) list, headed by Bruno Magras, won a clear majority of 72.2% of total votes cast, thereby obviating the need for a second round. The election was also contested by three other groupings: the Tous unis pour St-Barthélémy list, lead by Karine Miot-Richard, the Action Equilibre et Transparence list headed by Maxime Desouches—each of which secured 9.9% of the ballot—and Benoît Chauvin's Ensemble pour St-Barthélémy, which attracted the remining 7.9% of votes cast. Some 70.6% of the electorate exercised their right to vote. The Saint-Barth d'abord/UMP list obtained 16 of the 19 legislative seats, while the three other contenders were allocated one seat each. On 15 July Magras assumed the presidency of the Territorial Council and Saint-Barthélemy was officially installed as an Overseas Collectivity. Pending the election of one representative to the French Sénat (in 2008) and one deputy to the Assemblée nationale (in 2012), the territory was to continue to be represented by the Guadeloupean delegates.

Conseil Territorial
Gustavia.

President: BRUNO MAGRAS (Saint-Barth d'abord/UMP).

Election, 1 July 2007

	Seats
Saint-Barth d'abord/Union pour un Mouvement Populaire	16
Tous unis pour St-Barthélémy	1
Action Equilibre et Transparence	1
Ensemble pour St-Barthélémy	1
Total	**19**

SAINT-MARTIN

The French Overseas Collectivity (Collectivité d'outre-mer) of Saint-Martin forms the northern half of the island of Saint Martin (the remainder, St (Sint) Maarten, being part of the Netherlands Antilles). The small volcanic island lies among the Leeward group of the Lesser Antilles in the Caribbean Sea, 265 km north-west of Guadeloupe. The 10.2-km border between the French and the Dutch regions of the island is the only land frontier in the Lesser Antilles and makes Saint Martin the smallest island in the world to be divided. Saint-Martin occupies about 60% of the island (52 sq km or 20 sq miles). In terms of international neighbours, Saint-Martin is only 8 km south of the British Overseas Territory of Anguilla. The climate is tropical and moderated by the sea. Saint-Martin normally receives about 1,000 mm (43 ins) of rain annually. Saint-Martin has a population of about 30,000. French is the official language, but a Créole patois is widely spoken, as well as English, Dutch and Spanish. The majority of the population profess Christianity, and belong to the Roman Catholic Church. The principal town is Marigot, in the south-west of the territory, on the north coast of the island, between the sea and the Simpson's Bay Lagoon.

On 7 December 2003 the Guadeloupean dependency of Saint-Martin participated in a Department-wide referendum on Guadeloupe's future constitutional relationship with France. Although the proposal to streamline administrative and political processes was defeated, a majority of those participating in Saint-Martin, 76.2%, elected to secede from Guadeloupe to form a separate Overseas Collectivity. The reorganization was subsequently approved by the French Sénat on 6 February 2007 and by the Assemblée nationale the following day. Two weeks later, on 21 February, the territory Saint-Martin was formally designated an Overseas Collectivity.

Legislative elections to form a 23-member legislative assembly to be known as the Conseil territorial (Territorial Council) were held in July 2007. At the first round ballot, held on 1 July, the Union pour le Progrès/Union pour un Mouvement Populaire (UPP/UMP) list, headed by Louis Constant Fleming, won 40.4% of total votes cast, while the Rassemblement, responsabilité et réussite (RRR) list, lead by Alain Richardson, secured 31.9%, and Jean-Luc Hamlet's Réussir Saint-Martin obtained 10.9% of the vote. The Alliance list, headed by Dominque Riboud, received 9.1% and Wendel Cocks' Alliance démocratique pour Saint-Martin attracted the remining 7.8% of the ballot. Some 46.4% of the electorate exercised their right to vote. As no list emerged with an absolute majority, a further round of voting was contested by the three parties that had secured more than 10% of the vote. At this second round, held on 8 July, the UPP/UMP list won 49.0% of the vote and obtained 16 of the 23 legislative seats, the RRR received 42.2% of the vote (six seats), and Réussir Saint-Martin 8.9% (one seat). Voter participation was slightly higher, at 50.8%. Fleming assumed the presidency of the Conseil territorial on 15 July and Saint-Martin was officially installed as an Overseas Collectivity. Pending the election of one representative to the French Sénat (in 2008) and one deputy to the Assemblée nationale (in 2012), the territory was to continue to be represented by the Guadeloupean delegates.

Conseil Territorial
Marigot.

President: LOUIS CONSTANT FLEMING (UPP/UMP).

Elections, 1 and 8 July 2007

	Seats
Union pour le Progrès/Union pour un Mouvement Populaire (UPP/UMP)	16
Rassemblement, responsabilité et réussite	6
Réussir Saint-Martin	1
Total	**23**

Two other lists contested the elections: Alliance, and Alliance démocratique pour Saint-Martin.

SAINT PIERRE AND MIQUELON

Introductory Survey

Location, Climate, Language, Religion, Capital

The territory of Saint Pierre and Miquelon (Iles Saint-Pierre-et-Miquelon) consists of a number of small islands which lie about 25 km (16 miles) from the southern coast of Newfoundland and Labrador, Canada, in the North Atlantic Ocean. The principal islands are Saint Pierre, Miquelon (Grande Miquelon) and Langlade (Petite Miquelon)—the last two being linked by an isthmus of sand. Winters are cold, with temperatures falling to −20°C (−4°F), and summers are mild, with temperatures averaging between 10° and 20°C (50° and 68°F). The islands are particularly affected by fog in June and July. The language is French, and the majority of the population profess Christianity and belong to the Roman Catholic Church. The capital is Saint-Pierre, on the island of Saint Pierre.

Recent History

The islands of Saint Pierre and Miquelon are the remnants of the once extensive French possessions in North America. They were confirmed as French territory in 1815, and gained departmental status in July 1976. The departmentalization proved unpopular with many of the islanders, since it incorporated the territory's economy into that of the European Community (EC, now European Union, see p. 244—EU), and was regarded as failing to take into account the islands' isolation and dependence on Canada for supplies and transport links. In March 1982 socialist and other left-wing candidates, campaigning for a change in the islands' status, were elected unopposed to all seats in the Conseil général (General Council). Saint Pierre and Miquelon was excluded from the Mitterrand administration's decentralization reforms, undertaken in 1982.

In 1976 Canada imposed an economic interest zone extending to 200 nautical miles (370 km) around its shores. Fearing the loss of traditional fishing areas and thus the loss of the livelihood of the fishermen of Saint Pierre, the French Government claimed a similar zone around the islands. Hopes of discovering valuable reserves of petroleum and natural gas in the area heightened the tension between France and Canada.

In December 1984 legislation was approved giving the islands the status of a Territorial Collectivity (collectivité territoriale) with effect from 11 June 1985. This was intended to allow Saint Pierre and Miquelon to receive the investment and development aid suitable for its position, while allaying Canada's fears of EC exploitation of its offshore waters. Local representatives, however, remained apprehensive about the outcome of negotiations between the French and Canadian Governments to settle the dispute over coastal limits. (France continued to claim a 200-mile fishing and economic zone around Saint Pierre and Miquelon, while Canada wanted the islands to have only a 12-mile zone.) The dispute was submitted to international arbitration. Discussions began in March 1987, and negotiations to determine quotas for France's catch of Atlantic cod over the period 1988–91 were to take place simultaneously. In the mean time, Canada and France agreed on an interim fishing accord, which would allow France to increase its cod quota. The discussions collapsed in October, however, and French trawlers were prohibited from fishing in Canadian waters. In February 1988 Albert Pen and Gérard Grignon, Saint Pierre's elected representatives to the French legislature, together with two members of the Saint Pierre administration and 17 sailors, were arrested for fishing in Canadian waters. This episode, and the arrest of a Canadian trawler captain in May for fishing in Saint Pierre's waters, led to an unsuccessful resumption of negotiations in September. An agreement was reached on fishing rights in March 1989, whereby France's annual quotas for Atlantic cod and other species were determined for the period until the end of 1991. At the same time the Governments agreed upon the composition of an international arbitration tribunal which would delineate the disputed maritime boundaries and exclusive economic zones.

In July 1991 the international arbitration tribunal began its deliberations in New York, USA. The tribunal's ruling, issued in June 1992, was generally deemed to be favourable to Canada. France was allocated an exclusive economic zone around the territory totalling 2,537 square nautical miles (8,700 sq km), compared with its demand for more than 13,000 square nautical miles. The French authorities claimed that the sea area granted would be insufficient to sustain the islands' fishing community. Talks on new fishing quotas for the area off Newfoundland (known as Newfoundland and Labrador from December 2001) failed, and, in the absence of a new agreement, industrial fishing in the area was effectively halted until November 1994, when the Governments of the two countries signed an accord specifying new quotas for a period of at least 10 years. In the following month deputies in the Assemblée nationale (National Assembly) expressed concern that the terms of the agreement would be detrimental to Saint Pierre and Miquelon's interests, although the Government asserted that the accord recognized the islanders' historic fishing rights in Canadian waters.

In September 1992 some 64% of voters approved ratification of the Treaty on European Union (see p. 244), although only a small percentage of the electorate participated in the referendum. At elections to the Sénat in September 1993, Albert Pen, representing the Parti Socialiste (PS), was narrowly defeated at a second round of voting by Victor Reux of the right-wing Rassemblement pour la République (RPR), since 1994 the Secretary of the islands' Economic and Social Council. Gérard Grignon, of the centre-right Union pour la Démocratie Française (UDF), was re-elected to the Assemblée nationale at a second round of voting in June 1997.

A number of government proposals regarding the socio-economic and institutional development of the Overseas Departments, certain provisions of which were also to be applied to Saint Pierre and Miquelon, were provisionally accepted by the Assemblée nationale in May 2000, and subsequently adopted by the Sénat (following a number of modifications). The proposals were definitively approved by the Assemblée nationale in November and were ratified by the Constitutional Council in December. Measures included provisions for improving and supporting the economic development of the islands, as well the introduction of proportional representation in elections to the Conseil général. In the June 2002 general election Grignon, representing an alliance of the Union pour la Majorité Présidentielle and the UDF, was re-elected to the Assemblée nationale, with 69% of the second-round votes.

In late March 2003, as part of a wider constitutional reform, the islands were given the status of an Overseas Collectivity (collectivité d'outre-mer). At elections to the Sénat in September 2004 the mayor of Miquelon, Denis Detcheverry, narrowly defeated the mayor of Saint-Pierre, Karine Claireaux, attracting 51.4% of the votes cast. In December Albert Dupuy replaced Claude Valleix as Prefect. In late May 2005 a national referendum was held on ratification of the European Union constitutional treaty: 62.7% of the local electorate voted in favour of adopting the treaty; however, voter turn-out was only 37.1%. The treaty was ultimately rejected by a majority of voters in metropolitan France. At elections to the Conseil général in late March 2006 Archipel Demain won 13 of Saint Pierre's 15 seats with 66.8% of the vote; the left-wing Cap sur l'Avenir (CSA) took the remaining two seats. Meanwhile, Archipel Demain Miquelon won three of the four available seats allocated to Miquelon with 60.9% of the vote; SPM Ensemble took the remaining seat. Stéphane Artano of Archipel Demain was elected President of the Conseil général. In August Dupuy was succeeded as Prefect by Yves Fauqueur.

Further provisions of the 2003 constitutional reform were effected in February 2007, following the approval by the French Sénat and the Assemblée nationale of an organic law that amended the statutes and institutions of French Overseas Possessions. The legislation redesignated the Conseil général as a Conseil territorial (Territorial Council) and granted local government wider fiscal powers and greater control over the operation of the exclusive economic zone. In the first round of the presidential election, held on 22 April, Ségolène Royal of the PS obtained 26.6% of the votes cast on the islands, ahead of Nicolas Sarkozy of the Union pour un Mouvement Populaire (UMP), who received 24.9%. Royal subsequently won 60.9% of the islands' votes in the second round, on 6 May; however, Sarkozy, who obtained 39.1%, was elected President nationally. In the second round of the elections to the Assemblée nationale on 17 June, Grignon was narrowly defeated by Annick Girardin, representing the Parti Radical de Gauche in association with CSA, who won 51.3% of votes cast.

Government

The French Government is represented in Saint Pierre by an appointed Prefect. There is a Conseil territorial (Territorial Council, known as Conseil général—General Council—until February 2007), with 19 members (15 for Saint Pierre and four for Miquelon), elected by adult universal suffrage for a period of six years. Saint Pierre and Miquelon elects one deputy to the Assemblée nationale and one representative to the Sénat in Paris.

Defence

France is responsible for the islands' defence.

Economic Affairs

The soil and climatic conditions of Saint Pierre and Miquelon do not favour agricultural production, which is mainly confined to smallholdings, except for market-gardening and the production of eggs and chickens.

The principal economic activity of the islands is traditionally fishing and related industries, which employed some 18.5% of the working population in 1996. However, the sector has been severely affected by disputes with Canada regarding territorial waters and fishing quotas. By 2005 the fishing fleet had been reduced to some 26 vessels, of which only 15 were considered to be active. New arrangements have been to the detriment of Saint Pierre and Miquelon, although there is some optimism regarding potential for the exploitation of shellfish, notably mussels and scallops; since 2000 Export Development Canada has been developing commercial scallop farms in the islands' waters. The total fish catch increased from 747 metric tons in 1996 to 6,485 tons in 2000, before falling to 3,802 tons in 2001. By 2004 the total catch had recovered to 4,311 tons, however, this subsequently declined to 3,084 tons in 2005.

Fish-processing—producing frozen and salted fish, and fish meal for fodder—provided the basis for industrial activity, employing around 100 people in 2006. Following a sharp decrease in production in the late 1980s, much of the fish processed is now imported. Electricity is generated by two thermal power-stations, with a combined capacity of 23 MW. Plans were well advanced for the construction of a wind power-station, which, it was hoped, would generate some 40% of the islands' electricity requirements. The resolution of a boundary dispute between the Canadian provinces of Nova Scotia and Newfoundland and Labrador in 2002 accorded the islands about 500 sq miles of waters over the Gulf of Saint Lawrence basin, believed to contain substantial reserves of petroleum and gas. In May 2005, following four years of negotiations, the Governments of France and Canada signed an agreement on the exploration and exploitation of 'transboundary' hydrocarbon fields. Two Canadian oil companies were given exclusive licences to explore the area until April 2006.

The replenishment of ships' (mainly trawlers') supplies was formerly an important economic activity, but has now also been adversely affected by the downturn in the industrial fishing sector. Efforts were made to promote tourism, and the opening of the Saint Pierre–Montréal air route in 1987 led to an increase in air traffic in the 1990s. In 1999 the completion of a new airport capable of accommodating larger aircraft further improved transport links. Tourist arrivals in 2001 were estimated at 14,293.

In 1997 Saint Pierre and Miquelon recorded a trade deficit of 356m. French francs. In 2005 the total value of exports was €5.4m.; the total value of imports in that year was €68.2m. Most trade is with Canada and France and other countries of the EU (see p. 244). The only significant exports are fish and fish meal. The principal imports in 2004 were motor vehicles, building supplies and food from Canada. Items such as clothing and other consumer goods are generally imported from France.

The annual rate of inflation averaged 6.0% in 1997–2005; consumer prices increased by 2.0% in 2004 and by 6.6% in 2005. Some 12.8% of the labour force were unemployed at the 1999 census. According to preliminary census figures, the rate of unemployment in 2006 was 10.0%.

Given the decline of the fishing sector, the development of the ports of Saint-Pierre and Miquelon and the expansion of tourism (particularly from Canada and the USA) are regarded locally as the principal means of maintaining economic progress. In December 2005 a report commissioned by the Sénat recommended expanding trade links with Canada. The report also identified hydrocarbon exploration as a future source of revenue, if not from direct exploitation of resources within Saint Pierre and Miquelon's own territory, then by providing services to companies operating in Canadian waters, where oil deposits were already being worked. The islands will, none the less, remain highly dependent on budgetary assistance from the French central Government. In June 2005 the French Government allocated some €1m. to Saint Pierre and Miquelon: €700,000 under the fund for overseas investment, and €300,000 from the Ministry of Agriculture and Fisheries.

Education

The education system is modelled on the French system, and education is compulsory for children between the ages of six and 16 years. In 2002 there were eight primary schools, two secondary schools (one of which is private and has a technical school annex) and one technical school. At the time of the 2006 census, 211 students of higher education were studying outside of Saint Pierre and Miquelon. Agreements with universities in New Brunswick, Newfoundland and Labrador and Nova Scotia allow students from Saint Pierre and Miquelon to enjoy the same rights as Canadian students.

Public Holidays

2008: 1 January (New Year's Day), 24 March (Easter Monday), 1 May (Labour Day and Ascension Day), 8 May (Victory Day), 12 May (Whit Monday), 14 July (National Day), 15 August (Assumption Day), 1 November (All Saints' Day), 11 November (Armistice Day), 25 December (Christmas Day).

2009: 1 January (New Year's Day), 13 April (Easter Monday), 1 May (Labour Day), 8 May (Victory Day), 21 May (Ascension Day), 1 June (Whit Monday), 14 July (National Day), 15 August (Assumption Day), 1 November (All Saints' Day), 11 November (Armistice Day), 25 December (Christmas Day).

Weights and Measures

The metric system is in use.

Statistical Survey

Source: Préfecture, pl. du Lieutenant-Colonel Pigeaud, BP 4200, 97500 Saint-Pierre; tel. 41-10-10; fax 41-47-38.

AREA AND POPULATION

Area: 242 sq km (93.4 sq miles): Saint Pierre 26 sq km, Miquelon-Langlade 216 sq km.

Population: 6,316 (males 3,147, females 3,169) at census of 8 March 1999; 6,125 (Saint Pierre 5,509, Miquelon-Langlade 616) at census of March 2006 (preliminary).

Density (2006 census): 25.3 per sq km.

Births, Marriages and Deaths (1997): Live births 92; Marriages 36; Deaths 51.

Economically Active Population (1992): Fish and fish-processing 540; Construction 333; Transport 192; Dockers 44; Trade 409; Restaurants and hotels 154; Business services 417; Government employees 727; Activities not adequately defined 106; *Total labour force* 2,922. *2006 census* (preliminary): Total employed 2,876; Registered unemployed 318; Total labour force 3,194 (males 1,751, females 1,443).

FISHING

Total Catch (all capture, metric tons, live weight, 2005): Atlantic cod 2,340; Yellowtail flounder 140; Haddock 113; Saithe (Pollock) 30; Lumpfish 71; Queen crab 157; American sea scallop 172; Total (incl. others) 3,084.

Source: FAO.

FINANCE

Currency and Exchange Rates: French currency was used until the end of 2001. Euro notes and coins were introduced on 1 January 2002, and the euro became the sole legal tender from 18 February. Some of the figures in this Survey are still in terms of French francs. For details of exchange rates, see French Guiana.

Expenditure by Metropolitan France (million francs, 1997): 280.

Budget (estimates, million francs, 1997): Expenditure 244 (current 128; capital 116).

Money Supply (million francs at 31 December 1997): Currency outside banks 281; Demand deposits at banks 897; Total money 1,178.

Cost of Living (Consumer Price Index; base: 2000 = 100): 104.8 in 2003; 106.9 in 2004; 114.0 in 2005 (Source: ILO).

EXTERNAL TRADE

Total (€ million, 2005): *Imports:* 68.2; *Exports:* 5.4 (Source: Institut d'Emission des Départements d'Outre-mer)

Note: Most trade is with Canada, France (imports), other countries of the European Union (exports) and the USA.

TRANSPORT

Road Traffic (1997): 3,876 motor vehicles in use.

Shipping (1995): Ships entered 884; Freight entered 56,363 metric tons. *1997:* Ships entered 918 (Source: Service des Douanes).

Civil Aviation (2006): Passengers carried 29,142; Freight carried 68.7 metric tons (Source: Service de l'Aviation Civile de Saint Pierre et Miquelon).

TOURISM

Tourist Arrivals (2001): 14,293 (Source: Institut d'Emission des Départements d'Outre-mer).

Tourist Arrivals by Country of Residence (2000): Canada 7,092; France 919; USA 3,185; Total (incl. others) 12,156 (Source: Service Loisirs Accueil).

COMMUNICATIONS MEDIA

Radio Receivers (estimate, '000 in use): 5.0 in 1997.

Television Receivers (estimate, '000 in use): 3.5 in 1997.

EDUCATION

Primary (2002): 8 institutions; 73 teachers; 736 students.
Secondary (2002): 2 institutions; 56 teachers; 329 students.
Technical (2002): 1 institution; 25 teachers; 134 students.

Source: Service de l'Education Nationale de Saint Pierre et Miquelon.

Note: At the time of the 2006 census, 211 students of higher education were studying outside of Saint Pierre and Miquelon.

Directory

The Government
(March 2008)

Prefect: YVES FAUQUEUR, pl. du Lieutenant-Colonel Pigeaud, BP 4200, 97500 Saint-Pierre; tel. 41-10-10; fax 41-47-38; e-mail courrier@saint-pierre-et-miquelon.pref.gouv.fr; internet www.saint-pierre-et-miquelon.pref.gouv.fr.

President of the Economic and Social Committee: MAX OLAISOLA, 4 rue Bordas, 97500 Saint-Pierre; tel. 41-45-50; fax 41-42-45; e-mail comite.ec.soc.spm@cheznoo.net; internet www.cesdefrance.fr.

Deputy to the French National Assembly: ANNICK GIRARDIN (PRG-SPM).

Representative to the French Senate: DENIS DETCHEVERRY (UMP).

Conseil Territorial

2 pl. de Monseigneur François Maurer, BP 4208, 97500 Saint-Pierre; tel. 41-01-02; fax 41-22-97; e-mail cgspm@wanadoo.fr.

The Conseil territorial (fmrly the Conseil général) has 19 mems: Saint Pierre 15, Miquelon four. As a result of elections held in late March 2006, the composition by party was as follows: Archipel Demain (incl. Archipel Demain Miquelon) 16, Cap sur l'Avenir two, SPM Ensemble one.

President: STÉPHANE ARTANO.

Political Organizations

Archipel Demain: 1 rue Amiral Muselier, BP 1179, 97500 Saint-Pierre; tel. 41-42-19; fax 41-48-06; e-mail archipel@cheznoo.net; internet www.archipeldemain.fr; f. 1985; Pres. NICOLAS GOURMELON; Sec.-Gen. GÉRARD GRIGNON; incl. Archipel Demain Miquelon (Leader CÉLINE GASPARD).

Cap sur l'Avenir (CSA): 7 rue René Autin, BP 4477, 97500 Saint-Pierre; tel. 41-99-08; fax 41-99-97; e-mail agirardin@assemblee-nationale.fr; internet www.capsurlavenir-expression.net; f. 2000; left-wing and green coalition; associated with the PRG-SPM; Pres. ANNICK GIRARDIN.

Parti Radical de Gauche SPM (PRG-SPM): 7 rue René Autin, BP 4477, 97500 Saint-Pierre; tel. 41-99-08; fax 41-99-97; local br. of the metropolitan party; associated with CSA; Pres. YANNICK CAMBRAY; Sec. TATIANA URTIZBEREA.

SMP Ensemble: c/o Mairie de Miquelon, 2 rue du Baron de l'espérance, Miquelon, 97500 Saint-Pierre; internet spmensemble.oldiblog.com; f. 2006; left-wing, independent; advocates parity between the islands of Saint-Pierre and Miquelon; STÉPHANE COSTE.

Union pour un Mouvement Populaire (UMP): 15 rue Ange Gautier, BP 113, 97500 Saint-Pierre; tel. 41-35-73; fax 41-29-97; e-mail gerardgrignon@ump975.org; centre-right; local br. of the metropolitan party; Pres., Departmental Cttee RODRIQUE GIRARDIN; Departmental Sec. GÉRARD GRIGNON.

Judicial System

Tribunal Supérieur d'Appel: 14 rue Emile Sasco, BP 4215, 97500 Saint-Pierre; tel. 41-03-20; fax 41-03-23; e-mail francois.billon@justice.fr; Presiding Magistrate CLAUDINE BULLE; Procurator HERVÉ LEROY.

Tribunal de Première Instance: 14 rue Emile Sasco, BP 4215, 97500 Saint-Pierre; tel. 41-03-20; fax 41-41-03-23; Presiding Magistrate BRUNO MARCELIN.

Religion

Almost all of the inhabitants are adherents of the Roman Catholic Church.

CHRISTIANITY
The Roman Catholic Church

The islands form the Apostolic Vicariate of the Iles Saint-Pierre et Miquelon. At 31 December 2005 there were an estimated 6,271 adherents.

Vicar Apostolic: LUCIEN FISCHER (Titular Bishop of Avioccala), Vicariat Apostolique, BP 4245, 97500 Saint-Pierre; tel. 41-02-40; fax 41-47-09; e-mail mission-catho.spm@wanadoo.fr.

Other Churches

Eglise Evangélique de Saint-Pierre et Miquelon: 5 bis rue Paul Lebailly, BP 4325, 97500 Saint-Pierre; tel. 41-92-39; fax 41-59-75; e-mail pasteurspm@cheznoo.net; internet www.cheznoo.net/eglise_evangelique.spm; f. 1995; affiliated to the Fédération Nationale des Assemblées de Dieu de France and Commission des Eglises Evangéliques d'Expression Française à l'Extérieure; Pastor FRANCIS NOVERT.

The Press

L'Echo des Caps Hebdo: rue Georges Daguerre, BP 4213, 97500 Saint-Pierre; tel. 41-10-90; fax 41-49-33; e-mail echohebd@cheznoo.net; f. 1982; weekly; Editor-in-Chief DIDIER GIL; circ. 2,500.

Recueil des Actes Administratifs: 4 rue du Général Leclerc, BP 4233, 97500 Saint-Pierre; tel. 41-24-50; fax 41-20-85; e-mail imprimeriepref@cheznoo.net; f. 1866; monthly; Dir DANIEL KOELSCH.

Le Vent de la Liberté: 1 rue Amiral Muselier, BP 1179, 97500 Saint-Pierre; tel. 41-42-19; fax 41-48-06; e-mail archipel@cheznoo.net; f. 1986; monthly; Dir GÉRARD GRIGNON; circ. 550.

Broadcasting and Communications

TELECOMMUNICATIONS

SPM Telecom: 6 pl. du Général de Gaulle, BP 4253, 97500 Saint Pierre; tel. 41-00-15; fax 41-00-19; e-mail accueil@spmtelecom.com; internet www.spmtelecom.com.

RADIO AND TELEVISION

Réseau France Outre-mer (RFO): BP 4227, 97500 Saint-Pierre; tel. 41-11-11; fax 41-22-19; internet www.rfo.fr; acquired by Groupe France Télévisions in 2004; fmrly Société Nationale de Radio-Télévision Française d'Outre-mer, present name adopted in 1998; broadcasts 24 hours of radio programmes daily and 195 hours of television programmes weekly on two channels; Gen. Man. FRANÇOIS GUILBEAU; Regional Dir LAURENCE MAYERFELD.

Radio Atlantique: BP 1282, 97500 Saint-Pierre; tel. 41-24-93; fax 41-56-33; e-mail adlian@cheznoo.net; internet www.cheznoo.net/radioatlantique; f. 1982; private; broadcasts 24 hours of radio programmes daily; Pres. PHILLIPE BURY; Sec. JÉRÔME JANIL.

Finance

(cap. = capital, res = reserves, dep. = deposits; m. = million; amounts in euros)

BANKING
Central Bank

Institut d'Emission des Départements d'Outre-mer (IEDOM): 4 rue de la Roncière, BP 4202, 97500 Saint-Pierre; tel. 41-43-57; fax 41-58-55; internet www.iedom.fr; Dir BERNARD RATAFIKA.

Commercial Banks

Banque des Iles Saint-Pierre-et-Miquelon: 2 rue Jacques Cartier, BP 4223, 97500 Saint-Pierre; tel. 41-01-40; fax 41-01-52; f. 1889; subsidiary of Financière Océor, France; cap. 9.3m., res –3.3m., dep. 74.2m. (Dec. 2006); Pres. JEAN-MARC VARGEL; Gen. Man. PIERRE BALSAN; 2 brs.

Crédit Saint Pierrais: 20 pl. du Général de Gaulle, BP 4218, 97500 Saint-Pierre; tel. 41-22-49; fax 41-25-96; internet www.credit-sp.com; f. 1962; subsidiary of Financière Océor, France; cap. 5.7m., res 1.6m., dep. 56.2m. (Dec. 2005); Pres. ROBERT HARDY; Gen. Man. HERVÉ LOMBARD; 1 br.

INSURANCE

Cabinet Paturel Assurances, Agent Général AGF: 31 rue Maréchal Foch, BP 4288, 97500 Saint-Pierre; tel. 41-04-40; fax 41-51-65; internet www.agfspm.com; Gen. Agent GUY PATUREL; Man. NATHALIE PATUREL.

Mutuelle des Iles: 52 rue Maréchal Foch, BP 1112, 97500 Saint-Pierre; tel. 41-28-69; fax 41-51-13.

FRENCH OVERSEAS POSSESSIONS

Trade and Industry

DEVELOPMENT AGENCIES

Agence Française de Développement (AFD): 4 rue de la Roncière, BP 4202, 97500 Saint-Pierre; tel. 41-06-00; fax 41-25-98; e-mail iedom-spm@iedom-spm.fr; internet www.afd.fr; fmrly Caisse Française de Développement; Man. VICTOR-ROBERT NUGENT.

Société de Développement et de Promotion de l'Archipel (SODEPAR): Palais Royal, rue Borda, BP 4365, 97500 Saint-Pierre; tel. 41-15-15; fax 41-15-16; e-mail sodepar.spm@sodepar.com; internet www.sodepar.com; f. 1989; economic devt agency; Chair. STÉPHANE ARTANO; Dir THIERRY BASLE.

CHAMBER OF COMMERCE

Chambre d'Agriculture, de Commerce, d'Industrie et de Métiers (CACIM): 4 rue Constant-Colmay, BP 4207, 97500 Saint-Pierre; tel. 41-45-12; fax 41-32-09; e-mail cacim@ccimspm.org; internet cacim.apcma.fr/charte1/default.asp?id=230; Pres. MONIQUE WALSH; Dir-Gen. BERNARD LLINARES.

TRADE UNIONS

Syndicat des Armateurs à la Pêche Côtière: BP 937, 97500 Saint-Pierre; tel. 41-30-13; fax 41-73-89; e-mail kenavo@cheznoo.net; Pres. JEAN BEAUPERTUIS.

Syndicat CFDT (Union Interprofessionnelle SPM): 15 rue du Docteur Dunan, BP 4352, 97500 Saint-Pierre; tel. 41-23-20; fax 41-27-99; affiliated to the Confédération Française Démocratique du Travail; Sec.-Gen. PHILIPPE GUILLAUME.

Union Départementale Confédération Française des Travailleurs Chrétiens Saint Pierre et Miquelon (UD CFTC): 15 rue du Docteur Dunan, BP 1117, 97500 Saint-Pierre; tel. 41-37-19; fax 41-44-71.

Union Départementale Force Ouvrière: 15 rue du Docteur Dunan, BP 4241, 97500 Saint-Pierre; tel. 41-25-22; fax 41-46-55; e-mail max.claude.olaisola@wanadoo.fr; affiliated to the Confédération Générale du Travail-Force Ouvrière; Sec.-Gen. MAX OLAISOLA.

Union Intersyndicale CGT de Saint-Pierre et Miquelon: rue du 11 Novembre, 97500 Saint-Pierre; tel. 41-41-86; fax 41-30-21; e-mail cgtsp@cheznoo.net; affiliated to the Confédération Générale du Travail; Sec.-Gen. RONALD MANET.

UNSA-Education: rue du Docteur Dunan, 97500 Saint-Pierre; tel. 41-38-05; fax 41-34-08; e-mail 975@se-unsa.org; represents teaching staff; Sec.-Gen. ANDRÉ URTIZBEREA.

Transport

SHIPPING

Packet boats and container services operate between Saint-Pierre, Halifax, Nova Scotia, Boston, MA, and France. There is a ferry service between Saint-Pierre, Miquelon and Newfoundland and Labrador. The seaport at Saint-Pierre has three jetties and 1,200 metres of quays. In 2005 the cost of repairs and development of the port at Miquelon was estimated at almost €12.4m.

Alliance Europe Le Havre: 1 rue Abbé Pierre Gervain, 97500 Saint-Pierre; tel. 20-53-53; fax 20-53-86; e-mail lh.spm@alliance-europe.fr; internet alliance-europe.fr; f. 2004 as successor to Compagnie Maritime des Transports Frigorifiques (f. 1980); operates weekly container and ro-ro shipping services between Saint Pierre and Miquelon and ports in northern Europe; also operates air freight service; Gen. Man. ALAIN CHATEL.

SPM Express: Quai Mimosa, 97500 Saint-Pierre; tel. 41-44-00; fax 41-16-62; passenger ferry service between Saint-Pierre, Miquelon and Newfoundland and Labrador.

CIVIL AVIATION

There is an airport on Saint Pierre, served by airlines linking the territory with five destinations in Canada. Construction of a new airport, able to accommodate larger aircraft and thus improve air links, was completed in 1999.

Service de l'Aviation Civile de Saint-Pierre et Miquelon: Aérodrome Saint-Pierre Pointe Blanche, 97500 Saint-Pierre; tel. 41-18-00; fax 41-18-18; e-mail sacspm@aviation-civile.gouv.fr.

Air Saint-Pierre: 18 rue Albert Briand, Saint-Pierre, BP 4225, 97500 Saint-Pierre; tel. 41-00-00; fax 41-00-02; internet www.airsaintpierre.com; f. 1964; connects the territory directly with Newfoundland and Labrador, Nova Scotia and Québec; Pres. RÉMY L. BRIAND; Man. THIERRY BRIAND.

Tourism

There were an estimated 13,000 tourist arrivals in 2005. In that year there were 160 hotel rooms.

Comité Régional du Tourisme: pl. du Général de Gaulle, BP 4274, 97500 Saint-Pierre; tel. 41-02-00; fax 41-33-55; e-mail info@st-pierre-et-miquelon.info; internet www.st-pierre-et-miquelon.info; f. 1989; fmrly Service Loisirs Accueil; Dir. PIERRE-YVES CASTAING.

THE WALLIS AND FUTUNA ISLANDS

Introductory Survey

Location, Climate, Language, Religion, Capital

Wallis and Futuna comprises two groups of islands: the Wallis Islands, including Wallis Island (also known as Uvea) and 10 islets (*motu*) on the surrounding reef, and Futuna (or Hooru) to the south-west, comprising the two small islands of Futuna and Alofi. The islands are located north-east of Fiji and west of Samoa. Temperatures are generally between about 23°C (73°F) and 30°C (86°F), and there is a cyclone season between December and March. French and the indigenous Polynesian languages Wallisian (Uvean) and Futunian are spoken throughout the islands. Nearly all of the population is nominally Roman Catholic. The capital is Mata'Utu, on Wallis Island.

Recent History

The Wallis and Futuna Islands were settled first by Polynesian peoples, Wallis from Tonga and Futuna from Samoa. Futuna was subsequently discovered by the Dutch navigators, Schouten and Le Maire, in 1616, and Uvea was discovered by Samuel Wallis in 1767. Three kingdoms later emerged, and in 1837 the first Marist missionaries arrived. By 1842 the majority of the population had been converted to Christianity. In April 1842 the authorities requested French protection, coinciding with a similar proclamation in Tahiti (now French Polynesia). In 1851 a *fakauvea* war between the Catholic majority and the Methodist minority assisted by Tonga (which had commenced in 1843) came to an end when 500 Wallisians left for Tonga. Protectorate status was formalized in 1887 for Wallis and in 1888 for the two kingdoms of Futuna, but domestic law remained in force. Wallis and Futuna were never formally annexed, and nor were French law or representative institutions introduced, although the islands were treated as a dependency of New Caledonia. During the Second World War, Wallis was used as an air force base by the USA. In 1959 the traditional Kings and chiefs requested integration into the French Republic. The islands formally became an Overseas Territory in July 1961, following a referendum in December 1959, in which 94.4% of the electorate requested this status (almost all the opposition was in Futuna, which itself recorded dissent from only 22.2% of the voters; Wallis was unanimous in its acceptance).

Although there was no movement in Wallis and Futuna seeking secession of the Territory from France (in contrast with the situation in the other French Pacific Territories, French Polynesia and New Caledonia), the two Kings whose kingdoms share the island of Futuna requested in November 1983, through the Territorial Assembly, that the island groups of Wallis and Futuna become separate Overseas Territories of France, arguing that the administration and affairs of the Territory had become excessively concentrated on Uvea (Wallis Island).

At elections to the 20-member Territorial Assembly in March 1982, the Rassemblement pour la République (RPR) and its allies won 11 seats, while the remaining nine were secured by candidates belonging to, or associated with, the Union pour la Démocratie Française (UDF). Later that year one member of the Lua Kae Tahi, a group affiliated to the metropolitan UDF, defected to the RPR group. In November 1983, however, three of the 12 RPR members joined the Lua Kae Tahi, forming a new majority. In the subsequent election for President of the Territorial Assembly, this 11-strong bloc of UDF-associated members supported the ultimately successful candidate, Falakiko Gata, even though he had been elected to the Territorial Assembly in 1982 as a member of the RPR.

In April 1985 Falakiko Gata formed a new political party, the Union Populaire Locale (UPL), which was committed to giving priority to local, rather than metropolitan, issues.

In 1987 a dispute broke out between two families both laying claim to the throne of Sigave, the northern kingdom on the island of Futuna. The conflict arose following the deposition of the former King, Sagato Keletaona, and his succession by Sosefo Vanaï. The intervention of the island's administrative authorities, who attempted to ratify Vanaï's accession to the throne, was condemned by the Keletaona family as an interference in the normal course of local custom, according to which such disputes are traditionally settled by a fight between the protagonists.

At elections to the Territorial Assembly held in March 1987, the UDF (together with affiliated parties) and the RPR each won seven seats. However, by forming an alliance with the UPL, the RPR maintained its majority, and Falakiko Gata was subsequently re-elected President. At elections to the French Assemblée nationale (National Assembly) in June 1988, Benjamin Brial was re-elected Deputy. However, when the result was challenged by an unsuccessful candidate, Kamilo Gata, the election was investigated by the French Constitutional Council and the result declared invalid, owing to electoral irregularities. When the election was held again in January 1989, Kamilo Gata was elected Deputy, obtaining 57.4% of total votes.

Statistical information, gathered in 1990, showed that the emigration rate of Wallis and Futuna islanders had risen to over 50%. In October of that year 13,705 people (of whom 97% were Wallisians and Futunians) lived in the Territory, while 14,186 were resident in New Caledonia. At the 1996 census the number of Wallisians and Futunians resident in New Caledonia had increased to 17,563. According to the results, a proportion of the islanders had chosen to emigrate to other French Overseas Possessions or to metropolitan France. The principal reason for the increase was thought to be the lack of employment opportunities in the islands.

At elections to the Territorial Assembly in March 1992 the newly founded Taumu'a Lelei secured 11 seats, while the RPR won nine. The new Assembly was remarkable for being the first since 1964 in which the RPR did not hold a majority. At elections to the French Assemblée nationale in March 1993, Kamilo Gata was re-elected Deputy, obtaining 52.4% of total votes cast to defeat Clovis Logologofolau. In June 1994 the Union Locale Force Ouvrière organized a general strike in protest at the increasing cost of living in the Territory and the allegedly inadequate education system. It was reported that demonstrations continued for several days, during which the Territorial Assembly building was damaged in an arson attack.

In October 1994 it was reported that the King of Sigave, Lafaele Malau, had been deposed by a unanimous decision of the kingdom's chiefs. The action followed the appointment of two customary leaders to represent the Futunian community in New Caledonia, which had led to unrest among the inhabitants of Sigave. He was succeeded by Esipio Takasi.

At elections to the Territorial Assembly in December 1994 the RPR secured 10 seats, while a coalition group, Union Populaire pour Wallis et Futuna (UPWF), won seven, and independent candidates three. Mikaele Tauhavili was subsequently elected President of the Assembly.

The refusal by 10 of the 20 members of the Territorial Assembly to adopt budgetary proposals in January 1996, led to appeals for the dissolution of the Government by France and the organization of new elections. The budget (which, at US $20m., was some $4.5m. smaller than the previous year) aroused opposition for its apparent lack of provision for development funds, particularly for the islands' nascent tourist industry.

Elections to the Territorial Assembly took place on 16 March 1997. A participation rate of 87.2% was recorded at the poll, in which RPR candidates secured 14 seats and left-wing candidates (including independents and members of various political groupings) won six seats. Victor Brial, a representative of the RPR, was elected President of the Territorial Assembly. At the second round of elections to the French Assemblée nationale, on 1 June, Brial defeated Kamilo Gata, obtaining 3,241 votes (51.3% of the total).

Allegations that electoral irregularities had occurred in the elections to the Territorial Assembly of March 1997 were investigated and upheld for 11 of the seats. As a result, new elections were organized for the 11 seats on 6 September 1998, at which the RPR's representation in the Assembly was reduced to 11 seats overall, while left-wing and independent members increased their share of seats to nine. Also in September 1998, in a second round of voting, Fr Robert Laufoaulu was elected to the French Sénat (Senate), defeating Kamilo Gata in a vote by the Territorial Assembly. Laufoaulu, a priest and director of Catholic education in the islands, stood as a left-wing candidate, nominated by RPR candidates, but was elected with the support of right-wing politicians.

In late March 1999 festivities were held to commemorate the 40th anniversary of the accession of the King of Wallis Island, Lavelua Tomasi Kulimoetoke. From March 2000 delegations from Wallis and Futuna visited New Caledonia to discuss mutual arrangements concerning free trade and employment rights between the two Territories.

In January 2001 two candidates of the RPR contested the presidency of the Territorial Assembly. Patalione Kanimoa was elected by the majority of the RPR (eight votes) and of the UPWF (four votes). Soane Muni Uhila, the previous President of the Territorial Assembly, then formed a new party, La Voix des Peuples Wallisiens et Futuniens, along with five other RPR dissidents. The new majority RPR-UPWF grouping elected Albert Likuvalu (of the UPWF) president of the permanent commission.

In June 2001 senior officials from Wallis and Futuna and from New Caledonia agreed on a project to redefine their bilateral relationship under the Nouméa Accord (see the chapter on New Caledonia) on greater autonomy, signed in 1998. The Accord gave the New Caledonian authorities the power to control immigration from Wallis and Futuna; following decades of migration, the population of Wallis and Futuna was 15,000, while the number of migrants and descendants from the islands in New Caledonia had risen to 20,000. In exchange for controlling immigration, New Caledonia stated that it would make a financial contribution to economic development in Wallis and Futuna. The Nouméa Accord also envisaged a separate arrangement allowing for open access to New Caledonia for residents of Wallis and Futuna. The French State was to address the issue of financial aid before the two territories' assemblies approved the arrangement.

In January 2002 a delegation from Wallis and Futuna met President Jacques Chirac in Paris to discuss the situation of members of their community living in New Caledonia. Under the Nouméa Accord, New Caledonia was to have signed a separate agreement with Wallis and Futuna better to define the islanders' status, with particular regard to the job market.

An election was held on 10 March 2002 for the 20 seats of the Territorial Assembly. The RPR won 12 of the seats, whilst socialist candidates, or affiliated independents, won eight. An unprecedented 82.7% of some 9,500 registered voters cast their vote. The election campaign was the first to give parties coverage on television and radio, provided by the national broadcasting company. The Territory's only newspaper, *Te-Fenua Fo'ou*, ceased publication in April, following a dispute over the King of Wallis's alleged support for an electoral candidate, Make Pilioko. The paper contested that Pilioko, a former member of the Territorial Assembly, was unfit for office, having been convicted in 1999 of misuse of public funds. The publisher and editor of the newspaper, respectively Michel Boudineau and Laurent Gourlez (both of whom were French), were summoned before the King and ordered not to publish any further articles on the matter. However, the paper asserted its right to freedom of expression and, in defiance of the King, printed and distributed its next edition from New Caledonia. The police subsequently removed computers and other equipment from the newspaper's office in Mata'Utu. Boudineau filed a complaint with the French authorities for theft and obstruction of press freedom but was forced to close the paper and to dismiss its staff.

At elections to the Assemblée nationale in June 2002, Victor Brial, representing a coalition of the Union pour la Majorité Présidentielle (subsequently Union pour un Mouvement Populaire—UMP) and the RPR, was re-elected as the Wallis and Futuna deputy to the French legislature, winning 50.4% of the votes cast in the first round. (The RPR was fully absorbed into the UMP structure that year.) However, in December the Constitutional Council ruled that the result was invalid as certain ballot papers had been improperly marked; Brial (now representing the UMP) subsequently won the by-election in March 2003. Meanwhile, Christian Job replaced Alain Waquet as Chief Administrator of the islands in August 2002. In late November Soane Patita Maituka was enthroned as King of Alo following the deposition of Sagato Alofi in the previous month. In December the French Sénat approved a bill providing for a constitutional amendment that would allow Wallis and Futuna (along with French Polynesia) to be designated as an Overseas Country (pays d'outre-mer); both houses of the French legislature in Paris ratified the amendments to the Constitution in March 2003. Wallis and Futuna was given the status of an Overseas Collectivity (collectivité d'outre-mer). In July, during an official visit to New Caledonia, President Chirac received a delegation from Wallis and Futuna.

In October 2003 Pasilio Keletaona was deposed as King of Sigave by members of his own clan. He was succeeded in mid-March 2004 by Visesio Moeliku. In December 2003 the President of New Caledonia signed a special accord governing relations between France, New Caledonia and Wallis and Futuna. The signing of the accord, which had been agreed two years previously in an attempt to address the situation of the 20,000 Wallis and Futuna islanders permanently resident in New Caledonia, had been delayed by the continuing ethnic tensions there. Under the agreement, Wallis and Futuna and New Caledonia were henceforth to deliver separate public services. Concerns had been raised by the former's increasing debt (estimated to total 2,500m. francs CFP) to the Government of New Caledonia, a major creditor being the New Caledonian hospital. It was therefore hoped that Wallis and Futuna would become more self-sufficient in the areas of health and secondary education and that the islanders would be encouraged to remain on Wallis and Futuna, while those already settled in New Caledonia would become more integrated.

Between February and April 2003 the postal service was affected by strike action, which was resolved in favour of the striking workers. During May–June 2004 a strike prevented television and radio transmissions from the Territory's main broadcasting company, and again the dispute was resolved in favour of the striking employees, whose demands included the resignation of the station manager.

In January 2005 Xavier de Fürst replaced Christian Job as Chief Administrator of the islands. In February Albert Likuvalu, representing the newly formed Alliance grouping, a coalition of UDF members and left-wing independents, was elected President of the Territorial Assembly by 11 votes to nine, replacing Patalione Kanimoa of the UMP grouping. The Alliance comprised three members of the UDF and two left-wing ministers, including Likuvalu himself; they were supported by the UPWF grouping.

In January 2005 the local court found the Lavelua's grandson, Tomasi Tuugahala, guilty of unintentional homicide while driving under the influence of alcohol. Tuugahala took refuge in the Lavelua's palace and refused to surrender himself to the police. The Lavelua and his chiefs claimed that the matter had been settled in accordance with traditional custom but the incident brought them into confrontation with the French authorities and with pro-reform groups in Wallis and Futuna who wished to depose the Lavelua. In May the King's Prime Minister, Kapeliele Faupala, criticized de Fürst for interfering in traditional affairs and urged him to leave the island. Later in the month Tuugahala gave himself up to the authorities and was flown to New Caledonia to begin an 18-month prison sentence. However, in June de Fürst suspended allowances and salaries to the Lavelua and his Council of Ministers, while officially recognizing an alternative council composed of members of rival royal families from Futuna, headed by Clovis Logologofolau, whose previous posts had included that of President of the Territorial Assembly.

In August 2005 the Lavelua reiterated a pledge of allegiance to France but maintained that the crisis was the result of de Fürst's interference. In September the alternative council of ministers announced its intention to install Chief Sosefo Mautamakia as King of Wallis. Supporters of the Lavelua took to the streets in protest, mounting blockades and occupying the international airport; meanwhile, in the New Caledonian capital of Nouméa, a group of some 500 supporters marched to the French High Commission to present a petition demanding the intervention of France. The Secretary-General of the French High Commission in New Caledonia, Louis Lefranc, was dispatched to undertake negotiations; he reaffirmed France's recognition of Tomasi Kulimoetoke as Lavelua and overruled de Fürst's earlier decisions. As a result of negotiations among the royal clans themselves, no attempt was made to install a new King at the end of that month. In late November Emeni Simete of the UMP replaced Albert Likuvalu as President of the Territorial Assembly.

In March 2006 the two Kings of Futuna, accompanied by ministers of the kingdoms and members of the local assembly, travelled to France to meet President Jacques Chirac, Prime Minister Dominique de Villepin and other senior government officials. The delegation emphasized the need for improved transport links between Futuna and Wallis. The most recent examples of these inadequacies were the disruption caused on Futuna by severe weather conditions in January and February and the temporary halt to flights between the two islands because of a faulty aircraft, which had resulted in a delay to the beginning of the school year. The Futuna delegation reportedly claimed that President Chirac had assured them that their island would be designated as a sub-prefecture. At the end of July Wallis and Futuna commemorated the 45th anniversary of its status as a French Overseas Territory. In the following month Xavier de Fürst was replaced by Richard Didier as Chief Administrator. From August the health of the Lavelua deteriorated to the extent that he was unable to attend official events. He died in May 2007. The subject of his successor was declared taboo for six months. It emerged in August that the Tu'i Agaifo (King of Alo) was in hospital in New Caledonia with a serious illness. In February 2008 the Tu'i Agaifo was removed from office.

In January 2007 it was announced that the next election for the Territorial Assembly would be held at the beginning of April. Later in January a delegation from Wallis visited Futuna, amid reported tensions between the islands, to present a memorandum of understanding encompassing the three kingdoms, the details of which were not immediately publicized. At the legislative election conducted on 1 April, the level of participation reached an estimated 74% of registered voters. Three new members were elected, with many votes reportedly cast according to clan loyalties. Pesamino Taputai was subsequently selected to succeed Emeni Simete as the Assembly's President, receiving the support of 12 of the 20 members. In his inaugural speech Taputai urged the islands' leaders to address the various issues that continued to impede good relations between Wallis and Futuna.

The results of Wallis and Futuna's participation in the second round of the French presidential election in May 2007 showed similar levels of support for the two candidates: Nicolas Sarkozy of the UMP, who secured a majority overall, received 50.2% of votes cast locally, while the Parti Socialiste (PS) candidate, Ségolène Royal, received 49.8%. Elections to the French Assemblée nationale were held in June, with the incumbent UMP deputy, Victor Brial, winning the first round with 33.7% of the votes cast. However, in the second round Brial was defeated by the PS-affiliated candidate, Albert Likuvalu, who received 51.8% of the votes. In September it was announced that the 2013 South Pacific Mini Games were to be held in Wallis and Futuna; it was envisaged that the event would require significant development of the islands' infrastructure. In early October 2007 the King of Tonga, George Tupou V, paid a personal visit to Wallis and Futuna. Later in the month the French Minister-Delegate for the Overseas Possessions, Christian Estrosi, also visited the islands; the hosting of the South Pacific Mini Games was discussed during his three-day visit. In December the islands' former deputy to the Assemblée nationale, Victor Brial, was elected President of the Territorial Assembly. Brial received 13 out of 20 votes, including those of members affiliated with the UMP and the Mouvement Démocrate (MoDem—formerly known as the UDF), while his only opponent, Siliako Lauhea, received six.

Government

The Overseas Collectivity (collectivité d'outre-mer) of Wallis and Futuna is administered by a representative of the French Government, the Chief Administrator, who is assisted by the Territorial Assembly. The Assembly has 20 members and is elected for a five-year term. The three traditional kingdoms, one on Wallis and two sharing Futuna, have equal rights, although the kings' powers are limited. In addition, Wallis and Futuna elects one Deputy to the French Assemblée nationale (National Assembly) in Paris and one representative to the French Sénat (Senate). The islands may also be represented at the European Parliament.

Economic Affairs

In 1995 it was estimated that Wallis and Futuna's gross domestic product (GDP) was US $28.7m., equivalent to some $2,000 per head. Most monetary income in the islands is derived from government employment and from remittances sent home by islanders employed in New Caledonia and metropolitan France.

Agricultural activity is of a subsistence nature. Yams, taro, bananas, cassava and other food crops are also cultivated. Tobacco is grown for local consumption. Pigs, goats and chickens are reared on the islands. Apiculture was revived in 1996, and in 2000 honey production was sufficient to meet the demands of the local market. Fishing activity in the exclusive economic zone of Wallis and Futuna increased during the 1990s; the total catch was estimated at 300 metric tons in 2005, compared with 70 tons in 1991.

Mineral fuels are the main source of electrical energy, although it is hoped that hydroelectric power can be developed, especially on Futuna. There is a 4,000-kW thermal power station on Wallis, and a 2,600-kW thermal power station was completed on Futuna in 2000. The hydroelectric power station on the Vainifao river, on Futuna, provided 10% of the production needed. Total electricity output in 2006 reached 19.7m. kWh.

There were 291 businesses in Wallis and Futuna in 2000, of which 24 were in the industrial and artisanal sector, 68 in construction and 199 in the service and commercial sectors; 47 of those businesses were located on Futuna. A new commercial centre opened in Wallis in 2002. The tourism sector is very limited. In 2002 Wallis had four hotels and Futuna two. In November 2005 the French Government agreed to provide some €8m. towards expanding the domestic airport at Vele, on Futuna, to receive international traffic.

In 2006 the cost of the islands' imports reached 4,977.9m. francs CFP. Food products accounted for 27.0% of the total value of imports; followed by transport equipment (13.5%); electrical machinery and sound and television apparatus (11.2%); mineral products (10.7%); and building and public works supplies (10.7%). Export revenue reached only 4.6m. francs CFP in 2004. Traditional food products, mother of pearl (from the Trochus shell) and handicrafts are the only significant export commodities. Exports of copra from Wallis ceased in 1950, and from Futuna in the early 1970s. The principal sources of imports in 2004 were France, which supplied 32.5% of the total, and Australia (22.3%). Most of the islands' exports were purchased by Italy. In August 2001 the frequency of supplies to Wallis and Futuna was significantly improved when the Sofrana shipping company, based in Auckland, began operating a new route linking New Zealand, Tonga and the Samoas to Wallis and Futuna.

The islands' budgetary expenditure decreased from an estimated 2,862m. francs CFP in 2004, to an estimated 2,623m. francs CFP in 2005. Operational expenditure was projected at 2,750m. francs CFP in 2006. French aid to Wallis and Futuna increased from a total of 7,048m. francs CFP in 1999 to 10,461.3m., francs CFP, including investment expenditure of 949.2m. francs CFP, in 2005. In December

2002 France proposed a broad 15-year sustainable development strategy for Wallis and Futuna.

The annual rate of inflation in 1989–2007 averaged 1.7%. The rate of inflation in 2007 reached 2.1%. The high level of unemployment remains a major economic and social issue. More than 50% of those in formal employment are engaged in the public sector.

Wallis and Futuna forms part of the Franc Zone (see p. 306). Although France is also a member of the organization, Wallis and Futuna has membership in its own right of the Pacific Community (see p. 377), which is based in New Caledonia and provides technical advice, training and assistance in economic, cultural and social development to the region. Wallis and Futuna was granted observer status at the Pacific Islands Forum (see p. 380) in 2006.

In mid-2003 the Assemblée nationale in Paris approved the Overseas Territories Development Bill, providing support for economic and social development in Wallis and Futuna (together with French Polynesia and New Caledonia) by attracting foreign investment, and among other benefits allowing for overseas French residents to travel to mainland France to take advantage of free education. In early 2007 France concluded an agreement with Wallis and Futuna to provide US $50m. over the period 2007–11 for the purposes of infrastructural development. Projects included the upgrading of the airport on Futuna. This extension was scheduled for completion in December 2008, at a cost of $8.5m. Priority was also to be given to the areas of health, education and vocational training, with the sum of $8.5m. being allocated to the reorganization of the islands' health service. In March 2008 it was announced that the European Union (EU, see p. 244) had allocated the sum of €16.49m. to development projects in Wallis and Futuna, under the 10th European Development Fund (EDF) encompassing the period 2008–13. Areas of focus were expected to include sources of renewable energy, improved management of the islands' natural resources and sustainable development, in addition to the priority sectors of education and health, while the delays in the programme to upgrade facilities for fishing vessels in the harbour at Halalo, south of Wallis Island, which was originally scheduled to commence in 2006, were to be addressed. Meanwhile, in December 2004 discussions began regarding the replacement of the franc CFP with the euro. The eventual introduction of the new currency, however, would depend upon Wallis and Futuna, New Caledonia and French Polynesia all reaching a consensus.

Education

The Catholic Mission is responsible for state primary education; secondary education is entirely within the state system. In 2006 there were 15 primary schools and seven secondary schools (including two vocational schools) in Wallis and Futuna; primary and pre-primary pupils totalled 2,471 and secondary students 2,355. In 2005/06 a total of 80 students were attending various universities overseas.

Public Holidays

2008: 1 January (New Year's Day), 5 March (Missionary Day), 24 March (Easter Monday), 1 May (Ascension Day, Labour Day), 8 May (Liberation Day), 12 May (Whit Monday), 14 July (Fall of the Bastille), 8 September (Internal Autonomy Day), 24 September (anniversary of possession by France), 1 November (All Saints' Day), 11 November (Armistice Day), 25 December (Christmas Day).

2009: 1 January (New Year's Day), 5 March (Missionary Day), 13 April (Easter Monday), 1 May (Labour Day), 8 May (Liberation Day), 21 May (Ascension Day), 1 June (Whit Monday), 14 July (Fall of the Bastille), 8 September (Internal Autonomy Day), 24 September (anniversary of possession by France), 1 November (All Saints' Day), 11 November (Armistice Day), 25 December (Christmas Day).

Weights and Measures

The metric system is in force.

Statistical Survey

Source (unless otherwise indicated): Service Territorial de la Statistique et des Etudes Economiques, Immeuble Pukavila, RT1, BP 638, Mata'Utu, Falaleu, 98600 Wallis; tel. and fax 722403; fax 722487; e-mail stats@wallis.co.nc; internet www.spc.int/prism/country/wf/stats/index.htm.

AREA AND POPULATION

Area (sq km): 160. *By Island:* Uvea (Wallis Island) 78; Other Wallis Islands 18; Futuna Island 45; Alofi Island 19.

Population: Total population 14,166 (males 6,984, females 7,182) at census of 3 October 1996; 17,563 Wallisians and Futunians resided in New Caledonia. Total population 14,944 (males 7,494, females 7,450) at census of 22 July 2003: Wallis Islands 10,071; Futuna Island 4,873 (Alo 2,993, Sigave 1,880). *2008* (estimate): 15,546.

Density (census of July 2003): 93.4 per sq km.

Principal Town (census of July 2003): Mata'Utu (capital), population 1,191.

Births and Deaths (2003): Registered live births 290 (birth rate 19.4 per 1,000); Registered deaths 88 (death rate 5.9 per 1,000). *2006:* Registered live births 220; Registered deaths 77.

Expectation of Life (years at birth): 74.3 (males 73.1; females 75.5) in 2003.

Economically Active Population (census of July 2003): Total employed 3,104 (males 1,730, females 1,374); Unemployed persons seeking work 556 (males 319, females 237); Total labour force 3,660.

HEALTH AND WELFARE
Key Indicators

Total Fertility Rate (children per woman, census of July 2003): 3.1.

Under-5 Mortality Rate (per 1,000 live births, census of July 2003): 5.5.

Physicians (per 1,000 head, 2003): 0.7 (Source: World Health Organization).

Access to Sanitation (% of persons, census of July 2003): 80.0 (Source: World Health Organization).

For definitions, see explanatory note on p. vi.

AGRICULTURE, ETC.

Principal Crops ('000 metric tons, 2006, FAO estimates): Cassava 2.4; Taro (coco yam) 1.6; Yams 0.5; Other roots and tubers 1.0; Coconuts 2.3; Vegetables and melons 0.6; Bananas 4.1; Other fruits (excl. melons) 4.6.

Livestock ('000 head, year ending September 2006, FAO estimates): Pigs 25; Goats 7; Chickens 63.

Livestock Products (metric tons, 2006, FAO estimates): Pig meat 319; Goat meat 15; Chicken meat 47; Cows' milk 30; Hen eggs 33; Honey 11.

Fishing (metric tons, live weight, 2005): Total catch 300 (Marine fishes 296) (FAO estimates). Figures exclude Trochus shells (metric tons) 16.

Source: FAO.

INDUSTRY

Selected Products (metric tons unless otherwise indicated, 2006): Coconut oil 164.1 (FAO estimate); Copra 252.5 (FAO estimate); Electric energy 19.7m. kWh. Sources: FAO; Institut d'Emission d'Outre-Mer.

FINANCE

Currency and Exchange Rates: see French Polynesia.

Territorial Budget (million francs CFP, provisional figures): 2,551 in 2003; 2,862 in 2004; 2,623 in 2005.

Operating Budget (million francs CFP, 2006, provisional): Revenue 2,750; Expenditure 2,750.

Public Expenditure (million francs CFP, 2003): Operational expenditure 6,616.0 (Agriculture and fisheries department 95.5, Education 4,629.3, Economy, finance and industry department 265.7, Interior and decentralization department 99.2, Justice 39.5, Overseas affairs 864.1, Transport and communications 10.9, Maritime department 0.8, Youth and sports department 49.1, Health and welfare 501.6, Labour 58.6, Environment 1.7); Investment expenditure 603.4; Special Treasury accounts 24.0; Extra-budgetary expenditure 16.1; Total expenditure 7,259.6.

Aid from France (million francs CFP, 2005): Operational expenditure 8,717.7; Investment expenditure 949.2; Special accounts and extraordinary expenditure 25.4; *Total expenditure* (incl. others) 10,461.3. Source: Institut d'Emission d'Outre-mer.

Money Supply (million francs CFP at 31 December 2006): Currency in circulation 1,679; Demand deposits 2,310; *Total money* 3,989. Source: Institut d'Emission d'Outre-Mer.

Cost of Living (Consumer Price Index at January–March; base: July–Sept. 1989 = 100): All items 128.9 in 2005; 132.7 in 2006; 135.5 in 2007.

EXTERNAL TRADE

Principal Commodities (million francs CFP, provisional figures): *Imports c.i.f.* (2006): Food products 1,342.2; Transport equipment 671.6; Mineral products 533.3; Building and public works supplies 533.3; Electrical machinery, equipment and parts, sound and television apparatus 557.9; Chemicals 417.5; Clothes and accessories 259.3; Miscellaneous goods and products 142.4; Paper, cardboard 105.6; Optical instruments and equipment 163.6; Total (incl. others) 4,977.9. Source: Institut d'Emission d'Outre-Mer. *Exports f.o.b.* (2001): Preparations of molluscs and other aquatic invertebrates 0.3; Coral and shells 5.5; Braids and mats of vegetable material 0.9; Total 5.6. *2004:* Total exports 4.6.

Principal Trading Partners (million francs CFP): *Imports c.i.f.* (2004): Australia 1,313.8; China 172.8; France (incl. Monaco) 1,909.5; Italy 105.6; Japan 165.4; New Caledonia 471.2; Thailand 105.5; Total (incl. others) 5,879.1. *Exports f.o.b.* (2004): Italy 4.6; Total 4.6.

TRANSPORT

Road Traffic (vehicles in use, 2001): Scooters 1,093; Cars 1,293. Source: Ministère de l'Agriculture, de l'Alimentation, de la Pêche et des Affaires Rurales, *Recensement agricole du territoire 2001.*

Shipping: *Merchant Fleet* (31 December 2006): Vessels registered 8; Displacement ('000 grt): 92.3. Source: Lloyd's Register-Fairplay, *World Fleet Statistics.*

Civil Aviation (2005): *Domestic Traffic:* Aircraft movements 1,161; Passenger movements 12,397; Freight handled 23.2 metric tons; Mail handled 9.4 metric tons. *International Traffic:* Aircraft movements 226; Passenger arrivals 10,841; Passenger departures 11,716; Freight unloaded 149.2 metric tons; Freight loaded 23.2 metric tons; Mail handled 58.3 metric tons. Source: Institut d'Emission d'Outre-Mer.

TOURISM

Foreign Visitors (2006): *Total Arrivals:* 2,456. *Overnight Stays in Hotel Establishments:* 607.

Foreign Visitor Arrivals by Nationality (2006): Australia 37; Fiji 45; France 674; French Polynesia 62; New Caledonia 1,310; Total (incl. others) 2,456.

COMMUNICATIONS MEDIA

Telephones (at 31 March 2006): 1,826 main lines installed.

Facsimile Machines (1993): 90 in use (Source: UN, *Statistical Yearbook*).

Internet Subscribers (at 31 March 2006): 532.

EDUCATION

Pre-primary (2005): 3 institutions; 260 pupils.

Primary (2006): 15 institutions; 2,471 pupils (incl. pre-primary). Source: Institut d'Emission d'Outre-Mer.

Secondary (2006): 7 institutions (2 vocational); 2,355 students. Source: Institut d'Emission d'Outre-Mer.

Higher (students, 2005/06): 14 in New Caledonia; 60 in metropolitan France; 6 in French Polynesia. Source: Institut d'Emission d'Outre-Mer.

Teachers (2003): Pre-primary and primary 168; Secondary 209.

Adult Literacy Rate (census of July 2003): 78.8% (males 78.2%; females 79.3%).

Directory

The Constitution

The Territory of the Wallis and Futuna Islands has been administered according to a statute of 1961, and subsidiary legislation, under the Constitution of the Fifth Republic. The Statute declared the Wallis and Futuna Islands to be an Overseas Territory of the French Republic, of which they remain an integral part. The Statute established an administration, a Council of the Territory, a Territorial Assembly and national representation. The administrative, political and social evolution envisaged by, and enacted under, the Statute was intended to effect a smooth integration of the three customary kingdoms with the new institutions of the Territory. The Kings are assisted by ministers and the traditional chiefs. The Chief Administrator, appointed by the French Government, is the representative of the State in the Territory and is responsible for external affairs, defence, law and order, financial and educational affairs. The Chief Administrator is required to consult with the Council of the Territory, which has six members: three by right (the Kings of Wallis, Sigave and Alo) and three appointed by the Chief Administrator upon the advice of the Territorial Assembly. This Assembly assists in the administration of the Territory; there are 20 members elected on a common roll, on the basis of universal adult suffrage, for a term of up to five years. The Territorial Assembly elects, from among its own membership, a President to lead it. Wallis and Futuna elects national representatives—one Deputy to the Assemblée nationale (National Assembly), one Senator and one Economic and Social Councillor—and votes for representatives to the European Parliament in Strasbourg. In 2003 both the Assemblée nationale and Sénat (Senate) in Paris ratified amendments to the Constitution providing for Wallis and Futuna (along with French Polynesia) to be designated as an Overseas Country (pays d'outre-mer). Following the constitutional revisions of 2003, the official status of Wallis and Futuna became that of an Overseas Collectivity (collectivité d'outre-mer).

The Government

(April 2008)

Chief Administrator (Administrateur Supérieur): RICHARD DIDIER (took office 14 August 2006).

CONSEIL DU TERRITOIRE

Chair: Chief Administrator.

Members by Right: King of Wallis, King of Sigave, King of Alo.

Appointed Members: MIKAELE HALAGAHU (Faipule), ATOLOTO UHILA (Kulitea), KELETO LAKALAKA (Sous réserves).

GOVERNMENT OFFICES

Government Headquarters: Bureau de l'Administrateur Supérieur, BP 16, Mata'Utu, Havelu, Hahake, 98600 Uvea, Wallis Islands; tel. 722727; fax 722300; e-mail adsupwf@wallis.co.nc; internet www.adsupwf.org.

Department of Catholic Schools: Direction Diocésaine de l'Enseignement Catholique, BP 80, Mata'Utu, 98600 Uvea, Wallis Islands; tel. 722766; e-mail decwf.wallis@wallis.co.nc; internet www.wallis.co.nc/decwf; responsible for pre-primary and primary education since 1969.

Department of Cultural Action: BP 131, Mata'Utu, Aka'aka, 98600 Uvea, Wallis Islands; tel. 722667; fax 722563; e-mail usc@wallis.co.nc; internet www.wallis.co.nc/affcult.wf.

Department of the Environment: BP 294, Mata'Utu, Havelu, Hahake, 98600 Uvea, Wallis Islands; tel. 720351; fax 720597; e-mail senv@wallis.co.nc; internet www.wallis.co.nc/envwf.

Department of Justice: BP 12, Mata'Utu, Havelu, Hahake, 98600 Uvea, Wallis Islands; tel. 722715; fax 722531; e-mail tpi@wallis.co.nc.

Department of Labour and Social Affairs Inspection (SITAS): BP 385, Mata'Utu, Hahake, 98600 Uvea; tel. 722288; fax 722209; e-mail sitaswf@wallis.co.nc; internet www.wallis.co.nc/sitas.

Department of Public Works and Rural Engineering: BP 13, Mata'Utu, Kafika, Hahake, 98600 Uvea, Wallis Islands; tel. 722626; fax 722115; e-mail tpwallis@wallis.co.nc.

Department of Rural Affairs and Fisheries: BP 19, Mata'Utu, Aka'aka, 98600 Uvea, Wallis Islands; tel. 720400; fax 720404; e-mail ecoru@wallis.co.nc; e-mail ecoru.futuna@wallis.co.nc.

Department of Youth and Sports: BP 51, Mata'Utu, Kafika, Hahake, 98600 Uvea; tel. 722188; fax 722322; e-mail jeusport@wallis.co.nc; internet www.wallis.co.nc/jeusport.

Health Agency: Agence de Santé, BP 4G, 98600 Uvea, Wallis Islands; tel. 720700; fax 723399; e-mail sante@adswf.org; internet www.wallis.co.nc/adswf; operates two hospitals at Sia on Uvea and Kaleveleve on Futuna, respectively.

Legislature

ASSEMBLÉE TERRITORIALE

The Territorial Assembly has 20 members and is elected for a five-year term. Within the Assembly, ministers may form political groupings of five members or more. These groupings are not necessarily formed along party lines, and alliances may be made in support of a common cause. The most recent general election took place on 1 April 2007, at which three new members were elected.

President: VICTOR BRIAL (UMP).

Territorial Assembly: Assemblée Territoriale, BP 31, Mata'Utu, Havelu, Hahake, 98600 Uvea, Wallis Islands; tel. 722004; fax

721807; e-mail cab-pres.at@wallis.co.nc; internet www.wallis.co.nc/assemblee.ter.

PARLEMENT

Deputy to the French National Assembly: ALBERT LIKUVALU (PS).

Representative to the French Senate: Fr ROBERT LAUFOAULU (UMP).

The Kingdoms

WALLIS
(Capital: Mata'Utu on Uvea)

Lavelua, King of Wallis: (vacant).

Council of Ministers (Aliki Fau): The Council is composed of six ministers who assist the King:

Kivalu: the Prime Minister and King's spokesman at official meetings.

Mahe: the second Prime Minister and King's counsel.

Kulitea: responsible for cultural and customary matters.

Uluimonoa: responsible for the sea.

Fotuatamai: responsible for health and hygiene.

Mukoifenua: responsible for land and agriculture.

In addition, the Puliuvea is responsible for the King's security and the maintenance of public order.

The Kingdom of Wallis is divided into three administrative districts (Hihifo, Hahake, Mua), and its traditional hierarchy includes three district chiefs (Faipule), 20 village chiefs (Pule) and numerous hamlet chiefs (Lagiaki).

SIGAVE
(Capital: Leava on Futuna)

Keletaona, King of Sigave: VISESIO MOELIKU.

Council of Ministers: six ministers, chaired by the King.

The Kingdom of Sigave is located in the north of the island of Futuna; there are five village chiefs.

ALO
(Capital: Ono on Futuna)

Tu'i Agaifo, King of Alo: (vacant).

Council of Ministers: five ministers, chaired by the King.

The Kingdom of Alo comprises the southern part of the island of Futuna and the entire island of Alofi. There are nine village chiefs.

Political Organizations

Alliance: c/o Assemblée Territoriale; f. 2005; coalition of UDF mems and left-wing independents; Pres. APITONE MUNIKIHAAFATA.

Mouvement Démocrate (MoDem): c/o Assemblée Territoriale; fmrly known as Union pour la Démocratie Française; name changed as above in 2007; centrist; based on Uvean (Wallisian) support.

Union pour un Mouvement Populaire (UMP): c/o Assemblée Territoriale; f. 2002 as Union pour un Majorité Présidentielle incl. fmr mems of Rassemblement pour la République; centre-right; local branch of the metropolitan party; includes fmr mems of the NI party; Territorial Leader CLOVIS LOGOLOGOFOLAU.

Union pour Wallis et Futuna (UPWF): c/o Assemblée Territoriale; f. 1994 as Union Populaire pour Wallis et Futuna; affiliated to the Parti Socialiste of France since 1998; Leader SILIAKO LAUHEA.

Judicial System

The Statute provided for two parallel judicial systems: customary law, which applied to the indigenous population; and French State law. The competencies of the respective systems are not always clearly defined, which has been a cause of tensions between the indigenous monarchy and the French authorities. On Uvea, under customary law there are separate courts for civil matters (Fono Puleaga) and village matters (Fono Fenua). Disputes over land are dealt with by the Council of the Territory, presided over by the King. A similar system exists on Futuna. Judgments may be referred to a Chambre d'Annulation at the Court of Appeal at Nouméa, New Caledonia.

Court of the First Instance: Tribunal de Première Instance, BP 12, Havelu, Mata'Utu, Hahake, 98600 Uvea, Wallis Islands; tel. 722715; fax 722531; e-mail pr.tpi@wallis.co.nc; f. 1983; Pres. FRANCIS ALARY.

Religion

Almost all of the inhabitants profess Christianity and are adherents of the Roman Catholic Church.

CHRISTIANITY

The Roman Catholic Church

The Territory comprises a single diocese, suffragan to the archdiocese of Nouméa (New Caledonia). The diocese estimated that there were 14,400 adherents at 31 December 2005. The Bishop participates in the Catholic Bishops' Conference of the Pacific, currently based in Fiji.

Bishop of Wallis and Futuna: GHISLAIN MARIE RAOUL SUZANNE DE RASILLY, Evêché Lano, BP G6, Mata'Utu, 98600 Uvea, Wallis Islands; tel. 722932; fax 722783; e-mail eveche.wallis@wallis.co.nc.

The Press

'Uvea Mo Futuna: Tuku'atu Ha'afuasia, Uvea, Wallis Islands; e-mail filihau@uvea-mo-futuna.com; internet www.uvea-mo-futuna.com; f. 2002; daily; electronic; Editor FILIHAU ASI TALATINI.

The territory's only newspaper, *Te-Fenua Fo'ou*, was forced to close in April 2002, following a dispute with the King of Wallis. *Fenua Magazine* was launched by a group of local business people in September 2002 but closed in September 2003 owing to a lack of advertising revenue. There is currently no printed press in Wallis and Futuna.

Broadcasting and Communications

TELECOMMUNICATIONS

France Telecom (FCR): Télécommunications Extérieures de Wallis et Futuna, BP 54, Mata'Utu, 98600 Uvea, Wallis Islands; tel. 722436; fax 722255; e-mail fcr@wallis.co.nc.

Service des Postes et Télécommunications: BP 00, Mata'Utu, 98600 Uvea, Wallis Islands; tel. 720809; fax 722662; e-mail pio.tui@wallis.co.nc; Dir MANUELE TAOFIFENUA; Head of Postage Stamp Section PIO TUI.

BROADCASTING

Radio and Television

Réseau France Outre-mer (RFO): BP 102, Pointe Matala, Mata'Utu, 98600 Uvea, Wallis Islands; tel. 721300; fax 722446; e-mail rfo.wallis@wallis.co.nc; internet wallisfutuna.rfo.fr; f. 1979; acquired by Groupe France Télévisions in 2004; fmrly Radiodiffusion Française d'Outre-mer, present name adopted in 1998; transmitters at Mata'Utu (Uvea) and Alo (Futuna); programmes broadcast 24 hours daily in Uvean (Wallisian), Futunian and French; a television service on Uvea, transmitting for 12 hours daily in French, began operation in 1986; a television service on Futuna was inaugurated in December 1994; satellite television began operation in March 2000; Regional Dir GÉRARD CHRISTIAN HOARAU; Station Man. LUSIA KAVAKAVA; Editor-in-Chief MICHEL-CLAUDE ADNOT.

Finance

BANKING

Bank of Issue

Institut d'Emission d'Outre-Mer: BP G5, Mata'Utu, Havelu, Hahake, 98600 Uvea, Wallis Islands; tel. 722505; fax 722003; e-mail direction@ieomwf.fr; internet www.ieom.fr; f. 1998; Dir RAYMOND COFFRE.

Other Banks

Agence Française de Développement: BP G5, Mata'Utu, 98600 Uvea, Wallis Islands; tel. 722505; fax 722003; e-mail afdmatautu@groupe-afd.org; fmrly Caisse Française de Développement; devt bank; Man. DIDIER SIMON.

Banque de Wallis et Futuna: BP 59, Mata'Utu, 98600 Uvea, Wallis Islands; tel. 722124; fax 722156; e-mail maurice.j.lasante@bnpparibas.com; internet nc.bnpparibas.net; f. 1991; 51% owned by BNP Paribas (New Caledonia); CEO MAURICE LASANTE.

Paierie de Wallis et Futuna: Mata'Utu, 98600 Uvea, Wallis Islands.

Insurance

GAN Assurances: BP 52, Mata'Utu, Hahake, 98600 Uvea, Wallis Islands; subsidiary of GAN Assurances, France; general non-life insurance.

Poe-ma Insurances: Matala'a, Utufua, Mua, BP 728, Vaitupu, 98600 Uvea, Wallis Islands; tel. 450096; fax 450097; e-mail poema@mail.pf.

Trade and Industry

UTILITIES

Electricité et Eau de Wallis et Futuna (EEWF): BP 28, Mata'Utu, 98600 Uvea, Wallis Islands; tel. 721500; fax 721196; e-mail eewf@wallis.co.nc; 32.4% owned by the territory and 66.6% owned by Electricité et Eau de Calédonie (Groupe Suez, France); production and distribution of electricity on Wallis and Futuna; production and distribution of potable water on Wallis since 1986; Dir JEAN-MARC PETIT.

TRADE UNIONS

Union Interprofessionnelle CFDT Wallis et Futuna (UI CFDT): BP 178, Mata'Utu, 98600 Uvea, Wallis Islands; tel. 721880; Sec.-Gen. KALOLO HANISI.

Union Territoriale Force Ouvrière: BP 325, Mata'Utu, 98600 Uvea, Wallis Islands; tel. 721732; fax 721732; Sec.-Gen. CHRISTIAN VAAMEI.

Transport

ROADS

Uvea has a few kilometres of road, one route circling the island, and there is also a partially surfaced road circling the island of Futuna; the only fully surfaced roads are in Mata'Utu.

SHIPPING

There are two wharfs on Uvea for bulk goods, at Mata'Utu, and liquid fuels, at Halalo, respectively. There is one wharf at Leava on Futuna. Wallis and Futuna is served by two container ships: the Southern Moana, operated jointly by Moana Services of New Caledonia and Pacific Direct Line of New Zealand between Auckland (New Zealand), Nouméa (New Caledonia) and the islands; and the Sofrana Bligh, operated by Sofrana between Auckland and the islands. Plans to expand the harbour facilities at Mata'Utu and to make improvements to the fishing port of Halalo have been subject to delay.

Société Française Navigation (SOFRANA): BP 24, Mata'Utu, 98600 Uvea, Wallis Islands; f. 1986; subsidiary of Sofrana Unilines, New Zealand; 1 vessel.

CIVIL AVIATION

There is an international airport in Hihifo district on Uvea, about 5 km from Mata'Utu. Air Calédonie International (Aircalin—New Caledonia) is the only airline to serve Wallis and Futuna. The company operates five flights a week from Wallis to Futuna, one flight a week from Wallis to Tahiti (French Polynesia) and two flights a week from Wallis to Nouméa (New Caledonia). The airport on Futuna is at Pointe Vele, in the south-east, in the Kingdom of Alo; work began in 2005 to upgrade Vele airport to receive international traffic, scheduled to be completed by 2008. The Compagnie Aérienne de Wallis et Futuna (Air Wallis) was established in 2004, as a joint venture between the Government and local business interests; however, the project was delayed in 2005.

Office of Civil Aviation: BP 01, Mata'Utu, Malae, Hihifo, 98600 Uvea, Wallis Islands; tel. 721200; fax 722954; e-mail aviation.civile@wallis.co.nc.

Tourism

Tourism remains undeveloped. There are four small hotels on Uvea, Wallis Islands. In 2006 foreign visitors to the islands totalled 2,456. The number of hotel rooms available was expected to increase to 60 in 2006. There are two small guest-houses for visitors on Futuna.

Other French Overseas Territories

The other French territories are the French Southern and Antarctic Territories, and New Caledonia. The latter has a unique status as a collectivité *sui generis* within the framework of the French Republic. Powers are devolved to New Caledonia under the terms of the 1998 Nouméa Accord.

THE FRENCH SOUTHERN AND ANTARCTIC TERRITORIES

Introduction

The French Southern and Antarctic Territories (Terres australes et antarctiques françaises) are administered under a special statute. The territory comprises Adélie Land, a narrow segment of the mainland of Antarctica together with a number of offshore islets, three groups of sub-Antarctic islands (the Kerguelen and Crozet Archipelagos, and Saint-Paul and Amsterdam Islands) in the southern Indian Ocean, and the Iles Eparses, in the Indian Ocean, comprising Bassas da India, Juan da Nova, Europa and Les Glorieuses, which are also claimed by Madagascar, and Tromelin, also claimed by Madagascar and Mauritius.

Under the terms of legislation approved by the French Government in 1955, the French Southern and Antarctic Territories were placed under the authority of a chief administrator, responsible to the government member for the overseas possessions. The Prefect, Chief Administrator is assisted by a Consultative Council, which meets at least twice annually. The Council is composed of seven members who are appointed for five years by the government member for the overseas possessions (from among members of the Office of Scientific Research and from those who have participated in scientific missions in the sub-Antarctic islands and Adélie Land). Under the terms of a decree promulgated in 1997, administration of the French Southern and Antarctic Territories was formally transferred from Paris to Saint-Pierre, Réunion, in April 2000. The Iles Eparses, administrative control of which was transferred from the Prefect of Réunion to the Prefect, Chief Administrator of the French Southern and Antarctic Territories in January 2005, became an integral part of the French Southern and Antarctic Territories under an organic law promulgated in February 2007.

From 1987 certain categories of vessels were allowed to register under the flag of the Kerguelen Archipelago, provided that 25% of their crew (including the captain and at least two officers) were French. These specifications were amended to 35% of the crew and at least four officers in April 1990. Under new legislation enacted in May 2005 this 'Kerguelen Register' was replaced with a new French International Register, whereby, *inter alia*, the captain and one officer would be required to be a French national, and 35% of the crew would be required to be from member countries of the European Union. At 31 December 2005 there were 145 registered vessels.

A permanent French base was established in 1950 at Martin de Viviès, on Amsterdam Island, followed by a second at Port-aux-Français, in the Kerguelen Archipelago, in 1951. The first permanent French base on the mainland was built in 1952 at Port Martin. Having been destroyed by fire, it was replaced in 1956 by a new permanent base at Dumont d'Urville. A fourth base was opened in 1964 at Alfred Faure on Ile de la Possession, in the Crozet Archipelago. In 1992 the French Government created a Public Interest Group, the Institut Français pour la Recherche et la Technologie Polaires (IFRTP—renamed the Institut Polaire Français Paul Emile Victor—IPEV—in 2002), to assume responsibility for the organization of scientific and research programmes in the French Southern and Antarctic Territories. Under an agreement between the IFRTP and Italy's Programma Nazionale di Ricerche in Antartide in 1993, work began on a joint project, Concordia, with a permanent base to be established at Dome C. Concordia was officially opened for winter operation in 2005. France is a signatory to the Antarctic Treaty (see p. 575).

Fishing for crayfish and Patagonian toothfish in the territories' Exclusive Economic Zone is strictly regulated by quotas (see Statistical Survey). During 2005/06 six companies were licensed to fish in the zone. Following the implementation of a new satellite surveillance system in February 2004, illegal fishing incursions were believed to have been reduced by some 90% by November 2005.

Limited numbers of tourists have since 1994 been permitted to visit Crozet, Kerguelen and Amsterdam: about 60 tourists travel to the territories each year aboard the supply and oceanographic vessel *Marion Dufresne II*.

Statistical Survey

Area (sq km): Kerguelen Archipelago 7,215, Crozet Archipelago 515, Amsterdam Island 58, Saint-Paul Island 8, Adélie Land (Antarctica) 432,000, Iles Eparses 44 (Bassas da India 1, Europa 30, Juan de Nova 5, Les Glorieuses 7, Tromelin 1).

Population (the population, comprising members of scientific missions, fluctuates according to season, being higher in the summer, but the average is around 200; the figures given are approximate): Kerguelen Archipelago, Port-aux-Français 80; Amsterdam Island at Martin de Viviès 30; Adélie Land at Base Dumont d'Urville 27; the Crozet Archipelago at Alfred Faure (on Ile de la Possession) 35; Saint-Paul Island is uninhabited; Total population (April 2000): 172. *2003/04:* Adélie Land at Base Concordia 41 (joint French-Italian team).

Fishing (catch quotas in metric tons, 2005/06): Crayfish (spiny lobsters) in Amsterdam and Saint-Paul: 390; Patagonian toothfish (caught by French and foreign fleets) in the Kerguelen and Crozet Archipelagos: 6,150.

Currency: French currency was used until the end of 2001. Euro notes and coins were introduced on 1 January 2002, and the euro became the sole legal tender from 18 February. For details of exchange rates, see French Guiana.

Budget: €33.4m. in 2005, of which official subventions comprised €281,800.

External Trade: Exports consist mainly of crayfish and other fish to France and Réunion. The Territories also derive revenue from the sale of postage stamps and other philatelic items.

Directory

Government: e-mail taaf.com@wanadoo.fr; internet www.taaf.fr; the central administration is in Saint-Pierre, Réunion; Prefect, Chief Administrator Eric Pilloton.

Consultative Council: Pres. Jean-Pierre Charpentier.

Publications: The central administration in Réunion produces two quarterly publications relating to the French Southern and Antarctic Territories: the legal bulletin *Journal officiel des Terres australes et antarctiques françaises* and a newsletter, *Terres Extrêmes*.

Institut Polaire Français Paul Emile Victor (IPEV): Technopôle de Brest-Iroise, BP 75, 29280 Plouzané, France; tel. 2-98-05-65-00; fax 2-98-05-65-55; e-mail infoipev@ipev.fr; internet www.institut-polaire.fr; f. 1992 as Institut Français pour la Recherche et la Technologie Polaires, name changed 2002; Dir Gérard Jugie; 5 permanent bases.

Research Stations: There are meteorological stations and geophysical research stations on Kerguelen, Amsterdam, Adélie Land and Crozet. Research in marine microbiology is conducted from the Crozet and Kerguelen Archipelagos, and studies of atmospheric pollution are carried out on Amsterdam Island. Additionally, a joint French-Italian research station, Concordia, operates at Dome C. The French atomic energy authority, the Commissariat à l'énergie atomique, also maintains a presence on Crozet, Kerguelen and Adélie Land.

Transport: An oceanographic and supply vessel, the *Marion Dufresne II*, operated by the French Government, provides regular links between Réunion and the sub-Antarctic islands. A polar research vessel, *Astrolabe*, owned by the Groupe Bourbon and operating from Hobart, Tasmania, calls five times a year at the Antarctic mainland. The IPEV also has a coastal research vessel, *Curieuse*, based at Cemetery Island, in the Kerguelen Archipelago.

NEW CALEDONIA

Introductory Survey

Location, Climate, Language, Religion, Capital

New Caledonia comprises one large island and several smaller ones, lying in the South Pacific Ocean, about 1,500 km (930 miles) east of Queensland, Australia. The main island, New Caledonia (Grande Terre), is long and narrow, and has a total area of 16,372 sq km. Rugged mountains divide the west of the island from the east, and there is little flat land. The nearby Loyalty Islands, which are administratively part of New Caledonia, are 1,981 sq km in area, and a third group of islands, the uninhabited Chesterfield Islands, lies about 400 km north-west of the main island. The islands are surrounded by the world's largest continuous coral barrier reef, encompassing some 40,000 sq km. The climate is generally mild, with an average temperature of about 24°C (75°F) and a rainy season between December and March. The average rainfall in the east of the main island is about 2,000 mm (80 ins) per year, and in the west about 1,000 mm (40 ins). French is the official language and the mother tongue of the Caldoches (French settlers). The indigenous Kanaks (Melanesians) also speak Melanesian languages: 29 languages were taken into account at the census of 1996, when it was recorded that 38% of the total indigenous Kanak population spoke a Melanesian language. Other immigrants speak Polynesian and Asian languages. New Caledonians almost all profess Christianity; about 59% are Roman Catholics, and there is a substantial Protestant minority. The capital is Nouméa, on the main island.

Recent History

New Caledonia became a French possession in 1853, when the island was annexed as a dependency of Tahiti. In 1860 a separate administration was established, and in 1885 a conseil général was elected to defend the local interests before metropolitan France. France took possession of Melanesian land and began mining nickel and copper in 1864, displacing the indigenous Kanak population. This provoked a number of rebellions, including the Kanak revolt of 1878. From 1887 two separate administrations existed, for Melanesian Kanaks and expatriates, until New Caledonia became an Overseas Territory of the French Republic in 1946. In 1956 the first Territorial Assembly, with 30 members, was elected by universal adult suffrage, although the French Governor effectively retained control of the functions of government. New Caledonian demands for a measure of self-government were answered in 1976 by a new statute, which gave the Council of Government, elected from the Territorial Assembly, responsibility for certain internal affairs. The post of Governor was replaced by that of French High Commissioner to the Territory. In 1978 the Kanak-supported, pro-independence parties obtained a majority of the posts in the Council of Government. In early 1979, however, the French Government dismissed the Council, following its failure to support a proposal for a 10-year 'contract' between France and New Caledonia, because the plan did not acknowledge the possibility of New Caledonian independence. The Territory was then placed under the direct authority of the High Commissioner. A general election was held in July, but a new electoral law, which affected mainly the pro-independence parties, ensured that minor parties were not represented in the Assembly. Two parties loyal to France (Rassemblement pour la Calédonie dans la République—RPCR—and Fédération pour une Nouvelle Société Calédonienne—FNSC) together won 22 of the 36 seats.

Following the election of François Mitterrand as President of France, tension increased in September 1981 after the assassination of Pierre Declercq, the Secretary-General of the pro-independence party, Union Calédonienne (UC). In December of that year the French Government made proposals for change that included equal access for all New Caledonians to positions of authority, land reforms and the fostering of Kanak cultural institutions. To assist in effecting these reforms, the French Government simultaneously announced that it would rule by decree for a period of at least one year. In 1982 the FNSC joined with the opposition grouping, Front Indépendantiste (FI), to form a government that was more favourable to the proposed reforms.

In November 1983 the French Government proposed a five-year period of increased autonomy from July 1984 and a referendum in 1989 to determine New Caledonia's future. The statute was opposed in New Caledonia, both by parties in favour of earlier independence and by those against, and it was rejected by the Territorial Assembly in April 1984. However, the proposals were approved by the French Assemblée nationale (National Assembly) in September 1984. Under the provisions of the statute, the Territorial Council of Ministers was given responsibility for many internal matters of government, its President henceforth being an elected member instead of the French High Commissioner; a second legislative chamber, with the right to be consulted on development planning and budgetary issues, was created at the same time. All of the main parties seeking independence (except the Libération Kanak Socialiste—LKS—party, which left the FI) boycotted elections for the new Territorial Assembly in November 1984 and, following the dissolution of the FI, formed a new movement called the Front de Libération Nationale Kanak Socialiste (FLNKS). On 1 December the FLNKS Congress established a 'provisional' Government, headed by Jean-Marie Tjibaou. The elections to the Territorial Assembly attracted only 50.1% of the electorate, and the anti-independence party RPCR won 34 of the 42 seats. An escalation of violence began in November, and in the following month three settlers were murdered by pro-independence activists and 10 Kanaks were killed by *métis* (mixed race) settlers.

In January 1985 Edgard Pisani, the new High Commissioner, announced a plan by which the Territory might become independent 'in association with' France on 1 January 1986, subject to the result of a referendum in July 1985. Kanak groups opposed the plan, insisting that the indigenous population be allowed to determine its own fate. At the same time, the majority of the population, which supported the RPCR, demonstrated against the plan and in favour of remaining within the French Republic. A resurgence of violence followed the announcement of Pisani's plan, and a state of emergency was declared after two incidents in which a leading member of the FLNKS was killed by security forces and the son of a French settler was killed by Kanak activists.

In April 1985 the French Prime Minister, Laurent Fabius, put forward new proposals for the future of New Caledonia, whereby the referendum on independence was deferred until an unspecified date not later than the end of 1987. Meanwhile, the Territory was to be divided into four regions, each to be governed by its own elected autonomous council, which would have extensive powers in the spheres of planning and development, education, health and social services, land rights, transport and housing. The elected members of all four councils together would serve as regional representatives in a Territorial Congress (to replace the Territorial Assembly).

The 'Fabius plan' was well received by the FLNKS, although the organization reaffirmed the ultimate goal of independence. It was also decided to maintain the 'provisional Government' under Jean-Marie Tjibaou at least until the end of 1985. The RPCR, however, condemned the plan, and the proposals were rejected by the predominantly anti-independence Territorial Assembly in May. However, the necessary legislation was approved by the French Assemblée nationale in July, and the Fabius plan came into force. Elections were held in September, and as expected only in the region around Nouméa, where the bulk of the population is non-Kanak, was an anti-independence majority recorded. However, the pro-independence Melanesians, in spite of their majorities in the three non-urban regions, would be in a minority in the Territorial Congress.

The FLNKS boycotted the general election to the French Assemblée nationale in March 1986, in which only about 50% of the eligible voters in New Caledonia participated. In May the French Council of Ministers approved a draft law providing for a referendum to be held in New Caledonia within 12 months, whereby voters would choose between independence and a further extension of regional autonomy. In December, in spite of strong French diplomatic opposition, the UN General Assembly voted to reinscribe New Caledonia on the UN list of non-self-governing territories, thereby affirming the population's right to self-determination.

The FLNKS decided to boycott the referendum on 13 September 1987, at which 98.3% of the votes cast were in favour of New Caledonia's continuation as part of the French Republic and only 1.7% of those cast favoured independence. Of the registered electorate, almost 59% voted, a higher level of participation than was expected, although 90% of the electorate abstained in constituencies inhabited by a majority of Kanaks.

In October 1987 seven pro-French loyalists were acquitted on a charge of murdering 10 Kanak separatists in 1984. Jean-Marie Tjibaou, who reacted to the ruling by declaring that his followers would have to abandon their stance of pacifism, and his deputy, Yeiwéné Yeiwéné, were indicted for 'incitement to violence'. In April 1988 four gendarmes were killed, and 27 held hostage in a cave on the island of Uvéa (the neighbouring Wallis Island), by supporters of the FLNKS. Two days later, Kanak separatists prevented about one-quarter of the Territory's polling stations from opening when local elections were held. The FLNKS boycotted the elections. Although 12 of the gendarmes taken hostage were subsequently released, six members of a French anti-terrorist squad were captured. French security forces immediately laid siege to the cave, and in the following month made an assault upon it, leaving 19 Kanaks and two gendarmes dead. Following the siege, allegations that three Kanaks had been executed or left to die, after being arrested, led to an announcement by the new French Socialist Government that a judicial inquiry into the incident was to be opened.

At the elections to the French Assemblée nationale in June 1988, both New Caledonian seats were retained by the RPCR. Michel

Rocard, the new French Prime Minister, chaired negotiations in Paris, between Jacques Lafleur (leader of the RPCR) and Jean-Marie Tjibaou, who agreed to transfer the administration of the Territory to Paris for 12 months. Under the provisions of the agreement (known as the Matignon Accord), the Territory was to be divided into three administrative Provinces prior to a territorial plebiscite on independence to be held in 1998. Only people resident in the Territory in 1988, and their direct descendants, would be allowed to vote in the plebiscite. The agreement also provided for a programme of economic development, training in public administration for Kanaks, and institutional reforms. The Matignon Accord was presented to the French electorate in a referendum, held on 6 November 1988, and approved by 80% of those voting (although an abstention rate of 63% of the electorate was recorded). The programme was approved by a 57% majority in New Caledonia, where the rate of abstention was 37%. In November, under the terms of the agreement, 51 separatists were released from prison, including 26 Kanaks implicated in the incident on Uvéa.

In May 1989 the leaders of the FLNKS, Jean-Marie Tjibaou and Yeiwéné Yeiwéné, were murdered by separatist extremists, alleged to be associated with the Front Uni de Libération Kanak (FULK), a grouping which had until then formed part of the FLNKS, but which opposed the Matignon Accord on the grounds that it conceded too much to the European settlers. The assassinations were regarded as an attempt to disrupt the implementation of the Accord. Elections to the three Provincial Assemblies were nevertheless held, as scheduled, in June: the FLNKS won a majority of seats in the North Province and the Loyalty Islands Province, while the RPCR obtained a majority in the South Province, and also emerged as the dominant party in the Territorial Congress, with 27 of the 54 seats; the FLNKS secured 19 seats.

The year of direct rule by France ended, as agreed, on 14 July 1989, when the Territorial Congress and Provincial Assemblies assumed the administrative functions allocated to them in the Matignon Accord (see Government, below). In November the French Assemblée nationale approved an amnesty (as stipulated in the Matignon Accord) for all who had been involved in politically-motivated violence in New Caledonia before August 1988, despite strong opposition from the right-wing French parties.

In April 1991 the LKS announced its intention to withdraw from the Matignon Accord, accusing the French Government, as well as several Kanak political leaders, of seeking to undermine Kanak culture and tradition. The RPCR's policy of encouraging the immigration of skilled workers from mainland France and other European countries continued to be a source of conflict between the conservative coalition and the FLNKS.

At elections for the New Caledonian representative to the French Sénat (Senate) in September 1992, the RPCR's candidate, Simon Loueckhote, narrowly defeated Roch Wamytan, the Vice-President of the FLNKS.

Debate concerning the political future of the Territory continued in 1994. In October Jacques Lafleur proposed that New Caledonia abandon the planned 1998 referendum on self-determination, in favour of a 30-year agreement with France, similar to the Matignon Accord, but with provision for greater autonomy in judicial matters. The UC, however, rejected the proposal and reiterated its demand for a gradual transfer of power from France to New Caledonia, culminating in a return to sovereignty in 1998.

French presidential elections took place in April–May 1995. During the second round of voting in the Territory, the socialist candidate, Lionel Jospin, received 25.9% of the total votes, while the candidate of the Gaullist Rassemblement pour la République (RPR), Jacques Chirac, won 74.1%. (Chirac was elected to the presidency with 52.6% of votes cast throughout the republic.)

At provincial elections in July 1995 the RPCR remained the most successful party, although its dominance was reduced considerably. The FLNKS remained in control of the North Province and the Loyalty Islands, while the RPCR retained a large majority in the South Province. The RPCR retained an overall majority in the Territorial Congress, while the FLNKS remained the second largest party. Considerable gains were made by a newly-formed party led by Nouméa businessman Didier Leroux, Une Nouvelle-Calédonie pour Tous (UNCT), which secured seven seats in the Territorial Congress and seven seats in the Provincial Government of the South. An estimated 67% of the electorate participated in the elections. However, a political crisis subsequently arose as a result of the UNCT's decision to align itself with the FLNKS, leaving the RPCR with a minority of official positions in the congressional committees. Jacques Lafleur would not accept a situation in which the UNCT appeared to be the dominant party in the chamber, and Pierre Frogier, the RPCR's President of Congress, refused to convene a congressional sitting under such circumstances. The deadlock was broken only when the FLNKS released a statement in October, reiterating the importance of the relationship between the FLNKS and the RPCR as signatories of the Matignon Accord, and proposing the allocation of congressional positions on a proportional basis.

Negotiations between the French Government and delegations from the FLNKS and the RPCR were held in Paris in late 1995. It was agreed that further discussions would take place in early 1996, involving representatives from numerous interest groups in the Territory, to examine the possibility of achieving a consensus solution on the future of the islands. Thus, the major political groups in New Caledonia sought to achieve a consensus solution on the Territory's future, which could be presented to the electorate for approval in the 1998 referendum. It was widely believed that this was preferable to a simple 'for' or 'against' vote on independence, which would necessarily polarize the electorate and create a confrontational political climate.

Elections to the French Assemblée nationale in May–June 1997 were boycotted by the pro-independence FLNKS and LKS, resulting in a relatively low participation rate among the electorate. Jacques Lafleur and Pierre Frogier, both RPCR candidates, were elected to represent New Caledonia. Intensive negotiations involving the RPCR, the FLNKS and the French Government took place throughout early 1996. The process, however, was disrupted by a dispute over the disclosure of confidential information regarding the talks to the French press (responsibility for which was later admitted by Lafleur) and the belief by pro-independence leaders that France had apparently reneged on its promise to consider all available options for the Territory's political future by discounting the possibility of outright independence. France's refusal to grant final approval for a large-scale nickel smelter project in the North Province (see Economic Affairs, below) until the achievement of consensus in the discussions on autonomy prompted accusations of blackmail from several sources within the Territory and fuelled suspicions that metropolitan France would seek to retain control of the islands' valuable mineral resources in any settlement on New Caledonia's future status. The issue proved to be a serious obstacle in the negotiations and resulted in the virtual cessation of discussions between the two sides during the remainder of 1996. The FLNKS argued that the smelter project should be administered by local interests, consistent with the process of reallocating responsibility for the economy from metropolitan France to the Territory as advocated in the Matignon Accord. Their demands were supported by widespread industrial action in the mining sector during late 1996.

In February 1997 the French Minister for Overseas Territories, Jean-Jacques de Peretti, travelled to New Caledonia in an attempt to achieve an exchange agreement on nickel between the Société Minière du Sud Pacifique (SMSP), controlled by the North Province, and a subsidiary of the French mining conglomerate Eramet, Société Le Nickel (SLN). The minister failed to resolve the dispute during his visit; however, at the end of the month, in a complete reversal of its previous position, the French Government announced its decision not to compensate SLN for any losses incurred. The decision provoked strong criticism from SLN and Eramet, and attracted protests from shareholders and employees of the company. During March large-scale demonstrations were held by the UC and the pro-independence trade union, the Union Syndicale des Travailleurs Kanak et des Exploités (USTKE), in support of SMSP's acquisition of the smelter. Meanwhile, another trade union, USOENC (which represented a high proportion of SLN employees), organized a protest rally against the unequal exchange of mining sites. Frustrated at SLN's seemingly intransigent position during the negotiations, the FLNKS organized protests and blockades at all the company's major mining installations. Supporters of the pro-independence organization also restricted shipments of ore around New Caledonia. Consequently, four mines were forced to close, while a 25% reduction in working hours was imposed on 1,500 mine workers, prompting protests by SLN employees and demands from USOENC that the blockades be removed. In January 1998 Roch Wamytan urged the French Prime Minister, Lionel Jospin, to settle the dispute by the end of the month in order that official negotiations on the political future of New Caledonia, in preparation for the referendum, might begin. The position of the FLNKS had been somewhat undermined by the decision, in the previous month, of a breakaway group of pro-independence politicians—including prominent members of the UC, the Parti de Libération Kanak (PALIKA), and the LKS—to begin negotiations with the RPCR concerning the dispute. These moderate supporters of independence formed the Fédération des Comités de Coordination des Indépendantistes (FCCI) in 1998.

In February 1998, in response to the demands of Kanak political leaders, the French Government, Eramet, SMSP and others signed the Bercy Accord, whereby Eramet was to relinquish control of its site at Koniambo, located in the North Province, in exchange for the Poum mine, operated by SMSP, in the South Province. (The Bercy Accord was the foundation for the 'rebalancing' of New Caledonia's economy under the Nouméa Accord—see below—by creating wealth beyond the South Province.) In April SMSP formed a joint venture with the Canadian mining company Falconbridge to develop the Koniambo nickel deposits. If construction of a nickel smelter had not begun by the end of 2005, control of the nickel deposits was to revert from SMSP to SLN. Meanwhile, the French Government agreed to pay compensation of some 1,000m. French francs to Eramet for the reduction in the company's reserves. An agreement was concluded in February 1999 to enable the transfer of 30% of SLN's share capital (and 8% of Eramet's capital) to a newly created company representing local interests, the Société Territoriale Calédonienne de Participation Industrielle (STCPI), to be owned by the development companies of the three New Caledonian provinces. In July 2000, following two years of negotiations, New Caledonia's political leaders signed an agreement on the formation of the STCPI, the new company to be owned equally by PROMOSUD (representing the South Province) and NORDIL (combining the interests of the North Province and the Loyalty Islands). In September shares in SLN and Eramet were transferred to the STCPI, reducing Eramet's interest in SLN from 90% to 60%.

Tripartite talks on the constitutional future of New Caledonia resumed in Paris in late February 1998. Discussions involving representatives of the French Government, the FLNKS and the RPCR continued in March, despite a temporary boycott of the talks by the RPCR delegation, which requested the inclusion of various other minor political groups in the negotiations, including the FCCI. On 21 April, following a final round of talks in Nouméa, an agreement was concluded by the three sides. The agreement, which became known as the Nouméa Accord, postponed the referendum on independence for a period of between 15 and 20 years but provided for a gradual transfer of powers to local institutions. The document also acknowledged the negative impact of many aspects of French colonization on New Caledonia and emphasized the need for greater recognition of the importance of the Kanak cultural identity in the political development of the islands. The Nouméa Accord was signed on 5 May.

On 6 July 1998 both chambers of the French legislature voted in favour of adopting the proposed changes regarding the administration of New Caledonia, which were to be incorporated in an annex to the French Constitution. The following month the French Minister for Overseas Territories, Jean-Jack Queyranne, returned to New Caledonia for discussion on draft legislation for the devolution process. In September a new political group, the Comité Provisoire pour la Défense des Principes Républicains de la Nouvelle-Calédonie Française, was formed in opposition to the Nouméa Accord, with support from members of the Front National and other right-wing parties. The UNCT, which was dissatisfied with several aspects of the accord, also urged its supporters to vote against the agreement.

The Nouméa Accord, which designated New Caledonia as an Overseas Country (pays d'outre-mer) of France, was presented to the electorate in a referendum on 8 November 1998, when it was decisively approved, with 71.9% of votes cast in favour of the agreement. The North Province registered the strongest vote in favour of the agreement (95.5%), while the South Province recorded the most moderate level of approval (62.9%). In late December the French Assemblée nationale unanimously approved draft legislation regarding the definitive adoption of the accord. The Sénat similarly approved the legislation in February 1999. In March of that year, however, the French Constitutional Council declared its intention to allow any French person who had resided in New Caledonia for 10 years or more to vote in provincial elections. This decision was criticized by Roch Wamytan, leader of the FLNKS, as well as by politicians in the French Assemblée nationale and Sénat, who claimed that this was in breach of the Nouméa Accord, whereby only those residing in New Caledonia in 1998 would be permitted to vote in provincial elections. Pro-independence groups threatened to boycott the elections (to be held in May). In response to this, the French Government announced that the Accord would be honoured, claiming that the Constitutional Council had breached the Nouméa Accord, and stating that this contravention would be rectified. In June the French Council of Ministers announced that it had drafted legislation restricting eligibility for voting in provincial elections and in any future referendums on sovereignty, to those who had been eligible to vote in the November 1998 referendum on the Nouméa Accord, and to their children upon reaching the age of majority. This decision was condemned by the right-wing Front National, and by Jacques Lafleur, leader of the RPCR. In January 2005 the European Court of Human Rights upheld the ruling, but the matter was expected to be discussed at talks in Paris later that month as part of the follow-up process to the Nouméa Accord; Lafleur, who had since been replaced as leader of Rassemblement-UMP (the successor party to the RPCR—see below) by Pierre Frogier, had already proposed reducing to three years the period of residence required before one would be allowed to vote and was threatening to boycott the talks.

At the general election held on 9 May 1999, no party gained an absolute majority. However, Jacques Lafleur's anti-independence RPCR won 24 of the 54 seats in the Congress and formed a coalition with the recently-established FCCI and, on an informal level, with the Front National, thus creating an anti-independence block of 31 seats in the chamber. The pro-independence FLNKS won 18 seats. Simon Loueckhote was re-elected as President of the Congress in late May. Results of the elections in the Loyalty Islands were officially challenged by the moderate independence parties, LKS and FCCI, as well as by the RPCR, following the issue by the electoral commissioner for the Province of a report claiming that a large number of irregularities had occurred. A new election was held in June 2000, at which a coalition of the RPCR, FCCI, LKS and FULK obtained 44.8% of votes and six seats. The FLNKS obtained 37.3% of votes and six seats, and PALIKA 17.8% of votes and two seats. The composition of the Congress therefore remained unchanged. Robert Xowie was re-elected as President of the Province.

On 28 May 1999 the Congress elected Jean Lèques as the first President of the Government of New Caledonia, under the increased autonomy terms of the Nouméa Accord. The new Government was elected on the basis of proportional representation and replaced the French High Commissioner as New Caledonia's executive authority. The election of Léopold Jorédié, leader of the FCCI, as Vice-President was denounced by the FLNKS, which argued that, as it was the second largest party in Congress and had been a joint negotiator in the Nouméa Accord, the post should have gone to its leader, Roch Wamytan. In the formation of the Government the RPCR-FCCI was awarded seven positions and the FLNKS four.

In October 1999 Wamytan threatened to withdraw from the Government, in protest at the lack of co-operation among parties. He claimed that sections of the Nouméa Accord requiring power to be distributed among the various political parties had not been observed (see above). In December Vice-President Léopold Jorédié received a one-year suspended prison sentence following accusations of misuse of public funds. Jorédié was charged with illegally obtaining grants totalling an estimated 5.5m. francs CFP, for the benefit of his son.

In July 2000 concern was expressed by the French Government over the implementation of the 'collegiality' clause in the Nouméa Accord, which provided for greater political co-operation among parties. Repeated threats by the FLNKS to withdraw from the Government because of its discontent with the RPCR's lack of power-sharing led to the establishment of an agreement between New Caledonia and the French State detailing the role of the two Governments in areas such as education and foreign policy; the role of the traditional chiefs in legal matters was also specified. In August Jacques Lafleur threatened to resign from his seat in the French Assemblée nationale, following the decision to uphold a ruling that convicted him of slander against Bruno Van Peteghem, an activist opposing construction plans for a complex near Nouméa. However, in early September Lafleur retracted his threat, following pleas by RPCR members.

At the FLNKS's annual conference, held in November 2000, Roch Wamytan was re-elected President of the party (Wamytan was also narrowly re-elected leader of the UC); at the same time a new pro-independence party, the Groupe UC du Congrès, formed by a break-away faction of the UC, was officially recognized by both the UC and the FLNKS.

Municipal elections held in March 2001 confirmed the predominance of the RPCR in the south, when it won 39 of the 49 seats in Nouméa. However, overall the RPCR controlled only 14 of the 33 municipalities in New Caledonia, while pro-independence parties, principally the UC, PALIKA, LKS and FLNKS, held 19. The FLNKS won a majority in the north and took all three communes in the Loyalty Islands. Jean Lèques resigned as President and was replaced by fellow RPCR politician, Pierre Frogier, in April. Déwé Gorodey of the FLNKS was elected Vice-President. The election to the two most senior posts took place after the Congress had elected an 11-member Government consisting of seven RPCR-FCCI coalition members, three from the FLNKS and one from the UC.

In October 2001 the French Conseil d'état (State Council) ruled that the 11th seat in the New Caledonian Government had been incorrectly allocated to the FLNKS following the local elections of April 2001. As a result, FCCI leader Raphaël Mapou replaced Aukusitino Manuohalalo of the FLNKS as Minister for Social Security and Health. Roch Wamytan, threatened to resign from the Government in protest. In the same month, however, Wamytan was replaced as President of the UC by his deputy, Pascal Naouna; many members believed that Wamytan's dual role as President of both the UC and the FLNKS was weakening the party. Then, in November, Wamytan lost the presidency of the FLNKS following a leadership struggle between its two main factions, the UC and PALIKA. The political bureau of the FLNKS was to lead the party until its internal disputes were settled. Wamytan was subsequently replaced as Minister for Customary Affairs and Relations with the Senate by Mapou, who was in turn replaced as Minister for Social Security and Health by Manuohalalo.

In June 2001, as a result of the failure to resolve industrial action over the dismissal of 12 employees from public works company Lefèbvre Pacifique, USTKE extended its strike to 24-hour blockades of supermarkets, petrol stations, state radio and television companies, schools, the port and the airport. In July 2001 a 100,000 francs CFP monthly minimum wage, as provided for in a 'social pact' negotiated in September 2000, was implemented. Further strike action affected the tourist industry when, in December, USTKE launched a strike and occupation of the Château Royal complex, following Club Med's announcement of the Nouméa holiday resort's closure.

Meanwhile, a long-standing dispute over the ownership of a Wallisian settlement—Ave Maria, near Nouméa—had led to intense fighting between Wallisian and Kanak communities from December 2001. The Kanak community in neighbouring Saint Louis demanded the departure of all Wallisians from Ave Maria by March 2002. The French High Commissioner mediated at several meetings in January 2002 in an attempt to resolve the issue, leading to the Wallisian spokesman's suggestion that his community might be prepared to leave Ave Maria, provided it was offered an alternative 25 ha of land on which to resettle. Four working groups were established in April to rehouse Wallisians, to improve the area's public facilities, and to reintegrate youths who had abandoned the education system. In November the Kanak and Wallisian communities signed an agreement, mediated by the High Commissioner, to end the violence, which had claimed three lives in total. About half of the 140 Wallisian families present in Saint Louis had left by the end of 2002; under the terms of the agreement, the remainder were to be resettled in 2003. In June of that year some 100 Wallisians were forced to flee Ave Maria and take up residence in temporary housing, following another outbreak of racial violence with the Kanak community. By mid-September the remaining 30 Wallisian families had left the area to be resettled in and around Nouméa. The leader of the opposition Alliance pour la Calédonie, Didier Leroux, condemned the failure of the French Government to intervene as tantamount to 'ethnic cleansing'. In late December 2005 an agreement was reached by the authorities of the South Province to make funds available to some 171 families who had been evacuated to the area.

In the first round of the presidential election, held on 21 April 2002, Jacques Chirac obtained 48.4% of the vote on the islands, followed by Lionel Jospin, who won 22.4%, and was eliminated nationally. In the second round, held on 5 May, Chirac overwhelmingly defeated Jean-Marie Le Pen of the extreme right-wing Front National, with 80.4% of the vote. Elections to the French Assemblée nationale were held in June 2002. Prior to the elections RCPR became affiliated to the metropolitan Union pour la Majorité Presidentielle—latterly Union pour un Mouvement Populaire—to form Rassemblement-UMP. The UC and PALIKA could not agree upon their choice of President for the FLNKS. The UC therefore refused to take part in the elections and urged its supporters to abstain from the poll, thereby depriving the President of PALIKA, Paul Néaoutyine, of any chance of re-election to the Assemblée nationale in Paris. Jacques Lafleur, now representing Rassemblement-UMP, was thus re-elected as a deputy, winning 55.7% of the votes cast in the second round of polling; fellow Rassemblement-UMP member Pierre Frogier was also re-elected, with 55.7% of the votes cast; the rate of abstention, however, was almost 60%. In December Lafleur announced his 'progressive retirement' from politics, although he gave no precise date.

Following two resignations in July 2002, a series of ministerial reorganizations took place. The Minister for Employment and Public Services, Françoise Horhant, resigned and was replaced by a fellow Rassemblement-UMP member, Georges Naturel. In late July Raphaël Mapou resigned, following his criticism of the tendering of mining and prospecting rights in the South Province to a Canadian mining company. He was replaced by Corinne Fuluhea of Rassemblement-UMP. Shortly afterwards, her portfolio was altered to that of Professional Training. In November the sole UC member of the Government, Gerald Cortot, resigned, prompting the immediate dissolution of the Government, as stipulated in the Nouméa Accord. Later that month the size of the Council of Ministers was reduced to 10 members, and the Congress appointed a new administration, with Pierre Frogier reappointed as President; the incoming Government contained seven members of the Rassemblement-UMP–FCCI coalition, two from the FLNKS and one from the UC.

In May 2003 it was announced that New Caledonia (together with French Polynesia) would be granted one additional seat in the French Sénat, probably effective from the next senatorial elections (scheduled for 2008). Also in May 2003, at a congress of the FLNKS, officials of the party reportedly claimed that the terms of the Nouméa Accord were not being fully observed by the French Government. In July the USTKE called a general strike to coincide with a visit to New Caledonia by President Chirac. A rally organized by the mainly Kanak trade union was attended by 2,000 protesters. Chirac's four-day visit also provoked demonstrations by several hundred members of the UC. Police used tear gas in an attempt to disperse the pro-independence protesters, who had gathered near an official ceremony in honour of the visiting head of state. Kanak representatives, meanwhile, expressed dismay at their exclusion from meetings with the French President. During his visit Chirac refrained from making any direct comment on the status of New Caledonia.

Legislative elections took place on 9 May 2004. Rassemblement-UMP lost its majority in both the Congress of New Caledonia and in the South Province. The results demonstrated an increase in support for the pro-independence movements, notably the recently formed Avenir Ensemble. Each Provincial Assembly in turn elected its President: Philippe Gomès of Avenir Ensemble became President of the South Province, replacing Jacques Lafleur; Paul Néaoutyine of the UNI-FLNKS was re-elected in the North Province; and Néko Hnépeune, also of the UNI-FLNKS, was elected President in the Loyalty Islands. At its inaugural meeting in late May the incoming Congress elected Harold Martin of Avenir Ensemble as its President and began the process of appointing a new Government. In early June Marie-Noëlle Thémereau of Avenir Ensemble and Déwé Gorodey of the UNI-FLNKS were respectively nominated President and Vice-President. However, the Government disintegrated within hours following the resignation of three Rassemblement-UMP cabinet ministers, who claimed that they were entitled to four seats under power-sharing terms set out in the Nouméa Accord. Congress granted Rassemblement-UMP the seats but with the result that the decision of the Council of Ministers on its leadership reached a stalemate. In late June, following negotiations that also involved the French High Commissioner in New Caledonia and discussions in Paris between Harold Martin and the French Government, a new vote returned Thémereau and Gorodey to their elected posts. The incoming Government endorsed a code of conduct that emphasized the importance of consensus-building among the parties and 'collegiality' in the decision-making process, in compliance with the Nouméa Accord (see above). In late January 2005 representatives of Avenir Ensemble for the first time took part in talks with the French Government in Paris as part of the follow-up process to the Nouméa Accord.

In late July 2004 USTKE members blockaded the harbour wharf in protest at moves by stevedoring companies to consolidate cargo-handling activities, which it was believed would lead to redundancies. Police intervention provoked a 'roving' general strike by some 5,000 workers which disrupted freight services at the wharf and airport, and refuse collections. Nickel-mining companies were affected by the action, as was the principal flour mill, leading to a shortage of bread. Blockades of fuel depots forced the closure of service stations and brought school bus services to a standstill. The RFO radio and television network was unable to broadcast. After three days the cargo-handling agreement was reversed and the USTKE withdrew its pickets in early August. However, in an unrelated strike over contractual terms, the USTKE forced RFO off the air again in mid-August; the strike action spread in September, halting production for two weeks at the newspaper *Les Nouvelles Calédoniennes*. (The strike at RFO was finally resolved in December and led to the replacement of the station manager.)

In September 2004 politicians from across the political spectrum urged a boycott of the population census on the grounds that it would not record individuals' ethnic identity. During his visit to New Caledonia in July 2003 President Chirac had declared his opposition to the inclusion of such details, taking the position that France recognized French citizens without regard to specific ethnicity. However, some 10% of the population were believed to have abstained from the census. An additional survey of ethnicity was scheduled to take place in April 2005 at a cost of some US $1.5m.

In October 2004 an operating licence was granted to the Canadian mining company Inco for the development of a proposed nickel-cobalt plant at Goro in the South Province (see Economic Affairs). Concerns about the disposal of industrial waste into the sea had been raised in a public inquiry in the previous August and in February 2005 protesters from a Kanak environmental organization, Rééhbù Nùù, blockaded the Goro site. In that month an agreement was reached between Inco and the newly formed Société de Participation Minière du Sud Calédonien (a shareholding company representing the three New Caledonia provinces) to acquire a 10% share in the Goro development. In November a prospecting licence granted to Inco in early 2004 was ruled null and void by the Court of Administrative Law on the grounds that the proper procedure had not been followed. In mid-December Goro was again blockaded, this time by protesters from another Kanak organization, the Conseil Autochtone pour la Gestion des Ressources Naturelles en Kanaky Nouvelle-Calédonie (CAUGERN), which had been formed in July. CAUGERN received the support of USTKE and the local Customary Senate in raising concerns relating to the socio-economic and political impact of nickel-mining activities, as well as with regard to the environmental repercussions.

In November 2005 the workers' union Confédération Syndicale des Travailleurs de Nouvelle-Calédonie (CSTNC) picketed SLN, demanding the reinstatement of two of its members who had been dismissed in the previous month. The strike spread to other sectors, including bakeries and banks, and blockades prevented access to three oil depots. The blockade was lifted following police intervention and the arrest of CSTNC leader Sylvain Néa. SLN eventually agreed to allow the two dismissed men to return to work at the end of February 2006; it was estimated that the strike action had cost the company some US $50m.

In early December 2005 Eramet instigated a legal challenge at the Tribunal de grande instance, in Paris, over the transfer of control of the Koniambo mine to Falconbridge and SMSP. Under the terms of the Bercy Accord (see above), the transfer was to be completed by the end of the year. However, Eramet claimed that Falconbridge had not fulfilled certain conditions, as a result of which control of the mine would remain with Eramet's subsidiary, SLN. In mid-December some 2,000 protesters were reported to have demonstrated in Nouméa in support of the transfer, which was seen as empowering the indigenous Kanak population of the North Province. USTKE voiced the opinion that the delay in reaching a final agreement was the result of interference from the French Government. Initially the Government had promised financial and tax concessions to Falconbridge, but in late November it was announced that while the Government supported the project it would be unable to make a commitment until the drafting of the following year's budget. In early December, with the support of SMSP, Falconbridge undertook to finance the entire cost of the project. Later that month the French court rejected Eramet's challenge and the transfer was completed.

In 2006 plans for a merger between Inco and Falconbridge were cancelled; Falconbridge was subsequently acquired by a Swiss-based company, Xstrata PLC, while Inco became a wholly owned subsidiary of the Brazilian enterprise, Companhia Vale do Rio Doce (CVRD). In April the development of the Goro Nickel mine again became a major issue when Réébhù Nùù members, opposed to the project because of its environmental impact, blockaded access routes to the mining site and caused damage to equipment estimated at US $10m. Construction work at the nickel plant was halted owing to security fears, and more than 1,300 employees were dispatched on leave. Réébhù Nùù maintained that the dumping of large amounts of waste from the mine into the sea would cause unacceptable damage to the environment and demanded that Goro Nickel address this concern, as well as establish a system of royalty payments to the local community. In the following week negotiations between the company and the protesters failed to reach a solution; meanwhile, Goro Nickel remained committed to beginning operations in late 2007. In mid-April 2006 Pierre Frogier, who continued as New Caledonia's Deputy to the Assemblée nationale in Paris, submitted a request to the French Government for the deployment of additional police officers to manage the security situation. Several hundred Goro Nickel employees also staged a demonstration in Nouméa to demand intervention by the French Government to facilitate their return to work. The FLNKS assumed the role of mediator on behalf of Réébhù Nùù, Goro Nickel, the New Caledonian Government and community leaders, while the USTKE announced its support for the Réébhù Nùù campaign, having obstructed two boats bound for the mining site. Towards the end of the month Goro Nickel announced that it would restart construction work, following reassurances from the police and the French Government about the security of the site. Opposition to the project remained, however, and demonstrations continued. In mid-June the mining project suffered a set-back when a New Caledonian court ruled that the possible environmental consequences of the scheme had not been comprehensively investigated, and therefore cancelled its licence to operate. Although the company's construction licence remained intact, the ruling represented a significant advance for the Réébhù Nùù campaign. In July Réébhù Nùù, joined by CAUGERN, warned of further action if Goro Nickel failed to halt construction by a deadline of 24 September. On 25 September the CSTNC began a general strike. Among the CSTNC's demands were the expulsion of several hundred Filipino employees of Goro Nickel and the resignations of local government officials. Its tactics included blockades of mining operations, which also resulted in a decrease in productivity for SLN operations. In November Réébhù Nùù succeeded in gaining an injunction from a French court on Goro Nickel's construction of a waste facility. The CSTNC's strike action continued until January 2007, although at that time several issues remained unresolved. In February 2007 the court ruling that had halted construction of the waste facility was rescinded. In February 2008 the general manager of Goro Nickel announced that 70% of construction had been completed, and estimated that production at the site would begin in November 2008. This represented a significant delay to the original schedule, combined with an increase in the cost to an estimated US $3,200m., as at mid-2007.

According to an official report, overall some 33,000 working days were lost in New Caledonia in 2005 as a result of strike action, compared with 22,000 days in 2004. In early January 2006 the Congress approved legislation (superseding the previous 'social pact'—see above) aimed at reducing the number of unions, and thereby the incidence of strike action. As of 31 March unions would be required to obtain the votes of at least 5% of employees at local professional elections. Other factors that would be taken into account would be the number of members, the level of their contributions and the date of establishment of the organization (within the last two years).

In July 2006 Harold Martin was re-elected President of the Congress of New Caledonia. In the following month Jacques Lafleur brought attention to the new political party he had founded with Simon Loueckhote, the Rassemblement pour la Calédonie (Rally for Caledonia—RPC); initially Lafleur had linked the RPC to the metropolitan French UMP, but in January 2007 he resigned from the latter party. Also in January, the French Sénat approved a constitutional amendment that limited voting rights to those who had been resident in New Caledonia since 1998 or before. The proposed legislation, which was also approved by the Assemblée nationale in Paris, was due to enter into force in 2009 and would not cover the French legislative and presidential elections. Later in January 2007 a former President of the North Province, Léopold Jordi, was sentenced to two years' imprisonment for misuse of funds and barred from contesting elections for five years. At the first round of voting in the French presidential election, held on 22 April 2007, provisional results suggested that the UMP candidate, Nicolas Sarkozy, had secured almost 50% of the votes cast in New Caledonia, while Ségolène Royal of the Parti Socialiste received just under 24%. Sarkozy went on to defeat Royal in the second round, garnering 62.9% of the votes in New Caledonia (Royal received 37.1%). The discrepancy between their respective proportions of the vote was significantly smaller within France. Elections to the Assemblée nationale were held in June. Although the Rassemblement-UMP candidates, incumbent deputy Pierre Frogier and Gaël Yanno, received the largest number of votes in their respective constituencies, their failure to secure an absolute majority resulted in the scheduling of a second round. Avenir Ensemble candidates, along with former Rassemblement-UMP member Jacques Lafleur, did not receive enough votes to proceed to the next stage. In the second round, Yanno secured a decisive victory over FLNKS candidate Charles Washetine, the Minister for Education and Research, while Frogier was re-elected, defeating Charles Pidjot of the FLNKS by a smaller margin. The results prompted speculation over the future of the New Caledonian Government, led by Marie-Noëlle Thémereau of Avenir Ensemble. The possibility of a reconciliation between Avenir Ensemble and Rassemblement-UMP was also raised when a senior French government official urged the two parties to unite.

As had been widely anticipated, Thémereau resigned from the position of President in July 2007, although the Council of Ministers was to remain in place until the appointment of a new Government. Pierre Frogier was elected President of the Congress of New Caledonia in late July, following reports that Avenir Ensemble and Rassemblement-UMP had signed an agreement, a so-called 'majority accord', which the President of the RPC, Simon Loueckhote, had also entered into. An initial attempt to form a multi-party Council of Ministers in early August failed after the FLNKS, dissatisfied with the number of ministerial posts it had been allocated, withdrew its support. The resultant Council, comprising eight members and led by Harold Martin, was to govern for a period of two weeks, until the Congress could reconvene and stage a second vote. On 21 August Congress elected a new Council of Ministers, meeting the FLNKS's demand for four cabinet positions out of a total of 11. Harold Martin was subsequently elected President, with additional responsibility for mining and taxes, and Déwé Gorodey returned to the position of Vice-President, retaining the portfolios of culture, women's affairs and citizenship. Notable appointments included that of Annie Beustes of Rassemblement-UMP as Minister for Economy, Labour, Public Service, External Trade, and Money and Lending Issues.

In October 2007 the French High Commissioner in New Caledonia, Michel Mathieu, resigned amid reports of a disagreement with the French Minister-Delegate for the Overseas Possessions, Christian Estrosi, who had signalled a new approach to the issue of strike action in New Caledonia. The appointment of Yves Dassonville as Mathieu's replacement was approved in the same month, and Dassonville took office in November. In January 2008 a USTKE strike in Nouméa escalated into violence following police intervention; several people were injured. Municipal elections were held in March.

Between late December 2005 and early January 2006 more than 4,000 ha of tropical rainforest were destroyed by fire; the police suspected arson. In March 2006 the French Minister for Overseas Territories, François Baroin, and President Thémereau signed development contracts whereby France was to provide aid totalling €393.2m. during the period 2006–10 (see Economic Affairs).

Government

New Caledonia was designated as an Overseas Country (pays d'outre-mer) in 1999. Its status of collectivité *sui generis*, conferred following a constitutional revision of 2003, is unique within the French Republic in that the local assembly is permitted to pass its own laws and a local citizenship may be bestowed upon permanent residents. The French Government is represented in New Caledonia by its High Commissioner, and controls a number of important spheres, including external relations, defence, external trade and secondary education. In July 1989 administrative reforms were introduced, as stipulated in the Matignon Accord (which had been approved by national referendum in November 1988). New Caledonia was divided into three Provinces (North, South and Loyalty Islands), each governed by an assembly, which is elected on a proportional basis. The members of the three Provincial Assemblies together form the Congress. Members are subject to re-election every five years. The responsibilities of the Congress include New Caledonia's budget and fiscal affairs, infrastructure and primary education, while the responsibilities of the Provincial Assemblies include local economic development, land reform and cultural affairs. The Government of New Caledonia is elected by the Congress, and comprises between seven and 11 members. Under the terms of the Nouméa Accord (which was approved by a referendum in November 1998), the Government replaces the French High Commissioner as New Caledonia's executive authority. A gradual transfer of power from metropolitan France to local institutions was to be effected over a period of between 15 and 20 years under the terms of the Nouméa Accord.

In addition, New Caledonia elects two deputies to the French Assemblée nationale in Paris and one representative to the French Sénat (Senate) on the basis of universal adult suffrage; one Economic and Social Councillor is also nominated. (In 2003 it was announced that New Caledonia would be granted one additional seat in the French Sénat, probably effective from 2008.) New Caledonia may also be represented at the European Parliament.

Defence

As assessed at November 2007, France maintained a force of 1,540 military personnel in New Caledonia, including a gendarmerie.

Economic Affairs

In 2000, according to World Bank estimates, New Caledonia's gross national income (GNI) at average 1998–2000 prices totalled US $2,989.6m., equivalent to $14,060 per head (or $22,210 per head on an international purchasing-power parity basis). During 1996–2006, it was estimated, the population rose at an average annual rate of 1.9%. According to the UN Economic and Social Commission for Asia and the Pacific (ESCAP), gross domestic product (GDP) per head decreased, in real terms, by an annual average of 1.7% during 1995–2000 and by 1.0% in 2000–05. However, overall GDP increased at an average annual rate of 0.4% in 1995–2000, rising by 0.7% annually in 2000–05. In comparison with the previous year, GDP was estimated to have expanded by 0.8% in 2006, to reach $3,107m.

Agriculture, forestry and fishing contributed only an estimated 1.9% of GDP in 2003. In 2006 2.9% of the employed labour force were engaged in the sector. Maize, yams, sweet potatoes and coconuts have traditionally been the principal crops, and pumpkins (squash) became an important export crop for the Japanese market from the 1990s. Livestock consists mainly of cattle, pigs and poultry. The main fisheries products are albacore, tuna and shrimps (most of which are exported to Japan). The aquaculture industry has expanded steadily, with production of blue shrimp increasing from 691 metric tons in 1994 to 2,440 tons in 2005. In 2007, according to provisional figures, exports of marine products were worth 2,266m. francs CFP, thus accounting for some 1.3% of total exports. The GDP of the agricultural sector was estimated to have increased at an average annual rate of 6.0% in 1995–2000 and by an annual average of 1.1% in 2000–05. Compared with the previous year, agricultural GDP rose by 1.5% in 2006.

Industry (comprising mining, manufacturing, construction and utilities) provided an estimated 25.4% of GDP in 2003. The industrial sector employed 21.3% of the working population in 2006. The GDP of the industrial sector was estimated to have expanded at an average annual rate of 3.9% in 1995–2000, before contracting by an annual average of 1.4% in 2000–05. In comparison with the previous year, industrial GDP increased by 1.0% in 2006.

Although mining employed only 1.5% of New Caledonia's working population in 2006, it constitutes the most important industrial activity. In 2003 the mining and processing of nickel contributed an estimated 8.6% of GDP. New Caledonia is a major producer of ferronickel and is believed to possess about one-quarter of the world's nickel reserves. Output of nickel ore was estimated at 7.5m. wet tons in 2007. Compared with the previous year, metallurgical production increased by 4.7% in 2006, before declining by 8.2% in 2007. Export receipts from sales of nickel ore, ferro-nickel and nickel matte reached an estimated 172,172m. francs CFP in 2007, thus accounting for 96.3% of total export revenue. In December 2005 the transfer of the Koniambo mine to Falconbridge and Société Minière du Sud Pacifique (SMSP) was completed (see Recent History). Upon completion of the facility in 2011, annual nickel output from the Koniambo mine was projected to reach 60,000 metric tons within two years. The similarly controversial Goro Nickel plant (see Recent History) was expected to start production in late 2008. It was projected to reach full production capacity in 2012, when it was anticipated that 60,000 tons of nickel and 4,500 tons of cobalt would be produced annually. In 1999 a joint French and Australian research mission made an offshore discovery of what was believed to be the world's largest gas deposit, measuring an estimated 18,000 sq km. It was hoped that this might indicate the presence of considerable petroleum reserves.

The manufacturing sector, which engaged 9.2% of the employed labour force in 2006, consists mainly of small and medium-sized enterprises, most of which are situated around the capital, Nouméa, producing building materials, furniture, salted fish, fruit juices and perishable foods. Food-processing and other manufacturing activities accounted for an estimated 5.8% of GDP in 2003.

Electrical energy is provided mainly by thermal power stations (some 80% in 2004), by hydroelectric plants, and more recently by wind power. Fuels accounted for 15.9% of total imports in 2005. As part of the Government's plans to reduce expensive imports of diesel fuel, a target was set to provide 60,000 kWh of wind-generated electricity by 2010, equivalent to some 15% of New Caledonia's energy requirements. Plans for the Falconbridge nickel plant at Koniambo envisaged the construction of a 390-MW power station. In 2007 production of electric energy reached an estimated 1,926m. kWh.

Service industries contributed an estimated 72.7% of GDP in 2003 and engaged 75.8% of the employed labour force in 2006. The GDP of the services sector was estimated to have declined at an average annual rate of 0.8% in 1995–2000, rising by an annual average of 1.0% in 2000–05. The GDP of the services sector increased by 1.2% in 2006, compared with the previous year. The tourism sector in New Caledonia, however, has failed to witness an expansion similar to that experienced in many other Pacific islands, and tourist arrivals have been intermittently affected by political unrest. The majority of visitors come from France, Japan, Australia and New Zealand. In 2007 the number of tourist arrivals by air totalled 103,363, while the number of visiting cruise-ship passengers reached 121,393. Receipts from tourism were estimated at 17,562m. francs CFP in 2004.

In 2006 New Caledonia recorded a visible trade deficit of 70,281m. francs CFP, and there was a deficit of 47,198m. francs CFP on the current account of the balance of payments. The principal imports in 2007 were machinery and electrical equipment, foodstuffs and mineral products, while the principal exports remained nickel products, prawns and fish. France was the main supplier of imports in 2007 according to provisional data, accounting for 26.6% of the total. Other important suppliers of imports were Singapore (13.6%) and Australia (10.7%). The principal market for New Caledonia's exports was Japan, representing 22.3% of the total, while France (14.5%), Taiwan (12.1%) and the People's Republic of China (11.2%) were also important buyers.

The current budget surplus of 453.1m. francs CFP in 2006 was largely due to the strength of nickel prices. Budgetary expenditure by France in 2006 exceeded €907.6m. Of the total aid of €393.2m. to be provided by France under an agreement reached in March 2006 (see Recent History), over the period 2006–10 Grande Terre was to receive €40.2m. and the municipalities €88.5m. A further €26.4m. was allocated towards protection of natural heritage and as financial assistance in preparation for the 2011 Pacific Games, to be hosted by New Caledonia. The three provinces were to receive a total of €238.2m. (the South Province €69.2m., the North Province €116.2m., the Loyalty Islands €52.8m.). Key areas of investment included health, employment, social housing and economic development. In 2004 New Caledonia also received €13.8m. in aid from the European Union (EU, see p. 244) as part of the European Development Fund, which undertook to invest some €21m. in New Caledonia during 2004–09; principal beneficiaries were the education sector and the fishing industry.

The annual rate of inflation in Nouméa averaged 1.5% in 1996–2006. Consumer prices rose by 1.8% in 2007. In 2006 the total of those registered as unemployed averaged 7,049, equivalent to almost 9% of the labour force.

New Caledonia forms part of the Franc Zone (see p. 306), is an associate member of the UN Economic and Social Commission for Asia and the Pacific (ESCAP, see p. 35) and is a member, in its own right, of the Pacific Community (see p. 377). New Caledonia became an associate member of the Pacific Islands Forum (see p. 380) in 2006.

New Caledonia's economy is vulnerable to factors affecting the nickel industry, notably fluctuations in international prices for the commodity, as well as intermittent political and social unrest (see Recent History). Following a decline in the world nickel market in 2001, prices subsequently increased strongly to reach record levels in 2007. Discussions began in December 2004 on the replacement of the franc CFP with the euro. The eventual introduction of the new currency, however, would depend upon New Caledonia, French Polynesia and Wallis and Futuna all reaching a consensus. In November 2006, in response to continuing public protests at the high cost of living, the New Caledonian legislature approved measures to exempt from tax a total of 14 essential consumer items. This concession was expected to reduce government revenue by the equivalent of US $1.5m. In the same month the monthly minimum wage was raised to 120,000 francs CFP, with effect from January 2007. The budget for 2008, which envisaged total expenditure of 158,000m. francs CFP, placed continued emphasis on the implementation of the Nouméa Accord (see Recent History) and the redistribution of the islands' wealth, focusing on vocational training and higher education (including funding for the newly established academy of Kanak language). In early 2008 it was announced that the French Government was to grant tax rebates of $230m. to the Koniambo mining project (see above). Investment in the scheme was estimated to total $3,800m. The Koniambo project was to receive additional tax concessions for the first 15 years of its operation. Goro Nickel, the other major nickel-mining project, was to receive a similar tax rebate of as much as $500m.

FRENCH OVERSEAS POSSESSIONS

Education

Education is compulsory for 10 years between six and 16 years of age. Schools are operated by both the State and churches, under the supervision of three Departments of Education: the Provincial department responsible for primary level education, the New Caledonian department responsible for primary level inspection, and the State department responsible for secondary level education. The French Government finances the state secondary system. Primary education begins at six years of age, and lasts for five years; secondary education, beginning at 11 years of age, comprises a first cycle of four years and a second, three-year cycle. Overall, in 2004 some 71% of pupils were enrolled at state institutions. In 2006 a total of 13,262 pupils attended pre-primary school and 23,647 pupils were attending primary school. Some 1,883 teachers were employed in pre-primary and primary education in 2005. A total of 32,591 pupils attended secondary school in 2006. There were 2,727 teachers employed in secondary education in 2005. There were 21 technical and higher institutions and their annexes (of which 8 were private). In 1987 the French University of the Pacific (based in French Polynesia) was established, with a centre in Nouméa, and divided into two universities in 1999. In 2005 the University of New Caledonia had 70 teachers and researchers and some 2,200 students. Several other vocational tertiary education centres exist in New Caledonia, including a teacher-training college and two agricultural colleges. In 1989 the rate of adult illiteracy averaged 6.9% (males 6.0%, females 7.9%).

Public Holidays

2008: 1 January (New Year's Day), 5 March (Missionary Day), 24 March (Easter Monday), 1 May (Ascension Day, Labour Day), 8 May (Liberation Day), 12 May (Whit Monday), 14 July (Fall of the Bastille), 8 September (Internal Autonomy Day), 24 September (Anniversary of possession by France), 1 November (All Saints' Day), 11 November (Armistice Day), 25 December (Christmas Day).

2009: 1 January (New Year's Day), 5 March (Missionary Day), 13 April (Easter Monday), 1 May (Labour Day), 8 May (Liberation Day), 21 May (Ascension Day), 1 June (Whit Monday), 14 July (Fall of the Bastille), 8 September (Internal Autonomy Day), 24 September (Anniversary of possession by France), 1 November (All Saints' Day), 11 November (Armistice Day), 25 December (Christmas Day).

Weights and Measures

The metric system is in force.

Statistical Survey

Source (unless otherwise stated): Institut de la Statistique et des Etudes Economiques, BP 823, 98845 Nouméa; tel. 275481; fax 288148; internet www.isee.nc.

AREA AND POPULATION

Area (sq km): New Caledonia island (Grande Terre) 16,372; Loyalty Islands 1,981 (Lifou 1,207, Maré 642, Ouvéa 132); Isle of Pines 152; Belep Archipelago 70; Total 18,575 (7,172 sq miles).

Population: 196,836 at census of 16 April 1996; 230,789 (males 116,485, females 114,304) at census of 31 August 2004. *Population by Province* (census of 2004): Loyalty Islands 22,080; North Province 44,474; South Province 164,235. *1 January 2007* (official estimate): 240,390.

Density (1 January 2007): 12.9 per sq km.

Ethnic Groups (census of 1996): Indigenous Kanaks (Melanesians) 86,788; French and other Europeans 67,151; Wallisians and Futunians (Polynesian) 17,763; Tahitians (Polynesian) 5,171; Indonesians 5,003; Others 14,960.

Principal Towns (population of communes at census of 2004): Nouméa (capital), 91,386; Mont-Doré 24,195; Dumbéa 18,602; Païta 12,062.

Births, Marriages and Deaths (2006): Registered live births 4,268 (birth rate 17.7 per 1,000); Registered marriages 927 (marriage rate 3.9 per 1,000); Registered deaths 1,113 (death rate 4.7 per 1,000).

Expectation of Life (years at birth, 2006): 76.4 (males 72.9; females 80.2).

Employment (salaried workers at 31 December 2006): Agriculture, hunting, forestry and fishing 2,148; Mining and quarrying 1,139; Manufacturing 6,752; Electricity, gas and water 766; Construction 7,023; Trade (vehicle repairs and domestic goods) 8,710; Hotels and restaurants 3,579; Transport and communications 4,840; Financing activities 1,674; Real estate and business services 5,517; Education 184; Health and welfare 1,607; Domestic services for households 3,673; Community, social and personal services 2,101; Other market services 34; Non-market services 23,862; *Total employed* 73,609. *Unemployed* (annual average, 2006): 7,049.

HEALTH AND WELFARE
Key Indicators

Physicians (per 1,000 head, 2003): 2.1.

Hospital Beds (per 1,000 head, 2003): 3.7.

For definitions, see explanatory note on p. vi.

AGRICULTURE, ETC.

Principal Crops ('000 metric tons, 2006): Maize 5.7*; Potatoes 2.3; Sweet potatoes 3.1*; Cassava 3.1*; Yams 11.1*; Coconuts 16.3*; Vegetables (excl. melons) 6.1; Bananas 0.8*; Other fruits 3.0*.
* FAO estimate.

Livestock ('000 head, year ending September 2006, FAO estimates): Horses 11.5; Cattle 111.0; Pigs 28.5; Sheep 2.3; Goats 8.1; Poultry 600.

Livestock Products (metric tons, 2006): Cattle meat 2,992; Pig meat 1,965; Chicken meat 881 (FAO estimate); Cows' milk 789; Hen eggs 1,951.

Forestry ('000 cubic metres, 1994): *Roundwood Removals*: Sawlogs and veneer logs 2.8; Other industrial wood 2.0 (FAO estimate); Total 4.8. *Sawnwood Production*: 3.3 (all broadleaved). *1995–2006*: Annual output as in 1994 (FAO estimates).

Fishing (metric tons, live weight, 2005): Capture 3,465 (Albacore 1,590; Yellowfin tuna 448; marine fishes 753; Sea cucumbers 500; Trochus shells 150); Aquaculture 2,533 (Blue shrimp 2,440); Total catch 5,998.

Source: FAO.

MINING

Production: Nickel ore (metal content, '000 metric tons) 111.0 in 2005 (Source: US Geological Survey, provisional); Nickel ore ('000 wet tons) 7,508 in 2007 (provisional).

INDUSTRY

Production (2007, unless otherwise indicated, provisional): Ferronickel 43,372 metric tons (nickel content); Nickel matte 13,860 metric tons (nickel content); Electric energy 1,926 million kWh; Cement 119,302 metric tons (Source: US Geological Survey, 2005, provisional).

FINANCE

Currency and Exchange Rates: see French Polynesia.

French Government Budget Expenditure (million francs CFP): 100,387 in 2004; 105,735 in 2005; 108,310 in 2006 (provisional).

Territorial Budget (million francs CFP, 2006): *Revenue:* Current 126,935 (Direct taxes 44,578; Indirect taxes 41,417); Capital 1,122; Total 128,057. *Expenditure:* Current 122,404 (Transfers to provinces 53,842); Capital 5,221; Total 127,624.

Money Supply (million francs CFP at 31 December 2006): Currency in circulation 12,517; Demand deposits 177,763; Total money 190,280. Source: Institut d'Emission d'Outre-Mer.

Cost of Living (Consumer Price Index for Nouméa, December each year; base: December 1992 = 100): All items 123.4 in 2005; 125.2. in 2006; 127.5 in 2007.

Gross Domestic Product (US $ million at constant 1990 prices): 3,054 in 2004; 3,081 in 2005; 3,107 in 2006. Source: UN Statistics Division, National Accounts Main Aggregates Database.

Expenditure on the Gross Domestic Product (million francs CFP at current prices, 2006, estimates): Government final consumption expenditure 159,057; Private final consumption expenditure 396,942; Gross capital formation 198,827; *Total domestic expenditure* 754,826; Exports of goods and services 149,085; *Less* Imports of goods and services 256,898; *GDP in purchasers' values* 647,014.

Gross Domestic Product by Economic Activity (million francs CFP at current prices, 2003): Agriculture, hunting, forestry and fishing 9,041; Nickel mining and processing 40,995; Food processing 10,505; Miscellaneous manufacturing 16,979; Electricity, gas and water 8,332; Construction 44,346; Trade 62,141; Transport and telecommunications 35,270; Banks and insurance 17,786; Business services 32,574; Services to households 101,239; Public administration 98,449; *Sub-total* 477,657; *Less* Financial intermediation services indirectly measured 15,002; *Gross value added in basic prices* 462,654; Taxes and subsidies on products (net) 55,891; *GDP in market prices* 518,545. *2006* (estimates): Gross value added in basic prices 577,356; Taxes on products 70,636; *Less* Subsidies on products 977; GDP in market prices 647,014.

Balance of Payments (million francs CFP, 2006): Exports of goods 113,557; Imports of goods –183,837; *Trade balance* –70,281; Exports of services 52,730; Imports of services –111,704; *Balance on goods and services* –129,255; Other income received 56,916; Other income paid –15,482; *Balance on goods, services and income* –87,821; Current transfers received 61,509; Current transfers paid –20,887; *Current balance* –47,198; Capital account (net) 367; Direct investment (net) 68,351; Portfolio investment assets 68,098; Portfolio investment liabilities –72,299; Other investment assets 290,220; Other investment liabilities –309,123; *Overall balance* –1,584. Source: Institut d'Emission d'Outre-Mer.

EXTERNAL TRADE

Principal Commodities (million francs CFP, 2007, provisional): *Imports:* Food products, beverages and tobacco 26,513; Mineral products 35,750; Chemical products 14,972; Plastic and rubber articles 7,788; Paper and paper articles 4,497; Textiles and textile articles 5,555; Base metals and articles thereof 15,381; Machinery and mechanical appliances, and electrical equipment 47,784; Transport equipment 35,502; Total (incl. others) 244,105. *Exports:* Nickel ore 44,004; Ferro-nickel 103,462; Nickel matte 24,706; Marine products 2,266 (Prawns 1,527); Total (incl. others) 178,754.

Principal Trading Partners (million francs CFP, 2007, provisional): *Imports:* Australia 26,221; France 65,014; Japan 7,257; New Zealand 9,716; Singapore 33,219; USA 7,876; Total (incl. others) 244,105. *Exports:* Australia 8,515; China, People's Republic 20,035; France 25,843; Japan 39,819; South Africa 7,630; Taiwan 21,562; USA 4,261; Total (incl. others) 178,754.

TRANSPORT

Road Traffic (motor vehicles in use, 2001): Total 85,499.

Shipping (2005): *Domestic Traffic* ('000 metric tons): Freight unloaded 2,949; Freight loaded 89. *International Traffic:* Freight unloaded 1,566 metric tons; Freight loaded 3,643 metric tons. *Merchant Fleet* (vessels registered, '000 grt, at 31 December 1992): 14.

Civil Aviation (La Tontouta international airport, Nouméa, 2006): *Passenger Traffic:* Passengers arriving 208,606; Passengers departing 206,384. *Freight Traffic:* Freight unloaded 4,408 metric tons; Freight loaded 1,032 metric tons (Source: Department of Civil Aviation).

TOURISM

Foreign Arrivals: *Arrivals by Air:* 100,651 in 2005; 100,491 in 2006; 103,363 in 2007. *Cruise-ship Passenger Arrivals:* 81,215 in 2005; 118,898 in 2006; 121,393 in 2007.

Tourist Arrivals by Country of Residence (2007): Australia 16,352; France 29,104; Japan 26,755; New Zealand 9,475; Total (incl. others) 103,363.

Tourism Receipts (million francs CFP): 17,349 in 2002; 17,610 in 2003; 17,562 in 2004 (provisional figure).

COMMUNICATIONS MEDIA

Radio Receivers (1997): 107,000 in use*.

Television Receivers (2000): 106,000 in use†.

Telephones (2006): 55,300 main lines in use†.

Facsimile Machines (1994): 2,200 in use‡.

Mobile Cellular Telephones (2006): 134,300 subscribers†.

Internet Users (2006): 80,000†.

Broadband Subscribers (2006): 9,600†.

Daily Newspapers (1999): 1.

* Source: UNESCO, *Statistical Yearbook*.
† Source: International Telecommunication Union.
‡ Source: UN, *Statistical Yearbook*.

EDUCATION

Pre-primary (2007 unless otherwise indicated): 83 schools (2004); 12,931 pupils.

Primary (2007): 289 schools (incl. pre-primary); 1,958 teachers (incl. pre-primary); 24,080 pupils (incl. special education).

Secondary (2007): 71 schools; 2,758 teachers (incl. higher); 32,089 pupils (incl. vocational training 6,651).

Higher (2005): 4 institutions; 111 teaching staff.

Adult Literacy Rate (1989): Males 94.0%; Females 92.1%.

Directory

The Constitution

The constitutional system in New Caledonia is established under the Constitution of the Fifth French Republic and specific laws, including those enacted in July 1989 in accordance with the terms agreed by the Matignon Accord and the Transitional Provisions appended by legislation on 20 July 1998. A referendum on the future of New Caledonia (originally expected to be conducted in 1998) was postponed for a period of between 15 and 20 years while a gradual transfer of power from metropolitan France to local institutions is effected under the terms of the Nouméa Accord, concluded in 1998. Under the Nouméa Accord, New Caledonia is designated as an Overseas Country (pays d'outre-mer) of the French Republic, of which it remains an integral part. (Its official status is that of a collectivité *sui generis*.) The High Commissioner is the representative of the State in New Caledonia and is appointed by the French Government. The High Commissioner is responsible for external relations, defence, law and order, finance and secondary education. New Caledonia is divided into three Provinces, of the South, the North and the Loyalty Islands. Each is governed by a Provincial Assembly, which is elected on a proportional basis and is responsible for local economic development, land reform and cultural affairs. Members of the Assemblies (40 for the South, 22 for the North and 14 for the Loyalty Islands) are subject to re-election every five years. A proportion of the members of the three Provincial Assemblies together form the Congress of New Caledonia (32 for the South, 15 for the North and seven for the Loyalty Islands), which is responsible for the New Caledonian budget and fiscal affairs, infrastructure and primary education. The Assemblies and the Congress each elect a President as leader. The Government of New Caledonia is elected by the Congress, and comprises between seven and 11 members. Under the terms of the Nouméa Accord, it replaces the French High Commissioner as New Caledonia's executive authority. Provision is also made for the maintenance of Kanak tradition: there are eight custom regions, each with a Regional Consultative Custom Council. These eight Councils, with other appropriate authorities, are represented on the Customary Senate, which is composed of 16 members (two elected from each regional council for a six-year period); the local Senate is consulted by the Congress and the Government. Local government is conducted by 33 communes. New Caledonia also elects two deputies to the Assemblée nationale (National Assembly) in Paris and one representative to the Sénat (Senate), on the basis of universal adult suffrage. One Economic and Social Councillor is also nominated. New Caledonia may be represented in the European Parliament.

The Government

(April 2008)

STATE GOVERNMENT

High Commissioner: YVES DASSONVILLE (took office November 2007).

Secretary-General: JEAN-BERNARD BOBIN.

Deputy Secretary-General: BÉATRICE STEFFAN.

LOCAL GOVERNMENT

Secretary-General: ALAIN SWETSCHKIN.

Deputy Secretary-General: MARTINE MICHEL.

Deputy Secretary-General: LÉON WAMYTAN.

COUNCIL OF MINISTERS

President, responsible for Mining and Taxes: HAROLD MARTIN (AE).

Vice-President and Minister for Culture, Women's Affairs, Citizenship, and Customary Affairs and Relations with the Customary Senate: EPÉRI DÉWÉ GORODEY (UNI-FLNKS).

Minister for Agriculture, Fisheries and Sustainable Development: ERIC BABIN (AE).

Minister for Education and Research: CHARLES WASHETINE (UNI-FLNKS).

Minister for Vocational Training and Domestic Air Transport: PIERRE NGAIHONI (UNI-FLNKS).

Minister for Land and Maritime Transport, Energy, Road Safety and Public Infrastructure: GÉRALD CORTOT (UC).

Minister for Economy, Labour, Public Service, External Trade, Customs and Money and Lending Issues: ANNIE BEUSTES (Rassemblement-UMP).

FRENCH OVERSEAS POSSESSIONS

Minister for Budget and Finance, Audiovisual Communication, and Relations with the Economic and Social Council and the Congress: Pascal Vittori (AE).

Minister for International Air Transport, Communications, Social Dialogue, Francophone Matters and Relations with Municipalities: Jean-Claude Briault (Rassemblement-UMP).

Minister for Health, Social Affairs, Solidarity and the Disabled: Sylvie Robineau (AE).

Minister for Youth and Sports: Maurice Ponga (Rassemblement-UMP).

GOVERNMENT OFFICES

Office of the High Commissioner: Haut-commissariat de la République en Nouvelle-Calédonie, 1 ave Maréchal Foch, BP C5, 98844 Nouméa Cédex; tel. 266300; fax 272828; e-mail haussariat@hc.etat.nc; internet www.gouv.nc/static/pages/institutions/etat.htm.

New Caledonian Government: *Présidence du Gouvernement:* 8 route des Artifices, BP M2, 98849 Nouméa Cédex; *Congrès de la Nouvelle-Calédonie:* 1 blvd Vauban, BP P3, 98851 Nouméa Cédex; tel. 246536; fax 246580; tel. 273129; fax 277020; e-mail presidence@gouv.nc; e-mail courrier@congres.nc; internet www.gouv.nc.

Office of the Secretary-General of the Government of New Caledonia: 8 route des Artifices, BP M2, 98849 Nouméa Cédex; tel. 246532; fax 246620; e-mail alain.swetschkin@gouv.nc; internet www.gouv.nc.

GOVERNMENT DEPARTMENTS

Department of the Budget and Financial Affairs (DBAF): 18 ave Paul Doumer, BP M2, 98849 Nouméa Cédex; tel. 256083; fax 283133; e-mail dbaf@gouv.nc.

Department of Civil Aviation: 179 rue Gervolino, BP H01, 98849 Nouméa Cédex; tel. 265200; fax 265202; e-mail bpasqualini@canl.nc; Dir Y. Debouverie.

Department of Computer Technology (DTSI): 127 rue A. Daly, Ouemo, 98800 Nouméa; tel. 275888; fax 281919; e-mail dtsi@gouv.nc; Dir Paola Logli.

Department of Cultural and Customary Affairs (DACC): 8 rue de Sébastopol, BP 2685, Nouméa; tel. 269766; fax 269767; e-mail secretariat.dacc@gouv.nc; Dir Régis Vendegou.

Department of Culture: Mission aux Affaires Culturelles, 9 rue de la République, BP C5, Nouméa; tel. 242181; fax 242180; Dir Emmanuelle Charrier.

Department of Economic Affairs (DAE): 7 rue du Général Galliéni, BP 2672, 98846 Nouméa Cédex; tel. 232250; fax 232251; e-mail dae@gouv.nc.

Department of Education (DENC): Immeuble Foch, 19 ave du Maréchal Foch, BP 8244, 98807 Nouméa Cédex; tel. 239600; fax 272921; e-mail denc@gouv.nc; internet www.denc.gouv.nc.

Department of Employment (DT): 12 rue de Verdun, BP 141, 98845 Nouméa Cédex; tel. 275572; fax 270494; e-mail dt@gouv.nc; internet www.dtnc.gouv.nc.

Department of Fiscal Affairs (DSF): Hôtel des Impôts, 13 rue de la Somme, BP D2, 98848 Nouméa Cédex; tel. 257500; fax 251166; e-mail dsf@gouv.nc; internet www.dsf.gouv.nc.

Department of Health and Social Services (DASS): 5 rue Gallieni, BP N4, 98851 Nouméa Cédex; tel. 243700; fax 243704; e-mail dass@gouv.nc; internet www.dass.gouv.nc.

Department of Human Resources and Civil Service (DRHFPT): 18 ave Paul Doumer, BP M2, 98849 Nouméa Cédex; tel. 256000; fax 274700; e-mail drhfpt@gouv.nc; internet www.drhfpt.gouv.nc.

Department of Industry, Mines and Energy (DIMENC): 1 ter rue Edouard Unger, 1ère, Vallée du Tir, BP 465, 98845 Nouméa Cédex; tel. 270230; fax 272345; e-mail dimenc@gouv.nc; internet www.dimenc.gouv.nc.

Department of Infrastructure, Topography and Transport (DITTT): 1 bis rue Edouard Unger, 1ère, Vallée du Tir, BP A2, 98848 Nouméa Cédex; tel. 280300; fax 281760; e-mail dittt@gouv.nc; internet www.dittt.gouv.nc.

Department of Maritime Affairs: 2 bis rue Félix Russeil, BP 36, 98845 Nouméa Cédex; tel. 272626; fax 287286; e-mail affmar@gouv.nc; internet www.affmar.gouv.nc.

Department of Veterinary, Food and Rural Affairs (DAVAR): 209 rue Auguste Bénébig, Haut Magenta, BP 256, 98845 Nouméa Cédex; tel. 255100; fax 255129; e-mail davar@gouv.nc; internet www.davar.gouv.nc.

Department of Vocational Training (DFPC): 19 ave du Maréchal Foch, BP 110, 98845 Nouméa Cédex; tel. 246622; fax 281661; e-mail dfpc@gouv.nc; internet www.dfpc.gouv.nc.

Department of Youth and Sports (DJS): 23 rue Jean Jaurès, BP 810, 98845 Nouméa Cédex; tel. 252384; fax 254585; e-mail djsnc@gouv.nc; internet www.djs.gouv.nc.

Legislature

ASSEMBLÉES PROVINCIALES

Members of the Provincial Assemblies are elected on a proportional basis for a five-year term. Each Provincial Assembly elects its President. A number of the members of the Provincial Assemblies sit together to make up the Congress of New Caledonia. The Assembly of the North Province has 22 members (including 15 sitting for the Congress), the Loyalty Islands 14 members (including seven for the Congress) and the South Province has 40 members (including 32 for the Congress).

North Province: BP 41, 98860 Koné; tel. 417100; fax 472475; e-mail presidence@province-nord.nc; internet www.province-nord.nc; Pres. Paul Néaoutyine (UNI-FLNKS).

South Province: Hôtel de la Province Sud, Route des Artifices, Port Moselle, BP L1, 98849 Nouméa Cédex; tel. 258000; fax 274900; e-mail cabinet@province-sud.nc; internet www.province-sud.nc; Pres. Philippe Gomès (Avenir Ensemble).

Loyalty Islands Province: BP 50, Wé, 98820 Lifou; tel. 455100; fax 451440; e-mail presidence@loyalty.nc; internet www.province-iles.nc; Pres. Néko Hnépeune (UNI-FLNKS).

Election, 9 May 2004 (results by province)

Party	North	South	Loyalty Islands
Le Rassemblement-Union pour un Mouvement Populaire (UMP)	3	16	2
L'Avenir Ensemble (AE)	1	19	—
Union Nationale pour l'Indépendance-Front de Libération Nationale Kanak Socialiste (UNI-FLNKS)	11	—	2
Union Calédonienne (UC)	7	—	4
Front National (FN)	—	5	—
Fédération des Comités de Coordination des Indépendantistes (FCCI)	—	—	2
Libération Kanak Socialiste (LKS)-KAP Identité	—	—	2
Union Calédonienne Renouveau (UC Renouveau)	—	—	2
Total	22	40	14

CONGRÈS

A proportion of the members of the three Provincial Assemblies sit together, in Nouméa, as the Congress of New Caledonia. There are 54 members (out of a total of 76 sitting in the Provincial Assemblies).

President: Pierre Frogier.

Election, 9 May 2004 (results for New Caledonia as a whole)

Party	Votes	%	Seats
Le Rassemblement-UMP	21,880	24.43	16
AE	20,338	22.71	16
UNI-FLNKS	12,556	14.02	8
UC	10,624	11.86	7
FN	6,684	7.46	4
FCCI-FULK	2,864	3.20	1
LKS-KAP Identité	2,572	2.87	1
UC Renouveau	1,587	1.77	1
Others	10,467	11.69	—
Total	89,572	100.00	54

PARLEMENT

Deputies to the French National Assembly: Pierre Frogier (Rassemblement-UMP), Gaël Yanno (Rassemblement-UMP).

Representative to the French Senate: Simon Loueckhote.

Political Organizations

L'Avenir Ensemble (AE): 2 bis blvd Vauban, Nouméa; tel. 281179; fax 281011; e-mail avenirensemble@lagoon.nc; internet www.avenirensemble.nc; f. 2004; combined list incl. fmr mems of Rassemblement pour la Calédonie dans la République and Alliance pour la Calédonie; anti-independence party; supports unification of all ethnic groups; Pres. HAROLD MARTIN.

Fédération des Comités de Coordination des Indépendantistes (FCCI): f. 1998 by breakaway group of FLNKS; includes Front du Développement des Iles Loyauté and Front Uni de Libération Kanak; Leaders LÉOPOLD JORÉDIÉ, RAPHAËL MAPOU, FRANÇOIS BURCK.

Front Calédonien (FC): extreme right-wing; Leader M. SARRAN.

Front de Libération Nationale Kanak Socialiste (FLNKS): 9 rue Austerlitz, Immeuble SAM3, 98800 Nouméa Cédex; tel. 265880; fax 265887; f. 1984 following dissolution of Front Indépendantiste; pro-independence; Pres. PAUL NÉAOUTYINE; a grouping of the following parties:

Parti de Libération Kanak (PALIKA): f. 1975; Leader EPÉRI 'DÉWÉ' GORODEY.

Rassemblement Démocratique Océanien (RDO): Nouméa; f. 1994 by breakaway faction of Union Océanienne (UO, f. 1989); supports Kanak sovereignty; Pres. ALOISIO SAKO.

Union Calédonienne (UC): 4 rue de la Gazelle, Aérodrome de Magenta, Nouméa; tel. 272599; fax 276257; e-mail info@union-caledonienne.org; internet www.union-caledonienne.org; f. 1952; left FLNKS coalition prior to elections of 2004; subsequently returned; 11,000 mems; Pres. CHARLES PIDJOT; Sec.-Gen. DANIEL YEIWÉNÉ.

Union Progressiste Mélanésienne (UPM): f. 1974 as Union Progressiste Multiraciale; Pres. VICTOR TUTUGORO; Sec.-Gen. RENÉ POROU.

Front National (FN): BP 4198, 98846 Nouméa; tel. 258068; fax 258064; e-mail george@province-sud.nc; right-wing; Leader GUY GEORGE.

Génération Calédonienne: f. 1995; youth-based; aims to combat corruption in public life; Pres. JEAN-RAYMOND POSTIC.

Le Groupe MUR: BP 1211, 98845 Nouméa Cédex; tel. and fax 419385; a coalition of the Mouvement des Citoyens Calédoniens (MCC), Union Océanienne (UO—f. 1989) and Rassemblement des Océaniens dans la Calédonie (ROC); Jt Pres TINO MANUOHALALO (MCC), MICHEL HEMA (UO), MIKAELE TUIFUA (ROC).

Libération Kanak Socialiste (LKS): Maré, Loyalty Islands; moderate, pro-independence; Leader NIDOÏSH NAISSELINE.

Le Rassemblement-UMP: 13 rue de Sebastopol, BP 306, 98800 Nouméa; tel. 282620; fax 284033; e-mail contact@rassemblement.nc; internet www.rassemblement.nc; f. 1976 as Rassemblement pour la Calédonie dans la République; affiliated to the metropolitan Union pour un Mouvement Populaire (UMP); in favour of retaining the status quo in New Caledonia; Leader PIERRE FROGIER; Sec.-Gen. ERIC GAY.

A coalition of the following parties:

Centre des Démocrates Sociaux (CDS): f. 1971; Leader JEAN LÈQUES.

Parti Républicain (PR): Leader PIERRE MARESCA.

Rassemblement pour la Calédonie (RPC): Nouméa; f. 2006; Pres. SIMON LOUECKHOTE.

Union Calédonienne Renouveau (UC Renouveau): Hôtel de la province des îles Loyauté, BP 50, Wé Lifou; tel. 455100; fax 451440; Leader JACQUES LALIE.

Other political organizations participating in the elections of May 2004 included: Avance, Calédonie Mon Pays, Construire Ensemble l'Avenir, Le FLNKS pour l'Indépendance, Mouvement Chiraquien des Démocrates Chrétiens UMP, and Patrimoine et Environnement avec les Verts.

Judicial System

Court of Administrative Law: 85 ave du Général de Gaulle, Immeuble Carcopino 3000, 4ème étage, BP Q3, 98851 Nouméa Cédex; tel. 250630; fax 250631; e-mail greffe.ta-noumea@juradm.fr; internet www.ta-noumea.juradm.fr; f. 1984; Pres. GUY LAPORTE; Cllrs MICHEL M. BICHET, ARSÈNE IBO, MARIE-THÉRÈSE LACAU.

Court of Appeal: Palais de Justice, BP F4, 98848 Nouméa; tel. 279350; fax 269185; e-mail pp.ca-noumea@justice.fr; First Pres. GÉRARD FEY; Procurator-Gen. ANNIE BRUNET-FURSTER.

Court of the First Instance: 2 blvd Extérieur, BP F4, 98848 Nouméa; fax 276531; e-mail p.tpi-noumea@justice.fr; Pres. JEAN PRADAL; Procurator of the Republic ROBERT BLASER; there are two subsidiary courts, with resident magistrates, at Koné (North Province) and Wé (Loyalty Islands Province).

Customary Senate of New Caledonia: Conseil Consultatif Coutumier, 68 ave J. Cook, POB 1059, Nouville; tel. 242000; fax 249320; f. 1990; consulted by Local Assembly and French Govt on matters affecting land, Kanak tradition and identity; composed of 16 elected mems (two from the regional council of each of the eight custom areas) for a six-year period; Pres. Chief JEAN GUY M'BOUERI.

Religion

The majority of the population is Christian, with Roman Catholics comprising about 55% of the total in 2002. About 3% of the inhabitants, mainly Indonesians, are Muslims.

CHRISTIANITY

The Roman Catholic Church

The Territory comprises a single archdiocese, with an estimated 112,000 adherents in December 2005. The Archbishop participates in the Catholic Bishops' Conference of the Pacific, based in Fiji.

Archbishop of Nouméa: Most Rev. MICHEL-MARIE-BERNARD CALVET, Archevêché, 4 rue Mgr-Fraysse, BP 3, 98845 Nouméa; tel. 265353; fax 265352; e-mail archeveche@ddec.nc; internet www.ddec.nc/diocese.

The Anglican Communion

Within the Church of the Province of Melanesia, New Caledonia forms part of the diocese of Vanuatu. The Archbishop of the Province is the Bishop of Central Melanesia (resident in Honiara, Solomon Islands). At mid-2000 there were an estimated 160 adherents.

Protestant Churches

At mid-2000 there were an estimated 30,000 adherents.

Eglise évangélique en Nouvelle-Calédonie et aux Iles Loyauté: BP 277, Nouméa; f. 1960; Pres. Rev. SAILALI PASSA; Gen. Sec. Rev. TELL KASARHEROU.

Other churches active in the Territory include the Assembly of God, the Free Evangelical Church, the New Apostolic Church, the Pentecostal Evangelical Church, the Presbyterian Church and the Tahitian Evangelical Church. At mid-2000 there were an estimated 15,500 adherents professing other forms of Christianity.

The Press

L'Avenir Calédonien: 10 rue Gambetta, Nouméa; organ of the Union Calédonienne; Dir GABRIEL PAÏTA.

La Calédonie Agricole: BP 111, 98845 Nouméa Cédex; tel. 243160; fax 284587; quarterly; official publ. of the Chambre d'Agriculture; Pres. GÉRARD PASCO; Man. PATRICK LAUBREAUX; circ. 3,000.

Le Chien Bleu: BP 16018, Nouméa; tel. 288505; fax 261819; e-mail courrier@lechienbleu.nc; internet www.lechienbleu.nc; monthly; satirical; Man. Editor ETIENNE DUTAILLY.

Eglise de Nouvelle-Calédonie: BP 3, 98845 Nouméa; fax 265352; f. 1976; monthly; official publ. of the Roman Catholic Church; circ. 450.

Les Infos: 42 route de l'Anse-Vata, BP 8134, 98807 Nouméa; tel. 251808; fax 251882; e-mail lesinfos@lagoon.nc; weekly; Editor-in-Chief THIERRY SQUILLARIO.

Journal Officiel de la Nouvelle-Calédonie: Imprimerie administrative, BP M2, 98849 Nouméa Cédex; tel. 256013; fax 256021; e-mail webmestre.juridoc@gouv.nc; internet www.juridoc.gouv.nc; f. 1853 as *Bulletin Officiel de la Nouvelle-Calédonie*; present name adopted in 1988; only the paper version is official; twice a week; publ. by the Government of New Caledonia; record of state legislative developments in New Caledonia.

Mwà Véé: Centre Tjibaou, BP 378, 98845 Nouméa; tel. 414555; fax 414556; e-mail adck@adck.nc; f. 1993; quarterly; French; publ. by l'Agence de Développement de la Culture Kanak; Kanak history, culture and heritage; Publr EMMANUEL KASARHE'ROU; Editor GÉRARD DEL RIO.

Les Nouvelles Calédoniennes: 41–43 rue de Sébastopol, BP G5, 98848 Nouméa; tel. 272584; fax 281627; e-mail pminard@canl.nc; internet www.info.lnc.nc; f. 1971; daily; Publr ROBERT HERSANT; Gen. Man. THIERRY MASSÉ; Editor-in-Chief PHILIPPE MINARD; circ. 18,500.

Tazar: Immeuble Gallieni II, 12 rue de Verdun, 98800 Nouméa; tel. 282277; fax 283443; monthly; publ. by Mission d'Insertion des Jeunes de la Province Sud; youth.

Télé 7 Jours: Route de Vélodrome, BP 2080, 98846 Nouméa Cédex; tel. 284598; weekly.

NEWS AGENCY

Agence France-Presse (AFP): 15 rue Docteur Guégan, 98800 Nouméa; tel. 263033; fax 278699; Correspondent FRANCK MADOEUF.

Publishers

Editions d'Art Calédoniennes: 3 rue Guynemer, BP 1626, Nouméa; tel. 277633; fax 281526; art, reprints, travel.

Editions du Santal: 5 bis rue Emile-Trianon, 98846 Nouméa; tel. and fax 262533; history, art, travel, birth and wedding cards; Dir PAUL-JEAN STAHL.

Grain de Sable: BP 577, 98845 Nouméa; tel. and fax 273057; e-mail grainesable@canl.nc; internet www.pacific-bookin.com; literature, travel; Publr JEAN-BRICE PEIRANO.

Ile de Lumière: BP 8401, Nouméa Sud; tel. 289858; history, politics.

Savannah Editeur SNP: Yacht Marianne, BP 3086, 98846 Nouméa; e-mail savannahmarc@hotmail.com; f. 1994 as Savannah Editions; present name adopted in 2006; sports, travel, leisure; Publr JOËL MARC.

Société d'Etudes Historiques de la Nouvelle-Calédonie: BP 63, 98845 Nouméa; tel. 767155.

Broadcasting and Communications

TELECOMMUNICATIONS

France Câbles et Radio (FCR): Télécommunications Extérieures de la Nouvelle-Calédonie, BP A1, 98848 Nouméa Cédex; tel. 266600; fax 266666; e-mail contact.fcr-nc@orange-ftgroup.com; internet www.fcr.nc; announced withdrawal from New Caledonia Feb. 2007; Dir THIERRY MILARD.

Offices des Postes et Télécommunications (OPT): Le Waruna, 2 rue Monchovet, Port Plaisance, 98841 Nouméa Cédex; tel. 268217; fax 262927; e-mail direction@opt.nc; internet www.opt.nc; provides postal and fixed-line telephone services, and operates Mobilis mobile cellular telephone network (f. 2003); Dir-Gen. JEAN-YVES OLLIVAUD.

BROADCASTING
Radio

NRJ Nouvelle-Calédonie: 41–43 rue Sébastopol, BP G5, 98848 Nouméa; tel. 263434; fax 279447; e-mail nrj@nrj.nc; internet www.nrj.nc; f. 1984; Dir RICARDO GREMY.

Radio Djiido (Kanal K): 3 rue Sainte Cécile, Résidence La Caravelle Vallée du Tir, BP 14359, 98803 Nouméa Cédex; tel. 778768; fax 272187; e-mail radiodjiido@radiodjiido.nc; internet www.radiodjiido.nc; f. 1985; pro-independence community station; broadcasts in French; socio-cultural programmes; 60% local news, 30% regional, 10% international; Pres. CHARLES PIDGOT; Station Man. THIERRY KAMÉRÉMOIN; Editor-in-Chief CÉDRICK WAKAHUGNEME.

Radio Nouvelle-Calédonie: Réseau France Outre-mer (RFO), 1 rue Maréchal Leclerc, Mont Coffyn, BP G3, 98848 Nouméa Cédex; tel. 239999; fax 239975; e-mail internet.nc@rfo.fr; internet nouvellecaledonie.rfo.fr; f. 1942; fmrly Radiodiffusion Française d'Outre-mer (RFO); French; relays Radio Australia's French service; Dir-Gen. BENOÎT SAUDEAU; Gen. Man. FRANÇOIS GUILBEAU; Editor-in-Chief XAVIER ROBERT.

Radio Océane: 1 ave d'Auteuil, Lotissement FSH, Koutio, 98835 Dumbéa; tel. 410095; fax 410099; e-mail oceane.fm@lagoon.nc; Dir YANN DUVAL.

Radio Rythme Bleu: 8 ave Foch, BP 578, 98845 Nouméa; tel. 254646; fax 284928; e-mail rrb@lagoon.nc; f. 1984; music and local, national and international news; Pres. CHRISTIAN PROST; Dir ELIZABETH NOUAR.

Television

RFO-Télé Nouvelle-Calédonie: Réseau France Outre-mer (RFO), 1 rue Maréchal Leclerc, Mont Coffyn, BP G3, 98848 Nouméa Cédex; tel. 239999; fax 239975; internet www.rfo.fr; f. 1965; part of the France Télévisions group, France; three channels; Gen. Man. BENOÎT SAUDEAU; Editor-in-Chief GONZAGUE DE LA BOURDONNAYE.

Canal+ Calédonie: 30 rue de la Somme, BP 1797, 98845 Nouméa; tel. 265343; fax 265338; e-mail abonnement@canal-caledonie.com; internet www.canalcaledonie.com; subsidiary of Canal Plus, France; subscription service; broadcasts 24 hours daily; CEO SERGE LAMAGNÈRE.

Canal Outre-mer (Canal+): Nouméa; f. 1995; cable service.

Finance

(cap. = capital; res = reserves; dep. = deposits; m. = million; brs = branches; amounts in francs CFP unless otherwise stated)

BANKING

Agence Française de Développement: 5 rue Barleux, BP JI, 98849 Nouméa Cédex; tel. 242600; fax 282413; e-mail afdnoumea@nc.groupe-afd.org.

Banque Calédonienne d'Investissement (BCI): 54 ave de la Victoire, BP K5, 98848 Nouméa Cédex; tel. 256565; fax 274035; e-mail dg@bci.nc; internet www.bci.nc; f. 1988; cap. 7,500m. (Dec. 2003); Pres. DIDIER LEROUX; Gen. Man. ALAIN CELESTE.

Banque de Nouvelle-Calédonie: 25 ave de la Victoire, BP L3, 98849 Nouméa Cédex; tel. 257400; fax 274147; e-mail contact@bnc.nc; internet www.bnc.nc; f. 1974; adopted present name Jan. 2002; 95.8% owned by Financière Océor, France; cap. 3,858.3m., res 1,294.2m., dep. 66,873.0m. (Dec. 2004); Pres. JEAN-CLAUDE CLARAC; Gen. Man. JEAN-PIERRE FLOTAT; 7 brs.

BNP Paribas Nouvelle-Calédonie (France): 37 ave Henri Lafleur, BP K3, 98849 Nouméa Cédex; tel. 258400; fax 258459; e-mail bnp.nc@bnpparibas.com; internet nc.bnpparibas.net/fr; f. 1969 as Banque Nationale de Paris; present name adopted in 2001; cap. €28.0m., res €315.6m. (Dec. 2001); Pres. JEAN-PASCAL DUMANS; Gen. Man. JEAN-FRANCOIS ARACIL; 10 brs.

Société Générale Calédonienne de Banque: 44 rue de l'Alma, Siège et Agence Principale, BP G2, 98848 Nouméa Cédex; tel. 256300; fax 276245; e-mail svp.sgcb@canl.nc; internet www.sgcb.com; f. 1981; total assets 936m. (Dec. 2005); Gen. Man. FRANÇOIS TURCOT; Chair. JEAN-LOUIS MATTEI; 19 brs.

INSURANCE

AGF Vie & AGF IART Nouvelle-Calédonie: 99 ave du Générale de Gaulle, BP 152, 98845 Nouméa; tel. 283838; fax 281628; e-mail agfvienc@agfvie.nc; life and general non-life insurance.

GAN Pacifique: 58 bis ave de la Victoire, BP 223, 98845 Nouméa Cédex; tel. 243070; fax 278884; e-mail ganoumea@canl.nc; subsidiary of GAN Assurances, France; general non-life insurance; Chair. JEAN-FRANÇOIS LEMOUX; Gen. Man. DIDIER COURIER.

Poe-ma Insurances: 3 rue Sébastopol, BP 8069, 98807 Nouméa; tel. 274263; fax 274267; e-mail info@poema.nc.

Trade and Industry

DEVELOPMENT ORGANIZATIONS

Agence de Développement de la Culture Kanak (ADCK): Centre Culturel Tjibaou, rue des Accords de Matignon, BP 378, 98845 Nouméa Cédex; tel. 414555; fax 414546; e-mail adck@adck.nc; internet www.adck.nc; Pres. MARIE-CLAUDE TJIBAOU; Dir EMMANUEL KASARHEROU.

Agence de Développement Economique de la Nouvelle-Calédonie (ADECAL): 15 rue Guynemer, BP 2384, 98846 Nouméa Cédex; tel. 249077; fax 249087; e-mail adecal@offratel.nc; internet www.adecal.nc; f. 1995; promotes investment within New Caledonia; Dir JEAN-MICHEL ARLIE.

Agence de Développement Rural et d'Aménagement Foncier (ADRAF): 1 rue de la Somme, BP 4228, 98847 Nouméa Cédex; tel. 258600; fax 258604; e-mail adraf@adraf.nc; internet www.adraf.nc; f. 1986, reorganized 1989; acquisition and redistribution of land; Chair. MICHEL MATHIEU; Dir-Gen. JULES HMALOKO.

Agence pour l'Emploi de Nouvelle-Calédonie: 1 rue de la Somme, BP 497, 98845 Nouméa Cédex; tel. 281082; fax 272079; e-mail ape.nc@apenc.nc; internet www.apenc.nc; Dir PHILIPPE MARTIN.

Conseil Economique et Social: 30 route Baie des Dames, Immeuble Le Centre, Ducos, BP 4766, 98847 Nouméa Cédex; tel. 278517; fax 278509; e-mail ces@gouv.nc; internet www.ces.gouv.nc; represents trade unions and other orgs involved in economic, social and cultural life; Pres. ROBERT LAMARQUE; Sec.-Gen. FRANÇOIS-PAUL BUFNOR.

Institut Calédonien de Participation (ICAP): 1 rue Barleux, BP J1, 98849 Nouméa; tel. 276218; fax 282280; e-mail icap@icap.nc; internet www.icap.nc; f. 1989 to finance devt projects and encourage the Kanak population to participate in the market economy; Pres. PAUL NÉAOUTYINE; Man. YVES GOYETCHE.

Société de Développement et d'Investissement des Iles Loyauté (SODIL SA): 12 rue du Général Mangin, Immeuble Richelieu, BP 2217, 98846 Nouméa Cédex; tel. 276663; fax 276709; e-mail sodil@lagoon.nc; f. 1991; financing, promotion and sustainable devt of industry, tourism and artisanal cos; priority areas are transport, food processing, aquaculture, and regional and international tourism; Pres. HNAEJÉ HAMU; Man. SAMUEL HNEPEUNE.

Société d'Equipement de Nouvelle-Calédonie (SECAL): 28 rue du Général Mangin, BP 2517, 98846 Nouméa Cédex; tel. 270369; fax 281333; e-mail contact@secal.nc; f. 1971; urban management and devt, public-sector construction and civil engineering; Dir VINCENT SILVE.

Société de Financement et de Développement de la Province Sud (PROMOSUD): BP 295, 98845 Nouméa Cédex; tel. 241972; fax 271326; e-mail info@promosud.nc; f. 1991; financing, promotion and economic devt of cos in priority sectors, incl. tourism, fishing and aquaculture, and processing industries; Pres. ALAIN DESCOMBELS; Man. CHRISTIAN NEUZERET.

Société de Financement et d'Investissement de la Province Nord (SOFINOR): 85 ave du Général de Gaulle, BP 66, 98800

Nouméa; tel. 281353; fax 281567; e-mail dirgen@smsp.nc; internet www.sofinor.nc; f. 1990; economic devt, management and financing; priority areas include mining and metal production, aquaculture and fishing, tourism, transport, real estate and engineering; Pres. GUIGUI DOUNEHOTE; Man. LOUIS MAPOU.

CHAMBERS OF COMMERCE

Chambre d'Agriculture: 3 rue A. Desmazures, BP 111, 98845 Nouméa Cédex; tel. 243160; fax 284587; e-mail direction@canc.nc; f. 1909; Pres. GÉRARD PASCO; Dir PATRICK LAUBREAUX; 33 mems.

Chambre de Commerce et d'Industrie: 15 rue de Verdun, BP M3, 98849 Nouméa Cédex; tel. 243100; fax 243131; e-mail cci@cci.nc; internet www.cci.nc; f. 1879; Pres. ANDRÉ DESPLAT; Gen. Man. MICHEL MERZEAU; 29 mems.

Chambre des Métiers et de l'Artisanat: 10 ave James Cook, BP 4186, 98846 Nouméa Cédex; tel. 282337; fax 282729; e-mail cma@cma.nc; internet www.cma.nc; Pres. JEAN-CLAUDE MERLET; Sec.-Gen. PAUL SANCHEZ.

EMPLOYERS' ORGANIZATION

MEDEF de Nouvelle-Calédonie (Fédération Patronale des Chefs d'Entreprise en Nouvelle-Calédonie): 10 rue Jean Jaurès, 98800 Nouméa Cédex; tel. 273525; fax 274037; e-mail medefnc@medef.nc; internet www.medef.nc; f. 1936; represents the leading cos of New Caledonia in the defence of professional interests, co-ordination, documentation and research in socio-economic fields; affiliated to the Mouvement des Entreprises de France; Pres. JEAN-YVES BOUVIER; Vice-Pres. PIERRE ALLA.

UTILITIES

Electricity

Electricité et Eau de Nouvelle-Calédonie (EEC): 29 rue Jules Ferry, BP F3, 98848 Nouméa Cédex; tel. 273636; fax 275655; e-mail dr.elyo@eec.nc; f. 1929 as UNLECO; present name adopted in 1984; subsidiary of Elyo, France; producers and distributors of electricity; Gen. Man. FRANÇOIS GUICHARD.

Société Néo-Calédonienne d'Energie (ENERCAL): 87 ave du Général de Gaulle, BP C1, 98848 Nouméa Cédex; tel. 250250; fax 250253; e-mail jbegaud@canl.nc; f. 1955; 16% owned by EDEV, France; production and distribution of electricity; Chair. JEAN-CLAUDE HIREL; Gen. Man. JEAN BÉGAUD.

Water

Société Calédonienne des Eaux (CDE): 15 rue Edmond Harbulot, PK 6, BP 812, 98845 Nouméa Cédex; tel. 282040; fax 278128; e-mail patrick.chantre@cde.nc; water distribution; Gen. Man. PATRICK CHANTRE.

TRADE UNIONS

Confédération Générale des Travailleurs de Nouvelle-Calédonie (COGETRA): incorporates:

Syndicat de la Fonction Publique Territoriale (SFPT): 3 Edouard Unger, Maison des Syndicats, Vallée du Tir, BP 10453, 98805 Nouméa Cédex; tel. and fax 271820; e-mail cogetra_nc@yahoo.fr; f. 1998; Pres. FRANÇOISE ARMAND.

Union des Secteurs Généraux du Commerce et de l'Industrie de Nouvelle-Calédonie: 3 Edouard Unger, Maison des Syndicats, Vallée du Tir, BP 1612, 98845 Nouméa Cédex; tel. 245371; fax 245270; e-mail usgcinc@canl.nc; f. 1966; Pres. REYNALD FAHRNER.

Confédération Générale du Travail-Force Ouvrière de Nouvelle-Calédonie (CGT-FO NC): 13 rue Jules Ferry, BP R2, 98851 Nouméa Cédex; tel. 274950; fax 278202; e-mail cgtfonc@lagoon.nc; f. 1984; Sec.-Gen. JEAN-CLAUDE NÈGRE.

Confédération Syndicale des Travailleurs de Nouvelle-Calédonie (CSTNC): 49 rue Auer Ducos, 98800 Nouméa; tel. and fax 269648; e-mail cst-nc@laposte.net; Sec.-Gen. SYLVAIN NÉA; grouped with the following organizations.

Fédération des Fonctionnaires, Agents et Ouvriers de la Fonction Publique (FSFAOFP): 3 Edouard Unger, Maison des Syndicats, Vallée du Tir, BP 820, 98845 Nouméa Cédex; tel. and fax 273532; e-mail fsfaofp@lagoon.nc; f. 1946; represents civil servants and public-sector employees; Sec.-Gen. JOÃO D'ALMEIDA.

Union des Syndicats des Ouvriers et Employés de Nouvelle-Calédonie (USOENC): 3 Edouard Unger, Maison des Syndicats, Vallée du Tir, BP 2534, 98846 Nouméa; tel. 259640; fax 250164; e-mail usoenc@canl.nc; f. 1968; affiliated to the Int. Metalworkers' Fed; Sec.-Gen. DIDIER GUÉNANT-JEANSON; 4,011 mems (2005).

Union Syndicale des Travailleurs Kanak et des Exploités (USTKE): 2 rue Ali Raleb, Vallée du Tir, BP 4372, Nouméa; tel. 277210; fax 277687; e-mail contact@ustke.org; internet www.ustke.org; f. 1981; Pres. GÉRARD JODAR; Vice-Pres. ALAIN BOEWA.

Union Territoriale de la Confédération Française de l'Encadrement-Confédération Générale des Cadres (UT-CFE-CGC): Complexe Commercial La belle vie, 224 rue Jacques Ikékawé, PK 6, BP 30536, 98895 Nouméa Cédex; tel. and fax 410300; fax 410310; e-mail utcfecgc@utcfecgc.nc; internet www.utcfecgc.nc; f. 1996; territorial br. of the Confédération Française de l'Encadrement-Confédération Générale des Cadres; Pres. SONIA BACKES; Sec.-Gen. JEAN MARIE ARMAND.

Other unions include the Fédération des Cadres et Collaborateurs en Nouvelle-Calédonie (f. 1968), Syndicat Libre Unité Action (f. 1995), Syndicat National Personnel Navigant Commercial (f. 1984) and Syndicat des Ouvriers de Travaux Publics et Municipaux (f. 1962).

Transport

ROADS

In 2005 there was a total of 4,926 km of roads in New Caledonia; of these some 2,559 km were unsealed. There were some 410,680 km of urban roads and 890,450 km of rural tracks. There was a further estimated 350 km of unrecorded urban roads within Nouméa.

Société Anonyme des Voies Express à Péage (SAVEXPRESS): 15 rue de Verdun, BP M3, 98849 Nouméa Cédex; tel. 411930; fax 412899; e-mail savexpress@savexpress.nc; f. 1979; highway management and devt; Pres. GUY GEORGE; Man. MAXIME CHASSOT.

SHIPPING

Most traffic is through the port of Nouméa. Passenger and cargo services, linking Nouméa to other towns and islands, are regular and frequent. There is also a harbour for yachts and pleasure craft at Nouméa. There are plans to develop Nepoui, in the North Province, as a deep-water port and industrial centre.

Port Autonome de la Nouvelle-Calédonie: BP 14, 98845 Nouméa Cédex; tel. 255000; fax 275490; e-mail noumeaportnc@canl.nc; Port Man. PHILIPPE LAFLEUR; Harbour Master EDMUND MARTIN.

Moana Services: 2 bis rue Berthelot, BP 2099, 98846 Nouméa; tel. 273898; fax 259315; e-mail moana@canl.nc; internet www.moana.nc; shipping and logistics agency; representatives for Moana Shipping (Wallis), Maersk Line (Denmark), Canadian Steamship Lines (Canada) and BHP Billiton Marine (Australia); Man. LUCIEN BOURGADE.

SEM de la Baie de la Moselle (SODEMO): rue de la Frégate-Nivôse, BP 2960, 98846 Nouméa; tel. 277197; fax 277129; e-mail contact@sodemo.nc; internet www.sodemo.nc; f. 1987; operates Port Moselle for pleasure craft; Pres. JEAN-PIERRE GUILLEMARD; Man. FRANÇOIS LE BRUN.

Sofrana NC: 14 ave James Cook, BP 1602, 98845 Nouméa; tel. 275191; fax 272611; e-mail info@sofrana.nc; internet www.sofrana.nc; f. 1968; subsidiary of Sofrana Holding; shipping agents and stevedores; barge operators; Chair. JEAN-BAPTISTE LEROUX; Gen. Man. FRANÇOIS BURNOUF.

CIVIL AVIATION

There is an international airport, La Tontouta, 47 km from Nouméa, and an internal network, centred on Magenta airport, which provides air services linking Nouméa to other towns and islands. In November 2007 major expansion plans were announced for La Tontouta airport; work was scheduled to begin in January 2008 and to be completed in 2011. Air France, which formerly operated a service between Nouméa and Paris via Tokyo, Japan, ceased operations in New Caledonia in early 2003. The route to Tokyo was taken over by Air Calédonie International (Aircalin). Other airlines providing services to the island include Air New Zealand, Air Vanuatu and Qantas.

Air Calédonie: Aérodrome de Magenta, BP 212, 98845 Nouméa Cédex; tel. 250302; fax 254869; e-mail direction@air-caledonie.nc; internet www.air-caledonie.nc; f. 1954; services throughout mainland New Caledonia and its islands; operates four aircraft; Pres. NIDOÏSH NAISSELINE; CEO WILLIAM IHAGE; 300,000 passengers and c. 1,000 metric tons of freight carried in 2006/07.

Air Calédonie International (Aircalin): 8 rue Frédéric Surleau, BP 3736, 98846 Nouméa Cédex; tel. 265546; fax 272772; internet www.aircalin.com; f. 1983; 27% owned by Agence pour la Desserte Aérienne de la Nouvelle-Calédonie (NC Air Transport Agency), 72% by Caisse Nationale des Caisses d'Epargne et de Prévoyance, 1% by others; services to Sydney and Brisbane (Australia), Auckland (New Zealand), Nadi (Fiji), Papeete (French Polynesia), Wallis and Futuna Islands, Port Vila (Vanuatu) and Osaka and Tokyo (Japan); Chair. CHARLES LAVOIX; Pres. and CEO JEAN-MICHEL MASSON; 350,070 passengers in 2005/06.

Tontouta Air Service (TAS): La Tontouta International Airport, BP 2, 98840 La Tontouta; tel. 352600; fax 352601; e-mail tas@tas.nc; internet www.tas.nc; f. 1995; owned by Endel Group; operates

Tontouta airport and freight management services; Exec. Vice-Pres. PHILIPPE DARRASON.

Tourism

In 2007 there were 103,363 visitors to New Caledonia, of whom 28.2% came from France, 25.9% from Japan and 15.8% from Australia. A total of 2,643 hotel rooms were available in 2004. In that year the industry earned 17,562m. francs CFP.

GIE Tourisme Province Nord: Centre Commercial Le Village, 35 ave Foch, Nouméa; e-mail info@tourismeprovincenord.nc; internet www.tourismeprovincenord.nc.

New Caledonia Tourism South: Galerie Nouméa Centre, 20 rue Anatole France; BP 688, 98845 Nouméa Cédex; tel. 242080; fax 242070; e-mail info@nctps.com; internet www.visitnewcaledonia.com; f. 2001; international promotion of tourism in the South Province of New Caledonia; Chair. CHRISTIANE GAMBEY; Gen. Man. PATRICK MOISAN.

GABON

Introductory Survey

Location, Climate, Language, Religion, Flag, Capital

The Gabonese Republic is an equatorial country on the west coast of Africa, with Equatorial Guinea and Cameroon to the north and the Congo to the south and east. The climate is tropical, with an average annual temperature of 26°C (79°F) and an average annual rainfall of 2,490 mm (98 ins). The official language is French, but Fang (in the north) and Bantu dialects (in the south) are also widely spoken. About 60% of the population are Christians, mainly Roman Catholics. Most of the remainder follow animist beliefs. The national flag (proportions 3 by 4) has three equal horizontal stripes, of green, yellow and blue. The capital is Libreville.

Recent History

Formerly a province of French Equatorial Africa, Gabon was granted internal autonomy in November 1958, and proceeded to full independence on 17 August 1960. Léon M'Ba, the new Republic's President, established Gabon as a one-party state. Following his death in November 1967, M'Ba was succeeded by the Vice-President, Albert-Bernard (later Omar) Bongo, who organized a new ruling party, the Parti démocratique gabonais (PDG). Gabon enjoyed political stability and rapid economic growth in the 1970s, underpinned by substantial foreign investment in the development and exploitation of its petroleum reserves. However, the social and economic problems that accompanied the subsequent decline in world petroleum prices led to the emergence in 1981 of a moderate opposition group, the Mouvement de redressement national (MORENA), which demanded the restoration of a multi-party system and formed a government-in-exile in Paris, France, from which it unsuccessfully sought to put forward a candidate to challenge Bongo in the presidential election held in November 1986.

In May 1989 the Chairman of MORENA, Fr Paul M'Ba Abessole, visited Gabon and, after a meeting with Bongo, announced that he and many of his supporters would return to Gabon. In January 1990 representatives of MORENA announced that M'Ba Abessole had been dismissed from the leadership of the movement, following his declaration of support for the Government. M'Ba Abessole subsequently formed a breakaway faction, known as MORENA des bûcherons (renamed Rassemblement national des bûcherons—RNB—in 1991 to avoid confusion with the rival MORENA—originels).

A number of arrests took place in October 1989, following an alleged conspiracy to overthrow the Government. It was claimed that the plot had been initiated by Pierre Mamboundou, the leader of the Union du peuple gabonais (UPG, an opposition movement based in Paris). In early 1990 Bongo announced that extensive political reforms were to be introduced and that the ruling party was to be replaced by a new organization, the Rassemblement social-démocrate gabonais (RSDG).

In March 1990 the PDG announced that a multi-party system was to be introduced, under the supervision of the RSDG, at the end of a five-year transitional period. Later that month a national conference, attended by representatives of more than 70 political organizations, rejected Bongo's proposals for a transitional period of political reform under the aegis of the RSDG, and demanded the immediate establishment of a multi-party system and the formation of a new government, which would hold office only until legislative elections could take place. Bongo acceded to the decisions of the conference, and in late April Casimir Oyé Mba, the Governor of the Banque des états de l'Afrique centrale, was appointed Prime Minister of a transitional administration, which included several opposition members.

In May 1990 the Central Committee of the PDG and the legislature, the Assemblée nationale, approved constitutional changes that would facilitate the transition to a multi-party political system. The existing presidential mandate (effective until January 1994) was to be respected; thereafter, elections to the presidency would be contested by more than one candidate, and the tenure of office would be reduced to five years, renewable only once.

Legislative elections were scheduled for 16 and 23 September 1990. The first round of the elections was disrupted by violent protests by voters who claimed that the PDG was engaging in electoral fraud. Following further allegations of widespread electoral malpractices, results in 32 constituencies were declared invalid, although the election of 58 candidates (of whom 36 were members of the PDG) was confirmed. The interim Government subsequently conceded that electoral irregularities had taken place, and further voting was postponed until 21 and 28 October. At the elections the PDG won an overall majority in the 120-member Assemblée nationale, with 62 seats, while opposition candidates secured 55 seats.

On 27 November 1990 a Government of National Unity, under Oyé Mba, was formed. Sixteen posts were allocated to members of the PDG, while the remaining eight portfolios were distributed among members of five opposition parties. A new draft Constitution, which was promulgated on 22 December, endorsed reforms that had been included in the transitional Constitution, introduced in May. Further measures included the proposed establishment of an upper house, to be known as the Sénat, which was to control the balance and regulation of power. A Constitutional Council was to replace the administrative chamber of the Supreme Court, and a National Communications Council was to be formed to ensure the impartial treatment of information by the state media.

The final composition of the Assemblée nationale was determined in March 1991, when elections took place in five constituencies, where the results had been annulled, owing to alleged malpractice. Following the completion of the elections, the PDG held a total of 66 seats in the Assemblée nationale, while various opposition groups held 54 seats. The two most prominent opposition movements, the Parti gabonais du progrès (PGP) and the RNB, held 19 and 17 seats, respectively.

In May 1991 six opposition parties formed an alliance, known as the Co-ordination de l'opposition démocratique (COD), in protest at the delay in the implementation of the new Constitution. The COD also demanded the appointment of a new Prime Minister, the abolition of certain institutions under the terms of the Constitution, and the liberalization of the state-controlled media. Following a general strike, organized by the COD, Bongo announced the resignation of the Council of Ministers, and declared that he was prepared to implement fully the new Constitution. He also claimed that, in accordance with the Constitution, several institutions, including the High Court of Justice, had been dissolved, and that a Constitutional Court and a National Communications Council had been established. However, opposition parties within the COD refused to be represented in a new Government of National Unity, of which Oyé Mba was appointed as Prime Minister. In June Oyé Mba appointed a new coalition Government, in which 14 members of the previous Council of Ministers retained their portfolios. Members of MORENA–originels, the Union socialiste gabonaise (USG) and the Association pour le socialisme au Gabon (APSG) were also represented in the Government.

In November 1993 five political associations, the PDG, the USG, the APSG, the Cercle des libéraux réformateurs (CLR) and the Parti de l'unité du peuple gabonais, agreed to support Bongo's candidacy in the forthcoming presidential election, while eight opposition candidates established an informal alliance, known as the Convention des forces du changement. In early December, following sustained opposition protests against alleged electoral malpractice, the Government agreed to revise the electoral register in part, but rejected opposition demands that the election be postponed.

At the presidential election, which took place on 5 December 1993, Bongo was re-elected, winning 51.2% of votes cast, while M'Ba Abessole (the leader of the RNB) secured 26.5% of the votes. The official announcement of the results prompted rioting by opposition supporters. Five deaths were reported after security forces suppressed the unrest, and a national curfew and state of alert were subsequently imposed. M'Ba Abessole, however, claimed victory and formed a Haut conseil de la République, later redesignated as the Haut conseil de la résistance (HCR), which included the majority of opposition presidential candidates, and a parallel government. Despite the reports by international observers that the elections had been conducted fairly, the opposition appealed to the Constitutional Court to annul the results, on the grounds that the Government had perpetrated electoral malpractice. In December Bongo condemned M'Ba Abessole's actions and invited the other candidates who had contested the election to participate in a government of national consensus.

In mid-January 1994 the Constitutional Court ruled against the appeal by the opposition and endorsed the election results. On 22 January Bongo was officially inaugurated as President. In mid-February the national curfew and the state of alert, which had been in force since December 1993, were repealed, but later that month were reimposed, after a general strike, in support of demands for an increase in salaries to compensate for a devaluation of the CFA franc in January, degenerated into violence. Strike action was suspended after four days, following negotiations between the Government and trade unions; nine people had been killed during that period, according to official figures (although the opposition claimed that a total of 38 had died).

In March 1994 Oyé Mba resigned and dissolved the Council of Ministers. Later that month he was reappointed as Prime Minister, and, following the opposition's refusal to participate in a government of national unity, formed a 38-member administration, largely comprising representatives of the presidential majority. In the same month the Assemblée nationale approved a constitutional amendment that provided for the establishment of a Sénat (which the opposition had resisted) and repealed legislation prohibiting unsuccessful presidential candidates from participating in the Government within a period of 18 months. In June opposition parties agreed to a further postponement of the local government elections, to early 1995, and in August announced that they were prepared to participate in a coalition government, on condition that it was installed as a transitional organ pending legislative elections. In September negotiations between the Government and opposition took place in Paris, under the auspices of the Organization of African Unity (OAU, now the African Union—AU, see p. 164), in order to resolve remaining differences concerning the results of the presidential election and the proposed formation of a government of national unity.

At the end of September 1994 an agreement was reached whereby a transitional coalition government was to be installed, with local government elections scheduled to take place after a period of one year, followed by legislative elections six months later; the electoral code was to be revised and an independent electoral commission established, in an effort to ensure that the elections be conducted fairly. In early October Oyé Mba resigned from office and dissolved the Council of Ministers. Shortly afterwards Bongo appointed Dr Paulin Obame-Nguema, a member of the PDG who had served in former administrations, as Prime Minister. Obame-Nguema subsequently formed a 27-member Council of Ministers, which included six opposition members. The composition of the new Government was, however, immediately criticized by the opposition, on the grounds that it was entitled to one-third of ministerial portfolios in proportion to the number of opposition deputies in the Assemblée nationale; the HCR announced that the opposition would boycott the new administration, which, it claimed, was in violation of the Paris accord. Four opposition members consequently refused to accept the portfolios allocated to them, although two of these finally agreed to join the Government. (The portfolios that remained vacant were later assigned to a further two opposition members.)

In January 1995 controversy emerged over the extent of the authority vested in the Assemblée nationale, after members of the HCR refused to participate in the drafting of the new electoral code until the Paris agreement was ratified. The Constitutional Court subsequently ruled that the Assemblée nationale was not empowered, under the terms of the Constitution, to ratify the agreement. In February, however, opposition deputies ended a boycott of the Assemblée nationale, following a further ruling by the Constitutional Court that the Assemblée nationale was entitled to act as a parliamentary body, pending the installation of a Sénat after the legislative elections in 1996, but that the constitutional provisions adopted under the terms of the Paris accord would require endorsement by a referendum, which was scheduled for June. In the same month, in accordance with the Paris accord, the Cabinet approved legislation providing for the release of prisoners detained on charges involving state security. Later in April Gabon withdrew its ambassador in Paris, in protest at reports by the French media regarding Bongo's alleged liaisons with prostitutes; a number of demonstrations in support of Bongo took place in Libreville. Government efforts to prohibit two pro-opposition newspapers, which had published French press reports considered to be critical of Bongo, were rejected by the National Communications Council. At the national referendum (which had been postponed until 24 July), the constitutional amendments were approved by 96.5% of votes cast, with 63% of the electorate participating.

During early 1996 opposition parties criticized the Government for delaying the implementation of the electoral timetable contained in the Paris accord. At the beginning of May, following a meeting attended by all the officially recognized political parties, Bongo agreed to establish a Commission nationale électorale (National Election Commission—CNE) to formulate an electoral timetable, in consultation with all the official parties. It was also decided that access to state-controlled media and election funding should be equitably divided. On 20 May 1996 the Assemblée nationale's mandate expired, and Obame-Nguema's Government resigned at the beginning of June, in accordance with the Paris accord. Bongo, however, rejected the resignation on the grounds that the Government should, before leaving office, organize the elections and finalize pending agreements with the IMF and the World Bank. At the beginning of October the CNE adopted a timetable for legislative elections: the first round was to take place on 17 November, with a second round scheduled for 1 December. HCR representatives denounced the timetable, withdrew from the commission and demanded the postponement of the local and legislative elections.

Organizational problems disrupted the local elections, which were eventually held on 20 October 1996; according to reports, only 15% of the electorate participated. The PDG gained control of the majority of the municipalities, although the PGP secured victory in Port-Gentil, while the RNB was successful in the north of the country. Elections in Fougamou (where voting had not taken place) and Libreville (where the results had been invalidated) were eventually rescheduled for 24 November, although the RNB demanded the validation of the original results. On 24 November the RNB secured 62 of the 98 seats available in Libreville; M'Ba Abessole was subsequently elected mayor.

Legislative elections were rescheduled on several occasions, owing to the delay in the release of the local election results and the failure to revise electoral registers in time. The first round of the elections took place on 15 December 1996, without major incidents. Later that month it was reported that the PDG had obtained 47 of the 55 seats that were decided in the first round of voting. The opposition disputed the results, and there were demands for a boycott of the second round of voting. The PDG secured a substantial majority of the seats decided in the second round, which was held on 29 December, winning 84 seats, while the RNB obtained seven, the PGP six and independent candidates four, with the remaining 14 seats shared by the CLR, the UPG, the USG and others. Polling was unable to proceed for the five remaining seats, and results in a number of other constituencies were later annulled, owing to irregularities. (Following by-elections held in August 1997, during which five people were reportedly killed in violent incidents in north-east Gabon, the PDG held 88 seats, the PGP nine and the RNB five.) Guy Ndzouba Ndama was elected President of the new Assemblée nationale. Obame-Nguema was reappointed Prime Minister on 27 January, and a new Council of Ministers, dominated by members of the PDG, was announced on the following day. The PGP, the main opposition party represented in the Assemblée nationale, had refused to participate in the new Government.

Elections to the new Sénat took place on 26 January and 9 February 1997, with senators to be elected by members of municipal councils and departmental assemblies. The PDG won 53 of the Sénat's 91 seats, while the RNB secured 20 seats, the PGP four, the Alliance démocratique et républicaine (ADERE) three, the CLR one, and the RDP one, with independent candidates obtaining nine seats. The results for a number of seats were annulled, however, and in subsequent by-elections, held later that year, the PDG increased its representation to 58 seats, while the RNB held 20 seats and the PGP four.

In mid-April 1997 a congress of deputies and senators adopted constitutional amendments which extended the presidential term to seven years, provided for the creation of the post of Vice-President and formally designated the Sénat as an upper chamber of a bicameral legislature. Opposition demands that a referendum be held were ignored. The Vice-President was to deputize for the President as required, but was not to have any power of succession. In late May Didjob Divungui-di-N'Dingue, a senior member of the ADERE and a candidate in the 1993 presidential election, was appointed to the new post.

In September 1998 opposition parties withdrew their members from the CNE in protest at alleged irregularities in the voter registration process for the forthcoming presidential election. In October President Bongo confirmed that he was to seek re-election; his candidature was formally accepted later that month, together with those of Kombila, M'Ba Abessole and Alain Egouang Nze for the RNB, Pierre Mamboundou for the HCR, Maganga Moussavou for the PSD, and two independents.

At the presidential election, which was held on 6 December 1998, Bongo was re-elected with 66.6% of votes cast, while Mamboundou received 16.5% of the votes and M'Ba Abessole secured 13.4%. The reported rate of participation was 53.8%. Opposition parties rejected the results, again alleging electoral malpractice, and called for fresh elections to be held. None the less, Bongo was inaugurated as President on 21 January 1999, and a new 42-member Council of Ministers, headed by Jean-François Ntoutoume Emane, was subsequently appointed.

Elections to the Assemblée nationale took place on 9 and 23 December 2001. Three opposition parties accused the Government of falsely inflating voter registration lists and boycotted the elections, while others called for the first round to be annulled, as a result of reputed irregularities and high abstention rates, reported to have reached some 80% in urban areas. In the event, the elections were postponed in three districts until 6 January 2002, owing to violent incidents, and voting was repeated on 20 January in a further two constituencies where candidates had received the same number of votes and in a third district where violence had marred the initial ballot. An outbreak of the Ebola virus (see below) resulted in the indefinite postponement of voting in the north-eastern district of Zadie. The PDG won 86 seats in the Assemblée, which were supplemented by 19 seats secured by independents with links to the PDG and other parties affiliated to the ruling party. Opposition parties obtained a total of 14 seats (the Rassemblement pour le Gabon—RPG—as the RNB had been restyled, eight, the PSD two and the UPG one).

A new, enlarged 39-member Council of Ministers, which included four opposition representatives, was appointed in late January 2002. Ntoutoume Emane was reappointed as Prime Minister, while M'Ba Abessole was named Minister of State for Human Rights and Missions. The new Government's priorities were stated to be poverty alleviation, social reintegration and the eradication of corruption.

During March and April 2002 the Constitutional Court annulled the results of voting in the December 2001 elections to the Assemblée nationale in 12 constituencies, including eight in which the PDG had been successful, owing to irregularities. On 26 May and 9 June by-elections took place in these 12 constituencies and in Zadie (where voting had been postponed); the PDG won 10 of the 13 seats contested, increasing its representation to 88 seats.

Throughout late 2002 the ruling PDG formed a number of alliances with minor opposition parties. In November the Parti de l'unité du peuple gabonais and the Mouvement commun de développement agreed formally to join the PDG, and in the same month the Parti gabonais du centre indépendant resolved to support the 'presidential majority' in the local elections scheduled for December.

In late January 2003 Vice-President Divungui-di-N'Dingue was the target of an assassination attempt, perpetrated, his office claimed, by members of the PSD. Although Maganga Moussavou denied the accusations, Bongo dismissed him from the Council of Ministers in a reshuffle on the following day, promoting M'Ba Abessole to the post of Vice-Prime Minister. Elections to the Sénat took place on 9 February 2003; the PDG won more than 60 of the upper chamber's 91 seats, followed by the RPG, which secured eight seats.

In July 2003 the Assemblée nationale voted to revoke the Constitution's limit on the number of terms of office for which the President is eligible to seek re-election. Opposition politicians claimed that Bongo thus intended to become 'President-for-Life' by means of continuous fraud in future presidential elections. In September, in response to a series of strikes and protests, the Government and representatives of labour groups announced the signing of a so-called 'social truce', which included commitments to lower the prices of essential items and reduce the extent of political patronage over the following three years. However, renewed protests over reductions in state expenditure in early 2004 appeared to threaten the viability of the agreement.

In early September 2004 President Bongo Ondimba (who had added his father's name to his own in November 2003) carried out a minor cabinet reshuffle, in which several leading opposition figures were awarded ministerial portfolios in the newly enlarged 44-member Council of Ministers. Emane retained the post of Prime Minister and the key ministerial portfolios remained unchanged. It was widely believed that the inclusion of opposition leaders in the Government was intended to reduce the number of candidates opposing Bongo and the PDG in the presidential and legislative elections scheduled for 2005 and 2006, respectively. In October 2005 disquiet arose among opposition groups, following the decision of the CNE to exclude nine presidential candidates, two of whom subsequently appealed successfully against their exclusion, from contesting the election.

At the presidential election held on 27 November 2005 Bongo Ondimba was re-elected, receiving 79.18% of votes cast. Pierre Mamboundou, the candidate of the UPG, received 13.61%, while Zacharie Myboto, a former government minister representing the newly formed Union gabonaise pour la démocratie et le développement, received 6.58%. Augustin Moussavou King of the PSG and the independent candidate Christian Serge Maroga, received 0.33% and 0.30%, respectively. The rate of voter participation was recorded at 63.5%. Following the announcement of the results, both Mamboundou and Myboto disputed their validity, alleging electoral malpractice, and each claimed victory for himself. However, a delegation of international election observers, including a representative from the French Sénat, declared the elections to have been largely free and transparent. The ensuing unrest caused by supporters of the defeated candidates was broadly quelled following the deployment of security forces throughout the country in January 2006. On 20 January President Bongo Ondimba appointed Jean Eyéghé Ndong of the PDG as Prime Minister and later that month Ndong unveiled a new, expanded Council of Ministers composed overwhelmingly of PDG members.

Legislative elections took place on 17 December 2006, although voting in seven constituencies was postponed until 24 December for logistical reasons. The PDG retained control of the Assemblée nationale, winning 82 of the 120 seats, while parties allied to the PDG secured a further 17 seats; the opposition won 17 seats (the UPG secured the largest number of opposition seats with eight) and independents won four. Electoral observers endorsed the results and proclaimed that the polls had been held peacefully, but the opposition complained that it was not given adequate access to state media during the election campaign. In late January 2007 Ndong, who had been reappointed to the premiership, announced a largely unchanged 50-member Council of Ministers, which was again dominated by members of the PDG. Results in 20 constituencies were subsequently annulled owing to allegations of procedural irregularities and fraud. By-elections were held on 10 June 2007 at which the PDG won 11 of the 20 seats available. Parties allied to the PDG won six seats while the opposition took two; the remaining seat was secured by an independent candidate.

In July 2007 Louis-Gaston Mayila was dismissed from the post of Vice-Prime Minister, Minister of National Solidarity, Social Affairs, Welfare and the Fight against Poverty. Jean-François Ndongou subsequently assumed responsibility for those portfolios. Shortly before Mayila was dismissed he had announced the formation of a new political party, the Union pour la nouvelle République, and had therefore positioned himself as a potential challenger to Bongo Ondimba's presidency.

In December 2007 President Bongo Ondimba appointed a new reduced Government, retaining Jean Eyéghé Ndong as Prime Minister but dismissing Emmanuel Ondo Methogo, hitherto Vice-Prime Minister, Minister of Relations with Parliament and Constitutional Institutions. The new Government comprised just three Vice-Prime Ministers and 10 Ministers-delegate, reduced from 15 in the previous cabinet, in an attempt to increase efficiency within the administration. A further governmental reorganization was effected in February 2008, following the appointment of Jean Ping, hitherto Vice-Prime Minister, Minister of Foreign Affairs, Co-operation, Francophonie and Regional Integration, to the position of Chairperson of the Commission of the AU. Laure Olga Gondjout, formerly the Minister of Communication, Post and Telecommunications and New Information Technologies, Spokesperson for the Government replaced Ping, while Jean Boniface Asselé assumed Gondjout's vacated portfolio.

President Bongo has pursued a policy of close co-operation with France in the fields of economic and foreign affairs. Relations became strained in March 1997, however, when allegations that Bongo had been a beneficiary in an international fraud emerged during a French judicial investigation into the affairs of the petroleum company Elf Aquitaine (now part of Total). The Chairman of Elf-Gabon, André Tarallo, was temporarily detained, and overseas bank accounts, said to contain Gabonese government funds, were blocked. In response, Bongo cancelled a visit to France and reportedly threatened to impose economic sanctions on French oil interests in Gabon. In October 1999 a further judicial investigation into the affairs of Elf Aquitaine, carried out by Swiss authorities, revealed that Tarallo had used bank accounts in that country secretly to transfer large sums of money to several African heads of state, among them Bongo. Bongo denied personally receiving direct payments from Elf and maintained that such 'bonus' payments were made only to the Gabonese Government. However, a report released in November, following a separate investigation by the US Congress into money-laundering and corruption among political figures, alleged further improper financial dealing between Bongo and Elf. In March 2003 the trial commenced in Paris of 37 defendants accused of permitting the embezzlement of the equivalent of some €300m. of funds from Elf Aquitaine. In November Tarallo was sentenced to four years' imprisonment and fined €2m., while 29 others also received terms of imprisonment. Tarallo was released from prison on the grounds of ill-health in January 2004; however, his sentence was increased to seven years' imprisonment, following appeals by the prosecution in March 2005. In November the Government signed an agreement with France to increase co-operation between French and Gabonese small and medium-sized businesses.

Bongo has often acted as an intermediary in regional disputes, chairing the OAU ad hoc committee seeking to resolve the border dispute between Chad and Libya, and encouraging dialogue between Angola and the USA. In 1997 he mediated in civil conflicts in Zaire (now the Democratic Republic of the Congo—DRC), the Central African Republic (CAR) and the Republic of the Congo. In July of that year the Government expressed concern at the large numbers of refugees arriving in Gabon and subsequently announced plans for repatriation. Throughout late 1998 Bongo participated in discussions with other central African leaders in an attempt to find a solution to the political and military crisis in the DRC, which had been invaded by Rwandan and Ugandan troops in August of that year. At a summit meeting held in Libreville in September, it was decided that Bongo would chair a monitoring and consultations committee on the conflict.

At a meeting of the Communauté économique et monétaire de l'Afrique centrale (CEMAC, see p. 307) in Libreville in early December 2001, Bongo was appointed to chair a commission, also comprising Presidents Idriss Deby and Denis Sassou-Nguesso of Chad and the Republic of the Congo, respectively, to find a lasting solution to instability in the CAR (q.v.). In October 2002 a CEMAC summit in Libreville sought to defuse tensions between the CAR and Chad, following outbreaks of violence on their common border. In November Gabonese soldiers arrived in the CAR as part of a CEMAC peace-keeping force; the Gabonese contingent totalled some 139 troops in January 2004. In January 2005 Bongo Ondimba was influential in resolving a dispute over candidacies to the forthcoming presidential election in the CAR.

Following a visit to Gabon in February 2004 by the Chinese President, Hu Jintao, agreements were signed providing for greater economic co-operation between the two countries; most notably, the French oil corporation Total concluded an agreement to export Gabonese oil to the People's Republic of China. Relations were further strengthened following Bongo's visit to China in September, during which he secured some US $5m. in aid from the Jintao administration. In February 2005 it was announced that in 2004 Chinese exports to Gabon had increased by some 60%, compared with the previous year.

In March 2003 relations with Equatorial Guinea became tense, following Gabon's occupation of the uninhabited island of Mbagne (Mbañé, Mbanie), which lies in potentially oil-rich waters in Corisco Bay, north of Libreville. Both countries claimed sovereignty over the island. Equatorial Guinea rejected Bongo's proposal for joint exploitation of any petroleum reserves found in the vicinity of the island, despite an official visit to Libreville in early May by the Equato-Guinean President, Gen. (Theodoro) Obiang Nguema Mbasogo. Attempts to reach a negotiated settlement failed in December, although the two countries agreed to the appointment of a UN mediator in the dispute in January 2004. In July a provisional agreement was reached to explore jointly for petroleum in the disputed territories and at a meeting in Libreville in January 2005 Bongo Ondimba and Obiang Nguema expressed optimism that an amicable agreement would soon be finalized. In February 2006 both presidents agreed, under the auspices of UN Secretary-General Kofi Annan in Geneva, Switzerland, to work on an accord to resolve the dispute. Annan visited Gabon and Equatorial Guinea to meet Bongo Ondimba and Obiang Nguema, respectively, in March but no further progress on this issue was announced, and in late 2006 negotiations were suspended indefinitely. In 2007 the issue remained unresolved and in October the Gabonese Government requested the intervention of French President Nicolas Sarkozy in settling the dispute.

Government

The Constitution of March 1991 provides for a multi-party system, and vests executive power in the President, who is directly elected by universal suffrage for a period of seven years. The President appoints the Prime Minister, who is Head of Government and who (in consultation with the President) appoints the Council of Ministers. Legislative power is vested in the Assemblée nationale, comprising 120 members, who are elected by direct universal suffrage for a term of five years, and the 91-member Sénat, which is elected by members of municipal councils and departmental assemblies for a term of six years. The independence of the judiciary is guaranteed by the Constitution. Gabon is divided into nine provinces, each under an appointed governor, and 37 prefectures.

Defence

As assessed at November 2007, the army consisted of 3,200 men, the air force of 1,000 men, and the navy of an estimated 500 men. Paramilitary forces numbered 2,000. Military service is voluntary. France maintains a military detachment of 700 in Gabon. The defence budget for 2005 was estimated at 10,000m. francs CFA.

Economic Affairs

In 2006, according to estimates by the World Bank, Gabon's gross national income (GNI), measured at average 2004–06 prices, was US $7,032m., equivalent to $5,000 per head (or $5,310 per head on an international purchasing-power parity basis). During 1996–2006, it was estimated, the population increased at an average annual rate of 2.0%, while gross domestic product (GDP) per head declined, in real terms, by an average of 1.2% per year. Overall GDP increased, in real terms, at an average annual rate of 0.8% in 1996–2006; growth in 2006 was 1.2%.

Agriculture (including forestry and fishing) contributed an estimated 4.9% of GDP in 2006, according to the World Bank. About 31.6% of the labour force were employed in the agricultural sector in mid-2005, according to FAO estimates. Cocoa, coffee, oil palm and rubber are cultivated for export. Gabon has yet to achieve self-sufficiency in staple crops: imports of prepared foodstuffs accounted for 19.2% of the value of total imports in 2004. The principal subsistence crops are plantains, cassava and yams. The exploitation of Gabon's forests (which cover about 75% of the land area) is a principal economic activity. In 2004 timber accounted for an estimated 8.8% of total exports. Although Gabon's territorial waters contain important fishing resources, their commercial exploitation is minimal. Agricultural GDP increased at an average annual rate of 1.6% in 1996–2006; growth in 2006 was 2.0%.

Industry (including mining, manufacturing, construction and power) contributed an estimated 61.2% of GDP in 2006, according to World Bank figures. About 14.1% of the working population were employed in the sector in 1991. Industrial GDP decreased at an average annual rate of 1.5% in 1996–2006; it increased by 1.7% in 2005, but contracted by 4.6% in 2006.

Mining accounted for an estimated 48.5% of GDP in 2004 (with 46.6% contributed by the petroleum sector alone). In 2004 sales of petroleum and petroleum products provided an estimated 80.2% of export revenue. Production of crude petroleum was estimated at 232,000 barrels per day in 2006 and at the end of that year Gabon had proven petroleum reserves of 2,100m. barrels and proven natural gas reserves of 1,200,000m. cu ft. Gabon is among the world's foremost producers and exporters of manganese (which contributed an estimated 7.1% of export earnings in 2004). In 2004 some 2.7m. metric tons of manganese were exported. Major reserves of iron ore remain undeveloped, although in September 2004 a Chinese company signed an agreement to exploit some 1,000m. tons of Gabonese iron ore (see Recent History), and there are also substantial niobium (columbium) reserves at Mabounie. Small amounts of gold are extracted, and the existence of many mineral deposits, including talc, barytes, phosphates, rare earths, titanium and cadmium, has also been confirmed. In 1996–2002, according to the IMF, mining GDP declined at an estimated average annual rate of 6.5%. The IMF estimated a decline of 2.1% in mining GDP in 2002.

According to World Bank figures, the manufacturing sector contributed an estimated 4.1% of GDP in 2006. The principal activities are the refining of petroleum and the processing of other minerals, the preparation of timber and other agro-industrial processes. The chemicals industry is also significant. Manufacturing GDP increased at an average annual rate of 3.9% in 1996–2006. It grew by 6.8% in 2005, but declined by 1.5% in 2006.

In 2004 58.1% of electrical energy was provided by hydroelectric power, with the remainder provided by petroleum and natural gas. Imports of fuel and energy comprised an estimated 3.2% of the total value of merchandise imports in 2004.

Services engaged 18.8% of the economically active population in 1991 and, according to World Bank figures, provided an estimated 33.9% of GDP in 2006. The GDP of the services sector increased at an average annual rate of 2.8% in 1996–2006; services GDP increased by 6.0% in 2006.

According to preliminary estimates, in 2006 Gabon recorded a trade surplus of 2,338,000m. francs CFA, and there was a surplus of 920,000m. francs CFA on the current account of the balance of payments. In 2004 the principal source of imports (40.8%) was France; other major sources were Belgium, the USA and the Netherlands. The principal market for exports in that year was the USA (49.1%); France and the People's Republic of China were also important purchasers. The principal exports in 2004 were petroleum and petroleum products, timber and manganese. The principal imports in that year were machinery and mechanical appliances, prepared foodstuffs and consumption goods.

In 2006 there was a preliminary budgetary surplus of 460,500m. francs CFA. Gabon's external debt totalled US $3,902m. at the end of 2005, of which $3,582m. was long-term public debt. In 2004 the cost of debt-servicing was equivalent to 5.3% of the value of exports of goods and services. In 1996–2006 the average annual rate of inflation was 1.5%. Consumer prices increased by 4.0% in 2006. The Government estimated about 20% of the labour force to be unemployed in 1996.

Gabon is a member of the Central African organs of the Franc Zone (see p. 307), and of the Communauté économique des états de l'Afrique centrale (CEEAC, see p. 411).

Gabon's potential for economic growth is based on its considerable mineral and forestry resources. Petroleum provides the country's principal source of income, but production is estimated to be in long-term decline. Efforts to increase revenue from non-petroleum sectors, especially agriculture and tourism, were moderately successful in the mid-2000s, with non-petroleum sector GDP growth of 4.9% in 2006 and a projected 5.7% in 2007, according to the IMF, while in June 2006 the Government awarded a Chinese company exclusive rights to exploit iron ore reserves (estimated at more than 500m. metric tons) at Belinga in the north-east of the country. The first iron ore was expected to be extracted by 2010 and the project was also to include the construction of railways, a port and two hydroelectric power stations, and was predicted to lead to the creation of some 27,000 jobs. In May 2007 the IMF approved a US $117m. stand-by agreement, following a broadly positive review of government fiscal management, although the Fund continued to encourage further reforms to Gabon's economy and advised the Gabonese authorities to use higher petroleum prices to reduce domestic and external debt. To this end, in mid-2007 the Government concluded an agreement with the 'Paris Club' of creditors to repay $1,500m. of the $2,334m. debt owed to those lenders. The country's infrastructure remained underdeveloped and allegations of government corruption continued to threaten Gabon's financial credibility. Since 2005 the Government's objectives have included the regulation of public-sector salaries and improvements in tax collection, and revenues from the hydrocarbon sector in particular were to be subjected to closer scrutiny, in order that they be allocated in greater quantities to public spending. As a result of the continuing decline in oil production, real GDP growth was estimated by the IMF to have reached just 1.2% in 2006, before recovering to 4.8% in 2007.

Education

Education is officially compulsory for 10 years between six and 16 years of age. Primary and secondary education is provided by state and mission schools. Primary education begins at the age of six and lasts for six years. Secondary education, beginning at 12 years of age, lasts for up to seven years, comprising a first cycle of four years and a second of three years. According to UNESCO estimates, in 2000/01 77% of children in the relevant age-group (77% of boys; 77% of girls) attended primary schools, while in 2001/02 enrolment at secondary schools was equivalent to 50% of children in the relevant age-group. The Université Omar Bongo Ondimba is based at Libreville and the Université des Sciences et des Techniques de Masuku at Franceville. In 1998 7,473 students were enrolled at institutions providing tertiary education. The 1994 budget allocated 78,850m. francs CFA (19% of total administrative spending) to expenditure on education.

Public Holidays

2008: 1 January (New Year's Day), 12 March (Anniversary of Renovation, foundation of the Parti démocratique gabonais), 20 March* (Mouloud, Birth of Muhammad), 24 March (Easter Monday), 1 May (Labour Day), 12 May (Whit Monday), 17 August (Anniversary of Independence), 1 October* (Id al-Fitr, end of Ramadan), 1 November (All Saints' Day), 9 December* (Id al-Adha, Feast of the Sacrifice), 25 December (Christmas).

2009: 1 January (New Year's Day), 12 March (Anniversary of Renovation, foundation of the Parti démocratique gabonais), 9 March* (Mouloud, Birth of Muhammad), 13 April (Easter Monday), 1 May (Labour Day), 1 June (Whit Monday), 17 August (Anniversary of Independence), 20 September* (Id al-Fitr, end of Ramadan), 1 November (All Saints' Day), 27 November* (Id al-Adha, Feast of the Sacrifice), 25 December (Christmas).

* These holidays are dependent on the Islamic lunar calendar and may vary by one or two days from the dates given.

Weights and Measures

The metric system is in official use.

Statistical Survey

Source (unless otherwise stated): Direction Générale de la Statistique et des Etudes Economiques, Ministère de la Planification et de la Programmation du Développement, BP 2119, Libreville; tel. 72-13-69; fax 72-04-57; e-mail plan@dgsee.yahoo.fr; internet www.stat-gabon.ga.

Area and Population

AREA, POPULATION AND DENSITY

Area (sq km)	267,667*
Population (census results) 31 July 1993	
Males	501,784
Females	513,192
Total	1,014,976
1 December 2003	1,269,000†
Population (UN estimates at mid-year)‡	
2005	1,291,000
2006	1,311,000
2007	1,331,000
Density (per sq km) at mid-2007	5.0

* 103,347 sq miles.
† Provisional (Source: UN, *Population and Vital Statistics Report*).
‡ Source: UN, *World Population Prospects: The 2006 Revision*.

REGIONS
(1993 census)

Region	Area (sq km)	Population	Density (per sq km)	Chief town
Estuaire	20,740	463,187	22.3	Libreville
Haut-Ogooué	36,547	104,301	2.9	Franceville
Moyen-Ogooué	18,535	42,316	2.3	Lambaréné
N'Gounié	37,750	77,781	2.1	Mouila
Nyanga	21,285	39,430	1.9	Tchibanga
Ogooué-Ivindo	46,075	48,862	1.1	Makokou
Ogooué-Lolo	25,380	43,915	1.7	Koula-Moutou
Ogooué-Maritime	22,890	97,913	4.3	Port-Gentil
Woleu-N'Tem	38,465	97,271	2.5	Oyem
Total	267,667	1,014,976	3.8	

PRINCIPAL TOWNS
(population at 1993 census)

Libreville (capital)	419,596	Mouila	16,307
Port-Gentil	79,225	Lambaréné	15,033
Franceville	31,183	Tchibanga	14,054
Oyem	22,404	Koulamoutou	11,773
Moanda	21,882	Makokou	9,849

Mid-2007 (incl. suburbs, UN estimate): Libreville (capital) 576,000 (Source: UN, *World Urbanization Prospects: The 2007 Revision*).

BIRTHS AND DEATHS
(annual averages, UN estimates)

	1990–95	1995–2000	2000–05
Birth rate (per 1,000)	30.2	27.7	25.7
Death rate (per 1,000)	10.2	11.7	11.7

Source: UN, *World Population Prospects: The 2006 Revision*.

Expectation of life (years at birth, WHO estimates): 55.4 (males 54.1; females 56.9) in 2005 (Source: WHO, *World Health Statistics*).

ECONOMICALLY ACTIVE POPULATION
('000 persons, 1991, estimates)

	Males	Females	Total
Agriculture, etc.	187	151	338
Industry	62	9	71
Services	69	26	95
Total labour force	318	186	504

Source: UN Economic Commission for Africa, *African Statistical Yearbook*.

1993 (census figures, persons aged 10 years and over): Total employed 308,322; Unemployed 67,622; Total labour force 375,944.

Mid-2005 (estimates in '000): Agriculture, etc. 197; Total 624 (Source: FAO).

Health and Welfare

KEY INDICATORS

Total fertility rate (children per woman, 2005)	3.8
Under-5 mortality rate (per 1,000 live births, 2005)	91
HIV/AIDS (% of persons aged 15–49, 2005)	7.9
Physicians (per 1,000 head, 2004)	0.29
Hospital beds (per 1,000 head, 1990)	3.19
Health expenditure (2004): US $ per head (PPP)	264.2
Health expenditure (2004): % of GDP	4.5
Health expenditure (2004): public (% of total)	68.8
Access to water (% of persons, 2004)	88
Access to sanitation (% of persons, 2004)	36
Human Development Index (2005): ranking	119
Human Development Index (2005): value	0.677

For sources and definitions, see explanatory note on p. vi.

Agriculture

PRINCIPAL CROPS
('000 metric tons)

	2004	2005	2006
Maize*	31	30	30
Cassava (Manioc)*	230	232	232
Taro (Coco yam)	59*	n.a.	59*
Yams*	155	165	165
Sugar cane*	190	180	180
Groundnuts (in shell)*	20	20	20
Oil palm fruit*	32	32	32
Bananas*	12	13	13
Plantains*	270	274	274
Natural rubber*	11	n.a.	11

* FAO estimate(s).

Aggregate production ('000 metric tons, may include official, semi-official or estimated data): Total cereals 32 in 2004, 31 in 2005, 31 in 2006; Total roots and tubers 447 in 2004, 459 in 2005, 459 in 2006; Total vegetables (incl. melons) 354 in 2004, 354 in 2005, 354 in 2006; Total fruits (excl. melons) 294 in 2004, 298 in 2005, 298 in 2006.

Source: FAO.

GABON

Statistical Survey

LIVESTOCK
('000 head, year ending September, FAO estimates)

	2001	2002	2003
Cattle	36	36	35
Pigs	213	212	212
Sheep	198	195	195
Goats	90	90	90
Chickens	3,200	3,100	3,100
Rabbits	300	300	300

2004–06: Figures assumed to be unchanged from 2003 (FAO estimates).
Source: FAO.

LIVESTOCK PRODUCTS
('000 metric tons, FAO estimates)

	2003	2004	2005
Cattle meat	0.7	1.1	1.1
Pig meat	3.1	3.2	3.3
Chicken meat	3.6	3.9	4.0
Rabbit meat	2.0	1.9	2.0
Game meat	21.0	21.0	n.a.
Cows' milk	1.6	1.6	1.6
Hen eggs	2.0	2.0	n.a.

2006: Figures assumed to be unchanged from 2005 (FAO estimates).
Source: FAO.

Forestry

ROUNDWOOD REMOVALS
('000 cubic metres)

	2004	2005	2006
Sawlogs, veneer logs and logs for sleepers	3,500	3,200	3,500
Fuel wood	1,070	528	530
Total	4,570	3,728	4,030

Source: FAO.

SAWNWOOD PRODUCTION
('000 cubic metres, incl. railway sleepers)

	2004	2005	2006
Total	133	230	235

Source: FAO.

Fishing

('000 metric tons, live weight)

	2003	2004	2005
Capture	45.3	46.0	43.9
Tilapias	3.8	3.8	3.8
Other freshwater fishes	6.0	4.8	6.3
Barracudas	1.5	1.6	1.0
Bobo croakers	1.3	2.1	1.7
West African croakers	3.4	5.1	4.5
Lesser African threadfin	0.8	0.7	1.7
Bonga shad	12.0	10.6	8.6
Sardinellas	1.8	1.8	2.4
Penaeus shrimp	2.8	1.8	1.4
Aquaculture	0.1	0.1	0.1
Total catch	45.4	46.0	43.9

Source: FAO.

Mining

	2003	2004*	2005*
Crude petroleum ('000 barrels)	87,965	87,235†	85,469†
Natural gas (million cu metres)*	79	80	80
Diamonds (carats)*	500	500	500
Hydraulic cement ('000 metric tons)*	260	260	260
Manganese ore ('000 metric tons): gross weight‡	1,950*	2,400	2,800
Manganese ore ('000 metric tons): metal content§	50*	60	59
Gold (kilograms)*‡||	70	300	300

* Estimated production.
† Reported figure.
‡ Figures refer to the metal content of ore.
§ Figures refer to the weight of chemical-grade pellets.
|| Excluding production smuggled out of the country (estimated at more than 400 kg annually).
Source: US Geological Survey.

Industry

PETROLEUM PRODUCTS
('000 metric tons)

	2002	2003	2004
Butane	9.8	8.8	9.2
Motor spirit (petrol)	64.5	64.3	65.9
Kerosene	79.4	69.7	61.8
Distillate fuel oils	218.8	198.1	223.0
Residual fuel oils and asphalt	288.5	285.1	347.5

Source: IMF, *Gabon: Statistical Appendix* (May 2005).

2005 ('000 metric tons): Butane 9.5.

SELECTED OTHER PRODUCTS

	2003	2004	2005
Plywood ('000 cu metres)	37.8	52.8	68.1
Veneer sheets ('000 cu metres)	198.2	120.7	175.2
Cement ('000 metric tons)*	260	260	260
Alcoholic beverages ('000 hectolitres)	755.9	750.1	852.1
Soft drinks ('000 hectolitres)	568.4	537.9	587.0
Electric energy (million kWh)	1,314.6	1,337.1	1,363.7

* Estimated data from the US Geological Survey.

Finance

CURRENCY AND EXCHANGE RATES

Monetary Units
100 centimes = 1 franc de la Coopération financière en Afrique centrale (CFA).

Sterling, Dollar and Euro Equivalents (31 December 2007)
£1 sterling = 892.702 francs CFA;
US $1 = 445.593 francs CFA;
€1 = 655.957 francs CFA;
10,000 francs CFA = £11.20 = $22.44 = €15.24.

Average Exchange Rate (francs CFA per US $)
2005   527.47
2006   522.89
2007   479.27

Note: An exchange rate of 1 French franc = 50 francs CFA, established in 1948, remained in force until January 1994, when the CFA franc was devalued by 50%, with the exchange rate adjusted to 1 French franc = 100 francs CFA. This relationship to French currency remained in effect with the introduction of the euro on 1 January 1999. From that date, accordingly, a fixed exchange rate of €1 = 655.957 francs CFA has been in operation.

GABON

Statistical Survey

BUDGET
('000 million francs CFA)

Revenue*	2004	2005	2006†
Petroleum revenue	600.0	907.2	1,012.9
Non-petroleum revenue	511.5	525.0	569.7
Direct taxes	137.3	138.6	159.4
Indirect taxes	115.1	113.7	113.7
Value-added tax	82.6	80.5	78.4
Taxes on international trade and transactions	200.5	215.3	240.4
Import duties	172.9	179.6	210.1
Export duties	27.6	35.7	30.2
Other revenue	58.7	57.4	56.2
Total	**1,111.5**	**1,432.2**	**1,582.6**

Expenditure‡	2004	2005	2006†
Current expenditure	627.8	789.3	827.5
Wages and salaries	226.3	227.8	252.4
Other goods and services	125.1	153.2	167.2
Transfers and subsidies	125.6	279.1	291.3
Interest payments	150.8	129.2	116.6
Domestic	31.4	29.3	24.5
External	119.4	99.9	92.2
Capital expenditure	160.0	193.4	238.8
Domestically financed investment	142.2	146.1	190.0
Externally financed investment	17.8	47.3	48.8
Total	**787.8**	**982.7**	**1,066.3**

* Excluding grants received ('000 million francs CFA): 2.1 in 2004; 2.0 in 2005; nil in 2006 (preliminary).
† Preliminary figures.
‡ Excluding net lending, restructuring cost of public enterprises, and road maintenance and other special funds ('000 million francs CFA): 39.3 in 2004 (funds only); 58.4 in 2005; 55.8 in 2006 (funds only, preliminary).

Source: IMF, *Gabon: Request for Stand-By Arrangement - Staff Report; Staff Statement; Press Release on the Executive Board Discussion; and Statement by the Executive Director for Gabon* (May 2007).

INTERNATIONAL RESERVES
(US $ million at 31 December)

	2004	2005	2006
Gold*	5.63	6.59	8.14
IMF special drawing rights	6.26	0.12	0.88
Reserve position in IMF	0.28	0.31	0.37
Foreign exchange	436.88	668.13	1,112.19
Total	**449.05**	**675.15**	**1,121.58**

* Valued at market-related prices.

Source: IMF, *International Financial Statistics*.

MONEY SUPPLY
('000 million francs CFA at 31 December)

	2004	2005	2006
Currency outside banks	138.69	198.03	219.06
Demand deposits at commercial and development banks	248.06	326.41	396.99
Total money (incl. others)	**387.45**	**528.29**	**617.99**

Source: IMF, *International Financial Statistics*.

COST OF LIVING
(Consumer Price Index; base: 2000 = 100)

	2004	2005	2006
Food	105.1	105.5	112.2
Clothing	105.4	103.3	105.0
Rent	101.7	100.0	102.5
All items (incl. others)	**104.9**	**104.9**	**109.1**

Source: ILO.

NATIONAL ACCOUNTS
Expenditure on the Gross Domestic Product
(US $ million)

	2004	2005	2006
Government final consumption expenditure	940.21	999.30	1,046.65
Private final consumption expenditure	2,578.46	2,717.46	2,917.43
Gross fixed capital formation	1,997.07	2,010.82	2,151.00
Total domestic expenditure	**5,515.74**	**5,727.58**	**6,115.08**
Exports of goods and services	4,329.97	5,736.53	6,617.15
Less Imports of goods and services	2,667.58	2,798.37	3,241.41
GDP at market prices	**7,178.13**	**8,665.74**	**9,490.81**

Source: African Development Bank, *Selected Statistics on African Countries*.

Gross Domestic Product by Economic Activity
('000 million francs CFA at current prices)

	2002	2003	2004*
Agriculture, livestock, hunting and fishing	148.2	151.7	155.8
Forestry	60.0	59.6	58.8
Petroleum exploitation	1,380.4	1,416.6	1,654.7
Other mining	51.7	53.7	66.3
Manufacturing†	228.5	236.9	231.3
Electricity and water	45.2	47.0	51.3
Construction and public works	83.1	78.0	81.2
Trade	241.1	244.5	238.3
Transport	191.7	197.6	206.6
Financial services	20.4	20.9	20.0
Government services	293.4	301.0	308.6
Other services	459.9	461.3	475.2
GDP at factor cost	**3,203.6**	**3,268.7**	**3,548.0**
Indirect taxes	245.3	250.2	270.0
GDP in purchasers' values	**3,448.9**	**3,518.9**	**3,818.0**

* Estimates.
† Includes processing of primary products and research and oil services.

Source: IMF, *Gabon: Selected Issues and Statistical Appendix* (May 2005).

BALANCE OF PAYMENTS
('000 million francs CFA)

	2005*	2006†	2007‡
Exports of goods f.o.b.	2,989	3,166	3,101
Petroleum	2,489	2,602	2,480
Imports of goods f.o.b.	–716	–828	–953
Trade balance	**2,273**	**2,338**	**2,148**
Services and other income (net)	–1,275	–1,314	–1,238
Balance on goods, services and income	**998**	**1,024**	**910**
Current transfers (net)	–107	–103	–49
Current balance	**891**	**920**	**861**
Capital transfers (net)	3	3	0
Medium- and long-term capital	–361	–457	–322
Direct and portfolio investment	–146	–159	–86
Short-term capital	–435	–273	–340
Overall balance	**98**	**194**	**200**

* Preliminary.
† Estimates.
‡ Forecasts.

Source: IMF, *Gabon: Request for Stand-By Arrangement - Staff Report; Staff Statement; Press Release on the Executive Board Discussion; and Statement by the Executive Director for Gabon* (May 2007).

External Trade

PRINCIPAL COMMODITIES
('000 million francs CFA)

Imports	2002	2003	2004
Prepared foodstuffs (excl. beverages)	119.9	121.5	124.8
Beverages	12.6	11.0	9.5
Base metals and their manufactures	51.0	51.8	37.8
Machinery and mechanical appliances	145.6	106.4	130.8
Machines and electrical appliances	60.3	49.8	54.3
Vehicles	64.6	74.4	54.1
Consumption goods (excl. foodstuffs and beverages)	129.9	98.7	104.1
Intermediary products imported for construction and public works	20.6	17.1	18.2
Other	47.1	75.3	115.7
Total	**651.7**	**605.9**	**649.3**

Exports	2002	2003	2004*
Petroleum and petroleum products	1,430	1,499	1,801
Manganese	101	104	159
Timber	203	221	198
Total (incl. others)	**1,781**	**1,850**	**2,245**

* Estimates.

Source: IMF, *Gabon: Selected Issues and Statistical Appendix* (May 2005).

PRINCIPAL TRADING PARTNERS
(US $ million)

Imports c.i.f.	2002	2003	2004
Austria	12.4	10.6	1.8
Belgium	37.1	31.4	106.1
Brazil	0.0	7.9	16.4
Cameroon	0.0	31.7	30.1
China, People's Republic	0.0	8.6	14.5
Côte d'Ivoire	0.0	5.4	19.1
France (incl. Monaco)	443.8	308.4	393.8
Germany	31.3	21.2	14.1
India	0.0	4.1	10.3
Italy	34.1	25.3	26.5
Japan	0.0	40.4	29.1
Netherlands	44.8	34.2	40.0
Norway	33.9	6.8	1.1
Singapore	0.0	7.7	4.6
South Africa	0.0	7.6	20.3
Spain	34.2	10.8	21.9
Switzerland-Liechtenstein	12.1	3.4	2.4
Thailand	0.0	5.6	27.2
United Arab Emirates	0.0	3.4	9.8
United Kingdom	29.9	27.6	40.0
USA	0.0	105.8	44.2
Total (incl. others)	**745.2**	**770.0**	**964.9**

Exports f.o.b.	2001	2002	2004
Brazil	62.0	58.1	0.0
China, People's Republic	129.1	108.1	175.2
France (incl. Monaco)	350.2	183.7	246.2
Iceland	50.1	47.4	117.0
India	13.7	89.1	45.4
Italy	24.2	27.2	54.8
Japan	3.9	26.5	2.0
Korea, Republic	89.2	24.6	2.5
Nigeria	1.6	27.1	2.8
Norway	4.9	8.0	31.1
Portugal	33.2	8.0	13.0
Singapore	1.5	57.8	3.4
South Africa	61.2	52.9	38.4
Spain	35.6	14.0	33.6
Switzerland-Liechtenstein	96.0	39.8	53.4
Trinidad and Tobago	9.3	35.1	1.9
USA	1,418.9	1,430.0	1,363.6
Total (incl. others)	**2,521.5**	**2,411.1**	**2,780.0**

Note: data for exports for 2003 not available.

Source: UN, *International Trade Statistics Yearbook*.

Transport

RAILWAYS
(traffic)

	2003	2004	2005
Passengers carried ('000)	206.8	214.4	218.5
Freight carried ('000 metric tons)	2,967.7	3,455.8	3,923.8

ROAD TRAFFIC
(estimates, motor vehicles in use)

	1994	1995	1996
Passenger cars	22,310	24,000	24,750
Lorries and vans	14,850	15,840	16,490

Source: IRF, *World Road Statistics*.

SHIPPING

Merchant Fleet
(registered at 31 December)

	2004	2005	2006
Number of vessels	46	48	49
Total displacement ('000 grt)	12.8	13.5	13.8

Source: Lloyd's Register-Fairplay, *World Fleet Statistics*.

International Sea-borne Freight Traffic
('000 metric tons, Port-Gentil and Owendo)

	2002	2003	2004
Goods loaded	15,429	16,005	17,144
Goods unloaded	763	739	776

Source: IMF, *Gabon: Statistical Appendix* (May 2005).

CIVIL AVIATION
(traffic on scheduled services)

	2001	2002	2003
Kilometres flown (million)	7	7	8
Passengers carried ('000)	374	366	386
Passenger-kilometres (million)	637	643	655
Total ton-kilometres (million)	107	106	112

Source: UN, *Statistical Yearbook*.

Passengers carried ('000): 838.1 in 2002; 854.8 in 2003; 698.6 in 2004; 635.4 in 2005.

Tourism

	2001	2002	2003
Tourist arrivals	169,191	208,348	222,257
Tourism receipts (US $ million, incl. passenger transport)	46	77	84

Receipts from tourism (US $ million, incl. passenger transport): 74 in 2004.
Source: World Tourism Organization.

Communications Media

	2004	2005	2006
Telephones ('000 main lines in use)	38.7	39.1	36.5
Mobile cellular telephones ('000 subscribers)	489.4	652.3	764.7
Personal computers ('000 in use)	40	45	n.a.
Internet users ('000)	40	67	81
Broadband subscribers ('000)	0.6	1.5	1.2

1997: 501 facsimile machines in use.

1999: 600,000 radio receivers in use.

2001: 400,000 television receivers in use.

Daily newspapers: 2 (estimated average circulation 34,800 copies) in 1998; 1 in 2004.

Sources: UNESCO Institute for Statistics; UN, *Statistical Yearbook*; International Telecommunication Union.

Education

(2003/04 unless otherwise indicated, estimates)

			Pupils		
	Institutions	Teachers	Males	Females	Total
Pre-primary	9*	517†	7,784†	7,784†	15,568†
Primary	1,175*	7,807	142,268	139,103	281,371
Secondary:					
General	88§	3,102†	43,892‡	39,303‡	97,604†
Technical and vocational	11§	394†	5,025‖	2,562‖	7,587‖
Tertiary	2*	585¶	4,806¶	2,667¶	7,473¶

* 1991/92 figure.
† 2000/01 figure.
‡ 1999/2000 figure.
§ 1996 figure.
‖ 2002/03 figure.
¶ 1998/99 figure.

Source: UNESCO Institute for Statistics.

Adult literacy rate: 84.0% (males 88.0%; females 80.0%) in 2004 (Source: UNESCO Institute for Statistics).

Directory

The Constitution

The Constitution of the Gabonese Republic was adopted on 14 March 1991. The main provisions are summarized below.

PREAMBLE

Upholds the rights of the individual, liberty of conscience and of the person, religious freedom and freedom of education. Sovereignty is vested in the people, who exercise it through their representatives or by means of referendums. There is direct, universal and secret suffrage.

HEAD OF STATE*

The President is elected by direct universal suffrage for a five-year term, renewable only once. The President is Head of State and of the Armed Forces. The President may, after consultation with his ministers and leaders of the Assemblée nationale, order a referendum to be held. The President appoints the Prime Minister, who is Head of Government and who is accountable to the President. The President is the guarantor of national independence and territorial sovereignty.

EXECUTIVE POWER

Executive power is vested in the President and the Council of Ministers, who are appointed by the Prime Minister, in consultation with the President.

LEGISLATIVE POWER

The Assemblée nationale is elected by direct universal suffrage for a five-year term. It may be dissolved or prorogued for up to 18 months by the President, after consultation with the Council of Ministers and President of the Assemblée. The President may return a bill to the Assemblée for a second reading, when it must be passed by a majority of two-thirds of the members. If the President dissolves the Assemblée, elections must take place within 40 days.

The Constitution also provides for the establishment of an upper chamber (the Sénat), to control the balance and regulation of power.

POLITICAL ORGANIZATIONS

Article 2 of the Constitution states that 'Political parties and associations contribute to the expression of universal suffrage. They are formed and exercise their activities freely, within the limits delineated by the laws and regulations. They must respect the principles of democracy, national sovereignty, public order and national unity'.

JUDICIAL POWER

The President guarantees the independence of the judiciary and presides over the Conseil Supérieur de la Magistrature. Supreme judicial power is vested in the Supreme Court.

* A constitutional amendment, adopted by the legislature on 18 April 1997, extended the presidential term to seven years and provided for the creation of the post of Vice-President. On 29 July 2003 the Constitution was further amended to remove the restriction on the number of terms of office the President may serve.

The Government

HEAD OF STATE

President: El Hadj OMAR (ALBERT-BERNARD) BONGO ONDIMBA (took office 2 December 1967, elected 25 February 1973, re-elected December 1979, November 1986, December 1993, December 1998 and November 2005).

Vice-President: DIDJOB DIVUNGUI-DI-N'DINGUE.

COUNCIL OF MINISTERS
(February 2008)

Prime Minister and Head of Government: JEAN EYÉGHÉ NDONG (PDG).

Vice-Prime Minister, Minister of the Environment, Sustainable Development and the Protection of Nature: GEORGETTE KOKO.

Vice-Prime Minister, Minister of Culture, the Arts, Educating the Population, Reconstruction Projects and Human Rights: PAUL MBA ABESSOLE (RPG).

Vice-Prime Minister, Minister of State Control, Inspections, the Fight against Corruption and the Illegal Accumulation of Wealth: Honorine Doussou Naki (PDG).
Minister of State for Mining, Petroleum, Hydrocarbons, Energy, Hydraulics and the Promotion of New Energy Resources: Casimir Oyé Mba (PDG).
Minister of State for the Economy, Finance, the Budget and Privatization: Paul Toungui (PDG).
Minister of Foreign Affairs, Co-operation, Francophonie and Regional Integration: Laure Olga Gondjout.
Minister of Health and Public Hygiene, responsible for the Family and the Promotion of Women: Angélique Ngoma (PDG).
Minister of Tourism and National Parks: Gen. (retd) Idriss Ngari (PDG).
Minister of Technical Instruction, Professional Training and the Professional Integration of Youths: Prof. Pierre André Kombila.
Minister of the Merchant Navy and Port Equipment: Jacques Adiahénot (PDG).
Minister of National Defence: Ali Bongo Ondimba (PDG).
Minister of Agriculture and Rural Development: Faustin Boukoubi (PDG).
Minister of Commerce and Industrial Development, responsible for NEPAD: Paul Biyoghé-Mba (PDG).
Minister of the Interior, Local Communities, Decentralization, Security and Immigration: André Mba Obame (PDG).
Minister of Planning and Programme Development, responsible for the Evaluation of the Public Policies: Richard Auguste Onouviet (PDG).
Minister of Public Works, Infrastructure and Construction: Gen. Flavien Nziengui Nzoundou.
Minister of Forest Economy, Water Resources and Fishing: Emile Doumba (PDG).
Minister of Youth, Sports and Leisure, responsible for Community Life, Spokesperson for the Government: René Ndemezo Obiang.
Minister of Public Affairs and the Modernization of the State: Alain Mensah Zoguelet.
Minister of Justice, Keeper of the Seals: Martin Mabala (PDG).
Minister for Small and Medium-sized Businesses, the Social Economy and the Fight against Poverty: Vincent Essone Mengue.
Minister of Land Settlement and Town Policy: Pierre Claver Maganga Moussavou (PSD).
Minister of Labour, Employment and Social Security: Jean-François Ndoungou.
Minister of Higher Education: Dieudonné Pambou.
Minister of Accommodation, Housing and Town Planning: Patrice Tonda.
Minister of National Education and Civic Instruction: Michel Menga M'Essone (PDG).
Minister of Scientific Research and Technological Development: Fr Albert Ondo Ossa.
Minister of Communication, Post and Telecommunications and New Information Technologies: Jean Boniface Asséle.
Minister of Social Affairs, National Solidarity, the Protection of Widows and Orphans and the Fight against AIDS: Denise Mekame'Ne.
Minister of Relations with Parliament and Constitutional Institutions: José Mbadinga.
Minister of Transport and Civil Aviation: Dieudonné Mouri-Boussougou.
There were also 10 Ministers-delegate.

MINISTRIES

Office of the Prime Minister: BP 546, Libreville; tel. 77-89-81.
Ministry of Agriculture, Livestock and Rural Development: BP 551, Libreville; tel. 77-59-22; fax 76-38-34.
Ministry of Commerce and Industrial Development: Libreville.
Ministry of Decentralization and Territorial Administration: Libreville; tel. 72-29-83; fax 77-29-62.
Ministry of Economic Affairs, Finance, the Budget and Privatization: BP 165, Libreville; tel. 76-12-10; fax 76-59-74.
Ministry of the Environment, the Protection of Nature, Research and Technology: BP 2217, Libreville; tel. and fax 76-39-09.
Ministry of Family Affairs, the Protection of Children and the Promotion of Women: BP 5684, Libreville; tel. 77-50-32; fax 76-69-29.
Ministry for the Fight against AIDS and for the Protection of AIDS Orphans: Libreville.
Ministry of Foreign Affairs, Co-operation and Francophone Affairs: BP 2245, Libreville; tel. 72-95-21; fax 72-91-73.
Ministry of Government Auditing: Libreville.
Ministry of Housing, Urbanization and Cadastral Services: BP 512, Libreville; tel. 77-31-04; fax 74-04-62.
Ministry of the Interior, Public Security and Immigration: BP 2110, Libreville; tel. 74-35-06; fax 72-13-89.
Ministry of Justice: BP 547, Libreville; tel. 74-66-28; fax 72-33-84.
Ministry of Labour and Employment: BP 4577, Libreville; tel. 74-32-18.
Ministry of the Merchant Navy and Port Equipment: Libreville.
Ministry of Mining, Energy, Petroleum and Water Resources: BP 576, Libreville; tel. 77-22-39.
Ministry of National Defence: BP 13493, Libreville; tel. and fax 77-86-96.
Ministry of National and Higher Education: BP 6, Libreville; tel. 72-44-61; fax 72-19-74.
Ministry of National Solidarity, Social Affairs, Welfare and the Fight against Poverty: Libreville.
Ministry of Planning and Development: Libreville.
Ministry of Post and Telecommunications and New Technologies: Libreville.
Ministry for the Prevention and Management of Natural Disasters: Libreville.
Ministry for the Promotion of the Private Sector, the Social Economy and Crafts: BP 178, Libreville; tel. 76-34-62.
Ministry of Public Affairs, Administrative Reform and Modernization of the State: BP 496, Libreville; tel. 76-38-86.
Ministry of Public Health: BP 50, Libreville; tel. 76-36-11.
Ministry of Public Works, Equipment and Construction: BP 49, Libreville; tel. 76-38-56; fax 74-80-92.
Ministry of Reform, Human Rights, the Fight against Poverty and Illicit Enrichment: Libreville.
Ministry of Small and Medium-sized Businesses: BP 3096, Libreville; tel. 74-59-21.
Ministry of Technical Instruction, Professional Training and Reintegration and the Professional Integration of Youths: Libreville; tel. 73-37-35; fax 73-37-39.
Ministry of Territorial Waters, Forestry, Fishing and National Parks: BP 3974, Libreville; tel. 76-01-09; fax 76-61-83.
Ministry of Towns, the Promotion of Collective Life and Protection of Widows and Orphans: Libreville; tel. 31-68-98.
Ministry of Transport and Civil Aviation: BP 803, Libreville; tel. 74-71-96; fax 77-33-31.
Ministry of Youth and Sports: BP 2150, Libreville; tel. 74-00-19; fax 74-65-89.

President and Legislature

PRESIDENT

Presidential Election, 27 November 2005

Candidate	Votes	% of votes
El Hadj Omar (Albert-Bernard) Bongo Ondimba (PDG)	275,819	79.18
Pierre Mamboundou (UPG)	47,410	13.61
Zacharie Myboto (Ind.)	22,921	6.58
Augustin Moussavou King (PSG)	1,149	0.33
Christian Serge Maroga (RDD)	1,045	0.30
Total	**348,344**	**100.00**

ASSEMBLÉE NATIONALE

President: Guy Ndzouba Ndama.
Secretary-General: Jean-Baptiste Yama-Legnongo.

General Election, 17 December 2006*

Party	Seats
Parti démocratique gabonais (PDG)	82
Rassemblement pour le Gabon (RPG)	8
Union du peuple gabonais (UPG)	8
Union gabonaise pour la démocratie et le développement (UGDD)	4
Alliance démocratique et républicaine (ADERE)	3
Cercle des libéraux réformateurs (CLR)	2
Parti gabonais du progrès (PGP)	2
Parti social-démocrate (PSD)	2
Forum africain pour la reconstruction (FAR)	1
Rassemblement des démocrates républicains (RDR)	1
Congrès pour la démocratie et la justice (CDJ)	1
Mouvement africain de développement (MAD)	1
Rassemblement national des bûcherons—Democratique (RNB)	1
Independents	4
Total	**120**

* Elections in seven constituencies were postponed until 24 December 2006, owing to organizational difficulties. Results in 20 constituencies were annulled, following allegations of irregularities and fraud. By-elections were held on 10 June 2007 at which the PDG won 11 of the 20 seats available. Parties allied to the PDG won six seats, the opposition took two, and the remaining seat was secured by an independent candidate.

SÉNAT

President: René Radembino-Coniquet.
Secretary-General: Félix Owansango Deackeu.

Indirect elections to the 91-member Sénat were held on 9 February 2003. The PDG won more than 60 seats and the RPG secured eight seats.

Election Commission

Commission électorale nationale autonome et permanente (CENAP): Libreville; f. 2006 to replace the Commission nationale électorale; Pres. appointed by the Constitutional Court; Pres. René Aboghé Ella.

Political Organizations

Alliance démocratique et républicaine (ADERE): Pres. Mboumbou Ngoma; Sec.-Gen. Didjob Divungui-di-N'Dingue.

Cercle des libéraux réformateurs (CLR): f. 1993 by breakaway faction of the PDG; Leader Jean-Boniface Assele.

Congrès pour la démocratie et la justice (CDJ): Pres. Jules Bourdes Ogouliguende.

Forum africain pour la reconstruction (FAR): f. 1992; Leader Prof. Léon Mbou-Yembi.

Parti socialiste gabonais (PSG): f. 1991; Leader Augustin Moussavou King.

Union socialiste gabonais (USG): Leader Dr Serge Mba Bekale.

Front national (FN): f. 1991; Leader Martin Efayong.

Mouvement africain de développement (MAD): Leader Pierre Claver Nzeng Ebome.

Mouvement pour la démocratie, le développement et la réconciliation nationale (Modern): Libreville; f. 1996; Leader Gaston Mozogo Ovono.

Mouvement d'emancipation socialiste du peuple: Leader Mouanga Mbadinga.

Parti démocratique gabonais (PDG): BP 268, Libreville; tel. 70-31-21; fax 70-31-46; f. 1968; sole legal party 1968–90; Leader Omar Bongo Ondimba; Sec.-Gen. Simplice Guedet Manzela.

Parti gabonais du centre indépendant (PGCI): allied to the PDG; Leader Jérôme Okinda.

Parti gabonais du progrès (PGP): f. 1990; Pres. (vacant); Vice-Pres. Joseph-Benoît Mouity; Sec.-Gen. Pierre Louis Agondjo Okawe.

Parti radical des républicains indépendants (PARI): Leader Anaclé Bissielo.

Parti social-démocrate (PSD): f. 1991; Leader Pierre-Claver Maganga Moussavou.

Rassemblement des démocrates (RDD): f. 1993; Leader Christian Serge Maroga.

Rassemblement des démocrates républicains (RDR): Leader Max Mebale m'Obame.

Rassemblement pour la démocratie et le progrès (RDP): Pres. Pierre Emboni.

Rassemblement pour le Gabon (RPG): f. 1990 as MORENA des bûcherons; renamed Rassemblement national des bûcherons in 1991, name changed as above in 2000; allied to the PDG; Leader Fr Paul M'Ba Abessole; Vice-Pres. Prof. Vincent Moulengui Boukosso.

Rassemblement national des bûcherons—Démocratique (RNB): Libreville; f. 1991; Leader Pierre André Kombila.

Rassemblement national des républicains (RNR): Libreville; f. 2002; Pres. Gérard Ella Nguema; Sec-Gen. Christian Abiaghe Ngomo.

Union démocratique et sociale (UDS): f. 1996; Leader Hervé Assamanet.

Union gabonaise pour la démocratie et le développement (UGDD): Libreville; e-mail ugdd@ugdd.org; internet www.ugdd.org; f. 2005; Pres. Zacharie Myboto.

Union nationale pour la démocratie et le développement (UNDD): f. 1993; supports President Bongo.

Union pour la nouvelle République: f. 2007 following the merger of the Front pour l'unité nationale (FUNDU) and the Rassemblement des républicains indépendants (RRI); Leader Louis-Gaston Mayila.

Union du peuple gabonais (UPG): f. 1989 in Paris, France; Leader Pierre Mamboundou; Sec.-Gen. David Badinga.

Union pour le progrès national (UPN): Leader Daniel Tengue Nzoundo.

Diplomatic Representation

EMBASSIES IN GABON

Algeria: Batterie 4, BP 4008, Libreville; tel. 73-23-18; fax 73-14-03; e-mail ambalgabon@komo.tiggabon.com; Ambassador (vacant).

Angola: BP 4884, Libreville; tel. 73-04-26; fax 73-78-24; Ambassador Emilio José de Carvalho Guerra.

Belgium: Quartier Bas de Gué-Gué, Bord de Mer à côté de la Délégation de la Commission Européenne, BP 4079, Libreville; tel. 73-29-92; fax 73-96-94; e-mail libreville@diplobel.org; internet www.diplomatie.be/libreville; Ambassador Ivo Goemans.

Benin: BP 3851, Akebe, Libreville; tel. 73-76-82; fax 73-77-75; Ambassador El Hadj Lassissi Adébo.

Brazil: blvd de l'Indépendance, BP 3899, Libreville; tel. 76-05-35; fax 74-03-43; e-mail emblibreville@inet.ga; internet www.ambassadedubresil-gabon.org; Ambassador Carlos A. Ferreira Guimarães.

Cameroon: BP 14001, Libreville; tel. 73-28-00; Ambassador Jean Koé Ntonga.

Central African Republic: Libreville; tel. 72-12-28; Ambassador (vacant).

China, People's Republic: blvd Triomphale Omar Bongo, BP 3914, Libreville; tel. 74-32-07; fax 74-75-96; e-mail gzy@internetgabon.com; Ambassador Xue Jinwei.

Congo, Democratic Republic: BP 2257, Libreville; tel. 74-32-53; Ambassador Kabangi Kaumbu Bula.

Congo, Republic: BP 269, Libreville; tel. 07-85-26-11; e-mail ambacobrazzalibreville@yahoo.fr; Ambassador Edouard Roger Okoula.

Côte d'Ivoire: Charbonnages, BP 3861, Libreville; tel. 73-82-70; fax 73-82-87; Ambassador Claudine Yapobi Ricci.

Egypt: Immeuble Floria, 1 blvd de la Mer, Quartier Batterie IV, BP 4240, Libreville; tel. 73-25-38; fax 73-25-19; Ambassador Ahmed Muhammad Taha Awad.

Equatorial Guinea: BP 1462, Libreville; tel. 75-10-56; Ambassador José Esono Bacale.

France: 1 rue du pont Pirah, BP 2125, Libreville; tel. 79-70-00; fax 79-70-09; e-mail ambafran@inet.ga; internet www.ambafrance-ga.org; Ambassador Jean Marc Simon.

Germany: blvd de l'Indépendance, Immeuble les Frangipaniers, BP 299, Libreville; tel. 76-01-88; fax 72-40-12; e-mail amb-allegmagne@inet.ga; Ambassador Hans-Dietrich Bernhard.

Guinea: BP 4046, Libreville; tel. 73-85-09; Ambassador Mohamed Sampil.

Holy See: blvd Monseigneur Bessieux, BP 1322, Libreville (Apostolic Nunciature); tel. 74-45-41; e-mail nonapcg@yahoo.com; Apos-

GABON

tolic Nuncio Mgr ANDRÉS CARRASCOSA COSO (Titular Archbishop of Elo).

Italy: Immeuble Personnaz et Gardin, rue de la Mairie, BP 2251, Libreville; tel. 74-28-92; fax 74-80-35; e-mail ambasciata.libreville@esteri.it; internet www.amblibreville.esteri.it; Ambassador RAFFAELE DE BENEDICTIS.

Japan: blvd du Bord de Mer, BP 2259, Libreville; tel. 73-22-97; fax 73-60-60; Ambassador SADAMU FUJIWARA.

Korea, Democratic People's Republic: Ambassador KIM RYONG YONG.

Korea, Republic: BP 2620, Libreville; tel. 73-40-00; fax 73-99-05; e-mail gabon-ambcoree@mofat.go.kr; internet gab.mofat.go.kr; Ambassador EOM SUNG-JUN.

Lebanon: BP 3341, Libreville; tel. 73-14-77; Ambassador MICHELIN BAZ.

Mali: BP 4007, Quartier Batterie IV, Libreville; tel. 82-73-82; fax 73-82-80; e-mail ambamaga@yahoo.fr; Ambassador TRAORÉ ROKIATOU GUIKINE.

Mauritania: BP 3917, Libreville; tel. 74-31-65; Ambassador El Hadj THIAM.

Morocco: blvd de l'indépendance, Immeuble CK 2, BP 3983, Libreville; tel. 77-41-51; fax 77-41-50; e-mail sifamalbv@inet.ga; Ambassador ALI BOJI.

Nigeria: ave du Président Léon-M'Ba, Quartier blvd Léon-M'Ba, BP 1191, Libreville; tel. 73-22-03; fax 73-29-14; e-mail nigeriamission@internetgabon.com; Ambassador Chief IGNATIUS H. AJURU.

Russia: BP 3963, Libreville; tel. 72-48-69; fax 72-48-70; Ambassador VSEVOLOD SOUKHOV.

São Tomé and Príncipe: BP 489, Libreville; tel. 72-09-94; Ambassador URBINO JOSÉ GONHALVES BOTELÇO.

Senegal: Quartier Sobraga, BP 3856, Libreville; tel. 77-42-67; fax 77-42-68; e-mail ambasengab@yahoo.fr; Ambassador IBRAHIMA CABA.

South Africa: Immeuble les Arcades, 142 rue des Chavannes, BP 4063, Libreville; tel. 77-45-30; fax 77-45-36; e-mail saegabon@internetgabon.com; Ambassador MAHLOMOLA JOMO KHASU.

Spain: Immeuble Diamant, 2ème étage, blvd de l'Indépendance, BP 1157, Libreville; tel. 72-12-64; fax 74-88-73; e-mail ambespga@mail.mae.es; Ambassador Dr RAMIRO FERNÁNDEZ BACHILLER.

Togo: BP 14160, Libreville; tel. 73-29-04; fax 73-32-61; Ambassador AHLONKO KOFFI AQUEREBURU.

Tunisia: BP 3844, Libreville; tel. 73-28-41; Ambassador EZZEDINE KERKENI.

USA: blvd du Bord de Mer, BP 4000, Libreville; tel. 76-20-03; fax 74-55-07; e-mail clolibreville@state.gov; internet libreville.usembassy.gov; Ambassador R. BARRIE WALKLEY.

Judicial System

Supreme Court: BP 1043, Libreville; tel. 72-17-00; three chambers: judicial, administrative and accounts; Pres. BENJAMIN PAMBOU-KOMBILA.

Constitutional Court: Libreville; tel. 72-57-17; fax 72-55-96; Pres. MARIE MADELEINE MBORANTSUO.

Courts of Appeal: Libreville and Franceville.

Court of State Security: Libreville; 13 mems; Pres. FLORENTIN ANGO.

Conseil Supérieur de la Magistrature: Libreville; Pres. El Hadj OMAR BONGO ONDIMBA; Vice-Pres. BENJAMIN PAMBOU-KOMBILA (ex officio).

There are also Tribunaux de Première Instance (County Courts) at Libreville, Franceville, Port-Gentil, Lambaréné, Mouila, Oyem, Koula-Moutou, Makokou and Tchibanga.

Religion

About 60% of Gabon's population are Christians, mainly adherents of the Roman Catholic Church. About 40% are animists and fewer than 1% are Muslims.

CHRISTIANITY

The Roman Catholic Church

Gabon comprises one archdiocese, four dioceses and one apostolic prefecture. At 31 December 2005 the estimated number of adherents in the country was equivalent to 50.6% of the total population.

Bishops' Conference

Conférence Episcopale du Gabon, BP 2146, Libreville; tel. 72-20-73; f. 1989; Pres. Most Rev. TIMOTHÉE MODIBO-NZOCKENA (Bishop of Franceville).

Archbishop of Libreville: Most Rev. BASILE MVÉ ENGONE, Archevêché, Sainte-Marie, BP 2146, Libreville; tel. and fax 72-20-73; e-mail basilemve@yahoo.fr.

Protestant Churches

Christian and Missionary Alliance: Gabon Field, BP 13021, Libreville; active in the south of the country; Field-Dir Rev. ALBERT STOMBAUGH; 16,000 mems.

Eglise Evangélique du Gabon: BP 10080, Libreville; tel. 72-41-92; f. 1842; independent since 1961; 120,000 mems; Pres. Pastor SAMUEL NANG ESSONO; Sec. Rev. EMILE NTETOME.

The Evangelical Church of South Gabon and the Evangelical Pentecostal Church are also active in Gabon.

The Press

Afric'Sports: BP 3950, Libreville; tel. 76-24-74; monthly; sport; CEO SERGE ALFRED MPOUHO; Man. YVON PATRICE AUBIAN; circ. 5,000.

Le Bûcheron: BP 6424, Libreville; tel. 72-50-20; f. 1990; weekly; official publ. of the Rassemblement pour le Gabon; Editor DÉSIRÉ ENAME.

Bulletin Evangélique d'Information et de Presse: BP 80, Libreville; monthly; religious.

Bulletin Mensuel de Statistique de la République Gabonaise: BP 179, Libreville; monthly; publ. by Direction Générale de l'Economie.

La Concorde: Libreville; f. 2005; owned by TV+ group; daily; Dir FRANÇOIS ONDO EDOU; circ. 10,000.

L'Economiste Gabonais: BP 3906, Libreville; quarterly; publ. by the Centre gabonais du commerce extérieur.

Gabon d'Aujourd'hui: BP 750, Libreville; weekly; publ. of the Ministry of Culture, the Arts and Popular Education.

Gabon Libre: BP 6439, Libreville; tel. 72-42-22; weekly; Dir DZIME EKANG; Editor RENÉ NZOVI.

Gabon-Matin: BP 168, Libreville; daily; publ. by Agence Gabonaise de Presse; Man. HILARION VENDANY; circ. 18,000.

Gabon Show: Libreville; f. 2004; independent; satirical; printed in Cameroon; Man. Editor FULBERT WORA; weekly; circ. 3,000.

Gris-Gris International: Paris; f. 1990; weekly; independent; satirical; distribution forbidden in 2001; Editor-in-Chief RAPHAEL NTOUTOUME NKOGHE; Editor MICHEL ONGOUNDOU.

Journal Officiel de la République Gabonaise: BP 563, Libreville; f. 1959; fortnightly; Man. EMMANUEL OBAMÉ.

Le Misamu: BP 887, Libreville; tel. 74-74-59; fortnightly; Founder NOËL NGWA NGUEMA.

Ngondo: BP 168, Libreville; monthly; publ. by Agence Gabonaise de Presse.

Le Progressiste: blvd Léon-M'Ba, BP 7000, Libreville; tel. 74-54-01; f. 1990; Dir BENOÎT MOUITY NZAMBA; Editor JACQUES MOURENDE-TSIOBA.

La Relance: BP 268, Libreville; tel. 72-93-08; weekly; publ. of the Parti démocratique gabonais; Pres. JACQUES ADIAHÉNOT; Dir RENÉ NDEMEZO'O OBIANG.

Le Réveil: BP 20386, Libreville; tel. and fax 73-17-21; weekly; Man. ALBERT YANGARI; Editor RENÉ NZOVI; circ. 8,000.

La Sagaie: tel. Libreville; fortnightly; satirical; distribution suspended September 2003.

Sept Jours: BP 213, Libreville; weekly.

Sub-Version: Libreville; fortnightly; f. 2003; independent; satirical; printed in Douala, Cameroon; publ. suspended in 2003.

La Tribune des Affaires: BP 2234, Libreville; tel. 72-20-64; fax 74-12-20; monthly; publ. of the Chambre de Commerce, d'Agriculture, d'Industrie et des Mines du Gabon.

L'Union: Sonapresse, BP 3849, Libreville; tel. 73-58-61; fax 73-58-62; e-mail mpg@inet.ga; f. 1974; 75% state-owned; daily; official govt publ.; Dir-Gen. ALBERT YANAGRI; circ. 20,000.

La Voix du Peuple: BP 4049, Libreville; tel. 76-20-45; f. 1991; weekly; Editor-in-Chief JEAN KOUMBA; Editor MAURICE-BLAISE NDZADIENGA MAYILA; circ. 4,000.

Zoom Hebdo: Carrefour London, BP 352, Libreville; tel. 76-44-54; fax 74-67-50; e-mail actismedia@inet.ga; internet www.zoomhebdo.com; Friday; f. 1991; Dir-Gen. HANS RAYMOND KWAAITAAL; circ. 12,000–20,000.

NEWS AGENCIES

Agence Gabonaise de Presse (AGP): BP 168, Libreville.

Association Professionnelle de la Presse Ecrite Gabonaise (APPEG): BP 3849, Libreville; internet www.gabon-presse.org.

BERP International: BP 8483, Libreville; tel. 33-80-16; fax 77-58-81; e-mail berp8483@hotmail.com; f. 1995; Dir ANTOINE LAWSON.

Publishers

Gabonaise d'Imprimerie (GABIMP): BP 154, Libreville; tel. 70-22-55; fax 70-31-85; e-mail gabimp@inet.ga; f. 1973; Dir BÉATRICE CAILLOT.

Multipress Gabon: blvd Léon-M'Ba, BP 3875, Libreville; tel. 73-22-33; fax 73-63-72; e-mail mpg@inet.ga; monopoly distributors of magazines and newspapers; f. 1973; Chair. PAUL BORY.

Société Imprimerie de Gabon: BP 9626, Libreville; f. 1977; Man. Dir AKWANG REX.

Société nationale de Presse et d'Edition (SONAPRESSE): BP 3849, Libreville; tel. and fax 73-58-60; e-mail unionplus@intergabon.com; f. 1975; Pres. and Man. Dir NARCISSE MASSALA-TSAMBA.

Broadcasting and Communications

TELECOMMUNICATIONS

Celtel Gabon: 124 ave Bouët, Montagne Sainte, BP 9259, Libreville; tel. 74-00-00; e-mail serviceclients@ga.celtel.com; internet www.ga.celtel.com; f. 2000; Dir-Gen. JEAN-YVES KOUASSI-GOLY.

Gabon Télécom: Immeuble du Delta Postal, BP 20000, Libreville; tel. 78-70-00; fax 78-67-70; e-mail gabontelecom@gabontelecom.ga; f. 2001; provider of telecommunications, incl. satellite, internet and cellular systems; 51% owned by Maroc Telecom; Dir-Gen. HERVÉ FULGENCE OSSAMY.

  Libertis: Immeuble du Delta Postal, BP 20000, Libreville; tel. 22-22-22; e-mail contact@libertis.ga; internet www.libertis.ga; f. 1999; mobile celluler telephone operator; Dir-Gen. MOSTAPHA LAARABI; 250,000 subscribers in 2006.

Société des Télécommunications Internationales Gabonaises (TIG): BP 2261, Libreville; tel. 78-77-56; fax 74-19-09; f. 1971; cap. 3,000m. francs CFA; 61% state-owned; privatization pending; planning and devt of int. telecommunications systems; Man. Dir A. N'GOUMA MWYUMALA.

Telecel Gabon: BP 12470; tel. 76-83-83; fax 76-83-88; f. 2000.

BROADCASTING

Radio

The national network, 'La Voix de la Rénovation', and a provincial network broadcast for 24 hours each day in French and local languages.

Africa No. 1: BP 1, Libreville; tel. 76-11-52; fax 74-21-33; e-mail africa@africa1.com; internet www.africa1.com; f. 1980; 35% state-controlled; int. commercial radio station; daily programmes in French and English; Pres. LOUIS BARTHÉLEMY MAPANGOU; Sec.-Gen. MICHEL KOUMBANGOYE.

Radiodiffusion-Télévision Gabonaise (RTG): BP 150, Libreville; tel. 73-20-25; fax 73-21-53; f. 1959; state-controlled; Dir-Gen. DAVID MINTSA; Dir of Radio GILLES TERENCE NZOGHE.

Radio Fréquence 3: f. 1996.

Radio Génération Nouvelle: f. 1996; Dir JEAN-BONIFACE ASSELE.

Radio Mandarine: f. 1995.

Radio Soleil: f. 1995; affiliated to Rassemblement pour le Gabon.

Radio Unité: f. 1996.

Television

Radiodiffusion-Télévision Gabonaise (RTG): BP 10150, Libreville; tel. 73-21-52; fax 73-21-53; f. 1959; state-controlled; Dir-Gen. JOHN JOSEPH MBOUROU; Dir of Television JULES CÉSAR LEKOGHO.

Télé-Africa: BP 4269, Libreville; tel. 72-49-22; fax 76-16-83; f. 1985; private channel; daily broadcasts in French.

Télédiffusion du Gabon: f. 1995.

TV Sat (Société de Télécommunications Audio-Visuelles): Immeuble TV SAT BP 184, Libreville; tel. 72-49-22; fax 76-16-83; f. 1994.

Finance

(cap. = capital; res = reserves; dep. = deposits; m. = million; brs = branches; amounts in francs CFA)

BANKING

Central Bank

Banque des Etats de l'Afrique Centrale (BEAC): BP 112, Libreville; tel. 76-13-52; fax 74-45-63; e-mail beaclbv@beac.int; internet www.beac.int; HQ in Yaoundé, Cameroon; f. 1973; bank of issue for mem. states of the Communauté économique et monétaire de l'Afrique centrale (CEMAC, fmrly Union douanière et économique de l'Afrique centrale), comprising Cameroon, the Central African Repub., Chad, the Repub. of the Congo, Equatorial Guinea and Gabon; cap. 45,000m., res 176,661m., total assets 2,144,626m. (Nov. 2003); Gov. JEAN-FÉLIX MAMALEPOT; Dir in Gabon PHILIBERT ANDZEMBÉ; 4 brs in Gabon.

Commercial Banks

Banque Internationale pour le Commerce et l'Industrie du Gabon, SA (BICIG): ave du Colonel Parant, BP 2241, Libreville; tel. 77-26-13; fax 74-40-34; e-mail bicigdoi@inet.ga; internet bicig-gabon.com; f. 1973; 26.30% state-owned, 46.67% owned by BNP Paribas SA; cap. and res 23,673.0m., total assets 268,199.0m. (Dec. 2003); Pres. ETIENNE GUY MOUVAGHA TCHIOBA; Dir-Gen. CLAUDE AYO-IGUENDHA; 9 brs.

Banque Internationale pour le Gabon: Immeuble Concorde, blvd de l'Indépendance, BP 106, Libreville; tel. 76-26-26; fax 76-20-53.

BGFIBANK: blvd du Bord de Mer, BP 2253, Libreville; tel. 76-40-35; fax 76-08-94; e-mail bgfi@internet.com; internet www.bgfi.com; f. 1972 as Banque Gabonaise et Française Internationale (BGFI); name changed as above in March 2000; 8% state-owned; cap. 25,065.4m., res 27,683.0m., dep. 309,751.4m. (Dec. 2005); Chair. PATRICE OTHA; Gen. Man. HENRI-CLAUDE OYIMA; 3 brs.

Citibank: 810 blvd Quaben, rue Kringer, BP 3940, Libreville; tel. 73-19-16; fax 73-37-86; total assets 1,000m. (Dec. 2004); Dir-Gen. FUNMI ADE AJAYI; Dep. Dir-Gen. JULIETTE WEISTFLOG.

Financial Bank Gabon: Immeuble des Frangipaniers, blvd de l'Indépendance, BP 20333, Libreville; tel. 77-50-78; fax 72-41-97; e-mail financial.gabon@financial-bank.com; cap. and res 719.0m., total assets 5,342.0m. (Dec. 2004); 69.78% owned by Financial BC, SA (Togo), 1.58% state-owned; Pres. RENÉ-HILAIRE ADIAHENO; Dir-Gen. PIERRE LECLAIRE.

Union Gabonaise de Banque, SA (UGB): ave du Colonel Parant, BP 315, Libreville; tel. 77-70-00; fax 76-46-16; e-mail ugbdio@internetgabon.com; internet ugb-interactif.com; f. 1962; 26.09% state-owned, 58.71% owned by Crédit Lyonnais (France); cap. 7,400.0m., res 6,076.1m., dep. 204,541.4m. (Dec. 2006); Chair. MARCEL DOUPAMBY-MATOKA; Man. Dir FRANÇOIS HOFFMANN; 6 brs.

Development Banks

Banque Gabonaise de Développement (BGD): rue Alfred Marche, BP 5, Libreville; tel. 76-24-29; fax 74-26-99; e-mail bdg@internetgabon.com; internet www.bgd-gabon.com; f. 1960; 69.01% state-owned; cap. and res 33,238.5m., total assets 52,339.0m. (Dec. 2003); Pres. MICHEL ANCHOVEY.

Banque Nationale de Crédit Rural (BNCR): ave Bouet, BP 1120, Libreville; tel. 72-47-42; fax 74-05-07; f. 1986; 74% state-owned; under enforced administration since March 2002; total assets 5,601m. (Dec. 2000); Pres. GÉRARD MEYO M'EMANE; Man. JOSEPH KOYAGBELE.

Banque Populaire du Gabon: 413 blvd de l'Indépendance, BP 6663, Libreville; tel. 72-86-89; fax 72-86-91.

BICI-Bail Gabon: Immeuble BICIG, 5ème étage, ave du Colonel Parant, BP 2241, Libreville; tel. 77-75-52; fax 77-48-15; internet www.bicig.ga/bicibail.htm; BNP Paribas-owned.

Société Financière Transafricaine (FINATRA): blvd de l'Indépendance, BP 8645, Libreville; tel. and fax 77-40-87; e-mail bgfi@internetgabon.com; internet www.bgfi.com; 50% owned by BGFI-BANK; cap. 2,000m., total assets 14,613m. (Dec. 2003); Dir-Gen. MARIE CÉLINE NTSAME-MEZUI.

Société Gabonaise de Crédit Automobile (SOGACA): Immeuble SOGACA, BP 63, Libreville; tel. 76-08-46; fax 76-01-03; car finance; 43% owned by CFAO Gabon, 10% state-owned; cap. and res 2,828.0m., total assets 18,583.0m. (Dec. 2003); Pres. THIERRY DE LAPLAGNOLLE; Dir-Gen. M. DE PAPILLION.

Société Gabonaise de Crédit-Bail (SOGABAIL): Immeuble Sogaca, BP 63, Libreville; tel. 77-25-73; fax 76-01-03; e-mail sogaca@assala.net; 25% owned by CFAO Gabon, 14% state-owned; cap. and res 2,980.4m., total assets 4,123.2m.; Pres. M. LAPLAGNOLLE; Dir-Gen. THIERRY PAPILLON.

Société Nationale d'Investissement du Gabon (SONADIG): BP 479, Libreville; tel. 72-09-22; fax 74-81-70; f. 1968; state-owned; cap. 500m.; Pres. Antoine Oyieye; Dir-Gen. Narcisse Massala Tsamba.

Financial Institution

Caisse Autonome d'Amortissement du Gabon: BP 912, Libreville; tel. 74-41-43; management of state funds; Dir-Gen. Maurice Eyamba Tsimat.

INSURANCE

Agence Gabonaise d'Assurance et de Réassurance (AGAR): BP 1699, Libreville; tel. 74-02-22; fax 76-59-25; f. 1987; Dir-Gen. Ange Gouloumes.

Assinco: BP 7812, Libreville; tel. 72-19-25; fax 72-19-29; e-mail assinco@internetgabon.com; Dir Eugénie Dendé.

Assurances Mutuelles du Gabon (AMG): Libreville; tel. 72-13-90; fax 74-17-02; Dir-Gen. M. Veron.

Assurances Nouvelles du Gabon: ave du Colonel Parant, BP 2225, Libreville; tel. 72-13-90; fax 74-17-02; fmrly Mutuelle Gabonaise d'Assurances; Dir-Gen. Ekomie Césare Afene.

Assureurs Conseils Franco-Africains du Gabon (ACFRA-GABON): BP 1116, Libreville; tel. 72-32-83; Chair. Frédéric Marron; Dir M. Garnier.

Assureurs Conseils Gabonais (ACG): Immeuble Shell-Gabon, rue de la Mairie, BP 2138, Libreville; tel. 74-32-90; fax 76-04-39; e-mail acg@ascoma.com; represents foreign insurance cos; Dir Michelle Valette.

Axa Assurances Gabon: BP 4047, Libreville; tel. 76-28-97; fax 76-03-34; e-mail axa.gabon@inet.ga; internet www.axa.com; Dir Bernard Bartoszek.

Commercial Union: Libreville; tel. 76-43-00; Exec. Dir M. Milan.

Fédération gabonaise des assureurs (FEGASA): BP 4005, Libreville; tel. 74-45-29; fax 77-58-23; Pres. Jacques Amvamé.

Gras Savoye Gabon: ave du Colonel Parant, BP 2148, Libreville; tel. 76-09-73; fax 76-57-41; e-mail contact@ga.grassavoye.com; internet www.ga.grassavoye.com; Dir Christophe Roudaut.

Groupement Gabonais d'Assurances et de Réassurances (GGAR): Libreville; tel. 74-28-72; f. 1985; Chair. Rassaguiza Akerey; Dir-Gen. Denise Ombagho.

OGAR Gabon: BP 201, Libreville; tel. 76-15-96; fax 76-58-16; e-mail ogar@inet.ga; Dir Edouard Valentin.

Omnium Gabonais d'Assurances et de Réassurances (OGAR): 1811 blvd de l'Indépendance, BP 201, Libreville; tel. 76-15-96; fax 76-58-16; e-mail ogar@inet.ga; internet www.assurances-gabon.com; f. 1976; owned by Assurances Générales de France; general; Pres. Marcel Doupamby-Matoka; Exec. Dir Blaise Noyon.

Sécurité Gabonaise Assureurs Conseils (SGAC): Libreville; tel. 74-24-85; fax 74-60-07.

Société Librevilloise de Courtage d'Assurance et de Réassurance (SOLICAR): Libreville; tel. 74-01-23; fax 76-08-03.

Société Nationale Gabonaise d'Assurances et de Réassurances (SONAGAR): ave du Colonel Parant, BP 3082, Libreville; tel. 72-28-97; f. 1974; owned by l'Union des Assurances de Paris (France); Dir-Gen. Jean-Louis Messan.

SOGERCO-Gabon: BP 2102, Libreville; tel. 76-09-34; f. 1975; general; Dir M. Rabeau.

UAG-Vie: ave du Colonel Parant, Libreville; tel. 72-48-58; fax 72-48-57; life insurance; Chair. François Simon; Dir Laurent Argouet.

L'Union des Assurances pour le Gabon (UAPG): ave du Colonel Parant, BP 2141, Libreville; tel. 76-28-97; fax 74-18-46; f. 1976; Chair. Gaston Olouna; Dir-Gen. Jacques Bardoux.

Trade and Industry

GOVERNMENT AGENCIES

Conseil Economique et Social de la République Gabonaise: BP 1075, Libreville; tel. 73-19-46; fax 73-19-44; comprises representatives from salaried workers, employers and Govt; commissions on economic, financial and social affairs and forestry and agriculture; Pres. Louis Gaston Mayila.

Agence de Promotion des Investissements Privés (APIP): BP 13740, Front de Mer, Libreville; tel. 76-87-65; fax 76-87-64; e-mail apip@netcourrier.com; internet www.invest-gabon.com; f. 2002; promotes private investment; Dir-Gen. Ludovic Ognagna Ockogho.

DEVELOPMENT ORGANIZATIONS

Agence Française de Développement (AFD): BP 64, Libreville; tel. 74-33-74; fax 74-51-25; e-mail afdlibreville@ga.groupe-afd.org; internet www.afd.fr; fmrly Caisse Française de Développement; Dir Yves Boudot.

Agence Nationale de Promotion de la Petite et Moyenne Entreprise (PROMOGABON): BP 2111, Libreville; tel. 26-79-19; fax 74-89-59; f. 1964; state-controlled; promotes and assists small and medium-sized industries; Pres. Simon Boulamatari; Man. Dir Jean-Fidèle Otando.

Centre Gabonais de Commerce Extérieur (CGCE): Immeuble Rénovation, 3ème étage, BP 3906, Libreville; tel. 72-11-67; fax 74-71-53; promotes foreign trade and investment in Gabon; Gen. Dir Pierre Sockat.

Commerce et Développement (CODEV): BP 2142, Libreville; tel. 76-06-73; f. 1976; 95% state-owned; import and distribution of capital goods and food products; Chair. and Man. Dir Jérôme Ngoua-Bekale.

Conservation et Utilisation Rationelle des Ecosystèmes Forestiers en Afrique Centrale (ECOFAC): BP 15115, Libreville; tel. 73-23-43; fax 73-23-45; e-mail coordination@ecofac.org; internet www.ecofac.org.

Groupes d'Etudes et de Recherches sur la Démocratie et le Développement Economique et Social (GERDDES): BP 13114, Libreville; tel. 76-62-47; fax 74-08-94; e-mail gerddes@firstnet1.com; internet www.gerddes.org; Pres. Maryvonne Ntsame Ndong.

Institut Gabonais d'Appui au Développement (IGAD): BP 20423, Libreville; tel. and fax 74-52-47; e-mail igad@inet.ga.

Mission Française de Coopération: BP 2105, Libreville; tel. 76-10-56; fax 74-55-33; administers bilateral aid from France; Dir Jean-Claude Quirin.

Office Gabonais d'Amélioration et de Production de Viande (OGAPROV): BP 245, Moanda; tel. 66-12-67; f. 1971; devt of private cattle farming; manages ranch at Lekedi-Sud; Pres. Paul Kounda Kiki; Dir-Gen. Veyrant Ombé Epigat.

Palmiers et Hévéas du Gabon (PALMEVEAS): BP 75, Libreville; f. 1956; state-owned; palm-oil devt.

Programme Régionale de Gestion de l'Information Environnementale en Afrique Centrale (PRGIE): BP 4080, Libreville; tel. 76-30-19; fax 77-42-61; e-mail urge@adie-prgie.org; internet www.adie-prgie.org.

Société de Développement de l'Agriculture au Gabon (AGRO-GABON): BP 2248, Libreville; tel. 76-40-82; fax 76-44-72; f. 1976; 93% state-owned; acquired by the Société Industrielle Agricole du Tabac Tropical in April 2004; Man. Dir André Paul-Apandina.

Société de Développement de l'Hévéaculture (HEVEGAB): BP 316, Libreville; tel. 72-08-29; fax 72-08-30; f. 1981; acquired by the Société Industrielle Agricole du Tabac Tropical in April 2004; devt of rubber plantations in the Mitzic, Bitam and Kango regions; Chair. François Owono-Nguema; Man. Dir Janvier Essono-Assoumou.

Société Gabonaise de Recherches et d'Exploitations Minières (SOGAREM): Libreville; state-owned; research and devt of gold mining; Chair. Arsène Bounguenza; Man. Dir Serge Gassita.

Société Gabonaise de Recherches Pétrolières (GABOREP): BP 564, Libreville; tel. 75-06-40; fax 75-06-47; exploration and exploitation of hydrocarbons; Chair. Hubert Perrodo; Man. Dir P. F. Leca.

Société Nationale de Développement des Cultures Industrielles (SONADECI): Libreville; tel. 76-33-97; f. 1978; state-owned; agricultural devt; Chair. Paul Kounda Kiki; Man. Dir Georges Bekalé.

CHAMBER OF COMMERCE

Chambre de Commerce, d'Agriculture, d'Industrie et des Mines du Gabon: BP 2234, Libreville; tel. 72-20-64; fax 74-12-20; f. 1935; regional offices at Port-Gentil and Franceville; Pres. Joachim Boussamba-Mapaga; Sec.-Gen. Dominique Mandza.

EMPLOYERS' ORGANIZATIONS

Confédération Patronale Gabonaise: Immeuble les Frangipaniers, BP 410, Libreville; tel. 76-02-43; fax 74-86-52; e-mail infocpg@confederation-patronale-gabonaise.org; internet www.confederation-patronale-gabonaise.org; f. 1959; represents industrial, mining, petroleum, public works, forestry, banking, insurance, commercial and shipping interests; Pres. Henri-Claude Oyima; Sec.-Gen. Christiane Quinio.

Conseil National du Patronat Gabonais (CNPG): Libreville; Pres. Rahandi Chambrier; Sec.-Gen. Thomas Franck Eya'a.

Syndicat des Entreprises Minières du Gabon (SYNDIMINES): BP 260, Libreville; Pres. André Berre; Sec.-Gen. Serge Gregoire.

Syndicat des Importateurs Exportateurs du Gabon (SIMPEX): Libreville; Pres. Albert Jean; Sec.-Gen. R. Tyberghein.

Syndicat des Industries du Gabon: BP 2175, Libreville; tel. 72-02-29; fax 74-52-13; e-mail sociga@ga.imptob.com; Pres. JACQUES-YVES LAUGE.

Syndicat des Producteurs et Industriels du Bois du Gabon: BP 84, Libreville; tel. 72-26-11; fax 77-44-43.

Syndicat Professionnel des Usines de Sciages et Placages du Gabon: Port-Gentil; f. 1956; Pres. PIERRE BERRY.

Union des Représentations Automobiles et Industrielles (URAI): BP 1743, Libreville; Pres. M. MARTINENT; Sec. R. TYBERGHEIN.

Union Nationale du Patronat Syndical des Transports Urbains, Routiers et Fluviaux du Gabon (UNAPASY-TRUFGA): BP 1025, Libreville; f. 1977; represents manufacturers of vehicle and construction parts; Pres. LAURENT BELLAL BIBANG-BI-EDZO; Sec.-Gen. AUGUSTIN KASSA-NZIGOU.

UTILITIES

Société d'Energie et d'Eau du Gabon (SEEG): BP 2187, Libreville; tel. 76-78-07; fax 76-11-34; e-mail laroche.lbv@inet.ga; internet www.seeg-gabon.com; f. 1950; 51% owned by Vivendi (France); controls 35 electricity generation and distribution centres and 32 water production and distribution centres; Pres. FRANÇOIS LAROCHE.

TRADE UNIONS

Confédération Gabonaise des Syndicats Libres (CGSL): BP 8067, Libreville; tel. 77-37-82; fax 74-45-25; e-mail c.libres@voila.fr; f. 1991; Sec.-Gen. FRANCIS MAYOMBO; 16,000 mems.

Confédération Syndicale Gabonaise (COSYGA): BP 14017, Libreville; tel. 68-07-26; fax 74-21-70; e-mail mintsacosyga@yahoo.fr; f. 1969 by the Govt, as a specialized organ of the PDG, to organize and educate workers, to contribute to social peace and economic devt, and to protect the rights of trade unions; Gen. Sec. MARTIN ALLINI.

Transport

RAILWAYS

The construction of the Transgabonais railway, which comprises a section running from Owendo (the port of Libreville) to Booué (340 km) and a second section from Booué to Franceville (357 km), was completed in 1986. By 1989 regular services were operating between Libreville and Franceville. Some 2.9m. metric tons of freight and 215,000 passengers were carried on the network in 1999, which in that year totalled 814 km. In 1998 the railways were transferred to private management.

Société d'Exploration du Chemin de Fer Transgabonais (SETRAG): BP 578, Libreville; tel. 70-24-78; fax 70-20-38; operates Transgabonais railway; 84% owned by COMILOG; Chair. MARCEL ABEKE.

ROADS

In 2004 there were an estimated 9,170 km of roads, including 2,793 km of main roads and 6,377 km of secondary roads; about 10.2% of the road network was paved.

AGS Frasers: BP 9161, Libreville; tel. 70-23-16; fax 70-41-56; e-mail ags-gabon@ags-demenagement.com; internet www.agsfrasers.com; Dir CHRISTIAN POITTIER.

APRETRAC: BP 4542, Libreville; tel. 72-84-93; fax 74-40-45; e-mail apretrac@assala.net; Dir CHRISTOPHE DISSOU.

A.R.T.: BP 9391, Libreville; tel. 70-57-26; fax 70-57-28; freight; Dir-Gen. PHILIPPE BERGON.

Compagnie Internationale de Déménagement Transit (CIDT): BP 986, Libreville; tel. 76-44-44; fax 76-44-55; e-mail cidg@internetgabon.com; Dir THIERRY CARBONIE.

GETMA Gabon: BP 7510, Libreville; tel. 70-28-14; fax 70-40-20; e-mail claude.barone@assala.net; Dir CLAUDE BARONE.

Transform: BP 7538, Libreville; tel. 70-43-95; fax 70-21-91; e-mail transform@voila.fr; Dir J. P. POULAIN.

Transitex: BP 20323, Libreville; tel. 77-84-26; fax 77-84-35; e-mail helenepedemonte@transitex.ga; freight; Man. FRÉDÉRIC GONZALEZ.

INLAND WATERWAYS

The principal river is the Ogooué, navigable from Port-Gentil to Ndjolé (310 km) and serving the towns of Lambaréné, Ndjolé and Sindara.

Compagnie de Navigation Intérieure (CNI): BP 3982, Libreville; tel. 72-39-28; fax 74-04-11; f. 1978; scheduled for privatization; responsible for inland waterway transport; agencies at Port-Gentil, Mayumba and Lambaréné; Chair. JEAN-PIERRE MENGWANG ME NGYEMA; Dir-Gen. JEAN LOUIS POUNAH-NDJIMBI.

SHIPPING

The principal deep-water ports are Port-Gentil, which handles mainly petroleum exports, and Owendo, 15 km from Libreville, which services mainly barge traffic. The main ports for timber are at Owendo, Mayumba and Nyanga, and there is a fishing port at Libreville. The construction of a deep-water port at Mayumba is planned. A new terminal for the export of minerals, at Owendo, was opened in 1988. In 2006 the merchant shipping fleet numbered 49 and had a total displacement of 13,770 grt. In 1997 the Islamic Development Bank granted a loan of 11,000m. francs CFA for the rehabilitation of Gabon's ports.

Compagnie de Manutention et de Chalandage d'Owendo (COMACO): BP 2131, Libreville; tel. 70-26-35; f. 1974; Pres. GEORGES RAWIRI; Dir in Libreville M. RAYMOND.

Office des Ports et Rades du Gabon (OPRAG): BP 1051, Libreville; tel. 70-00-48; fax 70-37-37; f. 1974; 25-year management concession acquired in April 2004 by the Spanish PIP group; national port authority; Pres. ALI BONGO; Dir-Gen. JEAN PIERRE OYIBA.

SAGA Gabon: Zone OPRAG, BP 518, Port-Gentil; tel. 55-58-19; fax 55-21-71; e-mail sagalbv@internetgabon.com; Chair. G. COGNON; Man. Dir DANIEL FERNÁNDEZ.

SDV Gabon: Zone Portuaire d'Owendo, BP 77, Libreville; tel. 70-26-36; fax 70-23-34; e-mail shipping.lbv@ga.dti.bollore.com; internet www.sdv.com; freight by land, sea and air.

Société Nationale d'Acconage et de Transit (SNAT): BP 3897, Libreville; tel. 70-04-04; fax 70-13-11; e-mail marc.gérard@ga.dti.bollore.com; freight transport and stevedoring; Dir-Gen. MARC GÉRARD.

Société Nationale de Transports Maritimes (SONATRAM): BP 3841, Libreville; tel. 74-44-04; fax 74-59-87; f. 1976; relaunched 1995; 51% state-owned; river and ocean cargo transport; Man. Dir RAPHAEL MOARA WALLA.

Société du Port Minéralier d'Owendo: f. 1987; majority holding by Cie Minière de l'Ogooué; management of a terminal for minerals at Owendo.

SOCOPAO–Gabon: Immeuble Socapao, Zone Portuaire d'Owendo, BP 4, Libreville; tel. 56-09-13; fax 55-45-43; e-mail socopaolibreville@vpila.fr; f. 1983; freight transport and storage; Dir DANIEL BECQUERELLE.

CIVIL AVIATION

There are international airports at Libreville, Port-Gentil and Franceville, and 65 other public and 50 private airfields, linked mostly with the forestry and petroleum industries.

Air Affaires Gabon: BP 3962, Libreville; tel. 73-25-13; fax 73-49-98; e-mail ops@snzag.com; f. 1975; domestic passenger chartered and scheduled flights; Chair. RAYMOND BELLANGER.

Air Service Gabon (ASG): BP 2232, Libreville; tel. 73-24-08; fax 73-60-69; f. 1965; charter flights; Chair. JEAN-LUC CHEVRIER; Gen. Man. FRANÇOIS LASCOMBES.

Gabon Airlines SA: Aéroport International Léon M'ba, BP 12913, Libreville; tel. 72-02-02; internet www.gabonairlines.com; f. 2006; internal and international cargo and passenger services.

Gabon Fret: BP 20384, Libreville; tel. 73-20-69; fax 73-44-44; e-mail gabonfret.gf@gabonfret.com; internet www.gabonfret.com; f. 1995; air freight handlers; Dir DOMINIQUE OYINAMONO.

Société de Gestion de l'Aéroport de Libreville (ADL): BP 363, Libreville; tel. 73-62-44; fax 73-61-28; e-mail adl@inet.ga; f. 1988; 26.5% state-owned; management of airport at Libreville; Pres. CHANTAL LIDJI BADINGA; Dir-Gen. PIERRE ANDRÉ COLLET.

Tourism

Tourist arrivals were estimated at 222,257 in 2003, and receipts from tourism totalled US $74m. in 2004. The tourism sector is being extensively developed, with new hotels and associated projects and the promotion of national parks.

Centre Gabonais de Promotion Touristique (GABONTOUR): ave du Colonel Parant, BP 2085, Libreville; tel. 72-85-04; fax 72-85-03; e-mail gabontour2006@yahoo.fr; f. 1988; Dir-Gen. LOUIS BARRY OGOULA OLINGO.

Office National Gabonais du Tourisme: BP 161, Libreville; tel. 72-21-82.

THE GAMBIA

Introductory Survey

Location, Climate, Language, Religion, Flag, Capital

The Republic of The Gambia is a narrow territory around the River Gambia on the west coast of Africa. Apart from a short coastline on the Atlantic Ocean, the country is a semi-enclave in Senegal. The climate is tropical, with a rainy season from July to September. Away from the river swamps most of the terrain is covered by savannah bush. Average temperatures in Banjul range from 23°C (73°F) in January to 27°C (81°F) in July, while temperatures inland can exceed 40°C (104°F). English is the official language, while the principal vernacular languages are Mandinka, Fula and Wolof. About 85% of the inhabitants are Muslims; most of the remainder are Christians, and there are a small number of animists. The national flag (proportions 2 by 3) has red, blue and green horizontal stripes, with two narrow white stripes bordering the central blue band. The capital is Banjul.

Recent History

Formerly administered with Sierra Leone, The Gambia became a separate British colony in 1888. Party politics rapidly gained momentum following the establishment of a universal adult franchise in 1960. Following legislative elections in May 1962, the leader of the People's Progressive Party (PPP), Dr (later Sir) Dawda Kairaba Jawara, became Premier. Full internal self-government followed in October 1963. On 18 February 1965 The Gambia became an independent country within the Commonwealth, with Jawara as Prime Minister. The country became a republic on 24 April 1970, whereupon Jawara took office as President. He was re-elected in 1972 and again in 1977.

In July 1981 a coup was attempted while Jawara was visiting the United Kingdom. Left-wing rebels formed a National Revolutionary Council and proclaimed their civilian leader, Kukoi Samba Sanyang, as Head of State. Under the terms of a mutual defence pact, Senegalese troops assisted in suppressing the rebellion.

The first presidential election by direct popular vote was held in May 1982. Jawara was re-elected, with 72% of the votes cast; he was opposed by the leader of the National Convention Party (NCP), Sheriff Mustapha Dibba. In the concurrent legislative elections the PPP won 27 of the 35 elective seats in the House of Representatives. At legislative elections in March 1987 the PPP took 31 of the 36 directly elected seats in the House of Representatives. In the presidential election Jawara was re-elected with 59% of the votes cast; Dibba received 27% of the votes, and Assan Musa Camara, a former Vice-President who had recently formed the Gambian People's Party (GPP), won 14%. Rumours of financial impropriety, corruption and the abuse of power at ministerial level persisted throughout the decade.

Plans were announced in August 1981 for a confederation of The Gambia and Senegal, to be called Senegambia. The confederal agreement came into effect in February 1982; a Confederal Council of Ministers, headed by President Abdou Diouf of Senegal (with President Jawara as his deputy), held its inaugural meeting in January 1983, as did a 60-member Confederal Assembly. Agreements followed on co-ordination of foreign policy, communications, defence and security, but Jawara was reluctant to proceed towards full economic and political integration. In August 1989 Diouf announced that Senegalese troops were to leave The Gambia, apparently in protest at a request by Jawara that The Gambia be accorded more power within the confederal structures. The confederation was dissolved in September, and a period of tension between the two countries followed: The Gambia alleged that the Senegalese authorities had introduced trade and travel restrictions, while Senegal accused The Gambia of harbouring rebels of the Mouvement des forces démocratiques de la Casamance (MFDC), an organization seeking independence for the Casamance region—which is virtually separated from the northern segment of Senegal by the enclave of The Gambia. In January 1991 the two countries signed an agreement of friendship and co-operation.

Jawara was elected for a sixth time in April 1992, receiving 58% of the votes cast, while Dibba took 22%. In elections to the House of Representatives the PPP retained a clear majority, with 25 elected members. The NCP secured six seats, the GPP two and independent candidates the remaining three.

On 22 July 1994 Jawara was deposed by a self-styled Armed Forces Provisional Ruling Council (AFPRC), a group of five young army officers led by Lt (later Col) Yahya Jammeh, in a bloodless coup. The AFPRC suspended the Constitution and banned all political activity. Jammeh pronounced himself Head of State and appointed a mixed civilian and military Government. Purges of the armed forces and public institutions were implemented, and in November it was announced that 10 of Jawara's former ministers would be tried on charges of corruption.

The AFPRC's timetable for a transition to civilian rule, published in October 1994, envisaged a programme of reform culminating in the inauguration of new elected institutions in December 1998. The length of the transition period prompted criticism both internationally and domestically. In November 1994 Jammeh commissioned a National Consultative Committee (NCC) to make recommendations regarding a possible shortening of the period of transition to civilian rule; the NCC proposed a return to civilian government in 1996.

The death penalty, abolished in April 1993, was restored by governmental decree in August 1995, reportedly in response to an increase in the murder rate. In November a government decree conferring wide powers of arrest and detention on the Minister of the Interior was issued. Although the AFPRC stated its commitment to freedom of expression, a ban on the publication of journals by political organizations was introduced shortly after the July 1994 coup. Subsequent periodic incidents of the arrest of, or fines against, journalists provoked considerable international concern, while several non-Gambian journalists were deported.

The draft of a report by a Constitutional Review Commission (established in April 1995) was published in March 1996. Despite demands by the European Union (EU, see p. 244) and the Commonwealth, as well as by individual countries that had previously been major donors to The Gambia, for an expedited return to civilian rule, the AFPRC continued to assert that it would adhere to its revised timetable. In April, however, it was announced that it would be impossible to complete the return to elected civilian government by July, and in May new dates were set for the constitutional referendum, and for presidential and legislative elections, which would now take place in August, September and December, respectively. Opponents of the AFPRC criticized provisions of the Constitution that, they alleged, had been formulated with the specific intention of facilitating Jammeh's election to the presidency (although the Head of State had frequently asserted that he would not seek election).

The constitutional referendum took place on 8 August 1996. The rate of participation was high (85.9%), and 70.4% of voters endorsed the new document. A presidential decree was issued in the following week reauthorizing party political activity. Shortly afterwards, however, a further decree (Decree 89) was promulgated, according to which all holders of executive office in the 30 years prior to July 1994 were to be prohibited from seeking public office, with the PPP, the NCP and the GPP barred from contesting the forthcoming presidential and parliamentary elections. Thus, the only parties from the Jawara era authorized to contest the elections were the People's Democratic Organization for Independence and Socialism (PDOIS) and the People's Democratic Party. The effective ban on the participation of all those associated with political life prior to the military take-over in the restoration of elected institutions was strongly criticized by the Commonwealth Ministerial Action Group on the Harare Declaration (CMAG, see p. 208), which had hitherto made a significant contribution to the transition process. At the same time the AFPRC announced that the presidential poll was to be postponed until 26 September 1996.

Jammeh formally announced his intention to contest the presidency in mid-August 1996. At the end of the month the establishment of a political party supporting Jammeh, the Alliance for Patriotic Reorientation and Construction (APRC), was reported. In early September Jammeh resigned from the army, in order to contest the presidency as a civilian, as required by the Constitution. The presidential election proceeded on 26 September. According to official results, Jammeh secured the presidency with 55.8% of the votes cast, ahead of Ousainou Darboe, the leader of the United Democratic Party (UDP), who received 35.8%. The rate of participation by voters was again high, especially in rural areas, although observers, including CMAG, expressed doubts as to the credibility of the election results. The dissolution of the AFPRC was announced the same day. Jammeh was inaugurated as President on 18 October.

Legislative elections took place on 2 January 1997 and the Gambian authorities, opposition groups and most international observers expressed broad satisfaction at the conduct of the poll. (The Commonwealth did not send observers, owing to the continued ban on former members of Jawara's administration from seeking public office.) As expected, the APRC won an overwhelming majority of seats, securing 33 elective seats (including five in which the party was unopposed). The UDP obtained seven elective seats, the National Reconciliation Party (NRP) two, the PDOIS one and independent candidates two. The overall rate of participation by voters was 73.2%. As Head of State, Jammeh was empowered by the Constitution to nominate four additional members of parliament, from whom the Speaker and Deputy Speaker would be chosen. The opening session of the National Assembly, on 16 January, denoted the full entry into force of the Constitution and thus the inauguration of the Second Republic.

Under the new Constitution, ministers of cabinet rank were designated Secretaries of State, and the Government was re-organized to this effect in March 1997. Isatou Njie-Saidy, Secretary of State for Health, Social Welfare and Women's Affairs, was appointed Vice-President. However, most of the responsibilities hitherto associated with this post were transferred to the Secretary of State for the Office of the President, a position now held by Edward Singhateh: although Singhateh had succeeded Sabally as AFPRC Vice-President in early 1995, he was, under the terms of the new Constitution, too young (at 27 years of age) to assume the office of Vice-President.

In January 1999 four cabinet members were dismissed, as was the Managing Director of the National Water and Electricity Company, amid allegations that financial mismanagement had occurred in certain government departments. In January 2000 further allegations of government corruption emerged after the disclosure in legal proceedings in the United Kingdom that significant sums of money generated by the sale of crude petroleum had been paid into an anonymous Swiss bank account. The crude petroleum had been granted to The Gambia for trading purposes by the Nigerian Government between August 1996 and June 1998, reportedly in recognition of Jammeh's opposition in 1995 to the imposition of sanctions by the Commonwealth against Nigeria. Jammeh vigorously denied any involvement in the matter.

In January 2000 the security forces announced that they had forestalled an attempted military coup, while in May five men were detained by the National Intelligence Agency in connection with an alleged plot to assassinate Jammeh and overthrow the APRC Government. After their arrest without trial was declared unconstitutional by the High Court, a total of seven men were subsequently charged with treason. The trial, which opened in December, was adjourned several times, recommencing in February 2003. By October four of the seven men had been acquitted. In July 2004 the remaining three were acquitted. Lawyers for the Government subsequently appealed against the ruling.

In August 2000 the APRC suggested that it would not be possible to hold local government elections in November, as scheduled, as the National Assembly had yet to approve the local government act. In December Jammeh dismissed Anglican Bishop Solomon Tilewa Johnson from his position as Chairman of the Independent Electoral Commission (IEC). Johnson's predecessor, Gabriel Roberts, was reappointed, despite allegations that he had been involved in fraudulent behaviour to benefit the APRC at the elections of 1996 and 1997. The dismissal of Johnson, which the opposition described as unconstitutional, followed his instigation of a court case in response to the Government's failure to enact the local government act.

In May 2001 the National Assembly and the President approved a number of constitutional amendments, which were to be submitted to a referendum. The opposition protested that the proposed changes, including the extension of the presidential term from five to seven years, the introduction of a presidential prerogative to appoint local chiefs, and the replacement of the permanent IEC with an ad hoc body, would further increase the powers of the President and precipitate acts of electoral fraud at the forthcoming parliamentary and presidential elections.

In July 2001 Jammeh announced the abrogation of Decree 89, although several prominent individuals who had participated in pre-1994 administrations, including Jawara and Sabally, remained prohibited from seeking public office. None the less, the PPP, the NCP and the GPP were subsequently re-established. In August the UDP, the PPP and the GPP formed a coalition and announced that Darboe would be its presidential candidate in the election scheduled for October. Opposition supporters and other observers claimed that the compilation of voters' lists had been accompanied by widespread fraud. In particular, concern was expressed that foreign citizens (notably Senegalese nationals of the Diola ethnic group) resident in The Gambia had been registered as eligible to vote. In the same month the Secretary of State for Foreign Affairs, Sedate Jobe, resigned, reportedly in connection with the recent expulsion from The Gambia of a British diplomat (see below). Blaise Baboucar Jagne, Secretary of State for Foreign Affairs in 1995–96, was reappointed to the post.

A number of violent incidents were reported during the week before the presidential election. In Serrekunda, a suburb of Banjul, members of the security forces fired shots in order to disperse a rally by supporters of Darboe, and one person was killed during clashes between opposition supporters and soldiers. Nevertheless, the presidential election was held, as scheduled, on 18 October 2001. Controversy was provoked by a reported relaxation in identification requirements for voters, and a turn-out of some 90% was recorded. Jammeh was re-elected to the presidency, with 52.8% of the votes cast, according to official results, ahead of Darboe, who won 32.6% of the votes. Although Darboe conceded defeat, members of the opposition subsequently disputed the legitimacy of the results, reiterating claims of incorrect practice in the distribution of voting credentials and in the counting of ballots. None the less, international observers described the poll as being largely free and fair.

Following the election, a number of eminent opposition figures were arrested. In October 2001 a leading Gambian human rights activist, Lamin Sillah, was detained after he alleged that members of the opposition had been subject to harassment and sustained detention. Subsequent reports suggested that up to 60 opposition supporters had been arrested in the week after the election, and that the homes of prominent members of the UDP had been attacked, allegedly by members of the youth wing of the APRC. Following pressure from international human rights campaigners, Sillah was released. In early November Darboe announced his party's intention to take legal action to secure the release of UDP activists who remained in prison. Meanwhile, the IEC announced the postponement of the referendum on proposed constitutional changes. In late December, at his inauguration, President Jammeh granted an unconditional amnesty to Jawara, guaranteeing the former President's security should he decide to return to The Gambia.

In December 2001 the UDP-PPP-GPP coalition announced that it would boycott legislative elections scheduled for January 2002, as a result of the alleged addition of some 50,000 foreign citizens to electoral lists and the reputed transfer of voters between the electoral lists of different constituencies. Having denied these accusations, the IEC announced that the APRC had secured 33 of the 48 elective seats in the enlarged National Assembly, in constituencies where the party was unopposed owing to the boycott. At the elections, which took place on 17 January, the APRC won 12 of the 15 contested seats, giving the party an overall total of 45 elective seats; the PDOIS obtained two seats, and the NRP one. Electoral turn-out was reportedly low. An additional five members of parliament were appointed by President Jammeh, in accordance with the Constitution. Dibba, whose NCP had formed an alliance with the APRC prior to the elections, was appointed Speaker of the new National Assembly.

The long-delayed municipal elections, which were finally held in April 2002, were boycotted by the UDP and the PDOIS; consequently, the APRC was unopposed in some 85 of the 113 local seats, and won a total of 99 seats, securing control of all seven regional authorities. The NRP was the only other political organization to gain representation in local government in the elections, winning five seats; the remaining nine seats were secured by independent candidates. In early May the National Assembly approved legislation that imposed stricter regulations over the print media, in accordance with which all journalists not working for the state-controlled media would be required to register with a National Media Commission. The law was condemned by the Gambia Press Union, which announced that it would not co-operate with the Commission. In early June Jawara returned to The Gambia from exile; at the end of the month he was officially received by Jammeh and later tendered his resignation as leader of the PPP. In July legislation was adopted that allowed Jammeh to appoint up to 20 secretaries of state to his Cabinet, instead of 15.

In August 2002 a senior member of the UDP, Lamine Wa Juwara, alleged that the party's campaign funds had been diverted prior to the April elections to pay for Darboe's outstanding income-tax debts. The UDP expelled Juwara, accusing him of trying to challenge Darboe for the leadership, and in mid-October Juwara formed a new party, the National Democratic Action Movement (NDAM). In November the opposition UDP-PPP-GPP coalition split, following the resignation of its Chairman, Assan Musa Camara, while President Jammeh dismissed a number of members of his Cabinet, accusing them of lacking seriousness.

In September 2003 Joseph Henry Joof resigned as Secretary of State for Justice and Attorney-General, and President Jammeh dismissed Badjie and Famara Jatta, the Secretary of State for Finance and Economic Affairs. Bakary Njie, the Secretary of State for Communication, Information and Technology, was removed from his post in October. In the same month the President launched an anti-corruption drive, named 'Operation No Compromise', which led to a number of high-profile arrests. In November Baba Jobe, the leader of the APRC in the National Assembly, was charged with fraud. (In April 2004 he was sentenced to nine years in prison.) In December 2003 Yankuba Touray, appointed to replace Njie as Secretary of State for Communication, Information and Technology, was dismissed from the Government.

In June 2003 the National Media Commission was created, despite continuing opposition from journalists, and was given far-reaching powers, including the authority to imprison journalists for terms of up to six months. It was originally envisaged that media organizations would have to register with the Commission by 14 May 2004; however, following a self-imposed week-long media blackout, the deadline was extended by three months. Reports continued throughout 2003 and 2004 of journalists being arrested or subjected to harassment. In September 2003 the editor-in-chief of *The Independent*, Abdoulaye Sey, was reportedly detained for four days, shortly after the newspaper published an article criticizing Jammeh. In October the newspaper's offices in Banjul were set on fire and in April 2004 the printing press was destroyed. In early December legislation providing for terms of imprisonment of up to three years for journalists found guilty of libel or sedition, and obliging members of the media to re-register with the state, was approved by the National Assembly, despite protests by members of the Gambian and international media. In mid-December Deyda Hydara, the editor of the independent newspaper *The Point*, who had been severely critical of the new legislation, was murdered in Banjul. The incident precipitated a demonstration in the capital, reportedly attended by several hundred journalists, and later that month a one-week media strike was observed. In January 2005 Reporters sans frontières called for an independent commission to be established to investigate the murder of Hydara and maintained that it had been carried out by a contract killer. In March it was claimed that the new legislation had been signed into law by Jammeh on 28 December 2004, although not published until March 2005, thus contravening the Constitution, which stated that legislation must be published within 30 days of promulgation.

Meanwhile, in October 2003 Juwara was arrested on a charge of sedition, after urging Gambians to demonstrate in protest at price rises. Although his arrest was later ruled to be illegal, in mid-December his bail was revoked, and he was once again taken into custody. In mid-February 2004 Juwara was sentenced to six months' imprisonment; an appeal against the ruling was filed later that month and he was eventually released in June.

In March 2005 a report by the Presidential Anti-Corruption Commission of Inquiry led to the dismissal of government officials and the establishment of the Public Accountability and Anti-Corruption Unit, the purpose of which was to monitor and control corruption.

Meanwhile, in January 2005 the National Alliance for Democracy and Development (NADD), a coalition of five opposition parties comprising the UDP, the NRP, the NDAM, the PDOIS and the PPP, was formed with the aim of presenting a single candidate to contest the presidential election scheduled to take place in late 2006. In June 2005 four deputies, among them three opposition leaders—Hamat Bah of the NRP and Sidia Jatta and Halifa Sallah of the PDOIS—were expelled from the National Assembly following their registration as members of the NADD. According to Gambian law, deputies are not permitted to switch allegiance between political parties during the term of a parliament. By-elections to the vacant seats were held in September at which the NADD retained three of the contested constituencies, while the APRC took the remaining seat. In November Bah and Sallah, along with another senior member of the NADD, Omar Jallow, were arrested and charged with sedition. They were released on bail in mid-December and in February 2006 all charges against them were dropped. However, in the same month a rift in the NADD became apparent, with the NRP and the UDP withdrawing and forming a new coalition.

In March 2006 it was reported that the security forces had discovered plans to stage a coup. The Chief of Staff of the Armed Forces, Lt-Col Ndure Cham, was implicated in the plot, and was subsequently reported to have fled to Senegal. It was alleged that other current and former government officials as well as members of the military and the security forces were involved, and at least 27 people were arrested. (Five of the suspects were reported to have escaped in the following month, although it was speculated that they may have been executed.) The Chairman of the National Assembly, Sheriff Dibba, was among those implicated and was succeeded in that office by Belinda Bidwell. In October the trial for treason of several of the accused plotters was transferred to a military tribunal; in May 2007 10 of the accused were convicted and sentenced to terms ranging from 10 years to life imprisonment.

In mid-July 2006 the Chairman of the IEC was unexpectedly dismissed from office. It was subsequently announced that a presidential election was to be held on 22 September. President Jammeh won 67.33% of the votes cast, with a voter participation rate of 59%. His nearest rival was Darboe (candidate for the UDP, the NRP and the Gambia Party for Democracy and Progress) with 26.69%, while Halifa Sallah of the NADD was placed third with some 5.98%. As occurred during previous presidential elections, unrest erupted in neighbouring regions of Senegal and refugees from there—who were of the same ethnicity as Jammeh—were permitted to register and vote in The Gambia. In late October a new Cabinet, appointed by Jammeh, was sworn into office; Jammeh was inaugurated as President on 15 December.

Legislative elections took place on 25 January 2007, at which the ruling APRC won 42 seats, the UDP took four seats, the NADD one seat and an independent candidate one seat. Halifa Sallah of the NADD and Hamat Bah of the NRP failed to be re-elected to the National Assembly. The rate of voter participation was officially recorded at 41.7%. In the following month Belinda Bidwell was replaced as Chairman of that body by Fatoumata Jahumpa-Ceesay, and Susan Waffa-Ogoo was relieved of her duties as Secretary of State for Trade, Industry and Employment. In April the NDAM withdrew from the NADD.

A Cabinet reorganization was effected in September 2007 in which Crispin Grey-Johnson was appointed Secretary of State for Foreign Affairs and National Assembly Matters, while Ousman Jammeh assumed the newly created petroleum, energy and mineral resources portfolio. Further governmental changes were implemented in November when Secretary of State for Health and Social Welfare Dr Tamsir Mbowe was dismissed. Although no official reason was given, Mbowe was earlier reported to have made controversial claims that President Jammeh had succeeded in finding a cure for HIV/AIDS. The relationship between the two had become increasingly strained in the period leading to Mbowe's removal. The following month Maj. Dr Malick Njie was named as Mbowe's successor.

After the 1994 coup The Gambia's traditional aid donors and trading partners suspended much co-operation, although vital aid projects generally continued. The Jammeh administration therefore sought new links: diplomatic relations with Libya, severed in 1980, were restored in November 1994, and numerous co-operation agreements ensued. Links with the Republic of China (Taiwan), ended in 1974, were re-established in July 1995, whereupon Taiwan became one of The Gambia's major sources of funding.

Despite the presence in Senegal of prominent opponents of his Government, Jammeh also sought to improve relations with that country, and in January 1996 the two countries signed an agreement aimed at increasing bilateral trade and at minimizing cross-border smuggling; a further trade agreement was concluded in April 1997. In June the two countries agreed to take joint measures to combat insecurity, illegal immigration, arms-trafficking and drugs-smuggling. In January 1998 the Government of Senegal welcomed an offer by Jammeh to mediate in the conflict in the southern province of Casamance: the separatist MFDC is chiefly composed of the Diola ethnic group, of which Jammeh is a member. In December 2000 the Gambian Government sent a delegation to participate in talks between the MFDC and the Senegalese Government. At the end of 2002 there were some 4,230 refugees from Casamance resident in The Gambia, although by late 2004 only 500 were registered with the Office of the UN High Commissioner for Refugees. A dispute between the two countries arose in August 2005 when Gambian authorities increased the price of the ferry across the Gambia river at Banjul and in retaliation Senegalese lorry drivers commenced a blockade of the common border. The conflict was resolved in October, under the mediation of the Nigerian President, Olusegun Obasanjo, and an agreement was reached to build a bridge over the Gambia river. However, renewed fighting in Senegal's Casamance province from March 2006 resulted in the movement of some 10,000 refugees into The Gambia, including a number of rebel leaders sought by the Senegalese authorities.

In June 1998 Jammeh offered to mediate in the conflict between the Government and rebel forces in Guinea-Bissau (q.v.); the rebel leader, Brig. Ansumane Mané, was a Diola of Gambian extraction. In January 1999 The Gambia agreed to provide troops for an ECOMOG peace-keeping mission of the Economic Community of West African States (see p. 232) in Guinea-Bissau. After the defeat of government forces in Guinea-Bissau in May 1999, the Gambian authorities secured the safe passage of former President Vieira to The Gambia, from where he departed for Portugal. The killing of Mané in December 2000 was widely regarded as a serious set-back for Gambian foreign policy. In June 2002 relations with Guinea-Bissau were strained after President Kumba Yalá of Guinea-Bissau threatened to invade The Gambia, accusing Jammeh of involvement in a failed coup attempt in May and of support for the Casamance rebels. An exchange of visits by the foreign ministers of the two countries, followed by UN intervention in July, relieved the tension, however; relations had improved further by September, when Yalá visited Banjul.

Relations with the United Kingdom were strained in 2001, following the expulsion of the British Deputy High Commissioner, Bharat Joshi, from The Gambia in late August. The Gambian authorities alleged that the diplomat had interfered in the country's internal affairs, following his attendance at an opposition meeting, but emphasized the action had been taken against Joshi, and not the United Kingdom. However, in late September the Gambian Deputy High Commissioner in London was expelled from the United Kingdom, and further retaliatory measures were implemented against The Gambia. Relations were restored during 2002, although in January of that year the EU representative, George Marc-André, was declared *persona non grata* by the Gambian authorities and requested to leave the country.

The Gambia is a member of the Community of Sahel-Saharan States—CEN-SAD (see p. 411).

Government

The Constitution of the Second Republic of The Gambia, which was approved in a national referendum on 8 August 1996, entered into full effect on 16 January 1997. Under its terms, the Head of State is the President of the Republic, who is directly elected by universal adult suffrage. No restriction is placed on the number of times a President may seek re-election. Legislative authority is vested in the National Assembly, elected for a five-year term and comprising 48 members elected by direct suffrage and five members nominated by the President of the Republic. The President appoints government members, who are responsible both to the Head of State and to the National Assembly. The Gambia is divided into eight local government areas.

Defence

As assessed at November 2007, the Gambian National Army comprised 800 men (including a marine unit of about 70 and a presidential guard) in active service. At that time Gambian observers and/or troops were deployed in UN missions in Côte d'Ivoire, Ethiopia, Eritrea, Liberia, Nepal and Sudan. Military service has been mainly voluntary; however, the Constitution of the Second Republic, which entered into full effect in January 1997, makes provision for compulsory service. The defence budget for 2006 was estimated at D45m.

Economic Affairs

In 2006, according to estimates by the World Bank, The Gambia's gross national income (GNI), measured at average 2004–06 prices, was US $488m., equivalent to $310 per head (or $1,970 on an international purchasing-power parity basis). During 1996–2006, it was estimated, the population increased at an average annual rate of 3.0%, while gross domestic product (GDP) per head increased by 1.4%. Overall GDP increased, in real terms, at an average annual rate of 4.4% in 1996–2006; GDP increased by 4.5% in 2006.

Agriculture (including forestry and fishing) contributed an estimated 33.0% of GDP in 2005. About 77.3% of the labour force were employed in the sector in mid-2005. The dominant agricultural activity has traditionally been the cultivation of groundnuts and exports of that commodity accounted for an estimated 68.2% of domestic export earnings in 1999. However, according to the IMF, that figure declined to an estimated 13.3% of total exports (including re-exports) in 2004, following a drought which destroyed over 50% of the 2001/02 harvest. Groundnuts accounted for just 1.3% of total exports in 2005. The significant decline was attributed to poor production (owing to transport problems) and a change in licensing requirements that left just one company in operation in the sector. A significant proportion of the groundnut crop is frequently smuggled for sale in Senegal. Cotton, citrus fruits, mangoes, avocados and sesame seed are also cultivated for export. The principal staple crops are millet, maize, rice and sorghum, although The Gambia remains heavily dependent on imports of rice and other basic foodstuffs. Fishing makes an important contribution to the domestic food supply. In 2001 the Government announced the construction of a major new fishing port in Banjul, at a cost of US $10m. According to the World Bank, agricultural GDP increased at an average annual rate of 5.7% in 1996–2006; growth of 4.5% was recorded in 2006.

Industry (including manufacturing, construction, mining and power) contributed an estimated 13.0% of GDP in 2005. About 9.7% of the labour force were employed in the sector at the time of the 1993 census. According to African Development Bank (ADB) figures, industrial GDP increased at an average annual rate of 4.8% in 1996–2006; growth in 2006 was 5.9%.

The Gambia has no economically viable mineral resources, although seismic surveys have indicated the existence of petroleum deposits off shore. Deposits of kaolin and salt are currently unexploited.

Manufacturing contributed an estimated 5.1% of GDP in 2005, and employed about 6.3% of the labour force in 1993. The sector is dominated by agro-industrial activities, most importantly the processing of groundnuts and fish. Beverages and construction materials are also produced for the domestic market. According to the ADB, manufacturing GDP increased at an average annual rate of 3.0% in 1996–2006; growth in 2006 was 6.0%.

The Gambia is highly reliant on imported energy. According to the IMF, imports of fuel and energy comprised an estimated 10.1% of the value of total merchandise imports in 2004.

The services sector contributed an estimated 53.9% of GDP in 2005. The tourism industry is of particular significance as a generator of foreign exchange. Tourism contributed about 10% of annual GDP in the early 1990s, and employed about one-third of workers in the formal sector at that time. The international response to the 1994 coup and its aftermath had a severe impact on tourism, although the industry recovered strongly from 1996 onwards. The Jammeh administration has expressed its intention further to exploit the country's potential as a transit point for regional trade and also as a centre for regional finance and telecommunications. The GDP of the services sector increased at an average annual rate of 5.2% in 1996–2006; growth in 2006 was 4.5%.

In 2006 The Gambia recorded an estimated visible trade deficit of US $113.2m., while there was a deficit of $72.3m. on the current account of the balance of payments. In 2005 the principal source of imports was the People's Republic of China, which supplied an estimated 21.3% of total imports; other major sources were Senegal, Côte d'Ivoire and the USA. The largest market for exports in that year was India (an estimated 40.4% of total exports). The Gambia's principal domestic exports in 2005 were cotton and groundnut products. The principal imports in 2004 were food and live animals, machinery and transport equipment, mineral fuels and lubricants, chemicals and beverages and tobacco.

THE GAMBIA

In 2006, according to the IMF, there was an overall budget deficit of D879m. (equivalent to 6.2% of GDP). The Gambia's total external debt was US $671.7m. at the end of 2005, of which $626.4m. was long-term public debt. In that year the cost of debt-servicing was equivalent to 12.0% of the value of exports of goods and services. The average annual rate of inflation was 9.4% in 2000–05; consumer prices increased by an average of 3.1% in 2005. The rate of unemployment was estimated at some 26% of the labour force in mid-1994.

The Gambia is a member of the Economic Community of West African States (ECOWAS, see p. 232), of the Gambia River Basin Development Organization (OMVG, see p. 412), of the African Groundnut Council (see p. 407), of the West Africa Rice Development Association (WARDA, see p. 410), and of the Permanent Inter-State Committee on Drought Control in the Sahel (CILSS, see p. 414).

Although the installation of elected civilian institutions in early 1997 prompted the international economic community to recommence full support, which had been partially suspended following the military coup of July 1994, in December 2003 the IMF suspended Poverty Reduction and Growth Facility (PRGF) assistance due to concerns at the deteriorating economic situation and alleged inaccuracies in economic data provided by the Gambian authorities. Additionally, in 2004 and 2005 IMF missions were critical of the Government's lack of macroeconomic policies, and recommended the introduction of a comprehensive economic programme. However, in early 2007 the Gambian authorities were praised by the IMF for stabilizing the economy over the previous three years, with greater control of monetary policy aiding inflation and exchange rate stability. The IMF therefore approved a three-year arrangement under the PRGF for US $21m. In October 2007 the World Bank approved a grant worth some $3m. for the Capacity Building for Economic Change Project, while later that year the African Development Fund approved a grant worth $2.2m. for the Institutional Support Project for Economic and Financial Governance, which aims to reduce poverty through measures to increase capacity in public bodies. The Gambia's overriding dependence on the largely unmodernized groundnut sector remains an obstacle to sustained growth, although the gradual introduction of reforms, which sought to improve relations between public- and private-sector interests, and between production and marketing interests, in the sector, commenced in 2000. Poor export figures for groundnuts in 2005 led to reduced GDP growth of 5.1%, compared with 7.0% in the previous year, although in 2004–06 growth still averaged 6.2% annually, driven by the tourism, construction and communications sectors. None the less, concern remains at the level of borrowing incurred by the Jammeh Government to finance its extensive infrastructural programme.

The 2007 budget projected a surplus—the first in several years—of D472m., with 87.5% of total revenue derived from taxation. GDP growth for 2007 was estimated at 7.0%, with growth in 2008 forecast to slow to 6.0%, according to IMF figures.

Education

Primary education, beginning at seven years of age, is free but not compulsory and lasts for nine years. It is divided into two cycles of six and three years. Secondary education, from 16 years of age, comprises two cycles, lasting three and two years. According to UNESCO estimates, in 2003/04 total enrolment at primary schools included 75% of children in the relevant age-group (boys 73%; girls 77%), while secondary enrolment included 45% of the appropriate age-group (boys 49%; girls 41%). The Jammeh administration has, since 1994, embarked on an ambitious project to improve educational facilities and levels of attendance and attainment. A particular aim has been to ameliorate access to schools for pupils in rural areas. Post-secondary education is available in teacher training, agriculture, health and technical subjects. Some 1,591 students were enrolled at tertiary establishments in 1994/95. The University of The Gambia, at Banjul, was officially opened in 2000. In 1977 The Gambia introduced Koranic studies at all stages of education, and many children attend Koranic schools (daara). In 2004 current expenditure by the central Government on education was an estimated D224.3m., equivalent to 17.5% of non-interest current expenditure.

Public Holidays

2008: 1 January (New Year's Day), 19 January (Ashoura), 18 February (Independence Day), 20 March* (Eid al-Moulid, Birth of the Prophet), 21 March (Good Friday), 24 March (Easter Monday), 1 May (Workers' Day), 22 July (Anniversary of the Second Republic), 15 August (Assumption/St Mary's Day), 1 October* (Eid al-Fitr, end of Ramadan), 9 December* (Eid al-Kebir, Feast of the Sacrifice), 25 December (Christmas).

2009: 1 January (New Year's Day), 7 January (Ashoura), 18 February (Independence Day), 9 March* (Eid al-Moulid, Birth of the Prophet), 10 April (Good Friday), 13 April (Easter Monday), 1 May (Workers' Day), 22 July (Anniversary of the Second Republic), 15 August (Assumption/St Mary's Day), 20 September* (Eid al-Fitr, end of Ramadan), 27 November* (Eid al-Kebir, Feast of the Sacrifice), 25 December (Christmas).

* These holidays are dependent on the Islamic lunar calendar and may vary by one or two days from the dates given.

Weights and Measures

Imperial weights and measures are used. Importers and traders also use the metric system.

Statistical Survey

Sources (unless otherwise stated): Department of Information Services, 14 Daniel Goddard St, Banjul; tel. 4225060; fax 4227230; Central Statistics Department, Central Bank Building, 1/2 Ecowas Ave, Banjul; tel. 4228364; fax 4228903; e-mail director@csd.gm; internet www.gambia.gm/Statistics/statistics.html.

Area and Population

AREA, POPULATION AND DENSITY

Area (sq km)	11,295*
Population (census results)	
15 April 1993	1,038,145
15 April 2003†	
Males	687,781
Females	676,726
Total	1,364,507
Population (UN estimate at mid-year)‡	
2005	1,617,000
2006	1,663,000
2007	1,709,000
Density (per sq km) at mid-2007	151.3

* 4,361 sq miles.
† Provisional.
‡ Source: UN, *World Population Prospects: The 2006 Revision*.

ETHNIC GROUPS

1993 census (percentages): Mandinka 39.60; Fula 18.83; Wolof 14.61; Jola 10.66; Serahule 8.92; Serere 2.77; Manjago 1.85; Bambara 0.84; Creole/Aku 0.69; Others 1.23.

ADMINISTRATIVE DIVISIONS
(population at 2003 census, provisional results)

Banjul	34,828	Kanifing	322,410
Basse	183,033	Kerewan	172,806
Brikama	392,987	Kuntaur	79,098
Georgetown	106,799	Mansakonko	72,546

THE GAMBIA

PRINCIPAL TOWNS
(population at 1993 census)

Serrekunda	151,450	Lamin		10,668
Brikama	42,480	Gunjur		9,983
Banjul (capital)	42,407	Basse		9,265
Bakau	38,062	Soma		7,925
Farafenni	21,142	Bansang		5,405
Sukuta	16,667			

Mid-2007 (incl. suburbs, UN estimate): Banjul 406,000 (Source: UN, *World Urbanization Prospects: The 2007 Revision*).

BIRTHS AND DEATHS
(annual averages, UN estimates)

	1990–95	1995–2000	2000–05
Birth rate (per 1,000)	42.7	40.6	38.1
Death rate (per 1,000)	14.1	12.3	11.2

Source: UN, *World Population Prospects: The 2006 Revision*.

Expectation of life (years at birth, WHO estimates): 55.1 (males 53.4; females 56.8) in 2005 (Source: WHO, *World Health Statistics*).

ECONOMICALLY ACTIVE POPULATION*
(persons aged 10 years and over, 1993 census)

	Males	Females	Total
Agriculture, hunting and forestry	82,886	92,806	175,692
Fishing	5,610	450	6,060
Mining and quarrying	354	44	398
Manufacturing	18,729	2,953	21,682
Electricity, gas and water supply	1,774	84	1,858
Construction	9,530	149	9,679
Wholesale and retail trade; repair of motor vehicles, motorcycles and personal and household goods	33,281	15,460	48,741
Hotels and restaurants	3,814	2,173	5,987
Transport, storage and communications	13,421	782	14,203
Financial intermediation	1,843	572	2,415
Other community, social and personal service activities	25,647	15,607	41,254
Activities not adequately defined	10,421	6,991	17,412
Total labour force	207,310	138,071	345,381

* Figures exclude persons seeking work for the first time, but include other unemployed persons.

Mid-2005 (estimates in '000): Agriculture, etc. 597; Total labour force 772 (Source: FAO).

Health and Welfare

KEY INDICATORS

Total fertility rate (children per woman, 2005)	4.5
Under-5 mortality rate (per 1,000 live births, 2005)	137
HIV/AIDS (% of persons aged 15–49, 2005)	2.4
Physicians (per 1,000 head, 2003)	0.11
Hospital beds (per 1,000 head, 2005)	0.8
Health expenditure (2004): US $ per head (PPP)	87.5
Health expenditure (2004): % of GDP	6.8
Health expenditure (2004): public (% of total)	27.1
Access to water (% of persons, 2004)	82
Access to sanitation (% of persons, 2004)	53
Human Development Index (2005): ranking	155
Human Development Index (2005): value	0.502

For sources and definitions, see explanatory note on p. vi.

Agriculture

PRINCIPAL CROPS
('000 metric tons)

	2004	2005	2006*
Rice (paddy)	32.6†	17.9	31.0
Maize	29.2	29.0	45.0
Millet	132.5	127.6	153.1
Sorghum	29.0	30.5	26.7
Cassava (Manioc)*	7.5	7.6	7.5
Groundnuts (in shell)	135.7	107.0†	100.0
Oil palm fruit*	35.0	35.0	35.0
Guavas, mangoes and mangosteens*	0.7	0.7	0.6

* FAO estimates.
† Unofficial estimate.

Aggregate production ('000 metric tons, may include official, semi-official or estimated data): Total cereals 223.9 in 2004, 205.6 in 2005, 256.4 in 2006; Total pulses 3.2 in 2004, 3.2 in 2005, 3.2 in 2006; Total vegetables (incl. melons) 9.0 in 2004, 9.0 in 2005, 9.0 in 2006; Total fruits (excl. melons) 4.3 in 2004, 4.3 in 2005, 4.2 in 2006.

Source: FAO.

LIVESTOCK
('000 head, year ending September, FAO estimates)

	2003	2004	2005
Cattle	327.0	328.0	330.0
Goats	262.0	265.0	270.0
Sheep	146.0	147.0	148.0
Pigs	17.5	17.8	19.0
Asses, mules or hinnies	35.0	35.0	35.0
Horses	17.0	17.0	17.0
Chickens	600	620	650

2006: Figures assumed to be unchanged from 2005 (FAO estimates).

Source: FAO.

LIVESTOCK PRODUCTS
('000 metric tons, FAO estimates)

	2004	2005	2006
Cattle meat	3.2	3.2	3.3
Goat meat	0.7	0.7	0.8
Sheep meat	0.4	0.4	0.4
Chicken meat	0.9	1.0	1.0
Game meat	1.0	1.0	1.1
Cows' milk	7.6	7.7	7.8
Hen eggs	0.7	0.7	0.8

Source: FAO.

Forestry

ROUNDWOOD REMOVALS
('000 cubic metres, excluding bark, FAO estimates)

	2004	2005	2006
Sawlogs, veneer logs and logs for sleepers*	106	106	106
Other industrial wood†	7	7	7
Fuel wood	638	647	656
Total	751	760	769

* Assumed to be unchanged since 1994.
† Assumed to be unchanged since 1993.

Source: FAO.

THE GAMBIA

Fishing

('000 metric tons, live weight of capture)

	2003	2004	2005
Tilapias	1.1	1.1	1.1
Hairtails, scabbardfishes, etc.	0.0	4.0	3.0
Sea catfishes	0.7	0.8	0.8
Bonga shad	22.1	16.8	18.0
Sharks, rays, skates	1.1	0.5	0.5
Total catch*	36.9	31.4	32.0

* FAO estimates.
Source: FAO.

Mining

	2003	2004*	2005*
Clay (metric tons)	12,375	13,655	13,700
Laterites (metric tons)	227	245	250
Silica sand ('000 metric tons)	1,534	1,389	1,390
Zircon (metric tons)	13†	—	—

* Estimate.
† Data derived from sales figures.
Source: US Geological Survey.

Industry

SELECTED PRODUCTS
('000 metric tons, unless otherwise stated)

	2003	2004	2005
Palm oil—unrefined*	2.5	2.5	2.5
Groundnut oil*	24.0	38.5	34.8
Beer of millet*	50.4	55.4	55.4
Electric energy (million kWh)†	150.3	128.1	156.3

* FAO estimates.
† State Department for Trade, Industry and Employment.
Source: mainly FAO.

Finance

CURRENCY AND EXCHANGE RATES

Monetary Units
100 butut = 1 dalasi (D).

Sterling, Dollar and Euro Equivalents (31 December 2007)
£1 sterling = 45.1555 dalasi;
US $1 = 22.5394 dalasi;
€1 = 33.1802 dalasi;
1,000 dalasi = £22.15 = $44.37 = €30.14.

Average Exchange Rate (dalasi per US $)
2005   28.575
2006   28.066
2007   24.875

Statistical Survey

BUDGET
(million dalasi)

Revenue*	2005	2006	2007†
Tax revenue	2,263	2,691	3,093
Direct taxes	682	803	929
Domestic taxes on goods and services	375	475	576
Taxes on international trade	1,206	1,413	1,588
Non-tax revenue	340	330	441
Total	2,603	3,021	3,535

Expenditure‡	2005	2006	2007†
Current expenditure	2,420	2,584	2,653
Wages and salaries	554	653	724
Other goods and services	736	1,010	1,147
Interest payments	1,131	921	782
Internal	890	689	585
External	241	232	197
Capital expenditure	1,450	1,493	1,339
Gambia Local Fund	106	77	151
External loans	1,138	1,176	634
External grants	203	240	554
Total	3,870	4,077	3,992

* Excluding grants received (million dalasi): 220 in 2005; 240 in 2006; 1,001 in 2007.
† Projected figures.
‡ Excluding lending minus repayments (million dalasi): –30 in 2005; 63 in 2006; 72 in 2007.

Source: IMF, *The Gambia: Second Review Under the Three-Year Arrangement Under the Poverty Reduction and Growth Facility, and Request for Waiver and Modification of Performance Criteria - Staff Report; Press Release on the Executive Board Discussion; and Statement by the Executive Director for The Gambia* (February 2008).

INTERNATIONAL RESERVES
(US $ million at 31 December)

	2004	2005	2006
IMF special drawing rights	0.75	0.16	1.46
Reserve position in IMF	2.31	2.12	2.23
Foreign exchange	80.72	96.03	116.92
Total	83.77	98.31	120.61

Source: IMF, *International Financial Statistics*.

MONEY SUPPLY
(million dalasi at 31 December)

	2004	2005	2006
Currency outside banks	1,416.27	1,424.20	1,937.30
Demand deposits at commercial banks	1,691.34	1,896.41	2,248.10
Total money	3,107.61	3,320.61	4,185.40

Source: IMF, *International Financial Statistics*.

COST OF LIVING
(Consumer Price Index for Banjul and Kombo St Mary's; base: 1974 = 100)

	1997	1998	1999
Food	1,511.8	1,565.8	1,628.8
Fuel and light	2,145.8	1,854.9	2,076.0
Clothing*	937.5	981.8	999.9
Rent	1,409.6	1,431.3	1,428.6
All items (incl. others)	1,441.5	1,457.3	1,512.8

* Including household linen.

All items (Consumer Price Index for Banjul and Kombo St Mary's; base: 2000 = 100): 132.8 in 2003; 151.7 in 2004; 156.5 in 2005. (Source: ILO).

THE GAMBIA

NATIONAL ACCOUNTS
(million dalasi at current prices)

Expenditure on the Gross Domestic Product

	2003	2004	2005
Government final consumption expenditure	877.7	986.2	1,310.9
Private final consumption expenditure	8,121.6	9,913.7	10,999.7
Increase in stocks	1,953.6	3,259.7	3,464.7
Gross fixed capital formation			
Total domestic expenditure	10,952.9	14,159.5	15,775.3
Exports of goods and services	4,739.3	6,067.5	6,815.8
Less Imports of goods and services	5,666.3	8,190.5	9,215.3
Statistical discrepancy	—	—	195.9
GDP in purchasers' values	10,025.9	12,036.6	13,179.9
GDP at constant 1976/77 prices	809.1	850.1	892.4

Gross Domestic Product by Economic Activity

	2003	2004	2005
Agriculture, hunting, forestry and fishing	2,822.4	3,610.0	3,899.6
Manufacturing	485.4	582.8	617.9
Electricity and water	123.7	117.4	128.9
Construction and mining	665.1	751.0	818.5
Trade	1,012.7	1,151.3	1,230.4
Restaurants and hotels	611.4	753.1	836.3
Transport and communications	1,740.8	2,073.9	2,404.7
Real estate and business services	567.1	658.6	714.2
Government services	712.9	810.0	872.5
Other services	344.8	400.5	421.6
GDP at factor cost	9,086.3	10,908.5	11,944.7
Indirect taxes, *less* subsidies	939.7	1,128.1	1,235.3
GDP in purchasers' values	10,025.9	12,036.6	13,179.9

Source: IMF, *The Gambia: Selected Issues and Statistical Appendix* (March 2007).

BALANCE OF PAYMENTS
(US $ million, year ending 30 June)

	2004	2005	2006
Exports of goods f.o.b.	109.16	100.98	108.68
Imports of goods f.o.b.	−207.24	−215.47	−221.84
Trade balance	−98.08	−114.49	−113.16
Exports of services	73.14	79.58	91.92
Imports of services	−45.72	−45.38	−93.92
Balance on goods and services	−70.66	−80.30	−115.15
Other income received	1.78	3.13	4.48
Other income paid	−29.57	−35.37	−42.35
Balance on goods, services and income	−98.45	−112.54	−153.02
Current transfers received	78.23	88.01	107.42
Current transfers paid	−24.24	−25.90	−26.70
Current balance	−44.46	−50.44	−72.30
Capital account (net)	5.15	0.58	—
Direct investment from abroad	56.75	51.93	82.07
Other investment assets	−15.37	13.60	−14.08
Investment liabilities	5.56	2.93	10.44
Net errors and omissions	−8.88	−54.32	−6.23
Overall balance	−1.24	−35.73	−0.09

Source: IMF, *International Financial Statistics*.

External Trade

PRINCIPAL COMMODITIES
(US $ '000)

Imports c.i.f.	2002	2003	2004
Food and live animals	37,581	40,456	64,687
Beverages and tobacco	8,231	8,592	12,374
Mineral fuels, lubricants, etc.	17,008	21,777	23,921
Animal and vegetable oils	6,078	6,104	11,404
Chemicals	16,201	9,965	17,414
Machinery and transport equipment	27,262	26,325	42,778
Miscellaneous manufactured articles	15,563	14,559	24,536
Total (incl. others)	160,105	152,607	236,604

2005: Total imports (US $ '000) 279,657.

Exports f.o.b.	2003	2004	2005*
Groundnut products	9,143	16,896	1,860
Fruit and vegetables	5,100	6	77
Fish and fish products	421	—	—
Cotton products	235	6,045	6,683
Total (incl. others†)	106,986	127,044	144,465

* Preliminary figures.
† Of which, re-exports: 83,454 in 2003; 101,190 in 2004; 132,733 in 2005.

Source: IMF, *The Gambia: Selected Issues and Statistical Appendix* (March 2007).

PRINCIPAL TRADING PARTNERS
(US $ million)

Imports c.i.f.	2001	2002	2003
Belgium	6.1	4.1	4.3
Brazil	5.4	7.9	5.9
China, People's Repub.	8.6	6.6	8.3
Côte d'Ivoire	10.7	5.7	5.1
Cyprus	2.1	0.5	1.8
Denmark	1.2	1.3	3.3
France (incl. Monaco)	8.2	8.0	10.2
Germany	34.3	61.2	58.8
Hong Kong	3.7	2.2	3.9
India	2.7	3.8	5.7
Italy	2.1	2.1	2.9
Japan	2.8	4.0	2.4
Netherlands	7.9	3.3	4.5
Senegal	2.4	6.9	7.5
Singapore	0.3	0.9	2.2
Spain	3.1	3.8	3.2
Thailand	0.3	3.2	0.5
Turkey	0.8	0.5	1.8
United Arab Emirates	1.1	0.9	2.3
United Kingdom	13.7	15.9	16.8
USA	3.9	7.2	3.4
Viet Nam	1.6	0.0	0.0
Total (incl. others)	132.3	156.3	162.6

THE GAMBIA

Exports f.o.b.	2001	2002	2003
Belgium	0.8	0.1	0.0
China, People's Repub.	0.0	0.0	0.5
France (incl. Monaco)	2.2	0.0	0.1
Germany	0.1	0.1	0.5
Guinea	0.4	0.1	0.0
Guinea-Bissau	0.0	0.1	0.0
Hong Kong	0.0	0.0	0.1
Italy	0.0	0.4	0.9
India	0.0	0.0	0.1
Netherlands	0.0	0.1	0.4
Portugal	0.1	0.0	0.0
Senegal	0.2	0.3	0.2
Sierra Leone	0.1	0.4	0.1
Spain	0.5	0.2	0.2
Switzerland-Liechtenstein	0.0	1.2	0.0
United Kingdom	1.7	0.5	1.2
Total (incl. others)	6.3	3.8	5.1

Source: UN, *International Trade Statistics Yearbook*.

2005 (percentage of total): *Imports:* China, People's Republic 21.3; Côte d'Ivoire 8.4; Hong Kong 1.5; India 2.9; Japan 0.6; Senegal 11.3; Thailand 2.5; USA 5.3. *Exports* China, People's Republic 0.6; Ghana 1.3; Guinea 1.0; Guinea-Bissau 2.1; Hong Kong 0.6; India 40.4; Japan 2.2; Senegal 4.6; Thailand 3.7; USA 1.0 (Source: IMF, *The Gambia: Selected Issues and Statistical Appendix*—March 2007).

Transport

ROAD TRAFFIC
(motor vehicles in use, estimates)

	2002	2003	2004
Passenger cars	7,919	8,168	8,109
Buses	2,261	1,300	1,200
Lorries and vans	1,531	1,862	1,761

Source: IRF, *World Road Statistics*.

SHIPPING
Merchant Fleet
(registered at 31 December)

	2004	2005	2006
Number of vessels	13	13	15
Total displacement (grt)	33,159	33,159	34,635

Source: Lloyd's Register-Fairplay, *World Fleet Statistics*.

International Sea-borne Freight Traffic
('000 metric tons)

	1996	1997	1998
Goods loaded	55.9	38.1	47.0
Goods unloaded	482.7	503.7	493.2

CIVIL AVIATION
(traffic on scheduled services)

	1992	1993	1994
Kilometres flown (million)	1	1	1
Passengers carried ('000)	19	19	19
Passenger-km (million)	50	50	50
Total ton-km (million)	5	5	5

Source: UN, *Statistical Yearbook*.

Tourism

FOREIGN VISITORS BY COUNTRY OF ORIGIN*

	2002	2003	2004
Belgium	4,268	1,707	4,961
Denmark	2,260	2,616	1,997
Germany	3,707	4,253	2,891
Netherlands	10,419	7,262	13,112
Norway	711	999	5,513
Sweden	5,594	4,205	3,954
United Kingdom	48,894	40,872	48,297
USA	866	445	3,059
Total (incl. others)	81,005	73,485	90,095

* Air charter tourist arrivals.

Receipts from tourism (US $ million, incl. passenger transport): 58 in 2003; 51 in 2004; 57 in 2005.

Source: World Tourism Organization.

2005: Total foreign visitors 110,815 (Source: Source: IMF, *The Gambia: Selected Issues and Statistical Appendix*—March 2007).

Communications Media

	2004	2005	2006
Telephones ('000 main lines in use)	43.0	44.0	52.9
Mobile cellular telephones ('000 subscribers)	175.0	247.5	404.3
Personal computers ('000 in use)	23	23	n.a.
Internet users ('000)	49	58	n.a.

Television receivers (number in use): 4,000 in 2000.

Radio receivers ('000 in use): 196 in 1997.

Facsimile machines (number in use, year ending 31 March): 1,149 in 1997/98.

Daily newspapers: 1 in 1998 (average circulation 2,100 copies).

Non-daily newspapers: 4 in 1996 (estimated average circulation 6,000 copies).

Book production: 10 titles in 1998 (10,000 copies).

Broadband subscribers: 100 in 2005.

Sources: UNESCO Institute for Statistics; UNESCO, *Statistical Yearbook*; UN, *Statistical Yearbook*; International Telecommunication Union.

Education

(2004/05)

	Institutions	Teachers	Students Males	Females	Total
Primary	402	4,819	91,741	89,241	180,982
Junior Secondary	160	1,004	30,173	26,892	57,065
Senior Secondary	49	409	16,740	11,795	28,535

Source: Department of State for Education, Banjul.

Adult literacy rate (UNESCO estimates): 37.8% (males 45.0%; females 30.9%) in 2002 (Source: UN Development Programme, *Human Development Report*).

Directory

The Constitution

Following the *coup d'état* of July 1994, the 1970 Constitution was suspended and the presidency and legislature, as defined therein, dissolved. A Constitutional Review Commission was inaugurated in April 1995; the amended document was approved in a national referendum on 8 August. The Constitution of the Second Republic of The Gambia entered into full effect on 16 January 1997.

Decrees issued during the transition period (1994–96) are deemed to have been approved by the National Assembly and remain in force so long as they do not contravene the provisions of the Constitution of the Second Republic.

The Constitution provides for the separation of the powers of the executive, legislative and judicial organs of state. The Head of State is the President of the Republic, who is directly elected by universal adult suffrage. No restriction is placed on the number of times a President may seek re-election. Legislative authority is vested in the National Assembly, comprising 48 members elected by direct universal suffrage and five members nominated by the President of the Republic. The Speaker and Deputy Speaker of the Assembly are elected, by the members of the legislature, from among the President's nominees. The Constitution upholds the principle of executive accountability to parliament. Thus, the Head of State appoints government members, but these are responsible both to the President and to the National Assembly. Ministers of cabinet rank take the title of Secretary of State. Committees of the Assembly have powers to inquire into the activities of ministers and of government departments, and into all matters of public importance.

In judicial affairs, the final court of appeal is the Supreme Court. Provision is made for a special criminal court to hear and determine all cases relating to the theft and misappropriation of public funds.

The Constitution provides for an Independent Electoral Commission, an Independent National Audit Office, an Office of the Ombudsman, a Lands Commission and a Public Service Commission, all of which are intended to ensure transparency, accountability and probity in public affairs.

The Constitution guarantees the rights of women, of children and of the disabled. Tribalism and other forms of sectarianism in politics are forbidden. Political activity may be suspended in the event of a state of national insecurity.

The Government

HEAD OF STATE

President: Col (retd) Alhaji YAHYA A. J. J. JAMMEH (proclaimed Head of State 26 July 1994; elected President 26 September 1996, re-elected 18 October 2001 and 22 September 2006).

Vice-President: ISATOU NJIE-SAIDY.

THE CABINET
(March 2008)

President: Col (retd) Alhaji YAHYA A. J. J. JAMMEH.

Vice-President and Secretary of State for Women's Affairs: ISATOU NJIE-SAIDY.

Secretary of State for Finance and Economic Affairs: MUSA GIBRIL BALA GAYE.

Secretary of State for Foreign Affairs and National Assembly Matters: Dr OMAR TOURAY.

Secretary of State for the Interior: Maj. (retd) OUSMAN SONKO.

Secretary of State for Justice and Attorney-General: MARIE SAINE-FIRDAUS.

Secretary of State for Agriculture: (vacant).

Secretary of State for Fisheries and Water Resources: YANKOUBA TOURAY.

Secretary of State for Forestry and the Environment: MOMODOU KOTU CHAM.

Secretary of State for Health and Social Welfare: Maj. Dr MALICK NJIE.

Secretary of State for Local Government, Lands and Religious Affairs: ISMAILA K. SAMBOU.

Secretary of State for Education: FATOU L. FAYE.

Secretary of State for Higher Education, Research, Science and Technology: CRISPIN GREY-JOHNSON.

Secretary of State for Tourism and Culture: NANCY NJIE.

Secretary of State for Communication, Information and Technology: FATIM BADJIE.

Secretary of State for Trade, Industry and Employment: ABDOU KOLLEY.

Secretary of State for Youth, Sports and Religious Affairs: MASS AXI GYE.

Secretary of State for Works, Construction and Infrastructure: LAMIN BOJANG.

Secretary of State for Petroleum, Energy and Mineral Resources: OUSMAN JAMMEH.

DEPARTMENTS OF STATE

Office of the President: PMB, State House, Banjul; tel. 4223811; fax 4227034; e-mail info@statehouse.gm; internet www.statehouse.gm.

Office of the Vice-President: State House, Banjul; tel. 4227605; fax 4224012; e-mail vicepresident@statehouse.gm.

Department of State for Agriculture: The Quadrangle, Banjul; tel. 228291; fax 223578.

Department of State for Communication, Information and Technology: Half-Die, Banjul; tel. 4227668; e-mail amjanneh@aol.com.

Department of State for Education: Willy Thorpe Bldg, Banjul; tel. 4227236; fax 4224180; internet www.edugambia.gm.

Department of State for Finance and Economic Affairs: The Quadrangle, POB 9686, Banjul; tel. 4228291; fax 4227954.

Department of State for Fisheries and Water Resources: 5 Marina Parade, Banjul; tel. 4228702; fax 4228628.

Department of State for Foreign Affairs: 4 Col. Muammar Ghadaffi Ave, Banjul; tel. 4223577; fax 4223578.

Department of State for Health and Social Welfare: The Quadrangle, Banjul; tel. 4225712; fax 4223178; e-mail dpi@dosh.gm.

Department of State for Higher Education and Research: Banjul.

Department of State for the Interior: ECOWAS Ave, Banjul; tel. 4228511; fax 4223063.

Department of State for Justice and Attorney-General's Chambers: Marina Parade, Banjul; tel. 4228181; fax 4225352; e-mail sthydara@hotmail.com.

Department of State for Local Government and Lands: The Quadrangle, Banjul; tel. 4228291.

Department of State for Petroleum, Energy and Mineral Resources: Banjul.

Department of State for Tourism and Culture: New Administrative Bldg, The Quadrangle, Banjul; tel. 4227593; fax 4227753; e-mail masterplan@gamtel.gm.

Department of State for Trade, Industry and Employment: Central Bank Bldg, Independence Dr., Banjul; tel. 4228868; fax 4227756; e-mail tiewebmaster@qanet.gm; internet www.gambia.gm.

Department of State for Works, Construction and Infrastructure: Banjul.

Department of State for Youth, Sports and Religious Affairs: The Quadrangle, Banjul; tel. 4225264; fax 4225267; e-mail dosy-s@qanet.gm.

President and Legislature

PRESIDENT

Presidential Election, 22 September 2006

Candidate	Votes	% of votes
Yahya A. J. J. Jammeh (APRC)	264,404	67.33
Ousainou N. Darboe (UDP)	104,808	26.69
Halifa Sallah (NADD)	23,473	5.98
Total	392,685	100.00

NATIONAL ASSEMBLY

Speaker: FATOUMATA JAHUMPA-CEESAY.

National Assembly: Parliament Buildings, Independence Dr., Banjul; tel. 4227241; fax 4225123; e-mail assemblyclerk@yahoo.com; internet www.nationalassembly.gm.

THE GAMBIA

General Election, 25 January 2007

Party	Votes	% of votes	Seats
Alliance for Patriotic Reorientation and Construction (APRC)	156,573	59.77	42
United Democratic Party (UDP)	57,368	21.90	4
National Reconciliation Party (NRP)	14,932	5.70	—
National Alliance for Democracy and Development (NADD)	13,990	5.34	1
Independents	19,111	7.29	1
Total	**261,974**	**100.0**	**48***

* The President of the Republic is empowered by the Constitution to nominate five additional members of parliament. The total number of members of parliament is thus 53.

Election Commission

Independent Electoral Commission (IEC): 7 Kairaba Ave, Latrikunda, Kanifing, POB 793, Banjul; tel. 4373804; fax 4373803; e-mail info@iec.gm; internet www.iec.gm; f. 1997; Chair. Alhaji MUSTAPHA CARAYOL.

Political Organizations

In 2006 eight parties were registered with the Independent Electoral Commission.

Alliance for Patriotic Reorientation and Construction (APRC): Gambisara White House, Kairaba Ave, Banjul; tel. 4377550; fax 4377552; f. 1996; governing party; Chair. President YAHYA A. J. J. JAMMEH.

Gambia People's Party (GPP): Banjul; f. 1986; socialist; not registered with the IEC; Leader ASSAN MUSA CAMARA.

The Gambia Party for Democracy and Progress (GPDP): POB 4014, Kombo St Mary, Serrekunda; tel. 9955226; f. 2004; Sec.-Gen. HENRY GOMEZ.

National Alliance for Democracy and Development (NADD): Banjul; f. Jan. 2005 to contest 2006 elections; Co-ordinator HALIFA SALLAH; comprises parties listed below.

People's Democratic Organization for Independence and Socialism (PDOIS): POB 2306, 1 Sambou St, Churchill, Serrekunda; tel. and fax 4393177; e-mail foroyaa@qanet.gm; f. 1986; socialist; Leaders HALIFA SALLAH, SAM SARR, SIDIA JATTA.

People's Progressive Party (PPP): c/o Omar Jallow, Ninth St East, Fajara M Section, Banjul; tel. and fax 4392674; f. 1959; fmr ruling party in 1962–94; centrist; Chair. OMAR JALLOW.

National Convention Party (NCP): 47 Antouman Faal St, Banjul; tel. 4229440; f. 1977; left-wing; Leader SHERIFF MUSTAPHA DIBBA.

National Democratic Action Movement (NDAM): 1 Box Bar Rd, Nema, Brikama Town, Western Division, Banjul; tel. 4484990; e-mail ndam_gambia@hotmail.com; f. 2002; reformist; Leader and Sec.-Gen. LAMIN WAA JUWARA.

National Reconciliation Party (NRP): 69 Daniel Goddard St, Banjul; tel. 4201371; fax 4201732; f. 1996; formed an alliance with the UDP in 2006; Leader HAMAT N. K. BAH.

United Democratic Party (UDP): 1 ECOWAS Ave, Banjul; tel. 4221730; fax 4224601; e-mail info@udpgambia.org; f. 1996; formed an alliance with the NRP in 2006; reformist; Sec.-Gen. and Leader OUSAINOU N. DARBOE; Nat. Pres. Col (retd) SAM SILLAH.

Diplomatic Representation

EMBASSIES AND HIGH COMMISSIONS IN THE GAMBIA

China (Taiwan): 26 Radio Gambia Rd, Kanifing South, POB 916, Banjul; tel. 4374046; fax 4374055; e-mail rocemb@gamtel.gm; Ambassador PATRICK CHANG PEI-CHI.

Cuba: C/801, POB 1487, Banjul; tel. and fax 4460789; e-mail embacuba@ganet.gm; Ambassador JORGE MARTÍNEZ SALSAMENDI.

Libya: Independence Dr., Banjul; tel. 4223213; fax 4223214; Chargé d'affaires a.i. TAHER S. DALOUB.

Nigeria: 52 Garba Jalumpa Ave, Bakau, POB 630, Banjul; tel. 4495803; fax 4496456; e-mail nigeriahc@qanet.gm; High Commissioner MARIAM MUHAMMED.

Senegal: 159 Kairaba Ave, POB 385, Banjul; tel. 4373752; fax 4373750; Ambassador MAMADOU FALL.

Sierra Leone: 67 Daniel Goddard St, Banjul; tel. 4228206; fax 4229819; e-mail mfodayyumkella@yahoo.co.uk; High Commissioner MOHAMMED FODAY YUMKELLA.

United Kingdom: 48 Atlantic Rd, Fajara, POB 507, Banjul; tel. 4495133; fax 4496134; e-mail bhcbanjul@fco.gov.uk; internet www.britishhighcommission.gov.uk/thegambia; High Commissioner PHILIP SINKINSON.

USA: The White House, Kairaba Ave, Fajara, PMB 19, Banjul; tel. 4392856; fax 4392475; e-mail consularbanjul@state.gov; internet www.usembassybanjul.gm; Ambassador BARRY LEON WELLS.

Judicial System

The judicial system of The Gambia is based on English Common Law and legislative enactments of the Republic's Parliament which include an Islamic Law Recognition Ordinance whereby an Islamic Court exercises jurisdiction in certain cases between, or exclusively affecting, Muslims.

The Constitution of the Second Republic guarantees the independence of the judiciary. The Supreme Court is defined as the final court of appeal. Provision is made for a special criminal court to hear and determine all cases relating to theft and misappropriation of public funds.

Supreme Court of The Gambia

Law Courts, Independence Dr., Banjul; tel. 4227383; fax 4228380. Consists of the Chief Justice and up to six other judges.

Chief Justice: ABDOU KARIM SAVAGE.

The **Banjul Magistrates Court**, the **Kanifing Magistrates Court** and the **Divisional Courts** are courts of summary jurisdiction presided over by a magistrate or in his absence by two or more lay justices of the peace. There are resident magistrates in all divisions. The magistrates have limited civil and criminal jurisdiction, and appeal from these courts lies with the Supreme Court. **Islamic Courts** have jurisdiction in matters between, or exclusively affecting, Muslim Gambians and relating to civil status, marriage, succession, donations, testaments and guardianship. The Courts administer Islamic *Shari'a* law. A cadi, or a cadi and two assessors, preside over and constitute an Islamic Court. Assessors of the Islamic Courts are Justices of the Peace of Islamic faith. **District Tribunals** have appellate jurisdiction in cases involving customs and traditions. Each court consists of three district tribunal members, one of whom is selected as president, and other court members from the area over which it has jurisdiction.

Attorney-General: Sheikh TIJAN HYDARA.

Solicitor-General: HENRY D. R. CARROLL.

Religion

About 85% of the population are Muslims. The remainder are mainly Christians, and there are a few animists, mostly of the Diola and Karoninka ethnic groups.

ISLAM

Banjul Central Mosque: King Fahd Bun Abdul Aziz Mosque, Box Bar Rd, POB 562, Banjul; tel. 4228094; Imam Ratib Alhaji ABDOULIE M. JOBE; Dep. Imam Ratib Alhaji TAFSIR GAYE.

Supreme Islamic Council: Banjul; Chair. Alhaji BANDING DRAMMEH; Vice-Chair. Alhaji OUSMAN JAH.

CHRISTIANITY

Christian Council of The Gambia: MDI Rd, Kanifing, POB 27, Banjul; tel. 4392092; f. 1966; seven mems (churches and other Christian bodies); Chair. Rt Rev. ROBERT P. ELLISON (Roman Catholic Bishop of Banjul); Sec.-Gen. Rev. WILLIE E. E. CARR.

The Anglican Communion

The diocese of The Gambia, which includes Senegal and Cape Verde, forms part of the Church of the Province of West Africa. The Archbishop of the Province is the Bishop of Koforidua, Ghana. There are about 1,500 adherents in The Gambia.

Bishop of The Gambia: Rt Rev. SOLOMON TILEWA JOHNSON, Bishopscourt, POB 51, Banjul; tel. 4227405; fax 4229495; e-mail anglican@qanet.gm.

The Roman Catholic Church

The Gambia comprises a single diocese (Banjul), directly responsible to the Holy See. At 31 December 2005 there were an estimated 42,400 adherents of the Roman Catholic Church in the country, equivalent to 2.4% of the population. The diocese administers a development organization (Caritas, The Gambia), and runs 63 schools and training centres. The Gambia participates in the Inter-territorial Catholic Bishops' Conference of The Gambia and Sierra Leone (based in Freetown, Sierra Leone).

Bishop of Banjul: Rt Rev. ROBERT PATRICK ELLISON, Bishop's House, POB 165, Banjul; tel. 4391957; fax 4390998.

Protestant Churches

Abiding Word Ministries (AWM): 156 Mosque Rd, PMB 207, Serrekunda Post Office, Serrekunda; tel. 4392569; fax 4394035; e-mail info@awmgambia.com; internet www.awmgambia.com; f. 1988; Senior Pastor Rev. FRANCIS FORBES.

Methodist Church: 1 Macoumba Jallow St, POB 288, Banjul; tel. 4227506; fax 4228510; f. 1821; Chair. and Gen. Supt Rev. NORMAN A. GRIGG.

BAHÁ'Í FAITH

National Spiritual Assembly: POB 583, Banjul; tel. 4229015; e-mail alsalihi@commit.gm.

The Press

All independent publications are required to register annually with the Government and to pay a registration fee.

The Daily Express: Banjul; f. 2006; independent; Man. Dir SAM OBI.

The Daily Observer: POB 131, Banjul; tel. 4496608; fax 4496878; e-mail webmaster@observer.gm; internet www.observer.gm; f. 1992; daily; pro-Govt; Gen. Man. Dr SAJA TAAL.

Foroyaa (Freedom): 1 Sambou St, Churchill's Town, POB 2306, Serrekunda; tel. and fax 4393177; e-mail foroyaa@qanet.gm; internet www.foroyaa.com; 2 a week; publ. by the PDOIS; Editors HALIFA SALLAH, SAM SARR, SIDIA JATTA.

The Gambia Daily: Dept of Information, 14 Daniel Goddard St, Banjul; tel. 4225060; fax 4227230; e-mail gamna@gamtel.gm; f. 1994; govt organ; Dir of Information EBRUMA COLE; circ. 500.

The Independent: next to A–Z Supermarket, Kairaba Ave, Banjul; f. 1999; 2 a week; independent; Gen. Man. MADI CEESAY; Editor-in-Chief MUSA SAIDYKHAN.

The Point: 2 Garba Jahumpa Rd, Fajara, Banjul; tel. 4497441; fax 4497442; e-mail thepoint13@yahoo.com; internet www.thepoint.gm; f. 1991; 3 a week; Editor-in-Chief PAP SAINE; circ. 3,000.

The Toiler: 31 OAU Blvd, POB 698, Banjul; Editor PA MODOU FALL.

The Worker: 6 Albion Place, POB 508, Banjul; publ. by the Gambia Labour Union; Editor MOHAMED M. CEESAY.

NEWS AGENCY

The Gambia News Agency (GAMNA): Dept of Information, 14 Daniel Goddard St, Banjul; tel. 4225060; fax 4227230; e-mail gamna@gamtel.gm; Dir EBRIMA COLE.

PRESS ASSOCIATION

The Gambia Press Union (GPU): 78 Mosque Rd, Serrekunda, POB 1440, Banjul; tel. and fax 4377020; affiliated to West African Journalists' Association; Pres. MADI CEESAY.

Publishers

National Printing and Stationery Corpn: Sankung Sillah St, Kanifing; tel. 4374403; fax 4395759; f. 1998; state-owned.

Baroueli: 73 Mosque Rd, Serrekunda, POB 976, Banjul; tel. 4392480; e-mail baroueli@qanet.gm; f. 1986; educational.

Observer Company: Bakau New Town Rd, Kanifing, PMB 131, Banjul; tel. 4496087; fax 4496878; e-mail webmaster@observer.gm; internet www.observer.gm; f. 1995; indigenous languages and non-fiction.

Sunrise Publishers: POB 955, Banjul; tel. 4393538; e-mail sunrisepublishers@yahoo.com; internet www.sunrisepublishers.net; f. 1985; regional history, politics and culture; Man. PATIENCE SONKO-GODWIN.

Broadcasting and Communications

TELECOMMUNICATIONS

Africell (Gambia): 43 Kairaba Ave, POB 2140, Banjul; tel. 4376022; fax 4376066; e-mail mmakkaoui@africell.gm; internet www.africell.gm; f. 2001; provider of mobile cellular telecommunications; CEO MEKIEDDIUE MAKKAOUI.

The Gambia Telecommunications Co Ltd (GAMTEL): Gamtel House, 3 Nelson Mandela St, POB 387, Banjul; tel. 4225262; fax 4224511; e-mail gen-info@gamtel.gm; internet www.gamtel.gm; f. 1984; state-owned; also operates mobile cellular telecommunications network, Gamcel, www.gamcel.gm; Man. Dir KATIM TOURAY.

BROADCASTING
Radio

The Gambia Radio and Television Services (GRTS): GRTV Headquarters, MDI Rd, Kanifing, POB 158, Banjul; tel. 4373913; fax 4374242; e-mail bora@gamtel.gm; f. 1962; state-funded, non-commercial broadcaster; radio broadcasts in English, Mandinka, Wolof, Fula, Diola, Serer and Serahuli; Dir-Gen. Alhaji MODOU SANYANG.

Citizen FM: Banjul; independent commercial broadcaster; broadcasts news and information in English, Wolof and Mandinka; rebroadcasts selected programmes from the British Broadcasting Corpn; operations suspended in Oct. 2001; Propr BABOUCAR GAYE; News Editor EBRIMA SILLAH.

Farafenni Community Radio: Farafenni; tel. 5735527.

FM B Community Radio Station: Brikama; tel. 4483000; FM broadcaster.

Radio 1 FM: 44 Kairaba Ave, POB 2700, Serrekunda; tel. 4396076; fax 4394911; e-mail george.radio1@qanet.gm; f. 1990; private station broadcasting FM music programmes to the Greater Banjul area; Dir GEORGE CHRISTENSEN.

Radio Gambia: Mile 7, Banjul; tel. 4495101; fax 4495923; e-mail semafye@hotmail.com.

Radio Syd: POB 279, Banjul; tel. 4228170; fax 4226490; e-mail radiosyd@gamtel.gm; f. 1970; commercial station broadcasting mainly music; programmes in English, French, Wolof, Mandinka and Fula; also tourist information in Swedish; not broadcasting at present, due to antenna problems; Dir CONSTANCE WADNER ENHÖRNING; Man. BENNY HOLGERSON.

Sud FM: Buckle St, POB 64, Banjul; tel. 4222359; fax 4222394; e-mail sudfm@gamtel.gm; licence revoked in 2005; Man. MAMADOU HOUSSABA BA.

West Coast Radio: Manjai Kunda, POB 2687, Serrekunda; tel. 4460911; fax 4461193; e-mail info@westcoast.gm; internet www.westcoast.gm; FM broadcaster.

The Gambia also receives broadcasts from Radio Democracy for Africa (f. 1998), a division of the Voice of America, and the British Broadcasting Corpn.

Television

The Gambia Radio and Television Services (GRTS): see Radio; television broadcasts commenced 1995.

There is also a private satellite channel, Premium TV.

Finance

(cap. = capital; res = reserves; dep. = deposits; m. = million; br(s). = branch(es); amounts in dalasi)

BANKING
Central Bank

Central Bank of The Gambia: 1–2 ECOWAS Ave, Banjul; tel. 4228103; fax 4226969; e-mail info@cbg.gm; internet www.cbg.gm; f. 1971; bank of issue; monetary authority; cap. 1.0m., res 3.0m., dep. 993.6m. (Dec. 1998); Gov. M. B. SAHO.

Other Banks

Arab-Gambian Islamic Bank: 7 ECOWAS Ave, POB 1415, Banjul; tel. 4222222; fax 4223770; e-mail agib@qanet.gm; internet www.agib.gm; f. 1996; 21.1% owned by The Gambia National Insurance Co Ltd, 20.0% owned by Islamic Development Bank (Saudi Arabia); cap. and res 9.0m., total assets 116.9m. (Dec. 2001); Man. Dir MAMOUR MALICK JAGNE; 1 br.

First International Bank Ltd: 2 Kairaba Ave, Kanifing; tel. and fax 4396580; fax 4396662; e-mail admin@fibgm.com; internet www.fibgm.com; f. 1999; 61.9% owned by Slok Ltd (Nigeria); cap. 29.4m., dep. 88.3m. (Dec. 2004); Chair. Dr OGALA OSAKA; Man. Dir and CEO MOMODOU S. MUSA.

Guaranty Trust Bank (Gambia): 55 Kairaba Ave, Fajara, POB 1958, Banjul; tel. 4376371; fax 4376398; e-mail webmaster@gambia.gtbplc.com; internet www.gambia.gtbplc.com; f. 2002; subsidiary of Guaranty Trust Bank PLC (Nigeria); Man. Dir AYO RICHARDS.

International Bank for Commerce (Gambia) Ltd: 11A Liberation Ave, POB 211, Banjul; tel. 4228144; fax 4229312; f. 1968; owned by Banque Mauritanienne pour le Commerce International; cap. and res 58,170m., dep. 307.0m. (Dec. 2003); Man. Dir MORY GUEBA CISSÉ; 2 brs.

International Commercial Bank (Gambia) Ltd: 48 Kairaba Ave, Serrekunda, KMC, POB 1600, Banjul; tel. 4377878; fax 4377880; e-mail yiphean01@yahoo.com; CEO TAN YIP HEAN.

Standard Chartered Bank (Gambia) Ltd: 8 ECOWAS Ave, POB 259, Banjul; tel. 4227744; fax 4227714; e-mail stsik@scbgamb.mhs.compuserve.com; internet www.standardchartered.com; f. 1978; 75% owned by Standard Chartered Holdings BV, Amsterdam; cap. 8.9m., res 62.8m., dep. 1,843.2m. (Dec. 2004); Chair. MOMODOU B. A. SENGHORE; 5 brs.

Trust Bank Ltd (TBL): 3–4 ECOWAS Ave, POB 1018, Banjul; tel. 4225777; fax 4225781; e-mail info@trustbank.gm; internet www.trustbank.gm; f. 1992; fmrly Meridien BIAO Bank Gambia Ltd; 30% owned by Data Bank, 25% by Social Security and Housing Finance Corpn, 10% by Boule & Co Ltd; cap. 40.0m., res 55.0m., dep. 1,358.2m. (Dec. 2004); Chair. KEN OFORI ATTA; Man. Dir PA MACOUMBA NJIE; 4 brs.

INSURANCE

Capital Insurance Co Ltd: 22 Anglesea St, POB 268, Banjul; tel. 4227480; fax 4229219; e-mail capinsur@gamtel.gm; f. 1985; CEO DODOU TAAL.

The Gambia National Insurance Co Ltd (GNIC): 19 Kairaba Ave, Fajara, KSMD, POB 750, Banjul; tel. 4395725; fax 4395716; e-mail info@gnic.gm; internet www.gnic.gm; f. 1974; privately owned; Chair. M. O. DRAMMEH; Man. Dir WILLIAM B. COKER; 3 brs.

Gamstar Insurance Co Ltd: 79 Daniel Goddard St, POB 1276, Banjul; tel. 4228610; fax 4229755; internet www.gamstarinsurance.net; f. 1991; Man. Dir BAI NDONGO FAAL.

Global Security Insurance Co Ltd: 73A Independence Dr., POB 1400, Banjul; tel. 4223716; fax 4223715; e-mail global@gamtel.gm; f. 1996; Man. Dir KWASU DARBOE.

Great Alliance Insurance Co: 10 Nelson Mandela St, POB 1160, Banjul; tel. 4227839; fax 4229444; f. 1989; Pres. BAI MATARR DRAMMEH; Man. Dir DEBORAH H. FORSTER.

Londongate (Gambia) Insurance Co: 1–3 Liberation Ave, POB 602, Banjul; tel. 4201740; fax 4201742; e-mail izadi@londongate.gm; internet www.londongate.co.uk/gambia_profile.htm; f. 1999; owned by Boule & Co Ltd; Marketing Man. T. OGOH.

New Vision Insurance Co. Ltd: 3–4 ECOWAS Ave, POB 239, Banjul; tel. 4223045; fax 4223040; Dir ANTHONY G. CARVALHO.

Prime Insurance Co Ltd: 10C Nelson Mandela St, POB 277, Banjul; tel. 4222476; e-mail prime@qanet.gm; f. 1997; Exec. Dir JARREH F. M. TOURAY; Man. Dir PA ALASSAN JAGNE.

Insurance Association

Insurance Association of The Gambia (IAG): Banjul.

Trade and Industry

GOVERNMENT AGENCIES

The Gambia Divestiture Agency (GDA): 80 OAU Blvd, POB 391, Banjul; tel. 4202530; fax 4202533; e-mail gda@gda.gm; internet www.gda.gm; f. 2001; advisory body; Man. Dir (vacant).

The Gambia Investment Promotion and Free Zones Agency (GIPFZA): 48 Kairaba Ave, Serrekunda, KMC, POB 757, Banjul; tel. 4377377/8; fax 4377379; e-mail info.gipfza@qanet.gm; internet www.gipfza.gm; f. 2001; the implementing agency of the Gateway Project, funded by the World Bank and the Gambian Government, responsible for fostering local and foreign direct investment funded; CEO KEBBA A. TOURAY.

Indigenous Business Advisory Services (IBAS): POB 2502, Bakau; tel. 4496098; e-mail payibas@gamtel.gm.

National Investment Promotion Authority (NIPA): Independence Dr., Banjul; tel. 4228332; fax 4229220; f. 1994 to replace the National Investment Bd; CEO S. M. MBOGE.

DEVELOPMENT AGENCY

The Gambia Rural Development Agency (GARDA): Soma Village, Jarra West, PMB 452, Serrekunda; tel. 4496676; fax 4390095.

CHAMBER OF COMMERCE

The Gambia Chamber of Commerce and Industry (GCCI): 55 Kairaba Ave, KSMD, POB 3382, Serrekunda; tel. 4378929; fax 4378936; e-mail gcci@gambiachamber.com; internet www.gambiachamber.com; f. 1967; Pres. BAI MATARR DRAMMEH; CEO MAM CHERNO JALLOW.

INDUSTRIAL AND TRADE ASSOCIATIONS

Association of Gambian Entrepreneurs (AGE): POB 200, Banjul; tel. 4393494.

Gambia Produce Marketing Board (GPMB): Marina Foreshore, POB 284 Banjul; tel. 4227278; fax 4228037.

UTILITIES

Public Utilities Regulatory Authority (PURA): 1 Paradise Beach Pl., Bertil Harding Highway, Kololi; tel. 4465180; e-mail pura@pura.gm; internet www.pura.gm; f. 2001; monitors and enforces standards of performance by public utilities; Chair. ABDOULIE TOURAY; Dir-Gen. ALAGI B. GAYE.

National Water and Electricity Co Ltd (NAWEC): POB 609, Banjul; tel. 4496430; fax 4496751; f. 1996; in 1999 control was transferred to the Bassau Development Corpn, Côte d'Ivoire, under a 15-year contract; electricity and water supply, sewerage services; Chair. MOMODOU A. JENG; Man. Dir BABOUCAR M. JOBE.

CO-OPERATIVES

Federation of Agricultural Co-operatives: Banjul.

The Gambia Co-operative Union (GCU): Dept of Co-operatives, 14 Marina Parade, Banjul; tel. 4227507; fax 4392582; Chief Officer BAKARY SONKO.

TRADE UNIONS

Agricultural Workers' Association (AWA): Banjul; Pres. Sheikh TIJAN SOSSEH; 247 mems.

Association of Gambian Sailors: c/o 31 OAU Blvd, POB 698, Banjul; tel. 4223080; fax 4227214.

Dock Workers' Union: Albert Market, POB 852, Banjul; tel. 4229448; fax 4225049.

The Gambia Labour Union: 6 Albion Pl., POB 508, Banjul; f. 1935; Pres. B. B. KEBBEH; Gen. Sec. MOHAMED M. CEESAY; 25,000 mems.

The Gambia National Trades Union Congress (GNTUC): Trade Union House, 31 OAU Blvd, POB 698, Banjul; Sec.-Gen. EBRIMA GARBA CHAM.

Gambia Teachers' Union (GTU): POB 133, Banjul; tel. and fax 4392075; e-mail gtu@gamtel.gm; f. 1937; Pres. OMAR J. NDURE.

The Gambia Workers' Confederation: Trade Union House, 72 OAU Blvd, POB 698, Banjul; tel. and fax 4222754; e-mail gambiawc@hotmail.com; f. 1958 as The Gambia Workers' Union; present name adopted in 1985; Sec.-Gen. PA MOMODOU FAAL; 30,000 mems (2001).

Transport

The Gambia Public Transport Corpn: Factory St, Kanifing Housing Estate, POB 801, Kanifing; tel. 4392230; fax 4392454; f. 1975; operates road transport and ferry services; Man. Dir BAKARY HUMA.

RAILWAYS

There are no railways in The Gambia.

ROADS

In 2004 there were an estimated 3,742 km of roads in The Gambia, of which 1,652 km were main roads, and 1,300 km were secondary roads. In that year only 19.3% of the road network was paved. Some roads are impassable in the rainy season. The expansion and upgrading of the road network is planned, as part of the Jammeh administration's programme to improve The Gambia's transport infrastructure. Among intended schemes is the construction of a motorway along the coast, with the aid of a loan of US $8.5m. from Kuwait. In early 1999 Taiwan agreed to provide $6m. for road construction programmes, and in early 2000 work began on the construction of a dual carriageway between Serrekunda, Mandina and Ba, supported by funds from the Islamic Development Fund and the Organization of the Petroleum Exporting Counties. In 2006 the European Union provided a grant of €44m. to rehabilitate five roads.

SHIPPING

The River Gambia is well suited to navigation. A weekly river service is maintained between Banjul and Basse, 390 km above Banjul, and a ferry connects Banjul with Barra. Small ocean-going vessels can reach Kaur, 190 km above Banjul, throughout the year. Facilities at the port of Banjul were modernized and expanded during the mid-1990s, with the aim of enhancing The Gambia's potential as a transit point for regional trade. In 1999 three advanced storage warehouses were commissioned with total storage space of 8,550 sq m. The Gambia's merchant fleet consisted of 15 vessels, totalling 34,635 grt, at 31 December 2005.

The Gambia Ports Authority: 34 Liberation Ave, POB 617, Banjul; tel. 4227269; fax 4227268; e-mail info@gamport.gm; internet www.gamport.gm; f. 1972; Man. Dir ADAMA M. DEEN.

Gambia River Transport Co Ltd: 61 Wellington St, POB 215, POB 215, Banjul; tel. 4227664; river transport of groundnuts and general cargo; Man. Dir LAMIN JUWARA; 200 employees.

The Gambia Shipping Agency Ltd: 1A Cotton St, POB 257, Banjul; tel. and fax 4227518; e-mail otal@gamship.gm; f. 1984; shipping agents and forwarders; Man. Dir N. LANGGAARD-SORENSEN; 30 employees.

Interstate Shipping Co (Gambia) Ltd: 43 Buckle St, POB 220, Banjul; tel. 4229388; fax 4229347; e-mail interstate@gamtel.gm; transport and storage; Man. Dir B. F. SAGNIA.

Maersk Gambia Ltd: 80 OAU Blvd, POB 1399, Banjul; tel. 4224450; fax 4224025; e-mail gamsalimp@maersk.com; f. 1993; owned by Maersk Line.

CIVIL AVIATION

Banjul International Airport, is situated at Yundum, 27 km from the capital. Construction of a new terminal, at a cost of some US $10m., was completed in late 1996. Facilities at Yundum have been upgraded by the US National Aeronautics and Space Administration (NASA), to enable the airport to serve as an emergency landing site for space shuttle vehicles.

The Gambia Civil Aviation Authority (GCAA): Banjul International Airport, Yundum; tel. 4472831; fax 4472190; e-mail dggcaa@qanet.gm; internet www.gambia.gm/gcaa; f. 1991; Dir-Gen. FANSU BOJANG.

The Gambia International Airlines: PMB 353, Banjul; tel. 4472770; fax 4223700; internet www.gia.gm; f. 1996; state-owned; sole handling agent at Banjul, sales agent; Chair. (vacant); Man. Dir (vacant).

Slok Air International (Gambia) Ltd: Banjul International Airport, Yundum; internet www.slokairinternational.com; commenced operations in The Gambia in 2004; Chair. AMADOU SAMBA; Man. Dir Capt. ERNEST I. BELL.

Tourism

Tourists are attracted by The Gambia's beaches and also by its abundant birdlife. A major expansion of tourism facilities was carried out in the early 1990s. Although there was a dramatic decline in tourist arrivals in the mid-1990s (owing to the political instability), the tourism sector recovered well. In 2005 some 118,815 tourists visited The Gambia. In 2005 estimated earnings from tourism were US $57m. An annual 'Roots Festival' was inaugurated in 1996, with the aim of attracting African-American visitors to The Gambia.

The Gambia Hotels' Association: c/o The Bungalow Beach Hotel, POB 2637, Serrekunda; tel. 4465288; fax 4466180; e-mail bbhotel@qanet.gm; Chair. ARDY SARGE.

The Gambia Tourist Authority: Kololi, POB 4085, Bakau; tel. 4462491; fax 4462487; e-mail info@gta.gm; internet www.visitthegambia.gm; f. 2001; Dir ALIEU MBOGE.

GEORGIA

Introductory Survey

Location, Climate, Language, Religion, Flag, Capital

Georgia is situated in west and central Transcaucasia, on the southern foothills of the Greater Caucasus mountain range. There is a frontier with Turkey to the south-west and a western coastline on the Black Sea. The northern frontier with Russia follows the axis of the Greater Caucasus. To the south lies Armenia, and to the south-east is Azerbaijan. Georgia includes two autonomous republics (Abkhazia and Adjara), of which the former remained outside central government control in early 2008; additionally, the territories of South Ossetia were only under partial control of the central Government at that time. The Black Sea coast and the Rion plains have a warm, humid, subtropical climate, with annual rainfall of more than 2,000 mm and average temperatures of 6°C (42°F) in January and 23°C (73°F) in July. Eastern Georgia has a more continental climate, with cold winters and hot, dry summers. The official language is Georgian, a member of the South Caucasian (Kartavelian) language group, which is written in the Georgian script. Most of the population are adherents of Christianity; the principal denomination is the Georgian Orthodox Church. Islam is professed by Ajarians, Azeris, Kurds and some others. The national flag (proportions 100 by 147) consists of a white field, with a centred red cross and a smaller red cross in each quarter. The capital is Tbilisi.

Recent History

A powerful kingdom in medieval times, Georgia subsequently came under periods of foreign domination, and was annexed by the Russian Empire from the 19th century, until its collapse in 1917. An independent Georgian state was established on 26 May 1918, ruled by a Menshevik Socialist Government. Although it received recognition from the Bolshevik Government of Soviet Russia in May 1920, Bolshevik troops invaded Georgia and proclaimed a Georgian Soviet Socialist Republic (SSR) on 25 February 1921. In December 1922 it was absorbed into the Transcaucasian Soviet Federative Socialist Republic (TSFSR), which, on 22 December, became a founder member of the USSR. In 1936 the TSFSR was disbanded and Georgia reverted to the status of a SSR.

During the 1930s Georgians suffered persecution under the Soviet leader, Stalin (Iosif V. Dzhugashvili), himself an ethnic Georgian. Most members of the Georgian leadership were dismissed after Stalin's death in 1953. There was a further purge in 1972, when Eduard Shevardnadze became First Secretary of the Communist Party of Georgia (CPG) and attempted to remove officials who had been accused of corruption. Shevardnadze remained leader of the CPG until 1985, when he became Minister of Foreign Affairs of the USSR.

The increased freedom of expression that followed the election of Mikhail Gorbachev as the Soviet leader in 1985 allowed the formation of 'unofficial groups', which were prominent in organizing demonstrations in November 1988 against russification in Georgia. In February 1989 Abkhazians renewed a campaign, begun in the 1970s, for secession of their (nominally) autonomous republic from the Georgian SSR (see below). Counter-demonstrations were staged in the Georgian capital, Tbilisi, to demand that Georgia's territorial integrity be preserved. On the night of 8–9 April 1989 Soviet security forces attacked demonstrators in Tbilisi, who were advocating Georgian independence, killing 16 people and injuring many more. Despite the subsequent resignation of state and party officials (including the First Secretary of the CPG, Jumber Patiashvili), anti-Soviet sentiment increased sharply. In November the Georgian Supreme Soviet (Supreme Council—legislature), which was dominated by CPG members, declared the supremacy of Georgian laws over all-Union (USSR) laws. In February 1990 the same body declared Georgia 'an annexed and occupied country', and in the following month abolished the CPG's monopoly on power. Legislation permitting full multi-party elections was adopted in August.

In early 1990 principal political parties formed the Round Table–Free Georgia coalition, which aimed to achieve independence by parliamentary means. More radical parties, however, united in the National Forum, announced their intention to boycott the elections to the Georgian Supreme Soviet and, instead, elect a rival parliament, the 'National Congress'. However, at the elections to the National Congress, held on 30 September, only 51% of the electorate participated, and many parties did not present candidates.

In the elections to the Supreme Soviet, held on 28 October and 11 November 1990, the Round Table–Free Georgia coalition, led by Zviad Gamsakhurdia, a former dissident, won 155 seats in the 250-seat chamber, and 64% of the votes cast. The CPG won 64 seats, while the remainder were won by the Georgian Popular Front (GPF), smaller coalitions and independents. All 14 of the political parties and coalitions involved in the election campaign, including the CPG, declared their support for Georgia's independence. The elections were boycotted by many non-ethnic Georgians, since parties limited to one area of the country were prevented from participating.

The new Supreme Soviet convened for the first time on 14 November 1990 and elected Gamsakhurdia as its Chairman. Two symbolic gestures of independence were adopted: the territory was, henceforth, to be called the Republic of Georgia and the white, black and cornelian red-coloured flag of the 1918–21 Georgian state (and of the Menshevik Party of that period) was officially adopted. Tengiz Sigua was appointed Chairman of the Council of Ministers. At its first session the new Supreme Soviet declared illegal the conscription of Georgians into the Soviet armed forces. Many young men were reported to have joined nationalist paramilitary groups or were ready to join the National Guard (a de facto republican army), which the Supreme Soviet established in January 1991.

The Georgian authorities officially boycotted the all-Union referendum on the future of the USSR, held in nine other Soviet republics in March 1991, but polling stations were opened in Abkhazia, in local military barracks and in the territories of the former autonomous oblast of South Ossetia (which had been abolished in December 1990). It was reported that in Abkhazia almost the entire non-Georgian population voted to preserve the Union, and that in the territories formerly included in South Ossetia only nine people voted against the preservation of the USSR. On 31 March the Government conducted a referendum asking whether 'independence should be restored on the basis of the act of independence of 26 May 1918'. Of those eligible to vote, 95% participated in the referendum, 93% of whom voted for independence, according to official figures. On 9 April 1991 the Georgian Supreme Council approved a decree formally restoring Georgia's independence. Georgia thus became the first republic to secede from the USSR. Direct elections to the newly established post of executive President, held in May, were won by Gamsakhurdia, who received 86.5% of the votes cast. Voting did not take place in Abkhazia or South Ossetia.

Gamsakhurdia's actions during the failed Soviet coup in Moscow, the Russian and Soviet capital, in August 1991 were strongly criticized, as he initially refrained from publicly condemning the conservative communist coup leaders (although the CPG was subsequently disbanded). After the coup collapsed, Gamsakhurdia's position became tenuous. Tengiz Kitovani, the former leader of the National Guard (who had been dismissed by Gamsakhurdia on 19 August, when the Soviet coup attempt began), announced that 15,000 of his men were no longer subordinate to the President. Kitovani was joined in opposition to Gamsakhurdia by Sigua, who resigned as Chairman of the Council of Ministers in mid-August. In September 30 opposition parties united and organized a series of demonstrations to demand the resignation of Gamsakhurdia. Opposition supporters occupied the television station in Tbilisi, and several people were killed in clashes between Kitovani's troops and those forces loyal to Gamsakhurdia. Gamsakhurdia ordered the arrest of prominent opposition leaders and imposed a state of emergency in Tbilisi, while his effective monopoly of the republican media further strengthened his position.

In December 1991 armed conflict broke out in Tbilisi, as the opposition, led by Kitovani and by Jaba Ioseliani, the leader of the paramilitary *Mkhedrioni* (Horsemen), resorted to force to oust the President. More than 100 people were believed to have been killed. Gamsakhurdia and some of his supporters (or 'Zviadists') fled Georgia on 6 January 1992. A few days previously the opposition had declared Gamsakhurdia deposed and formed a Military Council, which appointed Sigua as acting Chairman of the Council of Ministers. The office of President was abolished, and the functions of Head of State were, instead, to be exercised by the Chairman of the Supreme Council.

In mid-January 1992 Sigua began the formation of a new Government. In early March Shevardnadze returned to Georgia, and a State Council was created to replace the Military Council in legislative and executive matters. The State Council, of which Shevardnadze was designated Chairman, comprised 50 members, drawn from all the major political organizations, and included Sigua, Ioseliani and Kitovani. Shevardnadze succeeded in reconciling the various factions of the State Council and by April government troops had re-established control in the rebellious areas. In July, however, a deputy premier was taken hostage by Zviadists in western Georgia. This was followed by the kidnapping of the Minister of Internal Affairs, and several other officials. In response, the State Council dispatched more than 3,000 National Guardsmen to Abkhazia, where the hostages were believed to be held, prompting armed resistance by Abkhazian militia. By August several of the hostages had been released.

Elections to the Supreme Council were held on 11 October 1992. Voting did not take place in South Ossetia, Mingrelia (south-east of Abkhazia) and parts of Abkhazia. An estimated 75% of the total electorate participated. Of the more than 30 parties and alliances contesting the elections, none succeeded in obtaining a significant representation in the 235-seat legislature. The largest number of seats (29) was won by the centrist Peace bloc. Of greater consequence, however, was the direct election of the legislature's Chairman—effectively a presidential role—which was held concurrently. Shevardnadze was the sole candidate for the post, winning more than 95% of the total votes cast. The new Supreme Council convened in early November. One of the principal aims of the new Government, headed by Sigua, was to create a unified army. A comprehensive programme of economic reform was also initiated.

Almost immediately, Shevardnadze was confronted by opposition from within his own administration. In response to allegations that Kitovani was plotting to overthrow him, in May Shevardnadze dismissed Kitovani as Minister of Defence. In August the Council of Ministers tendered its resignation, following the legislature's rejection of the proposed budget. In September Shevardnadze appointed a new Council of Ministers, which was headed by Otar Patsatsia, a former CPG official. Shevardnadze tendered his resignation as Head of State in mid-September, in response to accusations of dictatorial methods. However, crowds blockaded the parliament building, demanding his reinstatement, and the Supreme Council rejected Shevardnadze's resignation. By late September Georgia appeared ungovernable: confronted by the growing political and economic crisis and military defeat in Abkhazia (see below), Shevardnadze's position was made more precarious by the resurgence of Zviadists in western Georgia. In early October Gamsakhurdia's forces captured the Black Sea port of Poti as well as the strategic town of Samtredia, blocking all rail traffic to Tbilisi. As the rebel forces advanced eastwards, Shevardnadze persuaded the Supreme Council to agree to Georgia's immediate membership of the Commonwealth of Independent States (CIS, see p. 215), established in December 1991 by 11 former Soviet republics. In late October 1993 Russian troops were dispatched to Georgia, and by early November the Zviadists had been entirely routed from the republic. (Georgia's formal admittance to the CIS was delayed until early December 1993, when all of the member states finally granted their approval.) In early January 1994 it was reported that Gamsakhurdia had committed suicide, although the exact circumstances of his death remained obscure.

Meanwhile, following the restoration of some measure of stability in Georgia (excluding Abkhazia), Shevardnadze created his own party, the Citizens' Union of Georgia (CUG). Throughout 1994 Shevardnadze sought to curb organized crime; however, assassinations and other acts of political violence remained widespread. New opposition parties emerged: a National Liberation Front (NLF) was established by Sigua and Kitovani with the declared aim of regaining control of Abkhazia, although the organization was banned after Kitovani led an armed convoy of some 350 NLF supporters towards Abkhazia in January 1995 in an apparent attempt to 'liberate' the region.

In August 1995 the Supreme Council adopted Georgia's new Constitution. The document provided for a strong executive presidency and a 235-member unicameral legislature, the Sakartvelos Parlamenti (Parlamenti—Georgian Parliament). The Government was to be directly subordinate to the President, the post of Prime Minister was abolished; the most senior position in the Government was henceforth to be that of the Minister of State. The country (the official title of which was changed from the Republic of Georgia to Georgia) was described as 'united and undivided'; however, the territorial status of Abkhazia and Adjara was not defined, while the incorporation of the former South Ossetian territories into various other, non-ethnically based regions, was confirmed. It was stated that, following the eventual resumption of central government control across the entire territory of Georgia, Parlamenti would be transformed into a bicameral body.

The Constitution was due to be signed at an official ceremony on 29 August 1995, but, following an assassination attempt on Shevardnadze, the signing was postponed until 17 October. Igor Giorgadze, the Minister of State Security, was subsequently named by state prosecutors as the chief instigator of the plot. Giorgadze, along with two other alleged plotters, fled abroad.

A presidential election was held on 5 November 1995, in which Shevardnadze won almost 75% of the votes cast. His closest rival (with 19%) was Patiashvili. The election of Parlamenti was held concurrently with the presidential election. A mixed system of voting was employed: 150 seats were to be filled by proportional representation, while 85 deputies were to be elected by majority vote in single-member constituencies. The elections were boycotted in Abkhazia and in parts of South Ossetia. Only three parties contesting the proportional seats succeeded in obtaining the 5% of the votes required to obtain representation on this basis. Of these, Shevardnadze's CUG won the largest number of seats (90), followed by the National Democratic Party of Georgia (31) and the All-Georgian Union of Revival, chaired by Aslan Abashidze, the leader of the Autonomous Republic of Adjara (25 seats). Only about one-half of the single-mandate seats were filled; however, following a further two rounds of voting, all 85 deputies were elected. The CUG held a total of 107 seats, but it was supported by many of the other parties that obtained representation. Approximately 64% of the registered electorate was reported to have participated in the legislative elections.

Parlamenti convened for the first time in late November 1995 and elected as its Chairman Zurab Zhvania, the General Secretary of the CUG. In December Shevardnadze formed a new Government, with Nikoloz Lekishvili, formerly Mayor of Tbilisi, as Minister of State.

Meanwhile, in late 1995 criminal proceedings commenced in Tbilisi against Kitovani, in connection with the NLF's attempted raid on Abkhazia in early 1995. In May 1996 Ioseliani was convicted of complicity in the assassination attempt against Shevardnadze in August 1995. (He was released in April 2000 and died in March 2003.) In June 1996 supporters of Gamsakhurdia received lengthy prison sentences for their roles in the civil conflict of 1993. In September 1996 Kitovani was convicted on charges of establishing an illegal armed formation and was sentenced to eight years' imprisonment. (He was released in May 1999.)

In February 1998 Shevardnadze survived a further attempt on his life. In March Guram Absandze, Minister of Finance under Gamsakhurdia, was arrested in Moscow and returned to Georgia to stand trial on charges of organizing the attempted assassination. Absandze was sentenced to 17 years' imprisonment in August 2001 (although he was later pardoned). Further arrests were made in May 1999, following the discovery of a new plot to overthrow Shevardnadze. All of those arrested were reported to have links with Giorgadze; one of the accused died in detention, and 10 others were sentenced to terms of imprisonment in November 2001. In July 1998 most of the Government, including the Minister of State resigned, to permit the President to carry out a major ministerial reorganization. In August the former ambassador to Russia, Vazha Lortkipanidze, was appointed Minister of State. In October a two-day armed insurrection in western Georgia ended when the Zviadist rebel troops surrendered to government forces at Kutaisi. Following this incident and the subsequent escape of the rebel leaders, the Minister of State Security, Jemal Gakhokidze, resigned in late October.

In July 1999 Parlamenti approved a constitutional amendment, increasing the minimum requirement for parliamentary representation from 5% to 7% of the votes cast under the system of proportional representation. Legislative elections, held in two rounds, on 31 October and 14 November, were contested by 32 parties and blocs, with the participation of 68% of the electorate. According to the final results, the CUG obtained 130 seats. The Union for the Revival of Georgia bloc, led by Abashidze, and the Industry Will Save Georgia bloc secured 58 seats and 15 seats, respectively. Despite opposition allegations of irregularities, observers from the Organization for Security and Co-operation in Europe (OSCE, see p. 354) declared the elections lawful. The new Parlamenti re-elected Zhvania as Chairman. In late November Lortkipanidze was awarded presidential powers for the settlement of conflicts in Georgia, and in the following month the President expanded the responsibilities of the Minister of State.

In the presidential election of 9 April 2000, Shevardnadze demonstrated the strength of his position against the fragmented opposition, securing 79.8% of the votes cast. Patiashvili was again second, with 16.7%. Electoral violations were noted by the OSCE, but the Parliamentary Assembly of the Council of Europe (PACE, see p. 225) and the Central Electoral Commission (CEC) reported no major infringements of voting procedure. On 11 May Parlamenti endorsed the appointment of Giorgi Arsenishvili as Minister of State, and the Council of Ministers was approved three days later.

In September 2001 the Minister of Justice, Mikheil Saakashvili, resigned, apparently in response to a perceived lack of support for his anti-corruption campaign; he subsequently founded a new political party, the National Movement. In that month Shevardnadze resigned as Chairman of the CUG. In late October public discontent culminated in large-scale protests in Tbilisi, after Rustavi 2, an independent television station that had been critical of the Government, was raided by security officials during a live broadcast. (In July a journalist for the station, who had been carrying out an investigation into official corruption, had been murdered.) Zhvania, as parliamentary Chairman, urged both the Minister of State Security and the Minister of Internal Affairs to resign in order to avert further protests. However, the latter refused to comply with this request, and the popular protests intensified, with demands for further resignations, including that of Shevardnadze. Consequently, on 1 November Shevardnadze dismissed the entire Government. The Prosecutor-General subsequently resigned, as did Zhvania, who stated that Shevardnadze no longer understood the needs of the public; he was replaced as parliamentary Chairman by Nino Burjanadze. Later in the month, a new Government, with Avtandil Jorbenadze, hitherto Minister of Labour, Health and Social Welfare, as Minister of State, was formed.

Following divisions within the CUG, in late May 2002 the Supreme Court ruled that the faction of the CUG that continued to support President Shevardnadze was the legitimate grouping, rather than an opposing 'reformist' faction led by Zhvania; in June Zhvania founded a new political party, the United Democrats. At municipal elections, held in early June, the CUG suffered a serious reverse, while the New Conservative Party, another party composed of former CUG members, won the largest number of seats nation-wide. Jorbenadze was subsequently elected as Chairman of the CUG.

From April 2003 a student-based protest organization, Kmara (Enough), co-ordinated anti-Government rallies to demand free and fair elections and the resignation of Shevardnadze. In early June the country's principal opposition parties also organized demonstrations outside Parlamenti to demand the appointment of a new CEC and the replacement of the Georgian leadership. In August Zhvania and Burjanadze announced the formation of an electoral alliance known as the Burjanadze-Democrats bloc.

On 2 November 2003 elections were held to Parlamenti. Preliminary results indicated that the pro-presidential For a New Georgia bloc had obtained the majority of the votes cast. However, international monitors from the Council of Europe and the OSCE noted electoral irregularities, and there were widespread allegations of electoral malpractice and the falsification of results. On 4 November thousands of people assembled in Tbilisi to protest against the conduct of the elections, and Saakashvili (who claimed that his National Movement had attracted the most support) led demands for Shevardnadze's resignation. Further large-scale protest demonstrations subsequently took place in Tbilisi and elsewhere in the country. Shevardnadze warned against an escalation into civil conflict, and held talks with opposition leaders in an attempt to stabilize the situation. On 20 November the CEC announced the final results of the elections (although five members of the Committee refused to endorse the results). According to the official results, the For a New Georgia bloc had received a total of 57 seats in Parlamenti (including 38 of the 150 seats allocated by proportional representation), followed by Abashidze's Democratic Union of Revival, with 39 seats (33 on a proportional basis), and the National Movement, with 36 seats (32 on a proportional basis). The Georgian Labour Party obtained 21 seats, the Burjanadze-Democrats bloc 16, the New Right bloc 15 and the Industry Will Save Georgia bloc two; 16 seats were won by independents, and repeat elections were scheduled to be held in other constituencies. The leaders of the National Movement and the Burjanadze-Democrats bloc reiterated their claims that the results were invalid, while international critics of the conduct of the election notably included the USA. A referendum, held concurrently with the parliamentary elections, approved an eventual reduction in the number of parliamentary deputies to a maximum of 150. Saakashvili announced his intention to organize a peaceful protest march on 22 November, in an attempt to prevent the new legislature from convening for its opening session. On 21 November the Secretary of the National Security Council, Tedo Japaridze, acknowledged the legitimacy of criticism levelled at the conduct of the elections and proposed that new polls be scheduled once Parlamenti had convened. However, the next day some 30,000 demonstrators proceeded to the parliament building, precipitating what became known as the 'rose revolution'. Troops attached to the Ministry of Internal Affairs failed to prevent protesters from besieging the main parliamentary chamber, and Shevardnadze was evacuated from the building. He subsequently declared a nation-wide state of emergency. The Russian Minister of Foreign Affairs, Igor Ivanov, was dispatched to Tbilisi, and on 23 November Shevardnadze and Saakashvili attended a meeting, mediated by Ivanov, at which Shevardnadze agreed to tender his resignation, in return for guarantees of immunity from prosecution. Burjanadze immediately assumed the presidency in an interim capacity, pending a presidential election, and the state of emergency was lifted the following day.

Jorbenadze and several other senior ministers resigned on 25 November 2003, and on the same day the Supreme Court annulled the results of the legislative elections for the 150 mandates allocated by proportional representation. (The single-member constituency mandates, were, however, to remain valid.) On 27 November Zhvania was approved as Minister of State, and new appointments were made to the posts of Minister of Internal Affairs, Minister of Foreign Affairs, Minister of Finance and Chairman of the CEC. In early December Guram Absandze was appointed as a Deputy Minister of State, with responsibility for national reconciliation.

In the presidential election, held on 4 January 2004, Mikheil Saakashvili obtained 96.3% of the votes cast, and the electoral turn-out was 88.0%. On 14 January the legislature adopted a new national flag, hitherto the party flag of the National Movement, and a new Prosecutor-General was appointed. On 25 January Saakashvili was inaugurated as President; following his confirmation in office, the interim Government submitted its resignation, as stipulated by the Constitution. Saakashvili immediately announced that he intended to pursue those suspected of large-scale corruption. In early February Parlamenti adopted several constitutional amendments, proposed by Saakashvili, which provided for, *inter alia*, the reintroduction of the post of prime minister and the removal of the government by means of two consecutive legislative votes of no confidence. On 17 February Parlamenti approved the composition of a new Government, headed by Zhvania as Prime Minister. The members of the Government, none of whom had served in the Shevardnadze administration, were predominantly young and western-educated. In mid-March Saakashvili announced the appointment of Salomé Zurabishvili, hitherto the French ambassador to Georgia, as Minister of Foreign Affairs.

Elections to fill the 150 proportional seats in Parlamenti were held on 28 March 2004. A coalition of the National Movement and the United Democrats won 67.3% of the votes cast and 135 seats (giving them a total of 152 seats of the 235 in Parlamenti, taking into account their single-member constituency mandates). Although international observers commended the overall conduct of the elections, some violations were reported and the Government attracted criticism from the Council of Europe for its refusal to reduce the threshold for representation in Parlamenti under the proportional system from 7% of the votes to 5%. The Rightist Opposition (an alliance of Industry Will Save Georgia and the New Conservative Party) was the only other grouping to secure seats in the legislature on a party-list basis (with 7.5% of the votes and 15 seats—giving them 23 seats overall). Abashidze, whose Democratic Union of Revival obtained 6.0% of the proportional votes, subsequently claimed that the results had been falsified. On 22 April Burjanadze was re-elected as Chairman of Parlamenti. In June Zhvania's proposals for a ministerial reorganization were approved by Parlamenti. The hitherto Minister of Internal Affairs, Giorgi Baramidze, became Minister of Defence, being replaced in his former capacity by Irakli Okruashvili, the former Prosecutor-General. Vano (Ivane) Merabishvili was appointed Deputy Prime Minister and Minister of State Security, succeeding Zurab Adeishvili, who became Prosecutor-General. Kakha Bendukidze, a prominent Georgian industrialist with major business interests in Russia, was appointed Minister of the Economy. In the same month the Republican Party of Georgia announced that it would no longer co-operate with the National Movement–United Democrats bloc, becoming an opposition party; however, this depleted the pro-presidential parliamentary faction by only four, with two of the party's deputies continuing to support the Government. In November the National Movement and the United Democrats merged to form the United National Movement (UNM), headed by Saakashvili. In December Parlamenti approved a further government reorganization. Okruashvili was appointed as Minister of Defence, while Baramidze became Deputy Prime Minister with responsibility for European Integration; the Ministry of State Security was merged with the Ministry of Internal Affairs, and Bendukidze was appointed to the more senior position of State Minister, responsible for Economic Reform.

On 3 February 2005 Prime Minister Zhvania and a junior government official were discovered dead, apparently from poisoning attributed to a domestic gas leak. On 17 February Parlamenti approved a reorganized Government, headed by the hitherto Minister of Finance, Zurab Noghaideli; Valeri Chechelashvili, hitherto ambassador to Russia, succeeded him in his former role, while Konstantine Kemularia, hitherto Chairman of the Supreme Court, became Deputy Prime Minister and Minister of Justice. On 23 February Parlamenti endorsed the constitutional amendments providing for a reduction in the number of parliamentary deputies that had been approved by referendum in November 2003; the new measures were to take effect from the legislative elections scheduled for 2008. Meanwhile, in June 2005 Lekso (Aleksi) Aleksishvili—hitherto Minister of Economic Development—was appointed as Minister of Finance, following the dismissal of Chechelashvili, who was accused of bribery. On 1 July legislation was approved by Parlamenti, providing for the election of the mayor of Tbilisi by the Tbilisi City Council, rather than directly by the electorate, thereby contravening the policy of direct election for which Saakashvili's National Movement had campaigned while in opposition.

On 13 October 2005 Parlamenti ratified the Framework Convention for the Protection of National Minorities (with a number of modifications), honouring one of its commitments on joining the Council of Europe in 1999. However, delays in the preparation and submission of the document prompted a number of deputies to demand the dismissal of Minister of Foreign Affairs Zurabishvili; her removal on 19 October prompted protest rallies by some 4,000–5,000 of her supporters. She was replaced by Gela Bezhuashvili. In November Zurabishvili announced that she was to establish a new political movement; the grouping, Georgia's Way, was officially established in March 2006.

In late March 2006 three opposition factions—the Democratic Front (comprising the Conservative Party of Georgia and the Republican Party of Georgia), the New Conservative Party and Industry Will Save Georgia—launched a boycott of parliamentary proceedings, in protest at Parlamenti's decision to remove the mandate of Valery Gelashvili, of the Republican Party of Georgia, owing to his suspect business activities. In early April the parties announced a number of preconditions for an end to the boycott, including the resignation of Merabishvili from the position of Minister of Internal Affairs, the creation of a special parliamentary commission to investigate crimes committed by the Ministry of Internal Affairs's special police force and amendments to electoral legislation to ensure secret ballots. Meanwhile, in March a protest against the apparently routine use of violence by police was staged outside the parliament building in Tbilisi. Four officers belonging to the interior ministry's special police force were arrested on suspicion of the killing of a bank employee, Sandro Girgvliani, and in July they were convicted and sentenced to between seven and eight years. On 21 July Giorgi Khaindrava was dismissed as State Minister, responsible for Conflict Resolution, having become increasingly critical in preceding weeks of what he regarded as Merabishvili's inadequate response to the killing of Girgvliani. As one-third (6 members) of the Government had now been dismissed since its formation, the entire administration was constitutionally compelled to resign. A new Government, to which only two changes had been made—the appointment of Merab Antadze as Khaindrava's replacement and that of Davit Tkeshelashvili as Minister of the Environment—was approved in Parlamenti later that month.

On 28 August 2006 President Saakashvili issued a decree stating that municipal elections, which had been scheduled to take place in December, were to be brought forward to 5 October; the deadline for candidates to submit their applications was later that day, which also happened to be a public holiday, provoking outrage from the opposition, which alleged that the presidential decree represented a deliberate ploy to impede the opposition. In response to this development, the chairman of the New Conservative Party, Davit Gamkrelidze, announced in September that the party was to boycott the elections. Also in September 29 members of the Justice Party and other affiliated organizations were arrested on suspicion of plotting a coup to effect the return to Georgia of Giorgadze; 13 of those arrested were subsequently charged. At the municipal elections on 5 October 2006, the UNM secured a resounding victory, attracting 66.5% of the total votes cast; a coalition of the Conservative Party of Georgia and the Republican Party of Georgia won 12.0% of the votes, the Georgian Labour Party 10.7% and Industry Will Save Georgia 6.1%. There were numerous allegations of electoral irregularities and malpractice, and elections were repeated in 10 electoral districts, owing to procedural violations. On 10 November Okruashvili was dismissed as Minister of Defence, after he made controversial comments to the effect that he wished Georgia to have obtained full control over South Ossetia by the end of the year; he was replaced by Davit Kezerashvili and instead appointed as Minister of Economic Development. One week later Okruashvili, who was regarded as one of the most popular politicians in the country, resigned as Minister of Economic Development.

In January 2007 President Saakashvili signed into force a series of constitutional amendments, as a result of which the President would no longer be authorized to dismiss or appoint judges, nor be involved in the activities of the High Council of Justice. The amendments also stipulated that presidential and legislative elections were henceforth to be conducted simultaneously; this had the effect of bringing forward the next presidential election, hitherto scheduled for early 2009, to late 2008.

In early September 2007 a government reorganization, effected by Saakashvili at the end of August, was approved by Parlamenti; changes included the appointment of the Minister of Finance, Lekso Aleksishvili, to the presidency of the National Bank, while the Minister of Energy, Nikoloz Gilauri, received the finance portfolio. Later in September Okruashvili, who established a new opposition party, the Movement for a United Georgia, publicly accused Saakashvili of corruption and of conspiring to kill a prominent Georgian businessman resident in the United Kingdom, Arkadi (Badri) Patarkatsishvili, who owned several media organizations in Georgia, including the Imedi television channel. Two days later Okruashvili was arrested on charges of financial malpractice and misuse of office while serving as Minister of Defence, prompting a large rally staged outside the parliamentary building to demand his release and early legislative elections. Early in October Okruashvili withdrew the accusations of criminal behaviour he had made against Saakashvili, and also confessed to criminal charges against him; he was released on bail and subsequently announced that he had left active politics. In November he stated that he had been forced to retract the accusations while in detention, and left Georgia. Later that month he was arrested and detained in Germany in response to a request of the Georgian authorities, but was transferred to France on the grounds that the visa on which he had been permitted to travel to Germany had been issued by France; he was released on bail in January 2008. In March a Georgian court found Okruashvili was found guilty of embezzlement, and sentenced him *in absentia* to 11 years' imprisonment. In late April it was announced that France had granted Okruashvili political asylum.

In October 2007 a 10-party opposition alliance presented a joint manifesto to the authorities, demanding that elections to Parlamenti be conducted in early 2008, the electoral system be reformed, new election bodies established owing to the party affiliation of the existing CEC, and political prisoners released.

In early November the alliance announced a campaign of rallies in support of its demands, while Patarkatsishvili declared that he would provide funding to the opposition for organized protests. In early November the opposition organized its largest rally outside the parliamentary building; however, Burjanadze and other government leaders insisted that the authorities would not revise the electoral schedule. Protests continued, and the opposition issued a demand for Saakashvili's resignation. On 7 November, after protesters clashed with police, special forces violently dispersed opposition supporters; later that day the Government declared a national state of emergency, under the terms of which broadcasts of the Imedi television channel were suspended by the police. On the following day Saakashvili announced that a presidential election would be held on 5 January 2008, and a referendum early that year to determine whether legislative elections should be brought forward. The authorities announced that the Chairman of the Georgian Labour Party, Shalva Natelashvili, together with another opposition leader, had been charged with espionage and conspiring to overthrow the Government with Russian support, and that Patarkatsishvili was suspected of complicity. On 16 November the state of emergency was ended by parliamentary decree; on the same day Saakashvili dismissed Noghaideli and nominated Vladimer (Lado) Gurgenidze, hitherto the Chairman of the Bank of Georgia, to the premiership. A reorganized Government (with only two new ministers) was subsequently approved by Parlamenti. On 25 November Saakashvili resigned the presidency, as required by the Constitution, in order to campaign for the forthcoming election; Burjanadze replaced him in an interim capacity. In early December Imedi resumed broadcasts.

The alliance of nine opposition parties agreed to nominate Levan Gachechiladze, a parliamentary deputy with no party affiliation, to contest the presidential election. (The Georgian Labour Party, formerly part of the coalition, had announced its intention to present Natelashvili.) In late December Patarkatsishvili, who had registered to contest the election, announced his withdrawal from the poll (although his name remained on the ballot) and returned to the United Kingdom, claiming that the Georgian authorities planned his assassination. At the presidential election, which was contested by seven candidates on 5 January 2008, Saakashvili was re-elected with 53.5% of votes cast; Gachechiladze secured 25.7% of votes. At the concurrent referendum some 79.9% of votes cast were in favour of bringing forward legislative elections to be conducted early that year. Despite opposition claims of electoral malpractice and demands for a second round, the presidential results were officially recognized by the CEC on 13 January. Saakashvili was inaugurated on 20 January. A reorganized administration was approved by Parlamenti at the end of January (with opposition deputies boycotting the session); government changes included the appointment of new Ministers of Justice and the Economy. In February the death of Patarkatsishvili at his British residence prompted immediate speculation that he had been assassinated; however, initial medical investigations concluded that he had died from natural causes. On 26 February Parlamenti adopted constitutional amendments providing for legislative elections to be brought forward to May, and for certain changes to government organization; however, voting on other significant reforms (including the reduction of the minimum percentage of the votes required for parliamentary representation from 7% to 5%) was postponed, owing to the continued boycott by opposition parties. On 12 March Parlamenti adopted further constitutional amendments, which reduced the number of legislative deputies from 235 to 150, of whom 75 were to be elected on the basis of proportional representation and 75 in single-member constituencies.

Following his return to Georgia in March 1992, Eduard Shevardnadze struggled to resolve the inter-ethnic tensions in several regions of Georgia that had enjoyed a nominally autonomous status during the Soviet period. These tensions had intensified following the election of Gamsakhurdia's nationalist Government in 1990, and had led to serious armed conflict in South Ossetia and Abkhazia.

The Autonomous Republic of Adjara, in south-west Georgia, proved to be the least troubled of the country's three autonomous territories. Despite being of ethnic Georgian origin, the Ajars, whose autonomous status was the result of a Soviet-Turkish Treaty of Friendship (1921), retained a sense of separate identity, owing to their adherence to Islam. In April 1991 there were prolonged demonstrations in protest against proposals to abolish Adjaran autonomy. Elections to the Supreme Council (legislature) of Adjara were held in September 1996, and Aslan Abashidze was re-elected Chairman of the Adjaran Supreme Council (regional leader), a position he had held since 1991. (Abashidze had concurrently been a Deputy Chairman of the Georgian Supreme Council in 1991–95.) In December the deployment of armoured vehicles, allegedly from Russian military units, on the streets of Batumi, the republic's capital, led to tension between the Georgian authorities and the leadership of Adjara; Abashidze denied reports that a state of emergency had been declared, and announced that the military units were carrying out deployment exercises.

In November 2001 Abashidze stood as the only candidate in a direct election to the new post of Head of the Republic, which replaced that of Chairman of the Adjaran Supreme Council. In the same month he was appointed as President Shevardnadze's personal representative for conflict resolution in Abkhazia. In early December Adjara's new bicameral legislature (composed of the Council of the Republic and the Senate), held its inaugural session, following the implementation of amendments to the region's Constitution, which had been agreed in July.

Following the disputed Georgian legislative elections of early November 2003 (see above), Abashidze announced the dispatch of hundreds of supporters to Tbilisi, in an attempt to prevent the overthrow of Shevardnadze's regime. (According to the official results of the national elections, which were declared invalid on 25 November, Abashidze's Democratic Union of Revival had been the second-placed party nationally.) In response to Shevardnadze's resignation on 23 November, Abashidze declared an immediate state of emergency in Adjara. He subsequently pledged to boycott the national presidential election due to be held in early January 2004, condemning it as unconstitutional. In the event, following US pressure, the region did participate in the election, but the state of emergency, which had been lifted the day before the election took place, was swiftly reimposed, prompting criticism from the Georgian Government. Meanwhile, a number of opposition movements (in particular, Our Adjara and a regional branch of the student organization *Kmara*) had became active in the region, with the clear aim of replicating the peaceful transfer of power that had taken place within the central Government, amid reports of their repression by the local authorities.

Further tensions between Abashidze and the Georgian Government emerged in early 2004. On 13 March the Georgian Minister of Finance, Zurab Noghaideli, was briefly detained by the Adjaran security services while visiting Batumi, and the following day the recently elected Georgian President, Mikheil Saakashvili, was prevented from entering the region. He subsequently issued an ultimatum, demanding that Adjara: allow members of the central Government freedom of movement; ensure that the national parliamentary elections, due to take place on 28 March, were conducted freely and fairly in the region; disarm all illegal armed formations; and cede to the central Government supervision of finance and communications (including borders and customs controls). Economic sanctions were subsequently imposed on the region. Following Russian mediation, talks between Saakashvili and Abashidze took place in Batumi on 18 March, at which Abashidze agreed to permit free campaigning for the national legislative elections, in return for a pledge by the Georgian President to remove the economic blockade. Abashidze gave assurances that a state of emergency, imposed at the beginning of the crisis, would be lifted once Georgian troops, deployed along the border between Adjara and the rest of the country, had been withdrawn.

However, tensions subsequently escalated on 2 May 2004, when Abashidze ordered the destruction of bridges linking Adjara with neighbouring regions of Georgia, following military manoeuvres by government troops close to the border, despite assurances by Saakashvili that the Government did not intend to take military action against the region. Saakashvili immediately threatened to dismiss Abashidze and schedule new elections in the region, unless the Adjaran leader disarmed his security forces and agreed to comply with the 'framework of the Georgian Constitution' within a period of 10 days. Large public demonstrations against Abashidze ensued. Following discussions with the Chairman of the Security Council of the Russian Federation (and former Minister of Foreign Affairs), Igor Ivanov, on 5 May Abashidze resigned from office and departed for Russia. Saakashvili immediately imposed presidential rule on the region and on 6 May Parlamenti voted to approve the President's authority to dismiss the Parliament and the Government of the Autonomous Republic of Adjara and to schedule new elections. The Adjaran Supreme Council also voted to abolish the post of Head of the Republic, scheduled new parliamentary elections and dissolved itself. Immunity from prosecution was extended to armed groups that surrendered their weapons within seven days. Levan Varshalomidze was appointed as the head of an interim council to rule the region. On 20 June elections to the new republican unicameral legislature, the Supreme Council, took place. The Saakashvili—Victorious Adjara party received some 75% of the votes cast and 28 of the 30 seats in the Council; the Republican Party won the remaining two seats. On 1 July Parlamenti approved legislation, whereby the President of Georgia would be empowered to dismiss the Adjaran Government, dissolve the parliament and annul legislation. The legislation also prescribed which ministries the Adjaran Government should comprise, specifically excluding those of security and defence. Mikheil Makharadze was elected Chairman of the newly elected Supreme Council; Levan Varshalomidze was the sole candidate for Chairman of the Government. Abashidze's personal fortune and estate was confiscated by the authorities on the grounds that it had been acquired illegally. In January 2005 PACE issued a resolution that commended the peaceful reintegration of Adjara but declared the region to be an inadequate model of autonomy, on the basis that the leader of the republic should be directly elected (rather than selected by the President of Georgia for the approval of the Adjaran parliament). In December a warrant was issued for Abashidze's arrest on charges of abuse of office, terrorist offences and embezzlement, despite claims that Abashidze's resignation had taken place under a guarantee of immunity from prosecution. The relocation of the Constitutional Court of Georgia from Tbilisi to Batumi took effect from September 2006; this move, and the new location of the court, in Abashidze's former residence, was described as a highly symbolic measure by supporters of the Saakashvili administration.

A movement for secession from Georgia had been revived in the Autonomous Republic of Abkhazia (Apsny), in the north-west of Georgia, in 1989. The Abkhaz are a predominantly Muslim people and their region had enjoyed virtual sovereignty within Georgia during the 1920s. In 1930 Abkhazia was made an autonomous republic subordinate to, and within, Georgia and, on Stalin's orders, large numbers of ethnic Georgians were resettled in the region. By 1989 Abkhaz comprised only 18% of the area's population, and Georgians constituted the largest ethnic group (46%). The Georgian Government repeatedly rejected Abkhazian secessionist demands on these demographic grounds, and the movement for Abkhazian independence was also fiercely resisted by the local Georgian population. In July 1989 violent clashes erupted between ethnic Georgians and Abkhaz in Sukhumi (Sukhum or Sokhumi), the republic's capital, resulting in 14 deaths. A state of emergency was imposed throughout Abkhazia, but troops did not succeed in preventing further inter-ethnic violence.

In August 1990 the Abkhazian Supreme Soviet voted to declare independence from Georgia. This declaration was pronounced invalid by the Georgian Supreme Soviet, and ethnic Georgians in Abkhazia staged protests and began a rail blockade of Sukhumi. In late August Georgian deputies in the Abkhazian legislature succeeded in reversing the declaration of independence. Inter-ethnic unrest continued during late 1990 and in 1991. Following the overthrow of Zviad Gamsakhurdia as President of Georgia in January 1992, there was renewed unrest in Abkhazia, as large numbers of ethnic Georgians demonstrated in support of Gamsakhurdia. In July the Abkhazian legislature declared Abkhazia's sovereignty as the 'Republic of Abkhazia'.

A period of violent armed conflict began in August 1992, when the Georgian Government dispatched some 3,000 members of the National Guard to the republic, allegedly in order to release senior officials who had been taken hostage by Zviadists and who were apparently being held in Abkhazia (see above). The Chairman of the Abkhazian legislature and leader of the independence campaign, Vladislav Ardzinba, retreated north with his forces. The situation was complicated by the dispatch of Russian paratroopers to the region to protect Russian (former Soviet) military bases, and relations between Georgia and Russia became strained, amid reports of Russian complicity in supplying military assistance to the separatists. In October 1992 an Abkhazian counter-offensive resulted in separatist forces regaining control of northern Abkhazia; hostilities intensified further in the first half of 1993. None the less, a provisional peace agreement was signed in July by Georgian and Abkhazian leaders. The cease-fire held until September, when a series of attacks by Abkhazian forces resulted in the recapture of Sukhumi after 11 days of intense fighting. Shevardnadze, who had arrived in Sukhumi at the beginning of the offensive, was forced to flee by air, under heavy bombardment. By late September almost all Georgian forces had been expelled from Abkhazia.

Several hundred people were believed to have been killed during the fighting, and more than 200,000 people (mostly ethnic Georgians) fled Abkhazia. Many thousands of the refugees were subsequently stranded, in freezing conditions, near the mountainous south-eastern border region of Abkhazia, where large numbers perished. The situation in Abkhazia following the rout of the Georgian forces was reported to be close to anarchy. Nevertheless, in early December 1993 Georgian and Abkhazian officials signed an eight-point 'memorandum of understanding' at UN-sponsored talks in Geneva, Switzerland. A small number of UN military personnel, part of the UN Observer Mission in Georgia (UNOMIG, see p. 86) were subsequently dispatched to Sukhumi in a peace-keeping capacity.

Outbreaks of violence continued in Abkhazia throughout 1994, although peace talks were held at regular intervals. The fundamental disagreement between the Georgian and Abkhazian delegations concerned the future status of Abkhazia: Ardzinba demanded full independence for Abkhazia, while the Georgian Government insisted on the preservation of Georgia's territorial integrity. However, hope for a peaceful solution was raised in May, by the declaration of a full cease-fire. Under the accord, a contingent of some 2,500 CIS (mainly Russian) peace-keepers was deployed in June, joining an augmented UN observer force in Abkhazia. Nevertheless, hostilities continued.

In November 1994 the Abkhazian legislature adopted a new Constitution, which declared the 'Republic of Abkhazia' to be a sovereign state. Ardzinba was elected to the new post of 'President'. The declaration of sovereignty was condemned by the Georgian Government, and the peace negotiations were suspended. Protests were also expressed by the USA, Russia and the UN Security Council, all of which reaffirmed their recognition of Georgia's territorial integrity. Peace talks were resumed in 1995, despite periodic outbreaks of violence. In January 1996, at a summit meeting of CIS leaders in Moscow, it was agreed to implement Shevardnadze's request for economic sanctions to be imposed against Abkhazia until it consented to rejoin Georgia.

On 23 November 1996 elections to the secessionist Abkhazian 'legislature', the People's Assembly, were held. The UN and the OSCE severely criticized the holding of the elections, which were not recognized by the Georgian authorities. The mandate of the CIS peace-keeping forces in Abkhazia was the focus of much controversy in 1997, and members of the Abkhazian faction in Parlamenti staged a hunger strike in March, demanding their withdrawal. However, the peace-keepers' mandate was repeatedly extended. In July violent clashes took place in the Kodori Gorge region of Abkhazia. Peace talks sponsored by the UN were subsequently held in Geneva, but no formal conclusion was reached. The UN observers' mandate, which expired on 31 July, was subsequently granted successive six-monthly extensions. Russian proposals for a settlement of the conflict, which provided for substantial autonomy for Abkhazia, while retaining Georgia's territorial integrity, were welcomed by Shevardnadze, but rejected by Ardzinba. In August, for the first time since 1992, Ardzinba visited Tbilisi, together with the Russian Minister of Foreign Affairs, Yevgenii Primakov. Talks were held with Shevardnadze and a reaffirmation of both sides' commitment to a peaceful resolution of the conflict was made. In mid-November 1997 UN-sponsored talks were convened, at which it was agreed to establish a joint Co-ordinating Council, in which representatives of the parties to the conflict, as well as Russian, UN and European Union (EU, see p. 244) delegates, were to participate.

In May 1998 there was a brief renewal of hostilities, following an attempt by Abkhazian troops to enter the neutral zone between Abkhazia and the remainder of Georgia in order to force ethnic Georgians out of the district of Gali, in south-eastern Abkhazia. Georgian forces were put on full combat alert, and tens of thousands of ethnic Georgian refugees fled the region. Negotiations resumed in June; Georgia's principal demand was the prompt and unconditional repatriation to Gali of some 35,000 ethnic Georgians who had been forced to flee. In January 1999 Ardzinba agreed to permit ethnic Georgian refugees to return to Gali from 1 March. However, their return and the convening of proposed peace talks in Gali were hindered by a one-month blockade of the road bridge permitting access to Abkhazia by refugees demanding, *inter alia*, that Georgia leave the CIS and that persecution of ethnic Georgian guerrillas be halted.

On 3 October 1999 Ardzinba, the sole candidate, was re-elected 'President', reportedly with 99% of the votes cast; the rate of participation was 87.7%. The election was declared illegal by international observers. In a referendum held concurrently, 97% of the votes cast were reported to have upheld the 1994 Constitution that proclaimed Abkhazia as an independent, democratic republic. Shortly afterwards the Abkhazian legislature unanimously passed the State Independence Act. None the less, Georgia remained determined to pursue peace talks, and in July 2000 a UN-sponsored protocol on stabilization measures was signed by Abkhazia and Georgia. However, violent incidents continued.

In March 2001, at a summit meeting held in Yalta, Crimea, Ukraine, under UN auspices, Abkhazia and Georgia signed an accord renouncing the use of force. However, hostilities resumed in Abkhazia in early October, when a UN helicopter was shot down over the Kodori Gorge, killing all nine of its passengers. The UN mission was subsequently suspended, and violence in the region intensified; Abkhazian officials blamed the attack on pro-Georgian guerrillas and on dissidents from the separatist Chechen Republic within Russia. The Abkhazian authorities blamed Georgia for subsequent aerial attacks on villages in the Kodori Gorge; Georgia, in turn, attributed responsibility for the attacks to Russia, and made repeated allegations of violations of Georgian airspace by Russian aircraft in October–November. The Georgian Government dispatched troops to the region in October, ostensibly to protect the ethnic Georgian population there, in what was deemed by the UN to be a violation of the cease-fire agreement of 1994.

In October 2001 Parlamenti voted to request the immediate withdrawal of the CIS peace-keeping forces from Abkhazia; however, Shevardnadze argued against their removal, as no substitute force was forthcoming. In January 2002 the Georgian and Abkhazian authorities signed a protocol, according to which Georgia agreed to withdraw the troops deployed in the Kodori Gorge; the two sides signed a further protocol in early April, and later that month the Georgian Ministry of Defence announced that the withdrawal of its military forces had taken place as agreed. However, in the same month the Abkhazian authorities suspended their participation in the UN-sponsored Co-ordinating Council. Meanwhile, UNOMIG resumed its activities in February, recommencing patrols of the Kodori Gorge, together with the Russian-led peace-keeping forces, in late March, following the extension of their mandate. At a CIS summit meeting held in March Shevardnadze and the Russian President, Vladimir Putin, agreed to amend the mandate of the CIS peace-keeping forces, to satisfy Georgian demands that they withdraw to a more northerly position, undertake policing duties and include forces from countries other than Russia. Legislative elections, which were held in Abkhazia on 2 March, were deemed to be illegal by the Georgian Government. In late July the UN Security Council adopted Resolution 1427, which urged the resumption of negotiations on Abkhazia's status within Georgia.

In late January 2003 the Georgian National Security Council ruled that the country would not approve a renewal of the CIS peace-keepers' mandate (which had expired at the end of December 2002) until, *inter alia*, the definition of the conflict zone was extended and a recently resumed railway service from the Russian Black Sea port of Sochi to Tbilisi, via Sukhumi, was halted; the Government objected to the operation of the railway link prior to the repatriation of the ethnic Georgian refugees from Abkhazia. In mid-February the National Security Council finally agreed to remove all objections to the renewal of the peace-keepers' mandate, and in early March, following talks in Sochi, Presidents Shevardnadze and Putin issued a joint statement, according to which they agreed to expedite the repatriation of displaced persons to Abkhazia, prior to the resumption of the railway service. In addition, they agreed to extend indefinitely the mandate of the CIS peace-keeping forces, until either Georgia or Abkhazia explicitly demanded their withdrawal.

Following Shevardnadze's removal from power in late 2003 (see above), there were demands for the resignation of Gen. Tamaz Nadareishvili, the Chairman of the Tbilisi-based Abkhazian parliament-in-exile (comprising deputies elected to the Abkhazian parliament in 1991), who was accused of corruption. Nadareishvili eventually resigned in mid-January 2004, and was replaced by a member of President Mikheil Saakashvili's National Movement in mid-March.

An internationally unrecognized presidential election took place on 3 October 2004, in which former 'Prime Minister' of Abkhazia Raul Khadzhimba, the candidate endorsed by Ardzinba and supported by Russia, was initially declared the winner. However, Khadzhimba's rival Sergei Bagapsh (the head of the Chernomorenergo energy company) was ultimately judged to have received the most votes, by a narrow margin. Khadzhimba disputed this result, demanding the annulment of the ballot. (In early December Russia suspended the rail link with the region, which had only been resumed from September, on the basis of security concerns.) An agreement was reached on 6 December, under the mediation of Russian officials, according to which the two candidates were to participate jointly in a new election. Bagapsh was to contest the presidency, with Khadzhimba as his Vice-President, and with the powers of the latter role to be augmented by an amendment to the separatist territory's 'constitution'. In the repeat election held on 12 January 2005 Sergei Bagapsh was elected as 'President' with some 90% of the votes cast; following his inauguration in February, Bagapsh nominated Aleksandr Ankvab, a close ally, as 'Prime Minister'. Ankvab survived assassination attempts in February and April, which were officially attributed to criminal groups. Despite Russia's apparent preference for Khadzhimba's presidential candidacy, Bagapsh also sought a strategic union with Russia. In February Saakashvili appointed Irakli Alasania, the head of the Tbilisi-based Abkhazian Government-in-exile, as special envoy for negotiations with the separatist authorities; however, the authorities refused to conduct talks with him on the basis that they did not recognize his official title as legitimate.

In mid-2005 the Georgian authorities indicated that they might cease to link the reopening of the Sochi–Tbilisi railway with the return of displaced persons, and in December the Georgian Prime Minister Noghaideli and the Russian Minister of Transport Igor Levitin signed a protocol on the establishment of an international consortium to fund the restoration and operation of the railway. In October Parlamenti adopted a resolution establishing a deadline of 15 June 2006 for the Russian peace-keeping forces in the region to demonstrate compliance with their mandate. In February 2006 negotiations took place in Geneva between representatives of the Georgian and Abkhazian authorities. Although Bagapsh had expressed willingness to discuss all aspects of the conflict except for the issue of Abkhazia's status, UN representatives (from France, Germany, Russia, the United Kingdom and the USA) asserted that in addition to making progress on confidence-building measures, including the preparation of a document on the non-resumption of hostilities and the facilitation of the return of refugees, the two sides should address 'core political issues' relating to the conflict. In May officials from Abkhazia, Georgia, Armenia and Russia signed a protocol establishing the Black Sea Railways consortium, which was charged with rebuilding the section of the railway in Abkhazia.

Meanwhile, at the end of March 2006 the UN Security Council voted to extend UNOMIG's mandate for a further six-month period. In the same month the Georgian Government announced that it would reopen negotiations with Abkhazian officials; in May the UN-sponsored Co-ordinating Council convened in Tbilisi to oversee talks between the two sides, which focused on security and socio-economic issues and the repatriation of Georgian refugees. In late July Georgian government forces launched an operation to disarm an armed militia group, *Monadire* (Hunter), in the upper Kodori Gorge, and capture its leader, Emzar Kvitsiani, and 'restore constitutional order' to the region. Despite claims to the contrary, the Georgian Government insisted that its forces comprised only police and security personnel and that no military troops were involved. On 27 July President Saakashvili announced that Georgian forces had, for the first time in 13 years, regained full control of the Kodori Gorge and surrounding regions; on the following day Saakashvili ordered the Abkhazian parliament-in-exile to relocate to Chkhalta, in the newly captured region, which was henceforth to be officially known as Upper Abkhazia, as part of efforts to ensure that eventual central control over the republic be restored. In an address at a session of the UN General Assembly in September, Saakashvili stated that Georgia would acquiesce to an agreement on the non-resumption of hostilities and the safe return of refugees only if Russian peace-keeping troops in Abkhazia were replaced by a multinational police force. On 13 October the UN Security Council adopted a resolution that urged Georgia to refrain from 'provocative' actions in Abkhazia and underlined the significance of Russian peace-keeping forces therein; the Council also voted to extend the mandate of UNOMIG for another six months. Also in October US ambassador to the UN John Bolton affirmed his country's support for Georgia's sovereign integrity and declared that the Georgian Government had acted within its rights during attempts to quell the militant uprising in the Kodori Gorge.

On 11 February 2007 local elections were held in Abkhazia. On 4 March some 108 candidates contested the elections for the republic's 35-member legislature; however, the initial poll produced an outright victor in only 18 constituencies. On the following day the Abkhazian 'Central Election Committee' upheld the parliamentary elections as legitimate, on the grounds that 48% of the electorate had participated, comfortably surpassing the turn-out of 25% required to render the process valid. However, the Georgian Government denounced both sets of elections as illegal. On 18 March a second round of voting was held for the 17 seats not filled in the first round. Meanwhile, in mid-March three military helicopters made a series of aerial bombings in the Kodori Gorge area of Georgian-controlled Upper Abkhazia, although no casualties ensued. Both the Russian and separatist Abkhazian authorities denied any involvement in the attacks, although some reports stated that the helicopters had entered the territory from Russian airspace. Following the announcement in July that Russia was to host the 2014 Winter Olympic Games in the Black Sea resort of Sochi, reports that Russian enterprises intended to import materials for the construction of sports facilities from nearby Abkhazia (with considerable potential benefit to the local economy) prompted strong protests from Georgian officials. The widespread granting of Russian passports to residents of Abkhazia (and of South Ossetia) was also a further source of tension between Georgia and Russia in the mid-2000. This tension intensified in early 2008; in March Russia announced that it was to lift CIS sanctions against the separatist Abkhazian regime; one consequence of this decision would be that military assistance could more readily be granted to the de facto administration there. In the same month the separatist Abkhazian authorities rejected a new proposal for a resolution of the status of the territory presented by Georgian President Saakashvili; the proposals included the maintenance of extensive autonomy for the territory within Georgia, and the establishment of a Georgian vice-presidential post to represent Abkhazia that would hold the power to veto governmental decisions relating to the region. The announcement, in April, that Russia was to establish closer relations with the separatist territories, was described by the Georgian Minister of Foreign Affairs, Davit Bakradze, as effectively constituting the annexation of part of the country.

Ossetia (Osetiya), the original inhabitants of which are an East Iranian people, was divided into two parts under Stalin, with North Osetiya (later North Osetiya—Alaniya) falling under Russian jurisdiction as a nominally autonomous republic and South Ossetia assuming the lesser status of an autonomous oblast (region) within Georgia. At the census of 1979 ethnic Ossetians comprised 66% of the oblast's population. The longstanding Georgian animosity towards the Ossetians was exacerbated by the Ossetians' traditional pro-Russian stance. The current dispute began in 1989, when Ossetian demands for greater autonomy and eventual reunification with North Osetiya (and thus integration into Russia) led to violent clashes between local Georgians and Ossetians. Troops of the Soviet Ministry of Internal Affairs were dispatched to South Ossetia in January 1990, but in September the South Ossetian Supreme Soviet (legislature) proclaimed South Ossetia's independence from Georgia (as the 'South Ossetian Soviet Democratic Republic') and state sovereignty within the USSR. This decision was declared unconstitutional by the Georgian Supreme Soviet, which in December revoked the region's nominally autonomous status. Following renewed violence, the Georgian legislature declared a state of emergency in Tskhinvali, the principal city in South Ossetia (by which name the Georgian authorities now referred to the entire region).

In January 1991 Soviet President Gorbachev annulled both South Ossetia's declaration of independence and the Georgian Supreme Soviet's decision of December 1990. However, violence continued throughout 1991, with the resulting displacement of many thousands of refugees, both prior and subsequent to Georgia's declaration of independence, despite a series of short-lived cease-fires. In December the South Ossetian Supreme Soviet declared a state of emergency and a general mobilization, in response to the Georgian Government's dispatch of troops to the region. In the same month the South Ossetian legislature adopted a second declaration of the region's independence, as well as a resolution in favour of its integration into Russia. The resolutions were endorsed at a referendum held in the region in January 1992. Hostilities continued, compounded by the intervention of Georgian government troops. The situation was further complicated by the arrival of volunteer fighters from North Osetiya, in support of their South Ossetian neighbours.

In June 1992 negotiations between Shevardnadze and President Boris Yeltsin of Russia led to an agreement to secure a lasting cease-fire and a peaceful solution to the conflict (in which more than 400 Georgians and 1,000 Ossetians had been killed since 1989). Peace-keeping monitors (comprising Georgians, Ossetians and Russians) were deployed during July, with the simultaneous withdrawal of all armed forces from the region. The return of refugees began in that month. However, no political settlement to the conflict was reached, and some parts of South Ossetia remained effectively a seceded territory; on 23 December 1993 the separatist authorities introduced a new 'Constitution', which referred to the territory as the 'Republic of South Ossetia'. (However, separatists failed to gain control over the full territorial extent of the former Autonomous Oblast, and the region was characterized by the existence of discrete areas controlled either by supporters of the central Government in Tbilisi, or of the separatist 'Republic', a situation that continued to prevail in early 2008.) The lack of a formal settlement delayed the repatriation of refugees: in early 1994 some 11,000 South Ossetians remained in North Osetiya, while some 7,000 ethnic Georgians had yet to return to their homes. In July 1995 representatives from Georgia, Russia, North Osetiya and South Ossetia reopened talks on a political settlement, under the aegis of the OSCE. In April 1996 a memorandum 'on strengthening mutual trust and security measures' was initialled in Tskhinvali; it was signed in Moscow in the following month. Meetings were subsequently held between President Shevardnadze and Ludvig Chibirov, the Chairman of the South Ossetian 'legislature', to negotiate South Ossetia's political status. In September, however, the separatist legislature approved an amendment to its Constitution to allow the introduction of a presidential system of government. Despite the Georgian leadership's declaration that the results of any election would be considered illegitimate, an election to the post of 'President' of South Ossetia was held on 10 November, and was won by Chibirov.

Quadripartite negotiations were held throughout 1997, and it was agreed that the policing role of peace-keeping forces deployed in South Ossetia was to be transferred to regional law-enforcement bodies. Talks held in Moscow in March confirmed the principle of Georgia's territorial integrity, while allowing a measure of self-determination for South Ossetia. In September Shevardnadze and Chibirov signed an agreement on the return of refugees to South Ossetia. Legislative elections took place in the regions of South Ossetia controlled by separatists in May 1999; the local Communist Party secured about 39% of the votes cast. The elections were not recognized by the OSCE or by the Georgian authorities. In April 2001 a referendum was held in South Ossetia, at which 69% of those who participated voted in favour of adopting amendments to the 1993 'Constitution', which included the designation of both Georgian and Russian as official languages, in addition to Ossetian. The plebiscite was not recognized as legal by the Georgian Government, and it was boycotted by South Ossetia's ethnic Georgian population. In a presidential election held in November–December 2001 a Russian-based businessman, Eduard Kokoyev (Kokoiti), emerged as the victor, after a second round of voting, securing 55% of the votes cast. Although Kokoyev declared himself to be willing to resume talks with the Georgian Government, he also expressed an interest in developing closer ties with Russia, particularly with North Osetiya. Kokoyev was inaugurated on 18 December; in subsequent months he oversaw a policy of granting Russian citizenship to many residents of the regions of South Ossetia under separatist control. Kokoyev's Unity Party won a majority of seats in legislative elections held on 23 May 2004.

Proposals for the granting to South Ossetia of broad autonomy, including the right to directly elected self-governance, which were presented by the Georgian authorities in 2004–05, were repeatedly rejected by the separatist leadership. In December 2005 Kokoyev submitted his own proposals, which endorsed President Saakashvili's planned three-stage format for resolving the conflict (focusing on demilitarization, confidence-building, and social and economic reconstruction, prior to a decision on South Ossetia's political status), but without imposing a timetable. Meanwhile, in October Parlamenti had approved a resolution establishing a deadline of 10 February 2006 for the Russian peace-keeping force deployed in South Ossetia to demonstrate their compliance with the terms of their mandate. In early February the commander of the peace-keeping troops reportedly stated that their mandate could not be revoked without the agreement of all four parties to the Joint Control Commission charged with monitoring the security situation. Nevertheless, on 15 February Parlamenti unanimously adopted a second resolution, which demanded that the Government replace the peace-keepers with international forces, but without stipulating a deadline. Amid rising tensions in South Ossetia and deteriorating relations with Russia, Georgia subsequently announced proposals for the demilitarization of the conflict zone, and a willingness to participate in talks with the aim of resolving the conflict through peaceful means.

In July 2006 Oleg Alborov, secretary of South Ossetia's self-styled 'National Security Council', was killed when a bomb exploded outside his residence in Tskhinvali; another bomb attack in Tskhinvali, at the home of Bala Bestayev, a well-known South Ossetian militia leader, killed two people and injured two others. South Ossetian officials alleged that the attacks had been carried out by the Georgian Government. In the same month three South Ossetian residents were sentenced to life imprisonment, following convictions for a car bombing in February 2004 at a Georgian police station. In August South Ossetian officials began issuing Russian passports to residents of the territory, provoking outrage from the Georgian Government, which branded the introduction of the new passports an illegitimate act of provocation; it was reported in the following year that a majority of citizens in those regions under South Ossetian control had been issued with Russian passports.

On 12 November 2006 presidential elections were held in those areas of South Ossetia controlled by the separatist authorities. Kokoyev was overwhelmingly elected to a second term in office, reportedly attracting 98.1% of the votes cast. The poll coincided with a referendum, in which voters were asked whether or not South Ossetia should preserve its de facto independent status. Results released by the 'South Ossetian Central Election Commission' indicated that 99% of those who voted had cast their ballots in favour of independence from Georgia; voter turn-out was reported to be 95.2% of the registered electorate. However, what was termed an 'alternative election' for a regional 'President' was held concurrently in those South Ossetian territories that remained under control of the Georgian state; this poll was reported to have been won by an opponent of Kokoyev, Dmitry Sanakoyev, a former rebel leader. A referendum held in these territories also expressed approval, by a resounding majority, for the commencement of negotiations with the central authorities in Tbilisi on the establishment of a federal Georgian state, of which South Ossetia would form a unit. Although these polls were not officially recognized, nationally or internationally, Sanakoyev adopted the title 'President of South Ossetia' and announced the formation of an alternative 'Government', based in the village of Kurta, outside Tskhinvali, at the start of December. Also in December Parlamenti approved draft legislation concerning restitution for victims of the South Ossetian conflict; the new laws recognized the right of fugitives of the conflict to return to their abandoned homes and assured victims of financial compensation for material damage caused to property. In mid-March 2007 President Saakashvili visited Kurta, and extended an offer to rebuild infrastructure damaged by the fighting in the early 1990s. However, the President's visit was not welcomed by the South Ossetian authorities led by Kokoyev, who accused Saakashvili of attempting to fuel tensions in the region. In early April 2007 Parlamenti approved the formation of an interim South Ossetian administrative unit, among the principal purposes of which would be the promotion of a peaceful resolution of the conflict, the restoration of constitutional order and the creation of the conditions for the holding of democratic elections. On 10 May Sanakoyev became head of the new Provisional Administration of South Ossetia, officially established under a resolution by Parlamenti on 8 May. In July President Saakashvili established a new Joint Control Committee, which was to initiate dialogue between all authorities for settlement of the conflict in South Ossetia. The EU and OSCE expressed support for this initiative.

Georgia was one of only four republics of those that had constituted the USSR not to join the CIS at its formation in December 1991. However, as civil and separatist conflicts threatened to destroy the country, Shevardnadze was forced to reverse official policy on the CIS, and in late 1993 the republic was admitted to that body. In May 1999, however, Georgia failed to renew its adherence to the Collective Security Treaty. Georgia's relations with Russia were strained by developments in secessionist Abkhazia from 1992 and by Georgian accusations of Russian support for the separatists. However, in February 1994 Georgia and Russia signed a 10-year treaty of friendship and co-operation, which provided, *inter alia*, for the establishment of Russian military bases in Georgia. In 1996 President Shevardnadze and the Georgian legislature threatened to close the military bases, unless Russia adopted a firmer stance against the separatists in South Ossetia and Abkhazia.

The lifting of customs and travel restrictions on the Russian–Abkhazian border in September 1999 angered Georgia, and further tension occurred later in the year, owing to the renewed conflict in Russia's Chechen Republic. Georgia denied allegations that it was harbouring Chechen soldiers and selling arms to the breakaway republic. In August 2000, following an accidental bomb attack by Russia on the border with Chechnya, it was agreed that all Russian border guards deployed in Abkhazia and Adjara would be withdrawn by the beginning of November. Furthermore, in November it was agreed that two of the four Russian military bases on Georgian territory would be closed in 2001. Russia repeatedly failed to agree to a deadline for the closure of the two remaining military bases, but in May 2005 it finally announced that the bases would be closed by the end of 2008. An agreement on the closure of the bases was signed by Georgia and Russia at the end of March 2006, and ratified by Parlamenti in mid-April (see below).

In 2000 there were violent disturbances and repeated kidnappings in the Pankisi Gorge, close to the Chechen border, which was inhabited by both ethnic Chechens and Chechen refugees. Despite this, in December Shevardnadze reiterated Georgia's refusal to carry out joint operations in the area with Russian troops. Russia's decision to implement a full visa regime for Georgian citizens entering its territory from January 2001 caused further antagonism between the two countries, particularly since citizens of the separatist republics in Abkhazia and South Ossetia were to be exempt from the requirement. In January 2002 Georgian security forces launched a campaign to reassert government authority and restore order to the Pankisi region, prompting speculation that the operation had been undertaken in an attempt to forestall direct military intervention by Russia. At the end of January Georgia's Deputy Minister of State Security was shot and killed in the Pankisi Gorge, and four police officers were taken hostage in the Gorge in February, prompting élite government security forces to be dispatched to the region; the hostages were released after three days. In the same month the US chargé d'affaires in Georgia announced that international Islamist militants were believed to have established bases in the Pankisi Gorge, a claim that the Georgian authorities appeared unable to refute. In May a US-led military-training programme commenced in Georgia, to equip the armed forces for operations in the Pankisi Gorge.

Relations between Georgia and Russia deteriorated later in 2002. In late August Georgia accused Russia of perpetrating an act of aggression, and announced its preparedness to repel subsequent attacks, when the aerial bombardment of the Pankisi Gorge by unmarked aircraft led to at least one death; Russia denied responsibility for the attack. Some 1,000 Georgian troops consequently attempted to impose control over the region. In September Russian President Vladimir Putin wrote to the UN Secretary-General, warning that unless the Georgian Government was prepared to take direct action to eliminate the Chechen rebels alleged to be operating from its territory, Russia would take unilateral action to counteract the perceived terrorist threat. In early October Georgia extradited five suspected Chechen militants to Russia, although this prompted demonstrations by Chechen refugees living in the Pankisi region. Relations with Russia subsequently improved when, later in the month, Presidents Shevardnadze and Putin reached an agreement, according to which the two countries were to resume joint patrols of their common border, and seek to resolve border issues by diplomatic means.

In February 2004 Presidents Saakashvili and Putin met in Moscow, where progress was made towards the planned signature of a framework agreement on issues of significance for the two countries, including energy, the Abkhazian conflict and co-operation in efforts to combat terrorism. Relations with Russia, which were already strained, deteriorated in January 2006, when two natural gas pipelines and a power line supplying power to Georgia from Russia were damaged by a series of explosions. Saakashvili reportedly accused the Russian Government of sabotage, in retaliation for attempts by Georgia to reduce dependency on Russian gas. The decision of the Georgian Parlamenti, in mid-February, to request the replacement of Russian peace-keepers in South Ossetia with international forces (see above), threatened to lead to further tensions between the two countries. Also in February Russia suspended its visa arrangements with Georgia, in protest at Georgia's perceived obstruction of the provision of visas for military personnel, and a visit to Russia by Georgian Prime Minister Zurab Noghaideli was postponed by the Russian authorities. In March Russia banned the import of wine from Georgia, apparently owing to suspected contamination with pesticides (exports to Russia accounted for approximately 80% of Georgian wine exports). The Georgian Government railed against the decision, which it claimed was politically motivated. A popular brand of Georgian mineral water was banned from Russian shops and restaurants in May, again on the grounds of alleged health concerns, provoking further claims of Russian political machinations aimed at damaging the economy of its neighbour. In late September Georgian security forces detained four Russian military officers on suspicion of espionage. In early October President Saakashvili announced that the officers had been transferred to the authority of the OSCE, which arranged for their return to Russia. In response to the detention of the officers, Russia withdrew its ambassador from Georgia, cut all transport and postal links between the two countries, and expelled several hundred ethnic Georgians (whom the Russian authorities stated were illegal immigrants) from Russia. Russia's ambassador returned to Tbilisi in January 2007, although economic sanctions imposed by Russia against Georgia remained in place. In late March Georgia lodged a case at the European Court of Human Rights in response to the expulsions. In March 2006 Georgia and Russia signed an agreement providing for a Russian withdrawal from the military base that it maintained at Akhalkalaki and headquarters at Tbilisi by the end of 2007, and from the second base at Batumi in 2008. In the event, the withdrawal of Russian forces from the military bases was completed in November 2007, earlier than scheduled, although, the continued deployment of Russian peace-keeping forces in Abkhazia and South Ossetia remained a source of tension.

In August 2007 the Georgian authorities issued an announcement urging the international community to condemn the alleged violation of Georgian airspace by two military aircraft originating from Russia, and the apparent launch of a missile near South Ossetia. The Russian Government strongly denied the allegations; however, international experts subsequently confirmed that at least one aircraft had entered Georgian airspace from Russia. Following the imposition of a national state of emergency in early November (see above), Georgia expelled three Russian embassy staff, on the grounds that they were engaged in subversive activities against the Government, prompting Russia to expel three Georgian diplomats in retaliation. Tensions heightened further in early 2008, as Russia announced its intension of establishing closer relations with the separatist authorities in Abkhazia and South Ossetia (see above).

Relations with the USA became increasingly cordial in the mid-2000s. The USA openly condemned the conduct of the parliamentary elections of November 2003, and the US Secretary of State, Colin Powell, attended US-educated Saakashvili's inauguration as President in January 2004. In February Saakashvili visited Washington, DC, where he attended talks with US President George W. Bush. In May 2005 President Bush made a brief state visit to Georgia, during which he praised the 'rose revolution' and endorsed the Government's efforts to bring about reform. In September 2005 Saakashvili and the US Secretary of State, Condoleezza Rice, signed an agreement, according to which the USA was to disburse some US $300m. in aid to Georgia over a period of five years. In February 2006 Georgian and US representatives signed a further agreement, pledging to increase co-operation in combating the smuggling of nuclear and radioactive materials, which had been a persistent source of concern in Georgia and the wider Caucasus region. In July Saakashvili visited Washington, DC, whereupon he met with President Bush and Condoleezza Rice to discuss the political situation in Georgia, energy co-operation and Georgia's uneasy relationship with Russia. President Bush affirmed his country's support for Georgian ambitions of NATO membership and praised the Georgian Government for its progress towards democratic reform. In September the USA pledged to provide Georgia with $40m. as part of a wider programme of US military assistance intended to improve Georgian defence capabilities. In 2007 Georgia's presence in Iraq was increased from 850 personnel to 2,000.

In January 2005 President Saakashvili visited the newly inaugurated President Viktor Yushchenko in Ukraine (see the chapter on Ukraine), and signed a document known as the Carpathian Declaration, which referred to the events that had led to both leaders coming to power as marking a 'new wave of the liberation of Europe, that would lead to the final victory of freedom and democracy on the European continent'. In August the two Presidents, meeting in Borjmi, Georgia, signed another declaration (the Borjomi Declaration), on the creation of a new Community of Democratic Choice, an alliance that was intended to remove divisions and resolve conflicts in the Baltic, Black Sea and Caspian regions. The new, nine-country grouping was officially launched in December, at a meeting in Kyiv, Ukraine.

In April 1996 Georgia (together with Armenia and Azerbaijan) signed an agreement on partnership and co-operation with the EU, and in January 1999 it joined the Council of Europe. In March 2005 the European Commission recommended strengthening relations with Georgia under its European Neighbourhood Policy, in which Georgia had been included in June 2004. In November 2002 Georgia formally applied for membership of the North Atlantic Treaty Organization (NATO, see p. 340). In October 2004 NATO approved a two-year Individual Partnership Action Plan with Georgia, the intention of which was to enhance dialogue and consultation between the parties. At a NATO summit meeting in Rīga, Latvia, in November 2006, Georgia received formal acknowledgement and praise for its efforts in conducting an 'intensified dialogue' with the Organization, as well as for its contribution to international peace-keeping and security operations. During the summit NATO also reaffirmed its support for the territorial integrity of Georgia.

Government

Under the Constitution of August 1995, the President of Georgia is Head of State and the head of the executive, and also Commander-in-Chief of the Armed Forces. The President is directly elected for a five-year term (and may not hold office for more than two consecutive terms). The Government is accountable to the President, to whom it acts as an advisory body. Following the adoption of constitutional amendments in February 2004, the Government is headed by the Prime Minister. The supreme legislative body is the unicameral Sakartvelos Parlamenti (Georgian Parliament), which is directly elected for four years. In March 2008 constitutional amendments reduced the number of deputies in Parlamenti from 235 to 150, of whom 75 were to be elected on the basis of proportional representation and 75 in single-member constituencies. (The Constitution provides for a future bicameral Parliament, comprising a Council of the Republic and a Senate, following the eventual restoration of Georgia's territorial integrity.) Georgia contains two nominally autonomous territories: the Autonomous Republic of Adjara; and Abkhazia. The status of Abkhazia and South Ossetia were both disputed, with the former remaining almost entirely outside of central government control. Those parts of the country under central government control are divided into nine mkharebi (regions—singular mkhare) headed by trustees (governors) appointed by the President, and the city of Tbilisi, headed by a mayor. A second tier of local government comprises seven cities of special status and 60 districts (raions), and a third tier comprises a total of 966 villages and settlements.

Defence

One of the principal objectives of the Government following independence in 1991 was to create a unified army from the various existing paramilitary and other groups. A National Security Council (headed by the President of Georgia) was established in early 1996 as a consultative body co-ordinating issues related to defence and security. As assessed at November 2007, the country's total armed forces numbered some 21,150: an army of 17,767, a navy of 495, an air force of 1,310 and a national guard of 1,578. There were also 11,700 paramilitary forces, comprising a border guard of 5,400 and 6,300 troops controlled by the Ministry of Internal Affairs. Military service lasts for 18 months. In March 1994 Georgia joined NATO's 'Partnership for Peace' (see p. 342) programme of military co-operation. President Mikheil Saakashvili planned to implement far-reaching military reform, involving increased expenditure, in conformity with NATO guide-lines. In February 2006 President Saakashvili ended Georgia's participation in the Defence Council of the Commonwealth of Independent States (CIS, see p. 215). A 1,500-member Joint Peace-keeping Force, comprising 500 Russian, Georgian and Ossetian troops, was established in 1992 to maintain a cease-fire in South Ossetia. A Commonwealth of Independent States (CIS) Peace-keeping Force of some 3,000 troops in Abkhazia, was established under a 1994 agreement. In addition, the UN Observer Mission in Georgia (UNOMIG), created in 1993 for deployment in Abkhazia, comprised 131 military observers and 18 police at the end of January 2008. The 2007 budget allocated some 957m. lari to defence.

Economic Affairs

In 2006, according to estimates by the World Bank, Georgia's gross national income (GNI), measured at average 2004–06 prices, was US $6,938m., equivalent to $1,560 per head (or $3,690 per head on an international purchasing-power parity basis). During 1996–2006, it was estimated, the population decreased by an average of 1.1% per year, while gross domestic product (GDP) per head increased, in real terms, by an annual average of 7.6%. Overall GDP increased, in real terms, by an average of 6.4% annually during 1996–2006. Real GDP increased by 9.3% in 2005 and by 9.4% in 2006.

Agriculture contributed 12.7% of GDP in 2006, and the sector (including hunting and forestry) provided 54.3% of the total employed labour force in 2005. Georgia's favourable climate allows the cultivation of subtropical crops, such as tea and oranges. Other fruits (including wine grapes), flowers, tobacco and grain are also cultivated. The mountain pastures are used for sheep- and goat-farming. In 2002 private farms accounted for 94% of the agricultural crop harvest. Production of hazelnuts—which increased by an estimated 28% in 2007, to 30,000 tons—was expected to increase further as a result of investment in the sector by the Italian confectionary firm, Ferrero, which announced plans to purchase 2,000 ha of arable land for cultivation of the crop in early 2008 and were also intending to construct a hazelnut processing facility in the western Samegrelo-Zemo Svaneti region. During 1996–2006, according to the World Bank, agricultural GDP decreased, in real terms, by an average of 0.1% per year. Real agricultural GDP decreased by 12.0% in 2005, but declined by 9.3% in 2006.

Industry contributed 24.6% of GDP in 2006, and the sector (comprising mining, manufacturing, utilities and construction) provided 9.3% of the total employed labour force in 2005. The most significant parts of the sector are the agro-processing and energy industries. According to the World Bank, industrial GDP increased, in real terms, by an annual average of 8.5% in 1996–2006. Construction work on two international pipelines (see below) contributed to significant expansion in the construction, industrial and services sectors in the early 2000s. Real GDP in the sector increased by 14.5% in 2005 and by 14.4% in 2006.

Mining and quarrying accounted for just 1.1% of GDP in 2006 and provided 0.3% of the total employed labour force in 2005. The principal minerals extracted are manganese ore, petroleum and coal, but reserves of high-grade manganese ore are largely depleted. There are also deposits of copper, gold and silver. Substantial natural gas deposits were discovered in 1994–96.

The manufacturing sector contributed 9.8% of GDP in 2006, and it provided 5.1% of the total employed labour force in 2005. Although the machinery and metal-working industries, traditionally the most important parts of the sector, were in decline in the late 1990s, manufacturing GDP increased, in real terms, by an average of 5.3% per year in 1996–2006. Real manufacturing GDP increased by 10.7% in 2005 and by 17.0% in 2006.

Hydroelectric power provided 87.4% of the country's electricity in 2004. However, the country's largest hydroelectric power station was located in the secessionist region of Abkhazia, and the IMF estimated that more than one-third of the power it produced was consumed without payment. Imports of fuel and energy comprised 19.9% of total imports in 2005. In April 1999 a pipeline transporting petroleum to Supsa, on Georgia's Black Sea coast, from Baku, Azerbaijan, officially entered into service. Construction work on a 1,768-km pipeline to carry petroleum from Baku to Ceyhan, Turkey, via Tbilisi (the BTC pipeline) commenced in April 2003, and the Georgian section of the pipeline (measuring some 248 km) was officially inaugurated in October 2005, and commenced operations in July 2006. The South Caucasus Gas Pipeline Project (SCP), which was to transport natural gas from Baku to Erzurum, Turkey, via Tbilisi, running parallel with much of the BTC pipeline, was scheduled to make its first shipments by the end of 2007, Georgia was to receive 5% of the gas transported by the pipeline, as a transit fee.

However, Georgia hoped to develop its own energy resources. New gas-turbine electricity generators commenced operations in early 2006, and the country intended to reconstruct several hydroelectric power plants, as part of measures intended to make the country self-sufficient in electricity.

The services sector contributed 62.7% of GDP in 2006, and it engaged 36.4% of the employed labour force in 2005. Trade and transport and communications are the sector's most significant areas of activity, with telecommunications and hotels and restaurants demonstrating the greatest growth in 2000–03. According to the World Bank, the GDP of the services sector increased, in real terms, by an annual average of 8.4% in 1996–2006. Real sectoral GDP increased by 7.4% in 2005 and by 15.3% in 2006.

In 2006 Georgia recorded a visible trade deficit of US $2,019.4m., and there was a deficit of $1,235.5m. on the current account of the balance of payments. In 2007 Turkey was the principal source of imports (accounting for 20.2% of the total), followed by Russia (16.3%); other major sources were Ukraine, Germany and Azerbaijan. Turkey was also the principal market for exports in that year (accounting for 22.2% of the total), followed by the USA (19.3%); other important purchasers were Azerbaijan and Ukraine. The principal exports in 2006 were Portland cement, ferro-alloys, copper ore and concentrates, and motor cars. The principal imports in that year were petroleum and petroleum oils, motor cars, petroleum gases and other gaseous hydrocarbons, and wheat.

In 2006 there was a budgetary deficit of 34.3m. lari (equivalent to 0.2% of GDP). At the end of 2005 Georgia's total external debt was US $1,911m., of which $1,494m. was long-term public debt. The cost of debt-servicing in that year was equivalent to 7.4% of the value of exports of goods and services. The annual rate of inflation averaged 20.5% during 1995–2005. Consumer prices increased by 6.1% in 2005 and by 8.8% in 2006. In 2005 the average rate of unemployment was 13.8%.

In 1992 Georgia became a member of the IMF and the World Bank, and also joined the European Bank for Reconstruction and Development (EBRD, see p. 239). Georgia is a member of the Organization of the Black Sea Economic Co-operation (see p. 367), and it became a full member of the World Trade Organization (WTO, see p. 396) in 2000.

The collapse of the USSR and the de facto secession of Abkhazia and South Ossetia adversely affected Georgia's economy. The administration of President Mikheil Saakashvili (2004–) announced wide-ranging institutional reforms and the implementation of measures intended to reduce corruption. The Government negotiated international assistance of some US $1,100m. in aid at a donors' meeting held in June 2004; the lending programmes of the IMF and the World Bank resumed in the same month and the 'Paris Club' of creditors restructured $161m. of the country's debt. A financial amnesty programme for illegally acquired property and assets of former state officials generated $500m. by October of that year. Parlamenti subsequently approved a new tax code, introducing a uniform-rate system of personal income tax (of 12%) and reducing the rate of value-added tax from 20% to 18%. A wide-ranging privatization programme was announced in 2004. In 2005 a programme to tackle the energy crisis in the country was launched, focusing on security and diversification of supplies and improving the profitability of the sector. Meanwhile, the Russian state-controlled natural gas supplier Gazprom announced a four-fold increase in the price of gas available for purchase by Georgia, prompting the country to begin sourcing supplies from Iran and Azerbaijan. In February 2007 Energo-Pro (of the Czech Republic) completed its acquisition of 62.5% of Georgia's electricity-distribution market, including the purchase of six hydro-electric power plants. Meanwhile, the imposition of economic sanctions against Georgia by Russia (see recent history), was expected to result in a slowdown in Georgian economic growth, although to some extent this would be counterbalanced by the receipt of transit fees for use of the SCP and the BTC pipeline. Foreign Direct Investment (FDI) was estimated to have totalled US $1,682m. in 2007, representing a 41% increase on the previous year. Rapidly increasing capital inflows provided the economy with its main source of growth in 2007, when real GDP was estimated to have risen by 11.0%. Concerns about political stability, and the worsening of relations with Russia in 2007–08, however, threatened to constrain Georgia's economic progress. Meanwhile, the economy continued to adjust to escalating energy costs which resulted in an overall rise in consumer prices of 8.5% in 2007, according to the IMF.

Education

Education is officially compulsory for nine years. Primary education begins at six years of age and lasts for four years. Secondary education, beginning at the age of 10, lasts for a maximum of seven years, comprising a first cycle of five years and a second cycle of two years. Free secondary education is available for the highest-achieving 30% of primary-school pupils. In 2004/05 pre-primary enrolment was equivalent to 49% of children in the relevant age-group, 86.4% of whom were instructed solely in Georgian. In 2004/05 primary enrolment was equivalent to 95% of the relevant age-group, and the comparable ratio for secondary enrolment was 82%. In 2004/05 there were 1,816 secondary day schools, with a total enrolment of 565,900 pupils. In 2004/05 some 85.5% of primary- and secondary-school pupils were taught in Georgian-language schools, while 5.5% were taught in Russian-language schools, 5.4% in Azerbaijani-language schools and 3.5% in Armenian-language schools. In 2005/06 some 144,313 students were enrolled at institutions of higher education (including universities), of which there were 146 in that academic year; enrolment was equivalent to 42% of the relevant age-group in 1996/97. Government expenditure on education amounted to a total of 288.7m. lari (equivalent to 8.8% of total spending) in 2005.

Public Holidays

2008: 1–2 January (New Year), 7 January (Christmas), 19 January (Epiphany), 3 March (Mothers' Day), 8 March (International Women's Day), 9 April (Restoration of Independence Day), 26–29 April (Easter and Commemoration of the Deceased), 9 May (Victory Day), 12 May (St Andrew's Day), 26 May (Independence Day), 28 August (Assumption), 14 October (Mtskhetoba), 23 November (St George's Day).

2009: 1–2 January (New Year), 7 January (Christmas), 19 January (Epiphany), 3 March (Mothers' Day), 8 March (International Women's Day), 18–21 April (Easter, Restoration of Independence Day and Commemoration of the Deceased), 9 May (Victory Day), 12 May (St Andrew's Day), 26 May (Independence Day), 28 August (Assumption), 14 October (Mtskhetoba), 23 November (St George's Day).

Weights and Measures

The metric system is in force.

Statistical Survey

Source (unless otherwise indicated): State Department for Statistics, 0115 Tbilisi, K. Gamsakhurdia 4; tel. (32) 33-05-40; fax (32) 93-89-36; e-mail info@statistics.gov.ge; internet www.statistics.ge.

Area and Population

AREA, POPULATION AND DENSITY

Area (sq km)	69,700*
Population (census results)†	
12 January 1989	5,400,841
17 January 2002‡	
Males	2,061,753
Females	2,309,782
Total	4,371,535
Population (official estimates at 1 January)§	
2005	4,321,500
2006	4,401,300
2007	4,394,700
Density (per sq km) at 1 January 2007	63.1

* 26,911 sq miles.
† Population is *de jure*. The *de facto* total at the 2002 census was 4,355,700.
‡ Those territories of the former autonomous oblast (district) of South Ossetia that remained outside Georgian government control, as well as those of the separatist 'Republic of Abkhazia', were not included in the census of 2002. It was estimated that around 230,000 people lived in these territories.
§ Including the territories not under the control of the central Government.

POPULATION BY ETHNIC GROUP

(2002 census result, excl. areas outside Georgian government control)

	Number ('000)	% of total population
Georgian	3,661.2	83.8
Azeri	284.8	6.5
Armenian	248.9	5.7
Russian	67.7	1.5
Ossetian	38.0	0.9
Kurdish	20.8	0.5
Others	50.1	1.1
Total (incl. others)	4,371.5	100.0

ADMINISTRATIVE DIVISIONS
(1 January 2007, '000, rounded figures*)

Territory	Population	Principal city†
Autonomous Republic		
Adjara	378.8	Batumi (122.0)
Mkharebi (Regions)		
Guria	139.0	Ozurgeti (77.4)
Imereti	697.6	Kutaisi (189.7)
Kakheti	403.6	Telavi (70.4)
Kvemo Kartli	508.3	Rustavi (117.9)
Mtskheta-Mtianeti	124.1	Mtskheta (65.0)
Racha-Lechkumi and Kvemo-Svaneti	48.6	Ambrolauri (15.1)
Samegrelo-Zemo Svaneti‡	471.7	Zugdidi (172.1)
Samstkhe-Javakheti	208.3	Akhaltsikhe (46.9)
Shida Kartli‖	313.6	Gori (148.8)
Capital City		
Tbilisi	1,101.1	—

* These figures exclude the population of the 'Republic of Abkhazia'.
† With official estimate of population at 1 January 2007 ('000, rounded figures).
‡ Including population of Kodori gorge (Upper Abkhazia).
‖ Most of the territories of South Ossetia are included in Shida Kartli Mkhare.

PRINCIPAL TOWNS
(estimates at 1 January 2007, unless otherwise indicated)

Tbilisi (capital)	1,101,100	Batumi	122,200
Kutaisi	189,700	Marneuli*	121,800
Zugdidi*	172,100	Rustavi	117,900
Gori*	148,800	Gardabani*	116,500

* Figures refer to the population of the municipality.

GEORGIA

BIRTHS, MARRIAGES AND DEATHS

	Registered live births Number	Rate (per 1,000)	Registered marriages Number	Rate (per 1,000)	Registered deaths Number	Rate (per 1,000)
1999	48,695	10.9	13,845	3.1	47,184	10.6
2000	48,800	11.0	12,870	2.9	47,410	10.7
2001	47,589	10.8	13,336	3.0	46,218	10.5
2002	46,605	10.7	12,535	2.9	46,446	10.7
2003	46,194	10.7	12,696	2.9	46,055	10.6
2004	49,572	11.5	14,866	3.4	48,793	11.3
2005	46,512	10.7	18,012	4.1	42,984	9.9
2006	47,795	10.9	21,845	5.0	42,255	9.6

Expectation of life (years at birth, WHO estimates): 71.5 (males 67.6; females 75.2) in 2005 (Source: WHO, *World Health Statistics*).

ECONOMICALLY ACTIVE POPULATION
(annual averages, '000 persons)*

	2003	2004	2005
Agriculture, hunting and forestry	995.6	962.4	947.8
Fishing	0.7	0.4	n.a.
Mining and quarrying	2.8	3.9	5.8
Manufacturing	88.8	90.8	89.8
Electricity, gas and water supply	19.8	20.7	23.4
Construction	40.1	42.1	43.1
Wholesale and retail trade; repair of motor vehicles and personal and household goods	198.5	196.9	188.2
Hotels and restaurants	16.6	18.7	16.3
Transport, storage and communications	76.9	74.3	69.3
Financial intermediation	9.8	12.8	13.3
Real estate, renting and business activities	32.3	28.4	25.9
Public administration and defence; compulsory social security	91.4	86.8	81.8
Education	135.6	134.1	130.9
Health and social work	49.0	54.8	58.0
Other community, social and personal service activities	45.2	42.7	38.2
Private households with employed persons	7.8	8.4	9.2
Extra-territorial organizations and bodies	3.5	4.4	3.3
Activities not adequately defined	0.1	1.4	0.3
Total employed	**1,814.5**	**1,783.3**	**1,744.6**
Unemployed	235.9	257.6	279.3
Total labour force	**2,050.4**	**2,041.0**	**2,023.9**
Males	1,081.7	1,069.7	1,074.4
Females	968.7	971.3	949.5

* Figures exclude employment in the informal sector, estimated to total about 750,000 persons at the end of 1997.

Health and Welfare

KEY INDICATORS

Total fertility rate (children per woman, 2005)	1.4
Under-5 mortality rate (per 1,000 live births, 2005)	45
HIV/AIDS (% of persons aged 15–49, 2005)	0.2
Physicians (per 1,000 head, 2003)	4.09
Hospital beds (per 1,000 head, 2005)	3.8
Health expenditure (2004): US $ per head (PPP)	171.0
Health expenditure (2004): % of GDP	5.3
Health expenditure (2004): public (% of total)	27.4
Human Development Index (2005): ranking	96
Human Development Index (2005): value	0.754

For sources and definitions, see explanatory note on p. vi.

Agriculture

PRINCIPAL CROPS
('000 metric tons)

	2004	2005	2006
Wheat	185.8	190.1	160.0
Barley	61.4	65.4	47.3
Maize	410.6	421.3	217.6
Potatoes	419.5	432.2	208.3
Sunflower seed	22.3	22.3	10.7
Cabbages and other brassicas	104.0	113.5*	53.0*
Tomatoes	116.0	126.5*	59.0*
Cucumbers and gherkins†	90.0	98.0	46.0
Dry onions	26.0	28.5*	13.5*
Watermelons	109.5	119.6	53.5
Oranges	38.2	122.4	137.0*
Apples	76.3	104.3	116.5*
Pears	25.4	35.7	40.0*
Sour (Morello) cherries	12.4	20.0	22.0*
Peaches and nectarines	2.9	10.2	12.0*
Plums and sloes	14.8	19.0	21.0*
Grapes	180.0	250.3	280.0*
Tea (made)	20.0	22.8	28.0*
Tobacco (leaves)	1.5	1.1	1.4

* FAO estimate.
† Unofficial figures.

Aggregate production ('000 metric tons, may include official, semi-official or estimated data): Total cereals 662.7 in 2004, 679.7 in 2005, 427.9 in 2006; Total nuts 14.7 in 2004, 30.9 in 2005, 32.0 in 2006; Total roots and tubers 419.5 in 2004, 432.2 in 2005, 208.3 in 2006; Total vegetables (incl. melons) 510.0 in 2004, 556.3 in 2005, 257.2 in 2006; Total fruits (excl. melons) 378.4 in 2004, 637.5 in 2005, 708.1 in 2006.

Source: FAO.

LIVESTOCK
('000 head at 1 January)

	2004	2005	2006
Horses	43.4	44.4	42.8
Cattle	1,242.5	1,250.7	1,260.4
Buffaloes	32.7	33.2	33.2*
Pigs	473.8	483.9	455.3
Sheep	628.8	689.2	719.8
Goats	93.4	115.7*	95.5
Chickens	8,500†	8,650*	6,850*
Turkeys	706†	705*	650*

* FAO estimate.
† Unofficial figure.
Source: FAO.

LIVESTOCK PRODUCTS
('000 metric tons)

	2004	2005	2006*
Cattle meat	49.8	49.2	47.0
Sheep meat	9.2	9.6	9.2
Pig meat	34.7	33.3	32.0
Chicken meat	15.2	16.9	16.5
Cows' milk	755.0	760.8	690.0
Hen eggs	15.0	15.3	11.3

* FAO estimates.
Source: FAO.

Forestry

ROUNDWOOD REMOVALS
('000 cubic metres, excl. bark)

	2003	2004	2005
Sawlogs, veneer logs and logs for sleepers	41.2	49.8	81.0
Other industrial wood	41.2	49.8	81.0
Fuel wood	367.3	443.3	453.9
Total	449.7	542.9	615.9

2006: Figures assumed to be unchanged from 2005 (FAO estimates).
Source: FAO.

SAWNWOOD PRODUCTION
('000 cubic metres, incl. railway sleepers)

	2003	2004*	2005†
Coniferous (softwood)	7.1	6.9	6.9
Broadleaved (hardwood)	64.0	62.5	62.5
Total	71.1	69.4	69.4

* Unofficial figures.
† FAO estimates.
2006: Figures assumed to be unchanged from 2005 (FAO estimates).
Source: FAO.

Fishing

(metric tons, live weight)

	2003	2004	2005*
Capture	3,306	2,951	3,000
Mullets	80	68	70
Surmullets	50	35	40
European anchovy	2,665	2,562	2,600
Sharks, rays, skates, etc.	40	31	35
Sea snails	295	65	70
Aquaculture	56	72	72
Total catch	3,362	3,023	3,072

* FAO estimates.
Source: FAO.

Mining

('000 metric tons, unless otherwise indicated)

	2003	2004	2005
Coal	8.0	8.0	8.0
Crude petroleum	139.7	97.6	66.7
Natural gas (million cu m)	17.8	6.1	14.8
Manganese ore	173.5	218.7	251.8
Cement	344.8	424.6	450.0*

* Estimated production.
Source: US Geological Survey.

Industry*

SELECTED PRODUCTS
('000 metric tons, unless otherwise indicated)

	2002	2003	2004
Refined sugar	47.9	91.8	n.a.
Wine ('000 hectolitres)	201	231	n.a.
Beer ('000 hectolitres)	273	284	476
Vodka and liqueurs ('000 hectolitres)	21	26	62
Soft drinks ('000 hectolitres)	379	678	918
Mineral water ('000 hectolitres)	596	691	818
Cigarettes (million)	1,894	2,972	2,808
Mineral fertilizers	83.2	n.a.	n.a.
Synthetic ammonia	111.3	n.a.	n.a.
Residual fuel oil	12	13	14
Building bricks (million)	6.0	9.0	9.0
Electric energy (million kWh)	7,257	7,116	6,924

Source: mainly UN, *Industrial Commodity Statistics Yearbook*.
* Data for those areas of South Ossetia outside of central Government control and for the separatist 'Republic of Abkhazia' are not included.

Finance

CURRENCY AND EXCHANGE RATES

Monetary Units
100 tetri = 1 lari.

Sterling, Dollar and Euro Equivalents (31 December 2007)
£1 sterling = 3.189 lari;
US $1 = 1.592 lari;
€1 = 2.343 lari;
100 lari = £31.36 = $62.83 = €42.68.

Average Exchange Rate (lari per US $)
2005 1.8127
2006 1.7804
2007 1.6075

Note: On 25 September 1995 Georgia introduced the lari, replacing interim currency coupons at the rate of 1 lari = 1,000,000 coupons. From April 1993 the National Bank of Georgia had issued coupons in various denominations, to circulate alongside (and initially at par with) the Russian (formerly Soviet) rouble. From August 1993 coupons became Georgia's sole legal tender, but their value rapidly depreciated. The transfer from coupons to the lari lasted one week, and from 2 October 1995 the lari became the only permitted currency in Georgia.

BUDGET
(million lari)*

Revenue†	2002	2003	2004
Tax revenue	1,054.7	1,186.8	1,811.2
Taxes on income	142.9	152.9	268.7
Taxes on profits	82.2	101.1	161.6
Value-added tax	404.6	406.8	628.2
Excise	86.7	100.1	163.8
Customs duties	59.0	70.3	100.1
Other taxes	114.0	128.0	134.1
Other current revenue	80.6	86.1	274.4
Total‡	1,135.3	1,272.9	2,085.6

GEORGIA

Statistical Survey

Expenditure§	2002	2003	2004
General state services	258.6	301.1	356.9
Defence	48.9	61.2	160.4
Civil order and security	100.0	113.6	274.2
Education	166.6	164.1	289.1
Health	64.3	29.5	97.2
Social insurance and social care	302.7	342.5	473.0
Recreation, culture, sports and religion	59.6	49.7	90.2
Fuel-energy services	16.9	36.8	78.8
Agriculture, forestry, fisheries and hunting	11.3	16.0	32.0
Transport and communications	43.7	50.2	70.5
Other expenditures	336.9	445.2	489.9
Total	**1,409.5**	**1,609.9**	**2,412.2**

* Figures represent a consolidation of the State Budget (covering the central Government and local administrations) and extrabudgetary funds.
† Excluding grants received (million lari): 22.6 in 2002; 47.7 in 2003; 123.9 in 2004.
‡ Excluding extrabudgetary revenue (comprising the revenues of the Social Protection Fund, the Single State Employment Fund and the State Road Fund) (million lari): 165 in 2002; 254 in 2003; 337 in 2004.
§ Including net lending.

2005 (million lari): Total revenue (excl. grants) 3,152.7 (Tax revenue 2,411.5, Non-tax current revenue 321.8, Capital revenue 419.4); Grants received from abroad 104.6; Total expenditure and net lending 3,280.8 (Financial aid issued from state budget 176.7).

2006 (million lari): Total revenue (excl. grants) 4,235.5 (Tax revenue 3,149.4, Non-tax current revenue 521.7, Capital revenue 564.5); Grants received from abroad 194.3; Total expenditure and net lending 4,464.1 (Financial aid issued from state budget 217.3).

2007 (million lari): Total revenue (excl. grants) 5,915.6 (Tax revenue 4,391.1, Non-tax current revenue 880.7, Capital revenue 643.8); Grants received from abroad 116.9; Total expenditure and net lending 6,083.1 (Financial aid issued from state budget 178.6).

INTERNATIONAL RESERVES
(excl. gold, US $ million at 31 December)

	2004	2005	2006
IMF special drawing rights	11.22	1.02	0.90
Reserve position in the IMF	0.02	0.01	0.02
Foreign exchange	375.44	477.61	929.91
Total	**386.68**	**478.64**	**930.83**

Source: IMF, *International Financial Statistics*.

MONEY SUPPLY
(million lari at 31 December)

	2004	2005	2006
Currency outside banks	615.99	736.28	827.36
Demand deposits	202.68	263.25	439.45
Total money (incl. others)	**818.67**	**999.54**	**1,266.80**

Source: IMF, *International Financial Statistics*.

COST OF LIVING
(Consumer Price Index for five cities*; base: December 2003 = 100)

	2004	2005	2006
Food and non-alcoholic beverages	112.1	116.7	132.3
Alcoholic beverages and tobacco	121.2	166.7	149.2
Clothing and footwear	100.5	104.7	107.6
Housing, utilities and other fuels	104.5	110.7	135.3
Household furnishings and maintenance	103.7	106.2	107.9
Health	98.7	99.5	115.4
Transport	105.7	113.0	115.9
Education	93.2	96.1	98.2
Recreation and culture	99.8	101.8	101.4
All items (incl. others)	**107.5**	**114.1**	**124.1**

* Tbilisi, Kutaisi, Batumi, Gori and Telavi.

NATIONAL ACCOUNTS
(million lari at current prices)

National Income and Product

	2004	2005	2006
Compensation of employees	1,641.1	1,977.4	2,293.2
Net operating surplus	3,303.6	2,186.0	2,647.9
Net mixed income	2,934.0	4,923.2	5,680.5
Domestic primary incomes	**7,878.7**	**9,086.6**	**10,621.6**
Consumption of fixed capital	976.8	1,113.5	1,306.4
Gross domestic product (GDP) at factor cost	**8,855.5**	**10,200.1**	**11,928.0**
Taxes on production and imports	1,026.2	1,481.7	1,919.5
Less Subsidies	57.3	60.8	57.6
GDP in market prices	**9,824.4**	**11,621.0**	**13,789.9**
Primary incomes received from abroad	478.2	477.6	598.5
Less Primary incomes paid abroad	297.7	306.8	286.0
Gross national income (GNI)	**10,004.9**	**11,791.8**	**14,102.4**
Less Consumption of fixed capital	976.8	1,113.5	1,306.4
Adjustment to consumption of fixed capital	−3.2	−8.9	3.0
Net national income	**9,024.9**	**10,669.4**	**12,799.0**
Current transfers from abroad	881.4	747.9	1,029.1
Less Current transfers paid abroad	97.9	98.5	111.7
Net disposable income	**9,808.3**	**11,318.9**	**13,716.4**

EXPENDITURE ON THE GROSS DOMESTIC PRODUCT

	2004	2005	2006
Government final consumption expenditure	1,379.1	2,014.0	2,116.0
Private final consumption expenditure	7,194.7	7,780.2	10,855.9
Increase in stocks	78.4	60.5	156.2
Gross fixed capital formation	2,697.3	3,261.4	3,524.2
Total domestic expenditure	**11,349.5**	**13,116.1**	**16,652.3**
Exports of goods and services	3,100.1	3,921.9	4,532.1
Less Imports of goods and services	4,733.6	5,992.7	7,862.6
Statistical discrepancy	108.2	575.7	468.0
GDP in market prices	**9,824.3**	**11,621.0**	**13,789.9**
GDP at constant 1996 prices	**6,001.4**	**6,577.5**	**7,194.7**

Gross Domestic Product by Economic Activity

	2004	2005	2006
Agriculture, forestry and fishing	1,610.7	1,716.4	1,544.3
Mining and quarrying	77.0	91.3	138.8
Manufacturing	803.9	998.7	1,194.3
Electricity, gas and water supply	304.2	326.2	375.1
Processing of products by households	396.8	406.8	338.9
Construction	793.2	937.9	947.3
Wholesale and retail trade; repair of motor vehicles, motorcycles and personal and household goods	1,247.2	1,388.8	1,878.6
Hotels and restaurants	266.2	330.3	317.4
Transport, storage and communications	1,313.1	1,443.0	1,594.5
Financial intermediation	130.3	231.7	292.8
Real estate, renting and business activities*	570.1	620.6	788.6
Public administration and defence; compulsory social security	573.8	750.5	1,174.5

GEORGIA

Statistical Survey

—continued	2004	2005	2006
Education	344.1	385.2	511.2
Health and social services	345.8	404.0	597.5
Other community, social and personal services	279.0	373.3	450.1
Private households with employed persons	8.9	9.6	10.2
Sub-total	9,064.3	10,414.2	12,154.1
Less Financial intermediation services indirectly measured	74.8	129.7	107.3
Gross value added in basic prices	8,989.6	10,284.5	12,046.9
Taxes on products	892.1	1,397.3	1,800.6
Less Subsidies on products	57.3	60.8	57.6
GDP in market prices	9,824.3	11,621.0	13,789.9

* Including imputed rent of owner-occupied dwellings.

BALANCE OF PAYMENTS
(US $ million)

	2004	2005	2006
Exports of goods f.o.b.	1,092.1	1,472.4	1,666.5
Imports of goods f.o.b.	−2,007.7	−2,686.6	−3,685.9
Trade balance	−915.5	−1,214.2	−2,019.4
Exports of services	552.1	711.1	900.9
Imports of services	−484.8	−631.5	−727.0
Balance on goods and services	−848.2	−1,134.6	−1,845.5
Other income received	251.7	263.3	339.5
Other income paid	−161.2	−188.2	−170.6
Balance on goods, services and income	−758.2	−1,059.5	−1,676.6
Current transfers received	389.1	351.2	504.1
Current transfers paid	−51.5	−54.4	−63.0
Current balance	−420.6	−762.6	−1,235.5
Capital account (net)	40.8	58.6	168.7
Direct investment abroad	−9.6	89.5	15.8
Direct investment from abroad	492.3	452.8	1,059.8
Portfolio investment assets	−13.1	13.1	−2.2
Portfolio investment liabilities	—	2.5	117.8
Other investment assets	−27.4	−15.5	−45.7
Other investment liabilities	4.1	123.6	193.6
Net errors and omissions	1.5	18.6	58.4
Overall balance	68.0	−19.4	330.7

Source: IMF, *International Financial Statistics*.

External Trade

PRINCIPAL COMMODITIES
(US $ million)

Imports	2005	2006	2007
Wheat	45.1	99.1	139.2
Sugar	78.2	65.6	90.5
Petroleum and petroleum oils	336.3	443.1	556.3
Petroleum gases and other gaseous hydrocarbons	90.8	213.1	293.7
Medicaments	92.5	114.5	144.0
Bars and rods of iron or non-alloy steel	14.6	33.1	71.9
Automatic data-processing machines	22.4	46.4	78.0
Transmission apparatus	27.1	58.7	105.2
Motor cars	178.5	295.3	369.7
Total (incl. others)	2,490.0	3,677.8	5,216.7

Exports	2005	2006	2007
Alcohol and other spirituous beverages	29.2	30.1	57.4
Edible fruits and nuts	70.3	56.6	65.1
Mineral or chemical fertilizers, nitrogenous	35.8	46.6	57.0
Portland cement	17.7	28.8	64.0
Copper ores and concentrates	36.4	79.5	79.2
Gold, unwrought or in semi-manufactured forms	34.7	49.4	69.4
Ferrous waste and scrap; remelting scrap ingots of iron or steel	84.2	72.4	96.9
Ferro-alloys	80.2	89.8	159.6
Motor cars	17.9	50.6	70.2
Total (incl. others)	865.5	936.2	1,240.2

PRINCIPAL TRADING PARTNERS
(US $ million)

Imports c.i.f.	2003	2004	2005
Armenia	11.2	26.2	39.3
Austria	11.3	22.3	19.0
Azerbaijan	93.7	156.4	233.4
Belgium	9.9	15.5	25.6
Brazil	11.2	23.7	33.0
Bulgaria	19.3	38.9	72.3
China, People's Repub.	23.2	28.9	46.7
France	55.7	63.2	97.3
Germany	82.8	151.1	206.8
Italy	36.5	61.6	64.4
Iran	7.0	15.2	26.0
Kazakhstan	9.8	21.4	11.6
Netherlands	23.8	34.6	53.1
Romania	10.5	14.0	40.7
Russia	161.1	257.8	384.3
Switzerland	14.3	26.1	17.5
Turkey	112.0	202.1	283.0
Turkmenistan	9.8	32.7	95.1
Ukraine	80.2	142.4	219.4
United Arab Emirates	19.8	46.7	73.0
United Kingdom	145.6	171.8	70.2
USA	90.7	110.9	146.8
Total (incl. others)	1,141.2	1,847.9	2,490.9

Exports f.o.b.	2003	2004	2005
Armenia	30.8	54.5	39.9
Azerbaijan	16.4	25.3	83.4
Bulgaria	0.1	15.6	42.8
Canada	0.2	3.7	35.6
France	4.9	9.6	11.5
Germany	9.8	15.9	28.5
Greece	5.2	7.3	10.4
India	6.4	6.0	2.3
Italy	8.7	11.6	33.6
Kazakhstan	4.3	7.6	9.8
Netherlands	9.9	9.8	11.3
Romania	1.0	1.3	8.8
Russia	83.9	104.5	153.9
Seychelles	0.0	2.1	12.6
Spain	7.0	9.5	14.2
Switzerland	33.3	17.8	3.2
Turkey	82.5	118.6	121.8
Turkmenistan	54.9	113.4	75.8
Ukraine	30.1	15.6	37.3
United Kingdom	27.9	31.7	31.9
USA	15.4	21.2	26.7
Total (incl. others)	461.4	647.0	866.2

2005 (US $ million, revised): Total imports 2,490.0; Total exports 865.5.

2006 (US $ million): Total imports 3,677.8 (Azerbaijan 318.5; Bulgaria 115.5; China, People's Republic 103.3; Germany 351.2; Italy 102.1; Russia 558.8; Ukraine 320.1; United Arab Emirates 109.1; USA 129.6); Total exports 992.5 (Armenia 73.6; Azerbaijan 92.2; Canada 48.9; Germany 45.4; Kazakhstan 15.4; Russia 75.7; Spain 16.6; Turkey 124.9; USA 58.9).

2007 (US $ million): Total imports 5,216.7 (Azerbaijan 382.0; Bulgaria 184.0; China, People's Republic 206.7; Germany 387.3; Russia 578.8; Turkey 727.9; Ukraine 574.9; United Arab Emirates 214.7; USA 203.9); Total exports 1,240.2 (Azerbaijan 137.3; Bulgaria 59.4; Germany 56.2; Russia 53.0; Turkey 171.8; Ukraine 94.2; USA 149.6).

GEORGIA

Transport

RAILWAYS
(traffic)

	2002	2003	2004
Passengers carried (million)	2.1	2.2	3.0
Passenger-km (million)	400.6	387.4	614.0
Freight ('000 tons)	14,951.5	16,558.7	15,408.4
Freight net ton-km (million)	5,074.5	5,538.7	4,855.8

ROAD TRAFFIC
('000 motor vehicles in use)

	2001	2002	2003
Passenger cars	247.8	252.0	255.2
Buses	22.7	24.1	25.7
Lorries and vans	47.0	45.5	42.9
Total (incl. others)	319.6	323.6	325.0

SHIPPING
Merchant Fleet
(registered at 31 December)

	2004	2005	2006
Number of vessels	327	375	386
Total displacement ('000 grt)	974.3	1,091.9	1,129.3

Source: Lloyd's Register-Fairplay, *World Fleet Statistics*.

CIVIL AVIATION
(traffic on scheduled services)

	2002	2003	2004
Passengers carried ('000)*	100	200	200
Passenger-km (million)	297.3	400.3	483.3
Total ton-km (million)	29	27	37

* Figures are rounded.

Tourism

FOREIGN TOURIST ARRIVALS

Country of residence	2003	2004	2005
Armenia	61,351	71,261	100,508
Azerbaijan	42,790	63,663	153,467
Germany	6,533	7,208	8,840
Greece	4,646	4,148	7,098
Israel	3,469	5,167	6,318
Russia	46,699	61,400	90,277
Turkey	71,751	74,700	109,796
Ukraine	15,354	14,721	12,431
United Kingdom	4,519	6,397	6,677
USA	7,486	9,609	12,928
Total (incl. others)	313,442	368,312	560,021

Tourism receipts (US $ million, incl. passenger transport): 172 in 2003; 209 in 2004; 288 in 2005.

Source: World Tourism Organization.

Communications Media

	2004	2005	2006
Telephones ('000 main lines in use)	683.2	570.2	553.1
Mobile cellular telephones ('000 subscribers)	840.6	1,174.3	1,703.9
Internet users ('000)	175.6	271.4	332.0
Broadband subscribers ('000)	1.9	2.4	27.0
Personal computers (in use, '000)	192	n.a.	n.a.
Newspapers: titles	122	88	n.a.
Newspapers: circulation ('000)	600	400	n.a.

Radio receivers ('000 in use): 3,020 in 1997.

Television receivers ('000 in use): 2,590 in 2000.

Facsimile machines (number in use): 500 in 1996.

Book production (incl. pamphlets): 581 titles in 1996 (834,000 copies); 697 titles in 1999.

Sources: UN, *Statistical Yearbook*; UNESCO, *Statistical Yearbook*; and International Telecommunication Union.

Education

(2006/07 unless otherwise indicated)

	Institutions	Students†
Pre-primary schools	1,197	77,922
General education: schools (primary)*	2,539	322,249
General education: schools (secondary)		313,739
General education: evening schools‡	14	n.a.
State secondary professional schools	79	18,242
Private secondary professional schools	26	6,658
State higher schools (incl. universities)	18	110,846
Private higher schools (incl. universities)	148	29,961

* Including primary schools covering part of the secondary syllabus.
† Some figures are rounded.
‡ Data for 2005/06.

Teachers (2005/06 unless otherwise indicated): Pre-primary 7,783 (2004/05); Total in general day schools 68,992 (primary, basic 8,467, secondary 59,856); Total in secondary professional schools 4,673 (3,462 public, 1,211 private); Total in institutes of higher education 20,960 (13,288 in public institutions, 7,672 in non-state institutions).

Directory

The Constitution

A new Constitution was approved by the Georgian legislature on 24 August 1995; it entered into force on 17 October. The following is a summary of the Constitution's main provisions, as subsequently amended:

GENERAL PROVISIONS

Georgia is an independent, united and undivided state and a democratic republic.

All state power belongs to the people, who exercise this power through referendums, other forms of direct democracy and through their elected representatives. The State recognizes and defends universally recognized human rights and freedoms. The official state language is Georgian; in Abkhazia both Georgian and Abkhazian are recognized as state languages. While the State recognizes the exceptional role played by the Georgian Orthodox Church in Georgian history, it declares the complete freedom of faith and religion as well as the independence of the Church from the State. The capital is Tbilisi.

FUNDAMENTAL HUMAN RIGHTS AND FREEDOMS

Georgian citizenship is acquired by birth and naturalization. A Georgian citizen may not be a citizen of another state concurrently. Every person is equal before the law. No one may be subjected to torture or inhuman, cruel or humiliating treatment or punishment.

Freedom of speech and conscience are guaranteed. The mass media are free. The right to assemble publicly is guaranteed, as is the right to form public associations, including trade unions and political parties. Every citizen who has attained the age of 18 years has the right to participate in referendums and elections for state and local administrative bodies.

PARLAMENTI

Parlamenti (Sakartvelos Parlamenti, or the Georgian Parliament) is the supreme representative body. It is elected on the basis of universal, equal and direct suffrage by secret ballot, for a term of four years. It is composed of 235 members: 150 elected by proportional representation and 85 by majority vote in single-member constituencies. Under constitutional amendments adopted in March 2008, the number of deputies in Parlamenti was reduced from 235 to 150, with effect from early legislative elections in May: 75 were to be elected by proportional representation (with a minimum requirement of 5% of the votes cast to secure parliamentary representation) and 75 by majority vote in single-member constituencies. Any citizen who has attained the age of 25 years and has the right to vote may be elected to Parlamenti.

Parlamenti elects a Chairman and Deputy Chairmen (including one Deputy Chairman each from deputies elected in Abkhazia and Adjara), for the length of its term of office. Members of Parlamenti may unite to form parliamentary factions of no fewer than 10 members.

Following the creation of the appropriate conditions throughout the territory of Georgia and the formation of bodies of local self-government, Parlamenti will be composed of two chambers: the Council of the Republic and the Senate. The Council of the Republic will be composed of deputies elected according to the proportional system. The Senate will be composed of deputies elected in Abkhazia, Adjara and other territorial units of Georgia, and five members appointed by the President of Georgia.

THE PRESIDENT OF GEORGIA AND THE GOVERNMENT

The President of Georgia is Head of State and the head of executive power. The President is elected on the basis of universal, equal and direct suffrage by secret ballot, for a period of five years. The President may not be elected for more than two consecutive terms. Any citizen of Georgia who has the right to vote and who has attained the age of 35 years and lived in Georgia for no less than 15 years is eligible to be elected President.

The President of Georgia concludes international treaties and agreements and conducts negotiations with foreign states; with the consent of Parlamenti, appoints members of the Government and Ministers; is empowered to remove Ministers from their posts; submits to Parlamenti the draft state budget; declares a state of war, and concludes peace; declares a state of emergency; signs and promulgates laws; grants pardons; schedules elections to Parlamenti and other representative bodies; is the Commander-in-Chief of the Armed Forces, and appoints and dismisses military commanders.

The President enjoys immunity from arrest and criminal proceedings. In the event that the President violates the Constitution, betrays the State or commits other crimes, Parlamenti may remove him/her from office with the approval of the Constitutional Court or the Supreme Court.

Parlamenti appoints and dismisses a Prime Minister. Members of the Government may be removed from their posts by the President or by Parlamenti, or by two successive legislative votes expressing 'no confidence' adopted by a two-thirds' majority in Parlamenti. Ministries perform state management in specific spheres of state and public life.

JUDICIAL POWER

Judicial power is independent. Court proceedings are held in public (except for certain specified instances). It is prohibited to instigate criminal proceedings against a judge or to detain or arrest him, without the consent of the Chairman of the Supreme Court.

The Constitutional Court is the legal body of constitutional control. It is composed of nine judges, three of whom are appointed by the President, three elected by Parlamenti, and three appointed by the Supreme Court. The term of office of members of the Constitutional Court is 10 years.

The Supreme Court supervises legal proceedings in general courts and, as the court of first instance, examines cases determined by law. On the recommendation of the President of Georgia, the Chairman and judges of the Supreme Court are elected by Parlamenti for a period of at least 10 years.

The Procurator's Office is an institution of judicial power, which carries out criminal prosecution, supervises preliminary investigations and the execution of a punishment, and supports the state prosecution. On the recommendation of the President of Georgia, the Procurator-General is appointed by Parlamenti for a term of five years. Lower-ranking procurators are appointed by the Procurator-General.

The Government

HEAD OF STATE

President: MIKHEIL SAAKASHVILI (elected 4 January 2004; re-elected 5 January 2008; inaugurated 20 January 2008).

GOVERNMENT
(March 2008)

Prime Minister: VLADIMER (LADO) GURGENIDZE.

Deputy Prime Minister and State Minister, responsible for European and Euro-Atlantic Integration: GIORGI BARAMIDZE.

State Minister, responsible for Regional Affairs: DAVIT TKESHELASHVILI.

State Minister, responsible for Diaspora Affairs: IULON GAGOSHIDZE.

State Minister, responsible for Reintegration Affairs: TEMUR IAKOBASHVILI.

Minister of Foreign Affairs: DAVIT BAKRADZE.

Minister of Education and Science: GIA NODIA.

Minister of Economic Development: EKATERINE SHARASHIDZE.

Minister of Finance: NIKOLOZ GILAURI.

Minister of Defence: DAVIT KEZERASHVILI.

Minister of Internal Affairs: IVANE MERABISHVILI.

Minister of Justice: NIKA GVARAMIA.

Minister of Agriculture: PETRE TSISKARISHVILI.

Minister of the Environmental Protection and Natural Resources: ZAAL GAMTSEMLIDZE.

Minister of Energy: ALEXANDER KHETAGURII.

Minister of Culture, the Protection of Monuments and Sport: NIKA VACHEISHVILI.

Minister of Refugee and Resettlement Affairs: KOBA SUBELIANI.

Minister of Health, Labour, and Social Protection: SANDRO KVITASHVILI.

MINISTRIES

Office of the President: 0105 Tbilisi, P. Ingorovka 7; tel. (32) 99-00-70; fax (32) 99-88-87; e-mail secretariat@admin.gov.ge; internet www.president.gov.ge.

Chancellery of the Government: 0105 Tbilisi, P. Ingorovka 7; tel. (32) 92-22-43; fax (32) 92-10-69; e-mail primeminister@geo.gov.ge; internet www.government.gov.ge.

Office of the Deputy Prime Minister, State Minister, responsible for Euro-Atlantic Integration: 0105 Tbilisi, P. Ingorovka 7; tel. (32) 93-28-67; fax (32) 93-27-22; internet www.eu-nato.gov.ge.

Office of the State Minister, responsible for Diaspora Affairs: 0105 Tbilisi, P. Ingorovka 7.

Office of the State Minister, responsible for Regional Affairs: 0105 Tbilisi, P. Ingorovka 7.

Office of the State Minister, responsible for Reintegration Affairs: 0105 Tbilisi, P. Ingorovka 7.

Ministry of Agriculture: 0179 Tbilisi, Kostava 41; tel. and fax (32) 93-23-25; e-mail ministry@maf.ge; internet www.maf.ge.

Ministry of Culture, the Protection of Monuments and Sport: 0108 Tbilisi, Rustaveli 37; tel. (32) 93-22-55; fax (32) 99-90-37; e-mail info@mcs.gov.ge; internet www.mcs.gov.ge.

Ministry of Defence: 0112 Tbilisi, Gen. Kvinitadze 20; tel. (32) 91-19-63; fax (32) 91-06-45; e-mail pr@mod.gov.ge; internet www.mod.gov.ge.

Ministry of Economic Development: 0108 Tbilisi, Chanturia 12; tel. (32) 93-16-33; fax (32) 92-15-34; e-mail ministry@econom.ge; internet www.economy.ge.

GEORGIA

Ministry of Education and Science: 0102 Tbilisi, D. Uznadze 52; tel. (32) 95-70-10; fax (32) 91-04-47; e-mail pr@mes.gov.ge; internet www.mes.gov.ge.

Ministry of Energy: 0105 Tbilisi, Lermontov 10; tel. and fax (32) 98-31-94; internet www.minenergy.gov.ge.

Ministry of the Environment Protection and Natural Resources: 0114 Tbilisi, G. Gulua 6; tel. (32) 27-57-00; fax (32) 33-39-52; e-mail gmep@access.sanet.ge; internet www.moe.gov.ge.

Ministry of Finance: 0162 Tbilisi, Irakli Abashidze 70; tel. (32) 22-68-05; fax (32) 93-19-22; e-mail minister@mof.ge; internet www.mof.ge.

Ministry of Foreign Affairs: 0108 Tbilisi, Sh. Chitadze 4; tel. (32) 28-47-47; fax (32) 28-46-78; e-mail inform@mfa.gov.ge; internet www.mfa.gov.ge.

Ministry of Health, Labour and Social Protection: 0102 Tbilisi, K. Gamsakhurdia 30; tel. (32) 38-75-10; fax (32) 38-00-23; internet www.healthministry.ge.

Ministry of Internal Affairs: 0114 Tbilisi, Gulua 10; tel. (32) 75-55-56; fax (32) 75-20-27; e-mail press_center@pol.ge; internet www.police.ge.

Ministry of Justice: 0146 Tbilisi, Rustaveli 30; tel. (32) 75-82-20; fax (32) 75-82-22; e-mail justice@justice.gov.ge; internet www.justice.gov.ge.

Ministry of Refugees and Resettlement Affairs: 0180 Tbilisi, Ts. Dadiani 30; tel. (32) 92-13-05; fax (32) 92-14-27; e-mail presscentre@mra.gov.ge; internet www.mra.gov.ge.

President

Presidential Election, 5 January 2008

Candidates	Votes	%
Mikheil Saakashvili	1,060,042	53.47
Levan Gachechiladze	509,234	25.69
Arkadi (Badri) Patarkatsishvili	140,826	7.10
Shalva Natelashvili	128,589	6.49
David Gamkrelidze	79,747	4.02
Others	18,491	0.93
Total*	**1,982,318**	**100.00**

*Including invalid votes (2.29% of the total).

Legislature

**Sakartvelos Parlamenti
(Georgian Parliament)**

0118 Tbilisi, Rustaveli 8; tel. (32) 93-61-70; fax (32) 99-93-86; e-mail hdstaff@parliament.ge; internet www.parliament.ge.

Chairman: NINO BURJANADZE.

General Election, 2 November 2003 and 28 March 2004*

Parties and blocs	% of votes	Seats (Party lists)	Constituency seats	Total seats
National Movement-United Democrats	67.32	135	17	152
Rightist Opposition†	7.51	15	8	23
Democratic Union of Revival	6.03	—	6	6
Georgian Labour Party	5.97	—	4	4
Freedom	4.31	—	—	—
Citizens' Union of Georgia	—	—	19	19
Independents	—	—	20	20
Vacant‡	—	—	11	11
Total (incl. others)	**100.00**	**150**	**85**	**235**

*Final preliminary results. Seventy-four of the single-member constituency seats were filled on 2 November 2003. New elections for deputies elected on the basis of party lists were held on 28 March 2004, following the annulment of the earlier results.

†An electoral alliance of Industry Will Save Georgia and the New Conservative Party.

‡One single-member constituency seat remained vacant, while the remaining 10 mandates (representing the secessionist region of Abkhazia: the terms of those members elected to them in 1992 having been renewed) were revoked on 30 April 2004.

Election Commission

Central Electoral Commission of Georgia (CEC): 0108 Tbilisi, Rustaveli 29, 3rd Floor; tel. (32) 98-70-10; fax (32) 98-70-00; e-mail cec@cec.gov.ge; internet www.cec.gov.ge; Chair. LEVAN TARKHNISHVILI.

Political Organizations

In early 2008 some 190 political parties and alliances were registered with the Central Electoral Commission. The following were among the most prominent parties in Georgia at that time:

Christian Democratic Union of Georgia: 0177 Tbilisi, Kazbegi 37; tel. (32) 48-20-01; fax (32) 48-20-04; e-mail cdu@cdu.ge; internet www.cdu.ge; f. 1990; centre-right; contested (subsequently annulled) 2003 legislative elections as mem. of the For a New Georgia bloc; Leader VAZHA LORTKIPANIDZE.

Citizens' Union of Georgia (CUG) (SMK): 0179 Tbilisi, Chavchavadze 55; tel. (32) 99-94-79; fax (32) 93-15-84; e-mail cug@access.sanet.ge; f. 1993; contested (subsequently annulled) 2003 legislative elections as mem. of the For a New Georgia bloc; Chair. AVTANDIL JORBENADZE.

Conservative Party of Georgia (Sakartvelos konservatorebi): 0108 Tbilisi, Kutateladze 4; tel. and fax (32) 28-12-25; e-mail kukava@parliament.ge; internet www.conservators.ge; f. 2001; Chair. ZVIAD DZIDZIGURI.

Freedom (Tavisupleba): Tbilisi; f. 2004 by a son of former President Zviad Gamsakhurdia; nationalist; Leader KONSTANTINE GAMSAKHURDIA.

Georgian Social Democratic Party: 0108 Tbilisi, Tskhra Aprilis 2; tel. (32) 99-95-50; fax (32) 98-42-57; f. 1990; contested (subsequently annulled) 2003 legislative elections as mem. of the Jumber Patiashvili-Unity bloc; Chair. Prof. JEMAL KAKHNIASHVILI.

Georgia's Way: 0108 Tbilisi, Rustaveli 40; f. 2006; Leader SALOMÉ ZURABISHVILI; Chair. of Political Council GIA TORTLADZE.

Green Party (Mtsvanta Partia): 0112 Tbilisi, D. Aghmashenebeli 182; tel. (32) 35-19-14; fax (32) 35-16-74; e-mail info@greensparty.ge; internet www.greensparty.ge; f. 1990; contested (subsequently annulled) 2003 legislative elections as mem. of the For a New Georgia bloc; Chair. GIORGI GACHECHILADZE.

Hope (Imedi): Tbilisi; f. 2006; opposition; supports exiled former minister Igor Giorgadze; Leader IRINA SARISHVILI-CHANTURIA.

Industry Will Save Georgia (Mretsveloba Gadaarchens Sakartvelos): 0105 Tbilisi, Marjvena Sanapiro 7; tel. (32) 94-09-81; f. 1999; contested 2004 legislative elections as mem. of Rightist Opposition bloc; Chair. ZURAB TKEMALADZE; Leader GIORGI TOPADZE.

Justice (Samartlianoba): 0108 Tbilisi, Rustaveli 24; tel. (32) 99-63-48; fax (32) 99-08-76; f. 2003; supports closer relations between Georgia and Russia; Chair. IGOR GIORGADZE (in exile).

Movement for a United Georgia: Tbilisi; f. 2007; Leader IRAKLI OKRUASHVILI.

National Forum: Tbilisi; f. 2006; Leader KAKHA SHARTAVA.

New Conservative Party (Axali Memarjveneebi—Axlebi): 0114 Tbilisi, Bevreti 3; tel. (32) 92-03-13; fax (32) 92-38-58; e-mail ncp@ncp.ge; internet www.ncp.ge; f. 2001; contested 2004 legislative elections as mem. of Rightist Opposition bloc; Chair. Dr DAVIT GAMKRELIDZE; Gen. Sec. DAVIT SAGANELIDZE.

People's Front of Georgia: 0105 Tbilisi, Pushkin 5; tel. (32) 93-17-10; f. 1989; Chair. NODAR NATADZE.

People's Party (Didgori): 0102 Tbilisi, D. Uznadze 56; tel. (32) 96-03-69; fax (32) 93-57-98; f. 1996; Chair. MAMUKA GIORGIADZE.

Republican Party of Georgia: 0108 Tbilisi, Griboedov 13; tel. and fax (32) 92-00-58; fax (32) 93-39-96; e-mail republicans@republicans.ge; internet www.republicans.ge; f. 1995; absorbed Georgian Popular Front (f. 1989); politically, economically and socially liberal; Chair. DAVID USUPASHVILI.

Socialist Party of Georgia: 0105 Tbilisi, Leselidze 41; tel. (32) 93-10-21; fax (32) 93-27-09; e-mail spg@geo-plus.net; f. 1995; contested (subsequently annulled) 2003 legislative elections as mem. of the For a New Georgia bloc; Chair. IRAKLI MINDELI.

Union of Georgian Traditionalists: 0108 Tbilisi, Virsaladze 10; tel. (32) 98-39-55; f. 1990; contested (subsequently annulled) 2003 legislative elections as mem. of the Burjanadze-Democrats bloc; alliance with the National Democratic Party of Georgia announced in Dec. 2003; founded the People's Forum for Welfare and Democracy in 2005, to campaign for the direct election of city mayors and regional governors; Chair. AKAKI ASATIANI.

United National Movement (UNM): 0118 Tbilisi, Lesya Ukrainka 1; tel. (32) 92-30-84; fax (32) 92-30-91; e-mail international@unm.ge; internet www.unm.ge; f. Nov. 2004 by merger of National Movement and United Democrats; nationalist; Chair. MIKHEIL SAAKASHVILI; Sec.-Gen. DAVID KIRKITADZE.

GEORGIA

Unity (Ertoba): 0105 Tbilisi, Tavisuplebis Moedani; tel. (32) 92-30-65; fax (32) 93-46-94; e-mail ertoba@post.com; f. 2001; contested (subsequently annulled) 2003 legislative elections as mem. of the Jumber Patiashvili-Unity bloc; Co-Chair. JUMBER PATIASHVILI, ALEKSANDER CHACHIA.

Diplomatic Representation

EMBASSIES IN GEORGIA

Armenia: 0102 Tbilisi, Tetelashvili 4; tel. (32) 95-17-23; fax (32) 96-42-87; e-mail armemb@caucasus.net; Ambassador HRACH SILVANIAN.

Azerbaijan: 0177 Tbilisi, Nutsubidze 47; tel. (32) 25-26-39; fax (32) 25-00-13; e-mail secretariat@azembassy.ge; internet www.azembassy.ge; Ambassador NAMIQ ALIYEV.

Bulgaria: 0102 Tbilisi, D. Aghmashenebeli 61; tel. (32) 91-01-94; fax (32) 91-02-70; e-mail bgembassy.georgia@gol.ge; internet www.mfa.bg/tbilisi; Chargé d'affaires a.i. IAHOR SAHARIEV.

China, People's Republic: 0108 Tbilisi, Barnov 52, POB 224; tel. (32) 25-26-71; fax (32) 44-13-83; e-mail yfarm@access.sanet.ge; internet ge.china-embassy.org; Ambassador WANG KAIWEN.

Czech Republic: 0162 Tbilisi, Chavchavadze 37/6; tel. (32) 91-67-40; fax (32) 91-67-44; e-mail tbilisi@embassy.mzv.cz; internet www.mzv.cz/tbilisi; Ambassador JOZEF VRABEC.

Estonia: 0171 Tbilisi, Saburtalo, Likhauri 4; tel. (32) 36-51-22; fax (32) 36-51-38; e-mail tbilisisaatkond@mfa.ee; Chargé d'affaires a.i. HARRY LAHTEIN.

France: 0108 Tbilisi, Gogebashvili 15; tel. (32) 99-99-76; fax (32) 95-33-75; e-mail ambafrance@access.sanet.ge; internet www.ambafrance-ge.org; Ambassador ERIC FOURNIER.

Germany: 0103 Tbilisi, Telavi 20, Sheraton Metekhi Palace Hotel; tel. (32) 44-73-00; fax (32) 44-73-64; e-mail info@tiflis.diplo.de; internet www.tiflis.diplo.de; Ambassador Dr PATRICIA FLOR.

Greece: 0179 Tbilisi, T. Tabldze 37D; tel. and fax (32) 91-49-70; fax (32) 91-49-80; e-mail grembgeo@access.sanet.ge; internet www.greekembassy.ge; Ambassador GEORGIOS CHATZIMIHELAKIS.

Holy See: 0108 Tbilisi, Jenti 40, Nutsubidze Plateau; tel. (32) 53-76-01; fax (32) 53-67-04; e-mail nuntius@access.sanet.ge; Apostolic Nuncio Most Rev. CLAUDIO GUGEROTTI (Titular Archbishop of Ravello).

Iran: 0160 Tbilisi, Zovreti 16; tel. (32) 98-69-90; fax (32) 98-69-93; e-mail iranemb@caucasus.net; Ambassador MOJTABA DAMIRCHILOU.

Israel: 0102 Tbilisi, D. Aghmashenebeli 61; tel. (32) 94-27-05; fax (32) 95-52-09; e-mail press@tbilisi.mfa.gov.il; internet tbilisi.mfa.gov.il; Ambassador SHABTAI TSUR.

Italy: 0108 Tbilisi, Chitadze 3A; tel. (32) 99-64-18; fax (32) 99-64-15; e-mail embassy.tbilisi@esteri.it; internet www.ambtbilisi.esteri.it; Chargé d'affaires a.i. VITTORIO SANDALLI.

Latvia: 0160 Tbilisi, Odessa 60; tel. (32) 24-48-58; fax (32) 38-14-06; e-mail embassy.georgia@mfa.gov.lv.

Lithuania: 0162 Tbilisi, T. Abuladze 27; tel. (32) 91-29-33; fax (32) 22-17-93; e-mail amb.ge@urm.lt; Ambassador RIČARDAS DEGUTIS.

Netherlands: 0103 Tbilisi, Telavi 20, Sheraton Metekhi Palace Hotel; tel. (32) 27-62-00; fax (32) 27-62-32; e-mail tbi@minbuza.nl; internet www.dutchembassy.ge; Ambassador O. F. G. ELDERENBOSCH.

Poland: 0108 Tbilisi, Zubalashvili 19; tel. (32) 92-03-98; fax (32) 92-03-97; e-mail ambpolgruzja@access.sanet.ge; internet www.tbilisi.polemb.net; Ambassador JACEK MULTANOWSKI.

Romania: 0108 Tbilisi, Lvovi 7; tel. (32) 38-53-10; fax (32) 38-52-10; e-mail roembtbl@caucasus.net; Ambassador DAN MIHAI BÂRLIBA.

Russia: 0162 Tbilisi, Chavchavadze 51; tel. (32) 91-24-06; fax (32) 91-27-38; e-mail russianembassy@caucasus.net; internet www.georgia.mid.ru; Ambassador VYACHESLAV YE. KOVALENKO.

Switzerland: 0114 Tbilisi, Krtsanisi 11; tel. (32) 75-30-01; fax (32) 75-30-06; e-mail tif.vertretung@eda.admin.ch; internet www.eda.admin.ch/tbilisi; Ambassador Dr LORENZO AMBERG.

Turkey: 0102 Tbilisi, D. Aghmashenebeli 61; tel. (32) 25-20-72; fax (32) 22-06-66; e-mail tiblisbe@dsl.ge; Ambassador ERTAN TEZGOR.

Ukraine: 0160 Tbilisi, Oniashvili 75; tel. (32) 31-11-61; fax (32) 31-11-81; e-mail emb_ge@mfa.gov.ua; internet www.uaembassy.ge; Ambassador MYKOLA M. SPYS.

United Kingdom: 0105 Tbilisi, Tavisuplebis Moedani 4; tel. (32) 27-47-47; fax (32) 27-47-92; e-mail british.embassy.tbilisi@fco.gov.uk; internet www.britishembassy.gov.uk/georgia; Ambassador DENIS KEEFE.

USA: 0131 Tbilisi, G. Balanchine 11; tel. (32) 27-70-00; fax (32) 53-23-10; e-mail consulate-tbilisi@state.gov; internet georgia.usembassy.gov; Ambassador JOHN F. TEFFT.

Judicial System

Constitutional Court: 6000 Adjara, Batumi; tel. (222) 7-00-99; fax (222) 7-01-44; e-mail court@const.gov.ge; internet www.constcourt.gov.ge; f. 1996; consists of 9 members; Pres. GIORGI PAPUASHVILI.

Supreme Court

0110 Tbilisi, Zubalashvili 32; tel. (32) 93-12-62; fax (32) 92-08-76; e-mail reception@supremecourt.ge; internet www.supremecourt.ge; Chair. KONSTANTIN KUBLASHVILI.

Procurator-General: EKA TKESHELASHVILI.

High Council of Justice: 0144 Tbilisi, Bochorma 12; tel. (32) 27-31-00; fax (32) 27-31-01; e-mail justice@caucasus.net; internet www.hcoj.gov.ge; f. 1997; 15-member council that co-ordinates the appointment of judges and their activities; Chair. Chairman of the Supreme Court KONSTANTIN KUBLASHVILI; Exec. Sec. VALERIAN TSERTSVADZE.

Religion

CHRISTIANITY

The Georgian Orthodox Church

The Georgian Orthodox Church is divided into 27 dioceses, and includes not only Georgian parishes, but also several Russian, Greek and Armenian Orthodox communities, which are under the jurisdiction of the Primate of the Georgian Orthodox Church. There are 40 monasteries and convents, two theological academies and four seminaries.

Georgian Patriarchate: 0105 Tbilisi, Erekle II Moedani 1; tel. (32) 99-03-78; fax (32) 98-71-14; e-mail orthodox@patriarchate.ge; internet www.patriarchate.ge; Catholicos-Patriarch of All Georgia ILIA II.

The Roman Catholic Church

The Apostolic Administrator of the Caucasus for Roman Catholics of the Latin Rite is resident in Tbilisi. At 31 December 2005 there were some 50,140 adherents within the territory covered by the Administration (which includes Armenia in addition to Georgia).

Apostolic Administrator: Most Rev. GIUSEPPE PASOTTO (Titular Bishop of Musti), 0105 Tbilisi, G. Abesadze 6; tel. and fax (32) 99-60-50; e-mail ammapost@geo.net.ge.

ISLAM

The Meshketian population, which formerly constituted one of the principal Muslim groups in Georgia, was deported to Central Asia in 1944 at Stalin's behest. The principal Islamic communities in Georgia are those among the Ajars and Abkhaz (who are Sunni Muslims) and Azeris (who are Shi'ite).

The Press

PRINCIPAL NEWSPAPERS

In 2005 88 newspaper titles were printed. Those listed below appear in Georgian, except where otherwise stated.

Axali Taoba (New Generation): 0102 Tbilisi, D. Aghmashenebeli 89/24; tel. (32) 95-25-89; fax (32) 94-06-91; e-mail akhtao@geo.net.ge; internet www.opentext.org.ge/akhalitaoba; f. 1993; Editor SOSO GONIASHVILI.

Axali Versia (New Possibility): 0154 Tbilisi, Agladze 39; tel. (32) 95-69-38; internet versia-online.com; Editor-in-Chief ALEKO TSKITISHVILI.

Dilis Gazeti (Morning Newspaper): 0102 Tbilisi, Marjanishvili 5; tel. (32) 96-91-88; fax (32) 96-91-81; e-mail dilgazet@access.sanet.ge; Editor MANANA KARTOZIA.

Droni (The Times): 0108 Tbilisi, Kostava 14; tel. (32) 99-56-54; e-mail newspdroni@usa.net; 2 a week; Editor-in-Chief GIORGI CHOCHISHVILI.

Georgia Today: 0179 Tbilisi, Irakli Abishidze 41/45; tel. (32) 91-48-92; fax (32) 91-72-75; e-mail info@georgiatoday.ge; internet www.georgiatoday.ge; f. 2000; weekly; in English; Gen. Man. GEORGE SHARASHIDZE.

Georgian Messenger: 0162 Tbilisi, Barnov 28; tel. and fax (32) 93-91-69; e-mail gtze@messenger.com.ge; internet www.messenger.com.ge; f. 1990; daily; in English; Editor-in-Chief ZAZA GACHECHILADZE.

Georgian Times: 0107 Tbilisi, Kikodze 12; tel. and fax (32) 93-44-05; e-mail geotimes@geotimes.ge; internet www.geotimes.ge; f. 1993; weekly, Mondays; in English, Georgian and Russian; Editor-in-Chief ZVIAD POCHKHUA.

Iberia Spektri (Iberian Spectrum): 0105 Tbilisi, Machabeli 11; tel. (32) 98-73-87; fax (32) 98-73-88; Editor IRAKLI GOTSIRIDZE.

GEORGIA — Directory

Literaturuli Sakartvelo (Literary Georgia): 0105 Tbilisi, Gudiashvili Moedani 2; tel. (32) 99-84-04; internet www.opentext.org.ge/literaturulisakartvelo; weekly; organ of the Union of Writers of Georgia; Editor TAMAZ TSIVTSIVADZE.

Respublika (Republic): 0196 Tbilisi, Kostava 14; tel. and fax (32) 93-43-91; f. 1990; weekly; independent; Editor J. NINUA; circ. 40,000.

Rezonansi (Resonance): 0102 Tbilisi, D. Aghmashenebeli 89/24; tel. (32) 37-79-69; fax (32) 95-06-42; e-mail resonance01@caucasus.net; internet www.resonance.ge; f. 1990; daily; Group Editor-in-Chief ZURAB MATCHARADZE; circ. 7,000.

Sakartvelo (Georgia): 0196 Tbilisi, Kostava 14; tel. (32) 99-92-26; 5 a week; organ of the Georgian Parliament; Editor SERGO JANASHIA.

Shvidi Dghe (Seven Days): 0102 Tbilisi, Krilov 5; tel. (32) 94-35-52; fax (32) 95-40-76; e-mail dge7@caucasus.net; internet www.opentext.org.ge/7_dge/default.htm; f. 1991; weekly; Editor KOBA AKHALBEDASHVILI.

Svobodnaya Gruziya (Free Georgia): 0108 Tbilisi, Rustaveli 42; tel. (32) 93-11-58; e-mail new@caucasus.net; internet www.svobodnaya-gruziya.com; f. 1922 as *Zarya Vostoka* (Dawn of the East); present name adopted 1991; in Russian; Editor-in-Chief TATO LASKHISHVILI; circ. 5,000.

PRINCIPAL PERIODICALS

Dila (The Morning): 0196 Tbilisi, Kostava 14; tel. (32) 93-41-30; internet www.dila.ge; f. 1904; present name adopted 1947; fortnightly; illustrated; for 5-to–12 year-olds; Editor-in-Chief DODO TSIVTSIVADZE; circ. 4,500.

Literaturnaya Gruziya (Literary Georgia): 0108 Tbilisi, Kostava 5; tel. (32) 99-06-59; fax (32) 22-47-37; e-mail abzianidze@hotmail.com; f. 1957; quarterly journal; politics, art and fiction; in Russian; Editor Prof. ZAZA ABZIANIDZE.

Metsniereba da Tekhnologiebi (Science and Technologies): 0108 Tbilisi, Rustaveli 52, Georgian Academy of Sciences; internet tech@gw.acnet.ge; internet www.acnet.ge/mectechnology; f. 1949; monthly; journal of the Georgian Academy of Sciences; popular; Editor V. CHAVCHANIDZE.

Nakaduli (Stream): 0108 Tbilisi, Kostava 14; tel. (32) 93-31-81; f. 1926; fmrly *Pioneri*; monthly journal of the Ministry of Education; illustrated; for 10-to-15-year-olds; Editor MANANA GELASHVILI; circ. 5,000.

Sakartvelos Metsnierebata Akademiis Moambe/Bulletin of Georgian Academy of Sciences: 0108 Tbilisi, Rustaveli 52; tel. (32) 99-75-93; fax (32) 99-88-23; e-mail bulletin@gw.acnet.ge; internet www.acnet.ge/moambe/index1.htm; f. 1940; 6 a year; in Georgian and English; Editor-in-Chief THOMAS V. GAMKRELIDZE.

Saunje (Treasure): 0107 Tbilisi, Dadiani 2; tel. (32) 72-47-31; f. 1974; 6 a year; organ of the Union of Writers of Georgia; foreign literature in translation; Editor S. NISHNIANIDZE.

Tsiskari (Dawn): 0107 Tbilisi, Khidis 1/29; tel. (32) 99-85-81; f. 1957; monthly; organ of the Union of Writers of Georgia; fiction; Editor ZAUR KALANDIA.

NEWS AGENCIES

Inter-Press: 0193 Tbilisi, M. Aleksidze 3; tel. (32) 99-67-72; fax (32) 93-56-39; e-mail ipcommerce@interpress.ge; internet www.interpressnews.ge; f. 2000; in Georgian, Russian and English.

Kavkasia-Press (Caucasus Press): 0108 Tbilisi, Rustaveli 42; tel. (32) 92-29-19; fax (32) 98-53-57; e-mail en-edit@caucasus.net.

Prime News Agency (PNA): 0105 Tbilisi, Leselidze 28; tel. (32) 92-32-63; fax (32) 93-91-35; e-mail info@primenewsonline.com; internet www.primenewsonline.com; f. 1997; news on Armenia, Azerbaijan and Georgia; Gen. Man. DEMNA CHAGELISHVILI.

Sarke Information Agency: 0102 Tbilisi, D. Aghmashenebeli 54; tel. (32) 95-06-59; fax (32) 95-08-37; e-mail info@sarke.com; internet www.sarke.com; f. 1992; professional agency for economic and business news in Georgia; privately owned; Dir VALERIAN KHUKHUNASHVILI; Editor-in-Chief VICTORIA GUJELASHVILI.

JOURNALISTS' ASSOCIATIONS

Independent Association of Georgian Journalists: 0105 Tbilisi, Lermontov 10; tel. (99) 96-52-52; fax (32) 93-44-05; e-mail iagj@ip.osgf.ge; internet www.iagj.org.ge; f. 2000; Pres. ZVIAD POCHKHUA.

Journalists' Federation of Georgia: 0105 Tbilisi, Erekle II Moedani 6; tel. (32) 98-24-47; e-mail foraf@geotvr.ge; Chair. AKAKI SIKHARULIDZE.

Publishers

Bakur Sulakauri Publishing: 0112 Tbilisi, D. Agmashenebeli 150; tel. and fax (32) 91-09-54; e-mail book@access.sanet.ge; internet www.sulakauri.ge; f. 1998; reference, fiction and children's literature; Dir BAKUR SULAKAURI.

Ganatleba (Education): 0164 Tbilisi, Chubinashvili 50; tel. (32) 95-50-97; f. 1957; educational, literature; Dir L. KHUNDADZE.

Georgian National Universal Encyclopedia: 0108 Tbilisi, Rustaveli 52; Editor-in-Chief Z. ABASHIDZE.

Khelovneba (Art): 0102 Tbilisi, D. Aghmashenebeli 179; f. 1947; Dir N. JASHI.

Merani (Writer): 0108 Tbilisi, Rustaveli 42; tel. (32) 99-64-92; fax (32) 93-46-75; e-mail hmerani@iberiapac.ge; f. 1921; fiction; Dir G. GVERDTSITELI.

Meridian Publishing Co: 0192 Tbilisi, Grmagele 22/10A; tel. (32) 61-27-98; fax (32) 95-56-35; e-mail info@meridianpub.com; internet www.meridianpub.com; f. 1994; academic and schools; Editor-in-Chief GIORGI GIGINEISHVILI.

Metsniereba (Sciences): 0160 Tbilisi, Gamrekeli 19; tel. and fax (32) 37-22-97; e-mail publicat@gw.acnet.ge; f. 1941; owned by Georgian Academy of Sciences; Dir DAVID KOLOTAURI; Editor CISANA KARTOZIA.

Nakaduli (Stream): 0194 Tbilisi, Gamsakhurdia 28; tel. (32) 38-69-12; f. 1938; books for children and youth.

Sakartvelo (Georgia): 0102 Tbilisi, Marjanishvili 5; tel. (32) 95-42-01; f. 1921; fmrly *Sabchota Sakartvelo* (Soviet Georgia); political, scientific and fiction; Dir JANSUL GVINJILIA.

Tbilisi State University Publishing House: 0128 Tbilisi, Chavchavadze 14; f. 1933; scientific and educational literature; Editor V. GAMKRELIDZE.

Broadcasting and Communications

TELECOMMUNICATIONS

Georgian National Communications Commission: 0177 Tbilisi, Al. Kazbegi 42; tel. (32) 92-16-67; fax (32) 92-16-25; e-mail post@gncc.ge; internet www.gncc.ge; f. 2000; Chair. GIORGI ARVEL.

Geocell: 0102 Tbilisi, POB 48; tel. (32) 77-01-00; fax (32) 77-01-01; e-mail cc@geocell.com.ge; internet www.geocell.com.ge; f. 1996; mobile cellular communications.

Magti: 0186 Tbilisi, Jikia 5; tel. (32) 32-23-31; fax (32) 32-18-83; e-mail office@magtigsm.ge; internet www.magticom.ge; f. 1997; fmrly known as Magti GSM; name changed as above 2006; mobile cellular communications; launched 3G mobile services July 2006; Dir DAVID LEE.

Telecom Georgia (Sakartvelos Telekomi): 0108 Tbilisi, Rustaveli 31; tel. (32) 44-19-19; fax (32) 44-29-29; e-mail tamta@telecom.ge; internet www.telecom.ge; f. 1994; provides international telecommunications services; 100% owned by Metromedia International Group Inc (USA); Gen. Dir OTAR ZUMBURIDZE.

United Telecommunications Company of Georgia (United Telecom): 0107 Tbilisi, Tsinamdzgvrishvili 95; tel. (32) 99-55-99; fax (32) 00-10-55; e-mail unitedtelecom@utg.ge; fmrly Sakelektrokavshiri; privatized in 2006; owned by Bank TuranAlem (Kazakhstan).

BROADCASTING

Television

Georgian Public Broadcasting: 0171 Tbilisi, Kostava 68; tel. and fax (32) 40-93-30; e-mail tamuna@gpb.geoffice@geotvr.ge; internet www.gpb.ge; f. 2005; comprises 2 television channels: Public TV (f. 1956) and Second Channel (f. 1971), and two radio stations: Public Radio (f. 1925) and Radio Two (f. 1995); Dir-Gen. TAMAR KINTSURASHVILI.

Adjara TV: 6000 Adjara, Batumi, M. Abashidze 41; tel. (222) 74-370; fax (222) 74-384; internet www.adjaratv.com; Chief Exec. TEA TSETSKHLADZE.

Imedi TV: 0159 Tbilisi, Lubliana 5; tel. (32) 91-93-12; fax (32) 91-90-41; e-mail info@imedi.ge; internet www.imedi.ge; partnership agreement concluded between Imedi Media Holding and News Corpn (USA) in Sept. 2006; Chair. (vacant); Man. Dir BIDZINA BARATASHVILI.

Mze TV (Sun TV): 0171 Tbilisi, Kostava 75B; tel. (32) 33-55-98; e-mail reklama@mze.ge; internet www.mze.ge; f. 2003; 78% owned by Rustavi 2; Dir ZAZA TANANASHVILI (acting).

Rustavi 2: 0177 Tbilisi, Vazha-Pshavela 45; tel. (32) 20-11-11; fax (32) 20-00-12; e-mail tv@rustavi2.com; internet www.rustavi2.com; f. 1994; independent; Gen. Dir KOBA DAVARASHVILI.

Radio

Georgian Public Broadcasting: see Television.

Radio Imedi: 0159 Tbilisi, Lubliana 5; e-mail info@radio-imedi.ge; internet www.radio-imedi.ge; f. 2001; national broadcasting, 24 hours; news; Dir IRAKLI KHETERELI.

GEORGIA

Radio Sakartvelo (Radio Georgia): 0159 Tbilisi, Marshal Gelovani 2; tel. (32) 38-30-30; fax (32) 33-60-60; e-mail tamara@fortuna.ge; internet www.fortuna.ge; f. 1999; owns and operates 4 stations, incl. Radio Fortuna and Radio Fortuna Plus; popular and classical music; Gen. Dir GURAM CHIGOGIDZE.

Finance

(cap. = capital; res = reserves; dep. = deposits; m. = million; brs = branches; amounts in lari, unless otherwise indicated)

BANKING

Central Bank

National Bank of Georgia: 0105 Tbilisi, Leonidze 3–5; tel. (32) 99-65-05; fax (32) 99-93-46; e-mail info@nbg.gov.ge; internet www.nbg.gov.ge; f. 1991; cap. 15.0m., res 55.9m., dep. 1,003.8m. (Dec. 2006); Pres. and Chair. of Bd ROMAN GOTSIRIDZE; 9 brs.

Other Banks

Agro-Business Bank: Tbilisi, 0160 Budapeshti 10; tel. (32) 32-96-68; fax (32) 93-28-80; e-mail abg@caucasus.net; internet www.abg.com.ge; f. 2000; 100% owned by the European Commission; cap. 6.9m., dep. 0.7m. (Dec. 2003); Gen. Dir GEORGE KALANDARISHVILI.

Bank of Georgia (Sakartvelos Banki): 0105 Tbilisi, Pushkin 3; tel. (32) 44-44-44; fax (32) 44-42-47; e-mail welcome@bog.ge; internet www.bog.ge; f. 1991; present name adopted 1994; cap. 25.2m., res 281.7m., dep. 785.1m. (Dec. 2006); Chair. NICHOLAS ENUKIDZE (acting); Chief Exec. IRAKLI GILAURI; 25 brs.

Bank Republic: 0179 Tbilisi, Gr. Abashidze 2; tel. (32) 92-55-55; fax (32) 92-55-44; e-mail info@republic.ge; internet www.republic.ge; f. 1991; 60% owned by Société Générale (France); cap. 22.0m., res 8.5m., dep. 278.8m. (Dec. 2006); Pres. LASHA PAPASHVILI; Gen. Dir GILBERT HIE.

Basisbank: 0103 Tbilisi, K. Tsamebuli 1; tel. (32) 92-29-22; fax (32) 98-65-48; e-mail info@basisbank.ge; internet www.basisbank.ge; f. 1993; cap. 5.0m., dep. 38.7m., total assets 50,688.0m. (Dec. 2005); Gen. Dir ZURAB TSIKHISTAVI.

Cartu Bank: 0162 Tbilisi, Chavchavadze 39A; tel. (32) 92-55-92; fax (32) 91-22-79; e-mail cartubank@cartubank.ge; internet www.cartubank.ge; f. 1996; cap. 54.7m., res 23.1m., dep. 74.2m. (Dec. 2005); Pres. GEORGE LOMAIA; Chair. of Bd GEORGE CHRDILELI; 5 brs.

Cascade Bank—Georgia: 0108 Tbilisi, Chanturia 14; tel. (32) 92-23-76; fax (32) 92-24-33; e-mail info@cascadebanking.ge; internet www.cascadebanking.com; f. 1996 as International Commercial Black Sea Bank; present name adopted in 2006; owned by Cascade Bank (Armenia); cap. 9.7m., res 0.08m., dep. 5.3m. (Dec. 2005); Man. Dir KONSTANTIN GORDEZIANI.

Investbank: 0108 Tbilisi, Lesya Ukrainka 3; tel. (32) 92-25-36; fax (32) 92-25-37; e-mail info@investbank.ge; internet www.investbank.ge; f. 2003; Gen. Dir IRAKLI KAKABADZE.

People's Bank of Georgia: 0162 Tbilisi, Chavchavadze 74; tel. (32) 91-22-45; fax (32) 93-64-68; e-mail info@peobge.com; internet www.peoplesbank.ge; f. 2002; cap. 10.0m., res 0.7m., dep. 64.8m. (Dec. 2005); Gen. Dir GIORGI GOGUADZE; 70 brs.

ProCredit Bank, Georgia: 0112 Tbilisi, Tamar Mepis 18; tel. (32) 20-22-22; fax (32) 25-05-80; e-mail info@procreditbank.ge; internet www.procreditbank.ge; f. 1999; present name adopted 2003; 39% owned by Internationale Micro Investitionen AG (Germany); cap. 48.9m., res 6.3m., dep. 341.4m. (Dec. 2006); Chief Exec. PHILIPP POTT.

Standard Bank (Standartbank): 0162 Tbilisi, Chavchavadze 43; tel. (32) 50-77-01; fax (32) 50-77-07; e-mail mail@standardbank.ge; internet www.standardbank.ge; f. 2000; name changed from Agro-Business Bank (ABG) in 2005; development bank; cap. 6.9m., dep. 16.1m., total assets 23.5m. (Dec. 2005); wholly owned by the European Commission; Gen. Dir GEORGE KALANDARISHVILI; 61 brs.

TaoPrivatBank: 0119 Tbilisi, Tsereteli 114; tel. (32) 35-05-00; fax (32) 35-50-80; e-mail info@taobank.ge; internet www.taobank.ge; f. 1992; cap. 52.0m., dep. 9.8m. (July 2007); Chair. VLADIMER UGULAVA.

TBC Bank: 0102 Tbilisi, Marjanishvili 7; tel. (32) 77-70-00; fax (32) 77-27-74; e-mail info@tbcbank.com.ge; internet www.tbcbank.com.ge; f. 1992; 30.95% owned by International Finance Corpn (USA); cap. 5.4m., res 14.7m., dep. 819.8m. (Dec. 2006); Pres. of Bd of Dirs VAKHTANG BUTSKHRIKIDZE; 13 brs.

VTB Georgia (VneshTorgBank Georgia): 0108 Tbilisi, Chanturia 14; tel. (32) 50-55-05; fax (32) 99-91-39; e-mail info@vtb.com.ge; internet www.vtb.com.ge; f. 1995 as United Georgian Bank; name changed as above 2006; 53% owned by the VneshTorgBank Group (Russia); 19% owned by European Bank for Reconstruction and Development; cap. 41.0m., res 0.2m., dep. 287.9m. (Dec. 2006); Chair. of Supervisory Bd ZAZA SIORIDZE; Man. Dir IUZA TAVDIDISHVILI; 19 brs.

STOCK EXCHANGE

Georgian Stock Exchange: 0162 Tbilisi, Chavchavadze 74A; tel. (32) 22-07-18; fax (32) 25-18-76; e-mail info@gse.ge; internet www.gse.ge; f. 1999; Chair. of Supervisory Bd GEORGE LOLADZE; Gen. Dir VAKHTANG SVANADZE.

INSURANCE

At the end of 2004 there were 14 insurance companies in Georgia.

State Insurance Supervision Service: 0164 Tbilisi, G. Chitaia 21; tel. (32) 95-64-89; fax (32) 95-71-42; e-mail isssg@inbox.ge; internet www.insurance.caucasus.net; f. 1997; provides state regulation of insurance activity; Dir ARCHIL TSERTSVADZE.

Aldagi Insurance Co: 0179 Tbilisi, Melikishvili 16; tel. (32) 92-44-11; fax (32) 29-49-05; e-mail aldagi@aldagi.com.ge; internet www.aldagi.com; f. 1990; 50% owned by Bank Republic; Chair. GURAM ASSATHIANY; Gen. Dir EVA IASHVILI.

Anglo-Georgian Insurance Co (AGIC): 0130 Tbilisi, I. Abashidze 29; tel. (32) 25-03-51; fax (32) 25-03-50; e-mail post@agic.com.ge; internet www.agic.com.ge; f. 1998 as a joint-stock co; all types of insurance; Gen. Dir FRANCIS MATHEW.

British-Caucasian Insurance Co: 0108 Tbilisi, Rustaveli 27; tel. (32) 98-89-98; fax (32) 25-28-08; e-mail bci@bci.ge; internet www.bci.ge; Dir RAMAZ KUKULADZE.

Europace: 0112 Tbilisi, Aghmashenebeli 150; tel. (32) 91-06-04; fax (32) 91-06-08; e-mail info@europace.com; internet www.europace.ge; f. 1998; fmrly Nabati Ltd; Dir VASIL AKHRAKHADZE.

Georgian Pension and Insurance Holding Co: 0162 Tbilisi, Chavchavadze 1/5; tel. (32) 92-01-20; internet www.gpih.ge; Gen. Dir PAATA GADZADZE.

Trade and Industry

GOVERNMENT AGENCIES

National Investment Agency: Invest In Georgia: 0108 Tbilisi, Chanturia 12; tel. (32) 43-34-33; fax (32) 98-27-55; e-mail info@investingeorgia.org; internet www.investingeorgia.org; f. 2002 to promote foreign direct investment; Dir-Gen. OTAR NISHNIANIDZE.

State Property Management Agency: 0108 Tbilisi, Chanturia; tel. (32) 99-74-16; e-mail info@privatization.ge; internet www.privatization.ge; responsible for divestment of state-owned enterprises.

CHAMBER OF COMMERCE

Georgian Chamber of Commerce and Industry: 0179 Tbilisi, Chavchavadze 11; tel. (32) 23-00-45; fax (32) 23-57-60; e-mail info@gcci.ge; internet www.gcci.ge; f. 1963; brs in Sukhumi and Batumi; Chair. JEMAL INAISHVILI.

Chamber of Commerce and Industry of the Autonomous Republic of Adjara: 6010 Adjara, Batumi, Melashvili 26; tel. (222) 728-41; fax (222) 728-42; e-mail cci@ajcci.ge; internet ajcci.ge; f. 2004; Pres. TENGIZ BAKURIDZE; Dir-Gen. IASON TSERTSVADZE.

TRADE ASSOCIATIONS

Association of Georgian Exporters: 0177 Tbilisi, Jikia 5; tel. (32) 24-43-02; fax (32) 24-43-03; e-mail gea@gepa.org.ge; Gen. Dir TAMAZ AGLADZE.

Agricultural Development Association of Georgia (ADA): 0102 Tbilisi, Doki 2; tel. (99) 58-86-28; e-mail ada@access.sanet.ge; Chair. ALEXANDER LAZASHVILI.

Employers' Association of Georgia: 0108 Tbilisi, R. Tabukashvili 15/4; tel. (32) 92-03-30; fax (32) 23-21-71; e-mail employer@gol.ge; Dir ELGUJA MELADZE.

Federation of Georgian Businessmen: 0105 Tbilisi, Gergeti 3; tel. (32) 94-04-72; fax (32) 92-30-15; e-mail admin@fgb.ge; internet www.fgb.ge; f. 2004; 150 mems; Pres. (vacant); Exec. Dir GIORGI ISAKADZE.

Small and Medium Enterprise Development Agency (SMEDA): 0162 Tbilisi, Chavchavadze 80; tel. (32) 99-90-77; fax (32) 93-35-39; e-mail smeda@caucasus.net; internet www.abco.caucasus.net/smeda; Dir ALEKO GOGOBERIDZE.

UTILITIES

Regulatory Authorities

Georgian National Energy Regulation Committee (Semeki): 0177 Tbilisi, Al. Kazbegi 45; tel. (32) 24-10-40; fax (32) 24-10-42;

e-mail mail@gnerc.org; internet www.gnerc.org; f. 1997; Chair. GURAM CHALAGASHVILI.

State Agency for the Regulation of Oil and Gas Resources (SAROGR): 0177 Tbilisi, Al. Kazbegi 45; tel. and fax (32) 25-33-11; e-mail sarogr@access.sanet.ge; internet www.sarogr.ge; f. 1999; Pres. ANDRIA KOTETISHVILI.

Electricity

In February 2007 Energo-Pro (Czech Republic) completed its purchase of 62.5% of Georgia's electricity distribution market, including six hydro-electric power plants (Ats, Dzevrula, Gumati, Lajanuri, Rioni and Shaori) and two distribution companies (UEDC and Energy Company of Adjara—ECA), with a total of 875,000 customers. The company pledged to invest US $285m. in the sector, including the construction of a new 100-MW hydro-electric plant.

Electricity System Commercial Operator (ESCO): 0177 Tbilisi, Al. Kazbegi 45; tel. (32) 31-14-70; fax (32) 31-17-49; e-mail office@esco.ge; internet www.esco.ge; f. 2006; state owned; scheduled for privatization; trades electricity and reserve capacity in order to maintain the balance of supply and demand; Gen. Dir BIDZINA CHKHONIA (acting).

Georgian State Electrosystem (GSE): 0105 Tbilisi, Baratashvili 2; tel. and fax (32) 20-17-00; fax (32) 92-31-42; internet www.gse.com.ge; f. 2002 from the merger of Electrodispetcherizatsia and Elektrogadatsema, formerly part of Sakenergo; operator of electricity transmission grid; state-owned; managed from March 2003 by ESBI Georgia, a subsidiary of ESBI International (Ireland); Gen. Dir SULKHAN ZUMBURIDZE.

Georgian United Energy Distribution Co (GUDC): 0107 Tbilisi, Lermontov 10; tel. (32) 93-13-84; internet www.uedc.ge; f. 2002 by amalgamation of the majority of regional electricity cos, excluding the regions of Tbilisi, Adjara and Kakheti; privatized in 2006; owned by Energo-Pro (Czech Rep.); Dirs DEAN WHITE, GIVI VARDIASHVILI; 5,000 employees.

Kakhati Energy Distribution (KED): 2120 Samegrelo-Zemo Svaneti Mkhare, Zugdidi rajon, Kakhati; comprising eight distributors; owned by TBC Energy.

Sakenergo: 0105 Tbilisi, V. Vekua 1; tel. (32) 98-98-14; fax (32) 98-31-97; formerly state-owned energy supplier; in 1996 restructured into three cos (generation, transmission and distribution); further restructured in 1998, see Georgian United Energy Distribution Co and Sakenergogeneratsia; Gen. Dir VAZHA METREVELI.

Sakenergogeneratsia: 0105 Tbilisi, V. Vekua 1; tel. and fax (32) 98-98-13; f. 1996; state power-generating co; Gen. Dir G. BADURASHVILI.

Telasi: 0154 Tbilisi, Vani 3; tel. (32) 25-52-11; fax (32) 77-99-78; privatized in 1999; 75% owned by Unified Energy Systems (Russia); Tbilisi distribution grid; 412,000 customers; owns two hydro-electric plants and two gas-fuelled generation plants; Gen. Dir YURI PIMONOV.

Gas

Georgian Oil and Gas Corpn (GOGC): Tbilisi, Kakheti Highway 21; tel. (32) 24-40-40; fax (32) 24-40-42; e-mail public@gogc.ge; internet www.gogc.ge; f. 1997; state-owned; fmrly Georgian International Gas Corpn, reorganized in 2006, merged with Georgian International Oil Corpn and Saknavtobi; exclusive operator, owner, user, disposer, and manager of natural and liquid gas import and transit in Georgia; Gen. Dir ZURAB JANJGAVA.

KazTransGaz Tbilisi (Tbilgazi): 0194 Tbilisi, Mitskevich 18A; tel. (32) 38-76-25; fax (32) 37-56-51; e-mail info@ktg-tbilisi.ge; internet www.tbilgazi.ge; fmrly Tbilgazi; gas distribution co for the Tbilisi region; privatized in 2006; 100% owned by KazTransGaz (Kazakhstan); Dir-Gen. GIORGI KOIAVA.

Water

Tbilisi Water Utility (Tbilisis Tskali): 0179 Tbilisi, M. Kostava 1st Alley 33; tel. (32) 48-71-10; scheduled for privatization; fmrly Tbiltskalkanali; water supply and sewerage system; Dir GIORGI GELBAKIANI.

TRADE UNION CONFEDERATION

Amalgamation of Trade Unions of Georgia (GTUA): 0122 Tbilisi, Shartava 7; tel. (32) 38-29-95; fax (32) 22-46-63; e-mail gtua@geo.net.ge; f. 1995 as Confederation of Trade Unions of Georgia, name changed as above in 2000; comprises branch unions with a total membership of approx. 800,000; in February 2005 the association ceded 90% of its property to the state; following legislative amendments all members were required to re-register; Chair. IRAKLI PETRIASHVILI.

Transport

RAILWAYS

In 2004 Georgia's rail network (including the sections within the secessionist republic of Abkhazia) totalled approximately 1,554 km. There are rail links with Azerbaijan, Armenia and Iran. Services on the railway line to Russia, along the Black Sea coast, have been disrupted and suspended as a result of the conflict in Abkhazia, although local services linking Abkhazia with the Black Sea region of Russia had been restored by the mid-2000s. In December 2004 an agreement was signed on the construction of a rail link between Kars, in Turkey, and Akhalkalaki, in Georgia, continuing to Azerbaijan, and the rehabilitation of the line between Akhalkalaki and Tbilisi.

The first section of the Tbilisi Metro was opened in 1966; by 2005 the system comprised two lines with 22 stations, totalling 26.4 km in length. Three extensions, totalling 15 km, were under construction; Tbilisi City Council's budget for 2006 allocated 16m. lari to the project.

Georgian Railway Co: 0112 Tbilisi, Tamar Mepis 15; tel. (32) 56-48-82; fax (32) 56-41-82; e-mail sag@railway.ge; internet www.railway.ge; f. 1872; Chair. and Dir-Gen. IRAKLI EZUGBAIA.

Tbilisi Metro (Tbilisi Metropolitena): 0112 Tbilisi, Tavisuplebis Moedani 2; tel. (32) 34-14-71; fax (32) 93-41-86; e-mail info@tbilmetro.com.ge; f. 1966; Gen. Dir ZURAB KIKALISHVILI.

ROADS

In 2004 the total length of roads in use was an estimated 20,247 km (including 1,474 km of main roads and 3,326 km of secondary roads). In that year 93.8% of the road network was paved.

SHIPPING

There are international shipping services to and from Black Sea and Mediterranean ports. The main ports are at Batumi and Poti.

Georgian Ocean Shipping Co (OSCO): 0160 Tbilisi, Al. Kazbegi 12A; tel. (32) 25-18-95; fax (32) 25-18-97; e-mail osco@wanex.net; f. 1999; privatized in 2005; owns 15 petroleum product and chemical carrier tankers; Chair. GURAM DOLBAIA.

Port of Batumi (Batumi Sea Trading Port Ltd): 6003 Adjara, Batumi, Kutaisi 1; tel. (222) 76-261; fax (222) 76-958; e-mail bsport@batumiport.com; internet www.batumiport.com; operates five terminals: petroleum terminal, container terminal, railway ferry, dry cargo terminal and passenger terminal; privatized in 2006; owned by Greenoak Group (United Kingdom); Gen. Dir PHRIDON SURMANIDZE.

Poti Sea Port: 4401 Samegrelo-Zemo Svaneti Mkhare, Poti, D. Agmashenebeli 52; tel. (393) 20-660; fax (393) 22-888; e-mail administration@potiseaport.com; internet www.potiseaport.com; f. 1858; commercial port; Gen. Dir LASHA AKHALADZE.

CIVIL AVIATION

Georgia's primary airport is Tbilisi International Airport, Lochini. There are three other airports in operation in Batumi, Kutaisi and Senaki.

Civil Aviation Authority: 0160 Tbilisi, Al. Kazbegi 12; tel. (32) 93-30-92; fax (32) 99-74-80; e-mail inspect@access.sanet.ge; f. 2002; Dir GIORGI MZHAVANADZE.

Georgian Airways: 0108 Tbilisi, Rustaveli 12; tel. (32) 99-97-30; fax (32) 99-96-60; e-mail info@georgian-airways.com; internet www.georgian-airways.com; f. 1999; present name adopted 2004; privately owned; flights to various destinations in Europe and the Middle East; Chair. of Bd of Dirs TAMAZ GAIASHVILI.

Georgian National Airlines: 0119 Tbilisi, Bakradze 6; tel. (32) 35-58-02; fax (32) 35-58-01; e-mail info@national-avia.com; internet www.national-avia.com; f. 1998 as Air Bisec; present name adopted 2004; Pres. GIORGI KODUA.

Tourism

Prior to the disintegration of the USSR, Georgia attracted some 1.5m. tourists annually (mainly from other parts of the USSR). However, following the outbreak of civil conflict in the early 1990s in South Ossetia and Abkhazia, there was an almost complete cessation in tourism. Efforts to regenerate the sector were made in the late 1990s, with the historic buildings of Tbilisi and the surrounding area one of the primary attractions. According to the World Tourism Organization, there were 560,021 tourist arrivals in 2005, compared with 313,442 in 2003, and receipts from tourism (including passenger transport) totalled US $288m. in 2005.

Department of Tourism and Resorts of Georgia: 0162 Tbilisi, Chavchavadze 80; tel. (32) 22-61-25; fax (32) 29-40-52; e-mail georgia@tourism.gov.ge; internet www.tourism.gov.ge; forms part of the Ministry of Economic Development; Chair. SABA KIKNADZE.

GERMANY

Introductory Survey

Location, Climate, Language, Religion, Flag, Capital

The Federal Republic of Germany, which was formally established in October 1990 upon the unification of the Federal Republic of Germany (FRG, West Germany) and the German Democratic Republic (GDR, East Germany), lies in the heart of Europe. Its neighbours to the west are the Netherlands, Belgium, Luxembourg and France, to the south Switzerland and Austria, to the east the Czech Republic and Poland, and to the north Denmark. The climate is temperate, with an annual average temperature of 9°C (48°F), although there are considerable variations between the North German lowlands and the Bavarian Alps. The language is German. There is a small Sorbian-speaking minority (numbering about 100,000 people). About 33% of the population are Protestants and a further 32% are Roman Catholics. The national flag (proportions 3 by 5) consists of three equal horizontal stripes, of black, red and gold. The capital is Berlin.

Recent History

Following the defeat of the Nazi regime and the ending of the Second World War in 1945, Germany was divided, according to the Berlin Agreement, into US, Soviet, British and French occupation zones. Berlin was similarly divided. The former German territories east of the Oder and Neisse rivers, with the city of Danzig (now Gdańsk), became part of Poland, while the northern part of East Prussia, around Königsberg (now Kaliningrad), was transferred to the USSR. After the failure of negotiations to establish a unified German administration, the US, French and British zones were integrated economically in 1948. In May 1949 a provisional Constitution, the Grundgesetz (Basic Law), came into effect in the three zones (except in Saarland—see below), and federal elections were held in August. On 21 September 1949 a new German state, the Federal Republic of Germany (FRG), was established in the three Western zones. The FRG was governed from Bonn in Nordrhein-Westfalen. (Saarland was not incorporated into the FRG until 1957.) In October 1949 Soviet-occupied Eastern Germany declared itself the German Democratic Republic (GDR), with the Soviet zone of Berlin as its capital. This left the remainder of Berlin (West Berlin) as an enclave of the FRG within the territory of the GDR.

The FRG and GDR developed sharply divergent political and economic systems. The leaders of the GDR created a socialist state, based on the Soviet model. As early as 1945 large agricultural estates in eastern Germany were nationalized, followed in 1946 by major industrial concerns. Exclusive political control was exercised by the Sozialistische Einheitspartei Deutschlands (SED, Socialist Unity Party of Germany), which had been formed in April 1946 by the merger of the Communist Party of Germany and the branch of the Sozialdemokratische Partei Deutschlands (SPD, Social Democratic Party of Germany) in the Soviet zone. Other political parties in eastern Germany were under the strict control of the SED, and no independent political activity was permitted. In 1950 Walter Ulbricht was appointed Secretary-General (later restyled First Secretary) of the SED.

The transfer, as war reparations, of foodstuffs, livestock and industrial equipment to the USSR from eastern Germany had a devastating effect on the area's economy in the immediate post-war period. In June 1953 increasing political repression and severe food shortages led to uprisings and strikes, which were suppressed by Soviet troops. The continued failure of the GDR to match the remarkable economic recovery of the FRG prompted a growing number of refugees to cross from the GDR to the FRG (between 1949 and 1961 an estimated 2.5m. GDR citizens moved permanently to the FRG). Emigration was accelerated by the enforced collectivization of many farms in 1960, and in August 1961 the GDR authorities hastily constructed a guarded wall between East and West Berlin (the Berlin Wall).

In May 1971 Ulbricht was succeeded as First Secretary (later restyled General Secretary) of the SED by Erich Honecker. Ulbricht remained Chairman of the Council of State (Head of State), a post that he had held since 1960, until his death in August 1973. He was initially succeeded in this office by Willi Stoph, but in October 1976 Stoph returned to his previous post as Chairman of the Council of Ministers, and Honecker became Chairman of the Council of State. Under Honecker, despite some liberalization of relations with the FRG, there was little relaxation of repressive domestic policies. Honecker strongly opposed the political and economic reforms that began in the USSR and some other Eastern European countries in the mid-1980s.

The 1949 elections in the FRG resulted in victory for the conservative Christlich-Demokratische Union Deutschlands (CDU, Christian Democratic Union of Germany), together with its sister party in Bavaria, the Christlich-Soziale Union (CSU, Christian Social Union). The SPD was the largest opposition party. Dr Konrad Adenauer, the leader of the CDU, was elected Federal Chancellor by the Bundestag (Federal Assembly); Theodor Heuss became the first President of the Republic. Under Adenauer's chancellorship (which lasted until 1963) and the direction of Dr Ludwig Erhard, his Minister of Economics (and successor as Chancellor), the FRG rebuilt itself rapidly to become one of the most affluent and economically dynamic states in Europe, as well as an important strategic ally of other Western European states and the USA. The Paris Agreement of 1954 gave full sovereign status to the FRG from 5 May 1955, and also granted it membership of the North Atlantic Treaty Organization (NATO, see p. 340).

The CDU/CSU held power in coalition with the SPD from 1966 to 1969, under the chancellorship of Dr Kurt Kiesinger, but lost support at the 1969 general election, allowing the SPD to form a coalition Government with the Freie Demokratische Partei (FDP, Free Democratic Party), under the chancellorship of Willy Brandt, the SPD leader. Following elections in November 1972, the SPD became, for the first time, the largest party in the Bundestag. In May 1974, however, Brandt resigned as Chancellor, after the discovery that his personal assistant had been a clandestine agent of the GDR. He was succeeded by Helmut Schmidt of the SPD, hitherto the Minister of Finance. A deteriorating economic situation was accompanied by a decline in the popularity of the Government and increasing tension between the coalition partners. In the general election of October 1976 the SPD lost its position as the largest party in the Bundestag, but the SPD-FDP coalition retained a slender majority.

At the general election of October 1980 the SPD-FDP coalition secured a 45-seat majority in the Bundestag. However, over the next two years the coalition became increasingly unstable, with the partners divided on issues of nuclear power, defence and economic policy. In September 1982 the coalition collapsed when the two parties failed to agree on budgetary measures. In October the FDP formed a Government with the CDU/CSU, under the chancellorship of the CDU leader, Dr Helmut Kohl. This new partnership was consolidated by the results of the general election of March 1983, when the CDU/CSU substantially increased its share of the vote. An environmentalist party, Die Grünen (The Greens), gained representation in the Bundestag for the first time. In July 1984 Prof. Karl Carstens, who had held the post of Federal President since 1979, was succeeded by Dr Richard von Weizsäcker, also of the CDU. The CDU/CSU-FDP coalition retained office after the general election of January 1987, although with a reduced majority; Kohl was reappointed Chancellor by the Bundestag.

During 1949–69 the FRG, under the CDU/CSU, remained largely isolated from Eastern Europe, owing to the FRG Government's refusal to recognize the GDR as an independent state or to maintain diplomatic relations with any other states that recognized the GDR. When Brandt became Chancellor in 1969, he adopted a more conciliatory approach to relations with Eastern Europe and, in particular, towards the GDR, a policy which came to be known as Ostpolitik. In 1970 formal discussions were conducted between representatives of the GDR and the FRG for the first time, and there was a significant increase in diplomatic contacts between the FRG and the other countries of Eastern Europe. In 1970 treaties were signed with the USSR and Poland, in which the FRG formally renounced claims to the eastern territories of the Third Reich and recognized the 'Oder–Neisse Line' as the border between Germany (actually the GDR) and Poland. Further negotiations between the GDR and the

FRG, following a quadripartite agreement on West Berlin in September 1971, clarified access rights to West Berlin and also allowed West Berliners to visit the GDR. In December 1972 the two German states signed a 'Basic Treaty', agreeing to develop normal, neighbourly relations with each other, to settle all differences without resort to force, and to respect each other's independence. The Treaty permitted both the FRG and the GDR to join the UN in September 1973, and allowed many Western countries to establish diplomatic relations with the GDR, although both German states continued to deny formal diplomatic recognition to each other.

In December 1981 the first official meeting for 11 years took place between the two countries' leaders, when Chancellor Schmidt travelled to the GDR for discussions with Honecker. Inter-German relations deteriorated following the deployment, in late 1983, of US nuclear missiles in the FRG, and the subsequent siting of additional Soviet missiles in the GDR. Nevertheless, official contacts were maintained, and Honecker made his first visit to the FRG in September 1987.

Relations between the two German states were dramatically affected by political upheavals that occurred in the GDR in late 1989 and 1990. In the latter half of 1989 many thousands of disaffected GDR citizens emigrated illegally to the FRG, via Czechoslovakia, Poland and Hungary. The exodus was accelerated by the Hungarian Government's decision, in September 1989, to permit citizens of the GDR to leave Hungary without exit visas. Meanwhile, there was a growth in popular dissent within the GDR, led by Neues Forum (New Forum), an independent citizens' action group which had been established to encourage discussion of democratic reforms, justice and environmental issues.

In early October 1989, following official celebrations to commemorate the 40th anniversary of the foundation of the GDR, anti-Government demonstrations erupted in East Berlin and other large towns. Eventually, as the demonstrations attracted increasing popular support, intervention by the police ceased. (It was later reported that the SED Politburo had voted narrowly against the use of the armed forces to suppress the civil unrest.) In mid-October, as the political situation became more unsettled, Honecker resigned as General Secretary of the SED, Chairman of the Council of State and Chairman of the National Defence Council, citing reasons of ill health. He was replaced in all these posts by Egon Krenz, a senior member of the SED Politburo. Krenz immediately initiated a dialogue with Neues Forum (which was legalized in November) and with church leaders. There was also a noticeable liberalization of the media, and an amnesty was announced for all persons who had been detained during the recent demonstrations and for those imprisoned for attempting to leave the country illegally. However, large demonstrations, to demand further reforms, continued in many towns throughout the GDR.

On 7 November 1989, in a further attempt to placate the demonstrators, the entire membership of the GDR Council of Ministers resigned. On the following day the SED Politburo also resigned. On 9 November restrictions on foreign travel for GDR citizens were ended, and all border crossings to the FRG were opened. During the weekend of 10–11 November an estimated 2m. GDR citizens crossed into West Berlin, and the GDR authorities began to dismantle sections of the Berlin Wall. Dr Hans Modrow, a leading member of the SED who was regarded as an advocate of greater reforms, was appointed Chairman of a new Council of Ministers. The new Government pledged to introduce comprehensive political and economic reforms and to hold free elections in 1990.

In early December 1989 the Volkskammer (the GDR's legislature) voted to remove provisions in the Constitution that protected the SED's status as the single ruling party. However, the mass demonstrations continued, prompted by revelations of corruption and personal enrichment by the former leadership and of abuses of power by the state security service (Staatssicherheitsdienst, known colloquially as the Stasi, which was subsequently disbanded). A special commission was established to investigate such charges, and former senior officials, including Honecker and Stoph, were expelled from the SED and placed under house arrest, pending legal proceedings. As the political situation became increasingly unstable, the entire membership of the SED Politburo and Central Committee, including Krenz, resigned, and both bodies, together with the post of General Secretary, were abolished. Shortly afterwards, Krenz also resigned as Chairman of the Council of State; he was replaced by Dr Manfred Gerlach, the Chairman of the Liberal-Demokratische Partei Deutschlands (LDPD, Liberal Democratic Party of Germany). Dr Gregor Gysi, a prominent defence lawyer who was sympathetic to the opposition, was elected to the new post of Chairman of the SED (restyled the Partei des Demokratischen Sozialismus—PDS, Party of Democratic Socialism, in February 1990).

In December 1989 and January 1990 all-party talks took place in the GDR, resulting in the formation, in early February, of a new administration, designated the Government of National Responsibility (still led by Modrow), to remain in office until elections were held. The GDR's first free legislative elections took place on 18 March 1990, with the participation of 93% of those eligible to vote. The East German CDU obtained 40.8% of the total votes cast, while the newly re-established East German SPD and the PDS secured 21.8% and 16.4% respectively. In April a coalition Government was formed, headed by Lothar de Maizière, leader of the Eastern CDU. Five parties were represented in the new Government: the CDU, the SPD, the Liga der Freien Demokraten (League of Free Democrats) and two smaller parties—the Deutsche Soziale Union (German Social Union) and Demokratische Aufschwung (Democratic Departure). The PDS was not invited to join the coalition.

As a result of the changes within the GDR and the subsequent free contact between Germans of east and west, the issue of possible unification of the two German states inevitably emerged. In November 1989 Chancellor Kohl proposed a plan for the eventual unification of the two countries by means of an interim confederal arrangement. In December Kohl made his first visit to the GDR, where he held discussions with the East German leadership. The two sides agreed to develop contacts at all levels and to establish joint economic, cultural and environmental commissions. However, the GDR Government initially insisted that the GDR remain a sovereign, independent state. Nevertheless, in February 1990, in response to growing popular support among GDR citizens for unification, Modrow publicly advocated the establishment of a united Germany. Shortly afterwards, Kohl and Modrow met in Bonn, where they agreed to establish a joint commission to achieve full economic and monetary union between the GDR and the FRG. The new coalition Government of the GDR, formed in April, pledged its determination to achieve German unification in the near future. In mid-May the legislatures of the GDR and the FRG approved the Treaty Between the FRG and the GDR Establishing a Monetary, Economic and Social Union, which came into effect on 1 July. Later in July the Volkskammer approved the re-establishment on GDR territory of the five Länder (states)—Brandenburg, Mecklenburg-Western Pomerania (Mecklenburg-Vorpommern), Saxony (Sachsen), Saxony-Anhalt (Sachsen-Anhalt) and Thuringia (Thüringen)—which had been abolished by the GDR Government in 1952 in favour of 14 districts (Berzirke). On 31 August 1990 the Treaty Between the FRG and the GDR on the Establishment of German Unity was signed in East Berlin by representatives of the two Governments. The treaty stipulated, *inter alia*, that the newly restored Länder would accede to the FRG on 3 October 1990, and that the 23 boroughs of East and West Berlin would jointly form the Land (state) of Berlin.

Owing to the complex international status of the FRG and the GDR and the two countries' membership of opposing military alliances (respectively, NATO and the now-defunct Warsaw Pact), the process of German unification also included negotiations with other countries. In February 1990 representatives of 23 NATO and Warsaw Pact countries agreed to establish the so-called 'two-plus-four' talks (the FRG and the GDR, plus the four countries that had occupied Germany after the Second World War—France, the USSR, the United Kingdom and the USA) to discuss the external aspects of German unification. In June both German legislatures approved a resolution recognizing the inviolability of Poland's post-1945 borders, stressing that the eastern border of a future united Germany would remain along the Oder–Neisse line. In July, at bilateral talks in the USSR with Chancellor Kohl, the Soviet leader, Mikhail Gorbachev, agreed that a united Germany would be free to join whichever military alliance it wished, thus permitting Germany to remain a full member of NATO. The USSR also pledged to withdraw its armed forces (estimated at 370,000 in 1990) from GDR territory within four years, and it was agreed that a united Germany would reduce the strength of its armed forces to 370,000 within the same period. This agreement ensured a successful result to the 'two-plus-four' talks, which were concluded in September in the Soviet capital, Moscow, where the Treaty on the Final Settlement with Respect to Germany was signed. In late September the GDR withdrew from the Warsaw Pact.

On 1 October 1990 representatives of the four countries that had occupied Germany after the Second World War met in New York, USA, to sign a document in which Germany's full sovereignty was recognized. Finally, on 3 October, the two German states were formally unified. On the following day, at a session of the Bundestag (which had been expanded to permit the representation of former deputies of the GDR Volkskammer), five prominent politicians from the former GDR were sworn in as Ministers without Portfolio in the Federal Government.

Prior to unification, the CDU, the SPD and the FDP of the GDR had merged with their respective counterparts in the FRG to form three single parties. At state elections in the newly acceded Länder, held in mid-October 1990, the CDU obtained an average of 41% of the total votes cast and won control of four Land legislatures, while the SPD received an average of 27% of the total votes cast and gained a majority only in Brandenburg. This surge of support for Chancellor Kohl and the CDU was confirmed by the results of elections to the Bundestag in early December (the first all-German elections since 1933). The CDU (together with the CSU) secured a total of 319 seats in the 662-member Bundestag. The SPD achieved its poorest result in a general election since 1957, winning 239 seats in the legislature (a result attributed, in large part, to the party's cautious stance on unification). The FDP won 79 seats in the Bundestag, its most successful result in legislative elections since 1961. Unexpectedly, the West German Grünen lost the 42 seats that they had previously held in the legislature, having failed to obtain the necessary 5% of the votes cast in the area formerly constituting the FRG. However, as a result of a special clause in the electoral law (valid only for the legislative elections of December 1990), which permitted representation in the Bundestag for parties of the former GDR that received at least 5% of the total votes cast in former GDR territory, the party's eastern German counterpart, in coalition with Bündnis 90 (Alliance 90), secured eight seats in the legislature. Under the same ruling, the PDS won 17 seats in the Bundestag (having received almost 10% of the total votes cast in the area formerly constituting the GDR).

Dr Kohl was formally re-elected to the post of Federal Chancellor in mid-January 1991, immediately after the formation of the new Federal Government. This comprised 20 members, but included only three politicians from the former GDR. The FDP's representation was increased from four to five ministers, reflecting the party's recent electoral success.

Investigations into the abuse of power by the former GDR administration, conducted during the early 1990s, prompted the dismissal or resignation from government posts of several former SED politicians. In January 1991 the German authorities temporarily suspended efforts to arrest Honecker on charges of manslaughter (for complicity in the deaths of people who had been killed while attempting to escape from the GDR), owing to the severe ill health of the former GDR leader. In March it was announced that Honecker had been transferred, without the permission of the German authorities, to the USSR, and in December he took refuge in the Chilean embassy in Moscow.

One of the most serious problems confronting the Government following unification was that of escalating unemployment in eastern Germany, as a result of the introduction of market-orientated reforms intended to integrate the economic system of the former GDR with that of the rest of the country. A substantial increase in the crime rate in eastern Germany was also recorded. A further disturbing social issue, particularly in the eastern Länder, was the resurgence of extreme right-wing and neo-Nazi groups. Moreover, there were also fears of a resurgence of political violence, following a series of terrorist acts culminating in the assassination, in April 1991, of Detlev Rohwedder, the executive head of the Treuhandanstalt (the trustee agency that had been established in March 1990 to supervise the privatization of state-owned enterprises in the former GDR). Responsibility for this and other attacks was claimed by the Rote Armee Fraktion (Red Army Faction), an extreme left-wing terrorist organization that had been active in the FRG during the 1970s. (The Red Army Faction eventually disbanded in 1998.)

Increasing popular discontent with the Government's post-unification policies was reflected in successive victories for the SPD in Land elections in the first half of 1991, enabling the SPD to regain its majority in the Bundesrat (Federal Council). In June 1991 the Bundestag voted in favour of Berlin as the future seat of the legislature and of government; it was envisaged that the transfer of organs of government from Bonn to Berlin would be completed by 2000.

In January 1992 some 2m. Stasi files were opened to public scrutiny. In February Erich Mielke, the former head of the Stasi, was brought to trial on charges of murder, and in September Markus Wolf, the former head of East Germany's intelligence service, was charged with espionage, treason and corruption; both were subsequently found guilty and each was sentenced to six years' imprisonment. Meanwhile, Honecker returned to Germany from Russia in July 1992. He was brought to trial in November, together with five other defendants (among them Mielke and Stoph), on charges of manslaughter and embezzlement. In April 1993, however, the charges against Honecker were suspended. (The former East German leader, who was terminally ill, had been allowed to leave for Chile in January of that year; he died in May 1994.) Stoph was also released on grounds of ill health.

The issue of asylum seekers dominated domestic politics during the early 1990s. At Land elections in April 1992, both the CDU and the SPD lost considerable support to right-wing extremist parties. In June the Bundestag approved controversial legislation which aimed to accelerate the processing of applications by refugees and introduced stricter rules for the granting of asylum. A six-week limit was imposed on the time that could be devoted to the consideration of each case, during which period applicants would be required to stay in special camps. Extreme nationalistic sentiment in some quarters led to an escalation in brutal attacks against asylum seekers and foreign workers during the early 1990s. In August 1992 neo-Nazi youths attacked refugee centres in more than 15 towns and bombed a memorial to the Holocaust (the Nazis' extermination of an estimated 6m. Jews) in Berlin. Sporadic attacks continued throughout Germany (though mainly in the east) in September and October. Several neo-Nazi vandals were arrested, but there was criticism of the lenient sentences imposed on those convicted. The murder in November of three Turkish immigrants in an arson attack in Mölln, Schleswig-Holstein, prompted the Government to ban several right-wing extremist groups that were believed to have been responsible for co-ordinating attacks on foreigners. In December the main political parties reached agreement on the terms of a constitutional amendment to the law of asylum, and the new provisions, empowering immigration officials to refuse entry to economic migrants while still facilitating the granting of asylum to persons who were deemed to be political refugees, were approved by the Bundestag and the Bundesrat in May 1993. The Ministry of the Interior estimated that a record total of 438,191 people had sought asylum in Germany during 1992. By 1998, however, mainly as a result of the 1993 legislation, the number of applications had fallen to 98,644. During May 1993 the deaths of five Turkish women in an arson attack near Cologne (Köln) precipitated protest demonstrations throughout Germany and widespread condemnation in the international media. In May 1994 the Bundesrat approved measures to impose stricter penalties on perpetrators of right-wing extremist violence and on those who denied the existence of the Holocaust; further strong measures against nationalist extremists were adopted in September.

The CDU/CSU-FDP coalition was re-elected at a general election held in October 1994; its majority in the Bundestag (enlarged to 672 seats) was, however, sharply reduced, from 134 to 10 seats. The CDU (with the CSU) won 294 seats, the SPD 252 seats, Bündnis 90/Die Grünen 50 seats, the FDP (which had lost representation at several Land parliament elections during 1994) 47 seats, and the PDS 30 seats. The right-wing extremist organizations did not attract strong support. In early November the ruling coalition negotiated a new political programme, with the creation of jobs a priority. Shortly afterwards Dr Kohl was formally re-elected as the Federal Chancellor, by a margin of five votes.

In May 1995 the Federal Constitutional Court ruled that alleged former East German spies should not be prosecuted by federal courts regarding crimes that were committed against the Federal Republic on behalf of the former GDR prior to unification; consequently, in October the 1992 conviction of Markus Wolf was overturned. In November 1996 the Federal Constitutional Court ruled that the legal principles of the FRG regarding human rights could be retroactively applied to actions carried out within the former GDR. Thus, in May 1997 Wolf was convicted on charges of abduction, coercion and assault, receiving a suspended sentence of two years' imprisonment. In August Egon Krenz and two other former senior SED members, Günther

Schabowski and Günther Kleiber, were found guilty of the manslaughter and attempted manslaughter of people who had sought to flee the former GDR; all three were sentenced to terms of imprisonment. The convictions were upheld in November 1999, following unsuccessful appeals. Krenz's conviction was again upheld in 2001, following an unsuccessful appeal to the European Court of Human Rights. Schabowski and Kleiber were pardoned in September 2000.

The activities of extreme right-wing organizations increased significantly in 1997, and during the latter half of the year a series of incidents was reported that suggested the infiltration of some sections of the armed forces by neo-Nazi interests. In April 1998 the extreme right-wing and openly xenophobic Deutsche Volksunion (DVU, German People's Union) won unprecedented support at an election to the Land parliament for the economically depressed region of Sachsen-Anhalt in eastern Germany, securing 12.9% of the votes cast.

Tensions within the CDU/CSU-FDP coalition became apparent in 1997, mainly concerning the desirability and means of meeting the so-called 'convergence criteria' for participation in European Economic and Monetary Union (EMU) by 1999. Record levels of unemployment continued to cause concern, as well as an unexpectedly large deficit on the 1997 budget. In April 1998, despite evidence of widespread opposition to the new single European currency, the Bundestag voted strongly in favour of Germany's participation in EMU.

At the general election held in late September 1998 the CDU/CSU-FDP coalition was decisively defeated by the SPD, which won 298 of the total seats in the Bundestag (reduced to 669). The CDU took 198 seats, both the CSU and Bündnis 90/Die Grünen secured 47, the FDP 43 and the PDS 36. Neither the right-wing Republikaner nor the DVU gained representation in the federal legislature. Following the election, Kohl resigned as Chairman of the CDU; he was replaced by the party's parliamentary leader, Dr Wolfgang Schäuble. Meanwhile, the SPD and Bündnis 90/Die Grünen swiftly negotiated a coalition pact. In late October Gerhard Schröder of the SPD, formerly the Minister-President of Lower Saxony (Niedersachsen), was elected Federal Chancellor by a large majority of Bundestag members. The new Federal Government included three ministers representing Bündnis 90/Die Grünen, the most prominent of whom was the new Federal Vice-Chancellor and Minister of Foreign Affairs, Joschka Fischer, who was formerly the parliamentary leader of the ecological parties. Oskar Lafontaine, the Chairman of the SPD, was appointed Minister of Finance, charged with guiding Germany into EMU. The SPD-Bündnis 90/Die Grünen coalition held a 21-seat majority in the Bundestag.

In early November 1998 Schröder delivered his first major policy statement, placing high priority on reducing the rising level of unemployment; measures were also planned to expedite the economic reconstruction of the eastern Länder, to reform the pension system, to impose an 'ecological' tax on energy consumption and gradually to curtail the country's nuclear energy programme. It soon became apparent, however, that the two coalition partners envisaged very different time-scales for the abandonment of atomic power. While the SPD favoured phased closure over a period of 25 years, the ecological parties aimed to act far more swiftly. In mid-December Schröder overruled the Minister of the Environment, Nature Conservation and Nuclear Safety, Jürgen Trittin of Bündnis 90/Die Grünen, when Trittin unilaterally attempted both to cancel contracts for the reprocessing of German nuclear waste and to dismiss the chiefs of the national atomic power safety commissions.

In early March 1999 Lafontaine resigned as Minister of Finance, apparently in protest at an evident lack of support for his economic policies and management from within both the business community and the Government; he also vacated his seat in the Bundestag and the chairmanship of the SPD. Hans Eichel of the SPD, hitherto the Minister-President of Hesse (Hessen), was appointed as the new Minister of Finance. In the following month Schröder was elected to the post of Chairman of the SPD. In May the Government approved legislation that enabled people born in Germany of resident foreign parents to hold both German citizenship (hitherto denied them) and the nationality of one parent until adulthood, whereupon they would be required to relinquish one. This represented a significant departure from previous ethnically orientated citizenship legislation, and was intended to encourage the social assimilation of Germany's foreign population (numbering some 7m. in 1999). The opposition CDU had strongly opposed an initial proposal to grant a full right of dual nationality.

In June 1999 Dr Roman Herzog of the CDU was replaced as Federal President by Prof. Dr Johannes Rau of the SPD, formerly Minister-President of Nordrhein-Westfalen (North Rhine-Westphalia). During mid-1999 most organs of government moved from Bonn to the capital, Berlin. Both the Bündnis 90/Die Grünen alliance (which was becoming increasingly polarized between idealist and more pragmatic elements) and the SPD (which was popularly regarded as having betrayed its avowed commitment to social justice following the announcement in June of a package of economic austerity measures designed to redress the decelerating economic growth rate and to appease the alienated business sector) performed poorly at elections to several Land legislatures during the second half of 1999; by late 1999 the ruling coalition controlled less than two-fifths of votes in the Bundesrat.

During November 1999 the opposition CDU became embroiled in a scandal concerning the discovery of a system of secret bank accounts, which had been used to deposit undisclosed donations to the party throughout the 1990s. (In accordance with the Grundgesetz, all substantial funding of political parties must be declared.) Allegations subsequently emerged that the CDU leadership had covertly accepted a large bribe from the then state-owned French oil company Elf Aquitaine, in connection with its purchase in 1992 of an eastern German oil refinery. It was also alleged that, in 1998, the CDU had granted an export licence to an arms exporting interest in return for an undeclared party donation. The former Chancellor, Kohl, admitted knowledge of some secret party funding, but repeatedly refused to name any sources; in January 2000 Kohl was forced to resign his honorary chairmanship of the CDU after he became the subject of a criminal investigation. The incumbent CDU leadership was also implicated in the scandal, including Schäuble, who was, none the less, confirmed as party Chairman later in the month, despite his confession that in 1994 he had accepted a cash donation from an arms dealer who was implicated in the funding scandal. Schäuble established a CDU independent inquiry into the funding scandal in January 2000, which subsequently revealed that irregularities had persisted for decades in German politics. Throughout January further revelations emerged, including the secretion of more than DM 13m. in illegal foreign accounts by the Hesse regional branch of the CDU. In February 2000 the CDU was fined DM 41m. for irregularities in the Hesse accounts for 1998. The following day Schäuble resigned as Chairman of the CDU, accepting responsibility for mishandling the funding scandal. By January 2002 another funding scandal had emerged when the Bundestag and state prosecutors launched preliminary investigations into allegations that the CSU had improperly obtained funds from federal authorities by incorrectly classifying its income.

Meanwhile, following the withdrawal from contention in March 2000 of the former Minister of Defence, Volke Rühe (owing to the party's poor performance under his leadership in the state legislative election in Schleswig-Holstein in late February), the CDU's Secretary-General, Angela Merkel, was elected Chairman at the party congress in April. Merkel, who had secured significant support as a result of her determination to expose the CDU's financial irregularities, was considered more liberal than her predecessors. In March excerpts from transcripts of telephone conversations of CDU officials, which had been illegally recorded by the Stasi, appeared to indicate that Kohl had been aware of the irregular party funding earlier than he had previously admitted. Following a campaign by Kohl, the leaders of the principal parties agreed in May to forbid the use of the transcripts by the parliamentary committee investigating financial irregularities in the CDU, and, in July 2001, Kohl secured a court ruling banning the publication of the transcripts. However, in May 2000 the state prosecutor concluded that there were sufficient grounds for the criminal prosecution of Kohl on charges of fraud and bribery (although, as an incumbent member of the legislature, Kohl was immune from prosecution). In his testimony in June to the parliamentary committee Kohl continued to admit accepting illegal secret contributions to party funds, but denied allegations that such donations had influenced government policy decisions (including the sale of the oil refinery to Elf Aquitaine).

In September 2000 Kohl resumed his seat in the legislature for the first time since December 1999. He declined an invitation to the 10th anniversary celebration of unification in October 2000 on the grounds that, despite his central role in achieving German unification, he had not been invited to speak. In December another fine, of DM 7.7m., was imposed on the CDU by the

Speaker of the Bundestag, Wolfgang Thierse, as a consequence of illegal fund-raising. Kohl had transferred DM 8m. (largely raised through donations) to the CDU in June to contribute to the payment of fines. The CDU's appeal against the previous DM 41m. fine was upheld by a court in January 2001, although Thierse announced his intention to appeal against the ruling. In February Kohl accepted the proposal of the state prosecutor that he should pay a fine of DM 300,000 in exchange for the abandonment of the criminal investigation into his acceptance of illegal contributions to the CDU in the 1990s; this arrangement subsequently gained judicial approval. The parliamentary inquiry continued, however, as did Kohl's refusal to name the illegal contributors to his party.

In December 1999 the German Government agreed to pay a substantial sum in compensation to people who had worked as forced labourers for German companies or been deprived of their assets under the Nazi regime; it was hoped that this would forestall a growing number of lawsuits taken out against German industrial interests and banks by survivors of the Holocaust. Chancellor Schröder announced that the Government would provide DM 5,000m. of the proposed DM 10,000m. fund; the other DM 5,000m. was to be raised by Germany's largest banks and companies. The Government's share was to be financed by state privatizations and contributions from the Länder. The USA agreed to contribute US $10m. as a gesture of solidarity. In March 2000 Schröder announced an improved agreement, which resolved differences between categories of victims and added a further DM 200m. to the compensation fund, to be derived from interest income and from a separate settlement between Swiss banks and Holocaust victims. The larger German insurers declined to contribute to the fund being raised by industry because of potentially overlapping claims from separate negotiations involving many leading European insurers. The compensation agreement was eventually signed in July, and, following the resolution of legal difficulties, payments began in May 2001.

In June 2000, following months of negotiations between the Government and the nuclear industry, Schröder announced that an agreement had been concluded to decommission the country's 19 nuclear power plants (which accounted for almost one-third of power requirements) without compensation by 2021. Under the accord, the reprocessing of nuclear fuel would end by 2005 (although the transportation of spent fuel for reprocessing elsewhere could continue under certain conditions). Despite some reservations on the part of a significant number of members of Bündnis 90/Die Grünen who had favoured an immediate cessation of nuclear power generation, the agreement was endorsed at a party conference later that month. Rioting erupted over three days in March 2001 as thousands of anti-nuclear protesters attempted to halt the transportation of a consignment of nuclear waste to a storage site in Lower Saxony. Around 20,000 riot police and other security units were deployed to remove the activists, some of whom had chained and cemented themselves to the rail track; about 600 protesters were arrested. The police action constituted the largest police deployment in Germany's post-war history. In September the Federal Government adopted a bill regulating the phasing out of nuclear power, which was subsequently approved by the Bundestag. The first closure took place in November 2003, when Germany's second oldest nuclear reactor, in Stade, near Hamburg, was shut down. The reactor at Obrigheim in Baden-Württemberg, Germany's oldest, was closed in May 2005.

In August 2000, in response to growing fears concerning the escalation of neo-Nazi violence against immigrants, the Government announced a series of measures to combat racist attacks. An application to the Constitutional Court to ban the extremist right-wing Nationaldemokratische Partei Deutschlands (NPD, National Democratic Party) on the grounds that it was anti-Semitic, racist and supported violence was approved by the Bundesrat in November and by the Bundestag in December. In January 2002, however, the Court postponed hearing the case when it emerged that one of the senior NPD activists whose statements were to be used in evidence against the party was an informant for the Bundesamt für Verfassungsschutz (BfV, Office for the Protection of the Constitution); the Court dismissed the case in March 2003. Meanwhile, in the latter half of 2000 Schröder demanded stricter application of existing legislation and tougher sentencing from the courts when dealing with right-wing extremists. In August 2000 the Government approved the expenditure of DM 75m. over three years to support local youth initiatives committed to fighting racism, anti-Semitism and xenophobia, and in January 2001 it was announced that the Ministry of Justice would provide DM 10m. to compensate the victims of far-right violence, threats or insults.

In late September 2001, following the attacks in the USA by suspected Islamist extremists, the Federal Government abolished the so-called 'religious privilege', thus removing legal protection for and allowing the banning of any religious organizations suspected of promoting terrorism. In early December police raided the premises of 20 militant Islamist groups throughout Germany, some of which were suspected of having links with the al-Qa'ida (Base) organization of the Saudi-born militant Islamist Osama bin Laden (which was widely believed to have organized the attacks in the USA in September). Evidence subsequently emerged that at least three of the presumed perpetrators of the US atrocities had recently lived in Hamburg and other German cities. Plans to introduce more liberal immigration laws were abandoned, and further new legislation was introduced to increase national security, including the extension of existing anti-terrorism legislation, which had hitherto only covered terrorist acts in Germany, to apply, in addition, to such acts committed in other countries. Measures to block funding channels for militant activists allowed the police access to bank account details of alleged terrorists. Further steps to control money-laundering were introduced, including the foundation of a centralized Financial Intelligence Unit, and the burden of proof regarding the authenticity of suspicious funds was moved from the banks and police to the client. Controls on employees with access to high-security areas of airports were made more stringent. All of these measures were to be funded by an immediate increase in tax on cigarettes and insurance policies.

In August 2002 a Moroccan national, Mounir al-Motassadek, was charged with offences under anti-terrorism legislation relating to the suicide attacks of 11 September 2001 in the USA; prosecutors claimed that al-Motassadek had been involved in financing the attacks. He stood trial in Hamburg, was convicted as an accessory to 3,066 murders, and was sentenced to 15 years' imprisonment. In August 2003 the trial began of a second Moroccan national, Abdelghani Mzoudi, who was also accused of helping to plan the attacks. However, Mzoudi was freed from custody in December after the Bundeskriminalamt (BKA—the Federal Office of Criminal Investigation) submitted testimony from an unnamed source—believed to be the suspected al-Qa'ida activist Ramzi bin ash-Shibh, who was in US custody—that the Hamburg cell had comprised only four members: three suicide pilots and one other man, an alleged senior al-Qa'ida operative who was already in US custody. The prosecutors appealed against the decision to free the defendant, citing the alleged unreliability of the evidence. Within minutes of the collapse of the case against Mzoudi, lawyers acting on behalf of al-Motassadek stated that they would appeal against their client's conviction; they sought access to the testimony, but their application was rejected. Despite his release from custody, Mzoudi's prosecutors continued the trial against him; he was acquitted, however, in February 2004 owing to lack of incriminating evidence. The following month the Federal Criminal Court overturned al-Motassadek's conviction on the grounds that he had not received a fair trial, principally because the Hamburg court had not had access to transcripts of ash-Shibh's interrogation by the US authorities. Al-Motassadek's retrial began in August. The US authorities again refused defence requests for access to certain al-Qa'ida suspects in US custody, although partial transcripts of the interrogations of three detainees (including ash-Shibh) were provided. The retrial concluded in August 2005, when judges ruled that there was insufficient evidence to convict al-Motassadek of involvement in the attacks. He was, however, found guilty of membership of a terrorist organization, and sentenced to seven years' imprisonment. Al-Motassadek appealed against his conviction, while prosecutors appealed to have his sentence increased. Al-Motassadek was imprisoned, but released in February 2006 when the Federal Constitutional Court ruled that he should not have been returned to custody while appeals were still pending. In mid-November 2006 the Federal Court of Justice upheld the decision to convict al-Motassadek of membership of a terrorist organization. Judges also ruled that the decision to overturn his original conviction as an accessory to murder had been flawed and found him guilty of abetting 246 murders. In early January 2007 a court in Hamburg sentenced al-Motassadek to 15 years' imprisonment. Al-Motassadek immediately announced that he intended to appeal against the ruling. Days later the Federal

Constitutional Court rejected an appeal launched by al-Motassadek in November following the decision in that month to convict him anew.

In August 2002 the German authorities banned 16 Islamist groups linked to the Köln-based 'Kalifatsstaat' ('Caliphate State'), an extremist Islamist group dedicated to the overthrow of Turkey's secular Government which had been banned, together with 20 related associations, in December 2001. Police raids against the Kalifatsstaat and other Islamist groups continued throughout 2002 and 2003. Several men were arrested on suspicion of recruiting 'suicide bombers' for operations in Iraq, following the removal from power of the Iraqi President, Saddam Hussain, by US-led military action in March–April 2003. Following the release from a German prison in March 2003 of the leader of the Kalifatsstaat, Metin Kaplan, Turkey requested his extradition to face treason charges. Germany had previously refused such requests as Kaplan would have thus faced the death sentence in Turkey. Following Turkey's abolition of the death sentence, however, and promises that Kaplan would receive a fair trial, a court in Köln ruled in May 2004 that Kaplan's extradition to Turkey should proceed. Despite his temporary disappearance and attempts to appeal against the decision, Kaplan was deported to Turkey in October.

At the general election held on 22 September 2002 the SPD won 251 seats in the Bundestag. The CDU secured 190 seats, the CSU 58 seats, Die Grünen 55 seats, the FDP 47 seats and the PDS two seats. The SPD-Bündnis 90/Die Grünen coalition remained in government. The SPD's position was, however, severely weakened and the Government's popularity suffered as a result of financial austerity measures adopted in an attempt to ward off economic recession. Elections were held in Lower Saxony and Hesse in February 2003, at which the SPD suffered emphatic defeats at the hands of the CDU, which strengthened its majority in the Bundesrat to such an extent that it was able to block government legislation.

On 27 January 2003 (the 58th anniversary of the liberation of the Nazi concentration camp at Auschwitz) the Government signed an agreement establishing a formal partnership with the Jewish population in Germany, according the Jewish faith the same legal status as the Protestant and Roman Catholic churches in Germany. Later that year the police engaged in a campaign to prevent the staging of violence by far-right extremists to mark the anniversary of *Kristallnacht*—the Nazi pogrom of November 1938 in which dozens of Jews were murdered and hundreds of synagogues burnt down throughout Germany. In September 10 members of the neo-Nazi group Southern Brotherhood were arrested on suspicion of plotting to detonate a bomb during the inauguration of a synagogue in Munich that President Rau and Paul Spiegel, the head of the German Jewish community, were due to attend. The following month police officers carried out raids on more than 50 premises in Kiel and Flensburg, confiscating weapons and illegal Nazi insignia, and arresting 10 members of the neo-Nazi group Combat 18.

In August 2003 the Federal Government approved the 12 bills that comprised Schröder's so-called Agenda 2010 package of economic reforms. The proposed reforms, the main aims of which were to reduce the rate of unemployment and to revive Germany's stagnant economy, constituted the most extensive overhaul of the country's welfare state since the founding of the Federal Republic. The proposals were, however, deeply unpopular among the general public, trade unions and many members of the SPD, and the passage of the legislation through both chambers of the legislature was expected to prove difficult. With a majority in the Bundestag of just four and no majority at all in the Bundesrat, it was widely forecast that Schröder would ultimately be forced to rely on the CDU-controlled Bundesrat to pass the legislation.

The first bill to be voted on by the Bundestag, in late September 2003, was a health reform bill, which had been drawn up jointly with CDU/CSU members and which was intended to reduce annual health-care costs by €23,000m. by 2007. In order to instil discipline for future Agenda 2010 votes, which were expected to be more divisive, Schröder insisted on passing the bill without having to rely on votes from the CDU. Several SPD members had threatened to vote against the bill, but, following Schröder's threats to resign unless the bill were passed by votes from the governing coalition alone, only six coalition members carried out their threat and the bill was passed. On the same day legislation to amend labour regulations (and consequently reduce the level of unemployment) was also passed by the Bundestag. The reforms contained in the bill were, however, particularly unpopular with the trade unions, which had long been traditional allies of the SPD, and their introduction was widely viewed as an act of betrayal on the part of the Government.

In mid-October 2003 the Bundestag voted on welfare and tax reforms. Most notably, the welfare legislation proposed the merging of unemployment benefit and social welfare payments (which, in effect, amounted to a reduction in the level of benefits paid). As part of the tax reforms, tax reductions of some €22,000m. were proposed, which, it was hoped, would stimulate consumption and thereby reduce public indebtedness (which was at its highest level in Germany's post-war history). For the majority, however, most of the benefits accrued from these reductions were likely to be swiftly cancelled out by a lowering of tax concessions and subsidies; additionally, there was to be an increase in tax on tobacco. Despite a backbench revolt, the bills were passed by 306 votes to 291, although, to achieve this, Schröder was forced to summon a number of seriously ill SPD members to vote and he himself left a summit meeting of the European Union (EU, see p. 244) early in order to attend the vote. Schröder had once again threatened to resign if the bills were not passed. Polls revealed that the SPD was losing support throughout Germany, largely owing to the unpopularity of the reforms.

A few days after the passage of the welfare and tax legislation through the Bundestag, Schröder announced a 'freeze' on pensions. This was one of five emergency measures approved by the Government to cover the €8,000m. shortfall in government 'pay-as-you-go' pension schemes expected in 2004 without raising contributions, and to reduce Germany's prohibitively high non-wage labour costs. The move alienated many within the SPD and was thought likely to complicate subsequent Agenda 2010 votes. The Government endorsed longer-term pension reform measures, which were to be presented to the legislature before the end of 2003, under which workers were to be encouraged to take up private pension cover, greater benefits were to be paid to those who retired later, and the age of retirement was to be raised to 67 years.

On 1 November 2003 some 100,000 people demonstrated against the reforms. Public discontent at the measures was also reflected in the SPD's poor performance in local elections in Bavaria. Nevertheless, Schröder vowed to pursue the reforms. On 7 November the CDU used its majority in the Bundesrat to block the legislation on debt-financed tax reductions (passed by the Bundestag in October), fearing the debt burden would overwhelm the economy rather than revive it; the chamber voted to assemble a cross-party mediation committee in an attempt to reach a compromise on Agenda 2010. The tax legislation was eventually passed (with amendments) in mid-December; the tax reductions were to be implemented in two stages, with only one-quarter of them to be financed by debt—the remainder were to be financed by the sale of government holdings in Deutsche Telekom and Deutsche Post. The tax cuts were also to be reduced from an original total of some €22,000m. to approximately €15,000m.

At the SPD conference held in mid-November 2003, Schröder was re-elected Chairman of the party, with 80.8% of votes cast (8% less than two years previously); this result was widely attributed, however, to a reluctance on the part of the SPD delegates to undermine their Chancellor. The party's General Secretary, Olaf Scholz, was also re-elected at the conference, but with just 53% of the votes cast, compared with 91% in 2001. Many SPD members felt that the Agenda 2010 reforms were a betrayal of the party's core values, and during 2003 the party lost some 5% of its membership (about 26,400 people—most of them long-time members). Conversely, some members of more right-wing parties believed that the reforms did not go far enough.

On 19 December 2003 the various bills comprising Agenda 2010, including the amended tax reductions, were finally passed by both houses of the legislature, despite some dissent among members of the governing coalition. Schröder had repeated his threat to resign in the event of the reforms not being approved. Bitterness and divisions remained within the SPD, however, following the approval of Agenda 2010, with the party leadership increasingly being seen as isolated from the rest of the membership. Consequently, on 6 February 2004, Schröder announced his resignation as Chairman of the SPD; he was, however, to remain in his post as Chancellor. The SPD elected Franz Müntefering as its new leader at a special party conference in March.

On 23 May 2004 the Bundesversammlung—a specially convened Federal Convention consisting of the members of the

Bundestag and an equal number of delegates from the legislatures of the 16 Länder—elected Dr Horst Köhler, the joint candidate of the CDU and the FDP, as the new Federal President; he was inaugurated on 1 July.

In May 2004 the governing SPD-Bündnis 90/Die Grünen coalition reached a compromise agreement with the CDU on the content of a bill to regulate immigration, the previous version of which had been rejected by the CDU-dominated Bundesrat in June 2003. The bill provided for the admission of a controlled number of skilled workers, self-employed persons and students who had completed their studies in Germany; government proposals for a general points system for would-be immigrants were abandoned at the CDU's insistence. The bill also strengthened the Government's powers to combat illegal immigration and to deport failed asylum seekers, as well as foreign religious leaders who engaged in extremist preaching in Germany. It was adopted by the Bundesrat on 9 July. The CDU announced that it intended to propose additional legislation to allow the detention of terrorist suspects without trial for up to two years.

In June 2004 the Bundesverwaltungsgericht (Federal Administrative Court) ruled that Stasi files on former Chancellor Kohl (see above) could be released with the consent of those affected where the information was not already public and where the files related to Kohl's public life only. Files containing personal information were to be released for research purposes alone, on the condition that they did not fall into the wrong hands or be published. Consequently the majority of the Stasi files on Kohl were expected to remain sealed for the foreseeable future.

In August 2004 two former members of the GDR Politburo were convicted of abetting the killing of three persons attempting to escape over the Berlin Wall in 1986–89, each receiving suspended prison sentences of 15 months. This was the final 'Berlin Wall' trial; a total of 126 former GDR officials had been convicted of such charges since reunification.

In mid-2004 the Agenda 2010 reforms again dominated the political arena in Germany. In July the Bundesrat passed the 'Hartz IV' bill, which legislated for reform (and ultimately a reduction) of unemployment and social welfare benefits; the law took effect on 1 January 2005. Opposition to Hartz IV was strong throughout Germany, but particularly so in the Länder of the former GDR, where long-term unemployment was endemic. Many thousands regularly took to the streets in *Montagsdemos* (Monday protests), which were intended to mirror the demonstrations that led to the fall of the Berlin Wall. For six weeks the weekly protests were held in Berlin and several other cities throughout Germany. The *Montagsdemos* were small compared with protests staged against other Agenda 2010 reforms earlier that year, but they were increasingly aggressive: Schröder had eggs and stones thrown at him. At their height it appeared that they might precipitate a political crisis; Lafontaine, the former Minister of Finance, demanded Schröder's resignation, openly revolt within the SPD and threatened to support a left-wing political movement composed of disaffected SPD members and trade unionists. Support for the SPD fell dramatically in mid-2004, reflecting not only the widespread anger at the reforms, but also the long-standing frustration of many east Germans at the failure to achieve economic integration of the east since reunification.

At local elections held in mid-September 2004 in Brandenburg and Sachsen (Saxony), extreme right-wing parties performed well, largely at the expense of the SPD. The DVU won six seats in Brandenburg, and the NPD won 12 seats in Sachsen. This surge in support was largely attributed to protest votes against Hartz IV, but the two parties' co-operation agreement and the less radical image adopted by their candidates were also believed to be contributory factors. Following the elections, the DVU and the NPD announced their intention to merge in order to contest the federal legislative elections in 2006.

By late September 2004 the *Montagsdemos* had virtually ceased, as resignation set in amongst the protestors. The Government offered some concessions, but the basic structure of the benefit reforms remained unchanged. Over a short period of time Schröder's support in opinion polls recovered from a nadir of 23% to 33%. Moreover, the opposition parties were unable to agree on a viable alternative to the reforms or on other important issues such as the restructuring of Germany's health system and Turkey's possible accession to the EU. However, when the reforms to the benefits system came into force in January 2005 the number of unemployed rose, partly owing to new methods of calculation, to 5m., which once again jeopardized the SPD's popular support.

Public disaffection with the SPD was evident when local elections were held in Schleswig-Holstein in February 2005. The SPD had held office in the Land since 1993, but on this occasion suffered heavy losses and was finally compelled to form a governing 'grand' coalition with the CDU, headed by a CDU Minister-President. In May 2005 the CDU won a decisive victory in state elections in Nordrhein-Westfalen and assumed control of the Land Government, which the SPD had hitherto led since 1965.

Following the SPD's defeat in Nordrhein-Westfalen, Schröder announced his intention to call an early general election, ostensibly because the CDU's increased majority in the Bundesrat rendered his Government unviable. However, as the CDU was still short of the two-thirds' majority required to block all government plans, observers suggested that Schröder was in fact trying to regain some political initiative and perhaps profit from the CDU's apparent lack of preparedness for the election. (Although Merkel had been re-elected as the CDU's leader in December 2004, she had lost support within her party and her candidacy for the chancellorship appeared to be in some doubt.) As the Grundgesetz does not technically allow early elections, Schröder called and deliberately lost a vote of confidence in his administration on 1 July 2005, thereby enabling President Köhler to dissolve the Bundestag. Two legal challenges against this process were dismissed by the Federal Constitutional Court in August, and the election was confirmed for 18 September.

Schröder's stratagem entailed considerable risk. The CDU rallied behind Merkel and endorsed her as its candidate in late May 2005, and opinion polls indicated that it had the majority of public support. Moreover, Schröder's confidence was not shared by his party, with many SPD members openly declaring victory in the election impossible. As the rift between Schröder and the left wing of the SPD deepened, Lafontaine left the party and, in July, established a new party with the PDS and other defectors from the SPD, known as Linkspartei.PDS (Die Linke—Left Party.PDS). Die Linke formed an electoral alliance with another left-wing grouping, Wahlalternative Arbeit und soziale Gerechtigkeit (WASG—Electoral Alternative Jobs and Social Justice). Its manifesto included the repeal of social reforms, an increase in the minimum wage and the imposition of higher taxes on the rich. The party swiftly gained considerable support, according to opinion polls, particularly in the east, although its alliance with the WASG undoubtedly broadened its appeal. (In June 2007, at a special conference in Berlin, the two parties completed a formal merger, as Die Linke, under the joint leadership of Lafontaine and Prof. Lothar Bisky.)

At the election, held on 18 September 2005, the CDU/CSU won a total of 225 seats (later increased to 226 following a delayed ballot in one constituency, the CDU taking 180 and the CSU 46), while the SPD secured 222. Despite neither party winning a majority, both Merkel and Schröder asserted their claims to the chancellorship. Owing to the strong performance of Die Linke, which won 54 seats, neither the CDU/CSU nor the SPD could form a majority government with their preferred coalition partners (respectively the FDP, with 61 seats, and Bündnis 90/Die Grünen, with 51 seats). Moreover, neither party was willing to form a coalition with Die Linke. In the days following the election coalitions involving the FDP and Bündnis 90/Die Grünen with either the CDU/CSU or the SPD were mooted and rejected, and by the end of September a 'grand coalition' of the CDU/CSU and the SPD seemed most likely.

Following three weeks of negotiations, Merkel was designated Chancellor on 10 October 2005 and the 'grand coalition' confirmed. The coalition agreement focused on a programme of job creation, economic reform and reform of the federal system. Many of the more radical reforms proposed by the CDU in its election campaign, including plans for a reduction in income tax for those earning high salaries and the liberalization of employment legislation, were abandoned. Indeed, increases in the rate of taxation were envisaged. There was no role for Schröder in the Government, but the SPD retained control of eight of the 14 ministries, including those of foreign affairs, finance, labour and social affairs and justice. Merkel was formally elected as Federal Chancellor by the Bundestag on 22 November, becoming both the first female and the first former citizen of the GDR to lead the country.

In April 2006 Matthias Platzeck, who had assumed the role of Chairman of the SPD in November 2005, unexpectedly announced his resignation from the post owing to ill health. He was replaced by Kurt Beck, the Minister-President of Rheinland-Palatinate (Rheinland-Pfalz). Amendments to 25 articles of the Grundgesetz were approved by the Bundestag on 30 June 2006 and by the Bundesrat on 7 July. The amendments were intended to simplify relations between the two legislative houses, as well as between the Federal and Land Governments, and to define their respective responsibilities more clearly. The reforms were intended to expedite the legislative process since the amendments substantially reduced the number of bills needing approval from the Bundesrat. Conversely, the Land Governments represented in the Bundesrat gained increased authority over services, including schools and prisons. In early July the coalition partners reached an agreement on the reform of health care provision in Germany, which was intended to reduce rising costs and to limit reliance on employers' contributions to finance health-insurance schemes. Despite opposition among members of both the CDU and the SPD, the proposals were formally approved by the Government in October and, subject to parliamentary approval, were expected to take effect in April 2007.

In mid-July 2006 anti-terrorism legislation adopted following the 11 September 2001 attacks in the USA was renewed for a five-year period by the Government. Under the renewed legislation, the Bundesnachrichtendienst (BND—the German intelligence service) was given greater powers, including access to information regarding passengers on international flights. On 1 August 2006 two explosive devices concealed in suitcases were discovered on trains in Dortmund and Koblenz in western Germany. The devices had, however, failed to detonate. Later that month four men were arrested in Lebanon and later charged with attempted murder and arson. The four stood trial in Lebanon in April 2007. In early 2007 another Lebanese man and a Syrian were also being held in Germany on suspicion of involvement in the failed bombings. On 18 December one of the men arrested in Lebanon, Jihad Hamad, was convicted of attempted murder and received a sentence of 12 years' imprisonment, while the Lebanese man arrested in Germany, Youssef al-Hajdib, was convicted *in absentia* and sentenced to life imprisonment for his role in the failed bombings; the three remaining defendants were acquitted. On the same day, the trial of al-Hajdib on charges of attempted murder began at a court in Düsseldorf.

At regional elections held in mid-September 2006 the CDU suffered a notable decline in support, reportedly as a result of public discontent with the slow progress of the Government's reform programme. In Merkel's home state of Mecklenburg-Western Pomerania, the right-wing extremist NPD won six seats (with 7.3% of the votes cast). The result was attributed to the NPD's strongly anti-immigrant stance in a region where the level of unemployment, at 18%, was the highest in Germany. In Berlin the SPD secured 30% of the votes cast, while the CDU took just 21%.

In mid-February 2007 a court in Stuttgart ordered the release from prison on parole of a former member of the Red Army Faction, Brigitte Mohnhaupt, who had been sentenced to life imprisonment in 1985 for her role in a series of murders carried out by the group during the late 1970s. Under the terms of her sentence, Mohnhaupt was eligible for parole in March 2007, after serving 24 years in prison. Another former senior member of the group, Christian Klar, who had been convicted of nine murders and 11 attempted murders and was sentenced to life imprisonment in 1985, had appealed to President Köhler to grant him a pardon. However, in May 2007 Köhler refused to grant a pardon after several right-wing politicians and commentators expressed vehement opposition to Klar's request. In August 2007 a court in Frankfurt am Main ordered the release of Eva Haule, who had originally been sentenced to 15 years' imprisonment in 1988 for her role in a bomb attack on a NATO college in Bayern. (In 1994 Haule was sentenced to life imprisonment for her involvement in a bomb attack on a US air base in Frankfurt am Main in 1985, in which three people were killed.) However, in early January 2008 the Federal Court of Justice ordered Mohnhaupt, Klar and another former Red Army Faction member, Knut Folkerts, to serve sentences of six months' imprisonment for refusing to provide evidence to an inquiry into the murder in 1977 of the Federal Prosecutor-General, Siegfried Buback.

In September 2007 three men were arrested by the German security services on suspicion of planning to carry out car bomb attacks against targets within Germany, including Frankfurt Airport and the US Air Force base near Ramstein-Miesenbach in Rheinland-Palatinate. It was subsequently reported that the three men, two of whom were German citizens, had previously travelled to Pakistan to participate in training camps organized by the militant Islamist group Islamic Jihad Union.

At a party conference held in Hamburg in late October 2007, Beck was re-elected as SPD Chairman, receiving some 95.5% of votes cast. Party members also voted to approve a policy programme that appeared to move the party toward the left in advance of the federal election scheduled for September 2009. Prior to the conference, some senior members of the party, including the Vice-Chancellor and Minister of Labour and Social Affairs, Franz Müntefering, had criticized proposals to relax some of the measures included in the Agenda 2010 programme, which had been introduced by the Schröder Government, in particular an initiative to increase the period during which those aged over 55 years were eligible to receive unemployment benefits, from 18 to 24 months. Following weeks of speculation over tensions within the party leadership, in mid-November 2007 Müntefering announced his resignation from the Government, citing personal reasons. Olaf Scholz was appointed to replace him as Minister of Labour and Social Affairs, while the Minister of Foreign Affairs, Frank-Walter Steinmeier, assumed the additional role of Vice-Chancellor.

Relations between the partners in the governing 'grand coalition' became increasingly strained in early 2008, as both the CDU and the SPD attempted to position themselves prior to regional elections in three Länder during the first two months of that year. In late January elections were held in Hesse and Lower Saxony, both of which had hitherto been governed by the CDU. In Hesse, following controversial remarks by the Minister-President, Koch, regarding the involvement of adolescents of immigrant origin in a series of criminal incidents within that Land, the CDU suffered a notable decline in support, mainly in favour of the SPD. None the less, neither of the two main parties secured a majority in the regional legislature (Landtag), both winning 37% of the votes cast. In Lower Saxony, however, the CDU retained its position as the largest party, with 43% of the votes cast. At an election to the Senate in Hamburg in late February 2008, the CDU remained the largest party (with 43% of the votes cast), but failed to achieve a majority, and subsequently began talks with Bündnis 90/Die Grünen over the formation of a coalition administration. At the elections Die Linke emerged as a significant political force in western Germany, a development which threatened to provoke internecine strife within the SPD. Following the election in Hesse, the SPD attempted to negotiate an agreement to form a minority coalition government in that region with Bündnis 90/Die Grünen, relying upon parliamentary support from Die Linke, despite having ruled out such an alliance prior to the election. However, in early March the SPD abandoned coalition talks after an SPD member of the Landtag announced her intention to vote against the proposed alliance with Die Linke. The failed proposal also prompted criticism of Beck, who had approved the alliance with Die Linke in Hesse, despite ruling out any such agreement at the federal level.

The orientation of Germany's foreign policy after unification broadly followed that of the FRG. The united Germany remained committed to a leading role in the European Community (EC—now EU), of which the FRG was a founding member, and NATO, while placing greater emphasis on defence co-operation with France. The country was also strongly committed to close relations with Eastern Europe, in particular with the USSR and, subsequently, its successor states.

Following the Iraqi invasion and annexation of Kuwait in August 1990, the German Government expressed support for the deployment of US-led allied forces in the region of the Persian (Arabian) Gulf, and contributed substantial amounts of financial and technical aid to the effort to liberate Kuwait, although there were mass demonstrations against the allied action in many parts of Germany. Despite criticism from certain countries participating in the alliance, Germany did not contribute troops to the allied force, in accordance with a provision in the Grundgesetz that was widely interpreted as prohibiting intervention outside the area of NATO operations. In July 1992, however, the Government announced that it was to send a naval destroyer and reconnaissance aircraft to the Adriatic Sea to participate in the UN force monitoring the observance of UN sanctions on the Federal Republic of Yugoslavia (FRY). This deployment was subsequently approved by the Bundestag. In April 1993 the Constitutional Court ruled that German forces could join the UN operation to enforce an air exclusion zone over Bosnia and Herzegovina. Germany dispatched troops to assist the UN relief effort in Somalia in mid-1993. In May 1994 the Constitutional Court declared the participation of German military units in collective international defence and security operations, with the approval of the Bundestag in each instance, to be compatible with the Grundgesetz. In March 1997, while supervising the evacuation from Albania of citizens of western European states, German troops opened fire on hostile forces for the first time since 1945. From March to early June 1999 Germany participated in the ongoing NATO military offensive against the FRY, despite misgivings from left-wing elements within the ruling SPD-Bündnis 90/Die Grünen coalition.

In May 1992 Germany and France reached agreement on the establishment of a combined defence corps, which, they envisaged, would provide the basis for a pan-European military force under the aegis of Western European Union (WEU, see p. 426). The so-called Eurocorps became operational in November 1995. In December 2000 the heads of government of the EU (except Denmark) endorsed the plan for a 60,000-strong European Rapid Reaction Force, which had been adopted by EU ministers in November (although NATO was to remain central to European defence). In November 2004 the EU defence ministers agreed to create 13 'battlegroups', each numbering 1,000–1,500 men, two of which would be ready for deployment at any one time within 10 days and be sustainable for 30 days, to carry out peace-keeping activities at crisis points around the world from January 2007. The German Government was committed to contribute to three battlegroups.

In early September 2001 German troops were dispatched to participate in a NATO peace-keeping mission in the former Yugoslav republic of Macedonia, despite opposition to the deployment by members of Bündnis 90/Die Grünen. In the aftermath of the terrorist attacks in the USA on 11 September, Schröder pledged 'unlimited solidarity' to the US Administration, and announced plans to send 3,900 troops to take part in the US-led military action in Afghanistan. These plans were strongly opposed by the majority of members of Bündnis 90/Die Grünen, although Schröder enjoyed the support of the Minister of Foreign Affairs, Joschka Fischer. Opposition to the proposed deployment increased to such an extent that by early November the governing coalition appeared close to collapse. Schröder embarked on the high-risk strategy of linking the parliamentary vote on the troop deployment to a vote of confidence in his Government; the Chancellor won the confidence vote, which was held on 16 November, albeit by a narrow majority. In November 2002 the Bundestag voted to extend the deployment of troops in Afghanistan by a further year. In June 2003 Germany announced that its troops would remain in Afghanistan for at least another year; in October Germany extended its peacekeeping mission beyond the capital, Kabul, by dispatching troops to form part of a 'provincial reconstruction team' in the northern city of Kunduz. In September 2004 the Bundestag overwhelmingly approved a motion authorizing the deployment of 2,250 German peace-keeping troops in Afghanistan for a further 12 months. In September 2005 the Bundestag extended the mandate of German troops in Afghanistan for a further 12 months, increasing the size of the contingent to 3,000. In September 2006 the Bundestag voted overwhelmingly to send around 2,400 German navy personnel and eight warships to participate in an international force under UN auspices in Lebanon. The German contingent conducted patrols along the coast of Lebanon, in an attempt to prevent the clandestine transportation of weapons to fighters from the Iranian-backed radical Shi'ite Hezbollah organization. In October 2007 the Bundestag voted to extend the mandate of German troops in Afghanistan for a further 12 months, increasing the size of the contingent to 3,500. Nevertheless, in February 2008 the US Secretary of Defense, Robert M. Gates, urged Germany to deploy further troops to southern Afghanistan, where NATO forces were increasingly engaged in direct combat with supporters of the former militant Islamist regime. The German Government rejected the demand, citing its increased contingent in northern Afghanistan and its commitment to reconstruction efforts. Later that month the Minister of Defence, Franz Jozef Jung, announced the deployment of a contingent of 250 combat troops to northern Afghanistan, but rejected the possibility of their involvement in combat in the south of the country.

In late 2002 and early 2003 the Franco-German *entente* was renewed, largely owing to the two countries' shared opposition to the US-led military action in Iraq. In February Germany and France, together with Belgium, vetoed proposals to deploy NATO troops in Turkey; they later ended their vetoes on the condition that the troops be deployed only to defend Turkey, and not to attack Iraq. Relations between Germany and the USA were strained during most of 2003, although in May of that year Germany did support the USA in calling for the UN to lift sanctions against Iraq. Germany opposed US plans for the reconstruction of Iraq following the removal of Saddam Hussain in March/April and advocated instead greater UN involvement and the swifter transfer of governing powers to Iraqis. Relations with the USA improved to a certain extent in September, however, when Chancellor Schröder offered to provide resources for the training of Iraqi police, security staff and military personnel (whilst continuing to refuse to send German peacekeeping troops to Iraq). The US President, George W. Bush, held talks with Schröder during the former's official visit to various European destinations in February 2005; in the course of these negotiations the Chancellor reiterated his Government's opposition to dispatching German peace-keepers to Iraq.

The continuing 'war on terror' precipitated further tensions in late 2005, amid reports that the USA's Central Intelligence Agency (CIA) had routed over 400 flights through German airports as part of its programme of 'extraordinary rendition'. Under this programme, it was alleged, suspected Islamist militants were secretly transferred to third countries, some of which were suspected of practising torture, for interrogation. When the US Secretary of State, Condoleezza Rice, visited Germany in December she admitted that suspects were flown abroad for interrogation but denied that they were tortured. She refused to confirm or deny claims that the CIA had established secret prisons throughout the world for this purpose. It was also alleged that Otto Schily, the former Minister of the Interior, had been informed about the flights and in particular about a German citizen who had been seized in the former Yugoslav republic of Macedonia in late 2003 and flown to a prison in Afghanistan, where he was reportedly held for five months. Schily refused to comment on the allegations, which the Ministry of the Interior was investigating. Further controversy arose in January 2006 when it emerged that two agents of the BND had remained in the Iraqi capital, Baghdad, in March 2003, despite the evacuation of the German diplomatic corps from the city and the opposition of the German Government to the US-led military action in Iraq. It was alleged that the BND agents provided geographical co-ordinates to the US military that were used to locate targets for bombs. The Minister of Foreign Affairs, Steinmeier, insisted that the agents had only provided co-ordinates for civilian sites that were to be avoided in bombing raids, not for military targets. Nevertheless, Germany's relations with the USA did improve after Merkel took office, and the importance of bilateral co-operation was emphasized during her first official visit to the USA in January 2006. A two-day visit to Germany by President Bush in mid-July signalled increasingly cordial relations between the two countries. Merkel met President Bush for talks in Washington, DC, in January 2007 and visited the USA again in November for discussions at President Bush's private estate in Texas.

In December 1992 the Bundestag ratified the Treaty on European Union (the Maastricht Treaty). At the same time the lower house approved an amendment to the Grundgesetz (negotiated in May 1992 with the Länder), whereby the state assemblies would be accorded greater involvement in the determination of German policy within the EC. The Bundesrat ratified the Maastricht Treaty later in December 1992. In April 1998 the Bundestag approved Germany's participation in EMU, which took effect in January 1999. Following the eventual approval of the draft EU constitutional treaty on 18 June 2004 by the Heads of State and of Government of the member countries of the EU, the German Government expressed its desire that Germany ratify the document as soon as possible. Legislative ratification, which required a two-thirds' majority in both houses, was secured in May 2005. (Germany's Grundgesetz prevented the holding of a national referendum on the issue.) However, following the subsequent rejection of the proposed constitution at public referendums in France and the Netherlands, the process of ratification in other member countries stalled. In January 2007 Germany assumed the presidency of the EU and, concurrently, the chairmanship of the Group of Eight industrialized nations (G-8). Chancellor Merkel stated her intention to revive stalled discussions on the EU constitution and to reach agreement on a common energy policy; energy security was also considered a priority for the G-8. Following a summit meeting of EU leaders in Brussels in early March, an agreement on the reduction of greenhouse gas emissions was signed, which envisaged a 20% reduction from 1990 levels by EU member countries to be achieved by 2020. A further agreement was subsequently announced, under which 20% of all energy consumed by member countries was to come from renewable sources by 2020. On 6–8 June 2007 a summit meeting of the leaders of the G-8 countries took place in Heiligendamm on Germany's Baltic coast. On 21–22 June Merkel hosted an EU summit meeting in Brussels, at which a preliminary agreement was reached for a reform treaty to replace the constitutional treaty that had been rejected at referendums in France and the Netherlands in 2005. The reform treaty was signed by EU leaders, including Merkel, in Lisbon, Portugal, on 13 December 2007. Parliament was expected to ratify the Treaty of Lisbon by late 2008.

From late 2002 Germany and France began a phase of markedly good bilateral relations, partly owing, as mentioned above, to both countries' opposition to the US-led military action in Iraq. The two countries were also united in their attitude towards the proposed EU constitution, and in the defence of their budgetary deficits, which were in breach of the EU's Stability and Growth Pact (see Economic Affairs). While close relations with France remained a priority following Merkel's election as Chancellor in November 2005 (as reflected in her decision to make her first foreign visit to that country), Merkel believed that Germany had worked too exclusively with France in the past and announced her intention to strengthen relations with smaller EU states and the USA. Following the election in May 2007 of Nicolas Sarkozy as French President, relations between the two countries deteriorated, as the attitudes of the two leaders appeared to diverge, especially with regard to a series of agreements signed by Sarkozy during late 2007 for the sale of nuclear technology to countries in the Middle East and French proposals regarding the formation of a so-called Mediterranean Union, membership of which was to be limited to the six EU member states that bordered the Mediterranean and Middle Eastern and African littoral countries. The German Government, which was thus excluded from the grouping, opposed the project on the grounds that it could undermine the influence of the ongoing Euro-Mediterranean Partnership (the Barcelona Process—a framework launched in 1995 for co-operation between all EU member states and 10 other Mediterranean states). However, in early March 2008, following negotiations between French and German representatives, Merkel and Sarkozy announced an agreement on the formation of the new union, which was restyled the Union for the Mediterranean, and which would incorporate all EU member states.

Germany's relations with Poland were for a long time influenced by the Second World War. In the course of the negotiations on EU enlargement during the 1990s, Germany strongly supported Poland's accession, citing the need for an historic conciliation with its eastern neighbour. Following Poland's accession to the EU in May 2004, German diplomacy shifted to the position that its past debts had thus been repaid, and began to work towards closer relations within the EU. In early 2004 Chancellor Schröder visited the Polish Prime Minister, Leszek Miller, to put the case against Poland's opposition to the proposed EU constitution. In August Schröder attended a ceremony in Warsaw to mark the 60th anniversary of the failed uprising there, during which he acknowledged the 'immeasurable suffering' inflicted by Nazi troops on Poland. This *rapprochement* was threatened, however, by the right-wing Preussische Treuhand (Prussian Trust), which launched a series of lawsuits claiming compensation and the restitution of property on behalf of the families of Germans expelled from Poland following the Second World War. In September Schröder and the new Polish Prime Minister, Marek Belka, jointly announced the creation of a commission to ensure that such claims would be stripped of any legal basis. In February 2005 President Köhler attended a ceremony in Poland to mark the 60th anniversary of the liberation of the Nazi concentration camp at Auschwitz. The Polish Government opposed the construction of a pipeline to transport natural gas to Germany from Russia (see below), fearing that it could be used to divert energy away from Poland for political reasons. Estonia, Latvia, Lithuania and Ukraine also expressed concern that the pipeline posed a potential threat to their own gas supplies from Russia. In October 2006 the new Polish Prime Minister, Jarosław Kaczyński, visited Berlin for talks with Chancellor Merkel. Relations between the two countries had deteriorated owing to the proposed gas pipeline and ongoing claims of compensation for families of Germans expelled from Poland following the Second World War. Relations had been further strained in July after the publication in a German newspaper of an article that was deemed offensive to Prime Minister Kaczyński and his twin brother, the Polish President, Lech Kaczyński. Relations deteriorated further still in June 2007 after the Polish Government objected to proposals supported by Germany for the reform of voting procedures within the EU institutions. However, the appointment in November of a new, largely pro-EU Government in Poland signalled an improvement in relations between the two countries. Indeed, the new Polish Prime Minister, Donald Tusk, visited Berlin in mid-December for a meeting with Merkel, following which the two leaders affirmed the friendly nature of relations between Germany and Poland, and promised close co-operation over the planned gas pipeline between Russia and Germany (see below) and a proposal to create a memorial in Berlin to German refugees expelled from Poland and other central European countries after the Second World War.

In October 2005 preliminary negotiations for the possible accession of Turkey to the EU began. Germany has a substantial Turkish population, and Schröder was supportive of its bid for EU membership. However, with the election of Merkel, who was opposed to Turkey's accession, as Chancellor in November 2005, Germany's continued support became more doubtful. In February 2008 the Turkish Prime Minister, Reçep Tayyip Erdoğan, visited Germany for talks with Merkel. However, a speech given in Turkish at a rally in Köln, during which Erdoğan urged the sizable Turkish population within Germany to retain their 'ethnic identity', provoked an angry reaction from several German politicians, who expressed fears that such remarks by their Turkish counterparts could undermine efforts to integrate people of Turkish origin into German society.

Germany's relations with Russia became increasingly important in the early 21st century as the latter supplied around one-third of Germany's natural gas requirement. During a visit to Germany in September 2005 the Russian President, Vladimir Putin, finalized an agreement with Chancellor Schröder on the construction of a pipeline directly linking Russia and Germany under the Baltic Sea. The pipeline was intended to transport up to 27,500m. cu m of Russian natural gas per year to Western Europe beginning in 2010. Schröder's appointment, in December, as Chairman of the shareholder committee of the Russian-led consortium constructing the pipeline proved controversial, given his role in approving the project. Chancellor Merkel visited Putin in Moscow in January 2006, declaring her support for the 'strategic partnership' developed under Schröder. Schröder came under further pressure in April when it emerged that his Government had agreed to provide a substantial loan guarantee to the Russian energy supplier Gazprom, which led the consortium constructing the gas pipeline, days before leaving office. In October Putin visited Dresden for talks with Chancellor Merkel. In late January 2007 Merkel travelled to Russia for talks with Putin, chiefly regarding energy security. Merkel expressed concerns that ongoing disputes between Russia and neighbouring countries (through which oil and gas are transported to Germany) over energy prices could lead to shortages of oil and gas in Germany. Indeed, despite the two leaders conducting regular meetings after Merkel became Chancellor, relations were slightly less cordial than under Schröder, with Merkel adopting a tougher position regarding human rights issues in Russia. In mid-October 2007 Putin visited Wiesbaden, in western Germany, for talks with Merkel. On 8 March 2008 Merkel became the first EU leader to visit Russia after the election of Dmitrii Medvedev as Russian President earlier in that month. Following talks with the outgoing President, Putin, Merkel expressed a desire to repair damaged relations between the two countries. Nevertheless, Putin hinted that the policies of his successor toward Germany would not differ substantially from his own.

Government

Germany is composed of 16 Länder (states), each Land having its own constitution, legislature and government.

The country has a parliamentary regime, with a bicameral legislature. The Upper House is the Bundesrat (Federal Council), with 69 seats. Each Land has between three and six seats, depending on the size of its population. The term of office of Bundesrat members varies in accordance with Land election dates. The Lower House, and the country's main legislative organ, is the Bundestag (Federal Assembly), with 669 deputies, who are elected for four years by universal adult suffrage (using a mixed system of proportional representation and direct voting).

Executive authority rests with the Federal Government (Bundesregierung), led by the Federal Chancellor (Bundeskanzler), who is elected by an absolute majority of the Bundestag and appoints the other Ministers. The Federal President (Bundespräsident) is elected by a Federal Convention (Bundesversammlung), which meets only for this purpose and consists of the Bundestag and an equal number of members elected by Land parliaments. The President is a constitutional Head of State with little influence on government.

Each Land has its own legislative assembly, with the right to enact laws except on matters that are the exclusive right of the Federal Government, such as defence, foreign affairs and finance. Education, police, culture and environmental protection are in the control of the Länder. Local responsibility for the execution of Federal and Land laws is undertaken by the Gemeinden (communities).

Defence

Germany is a member of the North Atlantic Treaty Organization (NATO, see p. 340). Military service is compulsory and lasts for nine months. In January 2004 it was announced that the size of the Bundeswehr (armed forces) was to be reduced, and that by around 2010 it was to be reorganized into a rapid reaction force of 35,000 troops, a second force of 70,000 troops for low- and medium-intensity conflict and a third force of 137,500 civilians providing medical and logistical support; more than 100 army bases were also to be closed as part of the streamlining process and the number of conscripts was to be decreased to 55,000. Germany's special forces, the Kommando Spezial Kräfte (KSK), were to be increased from 450 to 1,000. In October 2006 the Government endorsed a review of German defence policy, which contained proposals to redefine the primary role of the Bundeswehr from border defence to intervention in international conflicts. Under the proposals, the Bundeswehr would be expanded to allow for the deployment of up to 14,000 troops in five international missions simultaneously. As assessed at November 2007 Germany's armed forces totalled some 245,702, including 56,624 conscripts. The strength of the army stood at 160,794, including 42,566 conscripts. The navy numbered 20,540 (including 3,788 conscripts), and there were 50,310 in the air force (10,270 conscripts). There was also a reserve of 161,812 (army 144,548; navy 3,304; and air force 13,960). The defence budget for 2007 was set at €28,400m. In November 2007 the USA and the United Kingdom had 82,728 troops stationed in Germany, while France and the Netherlands maintained, respectively, forces of 2,800 and 2,300 men. Italy had 91 troops from its air force stationed in Germany. In November 2004 the European Union (EU, see p. 244) ministers responsible for defence agreed to create 13 'battlegroups' (each numbering about 1,500 men), which could be deployed at short notice to crisis areas around the world. The EU battlegroups, two of which were to be ready for deployment at any one time, following a rotational schedule, reached full operational capacity from 1 January 2007. Germany was committed to participate in three battlegroups.

Economic Affairs

In 2006, according to estimates by the World Bank, Germany's gross national income (GNI), measured at average 2004–2006 prices, was US $3,018,036m., equivalent to $36,620 per head (or $31,830 per head on an international purchasing-power parity basis). During 1996–2006, it was estimated, the population increased by an average of 0.1% per year, while Germany's gross domestic product (GDP) per head grew, in real terms, by an average of 1.5% annually. Overall GDP expanded, in real terms, at an average annual rate of 1.6% in 1996–2006; GDP increased by 2.8% in 2006.

Agriculture (including hunting, forestry and fishing) engaged 2.3% of the employed labour force in 2006, and provided 0.9% of Germany's GDP in 2007. The principal crops are wheat, sugar beet, barley and potatoes. Wine production is also important in western Germany. Agricultural GDP increased, in real terms, at an average annual rate of 1.7% in 1996–2005; it declined by 3.2% in 2006, before increasing by 2.9% in 2007.

Industry (including mining, power, manufacturing and construction) engaged 29.6% of the employed labour force in 2006, and contributed 30.1% of GDP in 2007. Industrial GDP declined at an average annual rate of 1.3% in 1996–2005; it increased by 5.5% in 2006 and by 4.8% in 2007.

The mining sector engaged 0.3% of the employed labour force in 2006 and, with energy, gas and water supply, contributed 2.6% of GDP in 2007. The principal mining activities are the extraction of lignite (low-grade brown coal), hard coal and salts.

The manufacturing sector employed 21.9% of the employed labour force in 2006, and provided 23.4% of GDP in 2007. Measured by value of output, the principal branches of manufacturing in 2004 were motor vehicles and parts (accounting for 20.1% of the total), non-electric machinery (11.4%), chemical products (9.7%) and food products (9.0%). Real manufacturing GDP increased at an average annual rate of 2.3% in 1996–2004; it increased by 5.8% in 2006 and 6.3% in 2007.

Of the total energy produced in 2004, coal accounted for 50.5%, nuclear power accounted for 27.4%, natural gas for 10.1% and hydroelectric power for 3.5%. In 2000 the Government announced plans to abandon the use of nuclear power by 2021; the closure of nuclear reactors began in 2003 (see Recent History). In 2006 imports of mineral fuels accounted for 12.3% of Germany's total imports.

Services engaged 68.2% of the employed labour force in 2006, and contributed 69.0% of GDP in 2007. The GDP of the services sector increased, in real terms, at an average annual rate of 1.% in 1996–2005: it grew by 2.0% in 2006 and 1.9% in 2007.

In 2006 Germany recorded a visible trade surplus of US $197,330m., and there was a surplus of $147,820m. on the current account of the balance of payments. Germany was the world's largest exporter of goods in the years 2004–07, although exports from the People's Republic of China were expected to exceed those from Germany by the end of 2008. More than one-half of Germany's total trade in 2006 was conducted with other countries of the European Union (EU, see p. 244). France is the most significant individual trading partner, supplying 8.7% of imports and purchasing 9.6% of exports, according to preliminary figures, in 2006. Other principal sources of imports in that year were the Netherlands (8.3%), China (6.7%) and the USA (6.6%); the other major purchasers of exports were the USA (8.7%), the United Kingdom (7.3%) and Italy (6.7%). The principal imports in 2006 were machinery and transport equipment (accounting for 35.6% of the total, with road vehicles and parts comprising 8.5%), basic manufactures (13.1%), chemicals and related products (11.1%), and miscellaneous manufactured articles (10.2%). The principal exports were machinery and transport equipment (accounting for 49.2% of the total, with road vehicles and parts comprising 16.9%), basic manufactures (13.9%), chemicals and related products (13.7%), and miscellaneous manufactured articles (9.4%).

The budgetary deficit for 2005 was equivalent to 3.4% of GDP—breaching the 3.0% higher limit permitted under the EU's Stability and Growth Pact for the fourth consecutive year. In 2006, however, the deficit was equivalent to just 1.6% of GDP. In 2006 general government gross debt totalled €1,568,490m., equivalent to 67.5% of GDP. Annual inflation averaged 1.5% during 1996–2006. Consumer prices rose by an annual average of 2.2% in 2007. Some 7.8% of the labour force were unemployed in December 2007.

Germany is a member of the EU and of the Organisation for Economic Co-operation and Development (OECD, see p. 347).

The German social market economy model that led to Germany's overwhelming economic success in the post-war era began adversely to affect economic growth in the 1980s. Underlying structural problems, including high levels of social protection and an inflexible labour market, coupled with the high cost of reunification, led to weak GDP growth during the 1990s and early 2000s and a large budget deficit. However, from 2004 the German economy experienced a resurgence that was largely attributed to restructuring in the corporate sector at company level, facilitated by the Agenda 2010 labour reforms introduced in 2003. Productivity rose sharply during 2006–07, aided by an increase in inward investment. The rise in competitiveness, coupled with the high demand for German machinery from emerging market economies, facilitated the continued rapid growth of exports in those years. The high rate of economic growth in 2006 was also, however, partly attributable to tax rises that came into effect in January 2007, when value-added tax (VAT) was raised by 3%, to 19%, and the top rate of income tax was increased by 3%, to 45%, causing companies and individuals to bring forward income and spending to 2006 to take advantage of lower taxes. Tax revenue grew faster than expected in 2006, enabling a reduction of the public sector deficit to within the limit of 3.0% permitted under the terms of the EU's Stability and Growth Pact (which Germany had breached in 2002–05) a year earlier than expected. In 2007 a budgetary surplus was achieved as tax revenues increased further, as a result of strong economic growth and the effects of tax increases. The fiscal surplus provided for a continuing decline in the ratio of public debt to GDP. Although unemployment declined steadily from late 2005, largely owing to high levels of job creation, real wage increases were slow to rise, thus enhancing the competitiveness of German exports. The German banking sector remained relatively unaffected by the international credit crisis which began in 2007. In

August, however, the regional bank Sachsen LB (partly owned by the Land Government of Saxony) was acquired by Landesbank Baden-Württemberg, after significant losses on its investment in the precarious sub-prime mortgage market in the USA threatened to precipitate its collapse. In February 2008 the Federal Government agreed to provide emergency funding totalling some €1,000m. to the IKB Deutsche Industriebank, which had suffered from a lack of liquidity resulting from the sub-prime crisis. In an attempt to stimulate domestic and foreign investment, in July 2007 the 'grand coalition' Government led by Angela Merkel introduced legislation providing for a reduction in the rate of corporation tax, from 25% to 15%, with effect from January 2008. However, further structural reform during that year was considered by analysts to be unlikely, owing largely to tensions within the 'grand coalition' Government, particularly over social provisions and wage policy. In 2008 low levels of household debt, higher real wages and strong employment creation were expected to encourage growth in private consumption, which had slowed in 2007. However, GDP growth was predicted to decline to less than 2.0% in 2008, owing mainly to the slowing of the global economy, which, in conjunction with the high exchange rate of the euro, was likely to have an adverse impact on exports.

Education

The Basic Law assigns the control of important sectors of the education system to the governments of the Länder. These do, however, co-operate quite closely to ensure a large degree of conformity in the system. Enrolment at pre-primary level was equivalent to 97% of children in the relevant age-group in 2005/06 (97% for boys; 96% for girls). Compulsory schooling begins at six years of age and continues for nine years (in some Länder for 10). Until the age of 18, all young people who do not continue to attend a full-time school must attend the Berufsschule (part-time vocational school). Primary education lasts four years (six years in some Länder) and is provided free of charge. In 2002/03 enrolment at primary level was equivalent to 99% of children in the relevant age-group (100% of boys; 99% of girls). Attendance at the Grundschule (elementary school) is obligatory for all children, after which their education continues at one of four types of secondary school. Enrolment at secondary level included 88% of both boys and girls in the relevant age-group in 2002/03. Approximately one-third of this age-group attend the Hauptschule (general school) for five or six years, after which they may enter employment, but continue their education part-time for three years at a vocational school. Alternatively, pupils may attend the Realschule (intermediate school) for up to nine years, the Gymnasium (grammar school) for nine years (eight years in some Länder), or the Gesamtschule (comprehensive school, not available in all parts of the country) for up to nine years. The Abitur (grammar school leaving certificate) is a prerequisite for entry into university education. According to UNESCO, a total of 2,268,741 students were enrolled in higher education in 2004/05.

In 2006 government expenditure on education amounted to €93,980m. (8.9% of total expenditure).

Public Holidays

2008: 1 January (New Year's Day), 6 January (Epiphany)*, 21 March (Good Friday), 24 March (Easter Monday), 1 May (Labour Day and Ascension Day), 12 May (Whit Monday), 22 May (Corpus Christi)*, 15 August (Assumption)*, 3 October (Day of Unity), 31 October (Reformation Day)*, 1 November (All Saints' Day)*, 25–26 December (Christmas), 31 December (New Year's Eve).

2009: 1 January (New Year's Day), 6 January (Epiphany)*, 10 April (Good Friday), 13 April (Easter Monday), 1 May (Labour Day), 21 May (Ascension Day), 1 June (Whit Monday), 11 June (Corpus Christi)*, 15 August (Assumption)*, 3 October (Day of Unity), 31 October (Reformation Day)*, 1 November (All Saints' Day)*, 25–26 December (Christmas), 31 December (New Year's Eve).

* Religious holidays observed in certain Länder only.

Weights and Measures

The metric system is in force.

Statistical Survey

Source (unless otherwise indicated): Statistisches Bundesamt, 65180 Wiesbaden; tel. (611) 752405; fax (611) 753330; e-mail info@destatis.de; internet www.destatis.de.

Area and Population

AREA, POPULATION AND DENSITY

Area (sq km)*	357,093
Population (official estimates at 31 December)†	
2004	82,500,800
2005	82,438,000
Males	40,340,000
Females	42,098,000
2006	82,351,000
Density (per sq km) at 31 December 2006	230.6

* 137,874 sq miles.
† Figures are rounded to nearest 100 persons.

LÄNDER

	Area (sq km)	Population ('000) at 31 Dec. 2006	Density (per sq km)	Capital
Baden-Württemberg	35,751.7	10,744	300.5	Stuttgart
Bayern (Bavaria)	70,551.6	12,493	177.1	München
Berlin	891.9	3,405	3,817.7	Berlin
Brandenburg	29,478.6	2,549	86.5	Potsdam
Bremen	404.3	665	1,644.8	Bremen
Hamburg	755.2	1,754	2,322.6	Hamburg
Hessen (Hesse)	21,114.8	6,078	287.9	Wiesbaden
Mecklenburg-Vorpommern (Mecklenburg-Western Pomerania)	23,180.1	1,696	73.2	Schwerin
Niedersachsen (Lower Saxony)	47,624.2	7,985	167.7	Hannover
Nordrhein-Westfalen (North Rhine-Westphalia)	34,085.3	18,036	529.1	Düsseldorf
Rheinland-Pfalz (Rhineland-Palatinate)	19,853.4	4,053	204.1	Mainz
Saarland	2,568.7	1,045	406.8	Saarbrücken
Sachsen (Saxony)	18,415.5	4,254	231.0	Dresden
Sachsen-Anhalt (Saxony-Anhalt)	20,446.3	2,446	119.6	Magdeburg
Schleswig-Holstein	15,799.4	2,834	179.4	Kiel
Thüringen (Thuringia)	16,172.1	2,315	143.1	Erfurt
Total	357,092.9	82,351	230.6	—

GERMANY

PRINCIPAL TOWNS
(estimated population at 31 December 2005, '000)

Berlin (capital)	3,395.2	Mannheim	307.9
Hamburg	1,743.6	Karlsruhe	285.3
München (Munich)	1,259.7	Wiesbaden	274.6
Köln (Cologne)	983.3	Münster	270.9
Frankfurt am Main	651.9	Gelsenkirchen	268.1
Stuttgart	592.6	Augsburg	262.7
Dortmund	588.2	Mönchengladbach	261.4
Essen	585.4	Aachen (Aix-la-Chapelle)	258.2
Düsseldorf	574.5	Chemnitz	246.6
Bremen	546.9	Braunschweig (Brunswick)	245.3
Hannover (Hanover)	515.7	Krefeld	237.7
Leipzig	502.7	Halle an der Saale*	237.2
Duisburg	501.6	Kiel	234.4
Nürnberg (Nuremberg)	499.2	Magdeburg	229.1
Dresden	495.2	Oberhausen	218.9
Bochum	385.6	Freiburg im Breisgau	216.0
Wuppertal	359.2	Lübeck	211.8
Bielefeld	326.9	Erfurt	202.8
Bonn	312.8		

* Including Halle-Neustadt.

BIRTHS, MARRIAGES AND DEATHS

	Registered live births Number	Rate (per 1,000)	Registered marriages Number	Rate (per 1,000)	Registered deaths Number	Rate (per 1,000)
1999	770,744	9.4	430,674	5.2	846,330	10.3
2000	766,999	9.3	418,550	5.1	838,797	10.2
2001	734,475	8.9	389,591	4.7	828,541	10.1
2002	719,250	8.7	391,963	4.8	841,686	10.2
2003	706,721	8.6	382,911	4.6	853,946	10.3
2004	705,622	8.5	395,992	4.8	818,271	9.9
2005	685,795	8.3	388,451	4.7	830,270	10.1
2006	672,724	8.2	373,681	4.5	821,627	10.0

Expectation of life (years at birth, WHO estimates): 79.3 (males 76.5; females 82.0) in 2005 (Source: WHO, *World Health Statistics*).

IMMIGRATION AND EMIGRATION
('000 persons)

	2004	2005	2006
Immigrant arrivals	780.2	707.4	661.9
Emigrant departures	698.0	628.4	639.1

ECONOMICALLY ACTIVE POPULATION
(sample surveys, '000 persons aged 15 years and over, at March unless otherwise indicated)

	2004	2005*	2006
Agriculture, hunting and forestry	827	861	837
Fishing	5	7	6
Mining and quarrying	120	123	116
Manufacturing	8,135	8,032	8,157
Electricity, gas and water	296	315	316
Construction	2,435	2,400	2,446
Wholesale and retail trade; repair of motor vehicles, motorcycles and personal and household goods	5,010	5,257	5,281
Hotels and restaurants	1,206	1,295	1,381
Transport, storage and communications	1,971	1,949	2,060
Financial intermediation	1,296	1,307	1,306
Real estate, renting and business activities	3,276	3,522	3,735
Public administration and defence; compulsory social security	2,896	2,879	2,901
Education	2,033	2,100	2,174
Health and social work	4,063	4,150	4,264
Other community, social and personal service activities	1,911	2,153	2,125
Private households with employed persons	152	179	187
Extra-territorial organizations and bodies	26	34	29
Total employed	35,659	36,566	37,322
Unemployed	4,388	4,583	4,279
Total labour force	40,047	41,150	41,601
Males	22,232	22,709	22,820
Females	17,814	18,441	18,781

*Data not wholly comparable with other years owing to amended methodology.

Source: ILO.

Health and Welfare

KEY INDICATORS

Total fertility rate (children per woman, 2005)	1.3
Under-five mortality rate (per 1,000 live births, 2005)	5
HIV/AIDS (% of persons aged 15–49, 2005)	0.1
Physicians (per 1,000 head, 2003)	3.37
Hospital beds (per 1,000 head, 2005)	8.4
Health expenditure (2004): US $ per head (PPP)	3,171.3
Health expenditure (2004): % of GDP	10.6
Health expenditure (2004): public (% of total)	76.9
Human Development Index (2005): ranking	22
Human Development Index (2005): value	0.935

For sources and definitions, see explanatory note on p. vi.

Agriculture

PRINCIPAL CROPS
('000 metric tons)

	2004	2005	2006
Wheat	25,427	23,693	22,428
Barley	12,993	11,614	11,967
Maize	4,200	4,083	3,220
Rye	3,830	2,794	2,644
Oats	1,186	964	830
Triticale (wheat-rye hybrid)	3,290	2,676	2,371
Potatoes	13,044	11,624	10,031
Sugar beet	27,159	25,285	20,647
Dry broad beans	64	60	49
Sunflower seed	70	67	62
Rapeseed	5,277	5,052	5,337
Cabbages and other brassicas	795	722	737
Cauliflowers and broccoli	182	177	159
Cucumbers and gherkins	205	220	221
Dry onions	426	365	337
Green beans	47	43	42
Carrots and turnips	554	516	504
Grapes*	1,332	1,326	1,326
Apples	980	891	948
Pears	79	38	49
Cherries	39	28	32
Plums and sloes	78	40	52
Strawberries	119	147	173
Currants	n.a.	n.a.	11

* FAO estimates.

Aggregate production ('000 metric tons, may include official, semi-official or estimated data): Total cereals 51,097 in 2004, 45,980 in 2005, 43,475 in 2006; Total roots and tubers 13,044 in 2004, 11,624 in 2005, 10,031 in 2006; Total vegetables (incl. melons) 3,269 in 2004, 3,158 in 2005, 3,157 in 2006; Total fruits (excl. melons) 2,781 in 2004, 2,578 in 2005, 2,691 in 2006.

Source: FAO.

GERMANY

LIVESTOCK
('000 head at December, unless otherwise indicated)

	2004	2005	2006
Horses	525.0*	500.4	500.4
Cattle†	13,195.8	13,034.5	12,747.9
Pigs†	25,659.3	26,857.8	26,521.3
Sheep	2,697.0	2,713.5	2,560.3
Goats	165	170	170
Chickens	110,000‡	107,267	107,267†
Geese and guinea fowls	400‡	329	329†
Ducks	2,300‡	2,352	2,352†
Turkeys	9,000‡	10,611	10,611†

* At May.
† At November.
‡ FAO estimate.

LIVESTOCK PRODUCTS
('000 metric tons)

	2004	2005	2006
Cattle meat	1,258.0	1,166.9	1,166.9†
Sheep meat	48.4	49.2	49.2†
Pig meat	4,323.4	4,500.0	4,500.0†
Chicken meat	609.4	605.1	608.4
Cows' milk	28,244.7	28,453.0	28,453.0†
Goats' milk†	35.0	35.0	35.0
Hen eggs	765.9	745.8	745.8†
Honey	25.6	21.2	21.2†
Wool: greasy†	15.0	15.0	15.0

* FAO estimate(s).
Source: FAO.

Forestry

ROUNDWOOD REMOVALS
('000 cubic metres, excluding bark)

	2004	2005	2006
Sawlogs, veneer logs and logs for sleepers	32,241	34,432	38,281
Pulpwood	12,695	12,964	12,888
Other industrial wood	3,721	3,509	2,831
Fuel wood	5,847	6,041	8,290
Total	54,504	56,946	62,290

Source: FAO.

SAWNWOOD PRODUCTION
('000 cubic metres, including railway sleepers)

	2004	2005	2006
Coniferous (softwood)	18,449	20,803	23,242
Broadleaved (hardwood)*	1,089	1,128	1,178
Total	19,538	21,931	24,420

* Unofficial figures.
Source: FAO.

Fishing
('000 metric tons, live weight)

	2003	2004	2005
Capture	260.9	262.1	285.7
Freshwater fishes	20.4	20.2	19.7
Atlantic cod	15.1	17.0	18.1
Saithe (Pollock)	12.1	12.1	15.0
Blue whiting (Poutassou)	27.0	15.3	22.8
Atlantic redfishes	11.9	4.4	3.9
Atlantic horse mackerel	18.8	22.9	19.4
Atlantic herring	74.8	70.6	92.6
European sprat	18.0	26.4	29.0
Atlantic mackerel	24.1	23.4	19.1
Common shrimp	16.3	19.2	22.6
Aquaculture	74.3	57.2	44.7
Common carp	16.2	16.0	12.0
Rainbow trout	23.3	22.0	19.3
Blue mussel	28.5	12.5	9.5
Total catch	335.1	319.3	330.4

Note: Figures exclude aquatic mammals, recorded by number rather than by weight. The number of harbour porpoises caught was: 10 in 2003; 5 in 2004; 4 in 2005.

Source: FAO.

Mining
('000 metric tons, unless otherwise indicated)

	2004	2005	2006
Hard coal	25,859	24,907	20,882
Brown coal	181,903	177,875	176,290
Crude petroleum	3,516	3,573	3,514
Salt (unrefined)	8,242	n.a.	n.a.

Natural gas (petajoules) (2004): 685 (Source: UN, *Industrial Commodity Statistics Yearbook*).

Industry

SELECTED PRODUCTS
('000 metric tons, unless otherwise indicated)

	2004	2005	2006
Margarine	441	433	424
Flour	4,762	4,823	4,895
Refined sugar	4,588	3,998	3,564
Beer ('000 hl)	97,615	94,806	96,937
Cigarettes (million)	208,347	212,428	216,042
Cotton yarn (pure and mixed)	53	40	39
Woven cotton fabrics ('000 sq metres)	316,239	283,900	268,112
Newsprint	2,242	2,712	2,711
Brown-coal briquettes	1,435	n.a.	n.a.
Pig-iron	30,018	n.a.	n.a.
Crude steel	46,374	n.a.	n.a.
Motor spirit (petrol)	24,936	25,584	25,061
Diesel oil*	31,893	34,730	34,281
Cement	32,064	31,231	33,317
Sulphuric acid	1,916	1,982	2,013
Nitrogenous fertilizers (N)	1,245	1,246	1,332
Artificial resins and plastics	16,025	16,791	17,213
Synthetic rubber	843	n.a.	1,112
Soap	159	199	210

GERMANY

—continued	2004	2005	2006
Aluminium (unwrought):			
primary	462	413	389
secondary	702	863	1,110
Refined lead (unwrought)	321	319	284
Refined zinc (unwrought)	361	n.a.	287
Refined copper	540	553	n.a.
Passenger cars and minibuses ('000)	5,773	5,912	5,932
Bicycles ('000)	2,319	2,116	1,913
Clocks, watches and non-electronic time-measuring instruments ('000)	10,782	n.a.	n.a.
Footwear ('000 pairs)†	19,159	n.a.	n.a.
Electricity (million kWh)	581,584	n.a.	n.a.

* Including light heating oil.
† Excluding rubber and plastic footwear.

Finance

CURRENCY AND EXCHANGE RATES

Monetary Units
100 cent = 1 euro (€).

Sterling and Dollar Equivalents (31 December 2007)
£1 sterling = 1.3609 euros;
US $1 = 0.6793 euros;
€10 = £7.35 = $14.72.

Average Exchange Rate (euros per US $)
2005 0.8041
2006 0.7971
2007 0.7306

Note: The national currency was formerly the Deutsche Mark (DM). From the introduction of the euro, with German participation, on 1 January 1999, a fixed exchange rate of €1 = 1.95583 DM was in operation. Euro notes and coins were introduced on 1 January 2002. The euro and local currency circulated alongside each other until 28 February, after which the euro became the sole legal tender.

GOVERNMENT FINANCE
(general government transactions, non-cash basis, € '000 million)

Summary of Balances

	2004	2005	2006
Revenue	958.13	977.02	1,017.57
Less Expense	1,047.07	1,059.13	1,059.59
Net operating balance	−88.94	−82.11	−42.02
Less Net acquisition of non-financial assets	−5.38	−6.54	−5.10
Net lending/borrowing	−83.56	−75.57	−36.92

Revenue

	2004	2005	2006
Taxes	485.57	497.14	534.57
Taxes on income, profits and capital gains	242.80	252.28	280.88
Taxes on goods and services	224.90	226.74	234.50
Social contributions	396.89	396.89	401.08
Grants	4.08	5.03	4.78
Other revenue	71.59	77.96	77.14
Total	958.13	977.02	1,017.57

Statistical Survey

Expense/Outlays

Expense by economic type	2004	2005	2006
Compensation of employees	169.50	168.45	167.74
Use of goods and services	91.23	96.90	97.80
Consumption of fixed capital	35.55	35.76	36.44
Interest	62.39	62.52	64.86
Subsidies	28.67	27.22	26.77
Grants	18.58	20.64	19.23
Social benefits	592.66	598.18	600.06
Other expense	48.49	49.46	46.69
Total	1,047.07	1,059.13	1,059.59

Outlays by functions of government*	2004	2005	2006
General public services	134.46	137.48	140.14
Defence	24.70	24.73	24.75
Public order and safety	36.53	36.73	36.65
Economic affairs	81.00	79.39	75.60
Environmental protection	10.76	10.96	11.31
Housing and community amenities	23.64	23.11	21.92
Health	135.42	139.81	143.33
Recreation, culture and religion	14.06	14.15	14.22
Education	94.19	94.41	93.98
Social protection	486.93	491.82	492.59
Total	1,041.69	1,052.59	1,054.49

* Including net acquisition of non-financial assets.

Source: IMF, *Government Finance Statistics Yearbook*.

INTERNATIONAL RESERVES
(US $ million at 31 December)

	2004	2005	2006
Gold (national valuation)	48,347	56,536	69,951
IMF special drawing rights	2,061	1,892	2,010
Reserve position in IMF	6,863	3,483	1,958
Foreign exchange	39,899	39,765	37,719
Total	97,170	101,676	111,638

Source: IMF, *International Financial Statistics*.

MONEY SUPPLY
(€ '000 million at 31 December)

	2004	2005	2006
Currency issued*	141.3	159.1	176.7
Demand deposits at banking institutions	655.0	725.4	759.6

* Currency put into circulation by the Deutsche Bundesbank totalled (€ '000 million): 204.7 in 2004, 234.2 in 2005 and 261.0 in 2006.

Source: IMF, *International Financial Statistics*.

COST OF LIVING
(Consumer Price Index for all private households; base: 2000 = 100)

	2005	2006	2007
Food	105.3	107.3	110.5
Alcohol and tobacco	129.2	133.7	137.8
Clothes and shoes	98.1	97.2	98.1
Housing, energy and fuel	109.5	112.7	114.6
All items (incl. others)	108.3	110.1	112.5

GERMANY

NATIONAL ACCOUNTS
(€ million at current prices, rounded to nearest €10m.)

National Income and Product

	2005	2006	2007
Compensation of employees	1,129,900	1,149,360	1,181,030
Net operating surplus/mixed income	561,250	601,870	643,180
Domestic primary incomes	1,691,150	1,751,230	1,824,210
Consumption of fixed capital	335,580	339,480	345,220
Gross domestic product (GDP) at factor cost	2,026,730	2,090,710	2,169,430
Net taxes on production and imports*	217,870	231,490	254,370
GDP in market prices	2,244,600	2,322,200	2,423,800
Balance of primary income from abroad	20,400	22,170	22,610
Gross national income (GNI)	2,265,000	2,344,370	2,446,410
Less Consumption of fixed capital	335,580	339,480	345,220
Net national income	1,929,420	2,004,890	2,101,190
Current transfers from abroad	10,320	11,160	12,520
Less Current transfers paid abroad	38,330	38,260	39,820
Net national disposable income	1,901,410	1,977,790	2,073,890

* Data obtained as residuals.

Expenditure on the Gross Domestic Product

	2005	2006	2007
Government final consumption expenditure	421,510	425,880	436,050
Private final consumption expenditure	1,326,400	1,357,500	1,374,390
Increase in stocks	−7,460	−4,670	−7,050
Gross fixed capital formation	390,820	417,110	449,560
Total domestic expenditure	2,131,270	2,195,820	2,252,950
Exports of goods and services	917,980	1,046,480	1,133,040
Less Imports of goods and services	804,650	920,100	962,190
GDP in purchasers' values	2,244,600	2,322,200	2,423,800

Gross Domestic Product by Economic Activity

	2005	2006	2007
Agriculture, hunting, forestry and fishing	17,800	17,840	19,930
Mining and quarrying*; Electricity, gas and water supply†	51,930	57,100	55,940
Manufacturing	455,030	474,310	508,730
Construction	79,850	83,890	88,530
Wholesale and retail trade; repair of motor vehicles, motorcycles and personal and household goods; and transport and communications	357,970	375,030	385,270
Financial intermediation; Real estate, renting and business activities†	601,410	618,050	637,830
Public administration and defence; compulsory social security; Education; Health and social work; Other community, social and personal service activities, incl. hotels and restaurants; Private households with employed persons	462,410	468,000	475,950
Gross value added in basic prices	2,026,400	2,094,220	2,172,180
Taxes on products	225,000	234,390	258,080
Less Subsidies on products	6,800	6,410	6,460
GDP in market prices	2,244,600	2,322,200	2,423,800

* Data obtained as residuals.
† Including deduction for financial intermediation services indirectly measured.

BALANCE OF PAYMENTS
(US $ '000 million)

	2004	2005	2006
Exports of goods f.o.b.	903.45	978.18	1,131.36
Imports of goods f.o.b.	−718.05	−789.77	−934.04
Trade balance	185.40	188.41	197.33
Exports of services	145.96	157.58	174.45
Imports of services	−195.27	−207.22	−219.38
Balance on goods and services	136.09	138.76	152.39
Other income received	164.44	192.81	236.03
Other income paid	−148.02	−167.12	−207.22
Balance on goods, services and income	152.51	164.45	181.19
Current transfers received	20.17	22.15	25.15
Current transfers paid	−54.76	−57.64	−58.52
Current balance	117.93	128.96	147.82
Capital account (net)	0.51	−1.69	−0.26
Direct investment abroad	−14.10	−56.94	−78.95
Direct investment from abroad	−8.86	35.30	43.42
Portfolio investment assets	−126.43	−253.76	−199.09
Portfolio investment liabilities	144.82	225.78	200.92
Financial derivatives liabilities	−9.14	−9.42	−7.74
Other investment assets	−180.53	−161.31	−259.94
Other investment liabilities	47.34	69.20	114.55
Net errors and omissions	26.65	21.30	35.61
Overall balance	−1.81	−2.60	−3.65

Source: IMF, *International Financial Statistics*.

OVERSEAS DEVELOPMENT AID
(€ million)

	2003	2004	2005
Bilateral	3,593	3,077	5,992
Multilateral	2,411	2,988	2,120
Total	6,005	6,064	8,112

GERMANY

Statistical Survey

External Trade

(Note: Figures include trade in second-hand ships, and stores and bunkers for foreign ships and aircraft. Imports exclude military supplies under the offshore procurement programme and exports exclude war reparations and restitutions, except exports resulting from the Israel Reparations Agreement)

PRINCIPAL COMMODITIES
(distribution by SITC, € million)

Imports c.i.f.	2004	2005	2006
Food and live animals	33,928	35,742	35,945
Crude materials (inedible) except fuels	18,945	20,413	24,594
Mineral fuels, lubricants, etc.	52,487	72,209	89,833
Petroleum, petroleum products, etc.	34,772	49,334	59,238
Chemicals and related products	66,424	73,466	81,396
Organic chemicals	14,247	15,734	17,974
Medicinal and pharmaceutical products	21,991	24,646	26,699
Basic manufactures	78,010	84,299	96,046
Machinery and transport equipment	226,521	239,399	260,105
Power-generating machinery and equipment	20,539	21,918	24,140
General industrial machinery, equipment and parts	20,604	22,105	24,573
Office machines and automatic data-processing equipment	28,884	31,087	31,497
Telecommunications and sound equipment	22,939	25,556	27,788
Other electrical machinery, apparatus and appliances	44,711	45,492	49,182
Road vehicles (incl. air-cushion vehicles) and parts	57,947	57,799	61,837
Other transport equipment	17,799	20,846	25,322
Miscellaneous manufactured articles	68,734	71,993	74,396
Articles of apparel and clothing accessories (excl. footwear)	19,983	20,254	21,148
Total (incl. others)	575,448	628,087	731,479

Exports f.o.b.	2004	2005	2006
Food and live animals	25,907	28,326	28,921
Chemicals and related products	100,646	109,274	122,785
Medical and pharmaceutical products	27,334	30,697	35,100
Basic manufactures	101,581	109,335	124,117
Machinery and transport equipment	381,226	404,925	440,932
Power-generating machinery and equipment	27,524	30,622	34,130
Machinery specialized for particular industries	35,100	37,642	40,935
General industrial machinery and equipment	49,585	53,567	60,177
Office machines and automatic data-processing equipment	23,185	23,311	23,939
Telecommunications and sound equipment	22,916	24,534	23,854
Electrical machinery, apparatus and appliances	58,523	61,193	65,988
Road vehicles (incl. air-cushion vehicles) and parts	132,393	140,969	151,509
Other transport equipment	21,039	20,979	26,799
Miscellaneous manufactured articles	72,327	77,372	83,875
Total (incl. others)	731,544	786,266	896,048

PRINCIPAL TRADING PARTNERS
(€ million)

Imports c.i.f.	2004	2005	2006*
Austria	24,019.6	26,048.4	29,895.1
Belgium	26,524.5	28,848.9	35,499.7
China, People's Republic	32,791.4	40,845.1	48,750.9
Czech Republic	16,493.4	17,679.9	22,074.8
Denmark	9,669.4	10,127.6	10,215.6
Finland	6,124.0	7,846.4	8,562.4
France	51,534.5	53,700.3	63,490.4
Hungary	13,412.1	14,209.1	16,022.3
Ireland	14,772.3	15,035.0	17,030.5
Italy	35,676.5	36,348.5	40,325.8
Japan	21,583.4	21,772.1	23,719.6
Korea, Republic	7,727.9	9,600.2	9,702.7
Netherlands	46,203.6	51,822.7	60,518.9
Norway	12,270.1	15,101.9	19,637.8
Poland	15,973.4	16,769.7	20,626.8
Russia	16,335.1	22,283.9	30,181.8
Spain	17,425.5	18,069.8	19,520.4
Sweden	10,197.3	11,306.1	12,873.4
Switzerland-Liechtenstein	21,751.3	22,903.3	25,507.4
Turkey	7,982.1	8,400.2	9,127.9
United Kingdom	34,465.5	39,069.0	42,829.0
USA	40,708.9	41,797.7	48,517.0
Total (incl. others)	575,448.0	628,086.8	731,478.8

Exports f.o.b.	2004	2005	2006*
Austria	40,244.0	43,304.5	48,921.1
Belgium	40,307.8	43,613.1	49,249.2
China, People's Republic	20,991.7	21,234.8	27,520.6
Czech Republic	17,765.6	19,160.7	22,255.3
Denmark	11,358.0	12,483.3	14,020.4
Finland	7,321.6	8,143.4	9,299.6
France	74,359.6	79,038.9	86,093.0
Hungary	12,815.7	13,646.0	15,870.8
Italy	51,479.2	53,855.3	59,971.4
Japan	12,718.6	13,338.4	13,860.9
Netherlands	46,729.7	49,033.4	55,876.5
Poland	18,776.3	22,348.8	28,820.4
Portugal	6,720.4	7,355.2	7,460.5
Russia	14,988.1	17,277.5	23,371.8
Spain	36,248.7	40,017.7	42,159.2
Sweden	15,729.5	17,238.3	18,881.2
Switzerland-Liechtenstein	28,373.5	30,099.2	35,249.3
Turkey	11,787.9	12,802.6	14,389.9
United Kingdom	59,985.8	60,393.6	65,340.5
USA	64,860.4	69,299.1	78,011.4
Total (incl. others)	731,543.8	786,265.9	896,048.1

*Preliminary.

Transport

FEDERAL RAILWAYS
(traffic)

	2004	2005	2006
Passengers (million)	2,071	2,131	2,212
Passenger-km (million)	72,562	74,946	77,803
Freight net ton-km (million)	91,921	95,421	105,759

ROAD TRAFFIC
('000 licensed vehicles at 1 January)

	2004	2005	2006
Passenger cars	45,022.9	45,375.5	46,090.3
Lorries	2,856.3	2,572.1	2,573.1
Buses	86.5	85.5	83.9
Motorcycles	3,745.0	3,827.9	3,902.5
Trailers	5,317.4	5,449.1	5,570.0

GERMANY

SHIPPING
Inland Waterways

	2001	2002	2003
Freight ton-km (million)	64,818	64,166	58,154

Merchant Fleet
(registered at 31 December)

	2004	2005	2006
Number of vessels	826	894	881
Displacement ('000 grt)	8,246.4	11,497.2	11,364.3

Source: Lloyd's Register-Fairplay, *World Fleet Statistics*.

Sea-borne Traffic

	1997	1998	1999
Vessels entered ('000 net registered tons):*			
domestic (coastwise)	19,785	43,667	21,213
international	260,553	263,470	269,637
Vessels cleared ('000 net registered tons):*			
domestic	19,664	67,036	20,529
international	235,110	237,071	246,887
Freight unloaded ('000 metric tons):†			
international	136,249	140,846	137,759
Freight loaded ('000 metric tons):†			
international	69,058	69,098	73,858
Total domestic freight ('000 metric tons)	8,011	7,444	10,005

* Loaded vessels only.
† Including transhipments.

CIVIL AVIATION
(traffic on scheduled services)

	2001	2002	2003
Kilometres flown (million)	861	927	1,070
Passengers carried ('000)	56,389	61,890	72,693
Passenger-km (million)	111,303	124,246	149,672
Total ton-km (million)	18,004	19,425	21,937

Source: UN, *Statistical Yearbook*.

Tourism

FOREIGN TOURIST ARRIVALS
('000)*

Country of residence	2004	2005	2006
Austria	920.4	995.3	1,066.3
Belgium and Luxembourg	923.6	994.7	1,093.3
Denmark	785.5	885.7	960.1
France	996.3	1,040.5	1,128.6
Italy	1,188.7	1,291.1	1,358.1
Japan	715.2	730.2	760.0
Netherlands	2,883.7	3,105.7	3,275.0
Poland	368.8	397.0	475.0
Spain	561.4	653.5	713.0
Sweden	815.4	827.8	877.3
Switzerland	1,416.6	1,561.4	1,657.2
United Kingdom	1,787.9	1,877.9	2,106.7
USA	1,925.6	1,949.8	2,118.6
Total (incl. others)	20,137.0	21,500.1	23,569.0

* Figures refer to arrivals at all accommodation types.

Tourism receipts (€ million): 22,243 in 2004; 23,449 in 2005; 26,091 in 2006.

Communications Media

	2004	2005	2006
Telephones ('000 main lines in use)	54,574	54,700	54,200
Mobile cellular telephones ('000 subscribers)	71,300	79,200	84,300
Personal computers ('000 in use)	40,000	45,000	n.a.
Internet users ('000)	35,200	35,700	38,600
Broadband subscribers ('000)	6,900.0	10,700.0	14,085.2

Source: International Telecommunication Union.

Television receivers ('000 in use, 2000): 48,170.
Facsimile machines ('000 in use, 1998): 6,000.
Radio receivers ('000 in use, 1997): 77,800.
Book production (titles, including pamphlets, 1996): 71,515.
Daily newspapers (2004): 347, average circulation ('000 copies) 22,100.
Non-daily newspapers (2004): 34, average circulation ('000 copies) 6,100.

Sources: UNESCO, *Statistical Yearbook*; UN, *Statistical Yearbook*.

Education

(2004/05)

	Teachers	Students
Pre-primary	189,780	2,178,123
Primary	234,107	3,306,136
Secondary:		
lower secondary	418,898	5,430,500
upper secondary:		
general	92,122	1,127,527
vocational	84,615	1,709,609
Post-secondary non-tertiary:		
general	7,096	491,449
vocational	15,334	
Higher:		
non-university institutions	287,251	341,442
universities and equivalent institutions		1,927,299
Total	1,329,203	16,512,085

Source: UNESCO Institute for Statistics.

Directory

The Constitution

The Basic Law (Grundgesetz), which came into force in the British, French and US Zones of Occupation in Germany (excluding Saarland) on 23 May 1949, was intended as a provisional Constitution to serve until a permanent one for Germany as a whole could be adopted. (Saarland was incorporated into the Federal Republic of Germany in 1957.) The Parliamentary Council which framed the Basic Law intended to continue the tradition of the Constitution of 1848–49, and to preserve some continuity with subsequent German constitutions (with Bismarck's Constitution of 1871, and with the Weimar Constitution of 1919), while avoiding the mistakes of the past.

With the accession of the five newly re-established eastern Länder and East Berlin to the Federal Republic on 3 October 1990, the Basic Law became the Constitution of the entire German nation.

Amendments to 25 articles of the Basic Law were adopted by the Bundestag on 30 June 2006 and by the Bundesrat on 7 July 2006. The reforms, which were to take effect in stages, were intended to simplify relations between the Bundestag and the Bundesrat, as well as those between the Federal and Land Governments, and to define their respective responsibilities more clearly. The number of bills requiring the approval of the Bundesrat was to be reduced from around 60% of the total to 35%–40%, although the upper house's powers over public services such as schools and prisons were to be increased.

The Basic Law has 182 articles, divided into 14 sections, and is introduced by a short preamble.

I. BASIC RIGHTS

The opening articles of the Constitution guarantee the dignity of man, the free development of his personality, the equality of all persons before the law, and freedom of faith and conscience. Men and women shall have equal rights, and no one shall suffer discrimination because of sex, descent, race, language, homeland and origin, faith or religion or political opinion (Article 3).

No one may be compelled against his conscience to perform war service as a combatant (Article 4). Everyone has the right freely to express and to disseminate his opinion through speech, writing or pictures. Freedom of the press and freedom of reporting by radio and motion pictures are guaranteed. Censorship is not permitted (Article 5).

The State shall protect marriage and the family, property and the right of inheritance. The care and upbringing of children is the natural right of parents. Illegitimate children shall be given the same conditions for their development and their position in society as legitimate children (Article 6). Schools are under the supervision of the State. Religion forms part of the curriculum in the State schools, but parents have the right to decide whether the child shall receive religious instruction (Article 7).

All Germans have the right to assemble peacefully and unarmed and to form associations and societies without permission or hindrance (Article 8).

A citizen's dwelling is inviolable; house searches may be made only by Court Order. No German may be deprived of his citizenship if he would thereby become stateless. The politically persecuted enjoy the right of asylum (Article 16A).

II. THE FEDERATION AND THE LÄNDER

Article 20 describes the Federal Republic (Bundesrepublik Deutschland) as a democratic and social federal state. The colours of the Federal Republic are black-red-gold, the same as those of the Weimar Republic. Each Land within the Federal Republic has its own Constitution, which must, however, conform to the principles laid down in the Basic Law. All Länder, districts and parishes must have a representative assembly resulting from universal, direct, free, equal and secret elections (Article 28). The exercise of governmental powers is the concern of the Länder, in so far as the Basic Law does not otherwise prescribe. Where there is incompatibility, Federal Law overrides Land Law (Article 31). Every German has in each Land the same civil rights and duties.

Political parties may be freely formed in all the states of the Federal Republic, but their internal organization must conform to democratic principles, and they must publicly account for the sources of their funds. Parties that seek to impair or abolish the free and democratic basic order or to jeopardize the existence of the Federal Republic of Germany are unconstitutional (Article 21). So are activities tending to disturb the peaceful relations between nations, and, especially, preparations for aggressive war, but the Federation may join a system of mutual collective security in order to preserve peace (Articles 26 and 24). The rules of International Law shall form part of Federal Law and take precedence over it and create rights and duties directly for the inhabitants of the Federal territory (Article 25).

The territorial organization of the Federation may be restructured by Federal Law, subject to regional plebiscites and with due regard to regional, historical and cultural ties, economic expediency and the requirements of regional policy and planning.

III. THE BUNDESTAG

The Federal Assembly (Bundestag) is the Lower House. Its members are elected by the people in universal, free, equal, direct and secret elections, for a term of four years*. Any person who has reached the age of 18 is eligible to vote and any person who has reached the age of 18 is eligible for election (Articles 38 and 39). A deputy may be arrested for a punishable offence only with the permission of the Bundestag, unless he be apprehended in the act or during the following day. (Article 46)

The Bundestag elects its President and draws up its Standing Orders. Most decisions of the House require a majority vote. Its meetings are public, but the public may be excluded by the decision of a two-thirds' majority. Upon the motion of one-quarter of its members the Bundestag is obliged to set up an investigation committee.

* The elections of 1949 were conducted on the basis of direct election, with some elements of proportional representation. In January 1953 the draft of a new electoral law was completed by the Federal Government and was approved shortly before the dissolution. The new law represents a compromise between direct election and proportional representation, and is designed to prevent the excessive proliferation of parties in the Bundestag.

IV. THE BUNDESRAT

The Federal Council (Bundesrat) is the Upper House, through which the Länder participate in the legislation and the administration of the Federation, and in matters relating to the European Union (EU). The Bundesrat consists of members of the Land governments, which appoint and recall them (Article 51). Each Land has at least three votes; Länder with more than two million inhabitants have four, and those with more than six million inhabitants have five. Länder with more than seven million inhabitants have six votes. The votes of each Land may only be given as a block vote. The Bundesrat elects its President for one year. Its decisions are taken by simple majority vote. Meetings are public, but the public may be excluded. The members of the Federal Government have the right, and, on demand, the obligation, to participate in the debates of the Bundesrat.

V. THE FEDERAL PRESIDENT

The Federal President (Bundespräsident) is elected by the Federal Convention (Bundesversammlung), consisting of the members of the Bundestag and an equal number of members elected by the Land Parliaments (Article 54). Every German eligible to vote in elections for the Bundestag and over 40 years of age is eligible for election. The candidate who obtains an absolute majority of votes is elected, but if such majority is not achieved by any candidate in two ballots, whoever receives most votes in a further ballot becomes President. The President's term of office is five years. Immediate re-election is permitted only once. The Federal President must not be a member of the Government or of any legislative body or hold any salaried office. Orders and instructions of the President require the counter-signature of the Federal Chancellor or competent Minister, except for the appointment or dismissal of the Chancellor or the dissolution of the Bundestag.

The President represents the Federation in its international relations and accredits and receives envoys. The Bundestag or the Bundesrat may impeach the President before the Federal Constitutional Court on account of wilful violation of the Basic Law or of any other Federal Law (Article 61).

VI. THE FEDERAL GOVERNMENT

The Federal Government (Bundesregierung) consists of the Federal Chancellor (Bundeskanzler) and the Federal Ministers (Bundesminister). The Chancellor is elected by an absolute majority of the Bundestag on the proposal of the Federal President (Article 63). Ministers are appointed and dismissed by the President upon the proposal of the Chancellor. Neither he nor his Ministers may be a member of any other executive body or hold any other salaried office. The Chancellor determines general policy and assumes responsibility for it, but within these limits each Minister directs his department individually and on his own responsibility. The Bundestag may express its lack of confidence in the Chancellor only by electing a successor with the majority of its members; the President must then appoint the person elected (Article 67). If a motion of the Chancellor for a vote of confidence does not obtain the support of the majority of the Bundestag, the President may, upon the proposal of the Chancellor, dissolve the House within 21 days, unless it elects another Chancellor within this time (Article 68).

VII. THE LEGISLATION OF THE FEDERATION

The right of legislation lies with the Länder in so far as the Basic Law does not specifically accord legislative powers to the Federation. Distinction is made between fields within the exclusive legislative powers of the Federation and fields within concurrent legislative powers. In the field of concurrent legislation the Länder may legislate so long and so far as the Federation makes no use of its legislative right. The Federation has this right only in matters relating to the creation of equal living conditions throughout the country and in cases where the preservation of legal and economic unity is perceived to be in the national interest. Exclusive legislation of the Federation is strictly limited to such matters as foreign affairs, Federal finance, citizenship, migration, currency, copyrights, customs, civil aviation, railways, waterways, shipping and post and telecommunications. In most other fields, as enumerated (Article 74), concurrent legislation exists.

The legislative organ of the Federation is the Bundestag, to which Bills are introduced by the Government, by members of the Bundestag or by the Bundesrat (Article 76). After their adoption they must be submitted to the Bundesrat, which may demand, within three weeks, that a committee of members of both houses be convened to consider the Bill (Article 77). In so far as its express approval is not needed, the Bundesrat may veto a law within two weeks. This veto can be overruled by the Bundestag, with the approval of a majority of its members. When the Bill requires the consent of the Bundesrat, such an overruling may not take place.

An amendment of the Basic Law requires a majority of two-thirds in both houses, but an amendment affecting the division of the Federation into Länder and the basic principles contained in Articles 1 and 20 is inadmissible (Article 79).

VIII. THE EXECUTION OF FEDERAL LAWS AND THE FEDERAL ADMINISTRATION

The Länder execute Federal Laws as matters of their own concern in so far as the Basic Law does not otherwise determine. In doing so, they regulate the establishment of the authorities and the administrative procedure, but the Federal Government exercises supervision in order to ensure that the Länder execute Federal Laws in an appropriate manner.

In order to avert imminent danger to the existence of the democratic order, a Land may call in the police forces of other Länder; and if the Land in which the danger is imminent is itself not willing or able to fight the danger, the Federal Government may place the police in the Land, or the police forces in other Länder, under its instructions (Article 91).

IX. THE ADMINISTRATION OF JUSTICE

Judicial authority is vested in independent judges, who are subject only to the law and who may not be dismissed or transferred against their will (Article 97).

Justice is exercised by the Federal Constitutional Court, by the Superior Federal Courts and by the Courts of the Länder. The Federal Constitutional Court decides on the interpretation of the Basic Law in cases of doubt, on the compatibility of Federal Law or Land Law with the Basic Law, and on disputes between the Federation and the Länder or between different Länder. Superior Federal Courts are responsible for the spheres of ordinary, administrative, fiscal, labour and social jurisdiction. If a Superior Federal Court intends to judge a point of law in contradiction to a previous decision of another Superior Federal Court, it must refer the matter to a special senate of the Superior Courts. Extraordinary courts are inadmissible.

The freedom of the individual may be restricted only on the basis of a law. No one may be prevented from appearing before his lawful judge (Article 101). Detained persons may be subjected neither to physical nor to mental ill-treatment. The police may hold no one in custody longer than the end of the day following the arrest without the decision of a court. Any person temporarily detained must be brought before a judge who must either issue a warrant of arrest or set him free, at the latest on the following day. A person enjoying the confidence of the detainee must be notified forthwith of any continued duration of a deprivation of liberty. An act may be punished only if it was punishable by law before the act was committed, and no one may be punished more than once for the same criminal act. A criminal act may not be punished by sentence of death.

X. FINANCE

The Federation has the exclusive power to legislate only on customs and fiscal monopolies; on most other taxes, especially on income, property and inheritance, it has concurrent power to legislate with the Länder (see VII, above).

Customs, fiscal monopolies, excise taxes (with the exception of the beer tax) and levies within the framework of the EU are administered by Federal finance authorities, and the revenues thereof accrue to the Federation. The remaining taxes are administered, as a rule, by the Länder and the Gemeinden (communities) to which they accrue. Income tax, corporation tax and value-added tax are shared taxes, accruing jointly to the Federation and the Länder (after deduction of a proportion of income tax for the municipalities; Article 106). The Federation and the Länder shall be self-supporting and independent of each other in their fiscal administration (Article 109). In order to ensure the working efficiency of the Länder with low revenues and to equalize their differing burdens of expenditure, there exists a system of revenue-sharing among the Länder; in addition, the Federation may make grants, out of its own funds, to the poorer Länder. All revenues and expenditures of the Federation must be estimated for each fiscal year and included in the budget, which must be established by law before the beginning of the fiscal year. Decisions of the Bundestag or the Bundesrat that increase the budget expenditure proposed by the Federal Government require its approval (Article 113).

XI. TRANSITIONAL AND CONCLUDING PROVISIONS

Articles 116–146 regulate a number of unrelated matters of detail, such as the relationship between the old Reich and the Federation. Article 143 contains divergences from the Basic Law, with regard to the newly acceded Länder, as stipulated in the Unification Treaty.

The Government

HEAD OF STATE

Federal President: Prof. Dr Horst Köhler (inaugurated 1 July 2004).

THE FEDERAL GOVERNMENT
(March 2008)

A coalition of the Christlich-Demokratische Union Deutschlands, with its sister party in Bavaria, the Christlich-Soziale Union Deutschlands (CDU/CSU, Christian-Democratic Union and Christian Social Union) and the Sozialdemokratische Partei Deutschlands (SPD, Social Democratic Party).

Federal Chancellor: Angela Merkel (CDU).

Federal Vice-Chancellor and Federal Minister of Foreign Affairs: Frank-Walter Steinmeier (SPD).

Federal Minister of the Interior: Wolfgang Schäuble (CDU).

Federal Minister of Justice: Brigitte Zypries (SPD).

Federal Minister of Finance: Peer Steinbrück (SPD).

Federal Minister of Economics and Technology: Michael Glos (CSU).

Federal Minister of Labour and Social Affairs: Olaf Scholz (SPD).

Federal Minister of Food, Agriculture and Consumer Protection: Horst Seehofer (CSU).

Federal Minister of Defence: Franz Josef Jung (CDU).

Federal Minister of Family Affairs, Senior Citizens, Women and Youth: Ursula von der Leyen (CDU).

Federal Minister of Health: Ulla Schmidt (SPD).

Federal Minister of Transport, Building and Urban Affairs: Wolfgang Tiefensee (SPD).

Federal Minister of the Environment, Nature Conservation and Nuclear Safety: Sigmar Gabriel (SPD).

Federal Minister of Education and Research: Annette Schavan (CDU).

Federal Minister of Economic Co-operation and Development: Heidemarie Wieczorek-Zeul (SPD).

Head of the Federal Chancellery and Minister for General Affairs: Thomas de Maizière (CDU).

MINISTRIES

Office of the Federal President: 11010 Berlin; Bundespräsidialamt, Spreeweg 1, 10557 Berlin; tel. (30) 20000; fax (30) 20001999; e-mail poststelle@bpra.bund.de; internet www.bpra.bund.de.

Federal Chancellery: Bundeskanzler-Amt, Willy-Brandt Str. 1, 10557 Berlin; tel. (30) 40000; fax (30) 40002357; e-mail internetpost@bundeskanzlerin.de; internet www.bundeskanzlerin.de.

Press and Information Office of the Federal Government: 11044 Berlin; Dorotheenstr. 84, 10117 Berlin; tel. (180) 2720000; fax (1888) 2722555; e-mail internetpost@bundesregierung.de; internet www.bundesregierung.de.

GERMANY

Federal Ministry of Defence: Stauffenbergstr. 18, 10785 Berlin; tel. (1888) 24000; fax (1888) 242129; e-mail poststelle@bmvg.bund400.de; internet www.bmvg.de.

Federal Ministry of Economic Co-operation and Development: Europahaus, Stresemannstr. 94, 10963 Berlin; tel. (30) 185350; fax (30) 185352595; e-mail info@bmz.bund.de; internet www.bmz.de.

Federal Ministry of Economics and Technology: Scharnhorststr. 34–37, 10115 Berlin; tel. (30) 186150; fax (30) 186157010; e-mail info@bmwi.bund.de; internet www.bmwi.de.

Federal Ministry of Education and Research: Hannoversche Str. 28–30, 10115 Berlin; tel. (30) 18570; fax (30) 185783601; e-mail bmbf@bmbf.bund.de; internet www.bmbf.de.

Federal Ministry of the Environment, Nature Conservation and Nuclear Safety: Alexanderstr. 3, 10178 Berlin; tel. (30) 183050; fax (30) 183054375; internet www.bmu.de.

Federal Ministry of Family Affairs, Senior Citizens, Women and Youth: 11018 Berlin; Alexanderstr. 3, 10178 Berlin; tel. (30) 185550; fax (30) 185554400; e-mail poststelle@bmfsfj.bund.de; internet www.bmfsfj.de.

Federal Ministry of Finance: 11016 Berlin; Wilhelmstr. 97, 10117 Berlin; tel. (30) 186820; fax (30) 186823260; e-mail poststelle@bmf.bund.de; internet www.bundesfinanzministerium.de.

Federal Ministry of Food, Agriculture and Consumer Protection: Postfach 42, 10177 Berlin; Wilhelmstr. 54, 10117 Berlin; tel. (30) 185290; fax (30) 185293179; e-mail poststelle@bmelv.bund.de; internet www.bmelv.bund.de.

Federal Ministry of Foreign Affairs: 11013 Berlin; Werderscher Markt 1, 10117 Berlin; tel. (30) 18170; fax (30) 18173402; internet www.auswaertiges-amt.de.

Federal Ministry of Health: 11055 Berlin; Friedrichstr. 108, 10117 Berlin; tel. (30) 184410; fax (30) 184411921; e-mail info@bmg.bund.de; internet www.bmg.bund.de.

Federal Ministry of the Interior: Alt-Moabit 101D, 10559 Berlin; tel. (30) 186810; fax (30) 186812926; e-mail poststelle@bmi.bund.de; internet www.bmi.bund.de.

Federal Ministry of Justice: Mohrenstr. 37, 10117 Berlin; tel. (30) 185800; fax (30) 185809525; e-mail presse@bmj.bund.de; internet www.bmj.bund.de.

Federal Ministry of Labour and Social Affairs: Wilhelmstr. 49, 10117 Berlin; tel. (30) 185270; fax (30) 185271830; e-mail info@bmas.bund.de; internet www.bmas.bund.de.

Federal Ministry of Transport, Building and Urban Affairs: Invalidenstr. 44, 10115 Berlin; tel. (30) 183003060; fax (30) 183001942; e-mail buergerinfo@bmvbs.bund.de; internet www.bmvbs.de.

Legislature

BUNDESTAG
(Federal Assembly)

Pl. der Republik 1, 11011 Berlin; tel. (30) 2270; fax (30) 22736878; e-mail mail@bundestag.de; internet www.bundestag.de.

President: Dr NORBERT LAMMERT (CDU).

Vice-Presidents: GERDA HASSELFELDT (CSU), Dr WOLFGANG THIERSE (SPD), Dr SUSANNE KASTNER (SPD), Dr HERMANN OTTO SOLMS (FDP), KATRIN GÖRING-ECKARDT (Bündnis 90/Die Grünen), PETRA PAU (Die Linke).

General Election, 18 September 2005

Parties and Groups	Votes*	% of votes*	Seats
Christlich-Demokratische Union Deutschlands/Christlich-Soziale Union Deutschlands (CDU/CSU)†	16,631,049	35.17	226
Sozialdemokratische Partei Deutschlands (SPD)	16,194,665	34.25	222
Freie Demokratische Partei (FDP)	4,648,144	9.83	61
Linkspartei.PDS (Die Linke)	4,118,194	8.71	54
Bündnis 90/Die Grünen	3,838,326	8.12	51
Others	1,857,610	3.93	—
Total	**47,287,988**	**100.00**	**614**

*Figures refer to valid second votes (i.e. for state party lists). The total number of valid first votes (for individual candidates) was 47,194,062.

†Of which the CDU received 13,136,740 votes (27.78%—180 seats) and the CSU received 3,494,309 votes (7.39%—46 seats).

BUNDESRAT
(Federal Council)

President: OLE VON BEUST (CDU).

The Bundesrat has 69 members. Each Land (state) has three, four, five or six votes, depending on the size of its population, and may send as many members to the sessions as it has votes. The head of government of each Land is automatically a member of the Bundesrat. Members of the Federal Government attend the sessions, which are held every two to three weeks.

Länder	Seats
Nordrhein-Westfalen (North Rhine-Westphalia)	6
Bayern (Bavaria)	6
Baden-Württemberg	6
Niedersachsen (Lower Saxony)	6
Hessen (Hesse)	5
Sachsen (Saxony)	4
Rheinland-Pfalz (Rhineland-Palatinate)	4
Berlin	4
Schleswig-Holstein	4
Brandenburg	4
Sachsen-Anhalt (Saxony-Anhalt)	4
Thüringen (Thuringia)	4
Hamburg	3
Mecklenburg-Vorpommern (Mecklenburg-Western Pomerania)	3
Saarland	3
Bremen	3
Total	**69**

The Land Governments

The 16 Länder of Germany are autonomous but not sovereign states, enjoying a high degree of self-government and extensive legislative powers. Thirteen of the Länder have a Landesregierung (Government) and a Landtag (Assembly). The equivalent of the Landesregierung in Berlin, Bremen and Hamburg is the Senate. The equivalent of the Landtag is the House of Representatives in Berlin and the City Council in Bremen and Hamburg.

BADEN-WÜRTTEMBERG

The Constitution was adopted by the Assembly in Stuttgart on 11 November 1953 and came into force on 19 November. The Minister-President, who is elected by the Assembly, appoints and dismisses Ministers. The current Government is formed by a coalition of the CDU and the FDP/DVP.

Minister-President: GÜNTHER OETTINGER (CDU).

Landtag von Baden-Württemberg: Haus des Landtags, Konrad-Adenauer-Str. 3, 70173 Stuttgart; tel. (711) 20630; fax (711) 2063299; e-mail post@landtag-bw.de; internet www.landtag-bw.de.

The composition of the Assembly, as a result of elections held on 26 March 2006, is as follows:

President of Assembly: PETER STRAUB (CDU).

Party	Seats
Christlich-Demokratische Union Deutschlands (CDU)	69
Sozialdemokratische Partei Deutschlands (SPD)	38
Bündnis 90/Die Grünen	17
Freie Demokratische Partei/Demokratische Volkspartei (FDP/DVP)	15

The Land is divided into four administrative districts: Stuttgart, Karlsruhe, Tübingen and Freiburg.

BAYERN (BAVARIA)

The Constitution of Bavaria provides for a unicameral Assembly and a Constitutional Court. Provision is also made for referendums. The Minister-President, who is elected by the Assembly for four years, appoints the Ministers and Secretaries of State with the consent of the Assembly. The Government is currently formed by the majority party (CSU).

Minister-President: Dr GÜNTHER BECKSTEIN (CSU).

Bayerischer Landtag: Landtagsamt, Maximilaneum, 81627 München; tel. (89) 41260; fax (89) 41261392; e-mail landtag@bayern.landtag.de; internet www.bayern.landtag.de.

The composition of the Assembly, as a result of elections held on 21 September 2003, is as follows:

President of Assembly: ALOIS GLÜCK (CSU).

Party	Seats
Christlich-Soziale Union Deutschlands (CSU)	124
Sozialdemokratische Partei Deutschlands (SPD)	41
Bündnis 90/Die Grünen	15

Bayern is divided into seven districts: Mittelfranken, Oberfranken, Unterfranken, Schwaben, Niederbayern, Oberpfalz and Oberbayern.

BERLIN

The House of Representatives (Abgeordnetenhaus) is the legislative body. The executive agency is the Senate, which is composed of the Governing Mayor (Regierender Bürgermeister) and up to 10 Senators, from among whom the deputy mayor is elected. The Governing Mayor and the senators are elected by a majority of the House of Representatives. The Senate is responsible to the House of Representatives and dependent on its confidence. The Senate is currently composed of a coalition of the SPD and Die Linke.

Regierender Bürgermeister: KLAUS WOWEREIT (SPD).

Abgeordnetenhaus von Berlin: Niederkirchnerstr. 5, 10117 Berlin; tel. (30) 23250; e-mail verwaltung@parlament-berlin.de; internet www.parlament-berlin.de.

The composition of the House of Representatives, as the result of elections held on 17 September 2006, is as follows:

President of House of Representatives: WALTER MOMPER (SPD).

Party	Seats
Sozialdemokratische Partei Deutschlands (SPD)	53
Christlich-Demokratische Union Deutschlands (CDU)	37
Die Linke	23
Bündnis 90/Die Grünen	23
Freie Demokratische Partei (FDP)	13

BRANDENBURG

The Constitution of Brandenburg was adopted on 14 June 1992 and came into force on 20 August. It was amended on 7 April 1999. The Government is currently formed from a coalition of the SPD and the CDU.

Minister-President: MATTHIAS PLATZECK (SPD).

Landtag Brandenburg: Postfach 601064, 14410 Potsdam; Am Havelblick 8, 14473 Potsdam; tel. (331) 9660; fax (331) 9661210; e-mail poststelle@landtag.brandenburg.de; internet www.landtag.brandenburg.de.

The composition of the Assembly, as a result of elections held on 19 September 2004, is as follows:

President of Assembly: GUNTER FRITSCH (SPD).

Party	Seats
Sozialdemokratische Partei Deutschlands (SPD)	33
Partei des Demokratischen Sozialismus (PDS)*	29
Christlich-Demokratische Union Deutschlands (CDU)	20
Deutsche Volksunion (DVU)	6

*Restyled Die Linke in June 2007.

BREMEN

The Constitution of the Free Hanseatic City of Bremen was sanctioned by referendum of the people on 12 October 1947. The main constitutional organs are the City Council (legislature), the Senate (government) and the Constitutional Court. The Senate is the executive organ elected by the Council for the duration of its own tenure of office. The Senate elects from its own ranks two Mayors (Bürgermeister), one of whom becomes President of the Senate. Decisions of the Council are subject to the delaying veto of the Senate. The Government is currently formed from a coalition of the SPD and Bündnis 90/Die Grünen.

First Bürgermeister and President of the Senate: JENS BÖHRNSEN (SPD).

Bremische Bürgerschaft: Am Markt 20, 28195 Bremen; tel. (421) 3614555; fax (421) 36112492; e-mail geschaeftsstelle@buergerschaft.bremen.de; internet www.bremische-buergerschaft.de.

The City Council was elected on 13 May 2007, and is composed as follows:

President of the City Council: CHRISTIAN WEBER (SPD).

Party	Seats
Sozialdemokratische Partei Deutschlands (SPD)	33
Christlich-Demokratische Union Deutschlands (CDU)	23
Bündnis 90/Die Grünen	14
Die Linke	7
Freie Demokratische Partei (FDP)	5
Deutsche Volksunion (DVU)	1

HAMBURG

The Constitution of the Free and Hanseatic City of Hamburg was adopted in June 1952. The City Council (legislature) elects the members of the Senate (government), which in turn elects the President and the President's deputy from its own ranks. The President remains in office for one year, but may stand for re-election. The Senate is currently formed by the majority party (CDU).

President of Senate and First Bürgermeister: OLE VON BEUST (CDU).

Bürgerschaft der Freien und Hansestadt Hamburg: Rathaus, Rathausmarkt 1, 20095 Hamburg; tel. (40) 428312408; fax (40) 428312558; e-mail oeffentlichkeitsservice@bk.hamburg.de; internet www.hamburgische-buergerschaft.de.

The City Council was elected on 24 February 2008, and is composed as follows:

President: BERNDT RÖDER (CDU).

Party	Seats
Christlich-Demokratische Union Deutschlands (CDU)	56
Sozialdemokratische Partei Deutschlands (SPD)	45
Bündnis 90/Die Grünen	12
Die Linke	8

HESSEN (HESSE)

The Constitution of this Land dates from 1 December 1946. The Minister-President is elected by the Assembly, and appoints and dismisses Ministers with its consent. The Assembly can force the resignation of the Government by a vote of 'no confidence'. The Government is currently formed by the majority party (CDU).

Minister-President: ROLAND KOCH (CDU).

Hessischer Landtag: Schlosspl. 1–3, 65183 Wiesbaden; tel. (611) 3500; fax (611) 350434; e-mail poststelle@ltg.hessen.de; internet www.hessischer-landtag.de.

The Assembly, elected on 27 January 2008, is composed as follows:

President of Assembly: NORBERT KARTMANN (CDU).

Party	Seats
Christlich-Demokratische Union Deutschlands (CDU)	42
Sozialdemokratische Partei Deutschlands (SPD)	42
Freie Demokratische Partei (FDP)	11
Bündnis 90/Die Grünen	9
Die Linke	6

Hessen is divided into three governmental districts: Kassel, Giessen and Darmstadt.

MECKLENBURG-VORPOMMERN (MECKLENBURG-WESTERN POMERANIA)

The Constitution was adopted by the Assembly on 14 May 1993. The Government is currently formed from a coalition of the SPD and CDU.

Minister-President: Dr HARALD RINGSTORFF (SPD).

Landtag Mecklenburg-Vorpommern: Schloss, Lennéstr. 1, 19053 Schwerin; tel. (385) 5250; fax (385) 5252141; e-mail poststelle@landtag-mv.de; internet www.landtag-mv.de.

The composition of the Assembly, as a result of elections held on 17 September 2006, is as follows:

GERMANY

President of Assembly: SYLVIA BRETSCHNEIDER (SPD).

Party	Seats
Sozialdemokratische Partei Deutschlands (SPD)	23
Christlich-Demokratische Union Deutschlands (CDU)	22
Die Linke	13
Freie Demokratische Partei (FDP)	7
Nationaldemokratische Partei Deutschlands (NPD)	6

NIEDERSACHSEN (LOWER SAXONY)

The Constitution was adopted by the Assembly on 19 May 1993 and came into force on 1 June. The Government is currently formed from a coalition of the CDU and the FDP.

Minister-President: CHRISTIAN WULFF (CDU).

Landtag Niedersachsen: Hinrich-Wilhelm-Kopf-Pl. 1, 30159 Hannover; tel. (511) 30300; fax (511) 30302806; e-mail poststelle@lt.niedersachsen.de; internet www.landtag-niedersachsen.de.

As a result of elections held on 27 January 2008, the Assembly is composed as follows:

President of Assembly: HERMANN DINKLA (CDU).

Party	Seats
Christlich-Demokratische Union Deutschlands (CDU)	68
Sozialdemokratische Partei Deutschlands (SPD)	48
Freie Demokratische Partei (FDP)	13
Bündnis 90/Die Grünen	12
Die Linke	11

Niedersachsen is divided into four governmental districts: Braunschweig, Hannover, Lüneburg and Weser-Ems.

NORDRHEIN-WESTFALEN (NORTH RHINE-WESTPHALIA)

The present Constitution was adopted by the Assembly on 6 June 1950, and was endorsed by the electorate in the elections held on 18 June. The Government is presided over by the Minister-President, who appoints Ministers. The Government is currently formed from a coalition of the CDU and the FDP.

Minister-President: Dr JÜRGEN RÜTTGERS (CDU).

Landtag von Nordrhein-Westfalen: Postfach 101143, 40002 Düsseldorf; Pl. des Landtags 1, 40221 Düsseldorf; tel. (211) 8840; fax (211) 8842258; e-mail email@landtag.nrw.de; internet www.landtag.nrw.de.

The Assembly, elected on 22 May 2005, is composed as follows:

President of Assembly: REGINA VAN DINTHER (CDU).

Party	Seats
Christlich-Demokratische Union Deutschlands (CDU)	89
Sozialdemokratische Partei Deutschlands (SPD)	74
Freie Demokratische Partei (FDP)	12
Bündnis 90/Die Grünen	11
Independent	1

The Land is divided into five governmental districts: Düsseldorf, Münster, Arnsberg, Detmold and Köln.

RHEINLAND-PFALZ (RHEINLAND-PALATINATE)

The three chief agencies of the Constitution of this Land are the Assembly, the Government and the Constitutional Court. The Minister-President is elected by the Assembly, with whose consent he/she appoints and dismisses Ministers. The Government, which is dependent on the confidence of the Assembly, is currently formed by the majority party (SPD).

Minister-President: KURT BECK (SPD).

Landtag Rheinland-Pfalz: Postfach 3040, 55020 Mainz; Deutschhauspl. 12, 55116 Mainz; tel. (6131) 2080; fax (6131) 2082447; e-mail poststelle@landtag.rlp.de; internet www.landtag.rlp.de.

The members of the Assembly are elected according to a system of proportional representation. Its composition, as a result of elections held on 26 March 2006, is as follows:

President of Assembly: JOACHIM MERTES (SPD).

Party	Seats
Sozialdemokratische Partei Deutschlands (SPD)	53
Christlich-Demokratische Union Deutschlands (CDU)	38
Freie Demokratische Partei (FDP)	10

Rheinland-Pfalz is divided into three districts: Koblenz, Rheinhessen-Pfalz (Rheinhessen-Palatinate) and Trier.

SAARLAND

Under the Constitution, which came into force on 1 January 1957, Saarland was politically integrated into the FRG as a Land. It was economically integrated into the FRG in July 1959. The Minister-President is elected by the Assembly. The Government is currently formed by the majority party (CDU).

Minister-President: PETER MÜLLER (CDU).

Landtag des Saarlandes: Postfach 101833, 66018 Saarbrücken; Franz-Josef-Röder Str. 7, 66119 Saarbrücken; tel. (681) 50020; fax (681) 5002546; e-mail r.riemann@landtag-saar.de; internet www.landtag-saar.de.

The composition of the Assembly, as a result of elections held on 5 September 2004, is as follows:

President of the Assembly: HANS LEY (CDU).

Party	Seats
Christlich-Demokratische Union Deutschlands (CDU)	27
Sozialdemokratische Partei Deutschlands (SPD)	18
Freie Demokratische Partei (FDP)	3
Bündnis 90/Die Grünen	2
Independent	1

SACHSEN (SAXONY)

The Constitution of Sachsen was adopted on 26 May 1992 and came into force on 6 June. The Government is formed from a coalition of the CDU and SPD.

Minister-President: Prof. Dr GEORG MILBRADT (CDU).

Sächsischer Landtag: Postfach 120705, 01008 Dresden; Bernhard-von-Lindenau Pl. 1, 01067 Dresden; tel. (351) 49350; fax (351) 4935900; e-mail info@slt.sachsen.de; internet www.landtag.sachsen.de.

The composition of the Assembly, as a result of elections held on 19 September 2004, is as follows:

President of Assembly: ERICH ILTGEN (CDU).

Party	Seats
Christlich-Demokratische Union Deutschlands (CDU)	55
Partei des Demokratischen Sozialismus (PDS)*	31
Sozialdemokratische Partei Deutschlands (SPD)	13
Nationaldemokratische Partei Deutschlands (NPD)	12†
Freie Demokratische Partei (FDP)	7
Bündnis 90/Die Grünen	6

* Restyled Die Linke in June 2007.
† Three of the NPD's 12 representatives resigned from the party in December 2005, opting to become independents.

SACHSEN-ANHALT (SAXONY-ANHALT)

The Constitution of Sachsen-Anhalt was adopted on 16 July 1992. The Government is formed by a coalition of the CDU, the SPD and one independent.

Minister-President: Prof. Dr WOLFGANG BÖHMER (CDU).

Landtag von Sachsen-Anhalt: Dompl. 6–9, 39104 Magdeburg; tel. (391) 5600; fax (391) 5601123; e-mail kontakt@lt.sachsen-anhalt.de; internet www.landtag.sachsen-anhalt.de.

The composition of the Assembly, as a result of elections held on 26 March 2006, is as follows:

GERMANY

President of Assembly: DIETER STEINECKE (CDU).

Party	Seats
Christlich-Demokratische Union Deutschlands (CDU)	40
Die Linke	26
Sozialdemokratische Partei Deutschlands (SPD)	24
Freie Demokratische Partei (FDP)	7

Sachsen-Anhalt is divided into three governmental districts: Magdeburg, Halle and Dessau.

SCHLESWIG-HOLSTEIN

The Provisional Constitution was adopted by the Assembly on 13 December 1949. The Government consists of the Minister-President and the Ministers appointed by the Minister-President. The Government is formed by a coalition of the CDU and the SPD.

Minister-President: PETER HARRY CARSTENSEN (CDU).

Landtag Schleswig-Holstein: Düsternbrooker Weg 70, 24105 Kiel; tel. (431) 9880; fax (431) 9881119; e-mail annette.wiese-krukowska@landtag.ltsh.de; internet www.sh-landtag.de.

The composition of the Assembly, as the result of elections held on 20 February 2005, is as follows:

President of Assembly: MARTIN KAYENBURG (CDU).

Party	Seats
Christlich-Demokratische Union Deutschlands (CDU)	30
Sozialdemokratische Partei Deutschlands (SPD)	29
Freie Demokratische Partei (FDP)	4
Bündnis 90/Die Grünen	4
Südschleswigscher Wählerverband (SSW)*	2

*Represents the Danish minority in Schleswig-Holstein.

THÜRINGEN (THURINGIA)

The Constitution of Thüringen was adopted on 25 October 1993. The Assembly Government is currently formed by the majority party (CDU).

Minister-President: DIETER ALTHAUS (CDU).

Thüringer Landtag: Jürgen-Fuchs Str. 1, 99096 Erfurt; tel. (361) 3772006; fax (361) 3772004; e-mail pressestelle@landtag.thueringen.de; internet www.thueringen.de/tlt.

The composition of the Assembly, as a result of elections held on 13 June 2004, is as follows:

President of Assembly: Prof. Dr DAGMAR SCHIPANSKI (CDU).

Party	Seats
Christlich-Demokratische Union Deutschlands (CDU)	45
Partei des Demokratischen Sozialismus (PDS)*	28
Sozialdemokratische Partei Deutschlands (SPD)	15

*Restyled Die Linke in June 2007.

Election Commission

Bundeswahlleiter (Federal Returning Officer): Statistisches Bundesamt, 65180 Wiesbaden; tel. (611) 751; fax (611) 724000; e-mail bundeswahlleiter@destatis.de; internet www.bundeswahlleiter.de; Federal Returning Officer WALTER RADERMACHER (Pres., Federal Office of Statistics); Deputy Federal Returning Officer PETER WEIGL.

Political Organizations

Bündnis 90/Die Grünen (Alliance 90/Greens): Pl. vor dem Neuen Tor 1, 10115 Berlin; tel. (30) 284420; fax (30) 28442210; e-mail info@gruene.de; internet www.gruene.de; f. 1993; merger of Bündnis 90 (f. 1990, as an electoral political asscn of citizens' movements of the former GDR) and Die Grünen (f. 1980, largely composed of the membership of the Grüne Aktion Zukunft, the Grüne Liste, Umweltschutz and the Aktionsgemeinschaft Unabhängiger Deutscher, also including groups of widely varying political views); essentially left-wing party programme includes ecological issues, democratization of society at all levels, social justice, comprehensive disarmament; Chair. CLAUDIA ROTH, REINHARD BÜTIKOFER; Parliamentary Leaders RENATE KÜNAST, FRITZ KUHN; Sec.-Gen. STEFFI LEMKE.

Christlich-Demokratische Union Deutschlands/Christlich-Soziale Union Deutschlands (CDU/CSU) (Christian Democratic and Christian Social Union):

CDU: Konrad-Adenauer-Haus, Klingelhöferstr. 8, 10785 Berlin; tel. (30) 220700; fax (30) 22070111; e-mail info@cdu.de; internet www.cdu.de; f. 1945; became a federal party in 1950; advocates united action between Catholics and Protestants for rebuilding German life on a Christian-Democratic basis, while guaranteeing private property and the freedom of the individual, and for a 'free and equal Germany in a free, politically united and socially just Europe'; other objectives are to guarantee close ties with allies within NATO and the EU; c. 540,000 mems; Chair. Dr ANGELA MERKEL; Parliamentary Leader VOLKER KAUDER; Sec.-Gen. RONALD POFALLA.

CSU: Franz Josef Strauß-Haus, Nymphenburger Str. 64, 80335 München; tel. (89) 12430; fax (89) 1243299; e-mail info@csu-bayern.de; internet www.csu.de; f. 1946; Christian Social party, aiming for a free-market economy 'in the service of man's economic and intellectual freedom'; also combines national consciousness with support for a united Europe; 181,000 mems; Chair. ERWIN HUBER; Sec.-Gen. CHRISTINE HADERTHAUER.

Deutsche Kommunistische Partei (DKP) (German Communist Party): Hoffnungstr. 18, 45127 Essen; tel. (201) 1778890; fax (201) 17788929; e-mail pv@dkp-online.de; internet www.dkp.de; Chair. HEINZ STEHR.

Deutsche Volksunion (DVU) (German People's Union): Postfach 600464, 81204 München; tel. (89) 89608568; fax (89) 8341534; e-mail info@dvu.de; internet www.dvu.de; f. 1987; extreme right-wing; Chair. Dr GERHARD FREY.

Freie Demokratische Partei (FDP) (Free Democratic Party): Reinhardtstr. 14, 10117 Berlin; tel. (30) 28495820; fax (30) 28495822; e-mail fdp-point@fdp.de; internet www.fdp.de; f. 1948; represents democratic liberalism and makes the individual the focal point of the State and its laws and economy; in Aug. 1990 incorporated the three liberal parties of the former GDR—the Association of Free Democrats, the German Forum Party and the FDP; publishes Elde; c. 64,880 mems (Dec. 2006); Chair. Dr GUIDO WESTERWELLE; Sec.-Gen. DIRK NIEBEL.

Freie Demokratische Partei/Demokratische Volkspartei (FDP/DVP): Konrad Adenauer-Str. 12, 70173 Stuttgart; tel. (711) 2063625; fax (711) 2063610; e-mail post@fdp.landtag-bw.de; internet www.fdp-dvp-fraktion.de; f. 1948; Chair. Dr ULRICH NOLL.

Die Linke (Left Party): Karl-Liebknecht-Haus, Kleine Alexanderstr. 28, 10178 Berlin; tel. (30) 24009520; fax (30) 24009310; e-mail bundesgeschaeftsstelle@die-linke.de; internet www.die-linke.de; successor to the Sozialistische Einheitspartei Deutschlands (SED—Socialist Unity Party, f. 1946 as a result of the unification of the Social Democratic Party and the Communist Party in Eastern Germany), which had been the dominant political force in the GDR until late 1989; renamed Partei des Demokratischen Sozialismus Feb. 1990; restyled Linkspartei.PDS 2005; adopted present name 2007 following merger with Wahlalternative Arbeit und soziale Gerechtigkeit (WASG—Electoral Alternative Jobs and Social Justice); has renounced Stalinism, opposes fascism, right-wing extremism and xenophobia, advocates a socially and ecologically sustainable market economy with public, collective and private ownership of the means of production, opposes terrorism, supports international disarmament and peaceful solutions to international conflicts; Chair. Prof. LOTHAR BISKY, OSKAR LAFONTAINE.

Nationaldemokratische Partei Deutschlands (NPD) (National Democratic Party of Germany): Postfach 840157, 12531 Berlin; Seelenbinderstr. 42, 12555 Berlin; tel. (30) 650110; fax (30) 65011140; e-mail bgst@npd.de; internet www.npd.de; f. 1964; right-wing; 15,000 mems; youth organization Junge Nationaldemokraten (JN), 6,000 mems; Chair. UDO VOIGT; Sec.-Gen. PETER MARX.

Neues Forum (New Forum): Winsstr. 60, 10405 Berlin; tel. (30) 2479404; fax (30) 24725605; e-mail info@neuesforum.de; internet www.neuesforum.de; f. 1989; as a citizens' action group; played prominent role in democratic movement in former GDR; campaigns for peace, social justice and protection of the environment; Leaders SABINE SCHAAF, REINHARD SCHULT, KLAUS TONNDORF.

Die Republikaner (REP) (Republican Party): Berliner Str. 9, 13187 Berlin; tel. (1805) 737000; fax (1805) 737111; e-mail info@rep.de; internet www.rep.de; f. 1983; conservative right-wing; c. 15,000 mems; Chair. Dr ROLF SCHLIERER.

Sozialdemokratische Partei Deutschlands (SPD) (Social Democratic Party of Germany): Willy-Brandt-Haus, Wilhelmstr. 141, 10963 Berlin; tel. (30) 259910; fax (30) 25991410; e-mail parteivorstand@spd.de; internet www.spd.de; f. 1863; maintains that a vital democracy can be built only on the basis of social justice; advocates for the economy as much competition as possible, as much planning as necessary to protect the individual from uncontrolled

GERMANY

economic interests; favours a positive attitude to national defence, while supporting controlled disarmament; rejects any political ties with Communism; 548,491 mems (July 2007); Chair. KURT BECK; Parliamentary Leader Dr PETER STRUCK; Sec.-Gen. HUBERTUS HEIL. There are also numerous other small parties, none of which is represented in the Bundestag, covering all shades of the political spectrum and various regional interests.

Diplomatic Representation

EMBASSIES IN GERMANY

Afghanistan: Taunusstr. 3, Ecke Kronbergerstr. 5, 14193 Berlin; tel. (30) 2067350; fax (30) 2291510; e-mail info@botschaft-afghanistam.de; internet www.botschaft-afghanistan.de; Ambassador Prof. Dr MALIHA ZULFACAR.

Albania: Friedrichstr. 231, 10969 Berlin; tel. (30) 2593040; fax (30) 25931890; e-mail kanzlei@botschaft-albanien.de; internet www.botschaft-albanien.de; Ambassador GAZMEND TURDIU.

Algeria: Görschstr. 45–46, 13187 Berlin; tel. (30) 437370; fax (30) 48098716; e-mail info@algerische-botschaft.de; internet www.algerische-botschaft.de; Ambassador HOCINE MEGHAR.

Angola: Wallstr. 58, 10179 Berlin; tel. (30) 2408970; fax (30) 24089712; e-mail botschaft@botschaftangola.de; internet www.botschaftangola.de; Ambassador ALBERTO DO CARMO BENTO RIBEIRO.

Argentina: Kleiststr. 23–26, 10787 Berlin; tel. (30) 2266890; fax (30) 2291400; e-mail info@argentinische-botschaft.de; internet www.argentinische-botschaft.de; Chargé d'affaires a.i. MAGDALENA DOLORES SUSANA VON BECKH WIDMANSTETTER.

Armenia: Nussbaumallee 4, 14050 Berlin; tel. (30) 4050910; fax (30) 40509125; e-mail armgermanyembassy@mfa.am; Ambassador KARINE KAZINIAN.

Australia: Wallstr. 76–79, 10179 Berlin; tel. (30) 8800880; fax (30) 880088210; e-mail info.berlin@dfat.gov.au; internet www.germany.embassy.gov.au; Ambassador IAN FERGUSON KEMISH.

Austria: Stauffenbergstr. 1, 10785 Berlin; tel. (30) 202870; fax (30) 2290569; e-mail berlin-ob@bmeia.gv.at; internet www.oesterreichische-botschaft.de; Ambassador Dr CHRISTIAN PROSL.

Azerbaijan: Hubertusallee 43, 14193 Berlin; tel. (30) 2191613; fax (30) 21916152; e-mail office@azembassy.de; internet www.azembassy.de; Ambassador PARVIZ SHAHBAZOV.

Bahrain: Klingelhöfer Str. 7, 10785 Berlin; tel. (30) 86877777; fax (30) 86877788; Chargé d'affaires a.i. KHALIL IBRAHIM MUHAMMAD BUTARADA.

Bangladesh: Dovestr. 1, 5th Floor, 10587 Berlin; tel. (30) 3989750; fax (30) 39897510; e-mail bdootbn@aol.com; internet www.bangladeshembassy.de; Chargé d'affaires a.i. ZAKIR AHMED.

Belarus: Am Treptower Park, 12345 Berlin; tel. (30) 5363590; fax (30) 53635923; e-mail info@belarus-botschaft.de; internet www.belarus-botschaft.de; Ambassador VLADIMIR SKVORTSOV.

Belgium: Jägerstr. 52–53, 10117 Berlin; tel. (30) 206420; fax (30) 20642200; e-mail berlin@diplobel.org; internet www.diplomatie.be/berlin; Ambassador MARK GELEYN.

Benin: Englerallee 23, 14195 Berlin; tel. (30) 23631470; fax (30) 236314740; Ambassador ISSA KPARA.

Bolivia: Wichmannstr. 6, 10787 Berlin; tel. (30) 2639150; fax (30) 26391515; e-mail embajada.bolivia@berlin.de; internet www.bolivia.de; Ambassador WALTER PRUDENCIO MAGNE VÉLIZ.

Bosnia and Herzegovina: Ibsenstr. 14, 10439 Berlin; tel. (30) 81471210; fax (30) 81471211; Ambassador MITAR KUJUNDŽIĆ.

Brazil: Wallstr. 57, 10179 Berlin; tel. (30) 726280; fax (30) 72628320; e-mail brasil@brasemberlin.de; internet www.brasilianische-botschaft.de; Ambassador LUIZ FELIPE DE SEIXAS CORRÊA.

Brunei: Kronenstr. 55–58, 10117 Berlin; tel. (30) 2060760; fax (30) 20607666; e-mail berlin@brunei-embassy.de; Ambassador Dato' Paduka Haji ALI Haji HASSAN.

Bulgaria: Mauerstr. 11, 10117 Berlin; tel. (30) 2010922; fax (30) 2086838; e-mail info@botschaft-bulgarien.de; internet www.botschaft-bulgarien.de; Ambassador MEGLENA IVANOVA PLUGTSCHIEVA-ALEXANDROVA.

Burkina Faso: Karolingerpl. 10–11, 14052 Berlin; tel. (30) 30105990; fax (30) 301059920; e-mail embassy_burkina_faso@t-online.de; Ambassador XAVIER NIODOGO.

Burundi: Berliner Str. 36, 10715 Berlin; tel. (30) 2345670; fax (30) 23456720; e-mail info@burundi-embassy-berlin.com; internet www.burundi-embassy-berlin.de; Ambassador DOMITILLE BARANCIRA.

Cambodia: Benjamin-Vogelsdorf-Str., 13187 Berlin; tel. (30) 48637901; fax (30) 48637973; e-mail rec-berlin@t-online.de; internet www.kambodscha-botschaft.de; Ambassador WIDHYA CHEM.

Cameroon: Rheinallee 76, 53173 Bonn; tel. (228) 356038; fax (228) 359058; e-mail botschaftkamerun@yahoo.fr; Ambassador JEAN MELAGA.

Canada: Leipziger Pl. 17, 10117 Berlin; tel. (30) 203120; fax (30) 20312590; e-mail brlin@international.gc.ca; internet www.kanada-info.de; Ambassador PAUL DUBOIS.

Cape Verde: Stavangerstr. 16, 10439 Berlin; tel. (30) 20450955; fax (30) 20450966; e-mail info@embassy-capeverde.de; internet www.embassy-capeverde.de; Ambassador JORGE HOMERO TOLENTINO ARAÚJO.

Central African Republic: Johanniterstr. 19, 53113 Bonn; tel. (228) 233564; fax (228) 6195928; e-mail rca@botschaft-zentralafrika.de; internet www.botschaft-zentralafrika.de; Ambassador (vacant).

Chile: Mohrenstr. 42, 10117 Berlin; tel. (30) 7262035; fax (30) 726203603; e-mail comunicaciones@echilealemania.de; internet www.embajadaconsuladoschile.de; Ambassador ÁLVARO ROJAS MARÍN.

China, People's Republic: Märkisches Ufer 54, 10179 Berlin; tel. (30) 275880; fax (30) 27588221; e-mail chinesischebotschaft@debital.net; internet www.china-botschaft.de; Ambassador MA CANRONG.

Colombia: Kurfürstenstr. 84, 10787 Berlin; tel. (30) 2639610; fax (30) 26396125; e-mail info@botschaft-kolumbien.de; internet www.botschaft-kolumbien.de; Ambassador Dr MARÍA DORA VICTORIANA MEJÍA MARULANDA.

Congo, Democratic Republic: Im Meisengarten 133, 53179 Bonn; tel. (228) 858160; fax (228) 349989; Chargé d'affaires a.i. PIERRE YVON MALAMBA OSANG-A-BULL.

Congo, Republic: Grabbeallee 47, 13156 Berlin; tel. (30) 49400753; fax (30) 49918063; e-mail botschaftkongobrzv@thotmail.de; Chargé d'affaires a.i. SERGE MICHEL ODZOCKI.

Costa Rica: Dessauer Str. 28–29, 10963 Berlin; tel. (30) 26398990; fax (30) 26557210; e-mail emb@botschaft-costarica.de; internet www.botschaft-costarica.de; Ambassador Dr BERND NIEHAUS QUESADA.

Côte d'Ivoire: Schinkelstr. 10, 14193 Berlin; tel. (30) 8906960; fax (30) 890696206; e-mail ambic@t-online.de; internet www.ambaci.de; Chargé d'affaires a.i. SERGES GBA.

Croatia: Ahornstr. 4, 10787 Berlin; tel. (30) 21915514; fax (30) 23628965; e-mail info@kroatische-botschaft.de; internet de.mfa.hr; Ambassador Dr VESNA CVJETKOVIĆ KURELEC.

Cuba: Stavangerstr. 20, 10439 Berlin; tel. (30) 44717319; fax (30) 9164553; e-mail embacuba-berlin@t-online.de; internet www.botschaft-kuba.de; Ambassador GERARDO PEÑALVER PORTAL.

Cyprus: Wallstr. 27, 10179 Berlin; tel. (30) 3086830; fax (30) 27591454; e-mail info@botschaft-zypern.de; internet www.botschaft-zypern.de; Ambassador PANTELAKIS ELIADES.

Czech Republic: Wilhelmstr. 44, 10117 Berlin; tel. (30) 226380; fax (30) 2294033; e-mail berlin@embassy.mzv.cz; internet www.mfa.cz/berlin; Ambassador RUDOLF JINDRÁK.

Denmark: Rauchstr. 1, 10787 Berlin; tel. (30) 50502000; fax (30) 50502050; e-mail beramb@um.dk; internet www.ambberlin.um.dk; Ambassador CARSTEN SØNDERGAARD.

Dominican Republic: Dessauer Str. 28–29, 10963 Berlin; tel. (30) 25757760; fax (30) 25757761; e-mail embajadomal@t-online.de; Ambassador PEDRO LUCIANO VERGES CIMAN.

Ecuador: Joachimstaler Str. 10–12, 10719 Berlin; tel. (30) 8009695; fax (30) 800969699; e-mail alemania@embassy-ecuador.org; Ambassador HORACIO HERNÁN SEVILLA BORJA.

Egypt: Stauffenbergstr. 6–7, 10785 Berlin; tel. (30) 4775470; fax (30) 4771049; e-mail embassy@egyptian-embassy.de; internet www.egyptian-embassy.de; Ambassador MUHAMMAD ABD AL-HAY M. AL-ORABI.

El Salvador: Joachim-Karnatz-Allee 47, 10557 Berlin; tel. (30) 2064660; fax (30) 22488244; e-mail embasalvarfa@googlemail.com; internet www.botschaft-elsalvador.de; Ambassador EDGARDO CARLOS SUÁREZ MALLAGRAY.

Equatorial Guinea: Rohlfsstr. 17–19, 14195 Berlin; tel. (30) 88663877; fax (30) 88663879; e-mail botschaft@guinea-ecuatorial.de; internet www.botschaft-aequatorialguinea.de; Ambassador CÁNDIDO MUATETEMA RIVAS.

Eritrea: Stavangerstr. 18, 10439 Berlin; tel. (30) 4467460; fax (30) 44674621; e-mail embassyeritrea@t-online.de; internet www.botschaft-eritrea.de; Ambassador PETROS TSEGGAI ASGHEDOM.

Estonia: Hildebrandstr. 5, 10785 Berlin; tel. (30) 25460600; fax (30) 25460601; e-mail embassy.berlin@mfa.ee; internet www.estemb.de; Ambassador CLYDE KULL.

Ethiopia: Boothstr. 20A, 12207 Berlin; tel. (30) 772060; fax (30) 7720626; e-mail emb.ethiopia@t-online.de; internet www.aethiopien-botschaft.de; Ambassador KASSAHUN AYELE TESEMMA.

GERMANY

Finland: Rauchstr. 1, 10787 Berlin; tel. (30) 505030; fax (30) 5050333; e-mail sanomat.ber@formin.fi; internet www.finnland.de; Ambassador ERNST RENÉ ANSELM NYBERG.

France: Pariser Pl. 5, 10117 Berlin; tel. (30) 590039000; fax (30) 590039110; e-mail info@botschaft-frankreich.de; internet www.ambafrance-de.org; Ambassador BERNARD DE MONTFERRAND.

Gabon: Hohensteinerstr. 16, 14197 Berlin; tel. (30) 89733440; fax (30) 89733444; e-mail info@botschaft-gabun.de; internet www.botschaft-gabun.de; Ambassador JEAN-CLAUDE BOUYOBART.

Georgia: Heinrich-Mann-Str. 32, 13156 Berlin; tel. (30) 4849070; fax (30) 48490720; e-mail info@botschaftvongeorgien.de; internet www.botschaftvongeorgien.de; Ambassador LEVAN DUCHIDZE.

Ghana: Stavangerstr. 17 and 19, 10439 Berlin; tel. (30) 5471490; fax (30) 44674063; e-mail chancery@ghanaemberlin.de; internet www.ghanaemberlin.de; Ambassador GRANT OHEMENG KESSE.

Greece: Jägerstr. 55, 3rd Floor, 10117 Berlin; tel. (30) 206260; fax (30) 20626444; e-mail greekembassyberlin@t-online.de; internet www.griechenland-botschaft.de; Ambassador ANASTASSIOS KRIEKOUKIS.

Guatemala: Joachim-Karnatz-Allee 45–47, 10557 Berlin; tel. (30) 2064363; fax (30) 20643659; e-mail embaguate.alemania@t-online.de; internet www.botschaft-guatemala.de; Chargé d'affaires a.i. NELSON RAFAEL OLIVERO GARCIA.

Guinea: Jägerstr. 67–69, 10117 Berlin; tel. (30) 20074330; fax (30) 200743333; e-mail berlin@embaguinee.de; Ambassador ALEXANDRE CECE LOUA.

Haiti: Uhlandstr. 14, 10623 Berlin; tel. (30) 88554134; fax (30) 88554135; e-mail haibot@aol.com; Ambassador JEAN ROBERT SAGET.

Holy See: Lilienthalstr. 3A, 10965 Berlin; tel. (30) 616240; fax (30) 61624300; e-mail apostolische@nuntiatur.de; internet www.nuntiatur.de; Apostolic Nuncio Most Rev. JEAN-CLAUDE PÉRISSET (Titular Archbishop of Iustiniana Prima).

Honduras: Cuxhavenerstr. 14, 10555 Berlin; tel. (30) 39743711; fax (30) 39749712; e-mail embahonduras@ngi.de; Ambassador ROBERTO AUGUSTO MARTÍNEZ CASTAÑEDA.

Hungary: Unter den Linden 74–76, 10117 Berlin; tel. (30) 203100; fax (30) 2291314; e-mail infober@kum.hu; internet www.mfa.gov.hu/kulkepviselet/de; Ambassador Dr SÁNDOR PEISCH.

Iceland: Rauchstr. 1, 10787 Berlin; tel. (30) 50504000; fax (30) 50504300; e-mail icemb.berlin@utn.stjr.is; internet www.botschaft-island.de; Ambassador OLAFUR DAVIĐSSON.

India: Tiergartenstr. 17, 10785 Berlin; tel. (30) 257950; fax (30) 25795102; e-mail infowing@indianembassy.de; internet www.indianembassy.de; Ambassador MEERA SHANKAR.

Indonesia: Lehrter Str. 16–17, 10557 Berlin; tel. (30) 478070; fax (30) 44737142; internet www.botschaft-indonesien.de; Ambassador MAKMUR WIDODO.

Iran: Podbielskiallee 65–67, 14195 Berlin; tel. (30) 843530; fax (30) 54353535; e-mail iran.botschaft@t-online.de; internet berlin.mfa.gov.ir; Ambassador MUHAMMAD MEHDI AKHOUNDZADEH BASTI.

Iraq: Riemeisterstr. 20, 14169 Berlin; tel. (30) 814880; fax (30) 81488222; e-mail info@iraqiembassy-berlin.de; internet www.iraqiembassy-berlin.de; Ambassador ALAA A. HUSSAIN AL-HASHIMI.

Ireland: Friedrichstr. 200, 10117 Berlin; tel. (30) 220720; fax (30) 22072299; e-mail berlin@dfa.ie; Ambassador DAVID DONOGHUE.

Israel: Auguste-Viktoria-Str. 74–76, 14193 Berlin; tel. (30) 89045500; fax (30) 89045222; e-mail botschaft@israel.de; internet www.israel.de; Ambassador YORAM BEN ZEEV.

Italy: Hiroshimastr. 1, 10785 Berlin; tel. (30) 254400; fax (30) 25440116; e-mail segreteria.berlino@esteri.it; internet www.ambberlino.esteri.it; Ambassador ANTONIO PURI PURINI.

Jamaica: Schmargendorfer Str. 32, 12159 Berlin; tel. (30) 85994511; fax (30) 85994540; e-mail info@jamador.de; internet www.jamador.de; Ambassador JOY ELFREDA WHEELER.

Japan: Hiroshimastr. 6, 10785 Berlin; tel. (30) 210940; fax (30) 21094222; e-mail info@botschaft-japan.de; internet www.botschaft-japan.de; Ambassador TOSHIYUKI TAKANO.

Jordan: Heerstr. 201, 13595 Berlin; tel. (30) 36996051; fax (30) 36996011; e-mail jordan@jordanembassy.de; internet www.jordanembassy.de; Ambassador ISSA NASSER TAWFIQ AYYOUB.

Kazakhstan: Nordendstr. 14–17, 13156 Berlin; tel. (30) 47007111; fax (30) 47007125; e-mail info@botschaft-kaz.de; internet www.botschaft-kasachstan.de; Ambassador NURLAN ONZHANOV.

Kenya: Markgrafenstr. 63, 10969 Berlin; tel. (30) 2592660; fax (30) 25926650; e-mail office@kenyaembassyberlin.de; internet www.kenyaembassyberlin.de; Ambassador HARRY MUTUMA KATHURIMA.

Korea, Democratic People's Republic: Glinkastr. 5–7, 10117 Berlin; tel. (30) 2293189; fax (30) 2293191; Ambassador HONG CHANG IL.

Korea, Republic: Stülerstr. 8–10, 10787 Berlin; tel. (30) 260650; fax (30) 2606551; e-mail koremb-ge@mofat.go.kr; internet www.koreaemb.de; Ambassador JUNG-IL CHOI.

Kuwait: Griegstr. 5–7, 14193 Berlin; tel. (30) 8973000; fax (30) 89730010; e-mail info@kuwait-botschaft.de; internet www.kuwait-botschaft.de; Ambassador ABD AL-HAMID ABDULLAH AL-AWADHI.

Kyrgyzstan: Otto-Suhr-Allee 146, 10585 Berlin; tel. (30) 34781338; fax (30) 34781362; e-mail info@botschaft-kirgisien.de; internet www.botschaft-kirgisien.de; Ambassador MARATBEK BAKIEV.

Laos: Bismarckallee 2A, 14193 Berlin; tel. (30) 89060647; fax (30) 89060648; Ambassador BOUNTHONG VONGSALY.

Latvia: Reinerzstr. 40–41, 14193 Berlin; tel. (30) 82600222; fax (30) 82600233; e-mail embassy.germany@mfa.gov.lv; internet www.mfa.gov.lv/berlin; Ambassador Dr MĀRTIŅŠ VIRSIS.

Lebanon: Berliner Str. 127, 13187 Berlin; tel. (30) 4749860; fax (30) 47487858; e-mail lubnan@t-online.de; internet www.libanesische-botschaft.info; Chargé d'affaires a.i. RAMEZ DIMECHKIÉ.

Lesotho: Kurfürstenstr. 84, 10787 Berlin; tel. (30) 2575720; fax (30) 25757222; e-mail embleso@yahoo.com; Ambassador Dr MAKASE NYAPHISI.

Liberia: Kurfürstenstr. 84, 10787 Berlin; tel. (30) 26391194; Ambassador SEDIA MASSAQUOI-BANGOURA.

Libya: Podbielskiallee 42, 14195 Berlin; tel. (30) 2005960; fax (30) 20059699; e-mail info@libysche-botschaft.de; internet www.libysche-botschaft.de; Chargé d'affaires a.i. HASSAN A. H. MAAWAL.

Liechtenstein: Mohrenstr. 42, 10117 Berlin; tel. (30) 52000630; fax (30) 52000631; e-mail vertretung@ber.rep.llv.li; internet www.berlin.liechtenstein.li; Ambassador Prince STEFAN OF LIECHTENSTEIN.

Lithuania: Charitéstr. 9, 10117 Berlin; tel. (30) 8906810; fax (30) 89068115; e-mail info@botschaft-litauen.de; internet de.mfa.lt; Ambassador EVALDAS IGNATAVIČIUS.

Luxembourg: Klingelhöfer Str. 7, 10785 Berlin; tel. (30) 2639570; fax (30) 26395727; e-mail berlin.amb@mae.etat.lu; Ambassador JEAN AUGUSTE JOSEPH WELTER.

Macedonia, former Yugoslav republic: Koenigsallee 2–4, 14193 Berlin; tel. (30) 89069522; fax (30) 89541194; e-mail amba.berlin@t-online.de; Ambassador GJORGJI FILIPOV.

Madagascar: Seepromenade 92, 14612 Falkensee (Brandenburg); tel. (3322) 23140; fax (3322) 231429; e-mail info@botschaft-madagaskar.de; internet www.botschaft-madagaskar.de; Ambassador ALPHONSE SEM RALISON.

Malawi: Westfälische Str. 86, 10709 Berlin; tel. (30) 8431540; fax (30) 84315430; e-mail malawibonn@aol.com; internet www.malawi-botschaft.de; Ambassador ISSAC CHIKWEKWERE LAMBA.

Malaysia: Klingelhöferstr. 6, 10785 Berlin; tel. (30) 8857490; fax (30) 88574950; e-mail info@malemb.de; internet www.malemb.de; Ambassador ZAKARIA BIN SULONG.

Mali: Kurfürstendamm 72, 10709 Berlin; tel. (30) 3199883; fax (30) 31998848; e-mail ambmali@1019freenet.de; internet www.ambamali.de; Ambassador FATOUMATA SIRE DIAKITE.

Malta: Klingelhöfer Str. 7, 10785 Berlin; tel. (30) 2639110; fax (30) 26391123; e-mail maltaembassy.berlin@gov.mt; Ambassador JOHN PAUL GRECH.

Mauritania: Kommandantenstr. 80, 10117 Berlin; tel. (30) 2065863; fax (30) 20674750; e-mail ambarim.berlin@gmx.de; Ambassador MAMADOU DIAKITÉ.

Mauritius: Kurfürstenstr. 84, 10787 Berlin; tel. (30) 2639360; fax (30) 26558323; e-mail berlin@mauritius-embassy.de; internet www.mauritius-embassy.de; Ambassador MARIE GHISELAINE HENRISON.

Mexico: Klingelhöfer Str. 3, 10785 Berlin; tel. (30) 2693230; fax (30) 269323700; e-mail mail@embamexale.de; internet www.embamex.de; Ambassador JORGE CASTRO-VALLE KUEHNE.

Moldova: Gotlandstr. 16, 10439 Berlin; tel. (30) 44652970; fax (30) 44652972; e-mail office@botschaft-moldau.de; internet www.botschaft-moldau.de; Ambassador IGOR CORMAN.

Monaco: Klingelhöferstr. 7, 10785 Berlin; tel. (30) 2639033; fax (30) 2690344; e-mail ambassademonaco@aol.com; Ambassador CLAUDE JOËL GIORDAN.

Mongolia: Dietzgenstr. 31, 13156 Berlin; tel. (30) 4748060; fax (30) 47480616; e-mail mongolbot@aol.com; internet www.botschaft-mongolei.de; Ambassador TUVDENDORJ GALBAATAR.

Montenegro: Dessauerstr. 28–29, 10963 Berlin; tel. (30) 25291996; fax (30) 25292334; Chargé d'affaires a.i. ABID CRNOVRŠANIN.

Morocco: Niederwallstr. 39, 10117 Berlin; tel. (30) 2061240; fax (30) 20612420; e-mail marokko-botschaft@t-online.de; internet www.maec.gov.ma/berlin; Ambassador MUHAMMAD RACHAD BOUHLAL.

Mozambique: Stromstr. 47, 10551 Berlin; tel. (30) 39876506; fax (30) 39876503; e-mail emoza@aol.com; Ambassador CARLOS DOS SANTOS.

GERMANY

Myanmar: Thielallee 19, 14195 Berlin; tel. (30) 2061570; fax (30) 20615720; e-mail info@botschaft-myanmar.de; internet www.botschaft-myanmar.de; Ambassador U TIN WIN.

Namibia: Wichmannstr. 5, 10787 Berlin; tel. (30) 2540950; fax (30) 25409555; e-mail namibia@home.ivm.de; internet www.namibia-botschaft.de; Ambassador Prof. PETER KATJAVIVI.

Nepal: Guerickestr. 27, 2nd Floor, 10587 Berlin; tel. (30) 34359920; fax (30) 34359906; e-mail neberlin@t-online.de; internet www.nepalembassy-germany.com; Ambassador MADAN KUMAR BHATTARAI.

Netherlands: Klosterstr. 50, 10179 Berlin; tel. (30) 209560; fax (30) 20956441; e-mail nlgovbln@bln.nlamb.de; internet www.niederlandeweb.de; Ambassador Dr PETER PAUL VAN WULFFTEN PALTHE.

New Zealand: Atrium, Friedrichstr. 60, 10117 Berlin; tel. (30) 206210; fax (30) 20621114; e-mail nzembassy.berlin@t-online.de; internet www.nzembassy.com/germany; Ambassador ALAN HOWARD COOK.

Nicaragua: Joachim-Karnatz-Allee 45, 10557 Berlin; tel. (30) 2064380; fax (30) 22487891; e-mail embajada.berlin@embanic.de; Chargé d'affaires a.i. KARLA LUZETTE BETETA BRENES.

Niger: Machnower Str. 24, 14165 berlin; tel. (30) 80589660; fax (30) 80589662; e-mail ambaniger@t-online.de; Ambassador DJIBO ALI AMINA BAZINDRE.

Nigeria: Neue Jakobstr. 4, 10179 Berlin; tel. (30) 212300; fax (30) 21230212; e-mail info@nigeriaembassygermany.org; internet www.nigeriaembassygermany.org; Ambassador ABDULKADIR BIN RIMDAP.

Norway: Rauchstr. 1, 10787 Berlin; tel. (30) 505050; fax (30) 505055; e-mail emb.berlin@mfa.no; internet www.norwegen.no; Ambassador SVEN SVEDMAN.

Oman: Clayallee 82, 14195 Berlin; tel. (30) 84416970; fax (30) 81005199; Ambassador KHALIFA ALI ISSA AL-HARTHI.

Pakistan: Schaperstr. 29, 10719 Berlin; tel. (30) 212440; fax (30) 21244210; e-mail pakemb.berlin@t-online.de; Ambassador SHAHID AHMAD KAMAL.

Panama: Joachim-Karnatz-Allee 45, 10557 Berlin; tel. (30) 22605811; fax (30) 22605812; e-mail panaemba@t-online.de; Ambassador DARÍO E. CHIRÚ OCHOA.

Paraguay: Hardenbergstr. 12, 10623 Berlin; tel. (30) 31998612; fax (30) 31998617; e-mail embapyde@t-online.de; Ambassador LILIANE LEBRON DE WENGER.

Peru: Mohrenstr. 42, 10117 Berlin; tel. (30) 2064103; fax (30) 20641077; e-mail gabinete@embaperu.de; internet www.botschaft-peru.de; Ambassador Prof. Dr FEDERICO AUGUSTO KAUFFMANN DOIG.

Philippines: Uhlandstr. 97, 10715 Berlin; tel. (30) 8649500; fax (30) 8732551; e-mail info@philippine-embassy.de; internet www.philippine-embassy.de; Ambassador DELIA DOMINGO-ALBERT.

Poland: Lassenstr. 19–21, 14193 Berlin; tel. (30) 223130; fax (30) 2213155; e-mail info@botschaft-polen.de; internet www.berlin.polemb.net; Ambassador Dr MAREK WŁADYSŁAW PRAWDA.

Portugal: Zimmerstr. 56, 10117 Berlin; tel. (30) 590063500; fax (30) 590063600; e-mail mail@botschaftportugal.de; internet www.botschaftportugal.de; Ambassador JOSÉ CAETANO DE CAMPOS ANDRADA DA COSTA PEREIRA.

Qatar: Hagenstr. 56, 14193 Berlin; tel. (30) 862060; fax (30) 86206150; e-mail berlin@mofa.gov.qa; Ambassador SALEH MUHAMMAD SALEH AN-NASIF.

Romania: Dorotheenstr. 62–66, 10117 Berlin; tel. (30) 21239202; fax (30) 21239399; e-mail office@rumaenische-botschaft.de; internet berlin.mae.ro; Ambassador BOGDAN MAZURU.

Russia: Unter den Linden 63–65, 10117 Berlin; tel. (30) 2291110; fax (30) 2299397; e-mail info@russische-botschaft.de; internet www.russische-botschaft.de; Ambassador VLADIMIR V. KOTENEV.

Rwanda: Jägerstr. 67–69, 10117 Berlin; tel. (30) 20916590; fax (30) 209165959; e-mail info@rwanda-botschaft.de; internet www.rwanda-botschaft.de; Ambassador EUGENE RICHARD GASANA.

Saudi Arabia: Kurfürstendamm 63, 10787 Berlin; tel. (30) 889250; fax (30) 88925179; Ambassador Prof. Dr OSAMA ABD AL-MAJID ALI SHOBOKSHI.

Senegal: Dessauerstr. 28–29, 10963 Berlin; tel. (30) 8562190; fax (30) 85621921; internet www.botschaft-senegal.de; Ambassador CHEIKH SYLLA.

Serbia: Taubertstr. 18, 14193 Berlin; tel. (30) 8957700; fax (30) 8252206; e-mail info@botschaft-smg.de; internet www.konzulatiscg.de; Ambassador OGNJEN PRIBIĆEVIĆ.

Sierra Leone: Rheinallee 20, 53173 Bonn; tel. (228) 352001; fax (228) 364269; e-mail secretariat@sierraleone-embassy.de; internet www.sierraleone-embassy.de; Ambassador FODAY MOHAMED DURAMANY SEISAY.

Singapore: Friedrichstr. 200, 10117 Berlin; tel. (30) 2263430; fax (30) 22634355; e-mail singemb_ber@sgmfa.gov.sg; internet www.mfa.gov.sg/berlin; Ambassador A. SELVERAJAH.

Slovakia: Friedrichstr. 60, 10117 Berlin; tel. (30) 8892620; fax (30) 88926222; e-mail presse@botschaft-slowakei.de; internet www.berlin.mfa.sk; Ambassador IVAN KORČOK.

Slovenia: Hausvogteipl. 3–4, 10117 Berlin; tel. (30) 2061450; fax (30) 20614570; e-mail vbn@mzz-dkp.gov.si; Ambassador DRAGOLJUBA BENČINA.

South Africa: Tiergartenstr. 18, 10785 Berlin; tel. (30) 220730; fax (30) 22073190; e-mail berlin.info@foreign.gov.za; internet www.suedafrika.org; Chargé d'affaires a.i. GEORGE HENRY JOHANNES.

Spain: Lichtensteinallee 1, 10787 Berlin; tel. (30) 2540070; fax (30) 25799557; e-mail embespde@mail.mae.es; internet www.maec.es/subwebs/embajadas/berlin; Ambassador GABRIEL BUSQUETS APARICIO.

Sri Lanka: Niklasstr. 19, 14163 Berlin; tel. (30) 80909749; fax (30) 80909757; e-mail info@srilanka-botschaft.de; internet www.srilanka-botschaft.de; Ambassador TIKIRI BANDARA MADUWEGEDERA.

Sudan: Kurfürstendamm 151, 10709 Berlin; tel. (30) 8906980; fax (30) 89409693; e-mail poststelle@sudan-embassy.de; internet www.botschaftsudan.de; Ambassador Dr BAHA AD-DIN HANAFI MANSOUR WAHEESH.

Sweden: Rauchstr. 1, 10787 Berlin; tel. (30) 505060; fax (30) 50506789; e-mail ambassaden.berlin@foreign.ministry.se; internet www.swedenabroad.com/berlin; Ambassador RUTH EVELYN JACOBY.

Switzerland: Otto-von-Bismarck-Allee 4A, 10557 Berlin; tel. (30) 3904000; fax (30) 3911030; e-mail ber.vertretung@eda.admin.ch; internet www.eda.admin.ch/berlin; Ambassador Dr CHRISTIAN BLICKENSTORFER.

Syria: Rauchstr. 25, 10787 Berlin; tel. (30) 501770; fax (30) 50177311; e-mail info@syrianembassy.de; internet www.syrianembassy.de; Ambassador HUSSEIN OMRAN.

Tajikistan: Otto-Suhr-Allee 84, 10585 Berlin; tel. (30) 3479300; fax (30) 34793029; e-mail info@botschaft-tadschikistan.de; Ambassador IMOMUDIN M. SATTOROV.

Tanzania: Eschenallee 11, 14050 Berlin; tel. (30) 3030800; fax (30) 30308020; e-mail info@tanzania-gov.de; internet www.tanzania-gov.de; Ambassador AHMADA RWEYEMAMU NGEMERA.

Thailand: Lepsiusstr. 64–66, 12163 Berlin; tel. (30) 794810; fax (30) 79481511; e-mail general@thaiembassy.de; internet www.thaiembassy.de; Ambassador SORAYOUTH PROMPOJ.

Togo: Grabbeallee 43, 13156 Berlin; tel. (30) 49908968; fax (30) 49908967; e-mail bbotschafttogo@web.de; internet www.botschaft-togo.de; Ambassador ESSOHANAM COMLA PAKA.

Tunisia: Lindenallee 16, 14050 Berlin; tel. (30) 3641070; fax (30) 30820683; Ambassador MONCEF BEN ABDALLAH.

Turkey: Rungestr. 9, 10179 Berlin; tel. (30) 275850; fax (30) 27590915; e-mail turk.em.berlin@t-online.de; internet www.tuerkischebotschaft.de; Ambassador MEHMET ALI IRTEMÇELIK.

Turkmenistan: Langobardenallee 14, 14052 Berlin; tel. (30) 30102452; fax (30) 30102453; e-mail info@botschaft-turkmenistan@t-online.de; Ambassador BERDYMURAT REDJEPOV.

Uganda: Axel-Springer-Str. 54A, 10117 Berlin; tel. (30) 24047556; fax (30) 24047557; e-mail ugembassy@yahoo.de; Ambassador NYINE SAMSON BITAHWA.

Ukraine: Albrechtstr. 26, 10117 Berlin; tel. (30) 288870; fax (30) 28887163; e-mail ukremb@t-online.de; internet www.mfa.gov.ua/germany; Ambassador IHOR DOLHOV.

United Arab Emirates: Hiroshimastr. 18–20, 10787 Berlin; tel. (30) 516516; fax (30) 51651900; e-mail uae@uaeembassy.de; internet www.uae-embassy.de; Ambassador MUHAMMAD AHMAD AL-MAHMUD.

United Kingdom: Wilhelmstr. 70–71, 10117 Berlin; tel. (30) 204570; fax (30) 20457594; e-mail info@britischebotschaft.de; internet www.britischebotschaft.de; Ambassador Sir MICHAEL ARTHUR.

USA: Neustädtische Kirchestr. 4–5, 10117 Berlin; tel. (30) 2385174; fax (30) 83051215; internet germany.usembassy.gov; Ambassador WILLIAM ROBERT TIMKEN, Jr.

Uruguay: Budapester Str. 39, 10787 Berlin; tel. (30) 2639016; fax (30) 26390170; e-mail urubrande@t-online.de; Ambassador PELAYO JOAQUÍN DÍAZ MUGUERZA.

Uzbekistan: Perleberger Str. 62, 10559 Berlin; tel. (30) 3940980; fax (30) 39409862; e-mail botschaft@uzbekistan.de; internet www.uzbekistan.de; Ambassador BAKHTIYAR GULYAMOV.

Venezuela: Schillstr. 9–10, 10785 Berlin; tel. (30) 8322400; fax (30) 83224020; e-mail embavenez.berlin@botschaft-venezuela.de; internet www.botschaft-venezuela.de; Ambassador BLANCA NIEVES PORTOCARRERO.

GERMANY

Viet Nam: Elsenstr. 3, 12435 Berlin; tel. (30) 53630108; fax (30) 53630200; e-mail info@vietnambotschaft.org; internet www.vietnambotschaft.org; Ambassador Duc Mau Tran.

Yemen: Budapester Str. 37, 10787 Berlin; tel. (30) 8973050; fax (30) 89730562; e-mail info@botschaft-jemen.de; internet www.botschaft-jemen.de; Ambassador Dr Muhammad Lutf Muhammad al-Eryani.

Zambia: Axel-Springer Str. 54A, 10117 Berlin; tel. (30) 2062940; fax (30) 20629419; e-mail botschaftvonsambia@t-online.de; internet www.sambia-botschaft.de; Ambassador Gen. (retd) Godwin Kingsley Chinkuli.

Zimbabwe: Kommandantenstr. 80, 10117 Berlin; tel. (30) 2062263; fax (30) 20455062; e-mail zimberlin@t-online.de; Ambassador Cuthbert Zhakata.

Judicial System

Justice is administered in accordance with the federal structure through the courts of the Federation and the Länder, as well as the Federal Constitutional Court and the Constitutional Courts of the Länder. Judges are independent and responsible to the law. They are not removable except by the decision of a court. One-half of the judges of the Federal Constitutional Court are elected by the Bundestag and the other half by the Bundesrat. A committee for the selection of judges participates in the appointment of judges of the Superior Federal Courts.

FEDERAL CONSTITUTIONAL COURT

Bundesverfassungsgericht

Postfach 1771, 76006 Karlsruhe; Schlossbezirk 3, 76131 Karlsruhe; tel. (721) 91010; fax (721) 9101382; e-mail bverfg@bundesverfassungsgericht.de; internet www.bundesverfassungsgericht.de.

President: Prof. Dr Hans-Jürgen Papier.

Vice-President: Prof. Dr Winfried Hassemer.

Director: Dr Elke Luise Barnstedt.

Judges of the First Senate: Dr Christine Hohmann-Dennhardt, Dr Wolfgang Hoffmann-Riem, Prof. Dr Brun-Otto Bryde, Dr Reinhard Gaier, Prof. Dr Michael Eichberger, Wilhelm Schluckebier, Prof. Dr Ferdinand Kirchhof.

Judges of the Second Senate: Prof. Dr Siegfried Bross, Prof. Dr Lerke Osterloh, Prof. Dr Udo di Fabio, Dr Rudolf Mellinghoff, Prof. Dr Gertrude Lübbe-Wolff, Dr Michael Gerhardt, Prof. Herbert Landau.

SUPERIOR FEDERAL COURTS

Bundesarbeitsgericht
(Federal Labour Court)

Hugo-Preuss-Pl. 1, 99084 Erfurt; tel. (361) 26360; fax (361) 26362000; internet www.bundesarbeitsgericht.de.

President: Ingrid Schmidt.

Vice-President: Hans-Jürgen Dörner.

Bundesgerichtshof
(Federal Court of Justice)

Herrenstr. 45A, 76133 Karlsruhe; tel. (721) 1590; fax (721) 1592512; e-mail poststelle@bgh.bund.de; internet www.bundesgerichtshof.de.

President: Prof. Dr Klaus Tolksdorf.

Vice-President: Dr Gerda Müller.

Presidents of the Senate: Prof. Dr Joachim Bornkamm, Prof. Dr Wulf Goette, Wolfgang Schlick, Wilfried Terno, Dr Wolf-Dieter Dressler, Wolfgang Ball, Dr Gero Fischer, Dr Klaus Mellulis, Gerd Nobbe, Dr Meo-Micaela Hahne, Armin Nack, Dr Ingeborg Tepperwien, Dr Ruth Rissing-van Saan, Clemens Basdorf.

Federal Prosecutor-General: Monika Harms.

Federal Prosecutors: Dr Karl Heinz Schnarr, Volkhard Wache, Dr Hans-Joachim Kurth.

Bundessozialgericht
(Federal Social Court)

Graf-Bernadotte-Pl. 5, 34119 Kassel; tel. (561) 3107460; fax (561) 3107475; e-mail presse@bsg.bund.de; internet www.bsg.bund.de.

President: Peter Masuch.

Vice-President: Dr Ruth Wetzel-Steinwedel.

Bundesverwaltungsgericht
(Federal Administrative Court)

Postfach 100854, 04008 Leipzig; Simsonpl. 1, 04107 Leipzig; tel. (341) 20070; fax (341) 20071000; e-mail pressestelle@bverwg.bund.de; internet www.bverwg.de.

President: Dr Marion Eckertz-Höfer.

Vice-President: Michael Hund.

Presidents of the Senate: Dr Horst Säcker, Prof. Dr Hans-Joachim Driehaus, Dr Stefan Paetow, Hartmut Albers, Dr Franz Bardenhewer, Prof. Dr Rainer Pietzner, Wolfgang Sailer, Christoph Gödel, Dr Ulrich Storost.

Bundesfinanzhof
(Federal Financial Court)

Postfach 860240, 81629 München; Ismaninger Str. 109, 81675 München; tel. (89) 92310; fax (89) 9231201; e-mail bundesfinanzhof@bfh.bund.de; internet www.bundesfinanzhof.de.

President: Wolfgang Spindler.

Vice-President: Hermann-Ulrich Viskorf.

Presidents of the Senate: Dr Gerhard Mösslang, Heide Boeker, Christian Herden, Dr Hans Joachim Herrmann, Dr Georg Grube, Dr Dietmar Gosch, Monika Völlmeke, Dr Klaus-Peter Müller-Eiselt, Prof. Dr Hans-Joachim Kanzler, Prof. Dr Heinrich Weber-Grellet, Dr Suse Martin.

Religion

CHRISTIANITY

Arbeitsgemeinschaft Christlicher Kirchen in Deutschland (Council of Christian Churches in Germany): Postfach 900617, 60446 Frankfurt a.M.; Ludolfusstr. 2–4, 60487 Frankfurt a.M.; tel. (69) 2470270; fax (69) 24702730; e-mail info@ack-oec.de; internet www.oekumene-ack.de; 23 affiliated Churches, including the Roman Catholic Church and the Orthodox Church in Germany.

The Roman Catholic Church

Germany comprises seven archdioceses and 20 dioceses. At 31 December 2005 there were an estimated 25,926,788 adherents (about 32% of the population).

Bishops' Conference

Deutsche Bischofskonferenz, Postfach 2962, 53019 Bonn; Kaiserstr. 161, 53113 Bonn; tel. (228) 103290; fax (228) 103299; e-mail sekretariat@dbk.de; Pres. Dr Robert Zollitsch (Archbishop of Freiburg im Breisgau); Sec. Pater Dr Hans Langendörfer.

Archbishop of Bamberg: Prof. Dr Ludwig Schick, Dompl. 3, 96049 Bamberg; tel. (951) 5020; fax (951) 502250.

Archbishop of Berlin: Cardinal Georg Sterzinsky, Postfach 040856, 10064 Berlin; tel. (30) 326840; fax (30) 32684276.

Archbishop of Freiburg im Breisgau: Dr Robert Zollitsch, Herrenstr. 9, 79098 Freiburg i. Br.; tel. (761) 21880; fax (761) 2188505; e-mail erzbischof@ordinariat-freiburg.de; internet www.erzbistum-freiburg.de.

Archbishop of Hamburg: Dr Werner Thissen, Postfach 101925, 20013 Hamburg; Danzigerstr. 52A, 20099 Hamburg; tel. (40) 248770; fax (40) 24877233; e-mail brune@egv-erzbistum-hh.de; internet www.erzbistum-hamburg.de.

Archbishop of Köln: Cardinal Dr Joachim Meisner, Generalvikariat, Marzellenstr. 32, 50668 Köln; tel. (221) 16420; fax (221) 16421700.

Archbishop of München and Freising: Dr Reinhard Marx, Postfach 100551, 80079 München; Rochsusstr. 5–7, 80333 München; tel. (89) 21370; fax (89) 21371478.

Archbishop of Paderborn: Hans-Josef Becker, Erzbischöfliches Generalvikariat, Dompl. 3, 33098 Paderborn; tel. (5251) 1250; fax (5251) 1251470.

Commissariat of German Bishops—Catholic Office: Postfach 040660, 10063 Berlin; Hannoversche Str. 5, 10115 Berlin; tel. (30) 288780; fax (30) 28878108; e-mail post@kath-buero.de; represents the German Conference of Bishops before the Federal Govt and international institutions on political issues; Leader Prälat Dr Karl Jüsten.

Central Committee of German Catholics: Hochkreuzallee 246, 53175 Bonn; tel. (228) 382970; fax (228) 3829744; e-mail info@zdk.de; internet www.zdk.de; f. 1868; represents Catholic laymen and lay-organizations in Germany; Pres. Prof. Dr Hans Joachim Meyer; Gen. Sec. Dr Stefan Vesper.

GERMANY

Evangelical (Protestant) Churches

In 2005 the Evangelische Kirche in Deutschland, which includes the Lutheran, Uniate and Reformed Protestant Churches, had some 25m. members, amounting to about 30.8% of the population.

Evangelische Kirche in Deutschland (EKD) (Evangelical Church in Germany): Herrenhäuser Str. 12, 30419 Hannover; tel. (511) 27960; fax (511) 2796707; e-mail presse@ekd.de; internet www.ekd.de; the governing bodies of the EKD are its Synod of 120 clergy and lay members, which meets at regular intervals, the Conference of member churches, and the Council, composed of 15 elected members; the EKD has an ecclesiastical secretariat of its own (the Evangelical Church Office), including a special office for foreign relations; Chair. of the Council Right Rev. Prof. Dr WOLFGANG HUBER; Pres. of the Office Dr HERMANN BARTH.

Synod of the EKD: Herrenhäuser Str. 12, 30419 Hannover; tel. (511) 2796114; fax (511) 2796707; e-mail synode@ekd.de; Pres. BARBARA RINKE.

Deutscher Evangelischer Kirchentag (German Evangelical Church Convention): Postfach 1555, 36005 Fulda; Magdeburger Str. 59, 36037 Fulda; tel. (661) 969500; fax (661) 9695090; e-mail fulda@kirchentag.de; internet www.kirchentag.de; Pres. (vacant); Gen. Sec. Dr ELLEN VEBERSCHÄR.

Churches and Federations within the EKD:

Union Evangelischer Kirchen in der EKD (UEK): Jebensstr. 3, 10623 Berlin; tel. (30) 310010; fax (30) 31001200; e-mail postfach@kirchenkanzlei.de; internet www.uek-online.de; f. 2003; merger of Arnoldshainer Konferenz and Evangelische Kirche der Union; union of 14 regional churches (11 United, two Reformed and one Lutheran) with approx. 13.4m. mems; promotes unity among churches in the EKD; Chair. Vollkonferenz and Presidium Bishop Dr ULRICH FISCHER (Evangelical Church of Baden); Vice-Chairs CHRISTIAN DRÄGERT (Evangelical Church in the Rhineland), Dr HANS-WILHELM PIETZ (Evangelical Church in the Silesian Oberlausitz); Pres. of Administration Dr WILHELM HÜFFMEIER.

Bremen Evangelical Church: Postfach 106929, Franziuseck 2–4, 28199 Bremen; tel. (421) 55970; Pres. BRIGITTE BOEHME.

Church of Lippe: Leopoldstr. 27, 32756 Detmold; tel. (5231) 97660; fax (5231) 976850; e-mail oeff@lippische-landeskirche.de; internet www.lippische-landeskirche.de; Landessuperintendent Dr MARTIN DUTZMANN.

Evangelical Church in Baden: Postfach 2269, 76010 Karlsruhe; Blumenstr. 1, 76133 Karlsruhe; tel. (721) 91750; fax (721) 9175550; e-mail info@ekiba.de; internet www.ekiba.de; Landesbischof Dr ULRICH FISCHER.

Evangelical Church in Berlin-Brandenburg schlesiche Oberlausitz: Georgenkirchstr. 69/70, 10249 Berlin; tel. (30) 2434400; fax (30) 24344500; e-mail info@ekbo.de; internet www.ekbo.de; Bischof Prof. Dr WOLFGANG HUBER.

Evangelical Church in Hessen and Nassau: Pauluspl. 1, 64285 Darmstadt; tel. (6151) 4050; fax (6151) 405220; e-mail info@ekhn.de; internet www.ekhn.de; Pres. Prof. Dr PETER STEINACKER.

Evangelical Church in the Rhineland: Postfach 300339, 40403 Düsseldorf; Hans-Böckler-Str. 7, 40476 Düsseldorf; tel. (211) 45620; fax (211) 4562490; e-mail pressestelle@ekir.de; internet www.ekir.de; Pres. NIKOLAUS SCHNEIDER.

Evangelical Church of Kurhessen-Waldeck: Postfach 410260, 34114 Kassel-Wilhelmshöhe; Wilhelmshöher Allee 330, 34131 Kassel; tel. (561) 93780; fax (561) 9378400; e-mail landeskirchenamt@ekkw.de; internet www.ekkw.de; Bischof Prof. Dr MARTIN HEIN.

Evangelical Church of the Palatinate: Dompl. 5, 67346 Speyer; tel. (6232) 6670; fax (6232) 667228; e-mail kirchenpraesident@evkirchepfalz.de; internet www.evpfalz.de; Pres. EBERHARD CHERDRON.

Evangelical Church of Westfalen: Altstädter Kirchpl. 5, 33602 Bielefeld; tel. (521) 5940; fax (521) 594129; e-mail landeskirchenamt@lka.ekvw.de; internet www.ekvw.de; Präses ALFRED BUSS.

Evangelical-Lutheran Church in Württemberg: Postfach 101342, 70012 Stuttgart; tel. (711) 21490; fax (711) 2149236; e-mail komm.emh@elk.wue.de; internet www.elk-wue.de; Landesbischof FRANK OTFRIED JULY.

Reformierter Bund (Reformed Alliance): Vogelsangstr. 20, 42109 Wuppertal; tel. (202) 755111; fax (202) 754202; e-mail info@reformierter-bund.de; f. 1884; unites the Reformed Territorial Churches and Congregations of Germany (with an estimated 2m. mems). The central body of the Reformed League is the 'Moderamen', the elected representation of the various Reformed Churches and Congregations; Moderator Rev. PETER BUKOWSKI; Gen. Sec. Rev. HERMANN SCHAEFER.

Vereinigte Evangelisch-Lutherische Kirche Deutschlands (VELKD) (The United Evangelical-Lutheran Church of Germany): Postfach 210220, 30419 Hannover; Herrenhäuserstr. 12, 30419 Hannover; tel. (511) 27960; fax (511) 2796182; e-mail zentrale@velkd.de; internet www.velkd.de; f. 1948; 10.4m. mems; unites all but three of the Lutheran territorial Churches within the Evangelical Church in Germany; Presiding Bishop Landesbischof Dr JOHANNES FRIEDRICH (Munich).

Evangelical-Lutheran Church in Bavaria: Meiserstr. 11–13, 80333 München; tel. (89) 55950; fax (89) 5595444; e-mail poep@elkb.de; internet www.bayern-evangelisch.de; Landesbischof Dr JOHANNES FRIEDRICH.

Evangelical-Lutheran Church of Hannover: Haarstr. 6, 30169 Hannover; tel. (511) 5635830; fax (511) 56358311; e-mail landesbischoefin@evlka.de; internet www.evlka.de; Landesbischöfin Dr MARGOT KÄSSMANN.

Evangelical-Lutheran Church of North Elbe: Bischof Dr HANS CHRISTIAN KNUTH (Plessenstr. 5a, 24837 Schleswig; tel. (4621) 22056; fax (4621) 22194); Bischof BÖRBEL VON WARLENBERG-POFLER (Bädenstr. 3–5, 23564 Lübeck; tel. (451) 790201); Bischöfin MARIA JEPSEN (20457 Hamburg, Neue Burg 1; tel. (40) 373050); Pres. of North Elbian Church Administration Bischöfin BÄRBEL WARTENBERG-POTTER.

Evangelical-Lutheran Church of Schaumburg-Lippe: Herderstr. 27, 31675 Bückeburg; tel. (5722) 9600; e-mail lka@landeskirche-schaumburg-lippe.de; Landesbischof JÜRGEN JOHANNESDOTTER.

Also affiliated to the EKD:

Bund Evangelisch-Reformierter Kirchen (Association of Evangelical Reformed Churches): Wieblingenweg 6, 38112 Braunschweig; tel. (531) 312640; e-mail dresler-krommingen@reformierte.de; Chair. Präses SABINE DRESSLER-KROMMINGA.

Evangelical-Lutheran Church in Braunschweig: Dietrich-Bonhoeffer-Str. 1, 38300 Wolfenbüttel; tel. (5331) 8020; fax (5331) 802707; e-mail info@luth-braunschweig.de; internet www.landeskirche-braunschweig.de; Landesbischof Dr FRIEDRICH WEBER.

Evangelical-Lutheran Church in Oldenburg: Philosophenweg 1, 26121 Oldenburg; tel. (441) 77010; fax (441) 7701299; e-mail presse@ev-kirche-ol.de; internet www.ev-kirche-oldenburg.de; Bischof PETER KRUG.

Evangelical-Lutheran Church in Thuringia: Dr-Moritz-Mitzenheim Str. 2A, 99817 Eisenach; tel. (3691) 67899; fax (3691) 678355; e-mail kirchenamt.eisenach@ekmd.de; internet www.elkth-online.de; Landesbischof Prof. Dr CHRISTOPH KÄHLER.

Evangelical-Lutheran Church of Mecklenburg: Münzstr. 8, Postfach 111063, 19010 Schwerin; tel. (385) 51850; fax (385) 5185170; e-mail okr@ellm.de; internet www.kirche-mv.de; Landesbischof HERMANN BESTE.

Evangelical-Lutheran Church of Saxony: Postfach 120552, 01006 Dresden; Lukasstr. 6, 01069 Dresden; tel. (351) 46920; fax (351) 4692109; e-mail kirche@evlks.de; internet www.evlks.de; Landesbischof JOCHEN BOHL.

Evangelical-Reformed Church: Saarstr. 6, 26789 Leer; tel. (491) 91980; fax (491) 9198251; e-mail info@reformiert.de; internet www.reformiert.de; Moderator Rev. JANN SCHMIDT; Synod Clerk Dr JOHANN WEUSMANN.

Herrnhuter Brüdergemeine/Europäisch-Festländische Brüder-Unität (European Continental Province of the Moravian Church): Badwasen 6, 73087 Bad Boll; tel. (7164) 94210; fax (7164) 942199; f. 1457; there are 25 congregations in Germany, Denmark, Estonia, Latvia, the Netherlands, Sweden and Switzerland, with approx. 18,000 mems; Chair. FRIEDER VOLLPRECHT.

Other Evangelical (Protestant) Churches

Arbeitsgemeinschaft Mennonitischer Gemeinden in Deutschland (Assen of Mennonite Congregations in Germany): Ringstr. 3, 67677 Enkenbach-Alsenborn; tel. (6303) 3883; fax (6303) 983739; e-mail amg.werner.funck@mennoniten.de; internet www.mennoniten.de; f. 1886; re-organized 1990; Chair. WERNER FUNCK.

Bund Evangelisch-Freikirchlicher Gemeinden in Deutschland K.d.ö.R. (Union of Evangelical Free Churches (Baptists) in Germany): Johann-Gerhard-Oncken-Str. 7, 14641 Wustermark; tel. (33234) 74105; fax (33234) 74199; e-mail befg@baptisten.org; internet www.baptisten.org; f. 1849; Pres. EMANUEL BRANDT; Vice-Pres. CHRISTOPH STIBA; Gen. Sec. REGINA CLAAS.

Bund Freier evangelischer Gemeinden (Covenant of Free Evangelical Churches in Germany): Postfach 4005, 58426 Witten; Goltenkamp 4, 58452 Witten; tel. (2302) 9370; fax (2302) 93799; e-mail bund@feg.de; internet www.feg.de; f. 1854; Pres. PETER STRAUCH; Administrator KLAUS KANWISCHER; 36,000 mems.

GERMANY

Evangelisch-altreformierte Kirche von Niedersachsen (Evangelical Reformed Church of Lower Saxony): Boenster Str. 20, 26831 Bunde; tel. (4953) 922599; e-mail gerdschrader@compuserve.de; Sec. Rev. GERHARD SCHRADER.

Evangelisch-methodistische Kirche (United Methodist Church): Ludolfusstr. 2–4, 60487 Frankfurt a.M.; tel. (69) 2425210; fax (69) 24252129; e-mail kirchenkanzlei@emk.de; internet www.emk.de; f. 1968; Presiding Bishop ROSEMARIE WENNER.

Gemeinschaft der Siebenten-Tags-Adventisten (Seventh-Day Adventist Church): Postfach 4260, 73745 Ostfildern; Senefelderstr. 15, 73760 Ostfildern; tel. (711) 448190; fax (711) 4481960; e-mail sdv.zentrale@adventisten.de.

Die Heilsarmee in Deutschland (Salvation Army in Germany): Salierring 23–27, 50677 Köln; tel. (221) 208190; fax (221) 2081951; e-mail pr@heilsarmee.de; internet www.heilsarmee.de; f. 1886; Leader Col HORST CHARLET.

Mülheimer Verband Freikirchlich-Evangelischer Gemeinden (Pentecostal Church): Habenhauser Dorfstr. 27, 28279 Bremen; tel. (421) 8399130; fax (421) 8399136; e-mail mv-bremen@t-online.de; f. 1913.

Selbständige Evangelisch-Lutherische Kirche (Independent Evangelical-Lutheran Church): Schopenhauerstr. 7, 30625 Hannover; tel. (511) 557808; fax (511) 551588; e-mail selk@selk.de; internet www.selk.de; f. 1972; Bishop HANS JOERG VOIGT; Exec. Sec. Rev. MICHAEL SCHAETZEL.

Other Christian Churches

Other Christian churches had 4.5m.–5m. members in 2005, of whom 1.5m.–2m. persons were members of Orthodox churches.

Alt-Katholische Kirche (Old Catholic Church): Gregor-Mendel-Str. 28, 53115 Bonn; tel. (228) 232285; fax (228) 238314; e-mail ordinariat@alt-katholisch.de; internet www.alt-katholisch.de; seceded from the Roman Catholic Church as a protest against the declaration of Papal infallibility in 1870; belongs to the Utrecht Union of Old Catholic Churches; in full communion with the Anglican Communion; Pres. Bischof JOACHIM VOBBE (Bonn); 25,000 mems.

Apostelamt Jesu Christi: Madlower Hauptstr. 38, 03050 Cottbus; tel. (355) 541227; Pres. WALDEMAR ROHDE.

Armenisch-Apostolische Orthodoxe Kirche in Deutschland: Allensteiner Str. 5, 50735 Köln; tel. (221) 7126223; fax (221) 7126267; e-mail armenische_diozese@hotmail.com; Archbishop KAREKIN BEKDJIAN.

Griechisch-Orthodoxe Metropolie von Deutschland (Greek Orthodox Metropolitanate of Germany): Postfach 300555, 53185 Bonn; Dietrich-Bonhoeffer-Str. 2, 53227 Bonn; tel. (228) 462041; fax (228) 464989; e-mail sekretariat@orthodoxie.net; internet www.orthodoxie.net; Metropolit von Deutschland und Exarch von Zentraleuropa AUGOUSTINOS LABARDAKIS.

Religiöse Gesellschaft der Freunde (Quäker) (Society of Friends): Planckstr. 20, 10117 Berlin; tel. (30) 2082284; fax (30) 20458142; f. 1925; 270 mems.

Russische Orthodoxe Kirche—Berliner Diözese (Russian Orthodox Church): Postfach 17, 10267 Berlin; Wildensteiner Str. 10, 10318 Berlin; tel. (30) 50379488; fax (30) 5098153; e-mail red.stimme@snafu.de; Archbishop FEOFAN.

ISLAM

An estimated 3.3m. Muslims were living in Germany in 2005.

Zentralrat der Muslime in Deutschland eV (Central Council of Muslims in Germany): Postfach 1224, 52232 Eschweiler; Indestr. 93, 52249 Eschweiler; tel. (2403) 702075; fax (2403) 702076; e-mail sekretariat@zentralrat.de; internet www.zentralrat.de; f. 1994; 19 mem. asscns; Chair. Dr NADEEM ELYAS.

JUDAISM

The membership of Jewish synagogues in Germany numbered some 108,000 in 2005.

Zentralrat der Juden in Deutschland (Central Council of Jews in Germany): Tucholskystr. 9, Leo-Baeck-Haus, 10117 Berlin; tel. (30) 2844560; fax (30) 28445613; e-mail info@zentralratdjuden.de; internet www.zentralratdjuden.de; Pres. CHARLOTTE KNOBLOCH; Sec.-Gen. STEPHAN J. KRAMER.

Jüdische Gemeinde zu Berlin (Jewish Community in Berlin): Fasanenstr. 79–80, 10623 Berlin; e-mail vorstand@jg-berlin.org; Pres. LALA SÜSSKIND.

The Press

The German Press Council was founded in 1956 as a self-regulatory body, and is composed of publishers and journalists. It formulates guidelines and investigates complaints against the press.

In 1968 a government commission stipulated various limits on the proportions of circulation that any one publishing group should be allowed to control: (1) 40% of the total circulation of newspapers or 40% of the total circulation of magazines; (2) 20% of the total circulation of newspapers and magazines together; (3) 15% of the circulation in one field if the proportion owned in the other field is 40%.

Deutscher Presserat (German Press Council): Gerhard-von-Are-Str. 8, 53111 Bonn; tel. (228) 985720; fax (228) 9857299; e-mail info@presserat.de; internet www.presserat.de; Dir LUTZ TILLMANNS.

The principal newspaper publishing groups are:

Axel Springer Verlag AG: Axel-Springer-Str. 65, 10888 Berlin; and Axel-Springer-Pl. 1, 20355 Hamburg; tel. (30) 25910; fax (30) 251606; tel. (40) 34700; fax (40) 345811; internet www.asv.de; f. 1946; the largest newspaper publishing group in continental Europe; includes five major dailies *Die Welt*, *Hamburger Abendblatt*, *Bild*, *Berliner Morgenpost*, *BZ*, three Sunday papers *Welt am Sonntag*, *Bild am Sonntag*, *BZ am Sonntag*, and radio, television, women's and family magazines; Chair. AUGUST A. FISCHER.

Gruner + Jahr AG & Co Druck- und Verlagshaus: Am Vossbarg, 25524 Itzehoe; and Am Baumwall 11, 20459 Hamburg; tel. (4821) 7771; fax (4821) 777449; tel. (40) 37030; fax (40) 3703600; internet www.co.guj.de; owns, amongst others, *Stern*, *Brigitte*, *Capital*, *Eltern*, *Schöner Wohnen*, *Hamburger Morgenpost*; *Financial Times Deutschland*, a jt venture with *Financial Times* (UK) was launched in Feb. 2000.

JahreszeitenVerlag GmbH: Possmoorweg 5, 22301 Hamburg; tel. (40) 27170; fax (40) 27172056; f. 1948; owns, amongst others, the periodicals *Für Sie* and *Petra*; Pres. THOMAS GANSKE.

Süddeutscher-Verlag GmbH: Sendlingerstr. 80, 80331 München; tel. (89) 21830; fax (89) 2183787; internet www.sueddeutsche.de; f. 1945; owns *Süddeutsche Zeitung*, special interest periodicals.

Verlag Aenne Burda GmbH & Co KG: Am Kesterdamm 1, 77652 Offenburg; tel. (781) 840; fax (781) 843291; internet www.burda.de; f. 1908; publs incl. *Burda Modemagazin*, *Bild + Funk*, *Focus*, *Freundin*, *Meine Familie & ich* and *Schweriner Volkszeitung*; 10 Mans.

Verlagsgruppe Bauer: Postfach 4660, 20077 Hamburg; Burchardstr. 11, 20095 Hamburg; and Charles-de-Gaulle-Str. 8, 81737 München; tel. (40) 30190; fax (40) 30191043; tel. (89) 67860; fax (89) 6767137; internet www.bauerverlag.de; owns 125 popular illustrated magazines, including *Bravo* (München), *Neue Revue* (Hamburg), *Maxi*, *Neue Post*, *TV Horen + Sehen* and *TV Movie*; Pres. HEINRICH BAUER.

PRINCIPAL DAILIES

Aachen

Aachener Nachrichten: Postfach 110, 52002 Aachen; Dresdner Str. 3, 52068 Aachen; tel. (241) 51010; fax (241) 5101399; internet www.an-online.de; f. 1872; circ. 67,000.

Aachener Zeitung: Postfach 500110, 52085 Aachen; Dresdner Str. 3, 52068 Aachen; tel. (241) 51010; fax (241) 5101399; internet www.aachener-zeitung.de; f. 1946; Editor-in-Chief BERND MATHIEU; circ. 106,000.

Ansbach

Fränkische Landeszeitung: Postfach 1362, 91504 Ansbach; Nürnberger Str. 9–17, 91522 Ansbach; tel. (981) 95000; fax (981) 13961; Editor-in-Chief PETER M. SZYMANOWSKI; circ. 50,000.

Aschaffenburg

Main-Echo: Postfach 548, 63736 Aschaffenburg; Weichertstr. 20, 63739 Aschaffenburg a.M.; tel. (6021) 3960; fax (6021) 396499; e-mail redaktionssekretariat@main-echo.de; internet www.main-echo.de; Editors HELMUT WEISS, Dr HELMUT TEUFEL; circ. 93,000.

Augsburg

Augsburger Allgemeine: Curt-Frenzel-Str. 2, 86167 Augsburg; tel. (821) 7770; fax (821) 7772039; e-mail chefredaktion@augsburger-allgemeiner.de; internet www.augsburger-allgemeine.de; daily (Mon. to Sat.); Editor-in-Chief RAINER BONHORST; circ. 370,000.

Baden-Baden

Badisches Tagblatt: Badisches Tagblatt GmbH, Postfach 100033, 76481 Baden-Baden; Stefanienstr. 1–3, 76530 Baden-Baden; tel.

(7221) 2151241; fax (7221) 2151440; Editor-in-Chief Markus Langer; circ. 38,000.

Bamberg

Fränkischer Tag: Gutenbergstr. 1, 96050 Bamberg; tel. (951) 1880; fax (951) 188118; internet www.fraenkischer-tag.de; Publr Dr Helmuth Jungbauer; circ. 75,800.

Bautzen

Serbske Nowiny: Tuchmacher Str. 27, 02625 Bautzen; tel. (3591) 577232; e-mail redaktion@serbske-nowiny.de; internet www.serbske-nowiny.de; evening; Sorbian language paper; Editor Benedikt Dyrlich; circ. 1,900.

Berlin

Berliner Kurier: Karl-Liebknecht-Str. 29, 10178 Berlin; tel. (30) 23279; fax (30) 23275533; e-mail bk-online@berliner-kurier.de; internet www.berliner-kurier.de; f. 1990; evening; publ. by Berliner Verlag GmbH; Editor-in-Chief Hans-Peter Buschheuer; circ. 126,989 (June 2007).

Berliner Morgenpost: Axel-Springer-Str. 65, 10888 Berlin; tel. (30) 25910; fax (30) 2516071; e-mail redaktion@morgenpost.de; internet www.morgenpost.de; f. 1898; publ. by Ullstein GmbH; Editor-in-Chief Carsten Erdmann; circ. 139,731 (June 2007).

Berliner Zeitung: Karl-Liebknecht-Str. 29, 10178 Berlin; tel. (2) 23279; fax (30) 23275533; e-mail berliner-zeitung@berliner-zeitung.de; internet www.berliner-zeitung.de; f. 1945; morning (except Sun.); publ. by Berliner Verlag GmbH; Editor Josef Depenbrock; circ. 173,185 (June 2007).

BZ (Berliner Zeitung): BZ Ullstein GmbH, Kurfürstendamm 21–22, 10719 Berlin; tel. (30) 25910; fax (30) 259173006; e-mail redaktion@bz-berlin.de; internet www.bz-berlin.de; f. 1877; Editor-in-Chief Wolfgang Saurin.

Junge Welt: Torstr. 6, 10119 Berlin; tel. (30) 5363550; fax (30) 53635544; e-mail redaktion@jungewelt.de; internet www.jungewelt.de; f. 1947; morning; Editor Arnold Schölzel; circ. 20,000.

Neues Deutschland: Alt-Stralau 1–2, 10245 Berlin; tel. (30) 293905; fax (30) 29390600; e-mail redaktion@nd-online.de; internet www.neues-deutschland.de; f. 1946; morning; independent; Editor Dietmar Bartsch; circ. 52,000.

Der Tagesspiegel: Verlag der Tagesspiegel GmbH, 10876 Berlin; tel. (30) 260090; fax (30) 26009332; e-mail infotsp@tagesspiegel.de; internet www.tagesspiegel.de; f. 1945; circ. 151,000.

Die Welt: Axel-Springer-Str. 65, 10888 Berlin; tel. (30) 25910; fax (30) 251606; internet www.welt.de; f. 1946; publ. by Axel Springer Verlag AG; Editor-in-Chief Dr Thomas Löffelholz; circ. 276,670 (June 2007).

Bielefeld

Neue Westfälische: Postfach 100225, 33502 Bielefeld; Niederstr. 21–27, 33602 Bielefeld; tel. (521) 5550; fax (521) 555520; internet www.nw-news.de; f. 1967; circ. 254,753.

Westfalen-Blatt: Postfach 8740, 33531 Bielefeld; Südbrackstr. 14–18, 33611 Bielefeld; tel. (521) 5850; fax (521) 585370; internet www.westfalen-blatt.de; f. 1946; Editor Carl-W. Busse; circ. 147,400.

Bonn

General-Anzeiger: Justus-von-Liebig-Str. 15, 53121 Bonn; tel. (228) 66880; fax (228) 6688170; internet www.general-anzeiger-bonn.de; f. 1725; independent; Publr Hermann Neusser; circ. 90,000.

Braunschweig
(Brunswick)

Braunschweiger Zeitung: Postfach 8052, 38130 Braunschweig; Hamburger Str. 277, 38114 Braunschweig; tel. (531) 39000; fax (531) 3900610; internet www.newsclick.de; circ. 150,226 (Mon.–Fri.), 174,732 (Sat.).

Bremen

Bremer Nachrichten: Postfach 107801, 28078 Bremen; Martinistr. 43, 28195 Bremen; tel. (421) 36710; fax (421) 3379233; f. 1743; Publr Herbert C. Ordemann; Editor Dietrich Ide; circ. 30,000.

Weser-Kurier: Postfach 107801, 28078 Bremen; Martinistr. 43, 28195 Bremen; tel. (421) 36710; fax (421) 3379233; internet www.weser-kurier.de; f. 1945; Publr Herbert C. Ordemann; Editor Volker Weise; circ. 160,000.

Bremerhaven

Nordsee-Zeitung: Postfach 27512, 27512 Bremerhaven; Hafenstr. 140, 27576 Bremerhaven 1; tel. (471) 5970; fax (471) 597567; internet www.nordsee-zeitung.de; Chief Editor Jörg Jung; circ. 77,500.

Chemnitz

Freie Presse: Postfach 261, Brückenstr. 15, 09111 Chemnitz; tel. (371) 6560; fax (371) 643042; internet www.freiepresse.de; f. 1963; morning; Editor Dieter Soika; circ. 360,000.

Cottbus

Lausitzer Rundschau: Postfach 100279, 03002 Cottbus; Str. der Jugend 54, 03050 Cottbus; tel. (355) 4810; fax (355) 481245; internet www.lr-online.de; independent; morning; Chief Officers Frank Lüdecke, B. Liske; circ. 160,000.

Darmstadt

Darmstädter Echo: Postfach 100155, 64276 Darmstadt; Holzhofallee 25–31, 64295 Darmstadt; tel. (6151) 3871; fax (6151) 387448; internet www.echo-online.de; f. 1945; Publrs Dr Hans-Peter Bach, Horst Bach; Editor-in-Chief Roland Hof; circ. 87,300.

Dortmund

Ruhr-Nachrichten: Postfach 105051, Westenhellweg 86–88, 44047 Dortmund; internet www.westline.de; f. 1949; Editor Florian Lensing-Wolff; circ. 215,400.

Westfälische Rundschau: Postfach 105067, 44047 Dortmund; Brüderweg 9; Dortmund 44135; tel. (201) 8040; fax (201) 8042841; e-mail zentralredaktion@westfaelische-rundschau.de; internet www.westfaelische-rundschau.de; Editor Frank Bünte; circ. 250,000.

Dresden

Dresdner Morgenpost: Ostra-Allee, 01067 Dresden; tel. (51) 4864; fax (51) 4951116; circ. 126,700.

Dresdner Neueste Nachrichten/Union: Hauptstr. 21, 01097 Dresden; tel. (351) 8075210; fax (351) 8075212; internet www.dnn-online.de; morning; Editor-in-Chief Dirk Birgel; circ. 35,000.

Sächsische Zeitung: Haus der Presse, Ostra-Allee 20, 01067 Dresden; tel. (351) 48640; fax (351) 48642354; e-mail redaktion@sz-online.de; internet www.sz-online.de; f. 1946; morning; publ. by Gruner + Jahr AG; Editor-in-Chief Thomas Schultz-Homberg; circ. 397,700.

Düsseldorf

Düsseldorf Express: Postfach 1132, 40002 Düsseldorf; Königsallee 27, 40212 Düsseldorf; tel. (211) 13930; fax (211) 324835.

Handelsblatt: Postfach 102741, 40018 Düsseldorf; Kasernenstr. 67, 40213 Düsseldorf; tel. (211) 8870; fax (211) 329954; e-mail handelsblatt@vhb.de; internet www.handelsblatt.de; 5 a week; Publr Dieter von Holtzbrinck; circ. 156,473.

Rheinische Post: Zülpicherstr. 10, 40549 Düsseldorf; tel. (211) 5050; fax (211) 5052575; internet www.rp-online.de; f. 1946; Editor Ulrich Reitz; circ. 349,200.

Westdeutsche Zeitung: Postfach 101132, 40002 Düsseldorf; Königsallee 27, 40212 Düsseldorf; tel. (211) 83820; fax (211) 83822392; e-mail wzn@wz-newsline.de; internet www.wz-newsline.de; Editor-in-Chief Friedrich Roeingh; Publr Dr M. Girardet; circ. 176,800.

Erfurt

Thüringer Allgemeine: Gottstedter Landstr. 6, 99092 Erfurt; tel. (361) 2274; fax (361) 2275144; e-mail redaktion@thueringer-allgemeine.de; internet www.thueringer-allgemeine.de; f. 1946; morning; Editor-in-Chief Sergej Lochthofen; circ. 330,000.

Essen

Neue Ruhr Zeitung: Friedrichstr. 34–38, 45128 Essen; tel. (201) 8042605; fax (201) 8042121; Editor-in-Chief Dr Richard Kiessler; circ. 215,000.

Westdeutsche Allgemeine Zeitung: Friedrichstr. 34–38, 45128 Essen; tel. (201) 8040; fax (201) 8042841; Editor Ulrich Reitz; circ. 650,000.

Flensburg

Flensburger Tageblatt: Postfach 1553, 25804 Flensburg; Nikolaistr. 7, 24937 Flensburg; tel. (461) 8080; fax (461) 8082121.

Frankfurt am Main

Frankfurter Allgemeine Zeitung: Hellerhofstr. 2–4, 60327 Frankfurt a.M.; tel. (69) 75910; fax (69) 75911743; internet www.faz.net; f. 1949; Editors WERNER D'INKA, BERTHOLD KOHLER, Dr GÜNTHER NONNENMACHER, Dr FRANK SCHIRRMACHER, HOLGER STELTZNER; circ. 355,133 (June 2007).

Frankfurter Neue Presse: Postfach 100801, 60008 Frankfurt a.M.; Frankenallee 71–81, 60327 Frankfurt a.M.; tel. (69) 75010; fax (69) 75014330; internet www.fnp.de; independent; Editor GERHARD MUMME; circ. 110,440.

Frankfurter Rundschau: Walther-von-Cronberg Pl. 2–18, 60594 Frankfurt a.M.; tel. (69) 21991; fax (69) 21993720; e-mail politik@fr-online.de; internet www.fr-online.de; Editors-in-Chief Dr UWE VORKÖTTER, STEPHAN HEBEL, ROUVEN SCHELLENBERGER; circ. 150,000.

Frankfurt an der Oder

Märkische Oderzeitung: Postfach 178, 15201 Frankfurt a.d. Oder; Kellenspring 6, 15230 Frankfurt a.d. Oder; tel. (335) 55300; fax (335) 23214; morning; Editor HEINZ KURTZBACH; circ. 150,633.

Freiburg im Breisgau

Badische Zeitung: Pressehaus, Basler Str. 88, 79115 Freiburg i. Br.; tel. (761) 4960; fax (761) 4965008; e-mail redaktion@badische-zeitung.de; internet www.badische-zeitung.de; f. 1946; Editor THOMAS HAUSER; circ. 171,990.

Gera

Ostthüringer Zeitung: De-Smit-Str. 18, 6500 Gera; tel. (70) 6120; fax (70) 51233; morning; Editor-in-Chief ULLRICH ERZIGKEIT; circ. 237,537.

Göttingen

Göttinger Tageblatt: 37070 Göttingen; Dransfelder Str. 1, 37079 Göttingen; tel. (551) 9011; fax (551) 901229; e-mail info@goettinger-tageblatt.de; internet www.goettinger-tageblatt.de; f. 1889; Man. Dirs HERBERT FLECKEN, GÜNTER GIFFELS; Editor-in-Chief ILSE STEIN; circ. 50,000.

Hagen

Westfalenpost: Schürmannstr. 4, 58097 Hagen; tel. (2331) 9170; fax (2331) 9174206; e-mail westfalenpost@cityweb.de; f. 1946; Chief Editor BODO ZAPP; circ. 155,000.

Halle

Haller Kreisblatt: Postfach 1452, 33779 Halle; Gutenbergstr. 2, 33790 Halle.

Hamburg

Bild: Axel-Springer-Pl. 1, 20355 Hamburg; tel. (40) 34700; fax (40) 345811; internet www.bild.de; f. 1952; publ. by Axel Springer Verlag AG; Chief Editor KAI DIEKMANN; circ. 3,540,785 (June 2007).

Financial Times Deutschland: Stubbenhuk 3, 20459 Hamburg; tel. (40) 31990-0; fax (40) 31990-310; e-mail leserservice@ftd.de; internet www.ftd.de; f. 2000; publ. by Grüner + Jahr AG & Co KG; Editor-in-Chief STEFFEN KLUSMANN; circ. 103,284 (June 2007).

Hamburger Abendblatt: Axel-Springer-Pl. 1, 20355 Hamburg; tel. (40) 34700; fax (40) 345811; internet www.abendblatt.de; publ. by Axel Springer Verlag AG; Editor-in-Chief KLAUS KRUSE; circ. 315,600.

Hamburger Morgenpost: Griegstr. 75, 22763 Hamburg; tel. (40) 8090570; fax (40) 88303237; e-mail verlag@mopo.de; internet www.mopo.de; publ. by Morgenpost Verlag; circ. 110,000.

Hannover
(Hanover)

Hannoversche Allgemeine Zeitung: Bemeroder Str. 58, 30148 Hannover; tel. (511) 5180; fax (511) 527328; internet www.niedersachsen.com; circ. 269,600.

Neue Presse: Postfach 149, 30001 Hannover; Bemeroder Str. 58, 30559 Hannover; tel. (511) 51010; fax (511) 524554.

Heidelberg

Rhein-Neckar-Zeitung: Postfach 104560, 69035 Heidelberg; Hauptstr. 23, 69117 Heidelberg; tel. (6221) 5191; fax (6221) 519217; e-mail rnz-kontakt@rnz.de; internet www.rnz.de; f. 1945; morning; Publrs Dr LUDWIG KNORR, WINFRIED KNORR, Dr RUPRECHT SCHULZE; circ. 102,500.

Heilbronn

Heilbronner Stimme: Allee 2, 74072 Heilbronn; tel. (7131) 6150; fax (7131) 615200; e-mail servicecentre@stimme.de; internet www.stimme.de; f. 1946; Editor-in-Chief Dr WOLFGANG BOK; circ. 105,631.

Hof-Saale

Frankenpost: Postfach 1320, 95012 Hof-Saale; Poststr. 9–11, 95028 Hof-Saale; tel. (9281) 8160; fax (9281) 816283; e-mail fp-redaktion@frankenpost.de; internet www.frankenpost.de; publ. by Frankenpost Verlag GmbH; Editor-in-Chief MALTE BUSCHBECK; circ. 85,000.

Ingolstadt

Donaukurier: Postfach 100259, 85002 Ingolstadt; Stauffenbergstr. 2A, 85051 Ingolstadt; tel. (841) 96660; fax (841) 9666255; e-mail redaktion@donaukurier.de; internet www.donaukurier.de; f. 1872; Publr ELIN REISSMÜLLER; circ. 84,700.

Kassel

Hessische/Niedersächsische Allgemeine: Postfach 101009, 34010 Kassel; Frankfurter Str. 168, 34121 Kassel; tel. (561) 20300; fax (561) 2032116; internet www.hna.de; f. 1959; independent; circ. 189,200.

Kempten

Allgäuer Zeitung: Postfach 3155, 87440 Kempten; Heisinger Str. 14, 87437 Kempten; tel. (831) 2060; fax (831) 206379; internet www.all-in.de; f. 1945; Publrs GEORG FÜRST VON WALDBURG-ZEIL, GÜNTER HOLLAND, ELLINOR HOLLAND; circ. 117,900.

Kiel

Kieler Nachrichten: Postfach 1111, 24100 Kiel; Fleethörn 1–7, 24103 Kiel; tel. (431) 9030; fax (431) 903935; internet www.kn.online.de; publ. by Axel Springer Verlag; Chief Editor JÜRGEN HEINEMANN; circ. 113,400.

Koblenz

Rhein-Zeitung: Postfach 1540, August-Horch-Str. 28, 56070 Koblenz; tel. (261) 89200; fax (261) 892770; internet www.rhein-zeitung.de; Editors JOACHIM TÜRK, CHRISTIAN LINDNER; circ. 223,200.

Köln
(Cologne)

Express: Postfach 100410, 50450 Köln; Breite Str. 70, 50667 Köln; tel. (221) 2240; fax (211) 2242524; internet www.express.de; f. 1964; Publr ALFRED NEVEN DUMONT; circ. 370,000.

Kölner Stadt-Anzeiger: Amsterdamer Str. 192, 50735 Köln; tel. (221) 2240; fax (221) 2242524; internet www.ksta.de; f. 1876; Publr ALFRED NEVEN DUMONT; Editor FRANZ SOMMERFELD; circ. 294,400.

Kölnische Rundschau: Postfach 102145, 50461 Köln; Stolkgasse 25–45, 50667 Köln; tel. (221) 16320; fax (221) 1632491; e-mail jost.springensguth@kr-redaktion.de; internet www.rundschau-online.de; f. 1946; Publr HELMUT HEINEN; Editor-in-Chief JOST SPRINGENSGUTH; circ. 155,100.

Konstanz

Südkurier: Postfach 102001, Presse- und Druckzentrum, 78420 Konstanz; Max-Stromeyer-Str. 178, 78467 Konstanz; tel. (7531) 9990; fax (7531) 991485; e-mail redaktion@suedkurier.de; internet www.skol.de; f. 1945; circ. 148,990.

Leipzig

Leipziger Volkszeitung: Peterssteinweg 19, 04107 Leipzig; tel. (341) 21810; fax (341) 310992; internet www.lvz-online.de; f. 1894; morning; publ. by Verlagsgesellschaft Madsach and Axel Springer Verlag AG; circ. 264,000.

Leutkirch im Allgäu

Schwäbische Zeitung: Postfach 1145, 88291 Leutkirch im Allgäu; Rudolf-Roth-Str. 18, 88299 Leutkirch im Allgäu; tel. (7561) 800; fax (7561) 80134; e-mail redaktion@schwaebische-zeitung.de; internet www.schwaebische-zeitung.de; f. 1945; Editor JOACHIM UMBACH; circ. 196,000.

Lübeck

Lübecker Nachrichten: Herrenholz 10–12, 23556 Lübeck; tel. (451) 1440; fax (451) 1441022; internet www.ln-online.de; f. 1945; publ. by Axel Springer Verlag AG; Chief Editor MANFRED VON THIEN; circ. 115,900.

GERMANY

Ludwigshafen

Die Rheinpfalz: Postfach 211147, 67011 Ludwigshafen; Amtsstr. 5–11, 67059 Ludwigshafen; tel. (621) 590201; fax (621) 5902336; Dir Dr THOMAS SCHAUB; circ. 249,410.

Magdeburg

Magdeburger Volksstimme: Bahnhofstr. 17, 39104 Magdeburg; tel. (391) 59990; fax (391) 388400; f. 1890; morning; publ. by Magdeburger Verlags- und Druckhaus GmbH; Editor-in-Chief Dr HEINZ-GEORG OETTE; circ. 316,900.

Mainz

Allgemeine Zeitung: Postfach 3120, 55021 Mainz; Erich-Dombrowski-Str. 2, 55127 Mainz; tel. (6131) 1440; fax (6131) 144504; internet www.main-rheiner.de; publ. by Rhein-Main-Presse; circ. 134,000.

Mannheim

Mannheimer Morgen: Postfach 102164, 68021 Mannheim; Dudenstr. 12–26, 68167 Mannheim; tel. (621) 39201; fax (621) 3921376; e-mail redaktion@mamo.de; internet www.morgenweb.de; f. 1946; Publr R. VON SCHILLING; Chief Editor HORST ROTH; circ. 148,994.

München
(Munich)

Abendzeitung: Sendlingerstr. 10, 80331 München; tel. (89) 23770; fax (89) 2377478; internet www.abendzeitung.de; f. 1948; Dir CHRISTOPH MATTES; Editor-in-Chief MICHAEL RADTKE; circ. 160,098.

Münchner Merkur: Paul-Heyse-Str. 2–4, 80336 München; tel. (89) 53060; fax (89) 53068651; internet www.merkur-online.de; Publr Dr DIRK IPPEN; Editor KARL SCHERMANN; circ. 283,000.

Süddeutsche Zeitung: Sendlingerstr. 8, 80331 München; tel. (89) 21830; fax (89) 2183787; e-mail wir@sueddeutsche.de; internet www.sueddeutsche.de; f. 1945; publ. by Süddeutscher-Verlag GmbH; Editors-in-Chief HANS-WERNER KILZ, Dr GERNOT SITTNER; circ. 424,250 (June 2007).

TZ: Paul-Heyse-Str. 2–4, 80336 München; tel. (89) 53060; fax (89) 5306552; e-mail sekretariat@tz-online.de; f. 1968; Editor RUDOLF BÖGEL; circ. 154,695.

Münster

Münstersche Zeitung: Postfach 5560, 48030 Münster; Neubrückenstr. 8–11, 48143 Münster; tel. (251) 5920; fax (251) 592212; e-mail mz-redaktion@westline.de; internet www.westline.de; f. 1871; independent; Editor Dr GREGOR BOTHE; circ. 46,860.

Westfälische Nachrichten: Soester Str. 13, 48155 Münster; tel. (251) 690700; fax (251) 690705; internet www.westline.de; Chief Editor Dr NORBERT TIEMANN; circ. 121,211.

Neubrandenburg

Nordkurier: Flurstr. 2, 17034 Neubrandenburg; tel. (395) 45750; fax (395) 4575694; internet www.nordkurier.de; Editor-in-Chief Dr ANDRÉ UZULIS; circ. 250,000.

Nürnberg
(Nuremberg)

Nürnberger Nachrichten: Marienstr. 9–11, 90402 Nürnberg; tel. (911) 2160; fax (911) 2162326; internet www.nn-online.de; f. 1945; Editor FELIX HARTLIEB; circ. 344,000.

Oberndorf-Neckar

Schwarzwälder Bote: Postfach 1380, 78722 Oberndorf-Neckar; Kirchtorstr. 14, 78727 Oberndorf-Neckar; tel. (7423) 780; fax (7423) 7873; internet www.swol.de; circ. 104,300.

Oelde

Die Glocke: Engelbert-Holterdorf-Str. 4–6, 59302 Oelde; tel. (2522) 730; fax (2522) 73216; f. 1880; Editors FRIED GEHRING, ENGELBERT HOLTERDORF; circ. 65,500.

Offenbach

Offenbach Post: Postfach 100263, 63002 Offenbach; Waldstr. 226, 63071 Offenbach; tel. (69) 850080; fax (69) 85008198; internet www.op-online.de; f. 1947; Publr UDO BINTZ; circ. 53,200.

Oldenburg

Nordwest-Zeitung: Postfach 2527, 26015 Oldenburg; Peterstr. 28–34, 26121 Oldenburg; tel. (441) 998801; fax (441) 99882029; internet www.nwz-online.de; publ. by Nordwest-Zeitung Verlagsgesellschaft mbH & Co KG; Editor ROLF SEELHEIM; circ. 130,000.

Osnabrück

Neue Osnabrücker Zeitung: Postfach 4260, 49032 Osnabrück; Breiter Gang 10–16 and Grosse Str. 17–19, 49074 Osnabrück; tel. (541) 3100; fax (541) 310485; e-mail redaktion@neue-oz.de; internet www.neue-oz.de; f. 1967; Editors-in-Chief EWALD GELDING, Dr JÜRGEN WERMSER; circ. 172,059.

Passau

Passauer Neue Presse: Medienstr. 5, 94036 Passau; tel. (851) 8020; fax (851) 802256; internet www.pnp.de; f. 1946; circ. 177,282.

Potsdam

Märkische Allgemeine: Postfach 601153, 14411 Potsdam; Friedrich-Engels-Str. 24, 14473 Potsdam; tel. (331) 28400; fax (331) 2840310; e-mail chefredaktion@mazonline.de; internet www.maerkischeallgemeine.de; f. 1990; morning; independent; Chief Editor Dr KLAUS ROST; circ. 160,000.

Regensburg

Mittelbayerische Zeitung: Margaretenstr. 4, 93047 Regensburg; tel. (941) 207270; fax (941) 207307; e-mail gf@mittelbayerische.de; internet www.mittelbayerische.de; f. 1945; Editors PETER ESSER, THOMAS ESSER; circ. 142,070.

Rostock

Ostsee-Zeitung: Richard-Wagner-Str. 1A, 18055 Rostock; tel. (81) 3650; fax (81) 365244; internet www.ostsee-zeitung.de; f. 1952; publ. by Axel Springer Verlag AG; Editor GERD SPILKER; circ. 214,300.

Saarbrücken

Saarbrücker Zeitung: Gutenbergstr. 11–23, 66117 Saarbrücken; tel. (681) 5020; fax (681) 5022500; internet www.sol.de; f. 1761; Editor PETER STEGAN HERBST; circ. 167,184.

Schwerin

Schweriner Volkszeitung: Gutenbergstr. 1, 19061 Schwerin; tel. (385) 63780; fax (385) 3975140; internet www.svz.de; f. 1946; Editor THOMAS SCHUNCK; circ. 115,000.

Straubing

Straubinger Tagblatt: Ludwigspl. 30, 94315 Straubing; tel. (9421) 940115; fax (9421) 940155; e-mail service@idowa.de; internet www.idowa.de; f. 1860; morning; Chief Editor Dr HERMANN BALLE; circ. 140,000.

Stuttgart

Stuttgarter Nachrichten: Postfach 104452, 70039 Stuttgart; Plieninger Str. 150, 70567 Stuttgart; tel. (711) 72050; fax (711) 72057138; internet www.stuttgarter-nachrichten.de; f. 1946; Editor-in-Chief JÜRGEN OFFENBACH; circ. 332,000.

Stuttgarter Zeitung: Postfach 106032, 70049 Stuttgart; Plieninger Str. 150, 70567 Stuttgart; tel. (711) 72050; fax (711) 72051234; e-mail redaktion@stz.zgs.de; internet www.stuttgarter-zeitung.de; f. 1945; Chief Editor PETER CHRIST; circ. 151,600.

Trier

Trierischer Volksfreund: Postfach 3770, 54227 Trier; Hanns-Martin-Schleyer-Str. 8, 54294 Trier; tel. (651) 71990; fax (651) 7199990; e-mail redaktion@intrinet.de; internet www.intrinet.de; Chief Editor WALTER W. WEBER; circ. 100,000.

Ulm

Südwest Presse: Frauenstr. 77, 89073 Ulm; tel. (731) 1560; fax (731) 156308; internet www.suedwest-presse.de; circ. 107,800.

Weiden

Der Neue Tag: Postfach 1340, 92603 Weiden; Weigelstr. 16, 92637 Weiden; tel. (961) 850; fax (961) 44499; Editor-in-Chief HANS KLEMM; circ. 87,400.

Weimar

Thüringische Landeszeitung: Marienstr. 14, 99423 Weimar; tel. (3643) 206411; fax (3643) 206413; f. 1945; morning; Editor HANS HOFFMEISTER; circ. 62,000.

GERMANY

Wetzlar

Wetzlarer Neue Zeitung: Elsa-Brandström-Str. 18, 35578 Wetzlar; tel. (6441) 9590; fax (6441) 71684; f. 1945; Editor Wulf Eigendorf; circ. 75,000.

Wiesbaden

Wiesbadener Kurier: Postfach 6029, 65050 Wiesbaden; Langgasse 21, 65183 Wiesbaden; tel. (611) 3550; fax (611) 355377; internet www.main-rheiner-de; Chief Editors Matthias Friedrich, Friedrich Roeingh; circ. 86,700.

Würzburg

Main-Post: Berner Str. 2, 97084 Würzburg; tel. (931) 60010; fax (931) 6001242; internet www.mainpost.de; f. 1883; independent; Publrs David Brandstätter, Knut Müller; Editor-in-Chief Michael Reinhard; circ. 143,300.

SUNDAY AND WEEKLY PAPERS

Bayernkurier: Nymphenburger Str. 64, 80636 München; tel. (89) 120041; e-mail redaktion@bayernkurier.de; internet www.bayernkurier.de; weekly; organ of the CSU; Chief Editor Peter Schmalz; circ. 71,610.

Bild am Sonntag: Axel-Springer-Pl. 1, 20350 Hamburg; tel. (40) 34700; fax (40) 34726110; internet www.bild-am-sonntag.de; f. 1956; Sunday; publ. by Axel Springer Verlag AG; Chief Editor Claus Strunz; circ. 1,891,139 (June 2007).

BZ am Sonntag: Axel-Springer-Str. 65, 10888 Berlin; tel. (30) 25910; fax (30) 259173131; e-mail redaktion@bz-berlin.de; internet www.bz-berlin.de; f. 1992; publ. by Ullstein GmbH; Editor-in-Chief Florian V. Heintze; circ. 129,636.

Frankfurter Allgemeine Sonntagszeitung: Hellerhofstr. 2–4, 60327 Frankfurt a.M.; tel. (69) 75910; fax (69) 75911773; e-mail sonntagszeitung@faz.de; internet www.faz.de; Sunday; Publrs Werner D'Inka, Berthold Kohler, Günther Nonnenmacher, Frank Schirrmacher, Holger Steltzner; circ. 322,521 (June 2007).

Rheinischer Merkur: Postfach 201164, 53141 Bonn; Godesberger Allee 91, 53175 Bonn; tel. (228) 8840; fax (228) 884299; e-mail anzeigen@merkur.de; internet www.merkur.de; f. 1946; weekly; circ. 106,000.

Sonntag Aktuell: Plieninger Str. 150, 70567 Stuttgart; tel. (711) 72050; fax (711) 72053509; e-mail redaktion@soak.zgs.de; Sunday; circ. 869,500.

Welt am Sonntag: Axel-Springer-Str. 65, 10888 Berlin; tel. (30) 259100; e-mail leserbriefe@wams.de; internet www.weltamsonntag.de; Sunday; publ. by Axel Springer Verlag AG; Editor-in-Chief Christoph Keese; circ. 404,343 (June 2007).

Die Zeit: Speersort 1, Pressehaus, 20095 Hamburg; tel. (40) 32800; fax (40) 327111; internet www.zeit.de; f. 1946; weekly; Editor-in-Chief Giovanni di Lorenzo; circ. 455,000.

SELECTED PERIODICALS

Agriculture

Bauernzeitung: Postfach 310448, 10634 Berlin; Wilhelmsaue 37, 10713 Berlin; tel. (30) 46406-301; fax (30) 46406-319; e-mail bauernzeitung@bauernverlag.de; internet www.bauernzeitung.de; f. 1960; agricultural weekly; Editor-in-Chief Ralf Stephan; circ. 24,441 (June 2007).

Bayerisches Landwirtschaftliches Wochenblatt: Postfach 200523, 80005 München; Bayerstr. 57, 80335 München; tel. (89) 53098901; fax (89) 5328537; e-mail blw@dlv.de; internet www.wochenblatt-dlv.de; f. 1810; weekly; organ of the Bayerischer Bauernverband; Editor-in-Chief Johannes Urban; circ. 101,776 (June 2007).

dlz agrarmagazin: Postfach 400580, 80705 München; Lothstr. 29, 80797 München; tel. (89) 12705276; fax (089) 12705546; e-mail reddlz@dlv.de; internet www.dlz-agrarmagazin.de; publ. by Deutscher Landwirtschaftsverlag GmbH; Editor-in-Chief Detlef Steinert; circ. 66,771 (June 2007).

Eisenbahn-Landwirt: Ostring 6, 76131 Karlsruhe; tel. (721) 62830; fax (721) 628310; e-mail info@druck-verlag-sw.de; internet www.druck-verlag-sw.de; f. 1918; monthly; publ. by Druckhaus Karlsruhe, Druck + Verlagsgesellschaft Südwest mbH; Dir Rolf Haase; circ. 83,117 (June 2007).

Landpost: Wollgrasweg 31, 70599 Stuttgart; tel. (711) 16779-0; fax (711) 4586093; e-mail murschel@vdaw.de; internet www.vdaw.de; f. 1945; weekly; agriculture and gardening; Editor Erich Reich; circ. 14,727 (June 2007).

The Arts

Art. Das Kunstmagazin: Am Baumwall 11, 20459 Hamburg; tel. (40) 37030; fax (40) 37035618; e-mail kunst@art-magazin.de; internet www.art-magazin.de; f. 1979; monthly; publ. by Gruner + Jahr AG & Co KG; Editor-in-Chief Tim Sommer; circ. 69,704 (June 2007).

Intelligente Architektur: Fasanenweg 18, 70771 Leinfelden-Echterdingen; tel. (711) 7591286; fax (711) 7591410; e-mail ait-red@ait-online.de; internet www.xia-online.de; f. 1890; quarterly; Editor Dr D. Danner; circ. 17,500.

Theater der Zeit: Klosterstr. 68–70, 10179 Berlin; tel. (30) 24722414; fax (30) 24722415; e-mail redaktion@theaterderzeit.de; internet www.theaterderzeit.de; f. 1946; monthly; theatre, drama, opera, children's theatre, puppet theatre, dance; Editors Anja Dürrschmidt, Nina Peters, Dirk Pilz; circ. 8,000.

Theater heute: Reinhardtstr. 29, 10117 Berlin; tel. (30) 25449510; fax (30) 25449512; e-mail redaktion@theaterheute.de; internet www.theaterheute.de; f. 1960; monthly; Editors Barbara Burckhardt, Eva Behrendt, Dr Michael Merschmeier, Dr Franz Wille.

Economics, Finance and Industry

Absatzwirtschaft: Postfach 101102, 40002 Düsseldorf; Kasernenstr. 67, 40213 Düsseldorf; tel. (211) 8871422; fax (211) 8871420; e-mail absatzwirtschaft@fachverlag.de; internet www.absatzwirtschaft.de; f. 1958; monthly; marketing; Dirs Johannes Höfer, Dr Tobias Schulz-Isenbeck; Editor Christoph Berdi; circ. 25,000.

Atw—Internationale Zeitschrift für Kernenergie: Informationskreis KernEnergie, Robert-Koch-Pl. 4, 10115 Berlin; tel. (30) 49855530; fax (30) 49855518; e-mail w.liebholz@vhb.de; internet www.kernenergie.net/atw/de; f. 1956; monthly; technical, scientific and economic aspects of nuclear engineering and technology; Editor Volker Wasgindt; circ. 4,500.

Der Betrieb: Postfach 101102, 40002 Düsseldorf; Kasernenstr. 67, 40213 Düsseldorf; tel. (211) 8871451; fax (211) 8871450; e-mail der-betrieb@vhb.de; weekly; business administration, revenue law, corporate law, labour and social legislation; Editor-in-Chief Dr Günther Ackermann; circ. 24,300.

Börse: Postfach 800227, 81602 München; Weihenstephaner Str. 7, 81673 München; tel. (89) 4152200; fax (89) 4152383; e-mail leserbriefe@boerse-online.de; internet www.boerse-online.de; f. 1987; weekly; German and international stocks and stock-related investments; publ. by BÖRSE ONLINE Verlag GmbH & Co KG; Editor-in-Chief Stefanie Burgmaier; circ. 115,990.

Capital: Das Wirtschaftsmagazin Verlagsgruppe Köln, G+J Wirtschaftspresse, Eupener Str. 70, 50933 Köln; tel. (221) 490800; fax (221) 4908285; e-mail capital@capital.de; internet www.capital.de; f. 1962; fortnightly; business magazine; publ. by Gruner + Jahr AG & Co KG; circ. 218,293.

Creditreform: Postfach 101102, 40002 Düsseldorf; Kasernenstr. 67, 40213 Düsseldorf; tel. (211) 8871461; fax (211) 8871463; e-mail k.ernst@vhb.de; internet www.creditreform-magazin.de; f. 1879; Editor Klaus-Werner Ernst; circ. 120,825.

H&V Journal Handelsvermittlung und Vertrieb: Mainzer-Land-Str. 238, 60326 Frankfurt a.M.; Siegel-Verlag Otto Müller GmbH; tel. (69) 75890950; fax (69) 75890960; e-mail info@svffm.de; internet www.svffm.de; f. 1949; monthly; Editor Dr Andreas Paffhausen; circ. 14,956.

Impulse: Eupener Str. 70, 50933 Köln; tel. (221) 490801; fax (221) 4908285; e-mail leserservice@impulse.de; internet www.impulse.de; f. 1980; monthly; business and entrepreneurship; publ. by Gruner + Jahr AG & Co KG; Editor-in-Chief Dr Klaus Schweinsberg; circ. 135,531.

Industrie-Anzeiger: Postfach 100252, 70746 Leinfelden-Echterdingen; tel. (711) 7594451; internet www.industrieanzeiger.de; f. 1879; weekly; Editor-in-Chief Werner Götz; circ. 45,000.

Management International Review: Abraham-Lincoln-Str. 46, 65189 Wiesbaden; tel. (611) 7878230; fax (611) 7878411; e-mail mir@bwl.uni-kiel.de; internet www.bwl.uni-kiel.de/mir; six published issues; English; publ. by Gabler Verlag; Editors Prof. Dr M.-J. Oesterle (Bremen), Prof. Dr J. Wolf (Kiel).

VDI Nachrichten: Postfach 101054, Heinrichstr. 24, 40001 Düsseldorf; tel. (211) 61880; fax (211) 6188112; e-mail redaktion@vdi-nachrichten.com; internet www.vdi-nachrichten.com; f. 1946; weekly; technology and economics; circ. 165,000.

Versicherungswirtschaft: Klosestr. 20–24, 76137 Karlsruhe; tel. (721) 35090; fax (721) 3502-201; e-mail knippenberg@vvw.de; internet www.vvw.de; f. 1946; fortnightly; Editor Hubert Clemens; circ. 10,000.

WirtschaftsWoche: Kasernenstr. 67, 40213 Düsseldorf; tel. (211) 8870; fax (211) 887972114; e-mail wiwo@wiwo.de; internet www.wiwo.de; weekly; business; Editor Stefan Baron; circ. 183,000.

Education and Youth

Bravo: Charles-de-Gaulle-Str. 8, 81737 München; tel. (89) 6786700; fax (89) 6702033; e-mail post@bravo.de; internet www.bravo.de; weekly; for young people; circ. 500,000.

Computer Bild: Axel-Springer-Pl. 1, 20350 Hamburg; tel. (40) 34724300; fax (40) 34724683; e-mail redaktion@computerbild.de; internet www.computerbild.de; f. 1996; publ. by Axel Springer Verlag AG; circ. 947,807.

Erziehung und Wissenschaft: Goldammerweg 16, 45134 Essen; tel. (201) 843000; fax (201) 472590; e-mail info@stamm.de; internet www.stamm.de; f. 1948; monthly; Editor-in-Chief ULF RÖDDE; circ. 255,775.

PÄDAGOGIK: Werderstr. 10, 69469 Weinheim; tel. (6201) 6007349; fax (6201) 6007354; e-mail p.e.kalb@beltz.de; internet www.beltz.de/html/frm_paedagogikZ.htm; f. 1949; monthly, double issue for July/August; Editor Prof. Dr J. BASTIAN; circ. 15,000.

Praxis Deutsch: Im Brande 17, 30926 Seelze/Velber; tel. (511) 40004139; fax (511) 40004219; e-mail redaktion.pd@friedrich-verlag.de; internet www.friedrich-verlag.de; six a year; German language and literature; publ. by Erhard Friedrich Verlag GmbH; circ. 17,000.

Law

Deutsche Richterzeitung: Kronenstr. 73/74, 10117 Berlin; tel. (206) 125-0; fax (206) 125-25; internet www.driz.de; f. 1909; monthly; circ. 11,000.

Juristenzeitung: Postfach 2040, 72010 Tübingen; Wilhelmstr. 18, 72074 Tübingen; tel. (7071) 9230; fax (7071) 92367; e-mail jz@mohr.de; internet www.mohr.de/jz.html; f. 1944; fortnightly; Editor HEIDE SCHAPKA; circ. 5,400.

Juristische Rundschau: Postfach 303421, 10728 Berlin; Lützowstr. 33, 10785 Berlin; tel. (30) 26005123; fax (30) 26005329; e-mail jr@degruyter.de; internet www.degruyter.de; f. 1922; monthly; publ. by De Gruyter Rechtswissenschaften Verlags GmbH; Editors-in-Chief Prof. Dr DIRK OLZEN, Dr GERHARD SCHÄFER.

Neue Juristische Wochenschrift: Postfach 110241, 60037 Frankfurt a.M.; Beethovenstr. 7B, 60325 Frankfurt a.M.; tel. (69) 7560910; fax (69) 75609149; e-mail redaktion@beck-frankfurt.de; internet www.njw.de; f. 1947; weekly; Editor-in-Chief Prof. Dr ACHIM SCHÜNDER; circ. 55,000.

Rabels Zeitschrift für ausländisches und internationales Privatrecht: Mittelweg 187, 20148 Hamburg; tel. (40) 41900263; fax (40) 41900288; e-mail heinrich@mpipriv.de; internet www.mpipriv-hh.mpg.de; f. 1927; quarterly; German and English editions; Editors JÜRGEN BASEDOW, KLAUS J. HOPT, REINHARD ZIMMERMANN.

Versicherungsrecht: Klosestr. 20–24, 76137 Karlsruhe; tel. (721) 35090; fax (721) 3509206; e-mail redaktion-versr@vvw.de; internet www.vvw.de; f. 1950; insurance law; three a month; Editor Prof. Dr EGON LORENZ; circ. 6,600.

Zeitschrift für die gesamte Strafrechtswissenschaft: Postfach 303421, 10728 Berlin; Lützowstr. 33, 10785 Berlin; tel. (30) 26005123; fax (30) 26005329; e-mail recht@degruyter.com; internet www.degruyter.de; f. 1881; quarterly; publ. by De Gruyter Rechtswissenschaften Verlags GmbH; Editors-in-Chief Prof. Dr KRISTIAN KÜHL, Prof. Dr JOACHIM VOGEL.

Politics, Literature, Current Affairs

Akzente: Vilshofener Str. 10, 81679 München; tel. (89) 998300; fax (89) 99830460; e-mail zeller@hanser.de; internet www.hanser.de; f. 1954; Editor MICHAEL KRÜGER.

Eulenspiegel: Gubener Str. 47, 10243 Berlin; tel. (30) 29346311; fax (30) 29346322; e-mail redaktion@eulenspiegel-zeitschrift.de; internet www.eulenspiegel-zeitschrift.de; f. 1946; political, satirical and humorous monthly; Editors JÜRGEN NOWAK, HARTMUT BERLIN; circ. 100,000.

Focus: Arabellastr. 23, 81925 München; tel. (89) 92500; fax (89) 92502026; e-mail anzeigen@focus.de; internet www.focus.de; f. 1993; weekly; political, general; publ. by Burda GmbH & Co KG; circ. 779,866.

Gesellschaft-Wirtschaft-Politik (GWP): Sürderstr. 22A, 51375 Leverkusen; tel. (2171) 344594; fax (2171) 344693; e-mail redaktion@gwp-pb.de; internet www.gwp-pb.de; quarterly; economics, politics, education; publ. by Verlag Barbara Budrich; Editors Prof. Dr SIBYLLE REINHARDT, Prof. Dr STEFAN HRADIL, Prof. Dr ROLAND STURM.

Internationale Politik: Rauchstr. 17/18, 10787 Berlin; tel. (30) 25423146; fax (30) 25423167; e-mail ip@dgap.org; internet www.internationalepolitik.de; f. 1946; monthly; journal of the German Council on Foreign Relations; edns in English (*IP International Edition*, quarterly) and Russian (bimonthly); publ. by Frankfurts Societäts-Druckerei GmbH, Frankfurt a.M; Exec. Editor SABINE ROSENBLATT; circ. 5,000.

Literarische Welt: Axel-Springer-Str. 65, 10888 Berlin; tel. (30) 259172916; fax (30) 259172939; e-mail literaturwelt@welt.de; f. 1971; weekly; literary supplement of Die Welt.

Merian Jahreszeiten Verlag: Berg-am-Laim-Str. 47, 81673 München; tel. (89) 4500070; fax (89) 450007222; e-mail redaktion@merian.de; internet www.merian.de; f. 1948; monthly; every issue deals with a country or a city; Chief Editor ANDREAS HALLASCHKA; circ. 150,000.

Merkur (Deutsche Zeitschrift für europäisches Denken): Mommsenstr. 27, 10629 Berlin; tel. (30) 32709414; fax (30) 32709415; e-mail merkur.zeitschrift@snafu.de; internet www.online-merkur.de; f. 1947; 10 monthly issues, double issue Sept./Oct.; literary, political; Editors KARL HEINZ BOHRER, KURT SCHEEL; circ. 4,800.

Neue Gesellschaft—Frankfurter Hefte: c/o Friedrich-Ebert-Stiftung Berlin, Hiroshimastr. 17, 10785 Berlin; tel. (30) 26935819; fax (30) 26935855; e-mail norbert.seitz@fes.de; internet www.ngfh.de; f. 1946; monthly; cultural, political; Editor-in-Chief PETER GLOTZ; circ. 6,000.

Neue Rundschau: Hedderichstr. 114, 60596 Frankfurt a.M.; tel. (69) 60620; fax (69) 6062319; e-mail neuerundschau@fischerverlage.de; f. 1890; quarterly; literature and essays; Editors HANS-JÜRGEN BALMES, JÖRG BONG, ALEXANDER RÖSLER, OLIVER VOGEL; circ. 3,000.

Sozialdemokrat Magazin: Stresemannstr. 30, 10963 Berlin; tel. (255) 94300; fax (255) 94390; publ. by Berliner vorwärts-Verlagsgesellschaft mbH; circ. 834,599.

Der Spiegel: Brandstwiete 19/Ost-West-Str. 23, 20457 Hamburg; tel. (40) 30070; fax (40) 30072247; e-mail spiegel@spiegel.de; internet www.spiegel.de; f. 1947; weekly; political, general; Editor-in-Chief STEFAN AUST; circ. 1,050,000.

Universitas: Postfach 101061, 70009 Stuttgart; Birkenwaldstr. 44, 70191 Stuttgart; tel. (711) 25820; fax (711) 2582290; e-mail universitas@hirzel.de; internet www.hirzel.de/universitas; f. 1946; monthly; scientific, literary and philosophical; Editors Dr CHRISTIAN ROTTA, DIRK KATZSCHMANN; circ. 4,500.

VdK-Zeitung: Wurzerstr. 4A, 53175 Bonn; tel. (228) 820930; fax (228) 8209343; e-mail info@vdk.de; internet www.vdk.de; f. 1950; monthly; publ. by Sozialverband VdK Deutschland eV; Editors ULRICH LASCHET, SABINE KOHLS, MICHAEL PAUSDER, TANJA SCHÄFER, THOMAS A. SEEHUBER; circ. 1,300,000.

VdK-Zeitung, Bayern: Schellingstr. 31, 80799 München; tel. (89) 2117217; fax (89) 2117280; e-mail info@vdk.de; internet www.vdk-bayern.de; f. 1948; monthly; publ. by Sozialverband VdK Deutschland eV; Editor ALBRECHT ENGEL; circ. 1,100,000.

Popular

Anna: Arabellastr. 23, 81925 München; tel. (89) 92502772; fax (89) 92502745; f. 1974; monthly; publ. by Burda GmbH & Co KG; knitting and needlecrafts; Editor AENNE BURDA; circ. 81,046.

AUTO BILD: Axel-Springer-Pl. 1, 20350 Hamburg; tel. (40) 34700; fax (40) 345660; e-mail redaktion@autobild.de; internet www.autobild.de; f. 1986; weekly; publ. by Axel Springer Verlag AG; Man. Editors RALF BIELEFELDT, JAN MEIBOHM; circ. 735,000.

Bild der Frau: Axel-Springer-Pl. 1, 20355 Hamburg; tel. (40) 34700; f. 1983; publ. by Axel Springer Verlag AG; circ. 1,858,711.

Bild + Funk: München; tel. (89) 92502772; fax (89) 92502745; internet www.burda.de; publ. by Burda GmbH & Co KG; radio and television weekly; Editor GÜNTER VAN WAASEN; circ. 1,040,829.

Brigitte: Am Baumwall 11, 20459 Hamburg; tel. (40) 37030; fax (40) 37035679; e-mail infoline@brigitte.de; internet www.brigitte.de; f. 1954; fortnightly; women's magazine; also publishes Brigitte Balance (2 a year; circ. 128,000), Brigitte Cookie (quarterly; cooking; circ. 300,000), Brigitte Woman (6 a year; 380,000) and Brigitte Young Miss (monthly; circ. 163,787); publ. by Gruner + Jahr AG & Co KG; Editor-in-Chief ANDREAS LEBERT; circ. 822,278.

Bunte: Arabellastr. 23, 81925 München; tel. (89) 92500; fax (89) 92503427; internet www.bunte.de; f. 1948; weekly family illustrated; publ. by Bunte Entertainment Verlag GmbH; circ. 780,238.

Burda Modemagazin: Am Destendamm 1, 77652 Offenburg; tel. (781) 840; fax (781) 843291; e-mail burdamoden@vab.burda.com; internet www.burdamode.com; f. 1949; monthly; fashion, beauty; publ. by Verlag Aenne Burda GmbH & Co KG; circ. 1,000,000.

Deutschland: Postfach 10081, 60008 Frankfurt a.M.; Frankenallee 71–81, 60628 Frankfurt a.M.; tel. (69) 75014272; fax (69) 75014502; e-mail vertrieb.deutschland@fsd.de; internet www.magazine-deutschland.de; six a year; edns in German, Arabic, Chinese, English, French, Hebrew, Hungarian, Japanese, Portuguese, Russian, Spanish, Turkish; Editor-in-Chief PETER HINTEREDER; circ. 400,000.

Elle: Arabellastr. 23, 81925 München; tel. (89) 92500; fax (89) 92503332; e-mail elle@elle.burda.com; internet www.elle.de;

GERMANY

monthly; publ. by ELLE Verlag GmbH; Editor-in-Chief SABINE NEDELCHEV-BRANDT; circ. 221,000.

Eltern: Weihenstephanerstr. 7, 81673 München; tel. (89) 41520; fax (89) 4152666; e-mail lewicki.marie-luise@muc.guj.de; internet www.eltern.de; f. 1966; monthly; for parents of young children; publ. by Gruner + Jahr AG & Co KG; Editor MARIE-LUISE LEWICKI; circ. 385,906.

Eltern for family: internet www.eltern.de/forfamily; f. 1996; monthly; for parents of older children; circ. 162,046.

Essen & Trinken: Am Baumwall 11, 20459 Hamburg; tel. (40) 37032724; fax (40) 37035677; internet www.essen-und-trinken.de; f. 1972; monthly; food and drink; publ. by Gruner + Jahr AG & Co KG; circ. 215,062.

Essen & Trinken Für Jeden Tag: internet www.fuerjedentag.de; f. 2003; 10 a year; small-format; recipes; circ. 457,445.

Familie & Co: Kaiser-Joseph-Str. 263, 79098 Freiburg i.Br.; tel. (761) 705780; fax (761) 70578656; e-mail redaktion@familie.de; internet www.familie.de; f. 1996; monthly; publ. by Family Media GmbH & Co; circ. 215,785.

FF: Mauerstr. 86–88, 10117 Berlin; tel. (30) 231010; fax (30) 23101265; weekly; Editor ALFRED WAGNER; circ. 610,000.

Flora Garten: Am Baumwall 11, 20459 Hamburg; tel. (40) 37033771; fax (40) 37035682; internet www.floragarten.de; f. 1985; monthly; gardening; publ. by Gruner + Jahr AG & Co KG; circ. 240,611.

Frau aktuell: Adlerstr. 22, Düsseldorf; tel. (211) 36660; fax (211) 3666231; e-mail frauaktuell@waso.de; f. 1965; Editor INGRID THEIS; circ. 450,000.

Frau im Spiegel: Postfach 500445, 22704 Hamburg; Griegstr. 75, 22763 Hamburg; tel. (40) 883030654; fax (40) 88303467; e-mail serviceredaktion@frau-im-spiegel.de; internet www.frau-im-spiegel.de; f. 1947; weekly; aimed at women over 35; also publishes Frau Im Spiegel Legenden, a quarterly special edition concentrating on the life of a particular celebrity (circ. 80,000); publ. by Verlag Ehrlich & Sohn GmbH & Co KG; Editor-in-Chief SABINE INGWERSEN; circ. 400,709.

Freundin: Arabellastr. 23, 81925 München; tel. (89) 92500; fax (89) 92503991; e-mail freundin@burda.com; internet www.freundin.com; f. 1948; fortnightly; for young women; publ. by Burda GmbH & Co KG; Chief Editor RENATE ROSENTHAL; circ. 517,280.

Funk Uhr: Axel-Springer-Pl. 1, 20355 Hamburg; tel. (40) 34726315; fax (40) 34722601; f. 1952; television weekly; publ. by Axel Springer Verlag AG; Editor JAN VON FRENDELL; circ. 1,000,000.

Für Dich: Karl-Liebknecht-Str. 29, 10178 Berlin; tel. (2) 2440; fax (2) 2443327; f. 1962; women's weekly; Editors Dr HANS EGGERT, PETER PANKAU; circ. 350,000.

Für Sie: Possmoorweg 5, 22301 Hamburg; tel. (40) 27172300; fax (40) 27172048; e-mail anzeigen@fuer-sie.de; internet www.fuer-sie.de; fortnightly; women's magazine; circ. 572,159.

Gala: Schaarsteinweg 14, 20459 Hamburg; tel. (40) 37030; fax (40) 37035744; e-mail redaktion@gala.de; internet www.gala.de; f. 1994; weekly; celebrities; publ. by Norddeutsche Verlagsgesellschaft mbH; Editor-in-Chief PETER LEWANDOWSKI; circ. 385,372.

Geo: Am Baumwall 11, 20459 Hamburg; tel. (40) 37030; fax (40) 37035648; e-mail briefe@geo.de; internet www.geo.de; f. 1976; monthly; reports on science, politics and religion; publ. by Gruner + Jahr AG & Co KG; Editor-in-Chief PETER-MATTHIAS GAEDE; circ. 457,317.

Geo Epoche: f. 1999; quarterly; history; circ. 86,108.

Geo Saison: f. 1989; 10 a year; travel; circ. 125,877.

Geo Saison für Geniesser: f. 1999; 2 a year; luxury travel and lifestyle; circ. 70,000.

Geo Special: f. 1981; 6 a year; travel, each issue on a particular country, region or city; circ. 106,288.

Geo Wissen: f. 1987; 2 a year; developments and trends in human and natural sciences, each issue dedicated to a particular topic; circ. 140,000.

Geokompakt: f. 2004; quarterly; each issue dedicated to a particular general education topic; circ. 180,000.

Geolino: f. 1996; monthly; general interest magazine for boys and girls aged 8–14; supplemented game tips, puzzles, crafts, events and posters; circ. 272,418.

Gong: Postfach 400748, 80707 München; GONG Verlag GmbH & Co KG, Münchner Str. 101/09, 85737 Ismaning; tel. (89) 272700; fax (89) 272707490; e-mail kontakt@gongverlag.de; internet www.gong.de; f. 1948; radio and TV weekly; Editor CARSTEN PFEFFERKORN.

Guter Rat: Superillu Verlag GmbH & Co KG, Zimmerstr. 28, 10969 Berlin; tel. (30) 23876600; fax (30) 23876395; e-mail redaktion@guter-rat.de; f. 1945; monthly; consumer magazine; Editor-in-Chief WERNER ZEDLER; circ. 260,000.

Hörzu: Postfach 4110, Axel-Springer-Pl. 1, 20355 Hamburg; tel. (40) 34700; fax (40) 34722628; f. 1946; radio and television; publ. by Axel Springer Verlag AG; Editor MICHAEL HOHMANN; circ. 2,300,000.

How To Spend It: Stubbenhuk 3, 20459 Hamburg; tel. (40) 319900; fax (40) 31990310; f. 2001; 10 a year; luxury lifestyle; publ. by Financial Times Deutschland GmbH & Co KG; circ. 98,892.

Journal für die Frau: Axel-Springer-Pl. 1, 20350 Hamburg; tel. (40) 34700; fax (40) 34724201; e-mail chefredaktion@journal.de; f. 1978; fortnightly; women's magazine; publ. by Axel Springer Verlag AG; circ. 270,000.

Kicker-Sportmagazin: Badstr. 4–6, 90402 Nürnberg; tel. (911) 2160; e-mail info@kicker.de; internet www.kicker.de; f. 1920; two a week; illustrated sports magazine; publ. by Olympia Verlag; Man. Dir DIETRICH PUSCHMANN; circ. 246,669 (Mon.), 209,523 (Thurs.) (2004).

Living At Home: Mönkedamm 11, 20457 Hamburg; tel. (40) 37034267; fax (40) 37035838; internet www.livingathome.de; f. 2000; monthly; lifestyle magazine covering furnishing, decorating, cooking, entertaining and gardening; publ. by LaH Multimedia GmbH; Editor-in-Chief NADJA STAVENHAGEN; circ. 217,836.

Meine Familie & ich: Arabellastr. 23, 81925 München; tel. (89) 92500; fax (89) 92503030; publ. by Burda GmbH & Co KG; circ. 620,000.

Neue Post: Postfach 2427, Burchardstr. 11, 20095 Hamburg; weekly; circ. 1,728,750.

Neue Revue: Postfach 2411, Ost-West-Str. 20, 20077 Hamburg; tel. (40) 30190; fax (40) 30194401; e-mail neue-revue@hbv.de; f. 1946; illustrated weekly; Editor-in-Chief PETER BARTEL; circ. 1,121,184.

Petra: Jahreszeiten Verlag, Possmoorweg 5, 22301 Hamburg; tel. (40) 27173009; fax (40) 27173020; e-mail redaktion@petra.de; internet www.petra.de; monthly; circ. 253,744.

Praline: Hammerbrookstr. 5, 20097 Hamburg; fax (40) 24870190; weekly; women's magazine; circ. 569,300.

Readers Digest Deutschland: Postfach 106020, 70049 Stuttgart; Augustenstr. 1, 70178 Stuttgart; tel. (711) 66020; fax (711) 6602547; e-mail verlag@readersdigest.de; internet www.readersdigest.de; f. 1948; owned by Reader's Digest Assen Inc., Pleasantville NY (USA); magazines, general, serialized and condensed books, music and video programmes; Man. Dir WERNER NEUNZIG; circ. 800,000.

Schöner Essen: Am Baumwall 11, 20459 Hamburg; tel. (40) 37032724; fax (40) 37035677; internet www.schoener-essen.de; f. 1985; monthly; food; publ. by Gruner + Jahr AG & Co KG; circ. 91,472.

Schöner Wohnen: Am Baumwall 11, 20459 Hamburg; tel. (40) 37030; fax (40) 37035676; f. 1960; monthly; homes and gardens; publ. by Gruner + Jahr AG & Co KG; Editor ANGELIKA JAHR; circ. 320,000.

Schöner Wohnen Decoration: Hamburg; tel. (40) 37030; fax (40) 37035645; f. 1989; 6 a year; home decoration and furnishing; circ. 41,126.

7 Tage: Postfach 2071, 76490 Baden-Baden; Rotweg 8, 76532 Baden-Baden; tel. (7221) 3501501; fax (7221) 3501599; e-mail 7tage@klambt.de; internet www.klambt.de; f. 1843; weekly; Chief Editor PETER VIKTOR KULIG; circ. 480,000.

Sport Bild: Axel-Springer-Pl. 1, 20350 Hamburg; tel. (40) 34700; fax (40) 34722085; e-mail sportbild@asv.de; internet www.sportbild.de; f. 1988; weekly; publ. by Axel Springer Verlag AG; circ. 522,717.

Stern: 20444 Hamburg; Am Baumwall 11, 20459 Hamburg; tel. (40) 37030; fax (40) 37035631; e-mail stern@stern.de; internet www.stern.de; f. 1948; weekly; publ. by Gruner + Jahr AG & Co KG; Editors-in-Chief THOMAS OSTERKORN, ANDREAS PETZOLD; circ. 1,306,244.

Stern Biografie: f. 2002; quarterly; biographies; circ. 120,000.

Stern Fotografie: f. 1996; quarterly; photography; circ. 10,000.

Stern Gesund Leben: f. 2003; 6 a year; healthy living; 160 pages in four sections: prevention, nutrition, fitness and wellbeing; circ. 130,363.

TV Hören + Sehen: Burchardstr. 11, 20095 Hamburg; tel. (40) 30190; fax (40) 30194081; f. 1962; weekly; Chief Editor MARION HORN; circ. 2,936,670.

TVneu: Axel-Springer-Pl. 1, 20355 Hamburg; tel. (40) 34700; fax (40) 345811; publ. by Axel Springer Verlag AG; circ. 917,293.

Wochenend: Burchardstr. 11, 20095 Hamburg; tel. (40) 30190; fax (40) 30194081; f. 1948; weekly; Editor GERD ROHLOF; circ. 668,278.

Woman: Postfach 40, 20444 Hamburg; Kehrwieder 8, 20457 Hamburg; tel. (40) 37030; fax (40) 37035802; e-mail service@woman-magazin.de; internet www.woman-magazin.de; f. 2002; fortnightly; aimed at women aged around 30 years; Editor-in-Chief CHRISTINE ELLINGHAUS; circ. 330,509.

GERMANY

Religion and Philosophy

Chrismon plus rheinland: Postfach 302255, 40402 Düsseldorf; tel. (211) 43690150; fax (211) 43690100; e-mail redaktion@chrismon-rheinland; f. 2004; monthly; Protestant; Editor-in-Chief JUDITH WEBER; circ. 18,000.

Christ in der Gegenwart: Hermann-Herder-Str. 4, 79104 Freiburg i. Br.; tel. (761) 2717276; fax (761) 2717243; e-mail cig@herder.de; internet www.christ-in-der-gegenwart.de; f. 1948; weekly; Editor JOHANNES RÖSER; circ. 34,000.

Christlicher Digest: Okenstr. 23, 77652 Offenburg; tel. (781) 28428940; fax (781) 28428950; e-mail redaktion@christlicherdigest.de; internet www.christlicherdigest.de; f. 2002 by merger of Evangelischer Digest (f. 1958), Katholischer Digest (f. 1949) and Der Sonntagsbrief (f. 1974); monthly; publ. by Verlag Christlicher Digest GmbH & Co KG; Editor FRED HEINE.

Der Dom: Karl-Schurz-Str. 26, 33100 Paderborn; tel. (5251) 1530; fax (5251) 153104; e-mail karl.wegner@bonifatius.de; internet www.derdom.org; f. 1946; weekly; Catholic; publ. by Bonifatius GmbH, Druck-Buch-Verlag; circ. 65,000.

Katholisches Sonntagsblatt: Senefelderstr. 12, 73760 Ostfildern; tel. (711) 44060; fax (711) 4406101; e-mail ks@schwabenverlag.de; internet www.schwabenverlag.de; f. 1848; weekly; publ. by Schwabenverlag AG; circ. 71,500.

Katholische Sonntagszeitung für Deutschland: Verlag Christliche Familie GmbH, Komödienstr. 48, 50667 Köln; tel. (821) 502420; fax (821) 5024241; e-mail voss@suv.de; internet www.katolische-sonntagszeitung.de; f. 1885; weekly; Publr Dr DIRK HERMANN VOSS; Chief Editor Dr GERDA RÖDER.

Kirche und Leben: Postfach 4320, 48024 Münster; Breul 27, 48143 Münster; tel. (251) 48390; fax (251) 4839122; e-mail k-und-l@muenster.de; internet www.kirche-und-leben.muenster.de; f. 1945; weekly; Catholic; Chief Editor Dr HANS-JOSEF JOEST; circ. 160,000.

Kirchenzeitung für das Erzbistum Köln: Postfach 102041, 50460 Köln; Ursulapl. 1, 50668 Köln; tel. (221) 1619131; fax (221) 1619216; weekly; Chief Editor Mgr ERICH LÄUFER; circ. 120,000.

Philosophisches Jahrbuch: Ludwig-Maximilians-Universität, Geschwister-Scholl-Pl. 1, 80539 München; f. 1893; two a year.

Science and Medicine

Angewandte Chemie: Postfach 101161, 69451 Weinheim; Boschstr. 12, 69469 Weinheim; tel. (6201) 606315; fax (6201) 602328; e-mail angewandte@wiley-vch.de; internet www.angewandte.de; f. 1888; applied chemistry; weekly, 48 a year; publ. by Wiley-VCH Verlag GmbH & Co KGaA; circ. 3,580; international edition in English, f. 1962; circ. 3,600.

Ärztliche Praxis: Gabrielenstr. 9, 80636 München; tel. (89) 89817404; fax (89) 89817400; e-mail khp@rbi.de; internet www.aerztlichepraxis.de; two a week; publ. by Reed Business Information GmbH; Editor-in-Chief KARL-HEINZ PATZER; circ. 60,000.

Berichte der Bunsen-Gesellschaft für physikalische Chemie: VCH Verlagsgesellschaft mbH, Postfach 101161, Pappelallee 3, 69451 Weinheim/Bergstr.; tel. (6201) 6060; f. 1894; monthly; Editors R. AHLRICHS, W. FREYLAND, M. KAPPES, P. C. SCHMIDT; circ. 2,300.

Chemie-Ingenieur-Technik: Postfach 101161, 69451 Weinheim; tel. (6201) 606520; fax (6201) 606500; e-mail cit@wiley-vch.de; f. 1928; monthly; Editor B. BOECK; circ. 7,807.

Der Chirurg: Kirschnerstr. 1 (INF 110), 69120 Heidelberg; tel. (6221) 402813; fax (6221) 402014; f. 1928; surgery; monthly; Editor Prof. Dr Ch. HERFARTH; circ. 7,650.

Deutsche Apotheker Zeitung: Postfach 101061, 70009 Stuttgart; Birkenwaldstr. 44, 70191 Stuttgart; tel. (711) 2582238; fax (711) 2582291; e-mail daz@deutscher-apotheker-verlag.de; internet www.deutscher-apotheker-verlag.de; f. 1861; weekly; Editor PETER DITZEL; circ. 34,000.

Deutsche Medizinische Wochenschrift: Rüdigerstr. 14, 70469 Stuttgart; tel. (711) 8931232; fax (711) 8931235; e-mail dmw@thieme.de; internet www.thieme.de/dmw; f. 1875; weekly; Editor-in-Chief M. MIDDEKE; circ. 30,000.

Deutsche Zahnärztliche Zeitschrift: Deutscher Ärzte-Verlag, Dieselstr. 2, 50859 Köln; tel. (2234) 7011242; fax (2234) 7011515; e-mail dey@aerzteverlag.de; internet www.zahnheilkunde.de; f. 1945; monthly; dental medicine; Editors Prof. Dr GEURTSEN, Prof. Dr TH. KERSCHBAUM, Dr G. MASCHINSKI, Prof. Dr TH. HOFFMANN, Dr W. BENGEL; circ. 16,000.

Elektro Automation: Ernst-Mey-Str. 8, 70771 Leinfelden-Echterdingen; tel. (711) 7594279; fax (711) 7594221; e-mail ea.redaktion@konradin.de; internet www.ea-online.de; f. 1948; monthly; Editor-in-Chief STEFAN ZIEGLER; circ. 21,100.

Geographische Rundschau: Georg-Westermann-Allee 66, 38104 Braunschweig; tel. (531) 708385; fax (531) 708329; e-mail info@g-v.de; internet www.geographischerundschau.de; f. 1949; monthly; Man. Editor REINER JUENGST; circ. 12,000.

Geologische Rundschau (International Journal of Earth Sciences): Geologische Vereinigung e.V., Vulkanstr. 23, 56743 Mendig; tel. (2652) 989360; fax (2652) 989361; e-mail geol.ver@t-online.de; internet www.g-v.de; f. 1910; six a year; general, geological; Pres. Prof. Dr GEROLD WEFER; circ. 1,700.

Handchirurgie, Mikrochirurgie, Plastische Chirurgie: Postfach 300504, 70445 Stuttgart; Rüdigerstr. 14, 70469 Stuttgart; tel. (711) 89310; fax (711) 8931453; six a year; Editors Prof. Dr D. BUCK-GRAMCKO, Prof. Dr W. SCHNEIDER.

International Journal of Materials Research: Heisenbergstr. 3, 70569 Stuttgart; tel. (711) 6893525; fax (711) 6893653; e-mail ruehle@mf.mpg.de; f. 1911; monthly; fmrly Zeitschrift für Metallkunde; Editors M. RÜHLE, G. PETZOW, P. P. SCHEPP.

Journal of Neurology: Steinkopff Verlag, Poststr. 9, 64293 Darmstadt; tel. (6151) 828990; fax (6151) 8289940; e-mail tschech.steinkopff@springer.de; internet www.steinkopff.springer.de; f. 1891; official journal of the European Neurological Society; Editors-in-Chief T. BRANDT, D. H. MILLER.

Mund-, Kiefer- und Gesichtschirurgie: Glückstr. 11, 91054 Erlangen; tel. (9131) 8533601; fax (9131) 8536288; e-mail friedrich.neukam@uk-erlangen.de; internet www.mkg.uni-erlangen.de; seven a year; oral and maxillofacial surgery and oral pathology; Editor Prof. Dr FRIEDRICH W. NEUKAM.

Medizinische Klinik: Neumarkter Str. 43, 81673 München; tel. (89) 532920; fax (89) 53292100; e-mail verlag@urban-vogel.de; internet www.urban-vogel.de; f. 1904; monthly; Editor ANNA-MARIA WORSCH; circ. 14,000.

Nachrichten aus der Chemie: Postfach 900440, 60444 Frankfurt a.M.; tel. (69) 7917462; fax (69) 7917463; e-mail nachrichten@gdch.de; internet www.gdch.de/nch; f. 1953; monthly; journal of the German Chemical Society; Editor-in-Chief Dr ERNST GUGGOLZ; circ. 27,000.

National Geographic Deutschland: Am Baumwall 11, 20459 Hamburg; tel. (40) 37030; fax (40) 37035598; internet www.nationalgeographic.de; f. 1999; monthly; culture, history, nature, the Earth, the universe, people, animals, archaeology, paleontology, travel, research, expeditions; Editor-in-Chief KLAUS LIEDTKE; circ. 250,044.

NG World: Kehrwieder 8, 20457 Hamburg; tel. (40) 37030; fax (40) 37035598; e-mail pr@nationalgeographic-world.de; internet www.nationalgeographic-world.de; f. 2003; monthly; bilingual (German and English); for children aged 8–12 years; Editor SIEBO HEINKEN; circ. 180,000.

Natur + Kosmos: Konradin Medien GmbH, Bretonischer Ring 13, 85630 Grasbrunn; tel. (89) 45616220; fax (89) 45616300; internet www.natur.de; f. 1904; monthly; popular nature journal; Editor-in-Chief ILONA JERGER; circ. 100,000.

Naturwissenschaftliche Rundschau: Postfach 101061, 70009 Stuttgart; Birkenwaldstr. 44, 70191 Stuttgart; tel. (711) 2582295; fax (711) 2582283; e-mail nr@wissenschaftliche-verlagsgesellschaft.de; internet www.naturwissenschaftliche-rundschau.de; f. 1948; publ. by Gesellschaft Deutscher Naturforscher und Ärzte; monthly; scientific; Editor KLAUS REHFELD; circ. 5,000.

Planta Medica: Postfach 301120, 70451 Stuttgart; Georg Thieme Verlag, Rüdigerstr. 14, 70469 Stuttgart; tel. (711) 89310; fax (711) 8931298; e-mail custserv@thieme.com; internet www.thieme.com/plantamedica; f. 1952; 15 a year; journal of the Society of Medicinal Plant Research; Editor Prof. Dr LUC PEETERS.

P.M.: Weihenstephaner Str. 7, 81673 München; tel. (89) 41520; fax (89) 4152565; internet www.pm-magazin.de; f. 1978; monthly; technology, natural sciences, medicine, psychology, nature and the environment, history, philosophy, anthropology, culture, multimedia, the internet; publ. by Gruner + Jahr AG & Co KG; Publr HANS-HERMANN SPRADO; Man. Editor MICHAEL S. BUHL; circ. 406,466.

P.M. Fragen & Antworten: f. 2000; 6 a year; readers' questions and answers on science, technology, multimedia, economics, politics, health, medicine, nature, sex, relationships, history, culture, sports and entertainment.

P.M. History: f. 1993; monthly; circ. 76,232.

P.M. Intelligenz-trainer: f. 1997; monthly; problems to sharpen logic and enhance concentration, memory and patience.

P.M. Kreativ-trainer: f. 2000; monthly; creative puzzles.

P.M. Logik-trainer: f. 1988; monthly; logic exercises and puzzles; circ. 54,856.

P.M. Perspektive: f. 1986; quarterly; in each issue one topic from editorial spectrum of *P.M.* magazine (q.v.) is treated comprehensively and in-depth.

rfe: Am Friedrichshain 22, 10407 Berlin; tel. (30) 42151313; fax (30) 42151208; e-mail rfe.redaktion@hussberlin.de; internet www.rfe-online.de; f. 1952; monthly; technology and marketing of consumer goods electronics, digital imaging, multimedia, audio, video, broadcasting, TV; circ. 25,000.

Zeitschrift für Allgemeinmedizin: Postfach 301120, 70451 Stuttgart; Rüdigerstr. 14, 70469 Stuttgart; tel. (711) 89310; fax (711) 8931706; e-mail volker.niem@thieme.de; internet www.thieme.de/zfa; f. 1924; monthly; general and family medicine; publ. by Georg Thieme Verlag KG, Stuttgart; Editors Prof. Dr M. Kochen, Prof. Dr H.-H. Abholz, Prof. Dr W. Niebling; circ. 4,000.

Zeitschrift für Zahnärztliche Implantologie: Deutscher Zahnärzte-Verlag, Dieselstr. 2, 50859 Köln; tel. (2234) 7011242; fax (2234) 7011515; e-mail dey@aerzteverlag.de; internet www.zahnheilkunde.de; f. 1984; quarterly; dental medicine; Editors Prof. Dr H. Schliephake, Dr S. Schmidinger; circ. 7,200.

Zentralblatt für Neurochirurgie: Friedrich-Wilhelms Universität, Sigmund-Freud-Str. 25, 53127 Bonn; tel. (228) 2876501; fax (228) 2876573; e-mail zblatt.nch@ukb.uni-bonn.de; f. 1936; four a year; neuro-surgery, spine surgery, traumatology; Editor Prof. Dr J. Schramm; circ. 1,200.

NEWS AGENCIES

ddp (Deutscher Depeschendienst GmbH): Panoramastr. 1A, 10178 Berlin; tel. (30) 231220; fax (30) 23122182; e-mail info@ddp.de; internet www.ddp.de; f. 1971; merged with fmr official news agency of the GDR (Allgemeiner Deutscher Nachrichtendienst) 1992; maintains 22 branch offices in Germany; provides a daily news service and features in German; Man. Dir Dr Matthias Schulze; Editor-in-Chief Joachim Widmann.

dpa (Deutsche Presse-Agentur GmbH): Mittelweg 38, 20148 Hamburg; tel. (40) 41130; fax (40) 41132219; e-mail info@hbg.dpa.de; internet www.dpa.de; f. 1949; supplies all the daily newspapers, broadcasting stations and more than 1,000 further subscribers throughout Germany with its international, national and regional text, photo, audio, graphics and online services; English, Spanish, Arabic and German language news is also transmitted via direct satellite and the internet to press agencies, newspapers, radio and television stations, online services and non-media clients in more than 100 countries; Dir-Gen. Malte von Trotha; Editor-in-Chief Dr Wilm Herlyn.

vwd (Vereinigte Wirtschaftsdienste GmbH): Tilsiter Str. 1, 60487 Frankfurt am Main; tel. (69) 507010; fax (69) 50701126; e-mail sales@vwd.com; internet www.vwd.com; f. 1949; economic and financial news; Man. Dirs Edmund J. Keferstein, Spencer Bosse, Joachim Lauterbach.

PRESS AND JOURNALISTS' ASSOCIATIONS

Bundesverband Deutscher Zeitungsverleger eV (German Newspaper Publishers' Association): Markgrafenstr. 15, 10969 Berlin; tel. (30) 7262980; fax (30) 726298299; e-mail bdzv@bdzv.de; internet www.bdzv.de; 11 affiliated Land Asscns; Pres. Helmut Heinen; Chief Sec. Dr Volker Schulze.

Deutscher Journalisten-Verband (German Journalists' Association): Bennauerstr. 60, 53115 Bonn; tel. (228) 201720; fax (228) 2017233; e-mail djv@djv.de; internet www.djv.de; Chair. Prof. Dr Sigfried Weischenberg; Man. Dir Hubert Engeroff; 16 Land Asscns.

Verband Deutscher Zeitschriftenverleger eV (VDZ) (Association of German Magazine Publishers): Haus der Presse, Markgrafenstr. 15, 10969 Berlin; tel. (30) 726298101; fax (30) 7262898103; e-mail info@vdz.de; internet www.vdz.de; seven affiliated Land Asscns; Pres. Dr Hubert Burda; Chair., Exec. Bd Wolfgang Fürstner.

Verein der Ausländischen Presse in Deutschland eV (VAP) (Foreign Press Association): Pressehaus/1306, Schiffbauerdamm 40, 10117 Berlin; tel. (30) 22489547; fax (30) 22489549; e-mail info@vap-deutschland.org; internet www.vap-deutschland.org; f. 1906; Chair. Rozalia Romaniec.

Publishers

The following is a selection of the most prominent German publishing firms:

ADAC Verlag GmbH: Am Westpark 8, 81373 München; tel. (89) 76760; fax (89) 76764621; e-mail bettina.volk@adac.de; internet www.adac.de; f. 1958; guidebooks, legal brochures, maps, magazines; Man. Dir Dr Ralf Ueding.

Ariston Verlag GmbH & Co KG: München; tel. (89) 7241034; fax (89) 7241718; f. 1964; medicine, psychology; Man. Dir Frank Auerbach.

Aufbau Verlagsgruppe GmbH: Neue Promenade 6, 10178 Berlin; tel. (30) 283940; fax (30) 28394100; e-mail info@aufbau-verlag.de; f. 1945; fiction, non-fiction, classical literature; Dirs René Strien, Tom Erben.

J. P. Bachem Verlag GmbH: Ursulapl. 1, 50668 Köln; tel. (221) 16190; fax (221) 1619159; e-mail info@bachem-verlag.de; internet www.bachem-verlag.de; f. 1818; history, dialect, art history, architecture, sociology and walking/cycling tours of the Cologne and Rhine area; church and society; Dirs Lambert Bachem, Claus Bachem.

Bauverlag BV GmbH: Avenwedderstr. 55, 33311 Gütersloh; tel. (1805) 5522533; fax (1805) 5522535; e-mail leserservice@bauverlag.de; internet www.bauverlag.de; f. 1929; civil engineering, architecture, environment, energy, etc.; Dir Stefan Rühling.

Verlag C. H. Beck oHg: Postfach 400340, 80703 München, Wilhelmstr. 9, 80801 München; tel. (89) 381890; fax (89) 38189398; e-mail info@beck.de; internet www.beck.de; f. 1763; law, science, theology, archaeology, philosophy, philology, history, politics, art, literature; Dirs Dr Hans Dieter Beck, Wolfgang Beck.

Bibliographisches Institut und F. A. Brockhaus GmbH: Postfach 100311, 68167 Dudenstr. 6, 68003 Mannheim; tel. (621) 39010; fax (621) 3901391; internet www.bifab.de; f. 1805; encyclopaedias, dictionaries, atlases, textbooks, calendars; Chair. Dr Alexander Bob; Dirs Dr Hans-Jörg Dullmann, Ulrich Granseyer.

BLV Buchverlag GmbH & Co KG: Lothstr. 19, 80797 München; tel. (89) 127050; fax (89) 120212121; e-mail blv-verlag@blv.de; internet www.blv.de; f. 1946; gardening, nature, sports, fitness, equestrian, hunting, fishing, travel, food and drink, agriculture; Man. Dirs Hartwig Schneider, Hans Müller.

Breitkopf & Härtel: Postfach 1707, Walkmühlstr. 52, 65195 Wiesbaden; tel. (611) 450080; fax (611) 4500859; e-mail info@breitkopf.com; internet www.breitkopf.com; f. 1719; music and music books; Dirs Lieselotte Sievers, Gottfried Möckel.

Verlag Bruckmann München: Innsbrucker Ring 15, 81673 München; tel. (89) 1306990; fax (89) 13069930; f. 1858; travel guides, illustrated travel books, video cassettes; Man. Dir Clemens Schüssler.

Bund-Verlag GmbH: Postfach, 60424 Frankfurt; Heddernheimer Landstr. 144, 60439 Frankfurt; tel. (69) 7950100; fax (69) 79501010; e-mail kontakt@bund-verlag.de; internet www.bund-verlag.de; f. 1947; labour and social law; Man. Dirs Christian Paulsen, Rainer Jöde.

Verlag Georg D. W. Callwey GmbH & Co: Streitfeldstr. 35, 81673 München; tel. (89) 4360050; fax (89) 436005113; e-mail buch@callwey.de; internet www.callwey.de; f. 1884; architecture, gardens, crafts; Man. Dir Lutz Bandte.

Carlsen Verlag GmbH: Postfach 500380, 22703 Hamburg; Völckersstr. 14–20, 22765 Hamburg; tel. (40) 398040; fax (40) 39804390; e-mail info@carlsen.de; internet www.carlsen.de; f. 1953; children's and comic books; Dirs Klaus Humann, Klaus Kämpfe-Burghardt.

Cornelsen Verlag GmbH & Co: Mecklenburgische Str. 53, 14197 Berlin; tel. (30) 897850; fax (30) 89786299; e-mail c-cornelsen@cornelsen.com; internet www.cornelsen.com; f. 1946; school textbooks, educational software; Man. Dirs Alfred Grüner, Wolf-Rüdger Feldmann, Martin Hüppe, Dr Tilmann Michaletz.

Delius Klasing Verlag: Siekerwall 21, 33602 Bielefeld; tel. (521) 5590; fax (521) 559113; e-mail info@delius-klasing.de; internet www.delius-klasing.de; f. 1911; yachting, motor boats, surfing, mountain biking, race biking, basketball, motor cars; Dir Konrad Delius.

Deutsche Verlags-Anstalt (DVA): Bayerstr. 71–73, 80335 München; tel. (89) 41360; fax (89) 41363721; e-mail markus.desaga@dva.de; internet www.randomhouse.de/dva; f. 1831; general; owned by Random House Group Ltd (United Kingdom).

Deutscher Taschenbuch Verlag GmbH & Co KG (DTV): Postfach 400422, 80704 München; Friedrichstr. 1A, 80801 München; tel. (89) 381670; fax (89) 346428; e-mail verlag@dtv.de; internet www.dtv.de; f. 1961; general fiction, history, music, reference, children, natural and social science, medicine, textbooks; Man. Dirs Wolfgang Balk, Bernd Blüm.

Verlag Moritz Diesterweg: Waldschmidtstr. 39, 60316 Frankfurt a.M.; tel. (69) 420810; fax (69) 42081200; internet www.diesterweg.de; f. 1860; text books, languages, social sciences, sciences, pedagogics; Dirs Ralf Meier, Ulrich Pokern.

DuMont Monte GmbH & Co KG: Amsterdamer Str. 192, 50735 Köln; tel. (221) 2241831; fax (221) 2241878; e-mail montevertrieb@dumontverlag.de; internet www.dumontverlag.de; f. 1956; art, garden, cookery, calendars; Publr Helena Bommetsheim.

Egmont Pestalozzi Verlag GmbH: Schleissheimer Str. 267, 80809 München; tel. (89) 358116; fax (89) 35811869; internet www.pestalozzi-verlag.de; f. 1844; children's books; Man. Dirs Rehné Herzig, Frank Knau.

Egmont vgs Verlagsgesellschaft mbH: Gertrudenstr. 30–36, 50667 Köln; tel. (221) 208110; fax (221) 208166; e-mail info@vgs.de; internet www.vgs.de; f. 1970; fiction, hobbies, natural sciences,

GERMANY

culture, popular culture, cinema, television, history; Dir Dr MICHAEL SCHWEINS.

Eichborn Verlag: Kaiserstr. 66, 60329 Frankfurt a.M.; tel. (69) 2560030; fax (69) 25600330; f. 1980; literature, non-fiction, guidebooks, humour, cartoons; Man. Dir Dr MATTHIAS KIERZEK.

Bildungsverlag EINS GmbH: Sieglarer Str. 2, 53842 Troisdorf; tel. (41) 39-76-0; fax (41) 39-76-990; e-mail service@bildungsverlag1.de; internet www.bildungsverlag1.de; f. 2001 by merger of Gehlen, Kieser, Stam Verlag, Wolf, Dürr+Kessler and Konkordia; educational.

Elsevier GmbH: Postfach 100537, 07705 Jena; Löbdergraben 14A, 07745 Jena; tel. (3641) 6263; fax (3641) 626500; e-mail journals@elsevier.com; internet www.elsevier.de/journals; f. 1878; biological science, medical science; Dir BERND ROLLE.

Europaverlag: Neuer Wall 10, 20354 München; tel. (40) 3554340; fax (40) 35543466; e-mail info@europaverlag.de; internet www.europaverlag.de; fiction, non-fiction, poetry, biography and current events; Dirs GISELA ANNA STÜMPEL, WOLFGANG WEIDMANN.

S. Fischer Verlag GmbH: Postfach 700355, 60553 Frankfurt a.M.; Hedderichstr. 114, 60596 Frankfurt a.M.; tel. (69) 60620; fax (69) 6062319; e-mail info@fischerverlage.de; internet www.fischerverlage.de; f. 1886; general, paperbacks; Publrs PETER LOHMANN, Dr JÖRG BORG; Man. Dirs LOTHAR KLEINER, JOERG BONG, PETER LOHMANN.

Franzis Verlag GmbH: Gruber Str. 46, 85586 Poing; tel. (8121) 950; fax (8121) 951696; internet www.franzis.de; f. 1924; Gen. Mans THOMAS KÄSBOHRER, WERNER MÜTZEL.

GRÄFE UND UNZER Verlag GmbH: Grillparzerstr. 12, 81675 München; tel. (89) 41981140; fax (89) 41981406; e-mail beetz@graefe-und-unzer.de; internet www.graefe-und-unzer.de; f. 1722; cookery and wine, fitness, health and wellbeing, living and learning, gardening, nature, pets; Man. Dirs URBAN MEISTER, GEORG KESSLER, GÜNTER KOPIETZ.

Walter de Gruyter GmbH & Co KG Verlag: Postfach 303421, 10728 Berlin; Genthiner Str. 13, 10785 Berlin; tel. (30) 260050; fax (30) 26005251; e-mail wdg-info@degruyter.com; internet www.degruyter.com; f. 1919; humanities and theology, literary studies, linguistics, law, natural sciences, medicine, mathematics; Man. Dir KLAUS G. SAUR.

Carl Hanser Verlag: Kolbergerstr. 22, 81679 München; tel. (89) 998300; fax (89) 984809; e-mail info@hanser.de; internet www.hanser.de; f. 1928; modern literature, plastics, technology, chemistry, science, economics, computers, children's books; Man. Dirs WOLFGANG BEISLER, STEPHAN D. JOSS, MICHAEL KRÜGER.

Harenberg Kommunikation Verlags- und Mediengesellschaft mbH & Co KG: Postfach 101852, 44018 Dortmund; Königswall 21, 44137 Dortmund; tel. (231) 90560; fax (231) 9056110; e-mail post@harenberg.de; internet www.harenberg.de; f. 1973; almanacs, encyclopaedias, calendars, periodicals; Man. Dir BODO HARENBERG.

Rudolf Haufe Verlag GmbH & Co KG: Hindenburgstr. 64, 79102 Freiburg i. Br.; tel. (761) 36830; fax (761) 3683195; e-mail online@haufe.de; internet haufe.de; f. 1934; business, law, taxation, information management, finance, social science; Man. Dirs UWE RENALD MÜLLER, MARTIN LAQUA, HELMUTH HOPFNER.

Verlag Herder GmbH: Hermann-Herder-Str. 4; 79104 Freiburg i. Br.; tel. (761) 27170; fax (761) 2717520; e-mail info@herder.de; internet www.herder.de; f. 1801; religion, philosophy, psychology, history, education, art, encyclopaedias, children's books, gift books, periodicals; Proprs Dr HERMANN HERDER, MANUEL GREGOR HERDER.

Wilhelm Heyne Verlag: Bayerstr. 71–73, 80335 München; tel. (01805) 990505; e-mail vertrieb.verlagsgruppe@randomhouse.de; internet www.heyne.de; f. 1934; fiction, biography, history, cinema, etc.; Publr ULRICH GENZLER.

Hoffmann und Campe Verlag: Postfach 1304445, 20139 Hamburg; Harvestehuder Weg 42, 20149 Hamburg; tel. (40) 441880; fax (40) 44188202; e-mail presse@hoca.de; internet www.hoffmann-und-campe.de; f. 1781; biography, fiction, history, economics, science; Man. Dirs GÜNTER BEG, MARKUS GLOSE.

Dr Alfred Hüthig Verlag GmbH: Im Weiher 10, 6900 Heidelberg; tel. (6221) 4890; fax (6221) 489279; f. 1925; chemistry, chemical engineering, metallurgy, dentistry, etc.

Axel Juncker Verlag GmbH: Postfach 401120, 80711 München; Mies-van-der-Rohe-Str. 1, 80807 München; tel. (89) 360960; fax (89) 36096222; e-mail redaktion@axel-juncker.de; internet www.langenscheidt.de; f. 1972; dictionaries, language courses, reference; Man. Dir ANDREAS LANGENSCHEIDT.

S. Karger GmbH: Lörracherstr. 16A, 79115 Freiburg i. Br.; tel. (761) 452070; fax (761) 4520714; f. 1890; medicine, psychology, natural science; Man. Dir S. KARGER.

Verlag Kiepenheuer & Witsch GmbH & Co KG: Rondorferstr. 5, 50968 Köln 51; tel. (221) 376850; fax (221) 388595; e-mail info@kiwi-verlag.de; internet www.kiwi-verlag.de; f. 1948; general fiction, biography, history, sociology, politics; Man. Dirs HELGE MANCHOW, PETER ROIK.

Ernst Klett Verlag GmbH: Postfach 106016, 70049 Stuttgart; Rotebühlstr. 77, 70178 Stuttgart; tel. (711) 66720; fax (711) 6672800; internet www.klett.de; f. 1844; secondary school and university textbooks (especially German as a foreign language), dictionaries, atlases, teaching aids; Dirs MICHAEL KLETT, ROLAND KLETT, Dr THOMAS KLETT.

Verlag W. Kohlhammer GmbH: Hessbrühlstr. 69, 70565 Stuttgart; tel. (711) 78630; fax (711) 78638263; e-mail info@kohlhammer.de; internet www.kohlhammer.de; f. 1866; periodicals, general textbooks; Man. Dirs Dr JÜRGEN GUTBROD, LEOPOLD FREIHERR VON UND ZU WEILER.

Kösel-Verlag: Flüggenstr. 2, 80639 München; tel. (89) 178010; fax (89) 17801111; e-mail info@koesel.de; internet www.koesel.de; f. 1593; philosophy, religion, psychology, spirituality, family and education; Dir WINFRIED NONHOFF.

Kreuz Verlag GmbH: Postfach 800669; Breitwiesenstr. 30, 70565 Stuttgart; tel. (711) 788030; fax (711) 7880310; f. 1983; theology, psychology, pedagogics; Man. Dir Dr SABINE SCHUBERT.

Verlag der Kunst GmbH: Rosa-Menzer-Str. 12, 01309 Dresden; tel. (351) 3100052; fax (351) 3105245; e-mail verlag-der-kunst.dd@t-online.de; internet www.txt.de/vdk; f. 1952; art books and reproductions; Dir ROGER N. GREENE.

Peter Lang GmbH—Internationaler Verlag der Wissenschaften: Postfach 940225, 60460 Frankfurt a.M.; Eschborner Landstr. 42–50, 60489 Frankfurt a.M.; tel. (69) 7807050; fax (69) 78070550; e-mail zentrale.frankfurt@peterlang.com; internet www.peterlang.de; sociology, politics, communications, linguistics, science of law, literature, theology, economics, education.

Langenscheidt-Verlag: Postfach 401120, 80711 München; Mies-van-der-Rohe Str. 1, 80807 München; tel. (89) 360960; fax (89) 36096222; e-mail mail@langenscheidt.de; internet www.langenscheidt.de; f. 1856; foreign languages, German for foreigners, dictionaries, textbooks, language guides, CDs, CD-ROMs, cassettes, software, electronic dictionaries; Man. Dir ANDREAS LANGENSCHEIDT.

Verlagsgruppe Lübbe GmbH & Co KG: Scheidtbachstr. 23–31, 51469 Bergisch Gladbach; tel. (2202) 1210; internet www.luebbe.de; f. 1964; general fiction and non-fiction, biography, history, etc.; Publr STEFAN LÜBBE; Man. Dir THOMAS SCHIERACK.

Hermann Luchterhand Verlag GmbH: Postfach 2352, 56513 Neuwied; Heddesdorfer Str. 31, 56564 Neuwied; tel. (2631) 8012000; fax (2631) 8012204; e-mail info@wolterskluwer.de; internet www.luchterhand-fachverlag.de; f. 1924; insurance, law, taxation, labour; imprint of Wolters Kluwer Deutschland GmbH; Man. Dir Dr ULRICH HERMANN.

Mairdumont: Marco-Polo-Zentrum, 73760 Ostfildern; tel. (711) 45020; fax (711) 4502310; internet www.mairdumont.com; f. 1848; road maps, atlases, tourist guides; Man. Dir Dr VOLKMAR MAIR.

J. B. Metzler Verlag: Postfach 103241, 70028 Stuttgart; Werastr. 21–23, 70182 Stuttgart; tel. (711) 21940; fax (711) 2194249; e-mail info@metzlerverlag.de; internet www.metzlerverlag.de; f. 1682; literature, music, linguistics, history, cultural studies, philosophy, textbooks; Dir MICHAEL JUSTUS.

Verlag Moderne Industrie AG & Co KG: Justus-von-Liebig-Str. 1, 86895 Landsberg; tel. (8191) 1250; fax (8191) 125211; f. 1952; management, investment, technical; Man. Dir JOHANNES SEVKET GÖZALAN.

Verlagsgesellschaft Rudolf Müller GmbH & Co KG: Stolberger Str. 84, 50933 Köln; tel. (221) 54970; fax (221) 5497326; e-mail gf@rudolf-mueller.de; internet www.rudolf-mueller.de; f. 1840; architecture, construction, engineering, education; Publrs Dr CHRISTOPH MÜLLER, RUDOLF M. BLESER.

MVS Medizinverlage Stuttgart GmbH & Co KG: Oswald-Hesse-Str. 50, 70469 Stuttgart; tel. (711) 89310; fax (711) 8931706; e-mail kunden.service@thieme.de; internet www.medizinverlage.de; imprints are Karl F. Haug, Hippokrates, Sonntag, Enke, Parey and TRIAS und Haug Sachbuch; CEO Dr THOMAS SCHERB.

Verlag Friedrich Oetinger: Poppenbütteler Chaussee 53, 22397 Hamburg; tel. (40) 60790902; fax (40) 6072326; e-mail oetinger@verlagsgrupper-oetinger.de; internet www.oetinger.de; juvenile, illustrated books; Man. Dirs SILKE WEITENDORF, THOMAS HUGGLE, JAN WEITENDORF.

Oldenbourg Verlage: Rosenheimerstr. 145, 81671 München; tel. (89) 450510; fax (89) 45051333; internet www.oldenbourg.de; f. 1858; technology, science, history, textbooks, mathematics, economics, dictionaries, periodicals; Dirs Dr D. HOHM, WOLFGANG DICK, JOHANNES OLDENBOURG.

Pabel-Moewig Verlag KG: Karlsruher Str. 31, 76437 Rastatt; tel. (7222) 130; fax (7222) 13301; Gen. Man. GERHARD STEDTFELD.

GERMANY   Directory

Piper Verlag GmbH: Postfach 430861, Georgenstr. 4, 80799 München; tel. (89) 3818010; fax (89) 338704; e-mail info@piper.de; internet www.piper.de; f. 1904; literature, philosophy, theology, psychology, natural sciences, political and social sciences, history, biographies, music; Dir VIKTOR NIEMANN.

Verlagsgruppe Random House GmbH: Neumarkter Str. 28, 81673 München; tel. (01805) 990505; e-mail vertrieb.verlagsgruppe@randomhouse.de; internet www.randomhouse.de; f. 1994; general, reference; Chair. Dr JOERG PFUHR.

Ravensburger Buchverlag Otto Maier GmbH: Postfach 1860, Marktstr. 22–26, 88188 Ravensburg; tel. (751) 860; fax (751) 861289; e-mail info@ravensburger.de; internet www.ravensburger.de; f. 1883; Man. Dirs RENATE HERRE, JOHANNES HAUENSTEIN.

Philipp Reclam jun. Verlag GmbH: Siemensstr. 32, 71254 Ditzingen bei Stuttgart; tel. (7156) 1630; fax (7156) 163197; e-mail werbung@reclam.de; internet www.reclam.de; f. 1828; literature, literary criticism, fiction, history of culture and literature, philosophy and religion, biography, fine arts, music; Dirs FRANK R. MAX, FRANZ SCHÄFER.

Rowohlt Verlag GmbH: Hamburgerstr. 17, 21465 Reinbek bei Hamburg; tel. (40) 72720; fax (40) 7272319; internet www.rowohlt.de; f. 1908/1953; politics, science, fiction, translations of international literature; Dirs Dr HELMUT DÄHNE, ALEXANDER FEST, LUTZ KETTMANN.

K. G. Saur Verlag GmbH: Postfach 701620, 81316 München; Ortlerstr. 8, 81373 München; tel. (89) 769020; fax (89) 76902150; e-mail saur.info@thomson.com; internet www.saur.de; f. 1949; library science, reference, dictionaries, encyclopaedias, books, journals, microfiches, CD-ROMs, DVDs, online databases; brs in Leipzig, Thübingen and Osnabrück; part of Thomson Corpn.

Schattauer GmbH: Postfach 104543, 70040 Stuttgart; Hoelderlinstr. 3, 70174 Stuttgart; tel. (711) 229870; fax (711) 2298750; e-mail info@schattauer.de; internet www.schattauer.de; f. 1949; medicine and related sciences; Man. Dirs DIETER BERGEMANN, Dr WULF BERTRAM.

Verlag Dr Otto Schmidt KG: Unter den Ulmen 96–98, 50968 Köln; tel. (221) 9373801; fax (221) 93738943; f. 1905; university textbooks, jurisprudence, tax law; Man. Dir K. P. WINTERS.

Egmont Franz Schneider Verlag GmbH: Schleissheimer Str. 267, 80809 München; tel. (89) 358116; fax (89) 35811755; e-mail postmaster@schneiderbuch.de; internet www.schneiderbuch.de; f. 1913; children's books; Man. Dir FRANK KNAU.

Schroedel Schulbuchverlag GmbH: Georg-Westermann-Allee 66, 38104 Braunschweig; tel. (531) 7080; fax (531) 708209; e-mail sco@schroedel.de; internet www.schroedel.de; f. 1982; school textbooks and educational software; Man. Dirs THOMAS BAUMANN, Dr WERNER KUGEL.

Springer Science and Business Media Deutschland GmbH: Heidelberger Pl. 3, 14197 Berlin; tel. (30) 827870; fax (30) 8214091; f. 1842; wholly owned subsidiary of Springer Science+Business Media Netherlands BV; CEO DERK HAANK.

Stollfuss Verlag Bonn GmbH & Co KG: Dechenstr. 7, 53115 Bonn; tel. (228) 7240; fax (228) 659723; reference, fiscal law, economics, investment, etc.; Man. Dir WOLFGANG STOLLFUSS.

Suhrkamp Verlag GmbH & Co KG: Postfach 101945, 60019 Frankfurt a.M.; Suhrkamp Haus, Lindenstr. 29–35, 60325 Frankfurt a.M.; tel. (69) 756010; fax (69) 75601522; e-mail geschaeftsleitung@suhrkamp.de; internet www.suhrkamp.de; f. 1950; modern German and foreign literature, philosophy, poetry; Chair. ULLA UNSELD-BERKÉWICZ.

SYBEX Verlags- und Vertriebs-GmbH: Emil-Hoffmann-Str. 1, 50996 Köln; tel. (2236) 3999700; fax (2236) 3999229; e-mail sybex@sybex.de; internet www.sybex.de; f. 1981; computer books and software; Man. Dirs HOLGER SCHNEIDER, ANJA SCHRIEVER.

Georg Thieme Verlag: Postfach 301120, 70451 Stuttgart; Rüdigerstr. 14, 70469 Stuttgart; tel. (711) 89310; fax (711) 8931298; e-mail info@thieme.com; internet www.thieme.com; f. 1886; medicine and natural science; Man. Dirs Dr ALBRECHT HAUFF, Dr WOLFGANG KNÜPPE.

Thienemann Verlag GmbH: Blumenstr. 36, 70182 Stuttgart; tel. (711) 210550; fax (711) 2105539; e-mail info@thienemann.de; internet www.thienemann.de; f. 1849; picture books, children's books, juveniles; Dir KLAUS WILLBERG.

Transpress Verlagsgesellschaft mbH: Borkumstr. 2, 13181 Berlin; tel. (30) 47805151; fax (30) 47805160; f. 1990; specialized literature on transport and marketing; Man. Dr HARALD BÖTTCHER.

Verlag Eugen Ulmer GmbH & Co: Postfach 700561, 70574 Stuttgart; tel. (711) 45070; fax (711) 4507120; e-mail info@ulmer.de; f. 1868; agriculture, horticulture, science, periodicals; Dir ROLAND ULMER.

Verlag Ullstein GmbH: Charlottenstr. 13, 10969 Berlin; tel. (30) 25913570; fax (30) 25913523; f. 1894; literature, art, music, theatre, contemporary history, biography; Pres. Dr JÜRGEN RICHTER.

Ullstein Buchverlage GmbH: Friedrichstr. 16, 10117 Berlin; tel. (30) 23456300; fax (30) 23456303; e-mail info@ullstein-buchverlage.de; internet www.ullsteinbuchverlage.de; f. 1894; general fiction, history, art, philosophy, religion, psychology; Editorial Dir VIKTOR NIEMANN.

Georg Westermann Verlag GmbH: Postfach 3320, Georg-Westermann-Allee 66, 38023 Braunschweig; tel. (531) 7080; fax (531) 708248; f. 1838; non-fiction, paperbacks, periodicals; Dir Dr HANS-DIETER MÖLLER.

Wiley-VCH Verlag GmbH & Co KGaA: Boschstr. 12, 69469 Weinheim; tel. (6201) 6060; fax (6201) 606328; e-mail service@wiley-vch.de; internet www.wiley-vch.de; f. 1921; natural sciences, especially chemistry, chemical engineering, civil engineering, architecture, biotechnology, materials science, life sciences, information technology and physics, scientific software, business, management, computer science, finance and accounting; Man. Dir Dr MANFRED ANTONI.

Verlag Klaus Wingefeld: Lindenstr. 12, 71686 Remseck; fax (7146) 871881; e-mail kinderbuchverlag@t-online.de.

PRINCIPAL ASSOCIATION OF BOOK PUBLISHERS AND BOOKSELLERS

Börsenverein des Deutschen Buchhandels eV (German Publishers and Booksellers Association): Postfach 100442, 60004 Frankfurt a.M.; Grosser Hirschgraben 17–21, 60311 Frankfurt a.M.; tel. (69) 13060; fax (69) 1306201; e-mail info@boev.de; internet www.boersenverein.de; f. 1825; Chair. Dr GOTTFRIED HONNEFELDER; Man. Dir ALEXANDER SKIPIS.

Broadcasting and Communications

TELECOMMUNICATIONS

Arcor AG: Alfred-Herrhausen-Allee 1, 65760 Eschborn; tel. (18) 1070010; e-mail info@arcor.net; internet www.arcor.de; f. 1997 as Mannesmann Arcor AG; present name adopted 1998; operates fixed line telephone network; 73.65% owned by Vodafone Group PLC (United Kingdom), 18.17% by Deutsche Bahn AG, 8.18% by Deutsche Bank AG; Chair. HARALD STÖBER.

debitel AG: Gropiuspl. 10, 70545 Stuttgart; tel. (180) 5123123; e-mail tanja.wilcke@de.debitel.com; internet www.debitel.de; mobile telecommunications and internet service provider; 13m. subscribers (2007); owned by Swisscom AG; Chair. AXEL RÜCKERT.

Deutsche Telekom AG: Postfach 2000, 53105 Bonn; Friedrich-Ebert-Allee 140, 53113 Bonn; tel. (228) 1810; fax (228) 18171915; e-mail info@telekom.de; internet www.telekom.de; f. 1989; partially privatized 1995 with further privatization pending; 25% state-owned, 12% owned by Kreditanstalt für Wiederaufbau, 63% owned by private shareholders; fmr monopoly over national telecommunications network removed Jan. 1998; Chair., Supervisory Bd Dr KLAUS ZUMWINKEL; Chair., Management Bd and CEO RENÉ OBERMANN.

E-plus Mobilfunk GmbH: Postfach 300307, 40403 Düsseldorf; E-Plus-Pl. 1, 40468 Düsseldorf; tel. (211) 4480; fax (211) 4482222; e-mail kundenservice@eplus.de; internet www.eplus.de; f. 1993; 13.6m. subscribers (June 2007); owned by KPN Mobile NV (Netherlands); Chair., Supervisory Bd STAN MILLER; Chair., Management Bd and CEO THORSTEN DIRKS.

mobilCom Communicationstecknik AG: Hollerstr. 126, 24782 Büdelsdorf; tel. and fax (900) 1550250; e-mail info@mobilcom.de; internet www.mobilcom.de; f. 1991; Mans ECKHARD SPOERR, STEPHAN BRAUER, AXEL KRIEGER, STEPHAN ESCH.

O2 (Germany) GmbH & Co OHG: Georg-Brauchle-Ring 23–25, 80992 München; tel. (89) 24421201; fax (89) 24421201; internet www.de.02.com; f. 1995; owned by Telefónica SA (Spain); 11.6m. subscribers (June 2007); CEO JAIME SMITH BASTERRA.

T-Mobile Deutschland GmbH: POB 300463, 53184 Bonn; Landgrabenweg 151, 53227 Bonn; tel. (228) 93631717; fax (228) 93631719; internet www.t-mobile.de; f. 1993; 34.3m. subscribers (June 2007); subsidiary of T-Mobile International AG & Co KG; Man. Dir PHILIPP HUMM.

Vodafone D2 GmbH: Am Seestern 1, 40547 Düsseldorf; tel. (211) 5330; fax (211) 5332200; e-mail kontakt@vodafone.com; internet www.vodafone.de; f. 1992 as Mannesmann Mobilfunk GmbH; present name adopted 2000; operates D2 mobile telephone network; 31m. subscribers (June 2007); subsidiary of Vodafone Group PLC (United Kingdom); Chair., Management Bd and CEO FRIEDRICH JOUSSEN.

GERMANY   *Directory*

Associations

Bundesverband Digitale Wirtschaft eV: Kaistr. 14, 40221 Düsseldorf; tel. (211) 6004560; fax (211) 60045633; e-mail kehlen@dmmv.de; internet www.bvdw.org; fmrly Deutscher Multimedia Verband (dmmv); 900 mems (Aug. 2004).

Verband Privater Rundfunk und Telemedien eV (VPRT) (Ascn of Commercial Broadcasters and Audiovisual Cos): Stromstr. 1, 10555 Berlin; tel. (30) 398800; fax (30) 39880148; e-mail info@vprt.de; internet www.vprt.de; f. 1984; 160 mems (July 2007); Man. Dir URSULA K. ADELT.

Regulatory Authority

Bundesnetzagentur für Elektrizität, Gas, Telekommunikation, Post und Eisenbahnen (Bundesnetzagentur) (Federal Network Agency for Electricity, Gas, Telecommunications, Post and Railways): Tulpenfeld 4, 53113 Bonn; tel. (228) 140; fax (228) 148872; e-mail poststelle@bnetza.de; internet www.bundesnetzagentur.de; f. 1997; fmrly Regulierungsbehörde für Telekommunikation und Post, renamed 2005; responsible for supervising the liberalization and deregulation of the post and telecommunications sector, as well as electricity, gas and railways; Pres. MATTHIAS KURTH.

BROADCASTING

Radio

Regional public radio stations are co-ordinated by the ARD (see below). There are also numerous regional commercial radio stations.

In 2005 Digital Audio Broadcast (DAB) services were available to approximately 80% of the population. In that year there were around 80 stations on the air. DAB was first introduced in Germany in Sachsen-Anhalt in 1999. Since then DAB has been implemented in all Länder, although coverage in Schleswig-Holstein and Mecklenburg-Vorpommern is still considerably less extensive than in other Länder.

Public Stations

Arbeitsgemeinschaft der öffentlich-rechtlichen Rundfunkanstalten der Bundesrepublik Deutschland (ARD) (Association of Public Law Broadcasting Organizations): Bertramstr. 8, 60320 Frankfurt a.M.; tel. (69) 590607; fax (69) 1552075; e-mail info@ard.de; internet www.ard.de; f. 1950; Chair. FRITZ RAFF; the co-ordinating body of Germany's public service radio and television organizations; each of the following radio stations broadcasts 3–5 channels:

Bayerischer Rundfunk: Rundfunkpl. 1, 80300 München; tel. (89) 590001; fax (89) 59002375; internet www.bronline.de; Dir-Gen. Prof. ALBERT SCHARF; Chair., Broadcasting Council Prof. Dr WILHELM WIMMER; Chair., Admin. Bd JOHANN BÖHM.

Deutsche Welle: Kurt-Schumacher-Str. 3, 53113 Bonn; tel. (228) 4290; fax (228) 4293000; e-mail info@dw-world.de; internet www.dw-world.de; f. 1953; German short-wave radio and satellite television service; broadcasts daily in 30 languages for Europe and overseas; Dir-Gen. ERIK BETTERMANN.

DeutschlandRadio: Hans Rosenthal Pl., 10825 Berlin; tel. (30) 85030; internet www.deutschlandradio.de; Dir-Gen. ERNST ELLITZ.

Hessischer Rundfunk: Bertramstr. 8, 60320 Frankfurt a.M.; tel. (69) 1551; fax (69) 1552900; internet www.hr-online.de; Dir-Gen. Dr HELMUT REITZE.

Mitteldeutscher Rundfunk: Kanstr. 71–73, 04275 Leipzig; tel. (341) 3000; fax (341) 3005544; internet www.mdr.de; f. 1992; Dir-Gen. Prof. Dr UDO REITER.

Norddeutscher Rundfunk: Rothenbaumchaussee 132, 20149 Hamburg; tel. (40) 41560; fax (40) 447602; internet www.ndr.de; f. 1956; Dir-Gen. JOBST PLOG.

Radio Bremen: Diepenau 10, 28198 Bremen; tel. (421) 2460; fax (421) 2461010; internet www.radiobremen.de; f. 1945; radio and television; Dir-Gen. Prof. Dr HEINZ GLÄSSGEN.

Rundfunk Berlin-Brandenburg (rbb): Masurenallee 8–14, 14057 Berlin; tel. (30) 97993-0; fax (30) 97993-19; e-mail presse@rbb-online.de; internet www.rbb-online.de; f. 2003; Dir-Gen. DAGMAR REIM.

Saarländischer Rundfunk: Funkhaus Halberg, 66100 Saarbrücken; tel. (681) 6020; fax (681) 6023874; internet www.sr-online.de; f. 1952; Dir-Gen. FRITZ RAFF.

Südwestrundfunk: Neckarstr. 230, 70150 Stuttgart; tel. (49) 9290; fax (49) 9292600; internet www.swr.de; Dir-Gen. PETER BOUDGOUST.

WDR (Westdeutscher Rundfunk): Appellhofpl. 1, 50667 Köln; tel. (221) 2200; fax (221) 2204800; internet www.wdr.de; Dir-Gen. FRITZ PLEITGEN.

Commercial Radio

Verband Privater Rundfunk und Telemedien eV (VPRT): see under Telecommunications; represents privately owned radio stations.

Television

There are three public-service television channels. The autonomous regional broadcasting organizations combine to provide material for the First Programme, which is produced by ARD. The Second Programme (Zweites Deutsches Fernsehen/ZDF) is completely separate and is controlled by a public corporation of all the Länder. It is partly financed by advertising. The Third Programme (also produced by ARD) provides a cultural and educational service in the evenings only, with contributions from both ARD and ZDF. Commercial television channels also operate.

Digital Video Broadcasting (DVB) was introduced in Germany in 2002. Analogue broadcasting was due to be abandoned by 2010. By 2005 Berlin and Brandenburg had already switched off analogue broadcasting.

Public Stations

ARD: Programmdirektion Deutsches Fernsehen: Arnulfstr. 42, 80335 München; tel. (89) 590001; fax (89) 59003249; e-mail info@daserste.de; internet www.daserste.de; co-ordinates the following regional public-service television organizations: Bayerischer Rundfunk, Hessischer Rundfunk, MDR, NDR, Radio Bremen, Saarländischer Rundfunk, Rundfunk Berlin-Brandenburg, Südwestrundfunk, WDR; Chair. FRITZ RAFF; Dir of Programmes Dr GUENTER STRUVE.

ARTE Deutschland TV GmbH: Postfach 100213, 76483 Baden-Baden; tel. (7221) 9369-0; fax (7221) 9369-70; internet www.arte.tv; f. 1991; arts, cultural programmes, in French and German; Pres. Dr ANDREAS FUCHS.

Zweites Deutsches Fernsehen (ZDF): 55100 Mainz; tel. (6131) 702050; fax (6131) 702052; e-mail ia@zdf.de; internet www.zdf.de; f. 1961 by the Länder Govts as a second television channel; 104 main transmitters; Dir-Gen. MARKUS SCHÄCHTER; Dir of Programmes Dr THOMAS BELLUT.

Commercial Television

Premiere Fernsehen GmbH & Co KG: Medienallee 4, 85774 Unterföhring; tel. (89) 995802; fax (89) 99586239; e-mail info@premiere.de; internet www.premiere.de; f. 1988; subscriber service offering 28 television and 21 digital audio channels; CEO MICHAEL BÖRNICKE.

ProSiebenSat.1 Media AG: Medienallee 7, 85774 Unterföhring; tel. (89) 950710; fax (89) 95071122; e-mail info@prosiebensat1.com; internet www.prosiebensat1.com; f. 2000 by merger of ProSieben Media AG (f. 1989) and Sat.1 (f. 1984); operates Sat. 1, ProSieben, Kabel eins and N24; Chair., Management Bd GUILLAUME DE POSCH; Chair., Supervisory Bd GÖTZ MÄUSER.

RTL Television GmbH: Aachener Str. 1044, 50858 Cologne; tel. (49) 2214560; fax (49) 2214561690; internet www.rtl-television.de; f. 1984; subsidiary of RTL Group (Luxembourg); CEO ANKE SCHÄFERKORDT.

Verband Privater Rundfunk und Telemedien eV (VPRT): see under Telecommunications; represents privately owned satellite, cable and digital television cos.

Finance

(cap. = capital; res = reserves; dep. = deposits; m. = million; brs = branches; amounts in euros (€))

The Deutsche Bundesbank, the central bank of Germany, consists of the central administration in Frankfurt am Main (considered to be the financial capital of the country) and nine main offices (Hauptverwaltungen) with 58 branches. In carrying out its functions as determined by law the Bundesbank is independent of the Federal Government, but is required to support the Government's general economic policy. As a member of the European System of Central Banks (ESCB), the Bundesbank implements the single monetary policy determined by the Governing Council of the European Central Bank (ECB).

All credit institutions other than the Bundesbank are subject to supervision through the Federal Financial Supervisory Authority (Bundesanstalt für Finanzdienstleistungsaufsicht) in Bonn. Banks outside the central banking system are divided into three groups: private commercial banks, credit institutions incorporated under public law and co-operative credit institutions. All these commercial banks are 'universal banks', conducting all kinds of customary banking business. There is no division of activities. As well as the

GERMANY

commercial banks there are a number of specialist banks, such as private or public mortgage banks.

The group of private commercial banks includes all banks incorporated as a company limited by shares (Aktiengesellschaft—AG, Kommanditgesellschaft auf Aktien—KGaA) or as a private limited company (Gesellschaft mit beschränkter Haftung—GmbH) and those which are known as 'regional banks' because they do not usually function throughout Germany; and those banks which are established as sole proprietorships or partnerships and mostly have no branches outside their home town. The main business of all private commercial banks is short-term lending. The private bankers fulfil the most varied tasks within the banking system.

The public law credit institutions are the savings banks (Sparkassen) and the Landesbank-Girozentralen. The latter act as central banks and clearing houses on a national level for the savings banks. Laws governing the savings banks limit them to certain sectors—credits, investments and money transfers—and they concentrate on the areas of home financing, municipal investments and the trades. In 2002 there were 534 savings banks and 13 Landesbank-Girozentralen in Germany.

The head institution of the co-operative system is the DZ BANK Deutsche Zentrale-Genossenschaftsbank AG. In 2006 there were 1,250 credit co-operatives, including central institutions.

In 1990 there was a total of 4,700 banks in Germany; by early 2008 this number had decreased to 2,079.

SUPERVISORY BODY

Bundesanstalt für Finanzdienstleistungsaufsicht (BaFin) (Federal Financial Supervisory Authority): Graurheindorfer Str. 108, 53117 Bonn; tel. (228) 41080; fax (228) 41081550; e-mail poststelle@bafin.de; internet www.bafin.de; f. 2002; independent body within Federal administration; supervises credit institutions and financial services providers, insurance providers and securities trading; Pres. JOCHEN SANIO.

BANKS

The Central Banking System

Germany participates in the ESCB, which consists of the ECB and the national central banks of all European Union (EU) member states. Stage III of European Monetary Union (EMU), the launch of the euro, commenced (with 11 initial participants) on 1 January 1999. Euro banknotes and coins were issued on 1 January 2002; the Deutsche Mark remained legal tender until 28 February 2002.

Deutsche Bundesbank: Postfach 100602, 60006 Frankfurt a.M.; Wilhelm-Epstein-Str. 14, 60431 Frankfurt a.M.; tel. (69) 95661; fax (69) 95663077; e-mail presse-information@bundesbank.de; internet www.bundesbank.de; f. 1957; aims, in conjunction with the other members of the ESCB, to maintain price stability in the euro area. The Bundesbank, *inter alia*, holds and maintains foreign reserves of the Federal Republic of Germany, arranges for the execution of domestic and cross-border payments and contributes to the stability of payment and clearing systems. The Bundesbank (which has nine regional offices—Hauptverwaltungen—and 58 smaller branches) is the principal bank of the Federal Länder Govts, carrying accounts for public authorities, executing payments and assisting with borrowing on the capital market. The Bundesbank has reserve positions in, and claims on, the IMF and the ECB. The Executive Board determines the Bundesbank's business policy; members of the Federal Govt may take part in the deliberations of the Board but may not vote; cap. 2,500m., res 2,500m., dep. 53,170m. (Dec. 2006); Pres. Prof. Dr AXEL A. WEBER; Vice-Pres. Prof. Dr FRANZ-CHRISTOPH ZEITLER.

Hauptverwaltung Berlin: Leibnizstr. 10, 10625 Berlin; tel. (30) 34750; fax (30) 34751990; e-mail pressestelle.hv-berlin@bundesbank.de; internet www.bundesbank.de/hv/hv_berlin.php; Pres. NORBERT MATYSIK.

Hauptverwaltung Düsseldorf: Berliner Allee 14, 40212 Düsseldorf; tel. (211) 8740; fax (211) 8742424; e-mail stab.hv-duesseldorf@bundesbank.de; internet www.bundesbank.de/hv/hv_duesseldorf.php; Pres. HANS PETER WESER.

Hauptverwaltung Frankfurt: Taunusanlage 5, 60329 Frankfurt a.M.; tel. (69) 23880; fax (69) 23882130; e-mail pressestelle.hv-frankfurt@bundesbank.de; internet www.bundesbank.de/hv/hv_frankfurt.php; Pres. JÜRGEN HETTINGER.

Hauptverwaltung Hamburg: Willy-Brandt-Str. 73, 20459 Hamburg; tel. (40) 37070; fax (40) 37073342; e-mail pressestelle.hv-hamburg@bundesbank.de; internet www.bundesbank.de/hv/hv_hamburg.php; Pres. Prof. Dr ROLF EGGERT.

Hauptverwaltung Hannover: Georgspl. 5, 30159 Hannover; tel. (511) 30330; fax (511) 30332500; e-mail pressestelle.hv-hannover@bundesbank.de; internet www.bundesbank.de/hv/hv_hannover.php; Pres. GERD-ALEXANDER LOCH.

Hauptverwaltung Leipzig: Str. des 18. Oktober 48, 04103 Leipzig; tel. (341) 8600; fax (341) 8602389; e-mail pressestelle.hv-leipzig@bundesbank.de; internet www.bundesbank.de/hv/hv_leipzig.php; Pres. HANS CHRISTOPH POPPE.

Hauptverwaltung Mainz: Hegelstr. 65, 52122 Mainz; tel. (6131) 3770; e-mail pressestelle.hv-mainz@bundesbank.de; internet www.bundesbank.de/hv/hv_mainz.php; Pres. PETRA PALTE.

Hauptverwaltung München: Ludwigstr. 13, 80539 München; tel. (89) 28895; fax (89) 28893598; e-mail pressestelle.hv-muenchen@bundesbank.de; internet www.bundesbank.de/hv/hv_muenchen.php; Pres. Prof. WOLFGANG SIMLER.

Hauptverwaltung Stuttgart: Marstallstr. 3, 70173 Stuttgart; tel. (711) 9440; fax (711) 9441903; e-mail hv-stuttgart@bundesbank.de; internet www.bundesbank.de/hv/hv_stuttgart.php; Pres. BERNHARD SIBOLD.

Private Commercial Banks

In December 2002 354 private commercial banks were operating in Germany. The most prominent of these are listed below:

Bayerische Hypo- und Vereinsbank AG (HypoVereinsbank): Postfach 100101, 80333 München; Am Tucherpark 16, 80538 München; tel. (89) 3780; fax (89) 378113422; e-mail info@hypovereinsbank.de; internet www.hypovereinsbank.de; f. 1998 by merger of Bayerische Hypotheken- und Wechsel Bank AG (f. 1835) and Bayerische Vereinsbank AG (f. 1869); 93.93% owned by UniCredito Italiano SpA; cap. 2,252m., res 13,816m., dep. 314,708m. (Dec. 2006); Chair., Supervisory Bd ALESSANDRO PROFUMO; Chair., Bd of Management Dr WOLFGANG SPRISSLER; 1,426 brs.

Berliner Volksbank eG: Budapester Str. 35, 10787 Berlin; tel. (30) 30630; fax (30) 30631550; e-mail service@berliner-volksbank.de; internet www.berliner-volksbank.de; f. 1880; cap. 260m., res 255m., dep. 9,535m. (Dec. 2006); Chair. Prof. Dr DIETMAR WINJE; 109 brs.

BHF-Bank Aktiengesellschaft: Bockenheimer Landstr. 10, 60323 Frankfurt a.M.; tel. (69) 7180; fax (69) 7182296; e-mail kontakt@bhf-bank.com; internet www.bhf-bank.com; f. 1856; current name adopted 2005; cap. 200m., res 491m., dep. 16,515m. (Dec. 2006); Man. Dir MATTHIAS GRAF VON KROCKOW; 11 brs.

Citibank Privatkunden AG & Co KGaA: Postfach 101818, 40009 Düsseldorf; Kasernenstr. 10, 40213 Düsseldorf; tel. (211) 89840; fax (211) 8984222; internet www.citibank.de; f. 1926 as KKB Bank KGaA; present name adopted 1991; cap. 135m., res 601m., dep. 10,152m. (Dec. 2004); Man. SUSAN S. HARNETT; 286 brs.

Citigroup Global Markets Deutschland AG & Co KGaA: Postfach 110333, 60038 Frankfurt a.M.; Reuterweg 16, 60323 Frankfurt a.M.; tel. (69) 13660; fax (69) 13661113; internet www.citigroup.com; f. 1976 as Citibank AG; current name adopted 2003; cap. 333m., res 254m., dep. 10,123m. (Dec. 2006); Chair., Bd of Management Dr MICHAEL ZITZMANN; 2 brs.

Commerzbank AG: Kaiserpl., 60311 Frankfurt a.M.; tel. (69) 13620; fax (69) 285389; e-mail info@commerzbank.de; internet www.commerzbank.de; f. 1870; cap. 1,705m., res 12,064m., dep. 495,792m. (Dec. 2006); Chair., Bd of Management KLAUS-PETER MÜLLER; 964 brs.

Crown Westfalen Bank AG: Postfach 102710, 44727 Bochum; Huestr. 21–25, 44787 Bochum; tel. (234) 6160; fax (234) 6164400; e-mail info@westfalenbank.de; internet www.westfalenbank.de; f. 1921; cap. 51m., res 21m., dep. 1,082m. (Dec. 2005); owned by Crown Northcorp, Inc (USA); Man. Dirs Dr JOACHIM PAULUS, Dr CHRISTIAN VON VILLIEZ.

Deutsche Bank AG: Taunusanlage 12, 60325 Frankfurt a.M.; tel. (69) 91000; fax (69) 91034225; e-mail deutsche.bank@db.com; internet www.deutsche-bank.de; f. 1870; cap. 1,343m., res 6,396m., dep. 857,798m. (Dec. 2006); Chair., Supervisory Bd ROLF E. BREUER; Chair., Bd of Management JOSEF ACKERMANN; 133 brs.

Dresdner Bank AG: Jürgen-Ponto-Pl. 1, 60329 Frankfurt a.M.; tel. (69) 2630; fax (69) 634004; e-mail webmaster@dresdner-bank.com; internet www.dresdner-bank.de; f. 1872; owned by Allianz AG; cap. 1,503m., res 10,415m., dep. 464,510m. (Dec. 2006); Chair., Supervisory Bd MICHAEL DIEKMANN; Chair., Bd of Management Dr HERBERT WALTER; 960 brs.

HSBC Trinkaus & Burkhardt AG: Postfach 101108, 40002 Düsseldorf; Königsallee 21–23, 40212 Düsseldorf; tel. (211) 9100; fax (211) 910616; internet www.hsbctrinkhaus.de; f. 1785; current name adopted 2006; cap. 70m., res 693m., dep. 10,594m. (Dec. 2006); Chair. and Man. Dir ANDREAS SCHMITZ; 6 brs.

Merck Finck & Co oHG: Pacellistr. 16, 80333 München; tel. (89) 21040; fax (89) 299814; e-mail info@merckfinck.de; internet www.merckfinck.de; f. 1870; cap. 155m., res 9m., dep. 884m. (Dec. 2004); Partners ALEXANDER METTENHEIMER, MICHAEL KRUME, GEORG FREIHERR VON BOESELAGER; 5 brs.

J. P. Morgan AG: Junghofstr. 14, 60311 Frankfurt a.M.; tel. (69) 71240; fax (69) 71242209; f. 1947; cap. 60m., res 84m., dep. 9,896m. (Dec. 2006); Chair. THOMAS MEYER.

GERMANY

Oldenburgische Landesbank AG: Postfach 2605, 26016 Oldenburg; Stau 15–17, 26122 Oldenburg; tel. (441) 2210; fax (441) 2212410; e-mail olb@olb.de; internet www.olb.de; f. 1868; cap. 60m., res 376m., dep. 8,050m. (Dec. 2006); Chair., Bd of Management Dr JÖRG BLECKMANN.

Sal. Oppenheim Jr & Cie KGaA: Postfach 102743, 50467 Köln; Unter Sachsenhausen 4, 50667 Köln; tel. (221) 14501; fax (221) 1451512; e-mail info@oppenheim.de; internet www.oppenheim.de; f. 1789; cap. 900m., res 873m., dep. 13,020m. (Dec. 2006); Chair. MATTHIAS GRAF VON KROCKOW; 16 brs.

SEB AG: Ulmenstr. 30, 60283 Frankfurt a.M.; tel. (69) 2580; fax (69) 2587578; e-mail info@seb.de; internet www.seb.de; f. 1958 as BfG Bank AG; adopted current name 2001; owned by Skandinaviska Enskilda Banken AB (Sweden); cap. 775m., res 1,448m., dep. 47,116m. (Dec. 2006); Chair. PETER BUSCHBECK; 175 brs.

UBS Deutschland AG: Stephanstr. 14–16, 60313 Frankfurt a.M.; tel. (69) 21790; fax (69) 21796511; internet www.ubs.com/deutschland; f. 1998 as Warburg Dillon Read AG by merger of Schweizerischer Bankverein (Deutschland) and Union Bank of Switzerland (Deutschland) AG; present name adopted 2005; cap. 125m., res 166m., dep. 21,795m. (Dec. 2002); Chair. JÜRG ZELTNER; 11 brs.

Weberbank Aktiengesellschaft: Postfach, 10893 Berlin; Hohenzollerndamm 134, 14199 Berlin; tel. (30) 897980; fax (30) 89798900; e-mail info@weberbank.de; internet www.weberbank.de; f. 1949 as Weberbank Berliner Industriebank; current name adopted 2005; owned by WestLB AG; cap. 52m., res 126m., dep. 3,868m. (Dec. 2004); Gen. Mans KARSTEN BICH, KLAUS SIEGERS; 3 brs.

Public-Law Credit Institutions

Together with the private banks, the banks incorporated under public law (savings banks—Sparkassen—and their central clearing houses—Landesbank-Girozentralen) play a major role within the German banking system. In 2002 there were 534 savings banks and 13 central clearing houses.

BayernLB: Brienner Str. 18, 80333 München; tel. (89) 217101; fax (89) 217123579; e-mail info@bayernlb.de; internet www.bayernlb.de; f. 1972 as Bayerische Landesbank; present name adopted 2005; cap. 4,818m., res 5,877m., dep. 317,853m. (Dec. 2006); Chair. WERNER SCHMIDT.

Bremer Landesbank Kreditanstalt Oldenburg: Domshof 26, 28195 Bremen; tel. (421) 3320; fax (421) 3322322; e-mail kontakt@bremerlandesbank.de; internet www.bremerlandesbank.de; f. 1983; cap. 748m., res 411m., dep. 28,930m. (Dec. 2006); Chair. Dr STEPHAN ANDREAS KAULVERS.

DekaBank Deutsche Girozentrale: Mainzer Landstr. 16, 60325 Frankfurt am Main; tel. (69) 71470; fax (69) 71471376; e-mail konzerninfo@dekabank.de; internet www.dekabank.de; f. 1999 by merger of Deutsche Girozentrale-Deutsche Kommunalbank and Dekabank GmbH; present name adopted 2002; central institution of Sparkassen organization; issues Pfandbriefe (bonds); cap. 286m., res 2,609m., dep. 89,461m. (Dec. 2006); Chair., Bd of Management FRANZ S. WAAS.

HSH Nordbank AG: Gerhart-Hauptmann-Pl. 50, 20095 Hamburg; tel. (40) 33330; fax (40) 333334001; e-mail info@hsh-nordbank.com; internet www.hsh-nordbank.com; f. 2003 by merger of Hamburgische Landesbank-Girozentrale and Landesbank Schleswig-Holstein Girozentrale; cap. 4,545m., res 2,276m., dep. 167,094m. (Dec. 2006); CEO HANS BERGER.

Landesbank Baden-Württemberg (LBBW): Postfach 106049, 70049 Stuttgart; tel. (711) 1270; fax (711) 12743544; e-mail kontakt@lbbw.de; internet www.lbbw.de; f. 1999 by merger of Landesgirokasse, L-Bank Landeskreditbank Baden-Württemberg and Südwestdeutsche Landesbank Girozentrale; cap. 4,921m., res 6,251m., dep. 401,361m. (Dec. 2006); Chair., Bd of Management Dr SIEGFRIED JASCHINSKI.

Landesbank Berlin AG: Alexanderpl. 2, 10178 Berlin; tel. (30) 869801; fax (30) 86983074; e-mail information@lbb.de; internet www.lbb.de; f. 1818; cap. 2,300m., res 602m., dep. 100,196m. (Dec. 2006); Chair., Bd of Management HANS-JÖRG VETTER; 150 brs.

Landesbank Hessen-Thüringen Girozentrale (Helaba): Main Tower, Neue Mainzer Str. 52–58, 60297 Frankfurt a.M.; tel. (69) 913201; fax (69) 291517; e-mail presse@helaba.de; internet www.helaba.de; f. 1953; cap. 3,501m., res 1,395m., dep. 151,928m. (Dec. 2006); Chair. Dr GÜNTHER MERL; 5 brs.

Landesbank Saar (SaarLB): Ursulinenstr. 2, 66111 Saarbrücken; tel. (681) 38301; fax (681) 3831295; e-mail service@saarlb.de; internet www.saarlb.de; f. 1941; cap. 388m., res 154m., dep. 18,007m. (Dec. 2006); Chair., Management Bd THOMAS-CHRISTIAN BUCHBINDER.

LRP Landesbank Rheinland-Pfalz: Grosse Bleiche 54–56, 55098 Mainz; tel. (6131) 1301; fax (6131) 132724; e-mail lrp@lrp.de; internet www.lrp.de; f. 1958; wholly owned by LBBW; cap. 919m., res 577m., dep. 68,654m. (Dec. 2006); Chair. and CEO Dr FRIEDHELM PLOGMANN.

Norddeutsche Landesbank Girozentrale (NORD/LB): Friedrichswall 10, 30159 Hannover; tel. (511) 3610; fax (511) 3612502; e-mail info@nordlb.de; internet www.nordlb.de; f. 1970 by merger of several north German banks; cap. 2,290m., res 3,005m., dep. 132,749m. (Dec. 2006); Chair. Dr HANNES REHM; 108 brs.

Sachsen Bank: Humboldtstr. 25, 04105 Leipzig; tel. (341) 979-0; fax (341) 979-7979; e-mail info@sachsenlb.de; internet www.sachsenlb.de; acquired by LBBW in 2008; Chair., Supervisory Bd MICHAEL HORN; Chair., Management Bd HARALD R. PFAB.

WestLB AG: Herzogstr. 15, 40217 Düsseldorf; tel. (211) 82601; fax (211) 8266119; e-mail presse@westlb.de; internet www.westlb.de; f. 1969; cap. 2,210m., res 4,535m., dep. 143,000m. (Dec. 2006); Chair. ALEXANDER STUHLMANN; 20 brs.

Central Bank of Co-operative Banking System

DZ BANK AG (Deutsche Zentral-Genossenschaftsbank): Pl. der Republik, 60265 Frankfurt a.M.; tel. (69) 744701; fax (69) 74471685; e-mail mail@dzbank.de; internet www.dzbank.de; f. 1949; cap. 3,028m., res 6,176m., dep. 365,455m. (Dec. 2006); Chair., Supervisory Bd Dr CHRISTOPHER PLEISTER; Chair., Bd of Management WOLFGANG KIRSCH; 46 brs.

DZ BANK is a specialist wholesale bank and is the central institution in the German co-operative banking sector, which comprises local co-operative banks, three regional central banks and a number of specialist financial institutions. In 2006 there were 1,250 credit co-operatives, including central institutions.

Specialist Banks

Although Germany is considered the model country for universal banking, banks that specialize in certain types of business are also extremely important. In December 1998 there were 51 specialist banks. A selection of the most prominent among these is given below:

Aareal Bank AG: Postfach 2169, 65011 Wiesbaden; Paulinenstr. 15, 65189 Wiesbaden; tel. (611) 3480; fax (611) 3482549; e-mail aareal@aareal-bank.com; internet www.aareal-bank.com; f. 1923; fmrly DePfa Deutsche Pfandbriefbank AG; cap. 128m., res 893m., dep. 34,767m. (Dec. 2006); Chair. Dr WOLF SCHUMACHER.

Berlin-Hannoversche Hypothekenbank AG: Budapester Str. 1, 10787 Berlin; tel. (30) 259990; fax (30) 25999131; e-mail kommunikation@berlinhyp.de; internet www.berlinhyp.de; f. 1996 by merger; cap. 573m., res 67m., dep. 39,029m. (Dec. 2006); Chair., Supervisory Bd HANS-JÖRG VETTER; Chair., Bd of Management JAN BETTINK.

COREALCREDIT BANK AG: Postfach 170162, 60075 Frankfurt a.M.; Grüneburgweg 58-62, 60322 Frankfurt a.M.; tel. (69) 71790; fax (69) 7179100; e-mail info@corealcredit.de; internet www.corealcredit.com; f. 1962 as Allgemeine Hypotheken Bank AG; name changed to Allgemeine HypothekenBank Rheinboden in 2001; present name adopted 2007; specializes in commercial property market; Chair. Dr CLAUS NOLTING.

Deutsche Hypothekenbank AG: Georgspl. 8, 30159 Hannover; tel. (511) 30450; fax (511) 3045459; e-mail mail@deutsche-hypo.de; internet www.deutsche-hypo.de; f. 1872; cap. 81m., res 398m., dep. 33,567m. (Dec. 2006); Chair., Supervisory Bd ALEXANDER STUHLMANN; 4 brs.

Deutsche Postbank AG: Friedrich-Ebert-Allee 114–126, 53113 Bonn; tel. (228) 9200; fax (228) 92035151; e-mail banks@postbank.de; internet www.postbank.de; f. 1990; 50.01% owned by Deutsche Post AG; cap. 410m., res 4,100m., dep. 164,521m. (Dec. 2006); Chair. Prof. Dr WULF VON SCHIMMELMANN.

Eurohypo AG: Helfmann-Park 5, 65760 Eschborn; tel. (69) 25480; fax (69) 254888888; e-mail info@deutschehyp.de; internet www.eurohypo.com; f. 2002 by merger of Deutsche Hyp (f. 1862), Eurohyp (f. 1862) and Rheinhyp (f. 1871); 98.04% owned by Commerzbank AG; cap. 914m., res 5,767m., dep. 206,569m. (Dec. 2006); CEO and Chair., Management Bd BERND KNOBLOCH; 16 brs.

Hypo Real Estate Bank AG: Von-der-Tann-Str. 2, 80539 München; tel. (89) 28800; fax (89) 288010319; e-mail info@hyporealestate.de; internet www.hyporealestatebank.de; f. 2001 by merger of Bayerische Handelsbank AG, Süddeutsche Bodencreditbank AG and Nürnberger Hypothekenbank AG; part of Hypo Real Estate Group; cap. 133m., res 1,703m., dep. 70,324m. (Dec. 2006); Chair., Supervisory Bd GEORG FUNKE; Chair., Management Bd FRANK LAMBY.

IKB Deutsche Industriebank AG: Postfach 101118, 40002 Düsseldorf; Willhelm-Bötzkes-Str. 1, 40474 Düsseldorf; tel. (211) 82210; fax (211) 82213959; e-mail info@ikb.de; internet www.ikb.de; f. 1949; cap. 225m., res 1,544m., dep. 48,750m. (March 2007); Gen. Mans JOACHIM NEUPEL, STEFAN ORTSEIFEN, CLAUS MOMBURG, Dr MARKUS GUTHOFF, Dr FRANK SCHÖNHERR; 7 brs.

GERMANY   *Directory*

KfW Bankengruppe (Kreditanstalt für Wiederaufbau): Postfach 111141, 60046 Frankfurt a.M.; Palmengartenstr. 5–9, 60325 Frankfurt a.M.; tel. (69) 74310; fax (69) 74312944; e-mail info@kfw.de; internet www.kfw.de; f. 1948; cap. 3,300m., res 5,877m., dep. 323,807m. (Dec. 2006); Chair. INGRID MATTHÄUS-MAIER.

Münchener Hypothekenbank eG: Karl-Scharnagl-Ring 10, 80539 München; tel. (89) 5387800; fax (89) 5387900; e-mail serviceteam800@muenchenerhyp.de; internet www.muenchenerhyp.de; f. 1896; cap. 368m., res 268m., dep. 30,882m. (Dec. 2006); Chair., Supervisory Bd Prof. Dr WILLIBALD J. FOLZ; Chair., Management Bd ERICH RÖDEL; 12 brs.

Bankers' Organizations

Bankenverband—Bundesverband deutscher Banken (Association of German Banks): Postfach 040307, 10062 Berlin; Burgstr. 28, 10178 Berlin; tel. (30) 16630; fax (30) 16631399; e-mail bankenverband@bdb.de; internet www.bdb.de; f. 1951; Gen. Man. Prof. Dr MANFRED WEBER.

Bundesverband der Deutschen Volksbanken und Raiffeisenbanken eV (BVR) (Federal Association of German Co-operative Banks and Agricultural Credit Co-operatives): Schellingstr. 4, 10785 Berlin; tel. (30) 20210; fax (30) 20211900; e-mail info@bvr.de; internet www.bvr.de; f. 1972; Pres. Dr CHRISTOPHER PLEISTER; 1,255 mems (2006).

Bundesverband Öffentlicher Banken Deutschlands eV (VÖB) (Association of German Public Sector Banks): Lennéstr. 11, 10785 Berlin; tel. (30) 81920; fax (30) 8192222; e-mail presse@voeb.de; internet www.voeb.de; 34 mems and 28 assoc. mems; Chair. Dr SIEGFRIED JASCHINSKI.

Deutscher Sparkassen- und Giroverband eV (German Savings Banks Association): Postfach 110180, 10831 Berlin; Charlottenstr. 47, 10117 Berlin; tel. (30) 202250; fax (30) 20225250; e-mail info@dsgv.de; internet www.dsgv.de; Pres. HEINRICH HAASIS.

STOCK EXCHANGES

Berlin: Börse Berlin AG, Fasanenstr. 85, 10623 Berlin; tel. (30) 3110910; fax (30) 31109179; e-mail kundenbetreuung@boerse-berlin.de; internet www.boerse-berlin.de; f. 1685; 109 mems; Pres. Dr JÖRG WALTER.

Düsseldorf: Börse Düsseldorf AG, Ernst-Schneider-Pl. 1, 40212 Düsseldorf; e-mail kontakt@boerse-duesseldorf.de; internet www.boerse-duesseldorf.de; tel. (211) 13890; fax (211) 133287; f. 1935; 110 mem. firms; Chair. DIRK ELBERSKIRCH.

Frankfurt am Main: Deutsche Börse AG, Börsenplatz 4, 60313 Frankfurt a.M.; tel. (69) 2110; fax (69) 21111021; internet www.exchange.de; f. 1585 as Frankfurter Wertpapierbörse; 269 mems; CEO RETO FRANCIONI; Chair., Supervisory Bd KURT F. VIERMETZ.

München: Bayerische Börse AG, Hopfenstr. 4A, 80335 München; tel. (89) 5490450; fax (89) 54904531; e-mail info@boerse-muenchen.de; internet www.boerse-muenchen.de; f. 1830; 81 mems; Chair., Supervisory Bd DIETER RAMPL; Chair., Bd of Management UTO BAADER.

North Germany (Hamburg): BÖAG Börsen AG, Kleine Johannisstr. 2–4, 20457 Hamburg; tel. (40) 3613020; fax (40) 36130223; internet www.boersenag.de; f. 1999 by merger of Hanseatische Wertpapierbörse Hamburg and Niedersächsische Börse zu Hannover; 109 mems; Pres. UDO BANDOW; Chair. Dr THOMAS LEDERMANN.

North Germany (Hannover): BÖAG Börsen AG, Rathenaustr. 2, 30159 Hannover; tel. (511) 327661; fax (511) 324915; e-mail s.lueth@boersenag.de; internet www.boersenag.de; f. 1999 by merger of Hanseatische Wertpapierbörse Hamburg and Niedersächsische Börse zu Hannover; 81 mems; Chair. Prof. Dr HANS HEINRICH PETERS.

Stuttgart: boerse-Stuttgart AG, Börsenstr. 4, 70174 Stuttgart; tel. (711) 2229850; fax (711) 22298555; e-mail info@boerse-stuttgart.de; internet www.boerse-stuttgart.de; f. 1861; 121 mems; Pres. ROLF LIMBACH; Man. Dir Dr CHRISTOPH MURA.

INSURANCE

German law specifies that property and accident insurance may not be jointly underwritten with life, sickness, legal protection or credit insurance by the same company. Insurers are therefore obliged to establish separate companies to cover the different classes of insurance.

Aachener und Münchener Lebensversicherung AG: Robert-Schuman-Str. 51, 52066 Aachen; tel. (241) 600101; fax (241) 60015138; internet www.aachenerundmuenchener.de; f. 1868; Chair. Dr WOLFGANG KASKE; Gen. Man. Dr MICHAEL KALKA.

Albingia Versicherungs-AG: Ballindamm 39, 20095 Hamburg; tel. (40) 30220; fax (40) 30222585; e-mail infoa@albingia.de; internet www.albingia.de; f. 1901; Chair. Dr K. ASCHER; Gen. Man. V. BREMKAMP.

Allianz AG: Königinstr. 28, 80802 München; tel. (89) 38000; fax (89) 349941; internet www.allianz.com; f. 1890; Chair., Supervisory Bd Dr KLAUS LIESEN; Chair., Bd of Management Dr HENNING SCHULTE-NOELLE.

Allianz Lebensversicherungs-AG: Reinsburgstr. 19, 70178 Stuttgart; tel. (711) 6630; fax (711) 6632654; internet www.allianzgroup.com; f. 1922; Chair., Supervisory Bd MICHAEL DIEKMANN; Chair., Bd of Management Dr G. RUPPRECHT.

Allianz Private Krankenversicherungs AG: Königinstr. 28, 80802 München; tel. (89) 38000; fax (89) 38003425; e-mail info@allianz.de; internet www.gesundheit.allianz.de; f. 1925; Chair. Dr ULRICH RUMM.

Allianz Versicherungs AG: Elsa-Brandström-Str. 10–12, 80802 München; tel. (89) 38000; fax (89) 349941; e-mail medienzentrale@allianz.de; f. 1985; Chair. Dr H. SCHULTE-NOELLE; Gen. Man. Dr R. HAGEMANN.

AXA Colonia Krankenversicherung AG: 50592 Köln; tel. (221) 148125; fax (221) 14832602; f. 1962; Chair. CLAAS KLEYBOLDT; Gen. Man. Dr CARL HERMANN SCHLEIFFER.

AXA Lebensversicherung AG: Colonia-Allee 10–20, 51067 Köln; tel. (1803) 556622; fax (221) 14822750; e-mail service@axa.de; internet www.axa.de; f. 1853; Chair., Supervisory Bd CLAAS KLEYBOLDT; Chair., Bd of Management Dr CLAUS-MICHAEL DILL.

AXA Versicherung AG: Colonia-Allee 10–20, 50670 Köln; tel. (1803) 556622; fax (221) 14822740; e-mail service@axa.de; internet www.axa.de; f. 1839 as Colonia Kölnischer Freuer Versicherung AG; present name adopted 2001; non-life insurance; Chair., Supervisory Bd CLAAS KLEYBOLDT; Chair., Bd of Management Dr CLAUS-MICHAEL DILL.

Continentale Krankenversicherung AG: Postfach 105032, 44047 Dortmund; tel. (231) 9190; fax (231) 9191799; f. 1926; Chair. F. LENSING-WOLFF; Gen. Man. Dr H. HOFFMANN.

DBV-Winterthur Lebensversicherung AG: Frankfurter Str. 50, 65178 Wiesbaden; tel. (611) 3630; fax (611) 3636565; e-mail info@dbv-winterthur.de; f. 1872; Chair. T. SCHULTE; Man. Dir H. FALK.

Debeka Krankenversicherungsverein AG: Ferdinand-Sauerbruch-Str. 18, 56058 Koblenz; tel. (261) 4980; fax (261) 41402; f. 1905; Chair. P. GREISLER; Gen. Man. UWE LAUE.

Deutsche Krankenversicherung AG: Postfach 100865, 50448 Köln; Aachener Str. 300, 50933 Köln; tel. (1801) 358100; fax (1801) 5786000; e-mail service@dkv.com; internet www.dkv.com; f. 1927; Chair. Dr NIKOLAUS VON BOMHARD; Gen. Man. GÜNTHER DIBBERN.

Frankfurter Versicherungs-AG: Theodor-Stern-Kai 1, 60596 Frankfurt a.M.; tel. (69) 71260; fax (69) 712684455; internet www.frankfurter-alliance.de; f. 1929; Chair. Dr R. HAGEMANN; Gen. Man. Dr KARL LUDWIG FRHR VON FREYBERG.

Gerling-Konzern Allgemeine Versicherungs-AG: Postfach 100808, 50448 Köln; Von-Werth-Str. 4–14, 50670 Köln; tel. (221) 1441; fax (221) 1445473; internet www.gerling.com; f. 1918; Chair., Supervisory Bd B. JANSLI; Chair., Bd of Management Dr W. BREUES.

Gothaer Versicherungsbank Versicherungsverein AG: Arnoldipl. 1, 50598 Köln; tel. (221) 30800; fax (221) 308103; internet www.gothaer.de; f. 1820; Chair., Supervisory Bd Dr KLAUS MURMANN; Chair., Bd of Management Dr WOLFGANG PEINER.

Haftpflicht-Unterstützungs-Kasse kraftfahrender Beamter Deutschlands AG in Coburg (HUK-COBURG): Bahnhofspl., 96444 Coburg; tel. (9561) 960; fax (9561) 963636; e-mail info@huk-coburg.de; internet www.huk.de; f. 1933; CEO ROLF-PETER HOENEN.

Hamburg-Mannheimer Versicherungs-AG: Überseering 45, 22297 Hamburg; tel. (40) 63760; fax (40) 63762885; e-mail prr@hamburg-mannheimer.de; internet www.hamburg-mannheimer.de; subsidiary of ERGO Versicherungsgruppe AG; f. 1899; Chair. Dr EDGAR JAMMOTT; Gen. Man. Dr GÖTZ WRICKE.

HDI Direkt Versicherung AG: Riethorst 2, 30659 Hannover; tel. (511) 6450; fax (511) 6454545; internet www.hdi-gerling.de; Chair. Dr CHRISTIAN HINSCH; CEO Dr WOLFGANG BREUER.

HDI—Gerling Industrie Versicherung AG: Postfach 510369, 30633 Hannover; tel. (511) 6450; fax (511) 6454545; internet www.hdi-gerling.de; f. 2001; Chair. H. K. HAAS; CEO Dr C. HINSCH.

IDUNA Vereinigte Lebensversicherung AG für Handwerk, Handel und Gewerbe: Neue Rabenstr. 15–19, 20354 Hamburg; tel. (40) 41240; e-mail info@signal-iduna.de; internet www.signal-iduna.de; f. 1914; Chair., Supervisory Bd G. KURTZ; Gen. Man. REINHOLD SCHULTE.

LVM Versicherungen: Kolde-Ring 21, 48126 Münster; tel. (251) 7020; fax (251) 7021099; e-mail info@lvm.de; internet www.lvm.de; f. 1896; Chair. JOCHEN BORCHERT; Gen. Man. G. KETTLER.

SIGNAL Krankenversicherung AG: Joseph-Scherer-Str. 3, 44139 Dortmund; tel. (231) 1350; fax (231) 1354638; e-mail info@

signal-iduna.de; internet www.signal-iduna.de; f. 1907; Chair., Supervisory Bd G. KUTZ; Gen. Man. REINHOLD SCHULTE.

Talanx AG: Riethorst 2, 30659 Hannover; tel. (511) 37470; fax (511) 37472525; e-mail info@talanx.com; internet www.talanx.com; f. 1996; HDI Haftpflichtverband der Deutschen Industrie VaG; CEO HERBERT K. HAAS.

Victoria Lebensversicherung AG: Victoriapl. 1–2, 40198 Düsseldorf; tel. (211) 4770; fax (211) 4772222; e-mail info@victoria.de; internet www.victoria.de; subsidiary of ERGO Versicherungsgruppe AG; f. 1929; Chair. Dr E. JANNOTT; Gen. Man. MICHAEL ROSENBERG.

Victoria Versicherung AG: Victoriapl. 1–2, 40198 Düsseldorf; tel. (221) 4770; fax (211) 4772222; e-mail info@victoria.de; internet www.victoria.de; subsidiary of ERGO Versicherungsgruppe AG; f. 1904; Chair. Dr E. JANNOTT; Gen. Man. HORST DÖRING.

Volksfürsorge Deutsche Lebensversicherung AG: Postfach 106420, 20043 Hamburg; tel. (40) 28650; fax (40) 28653369; f. 1913; Chair. Dr WOLFGANG KASKE; Gen. Man. Dr H. JÄGER.

Württembergische AG Versicherungs-Beteiligungsgesellschaft: Gutenbergstr. 30, 70176 Stuttgart; tel. (711) 6620; fax (711) 6622520; e-mail keu@wuerttembergische.de; internet www.wuerttembergische.de; f. 1828; Chair., Supervisory Bd Dr G. BÜCHNER; Chair., Bd of Management G. MEHL.

Reinsurance

DARAG Deutsche Versicherungs- und Rückversicherungs-AG: Postfach 10, 13062 Berlin; Gustav-Adolf-Str. 130, 13086 Berlin; tel. (30) 477080; fax (30) 47708100; e-mail info@darag.de; internet www.darag.de; f. 1958; re-formed 1990; fire and non-life, technical, cargo transport, marine hull, liability, aviation insurance and reinsurance; Chair., Supervisory Bd Dr WERNER SCHIMMING; Chair., Bd of Management VOLKER REIFENSCHEID; Gen. Man. Dr INGO WELTHER.

Deutsche Rückversicherung AG: Düsseldorf; tel. (211) 455401; fax (211) 4554199; f. 1951; Chair. Dr HEIKO WINKLER; Gen. Man. JÜRGEN REHMANN.

ERC-Aachener Rückversicherungs-Gesellschaft AG: Postfach 25, 52001 Aachen; tel. (241) 93690; fax (241) 9369205; f. 1853; Chair., Supervisory Bd KAJ AHLMANN; Chair., Bd of Management BERNHARD C. FINK.

GE Frankona Rückversicherungs-AG: Postfach 860380, 81630 München; Maria-Theresa-Str. 35, 81675 München; tel. (89) 92280; fax (89) 92287395; internet www.geercgroup.com/gpc; f. 1886; Chair. RICHARD F. SMITH; Gen. Man. KENNETH BRANDT.

Hamburger Internationale Rückversicherung AG: Postfach 1161, 25452 Rellingen; Halstenbeker Weg 96A, 25462 Rellingen; tel. (4101) 4710; fax (4101) 471298; f. 1965; Chair., Supervisory Bd REINER SOLL; Chair., Exec. Bd Dr WOLFGANG EILERS.

Hannover Rückversicherung AG: Postfach 610369, 30603 Hannover; Karl-Wiechert-Allee 50, 30625 Hannover; tel. (511) 56040; fax (511) 56041188; e-mail info@hannover-re.com; internet www.hannover-re.com; f. 1966; Chair., Supervisory Bd W. BAUMGARTL; Chair., Bd of Management W. ZELLER.

Kölnische Rückversicherungs-Gesellschaft AG: Postfach 102244, 50668 Köln; Theodor-Heuss-Ring 11, 50462 Köln; tel. (221) 3780; fax (221) 9738494; e-mail contact@genre.com; internet www.genre.com; f. 1846; Chair. Dr PETER LÜTKE-BORNEFELD.

Münchener Rückversicherungs-Gesellschaft AG: Königinstr. 107, 80802 München; tel. (89) 38910; fax (89) 399056; e-mail info@munichre.com; internet www.munichre.com; f. 1880; all classes of reinsurance; Chair. ULRICH HARTMANN; Gen. Man. NICKOLAUS VON BOMHARD.

R + V Versicherung-AG Reinsurance: Sonnenberger Str. 44, 65193 Wiesbaden; tel. (611) 533940; fax (611) 529610; f. 1935; all classes of reinsurance; Chair. W. GRÜGER; Gen. Man. Dr J. FÖRTERER.

Swiss Re Germany AG: Dieselstr. 11, 85774 Unterföhring bei München; tel. (89) 38440; fax (89) 38442279; e-mail info.srmuc@swissre.com; internet www.swissre.com; Chair. Dr RÜDGER ARNDO-LÜSSEN; Gen. Man. M. LIES.

Principal Insurance Association

Gesamtverband der Deutschen Versicherungswirtschaft eV (German Insurance Assen): Friedrichstr. 191, 10117 Berlin; tel. (30) 20205000; fax (30) 20206000; e-mail berlin@gdv.org; internet www.gdv.de; f. 1948; affiliating three mem. asscns and 443 mem. cos; Pres. Dr BERNHARD SCHARECK (Karlsruhe); CEO Dr FRANK VON FÜRSTENWERTH.

Trade and Industry

GOVERNMENT AGENCIES

Bundesagentur für Aussenwirtschaft (German Office for Foreign Trade): Postfach 100522, 50445 Köln; Agrippastr. 87–93, 50676 Köln; tel. (221) 20570; fax (221) 2057212; e-mail info@bfai.de; internet www.bfai.de.

Bundesverband des Deutschen Gross- und Aussenhandels eV: Bonn; tel. (228) 260040; fax (228) 2600455; f. 1949; Dir-Gen. Dr PETER SPARY; 77 mem. asscns.

Hauptverband des Deutschen Einzelhandels eV: Berlin; tel. (30) 7262500; fax (30) 72625099; e-mail hde@einzelhandel.de; internet www.einzelhandel.de; f. 1947; Chair. HERMANN FRANZEN; Exec. Dir HOLGER WENZEL.

Industrial Investment Council (IIC): Friedrichstr. 60, 10117 Berlin; tel. (30) 20945660; fax (30) 20945666; e-mail info@iic.de; internet www.iic.de; promotes investment in eastern Germany; Chair. Dr HORST DIETZ.

Zentralverband Gewerblicher Verbundgruppen: Haus des Handels, Am Weidendamm 1A, 10117 Berlin; tel. (30) 590099663; fax (30) 59099617; e-mail info@zgv-online.de; internet www.zgv-online.de; f. 1992; Pres. JOACHIM SIEBERT; c. 400 mems.

CHAMBERS OF COMMERCE

Deutscher Industrie- und Handelskammertag (Association of German Chambers of Industry and Commerce): Breite Str. 29, 10178 Berlin; tel. (30) 203080; fax (30) 203081000; internet www.diht.de; Pres. HANS PETER STIHL; Sec.-Gen. Dr FRANZ SCHOSER; affiliates 83 Chambers of Industry and Commerce.

There are Chambers of Industry and Commerce in all the principal towns and also 14 regional associations including:

Arbeitsgemeinschaft der Industrie- und Handelskammern in Mecklenburg-Vorpommern: Schlossstr. 17, 19053 Schwerin; tel. (385) 51030; fax (385) 5103136; e-mail info@schwerin.ihk.de; internet www.ihkzuschwerin.de; Pres. JOERGEN THIELE; Man. Dir KLAUS-MICHAEL ROTHE.

Arbeitsgemeinschaft der Thüringer Industrie- und Handelskammern: Aurustädter Str. 34, 99096 Erfurt; tel. (361) 34840; fax (361) 3485972; f. 1991; Pres. NIELS LUND CHRESTENSEN.

Arbeitsgemeinschaft Hessischer Industrie- und Handelskammern: Börsenpl. 4, 60313 Frankfurt a.M.; tel. (69) 21971384; fax (69) 21971448; internet www.ihk-hessen.de; Chair. HANS-JOACHIM TONNELLIER; Sec.-Gen. MATTHIAS GRÄSSLE; 11 mems.

Arbeitsgemeinschaft Norddeutscher Industrie- und Handelskammern: Adolphspl. 1, 20457 Hamburg; tel. (40) 366382; Vice-Pres. Dr MARTIN WILLICH; Sec. Dr UWE CHRISTIANSEN.

Baden-Württembergischer Industrie- und Handelskammertag: Jägerstr. 40, 70174 Stuttgart; tel. (711) 22550060; fax (711) 22550077; e-mail info@bw.ihk.de; internet www.bw.ihk.de; Chair. BERND BECHTOLD.

Bayerischer Industrie- und Handelskammertag: Max-Joseph-Str. 2, 80333 München; tel. (89) 51160; fax (89) 5116290; e-mail iszihkmail@muenchen-ihk.de; Pres. Prof. Dr ERICH GREIPL; Sec.-Gen. Dr REINHARD DÖRFLER; 310,000 mems.

IHK-Arbeitsgemeinschaft Rheinland-Pfalz: Herzogenbuscher Str. 12, 54292 Trier; tel. (651) 9777101; fax (651) 9777105; e-mail info@trier.ihk.de; Sec. PETER ADRIAN; four mems.

IHK-Vereinigung Schleswig-Holstein: Bergstr. 2, 24103 Kiel; tel. (431) 5194215; fax (431) 5194515; e-mail ihk@kiel.ihk.de; internet www.kiel-ihk.de; Chair. Prof. Dr HANS HEINRICH DRILLMANN; Sec.-Gen. WOLF-RÜDIGER JANZEN.

Industrie- und Handelskammer in Südwestsachsen (Chemnitz, Plauen, Zwickau): Str. der Nationen 25, 09111 Chemnitz; tel. (371) 69001242; fax (371) 6900191210; e-mail reichelt@chemnitz.ihk.de; internet www.chemnitz.ihk24.de.

Industrie- und Handelskammer Magdeburg: Postfach 1840, Alter Markt 8, 39104 Magdeburg; tel. (391) 56930; fax (391) 5693193; e-mail internet@magdeburg.ihk.de; internet www.magdeburg.ihk.de; f. 1825; Pres. KLAUS OLBRICHT.

Industrie- und Handelskammer Potsdam: Breite Str. 2A–C, 14467 Potsdam; tel. (331) 2786251; fax (331) 2786190; e-mail ullmann@potsdam.ihk.de; internet www.potsdam.ihk24.de; f. 1990; 67,000 cos; Pres. Dr VICTOR STIMMING; CEO RENÉ KOHL.

Niedersächsische IHK-Arbeitsgemeinschaft Hannover-Braunschweig (Nds. IHK-AG): Schiffgraben 49, 30175 Hannover; tel. (511) 3107237; fax (511) 3107444; e-mail ihk-ag@hannover.ihk.de; f. 1899; Pres. Prof. Dr KLAUS E. GOEHRMANN; Man. Dir Dr WILFRIED PREWO; 2 mems.

Vereinigung der Industrie- und Handelskammern in Nordrhein-Westfalen: Postfach 240120, 40090 Düsseldorf; tel. (211)

367020; fax (211) 3670221; CEO Hans Georg Crone-Erdmann; Pres. Dr Jörg Mittelsten Scheid; 16 mems.

INDUSTRIAL AND TRADE ASSOCIATIONS

Bundesverband der Deutschen Industrie eV (Federation of German Industry): Breite Str. 29, 10178 Berlin; tel. (30) 20281566; fax (30) 20282566; e-mail presse@bdi.eu; internet www.bdi.eu; Pres. Jürgen R. Thümann; Chair., Management Cttee Klaus Bräunig.

Arbeitsgemeinschaft Keramische Industrie eV (Ceramics): Postfach 1624, 95090 Selb; Schillerstr. 17, 95100 Selb; tel. (9287) 8080; fax (9287) 70492; e-mail info@keramverband.de; internet www.keramverbaende.de; Pres. Franz Kook; Man. Peter Frischholz.

Bundesverband Baustoffe—Steine und Erden eV (Building Materials): Postfach 610486, 10928 Berlin; Kochstr. 6–7, 10969 Berlin; tel. (30) 72619990; fax (30) 726199912; e-mail info@bvbaustoffe.de; internet www.baustoffindustrie.de; f. 1948; Pres. Dr Gernot Schaefer; Chief Dir Dr Michael Weissenhorn.

Bundesverband der Deutschen Entsorgungswirtschaft (BDE) (Waste Disposal and Recycling): Behrenstr. 29, 10117 Berlin; tel. (30) 59003350; fax (30) 590033599; e-mail info@bde-berlin.de; internet www.bde-berlin.de; Pres. Peter Hoffmeyer; Dir-Gen. Dr Stephan Harmening.

Bundesverband der Deutschen Luft- und Raumfahrtindustrie eV (BDLI) (German Aerospace Industries Asscn): Friedrichstr. 60, 10117 Berlin; tel. (30) 2061400; fax (30) 20614090; e-mail info@bdli.de; internet www.bdli.de; f. 1955; Pres. Dr Thomas Enders; Man. Dir Dietmar Schrick.

Bundesverband Druck und Medien eV (Printing and Media): Postfach 1869, 65008 Wiesbaden; Biebricher Allee 79, 65187 Wiesbaden; tel. (611) 8030; fax (611) 803113; e-mail info@bvdm-online.de; f. 1947; Pres. Manfred Adrian; Man. Dir Thomas Mayer; 12 mem. asscns.

Bundesverband Glasindustrie eV (Glass): Postfach 101753, 40008 Düsseldorf; Am Bonneshof 5, 40474 Düsseldorf; tel. (211) 4796134; fax (211) 9513751; e-mail info@bvglas.de; internet www.bvglas.de; Chair. Paul Neeteson; 4 mem. asscns.

Bundesverband Schmuck, Uhren, Silberwaren und Verwandte Industrien eV (Jewellery, Clocks and Silverware): Zerrenstr. 32, 75172 Pforzheim; tel. (7231) 33041; fax (7231) 355887; e-mail info@bv-schmuck-uhren.de; internet www.bv-schmuck-uhren.de; Pres. Lothar Keller; Man. Dir Dr Alfred Schneider.

Bundesvereinigung der Deutschen Ernährungsindustrie eV (BVE) (Food): Claire-Waldorf-Str. 7, 10117 Berlin; tel. (30) 2007860; fax (30) 200706299; e-mail bve@bve-online.de; internet www.bve-online.de; f. 1949; Chair. Jürgen Abraham; Chief Gen. Man. Prof. Dr Matthias Horst.

Centralvereinigung Deutscher Wirtschaftsverbände für Handelsvermittlung und Vertrieb (Trade and Marketing): Am Weidendamm 1A, 10117 Berlin; tel. (30) 72625600; fax (30) 72625699; e-mail centralvereinigung@cdh.de; internet www.cdh.de; f. 1902; Pres. Heinrich Schmidt; Gen. Sec. Dr Andreas Paffhausen; 18,000 mems.

Deutscher Giessereiverband (Foundries): Postfach 101961, 40010 Düsseldorf; Sohnstr. 70, 40237 Düsseldorf; tel. (211) 6871215; fax (211) 6871205; e-mail info@dgv.de; internet www.dgv.de; f. 1865; Pres. Dr Arnold Kawlath; Man. Dir Dr Klaus Urbat.

Deutscher Hotel- und Gaststättenverband eV (DEHOGA): Am Weidendamm 1A, 10117 Berlin; tel. (30) 7262520; fax (30) 72625242; f. 1949; Pres. Ernst Fischer; Gen. Sec. Ingrid Hartges; over 75,000 mems.

Gemeinschaftsausschuss der Deutschen gewerblichen Wirtschaft (Joint Committee for German Industry and Commerce): Köln; tel. (221) 370800; fax (221) 3708730; f. 1950; a discussion forum for the principal industrial and commercial orgs; Pres. Dr Tyll Necker; 16 mem. orgs.

GermanFashion Modeverband Deutschland eV: An Lyskirchen 14, 50676 Köln; tel. (221) 77440; fax (221) 7744137; e-mail info@germanfashion.net; internet www.germanfashion.net; f. by merger of Bundesverband Bekleidungsindustrie eV and Bundesvereinigung der Arbeitgeber im Bundesverband Bekleidungsindustrie eV.

Gesamtverband kunststoffverarbeitende Industrie eV (GKV) (Plastics): Am Hauptbahnhof 12, 60329 Frankfurt a.M.; tel. (69) 271050; fax (69) 232799; e-mail tenhagen-gkv@t-online.de; internet www.gkv.de; f. 1950; Chair. Günter Schwank; Sec.-Gen. Joachim den Hagen; 750 mems.

Gesamtverband der deutschen Textil und Modeindustrie eV (Textiles and Clothing): Postfach 5340, 65728 Eschborn; Frankfurter Str. 10–14, 65760 Eschborn; tel. (6196) 9660; fax (6196) 42170; e-mail info@textil-mode.de; internet www.textil-online.de; f. 1948; Dir-Gen. Dr Wolf R. Baumann.

Hauptverband der Deutschen Bauindustrie eV (Building): Kurfürstenstr. 129, 10785 Berlin; tel. (30) 212860; fax (30) 21286240; e-mail bauind@bauindustrie.de; internet www.bauindustrie.de; f. 1948; Pres. Dr Hans-Peter Keitel; Dir-Gen. Michael Knipper; 23 mem. asscns.

Hauptverband der Deutschen Holz und Kunststoffe verarbeitenden Industrie und verwandter Industriezweige eV (HDH) (Woodwork and Plastic): Flutgraben 2, 53604 Bad-Honnef; tel. (2224) 93770; fax (2224) 937777; e-mail info@hdh-ev.de; internet www.hdh-ev.de; f. 1948; Pres. Helmut Lübke; Man. Dir Dirk-Uwe Klaas; 24 mem. asscns.

Hauptverband der Papier, Pappe und Kunststoffe verarbeitenden Industrie eV (HPV) (Paper, Board and Plastic): Strubbergstr. 70, 60489 Frankfurt a.M.; tel. (69) 9782810; fax (69) 97828130; e-mail info@hpv-ev.org; internet www.hpv-ev.org; f. 1948; 10 regional groups, 20 production groups; Pres. Lutz Boeder; Dir-Gen. Thomas Beck; 1,300 mems.

Kaliverein eV (Potash): Postfach 410554, 34067 Kassel; Wilhelmshöher Allee 239, 34121 Kassel; tel. (561) 318270; fax (561) 3182716; e-mail kaliverein@k-plus-s.com; internet www.kaliverein.de; f. 1905; Pres. Dr Ralf Bethke; Man. Dir Dr Arne Brockhoff.

Mineralölwirtschaftsverband eV (Petroleum): Steindamm 55, 20099 Hamburg; tel. (40) 248490; fax (40) 24849253; e-mail mwv@mwv.de; internet www.mwv.de; f. 1946; Chair. Dr Josef Waltl; Man. Dir Dr Klaus Picard.

SPECTARIS—Deutscher Industrieverband für optische, medizinische und mechatronische Technologien eV (German Industrial Asscn for Optical, Medical and Mechatronical Technologies): Saarbrücker Str. 38, 10405 Berlin; tel. (30) 4140210; fax (30) 41402133; e-mail info@spectaris.de; internet www.spectaris.de; f. 1949; Chair. Dr Michael Kaschke; Dir Sven Behrens.

Verband der Automobilindustrie eV (Motor Cars): Postfach 170563, 60079 Frankfurt a.M.; Westendstr. 61, 60325 Frankfurt a.M.; tel. (69) 975070; fax (69) 97507261; e-mail info@vda.de; internet www.vda.de; Pres. Prof. Dr Bernd Gottschalk.

Verband der Chemischen Industrie eV (Chemical Industry): Karlstr. 21, 60329 Frankfurt a.M.; tel. (69) 25560; fax (69) 25561471; e-mail info@vci.de; internet www.chemische-industrie.de; f. 1877; Pres. (vacant); Dir-Gen. Dr Wilfried Sahm; 1,619 mems.

Verband der Cigarettenindustrie (Cigarettes): Neustädtische Kirchstr. 8, 10117 Berlin; tel. (30) 206050; fax (30) 20605250; e-mail vdc@vdc.berlin.de; internet www.vdc-berlin.de; Chair. Wolfgang Hainer.

Verband Deutscher Maschinen- und Anlagenbau eV (VDMA) (German Engineering Federation): Postfach 710864, 60498 Frankfurt a.M.; Lyoner Str. 18, 60528 Frankfurt a.M.; tel. (69) 66030; fax (69) 66031511; e-mail puoe@vdma.org; internet www.vdma.org; f. 1892; Pres. Dieter Brucklacher; Gen. Man. Dr Hannes Hesse.

Verband Deutscher Papierfabriken eV (Paper): Adenauerallee 55, 53113 Bonn; tel. (228) 267050; fax (228) 2670562; Pres. Hans-Michael Gellenkamp; Dir-Gen. Klaus Windhagen.

Verband für Schiffbau und Meerestechnik eV (German Shipbuilding and Ocean Industries Asscn): Steinhoeft 11, 20459 Hamburg; tel. (40) 2801520; fax (40) 28015230; e-mail info@vsm.de; internet www.vsm.de; f. 1884; Man. Dirs Dr Werner Lundt, Dr Ralf Soeren Marquardt.

Verein der Zuckerindustrie (Sugar): Am Hofgarten 8, 53113 Bonn; tel. (228) 22850; fax (228) 2285100; e-mail wvz-vdz@zuckerverbaende.de; internet www.zuckerverbaende.de; f. 1850; Chair. Horst W. Mewis; Dir-Gen. Dr Dieter Langendorf.

Vereinigung Rohstoffe und Bergbau eV (Mining): Postfach 120736, 10597 Berlin; Am Schillertheater 4, 10625 Berlin; tel. (30) 31518242; fax (30) 31518235; e-mail info@v-r-b.de; internet www.v-r-b.de; Pres. Matthias Hartung; Gen. Man. Dr Heinz-Norbert Schächter; 9 mem. asscns.

Wirtschaftsverband der Deutschen Kautschukindustrie eV (WDK) (Rubber): Zeppelinallee 69, 60487 Frankfurt a.M.; tel. (69) 79360; fax (69) 7936165; e-mail info@wdk.de; internet www.wdk.de; f. 1894; Pres. Paul Eberhard-Krug; Gen. Man. Fritz Katzensteiner; 87 mems.

Wirtschaftsverband Erdöl- und Erdgasgewinnung eV (Association of Crude Oil and Gas Producers): Brühlstr. 9, 30169 Hannover; tel. (511) 121720; fax (511) 1217210; e-mail info@erdoel-erdgas.de; internet www.erdoel-erdgas.de; f. 1945; Pres. Dr Cernot Kalkoffen; Gen. Man. Josef Schmid.

Wirtschaftsverband Stahlbau und Energietechnik (SET) (Steel and Energy): Postfach 320420, 40419 Düsseldorf; Sternstr. 36, 40479 Düsseldorf; tel. (211) 4987092; fax (211) 4987036; e-mail info@set-online.de; internet www.set-online.de; Chair. Klaus Dieter Rennert; Dir-Gen. R. Maass.

WSM—Wirtschaftsverband Stahl- und Metallverarbeitung eV (Steel and Metal-Processing Industry): Kaiserwerther Str. 135,

GERMANY

40474 Düsseldorf; tel. (211) 4564108; fax (211) 4564169; e-mail hwolff@wsm-net.de; internet www.wsm-net.de; Pres. JÜRGEN R. THUMANN; Dir-Gen. Dr ANDREAS MOEHLENKAMP.

WirtschaftsVereinigung Metalle (Metal): Postfach 105463, 40045 Düsseldorf; Am Bonneshof 5, 40474 Düsseldorf; tel. (211) 47960; fax (211) 4796400; e-mail info@wvmetalle.de; internet www.wvmetalle.de; Pres. Dr KARL-HEINZ DÖRNER; Dir-Gen. MARTIN KNEER.

Wirtschaftsvereinigung Stahl (Steel): Postfach 105464, 40045 Düsseldorf; Sohnstr. 65, 40237 Düsseldorf; tel. (211) 67070; fax (211) 6707310; e-mail wvstahl@wvstahl.de; internet www.stahl-online.de; Pres. Prof. Dr DIETER AMELING; Dir ALBRECHT KORMANN.

Wirtschaftsvereinigung Ziehereien und Kaltwalzwerke eV (Metal): Drahthaus, Kaiserswerther Str. 137, 40474 Düsseldorf; tel. (211) 478060; fax (211) 4780622; Chair. and Gen. Man. Dr FRIEDRICH UENHAUS.

Zentralverband des Deutschen Handwerks: Mohrenstr. 20/21, 10117 Berlin; tel. (30) 206190; fax (30) 20619460; e-mail info@zdh.de; internet www.zdh.de; f. 1949; Pres. OTTO KENTZLER; Gen. Sec. HANNS-EBERHARD SCHLEYER; 54 mem. chambers, 38 asscns.

Zentralverband Elektrotechnik- und Elektronikindustrie eV (ZVEI) (Electrical and Electronic Equipment): Postfach 701261, 60591 Frankfurt a.M.; Stresemannallee 19, 60596 Frankfurt a.M.; tel. (69) 63020; fax (69) 6302317; e-mail zvei@zvei.org; internet www.zvei.org; f. 1918; Chair. Prof. Dr EDWARD G. KRUBASIK; Dirs GOTTHARD GRASS, Dr OLIVER BLANK, Dr HORST GERLACH; 1,400 mems.

EMPLOYERS' ORGANIZATIONS

Bundesvereinigung der Deutschen Arbeitgeberverbände (BDA) (Confederation of German Employers' Associations): im Haus der Deutschen Wirtschaft, 11054 Berlin; tel. (30) 20330; fax (30) 20331055; e-mail info@bda-online.de; internet www.bda-online.de; f. 1904; represents the professional and regional interests of German employers in the social policy field, affiliates 14 regional asscns and 53 branch asscns, of which some are listed under industrial asscns; Pres. Dr DIETER HUNDT; Dirs Dr REINHARD GÖHNER, ALEXANDER GUNKEL, PETER CLEVER.

Affiliated associations:

Arbeitgeberverband der Cigarettenindustrie (Employers' Association of Cigarette Manufacturers): Harvestehuder Weg 88, 20149 Hamburg; tel. (40) 445739; fax (40) 443039; f. 1949; Pres. SIEGFRIED HANKE; Dir LUTZ SANNIG.

Arbeitgeberverband der Deutschen Binnenschiffahrt eV (Employers' Association of German Inland Waterway Transport): Dammstr. 15–17, 47119 Duisburg; tel. (203) 8000631; fax (203) 8000628; e-mail info@adb-ev.de; internet www.schulschiffrhein-adb.de; f. 1974; Pres. Dr WOLFGANG HÖNEMANN; Dir J. RUSCHE.

Arbeitgeberverband der Deutschen Glasindustrie eV (German Glass Industry Employers' Association): Postfach 200219, 80002 München; Max-Joseph-Str. 5, 80333 München; tel. (89) 55178400; fax (89) 55178444; e-mail info@agvglas.de; internet www.agvglas.de; Pres. THOMAS KIETSCHMANN; Gen. Man. GERNOT STEINBACHER.

Arbeitgeberverband der Deutschen Kautschukindustrie (ADK) eV (German Rubber Industry Employers' Association): Schiffgraben 36, 30175 Hannover; tel. (511) 85050; fax (511) 8505201; e-mail agv-hannover@vmn.de; internet www.adk-ev.de; Pres. JÜRGEN KREBAUM; Gen. Man. DIETRICH KRÖNCKE.

Arbeitgeberverband Deutscher Eisenbahnen eV (German Railway Employers' Association): Volksgartenstr. 54A, 50677 Köln; tel. (221) 9318450; fax (221) 93184588; Pres. Dr JENS JAHNKE; Dir Dr HANS-PETER ACKMANN.

Arbeitgeberverband des Gesamtverbandes der deutschen Textil- und Modeindustrie eV (General Textile Employers' Organization): Frankfurter Str. 10–14, 65760 Eschborn; tel. (6196) 9660; fax (6196) 42170; internet www.textil-online.de; Chair. WOLFGANG BRINKMANN; Gen. Man. HELGE MARTIN KROLL-MANN; 13 mem. asscns.

Arbeitgeberverband des Privaten Bankgewerbes eV (Private Banking Employers' Association): Burgstr. 28, 10178 Berlin; tel. (30) 590011270; e-mail service@agvbanken.de; f. 1954; 120 mems; Pres. HEINZ LABER; Dir GERD BENRATH.

Arbeitgeberverband der Versicherungsunternehmen in Deutschland (Employers' Association of Insurance Companies): Arabellastr. 29, 81925 München; tel. (89) 9220010; fax (89) 92200150; e-mail agvvers@agv-vers.de; internet www.agv-vers.de; f. 1950; Pres. Dr JOSEF BEUTELMANN; Dir-Gen. Dr JÖRG MÜLLER-STEIN.

Bundesarbeitgeberverband Chemie eV (Federation of Employers' Associations in the Chemical Industry): Postfach 1280, 65002 Wiesbaden; Abraham-Lincoln-Str. 24, 65189 Wiesbaden; tel. (611) 778810; fax (611) 7788123; e-mail info@bavc.de; internet www.bavc.de; Pres. Dr RÜDIGER ERCKEL; Dir HANS PAUL FREY; 11 mem. asscns.

Gesamtmetall—Gesamtverband der Arbeitgeberverbände der Metall- und Elektro-Industrie eV (Federation of the Metal Trades Employers' Associations): Postfach 060249, 10052 Berlin; Vossstr. 16, 10117 Berlin; tel. (30) 551500; e-mail info@gesamtmetall.de; internet www.gesamtmetall.de; Pres. MARTIN KANNEGIESSER; 22 mem. asscns.

Gesamtverband der Deutschen Land- und Forstwirtschaftlichen Arbeitgeberverbände eV (Federation of Agricultural and Forestry Employers' Associations): Claire-Waldoff-Straße 7, Berlin; tel. (30) 31904250; fax (30) 31904204; e-mail glfa@bauernverband.net; Pres. LOTHAR LAMPE; Sec. BURKHARD MÖLLER.

Vereinigung der Arbeitgeberverbände der Deutschen Papierindustrie eV (Federation of Employers' Associations of the German Paper Industry): Adenauerallee 55, 53113 Bonn; tel. (228) 2672810; fax (228) 215270; e-mail info@vap-papier.de; internet www.vap-papier.de; Pres. EBERHARD POTEMPA; Dir HANS-JOACHIM BLÖMEKE; 8 mem. asscns.

Vereinigung der Arbeitgeberverbände energie- und versorgungswirtschaftlicher Unternehmungen (Employers' Federation of Energy and Power Supply Enterprises): Theaterstr. 3, 30159 Hannover; tel. (511) 911090; fax (511) 9110940; f. 1962; Pres. HARTMUT GELDMACHER; Dir JOBST KLEINEBERG; 7 mem. asscns.

Regional employers' associations:

Landesvereinigung Baden-Württembergischer Arbeitgeberverbände eV: Postfach 700501, 70574 Stuttgart; Löffelstr. 22–24, 70597 Stuttgart; tel. (711) 76820; fax (711) 7651675; e-mail info@suedwestmetall.de; internet www.agv-bw.de; Pres. Dr DIETER HUNDT; Dir Dr ULRICH BROCKER; 42 mem. asscns.

Vereinigung der Bayerischen Wirtschaft (Federation of Employers' Associations in Bavaria): Postfach 202061, 80020 München; Max-Joseph-Str. 5, 80333 München; tel. (89) 55178100; fax (89) 55178111; e-mail info@vbw-bayern.de; internet www.vbw-bayern.de; Pres. RANDOLF RODENSTOCK; Gen. Man. STEPHAN GÖTZL; 76 mem. asscns.

Vereinigung der Unternehmensverbände in Berlin und Brandenburg eV (Federation of Employers' Associations in Berlin and Brandenburg): Am Schillertheater 2, 10625 Berlin; tel. (30) 310050; fax (30) 31005166; e-mail uvb@uvb-online.de; internet www.uvb-online.de; Pres. GERD VON BRANDENSTEIN; Dir Dr HARTMANN KLEINER; 62 mem. asscns.

Die Unternehmensverbände im Lande Bremen eV (Federation of Employers' Associations in the Land of Bremen): Postfach 100727, 28007 Bremen; Schillerstr. 10, 28195 Bremen; tel. (421) 368020; fax (421) 3680249; Pres. INGO KRAMER; Dir ORTWIN BAUM; 17 mem. asscns.

UVNord—Vereinigung der Unternehmensverbände in Hamburg und Schleswig-Holstein eV (Federation of Employers' Associations in Hamburg and Schleswig-Holstein): Postfach 601969, 22219 Hamburg; Kapstadtring 10, 22297 Hamburg; tel. (40) 63785100; fax (40) 63785075; e-mail kemmet@uvnord.de; internet www.uvnord.de; Pres. Prof. Dr HANS HEINRICH DRIFTMANN; Dir Dr KLAUS KEMMET; 58 mem. asscns.

Vereinigung der Hessischen Unternehmerverbände eV (Hessian Federation of Enterprise Associations): Postfach 500561, 60394 Frankfurt a.M.; Emil-von-Behring-Str. 4, 60439 Frankfurt a.M.; tel. (69) 958080; fax (69) 95808126; e-mail info@vhu.de; internet www.vhu.de; f. 1947; Pres. Prof. DIETER WEIDEMANN; Dir and Sec. VOLKER FASBENDER; 50 mem. asscns.

Vereinigung der Unternehmensverbände für Mecklenburg-Vorpommern eV (Federation of Employers' Associations of Mecklenburg-Western Pomerania): Eckdrift 93, 19061 Schwerin; tel. (385) 6356100; fax (385) 6356151; e-mail info@vumv.de; internet www.vumv.de; Pres. KLAUS HERING; Dir Dr THOMAS KLISCHAN; 29 mem. asscns.

Unternehmensverbände Niedersachsen eV (Federation of Employers' Associations in Lower Saxony): Schiffgraben 36, 30175 Hannover; tel. (511) 8505243; fax (511) 8505268; e-mail uvn@uvn-online.de; internet www.uvn-online.de; f. 1951; Pres. GOETZ VON ENGELBRECHTEN; Dir Dr VOLKER MÜLLER; 67 mem. asscns.

Landesvereinigung der Arbeitgeberverbände Nordrhein-Westfalen eV (North Rhine-Westphalia Federation of Employers' Associations): Postfach 300643, 40406 Düsseldorf; Uerdingerstr. 58–62, 40474 Düsseldorf; tel. (211) 45730; fax (211) 4573206; e-mail arbeitgebernrw@arbeitgebernrw.de; internet www.arbeitgebernrw.de; Pres. Dr JOCHEN F. KIRCHHOFF; Dir Dr HANSJÖRG DÖPP; 92 mem. asscns.

Landesvereinigung Unternehmerverbände Rheinland-Pfalz eV (LVU) (Federation of Employers' Associations in the

GERMANY

Rhineland Palatinate): Postfach 2966, 55019 Mainz; Hindenburgstr. 32, 55118 Mainz; tel. (6131) 55750; fax (6131) 557539; e-mail contact@lvu.de; internet www.lvu.de; f. 1963; Pres. Dr GERHARD F. BRAUN; Gen. Man. WERNER SIMON; 25 mem. asscns.

Vereinigung der Saarländischen Unternehmensverbände eV (Federation of Employers' Associations in Saarland): Postfach 650433, 66143 Saarbrücken; Harthweg 15, 66119 Saarbrücken; tel. (681) 954340; fax (681) 9543474; e-mail kontakt@vsu.de; internet www.vsu.de; Pres. Dr WALTER KOCH; Dir Dr JOACHIM MALTER; 18 mem. asscns.

Vereinigung der Sächsischen Wirtschaft eV (VSW) (Federation of Employers' Associations in Saxony): Postfach 300200, 01131 Dresden; Washingtonstr. 16/16A, 01139 Dresden; tel. (351) 255930; fax (351) 2559378; e-mail info@wirtschaftsverbaende-sachsen.de; internet www.wirtschaftsverbaende-sachsen.de; Pres. WOLFGANG HEINZE; Gen. Man. Dr ANDREAS WINKLER; 40 mem. asscns.

Landesvereinigung der Arbeitgeber-und-Wirtschaftsverbände Sachsen-Anhalt eV (Provincial Federation of Employers' and Managers' Associations of Saxony-Anhalt): Lorenzweg 56, 39128 Magdeburg; tel. (391) 5981710; fax (391) 5981716; e-mail info@lvsa.org; internet www.lvsa.org; Pres. Dr HELGE FÄNGER; Gen. Man. KLAUS LIEDKE; 31 mem. asscns.

Verband der Wirtschaft Thüringens eV (Association of Thuringian Management): Postfach 900353, 99007 Erfurt; Lossiusstr. 1, 99094 Erfurt; tel. (361) 67590; fax (361) 6759222; e-mail info@vwt.de; internet www.vwt.de; Pres. WALTER BOTSCHATZKI; Dir LOTAR SCHMIDT; 44 mem. asscns.

UTILITIES
Electricity

Bewag AG: 12432 Berlin; tel. (30) 26711077; fax (30) 26714667; e-mail bewag@bewag.com; internet www.bewag.de; f. 1884; supplies Berlin; promotes development of urban utilization of renewable energy resources.

E.ON Energie AG: Brienner Str. 40, 80333 München; tel. (89) 125401; fax (89) 12541401; e-mail info@eon-energie.de; internet www.eon-energie.de; f. 2000 by merger of Bayernwerk AG and Preussenelektra AG; Chair. Dr JOHANNES TEYSSEN.

Energie Baden-Württemberg (EnBW): Durlacher Allee 93; tel. (49) 7216306; e-mail info@enbw.com; internet www.enbw.com.

Hamburgische Electrizitäts-Werke AG (HEW): Überseering 12, 22297 Hamburg; tel. (40) 63960; fax (40) 63962770; e-mail hew@hew.de; internet www.hew.de; 73% owned by regional Govt; supplies Hamburg region.

RWE Energie AG: Postfach 103165, 45031 Essen; Kruppstr. 5, 45128 Essen; tel. (201) 1851; fax (201) 1854313; internet www.rweenergie.de; acquired Thames Water Utilities Ltd (UK) in 2000 and American Water Works Asscn (USA) in 2001; Pres. DIETMAR KUHNT; CEO HARRY ROELS.

VDEW—Verband der Elektrizitätswirtschaft eV: Robert-Kock-Pl. 4, 10115 Berlin; tel. (30) 7261470; fax (30) 726147140; e-mail info@vdew.net; internet www.strom.de; asscn of electricity supply cos; Dir-Gen. Dr EBERHARD MELLER.

Vereinigte Energiewerke AG (VEAG): Chaussestr. 23, 10115 Berlin; tel. (30) 51512521; fax (30) 51502220; e-mail info@veag.de; internet www.veag.de; serves eastern Germany.

Gas

Bundesverband der Deutschen Gas- und Wasserwirtschaft eV (BGW): Reinhardstr. 14, 10117 Berlin; tel. (30) 280410; fax (30) 28041520; e-mail info@bgw.de; internet www.bgw.de; asscn of gas and water cos; Pres. Dr WOLF PLUGE.

E.ON Ruhrgas AG: Huttropstr. 60, 45138 Essen; tel. (201) 18400; fax (201) 1843766; e-mail info@eon-ruhrgas.com; internet www.eon-ruhrgas.de; f. 1926; Chair. Dr BURCKHARD BERGMANN.

GASAG Berliner Gaswerke AG: 10703 Berlin; tel. (30) 78720; fax (30) 78723044; e-mail service@gasag.de; internet www.gasag.de; Chair., Supervisory Bd Dr KARL KAUERMANN.

Gasversorgung Süddeutschland GmbH (GVS): Stuttgart; internet www.gvs-erdgas.de; f. 1961; Chair., Supervisory Bd GERHARD WIDDER.

TRADE UNIONS

Following German unification in October 1990, the trade unions of the former GDR were absorbed into the member unions of the DGB (see below).

Deutscher Gewerkschaftsbund (DGB): Henriette-Herz-Pl. 2, 10178 Berlin; tel. (30) 240600; fax (30) 24060324; e-mail info.bvv@dgb.de; internet www.dgb.de; f. 1949; Pres. MICHAEL SOMMER; Vice-Pres. INGRID SEHRBROCK.

The following unions, with a total of 6,585,774 members (December 2006), are affiliated to the DGB:

Gewerkschaft Erziehung und Wissenschaft (GEW) (Education and Sciences): Reifenberger Str. 21, 60489 Frankfurt a.M.; tel. (69) 789730; fax (69) 78973201; e-mail info@gew.de; internet www.gew.de; Pres. ULRICH THÖNE; 249,462 mems (Dec. 2006).

Gewerkschaft Nahrung-Genuss-Gaststätten (Food, Beverages, Tobacco, Hotel and Catering and allied Workers): Haubachstr. 76, 22765 Hamburg; tel. (40) 380130; fax (40) 3892637; e-mail hauptverwaltung@ngg.net; internet www.ngg.net; f. 1949; Pres. FRANZ-JOSEF MÖLLENBERG; 211,573 mems (Dec. 2006).

Gewerkschaft der Polizei (Police Union): Stromstr. 4, 10555 Berlin; tel. (30) 3999210; fax (30) 39921211; e-mail gdp-bund-berlin@gdp-online.de; internet www.gdp.de; f. 1950; Chair. KONRAD FREIBERG; Sec. FRANK RICHTER; 170,835 mems (Dec. 2006).

IG Bau—Industriegewerkschaft Bauen-Agrar-Umwelt (Building and Construction Trade): Olof-Palme-Str. 19, 60439 Frankfurt a.M.; tel. (69) 957370; fax (69) 95737800; e-mail presse@igbau.de; internet www.igBAU.de; Pres. KLAUS WIESEHÜGEL; 368,768 mems (Dec. 2006).

IG BCE—Industriegewerkschaft Bergbau, Chemie, Energie (Mining, Chemical and Energy): Postfach 3047, 30030 Hannover; Königsworther Pl. 6, 30167 Hannover; tel. (511) 76310; fax (511) 7631715; e-mail abt.internationales.europa@igbce.de; internet www.igbce.de; Pres. HUBERTUS SCHMOLDT; 728,702 mems (Dec. 2006).

IG Metall—die Gewerkschaft in Produktion und Dienstleistung der Bereiche Metall-Elektro, Textil-Bekleidung, Holz-Kunststoff (Metal, Textiles, Clothing, Wood and Plastics Workers' Union): Wilhelm-Leuschner-Str. 79, 60329 Frankfurt a.M.; tel. (69) 66930; fax (69) 66932843; e-mail presse.igm@igmetall.de; internet www.igmetall.de; Chair. JÜRGEN PETERS; 2,332,720m. mems (Dec. 2006).

Transnet (Transport Workers): Chausseestr. 84, 10115 Berlin; tel. (30) 42439075; fax (30) 42439071; e-mail presse@transnet.org; internet www.transnet.org; Pres. NORBERT HANSEN; 248,983 mems (Dec. 2006).

Ver.di—Vereinte Dienstleistungsgewerkschaft (United Services Union): Paula-Thiede-Ufer 10, 10179 Berlin; tel. (30) 69560; fax (30) 69563141; e-mail info@verdi.de; internet www.verdi.de; f. 2001 by a merger of Gewerkschaft Handel, Banken und Versicherungen, Industriegewerkschaft Medien, Gewerkschaft Öffentliche Dienste, Transport und Verkehr, Deutsche Postgewerkschaft and Deutsche Angestellten-Gewerkschaft; Chair. FRANK BSIRSKE; 2,274,731m. mems (Dec. 2006).

DBB—Beamtenbund und Tarifunion (Civil Servants' Federation and Tariff Union): Friedrichstr. 169–170, 10117 Berlin; tel. (30) 408140; fax (30) 40814999; e-mail post@dbb.de; internet www.dbb.de; f. 1918; Pres. PETER HEESEM; 1.3m. mems (2007).

Forty member unions, of which the following is one of the largest:

Verkehrsgewerkschaft GDBA: Westendstr. 52, 60325 Frankfurt a.M.; tel. (69) 714001-0; fax (69) 71400141; e-mail verkehrsgewerkschaft@gdba.de; internet www.gdba.de; represents employees in the transportation, service and telecommunications sectors; Pres. KLAUS-DIETER HOMMEL.

GDL—Gewerkschaft Deutscher Lokomotivführer (Train Drivers' Union): Baumweg 45, 60316 Frankfurt a.M.; tel. (69) 4057090; fax (69) 40579040; e-mail info@gdl.de; internet www.gdl.de; f. 1867; Pres. MANFRED SCHELL.

Transport

RAILWAYS

At 31 December 2004 the length of state-owned track in Germany was 34,700 km, of which 19,300 km were electrified. There were a further 5,900 km of privately owned track, of which 2,000 km were electrified. In June 2001 new inter-city express rail links were opened on the Berlin–Hamburg, München–Zürich and Nürnberg–Dresden routes.

Regulatory Bodies

Eisenbahn-Bundesamt (EBA) (Federal Railway Authority): Vorgebirgsstr. 49, 53119 Bonn; tel. (228) 98260; fax (228) 9826119; e-mail poststelle@eba.bund.de; internet www.eisenbahn-bundesamt.de; supervisory and authorizing body; ensures safety of railway passengers; supervises construction; inspects and approves vehicles and monitors safe condition of railway operational network and railway operations; also supervises non-federal railways for 13 Länder; Pres. ARMIN KEPPEL.

Bundeseisenbahnvermögen (BEV) (Federal Railroad Assets): Kurt-Georg-Kiesinger-Allee 2, 53175 Bonn; tel. (228) 30770; fax

GERMANY

(228) 3077160; e-mail bonn@bev.bund.de; internet www.bev.bund.de; Pres. ARMIN KEPPEL.

Federal Railway

Deutsche Bahn AG (German Railways): Potsdamer Pl. 2, 10785 Berlin; tel. (30) 29761131; fax (30) 29761919; e-mail medienbetreuung@bku.db.de; internet www.db.de; f. 1994 by merger of Deutsche Bundesbahn and Deutsche Reichsbahn; state-owned; sale of 25% stake due 2008; CEO and Chair., Management Bd HARTMUT MEHDORN; Chair., Supervisory Bd Dr WERNER MÜLLER.

Metropolitan Railways

Berliner Verkehrsbetriebe (BVG) (Berlin Transport Authority): Postfach 303131, 10773 Berlin; Anstalt des öffentlichen Rechts, 10783 Berlin; Potsdamer Str. 188, 10729 Berlin; tel. (30) 2560; fax (30) 25649256; e-mail info@bvg.de; internet www.bvg.de; f. 1929; operates 144.9 km of underground railway; also runs tram and bus services; Chair., Management Bd ANDREAS STURMOWSKI.

Hamburger Hochbahn AG: Steinstr. 20, 20095 Hamburg; tel. (40) 32880; fax (40) 326406; e-mail info@hochbahn.de; internet www.hochbahn.de; f. 1911; operates 100.7 km of underground railway on 3 lines; fourth line under construction, scheduled for completion in 2011; also operates 120 bus routes; Chair., Management Bd GÜNTER ELSTE; Chair., Supervisory Bd Dr MICHAEL FREYTAG.

Münchner Verkehrsgesellschaft mbH (MVG): Emmy-Noether-Str. 2, 80287 München; tel. (89) 21910; fax (89) 21912405; e-mail info@swm.de; internet www.mvg-mobil.de; subsidiary of Stadtwerke München GmbH; operates underground railway (6 lines totalling 91 km), tramway (10 lines totalling 71 km), 67 bus lines (452 km); Chair., Management Bd HERBERT KÖNIG.

VAG Verkehrs-Aktiengesellschaft Nürnberg: 90338 Nürnberg; Südliche Fürther Str. 5, 90429 Nürnberg; tel. (911) 2830; fax (911) 2834800; e-mail vag@vag.de; internet www.vag.de; wholly owned subsidiary of Städtische Werke Nürnberg GmbH; operates underground railway (2 lines totalling 31 km), tramway (6 lines totalling 43 km) and bus services (80 routes); Chair., Management Bd HERBERT DOMBROWSKY; Chair., Supervisory Bd JÜRGEN FISCHER.

Association

Verband Deutscher Verkehrsunternehmen (VDV) (Association of German Transport Undertakings): Kamekestr. 37–39, 50672 Köln; tel. (221) 579790; fax (221) 514272; e-mail info@vdv.de; internet www.vdv.de; f. 1895; public transport, freight transport by rail; publishes *Der Nahverkehr* (10 a year), *Bus + Bahn* (monthly) and *Güterbahnen* (quarterly); Pres. GÜNTER ELSTE; Exec. Dir Prof. Dr ADOLF MÜLLER-HELLMANN.

ROADS

At 1 January 2005 there were 11,515 km of motorway, 41,321 km of other main roads and 177,899 km of secondary roads. A new 200-km motorway connecting Lübeck, via Rostock, to Stettin (Szczecin, in Poland) was completed in 2005, at a cost of €2,300m.

INLAND WATERWAYS

There are around 7,500 km of navigable inland waterways, including the Main–Danube Canal, linking the North Sea and the Black Sea, which was opened in 1992. Inland shipping accounts for about 20% of total freight traffic.

Associations

Bundesverband der Deutschen Binnenschiffahrt eV (BDB): Dammstr. 15–17, 47119 Duisburg; tel. (203) 8000650; fax (203) 8000621; e-mail infobdb@binnenschiff.de; internet www.binnenschiff.de; f. 1978; central Inland Waterway Association to further the interests of operating firms; Pres. Dr GÜNTHER JAEGERS; Man. Dirs JENS SCHWANEN, JÖRG RUSCHE.

Bundesverband Öffentlicher Binnenhäfen eV: Str. des 17. Juni 114, 10623 Berlin; tel. (30) 39802870; fax (30) 39802880; e-mail info-boeb@binnenhafen.de; internet www.binnenhafen.de; Chair. ERICH STAAKE.

Bundesverband der Selbstständigen Abteilung Binnenschiffahrt eV (BDS): August-Bier-Str. 18, 53129 Bonn; tel. (228) 746337; fax (228) 746569; e-mail infobds@binnenschiff.de; Man. Dir ANDREA BECKSCHÄFER.

Deutsche Binnenreederei Binnenschiffahrt Spedition Logistik GmbH: Revaler Str. 100, 10243 Berlin; tel. (30) 293760; fax (30) 29376201; e-mail dbr@binnenreederei.de; internet www.binnenreederei.de; f. 1949; Dir-Gen. HANS-WILHELM DÜNNER.

Hafenschiffahrtsverband Hamburg eV: Mattentwiete 2, 20457 Hamburg; tel. (40) 37890090; fax (40) 37890970; e-mail info@uvhh.de; internet www.uvhh.de.

Verein für europäische Binnenschiffahrt und Wasserstrassen eV (VBW): Dammstr. 15–17, 47119 Duisburg; tel. (203) 8000627; fax (203) 8000628; e-mail info@vbw-ev.de; internet www.vbw-ev.de; f. 1877; represents all brs of the inland waterways; Pres. Dr PHILIPPE GRULOIS.

SHIPPING

The principal ports for freight are Bremerhaven, Hamburg, Rostock-Überseehafen and Wilhelmshaven. Some important shipping companies are:

Argo Reederei Richard Adler & Söhne: Postfach 107529, 28075 Bremen; Am Wall 187–189, 28195 Bremen; tel. (421) 363070; fax (421) 321575; e-mail argo@argo-adler.de; internet www.argo-adler.de; f. 1896; shipowners; Propr MAX ADLER.

Aug. Bolten, Wm. Miller's Nachfolger GmbH & Co KG: Mattentwiete 8, 20457 Hamburg; tel. (40) 36010; fax (40) 3601423; e-mail info@aug-bolten.de; internet www.aug-bolten.de; ship-owner, manager and broker, port agent; Man. Dirs GERHARD BINDER, MICHAEL SAY.

Bugsier- Reederei- und Bergungs-Gesellschaft mbH & Co: Postfach 112273, 20422 Hamburg; Johannisbollwerk 10, 20459 Hamburg; tel. (40) 311110; fax (40) 313693; e-mail info@bugsier.de; internet www.bugsier.de; salvage, towage, tugs, ocean-going heavy lift cranes, submersible pontoons, harbour tugs; Man. Dirs B. J. SCHUCHMANN, J. W. SCHUCHMANN, A. HUETTMANN.

Christian F. Ahrenkiel GmbH & Co KG: Postfach 100220, 20001 Hamburg; Burchardstr. 8, 20095 Hamburg; tel. (40) 248380; fax (40) 24838375; e-mail info@ahrenkiel.net; internet www.ahrenkiel.net; f. 1950; shipowners, operators and managers.

DAL Deutsche Afrika-Linien GmbH & Co KG: Palmaille 45, 22767 Hamburg; tel. (40) 380160; fax (40) 38016663; Europe and South Africa; Man. Dirs Dr E. VON RANTZAU, H. VON RANTZAU.

Deutsche Seereederei GmbH: Silo4plus5, Business-Center am Stadthafen, Am Strande 3E, 18055 Rostock; tel. (381) 4584043; fax (381) 4584001; e-mail info@deutsche-seereederei.de; internet www.deutsche-seereederei.de; shipping, tourism, real estate, industry and finance.

Döhle, Peter, Schiffahrts–KG: Postfach 500440, 22704 Hamburg; Palmaille 33, 22767 Hamburg; tel. (40) 381080; fax (40) 38108255; internet www.doehle.de; shipbrokers, chartering agent, shipowners; Man. Dir JOCHEN DÖHLE.

Ernst Russ GmbH: Alsterufer 10, 20354 Hamburg; tel. (40) 414070; fax (40) 41407111; f. 1893; world-wide.

F. Laeisz Schiffahrtsgesellschaft mbH & Co KG: Postfach 111111, 20411 Hamburg; Trostbrücke 1, 20457 Hamburg; tel. (40) 368080; fax (40) 364876; e-mail info@laeisz.de; internet www.laeisz.de; f. 1983; Dirs NIKOLAUS W. SCHÜES, NIKOLAUS H. SCHÜES, VOLKER REDERSBORG.

Hamburg Südamerikanische Dampfschiffahrts-Gesellschaft KG: Willy-Brandt-Str. 59–61, 20457 Hamburg; tel. (40) 37050; fax (40) 37052400; e-mail central@ham.hamburgsud.com; internet www.hamburgsud.com; f. 1871; world-wide services.

Hapag-Lloyd AG: Ballindamm 25, 20095 Hamburg; tel. (40) 30010; fax (40) 336432; e-mail info@hapag-lloyd.de; internet www.hapag-lloyd.com; f. 1970; North, Central and South America, Middle East, Asia, Australasia; Chair. MICHAEL BEHRENDT.

John T. Essberger GmbH & Co KG: Postfach 500429, Palmaille 45, 22767 Hamburg; tel. (40) 380160; fax (40) 38016579; f. 1924; Man. Dirs Dr E. VON RANTZAU, H. VON RANTZAU.

KG Fisser & v. Doornum GmbH & Co: Postfach 130365, Feldbrunnenstr. 43, 20148 Hamburg; tel. (40) 441860; fax (40) 4108050; e-mail management@fissership.com; internet www.fissership.com; f. 1879; tramp; Man. Dirs CHRISTIAN FISSER, Dr MICHAEL FISSER.

Oldenburg-Portugiesische Dampfschiffs-Rhederei GmbH & Co KG: Postfach 110869, 20408 Hamburg; Kajen 10, 20459 Hamburg; tel. (40) 361580; fax (40) 364131; e-mail info@opdr.de; internet www.opdr.de; f. 1882; Gibraltar, Spain, Portugal, Madeira, North Africa, Canary Islands; Man. Dirs G. KEMPF, J. BERGMANN.

Oldendorff Carriers GmbH & Co KG: Willy-Brandt-Allee 6, 235544 Lübeck; tel. (451) 15000; fax (451) 73522; internet www.oldendorff.com; formerly Egon Oldendorff; Chair. HENNING OLDENDORFF; CEO PETER TWISS.

Rhein-, Maas und See-Schiffahrtskontor GmbH: Krausstr. 1A, 47119 Duisburg; tel. (203) 8040; fax (203) 804330; e-mail rms-team@rheinmaas.de; internet www.rheinmaas.de; f. 1948.

Sloman Neptun Schiffahrts-AG: Postfach 101469, 28014 Bremen; Langenstr. 44, 28195 Bremen; tel. (421) 17630; fax (421) 1763321; e-mail info@sloman-neptun.com; internet www.sloman-neptun.com; f. 1873; liner services from Northern Europe and Mediterranean to North Africa; gas carriers; agencies; Mans SVEN-MICHAEL EDYE, DIRK LOHMANN.

GERMANY

Walther Möller & Co: Gr. Elbstr. 14, 22767 Hamburg; tel. (40) 3803910; fax (40) 38039199; e-mail chartering@wmco.de; internet www.wmco.de.

Shipping Organizations

Verband Deutscher Reeder eV (German Shipowners' Association): Postfach 305580, 20317 Hamburg; Esplanade 6, 20354 Hamburg; tel. (40) 350970; fax (40) 35097211; e-mail vdr@reederverband.de; internet www.reederverband.de; Pres. FRANK LEONHARDT; Man. Dirs Dr HANS-HEINRICH NOELL, UTA ORDEMANN.

Zentralverband der Deutschen Seehafenbetriebe eV (Federal Association of German Seaport Operators): Am Sandtorkai 2, 20457 Hamburg; tel. (40) 366203; fax (40) 366377; e-mail info@zds-seehaefen.de; internet www.zds-seehaefen.de; f. 1934; Chair. DETTHOLD ADEN; 196 mems.

CIVIL AVIATION

There are two international airports in the Berlin region (a third, Tempelhof airport, was due to close in October 2008) and further international airports at Dresden, Düsseldorf, Frankfurt, Hamburg, Hannover, Köln-Bonn, Leipzig, München and Stuttgart. Construction of a major new international airport at Schönefeld, south-east of Berlin, commenced in 2006. The Berlin-Brandenburg International Airport was scheduled to be operational by November 2011.

Air Berlin GmbH & Co Luftverkehrs KG: Saatwinkler Damm 42-43, 13627 Berlin; tel. (1805) 737800; fax (30) 41021003; e-mail serviceteam@airberlin.com; internet www.airberlin.com; f. 1979; offers flights to 97 destinations in Germany and other European countries; CEO JOACHIM HUNOLD.

BFR Berliner Flug Ring GmbH: Rheinstr. 16, 12159 Berlin; tel. (30) 254020; fax (30) 25402263; e-mail info@germaniaairline.de; internet www.germania-flug.de; f. 1978; operates as Germania; charter and scheduled flights; Man. HEINZ RUMMLER.

Condor Flugdienst GmbH: Am Grünen Weg 3, 65440 Kelsterbach; tel. (6107) 9390; fax (6107) 939440; internet www.condor.com; f. 1955; subsidiary of Thomas Cook AG; low-cost airline; Chair., Management Bd RALF TECKENTRUP; Chair., Supervisory Bd HEINER WILKENS.

Deutsche Lufthansa AG: Flughafen-Bereich West, 60546 Frankfurt a.M.; tel. (69) 6960; fax (69) 69633022; internet konzern.lufthansa.com; f. 1953; extensive world-wide network; Chair., Supervisory Bd Dr JÜRGEN WEBER; Chair., Exec. Bd WOLFGANG MAYRHUBER.

Germanwings GmbH: Waldstr. 224, 51147 Köln; tel. (900) 1919100; fax (220) 31027-300; e-mail kontakt@germanwings.com; internet www.germanwings.com; f. 2002; low-cost airline, offers flights to 60 destinations within Europe; owned by Eurowings Luftverkehrs AG; Mans THOMAS WINKELMANN, Dr JOACHIM KLEIN.

Hapag-Lloyd Flug-GmbH: Postfach 420240, Flughafenstr. 10, 30855 Langenhagen; tel. (511) 97270; fax (511) 9727739; e-mail info@hlag.de; internet www.hapag-lloyd.de; f. 1972; charter and scheduled passenger services; Exec. Chair. MICHAEL BEHRENDT.

LTU Lufttransport-Unternehmen GmbH: Flughafen, Halle 8, 40474 Düsseldorf; tel. (211) 9418888; fax (211) 9418881; e-mail internet@ltu.de; internet www.ltu.de; f. 1955; charter and scheduled services; owned by Air Berlin GmbH & Co. Luftverkehrs KG; CEO HELMUT WEIXLER.

Lufthansa Cargo AG: Flughafen-Bereich West, 60546 Frankfurt a.M.; tel. (69) 6960; fax (69) 69691185; e-mail lhcargo@dlh.de; internet www.lufthansa-cargo.de; f. 1994; wholly owned subsidiary of Deutsche Lufthansa AG; freight-charter world-wide; Chair., Management Bd CARSTEN SPOHR; Chair., Supervisory Bd STEFAN H. LAUER.

Lufthansa CityLine GmbH: Flughafen Köln/Bonn, Heinrich-Steinmann-Str., 51147 Köln; tel. (2203) 5960; fax (2203) 596801; e-mail lh-cityline@dlh.de; internet www.lufthansacityline.com; scheduled services; subsidiary of Deutsche Lufthansa AG; Man. Dirs CHRISTIAN TILLMANS, Dr KLAUS FROESE.

Tourism

Germany's tourist attractions include spas, summer and winter resorts, mountains, medieval towns and castles, and above all a variety of fascinating cities. The North and Baltic Sea coasts, the Rhine Valley, the Black Forest, the mountains of Thuringia, the Erzgebirge and Bavaria are the most popular areas. The total number of foreign visitors was 23.6m. in 2006; receipts from tourism totalled €26,091m. in that year.

Deutsche Zentrale für Tourismus eV (DZT) (German National Tourist Board): Beethovenstr. 69, 60325 Frankfurt a.M.; tel. (69) 974640; fax (69) 751903; e-mail info@d-z-t.com; internet www.germany-tourism.de; f. 1948; CEO PETRA HEDORFER.

GHANA

Introductory Survey

Location, Climate, Language, Religion, Flag, Capital

The Republic of Ghana lies on the west coast of Africa, with Côte d'Ivoire to the west and Togo to the east. It is bordered by Burkina Faso to the north. The climate is tropical, with temperatures generally between 21°C and 32°C (70°–90°F) and average annual rainfall of 2,000 mm (80 ins) on the coast, decreasing inland. English is the official language, but there are 10 major national languages (each with more than 250,000 speakers), the most widely spoken being Akan, Ewe, Mole-Dagomba and Ga. Many of the inhabitants follow traditional beliefs and customs. Christians comprise an estimated 69% of the population. The national flag (proportions 2 by 3) has three equal horizontal stripes, of red, yellow and green, with a five-pointed black star in the centre of the yellow stripe. The capital is Accra.

Recent History

Ghana was formed as the result of a UN-supervised plebiscite in May 1956, when the British-administered section of Togoland, a UN Trust Territory, voted to join the Gold Coast, a British colony, in an independent state. Ghana was duly granted independence, within the Commonwealth, on 6 March 1957 and Dr Kwame Nkrumah, the Prime Minister of the former Gold Coast since 1952, became Prime Minister of the new state. Ghana became a republic on 1 July 1960, with Nkrumah as President. In 1964 the Convention People's Party, led by Nkrumah, was declared the sole authorized party.

In February 1966 Nkrumah was deposed in a military coup, the leaders of which established a governing National Liberation Council, led by Gen. Joseph Ankrah. In April 1969 Ankrah was replaced by Brig. (later Lt-Gen.) Akwasi Afrifa, and a new Constitution was introduced. Power was returned in October to an elected civilian Government, led by Dr Kofi Busia. However, in reaction to increasing economic and political difficulties, the army again seized power in January 1972, under the leadership of Lt-Col (later Gen.) Ignatius Acheampong. In July 1978 Acheampong was deposed by his deputy, Lt-Gen. Frederick Akuffo, who assumed power in a bloodless coup. Tensions within the army became evident in May 1979, when junior military officers staged an unsuccessful coup attempt. The alleged leader of the conspirators, Flight-Lt Jerry Rawlings, was imprisoned, but was subsequently released by other officers. On 4 June he and his associates successfully seized power, amid popular acclaim, established the Armed Forces Revolutionary Council, and introduced measures to eradicate corruption. Acheampong and Akuffo were among nine senior officers who were convicted on charges of corruption and executed.

At elections held in June 1979 the People's National Party, led by Dr Hilla Limann, emerged with the largest number of parliamentary seats and formed a coalition Government with support from the smaller United National Convention. Civilian rule was restored in September when Limann took office as President. However, dissatisfaction with measures taken by the Government to improve the economy provoked widespread civil unrest.

On 31 December 1981 Rawlings seized power for a second time, and established a governing Provisional National Defence Council (PNDC), with himself as Chairman. The PNDC's policies initially received strong support, but discontent with the regime and with the apparent ineffectiveness of its economic policies was reflected by a series of coup attempts. In July 1987 the PNDC announced that elections for district assemblies, scheduled for mid-1987, were to be postponed until late 1988, and that the ban on political parties was to remain. Elections for the district assemblies were held between December 1988 and February 1989. Although one-third of the 7,278 members of the district assemblies were appointed by the PNDC, the establishment of the assemblies was envisaged as the first stage in the development of a new political system of national democratic administration.

In July 1990, in response to pressure from Western aid donors to introduce further democratic reforms, the PNDC announced that a National Commission for Democracy (NCD) would organize a series of regional debates to consider Ghana's political and economic future. In August the newly formed Movement for Freedom and Justice (MFJ) criticized the NCD, claiming that it was too closely associated with the PNDC, and issued a series of demands, including the abolition of legislation prohibiting political associations and the release of all political prisoners. In September the MFJ accused the PNDC of intimidation, after its inaugural meeting was suppressed by security forces. In October the PNDC pledged to accept the conclusions of any national consensus on future democracy in the country.

In December 1990 Rawlings announced proposals for the introduction of a constitution by the end of 1991; the PNDC was to consider recommendations presented by the NCD, and subsequently to convene a consultative body to determine constitutional reform. However, the MFJ, the Christian Council of Ghana and the Ghana Bar Association objected to the proposals, on the grounds that no definite schedule for political reform had been presented, and that no criteria had been established for the composition of the consultative body.

In March 1991 the NCD presented a report on the democratic process, which recommended the election of an executive President for a fixed term, the establishment of a legislature and the creation of the post of Prime Minister. In May the PNDC endorsed the restoration of a multi-party system and approved the NCD's recommendations, although it was emphasized that the formation of political associations remained prohibited. Later in May the Government announced the establishment of a 260-member Consultative Assembly, which was to present a draft constitution to the PNDC by the end of 1991. The Government also appointed a nine-member committee of constitutional experts, who, in August, submitted a series of recommendations for constitutional reform, which included the establishment of a parliament and a council of state. It was proposed that the President, who would also be Commander-in-Chief of the Armed Forces, would be elected by universal suffrage for a four-year term of office, while the leader of the party that commanded a majority in the legislature would be appointed as Prime Minister. However, the subsequent review of the draft Constitution by the Consultative Assembly was impeded by opposition demands for a boycott, on the grounds that the number of government representatives in the Assembly was too high. Later in August Rawlings announced that presidential and legislative elections were to take place in late 1992.

In December 1991 the Government established an Interim National Electoral Commission (INEC), which was to be responsible for the demarcation of electoral regions and the supervision of elections and referendums. In January 1992 the Government extended the allocated period for the review of the draft Constitution to the end of March. In March Rawlings announced a programme for transition to a multi-party system, which was to be completed on 7 January 1993.

At the end of March 1992 the Consultative Assembly approved the majority of the constitutional recommendations that had been submitted to the PNDC. However, the proposed creation of the post of Prime Minister was rejected by the Assembly; executive power was to be vested in the President, who would appoint a Vice-President. Opposition groups subsequently objected to a provision in the draft Constitution that members of the Government be exempt from prosecution for human rights violations allegedly committed during the PNDC's rule. At a national referendum on 28 April, however, the draft Constitution was approved by 92% of votes cast, with 43.7% of the electorate voting.

On 18 May 1992 the Government introduced legislation permitting the formation of political associations; political parties were henceforth required to apply to the INEC for legal recognition, although emergent parties were not permitted to use names or slogans associated with 21 former political organizations that remained proscribed. Later in May the High Court rejected an application for an injunction against the legislation by opposition leaders, who claimed that it was biased in favour of the PNDC.

In June 1992 a number of political associations were established, many of which were identified with supporters of former

President Nkrumah; six opposition movements, including the People's National Convention (PNC), led by ex-President Limann, were subsequently granted legal recognition. In the same month a coalition of pro-Government organizations, the National Democratic Congress (NDC), was formed to contest the forthcoming elections on behalf of the PNDC. However, an existing alliance of Rawlings' supporters, the Eagle Club, refused to join the NDC, and created its own political organization, the Eagle Party (later known as the EGLE—Every Ghanaian Living Everywhere—Party). In July Rawlings rejected the EGLE Party's nomination as its candidate for the presidential election. In August the Government promulgated a new electoral code, which included a provision that in the event that no presidential candidate received more than 50% of votes cast the two candidates with the highest number of votes would contest a second round within 21 days. In September Rawlings officially retired from the air force (although he retained the post of Commander-in-Chief of the Armed Forces in his capacity as Head of State), in accordance with the new Constitution, and accepted a nomination to contest the presidential election as a candidate of the NDC. The NDC, the EGLE Party and the National Convention Party (NCP) subsequently formed a pro-Government electoral coalition, known as the Progressive Alliance.

Rawlings was elected President on 3 November 1992, securing 58.3% of the votes cast. The four opposition parties that had presented candidates, the PNC, the New Patriotic Party (NPP), the National Independence Party (NIP) and the People's Heritage Party (PHP), claimed that there had been widespread electoral malpractice, although international observers maintained that, despite isolated irregularities, the election had been conducted fairly. Later in November these four parties withdrew from the forthcoming legislative elections (scheduled for 8 December), in protest at the Government's refusal to comply with their demands for the compilation of a new electoral register and the investigation of alleged misconduct during the presidential election. As a result, the legislative elections were postponed until 22 December, and subsequently by a further week, and the nomination of new candidates permitted. In December the opposition claimed that many of its members had left Ghana, as a result of widespread intimidation by the Government. In the legislative elections, which took place on 29 December, the NDC secured 189 of the 200 seats in the Parliament, while the NCP obtained eight seats, the EGLE Party one seat and independent candidates the remaining two. According to official figures, however, only 29% of the electorate voted in the elections.

On 7 January 1993 Rawlings was sworn in as President of what was designated the Fourth Republic, the PNDC was dissolved and the new Parliament was inaugurated. Later that month Rawlings began to submit nominations for members of the Council of Ministers and the Council of State for approval by the Parliament. However, he announced that members of the existing Government were to remain in office in an interim capacity, pending the appointment of a Council of Ministers and other officials. In May a 17-member Council of Ministers, which included several ministers who had served in the former PNDC administration, was inaugurated. In December the PHP, the NIP and a faction of the PNC, all of which comprised supporters of ex-President Nkrumah, merged to form a new organization, known as the People's Convention Party (PCP).

In May 1995 the National Executive Committee of the NCP decided to withdraw the party from the government coalition, claiming that the NDC had dominated the alliance. However, the Vice President, Kow Nkesen Arkaah, a member of the NCP, announced that he was to retain that office, as his mandate remained valid.

In 1996 April presidential and parliamentary elections were scheduled for December and a consolidation of the opposition parties took place prior to the deadline for the nomination of candidates in September. In May the Popular Party for Democracy and Development merged with the PCP and declared its support for unity with the NPP. In July the NCP announced that it had removed Arkaah as its leader, following his selection as presidential candidate by the PCP. In August the NPP and the PCP formed an electoral coalition, the Great Alliance; it was subsequently announced that John Kufuor, of the NPP, was to be the Great Alliance's presidential candidate, with Arkaah as the candidate for the vice-presidency. The NCP stated that it would support the NDC in the forthcoming elections, while the PNC announced its intention to contest the elections alone, with Edward Mahama as its presidential candidate. In September the NDC nominated Rawlings as its presidential candidate. By 18 September, the official deadline for the nomination of candidates, only the Great Alliance, the Progressive Alliance (the NDC, the EGLE party and the Democratic People's Party—DPP) and the PNC had succeeded in having their nomination papers accepted. In October the NCP, which, according to the Electoral Commission (EC), had not presented the appropriate papers, declared its intention to take legal action against the Commission. In November a network of independent Domestic Election Observers was created to oversee the elections.

In the presidential election, which took place on 7 December 1996, Rawlings was re-elected, with 57.2% of the votes cast, while Kufuor secured 39.8%. In the parliamentary elections the NDC's representation was reduced to 133 seats, while the NPP won 60 seats, the PCP five and the PNC one seat. Voting was postponed in one constituency, owing to a legal dispute concerning the eligibility of candidates. (The seat was subsequently won by the NPP in a by-election in June 1997.) Despite opposition claims of malpractice, international observers declared that the elections had been conducted fairly, and an electoral turn-out of 76.8% was reported. At the end of December the PCP announced that the Great Alliance had broken down. On 7 January 1997 Rawlings was sworn in as President.

The appointment of a new Council of Ministers led to a protracted dispute between the NDC and the opposition, prompting a series of parliamentary boycotts by the NPP, which insisted that all ministerial appointees be approved by the parliamentary appointments committee prior to assuming their duties. Owing to the NDC's parliamentary majority, however, procedures were approved to allow those ministers who had been retained from the previous Government to avoid the vetting process. The majority of ministerial appointments had been made by April, although a number of posts were not filled until June. In early June the Supreme Court ruled that all presidential nominees for ministerial positions had to be approved by Parliament, even if they had served in the previous Government and the Government subsequently announced that it was prepared to submit all ministers to vetting procedures.

In August 1998 the NCP and the PCP merged to form the Convention Party. An earlier attempt by the party to register as the Convention People's Party (CPP) had been rejected on the grounds that the use of the name of a proscribed party was unconstitutional. (This decision was reversed in 2000, however, when the Convention Party was permitted to adopt the name and logo of Nkrumah's former party.) In October 1998 the NPP nominated Kufuor to stand as its presidential candidate, in elections due to be held in 2000. At an NDC congress in December 1998 the position of 'Life Chairman' of the party was created for Rawlings, who confirmed that he would comply with the terms of the Constitution and not stand for a third term as President, and subsequently announced that the incumbent Vice-President, Prof. John Evans Atta Mills, was to contest the election on behalf of the NDC. In June 1999, owing to dissatisfaction within the NDC at the changes carried out at the party congress and at Rawlings' pronouncement regarding his successor, a group of party members broke away to form a new political organization, the National Reform Party (NRP). At the end of April Mills had been elected unopposed as the NDC presidential candidate. Seven parties had submitted presidential candidates by the closure of nominations in September. In addition to Mills and Kufuor, the candidates included Mahama, for the PNC, and George Hagan, for the CPP. The EGLE Party and the DPP announced their support for Mills.

An estimated 62% of the electorate voted in the elections, which took place on 7 December 2000 (although, as a result of the inaccurate voters' register, it was claimed that the real rate of participation could have been as high as 80%). Observers from the Organization of African Unity (now the African Union, see p. 164) declared the elections to have been held in an orderly and fair manner. In the elections to the 200-seat Parliament the NPP won 100 seats, while the NDC obtained 92 seats, the PNC three, the CPP one, and independent candidates four. The NPP thus became the largest parliamentary party for the first time, gaining an unprecedented degree of support in rural areas. In the presidential election Kufuor won 48.2% of the valid votes cast, and Mills 44.5%, thus necessitating a second round, which proceeded on 28 December; Kufuor was elected to the presidency, with 56.9% of the valid votes cast.

On 7 January 2001 Kufuor was inaugurated as President and subsequently appointed a new Government, which notably included one member from each of the CPP, the NRP and the

PNC. The stated priority of the new Government was the creation of wealth, which was to be encouraged by greater promotion of the private sector and through the eradication of corruption within government and in the parastatal sector. To this effect, Vice-President Alhaji Aliu Mahama announced that a code of conduct for ministers and government appointees would be implemented. In February it was announced that members of the military were to be forbidden from celebrating the anniversaries of the coups staged by Rawlings in 1979 and 1981, and that their participation in quasi-political organizations was also to be prohibited. In addition, Kufuor ordered the suspension of the heads of six public sector financial institutions, to facilitate an investigation into allegations of embezzlement.

Also in February 2001 Kufuor announced that a National Reconciliation Commission (NRC) was to be established to investigate allegations of human rights abuses and other violations committed by state representatives. According to proposed legislation, the NRC, which would operate for a period of one year (with a provision permitting its operation to be extended by a further six months), would be charged with investigating three periods of military rule and unconstitutional government since independence: 24 February 1966–21 August 1969, 13 January 1972–23 September 1979 and 31 December 1981–6 January 1983, although the NRC would also be permitted to investigate complaints relating to events outside these periods. Despite protests by the NDC, which had sought to ensure that the mandate of the proposed NRC would incorporate the entire period from independence in 1957 until January 1993, in January 2002 Kufuor endorsed the creation of the Commission. The NRC was officially launched in May, although it did not commence work until September. The NRC commenced public hearings in January 2003, by which time some 2,800 complaints had been received, mostly relating to events that took place under military regimes.

In December 2001 violent clashes between members of the Mamprusi and Kusasi ethnic groups in Bawku reportedly resulted in some 50 deaths. A curfew was imposed in the town, and a delegation of ministers and military officials visited the region and announced the establishment of a commission of inquiry into the dispute. In March 2002 the Minister of the Interior and the Minister for the Northern Region both resigned, following the deaths of some 40 people during inter-ethnic clashes in the north of Ghana, which had been prompted by the abduction and murder of Ya-na Yakuba Andani, king of the Dagomba, in Yendi. A commission of inquiry was established, headed by traditional leaders, and a state of emergency was declared. The state of emergency ended in the majority of districts in October 2003, but remained in place in Tamale municipality and Yendi district until August 2004. Unrest, however, continued during 2005.

Meanwhile, in April 2002 the election of Dr Obed Asamoah as the new Chairman of the NDC created divisions within the party between supporters of Asamoah and Rawlings. During August Rawlings accused the Kufuor Government of incompetence, urging 'positive defiance' from the Ghanaian people; he was subsequently summoned for questioning by the Bureau of National Investigations. In September a number of accusations of financial impropriety were made against Rawlings and his former associates. In November, following the arrest of three NDC deputies on charges of fraud and the reckless loss of state revenues, the NDC boycotted the Parliament in protest; this followed an earlier boycott over a controversial US $1,000m. development loan.

In February 2004 Rawlings appeared briefly before the NRC to answer questions about the murders of three high court judges and a retired military officer in 1982 and about extrajudicial military killings in 1984. In July 2004 the NRC ended its hearings, prior to the submission of its report in October, which recommended that victims of state brutality receive compensation and that state institutions, including the security services, be reformed.

In October 2004 four presidential candidates submitted their nominations to the Chairman of the EC. As expected, Kufuor represented the NPP, while Mills was selected as the candidate for the NDC. Also contesting the election were George Aggudey of the CPP and Edward Mahama of the PNC for the Grand Coalition, which comprised the PNC and EGLE. (The Great Consolidated People's Party, led by Dan Lartey, had withdrawn from the coalition in late September over the election of the coalition's presidential candidate.)

The parliamentary and presidential elections were held as scheduled on 7 December 2004 and were conducted in a largely peaceful atmosphere. Kufuor was declared the winner of the presidential election on 9 December, after votes in 225 of the 230 constituencies had been counted. Final results, released by the EC on 1 January 2005, indicated that Kufuor had secured 52.4% of the valid votes cast, while Mills won 44.6%. Mahama and Aggudey took 1.9% and 1.0%, respectively. In the parliamentary election the NPP won 128 seats, with 55.6% of the vote, while the NDC won 94 seats, the PNC four and the CPP three. The remaining seat was taken by an independent candidate. Voter turn-out at the elections was recorded at 85.1%. International and independent internal observers praised the elections as being free, fair and peaceful.

The new Parliament was inaugurated on 7 January 2005; Ebenezer Begyina Seki Hughes was elected to the post of Speaker. On the same day Kufuor and Aliu Mahama were sworn in as President and Vice-President, respectively, following which Kufuor reorganized the Government. After being approved by the Parliament, 29 ministers were inaugurated on 1 February; the remaining nine were inaugurated later that month. The most notable changes included the appointments of Kwadwo Baah-Wiredu as Minister of Finance and Economic Planning (Yaw Osafu-Maafo, his predecessor, became the Minister of Education and Sports), Nii Ayikoi Otoo as Minister of Justice and Attorney-General and Papa Owusu Ankomah as Minister of the Interior. In December Peter Mac Manu was elected Chairman of the NPP, while Dr Kwabena Adjei was elected Chairman of the NDC.

In January 2006 the African Peer Review Mechanism, a programme of voluntary assessment organized by the New Partnership for Africa's Development (see p. 169), published its report on Ghana. The report, while commending overall development, criticized endemic corruption and the ongoing civil unrest in the north of the country. In late April President Kufuor effected an extensive government reshuffle. Notably, Joseph Ghartey was appointed Attorney-General and Minister of Justice, while Albert Kan Dapaah assumed responsibility for the interior portfolio, and portfolios for aviation and national security were created. In October Kufuor alleged that former President Rawlings had been seeking foreign support in order to overthrow the Government. At a party congress in December Mills was elected once again to be the NDC's presidential candidate in the election scheduled to take place in 2008.

In May 2007 the EC convened a meeting to discuss a proposal that would allow Ghanaians living abroad to vote in national elections. The controversial proposed amendment to the Representation of the People Act resulted in public protests and the NDC boycotting Parliament; the opposition party also threatened to reject the results of the forthcoming legislative and presidential elections, scheduled for December 2008, should the law be promulgated. In July 2007 eight cabinet ministers tendered their resignation, having declared their intention to contest the presidential election. Among those to step down was Minister of Defence Dr Kwame Addo Kufuor; a governmental reorganization was subsequently effected in which Akwasi Osei-Adjai was named Minister of Foreign Affairs, Regional Integration and NEPAD; Dapaah was later appointed to the Ministry of Defence.

In December 2007 nominations for candidates to the presidency were announced; Nana Addo Dankwa Akufuo-Addo, who had held the foreign affairs portfolio until July, was to represent the NPP, while Mills was again selected as the candidate of the NDC and Mahama was to contest the election on behalf of the PNC. Dr Kwesi Ndoum of the CPP also presented his candidacy.

Ghana enjoys a reputation as a peace-keeper in the region, and in February 2008 was the seventh largest contributor to UN peace-keeping missions world-wide. The Kufuor administration has sought to increase Ghanaian involvement in conflict resolution within west and central Africa. In late 2005 Ghana was elected as a non-permanent member of the UN Security Council.

In 1986 relations between Ghana and Togo became strained due to subversive activity by Ghanaian dissidents based in Togo, and an attempted coup in Togo, which was allegedly initiated from Ghanaian territory. In October 1992 Ghana denied claims that it was implicated in subversive activity by Togolese dissidents based in Ghana and in March 1993 the Rawlings administration denied allegations, made by the Togolese Government, of Ghanaian complicity in an armed attack on the residence of Togo's President, Gen. Gnassingbé Eyadéma. In January 1994 relations with Togo deteriorated further, following an attempt to overthrow the Togolese Government, which the

Togolese authorities claimed had been staged by armed dissidents based in Ghana. The Ghanaian chargé d'affaires in Togo was arrested, and Togolese forces killed 12 Ghanaians and attacked a customs post and several villages near the border. Ghana, however, denied any involvement in the coup attempt, and threatened to retaliate against further acts of aggression. Later that year, however, relations improved, and in November full diplomatic links were formally restored. In December Togo's border with Ghana (which had been closed in January 1994) was reopened. Following the death of Eyadéma in early 2005 and the subsequent unrest in Togo precipitated by the assumption of power by Eyadéma's son, Faure Gnassingbé, some 15,000 Togolese refugees were reported to have registered in Ghana.

During the conflict in Liberia (q.v.), which commenced in December 1989, Ghana contributed troops to the Monitoring Group (ECOMOG) of the Economic Community of West African States (ECOWAS, see p. 232). As Chairman of the ECOWAS Conference of Heads of State and Government, Rawlings mediated negotiations between the warring Liberian factions in the mid-1990s, and by mid-1997 some 17,000 Liberian refugees had arrived in Ghana. In 2003 Ghana also hosted peace negotiations concerning Liberia, and from September contributed troops to the ECOWAS Mission in Liberia (ECOMIL). In October the Ghanaian troops were transferred to a longer-term UN stabilization force, the UN Mission in Liberia (UNMIL, see p. 83), which replaced ECOMIL, with a mandate to support the implementation of a comprehensive peace agreement in that country. In late 2005 there were some 40,000 Liberian refugees registered in Ghana, a number of whom were in the process of repatriation, and by the end of 2006 the number of Liberian refugees remaining in Ghana was 35,653.

In June 1997 Ghana, Côte d'Ivoire, Guinea and Nigeria formed the 'committee of four', which was established by ECOWAS to monitor the situation in Sierra Leone, following the staging of a military coup; troops were dispatched to participate in a peace-keeping force. It was reported in February 1998 that Ghana had opposed the use of force by the Nigerian contingent of this peace-keeping unit to overthrow the military government in Sierra Leone. Following the reinstatement of the democratically elected Government in March, ECOMOG units remained in the country and continued to launch attacks against rebel forces, which still retained control of a number of areas. In December 2005 the Ghanaian troops participating in the UN Mission in Sierra Leone (UNAMSIL) returned to Ghana on the termination of the peace-keeping mission.

In November 2001 some 400 Ghanaian troops were dispatched to participate in peace-keeping duties in the Democratic Republic of the Congo, under the auspices of the UN Mission in the Democratic Republic of the Congo (MONUC, see p. 85). By November 2007 some 461 Ghanaian troops were participating in MONUC.

After the outbreak of an armed rebellion in Côte d'Ivoire (q.v.) in September 2002, Ghana denied accusations by the Ivorian rebels that it had intervened in support of President Laurent Gbagbo. At the end of September an emergency ECOWAS summit on the conflict was convened in Accra. In late October Ghana pledged to provide troops to an ECOWAS military mission in Côte d'Ivoire (ECOMICI), and the first contingent of the 266 Ghanaian soldiers to be contributed was deployed in February 2003. Further ECOWAS summit meetings on Côte d'Ivoire took place in Accra in March and November 2003. Ghanaian troops in Côte d'Ivoire were to be transferred to a UN Operation in Côte d'Ivoire (UNOCI, see p. 87), which was deployed from April 2004. A conference held in Accra in August 2004 led to the signing of a peace accord between rival Ivorian factions, known as Accra III. In November 2007 there were 542 Ghanaian troops stationed in Côte d'Ivoire as part of UNOCI.

In May 2004 Ghana became a full member of the Community of Sahel-Saharan States (see p. 411).

Government

Under the terms of the Constitution, which was approved by national referendum on 28 April 1992, Ghana has a multi-party political system. Executive power is vested in the President, who is the Head of State and Commander-in-Chief of the Armed Forces. The President is elected by direct universal suffrage for a maximum of two four-year terms of office. Legislative power is vested in a 230-member unicameral Parliament, which is elected by direct universal suffrage for a four-year term. The President appoints a Vice-President, and nominates a Council of Ministers, subject to approval by the Parliament. The Constitution also provides for a 25-member Council of State, principally comprising regional representatives and presidential nominees, and a 20-member National Security Council, chaired by the Vice-President, which act as advisory bodies to the President.

Ghana has 10 regions, each headed by a Regional Minister, who is assisted by a regional co-ordinating council. The regions constitute 110 administrative districts, each with a District Assembly, which is headed by a District Chief Executive. Regional colleges, which comprise representatives selected by the District Assemblies and by regional Houses of Chiefs, elect a number of representatives to the Council of State.

Defence

As assessed at November 2007, Ghana had total armed forces of 13,500 (army 10,000, navy 2,000 and air force 1,500). At that time Ghanaian troops were deployed in nine overseas peace-keeping missions. In January 2004 a peace-keeping training centre, which was primarily to be used by ECOWAS, was established in Accra. The defence budget for 2007 was estimated at 980,000m. new cedis.

Economic Affairs

In 2006, according to estimates by the World Bank, Ghana's gross national income (GNI), measured at average 2004–06 prices, was US $11,778m., equivalent to $520 per head (or $2,640 on an international purchasing-power parity basis). During 1996–2006, it was estimated, the population increased at an average annual rate of 2.2%, while gross domestic product (GDP) per head increased, in real terms, by an average of 2.6% per year. Overall GDP increased at an average annual rate of 4.8% in 1996–2006; growth in 2006 was 6.2%.

Agriculture (including forestry and fishing) contributed 39.3% of GDP (at constant 1993 prices) in 2006. An estimated 55.7% of the economically active population were employed in the sector in mid-2005, according to FAO. The principal cash crop is cocoa beans, contributing 5.1% of GDP in 2006. Ghana is the world's second largest producer after Côte d'Ivoire, and the cocoa harvest amounted to a record 740,000 metric tons in 2005/06. However, poor weather resulted in a reduction of the 2006/07 crop to 615,000 tons. Coffee, bananas, cassava, oil palm, coconuts, limes, kola nuts and shea-nuts (karité nuts) are also produced. The development of the palm oil and cassava sectors was underway. Timber production is also important, with the forestry sector accounting for 3.8% of GDP in 2006, and cork and wood, and manufactures thereof, contributing 4.8% of total export earnings in 2004. Fishing satisfies more than three-quarters of domestic requirements, and contributed 4.4% of GDP in 2006. During 1996–2006, according to the World Bank, agricultural GDP increased at an average annual rate of 4.6%; growth in 2006 was 6.6%.

Industry (including mining, manufacturing, construction and power) contributed 27.8% of GDP (at constant 1993 prices) in 2006, and employed 12.8% of the working population in 1984. According to the World Bank, industrial GDP increased at an average annual rate of 5.0% in 1996–2006; growth in 2006 was 6.2%.

Mining contributed 5.4% of GDP (at constant 1993 prices) in 2006, and employed 0.5% of the working population in 1984. Gold and diamonds are the major minerals exported (in 2005 gold production was 66.9 metric tons), although Ghana also exploits large reserves of bauxite and manganese ore. The Government is attempting to increase exploitation of salt, bauxite and clay. According to the Bank of Ghana, the GDP of the mining sector increased by an average of 3.3% per year in 2000–06; growth in 2004 was 4.8%.

Manufacturing contributed 9.6% of GDP in 2006, and employed 10.9% of the working population in 1984. The most important sectors are food processing, textiles, vehicles, cement, paper, chemicals and petroleum. According to the Bank of Ghana, manufacturing GDP increased at an average annual rate of 4.4% in 2000–2006; the GDP of the sector increased by 3.7% in 2006.

According to figures published by the World Bank, some 87.4% of Ghana's production of electricity was from hydroelectric power in 2004, with the Akosombo and Kpong plants being the major sources, and 12.6% from petroleum (an increase from 8.5% in 2000). In mid-2004 it was announced that the World Bank was providing a loan of US $60m. to increase the production of the thermal power generator, Takoradi II. In November 2004 the World Bank agreed to finance the construction of the West African Gas Pipeline, which was to supply natural gas from Nigeria to Ghana, Benin and Togo; this was expected to come on stream in 2008. Imports of petroleum comprised 18.6% of the total value of merchandise imports in 2004. Electricity is exported to Benin and Togo.

The services sector contributed 32.9% of GDP in 2006, and engaged 26.1% of the working population in 1984. According to the World Bank, the GDP of the services sector increased at an average annual rate of 5.0% in 1996–2006; growth in 2005 was 5.9%.

In 2006 Ghana recorded a visible trade deficit of US $3,027.0m., and there was a deficit of $1,040.2m. on the current account of the balance of payments. In 2004 the principal source of imports was the People's Republic of China (9.0%); other major sources were the USA, Germany, Belgium, the United Kingdom, South Africa and the Netherlands. The latter was the principal market for exports (taking 25.4% of the total) in that year; other important purchasers were the United Kingdom, Belgium, France and South Africa. The principal exports in 2004 were cocoa beans (which accounted for 56.4% of total export earnings), gold and timber and timber products. The principal imports in 2004 were machinery and transport equipment, food and live animals, basic manufactures, chemical and related products and petroleum products.

Ghana's overall budget deficit for 2006 was 6,824.6m. new cedis. Ghana's external debt totalled US $6,739m. at the end of 2005, of which $5,734m. was long-term public debt. In that year the cost of debt-servicing was equivalent to 7.1% of exports of goods and services. In 1997–2006 the average annual rate of inflation was 18.4%. Consumer prices increased by 10.6% in 2006. In 1995 some 41,000 people were registered as unemployed in Ghana.

Ghana is a member of the Economic Community of West African States (ECOWAS, see p. 232), of the International Cocoa Organization (ICCO, see p. 408), and of the International Coffee Organization (ICO, see p. 408).

Although Ghana's economy has made steady progress since the transfer to civilian rule in 1992, it remains vulnerable to unfavourable weather conditions and to fluctuations in international commodity prices. In May 2003 the IMF approved a three-year arrangement under the Poverty Reduction and Growth Facility (PRGF), amounting to some US $258m., and in July 2004 the Minister of Finance and Economic Planning announced that Ghana had complied with the criteria set for the heavily indebted poor countries initiative; following a meeting of the Ghana's 'Paris Club' creditors, it was agreed to reduce the country's debt to those countries from $1,940,000m. to $300m. In mid-2005 a further $125m. was made available by the World Bank as part of the three-year poverty-reduction programme, while in June the Group of Eight industrialized nations (G-8) announced that Ghana's multilateral debts to the World Bank, the IMF and the African Development Bank (ADB) would be forgiven, with immediate effect. With the country experiencing relative macroeconomic stability since the early 2000s, and the cedi's role as a store of value having been restored, in mid-2007 Ghana redenominated its currency by removing four zeros from its value. The old cedi notes and coins were withdrawn from circulation in December. Meanwhile in 2006 the World Bank's annual *Doing Business* survey reported a greater improvement in Ghana's attractiveness as an investment destination than any other African country and the rate of corporation tax was reduced from 32.5% to 25.0% in order further to promote foreign direct investment. In March 2008 the ADB agreed to provide a loan to the value of $63.8m. to fund some 60% of the costs incurred by the Northern Rural Growth Programme, aimed at addressing the nation's poverty and boosting sustainable agricultural production. Crop harvests and livestock numbers had been greatly reduced by severe flooding in 2007, although strong economic performance was nevertheless recorded in that year, eliciting praise from the IMF; the Ghanaian economy experienced the highest growth figures, and the lowest inflation in nearly 30 years. GDP was estimated to have increased by 6.3% in 2007, with growth of 6.9% projected for 2008, while inflation was anticipated to continue to decline, from 9.4% in 2007 to 8.8% in 2008.

Education

Education is officially compulsory for eight years between the ages of six and 14. Primary education begins at the age of six and lasts for six years. Secondary education, beginning at the age of 12, lasts for a further seven years, comprising a first, compulsory, cycle lasting three years and a second cycle also of three years. Following three years of junior secondary education, pupils are examined to determine admission to senior secondary school courses, or to technical and vocational courses. In 2004/05, according to UNESCO, primary enrolment included 65% of children in the relevant age-group (boys 65%; girls 65%), while the comparable ratio for secondary enrolment in that year was estimated at 37% (boys 39%; girls 35%). Some 82,346 students were enrolled in higher education in 1996/97, with 23,126 students attending the country's five universities. By 1998/99 there were seven universities in Ghana, and other tertiary institutions included 38 teacher-training colleges, eight polytechnics and 61 technical colleges. Expenditure on education by the central Government in 1998 was 608,000m. new cedis (18.2% of total spending). In late 2003 the Government was granted US $27m. by donor agencies for the improvement of the education system and in early 2004 the World Bank granted credit of $78m. for educational development.

Public Holidays

2008: 1 January (New Year's Day), 6 March (Independence Day), 21–24 March (Easter), 1 May (Labour Day), 25 May (African Union Day), 1 July (Republic Day), 1 October* (Eid-al-Fitr, end of Ramadan), 5 December (National Farmers' Day), 9 December* (Eid-al-Adha, Feast of the Sacrifice), 25–26 December (Christmas).

2009: 1 January (New Year's Day), 6 March (Independence Day), 10–13 April (Easter), 1 May (Labour Day), 25 May (African Union Day), 1 July (Republic Day), 20 September* (Eid-al-Fitr, end of Ramadan), 27 November* (Eid-al-Adha, Feast of the Sacrifice), 4 December (National Farmers' Day), 25–26 December (Christmas).

*These holidays are dependent on the Islamic lunar calendar and may vary by one or two days from the dates given.

Weights and Measures

The metric system is in force.

GHANA

Statistical Survey

Source (except where otherwise stated): Ghana Statistical Service, POB GP1098, Accra; tel. (21) 671732; fax (21) 671731; internet www.bog.gov.gh.

Area and Population

AREA, POPULATION AND DENSITY

Area (sq km)	238,537*
Population (census results)	
11 March 1984	12,296,081
26 March 2000	
Males	9,320,794
Females	9,524,471
Total	18,845,265
Population (UN estimates at mid-year)†	
2005	22,535,000
2006	23,008,000
2007	23,478,000
Density (per sq km) at mid-2007	98.4

* 92,100 sq miles.
† Source: UN, *World Population Prospects: The 2006 Revision*.

POPULATION BY REGION
(2000 census)

Region	Population	Capital
Ashanti	3,600,358	Kumasi
Brong-Ahafo	1,798,058	Sunyani
Central	1,593,888	Cape Coast
Eastern	2,101,650	Koforidua
Greater Accra	2,903,753	Accra
Northern	1,805,428	Tamale
Upper East	919,549	Bolgatanga
Upper West	575,579	Wa
Volta	1,630,254	Ho
Western	1,916,748	Takoradi
Total	**18,845,265**	

PRINCIPAL TOWNS
(population at 1984 census)

Accra (capital)	867,459	Takoradi	61,484
Kumasi	376,249	Cape Coast	57,224
Tamale	135,952	Sekondi	31,916
Tema	131,528		

Mid-2007 ('000, incl. suburbs, UN estimate): Accra 2,121 (Source: UN, *World Urbanization Prospects: The 2007 Revision*).

BIRTHS AND DEATHS
(annual averages, UN estimates)

	1990–95	1995–2000	2000–05
Birth rate (per 1,000)	37.8	34.3	32.2
Death rate (per 1,000)	10.7	10.0	10.0

Source: UN, *World Population Prospects: The 2006 Revision*.

Expectation of life (years at birth, WHO estimates): 57.0 (males 56.3; females 57.7) in 2005 (Source: WHO, *World Health Statistics*).

ECONOMICALLY ACTIVE POPULATION
(1984 census)

	Males	Females	Total
Agriculture, hunting, forestry and fishing	1,750,024	1,560,943	3,310,967
Mining and quarrying	24,906	1,922	26,828
Manufacturing	198,430	389,988	588,418
Electricity, gas and water	14,033	1,404	15,437
Construction	60,692	3,994	64,686
Trade, restaurants and hotels	111,540	680,607	792,147
Transport, storage and communications	117,806	5,000	122,806
Financing, insurance, real estate and business services	19,933	7,542	27,475
Community, social and personal services	339,665	134,051	473,716
Total employed	2,637,029	2,785,451	5,422,480
Unemployed	87,452	70,172	157,624
Total labour force	2,724,481	2,855,623	5,580,104

2000 census ('000 persons aged 7 years and over): Total economically active population 9,039.3.

Source: ILO.

Mid-2005 (estimates in '000): Agriculture, etc. 6,245; Total 11,203 (Source: FAO).

Health and Welfare

KEY INDICATORS

Total fertility rate (children per woman, 2005)	4.1
Under-5 mortality rate (per 1,000 live births, 2005)	112
HIV/AIDS (% of persons aged 15–49, 2005)	2.3
Physicians (per 1,000 head, 2004)	0.15
Hospital beds (per 1,000 head, 2005)	0.90
Health expenditure (2004): US $ per head (PPP)	94.7
Health expenditure (2004): % of GDP	6.7
Health expenditure (2004): public (% of total)	42.2
Access to water (% of persons, 2004)	75
Access to sanitation (% of persons, 2004)	18
Human Development Index (2005): ranking	135
Human Development Index (2005): value	0.553

For sources and definitions, see explanatory note on p. vi.

Agriculture

PRINCIPAL CROPS
('000 metric tons)

	2004	2005	2006*
Rice (paddy)	241.8	287.0	250.0
Maize	1,157.6	1,171.0	1,189.0
Millet	143.8	185.0	165.0
Sorghum	287.0	305.0	315.0
Sweet potatoes*	92.8	94.6	90.0
Cassava (Manioc)	9,738.8	9,567.0	9,638.0
Taro (Coco yam)	1,716.0	1,686.0	1,660.0
Yams	3,892.3	4,101.6*	3,600.0
Sugar cane	140.0	140.0*	140.0
Groundnuts (in shell)	389.6	420.0	520.0
Coconuts†	315.0	315.0	315.0
Copra†	11.0	11.7	11.0
Oil palm fruit	1,955.3	2,024.6	2,097.4
Tomatoes*	200.0	200.3	176.3
Chillies and green peppers*	306.4	328.6	277.0
Dry onions*	38.5	38.5	42.5

GHANA

Statistical Survey

—continued	2004	2005	2006*
Green beans*	20.0	20.0	22.0
Okra*	100.0	100.0	105.0
Bananas	10.0*	52.6	56.0
Plantains	2,380.9	2,792.0	2,900.0
Oranges	396.2*	500.0	470.0
Lemons and limes*	30.0	30.0	36.0
Pineapples*	66.7	71.2	66.0
Cottonseed†	9.5	12.5	11.4
Cocoa beans	737.0†	740.0	734.0
Natural rubber†	9.3	8.6	9.0

* FAO estimate(s).
† Unofficial figure(s).

Aggregate production ('000 metric tons, may include official, semi-official or estimated data): Total cereals 1,830 in 2004, 1,948 in 2005, 1,919 in 2006; Total roots and tubers 15,440 in 2004, 15,449 in 2005, 14,988 in 2006; Total vegetables (incl. melons) 679 in 2004, 701 in 2005, 636 in 2006; Total fruits (excl. melons) 2,938 in 2004, 3,503 in 2005, 3,591 in 2006.

Source: FAO.

LIVESTOCK
('000 head, year ending September)

	2003	2004	2005
Horses*	3.0	3.0	3.0
Asses, mules or hinnies*	13.5	13.7	13.7
Cattle	1,344.0	1,365.0*	1,385.0*
Pigs	303.0	300.0	305.0*
Sheep	3,015.0	3,111.5*	3,211.1*
Goats	3,560.0	3,595.6*	3,631.6*
Chickens	26,395	29,500*	30,000*

* FAO estimate(s).
2006: Figures unchanged from 2005.
Source: FAO.

LIVESTOCK PRODUCTS
('000 metric tons)

	2004	2005	2006*
Cattle meat	23.1	25.4	23.9
Sheep meat	10.3	9.9	10.4
Goat meat	12.1	11.8	11.2
Pig meat	4.8	4.8	3.7
Chicken meat*	28.3	28.8	30.0
Game meat*	57.0	57.0	57.0
Cows' milk*	35.5	36.0	36.5
Hen eggs*	25.2	25.2	25.7

* FAO estimate(s).
Source: FAO.

Forestry

ROUNDWOOD REMOVALS
('000 cubic metres, excl. bark)

	2004	2005	2006
Sawlogs, veneer logs and logs for sleepers	1,350	1,200	1,304
Fuel wood*	20,678	20,678	33,040
Total	22,028	21,878	34,344

* FAO estimates.
Source: FAO.

SAWNWOOD PRODUCTION
('000 cubic metres, incl. railway sleepers)

	2004	2005	2006
Total (all broadleaved)	480	520	527

Source: FAO.

Fishing

('000 metric tons, live weight)

	2003	2004	2005
Capture	390.8	399.4*	392.3*
Freshwater fishes	75.0	75.0*	75.0*
Bigeye grunt	7.7	26.5	16.8
Round sardinella	78.8	82.4	64.4
Madeiran sardinella	15.6	27.0	14.2
European anchovy	82.9	52.6	36.4
Skipjack tuna	32.8	33.6	54.3
Yellowfin tuna	19.0	15.1	19.8
Aquaculture	0.9	1.0	1.2
Total catch	391.7	400.3*	393.4*

* FAO estimate.
Source: FAO.

Mining

('000 metric tons, unless otherwise indicated)

	2003	2004	2005
Crude petroleum ('000 barrels)*	3,000	3,000	2,190
Natural gas (million cu m)	112	112*	100*
Bauxite	495	498	726
Manganese ore: gross weight	1,509	1,597	1,715
Manganese ore: metal content	528	559	600*
Silver (kilograms)†	3,379	3,329	3,300*
Gold (kilograms)‡	70,749	63,139	66,852
Salt (unrefined)*	250	265	300
Diamonds ('000 carats)§	904	905	1,063

* Estimated production.
† Silver content of exported doré.
‡ Gold content of ores and concentrates, excluding smuggled or undocumented output.
§ Of the total, the estimated production of gemstones (in '000 carats) was: 724 in 2003; 725 in 2004; 850 in 2005.
Source: US Geological Survey.

Industry

SELECTED PRODUCTS
('000 metric tons, unless otherwise indicated)

	2002	2003	2004
Groundnut oil*	98.9	76.4	61.5
Coconut oil	6.5*	7.0†	7.0†
Palm oil†	108.0	108.4	114.0
Palm kernel oil*	10.8	13.4	13.4
Butter of karité nuts (shea butter)*	8.4	9.8	18.3
Beer of barley*	100.0	100.0	100.0
Beer of millet*	66.6	73.8	60.2
Beer of sorghum*	234.6	258.3	340.7
Gasoline (petrol)	5,850	5,580	5,580†
Jet fuel	625	625	625†
Kerosene	1,950	1,950	1,950†
Distillate fuel oil	4,450	4,450	4,450†
Residual fuel oil	1,250	1,250	1,250†
Cement	1,900	1,900	1,900†
Aluminium (unwrought)‡	117	16	n.a.
Electric energy ('000 million kWh)	7,296	5,901	n.a.

* FAO estimate(s).
† Provisional or estimated figure(s).
‡ Primary metal only.

2005: Groundnut oil 7.0 (unofficial figure); Coconut oil 46.0 (FAO estimate); Palm oil 117.0 (unofficial figure); Palm kernel oil 14.6 (unofficial figure).

Sources: FAO; US Geological Survey; Energy Commission of Ghana.

GHANA

Finance

CURRENCY AND EXCHANGE RATES

Monetary Units
100 pesewas = 1 Ghana cedi.

Sterling, Dollar and Euro Equivalents (31 December 2007)
£1 sterling = 1.9441 Ghana cedis;
US $1 = 0.9704 Ghana cedis;
€1 = 1.4285 Ghana cedis;
10 Ghana cedis = £5.14 = $10.31 = €7.00.

Average Exchange Rate (Ghana cedis per US $)
2005   0.9068
2006   0.9169
2007   0.9355

Note: A new currency, the Ghana cedi, equivalent to 10,000 new cedis (the former legal tender), was introduced over a six-month period beginning in July 2007. Some statistical data in this survey are still presented in terms of the former currency, the new cedi.

GENERAL BUDGET
('000 million new cedis)

Revenue*	2004	2005	2006
Tax revenue	17,861.7	21,302.1	24,646.1
Income and property	5,344.0	6,615.1	7,183.3
Personal (PAYE)	1,908.2	2,435.1	3,111.5
Company tax	2,340.3	3,108.3	3,013.3
Domestic goods and services	3,734.6	4,429.3	4,776.8
Petroleum tax	3,119.4	3,751.0	4,071.3
International trade	3,988.0	4,114.0	5,418.4
Import duties	3,002.2	3,795.7	4,169.8
Cocoa export duty	931.1	615.1	1,248.6
Non-tax revenue	1,136.3	1,854.1	923.0
Total	18,998.0	23,156.2	25,569.1

Expenditure†	2004	2005	2006
Recurrent expenditure	16,278.0	18,032.8	24,734.9
Wages and salaries	6,946.7	8,920.8	11,069.5
Goods and services	2,360.3	3,305.9	4,049.1
Transfers to households	3,498.6	3,332.4	5,682.6
Interest payments	3,472.4	3,473.8	3,933.7
Domestic (accrual)	2,545.0	2,622.5	3,030.9
External (accrual)	927.4	851.3	902.8
Capital expenditure	8,081.9	9,726.8	10,961.8
Domestic	3,470.8	3,780.8	5,683.2
External	4,611.1	5,946.1	5,278.6
HIPC-financed expenditure	1,869.6	1,946.6	1,791.6
Adjustment	—	—	1,246.4
Total	26,229.5	29,706.2	38,734.7

* Excluding grants received ('000 million new cedis): 4,940.3 in 2004; 5,100.2 in 2005; 6,348.6 in 2006.
† Including net lending ('000 million new cedis): 182.9 in 2004; 72.8 in 2005; 7.6 in 2006.

Source: Bank of Ghana.

INTERNATIONAL RESERVES
(US $ million at 31 December)

	2004	2005	2006
Gold (national valuation)	122.6	144.5	177.9
IMF special drawing rights	20.7	1.1	1.2
Foreign exchange	1,605.9	1,751.8	2,089.1
Total	1,749.2	1,897.4	2,268.2

Source: IMF, *International Financial Statistics*.

MONEY SUPPLY
('000 million new cedis at 31 December)

	2004	2005	2006
Currency outside banks	7,306.5	8,032.3	10,207.8
Demand deposits at deposit money banks	6,358.0	6,614.3	9,781.1
Total money (incl. others)	13,745.3	14,707.5	20,045.2

Source: IMF, *International Financial Statistics*.

COST OF LIVING
(Consumer Price Index; prices at December; base: 1997 = 100)

	2004	2005	2006
Food and beverages	317.1	364.6	387.8
Clothing and footwear	341.5	372.1	389.9
Housing and utilities	756.5	883.7	1,030.4
Medical care and health expenses	257.0	314.9	342.6
Transport and communications	516.1	691.4	916.8
All items	360.7	414.2	457.9

Source: Bank of Ghana.

NATIONAL ACCOUNTS

National Income and Product
('000 million new cedis at current prices)

	2002	2003	2004
GDP at market prices	48,862	66,158	79,865
Net primary income from abroad	–797	–774	–872
Gross national income	48,065	65,384	78,993
Less Consumption of fixed capital	1,917	1,918	1,919
Net national income	46,148	63,466	77,074
Net transfers from abroad	3,528	6,197	7,158
Net national disposable income	49,676	69,663	84,232

Expenditure on the Gross Domestic Product
('000 million new cedis at current prices, estimates)

	2002	2003	2004
Government final consumption expenditure	8,595	11,722	12,780
Private final consumption expenditure	36,677	47,234	61,304
Increase in stocks	244	0	0
Gross fixed capital formation	9,391	15,175	22,278
Total domestic expenditure	54,907	74,131	96,362
Exports of goods and services	20,758	26,922	29,574
Less Imports of goods and services	26,803	34,895	46,071
GDP in purchasers' values	48,862	66,158	79,865
GDP at constant 1993 prices	5,601	5,895	6,236

2005 (US $ million at current prices): Government final consumption expenditure 1,641.09; Private final consumption expenditure 8,689.09; Gross capital formation 3,104.59; Total domestic expenditure 13,434.77; Exports of goods and services 3,868.59; *Less* Imports of goods and services 6,609.73; GDP at current market prices 10,693.62 (Source: African Development Bank).

2006 (US $ million at current prices): Government final consumption expenditure 1,803.19; Private final consumption expenditure 9,998.14; Gross capital formation 3,674.35; Total domestic expenditure 15,475.68; Exports of goods and services 4,824.95; *Less* Imports of goods and services 8,057.95; GDP at current market prices 12,242.68 (Source: African Development Bank).

GHANA

Statistical Survey

Gross Domestic Product by Economic Activity
('000 million new cedis at constant 1993 prices)

	2004	2005*	2006*
Agriculture and livestock	1,533.1	1,625.1	1,662.7
Cocoa	265.0	300.0	326.1
Forestry and logging	225.0	237.6	240.0
Fishing	265.4	275.0	278.9
Mining and quarrying	321.7	331.4	347.3
Manufacturing	560.8	591.7	613.6
Electricity and water	155.1	165.4	214.4
Construction	504.6	539.9	600.5
Transport, storage and communications	305.1	323.4	351.6
Wholesale and retail trade, restaurants and hotels	429.7	455.9	513.4
Finance, insurance, real estate and business services	267.4	282.4	309.6
Government services	667.1	700.5	740.4
Community, social and personal services	117.3	122.3	127.5
Private non-profit services	53.2	55.1	54.6
Sub-total	5,670.3	6,005.5	6,383.5
Indirect taxes, *less* subsidies	565.5	590.6	617.0
GDP at market prices	6,235.8	6,596.1	7,000.5

* Preliminary.

Source: Bank of Ghana.

BALANCE OF PAYMENTS
(US $ million)

	2004	2005	2006
Exports of goods f.o.b.	2,704.5	2,802.2	3,726.7
Imports of goods f.o.b.	−4,297.3	−5,347.3	−6,753.7
Trade balance	−1,592.8	−2,545.1	−3,027.0
Exports of services	702.3	1,106.5	1,398.7
Imports of services	−1,058.5	−1,273.1	−1,532.8
Balance on goods and services	−1,949.0	−2,711.7	−3,161.1
Other income received	44.5	43.3	73.3
Other income paid	−242.3	−230.4	−200.6
Balance on goods, services and income	−2,146.8	−2,898.8	−3,288.5
Current transfers (net)	1,579.9	1,794.2	2,248.3
Current balance	−566.9	−1,104.6	−1,040.2
Capital account (net)	251.0	331.2	229.9
Direct investment from abroad	139.3	145.0	434.5
Other investment assets	86.7	106.7	135.0
Other investment liabilities	−24.4	582.9	483.9
Net errors and omissions	115.2	25.6	174.2
Overall balance	1.0	86.7	417.4

Source: IMF, *International Financial Statistics*.

External Trade

PRINCIPAL COMMODITIES
(distribution by SITC, US $ million)

Imports c.i.f.	2002	2003	2004
Food and live animals	491.7	468.5	793.4
Fish, crustaceans and molluscs, and preparations thereof	115.4	56.2	116.7
Fish, fresh, chilled or frozen	102.2	49.5	105.4
Fish, frozen, excluding fillets	82.5	15.3	21.4
Cereals and cereal preparations	193.1	190.4	350.0
Rice	104.0	117.3	185.2
Sugar and honey	70.8	88.5	137.0
Crude materials (inedible), except fuels	109.2	65.7	68.4
Mineral fuels, lubricants, etc.	233.6	596.7	65.2
Petroleum, petroleum products, etc.	206.0	596.1	65.1
Crude petroleum and oils obtained from bituminous materials	151.1	576.5	0.0

Imports c.i.f.—*continued*	2002	2003	2004
Petroleum products, refined	35.3	8.6	49.6
Chemicals and related products	331.4	404.7	548.3
Basic manufactures	485.4	491.1	679.3
Non-metallic mineral manufactures	96.5	83.9	143.9
Iron and steel	70.4	89.2	113.3
Machinery and transport equipment	865.0	947.3	1,601.4
Power-generating machinery and equipment	38.7	47.5	76.0
Machinery specialized for particular industries	126.9	151.9	239.1
General industrial machinery and equipment, and parts thereof	108.8	122.0	194.4
Telecommunications, sound recording and reproducing equipment	49.2	74.3	169.3
Other electric machinery, apparatus and appliances, and parts thereof	88.7	100.0	178.5
Road vehicles and parts*	413.1	397.3	675.4
Passenger motor vehicles (excluding buses)	234.7	222.3	0.0
Motor vehicles for the transport of goods or materials	122.7	111.3	242.7
Miscellaneous manufactured articles	148.7	187.7	264.7
Total (incl. others)	2,720.1	3,210.2	4,073.9

* Data on parts exclude tyres, engines and electrical parts.

Exports f.o.b.	2003	2004
Food and live animals	1,046.2	1,246.9
Fish, crustaceans and molluscs, and preparations thereof	120.2	93.8
Fish, prepared or preserved	100.6	70.3
Vegetables and fruit	61.4	65.5
Fruit and nuts, fresh, dried	43.8	43.2
Fruit, fresh or dried	37.9	33.2
Pineapples, fresh or dried	33.4	0.0
Coffee, tea, cocoa, spices and manufactures thereof	846.6	1,074.3
Cocoa	838.0	1,070.3
Cocoa beans, raw, roasted	676.1	1,003.5
Cocoa butter and paste	126.1	34.4
Cocoa butter (fat or oil)	25.4	28.4
Crude materials (inedible) except fuels	215.3	130.1
Cork and wood	97.9	55.8
Wood, non-coniferous species, sawn, planed, tongued, grooved, etc.	93.8	55.3
Wood, non-coniferous species, sawn lengthwise, sliced or peeled	87.9	42.1
Mineral fuels, lubricants, etc.	1.1	55.4
Basic manufactures	150.6	108.9
Cork and wood manufactures (excl. furniture)	81.6	84.6
Veneers, plywood, 'improved' wood and other wood, worked	76.9	75.4
Wood sawn lengthwise, veneer sheets, etc., up to 5 mm in thickness	60.5	35.1
Aluminium and aluminium alloys, unwrought	10.2	2.3
Machinery and transport equipment	17.7	38.4
Gold, non-monetary, unwrought or semi-manufactured	829.6	125.3
Total (incl. others)	2,324.3	1,779.1

Source: UN, *International Trade Statistics Yearbook*.

Imports f.o.b. (US $ million): Total 5,345.4 (Petroleum 1,127.5, Non-petroleum 4,217.9) in 2005; Total 6,523.6 (Petroleum 1,416.1, Non-petroleum 5,107.5) in 2006 (preliminary) (Source: Bank of Ghana).

Exports f.o.b. (US $ million): Total 2,802.2 (Cocoa beans and products thereof 908.4, Gold 945.8, Timber and products thereof 226.5, Other 721.5) in 2005; Total 3,735.1 (Cocoa beans and products thereof 1,187.4, Gold 1,277.3, Timber and products thereof 199.5, Other 1,070.9) in 2006 (preliminary) (Source: Bank of Ghana).

GHANA

Statistical Survey

PRINCIPAL TRADING PARTNERS
(US $ million)

Imports c.i.f.	2002	2003	2004
Belgium	143.2	145.8	251.6
Brazil	46.8	78.2	156.3
Burkina Faso	89.5	0.3	0.0
Canada	57.1	66.5	119.5
China, People's Republic	128.9	179.6	364.8
Côte d'Ivoire	41.8	13.4	31.3
France (incl. Monaco)	104.7	118.4	164.0
Germany	190.0	218.8	314.8
India	69.9	99.4	150.1
Italy (incl. San Marino)	124.2	98.1	155.0
Japan	66.4	99.5	150.5
Korea, Republic	61.0	51.5	98.7
Nigeria	194.9	599.7	35.2
Netherlands	137.9	161.9	206.5
South Africa	101.6	145.8	224.1
Spain	56.0	67.6	94.6
Thailand	47.0	81.8	135.2
United Kingdom	239.3	218.9	234.0
USA	202.4	225.8	362.7
Total (incl. others)	2,720.1	3,210.2	4,073.9

Exports f.o.b.	2003	2004
Belgium	113.9	130.5
Benin	42.4	14.6
China, People's Republic	32.3	20.1
Côte d'Ivoire	18.9	2.5
France (incl. Monaco)	109.7	109.7
Germany	113.3	37.7
Ireland	5.6	14.1
Italy (incl. San Marino)	110.7	62.9
Japan	58.3	59.5
Netherlands	274.1	452.4
Nigeria	24.4	11.7
South Africa	87.8	106.4
Spain	49.4	44.0
Switzerland-Liechtenstein	587.9	34.9
Togo	30.0	0.0
Turkey	0.0	52.5
United Kingdom	464.7	239.5
USA	67.7	66.7
Total (incl. others)	2,324.3	1,779.1

Source: UN, *International Trade Statistics Yearbook*.

Transport

RAILWAYS
(traffic)

	2001	2002	2003
Passenger-km (million)	238	242	245
Net ton-km (million)	168	170	173

Source: UN, *Statistical Yearbook*.

ROAD TRAFFIC
(motor vehicles in use at 31 December)

	2001	2002	2003
Passenger cars	90,800	91,200	91,000
Lorries and vans	121,100	123,500	124,300

Source: UN, *Statistical Yearbook*.

SHIPPING
Merchant Fleet
(registered at 31 December)

	2004	2005	2006
Number of vessels	210	211	224
Total displacement ('000 grt)	116.7	115.2	116.3

Source: Lloyd's Register-Fairplay, *World Fleet Statistics*.

International Sea-borne Freight Traffic
(estimates, '000 metric tons)

	1991	1992	1993
Goods loaded	2,083	2,279	2,424
Goods unloaded	2,866	2,876	2,904

Source: UN Economic Commission for Africa, *African Statistical Yearbook*.

CIVIL AVIATION
(traffic on scheduled services)

	2001	2002	2003
Kilometres flown (million)	18	12	12
Passengers carried ('000)	301	256	241
Passenger-km (million)	1,233	912	906
Total ton-km (million)	157	107	101

Source: UN, *Statistical Yearbook*.

Tourism

ARRIVALS BY NATIONALITY

	2003	2004	2005
Côte d'Ivoire	25,521	28,069	25,155
France	19,181	21,096	10,089
Germany	25,611	28,168	14,094
Liberia	13,920	15,310	14,472
Netherlands	12,850	14,133	13,663
Nigeria	72,857	80,131	74,983
Togo	15,886	17,472	11,888
United Kingdom	45,959	50,547	36,747
USA	35,013	38,508	50,475
Total (incl. others)*	530,827	583,819	428,533

* Includes Ghanaian nationals resident abroad: 144,492 in 2003; 158,917 in 2004; 59,821 in 2005.

Receipts from tourism (US $ million, incl. passenger transport): 441 in 2003; 495 in 2004; 827 in 2005.

Source: World Tourism Organization.

Communications Media

	2004	2005	2006
Telephones ('000 main lines in use)	313.3	321.5	356.4
Mobile cellular telephones ('000 subscribers)	1,695.0	2,874.6	5,207.2
Personal computers ('000 in use)	112	112	n.a.
Internet users ('000)	368	401.3	609.8
Broadband subscribers ('000)	0.9	1.9	12.7

Source: International Telecommunication Union.

Radio receivers ('000 in use): 4,400 in 1997.

Television receivers ('000 in use): 2,390 in 2000.

Facsimile machines (number in use, estimate): 5,000 in 1995.

Daily newspapers: 4 titles in 1998 (average circulation 260,000).

Book production (titles, 1998): 7.

Sources: UNESCO Institute for Statistics; UNESCO, *Statistical Yearbook*; UN, *Statistical Yearbook*.

Education

(2004/05, unless otherwise indicated)

	Institutions	Teachers	Males	Females	Total
Pre-primary	n.a.	29,014	238.4	240.3	478.7
Primary	13,115*	88,461	1,525.5	1,404.0	2,929.5
Junior secondary	6,394*	56,485	548.1	462.1	1,010.2
Senior secondary	512*	17,381	194.3	145.9	340.2
Tertiary	n.a.	3,899	77.8	41.8	119.6

* 1998/99 figure.

1998/99: *Teacher training* 38 institutions; *Technical institutes* 61 institutions; *Polytechnics* 8 institutions; *Universities* 7 institutions.

Source: UNESCO and former Ministry of Education, Accra.

Adult literacy rate (UNESCO estimates): 57.9% (males 66.4%; females 49.8%) in 2000 (Source: UNESCO Institute for Statistics).

Directory

The Constitution

Under the terms of the Constitution of the Fourth Republic, which was approved by national referendum on 28 April 1992, Ghana has a multi-party political system. Executive power is vested in the President, who is Head of State and Commander-in-Chief of the Armed Forces. The President is elected by universal adult suffrage for a term of four years, and designates a Vice-President (prior to election). The duration of the President's tenure of office is limited to two four-year terms. It is also stipulated that, in the event that no presidential candidate receives more than 50% of votes cast, a new election between the two candidates with the highest number of votes is to take place within 21 days. Legislative power is vested in a 230-member unicameral Parliament, which is elected by direct adult suffrage for a four-year term. (This number was increased from 200 at the general election of December 2004.) The Council of Ministers is appointed by the President, subject to approval by the Parliament. The Constitution also provides for a 25-member Council of State, principally comprising presidential nominees and regional representatives, and a 20-member National Security Council (chaired by the Vice-President), both of which act as advisory bodies to the President.

The Government

HEAD OF STATE

President and Commander-in-Chief of the Armed Forces: JOHN AGYEKUM KUFUOR (inaugurated 7 January 2001; re-elected 7 December 2004 and inaugurated 7 January 2005).

Vice-President: Alhaji ALIU MAHAMA.

CABINET
(February 2008)

Minister of Defence: ALBERT KAN DAPAAH.
Minister of the Interior: KWAMENA BARTELS.
Minister of Education, Science and Sports: Prof. DOMINIC FOBIH.
Minister of Water Resources, Works and Housing: Alhaji ABUBAKAR SADDIQUE BONIFACE.
Minister of Lands, Forestry and Mines: ESTHER OBENG DAPAAH.
Minister of Tourism and Diasporan Relations: STEPHEN ASAMOAH-BOATENG.
Minister of Local Government, Rural Development and the Environment: KWADWO ADJEI-DARKO.
Minister of Finance and Economic Planning: KWADWO BAAH-WIREDU.
Minister of National Security: (vacant).
Minister of Health: Maj. (retd) COURAGE QUASHIGAH.
Attorney-General, Minister of Justice: JOSEPH GHARTEY.
Minister of Food and Agriculture: ERNEST AKUBOUR DEBRAH.
Minister of Energy: JOSEPH KOFI ADDA.
Minister of Foreign Affairs, Regional Integration and NEPAD: AKWASI OSEI-ADJAI.
Minister of Fisheries: GLADYS ASMAH.
Minister of Parliamentary Affairs: ABRAHAM OSEI-AIDOOH.
Minister of Trade and Industry: JOE BAIDOO-ANSAH.
Minister of Manpower, Youth and Employment: NANA AKOMEA.
Minister of Information and National Orientation: OBOSHIE SAI-COFIE.
Minister of Communication: Dr BENJAMIN AGGREY-NTIM.
Minister of Women's and Children's Affairs: Hajia ALIMA MAHAMA.
Minister of Ports, Harbours and Railways: Prof. CHRISTOPHER AMEYAW-AKUMFI.

MINISTERS OF STATE
(February 2008)

Minister of State for Finance and Economic Planning: Dr ANTHONY AKOTO OSEI.
Minister of State for Justice and the Attorney-General: AMBROSE DERY.
Minister of State for Culture and Chieftaincy: SAMPSON KWAKU BOAFO.
Minister of State for Aviation: GLORIA AKUFFO.
Minister of State for Public Sector Reform: SAMUEL OWUSU-ADJEI.
Minister of State for Education: ELIZABETH OHENE.
Minister of State for the Interior: NANA OBIRI BOAHEN.
Minister of State for Water Resources, Works and Housing: CECILIA ABENA DAPAAH.
Minister of State for Transportation: GODFRED T. BONYON.
Ministers of State at the Presidency: CHARLES BINTIMYAW BARIMAH.

REGIONAL MINISTERS
(February 2008)

Ashanti: EMMANUEL OWUSU-ANSAH.
Brong Ahafo: IGNATIUS BAFFOUR AWUAH.
Central: NANA ATO ARTHUR.
Eastern: KWADWO AFRAM ASIEDU.
Greater Accra: Sheikh IBRAHIM CUDJOE QUAYE.
Northern: Alhaji MUSTAPHA ALI IDRIS.
Upper East: ALHASSAN SAMARI.
Upper West: GEORGE HIKAH BENSON.
Volta: KOFI DZAMESI.
Western: EVANS A. AMOAH.

GHANA

MINISTRIES

Office of the President: POB 1627, Osu, Accra; tel. (21) 665415; internet www.ghanacastle.gov.gh.

Ministry of Aviation: POB M232, Accra.

Ministry of Communication: POB M38, Accra; tel. (21) 666465; fax (21) 667114; e-mail info@moc.gov.gh; internet www.moc.gov.gh.

Ministry of Culture and Chieftaincy: Accra.

Ministry of Defence: Burma Camp, Accra; tel. (21) 777611; fax (21) 778549; e-mail kaddok@internetghana.com.

Ministry of Education, Science and Sports: POB M45, Accra; tel. (21) 666070; fax (21) 664067.

Ministry of Energy: FREMA House, Spintex Rd, POB T40 (Stadium Post Office), Stadium, Accra; tel. (21) 667152; fax (21) 668262; e-mail moen@energymin.gov.gh; internet www.energymin.gov.gh.

Ministry of Finance and Economic Planning: POB M40, Accra; tel. (21) 686204; fax (21) 668879.

Ministry of Fisheries: State House, POB 1627, Accra; tel. (21) 776005; fax (21) 785670.

Ministry of Food and Agriculture: POB M37, Accra; tel. (21) 663036; fax (21) 668245; internet www.mofa.gov.gh.

Ministry of Foreign Affairs: Treasury Rd, POB M53, Accra; tel. (21) 664951; fax (21) 680017; e-mail ghmaf00@ghana.com.

Ministry of Health: POB M44, Accra; tel. (21) 666151; fax (21) 666810; internet www.moh-ghana.org.

Ministry of Information and National Orientation: POB M41, Accra; tel. (21) 228059; fax (21) 235800; internet www.ghana.gov.gh.

Ministry of the Interior: POB M42, Accra; tel. (21) 684400; fax (21) 684408.

Ministry of Justice and Attorney General's Department: POB M60, Accra; tel. (21) 665051; fax (21) 667609; e-mail info@mjag.gov.gh.

Ministry of Lands, Forestry and Mines: POB M212, Accra; tel. (21) 687314; fax (21) 666801; e-mail motgov@hotmail.com.

Ministry of Local Government, Rural Development and the Environment: POB M50, Accra; tel. (21) 664763; fax (21) 661015.

Ministry of Manpower, Youth and Employment: State House, POB M84, Accra; tel. (21) 684532; fax (21) 667251; e-mail info@mmde.gov.gh; internet www.mmde.gov.gh.

Ministry of National Security: Accra.

Ministry of Parliamentary Affairs: State House, POB 1627, Accra; tel. (21) 665349; fax (21) 667251.

Ministry of Ports, Harbours and Railways: Ministries Post Office, PMB M, Accra; tel. (21) 681780; fax (21) 681781; e-mail poharail@yahoo.com; internet www.mphrgh.org.

Ministry of Public Sector Reform: State House, POB 1627, Accra; tel. (21) 684086.

Ministry of Tourism and Diasporan Relations: POB 4386, Accra; tel. (21) 666701; fax (21) 666182; e-mail motgov@hotmail.com; internet www.ghanatourism.gov.gh.

Ministry of Trade and Industry: POB M47, Accra; tel. (21) 679283; fax (21) 665663; e-mail info@moti.gov.gh; internet www.moti-ghana.com.

Ministry of Transportation: POB M38, Accra; tel. (21) 661577; fax (21) 667114; e-mail info@mrt.gov.gh; internet www.mrt.gov.gh.

Ministry of Water Resources, Works and Housing: POB M43, Accra; tel. (21) 665940; fax (21) 667689; e-mail mwh@ighmail.com.

Ministry of Women's and Children's Affairs: POB M186, Accra; tel. (21) 255411; fax (21) 688182; e-mail barnes@africaonline.com.gh.

President and Legislature

PRESIDENT

Presidential Election, 7 December 2004

Candidate	Valid votes	% of valid votes
John Agyekum Kufuor (NPP)	4,524,074	52.45
John Evans Atta Mills (NDC)	3,850,368	44.64
Edward Nasigre Mahama (PNC)	165,375	1.92
George Aggudey (CPP)	85,968	1.00
Total	**8,625,785***	**100.00**

* Excluding 188,213 spoilt papers.

PARLIAMENT

Parliament: Parliament House, Accra; tel. (21) 664042; fax (21) 665957; e-mail clerk@parliament.gh; internet www.parliament.gh.

Speaker: EBENEZER BEGYINA SEKI HUGHES.

Legislative Elections, 7 December 2004

Party	% of votes	Seats
New Patriotic Party (NPP)	55.6	128
National Democratic Congress (NDC)	40.9	94
People's National Convention (PNC)	1.7	4
Convention People's Party (CPP)	1.3	3
Independents	0.4	1
Total	**100.0**	**230**

COUNCIL OF STATE

Chairman: Prof. DANIEL ADZEI BEKOE.

Election Commission

Electoral Commission (EC): Accra; internet www.ec.gov.gh; f. 1993; appointed by the President; Chair. Dr KWADWO AFARI-GYAN.

Political Organizations

Convention People's Party (CPP): 825/3 Mango Tree Ave, Asylum Down, POB 10939, Accra-North; tel. (21) 221773; f. 1998 as Convention Party by merger of the National Convention Party (f. 1992) and the People's Convention Party (f. 1993); present name adopted in 2000; Nkrumahist; Chair. Dr EDMUND DELLE; Sec.-Gen. Dr NII NOI DOWUONA.

Democratic Freedom Party (DFP): Accra; f. 2006; Leader Dr OBED YAO ASAMOAH.

Democratic People's Party (DPP): 698/4 Star Ave, Kokomlemle, Accra; tel. (21) 221671; f. 1992; Chair. THOMAS WARD-BREW; Gen. Sec. G. M. TETTEY.

EGLE (Every Ghanaian Living Everywhere) Party: Kokomlemle, POB 1859, Accra; tel. (21) 231873; f. 1992 as the Eagle Party; Chair. DANIEL OFFORI-ATTA.

Great Consolidated People's Party (GCPP): Citadel House, POB 3077, Accra; tel. (21) 311498; f. 1996; Nkrumahist; Chair. DAN LARTEY; Sec.-Gen. NICHOLAS MENSAH.

Grand Coalition: Accra; f. 2004 to contest general election; Chair. DAN LARTEY.

National Democratic Congress (NDC): 641/4 Ringway Close, POB 5825, Kokomlemle, Accra-North; tel. and fax (21) 230761; e-mail ndc2004@hotmail.com; internet www.ndc.org.gh; f. 1992; party of fmr Pres. Jerry Rawlings; Chair. Dr KWABENA ADJEI; Gen. Sec. JOHNSON ASEIDU NKETIAH.

National Reform Party (NRP): 31 Mango Tree Ave, Asylum Down, POB 19403, Accra-North; tel. (21) 228578; f. 1999 by a breakaway group from the NDC; Sec.-Gen. OPOKU KYERETWIE.

New Patriotic Party (NPP): C912/2 Duade St, Kokomlemle, POB 3456, Accra-North; tel. (21) 227951; fax (21) 224418; e-mail npp@africanonline.com.gh; internet www.nppghana.org; f. 1992; Chair. PETER MAC MANU; Sec.-Gen. NANA OHENE NTOW.

People's National Convention (PNC): Kokomlemle, near Sadisco, POB 7795, Accra; tel. (21) 236389; f. 1992; Nkrumahist; Leader Dr EDWARD MAHAMA; Chair. Dr MIKE MENSAH; Gen.-Sec. GABRIEL PWAMANG.

Reformed Patriotic Democrats (RPD): Accra; f. 2007 by former mems of the NPP; Leader KWABENA ADJEI (acting); Sec.-Gen. K. MANU SARPONG (acting).

United Ghana Movement (UGM): 1 North Ridge Cres., POB C2611, Cantonments, Accra; tel. (21) 225581; fax (21) 231390; e-mail info@ugmghana.org; f. 1996 by a breakaway group from the NPP; Chair. WEREKO BROBBY.

United Renaissance Party (URP): Accra; f. 2006; Chair. KOFI WAYO; Gen. Sec. ALHASSAN SAEED.

Diplomatic Representation

EMBASSIES AND HIGH COMMISSIONS IN GHANA

Algeria: 22 Josif Broz Tito Ave, POB 2747, Cantonments, Accra; tel. (21) 776719; fax (21) 776828; Ambassador LAKHAL BENKELAI.

GHANA

Directory

Angola: Accra; Ambassador EARISTO D. KIMBA.

Benin: 19 Volta St, Second Close, Airport Residential Area, POB 7871, Accra; tel. (21) 774860; fax (21) 774889; Ambassador PIERRE SADELER.

Brazil: Millennium Heights Bldg 2A, 14 Liberation Link, Airport Commercial Area, POB CT3859, Accra; tel. (21) 774908; fax (21) 778566; Ambassador LOUIS FERNANDO DE ANDRADI SERRA.

Bulgaria: 3 Kakramadu Rd, POB 3193, East Cantonments, Accra; tel. (21) 772404; fax (21) 774231; e-mail bulembgh@ghana.com; Chargé d'affaires a.i. GEORGE MITEV.

Burkina Faso: 772 Asylum Down, off Farrar Ave, POB 65, Accra; tel. (21) 221988; fax (21) 777490; e-mail ambafaso@ghana.com; Ambassador PIERRE SEM SANOU.

Canada: 42 Independence Ave, Sankara Interchange, POB 1639, Accra; tel. (21) 211521; fax (21) 211523; e-mail accra@international.gc.ca; internet www.accra.gc.ca; High Commissioner DARREN SCHEMMER.

China, People's Republic: 6 Agostino Neto Rd, Airport Residential Area, POB 3356, Accra; tel. (21) 777073; fax (21) 774527; e-mail chinaemb_gh@mfa.gov.cn; internet gh.china-embassy.org; Ambassador YU WENZHE.

Côte d'Ivoire: 9 18th Lane, off Cantonments Rd, POB 3445, Christiansborg, Accra; tel. (21) 774611; fax (21) 773516; e-mail acigh@ambaci-ghana.org; Ambassador PAUL KAKOULANGBA.

Cuba: 20 Amilcar Cabral Rd, Airport Residential Area, POB 9163 Airport, Accra; tel. (21) 775868; fax 774998; e-mail embghana@africaonline.com.gh; Ambassador MIGUEL PÉREZ GRUZ.

Czech Republic: C260/5, 2 Kanda High Rd, POB 5226, Accra-North; tel. (21) 223540; fax (21) 225337; e-mail accra@embassy.mzv.cz; internet www.mzv.cz/accra; Ambassador MIROSLAV KŘENEK.

Denmark: 67 Dr Isert Rd, North Ridge, POB CT 596, Accra; tel. (21) 253473; fax (21) 228061; e-mail accamb@um.dk; internet www.ambaccra.um.dk; Ambassador FLEMMING BJØRK PEDERSEN.

Egypt: 38 Senchi St, Airport Residential Area, Accra; tel. (21) 776795; fax (21) 777579; e-mail boustaneaccra@hotmail.com; Ambassador SEIF ALLAH MOSTAFA ABDUL MAGUID NOSEIR.

Ethiopia: 2 Milne Close, Airport Residential Area, POB 1646, Accra; tel. (21) 775928; fax (21) 776807; e-mail ethioemb@ghana.com; Ambassador Ato CHAM UGALA URIAT.

France: 12th Rd, off Liberation Ave, POB 187, Accra; tel. (21) 214550; fax (21) 214589; e-mail info@ambafrance-gh.org; internet www.ambafrance-gh.org; Ambassador PIERRE JACQUEMOT.

Germany: 6 Ridge St, North Ridge, POB 1757, Accra; tel. (21) 211000; fax (21) 221347; e-mail info@accra.diplo.de; internet www.accra.diplo.de; Ambassador Dr MARIUS HAAS.

Guinea: 11 Osu Badu St, Dzorwulu, POB 5497, Accra-North; tel. (21) 777921; fax (21) 760961; e-mail embagui@ghana.com; Ambassador MAMADOU FALILOU BAH.

Holy See: 8 Drake Ave, Airport Residential Area, POB 9675, Accra; tel. (21) 777759; fax (21) 774019; e-mail nuncio@ghana.com; Apostolic Nuncio Most Rev. GEORGE KOCHERRY (Titular Archbishop of Othona).

India: 9 Ridge Rd, Roman Ridge, POB 5708, Cantonments, Accra; tel. (21) 775601; fax (21) 772176; e-mail indiahc@ncs.com.gh; internet www.indiahc-ghana.com; High Commissioner RAJESH N. PRASAD.

Iran: 12 Arkusah St, Airport Residential Area, POB 12673, Accra-North; tel. (21) 774474; fax (21) 777043; Ambassador VALIOLLAH MOHAMMADI NASRABADI.

Italy: Jawaharlal Nehru Rd, POB 140, Accra; tel. (21) 775621; fax (21) 777301; e-mail ambasciata.accra@esteri.it; internet www.ambaccra.esteri.it; Ambassador FABRIZIO DE AGOSTINI.

Japan: Fifth Ave, POB 1637, West Cantonments, Accra; tel. (21) 765060; fax (21) 762553; Ambassador MASSAMICHI ISHIKAWA.

Korea, Democratic People's Republic: 139 Nortei Ababio Loop, Ambassadorial Estate, Roman Ridge, POB 13874, Accra; tel. (21) 777825; Ambassador KIM PYONG GI.

Korea, Republic: 3 Abokobi Rd, POB GP13700, East Cantonments, Accra-North; tel. (21) 776157; fax (21) 772313; Ambassador WI KEYEI-CHUI.

Lebanon: F864/1, off Cantonments Rd, Osu, POB 562, Accra; tel. (21) 776727; fax (21) 764290; e-mail lebanon@its.com.gh; Ambassador JAWDAT EL-HAJJAR.

Liberia: 10 Odoi Kwao St, Airport Residential Area, POB 895, Accra; tel. (21) 775641; fax (21) 775987; Ambassador RUDOLPH P. VON BALLMOOS.

Libya: 14 Sixth St, Airport Residential Area, POB 9665, Accra; tel. (21) 774819; fax (21) 774953; Secretary of People's Bureau MUHAMMAD AL-GAMUDI.

Malaysia: 18 Templesi Lane, Airport Residential Area, POB 16033, Accra; tel. (21) 763691; fax (21) 764910; e-mail mwaccra@africaonline.com.gh; Chargé d'affaires a.i. YAACOB AWANG CHIK.

Mali: 1st Bungalow, Liberia Rd, Airport Residential Area, POB 1121, Accra; tel. and fax (21) 666942; Ambassador MUPHTAH AG HAIRY.

Netherlands: 89 Liberation Rd, Ako Adjei Interchange, POB CT1647, Accra; tel. (21) 214350; fax (21) 773655; e-mail acc@minbuza.nl; internet www.ambaccra.nl; Ambassador LIDI REMMELZWAAL.

Niger: E104/3 Independence Ave, POB 2685, Accra; tel. (21) 224962; fax (21) 229011; Ambassador ABDOULKARIMOU SEINI.

Nigeria: 5 Tito Ave, POB 1548, Accra; tel. (21) 776158; fax (21) 774395; High Commissioner OLUTUNGI KOLAPO.

Russia: 856/1 Ring Rd East, 13 Lane, POB 1634, Accra; tel. (21) 775611; fax (21) 772699; e-mail russia@4u.com.gh; internet www.ghana.mid.ru; Ambassador ANDREY V. POKROVSKIY.

Sierra Leone: 83A Senchi St, Airport Residential Area, POB 55, Cantonments, Accra; tel. (21) 769190; fax (21) 769189; e-mail slhc@ighmail.com; High Commissioner MOKOWA ADU-GYAMFI.

South Africa: 10 Klotey Cres., Labone North, POB 298, Accra; tel. (21) 762380; fax (21) 762381; e-mail sahcgh@africaonline.com.gh; High Commissioner Dr R. S. MOLEKANE.

Spain: Drake Ave Extension, Airport Residential Area, PMB KA44, Accra; tel. (21) 774004; fax (21) 776217; e-mail emb.accra@mae.es; Ambassador JORGE MONTEALEGRE BUIRE.

Switzerland: Kanda Highway, North Ridge, POB 359, Accra; tel. (21) 228125; fax (21) 223583; e-mail acc.vertretung@eda.admin.ch; internet www.eda.admin.ch/accra; Ambassador GEORG ZUBLER.

Togo: Togo House, near Cantonments Circle, POB C120, Accra; tel. (21) 777950; fax (21) 765659; e-mail togamba@ighmail.com; Ambassador JEAN-PIERRE GBIKPI-BENISSAN.

United Kingdom: Osu Link, off Gamel Abdul Nasser Ave, POB 296, Accra; tel. and fax (21) 7010655; e-mail high.commission.accra@fco.gov.uk; internet www.britishhighcommission.gov.uk/ghana; High Commissioner Dr NICHOLAS WESTCOTT.

USA: Ring Rd East, POB 194, Accra; tel. (21) 775348; fax (21) 776008; e-mail prsaccra@pd.state.gov; internet accra.usembassy.gov; Ambassador PAMELA ETHEL BRIDGEWATER.

Judicial System

The civil law in force in Ghana is based on the Common Law, doctrines of equity and general statutes which were in force in England in 1874, as modified by subsequent Ordinances. Ghanaian customary law is, however, the basis of most personal, domestic and contractual relationships. Criminal Law is based on the Criminal Procedure Code, 1960, derived from English Criminal Law, and since amended. The Superior Court of Judicature comprises a Supreme Court, a Court of Appeal, a High Court and a Regional Tribunal; Inferior Courts include Circuit Courts, Circuit Tribunals, Community Tribunals and such other Courts as may be designated by law. In 2001 'fast-track' court procedures were established to accelerate the delivery of justice.

Supreme Court

Consists of the Chief Justice and not fewer than nine other Justices. It is the final court of appeal in Ghana and has jurisdiction in matters relating to the enforcement or interpretation of the Constitution.

Chief Justice: GEORGINA WOOD.

Court of Appeal: Consists of the Chief Justice and not fewer than five Judges of the Court of Appeal. It has jurisdiction to hear and determine appeals from any judgment, decree or order of the High Court.

High Court: Comprises the Chief Justice and not fewer than 12 Justices of the High Court. It exercises original jurisdiction in all matters, civil and criminal, other than those for offences involving treason. Trial by jury is practised in criminal cases in Ghana and the Criminal Procedure Code, 1960, provides that all trials on indictment shall be by a jury or with the aid of Assessors.

Circuit Courts: Exercise original jurisdiction in civil matters where the amount involved does not exceed 100,000 cedis. They also have jurisdiction with regard to the guardianship and custody of infants, and original jurisdiction in all criminal cases, except offences where the maximum punishment is death or the offence of treason. They have appellate jurisdiction from decisions of any District Court situated within their respective circuits.

District Courts: To each magisterial district is assigned at least one District Magistrate who has original jurisdiction to try civil suits in which the amount involved does not exceed 50,000 cedis. District Magistrates also have jurisdiction to deal with all criminal cases, except first-degree felonies, and commit cases of a more serious nature to either the Circuit Court or the High Court. A Grade I District Court can impose a fine not exceeding 1,000 cedis and sentences of imprisonment of up to two years and a Grade II District Court may impose a fine not exceeding 500 cedis and a sentence of imprisonment of up to 12 months. A District Court has no appellate jurisdiction, except in rent matters under the Rent Act.

Juvenile Courts: Jurisdiction in cases involving persons under 17 years of age, except where the juvenile is charged jointly with an adult. The Courts comprise a Chairman, who must be either the District Magistrate or a lawyer, and not fewer than two other members appointed by the Chief Justice in consultation with the Judicial Council. The Juvenile Courts can make orders as to the protection and supervision of a neglected child and can negotiate with parents to secure the good behaviour of a child.

National Public Tribunal: Considers appeals from the Regional Public Tribunals. Its decisions are final and are not subject to any further appeal. The Tribunal consists of at least three members and not more than five, one of whom acts as Chairman.

Regional Public Tribunals: Hears criminal cases relating to prices, rent or exchange control, theft, fraud, forgery, corruption or any offence which may be referred to them by the Provisional National Defence Council.

Special Military Tribunal: Hears criminal cases involving members of the armed forces. It consists of between five and seven members.

Attorney-General: JOSEPH GHARTEY.

Religion

According to the 2000 census, 69% of the population were Christians and 15.6% Muslims, while 6.9% followed indigenious beliefs.

CHRISTIANITY

Christian Council of Ghana: POB GP919, Accra; tel. (21) 776678; fax (21) 776725; e-mail christiancouncil@4u.com.gh; f. 1929; advisory body comprising 16 mem. churches and 2 affiliate Christian orgs (2005); Gen. Sec. Rev. Dr FRED DEEGBE.

The Anglican Communion

Anglicans in Ghana are adherents of the Church of the Province of West Africa, comprising 13 dioceses and a missionary region, of which nine are in Ghana.

Archbishop of the Province of West Africa and Bishop of Ho: Most Rev. ROBERT GARSHONG ALLOTEY OKINE, Bishop's Lodge, BT A167, Betom, POB 980, Koforidua; tel. (81) 22329; fax (21) 669125; e-mail archbishopwa@yahoo.com.

Bishop of Accra: Rt Rev. JUSTICE OFEI AKROFI, Bishopscourt, POB 8, Accra; tel. (21) 662292; fax (21) 669125; e-mail cpwa@ghana.com.

Bishop of Cape Coast: Rt Rev. DANIEL ALLOTEY, Bishopscourt, POB A233, Adisadel Estates, Cape Coast; tel. (42) 32502; fax (42) 32637.

Bishop of Koforidua: Rt Rev. FRANCIS QUASHIE, POB 980, Koforidua; tel. (81) 22329; fax (81) 22060; e-mail cpwa_gh@yahoo.com; internet koforidua.org.

Bishop of Kumasi: Rt Rev. DANIEL YINKAH SAFO, Bishop's Office, St Cyprian's Ave, POB 144, Kumasi; tel. and fax (51) 24117; e-mail kumangli@africaonline.com.gh.

Bishop of Sekondi: Rt Rev. JOHN KWAMINA OTOO, POB 85, Sekondi; tel. (31) 669125.

Bishop of Sunyani: Rt Rev. THOMAS AMPAH BRIENT, Bishop's House, POB 23, Sunyani, BA; tel. (61) 27213; fax (61) 27203; e-mail deegyab@ighmail.com.

Bishop of Tamale: Rt Rev. EMMANUEL ARONGO, POB 110, Tamale NR; tel. (71) 22906; fax (71) 22849.

The Roman Catholic Church

Ghana comprises four archdioceses and 14 dioceses. At 31 December 2005 there were 2,730,724 adherents in the country, equivalent to 12.7% of the total population.

Ghana Bishops' Conference

National Catholic Secretariat, POB 9712, Airport, Accra; tel. (21) 500491; fax (21) 500493; e-mail dscncs@africaonline.com.gh.
f. 1960; Pres. Rt Rev. LUCAS ABADAMLOORA APPIAH-TURKSON (Archbishop of Cape Coast).

Archbishop of Accra: Most Rev. GABRIEL CHARLES PALMER-BUCKLE, Chancery Office, POB 247, Accra; tel. (21) 222728; fax (21) 231619.

Archbishop of Cape Coast: Cardinal PETER KODWO APPIAH-TURKSON, Archbishop's House, POB 112, Cape Coast; tel. (42) 33471; fax (42) 33473; e-mail archcape@ghanacbc.com.

Archbishop of Kumasi: Most Rev. PETER KWASI SARPONG, POB 99, Kumasi; tel. (51) 24012; fax (51) 29395; e-mail cadiokum@ghana.com.

Archbishop of Tamale: Most Rev. GREGORY EBO KPIEBAYA, Archbishop's House, Gumbehini Rd, POB 42, Tamale; tel. and fax (71) 22425; e-mail tamdio2@yahoo.co.uk.

Other Christian Churches

African Methodist Episcopal Zion Church: POB MP522, Mamprobi, Accra; tel. (21) 669200; f. 1898; Pres. Rt Rev. WARREN M. BROWN.

Christian Methodist Episcopal Church: POB AN 7639, Accra; tel. (244) 630267; internet www.cmetenth.org/Ghana%20Regional%20Conference.htm; Pres. KENNETH W. CARTER; Mission Supervisor Rev. ADJEI K. LAWSON.

Church of Pentecost: POB 2194 Accra; tel. and fax (21) 772193; e-mail cophq@ghana.com; internet www1.thechurchofpentecost.com; Chair. Apostle M. K. NTUMY; Gen.-Sec. Apostle ALFRED KODUAH; 1,021,856 mems (July 2002).

Evangelical-Lutheran Church of Ghana: POB KN197, Kaneshie, Accra; tel. (21) 223487; fax (21) 220947; e-mail elcga@africaonline.com.gh; Pres. Rt Rev. Dr PAUL KOFI FYNN; 26,000 mems.

Evangelical-Presbyterian Church of Ghana: 19 Main St, Tesano, PMB, Accra-North; tel. (21) 220381; fax (21) 233173; f. 1847; Moderator Rev. Dr LIVINGSTON BUAMA; 295,000 mems.

Ghana Baptist Convention: PMB, Kumasi; tel. (51) 25215; fax (51) 28592; e-mail mail@gbconvention.org; internet www.gbconvention.org; f. 1963; Pres. Rev. Dr KOJO OSEI-WUSUH; Sec. Rev. KOJO AMO; 65,000 mems.

Ghana Mennonite Church: POB 5485, Accra; fax (21) 220589; f. 1957; Moderator Rev. THEOPHILUS TETTEH; Sec. JOHN ADETA; 5,000 mems.

Ghana Union Conference of Seventh-day Adventists: POB GP1016, Accra; tel. (21) 223720; fax (21) 227024; e-mail salarmie@compuserve.com; f. 1943; Pres. Pastor P. O. MENSAH; Sec. Pastor SAMUEL A. LARMIE; 23,700 mems.

Methodist Church of Ghana: E252/2, Liberia Rd, POB 403, Accra; tel. (21) 228120; fax (21) 227008; Pres. Rt Rev. Dr SAMUEL ASANTE ANTWI; Sec. Rev. MACLEAN AGYIRI KUMI; 341,000 mems.

Presbyterian Church of Ghana: POB 106, Accra; tel. (21) 662511; fax (21) 665594; f. 1828; Moderator Rt Rev. YAW FRIMPONG-MANSON; Sec. Rev. Dr D. N. A. KPOBI; 422,500 mems.

The African Methodist Episcopal Church, the Christ Reformed Church, the F"Eden Church, the Gospel Revival Church of God and the Religious Society of Friends (Quakers) are also active in Ghana.

ISLAM

In 2000 some 15.6% of the population of Ghana were Muslims, with a particularly large concentration in the Northern Region. The majority are Malikees.

Coalition of Muslim Organizations (COMOG): Accra; Pres. Alhaji Maj. MOHAMMED EASAH.

Ghana Muslim Representative Council: Accra.

Chief Imam: Sheikh USMAN NUHU SHARABUTU.

BAHÁ'Í FAITH

National Spiritual Assembly: POB 7098, Accra-North; tel. (21) 222127; e-mail bahaigh@africaonline.com.gh; Sec. KOBINA AMISSAH FYNN.

The Press

DAILY NEWSPAPERS

Accra Daily Mail: POB CT4910, Cantonments, Accra; e-mail mike@accra-mail.com; internet www.accra-mail.com; Man. Editor A.R. HARUNA ATTAH.

The Daily Dispatch: 1 Dade Walk, North Labone, POB C1945, Cantonments, Accra; tel. (21) 763339; e-mail ephson@usa.net; Editor BEN EPHSON.

Daily Graphic: Graphic Communications Group Ltd, POB 742, Accra; tel. (21) 684001; fax (21) 234754; e-mail info@graphicghana.com; internet www.graphicghana.com; f. 1950; state-owned; Editor YAW BOADU AYEBOAFO; circ. 100,000.

Daily Guide: Accra; owned by Western Publications Ltd; Editor GINA BLAY.

GHANA	*Directory*

The Ghanaian Times: New Times Corpn, Ring Rd West, POB 2638, Accra; tel. (21) 228282; fax (21) 229398; e-mail newtimes@ghana.com; f. 1958; state-owned; Editor AJOA YEBOAH-AFARI (acting); circ. 45,000.

The Telescope: Takoradi; f. 2005; Editor LOUIS HENRY DANSO.

PERIODICALS
Thrice Weekly

Ghanaian Chronicle: PMB, Accra-North; tel. (21) 222319; fax (21) 232608; e-mail chronicl@africaonline.com.gh; internet www.ghanaian-chronicle.com; Acting Editor JONATHAN ATO KOBBIE; circ. 60,000.

The Independent: Clear Type Press Bldg Complex, off Graphic Rd, POB 4031, Accra; tel. and fax (21) 661091; f. 1989; Editor ANDREW ARTHUR.

Network Herald: NBS Multimedia, PMB, OSU, Accra; tel. (21) 701184; fax (21) 762173; e-mail support@ghana.com; internet www.networkherald.gh; f. 2001; Editor ELVIS QUARSHIE.

Bi-Weekly

Ghana Palaver: Palaver Publications, POB WJ317, Wejia, Accra; tel. (21) 850495; e-mail editor@ghana-palaver.com; internet www.ghana-palaver.com; f. 1994; Editor JOJO BRUCE QUANSAH.

The Ghanaian Lens: Accra; Editor KOBBY FIAGBE.

The Ghanaian Voice: Newstop Publications, POB 514, Mamprobi, Accra; tel. (21) 324644; fax (21) 314939; Editor CHRISTIANA ANSAH; circ. 100,000.

Weekly

Business and Financial Times: POB CT16, Cantonments, Accra; tel. and fax (21) 223334; f. 1989; Editor JOHN HANSON; circ. 20,000.

The Crusading Guide: POB 8523, Accra-North; tel. (21) 763339; fax (21) 761541; internet www.ghanaweb.com/CrusadingGuide; Editor KWEKU BAAKO, Jr.

Free Press: Tommy Thompson Books Ltd, POB 6492, Accra; tel. (21) 225994; independent; Editor FRANK BOAHENE.

Ghana Life: Ghana Life Publications, POB 11337, Accra; tel. (21) 229835; Editor NIKKI BOA-AMPONSEM.

Ghana Market Watch: Accra; internet www.ghanamarketwatch.com; f. 2006; financial; CEO AMOS DOTSE.

Graphic Showbiz: Graphic Communications Group Ltd, POB 742, Accra; tel. (21) 228911; fax (21) 234754; e-mail info@graphicghana.com; internet www.graphicghana.info; state-owned; Editor NANA-BANYIN DADSON.

Graphic Sports: Graphic Communications Group Ltd, POB 742, Accra; tel. (21) 228911; fax (21) 234754; e-mail info@graphicghana.com; state-owned; Editor FELIX ABAYATEYE; circ. 60,000.

The Guide: Western Publications Ltd, POB 8253, Accra-North; tel. (21) 232760; Editor KWEKU BAAKO, Jr.

Gye Nyame Concord: Accra; internet www.ghanaweb.com/concord.

The Heritage: POB AD676, Arts Center, Accra; tel. (21) 236051; fax (21) 237156; e-mail heritagenewspaper@yahoo.co.uk; internet www.theheritagenews.com; Chair. STEPHEN OWUSU; Editor A. C. OHENE.

High Street Journal: POB 7974, Accra-North; tel. (21) 239835; fax (21) 239837; e-mail hsjaccra@ghana.com; Editor SHEIKH ABUTIATE.

The Mirror: Graphic Communications Group Ltd, POB 742, Accra; tel. (21) 228911; fax (21) 234754; e-mail info@graphicghana.com; internet www.graphicghana.info; f. 1953; state-owned; Sat.; Editor E. N. O. PROVENCAL; circ. 90,000.

The National Democrat: Democrat Publications, POB 13605, Accra; Editor ELLIOT FELIX OHENE.

Public Agenda: P. A. Communications, POB 5564, Accra-North; tel. (21) 238821; fax (21) 231687; e-mail isodec@ghana.com; f. 1994; Editor YAO GRAHAM; circ. 12,000.

The Standard: Standard Newspapers & Magazines Ltd, POB KA 9712, Accra; tel. (21) 513537; fax (21) 500493; e-mail snam.ncs@ghanacbc.org; internet www.ghanacbc.org; Roman Catholic; Editor ISAAC FRITZ ANDOH; circ. 10,000.

Statesman: Kinesic Communications, POB 846, Accra; tel. and fax (21) 233242; official publ. of the New Patriotic Party; Editor GABBY ASARE OTCHERE-DARKO.

The Vanguard: Accra; Editor OSBERT LARTEY.

The Weekend: Newstop Publications, POB 514, Mamprobi, Accra; tel. (21) 324644; fax (21) 314939; Editor EMMANUEL YARTEY; circ. 40,000.

Weekly Insight: Militant Publications Ltd, POB K272, Accra New Town, Accra; tel. (21) 660148; fax (21) 774338; e-mail insight93@yahoo.com; f. 1993; independent; English; Editor KWESI PRATT, Jr.

Weekly Spectator: New Times Corpn, Ring Rd West, POB 2638, Accra; tel. (21) 228282; fax (21) 229398; state-owned; f. 1963; Sun.; Editor WILLIE DONKOR; circ. 165,000.

Other

African Observer: POB 1171, Kaneshie, Accra; tel. (21) 231459; bi-monthly; Editor STEVE MALLORY.

The African Woman Magazine: Ring Rd West, POB AN 15064, Accra; tel. and fax (21) 241636; e-mail mail@theafricanwoman.com; internet www.theafricanwoman.com; f. 1957; monthly; Ed. NII ADUMUAH ORGLE.

AGI Newsletter: c/o Asscn of Ghana Industries, POB 8624, Accra-North; tel. (21) 779023; e-mail agi@agighana.org; internet www.agighana.org; f. 1974; monthly; Editor CARLO HEY; circ. 1,500.

AGOO: Newstop Publications, POB 514, Mamprobi, Accra; tel. (21) 324644; fax (21) 314939; monthly; lifestyle magazine; Publr KOJO BONSU.

Armed Forces News: General Headquarters, Directorate of Public Relations, Burma Camp, Accra; tel. (21) 776111; f. 1966; quarterly; Editor ADOTEY ANKRAH-HOFFMAN; circ. 4,000.

Boxing and Football Illustrated: POB 8392, Accra; f. 1976; monthly; Editor NANA O. AMPOMAH; circ. 10,000.

Business and Financial Concord: Sammy Tech Consult Enterprise, POB 5677, Accra-North; tel. (21) 232446; fortnightly; Editor KWABENA RICHARDSON.

Business Watch: Sulton Bridge Co Ltd, POB C3447, Cantonments, Accra; tel. (21) 233293; monthly.

Christian Messenger: Presbyterian Book Depot Bldg, POB 3075, Accra; tel. and fax (21) 663124; e-mail danbentil@yahoo.com; f. 1883; English-language; every two weeks; quarterly; Editor GEORGE MARTINSON; circ. 40,000.

Ghana Journal of Science: Ghana Science Asscn, POB 7, Legon; tel. (21) 500253; monthly; Editor Dr A. K. AHAFIA.

Ghana Official News Bulletin: Information Services Dept, POB 745, Accra; English; political, economic, investment and cultural affairs.

Ghana Review International (GRi): POB GP14307, Accra; tel. (21) 677437; fax (21) 677438; e-mail accra@ghanareview.com; internet www.ghanareview.com; publishes in Accra, London and New York; CEO NANA OTUO ACHEAMPONG; print circ. 100,000.

Ideal Woman (Obaa Sima): POB 5737, Accra; tel. (21) 221399; f. 1971; monthly; Editor KATE ABBAM.

Insight and Opinion: POB 5446, Accra; quarterly; Editorial Sec. W. B. OHENE.

Legon Observer: POB 11, Legon, Accra; fax (21) 774338; f. 1966; publ. by Legon Society on National Affairs; fortnightly; Chair. J. A. DADSON; Editor EBOW DANIEL.

Police News: Police HQ, Accra; monthly; Editor S. S. APPIAH; circ. 20,000.

The Post: Ghana Information Services, POB 745, Accra; tel. (21) 228011; f. 1980; monthly; current affairs and analysis; circ. 25,000.

Radio and TV Times: Ghana Broadcasting Corpn, Broadcasting House, POB 18167, Accra; tel. (21) 508927; fax (21) 773612; f. 1960; quarterly; Editor SAM THOMPSON; circ. 5,000.

Students World: POB M18, Accra; tel. (21) 774248; fax (21) 778715; e-mail afram@wwwplus.co.za; f. 1974; monthly; educational; Man. Editor ERIC OFEI; circ. 10,000.

The Teacher: Ghana National Asscn of Teachers, POB 209, Accra; tel. (21) 221515; fax (21) 226286; f. 1931; quarterly; circ. 30,000.

Truth and Life: Gift Publications, POB 11337, Accra-North; monthly; Editor Pastor KOBENA CHARM.

Uneek: POB 230, Achimota, Accra; tel. (21) 543853; fax (21) 231355; e-mail info@uneekmagazine.com; internet www.uneekmagazine.com; f. 1998; monthly; leisure, culture; CEO and Editor FRANCIS ADAMS.

The Watchman: Watchman Gospel Ministry, POB GP4521, Accra; tel. and fax (21) 500631; e-mail watchmannewspaper@yahoo.com; f. 1986; Christian news; fortnightly; Pres. and CEO DIVINE P. KUMAH; Chair. Dr E. K. OPUNI; circ. 5,000.

Other newspapers include **The Catalyst**, **The Crystal Clear Lens**, **The Enquirer** and **Searchlight**. There are also internet-based news sites, including **Ghana Today**, at www.ghanatoday.com and **ThisWeekGhana**, at www.thisweekghana.com.

NEWS AGENCY

Ghana News Agency: POB 2118, Accra; tel. (21) 215135; fax (21) 669841; e-mail ghnews@ncs.com.gh; f. 1957; Gen. Man. SAM B. QUAICOE; 10 regional offices and 110 district offices.

GHANA
Directory

PRESS ASSOCIATION

Ghana Journalists' Association: POB 4636, Accra; tel. (21) 234692; fax (21) 234694; e-mail info@ghanamedia.com; Pres. RANSFORD TETTEH.

Publishers

Advent Press: Osu La Rd, POB 0102, Osu, Accra; tel. (21) 777861; fax (21) 775327; e-mail eaokpoti@ghana.com; f. 1937; publishing arm of the Ghana Union Conference of Seventh-day Adventists; Gen. Man. EMMANUEL C. TETTEH.

Adwinsa Publications (Ghana) Ltd: Advance Press Bldg, 3rd Floor, School Rd, POB 92, Legon Accra; tel. and fax (21) 501515; e-mail adwinsa@yahoo.com; internet www.adwinsa.8k.com; f. 1977; general, educational; Man. Dir KWABENA AMPONSAH.

Afram Publications: C 184/22 Midway Lane, Abofu-Achimota, POB M18, Accra; tel. (21) 412561; e-mail aframpub@pubchgh.com; internet www.aframpublications.com.gh; f. 1973; textbooks and general; Man. Dir ERIC OFEI.

Africa Christian Press: POB 30, Achimota, Accra; tel. (21) 244147; fax (21) 220271; e-mail acpbooks@ghana.com; f. 1964; religious, fiction, theology, children's, leadership; Gen. Man. RICHARD A. B. CRABBE.

Allgoodbooks Ltd: POB AN10416, Accra-North; tel. (21) 664294; fax (21) 665629; e-mail allgoodbooks@hotmail.com; f. 1968; children's; Man. Dir MARY ASIRIFI.

Asempa Publishers: POB GP919, Accra; tel. (21) 233084; fax (21) 235140; e-mail asempa@ghana.com; f. 1970; religion, social issues, African music, fiction, children's; Gen. Man. SARAH O. APRONTI.

Black Mask Ltd: POB CT770, Cantonments, Accra; tel. (21) 234577; f. 1979; textbooks, plays, novels, handicrafts; Man. Dir YAW OWUSU ASANTE.

Catholic Book Centre: North Liberia Rd, POB 3285, Accra; tel. (21) 226651; fax (21) 237727.

Editorial and Publishing Services: POB 5743, Accra; general, reference; Man. Dir M. DANQUAH.

Educational Press and Manufacturers Ltd: POB 9184, Airport-Accra; tel. (21) 220395; f. 1975; textbooks, children's; Man. G. K. KODUA.

Encyclopaedia Africana Project: POB 2797, Accra; tel. (21) 776939; fax (21) 779228; e-mail eap@africaonline.com.gh; internet encyclopaediaafricana.org; f. 1962; reference; Dir GRACE BANSA.

Frank Publishing Ltd: POB MB414, Accra; tel. (21) 240711; f. 1976; secondary school textbooks; Man. Dir FRANCIS K. DZOKOTO.

Ghana Publishing Corpn: POB 124, Greater Accra.

  Ghana Publishing Corpn—Assembly Press Ltd: POB 124, Accra; tel. (21) 664338; fax (21) 664330; f. 1965; state-owned; textbooks and general fiction and non-fiction; Man. Dir F. K. NYARKO.

Ghana Universities Press: POB GP4219, Accra; tel. (21) 513401; fax (21) 513402; f. 1962; scholarly, academic and general and textbooks; CEO Dr K. M. GANU.

Golden Wings Publications: 26 Mantse Kwao St, POB 1337, Accra; educational and children's; Man. Editor GREGORY ANKRAH.

Sam-Woode Ltd: A.979/15 Dansoman High St, POB 12719, Accra-North; tel. (21) 305287; fax (21) 310482; e-mail samwoode@ghana.com; f. 1984; educational and children's; Chair. KWESI SAM-WOODE.

Sedco Publishing Ltd: Sedco House, 5 Tabon St, North Ridge, POB 2051, Accra; tel. (21) 221332; fax (21) 220107; e-mail sedco@africaonline.com.gh; f. 1975; educational; Chair. COURAGE K. SEGBAWU; Man. Dir FRANK SEGBAWU.

Sub-Saharan Publishers: PO Box 358, Legon, Accra; tel. and fax (21) 233371; e-mail sub-saharan@ighmail.com; Man. Dir AKOSS OFORI-MENSAH.

Unimax Macmillan Ltd: 42 Ring Rd South Industrial Area, POB 10722, Accra-North; tel. (21) 227443; fax (21) 225215; e-mail info@unimacmillan.com; internet www.unimacmillan.com; representative of Macmillan UK; atlases, educational and children's; Man. Dir EDWARD ADDO.

Waterville Publishing House: 4 Thorpe Rd, POB 195, Accra; tel. (21) 663124; f. 1963; general fiction and non-fiction, textbooks, paperbacks, Africana; Man. Dir E. ANIM-ANSAH.

Woeli Publishing Services: POB NT601, Accra New Town; tel. and fax (21) 229294; e-mail woeli@libr.ug.edu.gh; f. 1984; children's, fiction, academic; Dir W. A. DEKUTSEY.

PUBLISHERS' ASSOCIATIONS

Ghana Book Development Council: POB M430, Accra; tel. (21) 229178; f. 1975; govt-financed agency; promotes and co-ordinates writing, production and distribution of books; Exec. Dir D. A. NIMAKO.

Ghana Book Publishers' Association (GBPA): POB LT471, Laterbiokorshie, Accra; tel. (21) 229178; fax (21) 810641; e-mail stevebrob@yahoo.co.uk; f. 1976; Exec. Sec. STEPHEN BROBBEY.

Private Newspaper Publishers' Association of Ghana (PRINPAG): POB 125, Darkuman, Accra; Chair. NANA KOFI KOOMSON; Gen. Sec. K. AGYEMANG DUAH.

Broadcasting and Communications

TELECOMMUNICATIONS

Regulatory Authority

National Communication Authority (NCA): 1 Rangoon Close, POB 1568, Cantonments, Accra; tel. (21) 776621; fax (21) 763449; e-mail nca@nca.org.gh; internet www.nca.org.gh; f. 1996; regulatory body; Chair. JUDE ARTHUR; Dir-Gen. BERNARD AIDOO FORSON.

Major Telecommunications Companies

Ghana Telecom (GT): Telecom House, nr Kwame Nkrumah Circle, Accra-North; tel. (21) 200200; fax (21) 221002; e-mail info@ghanatel.net; internet www.ghanatelecom.com.gh; f. 1995; govt-owned; operates mobile cellular, fixed line networks and data services; Chair. NANA ANTWI BOASIAKO; CEO DICKSON ODURO-NYANING.

  gtOnetouch: Telecom House, nr Kwame Nkrumah Circle, Accra-North; tel. (21) 910128; fax (21) 253541; internet www.onetouch.com.gh; mobile cellular telephone provider; 1.0m. subscribers (Jan. 2007).

Millicom Ghana Ltd: Millicom Place, Barnes Rd, PMB 100, Accra; tel. (27) 7551000; fax (27) 7503999; e-mail info@tigo.com.gh; internet www.tigo.com.gh; f. 1990; mobile cellular telephone services through the network Tigo; Man. Dir GARETH TOWNLEY; 1.21m. subscribers (Dec. 2006).

Scancom (MTN): Auto Parts Bldg, 41A Graphic Rd, South Industrial Area, POB 281, International Trade Fair Lane, Accra; tel. (24) 4300000; fax (21) 231974; internet www.areeba.com.gh; f. 1994; Ghana's largest mobile cellular telephone provider, through the network MTN (formerly Areeba); 100% owned by MTN (South Africa); CEO BRETT GOSCHEN; 2.59m. subscribers (Dec. 2006).

Western Telesystems Co (WESTEL): Accra; f. 1997; state-owned; fixed line operator.

BROADCASTING

There are internal radio broadcasts in English, Akan, Dagbani, Ewe, Ga, Hausa and Nzema, and an external service in English and French. There are three transmitting stations, with a number of relay stations. The Ghana Broadcasting Corporation operates two national networks, Radio 1 and Radio 2, which broadcast from Accra, and four regional FM stations. In late 2004 128 radio stations and 24 television stations were registered in Ghana.

Ghana Broadcasting Corpn (GBC): Broadcasting House, Ring Rd Central, Kanda, POB 1633, Accra; tel. and fax (21) 768975; e-mail gbc@ghana.com; internet www.gbcghana.com; f. 1935; Acting Dir-Gen. YAW OWUSU-ADDO; Dir of TV KOFI BUCKNOR; Dir of Radio THEO AGBAM.

CitiFM: 11 Tettey Loop, Adabraka, Accra; tel. (21) 226171; fax (21) 224043; e-mail info@citifmonline.com; internet www.citifmonline.com; Man. Dir SAMUEL ATTA MENSAH.

Joy FM: 355 Faanofa St, Kokomlemle, POB 17202, Accra; tel. (21) 701199; fax (21) 224405; e-mail info@myjoyonline.com; internet www.myjoyonline.com; f. 1995; news, information and music broadcasts; Dir KWESI TWUM.

Metro TV: POB C1609, Cantonments, Accra; tel. (21) 765701; fax (21) 765702; e-mail webdesign@metrotv.com.gh; internet www.metrotv.com.gh.

Radio Ada: POB KA9482, Accra; tel. (21) 500907; fax (21) 516442; e-mail radioada@kalssinn.net; f. 1998; community broadcasts in Dangme; Dirs ALEX QUARMYNE, WILNA QUARMYNE.

Radio Gold FM: POB 17298, Accra; tel. (22) 779404; fax (22) 300284; Man. Dir BAFFOE BONNIE.

Sky Broadcasting Co, Ltd: 45 Water Rd, Kanda Overpass, North Ridge, POB CT3850, Cantonments, Accra; tel. (21) 225716; fax (21) 221983; e-mail vayiku@yahoo.com; internet www.spirit.fm; f. 2000; Chief Operations Officer VERONICA AYIKU; Gen. Man. ANDY GLOVER.

TV3: 12th Rd, Kanda, (opposite French embassy), Accra; tel. (21) 763458; fax (21) 763450; e-mail info@tv3.com.gh; internet www.tv3

GHANA

.com.gh; f. 1997; private television station; progamming in English and local languages; CEO SYED AHMAD ZAIDI SYED AKIL.

Vibe FM: Pyramid House, 3rd Floor, Ring Rd Central, Accra; internet www.vibefm.com.gh; educational; CEO MIKE COOKE.

Finance

(cap. = capital; res = reserves; dep. = deposits; m. = million; br(s). = branch(es); amounts in cedis)

BANKING

The commercial banking sector comprised 10 commercial banks, three development banks, five merchant banks and five foreign banks in 2004. There were also 115 rural banks and several non-banking financial institutions.

Central Bank

Bank of Ghana: 1 Thorpe Rd, POB 2674, Accra; tel. (21) 666902; fax (21) 662996; e-mail bogsecretary@bog.gov.gh; internet www.bog.gov.gh; f. 1957; bank of issue; cap. 100,000m., res 706,657m., dep. 16,642,274m. (Dec. 2004); Gov. PAUL A. ACQUAH.

Commercial Banks

Amalgamated Bank Ltd: 131–3 Farrar Ave, Cantonments, POB CT1541, Accra; tel. (21) 249690; fax (21) 249697; e-mail amalbank@amalbank.com.gh; internet www.amalbank.com.gh; f. 1999; Man. Dir WELBECK ABRA-APPIAH.

Fidelity Bank: Ridge Towers, PMB 43, Cantonments, Accra; tel. (21) 214490; fax (21) 678868; internet www.fidelitybank.com.gh; f. 2006; CEO EDWARD EFFAH.

Ghana Commercial Bank Ltd: Thorpe Rd, POB 134, Accra; tel. (21) 664914; fax (21) 662168; e-mail gcbmail@gcb.com.gh; internet www.gcb.com.gh; f. 1953; 46.8% state-owned; cap. 20,000m., res 5,607,047m., dep. 4,265,733m. (Dec. 2004); Chair. K. G. OSEI-BONSU; Man. Dir LAWRENCE NEWTON ADU-MANTE; 131 brs.

NTHC Ltd: Martco House, Okai Mensah Link, off Kwame Nkrumah Ave, POB 9563, Adabraka, Accra; tel. (21) 238492; fax (21) 229975; e-mail nthc@ghana.com; internet www.nthcghana.com; fmrly National Trust Holding Co Ltd; f. 1976 to provide stockbrokerage services, asset management and financial advisory services; cap. 9,000m. (2001); Chair. BENJAMIN ADU-AMANKWA; Man. Dir Dr A. W. Q. BARNOR.

Prudential Bank Ltd: 8 Nima Ave, Ring Rd Central, PMB GPO, Accra; tel. (21) 781201; fax (21) 781210; e-mail prudential@ghana.com; internet www.prudentialbank-ghana.com; f. 1996; Exec. Chair. JOHN SACKAH ADDO; Man. Dir STEPHEN SEKYERE-ABANKWA; 9 brs.

The Trust Bank Ltd: Re-insurance House, 68 Kwame Nkrumah Ave, POB 1862, Accra; tel. (21) 240049; fax (21) 240059; e-mail trust@ttbgh.com; internet www.ttbgh.net; f. 1996; 35% owned by Banque Belgolaise (Belgium), 33% owned by the Social Security and National Insurance Trust; cap. 10,000m., res 61,469m., dep. 692,266m. (Dec. 2004); Chair. ALBERT OSEI; Man. Dir PAUL CARDOEN; 6 brs.

uniBank (Ghana) Ltd: Royal Castle Rd, POB AN15367, Kokomlemle, Accra; tel. (21) 253696; fax (21) 253695; e-mail info@unibankghana.com; internet www.unibankghana.com; f. 2001; Man. Dir JOSEPH N. B. TETTEH.

Development Banks

Agricultural Development Bank (ADB): Cedi House, Liberia Rd, POB 4191, Accra; tel. (21) 662758; fax (21) 662846; e-mail adbweb@agricbank.com; internet www.agricbank.com; f. 1965; 51.8% state-owned, 48.2% owned by Bank of Ghana; credit facilities for farmers and commercial banking; cap. and res 390,064.5m., dep. 968,713.0m. (Dec. 2002); Chair. PAUL S. M. KORANTENG; Man. Dir EDWARD BOAKYE-AGYEMANG; 32 brs.

National Investment Bank Ltd (NIB): 37 Kwame Nkrumah Ave, POB 3726, Accra; tel. (21) 661701; fax (21) 661730; e-mail info@nib-ghana.com; internet www.nib-ghana.com; f. 1963; 86.4% state-owned; provides long-term investment capital, jt venture promotion, consortium finance man. and commercial banking services; cap. 3,260m., surplus & res 166,598m., dep. 446,703m. (Dec. 2004); Man. Dir DANIEL CHARLES GYIMAH; 23 brs.

Merchant Banks

CAL Bank Ltd: 23 Independence Ave, POB 14596, Accra; tel. (21) 680068; fax (21) 680081; e-mail calbank@calbank-gh.com; internet www.calbank-gh.com; f. 1990; cap. 70,588m., res 88,474m., dep. 542,687m. (Dec. 2004); Chair. GEORGE VICTOR OKOH; Man. Dir FRANK BRAKO ADU, Jr.

Databank: 61 Barnse Rd, Adabraka, PMB, Ministries Post Office, Accra; tel. (21) 681389; fax (21) 681443; e-mail info@databankgroup.com; internet www.databankgroup.com; f. 1990; Exec. Chair. KEN OFORI-ATTA; Exec. Dir YOFI GRANT; 3 brs.

Ecobank Ghana Ltd (EBG): 19 7th Ave, Ridge West, PMB-GPO, Accra; tel. (21) 681148; fax (21) 680428; e-mail ecobankgh@ecobank.com; internet www.ecobank.com; f. 1989; 92.2% owned by Ecobank Transnational Inc (Togo, operating under the auspices of the Economic Community of West African States); cap. 70,000m., res 168,958m., dep. 1,959,689m. (Dec. 2004); Chair. EDWARD PATRICK LARBI GYAMPOH; 7 brs.

First Atlantic Merchant Bank Ltd: Atlantic Pl., 1 Seventh Ave, Ridge West, POB C1620, Cantonments, Accra; tel. (21) 682203; fax (21) 479245; e-mail info@firstatlanticbank.com.gh; internet www.firstatlanticbank.com.gh; f. 1994; cap. 50,000.0m., res 18,167.1m., dep. 692,675.0m. (Dec. 2005); Chair. PHILIP OWUSU; Man. Dir JUDE ARTHUR.

Merchant Bank (Ghana) Ltd: Merban House, 44 Kwame Nkrumah Ave, POB 401, Accra; tel. (21) 666331; fax (21) 667305; e-mail merban_services@merbangh.com; internet www.merbankgh.com; f. 1972; cap. 70,000m., res 107,616m., dep. 1,490,187m. (Dec. 2005); Chair. SOLOMON KWAMI TETTEH; Man. Dir B. O. MANKWA; 9 brs.

Foreign Banks

Barclays Bank of Ghana Ltd (UK): Barclays House, High St, POB 2949, Accra; tel. (21) 664901; fax (21) 669254; e-mail barclays.ghana@barclays.com; internet www.africa.barclays.com/ghana.htm; f. 1971; 90% owned by Barclays Bank Plc; 10% owned by Govt of Ghana; res 389,484m., dep. 9,810m. (Dec. 2003); Chair. NANA WEREKO AMPEM II; Man. Dir K. QUANSAH; 26 brs.

Guaranty Trust Bank (Ghana) Ltd: 25A Castle Rd, Ambassadorial Area Ridge, Accra; tel. (21) 680662; fax (21) 662727; e-mail corporateaffairs@gtbghana.com; internet www.gtbghana.com; f. 2004; 70% owned by Guaranty Trust Bank Plc, 15% owned by Netherlands Development Finance Co (FMO), 15% owned by Alhaji Yusif Ibrahim; Man. Dir. DOLAPO OGUNDIMU.

International Commercial Bank (Ghana) Ltd (Taiwan): Meridian House, Ring Rd Central, PMB 16, Accra; tel. (21) 236133; fax (21) 238228; e-mail icb@icbank-gh.com; internet www.icbank-gh.com; f. 1996; cap. and res 31,205m., total assets 218,318m. (Dec. 2003); CEO LALGUDI KRISHNAMURTHY GANAPATHIRAMAN; 6 brs.

SG-SSB Bank Ltd: Ring Rd Central, POB 13119, Accra; tel. (21) 202001; fax (21) 248920; internet www.sg-ssb.com.gh; f. 1976 as Social Security Bank; 51.0% owned by Société Générale, France; cap. 70,000m., surplus and res 438,262m., dep. 2,367,711m. (Dec. 2006); Chair. GÉRALD LACAZE; Man. Dir ALAIN BELLISSARD; 37 brs.

Stanbic Bank Ghana: Valco Trust House, Castle Rd Ridge, POB CT2344, Cantonments, Accra; tel. (21) 234683; fax (21) 234685; e-mail stanbic@ghana.com; internet www.stanbic.com.gh; f. 1999; subsidiary of the Standard Bank of South Africa Ltd; cap. and res 14,981m., total assets 97,253m. (Dec. 2001); Chair. DENNIS W. KENNEDY; Man. Dir W. A. THOMAS; 1 br.

Standard Chartered Bank Ghana Ltd (UK): High St, POB 768, Accra; tel. (21) 664591; fax (21) 667751; internet www.standardchartered.com/gh; f. 1896 as Bank of British West Africa; cap. 131,313m., res 517,024m., dep. 3,718,469m. (Dec. 2005); Chair. PETER SULLIVAN; CEO VISHNU MOHAN; 18 brs.

Zenith Bank Ghana (Nigeria): Premier Towers, Liberia Rd, PMB CT393, Accra; tel. (21) 660075; fax (21) 660087; internet www.zenithbank.com.

Other banks include Fidelity Bank (www.fidelitybankplc.com).

STOCK EXCHANGE

Ghana Stock Exchange (GSE): Cedi House, 5th Floor, Liberia Rd, POB 1849, Accra; tel. (21) 669908; fax (21) 669913; e-mail info@gs.com.gh; internet www.gse.com.gh; f. 1990; 29 listed cos in early 2006; Chair. NORBERT KUDJAWU; Man. Dir KOFI YAMOAH.

INSURANCE

In 2004 there were 19 insurance companies.

Donewell Insurance Co Ltd: POB 2136, Accra; tel. (21) 760483; fax (21) 760484; e-mail donewell@africaonline.com.gh; internet www.donewellinsurance.com; f. 1992; Chair. JOHN S. ADDO.

Enterprise Insurance Co Ltd: Enterprise House, 11 Hight St, POB GP50, Accra; tel. (21) 666847; fax (21) 666186; e-mail quotes@eicghana.com; internet www.eicghana.net; f. 1972; Chair. TREVOR TREFGARNE; Man. Dir GEORGE OTOO.

Ghana Union Assurance Co Ltd: F828/1 Ring Rd East, POB 1322, Accra; tel. (21) 780627; fax (21) 780647; e-mail gua@ghanaunionassurancecompany.com; f. 1973; insurance underwriting; Man. Dir NANA AGYEI DUKU.

GHANA

Metropolitan Insurance Co Ltd: Caledonian House, Kojo Thompson Rd, POB GP20084, Accra; tel. (21) 220966; fax (21) 237872; e-mail met@metinsurance.com; internet www.metinsurance.com; f. 1991; Chair. ROBERT AHOMKA-LINDSAY; CEO KWAME-GAZO AGBENYADZIE.

Social Security and National Insurance Trust (SSNIT): Pension House, POB M149, Accra; tel. (21) 667731; e-mail infodesk@ssnit.org.gh; internet www.ssnit.com; f. 1972; covers over 650,000 contributors; Dir-Gen. KWASI OSEI.

Starlife Assurance Co Ltd: Accra; f. 2005; CEO Dr KWABENA DUFFUOR.

State Insurance Corpn of Ghana Ltd: 6 Kinbu Rd, POB 2363, Accra; tel. (21) 666961; fax (21) 662205; e-mail sic.info@ighmail.com; f. 1962; state-owned; privatization pending; all classes of insurance; Chair. LARRY ADJETEY; Man. Dir L. K. MOBILA.

Vanguard Assurance Co Ltd: Derby House, POB 1869, Accra; tel. (21) 666485; fax (21) 668610; e-mail vanguard@ghana.com; f. 1974; general accident, marine, motor and life insurance; Man. Dir A. E. B. DANQUAH; 7 brs.

Trade and Industry

GOVERNMENT AGENCIES

Divestiture Implementation Committee: F35, 5 Ring Rd East, North Labone, POB CT102, Cantonments, Accra; tel. (21) 772049; fax (21) 773126; e-mail dic@dic.com.gh; internet www.dic.com.gh; f. 1988; Chair. C. O. NYANOR; Exec. Sec. BENSON POKU-ADJEI.

Environmental Protection Agency (EPA): 91 Starlets Rd, POB M326, Accra; tel. (21) 664697; fax (21) 662690; e-mail epaed@africaonline.com.gh; internet www.epa.gov.gh; f. 1974; Exec. Dir JONATHAN A. ALLOTEY.

Export Development and Investment Fund (EDIF): POB M493, Accra; tel. (21) 570532; fax (21) 670536; e-mail info@edif.com.gh; f. 2000; part of Ministry of Trade, Industry, the Private Sector and Special Presidential Initiatives.

Forestry Commission of Ghana (FC): 4 3rd Ave Ridge, PMB 434, Accra; tel. (21) 221315; fax (21) 220818; e-mail info@hq.fcghana.com; internet www.fcghana.com; subsidiary of Ministry of Lands, Forestry and Mines; CEO JOHN OTOO.

Ghana Export Promotion Council (GEPC): Republic House, Tudu Rd, POB M146, Accra; tel. (21) 683153; fax (21) 677256; internet www.gepcghana.com; f. 1974; part of Ministry of Trade, Industry, the Private Sector and Special Presidential Initiatives; Exec. Sec. EDWARD BOATENG.

Ghana Free Zones Board: POB M626, Accra; tel. (21) 780534; fax (21) 785036; e-mail info@gfzb.com; internet www.gfzb.com; f. 1996; part of Ministry of Trade, Industry, the Private Sector and Special Presidential Initiatives; approves establishment of cos in export-processing zones; Exec.-Sec. E. DWOMOH APPIAH.

Ghana Heavy Equipment Ltd (GHEL): POB 1524, Accra; tel. (21) 680118; fax (21) 660276; fmrly subsidiary of Ghana National Trading Corpn; part of Ministry of Trade, Industry, the Private Sector and Special Presidential Initiatives; organizes exports, imports and production of heavy equipment; Chair. KOFI ASARE DARKWA POKU.

Ghana Investment Promotion Centre (GIPC): POB M193, Accra; tel. (21) 665125; fax (21) 663801; e-mail info@gipc.org.gh; internet www.gipc.org.gh; f. 1994; negotiates new investments, approves projects, registers foreign capital and decides extent of govt participation; Chair. PAUL VICTOR OBENG; Dir PETER ANKRAH.

Ghana Minerals Commission (MINCOM): 9 Switchback Rd Residential Area, POB M248, Cantonments, Accra; tel. (21) 772783; fax (21) 773324; e-mail mincom@mincomgh.org; internet www.mincomgh.org; f. 1986 to regulate and promote Ghana's mineral industry; CEO BENJAMIN NII AYI ARYEE.

Ghana National Petroleum Agency (NPA): Accra; internet www.energymin.gov.gh/npa.htm; f. 2005; oversees petroleum sector; Chair. Prof. IVAN ADDAE-MENSAH.

Ghana National Procurement Agency (GNPA): POB 15331, Accra; tel. (21) 228321; fax (21) 221049; e-mail info@gnpa-ghana.com; internet www.gnpa-ghana.com; f. 1976; part of Ministry of Trade, Industry, the Private Sector and Special Presidential Initiatives; imports essential commodities.

Ghana Standards Board: POB MB245, Accra; tel. (21) 500065; fax (21) 500092; e-mail gsbdir@ghanastandards.org; internet ghanastandards.org; f. 1967; establishes and promulgates standards; promotes standardization, industrial efficiency and devt and industrial welfare, health and safety; operates certification mark scheme; 402 mems; Chair. Prof. EMMANUEL KENNETH AGYEI; Exec. Dir ADU G. DARKWA.

Ghana Trade Fairs Co Ltd: Trade Fair Centre, POB 111, Accra; tel. (21) 776611; fax (21) 772012; e-mail gftc@ghana.com; f. 1989; part of Ministry of Trade, Industry, the Private Sector and Special Presidential Initiatives.

Ghana Trade and Investment Gateway Project (GHATIG): POB M47, Accra; tel. 663439; fax 773134; e-mail gateway1@ghana.com; promotes private investment and trade, infrastructural devt of free-trade zones and export-processing zones.

National Board for Small-scale Industries (NBSSI): POB M85, Accra; tel. (21) 668641; fax (21) 661394; e-mail nbssided@ghana.com; f. 1985; part of Ministry of Trade, Industry, the Private Sector and Special Presidential Initiatives; promotes small and medium-scale industrial and commercial enterprises by providing credit, advisory services and training; Exec. Dir Dr NANA BAAH BOAKYE.

In late 2004 the Ghana Trade Centre and the Ghana ECOWAS Trading Co were launched to facilitate trade by small and medium-sized enterprises.

DEVELOPMENT ORGANIZATIONS

Agence Française de Développement (AFD): 8th Rangoon Close, Ring Rd Central, POB 9592, Airport, Accra; tel. (21) 778755; fax (21) 778757; e-mail afdaccra@gh.groupe-afd.org; internet www.afd.fr; f. 1985; fmrly Caisse Française de Développement; Resident Man. JEAN-FRANÇOIS ARNAL.

Private Enterprise Foundation (PEF): POB C1671, Cantonments, Accra; tel. (21) 771504; fax (21) 771500; e-mail pet@ighmail.com; internet www.pefghana.org; promotes development of private sector; Pres. WILSON ATTA KROFAH.

CHAMBER OF COMMERCE

Ghana National Chamber of Commerce and Industry (GNCCI): 1st Floor, Tudu, 65 Kojo Thompson Rd, POB 2325, Accra; tel. (21) 662427; fax (21) 662210; e-mail gncc@ghana.com; internet www.ghanachamber.org; f. 1961; promotes and protects industry and commerce, organizes trade fairs; 2,500 individual mems and 10 mem. chambers; Pres. WILSON ATTA KROFAH; CEO SALATHIEL DOE AMEGAVIE.

INDUSTRIAL AND TRADE ORGANIZATIONS

Federation of Associations of Ghanaian Exporters (FAGE): POB M124, Accra; tel. (21) 232554; fax (21) 222038; e-mail fage@ighmail.com; internet www.ghana-exporter.org; non-governmental, not-for-profit org. for exporters of non-traditional exports; over 2,500 mems.

Forestry Commission of Ghana, Timber Industry Development Division (TIDD): 4 Third Ave, Ridge, POB MB434, Accra; tel. (31) 221315; fax (31) 220818; e-mail info@hq.fcghana.com; internet www.ghanatimber.org; f. 1985; promotes the development of the timber industry and the sale and export of timber.

Ghana Cocoa Board (COCOBOD): Cocoa House, Kwame Nkrumah Ave, POB 933, Accra; tel. (21) 661872; fax (21) 667104; internet www.cocobod.gh; f. 1985; monopoly purchaser of cocoa until 1993; responsible for purchase, grading and export of cocoa, coffee and shea nuts; also encourages production and scientific research aimed at improving quality and yield of these crops; controls all exports of cocoa; subsidiaries include the Cocoa Marketing Co (Ghana) Ltd and the Cocoa Research Institute of Ghana; CEO ISAAC OSEI.

Grains and Legumes Development Board: POB 4000, Kumasi; f. 1970; subsidiary of Ministry of Food and Agriculture; produces, processes and stores seeds and seedlings, and manages national seed security stocks.

EMPLOYERS' ORGANIZATION

Ghana Employers' Association (GEA): State Enterprises Commission Bldg, POB GP2616, Accra; tel. (21) 678455; fax (21) 678405; e-mail gea@ghanaemployers.com; internet www.ghanaemployers.com; f. 1959; 550 mems (2006); Pres. CHARLES ALEXANDER COFIE; Vice-Pres. JOYCE R. ARYEE.

Affiliated Bodies

Association of Ghana Industries (AGI): Trade Fair Centre, POB AN8624, Accra-North; tel. (21) 779023; fax (21) 773143; e-mail agi@agighana.org; internet www.agighana.org; f. 1957; Pres. Prince KOFI KLUDJESON; Exec. Dir ANDREW LAWSON; c. 500 mems.

Ghana Booksellers' Association: POB 10367, Accra-North; tel. (21) 773002; fax (21) 773242; e-mail minerva@ghana.com; Pres. FERD J. REIMMER; Gen. Sec. ADAMS AHIMAH.

Ghana Chamber of Mines: Minerals House 10, Sixth St, Airport Residential Area, POB 991, Accra; tel. (21) 760652; fax (21) 760653; e-mail ingo@ghanachamberofmines.org; internet ghanachamberofmines.org; f. 1928; Pres. JURGEN EIJGENDAAL; CEO JOYCE R. ARYEE.

GHANA

Ghana Timber Association (GTA): POB 1020, Kumasi; tel. and fax (51) 25153; f. 1952; promotes, protects and develops timber industry; Chair. TETTEH NANOR.

UTILITIES

Regulatory Bodies

Energy Commission (EC): FREMA House, Plot 40, Spintex Rd, PMB Ministries, Accra; tel. (21) 813756; fax (21) 813764; e-mail info@energycom.gov.gh; internet www.energycom.gov.gh; f. 2001; Chair. DAASEBRE OSEI BONSU; Exec. Sec. (vacant).

Public Utilities Regulatory Commission (PURC): 51 Liberation Rd, African Liberation Circle, POB CT3095, Cantonments, Accra; tel. (21) 244181; fax (21) 224188; e-mail info@purcghana.com; internet www.purcghana.com; f. 1997; Exec. Sec. STEPHEN N. ADU.

Electricity

Electricity Co of Ghana (ECG): Electro-Volta House, POB 521, Accra; tel. (21) 676727; fax (21) 666262; e-mail ecgho@ghana.com; internet www.electricitygh.com; Chair. KWAME SAARAH MENSAH; Man. Dir Chief MUSA B. ADAM.

Volta River Authority (VRA): Electro-Volta House, 28th February Rd, POB M77, Accra; tel. (21) 664941; fax (21) 662610; e-mail paffairs@vra.com; f. 1961; controls the generation and distribution of electricity; Northern Electricity Department of VRA f. 1997 to distribute electricity in northern Ghana; CEO JOSHUA OFEDIE.

Water

In mid-2006 the Volta Basin Authority (VBA) was created by Ghana, Benin, Burkina Faso, Côte d'Ivoire, Mali and Togo to manage the resources of the Volta River basin.

Ghana Water Co Ltd (GWCL): POB M194, Accra; tel. (21) 666781; fax (21) 663552; f. 1965 to provide, distribute and conserve water supplies for public, domestic and industrial use, and to establish, operate and control sewerage systems; jointly managed by Aqua Vitens (the Netherlands) and Rand Water (South Africa); Chair. A. R. MUSSAH; Man. Dir COBBIE KESSIE, Jr.

CO-OPERATIVES

Department of Co-operatives: POB M150, Accra; tel. (21) 666212; fax (21) 772789; f. 1944; govt-supervised body, responsible for registration, auditing and supervision of co-operative socs; Registrar R. BUACHIE-APHRAM.

Ghana Co-operatives Council Ltd (GACOCO): POB 4034, Accra; tel. (21) 686253; fax (21) 672014; e-mail ghacoco@ghana.com; f. 1951; co-ordinates activities of all co-operative socs and plays advocacy role for co-operative movement; comprises 11 active nat. asscns and two central orgs; Sec.-Gen. ALBERT AGYEMAN PREMPEH.

The national associations and central organizations include the Ghana Co-operative Marketing Asscn Ltd, the Ghana Co-operative Credit Unions Asscn Ltd, the Ghana Co-operative Distillers and Retailers Asscn Ltd, and the Ghana Co-operative Poultry Farmers Asscn Ltd.

TRADE UNIONS

Ghana Federation of Labour: POB Trade Fair 509, Accra; tel. (21) 252105; fax (21) 307394; e-mail gflgh@hotmail.com; Sec.-Gen. ABRAHAM KOOMSON; 10,540 mems.

Ghana National Association of Teachers (GNAT): POB 209, Accra; tel. (21) 221515; fax (21) 226286; e-mail info@ghanateachers.org; internet www.ghanateachers.org; f. 1962; Pres. JOSEPH KWEKU ADJEI; Gen. Sec. IRENE DUNCAN ADANUSA; 178,000 mems (2003).

Trades Union Congress (Ghana) (TUC): Hall of Trade Unions, POB 701, Accra; tel. (21) 662568; fax (21) 667161; e-mail tuc@ighmail.com; f. 1945; 17 affiliated unions; Chair. ALEX K. BONNEY; Sec.-Gen. KWASI ADU-AMANKWAH.

General Agricultural Workers' Union (GAWU): Hall of Trade Unions, 5th Floor, POB 701, Accra; tel. and fax (21) 672468; e-mail gawu@ghmail.com; affiliated to the TUC; Gen. Sec. SAMUEL KANGAH.

Teachers and Educational Workers' Union (TEWU): Hall of Trade Unions, Liberia Road, POB 701, Accra; tel. (21) 663050; fax (21) 662766; e-mail tewu@ghana.com; mem. of TUC; Chair. MICHAEL NYAME; Sec.-Gen. DANIEL AYIM ANTWI.

Transport

RAILWAYS

Ghana has a railway network of 947 km, which connects Accra, Kumasi and Takoradi. In late 2004 OPEC provided a loan of US $5m.

to upgrade the Accra–Tema railway. In 2006 the Government was undertaking negotiations to contract out the upgrading and operation of the rail network, and plans were underway regarding the construction of a rail link with Burkina Faso.

Ghana Railway Co Ltd (GRC): POB 251, Takoradi; f. 1901; responsible for the operation and maintenance of all railways; to be run under private concession from April 2004; 947 km of track in use in 2003; Chair HENRY BENYA; Acting Man. Dir RUFUS OKAI QUAYE.

Ghana Railway Development Authority (GRDA): Ministry of Ports and Railways, PMB, Accra; tel. (21) 681780; fax (21) 681781; f. 2005; regulatory and devt authority.

ROADS

In 2005 Ghana had a total road network of approximately 57,6134 km, of which just 15% was paved. Construction work on 36 bridges nation-wide, funded by the Japanese Government, commenced in 2003. In 2006 a comprehensive upgrade of the road network was underway; in 2005 €11m. was pledged by the European Union for upgrading the road network in key cocoa-producing areas.

Ghana Highway Authority: POB 1641, Accra; tel. (21) 666591; fax (21) 665571; e-mail eokonadu@highways.mrt.gov.gh; f. 1974 to plan, develop, administer and maintain trunk roads and related facilities; CEO E. ODURO-KONADI.

Vanef STC: POB 7384, 1 Adjuma Cres., Ring Rd West Industrial Area, Accra; tel. (21) 221912; fax (21) 221945; e-mail stc@ghana.com; f. 1965; fmrly State Transport Co, transferred to private-sector ownership in 2000; regional and international coach services; CEO JAMES OWUSU BONSU.

SHIPPING

The two main ports are Tema (near Accra) and Takoradi, both of which are linked with Kumasi by rail. There are also important inland ports on the Volta, Ankobra and Tano rivers. At 31 December 2006 the merchant fleet comprised 224 vesels, totalling 116,284 grt.

Ghana Maritime Authority (GMA): PMB 34, Ministries, Accra; tel. (21) 662122; fax (21) 677702; internet www.ghanamaritime.org; f. 2002; part of Ministry of Port and Railways; regulates shipping industry; Dir-Gen. ISSAKA PETER AZUMA.

Ghana Ports and Harbour Authority: POB 150, Tema; tel. (22) 202631; fax (22) 202812; e-mail ghpa@ghana.com; holding co for the ports of Tema and Takoradi; Dir-Gen. BEN OWUSU-MENSAH.

Alpha (West Africa) Line Ltd: POB 451, Tema; operates regular cargo services to West Africa, the United Kingom, the USA, the Far East and northern Europe; shipping agents; Man. Dir AHMED EDGAR COLLINGWOOD WILLIAMS.

Liner Agencies and Trading (Ghana) Ltd: POB 214, Tema; tel. (22) 202987; fax (22) 202989; e-mail enquiries@liner-agencies.com; international freight services; shipping agents; Dir J. OSSEI-YAW.

Maersk Ghana Ltd: Obourwe Bldg, Torman Rd, Fishing Harbour Area, POB 8800, Community 7, Tema; tel. (22) 206740; fax (22) 204114; e-mail gnamkt@maersk.com; internet www.maerskline.com/ghana; f. 2001; owned by Maersk Line (Denmark); offices in Tema, Takoradi and Kumasi; Man. Dir JEFF GOSCINIAK.

Scanship (Ghana) Ltd: CFAO Bldg, High St, POB 1705, Accra; tel. (21) 664314; shipping agents.

Shipping Association

Ghana Shippers' Council: Enterprise House, 5th Floor, High St, POB 1321, Accra; tel. (21) 555915; fax (21) 668768; e-mail scouncil@shippers-gh.com; internet www.ghanashipperscouncil.org; f. 1974; represents interests of 28,000 registered Ghanaian shippers; also provides cargo-handling and allied services; Chief Exec. KOFI MBIAH.

CIVIL AVIATION

The main international airport is at Kotoka (Accra). There are also airports at Kumasi, Takoradi, Sunyani, Tamale and Wa. The construction of a dedicated freight terminal at Kotoka Airport was completed in 1994. In 2001 622,525 passengers and 44,779 metric tons of freight passed through Kotoka Airport. The rehabilitation of Kumasi Airport was underway in 2006, while there were also plans to construct a further international airport at Kumasi.

Ghana Civil Aviation Authority (GCAA): PMB, Kotoka International Airport, Accra; tel. (21) 776171; fax (21) 773293; e-mail info@gcaagh.com; internet www.gcaa.com.gh; f. 1986; Chair. TIM PAPPOE; Dir-Gen. NII ADUMASA BADDOO.

Afra Airlines Ltd: 7 Nortei St, Airport Residential Area, Accra; tel. (244) 932488; e-mail lukebutler@afraairlines.com; f. 2005; CEO LUKE BUTLER.

Gemini Airlines Ltd (Aero Gem Cargo): America House, POB 7238, Accra-North; tel. (21) 771921; fax (21) 761939; e-mail aerogemcargo@hotmail.com; f. 1974; operates weekly cargo flight between Accra and London; Gen. Man. ENOCH ANAN-TABURY.

GHANA   Directory

Ghana International Airlines, Ltd (GIA): Silver Star Tower, PMB 78, Kotoka International Airport, Accra; tel. (21) 213555; fax (21) 767744; e-mail humanresources@fly-ghana.com; internet www.fly-ghana.com; f. 2005 to replace Ghana Airways; owned by Govt of Ghana and GIA-USA, Llc (US); flies to destinations in Africa and Europe; Pres. AZU MATE; CEO Dr CHARLES WEREKO.

Tourism

Ghana's attractions include fine beaches, game reserves, traditional festivals, and old trading forts and castles. In 2005 some 428,533 tourists visited Ghana, with revenue from tourism totalling US $827m.

Ghana Tourist Board: POB GP3106, Accra-North; tel. (21) 222153; fax (21) 244611; internet www.touringghana.com; f. 1968; Exec. Dir CHARLES OSEI-BONSU (acting).

Ghana Association of Tourist and Travel Agencies (GATTA): Swamp Grove, Asylum Down, POB 7140, Accra-North; tel. (21) 222398; fax (21) 231102; e-mail info@gattagh.com; internet www.gattagh.com; Pres. GODWIN PINTO; Exec. Sec. GIFTY KORANTENG-ADDO.

Ghana Tourist Development Co Ltd: POB 8710, Accra; tel. (21) 257244; fax (21) 772093; f. 1974; develops tourist infrastructure, incl. hotels, restaurants and casinos; operates duty-free shops; Man. Dir ALFRED KOMLADZEI.

2018   www.europaworld.com

GREECE

Introductory Survey

Location, Climate, Language, Religion, Flag, Capital

The Hellenic Republic lies in south-eastern Europe. The country consists mainly of a mountainous peninsula between the Mediterranean Sea and the Aegean Sea, bounded to the north by Albania, the former Yugoslav republic of Macedonia and Bulgaria, and to the east by Turkey. To the south, east and west of the mainland lie numerous Greek islands, of which the largest is Crete. The climate is Mediterranean, with mild winters and hot summers. The average temperature in the capital is 28°C (82°F) in July and 9°C (48°F) in January. The language is Greek, of which there are two forms—the formal language (katharevoussa) and the language commonly spoken and taught in schools (demotiki). Almost all of the inhabitants profess Christianity, and the Greek Orthodox Church, to which about 97% of the population adhere, is the established religion. The national flag (proportions 2 by 3) displays nine equal horizontal stripes of blue and white, with a white cross throughout a square canton of blue at the upper hoist. The capital is Athens (Athenai).

Recent History

The liberation of Greece from the German occupation (1941–44) was followed by a civil war, which lasted until 1949. The communist forces were defeated, and the constitutional monarchy re-established. King Konstantinos (Constantine) II acceded to the throne on the death of his father, King Pavlos (Paul), in 1964. A succession of weak governments and conflicts between the King and his ministers, and an alleged conspiracy involving military personnel, culminated in a coup, led by rightwing army officers, in April 1967. An attempted counter-coup, led by the King, failed, and he went into exile. Col Georgios Papadopoulos emerged as the dominant personality in the new regime, becoming Prime Minister in December 1967 and Regent in March 1972. The regime produced nominally democratic constitutional proposals, but all political activity was banned, and its opponents were expelled from all positions of influence.

Following an abortive naval mutiny, Greece was declared a republic in June 1973, and Papadopoulos was appointed President. Martial law was ended, and a civilian Government was appointed in preparation for a general election. However, a student uprising in Athens in November was violently suppressed by the army, and Papadopoulos was overthrown by another military coup. Lt-Gen. Phaidon Ghizikis was appointed President, and a mainly civilian Government, led by Adamantios Androutsopoulos, was installed, but effective power lay with a small group of officers and the military police under Brig.-Gen. Demetrios Ioannides. As a result of the failure of the military junta's attempt to overthrow President Makarios of Cyprus, and its inability to prevent the Turkish invasion of the island (see the chapter on Cyprus), the Androutsopoulos administration collapsed in July 1974. Ghizikis summoned from exile a former Prime Minister, Konstantinos Karamanlis, who was invited to form a civilian Government of National Salvation. Martial law was ended, the press was released from state control and political parties, including the communists, were allowed to operate freely. A general election in November resulted in victory for Karamanlis's New Democracy Party (ND), which won 220 of the 300 parliamentary seats. A referendum in December rejected proposals for a return to constitutional monarchy, and in June 1975 a new republican Constitution, providing for a parliamentary democracy, was promulgated. In the same month Prof. Konstantinos Tsatsos was elected President by the Vouli (Parliament).

In the general election of November 1977 ND was re-elected with a reduced majority. In May 1980 Karamanlis was elected President; Georgios Rallis subsequently assumed the leadership of ND and was appointed Prime Minister. Rallis encountered considerable opposition from the increasingly popular Panhellenic Socialist Movement (PASOK). On 1 January 1981 Greece acceded to the European Community (EC, now the European Union—EU, see p. 244). In the general election of October 1981 PASOK secured an absolute majority in the Vouli. The PASOK leader, Andreas Papandreou, became Prime Minister of the first ever socialist Government, which was initially committed to withdrawal from the EC, to the removal of US military bases from Greek territory and to the implementation of an extensive programme of domestic reform.

In March 1985 Papandreou unexpectedly withdrew support for President Karamanlis's candidature for a further five-year term. The Prime Minister planned to amend the 1975 Constitution to relieve the President of all executive power and render the Head of State's functions largely ceremonial. Karamanlis resigned in protest, and the Vouli elected Christos Sartzetakis, a judge, as President, in a vote that was widely considered to be unconstitutional. A general election was held in June 1985 to enable the Government to secure support for the proposed constitutional changes. PASOK was returned to power, winning 161 seats in the 300-member Vouli; ND secured 126 seats. In October the Government introduced a programme of economic austerity, provoking widespread industrial unrest, which continued throughout 1986. In March 1986, despite considerable opposition from ND, the Vouli approved a series of constitutional amendments limiting the powers of the President.

In May 1987, in response to numerous accusations made by ND of mismanagement and corruption on the part of the Government, Papandreou sought and won a parliamentary vote of confidence in his Government. The Government suffered a serious reverse in November 1988, when several prominent ministers were implicated in a major financial scandal involving alleged embezzlement, and were forced to resign.

In January 1989 the Greek Left Party, led by Leonidas Kyrkos, formed an electoral alliance with the 'Exterior' faction of the Communist Party of Greece (KKE), under the leadership of Charilaos Florakis, to create the Coalition of the Left and Progress (the Left Coalition). At a general election in June, ND won the largest proportion of the votes cast, but failed to attain an overall majority in the Vouli. Following the failure of both ND and PASOK to reach an agreement with the Left Coalition to form a coalition government, President Sartzetakis empowered the Left Coalition to seek a coalition agreement. The Left Coalition unexpectedly agreed to form an interim administration with ND, on the condition that the ND leader, Konstantinos Mitsotakis, renounced his claim to the premiership. Accordingly, Tzannis Tzannetakis, an ND deputy, was appointed Prime Minister in a new Government, which included two communist ministers. The unprecedented conservative-communist coalition announced its intention to govern for only three months, during which time it aimed to implement a *katharsis* (campaign of purification) of Greek politics. Accordingly, the administration resigned in early October, having initiated investigations into the involvement of officials of the former socialist Government, including Papandreou, in a number of scandals involving banking, armaments and financial transactions. (In March 1991 Papandreou and three of his former ministers were tried on charges of complicity in large-scale embezzlement during their terms of office; in January 1992 Papandreou was acquitted of all charges, and two of the former ministers received minor sentences; the third had died during the trial.) The President of the Supreme Court, Ioannis Grivas, was subsequently appointed Prime Minister in an interim Government comprising non-political figures, which was to oversee the second general election of the year. However, the results of the election, conducted in November, were again inconclusive. The political crisis was temporarily resolved in mid-November, when ND, PASOK and the Left Coalition agreed to form a coalition to administer the country pending the results of a further poll, to be conducted in April 1990. However, following a dispute over military promotions in February 1990, the Government collapsed, and the same non-political administration was reinstated to govern until the new general election. Attempts by the Vouli in February and March to elect a head of state by the required majority were unsuccessful, owing largely to a decision taken by ND representatives to abstain from voting, following the refusal of their candidate, Karamanlis, to contest the election. A general election, conducted in April, finally resolved the parliamentary impasse; ND secured 150 seats in the Vouli. Following the announcement of the results,

Mitsotakis secured the support of Konstantinos Stefanopoulos, the leader (and the one elected parliamentary representative) of the Party of Democratic Renewal, thereby enabling him to form the first single-party Government since 1981. In May 1990 Karamanlis took office as President for a five-year term, following his election by 153 of the 300 members of the Vouli. Stefanopoulos formally joined ND in June.

The unpopularity of austerity measures introduced by the new Government led to widespread industrial unrest during 1990. In November reforms to the electoral law, providing for a modified form of proportional representation, in which political parties wishing to appoint representatives to the Vouli would require a minimum of 3% of the votes in a general election, were finally ratified. Left-wing parties criticized the new electoral system, which also incorporated procedural disincentives to the formation of political alliances to contest elections, as unconstitutional.

In August 1991 Mitsotakis effected a comprehensive reorganization of the Government (including the removal of his daughter from the post of Under-Secretary to the Prime Minister), in response to public criticism of family involvement in politics. In April 1992 the Prime Minister successfully sought a vote of confidence from the Vouli, following the dismissal of the Minister of Foreign Affairs, Antonis Samaras, and Mitsotakis's assumption of the portfolio in order to address personally attempts by the former Yugoslav republic of Macedonia (FYRM—q.v.) to achieve international recognition as the Republic of Macedonia (see below). As part of a government reorganization effected in August (which included the reappointment of the Prime Minister's daughter to her previous post), Michalis Papakonstantinou, a staunch defender of national territorial integrity, was allocated the foreign affairs portfolio. Industrial unrest continued throughout 1992 and 1993, in protest at privatization plans and other government austerity measures.

In September 1993 two ND deputies resigned, following an appeal for support by Political Spring (POLAN), a centre-right party that had been established in July by Samaras. The consequent loss of Mitsotakis's one-seat majority in the Vouli obliged him to offer the Government's resignation and schedule an early general election. At the election, conducted in October, PASOK obtained 46.9% of the total votes cast and 170 of the 300 parliamentary seats, while ND received 39.3% of the votes and 111 seats, and POLAN secured 4.9% of the votes and 10 seats. In October Mitsotakis resigned as leader of ND. Following a reduction in electoral support for PASOK in elections to the European Parliament in June 1994, Papandreou undertook a government reorganization.

In March 1995 Stefanopoulos was elected President by 181 of the 300 members of the Vouli, having failed to secure the required two-thirds' majority in two earlier rounds of voting; jointly favoured by PASOK and POLAN, he took office on 10 March. From mid-1995 tensions within the governing PASOK became increasingly evident. Konstantinos Simitis, together with Theodhoros Pangalos, Vasiliki (Vasso) Papandreou, and Paraskevas Avgerinos constituted a group of 'dissident' PASOK deputies (referred to as the Group of Four) who urged the resignation of Papandreou, in view of his failing health, and the implementation of further reforms within the party. In November Papandreou was admitted to hospital; Apostolos-Athanassios (Akis) Tsohatzopoulos, a close associate of Papandreou, who had joined the Government in September, assumed his prime ministerial duties, in an acting capacity. In January 1996 a parliamentary motion of 'no confidence' in the Government was defeated, although on 15 January Papandreou submitted his resignation as Prime Minister, but remained leader of PASOK. Three days later Simitis was elected to the premiership by the members of the PASOK parliamentary party. Simitis awarded Pangalos the foreign affairs portfolio, but retained Tsohatzopoulos and Gerasimos Arsenis (two other contestants in the leadership election) in the Government in an attempt to unite the party. However, pro-European ministers who supported Simitis's desire for economic reform replaced the majority of Papandreou's former associates.

Almost immediately, Simitis was confronted by a sharp escalation in hostilities with Turkey (see below). Following his acceptance of a US-mediated compromise to defuse the situation, Simitis was condemned by all opposition parties. In February 1996 the Prime Minister dismissed the Chief of the General Staff of the armed forces, Adm. Christos Lyberis.

Following Papandreou's death in June 1996, Simitis was elected leader of PASOK, with 53.5% of the votes cast, defeating Tsohatzopoulos. In August Simitis announced that an early general election was to be held, in order to obtain a firm mandate to pursue the reforms needed to achieve the EU's economic and monetary union (EMU) targets. In the election, held on 22 September 1996, PASOK won 162 of the 300 parliamentary seats, with 41.5% of the votes cast, while ND obtained 108 seats (38.2%). Support for POLAN declined substantially, and the party lost all 10 of the seats obtained at the previous election. Principal ministers in the outgoing Government were retained in the new PASOK administration. In March 1997 Konstantinos (Kostas) Karamanlis (a nephew of the former President and ND party leader) was elected leader of ND.

A general strike was staged in November 1996, in protest against new austerity measures. Nevertheless, Simitis continued to implement austerity policies in accordance with his commitment to meeting the 'convergence' criteria of EMU. Industrial action continued to cause disruption in 1998. In May a widely observed general strike was organized in protest at the privatization plans, which were approved at the end of June. In late November, in response to criticism of its austerity programme, the Government sought and won a parliamentary vote of confidence; Simitis had threatened to expel PASOK deputies from the party if they failed to support the motion.

In February 1999 it emerged that Abdullah Öcalan, the leader of the proscribed Kurdistan Workers' Party (PKK), accused by Turkey of a number of terrorist charges, had been given refuge at the Greek embassy in Kenya before being captured by the Turkish authorities. Kenya officially denounced Greece for allowing Öcalan to enter the embassy without informing the Kenyan authorities. Kurdish groups demonstrated at Greek embassies across Europe, and the Ministers of the Interior, Public Administration and Decentralization, of Foreign Affairs, and of Public Order resigned, prompting a government reorganization. Vasso Papandreou was appointed Minister of the Interior, Public Administration and Decentralization, and Georgios Papandreou (the son of the late Andreas Papandreou) replaced Pangalos as Minister of Foreign Affairs.

At the beginning of February 2000 Prime Minister Simitis announced that early legislative elections were to be held on 9 April. On 9 February Stefanopoulos was re-elected President by 269 of the 300 members of the Vouli. At the general election PASOK was returned to office, winning 43.8% of the votes cast and 158 parliamentary seats, narrowly defeating ND, with 42.7% of the votes and 125 seats. On 12 April Simitis formed a new Government.

In April 2001 government plans to raise the retirement age and reform the pension system precipitated widely supported public protests, including a general strike. In October Simitis reorganized the Government, following his re-election as party leader at a PASOK congress.

In October 2002 Dora Bakoyanni, a member of ND and the daughter of former Prime Minister Mitsotakis, was elected Mayor of Athens, with almost 60% of the votes cast. In December Bakoyanni narrowly escaped assassination when a gunman opened fire on her car. In July 2003 PASOK elected a new executive bureau, following a decision by Simitis that its members should not simultaneously hold a position in the Government. Michalis Chrisochoidhis, hitherto Minister of Public Order, replaced Costas Laliotis as Secretary-General. In January 2004 Simitis announced his resignation from the leadership of PASOK, and declared that early legislative elections would take place on 7 March, asserting that an administration with a new mandate was necessary to address developments on the issue of Cyprus (see below). On 8 February, following amendments to the party charter (whereby the leader would be selected by members nationally), Georgios Papandreou was elected unopposed as the President of PASOK.

At the legislative elections held on 7 March 2003, ND secured 45.4% of the votes cast, thereby removing PASOK, which won 40.6% of the votes, from government. On 9 March Karamanlis formed a new administration, which was officially installed on the following day. The new Prime Minister, who also held the culture portfolio, pledged to expedite the preparations for the summer Olympic Games, which Greece was to host in August 2004. Although there were reports that many of the Olympic construction projects greatly exceeded cost projections, the staging of the Olympiad on 13–29 August, with 202 nations participating, was widely considered to be a success for the Government. In November the Government publicly conceded that the PASOK administration had significantly understated public-debt and budgetary-deficit figures for several years in order for Greece to qualify for membership of EMU in January

2001, after evidence to that effect emerged; it appeared that continued misrepresentation of defence expenditure had partially caused the discrepancies. The statement provoked a dispute between the ruling ND and PASOK, which criticized the revision of past official figures. The Government subsequently pledged to restrain the budgetary deficit to within the stipulated limit (of 3% of GDP) by the end of 2006, in compliance with EU criteria.

On 8 February 2005 Karolos Papoulias, a member of PASOK and a former Minister of Foreign Affairs, was elected unopposed as the new President, receiving 279 votes in the 300-member Vouli. Papoulias was inaugurated as President on 12 March, following the expiry of the second five-year term of Stefanopoulos. In mid-June the Government won a motion of confidence in the Vouli for its labour reform plans, although strike action was organized by banking and other public-sector workers later in the month.

In early February 2006 the Government revealed that mobile cellular telephones belonging to Karamanlis, to prominent government and opposition members, and to public officials had been clandestinely monitored between June 2004 and March 2005. A judicial inquiry was subsequently announced into the illegal surveillance (which was thought likely to be linked to security concerns relating to the holding of the summer Olympic Games in 2004). Later in February 2006 Karamanlis announced an extensive reorganization of the Government, which included the appointment of Bakoyanni as Minister of Foreign Affairs and of Evangelos Meimarakis as Minister of National Defence. Georgios Voulgarakis, who, as Minister of Public Order, had been held responsible for the controversy surrounding the illegal surveillance, was transferred to the Ministry of Culture. Local government elections took place on 15 and 22 October. ND retained control of some 30 prefectural councils and the municipalities of Athens and Thessaloníki, while PASOK increased its representation from 19 to 22 councils and gained control of the port towns of Piraeus and Patras. In December the mobile cellular telecommunications operator, Vodafone Greece, was ordered to pay €76m. by the independent Authority for the Assurance of Information and Communication Privacy and Security, after being held responsible for the clandestine surveillance and for obstructing the subsequent investigations (while the instigators of the monitoring remained unknown).

In early 2007 mass protests were staged by students and education-sector staff, in opposition to proposals to allow the establishment of private universities from 2008 as part of the Government's undertaking to improve higher education. The proposed reforms, which were supported by PASOK, but opposed by other opposition parties, required an amendment to the national Constitution. In early February PASOK withdrew from a parliamentary committee session during the constitutional debate, after accusing the Government of pressurizing ND dissenters to support reforms, and demanded the organization of early elections. A resultant parliamentary motion of censure in the Government was defeated. In early March a number of protesters were arrested, after a further demonstration in Athens against the education reforms escalated into violence.

On 25 August 2007 Karamanlis declared a state of emergency, after fires, exacerbated by drought conditions, caused widespread destruction throughout much of the country, particularly in the southern Peloponnese region, and resulted in the deaths of some 65 people. More than 30 suspects were subsequently detained, and seven were charged. In late August an estimated 10,000 people staged a protest in Athens at the Government's response to the emergency; it was alleged that poor control of forests had prompted arsonists to take action to clear land for unauthorized building, while opposition leaders accused the authorities of failing effectively to organize efforts to combat the fires. The popularity of Karamanlis, who earlier in August had scheduled legislative elections for 16 September, declined sharply as a result of the crisis. Nevertheless, at the elections ND was returned to power, securing 41.8% of the votes cast and 152 seats in the Vouli. PASOK, with 38.1% of the votes, won a reduced number of seats (102), followed by the KKE (with 8.2% of votes and 22 seats) and the Coalition of the Radical Left (5.0% of votes and 14 seats); an extreme nationalist organization, Popular Orthodox Rally, received 3.8% of the votes and 10 seats, obtaining parliamentary representation for the first time. The rate of participation by the electorate was some 74.1%. Karamanlis, who pledged to implement economic and social-sector reforms, subsequently established a smaller administration; following the criticism of the Government's management of the fires, the former Minister of Public Order was not reappointed, and the Ministry of Public Order was merged into the Ministry of the Interior.

In November 2007 students and university staff again demonstrated in Athens to demand improved funding for state education bodies and to contest the establishment of private universities. In December the country's two largest trade unions, the Greek General Confederation of Labour and the Supreme Administration of Greek Civil Servants' Trade Unions, organized a general strike, which resulted in the suspension of public transport and the closure of banks and government offices, in protest at the planned reform of the pension system, and demonstrations were staged in Athens and Thessaloníki. Further days of national strike action took place in February 2008, and continued in March. At the end of March the Vouli narrowly approved legislation on reform of the pension system; a subsequent opposition motion demanding that a referendum be held was rejected. Private- and public-sector unions pledged to continue strikes against the measures.

Throughout the 1990s numerous bomb attacks against military and commercial targets (particularly those associated with the USA) in Greece were carried out by dissident groups, in particular the extremist left-wing November 17 Revolutionary Organization (active since 1975) and the Revolutionary People's Struggle (ELA). Dissident activities continued into the early 2000s. In June 2000 a British defence attaché, Brig. Stephen Saunders, was assassinated by the November 17 group, which claimed that Saunders had helped to co-ordinate the bombing offensive by the North Atlantic Treaty Organization (NATO, see p. 340) of Serbia and Montenegro in 1999 (which had been strongly opposed in Greece—see below). Saunders' murder led to concern that Greece was failing to co-operate fully with international anti-terrorist efforts, although in July 2000 a series of anti-terrorist initiatives was agreed between Greece and the United Kingdom. In January 2001, however, a member of the Vouli was injured in a further attack that was attributed to November 17. In June the Vouli approved widespread changes to criminal legislation in an attempt to improve Greece's record on combating militant activity. The amendments, which introduced non-jury criminal trials, a limited right to appeal and broader police powers of surveillance, and which permitted the non-consensual DNA testing of suspects, provoked strong objections from legal associations and civil liberties groups.

In 2002 the Government made significant progress in combating terrorist activity. Notably, in July the authorities apprehended 14 suspected members of November 17. The arrest of Savvas Xiros, who had been injured in a bomb explosion, represented the first arrest of an alleged member of the organization, and the police were subsequently able to arrest the suspected leader of November 17, Alexandros Giotopoulos, and two of Xiros's brothers, one of whom had reportedly confessed to the assassination in 2000 of Brig. Saunders. Shortly afterwards, the Government announced that November 17 had been disbanded. In September 2002 Dimitris Koufodinas, believed to be the second highest-ranking member of November 17, surrendered to police in Athens. By January 2003 a total of 19 suspected members of November 17 had been apprehended, and in February the police arrested four suspected members of the ELA. The trial of all 19 alleged members of November 17 commenced in March. The two principal defendants were accused of over 1,000 criminal acts, including some 23 killings and numerous bomb attacks. The trial was concluded in December. Four of the defendants were acquitted owing to lack of evidence. Giotopoulos, Koufodinas and four others were sentenced to life imprisonment, and eight defendants received less severe custodial sentences. The remaining defendant, who had testified against the others, received a suspended sentence. In October, following an eight-month trial, five members of the ELA, including the movement's reputed leader, were each sentenced to 25 years' imprisonment on charges relating to more than 100 bomb attacks.

Meanwhile, another extremist, left-wing organization, Revolutionary Struggle (EA), had emerged. The EA was held responsible for a bomb attack in Athens on 5 May 2004 (100 days before the opening of the summer Olympic Games), and against two police vehicles in October. The organization also claimed responsibility for bomb attacks at the Ministry of Labour and Social Security in May 2005, and outside the Ministry of the Economy and Finance in December. In January 2007 the EA claimed responsibility for a rocket attack against the US embassy in Athens (which resulted in minor damage to the building). In

March the US and Greek Governments offered a reward totalling US $2m. for information resulting in the arrest of EA leaders.

Greece became a full member of the EC (now EU) in January 1981, having signed the Treaty of Accession in 1979.

Relations with Turkey have been characterized by long-standing disputes concerning Cyprus (q.v.) and sovereignty over the continental shelf beneath the Aegean Sea. The difficulties in relations with Turkey were exacerbated by the unilateral declaration of an 'independent' Turkish Cypriot state in Cyprus in November 1983 (the 'Turkish Republic of Northern Cyprus'—'TRNC'), together with various minor sovereignty disputes over islands in the Aegean Sea, which led to Greece's withdrawal from NATO military exercises in August 1984 and to a boycott of manoeuvres in subsequent years. In March 1987 a disagreement between Greece and Turkey over petroleum-prospecting rights in disputed areas of the Aegean Sea almost resulted in military conflict. In January 1988, however, the Greek and Turkish Prime Ministers, meeting in Davos, Switzerland, agreed that the two countries' premiers should meet annually in order to improve bilateral relations (the Davos meeting was the first formal contact between Greek and Turkish Heads of Government for 10 years), and that joint committees should be established to negotiate peaceful solutions to disputes.

In 1994 the issue of the demarcation of territorial waters in the Aegean Sea re-emerged as a major source of tension. Greece's right to extend its territorial waters from six to 12 nautical miles, as enshrined in the international Convention on the Law of the Sea (see the International Seabed Authority, p. 323), was strongly condemned by Turkey, which feared the loss of shipping access, via the Aegean Sea, to international waters. The dispute intensified prior to the scheduled entry into force of the Convention in mid-November, with both countries conducting concurrent military exercises in the Aegean. The concern surrounding the international Convention on the Law of the Sea re-emerged in June 1995, when the Vouli ratified the treaty; Turkey conducted further military exercises in the region. In early 1996 tensions were exacerbated by conflicting claims of sovereignty over Imia (Kardak), a group of uninhabited islands in the Aegean Sea. By late January Greek and Turkish military vessels were patrolling the islands and attempts were made to raise their respective national flags on the territory. The situation was defused when the new PASOK administration complied with a petition by the USA to withdraw from the area and to remove the national flags.

In February 1996 Greek opposition delayed the implementation of a financial protocol of the EU-Turkey customs union; Greece claimed that Turkey's aggressive action in the Aegean violated the terms of the customs union agreement. In July Greece finally withdrew its opposition to Turkey's participation in an EU-Mediterranean assistance programme, in response to a joint statement by EU Heads of Government urging an end to Turkey's 'hostile policy' towards Greece; however, the block on funds from the customs union agreement remained in effect.

In July 1997 the Greek Prime Minister, Konstantinos Simitis, and the Turkish President, Süleyman Demirel, held direct talks (the first such meeting for three years), which led to an agreement, the Madrid Declaration, pledging not to use violence or the threat of violence to resolve bilateral disputes. However, relations remained strained, particularly concerning Greek support for Cyprus's application for membership of the EU; Turkey threatened annexation of the 'TRNC' should Cyprus be admitted to the organization. Further tension was caused by frequent alleged violations of Greek airspace by Turkish military aircraft. In November Greece threatened to oppose Turkey's participation in a planned EU enlargement conference in London, United Kingdom, unless Turkey abandoned its attempts to prevent EU accession talks with Cyprus, and threatened to veto the admission to the EU of other applicant countries if Cyprus were rejected. As Cyprus began accession talks with the EU in March 1998, Greece reiterated its intention to veto the admission of other countries if Cyprus were not included, and maintained its refusal to lift its veto on EU financial aid to Turkey.

In July 1999 Greece alleged that two Turkish military aircraft had intercepted a Greek aircraft carrying the Minister of Transport to Cyprus and had forced it briefly to alter course. Relations between the two countries improved in August, however, when Greece offered both financial and material assistance to Turkey, following a severe earthquake in the north-west of that country; Greece also announced its intention to lift its veto on EU financial aid to Turkey. Turkey reciprocated Greece's provision of emergency assistance when an earthquake struck Athens in early September. At an EU summit, held in Helsinki, Finland, in December, a diplomatic impasse was finally ended when Greece formally lifted its objections to Turkey's membership of the EU, although the conditions for its accession depended on the resolution of both the Cyprus issue and of its dispute with Greece in the Aegean. The improvement in relations between Greece and Turkey was demonstrated in January 2000 when the Greek Minister of Foreign Affairs, Georgios Papandreou, visited Ankara, the Turkish capital, for talks with his Turkish counterpart, İsmail Cem, and the Turkish Prime Minister, in the first official visit by a Greek Minister of Foreign Affairs to Turkey since 1962. In February 2000 the *rapprochement* between Greece and Turkey continued with an official visit to Athens by the Turkish Minister of Foreign Affairs, during which further co-operation agreements (primarily relating to economic affairs) were signed. In October, however, Greece withdrew from a joint NATO military exercise in the Aegean Sea, after it accused Turkey of preventing Greek aircraft from flying over two disputed islands. Nevertheless, in April 2001 both Greece and Turkey announced significant reductions in their weapons-procurement programmes.

In November 2001 Greece and Turkey signed an agreement that allowed Greece to repatriate illegal Turkish immigrants. (The Greek Government believed that as many as 750,000 illegal immigrants had entered the country from Turkey since 1998.) None the less, the issue of Cyprus continued to overshadow bilateral relations. In February 2002 the Greek and Turkish Ministers of Foreign Affairs recommenced talks, following the resumption of negotiations between the Greek and Turkish Cypriot sides over the issue of Cyprus. In April 2003, after further efforts towards reaching a peace settlement ended in failure, the newly elected Cypriot President, Tassos Papadopoulos, signed Cyprus's Treaty of Accession to the EU in Athens, thereby confirming that Cyprus would join the organization on 1 May 2004. Following UN-mediated discussions in New York, USA, in mid-February 2004 agreement was reached on proposals for the resolution of the reunification issue, which would provide for Cyprus's accession to the EU as a single state. The final plan for reunification, submitted for approval in both the Republic of Cyprus and the 'TRNC' at referendums on 24 April, was endorsed in the latter with 64.9% of the votes cast, but rejected in the former with 75.8% of the votes (with the result that only that part of Cyprus administered by the principally Greek Cypriot Republic of Cyprus joined the EU). In early May the Turkish Prime Minister, Reçep Tayyip Erdoğan, made an official visit to Greece (the first by a Turkish premier in 16 years), in a demonstration of the improvement in bilateral relations. In July the Greek Minister of Public Order and his Turkish counterpart signed a security co-operation agreement in İstanbul. The EU opened accession talks with Turkey in October 2005; however, the Cypriot Government, supported by Greece, continued to criticize strongly Turkey's failure to open ports and airports to all EU members in accordance with a customs protocol, which in December 2006 resulted in a EU decision to suspend accession negotiations in several policy areas. In February 2008 the election of a new Greek Cypriot President, Demetris Christofias of the Progressive Party of the Working People, who immediately proposed the resumption of discussions with the 'TRNC' authorities, was welcomed by the international community.

In 1985 Greece and Albania reopened their borders, which had remained closed since 1940, and Greece formally annulled claims to North Epirus (southern Albania), where there is a sizeable Greek minority. In 1987 the Greek Government put a formal end to a legal vestige of the Second World War by proclaiming that it no longer considered Greece to be at war with Albania. In 1988 the two countries signed an agreement to promote trade between their border provinces. During the early 1990s, however, bilateral relations were severely strained by concerns relating to the treatment of ethnic Greeks residing in Albania (numbering an estimated 300,000) and to the illegal immigration of several thousand Albanians seeking work opportunities or political asylum in Greece. In March 1996 President Stefanopoulos signed a treaty of friendship and co-operation with Albania's President, Sali Berisha. Albania agreed to provide Greek-language education in schools serving the ethnic Greek population and Greece declared its willingness to issue temporary work permits for at least 150,000 seasonal workers from Albania.

Following a revolt in southern Albania in March 1997, the Greek Government mediated in negotiations with rebel leaders, in an effort to restore stability. Greece contributed 700 men to a multinational force led by Italy, which was established with a mandate to facilitate the distribution of humanitarian aid. In August Greece agreed to legitimize the status of tens of thousands of illegal Albanian immigrants by granting them temporary work permits in exchange for assistance from Albania in combating cross-border crime. In August 1998 the establishment was announced of a free border zone between the two countries to take effect in 2000; citizens of either country living in this area were to be given special entry documents for both Greece and Albania. A new border crossing was opened between Greece and Albania in May 1999. However, following the stabilization of the political situation in Albania, the influx of Albanians into Greece decreased considerably.

During the conflicts in the former Yugoslavia, Greece maintained close relations with the authorities of the Federal Republic of Yugoslavia (FRY—reconstituted as the State Union of Serbia and Montenegro in 2003–06) and advocated the removal of the UN-imposed trade embargo against the FRY. Greece's stance was shared, notably, by Bulgaria and Russia. Greece advocated a diplomatic solution to the conflict in the Serbian province of Kosovo (see the chapter on Serbia), and refused to participate in the March–June 1999 NATO air offensive against Serbian targets. A planned three-day visit by US President Bill Clinton in November was reduced to 24 hours' duration, following a series of protests (including two bombing incidents).

Attempts after 1991 by the FYRM to achieve international recognition as an independent state were strenuously opposed by the Greek Government, which insisted that 'Macedonia' was a purely geographical term (delineating an area that included a large part of northern Greece) and expressed fears that the adoption of such a name could imply ambitions on the Greek province of Macedonia and might foster a false claim to future territorial expansion. In early 1993 the Greek administration withdrew its former objection to the use of the word 'Macedonia', and its derivatives, as part of a fuller name for the new republic. At the end of March the Greek Government accepted a UN proposal that the title 'the former Yugoslav republic of Macedonia' should be used temporarily and agreed to hold direct talks with the FYRM to consider confidence-building measures. In late 1993 the newly elected PASOK Government strongly criticized recognition of the FYRM by several EU members and, despite assurances that it would adopt a more conciliatory attitude, in February 1994 the Government condemned a decision by the USA (the final permanent member of the UN Security Council to do so) to recognize the FYRM. At an emergency meeting in mid-February, the Government agreed to prevent any movement of goods, other than humanitarian aid, into the FYRM via the Greek port of Thessaloníki. The initiative was widely criticized by the international community as effectively constituting an illegal trade embargo, and the EU ministers responsible for foreign affairs urged Greece to revoke the measures, which, it was determined, violated EU law. In April the European Commission commenced legal proceedings against Greece at the Court of Justice of the European Communities. In April 1995 a preliminary opinion of the Court determined that the embargo was not in breach of Greece's obligations under the Treaty of Rome. In September the ministers responsible for foreign affairs of Greece and the FYRM, meeting in New York, under UN auspices, signed an interim accord to normalize relations between the two countries, which included recognition of the existing international border. Under the terms of the agreement, Greece was to grant access to the port facilities at Thessaloníki and to remove all obstructions to the cross-border movement of people and goods, while the FYRM was to approve a new state flag (removing the symbolic Vergina sun); the measures were successfully implemented by October. Negotiations were to be pursued regarding the issue of a permanent name for the FYRM, which would be acceptable to both sides. In March 1997 the Greek Minister of Foreign Affairs visited the FYRM for the first time since its independence from Yugoslavia. In the first half of 2001 armed insurrection by ethnic Albanian militants of the self-styled National Liberation Army in the FYRM (q.v.) caused alarm in Greece. However, following the deployment of a NATO force in June (which was replaced by an EU-led mission in March 2003) and the signature of a peace agreement in August, stability was gradually restored to the republic. Meanwhile, in 1999 work had commenced on the construction of a pipeline to carry petroleum from the FYRM's capital, Skopje, to Thessaloníki; the 214-km pipeline was inaugurated in July 2002. Greece strongly objected to the decision by the USA, announced in November 2004, that it would henceforth recognize the FYRM by its constitutional name of 'the Republic of Macedonia'.

Negotiations on the issue, mediated by the UN, continued, and in April 2005 a UN proposal for the adoption of the name 'Republic of Macedonia-Skopje' was rejected by both countries, although Greece welcomed it as a basis for further dialogue. The Greek Government repeatedly threatened to obstruct the FYRM's aspirations to NATO and EU accession, if it failed to agree to a compromise resolution. In January 2007 a UN envoy mediated a further bilateral meeting, after Greece protested at a decision by the FYRM Government to rename the international airport near Skopje after Alexander 'the Great' (who was considered by Greece to be integral to its cultural heritage). In January 2008 negotiations resumed between Greek and FYRM officials on a further proposal by the UN special envoy on the issue. Despite increased UN pressure on both Governments to reach a compromise resolution prior to a NATO conference in Bucharest, Romania, in early April, the continued impasse resulted in Greece's veto of the FYRM's application and a consequent decision to delay its membership invitation.

Government

Under the Constitution of June 1975, the President is Head of State and is elected by the Vouli (Parliament) for a five-year term. The President appoints the Prime Minister and, upon his recommendation, the other members of the Government. The unicameral Vouli has 300 members, directly elected by universal adult suffrage for four years. Greece comprises 13 administrative regions, and is divided into 54 prefectures (nomoi).

Defence

Greece returned to the military structure of the North Atlantic Treaty Organization (NATO, see p. 340) in 1980, after an absence of six years. Military service is compulsory, and lasts for up to 12 months. As assessed at November 2007, the armed forces numbered 156,600 (including conscripts), with an army of 93,500, a navy of 20,000, an air force of 31,500 and 11,600 joint-service troops; in addition, there was a coast guard and customs force of 4,000. Reservists, which included a national guard of 34,500, totalled 251,000. The USA occupied two military bases in Greece, with a total of 352 troops stationed there at November 2007. The budget for 2007 allocated €3,870m. to defence.

Economic Affairs

In 2006, according to estimates by the World Bank, Greece's gross national income (GNI), measured at average 2004–06 prices, was US $241,042m., equivalent to $21,690 per head (or $24,560 per head on an international purchasing-power parity basis). During 1996–2006, it was estimated, the population increased at an average annual rate of 0.4%, while gross domestic product (GDP) per head increased, in real terms, at an average annual rate of 3.7%. Overall GDP increased, in real terms, at an average annual rate of 4.1% in 1996–2006. Real GDP increased by 4.3% in 2006.

Agriculture (including hunting, forestry and fishing) contributed some 3.7% of GDP in 2006, and engaged 11.8% of the employed labour force in 2007. The principal cash crops are vegetables and fruit (which, together, accounted for 7.4% of total export earnings in 2004), cereals, sugar beet and tobacco. According to the World Bank, real agricultural GDP declined at an average annual rate of 0.9% during 1996–2005; the GDP of the sector rose by 0.7% in 2004, but decreased by 2.1% in 2005. Widespread destruction caused by forest fires, particularly in the southern Peloponnese region, in 2007, was expected to have a severe impact on agricultural production in that year.

Industry (including mining, manufacturing, utilities and construction) provided an estimated 24.2% of GDP in 2006, and engaged 22.5% of the employed labour force in 2007. According to the World Bank, during 1996–2005 real industrial GDP increased at an average annual rate of 3.4%; the GDP of the industrial sector declined by 0.1% in 2004, but increased by 1.2% in 2005.

Mining and quarrying contributed an estimated 0.5% of GDP in 2006, and engaged 0.4% of the employed labour force in 2007. Mineral fuels and lubricants, iron and steel, and aluminium and aluminium alloys are the major mineral and metal exports. Lignite, magnesite, silver ore and marble are also mined. In addition, Greece has small reserves of uranium, natural gas and gold.

Manufacturing provided an estimated 13.2% of GDP in 2006, and engaged 12.6% of the employed labour force in 2007. According to the World Bank, the GDP of the manufacturing sector increased, in real terms, by an annual average of 1.9% in

1996–2004; manufacturing GDP increased by 3.5% in 2003, but declined by 1.5% in 2004.

Energy is derived principally from lignite, which accounted for 60.2% of production in 2004, followed by natural gas (15.3%) and petroleum (14.3%). Greece is exploiting an offshore petroleum deposit in the north-eastern Aegean Sea. In March 2007 an agreement was concluded between the Governments of Russia, Greece and Bulgaria on the construction of a pipeline to transport Russian petroleum from the Bulgarian Black Sea port of Burgas to Alexandroupolis, on the Greek Aegean coast; work on the 288-km pipeline was expected to commence in 2008. Solar power resources are also being developed. Mineral fuels represented 17.9% of the total value of imports in 2005.

The services sector contributed 72.0% of GDP in 2006, and engaged 65.7% of the employed labour force in 2007. Tourism is an important source of foreign exchange. In 2005 there were 14.3m. visitor arrivals, and receipts from the tourist sector totalled US $13,697m. (an increase of 6.9%, compared with the previous year). According to the World Bank, during 1996–2005 the GDP of the services sector increased, in real terms, at an average annual rate of 4.1%; sectoral GDP increased by 3.5% in 2005.

In 2006 Greece recorded a visible trade deficit of US $44,285m., and there was a deficit of $29,565m. on the current account of the balance of payments. In 2004 the principal source of imports was Germany (13.4%), followed by Italy (12.9%); other major sources were France, the Netherlands and Russia. The principal market for exports in that year was also Germany (13.2%); other major purchasers were Italy, the United Kingdom, Bulgaria and the USA. The principal exports in that year were basic manufactures (in particular, non-ferrous metals), miscellaneous manufactured articles (especially clothing and accessories), food and live animals, machinery and transport equipment, chemicals, mineral fuels and lubricants, and crude materials. The principal imports were machinery and transport equipment, basic manufactures, chemicals, mineral fuels and lubricants (mainly petroleum and petroleum products), miscellaneous manufactured articles, and food and live animals.

According to government figures, the budgetary deficit was estimated to amount to €8,563m. (2.6% of GDP) in 2006. Greece's total external debt was estimated at €182,702m. at the end of 2004 (equivalent to 110.5% of GDP). In 1999 the cost of debt-servicing was equivalent to 9% of GDP. In 1996–2006 the average annual rate of inflation was 3.6%; consumer prices increased by 3.2% in 2006. The rate of unemployment was 9.1% in 2007.

Greece is a member of the European Union (EU, see p. 244), the Organisation for Economic Co-operation and Development (OECD, see p. 347) and the Organization of the Black Sea Economic Co-operation (see p. 367).

Greece qualified for full membership of the EU's economic and monetary union from 1 January 2001, and the common European currency, the euro, replaced the drachma as the country's legal tender from 1 January 2002. Greece's hosting of the summer Olympic Games in Athens in August 2004 resulted in an extended period of strong growth, and the tourism industry benefited. Later that year evidence emerged that the previous administration had significantly understated budgetary deficit and public debt figures since 1999, in order to qualify for EMU membership. Substantial revisions of data indicated that fiscal levels were considerably higher than presented, and the Government was obliged to conduct an immediate audit. Higher than projected expenditure on the Olympic Games contributed to the poor fiscal situation. Greece avoided legal proceedings, agreeing with the European Commission to reduce the budgetary deficit to below the 'euro zone' maximum level of 3% by the end of 2006. There were concerns that privatization measures would increase unemployment, and in December 2006 the public-sector trade unions initiated a strike in protest. In May 2007 the European Commission announced that it was to end budgetary supervision of Greece, after the Government made significant progress in reducing the deficit. In December and in early 2008 industrial action, affecting international flights, shipping movements and the provision of services, was organized in response to proposed reforms to the pension system (see Recent History), amid public concern that planned mergers of pension funds would lead to a lower per-head allocation, and result in an eventual increase in the national retirement age. Maintaining fiscal austerity remained a priority for the Government. Growth in GDP reached 4.1% in 2007, according to estimates released by the central bank. The annual rate of inflation exceeded the EU average of 2.1%, with IMF figures indicating that consumer prices increased by 3.0% in that year. Persistently high levels of inflation were attributed, in part, to the strong presence of trade unions, which continued to demand higher wages. Work was expected to commence in 2008 on the construction of a pipeline to transport Russian petroleum from the Bulgarian Black Sea port of Burgas to Alexandroupolis, on the Greek Aegean coast.

Education

Education is available free of charge at all levels, and is officially compulsory for all children between the ages of six and 15 years. Primary education begins at the age of six and lasts for six years. Secondary education, beginning at the age of 12, is generally for six years, divided into two equal cycles. The vernacular language (demotiki) has replaced the formal version (katharevoussa) in secondary education. Primary enrolment in 2004 included 100% of children in the relevant age-group, and the comparable ratio at secondary schools was 87%. There are 18 universities. In 2004 the equivalent of 70% of the relevant age-group were enrolled in tertiary education (males 60%; females 79%). In that year budgetary spending on education represented an estimated 7% of total expenditure.

Public Holidays

2008: 1 January (New Year's Day), 6 January (Epiphany), 10 March (Clean Monday), 25 March (Independence Day), 25–28 April (Greek Orthodox Easter), 1 May (Labour Day), 16 June (Whit Monday), 15 August (Assumption of the Virgin Mary), 28 October ('Ochi' Day, anniversary of Greek defiance of Italy's 1940 ultimatum), 25–26 December (Christmas).

2009: 1 January (New Year's Day), 6 January (Epiphany), 23 February (Clean Monday), 25 March (Independence Day), 10–13 April (Greek Orthodox Easter), 1 May (Labour Day), 8 June (Whit Monday), 15 August (Assumption of the Virgin Mary), 28 October ('Ochi' Day, anniversary of Greek defiance of Italy's 1940 ultimatum), 25–26 December (Christmas).

Weights and Measures

The metric system is in force.

GREECE

Statistical Survey

Source (unless otherwise stated): National Statistical Service of Greece, Odos Lykourgou 14–16, 101 66 Athens; tel. (210) 4852084; fax (210) 4852552; e-mail info@statistics.gr; internet www.statistics.gr.

Area and Population

AREA, POPULATION AND DENSITY

Area (sq km)	131,957*
Population (census results)†	
17 March 1991	10,259,900
March 2001	
Males	5,431,816
Females	5,532,204
Total	10,964,020
Population (official estimates at 1 January)	
2005	11,082,751
2006	11,125,179
2007	11,171,740
Density (per sq km) at 1 January 2007	84.7

* 50,949 sq miles.
† Including armed forces stationed abroad, but excluding foreign forces stationed in Greece.

PRINCIPAL TOWNS
(population at 2001 census*)

Athínai (Athens, the capital)	789,166	Pésterion	146,743
Thessaloníki (Salonika)	385,406	Iraklion	135,761
Piraeus	181,933	Larissa	131,095
Patras (Patrai)	168,530	Calithèa	115,150

* Population is *de jure*.
Source: UN, *Demographic Yearbook*.

BIRTHS, MARRIAGES AND DEATHS

	Registered live births		Registered marriages		Registered deaths	
	Number	Rate (per 1,000)	Number	Rate (per 1,000)	Number	Rate (per 1,000)
1999	100,643	9.3	61,165	5.6	103,304	9.5
2000	103,267	9.5	48,880	4.5	105,219	9.6
2001	102,282	9.3	58,491	5.3	102,559	9.4
2002	103,569	9.4	57,872	5.3	103,915	9.5
2003	104,420	9.5	61,081	5.5	105,529	9.6
2004	105,655	9.6	51,377	4.6	104,942	9.5
2005	107,545	9.7	61,043	5.5	105,091	9.5
2006	112,042	10.1	57,802	5.2	105,476	9.5

Expectation of life (years at birth, WHO estimates): 79.4 (males 76.9; females 82.1) in 2005 (Source: WHO, *World Health Statistics*).

ECONOMICALLY ACTIVE POPULATION
(sample surveys, '000 persons aged 15 years and over, January–March*)

	2005	2006	2007
Agriculture, hunting and forestry	532.1	523.0	511.0
Fishing	14.6	14.4	17.0
Mining and quarrying	16.8	17.3	16.8
Manufacturing	571.0	554.8	560.8
Electricity, gas and water supply	38.2	39.5	41.6
Construction	358.9	357.3	383.0
Wholesale and retail trade; repair of motor vehicles, motorcycles and personal and household goods	761.9	790.5	794.4
Hotels and restaurants	269.5	273.0	281.1
Transport, storage and communications	262.0	285.0	270.5
Financial intermediation	114.0	116.2	116.9
Real estate, renting and business activities	285.1	282.2	290.7

—continued	2005	2006	2007
Public administration and defence; compulsory social security	345.2	373.0	383.6
Education	313.1	328.6	328.3
Health and social work	219.7	223.0	241.3
Other community, social and personal service activities	152.8	149.8	152.9
Private households with employed persons	68.7	71.8	69.5
Extra-territorial organizations and bodies	1.4	0.6	1.6
Total employed	4,325.0	4,400.0	4,461.2
Unemployed	502.4	473.1	445.7
Total labour force	4,827.5	4,873.1	4,906.9
Males	2,869.1	2,887.7	2,905.6
Females	1,958.4	1,985.5	2,001.2

* Including members of the regular armed forces, but excluding persons on compulsory military service.

Health and Welfare

KEY INDICATORS

Total fertility rate (children per woman, 2005)	1.2
Under-5 mortality rate (per 1,000 live births, 2005)	5
HIV/AIDS (% of persons aged 15–49, 2005)	0.2
Physicians (per 1,000 head, 2001)	4.38
Hospital beds (per 1,000 head, 2004)	4.7
Health expenditure (2004): US $ per head (PPP)	2,179.4
Health expenditure (2004): % of GDP	7.9
Health expenditure (2004): public (% of total)	52.8
Human Development Index (2005): ranking	24
Human Development Index (2005): value	0.926

For sources and definitions, see explanatory note on p. vi.

Agriculture

PRINCIPAL CROPS
('000 metric tons)

	2004	2005	2006
Wheat	2,092	2,037	1,380
Rice (paddy)	188	159	201*
Barley	234	229	188
Maize	2,455	2,543	1,710
Oats	83	81	90
Potatoes	948	891	891*
Sugar beet	2,291	2,596	1,600
Olives	2,204	2,661	2,661*
Cottonseed†	645	670	520
Cabbages	175	180	180*
Lettuce	92	106	106*
Tomatoes	1,963	1,712	1,712*
Cauliflower and broccoli	89	86	86*
Pumpkins, squash and gourds	83	100	100*
Cucumbers and gherkins	156	136	136*
Aubergines (Eggplants)	73	68	68*
Chillies and green peppers	108	104	104*
Dry onions	203	187	187*
Green beans	72	68	68*
Watermelons	723	697	697*
Cantaloupes and other melons	175	169	169*
Oranges	698	952	952*

GREECE

Statistical Survey

—continued	2004	2005	2006
Tangerines, mandarins, clementines and satsumas	91	124	124*
Lemons and limes	68	88	88*
Apples	275	250	250*
Pears	76	79	79*
Apricots	90	73	73*
Peaches and nectarines	876	864	864*
Grapes	895	897	897*
Figs	22	24	24*
Tobacco (leaves)	134	126	126*
Cotton (lint)	391	430	400*

* FAO estimate.
† Unofficial figures.

Aggregate production ('000 metric tons, may include official, semi-official or estimated data): Total cereals 5,088 in 2004, 5,084 in 2005, 3,592 in 2006; Total roots and tubers 954 in 2004, 896 in 2005, 896 in 2006; Total vegetables (incl. melons) 4,254 in 2004, 3,939 in 2005, 3,939 in 2006; Total fruits (excl. melons) 3,360 in 2004, 3,615 in 2005, 3,615 in 2006.

Source: FAO.

LIVESTOCK
('000 head, year ending 30 September)

	2004	2005	2006
Horses	27	27	27*
Asses, mules or hinnies	73	69	69*
Cattle	603	603	617
Pigs	940	949	949*
Sheep	9,000	8,827	8,790
Goats	5,619	5,509	5,417
Chickens	30,391	31,371	31,371*

* FAO estimate.
Source: FAO.

LIVESTOCK PRODUCTS
('000 metric tons)

	2003	2004	2005
Cattle meat	61.8	77.0	72.4
Sheep meat*	80.0	93.5	92.6
Goat meat	47.2	57.8	57.4
Pig meat	111.1	107.5	109.4
Horse meat*	2.7	2.7	2.7
Chicken meat*	134.4	143.3	144.4
Other meat*	6.0	11.0	10.2
Cows' milk	797.8	774.2	790.8
Sheep's milk	735.0	744.7	790.8
Goats' milk	515.0	519.4	511.4
Hen eggs	105.6	100.5	100.1
Honey	15.7	15.9	16.3
Wool: greasy	9.0	9.1	9.1

* FAO estimates.
2006: Figures assumed to be unchanged from 2005.
Source: FAO.

Forestry

ROUNDWOOD REMOVALS
('000 cubic metres, excl. bark)

	2003	2004	2005
Sawlogs, veneer logs and logs for sleepers	528	381	420
Other industrial wood	71	88	99
Fuel wood	1,074	1,225	1,004
Total	1,673	1,694	1,523

2006: Figures assumed to be unchanged from 2005 (FAO estimates).
Source: FAO.

SAWNWOOD PRODUCTION
('000 cubic metres, incl. railway sleepers)

	2001*	2002	2003
Coniferous (softwood)	71	81	74
Broadleaved (hardwood)	52	115	117
Total	123	196	191

* FAO estimates.
2004–06: Figures assumed to be unchanged from 2003 (FAO estimates).
Source: FAO.

Fishing
('000 metric tons, live weight)

	2003	2004	2005
Capture	93.4	93.9	92.7
European pilchard (sardine)	8.7	9.2	11.3
European anchovy	13.8	13.4	11.3
Aquaculture	101.4	97.1	106.2
European seabass	27.3	25.8	31.0
Gilthead seabream	44.1	37.4	43.8
Mediterranean mussel	25.6	28.8	26.0
Total catch	194.8	191.0	199.0

Note: Figures exclude corals and sponges (metric tons, capture only): 2.2 in 2003; 1.0 in 2004; 1.8 in 2005.
Source: FAO.

Mining
('000 metric tons, unless otherwise indicated)

	2003	2004	2005*
Lignite	69,411	68,000*	68,000
Crude petroleum ('000 barrels)	1,026	1,100*	1,100
Natural gas (million cu m)*	36	30	30
Iron ore*†	600	575	575
Bauxite	2,442	2,444	3,315
Zinc†	30.4	—	—
Lead*†	20.0	—	—
Nickel†	21.4	21.7	22.0
Silver (metric tons)†	79.2	78.0*	78.0
Magnesite (crude)	549.0	550.0*	500.0
Salt (unrefined)	192.2	190.0*	190.0
Bentonite	1,156.6	1,160.0*	1,200.0
Kaolin	59.7	60.0*	60.0
Gypsum	731.8	735.0*	735.0
Feldspar	102.8	103.0*	105.0
Perlite (crude)	1,079.0	850.0*	1,000.0
Pozzolan	1,383.5	1,400.0*	1,400.0
Pumice	893.0	890.0*	800.0
Marble ('000 cu m)	233.4	230.0*	230.0

* Estimate(s).
† Figures refer to the metal content of ores and concentrates.
Source: US Geological Survey.

GREECE
Statistical Survey

Industry

SELECTED PRODUCTS
('000 metric tons, unless otherwise indicated)

	2003	2004	2005
Olive oil (virgin)	504	321	386
Raw sugar*	223	282	n.a.
Wine	387	443	437
Beer of barley	440*	420*	400†
Liquefied petroleum gas ('000 barrels)	8,932	8,900†	8,900†
Naphthas ('000 barrels)	7,905	8,000†	8,000†
Motor spirit (petrol) ('000 barrels)	32,725	32,000†	32,000†
Jet fuels ('000 barrels)	14,400	14,000†	14,000†
Distillate fuel oils ('000 barrels)	41,776	42,000†	42,000†
Residual fuel oils ('000 barrels)	49,617	50,000†	50,000†
Cement (hydraulic)†	15,300	15,000	15,000
Crude steel (incl. alloys)	1,701	1,967	2,266
Aluminium (primary, unwrought)	167.8	167.3	165.0†

* Unofficial figure(s).
† Estimate(s).

Sources: FAO; US Geological Survey.

2003 (metric tons, unless otherwise indicated): Cigarettes (million) 26,249; Cotton yarn 108,700; Woven cotton fabrics 14,000; Wool yarn 3,300; Yarn of artificial material 7,900; Leather footwear ('000 pairs) 3,563; Wrapping and packaging paper and paperboard ('000 metric tons) 94; Sulphuric acid ('000 metric tons) 484; Polyvinyl chloride ('000 metric tons) 77 (Source: UN, _Industrial Commodity Statistics Yearbook_).

Finance

CURRENCY AND EXCHANGE RATES

Monetary Units
100 cent = 1 euro (€).

Sterling, Dollar and Euro Equivalents (31 December 2007)
£1 sterling = 1.3609 euros;
US $1 = 0.6793 euros;
€10 = £7.35 = $14.72.

Average Exchange Rate (euros per US $)
2005 0.8041
2006 0.7971
2007 0.7306

Note: The national currency was formerly the drachma. Greece became a member of the euro area on 1 January 2001, after which a fixed exchange rate of €1 = 340.75 drachmae was in operation. Euro notes and coins were introduced on 1 January 2002. The euro and local currency circulated alongside each other until 28 February, after which the euro became the sole legal tender. Some of the figures in this Survey are still in terms of drachmae.

CENTRAL GOVERNMENT BUDGET
(€ million)*

Revenue	2005	2006†	2007‡
Ordinary budget	44,760	47,830	51,370
Tax revenue	42,093	44,820	48,030
Direct taxes	18,371	18,560	19,450
Personal income tax	8,292	9,100	9,720
Corporate income tax	4,730	4,500	4,620
Indirect taxes	23,722	26,260	28,580
Consumption taxes	7,077	7,535	8,210
Transaction taxes	15,817	17,675	19,375
Value-added tax	14,131	15,855	17,435
Non-tax revenue	2,667	3,010	3,340
Non-recurrent receipts	—	770	—
Tax refunds	−2,554	−2,200	−2,200
Investment budget	2,686	3,550	3,890
From EU	2,623	3,400	3,750
Total	48,892	49,950	53,060

Expenditure§	2005	2006†	2007‡
Ordinary budget	48,686	50,413	53,360
Salaries and pensions	18,347	19,555	20,799
Grants to social security and medical care	8,415	8,662	9,786
Operating expenditure	7,931	8,551	8,732
Returned resources	3,873	4,114	4,293
Interest payments	9,774	9,530	9,750
Investment budget	7,524	8,100	8,750
Total	56,210	58,513	62,110

* Figures refer to the budgetary transactions of the central Government, excluding the operations of social security funds and public entities (such as hospitals, educational institutions and government agencies) with individual budgets.
† Estimates.
‡ Forecasts.
§ Excluding amortization payments (€ million): 21,752 in 2005; 16,950 in 2006 (estimate); 24,247 in 2007 (forecast). Also excluded is expenditure on military procurement (€ million): 1,394 in 2005; 1,500 in 2006 (estimate); 1,700 in 2007 (forecast).

Source: Ministry of the Economy and Finance, Athens.

INTERNATIONAL RESERVES
(US $ million at 31 December)*

	2004	2005	2006
Gold†	1,516.8	1,780.6	2,284.1
IMF special drawing rights	27.0	29.1	29.5
Reserve position in IMF	420.2	168.3	128.1
Foreign exchange	743.7	309.1	408.3
Total	2,707.7	2,287.0	2,850.0

* Figures exclude deposits made with the European Monetary Institute.
† Gold reserves are valued at market-related prices.

Source: IMF, _International Financial Statistics_.

MONEY SUPPLY
(€ '000 million at 31 December)

	2004	2005	2006
Currency in circulation*	12.76	14.36	15.95
Demand deposits	91.10	98.96	99.67

* Currency put into circulation by the Bank of Greece (€ '000 million): 13.19 in 2004; 15.61 in 2005; 17.52 in 2006.

Source: IMF, _International Financial Statistics_.

COST OF LIVING
(Consumer Price Index; base: 2000 = 100)

	2004	2005	2006
Food	116.8	117.5	121.9
Fuel and light	110.9	131.2	n.a.
Clothing	113.6	119.0	121.9
Rent	120.9	126.0	n.a.
All items (incl. others)	114.1	118.2	122.0

Source: ILO.

GREECE

Statistical Survey

NATIONAL ACCOUNTS
(€ million at current prices, provisional figures)

National Income and Product

	2004	2005	2006
Compensation of employees	65,122	70,186	76,743
Net operating surplus/mixed income	80,105	85,991	91,970
Domestic primary incomes	145,227	156,177	168,713
Consumption of fixed capital	20,306	21,643	23,085
Gross domestic product (GDP) at factor cost	165,533	177,820	191,798
Taxes on production and imports	22,147	23,345	26,150
Less Subsidies	2,454	2,555	3,963
GDP in market prices	185,225	198,609	213,985
Primary incomes received from abroad	5,200	5,468	7,282
Less Primary incomes paid abroad	7,339	9,453	11,189
Gross national income (GNI)	183,086	194,624	210,077
Less Consumption of fixed capital	20,306	21,643	23,085
Net national income	162,780	172,981	186,992
Current transfers from abroad	2,626	2,552	2,735
Less Current transfers paid abroad	2,151	2,733	2,835
Net national disposable income	163,255	172,800	186,892

Expenditure on the Gross Domestic Product

	2004	2005	2006
Final consumption expenditure	162,405	173,800	185,813
Households	128,638	138,475	149,453
Non-profit institutions serving households	2,174	2,340	2,500
General government	31,594	32,986	33,860
Gross capital formation	45,773	47,261	55,056
Gross fixed capital formation	45,196	46,539	55,160
Changes in inventories	577	722	−104
Total domestic expenditure	208,178	221,061	240,869
Exports of goods and services	40,335	43,107	46,868
Less Imports of goods and services	63,289	65,560	73,752
GDP in purchasers' values	185,225	198,609	213,985

Gross Domestic Product by Economic Activity

	2004	2005	2006
Agriculture, hunting, forestry and fishing	7,812	7,698	7,061
Mining and quarrying	1,084	991	959
Manufacturing	18,995	22,170	25,050
Electricity, gas and water supply	3,542	3,572	3,767
Construction	12,724	12,729	16,317
Wholesale and retail trade; repair of motor vehicles and household goods	24,264	25,725	27,355
Hotels and restaurants	13,126	14,326	14,774
Transport, storage and communications	14,765	15,198	15,107
Financial intermediation	5,843	7,026	7,709
Real estate, renting and business activities	24,261	25,817	26,971
Public administration and defence; compulsory social security	14,501	15,093	15,793
Education	9,413	9,947	10,569
Health and social work	6,555	7,969	8,710
Other service activities	7,668	8,464	8,533
Private households with employed persons	1,223	1,293	1,424
Gross value added in basic prices	165,775	178,017	190,098
Taxes, less subsidies, on products	19,450	20,592	23,887
GDP in market prices	185,225	198,609	213,985

BALANCE OF PAYMENTS
(US $ million)

	2004	2005	2006
Exports of goods f.o.b.	15,739	17,631	20,300
Imports of goods f.o.b.	−47,360	−51,900	−64,585
Trade balance	−31,621	−34,268	−44,285
Exports of services	33,085	33,914	35,762
Imports of services	−14,020	−14,742	−16,367
Balance on goods and services	−12,556	−15,096	−24,889
Other income received	3,495	4,072	4,566
Other income paid	−8,920	−11,102	−13,524
Balance on goods, services and income	−17,980	−22,126	−33,847
Current transfers received	7,901	8,615	8,587
Current transfers paid	−3,396	−4,722	−4,305
Current balance	−13,476	−18,233	−29,565
Capital account (net)	2,990	2,563	3,822
Direct investment abroad	−1,028	−1,476	−4,226
Direct investment from abroad	2,105	658	5,401
Portfolio investment assets	−13,835	−23,194	−9,374
Portfolio investment liabilities	31,301	32,308	18,738
Financial derivatives liabilities	−429	13	920
Other investment assets	−7,463	−8,740	−7,336
Other investment liabilities	−3,813	16,064	21,539
Net errors and omissions	373	−67	361
Overall balance	−3,277	−104	279

Sources: IMF, *International Financial Statistics*.

External Trade

PRINCIPAL COMMODITIES
(US $ million)

Imports c.i.f.	2002	2003	2004
Food and live animals	3,329.9	4,150.7	4,833.6
Meat and meat preparations	759.8	919.4	1,050.7
Crude materials (inedible) except fuels	915.5	1,084.4	1,312.3
Mineral fuels, lubricants, etc.	4,514.5	6,161.2	6,693.6
Petroleum, petroleum products, etc.	4,150.9	5,657.6	6,100.3
Crude petroleum oils, etc.	3,373.7	4,140.7	4,650.7
Chemicals and related products	3,572.6	5,709.4	7,131.2
Medicinal and pharmaceutical products	859.3	2,181.8	2,796.6
Medicaments (incl. veterinary medicaments)	736.4	1,899.6	2,414.2
Basic manufactures	4,521.6	6,117.4	7,415.9
Textile yarn, fabrics, etc.	886.2	1,086.6	1,167.6
Iron and steel	901.5	1,226.0	1,648.3
Machinery and transport equipment	10,694.4	15,712.0	18,185.9
Machinery specialized for particular industries	668.1	966.0	1,042.8
General industrial machinery equipment and parts	1,026.4	1,405.1	1,787.6
Telecommunications and sound equipment	1,157.4	1,541.1	1,892.3
Other electrical machinery, apparatus, etc.	1,044.2	1,448.7	1,819.1
Road vehicles and parts*	2,748.4	3,935.4	5,594.2
Passenger motor cars (excl. buses)	1,685.4	2,464.8	3,618.8
Other transport equipment*	2,949.1	4,996.0	4,153.3
Ships, boats and floating structures	2,535.7	3,675.8	2,439.2
Miscellaneous manufactured articles	4,199.7	4,992.0	6,208.1
Clothing and accessories (excl. footwear)	888.0	1,303.5	1,634.9
Total (incl. others)	32,518.8	44,856.4	52,809.2

* Excluding tyres, engines and electrical parts.

GREECE

Statistical Survey

Exports f.o.b.	2002	2003	2004
Food and live animals	1,817.6	1,975.6	2,166.2
Vegetables and fruit	1,096.9	1,055.8	1,124.8
Fresh or dried fruit and nuts (excl. oil nuts)	399.7	409.4	435.1
Preserved fruit and fruit preparations	307.2	264.0	268.0
Beverages and tobacco	492.0	635.2	614.1
Tobacco and manufactures	374.4	481.7	445.4
Unmanufactured tobacco (incl. refuse)	241.6	319.8	282.2
Crude materials (inedible) except fuels	564.7	757.1	850.9
Textile fibres and waste	233.0	399.0	395.9
Cotton	225.3	392.5	388.1
Raw cotton (excl. linters)	211.2	374.4	365.1
Mineral fuels, lubricants, etc.	909.4	940.4	1,047.9
Petroleum, petroleum products, etc.	864.1	885.2	1,002.7
Refined petroleum products	857.9	874.4	986.2
Animal and vegetable oils, fats and waxes	217.7	355.4	199.8
Fixed vegetable oils and fats	212.5	347.9	189.9
Soft fixed vegetable oils	211.3	346.4	187.6
Olive oil	193.8	323.1	168.3
Chemicals and related products	1,052.6	1,674.1	2,036.0
Basic manufactures	2,203.0	2,834.1	3,373.8
Textile yarn, fabrics, etc.	484.5	632.1	694.6
Non-metallic mineral manufactures	275.6	329.5	319.2
Lime, cement, etc.	189.8	238.9	215.3
Non-ferrous metals	700.5	910.7	1,059.3
Aluminium	508.9	709.9	765.6
Worked aluminium and aluminium alloys	407.1	596.1	637.4
Machinery and transport equipment	1,426.3	1,746.9	2,052.9
Electrical machinery, apparatus, etc.	374.3	435.8	585.6
Miscellaneous manufactured articles	1,931.8	2,500.5	2,254.4
Clothing and accessories (excl. footwear)	1,420.9	1,819.6	1,804.5
Total (incl. others)	10,765.8	13,671.4	15,224.0

Source: UN, *International Trade Statistics Yearbook*.

2005 (€ million): Total imports 41,759.8 (Oil-related 6,055.8); Total exports 14,200.9 (Oil-related 2,257.7) (Source: Bank of Greece).

2006 (€ million): Total imports 51,440.6 (Oil-related 11,701.1); Total exports 16,154.3 (Oil-related 2,939.8) (Source: Bank of Greece).

PRINCIPAL TRADING PARTNERS
(US $ million)*

Imports c.i.f.	2002	2003	2004
Austria	251.7	445.0	561.8
Belgium	1,415.5	1,632.8	1,974.6
Bulgaria	323.5	419.5	574.5
China, People's Republic	1,006.5	1,383.1	1,764.6
Denmark	327.3	397.3	495.7
Finland	305.7	535.8	533.3
France (incl. Monaco)	1,847.7	3,004.2	3,382.0
Germany	3,962.4	5,654.0	7,054.7
Iran	479.1	973.6	1,436.0
Italy	3,746.0	5,625.0	6,803.0
Japan	981.8	1,918.6	1,537.3
Korea, Republic	1,938.2	2,479.5	2,143.7

Imports c.i.f.—continued	2002	2003	2004
Netherlands	1,813.2	2,371.6	2,933.6
Russia	2,386.3	2,688.5	2,863.8
Saudi Arabia	918.4	1,232.6	1,597.0
Spain	1,252.7	1,633.9	2,026.4
Sweden	384.6	581.9	775.5
Switzerland	492.9	636.5	753.1
Turkey	620.2	881.6	1,223.6
United Kingdom	1,322.9	1,856.3	2,199.8
USA	1,528.8	2,264.6	2,345.8
Total (incl. others)	32,518.8	44,856.4	52,809.2

Exports f.o.b.	2002	2003	2004
Albania	335.4	358.7	414.5
Austria	78.0	118.0	158.3
Belgium	113.9	204.7	242.2
Bulgaria	576.7	834.1	965.6
Cyprus	511.5	642.8	719.9
France (incl. Monaco)	384.4	581.7	647.6
Germany	1,123.1	1,757.3	2,009.0
Israel	126.8	119.3	120.7
Italy	916.1	1,470.3	1,536.6
Macedonia, former Yugoslav republic	341.3	364.4	382.0
Malta	109.8	77.7	34.0
Netherlands	254.3	357.3	409.2
Romania	292.7	350.4	479.1
Russia	305.2	344.8	326.7
Serbia and Montenegro†	187.0	242.2	n.a.
Spain	270.3	501.9	514.2
Sweden	97.2	140.9	159.7
Turkey	362.2	532.5	687.8
United Kingdom	670.1	999.6	1,155.8
USA	569.9	878.3	806.6
Total (incl. others)	10,765.8	13,671.4	15,224.0

* Imports by country of first consignment; exports by country of consumption.
† The Federal Republic of Yugoslavia prior to February 2003.

Source: UN, *International Trade Statistics Yearbook*.

Transport

RAILWAYS
(estimated traffic)

	2002	2003	2004
Passenger-kilometres (million)	1,836	1,574	1,669
Net ton-kilometres (million)	327	457	592

Source: UN, *Statistical Yearbook*.

ROAD TRAFFIC
(motor vehicles in use at 31 December)

	2004	2005	2006
Passenger cars	4,073,511	4,303,129	4,543,016
Buses and coaches	26,780	26,829	26,938
Lorries and vans	1,159,137	1,186,483	1,219,483
Motorcycles	1,042,605	1,124,172	1,205,816
Total	6,302,033	6,640,613	6,997,253

SHIPPING

Merchant Fleet
(registered at 31 December)

	2004	2005	2006
Number of vessels	1,540	1,491	1,455
Total displacement ('000 grt)	32,040.7	30,744.7	32,048.1

Source: Lloyd's Register-Fairplay, *World Fleet Statistics*.

GREECE

International Sea-borne Freight Traffic
('000 metric tons*)

	2002	2003	2004
Goods loaded	21,804	26,000	24,400
Goods unloaded	50,900	51,900	51,900

* Figures rounded to nearest 100,000 metric tons.

Source: UN, *Monthly Bulletin of Statistics*.

CIVIL AVIATION
(traffic on scheduled services)

	2001	2002	2003
Kilometres flown (million)	68	58	55
Passengers carried ('000)	3,320	3,015	2,855
Passenger-kilometres (million)	8,212	7,194	6,177
Total ton-kilometres (million)	879	760	640

Source: UN, *Statistical Yearbook*.

Tourism

FOREIGN TOURIST ARRIVALS BY NATIONALITY
(arrivals at national borders, excl. cruise ship passengers)

Country	2003	2004	2005
Albania	1,118,558	1,193,936	1,478,197
Austria	443,595	440,391	646,470
Belgium-Luxembourg	384,793	374,557	n.a.
Bulgaria	459,554	440,263	599,872
Denmark	294,076	282,340	288,858
France	714,821	621,407	676,658
Germany	2,267,063	2,189,222	2,241,942
Italy	865,730	898,208	1,128,506
Macedonia, former Yugoslav republic	443,319	411,103	n.a.
Netherlands	635,882	611,990	666,287
Sweden	352,905	334,150	316,042
United Kingdom	3,008,382	2,869,737	2,718,721
Total (incl. others)	13,969,393	13,312,629	14,276,465

Tourism receipts (US $ million, incl. passenger transport): 10,842 in 2003; 12,809 in 2004; 13,697 in 2005.

Source: World Tourism Organization.

Communications Media

	2004	2005	2006
Telephones ('000 main lines in use)	6,352.3	6,310.4	6,185.2
Mobile cellular telephones ('000 subscribers)	9,324.3	10,260.4	11,097.5
Personal computers ('000 in use)	986	n.a.	n.a.
Internet users ('000)	1,955.0	2,001.0	2,048.1
Broadband subscribers ('000)	51.5	160.1	487.9

Television receivers ('000 in use): 5,500 in 2001.
Radio receivers ('000 in use): 5,020 in 1997.
Facsimile machines (number in use, estimate): 40,000 in 1996.
Daily newspapers (1997): 207 (average circulation 1,389,000 copies).
Non-daily newspapers (2000): 14 (average circulation 441,000 copies).
Books (titles published): 4,225 in 1996.

Sources: UN, *Statistical Yearbook*, UNESCO, *Statistical Yearbook*, and International Telecommunication Union.

Education

(2005/06, unless otherwise indicated)

	Institutions	Teachers	Students
Pre-primary	5,715*	n.a.	143,401
Primary	5,753	58,376	639,685
Secondary: General	3,308	62,149	569,887
Secondary: Technical, vocational and ecclesiastical	660	16,066	123,436
Higher: Universities	21†	11,575	171,967†
Higher: Technical, vocational and ecclesiastical	75	12,021	147,715

* In addition there were 11,461 kindergartens.
† Excluding data from the Medical School of Athens.

Adult literacy rate (UNESCO estimates): 96.0% (males 97.8%; females 94.2%) in 2001 (Source: UNESCO Institute for Statistics).

Directory

The Constitution

A new Constitution for the Hellenic Republic came into force on 11 June 1975. The main provisions of this Constitution, as subsequently amended, are summarized below.

Greece shall be a parliamentary democracy with a President as Head of State. All powers are derived from the people and exist for the benefit of the people. The established religion is that of The Eastern Orthodox Church of Christ.

EXECUTIVE AND LEGISLATIVE

The President

In March 1986 a series of amendments to the Constitution was approved by a majority vote of Parliament, which relieved the President of his executive power and transferred such power to the legislature, thus confining the Head of State to a largely ceremonial role.

The President is elected by Parliament for a period of five years. The re-election of the same person shall be permitted only once. The President represents the State in relations with other nations, is Supreme Commander of the armed forces and may declare war and conclude treaties. The President shall appoint the Prime Minister and, on the Prime Minister's recommendation, the other members of the Government. The President shall convoke the Vouli (Parliament) once every year and in extraordinary session whenever he deems it reasonable. In exceptional circumstances the President may preside over the Cabinet, convene the Council of the Republic, and suspend the Vouli for a period not exceeding 30 days. The President can dissolve the Vouli only if the resignation of two Governments in quick succession demonstrates the absence of political stability. If no party has a majority in the Vouli, the President must offer an opportunity to form a government to the leader of each of the four biggest parties in turn, strictly following the order of their parliamentary strengths. If no party leader is able to form a government, the President may try to assemble an all-party government; failing that, the President must appoint a caretaker cabinet, led by a senior judge, to hold office until a fresh election takes place. The Constitution continues to reserve a substantial moderating role for the President, however, in that he retains the right to object to legislation and may request the Vouli to reconsider it or to approve it with an enlarged majority.

The Government

The Government consists of the Cabinet which comprises the Prime Minister and Ministers. The Government determines and directs the general policy of the State in accordance with the Constitution and the laws. The Cabinet must enjoy the confidence of the Vouli and may be removed by a vote of no confidence. The Prime Minister is to be the leader of the party with an absolute majority in the Vouli, or, if no such party exists, the leader of the party with a relative majority.

The Council of the Republic

The Council of the Republic shall be composed of all former democratic Presidents, the Prime Minister, the leader of the opposition

GREECE

and the parliamentary Prime Ministers of governments that have enjoyed the confidence of the Vouli, presided over by the President. It shall meet when the largest parties are unable to form a government with the confidence of the Vouli and may empower the President to appoint a Prime Minister who may or may not be a member of the Vouli. The Council may also authorize the President to dissolve the Vouli.

The Vouli

The Vouli (Parliament) is to be unicameral and composed of not fewer than 200 and not more than 300 deputies elected by direct, universal and secret ballot for a term of four years. The Vouli shall elect its own President (Speaker). It must meet once a year for a regular session of at least five months. Bills passed by the Vouli must be ratified by the President, and the President's veto can be nullified by an absolute majority of the total number of deputies. The Vouli may impeach the President by a motion signed by one-third and passed by two-thirds of the total number of deputies. The Vouli is also empowered to impeach present or former members of the Government. In these cases the defendant shall be brought before an ad hoc tribunal presided over by the President of the Supreme Court and composed of 12 judges. Certain legislative work, as specified in the Constitution, must be passed by the Vouli in plenum, and the Vouli cannot make a decision without an absolute majority of the members present, which under no circumstances shall be less than one-quarter of the total number of deputies. The Constitution provides for certain legislative powers to be exercised by not more than two Parliamentary Departments. The Vouli may revise the Constitution in accordance with the procedure laid down in the Constitution.

THE JUDICIAL AUTHORITY

Justice is to be administered by courts of regular judges, who enjoy personal and functional independence. The President, after consultations with a judicial council, shall appoint the judges for life. The judges are subject only to the Constitution and the law. Courts are divided into administrative, civil and penal and shall be organized by virtue of special laws. They must not apply laws which are contrary to the Constitution. The final jurisdiction in matters of judicial review rests with a Special Supreme Tribunal.

Certain laws, passed before the implementation of this Constitution and deemed not contrary to it, are to remain in force. Other specified laws, even if contrary to the Constitution, are to remain in force until repealed by further legislation.

INDIVIDUAL AND SPECIAL RIGHTS

All citizens are equal under the Constitution and before the law, having the same rights and obligations. No titles of nobility or distinction are to be conferred or recognized. All persons are to enjoy full protection of life, honour and freedom, irrespective of nationality, race, creed or political allegiance. Retrospective legislation is prohibited and no citizen may be punished without due process of law. Freedom of speech, of the press, of association and of religion are guaranteed under the Constitution. All persons have the right to a free education, which the state has the duty to provide. Work is a right and all workers, irrespective of sex or other distinction, are entitled to equal remuneration for rendering services of equal value. The right of peaceful assembly, the right of a person to property and the freedom to form political parties are guaranteed under the Constitution. The exercise of the right to vote by all citizens over 18 years of age is obligatory. No person may exercise his rights and liberties contrary to the Constitution.

MOUNT ATHOS

The district of Mount Athos shall, in accordance with its ancient privileged status, be a self-governing part of the Greek State and its sovereignty shall remain unaffected.

The Government

HEAD OF STATE

President: KAROLOS PAPOULIAS (inaugurated 12 March 2005).

GOVERNMENT
(March 2008)

Prime Minister: Dr KONSTANTINOS (KOSTAS) A. KARAMANLIS.

Minister of State and Government Spokesman: THEODOROS ROUSSOPOULOS.

Minister of the Economy and Finance: GEORGIOS ALOGOSKOUFIS.

Minister of Foreign Affairs: DORA BAKOYANNIS.

Minister of National Defence: EVANGELOS MEIMARAKIS.

Minister of the Interior: PROKOPIS PAVLOPOULOS.

Minister of Development: CHRISTOS FOLIAS.

Minister of the Environment, Physical Planning and Public Works: GEORGIOS SOUFLIAS.

Minister of Education and Religious Affairs: EVRIPIDIS STYLIANIDIS.

Minister of Employment and Social Protection: FANI PALLI-PETRALIA.

Minister of Health and Welfare: DIMITRIOS AVRAMOPOULOS.

Minister of Agricultural Development and Food: ALEXANDROS KONTOS.

Minister of Justice: SOTIRIOS HADJIGAKIS.

Minister of Culture: MICHALIS LIAPIS.

Minister of Transport and Communications: KONSTANTINOS HADJIDAKIS.

Minister of Merchant Marine: GEORGIOS VOULGARAKIS.

Minister of Macedonia and Thrace: MARGARITIS TZIMAS.

Minister of Tourism: ARIS SPILIOTOPOULOS.

MINISTRIES

Office of the President: Odos Vassileos Georgiou 2, 100 28 Athens; tel. (210) 7283111; fax (210) 7248938; e-mail publicrelationsoffice@presidency.gr; internet www.presidency.gr.

Office of the Prime Minister: Maximos Mansion, Herodou Atticou 19, 106 74 Athens; tel. (210) 7243333; fax (210) 7240762; e-mail mail@primeminister.gr; internet www.primeminister.gr.

Ministry of Agricultural Development and Food: Odos Acharnon 2, 104 32 Athens; tel. (210) 2124000; fax (210) 5240475; e-mail info@minagric.gr; internet www.minagric.gr.

Ministry of Culture: Odos Bouboulinas 42, 106 82 Athens; tel. (210) 8894800; fax (210) 8894805; e-mail dpse@hch.culture.gr; internet www.culture.gr.

Ministry of Development: Odos Mesogeion 119, 101 92 Athens; tel. (210) 6969218; fax (210) 7788279; e-mail grammatia@ypan.gr; internet www.ypan.gr.

Ministry of the Economy and Finance: Odos Nikis 5–7, 101 80 Athens; tel. (210) 3332000; e-mail ypetho@mnec.gr; internet www.mnec.gr.

Ministry of Education and Religious Affairs: Odos Metropoleos 15, 101 85 Athens; tel. (210) 3723000; fax (210) 3248264; e-mail webmaster@ypepth.gr; internet www.ypepth.gr.

Ministry of Employment and Social Protection: Odos Pireos 40, 104 37 Athens; tel. (210) 5295000; fax (210) 5249805; internet www.ypakp.gr.

Ministry of the Environment, Physical Planning and Public Works: Odos Trikoupi 182, 115 23 Athens; tel. (210) 6415700; fax (210) 6432589; e-mail minister@minenv.gr; internet www.minenv.gr.

Ministry of Foreign Affairs: Odos Akadimias 3, 106 71 Athens; tel. (210) 3682700; fax (210) 3624195; e-mail mfa@mfa.gr; internet www.mfa.gr.

Ministry of Health and Welfare: Odos Aristotelous 19, 104 33 Athens; tel. (210) 5232820; fax (210) 5231707; e-mail webmaster@mohaw.gr; internet www.mohaw.gr.

Ministry of the Interior: Odos Stadiou 27, 101 83 Athens; tel. (210) 3744000; fax (210) 3240631; e-mail info@ypes.gr; internet www.ypes.gr.

Ministry of Justice: Odos Mesogeion 96, 115 27 Athens; tel. (210) 7711019; fax (210) 7759879; e-mail minjust@otenet.gr; internet www.ministryofjustice.gr.

Ministry of Macedonia and Thrace: Administration Bldg, 541 23 Thessaloníki; tel. (2310) 379000; fax (2310) 263332; e-mail info@mathra.gr; internet www.mathra.gr.

Ministry of Merchant Marine: Odos Gregoriou Lambraki 150, 18 518 Piraeus; tel. (210) 4191700; fax (210) 4134286; e-mail egov@yen.gr; internet www.yen.gr.

Ministry of National Defence: Odos Mesogeion 227–231, 154 51 Athens; tel. (210) 6598607; fax (210) 6443832; e-mail minister@mod.mil.gr; internet www.mod.gr.

Ministry of Tourism: Odos Mesogeion 119, 101 92 Athens; tel. (210) 6969813; e-mail info@mintour.gr; internet www.mintour.gr.

Ministry of Transport and Communications: Odos Anastaseos 2, 101 91 Athens; tel. (210) 6508000; fax (210) 6508088; e-mail press@yme.gov.gr; internet www.yme.gr.

Legislature

Vouli
(Parliament)

Parliament Bldg, Leoforos Vassilissis Sofias 2, 100 21 Athens; tel. (210) 3707000; fax (210) 3692170; e-mail info@parliament.gr; internet www.parliament.gr.

President: DIMITRIS SIOUFAS.

General Election, 16 September 2007

Parties	Votes	% of votes	Seats
New Democracy Party	2,995,479	41.83	152
Panhellenic Socialist Movement	2,727,853	38.10	102
Communist Party	583,815	8.15	22
Coalition of the Radical Left*	361,211	5.04	14
Popular Orthodox Rally	271,764	3.80	10
Others	220,143	3.07	—
Total	7,160,265	100.00	300

*A coalition of left-wing parties, led by the Coalition of the Left of Movements and Ecology.

Election Commission

National Election Commission: 155 61 Athens; tel. (210) 6535522; fax (210) 6546886; e-mail elections@elections.gr; internet www.elections.gr; controlled by the Ministry of the Interior.

Political Organizations

Coalition of the Left of Movements and Ecology (Synaspismos Tis Aristeras Ton Kinimaton Kai Tis Oikologias): Pl. Eleftherias 1, 105 53 Athens; tel. (210) 3378633; fax (210) 3378634; e-mail alavanos@syn.gr; internet www.syn.gr; f. 1991 on the basis of an alliance (f. 1989) of the nine political groups comprising the Greek Left Party and the Communist Party of Greece ('of the Exterior'); present name adopted 2003; contested Sept. 2007 legislative elections as part of the Coalition of the Radical Left; Pres. ALEXIS TSIPRAS.

Communist Party of Greece (KKE) (Kommunistiko Komma Ellados): Leoforos Irakliou 145, Perissos, 142 31 Athens; tel. (210) 2592111; fax (210) 2592298; e-mail cpg@int.kke.gr; internet www.kke.gr; f. 1918; banned 1947, re-emerged 1974; Gen. Sec. ALEKA PAPARIGA.

Democratic Revival (Dimokratiki Anagenissi): Athens; internet www.danagennisi.eu; f. 2004; re-emerged 2007; nationalist; Leader STELIOS PAPATHEMELIS.

Democratic Social Movement (DIKKI) (Dimokratiko Koinoniko Kinima): Odos Halkokondili 9, 106 77 Athens; tel. (210) 5234288; fax (210) 5239856; e-mail info@dikki.org; internet www.dikki.org; f. 1995; leftist; contested Sept. 2007 legislative elections as part of the Coalition of the Radical Left.

Ecologist Greens: Odos Kolokotronis 31, 105 62 Athens; tel. (210) 3241001; e-mail ecogreen@otenet.gr; internet www.ecogreens.gr; f. 2002; mem. of European Federation of Green Parties; Leader NANOS VALAORITIS.

New Democracy Party (ND) (Nea Demokratia): Odos Rhigillis 18, 106 74 Athens; tel. (210) 7418000; fax (210) 7418119; e-mail ir@nd.gr; internet www.nd.gr; f. 1974; broadly-based centre-right party advocating social reform in the framework of a liberal economy; supports European integration and enlargement; Pres. Dr KONSTANTINOS (KOSTAS) KARAMANLIS; Sec. of the Central Committee LEFTERIS ZAGORITIS.

Panhellenic Socialist Movement (PASOK) (Panellinion Socialistikon Kinima): Odos Charilaou Trikoupi 50, 106 80 Athens; tel. (210) 3232049; e-mail pasok@pasok.gr; internet www.pasok.gr; f. 1974; incorporates Democratic Defence and Panhellenic Liberation Movement resistance organizations; supports social welfare, decentralization and self-management, aims at a Mediterranean socialist development through international co-operation; 500 local organizations, 30,000 mems; Pres. GEORGIOS PAPANDREOU; Sec.-Gen. MICHALIS CHRISOCHOIDHIS.

Popular Orthodox Rally (Laikos Orthodoxos Synagermos—LA.O.S): Eratosthenous and Vas. Konstantinou 1, 116 35 Athens; tel. (210) 7522700; fax (210) 7522704; e-mail pr@laos.gr; internet www.laos.gr; f. 2000; nationalist; Leader GEORGIOS KARATZAFERIS.

Union of Centrists (Enosi Kentroon): Odos Karolos 28, 122 42 Athens; tel. (210) 5220357; fax (210) 5246864; internet www.enosikentroon.gr; f. 1992; Leader VASSILIS LEVENTIS.

Union of Democratic Centre Party (EDIK) (Enosi Dimokratikou Kentrou): Odos Charilaou Trikoupi 18, 106 79 Athens; tel. (210) 3609711; fax (210) 3303313; e-mail edik@edik.gr; internet www.edik.gr; f. 1974; democratic socialist party; Chair. Prof. NEOKLIS SARRIS; Sec.-Gen. KARABELAS STAVROS.

Diplomatic Representation

EMBASSIES IN GREECE

Albania: Odos Vekiareli 7, Filothei, 152 37 Athens; tel. (210) 6876200; fax (210) 6876223; e-mail albem@ath.forthnet.gr; Ambassador VILI MINAROLLI.

Algeria: Leoforos Vassileos Konstantinou 14, 116 35 Athens; tel. (210) 7564191; fax (210) 7018681; e-mail ambdzath@otenet.gr; Ambassador AHMED BENYAMINA.

Argentina: Leoforos Vassilissis Sofias 59, 115 21 Athens; tel. (210) 7224753; fax (210) 7227568; e-mail egrecmrs@compulink.gr; Ambassador JORGE ALEJANDRO MASTROPIETRO.

Armenia: Leoforos Sygrou 159, 171 21 Athens; tel. (210) 9345727; fax (210) 9352187; Ambassador VAHRAN KAZGOIAN.

Australia: Thon Bldg, Odos Kifisias & Odos Alexandras, Ambelokipi, POB 14070, 115 10 Athens; tel. (210) 8704000; fax (210) 8704111; e-mail ae.athens@dfat.gov.au; internet www.ausemb.gr; Ambassador PAUL TIGHE.

Austria: Leoforos Vassilissis Sofias 4, 106 74 Athens; tel. (210) 7257270; fax (210) 7257292; e-mail athen-ob@bmeia.gv.at; Ambassador Dr MICHAEL LINHART.

Azerbaijan: Skoufa 10, Kolonaki, 106 73 Athens; tel. (210) 3632721; fax (210) 3639087; e-mail embassy@azembassy.gr; internet www.azembassy.gr; Ambassador MIR-HAMZA EFENDIYEV.

Belgium: Odos Sekeri 3, 106 71 Athens; tel. (210) 3617886; fax (210) 3604289; e-mail athens@diplobel.org; internet www.diplomatie.be/athens; Ambassador PIERRE VAESEN.

Bosnia and Herzegovina: Filaellinon 25, 105 57 Athens; tel. (210) 6410788; fax (210) 6411978; e-mail ambasbih@otenet.gr; Ambassador MILOVAN BLAGOJEVIĆ.

Brazil: Plateia Philikis Etairias 14, 106 73 Athens; tel. (210) 7213039; fax (210) 7244731; e-mail embragre@embratenas.gr; Ambassador AFFONSO EMILIO DE ALENCASTRO MASSOT.

Bulgaria: Odos Stratigou Kallari 33A, Palaio Psychiko, 154 52 Athens; tel. (210) 6478068; fax (210) 6478130; e-mail embassbg@otenet.gr; internet www.bulgaria.bg/Europe/Atina; Ambassador ANDREI KARASLAVOV.

Canada: Odos Ioannou Ghennadiou 4, 115 21 Athens; tel. (210) 7273400; fax (210) 7273480; e-mail athns@dfait-maeci.gc.ca; internet www.dfait-maeci.gc.ca/canadaeuropa/greece; Ambassador RENATE ELISABETH WIELGOSZ.

Chile: Odos Rigillis, 3rd Floor, 106 74 Athens; tel. (210) 7252574; fax (210) 7252536; e-mail embachilegr1@ath.forthnet.gr; Ambassador SOFIA PRATS.

China, People's Republic: Odos Demokratias 10, Palaio Psychiko, 154 52 Athens; tel. (210) 6723282; fax (210) 6723819; e-mail embchina@otenet.gr; Ambassador LUO LINQUAN.

Congo, Democratic Republic: Odos Iras 3A, Palaio Psychiko, 154 52 Athens; tel. (210) 6776123; fax (210) 6776124; e-mail ambathenes@minaffecirdc.cd; Chargé d'affaires a.i. MARIE-JEANNE NKALE KETA.

Croatia: Tzavela 4, Neo Psychiko, 154 51 Athens; tel. (210) 6777059; fax (210) 6711208; Ambassador NEVEN MADEY.

Cuba: Odos Sofokleos 5, Filothei, 152 37 Athens; tel. (210) 6855550; fax (210) 6842807; Ambassador HERMES HERRERA HERNANDEZ.

Cyprus: Odos Herodotou 16, 106 75 Athens; tel. (210) 7232727; fax (210) 4536373; Ambassador GEORGIOS GEORGIS.

Czech Republic: Odos Georgiou Seferis 6, Palaio Psychiko, 154 52 Athens; tel. (210) 6713755; fax (210) 6710675; e-mail athens@embassy.mzv.cz; internet www.mzv.cz/athens; Ambassador HANA MOTTLOVÁ.

Denmark: Mourouzilo 10, 106 74 Athens; tel. (210) 7256440; fax (210) 7256473; e-mail athamb@athamb.um.dk; internet www.ambathen.um.gr; Ambassador TOM HELGE NØRRING.

Egypt: Leoforos Vassilissis Sofias 3, 106 71 Athens; tel. (210) 3618612; fax (210) 3603538; Ambassador HAMDY SANAD LOZA.

Estonia: Patriarchou Ioakeim 48, 106 76 Athens; tel. (210) 7229803; fax (210) 7229804; e-mail estemb@otenet.gr; internet www.estemb.gr; Ambassador PEEP JAHILO.

GREECE

Finland: Odos Eratosthenous 1, 116 35 Athens; tel. (210) 7010444; fax (210) 7515064; e-mail sanomat.ate@formin.fi; internet www.finland.gr; Ambassador ERKKI VÄINÖ JUHANI HUITTINEN.

France: Leoforos Vassilissis Sofias 7, 106 71 Athens; tel. (210) 3391000; fax (210) 3391009; internet www.ambafrance-gr.org; Ambassador CHRISTOPHE FARNAUD.

Georgia: Odos Agiou Dimitriou 24, Palaio Psychiko, 154 52 Athens; tel. (210) 6716737; fax (210) 6716722; Ambassador IRAKLI TAVARTKILADZE.

Germany: Odos Karaoli & Dimitriou 3, 106 75 Athens; tel. (210) 7285111; fax (210) 7251205; e-mail boathens@internet.gr; internet www.athen.diplo.de; Ambassador Dr WOLFGANG SCHULTHEISS.

Holy See: POB 65075, Odos Mavili 2, Palaio Psychiko, 154 52 Athens; tel. (210) 6722728; fax (210) 6742849; e-mail nunate@ath.forthnet.gr; Apostolic Nuncio Most Rev. PATRICK COVENEY (Titular Archbishop of Satriano).

Hungary: Odos Karneadou 25–29, Kolonaki, 106 75 Athens; tel. (210) 7256800; fax (210) 7256840; e-mail mission.ath@kum.hu; internet www.hunembassy.gr; Ambassador JÓZSEF TÓTH.

India: Odos Kleanthous 3, 106 74 Athens; tel. (210) 7216227; fax (210) 7211252; e-mail indembassy@ath.forthnet.gr; internet www.indembassyathens.gr; Ambassador DILIP SINHA.

Indonesia: Odos Marathonodromou 99, Palaio Psychiko, 154 52 Athens; tel. (210) 6742345; fax (210) 6756955; Ambassador FAISHA H. SOEFTENDY.

Iran: Odos Kalari 16, Palaio Psychiko, 154 52 Athens; tel. (210) 6471436; fax (210) 6477945; e-mail irembatn@compulik.gr; Ambassador MEHDI MOHTASHAMI.

Iraq: Odos Mazaraki 4, Palaio Psychiko, 154 52 Athens; tel. (210) 6722330; fax (210) 6717185; e-mail iraqvia@otenet.gr; Ambassador HATIM ABDUL HASSAN AL-KHAWAM.

Ireland: Leoforos Vassileos Konstantinou 7, 106 74 Athens; tel. (210) 7232771; fax (210) 7293383; e-mail athensembassy@dfa.ie; Ambassador ANTÓIN MAC UNFRAIDH.

Israel: Odos Marathonodromou 1, Palaio Psychiko, 154 52 Athens; tel. (210) 6719530; fax (210) 6479510; e-mail info@athens.mfa.gov.il; internet athens.mfa.gov.il; Ambassador ALI YAHYA.

Italy: Odos Sekeri 2, 106 74 Athens; tel. (210) 3617260; fax (210) 3617330; e-mail ambasciata.atene@esteri.it; internet www.ambatene.esteri.it; Ambassador GIANPAOLO SCARANTE.

Japan: Odos Ethnikis Antistasseos, Halandri, 152 31 Athens; tel. (210) 6709900; fax (210) 6709980; e-mail embjapan@otenet.gr; internet www.embjapan.gr; Ambassador TAKANORI KITAMURA.

Jordan: Odos Papadiamnti 21, Palaio Psychiko, 154 52 Athens; tel. (210) 6744161; fax (210) 6740578; e-mail jor_embl@otenet.gr; Ambassador ZAID ABDULLAH ZURAIKAT.

Korea, Republic: Leoforos Kifissias 124, 115 26 Athens; tel. (210) 6984080; fax (210) 6984083; e-mail gremb@mofat.go.kr; Ambassador YOUNG-HAN BAE.

Kuwait: Odos Marathonodromou 27, Palaio Psychiko, 154 52 Athens; tel. (210) 6473593; fax (210) 6875875; e-mail kuwemath@otenet.gr; Ambassador KHALED MUTLAQ AL-DUWAILAH.

Latvia: Odos Irodotou 9, Kolonaki, 106 74 Athens; tel. (210) 7294483; fax (210) 7294479; e-mail latvia@otenet.gr; Ambassador LĪGA BERGMANE.

Lebanon: 6 Odos Maritou 25, Palaio Psychiko, 154 52 Athens; tel. (210) 6755873; fax (210) 6755612; e-mail grlibemb@otenet.gr; Ambassador GIBRAN SOUFAN.

Libya: Odos Vironos 13, Palaio Psychiko, 154 52 Athens; tel. (210) 6472120; Ambassador (vacant).

Lithuania: Leoforos Vassilissis Sofias 49, 106 76 Athens; tel. (210) 7294356; fax (210) 7294347; e-mail amb.gr@urm.lt; Ambassador ARTŪRAS ŽURAUSKAS.

Luxembourg: Leoforos Vassilissis Sofias 23A & Odos Neophytou Vamva 2, 10674 Athens; tel. (210) 7256400; fax (210) 7256405; e-mail athenes.amb@mae.etat.lu; internet www.mae.lu/grece; Ambassador CONRAD BRUCH.

Malta: Leoforos Vassilissis Sofias 96, 115 28 Athens; tel. (210) 7785138; fax (210) 7785242; e-mail maltaembassy.athens@gov.mt; Ambassador RICHARD VELLA LAURENTI.

Mexico: Plateia Philikis Etairias 14, 106 73 Athens; tel. (210) 7294780; fax (210) 7294783; e-mail embgrecia@sre.gob.mx; Ambassador MANUEL COSÍO DURÁN.

Morocco: Odos Marathonodromou 5, Palaio Psychiko, 154 52 Athens; tel. (210) 6744209; fax (210) 6749480; e-mail sifamath@otenet.gr; Ambassador MUHAMMAD LOFTI AOUAD.

Moldova: G. Bacu 20, 115 24 Athens; tel. (210) 699-0372; fax (210) 699-0371; e-mail atena@mfa.md; Ambassador IULIAN MAGALEAS.

Netherlands: Leoforos Vassileos Konstantinou 5–7, 106 74 Athens; tel. (210) 7239701; fax (210) 7248900; e-mail ath@minbuza.gr; internet www.dutchembassy.gr; Ambassador JOHANNES ANTHONIUS FRANCISCUS MARIA FORSTER.

Nigeria: Odos Dolianis 65, Maroussi, 151 24 Athens; tel. (210) 8021168; fax (210) 8024208; e-mail ngrathen@otenet.gr; Ambassador Prof. SUNDAY OLUWADARE AGBI.

Norway: Leoforos Vassilissis Sofias 23, 106 74 Athens; tel. (210) 7246173; fax (210) 7244989; e-mail emb.athens@mfa.no; internet www.norway.gr; Ambassador SVERRE STUB.

Pakistan: Odos Loukianou 6, Kolonaki, 106 75 Athens; tel. (210) 7290122; fax (210) 7257641; e-mail info@pak-embassy.gr; internet www.pak-embassy.gr; Ambassador IFTIKHAR HUSSAIN KAZMI.

Panama: Odos Praxitelous & Odos II Merarchias 192, 185 35 Athens; tel. (210) 4286441; fax (210) 4286448; e-mail panpir5@otenet.gr; internet crewlicense@hotmail.com; Ambassador ANTONIO FOTIS TAQUIS OCHOA.

Peru: Odos Semitelou 2, 115 28 Athens; tel. (210) 7792761; fax (210) 7792905; e-mail lepruate@compulink.gr; Ambassador LUIS FELIPE GÁLVEZ VILLARROEL.

Philippines: Odos Antheon 26, Palaio Psychiko, 154 52 Athens; tel. (210) 6721883; fax (210) 6721872; e-mail athensspe@otenet.gr; Ambassador RIGOBERTO D. TIGLAO.

Poland: Odos Chryssanthemon 22, Palaio Psychiko, 154 52 Athens; tel. (210) 6797700; fax (210) 6797711; e-mail info@poland-embassy.gr; internet www.poland-embassy.gr; Ambassador MICHAL KLINGER.

Portugal: Leoforos Vassilissis Sofias 23, 106 74 Athens; tel. (210) 7290096; fax (210) 7245122; e-mail embportg@otenet.gr; Ambassador CARLOS NEVES FERREIRA.

Romania: Odos Emmanuel Benaki 7, Palaio Psychiko, 154 52 Athens; tel. (210) 6728875; fax (210) 6728883; e-mail secretariat@romaniaemb.gr; internet www.atena.mae.ro; Ambassador GEORGE CIAMBA.

Russia: Odos Nikiforou Litra 28, Palaio Psychiko, 154 52 Athens; tel. (210) 6725235; fax (210) 6479708; e-mail embraf@otenet.gr; internet www.greece.mid.ru; Ambassador ANDREI VDOVIN.

Saudi Arabia: Odos Marathonodromou 71, Palaio Psychiko, 154 52 Athens; tel. (210) 6716911; e-mail gremb@mofa.gov.sa; Chargé d'affaires a.i. FALEH MOHAMMAD AR-RAHILI.

Serbia: Leoforos Vassilissis Sofias 106, 115 27 Athens; tel. (210) 7774344; internet www.embassyscg.gr; Ambassador LJILJANA BACEVIĆ.

Slovakia: Odos Georgiou Seferis 4, Palaio Psychiko, 154 52 Athens; tel. (210) 6771980; fax (210) 6771878; e-mail emb.athens@mzv.sk; internet www.mzv.sk/athens; Ambassador JÁN VODERADSKÝ.

Slovenia: Odos Mavili 10, Palaio Psychiko, 154 52 Athens; tel. (210) 6775683; fax (210) 6775680; e-mail vat@mzz-dkp.gov.si; Ambassador VLADIMIR KOLMANIČ.

South Africa: Leoforos Kifissias 60, 151 25 Athens; tel. (210) 6106645; fax (210) 6106640; e-mail embassy@southafrica.gr; internet www.southafrica.gr; Ambassador MANDISA DONA MARASHA.

Spain: Odos D. Areapagitou 21, 117 42 Athens; tel. (210) 9213123; fax (210) 9213090; e-mail emb-esp@otenet.gr; Ambassador JUAN RÁMON MARTINEZ SALAZAR.

Sweden: Leoforos Vassileos Konstantinou 7, 106 74 Athens; tel. (210) 7266100; fax (210) 7266150; e-mail ambassaden.athens@foreign.ministry.se; internet www.swedenabroad.com/athen; Ambassador MÅRTEN GRUNDITZ.

Switzerland: Odos Iassiou 2, 115 21 Athens; tel. (210) 7230364; fax (210) 7249209; e-mail vertretung@ath.rep.admin.ch; internet www.eda.admin.ch/athens; Ambassador PAUL KOLLER-HAUSER.

Syria: Diamandidou 61, Palaio Psychiko, 154 52 Athens; tel. (210) 6725577; fax (210) 6716402; e-mail syrembas@otenet.gr; Ambassador SOUAD M. AL-AYOUBI.

Thailand: Odos Marathonodromou & Odos Kyprou 25, Palaio Psychiko, 154 52 Athens; tel. (210) 6710155; fax (210) 6479508; e-mail thaiath@otenet.gr; Ambassador ASHA DVITIYANANDA.

Tunisia: Odos Antheon & Odos Marathonodromou 2, Palaio Psychiko, 154 52 Athens; tel. (210) 6717590; fax (210) 6713432; e-mail atathina@otenet.gr; Ambassador NACEUR MESTIRI.

Turkey: Odos Vassileos Gheorghiou 8B, 106 74 Athens; tel. (210) 7263000; fax (210) 7229597; e-mail atina.be@mfa.gov.tr; Ambassador AHMET OĞUZ ÇELIKKOL.

Ukraine: Odos Stefanou Delta 2–4, Filothei, 152 37 Athens; tel. (210) 6800230; fax (210) 6854154; e-mail ukrembas@otenet.gr; internet www.ukrembas.gr; Ambassador VALERIY TSYBUKH.

United Kingdom: Odos Ploutarchou 1, 106 75 Athens; tel. (210) 7272600; fax (210) 7272734; internet www.british-embassy.gr; Ambassador SIMON GASS.

USA: Leoforos Vassilissis Sofias 91, 106 60 Athens; tel. (210) 7212951; fax (210) 7226724; e-mail usembassy@usembassy.gr; internet www.usembassy.gr; Ambassador DANIEL V. SPECKHARD.

GREECE

Uruguay: Odos Likavitou I G, 106 72 Athens; tel. (210) 3602635; fax (210) 3613549; e-mail urugrec@otenet.gr; Ambassador Diana Espino de Papantonakis.

Venezuela: Odos Marathonodromou 19, Palaio Psychiko, 154 52 Athens; tel. (210) 6729169; fax (210) 6727464; internet users.hol.gr/~emvenath; Chargé d'affaires a.i. Maria Ines Fonseca.

Judicial System

The Constitution of 1975 provided for the establishment of a Special Supreme Tribunal. Other provisions in the Constitution provided for a reorganization of parts of the judicial system to be accomplished through legislation.

SUPREME ADMINISTRATIVE COURTS

Special Supreme Tribunal: Odos Patision 30, Athens; has final jurisdiction in matters of constitutionality.

Council of State

Odos Panepistimiou 47, 105 64 Athens; tel. (210) 3710098; fax (210) 3710097; e-mail s-epikr@otenet.gr.

Has appellate powers over acts of the administration and final rulings of administrative courts; has power to rule upon matters of judicial review of laws.

President: Georgios Panayiotopoulos.

Supreme Civil and Penal Court

Leoforos Alexandros 121, 115 22 Athens; tel. (210) 6411506; fax (210) 6433799; e-mail areios@otenet.gr.

Supreme court in the State, also having appellate powers; consists of six sections (four Civil, two Penal) and adjudicates in quorum.

President: Romylos Kedikoglou.

COURTS OF APPEAL

There are 12 Courts of Appeal with jurisdiction in cases of Civil and Penal Law of second degree, and, in exceptional penal cases, of first degree.

COURTS OF FIRST INSTANCE

There are 59 Courts of First Instance with jurisdiction in cases of first degree, and in exceptional cases, of second degree. They function both as Courts of First Instance and as Criminal Courts. For serious crimes the Criminal Courts function with a jury.

In towns where Courts of First Instance sit there are also Juvenile Courts. Commercial Tribunals do not function in Greece, and all commercial cases are tried by ordinary courts of law. There are, however, Tax Courts in some towns.

OTHER COURTS

There are 360 Courts of the Justice of Peace throughout the country. There are 48 Magistrates' Courts (or simple Police Courts).

In all the above courts, except those of the Justice of Peace, there are District Attorneys. In Courts of the Justice of Peace the duties of District Attorney are performed by the Public Prosecutor.

Religion

CHRISTIANITY

The Eastern Orthodox Church

The Greek branch of the Holy Eastern Orthodox Church is the officially established religion of the country, to which nearly 97% of the population profess adherence. The administrative body of the Church is the Holy Synod of 12 members, elected by the bishops of the Hierarchy.

Within the Greek State there is also the semi-autonomous Church of Crete, composed of seven Metropolitans and the Holy Archbishopric of Crete. The Church is administered by a Synod consisting of the seven Metropolitans under the Presidency of the Archbishop; it is under the spiritual jurisdiction of the Ecumenical Patriarchate of Constantinople (based in Istanbul, Turkey), which also maintains a degree of administrative control.

There are also four Metropolitan Sees of the Dodecanese, which are spiritually and administratively dependent on the Ecumenical Patriarchate and, finally, the peninsula of Athos, which constitutes the region of the Holy Mountain (Mount Athos) and comprises 20 monasteries. These are dependent on the Ecumenical Patriarchate of Constantinople, but are autonomous and are safeguarded constitutionally.

The Orthodox Church of Greece: Odos Ioannou Gennadiou 14, 115 21 Athens; tel. (210) 7218381; e-mail contact@ecclesia.gr; internet www.ecclesia.gr; f. 1850.

Primate of Greece: (vacant).

Archbishop of Crete: Archbishop Timotheos (whose See is in Heraklion).

The Roman Catholic Church

Latin Rite

Greece comprises four archdioceses (including two, Athens and Rhodes, directly responsible to the Holy See), four dioceses, one Apostolic Vicariate and one Apostolic Exarchate for adherents of the Byzantine Rite. There is also an Ordinariate for Armenian Catholics. At 31 December 2005 there were an estimated 129,950 adherents in the country.

Bishops' Conference

Katholiki Episkopi, 841 00 Syros; tel. (22810) 82768; fax (22810) 83924; e-mail syrensisi@otenet.gr.

f. 1967; Pres. Rt Rev. Papamanólis Franghískos (Bishop of Syros and Milos, and of Santorini).

Archbishop of Athens: Archbishop Most Rev. Nikólaos Fóskolos, Odos Homirou 9, 106 72 Athens; tel. (210) 3624311; fax (210) 3618632.

Archbishop of Corfu, Zante and Cefalonia: Most Rev. Ioannis Spiteris, Montzeníkhou 3, 491 00 Kérkyra; tel. (26610) 30277; fax (26610) 31675; e-mail cathepco@otenet.gr.

Archbishop of Naxos, Andros, Tinos and Mykonos: Most Rev. Nikólaos Printesis, 842 00 Tinos; tel. (22830) 22382; fax (22830) 24769; e-mail karantam@thn.forthnet.gr.

Archbishop of Rhodes: (vacant), Odos Ionos Dragoumi 5, 851 00 Rhodes; tel. (22410) 21845; fax (22410) 26688.

Apostolic Vicariate of Thessaloníki: Kolokotroni 19b, 564 30 Thessaloníki; tel. (2310) 654256; fax (2310) 835780; e-mail cathepco@otenet.gr; Apostolic Vicar (vacant).

Byzantine Rite

Apostolic Exarchate for Greek Catholics of the Byzantine Rite: Odos Akarnon 246, 112 53 Athens; tel. (210) 8670170; fax (210) 8677039; e-mail grcathex@hol.gr; 3 parishes; 2,300 adherents (31 Dec. 2005); Apostolic Exarch Rt Rev. Anárghyros Printesis (Titular Bishop of Gratianopolis).

Armenian Rite

Ordinariate for Catholics of the Armenian Rite in Greece: Odos René Pyo 2, 117 44 Athens; tel. (210) 9014089; fax (210) 9012109; e-mail ordarmcagr@yahoo.gr; 400 adherents (31 Dec. 2004); Ordinary (vacant); Apostolic Administrator Most Rev. Nechan Karakahian (Titular Archbishop of Adana of the Armenian Rite).

Protestant Church

Greek Evangelical Church (Reformed): Odos Markon Botsari 24, 117 41 Athens; tel. (210) 9222684; e-mail info@gec.gr; internet www.gec.gr; f. 1858; comprises 32 organized churches; 5,000 adherents (1996); Moderator Rev. Meletis Meletiadis.

ISLAM

The law provides as religious head of the Muslims a Chief Mufti; the Muslims in Greece possess a number of mosques and schools.

JUDAISM

The Jewish population of Greece, estimated in 1943 at 75,000 people, was severely reduced as a result of the Nazi German occupation. In 1994 there were about 5,000 Jews in Greece.

Central Board of the Jewish Communities of Greece: Odos Voulis 36, 105 57 Athens; tel. (210) 3244315; fax (210) 3313852; e-mail info@kis.gr; internet www.kis.gr; f. 1945; officially recognized representative body of the Jewish communities of Greece; Pres. Moses Konstantinis.

The Press

PRINCIPAL DAILY NEWSPAPERS

Morning papers are not published on Mondays, nor afternoon papers on Sundays. Afternoon papers are more popular than morning ones.

GREECE

Athens

Apogevmatini (The Afternoon): Odos Phidiou 12, 106 78 Athens; tel. (210) 6430011; fax (210) 3609876; internet www.apogevmatini.gr; f. 1956; independent; Editor P. KARAYANNIS; circ. 30,000.

Athens Daily Post: Odos Stadiou 57, Athens; tel. (210) 3249504; f. 1952; morning; English; Owner G. SKOURAS.

Athens News: Odos Christou Lada 3, 102 37 Athens; tel. (210) 3333555; fax (210) 3231384; e-mail athnews@dolnet.gr; internet www.athensnews.gr; f. 1952; morning; in English; Editor JOHN PSAROPOULOS; circ. 10,000.

Athlitiki Icho (Athletics Echo): Konstantinoupelos 161, 104 41 Athens; tel. (210) 5232201; fax (210) 5232433; e-mail text@athlitiki-iho.gr; f. 1945; morning; Editor DEMOSTHENES CHRISTOU; circ. 40,000.

Avgi (Dawn): Odos Ag. Konstantiou 12, 104 31 Athens; tel. (210) 5231831; fax (210) 5231830; e-mail editors@avgi.gr; internet www.avgi.gr; f. 1952; morning; independent newspaper of the left; Editor NIKOS PHILES; circ. 5,400.

Avriani (Tomorrow): Odos Dimitros 11, 177 78 Athens; tel. (210) 3424090; fax (210) 3452190; f. 1980; evening; Publr GEORGE KOURIS; circ. 51,317.

Dimokratikos Logos (Democratic Speech): Odos Dimitros 11, 177 78 Athens; tel. (210) 3424023; fax (210) 3452190; f. 1986; morning; Dir and Editor KOSTAS GERONIKOLOS; circ. 7,183.

Eleftherotypia (Press Freedom): Odos Minou 10–16, 117 43 Athens; tel. (210) 9296001; fax (210) 9028311; internet www.enet.gr; f. 1974; evening; Publr CHR. TEGOPOULOS; circ. 115,000.

Estia (Vesta): Odos Anthimou Gazi 7, 105 61 Athens; tel. (210) 3230650; fax (210) 3243071; e-mail estianews@otenet.gr; f. 1894; afternoon; Dir ALEXIS ZAOUSSIS; circ. 12,000.

Ethnos (Nation): Odos Benaki 152, Metamorfosi Chalandriou, 152 35 Athens; tel. (210) 6580640; fax (210) 6396515; internet www.ethnos.gr; f. 1981; evening; Dir TH. KALOUDIS; circ. 84,735.

Express: Odos Halandriou 39, Paradissos Amaroussiou, 151 25 Athens; tel. (210) 6850200; fax (210) 6852202; internet www.express.gr; f. 1963; morning; financial; publ. by Hellenews Publications; Editor D. G. KALOFOLIAS; circ. 28,000.

Filathlos: Odos Dimitros 31, 177 78 Athens; tel. (210) 3486000; fax (210) 3486450; e-mail info@filathlos.gr; internet www.filathlos.gr; f. 1982; morning; sports; Editor G. KOLOKOTRONIS; circ. 40,000.

Imerissia (Daily): Odos Benaki & Ag. Nektariou, Metamorfosi Chalandriou, 152 35 Athens; tel. (210) 6061000; fax (210) 6016563; e-mail imerissia@pegasus.gr; internet www.imerisia.gr; f. 1947; morning; financial; Editor ANTONIS DALIPIS; circ. 39,000.

Kathimerini (Every Day): Ethnarchou Makariou 185–47 & Odos Falireos 2, Athens; tel. and fax (210) 4808000; e-mail kathi-editor@ekathimerini.com; internet www.kathimerini.gr; f. 1919; morning; conservative; Editor CH. PANAGOPOULOS; circ. 34,085.

Kerdos (Profit): Leoforos Kifissias 178, Halandri, 152 31 Athens; tel. (210) 6747881; fax (210) 6747893; e-mail mail@kerdos.gr; internet www.kerdos.gr; f. 1985; morning; financial; Editor VASILIS STEFANAKADIS; circ. 18,000.

Naftemporiki (Daily Journal): Odos Lenorman 205, 104 42 Athens; tel. (210) 5198000; fax (210) 5146013; e-mail info@naftemporiki.gr; internet www.naftemporiki.gr; f. 1924; morning; non-political journal of finance, commerce and shipping; Editor D. KEFALAKOS; circ. 35,000.

Ora Gia Spor (Time for Sport): Ioannou Metaxa 8, 173 43 Athens; tel. (210) 9251200; fax (210) 9761211; f. 1991; sport; Editor C. SEMBOS.

Rizospastis (Radical): Lefkis 134, Perissos, 145 65 Athens; tel. (210) 6297000; fax (210) 6297999; e-mail mailbox@rizospastis.gr; internet www.rizospastis.gr; f. 1974; morning; Editor T. TSIGGAS; circ. 28,740.

Ta Nea (News): Odos Christou Lada 3, 102 37 Athens; tel. (210) 3333555; fax (210) 3228797; e-mail tanea@dolnet.gr; internet www.tanea.gr; f. 1944; liberal; evening; Editor HLIAS MATSIKAS; circ. 135,000.

To Vima (Tribune): Odos Michalakopoulou 80, 115 28 Athens; tel. (210) 3658000; fax (210) 3658004; e-mail tovima@dolnet.gr; internet www.tovima.dolnet.gr; f. 1922; liberal; Dir and Editor STAVROS R. PSYCHARIS; circ. 250,000.

Vradyni (Evening Press): L. Ionias 166, 111 44 Athens; tel. (210) 2113600; fax (210) 2113648; e-mail vradyni@otenet.gr; f. 1923; evening; right-wing; Editor PANOS TSIROS; circ. 71,914.

Patras

Peloponnesos: Maizonos 206, 262 22 Patras; tel. (2610) 312530; fax (2610) 312535; internet www.peloponnisos.com.gr; f. 1886; independent; conservative; Publr and Editor S. DOUKAS; circ. 7,000.

Thessaloníki

Thessaloníki: Odos Monastiriou 85, 546 27 Thessaloníki; tel. (2310) 521621; f. 1963; evening; Editor KATERINA VELLIDI; circ. 36,040.

SELECTED PERIODICALS

48 Ores (48 Hours): Leoforos Alexandras 19, 114 73 Athens; tel. (210) 6430313; fax (210) 6461361; weekly; Dir and Editor SP. KARATZAFERIS; circ. 9,127.

Aktines: Odos Karytsi 14, 105 61 Athens; tel. (210) 3235023; f. 1938; monthly; Christian publication on current affairs, science, philosophy, arts; circ. 10,000.

The Athenian: Athens; tel. (210) 3222802; fax (210) 3223052; f. 1974; monthly; English; Editor JOANNA STAVROPOULOS; circ. 14,000.

Computer Gia Olous (Computers for All): Leoforos Syngrou 44, Kallithea, 117 42 Athens; tel. (210) 9238672; fax (210) 9216847; internet www.cgomag.gr; monthly; Editor GEORGE CHRISTOPOULOS.

Deltion Diikiseos Epichiriseon Euro-Unial (Euro-Unial Business Administration Bulletin): Odos Rhigillis 26, 106 74 Athens; tel. (210) 7235736; fax (210) 7240000; e-mail busadmibul@otenet.gr; monthly; Editor I. PAPAMICHALAKIS; circ. 26,000 (2006).

Ekonomicos Tachydromos (Financial Courier): Odos Christou Lada 3, 102 37 Athens; tel. (210) 3333630; fax (210) 3238740; e-mail oikonomikos@dolnet.gr; internet oikonomikos.dolnet.gr; f. 1926; weekly; Man. Dir DENNIS ANTYPAS; circ. 23,000.

Epiloghi: Odos Stadiou 4, 105 64 Athens; tel. (210) 3238427; fax (210) 3235160; e-mail epilogi@mail.hol.gr; f. 1962; weekly; economics; Editor GEORGE MALOUHOS.

Greece's Weekly for Business and Finance: Odos Fokiodos 10, 115 26 Athens; tel. (210) 7707280; weekly; English; finance; Dir V. KORONAKIS.

Gynaika (Women): Odos Fragoklissias 7, Marousi, 151 25 Athens; tel. (210) 6199149; fax (210) 6104707; f. 1950; monthly; Publr CHRISTOS TERZOPOULOS; circ. 45,000.

Hellenews: Odos Halandriou 39, Marousi, 151 25 Athens; tel. (210) 6199400; fax (210) 6199421; weekly; English; finance and business; Editor J. M. GERMANOS.

Idaniko Spiti (Ideal Home): Odos St Nectarios, 152 35 Athens; tel. (210) 6061777; fax (210) 6011044; e-mail pa@pegasus.gr; internet www.idanikospiti.gr; f. 1990; monthly; interior decoration; Editor PETROS ANTONIADIS; circ. 60,000 (2002).

Klik: Odos Fragoklisias 7, 151 25 Athens; tel. (210) 6897945; fax (210) 6899153; internet www.klik.gr; f. 1987; monthly; popular music, media and fashion; Editor PETROS COSTOPOULOS.

Men: Odos Fragoklisias 7, 151 25 Athens; tel. (210) 6826680; fax (210) 6824730; e-mail mensynt@dolnet.gr; internet www.men.gr; six a year; men's fashion and general interest.

Oikonomiki Viomichaniki Epitheorissis (Industrial Review): Odos Zalokosta 4, 106 71 Athens; tel. (210) 3626360; fax (210) 3626388; e-mail editor@oikonomiki.gr; internet www.oikonomiki.gr; f. 1934; monthly; industrial and economic review; Editor D. KARAMANOS; circ. 25,000.

Pantheon: Odos Christou Lada 3, 102 37 Athens; tel. (210) 3230221; fax (210) 3228797; every two weeks; Publr and Dir N. THEOFANIDES; circ. 23,041.

Politika Themata: Odos Ypsilantou 25, 106 75 Athens; tel. (210) 7218421; weekly; Dir C. KYRKOS.

Pontiki (Mouse): Odos Massalias 10, 106 81 Athens; tel. (210) 3609531; weekly; humour; Dir and Editor K. PAPAIOANNOU.

Ptisi & Diastima (Flight & Space): Odos Helioupoleos 2–4, 172 37 Athens; tel. (210) 9792500; fax (210) 9792528; e-mail ptisi@techlink.gr; internet www.ptisi.gr; f. 1975; monthly; Editor FAITHON KARAIOSSIFIOIS; circ. 12,000 (2003).

Radiotileorassi (Radio-TV): Odos Rhigillis 4, 106 74 Athens; tel. (210) 7407032; fax (210) 7224812; e-mail radiotileorasi@ert.gr; weekly; circ. 55,000.

Technika Chronika (Technical Times): Odos Karageorgi Servias 4, 105 62 Athens; tel. (210) 3291200; fax (210) 3221772; e-mail intrel@central.tee.gr; internet www.tee.gr; f. 1932; every two months; general technical and economic subjects; Editor IOANNIS ALAVANOS; circ. 12,000.

Tilerama: Odos Voukourestiou 18, 106 71 Athens; tel. (210) 3607160; fax (210) 3607032; f. 1977; weekly; radio and television; circ. 189,406.

NEWS AGENCY

Athens News Agency (ANA): Odos Tsoha 36, 115 21 Athens; tel. (210) 6400560; fax (210) 6400581; e-mail ape@ana.gr; internet www.ana.gr; f. 1895; correspondents in leading capitals of the world and towns throughout Greece; Man. Dir NIKOLAS VOULELIS; Gen. Dir ANDREAS CHRISTODOULIDES.

GREECE

PRESS ASSOCIATIONS

Enosis Antapokriton Xenou Tipou (Foreign Press Association of Greece): Odos Akademias 23, 106 71 Athens; tel. (210) 3637318; fax (210) 3605035.

Enosis Syntakton Imerission Ephimeridon Athinon (Journalists' Union of Athens Daily Newspapers): Odos Akademias 20, 106 71 Athens; tel. (210) 3632601; fax (210) 3632608; e-mail info@esiea.gr; internet www.esiea.gr; f. 1914; Pres. FANI PETRALIA; Gen. Sec. ANASTASIA DAOUDAKI; 1,400 mems.

Enosis Syntakton Periodikou Tipou (Journalists' Union of the Periodical Press): Odos Valaoritou 9, 106 71 Athens; tel. (210) 3633427; fax (210) 3638627; e-mail espt@otenet.gr; internet www.espit.org; Pres. GIANNIS PLACHOURIS; 835 mems.

Publishers

Agkyra Publications: Leoforos Kifisou 85, Egaleo, 122 41 Athens; tel. (210) 3455276; fax (210) 3474732; f. 1890; general; Man. Dir DIMITRIOS PAPADIMITRIOU.

Akritas: Odos Efessou 24, 171 21 Athens; tel. (210) 9334554; fax (210) 9311436; e-mail akritaspublications@ath.forthnet.gr; f. 1979; history, spirituality, children's books.

D. I. Arsenidis & Co: Odos Akademias 57, 106 79 Athens; tel. (210) 3629538; fax (210) 3618707; f. 1952; biography, literature, children's books, history, philosophy, psychology, social sciences; Man. Dir JOHN ARSENIDIS.

Boukoumanis Editions: Odos Mavromichali 1, 106 79 Athens; tel. (210) 3618502; fax (210) 3630669; f. 1967; history, politics, sociology, psychology, belles-lettres, educational, arts, children's books, ecology; Man. ELIAS BOUKOUMANIS.

Dorikos Publishing House: Odos Charalabou Sotiriou 9–11, 114 72 Athens; tel. (210) 6454726; fax (210) 3301866; f. 1958; literature, fiction, history, politics; Editor ROUSSOS VRANAS.

Ekdotike Athenon: Odos Akademias 34, 106 72 Athens; tel. (210) 3608911; fax (210) 3606157; e-mail ekdath@aias.gr; internet www.add.gr/comp/ekdotiki; f. 1961; history, archaeology, art; Pres. GEORGE A. CHRISTOPOULOS.

G. C. Eleftheroudakis: Odos Panepistimiou 17, 105 64 Athens; tel. (210) 3314180; fax (210) 3239821; e-mail elebooks@netor.gr; internet www.books.gr; f. 1915; general, technical and scientific; Man. Dir VIRGINIA ELEFTHEROUDAKIS-GREGOU.

Exandas Publications: Odos Didotou 57, 106 81 Athens; tel. (210) 3804885; fax (210) 3813065; e-mail exandas@otenet.gr; internet www.exandasbooks.gr; f. 1974; fiction, literature, social sciences; Pres. MAGDA N. KOTZIA.

Govostis Publishing: Zoodohou Pigis 21, 106 81 Athens; tel. (210) 3815433; fax (210) 3816661; e-mail cotsos@compulink.gr; f. 1926; arts, fiction, politics; Pres. COSTAS GOVOSTIS.

Denise Harvey: Katounia, 340 05 Limni, Evia; tel. and fax (22270) 31154; e-mail denise@teledomenet.gr; f. 1972; modern Greek literature and poetry, belles-lettres, theology, translations, selected general list (English and Greek); Man. Dir DENISE HARVEY.

Hestia-I.D. Kollaros S.A. & Co: Odos Evripidou 84, 105 53 Athens; tel. (210) 3213704; fax (210) 3214610; e-mail info@hestia.gr; internet www.hestia.gr; f. 1885; literature, history, politics, psychoanalysis, philosophy, children's books, political and philosophical essays; Gen. Dir EVA-MARIA KARAITIDI.

Kastaniotis Editions: Odos Zalogou 11, 106 78 Athens; tel. (210) 3301208; fax (210) 3822530; e-mail info@kastaniotis.com; internet www.kastaniotis.com; f. 1969; fiction and non-fiction, including arts, social sciences and psychology, children's books; Man. Dir ATHANASIOS KASTANIOTIS.

Kritiki Publishing: Odos Patission 75, 104 34 Athens; tel. (210) 8211811; fax (210) 8211026; e-mail biblia@kritiki.gr; internet www.kritiki.gr; f. 1987; economics, politics, literature, philosophy, business management, popular science; Publisher THEMIS MINOGLOU.

Kronos: Odos Egnatia 33, 546 26 Thessaloníki; tel. (2310) 532077; fax (2310) 538158; Dir TH. GIOTAS.

Livani Publishing Organization: Odos Solonos 98, 106 80 Athens; tel. (210) 3661200; fax (210) 3617791; e-mail rights@livanis.gr; internet www.livanis.gr; f. 1972; general; Publr A. A. LIVANI.

Minoas: Odos Posseidonos 1, N. Iraklio, 141 21 Athens; tel. (210) 2711222; fax (210) 2711056; e-mail info@minoas.gr; internet www.minoas.gr; f. 1952; fiction, art, history; Man. Dir IOANNIS KONSTANTAROPOULOS.

Odos Panos: Odos Didotou 39, 106 08 Athens; tel. and fax (210) 3616782; poetry, drama, biography.

Papazissis Publishers: Nikitara 2, 106 78 Athens; tel. (210) 3822496; fax (210) 3809150; e-mail papazisi@otenet.gr; internet www.papzisi.gr; f. 1929; economics, politics, law, history, school books; Man. Dir VICTOR PAPAZISSIS.

Patakis Publications: Odos Valtetsiou 14, 106 80 Athens; tel. (210) 3650000; fax (210) 3650069; e-mail info@patakis.gr; internet www.patakis.gr; f. 1974; art, reference, fiction, educational, philosophy, psychology, sociology, religion, music, children's books, audiobooks; Pres. STEFANOS PATAKIS.

Pontiki Publications: Odos Massalias 10, 106 80 Athens; tel. (210) 3609531; fax (210) 3645406; f. 1979; govt, history, political science; Man. Dir KOSTAS TABANIS.

John Sideris: Odos Stadiou 44, 105 64 Athens; tel. (210) 3229638; fax (210) 3245052; f. 1898; school textbooks, general; Man. J. SIDERIS.

J. G. Vassiliou: Odos Hippokratous 15, 106 79 Athens; tel. (210) 3623382; fax (210) 3623580; f. 1913; fiction, history, philosophy, dictionaries, children's books; Pres. J. VASSILIOU.

PUBLISHERS' ASSOCIATIONS

Book Publishers' Association of Athens: Odos Themistokleus 73, 106 83 Athens; tel. (210) 3303268; fax (210) 3823222; e-mail info@seva.gr; internet www.seva.gr; f. 1945; Pres. STELIOS ELLINIADIS; Sec. LOUCAS RINOPOULOS.

Hellenic Federation of Publishers and Booksellers: Odos Themistokleus 73, 106 83 Athens; tel. (210) 3300924; fax (210) 3301617; e-mail poev@otenet.gr; f. 1961; Pres. GEORGE DARDANOS; Gen. Sec. TITOS MYLONOPOULOS.

Broadcasting and Communications

TELECOMMUNICATIONS

National Telecommunications Commission (NTC): Leoforos Kifissias 60, 151 25 Athens; tel. (210) 6151000; fax (210) 6805049; e-mail info@eet.gr; internet www.eet.gr; regulatory body; Chair. EMMANOUIL GIACOUMAKIS.

Ericsson Hellas S.A.: Odos Attiki 40/2, Peania, Athens; tel. (210) 6695100; fax (210) 6695315; internet www.ericsson.com; parent co based in Sweden; Man. Dir BILL ZIKOU.

Hellenic Telecommunications Organization (OTE) (Organismos Telepikoinonion tis Elladas): Leoforos Kifissias 99, 151 24 Maroussi, Athens; tel. (210) 8827015; fax (210) 6115825; internet www.ote.gr; f. 1949; 38.7% owned by the Government, 61.3% by public shareholders; 6m. lines in service; Chief Exec. and Chair. PANAGIS VOURLOUMIS.

COSMOTE: Leoforos Kifissias 44, 151 25 Athens; tel. (210) 6177700; fax (210) 6177594; e-mail customercare@cosmote.gr; internet www.cosmote.gr; f. 1998; 59% owned by OTE; mobile cellular telecommunications; Man. Dir EVANGELOS MARTIGOPOULOS.

Maritel: Odos Egaleo 8, 185 45 Piraeus; tel. (210) 4599500; fax (210) 4599600; e-mail maritel@maritel.gr; internet www.maritel.gr; OTE subsidiary; marine telecommunications; Chair. THEODOROS VENIAMIS; Man. Dir MICHALIS MICHAELIDES.

Telestet Hellas: Leoforos Alex. Papagoy 8, 157 71 Athens; tel. (210) 7772033; e-mail po@telestet.gr; internet www.telestet.gr; 75%-owned by STET International; mobile cellular telecommunications; Man. Dir GIACINTO CICCHESE.

Vodafone Greece: 1–3 Tzavella, 152 31 Halandri; tel. (210) 6702000; fax (210) 6703200; internet www.vodafone.gr; 55% owned by Vodafone Europe Holdings (United Kingdom); mobile cellular telecommunications; Chair. GEORGIOS KORONIAS.

RADIO

Elliniki Radiophonia Tileorassi (ERT) (Greek Radio-Television): Leoforos Messoghion 432, 153 42 Athens; tel. (210) 6066835; fax (210) 6009325; e-mail president@ert.gr; internet www.ert.gr; state-controlled; Chair. and Man. Dir A. STAGKOS.

Elliniki Radiophonia (ERA) (Greek Radio): POB 60019, Leoforos Messoghion 432, 153 42 Aghia Paraskevi, Athens; tel. (210) 6066835; fax (210) 6009325; e-mail president@ert.gr; internet www.ert.gr/radio; Pres. CHRISTOS PANAGOPOULOS.

ERT3—Macedonia Radio Station: Odos Angelaki 2, 546 21 Thessaloníki; tel. (2310) 299400; fax (2310) 299451; e-mail info@ert3.gr; internet www.ert3.gr.

TELEVISION

A television network of 17 transmitters is in operation.

State Stations

Elliniki Radiophonia Tileorassi (ERT, SA) (Greek Radio-Television): see Radio.

Elliniki Tileorassi 1 (ET1) (Greek Television 1): Leoforos Messoghion 136, 115 27 Athens; tel. (210) 7758824; fax (210) 7797776; e-mail kalavanos@ert.gr; internet www.ert.gr/et1; Dir-Gen. KONSTANTINOS ALAVANOS.

ET2: Leoforos Messoghion 136, 115 25 Athens; tel. (210) 7701911; fax (210) 7797776; Dir-Gen. PANAYOTIS PANAYOTOU.

ET3: Aggelaki 2, 546 21 Thessaloníki; tel. (2310) 299610; fax (2310) 299655; e-mail pr@ert3.gr; internet www.ert.gr/et3; Dir-Gen. DEMETRIS KATSANTONIS.

Private Stations

Antenna TV: Leoforos Kifissias 10–12, Maroussi, 151 25 Athens; tel. (210) 6886100; fax (210) 6834349; e-mail webmaster@antenna.gr; internet www.antenna.gr; Chair. M. X. KYRIAKOU.

City Channel: Leoforos Kastoni 14, 412 23 Larissa; tel. (241) 232839; fax (241) 232013.

Mega Channel: Leoforos Messoghion 117, 115 26 Athens; tel. (210) 6903000; fax (210) 6983600; e-mail ngeorgiou@megatv.com; internet www.megatv.com; f. 1989; Man. Dir ELIAS TSIGAS.

Serres TV: Nigritis 27, 621 24 Serres.

Skai TV: Phalereos & Ethnarchou 2, Macaroiu, N. Phaliro.

Star Channel: Odos Thermopylon 87, 351 00 Lamia; tel. (22310) 46725; fax (22310) 38903; e-mail starch@lam.forthnet.gr; f. 1988; Pres. VASILEIOS CHEIMONIDIS.

Tele City: Praxitelous 58, 176 74 Athens; tel. (210) 9429222; fax (210) 9413589.

Teletora: Lycabetous 17, 106 72 Athens; tel. (210) 3617285; fax (210) 3638712.

Traki TV: Central Sq., 671 00 Xanthi; tel. (25410) 20670; fax (25410) 27368.

TRT: Odos Zachou 5, 383 33 Volos; tel. (24210) 288013; fax (24210) 36888.

TV Macedonia: Nea Egnatia 222, 546 42 Thessaloníki; tel. (2310) 850512; fax (2310) 850513.

TV-100: Odos Aggelaki 16, 546 21 Thessaloníki; tel. (2310) 265828; fax (2310) 267532.

Finance

(cap. = capital; res = reserves; dep. = deposits; m. = million; br. = branch; amounts in euros, unless otherwise stated; SDR = Special Drawing Rights)

BANKING

In 2006 there were 62 banks in Greece, of which 24 were foreign-owned banks.

Central Bank

Bank of Greece: Leoforos E. Venizelos 21, 102 50 Athens; tel. (210) 3201111; fax (210) 3232239; e-mail sec.secretariat@bankofgreece.gr; internet www.bankofgreece.gr; f. 1927; state bank of issue; cap. 89.0m., res 559.2m., dep. 6,557.4m. (Dec. 2005); cap. and res 667.2m. (Dec. 2006); Gov. NICHOLAS C. GARGANAS; 23 brs.

Commercial Banks

Agricultural Bank of Greece: Odos Panepistimiou 23, 105 64 Athens; tel. (210) 3298407; fax (210) 3255079; e-mail ategt@ate.gr; internet www.atebank.gr; f. 1929; state-owned; cap. 651.9m., res 459.9m., dep. 18,342.2m. (Dec. 2006); Pres. and Gov. DIMITRIOS MILIAKOS; 472 brs.

Alpha Bank: Stadiou 40, 102 52 Athens; tel. (210) 3260000; fax (210) 3265438; e-mail secretariat@alpha.gr; internet www.alpha.gr; f. 1879; present name adopted 2000; cap. 1,591.3m., res 321.3m., dep. 42,969.2m. (Dec. 2006); Chair. and Gen. Man. IOANNIS S. COSTOPOULOS; 431 brs.

Aspis Bank: Odos Othonos 4, Syntagma, 105 57 Athens; tel. (210) 3364000; fax (210) 3243473; e-mail aspis@aspisbank.gr; internet www.aspisbank.gr; f. 1992; total assets 2,312.4m., dep. 2,078.5m. (Dec. 2006); Chair. and Man. Dir KONSTANTINOS KARATZAS.

Bank of Attica: Odos Omirou 23, 106 72 Athens; tel. (210) 3669000; fax (210) 3669413; e-mail georgiou.george@atticabank.gr; internet www.atticabank.gr; f. 1925; cap. 28.9m., res 114.6m., dep. 2,820.4m. (Dec. 2006); Chair. and CEO TRYPHON KOLLINTZAS; 62 brs.

Black Sea Trade and Development Bank: Odos Komninon 1, 546 24 Thessaloníki; tel. (2310) 290400; fax (2310) 221796; e-mail info@bstdb.org; internet www.bstdb.org; f. 1997; owned by 11 member states: Greece, Russian Federation, Turkey (16.5% each); Bulgaria, Romania, Ukraine (13.5% each); Albania, Armenia, Azerbaijan, Georgia, Moldova (2% each); cap. SDR 291.0m., res SDR 13.5m. (Dec. 2006); Pres. HAYRETTIN KAPLAN.

EFG Eurobank Ergasias SA: Odos Othonos 8, 105 57 Athens; tel. (210) 3337000; fax (210) 3337256; internet www.eurobank.gr; f. 1990; present name adopted 2000; cap. 1,242m., res 2,201m., dep. 35,546m. (Dec. 2006); Pres. X. NIKITAS; Man. Dir NIKOLAS NANOPOULOS; 393 brs.

FBB First Business Bank SA: Odos Michalakopoulou 91, 115 28 Athens; tel. (210) 7499700; fax (210) 7499766; e-mail info@fbbank.gr; internet www.fbbank.gr; f. 2001; 44.0% owned by Agricultural Bank of Greece; total assets 1,128.6m., dep. 1,019.0m. (Dec. 2006); Chair. DIMITRIOS MILIAKOS.

Geniki Bank—General Bank of Greece: Odos Messogeion 109–111, 115 10 Athens; tel. (210) 6975000; fax (210) 6975910; e-mail intdiv@geniki.gr; internet www.geniki.gr; f. 1937; present name adopted 1998; controlling stake acquired by Société Générale (France) in 2004; cap. 336.9m., res –206.1m., dep. 3,503.9m. (Dec. 2006); Chair. TRYFON KOUTALIDIS; Man. Dir JACQUES TOURNEBIZE; 118 brs.

Investment Bank of Greece: Leoforus Kifissias 24B, 151 25 Athens; tel. (210) 8171810; fax (210) 6851472; internet www.ibog.gr; f. 2000; cap. 89.6m., res 2.1m., dep. 175.4m. (Dec. 2005); CEO KYRIAKOS MAGIRAS.

Marfin Egnatia Bank: Odos Danaidon 4, 546 26 Thessaloníki; tel. (210) 9304811; fax (210) 6896306; e-mail info@marfinegnatiabank.gr; internet www.marfinegnatiabank.gr; f. 1991 as Egnatia Bank; present name adopted July 2007, after merger of Laiki Bank (Hellas) and Marfin Bank with Egnatia Bank; cap. 107.8m., res 155.7m., dep. 2,968.7m. (Dec. 2005); Pres. and Chair. VASSILIOS THEOCHARAKIS; 77 brs.

National Bank of Greece (NBG): Odos Aeoloυ 86, 102 32 Athens; tel. (210) 3341000; fax (210) 4806510; e-mail webmaster@nbg.gr; internet www.nbg.gr; f. 1841; state-controlled, but operates independently of the Government; cap. 2,376.4m., res 5,845.9m., dep. 60,693.4m. (Dec. 2006); Chair. and CEO TAKIS ARAPOGLOU; 594 brs.

Panellinia Bank: Mesogeion 290, Cholargos, Attica, 155 62 Athens; tel. (210) 6596200; fax (210) 6561922; e-mail mgmt@paneliniabank.gr; internet www.panelliniabank.gr; cap. 36.9m., res 10.3m., dep. 567.8m. (Dec. 2006); Chair. YIANNIS LEBIDAKIS.

Piraeus Bank: Odos Amerikis 4, 105 64 Athens; tel. (210) 3335000; fax (210) 3335080; e-mail investor-relations@piraeusbank.gr; internet www.piraeusbank.gr; f. 1916; cap. 1,288.8m., res 135.1m., dep. 25,598.9m. (Dec. 2006); Chair. MICHALIS G. SALLAS; 6 brs.

ProBank SA: Odos Amerikis 10, 106 71 Athens; tel. (210) 9540300; fax (210) 9595112; e-mail info@probank.gr; internet www.probank.gr; f. 2001; cap. 34.2m., res 190.5m., dep. 1,827.1m. (Dec. 2006); Pres. MILITIADIS DAMANAKIS.

Proton Bank: Amaliados and Eslin 20, Ampelokipi, Attica, 115 23 Athens; tel. (210) 6970000; fax (210) 6970111; e-mail protonbank@proton.gr; internet www.proton.gr; f. 2001 as Proton Investment Bank; name changed as above Oct. 2006 after merger with Omega Bank; cap. 281.5m., res 101.9m., dep. 1,161.4m. (Dec. 2006); Chair. ANGELIKI FRANGOU.

STOCK EXCHANGE

Athens Stock Exchange: Odos Sophokleous 10, 105 59 Athens; tel. (210) 3211301; fax (210) 3213938; e-mail webmaster@ase.gr; internet www.ase.gr; f. 1876; Pres. PANAYOTIS ALEXAKIS; Vice-Pres. THEODOROS PANTOLAKIS.

PRINCIPAL INSURANCE COMPANIES

The Greek insurance market underwent a period of some consolidation in the second half of the 1990s and the first half of the 2000s. Whereas there had been 139 insurance companies operating in Greece in 1995, by 2005 this number had been reduced to 95, of which 18 provided life insurance, 64 provided non-life insurance, and 13 provided both life and non-life insurance.

Agrotiki Hellenic Insurance Co: Leoforos Syngrou 163, 171 21 Kallithea, Athens; tel. (210) 9379100; fax (210) 9358924; internet www.agroins.com; Gen. Man. TR. LISIMACHOU.

Alpha Insurance: Odos Michalakopoulou 48, 115 28 Athens; tel. (210) 7268000; fax (210) 7268810; e-mail info@alpha-insurance.gr; internet www.alpha-insurance.gr; f. 1999 by merger; Chair. PHOTIS P. COSTOPOULOS; Man. Dir D. PALEOLOGOS; Gen. Man. NIKOLAOS GIANNOULAS.

Aspis Pronia General Insurance SA: Leoforos Kifissias 62, 151 25 Maroussi, Athens; tel. (210) 6198960; fax (210) 6198974; e-mail info@aspis.gr; internet www.aspis.gr; f. 1941; Pres. and Chief Exec. PAUL PSOMIADES.

GREECE — Directory

Atlantiki Enosis: Odos Messoghion 71 & Ilidos 36, 115 26 Athens; tel. (210) 7799211; fax (210) 7794446; e-mail atlantiki@atlantiki.gr; internet www.atlanticunion.gr; f. 1970; Pres. SARANDOS STASINOPOULOS; Man. Dir NOTIS LAPATAS.

Commercial Value: D. Aeropagitou & Makri 1, 117 42 Athens; tel. (210) 9290808; fax (210) 9231952; e-mail admin@nch.gz; internet www.commercialvalue.gr; f. 2002; Pres. D. DASKALOPOULOS; Man. Dir P. ATHENEOS.

Dynamis: Leoforos Syngrou 106, 117 41 Kallithea, Athens; tel. (210) 9227255; fax (210) 9237768; e-mail genka@asfgenka.gr; f. 1977; Man. Dir NIKOLAS STAMATOPOULOS.

Egnatia Co: Odos Fragon 1, 546 26 Thessaloníki; tel. (2310) 523325; fax (2310) 523555; Rep. P. MIGAS.

Emporiki Life: Odos Korai 6, 105 64 Athens; tel. (210) 3282346; fax (210) 3282441; e-mail mzanatta@emporikilife.gr; f. 1940; Chair. DIMITRIS FRANGETIS; Exec. Dir MICHAEL ZANATTA.

Ethniki Hellenic General Insurance Co SA: Odos Karageorgi Servias 8, 102 10 Athens; tel. (210) 3299000; fax (210) 3236101; internet www.ethniki-asfalistiki.gr; f. 1891; Gen. Man. C. PHILIPOU.

Galaxias Insurance Co: Leoforos Syngrou 40–42, 117 42 Kallithea, Athens; tel. (210) 9241082; fax (210) 9241698; f. 1967; Gen. Man. K. ANAGNOSTAKIS.

Gothaer Hellas: Odos Michalakopoulou 174, 115 27 Athens; tel. (210) 7750801; fax (210) 7757094; Gen. Man. S. GALANIS.

Hellas Insurance Co: Leoforos Kifissias 119, Marousi, 151 24 Athens; tel. (210) 8127600; fax (210) 8027189; e-mail nick.nardis@aig.com; internet www.aig-greece.gr; f. 1973; Gen. Man. N. NARDIS.

Hellenic Reliance General Insurances: Leoforos Kifissias 304, Halandri, 152 32 Athens; tel. (210) 6843733; fax (210) 6843734; f. 1990; Man. Dir S. F. TRIANTAFYLLAKIS.

Hellenobretanniki General Insurances: Leoforos Messoghion 2–4, 115 27 Athens; tel. (210) 7755301; fax (210) 7714768; f. 1988.

Helvetia General Insurance Co: Leoforos Kifissias 124, 115 26 Athens; tel. (210) 6980840; fax (210) 6923446; f. 1943; Gen. Man. J. DELENDAS.

Horizon General Insurance Co: Leoforos Amalias 26A, 105 57 Athens; tel. (210) 3227932; fax (210) 3225540; f. 1965; Gen. Mans THEODORE ACHIS, CHR. ACHIS.

Imperial Hellas: Leoforos Syngrou 253, N. Smirni, 171 22 Athens; tel. (210) 9426352; fax (210) 9426202; internet www.imperial.gr; f. 1971; Gen. Man. G. TZANIS.

Interamerican Hellenic Life Insurance Co: Interamerican Plaza, Leoforos Kifissias 117, Maroussi, 151 80 Athens; tel. (210) 6191111; fax (210) 6191877; e-mail moissism@interamerican.gr; internet www.interamerican.gr; f. 1971; 79.4% owned by Eureko (Netherlands); subsidiary cos provide medical, property, casualty, and automobile insurance; Pres. and Man. Dir DIMITRI KONTOMINAS.

Kykladiki Insurance Co: Leoforos Syngrou 80–88, Kallithea, 117 41 Athens; tel. (210) 9247664; fax (210) 9247344; f. 1919; Gen. Man. PAN. KATSIKOSTAS.

Phoenix General Insurance Co of Greece: Odos Omirou 2, 105 64 Athens; tel. (210) 3295111; fax (210) 3239135; e-mail phoenix@phoenix.gr; f. 1928; general insurance.

Poseidon: Odos Karaiskou 163, 185 35 Piraeus; tel. (210) 4522685; fax (210) 4184337; e-mail poseidon@otenet.gr; f. 1972; Gen. Man. THANOS J. MELAKOPIDES.

Sideris Insurance Co: Odos Lekka 3–5, 105 63 Athens; tel. (210) 3224484; fax (210) 3231066; e-mail siderisa@acci.gr; internet www.sideris-insurance.gr; Dir G. SIDERIS.

Syneteristiki General Insurance Co: Leoforos Syngrou 367, 175 64 Kallithea, Athens; tel. (210) 9491280; fax (210) 9403148; internet www.syneteristiki.gr; Gen. Man. D. ZORBAS.

Victoria General Insurance Co SA: Odos Tsimiski 21, 546 22 Thessaloníki; tel. (2310) 371100; fax (2310) 371392; e-mail victoria@victoria.gr; internet www.victoria.gr; f. 1972; Man. Dir G. ANDONIADIS.

Insurance Association

Hellenic Association of Insurance Companies: Odos Xenophontos 10, 105 57 Athens; tel. (210) 3334100; fax (210) 3334149; e-mail info@eaee.gr; internet www.eaee.gr; f. 1907; 77 mems; Gen. Man. MARGARITA ANTONAKI.

Trade and Industry

CHAMBERS OF COMMERCE

Athens Chamber of Commerce and Industry: Odos Akademias 7, 106 71 Athens; tel. (210) 3625342; fax (210) 3618810; e-mail info@acci.gr; internet www.acci.gr; f. 1919; Pres. DRACOULIS FOUNDOUKAKOS; Sec.-Gen. PANAGIOTIS KOUTSIKOS; 70,000 mems.

Athens Chamber of Small and Medium-sized Industries: Odos Akademias 18, 106 71 Athens; tel. (210) 3680700; fax (210) 3614726; internet www.acsmi.gr; f. 1940; Pres. D. CHARISIS; Sec.-Gen. ATH. PAVLOU; c. 60,000 mems.

Crafts Chamber of Piraeus: Odos Karaiscou 111, 185 32 Piraeus; tel. (210) 4110443; fax (210) 4179495; e-mail info@bep.gr; internet www.bep.gr; f. 1925; Pres. KONSTANTINOS MOSCHOLIOS; Sec.-Gen. PANTELIS ANTONIADIS; 18,500 mems.

Piraeus Chamber of Commerce and Industry: Odos Loudovikou 1, 185 31 Piraeus; tel. (210) 4177241; fax (210) 4178680; f. 1919; Pres. GEORGE KASSIMATIS; Sec.-Gen. KONSTANTINOS SARANTOPOULOS.

Thessaloníki Chamber of Commerce and Industry: Odos Tsimiski 29, 546 24 Thessaloníki; tel. (2310) 224438; fax (2310) 230237; f. 1919; Pres. PANTELIS KONSTANTINIDIS; Sec.-Gen. EMMANUEL VLACHOYANNIS; 14,500 mems.

INDUSTRIAL AND TRADE ASSOCIATIONS

Federation of Greek Industries (SEV): Odos Xenophontos 5, 105 57 Athens; tel. (210) 3237325; fax (210) 3222929; e-mail main@fgi.org.gr; internet www.fgi.org.gr; f. 1907; Chair. ELEFTHERIOS ANTONAKOPOULOS; 950 mems.

Federation of Industries of Northern Greece: Morihovou 1, 6th Floor, 546 35 Thessaloníki; tel. (2310) 539817; fax (2310) 541933; e-mail info@sbbe.gr; internet www.sbbe.gr; f. 1915; Pres. GEORGE MILONAS.

Hellenic Cotton Board: Leoforos Syngrou 150, 176 71 Kallithea, Athens; tel. (210) 9225011; fax (210) 9249656; f. 1931; state organization; Pres. P. K. MYLONAS.

Hellenic Organization of Small and Medium-sized Enterprises and Handicrafts (EOMMEX): Odos Xenias 16, 115 28 Athens; tel. (210) 7491100; fax (210) 7491146; e-mail interel@eommex.gr; internet www.eommex.gr; Pres. NICKOLAOS I. KAKOURIS.

UTILITIES

Electricity

Public Power Corpn (DEI): Odos Xalkokondyli 30, 104 32 Athens; tel. (210) 5230301; fax (210) 5238445; e-mail info@dei.gr; internet www.dei.gr; f. 1950; 84% state-owned; generating capacity of 96 power stations: 12,224 MW (2005); generation, transmission and distribution of electricity; Chief Exec. and Man. Dir KYRIAKOPOULOS KONSTANTINOS.

Gas

Public Gas Corpn (DEPA): Leoforos Messoghion 207, 115 25 Athens; tel. (210) 6793500; fax (210) 6749504; e-mail info@depa.gr; internet www.depa.gr; f. 1988; 35% owned by Hellenic Petroleum SA, 65% state-owned; began gas imports 1997, initially for industrial use; Man. Dir ARISTEIDIS VAKIRLIS.

Water

In 1980 a law was passed under which Municipal Enterprises for Water Supply and Sewerage (DEYA) were created to manage drinking water and sewerage throughout Greece. Since then some 90 DEYA have been established.

The Hellenic Union of Municipal Enterprises for Water Supply and Sewerage (EDEYA): Odos Anthimou Gaza 3, 412 22 Larissa; internet www.edeya.gr; f. 1989; 67 mems.

TRADE UNIONS

There are about 5,000 registered trade unions, grouped together in 82 federations and 86 workers' centres, which are affiliated to the Greek General Confederation of Labour.

Greek General Confederation of Labour (GSEE): Odos Patission 69, Athens; tel. (210) 8834611; fax (210) 8202156; e-mail info@gsee.gr; internet www.gsee.gr; f. 1918; Pres. IOANNIS PANAGOPOULOS; Gen. Sec. KOSTAS POUPAKIS; 700,000 mems.

Pan-Hellenic Federation of Seamen's Unions (PNO): Livanos Bldg, Akti Miaouli 47–49, 185 36 Piraeus; tel. (210) 4292960; fax (210) 4293040; f. 1920; confederation of 14 marine unions; Pres. IOANNIS CHELAS; Gen. Sec. JOHN HALAS.

Supreme Administration of Greek Civil Servants' Trade Unions (ADEDY): Odos Psylla Philellinon 2; tel. (210) 3227962; fax (210) 3246165; e-mail adedyed@otenet.gr; internet www.adedy.gr.

Transport

RAILWAYS

Construction of a 26.3 km electrified extension to the Athens–Piraeus line, in order to provide a three-line urban railway system for Athens, designated Metro Line 1, was completed in 2000. Metro Lines 2 and 3, each measuring some 9 km, opened prior to the holding of the summer Olympic Games in 2004.

Attiko Metro: Leoforos Messoghion 191–93, 115 25 Athens; tel. (210) 6792399; fax (210) 6726126; e-mail info@ametro.gr; internet www.ametro.gr; f. 1999; operates underground railway in Athens; Chair. IOANNIS CHRISSIKOPOULOS.

Ilektriki Sidirodromi Athinon–Pireos (ISAP) (Athens–Piraeus Electric Railways): Odos Athinas 67, 105 52 Athens; tel. (210) 3248311; fax (210) 3223935; internet www.isap.gr; state-owned; 25.6 km of electrified track; Chair. GEORGE PAPAVASSILIOU; Man. Dir DIONISSIOS RAPPOS.

Organismos Sidirodromon Ellados (OSE) (Hellenic Railways Organization Ltd): Odos Karolou 1–3, 104 37 Athens; tel. (210) 5248395; fax (210) 5243290; internet www.ose.gr; f. 1971; state railways; total length of track: 2,474 km; Chair. NIKOLAOS BALTAS; Dir-Gen. A. LAZARIS.

ROADS

In 1999 there were an estimated 117,000 km of roads in Greece. Of this total, an estimated 9,100 km were main roads, and 470 km were motorways. Construction of the 680 km Egnatia highway, extending from the Adriatic coast to the Turkish border, was one of the largest road projects in Europe and was scheduled for completion in 2008.

INLAND WATERWAYS

There are no navigable rivers in Greece.

Corinth Canal: built 1893; over six km long, links the Corinthian and Saronic Gulfs; shortens the journey from the Adriatic to the Piraeus by 325 km; spanned by three single-span bridges, two for road and one for rail; can be used by ships of a maximum draught of 22 ft and width of 60 ft; managed since June 2001 by Sea Containers Group (United Kingdom).

SHIPPING

In 2006 the Greek merchant fleet totalled 1,455 vessels, with a combined aggregate displacement of 32.1m. grt. Greece controls one of the largest merchant fleets in the world. The principal ports are Piraeus, Patras and Thessaloníki.

Union of Greek Shipowners: Akti Miaouli 85, 185 38 Piraeus; f. 1916; Pres. NICOS EFTHYMIOU.

Port Authorities

Port of Patras: Patras Port Authority, Central Port Office, Patras; tel. (2610) 316400; fax (2610) 327136; internet www.patrasport.gr; Pres. GEORGE LAZARIS; Harbour Master Capt. NIKOLAS RAFAILOVITS.

Piraeus Port Authority: Piraeus Port Authority, Akti Miaouli 10, 185 35 Piraeus; tel. (210) 4520911; fax (210) 4286843; e-mail olpdsx@otenet.gr; internet www.olp.gr; 25% privatized; Man. Dir HARILAOS PSARAFTIS.

Port of Thessaloníki: Thessaloníki Port Authority, POB 10467, 541 10 Thessaloníki; tel. (2310) 593129; fax (2310) 510500; e-mail secretariat@thpa.gr; internet www.thpa.gr; Chief Exec. IOANNIS TSARAS; Pres. LAZAROS KANAVOURAS.

Shipping Companies

The following are among the largest or most important shipping companies.

Anangel Shipping Enterprises: Akti Miaouli, POB 80004, 185 10 Piraeus; tel. (210) 4224500; fax (210) 4224819; Man. Dir J. PLATSIDAKIS.

Attika Shipping Co: Odos Voucourestion 16, 106 71 Athens; tel. (210) 3609631; fax (210) 3601439; Dir G. PRIOVOLOS.

Bilinder Marine Corpn: Odos Igias 1–3 & Akti Themistokleos, 185 36 Piraeus; tel. (210) 4287300; fax (210) 4287355; Gen. Man. V. ARMOGENI.

Blue Star Ferries: C. Karamanli 157, Voula, 166 73 Athens; tel. (210) 8919800; fax (210) 8919829; e-mail bluestarferries@bluestarferries.com; internet www.bluestarferries.com; Man. Dir G. STRINTZIS.

Ceres Hellenic Shipping Enterprises Co: Akti Miaouli 69, 185 37 Piraeus; tel. (210) 4591000; fax (210) 4283552; e-mail chse@ceres.gr; internet www.ceres.gr; Chief Exec. NIKOLAOS G. FISTES.

Chandris (Hellas) Co: POB 80067, Akti Miaouli 95, 185 38 Piraeus; tel. (210) 4290300; fax (210) 4290256; Man. Dirs A. C. PIPERAS, M. G. SKORDIAS.

Costamare Shipping Co: Odos Zephyrou 60, Kallithea, 175 64 Athens; tel. (210) 9390000; fax (210) 9409051; Pres. Capt. V. C. KONSTANTAKOPOULOS.

European Navigation Co: Odos Artemissiou 2, 166 75 Athens; tel. (210) 8981581; fax (210) 8946777; Dir P. KARNESSIS.

Glafki (Hellas) Maritime Co: Odos Mitropoleos 3, 105 57 Athens; tel. (210) 3244991; fax (210) 3228944; Dirs M. FRAGOULIS, G. PANAGIOTOU.

Golden Union Shipping Co: Odos Aegales 8, 185 45 Piraeus; tel. (210) 4061000; fax (210) 4061199; e-mail infgusc@goldenunion.gr; internet www.goldenunion.gr; f. 1977; Chair. THEODORE VENIAMIS.

M. Koutlakis & Co: Makras Stoas 5, 185 31 Piraeus; tel. (210) 4129428; fax (210) 4178755; Dir M. KOUTLAKIS.

Laskaridis Shipping Co: Odos Chimaras 5, Maroussi, 151 25 Athens; tel. (210) 6899090; fax (210) 6806762; Man. Dirs P. C. LASKARIDIS, A. C. LASKARIDIS.

Marmaras Navigation Co: Odos Filellinon 4–6, Okeanion Bldg, 185 36 Piraeus; tel. (210) 4294226; fax (210) 4294304; Dir D. DIAMANTIDES.

Minoan Lines Shipping Co: Odos 25 August 17, 712 02 Iraklion; tel. (2810) 399800; fax (2810) 330308; e-mail info@minoan.gr; internet www.minoan.gr; Pres. KONSTANTINOS KLIRONOMAS.

Naftomar Shipping and Trading Co: Leoforos Alkyonidon 243, 166 73 Voula; tel. (210) 8914200; fax (210) 8914235; e-mail naftomar@naftomar.gr; internet www.naftomar.gr; Man. Dir RIAD ZEIN.

Thenamaris (Ships Management) Co: Odos Athinas 16, Kavouri, 166 71 Athens; tel. (210) 8969111; fax (210) 8969653; e-mail thena@thenamaris.gr; internet www.thenamaris.gr; Dir K. MARTINOS.

Tsakos Shipping and Trading Co: Macedonia House, Leoforos Syngrou 367, POB 79141, 175 02 Athens; tel. (210) 9380700; fax (210) 9480710; e-mail mail@tsakoshellas.gr; Dirs P. N. TSAKOS, E. SAROGLOU.

United Shipping and Trading Co of Greece: Odos Iassonos 6, 185 37 Piraeus; tel. (210) 4283660; fax (210) 4283630; Dir CH. TSAKOS.

CIVIL AVIATION

There are international airports at Athens, Thessaloníki, Alexandroupolis, Corfu, Lesbos, Andravida, Rhodes, Kos and Heraklion/Crete, and 24 domestic airports (of which 13 are authorized to receive international flights). A new international airport, Eleftherios Venizelos, at Spata, some 25 km east of Athens, was opened in March 2001. The airport was expected to have a handling capacity of 16m. passengers per year.

Aegean Airlines: Leoforos Vouliagmenis 572, 164 51 Athens; tel. (210) 9988350; fax (210) 9957598; internet www.aegeanair.com; f. 1987; domestic and international services; Pres. and Chief Exec. THEODOROS VASSILAKIS.

Olympic Airlines: Leoforos Syngrou 96–100, 117 41 Kallithea, Athens; tel. (210) 9269111; fax (210) 9267154; e-mail ebusms@olympicairlines.com; internet www.olympicairlines.com; f. 1957 as Olympic Airways; state-owned; restructured and renamed as above in 2003; further restructuring pending; Chair. Prof. PETROS PAPAGEORGIOU; Chief Exec. LEONARDOS-ODYSSEAS VLAMIS.

Tourism

The sunny climate, the natural beauty of the country and its great history and traditions attract tourists to Greece. There are numerous islands and many sites of archaeological interest. The number of tourists visiting Greece increased from 1m. in 1968 to 14.3m. in 2005. Receipts from tourism, which totalled US $120m. in 1968, reached $13,697m. in 2005.

Ellinikos Organismos Tourismou (EOT) (Greek National Tourist Organization): Odos Tsoha 7, 115 21 Athens; tel. (210) 8707000; e-mail info@gnto.gr; internet www.visitgreece.gr; Pres. Dr ARISTIDIS S. CALOGEROPOULOS-STRATIS.

GRENADA

Introductory Survey

Location, Climate, Language, Religion, Flag, Capital

Grenada, a mountainous, heavily forested island, is the most southerly of the Windward Islands, in the West Indies. The country also includes some of the small islands known as the Grenadines, which lie to the north-east of Grenada. The most important of these are the low-lying island of Carriacou and its neighbour, Petit Martinique. The climate is semi-tropical, with an average annual temperature of 28°C (82°F) in the lowlands. Annual rainfall averages about 1,500 mm (60 ins) in the coastal area and 3,800 mm to 5,100 mm (150–200 ins) in mountain areas. Most of the rainfall occurs between June and December. The majority of the population speak English, although a French patois is sometimes spoken. According to the census of 1991, 82% of Grenada's population were of African descent, while 13% were of mixed ethnic origins. Most of the population profess Christianity, and the main denominations are Roman Catholicism (to which some 45% of the population adhered in 2006) and Anglicanism (about 14% of the population). The national flag (proportions 1 by 2) consists of a diagonally quartered rectangle (yellow in the upper and lower segments, green in the right and left ones) surrounded by a red border bearing six five-pointed yellow stars (three at the upper edge of the flag, and three at the lower edge). There is a red disc, containing a large five-pointed yellow star, in the centre, and a representation of a nutmeg (in yellow and red) on the green segment near the hoist. The capital is St George's.

Recent History

Grenada was initially colonized by the French but was captured by the British in 1762. The Treaty of Versailles recognized British control in 1783. Grenada continued as a British colony until 1958, when it joined the Federation of the West Indies, remaining a member until the dissolution of the Federation in 1962. Full internal self-government and statehood in association with the United Kingdom were achieved in March 1967. During this period, the political life of Grenada was dominated by Herbert Blaize, the leader of the Grenada National Party (GNP), and Eric Gairy, a local trade union leader, who in 1950 founded the Grenada United Labour Party (GULP), with the support of an associated trade union. Gairy became Premier after the elections of 1967 and again after those of 1972, which he contested chiefly on the issue of total independence. Grenada became independent, within the Commonwealth, on 7 February 1974, with Gairy as Prime Minister. Domestic opposition to Gairy was expressed in public unrest, and the formation by the three opposition parties—the GNP, the United People's Party and the New Jewel Movement (NJM)—of the People's Alliance, which contested the 1976 general elections and reduced GULP's majority in the Lower House.

The opposition regarded the rule of Sir Eric Gairy, as he became in June 1977, as increasingly autocratic and corrupt, and on 13 March 1979 he was replaced in a bloodless coup by the leader of the left-wing NJM, Maurice Bishop. The new People's Revolutionary Government (PRG) suspended the 1974 Constitution and announced the imminent formation of a People's Consultative Assembly to draft a new constitution. Meanwhile, Grenada remained a monarchy, with the British Queen as Head of State, represented in Grenada by a Governor-General. During 1980–81 there was an increase in repression, against a background of mounting anti-Government violence and the PRG's fears of an invasion by US forces.

By mid-1982 relations with the USA, the United Kingdom and the more conservative members of the Caribbean Community and Common Market (CARICOM, see p. 196) were becoming increasingly strained: elections had not been arranged, restrictions against the privately owned press had been imposed, many detainees were still awaiting trial, and Grenada was aligning more closely with Cuba and the USSR. Cuba was contributing funds and construction workers for the airport at Point Salines, a project which further strengthened the US Government's conviction that Grenada was to become a centre for Soviet manoeuvres in the area.

In March 1983 the armed forces were put on alert, in response to renewed fears that the USA was planning to invade. (The USA strenuously denied any such plans.) In June Bishop sought to improve relations with the USA, and announced the appointment of a commission to draft a new constitution. The more left-wing members of the PRG denounced this attempt at conciliation as an ideological betrayal. A power struggle developed between Bishop and his deputy, Bernard Coard, the Minister of Finance and Planning. In October Bishop was placed under house arrest, allegedly for his refusal to share power with Coard. The commander of the People's Revolutionary Army (PRA), Gen. Austin Hudson, subsequently announced that Bishop had been expelled from the NJM. On 19 October thousands of Bishop's supporters stormed the house, freed Bishop, and demonstrated outside the PRA headquarters. PRA forces responded by firing into the crowd. Later in the day, Bishop, three of his ministers and two trade unionists were executed by the PRA. The Government was replaced by a 16-member Revolutionary Military Council (RMC), led by Gen. Austin and supported by Coard and one other minister. The remaining NJM ministers were arrested and imprisoned, and a total curfew was imposed.

Regional and international outrage at the assassination of Bishop, in addition to fears of a US military intervention, were so intense that after four days the RMC relaxed the curfew, reopened the airport and promised a swift return to civilian rule. However, the Organisation of Eastern Caribbean States (OECS, see p. 425) resolved to intervene in an attempt to restore democratic order, and asked for assistance from the USA, which readily complied. (It is unclear whether the decision to intervene preceded or followed a request for help to the OECS by the Grenadian Governor-General, Sir Paul Scoon.) On 25 October 1983 some 1,900 US military personnel invaded the island, accompanied by 300 troops from Jamaica, Barbados and member countries of the OECS. Fighting continued for some days, and the USA gradually increased its troop strength, with further reinforcements waiting off shore with a US naval task force. The RMC's forces were defeated, while Coard, Austin and others who had been involved in the coup were detained.

On 9 November 1983 Scoon appointed a non-political interim Council to assume responsibility for the government of the country until elections could be held. Nicholas Brathwaite, a former Commonwealth official, was appointed Chairman of this Council in December. The 1974 Constitution was reinstated (although the country did not rejoin the East Caribbean Supreme Court), and an electoral commission was created. By mid-December the USA had withdrawn all its forces except 300 support troops who were to assist the 430 members of Caribbean forces remaining on the island. A 550-member police force, trained by the USA and the United Kingdom, was established, including a paramilitary body that was to be the new defence contingent.

Several political parties that had operated clandestinely or from exile during the rule of the PRG re-emerged and announced their intention of contesting the elections for a new House of Representatives. Sir Eric Gairy returned to Grenada in January 1984 to lead GULP, but stated that he would not stand as a candidate himself. In May three former NJM ministers formed the Maurice Bishop Patriotic Movement (MBPM) to contest the elections. A number of centrist parties emerged or re-emerged, including Blaize's GNP. Fears that a divided opposition would allow GULP to win a majority of seats in the new House resulted in an agreement by several of these organizations, in August 1984, to form the New National Party (NNP), led by Blaize.

At the general election held in December 1984 the NNP achieved a convincing victory by winning 14 of the 15 seats in the House of Representatives, with 59% of the popular votes. Both GULP and the MBPM claimed that the poll had been fraudulent, and the one successful GULP candidate, Marcel Peters, initially refused to take his seat in protest. He subsequently accepted the seat, but was expelled from the party and formed the Grenada Democratic Labour Party (GDLP). Blaize became Prime Minister. US and Caribbean troops remained in Grenada, at Blaize's request, until September 1985.

The trial of 19 detainees (including Coard, his wife, Phyllis, and Gen. Austin), accused of murder and conspiracy against

Bishop and six of his associates, opened in November 1984. However, repeated adjournments postponed the trial of 18 of the detainees until April 1986. One of the detainees agreed to give evidence for the State in return for a pardon. Eventually, in December, the jury returned verdicts on 196 charges of murder and conspiracy to murder. Fourteen of the defendants were sentenced to death, three received prison sentences of between 30 and 45 years, and one was acquitted. In July 1991 the Court of Appeal upheld the original verdicts that had been imposed in 1986 on the defendants in the Bishop murder trial, and further pleas for clemency were rejected. Preparations for the imminent hanging of the 14, however, provoked international outrage, and in August Brathwaite announced that the death sentences were to be commuted to terms of life imprisonment.

Internal differences gradually led to the disintegration of the NNP. In 1986 its parliamentary strength was reduced to 12 seats, following the resignation of two members who subsequently formed the Democratic Labour Congress (DLC). Three more government members resigned in April 1987, and joined forces with the DLC and the GDLP in July to form a united opposition, with six seats in the House of Representatives. In October they formally launched a new party, the National Democratic Congress (NDC), led by George Brizan, who had earlier been appointed parliamentary opposition leader.

During 1988–89 the actions of the Blaize Government, under provisions of the controversial Emergency Powers Act of 1987, gave rise to concerns both within the opposition and among regional neighbours. Deportation orders and bans were enforced by the administration against prominent left-wing politicians and journalists from the region, and a variety of books and journals were proscribed.

In January 1989 Blaize was replaced as party leader by his cabinet colleague, Dr Keith Mitchell, although he remained Prime Minister. In July, however, following allegations of corruption by the NDC, Blaize announced the dismissal of Mitchell and the Chairman of the NNP. Amid uncertainty as to whether the Blaize faction had formed a separate party, two more members of the Government resigned, thus reducing support for the Blaize Government to only five of the 15 members of the House of Representatives. Blaize did not officially announce the formation of a new party, The National Party (TNP), until late August, by which time he had advised the acting Governor-General to prorogue Parliament. (The Government thereby avoided being defeated in a motion of 'no confidence', the immediate dissolution of Parliament and the prospect of an early general election.) The term of the Parliament was due to expire at the end of December, and a general election had to be held within three months. However, Blaize died in mid-December, and the Governor-General appointed Ben Jones, Blaize's former deputy and the new leader of TNP, as Prime Minister. At the general election, held in March 1990, no party achieved an absolute majority in the House of Representatives. The NDC, with seven of the 15 legislative seats, achieved a working majority in Parliament when one of GULP's successful candidates announced his defection to the NDC. Nicholas Brathwaite, who had succeeded Brizan as NDC leader in 1989, subsequently became Prime Minister and appointed a new Cabinet.

Brathwaite resigned as leader of the NDC in September 1994 and was succeeded by George Brizan. In February 1995 Brathwaite resigned as Prime Minister, and was succeeded by Brizan. At the general election held in June the NNP secured eight of the 15 seats in the House of Representatives, while the NDC's representation was reduced to five seats. The remaining two seats were secured by GULP. Dr Keith Mitchell, leader of the NNP, became Prime Minister and appointed a Cabinet. The NNP subsequently undertook negotiations with GULP in an attempt to strengthen its single-seat majority and to secure the two-thirds' majority required to amend the Constitution. In July Francis Alexis resigned as deputy leader of the NDC; in November he and three other former NDC members announced the formation of a new opposition group, the Democratic Labour Party (DLP).

The appointment in August 1996 of Daniel (later Sir Daniel) Williams to the post of Governor-General provoked considerable controversy because of Williams' connections with the NNP (he had been deputy leader of the party during the 1980s) and his previous role as a cabinet minister in the Government of Herbert Blaize. Opposition members staged a walk-out at his inauguration ceremony, a protest that led to Brizan, the Leader of the Opposition, being suspended from the House of Representatives for one month.

In March 1997 the Government's Mercy Committee rejected a request made by the Conference of Churches of Grenada for the release, on the grounds of their deteriorating physical and mental health, of Phyllis Coard and another of those serving terms of life imprisonment for the murder of Maurice Bishop. None the less, the Committee gave assurances that the detainees' medical requirements would receive attention, and that conditions at the prison where they were being held would be improved.

In late November 1998 the resignation of the Minister of Foreign Affairs, Raphael Fletcher, from the Government and NNP in order to join GULP, resulted in an early general election being called. At the general election, held on 18 January 1999, the NNP achieved a comprehensive victory, obtaining all of the 15 seats in the House of Representatives. The NNP's return to power constituted the first time in the country's history that a political party had been given two successive terms in government.

In late September and early October 1999 two leading journalists were arrested on separate charges of alleged criminal libel. One of the detainees was the editor of *Grenada Today*, George Worme, who had published a letter accusing Mitchell of having bribed voters during the last election campaign. Opposition parties, human rights organizations and media associations claimed that the Government was seeking to intimidate independent journalists. In November 2000 the Grenada High Court ruled that the charge brought against Worme was unconstitutional, since it violated his right to free expression.

Also in early October 1999 Bernard Coard, the former Deputy Prime Minister serving a term of life imprisonment with 16 others for the 1983 murder of Prime Minister Maurice Bishop and a number of his associates (see above), issued a statement in which he accepted full responsibility for the crimes; it was, however, unclear as to whether he was speaking on behalf of all 17 prisoners. In February 2002 it was announced that three former soldiers jailed in 1986 for Bishop's murder and that of seven others during the 1983 coup attempt were to be released. A High Court judge deemed it unconstitutional that their multiple sentences for manslaughter should be served consecutively. Furthermore, in March 2004 the Court of Appeal ruled that the life sentences imposed on the 17 prisoners were unconstitutional; the prisoners were to receive new sentences, possibly resulting in their release from jail. However, on 26 April, the day before the prisoners were to be resentenced, the Court of Appeal of the OECS, based in Saint Lucia, overturned the ruling. This decision was confirmed after a further hearing in February 2005; lawyers for the men appealed against the judgment to the Privy Council, based in the United Kingdom, occasioning a ruling in February 2007 for the resentencing of 13 of the prisoners (three of their original number had been released in December 2006 after their sentences were commuted by one-third on grounds of good behaviour, while Phyllis Coard had secured early release in 2000 in order to seek life-saving medical treatment). Subsequently, in June 2007 the Supreme Court ordered the release of three of the prisoners and resentenced the remaining 10, whose prison terms were consequently due to end in 2010.

In June 2000 Mitchell dismissed Michael Baptiste from the Government after he was reported to have openly criticized Mitchell's running of the country. Baptiste subsequently left the NNP and became the sole opposition member in the House of Representatives. In January 2001 Baptiste formed a new opposition party, the United Labour Congress (ULC). Later in the year the ULC merged with GULP and, at the party's convention in December, Baptiste was elected opposition leader.

In February 2003 Gloria Payne-Banfield succeeded Baptiste as GULP leader, in preparation for the legislative election that was held on 27 November. The NNP secured a third successive term in office, although its parliamentary majority was reduced to just one seat. The NDC won the seven remaining seats in the 15-seat House of Representatives. Keith Mitchell was sworn in again as Prime Minister on 29 November. The electoral campaign was dominated by opposition claims that the Mitchell Government had allowed national debt and unemployment to increase to critical levels; the NNP, however, successfully argued that the party had guided the economy back to real growth.

On 16 December 2003 a defeated NDC candidate, George Prime, issued a legal challenge to the election result in the Carriacou/Petit Martinique seat, claiming that a number of irregularities had surrounded the voting there. In January 2004 the NNP responded by filing a petition challenging the results in two other seats, also citing voting irregularities. In

August the Prime Minister commenced legal proceedings against George Prime, as well as against a local company and a US-based publication after corruption allegations were made relating to the appointment of Eric Resteiner, a former Grenadian diplomat. Later in the same month an official inquiry into the allegations was established; Richard Cheltenham, a prominent Barbadian lawyer, was appointed to lead the investigation. Mitchell was finally cleared of the allegations in August 2007 and later in the year was granted immunity from prosecution by the US Government after Charles Howland, a US businessman, filed charges, seeking to recover monies allegedly misappropriated by Mitchell after meeting Resteiner.

Grenada was severely devastated by 'Hurricane Ivan', which struck the island in early September 2004. Some 39 Grenadians were killed and around 90% of the housing stock was destroyed; as a result of the infrastructural damage caused by the hurricane, the country's economy was expected to enter a recession lasting several years. According to the OECS, full rehabilitation would cost at least US $814m. Opposition MPs, who urged the NNP to establish an interim coalition Government, strenuously criticized the Government's relief efforts and the country's perceived slow recovery progress. In October Grenada established the Agency for Reconstruction and Development to implement and monitor reconstruction projects and to manage the receipt of grants from the numerous international donors. Widespread looting and violent crime was brought under effective control after intervention from regional (primarily Trinidadian) security forces. The island was struck by another huge storm, 'Hurricane Emily', in July 2005. The cost of the damage was tentatively estimated at $200m.; however, the misfortune was compounded by the impact of 'Emily' upon the recovery process from 'Hurricane Ivan'. Although Grenada quickly secured a $10m. reconstruction loan from the Caribbean Development Bank (see p. 201) in July, and further help from the World Bank in December, in January 2006 Mitchell announced that a 5% salary tax to help finance rebuilding efforts would be introduced in that year's budget, scheduled for April. The levy was strenuously opposed by the Grenada Trade Union Congress, which argued that Grenadians were already overburdened by costs associated with the recovery process. Further assistance was secured in January 2007 when the Japanese Government, together with the UN, announced that US $1.03m. was to be designated under the Trust Fund for Human Security for the restoration of livelihoods and enhancing disaster-preparedness. At the end of 2007 the IMF reported that the economy had recovered significantly owing to the measures detailed above and the positive impact of the Cricket World Cup held earlier in the year.

Meanwhile, in February 2005 the Government was embroiled in an argument with the Grenada Bar Association (GBA) over the former's nomination of Hugh Wildman, the Director of the Financial Intelligence Unit of the Grenada International Financial Services Authority, for the post of Attorney-General. Wildman attracted intense criticism from the GBA in his previous role as Director of Public Prosecutions and it was finally agreed that the Cabinet would review the nomination. The decision was passed to the Judicial and Legal Services Commission of the OECS, which has the power to adjudicate on senior judicial appointments, and in late February Wildman's appointment was rejected. The Government accepted the ruling and in March the position of Attorney-General was added to the responsibilities of Elvin Nimrod, who, in addition to holding several other portfolios, was also the Minister of Legal Affairs. Wildman, meanwhile, was given the apparently newly created role of legal adviser to the Cabinet, an appointment that opposition MPs regarded as a crude attempt by Mitchell to circumvent the Constitution and as a waste of resources.

In May 1996 Grenada signed two treaties with the USA, relating to mutual legal assistance and extradition, as part of a regional campaign to combat drugs-trafficking. Improved relations with Cuba, which had been severely strained since 1983 when diplomatic ties were suspended, resulted in offers of assistance with education, health and agriculture in Grenada in 1997. Diplomatic relations between the two countries were restored in December 1999, and in January 2003 a new hospital was opened in St George's, partly financed by the Cuban Government. In 2000 Grenada restored diplomatic relations with Libya, also suspended in 1983. In the following year Libya granted Grenada, along with other eastern Caribbean islands, access to a US $2,000m. development fund. It was also reported, in September, that Libya had agreed to purchase the entire output of Grenada's bananas and would provide the island with a set of grants and loans worth $4m., as well as cancelling a $6m. loan for the construction of Grenada's international airport in 1981.

From 1983 Grenada had maintained diplomatic relations with Taiwan instead of the People's Republic of China; however, in December 2004 Taiwan recalled its ambassador to Grenada after Mitchell visited mainland China. It was reported in the same month that the Chinese Government had promised Mitchell substantial funds for development projects in Grenada. Mitchell emphasized that the destruction caused by 'Hurricane Ivan' had forced the Government to reconsider its international relationships and on 20 January 2005 Grenada duly established official ties with the People's Republic of China. One week later Taiwan severed its relations with Grenada. However, the security of this still recent diplomatic determinism was threatened in February 2007 at the highly publicized opening of Grenada's new Queen Park National Stadium, funded by the People's Republic of China, when the Grenadian police band erroneously performed the Taiwanese national anthem, to the considerable embarrassment of government officials. Hasty apologies to the Chinese delegation ensued and a thorough inquiry into the debacle was launched. Meanwhile, in July 2005 diplomatic relations were established with Namibia in an effort to promote trade, tourism and economic co-operation between the two countries, and the Namibian embassy in Cuba was assigned responsibility for Grenada.

In January 2006 Mitchell indicated that Grenada would join CARICOM's Caribbean Single Market and Economy (CSME), which was established by six founding member states on 1 January, later in that year. The CSME was intended to enshrine the free movement of goods, services and labour throughout the CARICOM region, although no OECS countries were signatories to the new project from its inauguration. An intra-regional common passport initiative, designed to enhance a sense of community and facilitate travel for citizens of participating nations, was implemented in Grenada on 29 January 2007; use of the CARICOM passport, constituting an integral component of the regional shift towards economic union, was expected to have been introduced by all 15 member governments by early 2008. Successive Grenadian Governments have also participated in negotiations towards the establishment of the Caribbean Court of Justice (CCJ), which was intended to replace the Privy Council as the final court of appeal. By early 2008, however, legislation giving ultimate judicial power to the CCJ, which was inaugurated in Trinidad and Tobago in April 2005, had still to be approved by the Grenadian Parliament.

Government

Grenada has dominion status within the Commonwealth. The British monarch is Head of State and is represented locally by a Governor-General. The Cabinet, led by the Prime Minister, holds executive power. Parliament comprises the Senate, made up of 13 Senators appointed by the Governor-General on the advice of the Prime Minister and the Leader of the Opposition, and the 15-member House of Representatives, elected by universal adult suffrage. The Cabinet is responsible to Parliament.

Defence

A regional security unit was formed in 1983, modelled on the British police force and trained by British officers. A paramilitary element, known as the Special Service Unit and trained by US advisers, acts as the defence contingent and participates in the Regional Security System, a defence pact with other East Caribbean states.

Economic Affairs

In 2006, according to estimates by the World Bank, Grenada's gross national income (GNI), measured at average 2004–06 prices, was US $477.6m., equivalent to US $4,420 per head (or $7,810 per head on an international purchasing-power parity basis). In 1996–2006 Grenada's population increased at an average rate of 0.9% per year, while gross domestic product (GDP) per head increased, in real terms, by an average of 2.7% per year. Overall GDP increased, in real terms, at an average annual rate of 3.6% in 1996–2006. Real GDP increased by 6.5% in 2006.

According to preliminary figures, agriculture (including hunting, forestry and fishing) contributed 5.6% of GDP in 2006. The sector engaged an estimated 22.0% of the employed labour force in 2005, according to FAO. Grenada, known as the Spice Island of the Caribbean, is one of the world's largest producers of nutmeg (although Indonesia produces some 75% of the world's total). In 2004 sales of nutmeg and mace (the pungent red membrane around the nut) accounted for an estimated 33.5% of Grenada's domestic export earnings; in early 2004 the spice was planted on some 12,000 of the 19,708 acres under agricultural cultivation in the country. Exports of bananas were suspended in early 1997 by the Windward Islands Banana Development and Exporting Company (WIBDECO) because of poor quality, but were permitted to resume in late 1998, following a rehabilitation programme. Exports of bananas were still greatly reduced in 2005, particularly following the severe hurricane damage sustained by the agricultural sector in 2004 and 2005; however, production recovered in 2006 following the implementation of a crop recovery programme. Preliminary figures indicated that output grew by a further 29.3% in the first nine months of 2007, when banana production reached 891 metric tons. Since the demise of the banana industry, the other principal cash crop is cocoa, which accounted for an estimated 6.3% of domestic export earnings in 2004. Livestock production, for domestic consumption, is important on Carriacou. There are extensive timber reserves on the island of Grenada; forestry development is strictly controlled and involves a programme of reafforestation. Exports of fish contributed an estimated 9.5% of domestic export earnings in 2004. Agricultural GDP declined at an average annual rate of 1.4% in 1996–2006. The sector contracted by a devastating 41.2% in 2005, reflecting the impact of hurricane damage; however, the sector recovered by 28.1% in 2006.

Industry (mining, manufacturing, construction and utilities) provided an estimated 24.0% of GDP in 2006 and engaged 23.9% of the employed labour force in 1998. The mining sector accounted for only 0.2% of employment in 1998 and 0.7% of GDP in 2006. Manufacturing, which contributed 5.1% of GDP in 2006 and employed 7.4% of the working population in 1998, consists mainly of the processing of agricultural products and of cottage industries producing garments and spice-based items. Rum, soft drinks, paints and varnishes, household paper products and the tyre-retreading industries are also important. Manufacturing GDP increased by an average of 0.5% per year in 1998–2006; the sector's GDP increased by 16.9% in 2005, but decreased by 2.8% in 2006. The construction sector experienced an extraordinary 83.1% expansion in 2005, attributed, principally, to the extensive rehabilitation and investment projects commenced in the aftermath of hurricanes 'Ivan' and 'Emily'. Construction GDP decreased by 30.1% in 2006 following the completion of many of these commissions. Overall, industrial GDP increased by an annual average of 4.6% in 1998–2006. The sector increased by 43.2% in 2005; led by heightened activity in the construction sector (see above), but declined by 14.5% in 2006.

Grenada is dependent upon imports for its energy requirements, and in 2004 fuel accounted for an estimated 6.1% of the total cost of imports.

The services sector contributed 70.4% of GDP in 2006, when hotels and restaurants accounted for some 5.5% of GDP. From the mid-1980s until the late 1990s Grenada's tourism industry experienced a rapid expansion. However, total visitor arrivals declined dramatically in the first three years of the 21st century. The decrease was mainly owing to a massive fall in cruise-ship arrivals (26.6% in 2000, 18.2% in 2001 and 8.3% in 2002). Stop-over arrivals, however, remained relatively stable in all three years. Following a slight recovery in 2003, in 2004 there was a huge improvement (of 54.4%) in the number of cruise-ship passengers visiting Grenada, although there was a slight decrease (4.4%) in stop-over arrivals. According to preliminary figures, 2005 saw a considerable improvement (21.2%) in the number of cruise-ship passengers, while the number of stop-over arrivals decreased significantly, by 23.0%, partly attributed to the reduced operating capacity of visitor accommodation owing to storm damage. Cruise-ship arrivals declined by a further 20.5% in 2006 owing to a reduction in the number of cruise liners calling into port. None the less, there was some recovery in the tourism sector in that year, following the rehabilitation of hurricane-afflicted hotels and facilities. Stop-over and yacht arrivals increased in 2006 by a robust 20.4% and 8.7%, respectively. The Government hoped that the construction of a new port and marina in the northern parish of St Patrick would encourage a further increase in the number of yachts visiting Grenada. A full proposal detailing the construction of the new facilities (which would also include a dry dock facility, tourist accommodation and a shopping centre) was released in February 2008. The three-year project (scheduled for completion in 2011) was to be entirely financed by the Export and Import Bank of the People's Republic of China. The GDP of the services sector increased at an average annual rate of 3.0% in 1998–2006; the sector increased by 6.5% in 2005, and by 0.4% in 2006.

In 2006 Grenada reported a preliminary trade deficit of EC $569.5m. and there was a deficit of $417.1m. on the current account of the balance of payments. In 2004 the principal source of imports was the USA, accounting for 42.6% of the total. The USA is also the principal market for exports, taking 23.4% of the total in the same year. The principal export is nutmeg, accounting for 33.5% of total exports in 2004. The principal imports in that year were food and live animals, basic manufactures and machinery and transport equipment. The trade deficit is partly offset by earnings from tourism, capital receipts and remittances from the large numbers of Grenadians working abroad.

In 2006 there was an overall budgetary surplus of EC $98.1m. (equivalent to 6.5% of GDP). Grenada's total external debt was US $404.7m. at the end of 2005, of which US $390.0m. was long-term public debt. In that year the cost of debt-servicing was equivalent to 7.1% of the value of exports of goods and services. In December 2004 the Government, which was unable to meet its interest payment obligations, announced the country's external debt commitments were to be restructured; consequently, the value of total debt-servicing declined by 39.1% in 2005, to EC $92.8m. (equivalent to 25.8% of current revenue, representing a decline of 28.6% over the previous year). The average annual rate of inflation was 2.4% in 2000–06; consumer prices increased by 3.8% in 2006. According to estimates, 10.9% of the labour force were unemployed at the end of 2003, although the rate was presumed to have increased to over 25% in 2005 after 'Hurricane Ivan' destroyed much of the island's economic infrastructure.

Grenada is a member of CARICOM (see p. 196). It is also a member of the Economic Commission for Latin America and the Caribbean (ECLAC, see p. 38), the Organization of American States (OAS, see p. 360), the Organisation of Eastern Caribbean States (OECS, see p. 425) and is a signatory to the Cotonou Agreement (see p. 301), the successor arrangement to the Lomé Conventions between the African, Caribbean and Pacific (ACP) countries and the European Union. Grenada is a member of the Eastern Caribbean Securities Exchange (based in Saint Christopher and Nevis). In September 2005 Grenada became one of 13 Caribbean nations to sign the PetroCaribe accord, under which Grenada would be allowed to purchase petroleum from Venezuela at reduced prices. Grenada received its first shipment— 20,000 barrels of diesel oil—under this accord in October 2007.

From the late 1990s the Government attempted to diversify the economy partly through the expansion of the 'offshore' financial sector. In 2000, following Grenada's inclusion on Organisation for Economic Co-operation and Development's (OECD) tax havens blacklist and the Financial Action Task Force's (FATF) money-laundering blacklist, the Government introduced measures to strengthen regulation of the sector. Following the Government's commitment further to improve transparency in the tax sector, in March 2002 Grenada was removed from the OECD list. The country was also removed from the FATF's list in the following year. By the end of 2004 there was just one 'offshore' bank operating in Grenada; the 'offshore' sector also included 859 international business companies at that time, considerably fewer than at the sector's peak.

Grenada's economy remains fairly dependent upon agriculture, which is vulnerable to adverse weather conditions and infestation by pests. In September 2004 'Hurricane Ivan' destroyed that season's nutmeg, banana and cocoa crops; further damage, mainly to the banana crop (90% of which was estimated to have been destroyed), was sustained from the passage of 'Hurricane Emily' in July 2005. An Agriculture Emergency Resuscitation programme introduced by the Government in the wake of 'Ivan' met with only limited success in restoring agricultural production capacity and supply to domestic markets, the initial advances made being largely negated by 'Emily'. The need for further economic diversification was also emphasized by the loss in 2006 of preferential access to European markets for banana producers of the ACP countries. The most promising sector of the economy was tourism, from which revenue more than doubled between 1990 and 1999. After a contraction as a result of repercussions of the terrorist attacks in the USA in September 2001, the industry began to recover until the arrival of 'Hurricane Ivan'. After the successful reconstruction of most of the country's major hotels, in 2005 Grenada was 'relaunched' as an international tourist destination; the renas-

GRENADA

cent industry was spared the severe damage that 'Hurricane Emily' caused to the agriculture sector in July. According to the Government's 2007 budget address, the sector expanded by 65% in 2006 and it was hoped that the extensive development of tourism-related facilities undertaken in that year—notably including commencement of work on the ambitious EC $1,600m. Port Louis Project—together with a heightened international profile as a host nation of the 2007 Cricket World Cup, would further invigorate future tourism revenues. Plans for a value-added tax were expedited, with implementation anticipated in October 2007 (four months earlier than previously suggested), while a number of other taxes were to be repealed. Although deeply unpopular, the National Reconstruction Levy, introduced in May 2006 as part of the Government's three-year Economic Reform Programme, was expected to generate a further EC $12m. during 2007. Revised figures for 2006 suggested improved annual growth of 7.4%. Grenada's incorporation into an IMF Poverty Reduction and Growth Facility programme in 2006 included an estimated US $15.2m., to be disbursed over three years, and prescribed that stringent fiscal reforms be strictly observed in order that improvements in debt repayment, poverty alleviation and economic growth were sustained over the medium term. Although largely contingent upon adherence to these recommendations, GDP was projected to increase by some 4.0% in 2008, following growth of 3.0% in 2007.

Education

Education is free and compulsory for children between the ages of five and 16 years. Primary education begins at five years of age and lasts for seven years. Secondary education, beginning at the age of 12, lasts for a further five years. In 2004/05 enrolment at primary schools included 83.9% of children in the relevant age-group; there were 57 primary schools in 1995. There were 20 public secondary schools in 2002, with 10,603 pupils registered in 2003; enrolment at all secondary schools included 78.2% of pupils in the relevant age-group in 2004/05. In 2006 there were 2,710 full-time enrolled students at the T. A. Marryshow Community College, reportedly the largest tertiary education centre among OECS member countries. Technical Centres have been established in St Patrick's, St David's and St John's, and the Grenada National College, the Mirabeau Agricultural School and the Teachers' Training College have been incorporated into the Technical and Vocational Institute in St George's. The Extra-Mural Department of the University of the West Indies has a branch in St George's. A School of Medicine has been established at St George's University, where a School of Arts and Sciences was also founded in 1997, while there is a School of Fishing at Victoria. In May 2003 Grenada successfully completed negotiations with the World Bank and the Organisation of Eastern Caribbean States for an EC $11.3m. loan and credit agreement for educational development. A government-co-ordinated adult literacy initiative was launched in November 2006 and various other government training and education schemes were also implemented to address the skilled labour force deficit identified as a major impediment to Grenada's employment and economic development prospects. Total budgeted capital expenditure on education was $11.5m. in 2006 (equivalent to 5.0% of total capital expenditure).

Public Holidays

2008: 1 January (New Year's Day), 7 February (Independence Day), 21 March (Good Friday), 24 March (Easter Monday), 1 May (Labour Day), 12 May (Whit Monday), 22 May (Corpus Christi), 4–5 August (Emancipation Holidays), 11–12 August (Carnival), 25 October (Thanksgiving Day), 25–26 December (Christmas).
2009: 1 January (New Year's Day), 7 February (Independence Day), 10 April (Good Friday), 13 April (Easter Monday), 1 May (Labour Day), 1 June (Whit Monday), 11 June (Corpus Christi), 3–4 August (Emancipation Holidays), 10–11 August (Carnival), 25 October (Thanksgiving Day), 25–26 December (Christmas).

Weights and Measures

The metric system is in use.

Statistical Survey

AREA AND POPULATION

Area: 344.5 sq km (133.0 sq miles).
Population: 94,806 (males 46,637, females 48,169) at census of 12 May 1991 (excluding 537 persons in institutions and 33 persons in the foreign service); 100,895 at census of 25 May 2001 (preliminary). *2006* (mid-year estimate): 106,605 (Source: Eastern Caribbean Central Bank).
Density (mid-2006): 309.4 per sq km.
Principal Town (population at 2001 census, preliminary): St George's (capital) 3,908. *Mid-2007* (UN estimate, incl. suburbs): St George's 32,000 (Source: UN, *World Urbanization Prospects: The 2007 Revision*).
Births and Deaths (registrations, 2001, provisional): Live births 1,899 (birth rate 18.8 per 1,000); Deaths 727 (death rate 7.2 per 1,000); *2007*: Birth rate 18.0 per 1,000; Death rate 8.3 per 1,000 (Source: Pan American Health Organization).
Expectation of Life (years at birth, WHO estimates): 67.8 (males 66.1; females 69.5) in 2005. Source: WHO, *World Health Statistics*.
Employment (employees only, 1998): Agriculture, hunting, forestry and fishing 4,794; Mining and quarrying 58; Manufacturing 2,579; Electricity, gas and water 505; Construction 5,163; Wholesale and retail trade 6,324; Restaurants and hotels 1,974; Transport, storage and communications 2,043; Financing, insurance and real estate 1,312; Public administration, defence and social security 1,879; Community services 3,904; Other services 2,933; Activities not adequately defined 1,321; *Total employed* 34,789 (males 20,733, females 14,056). *Mid-2005* (estimates): Agriculture, etc. 11,000; Total labour force 50,000 (Source: FAO).

HEALTH AND WELFARE

Key Indicators

Total Fertility Rate (children per woman, 2005): 2.3.
Under-5 Mortality Rate (per 1,000 live births, 2005): 21.
Physicians (per 1,000 head, 1997): 0.50.
Hospital Beds (per 1,000 head, 2005): 4.8.
Health Expenditure (2004): US $ per head (PPP): 480.0.
Health Expenditure (2004): % of GDP: 6.9.
Health Expenditure (2004): public (% of total): 72.8.
Access to Water (% of persons, 2004): 95.
Access to Sanitation (% of persons, 2004): 96.
Human Development Index (2005): ranking: 82.
Human Development Index (2005): value: 0.777.

For sources and definitions, see explanatory note on p. vi.

AGRICULTURE, ETC.

Principal Crops ('000 metric tons, 2006, FAO estimates): Sugar cane 7.2; Pigeon peas 0.5; Coconuts 6.0; Bananas 1.0; Plantains 0.8; Oranges 0.9; Grapefruit and pomelos 2.0; Apples 0.6; Plums 0.7; Mangoes 1.9; Avocados 1.5; Cocoa beans 0.7; Nutmeg, mace and cardamons 3.0; *Aggregate Production* ('000 metric tons, may include official, semi-official or estimated data): Roots and tubers 4.1; Vegetables (incl. melons) 2.7; Fruits (excl. melons) 13.7.
Livestock ('000 head, year ending September 2006, FAO estimates): Cattle 4.5; Pigs 2.7; Sheep 13.2; Goats 7.2; Asses 0.7; Chickens 268.
Livestock Products ('000 metric tons, 2006, FAO estimates): Chicken meat 0.7; Cows' milk 0.5; Hen eggs 0.9.
Fishing (metric tons, live weight, 2005): Red hind 200 (FAO estimate); Coney 100 (FAO estimate); Snappers and jobfishes 90 (FAO estimate); Parrotfishes 140 (FAO estimate); Blackfin tuna 306; Yellowfin tuna 492; Atlantic sailfish 147; Swordfish 56; Common dolphinfish 160; *Total catch* (incl. others) 2,050 (FAO estimate).

Source: FAO.

INDUSTRY

Production (1994): Rum 300,000 litres; Beer 2,400,000 litres; Wheat flour 4,000 metric tons (1996); Cigarettes 15m.; Electricity 173.49 million kWh (2006). Source: partly UN, *Industrial Commodity Statistics Yearbook*.

GRENADA

FINANCE

Currency and Exchange Rates: 100 cents = 1 Eastern Caribbean dollar (EC $). *Sterling, US Dollar and Euro Equivalents* (31 December 2007): £1 sterling = EC $5.579; US $1 = EC $2.700; €1 = EC $3.985; EC $100 = £17.92 = US $37.04 = €25.09. *Exchange Rate:* Fixed at US $1 = EC $2.70 since July 1976.

Budget (EC $ million 2006, preliminary): *Revenue:* Tax revenue 360.0 (Taxes on income and profits 56.0, Taxes on property 22.6, Taxes on domestic goods and services 69.0, Taxes on international trade and transactions 212.3); Other current revenue 26.0; Capital revenue 0.1; Total 386.0, excluding grants received (104.7). *Expenditure:* Current expenditure 317.5 (Personal emoluments 154.0, Goods and services 66.1, Interest payments 29.0, Transfers and subsidies 68.4); Capital expenditure and net lending 271.3; Total 588.8. Source: Eastern Caribbean Central Bank. *2007* (EC $ million, budget estimates): Total revenue 441.1; Total expenditure 632.5 (incl. amortization 56.3). *2008* (EC $ million, budget estimates): Total revenue 460.1; Total expenditure 751.7 (incl. amortization 111.5).

International Reserves (US $ million at 31 December 2006): IMF special drawing rights 0.17; Foreign exchange 99.79; Total 99.96. Source: IMF, *International Financial Statistics*.

Money Supply (EC $ million at 31 December 2006): Currency outside banks 104.50; Demand deposits at deposit money banks 250.93; Total money (incl. others) 355.43. Source: IMF, *International Financial Statistics*.

Cost of Living (Consumer Price Index; base: 2000 = 100): 107.4 in 2004; 111.1 in 2005; 115.3 in 2006. Source: IMF, *International Financial Statistics*.

Gross Domestic Product (EC $ million at constant 1990 prices): 835.83 in 2004; 953.21 in 2005; 960.51 in 2006. Source: Eastern Caribbean Central Bank.

Expenditure on the Gross Domestic Product (EC $ million at current prices, 2006): Government final consumption expenditure 243.2; Private final consumption expenditure 1,068.2; Gross capital formation 664.7; *Total domestic expenditure* 1,976.2; Exports of goods and services 442.5; *Less* Imports of goods and services 908.2; Statistical discrepancy 5.2; *GDP in purchasers' values* 1,515.6. Source: Eastern Caribbean Central Bank.

Gross Domestic Product by Economic Activity (EC $ million at current prices, 2006): Agriculture 74.49; Mining and quarrying 9.33; Manufacturing 67.57; Electricity and water 72.15; Construction 170.86; Wholesale and retail trade 105.45; Hotels and restaurants 72.53; Transport and communication 247.21; Financial and business services 150.37; Government services 203.17; Other services 157.50; *Sub-total* 1,330.63; *Less* Financial intermediation services indirectly measured (FISIM) 96.35; *GDP at factor cost* 1,234.28; Taxes on products, less subsidies 281.33; *GDP in market prices* 1,515.61. Source: Eastern Caribbean Central Bank.

Balance of Payments (EC $ million, 2006, preliminary): Goods (net) –569.5; Services (net) 103.7; *Balance of goods and services* –465.7; Other income (net) –78.0; Current transfers (net) 126.6; *Current balance* –417.1; Capital account (net) 176.1; Direct investment 312.8; Portfolio investment 0.3; Other investments –56.8; *Overall balance* 15.2. Source: Eastern Caribbean Central Bank.

EXTERNAL TRADE

Principal Commodities (US $ million, 2004): *Imports c.i.f.:* Food and live animals 49.6; Crude materials (excl. fuel) 7.2; Mineral fuels and lubricants 15.4; Chemicals 15.4; Basic manufactures 58.8; Machinery and transport equipment 64.0; Miscellaneous manufactures 30.7; Total (incl. others) 250.5. *Exports f.o.b.:* Cocoa 2.0; Nutmeg and mace 10.6; Fish 3.0; Machinery and transport equipment 4.3; Paper products 2.1; Wheat flour 2.8; Total (incl. others) 31.6 (Source: UN, *International Trade Statistics Yearbook*). *2005* (EC $ million): Total imports c.i.f. 756.81; Total exports f.o.b. 102.61 (Source: Eastern Caribbean Central Bank). *2006* (EC $ million): Total imports c.i.f. 656.76; Total exports f.o.b. 87.31 (Source: Eastern Caribbean Central Bank).

Principal Trading Partners (US $ million, 2004): *Imports c.i.f.:* Barbados 8.3; Brazil 4.4; Canada 7.9; China, People's Republic 4.2; France 2.8; Germany 3.9; Honduras 3.1; Japan 12.2; Netherlands 3.2; Sweden 0.4; Trinidad and Tobago 47.4; United Kingdom 16.4; USA 106.8; Total (incl. others) 250.5. *Exports f.o.b.:* Antigua and Barbuda 0.6; Argentina 0.6; Barbados 1.5; Belgium 2.4; Canada 0.6; Dominica 0.8; Dominican Republic 0.2; France 1.7; Germany 1.5; Guyana 0.4; Jamaica 0.6; Japan 0.8; Netherlands 5.2; Saint Christopher and Nevis 1.6; Saint Lucia 2.0; Saint Vincent and the Grenadines 0.5; Trinidad and Tobago 0.5; United Kingdom 1.4; USA 7.4; Total (incl. others) 31.6. Source: UN, *International Trade Statistics Yearbook*.

TRANSPORT

Road Traffic ('000 motor vehicles in use, 2001): Passenger cars 15.8; Commercial vehicles 4.2. Source: UN, *Statistical Yearbook*.

Shipping: *Merchant Fleet* (registered at 31 December 2006) 11 vessels (total displacement 2,821 grt) (Source: Lloyd's Register-Fairplay, *World Fleet Statistics*). *International Sea-borne Freight Traffic* (estimates, '000 metric tons, 1995): Goods loaded 21.3; Goods unloaded 193.0. *Ship Arrivals* (1991): 1,254. *Fishing Vessels* (registered, 1987): 635.

Civil Aviation (aircraft arrivals, 1995): 11,310.

TOURISM

Visitor Arrivals: 269,204 (121,074 stop-over visitors, 4,094 excursionists, 8,975 yacht passengers, 135,061 cruise-ship passengers) in 2002; 292,275 (133,724 stop-over visitors, 4,931 excursionists, 6,695 yacht passengers, 146,925 cruise-ship passengers) in 2003; 366,054 (127,904 stop-over visitors, 6,146 excursionists, 5,034 yacht passengers, 226,970 cruise-ship passengers) in 2004 (preliminary). *2005:* 98,548 stop-over visitors, 5,823 excursionists, 4,353 yacht passengers, 275,085 cruise-ship passengers; *2006:* 118,653 stop-over visitors, 4,821 excursionists, 4,733 yacht passengers, 218,684 cruise-ship passengers. (Sources: Grenada Board of Tourism; Eastern Caribbean Central Bank).

Tourism Receipts (EC $ million): 225.4 in 2004; 192.8 in 2005; 252.4 in 2006.

Source: Eastern Caribbean Central Bank.

COMMUNICATIONS MEDIA

Radio Receivers (1997): 57,000 in use*.

Television Receivers (1999): 35,000 in use*.

Telephones (2005): 32,700 main lines in use†.

Facsimile Machines (1996): 270 in use‡.

Mobile Cellular Telephones (2006): 46,200 subscribers†.

Personal Computers (2004): 16,000 in use†.

Internet Users (2004): 19,000†.

Broadband Subscribeers (2006): 5,500†.

Non-daily Newspapers (2004): 4; circulation 14,000 (1996)*.

* Source: UNESCO, *Statistical Yearbook*.
‡ Source: International Telecommunication Union.
† Source: UN, *Statistical Yearbook*.

EDUCATION

Pre-primary (2003/04 unless otherwise indicated): 74 schools (1994); 330 teachers (2004/05); 3,339 pupils.

Primary (2004/05 unless otherwise indicated): 57 schools (1995); 909 teachers; 16,072 pupils.

Secondary (2004/05 unless otherwise indicated): 20 schools (2002); 886 teachers; 13,675 pupils.

Higher (excl. figures for the Grenada Teachers' Training College, 1993): 66 teachers; 651 students.

Source: partly UNESCO Institute for Statistics.

Adult Literacy Rate: 96.0% in 2003. Source: UN Development Programme, *Human Development Report*.

Directory

The Constitution

The 1974 independence Constitution was suspended in March 1979, following the coup, and almost entirely restored between November 1983, after the overthrow of the Revolutionary Military Council, and the elections of December 1984. The main provisions of this Constitution are summarized below:

The Head of State is the British monarch, represented in Grenada by an appointed Governor-General. Legislative power is vested in the bicameral Parliament, comprising a Senate and a House of Representatives. The Senate consists of 13 Senators, seven of whom are appointed on the advice of the Prime Minister, three on the advice of the Leader of the Opposition and three on the advice of the Prime Minister after he has consulted interests which he considers Senators should be selected to represent. The Constitution does not specify the number of members of the House of Representatives, but the country consists of 15 single-member constituencies, for which representatives are elected for up to five years, on the basis of universal adult suffrage.

The Cabinet consists of a Prime Minister, who must be a member of the House of Representatives, and such other ministers as the Governor-General may appoint on the advice of the Prime Minister.

There is a Supreme Court and, in certain cases, a further appeal lies to Her Majesty in Council.

The Government

HEAD OF STATE

Monarch: HM Queen ELIZABETH II (succeeded to the throne 6 February 1952).
Governor-General: Sir DANIEL WILLIAMS (appointed 8 August 1996).

THE CABINET
(March 2008)

Prime Minister and Minister of Finance, National Security, Information, Human Resource Development, Business and Private-Sector Development, Youth Development and Information Communications Technology: Dr KEITH CLAUDIUS MITCHELL.
Deputy Prime Minister and Minister of Agriculture, Lands, Forestry, Fisheries, Public Utilities, Energy and the Marketing and National Importing Board: Sen. GREGORY BOWEN.
Minister of Carriacou and Petit Martinique Affairs, of Foreign Affairs, and Attorney-General: Sen. ELVIN NIMROD.
Minister of Communications, Works and Transport: Sen. BRENDA HOOD.
Minister of Economic Development and Planning: ANTHONY BOATSWAIN.
Minister of Education, Labour and of Legal Affairs: CLARIS CHARLES.
Minister of Health, Social Security, the Environment and Ecclesiastical Relations: ANN DAVID ANTOINE.
Minister of Social Development: YOLANDE BAIN-HORSFORD.
Minister of Sports, Community Development and Co-operatives, with responsibility for Community Development and Co-operatives: ROLAND BHOLA.
Minister of Tourism, Civil Aviation, Culture and the Performing Arts: CLARICE MODESTE-CURWEN.
Minister of State in the Prime Minister's Office with responsibility for National Security and Information: Sen. EINSTEIN LOUISON.
Minister of State in the Prime Minister's Office with responsibility for Youth Development: Sen. EMMALIN PIERRE.

MINISTRIES

Office of the Governor-General: Government House, St George's; tel. 440-6639; fax 440-6688; e-mail patogg@caribsurf.com.
Office of the Prime Minister and Ministry of National Security, Information, Human Resource Development, Youth Development and Information Communications Technology: Ministerial Complex, 6th Floor, Botanical Gardens, St George's; tel. 440-2255; fax 440-4116; e-mail pmoffice@gov.gd; internet www.pmoffice.gov.gd.
Ministry of Agriculture, Lands, Forestry, Fisheries, Public Utilities and Energy: Ministerial Complex, 2nd and 3rd Floors, Botanical Gardens, St George's; tel. 440-2708; fax 440-4191; e-mail agriculture@gov.gd; internet www.agriculture.gov.gd.
Ministry of Carriacou and Petit Martinique Affairs: Beauséjour, Carriacou; tel. 443-6026; fax 443-6040; e-mail minccoupm@spiceisle.com.
Ministry of Communications, Works and Transport: Ministerial Complex, 4th Floor, Botanical Gardens, St George's; tel. 440-2181; fax 440-4122.
Ministry of Economic Development and Planning: Financial Complex, The Carenage, St George's; tel. 440-2731; fax 440-4115.
Ministry of Education and Labour: Ministry of Education Bldg, Ministerial Complex, Botanical Gardens, Tanteen, St George's; tel. 440-2737; fax 440-6650; internet www.grenadaedu.com.
Ministry of Finance: Financial Complex, The Carenage, St George's; tel. 440-2741; fax 440-4115; e-mail finance@gov.gd; internet finance.gov.gd.
Ministry of Foreign Affairs: Ministerial Complex, 4th Floor, Botanical Gardens, St George's; tel. 440-2640; fax 440-4184; e-mail foreignaffairs@gov.gd.
Ministry of Health, Social Security, the Environment and Ecclesiastical Relations: Ministerial Complex, 1st and 2nd Floors, Botanical Gardens, St George's; tel. 440-2649; fax 440-4127; e-mail min-healthgrenada@spiceisle.com.
Ministry of Legal Affairs: Progress House, Carenage, St George's; tel. 440-2962; fax 440-2964; e-mail legal@gov.gd.
Ministry of Social Development: Ministerial Complex, 1st Floor, Botanical Gardens, St George's; tel. 440-2269; fax 440-7990; e-mail mhousing@hotmail.com.
Ministry of Sports, Community Development and Co-operatives: Ministerial Complex, 3rd Floor, Botanical Gardens, St George's; tel. 440-6917; fax 440-6924; e-mail sports@gov.gd.
Ministry of Tourism, Civil Aviation, Culture and the Performing Arts: Ministerial Complex, 4th Floor, Botanical Gardens, St George's; tel. 440-0366; fax 440-0443; e-mail tourism@gov.gd; internet www.grenada.mot.gd.

Legislature

PARLIAMENT

Houses of Parliament: Botanical Gardens, POB 315, St George's; tel. 440-2090; fax 440-4138; e-mail order.order@caribsurf.com.

Senate

President: Sen. KENNY LALSINGH.
There are 13 appointed members.

House of Representatives

Speaker: LAWRENCE JOSEPH.
General Election, 27 November 2003

	Votes	%	Seats
New National Party (NNP)	22,566	47.78	8
National Democratic Congress (NDC)	21,445	45.40	7
Grenada United Labour Party (GULP)	2,243	4.75	—
People's Labour Movement (PLM)	933	2.00	—
Others	52	0.18	—
Total	47,239	100.00	15

Political Organizations

Grenada United Labour Party (GULP): St George's; internet www.gulpstar.org; f. 1950; merged with United Labour Congress in 2001; right-wing; Pres. WILFRED HAYES; Leader GLORIA PAYNE-BANFIELD.

National Democratic Congress (NDC): NDC Headquarters, Lucas St, St George's; tel. 440-3769; e-mail ndcgrenada@ndcgrenada.org; internet www.ndcgrenada.org; f. 1987 by fmr mems of the NNP and merger of Democratic Labour Congress and Grenada Democratic Labour Party; centrist; Leader TILLMAN THOMAS; Dep. Leader GEORGE PRIME.

GRENADA
Directory

New National Party (NNP): Upper Lucas St, St George's; tel. 440-1875; fax 440-1876; e-mail nnpadmin@spiceisle.com; internet nnpnews.com; f. 1984 following merger of Grenada Democratic Movement, Grenada National Party and National Democratic Party; centrist; Chair. ELVIN NIMROD; Leader Dr KEITH MITCHELL; Dep. Leader GREGORY BOWEN.

People's Labour Movement (PLM): St George's; f. 1995 by fmr mems of the NDC; fmrly known as the Democratic Labour Party; Leader Dr FRANCIS ALEXIS; Pres. Dr TERRANCE MARRYSHOW.

Diplomatic Representation

EMBASSIES AND HIGH COMMISSION IN GRENADA

China, People's Republic: Azar Villa, Calliste St, St George's; tel. 414-1228; fax 439-6231; internet gd.china-embassy.org; Ambassador QIAN HONGSHAN.

Cuba: L'Anse aux Epines, St George's; tel. 444-1884; fax 444-1877; e-mail embacubagranada@caribsurf.com; Ambassador MARGARITA DELGADO.

USA: POB 54, St George's; tel. 444-1173; fax 444-4820; e-mail usemb_gd@caribsurf.com; Ambassador MARY OURISMAN (resident in Barbados).

Venezuela: Upper Lucas St, POB 201, St George's; tel. 440-1721; fax 440-6657; e-mail embavengda@caribsurf.com; Ambassador EDNA FIGUERA CEDEÑO.

Judicial System

Justice is administered by the Eastern Caribbean Supreme Court, formerly styled the West Indies Associated States Supreme Court in Grenada, composed of a High Court of Justice and a Court of Appeal. The Itinerant Court of Appeal consists of three judges and sits three times a year; it hears appeals from the High Court and the Magistrates' Court. Two of the 16 puisne judges of the High Court are resident in Grenada. The Magistrates' Court administers summary jurisdiction.

Attorney-General: Sen. ELVIN NIMROD.

Puisne Judges: KENNETH ANDREW CHARLES BENJAMIN, CLAIRE HENRY.

Registrar of the Supreme Court: ROBERT BRANCH.

Acting Chief Justice of the Court of Appeal: HUGH ANTHONY RAWLINS (resident in Saint Lucia).

Office of the Attorney-General: Church St, St George's; tel. 440-2050; fax 440-6630; e-mail legalaffairs@caribsurf.com.

Religion

CHRISTIANITY

The Roman Catholic Church

Grenada comprises the single diocese of Saint George's, suffragan to the archdiocese of Castries (Saint Lucia). The Bishop participates in the Antilles Episcopal Conference (based in Port of Spain, Trinidad and Tobago). At 31 December 2005 there were an estimated 45,573 adherents in the diocese.

Bishop of St George's in Grenada: Rev. VINCENT DARIUS, Bishop's House, Morne Jaloux, POB 375, St George's; tel. 443-5299; fax 443-5758; e-mail bishopgrenada@caribsurf.com; internet www.stgdiocese.org.

The Anglican Communion

Anglicans in Grenada are adherents of the Church in the Province of the West Indies, and represented 14% of the population at the time of the 1991 census. The country forms part of the diocese of the Windward Islands (the Bishop, the Rt Rev. CALVERT LEOPOLD FRIDAY, resides in Kingstown, Saint Vincent).

Other Christian Churches

The Presbyterian, Methodist, Plymouth Brethren, Baptist, Salvation Army, Jehovah's Witness, Pentecostal (7.2% of the population in 1991) and Seventh-day Adventist (8.5%) faiths are also represented.

The Press

NEWSPAPERS

Barnacle: Frequente Industrial Park, St George's; tel. 440-5151; internet www.grenadabarnacle.com; bi-weekly; Editor IAN GEORGE.

The Grenada Informer: Market Hill, POB 622, St George's; tel. 440-1530; fax 440-4119; e-mail grenadainformer@yahoo.com; f. 1985; weekly; Editor CARLA-RAE A. BRIGGS; circ. 6,000.

Grenada Today: St John's St, POB 142, St George's; tel. 440-4401; internet www.belgrafix.com/gtoday98.htm; weekly; Editor GEORGE WORME.

The Grenadian Voice: Frequente Industrial Park, Bldg 1B, Maurice Bishop Highway, POB 633, St George's; tel. 440-1498; fax 440-4117; e-mail gvoice@caribsurf.com; weekly; Man. Editor LESLIE PIERRE; circ. 3,000.

Government Gazette: St George's; weekly; official.

PRESS ASSOCIATION

Press Association of Grenada: St George's; f. 1986; Pres. LESLIE PIERRE.

Publisher

Anansi Publications: Woodlands, St George's; tel. 440-0800; e-mail aclouden@spiceisle.com; f. 1986; Man. Dir ALVIN CLOUDEN.

Broadcasting and Communications

TELECOMMUNICATIONS

Regulatory Authorities

Eastern Caribbean Telecommunications Authority: Castries, Saint Lucia; f. 2000 to regulate telecommunications in Grenada, Dominica, Saint Christopher and Nevis, Saint Lucia and Saint Vincent and the Grenadines.

National Telecommunications Regulatory Commission: Suite 8, Grand Anse Shopping Centre, POB 854, St George's; tel. 435-6872; fax 435-2132; e-mail gntrc@caribsurf.com; internet www.ectel.int/grd; Chair. LINUS SPENCER THOMAS; Dir of Telecommunications ROBERT OLIVER FINLAY.

Major Service Providers

Cable & Wireless Grenada Ltd: POB 119, The Carenage, St George's; tel. 440-1000; fax 440-4134; e-mail cwcares@candw.gd; internet www.candw.gd; f. 1989; until 1998 known as Grenada Telecommunications Ltd (Grentel); 30% govt-owned; Chief Exec. IAN BLANCHARD.

Digicel Grenada Ltd: Point Salines, POB 1690, St George's; e-mail GREcustcare@digicelgroup.com; internet www.digicelgrenada.com; tel. 439-4463; fax 439-4464; f. 2003; began operating cellular telephone services in Oct. 2003; owned by an Irish consortium; Chair. DENIS O'BRIEN; Eastern Caribbean CEO KEVIN WHITE.

Grenada Postal Corporation (GPC): Burns Point, St George's; tel. 440-2526; fax 440-4271; e-mail grenadapost@grenadapost.net; internet www.spiceisle.com/gpc; Chair. MICHAEL PIERRE; Dir of Post LEO ROBERTS.

BROADCASTING

Grenada Broadcasting Network (GBN): Observatory Rd, POB 535, St George's; tel. 444-5521; fax 440-4180; e-mail gbn@spiceisle.com; internet www.klassicgrenada.com; f. 1972; 60% owned by One Caribbean Media Ltd, 40% govt-owned; Chair. CRAIG REYNALD; Gen. Man. RICHARD PURCELL.

Radio

Grenada Broadcasting Network (Radio): see Broadcasting.

Klassic AM: Observatory Rd, POB 535, St George's; tel. 444-5521; fax 440-4180; e-mail gbn@caribsurf.com; internet www.klassicgrenada.com.

HOTT FM: Observatory Rd, POB 535, St George's; tel. 444-5521; fax 440-4180; e-mail gbn@caribsurf.com; internet www.klassicgrenada.com; f. 1999; contemporary music.

The Harbour Light of the Windwards: Carriacou; tel. 443-7628; fax 443-6180; e-mail harbourlight@spiceisle.com; internet www.harbourlightradio.org; f. 1991; owned by Aviation Radio Missionary Services; Christian radio station; Station Man. RANDY CORNELIUS; Chief Engineer JOHN MCPHERSON.

Spice Capital Radio FM 90: Springs, St George's; tel. 440-0162.

GRENADA

Directory

Television

Television programmes from Trinidad and Tobago and Barbados can be received on the island.

Grenada Broadcasting Network (Television): see Broadcasting; two channels.

Finance

(cap. = capital; res = reserves; dep. = deposits; brs = branches; amounts in Eastern Caribbean dollars)

The Eastern Caribbean Central Bank, based in Saint Christopher, is the central issuing and monetary authority for Grenada.

Eastern Caribbean Central Bank—Grenada Office: Monckton St, St George's; tel. 440-3016; fax 440-6721; e-mail eccbgnd@caribsurf.com; Country Dir LINDA FELIX-BERKLEY.

BANKING

Regulatory Authority

Grenada International Financial Services Authority: Bldg 5, Financial Complex, The Carenage, POB 3973, St George's; tel. 440-8717; fax 440-4780; e-mail gifsa@caribsurf.com; f. 1999; revenue 4.2m. (2002); Chair. TIMOTHY ANTOINE; Exec. Dir STEVEN HORSFORD (acting).

Commercial Banks

FirstCaribbean International Bank (Barbados) Ltd: Church St, POB 37, St George's; tel. 440-3232; fax 440-4103; internet www.firstcaribbeanbank.com; f. 2002; 83.0% owned by Canadian Imperial Bank of Commerce (CIBC), after Barclays Bank PLC (United Kingdom) sold its 43.7% stake to CIBC in 2006; CEO CHARLES PINK; Exec. Dir SHARON BROWN; 4 brs.

Grenada Co-operative Bank Ltd: 8 Church St, POB 135, St George's; tel. 440-2111; fax 440-6600; e-mail info@grenadaco-opbank.com; internet www.grenadaco-opbank.com; f. 1932; Man. Dir and Sec. G. V. STEELE; brs in St Andrew's, St George's, St Patrick's and Hillsborough.

Grenada Development Bank: Melville St, POB 2300, St George's; tel. 440-2382; fax 440-6610; e-mail gdbbank@spiceisle.com; f. 1976 following merger; Chair. Dr BERNARD FRANCOIS; Man. JOHN M. DUMONT.

National Commercial Bank of Grenada Ltd: NCB House, POB 857, Grand Anse, St George's; tel. 444-2265; fax 444-5501; e-mail ncbgnd@caribsurf.com; internet www.ncbgrenada.com; f. 1979; 51% owned by Republic Bank Ltd, Port of Spain, Trinidad and Tobago; cap. 15.0m., res 31.5m., dep. 522.3m. (Sept. 2004); Chair. RONALD HARFORD; Man. Dir DANIEL ROBERTS; 9 brs.

RBTT Bank Grenada Ltd: Cnr of Cross and Halifax Sts, POB 4, St George's; tel. 440-3521; fax 440-4153; e-mail RBTTLTD@caribsurf.com; internet www.rbtt.com; f. 1983 as Grenada Bank of Commerce; name changed as above 2002; 10% govt-owned; national insurance scheme 15%; public 13%; RBTT Bank Caribbean Ltd, Castries 62%; cap. 11.1m., res 15.9m., dep. 425.9m. (31 Dec. 2004); Chair. PETER JULY; Man. Dir AMRIT SINANAN.

STOCK EXCHANGE

Eastern Caribbean Securities Exchange: based in Basseterre, Saint Christopher and Nevis; tel. (869) 466-7192; fax (869) 465-3798; e-mail info@ECSEonline.com; internet www.ecseonline.com; f. 2001; regional securities market designed to facilitate the buying and selling of financial products for the eight member territories—Anguilla, Antigua and Barbuda, Dominica, Grenada, Montserrat, Saint Christopher and Nevis, Saint Lucia and Saint Vincent and the Grenadines; Chair. K. DWIGHT VENNER; Man. Dir MICHAEL MORTON.

INSURANCE

Several foreign insurance companies operate in Grenada and the other islands of the group. Principal locally owned companies include the following:

Gittens Insurance Brokerage Co Ltd: Benoit Bldg, Grand Anse, POB 1696, St George's; tel. 439-4408; fax 439-4456; CEO PHILLIP A. GITTENS.

Grenada Motor and General Insurance Co Ltd: Scott St, St George's; tel. 440-3379.

Grenadian General Insurance Co Ltd: Cnr of Young and Scott Sts, POB 47, St George's; tel. 440-2434; fax 440-9296; e-mail clingren@caribsurf.com.

Trade and Industry

CHAMBERS OF COMMERCE

Grenada Chamber of Industry and Commerce, Inc (GCIC): POB 129, Frequente, St George's; tel. 440-2937; fax 440-6627; e-mail info@grenadachamber.org; internet www.grenadachamber.org; f. 1921; inc. 1947; 170 mems; Pres. YVONNE GELLINEAU-SIMON; Exec. Dir CHRISTOPHER DERIGGS.

Grenada Manufacturing Council: POB 129, St George's; tel. 440-2937; fax 440-6627; f. 1991 to replace Grenada Manufacturers' Asscn; Chair. CHRISTOPHER DEALLIE.

INDUSTRIAL AND TRADE ASSOCIATIONS

Grenada Cocoa Association (GCA): Lagoon Rd, POB 3649, St George's; tel. 440-2234; fax 440-1470; e-mail gca@spiceisle.com; f. 1987 following merger; changed from co-operative to shareholding structure in 1996; Chair. REGINALD BUCKMIRE; Man. ANDREW HASTICK.

Grenada Co-operative Nutmeg Association (GCNA): Lagoon Rd, POB 160, St George's; tel. 440-2117; fax 440-6602; e-mail gcna.nutmeg@caribsurf.com; f. 1947; processes and markets all the nutmeg and mace grown on the island; includes the production of nutmeg oil; Chair. DENIS FELIX; Gen. Man. TERRENCE MOORE.

Grenada Industrial Development Corporation (GIDC): Frequente Industrial Park, Frequente, St George's; tel. 444-1033-40; fax 444-4828; e-mail gidc@caribsurf.com; internet www.grenadaworld.com; f. 1985; Chair. R. ANTHONY JOSEPH; Man. SONIA RODEN.

Marketing and National Importing Board (MNIB): Young St, St George's retail outlet; tel. 440-1791; fax 440-4152; e-mail mnib@spiceisle.com; internet www.mnibgrenada.com; f. 1974; govt-owned; imports basic food items, incl. sugar, rice and milk; Chair. CHESTER PALMER; Gen. Man. FITZROY JAMES.

EMPLOYERS' ORGANIZATION

Grenada Employers' Federation: Mt Gay, POB 129, St George's; tel. 440-1832; fax 440-6627; e-mail gef@caribsurf.com; Pres. JOHN DUMONT; Exec. Dir CECIL EDWARDS; 60 mems.

There are several marketing and trading co-operatives, mainly in the agricultural sector.

UTILITIES

Public Utilities Commission: St George's.

Electricity

Grenada Electricity Services Ltd (Grenlec): Halifax St, POB 381, St George's; tel. 440-9425; fax 440-4106; e-mail customersupport@grenlec.com; internet www.grenlec.com; generation and distribution; 90% privately owned, 10% govt-owned; Chair. G. ROBERT BLANCHARD, Jr; Man. Dir and CEO VERNON LAWRENCE.

Water

National Water and Sewerage Authority (NAWASA): The Carenage, POB 392, St George's; tel. 440-2155; fax 440-4107; e-mail nawasa@caribsurf.com; internet www.spiceisle.com/nawasa; f. 1969; Chair. MICHAEL PIERRE; Man. ALLEN MCQUIRE.

TRADE UNIONS

Grenada Trade Union Council (GTUC): Green St, POB 411, St George's; tel. and fax 440-3733; e-mail gtuc@caribsurf.com; internet www.grenadatuc.org; Pres. MADONNA HARFORD (acting); Gen. Sec. RAY ROBERTS.

Bank and General Workers' Union (BGWU): Bain's Alley, POB 329, St George's; tel. and fax 440-3563; e-mail bgwu@caribsurf.com; Pres. DEREK ALLARD; Gen. Sec. JUSTIN CAMPBELL.

Commercial and Industrial Workers' Union: Bain's Alley, Grand Anse, POB 1791, St George's; tel. and fax 440-3423; e-mail cominwu@caribsurf.com; Pres. ELLIOT BISHOP; Gen. Sec. BARBARA FRASER; 492 mems.

Grenada Manual, Maritime and Intellectual Workers' Union (GMMIWU): c/o Birchgrove, POB 1927, St Andrew's; tel. and fax 442-7724; Pres. BERT LATOUCHE; Gen. Sec. OSCAR WILLIAMS.

Grenada Union of Teachers (GUT): Marine Villa, POB 452, St George's; tel. 440-2992; fax 440-9019; f. 1913; Pres. MARVIN ANDAL; Gen. Sec. ELIZABETH FORSYTH; 1,300 mems.

Media Workers' Association of Grenada (MWAG): St George's; f. 1999; Gen. Sec. RAE ROBERTS.

Public Workers' Union (PWU): Tanteen, POB 420, St George's; tel. 440-2203; fax 440-6615; e-mail pwu-cpsa@caribsurf.com; f. 1931; Pres. MADONNA HARFORD; Exec. Sec. ALVIN ST JOHN.

GRENADA

Seamen and Waterfront Workers' Union: Ottway House, POB 154, St George's; tel. 440-2573; fax 440-7199; e-mail swwu@caribsurf.com; f. 1952; Pres. ALBERT JULIEN; Gen. Sec. LYLE SAMUEL; 350 mems.

Grenada Technical and Allied Workers' Union (GTAWU): Green St, POB 405, St George's; tel. 440-2231; fax 440-5878; e-mail gtawu@spiceisle.com; f. 1958; Pres.-Gen. Sen. CHESTER HUMPHREY; Gen. Sec. BERT PATERSON.

Transport

RAILWAYS

There are no railways in Grenada.

ROADS

In 1999 there were approximately 1,127 km (700 miles) of roads, of which 61.3% were paved. Public transport is provided by small private operators, with a system covering the entire country.

SHIPPING

The main port is St George's, with accommodation for two ocean-going vessels of up to 500 ft. A number of shipping lines call at St George's. Grenville, on Grenada, and Hillsborough, on Carriacou, are used mostly by small craft. The first phase of a project to expand the port at St George's and enable the harbour to accommodate modern super-sized cruise ships was completed in July 2003, while the Melville Street Cruise Terminal phase became operational in November 2004. Work commenced in November 2006 upon an ambitious EC $1,600m. development at Port Louis, to include a 350-slipway marina with yachting facilities.

Grenada Ports Authority: POB 494, The Carenage, St George's; tel. 440-7678; fax 440-3418; e-mail grenport@spiceisle.com; internet www.grenadaports.com; f. 1981; state-owned; Chair. Dr SPENCER THOMAS; Gen. Man. AMBROSE PHILLIP.

CIVIL AVIATION

The Point Salines International Airport, 10 km (6 miles) from St George's, was opened in October 1984, and has scheduled flights to most East Caribbean destinations, including Venezuela, and to the United Kingdom and North America. There is an airfield at Pearls, 30 km (18 miles) from St George's, and Lauriston Airport, on the island of Carriacou, offers regular scheduled services to Grenada, Saint Vincent and Palm Island (Grenadines of Saint Vincent).

Grenada is a shareholder in the regional airline, LIAT (Antigua and Barbuda), which acquired another regional carrier, Caribbean Star, in October 2007.

Grenada Airports Authority: Point Salines Int. Airport, POB 385, St George's; tel. 444-4101; fax 444-4838; e-mail gaa@caribsurf.com; f. 1985; Man. Dir PHILIPPE BARIL; CEO RONALD O. CHARLES; Gen. Man. DONALD MCPHAIL.

Airlines of Carriacou: Point Salines Int. Airport, POB 805, St Georges; tel. 444-1475; fax 444-2898; e-mail info@travelgrenada.com; internet www.travelgrenada.com/aircarriacou.htm; f. 1992; acquired by St Vincent and Grenada Air in 1999; national airline, operates in asscn with LIAT; Man. Dir ARTHUR W. BAIN.

Tourism

Grenada has the attractions of both white sandy beaches and a scenic, mountainous interior with an extensive rainforest. There are also sites of historical interest, and the capital, St George's, is a noted beauty spot. In 2006 there were 118,653 stop-over arrivals and 218,684 cruise-ship passengers; in that year tourism earned some EC $252.4m.

Grenada Board of Tourism: Burns Point, POB 293, St George's; tel. 440-2279; fax 440-6637; e-mail gbt@spiceisle.com; internet www.grenadagrenadines.com; f. 1991; Chair. NIKOYAN ROBERTS; Dir JOCELYN SYLVESTER-GAIRY.

Grenada Hotel and Tourism Association Ltd: POB 440, St George's; tel. 444-1353; fax 444-4847; e-mail grenhota@spiceisle.com; internet www.grenadahotelsinfo.com; f. 1961; Pres. IAN DA BREO; Exec. Dir PANCY CHANDLER CROSS.

GUATEMALA

Introductory Survey

Location, Climate, Language, Religion, Flag, Capital

The Republic of Guatemala lies in the Central American isthmus, bounded to the north and west by Mexico, with Honduras and Belize to the east and El Salvador to the south. It has a long coastline on the Pacific Ocean and a narrow outlet to the Caribbean Sea. The climate is tropical in the lowlands, with an average temperature of 28°C (83°F), and more temperate in the central highland area, with an average temperature of 20°C (68°F). The official language is Spanish, but more than 20 indigenous languages are also spoken. Almost all of the inhabitants profess Christianity: the majority are Roman Catholics, while an estimated 30% are Protestants. A large proportion of the population also follows traditional Mayan beliefs. The national flag (proportions 5 by 8) has three equal vertical stripes, of blue, white and blue, with the national coat of arms (depicting a quetzal, the 'bird of freedom', and a scroll, superimposed on crossed rifles and sabres, encircled by a wreath) in the centre of the white stripe. The capital is Guatemala City.

Recent History

Under Spanish colonial rule, Guatemala was part of the Viceroyalty of New Spain. Independence was obtained from Spain in 1821, from Mexico in 1824 and from the Federation of Central American States in 1838. Subsequent attempts to revive the Federation failed and, under a series of dictators, there was relative stability, tempered by periods of disruption. A programme of social reform was begun by Juan José Arévalo (President in 1944–50) and his successor, Col Jacobo Arbenz Guzmán, whose policy of land reform evoked strong opposition from landowners. In 1954 President Arbenz was overthrown in a coup led by Col Carlos Castillo Armas, who invaded the country with US assistance. Castillo became President but was assassinated in July 1957. The next elected President, Gen. Miguel Ydígoras Fuentes, took office in March 1958 and ruled until he was deposed in March 1963 by a military coup, led by Col Enrique Peralta Azurdia. He assumed full powers as Chief of Government, suspended the Constitution and dissolved the legislature. A Constituent Assembly, elected in 1964, introduced a new Constitution in 1965. Dr Julio César Méndez Montenegro was elected President in 1966, and in 1970 the candidate of the Movimiento de Liberación Nacional (MLN), Col (later Gen.) Carlos Araña Osorio, was elected President. Despite charges of fraud in the elections of March 1974, Gen. Kjell Laugerud García of the MLN took office as President in July.

President Laugerud sought to discourage extreme right-wing violence and claimed some success, although it was estimated that 50,000–60,000 people were killed in political violence between 1970 and 1979. In March 1978 Gen. Fernando Romeo Lucas García was elected President. The guerrilla movement increased in strength in 1980–81, while the Government was accused of the murder and torture of civilians and, particularly, persecution of the country's indigenous Indian inhabitants, who comprise 60% of the population.

In the presidential election of March 1982, from which the left-wing parties were absent, the Government's candidate, Gen. Angel Aníbal Guevara, was declared the winner; however, the election was denounced as fraudulent by the other presidential candidates. Guevara was prevented from taking office in July by a coup on 23 March, in which a group of young right-wing military officers installed Gen. José Efraín Ríos Montt as leader of a three-man junta. The Congreso Nacional (National Congress) was closed, and the Constitution and political parties suspended. In June Gen. Ríos Montt dissolved the junta and assumed the presidency. He attempted to fight corruption, reorganized the judicial system and disbanded the secret police. The number of violent deaths diminished. However, after initially gaining the support of the national university, the Roman Catholic Church and the labour unions and hoping to enter into dialogue with the guerrillas, who refused to respond to an amnesty declaration in June, Ríos Montt declared a state of siege and imposed censorship of the press. In addition, the war against the guerrillas intensified, and a civil defence force of Indians was established. The efficiency and ruthlessness of the army increased. Whole villages were burnt, and many inhabitants killed, in order to deter the Indians from supporting the guerrillas. Ríos Montt's increasingly corporatist policies alienated all groups, and his fragile hold on power was threatened in 1982 by several attempted coups, which he managed to forestall.

The US Administration was eager to renew sales of armaments and the provision of economic and military aid to Guatemala, which had been suspended in 1977 as a result of serious violations of human rights. In January 1983 the US Government, satisfied that there had been a significant decrease in such violations during Ríos Montt's presidency, announced the resumption of arms sales to Guatemala. However, independent reports claimed that the situation had deteriorated, and revealed that 2,600 people had been killed during the first six months of Ríos Montt's rule. In March the army was implicated in the massacre of 300 Indian peasants at Nahulá, and there was a resurgence in the activity of both left- and right-wing 'death squads'. The President declared a 30-day amnesty for guerrillas and political exiles, and lifted the state of siege. Furthermore, he announced the creation of an electoral tribunal to oversee a proposed transfer from military rule to civilian government. The Government's 'guns and beans' policy provided food and medicine in exchange for recruitment to the Patrullas de Autodefensa Civil (PAC), a pro-Government peasant militia. There then followed the development of 'model villages', as well as an ambitious rural development scheme.

By mid-1983 opposition to the President was widespread. On 8 August Gen. Oscar Humberto Mejía Victores, the Minister of Defence, led a successful coup against President Ríos Montt. The new President ended press censorship. An amnesty for guerrillas was announced and subsequently extended. Urban and rural terrorism continued to escalate, however, and in November the Government was accused of directing a campaign of kidnappings against the Roman Catholic Church. Following the murder in northern Guatemala of six US aid workers, the USA suspended US $50m. in aid to Guatemala in 1984. Israel continued to supply weapons to Guatemala, and Israeli military advisers were reported to be active in the country. In accordance with the President's assurance of electoral reform, elections for a Constituent Assembly were held in July, at which the centre groups, including the newly formed Unión del Centro Nacional (UCN), obtained the greatest number of votes. Under the system of proportional representation, however, the right-wing coalition of the MLN and the Central Auténtica Nacionalista (CAN) together obtained a majority of seats in the Assembly.

Guatemala's new Constitution was promulgated in May 1985. Eight candidates participated in the presidential election in November, but the main contest was between Jorge Carpio Nicolle, the candidate of the UCN, and Mario Vinicio Cerezo Arévalo, the candidate of the Partido Democracia Cristiana Guatemalteca (PDCG). As neither of the leading candidates obtained the requisite majority, a second round of voting was held in December, when Cerezo secured 68% of the votes cast. The PDCG won the majority of seats in the concurrently held election to the new Congreso Nacional, and the party also won the largest proportion of mayoralties. The US Administration increased its allocation of economic aid and resumed military aid to Guatemala, in support of the new civilian Government.

Immediately prior to the transfer of power in January 1986, the outgoing military Government decreed a general amnesty to encompass those suspected of involvement in abuses of human rights since March 1982. In the following month, however, in an attempt to curb the continuing violence and to improve the country's poor record for the observance of human rights, the notorious Department of Technical Investigations was dissolved and replaced by a new criminal investigations unit. None the less, violence continued unabated. Cerezo claimed that not all murders were politically motivated, while his relations with the armed forces remained precarious. In April 1987 the creation of a government commission to investigate 'disappearances' was announced. Nevertheless, by mid-1988 there were frequent reports of torture and killings by right-wing 'death squads' as discontent with the Government's liberal policies increased. In

September 1989 the Consejo Nacional de Desplazados de Guatemala was created to represent the 1m. refugees who had fled their homes since 1980. According to the UN Commission for Human Rights, almost 3,000 complaints of human rights abuses were lodged in 1989.

In August 1987 a peace plan for the region was signed in Guatemala City by the Presidents of Costa Rica, El Salvador, Guatemala, Honduras and Nicaragua. Subsequently, a Commission of National Reconciliation (CNR) was formed in compliance with the terms of the accord. In October representatives of the Guatemalan Government and the main guerrilla grouping, the Unidad Revolucionaria Nacional Guatemalteca (URNG), met in Spain, but the peace negotiations ended without agreement. Right-wing pressure on the Government, and an attempted coup in May 1988, forced Cerezo to postpone further negotiations with the URNG. After another coup plot was discovered in July, Cerezo rejected the URNG's proposal for a truce.

During 1989 guerrilla activity by groups from both the right and the left intensified. Many political figures and labour leaders fled the country after receiving death threats from paramilitary groups. Meanwhile, Cerezo refused to negotiate with the URNG for as long as its members remained armed. In September the URNG made further proposals for negotiations, following the signing of the Tela Agreement (the Central American peace plan accord), but these were rejected. A major counter-insurgency operation was launched by the Government in December. In the same month, Cerezo accused the ruling party in El Salvador of supplying weapons to the right-wing death squads of Guatemala.

Despite Cerezo's promise to restrict the unlawful activities of the armed forces and right-wing death squads, the number of politically motivated assassinations and 'disappearances' escalated in 1990. In March the URNG and the CNR began discussions in Norway with a view to resolving the problem of reincorporating the armed movements into the country's political process. Further talks were held in Spain in June, as a result of which, the URNG pledged not to disrupt the upcoming presidential and legislative elections, and agreed to participate in a constituent assembly to reform the Constitution.

In the presidential election of November 1990 none of the presidential nominees obtained an absolute majority in the first round, leading to a second ballot on 6 January 1991 between the two leading candidates, which was won by Jorge Serrano Elías of the Movimiento de Acción Solidaria (MAS). The MAS failed to secure a majority in the legislative election, however, and in an effort to offset the imbalance in the Congreso, Serrano invited members of the Plan por el Adelantamiento Nacional (PAN) and the Partido Socialista Democrático (PSD) to participate in the formation of a coalition Government.

In April 1991 a fresh round of direct talks between the URNG and the Government began in Mexico City. However, in an attempt to destabilize the Government's efforts at national reconciliation, members of the state security forces, believed to be acting independently of their superiors, launched a campaign of violence, directing death threats against leaders of trade unions and human rights organizations, and murdering a PSD politician. These actions indicated a clear division within the military between those favouring a negotiated settlement and those regarding the talks merely as a political platform for the rebels. In late 1991 the ombudsman, Ramiro de León Carpio, secured the resignation of the Director of the National Police, Col Mario Enrique Paíz Bolanos, who was alleged to be responsible for the use of torture. Further peace talks at the end of the year failed to produce any agreement.

Negotiations between the Government and the URNG, which took place in Mexico City in August 1992, led to concessions by the Government, which agreed to curb the expansion of the PAC. These self-defence patrols played a major role in the army's counter-insurgency campaign and were widely accused of human rights violations. The URNG, which maintained that *campesinos* (peasants) were forcibly enlisted into the PAC, included in its conditions for a peace agreement the immediate dissolution of the patrols. In November the Government accepted renewed proposals by the URNG for the establishment of a commission on past human rights violations, but only on the condition that the rebels sign a definitive peace accord. In January 1993 Serrano announced his commitment to the negotiation and signing of a peace agreement with the URNG within 90 days. In response, the URNG called for a 50% reduction in the size of the armed forces, and repeated demands for the immediate dissolution of the PAC and the dismissal of military officials implicated in human rights violations. The Government rejected these proposals. Talks stalled in March, owing principally to government demands that the URNG disarm as a precondition to the implementation of procedures for the international verification of human rights in Guatemala, and were suspended in May, owing to the prevailing constitutional crisis (see below).

The URNG announced a unilateral cease-fire as a gesture of goodwill to the incoming President Ramiro de León Carpio in June 1993 (see below). In August, in a concession to the URNG, de León announced the reform of the Estado Mayor Presidencial, a military body widely accused of human rights offences. However, in the following month the army announced that it would be resuming military operations against the rebels, which had been suspended in June. In October the Government presented a revised peace plan to the UN, providing for the creation of a Permanent Forum for Peace and renewed cease-fire negotiations with a view to an eventual amnesty for the URNG; the plan was, however, rejected by the rebels. Preliminary talks were finally resumed in Mexico in January 1994.

Unrest at economic austerity measures escalated as public confidence in the Government declined in May 1993. With the MAS no longer able to effect a constructive alliance in the Congreso and the country's stability in jeopardy, on 25 May Serrano, with the support of the military, suspended parts of the Constitution and dissolved the Congreso and the Supreme Court. A ban was imposed on the media and Serrano announced that he would rule by decree pending the drafting of a new constitution by a constituent assembly, to be elected within 60 days. The constitutional coup provoked almost unanimous international condemnation, with the USA immediately suspending in excess of US $30m. in aid. Such pressure, in addition to overwhelming domestic opposition, led the military to reappraise its position and, opting to effect a return to constitutional rule, it forced the resignation of Serrano, who relinquished his post on 1 June and subsequently fled to El Salvador. (He was later granted political asylum in Panama.) The Minister of National Defence, Gen. José Domingo García Samayoa, assumed control of the country pending the election of a new president. The entire Cabinet, excluding García and the Minister of the Interior, Francisco Perdomo Sandoval, resigned two days later. On 5 June the Congreso reconvened following a constitutional court order, to conduct a presidential ballot. The Instancia Nacional de Consenso (INC), a broad coalition of political parties, business leaders and trade unions which had been instrumental in removing Serrano from office, proposed three candidates, of whom Ramiro de León Carpio, the former human rights ombudsman, was elected President in an uncontested second round of voting. The USA subsequently restored its aid programme to Guatemala.

In August 1993, as an initial measure in a campaign to eradicate corruption from state institutions and restore dwindling public confidence in his Government, de León requested the voluntary resignation of the Congreso and the Supreme Court. The request caused a serious division in the legislature, which separated into two main factions, the Gran Grupo Parlamentario (GGP), which included some 70 members of the MAS, UCN, PAN and the Frente Republicano Guatemalteco (FRG) and supported the dismissal of 16 deputies identified by the INC as corrupt, and a group of 38 deputies, including members of the PDCG and independents, who supported the voluntary resignation of all 116 deputies. In September, following the suspension of a congressional session by the President of the Congreso, Fernando Lobo Dubón (a member of the PDCG), the GGP defied the decision and elected a new congressional President. Although Lobo was temporarily reinstated by the Constitutional Court, the GGP threatened to boycott any further sessions convened by him. In order to resolve the impasse, de León requested the Supreme Electoral Tribunal to put the issue to a referendum. However, in November the Constitutional Court upheld a Supreme Court injunction of the previous month, suspending the referendum. Later in the same month a compromise was reached between the Government and the legislature, involving a series of constitutional reforms that were summarily approved by the Congreso and subsequently by a referendum. Fewer than 20% of the electorate participated in the voting, reflecting popular concern that more extensive reforms were necessary. The reforms took effect in April, and fresh legislative elections were to be held in August. The new Congreso, which was to serve until 14 January 1996, was to appoint the members of a new, enlarged Supreme Court. Other reforms included a reduction in the terms of office of the President, legislature and municipal authorities (from five to four years), and of the Supreme Court justices (from six to five years), and a reduction in the number of seats in the Congreso.

In March 1994 the Government and the URNG agreed a timetable of formal peace negotiations aimed at achieving a definitive peace agreement by the end of the year. In addition, a general human rights agreement was signed, providing guarantees, including a government commitment to eliminate illegal security corps, strengthen national human rights institutions and cease obligatory military recruitment. Agreement was also reached on the establishment of a UN deputation, the Human Rights Verification Mission in Guatemala (MINUGUA), to verify the implementation of the accord. Further talks in Oslo, Norway, resulted in the signing, in June, of agreements on the resettlement of people displaced by the civil war (estimated to number some 1m.), and on the establishment of a Comisión para el Esclarecimiento Histórico (CEH—Commission for Historical Clarification) to investigate human rights violations committed during the 33-year conflict.

In August 1994 the URNG withdrew from the peace negotiations and accused the Government of failing to observe the human rights provisions agreed in March. Talks resumed in November, but remained deadlocked until February 1995, when a new timetable for negotiations, achieved with UN mediation, was announced. The new agenda, which was formally agreed by the Government and the URNG in March, provided for a cease-fire agreement by June and the signing of a definitive peace accord in August. In March the issue of the identity and rights of indigenous peoples was finally resolved, but talks continued beyond the agreed deadline without agreement on other substantive issues, including agrarian and other socio-economic reform and the incorporation of URNG guerrillas into civilian life.

At the legislative election held in August 1994 only some 20% of the electorate exercised their vote, again reflecting widespread scepticism at the extent to which the reforms instigated by de León would serve to rid Guatemalan institutions of corruption. Despite winning the greatest number of seats in the 80-seat legislature, the FRG, led by Gen. (retd) José Efraín Ríos Montt, was excluded from the 12-member congressional directorate by an alliance of the PAN, PDCG, MLN and UD. However, in December the PDCG transferred its allegiance to the FRG and Ríos Montt was subsequently elected President of the Congreso. His inauguration in January 1995 provoked demonstrations by human rights organizations, which considered him responsible for the deaths of as many as 15,000 civilians as a result of counter-insurgency operations conducted during his period as de facto ruler in 1982–83.

In June 1995 Ríos Montt formally requested registration as a candidate in the forthcoming presidential election, despite the constitutional provision precluding the candidacy of anyone who had previously come to power by means of a coup, as Ríos Montt had done in 1982. In August the Supreme Electoral Tribunal confirmed that he was not eligible to stand for election and in the same month the Supreme Court ruled that he should be temporarily suspended from his position as President of the Congreso to answer charges of abuse of authority and violation of the Constitution. The charges concerned an attempt by Ríos Montt and several other FRG deputies to impeach the magistrates of the Supreme Electoral Tribunal without first securing congressional approval.

The presidential and legislative elections on 12 November 1995 were notable for the return to the electoral process, for the first time for more than 40 years, of the left wing, which was represented by the Frente Democrático Nueva Guatemala (FDNG). In addition, the URNG, which had boycotted all previous ballots, declared a unilateral cease-fire to coincide with the electoral campaign and urged people to exercise their vote. As no candidate received the necessary 50% of the votes to win the presidential election outright, the two leading candidates, Alvaro Enrique Arzú Irigoyen of the PAN and Alfonso Portillo of the FRG, contested a second round of voting on 7 January 1996, at which Arzú secured a narrow victory. At the legislative election the PAN also secured a majority of seats in the Congreso.

Shortly after assuming office in January 1996, Arzú implemented a comprehensive reorganization of the military high command, replacing those officers who were not in favour of a negotiated peace settlement. In March Congress ratified the International Labour Organization's Convention on the rights of indigenous peoples. However, the document, which had been before the Congreso since 1992 and had encountered strong opposition from landed interests, had been amended by the Congreso, prompting protests by Indian organizations. On 20 March the URNG announced an indefinite unilateral cease-fire. Arzú responded immediately by ordering the armed forces to suspend counter-insurgency operations. In May the Government and the URNG signed an agreement on agrarian and socio-economic reforms. In the following month the Congreso adopted legislation that made members of the armed forces accountable to civilian courts for all but strictly military crimes.

In September 1996 the Government and the URNG signed an agreement in Mexico City on the strengthening of civilian power and the role of the armed forces. Under the terms of the accord, all military and intelligence services were to be placed under the authority of the Government. The police force was to be reorganized, with the creation of a new National Civilian Police force (Policía Nacional Civil—PNC), which would replace the existing units from mid-1997. The armed forces were to be reduced in size by one-third and were to relinquish responsibility for internal security. Also confirmed in the accord was the abolition of the PAC. By December the demobilization of the PAC, estimated to number some 202,000 members, was officially concluded. Later that month a general amnesty law was approved by the Congreso. Whilst the law did not exonerate former combatants for human rights violations, the rebels expressed concern that the amnesty was too extensive and that atrocities committed by the armed forces would go unpunished.

On 29 December 1996 the Government and the URNG signed the definitive peace treaty in Guatemala City, bringing to an end some 36 years of civil war, during which an estimated 140,000 people had died. The demobilization of URNG guerrillas, estimated to number some 3,250, was to be supervised by MINUGUA. Earlier in the year the URNG had established a 44-member political council to prepare for the reconstitution of the organization as a broad-based political party. Demobilization was completed in May 1997. In the following month the URNG registered as a political party in formation and, in December 1998, formally engaged as a political party.

In April 1998 the auxiliary bishop of the metropolitan diocese of Guatemala City, Juan José Gerardi Conedera, was murdered. Gerardi had been a founder of the Roman Catholic Church's Oficina de Derechos Humanos del Arzobispado (ODHA—Archbishopric's Human Rights Office), and a prominent critic of the armed forces. Days before his death Gerardi had presented a report by the ODHA documenting human rights abuses committed during the civil conflict, of which army personnel were found responsible for some 80%. In July, in what the Church and human rights groups interpreted as an attempt to conceal the truth, a priest, Mario Orantes Nájera, was arrested. He was formally charged with Gerardi's murder in October. In February 1999 the presiding judge in the case, Henry Monroy, ordered the release of Orantes on grounds of insufficient evidence. However, in March Monroy withdrew from the case after allegedly receiving threats against his life. The case finally went to trial in 2001 and in June former intelligence chief Col (retd) Disrael Lima Estrada, his son, Capt. Byron Lima Oliva, and a former member of the presidential guard, José Obdulio Villanueva, were convicted of Bishop Gerardi's murder; Orantes was convicted of conspiring in his death. However, in October 2002 a Court of Appeal overturned the convictions and ordered a retrial, after accepting the defence's argument that there had been irregularities in the testimony of a key witness. At the retrial in February 2003 the sentences were upheld by the Supreme Court. Nevertheless, in March 2005 a Court of Appeal amended the convictions of Lima Estrada and Lima Oliva to accessory to murder, reducing their sentences from 30 years' to 20 years' imprisonment.

In August 1999, in what was widely regarded as a test case for the judicial system, 25 members of the armed forces convicted of the massacre in 1995 of 11 civilians in Xamán, Alta Verapaz, received minimum sentences of five years' imprisonment. The case was the first in which military personnel accused of killing civilians had been tried by a civilian court and the decision, which provoked public outrage, served greatly to undermine confidence in the courts' ability to administer justice in the remaining 625 cases of massacres attributed to the security forces. By contrast, in late 1998 death sentences had been passed on three members of the PAC found guilty of participating in massacres of civilians. In December 1999 MINUGUA issued a report stating that commitments made by the Arzú administration under the 1996 peace treaty to reduce the influence of the military remained unfulfilled. A MINUGUA report in the follow-

GUATEMALA

ing year stated that the number of extra-judicial executions had doubled between 1996 and 2000.

In February 1999 the CEH published its final report, in which it attributed more than 93% of human rights violations committed during the civil conflict to the armed forces and state paramilitaries. It announced that 200,000 people had been killed or had 'disappeared' between 1962 and 1996, the majority of them Mayan Indians. It also concluded that the USA had financed and trained Guatemalan forces responsible for atrocities. The report recommended that compensation be provided for the families of victims, that prosecutions be brought against those suspected of crimes against humanity and that a purge of the armed forces be implemented. The Government described the Commission's findings as 'controversial', and did not express any intention of pursuing its recommendations.

In October 1998 the Congreso approved constitutional reforms provided for in the 1996 peace accords. The reforms, which concerned the rights of indigenous peoples, the role of the armed forces and the police, and the strengthening of the courts, were subject to ratification in a referendum. However, at the referendum, on 16 May 1999, 55.6% of participating voters rejected the constitutional amendments. The turn-out was extremely low, with only 18.6% of the 4m. registered voters taking part, and observers attributed the result to a lack of information and to mistrust of the political establishment rather than to the rejection of the peace accords themselves. At presidential and legislative elections, conducted on 7 November, the voter turn-out, at some 40%, was greatly improved. As no candidate received the necessary 50% of the votes to win the presidential election outright, the two leading candidates, Alfonso Antonio Portillo Cabrera of the FRG and Oscar Berger Perdomo of the PAN, contested a second round of voting on 26 December, in which Portillo secured victory. The FRG secured an outright majority in the election to the newly enlarged legislature.

The new Government of President Portillo, which took office on 14 January 2000, immediately undertook the promised demilitarization of the upper echelons of government, and announced that one of its priorities was the narrowing of the fiscal deficit. A Governability Pact was introduced, intended to build consensus between the representatives of the state and the country's political and social leaderships. However, disputes between the Government and the Congreso Nacional resulted in virtual paralysis in policy-making throughout 2001. In mid-March two deputies defected from the FRG to join the Unidad Nacional de la Esperanza (UNE), a coalition established by the former presidential candidate Alvaro Colom Caballeros. Furthermore, throughout the year the Government was beset by allegations of corruption; the Ministers of Public Finance and of Communications, Transport and Public Works both left the Cabinet after irregular practices were uncovered in their ministries, while in November human rights groups claimed that the appointment of Brig.-Gen. (retd) Eduardo Arévalo Lacs, hitherto Minister of National Defence, as Minister of the Interior, was in contravention of the peace agreements. There were further protests in January 2002 when Gen. Lacs dismissed the director of the police force, Ennio Rivera Cardona, and replaced him with a former head of the disbanded national police, Luis Arturo Paniagua, who had been accused of human rights abuses.

In March 2002 a congressional commission was formed to investigate claims that President Portillo and Vice-President Francisco Reyes López had established bank accounts in Panama for the purpose of money-laundering. The Attorney-General and the Auditor-General's Office also began separate investigations. The allegations provoked mass protests in Guatemala City by trade-union members and socialist and religious groups, who demanded the President's resignation. However, at the end of the month the Auditor-General's Office declared that evidence used to support the claims had been fabricated, and in June the investigation by the congressional commission also collapsed, owing to a lack of evidence.

Meanwhile, violent attacks against public figures continued in 2002. In mid-March, days after he had given a speech at the anti-Portillo demonstrations, the leader of the opposition group Partido Patriótico, Jorge Rosal Zea, was assassinated. In October the US Assistant Secretary of State for the Western Hemisphere, Otto Reich, expressed his concern at levels of corruption, drugs-trafficking and continuing human rights abuses in Guatemala. President Portillo subsequently announced a number of reforms to the security forces, including the dissolution of the Departamento de Operaciones Antinarcóticos (Department of Anti-Narcotics Operations) and the creation of a new unit, Unidades

Introductory Survey

Móviles Operativas, to combat drugs-trafficking and terrorism. Nevertheless, in February 2003 the USA added Guatemala to the list of nations it considered unco-operative in combating drugs-trafficking.

In May 2003 the PAN's candidate in the forthcoming presidential election, Oscar José Rafael Berger Perdomo, announced he had left the party and would stand as the candidate of the Gran Alianza Nacional (GANA), a small, centre-right alliance supported by the private sector and comprising the Partido Progresista, the Partido Reformador Guatemalteco and the Partido Solidaridad Nacional. Nine PAN deputies followed suit. President Portillo supported the nomination of Ríos Montt as the FRG's nominee. However, constitutionally, Ríos Montt was barred from standing for presidential office, having come to power through unconstitutional means in 1982. In June 2003 the Supreme Electoral Tribunal rejected his candidature on these grounds, a decision supported by a supreme court ruling in early July. However, in mid-July the Constitutional Court overturned the ban, ruling that the former military leader could stand for re-election on the grounds that the pertinent legislation had been introduced in 1987, four years after Ríos Montt had left office. Nevertheless, the Supreme Court subsequently barred his candidacy, prompting violent protests. At the end of the month the Constitutional Court again overruled the supreme court decision and instructed the Electoral Tribunal to register Ríos Montt as a candidate.

Presidential and legislative elections took place on 9 November 2003. As no candidate secured more than 50% of the ballot in the first round of the presidential ballot, the two leading candidates, Berger and the UNE's Alvaro Colom, contested a second round of voting on 28 December, in which Berger narrowly secured the presidency. In the legislative elections, GANA secured the largest number of seats in the expanded assembly, although it failed to secure a congressional majority. Fears that the FRG or the PAC would interfere with the electoral process were not realized, although in the weeks preceding the elections some 20 party activists and regional leaders were murdered. Following the elections GANA was forced to enter into negotiations with other parties in order to establish a legislative majority. Eventually, in January 2004, the party agreed a two-year governability pact with the UNE and the PAN. The pact set out key legislative priorities, which included a programme of austere but transparent public expenditure, compliance with the peace accords, and political and electoral reform. President Berger took office on 14 January.

In February 2004 the Constitutional Court lifted the parliamentary immunity Ríos Montt had hitherto enjoyed. The following month Ríos Montt was charged with premeditated murder, coercion and threats in connection to the violence outside the Supreme Court in July 2003 and placed under house arrest; however, the charges were dismissed in January 2006. Also in February 2004, former President Portillo and former Vice-President Reyes similarly lost their parliamentary immunity from prosecution. Shortly after, Portillo left the country for Mexico. An injunction for his arrest on charges of money-laundering and misuse of public funds was subsequently requested and the US embassy revoked his visa. Reyes was arrested in July and charged with fraud, embezzlement and abuse of authority. He was released on bail in December pending further investigations. In July 2005 the warrant for Portillo's arrest was confirmed, and proceedings for his extradition from Mexico were initiated in October. In October 2006 Portillo's extradition was authorized by the Mexican Government. However, in late May 2007 the Constitutional Court ordered that the case against Portillo be abandoned, and in early June a Mexican federal judge accepted Portillo's appeal against his extradition.

On 11 August 2004 former members of the PAC held a protest outside the Congreso in an attempt to prevent legislators leaving the building until they had approved payment to the militias of the remainder of the compensation agreed during President Portillo's term in office. Portillo had decreed the payment of US $640 to former members of the PAC, but only $215 had been disbursed. During 2004 the Congreso approved legislation to compensate PAC members on three separate occasions, but each time human rights organizations successfully appealed to the Constitutional Court that the laws were unconstitutional. In December the Government announced it was to establish a social fund for housing, rural infrastructure and reforestation projects for the former militias; however, protests by PAC members continued in 2005, and in March President Berger agreed to resubmit compensation legislation to the Congreso. Further protest action, including road blockades, took place in July. The former PAC members were demanding monetary compensation rather than the proposed social fund. None the less, a reforestation project financed by the social fund, which employed former PAC members, commenced in mid-2006.

In March 2005 the Congreso ratified the Dominican Republic-Central American Free Trade Agreement (DR-CAFTA) with the USA, by a three-quarters' majority. Following the ratification, some 4,000 union members, farmers and students protested outside government buildings in Guatemala City to call for a referendum on the Agreement. However, in early April the Constitutional Court ruled that DR-CAFTA was in keeping with the Constitution; on the same day 10,000 people participated in protests co-ordinated by the Movimiento Indígena, Campesino, Sindical y Popular.

Domestic security was one of the most pressing problems facing the Berger Government. Gang rivalry and vigilante groups were widely held to be responsible for the rising rates of murder and violent crime. In the first six months of 2004 the incidence of violent crime increased by 13% on the previous year, prompting the resignation of the Minister of the Interior in July. Following the exposure of several senior police officers with links to criminal groups, in June Berger dismissed the head of the PNC. In July, in a campaign named 'Crusade against Violence', some 4,000 police and military officers were deployed in areas with particularly high crime rates. In spite of these initiatives, the murder rate increased by 25% in 2004, to 4,346, and in 2005 it climbed to 5,308, its highest rate since the civil war. The figure included a number of judges and lawyers investigating cases of drugs-trafficking. In mid-August 2005 riots took place simultaneously in at least three prisons between members of rival gangs, resulting in the deaths of 31 gang members. It was alleged that prison guards were involved in smuggling weapons into the gaols. In the following month a further 14 gang members were killed in a juvenile detention centre. In response, President Berger transferred the administration and security of these centres to the remit of the prison service and deployed the armed forces to patrol the perimeters. In October 19 inmates escaped from a prison in Escuintla; once again, it was alleged that prison guards were privy to the security breach. Four days later the Minister of Defence, Gen. Carlos Aldana Villanueva, announced that the armed forces would assume responsibility for the external security surrounding prisons. Berger subsequently dismissed Aldana Villanueva, appointing Gen. Francisco Bermúdez to succeed him.

Internal political conflicts and the defection of congressional deputies impeded the Berger Government's efforts to implement its legislative agenda. In an attempt to secure opposition support for proposed fiscal reforms, in May 2004 President Berger met with Ríos Montt. However, the meeting was criticized by Berger's allies: the UNE and the PAN withdrew from the governability pact and the Partido Patriota (PP) left GANA in protest, leaving the Government even more reliant on securing FRG support. Despite some success in addressing the problems of corruption, in late 2004 a MINUGUA report noted that government efforts to reform the criminal justice system had been largely ineffective and that the state remained unable to ensure that laws were observed. Upon its withdrawal from Guatemala in December, a MINUGUA report stated that the Government still had to overcome three major challenges: public security, judicial reform and discrimination against indigenous peoples. Following legislative approval, an office of the UN's High Commission for Human Rights was opened in Guatemala in July 2005, to replace MINUGUA in monitoring human rights.

During 3–5 October 2005 Guatemala was devastated by the effects of 'Hurricane Stan' and subsequent mudslides. Some 669 deaths were officially recorded, although the unofficial death toll was much higher, at 1,500. According to UN estimates, the hurricane caused losses totalling more than US $985m. The Government declared a state of emergency on 5 October, which was later extended to the end of November, in an attempt to expedite the reconstruction effort by circumventing the normal bidding process for government contracts and purchases.

Political tensions escalated into violence in early 2006. A number of political activists were assassinated, including a UNE deputy and the co-ordinator of the nascent political party Encuentro por Guatemala, Eleaza Tebalan, who were both murdered in early April. Later the same month four people were lynched in two separate attacks, prompting the mobilization of 11,000 members of the armed forces to assist the police in maintaining order. According to the Ministry of the Interior, in 2006 the murder rate increased to 5,629. In late September the Government disclosed that the controversial deployment of the armed forces to support the police was expected to continue for at least two further presidential terms.

Addressing drugs-related and violent crime remained a priority for Berger's Government throughout 2006. According to the US Administration, an estimated 150 metric tons of cocaine were trafficked through Guatemala each year. In January the Fuerza Interinstitucional de Tarea, a counter-narcotics task force operating with military assistance from the USA, initiated a campaign to destroy clandestine airstrips that were reportedly used by drugs-traffickers. By May the Government claimed to have rendered inoperable 90 of these strips. Legislation to strengthen the capacity of the police force to address organized crime, particularly drugs-smuggling, was approved by the Congreso Nacional in mid-July. The new law provided for the electronic surveillance of suspects and introduced the offence of 'association to commit crime', intended to discourage collusion in, *inter alia*, trafficking of drugs and people, money-laundering and murder. In a separate move to curb the trade in illicit drugs, in August and September an operation to destroy opium poppy plantations and apprehend drugs-smugglers resulted in the uprooting of some 583 ha of poppies.

There was significant upheaval in the Berger administration in the latter half of 2006 and early 2007. In July 2006 the Minister of Foreign Affairs, Jorge Briz Abularach, submitted his resignation. Then, in early September Bernardo de Jesús López Figueroa was appointed Minister of Agriculture, Livestock and Food, replacing Alvaro Aguilar Prado who relinquished his post in order to present his candidacy for the 2007 presidential election. In mid-September Dr Hugo Beteta Méndez-Ruiz was appointed Minister of Public Finance, replacing María Antonieta del Cid de Bonilla who was to assume the presidency of the Banco de Guatemala. Also in mid-September Minister of Public Health and Social Welfare Marco Tulio Sosa Ramírez tendered his resignation following two months of industrial action by doctors and other health sector employees in protest at the shortage of medical supplies and equipment. An independent deputy, Víctor Manuel Gutiérrez Longo, was promptly appointed in his stead. Negotiations between Gutiérrez Longo and representatives of the medical staff resulted in an agreement in early December to restructure the health service, thereby bringing to an end nearly five months of industrial action. However, in January 2007 Gutiérrez Longo resigned, citing a lack of support. He was replaced by Alfredo Antonio Privado Medrano. Meanwhile, in early October 2006 Minister of Employment and Social Security Jorge Francisco Gallardo Flores was replaced by deputy minister Rodolfo Colmenares Arandi and at the end of December Maj.-Gen. Ronaldo Cecilio Leiva succeeded Gen. Francisco Bermúdez Amado as Minister of National Defence. In early February 2007 Bermúdez Amado announced the creation of an auxiliary police unit, composed of former members of the armed forces, to be deployed in areas experiencing the highest rates of violent crime. Two further cabinet changes were made in January: Berger appointed Francisco Unda as Minister of Communications, Infrastructure and Housing, replacing Manuel Eduardo Castillo Arroyo, and Luis Oscar Estrada as Minister of Economy in succession to Marcio Ronaldo Cuevas Quezada.

In mid-February 2007 three Salvadorean deputies were found murdered on the outskirts of Guatemala City. Three days later four Guatemalan police officers who had confessed to the murders were arrested and imprisoned; however, they too were later assassinated. Following the incident 22 prison employees were arrested on suspicion of complicity in the crime. The Minister of the Interior, Carlos Roberto Vielmann Montes, and PNC Director Erwin Sperissen tendered their resignations; however, these were rejected by Berger. The issue highlighted the ongoing challenge of eradicating corruption in public institutions, particularly the PNC (in January 2006 some 1,500 members of the PNC had been dismissed for corrupt or criminal activities). Notwithstanding the arrest in mid-March of four further suspects in relation to the assassinations, a vote of 'no confidence' in Vielmann Montes in mid-March was approved by the Congreso Nacional. His resignation was accepted and he was replaced by Adela Camacho de Torrebiarte. In late July the Government revealed evidence that implicated an independent congressional deputy, Manuel Castillo, in the murders.

The crisis provoked by the assassinations facilitated, in early August 2007, the overwhelming approval by the Congreso Nacional of legislation to create the International Commission against Impunity in Guatemala (CICIG—Comisión Internacional contra la Impunidad en Guatemala), in fulfilment of an agreement between the Government and the UN signed in December 2006. The independent body was to comprise a panel of international experts who would assist the Guatemalan authorities in the investigation and dismantling of paramilitary security forces and other criminal organizations linked to state institutions. CICIG was established in early September, and later in that month Carlos Castresana Fernández, a Spanish judge, was appointed as its director.

Security issues dominated the campaign for the presidential and legislative elections held on 9 September 2007. More than 40 people were killed in the months preceding the vote, including candidates, their relatives and party activists, in the most violent electoral campaign since the end of the civil war. In the presidential ballot, the UNE's Colom—contesting his third consecutive presidential election—secured 28.2% of valid votes cast, followed by Gen. (retd) Otto Fernando Pérez Molina, the PP candidate, with 23.5%, and Alejandro Eduardo Giammattei Falla, representing GANA, who received 17.2%. As no candidate had obtained the required 50% of ballot, a second round of voting was contested by Colom and Pérez Molina on 4 November, as a result of which Colom was elected President with 52.8% of valid votes. In elections to the Congreso Nacional the UNE increased its representation to 50 out of 158 seats, thereby becoming the largest party in the legislature; GANA won 36 seats, the PP 29 and the FRG 15. Colom was sworn in on 14 January 2008, becoming the first centre-left President since 1954.

Until the return to civilian government in 1986, Guatemala remained steadfast in its claims to the neighbouring territory of Belize, a former British dependency. However, Guatemala's new Constitution, which took effect in January 1986, did not include Belize in its delineation of Guatemalan territory. In September 1991 Guatemala and Belize signed an accord under the terms of which Belize pledged to legislate to reduce its maritime boundaries and to allow Guatemala access to the Caribbean Sea and use of its port facilities. In return, Guatemala officially recognized Belize as an independent state and established diplomatic relations. Nevertheless, in March 1994 Guatemala formally reaffirmed its territorial claim to Belize. The Standing Committee of Ministers of Foreign Affairs of the Caribbean Community and Common Market (CARICOM, see p. 196) again confirmed its support for Belizean sovereignty. In September 1996 the Ministers of Foreign Affairs of Guatemala and Belize conducted preliminary talks on a resumption of negotiations on the territorial dispute. In August 2000 a panel of negotiators was established at the headquarters of the Organization of American States (OAS, see p. 360) in Washington, DC, to supervise the process of bilateral negotiations. Negotiations in 2001 focused on the issue of Guatemalans living in the disputed border area, who, according to Belize, were being used by Guatemala to assert sovereignty over the territory; an agreement was later reached to relocate the families.

In 2002 relations with Belize appeared to improve following further OAS-mediated discussions on the border issue; in September proposals were outlined for a solution to the dispute. These included the provision that Guatemala would recognize Belize's land boundary as set out in the Treaty of 1859, and the creation of a model settlement for peasants and landless farmers in the disputed area. The two countries were to hold simultaneous public referendums on the agreement by the end of November. However, the fatal shooting of a Guatemalan on the Belizean side of the border in October delayed the plebiscites. Following further conciliatory discussions, in February 2003 the foreign ministers of both countries signed a co-operation agreement pending a final settlement of the dispute. In May 2004 delegations from the two countries participated in OAS-sponsored negotiations to establish a series of initiatives designed to promote mutual confidence, including a free trade agreement, and in September 2005 Guatemala and Belize signed an Agreement on a Framework of Negotiation and Confidence Building Measures; negotiations towards final settlement of the dispute were in progress in 2008. Following almost two years of negotiations, in March 2006 representatives of the two countries signed a preliminary trade accord enabling 150 products to be traded duty-free.

Government

Guatemala is a republic comprising 22 departments. Under the 1986 Constitution (revised in 1994), legislative power is vested in the unicameral Congreso Nacional (National Congress), with 158 members elected for four years by universal adult suffrage. Of the total seats, 127 are filled by departmental representation and 31 according to national listing. Executive power is held by the President (also directly elected for four years), assisted by a Vice-President and an appointed Cabinet.

Defence

As assessed at November 2007, the armed forces totalled an estimated 15,500, of whom 13,444 were in the army, 986 in the navy and 1,070 in the air force. Reserve forces totalled 63,863. In addition, there were paramilitary forces of 19,000. Military service is by selective conscription for 30 months. Defence expenditure in 2007 was budgeted at 1,200m. quetzales (US $164m.).

Economic Affairs

In 2006, according to estimates by the World Bank, Guatemala's gross national income (GNI), measured at average 2004–06 prices, was US $34,089m., equivalent to $2,640 per head (or $4,800 per head on an international purchasing-power parity basis). During 1996–2006, it was estimated, the population increased by an average of 2.4% per year, while gross domestic product (GDP) per head increased, in real terms, by an average of 1.0% per year. Overall GDP increased, in real terms, at an average annual rate of 3.4% in 1996–2006; GDP grew by a preliminary 5.7% in 2007.

Agriculture, including hunting, forestry and fishing, contributed a preliminary 13.8% of GDP, measured in constant prices, in 2007. According to FAO estimates, 42.0% of the labour force were employed in this sector. The principal cash crops are coffee (which accounted for 8.3% of export earnings in 2007), sugar cane and bananas. The coffee sector has suffered various set-backs in recent years: following a drought in 2001, a regional crisis in the coffee industry blighted the sector in 2002 (leading to a 14.7% fall in exports in that year). Then, in October 2005, coffee-growing regions were particularly badly affected by 'Hurricane Stan'. Exports of shrimps are also significant. In recent years the country has successfully expanded production of less traditional crops, such as mangoes, berries and green beans. During 1996–2006 agricultural GDP increased, in real terms, by an estimated average of 2.7% per year. Growth in agricultural GDP was a preliminary 3.4% in 2007.

Industry, including mining, manufacturing, construction and power, contributed an estimated 27.0% of GDP, measured in constant prices, in 2007. This sector employed 20.6% of the working population in 2002. Industrial GDP increased by an estimated average of 2.9% per year in 1996–2006. Growth in industrial GDP was a preliminary 4.9% in 2007.

Mining contributed an estimated 0.7% of GDP, measured in constant prices, in 2007 and employed 0.2% of the working population in 2002. The most important mineral export is petroleum, which accounted for 3.6% of total export earnings in 2007. In addition, copper, antimony, lead, zinc and tungsten are mined on a small scale. There are also deposits of nickel, gold and silver. It was estimated that mining GDP increased by an average of 6.1% per year during 1995–2006. This sector expanded by a preliminary 9.0% in 2007.

Guatemala's industrial sector is the largest in Central America. Manufacturing contributed an estimated 19.2% of GDP, measured in constant prices, in 2007 and employed 13.4% of the working population in 2002. Manufacturing GDP increased by an average of 2.3% per year in 1996–2006. Growth in manufacturing GDP was estimated at 3.3% in 2007. Guatemala's clothing assembly, or *maquila*, manufacturing sector was an important economic contributor, although it contracted in the early 2000s. The advent of the Dominican Republic-Central America Free Trade Agreement (DR-CAFTA) with the USA from 2006 (see below) was expected to lead to growth in the *maquila* sector.

Energy is derived principally from mineral fuels and hydroelectric power. Petroleum provided 35.7% of electric energy in 2004. However, hydroelectric power was responsible for a decreasing proportion of total power output, accounting for 34.7% of electricity generation in 2004, compared with 57.6% in 1997, while power generation from coal sources increased from 0.7% in 1999 to 17.1% in 2004. Guatemala is a marginal producer of petroleum and, in 2006, produced on average 20,000 barrels per day. Proven petroleum reserves were estimated at 526m. barrels in January 2000. Reserves of natural gas were put at some 109,000m. cu ft in the same year. Imports of mineral products comprised 18.5% of the value of total imports in 2007.

In 2007 the services sector contributed a preliminary 59.2% of GDP, measured in constant prices, and in 2002 the sector employed 36.5% of the working population. The GDP of the

GUATEMALA

services sector increased by an average of 3.8% per year in 1996–2006; growth in the sector was a preliminary 7.4% in 2007.

In 2006 Guatemala recorded a visible trade deficit of US $5,043.6m., and there was a deficit of $1,592.1m. on the current account of the balance of payments. In 2007 the principal source of imports (34.2%) was the USA; other major suppliers were Mexico, the People's Republic of China, El Salvador, the Netherlands Antilles and the Republic of Korea. The USA was also the principal market for exports (taking 42.3% of exports in that year); other significant purchasers were El Salvador, Honduras, Mexico and Nicaragua. The main exports in 2007 were coffee, cardamom, sugar and bananas. The principal imports were mineral products, audiovisual equipment and chemicals and related products. Remittances from citizens working abroad represented the second largest hard currency inflow into the country after non-traditional exports. According to the central bank, Banco de Guatemala, in 2007 remittances from the USA totalled $4,128.4m.

In 2006 there was an estimated budgetary deficit of 4,497.6m. quetzales, equivalent to some 1.7% of GDP. At the end of 2005 Guatemala's total external debt stood at US $5,349m., of which $3,688m. was long-term public debt. In that year the cost of debt-servicing was equivalent to 5.8% of the value of exports of goods and services. In 1999–2006 the average annual rate of inflation was 7.2%. Consumer prices increased by an average of 5.8% in 2006. An estimated 3.4% of the labour force were unemployed in 2003.

Guatemala is a member of the Central American Common Market (CACM, see p. 201). In 2000 Guatemala, El Salvador and Honduras signed a free trade agreement with Mexico, which promised greater market access and increased bilateral trade. In May 2001 the Central American countries, including Guatemala, reached an agreement with Mexico to establish a series of joint transport, industry and tourism projects intended to integrate the region, called the 'Plan Puebla–Panamá'. Negotiations between Guatemala and the USA towards DR-CAFTA (to comprise Guatemala, Costa Rica, El Salvador, Honduras, Nicaragua, the Dominican Republic and the USA) were concluded in December 2003. The agreement, which was ratified by the Congreso in March 2005, entailed the gradual elimination of tariffs on most industrial and agricultural products over the next 10 and 20 years, respectively, and was expected to lead to an increase in exports. DR-CAFTA came into effect on 1 July 2006. In May 2004 the Presidents of Guatemala, El Salvador, Honduras and Nicaragua signed an agreement creating a Central American customs union. A free trade agreement between Guatemala and Taiwan came into effect in early 2006.

The implementation of DR-CAFTA was considered vital to the future development of the Guatemalan economy, which continued to suffer from large trade deficits. Much of the country's trade took place on commodity markets, with oil a major import. Given the price volatility of agricultural goods exported by Guatemala, the steady inflow of remittances from abroad (mainly the USA) tended to offset shortfalls in foreign exchange earnings; however any downturn in the US economy would adversely affect this flow of funds. In early 2008 the economy was still suffering the effects of 'Hurricane Stan', which struck in October 2005; as a result, the budget deficit in 2005 increased to 1.5% of GDP from just 0.3% the previous year and, despite increased inflows of remittances, expanded further, to 1.7% of GDP, in 2006. The 2007 deficit was estimated at 2.1% of GDP. Another major obstacle to economic growth was the high rate of violent crime in the country, which continued to deter foreign investment. Nevertheless, foreign investment did increase in 2007, contributing to a preliminary 5.7% increase in GDP. The implementation of DR-CAFTA was expected to bring greater access to US markets and encourage economic diversification. The centre-left Government of Alvaro Colom Caballeros, which took office in January 2008, pledged to address the problem of violent crime and reduce poverty levels without substantially increasing expenditure. However, the discovery of irregularities in the outgoing administration's accounting prompted fears that the new Government's spending plans might have to be curtailed. Furthermore, any requests for extra funding would have to be approved by the Congreso, in which Colom's party, the Unidad Nacional de la Esperanza, did not enjoy a majority.

Education

Elementary education is free and, in urban areas, compulsory between seven and 14 years of age. Primary education begins at the age of seven and lasts for six years. Secondary education, beginning at 13 years of age, lasts for up to six years, comprising two cycles of three years each. In 2000 there were 10,424 pre-primary schools, and in 2004/05 there were 16,609 primary schools and 3,585 secondary schools. In 2004 enrolment at primary schools was equivalent to 93.0% of children in the relevant age-group (males 95.4%; females 90.5%). The comparable ratio for secondary education in that year was 33.7% (males 35.1%; females 32.4%). There are 12 universities. The inauguration of Guatemala's first indigenous university, the Universidad Maya de Guatemala, took place in December 2004. Open to both indigenous and non-indigenous students, the institution offered courses in medicine, education, Mayan Law, art, architecture, community development and agriculture. In 2006 budgetary expenditure on education was an estimated 6,251.2m. quetzales, equivalent to 18.6% of total spending.

Public Holidays

2008: 1 January (New Year's Day), 20–23 March (Easter), 1 May (Labour Day), 30 June (Anniversary of the Revolution), 15 August (Assumption, Guatemala City only), 15 September (Independence Day), 12 October (Columbus Day), 20 October (Revolution Day), 1 November (All Saints' Day), 24 December (Christmas Eve, afternoon only), 25 December (Christmas Day), 31 December (New Year's Eve, afternoon only).

2009: 1 January (New Year's Day), 9–12 April (Easter), 1 May (Labour Day), 30 June (Anniversary of the Revolution), 15 August (Assumption, Guatemala City only), 15 September (Independence Day), 12 October (Columbus Day), 20 October (Revolution Day), 1 November (All Saints' Day), 24 December (Christmas Eve, afternoon only), 25 December (Christmas Day), 31 December (New Year's Eve, afternoon only).

Weights and Measures

The metric system is in official use.

GUATEMALA

Statistical Survey

Sources (unless otherwise stated): Banco de Guatemala, 7a Avda 22-01, Zona 1, Apdo 365, Guatemala City; tel. 230-6222; fax 253-4035; internet www.banguat.gob.gt; Instituto Nacional de Estadística, Edif. América 4°, 8a Calle 9-55, Zona 1, Guatemala City; tel. 2232-6212; e-mail info-ine@ine.gob.gt; internet www.ine.gob.gt.

Area and Population

AREA, POPULATION AND DENSITY

Area (sq km)	
Land	108,429
Inland water	460
Total	108,889*
Population (census results)†	
17 April 1994	8,322,051
24 November 2002	11,237,196
Population (UN estimates at mid-year)‡	
2005	12,710,000
2006	13,029,000
2007	13,354,000
Density (per sq km) at mid-2007	123.2

* 42,042 sq miles.
† Excluding adjustments for underenumeration.
‡ Source: UN, *World Population Prospects: The 2006 Revision*.

DEPARTMENTS
(population at census of November 2002)

Alta Verapaz	776,246	Quetzaltenango	624,716
Baja Verapaz	215,915	Quiché	655,510
Chimaltenango	446,133	Retalhuleu	241,411
Chiquimula	302,485	Sacatepéquez	248,019
El Progreso	139,490	San Marcos	794,951
Escuintla	538,746	Santa Rosa	301,370
Guatemala	2,541,581	Sololá	307,661
Huehuetenango	846,544	Suchitepéquez	403,945
Izabal	314,306	Totonicapán	339,254
Jalapa	242,926	Zacapa	200,167
Jutiapa	389,085		
Petén	366,735	**Total**	**11,237,196**

PRINCIPAL TOWNS
(population at census of November 2002)

Guatemala City	942,348	Cobán	144,461
Mixco	403,689	Quetzaltenango	127,569
Villa Nueva	355,901	Escuintla	119,897
San Juan Sacatepéquez	152,583	Jalapa	105,796
San Pedro Carcha	148,344	Totonicapán	96,392

Mid-2007 ('000, incl. suburbs, UN estimate): Guatemala City 1,024 (Source: UN, *World Urbanization Prospects: The 2007 Revision*).

BIRTHS, MARRIAGES AND DEATHS

	Registered live births		Registered marriages		Registered deaths	
	Number	Rate (per 1,000)	Number	Rate (per 1,000)	Number	Rate (per 1,000)
1998	378,438	35.0	52,499	4.9	69,633	6.4
1999	409,034	36.9	62,034	5.6	65,139	5.9
2000	425,410	37.4	58,311	5.1	67,284	5.9
2001	415,338	35.6	54,722	4.7	68,041	5.8
2002	387,287	32.3	51,857	4.3	66,089	5.5
2003	375,092	31.0	51,247	4.2	66,695	5.5
2004	383,704	31.0	53,860	4.3	66,991	5.4
2005	374,066	29.5	52,186	4.1	71,039	5.6

Source: partly UN, *Demographic Yearbook* and *Population and Vital Statistics Report*.

Expectation of life (years at birth, WHO estimates): 67.9 (males 64.8; females 70.8) in 2005 (Source: WHO, *World Health Statistics*).

ECONOMICALLY ACTIVE POPULATION
(at census of November 2002)

	Males	Females	Total
Agriculture, forestry, hunting and fishing	1,278,739	178,364	1,457,103
Mining and quarrying	5,313	756	6,069
Manufacturing	301,222	164,725	465,947
Construction	186,611	21,266	207,877
Electricity, gas, water and sanitary services	23,518	10,135	33,653
Commerce	343,586	228,114	571,700
Transport, storage and communications	96,410	16,913	113,323
Financial and property services	82,644	42,839	125,483
Public administration and defence	60,853	25,137	85,990
Education	42,366	59,796	102,162
Community and personal services	68,165	197,794	265,959
Activities not adequately described	18,256	9,875	28,131
Total	**2,525,683**	**937,714**	**3,463,397**

Mid-2005 (estimates in '000): Agriculture 1,929; Total labour force 4,595 (Source: FAO).

Health and Welfare

KEY INDICATORS

Total fertility rate (children per woman, 2005)	4.4
Under-5 mortality rate (per 1,000 live births, 2005)	43
HIV/AIDS (% of persons aged 15–49, 2005)	0.9
Physicians (per 1,000 head, 1999)	0.9
Hospital beds (per 1,000 head, 2005)	0.7
Health expenditure (2004): US $ per head (PPP)	256.2
Health expenditure (2004): % of GDP	5.7
Health expenditure (2004): public (% of total)	41.0
Access to water (% of persons, 2004)	95
Access to sanitation (% of persons, 2004)	86
Human Development Index (2005): ranking	118
Human Development Index (2005): value	0.689

For sources and definitions, see explanatory note on p. vi.

GUATEMALA

Agriculture

PRINCIPAL CROPS
('000 metric tons)

	2004	2005	2006
Maize	1,072.3*	1,079.8	1,183.9
Sugar cane	18,000.0	19,070.0*	18,721.4
Oil palm fruit†	580.0	600.0	600.0
Tomatoes†	189.2	192.2	192.2
Watermelons†	129.8	131.9	131.9
Cantaloupes and other melons†	207.8	221.5	221.5
Bananas†	1,028.5	1,070.5	1,070.5
Plantains†	270.5	272.4	272.4
Lemons and limes†	141.4	141.8	141.8
Guavas, mangoes and mangosteens†	205.6	216.9	216.9
Coffee (green)*	216.6	256.6	256.6

* Unofficial figure(s).
† FAO estimates.

Aggregate production ('000 metric tons, may include official, semi-official or estimated data): Total cereals 1,172.1 in 2004, 1,167.8 in 2005, 1,275.5 in 2006; Total pulses 132.3 in 2004, 132.5 in 2005, 132.5 in 2006; Total roots and tubers 300.0 in 2004, 286.5 in 2005, 286.5 in 2006; Total vegetables (incl. melons) 1,024.6 in 2004, 1,059.8 in 2005, 1,044.3 in 2006; Total fruits (excl. melons) 2,053.8 in 2004, 2,116.5 in 2005, 2,276.5 in 2006.

Source: FAO.

LIVESTOCK
('000 head, year ending September, FAO estimates)

	2002	2003	2004
Horses	122	124	124
Asses, mules or hinnies	48.6	48.6	48.6
Cattle	2,540	2,540	2,540
Sheep	250	260	260
Pigs	212	212	212
Goats	112	112	112
Chickens	25,500	24,300	27,000

2005: Cattle 2,453 (all other figures assumed to be unchanged from 2004—FAO estimates).

2006: Cattle 2,796 (all other figures assumed to be unchanged from 2004—FAO estimates).

LIVESTOCK PRODUCTS
('000 metric tons, FAO estimates)

	2002	2003	2004
Cattle meat	63.0	63.0	63.0
Pig meat	25.6	26.5	26.0
Chicken meat	155.0	155.0	167.7
Cows' milk	270.0	270.0	270.0
Hen eggs	85.0	85.0	85.0
Honey	n.a.	1.5	1.5

2005: Chicken meat 176.2 (all other figures assumed to be unchanged from 2004—FAO estimates).

2006: Figures assumed to be unchanged from 2004 (FAO estimates).

Source: FAO.

Forestry

ROUNDWOOD REMOVALS
('000 cubic metres, excl. bark)

	2004	2005	2006
Sawlogs, veneer logs and logs for sleepers	404	385	439
Other industrial wood	15	20	15
Fuel wood*	15,905	16,265	16,609
Total	16,324	16,670	17,063

* FAO estimates.
Source: FAO.

SAWNWOOD PRODUCTION
('000 cubic metres, incl. railway sleepers)

	2002	2003	2004*
Coniferous (softwood)	180*	251	251
Broadleaved (hardwood)	160	115	115
Total	340	366	366

* FAO estimate(s).
2005–06: Production assumed to be unchanged from 2004 (FAO estimates).

Fishing

('000 metric tons, live weight)

	2003	2004	2005
Capture*	26.1	13.3	12.2
Freshwater fishes*	7.1	7.1	7.1
Skipjack tuna	9.9	1.3	1.1
Yellowfin tuna	3.0	0.8	2.2
Bigeye tuna	1.7	0.4	—
Penaeus shrimps	0.7	0.8	0.6
Pacific seabobs	1.8	1.4	0.2
Aquaculture	6.3	4.5	4.5
Nile tilapia*	1.1	—	—
Other tilapias*	0.6	0.6	0.6
Penaeus shrimps	3.8	3.9	3.9*
Total catch*	32.5	17.8	16.8

* FAO estimate(s).
Source: FAO.

Mining

('000 metric tons, unless otherwise indicated, estimates)

	2003	2004	2005
Crude petroleum ('000 42-gallon barrels)	9,028	7,384	6,728
Gold (kg)	—	—	740
Limestone	3,773	4,270	7,600
Sand and gravel ('000 cubic metres)	296	90	367

Source: US Geological Survey.

Industry

SELECTED PRODUCTS
('000 metric tons, unless otherwise indicated)

	2000	2001	2002
Sugar (raw)	883	1,670	1,912
Motor spirit (petrol)	150	147	111
Cigarettes (million)	4,262	—	—
Tobacco (prepared leaf)	19	20	21
Cement	2,039	1,976	2,068
Electric energy (million kWh)	6,051	5,856	6,191

2003: Cement 1,900 (estimate); Electric energy (million kWh) 6,561.
2004: Cement 1,900 (estimate); Electric energy (million kWh) 7,009.
Source: UN, *Industrial Commodity Statistics Yearbook*.

GUATEMALA

Finance

CURRENCY AND EXCHANGE RATES

Monetary Units
100 centavos = 1 quetzal.

Sterling, Dollar and Euro Equivalents (31 December 2007)
£1 sterling = 15,288 quetzales;
US $1 = 7.671 quetzales;
€1 = 11.233 quetzales;
10,000 quetzales = £6.54 = $13.10 = €8.90.

Average Exchange Rate (quetzales per US dollar)
2005 7.6339
2006 7.6026
2007 7.6733

Note: In December 2000 legislation was approved to allow the circulation of the US dollar and other convertible currencies, for use in a wide range of transactions, from 1 May 2001.

GOVERNMENT FINANCE
(budgetary central government operations, cash basis, million quetzales)

Summary of Balances

	2004	2005	2006
Revenue	23,389.1	24,764.6	29,102.4
Less Expense	24,128.9	26,660.7	31,073.7
Net cash inflow from operating activities	−739.8	−1,896.1	−1,971.3
Less Purchases of non-financial assets	1,253.3	1,674.0	2,526.3
Sales of non-financial assets	0.6	—	—
Cash surplus/deficit	1,992.4	−3,570.1	−4,497.6

Revenue

	2004	2005	2006
Taxation	22,001.0	23,276.8	27,251.5
Taxes on income, profits and capital gains	5,739.6	6,438.8	8,156.8
Domestic taxes on goods and services	13,535.9	12,800.2	16,090.4
Sales, turnover or value-added taxes	10,482.3	10,752.7	4,473.3
Excises	2,445.6	1,371.6	2,880.6
Taxes on international trade and transactions	2,428.1	3,715.4	2,603.5
Social contributions	539.7	549.8	585.1
Grants	312.1	359.9	370.0
Other revenue	536.4	578.1	895.8
Total (incl. grants)	23,389.1	24,764.6	29,102.4

Expense/Outlays

Expense by economic type	2004	2005	2006
Compensation of employees	6,783.9	6,796.2	7,608.7
Use of goods and services	2,884.0	3,171.3	4,102.8
Interest	2,547.1	2,868.7	3,128.2
Subsidies	187.3	331.4	436.4
Grants	6,321.3	4,289.2	5,264.3
Social benefits	1,738.6	1,867.1	2,040.5
Other expense	3,666.8	7,336.8	8,492.8
Total	24,128.9	26,660.7	31,073.7

Outlays by function of government*	2004	2005	2006
General public services	7,301.6	5,283.7	6,301.8
Defence	775.5	683.1	821.9
Public order and safety	2,630.1	2,800.2	3,173.6
Economic affairs	6,077.4	6,246.9	8,270.8
Environmental protection	186.6	675.1	701.6
Housing and community amenities	1,250.7	4,357.7	4,628.5
Health	1,799.9	2,281.8	2,587.5
Recreation, culture and religion	399.9	462.4	542.1
Education	4,794.7	5,393.6	6,251.2
Social protection	166.0	151.3	328.0
Statistical discrepancy	−0.6	−1.1	−7.0
Total	25,381.6	28,334.7	33,600.0

* Including purchases of non-financial assets.

Source: IMF, *Government Finance Statistics Yearbook*.

INTERNATIONAL RESERVES
(US $ million at 31 December)

	2004	2005	2006
Gold*	9.3	9.3	9.3
IMF special drawing rights	8.0	6.5	5.6
Foreign exchange	3,418.3	3,657.3	3,909.3
Total	3,435.6	3,673.1	3,924.2

* Valued at US $42 per troy ounce.

Source: IMF, *International Financial Statistics*.

MONEY SUPPLY
(million quetzales at 31 December)

	2004	2005	2006
Currency outside banks	11,192.7	12,490.5	14,801.8
Demand deposits at deposit money banks	19,573.4	23,234.0	28,215.8
Total money (incl. others)	30,646.6	35,714.6	43,003.6

Source: IMF, *International Financial Statistics*.

COST OF LIVING
(Consumer Price Index; base: 2000 = 100)

	2004	2005	2006
Food and non-alcoholic beverages	146.1	164.2	174.8
Clothing and footwear	121.0	125.3	128.4
Housing, water and power	125.1	133.5	139.3
Health	127.7	135.3	144.3
Transport and communications	120.1	129.6	139.7
Recreation and culture	131.5	137.6	145.9
Education	135.2	144.1	150.1
All items (incl. others)	133.9	145.4	153.8

NATIONAL ACCOUNTS
(million quetzales at constant 2001 prices)

Expenditure on the Gross Domestic Product

	2005	2006*	2007†
Government final consumption expenditure	13,812.7	14,642.0	15,718.2
Private final consumption expenditure	142,537.0	149,070.0	156,802.0
Increase in stocks	2,462.8	1,254.6	−231.8
Gross fixed capital formation	29,356.7	34,271.8	37,329.0
Statistical discrepancy	10.9	124.2	86.3
Total domestic expenditure	188,180.1	199,362.6	209,703.7
Exports of goods and services	44,001.9	46,007.7	50,963.7
Less Imports of goods and services	65,460.0	69,934.4	75,151.6
GDP in purchasers' values	166,722.0	175,435.9	185,515.8

* Preliminary figures.
† Estimates.

GUATEMALA

Gross Domestic Product by Economic Activity

	2005	2006*	2007†
Agriculture, hunting, forestry and fishing	23,547.6	23,821.7	24,637.0
Mining and quarrying	967.9	1,138.6	1,241.5
Manufacturing	32,260.3	33,274.7	34,358.3
Electricity, gas and water	4,453.7	4,582.6	4,821.1
Construction	6,133.7	6,935.2	7,774.2
Trade, restaurants and hotels	20,858.5	21,640.9	22,520.8
Transport, storage and communications	11,932.4	14,155.2	16,809.7
Finance, insurance and real estate	5,825.9	6,781.9	7,869.2
Ownership of dwellings	17,413.6	17,875.6	18,577.9
General government services	10,725.6	11,294.0	11,775.2
Other community, social and personal services	25,477.5	26,833.3	28,274.4
Statistical discrepancy	−639.3	−595.8	−777.0
Sub-total	158,957.4	167,737.9	177,882.3
Less Financial intermediation services indirectly measured (FISIM)	5,069.5	5,845.1	6,714.6
Gross value added in basic prices	153,887.9	161,892.8	171,167.7
Taxes on imports, less subsidies	12,834.1	13,543.1	14,348.1
GDP in purchasers' values	166,722.0	175,435.9	185,515.8

* Preliminary figures.
† Estimates.

BALANCE OF PAYMENTS
(US $ million)

	2004	2005	2006
Exports of goods f.o.b.	3,367.6	5,380.9	6,025.2
Imports of goods f.o.b.	−7,175.3	−9,754.9	−11,068.7
Trade balance	−3,807.7	−4,374.0	−5,043.6
Exports of services	1,178.1	1,229.9	1,394.6
Imports of services	−1,307.7	−1,478.6	−1,681.5
Balance on goods and services	−3,937.2	−4,622.7	−5,330.5
Other income received	173.3	252.6	355.3
Other income paid	−491.5	−584.5	−734.0
Balance on goods, services and income	−4,255.4	−4,954.6	−5,709.2
Current transfers received	3,087.5	3,569.8	4,181.8
Current transfers paid	−42.9	−47.2	−64.7
Current balance	−1,210.8	−1,432.0	−1,592.1
Capital account (net)	135.3	113.1	259.3
Direct investment from abroad	154.7	226.7	353.8
Portfolio investment assets	111.1	—	—
Portfolio investment liabilities	349.1	−0.2	1,714.9
Other investment assets	252.0	328.4	308.6
Other investment liabilities	842.3	932.1	−678.0
Net errors and omissions	−25.3	87.0	−88.0
Overall balance	608.3	255.0	278.5

Source: IMF, *International Financial Statistics*.

External Trade

PRINCIPAL COMMODITIES
(US $ million)

Imports c.i.f.	2005	2006	2007
Live animals	207.9	202.1	235.4
Vegetables	340.6	394.3	507.4
Mineral products	1,673.0	1,958.6	2,512.8
Chemicals and related products	1,287.6	1,405.6	1,582.3
Plastic, rubber and related products	708.0	809.8	904.2
Wood, paper and related products	468.1	538.8	591.0
Textiles and related products	1,423.5	1,404.5	1,321.1
Metal and related products	704.8	829.4	974.2
Audiovisual machinery and equipment	1,607.8	2,018.2	2,306.3
Transport equipment	848.0	989.1	1,049.1
Equipment and precision instruments for optometry, photography, surgery and watchmaking, etc.	118.1	134.9	147.4
Total (incl. others)	10,498.8	11,914.5	13,578.1

Exports f.o.b.	2005	2006	2007
Coffee	464.1	464.0	577.6
Sugar	236.6	298.6	358.1
Bananas	238.1	216.8	312.5
Petroleum	225.1	233.2	249.1
Chemical and pharmaceutical products	217.5	212.8	242.3
Natural rubber	12.9	14.5	12.3
Cardamom	464.1	464.0	577.6
Flowers and plants	25.3	25.1	27.2
Fabrics and yarns	20.7	24.7	37.5
Manufactures of wood	12.3	20.3	15.1
Total (incl. others)	5,380.9	6,012.8	6,925.7

PRINCIPAL TRADING PARTNERS
(US $ million)

Imports c.i.f.	2006	2007
Argentina	207.4	215.1
Brazil	391.0	309.1
Canada	146.0	134.5
Chile	165.8	282.1
China, People's Republic	594.3	778.0
Colombia	196.3	214.8
Costa Rica	372.0	405.9
Ecuador	148.9	190.1
El Salvador	544.8	620.8
Germany	200.3	236.9
Honduras	183.3	279.7
Hong Kong	196.6	144.2
Italy	116.7	154.0
Japan	316.7	395.6
Korea, Republic	579.4	444.2
Mexico	950.8	1,184.2
Netherlands Antilles	222.0	448.6
Panama	401.5	400.2
Puerto Rico	125.0	88.0
Spain	140.0	162.7
Taiwan	141.5	126.9
USA	4,115.1	4,642.7
Total (incl. others)	11,914.5	13,578.1

GUATEMALA

Exports f.o.b.	2005	2006	2007
Canada	73.3	99.6	111.3
Costa Rica	205.2	227.8	257.8
Dominican Republic	49.1	78.5	92.0
El Salvador	653.0	699.6	842.1
Germany	73.8	75.1	85.6
Honduras	394.0	481.6	593.5
Korea, Republic	8.4	84.2	74.8
Mexico	215.8	354.4	464.0
Netherlands	47.4	87.3	69.5
Nicaragua	213.2	235.3	267.6
Panama	80.5	98.2	119.6
Switzerland	80.6	68.4	33.2
USA	2,686.4	2,783.2	2,932.4
Total (incl. others)	5,380.8	6,012.8	6,925.7

Transport

RAILWAYS
(traffic)

	1994	1995	1996
Passenger-km (million)	991	0	0
Freight ton-km (million)	25,295	14,242	836

Source: UN, *Statistical Yearbook*.

ROAD TRAFFIC
(motor vehicles in use at 31 December)

	1997	1998	1999
Passenger cars	470,016	508,868	578,733
Buses and coaches	9,843	10,250	11,017
Lorries and vans	34,220	37,057	42,219
Motorcycles and mopeds	111,358	117,536	129,664

Source: IRF, *World Road Statistics*.

SHIPPING

Merchant Fleet
(registered at 31 December)

	2004	2005	2006
Number of vessels	10	10	10
Total displacement ('000 grt)	5.5	5.5	5.5

Source: Lloyd's Register-Fairplay, *World Fleet Statistics*.

International Sea-borne Freight Traffic
('000 metric tons)

	1992	1993	1994
Goods loaded	2,176	1,818	2,096
Goods unloaded	3,201	3,025	3,822

CIVIL AVIATION
(traffic on scheduled services)

	1997	1998	1999
Kilometres flown (million)	5	7	5
Passengers carried ('000)	508	794	506
Passenger-km (million)	368	480	342
Total ton-km (million)	77	50	33

Source: UN, *Statistical Yearbook*.

Tourism

TOURIST ARRIVALS BY COUNTRY OF ORIGIN

	2003	2004	2005
Canada	27,048	20,510	24,820
Costa Rica	29,529	31,979	34,693
El Salvador	209,745	411,277	497,430
France	18,433	20,793	19,219
Germany	27,734	21,786	18,258
Honduras	64,242	93,975	106,473
Italy	17,272	17,708	16,467
Mexico	70,732	67,502	72,908
Nicaragua	29,815	42,876	46,936
Spain	24,869	22,824	21,182
USA	209,247	267,126	286,871
Total (incl. others)	880,223	1,181,526	1,315,646

Tourism receipts (US $ million, incl. passenger transport): 646 in 2003; 806 in 2004; 883 in 2005.

Source: World Tourism Organization.

Communications Media

	2004	2005	2006
Telephones ('000 main lines in use)	1,132	1,248.2	1,354.9
Mobile cellular telephones ('000 subscribers)	3,168	4,510.1	7,178.7
Personal computers ('000 in use)	231	231	n.a.
Internet users ('000)	760	1,000	1,320.0
Broadband subscribers ('000)	n.a.	27.1	n.a.

Source: International Telecommunication Union.

Radio receivers ('000 in use): 835 in 1997.

Television receivers ('000 in use): 680 in 1999 (Source: UN, *Statistical Yearbook*).

Daily newspapers (number): 7 in 1996.

Facsimile machines (number in use): 10,000 in 1996.

Education

(2004/05, unless otherwise indicated)

	Institutions	Teachers	Students
Pre-primary	10,424*	17,371	415,445
Primary	16,609	75,519	2,345,301
Secondary	3,585	47,904	754,496
Tertiary	1,946	4,147†	114,764†

*2000 data.
†2002/03 data.

Source: mainly UNESCO Institute for Statistics.

Adult literacy rate (UNESCO estimates): 69.1% (males 75.4%; females 63.3%) in 2002 (Source: UNESCO Institute for Statistics).

Directory

The Constitution

In December 1984 the Constituent Assembly drafted a new Constitution (based on that of 1965), which was approved in May 1985 and came into effect in January 1986. A series of amendments to the Constitution were approved by referendum in January 1994 and came into effect in April 1994. The Constitution's main provisions are summarized below:

Guatemala has a republican representative democratic system of government and power is exercised equally by the legislative, executive and judicial bodies. The official language is Spanish. Suffrage is universal and secret, obligatory for those who can read and write and optional for those who are illiterate. The free formation and growth of political parties whose aims are democratic is guaranteed. There is no discrimination on grounds of race, colour, sex, religion, birth, economic or social position or political opinions.

The State will give protection to capital and private enterprise in order to develop sources of labour and stimulate creative activity.

Monopolies are forbidden and the State will limit any enterprise which might prejudice the development of the community. The right to social security is recognized and it shall be on a national, unitary, obligatory basis.

Constitutional guarantees may be suspended in certain circumstances for up to 30 days (unlimited in the case of war).

CONGRESS

Legislative power rests with Congress, which is made up of 158 deputies, elected according to a combination of departmental and proportional representation. Congress meets on 15 January each year and ordinary sessions last four months; extraordinary sessions can be called by the Permanent Commission or the Executive. All Congressional decisions must be taken by absolute majority of the members, except in special cases laid down by law. Deputies are elected for four years; they may be re-elected after a lapse of one session, but only once. Congress is responsible for all matters concerning the President and Vice-President and their execution of their offices; for all electoral matters; for all matters concerning the laws of the Republic; for approving the budget and decreeing taxes; for declaring war; for conferring honours, both civil and military; for fixing the coinage and the system of weights and measures; for approving, by two-thirds' majority, any international treaty or agreement affecting the law, sovereignty, financial status or security of the country.

PRESIDENT

The President is elected by universal suffrage, by absolute majority for a non-extendable period of four years. Re-election or prolongation of the presidential term of office are punishable by law. The President is responsible for national defence and security, fulfilling the Constitution, leading the armed forces, taking any necessary steps in time of national emergency, passing and executing laws, international policy, and nominating and removing Ministers, officials and diplomats. The Vice-President's duties include co-ordinating the actions of Ministers of State and taking part in the discussions of the Council of Ministers.

ARMY

The Guatemalan Army is intended to maintain national independence, sovereignty and honour and territorial integrity. It is an indivisible, apolitical, non-deliberating body and is made up of land, sea and air forces.

LOCAL ADMINISTRATIVE DIVISIONS

For the purposes of administration the territory of the Republic is divided into 22 Departments and these into 330 Municipalities, but this division can be modified by Congress to suit interests and general development of the Nation without loss of municipal autonomy. Municipal authorities are elected every four years.

JUDICIARY

Justice is exercised exclusively by the Supreme Court of Justice and other tribunals. Administration of Justice is obligatory, free and independent of the other functions of State. The President of the Judiciary, judges and other officials are elected by Congress for five years. The Supreme Court of Justice is made up of 13 judges. The President of the Judiciary is also President of the Supreme Court. The Supreme Court nominates all other judges. Under the Supreme Court come the Court of Appeal, the Administrative Disputes Tribunal, the Tribunal of Second Instance of Accounts, Jurisdiction Conflicts, First Instance and Military, the Extraordinary Tribunal of Protection. There is a Court of Constitutionality presided over by the President of the Supreme Court.

The Government

HEAD OF STATE

President: Alvaro Colom Caballeros (took office 14 January 2008).

Vice-President: Dr Rafael Espada.

CABINET
(March 2008)

Minister of Foreign Affairs: Roger Haroldo Rodas Melgar.

Minister of the Interior: Vinicio Gómez.

Minister of National Defence: Brig.-Gen. Marco Tulio García Franco.

Minister of Public Finance: Juan Alberto Fuentes Knight.

Minister of the Economy: (vacant).

Minister of Public Health and Social Welfare: Eusebio del Cid.

Minister of Communications, Infrastructure and Housing: Luis Alejandro Alejos Olivero.

Minister of Agriculture, Livestock and Food: Raúl Robles.

Minister of Education: Ana Ordóñez de Molina.

Minister of Employment and Social Security: Edgar Alfredo Rodríguez.

Minister of Energy and Mines: Carlos Meany.

Minister of Culture and Sport: Jerónimo Lancerio Chingo.

Minister of the Environment and Natural Resources: Luis Alberto Ferrate.

MINISTRIES

Ministry of Agriculture, Livestock and Food: Edif. Monja Blanca, 7a Avda 12-90, Zona 13, Guatemala City; tel. 2362-4756; fax 2332-8302; e-mail infroagro@maga.gob.gt; internet www.maga.gob.gt.

Ministry of Communications, Infrastructure and Housing: Edif. Antiguo Cocesna, 8a Avda y 15 Calle, Zona 13, Guatemala City; tel. 2362-6051; fax 2362-6059; e-mail relpublicas@micivi.gob.gt; internet www.civ.gob.gt.

Ministry of Culture and Sport: 12 Avda 11-11, Zona 1, Guatemala City; tel. 2253-0543; fax 2253-0540; internet www.mcd.gob.gt.

Ministry of the Economy: 8a Avda 10-43, Zona 1, Guatemala City; tel. 2238-3330; fax 2238-2413; e-mail einteriano@mineco.gob.gt; internet www.mineco.gob.gt.

Ministry of Education: 6a Calle 1-87, Zona 10, Guatemala City; tel. 2360-0911; fax 2361-0350; e-mail info@mineduc.gob.gt; internet www.mineduc.gob.gt.

Ministry of Employment and Social Security: Edif. Torre Empresarial, 7a Avda 3-33, Zona 9, Guatemala City; tel. 2352-0100; fax 2251-3559; e-mail ministro@mintrabajo.gob.gt; internet www.mintrabajo.gob.gt.

Ministry of Energy and Mines: Diagonal 17, 29-78, Zona 11, Guatemala City; tel. 2477-0743; fax 2476-8506; e-mail informatica@mem.gob.gt; internet www.mem.gob.gt.

Ministry of the Environment and Natural Resources: Edif. MARN, 20 Calle 28-58, Zona 10, Guatemala City; tel. 2423-0500; e-mail marnguatemala@marn.gob.gt; internet www.marn.gob.gt.

Ministry of Foreign Affairs: 2a Avda La Reforma 4-47, Zona 10, Guatemala City; tel. 2331-8410; fax 2331-8510; e-mail webmaster@minex.gob.gt; internet www.minex.gob.gt.

Ministry of the Interior: 6a Avda 13-71, Zona 1, Guatemala City; tel. 2413-8888; fax 2362-0020; internet www.mingob.gob.gt.

Ministry of National Defence: Antigua Escuela Politécnica, Avda La Reforma 1-45, Zona 10, Guatemala City; tel. 2360-9890; fax 2360-9909; internet www.mindef.mil.gt.

Ministry of Public Finance: Centro Cívico, 8a Avda y 21 Calle, Zona 1, Guatemala City; tel. 2248-5005; fax 2248-5054; e-mail info@minfin.gob.gt; internet www.minfin.gob.gt.

Ministry of Public Health and Social Welfare: Escuela de Enfermería, 3°, 6a Avda 3-45, Zona 1, Guatemala City; tel. 2475-2121; fax 2475-2168; e-mail info@mspas.gob.gt; internet www.mspas.gob.gt.

GUATEMALA

President and Legislature

PRESIDENT

Presidential Election, 9 September and 4 November 2007

Candidate	First round % of votes	Second round % of votes
Alvaro Colom Caballeros (UNE)	28.25	52.81
Gen. (retd) Otto Fernando Pérez Molina (PP)	23.54	47.19
Alejandro Eduardo Giammattei Falla (GANA)	17.23	—
José Eduardo Suger Cofiño (CASA)	7.45	—
Luis Armando Rabbe Tejada (FRG)	7.30	—
Mario Amilcar Estrada Orellana (UCN)	3.16	—
Rigoberta Menchu Tum (EG)	3.06	—
Total valid votes (incl. others)	100.00	100.00

CONGRESO DE LA REPÚBLICA

President: Arturo Eduardo Meyer Maldonado.
Vice-Presidents: Aristides Baldomero Meyer Maldonado, Ferdy Noel Berganza Bojórquez, Pablo Manuel Duarte Sáenz de Tejada.

General Election, 9 September 2007

	% of votes	Seats
Unidad Nacional de la Esperanza	22.84	50
Gran Alianza Nacional	16.54	36
Partido Patriota	15.66	29
Frente Republicano Guatemalteco	9.71	15
Partido Unionista	6.10	8
Centro de Acción Social	4.88	5
Unión del Cambio Nacionalista	4.06	5
Encuentro por Guatemala	6.18	3
Partido de Avanzada Nacional	4.54	3
Unidad Revolucionaria Nacional Guatemalteca—Movimiento Amplio de Izquierdas	3.56	3
Unión Democrática	1.41	1
Total valid votes (incl. others)	100.00	158

Election Commission

Tribunal Supremo Electoral: 6a Avda 0-32, Zona 2, Guatemala City; tel. 2232-0382; e-mail tse@tse.org.gt; internet www.tse.org.gt; f. 1983; independent; Pres. Oscar Edmundo Bolaños Parada.

Political Organizations

Alianza Nueva Nación (ANN): 15 Avda 5-60, Zona 1, Guatemala City; tel. 2251-2514; e-mail corriente@intelnet.net.gt; Leader Pablo Monsanto; Sec.-Gen. Alfonso Bauer Paz.

Bienestar Nacional (BIEN): 8a Avda 6-30, Zona 2, Guatemala City; tel. 524-1448; internet www.bienestarnacional.org; Sec.-Gen. Fidel Reyes Lee.

Centro de Acción Social (CASA): Guatemala City; f. 2003; Leader José Eduardo Suger Cofiño.

Democracia Cristiana Guatemalteca (DCG): Avda Elena 20-66, Zona 3, Guatemala City; tel. 2238-4988; fax 2337-0966; e-mail vcerezo@congreso.go.gt; internet www.dgt.org.gt; f. 1955; Sec.-Gen. Marco Vinicio Cerezo Blandón.

Desarrollo Integral Auténtico (DIA): 12a Calle 'A' 2-18, Zona 1, Guatemala City; tel. and fax 2232-8044; e-mail morlain@guate.net; f. 1998; left-wing party; Sec.-Gen. Jorge Luis Ortega Torres.

Encuentro por Guatemala (EG): Edif. Tecún, 6°, 11 Calle 8-14, Zona 1, Guatemala City; tel. 2251-4780; fax 2230-6463; internet www.encuentroporguatemala.org.gt; f. 2006; centre-left; promotes indigenous interests; Sec.-Gen. Nineth Verenca Montenegro Cottom.

Frente Republicano Guatemalteco (FRG): 3a Calle 5-50, Zona 1, Guatemala City; tel. 2238-0826; internet www.frg.org.gt; f. 1988; right-wing group; Sec.-Gen. Gen. (retd) José Efraín Ríos Montt.

Gran Alianza Nacional (GANA): 7a Avda, 10-40, Zona 9, Guatemala City; tel. 2331-0121; fax 2331-0144; f. 2003 as electoral alliance of PP, MR and PSN; registered as a party in 2005 following withdrawal of PP; split into two factions in Jan. 2008, led by Alfredo Vila and Jaime Martínez, respectively; Sec.-Gen. Alfredo Vila.

Movimiento Reformador (MR): Vía 6, 4-09, Zona 4, Guatemala City; tel. 2360-0745; e-mail ruben@itelgua.com; f. 1995 as the Partido Laborista Guatemalteco; adopted present name in 2002; did not contest the 2007 elections; Sec.-Gen. Alfredo Skinner Klee Arenales.

Partido de Avanzada Nacional (PAN): 7a Avda 10-38, Zona 9, Guatemala City; tel. 2334-1702; fax 2331-9906; Leader Alvaro Enrique Arzú Yrigoyen; Sec.-Gen. Leonel Eliseo López Rodas.

Partido Patriota (PP): 11 Calle 11-54, Zona 1, Guatemala City; tel. 2230-6227; e-mail comunicacion@partidopatriota.org; internet www.partidopatriota.org; f. 2002; contested 2003 elections as part of GANA (q.v.); withdrew from GANA in May 2004; right-wing; Sec.-Gen. Gen. (retd) Otto Fernando Pérez Molina.

Partido Unionista (PU): 3a Avda 'A' 14-23, Zona 9, Guatemala City; tel. 2331-7468; fax 2331-6141; e-mail info@unionista.org; internet www.unionistas.org; f. 1917; Sec.-Gen. Fritz García-Gallont.

Unidad Nacional de la Esperanza (UNE): 2a Avda 5-11, Zona 9, Guatemala City; tel. 2232-4685; e-mail ideas@une.org.gt; internet www.une.org.gt; f. 2001 following a split within the PAN; centre-left; Founder and Pres. Alvaro Colom Caballeros.

Unidad Revolucionaria Nacional Guatemalteca—Movimiento Amplio de Izquierdas (URNG—MAIZ): Avda Simeón Cañas 8-01, Zona 2, Guatemala City; tel. 2288-4440; fax 2254-0572; e-mail prensaurng@guate.net; internet www.urng-maiz.com; f. 1982 following unification of principal guerrilla groups engaged in the civil war; formally registered as a political party in 1998, following the end of the civil war in Dec. 1996; Sec.-Gen. Alba Estela Maldonado Guevara.

Unión del Cambio Nacionalista (UCN): Guatemala City; e-mail administracion.ucn@gmail.com; internet www.ucnguatemala.com; f. 2006; Sec.-Gen. Sidney Shaw Arrivillaga.

Unión Democrática (UD): Vista Hermosa II, Of. E, 3°, 1a Calle 18-83, Zona 15, 01015 Guatemala City; tel. 2369-7074; fax 2369-3062; e-mail info@uniondemocratica.info; internet www.uniondemocratica.info; f. 1983; Sec.-Gen. Manuel Eduardo Conde Orellana.

Los Verdes (LV): Vista Hermosa II, 1a Calle 22-08, Zona 15, Guatemala City; Sec.-Gen. Rodolfo Rosales García Salas.

Diplomatic Representation

EMBASSIES IN GUATEMALA

Argentina: Edif. Europlaza 1703, 5 Avda 5-55, Zona 14, Apdo 120, Guatemala City; tel. and fax 2385-3786; e-mail embajadadeargentina@hotmail.com; Ambassador Aníbal Gabriel Gutiérrez.

Belize: Edif. El Reformador, Suite 803, 8°, Avda de la Reforma 1-50, Zona 9, Guatemala City; tel. 2334-5531; fax 2334-5536; e-mail info@embajadadebelize.org; internet www.embajadadebelize.org; Ambassador Alfredo Martín Martínez.

Brazil: 18a Calle 2-22, Zona 14, Apdo 196-A, Guatemala City; tel. 2337-0949; fax 2337-3475; e-mail braembx@intelnet.net.gt; internet www.embajadadebrasil.com.gt; Ambassador Renan Paes Barreto.

Canada: Edif. Edyma Plaza, 8°, 13a Calle 8-44, Zona 10, Apdo 400, Guatemala City; tel. 2363-4348; fax 2365-1210; e-mail gtmla@international.gc.ca; internet www.guatemala.gc.ca; Ambassador Kenneth M. Cook.

Chile: 14 Calle 15-21, Zona 13, Guatemala City; tel. 2334-8273; fax 2334-8276; e-mail echilegu@intelnet.net.gt; Ambassador Jorge Mario Saavedra Canales.

China (Taiwan): 4a Avda 'A' 13-25, Zona 9, Apdo 1646, Guatemala City; tel. 2339-0711; fax 2332-2668; e-mail echina@intelnet.net.gt; Ambassador Hong-lien Ou.

Colombia: Edif. Europlaza 1603, 5a Avda 5-55, Zona 14, Guatemala City; tel. 2385-3432; fax 2335-3603; e-mail eguatemala@minrelext.gov.co; Ambassador Eduardo López Sabogal.

Costa Rica: 15 Calle 5-59, Zona 10, Guatemala City; tel. 2366-9918; fax 2368-0705; e-mail embarica@intelnet.net.gt; Ambassador Lidiette Brenes Arguedas.

Cuba: Avda las Américas 20-72, Zona 13, Guatemala City; tel. 2332-4066; fax 2332-5525; e-mail embagua@intelnet.net.gt; Ambassador Omar Morales Bazo.

Dominican Republic: Edif. Géminis 10, Suite 804, Torre Sur, 12 Calle 1-25, Zona 10, Guatemala City; tel. 2338-2170; fax 2338-2171; e-mail embardom@intelnet.net.gt; Ambassador Teresa Migdalia Torres García.

Ecuador: 4 Avda 12-04, Zona 14, Guatemala City; tel. 2337-2994; fax 2368-1831; e-mail embecuad@guate.net; Ambassador Roberto Ponce Alvaredo.

GUATEMALA

Directory

Egypt: Edif. Cobella, 5°, 5 Avda 10-84, Zona 14, Apdo 502, Guatemala City; tel. 2333-6296; fax 2368-2808; e-mail egyptemb@gold.guate.net.gt; Ambassador MAHER IBRAHIM YOUSSEF BADAR.

El Salvador: Avda las Américas 16-40, Zona 13, Guatemala City; tel. 2360-7660; fax 2334-2069; e-mail emsalva@intelnet.net.gt; Ambassador Gen. (retd) JUAN ANTONIO MARTÍNEZ VARELA.

France: Edif. COGEFAR, 5a Avda 8-59, Zona 14, Apdo 971-A, 01014 Guatemala City; tel. 2421-7370; fax 2421-7409; e-mail ambfrguate@intelnet.net.gt; internet www.ambafrance.org.gt; Ambassador NORBERT CARRASCO-SAULNIER.

Germany: Edif. Plaza Marítima, 2°, 20 Calle 6-20, Zona 10, Guatemala City; tel. 2364-6700; fax 2333-6906; e-mail embalemana@intelnet.net.gt; internet www.guatemala.diplo.de; Ambassador PETER LINDER.

Holy See: 10a Calle 4-47, Zona 9, Apdo 22, Guatemala City (Apostolic Nunciature); tel. 2332-4274; fax 2334-1918; e-mail nuntius@c.net.gt; Apostolic Nuncio Most Rev. BRUNO MUSARÒ (Titular Archbishop of Abari).

Honduras: 19 Avda 'A', 20-19, Zona 10, Guatemala City; tel. 2366-5640; fax 2368-0062; e-mail embhond@intelnet.net.gt; Ambassador BESSY ROSSANA VALENZUELA ULLOA DE FUENTES.

Israel: 13a Avda 14-07, Zona 10, Guatemala City; tel. 2333-4624; fax 2333-6950; e-mail info@guatemala.mfa.gov.il; Ambassador ISAAC BACHMAN.

Italy: 12 Calle 6-49, Zona 14, Guatemala City; tel. 2337-4557; fax 2337-0795; e-mail ambasciata.guatemala@esteri.it; internet www.ambguatemala.esteri.it; Ambassador PIO LUIGI TEODORANI FABBRI POZZO.

Japan: Edif. Torre Internacional, 10°, Avda de la Reforma 16-85, Zona 10, Guatemala City; tel. 2367-2244; fax 2367-2245; e-mail embjpn@intelnet.net.gt; internet www.gt.emb-japan.go.jp; Ambassador KAZUMI SUZUKI.

Korea, Republic of: Edif. El Reformador, 7°, Avda de la Reforma 1-50, Zona 9, Apdo 1649, Guatemala City; tel. 2334-5480; fax 2334-5481; e-mail korembsy@mofat.go.kr; internet gtm.mofat.go.kr; Ambassador YU JI-EUN.

Mexico: 2a Avda 7-57, Zona 10, Apdo 1455, Guatemala City; tel. 2420-3400; fax 2420-3410; e-mail embamexguat@itelgua.com; internet www.sre.gob.mx/guatemala; Ambassador EDUARDO IBARROLA NICOLÍN.

Netherlands: Edif. Torre Internacional, 13°, 16 Calle 0-55, Zona 10, Guatemala City; tel. 2381-4300; fax 2381-4350; e-mail nlgovgua@intelnet.net.gt; internet www.embajadadeholanda-gua.org; Ambassador TEUNIS KAMPER.

Nicaragua: 10a Avda 14-72, Zona 10, Guatemala City; tel. 2368-0785; fax 2337-4264; e-mail embaguat@terra.com.gt; Ambassador SILVIO MORA MORA.

Norway: Edif. Murano Center, 15°, Of. 1501, 14 Calle 3-51, Zona 10, Apdo 1764, Guatemala City; tel. 2366-5908; fax 2366-5928; e-mail ambgua@norad.no; internet www.noruega.org.gt; Chargé d'affaires a.i. TOM TYRIHJELL.

Panama: 12 Calle 2-65, Zona 14, Apdo 929A, Guatemala City; tel. 2366-3331; fax 2366-3338; e-mail panguate@hotmail.com; Ambassador CELSO GUSTAVO CARRIZO.

Peru: 5a Avda 13-46, Zona 9, Guatemala City; tel. 2331-8558; fax 2334-3744; e-mail leprugua@concyt.gob.gt; internet www.embajadaperu-guatemala.org; Ambassador ALFREDO JOSÉ CASTRO PÉREZ-CANETTO.

Russia: 2 Avenida 12-85, Zona 14, Guatemala City; tel. 2367-2765; fax 2367-2766; e-mail embrusa@guate.net.gt; internet www.guat.mid.ru; Ambassador VALERY NIKOLAENKO (resident in San José, Costa Rica).

Spain: 6a Calle 6-48, Zona 9, Guatemala City; tel. 2379-3530; fax 2379-3533; e-mail emb.guatemala@mae.es; internet www.mae.es/embajadas/guatemala; Ambassador JUAN LÓPEZ-DORIGA PÉREZ.

Sweden: 8a Avda 15-07, Zona 10, Guatemala City; tel. 2384-7300; fax 2384-7350; e-mail ambassaden.guatemala@foreign.ministry.se; internet www.swedenabroad.com/guatemala; Ambassador EWA WERNER DAHLIN.

Switzerland: Edif. Torre Internacional, 14°, 16 Calle 0-55, Zona 10, Apdo 1426, Guatemala City; tel. 2367-5520; fax 2367-5811; e-mail vertretung@gua.rep.admin.ch; Ambassador JEAN-PIERRE VILLARD.

United Kingdom: Edif. Torre Internacional, 11°, Avda de la Reforma, 16 Calle, Zona 10, Guatemala City; tel. 2367-5425; fax 2367-5430; e-mail embassy@intelnett.com; Ambassador IAN N. HUGHES.

USA: Avda de la Reforma 7-01, Zona 10, Guatemala City; tel. 2331-1541; fax 2331-8885; internet guatemala.usembassy.gov; Ambassador STEPHEN MCFARLAND (designate).

Uruguay: Edif. Plaza Marítima, 3°, Of. 341, 6a Avda 20-25, Zona 10, Guatemala City; tel. 2368-0810; fax 2333-7553; e-mail uruguate@guate.net; Ambassador ESTELLA RUBY ARMAND-UGON SEPÚLVEDA.

Venezuela: Edif. Atlantis, Of. 601, 13 Calle 3-40, Zona 10, Apdo 152, Guatemala City; tel. 2366-9832; fax 2366-9838; e-mail embavene@concyt.gob.gt; Ambassador JENY FIGUEREDO FRÍAS.

Judicial System

Corte Suprema

Centro Cívico, 21 Calle 7-70, Zona 1, Guatemala City; internet www.oj.gob.gt.

The members of the Supreme Court are appointed by the Congress.

President of the Supreme Court: OSCAR HUMBERTO VÁSQUEZ OLIVA.

Members: R. E. HIGUEROS GIRÓN, L. FERNÁNDEZ MOLINA, A. E. LÓPEZ RODRÍGUEZ, B. O. DE LEÓN REYES, C. G. CHACÓN TORREBIARTE, E. R. PACAY YALIBAT, J. G. CABRERA HURTARTE, Dr V. M. RIVERA WÖLTKE, L. S. SECAIRA PINTO, C. E. DE LEÓN CÓRDOVA, R. DE LEÓN MOLINA, J. F. DE MATA VELA.

Civil Courts of Appeal: 20 courts, located in Guatemala City, Quetzaltenango, Jalapa, Zacapa, Antigua Guatemala, Retalhuleu, Cobán and Mazatenango.

Courts of the First Instance: 10 civil and 12 penal in Guatemala City, and at least one civil and one penal in each of the 21 remaining Departments of the Republic.

Religion

Almost all of the inhabitants profess Christianity, with a majority belonging to the Roman Catholic Church. In recent years the Protestant churches have attracted a growing number of converts.

CHRISTIANITY

The Roman Catholic Church

For ecclesiastical purposes, Guatemala comprises two archdioceses, 10 dioceses and the Apostolic Vicariates of El Petén and Izabal. At 31 December 2005 adherents represented about 78% of the total population.

Bishops' Conference

Conferencia Episcopal de Guatemala, Secretariado General del Episcopado, Km 15, Calzada Roosevelt 4-54, Zona 7, Mixco, Apdo 1698, Guatemala City; tel. 2433-1832; fax 2433-1834; e-mail ceg@quetzal.net; internet www.iglesiacatolica.org.gt.

f. 1973; Pres. Rev. ALVARO RAMAZZINI IMERI (Bishop of San Marcos).

Archbishop of Guatemala City: Cardinal RODOLFO QUEZADA TORUÑO, Arzobispado, 7a Avda 6-21, Zona 1, Apdo 723, Guatemala City; tel. 2232-9707; fax 2251-5068; e-mail curiaarzobispal@intelnet.net.gt.

Archbishop of Los Altos, Quetzaltenango-Totonicapán: OSCAR JULIO VIAN MORALES, Arzobispado, 11a Avda 6-27, Zona 1, Apdo 11, 09001 Quetzaltenango; tel. 7761-2840; fax 7761-6049.

The Anglican Communion

Guatemala comprises one of the five dioceses of the Iglesia Anglicana de la Región Central de América.

Bishop of Guatemala: Rt Rev. ARMANDO ROMÁN GUERRA SORIA, Avda Castellana 40-06, Zona 8, Apdo 58-A, Guatemala City; tel. 2473-6828; fax 2472-0764; e-mail diocesis@infovia.com.gt; diocese founded 1967.

Protestant Churches

The largest Protestant denomination in Guatemala is the Full Gospel Church, followed by the Assembly of God, the Central American Church, and the Prince of Peace Church. The Baptist, Presbyterian, Lutheran and Episcopalian churches are also represented.

The Baptist Church: Convention of Baptist Churches of Guatemala, 12a Calle 9-54, Zona 1, Apdo 322, 01901 Guatemala City; tel. and fax 2232-4227; e-mail cibg@intelnet.net.gt; f. 1946; Pres. JOSÉ MARROQUÍN R.; 43,876 mems.

Church of Jesus Christ of Latter-day Saints: 12a Calle 3-37, Zona 9, Guatemala City; e-mail contactos@mormones.org.gt; internet www.mormones.org.gt; 17 bishoprics, nine chapels; Pres. GORDON B. HINCKLEY.

Conferencia de Iglesias Evangélicas de Guatemala (CIEDEG) (Conference of Protestant Churches in Guatemala): 7a Avda 1-11, Zona 2, Guatemala City; tel. 2232-3724; fax 2232-1609; Pres. VITALINO SIMILOX.

GUATEMALA

Congregación Luterana La Epifanía (Evangelical Lutheran Congregation La Epifanía): 2a Avda 15-31, Zona 10, Apdo 651, 01010 Guatemala City; tel. 2368-0301; fax 2366-4968; e-mail schweikle@web.de; mem. of Lutheran World Federation; Pres. MÓNICA HEGEL; 200 mems.

Divine Saviour Lutheran Church: Zacapa; tel. 7941-0254; e-mail hogarluterano@hotmail.com; f. 1946; Pastor GERARDO VENANCIO VÁSQUEZ SALGUERO.

Iglesia Nacional Evangélica Menonita Guatemalteca: Guatemala City; tel. 2339-0606; e-mail AlvaradoJE@ldschurch.org; Contact JULIO ALVARADO; 6,673 mems (2003).

Iglesia Evangélica Nacional Presbiteriana de Guatemala: Avda Simeón Cañas 7-13, Zona 2, Apdo 655, Guatemala City; tel. 2288-4441; fax 2254-1242; e-mail ienpg@yahoo.com; f. 1962; mem. of World Alliance of Reformed Churches; Sec. Pastor IVAN HAROLDO PAZ ANDRADE; 25,000 mems.

Union Church: 12 Calle 7-37, Zona 9, 01009 Guatemala City; tel. 2361-2037; fax 2362-3961; e-mail unionchurch@guate.net.gt; internet www.unionchurchguatemala.org; f. 1943; English-speaking church; Pastor DAVID GINTER.

The Press

PRINCIPAL DAILIES

Al Día: Avda de la Reforma 6-64, Zona 9, Guatemala City; tel. 2339-7430; fax 2339-7435; e-mail aldia@notinet.com.gt; f. 1996; Pres. LIONEL TORIELLO NÁJERA; Dir GERARDO JIMÉNEZ ARDÓN; Editor OTONIEL MONROY HERNÁNDEZ.

Diario de Centroamérica: 18a Calle 6-72, Zona 1, Guatemala City; tel. 2222-4418; internet www.diariodecentroamerica.gob.gt; f. 1880; morning; official; circ. 15,000.

Guía Interamericana de Turismo: Edif. Plaza los Arcos, 3°, 20 Calle 5-35, Zona 10, Guatemala City; e-mail info@guiainter.com; monthly; Dir-Gen. LORELIA OREANI; Editor ALFREDO MAYORGA; circ. 5,000.

La Hora: 9a Calle 'A' 1-56, Zona 1, Apdo 1593, Guatemala City; tel. 2250-0447; fax 2251-7084; e-mail lahora@lahora.com.gt; internet www.lahora.com.gt; f. 1920; evening; independent; Dir ÓSCAR CLEMENTE MARROQUÍN; Editor ESWIN QUIÑONEZ FLORIÁN; circ. 18,000.

Nuestro Diario: 15 Avda 24-51, Zona 13, Guatemala City; tel. and fax 2361-6988; e-mail opinion@nuestrodiario.com.gt; internet www.nuestrodiario.com.gt; Dir RODOLFO MÓBIL.

El Periódico: 15a Avda 24-51, Zona 13, Guatemala City; tel. 2362-0242; fax 2332-9761; e-mail redaccion@elperiodico.com.gt; internet www.elperiodico.com.gt; f. 1996; morning; independent; Pres. JOSÉ RUBÉN ZAMORA; Editors JUAN LUIS FONT, SYLVIA GEREDA; circ. 50,000.

Prensa Libre: 13a Calle 9-31, Zona 1, Apdo 2063, Guatemala City; tel. 2230-5096; fax 2251-8768; e-mail nacional@prensalibre.com.gt; internet www.prensalibre.com.gt; f. 1951; morning; independent; Gen. Man. ENRIQUE SOLORZANO MOLINA; Editor GONZALO MARROQUÍN GODOY; circ. 120,000.

Siglo Veintiuno: 7a Avda 11-63, Zona 9, Guatemala City; tel. 2360-6724; fax 2331-9145; e-mail buzon21@sigloxxi.com; internet www.sigloxxi.com; f. 1990; morning; Dir GUILLERMO FERNÁNDEZ; Gen. Man. LUCIANA CISNEROS; circ. 65,000.

PERIODICALS

Amiga: 13 Calle 9-31, Zona 1, Guatemala City; e-mail revistas@prensalibre.com.gt; internet www.amigaonline-pl.com; health; Dir CAROLINA VÁSQUEZ ARAYA.

Control TV: 13 Calle 9-31, Zona 1, Guatemala City; e-mail revistas@prensalibre.com.gt; Dir CAROLINA VÁSQUEZ.

Crónica Semanal: Guatemala City; tel. 2235-2155; fax 2235-2360; f. 1988; weekly; politics, economics, culture; Publr FRANCISCO PÉREZ.

Especiales: Edif. El Gráfico, 14 Avda 4-33, Zona 1, Guatemala City; e-mail moneda@guate.net; international news magazine; Dir KATIA DE CARPIO.

Gerencia: La Asociación de Gerentes de Guatemala, 6 Avda 1-36, Zona 14, 01014 Guatemala City; tel. 2427-4900; fax 2367-5006; e-mail agg@guate.net; f. 1967; monthly; official organ of the Association of Guatemalan Managers.

Guatemala Business News: 10a Calle 3-80, Zona 1, Guatemala City; monthly; Editor RODOLFO GARCÍA; circ. 5,000.

Inforpress Centroamericana: Guatemala City; fax 2232-9034; e-mail inforpre@inforpressca.com; internet www.inforpressca.com; f. 1972; weekly; Spanish and English; regional political and economic news and analysis; Dir ARIEL DE LEÓN.

Magazine Business Guatemala: 6a Avda 14-77, Zona 10, Guatemala City; consumer magazine.

El Metropolitano: Plaza Morumbi 7 y 8, 2°, 3a Calle 15-29, Zona 8, San Cristóbal, Guatemala City; e-mail info@elmetropolitano.net; internet www.elmetropolitano.net; Editor JORGE GARCÍA MONTENEGRO.

Mundo Motor: 13 Calle 9-31, Zona 1, Guatemala City; e-mail evasquez@prensalibre.com.gt; Dir CAROLINA VÁSQUEZ; Editor NÉSTOR A. LARRAZÁBAL B.

Revista D: 13 Calle 9-31, Zona 1, Guatemala City; e-mail revistas@prensalibre.com.gt; internet www.prensalibre.com/pl/domingo/index.shtml; weekly; general interest; Dir CAROLINA VÁSQUEZ; Editor GERARDO JIMÉNEZ.

Revista Data Export: Edif. Camara de Industria, 5°, 6a Ruta 9-21, Zona 4, Guatemala; monthly; Editor REGINA CEREZO; circ. 1,500.

Revista Industria: 6a Ruta 9-21, Zona 4, Guatemala City; tel. 2331-9191; fax 2334-1091; e-mail contactemos@industriaguate.com; internet www.industriguate.com; monthly; official organ of the Chamber of Industry; Dir OSCAR VILLAGRÁN.

Revista Mundo Comercial: 10a Calle 3-80, Zona 1, 01001 Guatemala City; e-mail mundo@guatemala-chamber.org; internet www.guatemala-chamber.org; monthly; business; official organ of the Chamber of Commerce; circ. 11,000.

Tertulia: Guatemala City; e-mail tertulia@intelnett.com; internet www.la-tertulia.net; f. 1997; women's affairs; Editor LAURA E. ASTURIAS.

Usuario: 13 Calle 9-31, Zona 1, Guatemala City; e-mail revistas@prensalibre.com.gt; computing; Dir CAROLINA VÁSQUEZ.

Viajes: 13 Calle 9-31, Zona 1, Guatemala City; e-mail revistas@prensalibre.com.gt; tourism; Dir CAROLINA VÁSQUEZ.

Vida Médica: Edif. Reforma Montúfar, Torre A, Of. 1006, Avda Reforma 12-01, Zona 10, Guatemala City; tel. 2331-7679; fax 2331-7754; e-mail vidamed@infovia.com.gt; internet www.infovia.com.gt/vidamedica; health; Dir SERAPIO ALVARADO; Editorial Dir Dr CARLOS SALAZAR.

PRESS ASSOCIATIONS

Asociación de Periodistas de Guatemala (APG): 14a Calle 3-29, Zona 1, Guatemala City; tel. 2232-1813; fax 2238-2781; e-mail apege@intelnet.net.gt; f. 1947; Pres. ILEANA ALAMILLA; Sec. WALTER HERMOSILLA.

Cámara Guatemalteca de Periodismo (CGP): Guatemala City; Pres. MARIO FUENTES DESTARAC.

Círculo Nacional de Prensa (CNP): Guatemala City; Pres. FREDY AZURDIA AZURDI; Sec.-Gen. MIGUEL ÁNGEL MORALES.

NEWS AGENCIES

Inforpress Centroamericana: Calle Mariscal 6-58, Zona 11, 0100 Guatemala City; tel. and fax 2473-1704; e-mail inforpre@guate.net; internet www.inforpressca.com; f. 1972; independent news agency; publishes two weekly news bulletins, in English and Spanish.

Foreign Bureaux

ACAN-EFE (Central America): Edif. El Centro, 8°, Of. 8-21, 9a Calle y 7a Avda, Zona 1, Guatemala City; tel. 2251-9454; fax 2251-9484; Man. ANA CAROLINA ALPÍREZ A.

Agenzia Nazionale Stampa Associata (ANSA) (Italy): Torre Norte, Edif. Géminis 10, Of. 805, 12a Calle 1-25, Zona 10, Guatemala City; tel. 2335-3039; e-mail ansagua@guate.net; Chief ALFONSO ANZUETO LÓPEZ.

Deutsche Presse-Agentur (dpa) (Germany): 5a Calle 4-30, Zona 1, Apdo 2333, Guatemala City; tel. and fax 2251-7505; Correspondent JULIO CÉSAR ANZUETO.

Inter Press Service (IPS) (Italy): Edif. El Centro, 3°, Of. 13, 7a Avda 8-56, Zona 1, Guatemala City; tel. 2253-8837; fax 2251-4736; internet www.ipslatam.net; Correspondent GEORGE RODRÍGUEZ-OTEIZA.

United Press International (UPI) (USA): Guatemala City; tel. and fax 2251-4258; e-mail latam_desk@upi.com; Correspondent AMAFREDO CASTELLANOS.

Publishers

Cholsamaj: 7a Avda 9-25, Zona 1, Apdo 4, Guatemala City; tel. 2232-5959; e-mail cholsamaj@micro.com; internet www.cholsamaj.org.gt; Mayan language publications.

Ediciones Legales Comercio e Industria: 12a Avda 14-78, Zone 1, Guatemala City; tel. 2253-5725; fax 2220-7592; Man. Dir LUIS EMILIO BARRIOS.

GUATEMALA

Editorial Cultura: 10A Calle 10-14, Zona 1, Guatemala City; tel. 2232-5667; fax 2230-0591; e-mail cultuarte@intelnet.net.gt; part of the Ministry of Culture and Sport.

Editorial Nueva Narrativa: Edif. El Patrio, Of. 108, 7a Avda 7-07, Zona 4, Guatemala City; tel. 2360-0732; fax 5704-7895; e-mail maxaraujo@intelnet.gt; Man. Dir MAX ARAÚJO A.

Editorial Palo de Hormigo: Calle 16-40, Zona 15, Col. El Maestro, Guatemala City; tel. 2369-2080; fax 2369-8858; e-mail juanfercif@hotmail.com; f. 1990; Man. Dir JUAN FERNANDO CIFUENTES.

Editorial Universitaria: Edif. de la Editorial Universitaria, Universidad de San Carlos de Guatemala, Ciudad Universitaria, Zona 12, Guatemala City; tel. and fax 2476-9628; literature, social sciences, health, pure and technical sciences, humanities, secondary and university educational textbooks.

F & G Editores: 31 Avda 'C' 5-54, Zona 7, 01007 Guatemala City; tel. and fax 2433-2361; e-mail fgeditor@guate.net; internet www.fygeditores.com; f. 1990 as Figueroa y Gallardo; changed name in 1993; law, literature and social sciences; Editor RAÚL FIGUEROA SARTI.

Piedra Santa: 37 Avda 1-26, Zona 7, Guatemala City; tel. 2324-2331; fax 2334-6801; e-mail patricia@piedrasanta.com; internet www.piedrasanta.com; f. 1947; education, culture; Man. Dir IRENE PIEDRA SANTA.

Broadcasting and Communications

TELECOMMUNICATIONS

Regulatory Authority

Superintendencia de Telecomunicaciones de Guatemala: Edif. Murano Center, 16°, 14a Calle 3-51, Zona 10, 01010 Guatemala City; tel. 2366-5880; fax 2366-5890; e-mail supertel@sit.gob.gt; internet www.sit.gob.gt; f. 1996; Supt OSCAR STUARDO CHINCHILLA.

Major Service Providers

Comunicaciones Celulares (Comcel): Guatemala City; tel. 2428-0000; e-mail sugerencias@comcel.com.gt; internet www.tigo.com.gt; provider of mobile telecommunications; 55% owned by Millicom International Cellular (Luxembourg).

Telecomunicaciones de Guatemala, SA (Telgua): Edif. Central Telgua, 7 Avda 12-39, Zona 1, Guatemala City; internet www.telgua.com.gt; fmrly state-owned Empresa Guatemalteca de Telecomunicaciones (Guatel); name changed as above to facilitate privatization; 95% share transferred to private ownership in 1998; owned by América Móvil, SA de CV (Mexico); Dirs JULIO BELIZARIO MONTEPEQUE, MARVIN EMILIO PAR-GONZÁLEZ LÓPEZ.

Telefónica MoviStar Guatemala, SA: Blvd Los Próceres, 20-09 Torre Telefónica, 9°, Zona 10, Guatemala City; tel. 2379-7979; e-mail servicioalcliente@telefonica.com.gt; internet www.telefonica.com.gt; owned by TelefónicaMóviles, SA (Spain); acquired BellSouth Guatemala in 2004; wireless, wireline and radio paging communications services; 298,000 customers; Pres. CÉSAR ALIERTA IZUEL.

Other service providers include: Emergia, FT & T (Telered), Cablenet, Universal de Telecomunicaciones, Telefónica Centroamérica Guatemala, Servicios de Comunicaciones Personales Inalámbricas, A-tel Communications, Cybernet de Centroamérica, Teléfonos del Norte, Americatel Guatemala, Desarrollo Integral, BNA, TTI, Optel and Concert Global Networks.

BROADCASTING

Dirección General de Radiodifusión y Televisión Nacional: Edif. Tipografía Nacional, 3°, 18 de Septiembre 6-72, Zona 1, Guatemala City; tel. 2253-2539; e-mail info@radiotgw.gob.gt; internet www.radiotgw.gob.gt; f. 1931; govt supervisory body; Dir-Gen. JAVIER HERNÁNDEZ OSORIOS.

Radio

There are currently five government and six educational stations, including:

Radio Cultural TGN: 4a Avda y 30 Calle, Zona 3, Apdo 601, Guatemala City; tel. 2471-4378; fax 2440-0260; e-mail trgn@radiocultural.com; internet www.radiocultural.com; f. 1950; religious and cultural station; programmes in Spanish and English, Cakchiquel, Kekchí, Quiché and Aguacateco; Dir Dr STEPHEN ROBB SYWULKA BURGESS; Man. ANTHONY WAYNE BERGER WISEMAN.

Radio Nacional TGW (La Voz de Guatemala): 18a Calle 6-72, Zona 1, Guatemala City; tel. 2253-2539; e-mail info@radiotgw.gob.gt; internet www.radiotgw.gob.gt; govt station; Dir JAVIER HERNÁNDEZ OSORIOS.

There are some 80 commercial stations, of which the most important are:

Emisoras Unidas de Guatemala: 4a Calle 6-84, Zona 13, Guatemala City; tel. 2440-5133; fax 2440-5159; e-mail patrullajeinformativo@emisorasunidas.com; internet sites .emisorasunidas.com; f. 1964; 7 stations: Yo Sí Sideral, Supercadena, Kiss, Atmósfera, Fabustereo, Radio Estrella and La Grande; Pres. JORGE EDGARDO ARCHILA MARROQUÍN; Vice-Pres. ROLANDO ARCHILA MARROQUÍN.

La Marca: 30 Avda 3-40, Zona 11, Guatemala City; tel. 2434-7330; e-mail lamarca@94fm.com.gt.

Metro Stereo: Guatemala City; e-mail metrored@metrostereo.net; internet www.metrostereo.net.

Television

Canal 5—Televisión Cultural y Educativa, SA: 4a Calle 18-38, Zona 1, Guatemala City; tel. 2253-1913; fax 2232-7003; f. 1980; cultural and educational programmes; Dir ALFREDO HERRERA CABRERA.

Radio-Televisión Guatemala, SA: 30a Avda 3-40, Zona 11, Apdo 1367, Guatemala City; tel. 2434-6320; fax 2294-7492; e-mail canal3@canal3.co.gt; internet www.canal3.com.gt; f. 1956; commercial station; operates channels 3 and 10; Pres. MAX KESTLER FARNÉS; Vice-Pres. J. F. VILLANUEVA.

Teleonce: 20a Calle 5-02, Zona 10, Guatemala City; tel. 2368-2532; fax 2368-2221; e-mail jcof@canalonce.tv; internet canal11y13.homestead.com/20CALLE.html; f. 1968; commercial; channel 11; Gen. Dir JUAN CARLOS ORTIZ.

Televisiete, SA: 30a Avda 3-40, Zona 11, Apdo 1242, Guatemala City; tel. 2594-5320; fax 2369-1393; internet www.canal7.com.gt; f. 1988; commercial station, channel 7; Dir ABDÓN RODRÍGUEZ ZEA.

Trecevisión, SA: 20a Calle 5-02, Zona 10, Guatemala City; tel. 2368-2532; e-mail jcof@canaltrece.tv; internet canal11y13.homestead.com/20CALLE.html; commercial; channel 13; f. 1978; Dir JUAN CARLOS ORTIZ; Gen. Man. JUAN CARLOS GONZÁLEZ.

Finance

(cap. = capital; res = reserves; dep. = deposits; m. = million; brs = branches; amounts in quetzales)

BANKING

Superintendencia de Bancos: 9a Avda 22-00, Zona 1, Apdo 2306, Guatemala City; tel. 2232-0001; fax 2232-0002; e-mail info@sib.gob.gt; internet www.sib.gob.gt; f. 1946; Supt EDGAR BARQUÍN.

Central Bank

Banco de Guatemala: 7a Avda 22-01, Zona 1, Apdo 365, Guatemala City; tel. 2230-6222; fax 2253-4035; e-mail webmaster@banguat.gob.gt; internet www.banguat.gob.gt; f. 1946; state-owned; cap. 355.5m., res 2,842.4m., dep. 33,411.2m. (Dec. 2005); Pres. MARÍA ANTONIETA DEL CID NAVAS DE BONILLA; Gen. Man. MANUEL AUGUSTO ALONSO ARAUJO.

State Commercial Bank

Crédito Hipotecario Nacional de Guatemala (CHN): 7a Avda 22-77, Zona 1, Apdo 242, Guatemala City; tel. 2384-5222; fax 2238-2041; e-mail mercadeo@chn.com.gt; internet www.chn.com.gt; f. 1980; govt-owned; Pres. OSCAR FRANCISCO PINEDA GARAY; Gen. Man. JOSÉ FIDENCIO GARCÍA BELTETÓN; 44 agencies.

Private Commercial Banks

Banco Agromercantil de Guatemala, SA: 7a Avda 7-30, Zona 9, 01009 Guatemala City; tel. 2338-6565; fax 2232-5406; e-mail agromercantil@bam.com.gt; internet www.agromercantil.com.gt; f. 2000 as Banco Central de Guatemala; changed name to Banco Agrícola Mercantil in 1948; name changed as above in 2000, following merger with Banco del Agro; cap. 345.8m., res 69.4m., dep. 4,264.3m. (Dec. 2005); Pres. JOSÉ LUIS VALDÉS; Man. RAFAEL ANTONIO E. VIEJO RODRÍGUEZ; 78 agencies.

Banco de América Central, SA (BAC): Local 6-12, 1°, 7a Avda 6-26, Zona 9, Guatemala City; tel. 2360-9440; fax 2331-8720; internet www.bac.net; Gen. Man. JUAN JOSÉ VIAUD PÉREZ.

Banco Americano, SA: 11 Calle 7-44, Zona 9, 01009 Guatemala City; tel. 2386-1700; fax 2386-1753; e-mail grufin@infovia.com.gt; internet www.bancoamericano.com.gt.

Banco Corporativo, SA: 6a Avda 4-38, Zona 9, 01009 Guatemala City; tel. 2279-9999; fax 2279-9990; e-mail mcatalan@corpobanco.com.gt; internet www.corpobanco.com.gt; f. 1990.

Banco Cuscatlán de Guatemala, SA: Edif. Céntrica Plaza, 15 Calle 1-04, Zona 10, 01010 Guatemala City; tel. 2250-2000; fax 2250-2001; e-mail info@cuscatlanguate.com; internet www

.bancocuscatlan.com; acquired Guatemalan assets of Lloyds TSB in Dec. 2003; cap. 441.7m., total assets 7,982.0m. (June 2007).

Banco de Desarrollo Rural, SA: Avda La Reforma 2-56, Zona 9, Guatemala City; tel. 2334-1383; fax 2360-9740; e-mail internacional4@banrural.com.gt; internet www.banrural.com.gt; f. 1971 as Banco de Desarrollo Agrícola; name changed as above in 1998; cap. 346.5m., res 77.5m., dep. 9,669.6m. (Dec. 2005); Pres. JOSÉ ANGEL LÓPEZ CAMPOSECO; Gen. Man. ADOLFO FERNANDO PEÑA PÉREZ; 450 agencies.

Banco de Exportación, SA (BANEX): Avda de la Reforma 11-49, Zona 10, Guatemala City; tel. 2331-9861; fax 2332-2879; e-mail info@banexfigsa.com; internet www.banexfigsa.com; f. 1985; cap. 342.5m., res 68.9m., dep. 1,966.9m. (Dec. 2006); Pres. ALEJANDRO BOTRÁN; Man. ROBERTO ORTEGA HERRERA; 15 brs.

Banco Industrial, SA (BAINSA): Edif. Centro Financiero, Torre 1, 7a Avda 5-10, Zona 4, Apdo 744, Guatemala City; tel. 2334-5111; fax 2331-9437; e-mail webmaster@bi.com.gt; internet www.bi.com.gt; f. 1964 to promote industrial devt; total assets 7.91m. (1999); Gen. Man. DIEGO PULIDO ARAGÓN.

Banco Inmobilario, SA: 7a Avda 11-59, Zona 9, Apdo 1181, Guatemala City; tel. 2339-3777; fax 2332-1418; e-mail info@bcoinmob.com.gt; internet www.bcoinmob.com.gt; f. 1958; cap. 77.6m., res 0.4m., dep. 738.6m. (Dec. 2002); Pres. EMILIO ANTONIO PERALTA PORTILLO; 38 brs.

Banco Internacional, SA: Torre Internacional, Avda Reforma 15-85, Zona 10, Apdo 2588, Guatemala City; tel. 2366-6666; fax 2366-6743; e-mail info@bco.inter.com; internet www.bancointernacional.com.gt; f. 1976; cap. 223.8m., res –30.9m., dep. 1,559.8m. (Dec. 2005); Pres. CARLOS BARTOLOMÉ FERNÁNDEZ; Gen. Man. JUAN MANUEL VENTAS BENÍTEZ; 34 brs.

Banco Privado para el Desarrollo, SA: 7a Avda 8-46, Zona 9, Guatemala City; tel. 2361-7777; fax 2361-7217; e-mail atencionalpublico@bancosol.com.gt; internet www.bancasol.com.gt.

Banco del Quetzal, SA: Edif. Plaza El Roble, 7a Avda 6-26, Zona 9, Apdo 1001-A, 01009 Guatemala City; tel. 2331-8333; fax 2334-0613; e-mail negocios@banquetzal.com.gt; internet banquetzal.com.gt; f. 1984; Pres. MARIO ROBERTO LEAL PIVARAL; Gen. Man. ALFONSO VILLA DEVOTO.

Banco Reformador, SA: 7a Avda 7-24, Zona 9, 01009 Guatemala City; tel. 2362-0888; fax 2362-0847; internet www.bancoreformador.com; cap. 184.1m., res 188.5m., dep. 4,348.9m. (Dec. 2006); merged with Banco de la Construcción in 2000; Pres. MIGUEL AGUIRRE; Gen. Man. JAIME ABASCAL; 47 brs.

Banco SCI: Edif. SCI Centre, Avda La Reforma 9-76, Zona 9, 01009 Guatemala City; tel. 2331-7515; fax 2339-0755; e-mail atencion@sci.net.gt; internet www.sci.com.gt; f. 1967.

Banco de los Trabajadores: Avda Reforma 6-20, Zona 9, 01001 Guatemala City; tel. 2339-8600; fax 2339-4750; e-mail bantrab@terra.com.gt; internet www.bantrab.com.gt; f. 1966; deals with loans for establishing and improving small industries as well as normal banking business; cap. 263.4m., dep. 1,460.1m., total assets 1,932.6m. (Dec. 2005); Pres. CARLOS ALFREDO VILLEDA OLIVA; Gen. Man. CARLOS OSWALDO ESTRADA SARMIENTO.

Banco Uno: Edif. Unicentro, 1°, Blvd Los Próceres, 18 Calle 5-56, Zona 10, 01010 Guatemala City; tel. 2366-1777; fax 2366-1553; e-mail bancouno@gua.pibnet.com; internet www.bancouno.com.gt.

Banco G & T Continental, SA: Plaza Continental, 6a Avda 9-08, Zona 9, Guatemala City; tel. 2338-6801; fax 2332-2682; e-mail subanco@gytcontinental.com.gt; internet www.gytcontinental.com.gt; f. 2000 following merger of Banco Continental and Banco Granai y Townson; total assets 11.4m. (2000); 130 brs.

Finance Corporations

Corporación Financiera Nacional (CORFINA): 11a Avda 3-14, Zona 1, Guatemala City; tel. 2253-4550; fax 2232-5805; e-mail corfina@guate.net; internet www.guate.net/corfina; f. 1973; provides assistance for the devt of industry, mining and tourism.

Financiera Guatemalteca, SA (FIGSA): 1a Avda 11-50, Zona 10, Apdo 2460, Guatemala City; tel. 2338-8000; fax 2331-0873; e-mail figsa@figsa.com; internet www.banexfigsa.com; f. 1962; investment agency; Gen. Man. ROBERTO FERNÁNDEZ BOTRÁN.

Financiera de Inversión, SA: 11a Calle 7-44, Zona 9, Guatemala City; tel. 2332-4020; fax 2332-4320; f. 1981; investment agency; Pres. MARIO AUGUSTO PORRAS GONZÁLEZ; Gen. Man. JOSÉ ROLANDO PORRAS GONZÁLEZ.

Banking Association

Asociación Bancaria de Guatemala: Edif. Margarita 2, Of. 502, Diagonal 6, Zona 10, Guatemala City; tel. 2336-6080; fax 2336-6094; internet www.abg.org.gt; f. 1961; represents all state and private banks; Pres. LUIS LARA GROJEC.

STOCK EXCHANGE

Bolsa de Valores Nacional, SA: Centro Financiero, Torre II, 2°, 7 Avda 5-10, Zona 4, Guatemala City; tel. 2338-4400; fax 2332-1721; e-mail bvn@bvnsa.com.gt; internet www.bvnsa.com.gt; f. 1987; the exchange is commonly owned (one share per associate) and trades stocks from private companies, government bonds, letters of credit and other securities; Pres. JUAN CARLOS CASTILLO; Gen. Man. ROLANDO SAN ROMÁN.

INSURANCE

National Companies

Aseguradora La Ceiba, SA: 20 Calle 15-20, Zona 13, Guatemala City; tel. 2379-1800; fax 2334-8167; e-mail aceiba@aceiba.com.gt; internet www.aceiba.com.gt; f. 1978; Man. ALEJANDRO BELTRANENA.

Aseguradora General, SA: 10a Calle 3-71, Zona 10, Guatemala City; tel. 2332-5933; fax 2334-2093; e-mail generaliguate@generali.com.gt; internet www.aseguresemejor.com; f. 1968; subsidiary of Grupo Generali, Trieste, Italy; Pres. JUAN O. NIEMANN; Man. ENRIQUE NEUTZE A.

Aseguradora Guatemalteca, SA: Edif. Torre Azul, 10°, 4a Calle 7-53, Zona 9, Guatemala City; tel. 2361-0206; fax 2361-1093; e-mail aseguate@guate.net; f. 1974; Pres. Gen. FERNANDO ALFONSO CASTILLO RAMÍREZ; Man. JOSÉ GUILLERMO H. LÓPEZ CORDÓN.

Cía de Seguros El Roble, SA: Torre 2, 7a Avda 5-10, Zona 4, Guatemala City; tel. 2332-1702; fax 2332-1629; e-mail rerales@elroble.com; f. 1973; Gen. Man. HERMANN GIRON.

Departamento de Seguros y Previsión del Crédito Hipotecario Nacional: Centro Cívico, 7a Avda 22-77, Zona 1, Guatemala City; tel. 2250-0271; fax 2253-8584; e-mail vjsc@chn.com.gt; internet www.chn.com.gt; f. 1942; Pres. FREDDY A. MUÑOZ MORAN; Man. HUGO CRUZ MONTERROSO.

Empresa Guatemalteca Cigna de Seguros, SA: 5a Avda 5-55, Zona 14, Guatemala City; tel. 2384-5454; fax 2384-5400; e-mail cigna@starnet.com.gt; f. 1951; Gen. Man. REBECA CASTELLANOS DE AGUILAR.

La Seguridad de Centroamérica, SA: Edif. Etisa, 7a Avda 12-23, Plazuela España, Zona 9, Guatemala City; tel. 2285-5900; fax 2361-3026; e-mail servicios.cmg@aig.com; internet www.aig.com; f. 1967; Gen. Man. JUAN MANUEL FRIEDERICH; Legal Rep. MARTA DE TORIELLO.

Seguros Alianza, SA: Edif. Etisa, 6°, 7a Avda 12-23, Plazuela España, Zona 9, Guatemala City; tel. 2331-5475; fax 2331-0023; internet www.segurosalianza.com.gt; f. 1968; Pres. LUIS FERNANDO SAMAYOA.

Seguros G & T, SA: 36-09 Avda Petapa, Zona 12, Guatemala City; tel. 2334-1361; fax 2332-8970; e-mail seguros@gyt.co.gt; internet www.segurosgyt.com.gt; f. 1947; Pres. ERNESTO TOWNSON R.; Exec. Man. MARIO GRANAI FERNÁNDEZ; Gen. Man. ENRIQUE RODRÍGUEZ.

Seguros de Occidente, SA: 7a Calle 'A' 7-14, Zona 9, Guatemala City; tel. 2331-1222; fax 2334-2787; e-mail occidente@occidente.com.gt; internet www.occidente.com.gt; f. 1979; Pres. Lic. PEDRO AGUIRRE; Gen. Man. LUIS PEDRO CHÁVEZ BLANCO.

Seguros Panamericana, SA: Avda de la Reforma 9-00, Edif. Plaza Panamericana, Zona 9, Guatemala City; tel. 2332-5922; fax 2331-5026; e-mail sortega@exchange.palic.com; f. 1968; Pres. FRANK PURVIS; Gen. Man. SALVADOR ORTEGA.

Seguros Universales, SA: 4a Calle 7-73, Zona 9, Apdo 1479, Guatemala City; tel. 2277-2727; fax 2332-3372; e-mail info@segurosuniversales.net; internet www.segurosuniversales.net; f. 1962; Man. PEDRO NOLASCO SICILIA.

Insurance Association

Asociación Guatemalteca de Instituciones de Seguros (AGIS): Edif. Torre Profesional I, Of. 703, 4°, 6a Avda 0-60, Zona 4, Guatemala City; tel. 2335-2140; fax 2335-2357; e-mail agis@intelnet.net.gt; internet www.agis.com.gt; f. 1953; 12 mems; Pres. KEVIN M. LUCAS H.; Sec. Gen. RENÉ LÓPEZ CASTILLO.

Trade and Industry

DEVELOPMENT ORGANIZATIONS

Comisión Nacional Petrolera: Diagonal 17, 29-78, Zona 11, Guatemala City; tel. 2276-0680; fax 2276-3175; f. 1983; awards petroleum exploration licences.

Corporación Financiera Nacional (CORFINA): see Finance—Finance Corporations.

Instituto de Fomento de Hipotecas Aseguradas (FHA): Edif. Aristos Reforma, 2°, Avda Reforma 7-62, Zona 9, Guatemala City; tel. 2362-9434; fax 2362-9492; e-mail promocion@fha.com.gt; internet www.fha.com.gt; f. 1961; insured mortgage institution for the promotion of house construction; Pres. FRANCISO SANDOVAL; Man. SERGIO IRUNGARAY.

GUATEMALA

Instituto Nacional de Administración Pública (INAP): 5a Avda 12-65, Zona 10, Apdo 2753, Guatemala City; tel. 2366-3021; fax 2366-2655; e-mail webmaster@inapgt.com; internet www.inapgt.com; f. 1964; provides technical experts to assist the Govt in administrative reform programmes; provides in-service training for local and central govt staff; has research programmes in administration, sociology, politics and economics; provides postgraduate education in public administration; Pres. HARRIS WHITBECK PIÑOL; Man. SANDRA JIMÉNEZ.

Instituto Nacional de Transformación Agraria (INTA): 14a Calle 7-14, Zona 1, Guatemala City; tel. 2228-0975; f. 1962 to carry out agrarian reform; current programme includes devt of the 'Faja Transversal del Norte'; Pres. NERY ORLANDO SAMAYOA; Vice-Pres SÉRGIO FRANCISCO MORALES-JUÁREZ, ROBERTO EDMUNDO QUIÑÓNEZ LÓPEZ.

Secretaría de Planificación y Programación (SEGEPLAN): 9a Calle 10-44, Zona 1, Guatemala City; tel. 2251-4549; fax 2253-3127; e-mail segeplan@segeplan.gob.gt; internet www.segeplan.gob.gt; f. 1954; prepares and supervises the implementation of the national economic devt plan; Dir HUGO BETETA.

CHAMBERS OF COMMERCE AND INDUSTRY

Comité Coordinador de Asociaciones Agrícolas, Comerciales, Industriales y Financieras (CACIF): Edif. Cámara de Industria de Guatemala, 6a Ruta 9-21, Zona 4, Guatemala City; tel. 2231-0651; e-mail informacion@cacif.org.gt; internet www.cacif.org.gt; co-ordinates work on problems and organization of free enterprise; 6 mem. chambers; Pres. MARCO AUGUSTO GARCÍA NORIEGA; Sec.-Gen. RAFAEL POLA.

Cámara de Comercio de Guatemala: 10a Calle 3-80, Zona 1, Guatemala City; tel. 2253-5353; fax 2220-9393; e-mail info@camaradecomercio.org.gt; internet www.negociosenguatemala.com; f. 1894; Pres. EDGARDO WAGNER DURÁN; Exec. Dir Dr RICARDO RODRÍGUEZ AMADO.

Cámara de Industria de Guatemala: 6a Ruta 9-21, 12°, Zona 4, Apdo 214, Guatemala City; tel. 2334-0850; fax 2334-1090; e-mail cig@industriaguate.com; internet www.industriaguate.com; f. 1959; Exec. Dir OSCAR VILLAGRÁN.

Cámara Oficial Española de Comercio de Guatemala: Edif. Géminis, 10°, Torre Sur, Of. 1513, 12 Calle 1-25, Zona 10, Apdo 2480, Guatemala City; tel. 2335-2735; fax 2335-3380; e-mail camacoes@terra.com.gt; internet www.camacoes-guate.com; Pres. ANDRÉS SICILIA; Gen. Man. BEATRIZ SÁNCHEZ.

INDUSTRIAL AND TRADE ASSOCIATIONS

Asociación de Azucareros de Guatemala (ASAZGUA): Edif. Europlaza, 178°, 5a Avda 5-55, Zona 14, Guatemala City; tel. 2386-2299; fax 2386-2020; e-mail asazgua@azucar.com.gt; internet www.azucar.com.gt; f. 1957; sugar producers' asscn; 15 mems; Pres. FRATERNO VILA; Gen. Man. ARMANDO BOESCHE.

Asociación General de Agricultores (AGA): 9a Calle 3-43, Zona 1, Guatemala City; f. 1920; general farmers' asscn; 350 mems.

Asociación de Gremiales de Exportadores de Productos No Tradicionales (AGEXPRONT): 15 Avda 14-72, Zona 13, Guatemala City; tel. 2362-2002; fax 2362-1950; internet www.export.com.gt; f. 1982; devt of export of non-traditional products.

Asociación Nacional de Avicultores (ANAVI): Edif. Galerías Reforma, Torre 2, 9°, Of. 904, Avda de la Reforma 8-60, Zona 9, Guatemala City; tel. 2231-1381; fax 2234-7576; e-mail anavig@terra.com.gt; f. 1964; national asscn of poultry farmers; 60 mems; Pres. Dr MARIO A. MOTTA GONZÁLEZ.

Asociación Nacional de Fabricantes de Alcoholes y Licores (ANFAL): Guatemala City; tel. 2292-0430; e-mail guillermo.borja@ronesdeguatemala.com; f. 1947; distillers' asscn; Pres. JUAN GUILLERMO BORJA.

Asociación Nacional del Café—Anacafé: Edif. Etisa, Plazuela España, Zona 9, Guatemala City; tel. 2236-7180; fax 2234-7023; e-mail sellodepureza@anacafe.org; internet www.anacafe.org; f. 1960; national coffee asscn; Pres. CHRISTIAN RASCH.

Cámara del Agro: 15a Calle 'A' 7-65, Zona 9, Guatemala City; tel. 2226-1473; e-mail camagro@intelnet.net.gt; f. 1973; Pres. ROBERTO CASTAÑEDA.

Gremial de Huleros de Guatemala: Edif. Galerias España, 7 Avda 11-63, 3°, Guatemala City; tel. 2331-8269; fax 2332-1553; e-mail gremhuleger@guate.net.gt; f. 1970; rubber producers' guild; 125 mems; Man. ALEJANDRO SOSA BROL.

UTILITIES
Electricity

Empresa Eléctrica de Guatemala, SA: 6a Avda 8-14, Zona 1, Guatemala City; tel. 2277-7000; e-mail consultas@eegsa.com; internet www.eegsa.com; f. 1972; state electricity producer; 80% share transferred to private ownership in 1998; Commercial Man. LUIS ANTONIO MATÉ.

Instituto Nacional de Electrificación (INDE): Edif. La Torre, 7a Avda 2-29, Zona 9, Guatemala City; tel. (2) 2422-1800; e-mail gerencia.general@inde.gob.gt; internet www.inde.gob.gt; f. 1959; fmr state agency for the generation and distribution of hydroelectric power; principal electricity producer; privatized in 1998; Pres. MARCIO CUEVAS QUEZADA; Gen. Man. CARLOS EDUARDO COLOM BICKFORD.

CO-OPERATIVES

Instituto Nacional de Cooperativas (INACOP): 13 Calle 5-16, Zona 1, Guatemala City; tel. 2234-1097; fax 2234-7536; technical and financial assistance in planning and devt of co-operatives.

TRADE UNIONS

A number of unions exist without a national centre, including the Union of Chicle and Wood Workers, the Union of Coca-Cola Workers and the Union of Workers of the Enterprise of the United Fruit Company.

Central General de Trabajadores de Guatemala (CGTG): 3a Avda 12-22, Zona 1, Guatemala City; tel. 2232-1010; fax 2251-3212; e-mail cgtg@turbonett.com; f. 1987; Sec.-Gen. JOSÉ E. PINZÓN SALAZAR.

Central de Trabajadores del Campo y la Ciudad (CTC): 12 Calle 'A', 12-44, Zona 1, Guatemala City; tel. and fax 2232-6947; e-mail centracampo@yahoo.com; Sec.-Gen. MIGUEL ANGEL LUCAS GÓMEZ.

Federación Sindical de Trabajadores de la Alimentación Agro-Industrias y Similares de Guatemala (FESTRAS): 16 Avda 3-52, Zona 1, Guatemala City; tel. and fax 2338-3075; e-mail festras@terra.com.gt; affiliated to International Union of Food, Agricultural, Hotel, Restaurants, Catering, Tobacco and Allied Workers' Asscns; Sec.-Gen. JOSÉ DAVID MORALES C.

Unidad de Acción Sindical y Popular (UASP): 10 Avda 'A' 5-40, Zona 1, Guatemala City; f. 1988; broad coalition of leading labour and peasant orgs; includes:

  Comité de la Unidad Campesina (CUC) (Committee of Peasants' Unity): 31 Avda 'A' 14-46, Zona 7, Ciudad de Plata, Apdo 1002, Guatemala City; tel. and fax 2434-9754; e-mail cuc@guate.net; internet cuc.mundoweb.org.

  Confederación de Unidad Sindical de Guatemala (CUSG): 12 Calle 'A', Zona 1, Guatemala City; tel. and fax 2232-8154; e-mail cusg@itelgua.com; f. 1983; mem. of ITUC; Sec.-Gen. CARLOS H. CARBALLO.

  Federación Nacional de Sindicatos de Trabajadores del Estado de Guatemala (FENASTEG): 10 Avda 5-40, Zona 1, Guatemala City; tel. and fax 2232-2772; Sec. ARTURO MESÍAS.

  Sindicato de Trabajadores del Instituto Guatemalteco de Seguridad Social (STIGSS): 11 Calle 11-15, Zona 1, Guatemala City; f. 1953.

  Unión Sindical de Trabajadores de Guatemala (UNSITRAGUA): 9 Avda 1-43, Zona 1, Guatemala City; tel. 2238-2272; fax 2220-4121; e-mail unsitragua@hotmail.com; f. 1985; mem. unions are mostly from the private industrial sector and include STECSA, SITRALU and SCTM; Co-ordinator BYRON GRAMAJO.

Unión Guatemalteca de Trabajadores (UGT): 13 Calle 11-40, Zona 1, Guatemala City; tel. and fax 2251-1686; e-mail ugt.guatemala@yahoo.com; Sec.-Gen. CARLOS ENRIQUE MANCILLA.

Transport
RAILWAYS

In 2005 there were 886 km of railway track in Guatemala.

Ferrocarriles de Guatemala (FEGUA): 18 Calle 9-03, Zona 1, Guatemala City; tel. 2232-9270; fax 2238-3039; e-mail ferroguat@hotmail.com; f. 1968; 50-year concession to rehabilitate and operate railway awarded in 1997 to the US Railroad Devt Corpn; 784 km from Puerto Barrios and Santo Tomás de Castilla on the Atlantic coast to Tecún Umán on the Mexican border, via Zacapa, Guatemala City and Santa María. Branch lines: Santa María–San José; Las Cruces–Champerico. From Zacapa another line branches southward to Anguiatú, on the border with El Salvador; Interventor Dr ARTURO GRAMAJO MONDAL.

ROADS

In 2004 there were an estimated 23,379 km of roads, of which about 14,283 km were paved. The Guatemalan section of the Pan-American highway is 518.7 km long and totally asphalted. In 2002 plans were discussed for the construction of a highway between Huehuetenango and Izabal under the 'Plan Puebla–Panamá' at an estimated cost of

US $292m. The highway would take five years to complete. In May 2003 the World Bank approved a loan of $46.7m. to repair existing roads and construct new networks in rural areas.

SHIPPING

Guatemala's major ports are Puerto Barrios and Santo Tomás de Castilla, on the Gulf of Mexico, San José and Champerico on the Pacific Ocean, and Puerto Quetzal, which was redeveloped in the late 1990s. In June 2002 the Government announced plans for the expansion of shipping facilities at Puerto Quetzal and Santo Tomás de Castilla in the near future.

Armadora Marítima Guatemalteca, SA (ARMAGUA): Edif. Armagua, 5°, 14a Calle 8-30, Zona 1, Apdo 1008, Guatemala City; tel. 2230-4686; fax 2253-7464; e-mail infoarmagua@armagua.com; internet www.armagua.com; f. 1968; cargo services; Pres. and Gen. Man. L. R. CORONADO CONDE.

Comisión Portuaria Nacional: 6a Avda A 8-66, Zona 9, Apdo 01009, Guatemala City; tel. 2360-5632; fax 2360-5457; e-mail comportn@cpn.gob.gt; internet www.cpn.gob.gt; Exec. Dir MARÍA ISABEL FERNÁNDEZ COLÍNDRES.

Empresa Portuaria Nacional de Champerico: Avda del Ferrocarril, frente a la playa, 1000101 Champerico, Retalhuleu; tel. 7773-7225; fax 7773-7223; Man. OSCAR GUILLERMO CALZIA RODRÍGUEZ.

Empresa Portuaria Nacional Santo Tomás de Castilla: Calle Real de la Villa, 17 Calle 16-43, Zona 10, Guatemala City; tel. 2366-9413; fax 2366-9445; internet www.empornac.gob.gt; Man. Col OTTO GUILLERMO NOACK SIERRA.

Empresa Portuaria Quetzal: Edif. Torre Azul, 1°, 4a Calle 7-53, Zona 9, Guatemala City; tel. 2334-7101; fax 2334-8172; e-mail mercadeo@puerto-quetzal.com; internet www.puerto-quetzal.com; port and shipping co; Pres. RODOLFO NEUTZE; Gen. Man. EDUARDO GARRIDO.

Transportes Renegado: 49 Calle 16-25, Zona 12, Guatemala City; tel. 2479-2529; e-mail trenegado@intelnet.net.gt; Gen. Man. JORGE GUTIÉRREZ.

Several foreign lines link Guatemala with Europe, the Far East and North America.

CIVIL AVIATION

There are two international airports, 'La Aurora' in Guatemala City and 'Santa Elena' in Petén. Modernization of the Santa Elena airport began in 2006.

Aerolíneas de Guatemala (AVIATECA): Aeropuerto 'La Aurora', Avda Hincapié 12-22, Zona 12, Guatemala City; tel. 2331-0375; fax 2334-7846; internet www.grupotaca.com; f. 1945; internal services and external services to the USA, Mexico, and within Central America; transferred to private ownership in 1989; CEO ROBERTO KRIETE; Pres. ALFREDO SCHILDKNECHT.

Aeroquetzal: Avda Hincapié, Hangar EH-05, Zona 13, Guatemala City; tel. 2334-7689; fax 2232-1491; scheduled domestic passenger and cargo services, and external services to Mexico.

Aviones Comerciales de Guatemala (Avcom): Aeropuerto 'La Aurora', Avda Hincapié 18, Zona 13, Guatemala City; tel. 2331-5821; fax 2332-4946; domestic charter passenger services.

Tourism

Following the end of the civil war in 1996 the number of tourist arrivals rose steadily and were recorded at some 884,190 in 2002. By 2005 arrivals had reached 1,315,646. In 2005 receipts from tourism were US $883m.

Instituto Guatemalteco de Turismo (INGUAT) (Guatemala Tourist Commission): Centro Cívico, 7a Avda 1-17, Zona 4, Guatemala City; tel. 2331-1333; fax 2331-4416; e-mail informacion@inguat .gob.gt; internet www.visitguatemala.com; f. 1967; policy and planning council: 11 mems representing the public and private sectors; Pres. WILLI KALTSCHMITT; Dir JOSEPH DANIEL MOONEY DEL CARMEN.

Asociación Guatemalteca de Agentes de Viajes (AGAV) (Guatemalan Association of Travel Agents): Edif. El Reformador, Avda La Reforma 1-50, Zona 9, Apdo 2735, Guatemala City; tel. 2332-0782; fax 2334-5217; e-mail agav@intelnet.net.gt; f. 1958; Pres. RONALD E. CASTILLO; 61 mems.

GUINEA

Introductory Survey

Location, Climate, Language, Religion, Flag, Capital

The Republic of Guinea lies on the west coast of Africa, with Sierra Leone and Liberia to the south, Senegal and Guinea-Bissau to the north, and Mali and Côte d'Ivoire inland to the east. The climate on the coastal strip is hot and moist, with temperatures ranging from about 32°C (90°F) in the dry season to about 23°C (73°F) in the wet season (May–October). The interior is higher and cooler. The official language is French, but Soussou, Manika and six other national languages are widely spoken. Most of the inhabitants are Muslims, but some follow traditional animist beliefs. Around 2% are Roman Catholics. The national flag (proportions 2 by 3) consists of three equal vertical stripes, of red, yellow and green. The capital is Conakry.

Recent History

The Republic of Guinea (formerly French Guinea, part of French West Africa) became independent on 2 October 1958, after 95% of voters rejected the Constitution of the Fifth Republic under which the French colonies became self-governing within the French Community. The new state was the object of punitive reprisals by the outgoing French authorities: all aid was withdrawn, and the administrative infrastructure destroyed. The Parti démocratique de Guinée—Rassemblement démocratique africain (PDG—RDA) became the basis for the construction of new institutions. Its leader, Ahmed Sekou Touré, became President, and the PDG—RDA the sole political party.

Sekou Touré pursued vigorous policies of socialist revolution. Opposition was ruthlessly crushed, and Sekou Touré perpetuated rumours of a 'permanent conspiracy' by foreign powers to overthrow his regime. Notably, an abortive invasion by Portuguese troops and Guinean exiles in 1970 prompted the execution of many of those convicted of involvement.

In November 1978 it was announced that the functions of the PDG—RDA and the State were to be merged, and the country was renamed the People's Revolutionary Republic of Guinea. There was, none the less, a general move away from rigid Marxism and a decline in relations with the USSR, as Guinea sought a political and economic rapprochement with its African neighbours, with France and with other Western powers.

In March 1984 Sekou Touré died while undergoing surgery in the USA. On 3 April, before a successor had been chosen by the ruling party, the armed forces seized power in a bloodless coup. A Comité militaire de redressement national (CMRN) was appointed, headed by Col (later Gen.) Lansana Conté, and Col Diarra Traoré became Prime Minister. The PDG—RDA and the legislature were dissolved, and the Constitution was suspended. In May the 'Second Republic of Guinea' was proclaimed.

In December 1984 Conté, as President, assumed the posts of Head of Government and Minister of Defence; the post of Prime Minister was abolished, and Traoré was demoted to a lesser post. In July 1985 Traoré attempted to seize power while Conté was out of the country. Troops loyal to Conté suppressed the revolt, and Traoré was arrested, along with more than 200 suspected sympathizers. In May 1987 it was announced that 58 people, including nine former government ministers, had been sentenced to death in secret trials for crimes committed under Sekou Touré or following the 1985 coup attempt. The announcement did little to allay international suspicions that many detainees had been executed in the aftermath of the abortive coup, and in December 1987 Conté stated that Traoré had died in the hours following his arrest.

In late 1989 Conté announced that, following a referendum on a proposed new constitution, a joint civilian and military Comité transitoire de redressement national (CTRN) would replace the CMRN. After a transitional period of not more than five years, civilian rule would be established, with an executive and legislature directly elected within a two-party system. The draft Constitution of what was designated the Third Republic was reportedly endorsed by 98.7% of the 97.4% of the electorate who voted in a referendum on 23 December 1990; the CTRN was inaugurated in February 1991 under Conté's chairmanship.

In October 1991 Conté announced that a law authorizing the registration of an unlimited number of political parties would come into effect in April 1992, and that legislative elections would be held before the end of 1992. The Constitution was promulgated on 23 December 1991, and in January 1992 Conté ceded the presidency of the CTRN, in conformity with the constitutional separation of powers. In February most military officers and all those who had returned from exile after the 1984 coup (known as *Guinéens de l'extérieur*) were removed from the Council of Ministers.

In April 1992 some 17 political parties, including the Rassemblement populaire guinéen (RPG), led by Alpha Condé, were legalized; It was subsequently rumoured that the pro-Conté Parti pour l'unité et le progrès (PUP), established by prominent *Guinéens de l'extérieur*, was benefiting from state funds. In December the Government postponed indefinitely the legislative elections, which had been scheduled for later that month. Subsequent indications that the parliamentary elections would not take place until after a presidential election caused resentment among the opposition, which had hoped to present a single candidate (from the party that had performed best in the legislative elections) for the presidency.

In October 1993 the Supreme Court approved eight candidates for the forthcoming presidential election. Conté resigned from the army in order to contest the election as a civilian. The official rate of participation by voters in the election, held on 19 December, was 78.5%, and preliminary results indicated that Conté had secured an absolute majority of the votes cast, obviating the need for a second round of voting. However, the Supreme Court annulled the outcome of voting in the Kankan and Siguiri prefectures (in both of which Condé had won more than 95% of the votes). According to official results, Conté was elected with 51.7% of the votes cast; Condé took 19.6% of the votes, Mamadou Boye Bâ of the Union pour la nouvelle République (UNR) 13.4% and Siradiou Diallo of the Parti pour le renouveau et le progrès (PRP) 11.9%. Conté was inaugurated as President on 29 January 1994. A major restructuring of the Council of Ministers was implemented in August. In February 1995 Conté readopted his military title.

Some 846 candidates, from 21 parties, contested the 114 seats in the Assemblée nationale at the delayed legislative elections, held on 11 June 1995. As preliminary results indicated that the PUP had won an overwhelming majority in the legislature, the so-called 'radical' opposition (the RPG, the PRP and the UNR) announced their intention to boycott the assembly, protesting that voting had been conducted fraudulently. According to the final results, which were verified by the Supreme Court in July, the PUP won 71 seats—having taken 30 of the 38 single-member constituencies and 41 of the 76 seats elected on the basis of national lists. Of the eight other parties to win representation, the RPG secured 19 seats, while the PRP and the UNR each won nine seats. The rate of participation was reported to be 63%. In July the RPG, the PRP and the UNR joined with nine other organizations in a Coordination de l'opposition démocratique (Codem), which indicated its willingness to enter into a dialogue with the authorities. El Hadj Boubacar Biro Diallo, of the PUP, was elected as the Speaker of the Assemblée nationale, which was officially inaugurated on 30 August.

In February 1996 Conté was reportedly seized as he attempted to flee the presidential palace during a mutiny by disaffected elements of the military, and was held by rebels for some 15 hours until he made concessions including a doubling of salaries and immunity from prosecution for those involved in the uprising. The Minister of Defence, Col Abdourahmane Diallo, was dismissed, and Conté assumed personal responsibility for defence.

In February 1996 Codem withdrew from a parliamentary commission investigating the circumstances surrounding the coup attempt, in protest at Conté's allusions to opposition links with anti-Government elements within the military. In March it was announced that eight members of the military, including four senior officers, had been charged with undermining state security in connection with the coup attempt. The armed forces Chief of Staff and the military Governor of Conakry, both of whom had been regarded as close associates of the President, were replaced in April. In July Conté announced the appointment of a non-partisan economist, Sidya Touré, as Prime Minister, the first time that position had existed under the Third Republic. (The Constitution made no explicit provision for such a post.)

In June 1997 it was announced that a State Security Court was to be established to deal with matters of exceptional jurisdiction, and that its first task would be to try the alleged leaders of the 1996 mutiny, including Cmmdr Joseph Gbago Zoumanigui, a former member of the CMRN. A ministerial reorganization was effected in October 1997. Notably, Dorank Assifat Diasseny, hitherto Minister of Territorial Administration and Decentralization, was transferred to the higher education and scientific research portfolio, but shortly afterwards was appointed Minister of National Defence (thereby becoming the first civilian to hold this post since the 1984 *coup d'état*). In March 1998 Bâ and two other UNR deputies were arrested, following the deaths of nine people as a result of violence in Conakry. In September the State Security Court sentenced 38 of those charged with offences related to the 1996 attempted coup to custodial sentences of up to 15 years, some with hard labour (Zoumanigui was sentenced *in absentia*), while 51 defendants were acquitted.

Meanwhile, Codem denounced proposals for the establishment of an Haut conseil aux affaires électorales (HCE), which was to act in conjunction with the Ministry of the Interior and Decentralization in preparing and supervising the forthcoming presidential election. The 68-member HCE was to comprise representatives of the parliamentary majority, as well as opposition delegates, ministerial representatives and members of civil society. The opposition also protested that a ban on public demonstrations, in advance of polling, due to be held on 14 December 1998, would disadvantage candidates other than Conté. The arrest of Condé (one of the five candidates in the election) two days after the poll, near the border with Côte d'Ivoire, on the grounds that he was seeking to leave the country illegally and was plotting against the state, provoked an upsurge of violence, in which at least 12 people were reported to have been killed. In late December Condé was formally charged with having recruited mercenaries with the aim of overthrowing the Conté regime. Meanwhile, opposition representatives denounced the conduct of the election as fraudulent and withdrew from the HCE. The official results confirmed a decisive victory for Conté, with 56.1% of the valid votes cast; Bâ, contesting the election for the Union pour le progrès et le renouveau (UPR, formed in 1998 by a merger of the UNR and the PRP), won 24.6% and Condé (who had been outside Guinea since April 1997, owing to fears for his safety, for the RPG) 16.6%. The rate of participation by registered voters was 71.4%.

In March 1999 Lamine Sidimé, hitherto Chief Justice of the Supreme Court, was appointed Prime Minister of a new Government. An apparent purge of the military high command, in mid-March, included the removal from office of former Chief of Staff Col Oumar Sanko; 18 officers were dismissed, accused of high treason, and 13 retired early, on the grounds of what were termed 'serious faults' arising from the 1996 mutiny.

Opposition groups and human rights organizations campaigned throughout 1999 and 2000 for the release of Condé and other activists detained at the time of the 1998 presidential election. In September 2000 Condé was found guilty of sedition by the State Security Court and sentenced to five years' imprisonment, while seven other defendants were given custodial sentences of between 18 months and three years; 40 other defendants were acquitted. Two days prior to the conclusion of the trial, President Conté had accused Condé of having instigated fighting on Guinea's borders with Sierra Leone and Liberia.

In January 2000 a major government reshuffle was announced. Conté effected a further ministerial reshuffle in June. Legislative elections, scheduled for 25 June, were postponed, although delayed local elections, re-scheduled for the same date, were held, contested by eight parties. Prior to the announcement of the results (in which the PUP and its allies secured control of 33 of the 38 local authorities), a series of clashes between the security forces and UPR members resulted in at least five deaths. In November Conté issued a decree postponing the legislative elections indefinitely.

Meanwhile, in early September 2000 an armed rebellion in the forest region of south-east Guinea reportedly resulted in at least 40 deaths. Instability subsequently intensified in regions near the borders with Sierra Leone and Liberia. Fighting between armed groups and Guinean soldiers was reported to have led to around 360 deaths between early September and mid-October. The Government attributed the upsurge in violence to forces supported by the Governments of Liberia and Burkina Faso, and to members of the Sierra Leonean rebel group, the Revolutionary United Front (RUF, see the chapter on Sierra Leone), in alliance with Guinean dissidents. In October 2000 a previously unknown organization, the Rassemblement des forces démocratiques de Guinée, claimed responsibility for the armed attacks, which, it stated, were an attempt to overthrow President Conté. Following an attack on the town of Forécariah, the local Governor expelled some 32,000 refugees from the region, many of whom were subject to further attacks, particularly following a speech made by Conté, in which he accused refugees from Sierra Leone and Liberia of forming alliances with rebel groups seeking to destabilize Guinea. In late November a series of cross-border attacks were reportedly conducted by former members of a faction of a dissolved Liberian dissident group, the United Liberation Movement of Liberia for Democracy (ULIMO), ULIMO—K (see the chapter on Liberia), which President Conté had previously supported. In December rebel attacks on the southern towns of Guéckédou and Kissidougou led to more than 230 deaths, and the almost complete destruction of Guéckédou. The Government estimated that some 94,000 people had been displaced as a result of fighting in the region, and aid agencies withdrew from south-east Guinea later in the month, as a result of the heightened instability.

In January 2001 Conté assumed personal control of defence; Diasseny, hitherto Minister at the Presidency, in charge of National Defence, was, however, retained as a cabinet member, receiving the title of Minister, Special Adviser at the Presidency. As rebel attacks continued, it was reported that Guinean planes had launched minor air offensives on rebel-held border areas of Sierra Leone. In January–February more than 130 deaths were reported in a series of attacks around Macenta. Allegations persisted that an unofficial alliance between former ULIMO—K rebels and Guinean government forces had broken down, with the result that ULIMO—K forces were now attacking Guinean military and civilian targets. Renewed clashes around Guéckédou prevented the proposed deployment by the Economic Community of West African States (ECOWAS, see p. 232) of an ECOMOG force, which had been intended to monitor stability and border security in the region from mid-February. Meanwhile, in February the death penalty, which had been suspended in 1984, was officially restored, and four of five defendants sentenced to death in 1995 were executed by firing squad (the fifth had died in detention).

Alpha Condé and two of his co-defendants were unexpectedly released from prison in mid-May 2001, following the granting of a presidential pardon. Condé, none the less, was prohibited from participating in political activities for a period of unspecified duration. In mid-June President Conté announced his intention to hold a referendum on proposed constitutional amendments that would remove the restriction on the number of terms of office the President could serve and allow candidates aged over 70 years to contest the presidency. (These changes would enable Conté to contest a third term of office.) Additionally, Conté sought to increase the presidential mandate from five years to seven, to take effect from the presidential election of 2003.

In June 2001, in response to a court ruling, gendarmes enforced the closure of the headquarters of the Union des forces républicaines (UFR), the party led by former Prime Minister Sidya Touré, who had recently formed a group to oppose Conté's proposed constitutional amendments, the Mouvement contre le référendum et pour l'alternance démocratique (Morad). At the end of September Condé resumed his functions as a parliamentary deputy. Morad also announced its intention to prevent the holding of the overdue legislative elections, which were scheduled to take place on 27 December.

The constitutional referendum took place on 11 November 2001, following violent clashes between security forces and those opposed to the referendum. According to official results, 98.4% of those who voted approved the amendments, and 87.2% of the registered electorate participated. Opposition members disputed the results, alleging that less than 20% of the electorate had voted. The presidential term of office was thus extended from five years to seven, with effect from the presidential election due in 2003, and the constitutional provision restricting the President to two terms of office was rescinded. Moreover, the President was to be permitted to appoint local government officials, who were hitherto elected. At the end of November 2001 the legislative elections were again postponed indefinitely. Despite the official result, strong opposition to the referendum was expressed by Boubacar Biro Diallo (who remained Speaker of the reconvened Assemblée nationale, whose mandate had, officially, expired in July 2000) and by Jean-Marie Doré, the leader of the Union pour le progrès de la Guinée (UPG).

In April 2002 President Conté issued a decree, scheduling the repeatedly postponed elections to the Assemblée nationale for 30 June; a further presidential decree, issued later in April, established a Conseil national electoral, to be responsible for the supervision of the elections. However, concern was expressed that the short period between the establishment of the Conseil and the holding of elections would be insufficient to ensure transparency in the conduct of the polls, and the European Union (see p. 244) subsequently withheld funding towards the elections. In May four opposition parties, which had announced their intention to boycott the legislative elections, including the RPG and the UFR, announced the formation of a political alliance, the Front de l'alternance démocratique (FRAD). Notably, Boubacar Biro Diallo, who was not affiliated to any party, and Bâ, the honorary President of the UPR, pledged allegiance to the FRAD, and a split in the UPR became increasingly apparent between those, led by Siradiou Diallo, the President of the party, who sought to engage with the electoral process, and those, led by Bâ, who rejected any such engagement. In early June Conté appointed François Lonceny Fall, previously the representative of Guinea to the UN, as Minister at the Presidency, responsible for Foreign Affairs.

At elections to the Assemblée nationale, held on 30 June 2002, a turn-out of 71.6% was recorded, according to official figures. The PUP increased its majority in the legislature, winning a total of 85 seats. The party was unopposed in all 38 single-member constituency seats, and obtained 47 of the 76 seats allocated by proportional representation. Other pro-presidential parties secured five seats, while the UPR became the second largest party in the Assemblée, with 20 seats, and the UPG won three seats. Opposition parties, both those of the FRAD and those that contested the elections, alleged that fraudulent practice had been widespread in the conduct of the elections, and the US ambassador to Guinea expressed concern at apparent irregularities in the poll. In September the Secretary-General of the PUP, Aboubacar Somparé, was elected as Speaker of the Assemblée nationale. In October Bâ was elected as President of a new party, the Union des forces démocratiques de Guinée (UFDG), which largely comprised the faction of the UPR that had boycotted the elections to the Assemblée nationale.

In December 2002 Conté, whose health had been the subject of a number of rumours, made an unexpected public appearance, having reportedly returned from abroad, and announced a minor government reorganization; a Secretary of State for Security was appointed, and other reforms were made to the security apparatus. At the end of December it was confirmed that Conté was receiving medical treatment in Morocco. None the less, it was announced in January 2003 that Conté was to contest the forthcoming presidential election. Meanwhile, internal political tensions continued to be evident. Bâ publicly stated that a temporary take-over by the armed forces, prior to the preparation of free elections, would be a 'lesser evil' than allowing the PUP to produce its own successor to Conté; similar views were subsequently expressed by a number of principal opposition leaders.

In September 2003, several days after the formal nomination of Conté as the presidential candidate of the PUP, the FRAD announced that negotiations between the Government and opposition parties on the conduct of the presidential election had broken down. In October a rally in Conakry, organized by the FRAD in support of demands for Conté to withdraw his candidacy, attracted between 5,000 and 10,000 people. Although Doré and Sidya Touré, the leader of the UFR, had previously announced their intention to contest the presidential election, in November the FRAD announced that it was to boycott the polls. (Later in the month the UPR also announced that it would boycott the election.) Meanwhile, the Assemblée nationale approved legislation providing for an amnesty for those convicted of political crimes, including, most notably, Condé, who would thereby be permitted to contest the presidential election. However, in the event, the sole candidate approved to contest the election, apart from Conté, was Mamadou Bhoye Barry, the leader of the Union pour le progrès national—Parti pour l'unité et le développement. It was reported that the Supreme Court had rejected on technical grounds the nominations of six other candidates. At the end of November 2003 it was reported that several army officers and soldiers, including a senior member of the presidential guard, had been arrested in Conakry on suspicion of plotting a *coup d'état*. (The authorities did not admit to holding the men in custody until their trial began in October 2004.)

Voting in the presidential election proceeded, as scheduled, on 21 December 2003. In the absence of any significant opposition, Conté was re-elected to a further seven-year term of office, receiving 95.25% of the votes cast, according to official figures. Although the opposition claimed that turn-out had been as low as 15% of the electorate, official figures indicated a rate of participation of approximately 82%. Barry, meanwhile, alleged that the official results were fraudulent, and that he had, in fact, received a majority of the votes cast. On 23 February 2004 Conté dismissed Sidimé and appointed a substantially reorganized Government, headed by Fall as Prime Minister. Further changes were made to the Government on 1 March, when a new Minister of the Economy and Finance, Mady Kaba Camara, was appointed; the Governor of the central bank, Ibrahim Chérif Bah, was also dismissed, amid increasing concern at the country's economic performance. In mid-March Siradiou Diallo died; he was replaced as President of the UPR by Ousmane Bah

In July 2004 widespread rioting and looting was reported in Conakry, to protest at a recent substantial increase in the market price of rice, Guinea's staple foodstuff. In response, President Conté ordered merchants to reduce their prices, and also ordered the dismissal of five mayors (all of whom were members of the ruling PUP) in communes in which riots had taken place.

Meanwhile, in late April 2004 it was announced that Fall had resigned as Prime Minister and had fled Guinea; the former premier subsequently claimed that his Government had been obstructed in its attempts to implement economic and judicial reforms. The post of Prime Minister remained vacant until the appointment in December of Cellou Dalein Diallo, previously Minister of Fisheries and Aquaculture and a government minister since 1996. Diallo pledged to reopen dialogue with opposition parties and suggested that private ownership of radio stations, hitherto prohibited, could be legalized.

In late January 2005 it was announced that President Conté had survived an assassination attempt earlier that month. A number of people were arrested following the attack, including an Islamic religious leader, who later died in custody. In March Conté removed three senior members from the Council of Ministers. The Minister of Security, Moussa Sampil, was replaced by Ousmane Camara; also dismissed were the Minister of Foreign Affairs and Co-operation, Mamady Condé, whose portfolio was assumed by the former Guinean ambassador to Nigeria, Sidibé Fatoumata Kaba, and the Minister of Mines and Geology, Dr Alpha Mady Soumah, who was replaced by Ahmed Tidiane Souaré, hitherto Inspector-General at the Ministry of the Economy and Finance. It was rumoured that Sampil's dismissal was related to his handling of the investigation into the assassination attempt on Conté.

During 2005 President Conté's continuing ill-health continued to be a major source of concern, as did the lack of a clear process of succession for the appointment of a new leader in the event of his death. Indeed, a report by a Belgian-based non-governmental organization (NGO), International Crisis Group, published in June, stated that Guinea 'risked becoming West Africa's next failed state', largely as a result of the concentration of power around the President and the lack of any precedent for the democratic transfer of power. Meanwhile, in May further sharp increases in the prices of rice and, in particular, of fuel products precipitated a series of protests in Conakry and several other cities. In early July Alpha Condé returned to Guinea after two years in self-imposed exile in France.

In mid-September 2005 the parties of the FRAD held a press conference, stating that the President's imminent departure from office was necessary in order to prevent a national descent into chaos. In mid-October it was announced that municipal elections, which had initially been scheduled to be held in June, would be held on 18 December; most of the major opposition parties, including the RPG, subsequently presented candidates. According to official results, announced later in December, the PUP won control of 31 of the 38 municipalities and 241 of the 303 rural communes. Opposition parties condemned the results as fraudulent, and alleged that the rate of participation in the elections was markedly lower than the 57% reported, while observers reported a low turn-out. In early January 2006 the

UPR announced that it was to withdraw from the Assemblée nationale in protest at the conduct of the elections.

In early April 2006 Cellou Dalein Diallo announced the implementation of a comprehensive governmental reorganization, nominating new appointees to the overwhelming majority of ministerial positions. Notably, responsibility for the economy and finance, for planning and international co-operation and for economic and financial control was to be transferred to the office of the Prime Minister, with three Minister-delegates appointed to assume responsibilities over these matters. However, it emerged that President Conté (who is constitutionally Head of Government as well as Head of State) had not authorized the reorganization, and on 5 April he dismissed Diallo as Prime Minister, and issued a decree restoring the Government that had been in place prior to the aborted reorganization.

In late May 2006 Conté restructured the Government, nominating six Ministers of State—responsible for the key portfolios, including foreign affairs, economy and finance and presidential affairs—but, notably, no Prime Minister was appointed. In early June the country's two principal trade unions, the Confédération Nationale des Travailleurs de Guinée (CNTG) and the Union Syndicale des Travailleurs de Guinée (USTG), organized a widely observed general strike and demanded the reduction of the prices of fuel and rice. Clashes were subsequently reported between protesters and the security forces resulting in the deaths of some 20 people. The strike was brought to an end after nine days, following the Government's decision to increase public-sector salaries and allowances for rent and transportation, as well as to lower the cost of rice. The President carried out minor reorganizations of the Council of Ministers in October and December.

On 10 January 2007 the CNTG and the USTG commenced a further general strike, which was supported by a number of opposition parties, including the RPG and the UFR, and several NGOs and civil society groups. Initially their demands again focused on the lowering of the cost of basic foodstuffs and fuel, as well as the return to gaol of two former prominent politicians accused of financial impropriety whose release had been secured by the President in the previous month. However, following violent clashes between demonstrators and the security forces in mid-January, during which five people were killed and several hundred were arrested, the unions insisted on the resignation of Conté and his Government. The President's proposals to reduce the duty on fuel and to increase the salaries of teachers were rejected as insufficient by the union leaders. On 19 January Conté dismissed the Minister of State for Presidential Affairs, El Hadj Fodé Bangoura, but protests continued and further deaths were reported across the country. The Government's response to the strike was condemned by the UN and the African Union (AU, see p. 164) and both organizations urged the Government to commence negotiations with the trade unions. On 23 January the leaders of the CNTG, the USTG and the Organisation Nationale des Syndicats Libres de Guinea were briefly detained. They were released the following day and invited to talks with Conté, following which he indicated his willingness to appoint a 'consensus' Prime Minister. Nevertheless, nation-wide disturbances continued, and it was reported that as many as 60 people had been killed since the beginning of the strike.

On 27 January 2007 the trade unions ended the general strike after President Conté agreed to nominate a new Prime Minister, who would head and appoint the Council of Ministers and represent Guinea at international meetings, although they threatened the commencement of further industrial action if the premier was not selected by 11 February. On 9 February Conté announced that he had chosen Eugène Camara, who had succeeded Bangoura as Minister of State for Presidential Affairs, as Prime Minister. The President's decision was rejected by the trade unions and the political opposition and violence again broke out in Conakry and other cities, reportedly resulting in the deaths of eight people. On 12 February the unions recommenced the general strike and demanded the resignation of Conté, who, in response, declared a 'state of siege' and imposed martial law and a nation-wide curfew the following day. The AU condemned the Guinean authorities' use of excessive force to combat the protests and both the USA and France expressed grave concern at the prevailing situation. Negotiations between the Government and the trade unions took place on 19 February, at which the unions refused to acquiesce to Conté's proposal to maintain Camara as Prime Minister for a period of three months. As the strike continued, on 23 February the Assemblée nationale voted to terminate martial law and the curfew with effect from the end of that day, and, following further negotiations facilitated by an ECOWAS delegation led by former Nigerian President Gen. Ibrahim Babangida, on 26 February Conté announced that he would select a Prime Minister from a list of candidates supplied by the trade unions and opposition parties. Lansana Kouyaté, a career diplomat and the former Executive Secretary of ECOWAS, was duly appointed as Prime Minister and the industrial action was brought to an end on 27 February. In May 2007 provision was made for the establishment of an independent commission of inquiry to determine those responsible for the alleged human rights abuses committed during the crisis, in which an estimated 110 people were killed. Kouyaté named the members of the commission in October but by November they had yet to be sworn in and no progress had been made towards the commencement of an investigation.

Meanwhile, Kouyaté was sworn in as Prime Minister on 1 March 2007 and later that month unveiled a new, 22-member Council of Ministers, composed largely of technocrats and which did not include any ministers from the previous administration. Ousmane Doré, a senior IMF official, was appointed Minister of the Economy, Finance and Planning, Abdoul Kabèlè Camara, hitherto a judge at the Court of Appeal in Conakry, became Minister of Foreign Affairs, Co-operation, African Integration and Guineans Abroad, while the former Deputy Chief of Staff of the Armed Forces, Gen. Arafan Camara, assumed the national defence portfolio. In May members of the armed forces launched a widespread campaign of intimidation against civilians in protest at salary arrears, in some cases dating back as far as 11 years, and the appointment of several senior defence personnel earlier in the year. The two-week uprising was finally suppressed when Arafan Camara and Kerfalla Camara (the Chief of Staff of the Armed Forces) were dismissed. Gen. Bailo Diallo was subsequently named as the new Minister of National Defence, while and Brig.-Gen. Diarra Camara replaced Kefralla Camara.

In early January 2008 Conté dismissed the Minister of Communication and Information Technology, Justin Morel Junior, and appointed in his place Issa Condé, hitherto the head of the state news agency; Morel Junior had criticized the content of the President's New Year's address in which he referred to Kouyaté's administration as a 'disappointment'. The trade unions demanded Morel Junior's reinstatement, and maintained that his replacement was contrary to the agreement that had brought an end to the violence of early 2007. Protests again took place in Conakry, in which at least one death was reported, and on 9 January 2008 Kouyaté and a delegation of government ministers held lengthy negotiations with representatives from the trade unions and civil society organizations in an attempt to avert further industrial action that would threaten the recent economic recovery, and, potentially, the Poverty Reduction and Growth Facility agreed with the IMF the previous month. An accord was reached whereby the unions postponed a planned general strike until 31 March, pending the further discussion of a presidential decree issued in December 2007, which resulted in a reduction in the powers of the Prime Minister. It was widely believed that Conté intended to reclaim a number of the responsibilities that had passed to Kouyaté, following his appointment to the premiership.

Following the *coup d'état* in Sierra Leone in April 1992, ex-President Maj.-Gen. Joseph Momoh was granted asylum in Guinea. His successor, Capt. Valentine Strasser, also took refuge in Guinea after he was deposed in January 1996. President Ahmed Tejan Kabbah, in turn, fled to Guinea in May 1997, following the seizure of power in Sierra Leone by forces led by Maj. Johnny Paul Koroma. Some 1,500 Guinean troops were dispatched in support of the Nigerian-led ECOMOG (see ECOWAS) force in Sierra Leone (occupying in the process the Sierra Leonean border town of Yenga, see below). Guinea joined other members of the international community in condemning the subversion of constitutional order in Sierra Leone, prior to Kabbah's reinstatement, in March 1998, as President of Sierra Leone.

The Liberian Government formally protested to Guinea in April 1999, in response to what it termed an invasion from Guinea of the border town of Voinjama, although the Guinean Government denied the accusations. In August the Liberian Government declared a state of emergency, again claiming that an invasion force had entered Liberia from Guinea, and the border between the two countries was closed. In August ECOWAS ministers responsible for foreign affairs agreed to establish a commission in an effort to resolve the issue of border insecurity in this region. In September Guinea protested to the Organization of African Unity (now the AU), the UN and ECOWAS, after 28 people were allegedly killed in attacks by Liberian troops on villages in the Macenta region. None the less, at an extraordinary summit meeting of ECOWAS leaders in mid-September, Conté and President Charles Taylor of Liberia made pledges of good neighbourliness and non-aggression. The summit condemned the attacks, without apportioning blame. The functions of the Mano River Union (MRU, see p. 413), comprising Guinea, Liberia and Sierra Leone, were to be reactivated, and a joint committee on border security was to be established.

Liberia reopened the border with Guinea in February 2000, but in July the Liberian Government reported renewed fighting, apparently following an attack by rebel groups allegedly based in Guinea. The Liberian Government, which dispatched reinforcements to the border with Guinea, threatened to attack the bases of the rebel groups and accused the Guinean authorities of complicity with the rebels. Relations between Guinea and Liberia deteriorated as tensions in the border region intensified from early September (see above). In January 2001 Liberia accused the Guinean Government of having supported the recent shelling of towns in its Foya district and recalled its ambassador from Conakry. Conté boycotted an ECOWAS conference in Abuja, Nigeria, in April, which had been organized to discuss the conflict in the countries of the MRU, in protest at Taylor's attendance: Liberia had recently expelled the ambassadors of Guinea and Sierra Leone and also sealed its borders with the two countries. In mid-May Guinean forces fired artillery shells at RUF-held positions in northern Sierra Leone, as a UN-supported disarmament process commenced in that country. As the peace process in Sierra Leone advanced in mid-2001, violent unrest in Guinea also abated. In June Kabbah and Conté met in Kambia, in northern Sierra Leone, to discuss regional tensions; following the discussions it was announced that the commercial highway between Conakry and the Sierra Leonean capital, Freetown, closed since 1998, was to reopen. In August 2001 the Liberian authorities withdrew all restrictions imposed on the Guinean and Sierra Leonean diplomatic presences in the Liberian capital, Monrovia, and the ambassadors of the two countries resumed their duties. At the end of September Taylor announced that Liberia was to reopen its borders with Guinea and Sierra Leone.

In February 2002, as violence by rebel groups in Liberia escalated and extended to the outskirts of Monrovia, the Guinean authorities denied allegations, made by Taylor (and subsequently reiterated by Guinean opposition leader Jean-Marie Doré), that Guinea supported rebels of the Liberians United for Reconciliation and Democracy (LURD—see the chapter on Liberia). In late February Taylor, Conté and Kabbah participated in a summit in Rabat, Morocco, to discuss the cross-border insurgencies affecting the three countries. Following further meetings of ministers from the three countries, agreement was reached on the deployment of joint defence and security troops along the common borders to facilitate the return of refugees and to monitor the movement of small arms in the region. In mid-April it was reported that Guinea had begun to deploy troops along its border with Liberia in compliance with this initiative. Relations with Liberia improved markedly from August 2003, when Taylor was forced into exile and the incumbent Government, rebel factions, political opposition and civil organizations in Liberia reached a peace agreement providing for the formation of a transitional power-sharing government and legislature. Sekou Damate Conneh, the Chairman of LURD, who was reported to be an associate of President Conté, returned to Liberia from Guinea in September.

Relations between Guinea and Sierra Leone were complicated in the early 2000s by the ongoing dispute over ownership of the border town of Yenga, in a reportedly diamond-rich region of Sierra Leone, which Guinean troops had occupied in 1998. In a joint statement in September 2004, signed by Presidents Conté and Tabbah, it was announced that both countries recognised Yenga as belonging to Sierra Leone, on the basis of a border agreement of 1912 between the British and French colonial powers.

The protracted conflicts in Liberia and Sierra Leone, and the civil conflict in Côte d'Ivoire from 2002, have resulted in the presence in Guinea of large numbers of refugees, variously estimated to number 5%–15% of the total population. The office of the UN High Commissioner for Refugees (UNHCR) assessed the total number of refugees in Guinea at 501,544 at the beginning of 2000, of which 129,096 were Liberian and 370,631 Sierra Leonean. By the end of 2006, according to UNHCR, the refugee population of Guinea had declined to 31,468, including 21,816 from Liberia and 5,259 from Sierra Leone.

Relations with both the Government of France and with private French interests strengthened considerably in the 1990s: official assistance from, and trade with, France is of great importance to the Guinean economy, as is French participation in the mining sector and in newly privatized organizations. However, in the early 2000s military assistance from France to Guinea was reduced and, to some extent, supplanted by support from other sources: Guinea signed a pact of military co-operation with Russia in 2001, and received military aid from the People's Republic of China in 2002, while in mid-2002 the US military participated in the training of Guinean troops.

Government

Under the terms of the Constitution promulgated on 23 December 1991, and amended in April 1992 and November 2001, the President of the Republic, who is Head of State, is elected for seven years by universal adult suffrage, in the context of a multi-party political system. The 114-member Assemblée nationale, which holds legislative power, is elected by universal suffrage for a five-year term. The President of the Republic is also Head of Government, and in this capacity appoints the other members of the Council of Ministers. The Constitution does not explicitly provide for the position of Prime Minister, but in practice such a position has often existed following the enactment of the 1991 Constitution.

Local administration is based on eight administrative entities (the city of Conakry and seven administrative regions) each under the authority of an appointed Governor; the country is sub-divided into 33 prefectures. Conakry, which comprises a separate administrative unit, is divided into five communes. The 33 prefectures outside of Conakry are sub-divided into 303 communes.

Defence

As assessed at November 2007, Guinea's active armed forces totalled 9,700, comprising an army of 8,500, a navy of 400 and an air force of 800. Paramilitary forces comprised a Republican Guard of 1,600 and a 1,000-strong gendarmerie, as well as a reserve 'people's militia' of 7,000. Military service is compulsory (conscripts were estimated at some 7,500 in 2001) and lasts for two years. The defence budget for 2007 was estimated at 220,000m. FG.

Economic Affairs

In 2006, according to estimates by the World Bank, Guinea's gross national income (GNI), measured at average 2004–06 prices, was US $3,732m., equivalent to $410 per head (or $2,410 on an international purchasing-power parity basis). During 1996–2006, it was estimated, the population increased at an average annual rate of 2.0%, while gross domestic product (GDP) per head increased, in real terms, by an average of 1.4% per year. Overall GDP increased, in real terms, at an average annual rate of 3.4% in 1996–2006, with GDP growth of 2.8% recorded in 2006.

According to the IMF, agriculture (including hunting, forestry and fishing) contributed 20.3% of GDP in 2006. About 81.8% of the labour force were employed in the agricultural sector in mid-2005, according to FAO. The principal cash crops are fruits, oil palm, groundnuts and coffee. Important staple crops include cassava, rice and other cereals and vegetables. The attainment of self-sufficiency in rice and other basic foodstuffs remains a priority. The food supply is supplemented by the rearing of cattle and other livestock. The Government has made efforts towards the commercial exploitation of Guinea's forest resources (forests cover about two-thirds of the country's land area) and substantial fishing stocks. According to the World Bank, during 1996–2006 agricultural GDP increased at an average annual rate of 4.4%; growth in agricultural GDP in 2006 was 4.2%.

Industry (including mining, manufacturing, construction and power) contributed an estimated 32.5% of GDP in 2006. An estimated 1.9% of the employed labour force were engaged in the industrial sector in 1990. According to the World Bank, industrial GDP increased at an average annual rate of 4.1% in 1996–2006; growth in 2006 was 5.0%.

Mining contributed an estimated 16.3% of GDP in 2006. Only 0.7% of the employed labour force were engaged in the sector at the time of the 1983 census. Guinea is the world's foremost exporter of bauxite and the second largest producer of bauxite ore, possessing between one-quarter and one-third of known reserves of the mineral. In 2002 exports of aluminium ore and concentrates and aluminium hydroxide together provided 66.1% of export earnings. Despite the importance to the national economy of the extraction of bauxite, only a small proportion of output is processed into alumina in Guinea; various plans to increase the production of alumina have been proposed. Production of alumina increased by an average of 7.6% per year in 1998–2002, according to the US Geological Survey, although the mining of bauxite declined slightly during the same period. Gold and diamonds are also mined: in 2006 gold contributed 31.6% of export earnings. Exploitation of valuable reserves of high-grade iron ore at Mt Nimba, near the border with Liberia, has been impeded by political instability in the region. Of Guinea's other known mineral deposits, only granite is exploitable on a commercial scale. The GDP of the mining sector increased at an average annual rate of 2.8% in 1997–2002, according to the IMF; growth in 2003 was estimated at 2.6%.

The manufacturing sector remains largely undeveloped, contributing only an estimated 4.0% of GDP in 2006. In 1983 only 0.6% of the employed labour force were engaged in the manufacturing sector. Other than the country's one alumina smelter, most industrial companies are involved in import-substitution, including the processing of agricultural products and the manufacture of construction materials. According to the World Bank, manufacturing GDP increased at an average annual rate of 4.0% in 1996–2006. It increased by 5.2% in 2006.

Electricity generation is, at present, insufficient to meet demand, and power failures outside the mining and industrial sectors (in which the largest operators generate their own power supplies) have been frequent. However, Guinea possesses considerable hydroelectric potential. The 75-MW Garafiri dam project was inaugurated in 1999, and a further major scheme, at Kaléta, was scheduled for completion in the mid-2000s. In the mean time, some 600,000 metric tons of hydrocarbons are imported annually, and in 2003 imports of petroleum products accounted for 23.7% of the value of total merchandise imports.

The services sector contributed an estimated 47.2% of GDP in 2006. During 1996–2006, according to the World Bank, the sector's GDP increased at an average annual rate of 2.4%; growth in 2006 was 1.3%.

In 2006 Guinea recorded a visible trade surplus of US $69.2m., while there was a deficit of $184.7m. on the current account of the balance of payments. The principal suppliers of imports in 2006 were the People's Republic of China (which supplied 8.6% of the total) and France. The principal markets for exports in that year were Russia (which took 11.6% of exports), Ukraine, Spain, the Republic of Korea and France. The principal exports in 2006 were bauxite, gold and alumina. The principal imports included capital goods, intermediate goods and petroleum products.

In 2006 Guinea's overall budget deficit was 473,600m. FG, equivalent to 2.9% of GDP. The country's total external debt was US $3,247m. at the end of 2005, of which $2,931m. was long-term public debt. In 2004 the cost of debt-servicing was equivalent to 19.9% of the value of exports of goods and services. Annual inflation averaged 11.7% in 1996–2006, according to the IMF; consumer prices increased by an average of 34.7% in 2006.

Guinea is a member of the Economic Community of West African States (ECOWAS, see p. 232), of the Gambia River Basin Development Organization (OMVG, see p. 412), of the International Coffee Organization (see p. 408), of the West Africa Rice Development Association (WARDA, see p. 410) and of the Mano River Union (see p. 413).

Guinea's potential for the attainment of wealth is substantial, owing to its valuable mineral deposits, water resources and generally favourable climate; however, the economy remains over-dependent on revenue from bauxite reserves and on external assistance, while the country's infrastructure is inadequate and its manufacturing base narrow. The economy recorded steady growth during the 1990s, at which time both inflation and the fiscal deficit were relatively low, although growth was more modest in the early 2000s, chiefly as a result of insecurity in the region, a decline in the price of bauxite (Guinea's principal export) and an increase in the international prices of imports, most significantly petroleum products. A deterioration in the economic situation in Guinea from 2004, characterized in particular by a series of sharp rises in the price of rice and fuel products, high electricity costs, and unpaid public sector wages, provoked a series of strikes and violent disturbances across the country. These culminated in the replacement of the Government in early 2007 (see above) and the appointment of a new Prime Minister, whose immediate priorities included addressing corruption in the country and attempting to halt the alarming economic decline of recent years. According to the IMF, the rate of inflation was recorded at 23.4% in 2007 (it had reached 34.7% the previous year), negating any reduction in the price of fuel and basic foodstuffs, and it was estimated by international relief agencies that more than 60% of Guineans lived in poverty. Furthermore, Guinea's infrastructure has suffered from years of underinvestment and severe power shortages, unemployment and widespread disease continued adversely to affect the population. By late 2007 the new Government's performance in aiding the recovery of the economy had satisfied the IMF sufficiently to end the nation's six-year suspension from the Fund, and a new three-year Poverty Reduction and Growth Facility, totalling US $75.2m., was approved by the IMF in December, aimed at supporting the administration's economic programme. Meanwhile, the UN International Fund for Agricultural Development granted $10m. to Guinea in September to provide rural families with improved access to drinking water, health care and education. GDP growth was forecast to increase by 5.1% in 2008.

Education

Education is provided free of charge at every level in state institutions. Primary education, which begins at seven years of age and lasts for six years, is officially compulsory. According to UNESCO estimates, in 2003/04 enrolment at primary schools included 64% of children in the relevant age-group (males 69%; females 58%), while enrolment at secondary schools in that year included 21% of children in the appropriate age-group (boys 28%; girls 14%). Secondary education, from the age of 13, lasts for seven years, comprising a first cycle (collège) of four years and a second (lycée) of three years. There are universities at Conakry and Kankan, and other tertiary institutions at Manéyah, Boké and Faranah; some 14,000 students were enrolled at these institutions in 2000. Independent schools, which had been banned for 23 years under the Sekou Touré regime, were legalized in 1984. Budget estimates for 1999 allocated 62,300m. FG to education (equivalent to 8.1% of total budgetary expenditure).

Public Holidays

2008: 1 January (New Year's Day), 20 March* (Mouloud, Birth of Muhammad), 24 April (Easter Monday), 1 May (Labour Day), 27 August (Anniversary of Women's Revolt), 28 September (Referendum Day), 1 October* (Id al-Fitr, end of Ramadan), 2 October (Republic Day), 1 November (All Saints' Day), 22 November (Day of 1970 Invasion), 25 December (Christmas).

2009: 1 January (New Year's Day), 9 March* (Mouloud, Birth of Muhammad), 9 April (Easter Monday), 1 May (Labour Day), 27 August (Anniversary of Women's Revolt), 20 September* (Id al-Fitr, end of Ramadan), 28 September (Referendum Day), 2 October (Republic Day), 1 November (All Saints' Day), 22 November (Day of 1970 Invasion), 25 December (Christmas).

* These holidays are determined by the Islamic lunar calendar and may vary by one or two days from the dates given.

Weights and Measures

The metric system is in force.

Statistical Survey

Source (unless otherwise stated): Direction Nationale de la Statistique, BP 221, Conakry; tel. 21-33-12; e-mail dnstat@biasy.net; internet www.afristat.org/ins-guinee.

Area and Population

AREA, POPULATION AND DENSITY

Area (sq km)	245,857*
Population (census results)	
4–17 February 1983	4,533,240†
31 December 1996‡	
Males	3,497,551
Females	3,658,855
Total	7,156,406
Population (UN estimates at mid-year)§	
2005	9,003,000
2006	9,181,000
2007	9,370,000
Density (per sq km) at mid-2007	38.1

* 94,926 sq miles.
† Excluding adjustment for underenumeration.
‡ Including refugees from Liberia and Sierra Leone (estimated at 640,000).
§ Source: UN, *World Population Prospects: The 2006 Revision*.

ETHNIC GROUPS

1995 (percentages): Peul 38.7; Malinké 23.3; Soussou 11.1; Kissi 5.9; Kpellé 4.5; Others 16.5 (Source: La Francophonie).

ADMINISTRATIVE DIVISIONS
(1996 census)

Region	Area (sq km)	Population	Density (per sq km)	Principal city
Conakry	450	1,092,936	2,428.7	Conakry
Basse-Guinée	47,063	1,460,577	31.0	Kindia
Moyenne-Guinée	52,939	1,639,617	31.0	Labé
Haute-Guinée	99,437	1,407,734	14.2	Kankan
Guinée Forestière	45,968	1,555,542	33.8	N'Zérékoré
Total	245,857	7,156,406	29.1	

Note: The regions were subsequently reorganized. The new regions (which in each case share their name with the regional capital) are: Boké; Conakry; Faranah; Kankan; Kindia; Labé; Mamou; and N'Zérékoré.

PRINCIPAL TOWNS
(population at 1996 census)

Conakry (capital)	1,092,936	Kindia	96,074
N'Zérékoré	107,329	Guéckédou	79,140
Kankan	100,192	Kamsar	61,526

Mid-2007 ('000, incl. suburbs, UN estimate): Conakry 1,497 (Source: UN, *World Urbanization Prospects: The 2007 Revision*).

BIRTHS AND DEATHS
(annual averages, UN estimates)

	1990–95	1995–2000	2000–05
Birth rate (per 1,000)	45.6	43.7	42.0
Death rate (per 1,000)	17.4	15.2	13.5

Source: UN, *World Population Prospects: The 2006 Revision*.

Expectation of life (years at birth, WHO estimates): 53 (males 52; females 55) in 2004 (Source: WHO, *World Health Report*).

ECONOMICALLY ACTIVE POPULATION
('000 persons at 1996 census)

	Males	Females	Total
Agriculture, hunting and forestry	1,140,775	1,281,847	2,422,622
Fishing	9,969	889	10,858
Mining and quarrying	26,599	8,376	34,975
Manufacturing	84,974	5,911	90,885
Electricity, gas and water supply	4,366	324	4,690
Construction	59,802	724	60,526
Wholesale and retail trade; repair of motor vehicles and motorcycles and personal and household goods	176,527	191,230	367,757
Restaurants and hotels	3,162	2,790	5,952
Transport, storage and communications	75,374	1,696	77,070
Financial intermediation	1,728	626	2,354
Real estate, renting and business activities	877	209	1,086
Public administration and defence; compulsory social security	50,401	12,791	63,192
Education	15,044	3,773	18,817
Health and social work	4,762	3,522	8,284
Other community, social and personal service activities	44,897	48,292	93,189
Private households with employed persons	5,553	6,202	11,755
Extra-territorial organizations and bodies	3,723	1,099	4,822
Total employed	1,708,533	1,570,301	3,278,834

Mid-2005 ('000 persons): Agriculture, etc. 3,788; Total labour force 4,631 (Source: FAO).

Health and Welfare

KEY INDICATORS

Total fertility rate (children per woman, 2005)	5.7
Under-5 mortality rate (per 1,000 live births, 2005)	150
HIV/AIDS (% of persons aged 15–49, 2005)	1.5
Physicians (per 1,000 head, 2004)	0.11
Hospital beds (per 1,000 head, 1990)	0.55
Health expenditure (2004): US $ per head (PPP)	95.6
Health expenditure (2004): % of GDP	5.3
Health expenditure (2004): public (% of total)	13.2
Access to water (% of persons, 2004)	50
Access to sanitation (% of persons, 2004)	18
Human Development Index (2005): ranking	160
Human Development Index (2005): value	0.456

For sources and definitions, see explanatory note on p. vi.

GUINEA   *Statistical Survey*

Agriculture

PRINCIPAL CROPS
('000 metric tons)

	2004	2005	2006*
Rice (paddy)	1,208.0	1,272.4	1,340.3
Maize	461.0	502.1	546.8
Fonio	208.4	219.4	231.1
Sweet potatoes	187.7	201.0	208.1
Cassava (Manioc)	968.8	1,017.4	1,068.5
Taro (Coco Yam)*	30	30	31
Yams*	57.1	61.6	40.5
Sugar cane*	280	280	281
Pulses*	60	60	61
Groundnuts (in shell)	257.2	275.2	294.5
Coconuts	28.1†	28.1†	28.1
Oil palm fruit*	872.8	896.3	883.0
Bananas*	158.0	162.3	155.0
Plantains*	440.7	446.5	435.0
Guavas, mangoes and mangosteens*	147.0	145.0	164.0
Pineapples*	102.1	103.1	107.0
Cotton (lint)*	15	15	16
Cottonseed*	19.3	21.5	22.0
Coffee (green)*	20.2	21.4	16.5

* FAO estimates.
† Unofficial figure.

Aggregate production ('000 metric tons, may include official, semi-official or estimated data): Total cereals 2,136.2 in 2004, 2,039.3 in 2005, 2,445.2 in 2006; Total roots and tubers 1,243.7 in 2004, 1,310.0 in 2005, 1,347.7 in 2006; Total vegetables (incl. melons) 483.0 in 2004, 481.8 in 2005, 492.3 in 2006; Total fruits (excl. melons) 1,102.4 in 2004, 1,111.3 in 2005, 1,121.3 in 2006.

Source: FAO.

LIVESTOCK
('000 head, year ending September)

	2004	2005	2006*
Cattle	3,561	3,756	3,756
Sheep	1,096	1,169	1,169
Goats	1,308	1,396	1,396
Pigs	71.3	74.8	74.8
Chickens	14,967	15,865	15,865

* FAO estimates.
Source: FAO.

LIVESTOCK PRODUCTS
('000 metric tons, FAO estimates)

	2004	2005	2006
Cattle meat	35.5	36.8	38.9
Chicken meat	4.7	5.1	5.4
Sheep meat	4.3	4.5	4.8
Goat meat	5.6	6.0	6.5
Other meat	5.9	6.0	6.1
Cows' milk	81.8	84.6	88.0
Goats' milk	7.2	7.6	8.4
Hen eggs	17.3	18.6	19.7

Source: FAO.

Forestry

ROUNDWOOD REMOVALS
('000 cubic metres, excl. bark, FAO estimates)

	2004	2005	2006
Sawlogs, veneer logs and logs for sleepers	138	138	138
Other industrial wood	513	513	513
Fuel wood	11,635	11,687	11,738
Total	12,286	12,338	12,389

Source: FAO.

SAWNWOOD PRODUCTION
('000 cubic metres, incl. railway sleepers)

	1998	1999	2000
Total (all broadleaved)	26	26*	26*

* FAO estimate.
2001–06: Figures assumed to be unchanged from 2000 (FAO estimates).
Source: FAO.

Fishing

('000 metric tons, live weight)

	2003	2004	2005*
Freshwater fishes*	4.0	4.0	4.0
Sea catfishes	11.8	6.0	6.0
Bobo croaker	9.8	7.7	8.0
West African croakers	3.2	2.5	2.5
Sardinellas	3.7	1.4	1.5
Bonga shad	52.8	32.4	34.0
Total catch (incl. others)*	120.2	93.9	96.6

* FAO estimates.
Source: FAO.

Mining

('000 metric tons, unless otherwise indicated)

	2003	2004	2005*
Bauxite (dry basis)†	15,000	15,254	15,200
Gold (kilograms)‡	16,622	11,100	15,300
Salt (unrefined)*	15	15	15
Diamonds ('000 carats)‡	666	740	550

* Estimates.
† Estimated to be 3% water.
‡ Including artisanal production.
Source: US Geological Survey.

Industry

SELECTED PRODUCTS
('000 metric tons, unless otherwise indicated)

	2000	2001	2002
Salted, dried or smoked fish*	11.0	11.0	11.0
Palm oil (unrefined)*†	50	50	50
Beer of barley*†	11.5	7.8	7.8
Raw sugar*	25‡	25†	25†
Alumina (calcined equivalent)§	571	644	680
Electric energy (million kWh)†	569	796	798

* Data from FAO.
† Estimate(s).
‡ Unofficial figure.
§ Data from the US Geological Survey.

Alumina ('000 metric tons, calcined equivalent): 730 in 2003; 877 in 2004; 730 in 2005 (estimate) (Source: US Geological Survey).

Electric energy (million kWh): 801 in 2003; 801 in 2004.

Source: mainly FAO; UN, *Industrial Commodity Statistics Yearbook*.

Finance

CURRENCY AND EXCHANGE RATES

Monetary Units
100 centimes = 1 franc guinéen (FG or Guinean franc).

Sterling, Dollar and Euro Equivalents (29 September 2006)
£1 sterling = 10,465.643 Guinean francs;
US $1 = 5,596.000 Guinean francs;
€1 = 7,084.540 Guinean francs;
100,000 Guinean francs = £9.55 = $17.87 = €14.12.

Average Exchange Rate (Guinean francs per US $)
2003	1,984.9
2004	2,225.0
2005	3,644.3

BUDGET
('000 million Guinean francs)

Revenue*	2004	2005	2006
Mining-sector revenue	171.0	380.6	675.0
Other revenue	765.0	1,176.0	1,497.3
Tax revenue	702.3	1,052.7	1,336.8
Taxes on income and profits	117.6	180.6	280.0
Taxes on domestic production and trade	402.8	554.4	620.3
Taxes on international trade	181.9	317.7	436.5
Non-tax revenue	62.6	123.3	160.5
Total	936.0	1,556.6	2,172.3

Expenditure†	2004	2005	2006
Current expenditure	1,015.9	1,304.4	2,188.0
Wages and salaries	274.8	332.5	444.4
Other goods and services	255.7	396.1	809.6
Subsidies and transfers	260.4	246.7	397.5
Interest due on external debt	120.6	167.9	273.8
Interest due on domestic debt	104.3	161.3	262.7
Capital expenditure	444.0	500.4	672.3
Domestically financed	181.1	199.5	295.2
Externally financed	262.9	300.9	377.1
Total	1,459.9	1,804.8	2,860.3

* Excluding grants received ('000 million Guinean francs): 91.4 in 2004; 74.9 in 2005; 225.5 in 2006.
† Excluding lending minus repayments ('000 million Guinean francs): 4.3 in 2004; 3.1 in 2005; 11.1 in 2006.

Source: IMF, *Guinea: Selected Issues and Statistical Appendix* (January 2008).

INTERNATIONAL RESERVES
(US $ million at 31 December)

	2004	2005
Gold (national valuation)	1.29	1.27
IMF special drawing rights	—	0.02
Reserve position in IMF	0.12	0.11
Foreign exchange	110.37	94.93
Total	111.78	96.33

2006 (US $ million at 31 December): Reserve position in IMF 0.11.

Source: IMF, *International Financial Statistics*.

MONEY SUPPLY
(million Guinean francs at 31 December)

	2003	2004	2005
Currency outside banks	478,133	536,169	786,587
Demand deposits at commercial banks	386,359	518,469	590,420
Total (incl. others)	893,055	1,143,312	1,394,203

Source: IMF, *International Financial Statistics*.

COST OF LIVING
(Consumer Price Index for Conakry; base: 2002 = 100)

	2004	2005	2006
Foodstuffs, beverages and tobacco	147.1	201.6	287.3
Clothing and shoes	109.8	121.9	151.6
Housing, water, electricity and gas	114.0	142.7	174.7
All items (incl. others)	130.1	170.9	230.2

Source: IMF, *Guinea: Selected Issues and Statistical Appendix* (January 2008).

NATIONAL ACCOUNTS

Expenditure on the Gross Domestic Product
('000 million Guinean francs at current prices)

	2004	2005	2006
Government final consumption expenditure	568.9	750.0	1,227.2
Private final consumption expenditure	7,732.5	9,820.9	13,618.7
Gross fixed capital formation	1,014.5	1,668.4	2,242.3
Change in stocks	1.2	0.9	0.6
Total domestic expenditure	9,317.0	12,240.2	17,088.8
Exports of goods and services	1,880.1	3,363.9	5,705.1
Less Imports of goods and services	2,265.4	3,735.5	6,463.5
GDP at market prices	8,931.8	11,868.7	16,330.4

Gross Domestic Product by Economic Activity
('000 million Guinean francs at constant 1996 prices)

	2004	2005	2006
Agriculture, livestock, forestry and fishing	987.2	1,017.3	1,057.5
Mining	831.6	861.1	846.3
Manufacturing	198.6	201.6	206.6
Electricity and water	27.8	28.1	28.2
Construction	531.0	562.9	607.9
Trade	1,315.3	1,331.1	1,351.1
Transport	289.7	293.5	297.6
Administration	267.5	270.2	272.9
Other services	510.9	522.1	535.2
GDP at factor cost	4,959.6	5,087.8	5,203.2
Indirect taxes	200.2	243.6	243.8
GDP at constant prices	5,159.8	5,331.4	5,447.0

Source: IMF, *Guinea: Selected Issues and Statistical Appendix* (January 2008).

BALANCE OF PAYMENTS
(US $ million)

	2004	2005	2006
Exports of goods f.o.b.	748.3	841.4	1,011.1
Imports of goods f.o.b.	−721.0	−754.9	−942.0
Trade balance	27.3	86.4	69.2
Exports of services	80.7	82.8	86.0
Imports of services	−277.9	−271.3	−301.0
Balance on goods and services	−169.9	−102.1	−145.8
Other income received (net)	−59.8	−39.9	−41.7
Balance on goods, services and income	−229.7	−142.0	−187.5
Current transfers (net)	2.3	−4.7	2.9
Current balance	−227.3	−146.6	−184.7
Capital account (net)	25.6	7.6	24.9
Financial account (net)	114.9	52.2	26.6
Net errors and omissions	−12.9	56.6	47.7
Overall balance	−99.8	−30.2	−85.6

Source: IMF, *Guinea: Selected Issues and Statistical Appendix* (January 2008).

GUINEA

External Trade

PRINCIPAL COMMODITIES
(US $ million)

Imports c.i.f.	2000	2001	2002
Food and live animals	110.0	110.9	115.1
Cereals and cereal preparations	55.9	61.2	63.0
Rice	28.8	33.2	43.0
Rice, semi-milled or wholly milled	28.5	32.7	42.9
Rice, semi-milled or milled (unbroken)	17.0	20.3	16.2
Rice, broken	11.5	12.3	26.7
Sugar, sugar preparations and honey	15.5	18.1	21.3
Sugar and honey	13.8	17.1	19.9
Refined sugar, etc.	13.5	16.8	19.3
Beverages and tobacco	26.3	22.1	25.3
Tobacco and tobacco manufactures	23.6	19.2	22.3
Cigarettes	23.0	18.7	21.8
Mineral fuels, lubricants, etc.	152.8	112.0	144.3
Petroleum products, refined	151.6	111.1	139.9
Chemicals and related products	51.6	65.7	82.3
Inorganic chemicals	6.2	25.5	24.0
Inorganic chemical elements, oxides and halogen salts	4.1	17.2	16.7
Medicinal and pharmaceutical products	23.3	15.7	34.2
Medicaments (incl. veterinary medicaments)	21.6	14.2	33.6
Medicaments (incl. veterinary medicaments) containing other substances	21.5	14.0	29.1
Basic manufactures	81.5	83.4	102.8
Non-metallic mineral manufactures	19.0	28.4	37.0
Lime, cement and fabricated construction materials	13.7	22.4	30.7
Cement	12.7	19.2	27.9
Iron and steel	19.3	16.1	21.6
Machinery and transport equipment	116.2	149.7	127.2
General industrial machinery, equipment and parts	22.8	37.1	31.7
Road vehicles	53.1	61.8	49.8
Passenger motor vehicles (excl. buses)	26.3	36.6	32.1
Miscellaneous manufactured articles	51.0	39.2	42.5
Total (incl. others)	612.4	600.8	666.5

Statistical Survey

Exports f.o.b.	2000	2001	2002
Crude materials (inedible) except fuels	283.5	310.8	277.6
Aluminium ore and concentrate	269.9	309.8	257.3
Chemicals and related products	56.9	98.6	90.0
Aluminium hydroxide	56.9	98.4	89.9
Miscellaneous manufactured articles	61.9	15.5	8.4
Unused postage; stamp-impressed papers; stock; cheque books, etc.	61.3	14.7	8.1
Gold, non-monetary, (excl. gold ores and concentrates) unwrought or semi-manufactured	96.3	118.6	129.9
Total (incl. others)	522.4	574.9	525.4

Source: UN, *International Trade Statistics Yearbook*.

2004 (US $ million): *Imports:* Food products 160.4; Other consumption goods 133.6; Petroleum products 124.1; Intermediate goods 142.3; Capital goods 217.2; Total imports (incl. others) 721.0. *Exports:* Bauxite 292.4; Alumina 163.0; Diamonds 48.2; Gold 171.3; Coffee 15.8; Total exports (incl. others) 748.3 (Source: IMF, *Guinea: Selected Issues and Statistical Appendix—January 2008*).

2005 (US $ million): *Imports:* Food products 147.0; Other consumption goods 119.2; Petroleum products 181.8; Intermediate goods 167.6; Capital goods 232.7; Total imports (incl. others) 754.9. *Exports:* Bauxite 356.7; Alumina 116.7; Diamonds 35.2; Gold 252.0; Coffee 23.3; Total exports (incl. others) 841.4 (Source: IMF, *Guinea: Selected Issues and Statistical Appendix—January 2008*).

2006 (US $ million): *Imports:* Food products 165.0; Other consumption goods 124.7; Petroleum products 223.7; Intermediate goods 227.7; Capital goods 317.4; Total imports (incl. others) 942.0. *Exports:* Bauxite 404.7; Alumina 141.8; Diamonds 42.9; Gold 319.3; Coffee 31.8; Total exports (incl. others) 1,011.1 (Source: IMF, *Guinea: Selected Issues and Statistical Appendix—January 2008*).

PRINCIPAL TRADING PARTNERS
(US $ million)

Imports c.i.f.	2000	2001	2002
Australia	7.2	11.9	18.0
Belgium	47.4	78.9	42.6
Brazil	2.7	2.3	9.5
China, People's Republic	28.4	32.4	43.7
Côte d'Ivoire	130.9	76.4	96.9
Cyprus	9.6	0.3	n.a.
Denmark	4.1	9.5	1.3
France (incl. Monaco)	121.2	104.8	107.7
Gabon	7.3	3.6	9.6
Germany	19.2	13.6	21.8
Hong Kong	6.1	6.0	8.9
India	11.4	9.3	20.9
Indonesia	5.6	6.5	9.0
Italy	21.0	20.6	29.5
Japan	34.2	23.2	36.3
Netherlands	14.3	28.7	11.8
Senegal	4.0	6.8	2.8
South Africa	3.9	9.9	8.1
Spain	11.5	17.8	12.6
Switzerland-Liechtenstein	4.5	9.6	8.9
Thailand	5.8	11.4	7.5
Ukraine	4.6	3.7	10.0
United Arab Emirates	4.2	6.1	7.9
United Kingdom	9.2	15.8	15.7
USA	48.4	42.8	55.3
Total (incl. others)	612.4	600.8	666.5

Exports f.o.b.	2000	2001	2002
Australia	—	—	9.2
Belgium	2.7	16.0	20.5
Cameroon	9.6	15.5	4.2
Canada	17.2	15.8	21.6
China, People's Republic	—	—	9.8
France (incl. Monaco)	172.6	149.7	127.9
Germany	32.1	37.6	42.1
Hungary	5.8	—	—
Ireland	47.5	65.1	53.5
Malta	6.3	—	—

GUINEA

Exports f.o.b.—continued	2000	2001	2002
Morocco	7.3	5.6	1.7
Netherlands	0.3	7.3	6.6
Romania	1.8	—	7.0
Russia	21.6	44.6	33.8
Seychelles	5.8	0.3	—
Spain	50.1	54.6	53.4
Sudan	6.5	—	—
Switzerland-Liechtenstein	26.5	5.5	30.9
Ukraine	15.5	1.6	7.3
United Kingdom	17.4	32.3	29.1
USA	66.7	96.9	46.3
Total (incl. others)	522.4	574.9	525.4

Source: UN, *International Trade Statistics Yearbook*.

2004 (percentage of total): *Imports:* Belgium 5.9; China, People's Rep. 5.9; Côte d'Ivoire 15.1; France 8.7; Japan 2.2; South Africa 4.6; USA 3.4. *Exports:* Belgium 14.7; France 17.7; Switzerland 12.8; Ukraine 4.2; United Kingdom 14.7 (Source: IMF, *Guinea: Selected Issues and Statistical Appendix*—January 2008).

2005 (percentage of total): *Imports:* Belgium 4.1; China, People's Rep. 8.5; Côte d'Ivoire 5.2; France 7.2; India 3.1; Italy 4.7; Senegal 2.4; South Africa 2.2; United Kingdom 2.4; USA 7.3. *Exports:* Belgium 4.5; France 5.7; Germany 5.0; Ireland 6.0; Korea, Rep. 11.3; Romania 2.8; Russia 14.6; Spain 10.2; Ukraine 7.9; USA 6.1. (Source: IMF, *Guinea: Selected Issues and Statistical Appendix*—January 2008).

2006 (percentage of total): *Imports:* Belgium 4.5; China, People's Rep. 8.6; Côte d'Ivoire 3.5; France 8.0; Japan 2.3; United Kingdom 2.9; USA 3.2. *Exports:* Belgium 3.2; Canada 2.2; France 7.7; Germany 5.4; Ireland 5.0; Korea, Rep. 8.8; Russia 11.6; Spain 9.0; Ukraine 9.6; USA 7.7. (Source: IMF, *Guinea: Selected Issues and Statistical Appendix*—January 2008).

Transport

RAILWAYS
(estimated traffic)

	1991	1992	1993
Freight ton-km (million)	660	680	710

Source: UN Economic Commission for Africa, *African Statistical Yearbook*.

ROAD TRAFFIC
('000, motor vehicles in use, estimates)

	2001	2002	2003
Passenger cars	41.6	43.1	47.5
Buses and coaches	24.8	20.5	20.9
Lorries and vans	11.1	10.5	15.7

SHIPPING
Merchant Fleet
(registered at 31 December)

	2004	2005	2006
Number of vessels	38	41	40
Total displacement ('000 grt)	13.4	14.7	18.5

Source: Lloyd's Register-Fairplay, *World Fleet Statistics*.

International Sea-borne Freight Traffic
('000 metric tons)

	2001	2002	2003
Goods loaded	2,424	2,595	2,828
Goods unloaded	2,043	2,178	2,453

CIVIL AVIATION
(traffic on scheduled services)

	1997	1998	1999
Kilometres flown (million)	1	1	1
Passengers carried ('000)	36	36	59
Passenger-km (million)	55	55	94
Total ton-km (million)	6	6	10

Source: UN, *Statistical Yearbook*.

Tourism

FOREIGN VISITOR ARRIVALS*

Country of origin	2003	2004	2005
Belgium	1,067	973	1,353
Canada	914	969	1,144
China, People's Repub.	1,002	1,515	1,562
Côte d'Ivoire	4,504	3,397	3,434
France	10,654	9,168	9,783
Germany	879	920	1,160
Mali	1,659	1,287	1,382
Senegal	4,358	4,993	5,536
Sierra Leone	3,345	2,714	848
USA	2,987	3,121	3,925
Total (incl. others)	43,966	42,041	45,334

* Arrivals of non-resident tourists at national borders, by country of residence.

Receipts from tourism (US $ million): 31 in 2003; 30 in 2004; n.a. in 2005.

Source: World Tourism Organization.

Communications Media

	2004	2005	2006
Telephones ('000 main lines in use)	26.2	26.3	26.3
Mobile cellular telephones ('000 subscribers)	154.9	189.0	189.0
Personal computers ('000 in use)	44	46	n.a.
Internet users ('000)	46	50	50

Source: International Telecommunication Union.

Television receivers ('000 in use): 351 in 2000 (Source: UNESCO, *Statistical Yearbook*).

Radio receivers ('000 in use): 380 in 1999 (Source: UNESCO, *Statistical Yearbook*).

Facsimile machines (number in use, estimate): 3,186 in 1999 (Source: UNESCO, *Statistical Yearbook*).

Non-daily newspapers: 1 title in 1996 (average circulation 20,000) (Source: UNESCO, *Statistical Yearbook*).

Education

(2004/05, unless otherwise indicated)

	Institutions	Teachers	Males	Females	Total
Pre-primary	202*	2,436	35.5	33.8	69.3
Primary	5,765	26,897	674.7	532.0	1,206.7
Secondary	557	11,888	282.1	141.4	423.5
Technical	41	n.a.	3.3	3.9	7.2
University	7	860	13.5	2.7	16.4

Students ('000)

* 1996/97.

Source: partly UNESCO Institute for Statistics.

Adult literacy rate (UNESCO estimates): 29.5% (males 42.6%; females 18.1%) in 2003 (Source: UNESCO Institute for Statistics).

Directory

The Constitution

The Constitution (*Loi fondamentale*) of the Third Republic of Guinea was adopted in a national referendum on 23 December 1990 and promulgated on 23 December 1991. An 'organic law' of 3 April 1992, providing for the immediate establishment of an unlimited number of political parties, countermanded the Constitution's provision for the eventual establishment of a two-party political system. There was to be a five-year period of transition, overseen by a Comité transitoire de redressement national (CTRN), to civilian rule, at the end of which executive and legislative authority would be vested in organs of state elected by universal adult suffrage in the context of a multi-party political system. The CTRN was dissolved following the legislative elections of June 1995. Amendments to provisions concerning the President were approved by referendum in November 2001.

The Constitution defines the clear separation of the powers of the executive, the legislature and the judiciary. The President of the Republic, who is Head of State, must be elected by an absolute majority of the votes cast, and a second round of voting is held should no candidate obtain such a majority at a first round. The duration of the presidential mandate is seven years, and elections are by universal adult suffrage. Any candidate for the presidency must be more than 40 years old, must not be a serving member of the armed forces, and must be proposed by a political party. There are no restrictions on the number of terms of office the President may serve. The President is Head of Government, and is empowered to appoint ministers and to delegate certain functions. The legislature is the 114-member Assemblée nationale. One-third of the Assemblée's members are elected as representatives of single-member constituencies, the remainder being appointed from national lists, according to a system of proportional representation. The legislature is elected, by universal suffrage, with a five-year mandate.

The Government

HEAD OF STATE

President: Gen. LANSANA CONTÉ (took office 4 April 1984; elected 19 December 1993; re-elected 14 December 1998 and 21 December 2003).

COUNCIL OF MINISTERS
(February 2008)

Prime Minister: LANSANA KOUYATÉ.
Minister of the Economy, Finance and Planning: OUSMANE DORÉ.
Minister of Foreign Affairs, Co-operation, African Integration and Guineans Abroad: ABDOUL KABÈLÈ CAMARA.
Minister of National Defence: Gen. BAILO DIALLO.
Minister of the Interior and Security: MAMADOU M'BOH KEÏTA.
Minister of Justice and Human Rights: PAULETTE KOUROUMA.
Minister of Economic and Financial Control, Ethics and Transparency: SAIDOU DIALLO.
Minister of Mines and Geology: AHMED KANTÉ.
Minister of Energy and Water Resources: GOMOU GNANGA KOUMATA.
Minister of Agriculture, Livestock, the Environment, Water and Forests: Dr MAMADOU CAMARA.
Minister of Fishing and Aquaculture: MOHAMED YOULA.
Minister of Trade, Industry, Tourism and Handicrafts: MAMADI TRAORÉ.
Minister of Public Works, Town Planning and Housing: THIERNO OUMAR BAH.
Minister of Transport: BOUBACAR SOW.
Minister of Communication and Information Technology: ISSA CONDÉ.
Minister of National Education and Scientific Research: Dr OUSMANE SOUARÉ.
Minister of Youth, Culture and Sports: BAIDI ARIBOT.
Minister of Public Health: SANGARÉ MAÏMOUNA BAH.
Minister of Social Affairs and the Promotion of Women and Children: HADJA TETE NABE.
Minister of Employment, Public Service and Administrative Reform: AMADOU DIALLO.
Secretary-General at the Presidency: SAM MAMADOU SOUMAH.
Secretary-General of the Government: El Hadj OURY BAILO BAH.
Secretary-General of Religious Affairs: MAHMOUD CHÉRIF NABANIOU.

MINISTRIES

Office of the President: BP 1000, Boulbinet, Conakry; tel. 30-41-10-16; fax 30-41-16-73.
Office of the Prime Minister: BP 5141, Conakry; tel. 30-41-51-19; fax 30-41-52-82.
Office of the Secretary-General of the Government: Boulbinet, Conakry; tel. 30-41-11-27.
Office of the Secretary-General at the Presidency: Conakry.
Office of the Secretary-General of Religious Affairs: BP 386, Conakry; tel. 30-41-23-38.
Ministry of Agriculture, Livestock, the Environment, Water and Forests: face à la Cité du Port, BP 576, Conakry; tel. 30-41-11-81; fax 30-41-11-69.
Ministry of Communication and Information Technology: Conakry.
Ministry of Economic and Financial Control, Ethics and Transparency: Conakry.
Ministry of the Economy, Finance and Planning: Boulbinet, BP 221, Conakry; tel. 30-45-17-95; fax 30-41-30-59.
Ministry of Employment, Public Service and Administrative Reform: Boulbinet, Conakry; tel. 30-45-20-01.
Ministry of Energy and Water Resources: Conakry; tel. 30-41-31-90.
Ministry of Fishing and Aquaculture: face à la Cité du Port, BP 307, Conakry; tel. 30-41-35-23; fax 30-41-35-28.
Ministry of Foreign Affairs, Co-operation, African Integration and Guineans Abroad: face au Port, ex-Primature, BP 2519, Conakry; tel. 30-45-12-70; fax 30-41-16-21; internet www.mae.gov.gn.
Ministry of the Interior and Security: Coléah-Domino, Conakry; tel. 30-41-45-50.
Ministry of Justice and Human Rights: face à l'Immeuble 'La Paternelle', Almamya, Conakry; tel. 30-41-29-60.
Ministry of Mines and Geology: BP 295, Conakry; tel. 30-41-38-33; fax 30-41-49-13; internet www.cpdm.gov.gn.
Ministry of National Defence: Camp Samory-Touré, Conakry; tel. 41-11-54.
Ministry of National Education and Scientific Research: face à la Cathédrale Sainte-Marie, BP 964, Conakry; tel. 30-45-12-17; fax 30-41-20-12.
Ministry of Public Health: blvd du Commerce, BP 585, Conakry; tel. 30-41-20-32; fax 30-41-41-38.
Ministry of Public Works, Town Planning and Housing: Conakry; tel. 30-41-35-60.
Ministry of Social Affairs and the Promotion of Women and Children: Corniche-Ouest, face au Terminal Conteneurs du Port de Conakry, BP 527, Conakry; tel. 30-41-20-15; fax 30-41-46-60.
Ministry of Trade, Industry, Tourism and Handicrafts: BP 468, Conakry; tel. 30-44-26-06; fax 30-44-49-90.
Ministry of Transport: BP 715, Conakry; tel. 30-41-36-39; fax 30-41-35-77.
Ministry of Youth, Sports and Culture: ave du Port Secrétariat, BP 262, Conakry; tel. 30-41-19-59; fax 30-41-19-26.

President and Legislature

PRESIDENT

Election, 21 December 2003

Candidate	Votes	% of votes
Lansana Conté (PUP)	3,884,594	95.25
Mamadou Bhoye Barry (UPN—PUD)	193,579	4.75
Total	4,078,173	100.00

LEGISLATURE

Assemblée nationale
Palais du Peuple, BP 414, Conakry; tel. 30-41-28-04; fax 30-45-17-00; e-mail s.general@assemblee.gov.gn; internet www.assemblee.gov.gn.

GUINEA

Speaker: ABOUBACAR SOMPARÉ.

General Election, 30 June 2002

Party	% of votes	Seats
Parti de l'unité et du progrès (PUP)	61.57	85
Union pour le progrès et le renouveau (UPR)	26.63	20
Union pour le progrès de la Guinée (UPG)	4.11	3
Parti démocratique de Guinée—Rassemblement démocratique africain (PDG—RDA)	3.40	3
Alliance nationale pour le progrès (ANP)	1.98	2
Union pour le progrès national—Parti pour l'unité et le développement (UPN—PUD)	0.69	1
Others	1.61	—
Total	100.00	114*

*Comprising 76 seats allocated by proportional representation from national party lists and 38 seats filled by voting in single-member constituencies, all of which were won by the PUP.

Election Commission

Commission électorale nationale autonome (CENA): Villa 17, Cité des Nations, Conakry; f. 2005; comprises seven representatives of the parliamentary majority, seven representatives of the parliamentary opposition, five representatives of the state administration and three representatives of civil society; Pres. Dr RACHID TOURÉ.

Advisory Council

Conseil Économique et Social: Immeuble FAWAZ, Corniche Sud, Coléaah, Matam, BP 2947, Conakry; tel. 30-45-31-23; fax 30-45-31-24; e-mail ces@sotelgui.net.gn; f. 1997; 45 mems; Pres. MICHEL KAMANO; Sec.-Gen. MAMADOU BOBO CAMARA.

Political Organizations

There were 46 officially registered parties in mid-2007, of which the following are the most important:

Alliance nationale pour le progrès (ANP): Conakry; opposes Govt of Pres. Conté; Leader Dr SAGNO MOUSSA.

Front de l'alternance démocratique (FRAD): Conakry; f. 2002; opposes Govt of Pres. Conté; boycotted legislative elections in 2002 and presidential election in 2003; Pres. MAMADOU BOYE BÂ; affiliated parties include:

Alliance nationale pour le développement: Conakry; Sec.-Gen. ANTOINE GBOKOLO SOROMOU.

Parti démocratique africain (PDA): Conakry; Pres. MARCEL CROS.

Parti Dyama: Conakry; moderate Islamist party; Leader MOHAMED MANSOUR KABA.

Rassemblement du peuple de Guinée (RPG): Conakry; e-mail admin@rpgguinee.org; internet www.rpgguinee.org; socialist; Pres. ALPHA CONDÉ.

Union des forces démocratiques (UFD): Conakry; Pres. MAMADOU BAADIKKO BAH.

Union des forces démocratiques de Guinée (UFDG): BP 3036, Conakry; e-mail baggelmalal@yahoo.fr; internet www.ufdg.org; f. 2002 by faction of UPR (q.v.) in protest at that party's participation in elections to Assemblée nationale; Pres. CELLOU DALEIN DIALLO.

Union des forces républicaines (UFR): Immeuble 'Le Golfe', 4e étage, BP 6080, Conakry; tel. 30-45-42-38; fax 30-45-42-31; e-mail ufrguinee@yahoo.fr; internet www.ufrguinee.org; f. 1992; liberal-conservative; Pres. SIDYA TOURÉ; Sec.-Gen. BAKARY G. ZOUMANIGUI.

Union pour le progrès de la Guinée (UPG): Conakry; opposes Govt of Pres. Conté; Leader JEAN-MARIE DORÉ.

Parti démocratique de Guinée—Rassemblement démocratique africain (PDG—RDA): Conakry; f. 1946; revived 1992; supports Govt of Pres. Conté; Sec.-Gen. El Hadj ISMAËL MOHAMED GASSIM GHUSSEIN.

Parti écologiste de Guinée (PEG—Les Verts): BP 3018, Quartier Boulbinet, 5e blvd, angle 2e ave, Commune de Kaloum, Conakry; tel. 30-44-37-01; supports Govt of Pres. Conté; Leader OUMAR SYLLA.

Parti du peuple de Guinée (PPG): BP 1147, Conakry; socialist; opposes Govt of Pres. Conté; boycotted presidential election in 2003, following the Supreme Court's rejection of its nominated candidate; Leader CHARLES-PASCAL TOLNO.

Parti de l'unité et du progrès (PUP): Camayenne, Conakry; internet www.pupguinee.org; Pres. Gen. LANSANA CONTÉ; Sec.-Gen. El Hadj Dr SÉKOU KONATÉ.

Union pour le progrès et le renouveau (UPR): BP 690, Conakry; tel. 30-25-26-01; e-mail basusmane@mirinet.net.gn; internet www.uprguinee.org; f. 1998 by merger of the Parti pour le renouveau et le progrès and the Union pour la nouvelle République; opposes Govt of Pres. Conté; boycotted presidential election in 2003; Pres. OUSMANE BAH.

Union pour le progrès national—Parti pour l'unité et le développement (UPN—PUD): Conakry; Leader MAMADOU BHOYE BARRY.

Diplomatic Representation

EMBASSIES IN GUINEA

Algeria: Cité des Nations, Quartiers Kaloum, BP 1004, Conakry; tel. 30-44-15-05; fax 30-41-15-35.

China, People's Republic: Quartier Donka, Cité Ministérielle, Commune de Dixinn, BP 714, Conakry; tel. 30-41-48-35; fax 30-45-15-26; e-mail chinaemb_gn@mfa.gov.cn; internet gn.chineseembassy.org; Ambassador HUO ZHENGDE.

Congo, Democratic Republic: Quartier Almamya, ave de la Gare, Commune du Kaloum, BP 880, Conakry; tel. 30-45-15-01.

Côte d'Ivoire: blvd du Commerce, BP 5228, Conakry; tel. 30-45-10-82; fax 30-45-10-79; Ambassador JEANNOT ZORO BI BAH.

Cuba: rue DI 256, Corniche Nord, Conakry; tel. 30-46-95-25; fax 30-46-95-28; e-mail embagcon@sotelgui.net.gn; Ambassador MARCELLO CABALLERO TORRES.

Egypt: Corniche Sud, BP 389, Conakry; tel. and fax 30-41-23-94; e-mail ambconakry@hotmail.com; Ambassador MOHAMED ABD ELHAY HASSOUNA.

France: ave du Commerce, BP 373, Conakry; tel. 30-47-10-00; fax 30-47-10-15; internet www.ambafrance-gn.org; Ambassador JEAN-MICHEL BERRIT.

Germany: 2e blvd, Kaloum, BP 540, Conakry; tel. 30-41-15-06; fax 30-45-22-17; e-mail amball@sotelgui.net.gn; internet www.conakry.diplo.de; Ambassador KARL PRINZ.

Ghana: Immeuble Ex-Urbaine et la Seine, BP 732, Conakry; tel. 30-44-15-10; Ambassador LAMISI MBILAH.

Guinea-Bissau: Quartier Bellevue, Commune de Dixinn, BP 298, Conakry; Ambassador MALAM CAMARA.

Holy See: La Minière, BP 2016, Conakry; tel. 30-42-26-76; fax 30-46-36-71; e-mail nonce@biasy.net; Apostolic Nuncio Most Rev. GEORGE ANTONYSAMY (Titular Archbishop of Sulci).

Iran: Donka, Cité Ministerielle, Commune de Dixinn, BP 310, Conakry; tel. 30-22-01-97; fax 30-46-56-38; e-mail ambiran_guinea@yahoo.com; Ambassador BAKHTIAR ASADZADEH SHEIKHJANI.

Japan: Lanseboundji, Corniche Sud, Commune de Matam, BP 895, Conakry; tel. 30-46-85-10; fax 30-46-85-09; Ambassador KEIICHI KITABAN.

Korea, Democratic People's Republic: BP 723, Conakry; Ambassador RI KYONG SON.

Liberia: Cité Ministérielle, Donka, Commune de Dixinn, BP 18, Conakry; tel. 30-42-26-71; Chargé d'affaires a. i. SIAKA FAHNBULLEH.

Libya: Commune de Kaloum, BP 1183, Conakry; tel. 30-41-41-72; Ambassador B. AHMED.

Malaysia: Quartier Mafanco, Corniche Sud, BP 5460, Conakry; tel. 30-22-17-54; e-mail mwcky@sotelgui.net.gn; Ambassador (vacant).

Mali: rue D1–15, Camayenne, Corniche Nord, BP 299, Conakry; tel. 30-46-14-18; fax 30-46-37-03; e-mail ambamaliguinee@yahoo.fr; Ambassador HAMADOUN IBRAHIMA ISSEBERE.

Morocco: Cité des Nations, Villa 12, Commune du Kaloum, BP 193, Conakry; tel. 30-41-36-86; fax 30-41-38-16; e-mail ambargu@sotelgui.net.gn; Ambassador MOHAMED LASFAR.

Nigeria: Corniche Sud, Quartier de Matam, BP 54, Conakry; tel. 30-46-13-41; fax 30-46-27-75; Ambassador ABDULKADIR SANI.

Russia: Matam-Port, km 9, BP 329, Conakry; tel. 30-40-52-22; fax 30-46-57-81; e-mail ambrus@biasy.net; Ambassador DMITRII V. MALEV.

Saudi Arabia: Quartier Camayenne, Commune de Dixinn, BP 611, Conakry; tel. 30-46-24-87; fax 30-46-58-84; e-mail gnemb@mofa.gov.sa; Chargé d'affaires a.i. MOHAMMAD MAHMOUD HILAL.

GUINEA
Directory

Senegal: bâtiment 142, Coleah, Corniche Che Sud, BP 842, Conakry; tel. 30-44-61-32; fax 30-46-28-34; Ambassador Gen. CHARLES ANDRÉ NELSON.

Sierra Leone: Quartier Bellevue, face aux cases présidentielles, Commune de Dixinn, BP 625, Conakry; tel. 30-46-40-84; fax 30-41-23-64; Ambassador Dr SHEKU B. SACCOH.

Ukraine: Commune de Calum, Corniche Nord, Quartier Camayenne, BP 1350, Conakry; tel. 30-45-37-56; fax 30-45-37-95; e-mail ambgv@sotelgui.net.gn; Ambassador OLEKSANDR O. SHULHA.

United Kingdom: BP 6729, Conakry; tel. 30-45-58-07; fax 30-45-60-20; e-mail britcon.oury@biasy.net; Ambassador JOHN MCMANUS.

USA: Koloma, Ratoma, BP 603, Conakry; tel. 30-42-08-61; fax 30-42-08-73; e-mail Consularconkr@state.gov; internet conakry.usembassy.gov; Ambassador PHILLIP CARTER, III.

Judicial System

The Constitution of the Third Republic embodies the principle of the independence of the judiciary, and delineates the competences of each component of the judicial system, including the Higher Magistrates' Council, the Supreme Court, the High Court of Justice and the Magistrature.

Supreme Court
Corniche-Sud, Camayenne, Conakry; tel. 30-41-29-28; Pres. Me LAMINE SIDIMÉ

Director of Public Prosecutions: ANTOINE IBRAHIM DIALLO.

Note: A State Security Court was established in June 1997, with exceptional jurisdiction to try, 'in times of peace and war', crimes against the internal and external security of the State. Members of the court are appointed by the President of the Republic. There is no constitutional provision for the existence of such a tribunal.

President of the State Security Court: Commdr SAMA PANNIVAL BANGOURA.

Religion

It is estimated that 85% of the population are Muslims and 8% Christians, while 7% follow animist beliefs.

ISLAM

National Islamic League: BP 386, Conakry; tel. 30-41-23-38; f. 1988; Sec.-Gen. (vacant).

CHRISTIANITY

The Roman Catholic Church
Guinea comprises one archdiocese and two dioceses. At 31 December 2005 there were an estimated 236,848 Roman Catholics in Guinea, comprising about 3.5% of the total population.

Bishops' Conference
Conférence Episcopale de la Guinée, BP 1006 bis, Conakry; tel. and fax 30-41-32-70; e-mail dhewara@eti.met.gn; Pres. Most Rev. PHILIPPE KOUROUMA (Bishop of N'Zérékoré).

Archbishop of Conakry: Most Rev. VINCENT COULIBALY, Archevêché, BP 2016, Conakry; tel. and fax 30-43-47-04; fax 30-41-32-70; e-mail conakriensis@yahoo.fr.

The Anglican Communion
Anglicans in Guinea are adherents of the Church of the Province of West Africa, comprising 12 dioceses. The diocese of Guinea was established in 1985 as the first French-speaking diocese in the Province. The Archbishop and Primate of the Province is the Bishop of Koforidua, Ghana.

Bishop of Guinea: Rt Rev. ALBERT D. GÓMEZ, Cathédrale Toussaint, BP 105, Conakry; tel. 30-45-13-23.

BAHÁ'Í FAITH

Assemblée spirituelle nationale: BP 2010, Conakry 1; e-mail kouchek@sotelgui.net.gn.

The Press

REGULATORY AUTHORITY

Conseil National de la Communication (CNC): en face Primature, BP 2955, Conakry; tel. 30-45-54-82; fax 30-41-23-85; f. 1991; regulates the operations of the press, and of radio and television; regulates political access to the media; nine mems; Pres. TIBOU KAMARA.

NEWSPAPERS AND PERIODICALS

In early 2004 there were more than 200 periodicals and newspapers officially registered with the National Council of Communication, although only around 60 were believed to be in operation at that time.

Le Démocrate: Quartier Ratoma Centre, Commune de Ratoma, BP 2427, Conakry; tel. 60-20-01-01; e-mail mamadoudianb@yahoo.fr; weekly; Dir HASSANE KABA; Editor-in-Chief MAMADOU DIAN BOLOÉ.

Le Diplomate: BP 2427, Conakry; tel. and fax 30-41-23-85; f. 2002; weekly; Dir SANOU KERFALLAH CISSÉ.

L'Enquêteur: Conakry; e-mail habib@boubah.com; internet enqueteur.boubah.com; f. 2001; two a month; Editor HABIB YAMBERING DIALLO.

L'Evénement de Guinée: BP 796, Conakry; tel. 30-44-33-91; monthly; independent; f. 1993; Dir BOUBACAR SANKARELA DIALLO.

Fonike: BP 341, Conakry; daily; sport and general; state-owned; Dir IBRAHIMA KALIL DIARE.

La Guinée Actuelle: Sans Fils, près Le Makity, BP 3618, Conakry; tel. 30-69-36-20.

Le Guinéen: Conakry; f. 2002; Dir JEAN-MARIE MORGAN.

Horoya (Liberty): BP 191, Conakry; tel. 30-47-71-17; fax 30-45-10-16; e-mail info@horoyaguinee.net; internet www.horoyaguinee.net; govt daily; Dir OUSMANE CAMARA.

L'Indépendant: Quartier Ratoma Centre, Commune de Ratoma, BP 2427, Conakry; tel. 60-20-01-01; e-mail lindependant@afribone.net.gn; internet www.lindependant-gn.info; weekly; also *L'Indépendant Plus*; Publr ABOUBACAR SYLLA; Dir HASSANE KABA; Editor-in-Chief THIERNO DAYÉDIO BARRY.

Journal Officiel de Guinée: BP 156, Conakry; fortnightly; organ of the Govt.

La Lance: Immeuble Baldi Zaire, BP 4968, Conakry; tel. and fax 30-41-23-85; weekly; general information; Dir SOULEYMANE E. DIALLO.

Le Lynx: Immeuble Baldé Zaïre Sandervalia, BP 4968, Conakry; tel. 30-41-23-85; fax 30-45-36-96; e-mail le-lynx@afribone.net.gn; internet www.afribone.net.gn/lynx; f. 1992; weekly; satirical; Editor SOULEYMANE DIALLO.

La Nouvelle Tribune: blvd Diallo Tally, entre 5e et 6e ave, BP 35, Conakry; tel. 30-22-33-02; e-mail abdcond@yahoo.fr; weekly, Tuesdays; independent; general information and analysis; Dir of Publ. and Editing ABDOULAYE CONDÉ.

L'Observateur: Immeuble Baldé, Conakry; tel. 30-40-05-24; independent; Dir EL-BÉCHIR DIALLO.

L'Oeil du Peuple: BP 3064, Conakry; tel. 30-67-23-78; weekly; independent; Dir of Publishing ISMAËL BANGOURA.

Sanakou: Labé, Foutah Djallon, Moyenne-Guinée; tel. 30-51-13-19; e-mail sanakoulabe@yahoo.fr; f. 2000; monthly; general news; Publr IDRISSA SAMPIRING DIALLO; Editor-in-Chief YAMOUSSA SOUMAH; circ. 1,000.

3-P Plus (Parole-Plume-Papier) Magazine: 7e ave Bis Almamyah, BP 5122, Conakry; tel. 30-45-22-32; fax 30-45-29-31; e-mail 3p-plus@mirinet.net.gn; internet www.mirinet.net.gn/3p_plus; f. 1995; journal of arts and letters; supplements *Le Cahier de l'Economie* and *Mag-Plus: Le Magazine de la Culture*; monthly; Pres. MOHAMED SALIFOU KEÏTA; Editor-in-Chief SAMBA TOURÉ.

NEWS AGENCY

Agence Guinéenne de Presse: BP 1535, Conakry; tel. 30-41-14-34; e-mail info@agpguinee.net; internet www.agpguinee.net; f. 1960; Man. Dir MOHAMED CONDÉ.

PRESS ASSOCIATION

Association Guinéenne des Editeurs de la Presse Indépendante (AGEPI): Conakry; f. 1991; an asscn of independent newspaper publishers; Chair. BOUBACAR SANKARELA DIALLO.

Publishers

Les Classiques Guinéens (SEDIS sarl): 545 rue KA020, Mauquepas, BP 3697, Conakry; tel. 11-21-18-57; fax 13-40-92-62; e-mail cheick.sedis@mirinet.net.gn; f. 1999; art, history, youth literature; Dir CHEICK ABDOUL KABA.

Editions du Ministère de l'Education Nationale: Direction nationale de la recherche scientifique et technique, BP 561, Conakry; tel. 30-43-02-66; e-mail dnrst@mirinet.net.gn; f. 1959; general and educational; Deputy Dir Dr TAMBA TAGBINO.

Editions Ganndal (Knowledge): BP 542, Conakry; tel. and fax 30-46-35-07; e-mail ganndal@mirinet.net.gn; f. 1992; educational, youth

GUINEA

and children, general literature and books in Pular; Dir MAMADOU ALIOU SOW.

Société Africaine d'Edition et de Communication (SEAC): Belle-Vue, Commune de Dixinn, BP 6826, Conakry; tel. 30-29-71-41; e-mail dtniane@yahoo.fr; social sciences, reference, literary fiction; Editorial Assistant OUMAR TALL.

Broadcasting and Communications

TELECOMMUNICATIONS
Regulatory Bodies

Comité National de Coordination des Télécommunications (CNCT): BP 5000, Conakry; tel. 30-41-40-79; fax 30-45-31-16; Exec. Sec. SEKOU BANGOURA.

Direction Nationale des Postes et Télécommunications (DNPT): BP 5000, Conakry; tel. 30-41-13-31; fax 30-45-31-16; e-mail dnpt.dnr@biasy.net; f. 1997; regulates transport, postal and telecommunications services; Dir KOLY CAMARA.

Service Providers

Intercel: Quartier Coleah Larseboundji, près du pont du 8 Novembre, Immeuble le Golfe, BP 965, Conakry; tel. 30-45-57-44; fax 30-40-92-92; e-mail info@gn.intercel.net; mobile cellular telephone operator; fmrly Telecel Guinée; Dir FRANÇOIS DICK.

Société des Télécommunications de Guinée (SOTELGUI): 4e blvd, BP 2066, Conakry; tel. 30-45-27-50; fax 30-45-03-06; e-mail marzuki@sotelgui.net.gn; internet www.sotelgui.net; f. 1993; privatized 1995; 60% owned by Telekom Malaysia; 40% state-owned; also provides mobile cellular services (as Lagui); 161,800 subscribers (Sept. 2005); Dir El Hadj MARZUKI ABDULLAH.

Spacetel Guinée SA (Mobilis Guinée): BP 835, Conakry; tel. and fax 12-66-00-11; e-mail info@spacetelguinee.com; f. 1994; mobile cellular telephone operator; operates with a range of 70km around Conakry; 35,000 subscribers (2002); also operates GSM satellite telephone network; Chair. K. ABOU KHALIL.

BROADCASTING
Regulatory Authority

Conseil National de la Communication (CNC): see The Press.

In mid-2005 a presidential decree permitted the creation of private radio and television stations in Guinea, subject to certain conditions. Political parties and religious organizations were to be prohibited from creating broadcast media, however, while restrictions were to be placed on foreign ownership of radio and television stations.

Radio

Radiodiffusion-Télévision Guinéenne (RTG): BP 391, Conakry; tel. 30-44-22-01; fax 30-41-50-01; internet www.rtgguinee.net; broadcasts in French, English, Créole-English, Portuguese, Arabic and local languages; Dir-Gen. ALPHA KABINÉ KEITA; Dir of Radio ISSA CONDÉ.

Radio Rurale de Guinée: BP 391, Conakry; tel. 30-42-11-09; fax 30-41-47-97; e-mail ruralgui@mirinet.net.gn; network of rural radio stations.

Television

Radiodiffusion-Télévision Guinéenne (RTG): see Radio; transmissions in French and local languages; one channel; f. 1977.

Finance

(cap. = capital; res = reserves; m. = million; brs = branches; amounts in Guinean francs)

BANKING
Central Bank

Banque Centrale de la République de Guinée (BCRG): 12 blvd du Commerce, BP 692, Kaloum, Conakry; tel. 30-41-26-51; fax 30-41-48-98; e-mail gouv.bcrg@eti-bull.net; internet www.bcrg.gov.gn; f. 1960; bank of issue; Gov. ALKALY MOHAMED DAFFE; Dep. Gov. DAOUDA BANGOURA.

Commercial Banks

Banque Internationale pour le Commerce et l'Industrie de la Guinée (BICIGUI): ave de la République, BP 1484, Conakry; tel. 30-41-45-15; fax 30-41-39-62; e-mail dg.bicigui@africa.bnpparibas.com; internet www.bicigui.com; f. 1985; 38.1% state-owned, 18.8% owned by BNP Paribas BDDI Participations (France); cap. and res 37,989.3m., total assets 315,689.5m. (Dec. 2003); Pres. IBRAHIMA SOUMAH; Dir-Gen. BERNARD DELEUZE; 11 brs.

Banque Populaire Maroco-Guinéenne (BPMG): Immeuble BPMG, blvd du Commerce, Kaloum, BP 4400, Conakry 01; tel. 30-41-36-93; fax 30-41-32-61; e-mail bpmg@sotelgui.net.gn; f. 1991; 55% owned by Crédit Populaire du Maroc, 42% state-owned; cap. and res 9,936m., total assets 65,549m. (Dec. 2004); Pres. EMMANUEL GNAN; Dir-Gen. AHMED IRAQUI HOUSSAINI; 3 brs.

Ecobank Guinée: Immeuble Al Iman, ave de la République, BP 5687, Conakry; tel. 30-45-58-77; fax 30-45-42-41; internet www.ecobank.com; f. 1999; wholly owned by Ecobank Transnational Inc. (Togo); cap. and res 7.7m., total assets 78.7m. (Dec. 2006); Pres. SAIKOU BARRY; Man. Dir ASSIONGBON EKUE; 2 brs.

First American Bank of Guinea: blvd du Commerce, angle 9e ave, BP 4540, Conakry; tel. 30-41-34-32; fax 30-41-35-29; f. 1994; jtly owned by Mitan Capital Ltd, Grand Cayman and El Hadj Haidara Abdourahmane Chérif, Mali.

International Commercial Bank: 4e ave Boulbinet, Bâtiment 346, BP 3547, Conakry; tel. 30-41-25-89; fax 30-41-25-92; f. 1997; total assets 19.6m. (Dec. 1999); Pres. JOSÉPHINE PREMLA; Man. Dir HAMZA BIN ALIAS.

Société Générale de Banques en Guinée (SGBG): Immeuble Boffa, Cité du Chemin de Fer, BP 1514, Conakry; tel. 30-45-60-00; fax 30-41-25-65; e-mail contact@sgbg.net.gn; internet www.sgbg.net.gn; f. 1985; 53% owned by Société Générale (France); cap. and res 13,074m., total assets 228,196m. (Dec. 2003); Pres. GÉRALD LACAZE; 5 brs.

Union Internationale de Banques en Guinée (UIBG): 6e ave de la République, angle 5e blvd, BP 324, Conakry; tel. 30-41-43-09; fax 30-97-26-30; e-mail uibg@financial-bank.com; f. 1988; cap. and res 5,700m., total assets 104,000m. (Dec. 2004); Pres. ALPHA AMADOU DIALLO; Dir-Gen. JACQUES DE VIGNAUD.

Islamic Bank

Banque Islamique de Guinée: Immeuble Nafaya, 6 ave de la République, BP 1247, Conakry; tel. 30-41-50-86; fax 30-41-50-71; f. 1983; 51% owned by Dar al-Maal al-Islami Trust (Switzerland); cap. and res 2,368.5m., total assets 26,932.1m. (Dec. 2003); Pres. ADERRAOUF BENESSAIAH; Dir-Gen. AZHAR SALEEM KHAN.

INSURANCE

Gras Savoye Guinée: 4e ave, angle 4e blvd, Quartier Boulbinet, Commune de Kaloum, Conakry; tel. 30-45-58-43; fax 30-45-58-42; affiliated to Gras Savoye (France); Man. CHÉRIF BAH.

Société Guinéenne d'Assurance Mutuelle (SOGAM): Immeuble Sonia, BP 434, Conakry; tel. 30-44-50-58; fax 30-41-25-57; f. 1990; Chair. Dr M. K. BAH; Man. Dir P. I. NDAO.

Société Nouvelle d'Assurance de Guinée (SONAG): BP 3363, Conakry; tel. 30-41-49-77; fax 30-41-43-03.

Union Guinéenne d'Assurances et de Réassurances (UGAR): pl. des Martyrs, BP 179, Conakry; tel. 30-41-48-41; fax 30-41-17-11; e-mail ugar@ugar.com.gn; f. 1989; 40% owned by AXA (France), 35% state-owned; cap. 2,000m.; Man. Dir RAPHAËL Y. TOURÉ.

Trade and Industry

GOVERNMENT AGENCIES

Centre de Promotion et de Développement Miniers (CPDM): BP 295, Conakry; tel. 30-41-15-44; fax 30-41-49-13; e-mail cpdm@mirinet.net.gn; f. 1995; promotes investment and co-ordinates devt strategy in mining sector; Dir MOCIRÉ SYLLA.

Entreprise Nationale Import-Export (IMPORTEX): BP 152, Conakry; tel. 30-44-28-13; state-owned import and export agency; Dir MAMADOU BOBO DIENG.

Office de Développement de la Pêche Artisanale et de l'Aquaculture en Guinée (ODEPAG): 6 ave de la République, BP 1581, Conakry; tel. 30-44-19-48; devt of fisheries and fish-processing.

Office de Promotion des Investissements Privés-Guichet Unique (OPIP): BP 2024, Conakry; tel. 30-41-49-85; fax 30-41-39-90; e-mail dg@opip.org.gn; internet www.opip-guinee.org; f. 1992; promotes private investment; Dir-Gen. DIANKA KOEVOGUI.

DEVELOPMENT ORGANIZATIONS

Agence Française de Développement (AFD): 5e ave, KA022, BP 283, Conakry; tel. 30-41-25-69; fax 30-41-28-74; e-mail afdconakry@groupe-afd.org; internet www.afd.fr; Country Dir MARC DUBERNET.

Association Française des Volontaires du Progrès (AFVP): BP 570, Conakry; tel. 30-35-08-60; internet www.afvp.org; f. 1987; devt and research projects; Nat. Delegate FRANCK DAGOIS.

Mission Française de Coopération et d'Action Culturelle: BP 373, Conakry; tel. 30-41-23-45; fax 30-41-43-56; administers bilateral aid; Dir in Guinea ANDRÉ BAILLEUL.

CHAMBERS OF COMMERCE

Chambre de Commerce, d'Industrie et de l'Artisanat de la Guinée (CCIAG): BP 545, Conakry; tel. 30-45-45-16; fax 30-45-45-17; f. 1985; Pres. El Hadj MAMADOU SYLLA.

Chambre Economique de Guinée: BP 609, Conakry.

TRADE AND EMPLOYERS' ASSOCIATIONS

Association des Commerçants de Guinée: BP 2468, Conakry; tel. 30-41-30-37; fax 30-45-31-66; Sec.-Gen. OUMAR CAMARA.

Association des Femmes Entrepreneurs de Guinée (AFEG): BP 104, Conakry; tel. 60-28-02-95; e-mail afeguine@yahoo.fr; f. 1987; Pres. HADJA RAMATOULAYE SOW.

Conseil National du Patronat Guinéen (CNPG): Dixinn Bora, BP 6403, Conakry; tel. and fax 30-41-24-70; e-mail msylla@leland-gn.org; f. 1992; Pres. El Hadj MAMADOU SYLLA.

Fédération Patronale de l'Agriculture et de l'Elevage (FEPAE): BP 5684, Conakry; tel. 30-22-95-56; fax 30-41-54-36; Pres. El Hadj MAMDOU SYLLA; Sec.-Gen. MAMADY CAMARA.

Groupement des Importateurs Guinéens (GIG): BP 970, Conakry; tel. 30-42-18-18; fax 30-42-19-19; Pres. FERNAND BANGOURA.

UTILITIES

Electricity

Barrage Hydroélectrique de Garafiri: BP 1770, Conakry; tel. 30-41-50-91; inaugurated 1999.

Electricité de Guinée (EDG): BP 1463, Conakry; tel. 30-45-18-56; fax 30-45-18-53; e-mail di.sogel@biasy.net; f. 2001 to replace Société Guinéenne d'Electricité; majority state-owned; production, transport and distribution of electricity; Dir-Gen. NOUCTAR BARRY.

Water

Service National d'Aménagement des Points d'Eau (SNAPE): BP 2064, Conakry; tel. 30-41-18-93; fax 30-41-50-58; e-mail snape@mirinet.net.gn; supplies water in rural areas.

Société Nationale des Eaux de Guinée (SONEG): Belle-vue, BP 150, Conakry; tel. 30-45-44-77; e-mail oaubot@seg.org.gn; f. 1988; national water co; Dir-Gen. Dr OUSMANE ARIBOT; Sec.-Gen. MAMADOU DIOP.

TRADE UNIONS

Confédération Nationale des Travailleurs de Guinée (CNTG): Bourse du Travail, Corniche Sud 004, BP 237, Conakry; tel. 30-41-50-44; fax 11-45-49-96; e-mail cntg60@yahoo.fr; f. 1984; Sec.-Gen. RABIATOU SERAH DIALLO.

Organisation Nationale des Syndicats Libres de Guinée (ONSLG): BP 559, Conakry; tel. 30-41-52-17; fax 30-43-02-83; e-mail onslguinee@yahoo.fr; 27,000 mems (1996); Sec.-Gen. YAMOUDOU TOURÉ.

Union Syndicale des Travailleurs de Guinée (USTG): BP 1514, Conakry; tel. 30-41-25-65; fax 30-41-25-58; e-mail fofi1952@yahoo.fr; independent; 64,000 mems (2001); Sec.-Gen. IBRAHIMA FOFANA.

Transport

RAILWAYS

There are 1,086 km of railways in Guinea, including 662 km of 1-m gauge track from Conakry to Kankan in the east of the country, crossing the Niger at Kouroussa. The contract for the first phase of the upgrading of this line was awarded to a Slovak company in early 1997. Three lines for the transport of bauxite link Sangaredi with the port of Kamsar in the west, via Boké, and Conakry with Kindia and Fria, a total of 383 km.

Office National des Chemins de Fer de Guinée (ONCFG): BP 589, Conakry; tel. 30-44-46-13; fax 30-41-35-77; f. 1905; Man. Dir MOREL MARGUERITE CAMARA.

Chemin de Fer de Boké: BP 523, Boké; operations commenced 1973.

Chemin de Fer Conakry–Fria: BP 334, Conakry; operations commenced 1960; Gen. Man. A. CAMARA.

Chemin de Fer de la Société des Bauxites de Kindia: BP 613, Conakry; tel. 30-41-38-28; operations commenced 1974; Gen. Man. K. KEITA.

ROADS

The road network comprised 44,348 km of roads (of which 4,342 km were paved) in 2003. An 895-km cross-country road links Conakry to Bamako, in Mali, and the main highway connecting Dakar (Senegal) to Abidjan (Côte d'Ivoire) also crosses Guinea. The road linking Conakry to Freetown (Sierra Leone) forms part of the Trans West African Highway, extending from Morocco to Nigeria.

La Guinéenne-Marocaine des Transports (GUIMAT): Conakry; f. 1989; owned jtly by Govt of Guinea and Hakkam (Morocco); operates nat. and regional transport services.

Société Générale des Transports de Guinée (SOGETRAG): Conakry; f. 1985; 63% state-owned; bus operator.

SHIPPING

Conakry and Kamsar are the international seaports. Conakry handled 3.9m. metric tons of foreign trade in 1999.

Getma Guinée: Immeuble KASSA, Cité des Chemins de Fer, BP 1648, Conakry; tel. 30-41-32-05; fax 30-41-42-73; e-mail info@getmaguinee.com.gn; internet www.getma.com; f. 1979; fmrly Société Guinéenne d'Entreprises de Transports Maritimes et Aeriens; marine transportation; cap. 1,100m. FG; Chair. JEAN-JACQUES GRENIER; 135 employees.

Port Autonome de Conakry (PAC): BP 805, Conakry; tel. 30-41-27-28; fax 30-41-26-04; e-mail pac@eti-bull.net; internet www.biasy.net/~pac; haulage, porterage; Gen. Man. ALIOU DIALLO.

Société Navale Guinéenne (SNG): BP 522, Conakry; tel. 30-44-29-55; fax 30-41-39-70; f. 1968; state-owned; shipping agents; Dir-Gen. NOUNKÉ KEITA.

SOAEM: BP 3177, Conakry; tel. 30-41-25-90; fax 30-41-20-25; e-mail soaem.gn@mirinet.net.gn.

SOTRAMAR: Kamsar; e-mail sotramar@sotramar.com; f. 1971; exports bauxite from mines at Boké through port of Kamsar.

Transmar: 33 blvd du Commerce, Kaloum, BP 3917, Conakry; tel. 30-43-05-41; fax 30-43-05-42; e-mail transmar@eti.net.gn; shipping, stevedoring, inland transport.

CIVIL AVIATION

There is an international airport at Conakry-Gbessia, and smaller airfields at Labé, Kankan and Faranah. Facilities at Conakry have been upgraded, at a cost of US $42.6m.; the airport handled some 300,000 passengers in 1999.

Air Guinée Express: 6 ave de la République, BP 12, Conakry; tel. 30-44-46-02; fax 30-41-29-07; e-mail air-guinee@mirinet.net.gn; f. 2002 to replace Air Guinée (f. 1960); regional and internal services; Dir-Gen. ANTOINE CROS.

Guinée Air Service: Aéroport Conakry-Gbessia; tel. 30-41-27-61.

Guinée Inter Air: Aéroport Conakry-Gbessia; tel. 30-41-37-08.

Société de Gestion et d'Exploitation de l'Aéroport de Conakry (SOGEAC): BP 3126, Conakry; tel. 30-46-48-03; f. 1987; manages Conakry-Gbessia int. airport; 51% state-owned.

Union des Transports Aériens de Guinée (UTA): scheduled and charter flights to regional and int. destinations.

Tourism

Some 45,334 tourists visited Guinea in 2005; receipts from tourism in 2004 totalled US $30m., an increase from $14m. in 2001.

Office National du Tourisme: Immeuble al-Iman, 6e ave de la République, BP 1275, Conakry; tel. 30-45-51-63; fax 30-45-51-64; e-mail ibrahimabakaley@yahoo.fr; internet www.ontguinea.org; f. 1997; Dir-Gen. IBRAHIM A. DIALLO.

GUINEA-BISSAU

Introductory Survey

Location, Climate, Language, Religion, Flag, Capital

The Republic of Guinea-Bissau lies on the west coast of Africa, with Senegal to the north and Guinea to the east and south. The climate is tropical, although maritime and Sahelian influences are felt. The average temperature is 20°C (68°F). The official language is Portuguese, of which the locally spoken form is Creole (Crioulo). There are 19 local languages, of which the most widely spoken are Balanta-Kentohe, Pulaar (Fula), Mandjak, Mandinka and Papel. The principal religious beliefs are animism and Islam. There is a small minority of Roman Catholics and other Christian groups. The national flag (proportions 1 by 2) has two equal horizontal stripes, of yellow over light green, and a red vertical stripe, with a five-pointed black star at its centre, at the hoist. The capital is Bissau.

Recent History

Portuguese Guinea (Guiné) was colonized by Portugal in the 15th century. Nationalist activism began to emerge in the 1950s. Armed insurgency commenced in the early 1960s, and by 1972 the Partido Africano da Independência da Guiné e Cabo Verde (PAIGC) was in control of two-thirds of the country. The independence of the Republic of Guinea-Bissau was unilaterally proclaimed in September 1973, with Luís Cabral (the brother of the founder of the PAIGC, Amílcar Cabral) as President of the State Council. Hostilities ceased following the military coup in Portugal in April 1974, and on 10 September Portugal recognized the independence of Guinea-Bissau under the leadership of Luís Cabral.

The PAIGC regime introduced measures to establish a single-party socialist state. At elections in December 1976 and January 1977 voters chose regional councils from which a new National People's Assembly (Assembléia Nacional Popular—ANP) was later selected. In 1978 the Chief State Commissioner, Francisco Mendes, died; he was succeeded by Commander João Vieira, hitherto State Commissioner for the Armed Forces and President of the ANP.

The PAIGC initially supervised both Cape Verde and Guinea-Bissau, the Constitutions of each remaining separate but with a view to eventual unification. These arrangements were terminated in November 1980, when President Cabral was deposed in a coup organized by Vieira, who was installed as Chairman of the Council of the Revolution. Diplomatic relations between Guinea-Bissau and Cape Verde were restored after the release of Cabral from detention in 1982.

In 1983 Vieira established a commission to examine plans for the revision of the Constitution and the electoral code. In late March Vieira, after dismissing the Prime Minister, formally assumed the role of Head of Government, and elections to regional councils took place. In May the ANP, which had been dissolved following the 1980 coup, was re-established, and the Council of the Revolution was replaced by a 15-member Council of State (Conselho de Estado), selected from among the members of the ANP. Vieira was subsequently elected as President of the Conselho de Estado and Head of State. The ANP immediately ratified the new Constitution, and formally abolished the position of Prime Minister.

A campaign against corruption, initiated by Vieira in August 1985, apparently provoked a military coup attempt in November, led by Col Paulo Correia, the First Vice-President of the Conselho de Estado, and other senior army officers. Correia was subsequently executed. In November 1986 the PAIGC endorsed proposals for the liberalization of the economy and re-elected Vieira as party Secretary-General for a further four years. In February 1987 Vieira appointed Dr Vasco Cabral, hitherto Minister of Justice, as Permanent Secretary of the Central Committee of the PAIGC, in an attempt to reinforce party support for the programme of economic liberalization.

Regional elections took place in June 1989, at which 95.8% of those who voted endorsed the single PAIGC list. In mid-June the Regional Councils, in turn, elected the ANP, which subsequently elected the Conselho de Estado, of which Vieira was re-elected President. In December 1990 the Central Committee of the PAIGC agreed to the adoption of a multi-party system, following a period of transition, and the holding of a presidential election in 1993. In May 1991 a series of constitutional amendments ending one-party rule were approved by the ANP, terminating the political monopoly of the PAIGC. In addition, all links between the PAIGC and the armed forces were severed, and the introduction of a free-market economy was guaranteed. New legislation in October accorded greater freedom to the press and permitted the formation of new trade unions. In November the Frente Democrática (FD) became the first opposition party to obtain official registration.

In December 1991 a major government reshuffle took place, in which the office of Prime Minister was restored. Carlos Correia was appointed to the post. In late 1991 and early 1992 three further opposition parties obtained legal status: the Resistência da Guiné-Bissau—Movimento Bah-Fatah (RGB—MB), led by Domingos Fernandes Gomes; the Frente Democrática Social (FDS), led by Rafael Barbosa; and the Partido Unido Social Democrático (PUSD), led by Vítor Saúde Maria. Following a split in the FDS, a further party, the Partido para a Renovação Social (PRS), was established in January 1992 by the former Vice-Chairman of the FDS, Kumba Yalá. In the same month four opposition parties—the PUSD, FDS, RGB—MB and the Partido da Convergência Democrática (PCD), led by Victor Mandinga—agreed on the establishment of a 'democratic forum', whose demands included the dissolution of the political police, the creation of an electoral commission and an all-party consultation on the setting of election dates.

In May 1992 a dissident group, known as the 'Group of 121', broke away from the PAIGC to form the Partido de Renovação e Desenvolvimento (PRD). In July the Government agreed to establish a multi-party national transition commission to organize and oversee the democratic process. In November the Government announced the postponement of presidential and legislative elections until March 1993. Legislation preparing for the transition to a multi-party democracy was approved by the ANP in February, and in the following month a commission was appointed to supervise the forthcoming elections. However, reports in March of an attempted coup threatened to disrupt the transition to democracy. Initial reports indicated that Maj. Robalo de Pina, commander of the Forças de Intervenção Rápida (an élite guard responsible for presidential security), had been assassinated in what appeared to be an army rebellion, provoked by disaffection at poor standards of pay and living conditions. In July Vieira announced that multi-party presidential and legislative elections would be held in March 1994.

One week before the designated date of the elections, Vieira announced their postponement, owing to financial and technical difficulties. In May 1994 it was announced that the elections would be held in July. In early May six opposition parties, the FD, the FDS, the Movimento para a Unidade e a Democracia, the Partido Democrático do Progresso, the PRD and the Liga Guineense de Protecção Ecológica (LIPE), formed a coalition, the União para a Mudança (UM). The elections took place on 3 July, although voting was extended for two days, owing to logistical problems. The PAIGC secured a clear majority in the ANP, winning 62 of the 100 seats, while in the presidential election Vieira obtained 46.3% of the votes, and his nearest rival, Yalá, secured 21.9% of the votes. The two candidates contested a second round of polling on 7 August in which Yalá was narrowly defeated, securing 48.0% of the votes, compared with Vieira's 52.0%. International observers later declared the elections to have been free and fair. Vieira was inaugurated as President on 29 September and appointed Manuel Saturnino da Costa (the Secretary-General of the PAIGC) as Prime Minister in late October. The Council of Ministers was appointed in November, comprising solely members of the PAIGC.

Guinea-Bissau attained membership of the Union économique et monétaire ouest-africaine (see p. 307) in March 1997 and entered the Franc Zone in April. The national currency was replaced by the franc CFA, and the Banque centrale des états de l'Afrique de l'ouest assumed central banking functions.

In May 1997, in order to address what Vieira described as a serious political crisis that was undermining the functioning of the State, da Costa was dismissed. Carlos Correia was subsequently appointed Prime Minister, and a new 14-member Council of Ministers was inaugurated in June. In October Correia was dismissed, bringing to an end an institutional crisis that had lasted since his appointment. The legislative process had been obstructed by opposition deputies who claimed that, by omitting to consult those parties represented in the legislature on Correia's appointment, Vieira had acted unconstitutionally. In October the Supreme Court ruled that Vieira had indeed contravened the Constitution. Following consultations with party leaders, Vieira reappointed Correia, with the full support of the main opposition parties.

In March 1998, following protests by opposition parties at delays in the organization of legislative elections, an independent national elections commission was established. The elections were due to be held in July. In April a new political party, the União Nacional para a Democracia e o Progresso (UNDP) was established.

In June 1998 rebel troops, led by Brig. (later Gen.) Ansumane Mané, who had recently been dismissed as Chief of Staff of the Armed Forces, seized control of the Bra military barracks in the capital, as well as other strategic locations in the city, including the international airport. Mané subsequently formed a 'military junta for the consolidation of democracy, peace and justice' and demanded the resignation of Vieira and his administration. With the support of Senegalese and Guinean soldiers, troops loyal to the Government attempted unsuccessfully to regain control of rebel-held areas of the city, and heavy fighting ensued. Over the following days more than 3,000 foreign nationals were evacuated from the capital to Senegal. An estimated further 200,000 residents of Bissau fled the city. Fighting continued into July, with many members of the Guinea-Bissau armed forces reportedly defecting to the side of the rebels.

On 26 July 1998, following mediation by a delegation from the lusophone commonwealth body, the Comunidade dos Países de Língua Portuguesa (CPLP, see below), the Government and the rebels agreed to implement a truce. In August representatives of the Government and the rebels met, under the auspices of the CPLP and the Economic Community of West African States (ECOWAS, see p. 232), and an agreement was reached to transform the existing truce into a cease-fire. The accord provided for the deployment of international forces to maintain and supervise the cease-fire. In September talks between the Government and the rebels resumed. However, the rebels' demand that all Senegalese and Guinean forces be withdrawn from the country as a prerequisite to a definitive peace agreement was rejected by the Government and the following month the cease-fire collapsed. On 20 October the Government imposed a nationwide curfew, and on the following day Vieira declared a unilateral cease-fire. By that time almost all of the government troops had joined forces with the rebels, who were thought to control some 99% of the country. On 23 October Mané agreed to conform to a 48-hour truce to allow Vieira to clarify his proposals for a negotiated peace settlement, and agreement was subsequently reached for direct talks to be held. At the talks the rebels confirmed that they would not seek Vieira's resignation. Further talks, held under the aegis of ECOWAS, resulted in the signing of a peace accord on 1 November. Under the terms of the accord, the two sides reaffirmed the cease-fire of 25 August, and resolved that the withdrawal of Senegalese and Guinean troops from Guinea-Bissau be conducted simultaneously with the deployment of an ECOMOG (ECOWAS Cease-fire Monitoring Group) interposition force, which would guarantee security on the border with Senegal. It was also agreed that a government of national unity would be established, to include representatives of the rebel junta, and that presidential and legislative elections would be held no later than March 1999. In November 1998 agreement was reached on the composition of a Joint Executive Commission to implement the peace accord. In December Francisco José Fadul was appointed Prime Minister, and Vieira and Mané reached agreement on the allocation of portfolios to the two sides.

In January 1999 Fadul announced that presidential and legislative elections would not take place until the end of the year. Also in January agreement was reached between the Government, the rebel military junta and ECOWAS on the strength of the ECOMOG interposition force, which was to comprise some 710 troops. A timetable for the withdrawal of Senegalese and Guinean troops from the country was also established. However, at the end of January hostilities resumed in the capital. In February talks between the Government and the rebels produced agreement on a cease-fire and provided for the immediate withdrawal of Senegalese and Guinean troops. On 20 February the new Government of National Unity was announced. The disarmament of rebel troops and those loyal to the President began in March and the withdrawal of Senegalese and Guinean troops was completed that month. On 30 April the UN Secretary-General established the UN Peace-building Support Office in Guinea-Bissau (UNOGBIS), with a mandate to aid peace-building efforts, support the consolidation of democracy and the rule of law, encourage friendly relations with the country's neighbours and assist in the electoral process; its mandate was regularly extended in subsequent years. An extension until December 2008 was approved in late 2007 and Guinea-Bissau also became the third country on the agenda of the Peace-building Commission, the United Nations advisory body set up to help countries emerging from conflict avoid returning to war.

In early May 1999 Vieira announced that the elections would take place on 28 December. However, on 7 May, to widespread condemnation by the international community, Vieira was overthrown by the rebel military junta. Fighting had erupted in Bissau on the previous day when rebel troops seized stockpiles of weapons that had been at Bissau airport since the disarmament of the rival forces in March. The rebels, who claimed that their actions had been prompted by Vieira's refusal to allow his presidential guard to be disarmed, surrounded the presidential palace and forced its surrender. On 10 May Vieira signed an unconditional surrender. The President of the ANP, Malam Bacai Sanhá, was appointed acting President of the Republic pending a presidential election, and the Government of National Unity remained in office. Vieira was replaced as President of the PAIGC in an interim capacity by da Costa. At a meeting in late May of representatives of the Government, the military junta and the political parties, agreement was reached that Vieira should stand trial for his involvement in the trafficking of arms to separatists from the Senegalese region of Casamance and for political and economic crimes relating to his terms in office. Vieira agreed to stand trial, but only after receiving medical treatment abroad, after which, he pledged, he would return to Guinea-Bissau. ECOMOG forces were withdrawn from the country in June. That month Vieira went into exile in Portugal where he was offered political asylum. In July constitutional amendments were introduced limiting the tenure of presidential office to two terms and abolishing the death penalty. It was also stipulated that the country's principal offices of state could only be held by Guinea-Bissau nationals born of Guinea-Bissau parents. In September an extraordinary congress of the PAIGC voted to expel Vieira and six others from the party. The incumbent Minister of Defence and Freedom Fighters, Francisco Benante, was appointed President of the party. In October the Attorney-General, Amine Michel Saad, announced that he had sufficient evidence to prosecute Vieira for crimes against humanity and expressed his intention to seek Vieira's extradition from Portugal.

Presidential and legislative elections took place on 28 November 1999. Of the 102 seats in the enlarged legislature, the PRS secured 38, the RGB—MB 28, the PAIGC 24, the Aliança Democrática (AD, an alliance of the FD and the PCD) four, the UM three, the Partido Social Democrático (PSD) three, and the FDS and the UNDP one each. As no candidate received the necessary 50% of the votes to win the presidential election outright, the leading candidates, Yalá of the PRS and Sanhá of the PAIGC, contested a second round of voting on 16 January 2000, at which Yalá secured victory with 72% of the votes cast. Yalá was inaugurated on the following day and installed a new Council of Ministers, which included members of several former opposition parties, later that month. Caetano N'Tchama of the PRS was appointed Prime Minister. The election was subsequently judged by international observers to have been 'free and fair'. In May tensions were reported between Yalá and certain elements in the army who viewed Mané as the rightful leader of the country, on the grounds that it was he who had ousted Vieira from power. In October Yalá appointed a State Council, comprising members of all parliamentary political parties, which was to have an advisory role.

Demonstrations organized by the PAIGC, in support of demands for the resignation of the coalition Government, took place in Bissau in November 2000. In late November Mané declared himself Commander-in-Chief of the armed forces, following renewed violence in Bissau, instigated by soldiers loyal to him. However, government troops quickly suppressed the insurgency, and a number of opposition leaders were arrested.

Mané fled the capital, and was subsequently killed by the security forces.

In early 2000 the RGB—MB withdrew from the coalition Government (formed with the PRS). In March Yalá dismissed N'Tchama in an attempt to increase stability in the minority Government; the former Deputy Prime Minister and Minister of Foreign Affairs, Faustino Fudut Imbali, was appointed in his place and subsequently formed a new broad-based Government. In May the Government's programme was accepted by the ANP, with the support of the PAIGC.

In October 2001 a motion of no confidence in Yalá was approved by the ANP; the vote had been instigated by opposition parties in response to what they considered to be increasingly unconstitutional actions by the President. Yalá then threatened to suspend the ANP. A demonstration against Yalá in Bissau, attended by some 10,000 people, followed further demands for the President's resignation by a coalition of opposition parties. Prime Minister Imbali was dismissed in December and was replaced by Almara Nhassé, a member of the PRS and hitherto Minister of Internal Administration. Nhassé immediately formed a new Government, composed solely of members of the ruling coalition. Nhassé was subsequently elected President of the PRS, in place of Yalá.

In September 2002 Yalá dismissed Rui Sanhá as Minister of Internal Administration; he was replaced in October by António Man, erstwhile President of the Supreme Court. The developing political uncertainty in the country intensified in November, when Yalá dissolved the ANP and dismissed the Government, citing its incompetence in coping with the economic crisis. Legislative elections were scheduled initially for February 2003, although later delayed. Mario Pires was appointed as Prime Minister, to head a transitional Government, which was dominated by the PRS.

Further government changes were effected in December 2002 and January 2003. Several political coalitions opposing the PRS were formed in late 2002 and early 2003 in preparation for the legislative elections, which had been postponed until 20 April. In December 2002 the PSD, the LIPE, the Partido da Renovação e Progresso and the Partido Socialista Guineense created the União Eleitoral (UE). In February 2003 the Plataforma Unida—Mufunessa Larga Guiné (PU—MLG) was formed by the AD (comprising the FD and the PCD), the FDS, the Frente para a Libertação e Independência da Guiné and the Grupo de Democratas Independentes, which had been established by Vaz and other former members of the RGB—MB, following a court decision to award the leadership of that party to Salvador Tchongo.

In March 2003 Yalá announced that the elections were to be further delayed, until 6 July. Man was dismissed as Minister of Internal Administration in April. This was followed in early May by the dismissal and unexplained arrest of the Minister of Defence, Marcelino Cabral, and the Minister of the Presidency of the Council of Ministers, José de Piña; they were released in June. In May the army demanded the resignation of Prime Minister Pires, on the grounds that they had not been paid for six months. In April and May President Yalá held a series of meetings with ministers and opposition leaders in an attempt to broaden support for his increasingly isolated presidency. In June five new ministers, all with connections to opposition parties, were appointed to the Government. In the same month the elections were postponed until 12 October. In July the Minister of Foreign Affairs and the Secretary of State for Information were dismissed; the latter's replacement was himself dismissed in early September. The elections were again postponed in early September.

On 14 September 2003 President Yalá was detained by the armed forces in a bloodless *coup d'état*, which was widely welcomed within Guinea-Bissau. The Chief of Staff of the Armed Forces, Gen. Veríssimo Correia Seabra, who led the coup, stated that the seizure of power had been a response to increasing unrest in the army and the worsening political and economic situation. Seabra proclaimed himself interim President of Guinea-Bissau, and President of a Comité Militar para a Recuperação da Ordem Constitucional e Democrática (Military Committee for the Restoration of Constitutional and Democratic Order). On 17 September Yalá officially resigned the presidency, and on 28 September Henrique Pereira Rosa, a business executive, and Artur Sanhá were sworn in as interim President and Prime Minister, respectively. On 2 October a transitional civilian Government, comprising a further 11 ministers and five secretaries of state, was appointed, in accordance with an agreement signed by political organizations and the military authorities. Ministers were not permitted to hold posts in political organizations. It was envisaged that elections to the ANP (which had been dissolved in November 2002) would be held within six months, and a presidential election within 18 months. A 56-member National Transition Council (NTC), composed of representatives of political and civil groups and the army, was to monitor government policy.

In mid-October 2003 President Rosa dismissed ex-President Yalá's close aides and appointed five new advisers, with the rank of minister. At the beginning of November the Government began paying civil servants' salaries, but warned that the 11 months of arrears owed to them would only be paid when funds became available. In the same month schools were reopened, having been closed for much of the previous two years owing to a series of strikes by unpaid teachers, after the World Bank provided a loan of US $2.5m. to pay salaries. In early December the NTC announced that legislative elections would be held on 28 March 2004, with the presidential election expected to be held a year later.

Elections to the ANP took place on 28 and 30 March 2004; international observers declared themselves generally satisfied with the conduct of the elections, despite poor organization in the capital, and voter turn-out was estimated at 74.6%. The PAIGC won 45 of the 100 seats while the PRS secured 35 and the PUSD 17. The President of the PAIGC, Carlos Gomes Júnior, announced his intention to form a broad-based coalition government. Negotiations between the PAIGC and the PUSD were unsuccessful, however, and the PAIGC reached an agreement with the PRS, whereby the latter undertook to support the Government. In return for this commitment, members of the PRS were appointed to senior positions in the ANP, in governmental departments and other state institutions. The ANP was inaugurated on 7 May; Francisco Benante was subsequently elected President of the chamber. Gomes Júnior took office as Prime Minister on 10 May, and pledged to rehabilitate the country's infrastructure and improve conditions in the military. The new Council of Ministers, which comprised 16 ministers and seven secretaries of state, was sworn in on 12 May. In September President Rosa announced that a presidential election would be held in April or May 2005 (according to the Transitional Charter drafted in October 2003, the election was to take place no later than 12 months after the legislative elections); Rosa, however, stated that he would not stand.

On 6 October 2004 Seabra and another senior military official, Lt-Col Domingos de Barros, were taken hostage and killed by a group of disaffected soldiers, led by Maj. Buate Yanta Namam, in protest at their non-payment for a peace-keeping operation undertaken in Liberia. On 6 and 7 October the soldiers, who emphasized that they were not seeking to overthrow the Government, presented their demands, which included an improvement in army conditions, a salary increase and the payment of salary arrears, and on 7 October President Rosa announced that the soldiers had agreed to refrain from further acts of violence. Meanwhile, Gomes Júnior attributed the unrest to political forces dissatisfied with the outcome of the April elections (widely assumed as referring to members of the PRS). On 10 October a Memorandum of Understanding was signed by Gomes Júnior, Yanta Naman and Maj.-Gen. Baptista Tagmé Na Wai, representing the armed forces, according to which the soldiers would return to their barracks and salary arrears would be paid. An amnesty was to be granted to the mutineers and later in October Gomes Júnior announced that nearly all salary arrears had been settled. A new military high command, reportedly chosen by the mutineers, was also installed. Na Wai became Chief of Staff of the Armed Forces, while José Americo Bubo Na Tchuto was appointed Navy Chief of Staff.

In mid-January 2005 Gomes Júnior, in his capacity as President of the PAIGC, dismissed the parliamentary leader of the party, Cipriano Cassamá, who was alleged to have retained close links to former President Vieira. A new register of voters was scheduled for compilation in February, although, following negotiations between the Government and opposition parties, it was announced in early March that the presidential election would be postponed until mid-July, thus contravening the conditions stipulated in the Transitional Charter. In mid-March, however, it was announced that the presidential election would take place on 19 June and the registration of voters proceeded later in March. Malam Bacai Sanhá, who served as acting President in 1999, was chosen as the candidate for the PAIGC. Meanwhile, both Vieira (who was standing as an independent) and Yalá, representing the PRS, announced their candidacies. According to the Transitional Charter, both Yalá and Vieira were subject to five-year bans from political activity; however, in April their candidacies were approved by the Supreme Court. Also in that month, Gomes Júnior effected a major reorganization of the Council of Ministers.

The presidential election, in which 13 candidates participated, took place, as scheduled, on 19 June 2005, and was monitored by a number of international observers including Joaquim Chissano, the former President of Mozambique and the UN Secretary-General's special envoy to Guinea-Bissau. In the event, Sanhá secured 35.45% of the votes cast, while Vieira took 28.87% and Yalá 25.00%. As none of the candidates had won an outright majority there followed on 24 July a second round of voting, contested by Sanhá and Vieira, at which Vieira received 52.35% of valid votes cast, while Sanhá took 47.65%. The rate of voter participation was recorded at 87.6% in the first round and 78.6% in the second round, and international observers declared the election to have been free and fair.

Despite allegations of widespread electoral fraud and Sanhá's demands that the results of the election be annulled, the outcome was upheld by the Supreme Court and Vieira took office on 1 October 2005. Tensions continued, however, among the pro-Vieira members of the PAIGC and the pro-Sanhá, governing faction of the party, which announced that it would accept the election result only days before Vieira's inauguration. In mid-October 14 PAIGC deputies resigned from the party and declared themselves independents, and several members of that party, together with the PRS and the PUSD, formed a pro-Vieira alliance, the Forúm de Convergência para o Desenvolvimento (FCD), with the intention of precipitating the collapse of Gomes Júnior's Government. Members of the FCD claimed to have a majority in the ANP, while the PAIGC could count on the support of only 31 of the 100 members of the legislature.

In late October 2005, following continued demands by the FCD for the dismissal of the Prime Minister, Vieira dissolved the Government. Aristides Gomes, the former Vice-President of the PAIGC, was appointed Prime Minister on 2 November, and pledged to form a government of national unity, the appointment of which was, however, delayed. Meanwhile, civil unrest and criticism of the current political situation by NGOs active in Guinea-Bissau exacerbated tensions, resulting in the temporary allocation to Aristides Gomes of the economy and finance portfolios, in order to facilitate the payment of civil service salaries. The new 19-member Government was sworn in on 9 November and comprised members of five parties (the PAIGC, the PRS, the PUSD, the PCD and the UE) and independents, the majority of whom were former members of the PAIGC. Notably, Issufo Sanhá of the PAIGC was reappointed as Minister of the Economy, the only member of the previous Government to remain in office. Vítor Mandinga, the leader of the PCD, was named Minister of Finance, and an independent, Ernesto de Carvalho, was subsequently appointed Minister of the Interior. The PAIGC challenged the constitutional legitimacy of the appointment of Aristides Gomes, claiming that as the party that held the largest number of seats in the legislature, it had the right to propose the new Prime Minister; however, in January 2006 the Supreme Court ruled that Vieira had acted in accordance with the Constitution.

In November 2006 Kumba Yalá was re-elected as leader of the PRS, following one year's absence from the country; he announced that he no longer recognized the FCD and sought early elections. In the same month the President dismissed the Minister of the Interior, Ernesto de Carvalho—a close associate of Yalá's. In mid-March 2007 the PAIGC, the PRS and the PUSD announced that they had signed a National Stability Pact (NSP), which aimed to precipitate the formation of a new government of national unity. The PRS and the PUSD also confirmed their withdrawal from the FCD. President Vieira initially refused to accede to demands to dismiss the Government; however, on 19 March 54 deputies approved a motion of no confidence in Prime Minister Gomes, who tendered his resignation 10 days later. Also in late March it was reported that the PUSD had withdrawn its support for the NSP. On 10 April Vieira nominated Martinho N'Dafa Cabi, a senior member of the PAIGC, who had held the positions of Deputy Prime Minister and Minister of National Defence in the Gomes Júnior administration, as the new Prime Minister. Cabi stated that he would seek national reconciliation through dialogue with all political parties and pledged to work towards the holding of legislative elections in 2008. A new 29-member Government was installed in mid-April 2007. In October Maj. Baciro Dabó, hitherto Minister of Internal Administration, was appointed presidential adviser; Certorio Biote assumed his vacated portfolio.

In July 1996 Vieira made an official visit to Portugal, during which agreement was reached on improved bilateral relations. In the same month Guinea-Bissau was among the five lusophone African nations which, along with Brazil and Portugal, officially established the CPLP, a lusophone grouping intended to benefit each member state by means of joint co-operation in technical, cultural and social matters. Portugal provided considerable funding and other aid to Guinea-Bissau.

In 1989 a dispute arose between Guinea-Bissau and Senegal over the demarcation of maritime borders. Guinea-Bissau began proceedings against Senegal in the International Court of Justice (ICJ) after rejecting an international arbitration tribunal's ruling in favour of Senegal. Guinea-Bissau requested direct negotiations with Senegal, and enlisted the aid of President Mubarak of Egypt, then the President of the Organization of African Unity (now the African Union—AU, see p. 164), and President Soares of Portugal as mediators. In November 1991 the ICJ ruled that a 1960 agreement regarding the demarcation of maritime borders between Guinea-Bissau and Senegal remained valid. In December 1992, in retaliation for the deaths of two Senegalese soldiers, the Senegalese air force and infantry bombarded alleged Casamance separatist bases in the São Domingos area of Guinea-Bissau. In March 1993, in an apparent attempt to convince Senegal that it did not support the rebels, the Government handed over Abbé Augustin Diamacouné Senghor, one of the exiled leaders of the Casamance separatists, to the Senegalese authorities. In October the Presidents of Guinea-Bissau and Senegal signed an agreement providing for the joint management and exploitation of the countries' maritime zones. Petroleum resources were to be divided, with Senegal receiving an 85% share and Guinea-Bissau the remaining 15%. Fishing resources were to be divided according to the determination of a joint management agency. The agreement was renewable after a period of 20 years. In December 1995 the legislature authorized the ratification of the October 1993 accord. In the previous month the ICJ announced that Guinea-Bissau had halted all proceedings regarding the border dispute with Senegal.

In February 1995 the Senegalese air force bombarded a village in Guinea-Bissau, close to the border with Senegal. Despite an acknowledgement by the Senegalese authorities that the bombing had occurred as a result of an error, the Senegalese armed forces conducted a similar attack later that month. In March President Abdou Diouf of Senegal visited Guinea-Bissau to provide a personal apology for the two recent incidents and to offer a commitment that Senegal would respect Guinea-Bissau's sovereignty. In September agreement was reached on strengthening co-operation and establishing dialogue concerning security on the countries' joint border. However, a further attack by the Senegalese air force in October prompted the Guinea-Bissau legislature to form a commission of inquiry to investigate such border incidents.

In April 2000 there were renewed reports of incidents on the border between Senegal and Guinea-Bissau; however, the Senegalese Government denied accusations that its troops had entered Guinea-Bissau, and in May requested assistance from Guinea-Bissau to resolve the Casamance conflict. In August an agreement was signed by Yalá and Wade providing for the establishment of a joint military force to patrol the border area. It was also agreed that a joint commission would be set up to 'identify and return' goods allegedly stolen by Guinea-Bissau citizens in the area. In July 2001 Senegal and Guinea-Bissau issued a joint statement reaffirming their commitment to the agreement reached in August of the previous year. Improved security arrangements along the Casamance border were confirmed at a meeting in July, following a decline in border incidents. Following the signature of a peace accord between the Senegalese Government and the Casamance separatists in December 2004, security in the region improved. However, a dissident faction of the separatists renewed disruption and from mid-March 2006 further skirmishes occurred with Guinea-Bissau troops, causing the displacement of civilian population.

Relations between Guinea-Bissau and The Gambia were severely strained in June 2002, when President Yalá accused the Government of The Gambia of harbouring and training Casamance rebels and former associates of Gen. Mané, the leader of the coup of 1998 and attempted coup of 2000. With specific reference to the alleged attempted coup of May 2002, Yalá threatened invasion of The Gambia if support for the rebels

GUINEA-BISSAU

Introductory Survey

continued; President Jammeh of The Gambia denied any such support was being provided. A visit to The Gambia by Guinea-Bissau's Minister of Foreign Affairs in mid-June eased tensions somewhat, and was followed by UN intervention in July, which recommended the reactivation of a joint commission of the two countries. An improvement in relations was signalled by a visit by Yalá to The Gambia in October.

Despite being generally welcomed in Guinea-Bissau, the coup of September 2003 was officially condemned by the international community, and sanctions imposed by the USA were not lifted until August 2004, following the legislative elections. However, President Rosa visited Portugal and a number of West African countries in late 2003 in an effort to gain support and financial aid for the transitional Government, as well as the US headquarters of the UN, the IMF and the World Bank. Representatives from ECOWAS, the AU and the CPLP mediated in talks between the Government and soldiers during the mutiny of October 2004. In November a delegation from the CPLP visited Guinea-Bissau to conduct talks with political and military leaders with the aim of strengthening the country's fragile political structure. In January 2008 the IMF approved the Emergency Post-Conflict Assistance (EPCA) programme, which was to assist in Guinea-Bissau's economic recovery and to reintegrate the country in the wider international financial community.

The People's Republic of China was active in promoting good economic relations with Guinea-Bissau in the mid-2000s, as with numerous other African countries, and funded various public projects, such as the construction of a new parliament building in 2005. This was regarded as undermining the unified approach of the rest of the international donor community in eliciting commitments to reform in return for aid. China benefited from maritime treaties and fishing rights in Guinea-Bissau territorial waters.

In 2004 Guinea-Bissau became a member of the Community of Sahel-Saharan States (see p. 411).

Government

Under the terms of the 1984 Constitution (revised in 1991, 1996 and 1999), Guinea-Bissau is a multi-party state, although the formation of parties on a tribal or geographical basis is prohibited. Legislative power is vested in the Assembléia Nacional Popular, which comprises 100 members, elected by universal adult suffrage for a term of four years. Executive power is vested in the President of the Republic, who is Head of State and who governs with the assistance of an appointed Council of Ministers, led by the Prime Minister. The President is elected by universal adult suffrage for a term of five years.

Defence

As assessed at November 2007, the armed forces officially totalled an estimated 9,250 men (army 6,800, navy 350, air force 100 and paramilitary gendarmerie 2,000). Military service was to be compulsory from 2007, as part of a programme of reform for the armed forces. Expenditure on defence in 2007 was estimated at 7,400m. francs CFA.

Economic Affairs

In 2006, according to estimates by the World Bank, Guinea-Bissau's gross national income (GNI), measured at average 2004–06 prices, was US $307m., equivalent to $190 per head (or $830 on an international purchasing-power parity basis). During 1996–2006, it was estimated, the population increased at an average annual rate of 2.9%, while gross domestic product (GDP) per head decreased, in real terms, by an average of 3.7% per year. Overall GDP declined, in real terms, at an average annual rate of 0.9% in 1996–2006; however, it increased by 4.2% in 2006.

Agriculture (including forestry and fishing) contributed 61.8% of GDP in 2006, and employed an estimated 81.5% of the economically active population in mid-2005. The main cash crops are cashew nuts (production of which in 2006 was estimated by FAO at 85,200 metric tons, with export earnings in 2005 totalling US $93.5m.) and cotton. Other crops produced include rice, oil palm fruit, roots and tubers, millet, coconuts and maize. Livestock and timber production are also important. The fishing industry developed rapidly during the 1990s, and earnings from fishing exports and the sale of fishing licences are a significant source of government revenue (revenue from fishing licences was 7,515m. francs CFA in 2005, equivalent to 26.9% of total revenue). A study conducted in 2004 revealed that the potential annual fishing catch was 96,000 tons; in early 2006 the Minister of Fisheries and the Maritime Economy estimated that 40,000 tons of fish were stolen from Guinea-Bissau waters annually. According to the World Bank, agricultural GDP increased, in real terms, by an average of 2.2% per year in 1996–2006; it increased by 5.5% in 2006.

Industry (including mining, manufacturing, construction and power) employed an estimated 4.1% of the economically active population at mid-1994 and provided 11.5% of GDP in 2006. According to the World Bank, industrial GDP declined, in real terms, by an average of 1.6% per year in 1996–2006; however, growth of 6.0% was recorded in 2006.

The mining sector is underdeveloped, although Guinea-Bissau possesses reserves of bauxite, phosphates, diamonds and gold. A Canadian company was attempting to develop phosphate mining at Farim, in the north of the country, in the early 2000s. In late 2003 recoverable petroleum reserves were estimated at 2,000m. barrels per day.

The sole branches of the manufacturing sector are food-processing, brewing and timber- and cotton-processing, while there are plans to develop fish-processing. Manufacturing and power contributed 7.2% of GDP in 2006. Manufacturing GDP decreased, in real terms, by an average of 1.9% per year in 1995–2006; however, growth of 5.9% was recorded in 2006.

Energy is derived principally from thermal and hydroelectric power. Imports of petroleum and petroleum products comprised 13.3% of the value of total imports in 2005. Energy production since 1999 has been insufficient to supply demand in Bissau, mainly owing to fuel shortages caused by government-set low prices, and to equipment failures caused by poor maintenance. As a result, most energy is currently supplied by private generators. A hydroelectric plant due to commence operations in Guinea in 2009 was expected to improve Guinea-Bissau's power supply.

Services employed an estimated 19.4% of the economically active population at mid-1994, and provided 26.8% of GDP in 2006. According to the World Bank, the combined GDP of the service sectors declined by 1.0% in 1996–2006; growth in 2006 was 0.8%.

In 2007 Guinea-Bissau recorded an estimated trade deficit of US $18.5m., and there was a deficit of $2.9m. on the current account of the balance of payments. In 2005 the principal source of imports were Senegal (34.6%), Italy (20.4%) and Portugal (12.7%). In that year India was the principal market for exports (67.4%), while Nigeria was also a major purchaser; according to official figures, exports of cashew nuts to India were worth $60m. in 2003. In 2005 the principal export was cashew nuts. The principal imports in that year were construction materials, petroleum and petroleum products, foodstuffs, transport equipment, and electrical equipment and machinery.

In 2007 there was an estimated budgetary surplus of 16,500m. francs CFA. Guinea-Bissau's total external debt was US $693m. at the end of 2005, of which $671.3m. was long-term public debt. In 2003 the cost of debt-servicing was equivalent to 16.1% of the total value of exports of goods and services. In 1996–2006 the average annual rate of inflation was 6.5%. Consumer prices increased by 2.0% in 2006.

Guinea-Bissau is a member of the Economic Community of West African States (ECOWAS, see p. 232) and of the West African organs of the Franc Zone (see p. 307).

Guinea-Bissau is one of the world's poorest, and most indebted, countries. Its economy is largely dependent on the traditional rural sector, which employs the vast majority of the labour force and produces primarily for subsistence. Revenue from the export of cashew nuts is vital to the country's economy and foreign financing accounts for a significant part of budget revenue. Relations with donors have, however, been uneasy since the early 2000s. In May 2001 the IMF and the World Bank suspended the aid programme in support of the Government's 2000–03 programme of economic reform, pending an investigation into the disappearance of US $15m. in donor assistance, while in December 2006 the World Bank suspended its support for a rehabilitation project after concluding that a joint venture agreement between the Government and a foreign energy company was incompatible with the project it had envisaged, thus delaying the expected disbursement of $10m. in budgetary support. The European Union and the African Development Bank also withheld financial assistance to Guinea-Bissau. Nevertheless, in November a donor conference (repeatedly suspended owing to political instability in Guinea-Bissau) had finally been convened, at which some $262.5m. was pledged for the period 2006–11, although a number of conditions were

GUINEA-BISSAU

placed on the dispersal of funds. In 2005 GDP growth amounted to just 2.3%, as a result of parasite damage to the cashew nut crop and a generally poor rice crop. A slight improvement was recorded in 2006, with GDP growth of 2.8%, but reduced growth of 2.5% was estimated in 2007, and a further decline, to 2.1%, was projected for 2008. In recent years the increasing use of the country as a route for the trafficking of illegal narcotics between South America and Europe has become a considerable concern to the Guinea-Bissau authorities, and the UN Office on Drugs and Crime (UNODC) stated in late 2007 that the value of the drugs trade within the country had exceeded that of national income. With the country lacking the infrastructure and equipment effectively to counter crime, UNDOC appealed for assistance of some $19m. to be invested in the nation's security services, judicial system and police resources.

Education

Education is officially compulsory only for the period of primary schooling, which begins at seven years of age and lasts for six years. Secondary education, beginning at the age of 13, lasts for up to five years (a first cycle of three years and a second of two years). According to UNESCO estimates, in 2000/01 enrolment at primary schools included 45% of children in the relevant age-group (males 53%; females 37%), while enrolment at secondary schools was equivalent to only 9% of children in the relevant age-group (males 11%; females 6%). In 1999/2000 463 students were enrolled in tertiary education. Some 200 students completed their studies in Havana, Cuba, in 2002, while a further 186 had scholarships to study in Paris, France, and Dakar, Senegal. In November 2003 President Rosa opened the country's first public university, the Amílcar Cabral University; a private university, Colinas de Boe, had also opened in September. According to the 2005 budget, expenditure on education was forecast at 15.0% of total spending.

Public Holidays

2008: 1 January (New Year's Day), 20 January (Death of Amílcar Cabral), 8 March (International Women's Day), 1 May (Labour Day), 3 August (Anniversary of the Killing of Pidjiguiti), 24 September (National Day), 1 October* (Korité, end of Ramadan), 14 November (Anniversary of the Movement of Readjustment), 9 December* (Tabaski, Feast of the Sacrifice), 25 December (Christmas Day).

2009: 1 January (New Year's Day), 20 January (Death of Amílcar Cabral), 8 March (International Women's Day), 1 May (Labour Day), 3 August (Anniversary of the Killing of Pidjiguiti), 13 September (National Day), 20 September* (Korité, end of Ramadan), 14 November (Anniversary of the Movement of Readjustment), 27 November* (Tabaski, Feast of the Sacrifice), 25 December (Christmas Day).

* These holidays are dependent on the Islamic lunar calendar and may vary by one or two days from the dates given.

Weights and Measures

The metric system is used.

Statistical Survey

Area and Population

AREA, POPULATION AND DENSITY

Area (sq km)	36,125*
Population (census results)	
16–30 April 1979	753,313
1 December 1991	
Males	476,210
Females	507,157
Total	983,367
Population (UN estimates at mid-year)†	
2005	1,597,000
2006	1,646,000
2007	1,695,000
Density (per sq km) at mid-2007	46.9

* 13,948 sq miles.
† Source: UN, *World Population Prospects: The 2006 Revision*.

ETHNIC GROUPS

1996 (percentages): Balante 30; Fulani 20; Mandjak 14; Mandinka 12; Papel 7; Other 16 (Source: Comunidade dos Países de Língua Portuguesa).

POPULATION BY REGION
(1991 census)

Bafatá	143,377	Gabú	134,971
Biombo	60,420	Oio	156,084
Bissau	197,610	Quinara	44,793
Bolama/Bijagos	26,691	Tombali	72,441
Cacheu	146,980	**Total**	983,367

PRINCIPAL TOWNS
(population at 1979 census)

Bissau (capital)	109,214	Catió	5,170
Bafatá	13,429	Cantchungo†	4,965
Gabú*	7,803	Farim	4,468
Mansôa	5,390		

* Formerly Nova Lamego.
† Formerly Teixeira Pinto.

Mid-2007 (incl. suburbs, UN estimate): Bissau 330,000 (Source: UN, *World Urbanization Prospects: The 2007 Revision*).

BIRTHS AND DEATHS

	2004	2005	2006
Birth rate (per 1,000)	49.6	49.6	49.5
Death rate (per 1,000)	19.6	19.4	19.2

Source: African Development Bank.

Expectation of life (years at birth, WHO estimates): 46.8 (males 45.7; females 47.9) in 2005 (Source: WHO, *World Health Statistics*).

ECONOMICALLY ACTIVE POPULATION
('000 persons at mid-1994)

	Males	Females	Total
Agriculture, etc.	195	175	370
Industry	15	5	20
Services	80	14	94
Total	290	194	484

Source: UN Economic Commission for Africa, *African Statistical Yearbook*.

Mid-2005 (estimates in '000): Agriculture, etc. 551; Total labour force 676 (Source: FAO).

GUINEA-BISSAU

Health and Welfare

KEY INDICATORS

Total fertility rate (children per woman, 2005)	7.1
Under-5 mortality rate (per 1,000 live births, 2005)	200
HIV/AIDS (% of persons aged 15–49, 2005)	3.8
Physicians (per 1,000 head, 2004)	0.12
Hospital beds (per 1,000 head, 1990)	1.48
Health expenditure (2004): US $ per head (PPP)	28.4
Health expenditure (2004): % of GDP	4.8
Health expenditure (2004): public (% of total)	27.3
Access to water (% of persons, 2004)	59
Access to sanitation (% of persons, 2004)	35
Human Development Index (2005): ranking	175
Human Development Index (2005): value	0.374

For sources and definitions, see explanatory note on p. vi.

Agriculture

PRINCIPAL CROPS
('000 metric tons)

	2004	2005	2006*
Rice (paddy)	89.2	98.3	106.0
Maize	31.9	39.8	41.8
Millet	31.5	47.2	49.6
Sorghum	15.5	23.4	24.5
Cassava*	39.9	42.3	40.0
Sugar cane*	5.5	5.5	6.5
Cashew nuts*	90.9	97.3	85.2
Groundnuts (in shell)*	19.9	20.1	20.0
Coconuts†	45.5	45.5	45.5
Oil palm fruit*	82.4	83.9	80.0
Plantains*	39.8	40.6	39.0
Oranges*	5.1	5.1	5.0

* FAO estimates.
† Unofficial figures.

Aggregate production ('000 metric tons, may include official, semi-official or estimated data): Total cereals 171.4 in 2004, 212.5 in 2005, 225.3 in 2006; Total roots and tubers 107.9 in 2004, 110.3 in 2005, 112.0 in 2006; Total vegetables (incl. melons) 25.5 in 2004, 25.5 in 2005, 25.5 in 2006; Total fruits (excl. melons) 77.3 in 2004, 78.1 in 2005, 79.7 in 2006.

Source: FAO.

LIVESTOCK
('000 head, year ending September, FAO estimates)

	2003	2004	2005
Cattle	520	520	530
Pigs	360	360	370
Sheep	290	290	300
Goats	330	330	335
Chickens	1,500	1,550	1,600

2006: Figures assumed to be unchanged from 2005 (FAO estimates).
Source: FAO.

LIVESTOCK PRODUCTS
('000 metric tons, FAO estimates)

	2004	2005	2006
Cattle meat	5.1	5.2	5.4
Pig meat	11.2	11.5	11.9
Cows' milk	14.3	14.5	14.7
Goats' milk	3.0	3.1	3.1

Source: FAO.

Forestry

ROUNDWOOD REMOVALS
('000 cubic metres, excluding bark)

	1997	1998	1999
Sawlogs, veneer logs and logs for sleepers*	40	40	40
Other industrial wood	124	127	130
Fuel wood†	422	422	422
Total	586	589	592

* Assumed to be unchanged since 1971.
† Assumed to be unchanged since 1979.

2000–06: Production as in 1999 (FAO estimates).
Source: FAO.

SAWNWOOD PRODUCTION
('000 cubic metres, including railway sleepers, FAO estimates)

	1970	1971	1972
Total	10	16	16

1973–2006: Production assumed to be unchanged since 1972 (FAO estimates).
Source: FAO.

Fishing

(metric tons, live weight)

	2003	2004*	2005*
Freshwater fishes*	150	150	150
Sea catfishes	315	320	320
Meagre	337	340	340
Mullets*	1,500	1,500	1,500
Sompat grunt	202	200	200
Lesser African threadfin	498	500	500
Total catch (incl. others)*	6,153	6,200	6,200

* FAO estimates.
Source: FAO.

Industry

SELECTED PRODUCTS
('000 metric tons, unless otherwise indicated)

	2001	2002	2003
Hulled rice	69.1	68.4	67.7
Groundnuts (processed)	6.8	6.7	6.6
Bakery products	7.6	7.7	7.9
Frozen fish	1.7	1.7	1.7
Dry and smoked fish	3.6	3.7	3.8
Vegetable oils (million litres)	3.6	3.6	3.7
Beverages (million litres)	3.5	0.0	0.0
Dairy products (million litres)	1.1	0.9	0.9
Wood products	4.7	4.5	4.4
Soap	2.6	2.5	2.4
Electric energy (million kWh)	18.9	19.4	15.8

Source: IMF, *Guinea-Bissau: Selected Issues and Statistical Appendix* (March 2005).

2004 (million kWh): 61 (Source: UN, *Industrial Commodity Statistics Yearbook*).

GUINEA-BISSAU

Finance

CURRENCY AND EXCHANGE RATES

Monetary Units
100 centimes = 1 franc de la Communauté financière africaine (CFA).

Sterling, Dollar and Euro Equivalents (31 December 2007)
£1 sterling = 892.702 francs CFA;
US $1 = 445.593 francs CFA;
€1 = 655.957 francs CFA;
10,000 francs CFA = £11.20 = $22.44 = €15.24.

Average Exchange Rate (francs CFA per US $)
2005   527.468
2006   522.890
2007   479.267

Note: An exchange rate of 1 French franc = 50 francs CFA, established in 1948, remained in force until January 1994, when the CFA franc was devalued by 50%, with the exchange rate adjusted to 1 French franc = 100 francs CFA. This relationship to French currency remained in effect with the introduction of the euro on 1 January 1999. From that date, accordingly, a fixed exchange rate of €1 = 655.957 francs CFA has been in operation. Following Guinea-Bissau's admission in March 1997 to the Union économique et monétaire ouest-africaine, the country entered the Franc Zone on 17 April. As a result, the Guinea peso was replaced by the CFA franc, although the peso remained legal tender until 31 July. The new currency was introduced at an exchange rate of 1 franc CFA = 65 Guinea pesos. At 31 March 1997 the exchange rate in relation to US currency was $1 = 36,793.3 Guinea pesos.

BUDGET

Revenue (million francs CFA)	2003	2004	2005
Tax revenue	11,941	11,830	18,334
Income taxes	2,907	2,838	4,074
Corporate tax	2,139	1,596	1,973
Individual taxes	587	605	1,338
Consumption taxes	1,437	1,420	2,148
General sales tax	3,568	3,192	5,649
Taxes on international trade and transactions	3,745	4,047	6,429
Import duties	2,583	2,347	3,754
Export duties	1,171	1,699	2,010
Port service charges	—	—	662
Other taxes	—	50	77
Non-tax revenue	8,903	12,699	9,644
Fees and duties	8,142	9,101	7,558
Fishing licences	7,977	8,988	7,515
Other non-tax revenues	760	3,597	2,087
Total	20,844	24,529	27,978

Source: IMF, *Guinea-Bissau: Selected Issues and Statistical Appendix* (August 2006).

2006 ('000 million francs CFA): Total revenue and grants 50.6 (Tax revenue 18.5, Non-tax revenue 13.0, Grants 19.1). Source: *IMF, Guinea Bissau: Use of Fund Resources—Request for Emergency Post-Conflict Assistance; Press Release; and Statement by the Executive Director for Guinea-Bissau* (February 2008).

2007 ('000 million francs CFA, estimates): Total revenue and grants 54.3 (Tax revenue 19.7, Non-tax revenue 7.8, Grants 26.8). Source: *IMF, Guinea Bissau: Use of Fund Resources—Request for Emergency Post-Conflict Assistance; Press Release; and Statement by the Executive Director for Guinea-Bissau* (February 2008).

2008 ('000 million francs CFA, projections): Total revenue and grants 76.7 (Tax revenue 20.8, Non-tax revenue 16.9, Grants 39.1). Source: *IMF, Guinea Bissau: Use of Fund Resources—Request for Emergency Post-Conflict Assistance; Press Release; and Statement by the Executive Director for Guinea-Bissau* (February 2008).

Expenditure ('000 million francs CFA)	2006	2007*	2008†
Current expenditure	46.6	46.8	47.7
Wages and salaries	20.5	21.8	21.3
Goods and services	7.9	6.0	7.1
Transfers	8.3	9.3	11.2
Other current expenditures	4.9	4.7	3.3
Scheduled interest payments	5.0	5.1	4.7
Capital expenditure and net lending	19.7	23.9	27.8
Total	66.2	70.8	75.5

* Estimates.
† Projections.

Source: IMF, *Guinea Bissau: Use of Fund Resources—Request for Emergency Post-Conflict Assistance; Press Release; and Statement by the Executive Director for Guinea-Bissau* (February 2008).

CENTRAL BANK RESERVES
(US $ million at 31 December)

	2004	2005	2006
IMF special drawing rights	0.68	0.57	0.50
Foreign exchange	72.41	79.24	81.52
Total	73.09	79.81	82.02

Source: IMF, *International Financial Statistics*.

MONEY SUPPLY
(million francs CFA at 31 December)

	2004	2005	2006
Currency outside banks	32,570	40,661	39,679
Demand deposits at deposit money banks	10,277	10,868	13,436
Total money (incl. others)	42,964	51,679	53,260

Source: IMF, *International Financial Statistics*.

COST OF LIVING
(Consumer Price Index; base: 2003 = 100)

	2004	2005	2006
Food, beverages and tobacco	101.1	104.7	105.2
Clothing	98.9	99.0	n.a.
Rent, water, electricity, gas and other fuels	101.7	101.9	n.a.
All items (incl. others)	100.9	104.3	106.4

Source: ILO.

NATIONAL ACCOUNTS

Expenditure on the Gross Domestic Product
('000 million francs CFA at current prices)

	2003	2004	2005*
Government final consumption expenditure	22.5	24.8	22.4
Private final consumption expenditure	110.1	119.9	152.9
Increase in stocks / Gross fixed capital formation	23.9	22.8	14.4
Total domestic expenditure	156.5	167.5	189.7
Exports of goods and services	41.3	44.1	57.2
Less Imports of goods and services	58.9	67.2	86.1
GDP in purchasers' values	138.8	144.4	160.8

* Estimates.

Source: Banque de France, *Rapport Zone franc 2005*.

2006 (US $ million at current prices): Government final consumption expenditure 18.65; Private final consumption expenditure 345.21; Gross capital formation 42.77; Total domestic expenditure 406.63; Exports of goods and services 74.25; *Less* Imports of goods and services 153.01; GDP at current market prices 327.87 (Source: African Development Bank).

GUINEA-BISSAU

Gross Domestic Product by Economic Activity
(million francs CFA at current prices)

	2003	2004	2005
Agriculture, hunting, forestry and fishing	82,763	84,009	94,193
Manufacturing, electricity and water	12,186	12,515	13,605
Construction	4,039	4,190	4,647
Trade, restaurants and hotels	21,578	23,352	26,274
Transport, storage and communications	3,656	3,888	4,270
Finance, insurance, real estate, etc. / Community, social and personal services (excl. government)	484	504	559
Government services	10,485	11,849	12,757
GDP at factor cost	135,191	140,307	156,305
Indirect taxes	1,927	2,269	2,522
GDP at market prices	137,118	142,576	158,827

Source: IMF, *Guinea-Bissau: Selected Issues and Statistical Appendix* (August 2006).

2006 (US $ million at constant 2000 prices): Agriculture 93.13; Industry 33.84 (Manufacturing 25.18) Services 91.12; GDP at factor cost 218.08 (Source: African Development Bank).

BALANCE OF PAYMENTS
('000 million francs CFA)

	2005	2006	2007*
Exports of goods f.o.b.	47.2	31.6	46.3
Imports of goods f.o.b.	−55.9	−63.2	−64.8
Trade balance	−8.7	−31.5	−18.5
Exports of services	2.6	6.7	6.4
Imports of services	−20.7	−25.3	−19.5
Balance on goods and services	−26.8	−50.1	−31.6
Other income (net)	−6.3	−4.9	−4.4
Balance on goods, services and income	−33.1	−55.0	−36.0
Official current transfers	12.1	21.6	16.7
Private current transfers	12.9	15.3	16.4
Current balance	−8.0	−18.2	−2.9
Capital account (net)	23.7	17.6	12.3
Financial account (net)	−26.7	−19.6	−17.2
Overall balance	−11.1	−20.3	−7.8

* Estimates.

Source: IMF, *Guinea Bissau: Use of Fund Resources—Request for Emergency Post-Conflict Assistance; Press Release; and Statement by the Executive Director for Guinea-Bissau* (February 2008).

External Trade

PRINCIPAL COMMODITIES
(US $ million)

Imports c.i.f.	2003	2004	2005*
Foodstuffs	25.8	19.1	15.1
Rice	18.2	12.7	10.8
Wheat flour	2.5	1.8	0.9
Oil	2.1	1.0	1.2
Beverages and tobacco	5.5	4.9	6.0
Other consumer goods	5.0	9.8	15.0
Petroleum and petroleum products	8.7	12.4	15.8
Diesel fuel and gasoline	7.7	8.8	13.7
Construction materials	7.2	12.5	20.6
Transport equipment	4.9	10.2	13.2
Passenger vehicles	3.4	7.5	8.2
Freight vehicles	1.1	2.1	3.5
Electrical equipment and machinery	6.0	10.6	12.0
Non-registered trade	6.1	3.3	15.7
Total (incl. others)	70.8	83.0	119.1

* Estimates.

Exports f.o.b.	2003	2004	2005
Agricultural products	56.7	73.2	94.4
Cashew nuts	55.7	72.8	93.5
Total (incl. others)	62.2	75.8	100.8

Source: IMF, *Guinea-Bissau: Selected Issues and Statistical Appendix* (August 2006).

PRINCIPAL TRADING PARTNERS
(percentage of trade)

Imports	2003	2004	2005
France	2.7	2.2	2.5
India	2.0	0.8	0.6
Italy	8.0	3.7	20.4
Netherlands	2.9	4.0	3.0
Pakistan	0.3	1.9	1.4
Portugal	13.3	13.8	12.7
Senegal	36.2	44.5	34.6
Spain	4.4	2.3	1.2

Exports	2003	2004	2005
Guinea	1.9	0.2	0.3
India	62.3	52.2	67.4
Nigeria	15.7	13.2	19.0
Portugal	2.6	0.8	1.1
Senegal	0.9	1.1	1.5
USA	2.6	22.2	0.2

Source: IMF, *Guinea-Bissau: Selected Issues and Statistical Appendix* (August 2006).

Transport

ROAD TRAFFIC
(motor vehicles in use, estimates)

	1994	1995	1996
Passenger cars	5,940	6,300	7,120
Commercial vehicles	4,650	4,900	5,640

Source: International Road Federation, *World Road Statistics*.

SHIPPING

Merchant Fleet
(registered at 31 December)

	2004	2005	2006
Number of vessels	23	25	25
Total displacement (grt)	5,943	6,627	6,627

Source: Lloyd's Register-Fairplay, *World Fleet Statistics*.

International Sea-Borne Freight Traffic
(UN estimates, '000 metric tons)

	1991	1992	1993
Goods loaded	40	45	46
Goods unloaded	272	277	283

Source: UN Economic Commission for Africa, *African Statistical Yearbook*.

GUINEA-BISSAU

CIVIL AVIATION
(traffic on scheduled services)

	1996	1997	1998
Kilometres flown (million)	1	0	0
Passengers carried ('000)	21	21	20
Passenger-km (million)	10	10	10
Total ton-km (million)	1	1	1

Source: UN, *Statistical Yearbook*.

Tourism

TOURIST ARRIVALS BY NATIONALITY

	2005
Cape Verde	159
France	599
Italy	213
Libya	12
Portugal	1,552
Senegal	235
Spain	324
USA	57
Total (incl. others)	**4,978**

Receipts from tourism (US $ million, excl. passenger transport): 2 in 2002; 3 in 2003; 2 in 2004.

Source: World Tourism Organization.

Communications Media

	2004	2005	2006
Telephones ('000 main lines in use)	10.6	10.2	10.2
Mobile cellular telephones ('000 subscribers)	41.7	95.0	95.0
Internet users ('000)	26	31	37

Facsimile machines (number in use): 550 in 2000.

Radio receivers ('000 in use): 49 in 1997.

Daily newspapers: 1 (average circulation 6,200 copies) in 1998.

Sources: UNESCO Institute for Statistics; UNESCO, *Statistical Yearbook*; UN, *Statistical Yearbook*; International Telecommunication Union.

Education

(1999)

	Teachers	Students Males	Students Females	Students Total
Pre-primary	194	2,027	2,132	4,159
Primary	4,306	89,401	60,129	149,530
Secondary: general	1,913*	16,109	8,925	25,034
Secondary: technical and vocational	1,913*	208	72	280
Tertiary	n.a.	n.a.	n.a.	463

* UNESCO estimate.

Institutions (1999): Pre-primary 54; Primary 759.

Source: UNESCO Institute for Statistics.

Adult literacy rate (UNESCO estimates): 39.6% (males 55.2%; females 24.7%) in 2003 (Source: UN Development Programme, *Human Development Report*).

Directory

The Constitution

A new Constitution for the Republic of Guinea-Bissau was approved by the Assembléia Nacional Popular on 16 May 1984 and amended in May 1991, November 1996 and July 1999 (see below). The main provisions of the 1984 Constitution were:

Guinea-Bissau is an anti-colonialist and anti-imperialist Republic and a State of revolutionary national democracy, based on the people's participation in undertaking, controlling and directing public activities. The Partido Africano da Independência da Guiné e Cabo Verde (PAIGC) shall be the leading political force in society and in the State. The PAIGC shall define the general bases for policy in all fields.

The economy of Guinea-Bissau shall be organized on the principles of state direction and planning. The State shall control the country's foreign trade.

The representative bodies in the country are the Assembléia Nacional Popular and the regional councils. Other state bodies draw their powers from these. The members of the regional councils shall be directly elected. Members of the councils must be more than 18 years of age. The Assembléia Nacional Popular shall have 150 members, who are to be elected by the regional councils from among their own members. All members of the Assembléia Nacional Popular must be over 21 years of age.

The Assembléia Nacional Popular shall elect a 15-member Council of State (Conselho de Estado), to which its powers are delegated between sessions of the Assembléia. The Assembléia also elects the President of the Conselho de Estado, who is also automatically Head of the Government and Commander-in-Chief of the Armed Forces. The Conselho de Estado will later elect two Vice-Presidents and a Secretary. The President and Vice-Presidents of the Conselho de Estado form part of the Government, as do Ministers, Secretaries of State and the Governor of the National Bank.

The Constitution can be revised at any time by the Assembléia Nacional Popular on the initiative of the deputies themselves, or of the Conselho de Estado or the Government.

Note: Constitutional amendments providing for the operation of a multi-party political system were approved unanimously by the Assembléia Nacional Popular in May 1991. The amendments stipulated that new parties seeking registration must obtain a minimum of 2,000 signatures, with at least 100 signatures from each of the nine provinces. (These provisions were adjusted in August to 1,000 and 50 signatures, respectively.) In addition, the amendments provided for the Assembléia Nacional Popular (reduced to 100 members) to be elected by universal adult suffrage, for the termination of official links between the PAIGC and the armed forces, and for the operation of a free-market economy. Multi-party elections took place in July 1994.

In November 1996 the legislature approved a constitutional amendment providing for Guinea-Bissau to seek membership of the Union économique et monétaire ouest-africaine and of the Franc Zone.

In July 1999 constitutional amendments were introduced limiting the tenure of presidential office to two terms and abolishing the death penalty. It was also stipulated that the country's principal offices of state could only be held by Guinea-Bissau nationals born of Guinea-Bissau parents.

The Government

HEAD OF STATE

President: João Bernardo Vieira (took office 1 October 2005).

COUNCIL OF MINISTERS
(February 2008)

Prime Minister: Martinho N'Dafa Cabi.

Minister of the Presidency of the Council of Ministers and Parliamentary Affairs: Pedro da Costa.

GUINEA-BISSAU

Minister of National Defence: Marciano Silva Barbeiro.

Minister of Foreign Affairs, International Co-operation and Communities: Maria de Conceição Nobre Cabral.

Minister of Internal Administration: Certorio Biote.

Minister of the Economy and Regional Integration: Abubacar Demba Dahaba.

Minister of Finance: Issufo Sanhá.

Minister of Justice: Carmelita Babosa Rodrigues Pires.

Minister of Administrative Reform, the Civil Service and Labour: Pedro Morato Milaco.

Minister of Transport and Communications: Fernando Gomes.

Minister of Culture, Youth and Sports: Adja Djaló Nandinga.

Minister of Natural Resources: Soares Sambú.

Minister of Trade and Handicrafts: Henri Mané.

Minister of Social Solidarity, the Family and the Fight against Poverty: Alfredo António da Silva.

Minister of Public Health: Eugenia Saldanha.

Minister of National and Higher Education: Alfredo Gomes.

Minister of Agriculture and Rural Development: Daniel Sulemane Embalo.

Minister of Fisheries: Daniel Gomes.

Minister of Public Works and Urbanization: Rui Araújo Gomes.

Minister of Energy and Industry: Vença Mendes na Luac.

Minister of the Fight for the Freedom of the Homeland: Isabel Buscardine.

There are, in addition, nine Secretaries of State.

MINISTRIES

Office of the Prime Minister: Av. Unidade Africana, CP 137, Bissau; tel. 211308; fax 201671.

Ministry of Administrative Reform, the Civil Service and Labour: Bissau.

Ministry of Agriculture and Rural Development: Av. Amílcar Cabral, CP 102, Bissau; tel. 221200; fax 222483.

Ministry of Culture, Youth and Sports: Bissau.

Ministry of the Economy and Regional Integration: Rua Justino Lopes 74A, CP 67, Bissau; tel. 203670; fax 203496; e-mail info@mail.guine-bissau.org; internet www.guine-bissau.org.

Ministry of Energy and Industry: Bissau.

Ministry of the Fight for the Freedom of the Homeland: Bissau.

Ministry of Finance: Rua Justino Lopes 74A, CP 67, Bissau; tel. 203670; fax 203496; e-mail info@mail.guine-bissau.org; internet www.guine-bissau.org.

Ministry of Fisheries: Av. Amílcar Cabral, CP 102, Bissau; tel. 201699; fax 202580.

Ministry of Foreign Affairs, International Co-operation and Communities: Rua Gen. Omar Torrijo, Bissau; tel. 204301; fax 202378.

Ministry of Internal Administration: Av. Unidade Africana, Bissau; tel. 203781.

Ministry of Justice: Av. Amílcar Cabral, CP 17, Bissau; tel. 202185.

Ministry of National Defence: Amura, Bissau; tel. 223646.

Ministry of National and Higher Education: Rua Areolino Cruz, Bissau; tel. 202244.

Ministry of Natural Resources: CP 311, Bissau; tel. 215659; fax 223149.

Ministry of the Presidency of the Council of Ministers and Parliamentary Affairs: Bissau.

Ministry of Public Health: CP 50, Bissau; tel. 204438; fax 201701.

Ministry of Public Works and Urbanization: Bissau.

Ministry of Social Solidarity, the Family and the Fight against Poverty: Bissau; tel. 204785.

Ministry of Territorial Administration: Bissau.

Ministry of Trade and Handicrafts: Av. 3 de Agosto, CP 67, Bissau; tel. 202172; fax 202171.

Ministry of Transport and Communications: Bissau; fax 201137.

President and Legislature

PRESIDENT

Presidential Election, First Round, 19 June 2005

Candidate	Votes	% of votes
Malam Bacai Sanhá (PAIGC)	158,276	35.45
João Bernardo Vieira (Independent)	128,918	28.87
Kumba Yalá (PRS)	111,606	25.00
Francisco José Fadul (PUSD)	12,733	2.85
Aregado Mantenque Té (PT)	9,000	2.02
Mamadú Yaya Djaló (Independent)	7,112	1.59
Mário Lopes da Rosa (Independent)	4,863	1.09
Others	13,985	3.13
Total	**446,493**	**100.00**

Second Round, 24 July 2005

Candidate	Votes	% of votes
João Bernardo Vieira (Independent)	216,167	52.35
Malam Bacai Sanhá (PAIGC)	196,759	47.65
Total	**412,926**	**100.00**

LEGISLATURE

Assembléia Nacional Popular: Palácio Colinas de Boé, Bissau; tel. 201991; fax 206725.

President: Francisco Benante.

General Election, 28 and 30 March 2004

Party	Votes	% of votes	Seats
Partido Africano da Independência da Guiné e Cabo Verde (PAIGC)	141,455	31.45	45
Partido para a Renovação Social (PRS)	111,354	24.76	35
Partido Unido Social Democrático (PUSD)	72,362	16.09	17
União Eleitoral (UE)	18,253	4.06	2
Aliança Popular Unida (APU)	5,776	1.28	1
Total (incl. others)	**449,755**	**100.00**	**100**

Election Commission

Comissão Nacional de Eleições (CNE): Av. 3 de Agosto 44, CP 359, Bissau; tel. 203600; fax 203601; e-mail cne-info@guinetel.com; Pres. Alhaji Malam Mané.

Political Organizations

The legislative elections of March 2004 were contested by 12 parties and three coalitions or alliances. In mid-2006 a total of 31 political organizations were registered.

Aliança Popular Unida (APU): Bissau; f. 2003 as coalition to contest the legislative elections of March 2004; Leader Fernando Gomes.

  Aliança Socialista da Guiné-Bissau (ASG): Bissau; f. 2000; Leader Fernando Gomes.

  Partido Popular Guineense (PPG): Bissau; Leader João Tátis Sá.

Foro Cívico da Guiné/Social Democracia (FCG/SD): Bissau; Pres. Antonieta Rosa Gomes; Sec.-Gen. Carlos Vaiman.

Forúm de Convergência para o Desenvolvimento (FCD): Bissau; f. 2005; alliance comprising the PRS, the PUSD, dissident, pro-Vieira, mems of the PAIGC and other parties; the PRS and the PUSD announced their withdrawal from the movement in March 2007; Leader Francisco Fadul.

Frente Republicana Ampla (FRA): Bissau; f. 2006; anti-Vieira alliance comprising 11 parties, including the PAIGC, the FSG/SD, the LIPE, the PDG, the PP, the PRP, the PST, the UM and the UPG.

Partido Africano da Independência da Guiné e Cabo Verde (PAIGC): CP 106, Bissau; internet www.paigc.org; f. 1956; fmrly the ruling party in both Guinea-Bissau and Cape Verde; although Cape Verde withdrew from the PAIGC following the coup in Guinea-Bissau in Nov. 1980, Guinea-Bissau has retained the party name and initials; Pres. Carlos Domingos Gomes Júnior.

GUINEA-BISSAU

Partido Democrático Guineense (PDG): Lisbon, Portugal; f. 2002; Leader MANUEL CÁ.

Partido Democrático Socialista da Salvação Guineense (PDSSG): Bissau; Leader SERIFO BALDÉ.

Partido para a Nova Democracia (PND): Bissau; f. 2006; Pres. IBRAIMA DJALÓ.

Partido da Reconciliação Nacional (PRN): Bissau; f. 2004; Leader ALMARA NHASSÉ; Sec.-Gen. OLUNDO MENDES.

Partido para a Renovação Social (PRS): c/o Assembléia Nacional Popular, Bissau; f. 1992; Pres. KUMBA YALÁ.

Partido de Solidariedade e Trabalho (PST): Bissau; f. 2002; Leader IANCUBA INDJAI; Sec.-Gen. ZACARIAS BALDÉ.

Partido dos Trabalhadores da Guiné-Bissau (PT): Bissau; e-mail contact@nodjuntamon.org; internet www.nodjuntamon.org; f. 2002; left-wing; Pres. AREGADO MANTENQUE TÉ.

Partido da Unidade Nacional (PUN): Bissau; f. 2002; Leader IDRISSA DJALÓ.

Partido Unido Social Democrático (PUSD): Bissau; f. 1991; officially registered in Jan. 1992; Interim Pres. AUGUSTO BARAI MANGO FERNANDES.

Plataforma Unida—Mufunessa Larga Guiné: f. 2003 as coalition to contest legislative elections; comprises the following parties:

Aliança Democrática (AD): c/o Assembléia Nacional Popular, Bissau; Leader VICTOR MANDINGA.

Frente Democrática (FD): Bissau; f. 1991; officially registered in Nov. 1991; Pres. CANJURA INJAI; Sec.-Gen. MARCELINO BATISTA.

Frente Democrática Social (FDS): c/o Assembléia Nacional Popular, Bissau; f. 1991; legalized in Dec. 1991; Leader RAFAEL BARBOSA.

Frente para a Libertação e Independência da Guiné (FLING): Bissau; f. 1962 as an external opposition movement; legally registered in May 1992; Leader KATENGUL MENDY.

Grupo de Democratas Independentes (GDI): Bissau; f. 2003 by fmr mems of the RGB; Leader HELDER VAZ.

Partido da Convergência Democrática (PCD): Bissau; Leader VÍTOR MANDINGA.

Resistência da Guiné-Bissau (RGB): Bissau; f. 1986 in Lisbon, Portugal, as Resistência da Guiné-Bissau—Movimento Bafatá; adopted present name prior to official registration in Dec. 1991; changed name as above in 2003; maintains offices in Paris (France), Dakar (Senegal) and Praia (Cape Verde); Pres. Lic. SALVADOR TCHONGO; Sec.-Gen. MÁRIO USSUMANE BALDÉ.

União Eleitoral (UE): f. 2002; coalition; supported the PAIGC candidate, Malam Bacai Sanhá, in the 2005 presidential election; Leader JOAQUIM BALDÉ; comprises a group of RGB dissidents, and the following parties:

Liga Guineense de Protecção Ecológica (LIPE): Bairro Missirá 102, CP 1290, Bissau; tel. and fax 252309; f. 1991; ecology party; Pres. Alhaji BUBACAR DJALÓ.

Partido da Renovação e Progresso (PRP): Bissau; Leader MAMADÚ URI DJALÓ.

Partido Social Democrático (PSD): c/o Assembléia Nacional Popular, Bissau; f. 1995 by breakaway faction of the RGB—MB; Leader JOAQUIM BALDÉ; Sec.-Gen. GASPAR FERNANDES.

Partido Socialista Guineense (PSG): Bissau; Leader CIRÍLO VIEIRA.

União para a Mudança (UM): Bissau; f. 1994 as coalition to contest presidential and legislative elections; re-formed April 1995; Leader AMINE MICHEL SAAD; comprises the following parties:

Movimento para a Unidade e a Democracia (MUDE): Bissau; officially registered in Aug. 1992; Leader FILINTO VAZ MARTINS.

Partido Democrático do Progresso (PDP): Bissau; f. 1991; officially registered in Aug. 1992; Pres. of Nat. Council AMINE MICHEL SAAD.

Partido de Renovação e Desenvolvimento (PRD): Bissau; f. 1992 as the 'Group of 121' by PAIGC dissidents; officially registered in Oct. 1992; Leaders MANUEL RAMBOUT BARCELOS, AGNELO REGALA.

União Patriótica Guineense (UPG): Bissau; f. 2004 by dissident members of the RGB; Pres. FRANCISCA VAZ TURPIN.

Other parties included the **Partido Democrático Socialista (PDS)** and the **Partido para o Progresso (PP)**, led by IBRAHIMA SOW. The **Centro Democrático** was founded in late 2005 by PAULINO IMPOSSA IÉ.

Diplomatic Representation

EMBASSIES IN GUINEA-BISSAU

Brazil: Rua São Tomé, Esquina Rua Moçambique, CP 29, Bissau; tel. 201327; fax 201317; e-mail embaixada-brasil@bissau.net; internet www.guine.org; Ambassador JOÃO BATISTA CRUZ.

China, People's Republic: Av. Francisco João Mendes, Bissau; tel. 203637; fax 203590; e-mail chinaemb_gw@mail.mfa.gov.cn; Ambassador YAN BANGHUA.

Cuba: Rua Joaquim N'Com 1, y Victorino Costa, CP 258, Bissau; tel. 213579; fax 201301; e-mail embcuba@sol.gtelecom.gw; Ambassador PEDRO FÉLIZ DOÑA SANTANA.

France: Av. Immeuble des 8 logements, ave Francisco Mendez, Bissau; tel. 201312; fax 205094; e-mail chancellerie@ambafrance-gw.org; internet www.ambafrance-gw.org; Ambassador JEAN-FRANÇOIS PAROT.

The Gambia: 47 Victorino Costa, Chao de Papel, CP 529, 1037 Bissau; tel. 205085; fax 251099; e-mail gambiaembbissau@hotmail.com; Ambassador CHERNO B. TOURAY.

Guinea: Rua 14, no. 9, CP 396, Bissau; tel. 212681; Ambassador TAMBA TIENDO MILLIMONO.

Korea, Democratic People's Republic: Bissau; Ambassador KIM KYONG SIN.

Libya: Rua 16, CP 362, Bissau; tel. 212006; Representative DOKALI ALI MUSTAFA.

Portugal: Av. Cidade de Lisboa, CP 76, 1021 Bissau; tel. 201261; fax 201269; e-mail embaixada@bissau.dgaccp.pt; Ambassador JOSÉ MANUEL SOARES B. PAIS MOREIRA.

Russia: Av. 14 de Novembro, CP 308, Bissau; tel. 251036; fax 251028; e-mail ambrus-gui@mirinet.net.gn; Chargé d'affaires a.i. VIACHELAV ROZHNOV.

Senegal: Rua Omar Torrijos 43A, Bissau; tel. 212944; fax 201748; Ambassador Gen. ABDOULAYE DIENG.

Judicial System

The Supreme Court is the final court of appeal in criminal and civil cases and consists of nine judges. Nine Regional Courts serve as the final court of appeal for the 24 Sectoral Courts, and deal with felony cases and major civil cases. The Sectoral Courts hear minor civil cases.

President of the Supreme Court: MARIA DO CEU SILVA MONTEIRO.

Religion

According to the 1991 census, 45.9% of the population are Muslims, 39.7% are animists and 14.4% are Christians, mainly Roman Catholics.

ISLAM

Associação Islâmica Nacional: Bissau; Sec.-Gen. Alhaji ABDÚ BAIO.

Conselho Superior dos Assuntos Islâmicos da Guiné-Bissau (CSAI-GB): Bissau; Exec. Sec. MUSTAFA RACHID DJALÓ.

CHRISTIANITY

The Roman Catholic Church

Guinea-Bissau comprises two dioceses, directly responsible to the Holy See. The Bishops participate in the Episcopal Conference of Senegal, Mauritania, Cape Verde and Guinea-Bissau, currently based in Senegal. At 31 December 2005 there were an estimated 128,000 adherents in the country, equivalent to 9.4% of the total population.

Bishop of Bafatá: Rev. CARLOS PEDRO ZILLI, CP 17, Bafatá; tel. 411507; e-mail domzilli@yahoo.com.br.

Bishop of Bissau: JOSÉ CÂMNATE NA BISSIGN, Av. 14 de Novembro, CP 20, 1001 Bissau; tel. 251057; fax 251058; e-mail diocesebissau@yahoo.it.

The Press

REGULATORY AUTHORITY

Conselho Nacional de Comunicação Social (CNCS): Bissau; f. 1994; dissolved in 2003, recreated in November 2004; Pres. AUGUSTO MENDES.

NEWSPAPERS AND PERIODICALS

Banobero: Rua José Carlos Schwarz, CP 760, Bissau; tel. 230702; fax 230705; e-mail banobero@netscape.net; weekly; Dir FERNANDO JORGE PEREIRA.

Comdev Negócios (Community Development Business): Av. Domingos Ramos 21, 1° andar, Bissau; tel. 215596; f. 2006; weekly; independent; business; Editor FRANCELINO CUNHA.

Correio-Bissau: Bissau; weekly; f. 1992; Editor-in-Chief JOÃO DE BARROS; circ. 9,000.

Diário de Bissau: Rua Vitorino Costa 29, Bissau; tel. 203049; daily; Owner JOÃO DE BARROS.

Fraskera: Bairro da Ajuda, 1ª fase, CP 698, Bissau; tel. 253060; fax 253070.

Gazeta de Notícias: Av. Caetano Semeao, CP 1433, Bissau; tel. 254733; e-mail gn@mail.eguitel.com; f. 1997; weekly; Dir HUMBERTO MONTEIRO.

Journal Nô Pintcha: Av. do Brasil, CP 154, Bissau; tel. 213713; Dir SRA CABRAL; circ. 6,000.

Kansaré: Edifico Sitec, Rua José Carlos Schwazz, Bissau; tel. 4906547; e-mail kansare@eguitel.com; internet www.kansare.com; f. 2003; Editor FAFALI KOUDAWO.

Voz de Bissau: Rua Eduardo Mondlane, Apdo 155, Bissau; tel. 202546; twice weekly.

Wandan: Rua António M'Bana 6, CP 760, Bissau; tel. 201789.

NEWS AGENCIES

Agência Bissau Media e Publicações: Rua Eduardo Mondlane 52, CP 1069, Bissau; tel. 206147; e-mail agenciabissau@agenciabissau.com; internet www.agenciabissau.com.

Agência Noticiosa da Guiné-Bissau (ANG): Av. Domingos Ramos, CP 248, Bissau; tel. 212151; fax 202155.

Broadcasting and Communications

TELECOMMUNICATIONS

In June 2004 a 10-year agreement was signed by Guiné Telecom and Portugal Telecom to develop the telecommunications sector.

Instituto das Comunicações da Guiné-Bissau (ICGB): Av. Domingos Ramos 53, CP 1372, Bissau; tel. 204873; fax 204876; e-mail icgb@mail.bissau.net; internet www.icgb.org; regulatory authority; Pres. ANÉSIMO DA SILVA CARDOSO.

Guiné Telecom (GT): Bissau; tel. 202427; internet www.gtelecom.gw; f. 2003 to replace the Companhia de Telecomunicações da Guiné-Bissau (Guiné Telecom—f. 1989); 40% owned by Portugal Telecom.

Guiné Tel: Bissau; f. 2003; 55% owned by Portugal Telecom; mobile operator; not yet operational as of mid-2006; CEO JOÃO FREDERICO DE BARROS.

Two further mobile networks, Spacetel and Orange Bissau, began operating in 2004 and 2007, respectively.

RADIO AND TELEVISION

An experimental television service began transmissions in 1989. Regional radio stations were to be established at Bafatá, Cantchungo and Catió in 1990. In 1990 Radio Freedom, which broadcast on behalf of the PAIGC during Portuguese rule and had ceased operations in 1974, resumed transmissions. Other radio stations included Radio Televisão Portuguesa Africa (RTP/Africa), which broadcasts from Bissau, and Rádio Sintchã Oco.

Radiodifusão Nacional da República da Guiné-Bissau (RDN): Av. Domingos Ramos, Praça dos Martires de Pindjiguiti, CP 191, Bissau; tel. 212426; fax 253070; e-mail rdn@eguitel.com; f. 1974; govt-owned; broadcasts in Portuguese on short-wave, MW and FM; Dir-Gen. LAMINE DJATA.

Rádio Bafatá: CP 57, Bafatá; tel. 411185.

Rádio Bombolom: Bairro Cupelon, CP 877, Bissau; tel. 201095; f. 1996; independent; Dir AGNELO REGALA.

Rádio Mavegro: Rua Eduardo Mondlane, CP 100, Bissau; tel. 201216; fax 201265.

Rádio Pindjiguiti: Bairro da Ajuda, 1ª fase, CP 698; tel. 253070; f. 1995; independent.

Televisão da Guiné-Bissau (TGB): Bairro de Luanda, CP 178, Bissau; tel. 221920; fax 221941; Dir-Gen. EUSÉBIO NUNES.

Finance

(cap. = capital; res = reserves; m. = million; amounts in francs CFA)

BANKING

Central Bank

Banque centrale des états de l'Afrique de l'ouest (BCEAO): Av. Amílcar Cabral 124, CP 38, Bissau; tel. 215548; fax 201305; internet www.bceao.int; HQ in Dakar, Senegal; f. 1955; bank of issue for the mem. states of the Union économique et monétaire ouest-africaine (UEMOA, comprising Benin, Burkina Faso, Côte d'Ivoire, Guinea-Bissau, Mali, Niger, Senegal and Togo); cap. and res 859,313m., total assets 5,671,675m. (Dec. 2002); Gov. DAMO JUSTIN BARO (acting); Dir in Guinea-Bissau LUÍS CÂNDIDO LOPES RIBEIRO.

Other Banks

Banco da África Ocidental, SARL: Rua Guerra Mendes 18, CP 1360, Bissau; tel. 203418; fax 203412; e-mail bao-info@eguitel.com; f. 2000; International Finance Corporation 15%, Grupo Montepio Geral (Portugal) 15%, Carlos Gomes Júnior 15%; cap. and res 1,883m. (Dec. 2003); Chair. ABDOOL VAKIL; Man. Dir LUIS ALMEIDA.

Banco da União (BDU): Bissau; f. 2005; CEO HUGO BORGES.

Caixa de Crédito da Guiné: Bissau; govt savings and loan institution.

Caixa Económica Postal: Av. Amílcar Cabral, Bissau; tel. 212999; postal savings institution.

STOCK EXCHANGE

In 1998 a regional stock exchange, the Bourse Régionale des Valeurs Mobilières, was established in Abidjan, Côte d'Ivoire, to serve the member states of the UEMOA.

INSURANCE

Instituto Nacional de Seguros e Previdência Social: CP 62, Bissau; tel. and fax 201665; state-owned; Gen. Man. A. MONDES.

Trade and Industry

CHAMBER OF COMMERCE

Câmara de Comércio, Indústria e Agricultura da Guiné-Bissau (CCIA): Av. Amílcar Cabral 7, CP 361, Bissau; tel. 212844; fax 201602; f. 1987; Pres. MACÁRIA BARAI; Sec.-Gen. SALIU BA.

INDUSTRIAL AND TRADE ASSOCIATIONS

Associação Comercial, Industrial e Agricola (ACIA): CP 88, Bissau; tel. 222276.

Direcção de Promoção do Investimento Privado (DPIP): Rua 12 de Setembro, Bissau Velho, CP 1276, Bissau; tel. 205156; fax 203181; e-mail dpip@mail.bissau.net.

Fundaçao Guineense para o Desenvolvimento Empresarial Industrial (FUNDEI): Rua Gen. Omar Torrijos 49, Bissau; tel. 202470; fax 202209; e-mail fundei@fundei.bissau.net; internet www.fundei.net; f. 1994; industrial devt org.; Pres. MACÁRIA BARAI.

Procajú: Bissau; private sector association of cashew producers.

UTILITIES

Electricity and Water

Empresa de Electricidade e Águas da Guiné-Bissau (EAGB): CP 6, EAGB E.P., Bissau; tel. 215191; fax 202716; operated under contract by private management co; Dir-Gen. WASNA PAPAI DAFNA.

Gas

Empresa Nacional de Importação e Distribuição de Gás Butano: CP 269, Bissau; state gas distributor.

TRADE UNIONS

Sindicato Nacional dos Marinheiros (SINAMAR): Bissau.

Sindicato Nacional dos Professores (SINAPROF): CP 765, Bissau; tel. and fax 204070; e-mail ict@mail.bissau.net; Pres. VINÇA MENDES.

União Nacional dos Trabalhadores da Guiné (UNTG): 13 Av. Ovai di Vievra, CP 98, Bissau; tel. and fax 207138; e-mail untgcs.gb@hotmail.com; Pres. DESEJADO LIMA DA COSTA; Sec.-Gen. MÁRIO MENDES CORREIA.

Legislation permitting the formation of other trade unions was approved by the Assembléia Nacional Popular in 1991.

Transport

RAILWAYS

There are no railways in Guinea-Bissau. In March 1998 Guinea-Bissau and Portugal signed an agreement providing for the construction of a railway linking Guinea-Bissau with Guinea.

ROADS

In 2002, according to International Road Federation estimates, there were about 3,455 km of roads, of which 964 km were paved. A major road rehabilitation scheme is proceeding, and an international road, linking Guinea-Bissau with The Gambia and Senegal, is planned. In early 2006 the European Union announced that it would provide financing for the rehabilitation of 350 km of the road network.

SHIPPING

Under a major port modernization project, the main port at Bissau was to be renovated and expanded, and four river ports were to be upgraded to enable barges to load and unload at low tide. The total cost of the project was estimated at US $47.4m., and finance was provided by the World Bank and Arab funds. At 31 December 2006 the merchant fleet comprised 25 vessels, totalling 6,627 grt. In mid-2004 plans were announced to improve links with the Bijagós islands, by providing a regular ferry service.

Empresa Nacional de Agências e Transportes Marítimos: Rua Guerva Mendes 4–4A, CP 244, Bissau; tel. 212675; fax 213023; state shipping agency; Dir-Gen. M. LOPES.

CIVIL AVIATION

There is an international airport at Bissau, which there are plans to expand, and 10 smaller airports serving the interior.

Halcyon Air/Bissau Airways: Bissau; f. 2006; flights to Dakar, Senegal; Chair. BALTASAR CARDOSO.

Hifly: Av. 24 de Setembro, CP 665, Bissau; tel. 206422; fax 206433; e-mail hiflygb@hifly.aero; internet www.hifly.aero; f. 2003 as Air Luxor; name changed as above in 2005.

Air Sénégal International, TAP Portugal and Transportes Aéreos de Cabo Verde (TACV) also fly to Bissau.

Tourism

There were 4,978 tourist arrivals in 2005. Receipts from tourism totalled US $2m. in 2004.

Central de Informação e Turismo: CP 294, Bissau; tel. 213905; state tourism and information service.

Direcção Geral do Turismo: CP 1024, Bissau; tel. 202195; fax 204441.

GUYANA

Introductory Survey

Location, Climate, Language, Religion, Flag, Capital

The Republic of Guyana lies on the north coast of South America, between Venezuela to the west and Suriname to the east, with Brazil to the south. The narrow coastal belt has a moderate climate with two wet seasons, from April to August and from November to January, alternating with two dry seasons. Inland, there are tropical forests and savannah, and the dry season lasts from September to May. The average annual temperature is 27°C (80°F), with average rainfall of 1,520 mm (60 ins) per year inland, rising to between 2,030 mm (80 ins) and 2,540 mm (100 ins) on the coast. English is the official language but Hindi, Urdu and Amerindian dialects are also spoken. The principal religions are Christianity (which is professed by about 50% of the population), Hinduism (about 28%) and Islam (less than 10%). The national flag (proportions 3 by 5 when flown on land, but 1 by 2 at sea) is green, with a white-bordered yellow triangle (apex at the edge of the fly) on which is superimposed a black-bordered red triangle (apex in the centre). The capital is Georgetown.

Recent History

Guyana was formerly British Guiana, a colony of the United Kingdom, formed in 1831 from territories finally ceded to Britain by the Dutch in 1814. A new Constitution, providing for universal adult suffrage, was introduced in 1953. The elections of April 1953 were won by the left-wing People's Progressive Party (PPP), led by Dr Cheddi Bharat Jagan. In October, however, the British Government, claiming that a communist dictatorship was threatened, suspended the Constitution. An interim administration was appointed. The PPP split in 1955, and in 1957 some former members founded a new party, the People's National Congress (PNC), under the leadership of Forbes Burnham. The PNC drew its support mainly from the African-descended population, while PPP support came largely from the (Asian-descended) 'East' Indian community.

A revised Constitution was introduced in December 1956 and an election was held in August 1957. The PPP won and Dr Jagan became Chief Minister. Another Constitution, providing for internal self-government, was adopted in July 1961. The PPP won an election in August and Dr Jagan was appointed premier. In the election of December 1964, held under the system of proportional representation that had been introduced in the previous year, the PPP won the largest number of seats in the Legislative Assembly, but not a majority. A coalition Government was formed by the PNC and The United Force (TUF), with Burnham as Prime Minister. This coalition led the colony to independence, as Guyana, on 26 May 1966.

The PNC won elections in 1968 and in 1973, although the results of the latter, and every poll thenceforth until the defeat of the PNC in 1992, were disputed by the opposition parties. Guyana became a co-operative republic on 23 February 1970, and Arthur Chung was elected non-executive President in March. In 1976 the PPP, which had boycotted the National Assembly since 1973, offered the Government its 'critical support'. Following a referendum in July 1978 that gave the Assembly power to amend the Constitution, elections to the Assembly were postponed for 15 months. The legislature assumed the role of a constituent assembly, established in November 1978, to draft a new constitution. In October 1979 elections were postponed for a further year. In October 1980 Forbes Burnham declared himself executive President of Guyana, and a new Constitution was promulgated.

Internal opposition to the PNC Government had increased after the assassination in June 1980 of Dr Walter Rodney, leader of the Working People's Alliance (WPA). The Government was widely believed to have been involved in the incident; an official inquest in 1988 produced a verdict, rejected by the opposition, of death by misadventure. All opposition parties except the PPP and TUF boycotted the December 1980 elections to the National Assembly. The PNC received 78% of the votes, according to official results, although allegations of substantial electoral malpractice were made, both within the country and by international observers. None the less, Burnham was formally inaugurated as President in January 1981.

In 1981 arrests and trials of opposition leaders continued, and in 1982 the Government's relations with human rights groups, and especially the Christian churches, deteriorated further. Editors of opposition newspapers were threatened, political violence increased, and the Government was accused of interference in the legal process. Industrial unrest and public discontent continued in 1983 and 1984, as Guyana's worsening economic situation increased opposition to the Government, and led to growing disaffection within the trade union movement and the PNC.

Burnham died in August 1985 and was succeeded as President by Desmond Hoyte, hitherto the First Vice-President and Prime Minister. At a general election in December the PNC won 78% of the votes and 42 of the elective seats in the National Assembly. Opposition groups, including the PPP and WPA, denounced the poll as fraudulent and in January 1986 five of the six opposition parties formed the Patriotic Coalition for Democracy (PCD).

During 1988 the opposition expressed fears about the independence of the judiciary and claimed that the Government's continued recourse to the laws of libel against its critics was an abuse of the legal system. Social unrest and industrial disruption in that year continued to impede government efforts to reform the economy, while the Government's hold on power was further compromised, following a division within the trade union movement. Seven unions withdrew from the Trades Union Congress (TUC) in September, alleging that elections for TUC officials were weighted in favour of PNC-approved candidates. The seven independent unions formed a separate congress, the Federation of Independent Trade Unions in Guyana (FITUG), in October. However, the Government refused to negotiate with the FITUG, accusing it of being politically motivated. Furthermore, the severity of austerity measures contained in the budget of March 1989, which included a devaluation of the currency, prompted a six-week strike in the sugar and bauxite industries.

Outside the formal opposition of the political parties, the Government also experienced pressure from members of the Guyana Human Rights Association, business leaders and prominent religious figures. This culminated, in January 1990, in the formation of a movement for legal and constitutional change, Guyanese Action for Reform and Democracy (Guard), which initiated a series of mass protests, urging the Government to accelerate the process of democratic reform. To counter this civic movement, the PNC began mobilizing its own newly established Committees to Re-elect the President (Creeps). Guard accused the Creeps of orchestrating violent clashes at Guard's rallies, and of fomenting racial unrest in the country in an attempt to regain support from the Afro-Guyanese population.

In January 1991 the date of the forthcoming general election was postponed, following the approval of legislation by the PNC extending the term of office of the National Assembly by two months after its official dissolution date of 2 February. In March a further two-month extension of the legislative term provoked the resignation of TUF and PPP members from the National Assembly (in addition to the WPA members, who had resigned a month earlier). Similar extensions followed in May and July, owing to alleged continuing problems relating to electoral reforms. The National Assembly was finally dissolved in late September. The publication of a revised electoral register in that month, however, revealed widespread inaccuracies, including the omission of an estimated 100,000 eligible voters. In November several opposition parties announced a boycott of the general election, which had been rescheduled for mid-December. However, on 28 November Hoyte declared a state of emergency (subsequently extended until June 1992) in order to legitimize a further postponement of the election. Legislation restoring the opposition seats in the National Assembly followed, and the Assembly was reconvened. A further revised electoral register was finally approved by the Elections Commission in August 1992. The election took place on 5 October and resulted in a narrow victory for the PPP in alliance with the CIVIC movement (a social and political movement of businessmen and professionals), which secured 32 of the 65 elective seats in the National Assembly, while the PNC secured 31 elective seats. The result, which signified an end to the PNC's 28-year period in government, provoked riots by the mainly Afro-Guyanese PNC supporters in Georgetown, in which two people were killed. International observers were, however, satisfied that the elections had been fairly conducted, and on 9 October Dr Cheddi Bharat Jagan took office as President. Jagan appointed Samuel Hinds, an industrialist who was not a member of the PPP, as Prime Minister.

In August 1995 a serious environmental incident resulted in the temporary closure of Omai Gold Mines Ltd (OGML). The company, which began production in the Omai District of Essequibo province in 1993, was responsible for an increase of some 400% in Guyana's gold production in subsequent years and was Guyana's largest foreign investor. However, in August 1995 a breach in a tailings pond (a reservoir where residue from the gold extraction process is stored) resulted in the spillage of some 3.5m. cu m of cyanide-tainted water, of which a large volume flowed into the Omai river, a tributary of the Essequibo river. The National Assembly approved a resolution to close the mine for an indefinite period pending an inquiry into the incident. OGML resumed operations in February 1996 following the implementation of government-approved environmental safeguards.

In March 1997, following the death of Dr Cheddi Bharat Jagan, Prime Minister Hinds succeeded to the presidency, in accordance with the provisions of the Constitution. Hinds subsequently appointed Janet Jagan, the widow of the former President, to the post of Prime Minister.

At the general election of 15 December 1997 delays in the verification of votes prompted protest by PNC supporters who accused the Government of electoral fraud. With some 90% of the votes counted, the Chairman of the Elections Commission, Doodnauth Singh, declared that Jagan, who was the PPP/CIVIC alliance's nominee, had established an unassailable lead, and on 19 December she was inaugurated as President. Singh's actions were strongly criticized as being premature by opposition parties, and the PNC expressed its intention to appeal to the High Court to have Jagan's appointment annulled while PNC supporters began a series of public demonstrations. According to the final election results, the PPP/CIVIC alliance secured 36 seats, the PNC won 26, and TUF, the Alliance for Guyana and the Guyana Democratic Party each obtained one seat.

In January 1998 the Government accepted a proposal by private-sector leaders for an international audit of the election to be conducted. The PNC, however, rejected the proposal and demanded instead the holding of fresh elections. In mid-January the Chief Justice ruled that it was beyond the jurisdiction of the High Court to prohibit Jagan from exercising her presidential functions pending a judicial review of the election. The ruling provoked serious disturbances in Georgetown, which, in turn, prompted the Government to introduce a one-month ban on public assemblies and demonstrations in the capital. Public protests by PNC supporters continued in defiance of the ban, resulting in confrontation with the security forces. However, in mid-January, following mediation by a three-member Caribbean Community and Common Market (CARICOM, see p. 196) commission, it was announced that an accord (the Herdmanston Agreement) had been signed by Jagan and PNC leader Desmond Hoyte, which provided for the organization of fresh elections within 36 months and the creation of a constitutional commission to make recommendations on constitutional reform, subsequently to be submitted to a national referendum and a legislative vote. The agreement also made provision for an independent audit of the December election. Meanwhile, although the PNC had submitted the names of 22 deputies who would represent the party in an emergency, the party continued to boycott the National Assembly. In early June the CARICOM commission upheld the published results of the December poll. Nevertheless, Hoyte continued publicly to question the legitimacy of the Jagan administration. Later in the month increasing political frustration, arising from the National Assembly's informing the PNC that its deputies had effectively forfeited their legislative seats (having failed to attend six consecutive sittings), erupted onto the streets of Georgetown. PNC supporters congregated in the capital, where violent demonstrations against the Government escalated into riots that were dispersed by the security forces with rubber bullets and tear gas. However, renewed CARICOM mediation between the PPP and the PNC in early July produced fresh commitments from both sides to renew discussions on constitutional reform and reinstate full legislative participation. Legislation designed to enable the PNC deputies to recover their seats in the legislature was subsequently formulated by both sides, and the PNC (with the exception of Hoyte—who continued to deny the legitimacy of Jagan's authority) rejoined the National Assembly on 14 July.

In January 1999 a 20-member Constitutional Reform Commission was established, comprising representatives of the country's principal political parties and community groups. In July the Commission published its report. It included proposals (submitted by the PPP/CIVIC alliance) that the country should be renamed the Republic of Guyana, that the President should be limited to two consecutive terms of office, and that the President should no longer be empowered to dissolve the National Assembly should he/she be censured by the Assembly. The Commission further proposed that the President should no longer have the power to dismiss a public officer in the public interest, and the President and Cabinet should be collectively responsible to the National Assembly and should resign if defeated in a vote of 'no confidence'.

In late April 1999 the Guyana Public Service Union (GPSU) called a general strike over salary increases. Other public-sector unions later joined the GPSU in taking industrial action, and much of the country was paralysed. Tension was exacerbated following the serving of legal summonses to three prominent union leaders for having organized protest marches in defiance of a government ban, while in mid-May the police opened fire (with pellet guns) on an allegedly violent crowd of strikers, injuring 17 people. After 56 days of industrial action, an agreement was finally reached between the unions and the authorities in late June, which granted public-sector workers an interim pay rise of 4.6% prior to the full settlement of their claim by an arbitration tribunal. In September the arbitration tribunal awarded public-sector workers an increase of 31.6% in 1999 and 26.7% in 2000.

In early August 1999 President Jagan announced her retirement on the grounds of ill health. She was replaced as President by the erstwhile Minister of Finance, Bharrat Jagdeo. The appointment of Jagdeo, whose relative youth (he was 35 years of age), reported willingness to reach across the political divide, and strong background in economics all contributed to his popularity, was widely welcomed in Guyana and by the international community. Jagdeo, who announced that he was to continue the largely market-orientated policies of the Jagan administration, reappointed Samuel Hinds as Prime Minister (Hinds had earlier resigned in accordance with the requirements of the Constitution) and announced that there was to be no cabinet reorganization in the immediate future. There was, however, controversy at the absence of Hoyte and other PNC representatives from the President's inauguration ceremony; Hoyte, who had refused to recognize Jagan as President, was reported to have declined to recognize any successor nominated by her.

In December 1999 the National Assembly approved the establishment of a committee to supervise the revision of the Constitution prior to the general election scheduled for mid-January 2001. In July 2000 the National Assembly approved legislation creating a permanent electoral institution, to be known as the Guyana Elections Commission (GECOM). In October the legislature unanimously approved a constitutional amendment establishing a mixed system of proportional representation combining regional constituencies and national candidate lists. Also approved was the abolition of the Supreme Congress of the People of Guyana and the National Congress of Local Democratic Organs. In December an Ethnic Relations Commission was officially established.

On 17 November 2000 GECOM announced that the election that, according to the Herdmanston Agreement, was to be held on 17 January 2001, would be postponed, owing to delays in the enactment of the proposed reform. A dispute had arisen between the Government and the PNC over the number of parliamentary seats that were to be allocated by region. In December an all-party committee decided that the PPP/CIVIC was to remain in office until the revised election date of March 2001, but was to limit its powers. In the same month the National Assembly approved a constitutional amendment removing the President's immunity from prosecution and limiting his power to appoint only four ministers from outside the National Assembly.

The general and regional elections of 19 March 2001 were preceded by demonstrations over the late distribution of voter identification cards (despite the announcement, in mid-February, that voters would be allowed to use other forms of identification). The elections were contested by 11 political parties. The

PPP/CIVIC secured 53% of the votes cast. The party also obtained a majority in the National Assembly, with 34 seats, while the PNC (which contested the elections as the PNCReform) won 27 seats, the Guyana Action Party, in alliance with the WPA, won two seats; while Rise, Organize and Rebuild Guyana Movement and TUF each secured one seat. Some 90% of the registered electorate participated. International observers declared the elections to be generally free and fair, and on 23 March it was officially declared that Jagdeo had regained the presidency. None the less, the PNCReform alleged that there had been a number of breaches of electoral procedure and successfully obtained a High Court injunction postponing the presidential inauguration. However, in late March the Chief Justice ordered an immediate declaration of the official results and on 31 March Jagdeo was sworn in as President.

In May 2001 the Government announced the depolitization of the social service: a Ministry of Public Service Management was subsequently created, separate from the Office of the President. The following month the National Assembly approved legislation making the appointment of the Chancellor of Justice and Chief of Justice the joint responsibility of the President and the Leader of the Opposition. In September Dr Steve Surujbally was appointed Chairman of GECOM; the Commission was preparing for local elections, which had been last held in 1994 and had been due in 1997. However, in December 2003 the local elections were postponed for a further year, owing to a lack of progress on electoral reform (they were subsequently further delayed, to 2008).

On 15 March 2002 opposition parties walked out of a debate on the 2002 budget, in protest at the delay in the implementation of the recommendations of the various joint committees. The PNCReform and the PPP announced that they would pursue a policy of active non-co-operation with the Government. A period of social unrest ensued, accompanied by a high incidence of violent crime. The disorder culminated on 3 July in an attack by opposition protesters on the presidential offices during a meeting of CARICOM heads of government. The security forces opened fire on the protesters, killing two and wounding 15. The protesters had been participating in a demonstration organized by the recently formed People's Solidarity Movement. While condemning the violence, the PNCReform leadership announced their support for the demonstrators' grievances of racial discrimination and police brutality. Later in the month the leaders of the opposing parties began a series of consultations with representatives from the Church, trade unions, private sector companies and the judiciary, in an effort to ascertain their ideas of how shared governance could function in Guyana.

In August 2002 President Jagdeo announced plans for the creation of an additional special police force to combat the rising crime rate. In late September the National Assembly approved stricter laws for prosecuting crime; however, proposed further anti-terrorism legislation was criticized by senior members of the judiciary as well as by human rights groups, who feared a contravention of basic civil liberties guaranteed by the Constitution.

In February 2003 Robert Corbin was elected as the new leader of the PNCReform following the unexpected death of Hoyte in December 2002. Corbin pledged a policy of 'constructive engagement' with the PPP and, following negotiations between party leaders, in early May Jagdeo and Corbin signed an agreement on a number of issues, including local government reform and opposition representation on state bodies, particularly the government-owned media. In the same month the PNCReform ended its boycott of the National Assembly. A 'stakeholder group' was established to monitor the implementation of the accord. Progress was slow and acrimonious throughout the year; none the less, in December agreement was reached by the two parties on the establishment of four constitutional commissions to oversee reform of the judiciary, the police, the civil service and the teaching sector. Furthermore, in January 2004 President Jagdeo announced his intention to establish a constitutional commission to promote the rights of Guyana's indigenous people.

Crime, in particular violent crime, continued to increase under Jagdeo's presidency. Following an increase in the number of abductions in the first months of 2003, in June the National Assembly approved legislation to extend the terms of imprisonment for those convicted of kidnap. In December a parliamentary report by the Disciplined Forces Commission referred to the possible existence of a clandestine, government-run paramilitary group. It was claimed that the group targeted suspected criminals and persons linked to known criminals. The allegations were supported in the following month by George Bacchus, who claimed he had been an informant for the so-called 'death squad', which had been allegedly responsible for more than 40 extra-judicial killings in 2003. Bacchus alleged that the Minister of Home Affairs, Ronald Gajraj, had orchestrated the group's operations. As a result, in late January 2004 the Canadian and US Governments revoked Gajraj's visa. Gajraj subsequently took a leave of absence from his ministerial post pending a government inquiry into the allegations. The Minister of Culture, Youth and Sports, Gail Teixeira, was appointed acting Minister of Home Affairs. In May a three-member commission was appointed to investigate the allegations. However, on 24 June, the day that he was scheduled to testify before the commission, George Bacchus was shot and killed. The murder of Bacchus, the chief witness in the case, led to increased calls by the opposition for an independent inquiry into the matter.

In April 2005 a Presidential Commission of Inquiry cleared Gajraj of involvement in the activities of the 'death squads'. He was immediately reinstated to his cabinet post; however, following international pressure and vociferous criticism from the opposition PNCReform, at the end of the month Gajraj stepped down from office. Teixeira was again subsequently appointed Minister of Home Affairs, this time on a permanent footing. She was succeeded as Minister of Culture, Youth and Sports by (Carl) Anthony Xavier, hitherto Minister of Transport and Hydraulics. A further ministerial appointment was made in November when Harry Narine Nawbatt was given the public works and communications portfolio (as the transport and hydraulics portfolio had been restyled).

Heightened criminal activity continued to affect the business sector in 2005, discouraging investment and increasing the rate of migration of skilled workers. In an attempt to prevent attacks on private businesses, in September the Guyana Revenue Authority introduced tax concessions for companies that imported security and surveillance equipment to protect their premises. The number of murders fell to 122 in 2005, compared with 137 in 2004 and 160 in 2002. Nevertheless, the problem of violent crime remained a pressing concern in early 2006 ahead of the general election that was scheduled to take place later in the year. The high incidence of violent crime was brought into dramatic focus in April 2006 when Minister of Agriculture Satyadeow Sawh was shot dead at his home. Furthermore, in January 2008 11 people, including five children, were killed when gunmen fired shots into several houses in a village in the east coast region of Demerara. The incident constituted the worst mass killing in the country for more than 30 years and prompted angry protests from local residents. Villagers built barricades of burning tyres blocking the main highway to Georgetown, accusing the security forces of failing to protect their community and of responding inadequately to the massacre. Speculation over the motive for the killings included those of race (those killed were of ethnic Indian origin and the murderers were of African ethnicity), political allegiance and a personal vendetta; however, a definitive motive eluded investigators. Police subsequently recovered a gun involved in the shootings and ballistic tests implicated the gang suspected of responsibility for the murder of Sawh.

The PPP/CIVIC secured a comfortable victory at the general election that was held on 28 August 2006, delayed beyond the constitutional deadline of 4 August by GECOM on technical grounds. The party increased its representation in the National Assembly to 36 seats, having secured a majority 54.3% of the votes cast, while the People's National Congress Reform-One Guyana (PNCR-1G, as PNCReform was restyled ahead of the elections) obtained 22 seats and 34.0% of the ballot. The recently formed Alliance for Change won five seats, with 8.3% of the votes cast. Notwithstanding the political unrest in the preceding months, the election was conducted peacefully. However, the rate of voter participation was the lowest since independence: only an estimated 69% of the electorate exercised their right to vote.

Jagdeo was inaugurated as President on 2 September 2006. In the new Cabinet, which included nine new ministerial appointments, Jagdeo appointed two ministers to each of the Ministries of Finance, Health and Education. However, a number of cabinet members were retained, including Dr Henry Benfield Jeffrey, hitherto Minister of Education, who was transferred to the Ministry of Foreign Trade and International Co-operation, and Clement Rohee, previously Minister of Foreign Trade, who assumed responsibility for the home affairs portfolio. President Jagdeo pledged that the new executive would give priority to reforming the police force and addressing social problems.

Guyana has been involved in long-running border disputes with its neighbours, Venezuela and Suriname, although Suriname restored diplomatic representation in Guyana in 1979. In 1983 relations improved further as a result of increased trade links between the countries. In late 1998 it was announced that a joint border commission, created to negotiate the settlement of a territorial dispute between Suriname and Guyana, was to be revived, after a two-year suspension. The two countries were also expected to conclude an agreement on fishing rights. However, in May 2000 Suriname formally claimed that Guyana had violated its territorial integrity by granting a concession to the Canadian-based company, CGX Energy Inc, to explore for petroleum and gas. Negotiations to settle the dispute in 2001 ended inconclusively. In January 2002 the Presidents of the two countries met to discuss the possibility of a production-sharing agreement. However, relations deteriorated when, in June, the Surinamese navy forcibly ejected a rig that had been authorized by Guyana to drill in waters disputed by the two countries. In late October a further meeting of the joint border commission was held in Suriname. In February 2004 Guyana referred the dispute to arbitration at the UN's International Tribunal for the Law of the Sea (ITLOS), in Hamburg, Germany. In May representatives of the two countries participated in talks presided over by Judge Dolliver Nelson, ITLOS President. Guyana requested that gas and oil exploration be allowed to continue during the negotiations. In September 2007 the Tribunal ruled in favour of Guyana, granting sovereignty over 33,152 sq km (12,800 sq miles) of coastal waters; Suriname was awarded 17,891 sq km (6,900 sq miles). Guyana's subsequent claims for compensation of US $34m. for damage arising from the expulsion of the oil rig were dismissed by the UN Permanent Court of Arbitration, which ruled that Suriname had not used armed force.

In 1962 Venezuela renewed its claim to 130,000 sq km (50,000 sq miles) of land west of the Essequibo river (nearly two-thirds of Guyanese territory). The area was accorded to Guyana in 1899, on the decision of an international tribunal, but Venezuela based its claim on a papal bull of 1493, referring to Spanish colonial possessions. The Port of Spain Protocol of 1970 put the issue in abeyance until 1982. Guyana and Venezuela referred the dispute to the UN in 1983, and in August 1989 the two countries agreed to a mutually acceptable intermediary, suggested by the UN Secretary-General. In March 1999 Guyana and Venezuela established a joint commission, the High Level Binational Commission, which was intended to expedite the resolution of the territorial dispute and to promote mutual co-operation. However, in September the Venezuelan Government alleged that the Guyanese authorities had granted concessions to petroleum companies within the disputed areas, and in October President Lt-Col (retd) Hugo Chávez Frías of Venezuela, speaking on the 100th anniversary of the international tribunal's decision, announced his Government's intention to reopen its claim to the territory. Reports of Venezuelan troop movements near the border area caused alarm in Guyana, but were described by the Venezuelan authorities as part of a campaign against drugs-traffickers. In December an agreement was reached between the two countries on co-operation in the fisheries sector. Early in 2000 Guyana signed an agreement with the US-based Beal Aerospace Corpn to build the world's first private satellite-launching facility in the disputed territory of Essequibo. However, following objections by Venezuela and financial difficulties, the company abandoned the project. Nevertheless, in January 2001 Venezuela announced an oil exploration project in the same disputed zone. In February 2004 President Chávez visited Guyana and met with President Jagdeo with the aim of increasing bilateral co-operation. In mid-2005 Guyana signed the PetroCaribe energy accord with Venezuela, which extended the financing arrangements introduced by the Caracas agreement on special energy concessions and offered favourable terms should the price of petroleum exceed US $40 per barrel. Relations were strained in November 2007 when Guyana accused Venezuelan troops of crossing into its territory and blowing up two gold-mining dredges. The Venezuelan Government subsequently expressed regret for the incident and talks took place between the two countries to establish measures to prevent another military incursion.

Guyana's relations with Brazil continued to improve through trade and military agreements. In May 2003 the Government approved a request by the Brazilian authorities for a partial abolition of visas for both countries. On a visit to Guyana in February 2005, Brazil's President, Luiz Inácio ('Lula') da Silva, reiterated his Government's commitment to the construction of the bridge across the Takatu river between the two countries. During the visit bilateral agreements on health and education were also signed, as was a three-year agreement aimed at facilitating improved training and qualifications for foreign service personnel in both countries. Joint-venture oil and gas exploration was also announced.

Throughout the 1990s Guyana became more closely integrated with CARICOM (see p. 196). In September 2001 construction began in Georgetown on the new CARICOM headquarters. Guyana also joined CARICOM's Caribbean Single Market and Economy, which was established on 1 January 2006. The country was also a member of the World Trade Organization (see p. 396). In February 2001 the leaders of 11 Caribbean states signed an agreement to establish a jointly administered regional court to replace the existing highest judicial body, the Privy Council in the United Kingdom. The Caribbean Court of Justice (CCJ) was eventually inaugurated in Trinidad and Tobago on 16 April 2005. However, by the end of 2007 only Guyana and Barbados had instituted the Court as their supreme appellate body. Guyana also participated in the third meeting of South American Presidents in Cusco, Peru, in December 2004, which created the Comunidad Sudamericana de Naciones (South American Community of Nations, which was renamed Unión de Naciones Suramericanas, UNASUR—Union of South American Nations—in April 2007), intended to promote greater regional economic integration.

Government

Under the 1980 Constitution, legislative power is held by the unicameral National Assembly, with 65 members: 53 elected for five years by universal adult suffrage, on the basis of proportional representation; 40 members are elected from national lists, and a further 25 members are elected from regional constituency lists. Executive power is held by the President, who leads the majority party in the Assembly and holds office for its duration. The President appoints and heads a Cabinet, which includes the Prime Minister, and may include up to four Ministers who are not elected members of the Assembly. The Cabinet is collectively responsible to the National Assembly. Guyana comprises 10 regions.

Defence

As assessed at November 2007, the Combined Guyana Defence Force consisted of some 1,100 men (of whom 900 were in the army, 100 were in the air force and 100 in the navy). One-third of the combined forces are civilian personnel. In addition there were reserve forces numbering some 670 (army 500, navy 170). A paramilitary force, the People's Militia, totalled 1,500. Defence expenditure totalled an estimated $ G1,030m. (US $5.8m.) in 2004.

Economic Affairs

In 2006, according to estimates by the World Bank, Guyana's gross national income (GNI), measured at average 2004–06 prices, was US $849.1m., equivalent to US $1,130 per head (or US $4,680 per head on an international purchasing-power parity basis). During 1996–2006, it was estimated, the population increased at an average annual rate of 0.2%, while gross domestic product (GDP) per head increased, in real terms, by an average of 1.2% per year. Overall GDP increased, in real terms, at an average annual rate of 1.4% in 1996–2006; GDP decreased by 2.2% in 2005, but decreased by 4.8% in 2006.

Agriculture (including forestry and fishing) provided an estimated 34.9% of GDP in 2006 and employed an estimated 15.9% of the total labour force in mid-2005. The principal cash crops are sugar cane (sugar providing an estimated 22.8% of the value of total domestic exports in 2006) and rice (9.1%). The sugar industry alone accounted for an estimated 13.5% of GDP in 2006. At the beginning of the 21st century the sugar industry was threatened by the disappearing preferential markets and the increasing cost of employment. In July 2004 the European Commission announced long-anticipated plans to reform comprehensively the European Union's (EU) sugar regime, ending the preferential prices paid to Guyanese producers. The proposed measures would reduce, by degrees, the EU price paid for sugar, by an eventual 36%. Guyana and the other sugar-producing members of the African Caribbean Pacific (ACP) group of countries condemned the proposals, noting that they would adversely impact on rural development, employment and investment. The new import regime took effect from mid-2006. Meanwhile, it was announced that some €40m. would be made available for assistance to the ACP countries in that period. In late 2004 the Government announced that funding had been secured to upgrade the Skeldon sugar refinery in Berbice and to construct a 30 MW co-generation facility, of which 15 MW would be supplied to the state sugar company GuySuCo (Guyana Sugar Corpn Inc). The US $135m. project would be jointly financed by the Government, GuySuCo and international lending institutions. Vegetables and fruit are cultivated for the local market, and livestock-rearing is being developed. Fishing is also important (particularly shrimp fishing), which accounted for an estimated 6.7% of GDP in 2006. Agricultural production increased at an average annual rate of 0.4% during 1996–2006. Agricultural GDP decreased by some 10.5% in 2005, following extensive flooding at the beginning of that year. However, this sector recovered somewhat in 2006, when its GDP expanded by an estimated 6.0%.

Timber resources in Guyana are extensive and underdeveloped. In 2006 the forestry sector contributed 2.4% of GDP. About three-quarters of the country's total land area consists of forest and woodland. In 2006 timber shipments provided an estimated 11.7% of total domestic exports. Although foreign investment in Guyana's largely undeveloped interior continued to be encouraged by the Government, there was much popular concern at the extent of the exploitation of the rainforest. The forestry sector decreased at an average annual rate of 0.4% in 1996–2006; however, the sector increased by 11.1% in 2006.

Industry (including mining, manufacturing and construction) provided an estimated 19.4% of GDP in 2006 and engaged 21.4% of the employed labour force in 2002. Industrial GDP increased at an average annual rate of 0.3% in 1996–2006. Industrial GDP rose by 0.2% in 2006.

Mining contributed an estimated 9.3% of GDP in 2006, and employed 4.1% of the total working population in 2002. Bauxite, which is used for the manufacture of aluminium, is one of Guyana's most valuable exports, and accounted for an estimated 11.2% of total domestic exports in 2006. The value of bauxite exports decreased significantly following the withdrawal in January 2002 of the US-based aluminium company Alcoa from the Aroaima bauxite and aluminium mine: figures for 2002 indicated that bauxite production subsequently decreased by 18.5% and exports by 42.1%, compared with the previous year. In September the Government merged the Bermine and Aroaima bauxite companies in an effort to improve the performance of the sector. Bauxite exports increased from US $35.3m. in 2002 to US $62.8m. in 2005. Production of bauxite increased to 1.37m. metric tons in 2006, owing to the rehabilitation of the Aroaima plant. The registered production of gold accounted for 19.0% of domestic exports in 2006. In 2000 the gold industry was estimated directly to employ some 32,000 people. There are also some petroleum reserves and significant diamond resources. In 2006 diamond production stood at 340,500 metric carats, compared with 356,900 metric carats in 2005. The GDP of the mining sector was estimated to have declined by an average of 4.9% per year in 1996–2006. The sector's GDP decreased, in real terms, by 17.7% in 2005. The contraction was owing, in part, to the closure of the Omai gold mine at the end of 2005. The mining industry's GDP declined by a further 22.3% in 2006.

Manufacturing (including power) accounted for an estimated 8.1% of GDP in 2006 and, in 2002, employed 13.2% of the total working population. The main activities are the processing of bauxite, sugar, rice and timber. Manufacturing GDP decreased at an average annual rate of 0.5% in 1996–2006. The sector declined by 9.5% in 2005, but increased by 3.2% in 2006.

Energy requirements are almost entirely met by imported hydrocarbon fuels. In 2006 fuels and lubricants constituted 29.1% of the total value of imports (mainly from Venezuela and Trinidad and Tobago). Despite the border dispute, in early 2001 Venezuela granted Guyana, along with a number of other Caribbean nations, entry to the Caracas energy accord for special petroleum concessions. In November 2002 Venezuela agreed to supply oil at a discount of 25%, providing that the price on world markets remained above US $30 per barrel. In June 2005 Guyana was one of 13 Caribbean countries that signed the PetroCaribe agreement, under which Venezuela extended and expanded the terms of previous energy accords. In June 2002 the Inter-American Development Bank (IDB, see p. 308) approved a loan for US $27.4m. to fund the extension of electricity lines to the coastal regions. The Government of the People's Republic of China granted US $3.8m. in October 2004 for the renovation of the Moco Moco hydroelectric station. Construction began in mid-2002 on the 100 MW Amaila Falls hydroelectric power project. However, the project failed to gain the support of the state power company, Guyana Power and Light Inc (GPL), and construction was halted in early 2003. In April 2003 the Government assumed control of GPL for the nominal sum of US $1 from its partner A C Power and, one year later, 50% of GPL was offered for sale on the local market for US $30m. US firm Synergy Holdings signed a memorandum of understanding on construction of the Amaila project in mid-2006: the power-station was scheduled to come into operation in late 2010. The Government hoped that oil and gas exploration in the country would increase following the settlement of the territorial dispute with Suriname; the UN's International Tribunal for the Law of the Sea (ITLOS) ruled in favour of Guyana in September 2007 (see Recent History).

The services sector contributed an estimated 45.7% of GDP in 2006 and engaged 52.1% of the employed labour force in 2002. The GDP of the services sector increased by an average of 3.0% per year in 1996–2006. Services GDP increased, in real terms, by 7.3% in 2006.

In 2006 Guyana recorded a visible trade deficit of US $197.6m. and a deficit of US $111.8m. on the current account of the balance of payments. In 2004 the principal source of imports was the USA (29.5%), followed by Trinidad and Tobago, the Netherlands Antilles, and Japan. In the same year Canada was the principal market for exports (18.6% of total exports), followed by the USA, Belgium (14.0%) and the United Kingdom. The principal exports are gold, sugar, rice and bauxite, and the principal imports are consumer goods and fuel and lubricants.

In 2006 the overall budget deficit was an estimated G $21,499.8m. (equivalent to 11.9% of GDP). According to World Bank estimates, by the end of 2005 Guyana's external debt totalled US $1,196m., of which US $1,021m. was long-term public debt. The cost of debt-servicing in that year was US $33m., equivalent to 3.7% of exports of goods and services. The annual rate of inflation (Georgetown only) averaged 5.4% in 1996–2006. Consumer prices increased by 6.5% in 2006. According to census figures, the rate of unemployment in 2002 was 11.7%.

Guyana is a founder member of CARICOM (see p. 196). It was also one of the six founder members of CARICOM's Caribbean Single Market and Economy (CSME), established on 1 January 2006. The CSME was intended to enshrine the free movement of goods, services and labour throughout the CARICOM region. Guyana is a member of the UN Economic Commission for Latin America and the Caribbean (ECLAC, see p. 38) and of the International Sugar Organization (see p. 409).

In the 1990s, following the introduction of wide-ranging economic recovery plans, Guyana qualified for funds under three Enhanced Structural Adjustment Facilities (ESAF). In 1996 negotiations with the 'Paris Club' of official creditors and with Trinidad and Tobago resulted in the cancellation of 67% of Guyana's bilateral debt with five creditor nations (a total reduction of US $395m.). In 1999 the IMF and the World Bank declared that Guyana had become eligible for some US $410m. in nominal debt-service relief under the heavily indebted poor countries (HIPC) initiative and for an additional US $590m. under the Enhanced HIPC initiative in the following year. In November 2002 the IMF approved a US $64m. debt-relief programme for Guyana; and released a further tranche in January 2004, although the Fund recommended that the Government of Bharrat Jagdeo improve transparency in the banking sector and reform the state-owned sugar and bauxite companies. In July 2005 in Gleneagles, United Kingdom, it was announced that Guyana satisfied the criteria under the HIPC initiative to qualify for immediate debt-relief totalling some US $336m. Later that year, following a further review, the IMF approved the cancellation, from early January 2006, of all debt incurred prior to 2005. The IMF recommended that the savings made by the debt cancellation be directed towards poverty alleviation schemes. However, emergency aid and reconstruction of infrastructure following the extensive flooding in Guyana in January 2005 meant that resources were stretched. The reconstruction effort was limited by a shortfall in reserves and much of the equipment used to rebuild infrastructure had to be imported. Legislation introduced in 2006 was intended to strengthen fiscal accountability, and a public sector investment programme was initiated; as well as reform of the sugar, power and water sectors, the bauxite sector was privatized. In January 2007 the Jagedo Government introduced value-added tax (VAT), in an attempt to reduce the fiscal deficit. The exemption of basic goods from VAT was intended to allow development plans to proceed without inhibiting domestic demand, although implementation proved problematic, with businesses failing to tax commodities effectively. VAT (coupled with rising international prices for oil and food) substantially increased inflation in 2007, which rose by 9.6% according to the IMF. In the same year, real GDP was estimated to have expanded by 5.6%; the result attributed to improvements in the agricultural and mining sectors. Elsewhere, plans to develop Guyana's nascent tourism sector were augmented by a budget allocation of US $300m. in 2008. It was hoped that this outlay would engender growth in niche sectors of the market, including sports tourism and eco-tourism.

Education

Education is officially compulsory, and is provided free of charge, for eight years between six and 14 years of age. Primary education begins at six years of age and lasts for at least six years. Secondary education, beginning at 12 years of age, lasts for up to five years, comprising a first cycle of three years and a second cycle of two years. Net primary enrolment in 2002/03 was equivalent to an estimated 99.2% of children in the relevant age-group (males 100.0%; females 98.4%). Secondary enrolment in the same year was equivalent to an estimated 75.0% of children in the relevant age-group (males 58.4%; females 91.9%). There are also 14 technical, vocational, special and higher educational institutions. These include the University of Guyana in Georgetown and a teacher training college. In 2002 the IDB approved a loan of US $30m. to assist with the modernization of basic education in Guyana. In 2004 the Government announced the construction of 25 new schools. In 2006 the Cuban Government offered 365 scholarships to Guyanese students to pursue studies in Cuba, and announced that a further 150 scholarships would be made available each year until 2010. Overall, 715 places were to be provided on medical courses and 250 places offered on agricultural or engineering programmes. Projected expenditure on education by the central Government in 2007 was estimated at $ G15.6m.

Public Holidays

2008: 1 January (New Year's Day), 23 February (Mashramani, Republic Day), 20 March* (Yum an-Nabi, birth of the Prophet), 21 March (Good Friday), 24 March (Easter Monday), 1 May (Labour Day), 5 May (Indian Heritage Day), 3 July (CARICOM Day), 4 August (Freedom Day), 1 October* (Id al-Fitr, end of Ramadan), 8 December* (Id al-Adha, feast of the Sacrifice), 25–26 December (Christmas).

2009: 1 January (New Year's Day), 23 February (Mashramani, Republic Day), 9 March* (Yum an-Nabi, birth of the Prophet), 10 April (Good Friday), 13 April (Easter Monday), 1 May (Labour Day), 5 May (Indian Heritage Day), 6 July (CARICOM Day), 3 August (Freedom Day), 20 September* (Id al-Fitr, end of Ramadan), 27 November* (Id al-Adha, feast of the Sacrifice), 25–26 December (Christmas).

* These holidays are dependent on the Islamic lunar calendar and may vary by one or two days from the dates given.

In addition, the Hindu festivals of Holi Phagwah (usually in March) and Diwali (October or November) are celebrated. These festivals are dependent on sightings of the moon and their precise date is not known until two months before they take place.

Weights and Measures

The metric system has been introduced.

Statistical Survey

Sources (unless otherwise stated): Bank of Guyana, 1 Church St and Ave of the Republic, POB 1003, Georgetown; tel. 226-3261; fax 227-2965; e-mail communications@solutions2000.net; internet www.bankofguyana.org.gy; Bureau of Statistics, Ministry of Finance, Main and Urquhart Sts, Georgetown; tel. 227-1114; fax 226-1284; internet www.statisticsguyana.gov.gy.

AREA AND POPULATION

Area: 214,969 sq km (83,000 sq miles).

Population: 758,619 (males 375,481, females 382,778) at census of 12 May 1980; 701,704 (males 344,928, females 356,776) at census of 12 May 1991; 751,223 (males 376,034, females 375,189) at census of 15 September 2002. *2006* (official estimate at 31 December): 761,510.

Density (31 December 2006): 3.5 per sq km.

Ethnic Groups (at 2002 census): 'East' Indians 326,277; Africans 227,062; Mixed 125,727; Amerindians 68,675; Portuguese 1,497; Chinese 1,396; White 477; Total (incl. others) 751,223.

Regions (population at 2002 census): Barima–Waini 24,275; Pomeroon–Supenaam 49,253; Essequibo Islands–West Demerara 103,061; Demerara–Mahaica 310,320; Mahaica–Berbice 52,428; East Berbice–Corentyne 123,695; Cuyuni–Mazaruni 17,597; Potaro–Siparuni 10,095; Upper Takutu–Upper Essequibo 19,387; Upper Demerara–Berbice 41,112; Total 751,223.

Principal Towns (population at 2002 census): Georgetown (capital) 134,497; Linden 29,298; New Amsterdam 17,033; Corriverton 11,494. *Mid-2007* ('000, incl. suburbs, UN estimate): Georgetown 133 (Source: UN, *World Urbanization Prospects: The 2007 Revision*).

Births, Marriages and Deaths (per 1,000 population): Birth rate 24.5 in 1990–95, 24.2 in 1995–2000, 21.3 in 2000–05; Crude death rate 8.7 in 1990–95, 9.1 in 1995–2000, 9.1 in 2000–05 (Source: UN, *World Population Prospects: The 2006 Revision*). Marriage rate 3.8 per 1,000 in 2002.

Expectation of Life (years at birth, WHO estimates): 63.8 (males 63.1; females 64.3) in 2005. Source: WHO, *World Health Statistics*.

Economically Active Population (persons aged 15 years and over, census of 2002): Agriculture, hunting and forestry 45,378; Fishing 5,533; Mining and quarrying 9,374; Manufacturing 30,483; Electricity, gas and water 2,246; Construction 16,100; Trade, repair of motor vehicles and personal and household goods 37,690; Restaurants and hotels 5,558; Transport, storage and communications 16,790; Financial intermediation 3,074; Real estate, renting and business services 7,384; Public administration, defence and social security 14,995; Education 13,015; Health and social work 5,513; Other community, social and personal service activities 9,599; Private households with employed persons 6,156; Extra-territorial organizations and bodies 477; Activities not adequately defined 1,489; Total employed 230,854. *Mid-2005* ('000, estimates): Agriculture, etc. 52; Total labour force 328 (Source: FAO). *2006:* Central government 10,197; Rest of the public sector 17,926; Total public sector employment 28,123.

HEALTH AND WELFARE
Key Indicators

Total Fertility Rate (children per woman, 2005): 2.2.

Under-5 Mortality Rate (per 1,000 live births, 2005): 63.

HIV/AIDS (% of persons aged 15–49, 2005): 2.4.

Physicians (per 1,000 head, 2000): 0.48.

Hospital Beds (per 1,000 head, 2001): 2.9.

Health Expenditure (2004): US $ per head (PPP): 328.9.

Health Expenditure (2004): % of GDP: 5.3.

Health Expenditure (2004): public (% of total): 83.5.

Access to Water (% of persons, 2004): 83.

Access to Sanitation (% of persons, 2004): 70.

Human Development Index (2005): ranking: 97.

Human Development Index (2005): value: 0.750.

For sources and definitions, see explanatory note on p. vi.

AGRICULTURE, ETC.

Principal Crops ('000 metric tons, 2006, FAO estimates): Rice (paddy) 273; Cassava (Manioc) 33; Sugar cane 3,000; Coconuts 66; Bananas 17; Plantains 17. *Aggregate Production* ('000 metric tons, may include official, semi-official or estimated data): Vegetables (incl. melons) 29.9; Fruits (excl. melons) 64.9.

Livestock ('000 head, year ending September 2006, FAO estimates): Horses 2.4; Asses 1.2; Cattle 110; Sheep 130; Pigs 13; Goats 79; Chickens 20,000.

Livestock Products ('000 metric tons, 2006, FAO estimates): Cattle meat 1.8; Sheep meat 0.5; Pig meat 0.7; Chicken meat 22.0; Cows' milk 30; Hen eggs 0.5.

Forestry ('000 cubic metres, 2006, FAO estimates): *Roundwood Removals:* Sawlogs, veneer logs and logs for sleepers 462, Pulpwood 100, Other industrial wood 12, Fuel wood 860; Total 1,434. *Sawnwood Production:* Total (all broadleaved) 68.

Fishing ('000 metric tons, live weight, 2005): Capture 54.2 (Marine fishes 30.0; Atlantic seabob 14.9; Whitebelly prawn 2.5); Aquaculture 0.6 (FAO estimate); *Total catch* 54.8 (FAO estimate). Note: Figures exclude crocodiles: the number of spectacled caimans caught in 2005 was 8,455.

Source: FAO.

MINING

Production (2006): Bauxite 1,374,000 metric tons; Gold 6,406 kg; Diamonds 340,500 metric carats.

INDUSTRY

Selected Products (2006, unless otherwise indicated): Raw sugar 246,100 metric tons (2005); Rice 306,800 metric tons; Rum 117,000 hectolitres; Beer and stout 90,000 hectolitres; Margarine 2,265 metric tons; Biscuits 1,071 metric tons; Paint 2,404 hectolitres; Electric energy 514.9m. kWh (2004).

FINANCE

Currency and Exchange Rates: 100 cents = 1 Guyana dollar ($ G). Sterling, *US Dollar and Euro Equivalents* (30 November 2007): £1 sterling = $ G418.963; US $1 = $ G202.750; €1 = $ G299.279; $ G1,000 = £2.39 = US $4.93 = €3.34. *Average Exchange Rate:* ($ G per US $): 198.307 in 2004; 199.875 in 2005; 200.188 in 2006.

Budget ($ G million, 2006, estimates): *Revenue:* Tax revenue 58,447.0 (Income tax 26,859.4; Consumption tax 23,375.8; Trade taxes 5,204.4); Other current revenue 3,909.7; Capital revenue (incl. grants) 17,524.6; Total 79,881.3. *Expenditure:* Current expenditure 59,574.7 (Personnel emoluments 20,085.0, Other goods and services 35,023.5, Interest 4,466.3); Capital expenditure 41,806.4; Total (excl. lending minus repayments) 101,381.1.

International Reserves (US $ million at 31 December 2006): IMF special drawing rights 1.59; Foreign exchange 278.05; *Total* 279.64. Source: IMF, *International Financial Statistics*.

Money Supply ($ G million at 31 December 2006): Currency outside banks 25,737; Demand deposits at commercial banks 31,283; Total money (including private-sector deposits at the Bank of Guyana) 56,557. Source: IMF, *International Financial Statistics*.

Cost of Living (Consumer Price Index; all urban areas; base: January 1994 = 100): All items 208.3 in 2004; 230.7 in 2005; 248.2 in 2006.

Expenditure on the Gross Domestic Product ($ G million at current prices, 2006, estimates): Government final consumption expenditure 44,284; Private final consumption expenditure 116,685; Gross capital formation 82,818; *Total domestic expenditure* 243,787; Net exports of goods and services –63,506; *GDP in purchasers' values* 180,282.

Gross Domestic Product by Economic Activity ($ G million at current prices, 2006): Agriculture 39,093 (Sugar 20,457; Rice 8,222; Livestock 3,533); Forestry 3,590; Fishing 10,154; Mining and quarrying 14,133; Manufacturing (incl. utilities) 5,467; Engineering and construction 9,677; Distribution 7,961; Transport and communication 17,237; Rented dwellings 7,239; Financial services 6,088; Other services 3,219; Government 27,341; *GDP at factor cost* 151,198; Indirect taxes, less subsidies 29,084; *GDP in purchasers' values* 180,282.

Balance of Payments (US $ million, 2006): Exports of goods f.o.b. 594.8; Imports of goods f.o.b. –792.4; *Trade balance* –197.6; Exports of services 147.7; Imports of services –218.4; *Balance on goods and services* –268.3; Other income (net) –43.3; *Balance on goods, services and income* –311.6; Current transfers received (net) 199.9; *Current balance* –111.8; Capital account (net) 350.5; Financial account (net) –80.4; Net errors and omissions –118.6; *Overall balance* 39.8. Source: IMF, *International Financial Statistics*.

EXTERNAL TRADE

Principal Commodities (US $ million, 2006): *Imports c.i.f.:* Capital goods 191.2; Consumer goods 197.7; Fuel and lubricants 257.8; Other intermediate goods 226.9; Total (incl. others) 885.0. *Exports f.o.b.:* Bauxite 67.3; Sugar 137.0; Rice 54.6; Gold 114.4; Shrimps 64.8; Timber 70.3; Total (incl. others, excl. re-exports) 601.3.

Principal Trading Partners ($ G million, 2004): *Imports:* USA 37,263; Trinidad and Tobago 33,621; Netherlands Antilles 11,853; Japan 7,806; United Kingdom 5,839; China, People's Republic 4,975; Canada 2,017; Netherlands 1,905; Venezuela 1,574; Total (incl. others) 126,275. *Exports:* Canada 20,088; USA 17,579; Belgium 15,107; United Kingdom 12,813; Trinidad and Tobago 7,423; Jamaica 6,457; Portugal 4,178; Barbados 3,969; Netherlands 2,563; Netherlands Antilles 1,508; Total (incl. others) 107,665.

TRANSPORT

Road Traffic ('000 vehicles in use, 2002): Passenger cars 61.3; Commercial vehicles 15.5. Source: UN, *Statistical Yearbook*.

Shipping: *International Sea-borne Freight Traffic* ('000 metric tons, estimates, 1990): Goods loaded 1,730; Goods unloaded 673 (Source: UN, *Monthly Bulletin of Statistics*.). *Merchant Fleet* (at 31 December 2006): Vessels 107; Displacement 37,391 grt (Source: Lloyd's Register-Fairplay, *World Fleet Statistics*).

Civil Aviation (traffic on scheduled services, 2001): Kilometres flown (million) 1; Passengers carried ('000) 48; Passenger-km (million) 175; Total ton-km (million) 17. Source: UN, *Statistical Yearbook*.

TOURISM

Tourist Arrivals: 100,911 (USA 49,625) in 2003; 121,989 (USA 64,947) in 2004; 116,596 (USA 60,071) in 2005.

Tourism Receipts (US $ million, incl. passenger transport): 28 in 2003; 30 in 2004; 37 in 2005.

Source: World Tourism Organization.

COMMUNICATIONS MEDIA

Radio Receivers (1999): 400,000 in use.

Television Receivers (2000): 70,000 in use.

Telephones (2005): 110,100 main lines in use.

Facsimile Machines (1990): 195 in use.

Mobile Cellular Telephones (2005): 281,400 subscribers.

Personal Computers (2005): 29,000 in use.

Internet Users (2005): 160,000.

Daily Newspapers (2000): 2; estimated circulation 56,750.

Non-daily Newspapers (2000): 4; estimated circulation 47,700.

Book Production (1997): 25.

Sources: mainly UNESCO, *Statistical Yearbook*; UN, *Statistical Yearbook*; International Telecommunication Union.

EDUCATION

Pre-primary (1999/2000): Institutions 320; Teachers 2,218; Students 36,995.

Primary (1999/2000): Institutions 423; Teachers 3,951; Students 105,800.

General Secondary (1999/2000): Institutions 70; Teachers 1,972; Students 36,055.

Special Education (1999/2000): Institutions 6; Teachers 64; Students 617.

Technical and Vocational (1999/2000): Institutions 6; Teachers 215; Students 4,662.

Teacher Training (1999/2000): Institutions 1; Teachers 297; Students 1,604.

University (1999/2000): Institutions 1; Teachers 371; Students 7,496.

Private Education (1999/2000): Institutions 7; Teachers 120; Students 1,692.

Source: Ministry of Education.

2004/05 (estimates): *Pre-primary:* 27,613 pupils; 2,032 teachers. *Primary:* 116,756 pupils; 4,164 teachers. *Secondary:* 70,615 pupils; 3,915 teachers. *Tertiary:* 7,278 students; 578 teachers (Source: UNESCO Institute for Statistics).

Adult Literacy Rate (UNESCO estimates): 98.6% (males 99.0%; females 98.2%) in 2001. Source: UN Development Programme, *Human Development Report*.

Directory

The Constitution

Guyana became a republic, within the Commonwealth, on 23 February 1970. A new Constitution was promulgated on 6 October 1980, and amended in 1998, 2000 and 2001. Its main provisions are summarized below:

The Constitution declares the Co-operative Republic of Guyana to be an indivisible, secular, democratic sovereign state in the course of transition from capitalism to socialism. The bases of the political, economic and social system are political and economic independence, involvement of citizens and socio-economic groups, such as co-operatives and trade unions, in the decision-making processes of the State and in management, social ownership of the means of production, national economic planning and co-operativism as the principle of socialist transformation. Personal property, inheritance, the right to work, with equal pay for men and women engaged in equal work, free medical attention, free education and social benefits for old age and disability are guaranteed. Additional rights include equality before the law, the right to strike and to demonstrate peacefully, the right of indigenous peoples to the protection and preservation of their culture, and a variety of gender and work-related rights. Individual political rights are subject to the principles of national sovereignty and democracy, and freedom of expression to the State's duty to ensure fairness and balance in the dissemination of information to the public. Relations with other countries are guided by respect for human rights, territorial integrity and non-intervention.

THE PRESIDENT

The President is the supreme executive authority, Head of State and Commander-in-Chief of the armed forces, elected for a five-year term of office, with no limit on re-election. The successful presidential candidate is the nominee of the party with the largest number of votes in the legislative elections. The President may prorogue or dissolve the National Assembly (in the case of dissolution, fresh elections must be held immediately) and has discretionary powers to postpone elections for up to one year at a time for up to five years. The President may be removed from office on medical grounds, or for violation of the Constitution (with a two-thirds' majority vote of the Assembly), or for gross misconduct (with a three-quarters' majority vote of the Assembly if allegations are upheld by a tribunal).

The President appoints a First Vice-President and Prime Minister, who must be an elected member of the National Assembly, and a Cabinet of Ministers, which may include four non-elected members and is collectively responsible to the legislature. The President also appoints a Leader of the Opposition, who is the elected member of the Assembly deemed by the President most able to command the support of the opposition.

THE LEGISLATURE

The legislative body is a unicameral National Assembly of 65 members (66 in special circumstances), elected by universal adult suffrage in a system of proportional representation; 40 members are elected at national level, and a further 25 are elected from regional constituency lists. The Assembly passes bills, which are then presented to the President, and may pass constitutional amendments.

LOCAL GOVERNMENT

Guyana is divided into 10 Regions, each having a Regional Democratic Council elected for a term of up to five years and four months, although it may be prematurely dissolved by the President.

OTHER PROVISIONS

Impartial commissions exist for the judiciary, the public service and the police service. An Ombudsman is appointed, after consultation between the President and the Leader of the Opposition, to hold office for four years.

The Government

HEAD OF STATE

President: BHARRAT JAGDEO (sworn in 11 August 1999, 31 March 2001 and 2 September 2006).

CABINET
(April 2008)

Prime Minister: SAMUEL A. HINDS.
Minister of Foreign Affairs: Dr CAROLYN RODRIGUES.
Minister of Foreign Trade and International Co-operation: Dr HENRY BENFIELD JEFFREY.
Minister of Finance: Dr ASHNI KUMAR SINGH.
Minister in the Ministry of Finance: JENNIFER WEBSTER.
Minister of Agriculture and of Fisheries, Crops and Livestock: ROBERT MONTGOMERY PERSAUD.
Minister of Amerindian Affairs: PAULINE CAMPBELL-SUKHAI.
Minister of Home Affairs: CLEMENT J. ROHEE.
Minister of Legal Affairs and Attorney-General: DOODNAUTH SINGH.
Minister of Education: SHAIK K. Z. BAKSH.
Minister in the Ministry of Education: Dr DESREY FOX.
Minister of Health: Dr LESLIE RAMSAMMY.
Minister in the Ministry of Health: Dr BHERI RAMSARRAN.
Minister of Housing and Water: HARRY NARINE NAWBATT.
Minister of Labour: MANZOOR NADIR.
Minister of Human Services and Social Security: PRIYA DEVI MANICKCHAND.
Minister of Local Government and Regional Development: KELLAWAN LALL.
Minister of Public Service Management: Dr JENNIFER WESTFORD.
Minister of Transport and Hydraulics: ROBESON BENN.
Minister of Tourism, Industry and Commerce: MANNIRAM PRASHAD.
Minister of Culture, Youth and Sport: Dr FRANK ANTHONY.
Secretary to the Cabinet: Dr ROGER LUNCHEON.

MINISTRIES

Office of the President: New Garden St, Bourda, Georgetown; tel. 225-1330; fax 227-3050; e-mail opmed@op.gov.gy; internet www.op.gov.gy.

Office of the Prime Minister: Oranapai Towers, Wight's Lane, Kingston, Georgetown; tel. 227-3101; fax 226-7573; e-mail pmoffice@sdnp.org.gov.gy.

Ministry of Agriculture: Regent and Vlissengen Rds, POB 1001, Georgetown; tel. 226-5165; fax 227-2978; e-mail minister@agriculture.gov.gy; internet www.agriculture.gov.gy.

Ministry of Culture, Youth and Sport: 71–72 Main St, South Cummingsburg, Georgetown; tel. 227-7860; fax 225-5067; e-mail mincys@guyana.net.gy.

Ministry of Education: 21 Brickdam, Stabroek, POB 1014, Georgetown; tel. 223-7900; fax 225-8511; e-mail moegyweb@yahoo.com; internet www.sdnp.org.gy/minedu.

Ministry of Finance: Main and Urquhart Sts, Kingston, Georgetown; tel. 225-6088; fax 226-1284; e-mail asingh@inetguyana.net; internet www.finance.gov.gy.

Ministry of Fisheries, Crops and Livestock: Regent Road, Bourda, Georgetown; tel. 226-1565; fax 227-2978; e-mail minfcl@sdnp.org.gy.

Ministry of Foreign Affairs: Takuba Lodge, 254 South Rd and New Garden St, Bourda, Georgetown; tel. 226-1607; fax 225-9192; e-mail minfor@guyana.net.gy; internet www.sdnp.org.gy/minfor.

Ministry of Foreign Trade and International Co-operation: Takuba Lodge, 254 South Rd and New Garden St, Bourda, Georgetown; tel. 226-5064; fax 226-8426; e-mail moftic@moftic.gov.gy; internet www.moftic.gov.gy.

Ministry of Health: Brickdam, Stabroek, Georgetown; tel. 226-1560; fax 225-4505; e-mail moh@sdnp.org.gy; internet www.health.gov.gy.

Ministry of Home Affairs: 60 Brickdam St, Georgetown; tel. 225-7270; fax 227-4806; e-mail homemin@guyana.net.

Ministry of Housing and Water: 41 Brickdam, Stabroek, Georgetown; tel. 225-7192; fax 227-3455; e-mail mhwps@sdnp.org.gy.

Ministry of Labour, Human Services and Social Security: 1 Water St and Corhill St, Stabroek, Georgetown; tel. 225-0655; fax 227-1308; e-mail khadoo@networksgy.com; internet www.sdnp.org.gy/mohss.

Ministry of Legal Affairs and Office of the Attorney-General: 95 Carmichael St, North Cummingsburg, Georgetown; tel. 226-2616; fax 226-9721; e-mail attorneygeneral_guyana@yahoo.com; internet www.agmla.gov.gy.

GUYANA

Ministry of Local Government and Regional Development: De Winkle Bldg, Fort St, Kingston, Georgetown; tel. 225-8621; fax 226-5070; e-mail mlgrdps@telsnetgy.net.

Ministry of Public Service Management: 164 Waterloo St, North Cummingsburg, Georgetown; tel. 226-6528; fax 225-7899; e-mail psm@sdnp.org.gy; internet www.sdnp.org.gy/psm.

Ministry of Transport and Hydraulics: Wights Lane, Kingston, Georgetown; tel. 226-1875; fax 225-8395; e-mail minoth@networksgy.com.

Ministry of Tourism, Industry and Commerce: 229 South Rd, Lacytown, Georgetown; tel. 226-2505; fax 225-9898; e-mail ministry@mintic.gov.gy; internet www.mintic.gov.gy.

President and Legislature

NATIONAL ASSEMBLY

Speaker: HARI NARAYEN (RALPH) RAMKARRAN.
Deputy Speaker: CLARISSA RIEHL.
Clerk: SHERLOCK ISAACS.

Election, 28 August 2006

Party	% of votes	Seats
People's Progressive Party/CIVIC	54.3	36
People's National Congress Reform-One Guyana	34.0	22
Alliance for Change	8.3	5
Guyana Action Party/Rise, Organize and Rebuild Guyana Movement	2.5	1
The United Force	0.9	1
Total	100.0	65

Under Guyana's system of proportional representation, the nominated candidate of the party receiving the most number of votes is elected to the presidency. Thus, on 2 September 2006 the candidate of the PPP/CIVIC alliance, BHARRAT JAGDEO, was inaugurated as President for a further term.

Election Commission

Guyana Elections Commission (GECOM): 41 High and Cowan Sts, Kingston, Georgetown; tel. 225-0277; e-mail gecomfeedback@webworksgy.com; internet www.gecom.org.gy; f. 2000; appointed by the Pres., partly in consultation with the leader of the opposition; Chair. Dr STEVE SURUJBALLY.

Political Organizations

Alliance for Change (AFC): 56 Chalmers Pl and Hadfield St, Georgetown; tel. 225-0452; e-mail alliance4changegy@yahoo.com; internet www.afcguyana.com; f. 2005; Leaders KHEMRAJ RAMJATTAN, RAPHAEL TROTMAN.

Guyana Action Party (GAP): Georgetown; allied with ROAR in 2006 elections; Leader PAUL HARDY.

Guyana Democratic Party (GDP): Georgetown; f. 1996; Leaders ASGAR ALLY, NANDA K. GOPAUL.

Guyana National Congress (GNC): Georgetown; Leader SAMUEL HAMER.

Guyana Republican Party (GRP): Paprika East Bank, Essequibo; e-mail 103203.652@compuserve.com; internet guyanarepublicanparty.org; f. 1985; right-wing; Leader LESLIE PRINCE (resident in the USA).

Justice For All Party (JFAP): 73 Robb and Wellington Sts, Lacytown, Georgetown; tel. 226-5462; fax 227-3050; e-mail sharma@guyana.net.gy; Leader CHANDRA NARINE SHARMA.

People's National Congress Reform-One Guyana (PNCR-1G): Congress Place, Sophia, POB 10330, Georgetown; tel. 225-7852; fax 225-6055; e-mail pnc@guyana-pnc.org; internet www.guyanapnc.org; f. 1955 as People's National Congress Reform following split with the PPP; present name adopted in 2006; Reform wing established in 2000; Leader ROBERT H. O. CORBIN; Chair. WINSTON MURRAY; Gen. Sec. OSCAR E. CLARKE.

People's Progressive Party/CIVIC (PPP/CIVIC): Freedom House, 41 Robb St, Lacytown, Georgetown; tel. 227-2095; fax 227-2096; e-mail pr@ppp-civic.org; internet www.ppp-civic.org; f. 1950; Marxist-Leninist; Gen. Sec. DONALD RAMOTAR.

Directory

Rise, Organize and Rebuild Guyana Movement (ROAR): 186 Parafield, Leonora, West Coast Demerara, POB 101409, Georgetown; tel. 268-2452; fax 268-3382; e-mail guyroar@yahoo.com; f. 1999; allied with GAP in 2006 elections; Leader RAVI DEV; Sec. ROY SINGH.

The United Force (TUF): Unity House, 95 Robb and New Garden Sts, Bourda, Georgetown; tel. 226-2596; fax 225-2973; internet www.tufsite.com; f. 1960; right-wing; advocates rapid industrialization through govt partnership and private capital; allied with the PPP/CIVIC since 2001 but contested 2006 election under its own auspices; Leader MANZOOR NADIR; Dep. Leader MICHAEL ANTHONY ABRAHAM.

Unity Party: 77 Hadfield St, Georgetown; tel. 227-6744; fax 227-6745; e-mail info@unityparty.net; internet www.unitypartyguyana.com; f. 2005; promotes private enterprise and coalition politics; Pres. CHEDDI (JOEY) JAGAN, Jr.

Working People's Alliance (WPA): Walter Rodney House, 80 Croal St, Stabroek, Georgetown; tel. and fax 225-3679; originally popular pressure group, became political party 1979; independent Marxist; Collective Leadership Dr CLIVE THOMAS, Dr RUPERT ROOPNARINE.

Diplomatic Representation

EMBASSIES AND HIGH COMMISSIONS IN GUYANA

Brazil: 308 Church St, Queenstown, POB 10489, Georgetown; tel. 225-7970; fax 226-9063; e-mail guibrem@solutions2000.net; Ambassador ARTHUR V. C. MEYER.

Canada: High and Young Sts, POB 10880, Georgetown; tel. 227-2081; fax 225-8380; e-mail grgtn@international.gc.ca; internet www.dfait-maeci.gc.ca/guyana; High Commissioner CHARLES COURT.

China, People's Republic: Lot 2, Botanic Gardens, Mandella Ave, Georgetown; tel. 225-9228; fax 231-6602; e-mail prcemb@networks.gy.com; internet gy.china-embassy.org/eng; Ambassador ZHANG JUNGAO.

Cuba: 46 High St, POB 10268, Kingston, Georgetown; tel. 225-1881; fax 226-1824; e-mail emguyana@networksgy.com; internet www.cubanembassy.org.gy; Ambassador FRANCISCO ALEJANDRO MARCHANTE CASTELLANOS.

India: Bank of Baroda Bldg, 10 Ave of the Republic, POB 101148, Georgetown; tel. 226-3996; fax 225-7012; e-mail hoc.georgetown@mea.gov.in; High Commissioner AVINASH C. GUPTA.

Russia: 3 Public Rd, Kitty, Georgetown; tel. 226-9773; fax 227-2975; e-mail embrus.guyana@mail.ru; internet www.rusembassyguyana.org.gy; Ambassador VLADIMIR S. STARIKOV.

Suriname: 171 Peter Rose and Crown Sts, Queenstown, Georgetown; tel. 226-7844; fax 225-0759; e-mail surnemb@gol.net.gy; Ambassador MANORMA SOEKNANDAN.

United Kingdom: 44 Main St, POB 10849, Georgetown; tel. 226-5881; fax 225-0671; e-mail bhcguyana@networksgy.com; internet www.britishhighcommission.gov.uk/guyana; High Commissioner FRASER WILLIAM WHEELER.

USA: 100 Young and Duke Sts, POB 10507, Kingston, Georgetown; tel. 226-3938; fax 225-8497; internet georgetown.usembassy.gov; e-mail usembassy@hotmail.com; Chargé d'affaires a.i. KAREN WILLIAMS.

Venezuela: 296 Thomas St, South Cummingsburg, Georgetown; tel. 226-1543; fax 225-3241; e-mail embveguy@gol.net.gy; Ambassador DARÍO MORANDY.

Judicial System

The Judicature of Guyana comprises the Supreme Court of Judicature, which consists of the Court of Appeal and the High Court (both of which are superior courts of record), and a number of Courts of Summary Jurisdiction.

The Court of Appeal, which came into operation in 1966, consists of the Chancellor as President, the Chief Justice, and such number of Justices of Appeal as may be prescribed by the National Assembly.

The High Court of the Supreme Court consists of the Chief Justice as President of the Court and Puisne Judges. Its jurisdiction is both original and appellate. It has criminal jurisdiction in matters brought before it on indictment. A person convicted by the Court has a right of appeal to the Guyana Court of Appeal. The High Court of the Supreme Court has unlimited jurisdiction in civil matters and exclusive jurisdiction in probate, divorce and admiralty and certain other matters. Under certain circumstances, appeal in civil matters lies either to the Full Court of the High Court of the Supreme Court, which is composed of no fewer than two judges, or to the Guyana Court of Appeal. On 4 November 2004 the National Assembly approved legislation recognizing the Caribbean Court of Justice

(CCJ) as Guyana's highest court of appeal. The CCJ was inaugurated in Port of Spain, Trinidad and Tobago, on 16 April 2005.

A magistrate has jurisdiction to determine claims where the amount involved does not exceed a certain sum of money, specified by law. Appeal lies to the Full Court.

Chancellor of Justice: CARL SINGH (acting).

Chief Justice: CARL SINGH.

Justices of Appeal: CLAUDETTE SINGH, IAN CHANG, NANDRAM KISSOON.

High Court Justices: WINSTON HORATIO PATTERSON, ROXANNE GEORGE, BRASSINGTON REYNOLDS.

Religion

CHRISTIANITY

Guyana Council of Churches: 26 Durban St, Lodge, Georgetown; tel. 225-3020; e-mail bishopedghill@hotmail.com; f. 1967 by merger of the Christian Social Council (f. 1937) and the Evangelical Council (f. 1960); 15 mem. churches, 1 assoc. mem.; Chair. Rev. ALPHONSO PORTER; Sec. Rev. NIGEL HAZEL.

The Anglican Communion

Anglicans in Guyana are adherents of the Church in the Province of the West Indies, comprising eight dioceses. The Archbishop of the Province is the Bishop of the North Eastern Caribbean and Aruba, resident in St John's, Antigua. The diocese of Guyana also includes French Guiana and Suriname. According to the 2002 census Anglicans constituted 6.9% of the population.

Bishop of Guyana: Rt Rev. RANDOLPH OSWALD GEORGE, The Church House, 49 Barrack St, POB 10949, Georgetown 1; tel. and fax 226-4183; e-mail dioofguy@networksgy.com; internet www.anglican.bm/G/01.html.

The Baptist Church

The Baptist Convention of Guyana: POB 10149, Georgetown; tel. 226-0428; 33 mem. churches, 1,823 mems.

The Lutheran Church

The Evangelical Lutheran Church in Guyana: Lutheran Courts, Berbice, POB 88, New Amsterdam; tel. and fax 333-6479; e-mail lcg@guyana.net.gy; internet www.elcguyana.org; f. 1947; 11,000 mems; Pres. Rev. ROY K. THAKURDYAL.

The Roman Catholic Church

Guyana comprises the single diocese of Georgetown, suffragan to the archdiocese of Port of Spain, Trinidad and Tobago. At 31 December 2005 adherents of the Roman Catholic Church comprised about 8% of the total population. The Bishop participates in the Antilles Episcopal Conference Secretariat, currently based in Port of Spain, Trinidad.

Bishop of Georgetown: FRANCIS DEAN ALLEYNE, Bishop's House, 27 Brickdam, POB 101488, Stabroek, Georgetown; tel. 226-4469; fax 225-8519; e-mail rcbishop@networksgy.com.

Seventh-day Adventists

At the end of 2004 an estimated 6.1% of the population belonged to the Guyana Conference of Seventh-day Adventists. The Guyana Conference is a member of the Caribbean Union Conference and comprises two congregations and 137 churches.

Guyana Conference: 222 Peter Rose and Almond Sts, Queenstown, POB 10191, Georgetown; tel. 226-3313; fax 223-8142; e-mail guycon1@gol.net.gy; 50,291 mems in 2007; Pres. Pastor HILTON GARNETT.

Other Christian Churches

Other denominations active in Guyana include the African Methodist Episcopal Church, the African Methodist Episcopal Zion Church, the Church of God, the Church of the Nazarene, the Ethiopian Orthodox Church, the Guyana Baptist Mission, the Guyana Congregational Union, the Guyana Presbyterian Church, the Hallelujah Church, the Methodist Church in the Caribbean and the Americas, the Moravian Church and the Presbytery of Guyana.

HINDUISM

At the census of September 2002, Hindus constituted an estimated 28.4% of the population.

Guyana Hindu Dharmic Sabha (Hindu Religious Centre): 162 Lamaha St, POB 10576, Georgetown; tel. 225-7443; f. 1934; Gen. Sec. REEPU DAMAN PERSAUD.

ISLAM

Muslims in Guyana comprised 7.2% of the population in 2002.

The Central Islamic Organization of Guyana (CIOG): M.Y.O. Bldg, Woolford Ave, Thomas Lands, POB 10245, Georgetown; tel. 225-8654; fax 227-2475; e-mail contact@ciog.org.gy; internet www.ciog.org.gy; Pres. Alhaji FAZEEL M. FEROUZ; Dir of Education QAYS ARTHUR.

Guyana United Sad'r Islamic Anjuman: 157 Alexander St, Kitty, POB 10715, Georgetown; tel. 226-9620; e-mail khalid@gusia.org; internet www.gusia.org; f. 1936; 120,000 mems; Pres. Haji A. HAFIZ RAHAMAN.

BAHÁ'Í FAITH

National Spiritual Assembly: 220 Charlotte St, Bourda, Georgetown; tel. and fax 226-5952; e-mail nsaguy@networksgy.gy; internet www.sdnp.org.gy/bahai; incorporated in 1976.

The Press

DAILIES

Guyana Chronicle: 2A Lama Ave, Bel Air Park, POB 11, Georgetown; tel. 227-5204; fax 227-5208; e-mail gm@guyanachronicle.com; internet www.guyanachronicle.com; f. 1881; govt-owned; also produces weekly Sunday Chronicle (tel. 226-3243); Editor-in-Chief SHARIEF KHAN; circ. 23,000 (weekdays), 43,000 (Sundays).

Kaieteur News: 24 Saffon St, Charlestown; tel. 225-8465; fax 225-8473; e-mail kaieteurnews@yahoo.com; internet www.kaieteurnewsgy.com; f. 1994; independent; Editor ADAM HARRIS; Publr MOHAN GLEN LALL; daily circ. 19,000, Fridays 25,000, Sundays 32,000.

Stabroek News: E1/2 46–47 Robb St, Lacytown, Georgetown; tel. 227-5197; fax 226-2549; internet www.stabroeknews.com; f. 1986; also produces weekly Sunday Stabroek; liberal independent; Editor-in-Chief DAVID DE CAIRES; Editor ANAND PERSAUD; circ. 14,100 (weekdays), 26,400 (Sundays).

WEEKLIES AND PERIODICALS

The Catholic Standard: 293 Oronoque St, Queenstown, POB 10720, Georgetown; tel. 226-1540; f. 1905; weekly; Editor COLIN SMITH; circ. 4,000.

Diocesan Magazine: 144 Almond and Oronoque Sts, Queenstown, Georgetown; quarterly.

Guyana Journal: Georgetown; e-mail guyanajournal@verizon.net; internet www.guyanajournal.com; monthly; Editor GARY GIRDHARI.

Guyana Review: 143 Oronoque St, POB 10386, Georgetown; tel. 226-3139; fax 227-3465; e-mail guyrev@networksgy.com; f. 1993; taken over by Guyana Publs Inc in Jan. 2007; monthly.

Mirror: Lot 8, Industrial Estate, Ruimveldt, Greater Georgetown; tel. 226-2471; fax 226-2472; e-mail ngmirror@guyana.net.gy; internet www.mirrornewsonline.com; owned by the New Guyana Co Ltd; Sundays; Editor DAVID DE GROOT; circ. 25,000.

New Nation: Congress Pl., Sophia, Georgetown; tel. 226-7891; f. 1955; organ of the People's National Congress; weekly; Editor FRANCIS WILLIAMS; circ. 26,000.

The Official Gazette of Guyana: Guyana National Printers Ltd, Lot 1, Public Rd, La Penitence; weekly; circ. 450.

Thunder: Freedom House, 41 Robb St, Lacytown, Georgetown; tel. 227-2095; fax 227-2096; e-mail ppp@guyana.net.gy; internet www.ppp-civic.org; organ of the People's Progressive Party/CIVIC; quarterly.

PRESS ASSOCIATION

Guyana Press Association (GPA): 82C Duje St, Kingston, Georgetown; tel. 623-5430; fax 223-6625; e-mail gpaexecutive@gmail.com; internet www.gpa.org.gy; affiliated with the Association of Caribbean Media Workers; Pres. DENIS CHABROL.

NEWS AGENCIES

Guyana Information Agency: Area B, Homestretch Ave, D'Urban Backlands, Georgetown; tel. 225-3117; fax 226-4003; e-mail gina@gina.gov.gy; internet www.gina.gov.gy; f. 1993; Dir PREM MISIR.

Foreign Bureaux

Xinhua (New China) News Agency (People's Republic of China): 52 Brickdam, Stabroek, Georgetown; tel. 226-9965.

Associated Press (USA), French Press Agency (AFP) and ITAR—TASS (Information Telegraphic Agency of Russia—Telegraphic Agency of the Sovereign Countries, Russia) are also represented.

Publishers

Guyana Free Press: POB 10386, Georgetown; tel. 226-3139; fax 227-3465; e-mail guyrev@networksgy.com; books and learned journals.

Guyana National Printers Ltd: 1 Public Rd, La Penitence, POB 10256, Greater Georgetown; tel. 225-3623; e-mail gnpl@guyana.net.gy; f. 1939; govt-owned printers and publishers; privatization pending.

Guyana Publications Inc: E 1/2 46–47 Robb St, Lacytown, Georgetown; tel. 226-5197; fax 226-3237; e-mail info@stabroeknews.com; internet www.stabroeknews.com; Man. Dir DOREEN DECAIRES.

Broadcasting and Communications

TELECOMMUNICATIONS

The telecommunications sector was restructured and opened to competition in 2002.

Digicel Guyana: 56 High St, POB 101845, Kingston, Georgetown; tel. 223-6531; fax 223-6532; e-mail customercare.guyana@digicelgroup.com; internet www.digicelguyana.com; f. 1999 as Trans-World Telecom; acquired Cel Star Guyana in 2003; acquired by Digicel Group in Nov. 2006; GSM cellular telecommunications network; operates Celstar and U-Mobile brands; CEO TIM BAHRANI; Vice-Pres. GREGORY LIBERTINY.

Guyana Telephones and Telegraph Company (GT & T): 79 Brickdam, POB 10628, Georgetown; tel. 226-7840; fax 226-2457; e-mail pubcomm@gtt.co.gy; internet www.gtt.co.gy; f. 1991; fmrly state-owned Guyana Telecommunications Corpn; 80% ownership by Atlantic Tele-Network (USA); Chair. (vacant); CEO Maj. Gen. (retd) JOSEPH G. SINGH.

BROADCASTING

In May 2001 the Government implemented the regulation of all broadcast frequencies. Two private stations relay US satellite television programmes.

National Communications Network (NCN): Homestretch Ave, D'Urban Park, Georgetown; tel. 227-1566; fax 226-2253; e-mail feedback@ncnguyana.com; internet www.ncnguyana.com; f. 2004 following merger of Guyana Broadcasting Corpn (f. 1979) and Guyana Television and Broadcasting Co (f. 1993); govt-owned; operates three radio channels and six TV channels; Chair. ROBERT PERSAUD; CEO DESMOND MOHAMED SATTAUR; Editor-in-Chief MICHAEL GORDON.

Radio

National Communications Network (NCN): see Broadcasting; operates three channels: Hot FM, Radio Roraima and Voice of Guyana.

Television

CNS Channel Six: 43 Robb and Wellington Sts, Georgetown; tel. 226-5462; fax 227-3050; privately owned; Dir CHANDRA NARINE SHARMA.

Hoyte/Blackman Television Station (HBTV-9): Georgetown; Dir NOEL BLACKMAN.

National Communications Network: see Broadcasting; TV network covers channels 8, 11, 13, 15, 21 and 26.

Finance

(cap. = capital; res = reserves; dep. = deposits; m. = million; brs = branches; amounts in Guyana dollars)

BANKING

Central Bank

Bank of Guyana: 1 Church St and Ave of the Republic, POB 1003, Georgetown; tel. 226-3250; fax 227-2965; e-mail communications@bankofguyana.org.gy; internet www.bankofguyana.org.gy; f. 1965; cap. 1,000m., res 3,747.5m., dep. 81,691.3m. (Dec. 2006); central bank of issue; acts as regulatory authority for the banking sector; Gov. LAWRENCE T. WILLIAMS.

Commercial Banks

Bank of Baroda (Guyana) Inc (India): 10 Ave of the Republic and Regent St, POB 10768, Georgetown; tel. 226-4005; fax 225-1691; e-mail bobinc@networksgy.com; f. 1908; Man. Dir R. K. SHARMA.

Citizens' Bank Guyana Inc: 201 Camp St, Lacytown, Georgetown; tel. 226-1705; fax 226-1719; internet www.citizensbankgy.com; f. 1994; 51% owned by Banks DIH; total assets 18,773m. (Sept. 2007); Chair. CLIFFORD B. REIS; Man. Dir ETON M. CHESTER (acting); 4 brs.

Demerara Bank Ltd: 230 Camp and South Sts, POB 12133, Georgetown; tel. and fax 225-0610; e-mail banking@demerarabank.com; internet www.demerarabank.com; f. 1994; cap. 450.0m., res 261.7m., dep. 16,202.6m. (Sept. 2006); Chair. YESU PERSAUD; CEO PRAVINCHANDRA S. DAVE.

Guyana Bank for Trade and Industry Ltd: 47–48 Water St, POB 10280, Georgetown; tel. 226-8430; fax 227-1612; e-mail banking@gbtibank.com; internet www.gbtibank.com; f. 1987 to absorb the operations of Barclays Bank; cap. 800m., res 733m., dep. 31,326m. (Dec. 2006); CEO RADHA KRISHNA SHARMA; Dir JOHN TRACEY; 7 brs.

Republic Bank (Guyana): Promenade Court, 155–156 New Market St, Georgetown; tel. 223-7938; fax 227-4506; e-mail email@nbicgy.com; internet www.nbicgy.com; f. 1984; 51% owned by Republic Bank Ltd, Port of Spain, Trinidad and Tobago; acquired Guyana National Co-operative Bank in 2003; name changed from National Bank of Industry and Commerce in 2006; cap. 300m., res 406.5m., dep. 60,078.7m. (Sept. 2006); Chair. DAVID DULAL-WHITEWAY; Man. Dir MICHAEL B. ARCHIBALD; 5 brs.

Merchant Bank

Guyana Americas Merchant Bank (GBTI): GBTI Bldg, 138 Regent St, Lacytown, Georgetown; tel. 223-5193; fax 223-5195; e-mail gambi@networksgy.com; f. 2001; fmrly known as Guyana Finance Corpn Ltd; merchant bank; Man. Dir Dr GRAHAM SCOTT.

Foreign Banks

STOCK EXCHANGE

Guyana Association of Securities Companies and Intermediaries (GASCI): Hand-in-Hand Bldg, 1 Ave of the Republic, Georgetown; tel. 223-6176; fax 223-6175; e-mail info@gasci.com; internet www.gasci.com; f. 2001; Chair. NIKHIL RAMKARRAN; Operations Man. GEORGE EDWARDS.

INSURANCE

Supervisory Body

Office of the Commissioner of Insurance: Privatisation Unit Bldg, 126 Barrack St, Kingston, Georgetown; tel. 225-0318; fax 226-6426; e-mail mvanbeek@insurance.gov.gy; internet www.insurance.gov.gy; regulates insurance and pensions industries; Commr MARIA VAN BEEK.

Companies

CLICO: 191 Camp St, South Cummings, Georgetown; tel. 227-1330; e-mail info@clico.com; internet www.clico.com; Exec. Chair. LAWRENCE A. DUPREY; Man. RAMONA SINGH.

Demerara Mutual Life Assurance Society Ltd: 61–62 Robb St and Ave of the Republic, Georgetown; tel. 225-8991; fax 225-8995; e-mail demlife@demeraramutual.com; internet www.demeraramutual.com; f. 1891; Chair. RICHARD B. FIELDS; CEO KEITH N. CHOLMONDELEY.

Diamond Fire and General Insurance Inc: 44B High St, Kingston, Georgetown; tel. 223-9771; fax 223-9770; e-mail diamondins@solutions2000.net; f. 2000; privately owned; Man. TARA CHANDRA; cap. 100m.

Guyana Co-operative Insurance Service (GCIS): 47 Main St, Georgetown; tel. 225-9153; f. 1976; 67% owned by the Hand-in-Hand Group; Area Rep. SAMMY RAMPERSAUD.

Guyana and Trinidad Mutual Life Insurance Co Ltd: 27–29 Robb and Hinck St, Georgetown; tel. 225-7910; fax 225-9397; e-mail gtmgroup@gtm-gy.com; f. 1925; affiliated co: Guyana and Trinidad Mutual Fire Insurance Co Ltd; Chair. HAROLD B. DAVIS; Man. Dir R. E. CHEONG.

Hand-in-Hand Mutual Fire and Life Group: Hand-in-Hand Bldg, 1–4 Ave of the Republic, POB 10188, Georgetown; tel. 225-0462; fax 225-7519; f. 1865; fire and life insurance; Chair. J. A. CHIN; Gen. Man. K. A. EVELYN.

Association

Insurance Association of Guyana: 54 Robb St, Bourda, POB 10741, Georgetown; tel. 226-3514; f. 1968.

Trade and Industry

GOVERNMENT AGENCIES

Environmental Protection Agency, Guyana: University of Guyana Campus, Turkeyen, Greater Georgetown; tel. 222-5783;

fax 222-2442; e-mail epa@epaguyana.org; internet www.epaguyana.org; f. 1988 as Guyana Agency for the Environment; renamed 1996; formulates, implements and monitors policies on the environment; Exec. Dir DOORGA PERSAUD.

Guyana Energy Agency (GEA): 295 Quamina St, POB 903, Georgetown; tel. 226-0394; fax 226-5227; e-mail ecgea@guyana.net.gy; internet www.sdnp.org.gy/gea; f. 1998 as successor to Guyana National Energy Authority; CEO MAHENDRA SHARMA (acting).

Guyana Office for Investment (Go-Invest): 190 Camp and Church Sts, Georgetown; tel. 225-0653; fax 225-0655; e-mail goinvest@goinvest.gov.gy; internet www.goinvest.gov.gy; f. 1994; CEO GEOFFREY DA SILVA.

Guyana Marketing Corporation: 87 Robb and Alexander Sts, Lacytown, POB 10810, Georgetown; tel. 226-8255; fax 227-4114; internet www.newgmc.com; Gen. Man. NIZAM HASSAN.

DEVELOPMENT ORGANIZATION

Institute of Private Enterprise Development (IPED): 253 South Rd, Bourda, Georgetown; tel. 225-8949; fax 223-7834; e-mail iped@solutions2000.net; internet www.ipedgy.com; f. 1986 to help establish small businesses; total loans provided $ G870m. (2003); Chair. YESU PERSAUD; Exec. Dir Dr LESLIE CHIN.

CHAMBER OF COMMERCE

Georgetown Chamber of Commerce and Industry: 156 Waterloo St, Cummingsburg, POB 10110, Georgetown; tel. 225-5846; fax 226-3519; e-mail info@georgetownchamberofcommerce.org; internet www.georgetownchamberofcommerce.org; f. 1889; Pres. GERALD GOUVEIA; 122 mems.

INDUSTRIAL AND TRADE ASSOCIATIONS

Guyana Rice Development Board: 116–17 Cowan St, Kingston, Georgetown; tel. 225-8717; fax 225-6486; internet www.grdb.gy; f. 1994 to assume operations of Guyana Rice Export Board and Guyana Rice Grading Centre; Gen. Man. JAGNARINE SINGH.

National Dairy and Development Programme (NDDP): c/o Lands and Surveys Bldg, 22 Upper Hadfield St, Durban Backlands, POB 10367, Georgetown; tel. 225-7107; fax 226-3020; e-mail nddp@sdnp.org.gym; internet www.sdnp.org.gy/minagri/nddp/generalinfo.htm; f. 1984; aims to increase domestic milk and beef production; Dir Dr DWIGHT WALROND.

EMPLOYERS' ASSOCIATIONS

Consultative Association of Guyanese Industry Ltd: 157 Waterloo St, POB 10730, Georgetown; tel. 225-7170; fax 227-0725; e-mail cagi@guyana.net.gy; f. 1962; Chair. YESU PERSAUD; Exec. Dir DAVID YANKANA; 193 mems, 3 mem. asscns, 159 assoc. mems.

Forest Products Association of Guyana: 157 Waterloo St, Georgetown; tel. 226-9848; e-mail fpasect@sdnp.org.gy; f. 1944; 62 mem. cos; Pres. DAVID PERSAUD; Exec. Officer WARREN PHOENIX.

Guyana Manufacturing and Services Association Ltd (GMSA): National Exhibition Centre, Sophia, Georgetown; tel. 227-4295; e-mail gma_guyana@yahoo.com; internet www.gma.org.gy; f. 1967 as the Guyana Manufacturers' Asscn; name changed in 2005 to reflect growth in services sector; 190 mems; Pres. GEORGE LESLIE ROBINSON.

Guyana Rice Producers' Association (GRPA): 126 Parade and Barrack St, Georgetown; tel. 226-4411; fax 223-7249; e-mail grpa.riceproducers@networksgy.com; f. 1946; non-govt org.; 18,500 mems; Gen. Sec. DHARAMKUMAR SEERAJ.

UTILITIES

Electricity

Guyana Power and Light Inc (GPL): 40 Main St, POB 10390, Georgetown; tel. 225-4618; fax 227-1978; e-mail enquiries@gplinc.com; internet www.gplinc.com; f. 1999; fmrly Guyana Electricity Corpn; state-owned; Chair. (vacant); CEO BHARAT DINDYAL; 1,200 employees.

Water

Guyana Water Inc (GWI): 10 Fort St, Georgetown; tel. 227-8701; internet www.gwiguyana.com; f. 2002 following merger of Guyana Water Authority (GUYWA) and Georgetown Sewerage and Water Comm.; operated by Severn Trent Water International (United Kingdom); Chair. Dr CYRIL SOLOMON; Man. Dir SIZWE JACKSON (acting).

CO-OPERATIVE SOCIETIES

Chief Co-operatives Development Officer: Ministry of Labour, Human Services and Social Security, 1 Water and Cornhill Sts, Stabroek, Georgetown; tel. 225-8644; fax 227-1308; e-mail coopdept@telsnet.gy.net; f. 1948; Dir CLIVE NURSE.

TRADE UNIONS

Trades Union Congress (TUC): Critchlow Labour College, Woolford Ave, Non-pareil Park, Georgetown; tel. 226-1493; fax 227-0254; e-mail gtucorg@yahoo.com; f. 1940; national trade union body; 22 affiliated unions; 70,000 mems; merged with the Federation of Independent Trade Unions in Guyana in 1993; affiliated to the Internat. Trade Union Confederation; Pres. ANDREW GARNETT; Gen. Sec. LINCOLN LEWIS.

Amalgamated Transport and General Workers' Union: Transport House, 46 Urquhart St, Georgetown; tel. 226-6243; fax 225-6602; Pres. RICHARD SAMUELS; Gen. Sec. VICTOR JOHNSON.

Association of Masters and Mistresses: c/o Critchlow Labour College, Georgetown; tel. 226-8968; Pres. GANESH SINGH; Gen. Sec. T. ANSON SANCHO.

Clerical and Commercial Workers' Union (CCWU): Clerico House, 140 Quamina St, South Cummingsburg, POB 101045, Georgetown; tel. 225-2822; fax 227-2618; e-mail ccwu@guyana.net.gy; Pres. ROY HUGHES; Gen. Sec. GRANTLEY L. CULBARD.

Guyana Bauxite and General Workers' Union: 180 Charlotte St, Georgetown; tel. 225-4654; Pres. CHARLES SAMPSON; Gen. Sec. LEROY ALLEN (acting).

Guyana Labour Union: 198 Camp St, Cummingsburg, Georgetown; tel. 227-1196; fax 225-0820; e-mail glu@solutions2000.net; Pres. SAMUEL WALKER; Gen. Sec. CARVIL DUNCAN; 6,000 mems.

Guyana Local Government Officers' Union: c/o Abbatoir, Georgetown; tel. 227-2131; fax 227-6905; e-mail daleantford@yahoo.com; Pres. ANDREW GARNETT; Gen. Sec. SANDRA HOOPER.

Guyana Mining, Metal and General Workers' Union: 56 Wismar St, Linden, Demerara River; tel. 204-6822; Pres. ERIC TELLO; Gen. Sec. LESLIE GONSALVES; 5,800 mems.

Guyana Postal and Telecommunication Workers' Union: Postal House, 310 East St, POB 10352, Georgetown; tel. 226-7920; fax 225-1633; Pres. MORRIS WALCOTT; Gen. Sec. GILLIAN BURTON.

Guyana Teachers' Union: Woolford Ave, POB 738, Georgetown; tel. 226-3183; fax 227-0403; Pres. SYDNEY MURDOCK; Gen. Sec. SHIRLEY HOOPER.

National Mining and General Workers Union: 10 Church St, New Amsterdam, Berbice; tel. 203-3496; Pres. CYRIL CONWAY; Gen. Sec. MARILYN GRIFFITH.

National Union of Public Service Employees: 4 Fort St, Kingston, Georgetown; tel. 227-1491; Pres. ROBERT JOHNSON; Gen. Sec. RUDOLPH WELCH.

Printing Industry and Allied Workers' Union: c/o Guyana TUC, Georgetown; tel. 226-8968; Gen. Sec. PATRICIA HODGE (acting).

Public Employees' Union: Regent St, Georgetown; Pres. REUBEN KHAN.

Union of Agricultural and Allied Workers (UAAW): 10 Hadfield St, Werk-en-Rust, Georgetown; tel. 226-7434; Pres. JEAN SMITH; Gen. Sec. SEELO BAICHAN.

University of Guyana Workers' Union: POB 841, Turkeyen, Georgetown; tel. 222-3586; e-mail adeolaplus@yahoo.com; supports Working People's Alliance; Pres. CLIVE Y. THOMAS; Gen. Sec. A. ESOOP.

Guyana Agricultural and General Workers' Union (GAWU): 59 High St and Wight's Lane, Kingston, Georgetown; tel. 227-2091; fax 227-2093; e-mail gawu@bbgy.com; Pres. KOMAL CHAND; Gen. Sec. SEEPAUL NARINE; 20,000 mems.

Guyana Public Service Union (GPSU): 160 Regent and New Garden Sts, Georgetown; tel. 225-0518; fax 226-5322; e-mail gpsu@guyana.net.gy; internet www.guyanapsu.org; Pres. PATRICK YARDE; Gen. Sec. LAWRENCE MENTIS; 11,600 mems.

National Association of Agricultural, Commercial and Industrial Employees (NAACIE): 64 High St, Kingston, Georgetown; tel. 227-2301; f. 1946; Pres. KENNETH JOSEPH; Gen. Sec. KAISREE TAKECHANDRA; c. 2,000 mems.

Transport

RAILWAY

There are no public railways in Guyana. Until the early 21st century the 15-km Linmine Railway was used for the transportation of bauxite from Linden to Coomaka.

ROADS

The coastal strip has a well-developed road system. In 1999 there were an estimated 7,970 km (4,952 miles) of paved and good-weather roads and trails. In September 2001 a European Union-funded road improvement programme between Crabwood Creek and the Guyana–Suriname Ferry Terminal was completed; the project was intended to help integrate the region. In the same year construction began on a bridge across the Takutu river, linking Guyana to Brazil; construction was temporarily suspended in 2002, owing to difficulties with planning regulations and financing, but completion of the project was anticipated in early 2008. The US $40m. rehabilitation of the Mahaica–Rosignol road, partly funded by the Inter-American Development Bank (IDB), began in 2003. In the same year work began on a complementary project to remove and relocate both the Mahaica and Mahaicony bridges. Construction of a bridge over the Berbice river began in late 2006 and was expected to be completed in 2008. The IDB approved a 40-year loan of $24.3m. towards highway infrastructure rehabilitation under the supervision of the Ministry of Public Works and Communications in November 2006.

SHIPPING

Guyana's principal ports are at Georgetown and New Amsterdam. The port at Linden serves for the transportation of bauxite products. A ferry service is operated between Guyana and Suriname. Communications with the interior are chiefly by river, although access is hindered by rapids and falls. There are 1,077 km (607 miles) of navigable rivers. The main rivers are the Mazaruni, the Potaro, the Essequibo, the Demerara and the Berbice. In 2000 the Brazilian Government announced that it was to finance the construction of both a deep-water port and a river bridge.

Transport and Harbours Department: Battery Rd, Kingston, Georgetown; tel. 225-9350; fax 227-8545; e-mail t&hd@solutions2000.net; Gen. Man. KAREN BOWEN (acting); Deputy Gen. Man. DAVID JOHN.

Shipping Association of Guyana Inc (SAG): 10–11 Lombard St, Werk-en-Rust, Georgetown; tel. 226-2169; fax 226-9656; e-mail saginc@networksgy.com; internet www.shipping.org.gy; f. 1952; non-governmental forum; Chair. ANDREW ASTWOOD; Vice-Chair. BERNIE FERNANDES; members:

    Guyana National Industrial Company Inc (GNIC): 1–9 Lombard St, Charlestown, POB 10520, Georgetown; tel. 225-5398; fax 226-0432; e-mail gnicadmin@futurenetgy.com; metal foundry, ship building and repair, agents for a number of international transport cos; privatized 1995; CEO CLINTON WILLIAMS; Port Man. ALBERT SMITH.

Guyana National Shipping Corporation Ltd: 5–9 Lombard St, La Penitence, POB 10988, Georgetown; tel. 226-1840; fax 225-3815; e-mail gnsc@guyana.net.gy; internet www.gnsc.com; govt-owned; Man. Dir ANDREW ASTWOOD (acting).

John Fernandes Ltd: 24 Water St, POB 10211, Georgetown; tel. 227-3344; fax 226-1881; e-mail philip@jf-ltd.com; internet www.jf-ltd.com; ship agents, pier operators and stevedore contractors; part of the John Fernandes Group of Cos; Chair. and CEO CHRIS FERNANDES.

CIVIL AVIATION

The main airport, Cheddi Jaggan International Airport, is at Timehri, 42 km (26 miles) from Georgetown.

Roraima Airways: R8 Epring Ave, Bel Air Park, Georgetown; tel. 225-9648; fax 225-9646; e-mail ral@roraimaairways.com; internet www.roraimaairways.com; f. 1992; flights to Venezuela and 4 domestic destinations; Man. Dir Capt. GERALD GOUVEIA.

Trans Guyana Airways: Ogle Aerodrome, Ogle, East Coast Demerara; tel. 222-2525; e-mail commercial@transguyana.com; internet www.transguyana.com; f. 1956; internal flights to 22 destinations; Dir Capt. GERARD GONSALVES.

Tourism

Despite the beautiful scenery in the interior of the country, Guyana has limited tourist facilities, and began encouraging tourism only in the late 1980s. During the 1990s Guyana began to develop its considerable potential as an 'eco-tourism' destination. However, tourist arrivals declined towards the end of the decade. The total number of visitors to Guyana in 2005 was 116,596, of whom 51.5% were from the USA. In that year expenditure by tourists amounted to US $35m.

Guyana Tourism Authority: National Exhibition Centre, Sophia, Georgetown; tel. 219-0094; fax 219-0093; e-mail info@guyana-tourism.com; internet www.guyana-tourism.com; f. 2003; Chair. BRIAN JAMES.

Tourism and Hospitality Association of Guyana (THAG): 157 Waterloo St, Georgetown; tel. 225-0807; fax 225-0817; e-mail thag@networksgy.com; internet www.exploreguyana.com; f. 1992; Pres. CATHY HUGHES; Exec. Dir MAUREEN PAUL.

HAITI

Introductory Survey

Location, Climate, Language, Religion, Flag, Capital

The Republic of Haiti occupies the western part of the Caribbean island of Hispaniola (the Dominican Republic occupies the remaining two-thirds) and some smaller offshore islands. Cuba, to the west, is less than 80 km away. The climate is tropical but the mountains and fresh sea winds mitigate the heat. Temperatures vary little with the seasons, and the annual average in Port-au-Prince is about 27°C (80°F). The rainy season is from May to November. The official languages are French and Creole. About 65% of the population belong to the Roman Catholic Church, the country's official religion, and other Christian churches are also represented. The folk religion is voodoo, a fusion of beliefs originating in West Africa involving communication with the spirit-world through the medium of trance. In April 2003 the Government announced that, henceforth, voodoo was to be given the status of an official religion. The national flag (proportions variable) has two equal vertical stripes, of dark blue and red. The state flag (proportions 3 by 5) has, in addition, a white rectangular panel, containing the national coat of arms (a palm tree, surmounted by a Cap of Liberty and flanked by flags and cannons), in the centre. The capital is Port-au-Prince.

Recent History

Haiti was first colonized in 1659 by the French, who named the territory Saint-Domingue. French sovereignty was formally recognized by Spain in 1697. Following a period of internal unrest, a successful uprising, begun in 1794 by African-descended slaves, culminated in 1804 with the establishment of Haiti as an independent state, ruled by Jean-Jacques Dessalines, who proclaimed himself Emperor. Hostility between the negro population and the mulattos continued throughout the 19th century until, after increasing economic instability, the USA intervened militarily and supervised the government of the country from 1915 to 1934. Mulatto interests retained political ascendancy until 1946, when a negro President, Dumarsais Estimé, was installed following a military coup. Following the overthrow of two further administrations, Dr François Duvalier, a country physician, was elected President in 1957.

The Duvalier administration soon became a dictatorship, maintaining its authority by means of a notorious private army, popularly called the Tontons Macoutes (Creole for 'Bogeymen'), who used extortion and intimidation to crush all possible opposition to the President's rule. In 1964 Duvalier became President-for-Life, and at his death in April 1971 he was succeeded by his 19-year-old son and designated successor, Jean-Claude Duvalier.

At elections held in February 1979 for the 58-seat National Assembly, 57 seats were won by the official government party, the Parti de l'Unité Nationale. The first municipal elections for 25 years, which took place in 1983, were overshadowed by allegations of electoral fraud and Duvalier's obstruction of opposition parties. No opposition candidates were permitted to contest the elections for the National Assembly held in February 1984.

In April 1985 Duvalier announced a programme of constitutional reforms, including the eventual appointment of a Prime Minister and the formation of political parties, subject to certain limiting conditions. In September Roger Lafontant, the minister most closely identified with the Government's acts of repression, was dismissed. However, protests organized by the Roman Catholic Church and other religious groups gained momentum, and further measures to curb continued disorder were adopted in January 1986. The university and schools were closed indefinitely, and radio stations were forbidden to report on current events. Duvalier imposed a state of siege and declared martial law.

In February 1986, following intensified public protests, Duvalier and his family fled from Haiti to exile in France, leaving a five-member National Council of Government (Conseil National Gouvernemental—CNG), led by the Chief of Staff of the army, Gen. Henri Namphy, to succeed him. The interim military-civilian Council appointed a new Cabinet. The National Assembly was dissolved, and the Constitution was suspended. Later in the month, the Tontons Macoutes were disbanded. Prisoners from Haiti's largest gaol were freed under a general amnesty. However, renewed rioting occurred to protest against the inclusion in the new Government of known supporters of the former dictatorship. In March 1986 there was a cabinet reshuffle. The new, three-member, CNG comprised Gen. Namphy, Col (later Brig.-Gen.) Williams Régala and Jacques François.

In April 1986 Gen. Namphy announced a proposed timetable for elections to restore constitutional government by February 1988. The first of these elections, to select members of the Constituent Assembly, which was to revise the Constitution, took place in October 1986. However, the level of participation at the election was only about 5%. The new Constitution was approved by 99.8% of voters in a referendum held on 29 March 1987. An estimated 50% of the electorate voted. An independent Provisional Electoral Council (Conseil Electoral Provisoire—CEP) was appointed to supervise the presidential and legislative elections, which were scheduled for 29 November.

On 29 November 1987 the elections were cancelled three hours after voting had begun, owing to renewed violence and killings, for which former members of the Tontons Macoutes were believed to be responsible. The Government dissolved the CEP and took control of the electoral process. In December a new CEP was appointed by the Government, and elections were rescheduled for 17 January 1988. Leslie Manigat of the Rassemblement des Démocrates Nationalistes et Progressistes (RDNP), with 50% of the total votes cast, was declared the winner of the presidential election. Legislative and municipal elections were held concurrently. Opposition leaders alleged that there had been extensive fraud and malpractice.

The Manigat Government took office in February 1988, but was overthrown by disaffected members of the army in June. Gen. Namphy, whom Manigat had attempted to replace as army Chief of Staff, assumed the presidency and appointed a Cabinet comprising members of the armed forces. The Constitution of 1987 was abrogated, and Duvalier's supporters returned to prominence, as did the Tontons Macoutes.

On 18 September 1988 Gen. Namphy was ousted in a coup, led by Brig.-Gen. Prosper Avril (who became President), who advocated the introduction of radical reforms. In November an independent electoral body, the Collège Electoral d'Haïti (CEDA), was established to supervise future elections, to draft an electoral law and to ensure proper registration of voters.

In March 1989 President Avril partially restored the Constitution of 1987 and restated his intention to hold democratic elections. In the following month the Government survived two coup attempts by the Leopard Corps, the country's élite anti-subversion squadron, and the Dessalines battalion, based in Port-au-Prince. Both battalions were subsequently disbanded.

Avril resigned as President in March 1990, in response to sustained popular and political opposition, together with diplomatic pressure from the USA. Before entering temporary exile in the USA, Avril ceded power to the Chief of the General Staff, Gen. Hérard Abraham, who subsequently transferred authority to Ertha Pascal-Trouillot, a member of the Supreme Court. As President of a civilian interim Government, Pascal-Trouillot shared power with a 19-member Council of State, whose principal function was to assist in preparations for the elections that were to be held later in the year. In May a new CEP was established. In September the CEP announced the postponement, until mid-December, of the elections, owing to a delay in the arrival of necessary funds and materials from donor countries.

The presidential and legislative elections took place on 16 December 1990. Fr Jean-Bertrand Aristide, a left-wing Roman Catholic priest representing the Front National pour le Changement et la Démocratie (FNCD), won an overwhelming victory in the presidential election, securing some 67% of the votes cast. His closest rival was Marc Bazin, the candidate of the centre-right Mouvement pour l'Instauration de la Démocratie en Haïti (MIDH), who obtained about 14% of the poll. However, the results of the concurrent first round of legislative voting were less decisive. Aristide's FNCD won five of the 27 seats in the

Sénat (Senate), and 18 (of 83) seats in the Chambre des Députés (Chamber of Deputies), while the Alliance Nationale pour la Démocratie et le Progrès (ANDP) secured 16 seats in the lower house. Seven other seats in the Chambre des Députés were distributed among other political parties.

In January 1991, one month before Aristide was due to be sworn in as President, a group of army officers, led by Roger Lafontant, seized control of the presidential palace, and forced Pascal-Trouillot to announce her resignation. However, the army remained loyal to the Government and arrested Lafontant and his associates. (In July Lafontant was sentenced to life imprisonment for organizing the coup, and Pascal-Trouillot was later charged with complicity with the coup attempt. She left the country in September.) A low turn-out in the second round of legislative voting, on 20 January 1991, was attributed to popular unease as a result of the recent coup attempt. The most successful party, the FNCD, won a further nine seats in the Chambre des Députés, and an additional eight in the Sénat, thereby failing to secure an overall majority in the two legislative chambers.

Aristide was inaugurated as President on 7 February 1991. The new Head of State subsequently initiated proceedings to secure the extradition from France of ex-President Duvalier to face charges that included embezzlement, abuse of power and murder. Aristide also undertook the reform of the armed forces (in July Gen. (later Lt-Gen.) Raoul Cédras replaced Gen. Hérard Abraham as Commander-in-Chief). In February the new President nominated one of his close associates, René Garcia Préval, as Prime Minister.

On 30 September 1991 a military junta, led by Gen. Cédras, overthrew the Government. Following diplomatic intervention by the USA, France and Venezuela, Aristide was allowed to go into exile. The coup received international condemnation, and an almost immediate economic embargo was imposed on Haiti by the Organization of American States (OAS, see p. 360). Many hundreds of people were reported to have been killed during the coup, including the imprisoned Lafontant. On 7 October military units assembled 29 members of the legislature and coerced them into approving the appointment of Joseph Nerette as interim President, and several days later a new Cabinet was announced. The OAS, however, continued to recognize Aristide as the legitimate President.

During the following months the OAS attempted to negotiate a settlement. However, the two sides remained deadlocked over the conditions for Aristide's return, the main obstacles being Aristide's insistence that Cédras be imprisoned or exiled, and the legislature's demands for an immediate repeal of the OAS embargo and a general amnesty. In February 1992, following OAS-supervised talks in Washington, DC, USA, between Aristide and members of a Haitian legislative delegation, an agreement was signed providing for the installation of René Théodore, leader of the Mouvement pour la Reconstruction Nationale, as Prime Minister. He was to govern in close consultation with the exiled Aristide and facilitate his return. Aristide undertook to respect all decisions taken by the legislature since the coup of September 1991, and agreed to a general amnesty for the police and armed forces. The economic embargo imposed by the OAS was to be revoked on ratification of the agreement by the legislature. However, in mid-March 1992 politicians opposed to the accord were reportedly coerced into withdrawing from a joint session of the Sénat and the Chambre des Députés, leaving it inquorate. In late March, following an appeal by interim President Nerette, the Supreme Court declared the agreement null and void, on the grounds that it violated the Constitution by endangering the country's sovereignty. In response, the OAS increased economic sanctions against Haiti.

In May 1992, following a tripartite summit meeting involving the legislature, the Government and the armed forces, an agreement providing for a 'consensus government' was ratified by the Sénat. The agreement envisaged the appointment of a new Prime Minister and a multi-party government of national consensus to seek a solution to the political crisis and negotiate an end to the economic embargo. In June the legislature, in the absence of the FNCD (which boycotted the sessions), approved the nomination of Marc Bazin, of the MIDH, to be Prime Minister. Under the terms of the tripartite agreement, the presidency was left vacant, ostensibly to allow for Aristide's return, although commentators suggested that this was purely a political manoeuvre by the military-backed Government and that such an eventuality was unlikely. A Cabinet, comprising members of most major parties (with the exception of the FNCD), was installed, with the army retaining control of the interior and defence. The appointment of the new Government provoked world-wide condemnation.

In July 1992 a 10-member 'presidential commission' was appointed by Aristide to hold negotiations with what he termed the 'real forces' in Haiti, referring to the armed forces and the wealthy élite. In September the Government agreed to allow the presence of an 18-member OAS commission in Haiti to help to guarantee human rights, reduce violence and assess progress towards a resolution of the prevailing political crisis. In February 1993 a further agreement was reached with the OAS and the UN on sending another international civil commission comprising some 200 representatives.

In April 1993 the joint envoy of the UN and the OAS, Dante Caputo, visited Haiti to present a series of proposals for the restoration of democratic rule in Haiti. These provided for the resignation of the military high command in return for a full amnesty for those involved in the coup of 1991, and for the establishment of a government of consensus and the eventual reinstatement of Aristide. A sum of US $1,000m. in economic aid was to become available once democracy was restored. However, the proposals were rejected by Cédras.

In early June 1993 the USA imposed sanctions against Haiti. Shortly afterwards Bazin resigned as Prime Minister following a loss of support in the legislature. In late June, following the imposition of a world-wide petroleum and arms embargo by the UN Security Council, Cédras attended talks with Aristide on Governor's Island, New York, USA, under the auspices of the UN and the OAS. On 3 July the so-called Governor's Island peace accord was signed, delineating a 10-point agenda for Aristide's reinstatement. Under the terms of the accord the embargo was to be revoked following the installation of a new Prime Minister (to be appointed by Aristide), Cédras would retire and a new Commander-in-Chief of the armed forces would be appointed by Aristide, who would return to Haiti by 30 October. The accord was approved by Haiti's main political parties, and a six-month political 'truce' was agreed to facilitate the transition. Legislation providing for a series of political and institutional reforms, as required under the terms of the accord, was to be enacted, including provision for the transfer of the police force to civilian control.

In August 1993 the legislature ratified the appointment by Aristide of Robert Malval as Prime Minister. The UN Security Council subsequently suspended its petroleum and arms embargo. In September a concerted campaign of political violence and intimidation by police auxiliaries, known as 'attachés', threatened to undermine the Governor's Island accord. Demands made by Malval that the attachés be disbanded were ignored by the chief of police, Col Joseph Michel François. With the upsurge of a Duvalierist tendency, largely embodied by the attachés, a new political party, the Front Revolutionnaire pour l'Avancement et le Progrès d'Haïti (FRAPH), was founded in opposition to any attempt to reinstate Aristide. In late September the UN Security Council approved a resolution providing for the immediate deployment of a lightly armed UN Mission In Haiti (UNMIH, renamed UN Support Mission in Haiti in June 1996, UN Transition Mission in Haiti in July 1997, and UN Civilian Police Mission in Haiti—MIPONUH—in November 1997). A new unarmed mission, the International Civilian Support Mission in Haiti, superseded MIPONUH in March 2000, comprising 150 members, to advise in the creation of a new police force and the modernization of the army. The new mission's mandate ended on 6 February 2001.

In October 1993, in violation of the Governor's Island accord, Cédras and François refused to resign their posts, asserting that the terms of the amnesty offered by Aristide were not sufficiently broad. In that month the campaign of political violence by the attachés escalated. A US vessel transporting members of UNMIH was prevented from docking at Port-au-Prince, and its arrival prompted violent demonstrations of defiance by the attachés. Several days later the Minister of Justice, Guy Malary, was assassinated. In response, the US Government ordered six warships into Haitian territorial waters to enforce the reimposed UN embargo. As a result of the instability, the UN/OAS international civil commission and other foreign government personnel were evacuated to the Dominican Republic.

In December 1993 Malval officially resigned as Prime Minister. In discussions with the US Government held earlier in the month, Malval announced a new initiative for a National Salvation Conference, involving multi-sector negotiations (to include the military) on a return to democratic rule. However, Aristide rejected the plans, proposing instead a National Reconciliation Conference, excluding the military, which took place in Miami, USA, in mid-January 1994. Following the military regime's failure to meet the revised UN deadline of 15 January to comply with the terms of the Governor's Island accord, in late January the USA unilaterally imposed further sanctions denying officers of the military regime access to assets held in the USA and cancelling their travel visas. In that month members of the UN/OAS international civil commission began to return to Haiti.

In February 1994 a 13-member faction of the Sénat—including eight members elected in January 1993 in partial legislative elections condemned as illegal by the USA and UN and widely regarded as an attempt by the military regime to legitimize its rule—appointed Bernard Sansaricq as President of the Sénat. However, the incumbent President of the Sénat, Firmin Jean-Louis, did not relinquish his position and continued to be recognized by the international community. In the same month Aristide twice rejected peace plans drafted by the USA, demanding instead the implementation of the Governor's Island accord.

In April 1994 the US Government abandoned its attempts to effect a compromise solution to the crisis in Haiti in favour of the implementation of more rigorous economic sanctions with a view to forcing the military regime to relinquish power. In May the UN Security Council approved a resolution introducing sanctions banning all international trade with Haiti, excluding food and medicine, reducing air links with the country and preventing members of the regime from gaining access to assets held outside Haiti.

In early 1994 the 13-member faction of the Sénat led by Bernard Sansaricq declared the presidency of the Republic vacant, invoking Article 149 of the Constitution, which provides that, in case of prolonged absence by the Head of State, the position may be assumed by the President of the Court of Cassation. In May, with the support of the armed forces, the 13 Senators and 30 members of the Chambre des Députés—not a sufficient number to form a quorum—appointed the President of the Court of Cassation, Emile Jonassaint, provisional President of the Republic. He subsequently appointed a new Cabinet. The appointment of the Jonassaint administration was denounced as illegal by the international community and by the outgoing acting Prime Minister, Malval. In the following month, the USA increased sanctions against Haiti.

In July 1994 the Haitian junta issued an order providing for the expulsion of the UN/OAS international civil commission. The order was immediately condemned by the UN Security Council. On 31 July the UN Security Council passed a resolution authorizing 'all necessary means' to remove the military regime from power. The terms of the resolution also provided for a UN peace-keeping force to be deployed once stability had been achieved, to remain in Haiti until February 1996, when Aristide's presidential term expired. In August the UN officially abandoned efforts to effect a peaceful solution to the crisis in Haiti. In the same month leaders of the Caribbean Community and Common Market (CARICOM, see p. 196) agreed to support a US-led military invasion.

On 19 September 1994 a nominally multinational force composed almost entirely of US troops began a peaceful occupation of Haiti. The occupation followed the diplomatic efforts of a mission led by former US President Jimmy Carter, which resulted in a compromise agreement, thus narrowly avoiding a full-scale invasion. Under the terms of the agreement, the Haitian security forces were to co-operate with the multilateral force in effecting a transition to civilian rule. All sanctions were to be lifted and the military junta granted 'early and honourable retirement' following legislative approval of a general amnesty law, or by 15 October at the latest (the date when Aristide was to return from exile to resume his presidency). The agreement did not, however, require the junta's departure from Haiti, nor did it address the reform of the security forces. Those legislators elected illegally in January 1993 were replaced by legislators returning from exile in the USA. Following the occupation, acts of violence by the Haitian police against supporters of Aristide led to a modification of the rules of operation of the multinational force, allowing for intervention to curb the violence. In late September the USA announced the suspension of its unilateral sanctions, although the Haitian military's assets in the USA remained frozen. A few days later the UN Security Council approved a resolution ending all sanctions against Haiti with effect from the day after the return of Aristide.

In early October 1994 Aristide signed a decree authorizing legislation, approved by the legislature that month, for the amnesty of those involved in the coup of September 1991. Cédras and the Chief of Staff of the army, Brig.-Gen. Philippe Biamby, promptly went into exile in Panama, whilst François was reported to have already fled to the Dominican Republic, where he was granted asylum. Later that month the USA formally ended its freeze on the assets of the Haitian military regime, estimated to be worth some US $79m. On 12 October Robert Malval resumed office as interim Prime Minister following the resignation of the Jonassaint administration. Aristide returned to Haiti on 15 October to resume his presidency and on 25 October appointed Smarck Michel as premier. He also appointed Gen. Jean-Claude Duperval provisional Commander-in-Chief of the armed forces and Gen. Bernardin Poisson Chief of Staff of the army. A new Cabinet, comprising mainly members of the pro-Aristide Organisation Politique Lavalas (OPL), was inaugurated on 8 November. In mid-November Gen. Poisson succeeded Gen. Duperval as Commander-in-Chief of the armed forces. Later that month the legislature approved the separation of the police from the army.

In December 1994 the formation of a new CEP, responsible for organizing and supervising the forthcoming legislative, local and municipal elections, was completed. However, owing to procedural delays the elections were thought unlikely to be held until mid-1995, leaving a period of legislative inactivity between the end of the current legislative term, ending in January 1995, and the inauguration of a new legislature, at a time when reform would be vital to the successful transition to peaceful civilian rule. In mid-December 1994 Aristide authorized the creation of a national commission of truth and justice to investigate past human rights violations, and ordered the reduction of the armed forces to 1,500 (from an estimated combined army and police force of 7,000–7,500). In the following month two commissions were established for the restructuring of the armed forces and the new civilian police force.

In January 1995 US military commanders certified that the situation in Haiti was sufficiently stable to enable the transfer of authority to the UN. On 30 January the UN Security Council adopted a resolution authorizing the deployment of a UN force of 6,000 troops and 900 civil police to succeed the incumbent multinational force. The UN force, entitled (like that deployed in 1993) the UN Mission in Haiti (UNMIH), was to be led by a US commander and include some 2,400 US troops. It was to be responsible for reducing the strength of the army and training both the army and the 4,000-strong (subsequently increased to 6,000) civilian police force, as well as maintaining the 'secure and stable' environment.

On 31 March 1995, against a background of increasing violence and criticism at the inadequacy of the interim police force, authority was officially transferred from the multinational force to UNMIH. The security situation deteriorated further in April, revealing widespread discontent at high prices, unemployment and the planned privatization of state enterprises. In late April Aristide announced that, following the election of the new legislature, he would seek a constitutional amendment providing for the abolition of the armed forces. (The armed forces were subsequently disbanded, although the constitutional amendment providing for their official abolition could not be approved until the end of the new legislative term.)

The first round of legislative, local and municipal elections (including elections to 18 of the 27 seats in the Sénat, all 83 seats in the Chambre des Députés, 125 mayorships and 555 local councils) were held on 25 June 1995. Owing to administrative failures and isolated incidents of violence and intimidation, voting continued into the following day. Despite the extension, thousands of intending voters were unable to participate, and a further, complementary poll was to be scheduled. The widespread irregularities prompted several opposition parties to demand the annulment of the elections and the dissolution of the CEP, which many perceived as too closely associated with the OPL, the party with majority representation in the Government. The official election results, which were released in mid-July, indicated that all of the 21 seats so far decided had been won by the Plateforme Politique Lavalas (PPL), a three-party electoral alliance comprising the OPL, the Mouvement pour l'Organisation du Pays and the Pati Louvri Baryè. The results were rejected by the majority of opposition parties, which announced a boycott of the electoral process.

In early August 1995 the FNCD, MIDH and the Parti National Progressiste Révolutionnaire withdrew their respective representatives from the Government, in protest at the absence of a resolution to the electoral dispute. The Minister of Culture, Jean-Claude Bajeux, of the Congrès National des Movements Démocratiques (KONAKOM) resisted his party's demand that he resign, and remained the sole opposition member in the Cabinet. On 13 August, following successive postponements, the complementary elections, for voters who had been denied the opportunity to vote on 25 June, were conducted in 21 districts. A further 17 seats were decided, all of which were won by the PPL. In late August the US Government presented a plan aimed at resolving the electoral dispute. However, its proposals, which included the annulment of the first round elections in many areas, were rejected by the CEP. The second round of voting was held on 17 September, despite the boycott that was maintained by the main opposition parties, and resulted in further large gains for the PPL, which won 17 of the 18 contested seats in the 27-member Sénat and 68 seats in the 83-member Chambre des Députés. The remaining contested seats were won mainly by independent candidates. In October Michel resigned as Prime Minister, and was succeeded by the Minister of Foreign Affairs, Claudette Werleigh.

In November 1995, despite extensive popular support for Aristide to continue in office for a further three years (to compensate for those years spent in exile), the President confirmed that he would leave office in February 1996. At a presidential election held on 17 December 1995, which was boycotted by all the main opposition parties except KONAKOM, the candidate endorsed by Aristide, René Préval (Prime Minister between February and September 1991), was elected with some 88% of the votes cast. He was inaugurated as President on 7 February 1996, and later that month the legislature approved the appointment of Rosny Smarth as Prime Minister. A new Cabinet was sworn in on 6 March.

The months following the inauguration of the Smarth administration were marked by a high incidence of violence in the capital. In mid-August 1996, amid a climate of unrest and general hostility towards government economic policy, in particular plans for the privatization of state enterprises, a series of armed attacks were conducted against public buildings. The attacks followed the arrest that month, at the headquarters of the right-wing Mobilisation pour le Développement National (MDN), of some 20 former officers of the armed forces who were accused of plotting against the Government. In August two leading members of the MDN were murdered by unidentified gunmen. Opposition politicians accused the Government of responsibility for the killings, and evidence emerged implicating members of the presidential guard in the murders. In mid-September, on the advice of the US Government, Préval dismissed the head of the presidential guard and initiated a reorganization of the unit.

In November 1996, as a result of diverging interests within the PPL, Aristide officially established a new political party, La Fanmi Lavalas (FL), which, it was anticipated, would promote his candidacy for the next presidential election. Aristide had openly expressed his opposition to Préval's adoption of economic policies proposed by the IMF, notably the privatization of state enterprises. Unrest continued, and in mid-January 1997 a general strike, in support of demands for the resignation of the Smarth administration and the reversal of the planned divestment of state enterprises, received considerable support.

On 6 April 1997 partial legislative elections were held for nine of the 27 seats in the Sénat and two seats in the Chambre des Députés, as well as elections to local councils. The elections were boycotted by many opposition parties, and less than 5% of the electorate participated in the poll. Of the legislative seats contested only two, in the Sénat, were decided, both of which were secured by candidates of the FL. The OPL, the majority party in the governing coalition, alleged that members of the CEP had manipulated the election results in favour of Aristide's party, and demanded the resignation of the CEP and the conduct of a fresh ballot. OAS observers of the poll supported the claims of electoral irregularities, and, following strong international pressure, the CEP postponed indefinitely the second round of the elections. The OPL had announced that it would boycott the second round elections.

In the light of mounting popular opposition, on 9 June 1997 Smarth resigned from office, although he remained Prime Minister in a caretaker capacity pending the appointment of a replacement. Smarth criticized the CEP for failing to annul the results of the April elections and thus perpetuating the electoral impasse. In the following month Préval nominated Ericq Pierre as Smarth's replacement, but his nomination was rejected by the Chambre des Députés. In September supporters of Aristide announced the formation of a new 25-member Anti-Neoliberal Bloc in the lower house. In the light of Préval's failure to nominate a candidate for Prime Minister who was acceptable to the legislature, on 20 October Smarth announced that he was to cease his role as caretaker Prime Minister.

In November 1997, in an effort to resolve the political crisis, Préval nominated Hervé Y. Denis, an economist and former Minister of Information, Culture and Co-ordination in the Government of Robert Malval, as Prime Minister. In addition, Préval announced the establishment of an electoral commission, comprising three independent legal experts, to resolve the electoral deadlock, and the resignation of six of the nine members of the CEP. The OPL, however, continued to demand the annulment of the April elections and the replacement of the entire CEP. In January 1998 the legislature formally announced its decision to reject the nomination of Denis. The FL subsequently rejected a proposal by the OPL for the creation of a body to mediate in the legislature and thus facilitate the appointment of a new Prime Minister.

In March 1998, following negotiations with the Anti-Neoliberal Bloc, the OPL (renamed the Organisation du Peuple en Lutte in February) withdrew its demands for the annulment of the April 1997 elections as a precondition for the approval of a new Prime Minister, and proposed three candidates. However, Préval subsequently renominated Denis: his candidacy was rejected by the legislature for a second time in April. In July Préval finally agreed to replace the CEP. Préval subsequently received the support of the OPL for the nomination of the incumbent Minister of National Education, Jacques Edouard Alexis, for Prime Minister. Conversely, the Anti-Neoliberal Bloc opposed the nomination of Alexis, who, it maintained, favoured the structural adjustment policies advocated by the IMF. In August the FL announced that it had formally gone into opposition to the Préval administration.

In November 1998 the Sénat voted to extend the legislature's current term to October 1999; under electoral legislation adopted in 1995, the term of office of legislators elected in that year's delayed vote had been shortened by one year in order to restore the constitutional timetable of elections, and was thus scheduled to end in January 1999. In December 1998 Alexis was finally declared eligible to assume the office of Prime Minister, subject to his nomination being approved by the legislature (which did not occur until November 2000). The decision had been delayed by a report by the state auditing board, subsequently declared inaccurate, which found irregularities in Alexis' tenure as Minister of National Education. On 11 January 1999 Préval announced that he would no longer recognize the legislature, rejecting the Sénat's earlier decision to extend its mandate, and declared that he would install a new government by presidential decree. In mid-January Préval withdrew parliamentary funding, prompting the legislature to seek a Supreme Court ruling on the constitutionality of the 1995 electoral law. Préval also entered into consultations with opposition parties in an effort to reach agreement on the composition of a new CEP. In February the Supreme Court postponed indefinitely a decision concerning the electoral law.

On 25 March 1999 Préval appointed by decree a new Cabinet headed by Alexis and including representatives of five small opposition parties that had negotiated an agreement with the President to end the political impasse. The OPL, which had ceased negotiations following the murder, in early March, of one of its leaders, was not included in the new administration. The party, which alleged that the killing had been perpetrated by supporters of Aristide, also stated that it would boycott any elections organized by the new CEP, which was appointed in that month. In May the Supreme Court refused to rule on the legality of Préval's decision to end the funding of the outgoing parliament. The OPL subsequently announced that it had accepted that the parliamentary term had ended and that it would participate in the forthcoming elections. In June the CEP announced that it would disregard the results of the flawed partial legislative elections of April 1997, and presented draft electoral legislation that envisaged the holding of legislative elections in November and December 1999. Préval criticized the CEP's decision concerning the 1997 elections, but in July 1999 he signed a decree annulling them. A new electoral law set 28 November as a provisional date for the first round of legislative and local elections; however, the elections were subsequently postponed, for logistical and financial reasons, on several occasions, prompting violent protests in the capital.

On 21 May 2000 the first round of legislative and municipal elections was held; an estimated 60% of the electorate participated. Opposition parties alleged that the results had been manipulated in favour of the FL, claims supported by OAS observers, and demanded the annulment of the election and the conduct of a fresh ballot. The CEP rejected these claims, but in mid-June the CEP President, Léon Manus, fled to the Dominican Republic, claiming that he had received death threats following his refusal to validate the first round results. His flight prompted demonstrations by Aristide supporters, demanding the publication of the results. According to official first round results, the FL won 16 of the 19 contested seats in the Sénat, and 26 of the 83 seats in the lower house. The results were criticized as inaccurate by the UN, the OAS and numerous foreign governments. Nevertheless, a second round of voting went ahead on 9 July. Opposition protests and a boycott by the 15-party opposition coalition, the Convergence Démocratique (CD), resulted in a low voter turn-out (an estimated 10%) and a high incidence of violence. According to official results, the FL won 72 seats in the Chambre des Députés and 18 of the 19 seats contested in the 27-seat upper house (the Pati Louvri Baryè won one seat). The party also secured control of some 80% of the local councils. In September Préval announced that elections to the presidency and to renew the remaining eight senate seats would be held in November. The CD immediately announced its intention to boycott the elections.

In mid-October 2000 it was revealed that an attempt by members of the police force to overthrow the Government had been uncovered. The seven police officers accused of planning the coup fled to the Dominican Republic, and were subsequently granted asylum in Ecuador. The Government reacted by dismissing several senior police officers. In November a court sentenced Gen. Cédras and 36 other senior army officers to life imprisonment with hard labour, *in absentia*, for their role in the murders of 15 people in the shanty town of Raboteau in May 1994.

At the presidential election of 26 November 2000, Aristide was elected with some 92% of the votes cast; the remaining six candidates all won less than 2% of the ballot. According to official estimates some 61% of the electorate voted, although opposition leaders claimed a far lower participation. The only official observer mission, from CARICOM, estimated a 30% voter turn-out. In concurrently held partial legislative elections, the FL also won the remaining eight seats in the Sénat, and the one remaining seat in the Chambre des Députés.

An eight-member Transition Committee was established in December 2000 to oversee the smooth transfer of power to Aristide, who was to take office on 7 February 2001. However, on 7 December the CD announced the formation of an alternative, provisional Government, known as the Front Alternatif, with the intention of holding fresh elections within two years. The announcement provoked widespread violent demonstrations by Aristide supporters. In early February 2001 the CD further announced that this Front Alternatif was to be headed by Gérard Gourgue. Discussions between the President-elect and opposition leaders ended without agreement. On 15 February seven of the Senators controversially awarded seats in the May 2000 election resigned. Two days after his inauguration, President Aristide named Jean-Marie Chérestal, a former Minister of Finance, as Prime Minister, and in early March a new Cabinet was appointed. The CD responded by calling for a month of anti-Government protests. In the same month, in an attempt to end the political impasse, Aristide appointed a new nine-member CEP to investigate the results of the disputed May 2000 elections. The CD was not represented on the Council. In March it was announced that legislative elections would be held one year early, in November 2002, in order to satisfy international and opposition criticism and to restore the flow of foreign aid, suspended since May 2000. (As well as an end to the political crisis and a strengthening of the democratic process, the resumption of aid was also dependent on Haiti implementing anti-drugs-trafficking measures and improving its human rights record.) Three days later violent protests broke out in Port-au-Prince, in which three people died and dozens were injured. Violence continued over the following months and a number of opposition party members were arrested on treason and terrorism charges. In July, following further OAS mediation, the Government stated that legislative and local elections would be held in 2002, although a timetable remained to be agreed; an accord was also reached on the composition of the new CEP. The CEP would additionally organize an election to the seven Sénat seats vacated in February.

Political violence continued throughout 2001. In late July an attempted *coup d'état*, responsibility for which was attributed to former members of the armed forces, resulted in the deaths of six police officers. In October the FL announced the resumption of OAS-mediated talks with the opposition, but these again ended without a resolution. In early November three people were killed during violent demonstrations in the La Saline district of Port-au-Prince and one week later the CD organized a widely observed national strike in protest at the deteriorating economic situation. Then, on 18 December, an armed group, allegedly composed of former members of the armed forces, attacked the presidential palace. At least four people were killed in the coup attempt, which prompted further outbreaks of violence as hundreds of government supporters attacked the homes and offices of opposition leaders in retaliation. The Government announced that former police chief Guy Philippe was wanted in connection with the palace attack; he subsequently fled the country. The opposition claimed that the coup attempt had been staged by the Government in order to justify further repression, and demanded that a UN mission be deployed to monitor the situation. In July 2002 an OAS Commission of Inquiry reported that no attempted coup had taken place and chastised the Government for its reluctance to punish those of its supporters who engaged in violence against the opposition.

On 23 January 2002, amid continuing political and economic turmoil, Prime Minister Chérestal resigned his post, following allegations of corruption, and criticism over his inability to resolve the crisis. On 15 March Aristide appointed Sénat speaker and prominent FL member, Yvon Neptune, as Prime Minister. Neptune subsequently reshuffled his Cabinet, removing several ministers who had attracted controversy; he signalled his commitment to encouraging dialogue to end the political stalemate by appointing Marc Bazin as Minister without Portfolio with specific responsibility for negotiations with the opposition. (Bazin resigned in September of that year, claiming that his job had become impossible.) In June Aristide met with opposition leaders for the first time in two years, but the talks achieved little progress. Further OAS-mediated dialogue in the following month also failed to make any significant headway. Meanwhile, Haiti's accession to full membership of CARICOM in July increased international pressure on Aristide to bring about an end to political instability in the country and allow new elections to take place. In August violent demonstrations occurred in the northern city of Gonaïves when the political activist Amiot Métayer escaped from prison, together with over 100 other inmates. Métayer was one of several Government supporters imprisoned for damaging the homes of opposition members following the attack on the presidential palace in December 2001.

In late 2002 the ongoing political unrest in the country intensified as the November deadline for the creation of a new CEP passed unfulfilled. On 17 November some 15,000 people in Cap-Haïtien participated in the largest anti-Government rally held in the country since the re-election of President Aristide in 2000. Meanwhile, shortly afterwards supporters of Aristide rioted in Port-au-Prince to protest against the anti-Government rallies. President Aristide refused to resign, stating that he believed the crisis could best be resolved through the formation of a CEP and the holding of new elections. While the opposition continued to refuse to nominate representatives to the CEP, five of the nation's civil groups chose representatives in November, having initially refused to do so until the Government demonstrated its commitment to guaranteeing public safety. In early December a general strike led by the opposition was joined by members of Haiti's private sector. During an address to his supporters in Les Cayes, President Aristide accused the opposition of attempting to orchestrate a coup. Meanwhile, opposition parties united in calling for the resignation of Aristide as the demonstrations continued. In December 2002, frustrated by the continued political instability, some 184 business and civil society organizations, led by a local businessman, André Apaid, agreed to form the 'Group of 184'. The grouping subsequently emerged as a major element of the opposition to Aristide.

In 2003 the political stalemate between the Government and the opposition remained unresolved, despite further efforts by the OAS to mediate in the dispute. Most nominees to the nine-member CEP refused to assume their posts, claiming that they were unconvinced that the Government would not resort to fraudulent practices in future legislative elections, as it had done in 2000. The CD and other opposition groups continued to insist that their participation in any elections would be conditional upon the resignation of President Aristide. In June the newly appointed Chief of Police, Jean-Robert Faveur, resigned after only two weeks in the post, complaining of widespread corruption. He subsequently claimed that his life was in danger and fled to the USA. He was replaced by Jocelyne Pierre, the head of the Port-au-Prince civil court. In October clashes occurred between police and demonstrators in Gonaïves, following the murder of Amiot Métayer in the previous month; at least four people died as a result of the violence. In December three ministers resigned in protest at the Government's increasing use of violence to suppress the continuing demonstrations.

In November 2003, in an attempt to end the ongoing political crisis, the Roman Catholic Bishops' Conference of Haiti called for the legislature to appoint a broadly representative council to advise President Aristide and thus to enable new elections to be held. In January 2004 the USA declared its support for the proposal, which was, however, later withdrawn by the Bishops' Conference, owing to the deterioration of the political situation. Early in the same month the opposition organized a 48-hour general strike as violent anti-Government protests continued.

On 12 January 2004 the mandates of all the members of the Chambre des Députés and 12 of the 27 members of the Sénat expired, leaving Haiti effectively without a legislature and entitling President Aristide to rule by decree. The President subsequently pledged to hold legislative elections within six months, an offer quickly rejected by the Haitian opposition. Meanwhile, another general strike was held as public demonstrations demanding the President's resignation continued. Later in the same month, in an attempt to resolve the escalating political crisis, members of CARICOM met with leading members of the Haitian opposition in the Bahamas. CARICOM threatened to impose economic sanctions on Haiti unless President Aristide satisfied a number of conditions, including the formation of a new electoral council and the holding of legislative elections. Aristide appeared to accept the conditions, stating that he was prepared to enter into constructive dialogue with the opposition, and agreed to meet with opposition members and CARICOM leaders later that month. Following the meeting, which was held in Kingston, Jamaica, Aristide agreed to implement a number of reforms within the following two months, including: nominating an independent prime minister; reforming the police force; creating a neutral electoral council; releasing illegally imprisoned members of the opposition; and disarming his supporters.

In February 2004 Prime Minister Neptune accused the opposition of attempting to orchestrate a coup and demanded that opposition parties actively discourage the ongoing demonstrations. However, as violent protests escalated across the country, anti-Government forces, led by Buter Métayer, the brother of Amiot Métayer, took control of Gonaïves and, subsequently, several other cities in the north of the country. Shortly afterwards, former members of the Haitian armed forces, led by ex-police chief Guy Philippe and the former deputy commander of the FRAPH, Louis-Jodel Chamblain, returned from exile in the Dominican Republic to participate in the insurrection, joining with the rebels to form the Front pour la Libération et la Reconstruction Nationales (FLRN). President Aristide appealed to the international community for assistance in suppressing the rebellion. A plan to end the violence, proposed by France, CARICOM and the OAS, was subsequently accepted by Aristide but rejected by the opposition as it failed to provide for the President's departure. Meanwhile, the uprising continued to gather momentum as the insurgents advanced towards the capital, Port-au-Prince, insisting that they would attack unless Aristide tendered his resignation. Cap-Haïtien had been brought under rebel control on 22 February. At a meeting of the UN Security Council in late February, Caribbean nations called for a multilateral force to be sent to the country in an attempt to bring an end to the violence. However, the USA and France insisted that a political settlement would have to be reached before any forces were deployed to Haiti.

President Aristide finally resigned on 29 February 2004, largely owing to increasing international pressure, and fled to the Central African Republic, where he claimed he had been unconstitutionally removed from office by the USA. The USA maintained that Aristide had requested assistance to leave Haiti. In line with the provisions made by the Constitution, the President of the Supreme Court, Boniface Alexandre, was sworn in as interim President. On the same day the UN Security Council, acting in response to a request from Alexandre, authorized the establishment of a Multinational Interim Force (MIF) to help to secure law and order prior to the deployment of a larger peace-keeping mission. The MIF eventually comprised around 3,600 troops from the USA, France, Canada and Chile. On 9 March Alexandre and the recently established Council of Elders appointed Gérard Latortue, an economist who had briefly served as Minister of Foreign Affairs under Leslie Manigat in 1988, as Prime Minister. One week later Latortue appointed a new Government, which was composed of independents and technocrats and which excluded any members from the main political parties. The installation of the new Cabinet was generally welcomed by the international community, although CARICOM refused to recognize the Latortue Government, and subsequently suspended Haiti's participation in the councils of the Community. In mid-March Aristide arrived in Jamaica at the invitation of the Government of P. J. Patterson; his arrival prompted Latortue to suspend diplomatic relations with Jamaica in protest.

In early April 2004 Latortue, the seven members of the Council of Elders, representatives of the main political organizations (with the exception of the FL) and leaders of civil society organizations signed an agreement on political transition, which provided for the organization of presidential, legislative and municipal elections in 2005, leading to the inauguration of a new administration by February 2006. The agreement also provided for a new CEP, which was sworn in in May 2004, and envisaged the creation of an anti-corruption unit. The FL refused to designate a representative to the CEP, demanding that alleged persecution and repression of its supporters cease. In the same month Jocelerme Privert, the former Minister of the Interior, was arrested on suspicion of having ordered the killing of a number of anti-Aristide protesters in February.

Louis-Jodel Chamblain surrendered to the authorities in late April 2004 to be retried for crimes of which he had been convicted *in absentia*: the murder of Antoine Izmery, an associate of Aristide, in 1993 and involvement in the killings of several people in Raboteau in 1994. In August 2004 Chamblain and his co-defendant, Jackson Joanis, a former police chief in Port-au-Prince, were acquitted of the murder of Izmery. However, the US Department of State and human rights organizations were severely critical of the conduct of the retrial and the haste with which it had been organized.

In a report to the UN Security Council presented in April 2004, the Secretary-General of the organization, Kofi Annan, accused Aristide of having formed an alliance with armed groups, known as *chimères*, in order to reinforce his position in power and of having condoned their engagement in organized crime, including drugs-smuggling. Aristide went into exile in South Africa at the end of May, having been offered temporary political asylum by President Thabo Mbeki.

A UN peace-keeping force, the UN Stabilization Mission in Haiti (MINUSTAH), was officially established on 1 June 2004 and replaced the MIF later that month, following a transitional period. MINUSTAH, which had an authorized strength of 6,700 military personnel and 1,622 civilian police, was to assist the interim administration with preparations for elections and the disarmament and demobilization of armed militias. Meanwhile, the OAS General Assembly approved a resolution declaring Aristide's removal from power to be unconstitutional, although it continued to recognize Latortue's Government. In mid-June Latortue announced the Government's intention to hold local and legislative elections in September 2005, followed by a presidential election in November of that year.

Former Prime Minister Neptune was arrested in late June 2004 in connection with the deaths of demonstrators in the uprising against Aristide's administration in February. In July the Latortue Government issued a deadline of 15 September for armed groups to surrender their weapons. The disarmament of the rebels was one of CARICOM's principal demands, and a five-member ministerial delegation from the Community arrived in Port-au-Prince the day after the deadline was announced to discuss developments in Haiti. International donors at a conference sponsored by the World Bank in Washington, DC, in mid-July pledged US $1,080m. in development aid for Haiti over the period 2004–06. In August 2004 former President Manigat declared his intention to contest the forthcoming presidential election as the candidate of the RDNP. The 15 September deadline for the surrender of weapons passed unfulfilled. A few days earlier the UN Security Council had urged the Government to accelerate the establishment and implementation of a national disarmament, demobilization and reintegration programme. Latortue responded by accusing MINUSTAH of failing adequately to counter insecurity in the country. More than 2,000 people were killed in extensive flooding in September. Rescue efforts were reportedly hindered by the fact that many of the worst affected areas in the north of the country remained effectively under the control of armed groups.

At the end of September 2004 violence broke out between the police and supporters of Aristide at a rally in Port-au-Prince in support of the former President's return from exile. Clashes continued, and by early November at least 80 people had been killed. Tensions were exacerbated by the arrival in the capital of more than 200 former soldiers, who demanded to be allowed to confront the so-called *chimères*. Three members of the FL, including the former President of the Sénat, Yvon Feuillé, were arrested in early October on suspicion of inciting the violence and possessing illegal firearms, and 75 suspected members of the *chimères* were also detained by the national police and MINUSTAH troops in a joint operation. Latortue accused Aristide of co-ordinating the uprising from exile. By mid-October only around 2,100 troops of the 6,700-strong authorized MINUSTAH force had actually been deployed. The deteriorating security situation prompted the IMF to withdraw its country representative from Haiti and to postpone a planned mission to discuss the interim Government's request for emergency post-conflict assistance.

In early November 2004 the President of the CEP, Roselaure Julien, resigned, claiming that considerable pressure had been exerted on her, particularly by the 'Group of 184', to allow manipulation of the electoral process. In the middle of the month a five-member Anti-Corruption Commission was established within the Ministry of Economy and Finance to investigate alleged corruption between February 2001 and February 2004, as envisaged in the agreement on political transition signed in April. At the Rio Group summit in Brazil in early November 2004 the President of the Dominican Republic, Leonel Fernández Reyna, was one of several heads of state to propose Aristide's inclusion in talks on Haiti's political future, a suggestion that was strongly opposed by Latortue's administration, the USA and France. A few days later, following a meeting in Trinidad and Tobago, CARICOM issued a 'consensus statement' reaffirming its decision not to recognize Latortue's Government. In late November the UN Security Council approved the extension of MINUSTAH's mandate until 1 June 2005. In December 2004, amid continuing political violence and civil unrest, MINUSTAH troops entered the Cité Soleil area of Port-au-Prince, a stronghold of the pro-Aristide gangs, and successfully seized control of two police stations and other official buildings that had been occupied by the *chimères* for several months; it was reported that six people were killed during the operation. Meanwhile, following pressure from the UN Secretary-General to free politicians detained without formal charge, the authorities provisionally released the three FL members arrested in early October.

In early January 2005 CARICOM announced that Haiti's participation in the Community's councils would not resume until elections had been held and democracy restored. In late January the CEP, under its newly appointed President, Pierre-Richard Duchemin, announced a timetable for the forthcoming elections: the municipal elections were to take place on 9 October, followed by legislative and presidential elections in two rounds, on 13 November and 18 December. A permanent register of voters was to be compiled prior to the elections, and national identity cards were to be issued. It was hoped that proposed mediation by the African Union (see p. 164) would result in the participation of the FL, which continued to demand the release of former officials of the Aristide administration, such as Yvon Neptune and Jocelerme Privert, and other 'political' prisoners. Latortue had earlier announced that he and his cabinet ministers would not contest the presidency. In early February the Government created a National Disarmament Commission to facilitate and monitor the recovery of illegal weapons. (According to a report released by the National Coalition for Human Rights, 403 people—384 civilians and 19 police officers—had been shot dead in Port-au-Prince since the end of September 2004.) On the same day Latortue effected a minor cabinet reshuffle, notably appointing Georges Moïse as Minister of the Interior and National Security, to replace Gen. (retd) Hérard Abraham, who became Minister of Foreign Affairs and Religion.

A sharp escalation in fighting between MINUSTAH troops and rebel groups was evident from March 2005. Many of the rebels who had helped to oust Aristide from power had subsequently turned against the interim Government. In March two UN peace-keeping troops were killed in a gun battle with rebels. In April a UN peace-keeper from the Philippines was shot dead while helping to set up a checkpoint in Cité Soleil. In the same month two prominent rebel leaders, Remissainthe Ravix and Jean Anthony, were killed following an exchange of gunfire with police; in a separate confrontation a few days later at least 20 rebels were killed. The interim Government denied claims from local residents and human rights organizations alike that there had been any civilian fatalities. In April the UN Security Council dispatched a mission to Haiti to assess the situation therein; in the ensuing report, published in May, the Council reported that the security situation had 'gradually improved' since 2004, but highlighted the need for continued international assistance if social and political progress were to be maintained.

In May 2005 Yvon Neptune was formally charged, 11 months after being arrested, for his alleged role in political killings during the uprising against Aristide's administration; in the previous month Neptune had begun a hunger strike to protest against his detainment without charge. Human rights organizations claimed that hundreds of Aristide supporters had similarly been detained without charge for almost a year.

In early June 2005 Paul-Henri Mourral, the French honorary consul, was shot dead and numerous others were also killed as gangs ran amok in the capital. Later that month the Prime Minister effected a minor cabinet reorganization, in which three new government ministers were appointed. Henri Marge Dorléans was appointed Minister of Justice and Public Security in place of Bernard Gousse, who had resigned earlier in the month following prolonged and widespread criticism of both his harsh treatment of Aristide supporters and of his lenience towards rebels. Paul Gustave Magloire replaced Georges Moïse as Minister of the Interior and National Security, and Franck Charles was appointed Minister of Social Affairs, in place of Pierre Claude Calixte.

In late June 2005 the UN Security Council decided both to extend MINUSTAH's mandate by a further eight months and to deploy an additional 1,000 peace-keeping troops to the country. In June and July MINUSTAH appeared to react to international censure regarding the effectiveness of its presence in the country by intensifying military operations against the rebel gangs. There were also reports that innocent civilians had been killed by UN troops, an allegation that MINUSTAH adamantly denied. In July about 1,000 protesters marched through the capital to protest against the interim Government, MINUSTAH and the collective failure of both to address adequately the security situation within Haiti. (The protest was catalysed by the murder earlier that month of the prominent Haitian journalist Jacques Roche, at whose funeral the Minister of Culture and Communications, Magalie Comeau Denis, had alleged that Aristide supporters had orchestrated the killing in an attempt to disrupt the electoral process.)

In August 2005 local elections, scheduled to take place in October of that year, were postponed until December, so as to allow the authorities to concentrate on preparations for legislative and presidential elections, the scheduled date of which was brought forward by a week, to 6 November. In September, however, it was announced that legislative and presidential elections were to be delayed to 20 November, on account of extremely low voter registration, divisions in the electoral council and general disorganization. The elections were further postponed on three subsequent occasions, with a revised date of 7 February eventually being announced in January 2006; at the same time Latortue also announced that he was to resign as Prime Minister on 7 February, regardless of when elections were finally held.

Meanwhile, in October 2005 the CEP published its final list of 35 presidential candidates; one notable absentee from the list was Gérard Jean-Juste, a Roman Catholic priest imprisoned for his alleged role in the murder of Jacques Roche; the FL's attempt to register Jean-Juste as its presidential nominee had been denounced as 'unconstitutional' by the CEP as Jean-Juste had been unable to register in person. The FL had threatened to withdraw from the electoral process if Jean-Juste was not released from prison. However, Marc Bazin, supported by the FL leadership, and former President Préval, representing Fwon Lespwa—a self-created party—but supported by the FL's grassroots, were both included on the CEP's list of accepted candidates.

In January 2006 the chief of MINUSTAH, the Brazilian Gen. Urano Teixera Da Matta Bacellar, was found dead in his hotel room; he was believed to have committed suicide. Gen. José Elito

Carvalho de Siqueira, another Brazilian, was selected as his replacement. In the same month Préval's campaign headquarters, located in the town of St Marc, were set on fire, serving as a reminder to the authorities of the difficulties that they were likely to continue to face in the weeks preceding the elections. In late January Jean-Juste was temporarily released from prison to receive medical treatment in the USA; the murder charges against him were dismissed, but he still faced charges of involvement in illegal gang activity and of possessing illegal weapons.

On 7 February 2006 presidential and legislative elections were finally held, despite widespread fears that they would again have to be postponed, largely owing to poor administrative preparations and to the unstable security situation. Turn-out was higher than expected, at 60% of the total electorate, in the presidential poll, and the much-feared violence was largely avoided. Initial reports suggested that the favourite, Préval, had secured a convincing victory; however, after all the votes had been counted it was announced that he had obtained 49% of the vote—far more than any other candidate, but marginally short of the overall majority required to avoid a second round of voting. Incensed by what they perceived to be an attempt by the interim Government to force a run-off vote, and with tempers further inflamed by the discovery of thousands of burnt ballot papers (many of which were reported to be marked in favour of Préval) in a dump near Port-au-Prince, thousands of Préval supporters marched through the capital in protest; at least one man was killed and many others were wounded during clashes between protesters and UN troops. Préval warned of more violent protests from his supporters if a second poll was required. Following calls from the UN Security Council, and amid allegations of vote manipulation from two members of the CEP itself, the interim Government ordered that the publication of official results be halted until a full inquiry could be held into the allegations of electoral fraud. However, it was subsequently announced on 16 February that Préval had in fact secured an outright victory and was consequently to be declared President. The announcement followed emergency talks between the interim Government and electoral officials, during which it was agreed to share out the 91,219 blank ballots (4.4% of the total votes cast) proportionately among the candidates, thereby increasing Préval's percentage of the vote to 51.2%. The RDNP representative, former President Leslie Manigat—the second placed candidate (with only 12.4% of the vote)—denounced the outcome, as did the nominee of the Respè coalition, Charles Henri Baker, who was placed third (with 8.2% of the vote). The international community—including, significantly, the UN, CARICOM, the OAS and the USA—did, however, recognize Préval's victory. Following a delay to the scheduled inauguration date of 29 March, caused by the postponement of the second round of the legislative ballot (see below), Préval was formally sworn into office on 14 May.

Elections to a newly enlarged 30-seat Sénat and 99-seat Chambre des Députés were also held on 7 February 2006. However, most of the results were inconclusive, necessitating a second round of voting, to be held on 19 March. This was subsequently postponed until 21 April, a delay attributed by the CEP to the numerous claims of voting irregularities from the first round, which had to be investigated before a second ballot could proceed. According to partial, provisional results following the second round of voting, Préval's Fwon Lespa won the largest number of seats in both legislative chambers (13 in the Sénat and 24 in the Chambre des Députés), although the party failed to secure a majority in either house. The Fusion des Sociaux-Démocrates Haïtiens alliance was placed second, with four seats in the upper house and 18 in the lower chamber, while the OPL won three senate seats and 11 seats in the Chambre des Députés.

Following the proclamation of Préval's victory, in February 2006 former President Aristide announced his intention to return to Haiti at the earliest opportunity, although he ruled out the possibility of a return to the political arena. Préval stated publicly that as the Constitution decreed that no Haitian required a visa to enter the country, Aristide was free to return. International observers expressed doubts about the wisdom of the former leader's return, however, suggesting that his presence could further destabilize the country. In April the South African authorities declared that Aristide would not be returned to Haiti without agreement first having been reached between the Haitian and South African authorities.

Shortly after his inauguration, President Préval nominated Jacques-Edouard Alexis for the position of Prime Minister. The proposed return of Alexis to his former role was subsequently approved by both legislative chambers and on 9 June 2006 a new 18-member coalition cabinet, with representatives from six political parties, was sworn into office. Addressing the legislature in mid-June, Alexis declared that he would give close consideration to the plight of political prisoners enduring lengthy detentions without being put on trial. A few days later it was announced that Jocelerme Privert had been released on parole, and in late July Yvon Neptune was released on health and humanitarian grounds, although the charges against him were upheld. Meanwhile, the period of relative calm that had followed Préval's election victory was fractured in June, during which month a severe intensification of street violence and kidnappings prompted MINUSTAH to increase its presence in Port-au-Prince. Between June and August approximately 100 people were reported to have been killed in the capital, with a further 400 people thought to have been wounded. In mid-August the President and the Prime Minister issued an ultimatum to the gang leaders thought to be responsible for much of the violence, ordering them to hand in their weapons or be killed. In September the Government appointed a new commission designed to disarm gang members by offering them food, financial support and training.

During his election campaign, Préval had stated his desire for MINUSTAH to remain in the country for at least a further two years, and in August 2006 the UN Security Council voted unanimously to extend the mission's mandate until mid-February 2007. In November two Jordanian MINUSTAH peace-keepers were killed during clashes with armed gang members. In November and December angry protesters amassed in the streets of Cité Soleil to demonstrate against the continued presence of MINUSTAH in the country, accusing UN troops of using indiscriminate force to quell civil unrest and alleging that many innocent civilians had been killed or injured in the crossfire, claims that the UN mission adamantly refuted. Despite the opposition, in February MINUSTAH's mandate was extended for a further eight months, to October; in that month it was extended until October 2008. The UN Special Envoy to Haiti and Head of MINUSTAH, Luiz Carlos da Costa, stated in July that the force would need a further four years in order to guarantee the process of stabilization, including reform of the judicial and prison system and consolidation of the police force. Joint operations by MINUSTAH and Haitian police contributed to a significant improvement in security in Port-au-Prince during 2007, with a reported 70% reduction in kidnappings compared to the previous year; none the less, the UN reported an increase in abduction and violent crime in the first two months of 2008.

Municipal elections were held on 3 December 2006. Fwon Lespwa won 276 seats on the local Assemblés des Sections Communales (ASECS), while the Fusion des Sociaux-Démocrates Haïtiens secured 171 and the OPL obtained 159; Union Nationale Chrétienne pour la Reconstruction d'Haïti (UNCRH) and Alyans won 89 and 77 seats, respectively. Voter turn-out was poor, at less than 40% of the electorate. The system of ASECS had been established by the Constitution of 1987 as a mechanism for the election of judges, members of a permanent electoral council and other officials, but had never been fully implemented.

In late July 2007 the Chambre des Députés adopted a motion of censure against the Minister of Culture and Communication, Daniel Elie, who had been accused of the misuse of public funds. Elie resigned in early August, although he denied the allegations against him, and was replaced in late September by Eddy Lubin. In October elections to renew one-third of the seats in the Sénat, scheduled for 25 November, were postponed indefinitely following allegations of corruption against members of the CEP, including its President, Max Mathurin. A new electoral council, presided by Frantz-Gérard Verret, was appointed in December; In early 2008 the elections were yet to be rescheduled.

In early April 2008 several days of violent demonstrations against a sharp increase in the cost of food resulted in the deaths of five people and the murder of a Nigerian MINUSTAH peace-keeper. (It was reported that the prices of food staples had increased by some 50% in the previous year, making survival increasingly difficult for poor Haitians.) On 12 April President Préval held talks with food importers and announced a 15.7% reduction in the price of rice. However, on the same day the Sénat approved a motion to dismiss Alexis as Prime Minister over his handling of the crisis. On 27 April Préval nominated Ericq Pierre as Prime Minister, for which role he had previously been designated in 1997 under Préval's first administration but had been rejected by the Chambre des Députés. The new Prime Minister's appointment was to require ratification by both legislative chambers, following which it was expected that a new Cabinet would also be appointed.

International relations, although improved after 1971, continued to be strained because of Haiti's unpopular political regimes and government corruption. Relations between Haiti and its neighbour on the island of Hispaniola, the Dominican Republic, have traditionally been tense owing to the use of the border area by anti-Government guerrillas, smugglers and illegal migrants, resulting in the periodic closure of the border. In March 1996, following an official visit to the Dominican Republic by Préval, the first by a Haitian President since 1935, a joint communiqué was issued establishing a bilateral commission to promote improved co-operation between the two countries. In June 1998, following an official visit to Haiti by President Fernández of the Dominican Republic, agreement was reached to establish joint border patrols to combat the traffic of drugs and other contraband between the two countries. In November 1999 Préval submitted a formal protest to the Dominican Republic following a spate of summary deportations of Haitians from the neighbouring country; according to human rights observers, some 8,000 Haitians were forcibly repatriated in the first three weeks of that month. Following a direct meeting between representatives of the two Governments, a protocol was signed in early December limiting the repatriations. However, the number of Haitians entering the Dominican Republic increased in 2001, owing to the deteriorating economic situation in Haiti as a result of the continuing suspension of foreign aid. At the end of the year bilateral relations were strained when the Dominican Republic refused to extradite former Haitian police chief Guy Philippe, who was suspected of plotting the December attack on the presidential palace (see above). Nevertheless, in January 2002 President Aristide paid his first official visit to the Dominican Republic and held talks with President Rafael Mejía, during which agreements were signed on economic co-operation and border and immigration issues.

Relations between Haiti and the Dominican Republic suffered a marked deterioration in 2005. The Dominican Republic's army forcibly repatriated thousands of Haitian immigrants, a process that was intensified following the murder of a Dominican woman, allegedly at the hands of two Haitian men, in May of that year. Human rights organizations alleged that the Dominican army was acting indiscriminately and had deported not only illegal immigrants but also many Haitians of legal status and Dominicans of Haitian origin; the army strenuously denied such claims. Hopes for improved relations between the two countries were raised following a meeting between their respective chiefs of police in the border town of Jimaní in November; the two men agreed to increase collaboration, particularly with regard to the issue of border security. In another move intended to ameliorate relations, in December Haiti hosted a visit by Fernández (who had regained the Dominican presidency in 2004); however, his stay was abruptly curtailed after violent demonstrations in protest at the alleged abuse of Haitians in the Dominican Republic broke out around the presidential palace where he was meeting President Alexandre and Prime Minister Latortue. A large number of Dominican diplomatic staff resident in Port-au-Prince were temporarily withdrawn in the wake of the incident. In January 2006 at least 25 Haitians died from asphyxiation while being smuggled into the Dominican Republic in the back of a truck; however, some survivors of the incident alleged that the truck in which they were travelling came under fire from a passing vehicle. The Dominican authorities' returned the bodies of the Haitians to UN forces in Haiti, but the vehicle carrying the coffins was shot at by Haitians protesters, who demanded a full explanation for the circumstances surrounding the Haitians' deaths; at least two people were killed, the vehicle was forced to turn back, and the bodies were buried in a common grave in the Dominican border town of Dajabón. In early March Préval visited the Dominican Republic in his first foreign trip since securing victory in February's presidential election. The President-elect met with senior Dominican politicians and businessmen, and held talks with President Fernández, with whom he shared a pre-existing friendship, which it was hoped might facilitate an improvement in bilateral relations.

Following the coup of 30 September 1991, the USA came under international criticism for its forced repatriation of Haitian refugees fleeing the repressive military regime. In November, following an appeal by the Haitian Refugee Center in Miami a US federal judge ordered a temporary halt to the repatriation. However, at the end of January 1992 the US Supreme Court annulled the federal judge's ruling, and repatriation resumed. While a small percentage of refugees were considered for political asylum, the US Government insisted that the majority were economic refugees and therefore not eligible. In May 1994 a change in the US Government's policy regarding Haitian refugees (it agreed to hold hearings for all asylum applications, rather than repatriating all refugees intercepted at sea) prompted a renewed exodus of thousands of refugees, forcing a further change of US policy in July under which refugees granted asylum were henceforth to be held indefinitely in safe havens outside the USA. The USA contributed some 1,900 troops to the MIF deployed in Haiti following the resignation of Aristide in February 2004. In early February 2005 the USA despatched the first 50 marines of an intended 200-strong mission to Gonaïves in the north of Haiti to undertake humanitarian projects, largely related to damage caused by the severe flooding in September 2004. In March 2006 President-elect Préval made a three-day visit to the USA, during which he met with US President George W. Bush and addressed the UN Security Council. In his speech at the UN, he called for the international community to provide long-term aid with which Haiti might reinvigorate its economy and enhance the performance of its public institutions. Préval also urged the UN to afford priority to strengthening Haiti's national police force, rather than MINUSTAH. In October, in recognition of the Alexis Government's efforts to introduce peace and stability to the country, the USA partially lifted its arms embargo against Haiti, which had been imposed in 1991 in response to the overthrow of Aristide. As a result of the easing of restrictions, the Haitian Government would henceforth be able to obtain licences for the purchase of high-powered weapons and other items required by the national police force.

Government

The Constitution, approved by referendum in March 1987, provided for a bicameral legislature, comprising a 77-member Chambre des Députés (Chamber of Deputies—later enlarged to 83 members and again, in 2006, to 99 members) and a 27-member Sénat (Senate—later enlarged to 30 members). The Chambre des Députés was elected for a term of four years, while the Sénat was elected for a term of six years with one-third renewed every two years. Both houses were elected by universal adult suffrage. Executive power was held by the President, who was elected by universal adult suffrage for a five-year term and could not stand for immediate re-election. The President selected a Prime Minister from the political party commanding a majority in the legislature. The Prime Minister chose a Cabinet in consultation with the President. However, the Constitution was interrupted by successive coups, in June and September 1988 and September 1991. A return to constitutional rule was finally effected in October 1994, following the intervention of a US-led multinational force and the reinstatement of the exiled President Aristide. In January 2004, owing to the country's failure to hold legislative elections, the mandates of all 83 members of the Chambre des Députés and 12 members of the Sénat expired, entitling the President to rule by decree. Elections were finally held in February 2006.

There are 10 departments, subdivided into arrondissements and communes.

Defence

Following the return to civilian rule in 1994, measures providing for the separation of the armed forces from the police force were approved by the legislature. In December of that year two commissions were established for the restructuring of the armed forces and the formation of a new 4,000-strong civilian police force (later enlarged to 6,000). In 1995 the armed forces were effectively dissolved, although officially they remained in existence pending an amendment to the Constitution providing for their abolition. As assessed at November 2007, the national police force numbered an estimated 2,000. In June 2004 the UN Stabilization Mission in Haiti (MINUSTAH) commenced operations in Haiti. MINUSTAH, which had an authorized strength of 6,700 military personnel and 1,622 civilian police, was charged with assisting the interim administration with preparations for elections in early 2006 and the disarmament and demobilization of armed militias. Following the presidential and legislative elections in early 2006 MINUSTAH remained in the country to support a process of national dialogue and reconciliation and the implementation of measures to re-establish law and order. In August 2006 MINUSTAH's capacity was enlarged to a maximum of 7,200 military personnel and 1,951 civilian police. In October 2007 the mandate of MINUSTAH was extended to October 2008. In January 2008 MINUSTAH comprised 7,066 troops, 1,927 civilian police, 1,638 international and local civilian staff and 197 UN Volunteers. The security budget for 2003 was an estimated US $23m.

Economic Affairs

In 2006, according to estimates by the World Bank, Haiti's gross national income (GNI), measured at average 2004–06 prices, was US $4,119m., equivalent to $480 per head (or $1,490 per head on an international purchasing-power parity basis). In 1996–2006 the population increased at an average annual rate of 1.4%, while gross domestic product (GDP) per head decreased, in real terms, by an average of 0.7% per year. Overall GDP increased, in real terms, at an average annual rate of 0.7% in 1996–2006; according to official estimates, real GDP increased by 3.2% in 2006/07.

Agriculture (including hunting, forestry and fishing) contributed an estimated 26.0% of GDP, at constant prices, in 2006/07. About 59.6% of the total labour force were engaged in agricultural activities in mid-2005, according to FAO estimates. The principal cash crop was coffee. However, from 1998 coffee production decreased significantly, prompting the Government to announce plans for its revival in 2003; by that year coffee production had declined to 10,000 bags, from 450,000 bags in 1985 (it was believed that this decrease was largely attributable to the fact that much of the country's yield was smuggled into the Dominican Republic). In 2004/05 coffee accounted for only 0.8% of export earnings. The export of cocoa, and of oils for cosmetics and pharmaceuticals, was also important. However, the deteriorating security situation in the country meant that by 2005 virtually all exports had ceased. The main food crops are sugar, bananas, maize, sweet potatoes and rice. Falling quality and cheaper imports of sugar cane forced closure of all the country's major sugar factories during the years of unrest, although one of them, at Darbonne, near Léogane, reopened in January 2001. During 1995–2004, according to the World Bank, the real GDP of the agricultural sector increased at an average annual rate of 1.7%; according to official estimates, agricultural GDP increased by 3.1% in 2006/07.

Industry (including mining, manufacturing, construction and power) contributed 16.3% of GDP, at constant prices, in 2006/07. About 8.8% of the employed labour force were engaged in the sector in 1990. According to the World Bank, industrial GDP declined at an average annual rate of 6.5% in 1995–2004; according to official estimates, it increased by 2.4% in 2006/07.

Mining contributed 0.1% of GDP, at constant prices, in 2006/07. About 1% of the employed labour force were engaged in extractive activities in 1990. Marble, limestone and calcareous clay are mined. There are also unexploited copper, silver and gold deposits. In June 2006 a Canadian company commenced exploratory operations on copper and gold deposits in the north and north-east of the country.

Manufacturing contributed 7.9% of GDP, at constant prices, in 2006/07. Some 35,000 people were engaged in the sector in mid-2000. The most important branches of manufacturing were food products, textiles (including apparel, leather and fur products and footwear), chemicals (including rubber and plastic products) and tobacco. According to the World Bank, manufacturing GDP decreased by an average of 9.5% per year in 1995–2004; according to official estimates, manufacturing GDP increased by 1.5% in 2006/07.

Energy is derived principally from local timber and charcoal. In 2004 52.5% of the country's public electricity came from petroleum, while 47.5% of electricity came from hydroelectric power. Severe shortfalls of electricity in 2000–01 led the Government to contract a Dominican and a US-Haitian company to add 70 MW to the national supply, increasing it by one-third, but by 2004 overall production had declined to one-10th of the capital's requirements. Imports of mineral fuels and related products accounted for 28.4% of the total value of imports in 2006/07. Steep rises in global oil prices during 2005 severely exacerbated the power shortages.

The services sector contributed 57.7% of GDP, at constant prices, in 2006/07 and engaged 22.8% of the employed labour force in 1990. According to the World Bank, the GDP of the services sector increased by an average of 4.7% per year in 1995–2004. According to official estimates, it increased by 4.7% in 2006/07.

In 2006/07 Haiti recorded a visible trade deficit of US $1,091.8m., and there was a surplus of $10.1m. on the current account of the balance of payments. In 2004 the principal source of imports (35%) was the USA; the USA was also the principal market for exports (81%) in that year. Other significant trading partners in recent years include France, Canada, Japan and the Dominican Republic. The principal export in 2006/07 was manufactured goods (34.6%); agricultural products were also significant, predominantly cocoa (1.2%). The principal imports in that year were mineral fuels and lubricants (28.4%) and food products (25.8%). In 2000 smuggling was estimated to have accounted for two-thirds of Haiti's imports.

In the financial year ending 30 September 2007 there was a budgetary deficit of 4,804.2m. gourdes. At the end of 2005 Haiti's total external debt was US $1,323m., of which $1,276m. was long-term public debt. In 2005 the cost of debt-servicing was equivalent to 3.7% of the total value of exports of goods and services. The annual rate of inflation averaged 16.4% per year in 1997–2006. Consumer prices increased by an average of 19.2% in 2005 and by 12.3% in 2006. Some 60% of the labour force were estimated to be unemployed in 2001. Remittances from Haitians living abroad amounted to more than $1,000m. in 2005 (equivalent to approximately one-quarter of GDP in that year).

Haiti is a member of the International Coffee Organization (see p. 408), the Latin American Economic System (SELA, see p. 413) and the Caribbean Community and Common Market (CARICOM, see p. 196). Haiti is also a signatory to the European Union's (EU) Cotonou Agreement (see p. 301), which replaced the Lomé Convention from June 2000, although from 2000 the disbursement of funds under this accord was suspended while the political crisis continued (see Recent History).

In terms of average income, Haiti is the poorest country in the Western hemisphere, and there is extreme inequality of wealth. Economic growth slowed further from 2000, exacerbated by the ongoing political impasse, which continued to impede investment and private-sector confidence, as well as the implementation of the necessary structural adjustments that would allow economic development. However, it was the continuing suspension of international aid to Haiti that was the main reason for the economy's deterioration. Although humanitarian funds continued to be disbursed, the international community made it clear that confidence in Haiti's democratic process had to be restored before financial aid could be resumed. In an attempt to encourage foreign investment, the Government approved legislation offering incentives to foreign businesses prepared to invest in the country. In early 2003 the Government attempted to stabilize the country's fiscal situation by introducing a series of austerity measures and in mid-2003 an agreement was reached with the IMF. Shortly afterwards, in an attempt to secure further aid, the Government paid US $32m. in arrears to the Inter-American Development Bank (IDB), enabling the release of $146m. of 'frozen' loans from that body. Following the overthrow of the Aristide Government in February 2004, the interim administration of Gérard Latortue secured some $1,500m. in international aid. However, disbursement of the funding was slow and the crisis precipitated by the September floods meant that much of the aid received was redirected towards humanitarian causes. In January 2005 the IMF approved SDR 10.24m. (approximately $14.7m.) in Emergency Post-Conflict Assistance (EPCA) for the interim Government; this was supplemented by the approval in October of a second EPCA, which provided a further SDR 10.23m. In June 2006 the EU pledged to increase development aid for Haiti—intended primarily to support education and infrastructure projects and partially to cover the budget deficit—from $211m. for the period 2002–07 to $293m. for 2008–13. At an international donors' conference held in Port-au-Prince in July, a total of $750m. (of which $210m. was to be provided by the USA) was pledged for Haiti between August 2006 and September 2007. In late 2006 the IMF approved a new three-year arrangement under the Poverty Reduction and Growth Facility (PRGF), which would ultimately provide the Haitian Government with SDR 73.7m. (approximately $109.5m.). Although it commended the initial efforts of the Préval Government to enhance economic performance, the IMF identified high inflation, low fiscal revenues and ineffective budget management as key areas requiring significant attention if sustained improvement was to be achieved. In August 2007 the first review under a new IMF arrangement was published. In it the executive praised the Government for declining inflation, a stabilized currency and modest growth, though it considered that budget management needed further improvement. In the mean time, the telecommunications sector continued to perform strongly, particularly in the mobile telecommunications market. Haiti's readmission in June 2006 to CARICOM, membership of which had been revoked in 2004 following the overthrow of Aristide, augured well for the national economy. Formal ratification by Haiti of the Revised

Education

Education is provided by the state, by the Roman Catholic Church and by other religious organizations, but many schools charge for tuition, books or uniforms. Teaching is based on the French model, and French is the language of instruction. Primary education, which normally begins at six years of age and lasts for six years, is officially compulsory. Secondary education usually begins at 12 years of age and lasts for a further six years, comprising two cycles of three years each. In 1997 primary enrolment included only 19.4% of children in the relevant age-group (18.9% of boys; 19.9% of girls). Enrolment at secondary schools in 1997 was equivalent to only 34.2% of children in the relevant age-group (35.2% of boys; 33.2% of girls). In 1999 combined enrolment in primary, secondary and tertiary education was 52%. Higher education is provided by 18 vocational training centres and 42 domestic science schools, and by the Université d'Etat d'Haïti, which has faculties of law, medicine, dentistry, science, agronomy, pharmacy, economic science, veterinary medicine and ethnology. Government expenditure on education in 1990 was 216m. gourdes, equivalent to 20.0% of total government expenditure.

Public Holidays

2008: 1 January (Independence Day), 2 January (Heroes of Independence), 4 February (Shrove Monday, half-day), 5 February (Shrove Tuesday), 21 March (Good Friday), 14 April (Pan-American Day), 1 May (Labour and Agriculture Day), 18 May (Flag and University Day), 22 May (Corpus Christi), 15 August (Assumption), 17 October (Death of J.-J. Dessalines), 24 October (United Nations Day), 1 November (All Saints' Day), 2 November (All Souls' Day), 18 November (Army Day and Commemoration of the Battle of Vertières), 25 December (Christmas Day).

2009: 1 January (Independence Day), 2 January (Heroes of Independence), 23 February (Shrove Monday, half-day), 24 February (Shrove Tuesday), 10 April (Good Friday), 14 April (Pan-American Day), 1 May (Labour and Agriculture Day), 18 May (Flag and University Day), 11 June (Corpus Christi), 15 August (Assumption), 17 October (Death of J.-J. Dessalines), 24 October (United Nations Day), 1 November (All Saints' Day), 2 November (All Souls' Day), 18 November (Army Day and Commemoration of the Battle of Vertières), 25 December (Christmas Day).

Weights and Measures

Officially the metric system is in force, but many US measures are also used.

Statistical Survey

Sources (unless otherwise stated): Banque de la République d'Haïti, angle rues du Pavée et du Quai, BP 1570, Port-au-Prince; tel. 299-1200; fax 299-1045; e-mail webmaster@brh.net; internet www.brh.net; Ministère de l'Economie et des Finances, Palais des Ministères, rue Monseigneur Guilloux, Port-au-Prince; tel. 222-7113; fax 223-1247; Institut Haitien de Statistique et d'Informatique; e-mail ihsi@ihsi-ht.org.

Area and Population

AREA, POPULATION AND DENSITY

Area (sq km)	27,750*
Population (census results)†	
30 August 1982	5,053,792
7 July 2003‡	
Males	3,832,980
Females	4,096,068
Total	7,929,048
Population (UN estimates at mid-year)§	
2005	9,296,000
2006	9,446,000
2007	9,598,000
Density (per sq km) at mid-2007	345.9

* 10,714 sq miles.
† Excluding adjustment for underenumeration.
‡ Preliminary results.
§ Source: UN, *World Population Prospects: The 2006 Revision*.

DEPARTMENTS
(preliminary figures, 2003 census)

	Population	Capital
Ouest	3,093,699	Port-au-Prince
Sud-Est	449,585	Jacmel
Nord	773,546	Cap-Haitien
Grand'Anse*	603,894	Jérémie
Nord-Est	300,493	Fort Liberté
L'Artibonit (Artibonite)	1,070,397	Gonaïves
Centre	565,043	Hinche
Sud	627,311	Les Cayes
Nord-Ouest	445,080	Port-de-Paix
Total	**7,929,048**	—

* A new department, Nippes (with its capital at Miragoâne), was created from Grand'Anse later in 2003.

PRINCIPAL TOWNS
(estimated population at mid-1999)

Port-au-Prince (capital)	990,558	Delmas	284,079
Carrefour	336,222		

Source: UN Statistics Division.

Mid-2007 ('000, incl. suburbs, UN estimate): Port-au-Prince 1,998 (Source: UN, *World Urbanization Prospects: The 2007 Revision*).

BIRTHS AND DEATHS
(UN estimates)

	1990–95	1995–2000	2000–05
Crude birth rate (per 1,000)	35.5	32.7	29.8
Crude death rate (per 1,000)	12.5	11.4	10.5

Source: UN, *World Population Prospects: The 2006 Revision*.

Expectation of life (years at birth, WHO estimates): 54.7 (males 53.0; females 56.4) in 2005 (Source: WHO, *World Health Statistics*).

HAITI

ECONOMICALLY ACTIVE POPULATION
(official estimates, persons aged 10 years and over, mid-1990)

	Males	Females	Total
Agriculture, hunting, forestry and fishing	1,077,191	458,253	1,535,444
Mining and quarrying	11,959	12,053	24,012
Manufacturing	83,180	68,207	151,387
Electricity, gas and water	1,643	934	2,577
Construction	23,584	4,417	28,001
Trade, restaurants and hotels	81,632	271,338	352,970
Transport, storage and communications	17,856	2,835	20,691
Financing, insurance, real estate and business services	3,468	1,589	5,057
Community, social and personal services	81,897	73,450	155,347
Activities not adequately defined	33,695	30,280	63,975
Total employed	1,416,105	923,356	2,339,461
Unemployed	191,333	148,346	339,679
Total labour force	1,607,438	1,071,702	2,679,140

Source: ILO, *Yearbook of Labour Statistics*.

Mid-2005 (estimates in '000): Agriculture, etc. 2,239; Total labour force 3,759 (Source: FAO).

Health and Welfare

KEY INDICATORS

Total fertility rate (children per woman, 2005)	3.5
Under-5 mortality rate (per 1,000 live births, 2005)	120
HIV/AIDS (% of persons aged 15–49, 2005)	3.8
Physicians (per 1,000 head, 1998)	0.25
Hospital beds (per 1,000 head, 2000)	0.81
Health expenditure (2004): US $ per head (PPP)	82.3
Health expenditure (2004): % of GDP	7.6
Health expenditure (2004): public (% of total)	38.5
Access to water (% of persons, 2004)	54
Access to sanitation (% of persons, 2004)	30
Human Development Index (2005): ranking	146
Human Development Index (2005): value	0.529

For sources and definitions, see explanatory note on p. vi.

Agriculture

PRINCIPAL CROPS
('000 metric tons)

	2004	2005	2006
Rice (paddy)*	107	96	98
Maize*	202	206	195
Sorghum†	90	90	90
Sweet potatoes*	166	161	161
Cassava (Manioc)*	330	327	327
Yams*	204	207	207
Sugar cane	n.a.	n.a.	1,020*
Bananas*	312	322	322
Plantains*	286	287	287
Guavas, mangoes and mangosteens*	243	236	236

* Estimate(s).
† Unofficial figures.

Aggregate production ('000 metric tons, may include official, semi-official or estimated data): Total cereals 399.5 in 2004, 392.3 in 2005, 383.0 in 2006; Total roots and tubers 750.9 in 2004, 745.3 in 2005, 745.3 in 2006; Total vegetables (incl. melons) 200.5 in 2004, 200.6 in 2005, 200.6 in 2006; Total fruits (excl. melons) 999.4 in 2004, 1,000.0 in 2005, 1,000.0 in 2006.

Source: FAO.

LIVESTOCK
('000 head, year ending September, FAO estimates)

	2002	2003	2004
Horses	501	501	500
Asses and mules or hinnies	297	303	280
Cattle	1,450	1,455	1,456
Pigs	1,001	1,002	1,000
Sheep	153	154	154
Goats	1,943	1,944	1,900
Chickens	6,005	6,075	5,925

2005–06: Figures assumed to be unchanged from 2004 (FAO estimates).
Source: FAO.

LIVESTOCK PRODUCTS
('000 metric tons, FAO estimates)

	2003	2004	2005
Cattle meat	42.5	42.5	42.5
Goat meat	6.5	6.0	6.0
Pig meat	33.1	35.3	36.9
Horse meat	5.7	5.6	5.6
Chicken meat	8.5	8.2	8.3
Cows' milk	44.0	44.5	44.5
Goats' milk	25.2	25.2	25.2
Hen eggs	4.4	4.5	4.5

2006: Output assumed to be unchanged from 2005 (FAO estimates).
Source: FAO.

Forestry

ROUNDWOOD REMOVALS
('000 cubic metres, excl. bark, FAO estimates)

	2004	2005	2006
Sawlogs, veneer logs and logs for sleepers*	224	224	224
Other industrial wood*	15	15	15
Fuel wood	1,993	2,000	2,008
Total	2,232	2,239	2,247

* Output assumed to be unchanged since 1971.
Source: FAO.

SAWNWOOD PRODUCTION
('000 cubic metres, incl. railway sleepers)

	1969	1970	1971
Coniferous (softwood)	5	8	8
Broadleaved (hardwood)	10	5	6
Total	14	13	14

1972–2006: Annual production as in 1971 (FAO estimates).
Source: FAO.

Fishing

('000 metric tons, live weight, FAO estimates)

	2002	2003	2004
Freshwater fishes	0.4	0.4	0.3
Marine fishes	5.3	5.5	5.7
Marine crabs	0.2	0.2	0.3
Caribbean spiny lobster	0.6	0.8	1.0
Natantian decapods	0.5	0.6	0.8
Stromboid conchs	0.3	0.3	0.3
Total catch	7.3	7.8	8.3

Note: Figures exclude corals and madrepores (FAO estimates, metric tons): 10 in 2002; 10 in 2003; 10 in 2004.

2005: Figures assumed to be unchanged from previous year (FAO estimates).

Source: FAO.

Industry

SELECTED PRODUCTS
(metric tons, unless otherwise indicated, year ending 30 September)

	1999/2000
Edible oils	38,839.6
Butter	2,972.2
Margarine	2,387.4
Cornflour	104,542.6
Soap	30,069.9
Detergent	4,506.1
Beer ('000 cases of 24 bottles)	784.5
Beverages ('000 cases of 24 bottles)	1,807.7
Rum ('000 750ml bottles)	2,009.5
Electric energy (million kWh)	697.6

Cement ('000 metric tons): 203.8 in 2001; 290.3 in 2002 (Source: US Geological Survey).

Electric energy (million kWh): 470 in 2002; 512 in 2003; 547 in 2004 (Source: UN, *Industrial Commodity Statistics Yearbook*).

Finance

CURRENCY AND EXCHANGE RATES

Monetary Units
100 centimes = 1 gourde.

Sterling, Dollar and Euro Equivalents (31 October 2007)
£1 sterling = 75.397 gourdes;
US $1 = 36.360 gourdes;
€1 = 52.530 gourdes;
1,000 gourdes = £13.26 = $27.50 = €19.04.

Average Exchange Rate (gourdes per US $)
2004   38.352
2005   40.449
2006   40.409

Note: The official rate of exchange was maintained at US $1 = 5 gourdes until September 1991, when the central bank ceased all operations at the official rate, thereby unifying the exchange system at the 'floating' free market rate.

BUDGET
(million gourdes, year ending 30 September)

Current revenue	2005	2006*	2007*
Internal receipts	10,901.2	13,144.7	15,656.9
Customs	4,437.8	6,741.8	6,924.1
Total (incl. others)	16,252.8	20,413.7	23,667.2

Expenditure	2005	2006*	2007*
Current expenditure	17,253.4	19,366.8	22,428.4
Wages and salaries	5,853.0	6,871.2	8,830.8
Capital expenditure	1,994.0	1,837.0	6,043.0
Total	19,247.4	21,203.8	28,471.4

* Provisional figures.

INTERNATIONAL RESERVES
(US $ million at 31 December)

	2004	2005	2006
IMF special drawing rights	0.2	12.3	7.8
Reserve position in IMF	0.1	0.1	0.1
Foreign exchange	114.1	120.7	245.1
Total	114.4	133.1	253.0

Source: IMF, *International Financial Statistics*.

MONEY SUPPLY
(million gourdes at 31 December)

	2004	2005	2006
Currency outside banks	10,218.3	12,218.3	12,371.2
Demand deposits at commercial banks	7,145.5	8,355.9	8,941.7
Total money (incl. others)	17,975.8	21,302.2	22,603.2

Source: IMF, *International Financial Statistics*.

COST OF LIVING
(Consumer Price Index, year ending 30 September; base: 2000 = 100, metropolitan areas)

	2004	2005	2006
Food	223.2	263.2	300.1
Clothing and footwear	179.4	203.4	225.9
Rent	198.8	226.3	272.7
All items (incl. others)	214.3	255.4	286.9

Source: ILO.

NATIONAL ACCOUNTS
(million gourdes, year ending 30 September)

Expenditure on the Gross Domestic Product
(at current prices)

	2003/04	2004/05	2005/06
Final consumption expenditure	142,230	162,292	199,347
Gross capital formation	38,386	46,072	57,861
Total domestic expenditure	180,616	208,364	257,208
Exports of goods and services	21,555	24,222	28,660
Less Imports of goods and services	61,784	64,552	85,413
GDP in purchasers' values	140,387	168,034	200,456
GDP at constant 1987 prices	12,558	12,783	13,079

Source: IMF, *International Financial Statistics*.

HAITI

Statistical Survey

Gross Domestic Product by Economic Activity
(at constant 1986/87 prices)

	2004/05*	2005/06†	2006/07†
Agriculture, hunting, forestry and fishing	3,256	3,311	3,413
Mining and quarrying	14	15	15
Manufacturing	994	1,017	1,032
Electricity and water	75	58	57
Construction	977	1,005	1,042
Trade, restaurants and hotels	3,350	3,451	3,612
Transport, storage and communication	806	842	883
Business services	1,542	1,573	1,638
Other services	1,358	1,379	1,449
Sub-total	12,372	12,651	13,141
Less Imputed bank service charge	523	533	643
Import duties	934	961	1,000
GDP in purchasers' values	12,783	13,079	13,498

* Provisional.
† Estimates.

BALANCE OF PAYMENTS
(US $ million, year ending 30 September, provisional)

	2005	2006	2007
Exports of goods f.o.b.	458.9	494.4	522.1
Imports of goods f.o.b.	−1,308.5	−1,548.2	−1,613.9
Trade balance	−849.6	−1,053.8	−1,091.8
Exports of services	138.5	197.2	206.7
Imports of services	−451.1	−532.8	−628.6
Balance on goods and services	−1,162.3	−1,389.4	−1,513.7
Other income (net)	−36.7	6.6	10.2
Balance on goods, services and income	−1,198.9	−1,382.8	−1,503.6
Current transfers received	1,313.3	1,450.1	1,610.0
Current transfers paid	−59.3	−67.9	−96.4
Current balance	55.0	−0.6	10.1
Capital account (net)	—	—	5.7
Direct investment (net)	26.0	160.0	74.5
Other investment assets	−25.3	−23.8	65.8
Net errors and omissions	−5.1	−38.4	25.1
Overall balance	50.5	97.2	181.2

External Trade

PRINCIPAL COMMODITIES
(US $ million, year ending 30 September)

Imports c.i.f.	2005	2006	2007
Food products	330.7	367.6	369.8
Mineral fuels, lubricants, etc.	313.5	395.9	406.0
Machinery and transport equipment	156.6	260.2	224.8
Manufactured goods	241.8	249.6	132.3
Total (incl. others)	1,406.9	1,548.1	1,430.7

Exports f.o.b.	2005	2006	2007
Coffee	3.8	4.1	2.0
Cocoa	6.9	7.4	6.2
Manufactured goods	154.7	169.7	180.6
Total (incl. others)	458.8	491.2	522.1

PRINCIPAL TRADING PARTNERS
(US $ million, year ending 30 September)*

Imports c.i.f.	1989/90	1990/91	1991/92
Belgium	3.4	3.7	2.9
Canada	22.0	31.9	15.2
France	24.5	32.4	17.2
Germany, Federal Republic	14.6	19.2	10.0
Japan	23.6	31.2	17.7
Netherlands	11.2	13.9	8.7
United Kingdom	5.6	6.7	4.2
USA	153.1	203.2	126.7
Total (incl. others)	332.2	400.5	277.2

Exports f.o.b.†	1989/90	1990/91	1991/92
Belgium	15.9	19.5	6.0
Canada	4.5	4.7	2.3
France	17.4	21.6	6.1
Germany, Federal Republic	5.4	6.6	2.4
Italy	16.5	20.7	8.7
Japan	2.4	2.9	0.9
Netherlands	3.4	4.3	1.4
United Kingdom	2.3	2.3	0.7
USA	78.3	96.3	39.7
Total (incl. others)	163.7	198.7	74.7

* Provisional figures.
† Excluding re-exports.

Source: Administration Générale des Douanes.

Transport

ROAD TRAFFIC
('000 motor vehicles in use)

	1994	1995	1996
Passenger cars	30.0	49.0	59.0
Commercial vehicles	30.0	29.0	35.0

1999 ('000 motor vehicles in use): Passenger cars 93.0; Commercial vehicles 61.6.

Source: UN, *Statistical Yearbook*.

SHIPPING
Merchant Fleet
(registered at 31 December)

	2004	2005	2006
Number of vessels	5	5	5
Total displacement ('000 grt)	1.3	1.3	1.3

Source: Lloyd's Register-Fairplay, *World Fleet Statistics*.

International Sea-borne Freight Traffic
('000 metric tons)

	1988	1989	1990
Goods loaded	164	165	170
Goods unloaded	684	659	704

Source: UN, *Monthly Bulletin of Statistics*.

CIVIL AVIATION

Traffic (international flights, 1995): Passengers arriving 367,900; Passengers departing 368,330.

Tourism

TOURIST ARRIVALS BY COUNTRY OF ORIGIN

	2003	2004	2005
Canada	11,354	8,014	9,986
Dominican Republic	6,586	3,648	5,543
France	3,754	1,831	3,349
Jamaica	4,548	2,091	3,649
USA	94,515	72,895	77,047
Total (incl. others)	136,031	96,439	112,267

Receipts from tourism (US $ million, excl. passenger transport): 93 in 2003; 87 in 2004; 110 in 2005.

Source: World Tourism Organization.

Communications Media

	2003	2004	2005
Telephones ('000 main lines in use)	140.0	140.0	143.5
Mobile cellular telephones ('000 subscribers)	320.0	400.0	500.2
Internet users ('000)	150.0	500.0	600.0

Personal computers ('000 in use): 2.0 in 1999.

Source: International Telecommunication Union.

Radio receivers ('000 in use): 415 in 1997.

Television receivers ('000 in use): 42 in 1999.

Daily newspapers: 4 in 1996 (total circulation 20,000 copies); 2 in 2004.

Book production: 340 titles published in 1995.

Sources (unless otherwise indicated): UNESCO, *Statistical Yearbook*; UN, *Statistical Yearbook*.

Education

(1994/95)

	Institutions	Teachers	Students
Pre-primary	n.a.	n.a.	230,391*
Primary	10,071	30,205	1,110,398
Secondary	1,038	15,275	195,418
Tertiary	n.a.	654*	6,288*

* 1990/91 figure.

Adult literacy rate (UNESCO estimates): 51.9% (males 53.8%; females 50.0%) in 2003 (Source: UN Development Programme, *Human Development Report*).

Directory

The Constitution

The Constitution of the Republic of Haiti, which was approved by the electorate in a referendum held in March 1987, provided for a system of power-sharing between a President (who may not serve two consecutive five-year terms), a Prime Minister, a bicameral legislature (comprising a chamber of deputies elected for four years and a senate whose members serve six-year terms, one-third of whom are elected every two years) and regional assemblies. The army and the police were no longer to be a combined force. The death penalty was abolished. Official status was given to the Creole language spoken by Haitians and to the folk religion, voodoo (vaudou). Fr Jean-Bertrand Aristide was elected President in December 1990, but was deposed in September 1991 by a military coup. The US military returned him to Haiti to begin the restoration of constitutional government. He declared the army dissolved in April 1995 but a constitutional amendment formally abolishing it was never presented to the legislature as required and, after the fall of Aristide in February 2004, there were calls for its revival. The head of the Supreme Court, Boniface Alexandre, succeeded Aristide, and a Council of Elders appointed Gérard Latortue as Prime Minister. Presidential and legislative elections were held in February and April 2006 and constitutional rule was re-established when President René Garcia Préval took office in May. In 2005 the number of seats in both chambers was increased, from 27 to 30 in the Senate and from 83 to 99 in the Chamber of Deputies.

The Government

HEAD OF STATE

President: RENÉ GARCIA PRÉVAL (assumed office on 14 May 2006).

CABINET
(April 2008)

Prime Minister: ERICQ PIERRE (designate).

Minister of Agriculture, Natural Resources and Rural Development: FRANÇOIS SEVRIN.
Minister of Culture and Communication: EDDY LUBIN.
Minister of Economy and Finance: DANIEL DORSAINVIL.
Minister of the Environment: JEAN-MARIE CLAUDE GERMAIN.
Minister of Foreign Affairs and Religion: JEAN RENALD CLÉRISMÉ.
Minister of Haitians Residing Abroad: JEAN GÉNÉUS.
Minister of Public Health and the Population: Dr ROBERT AUGUSTE.
Minister of the Interior and Local Government: PAUL ANTOINE BIEN-AIMÉ.
Minister of Justice and Public Security: RENÉ MAGLOIRE.
Minister of Education and Professional Training: GABRIEL BIEN-AIMÉ.
Minister of Planning and External Co-operation: JEAN-MAX BELLERIVE.
Minister of Public Works, Transport and Communications: FRANTZ VÉRELLA.
Minister of Social Affairs and Labour: GÉRALD GERMAIN.
Minister of Tourism: PATRICK DELATOUR.
Minister of Trade and Industry: MAGUY DURCÉ.
Minister of Women's Affairs and Rights: MARIE LAURENCE JOCELYN LASSÈGUE.
Minister of Youth, Sports and Civic Activities: FRITZ BELIZAIRE.
Minister-delegate to the Prime Minister, in charge of Parliamentary Relations: JOSEPH JASMIN.

There are also four Secretaries of State.

MINISTRIES

Office of the President: Palais National, rue de la République, Port-au-Prince; tel. 222-3024; e-mail webmestre@palaisnational.info.

HAITI

Office of the Prime Minister: Villa d'Accueil, Delmas 60, Musseau, Port-au-Prince; tel. 245-0007; fax 245-1624.

Ministry of Agriculture, Natural Resources and Rural Development: BP 2162, Route Nationale 1, Damien, Port-au-Prince; tel. 222-3599; fax 222-3591.

Ministry of Culture and Communication: 31 rue Roy, Port-au-Prince; tel. 223-2382; fax 221-7318; e-mail dg1@haiticulture.org.

Ministry of Economy and Finance: Palais des Ministères, rue Monseigneur Guilloux, Port-au-Prince; tel. 223-7113; fax 223-1247.

Ministry of Education and Professional Training: rue Dr Audain, Port-au-Prince; tel. 222-1036; fax 245-3400.

Ministry of the Environment: Haut Turgeau 181, Port-au-Prince; tel. 245-7572; fax 245-7360; e-mail info@rehred-haiti.net.

Ministry of Foreign Affairs and Religion: blvd Harry S Truman, Cité de l'Exposition, Port-au-Prince; tel. 222-8482; fax 223-1668; e-mail webmaster@maehaitiinfo.org.

Ministry of Haitians Residing Abroad: 87 ave Jean-Paul II, Turgeau, Port-au-Prince; tel. 244-4321; fax 245-0287; e-mail infomhave@haiti2004lakay.org; internet www.mhave.gouv.ht; f. 1995.

Ministry of the Interior and Local Government: Palais des Ministères, rue Mgr Guilloux, Port-au-Prince; tel. 223-4491; fax 222-4429.

Ministry of Justice and Public Security: ave Charles Sumner 19, Port-au-Prince; tel. 245-9737; fax 245-0474.

Ministry of Planning and External Co-operation: Palais des Ministères, rue Mgr Guilloux, Port-au-Prince; tel. 223-0114; fax 222-0226; e-mail robert.jean@mpce-ht.net.

Ministry of Public Health and the Population: Palais de Ministères, rue Mgr Guilloux, Port-au-Prince; tel. 223-6248; fax 222-4066; e-mail janjang@caramail.com; internet mspp.ht.

Ministry of Public Works, Transport and Communications: Palais des Ministères, rue Mgr Guilloux, Port-au-Prince; tel. 222-2528; fax 222-3240; e-mail bmministre@haititptc.org.

Ministry of Social Affairs and Labour: 16 rue de la Révolution, Port-au-Prince; tel. 222-1244; fax 223-8084.

Ministry of Tourism: 8 rue Légitime, Port-au-Prince; tel. 223-2135; fax 223-5359; e-mail pdelatour@yahoo.com.

Ministry of Trade and Industry: rue Légitime, Champ-de-Mars, BP 200, Port-au-Prince; tel. 222-1628; fax 223-8402.

Ministry of Women's Affairs and Rights: Delmas 31, rue Louverture et Biassou 2, Port-au-Prince; tel. 249-5913.

Ministry of Youth, Sports and Civil Activities: angle rues Garoute et Pacot Turgeau, BP 2339, Port-au-Prince; tel. 245-5794.

Office of the Minister-delegate to the Prime Minister in charge of Parliamentary Relations: Delmas 48, 5 Rue François, Port-au-Prince; tel. 246-9912.

President and Legislature

PRESIDENT

Election, 7 February 2006*

Candidates	Votes†	%
René Garcia Préval	992,766	51.21
Leslie François Manigat	240,306	12.40
Charles Henri Baker	159,683	8.24
Jean Chavannes Jeune	108,283	5.59
Luc Mesadieu	64,850	3.35
Serge Gilles	50,796	2.62
Paul Denis	50,751	2.62
Evans Paul	48,232	2.49
Guy Philippe	37,303	1.92
Luc Fleurinord	36,912	1.90
Total (incl. others)	**1,938,641**	**100.00**

* After 95.8% of the votes had been counted.
† Total votes for each candidate include blank ballots. As no candidate attracted 50% of the valid votes cast, in order to avoid a second round of voting blank ballots were distributed among the candidates in proportion to their share of valid votes cast.

LEGISLATURE

Sénat
(Senate)

President: KELLY C. BASTIEN.

Elections, 7 February and 21 April 2006, provisional results

	Seats
Fwon Lespwa	13
Fusion des Sociaux-Démocrates Haïtiens	4
Organisation du Peuple en Lutte (OPL)	3
La Fanmi Lavalas (FL)	2
Union Nationale Chrétienne pour la Reconstruction d'Haïti (UNCRH)	2
Latibonit an Aksyon	2
Rassemblement des Démocrates Nationalistes et Progressistes (RDNP)	1
Alyans	1
Pont	1
Mouvement Indépendant pour la Réconcilation Nationale (MIRN)	1
Total	**30**

Chambre des Députés
(Chamber of Deputies)

President: PIERRE ERIC JEAN-JACQUES.

Elections, 7 February and 21 April 2006, partial results

	Seats
Fwon Lespwa	24
Fusion des Sociaux-Démocrates Haïtiens	18
Union Nationale Chrétienne pour la Reconstruction d'Haïti (UNCRH)	12
Organisation du Peuple en Lutte (OPL)	11
Alyans	10
Latibonit an Aksyon	5
Mouvement Chrétien pour une Nouvelle Haïti (MOCHRENHA)	3
Mobilization for Haïti's Development (MPH)	3
Co-operative Action to Build Haïti (KONBA)	2
Mouvement Démocratique et Renovateur d'Haïti (MODEREH)	1
Mouvement Indépendant pour la Réconcilation Nationale (MIRN)	1
Mouvement pour la Reconstruction Nationale (MRN)	1
Front de Reconstruction Nationale (FRN)	1
Action Démocratique pour Bâtir Haïti (ADEBHA)	1
La Fanmi Lavalas (FL)	1
Rassemblement des Démocrates Nationalistes et Progressistes (RDNP)	1
Total	**99***

* The results in four constituencies were not available.

Election Commission

Conseil Electoral Provisoire (CEP): 300 route de Delmas, Port-au-Prince; tel. 246-1733; e-mail info@cep-ht.org; internet www.cep-ht.org; f. 2004, dissolved Oct. 2007; Pres. FRANTZ-GÉRARD VERRET; Dir-Gen. PIERRE LOUIS OPONT.

Political Organizations

Action Démocratique pour Bâtir Haïti (ADEBHA): Delmas 60, 16, Port-au-Prince; tel. 558-1623; e-mail camilleleblanc@hotmail.com; f. 2004; Pres. CAMILLE LEBLANC.

Alliance pour la Libération et l'Avancement d'Haïti (ALAH): Haut Turgeau 95, BP 13350, Port-au-Prince; tel. 245-0446; fax 257-4804; e-mail reynoldgeorges@yahoo.com; f. 1975; Leader REYNOLD GEORGES.

Alyans (Alliance Démocratique): Port-au-Prince; contested the 2006 elections; centre-left coalition of Konvansyon Inite Demokratik (KID) and Popular Party for the Renewal of Haïti (PPRH); Leader EVANS PAUL.

Congrès National des Mouvements Démocratiques (KONAKOM): 101 Bois Verna, Port-au-Prince; tel. 245-6228; f. 1987; social-democratic; Leader VICTOR BENOÎT.

La Fanmi Lavalas: blvd 15 Octobre, Tabarre, Port-au-Prince; tel. 256-7208; internet www.lavalas.org; f. 1996 by Jean-Bertrand Aristide; formed a coalition with the MOP, the OPL and the PLB.

Front de Reconstruction Nationale (FRN): Gonaïves; f. 2004; Sec.-Gen. GUY PHILIPPE.

HAITI
Directory

Fusion des Sociaux-Democrates Haitiens: POB 381056, Miami, FL 33138, USA; e-mail fusion@pfsdh.org; internet www.pfsdh.org; Pres. VICTOR BENOÎT.

Fwon Lespwa (Front de l'Espoir): Port-au-Prince; internet frontespoir.org; f. 2005 to support René Garcia Préval's candidacy in 2006 presidential election; Leader RENÉ GARCIA PRÉVAL.

Grand Front de Centre Droit (GFCD): 21 blvd Harry S Truman, Cité de l'Exposition, Port-au-Prince; tel. 245-6251; e-mail hdr@mdnhaiti.org; internet www.gfcd.org; f. 2003; centre-right alliance; Pres. HUBERT DE RONCERAY.

Grand Parti Socialiste Haïtien (GPSH): Port-au-Prince; f. 2004; mem. of the GFCD; contested 2006 elections under Fusion des Sociaux Démocrates umbrella; Leader SERGE GILLES.

Grand Rassemblement pour l'Evolution d'Haïti (GREH): Port-au-Prince; Leader HIMMLER REBU.

Jeunesse Pouvoir Populaire (JPP): 410 rue Tiremasse, Port-au-Prince; tel. 558-1647; f. 1997; Leader RENÉ CIVIL.

Konbit pou Bati Ayiti (KONBA) (Co-operative Action to Build Haïti): Port-au-Prince; f. 2005; contested the 2006 elections; Leader CHAVANNES JEAN-BAPTISTE.

Koordinasyon Resistans Grandans (KOREGA-ESCANP): regionally based; radical left; Leader Fr JOACHIM SAMEDI.

Latibonit an Aksyon (LAAA) (L'Artibonite en Action): Port-au-Prince; contested the 2006 elections; Leader YOURI LATORTUE.

Mobilisation pour le Développement National (MDN): c/o CHISS, 33 rue Bonne Foi, BP 2497, Port-au-Prince; tel. 222-3829; e-mail info@mdnhaiti.org; internet www.mdnhaiti.org; f. 1986; Pres. HUBERT DE RONCERAY; Sec.-Gen. MAX CARRE.

Mobilization for Haïti's Development (MPH): Port-au-Prince; Leader SAMIR MOURRA.

Mouvement pour l'Avancement, le Développement, et l'Innovation de la Démocracie en Haïti (MADIDH): Port-au-Prince; Leader MARC ANTOINE DESTIN.

Mouvement Chrétien pour une Nouvelle Haïti (MOCHRENHA): rue M 7 Turgeau, Carrefour, Port-au-Prince; tel. 443-3120; e-mail mochrenha@hotmail.com; f. 1998; Leaders LUC MÉSADIEU, GILBERT N. LÉGER.

Mouvement Démocratique et Renovateur d'Haïti (MODEREH): Port-au-Prince; e-mail modereh@yahoo.com; Leaders DANY TOUSSAINT, PRINCE PIERRE SONSON.

Mouvement Indépendant pour la Réconcilation Nationale (MIRN): Port-au-Prince; contested the 2006 elections; Leader LUC FLEURINORD.

Mouvement pour l'Instauration de la Démocratie en Haïti (MIDH): 114 ave Jean Paul II, Port-au-Prince; tel. 245-8377; f. 1986; centre-right; Pres. MARC BAZIN.

Mouvement National et Patriotique du 28 Novembre (MNP-28): f. 1991; Leader JEAN BAPTISTE DE JEAN BÉLIZAIRE.

Mouvement pour l'Organisation du Pays (MOP): 9 rue Stella, Delmas 31, Port-au-Prince; tel. 249-3408; f. 1946; centre party; Leader JEAN MOLIÈRE.

Mouvement Patriotique pour le Sauvetage National (MPSN): f. 1998; right-wing coalition comprising 7 parties; Leader HUBERT DE RONCERAY.

Mouvement pour la Reconstruction Nationale (MRN): f. 1991; Leader JEAN-ENOL BUTEAU.

Mouvman Konbit Nasyonal (MKN): Leader VOLVICK RÉMY JOSEPH.

Nouveau Parti Communiste Haïtien (NPCH): Port-au-Prince; e-mail vanialubin@yahoo.fr; internet www.npch.net; Marxist-Leninist.

Organisation pour l'Avancement de d'Haïti et des Haïtiens (OLAHH): Port-au-Prince; Leader JOEL BORGELLA.

Organisation du Peuple en Lutte (OPL): 105 ave Lamartinière, Bois Verna, Port-au-Prince; tel. 245-4214; e-mail info@oplpeople.com; internet www.oplpeople.com/home.html; f. 1991 as Organisation Politique Lavalas; name changed as above 1998; Leader PAUL DENIS.

Parti Agricole et Industrie National (PAIN): f. 1956; Spokesman TOUSSAINT DESROSIERS.

Parti du Camp Patriotique et de l'Alliance Haïtienne (PACA-PALAH): Port-au-Prince; Leader FRANCK FRANÇOIS ROMAIN.

Parti des Démocrates Haïtiens (PADEMH): Leader JEAN-JACQUES CLARK PARENT.

Parti Démocratique et Chrétien d'Haïti (PDCH): 127 rue du Magasin de l'Etat, Port-au-Prince; tel. 550-7282; f. 1979; Christian Democrat party; Leaders OSNER FÉVRY, JOACHIN PIERRE.

Parti pour un Développement Alternatif (PADH): Leader GÉRARD DALVIUS.

Parti pour l'Evolution Nationale d'Haïti (PENH): Port-au-Prince; Leader YVES M. SAINT-LOUIS.

Parti des Industriels, Travailleurs, Commercants et Agents du Développement d'Haïti (PITACH): Port-au-Prince; Leader JEAN JACQUES SYLVAIN.

Parti National Progressiste Révolutionnaire (PANPRA): 5 rue Marcelin, Port-au-Prince; tel. 257-5359; f. 1989; social-democratic; Leader SERGE GILLES.

Parti National des Travailleurs (PNT): Port-au-Prince.

Parti Nationale Démocratique Progressiste d'Haïti (PNDPH): Port-au-Prince; Pres. TURNEB DELPÉ.

Parti Populaire Nationale (PPN): 11 rue Capois, Port-au-Prince; tel. 222-6513; f. 1987 as Assemblée Populaire Nationale (APN); name changed as above in 1999; radical left; Sec.-Gen. BEN DUPUY.

Parti Revolutionnaire Démocratique d'Haïti (PRDH): fmrly Mouvement Démocratique pour la Libération d'Haïti (MODELH); Leader FRANÇOIS LATORTUE.

Parti Social Chrétien d'Haïti (PSCH): BP 84, Port-au-Prince; f. 1979; Leader GRÉGOIRE EUGÈNE.

Parti Social Renove (PSR): Port-au-Prince; Leader BONIVERT CLAUDE.

Pati Louvri Baryè (PLB): f. 1992 by Renaud Bernardin; Sec.-Gen. FRANÇOIS PIERRE-LOUIS.

Pont (Bridge): Port-au-Prince; contested the 2006 elections.

Rassemblement des Démocrates Chrétiens (RDC): 177 rue du Centre, Port-au-Prince; tel. 234-4214; Leader EDDY VOLEL.

Rassemblement des Démocrates Nationaux Progressistes (RDNP): 234 route de Delmas, Delmas, Port-au-Prince; tel. 246-3313; f. 1979; centre party; Sec.-Gen. MIRLANDE MANIGAT.

Regroupement Patriotique pour le Renouveau National (REPAREN): Port-au-Prince; Leader JUDIE C. ROY.

Respè: Port-au-Prince; f. 2005; party of the wealthy élite; Leader CHARLES HENRI BAKER.

Union Démocrates Patriotiques (UDP): 30 rue Geffrard, Port-au-Prince; tel. 256-1953; Leader ROCKFELLER GUERRE.

Union Nationale Chrétienne pour la Reconstruction d'Haïti (UNCRH): contested the 2006 elections; Leader JEAN CHAVANNES JEUNE.

Diplomatic Representation

EMBASSIES IN HAITI

Argentina: 50 rue Lamarre, Pétionville, BP 1755, Port-au-Prince; tel. and fax 256-6414; e-mail embarghaiti@hainet.net; Ambassador ERNESTO LÓPEZ.

Bahamas: 12 rue Goulard, pl. Boyer, Pétionville, Port-au-Prince; tel. 257-8782; fax 256-5729; e-mail bahamasembassy@hainet.net; Ambassador Dr EUGENE NEWRY.

Brazil: Immeuble Héxagone, 3ème étage, angle des rues Clerveaux et Darguin, Pétion-Ville, BP 15845, Port-au-Prince; tel. 256-9662; fax 256-0900; e-mail haibrem@accesshaiti.com; Ambassador IGOR KIPMAN.

Canada: route de Delmas, entre Delmas 71 et 75, BP 826, Port-au-Prince; tel. 249-9000; fax 249-9920; e-mail prnce@international.gc.ca; internet www.dfait-maeci.gc.ca/haiti; Ambassador CLAUDE BOUCHER.

Chile: 2 rue Coutilien, Musseau, Port-au-Prince; tel. 256-7960; fax 257-0623; e-mail echileht@acn2.net; Ambassador ALAIN MARCEL YOUNG DEBEUF.

China (Taiwan): 16 rue Léon Nau, Pétionville, BP 655, Port-au-Prince; tel. 257-2899; fax 256-8067; e-mail haiti888@gmail.com; Ambassador YANG CHENG-TA.

Cuba: 18 rue Marion, Peguy Ville, POB 15702, Port-au-Prince; tel. 256-3812; fax 257-8566; e-mail embacuba@hughes.net; Ambassador RAÚL BARZAGA NAVAS.

Dominican Republic: rue Panaméricaine 121, BP 56, Pétionville, Port-au-Prince; tel. 257-0568; fax 221-8718; e-mail embrepdomhai@yahoo.com; Ambassador JOSÉ SERULLE RAMIA.

France: 51 pl. des Héros de l'Indépendance, BP 1312, Port-au-Prince; tel. 222-0952; fax 223-8420; e-mail ambafrance@hainet.net; internet www.diplomatie.gouv.fr/fr/pays-zones-geo_833/haiti_513/index.html; Ambassador CHRISTIAN CONNAN.

Germany: 2 impasse Claudinette, Bois Moquette, Pétionville, BP 1147, Port-au-Prince; tel. 257-7280; fax 257-4131; e-mail amballemagne@hainet.net; Ambassador Dr HUBERTUS THOMA.

Holy See: rue Louis Pouget, Morne Calvaire, BP 326, Port-au-Prince; tel. 257-6308; fax 257-3411; e-mail nonciature@haitiworld

HAITI

.com; Apostolic Nuncio Most Rev. MARIO GIORDANA (Titular Archbishop of Minora).

Japan: Villa Bella Vista, 2 Impasse Tulipe Desprez, BP 2512, Port-au-Prince; tel. 245-3333; fax 245-8834; Ambassador HARUO OKOMOTO.

Mexico: Delmas 60, 2, BP 327, Port-au-Prince; tel. 257-8100; fax 256-6528; e-mail embmxhai@yahoo.com; Ambassador ZADALINDA GONZÁLEZ Y REYNERO.

Panama: 29 rue Capois, Park Hotel, face Champs Mars, Port-au-Prince; tel. 763-4960; Ambassador ALEXIS ROGELIO CABRERA.

Spain: 54 rue Pacot, State Liles, BP 386, Port-au-Prince; tel. 245-4410; fax 245-3901; e-mail ampespht@mail.mae.es; Ambassador JUAN FERNÁNDEZ TRIGO.

USA: 5 blvd Harry S Truman, BP 1761, Port-au-Prince; tel. 222-0200; fax 223-9038; internet haiti.usembassy.gov; Ambassador JANET A. SANDERSON.

Venezuela: blvd Harry S Truman, Cité de l'Exposition, BP 2158, Port-au-Prince; tel. 443-4127; fax 223-7672; e-mail embavenezhaiti@hainet.net; Ambassador PEDRO ANTONIO CANINO GONZÁLEZ.

Judicial System

Law is based on the French Napoleonic Code, substantially modified during the presidency of François Duvalier.

Courts of Appeal and Civil Courts sit at Port-au-Prince and the three provincial capitals: Gonaïves, Cap-Haïtien and Port de Paix. In principle each commune has a Magistrates' Court. Judges of the Supreme Court and Courts of Appeal are appointed by the President.

Supreme Court: Port-au-Prince; tel. 222-3212; Pres. (vacant); Vice-Pres. PRADEL PÉAN.

Citizens' Rights Defender: NECKER DESSABLES.

Religion

Roman Catholicism and the folk religion voodoo (vaudou) are the official religions. There are various Protestant and other denominations.

CHRISTIANITY

The Roman Catholic Church

For ecclesiastical purposes, Haiti comprises two archdioceses and seven dioceses. At 31 December 2005 adherents represented some 65.6% of the population.

Bishops' Conference

Conférence Episcopale de Haïti, angle rues Piquant et Lammarre, BP 1572, Port-au-Prince; tel. 222-5194; fax 223-5318; e-mail ceh56@hotmail.com.
f. 1977; Pres. Most Rev. LOUIS KÉBREAU (Archbishop of Cap-Haïtien).

Archbishop of Cap-Haïtien: Most Rev. LOUIS KÉBREAU, Archevêché, rue 19–20 H, BP 22, Cap-Haïtien; tel. 262-0071; fax 262-1278.

Archbishop of Port-au-Prince: Most Rev. JOSEPH SERGE MIOT, Archevêché, rue Dr Aubry, BP 538, Port-au-Prince; tel. 222-2045; e-mail archevechepap@globalsud.com.

The Anglican Communion

Anglicans in Haiti fall under the jurisdiction of a missionary diocese of Province II of the Episcopal Church in the USA.

Bishop of Haiti: Rt Rev. JEAN ZACHÉ DURACIN, Eglise Episcopale d'Haïti, BP 1309, Port-au-Prince; tel. 257-1624; fax 257-3412; e-mail epihaiti@hotmail.com; internet www.egliseepiscopaledhaiti.org.

Protestant Churches

Baptist Convention: Route Nationale 1, Cazeau BP 2601, Port-au-Prince; tel. 262-0567; e-mail conventionbaptiste@yahoo.com; f. 1964; Pres. Rev. GÉDÉON EUGÈNE.

Evangelical Lutheran Church of Haiti: Eglise Evangélique Luthérienne d'Haïti, 144 rue Capitale, BP 15, Les Cayes; tel. 286-3398; f. 1975; Pres. THOMAS BERNARD; 9,000 mems.

Other denominations active in Haiti include Methodists and the Church of God 'Eben-Ezer'.

VOODOO

Konfederasyon Nasyonal Vodou Ayisyen (KNVA): f. 2008; Supreme Leader FRANÇOIS MAX GESNER BEAUVOIR.

The Press

DAILIES

Le Matin: 3 rue Goulard, Pétionville; tel. 256-4461; e-mail info@lematinhaiti.com; internet www.lematinhaiti.com; f. 1907; French; independent; Editor CLARENS FORTUNÉ; circ. 5,000.

Le Nouvelliste: 198 rue du Centre, BP 1013, Port-au-Prince; tel. 223-2114; fax 223-2313; internet www.lenouvelliste.com; f. 1898; evening; French; independent; Editor MAX CHAUVET; circ. 6,000.

PERIODICALS

Ayiti Fanm: 3 bis, rue Sapotille, Port-au-Prince; tel. 245-1930; publ. by The National and International Center for Documentation and Information on Women in Haiti; Creole; Dir MYRIAM MERLET.

Bon Nouvèl: 103 rue Pavée, étage Imprimerie La Phalange, BP 1594, Port-au-Prince; tel. 223-9186; fax 222-8105; e-mail bonnouvel@rehred-haiti.net; internet www.rehred-haiti.net/membres/bonouvel; f. 1967; monthly; Creole; Dir JEAN HOET; circ. 18,000.

Bulletin de Liaison: Centre Pedro-Arrupe, BP 1710, Port-au-Prince; tel. and fax 245-3132; e-mail gillesbeaucheminsj@hotmail.com; internet liaison.lemoyne.edu; f. 1996; 4 a year; Editors ANDRÉ CHARBONNEAU, GILLES BEAUCHEMIN, DONALD MALDARI.

Haïti en Marche: 74 bis, rue Capois, Port-au-Prince; tel. 245-2030; e-mail haiti-en-marche@direcway.com; internet www.haitienmarche.com; f. 1987; weekly; Editor MARCUS GARCIA.

Haïti Observateur: 98 ave John Brown, Port-au-Prince; tel. 228-0782; e-mail contact@haiti-observateur.ney; internet www.haiti-observateur.net; f. 1971; weekly; Editor LÉO JOSEPH; circ. 75,000.

Haïti Progrès: 1 Impasse Lavaud, no 22, Port-au-Prince; tel. 244-3264; fax 222-7022; e-mail editor@haiti-progres.com; internet www.haiti-progres.com; f. 1983; weekly; French, English and Creole; Dir KIM IVES.

Liaison: Centre Pedro-Arrupe, CP 1710, 6110 Port-au-Prince; tel. 245-3132; fax 245-3629; e-mail gillesbeaucheminsj@hotmail.com; internet liaison.lemoyne.edu; French; available in Creole as *Aksyon*; Editors ANDRÉ CHARBONNEAU, DONALD MALDARI, GILLES BEAUCHEMIN.

Le Messager du Nord-Ouest: Port-de-Paix; weekly.

Le Moniteur: rue du Centre, BP 214 bis, Port-au-Prince; tel. 222-1744; internet www.pressesnationales-dhaiti.com; f. 1845; 2 a week; French; official state gazette; circ. 2,000.

Optique: Institut Français d'Haiti, BP 1316, Port-au-Prince; tel. 245-7766; monthly; arts.

Le Septentrion: Cap-Haïtien; weekly; independent; Editor NELSON BELL; circ. 2,000.

Superstar Détente: 3 ruelle Chériez, Port-au-Prince; tel. 245-3450; fax 222-6329; cultural magazine; Dir CLAUDEL VICTOR.

NEWS AGENCIES

Agence Haïtienne de Presse (AHP): 6 rue Fernand, Port-au-Prince; tel. 245-7222; fax 245-5836; e-mail ahp@yahoo.com; internet www.ahphaiti.org; f. 1989; publishes daily news bulletins in French and English; Dir-Gen. GEORGES VENEL REMARAIS.

AlterPresse: 38 Delmas 8, BP 19211, Port-au-Prince; tel. 249-9493; e-mail alterpresse@medialternatif.org; internet www.alterpresse.org; f. 2001; independent; Dir GOTSON PIERRE.

Publishers

Editions des Antilles: route de l'Aéroport, Port-au-Prince.

Editions Caraïbes, SA: 57 rue Pavée, BP 2013, Port-au-Prince; tel. 222-0032; e-mail piereli@yahoo.fr; Man. PIERRE J. ELIE.

Editions du Soleil: rue du Centre, BP 2471, Port-au-Prince; tel. 222-3147; education.

L'Imprimeur Deux: Le Nouvelliste, 198 rue du Centre, Port-au-Prince.

Maison Henri Deschamps—Les Entreprises Deschamps Frisch, SA: 25 rue Dr Martelly Seïde, BP 164, Port-au-Prince; tel. 223-2215; fax 223-4976; e-mail entdeschamps@gdfhaiti.com; f. 1898; education and literature; Man. Dir JACQUES DESCHAMPS, Jr; CEO HENRI R. DESCHAMPS.

Natal Imprimerie: rue Barbancourt, Port-au-Prince; Dir ROBERT MALVAL.

Théodore Imprimerie: rue Dantes Destouches, Port-au-Prince.

HAITI

Broadcasting and Communications

TELECOMMUNICATIONS

Regulatory Body

Conseil National des Télécommunications (CONATEL): 16 ave Marie Jeanne, Cité de l'Exposition, BP 2002, Port-au-Prince; tel. 222-0300; fax 223-9229; e-mail conatel@haiticonatel.org; internet www.conatel.gouv.ht; f. 1969; govt communications licensing authority; Dir-Gen. JEAN MICHEL BOISROND.

Major Operators

Communication Céllulaire d'Haïti (Comcel): Port-au-Prince; tel. 400-1111; e-mail customer-care@comcelhaiti.com; internet www.comcelhaiti.com; f. 1998; Dir-Gen. JULIEN COUSTAURY.

Digicel Haiti: angle rues Darguin et Clerveau, étage Hexagone, Pétionville, BP 15516, Port-au-Prince; tel. 711-3444; e-mail customercarehaiti@digicelgroup.com; internet www.digicelhaiti.com; f. 2005; mobile telephone network provider; sole company licensed to operate a GSM network within Haiti; Group Chair. DENIS O'BRIEN.

Télécommunications d'Haïti (Téléco): blvd Jean-Jacques Dessalines, BP 814, Port-au-Prince; tel. 245-2200; fax 223-0002; e-mail info@haititeleco.com.

BROADCASTING

Radio

Radio Antilles International: 175 rue du Centre, BP 2335, Port-au-Prince; tel. 223-0696; fax 222-0260; f. 1984; independent; Dir-Gen. JACQUES SAMPEUR.

Radio Cacique: 5 Bellevue, BP 1480, Port-au-Prince; tel. 245-2326; f. 1961; independent; Dir JEAN-CLAUDE CARRIÉ.

Radio Canal du Christ: 175 rue du Centre, Port-au-Prince; tel. 223-9917; fax 222-0260; e-mail canalchrist93.5@mcm.net; f. 1998; Dir JACQUES SAMPEUR.

Radio Caraïbes: 19 rue Chavannes, Port-au-Prince; tel. 223-0644; fax 223-4955; e-mail caraibesfm@netcourrier.com; f. 1949; independent; Dir PATRICK MOUSSIGNAC.

Radio Céleste: 106 rue de la Réunion, Port-au-Prince; tel. 222-4714; fax 222-6636; f. 1991; Dir JEAN-EDDY CHARLEUS.

Radio Galaxie: 17 rue Pavée, Port-au-Prince; tel. 223-9942; fax 223-9941; e-mail rgalaxie@hotmail.com; f. 1990; independent; Dir YVES JEAN-BART.

Radio Ginen: 9 bis, Delmas 31, Port-au-Prince; tel. 249-1738; e-mail feedback@radyoginen.com; internet www.radyoginen.com; f. 1994; Dir LUCIEN BORGES.

Radio Kadans FM: 3 rue Neptune, Delmas 65, Port-au-Prince; tel. 249-4040; fax 245-2672; f. 1991; Dir LIONEL BENJAMIN.

Radio Kiskeya: 7 rue Pavée, Port-au-Prince; tel. 222-6002; fax 223-6204; f. 1994; Dir SONY BASTIEN.

Radio Lakansyèl: 285 route de Delmas, Port-au-Prince; tel. 246-2020; independent; Dir ALEX SAINT-SURIN.

Radio Lumière: Côte-Plage 16, BP 1050, Port-au-Prince; tel. 234-0330; fax 234-3708; e-mail rlumiere@starband.net; internet www.radiolumiere.org; f. 1959; Protestant; independent; Dir VARNEL JEUNE.

Radio Magic Stéreo: 346 route de Delmas, Port-au-Prince; tel. 245-5404; f. 1991; independent; Dir FRITZ JOASSIN.

Radio Mélodie: 74 bis, rue Capois, Port-au-Prince; tel. 221-8567; fax 221-1323; e-mail melodiefm@hotmail.com; f. 1998; Dir MARCUS GARCIA.

Radio Metropole: 18 Delmas 52, BP 62, Port-au-Prince; tel. 246-2626; fax 249-2020; e-mail informations@naskita.com; internet www.metropolehaiti.com; f. 1970; independent; Dir-Gen. RICHARD WIDMAIER.

Radio Nationale d'Haïti: 174 rue du Magasin de l'Etat, BP 1143, Port-au-Prince; tel. 223-5712; fax 223-5911; f. 1977; govt-operated; Dir-Gen. MICHEL FAVARD.

Radio Plus: 85 rue Pavée, BP 1174, Port-au-Prince; tel. 222-1588; fax 223-2288; f. 1988; independent; Dir GUY CÉSAR.

Radio Port-au-Prince: Stade Sylvio Cator, BP 863, Port-au-Prince; f. 1979; independent; Dir GEORGE L. HÉRARD.

Radio Sans Souci: 16 rue Malval, Turgeau, Port-au-Prince; tel. 262-5445; fax 262-5444; e-mail sanssoucifm@radiosanssouci.com; internet www.radiosanssouci.com; f. 1998; Dir IVES-MARIE CHANEL.

Radio Signal FM: 127 rue Louverture, Pétionville, BP 391, Port-au-Prince; tel. 256-4368; fax 256-4396; e-mail amisignal@yahoo.com; internet www.signalfmhaiti.com; f. 1991; independent; Dir-Gen. ANNE MARIE ISSA.

Radio Soleil: BP 1362, Archevêché de Port-au-Prince; tel. 222-3062; fax 222-3516; e-mail contact@radiosoleil.com; internet www.radiosoleil.com; f. 1978; Catholic; independent; educational; broadcasts in Creole and French; Dir Fr ARNOUX CHÉRY.

Radio Solidarité: 6 rue Fernand, Port-au-Prince; tel. 244-0469; fax 244-6698; e-mail solidarite@haitiwebs.com; Dir VENEL REMARAIS.

Radio Superstar: 38 rue Safran, Delmas 68, Port-au-Prince; tel. 257-7219; fax 257-3015; e-mail superstar1029fmfr@yahoo.fr; f. 1987; independent; Dir-Gen. ALBERT CHANCY.

Radio Timoun: 27 bis, rue Camille Léon, Port-au-Prince; tel. 245-1099; f. 1996; Dir MARIE KEMLY PERCY.

Radio Tropic FM: 6 ave John Brown, Port-au-Prince; tel. 223-6565; f. 1991; independent; Dir GUY JEAN.

Radio Tropicale Internationale: Delmas 27–29, Dubois Shopping Center, Port-au-Prince; tel. 249-1646; f. 1994; Dir JOEL BORGELLA.

Radio Vision 2000: 184 ave John Brown, Port-au-Prince; tel. 245-4914; e-mail info@radiovision2000.com; f. 1991; Dir LÉOPOLD BERLANGER.

Television

Galaxy 2: 6 rue Henri Christophe, Jacmel; tel. 288-2324; f. 1989; independent; Dir MILOT BERQUIN.

PVS Antenne 16: 137 rue Monseigneur Guilloux, Port-au-Prince; tel. and fax 222-1277; f. 1988; independent; Dir-Gen. RAYNALD DELERME.

Télé Eclair: 526 route de Delmas, Port-au-Prince; tel. 256-4505; fax 256-3828; f. 1996; independent; Dir PATRICK ANDRÉ JOSEPH.

Télé Express Continentale: rue de l'Eglise, Jacmel; tel. 288-2246; fax 288-2191; f. 1985; independent; Dirs JEAN-FRANÇOIS VERDIER, JACQUES JEAN-PIERRE.

Télé Haïti: blvd Harry S Truman, BP 1126, Port-au-Prince; tel. 222-3887; fax 222-9140; f. 1959; independent; pay-cable station with 33 channels; broadcasts in French, Spanish and English; Dir MARIE CHRISTINE MOURRAL BLANC.

Télé Smart: Hinche; tel. 277-0347; f. 1998; independent; Dir MOZART SIMON.

Télé Timoun: blvd 15 Octobre, Tabarre; tel. 250-1924; fax 250-9972; f. 1996; independent.

Télémax: 3 Delmas 19, Port-au-Prince; tel. 246-2002; fax 246-1155; f. 1994; independent; Dir ROBERT DENIS.

Télévision Nationale d'Haïti: Delmas 33, BP 13400, Port-au-Prince; tel. 246-2325; fax 246-0693; e-mail info@tnh.ht; internet www.tnh.ht; f. 1979; govt-owned; cultural; 4 channels in Creole, French and Spanish; administered by 4-mem. board; Dir PRADEL HENRIQUEZ.

Trans-America: ruelle Roger, Gonaïves; tel. 274-0113; f. 1990; independent; Dir-Gen. HÉBERT PELISSIER.

TV Magik: 16 rue Conty, Jacmel; tel. 288-2456; f. 1992; independent; Dirs LOUIS ANTONIN BLAISE, RICHARD CYPRIEN.

TVA: rue Liberté, Gonaïves; independent; cable station with 3 channels; Dir-Gen. GÉRARD LUC JEAN-BAPTISTE.

Finance

(cap. = capital; m. = million; res = reserves; dep. = deposits; brs = branches; amounts in gourdes)

BANKING

Central Bank

Banque de la République d'Haïti: angle rues du Pavée et du Quai, BP 1570, Port-au-Prince; tel. 299-1200; fax 299-1045; e-mail brh@brh.net; internet www.brh.net; f. 1911 as Banque Nationale de la République d'Haïti; name changed as above in 1979; bank of issue; administered by 5-mem. board; cap. 50m., res 2,308.7m., dep. 20,562.6m. (Sept. 2005); Gov. RAYMOND MAGLOIRE; Dir-Gen. CHARLES CASTEL.

Commercial Banks

Banque Industrielle et Commerciale d'Haïti: 158 rue Dr Aubry, Port-au-Prince; tel. 299-6800; fax 299-6804; f. 1974.

Banque Nationale de Crédit: angle rues du Quai et des Miracles, BP 1320, Port-au-Prince; tel. 299-4081; fax 299-4045; e-mail bnc@bnc-ht.com; f. 1979; cap. 25m., dep. 729.9m. (Sept. 1989); Pres. GUITEAU TOUSSAINT; Dir-Gen. LEVÊQUE VALBRUN.

Banque Populaire Haïtienne: angle rues des Miracles et du Centre, Port-au-Prince; tel. 299-6000; fax 222-4389; e-mail bphinfo@brh.net; f. 1973; state-owned; cap. and res 22m., dep. 614m.

(31 Dec. 2001); Dir-Gen. ERNST GILLES; Pres. RODNÉE DESCHINEAUX; 3 brs.

Banque de Promotion Commerciale et Industrielle, SA (PROMOBANK): 113 rue Faubert, Pétionville, Port-au-Prince; tel. 299-8000; fax 299-8125; e-mail info@promointer.net; internet www.promointer.net; f. 1974 as B.N.P. Haïti; name changed as above in 1994; cap. 60.4m., res 16.4m., dep. 1,183.4m. (Dec. 1998); Pres. and Chair. GILBERT BIGIO; Gen. Man. RUDOLPH BERROUET.

Banque de l'Union Haïtienne: angle rues du Quai et Bonne Foi, BP 275, Port-au-Prince; tel. 299-8500; fax 299-8517; e-mail buh@buhsa.com; internet www.buhsahaiti.com; f. 1973; cap. 30.1m., res 6.2m. (Sept. 1997), dep. 1,964.3m. (Sept. 2004); Pres. RICHARD SASSINE; 12 brs.

Capital Bank: 38 rue Flaubert, BP 2464, Port-au-Prince; tel. 299-6700; fax 299-6519; e-mail capitalbank@brh.net; f. 1985; fmrly Banque de Crédit Immobilier, SA; Pres. BERNARD ROY; Gen. Man. LILIANE C. DOMINIQUE.

Société Caraïbéenne de Banque, SA (SOCABANK): 37 rue Pavée, BP 80, Port-au-Prince; tel. 299-7000; fax 299-7022; e-mail socabankcard@usa.net; internet www.socabank.net; f. 1994; Pres. CHARLES A. BEAULIEU; Dir-Gen. CHARLES CLERMONT.

Sogebank, SA (Société Générale Haïtienne de Banque, SA): route de Delmas, BP 1315, Port-au-Prince; tel. 229-5000; fax 229-5022; internet www.sogebank.com; f. 1986; dep. 16,371.4m. (Dec. 2005); Pres. RALPH PERRY; 35 brs.

Sogebel (Société Générale Haïtienne de Banque d'Espargne et de Logement): route de l'Aéroport, BP 2409, Delmas; tel. 229-5353; fax 229-5352; internet www.sogebank.com/groupe/sogebel.html; f. 1988; cap. 15.1m., dep. 249.9m.; Gen. Man. CLAUDE PIERRE-LOUIS; 2 brs.

Unibank: 157 rue Flaubert, Pétionville, BP 46, Port-au-Prince; tel. 299-2057; fax 299-2070; e-mail info@unibankhaiti.com; internet www.unibankhaiti.com; f. 1993; cap. 100m., res 17.5m., dep. 3,366m. (Sept. 1999); Pres. F. CARL BRAUN; Dir-Gen. FRANCK HELMCKE; 20 brs.

Development Bank

Banque Haïtienne de Développement: 20 ave Lamartinière, Port-au-Prince; tel. 245-4422; fax 244-3737; f. 1998; Pres. RANDOLPH VOYARD; Dir-Gen. YVES LEREBOURS.

INSURANCE

National Companies

Compagnie d'Assurances d'Haïti, SA (CAH): étage Dynamic Entreprise, route de l'Aéroport, BP 1489, Port-au-Prince; tel. 250-0700; fax 250-0236; e-mail info@groupedynamic.com; internet www.groupedynamic.com/cah.php; f. 1978; merged with Multi Assurances SA in 2000; subsidiary of Groupe Dynamic SA; Group Chair. and CEO PHILIPPE R. ARMAND.

Excelsior Assurance, SA: rue 6, no 24, Port-au-Prince; tel. 245-8881; fax 245-8598; Dir-Gen. EMMANUEL SANON.

Générale d'Assurance, SA: Champ de Mars, Port-au-Prince; tel. 222-5465; fax 222-6502; f. 1985; Dir-Gen. ROLAND ACRA.

Haïti Sécurité Assurance, SA: 16 rue des Miracles, BP 1754, Port-au-Prince; tel. 223-2118; Dir-Gen. WILLIAM PHIPPS.

International Assurance, SA (INASSA): angle rues des Miracles et Pétion, Port-au-Prince; tel. 222-1058; Dir-Gen. RAOUL MÉROVÉ-PIERRE.

MAVSA Multi Assurances, SA: étage Dynamic Entreprise, route de l'Aéroport, BP 1489, Port-au-Prince; tel. 250-0700; fax 250-0236; e-mail info@groupedynamic.com; internet www.groupedynamic.com/mavsa.php; f. 1992; subsidiary of Groupe Dynamic SA; credit life insurance and pension plans; Group Chair. and CEO PHILIPPE R. ARMAND.

National d'Assurance, SA (NASSA): 25 rue Ferdinand Canapé-Vert, Port-au-Prince, HT6115; tel. 245-9800; fax 245-9701; e-mail nassa@nassagroup.com; f. 1989; specializing in property, medical and life insurance; Pres. FRITZ DUPUY.

Office National d'Assurance Vieillesse (ONA): Champ de Mars, rue Piquant, Port-au-Prince; tel. 223-9034; Dir-Gen. JEAN RONALD JOSEPH.

Société de Commercialisation d'Assurance, SA (SOCOMAS): étage Complexe STELO, 56 route de Delmas, BP 636, Port-au-Prince; tel. 246-4768; fax 246-4874; Dir-Gen. JEAN DIDIER GARDÈRE.

Foreign Companies

Les Assurances Léger, SA (ALSA) (France): 40 rue Lamarre, BP 2120, Port-au-Prince; tel. 222-3451; fax 223-8634; e-mail alsa@alsagroup.com; f. 1994; Pres. GÉRARD N. LÉGER.

Cabinet d'Assurances Fritz de Catalogne (USA): angle rues du Peuple et des Miracles, BP 1644, Port-au-Prince; tel. 222-6695; fax 223-0827; Dir FRITZ DE CATALOGNE.

Groupement Français d'Assurances (France): Port-au-Prince; Agent ALBERT A. DUFORT.

National Western Life Insurance (USA): 13 rue Pie XII, Cité de l'Exposition, Port-au-Prince; tel. 223-0734; e-mail intlmktg@globalnw.com; internet www.nationalwesternlife.com; Chair. and CEO ROBERT L. MOODY; Agent VORBE BARRAU DUPUY.

Sagicor Capital Life Insurance Company Ltd (Bahamas): angle rues du Peuple et des Miracles, BP 1644, Port-au-Prince; tel. 222-6695; fax 223-0827; e-mail capital@compa.net; internet www.sagicor.com; Agent FRITZ DE CATALOGNE.

Insurance Association

Association des Assureurs d'Haïti: 153 rue des Miracles, POB 1754, Port-au-Prince; tel. 223-0796; fax 223-8634; Dir FRITZ DE CATALOGNE.

Trade and Industry

GOVERNMENT AGENCY

Conseil de Modernisation des Entreprises Publiques (CMEP): Palais National, Port-au-Prince; tel. 222-4111; fax 222-7761; f. 1996; oversees modernization and privatization of state enterprises.

DEVELOPMENT ORGANIZATIONS

Fonds de Développement Industriel (FDI): Immeuble PROMOBANK, 4 étage, ave John Brown et rue Lamarre, BP 2597, Port-au-Prince; tel. 222-7852; fax 222-8301; e-mail FDI-Finance@globelsud.net; f. 1981; Dir-Gen. ROOSEVELT SAINT-DIC.

Société Financière Haïtienne de Développement, SA (SOFIHDES): 11 blvd Harry S Truman, BP 1399, Port-au-Prince; tel. 222-8904; fax 222-8997; f. 1983; industrial and agro-industrial project financing, accounting, data processing, management consultancy; cap. 7.5m. (1989); Dir-Gen. FAUBERT GUSTAVE; 1 br.

CHAMBERS OF COMMERCE

Chambre de Commerce et d'Industrie d'Haïti (CCIH): blvd Harry S Truman, Cité de l'Exposition, BP 982, Port-au-Prince; tel. 222-2475; fax 222-0281; e-mail ccih@compa.net; f. 1895; Pres. JEAN-ROBERT ARGANT.

Chambre de Commerce et d'Industrie Haïtiano-Américaine (HAMCHAM): 6 rue Oge, Pétionville, POP 13486, Port-au-Prince; tel. 511-3024; e-mail csjean@hamcham.org; f. 1979; Exec. Dir CHANTAL SALOMON-JEAN.

Chambre de Commerce et d'Industrie des Professions du Nord et du Nord-Est: 43 A–B rue 17, BP 244, Cap-Haïtien; tel. 262-2360; fax 262-2895.

Chambre de Commerce et d'Industrie Française en Haïti (CCIFH): Hôtel le Plaza, 10 rue Capois, Champ de Mars, BP 1429, Port-au-Prince; tel. and fax 511-3036; e-mail haiti@ccife.org; internet www.ccife.org/haiti; f. 1987; Pres. PATRICK ATTIE; First Vice-Pres. JOSSELINE COLIMON FÉTHIÈRE.

INDUSTRIAL AND TRADE ORGANIZATIONS

Association des Exportateurs de Café (ASDEC): rue Barbancourt, BP 1334, Port-au-Prince; tel. 249-2919; fax 249-2142; Pres. HUBERT DUPORT.

Association des Industries d'Haïti (ADIH): 199 route de Delmas, entre Delmas 31 et 33, étage Galerie 128, BP 2568, Port-au-Prince; tel. 246-4509; fax 246-2211; e-mail adih@acn2.net; f. 1980; Pres. MARYSE KEDAR-PENETTE.

Association Nationale des Distributeurs de Produits Pétroliers (ANADIPP): Centre Commercial Dubois, route de Delmas, Bureau 401, Port-au-Prince; tel. 246-1414; fax 245-0698; f. 1979; Pres. MAX ROMAIN.

Association Nationale des Importateurs et Distributeurs de Produits Pharmaceutiques (ANIDPP): blvd Harry S Truman, Port-au-Prince; tel. 222-0268; fax 222-7887; e-mail anidpp@direcway.com; Pres. RALPH EDMOND.

Association des Producteurs Agricoles (APA): BP 1318, Port-au-Prince; tel. 246-1848; fax 246-0356; f. 1985; Pres. REYNOLD BONNEFIL.

UTILITIES
Electricity

Electricité d'Haïti: rue Dante Destouches, Port-au-Prince; tel. 222-4600; state energy utility company; Dir-Gen. SERGE RAPHAEL.

Péligre Hydroelectric Plant: Artibonite Valley.

Saut-Mathurine Hydroelectric Plant: Les Cayes.

Water

Service Nationale d'Eau Potable (SNEP): 48 Delmas, Port-au-Prince; tel. 246-3044; fax 246-0881; e-mail Snep_eau_potable@hotmail.com; Dir-Gen. PÉTION ROY.

TRADE UNIONS

Association des Journalistes Haïtiens (AJH): f. 1954; Sec.-Gen. GUYLER C. DELVA.

Batay Ouvriye (Workers' Struggle): Delmas, BP 13326, Port-au-Prince; tel. 222-6719; e-mail batay@batayouvriye.org; internet www.batayouvriye.org; f. 2002; independent umbrella org. providing a framework for various autonomous trade unions and workers' asscns.

Centrale Autonome des Travailleurs Haïtiens (CATH): 37 route Delmas, Port-au-Prince; tel. 401-5820; e-mail fignole2000@yahoo.fr; f. 1980; Sec.-Gen. FIGNOLE SAINT-CYR.

Confédération Ouvriers Travailleurs Haïtiens (KOTA): 155 rue des Césars, Port-au-Prince.

Confédération Nationale des Educateurs d'Haïti (CNEH): impasse Noë 17, ave Magloire Ambroise, BP 482, Port-au-Prince; tel. 224-4482; fax 245-9536; e-mail lana14@caramail.com; f. 1986; Sec.-Gen. JEAN LAVAUD FRÉDÉRIC.

Confédération des Travailleurs Haïtiens (CTH): f. 1989; Sec.-Gen. JACQUES BELZIN.

Fédération Haïtienne de Syndicats Chrétiens (FHSC): BP 416, Port-au-Prince; Pres. LÉONVIL LEBLANC.

Fédération des Ouvriers Syndiques (FOS): angle rues Dr Aubry et des Miracles 115, BP 785, Port-au-Prince; tel. 222-0035; f. 1984; Pres. PIERRE CHARLES JOSEPH.

Organisation Générale Indépendante des Travailleurs et Travailleuses d'Haïti (OGITH): 2–3 étage, 121 angle route Delmas et Delmas 3, BP 1212, Port-au-Prince; tel. 249-0575; e-mail pnumas@yahoo.fr; f. 1988; Gen. Sec. PATRICK NUMAS.

Syndicat des Employés de l'EDH (SEEH): c/o EDH, rue Joseph Janvier, Port-au-Prince; tel. 222-3367.

Union Nationale des Ouvriers d'Haïti (UNOH): Delmas 11, 121 bis, Cité de l'Exposition, BP 3337, Port-au-Prince; f. 1951; Pres. MARCEL VINCENT; Sec.-Gen. FRITZNER ST VIL; 3,000 mems from 8 affiliated unions.

A number of unions are non-affiliated and without a national centre, including those organized on a company basis.

Transport

RAILWAYS

The railway service, for the transportation of sugar cane, closed during the early 1990s.

ROADS

In 1999, according to International Road Federation estimates, there were 4,160 km (2,585 miles) of roads, of which 24.3% was paved. There are all-weather roads from Port-au-Prince to Cap-Haïtien, on the northern coast, and to Les Cayes, in the south. In early 2008 the World Bank's International Development Association was financing a US $40m. road-improvement project in southern Haiti.

SHIPPING

Many European and American shipping lines call at Haiti. The two principal ports are Port-au-Prince and Cap-Haïtien. There are also 12 minor ports.

Autorité Portuaire Nationale: blvd La Saline, BP 616, Port-au-Prince; tel. 222-1942; fax 223-2440; e-mail apnpap@hotmail.com; internet www.apn.gouv.ht; f. 1978; Dir-Gen. JEAN EVENS CHARLES.

CIVIL AVIATION

The international airport, situated 8 km (5 miles) outside Port-au-Prince, is the country's principal airport, and is served by many international airlines linking Haiti with the USA and other Caribbean islands. There is an airport at Cap-Haïtien, and smaller airfields at Jacmel, Jérémie, Les Cayes and Port-de-Paix.

Office National de l'Aviation Civile (OFNAC): Aéroport International Mais Gate, BP 1346, Port-au-Prince; tel. 246-0052; fax 246-0998; e-mail lpierre@ofnac.org; Dir-Gen. JEAN-LEMERQUE PIERRE.

Caribintair: Aéroport International, Port-au-Prince; tel. 246-0778; scheduled domestic service and charter flights to Santo Domingo (Dominican Republic) and other Caribbean destinations.

Haiti Air Freight, SA: Aéroport International, BP 170, Port-au-Prince; tel. 246-2572; fax 246-0848; cargo carrier operating scheduled and charter services from Port-au-Prince and Cap-Haïtien to Miami (USA) and Puerto Rico.

Haiti International Airlines: Delmas 65, rue Zamor 2, Port-au-Prince; tel. 434-7201; f. 1996; scheduled passenger and cargo services from Port-au Prince to Miami and New York (USA); Pres. and Chair. KHAN RAHMAN.

Tourism

Tourism was formerly Haiti's second largest source of foreign exchange. However, as a result of political instability, the number of cruise ships visiting Haiti declined considerably, causing a sharp decline in the number of tourist arrivals. With the restoration of democracy in late 1994, the development of the tourism industry was identified as a priority by the Government. In 2005 tourist arrivals totalled 112,267. Receipts from tourism in that year totalled US $110m.

Association Haïtienne des Agences de Voyages: 17 rue des Miracles, Port-au-Prince; tel. 222-8855; fax 222-2054.

Association Touristique d'Haïti: rue Lamarre, BP 2562, Port-au-Prince; tel. 257-4647; fax 257-4134; Vice-Pres. RICHARD BUTEAU; Dir ELIZABETH SILVERA DUCASSE.

HONDURAS

Introductory Survey

Location, Climate, Language, Religion, Flag, Capital

The Republic of Honduras lies in the middle of the Central American isthmus. It has a long northern coastline on the Caribbean Sea and a narrow southern outlet to the Pacific Ocean. Its neighbours are Guatemala to the west, El Salvador to the south-west and Nicaragua to the south-east. The climate ranges from temperate in the mountainous regions to tropical in the coastal plains: temperatures in the interior range from 15°C (59°F) to 24°C (75°F), while temperatures in the coastal plains average about 30°C (86°F). There are two rainy seasons in upland areas, May–July and September–October. The national language is Spanish. Almost all of the inhabitants profess Christianity, and in 2005 about 82% of the population were adherents of the Roman Catholic Church. The national flag (proportions 1 by 2) has three horizontal stripes, of blue, white and blue, with five blue five-pointed stars, arranged in a diagonal cross, in the centre of the white stripe. The capital is Tegucigalpa.

Recent History

Honduras was ruled by Spain from the 16th century until 1821 and became a sovereign state in 1838. From 1939 the country was ruled as a dictatorship by Gen. Tiburcio Carías Andino, leader of the Partido Nacional (PN), who had been President since 1933. In 1949 Carías was succeeded as President by Juan Manuel Gálvez, also of the PN. In 1954 the leader of the Partido Liberal (PL), Dr José Ramón Villeda Morales, was elected President, but was immediately deposed by Julio Lozano Díaz, himself overthrown by a military junta in 1956. The junta organized elections in 1957, when the PL secured a majority in Congress and Villeda was re-elected President. He was overthrown in 1963 by Col (later Gen.) Oswaldo López Arellano, the Minister of Defence, who, following elections held on the basis of a new Constitution, was appointed President in June 1965.

A presidential election in March 1971 was won by Dr Ramón Ernesto Cruz Uclés, the PN candidate. In December 1972, however, Cruz was deposed in a bloodless coup, led by former President López. In March 1974, at the instigation of the Consejo Superior de las Fuerzas Armadas (Supreme Council of the Armed Forces), President López was replaced as Commander-in-Chief of the Armed Forces by Col (later Gen.) Juan Melgar Castro, who was appointed President in April 1975. President Melgar was forced to resign by the Consejo Superior de las Fuerzas Armadas in August 1978, and was replaced by a military junta. The Commander-in-Chief of the Armed Forces, Gen. Policarpo Paz García, assumed the role of Head of State, and the junta promised that elections would take place.

Military rule was ended officially when, in April 1980, elections to a Constituent Assembly were held. The PL won 52% of the votes but was unable to assume power. Gen. Paz was appointed interim President for one year. At a general election in November 1981 the PL, led by Dr Roberto Suazo Córdova, secured an absolute majority in the Congreso Nacional (National Congress). Suazo was sworn in as President in January 1982. However, real power lay in the hands of Col (later Gen.) Gustavo Alvarez Martínez, who was appointed Head of the Armed Forces in the same month. In November Gen. Alvarez became Commander-in-Chief of the Armed Forces, having brought about a constitutional amendment separating the posts of President and Commander-in-Chief of the Armed Forces. During 1982 and 1983 Gen. Alvarez suppressed increasing political unrest by authorizing the arrests of trade union activists and left-wing sympathizers; 'death squads' were allegedly also used to eliminate 'subversive' elements of the population. In March 1984 Gen. Alvarez was deposed as Commander-in-Chief by a group of army officers.

At the November 1985 presidential election the leading candidate of the PN, Rafael Leonardo Callejas Romero, obtained 42% of the individual votes cast, but the leading candidate of the PL, José Simeón Azcona del Hoyo (who had obtained only 27% of the individual votes cast), was declared the winner because, in accordance with a new electoral law, the combined votes of the PL's candidates secured the requisite majority of 51% of the total votes cast.

In February 1988 a report by the human rights organization Amnesty International gave evidence of an increase in violations of human rights by the armed forces and by right-wing 'death squads'. In August of that year, and again in 1989, the Inter-American Court of Human Rights (an organ of the Organization of American States—OAS, see p. 360) found the Honduran Government guilty of the 'disappearances' of Honduran citizens between 1981 and 1984, and ordered that compensation be paid to the families involved. In 1991 Amnesty International published a further report alleging the mistreatment, torture and killing of detainees by members of the Honduran security forces. In January 1989 Gen. Alvarez was killed by left-wing guerrillas in Tegucigalpa. The PL secured a majority of seats in the Congreso Nacional at the general election held in November, while Callejas of the PN won the concurrent presidential election, receiving 51% of the votes cast. Callejas assumed office in January 1990. The new administration promptly adopted economic austerity measures, which provoked widespread social unrest.

In March 1993, in response to increasing pressure by human rights organizations and criticism by the US Department of State, the Government established a special commission to investigate allegations of human rights violations by the armed forces. The commission recommended, *inter alia*, the replacement of the armed forces' much-criticized secret counter-intelligence organization, the División Nacional de Investigaciones (DNI), with a body under civilian control.

At presidential and legislative elections in November 1993 Carlos Roberto Reina Idiaquez, the candidate of the PL, was elected President, winning 52% of the votes cast. The PL also obtained a clear majority in the Congreso Nacional, with 71 seats, while the PN secured 55 seats and the Partido Innovación y Unidad—Social Demócrata (PINU-SD) won the remaining two seats. Legislation replacing the DNI with a new ministry, the Dirección de Investigación Criminal (DIC), was approved in December 1993. On taking office in January 1994 Reina, a former President of the Inter-American Court of Human Rights, expressed his commitment to the reform of the judicial system and the armed forces, reducing the latter's size and sphere of influence. In May the Congreso Nacional approved a constitutional reform abolishing compulsory military service (the amendment was ratified in April 1995). Also approved was the transfer of the police from military to civilian control.

In July 1994, following protracted demonstrations in the capital, 4,000 members of indigenous organizations occupied the Congreso Nacional building and succeeded in securing an agreement with the Government granting rights and social assistance to the country's indigenous community. The following months were characterized by growing social and political tension, including several bomb attacks. Concern was raised by human rights organizations that the climate of instability was being fomented by the armed forces in an attempt to stem the rapid diminution of its powers. In mid-August an increase in the incidence of crime and violent demonstrations resulting from the accumulating effect of austerity measures, a worsening energy crisis and food shortages, forced the Government to declare a state of national emergency and to deploy the armed forces to maintain order.

In July 1995, in an unprecedented development in the Government's efforts to investigate past human rights violations, a civilian court issued indictments against 10 senior officers of the security services. The charges concerned the kidnapping, torture and attempted murder in 1982 of six left-wing students. However, the officers refused to appear in court, invoking an amnesty granted in 1991 which, they claimed, afforded them immunity from prosecution. In January 1996 the Supreme Court ruled that the officers were not entitled to protection under the 1991 law, overturning an earlier decision by the Court of Appeal. In July 1996 the Human Rights Defence Committee (Codeh) claimed that the extra-judicial execution of five former military intelligence agents had occurred in recent months, and alleged that the killings were the responsibility of military officers who were attempting to prevent evidence of human rights violations from coming to light.

In February 1997 demonstrations by thousands of public-sector employees, who were protesting in support of demands for salary increases, culminated in violent clashes between demonstrators and the security forces. The Government subsequently signed a social pact with labour leaders, which included commitments to increased social spending and price controls on basic goods. In May, following the killing of two ethnic minority leaders in the previous month, more than 3,000 members of the indigenous community conducted a march from the western departments of Copán and Ocotepeque to the capital to protest outside the presidential palace. As a result, Reina signed an agreement to conduct a full investigation into the killings and to accelerate the distribution of some 7,000 ha of land to the indigenous community. However, the killing of a further two ethnic minority leaders later that month led to accusations by human rights groups that attempts were being made to eliminate minority autonomous organizations.

At the general election held on 30 November 1997 Carlos Roberto Flores Facussé, the candidate of the ruling PL, was elected President. The PL also obtained a majority in the Congreso Nacional. Flores was inaugurated on 27 January 1998.

In May 1998 control of the police force was transferred from the military to the civilian authorities. The Fuerza de Seguridad Pública, which had been under military control since 1963 and was widely suspected of perpetrating human rights abuses, was replaced by a new force, the Policía Nacional. Nevertheless, reports of human rights abuses continued.

In November 1998, in the wake of the devastation caused by 'Hurricane Mitch', which struck the country in late October, causing losses estimated at US $5,000m., President Flores declared a state of emergency and imposed a curfew in order to combat widespread looting. At least 6,600 people were estimated to have died, with a further 8,052 people reported missing, as a result of the storms, which left some 2.1m. homeless and caused widespread damage to the country's infrastructure, as well as destroying principal export crops.

In January 1999 the Congreso Nacional ratified a constitutional amendment abolishing the post of Commander-in-Chief of the Armed Forces and transferring its responsibilities to the Minister of National Defence and Public Security. The military's ruling body, the Consejo Superior de las Fuerzas Armadas, was also disbanded. In July, acting on intelligence reports of a plot by senior-ranking military officers to overthrow the Government, Flores implemented a number of changes to the military high command. The plot itself was believed to have been prompted by resentment in the officer corps at the determination of the Minister of National Defence, Edgardo Dumas Rodríguez, to exert civilian control over the armed forces, and in particular at his plans to investigate military expenditure and supervise the armed forces' extensive business activities.

In August 2001 the Government engaged a UN Special Rapporteur on extra-judicial, summary and arbitrary executions, Asama Jahangir, to investigate the alleged organized murder of street children in recent years. Jahangir concluded that since 1998, some 800 children had been killed by youth gangs and members of the police and private security forces. The Government subsequently announced an inquiry into police involvement in the killings. In March 2003 the Government announced that a special commission would be established to investigate the murders of street children. The Permanent Commission on Physical and Moral Integrity of Children would comprise church leaders and government officials.

Legislative and presidential elections were held on 25 November 2001. Five candidates contested the presidential election; the PN candidate, Ricardo Maduro Joest, emerged victorious, with 52% of valid votes cast, compared with 44% secured by the PL nominee, Rafael Piñeda Ponce. The PN also gained a majority in the Congreso Nacional, winning 61 seats, while the number of PL deputies was reduced to 55. On taking office in January 2002, President Maduro announced that the armed forces would play a greater role in the anti-crime effort, a declaration that was met with opposition domestically and internationally. Maduro affirmed his intention to reorganize the police force and to reform the criminal justice system, in order to reduce corruption. The number of supreme court judges was subsequently increased to 15 and the panel appointed to select the judges was depoliticized by the incorporation of lawyers and civilians. Another stated priority of Maduro was tax reform and a reduction in government expenditure, in an attempt to secure debt relief from the IMF.

Despite resistance from opposition parties, in May proposed fiscal reform legislation was approved in the Congreso Nacional.

President Maduro faced increasing industrial unrest during his term in office. In May 2002 teachers began a strike in protest at their wages and working conditions. A pay deal offered in August was rejected. Later in the same month coffee growers demonstrated in Tegucigalpa against the Government's alleged failure to make available a US $20m. loan granted by Taiwan to help stimulate the coffee sector. The demonstration escalated into violence and some 500 protesters were arrested. In November the Government announced a new housing initiative, which controversially involved borrowing funds from public-sector pensions. The programme placed further strain on relations between the Government and public-sector workers. Teachers, together with employees of the state water company, who objected to plans to transfer responsibility for water services from the state to the municipalities, held a two-day demonstration in Tegucigalpa. The protest resulted in violent clashes between protesters and the police, which left 20 injured. Public dissatisfaction with reductions in public expenditure culminated in August 2003 with a 'March for Dignity', in which some 10,000 people converged on Tegucigalpa in protest at, *inter alia*, the decentralization of water services and government plans for civil service reform. The demonstration escalated into violent clashes between protesters and the police; some 21 people were injured. In October some 30,000 public-sector employees held a one-day strike in protest at the Government's economic austerity measures. Intermittent unrest continued in 2004, including a six-day march in June that culminated in a demonstration in Tegucigalpa against deforestation and unregulated mining.

Despite the implementation of increased security measures by the Maduro administration, Honduras experienced rising levels of violent crime in the early 2000s. In January 2003, in response to increasing conflict between street gangs (*maras*), 10,000 army troops had been deployed on to the streets of Tegucigalpa, San Pedro Sula, La Ceiba and Choluteca. Controversial legislation approved by the Congreso Nacional in August introduced prison sentences of between nine and 12 years and substantial fines for members of the *maras*. These gangs were held to be responsible for much of the crime in Honduras. However, the continued high incidence of kidnappings of businessmen and foreigners in 2004–05 prompted many to flee the country; it was also feared that the high crime rate would deter foreign investment, particularly in the *maquila* sector. In December 2004 the Government introduced further legislation, increasing the maximum prison sentence for 'illicit association' from 20 to 30 years and extending the period of detention without charge to 72 hours. However, President Maduro's strict policies towards criminals also raised fears of human rights abuses regarding the conditions in which the prisoners were kept. In May 2004 more than 100 inmates, mainly gang members, died in a fire at a prison in San Pedro Sula. Representatives of the deceased claimed that police and prison guards started the fire and subsequently refused to free the prisoners. The incident echoed another in April 2003 when 69 people, mainly *mara* members, died in a riot and subsequent fire at a prison in La Ceiba. The riot had been in protest at overcrowding and poor conditions in the gaol. A government inquiry into the deaths at La Ceiba later concluded that 51 of the victims had been summarily executed by prison officials who then set the fire to conceal their actions. On 23 December 2004 the massacre of 28 people on a bus near San Pedro Sula was attributed to an organized street gang.

In October 2004 the Attorney-General, Ovidio Navarro, was accused of abusing his position to protect former President Callejas after he dismissed 10 public prosecutors and transferred a further six to different duties. The dismissed prosecutors had criticized an earlier decision by Navarro to abandon a number of corruption cases, including seven against the former PN President. The controversial decision prompted industrial action in the prosecution service and demonstrations. In November the Supreme Court ordered the investigations to be resumed. Following increasing public pressure in the ensuing months, as well as a congressional investigation into corruption allegations against him, Navarro submitted his resignation on 28 June 2005.

The presidential election held on 27 November 2005 was narrowly won by the PL's José Manuel (Mel) Zelaya Rosales, a prominent rancher and minister in the Flores Government, who won 49.9% of the votes cast. The PN candidate, Porfirio Lobo Sosa, obtained 46.2%. Juan Angel Almendárez Bonilla of the PUD attracted 1.5% of the total valid votes, while Juan Ramón Martínez of the PDCH secured 1.4% and Carlos Sosa Coello of the

PINU-SD won the remaining 1.0%. In the concurrently held legislative election the PL won 62 of the 128 seats in the Congreso Nacional, while the PN secured 55 seats. The remaining 11 seats were allocated to the PUD (five seats), the PDCH (four) and the PINU-SD (two). Voter turn-out was 57%. The delay in announcing the final results was severely criticized by observers, who denounced the electoral process as the worst in 25 years of democracy. A report by the Movimiento Cívico por la Democracia criticized the conduct of the Tribunal Supremo de Elecciones (TSE), particularly that body's President, Arístides Mejía, who announced Zelaya's victory after just 2.8% of the ballot had been counted.

Zelaya assumed the presidency on 27 January 2006 and a new Government was installed, which included five women and a number of experienced politicians. Notable among the appointments was Hugo Noé Pino, a former President of the Central Bank and former ambassador to the USA and the UN, who became Minister of Finance, and Mejía, the TSE President, who assumed the national defence portfolio. On taking office the new President reiterated his commitment to his campaign promises of creating 400,000 jobs, building 200,000 houses, eliminating corruption and improving domestic security. However, Zelaya's approach to domestic security was expected to differ from Maduro's hardline policies, placing more emphasis on the rehabilitation of *mara* members and on measures to improve employment and opportunities for young people in an attempt to decrease gang membership. None the less, the new Minister of Public Security, Gen. Alvaro Antonio Romero Salgado, announced plans to transfer 1,000 soldiers to the police force, and to expand the army by almost 50%. In July Noé was replaced as Minister of Finance by Rebeca Patricia Santos, who had been the World Bank representative in Honduras since 2003. Her stated priority on assuming office was to ensure that Honduras complied with the terms of its agreement with the IMF.

A lingering dispute among teachers over the failure by successive governments to deliver agreed pay increases re-emerged in July 2006. Despite initial optimism over reaching a settlement with the new Government, striking teachers blockaded the airport at Tegucigalpa in protest at the Government's offer, which was considerably lower than that made in the final days of the previous administration. Further unrest occurred in November when hundreds of peasants, demanding land titles, credit and other assistance from the Government, occupied regional offices of the Instituto Nacional Agrario. Negotiations began after the protesters threatened roadblocks and further disruption if their demands were not met.

The findings of an internal evaluation of the Government, carried out during 2006, led to the dismissal of the Minister of Public Education, Rafael Pineda Ponce, and the director of the Fondo Hondureño de Inversión Social (FHIS) in January 2007. The evaluation, which had been requested by Zelaya to monitor financial efficiency within the Government and the performance of ministers, had been carried out by a team of advisors working under the Minister of the Presidency, Yani Rosenthal. The process had led to division and recriminations among members of the Cabinet, culminating in the Vice-President, Elvin Santos, criticizing Rosenthal as having neither the authority nor the competence to carry out the assessment, and questioning why Rosenthal himself had not been subject to an evaluation. Marlon Brevé Reyes was appointed as Minister of Public Education and César Salgado replaced Marlon Lara as director of the FHIS.

The assassination, in early March 2007, of Rigoberto Aceituno, the second most senior police official in Honduras, served as a stark reminder of the continuing influence of the country's drugs gangs. Aceituno, who was believed to have been killed by the Cartel del Atlántico, had previously served as police chief in the Colón Department, the region of Honduras where the gang was most active. In May Zelaya strongly criticized the country's news media for its treatment of the Government and of the security situation, accusing it of exacerbating violent crime by reporting it in a sensationalist manner, and ordered radio and television stations to broadcast government propaganda for two hours a day for 10 days. He later reduced the amount of time that was to be dedicated to government-sponsored programming after the order was denounced as undemocratic by a journalism association and by the opposition.

In June 2007 the Minister of Industry and Commerce, Elizabeth Ancona, resigned for personal reasons; she was replaced in early August by Jorge Rosa. In December Rosenthal resigned as Minister of the Presidency, reportedly in order to campaign for the PL's nomination as its candidate in the presidential election that was due in November 2009; Enrique Flores Lanza was appointed in his stead. An extensive cabinet reorganization was prompted in early January 2008 by the revelation that the Minister of Foreign Affairs, Milton Jiménez Puerto, had assaulted a police officer after allegedly driving under the influence of alcohol. Jiménez resigned and was replaced by Angel Edmundo Orellana Mercado, hitherto Minister of the Interior and Justice, in which post he was succeeded by Víctor Meza. Four other new ministers were appointed, including Freddy Cerrato, who replaced Rosa as Minister of Industry and Commerce.

From the early 1980s former members of the Nicaraguan National Guard, regarded by the left-wing Sandinista Government of Nicaragua as counter-revolutionaries ('Contras'), established bases in Honduras, from which they conducted raids across the border between the two countries, allegedly with support from the Honduran armed forces. In 1983 the USA and Honduras initiated 'Big Pine', a series of joint military manoeuvres on Honduran territory that enabled the USA to construct permanent military installations in Honduras. In return for considerable military assistance from the USA, the Honduran Government permitted US military aid to be supplied to the Contras based in Honduras. Public opposition to US military presence in Honduras increased from 1984, and in December, following revelations that the USA had secretly sold weapons to the Government of Iran and that the proceeds had been used to finance the activities of the Contra rebels, President Azcona requested the departure of the Contras from Honduras.

In August 1987 Honduras, Costa Rica, El Salvador, Guatemala and Nicaragua signed a Central American peace plan, known as the 'Esquipulas agreement', the crucial provisions of which were the implementation of simultaneous cease-fires in Nicaragua and El Salvador, a halt to foreign assistance to rebel groups, democratic reform in Nicaragua, a ban on the use of foreign territory as a base for attack, and the establishment of national reconciliation commissions in each of the Central American nations. However, the Honduran Government opposed a clause in the agreement providing for the establishment of a committee to monitor the dismantling of Contra bases in Honduras. In December 1988 the International Court of Justice (ICJ) announced it would consider an application by the Nicaraguan Government, which contended that Honduras had breached international law by allowing the Contras to operate from its territory.

In February 1989 an agreement was reached whereby the Contra forces encamped in Honduras would demobilize, while President Ortega of Nicaragua guaranteed that free and fair elections would take place in his country by February 1990. The Honduran Government agreed to the establishment by the UN and the OAS of an international commission to oversee the voluntary repatriation or removal to a third country of the rebel forces by December 1989; in return, the Nicaraguan Government agreed to abandon the action that it had initiated against Honduras at the ICJ. The rebel units officially disbanded and left Honduras in June 1990.

In June 1995 Honduras and Nicaragua signed an accord providing for the visible demarcation of each country's territorial waters in the Gulf of Fonseca, and the establishment of a joint naval patrol to police the area. Despite the agreement, however, disputes concerning fishing rights continued, and the demarcation process did not begin until May 1998.

In December 1999 a further dispute arose with Nicaragua, prompting it to sever commercial ties with, and impose import taxes on, Honduras, in direct contravention of Central American free trade undertakings. The dispute stemmed from the Caribbean Sea Maritime Limits Treaty, which Honduras had signed with Colombia in 1986 and had finally ratified in November 1999, thereby granting Colombia territorial rights to areas of the Caribbean historically claimed by Nicaragua. In February 2000, following OAS mediation, the two countries agreed to establish a maritime exclusion zone in the disputed area. In the following month, representatives of Honduras and Nicaragua met in Washington, DC, where they signed an accord on joint patrols in the Caribbean, pending a ruling by the ICJ, and on combined operations in the Gulf of Fonseca, as well as the withdrawal of forces from the land border area. However, in February 2001 the Nicaraguan defence minister accused Honduras of violating the accords by carrying out military exercises in the area. Following further talks under OAS auspices, in June the foreign ministers of the two countries agreed to allow monitors into the disputed area to verify troop deployment. In August 2001, however, the Nicaraguan authorities again

HONDURAS

Introductory Survey

accused Honduras of moving troops and military equipment into the area, with the intention of launching an attack on their country. The Government denied the accusations. In July 2002 the situation further deteriorated when the Nicaraguan Government announced plans to sell oil-drilling rights in the disputed area. However, in November 2006 President Zelaya met the newly elected President of Nicaragua, Daniel Ortega, who offered to end the acrimonious border dispute, stating that resources should rather be channelled into poverty-reduction programmes. He also suggested that the maritime area disputed by Honduras, Nicaragua and El Salvador be jointly administered by the three countries. Ortega's remarks appeared to surprise some observers, including Nicaragua's defence minister, who asserted that Nicaragua's legitimate claims before the ICJ should not be jeopardized by 'imprudent' remarks. In October 2007 the ICJ brought an end to the dispute, ruling on a revised maritime border approximately mid-way between the two countries. Both Honduran and Nicaraguan Governments declared themselves satisfied with the outcome.

A long-standing dispute between Honduras and El Salvador, regarding the demarcation of the two countries' common border and rival claims to three islands in the Gulf of Fonseca, caused hostilities to break out between the two countries in 1969. Although armed conflict soon subsided, the Honduran and Salvadorean Governments did not sign a peace treaty until 1980. In September 1992 the ICJ awarded Honduras sovereignty over some two-thirds of the disputed mainland territory and over one of the disputed islands in the Gulf of Fonseca. However, in subsequent years disputes continued to arise concerning the legal rights of those people resident in the reallocated territory, particularly with regard to landownership. A convention governing the acquired rights and nationality of those people was finally signed by the Presidents of both countries in January 1998. An agreement was also signed providing for the demarcation of the countries' common border to be undertaken within one year. In December 2003 the ICJ rejected an application by El Salvador to review its 1992 decision. However, in April 2006 President Zelaya met his Salvadorean counterpart to ratify the border demarcation. The two heads of state also announced plans to revive a joint project for the construction of a 704-MW hydroelectric facility on the Lempa River.

In November 1991 the Presidents of Honduras and El Salvador signed an agreement to establish a free trade zone on their common border, and subsequently to seek economic union. In May 1992 the Governments of Honduras, El Salvador and Guatemala agreed to promote trade and investment between the three countries, and, in October of that year, agreed to the eventual establishment of a Central American political federation.

In May 2004 President Maduro announced the temporary withdrawal of Honduras from the Central American Court of Justice, declaring that the funding dedicated to the regional court would be more usefully invested in social, health and educational programmes. In September the Government announced the withdrawal of funding for the Central American parliament, known as Parlacen, for similar reasons. However, in November 2006 the Government announced its intention to rejoin the Central American Court of Justice and also pledged its support for Parlacen. President Zelaya described the parliament as an important symbol of integration and urged the organization to strive towards the introduction of a single passport and currency for member states.

In January 2002 Honduras restored diplomatic relations with Cuba, suspended since 1961. President Zelaya visited Cuba in October 2007 and met the country's acting President, Raúl Castro Ruz. In December 2001 the Government also concluded an agreement with the United Kingdom defining the maritime border between Honduras and the Cayman Islands.

In June 2006 President Zelaya and US President George W. Bush met in Washington, DC, to discuss security, immigration and trade. Zelaya requested the USA's assistance in converting the US military airbase at Palmerola into a commercial airport and in providing troops to combat drugs-trafficking along the Caribbean coast. Bush indicated that the USA might build a new military base in the Mosquitia region, near the Nicaraguan border, to serve as a replacement for Palmerola. Talks between the two leaders continued in September.

Government

Under the provisions of the Constitution approved by the Congreso Nacional in 1982, the President is elected by a simple majority of the voters. The President holds executive power and has a single four-year mandate. Legislative power is vested in the Congreso Nacional (National Congress), with 128 members elected by universal adult suffrage for a term of four years. The country is divided into 18 local Departments.

Defence

Military service is voluntary. Active service lasts eight months, with subsequent reserve training. As assessed at November 2007, the armed forces totalled 12,000, of whom 8,300 were in the army, 1,400 in the navy and 2,300 in the air force. Paramilitary forces numbered 8,000. In 2007 budgeted expenditure on defence totalled some 1,400m. lempiras (US $76m.). In early 2006 the incoming Government of President José Manuel Zelaya Rosales announced plans to expand the army by a further 4,000 troops. As assessed at November 2007, some 412 US troops were based in Honduras.

Economic Affairs

In 2006, according to estimates by the World Bank, Honduras' gross national income (GNI), measured at average 2004–06 prices, was US $8,838.7m., equivalent to $1,200 per head (or $3,540 per head on an international purchasing-power parity basis). During 1996–2006, it was estimated, the population increased at an average annual rate of 2.4%, while gross domestic product (GDP) per head increased, in real terms, by an average of 1.1% per year. Overall GDP increased, in real terms, at an average annual rate of 3.5% in 1996–2006; growth was 6.3% in 2007, according to central bank preliminary figures.

Agriculture (including hunting, forestry and fishing) contributed an estimated 12.8% of GDP in 2007, and employed 36.3% of the economically active population in 2006. The principal cash crop is traditionally coffee, which contributed 23.6% of the total value of exports in 2007, according to preliminary figures. Exports of bananas contributed 13.2% of total export earnings in 2007, according to preliminary figures. The main subsistence crops include maize, plantains, beans, rice, sugar cane and citrus fruit. Exports of shellfish make a significant contribution to foreign earnings (supplying, according to preliminary figures, 8.7% of total export earnings in 2007). According to the World Bank, agricultural GDP increased at an average annual rate of 2.4% during 1996–2006; the sector increased by 5.0% in 2007, according to preliminary central bank figures.

Industry (including mining, manufacturing, construction and power) contributed an estimated 26.8% of GDP in 2007, and employed 21.6% of the economically active population in 2006. According to the World Bank, industrial GDP increased at an average annual rate of 4.1% during 1996–2006; according to preliminary central bank figures, it increased by 4.4% in 2007.

Mining contributed an estimated 0.7% of GDP in 2007, and employed 0.2% of the economically active population in 2006. In 2006 gold was the major mineral export, contributing an estimated 4.1% of total export earnings. Lead, zinc, silver, copper and low-grade iron ore are also mined. In addition, small quantities of petroleum derivatives are exported. The GDP of the mining sector increased by an average of 2.8% per year in 1995–2006; it increased by an estimated 7.7% in 2006.

Manufacturing contributed an estimated 18.9% of GDP in 2007, and employed 14.9% of the economically active population in 2006. Value added by the *maquila* sector contributed an estimated 11,358m. lempiras to the economy in 2006. According to the World Bank, manufacturing GDP increased at an average annual rate of 4.5% during 1996–2006. Preliminary central bank figures indicated that the sector increased by 3.5% in 2007.

Petroleum accounted for 51.5% of electrical energy output in 2004, while the remainder was derived from hydroelectric power. Fuel wood remains a prime source of domestic energy. Imports of mineral fuels and lubricants accounted for 19.1% of the value of total imports in 2007, according to preliminary figures. Frequent power shortages prompted the new Government of President José Manuel Zelaya Rosales to invite international tenders in the energy sector in 2006. A further joint project with El Salvador, on the Lempa River, was announced in April of that year.

The services sector contributed an estimated 60.4% of GDP in 2007, and engaged 42.0% of the working population in 2006. The GDP of the services sector increased by an average of 4.6% per year in 1996–2006, according to the World Bank. Preliminary central bank figures indicated that the sector increased by 7.9% in 2007.

In 2006 Honduras recorded a visible trade deficit of US $1,993.2m., while there was a deficit of $194.6m. on the current account of the balance of payments. Workers' remittances from abroad constitute an important source of income:

according to central bank estimates, remittances totalled some $2,561.4m. in 2007. The majority of remittances came from the USA, home to an estimated 500,000 Hondurans. The USA was the principal market for exports (35.7%, according to preliminary figures, excluding *maquila* goods) in 2007; other significant purchasers were El Salvador, Guatemala and Germany. In the same year the principal source of imports (38.6%) was the USA; other major suppliers were Guatemala, El Salvador, Mexico and Costa Rica. The principal exports (excluding *maquila* goods) in 2007 were coffee, bananas and shellfish. The principal imports in 2007 were mineral fuels and lubricants, machinery and electrical equipment, and chemicals and related products.

In 2006 there was an estimated budgetary deficit of 2,244.4m. lempiras (equivalent to 1.1% of GDP). Honduras' external debt totalled US $5,242m. at the end of 2005, of which $4,152m. was long-term public debt. In that year the cost of debt-servicing represented 7.2% of the value of exports of goods and services. The annual rate of inflation averaged 7.7% in 2001–07. Consumer prices increased by an annual average of 9.0% in 2007. Some 4.1% of the labour force were registered as unemployed in 2005; it was estimated that around one-quarter of the work-force was underemployed.

Honduras is a member of the Central American Common Market (CACM, see p. 201). The Dominican Republic-Central American Free Trade Agreement (DR-CAFTA), between the Dominican Republic, the Central American countries of Costa Rica, Honduras, El Salvador, Guatemala, Nicaragua, and the USA, entered force in Honduras in 2006. DR-CAFTA, which aims to foster export-orientated growth in the region, was to entail the gradual elimination of tariffs on most industrial and agricultural products over a period of 10 and 20 years, respectively.

In terms of average income, Honduras is among the poorest nations in the Western hemisphere, with some 64% of the population living in poverty in 2004. Following the devastation caused by 'Hurricane Mitch' in 1998, in 1999 Honduras was admitted to the IMF and World Bank's heavily indebted poor countries (HIPC) initiative. In 2005 it was announced that Honduras satisfied the criteria under the HIPC initiative to qualify for immediate debt-relief. The Government of José Manuel (Mel) Zelaya Rosales, which took office in 2006, pledged to continue the IMF-prescribed macroeconomic policies of its predecessor; for 2008, these included a reduction in the rate of inflation, an increase in international reserves, and further strengthening of the energy sector. Honduras became an official signatory to the Venezuelan PetroCaribe initiative in January 2008. This would, it was hoped, reduce the cost of fuel imports and thus release funds for restructuring of energy sector; however, there were concerns that regulations enshrined in the agreement would deter much-needed private investment in hydroelectricity. Meanwhile, export revenue from bananas remained relatively stable in 2006–07, despite concerns regarding the impact on the market of the adoption by the European Union (see p. 244), from January 2006, of a new tariff regime for imports of bananas. The implementation of DR-CAFTA in 2006 strengthened foreign investment, which rose to an estimated US $815m. in 2007, largely in the manufacturing and telecommunications sectors. Moreover, DR-CAFTA precipitated a large increase in trade with the USA, particularly exports of Honduran textiles and clothing, although the USA's imposition of a 13.5% tariff on garments in late 2007 was expected to lower revenue. Furthermore, the end of a US import quota system at the end of 2008 was expected further to erode the comparative advantage of the Honduran textile and clothing sector, notably increasing exposure to competition from the People's Republic of China.

Education

Primary education, beginning at six years of age and comprising three cycles of three years, is officially compulsory and is provided free of charge. Secondary education, which is not compulsory, begins at the age of 15 and lasts for three years. In 2005 the enrolment at primary schools included 90.6% of children in the relevant age-group, while enrolment at secondary schools in that year was equivalent to 65.5% of children in the appropriate age-group. There are eight universities, including the Autonomous National University in Tegucigalpa. The education budget in 2004 was 8,779m. lempiras, representing 34.3% of total government expenditure.

Public Holidays

2008: 1 January (New Year's Day), 20–22 March (Easter), 14 April (Pan-American Day/Bastilla's Day), 1 May (Labour Day), 15 September (Independence Day), 3 October (Morazán Day), 12 October (Columbus Day), 21 October (Army Day), 25 December (Christmas).

2009: 1 January (New Year's Day), 9–11 April (Easter), 14 April (Pan-American Day/Bastilla's Day), 1 May (Labour Day), 15 September (Independence Day), 3 October (Morazán Day), 12 October (Columbus Day), 21 October (Army Day), 25 December (Christmas).

Weights and Measures

The metric system is in force, although some old Spanish measures are used, including: 25 libras = 1 arroba; 4 arrobas = 1 quintal (46 kg).

Statistical Survey

Sources (unless otherwise stated): Department of Economic Studies, Banco Central de Honduras, Avda Juan Ramón Molina, 1a Calle, 7a Avda, Apdo 3165, Tegucigalpa; tel. 237-2270; fax 238-0376; e-mail jreyes@bch.hn; internet www.bch.hn; Instituto Nacional de Estadística, Edif. Gómez, Blvd Suyapa, Col. Florencia Sur, Apdo 9412, Tegucipgalpa; e-mail info@ine.online.hn; internet www.ine-hn.org.

Area and Population

AREA, POPULATION AND DENSITY

Area (sq km)	112,492*
Population (census results)†	
29 May 1988	4,614,377
1 August 2001	
Males	3,230,958
Females	3,304,386
Total	6,535,344
Population (official estimates at mid-year)	
2005	7,168,717
2006	7,367,021
Density (per sq km) at mid-2006	65.5

* 43,433 sq miles.
† Excluding adjustments for underenumeration, estimated to have been 10% at the 1974 census.

PRINCIPAL TOWNS
(official projected population estimates, '000, 2006)

Tegucigalpa—Distrito Central (capital)	922.2	La Lima	59.8
San Pedro Sula	579.0	Danlí	56.0
Choloma	188.2	Siguatepeque	49.9
La Ceiba	156.4	Catacamas	46.0
El Progreso	110.9	Villanueva	45.4
Choluteca	85.1	Juticalpa	40.7
Comayagua	70.9	Tocoa	40.6
Puerto Cortés	61.6		

HONDURAS

BIRTHS AND DEATHS
(UN estimates)

	1990–95	1995–2000	2000–05
Birth rate (per 1,000)	37.2	33.5	30.2
Death rate (per 1,000)	6.7	6.1	6.0

Source: UN, *World Population Prospects: The 2006 Revision*.

Expectation of life (years at birth, WHO estimates): 67.2 (males 64.6; females 70.0) in 2005 (Source: WHO, *World Health Statistics*).

EMPLOYMENT
('000 persons)

	2004	2005	2006
Agriculture, hunting, forestry and fishing	851.1	997.2	989.0
Mining and quarrying	6.4	6.2	6.4
Manufacturing	385.5	378.1	406.6
Electricity, gas and water	10.0	11.1	11.2
Construction	143.5	135.5	165.6
Trade, restaurants and hotels	514.5	503.8	584.4
Transport, storage and communications	82.8	87.4	87.7
Financing, insurance, real estate and business services	69.8	81.7	85.5
Community, social and personal services	375.6	342.5	388.0
Total	**2,439.0**	**2,543.5**	**2,724.4**

Health and Welfare

KEY INDICATORS

Total fertility rate (children per woman, 2005)	3.5
Under-5 mortality rate (per 1,000 live births, 2005)	40
HIV/AIDS (% of persons aged 15–49, 2005)	1.5
Physicians (per 1,000 head, 2000)	0.57
Hospital beds (per 1,000 head, 2002)	1.0
Health expenditure (2004): US $ per head (PPP)	197.4
Health expenditure (2004): % of GDP	7.2
Health expenditure (2004): public (% of total)	54.9
Access to water (% of persons, 2004)	87
Access to sanitation (% of persons, 2004)	69
Human Development Index (2005): ranking	115
Human Development Index (2005): value	0.700

For sources and definitions, see explanatory note on p. vi.

Agriculture

PRINCIPAL CROPS
('000 metric tons)

	2004	2005	2006*
Maize	445	468	470
Sorghum	33	41	39
Sugar cane	5,466	5,625	5,000
Dry beans	79	63	75
Oil palm fruit*	1,135	1,233	1,233
Tomatoes	121*	153	153
Melons	241	246	246
Bananas	811	887	887
Plantains	270	285	285
Oranges	270	285	285
Pineapples	122	145	145
Coffee (green)	185	191	191

* FAO estimate(s).

Aggregate production ('000 metric tons, may include official, semi-official or estimated data): Total cereals 502.0 in 2004, 531.4 in 2005, 529.2 in 2006; Total vegetables (incl. melons) 586.7 in 2004, 634.4 in 2005, 634.4 in 2006; Total fruits (excl. melons) 1,564 in 2004, 1,696 in 2005, 1,696 in 2006.

Source: FAO.

LIVESTOCK
('000 head, year ending September)

	2003	2004	2005
Cattle	2,403	2,451	2,500
Sheep	15	15	15
Goats	25	24	24
Pigs	478	483	490
Horses*	181	181	181
Asses, mules or hinnies*	92,600	92,600	92,600
Chickens*	18,700	18,700	18,700

* FAO estimate(s).

2006: Figures assumed to be unchanged from 2005 (FAO estimates).

Source: FAO.

LIVESTOCK PRODUCTS
('000 metric tons)

	2003	2004	2005
Cattle meat	61.4	64.0	72.9
Pig meat	8.3	8.8	9.0
Chicken meat	116.8	128.8	140.7
Cows' milk	1,679.5	1,722.3	1,762.0
Hen eggs	40.0	40.5	40.9

2006: Figures assumed to be unchanged from 2005 (FAO estimates).

Source: FAO.

Forestry

ROUNDWOOD REMOVALS
('000 cubic metres, excl. bark)

	2004	2005	2006
Sawlogs, veneer logs and logs for sleepers	920	935	873
Fuel wood*	8,699	8,697	8,668
Total	**9,619**	**9,633**	**9,541**

* FAO estimates.

Source: FAO.

SAWNWOOD PRODUCTION
('000 cubic metres, incl. railway sleepers)

	2003	2004	2005
Total (all coniferous, softwood)	421	454*	400*

* FAO estimate.

2006: Figures assumed to unchanged from 2005 (FAO estimates).

Source: FAO.

Fishing

('000 metric tons, live weight)

	2003	2004	2005
Capture*	10.5	15.1	19.3
Marine fishes	4.8	4.6	4.6
Caribbean spiny lobster	1.0	1.0	1.0
Penaeus shrimps	3.5	3.2	3.1
Stromboid conches	1.0	0.1	0.1
Aquaculture	20.0	22.5	29.4
Nile tilapia	3.5	4.5	28.4
Penaeus shrimps	16.5	18.0	1.0
Total catch*	**30.6**	**37.7**	**48.7**

* FAO estimates.

Source: FAO.

HONDURAS

Mining

(metal content)

	2003	2004	2005
Lead (metric tons)	9,014	8,877	10,488
Zinc (metric tons)	43,766	41,413	42,698
Silver (kilograms)	43,766	48,218	53,617
Gold (kilograms)	4,484	3,677	3,600*

* Estimate.

Source: US Geological Survey.

Industry

SELECTED PRODUCTS

	2004	2005	2006
Raw sugar ('000 quintales)	8,141	7,817	8,508*
Cement ('000 bags of 42.5 kg)	32,749	32,552	39,246*
Cigarettes ('000 packets of 20)	320,556	319,958	342,591*
Beer ('000 12 oz bottles)	257,198	278,278	285,464*
Soft drinks ('000 12 oz bottles)	1,329,341	1,359,574	1,414,179*
Wheat flour ('000 quintales)	2,637	2,804	2,850*
Fabric ('000 yards)	198,347	197,727	192,052*
Liquor and spirits ('000 litres)	12,799	12,402	14,178*
Vegetable oil and butter ('000 libras)	171,054	160,947	157,508*
Electric energy (million kWh)	5,220.3	5,551.0	5,959.0

* Preliminary figure.

Finance

CURRENCY AND EXCHANGE RATES

Monetary Units
100 centavos = 1 lempira.

Sterling, Dollar and Euro Equivalents (31 December 2007)
£1 sterling = 37.854 lempiras;
US $1 = 18.895 lempiras;
€1 = 27.815 lempiras;
1,000 lempiras = £26.42 = $52.92 = €35.95.

Average Exchange Rate (lempiras per US $)
2005 18.8323
2006 18.8952
2007 18.8951

GOVERNMENT FINANCE
(budgetary central government, cash basis, million lempiras)

Summary of Balances

	2004	2005	2006*
Revenue	27,486.8	32,157.4	37,147.1
Less Expense	28,684.4	33,436.4	36,638.4
Net cash inflow from operating activities	−1,197.6	−1,278.9	508.6
Less Purchases of non-financial assets	3,860.8	3,436.0	2,802.4
Sales of non-financial assets	44.7	16.5	49.4
Cash surplus/deficit	−5,013.7	−4,698.5	−2,244.4

Statistical Survey

Revenue

	2004	2005	2006*
Taxes	23,417.3	26,711.8	31,438.2
Taxes of income, profits and capital gains	5,890.1	7,046.4	9,256.0
Taxes of goods and services	15,022.7	16,819.6	19,441.0
Social contributions	—	—	—
Grants	1,331.2	2,127.6	3,055.4
Other revenue	2,738.4	3,318.1	2,653.5
Total	27,486.8	32,157.4	37,147.1

Expense by economic type†

	2004	2005	2006*
Compensation of employees	13,595.8	14,874.7	16,743.9
Wages and salaries	12,413.8	13,577.0	15,268.5
Social contributions	1,182.0	1,297.6	1,475.4
Use of goods and services	3,226.1	4,559.2	5,518.4
Interest	2,160.9	2,246.2	1,760.7
Subsidies	621.7	689.9	999.4
Grants	6,368.8	8,030.5	7,033.7
Social benefits	96.5	64.5	186.2
Other expense	2,614.6	2,971.4	4,396.1
Total	28,684.4	33,436.4	36,638.4

* Preliminary figures.
† Including purchases of non-financial assets.

Source: IMF, *Government Finance Statistics Yearbook*.

CENTRAL BANK RESERVES
(US $ million at 31 December)

	2004	2005	2006
Gold (national valuation)	9.93	11.34	13.95
IMF special drawing rights	0.90	0.28	—
Foreign exchange	1,956.90	2,314.60	2,615.50
Reserve position in IMF	13.40	12.33	12.98
Total	1,981.13	2,338.55	2,642.43

Source: IMF, *International Financial Statistics*.

MONEY SUPPLY
(million lempiras at 31 December)

	2004	2005	2006
Currency outside banks	7,639	8,962	10,587
Demand deposits at commercial banks	9,840	12,020	15,301
Total money (incl. others)	17,827	21,316	26,082

Source: IMF, *International Financial Statistics*.

COST OF LIVING
(Consumer Price Index, December; base: 1999 = 100)

	2005	2006	2007
Food	147.1	155.3	176.6
Alcohol and tobacco	173.6	191.1	202.7
Rent, water, fuel and power	182.4	191.6	205.1
Clothing and footwear	156.5	167.9	180.8
Health	190.4	200.0	212.9
Transport	190.8	195.4	208.4
Communications	98.2	82.2	75.5
Culture and recreation	139.5	144.5	149.7
Education	226.9	250.9	269.1
Restaurants and hotels	157.9	169.8	187.7
All items (incl. others)	162.7	171.3	186.5

HONDURAS

NATIONAL ACCOUNTS
(million lempiras at current prices, preliminary figures)

Expenditure on the Gross Domestic Product

	2005	2006	2007
Government final consumption expenditure	28,522	31,908	38,059
Private final consumption expenditure	138,424	155,509	179,476
Increase in stocks	4,975	7,419	7,196
Gross fixed capital formation	45,780	56,676	70,749
Total domestic expenditure	217,701	251,512	295,480
Exports of goods and services	108,422	111,118	119,877
Less Imports of goods and services	142,375	157,945	182,539
GDP in purchasers' values	183,749	204,685	232,817
GDP at constant 2000 prices	133,886	142,290	151,255

Gross Domestic Product by Economic Activity

	2005	2006	2007
Agriculture, hunting, forestry and fishing	22,915	25,359	28,513
Mining and quarrying	1,184	1,389	1,584
Manufacturing	35,066	38,129	42,209
Electricity, gas and water	2,558	2,786	3,099
Construction	9,407	10,954	12,895
Wholesale and retail trade	25,227	28,380	31,892
Hotels and restaurants	5,049	5,625	6,338
Transport and storage	6,363	7,362	8,296
Communications	6,765	7,925	8,815
Finance and insurance	9,626	11,669	13,784
Owner-occupied dwellings	10,053	11,074	12,240
Business activities	8,062	9,283	10,478
Education services	11,795	13,453	17,061
Health	4,849	5,632	6,284
Public administration and defence	11,268	12,264	13,813
Other services	4,572	5,233	5,816
Sub-total	174,759	196,517	223,117
Less Financial intermediation services indirectly measured	6,912	8,246	10,081
GDP at factor cost	167,848	188,270	213,036
Indirect taxes, *less* subsidies	15,901	16,415	19,781
GDP in purchasers' values	183,749	204,685	232,817

BALANCE OF PAYMENTS
(US $ million)

	2004	2005	2006
Exports of goods f.o.b.	2,420.6	2,749.4	3,043.4
Imports of goods f.o.b.	−3,676.7	−4,239.1	−5,036.6
Trade balance	−1,256.1	−1,489.7	−1,993.2
Exports of services	682.9	743.7	752.6
Imports of services	−784.2	−875.4	−1,018.9
Balance on goods and services	−1,357.4	−1,621.4	−2,259.4
Other income received	50.7	104.6	178.1
Other income paid	−410.0	−444.6	−464.9
Balance on goods, services and income	−1,716.7	−1,961.4	−2,546.2
Current transfers received	1,368.8	1,984.5	2,531.3
Current transfers paid	−129.6	−154.7	−179.6
Current balance	−477.5	−131.6	−194.6
Capital account (net)	21.9	582.0	1,467.3
Direct investment from abroad	324.6	371.8	385.0
Portfolio investment assets	−4.3	−4.6	−4.9
Portfolio investment liabilities	—	−12.3	−10.0
Other investment assets	34.7	−30.9	3.1
Other investment liabilities	431.5	−515.6	−1,251.7
Net errors and omissions	42.4	−52.7	−93.4
Overall balance	373.3	206.1	300.8

Source: IMF, *International Financial Statistics*.

External Trade

PRINCIPAL COMMODITIES
(US $ million, preliminary figures, excluding *maquila* goods)

Imports c.i.f.	2005	2006	2007
Vegetables and fruit	208.5	237.5	304.8
Mineral fuels and lubricants	935.3	1,119.5	1,334.7
Chemicals and related products	654.0	742.8	897.1
Plastic and manufactures	299.2	339.5	393.3
Paper, paperboard and manufactures	259.4	292.1	289.3
Textile yarn, fabrics and manufactures	153.8	175.3	183.8
Metal and manufactures	359.8	426.2	491.5
Food products	432.5	514.4	615.5
Machinery and electrical appliances	838.3	968.2	1,179.4
Transport equipment	298.5	381.8	651.1
Total (incl. others)	4,852.5	5,964.6	6,983.4

Exports f.o.b.	2005	2006	2007
Bananas	260.3	251.9	289.6
Coffee	366.3	423.6	516.5
Lead and zinc	25.1	69.3	81.6
Palm oil	56.3	66.2	110.5
Shellfish	180.6	199.8	191.4
Soaps and detergents	42.5	42.6	41.7
Wood	43.3	44.0	46.4
Total (incl. others)	1,829.2	1,974.0	2,192.3

Gold exports (US $ million, preliminary figures): 63.3 in 2005; 80.0 in 2006.

PRINCIPAL TRADING PARTNERS
(US $ million, preliminary figures, excluding *maquila* goods)

Imports c.i.f.	2005	2006	2007
Brazil	126.8	127.1	150.4
Colombia	52.6	63.5	71.5
Costa Rica	237.3	282.2	333.7
El Salvador	266.2	325.9	404.6
Germany	95.6	63.5	89.8
Guatemala	400.8	521.0	651.8
Japan	109.4	155.6	200.7
Mexico	239.6	270.7	378.9
Nicaragua	88.7	108.5	119.2
Spain	62.6	68.5	69.6
USA	1,813.5	2,039.1	2,695.7
Venezuela	48.5	47.8	36.2
Total (incl. others)	4,852.5	5,694.6	6,983.4

Exports f.o.b.	2005	2006	2007
Belgium	113.1	181.8	115.6
Canada	44.3	24.8	37.1
Costa Rica	26.5	30.6	33.3
El Salvador	170.5	170.6	199.2
France	14.9	11.1	27.0
Germany	118.7	159.4	185.9
Guatemala	131.3	125.7	189.0
Italy	28.2	18.3	23.7
Japan	18.5	21.7	21.6
Mexico	53.9	75.9	124.8
Netherlands	48.1	46.8	54.4
Nicaragua	73.1	73.2	89.9
Spain	46.3	81.9	71.5
United Kingdom	30.5	60.7	14.6
USA	721.3	708.8	782.2
Total (incl. others)	1,829.1	1,974.0	2,192.3

Transport

ROAD TRAFFIC
(licensed vehicles in use)

	2001	2002	2003
Passenger cars	345,931	369,303	386,468
Buses and coaches	20,380	21,814	22,514
Lorries and vans	81,192	86,893	91,230
Motorcycles and bicycles	36,828	39,245	41,852

SHIPPING

Merchant Fleet
(registered at 31 December)

	2004	2005	2006
Number of vessels	1,094	1,093	1,072
Total displacement ('000 grt)	784.1	793.2	735.3

Source: Lloyd's Register-Fairplay, *World Fleet Statistics*.

International Sea-borne Freight Traffic
('000 metric tons)

	1988	1989	1990
Goods loaded	1,328	1,333	1,316
Goods unloaded	1,151	1,222	1,002

Source: UN, *Monthly Bulletin of Statistics*.

CIVIL AVIATION
(traffic on scheduled services)

	1993	1994	1995
Kilometres flown (million)	4	5	5
Passengers carried ('000)	409	449	474
Passenger-km (million)	362	323	341
Total ton-km (million)	50	42	33

Source: UN, *Statistical Yearbook*.

Tourism

TOURIST ARRIVALS BY COUNTRY OF ORIGIN

	2003	2004	2005
Canada	10,324	10,803	11,002
Costa Rica	19,621	20,740	20,855
El Salvador	130,547	137,084	159,546
Guatemala	99,894	104,725	92,612
Italy	10,020	10,376	11,975
Mexico	13,149	13,913	17,212
Nicaragua	94,174	98,735	76,646
Panama	7,104	7,516	8,394
Spain	7,335	7,694	8,536
USA	161,954	169,692	197,601
Total (incl. others)	610,535	640,981	673,035

Source: World Tourism Organization.

Total tourist arrivals: 738,700 (excluding 397,700 daytrippers) in 2006.

Receipts from tourism (US $ million): 373.2 in 2003; 401.2 in 2004 (preliminary figure); 431.3 in 2005 (estimate). Source: Instituto Hondureño de Turismo.

Communications Media

	2004	2005	2006
Telephones ('000 main lines in use)	365.8	395.3	476.5
Mobile cellular telephones ('000 subscribers)	707.2	1,281.5	2,240.8
Personal computers ('000 in use)*	110	n.a.	n.a.
Internet users ('000)	222.3	258.2	270.0

* Source: International Telecommunication Union.

Radio receivers ('000 in use): 2,450 in 1997 (Source: UN, *Statistical Yearbook*).

Television receivers ('000 in use): 640 in 2001 (Source: UN, *Statistical Yearbook*).

Daily newspapers: 4 in 2002; 4 in 2003.

Weekly newspapers: 3 in 2002; 3 in 2003.

Education

(2005/06)

	Institutions	Teachers	Students
Pre-primary*	5,357	15,232	197,408
Primary (grades 1 to 6)	11,069	46,308	1,293,333
Secondary (grades 7 to 9)			339,771
High school	1,049	23,750	195,741
Higher (incl. university)	16	6,457	145,171

* Figures for 2002/03.

Adult literacy rate (UNESCO estimates): 80.0% (males 79.8%; females 80.2%) in 2001 (Source: UNESCO Institute for Statistics).

Directory

The Constitution

Following the elections of April 1980, the 1965 Constitution was revised. The new Constitution was approved by the Congreso Nacional (National Congress) in November 1982, and amended in 1995. The following are some of its main provisions:

Honduras is constituted as a democratic Republic. All Hondurans over 18 years of age are citizens.

THE SUFFRAGE AND POLITICAL PARTIES

The vote is direct and secret. Any political party that proclaims or practises doctrines contrary to the democratic spirit is forbidden. A National Electoral Council will be set up at the end of each presidential term. Its general function will be to supervise all elections and to register political parties. A proportional system of voting will be adopted for the election of Municipal Corporations.

INDIVIDUAL RIGHTS AND GUARANTEES

The right to life is declared inviolable; the death penalty is abolished. The Constitution recognizes the right of habeas corpus and arrests may be made only by judicial order. Remand for interrogation may not last more than six days, and no-one may be held incommunicado for more than 24 hours. The Constitution recognizes the rights of free expression of thought and opinion, the free circulation of information, of peaceful, unarmed association, of free movement within and

HONDURAS

out of the country, of political asylum and of religious and educational freedom. Civil marriage and divorce are recognized.

WORKERS' WELFARE
All have a right to work. Day work shall not exceed eight hours per day or 44 hours per week; night work shall not exceed six hours per night or 36 hours per week. Equal pay shall be given for equal work. The legality of trade unions and the right to strike are recognized.

EDUCATION
The State is responsible for education, which shall be free, lay, and, in the primary stage, compulsory. Private education is liable to inspection and regulation by the State.

LEGISLATIVE POWER
Deputies are obliged to vote, for or against, on any measure at the discussion of which they are present. The Congreso Nacional has power to grant amnesties to political prisoners; approve or disapprove of the actions of the Executive; declare part or the whole of the Republic subject to a state of siege; declare war; approve or withhold approval of treaties; withhold approval of the accounts of public expenditure when these exceed the sums fixed in the budget; decree, interpret, repeal and amend laws, and pass legislation fixing the rate of exchange or stabilizing the national currency. The Congreso Nacional may suspend certain guarantees in all or part of the Republic for 60 days in the case of grave danger from civil or foreign war, epidemics or any other calamity. Deputies are elected in the proportion of one deputy and one substitute for every 35,000 inhabitants, or fraction over 15,000. Congress may amend the basis in the light of increasing population.

EXECUTIVE POWER
Executive power is exercised by the President of the Republic, who is elected for four years by a simple majority of the people. No President may serve more than one term.

JUDICIAL POWER
The Judiciary consists of the Supreme Court, the Courts of Appeal and various lesser tribunals. The nine judges and seven substitute judges of the Supreme Court are elected by the Congreso Nacional for a period of four years. The Supreme Court is empowered to declare laws unconstitutional.

THE ARMED FORCES
The Armed Forces are declared by the Constitution to be essentially professional and non-political. The President exercises direct authority over the military.

LOCAL ADMINISTRATION
The country is divided into 18 Departments for purposes of local administration, and these are subdivided into 290 autonomous Municipalities; the functions of local offices shall be only economic and administrative.

The Government

HEAD OF STATE
President: JOSÉ MANUEL (MEL) ZELAYA ROSALES (took office 27 January 2006).
Vice-President: ELVIN ERNESTO SANTOS ORDÓÑEZ.

CABINET
(March 2008)

Minister of the Interior and Justice: Dr VÍCTOR MEZA.
Minister of the Presidency: ENRIQUE FLORES LANZA.
Minister of Foreign Affairs: ANGEL EDMUNDO ORELLANA MERCADO.
Minister of Industry and Commerce: FREDDY CERRATO.
Minister of Finance: REBECA PATRICIA SANTOS RIVERA.
Minister of Labour and Social Welfare: MAYRA MEJÍA DEL CID.
Minister of National Defence: ARÍSTIDES MEJÍA CARRANZA.
Minister of Public Security: JORGE ALBERTO RODAS GAMERO.
Minister of Public Works, Transport and Housing: JOSÉ ROSARIO BONNANO.
Minister of Culture, Art and Sports: Dr RODOLFO PASTOR FASQUELLE.
Minister of Agriculture and Livestock: HÉCTOR HERNÁNDEZ AMADOR.
Minister of Natural Resources and the Environment: THOMAS VAQUERO.
Minister of Tourism: RICARDO ALFREDO MARTÍNEZ.
Minister for the Honduran Council for Science and Technology: MYRIAM ELIZABETH MEJÍA.
Minister of the International Co-operation and Technical Secretariat: KAREN LIZETH ZELAYA ORELLANA.
Minister of the National Institute for Women's Affairs: SELMA ESTRADA LÓPEZ.
Minister of State in the Ministry of Health: ELSA YOLANDA PALAU.
Minister of State in the Ministry of Education: MARLÓN BREVÉ REYES.

MINISTRIES

Office of the President: Palacio José Cecilio del Valle, Blvd Juan Pablo II, Tegucigalpa; tel. 232-6282; fax 231-0097; internet www.presidencia.gob.hn.

Ministry of Agriculture and Livestock: Tegucigalpa; tel. 235-7388; e-mail infoagro@sag.gob.hn; internet www.sag.gob.hn.

Ministry of Culture, Art and Sports: Avda La Paz, Apdo 3287, Tegucigalpa; tel. 236-9643; fax 236-9532; e-mail binah@sdnhon.org.hn.

Ministry of Education: 1a Avda, entre 2a y 3a Calle, Comayagüela, Tegucigalpa; tel. 222-8571; fax 237-4312; e-mail info@se.gob.hn; internet www.se.gob.hn.

Ministry of Finance: 5a Avda, 3a Calle, Tegucigalpa; tel. 222-1278; fax 238-2309; e-mail despacho@sefin.gob.hn; internet www.sefin.gob.hn.

Ministry of Foreign Affairs: Centro Cívico Gubernamental, Antigua Casa Presidencial, Blvd Kuwait, Contiguo a la Corte Suprema de Justicia, Tegucigalpa; tel. 234-1962; fax 234-1484; internet www.sre.hn.

Ministry of Health: 2a Calle, Avda Cervantes, Tegucigalpa; tel. 222-8518; fax 238-6787; internet www.salud.gob.hn.

Ministry of Industry and Commerce: Edif. Salame, 5a Avda, 4a Calle, Tegucigalpa; tel. 238-2025; fax 237-2836; internet www.sic.gob.hn.

Ministry of the Interior and Justice: Residencia La Hacienda, Calle La Estancia, Tegucigalpa; tel. 232-1892; fax 232-0226; e-mail atencionalpublico@gobernacion.gob.hn; internet www.gobernacion.gob.hn.

Ministry of Labour and Social Welfare: Edif. Olympus (STSS), Col. Puerta del Sol, Contiguo a SETCO, Intersección Bulevares Villa Olímpica, La Hacienda, Tegucigalpa; tel. 235-3455; fax 235-3456; e-mail info@trabajo.gob.hn; internet www.trabajo.gob.hn.

Ministry of National Defence: 5a Avda, 4a Calle, Tegucigalpa; tel. 238-3427; fax 238-0238.

Ministry of Natural Resources and the Environment: 100 m al sur del Estadio Nacional, Apdo 1389, Tegucigalpa; tel. 235-7833; fax 232-6250; e-mail sdespacho@yahoo.com; internet www.serna.gob.hn.

Ministry of Public Security: 5a Avda, 4a Calle, Tegucigalpa; tel. 220-4323; fax 220-4352.

Ministry of Public Works, Transport and Housing: Barrio La Bolsa, Comayagüela, Tegucigalpa; tel. 225-0489; fax 225-2227; e-mail jmtorres@soptravi.gob.hn; internet www.soptravi.gob.hn.

Ministry of Tourism: Edif. Europa, Col. San Carlos, Apdo 3261, Tegucigalpa; tel. and fax 222-2124; e-mail tourisminfo@iht.hn; internet www.hondurastourism.com.

Honduran Council for Science and Technology: Edif. CAD, Contiguo a CHIMINIKE, Blvd Fuerzas Armadas, Tegucigalpa; tel. 230-7673; fax 230-1664; e-mail memejia@cohcit.gob.hn; internet www.cohcit.gob.hn.

International Co-operation and Technical Secretariat: Edif. El Sol, Col. Puerta del Sol, 1 c. atrás del Blvd La Hacienda, Tegucigalpa; tel. 239-5545; fax 239-5277; e-mail cohara@setco.gob.hn; internet www.setco.gob.hn.

National Institute for Women's Affairs: Tegucigalpa; tel. 221-3637; fax 221-4827; e-mail dtecnica@inam.gob.hn; internet www.inam.gob.hn.

HONDURAS

President and Legislature

PRESIDENT
Election, 27 November 2005

Candidate	Votes cast	% of votes
José Manuel (Mel) Zelaya Rosales (PL)	999,006	49.90
Porfirio Lobo Sosa (PN)	925,243	46.22
Juan Angel Almendárez Bonilla (PUD)	29,754	1.49
Juan-Ramón Martínez (PDCH)	27,812	1.39
Carlos Alejandro Sosa Coello (PINU-SD)	20,093	1.00
Total	2,001,908	100.00

CONGRESO NACIONAL
President: ROBERTO MICHELETTI BAIN.
General Election, 27 November 2005

	Seats
Partido Liberal (PL)	62
Partido Nacional (PN)	55
Partido de Unificación Democrática (PUD)	5
Partido Demócrata Cristiano de Honduras (PDCH)	4
Partido Innovación y Unidad Social Demócrata (PINU-SD)	2
Total	128

Election Commission

Tribunal Supremo Electoral (TSE): Tegucigalpa; tel. 223-4577; e-mail centroinformacion@tse.hn; internet www.tse.hn; f. 2004 as successor to Tribunal Nacional de Elecciones; Pres. JACOBO HERNÁNDEZ CRUZ.

Political Organizations

Partido Demócrata Cristiano de Honduras (PDCH): Col. San Carlos, Tegucigalpa; tel. 236-5969; fax 236-9941; e-mail pdch@hondutel.hn; internet www.pdch.hn; legally recognized in 1980; Pres. Dr HERNÁN CORRALES PADILLA; Sec.-Gen. SAÚL ESCOBAR ANDRADE.

Partido Innovación y Unidad—Social Demócrata (PINU-SD): 2a Avda, entre 9 y 10 calles, Apdo 105, Comayagüela; tel. 220-4224; fax 220-4232; e-mail partido@pinu.org; internet www.pinu-sd.org; f. 1970; legally recognized in 1978; Pres. JORGE AGUILAR.

Partido Liberal (PL): Col. Miramonte, Tegucigalpa; tel. 232-0520; fax 232-0797; e-mail multimedia@partidoliberal.net; internet www.partidoliberal.net; f. 1891; factions within the party include the Movimiento Pinedista (Leader Dr RAFAEL PINEDA PONCE), the Movimiento LIBRE (Leader JAIME ROSENTHAL OLIVA) and the Movimiento Esperanza Liberal (Leader JOSÉ MANUEL (MEL) ZELAYA ROSALES); has a youth organization called the Frente Central de Juventud Liberal de Honduras (Pres. EDUARDO RAINA GARCÍA); Pres. Dr RAFAEL PINEDA PONCE; Sec.-Gen. JAIME ROSENTHAL OLIVA.

Partido Nacional (PN): Paseo el Obelisco, Comayagüela, Tegucigalpa; tel. 237-7310; fax 237-7365; e-mail partidonacional@partidonacional.hn; internet www.partidonacional.hn; f. 1902; traditional right-wing party; Pres. PORFIRIO LOBO SOSA; Sec.-Gen. JUAN ORLANDO HERNÁNDEZ.

Partido de Unificación Democrática (PUD): Barrio La Plazuela, Avda Cervantes, Tegucigalpa; tel. and fax 238-2498; e-mail colectivoparlud@hotmail.com; f. 1993; left-wing coalition comprising Partido Revolucionario Hondureño, Partido Renovación Patriótica, Partido para la Transformación de Honduras and Partido Morazanista; Sec.-Gen. HERMILIO SOTO.

Diplomatic Representation

EMBASSIES IN HONDURAS

Argentina: Calle Palermo 302, Col. Rubén Darío, Apdo 3208, Tegucigalpa; tel. 232-3376; fax 231-0376; e-mail ehond@mrecic.gov.ar; Chargé d'affaires a.i. ALEJANDRO JOSÉ AMURA.

Brazil: Col. Palmira, Calle República del Brasil, Apdo 341, Tegucigalpa; tel. 221-4432; fax 236-5873; e-mail brastegu@sigmanet.hn; Ambassador BRIAN MICHAEL FRASER NEELE.

Chile: Calle Oslo C-4242, Col. Lomas del Guijarro, Tegucigalpa; tel. 232-2114; fax 239-7925; e-mail echilehn@123.hn; Ambassador SERGIO VERDUGO NEIRA.

China (Taiwan): Col. Lomas del Guijarro, Calle Eucaliptos 3750, Apdo 3433, Tegucigalpa; tel. 239-5837; fax 232-5103; e-mail hnd@mofa.gov.tw; Ambassador LAI CHIEN-CHUNG.

Colombia: Edif. Palmira, 3°, Col. Palmira, Apdo 468, Tegucigalpa; tel. 239-9324; fax 232-9324; e-mail ehonduras@cancilleria.gov.co; internet www.embajadadecolombia.hn; Ambassador MIGUEL CAMILO RUIZ BLANCO.

Costa Rica: Residencial El Triángulo, 1a Calle, Lomas del Guijarro, Apdo 512, Tegucigalpa; tel. 232-1768; fax 232-1876; e-mail embacori@amnettgu.com; Ambassador JAVIER GUERRA LASPIUR.

Cuba: Col. Loma Linda Norte, Calle Diagonal Huri 2255, contiguo a Residencial Torres Blancas, Tegucigalpa; tel. 239-3778; fax 235-7624; e-mail embacuba@amnettgu.com; internet embacu.cubaminrex.cu/honduras; Ambassador JUAN CARLOS HERNÁNDEZ PADRÓN.

Dominican Republic: Calle Principal frente al Banco Continental, Col. Miramontes, Tegucigalpa; tel. 239-0130; fax 239-1594; e-mail embadom@compunet.hn; Ambassador JOSÉ DEL CARMEN ACOSTA CARRASCO.

Ecuador: Casa 2968, Sendero Senecio, Col. Castaños Sur, Apdo 358, Tegucigalpa; tel. 221-1049; fax 235-4074; e-mail mecuahon@multivisionhn.net; Ambassador FERNANDO CHÁVEZ DÁVILA.

El Salvador: Col. Altos de Miramontes, Casa 2952, Diagonal Aguan, Tegucigalpa; tel. 232-4947; fax 239-6556; e-mail embasalhonduras@rree.gob.sv; internet www.rree.gob.sv/embajadas/honduras.nsf; Ambassador SIGIFREDO OCHOA PÉREZ.

France: Col. Palmira, Avda Juan Lindo, Callejón Batres 337, Apdo 3441, Tegucigalpa; tel. 236-6800; fax 236-8051; e-mail info@ambafrance-hn.org; internet www.ambafrance-hn.org; Ambassador LAURENT DOMINATI.

Germany: Edif. Paysen, 3°, Blvd Morazán, Apdo 3145, Tegucigalpa; tel. 232-3161; fax 239-9018; e-mail embalema@amnettgu.com; internet www.tegucigalpa.diplo.de; Ambassador PAUL ALBERT RESCH.

Guatemala: Col. Lomas del Guijaro, Calle Alfonso XIII, Casa 3716, Tegucigalpa; tel. 232-5018; fax 232-1580; Ambassador ANGELA GAROZ CABRERA.

Holy See: Palacio de la Nunciatura Apostólica, Col. Palmira, Avda Santa Sede 412, Apdo 324, Tegucigalpa; tel. 232-6613; fax 239-8869; e-mail nunciature@amnettgu.com; Apostolic Nuncio Most Rev. ANTONIO ARCARI (Titular Archbishop of Ceciti).

Italy: Edif Plaza Azul, 4°, Col. Lomas Del Guijarro Sur, Apdo U-9093, Tegucigalpa; tel. 239-5790; fax 239-5737; e-mail ambasciata.tegucigalpa@esteri.it; internet www.ambtegucigalpa.esteri.it; Ambassador GIUSEPPE MAGNO.

Japan: Col. San Carlos, Calzada Rep. Paraguay, Apdo 3232, Tegucigalpa; tel. 236-2628; fax 236-6100; e-mail gerardo@graduate.chiba-u.jp; internet www.hn.emb-japan.go.jp; Ambassador TAKASHI KOEZUKA.

Korea, Republic: Edif. Plaza Azul, 5°, Col. Lomas del Guijarro Sur, Tegucigalpa; tel. 235-5561; fax 235-5564; e-mail info@koreaemb.hn; internet www.koreaemb.hn; Ambassador SUN KIU KIM.

Mexico: Col. Lomas del Guijarro, Avda Eucalipto 1001, Tegucigalpa; tel. 232-4039; fax 232-4719; e-mail embamexhonduras@gmail.com; internet www.sre.gob.mx/honduras; Ambassador TARCISIO NAVARRETE MONTES DE OCA.

Nicaragua: Col. Tepeyac, Bloque M-1, Avda Choluteca 1130, Apdo 392, Tegucigalpa; tel. 231-1977; fax 231-1412; e-mail embanic@amnettgu.com; Ambassador PIERO COEN MONTEALEGRE.

Panama: Edif. Palmira, 2°, Col. Palmira, Apdo 397, Tegucigalpa; tel. 239-5508; fax 232-8147; e-mail ephon@multivisionhn.net; Ambassador ROBERT JOVANÉ.

Peru: Col. La Reforma, Calle Principal 2618, Tegucigalpa; tel. 221-0596; fax 236-6070; e-mail embajdadelperu@cablecolor.hn; Ambassador GUSTAVO OTERO ZAPATA.

Spain: Col. Matamoros, Calle Santander 801, Apdo 3221, Tegucigalpa; tel. 236-6875; fax 236-8682; e-mail embesphn@correo.mae.es; Ambassador AUGUSTÍN NÚÑEZ MARTÍNEZ.

USA: Avda La Paz, Apdo 3453, Tegucigalpa; tel. 236-9320; fax 236-9037; internet honduras.usembassy.gov; Ambassador CHARLES A. FORD.

Venezuela: Col. Rubén Darío, 2116 Circuito Choluteca, Apdo 775, Tegucigalpa; tel. 232-1879; fax 232-1016; e-mail evenezue@multivisionhn.net; internet venezuelabolivariana.com; Chargé d'affaires a.i. CLAUDIO SORIO FERMÍN.

Judicial System

Justice is administered by the Supreme Court (which has 15 judges), five Courts of Appeal and departmental courts (which have their own local jurisdiction).

Tegucigalpa has two Courts of Appeal which have jurisdiction (1) in the department of Francisco Morazán, and (2) in the departments of Choluteca Valle, El Paraíso and Olancho.

The Appeal Court of San Pedro Sula has jurisdiction in the department of Cortés; that of Comayagua has jurisdiction in the departments of Comayagua, La Paz and Intibucá; and that of Santa Bárbara in the departments of Santa Bárbara, Lempira and Copán.

Supreme Court: Edif. Palacio de Justicia, contiguo Col. Miraflores, Centro Cívico Gubernamental, Tegucigalpa; tel. 233-9208; fax 233-6784; internet www.poderjudicial.gob.hn; Pres. VILMA CECILIA MORALES MONTALVÁN.

Attorney-General: ROSA AMÉRICA DE GALO.

Religion

The majority of the population are Roman Catholics; the Constitution guarantees toleration to all forms of religious belief.

CHRISTIANITY

The Roman Catholic Church

Honduras comprises one archdiocese and seven dioceses (the diocese of Yoro was created in 2005). At 31 December 2005 there were an estimated 5.8m. adherants, representing some 82% of the population.

Bishops' Conference

Conferencia Episcopal de Honduras, Blvd Estadio Suyapa, Apdo 3121, Tegucigalpa; tel. 229-1111; fax 229-1144; e-mail ceh@unicah.edu.

f. 1929; Pres. Cardinal OSCAR ANDRÉS RODRÍGUEZ MARADIAGA (Archbishop of Tegucigalpa).

Archbishop of Tegucigalpa: Cardinal OSCAR ANDRÉS RODRÍGUEZ MARADIAGA, Arzobispado, 3a y 2a Avda 1113, Apdo 106, Tegucigalpa; tel. 237-0353; fax 222-2337; e-mail orodriguez@unicah.edu.

The Anglican Communion

Honduras comprises a single missionary diocese, in Province IX of the Episcopal Church in the USA.

Bishop of Honduras: Rt Rev. LLOYD EMMANUEL ALLEN, Apdo 586, San Pedro Sula; tel. 556-6155; fax 556-6467; e-mail emmanuel@anglicano.hn.

The Baptist Church

Convención Nacional de Iglesias Bautistas de Honduras (CONIBAH): Apdo 2176, Tegucigalpa; tel. and fax 236-6717; internet www.ublaonline.org/paises/honduras.htm; Pres. Pastor TOMÁS MONTOYA; 24,142 mems.

Other Churches

Iglesia Cristiana Luterana de Honduras (Lutheran): Barrio Villa Adela, 19 Calle entre 5a y 6a Avda, Apdo 2861, Tegucigalpa; tel. and fax 225-4464; e-mail iclh@123.hn; internet www.iglesialuteranadehonduras.com; Pres. Rev. ARMINDO SCHMECHEL; 1,000 mems.

BAHÁ'Í FAITH

National Spiritual Assembly: Sendero de los Naranjos 2801, Col. Castaños, Apdo 273, Tegucigalpa; tel. 232-6124; fax 231-1343; internet www.bahaihon.org; Co-ordinator SOHEIL DOOKI; 40,000 mems resident in more than 500 localities.

The Press

DAILIES

La Gaceta: Tegucigalpa; f. 1830; morning; official govt paper; circ. 3,000.

El Heraldo: Avda los Próceres, Frente Instituto del Tórax, Barrio San Felipe, Apdo 1938, Tegucigalpa; tel. 236-6000; internet www.elheraldo.hn; f. 1979; morning; independent; Pres. JORGE CANAHUATI LARACH; Editor CARLOS MAURICIO FLORES; circ. 50,000.

El Nuevo Día: 3a Avda, 11–12 Calles, San Pedro Sula; tel. 552-4298; fax 557-9457; f. 1994; morning; independent; Pres. ABRAHAM ANDONIE; Editor ARMANDO CERRATO; circ. 20,000.

La Prensa: 3a Avda, 6a–7a Calles No 34, Apdo 143, San Pedro Sula; tel. 553-3101; fax 553-0778; internet www.laprensahn.com; f. 1964; morning; independent; Pres. JORGE CANAHUATI LARACH; Exec. Dir NELSON EDGARDO FERNÁNDEZ; circ. 50,000.

El Tiempo: 1a Calle, 5a Avda 102, Santa Anita, Apdo 450, San Pedro Sula; tel. 553-3388; fax 553-4590; e-mail tiempo@continental.hn; internet www.tiempo.hn; f. 1960; morning; left-of-centre; Pres. JAIME ROSENTHAL OLIVA; Editor MANUEL GAMERO; circ. 35,000.

La Tribuna: Col. Santa Bárbara, Comayagüela, Apdo 1501, Tegucigalpa; tel. 233-1138; fax 233-1188; e-mail tribuna@mail.latribuna.hn; internet www.latribuna.hn; f. 1977; morning; independent; Dir ADÁN ELVIR FLORES; Gen. Man. MANUEL ACOSTA MEDINA; circ. 45,000.

PERIODICALS

Comercio Global: Cámara de Comercio e Industrias de Tegucigalpa, Blvd Centroamérica, Apdo 3444, Tegucigalpa; tel. 232-4200; fax 232-0759; f. 1970; monthly; commercial and industrial news; Editor VANESSA BALDASSARRE.

Hablemos Claro: Edif. Torre Libertad, Blvd Suyapa, Tegucigalpa; tel. 232-8058; fax 239-7008; e-mail abrecha@hondutel.hn; internet www.hablemosclaro.com; f. 1990; weekly; Editor RODRIGO WONG ARÉVALO; circ. 9,000.

Hibueras: Apdo 955, Tegucigalpa; Dir RAÚL LANZA VALERIANO.

Honduras This Week: Centro Comercial Villa Mare, Blvd Morazán, Apdo 1323, Tegucigalpa; tel. 239-3654; fax 232-2300; e-mail hondweek@hondutel.hn; internet www.hondurasthisweek.com; f. 1988; weekly; English language; tourism, culture and the environment; Man. Editor GLADYS ACOSTA; Editor MARIO GUTIÉRREZ MINERA.

El Libertador: Tegucigalpa; Dir JHONY LAGOS.

Pregonero Evangélico: Tegucigalpa; e-mail mcm@sdnhon.org.hn; internet www.mcmhn.org/pregonero; f. 2000; quarterly; Christian magazine.

PRESS ASSOCIATION

Asociación de Prensa Hondureña: Casa del Periodista, Avda Gutemberg 1525, Calle 6, Barrio El Guanacaste, Apdo 893, Tegucigalpa; tel. and fax 378-345; f. 1930; Pres. MIGUEL OSMUNDO MEJÍA; Sec.-Gen. FELA ISABEL DUARTE.

Publishers

Centro Editorial: San Pedro Sula; tel. and fax 558-1282; Dir JULIO ESCOTO.

Ediciones Ramses: Edif. Torres Fiallos, Avda Jerez, Apdo 5600, Tegucigalpa; tel. 220-4248; fax 220-0833; e-mail servicioalcliente@edicionesramses.hn; internet edicionesramses.galeon.com; educational material.

Editora Fuego Nuevo: Col. Florencia Sur, Blvd Suyapa, Tegucigalpa; tel. 232-4638; fax 232-4964; e-mail mirna_detorres@yahoo.com; Dir MYRNA LANZA GONZÁLEZ.

Editorial Pez Dulce: 143 Paseo La Leona, Barrio La Leona, Tegucigalpa; tel. and fax 222-1220; e-mail pezdulce@yahoo.com.

Editorial Universitaria de la Universidad Nacional Autónoma de Honduras: Blvd Suyapa, Tegucigalpa; tel. and fax 231-4601; e-mail segisfredo@eudoramail.com; f. 1847.

Guaymuras: Apdo 1843, Tegucigalpa; tel. 237-5433; fax 238-4578; e-mail ediguay@123.hn; f. 1980; Dir ISOLDA ARITA MELZER.

Broadcasting and Communications

TELECOMMUNICATIONS

Regulatory Authority

Comisión Nacional de Telecomunicaciones (Conatel): Col. Modelo, 6a Avda Suroeste, Apdo 15012, Tegucigalpa; tel. 234-8600; fax 234-8611; e-mail conatel@conatel.hn; internet www.conatel.hn; Pres. RASEL ANTONIO TOMÉ.

Major Service Providers

The monopoly of the telecommunications sector by Hondutel ceased at the end of 2005, when the fixed line and international services market was opened to domestic and foreign investment. In 2007 in addition to Hondutel there were two private mobile cellular telephone operators. A fourth mobile telecommunications contract was expected to be awarded in 2008.

Claro Honduras: Col. San Carlos, Avda República de Colombia, Tegucigalpa; tel. 205-4222; e-mail ventascorporativas@alosercom.hn; internet www.alo.hn; f. 2003; operated by Servicios de

HONDURAS

Comunicaciones de Honduras (Sercom Honduras), a subsidiary of América Móvil, SA de CV (Mexico) since July 2004; mobile cellular telephone operator.

Empresa Hondureña de Telecomunicaciones (Hondutel): Apdo 1794, Tegucigalpa; tel. 221-6555; fax 236-7795; e-mail miguel.velez@hondutelnet.hn; internet www.hondutel.hn; scheduled for privatization; Dir JORGE ROSA; Gen. Man. JACOBO LAGOS.

Multifon: Tegucigalpa; tel. 206-0607; e-mail sac@multifon.net; internet www.multifon.net; f. 2003; subsidiary of MultiData; awarded govt contract with UT Starcom (q.v.) for fixed telephone lines in 2003; Pres. JOSÉ RAFAEL FERRARI; CEO JOSÉ LUIS RIVERA.

Telefónica Celular (CELTEL): Edif. Celtel, contiguo a la Iglesia Episcopal, Blvd Suyapa, Col. Florencia Norte Hondureña, Tegucigalpa; tel. 235-7966; fax 220-7060; e-mail info@mail.celtel.net; internet www.tigo.com.hn; f. 1996; mobile cellular telephone company; 66.7% owned by Millicom International Cellular (Luxembourg).

UT Starcom (USA): Edif. Plaza Azul, 6°, Calle Viena, Avda Berlin, Col. Lomas del Guijarro Sur, Tegucigalpa; tel. 239-8289; fax 239-9161; internet www.utstar.com; awarded govt contract with Multifon (q.v.) for fixed telephone lines in 2003; Pres. and CEO HONG LIANG LU; Gen. Man. JULIO LARIOS.

BROADCASTING

Radio

Estereo McIntosh: La Ceiba, Atlántida; tel. 440-0326; fax 440-0325; e-mail mcintosh@psinet.hn; internet www.psinet.hn/mcintosh; commercial channel.

HRN, La Voz de Honduras: Blvd Suyapa, Apdo 642, Tegucigalpa; internet www.radiohrn.hn; commercial station; f. 1933; broadcasts 12 channels; 23 relay stations; Gen. Man. NAHÚN VALLADARES.

Power FM: Tegucigalpa; tel. 552-4898; e-mail info@powerfm.hn; internet www.powerfm.hn; Gen. Man. XAVIER SIERRA.

Radio América: Col. Alameda, frente a la Droguería Mandofer, Apdo 259, Tegucigalpa; tel. 232-8338; fax 232-1009; e-mail emchimirri@hondutelnet.hn; internet www.hondutel.hn; commercial station; broadcasts Radio San Pedro, Radio Continental, Radio Monderna, Radio Universal, Cadena Radial Sonora, Super Cien Stereo, Momentos FM Stereo and 3 regional channels; f. 1948; 13 relay stations; Gen. Man. MARCELO CHIMIRRI.

Radio Club Honduras: Salida Chamelecon, Apdo 273, San Pedro Sula; tel. 556-6173; e-mail hr2rch@yahoo.com; internet www.qsl.net/hr2rch; amateur radio club; Pres. NORMA LEIVA.

Radio Esperanza: La Esperanza, Intibucá; tel. 783-0025; fax 783-0644; e-mail radioesperanza1@hotmail.com; internet www.honducontact.com/Radio%20Esperanza.htm; Dir J. M. DEL CID.

Radio la Voz del Atlántico: 12a Calle, 2–3 Avda, Barrio Copen, Puerto Cortés; tel. 665-5166; fax 665-2401; e-mail atlantico@sescomnet.com; internet radioatlantico.8m.com.

Radio Nacional de Honduras: Avda La Paz, contiguo a la Secretaría de Cultura, Artes y Deportes, Tegucigalpa; tel. 236-7551; fax 236-7359; e-mail radionacional@sdnhon.org.hn; f. 1976; official station, operated by the Govt; Gen. Man. JOSÉ ROLANDO SARMIENTO ROSA.

La Voz de Centroamérica: 9a Calle, 10a Avda 64, Apdo 120, San Pedro Sula; tel. 552-7660; fax 557-3257; f. 1955; commercial station.

Television

Televicentro: Edif. Televicentro, Blvd Suyapa, Apdo 734, Tegucigalpa; e-mail mercadeoventas@televicentro.hn; internet www.televicentro.hn; f. 1987; 11 relay stations; Pres. JOSÉ RAFAEL FERRARI SAGASTUME.

 Canal 5: tel. 232-7835; fax 232-0097; f. 1959; Gen. Man. JOSÉ RAFAEL FERRARI SAGASTUME.

 Telecadena 7 y 4: tel. 239-2081; fax 232-0097; f. 1959; Pres. JOSÉ RAFAEL FERRARI SAGASTUME; Gen. Man. RAFAEL ENRIQUE VILLEDA.

 Telesistema Hondureño, Canal 3 y 7: tel. 232-7064; fax 232-5019; f. 1967; Gen. Man. RAFAEL ENRIQUE VILLEDA.

VICA Television: 9a Calle, 10a Avda 64, Barrio Guamilito, Apdo 120, San Pedro Sula; tel. 552-4478; fax 557-3257; e-mail info@mayanet.hn; internet www.vicatv.hn; f. 1986; operates regional channels 2, 9 and 13; Pres. BLANCA SIKAFFY.

Finance

(cap. = capital; res = reserves; dep. = deposits; m. = million; brs = branches; amounts in lempiras unless otherwise stated)

BANKING

Central Bank

Banco Central de Honduras (BANTRAL): Avda Juan Ramón Molina, 7a Avda y 1a Calle, Apdo 3165, Tegucigalpa; tel. 237-2270; fax 237-1876; e-mail eanariba@mail.bch.hn; internet www.bch.hn; f. 1950; bank of issue; cap. 223.4m., res 2,148.7m., dep. 43,974m. (Dec. 2006); Pres. EDWIN ARAQUE BONILLA; Man. GERMÁN ENRIQUE MARTEL BELTRÁN; 4 brs.

Commercial Banks

Banco Atlántida, SA (BANCATLAN): Plaza Bancatlán, Blvd Centroamérica, Apdo 3164, Tegucigalpa; tel. 232-1050; fax 232-6120; e-mail webmaster@bancatlan.hn; internet www.bancatlan.hn; f. 1913; cap. 1,421.0m., res 158.0m., dep. 18,002.1m. (Dec. 2006); Exec. Pres. GUILLERMO BUESO; Exec. Vice-Pres GUSTAVO OVIEDO, ILDOIRA G. DE BONILLA; 132 brs.

Banco Continental, SA (BANCON): 9–10 Avda NO, Blvd Morazán, San Pedro Sula; tel. 550-0880; fax 550-2750; e-mail imontoya@continental.hn; internet www.bancon.hn; f. 1974; cap. 500.0m., res 14.5m., dep. 1,611.1m. (Dec. 2005); Pres., Chair. and Gen. Man JAIME ROSENTHAL OLIVA; 41 brs.

Banco Financiera Comercial Hondureña (Banco FICOHSA): Edif. Plaza Victoria, Col. Las Colinas, Blvd Miraflores, Tegucigalpa; tel. 239-6410; fax 239-6420; e-mail ficobanc@ficohsa.hn; internet www.ficohsa.com; Chair. JORGE ALEJANDRO FARAJ.

Banco de Honduras, SA: Blvd Suyapa, Col. Loma Linda Sur, Tegucigalpa; tel. 232-6122; fax 232-6167; internet www.bancodehonduras.citibank.com; f. 1889; subsidiary of Citibank NA (USA); total assets 15,106m. (1999); Gen. Man. MAXIMO R. VIDAL; 2 brs.

Banco Mercantil, SA: Blvd Suyapa, frente a Emisoras Unidas, Apdo 116, Tegucigalpa; tel. 232-0006; fax 239-4509; internet www.bamernet.hn; Pres. JOSÉ LAMAS BEZOS; Vice-Pres. MANUEL VILLEDA TOLEDO.

Banco de Occidente, SA (BANCOCCI): 6a Avda, Calle 2–3, Apdo 3284, Tegucigalpa; tel. 237-0310; fax 237-0486; e-mail bancocci@cybertelh.hn; f. 1951; cap. and res 69m., dep. 606m. (June 1994); Pres. and Gen. Man. JORGE BUESO ARIAS; Vice-Pres. EMILIO MEDINA R.; 146 brs.

Banco de los Trabajadores, SA (BANCOTRAB): 3a Avda, 13a Calle, Comayagüela, Apdo 3246, Tegucigalpa; tel. 238-0017; fax 238-0077; internet www.btrab.com; f. 1967; cap. 204.8m. (Dec. 2002); Pres. ROLANDO DEL CID VELÁSQUEZ; 13 brs.

Development Banks

Banco Centroamericano de Integración Económica: Edif. Sede BCIE, Blvd Suyapa, Apdo 772, Tegucigalpa; tel. 228-2182; fax 228-2183; e-mail cmartine@bcie.hn; internet www.bcie.org; f. 1960 to finance the economic devt of the Central American Common Market and its mem. countries; mems Costa Rica, El Salvador, Guatemala, Honduras, Nicaragua; cap. and res US $1,020.0m. (June 2003); Dir EDUARDO MEMBREÑO.

Banco Financiera Centroamericana, SA (FICENSA): Edif. La Interamericana, Blvd Morazán, Apdo 1432, Tegucigalpa; tel. 238-1661; fax 238-1630; e-mail rrivera@ficensa.com; internet www.ficensa.com; f. 1974; private org. providing finance for industry, commerce and transport; Pres. OSWALDO LÓPEZ ARELLANO; Gen. Man. ROQUE RIVERA RIBAS.

Banco Hondureño del Café, SA (BANHCAFE): Calle República de Costa Rica, Blvd Juan Pablo II, Col. Lomas del Mayab, Apdo 583, Tegucigalpa; tel. 232-8370; fax 232-8782; e-mail bcaferhu@hondutel.hn; internet www.banhcafe.com; f. 1981 to help finance coffee production; owned principally by private coffee producers; cap. 200.0m., res 69.2m., dep. 2,218.2m. (Dec. 2006); Pres. MIGUEL ALFONSO FERNÁNDEZ RÁPALO; Gen. Man. RENÉ ARDÓN MATUTE; 50 brs.

Banco Nacional de Desarrollo Agrícola (BANADESA): 4a Avda y 5a Avda, 13a y 14a Calles, Barrio Concepción, Apdo 212, Tegucigalpa; tel. 237-2201; fax 237-5187; e-mail info@banadesa.hn; tel. www.banadesa.hn; f. 1980; govt devt bank; loans to agricultural sector; cap. 34.5m., res 42.7m., dep. 126.9m. (March 1993); Gen. Man. ENRIQUE ALBERTO CASTELLON; 35 brs.

Banking Associations

Asociación Hondureña de Instituciones Bancarias (AHIBA): Edif. AHIBA, Blvd Suyapa, Apdo 1344, Tegucigalpa; tel. 235-6770; fax 239-0191; e-mail ahiba@ahiba.hn; internet www.ahiba.hn; f. 1957; 21 mem. banks; Pres. ROQUE RIBERA RIVAS; Exec. Dir MARÍA LYDIA SOLANO.

HONDURAS

Comisión Nacional de Bancos y Seguros (CNBS): Edif. Santa Fé, Col. Castaño Sur, Paseo Virgilio Zelaya Rubí Bloque C, Apdo 20074, Tegucigalpa; tel. 290-4500; fax 237-6232; e-mail fneda@cnbs.gov.hn; internet www.cnbs.gov.hn; Pres. GUSTAVO A. ALFARO.

STOCK EXCHANGE

Bolsa Centroamericana de Valores: Edif. Sonisa, Costado este Plaza Bancatlán, Apdo 2885, Tegucigalpa; tel. 239-1930; fax 232-2700; internet www.bcv.hn; Pres. JOSÉ RUBÉN MENDOZA.

INSURANCE

American Home Assurance Co: Edif. Los Castaños, 4°, Blvd Morazán, Apdo 3220, Tegucigalpa; tel. 232-3938; fax 232-8169; internet www.aig.com; f. 1958; Mans LEONARDO MOREIRA, EDGAR WAGNER.

Aseguradora Hondureña, SA: Edif. El Planetario, 4°, Col. Lomas del Guijarro Sur, Calle Madrid, Avda Paris, Apdo 312, Tegucigalpa; tel. 232-2729; fax 231-0982; e-mail gerencia@asegurahon.hn; internet www.laaseguradora.com.hn; f. 1954; Pres. GERARDO CORRALES.

Compañía de Seguros El Ahorro Hondureño, SA: Edif. Trinidad, Avda Colón, Apdo 3643, Tegucigalpa; tel. 237-8219; fax 237-4780; e-mail pbetanco@eahsa.hn; internet www.seguroselahorro.hn; f. 1917; Pres. DORIS PATRICIA HERNÁNDEZ VALERIANO.

Interamericana de Seguros, SA: Col. Los Castaños, Apdo 593, Tegucigalpa; tel. 232-7614; fax 232-7762; internet www.interamericanadeseguros.com; f. 1957; part of Grupo Financiero Ficohsa; Pres. LEONEL GIANNINI K.

Newcom Honduras: Edif. Hondutur, 5°, Col. Alameda, Avda Juan Manuel Gálvez, Tegucigalpa; tel. 264-1000; internet www.newcomamericas.net; Gen. Man. LUIS BÁTRES.

Pan American Life Insurance Co (PALIC): Edif. PALIC, Avda República de Chile 804, Tegucigalpa; tel. 216-0909; fax 232-3907; e-mail fnunez@panamericanlife.com; internet www.panamericanlife.com; f. 1944; Pres. JOSÉ S. SUQUET; Gen. Man. ALBERTO AGURCIA.

Previsión y Seguros, SA: Edif. Grupo Financiero IPM, 4°, Blvd Centroamérica, Apdo 770, Tegucigalpa; tel. 232-4119; fax 232-4113; internet www.previsahn.com; f. 1982; Gen. Man. GERARDO A. RIVERA.

Seguros Atlántida: Edif. Sonisa, Costado Este Plaza Bancatlán, Tegucigalpa; tel. 232-4014; fax 232-3688; e-mail info@seatlan.com; internet www.seatlan.com; f. 1986; Pres. GUILLERMO BUESO; Gen. Man. JUAN MIGUEL ORELLANA.

Seguros Continental, SA: Edif. Continental, 4°, 3a Avda SO, 2a y 3a Calle, Apdo 320, San Pedro Sula; tel. 550-0880; fax 550-2750; e-mail seguros@continental.hn; f. 1968; Pres. JAIME ROSENTHAL OLIVA; Gen. Man. MARIO R. SOLÍS DACOSTA.

Insurance Association

Cámara Hondureña de Aseguradores (CAHDA): Edif. Casa Real, 3°, Col. San Carlos, Tegucigalpa; tel. 221-5354; fax 221-5356; e-mail info@cahda.org; internet www.cahda.org; f. 1974; Man. JOSÉ LUIS MONCADA RODRÍGUEZ.

Trade and Industry

GOVERNMENT AGENCIES

Fondo Hondureño de Inversión Social (FHIS): Antiguo Edif. I.P.M., Col. Godoy, Comayagüela, Apdo 3581, Tegucigalpa; e-mail csalgado@fhis.hn; internet www.fhis.hn; tel. 234-5231; fax 534-5255; social investment fund; Dir CÉSAR SALGADO.

Fondo Social de la Vivienda (FOSOVI): Col. Kennedy, 5°, entrada antigua bodega del INVA, Tegucigalpa; tel. 230-2624; fax 230-2245; e-mail fosovi.hn@hotmail.com; social fund for housing, urbanization and devt.

DEVELOPMENT ORGANIZATIONS

Consejo Hondureño de la Empresa Privada (COHEP): Edif. 8, Calle Yoro, Col. Tepeyac, Apdo 3240, Tegucigalpa; tel. 235-3336; fax 235-3345; e-mail consejo@cohep.com; internet www.cohep.com; f. 1968; represents 52 private-sector trade asscns; Pres. JOSÉ MARÍA AGURCIA.

Corporación Hondureña de Desarrollo Forestal (COHDEFOR): Salida Carretera del Norte, Zona El Carrizal, Comayagüela, Apdo 1378, Tegucigalpa; tel. 223-7383; fax 223-3348; internet www.cohdefor.hn; f. 1974; control and management of the forestry industry; Gen. Man. GUSTAVO MORALES.

Dirección Ejecutiva de Fomento a la Minería (DEFOMIN): Edif. DEFOMIN, 3°, Blvd Miraflores, Apdo 981, Tegucigalpa; tel. 232-6721; fax 232-8635; promotes the mining sector; Dir-Gen. SANDRA MARLENE PINTO.

Instituto Hondureño del Café (IHCAFE): Edif. El Faro, Col. las Minitas, Apdo 40-C, Tegucigalpa; tel. 237-3131; e-mail ihcafe@cafesdehonduras.com; f. 1970; coffee devt programme; Gen. Man. FERNANDO D. MONTES M.

Instituto Hondureño de Mercadeo Agrícola (IHMA): Apdo 727, Tegucigalpa; tel. 235-3193; fax 235-5719; f. 1978; agricultural devt agency; Gen. Man. TULIO ROLANDO GIRÓN ROMERO.

Instituto Nacional Agrario (INA): Col. La Almeda, 4a Avda, entre 10a y 11a Calles, No 1009, Apdo 3391, Tegucigalpa; tel. 232-4893; fax 232-7398; agricultural devt programmes; Dir JOSÉ FRANCISCO FUNEZ.

CHAMBERS OF COMMERCE

Cámara de Comercio e Industrias de Copán: Edif. Comercial Romero, 2°, Barrio Mercedes, Santa Rosa de Copán; tel. 662-0843; fax 662-1783; e-mail info@camaracopan.com; internet www.camaracopan.com; f. 1940; Pres. EUDOCIO LEIVA AMAYA.

Cámara de Comercio e Industrias de Cortés (CCIC): Col. Trejo, 17a Avda, 10a Calle, Apdo 14, San Pedro Sula; tel. 553-0761; fax 553-3777; e-mail ccic@ccichonduras.org; internet www.ccichonduras.org; f. 1931; 812 mems; Pres. OSCAR GALEANO; Dir RAÚL REINA CLEAVES.

Cámara de Comercio e Industrias de Tegucigalpa: Blvd Centroamérica, Apdo 3444, Tegucigalpa; tel. 232-4200; fax 232-0159; e-mail ccit@ccit.hn; internet www.ccit.hn; Pres. AMÍLCAR BULNES; Exec. Dir MARIA MARGARITA QUIÑÓNEZ.

Federación de Cámaras de Comercio e Industrias de Honduras (FEDECAMARA): Edif. Castañito, 2°, 6a Avda, Col. Los Castaños, Apdo 3393, Tegucigalpa; tel. 232-1870; fax 232-6083; e-mail fedecamara.direccion@amnettgu.com; internet www.fedecamara.org; f. 1948; 1,200 mems; Pres. EDISON CARDENAS; Co-ordinator JUAN FERRERA LÓPEZ.

Fundación para la Inversión y Desarrollo de Exportaciones (FIDE) (Foundation for Investment and Export Development): Col. La Estancia, Plaza Marte, final del Blvd Morazán, POB 2029, Tegucigalpa; tel. 221-6303; fax 221-6318; internet www.hondurasinfo.hn; f. 1984; private, non-profit agency; Pres. VILMA SIERRA DE FONSECA.

Honduran American Chamber of Commerce (Amcham Honduras): Commercial Area Hotel Honduras Maya, POB 1838, Tegucigalpa; tel. 232-6035; fax 232-2031; e-mail amcham1@quikhonduras.com; internet www.amchamhonduras.org; f. 1981; Pres. ROBERTO ALVAREZ GUERRERO; Exec. Dir JUAN CARLOS CASCO.

INDUSTRIAL AND TRADE ASSOCIATIONS

Consejo Hondureño de la Empresa Privada (COHEP): Edif. 8, Col. Tepeyac, Calle Yoro, Apdo 3240, Tegucigalpa; tel. 235-3336; fax 235-3345; e-mail consejo@cohep.com; internet www.cohep.com; f. 1968; umbrella org. representing 54 industrial and trade asscns; Pres. JOSÉ MARÍA AGURCIA.

Asociación Hondureña de Productores de Café (AHPROCAFE) (Coffee Producers' Association): Edif. AHPROCAFE, Avda La Paz, Apdo 959, Tegucigalpa; tel. and fax 236-8286; e-mail ahprocafe@amnet.tgu.com; Pres. FREDY ESPINOZA MONDRADON; Gen. Man. PEDRO MENDOZA FLORES.

Asociación Nacional de Acuicultores de Honduras (Aquaculture Association of Honduras): Calle Vicente Williams, Barrio La Esperanza, Apdo 229, Choluteca; tel. 782-0986; fax 782-3848; e-mail andahn@hondutel.hn; f. 1986; 136 mems; Exec. Dir ALBERTO ZELAYA G.

Asociación Nacional de Exportadores de Honduras (ANEXHON) (National Association of Exporters): Local de la C.C.I.C, Tegucigalpa; tel. 553-3029; fax 557-0203; e-mail Roberto@itsa.com; comprises 104 private enterprises; Pres. ROBERTO PANAYOTTI.

Asociación Nacional de Industriales (ANDI) (National Association of Manufacturers): Edif. Fundación Covelo, 3°, Col. Castaño Sur, Blvd Morazán, Apdo 3447, Tegucigalpa; tel. 232-2221; fax 221-5199; e-mail andi@andi.hn; internet www.andi.hn; Pres. ADOLFO FACUSSÉ; Exec. Dir GUILLERMO MATAMOROS.

Federación Nacional de Agricultores y Ganaderos de Honduras (FENAGH) (Farmers and Livestock Breeders' Association): Apdo 3209, Tegucigalpa; tel. 239-1303; fax 231-1392; Pres. ROBERTO GALLARDO LARDIZÁBAL.

UTILITIES

Electricity

AES Honduras: Tegucigalpa; tel. 556-5563; fax 556-5567; e-mail carlospineda@aes.com; subsidiary of AES Corpn (USA); CEO CARLOS LARACH; Gen. Man. CARLOS V. PINEDA.

Empresa Nacional de Energía Eléctrica (ENEE) (National Electrical Energy Co): Edif. Autobanco Atlántida, 5°, Calle Real Comayagüela, Apdo 99, Tegucigalpa; tel. 238-5977; fax 239-9881; e-mail dirplan@enee.hn; internet www.enee.hn; f. 1957; state-owned electricity co; Pres. ALPHA CASTILLO; Man. RIXI MONCADA GODOY.

HONDURAS

Luz y Fuerza de San Lorenzo, SA (LUFUSA): Edif. Comercial Los Próceres, Final Avda Los Próceres 3917, Tegucigalpa; tel. 236-5159; fax 236-5826; e-mail eduardo.kafie@lufussa.com; internet www.lufussa.com; generates thermoelectric power; Pres. EDUARDO KAFIE.

TRADE UNIONS

Central General de Trabajadores de Honduras (CGTH) (General Confederation of Labour of Honduras): Barrio La Granja, antiguo Local CONADI, Apdo 1236, Comayagüela, Tegucigalpa; tel. 225-2509; fax 225-2525; e-mail cgt@david.intertel.hn; f. 1970; legally recognized from 1982; attached to Partido Demócrata Cristiano; Sec.-Gen. DANIEL A. DURÓN.

Federación Auténtica Sindical de Honduras (FASH): Barrio La Granja, antiguo Local CONADI, Apdo 1236, Comayagüela, Tegucigalpa; tel. 225-2509; affiliated to CGTH, CCT, CLAT, CMT.

Federación Sindical del Sur (FESISUR): Barrio La Ceiba, 1 c. al norte del Instituto Santa María Goretti, Apdo 256, Choluteca; tel. 882-0328; affiliated to CGT, CLAT, CMT; Pres. REINA DE ORDÓÑEZ.

Unión Nacional de Campesinos (UNC) (National Union of Farmworkers): antiguo Local CONADI, Barrio La Granja, Comayagüela, Tegucigalpa; tel. 225-1005; linked to CLAT; Sec.-Gen. VÍCTOR MANUEL CAMPO.

Confederación Hondureña de Cooperativas (CHC): 3001 Blvd Morazán, Edif. I.F.C., Apdo 3265, Tegucigalpa; tel. 232-2890; fax 231-1024; Pres. JOSÉ R. MORENO PAZ.

Confederación de Trabajadores de Honduras (CTH) (Workers' Confederation of Honduras): Edif. Beige, 2°, Avda Juan Ramón Molina, Barrio El Olvido, Apdo 720, Tegucigalpa; tel. 238-3178; fax 237-8575; e-mail cthhn@yahoo.com; f. 1964; affiliated to CTCA, ORIT, CIOSL, FIAET and ITUC; Sec.-Gen. (vacant); 200,000 mems.

Asociación Nacional de Campesinos Hondureños (ANACH) (National Association of Honduran Farmworkers): Edif. Chávez Mejía, 2°, Calle Juan Ramón Molina, Barrio El Olvido, Tegucigalpa; tel. 238-0558; f. 1962; affiliated to CTH, ORIT, CIOSL; Pres. BENEDICTO CÁRCAMO MEJÍA; 80,000 mems.

Federación Central de Sindicatos de Trabajadores Libres de Honduras (FECESITLIH) (Honduran Federation of Free Trade Unions): antiguo Edif. EUKZKADI, 3a Avda, 3a y 4a Calle No 336, Comayagüela, Tegucigalpa; tel. 237-3955; affiliated to CTH, ORIT, CIOSL; Pres. (vacant).

Federación Sindical de Trabajadores Nacionales de Honduras (FESITRANH) (Honduran Federation of Farmworkers): 10a Avda, 11a Calle, Barrio Los Andes, Apdo 245, Cortés, San Pedro Sula; tel. 557-2539; f. 1957; affiliated to CTH; Pres. MAURO FRANCISCO GONZÁLEZ.

Sindicato Nacional de Motoristas de Equipo Pesado de Honduras (SINAMEQUIPH) (National Union of HGV Drivers): Avda Juan Ramón Molina, Barrio El Olvido, Tegucigalpa; tel. 237-4415; affiliated to CTH, IFF; Pres. ERASMO FLORES.

Confederación Unitaria de Trabajadores de Honduras (CUTH): Barrio Bella Vista, 10a Calle, 8a y 9a Avda, Casa 829, Tegucigalpa; tel. and fax 220-4732; e-mail cuth@123.hn; f. 1992; Sec.-Gen. ISRAEL SALINAS.

Asociación Nacional de Empleados Públicos de Honduras (ANDEPH) (National Association of Public Employees of Honduras): Barrio Los Dolores, Avda Paulino Valladares, frente Panadería Italiana, atrás Iglesia Los Dolores, Tegucigalpa; tel. 237-4393; Pres. FAUSTO MOLINA CASTRO.

Federación Unitaria de Trabajadores de Honduras (FUTH): Barrio La Granja, contiguo Banco Atlántida, Casa 3047, frente a mercadito la granja, Apdo 1663, Comayagüela, Tegucigalpa; tel. 225-1010; f. 1981; linked to left-wing electoral alliance Frente Patriótico Hondureño; Pres. JUAN ALBERTO BARAHONA MEJÍA; 45,000 mems.

Federación de Cooperativas de la Reforma Agraria de Honduras (FECORAH): Casa 2223, antiguo Local de COAPALMA, Col. Rubén Darío, Tegucigalpa; tel. 232-0547; fax 225-2525; f. 1970; legally recognized from 1974; Pres. Ing. WILTON SALINAS.

Transport

RAILWAYS

The railway network is confined to the north of the country and most lines are used for fruit cargo. There are 995 km of railway track in Honduras, of which 349 km are narrow gauge. Only 255 km of track were in use in 2004.

Ferrocarril Nacional de Honduras (National Railway of Honduras): 1a Avda entre 1a y 2a Calle, Apdo 496, San Pedro Sula; tel. and fax 552-8001; f. 1870; govt-owned; Gen. Man. M. A. QUINTANILLA.

ROADS

In 2004 there were an estimated 13,720 km of roads in Honduras, of which 2,970 km were paved. A further 3,156 km of roads have been constructed by the Fondo Cafetero Nacional and some routes have been built by COHDEFOR in order to facilitate access to coffee plantations and forestry development areas. In November 2000 the World Bank approved a US $66.5m. loan to repair roads and bridges damaged or destroyed by 'Hurricane Mitch' in 1998. In March 2003 the Central American Bank for Economic Integration approved funding worth $22.5m. for the construction of a highway from Puerto Cortés to the Guatemalan border.

Dirección General de Caminos: Barrio La Bolsa, Comayagüela, Tegucigalpa; tel. 225-1703; fax 225-0194; e-mail dgc@soptravi.gob.hn; internet www.soptravi.gob.hn; f. 1915; highways board; Dir MARCIO ALVARADO ENAMORADO.

SHIPPING

The principal port is Puerto Cortés on the Caribbean coast, which is the largest and best-equipped port in Central America. Other ports include Tela, La Ceiba, Trujillo/Castilla, Roatán, Amapala and San Lorenzo; all are operated by the Empresa Nacional Portuaria. There are several minor shipping companies. A number of foreign shipping lines call at Honduran ports.

Empresa Nacional Portuaria (National Port Authority): Apdo 18, Puerto Cortés; tel. 665-0987; fax 665-1402; e-mail rbabun@enp.hn; internet www.enp.hn; f. 1965; has jurisdiction over all ports in Honduras; a network of paved roads connects Puerto Cortés and San Lorenzo with the main cities of Honduras, and with the principal cities of Central America; Gen. Man. ROBERTO BABUM.

CIVIL AVIATION

Local airlines in Honduras compensate for the deficiencies of road and rail transport, linking together small towns and inaccessible districts. There are four international airports: Golosón airport in La Ceiba, Ramón Villeda Morales airport in San Pedro Sula, Toncontín airport in Tegucigalpa and Juan Manuel Gálvaz airport in Roatán. In 2001 it was announced that San Francisco Airport, USA, was to invest some US $150m. in the four airports over two years. In 2000 plans for a new airport inside the Copán Ruinas archaeological park, 400 km west of Tegucigalpa, were announced.

Dirección General Aeronáutica Civil: Barrio La Bolsa, Comayagüela, Tegucigalpa; tel. 233-1115; e-mail soptravi@soptravi.gob.hn; internet www.dgac.gob.hn; airport infrastucture and security; Dir of Flight Safety SUE HAROLD-CLUB.

AeroHonduras: Edif. Corporativo, Hotel Real Clarion, Col. Alameda, 1521 Avda Juan Manuel Gálvez, Apdo 1861, Tegucigalpa; tel. 235-3737; fax 232-5005; internet www.aerohonduras.com; f. 2002 as Sol Air; name changed as above in 2004; flights to Managua, Nicaragua, and Miami, FL, USA; Pres. RICARDO MARTÍNEZ.

Atlantic Airlines de Honduras: Tegucigalpa; tel. 440-2343; fax 440-2347; e-mail atlantic@caribe.hn; f. 2001; affiliated to Atlantic Airlines (Nicaragua); scheduled domestic and international services.

Isleña Airlines: Avda San Isidro, frente al Parque Central, Barrio El Iman, Apdo 402, La Ceiba; tel. 443-0179; e-mail info@flyislena.com; internet www.flyislena.com; subsidiary of TACA, El Salvador; domestic service and service to the Cayman Islands; Pres. and CEO ARTURO ALVARADO WOOD.

Tourism

Tourists are attracted by the Mayan ruins, the fishing and boating facilities in Trujillo Bay and Lake Yojoa, near San Pedro Sula, and the beaches on the northern coast. There is an increasing eco-tourism industry. Honduras received around 673,035 tourists in 2005, while tourism receipts totalled an estimated US $431.3m.

Asociación Hotelera y Afines de Honduras (AHAH): Hotel Escuela Madrid, Suite 402, Col. 21 de Octubre-Los Girasoles, Tegucigalpa; tel. 221-4579; fax 221-1778; e-mail staynhonduras@123.hn; Pres. ANASTASIO ANASTASSIU; Exec. Dir KAREN BONILLA.

Asociación Nacional de Agencias de Viajes y Turismo de Honduras: Blvd Morazán, frente a McDonald's, Tegucigalpa; tel. 236-9455; e-mail travelex@multivisiohn.net; Pres. SCARLETT DE MONCADA.

Asociación de Tour Operadores de Honduras (OPTURH): Edif. Adobe, Local 3, Col. Tara, San Pedro Sula; tel. 551-8639; fax 551-8634; e-mail presidencia@opturh.com; f. 1997; Pres. JUAN ANGEL WELCHEZ.

Instituto Hondureño de Turismo: Edif. Europa, 5°, Col. San Carlos, Apdo 3261, Tegucigalpa; tel. and fax 222-2124; e-mail tourisminfo@iht.hn; internet www.letsgohonduras.com; f. 1972; Dir RICARDO ALFREDO MARTÍNEZ.

HUNGARY

Introductory Survey

Location, Climate, Language, Religion, Flag, Capital

The Republic of Hungary lies in central Europe, bounded to the north by Slovakia, to the east by Ukraine and Romania, to the south by Serbia and Croatia, and to the west by Slovenia and Austria. Its climate is continental, with long, dry summers and severe winters. Temperatures in Budapest are generally between −3°C (27°F) and 28°C (82°F). The language is Hungarian (Magyar). There is a large Romany community (numbering between 500,000 and 700,000 people), and also Croat, German, Romanian, Serb, Slovak, Slovene and Jewish minorities. Most of the inhabitants profess Christianity, and the largest single religious denomination is the Roman Catholic Church, representing about 62% of the population. Other Christian groups include Calvinists (20%), Lutherans (5%) and the Eastern Orthodox Church. The national flag (proportions 2 by 3) consists of three equal horizontal stripes, of red, white and green. The capital is Budapest.

Recent History

Although Hungary co-operated with Nazi Germany before the Second World War and obtained additional territory when Czechoslovakia was partitioned in 1938 and 1939, when it sought to break the alliance in 1944 the country was occupied by German forces. In January 1945 Hungary was liberated by Soviet troops and signed an armistice, restoring the pre-1938 frontiers. It became a republic in February 1946. Nationalization measures began in December, despite opposition from the Roman Catholic Church. In the 1947 elections, the communists became the largest single party, with 22.7% of the votes. The communists merged with the Social Democrats to form the Hungarian Workers' Party in June 1948. A People's Republic was established in August 1949.

As First Secretary of the Workers' Party, Mátyás Rákosi became the leading political figure, and opposition was removed by means of purges and political trials. Rákosi became Prime Minister in 1952, but after the death of the Soviet leader Stalin (Iosif V. Dzhugashvili) one year later, he was replaced by the more moderate Imre Nagy, and a short period of liberalization followed. Rákosi, however, remained as First Secretary, and in 1955 forced Nagy's resignation. Dissension between the Rákosi and Nagy factions increased in 1956; in July Rákosi was forced to resign but was replaced by a close associate, Ernő Gerő. The consequent discontent provoked demonstrations against communist domination, and in October fighting broke out. Nagy was reinstated as Prime Minister; he renounced membership of the Warsaw Pact (the defence grouping of the Soviet bloc) and promised other controversial reforms. In November Soviet troops, stationed in Hungary under the 1947 peace treaty, intervened, and the uprising was suppressed. A new Soviet-supported Government, led by János Kádár, was installed. Some 20,000 participants in the uprising were arrested, of whom 2,000 were subsequently executed, including Nagy and four associates. Many opponents of the regime were deported to the USSR. Kádár, who was appointed the leader of the renamed Hungarian Socialist Workers' Party (HSWP), held the premiership until January 1958, and from September 1961 until July 1965.

In March 1985 Kádár was re-elected as leader of the party, with the new title of General Secretary of the Central Committee. The legislative elections in June 1985 were the first to give voters a wider choice of candidates under the system of mandatory multiple nominations. In May 1988 Kádár was replaced as General Secretary of the Central Committee by Károly Grósz (Chairman of the Council of Ministers since June 1987), and promoted to the new and purely ceremonial post of HSWP President; he lost his membership of the Politburo (Political Bureau). About one-third of the members of the Central Committee were replaced by younger politicians. Grósz declared his commitment to radical economic and political change, but excluded the immediate possibility of a multi-party political system. In June 1988 Dr Brunó Ferenc Straub, who was not a member of the HSWP, was elected to the largely ceremonial post of President of the Presidential Council. In November Miklós Németh, a prominent member of the HSWP, replaced Grósz as Chairman of the Council of Ministers.

Following Grósz's appointment as leader of the HSWP, there was a relaxation of censorship laws, and independent political groups were formally established. In January 1989 the right to strike was fully legalized. In the same month the Országgyűlés (National Assembly) enacted legislation guaranteeing the right to demonstrate and to form associations and political parties independent of the HSWP. In February the HSWP agreed to abandon the constitutional clause upholding the party's leading role in society. In March an estimated 100,000 people took part in a peaceful anti-Government demonstration in Budapest, in support of demands for democracy, free elections, the withdrawal of Soviet troops and an official commemoration of the 1956 uprising and of the execution of Imre Nagy in 1958.

During 1989 there was increasing evidence of dissension within the HSWP between conservative and reformist members. (At least 100,000 members had tendered their resignations between late 1987 and early 1989.) In April the Politburo was replaced by a smaller body. In May the Council of Ministers declared its independence from the HSWP; Kádár was removed from the presidency and the Central Committee of the party, officially for health reasons. In June a radical restructuring of the HSWP was effected; although Grósz remained as General Secretary, the newly elected Chairman, Rezső Nyers, effectively emerged as the party's leading figure. At a provincial by-election in July 1989, a joint candidate of the centre-right Hungarian Democratic Forum (HDF), the liberal Alliance of Free Democrats (AFD) and the Federation of Young Democrats (FYD) became the first opposition deputy since 1947 to win representation in the legislature. Four of five further by-elections were won by opposition candidates in July–September. At an HSWP Congress in October, delegates voted to reconstitute the party as the Hungarian Socialist Party (HSP), with Nyers as Chairman. The HSP initially failed to attract a large membership, however, and in December HSWP activists declared that their party had not been dissolved, and elected a new leader.

On 23 October 1989 (the anniversary of the 1956 uprising) the Republic of Hungary was proclaimed. In preparation, the Országgyűlés approved fundamental amendments to the Constitution, including the removal of the clause guaranteeing one-party rule. A new electoral law was approved, and the Presidential Council was replaced by the post of President of the Republic. Mátyás Szűrös, the President (Speaker) of the Országgyűlés, was named President of the Republic, on an interim basis.

Hungary's first free multi-party elections since 1945 were held, in two rounds, on 25 March and 8 April 1990. The elections were held under a mixed system of proportional and direct representation and were contested by a total of 28 parties and groups. The HDF received the largest proportion of the total votes cast (42.7%) and 165 of the 386 seats in the Országgyűlés. The AFD obtained the second largest proportion of the votes (23.8%), winning 92 legislative seats. The Independent Smallholders' Party (ISP, which advocated the restoration to its original owners of land collectivized after 1947) and the Christian Democratic People's Party (CDPP), both of which contested the second round of polling in alliance with the HDF, secured 43 and 21 seats, respectively. The HSP secured 33 seats, while the FYD (which was closely aligned with the AFD) obtained 21 seats. The HSWP failed to secure the 4% of the votes required for representation.

A coalition Government was formed in May 1990, comprising members of the HDF (which held the majority of posts), the ISP, the CDPP and three independents. József Antall, the Chairman of the HDF, had earlier been elected to chair the new Council of Ministers. Among the declared aims of the new Government was membership of the European Community (now European Union—EU, see p. 244) and a full transition to a Western-style market economy. In the same month Gyula Horn, the outgoing Minister of Foreign Affairs, replaced Nyers as leader of the HSP. In August Árpád Göncz, a writer and member of the AFD, was elected President of the Republic by the legislature. At municipal and local elections in September and October a coalition of the

AFD and the FYD won control of Budapest and many other cities, while in rural areas independent candidates obtained a majority of the votes. The governing coalition's poor result was attributed, in large part, to its failure to redress a sharp increase in the rates of inflation and unemployment.

In May 1991 the Országgyűlés approved legislation to provide compensation for persons killed, imprisoned or deported, or whose property had been expropriated for political reasons in 1939–89. Further legislation was approved in early 1993 allowing for prosecutions in connection with crimes committed under the communist regime.

In February 1992 the Chairman of the ISP, József Torgyán, announced that his party was to withdraw from the Government, in protest at what he claimed to be a lack of political influence. However, most of the ISP's legislative deputies refused to withhold their support for the Government, thus causing divisions in the party. In April as many as 20,000 people were reported to have attended an anti-Government demonstration organized by Torgyán in Budapest. The split in the party was formalized in June, when members loyal to the Government formed what subsequently became the United Historic Smallholders' Party; the ISP subsequently renamed itself the Independent Smallholders' and Peasants' Party (ISPP).

In September 1992 some 50,000 people demonstrated in Budapest against extreme right-wing figures within the HDF, including the Vice-Chairman of the party, István Csurka. In July 1993 Csurka was expelled from the HDF, and subsequently founded the Hungarian Justice and Life Party (HJLP). Antall died in December, and was succeeded as Prime Minister by Dr Péter Boross, an independent and hitherto the Minister of the Interior. In February 1994 Lajos Für was elected Chairman of the HDF.

Elections to the Országgyűlés, held on 8 and 29 May 1994, resulted in a parliamentary majority for the HSP, which received 33.0% of the votes cast for regional party lists and won 209 of the 386 legislative seats. The AFD won 19.8% of the votes and 70 seats, while the HDF won only 11.7% of the votes and 37 seats. The ISPP, the CDPP and the FYD also secured parliamentary seats. The HSP and the AFD signed a coalition agreement in late June; the coalition held the two-thirds' majority necessary to institute constitutional reforms. Horn was invested as Prime Minister in July.

Meanwhile, controversy over alleged government interference in branches of the mass media had arisen in mid-1992. During 1992–94 senior media figures resigned or were dismissed, and there were demonstrations in Budapest to demand press freedom. In October 1994 the Constitutional Court declared government interference in the media to be unlawful.

In January 1995 the Minister of Finance, László Bekesi, resigned, following disagreements with Horn regarding economic reform; he was replaced by Lajos Bokros. A new President of the central bank was also appointed. Economic austerity measures, adopted in March, prompted strong domestic criticism, and the ministers responsible for public health and for national security resigned shortly afterwards. In May the Országgyűlés approved legislation that was designed to accelerate the privatization process. On 19 June Göncz was re-elected President of the Republic by the Országgyűlés. At the end of the month the Constitutional Court ruled that elements of the austerity programme (specifically those relating to welfare provisions) were unconstitutional. Accordingly, in late July the Országgyűlés approved adjustments. The economic programme continued to cause dissent within the Government, and the Minister of Labour tendered her resignation in October. Bokros resigned in mid-February 1996, and a banker, Péter Medgyessy, was appointed as the new Minister of Finance. Following the election of Sándor Lezsák to the HDF leadership, divisions within the party were reported in March 1996; denouncing what it regarded as an increasingly nationalistic tendency in the party, a faction led by the former Minister of Finance in the HDF Government formed a new organization, the Hungarian Democratic People's Party.

In September 1997 Horn rejected demands for his resignation, following claims that he had served with a paramilitary force that had restored communist power following the 1956 rebellion, and that he had used the security services to suppress political opposition. In December 1997 the HDF established an electoral alliance with the Federation of Young Democrats—Hungarian Civic Party (FYD—HCP, which had been reconstituted from the FYD) and the Hungarian Christian Democratic Federation, a newly formed association of breakaway members of the CDPP.

Legislative elections took place, in two rounds, on 10 and 24 May 1998. The FYD—HCP, with 147 seats, obtained the largest representation in the Országgyűlés; the HSP received 134 seats, the ISPP 48, the AFD 24, the HDF 18 and the HJLP 14. In June the FYD—HCP signed an agreement with the HDF and the ISPP, providing for the formation of a new coalition government. In July the Országgyűlés elected Viktor Orbán, the Chairman of the FYD—HCP, as Prime Minister; his Government comprised 11 representatives of the FYD—HCP, four of the ISPP (later renamed the Independent Smallholders' and Civic Party—ISCP), one of the HDF and one of the Hungarian Christian Democratic Federation. In September, following the resignation of Horn from the leadership of the HSP, a former minister, László Kovács, was elected Chairman. In January 2000 László Kövér replaced Orbán as leader of the FYD—HCP. Following two inconclusive rounds of voting in the Országgyűlés, on 6 June 2000 Ferenc Mádl, the sole candidate, finally secured the requisite two-thirds' majority. He took office on 4 August.

In June 2001 the Országgyűlés approved legislation that, with effect from January 2002, granted ethnic Hungarians living in adjacent countries education, employment and medical rights in Hungary. This legislation, widely referred to as the 'status' or 'benefit' law, prompted protests from Romania and Slovakia (see below) that the law discriminated against their non-ethnic Hungarian populations and constituted a violation of sovereignty.

In September 2001 the governing FYD—HCP and HDF signed a co-operation agreement for the forthcoming legislative elections; in December a number of ISCP deputies agreed to participate in the elections in co-operation with the FYD—HCP and the HDF. The legislative elections were held, as scheduled, on 7 and 21 April 2002. Although the FYD—HCP-HDF alliance won 48.7% of the total votes cast (188 seats), a left-wing coalition of the HSP (46.1% of the votes and 178 seats) and the AFD (5.2% of the votes and 20 seats) secured an overall majority in the Országgyűlés. Péter Medgyessy of the HSP was sworn in as Prime Minister on 27 May; the Council of Ministers comprised eight further members of the HSP, four members of the AFD and three independents.

In June 2002 media allegations prompted the new Prime Minister to reveal that he had served as a counter-intelligence agent at the Ministry of Finance in 1977–82. Medgyessy insisted that he had worked to protect sensitive economic information from the KGB (the Soviet secret service), in order to negotiate Hungarian membership of the IMF (which it joined in 1982); the AFD subsequently retracted a threat to withdraw from the governing coalition. In July two parliamentary commissions were established to investigate the past role of Medgyessy and the alleged links of other post-communist government officials with the Soviet-era security service. Meanwhile, in early July the leader of the FYD—HCP, Zoltán Pokorni, who had led demands for Medgyessy's resignation, had relinquished his own party and parliamentary posts, after his father's role as a communist informer was revealed. It subsequently emerged that several members of the FYD—HCP (which had emphasized its anti-communist past during campaigning for the legislative elections) had counter-intelligence associations, thereby severely damaging the party's reputation. Local elections took place on 20 October, in which the governing coalition consolidated its position; the results of the elections confirmed the FYD—HCP's diminishing popularity.

In mid-December 2002 the Országgyűlés voted to adopt a number of constitutional amendments, which were required to enable the country to become a full member of the EU (see below). In February 2003 a minor reorganization of the Council of Ministers was effected. Medgyessy's failure to consult the minority AFD before the reorganization temporarily led to tensions within the governing coalition. In May the FYD—HCP re-formed as a new right-wing alliance, Fidesz—Hungarian Civic Alliance (Fidesz), with former premier Orbán as its leader.

In January 2004 the Minister of Finance, Csaba László, left office when it was revealed that the fiscal results for 2003 had exceeded government targets and jeopardized the country's schedule for the adoption of the common European currency (see Economic Affairs). Tibor Draskovics (who was not a party member) succeeded László in mid-February, and implemented a financial-austerity plan shortly afterwards. On 1 May Hungary acceded to full membership of the EU.

On 18 August 2004 Medgyessy resigned as Prime Minister following a decline in support for his party and a severe dispute with the AFD over changes he wished to make to the Council of

Ministers, in particular the proposed dismissal of the AFD Minister of the Economy and Transport, István Csillag. On 24 August the HSP elected one of the country's wealthiest business executives, Ferenc Gyurcsány, hitherto the Minister of Children, Youth and Sports, as Prime Minister-designate. Gyurcsány, who secured 73% of the votes at a party congress, was chosen in preference to Péter Kiss, who had been widely regarded as Medgyessy's likely successor. Gyurcsány was inaugurated as Prime Minister on 4 October. The Prime Minister appointed seven new ministers in October, including a further Minister without Portfolio, Etele Baráth, with responsibility for EU issues. Kiss retained his position as Minister in charge of the Prime Minister's Office, but Csillag resigned from his post in order to avoid 'unnecessary conflict' in the new Government. He was succeeded by another wealthy business executive, János Kóka. The Council of Ministers comprised 12 members of the HSP, four AFD politicians and two independents. In February 2005 Gyurcsány appointed Andras Bozoki as Minister of Cultural Heritage. Bozoki's predecessor, István Hiller, had resigned from his ministerial duties after having been appointed Chairman of the HSP in October 2004. Gyurcsány made further adjustments to the Council of Ministers in April 2005. Draskovics was dismissed as Minister of Finance, and replaced by János Veres, a member of the executive committee of the HSP.

On 7 June 2005 László Sólyom, an independent politician endorsed by the main opposition parties, was elected as President, after three rounds of voting in the Országgyülés. Sólyom, who defeated the government-endorsed candidate, Katalin Szili, took office on 5 August, when the incumbent, Mádl, completed his five-year term. At the legislative elections, which were held on 9 and 23 April 2006, the governing HSP-AFD coalition secured 210 of the 386 seats in the Országgyülés and 54.4% of the votes, representing the first occasion in the history of the Republic of Hungary that an incumbent government had won re-election. A coalition of Fidesz and the CDPP secured 164 seats (with 42.5% of the votes), the HDF took 11 seats (with 2.9% of the votes) and the remaining seat was won by an independent candidate. Coalition negotiations between the HSP and the AFD commenced on 27 April, concerning the legislative programme of the new government and the composition of the Council of Ministers. In early June, after several weeks of negotiations, a new administration, led by Gyurcsány and comprising members of the HSP and the AFD, was formed. On the following day Gyurcsány announced stringent fiscal adjustment measures, which were designed to reduce the considerable budget deficit, in compliance with EU requirements.

On 17 September 2006 the media broadcast of a clandestine recording of a post-election speech by Gyurcsány to his party members, in which he admitted having repeatedly misled the electorate during the campaign over the country's fiscal situation, precipitated mass anti-Government riots in Budapest. Protesters surrounded government buildings and temporarily seized control of the state television headquarters; some 300 people were injured in the rioting and the ensuing confrontations with the police. On 27 September Gyurcsány issued a public apology at the Government's delay in addressing the economic situation. At municipal elections on 2 October Fidesz made significant gains, securing mayoralties in 15 of Hungary's 23 largest cities and majorities in 18 of the 19 county councils. Nevertheless, in early October a parliamentary motion of confidence in the Government, proposed by Gyurcsány, was supported by 207 votes in the Országgyülés.

Official celebrations on 23 October 2006, the 50th anniversary of the 1956 uprising against Soviet rule, were marred by anti-Government demonstrations, organized by the leadership of Fidesz, which boycotted commemorations attended by Gyurcsány and demanded his resignation. Security forces suppressed ensuing violent riots, in which about 170 people were injured, and a total of 130 protesters were arrested. Gyurcsány subsequently accused Orbán of inciting the rioting, and the Budapest municipal authorities implemented measures to restrain continuing anti-Government protests. In February 2007 a commission investigating the rioting issued a report strongly criticizing Fidesz for implying support for the protesters, who were predominantly associated with extreme right-wing political groups, and also concluding that the police had employed excessive force in suppressing the violence. Despite official efforts to maintain security on 15 March, another national holiday, the arrest during a rally of an extreme nationalist leader, György Budaházy, in connection with the disturbances in September of the previous year, prompted further violent clashes between his supporters and members of the security forces.

In April 2007 the Minister of Health tendered his resignation, following increasing criticism of planned health-care reforms, to be introduced as part of the Government's fiscal-austerity plan. In May the Minister of Justice and Law Enforcement also resigned; he was replaced by Albert Takács. In June Gyurcsány reorganized the Government in support of his reform programme. In August extreme nationalist political elements, with the support of Fidesz, established a 56-member paramilitary Hungarian Guard. In early December Csaba Kákossy became the new Minister of Economy and Transport, following the resignation of Janos Koka, who had been elected Chairman of the AFD in March. In February 2008 Tibor Draskovics succeeded Takács to become the new Minister of Justice and Law Enforcement.

On 23 October 2007 Fidesz supported a further mass demonstration to demand the resignation of Gyurcsány, which again resulted in violent clashes between police and extreme nationalist protesters. In November one of the principal trade union federations, the Democratic Confederation of Free Trade Unions, organized a widely observed strike by public-sector workers in protest against the Government's proposed health-care reforms. In December legislation on the disputed health-care reforms was approved in the Országgyülés, but was vetoed by President Sólyom on the grounds that many issues remained unresolved. On 11 February 2008 further demonstrations were staged outside the parliamentary building to coincide with the repeated approval by the Országgyülés of the health-care legislation, which Sólyom was constitutionally obliged to endorse; the reforms included, notably, the establishment of 22 partially private health insurance companies and the introduction of medical fees. Fidesz organized a national referendum to seek support for the abolition of the newly introduced fees for doctors visits and hospital stays and for state-subsidized university fees. At the referendum, held on 9 March, more than 80% of the votes, cast by some 50.5% of the electorate, were in favour of the abolition of fees. Gyurcsány duly announced that the fees would be abandoned from 1 April. At the end of March Gyurcsány dismissed the AFD Minister of Health, Agnes Horvath, prompting the AFD to announce that it intended to withdraw from the governing coalition in late April; in early April the HSP parliamentary group voted in support of a pledge by Gyurcsány to continue to implement reforms aimed at reducing the budgetary deficit as the leader of a minority Government.

There has been considerable activism within Hungary by the country's ethnic minorities for the protection of their rights. In July 1993 the Országgyülés adopted legislation guaranteeing the cultural, civil and political rights of 12 minority groups and prohibiting ethnic discrimination. Following the approval of this legislation, minority-rights activists launched a new campaign to change Hungary's electoral law, with the aim of securing the direct representation of ethnic groups in the legislature. In the 1994 municipal elections, ethnic minorities were able to elect their own local ethnic authorities, with consultative roles on cultural and educational issues affecting the community. In February 1995 Hungary signed the Council of Europe (see p. 225) Convention on the Protection of National Minorities. In April the Roma of Hungary elected their own governing body, the National Autonomous Authority of the Romany Minority (the first such body in the former Eastern bloc), which was empowered to administer funds and deliberate issues affecting the Roma.

In September 1996 Hungary and Romania signed a bilateral treaty, guaranteeing the inviolability of the joint border between the two countries and the rights of ethnic minorities. In May 1997 President Arpád Göncz made an official visit to Romania (the first by a Hungarian Head of State). In August 2001 a meeting between Viktor Orbán and Prime Minister Adrian Năstase of Romania failed to resolve the tensions arising from Hungary's status law (see above) applying to the ethnic Hungarian diaspora (there were some 1,432,000 ethnic Hungarians in Romania in 2002). However, a memorandum of understanding was signed by the two Prime Ministers in late December 2001, which extended the short-term employment rights offered to ethnic Hungarians under the terms of the law to all Romanian citizens. President Ferenc Mádl made a state visit to Romania in October 2002. Finally, in late September 2003 a bilateral agreement on the implementation of the status law in Romania was signed in the Romanian capital, Bucharest, by Péter Medgyessy and Năstase.

Apart from issues arising from the presence of a large ethnic Hungarian minority in Slovakia (numbering some 520,500 in 2001), relations between Hungary and Slovakia were strained by a dispute over the Gabčíkovo-Nagymaros hydroelectric project (a joint Hungarian-Czechoslovak scheme initiated in 1977), involving the diversion of a 222-km stretch of the River Danube and the construction of a twin-dam system. In November 1989 the Hungarian Government announced that it was to abandon the scheme, following pressure from environmentalists. In July 1991 Czechoslovakia decided to proceed unilaterally with the project; the resumption of work, in February 1992, prompted the Hungarian Government to abrogate the 1977 treaty. In April 1993 it was agreed to refer the case to the International Court of Justice (ICJ) and to operate a temporary water-management scheme in the mean time.

In March 1995 Prime Minister Horn and his Slovak counterpart, Vladimír Mečiar, signed a Treaty of Friendship and Co-operation, according to which the two countries undertook to guarantee the rights of ethnic minorities and recognized the inviolability of their joint border. The Treaty came into effect in May 1996, following its ratification by the Slovak President. In August 1997 discussions between Horn and Mečiar resulted in an agreement that a joint committee be established to monitor the standard of human rights of ethnic Hungarians resident in Slovakia and the Slovak community in Hungary. In September the ICJ concluded proceedings regarding the dispute over the Gabčíkovo-Nagymaros hydroelectric project, ruling that both countries had contravened international law: Hungary had breached the terms of the agreement by withdrawing from the project, and the former Czechoslovakia had continued work without the permission of the Hungarian Government. Both Hungary and Slovakia were required to pay compensation for damages incurred, and to resume negotiations regarding the further implementation of the agreement. In December 1999 Hungary submitted a document to the Slovak Government, in which it renounced any claim to a share of the hydroelectric energy produced by the dam project, but requested an increase in the flow of common water along the Danube, in order to maintain the ecological balance. In February 2001 Slovakia accepted that it had no legal means to compel Hungary to proceed with the project, but stated that it would seek compensation. In February 2006 it was announced that Slovakia and Hungary had agreed to implement the 1997 ICJ ruling on the Gabčíkovo-Nagymaros hydroelectric project. The two Governments were to draft an agreement on the implementation of the ruling and amend the agreement on the construction and operation of the system.

The entry into force of the Hungarian status law (see above) in January 2002 threatened to damage relations with Slovakia, although that country had in place a similar law, which granted privileges to the Slovak diaspora. In February the Slovak parliament voted to reject the Hungarian law, claiming that it abrogated the treaty of May 1996. In early March 2003 the Council of Europe drafted a resolution urging the Hungarian Government to amend the status law. Also in early March Hungary agreed to suspend the application of the law in Slovakia, pending the approval by the Országgyűlés of a draft amendment stipulating that the legislation was not to apply in EU member countries (Slovakia acceded to the EU in May 2004, along with Hungary—see below). Finally, in December 2003 the Ministers of Foreign Affairs of Hungary and Slovakia signed a bilateral agreement on the implementation of the status law in Slovakia.

In November 1990 Hungary was the first former Eastern bloc, European country to become a member of the Council of Europe. In March 1996 Hungary was admitted to the Organisation for Economic Co-operation and Development (OECD, see p. 347). Meanwhile, Hungary's associate membership of the EU came into effect on 1 February 1994, and in April Hungary became the first post-communist state to apply for full EU membership. In December 2002 Hungary was one of 10 countries formally invited to join the EU in May 2004. At a national referendum, held on 12 April 2003, Hungarian membership of the EU was endorsed by 83.8% of votes cast (with 45.6% of the electorate participating). In December 2007 Hungary, together with eight other nations, implemented the EU's Schengen Agreement, enabling its citizens to travel to and from other member states without border controls. In the same month Hungary became the first EU member state to ratify the draft Treaty of Lisbon by parliamentary vote.

Following a North Atlantic Treaty Organization (NATO, see p. 340) summit meeting in Madrid, Spain, in July 1997, Hungary was invited to enter into discussions regarding its application for membership of the Alliance. A national referendum on the country's entry into NATO was conducted in November, at which its accession was approved by 85.3% of the votes cast, with the participation of 49% of the electorate. Hungary was formally admitted to NATO in March 1999 (although it was subsequently subject to some criticism for failing to fulfil its financial commitments). In early 2003 an air base at Taszar, in south-western Hungary, was used by the USA for the training of Iraqi opposition forces, in relation to the US-led military campaign in Iraq (see the chapters on the USA and Iraq). Hungary subsequently contributed 300 soldiers to the international peace-keeping force in Iraq. Following considerable public and political opposition to the US-led operation in Iraq, these were withdrawn from the region in March 2005. Prior to a visit to the Russian capital, Moscow, in March 2007, Prime Minister Ferenc Gyurcsány declared support for plans of the Russian gas producer Gazprom to extend its 'South Stream' pipeline, linking Novorossiisk, Krasnodar Krai, in southern Russia, to Ankara, Turkey, further to central Europe, which would allow the wider expansion of Russian gas exports. In February 2008 Gyurcsány signed an agreement with Russian government leaders in Moscow, which provided for the construction of the 'South Stream' gas pipeline through Hungary.

Government

Legislative power is held by the unicameral Országgyűlés (National Assembly), comprising 386 members, who are elected for four years by universal adult suffrage under a mixed system of proportional and direct representation. The President of the Republic (Head of State) is elected by the Országgyűlés for a term of five years. The President, who is also Commander-in-Chief of the Armed Forces, may be re-elected for a second term. The Council of Ministers, the highest organ of state administration, is elected by the Assembly on the recommendation of the President. For local administrative purposes, Hungary is divided into 19 counties (*megyei*) and the capital city (with 23 districts). A 53-member National Autonomous Authority of the Romany Minority, first elected in April 1995, is empowered to administer funds disbursed by the central Government.

Defence

Military service begins at the age of 18 years and lasts for six months. Compulsory military service was abolished in November 2004. As assessed at November 2007, the active armed forces numbered 32,300, including an army of 23,950, an air force of 7,500 and 850 joint-forces troops. Reservists totalled 44,000. Paramilitary forces comprised 12,000 border guards. In March 1999 Hungary became a member of the North Atlantic Treaty Organization (NATO, see p. 340). The budget for 2007 allocated 319,000m. forint to defence.

Economic Affairs

In 2006, according to estimates by the World Bank, Hungary's gross national income (GNI), measured at average 2004–06 prices, was US $110,079m., equivalent to $10,950 per head (or $18,290 per head on an international purchasing-power parity basis). During 1996–2006, it was estimated, the population decreased at an average annual rate of 0.3%, while gross domestic product (GDP) per head increased, in real terms, by an average of 4.7% per year. Overall GDP increased, in real terms, at an average annual rate of 4.4% during 1996–2006; real GDP increased by 3.9% in 2006.

Agriculture (including hunting, forestry and fishing) contributed 4.3% of GDP in 2006, when the sector engaged some 4.9% of the employed labour force. The principal crops are maize, wheat, sugar beet, barley and potatoes. Viticulture is also important. During 1996–2006, according to the World Bank, real agricultural GDP increased at an average annual rate of 3.0%. The GDP of the sector decreased by some 10.7% in 2005, but increased by 2.6% in 2006.

Industry (including mining, manufacturing, construction and power) contributed 30.5% of GDP in 2006, and engaged 32.3% of the employed labour force. The World Bank estimated that real industrial GDP increased at an average annual rate of 5.7% in 1996–2006. Industrial GDP increased by 5.4% in 2006.

Mining and quarrying accounted for just 0.2% of GDP in 2003, and engaged 0.4% of the employed labour force in 2006. Hungary's most important mineral resources are lignite (brown coal) and natural gas. Petroleum, bauxite and hard coal are also exploited. In February 2008 Hungary signed an agreement with Russia, allowing the Russian gas producer Gazprom to extend its 'South Stream' pipeline, linking Novorossiisk, Krasnodar Krai, in southern Russia, with central Europe, via Ankara, Turkey. During 1990–98 the output of the mining sector declined at an average annual rate of 11.1%.

The manufacturing sector contributed 22.9% of GDP in 2006, when it engaged 22.0% of the employed labour force. Manufacturing GDP increased, in real terms, at an average annual rate of 7.5% in 1996–2006. Manufacturing GDP increased by 8.8% in 2006.

In 2004 some 34.8% of Hungary's electricity production was generated by natural gas, 35.3% by nuclear power and 24.7% by coal. Fuel imports represented 6.5% of the value of total imports in 2005.

The services sector has a significant role in the Hungarian economy, contributing 65.3% of GDP in 2006, when it engaged 62.8% of the employed labour force. According to the World Bank, the GDP of the services sector increased, in real terms, at an average rate of 3.4% per year in 1996–2006. The GDP of the services sector increased by 3.2% in 2006.

In 2006 Hungary recorded a visible trade deficit of US $508m., and there was a deficit of $6,212m. on the current account of the balance of payments. In 2006, according to preliminary figures, the principal source of imports was Germany (accounting for 27.4% of the total); other major sources were Russia, Austria and the People's Republic of China. Germany was also the principal market for exports in that year (29.4%); other important purchasers were Italy and Austria. The principal exports in 2006 were machinery and transport equipment, basic manufactures, and food, beverages and tobacco. The main imports in that year were machinery and transport equipment and basic manufactures.

In 2007 Hungary's overall budgetary deficit amounted to 1,389,800m. forint. The country's total external debt was an estimated US $66,119m. at the end of 2005, of which $21,216m. was long-term public debt. In that year the cost of debt-servicing was equivalent to 31.0% of the value of exports of goods and services. The annual rate of inflation averaged 8.5% in 1996–2006; consumer prices increased by 3.9% in 2006. The average rate of unemployment was 7.5% in 2006.

Hungary is a member of the European Bank for Reconstruction and Development (EBRD, see p. 239), and was admitted to the Organisation for Economic Co-operation and Development (OECD, see p. 347) in 1996. Hungary became a full member of the European Union (EU, see p. 244) in May 2004.

In 1990 the Government pledged to effect a full transition to a Western-style market economy, and by the late 1990s the Government's fiscal policy had resulted in a decline in both the public-sector deficit and the annual rate of inflation. In December 1999 it was announced that, as a result of the country's success in achieving economic stabilization, Hungary would be one of the first applicant nations to be admitted to the EU; in December 2002 it was invited to become a full member from May 2004. However, the Government, which intended to adopt the common European currency, the euro, by 2010, failed to reduce the country's budgetary deficit (the largest among EU member nations in 2006) to a level consistent with this objective; the EU's criteria for entry to the 'euro zone' stipulated that aspirant countries should record a budgetary deficit of no more than 3% of GDP in the preceding two years. In June 2006 a newly installed Government announced stringent fiscal adjustment measures, which were designed to reduce the considerable budget deficit in compliance with EU requirements. In September public hostility to the planned austerity measures precipitated mass anti-Government riots in the capital (see Recent History). The Government of Prime Minister Ferenc Gyurcsány narrowly survived a subsequent motion of confidence, but in 2007 continued demonstrations and strike action were staged in protest at planned reforms, particularly in the health sector. In late 2007 the Government indicated that it had abandoned its target date of 2010 for adoption of the euro, and hoped to adopt the single currency by 2014. Government plans to reduce taxes substantially in order to stimulate economic growth and employment were expected to be adopted in mid-2008, and enter into effect in 2009. In early 2008 the Government allowed the forint to 'float' against the euro in order to allow the central bank to focus on reducing inflation, in preparation for the adoption of the single currency. In March a national referendum, organized by the opposition, approved the abolition of newly introduced fees for medical treatment and higher education. Prime Minister Gyurcsány subsequently conceded that the fees would be abolished, but pledged to continue the Government's programme for fiscal restraint (see Recent History).

Education

Children under the age of three years attend crèches (bölcsődék), and those between the ages of three and six years attend kindergartens (óvodák). Education is compulsory between the ages of six and 16 years. Children attend basic or primary school (általános iskola) until the age of 14. In 2004 primary enrolment included 89% of children in the relevant age-group, while the comparable ratio for secondary education was 91%. In southern Hungary bilingual schools have been established to promote the languages of the national minorities. The majority of children continue with their education after 16 years of age. The most popular types of secondary school are the grammar school (gimnázium) and the vocational school (szakközépiskola). The gimnázium provides a four-year course of mainly academic studies, although some vocational training does feature on the curriculum. The szakközépiskola offers full vocational training together with a general education, emphasis being laid on practical work. Apprentice training schools (szakmunkásképző intézetek) are attached to factories, agricultural co-operatives, etc., and lead to full trade qualifications. In 1999–2000 the system of higher education underwent a major reorganization, as a result of which from 1 January 2000 there were 30 state-run universities and colleges, 26 church universities and colleges and six colleges run by foundations. In 2000 an estimated 25% of the relevant age-group continued into tertiary education. Expenditure on education in 2003 was some 1,070,400m. forint (equivalent to 12.2% of total government expenditure). In 2003 the Government allocated more than 1,000m. forint in grants to support Romany students pursuing higher education. Tuition fees for state-subsidized higher education were abolished by national referendum in March 2008.

Public Holidays

2008: 1 January (New Year's Day), 15 March (Anniversary of 1848 uprising against Austrian rule), 24 March (Easter Monday), 1 May (Labour Day), 12 May (Whit Monday), 15 August (Assumption), 20 August (Constitution Day), 23 October (Day of the Proclamation of the Republic), 1 November (All Saints' Day), 25–26 December (Christmas).

2009: 1 January (New Year's Day), 15 March (Anniversary of 1848 uprising against Austrian rule), 13 April (Easter Monday), 1 May (Labour Day), 1 June (Whit Monday), 15 August (Assumption), 20 August (Constitution Day), 23 October (Day of the Proclamation of the Republic), 1 November (All Saints' Day), 25–26 December (Christmas).

Weights and Measures

The metric system is in force.

Statistical Survey

Source (unless otherwise stated): Központi Statisztikai Hivatal (Hungarian Central Statistical Office), 1525 Budapest, Keleti Károly u. 5–7; tel. (1) 345-6136; fax (1) 345-6378; e-mail erzsebet.veto@office.ksh.hu; internet www.ksh.hu.

Area and Population

AREA, POPULATION AND DENSITY

Area (sq km)	93,030*
Population (census results)	
1 January 1990	10,374,823
1 February 2001	
Males	4,863,610
Females	5,333,509
Total	10,197,119
Population (official estimates at 1 January)	
2005	10,097,549
2006	10,076,581
2007	10,066,158
Density (per sq km) at 1 January 2007	108.2

* 35,919 sq miles.

Languages (2001 census): Magyar (Hungarian) 98.6%; Romany 0.5%; German 0.3%; Slovak 0.1%; Croatian 0.1%; Ukrainian 0.1%; Others 0.2%.

ADMINISTRATIVE DIVISIONS
(population at 1 January 2007)

	Area (sq km)	Population	Density (per sq km)	County town (with population)*
Counties:				
Bács-Kiskun	8,445	536,290	63.5	Kecskemét (105,464)
Baranya	4,430	398,215	89.9	Pécs (158,607)
Békés	5,631	382,190	67.9	Békéscsaba (63,958)
Borsod-Abaúj-Zemplén	7,247	718,951	99.2	Miskolc (173,629)
Csongrád	4,263	423,751	99.4	Szeged (159,133)
Fejér	4,359	428,711	98.4	Székesfehérvár (105,293)
Győr-Moson-Sopron	4,089	442,667	108.3	Győr (127,275)
Hajdú-Bihar	6,211	545,641	87.9	Debrecen (205,032)
Heves	3,637	319,460	87.8	Eger (57,891)
Jász-Nagykun-Szolnok	5,582	403,622	72.3	Szolnok (76,875)
Komárom-Esztergom	2,265	315,036	139.1	Tatabánya (72,054)
Nógrád	2,544	213,030	83.7	Salgótarján (44,404)
Pest	6,393	1,176,550	184.0	Budapest† (1,838,753)
Somogy	6,036	328,496	54.4	Kaposvár (66,826)
Szabolcs-Szatmár-Bereg	5,937	576,054	97.0	Nyíregyháza (112,882)
Tolna	3,703	240,966	65.1	Szekszárd (35,358)
Vas	3,337	263,251	78.9	Szombathely (82,074)
Veszprém	4,613	363,706	78.8	Veszprém (62,631)
Zala	3,784	293,443	77.5	Zalaegerszeg (61,033)
Capital city				
Budapest†	525	1,696,128	3,230.7	—
Total	93,030	10,066,158	108.2	—

* At 1 January 1999.
† Budapest has separate County status. The area and population of the city are not included in the larger County (Pest) that it administers.

PRINCIPAL TOWNS
(official estimates at mid-2003)

Budapest (capital)	1,712,326	Győr	128,742
Debrecen	205,302	Nyíregyháza	116,720
Miskolc	179,046	Kecskemét	107,635
Szeged	162,723	Székesfehérvár	102,224
Pécs	158,301		

Source: UN, *Demographic Yearbook*.

BIRTHS, MARRIAGES AND DEATHS

	Registered live births		Registered marriages		Registered deaths	
	Number	Rate (per 1,000)	Number	Rate (per 1,000)	Number	Rate (per 1,000)
1999	94,645	9.4	45,465	4.5	143,210	14.2
2000	97,597	9.6	48,110	4.7	135,601	13.3
2001	97,047	9.5	43,583	4.3	132,183	13.0
2002	96,804	9.5	46,008	4.5	132,833	13.1
2003	94,647	9.3	45,398	4.5	135,823	13.4
2004	95,137	9.4	43,791	4.3	132,492	13.1
2005	97,496	9.7	44,234	4.4	135,732	13.5
2006	99,871	9.9	44,528	4.4	131,603	13.1

Expectation of life (years at birth, WHO estimates): 72.9 (males 68.6; females 77.1) in 2005 (Source: WHO, *World Health Statistics*).

ECONOMICALLY ACTIVE POPULATION
(labour force surveys, '000 persons aged 15 years to 74 years)

	2004	2005	2006
Agriculture, hunting, forestry and fishing	204.9	194.0	190.8
Mining and quarrying	14.2	14.9	15.0
Manufacturing	893.9	869.4	865.2
Electricity, gas and water supply	63.7	64.6	67.6
Construction	308.7	315.1	321.6
Wholesale and retail trade; repair of motor vehicles, motorcycles and personal and household goods	545.7	585.9	582.0
Hotels and restaurants	148.8	154.3	157.2
Transport, storage and communications	296.1	285.4	301.3
Financial intermediation	80.1	80.3	80.3
Real estate, renting and business activities	272.5	275.8	282.8
Public administration and defence; compulsory social security	298.8	297.9	299.2
Education	333.0	323.4	322.9
Health and social work	269.4	262.7	269.5
Other community, social and personal service activities	170.6	177.8	174.7
Total employed	3,900.4	3,901.5	3,930.1
Unemployed	252.9	303.9	316.8
Total labour force	4,153.3	4,205.4	4,246.9
Males	2,254.1	2,275.2	2,302.0
Females	1,899.2	1,930.2	1,944.9

Source: ILO.

Health and Welfare

KEY INDICATORS

Total fertility rate (children per woman, 2005)	1.3
Under-5 mortality rate (per 1,000 live births, 2005)	8
HIV/AIDS (% of persons aged 15–49, 2005)	0.1
Physicians (per 1,000 head, 2003)	3.3
Hospital beds (per 1,000 head, 2005)	7.9
Health expenditure (2004): US $ per head (PPP)	1,307.9
Health expenditure (2004): % of GDP	7.9
Health expenditure (2004): public (% of total)	71.6
Access to water (% of persons, 2004)	99
Access to sanitation (% of persons, 2004)	95
Human Development Index (2005): ranking	36
Human Development Index (2005): value	0.874

For sources and definitions, see explanatory note on p. vi.

HUNGARY   Statistical Survey

Agriculture

PRINCIPAL CROPS
('000 metric tons)

	2004	2005	2006
Wheat	6,007.0	5,088.2	4,379.0
Barley	1,423.0	1,190.4	1,081.1
Maize	8,317.0	9,050.0	8,441.2
Rye	125.0	107.3	949.7
Oats	216.0	157.4	155.6
Triticale (wheat-rye hybrid)	622.0	567.7	448.4
Potatoes	767.0	656.7	574.4
Sugar beet	3,130.0	3,515.9	2,547.5
Dry peas	35.0	50.2	16.0*
Soybeans (Soya beans)	66.0	78.0	82.0
Sunflower seed	1,198.0	1,107.9	1,164.5
Rapeseed	287.0	282.7	333.9
Cabbages	215.9	136.6	136.6*
Tomatoes	269.0	188.4	116.5
Cucumbers and gherkins	83.0	70.9	70.9*
Chillies and green peppers	126.1	113.4	113.4*
Dry onions	109.4	92.2	72.8
Green peas	93.0	85.0	85.0*
Carrots and turnips	150.4	110.1	110.1*
Green corn	508.0	354.2	n.a.
Watermelons	251.0	214.2	214.2*
Apples	680.0	510.4	505.5
Sour (Morello) cherries	77.0	48.1	83.3
Peaches and nectarines	83.0	48.4	48.4
Plums	67.0	36.0	54.6
Grapes	789.0	536.4	551.3
Tobacco (leaves)	11.0	11.4	11.4*

* FAO estimate.
† Unofficial figure.

Aggregate production ('000 metric tons, may include official, semi-official or estimated data): Total cereals 16,779 in 2004, 16,212 in 2005, 14,673 in 2006; Total roots and tubers 7,486 in 2004, 6,567 in 2005, 5,744 in 2006; Total vegetables (incl. melons) 2,033 in 2004, 1,547 in 2005, 1,456 in 2006; Total fruits (excl. melons) 1,826 in 2004, 1,268 in 2005, 1,323 in 2006.

Source: FAO.

LIVESTOCK
('000 head, year ending September)

	2004	2005	2006
Cattle	739	723	708
Pigs	4,913	4,059	3,853
Sheep	1,296	1,397	1,405
Goats	80	74	80
Horses	62	67	71
Chickens	37,502	32,814	31,902
Ducks	2,709	2,797	3,389
Geese	2,801	2,127	1,370
Turkeys	4,256	3,529	4,415

Source: FAO.

LIVESTOCK PRODUCTS
('000 metric tons)

	2004	2005	2006
Cattle meat	46.2	40.9	42.2
Sheep meat	2.0	2.2	2.5
Pig meat	539.6	508.5	517.8
Chicken meat	253.1	246.2	240.8
Duck meat	48.1	53.1	39.7
Rabbit meat	8.6	9.7	10.7
Cows' milk	1,894.6	1,928.7	1,832.2
Sheep's milk	3.5	3.6	3.6*
Goats' milk	4.7	4.6	4.6*
Hen eggs	181.4	164.6	161.3
Other poultry eggs*	4.0	4.2	4.2
Honey	19.5	19.7	17.6
Wool: greasy	4.7	5.0	5.0*

* FAO estimate(s).
Source: FAO.

Forestry

ROUNDWOOD REMOVALS
('000 cu metres, excl. bark)

	2004	2005	2006
Sawlogs, veneer logs and logs for sleepers	1,575	1,248	1,166
Pulpwood	653	453	475
Other industrial wood	760	1,103	1,026
Fuel wood	2,672	3,136	3,246
Total	5,660	5,940	5,913

Source: FAO.

SAWNWOOD PRODUCTION
('000 cu metres, incl. railway sleepers)

	2004	2005	2006
Coniferous (softwood)	82	82	74
Broadleaved (hardwood)	123	133	112
Total	205	215	186

Source: FAO.

Fishing

(metric tons, live weight)

	2003	2004	2005
Capture	6,536	7,242	7,609
Common carp	2,930	3,502	3,475
Silver carp	534	767	1,143
Other cyprinids	2,057	1,931	1,900
Aquaculture	11,870	12,744	13,661
Common carp	7,924	8,688	9,739
Grass carp	479	565	607
Silver carp	1,373	1,401	978
North African catfish	986	1,228	1,412
Freshwater fishes	629	476	536
Total catch	18,406	19,986	21,270

Source: FAO.

Mining

('000 metric tons, unless otherwise indicated)

	2003	2004	2005
Hard coal	667	260	n.a.
Brown coal	4,128	2,495	1,426
Lignite	8,564	8,470	8,154
Crude petroleum	1,133	1,100	948
Bauxite	666	647	535
Natural gas (million cu metres)*	3,010	3,200	3,159

* Marketed production.

Source: US Geological Survey.

HUNGARY

Industry

SELECTED PRODUCTS
('000 metric tons, unless otherwise indicated)

	2001	2002	2003
Crude steel	2,065	2,138	2,045
Cement	3,452	3,510	3,575
Nitrogenous fertilizers*	269	210	198
Refined sugar	444	352	259
Buses (number)	870	372	160
Non-rubber footwear ('000 pairs)	15,536	15,175	12,581
Electric energy (million kWh)	36,418	36,156	30,254
Radio receivers ('000)	3,459	2,917	2,991

* Production in terms of nitrogen.

2004: Cement ('000 metric tons) 3,363; Radio receivers 2,840,000.

Source: mainly UN, *Industrial Commodity Statistics Yearbook*.

Electric energy (million kWh): 29,201 in 2004; 30,552 in 2005; 29,646 in 2006.

Finance

CURRENCY AND EXCHANGE RATES

Monetary Units
100 fillér = 1 forint.

Sterling, Dollar and Euro Equivalents (31 December 2007)
£1 sterling = 345.807 forint;
US $1 = 172.610 forint;
€1 = 254.099 forint;
1,000 forint = £2.89 = $5.79 = €3.94.

Average Exchange Rate (forint per US dollar)
2005 199.582
2006 210.390
2007 183.626

BUDGET
('000 million forint)

Revenue	2006	2007	2008*
Payments of economic units	996.8	1,119.2	1,169.6
Corporate taxes	468.7	510.8	530.6
Simplified business tax	50.9	178.6	170.6
Gambling tax	71,468	71,461	73,500
Taxes on consumption	2,681.2	2,891.4	3,068.2
Value-added tax	1,832.0	1,979.4	2,130.6
Excises and tax on consumption	849.2	912.0	937.6
Payments of households	1,698.2	1,945.3	2,101.8
Personal income tax revenue of the central budget	1,579.8	1,820.8	1,965.1
Fees	111.1	118.8	131.4
Central budgetary institutions and chapter-administered appropriations	1,267.8	1,268.9	1,207.5
Payments of general government sub-systems	208.1	196.7	147.3
Payments of extra-budgetary funds	82.0	113.3	119.3
Payments related to state property	33.0	48.8	96.4
Revenue related to debt service	87.2	96.4	61.5
Other revenues	20.7	20.3	6.2
Transfers from the European Union	16.9	9.2	40.9
Total	7,009.9	7,596.3	7,899.5

Expenditure	2006	2007	2008*
Subsidies to economic units	124.0	197.4	141.8
Supports to the media	46.6	52.2	53.4
Consumer price subsidy	117.9	111.9	117.0
Housing grants	223.5	228.5	190.7
Family benefits and social subsidies	646.0	686.3	694.5
Family benefits	471.0	508.1	507.2
Income-supplement benefits	147.6	151.7	159.7
Payments of central budgetary institutions and chapter-administered appropriations	3,896.5	4,228.1	3,876.5
Transfers to general government sub-systems	2,237.6	2,160.3	2,222.3
Contribution to social-security funds	890.6	777.8	841.3
Transfers to local governments	1,327.9	1,354.6	1,348.6
Transfer to non-profit organizations	5.1	5.2	5.2
Expenditures of international transactions	8.0	14.6	14.2
Debt service related expenditures and interest expenditures	983.3	1,006.1	1,110.8
Reserves	—	—	230.3
State property expenditures	—	—	88.2
Extraordinary and other expenditures	66.6	37.5	46.3
Government guarantees redeemed	10.8	10.3	19.3
Debt assumptions	420.0	58.2	1.2
Contribution to the European Union budget	185.6	189.5	205.3
Total	8,971.6	8,986.1	9,017.1

* Estimates.

INTERNATIONAL RESERVES
(US $ million at 31 December)

	2004	2005	2006
Gold (national valuation)	43	51	63
IMF special drawing rights	58	64	74
Reserve position in IMF	538	192	137
Foreign exchange	15,312	18,283	21,316
Total	15,951	18,590	21,590

Source: IMF, *International Financial Statistics*.

MONEY SUPPLY
('000 million forint at 31 December)

	2004	2005	2006
Currency outside banks	1,341.6	1,600.3	1,838.3
Demand deposits at commercial and savings banks	2,308.0	3,033.5	3,227.7
Total money (incl. others)	3,654.2	4,633.8	5,065.9

Source: IMF, *International Financial Statistics*.

COST OF LIVING
(Consumer Price Index; base: 2000 = 100)

	2004	2005	2006
Food	131.2	134.5	144.8
Fuel and power	242.4	151.3	160.9
Clothing	116.6	116.9	116.1
Rent	154.8	161.6	168.4
All items (incl. others)	128.5	133.1	138.3

Source: ILO.

HUNGARY

Statistical Survey

NATIONAL ACCOUNTS
('000 million forint at current prices)

Expenditure on the Gross Domestic Product

	2004	2005	2006
Government final consumption expenditure	2,082.7	2,191.0	2,374.6
Private final consumption expenditure*	13,902.9	14,988.4	15,779.9
Changes in inventories	748.3	157.8	40.3
Gross fixed capital formation	4,631.2	4,995.3	5,163.8
Total domestic expenditure	21,365.1	22,332.5	23,358.6
Exports of goods and services	13,166.9	14,626.2	18,371.6
Less Imports of goods and services	13,819.7	14,932.0	18,168.7
GDP in purchasers' values	20,712.3	22,026.8	23,561.5
GDP at constant 2000 prices	16,049.2	16,730.7	17,384.8

* Includes non-profit institutions serving households.

Source: IMF, *International Financial Statistics*.

Gross Domestic Product by Economic Activity

	2004	2005	2006
Agriculture, hunting, forestry and fishing	853.0	815.9	871.1
Mining, quarrying and power	580.6	589.4	580.3
Manufacturing	3,907.1	4,188.0	4,669.6
Construction	861.1	899.9	958.4
Wholesale and retail trade; repair; hotels and restaurants	2,266.8	2,356.4	2,541.3
Transport, storage and communications	1,392.0	1,438.4	1,545.3
Financial intermediation and real estate activities	3,678.9	4,152.4	4,572.7
Public administration; education; health; social work	3,364.9	3,580.0	3,725.6
Other community, social and personal service activities	745.1	844.9	918.6
Gross value added in basic prices *	17,649.5	18,865.3	20,382.9
Taxes *less* subsidies on products	3,062.8	3,161.5	3,178.6
GDP in market prices	20,712.3	22,026.8	23,561.5

* Since the introduction of new accounting regulations at the beginning of 2005, data for financial intermediation services indirectly measured (FISIM) have been allocated retrospectively to user sectors and industries.

BALANCE OF PAYMENTS
(US $ million)

	2004	2005	2006
Exports of goods f.o.b.	55,689	62,245	73,509
Imports of goods f.o.b.	−58,695	−64,041	−74,017
Trade balance	−3,006	−1,795	−508
Exports of services	10,890	12,810	13,460
Imports of services	−10,604	−11,902	−12,159
Balance on goods and services	−2,720	−887	793
Other income received	1,877	2,094	4,804
Other income paid	−8,013	−8,974	−12,142
Balance on goods, services and income	−8,856	−7,768	−6,545
Current transfers received	1,633	2,592	3,117
Current transfers paid	−1,338	−2,386	−2,784
Current balance	−8,561	−7,561	−6,212
Capital account (net)	328	881	781
Direct investment abroad	−1,116	−2,377	−7,405
Direct investment from abroad	4,521	7,539	10,344
Portfolio investment assets	−441	−1,137	−2,231
Portfolio investment liabilities	7,353	5,777	8,694
Financial derivatives assets	4,214	3,621	4,565
Financial derivatives liabilities	−3,802	−3,765	−4,382
Other investment assets	−1,940	−2,203	−5,166
Other investment liabilities	3,199	6,445	5,595
Net errors and omissions	−1,773	−2,315	−3,481
Overall balance	1,981	4,904	1,102

Source: IMF, *International Financial Statistics*.

External Trade

PRINCIPAL COMMODITIES
(distribution by SITC, US $ million)

Imports c.i.f.	2002	2003	2004
Mineral fuels, lubricants, etc.	2,771.6	2,655.2	4,357.5
Petroleum, petroleum products, etc.	1,306.4	554.1	2,018.0
Petroleum gases	1,199.8	1,690.0	1,759.0
Chemicals and related products	3,420.3	4,596.7	5,705.7
Basic manufactures	6,131.1	7,648.7	9,627.2
Textile yarn, fabrics, etc.	1,116.3	1,253.4	1,396.5
Metal manufactures	1,303.6	1,689.6	2,089.6
Machinery and transport equipment	19,406.0	24,489.0	31,890.5
Power-generating machinery and equipment	1,965.3	2,573.4	3,669.2
Specialized industrial machinery	1,041.4	1,439.2	1,391.9
General industrial machinery equipment and parts	2,083.6	2,909.3	3,138.9
Office machines and automatic data-processing machines	2,125.9	2,039.7	2,336.0
Telecommunications and sound equipment	2,337.7	3,303.1	4,996.3
Other electrical machinery apparatus, etc.	6,368.2	7,769.3	10,760.1
Road vehicles and parts (excl. tyres, engines and electrical parts)	3,039.2	3,909.2	4,957.2
Miscellaneous manufactured articles	3,539.1	4,494.4	5,068.6
Total (incl. others)	37,611.6	46,675.0	60,248.7

Exports f.o.b.	2002	2003	2004
Food and live animals	2,202.9	2,651.0	3,163.7
Chemicals and related products	2,118.1	2,878.3	4,118.4
Basic manufactures	3,471.3	4,423.2	5,626.3
Machinery and transport equipment	20,128.5	26,260.6	34,647.0
Power-generating machinery and equipment	3,723.2	4,801.9	5,988.2
General industrial machinery equipment and parts	1,044.1	1,500.8	2,218.7
Office machines and automatic data-processing machines	2,454.3	3,031.6	3,795.7
Telecommunications and sound equipment	5,351.7	7,368.9	11,031.4
Other electrical machinery apparatus, etc.	3,825.9	5,133.1	6,015.4
Road vehicles and parts (excl. tyres, engines and electrical parts)	2,979.3	3,520.4	4,392.7
Miscellaneous manufactured articles	4,420.5	4,547.6	5,301.4
Clothing and accessories (excl. footwear)	1,283.5	1,439.6	1,485.4
Total (incl. others)	34,336.6	43,007.8	55,468.3

Source: UN, *International Trade Statistics Yearbook*.

2005 (million forint): *Imports:* Food, beverages and tobacco 536.9; Crude materials 234.7; Basic manufactures 4,320.4; Machinery and transport equipment 6,714.3; Total (incl. others) 13,145.5. *Exports:* Food, beverages and tobacco 718.0; Crude materials 246.4; Basic manufactures 3,429.3; Machinery and transport equipment 7,692.7; Total (incl. others) 12,425.5.

2006 (million forint): *Imports:* Food, beverages and tobacco 636.9; Crude materials 273.3; Basic manufactures 5,217.8; Machinery and transport equipment 8,052.5; Total (incl. others) 15,966.7. *Exports:* Food, beverages and tobacco 851.4; Crude materials 295.6; Basic manufactures 4,267.0; Machinery and transport equipment 9,639.0; Total (incl. others) 15,444.4.

HUNGARY

Statistical Survey

PRINCIPAL TRADING PARTNERS
('000 million forint)*

Imports c.i.f.	2004	2005	2006†
Austria	995.4	868.3	992.6
Belgium	253.1	292.9	335.7
China, People's Republic	583.3	709.7	817.8
Czech Republic	348.1	377.9	468.0
France	561.5	651.2	754.2
Germany	3,580.6	3,634.7	4,375.3
Italy	684.1	640.4	731.0
Japan	369.8	446.7	468.1
Korea, Republic	183.2	241.9	299.8
Netherlands	601.7	573.4	683.9
Poland	392.5	501.1	680.0
Romania	184.4	221.2	363.6
Russia	690.8	970.4	1,314.8
Slovakia	243.3	298.3	435.7
Spain	174.1	182.8	221.2
Sweden	158.2	148.7	218.9
Switzerland-Liechtenstein	196.6	136.8	156.8
Ukraine	131.9	106.3	177.6
United Kingdom	327.1	327.9	368.7
USA	202.1	220.5	273.7
Total (incl. others)	12,218.9	13,145.5	15,966.7

Exports f.o.b.	2004	2005	2006†
Austria	814.1	694.8	747.8
Belgium	249.6	263.8	301.0
Croatia	143.2	178.7	235.5
Czech Republic	266.4	380.1	530.6
Finland	224.4	130.9	85.4
France	625.3	635.7	716.5
Germany	3,552.5	3,739.0	4,547.0
Italy	616.9	686.0	842.2
Netherlands	410.8	480.7	463.6
Poland	321.2	403.2	618.8
Romania	355.5	464.5	634.6
Russia	184.8	233.2	423.1
Slovakia	216.8	355.5	594.6
Slovenia	112.8	146.3	162.4
Spain	313.6	400.4	510.8
Sweden	254.6	167.3	168.7
Switzerland-Liechtenstein	124.3	137.9	147.2
Ukraine	124.7	163.9	275.8
United Kingdom	625.7	631.8	689.0
USA	336.2	376.9	429.2
Total (incl. others)	11,232.4	12,425.5	15,444.4

* Imports by country of origin; exports by country of destination.
† Preliminary.

Transport

RAILWAYS
(traffic)

	2002	2003	2004
Passenger-kilometres (million)	10,531	10,286	10,544
Net ton-kilometres (million)	7,752	8,109	8,749

Source: UN, *Statistical Yearbook*.

ROAD TRAFFIC
(motor vehicles in use at 31 December)

	2001	2002	2003
Passenger cars	2,611,770	2,629,526	2,777,219
Buses and coaches	17,817	17,873	17,877
Lorries and vans	355,221	369,295	377,111
Motor cycles and mopeds	93,088	97,593	108,538
Road tractors	25,220	26,786	29,752

2004: Passenger cars 2,828,433; Lorries and vans 378,088.
2005: Passenger cars 2,888,735; Lorries and vans 391,731.
2006: Passenger cars 2,953,737; Lorries and vans 404,888.

SHIPPING
Merchant Fleet
(registered at 31 December)

	2001	2002	2003
Number of vessels	1	1	2
Total displacement (grt)	1,901	3,784	7,568

Source: Lloyd's Register-Fairplay, *World Fleet Statistics*.

INLAND WATERWAYS
(traffic)

	2001	2002	2003
Freight carried ('000 metric tons)	2,903	3,006	2,105
Freight ton-km (million)	1,055	1,120	1,117

CIVIL AVIATION
(traffic)

	2001	2002	2003
Kilometres flown (million)	39	39	46
Passengers carried ('000)	2,075	2,134	2,362
Passenger-km (million)	3,146	3,116	3,130
Total ton-km	324	312	314

Source: UN, *Statistical Yearbook*.

Tourism

TOURISTS BY COUNTRY OF ORIGIN
('000 arrivals, including visitors in transit)

	2004	2005	2006
Austria	5,237	5,600	6,088
Croatia	1,280	1,195	1,307
Germany	3,136	3,199	3,222
Poland	1,007	1,176	1,303
Romania	7,435	7,445	8,651
Serbia and Montenegro	3,618	3,229	3,315
Slovakia	5,548	7,322	7,968
Ukraine	2,564	2,387	1,874
Total (incl. others)	36,635	38,555	40,963

Tourist receipts (US $ million): 4,119 in 2003; 4,129 in 2004; 4,581 in 2005 (Source: World Tourism Organization).

Communications Media

	2004	2005	2006
Telephones ('000 main lines in use)	3,577.3	3,356.1	3,350.4
Mobile cellular telephones ('000 subscribers)	8,727.2	9,320.0	9,965.0
Personal computers ('000 in use)	1,476	1,476	n.a.
Internet users ('000)	2,700	3,000	3,500
Broadband subscribers ('000)	411.1	651.7	967.7
Book production: titles	11,211	12,898	n.a.
Book production: copies	32,035	40,974	n.a.

Radio receivers ('000 in use): 7,245 in 1998; 7,231 in 1999.

Television receivers ('000 in use): 4,377 in 1998; 4,519 in 1999; 4,451 in 2000.

Facsimile machines ('000 in use): 180 in 1998.

Daily newspapers: 34 titles (average daily circulation 2,195,000) in 2004.

Non-daily newspapers: 97 titles (average daily circulation 1,368,000) in 2004.

Sources: partly UNESCO, *Statistical Yearbook*, and International Telecommunication Union.

Education

(2006/07, full and part-time education, estimates)

	Institutions	Teachers	Students
Pre-primary	4,524	30,550	327,644
Primary	3,592	83,607	831,342
Secondary	1,763	40,538	534,423
General	1,039	30,212	400,394
Vocational	724	10,326	134,029
Tertiary	71	22,076	416,348

Directory

The Constitution

A new Constitution was introduced on 18 August 1949, and the Hungarian People's Republic was established two days later. The Constitution was amended in April 1972 and December 1983. Further, radical amendments were made in October 1989. Shortly afterwards, the Republic of Hungary was proclaimed.

The following is a summary of the main provisions of the Constitution, as amended in October 1989.

GENERAL PROVISIONS

The Republic of Hungary is an independent, democratic constitutional state in which the values of civil democracy and democratic socialism prevail in equal measures. All power belongs to the people, which they exercise directly and through the elected representatives of popular sovereignty.

Political parties may, under observance of the Constitution, be freely formed and may freely operate in Hungary. Parties may not directly exercise public power. No party has the right to guide any state body. Trade unions, and other organizations for the representation of interests, safeguard and represent the interests of employees, members of co-operatives and entrepreneurs.

The State safeguards the people's freedom, the independence and territorial integrity of the country as well as the frontiers thereof, as established by international treaties. The Republic of Hungary rejects war as a means of settling disputes between nations and refrains from applying force against the independence or territorial integrity of other states, and from threats of violence.

The Hungarian legal system adopts the universally accepted rules of international law. The order of legislation is regulated by an Act of constitutional force.

The economy of Hungary is a market economy, availing itself also of the advantages of planning, with public and private ownership enjoying equal right and protection. State-owned enterprises and organs pursuing economic activities manage their affairs independently, in accordance with the mode and responsibility as provided by law.

The Republic of Hungary protects the institutions of marriage and the family. It provides for the indigent through extensive social measures, and recognizes and enforces the right of each citizen to a healthy environment.

GOVERNMENT

Legislature

The highest organ of state authority in the Republic of Hungary is the Országgyűlés (National Assembly), which exercises all the rights deriving from the sovereignty of the people and determines the organization, direction and conditions of government. The Országgyűlés enacts the Constitution and laws, determines the state budget, decides the socio-economic plan, elects the President of the Republic and the Council of Ministers, directs the activities of ministries, decides upon declaring war and concluding peace, and exercises the prerogative of amnesty.

The Országgyűlés is elected for a term of four years and members enjoy immunity from arrest and prosecution without parliamentary consent. It meets at least twice a year and is convened by the President of the Republic or by a written demand of the Council of Ministers or of one-fifth of the Assembly's members. It elects a President, Deputy Presidents and Recorders from among its own members, and it lays down its own rules of procedure and agenda. As a general rule, the sessions of the Országgyűlés are held in public.

The Országgyűlés has the right of legislation which can be initiated by the President of the Republic, the Council of Ministers or any committee or member of the Országgyűlés. Decisions are valid only if at least half of the members are present, and they require a simple majority. Constitutional changes require a two-thirds' majority. Acts of the Országgyűlés are signed by the President of the Republic.

The Országgyűlés may pronounce its dissolution before the expiry of its term, and in the event of an emergency may prolong its mandate or may be reconvened after dissolution. A new Országgyűlés must be elected within three months of dissolution and convened within one month of polling day.

Members of the Országgyűlés are elected on the basis of universal, equal and direct suffrage by secret ballot, and they are accountable to their constituents, who may recall them. All citizens of 18 years and over have the right to vote, with the exception of those who are unsound of mind, and those who are deprived of their civil rights by a court of law.

President of the Republic

The President of the Republic is the Head of State of Hungary. He/she embodies the unity of the nation and supervises the democratic operation of the mechanism of State. The President is also the Commander-in-Chief of the Armed Forces. The President is elected by the Országgyűlés for a period of five years, and may be re-elected for a second term. Any citizen of Hungary qualified to vote, who has reached 35 years of age before the day of election, may be elected President.

The President may issue the writ for general or local elections, convene the Országgyűlés, initiate legislation, hold plebiscites, direct local government, conclude international treaties, appoint diplomatic representatives, ratify international treaties, appoint higher civil servants and officers of the armed forces, award orders and titles, and exercise the prerogative of mercy.

Council of Ministers

The highest organ of state administration is the Council of Ministers, responsible to the Országgyűlés and consisting of the Prime Minister and other Ministers who are elected by the Országgyűlés on the recommendation of the President of the Republic. The Council of Ministers directs the work of the ministries (listed in a special enactment) and ensures the enforcement of laws and the fulfilment of economic plans; it may issue decrees and annul or modify measures taken by any central or local organ of government.

HUNGARY

Local Administration

The local organs of state power are the county, town, borough and town precinct councils, whose members are elected for a term of four years by the voters in each area. Local councils direct economic, social and cultural activities in their area, prepare local economic plans and budgets and supervise their fulfilment, enforce laws, supervise subordinate organs, maintain public order, protect public property and individual rights, and direct local economic enterprises. They may issue regulations and annul or modify those of subordinate councils. Local Councils are administered by an Executive Committee elected by and responsible to them.

JUDICATURE

Justice is administered by the Supreme Court of the Republic of Hungary, county and district courts. The Supreme Court exercises the right of supervising in principle the judicial activities and practice of all other courts.

All judicial offices are filled by election; Supreme Court, county and district court judges are all elected for an indefinite period; the President of the Supreme Court is elected by the Országgyűlés. All court hearings are public unless otherwise prescribed by law, and those accused are guaranteed the right of defence. An accused person must be considered innocent until proved guilty.

Public Prosecutor

The function of the Chief Public Prosecutor is to supervise the observance of the law. He is elected by the Országgyűlés, to which he is responsible. The organization of public prosecution is under the control of the Chief Public Prosecutor, who appoints the public prosecutors.

RIGHTS AND DUTIES OF CITIZENS

The Republic of Hungary guarantees for its citizens the right to work and to remuneration, the right of rest and recreation, the right to care in old age, sickness or disability, the right to education, and equality before the law; women enjoy equal rights with men. Discrimination on grounds of sex, religion or nationality is a punishable offence. The State also ensures freedom of conscience, religious worship, speech, the press and assembly. The right of workers to organize themselves is stressed. The freedom of the individual, and the privacy of the home and of correspondence are inviolable. Freedom for creative work in the sciences and the arts is guaranteed.

The basic freedoms of all workers are guaranteed, and foreign citizens enjoy the right of asylum.

Military service (with or without arms) and the defence of their country are the duties of all citizens.

The Government

HEAD OF STATE

President of the Republic: LÁSZLÓ SÓLYOM (elected by vote of the Országgyűlés 7 June 2005; took office 5 August 2005).

COUNCIL OF MINISTERS
(April 2008)

A coalition of the Hungarian Socialist Party (HSP) and the Alliance of Free Democrats (AFD).*

Prime Minister: FERENC GYURCSÁNY (HSP).
Minister of Foreign Affairs: KINGA GÖNCZ (HSP).
Minister of Defence: IMRE SZEKERES (HSP).
Minister of Finance: JÁNOS VERES (HSP).
Minister of Economy and Transport: CSABA KÁKOSY (AFD).
Minister of Municipalities and Regional Development: GORDON BAJNAI (HSP).
Minister of Agriculture and Rural Development: JÓZSEF GRÁF (HSP).
Minister of Health: (vacant).
Minister of Justice and Law Enforcement: TIBOR DRASKOVICS (Independent).
Minister of Labour and Social Affairs: MÓNIKA LAMPERTH (HSP).
Minister of Environmental Protection and Water Management: GÁBOR FODOR (AFD).
Minister of Education and Culture: ISTVÁN HILLER (HSP).
Minister in charge of the Prime Minister's Office: PÉTER KISS (HSP).
Minister without Portfolio: GYÖRGY SZILVÁSY (HSP).

* On 31 March 2008 the AFD announced its intention to withdraw from the Government with effect from 30 April.

MINISTRIES

Office of the President: 1014 Budapest, Szent György tér 1–2; tel. (1) 224-5009.
Office of the Prime Minister: 1055 Budapest, Kossuth Lajos tér 1–3; tel. (1) 441-4000; fax (1) 268-3050; e-mail webmaster@meh.hu; internet www.meh.hu.
Ministry of Agriculture and Rural Development: 1055 Budapest, Kossuth Lajos tér 11; tel. (1) 301-4000; fax (1) 302-0408; internet www.fvm.hu.
Ministry of Defence: 1055 Budapest, Balaton u. 7–11; tel. (1) 236-5111; fax (1) 474-1111; e-mail honvedelem@armedia.hu; internet www.honvedelem.hu.
Ministry of Economy and Transport: 1055 Budapest, Honvéd u. 13–15; tel. (1) 374-1700; fax (1) 374-2700; e-mail press@gkm.hu; internet www.gkm.hu.
Ministry of Education and Culture: 1055 Budapest, Szalay u. 10–14; tel. (1) 302-0600; fax (1) 302-2002; e-mail info@okm.gov.hu; internet www.okm.gov.hu.
Ministry of Environmental Protection and Water Management: 1011 Budapest, POB 351, Fő u. 44–50; tel. (1) 457-3300; fax (1) 201-2846; e-mail kozonsir@mail.ktm.hu; internet www.ktm.hu.
Ministry of Finance: 1051 Budapest, József Nádor tér 2–4; tel. (1) 318-2066; fax (1) 318-2570; e-mail kommunikacio@pm.gov.hu; internet www1.pm.gov.hu.
Ministry of Foreign Affairs: 1027 Budapest, Bem rkp. 47; tel. (1) 458-1000; fax (1) 212-5981; internet www.mfa.gov.hu.
Ministry of Health: 1051 Budapest, Arany János u. 6–8; tel. (1) 301-7800; fax (1) 302-0925; e-mail webmester@eum.hu; internet www.eum.hu.
Ministry of Justice and Law Enforcement: 1055 Budapest, Kossuth Lajos tér 4; tel. (1) 441-3003; fax (1) 441-3711; e-mail ugyfelszolgalat@irm.gov.hu; internet www.irm.hu.
Ministry of Labour and Social Affairs: 1054 Budapest, Alkotmány u. 3; tel. (1) 475-5700; fax (1) 475-5800; internet www.szmm.gov.hu.
Ministry of Municipalities and Regional Development: 1051 Budapest, József Attila u. 2–4; tel. (1) 441-1000; fax (1) 441-1437; e-mail ugyfelszolgalat@otm.gov.hu; internet www.bm.hu.

Legislature

Országgyűlés
(National Assembly)

1055 Budapest, Kossuth Lajos tér 1–3; 1357 Budapest, POB 2; tel. (1) 441-4000; fax (1) 441-5000; internet www.mkogy.hu.
President: KATALIN SZILI.

General Election, 9 and 23 April 2006

Parties	% of votes	Seats
Hungarian Socialist Party-Alliance of Free Democrats (HSP-AFD) coalition	54.40	210
Fidesz—Hungarian Civic Alliance-Christian Democratic People's Party (Fidesz-CDPP) coalition	42.49	164
Hungarian Democratic Forum (HDF)	2.85	11
Independent	0.26	1
Total	100.00	386

Election Commission

Országos Választási Iroda (OVI) (National Election Office): 1450 Budapest, pf. 81; fax (1) 456-6579; e-mail visz@mail.ahiv.hu; internet www.valasztas.hu; Chair. Dr LAJOS FICZERE; Deputy Chair. Dr MIKLÓS MOLNÁR.

Political Organizations

Alliance of Free Democrats (AFD) (Szabad Demokraták Szövetsége—SzDSz): 1143 Budapest, Gizella u. 36; tel. (1) 223-2050; fax (1) 222-3599; e-mail szerkesztoseg@szdsz.hu; internet www.szdsz.hu; f. 1988; formed an electoral alliance with the Hungarian Socialist Party (q.v.) to contest the 2006 legislative elections; 19,000 mems (2000); Chair. KÓKA JÁNOS.
Alliance of Green Democrats: 1054 Budapest, Vadász u. 29; tel. (1) 353-0100; fax (1) 354-1902; e-mail zd@zd.hu; internet www.zd.hu;

f. 2003 from the merger of the Alliance of Greens, the Hungarian Women's Party, the New Left and others; Chair. GYÖRGY DROPPA.

Association for Somogy (Somogyért Egyesület): 7400 Kaposvár, Szent Imre u. 14; tel. (82) 526-070; e-mail somogyert@axelero.hu; internet www.somogyert.hu; f. 1994; local party in Somogy county; contested 2006 legislative elections in coalition with the Hungarian Socialist Party; Chair. Dr ISTVÁN GYENESEI.

Christian Democratic People's Party (CDPP) (Kereszténydemokrata Néppárt—KDNP): 1078 Budapest, István u. 44; tel. and fax (1) 489-0878; e-mail elnok@kdnp.hu; internet www.kdnp.hu; re-formed 1989; formed an electoral alliance with the Federation of Young Democrats—Hungarian Civic Alliance (q.v.) to contest the 2006 legislative elections; Chair. SEMJÉN ZSOLT.

Fidesz—Hungarian Civic Alliance (Fidesz) (Fidesz—Magyar Polgári Szöevetség): 1089 Budapest, Visi Imre u. 6; tel. (1) 555-2000; fax (1) 269-5343; e-mail fidesz@fidesz.hu; internet www.fidesz.hu; f. 1988 as the Federation of Young Democrats; renamed April 1995; re-formed as an alliance in 2003, with a new charter; 10,000 mems; Chair. VIKTOR ORBÁN.

Hungarian Communist Workers' Party (HWP) (Magyar Munkáspárt—MMP): 1082 Budapest, Baross u. 61; tel. (1) 334-2721; fax (1) 313-5423; e-mail info@munkaspart.hu; internet www.munkaspart.hu; f. 1956 as Hungarian Socialist Workers' Party; dissolved and replaced by Hungarian Socialist Party (see above) in 1989; re-formed in 1989 as Hungarian Socialist Workers' Party, name changed to Workers' Party in 2003, name changed as above 2005, after breakaway faction formed Workers' Party of Hungary 2006; approx. 30,000 mems; Pres. Dr GYULA THÜRMER.

Hungarian Democratic Forum (HDF) (Magyar Demokrata Fórum—MDF): 1026 Budapest, Szilágyi Erszébet fasor 73; tel. (1) 225-2280; fax (1) 225-2290; e-mail velemeny@mdf.hu; internet www.mdf.hu; f. 1987; centre-right; 25,000 mems (2001); Chair. Dr DÁVID IBOLYA.

Hungarian National Front (Magyar Nemzeti Front): 1052 Budapest, Semmelweis u. 1–3; tel. (1) 267-4510; e-mail info@nemzetifront.hu; internet www.nemzetifront.hu; f. 2003 by fmr mems of the Hungarian Justice and Life Party; Chair. ERNO ROZGONYI (acting).

Hungarian Social Democratic Party (HSDP) (Magyarországi Szociáldemokrata Párt—MSzDP): Budapest; tel. (1) 214-9496; fax (1) 214-9497; internet www.mszdp.hu; f. 1890; absorbed by the Communist Party in 1948; revived 1988; affiliated with the Social Democratic Youth Movement; Chair. LÁSZLÓ KAPOLYI.

Hungarian Socialist Party (HSP) (Magyar Szocialista Párt—MSzP): 1081 Budapest, Köztársaság tér 26; tel. (1) 210-0046; fax (1) 210-0081; e-mail info@mszp.hu; internet www.mszp.hu; f. 1989 to replace the Hungarian Socialist Workers' Party; formed an electoral coalition with the Alliance of Free Democrats (q.v.) to contest the 2006 legislative elections; Leader FERENC GYURCSÁNY.

Independent Smallholders', Agrarian Workers' and Civic Party (ISCP) (Független Kisgazda-, Földmunkás- és Polgári Párt—FKgP): 1092 Budapest, Kinizsi u. 22; tel. and fax (1) 318-1824; internet www.fkgp.hu; f. 1988 as the Independent Smallholders' Party, name subsequently changed to the Independent Smallholders' and Peasants' Party; 60,000 mems; Chair. PÉTER HEGEDÜS.

Third Way: 1085 Budapest, Rökk Szilárd u. 19; tel. and fax (1) 3171-2692; internet www.miep.hu; f. 2005 by merger of Hungarian Justice and Life Party—HJLP (f. 1993) and Movement for a Better Hungary (Jobbik—f. 2003); extreme right-wing, nationalist party; Co-Chair. ISTVÁN CSURKA, DAVID KOVÁCS.

Diplomatic Representation

EMBASSIES IN HUNGARY

Albania: 1026 Budapest, Gábor Áron u. 55; tel. (1) 326-8905; fax (1) 326-8904; e-mail aalbemb@enternet.hu; Ambassador EDUARD SULO.

Algeria: 1121 Budapest, Zugligeti u. 27; tel. (1) 200-6860; fax (1) 200-6781; e-mail ambalbud@axelero.hu; Ambassador BACHIR ROUIS.

Argentina: 1023 Budapest, Vérhalom u. 12–16, II, 3A; tel. (1) 325-0492; fax (1) 326-0494; Ambassador DOMINGO SANTIAGO CULLEN.

Australia: 1126 Budapest, Királyhágó tér 8–9; tel. (1) 457-9777; fax (1) 201-9792; e-mail ausembbp@mail.datanet.hu; internet www.ausembbp.hu; Ambassador ALEX BROOKING.

Austria: 1068 Budapest, Benczúr u. 16; tel. (1) 479-7010; fax (1) 352-8795; e-mail budapest-ob@bmeia.gv.at; internet www.austrian-embassy.hu; Ambassador Dr FERDINAND MAYRHOFER-GRÜNBÜHEL.

Azerbaijan: 1054 Budapest, Szabadság tér 7, Bank Center, Platina Tower, 5th floor; tel. (1) 374-6070; fax (1) 302-3535; e-mail bakybudapest@azerembassy.hu; Ambassador HASAN HASANOV.

Belarus: 1126 Budapest, Agárdi u. 3B; tel. (1) 214-0553; fax (1) 214-0554; e-mail hungary@belembassy.org; internet belembassy.org/hungary; Ambassador ALENA KUPCHYNA.

Belgium: 1027 Budapest, Kapás u. 11–15; tel. (1) 457-9960; fax (1) 375-1566; e-mail budapest@diplobel.org; internet www.diplomatie.be/budapest; Ambassador MARC TRENTESEAU.

Bosnia and Herzegovina: 1026 Budapest, Pasaréti u. 48; tel. (1) 212-0106; fax (1) 212-0109; Ambassador BRANIMIR MANDIĆ.

Brazil: 1123 Budapest, Alkotás u. 50; tel. (1) 351-0060; fax (1) 351-0066; internet www.brazil.hu; Ambassador JOSÉ AUGUSTO LINDGREN ALVES.

Bulgaria: 1062 Budapest, Andrássy u. 115; tel. (1) 322-0824; fax (1) 322-5215; e-mail bgembhu@axelero.hu; Ambassador GIRNO GYAVROV.

Canada: 1027 Budapest, Ganz utca 12–14; tel. (1) 392-3360; fax (1) 392-3390; internet www.canadaeuropa.gc.ca/hungary; Ambassador PIERRE GUIMOND.

Chile: 1024 Budapest, Rózsahegy u. 1B; tel. (1) 326-3054; fax (1) 326-3056; e-mail echilehu@axelero.hu; internet www.chile.hu; Ambassador JOAQUÍN MONTES LARRAÍN.

China, People's Republic: 1068 Budapest, Benczúr u. 15; tel. (1) 413-2400; fax (1) 413-2451; e-mail chinaemb_hu@mfa.gov.cn; internet hu.chineseembassy.org/hu; Ambassador ZHANG CHUNXIANG.

Croatia: 1063 Budapest, Munkácsy Mihály u. 15; tel. (1) 354-1315; fax (1) 354-1319; e-mail croemb.bp@mvpei.hr; Ambassador IVAN BANDIĆ.

Cuba: 1026 Budapest, Harangivrág u. 5; tel. (1) 325-7290; fax (1) 438-5956; e-mail ildiko@embacuba.hu; internet www.embacuba.hu; Chargé d'affaires a.i. BLAS NABEL PÉREZ.

Cyprus: 1051 Budapest, Dorottya u. 3, III, 2–3u.; tel. (1) 266-1330; fax (1) 266-0538; Ambassador GEORGE SHIAKALLIS.

Czech Republic: 1064 Budapest, Rózsa u. 61; tel. (1) 351-0539; fax (1) 351-9189; e-mail budapest@embassy.mzv.cz; internet www.mzv.cz/wwwo/?zu=budapest; Ambassador JAROMÍR PLÍŠEK.

Denmark: 1122 Budapest, Határőr u. 37; tel. (1) 487-9000; fax (1) 487-9045; e-mail budamb@um.dk; internet www.ambbudapest.um.dk; Ambassador MADS SANDAU-JENSEN.

Ecuador: 1023 Budapest, Levél u. 4; tel. (1) 315-2114; fax (1) 315-2104; e-mail embajada@ecuador.hu; internet www.ecuador.hu; Ambassador Dr ALFONSO LÓPEZ ARAUJO.

Egypt: 1125 Budapest, Istenhegyi u. 7B; tel. (1) 225-2150; fax (1) 225-8596; e-mail egyemb@pronet.hu; Ambassador HISHAM EL-ZIMAITY.

Estonia: 1062 Budapest, Lendvay u. 12, Fsz. 3; tel. (1) 354-2570; fax (1) 354-2571; Ambassador TOIVO TASA.

Finland: 1118 Budapest, Kelenhegyi u. 16A; tel. (1) 279-2500; fax (1) 385-0843; e-mail sanomat.bud@formin.fi; internet www.finland.hu; Ambassador JARI VILÉN.

France: 1062 Budapest, Lendvay u. 27; tel. (1) 332-4980; fax (1) 311-8291; e-mail ambasfn-presse@matavnet.hu; internet www.ambafrance.hu; Ambassador RENÉ ROUDAUT.

Germany: 1014 Budapest, Úri u. 64–66; tel. (1) 488-3500; fax (1) 488-3523; e-mail info@deutschebotschaft-budapest.hu; internet www.deutschebotschaft-budapest.hu; Ambassador HANS PETER SCHIFF.

Greece: 1063 Budapest, Szegfű u. 3; tel. (1) 413-2600; fax (1) 342-1934; e-mail greekemb@axelero.hu; Ambassador DIMITRIS CONTUMAS.

Holy See: 1126 Budapest, Gyimes u. 1–3; tel. (1) 355-8979; fax (1) 355-6987; e-mail nunciatura@nunciatura.axelero.net; Apostolic Nuncio Most Rev. JULIUSZ JANUSZ (Titular Archbishop of Caprulae).

India: 1025 Budapest, Búzavirág u. 14; tel. (1) 325-7742; fax (1) 325-7745; e-mail chancery@indianembassy.hu; internet www.indianembassy.hu; Ambassador MANBIR SINGH.

Indonesia: 1068 Budapest, Városligeti fasor 26; tel. (1) 413-3800; fax (1) 322-8669; e-mail kbribud@indonesia.hu; internet www.indonesia.hu; Ambassador SAPARTINI SINGGIH KUNTJORO JAKTI.

Iran: 1143 Budapest, Stefánia u. 97; tel. (1) 460-9260; fax (1) 460-9430; e-mail embiran@iranembassy.hu; internet www.iranembassy.hu; Ambassador ABULFAZ RAHNAMA HEZAVEI.

Ireland: 1944 Budapest, Bank Center Gránit Torony, VII; tel. (1) 302-9600; fax (1) 302-9599; e-mail iremb@hu.inter.net; Ambassador MARTIN GREENE.

Israel: 1026 Budapest, Fullánk u. 8; tel. (1) 392-6200; fax (1) 200-0783; e-mail info@budapest.mfa.gov.il; internet budapest.mfa.gov.il; Ambassador DAVID ADMON.

Italy: 1143 Budapest, Stefánia u. 95; tel. (1) 460-6200; fax (1) 460-6260; e-mail ambasciata.budapest@esteri.it; internet www.ambitalia.hu; Ambassador PAOLO GUIDO SPINELLI.

Japan: 1125 Budapest, Zalai u. 7; tel. (1) 398-3100; fax (1) 275-1281; e-mail japan.embassy@mail.datanet.hu; internet www.hu.emb-japan.go.jp; Ambassador TERUYOSHI INAGAWA.

Kazakhstan: 1025 Budapest, II ker., Kapy u. 59; tel. (1) 275-1300; fax (1) 275-2092; e-mail kazak@axelero.hu; internet www.kazembassy.hu; Ambassador Rashid Ibraev.

Korea, Republic: 1062 Budapest, Andrássy u. 109; tel. (1) 351-1179; fax (1) 351-1182; e-mail hungary@mofat.go.kr; internet www.mofat.go.kr/hungary; Ambassador Lee Ho-Jin.

Lebanon: 1112 Budapest, Sasadi u. 160; tel. (1) 249-0900; fax (1) 249-0901; e-mail amblib@axelero.hu.

Libya: 1143 Budapest, Stefánia u. 111; tel. (1) 343-6076; fax (1) 343-1583; Head of People's Bureau (Ambassador) Omar Muftah Dallal.

Lithuania: 1124 Budapest, Dobsinai u. 4A; tel. (1) 224-7910; fax (1) 202-3995; e-mail litvania@litvania.hu; internet hu.mfa.lt; Ambassador Darius Jonas Semaška.

Macedonia, former Yugoslav republic: 1024 Budapest, Margit Körut u. 43-45; tel. (1) 336-0510; fax (1) 315-1921; e-mail macedonia.embassy@axelero.hu; Chargé d'affaires a.i. Sašo Veljanovski.

Malaysia: 1026 Budapest, Pasaréti u. 29; tel. (1) 488-0810; fax (1) 488-0824; e-mail mwbdpest@axelero.hu; Ambasssador Wan Yusof Embong.

Mexico: 1024 Budapest, Rómer Flóris u. 58; tel. (1) 326-0447; fax (1) 326-0485; e-mail embamexhu@axelero.hu; internet www.sre.gob.mx/hungria; Ambassador José Luis Martínez y Hernández.

Moldova: 1111 Budapest, Budafoki u. 9–11; tel. (1) 209-1191; fax (1) 209-1195; Ambassador Valeriu Bobutac.

Mongolia: 1022 Budapest II, K. Bogár u. 14C; tel. (1) 212-4579; fax (1) 212-5731; e-mail mnk@mail.matavnet.hu; Ambassador Omboos-rengiin Erdenechimeg.

Morocco: 1026 Budapest, Törökvész Lejtő u. 12A; tel. (1) 200-7855; fax (1) 275-1437; e-mail sifamabudap@axelero.hu; Ambassador Lemhouer al-Hassane.

Netherlands: 1022 Budapest, Füge u. 5–7; tel. (1) 336-6300; fax (1) 326-5978; e-mail bdp@minbuza.nl; internet www.netherlandsembassy.hu; Ambassador Ronald Alexander Mollinger.

Nigeria: 1022 Budapest, Árvácska u. 6; tel. (1) 212-2021; fax (1) 212-2025; e-mail embassy@nigerianembassy.hu; internet www.nigerianembassy.hu; Ambassador Adeola Adebisi Obileye.

Norway: 1015 Budapest, Ostrom u. 13, POB 32; tel. (1) 212-9400; fax (1) 212-9410; e-mail emb.budapest@mfa.no; internet www.norvegia.hu; Chargé d'affaires a.i. Kristin Marøy Stockman.

Pakistan: 1125 Budapest, Adonis u. 3A; tel. (1) 355-8017; fax (1) 375-1402; internet www.pakistanembassy.hu.

Panama: 1016 Budapest, Mihály u. 15; tel. and fax (1) 466-9817; e-mail embpanbu@freemail.c3.hu.

Peru: 1023 Budapest, Vérhalom u. 12–16; tel. (1) 326-0984; fax (1) 326-1087; e-mail peru1@axelero.hu; internet www.peru.hu; Ambassador Guillermo Russo Checa.

Philippines: 1026 Budapest, Gábor Áron u. 58; tel. (1) 391-4300; fax (1) 200-5528; e-mail phbuda@mail.datanet.hu; Ambassador Alejandro D. del Rosario.

Poland: 1068 Budapest, Városligeti fasor 16; tel. (1) 413-8200; fax (1) 351-1722; e-mail info@polishemb.hu; internet www.budapeszt.polemb.net; Ambassador Joanna Stempinska Urnő.

Portugal: 1126 Budapest, Edifício C. Alkotás u. 53; tel. (1) 201-7617; fax (1) 201-7619; e-mail embport@axelero.hu; Ambassador Luís Filipe Castro Mendes.

Qatar: 1026 Budapest, Gadonvi Geza u. 19; tel. (1) 392-1010; fax (1) 392-1019; e-mail qatarembassy@t-online.hu; Ambassador Mubarak Rashid al-Buainen.

Romania: 1146 Budapest, Thököly u. 72; tel. (1) 384-0271; fax (1) 384-5535; e-mail postmaster@roembbud.axelero.net; Ambassador Ireny Comarovschi.

Russia: 1062 Budapest, Bajza u. 35; tel. (1) 302-5230; fax (1) 353-4164; internet www.hungary.mid.ru; Ambassador Igor S. Savolskii.

Serbia: 1068 Budapest, Dózsa György u. 92 B; tel. (1) 322-9838; fax (1) 322-1438; e-mail ambjubp@mail.datanet.hu; internet budapest.mfa.gov.yu; Ambassador (vacant).

Slovakia: 1143 Budapest, Stefánia u. 22–24; tel. (1) 460-9010; fax (1) 460-9020; e-mail slovakem@matavnet.hu; Ambassador Juraj Migaš.

Slovenia: 1025 Budapest, Cseppkö u. 68; tel. (1) 438-5600; fax (1) 325-9187; e-mail vbp@mzz-dkp.gov.si; Ambassador Andrej Gerenčer.

South Africa: 1026 Budapest, Gárdonyi Géza u. 17; tel. (1) 392-0999; fax (1) 200-7277; e-mail saemb@sa-embassy.hu; internet www.sa-embassy.hu; Ambassador Dr Duduzile M. Khoza.

Spain: 1067 Budapest, Kapás u. 11–15; tel. (1) 342-9992; fax (1) 351-0572; e-mail embesphu@mail.mae.es; Ambassador Antonio Ortiz Garcia.

Sweden: 1146 Budapest, Ajtósi Dürer sor 27 A; tel. (1) 460-6020; fax (1) 460-6021; e-mail ambassaden.budapest@foreign.ministry.se; internet www.swedenabroad.com/budapest; Ambassador Cecilia Björner.

Switzerland: 1143 Budapest, Stefánia u. 107; tel. (1) 460-7040; fax (1) 343-9492; e-mail bud.vertretung@eda.admin.ch; internet www.swissembassy.hu; Ambassador Marc-André Salamin.

Syria: 1026 Budapest, Harangvirág u. 3; tel. (1) 200-8046; fax (1) 200-8048; e-mail hungary@syrianembassy.hu; Ambassador (vacant).

Thailand: 1025 Budapest, Verecke u. 79; tel. (1) 438-4020; fax (1) 438-4023; e-mail thaiemba@mail.datanet.hu; internet www.thaiembassy.org/budapest; Ambassador Piamsak Milintachinda.

Tunisia: 1025 Budapest, Pusztaszei u. 24 A; tel. (1) 336-1616; fax (1) 325-7291; e-mail at.budapest@axelero.hu; Chargé d'affaires Abdel-waheb Bouzouita.

Turkey: 1062 Budapest, Andrássy u. 123; tel. (1) 344-5025; fax (1) 344-5143; e-mail budapest@turkishembassy.hu; Ambassador Umur Apaydin.

Ukraine: 1143 Budapest, Stefania u. 77; tel. (1) 422-4122; fax (1) 220-9873; e-mail ukran.kovetseg@mail.datanet.hu; Ambassador Dr Yuriy Mushka.

United Kingdom: 1051 Budapest, Harmincad u. 6; tel. (1) 266-2888; fax (1) 266-0907; e-mail info@britemb.hu; internet www.britishembassy.hu; Ambassador Greg Dorey.

USA: 1054 Budapest, Szabadság tér 12; tel. (1) 475-4400; fax (1) 475-4764; e-mail postmaster@usembassy.hu; internet www.usembassy.hu; Ambassador April H. Foley.

Venezuela: 1023 Budapest, Vérhalom u. 12–16, I, 14; tel. (1) 326-0460; fax (1) 326-0450; e-mail embavenezhu@t-online.hu; Ambassador María Teresa González.

Viet Nam: 1062 Budapest, Déhibáb u. 29; tel. (1) 342-5583; fax (1) 352-8798; e-mail su_quan@hu.inter.net; Ambassador Dao Thi Tam.

Yemen: 1025 Budapest, Józsefhegyi u. 28-30, D/6; tel. (1) 212-3991; fax (1) 212-3883; e-mail al-yemen.al-saida@matavnet.hu.

Judicial System

The system of court procedure in Hungary is based on an act that came into effect in 1953 and has since been updated frequently. The system of jurisdiction is based on the local courts (district courts in Budapest, city courts in other cities), labour courts, county courts (or the Metropolitan Court) and the Supreme Court. In the legal remedy system of two instances, appeals against the decisions of city and district courts can be lodged with the competent county court and the Metropolitan Court of Budapest, respectively. Against the judgment of first instance of the latter, appeal is to be lodged with the Supreme Court. The Chief Public Prosecutor and the President of the Supreme Court have the right to submit a protest on legal grounds against the final judgment of any court.

By virtue of the 1973 act, effective from 1974 and modified in 1979, the procedure in criminal cases is differentiated for criminal offences and for criminal acts. In the first instance, criminal cases are tried, depending on their character, by a professional judge, and where justified by the magnitude of the criminal act, by a council composed of three members, a professional judge and two lay assessors, while in major cases the court consists of five members, two professional judges and three lay assessors. In the Supreme Court, second instance cases are tried only by professional judges. The President of the Supreme Court is elected by the Országgyülés. Judges are appointed by the President of the Republic for an indefinite period. Assessors are elected by the local municipal councils.

In the interest of ensuring legality and a uniform application of the law, the Supreme Court exercises a principled guidance over the jurisdiction of courts. In the Republic of Hungary, judges are independent and subject only to the law and other legal regulations.

The Minister of Justice supervises the general activities of courts. The Chief Public Prosecutor is elected by the Országgyülés. The Chief Public Prosecutor and the Prosecutor's Office provide for the consistent prosecution of all acts violating or endangering the legal order of society, the safety and independence of the state, and for the protection of citizens.

The prosecutors of the independent prosecuting organization exert supervision over the legality of investigations and the implementation of punishments, and assist with specific means in ensuring that legal regulations should be observed by state, economic and other organs and citizens, and they support the legality of court procedures and decisions.

Supreme Court (Legfelsőbb Bíróság): 1055 Budapest, Markó u. 16; tel. (1) 268-4500; fax (1) 268-4740; e-mail fotitkar@legfelsobb.birosag.hu; internet www.lb.hu; Pres. Zoltán Lomnici; Chief Public Prosecutor Péter Polt.

HUNGARY

Constitutional Court (Alkotmánybíróság): 1015 Budapest, Donáti u. 35–45; tel. (1) 488-3100; fax (1) 488-3149; internet www.mkab.hu; Pres. MIHÁLY BIHARI.

Religion

CHRISTIANITY

Ecumenical Council of Churches in Hungary (Magyarországi Egyházak Ökumenikus Tanácsa): 1117 Budapest, Magyar tudósok körútja 3; tel. (1) 371-2690; fax (1) 371-2691; e-mail oikumene@meot.hu; internet oikumene.meot.hu; f. 1943; member churches: Anglican, Baptist, Bulgarian Orthodox, Evangelical Lutheran, Hungarian Orthodox, Hungarian Orthodox Exarchate, Methodist, Reformed Church, Romanian Orthodox and Serbian Orthodox; Pres. Bishop Dr IMRE SZEBIK; Gen. Sec. Dr ZOLTÁN BÓNA.

The Roman Catholic Church

Hungary comprises four archdioceses, nine dioceses (including one for Catholics of the Byzantine rite) and one territorial abbacy (directly responsible to the Holy See). At 31 December 2005 the Church had an estimated 5,991,964 adherents in Hungary.

Bishops' Conference

1071 Budapest, Városligeti fasor 45, POB 79; tel. (1) 342-6959; fax (1) 342-6957; e-mail pkt@katolikus.hu; internet www.katolikus.hu; Pres. Cardinal Dr PÉTER ERDŐ (Archbishop of Esztergom-Budapest).

Archbishop of Eger: Most Rev. Dr ISTVÁN SEREGÉLY, 3301 Eger, Széchenyi u. 1; tel. (36) 517-589; fax (36) 517-751.

Archbishop of Esztergom-Budapest: Cardinal Dr PÉTER ERDŐ, 1014 Budapest, Úri u. 62; tel. (33) 510-120; fax (33) 411-085; e-mail egombp@katolikus.hu.

Archbishop of Kalocsa-Kecskemét: Most Rev. Dr BALÁZS BÁBEL, 6301 Kalocsa, Szentháromság tér 1; tel. (78) 462-166; fax (78) 462-130; e-mail hivatal@asztrik.hu.

Archbishop of Veszprém: Most Rev. Dr GYULA MÁRFI, 8201 Veszprém, Vár u. 19; tel. (88) 462-088; fax (88) 466-287; e-mail ersekseg@erseksek.veszprem.hu.

Apostolic Administrator of Miskolc for Catholics of the Byzantine Rite in the Hungarian Territories, Bishop of Hajdúdorog: SZILÁRD KERESZTES, 4400 Nyíregyháza, Bethlen Gábor u. 5; tel. (42) 415-901; fax (42) 415-911; e-mail eparchia@hajdudorog.axelero.net.

270,000 adherents in diocese of Hajdúdorog and 20,000 adherents in the Apostolic Exarchate of Miskolc (Dec. 2005).

Protestant Churches

Baptist Union of Hungary (Magyarországi Baptista Egyház): 1068 Budapest, Benczur u. 31; tel. (1) 343-0618; fax (1) 352-9707; e-mail baptist.convention@mail.datanet.hu; f. 1846; 11,310 mems (2004); Pres. Rev. Dr KÁLMÁN MÉSZÁROS; Gen. Sec. Rev. KORNÉL MÉSZÁROS.

Evangelical Lutheran Church in Hungary (Magyarországi Evangélikus Egyház): 1085 Budapest, Üllői u. 24; tel. (1) 483-2260; fax (1) 486-3554; e-mail orszagos@lutheran.hu; internet www.lutheran.hu; 430,000 mems (1992); Presiding Bishop JÁNOS ITTZÉS.

United Methodist Church in Hungary (Magyarországi Metodista Egyház): 1032 Budapest, Kiscelli u. 73; tel. (1) 250-1536; fax (1) 250-1849; e-mail office@metodista.hu; internet www.metodista.hu; f. 1898; Superintendent ISTVÁN CSERNÁK.

Reformed Church in Hungary—Presbyterian (Magyarországi Református Egyház): 1146 Budapest, Abonyi u. 21; tel. (1) 343-7870; Pres. of Gen. Synod Bishop Dr GUSZTÁV BÖLCSKEI.

Unitarian Church in Hungary (Magyarországi Unitárius Egyház): 1055 Budapest, Nagy Ignác u. 2–4; tel. (1) 311-2801; e-mail mke@unitarius.hu; internet www.unitarius.hu; Bishop Rev. RÁZMÁNY CSABA.

The Eastern Orthodox Church

Hungarian Orthodox Church (Magyar Ortodox Egyház): 1052 Budapest, Petőfi tér 2/1/2; tel. (1) 318-4813; Archbishop PAVEL (PONOMARJOV).

The Bulgarian, Romanian, Russian and Serbian Orthodox Churches are also represented.

ISLAM

There are about 3,000 Muslims in Hungary.

Hungarian Islamic Community (Magyar Iszlám Közösség): Budapest; tel. (1) 177-7602; Leader Dr BALÁZS MIHÁLFFY.

JUDAISM

The Jewish community in Hungary is estimated to number between 100,000 and 120,000 people. Some 80% of Hungary's Jewish community resides in Budapest.

Federation of Jewish Communities in Hungary (Magyarországi Zsidó Hitközségek Szövetsége): 1075 Budapest, Sip u. 12, Budapesti Zsidó Hitközség (Jewish Community of Budapest); tel. (1) 413-5575; fax (1) 342-1790; e-mail bzstitk@hotmail.com; internet www.zsido.hu; 120,000 mems; 40 active synagogues; Orthodox and Conservative; Pres. Dr PÉTER FELDMAJER; Chief Rabbi of Hungary ROBERT DEUTSCH.

The Press

Budapest dailies circulate nationally. The most popular are: *Népszabadság*, *Nemzeti Sport* and *Népszava*. *Népszabadság*, the most important daily, was formerly the central organ of the Hungarian Socialist Workers' Party, but is now independent.

PRINCIPAL DAILIES

Békéscsaba

Békés Megyei Hírlap (Békés County News): 5601 Békéscsaba, Munkácsy u. 4; tel. (66) 446-242; fax (66) 441-020; internet www.bmhirlap.hu; f. 1945; Editor-in-Chief ZOLTÁN ÁRPÁSI; circ. 49,000.

Budapest

Blikk: 1062 Budapest, Aradi u. 22. IV/1; internet www.blikk.hu; f. 1994; colour tabloid.

Magyar Hírlap (Hungarian Journal): 1087 Budapest, Kerepesi u. 29B; tel. (1) 210-0050; fax (1) 210-3737; internet www.magyarhirlap.hu; f. 1968; Editor-in-Chief MÁTYÁS VINCE; circ. 75,000.

Magyar Nemzet (Hungarian Nation): Budapest; tel. (1) 476-2131; internet www.mno.hu; Editor-in-Chief GÁBOR LISZKAY; circ. 100,000.

Mai Nap (Today): 1145 Budapest, Szugló u. 14; tel. (1) 470-1382; fax (1) 470-1351; e-mail info@mainap.hu; internet www.ringier.hu; f. 1988; Editor-in-Chief FERENC KŐSZEGI; circ. 100,000.

Metro: 1106 Budapest, Fehér u. 10, 21-es épület; tel. (1) 431-6464; fax (1) 431-6465; e-mail szerk@metro.hu; internet www.metro.hu; distributed free of charge; Editor IZBÉKI GÁBOR.

Napi Gazdaság (World Economy): 1135 Budapest, Csata u. 32; tel. (1) 350-4349; fax (1) 350-1117; e-mail napi@mail.eleuder.hu; internet www.napi.hu; Editor-in-Chief ADÁM DANKÓ; circ. 16,000.

Nemzeti Sport (National Sport): 1141 Budapest, Szugló u. 81-85; tel. (1) 460-2600; fax (1) 460-2612; e-mail szerkesztoseg@nemzetisport.hu; internet www.nemzetisport.hu; Editor-in-Chief ATTILA KÁLNOKI KIS; circ. 100,000.

Népszabadság (People's Freedom): 1960 Budapest, Bécsi u. 122–124; tel. (1) 436-4500; fax (1) 387-8699; e-mail eotvosp@nepszabadsag.hu; internet www.nepszabadsag.hu; f. 1942; independent; Editor-in-Chief (vacant); circ. 200,000.

Népszava (Voice of the People): 1022 Budapest, Törökvész u. 30A; tel. (1) 202-7788; fax (1) 202-7798; e-mail online@nepszava.hu; internet www.nepszava.hu; f. 1873; Editor ANDRÁS KERESZTY; circ. 120,000.

Reggel: 1122 Budapest, Városmajor u. 12–14; tel. (1) 488-5561; fax (1) 488-5727; e-mail reggelonline@reggel.hu; internet www.reggel.hu; f. 2005; publ. by Axel Springer (of Germany); Publr JÓZSEF BAYER.

Üzlet (Business): Budapest; tel. (1) 111-8260; Editor-in-Chief IVÁN ÉRSEK.

Debrecen

Hajdú-Bihari Napló (Hajdú-Bihar Diary): 4024 Debrecen, Dósa nádor tér 10; tel. (52) 413-395; fax (52) 412-326; e-mail naplo@iscomp.hu; internet www.naplo.hu; f. 1944; Editor-in-Chief ZSOLT PORCSIN; circ. 60,000.

Dunaújváros

A Hírlap (The Journal): 2400 Dunaújváros, Városháza tér 1; tel. (25) 16-010; Editor-in-Chief CSABA D. KISS.

Eger

Heves Megyei Hírlap (Heves County Journal): 3301 Eger, Barkóczy u. 7; tel. (36) 13-644; e-mail hmhirlap@axels.hu; internet www.agria.hu/hmhirlap; Editor-in-Chief LEVENTE KAPOSI; circ. 33,000.

HUNGARY

Győr

Kisalföld: 9021 Győr, Újlak u. 4A; tel. (96) 504-444; fax (96) 504-414; e-mail kisalfoldmail@matav.hu; internet www.kisalfold.hu; Editor-in-Chief NYERGES CSABA.

Kaposvár

Somogyi Hírlap (Somogy Journal): 7401 Kaposvár, Latinca Sándor u. 2A; tel. (82) 11-644; internet www.somogyihirlap.hu; Editor-in-Chief Dr IMRE KERCZA; circ. 59,000.

Kecskemét

Petőfi Népe: 6000 Kecskemét, Szabadság tér 1A; tel. (76) 481-391; internet www.petofinepe.hu; Editor-in-Chief Dr DÁNIEL LOVAS; circ. 60,000.

Miskolc

Déli Hírlap (Midday Journal): 3527 Miskolc, Bajcsy-Zsilinszky u. 15; tel. (46) 42-694; Editor-in-Chief DEZSŐ BEKES; circ. 20,000.

Észak-Magyarország (Northern Hungary): 3527 Miskolc, Bajcsy-Zsilinszky u. 15; tel. (46) 341-888; internet www.eszak.hu; Editor-in-Chief LÁSZLÓ GÖRÖMBÖLYI; circ. 45,000.

Nyíregyháza

Kelet-Magyarország (Eastern Hungary): 4401 Nyíregyháza, Zrínyi u. 3–5; tel. (42) 11-277; Editor-in-Chief Dr SÁNDOR ANGYAL; circ. 80,000.

Pécs

Új Dunántúli Napló: 7601 Pécs, Hunyadi u. 11; tel. (72) 15-000; internet www.dunantulinaplo.hu; Editor-in-Chief JENŐ LOMBOSI; circ. 84,000.

Salgótarján

Nógrád Megyei Hírlap (Nógrád County Journal): 3100 Salgótarján, Alkotmány u. 9; tel. (32) 416-455; fax (32) 423-931; e-mail nmeolia@axels.hu; internet www.nogradmegyeihirlap.hu; f. 1964; Editor-in-Chief MIKLÓS KOPKA; circ. 10,000.

Szeged

Délvilág (Southern World): 6740 Szeged, Tanácsköztársaság u. 10; tel. (62) 14-911; internet www.delvilag.hu; Editor-in-Chief ISTVÁN NIKOLÉNYI; circ. 20,000.

Délmagyarország (Southern Hungary): 6740 Szeged, Stefánia 10; tel. (62) 481-281; internet www.delmagyar.szeged.hu; Editor-in-Chief IMRE DLUSZTUS; circ. 70,000.

Székesfehérvár

Fejér Megyei Hírlap (Fejér County Journal): 8003 Székesfehérvár, Honvéd u. 8; tel. (22) 12-450; internet www.fmh.hu; Editor-in-Chief JÁNOS Á. SZABÓ; circ. 52,000.

Szekszárd

Tolnai Népújság (Tolna News): 7100 Szekszárd, Liszt Ferenc tér 3; tel. (74) 16-211; Editor-in-Chief GYÖRGYNÉ KAMARÁS; circ. 32,000.

Szolnok

Új Néplap (New People's Paper): 5001 Szolnok, Kossuth tér 1, I. Irodaház; tel. (56) 42-211; internet www.ujneplap.hu; Editor-in-Chief JÓZSEF HAJNAL; circ. 46,000.

Szombathely

Vas Népe (Vas People): 9700 Szombathely, Fő tér 3–5; tel. (94) 528-288; fax (94) 528-290; e-mail hirdetes.szhely@plt.hu; internet www.vasnepe.hu; Editor-in-Chief SÁNDOR LENGYEL; circ. 65,000.

Tatabánya

24 Óra (24 Hours): 2800 Tatabánya, Fö tér 4; tel. (34) 514-012; fax (34) 514-011; e-mail szerk.kom@axels.hu; internet www.24ora.hu; Editor-in-Chief FERENC SZTRAPÁK; circ. 23,000.

Veszprém

Napló (Diary): 8201 Veszprém, Szabadság tér 15; tel. (80) 27-444; Editor-in-Chief ELEMÉR BALOGH; circ. 58,000.

Zalaegerszeg

Zalai Hírlap (Zala Journal): 8901 Zalaegerszeg, Ady Endre u. 62; tel. (92) 12-575; Editor-in-Chief JÓZSEF TARSOLY; circ. 71,000.

WEEKLIES

The Budapest Sun: 1015 Budapest, Batthyány u. 49-7/6; tel. (1) 489-4343; fax (1) 489-4344; e-mail editor@bpsun.hu; internet www.budapestsun.com; f. 1993; majority-share owned by Associated Newspapers (United Kingdom); in English; Man. Editor ROBIN MARSHALL.

The Budapest Times/Budapester Zeitung: 1036 Budapest, Pacsirtamezö u. 41; tel. (1) 453-0752; fax (1) 240-7583; e-mail editor@budapesttimes.hu; internet www.budapesttimes.hu; internet www.budapester.hu; f. 1999 (*Budapester Zeitung*); f. 2003 (*The Budapest Times*); English and German edns; Editor ALLEN ALLEN (*The Budapest Times*), JAN MAINKA (*Budapester Zeitung*).

Élet és Irodalom (Life and Literature): 1089 Budapest, Rezsö tér 15; tel. (1) 210-2157; fax (1) 303-9211; e-mail es@es.hu; internet www.es.hu; f. 1957; literary and political; Editor ZOLTÁN KOVÁCS; circ. 22,000.

Élet és Tudomány (Life and Science): 1088 Budapest, Bródy Sándor u. 16; tel. and fax (1) 138-2472; f. 1946; popular science; Editor-in-Chief Dr HERCZEG JÁNOS; circ. 20,000.

Evangélikus Élet (Evangelical Life): 1085 Budapest, Üllői u. 24; tel. (1) 317-1108; fax (1) 486–1195; e-mail evelet@lutheran.hu; internet www.evelet.hu; f. 1933; Evangelical Lutheran Church newspaper; Editor KÁROLY T. PINTÉR; circ. 6,000 (2007).

Heti Világgazdaság (World Economy Weekly): 1124 Budapest, Németvölgy u. 62-64; tel. (1) 355-5411; fax (1) 355-5693; internet www.hvg.hu; f. 1979; Editor-in-Chief IVÁN LIPOVECZ; circ. 141,000.

Képes Újság (Illustrated News): 1085 Budapest, Gyulai Pál u. 14; tel. (1) 113-7660; f. 1960; Editor MIHÁLY KOVÁCS; circ. 400,000.

Ludas Matyi: Budapest; tel. (1) 133-5718; satirical; Editor JÓZSEF ÁRKUS; circ. 352,000.

L'udové Noviny (People's News): 1065 Budapest, Nagymező u. 49; tel. (1) 331-9184; fax (1) 332-3158; e-mail ludove@axelero.hu; internet www.luno.hu; in Slovak; for Slovaks in Hungary; Editor IMRICH FUL; circ. 1,700.

Magyar Mezőgazdaság (Hungarian Agriculture): 1355 Budapest, Kossuth Lajos tér 11; tel. (1) 112-2433; f. 1946; Editor-in-Chief Dr KÁROLY FEHÉR; circ. 24,000.

Magyar Nők Lapja (Hungarian Women's Journal): 1022 Budapest, Törökvész u. 30 A; tel. (1) 212-4020; fax (1) 326-8264; e-mail noklapja@noklapja.ekh.hu; f. 1949; Editor-in-Chief LILI ZÉTÉNYI; circ. 550,000.

Magyarország (Hungary): Budapest; tel. (1) 138-4644; f. 1964; news magazine; Editor DÉNES GYAPAY; circ. 200,000.

Narodne Novine (People's News): 1396 Budapest, POB 495; tel. (1) 112-4869; f. 1945; for Serbs and Montenegrins in Hungary; in Serbian, Croatian and Slovene; Chief Editor MARKO MARKOVIĆ; circ. 2,800.

Neue Zeitung (New Paper): 1062 Budapest, Lendvay u. 22; tel. (1) 302-6877; e-mail neueztg@hu.inter.net; internet www.neue-zeitung.hu; f. 1957; for Germans in Hungary; Editor JOHANN SCHUTH; circ. 4,500.

Reform: Budapest; tel. and fax (1) 122-4240; f. 1988; popular tabloid; 50% foreign-owned; Editor PÉTER TŐKE; circ. 300,000.

Reformátusok Lapja: 1395 Budapest, POB 424; tel. (1) 117-6809; fax (1) 117-8386; f. 1957; Reformed Church paper for the laity; Editor-in-Chief and Publr ATTILA P. KOMLÓS; circ. 30,000.

RTV Részletes (Radio and TV News): 1801 Budapest; tel. (1) 328-8114; fax (1) 328-7349; e-mail rturszer@axelero.hu; internet www.rtvreszletes.hu; f. 1924; Editor KATALIN MOLDOVAN; circ. 100,000.

Szabad Föld (Free Earth): 1087 Budapest, Könyves Kálmán krt 76; tel. and fax (1) 133-6794; f. 1945; Editor GYULA ECK; circ. 720,000.

Szövetkezet (Co-operative): 1054 Budapest, Szabadság tér 14; tel. (1) 131-3132; National Council of Hungarian Consumer Co-operative Societies; Editor-in-Chief ATTILA KOVÁCS; circ. 85,000.

Tallózó: 1133 Budapest, Visegrádi u. 110–112; tel. and fax (1) 149-8707; f. 1989; news digest; Editor-in-Chief GYÖRGY ANDAI; circ. 35,000.

Tőzsde Kurir (Hungarian Stock Market Courier): Budapest; tel. (1) 122-3273; fax (1) 142-8356; business; Editor-in-Chief ISTVÁN GÁBOR BENEDEK.

Új Ember (New Man): 1053 Budapest, Kossuth Lajos u. 1; tel. (1) 317-3933; fax (1) 317-3471; e-mail ujember@katolikus.hu; internet ujember.katolikus.hu; f. 1945; weekly; Roman Catholic; Editor TAMÁS PAPP; circ. 40,000.

OTHER PERIODICALS
(Published monthly unless otherwise indicated)

Beszélő (The Speaker): 1054 Budapest, Akadémia u. 1/48–50; tel. and fax (1) 302-1271; e-mail beszelo@enternet.hu; internet beszelo.c3.hu; f. 1991; cultural; Editor-in-Chief MINK ANDRÁS.

HUNGARY   *Directory*

Business Partner Hungary: 1081 Budapest, Csokonai u. 3; tel. (1) 303-9586; fax (1) 303-9582; e-mail nemeth@kopdat.hu; internet www.kopdat.hu; f. 1986; every two months; English and German; economic journal; Head of Dept ILONA NÉMETH.

Egyházi Krónika (Church Chronicle): 1052 Budapest, Petőfi tér 2,1,2; tel. and fax (1) 318-4813; f. 1952; every two months; Eastern Orthodox Church journal; Editor Archpriest Dr FERIZ BERKI.

Elektrotechnika (Electrical Engineering): 1055 Budapest, Kossuth Lajos tér 6–8; tel. (1) 353-0117; fax (1) 353-4069; e-mail lernyei@mee.hu; f. 1908; organ of Electrotechnical Association; Editor Dr JÁNOS BENCZE; circ. 6,500.

Élelmezési Ipar (Food Industry): 1372 Budapest, POB 433; tel. (1) 214-6691; fax (1) 214-6692; e-mail mail.mete@mtesz.hu; internet www.mete.mtesz.hu; f. 1947; publ. by MÉTE Scientific Society for Food Industry; in Hungarian, with summaries in English and German; monthly; Chief Editor Dr ZOLTÁN HERNÁDI.

Energia és Atomtechnika (Energy and Nuclear Technology): 1055 Budapest, Kossuth Lajos tér 6–8; tel. (1) 153-2751; fax (1) 156-1215; f. 1947; every two months; publ. by Scientific Society for Energy Economy; Editor-in-Chief Dr G. BŐKI.

Energiagazdálkodás (Energy Economy): 1055 Budapest, Kossuth Lajos tér 6; tel. (1) 153-2751; fax (1) 153-3894; publ. by Scientific Society for Energetics; Editor Dr ANDOR ANESINI.

Ezermester 2000 (Handyman 2000): 1145 Budapest, Mexikói u. 35A; tel. (1) 222-6392; fax (1) 220-9065; e-mail ezermester2000@axelero.hu; internet www.ezermester2000.hu; f. 1957; do-it-yourself magazine; Editor JÓZSEF PERÉNYI; circ. 50,000.

Gép (Machinery): 1027 Budapest, Fő u. 68; tel. (1) 135-4175; fax (1) 153-0818; f. 1949; Scientific Society of Mechanical Engineering; Editor Dr KORNÉL LEHOFER.

Ipar-Gazdaság (Industrial Economy): 1371 Budapest, POB 433; tel. (1) 202-1083; f. 1948; Editor Dr TAMÁS MÉSZÁROS; circ. 4,000.

Jogtudományi Közlöny (Law Gazette): 1015 Budapest, Donáti u. 35-45; tel. (1) 355-0330; fax (1) 355-0441; e-mail voros@mkab.hu; f. 1866; legal and administrative sciences; Editor-in-Chief Dr IMRE VÖRÖS; circ. 1,000.

Kortárs (Contemporary): 1426 Budapest, POB 108; tel. (1) 342-1168; f. 1957; literary; Editor-in-Chief IMRE KIS PINTÉR; circ. 5,000.

Közgazdasági Szemle (Economic Review): 1112 Budapest, Budaörsi u. 45; tel. (1) 319-3165; fax (1) 319-3166; e-mail kszemle@sparc.core.hu; internet www.kszemle.hu; f. 1954; publ. by Cttee for Economic Sciences of Hungarian Academy of Sciences; Editor KATALIN SZABÓ; circ. 1,000.

Magyar Hírek (Hungarian News): Budapest; tel. (1) 122-5616; fax (1) 122-2421; every two weeks; illustrated magazine primarily for Hungarians living abroad; Editor GYÖRGY HALÁSZ; circ. 70,000.

Magyar Jog (Hungarian Law): 1054 Budapest, Szemere u. 10; tel. (1) 311-4880; fax (1) 311-4013; f. 1953; Editor-in-Chief Dr JÁNOS NÉMETH; circ. 2,200.

Magyar Közlöny (Official Gazette): Budapest; tel. (1) 112-1236; Editor Dr ELEMÉR KISS; circ. 90,000.

Magyar Tudomány (Hungarian Science): Hungarian Academy of Sciences, 1051 Budapest, Nádor u. 7; tel. and fax (1) 317-9524; e-mail matud@hefka.iif.hu; internet www.matud.hu; f. 1846; multi-disciplinary science review; Editors VILMOS CSÁNYI, ZSUZSA SZENT-GYÖRGYI.

Pedagógusok Lapja (Teachers' Review): 1068 Budapest, Városligeti fasor 10; tel. (1) 322-8464; e-mail psz-seh@mail.matav.hu; internet www.deltasoft.hu/pszseh; f. 1945; published by the Hungarian Union of Teachers; Editor-in-Chief AROK ANTAL; circ. 10,000.

Református Egyház (Reformed Church): 1146 Budapest, Abonyi u. 21; tel. (1) 343-7870; f. 1949; official journal of the Hungarian Reformed Church; Editor-in-Chief Rev. ÁRON CSOMA; circ. 1,300.

Statisztikai Szemle (Statistical Review): 1525 Budapest, POB 51; tel. (1) 345-6908; fax (1) 345-6594; e-mail statszemle@ksh.hu; internet www.ksh.hu/statszemle; f. 1923; publ. by the Hungarian Central Statistical Office; statistical studies and reviews; Editor-in-Chief Dr LÁSZLÓ HUNYADI; circ. 800.

Technika (Technology): 1027 Budapest, Fö u. 68; tel. (1) 225-3105; fax (1) 201-6457; e-mail tcinfo@eqnet.hu; internet www.e-technika.hu; f. 1957; official journal of the Hungarian Academy of Engineering; monthly in Hungarian, annually in English, German and Russian; Editor-in-Chief MARGIT WELLEK.

Turizmus (Tourism): 1088 Budapest, Múzeum u. 11; tel. (1) 266-5853; fax (1) 338-4293; e-mail turizmus@mail.matav.hu; Editor ZSOLT SZEBENI; circ. 8,000.

Új Élet (New Life): 1075 Budapest, Síp u. 12; tel. (1) 322-2829; every two weeks; Jewish interest; Editor Dr PÉTER KARDOS; circ. 5,000.

Új Technika (New Technology): Budapest; tel. (1) 155-7122; f. 1967; popular industrial quarterly; circ. 35,000.

Vigilia: 1364 Budapest, POB 48; tel. (1) 317-7246; fax (1) 486-4444; e-mail vigilia@vigilia.hu; internet www.vigilia.hu; f. 1935; Catholic; Editor LÁSZLÓ LUKÁCS; circ. 3,500.

NEWS AGENCY

Hungarian News Agency Co (Magyar Távirati Iroda Rt—MTI): 1016 Budapest, Naphegy tér 8; tel. (1) 441-9000; fax (1) 318-8297; e-mail mtiadmin@mti.hu; internet www.mti.hu; f. 1880; 20 brs in Hungary; 10 bureaux abroad; Pres. MÁTYÁS VINCE.

PRESS ASSOCIATIONS

Hungarian Newspaper Publishers' Association: 1034 Budapest, Bécsi u. 122-124; tel. (1) 368-8674; fax (1) 388-6707; e-mail mle.peto@mail.matav.hu; f. 1990; Gen. Sec. JÁNOS PETŐ; 40 mems.

National Association of Hungarian Journalists (Magyar Újságírók Országos Szövetsége—MÚOSZ): 1062 Budapest, Andrássy u. 101; tel. (1) 322-1699; fax (1) 322-1881; e-mail szakoszt@muosz.hu; internet www.muosz.hu; f. 1896; Gen. Sec. GÁBOR BENCSIK; 7,000 mems.

Publishers

PRINCIPAL PUBLISHING HOUSES

Akadémiai Kiadó: 1117 Budapest, Prielle Kornélia u. 19/D; tel. (1) 464-8200; fax (1) 464-8201; e-mail ak@akkrt.hu; internet www.akkrt.hu; f. 1828; economics, humanities, social, political, natural and technical sciences, dictionaries, textbooks, and journals; Hungarian and English; Dir BUCSI SZABÓ ZSOLT.

Corvina Kiadó: 1072 Budapest, Rákóczi u. 16; tel. (1) 318-4148; fax (1) 318-4410; e-mail corvina@exelero.hu; f. 1955; art and educational books, fiction and non-fiction, tourist guides, cookery books, and musicology; Man. Dir LÁSZLÓ KUNOS.

EMB Music Publisher: 1132 Budapest, Victor Hugo u. 11–15; tel. (1) 236-1100; fax (1) 236-1101; e-mail emb@emb.hu; internet www.emb.hu; f. 1950; music publishing and books on musical subjects; Dir ANTAL BORONKAY.

Európa Könyvkiadó: 1055 Budapest, Kossuth Lajos tér 13–15; tel. (1) 353-2328; fax (1) 331-4162; e-mail info@europakiado.hu; internet www.europakiado.hu; f. 1946; world literature translated into Hungarian; Dir IMRE BARNA.

Gondolat Könyvkiadó Vállalat: Budapest; tel. (1) 138-3358; fax (1) 138-4540; f. 1957; popular scientific publications on natural and social sciences, art, encyclopedic handbooks; Dir GYÖRGY FEHÉR.

Helikon Kiadó: 1053 Budapest, Papnövelde u. 8; tel. (1) 117-4865; fax (1) 117-4865; bibliophile books; Dir KATALIN BERGER.

Képzőművészeti Kiadó: Budapest; tel. (1) 251-1527; fax (1) 251-1527; fine arts; Man. Dr ZOLTÁN KEMENCZEI.

Kossuth Kiadó: 1043 Budapest, Csányi László u. 36; tel. (1) 370-0607; fax (1) 370-0602; f. 1944; social sciences, educational and philosophy publications, information technology books; Man. ANDRÁS SÁNDOR KOCSIS.

Közgazdasági és Jogi Könyvkiadó: Budapest; tel. (1) 112-6430; fax (1) 111-3210; f. 1955; business, economics, law, sociology, psychology, tax, politics, education, dictionaries; Man. Dir DAVID G. YOUNG.

Magvető Könyvkiadó: 1806 Budapest, POB 123; tel. (1) 235-5032; e-mail magveto@lira.hu; f. 1955; literature; Dir GÉZA MORCSÁNYI.

Medicina Könyvkiadó: 1054 Budapest, Zoltan u. 8; tel. (1) 112-2650; fax (1) 112-2450; f. 1957; books on medicine, sport, tourism; Dir BORBÁLA FARKASVÖLGYI.

Mezőgazda Kiadó: 1165 Budapest, Koronafürt u. 44; tel. (1) 407-1018; fax (1) 407-1012; e-mail mezoig@mezogazdakiado.hu; internet www.mezogazdakiado.hu; ecology, natural sciences, environmental protection, food industry; Man. Dr LAJOS LELKES.

Móra Ferenc Ifjúsági Kiadó: 1134 Budapest, Váci u. 19; tel. (1) 320-4740; fax (1) 320-5382; f. 1950; youth and children's books; Man. Dr JÁNOS CS. TÓTH.

Műszaki Könyvkiadó: 1033 Budapest, Szentendre u. 89–93; tel. (1) 437-2405; fax (1) 437-2404; e-mail lakatosz@muszakikiado.hu; internet www.muszakikiado.hu; f. 1955; scientific and technical, vocational, and general textbooks; Man. SÁNDOR BÉRCZI.

Nemzeti Tankönyvkiadó (National Textbook Publishing House): 1143 Budapest, Szobránc u. 6–8; tel. (1) 460-1800; fax (1) 460-1869; e-mail public@ntk.hu; internet www.ntk.hu; f. 1949; school and university textbooks, pedagogical literature and language books; Gen. Man. JÓZSEF PÁLFI.

Népszava Lapés Könyvkiadó Vállalat: Budapest; tel. (1) 122-4810; publishing house of National Confederation of Hungarian Trade Unions; Man. Dr JENŐ KISS.

HUNGARY

Statiqum Kiadó és Nyomda: 1033 Budapest, Kaszásdülő u. 2; tel. (1) 250-0311; fax (1) 168-8635; f. 1991; publications on statistics, systems-management and computer science; Dir BENEDEK BELECZ.

Szépirodalmi Könyvkiadó: Budapest; tel. (1) 122-1285; f. 1950; modern and classical Magyar literature; Man. SÁNDOR Z. SZALAI.

Zrinyi Kiadó: 1087 Budapest, Kerepesi u. 29B; tel. (1) 133-9165; military literature; Man. MÁTÉ ESZES.

PUBLISHERS' ASSOCIATION

Hungarian Publishers' and Booksellers' Association (Magyar Könyvkiadók és Könyvterjesztők Egyesülése): Budapest; tel. (1) 343-2540; fax (1) 343-2541; e-mail mkke@mkke.hu; internet www.mkke.hu; f. 1795; most leading Hungarian publishers are members of the Association; Pres. ISTVÁN BART; Sec.-Gen. PÉTER ZENTAI.

Broadcasting and Communications

TELECOMMUNICATIONS

Regulatory Authority

National Communications Authority (Nemzeti Hírközlési Hatóság): 1525 Budapest, POB 75; tel. (1) 457-7100; fax (1) 356-5520; e-mail info@hif.hu; internet www.nhh.hu; Chair. DÁNIEL PATAKI.

Service Providers

Magyar Telekom: 1013 Budapest, Krisztina krt 55; tel. (1) 458-0000; fax (1) 458-7176; e-mail investor.relations@telekom.hu; internet www.magyartelekom.hu; f. 1991 as Matáv Hungarian Telecommunications Co; name changed as above in May 2005; 59.2% owned by Deutsche Telekom AG (Germany); merged with T-Mobile Magyarország in Dec. 2005; telecommunications service provider; Chair. and Chief Exec. CHRISTOPHER MATTHEISEN; 12,341 employees (2006).

Pannon GSM Telecommunications: 2040 Budaörs, Baross u. 165; tel. (1) 930-4000; fax (1) 930-4100; internet www.pgsm.hu; f. 1993; 100% owned by Telenor (Norway); mobile telecommunications; CEO OVE FREDHEIM.

Vodafone Hungary: Budapest; e-mail orsolya.ivanyi@partners.vodafone.hu; internet www.vodafone.hu; f. 1999; mobile cellular telecommunications; owned by Vodafone (United Kingdom); Chief Exec. GYÖRGY BECK; more than 2m. subscribers (May 2007).

BROADCASTING

Hungarian National Radio and Television Board (Országos Rádió és Televízió Testület—ORTT): 1088 Budapest, Reviczky u. 5; tel. (1) 429-8600; fax (1) 267-2612; internet www.ortt.hu; Dir GYÖRGY KOVACS.

Radio

Hungarian Radio (Magyar Rádió zrt): 1800 Budapest, Bródy Sándor u. 5–7; tel. (1) 328-7621; fax (1) 328-7004; internet www.radio.hu; f. 1924; Stations: Radio Kossuth, Radio Petőfi, Radio Bartók (mainly classical music), MR4 (Regional and Minority Programmes), MR5 (broadcasting Parliamentary Sessions); Pres. GYÖRGY SUCH.

Antenna Hungária Rt: 1119 Budapest, Petzvál József u. 31–33; tel. (1) 203-6060; fax (1) 203-6093; internet www.ahrt.hu; f. 1989; radio and television broadcasting; 100% owned by TDF, SA (France); Chief Exec. ISTVÁN MÁTÉ; 1,290 employees.

Radio C: 1086 Budapest, Teleki tér 7; tel. (1) 459-0095; fax (1) 459-0094; internet www.radioc.hu; f. 2001; Roma radio station; news and cultural programming suspended in April 2003 owing to lack of funds; Man. GYÖRGY KERENYI.

Radio Danubius: 1138 Budapest, Váci u. 141; tel. (1) 452-6115; e-mail bartucz.laszlo@danubius.hu; internet www.danubius.hu; f. 1986; privatized 1998; broadcasts news, music and information in Hungarian 24 hours a day; transmitting stations in Budapest, Lake Balaton region, Sopron, Szeged and Debrecen; Man. Dir BARTUCZ LÁSZLÓ.

Television

Hungarian Television Rt (Magyar Televízió): 1054 Budapest, Szabadság tér 17; tel. (1) 373-4303; fax (1) 373-4133; e-mail laszlo.martinak@mtv.hu; internet www.mtv.hu; f. 1957; owned by parliament; two channels; Pres. Dr ZOLTÁN RUDI.

Antenna Hungária Rt: see Radio.

Finance

(cap. = capital; res = reserves; dep. = deposits; m. = million; amounts in forint unless otherwise stated)

In 2005 there was a total of 30 commercial banks in operation in Hungary. Responsibility for bank supervision is divided between the Central Bank of Hungary and the Hungarian Financial Supervisory Authority. Under legislation introduced in January 1997, the supervisory responsibilities of the Central Bank were restricted to areas relating to the operation of monetary policy and the foreign-exchange system.

BANKING

Central Bank

Central Bank of Hungary (Magyar Nemzeti Bank): 1850 Budapest, Szabadság tér 8–9; tel. (1) 428-2600; fax (1) 428-2500; e-mail info@mnb.hu; internet www.mnb.hu; f. 1924; bank of issue; conducts international transactions; supervises banking system; cap. 10,000m., res 65,531m., dep. 2,065,864m. (Dec. 2006); Gov. ANDRÁS SIMOR; 2 regional directorates.

Other Banks

Bank of Hungarian Savings Co-operatives (Magyar Takarékszövetkezeti Bank): 1122 Budapest, Pethényi köz 10, POB 775; tel. (1) 355-3122; fax (1) 356-2649; e-mail info@tbank.hu; internet www.takarekbank.hu; f. 1989; 63.72% owned by Savings Co-operatives, 31.27% owned by DZ Bank AG (Germany); cap. 2,041m., res 6,071m., dep. 251,168m. (Dec. 2006); Pres. ANTAL VARGA; CEO PÉTER CSICSÁKY.

Budapest Credit and Development Bank: 1138 Budapest, POB 1852, Váci u. 188; tel. (1) 450-6000; fax (1) 450-6001; e-mail info@budapestbank.hu; internet www.budapestbank.hu; f. 1987; cap. 19,346m., res 47,668m., dep. 579,691m. (Dec. 2006); 99.7% owned by GE Capital International Financing Corpn (USA); Pres. and CEO MARK ARNOLD; 65 brs.

Central-European International Bank (CIB): 1027 Budapest, Medve u. 4–14, POB 394; tel. (1) 457-6800; fax (1) 489-6500; e-mail cib@cib.hu; internet www.cib.hu; f. 1979; 85.8% owned by Intesa Holding International SA (Luxembourg); cap. 34,750m., total assets 1,874,437m. (Dec. 2006); Chair. Dr GYÖRGY SURÁNYI; Chief Exec. Dr LÁSZLÓ TÖRÖK.

Citibank Zrt: 1367 Budapest, POB 123; tel. (1) 374-5000; fax (1) 374-5100; internet www.citibank.hu; f. 1986; wholly owned by Citibank Overseas Investment Corpn (USA); cap. 13,005m., res 7,295m., dep. 364,493m. (Dec. 2006); Country Chief Officer SAJJAD RAZVI.

Commerzbank Zrt: 1054 Budapest, Széchenyi rkp 8; tel. (1) 374-1000; fax (1) 269-4530; e-mail info.budapest@commerzbank.hu; internet www.commerzbank.hu; f. 1993; cap. 2,466.9m., res 16,393.4m., dep. 174,498.4m. (Dec. 2006); Pres. and Chair. of Supervisory Bd WILHELM NÜSE; Chair. and Chief Exec. KOZMA ANDRÁS.

Erste Bank Hungary Nyrt: 1138 Budapest, Népfürdo u. 24–26; tel. (1) 298–0221; fax (1) 272-5160; e-mail uszolg@erstebank.hu; internet www.erstebank.hu; f. 1987; present name adopted 1998; absorbed Postbank and Savings Bank Corpn—Postabank in 2004; 99.9% owned by Erste Bank der öesterreichischen Sparkassen AG (Austria); cap. 53,410m., res 37,068m., dep. 1,533,627m. (Dec. 2006); Chief Exec. EDIT PAPP; 186 brs.

General Banking and Trust Co (Általános Értékforgalmi Bank): 1068 Budapest, Városligeti fasor 34–36; tel. (1) 462-7600; fax (1) 462-7606; e-mail info@gbt.hu; internet www.gbt.hu; f. 1922; 25.5% owned by Gazprombank (Russia); cap. 11,754.5m., res 5,458.5m., dep. 116,469.9m. (Dec. 2005); Chair. and Chief Exec. MEGDET RAKHIMKULOV; 5 brs.

Hungarian Development Bank (Magyar Fejlesztési Bank—MFT): 1051 Budapest, Nádor u. 31; tel. (1) 428-1400; fax (1) 428-1490; e-mail bank@mfb.hu; internet www.mfb.hu; f. 1991 as an investment company; authorized as a bank 1993; state-owned; cap. 87,570m., res 23,990m., dep. 891,206m. (Dec. 2006); Chair. of Bd GYÖRGY ZDEBORSKY.

Hungarian Export-Import Bank (EXIMBANK): 1065 Budapest, Nagymező u. 46-48; tel. (1) 374-9100; fax (1) 269-4476; e-mail eximh@eximbank.hu; internet www.eximbank.hu; f. 1994; state-owned; cap. 10,100m., res 2,837m., dep. 129,001m. (Dec. 2005); CEO Dr ZOLTÁN BODNAR.

ING Bank Zrt: 1068 Budapest, Dózsa György u. 84B; tel. (1) 235-8700; fax (1) 269-6447; e-mail ing@ing.hu; internet www.ing.hu; f. 1992 as NMB Bank; present name adopted 1996; 100% owned by ING Bank NV (Netherlands); cap. 18,589m., res 18,224m., dep. 316,540m. (Dec. 2005); Man. Dir MARTIJN SCHOUTEN.

Inter-Európa Bank Zrt: 1054 Budapest, Szabadság tér 15; 1364 Budapest, POB 65; tel. (1) 373-6000; fax (1) 269-2526; e-mail ieb@ieb.hu; internet www.ieb.hu; f. 1981 as Interinvest; name changed as

HUNGARY

above in 1989; cap. 7,019m., res 7,593m., dep. 213,383m. (Dec. 2005); Chair. FERENC BARTHA; 35 brs.

Kereskedelmi és Hitelbank Nyrt (K&H Bank Nyrt): 1051 Budapest, Vigadó tér 1; tel. (1) 328-9000; fax (1) 328-9696; e-mail khbinfo@khb.hu; internet www.kh.hu; f. 1987; 59.1% owned by KBC Bank NV (Belgium), 40.2% owned by ABN Amro Bank NV (Netherlands); cap. 52,507m., res 53,011m. dep. 1,523.5m. (2005); Pres. and Chair. BÉLA SINGLOVICS; CEO MARKO VOLJC; 158 brs.

MKB Bank Nyrt: 1056 Budapest, Váci u. 38; tel. (1) 327-8600; fax (1) 327-8700; e-mail telebankar@mkb.hu; internet www.mkb.hu; f. 1950; commercial banking; 89.6% owned by Bayerische Landesbank (Germany); absorbed Konzumbank in 2003; present name adopted 2005; cap. 13,133m., res 165,889m., dep. 1,665,455m. (Dec. 2006); Chair. and CEO TAMÁS ERDEI; 68 brs.

National Savings and Commercial Bank (Országos Takarékpénztár és Kereskedelmi Bank—OTP Bank): 1051 Budapest, Nádor u. 16; tel. (1) 473-5000; fax (1) 473-5955; e-mail otpbank@otpbank.hu; internet www.otpbank.hu; f. 1949; savings deposits, credits, foreign transactions; privatized in 1996; cap. 28,000m., res 820,362m., dep. 4,231,300m. (Dec. 2006); Chair. and Chief Exec. Dr SÁNDOR CSÁNYI; 408 brs.

Raiffeisen Bank Zrt: 1054 Budapest, Akadémia u. 6; tel. (1) 484-4400; fax (1) 484-4444; e-mail info@raiffeisen.hu; internet www.raiffeisen.hu; f. 1986; present name adopted 1999; 100% owned by Raiffeisen Banking Group (Austria); cap. 29,769m., res 27,406m., dep. 1,389,141m. (Dec. 2006); Pres. Dr HERBERT STEPIC; Man. Dir Dr PÉTER FELCSUTI; 120 brs.

UniCredit Bank Hungary Zrt: 1054 Budapest, Szabadság tér 5–6; tel. (1) 269-0812; fax (1) 353-4959; e-mail info@unicreditbank.hu; internet www.unicreditbank.hu; f. 2001 by merger of Bank Austria Creditanstalt Hungary RT and Hypovereinsbank Hungary RT; 100% owned by Bank Austria Creditanstalt AG; cap. 24,118m., res 27,507m., dep. 1,153,028m. (Dec. 2006); CEO Dr MIHALY PATAI.

WestLB Hungaria Bank: 1075 Budapest, Madách Imre u. 13–14; tel. (1) 235-5900; fax (1) 235-5906; e-mail public@westlb.hu; internet www.westlb.de; f. 1985; owned by WestLB AG (Germany); cap. 4,485.8m., res 4,175.6m., dep. 63,390.7m. (Dec. 2005); Chair. and Man. Dir GÁBOR KURUTZ.

Supervisory Authority

Hungarian Financial Supervisory Authority (HFSA) (Pénzügyi Szervezetek Állami Felügyelete—PSZAF): 1535 Budapest, POB 777; tel. (1) 489-9100; fax (1) 489-9102; e-mail pszaf@pszaf.hu; internet www.pszaf.hu; Chair. of Supervisory Bd ISTVÁN FARKAS; Dir-Gen. ERIKA MARSI.

STOCK EXCHANGE

Budapest Stock Exchange (Budapesti Értéktőzsde—BET): 1052 Budapest, Deák Ferenc u. 5; tel. (1) 429-6700; fax (1) 429-6800; e-mail info@bse.hu; internet www.bse.hu; f. 1991; partly owned by a consortium comprising: HVB Bank Hungary (with a 25.2% stake), Wiener Börse (Vienna Stock Exchange, Austria, 12.5%), Österreichische Kontrollbank AG (Austria, 12.5%), Raiffeisen Zentralbank Österreich AG (Austria, 6.4%) and Erste Bank der österreichischen Sparkassen AG (Austria, 6.4%); allied with the Wiener Börse from May 2004; Pres. ATTILA SZALAY-BERZEVICZY; Chief Exec. ÁRPÁD PÁL.

INSURANCE

In 2005 there were 29 insurance companies.

AB-AEGON Általános Biztosító: 1091 Budapest, Üllői u. 1; tel. (1) 218-1866; fax (1) 217-7065; internet www.aegon.hu; f. 1949; present name adopted 1992; pensions, life and property insurance, insurance of agricultural plants, co-operatives, foreign insurance, etc.; Gen. Man. Dr GÁBOR KEPECS.

Garancia Insurance Co (Garancia Biztosító): 1054 Budapest, Vadász u. 12; tel. (1) 269-2533; fax (1) 269-2549; f. 1988; cap. 4,050m.; Gen. Man. and Chief Exec. Dr ZOLTÁN NAGY; 52 brs.

Hungária Insurance Co (Hungária Biztosító): 1054 Budapest, Bajcsy u. 52; tel. (1) 301-6565; fax (1) 301-6100; f. 1986; handles international insurance, industrial and commercial insurance, and motor car, marine, life, household, accident and liability insurance; cap. 4,266m.; Chair. and Chief Exec. Dr MIHÁLY PATAI.

QBE Atlasz Insurance Co (QBE Atlasz Biztosító): 1143 Budapest, Stefánia u. 51; tel. (1) 460-1400; fax (1) 460-1499; e-mail qbe-atlasz@qbeatlasz.hu; internet www.qbeatlasz.hu; f. 1988; cap. 1,000m.; Gen. Man. DORON GROSSMAN.

Directory

Trade and Industry

GOVERNMENT AGENCY

Hungarian Privatization and State Holding Co (Állami Privatizációs és Vagyonkezelő—APV Rt): 1133 Budapest, Pozsonyi u. 56; tel. (1) 237-4400; fax (1) 237-4100; e-mail apvrt@apvrt.hu; internet www.apvrt.hu; f. 1995; CEO MARTON VAGI.

NATIONAL CHAMBERS OF COMMERCE AND OF AGRICULTURE

Hungarian Chamber of Agriculture (Magyar Agrárkamara): 1119 Budapest, Etele u. 57; tel. (1) 371-5517; fax (1) 371-5510; e-mail info@agrarkamara.hu; internet www.agrarkamara.hu; Pres. MIKLÓS CSIKAI.

Hungarian Chamber of Commerce and Industry (Magyar Kereskedelmi és Iparkamara): 1055 Budapest, Kossuth Lajos tér 6–8; tel. (1) 474-5141; fax (1) 474-5105; internet www.mkik.hu; f. 1850; central organization of the 23 Hungarian county chambers of commerce and industry; based on a system of voluntary membership; over 46,000 mems; Pres. Dr LÁSZLÓ PARRAGH; Sec.-Gen. PÉTER DUNAI.

REGIONAL CHAMBERS OF COMMERCE

There are regional chambers of commerce in each of the 20 principal administrative divisions of Hungary (comprising the 19 counties and the City of Budapest). The following are among the most important:

Borsod-Abaúj-Zemplén County Chamber of Commerce and Industry (Borsod-Abaúj-Zemplén Kereskedelmi és Iparkamara): 3525 Miskolc, Szentpáli u. 1; tel. (46) 328-539; fax (46) 328-722; e-mail bokik@bokik.hu; internet www.bokik.hu; f. 1990; membership of 1,100 cos; Pres. TAMÁS BIHALL; Sec. ANNA BAÁN-SZILÀGYI.

Budapest Chamber of Industry and Commerce (Budapesti Kereskedelmi és Iparkamara): 1016 Budapest, Krisztina krt 99; tel. (1) 488-2173; fax (1) 488-2180; internet www.bkik.hu; f. 1850; Chair. LÁSZLÓ KOJI; Sec.-Gen. CSABA BAZSC.

Csongrád County Chamber of Commerce and Industry: 6721 Szeged, Tisza L. krt 2–4; tel. (62) 423-451; fax (62) 426-149; internet www.csmkik.hu; Chair. ISTVÁN SZERI; Sec. LAJOS HORVÁTH.

Hajdú-Bihar County Chamber of Commerce and Industry: 4025 Debrecen, Petőfi tér 10; tel. (52) 500-721; fax (52) 500-720; e-mail hbkik@hbkik.hu; internet www.hbkik.hu; Chair. FERENC MIKLÓSSY; Sec. Dr EVA SKULTÉTI.

Pécs-Baranya Chamber of Commerce and Industry: 7625 Pécs, Dr Majorossy I. u. 36; tel. (72) 507-149; fax (72) 507-152; e-mail pbkik@pbkik.hu; internet www.pbkik.hu; Pres. ISTVÁN KÉRI; Sec. TAMÁS SÍKFÔI.

Pest County Chamber of Commerce and Industry (Pest Megyei Kereskedelmi és Iparkamara): 1056 Budapest, Vàci u. 40; tel. (1) 317-7666; fax (1) 317-7755; e-mail titkarsag@pmkik.hu; internet www.pmkik.hu; Chair. Dr ZOLTÁN VERECZKEY; Sec.-Gen. Dr LAJOS KUPCSOK.

Szabolcs-Szatmár-Bereg County Chamber of Commerce and Industry: 4400 Nyíregyháza, Széchenyi u. 2; tel. (42) 311-544; fax (42) 311-750; e-mail szabkam@szabkam.hu; internet www.szabkam.hu; Chair. Dr JÁNOS VERES; Sec. NAGY KATALIN VARGA.

EMPLOYERS' ASSOCIATIONS

Confederation of Hungarian Employers and Industrialists (Munkaadók és Gyáriparosok Országos Szövetsége—MGYOSZ): 1055 Budapest, Kossuth L. tér 6–8; fax (1) 474-2065; e-mail mgyosz@mgyosz.hu; internet www.mgyosz.hu; f. 1902; re-est. 1990; 64 member organizations; Sec.-Gen. ISTVÁN WIMMER.

National Asscn of Entrepreneurs and Employers (Vállalkozók és Munkáltatók Országos Szövetsége—VOSZ): 1107 Budapest, Mázsa tér 2–6, Porta Office Bldg, 4th Floor; tel. (1) 414-2181; fax (1) 414-2180; e-mail center@vosz.hu; internet www.vosz.hu; Sec.-Gen. DÁVID FERENC.

INDUSTRIAL AND TRADE ASSOCIATIONS

HUNICOOP Foreign Trade Co for Industrial Co-operation: 1036 Budapest, Galagonya u. 7; tel. (1) 250-8117; fax (1) 250-8121; e-mail hunicoop@axelero.hu; internet www.hunicoop.hu; agency for foreign companies in Hungary, export and import; Dir GÁBOR TOMBÁCZ.

Hungarian Industrial Asscn (Magyar Iparszövetség—OKISZ): 1146 Budapest, Thököly u. 58–60; tel. (1) 343-5570; fax (1) 343-5521; e-mail okisz@okiszinfo.hu; safeguards interests of over 1,100 member enterprises (all private); Pres. LÁSZLÓ HÖRÖMPÖLY.

National Asscn of Industrial Corporations (Ipartestületek Országos Szövetsége—IPOSZ): 1054 Budapest, Kálmán Imre u. 20; tel. (1) 354-3140; e-mail titkarsag@iposz.hu; internet www.iposz.hu; Chair. GYÖRGY SZÜCS.

HUNGARY

National Co-operative Council (Országos Szövetkezeti Tanács—OSZT): 1054 Budapest, Szabadság tér 14; tel. (1) 312-7467; fax (1) 311-3647; e-mail losz@losz.hu; internet www.losz.hu; f. 1968; Pres. TAMÁS FARKAS; Sec. Dr JÓZSEF PÁL.

National Federation of Agricultural Co-operators and Producers (Mezőgazdasági Szövetkezők és Termelők Országos Szövetsége—MOSZ): 1054 Budapest, Akadémia u. 1–3; tel. and fax (1) 353-2552; e-mail mosztit@mosz.tvnet.hu; f. 1990; Pres. TAMÁS NAGY; Sec.-Gen. GÁBOR HORVÁTH; c. 1,300 mem. orgs.

National Federation of Consumer Co-operatives (Általános Fogyasztási Szövetkezetek Országos Szövetsége—ÁFEOSZ): 1054 Budapest, Szabadság tér 14; tel. (1) 353-4222; fax (1) 311-3647; internet www.afeosz.hu; safeguards interests of Hungarian consumer co-operative societies; organizes co-operative wholesale activities; Pres. Dr PÁL BARTUS; 800,000 mems.

UTILITIES

Supervisory Organization

Hungarian Energy Office (Magyar Energia Hivatal): 1081 Budapest, Köztársaság tér 7; tel. (1) 459-7777; fax (1) 459-7766; e-mail info@eh.gov.hu; internet www.eh.gov.hu; f. 1994; regulation and supervision of activities performed by gas and electricity companies, price regulation and protection of consumer interest; Pres. FERENC J. HORVÁTH.

Electricity

AES-Tisza Erőmű (AES-Tisza Power Plant Co): 3581 Tiszaújváros Pf 53; tel. (49) 547-333; fax (49) 341-756; e-mail info@aes.hu; internet www.aes.hu; f. 1992; owned by AES Corpn (USA); electricity generation and merchandising; Chair. ALLAN B. DWYER; Man. Dir PETER LITHGOW; 182 employees.

Budapest Electricity Co (Budapesti Elektromos Művek) (ELMŰ): 1132 Budapest, Váci u. 72–74; tel. (1) 238-1000; fax (1) 238-2822; internet www.elmu.hu; f. 1949; transmission and distribution of electricity; Chair. EMMERICH ENDRESZ; Pres. ANDREAS RADMACHER; 3,371 employees.

Démász (South Hungarian Power Supply Co): 6720 Szeged, Klauzál tér 9; tel. (62) 476-576; fax (62) 482-500; e-mail ugfelszolgalat@demasz.hu; internet www.demasz.hu; f. 1951; distributes electricity to south-eastern Hungary; Pres. JACQUES PITHOIS.

Dunamenti Hőerőmű (Power Plant) Co: 2440 Százhalombatta, Erőmű u. 2; tel. (23) 354-161; fax (23) 354-381; electricity generation; Chair. TIBOR KUHL.

Émász (North Hungarian Electricity Supply Co): 3525 Miskolc, Dózsa Gy. u. 13; tel. (46) 411-875; fax (46) 411-871; e-mail emasz@emasz.hu; internet www.emasz.hu.

E.ON Del-dunántúli Áramszolgáltató: 7626 Pécs, Rákóczi, u. 73B; tel. (72) 501-000; fax (72) 501-208; internet www.eon-deldunantul.com; fmrly Dédász (South-West Hungarian Electricity Supply Co); present name adopted 2004; wholly owned by E.ON Hungária Rt; Chair. ZOLTÁN PALUSKA.

E.ON Észak-dunántúli Áramszolgáltató: 9027 Győr, Kandó Kálmán u. 11–13; tel. (96) 521-000; fax (96) 521-888; e-mail webmaster@edasz.hu; internet www.eon-eszakdunantul.com; f. 1951; fmrly Édász (North-West Hungarian Electricity Co); present name adopted 2004; generates and supplies electricity; 98.57% owned by E.ON Hungária Rt; Chair. BÉLA KÜNSZLER; 2,272 employees.

E.ON Hungária Rt: 1054 Budapest, Széchenyi rkp. 8; tel. (1) 472-2300; e-mail info@eon-hungaria.com; internet www.eon-hungaria.com; f. 2000; 85.98% owned by E.ON Energie AG (Germany); Chair. of Bd of Dirs KONRAD KRAUSER.

E.ON Tiszántúli Áramszolgáltató: 4024 Debrecen, Kossuth Lajos u. 4; tel. (52) 410-011; fax (52) 414-031; internet www.eon-tiszantul.com; 97.2% owned by E.ON Hungária; fmrly Titász (North-East Hungarian Electricity Co); present name adopted 2004; Chair. FRANZ ERÉNYI.

Hungarian Power Companies Co (Magyar Villamos Művek R—MVM): 1255 Budapest, POB 77; 1011 Budapest, Vám u. 5–7; tel. (1) 224-6200; fax (1) 202-1246; e-mail mvm@mvm.hu; internet www.mvm.hu; Hungarian national electricity wholesaler and power-system controller; Chair. GYULA LENGYEL.

Mátrai Power Plant (Erőmű Részvénytársaság) Co: 3272 Visonta, Erőmű u. 11; tel. (37) 328-001; fax (37) 328-036; internet www.mert.hu; electricity generation; Chair. JÓZSEF VALASKA; 3,645 employees.

Paks Nuclear Plant Co (Paksi Atomerőmű): 7031 Paks, POB 71; tel. (75) 508-833; fax (75) 506-662; internet www.npp.hu; f. 1992; electrical energy production; Plant Man. SÁNDOR NAGY; 2,800 employees.

Vértesi Power Plant (Erőmű) Co: 2840 Oroszlány, POB 23; tel. (34) 360-255; fax (34) 360-882; e-mail vert@vert.hu; internet www.vert.hu; electricity and heat generation; Chair. KÁROLY TAKÁCS; 5,438 employees.

Gas

Dégáz—Delalfoldi Gázszolgáltató (South-Western Gas) Co: 6724 Szeged, Pulcz u. 44; tel. (62) 569-600; fax (63) 473-943; e-mail ugyfel@degas.hu; internet www.degaz.hu; gas supply and services in Bács-Kiskun, Békés and Csongrád counties; 99.8% owned by Gaz de France (France).

Főgáz—Fővárosi Gázművek (Budapest Gas) Co: 1081 Budapest, Köztársaság tér 20; tel. (1) 477-1111; fax (1) 477-1277; internet www.fogaz.hu; f. 1856; gas distribution; Chair. DEZSŐ VASANITS.

MOL—Magyar Olaj és Gázipari (Hungarian Oil and Gas Co): 1117 Budapest, Október huszonharmadika u. 18; tel. (1) 209-0000; fax (1) 209-0005; e-mail webmaster@mol.hu; internet www.mol.hu; f. 1991; privatized in 1995; the state retains a 12.2% share; petroleum and gas exploration, processing, transportation and distribution; 12,000 employees; Chair. and Chief Exec. ZSOLT HERNÁDI; Group Chief Exec. GYÖRGI MOSONYI.

Tigáz—Tiszántúli Gázszolgáltató (Tisza Gas) Co: 4200 Hajdúszoboszló, Rákóczi u. 184; tel. (52) 558-100; fax (52) 361-149; e-mail titkarsaga@tigaz.hu; internet www.tigas.hu; f. 1950; 40% owned by Italgas Gruppo (Italy); gas distribution in north-eastern regions of Hungary; Chair. MARINO BIAGIO.

TRADE UNIONS

From 1988, and particularly after the restructuring of the former Central Council of Hungarian Trade Unions (SzOT) as the National Confederation of Hungarian Trade Unions (MSzOSz) in 1990, several new union federations were created. Several unions are affiliated to more than one federation, and others are completely independent. In May 2000 a trade-unions co-operation council was established.

Trade Union Federations

Association of Hungarian Free Trade Unions (Magyar Szabad Szakszervezetek Szövetsége): Budapest; f. 1994; 200,000 mems.

Autonomous Trade Union Confederation (Autonóm Szakszervezetek Szövetsége): 1068 Budapest, Benczúr u. 45; tel. (1) 342-1776; Pres. LAJOS FŐCZE.

Democratic Confederation of Free Trade Unions (Független Szakszervezetek Demokratikus Ligája—FSzDL): 1068 Budapest, Benczúr u. 41; tel. (1) 321-5262; fax (1) 321-5405; e-mail info@liganet.hu; internet www.liganet.hu; f. 1988; Pres. ISTVÁN GASKÓ; 103,000 mems.

Principal affiliated unions include:

Democratic Trade Union of Scientific Workers (Tudományos Dolgozók Demokratikus Szakszervezete—TDDSz): 1068 Budapest, Városligeti fasor 38; tel. (1) 142-8438; f. 1988; Chair. PÁL FORGACS.

Federation of Unions of Intellectual Workers (Értelmiségi Szakszervezeti Tömörülés—ESzT): 1066 Budapest, Jókai u. 2; tel. (1) 473-1429; fax (1) 331-4577; e-mail eszt@eszt.hu; internet www.eszt.hu; Pres. Dr LÁSZLÓ VIGH; Gen. Sec. Dr GÁBOR BÁNK.

Forum for the Co-operation of Trade Unions (Szakszervezetek Együttműködési Fóruma—SzEF): 1068 Budapest VIII, Puskin u. 4; tel. (1) 138-2651; fax (1) 118-7360; f. 1990; Pres. Dr ENDRE SZABÓ.

Principal affiliated unions include:

Federation of Hungarian Public Service Employees' Unions (Közszolgálati Szakszervezetek Szövetsége): 1081 Budapest, Kiss u. 8; tel. (1) 313-5436; fax (1) 133-7223; f. 1945; Pres. PÉTER MICHALKO.

National Confederation of Hungarian Trade Unions (Magyar Szakszervezetek Országos Szövetsége—MSzOSz): 1086 Budapest, Magdolna u. 5–7; tel. (1) 323-2660; fax (1) 323-2662; e-mail gykiss@mszosz.hu; internet www.mszosz.hu; f. 1898; reorganized 1990; Pres. Dr LÁSZLÓ SÁNDOR; 405,000 mems in 41 mem. orgs.

Principal affiliated unions include:

Commercial Employees' Trade Union (Kereskedelmi Alkalmazottak Szakszervezete): 1066 Budapest, Jókai u. 6; tel. (1) 331-8970; fax (1) 332-3382; e-mail saling@axelero.hu; f. 1900; Pres. Dr JÓZSEF SÁLING; 80,000 mems.

Federation of Agricultural, Forestry and Water Supply Workers' Unions (Mezőgazdasági, Erdészeti és Vízügyi Dolgozók Szakszervezeti Szövetsége—MEDOSZ): 1066 Budapest, Jókai u. 2; tel. (1) 301-9050; fax (1) 331-4568; e-mail medosz.net@mail.datanet.hu; f. 1906; Gen. Sec. Dr ANDRÁS BERECZKY; 9,277 mems.

Federation of Chemical Workers' Unions of Hungary, Confederation Founding Section (Magyar Vegyipari Dolgozók Szakszervezeti Szövetsége, össz-szövetségi alapító tagozata):

Budapest; tel. (1) 342-1778; fax (1) 342-9975; Gen. Sec. György Paszternák; 12,000 mems.

Federation of Communal Service Workers' Unions (Kommunális Dalgozók Szakszervezete): 1068 Budapest, Benczur u. 43; tel. (1) 111-6950; Gen. Sec. Zsolt Pék; 28,000 mems.

Federation of Hungarian Artworkers' Unions (Müvészeti Szakszervezetek Szövetsége): 1068 Budapest, Városligeti fasor 38; tel. (1) 342-8927; fax (1) 342-8372; e-mail eji@mail.datanet.hu; f. 1957; Pres. László Gyimesi; 32,000 mems.

Federation of Hungarian Metalworkers' Unions (Vasas Szakszervezeti Szövetség): 1086 Budapest, Magdolna u. 5–7; tel. (1) 210-9610; fax (1) 210-0116; e-mail csurgo.s@vasasszakszervezet.hu; internet www.vasasszakszervezet.hu; f. 1877; Pres. Béla Balogh; 53,000 mems.

Federation of Local Industry and Municipal Workers' Unions (Helyiipari és Városgazdasági Dolgozók Szövetségének): 1068 Budapest, Benczúr u. 43; tel. (1) 311-6950; f. 1952; Pres. Józsefné Svever; Gen. Sec. Pál Bakányi; 281,073 mems.

Federation of Municipal Industries and Service Workers' Unions (Települési Ipari és Szolgáltatási Dolgozók Szakszervezete): 1068 Budapest, Benczur u. 43; tel. (1) 111-6950; Gen. Sec. Zoltán Szikszai; 20,000 mems.

Federation of Postal and Telecommunications Workers' Unions (Postai és Hirközlési Dolgozók Szakszervezeti Szövetsége): 1146 Budapest, Cházár András u. 13; tel. (1) 142-8777; fax (1) 121-4018; f. 1945; Pres. Enikő Heszky-Gricser; 69,900 mems.

Hungarian Federation of Food Industry Workers' Unions (Magyar Élelmezésipari Dolgozók Szakszervezeteinek Szövetsége): 1068 Budapest, Városligeti fasor 44; tel. (1) 122-5880; fax (1) 142-8568; f. 1905; Pres. Gyula Sóki; Gen. Sec. Béla Vanek; 226,243 mems.

Hungarian Union of Teachers (Magyar Pedagógusok Szakszervezete): 1068 Budapest, Városligeti fasor 10; tel. (1) 122-8456; fax (1) 142-8122; f. 1945; Gen. Sec. Istvánné Szőllősi; 200,000 mems.

Hungarian Union of Textile Workers (Magyar Textilipari Dolgozók Szakszervezete): 1068 Budapest, Rippl-Rónai u. 2; tel. (1) 428-196; fax (1) 122-5414; f. 1905; Gen. Sec. Tamás Keleti; 70,241 mems.

Union of Health Service Workers (Egészségügyben Dolgozók Szakszervezeteinek Szövetsége): 1051 Budapest, Nádor u. 32, POB 36; tel. (1) 110-645; f. 1945; Pres. Dr Zoltán Szabó; Gen. Sec. Dr Pálné Kállay; 280,536 mems.

Union of Clothing Workers (Ruházatipari Dolgozók Szakszervezete): 1077 Budapest, Almássy tér 2; tel. (1) 342-3702; fax (1) 122-6717; f. 1892; Gen. Sec. Tamás Wittich; 22,000 mems.

Workers' Unions of Mining and Energy (Bánya–és Energiaipari Dolgozók Szakszervezete): 1068 Budapest, Városligeti fasor 46–48; tel. (1) 322-1226; fax (1) 342-1942; e-mail bdsz@banyasz.hu; f. 1913; Pres. Ferenc Rabi; 80,000 mems.

Transport

RAILWAYS

In 2003 the rail network in Hungary amounted to a length of 8,137 km. In 2004 10,544m. passenger-km were travelled on the network. There is an underground railway in Budapest, which had a network of three lines, totalling 33 km in 2002; a fourth line was also planned. The European Union (EU) provided funding for several railway modernization projects from the late 1990s.

Budapest Transport Company (BKV): 1072 Budapest, Akácfa u. 15; tel. (1) 461-6500; fax (1) 461-6557; e-mail bkvzrt@bkv.hu; internet www.bkv.hu; f. 1968; operates metro system, suburban railway network, trams, trolley buses, and conventional buses; Chief Exec. Attila Antal; Pres. György Tóthfalusi.

Hungarian State Railways Co (Magyar Államvasutak—MÁV): 1940 Budapest, Andrássy u. 73–75; tel. (1) 322-0660; fax (1) 342-8596; internet www.mav.hu; f. 1868; total network 7,785 km, including 2,628 km of electrified lines (2000); Pres. and Chief Exec. Gyula Gaal; Gen. Dir Márton Kukely.

Railway of Győr–Sopron–Ebenfurth (Győr–Sopron–Ebenfurti-Vasút—GySEV/ROeEE): 1011 Budapest, Szilágyi Dezső tér 1; internet www.gysev.hu; Hungarian-Austrian-owned railway; 162 km in Hungary, 65 km in Austria, all electrified; transport of passengers and goods; Dir-Gen. Dr László Fehérvári.

ROADS

In 2003 there were 542 km of motorways and 30,536 km of national public roads. There are extensive long-distance bus services. In 2006 a development programme was under way for the construction of 420 km of roads (including 326 km of motorways), at a cost of 1,100m. forint. This programme was to be partly funded by loans from the European Bank for Reconstruction and Development and the European Investment Bank. The central budget for 2003 allocated 79,400m. forint for road development.

Hungarocamion: 1239 Budapest, Nagykőrösi u. 351; tel. (1) 421-6666; fax (1) 421-6699; e-mail info@waberers.com; internet www.waberers.com; f. 1966; privatized in 1998; 92% purchased by Volán Tefu Rt in 2002; holding group renamed Waberers Csoport in 2004; international road freight transport company; 17 offices in Europe and the Middle East; fleet of 1,100 units for general and specialized cargo; Gen. Man. Gabriella Szakál; 3,800 employees.

Volánbusz: 1091 Budapest, Üllői u. 131; tel. (1) 219-8000; e-mail info@volanbusz.hu; internet www.volanbusz.hu; f. 1925 as Mavart; 100% state-owned; operates local, national and international passenger coach services.

SHIPPING AND INLAND WATERWAYS

MAFRACHT Kft: 1139 Budapest, Váci u. 85; tel. (1) 452-8260; fax (1) 452-8259; e-mail mafracht@mafracht.hu; internet www.mafracht.hu; shipping agency.

MAHART—Magyar Hajózás (Hungarian Shipping) Co: 1366 Budapest, POB 58; tel. (1) 484-6421; fax (1) 484-6422; e-mail freeport@mahart.hu; f. 1895; transportation of goods on the Rhine–Main–Danube waterway; carries passenger traffic on the Danube; operates port activities at Budapest Csepel National and Free Port (port agency service, loading, storage, handling goods); management of multi-modal and combined transport (cargo booking, oversized goods, chartering); ship-building and ship-repair services; Dir-Gen. Capt. László Somlóvári.

CIVIL AVIATION

The Ferihegy international airport is 16 km from the centre of Budapest. In 1999 a new passenger terminal opened. Balatonkiliti airport, near Siófok in western Hungary, also serves international traffic. Other airports are located at Nyíregyháza, Debrecen, Szeged, Pécs, Szombathely and Győr. In December 2005 the Government sold its 75% share of Budapest Airport Rt, which operates Ferihegy airport, to BAA of the United Kingdom.

Civil Aviation Authority (Polgári Légiközlekedésigyi Hatóság): Budapest; tel. (1) 296-9502; fax (1) 296-8808; e-mail info@caa.hu; internet www.caa.hu; controls civil aviation; Dir-Gen. Zoltán Antal.

Hungarocontrol (Hungarian Air Navigation Services): 1185 Budapest, POB 80, Igló u. 33–35; tel. (1) 293-4444; fax (1) 293-4343; e-mail info@hungarocontrol.hu; internet www.hungarocontrol.hu; f. 2002; state-owned; operation of air traffic control in Hungary; Dir István Mudra; 700 employees.

Malév Hungarian Airlines: 1051 Budapest, Roosevelt tér 2, POB 122; tel. (1) 235-3535; fax (1) 266-2685; internet www.malev.hu; f. 1946; regular services from Budapest to Europe, North Africa, North America, Asia and the Middle East; proposed privatization postponed in 2005; joined the Oneworld airline alliance in the same year; Pres. Ferenc Szarvas; Chief Exec. Ferenc Kovács.

Wizz Air Hungary: 2220 Vescés, Lorinci u. 59; tel. (22) 351-9499; e-mail info@wizzair.com; internet www.wizzair.com; f. 2004; wholly-owned subsidiary of Wizz Air (United Kingdom); mem. of European Low Fares Airline Asscn; Chair. and Chief Exec. József Váradi.

Tourism

Tourism has developed rapidly and is an important source of foreign exchange. Lake Balaton is the main holiday centre for boating, bathing and fishing. Hungary's cities have great historical and recreational attractions, and the annual Budapest Spring Festival is held in March. Budapest has numerous swimming pools watered by thermal springs, which are equipped with modern physiotherapy facilities. Revenue from tourism totalled US $4,581m. in 2005, and there were 41.0m. foreign visitors in 2006.

Association of Hungarian Travel Agents and Tour Operators (Magyar Utazásszervezők és Utazásközvetítők Szövetsége—MUISZ): 1364 Budapest, PO Box 267; tel. (1) 302-2813; fax (1) 269-5557; e-mail muisz@mail.selectrade.hu; internet www.muisz.com; f. 1974; Pres. Gabriella Molnár.

Hungarian Tourism Office: 1052 Budapest, Sütő u. 2; tel. (1) 317-9800; fax (1) 317-9656; e-mail info@hungarytourism.hu; internet www.hungarytourism.hu; Gen. Man. Dr Gábor Galla.

Tourism Office of Budapest: 1056 Budapest, Március 15, tér 7; tel. (1) 266-0479; fax (1) 266-7477; e-mail info@budapestinfo.hu; internet www.budapestinfo.hu; Dir László Fekete.

ICELAND

Introductory Survey

Location, Climate, Language, Religion, Flag, Capital

The Republic of Iceland comprises one large island and numerous smaller ones, situated near the Arctic Circle in the North Atlantic Ocean. The main island lies about 300 km (190 miles) south-east of Greenland, about 1,000 km (620 miles) west of Norway and about 800 km (500 miles) north of Scotland. The Gulf Stream keeps Iceland warmer than might be expected, with average temperatures ranging from 10°C (50°F) in the summer to 1°C (34°F) in winter. Icelandic is the official language. Almost all of the inhabitants profess Christianity: the Evangelical Lutheran Church is the established church and embraces about 81% of the population. The civil flag (proportions 18 by 25) displays a red cross, bordered with white, on a blue background, the upright of the cross being towards the hoist; the state flag (proportions 9 by 16) bears the same design, but has a truncated triangular area cut from the fly. The capital is Reykjavík.

Recent History

Iceland became independent on 17 June 1944, when the Convention that linked it with Denmark, under the Danish crown, was terminated. Iceland became a founder member of the North Atlantic Treaty Organization (NATO, see p. 340) in 1949, joined the Council of Europe (see p. 225) in 1950, and has belonged to the Nordic Council (see p. 424) since its foundation in 1952. Membership of the European Free Trade Association (EFTA, see p. 412) was formalized in 1970.

From 1959 to 1971 Iceland was governed by a coalition of the Independence Party (IP) and the Social Democratic Party (SDP). Following the general election of June 1971, Olafur Jóhannesson, the leader of the Progressive Party (PP), formed a coalition Government with the left-wing People's Alliance (PA) and the Union of Liberals and Leftists. At the general election held in June 1974 voters favoured right-wing parties, and in August the IP and the PP formed a coalition Government under the leader of the IP, Geir Hallgrímsson. However, failure adequately to address economic difficulties resulted in a decline in the coalition's popularity and prompted the Government's resignation in June 1978, following extensive electoral gains by the PA and the SDP. Disagreements over economic measures, and over the PA's advocacy of Icelandic withdrawal from NATO, led to two months of negotiations before a new government could be formed. In September Jóhannesson formed a coalition of the PP with the PA and the SDP, but this Government, after addressing immediate economic necessities, resigned in October 1979, when the SDP withdrew from the coalition. An interim administration was formed by Benedikt Gröndal, the leader of the SDP. The results of a general election, held in December, were inconclusive, and in February 1980 Gunnar Thoroddsen of the IP formed a coalition Government with the PA and the PP.

In June 1980 Vigdís Finnbogadóttir, a non-political candidate who was favoured by left-wing groups owing to her opposition to the US military airbase at Keflavík, achieved a narrow victory in the election for the mainly ceremonial office of President. She took office on 1 August 1980, becoming the world's first popularly elected female Head of State. The coalition Government lost its majority in the Lower House of the Althingi/Alþingi (parliament) in September 1982, and a general election took place in April 1983. The IP received the largest share (38.7%) of the votes cast, but two new parties, the Social Democratic Alliance (SDA) and the Women's List, together won almost 13% of the votes cast. A centre-right coalition was formed by the IP and the PP, with Steingrímur Hermannsson (the leader of the PP) as Prime Minister. In May 1985 the Althingi unanimously approved a resolution declaring the country a 'nuclear-free zone', thus banning the entry of nuclear weapons.

A general election for an enlarged, 63-seat Althingi was held in April 1987. Both parties of the outgoing coalition suffered losses: the IP's representation decreased from 24 to 18 seats, and the PP lost one of its 14 seats. The right-wing Citizens' Party (CP, which had been formed only one month earlier by Albert Guðmundsson, following his resignation from the Government and from the IP) won seven seats. Ten seats were won by the SDP, which included former members of the SDA (disbanded in 1986). A coalition of the IP, the PP and the SDP was formally constituted in July 1987. Thorsteinn Pálsson, the leader of the IP since November 1983 and hitherto the Minister of Finance, was appointed Prime Minister.

In June 1988 President Finnbogadóttir (who had begun a second term in office, unopposed, in August 1984) was elected for a third term, receiving more than 90% of the votes cast. This was the first occasion on which an incumbent Icelandic President seeking re-election had been challenged. In June 1992 Finnbogadóttir was elected unopposed for a fourth term of office.

In September 1988 the SDP and the PP withdrew from the Government, following disagreements over economic policy. Later that month Hermannsson became Prime Minister in a centre-left coalition of the PP, the SDP and the PA. The new Government committed itself to a series of devaluations of the króna, and introduced austerity measures, with the aim of lowering the rate of inflation and stimulating the fishing industry.

Following the resignation of Guðmundsson as leader of the CP in January 1989, relations between this party and the left improved, and in September a new Government, based on a coalition agreement between the PP, the SDP, the PA, the CP and the Association for Equality and Social Justice, was formed. Hermannsson, who remained as Prime Minister, affirmed that the new Government would not change its policies, emphasizing the need to reduce inflation and to stimulate economic growth, as well as reiterating an earlier declaration of the Althingi that no nuclear weapons would be located in Iceland.

In March 1991 Davíð Oddsson, the mayor of Reykjavík, successfully challenged Pálsson for the leadership of the IP. At a general election in April the IP emerged as the largest single party, securing 26 seats (with 38.6% of the votes cast), mostly at the expense of the CP. Although the incumbent coalition would have retained an overall majority of seats, the SDP decided to withdraw from the coalition, chiefly as a result of the failure to reach agreement on Iceland's position in the discussions between EFTA and the European Community (EC, now European Union—EU, see p. 244), with regard to the creation of a European Economic Area (EEA, see p. 412). A new coalition Government was formed in late April by the IP and the SDP, with Oddsson as Prime Minister; the new administration promised economic liberalization and a strengthening of links with the USA and Europe (although no application for membership of the EC was envisaged), but was faced with a deteriorating economic situation.

In 1991 Iceland's Constitution was amended, ending the system whereby the Althingi was divided into an Upper House (one-third of the members) and a Lower House.

Although the IP secured the largest number of seats (25, with 37% of the votes cast) at a general election in April 1995, the SDP obtained only seven seats, three fewer than in the previous election. Later in the month a new coalition Government was formed, comprising the IP and the PP, with Oddsson continuing as Prime Minister. Halldór Ásgrímsson, the Chairman of the PP, became Minister of Foreign Affairs. Since both parties in the coalition opposed the Common Fisheries Policy of the EU, it was considered unlikely that Iceland would apply for full membership of the EU in the near future.

Following the decision by Finnbogadóttir not to seek re-election as President in 1996, the principal candidates were Ólafur Ragnar Grímsson, a former leader of the PA (who had previously opposed Iceland's membership of NATO), Pétur Hafstein, a justice in the Supreme Court, and Guðrún Agnarsdóttir of the Women's List. In the election, held in June 1996, Grímsson won 41% of the votes cast, while Hafstein won 29% and Agnarsdóttir 26%. Grímsson duly took office as President in August. He began a second term of office in August 2000, his candidacy being unopposed.

At a general election held in May 1999 the governing coalition retained its majority in the Althingi: the IP won 26 seats, while the PP won 12 seats. Meanwhile, a left-wing electoral grouping entitled The Alliance, which was composed of the PA, the SDP, the People's Movement and the Women's List, won 17 seats. Two new parties also secured representation in the legislature: the Left-Green Movement, established by three former PA deputies, six seats, while the Liberal Party, founded by the former IP minister Sverrir Hermannsson, won two seats. A new coalition Government comprising the IP and the PP, under Oddsson, took office at the end of the month.

At the general election held on 10 May 2003, the IP remained the party with the largest representation in the Althingi, winning 22 seats. The IP renewed its coalition with the PP, which had won 12 seats, with Oddsson remaining as Prime Minister. The two parties agreed that Oddsson would relinquish the premiership in September 2004 in favour of Ásgrímsson, who had been reappointed as Minister of Foreign Affairs. The Alliance won 20 seats, the Left-Green Movement five seats, and the Liberal Party four seats.

In May 2004 the Althingi narrowly passed a bill to limit media ownership. Although the legislation was drafted following the publication of a report by a government-appointed committee that expressed concerns regarding the increased consolidation of media corporations, it provoked uncharacteristic public protests as many perceived the bill to be directed against a particular company, the Baugur Group, which dominated Iceland's retail, financial and media sectors, and whose media outlets had been openly critical of Oddsson. A petition urging President Grímsson to veto the bill attracted 30,000 signatures, an amount roughly equivalent to 10% of the population. Grímsson, who favoured a more active role for the presidency, refused to sign the bill, stating that it lacked the necessary consensus. It was the first time the presidential power of veto had been used in the 60-year history of the Republic. Grímsson was re-elected President for a third four-year term on 26 June, with 85.6% of the votes cast. However, discontent at his deployment of the veto was perhaps manifested in the low participation rate at the election of 62.5% (compared with a turnout of 85.9% in 1996) and the significantly high proportion of blank ballots (20.7%). Under the terms of the Constitution, the media bill was to be subject to a referendum in August 2004, but Oddsson instead withdrew the legislation and presented an amended version to the Althingi. The Althingi, however, rejected this new version of the bill in July.

Oddsson's defeat, the only one during his 13 years as Prime Minister, was followed by a period of ill health. On 15 September 2004, in accordance with the post-election agreement between the IP and PP, Oddsson stood down as Prime Minister in favour of Ásgrímsson, whose post Oddsson assumed. Oddsson resigned from politics in September 2005 and assumed the chairmanship of the Central Bank of Iceland. He was replaced as Minister of Foreign Affairs by Geir Haarde, hitherto the Minister of Finance, who was also elected leader of the IP in October.

In December 2004 opposition parties attacked Ásgrímsson's claim, in a televised interview, that the Althingi had been consulted prior to Iceland's endorsement of the US-led invasion of Iraq in March 2003. Opposition leaders accused Ásgrímsson and Oddsson, an outspoken supporter of the war in Iraq, of making the decision for Iceland to join the 'coalition of the willing' unilaterally. Ásgrímsson and Oddsson stated that the decision was supported by a vote of the Foreign Affairs Committee; however, other committee members claimed they were unable to recall any deliberations on the issue. Despite suffering a decline in public support, Ásgrímsson was re-elected as Chairman of the PP at a party conference in March 2005.

In June 2006 Ásgrímsson resigned as Prime Minister, following the PP's poor performance in municipal elections, and was succeeded by Haarde. A former Minister of Industry and Commerce, Valgerður Sverrisdóttir of the PP, replaced Haarde as Minister of Foreign Affairs. Ásgrímsson also announced that he would resign as Chairman of the PP following the party conference in August; he was subsequently replaced by Jón Sigurðsson, whom Haarde had appointed Minister of Industry and Commerce in June.

The general election of May 2007 was dominated by public concerns regarding the rate of industrial development in Iceland. While the IP and PP supported the further expansion of smelter and power plant projects, which had led to rapid economic growth in Iceland, The Alliance and the Left-Green Movement campaigned in favour of a moratorium on further development, pending an assessment of the environmental and economic impact of the current projects. At the election, which was held on 12 May, the IP remained the largest party in the Althingi, extending its representation from 22 seats to 25, with 36.6% of the valid votes cast. The PP, however, suffered a significant decline in support, winning just seven seats (11.7% of the votes cast), compared with 12 in the 2003 election, reducing the previous governing coalition's majority in the Althingi to one seat. The Alliance won 18 seats (26.8% of the votes cast), compared with 20 seats in 2003, while the Left-Green Movement became the third largest party in the legislature, increasing its representation from five to nine seats (14.3%), and the Liberal Party won four seats (7.3%). Despite the narrow majority retained by the outgoing coalition, Haarde and Sigurðsson indicated that the coalition agreement between the IP and the PP would not be renewed. On 24 May a new coalition Government comprising the IP and The Alliance, which commanded the support of 43 of the 63 members of the Althingi, was sworn in. Haarde retained the post of Prime Minister, while the leader of The Alliance, Ingibjörg Sólrún Gísladóttir, who was known to be in favour of Iceland joining the EU, became Minister of Foreign Affairs. Meanwhile, Sigurðsson resigned as Chairman of the PP and announced his withdrawal from politics. He was succeeded as leader of the PP by Guðni Ágústsson, who had been Minister of Agriculture in the previous Government.

Iceland has historically been an active participant in international co-operation. It is a member of the Nordic Council (see p. 424), which includes Denmark, Sweden, Norway and Finland, and the Nordic Council of Ministers (see p. 424). It was a founding member of NATO, joined the UN in 1946, the Council of Europe (see p. 225) in 1950 and has been a member of the Organization for Security and Co-operation in Europe (see p. 354) since its inception in 1975. Iceland is a member the EU's Schengen Agreement on border controls by virtue of its membership in the Nordic passport union.

In May 2003 it emerged that the USA was planning to withdraw the four remaining F-15/F-16 fighter jet aircraft stationed at Keflavík airbase, near Reykjavík, following a review of its international military commitments. The Iceland Defence Force (IDF), which, in mid-2003, was composed of 1,658 US troops and which had been stationed in Iceland since 1951 when an agreement had been drawn up between Iceland and the USA, was traditionally viewed as providing protection for Iceland, which had no military of its own; moreover, many Icelanders in the nearby town of Reykjanesbær depended on the Keflavík airbase for their livelihood. Oddsson suggested that if the USA withdrew the aircraft it would have to end its military presence in Iceland altogether—an unpalatable proposition for the USA, which still regarded its reconnaissance of the North Atlantic as a high priority. The possibility of Iceland forming its own national guard was the topic of much debate amongst Icelandic government officials. Concern among Icelanders was such that the Government requested that the Secretary-General of NATO, Lord Robertson of Port Ellen, intervene on their behalf. Following Lord Robertson's subsequent non-partisan representations in July 2003, the US authorities announced that they had delayed their decision with regard to the aircraft at Keflavík, which would instead be taken as part of a later general review of its military presence in Europe. The USA had previously withdrawn eight fighter aircraft from Iceland in 1994, but had agreed to retain four aircraft on a permanent basis at the Keflavík airbase; this agreement had originally been due to be renegotiated in 2001, but this had been postponed following the terrorist attacks in the USA of 11 September of that year.

In November 2005 the Government began investigating claims that the USA's Central Intelligence Agency (CIA) had routed flights through Icelandic airports as part of its programme of 'extraordinary rendition'. Under this programme, it was alleged, suspected Islamist militants were secretly transferred to third countries where it was possible that they could face torture during interrogation. The Icelandic media reported that 67 such flights had landed in Iceland since 2001. The Icelandic Government (among others) demanded an explanation from the USA, but the US Department of State refused to comment on specific allegations, or to confirm or deny claims that the CIA had established secret prisons throughout the world for this purpose.

In late March 2006 the USA announced its intention to withdraw the remaining US troops from Keflavík airbase by October of that year. The decision was received unfavourably by the Government, with the Prime Minister, Ásgrímsson, criticizing the decision as a breach of trust. A subsequent offer by the Government to contribute one-half of the annual cost of maintaining the US mission was rejected. Following his appointment as Prime Minister in June, Haarde expressed disappointment at the decision to withdraw US troops, but declared his intention to negotiate with the US Administration regarding the proposed withdrawal. In late September the new coalition Government signed an agreement with the USA, under which the USA reaffirmed its commitment to defend Iceland as a NATO ally and agreed to return the Keflavík airbase to Icelandic ownership. For its part, Iceland would pay up to 5,000m. krónur to clean contaminated land at the former US airbase and return the site to civilian use. On 30 September the USA completed the withdrawal of its troops from Iceland.

At a meeting of the North Atlantic Council in July 2007 NATO members signed an agreement over the protection of Icelandic airspace, which had been proposed by Haarde in November 2006. Under the accord, the air forces of NATO member countries would undertake military exercises and patrols in Iceland on a rotating basis at intervals of no more than four months, while the Icelandic Government would pay for technical assistance and the use by visiting forces of the facilities at the Keflavík airbase.

The importance of fishing to Iceland's economy, and fears of excessive exploitation of the fishing grounds near Iceland by foreign fleets, caused the Icelandic Government to extend its territorial waters to 12 nautical miles (22 km) in 1964 and to 50 nautical miles (93 km) in 1972. British opposition to these extensions resulted in two 'cod wars'. In October 1975 Iceland unilaterally introduced a fishing limit of 200 nautical miles (370 km), both as a conservation measure and to protect Icelandic interests. The 1973 agreement on fishing limits between Iceland and the United Kingdom expired in November 1975, and failure to reach a new agreement led to the third and most serious 'cod war'. Casualties occurred, and in February 1976 Iceland temporarily severed diplomatic relations with the United Kingdom, the first diplomatic break between two NATO countries. In June the two countries reached an agreement, and in December the British trawler fleet withdrew from Icelandic waters. In June 1979 Iceland declared its exclusive rights to the 200-mile fishing zone. Following negotiations between the EC and EFTA on the creation of the EEA, an agreement was reached (in October 1991) allowing tariff-free access to the EC for 97% of Iceland's fisheries products by 1997, while Iceland was to allow EC vessels to catch 3,000 metric tons of fish per year in its waters, in return for some access to EC waters. The EEA agreement was ratified by the Althingi in January 1993 and entered into force in January 1994.

In August 1993 a dispute developed between Iceland and Norway over fishing rights in an area of the Barents Sea fished by Iceland, over which Norway claimed jurisdiction. The dispute continued throughout 1994, and in June the Norwegian coastguards cut the nets of Icelandic trawlers fishing for cod in the disputed region. Iceland's case was weakened in January 1995, when Canada officially recognized Norway's sovereign rights over the disputed area (a fisheries protection zone extending 200 km around the Svalbard archipelago). A similar dispute arose in August 1996 between Iceland and Denmark over fishing rights in an area of the Atlantic Ocean between Iceland and Greenland (a self-governing province of Denmark). The Danish Government claimed that an agreement had been concluded in 1988 to allow fishing boats that were in possession of a licence issued in Greenland to operate in the area. Iceland, however, denied the existence of such an agreement, and announced that Danish boats would not be permitted to fish in the disputed area.

Iceland strongly criticized the moratorium on commercial whaling, imposed (for conservation purposes) by the International Whaling Commission (IWC, see p. 404) in 1986, and continued to catch limited numbers of whales for scientific purposes. However, in 1989 Iceland halted whaling, following appeals by environmental organizations for an international boycott of Icelandic products. In 1991 Iceland announced its withdrawal from the IWC (with effect from June 1992), claiming that certain species of whales were not only too plentiful to be in danger of extinction, but were also threatening Iceland's stocks of cod and other fish. In 1994 a report, commissioned by the Government, recommended that limited hunting be resumed in the future. In March 1999 the Althingi voted to end the self-imposed 10-year ban on whaling and requested the Government to implement the ruling, urging a swift resumption of hunting.

Iceland's application to rejoin the IWC, with an unprecedented exemption that would allow it to disregard the moratorium on commercial whaling, was rejected in July 2001. However, it was granted permission to attend discussions as an observer without voting rights. Its bid for full membership was rejected again in May 2002, but in October of that year Iceland was readmitted, when the Government undertook not to allow the resumption of commercial whaling until at least 2006 and after that not to resume commercial whaling while negotiations on a revised management plan were in progress. In August 2003, however, Iceland resumed whaling, provoking widespread international criticism and renewed calls for a boycott of Icelandic products. The Government authorized the capture of 38 minke whales in 2003, 25 in 2004 and 39 in 2005, ostensibly for the purpose of scientific research.

In October 2006 Iceland resumed commercial whaling, announcing that it would license the capture of nine fin whales and 30 minke whales during the year to August 2007, in addition to the 39 minke whales permitted for research purposes. The Ministry of Fisheries insisted that this was within sustainable limits, representing only 0.2% of the estimated 25,800 minke whales in Icelandic waters and less than 0.1% of the 43,600 fin whales, despite the latter's endangered status. However, whaling was halted following the killing of seven minke whales and seven fin whales, owing to a lack of consumer demand. In August 2007 the Minister of Fisheries and Agriculture, Einar Kristinn Guðfinnsson, announced the suspension of commercial whaling quotas during the forthcoming fishing season, which was due to commence in September, since meat from the 2006–07 season remained unsold.

Along with four other Nordic countries (Denmark, Finland, Norway and Sweden), Iceland was a participant in the Sri Lankan Monitoring Mission (SLMM) observing the implementation of a cease-fire agreement signed by the Sri Lankan Government and Tamil separatists in February 2002. However, the SLMM ended its operations in January 2008 after the cease-fire agreement was terminated by the Sri Lankan Government.

Government

According to the Constitution, executive power is vested in the President (elected for four years by universal adult suffrage) and the Cabinet, consisting of the Prime Minister and other ministers appointed by the President. In practice, however, the President performs only nominally the functions ascribed in the Constitution to this office, and it is the Cabinet alone that holds real executive power. Legislative power is held jointly by the President and the unicameral Althingi (parliament), with 63 members elected by universal suffrage for four years (subject to dissolution by the President), using a system of proportional representation in eight multi-member constituencies. The Cabinet is responsible to the Althingi. Municipal governments are responsible for education, infrastructure and social services. Following municipal elections held in June 2006, the number of municipalities was reduced from 105 to 79.

Defence

Apart from a 130-strong coastguard, Iceland has no defence forces of its own, but it is a member of the North Atlantic Treaty Organization (NATO, see p. 340). Until 2006 there were units of US forces at Keflavík airbase, which was used for observation of the North Atlantic Ocean, under a bilateral agreement made in 1951 between Iceland and the USA. In late September 2006 the USA withdrew its forces from Iceland, but maintained its commitment to defend Iceland as a fellow member of NATO.

Economic Affairs

In 2006, according to estimates by the World Bank, Iceland's gross national income (GNI), measured at 2004–06 prices, was US $15,121.7m., equivalent to $50,580 per head (or $36,560 per head on an international purchasing-power parity basis). During 1996–2006, it was estimated, the population increased at an average annual rate of 1.0%, while gross domestic product (GDP) per head increased, in real terms, by an average of 3.0% per year. Iceland's overall GDP increased, in real terms, at an average annual rate of 4.1% during 1996–2006; growth was 2.6% in 2006.

Agriculture (including fishing) contributed 5.9% of GDP in 2006 (fishing contributed 4.6% of GDP and agriculture alone only 1.3%); in 2007 5.9% of the employed labour force were engaged in the agricultural and fishing sectors, with a further 1.6% employed in fish processing. The principal agricultural products are dairy produce and lamb. Marine products accounted for 60.2% of total export earnings in 2004. A cod quota system is in place to avoid the depletion of fish stocks through over-fishing as happened in previous years. The decline in the catch of cod has been offset by an increase in the catch of other species, such as haddock and redfish. However, cod remains the most valuable species, accounting for 41% of the value of the total catch in 2004. During 1996–2006 agricultural GDP (including fishing) increased at an average annual rate of 0.6%; agricultural GDP (excluding fishing) increased at an average annual rate of 3.1% during 1996–2006, while the GDP of the fishing sector declined by 1.9% per year. Agricultural GDP (including fishing) decreased, in real terms, by 1.8% in 2006; the GDP of the fishing sector declined by 5.3% in the same year.

Industry (including mining, manufacturing, construction and power) contributed 24.6% of GDP in 2006 and engaged 20.7% of the employed labour force (including the 1.6% employed in fish processing) in 2007. Mining activity is negligible. During 1996–2006 industrial GDP increased at an average annual rate of 1.5%; industrial GDP declined by 11.5% in 2006.

Manufacturing contributed 10.8% of GDP in 2006, and employed 9.2% of the labour force in 2007. The most important sectors are fish processing (which contributed 1.3% of GDP in 2005), the production of aluminium, medical equipment, pharmaceuticals and ferro-silicon. Aluminium and ferro-silicon processing contributed 1.3% of GDP in 2004. A new aluminium smelter, Alcoa Fjardaál, fuelled by hydroelectric power plants, opened in 2007, with a production capacity of 322,000 metric tons per year. Three more proposals for aluminium smelters with power plants were submitted in 2007, provoking protests from environmentalists, who had opposed the Alcoa project. Site preparation for a new aluminium smelter near Helguvik began in March 2008; the new facility was to be constructed in stages, with the first stage, with a production capacity of 150,000 tons per year, expected to be in production by late 2010. Manufacturing GDP (including fish processing) increased, in real terms, at an average annual rate of 3.1% in 1995–2005; it grew by 6.1% in 2004 but declined by 1.3% in 2005.

Iceland is potentially rich in hydroelectric and geothermal power, and both energy sources are significantly underexploited. It was estimated in 2005 that only 17% of Iceland's energy potential for generating electricity has been exploited. Hydroelectric power has promoted the development of the aluminium industry, while geothermal energy provides nearly all the country's heating and hot water. In 2004 hydroelectric power provided 82.7% of the country's electricity. Fuel imports comprised 9.4% of the value of merchandise imports in 2005. In 2001 Iceland announced its intention to develop the world's first economy free of carbon dioxide emissions by using hydrogen or methanol-powered fuel cells. Hydrogen-fuelled buses began operating in Reykjavík in 2003. Two new hydroelectric power plants in the east of the country, the Kárahnjúkar Hydroelectric Project, built amidst much controversy to fuel the Alcoa Fjardaál smelter, were officially opened in June 2007.

Services contributed 69.5% of GDP in 2006 and employed 73.3% of the labour force in 2007. GDP from services increased, in real terms, at an average annual rate of 6.7% during 1996–2006; it grew by 6.1% in 2006. Banking is an important sector in Iceland, with the financial sector providing 9.7% of GDP in 2005. The tourism sector is becoming an increasingly significant source of revenue; the number of overnight stays by foreign visitors in hotels and guest houses totalled 1,719,140 in 2006; receipts from tourism totalled US $631m. in 2005.

In 2006 Iceland recorded a visible trade deficit of US $2,097m., while there was a deficit of $4,365m. on the current account of the balance of payments. In 2006 the principal sources of imports were the USA (providing 13.1% of total imports), Germany (12.4%), Norway (7.2%) and Denmark (6.6%); the principal market for exports was the Netherlands (accounting for 16.6% of total exports), followed by the United Kingdom (15.6%), Germany (15.0%), and the USA (10.1%). In 2006 member countries of the European Economic Area—EEA (see p. 412) provided 68.7% of Iceland's merchandise imports and took 81.2% of its exports. The principal imports in 2004 were industrial products (25%), capital goods (22%) and transport equipment (17%, including road vehicles, which accounted for 11% of the total value of exports). The principal exports in the same year were marine products (60.2%), aluminium and ferro-silicon (21.1%), other manufactured goods (14.1%) and agricultural products (2.1%).

In 2007 there was a budgetary surplus of 66.6m. krónur. Iceland's net external debt was 153,900m. krónur at the end of 2007. The cost of debt-servicing was equivalent to 1.5% of GDP in 2005. The annual rate of inflation averaged 3.9% in 1996–2006; consumer prices increased by 5.0% in 2007. The unemployment rate was 2.3% in 2007.

Iceland is a member of the European Free Trade Association (EFTA, see p. 412) and the Organisation for Economic Co-operation and Development (OECD, see p. 347). Although Iceland is not a member of the European Union (EU, see p. 244), it joined the EEA (see p. 412) in 1994 and was thereby integrated into the EU internal market.

During the late 1990s the Icelandic economy expanded rapidly, partly as a result of the recovery of the fishing industry and the global economy, but largely owing to the liberalization of the economy through extensive deregulation and restructuring (begun in the early 1990s). The financial sector benefited from the liberalization of capital flows and a series of privatizations, while significant biotechnology and information technology industries were developed and the tourism sector expanded rapidly. The construction of a large aluminium smelting plant and associated hydroelectric power plants (including a controversial dam) in Kárahnjúkar in the Eastern Highlands, commenced in 2003 and was completed in 2007. Although these large projects, which were led by foreign investment, promoted strong GDP growth, they also threatened economic stability as they contributed to rising current account deficits, increased inflationary pressures and raised levels of foreign debt. Inflationary pressures caused by the construction work in Kárahnjúkar and high domestic demand led to a sharp increase in consumer prices, which was exacerbated by rapid rises in house prices, as a result of a significant increase in inexpensive mortgage credit. Despite the flexibility in the immigration system, labour shortages, which had been a problem for several years, owing to the high demand for labour for the construction of the aluminium and power projects, escalated further in 2007. The scarcity of labour contributed to a rapid increase in wages, which in addition to the effect of tax cuts, led to a significant increase in disposable incomes and thus a large growth in domestic demand. The growth in the Icelandic economy was also due to the rapid expansion of the three major commercial banks, Kaupþing Banki, Glitnir Banki and Landsbanki Islands. This growth resulted in an increase in foreign funding and a growing dependence on access to international capital markets, which became problematic in late 2007, owing to the global liquidity problem caused by defaults on US mortgages. The rapid growth of the economy in Iceland has created imbalances: an unsustainable deficit on the current account, large external debts and high levels of inflation. These factors undermined investor confidence in 2007 and early 2008, precipitating a decline in the value of the stock exchange and a dramatic depreciation of the currency, which caused inflation to rise further. Interest rates were raised to 15% in March 2008 in an attempt to restore confidence in the króna, which had declined by about 30% against the euro in that year. However, Iceland's current account deficit declined from 25.5% of GDP in 2006 to 16.0% in 2007, the budget remained in surplus and the banks were fundamentally healthy. The Prime Minister suggested in early 2008 that the banks should postpone their expansion strategy to ease concerns about the economy from investors. Iceland has benefited greatly from its membership of the EEA, but remained reluctant to join the EU, owing to the potentially adverse effects of the Common Fisheries Policy on the Icelandic fishing industry. An application by the Icelandic bank Kaupþing to record its financial accounts and statements in euros was refused by the central bank in early 2008. Other banks were also keen to switch currencies, claiming the euro would offer greater exchange rate certainty and reflect their expansion into Europe.

Education

Education is compulsory and free for 10 years between six and 16 years of age (primary and lower secondary levels). Upper secondary education begins at 16 years of age and usually lasts for four years. In 2006 93% of 16 year-olds were enrolled in upper secondary-level education. In 2004 Iceland had 17 institutions providing tertiary-level education. In 2006 16,738 students were enrolled in tertiary-level education. Budgetary expenditure by the Ministry of Education, Science and Culture was forecast at 46,252m. krónur in 2007, representing 12.6% of total estimated public expenditure. Municipalities are responsible for pre-primary and compulsory education, although institutions at those levels follow National Curriculum Guidelines formulated by the Ministry of Education, Science and Culture. The Government is responsible for upper secondary and higher education.

Public Holidays

2008: 1 January (New Year's Day), 20 March (Maundy Thursday), 21 March (Good Friday), 24 March (Easter Monday), 24 April (First Day of Summer), 1 May (Labour Day and Ascension Day), 12 May (Whit Monday), 17 June (National Day), 4 August (Bank Holiday), 24 December (Christmas Eve)*, 25 December (Christmas Day), 26 December (Boxing Day), 31 December (New Year's Eve)*.

ICELAND

2009: 1 January (New Year's Day), 9 April (Maundy Thursday), 10 April (Good Friday), 13 April (Easter Monday), 23 April (First Day of Summer), 1 May (Labour Day), 21 May (Ascension Day), 1 June (Whit Monday), 17 June (National Day), 3 August (Bank Holiday), 24 December (Christmas Eve)*, 25 December (Christmas Day), 26 December (Boxing Day), 31 December (New Year's Eve)*.

Note: Holidays falling on a Saturday or Sunday will not be taken on the following Monday.
* Afternoon only.

Weights and Measures
The metric system is in force.

Statistical Survey

Sources (unless otherwise stated): Statistics Iceland, Borgartúni 21A, 150 Reykjavík; tel. 5281000; fax 5281099; e-mail statice@statice.is; internet www.statice.is; Seðlabanki Íslands (Central Bank of Iceland), Kalkofnsvegur 1, 150 Reykjavík; tel. 5699600; fax 5699605; e-mail sedlabanki@sedlabanki.is; internet www.sedlabanki.is.

AREA AND POPULATION

Area: 103,000 sq km (39,769 sq miles).

Population: 311,396 (males 158,866, females 152,530) at 1 July 2007 (national population register).

Density (per sq km): 3.0 (at 1 July 2007).

Principal Towns (population at 1 July 2007): Reykjavík (capital) 117,598; Kópavogur 28,032; Hafnarfjörður 24,455; Akureyri 16,964; Þéttbýli í Reykjanesbæ 12,327.

Births, Marriages and Deaths (2006): Live births 4,415 (birth rate 14.3 per 1,000); Marriages 1,681 (marriage rate 5.5 per 1,000); Deaths 1,901 (death rate 6.2 per 1,000).

Expectation of Life (years at birth, WHO estimates): 81.0 (males 79.2; females 82.8) in 2005. Source: WHO, *World Health Statistics*.

Economically Active Population (2007, figures rounded to nearest 10 persons): Agriculture 6,000; Fishing 4,500; Manufacturing (excl. fish-processing) 16,300; Fish-processing 2,900; Electricity and water supply 1,700; Construction 15,700; Wholesale and retail trade, repairs 25,400; Restaurants and hotels 6,200; Transport, storage and communications 11,100; Financial intermediation 8,700; Real estate and business services 17,200; Public administration 8,900; Education 13,500; Health services and social work 26,000; Other services not specified 12,600; *Total employed* (incl. unclassified) 177,300; Unemployed 4,200; *Total labour force* 181,500.

HEALTH AND WELFARE
Key Indicators

Total Fertility Rate (children per woman, 2005): 1.9.

Under-5 Mortality Rate (per 1,000 live births, 2005): 3.

HIV/AIDS (% of persons aged 15–49, 2005): 0.2.

Physicians (per 1,000 head, 2004): 3.62.

Hospital Beds (per 1,000 head, 2002): 7.5.

Health Expenditure (2004): US $ per head (PPP): 3,294.4.

Health Expenditure (2004): % of GDP: 9.9.

Health Expenditure (2004): public (% of total): 83.4.

Human Development Index (2005): ranking: 1.

Human Development Index (20045): value: 0.968.

For sources and definitions, see explanatory note on p. vi.

AGRICULTURE, ETC.

Principal Crops (metric tons, 2006, unless otherwise indicated): Cereals 11,253; Carrots 398; Cabbages 398*; Tomatoes 1,724*; Cucumbers 1,124*; Cauliflower 83*; Turnips 666 (2004 figure); Pepper 130*; Chinese cabbage 219*; Mushrooms 488*.
* Estimate.

Livestock (2006): Cattle 68,670; Sheep 455,656; Horses 75,644; Goats 449; Pigs 4,218; Hens 181,857; Other poultry 27,992; Mink 41,957; Foxes 116; Rabbits 254.

Livestock Products (metric tons, unless otherwise indicated, 2006): Sheep meat 8,7; Cattle meat 3,540; Horse meat 762; Pig meat 5,300; Chicken meat 5,766; Milk ('000 litres, processed) 109,445; Eggs 2,800. Source: FAO.

Fishing (metric tons, live weight, 2006): Atlantic cod 199,375; Saithe 75,460; Haddock 96,591; Atlantic redfishes 82,595; Capelin 184,431; Atlantic herring 291,380; Total (incl. others) 1,322,914.

INDUSTRY

Selected Products ('000 metric tons, 2005, unless otherwise indicated): Frozen fish 292.6 (demersal catch, 2002); Salted, dried or smoked fish 110.7 (2002); Cement 132.4; Ferro-silicon 114.8; Aluminium (unwrought) 273.3; Electric energy 8,680 million kWh. Source: partly US Geological Survey.

FINANCE

Currency and Exchange Rates: 100 aurar (singular: eyrir) = 1 new Icelandic króna (plural: krónur). *Sterling, Dollar and Euro Equivalents* (31 December 2007): £1 sterling = 123.910 krónur; US $1 = 61.850 krónur; €1 = 91.049 krónur; 1,000 krónur = £8.07 = $16.17 = €10.98. *Average Exchange Rate* (krónur per US $): 62.982 in 2005; 70.195 in 2006; 64.088 in 2007.

Budget (general government finances, million krónur, 2007): *Revenue:* Tax revenue 487,730 (Taxes on income and profits 242,828, Taxes on payroll and workforce 1,380, Taxes on property 29,130, Taxes on goods and services 206,939, Taxes on international trade 5,865, Other taxes 1,588); Social contributions 40,493; Grants 1,463; Other revenue 87,851 (Property income 42,979, Sales of goods and services 40,059, Fines, penalties and forfeits 2,093, Voluntary transfers other than grants 1,646, Miscellaneous and unidentified revenue 1,074); Total 617,537. *Expenditure:* Current expenditure 519,076 (Compensation of employees 198,215, Use of goods and services 133,447, Consumption of fixed capital 22,829, Interest 29,127, Subsidies 21,056, Grants 2,863, Social benefits 75,790, Other expenditure 35,749); Non-financial assets 31,848; Total 550,924.

International Reserves (US $ million at 31 December 2006): Gold (national valuation) 40.9; Reserve position in IMF 28.0; Foreign exchange 2,273.2; Total 2,342.1. Source: IMF, *International Financial Statistics*.

Money Supply (million krónur at 31 December 2006): Currency outside banks 11,471; Demand deposits at commercial and savings banks 191,111; Total money 202,583. Source: IMF, *International Financial Statistics*.

Cost of Living (Consumer Price Index for Reykjavík; average of monthly figures; base: May 1988 = 100): 244.1 in 2005; 260.6 in 2006; 273.7 in 2007.

Gross Domestic Product (million krónur at constant 2000 prices): 843,029 in 2005; 880,365 in 2006; 914,212 in 2007.

National Income and Product (million krónur at current prices, 2006, estimates): Compensation of employees 685,993; Gross operating surplus 268,545; *Gross domestic product at factor cost* 954,538; Taxes on production and imports 206,392; *Less* Subsidies 19,182; *Gross domestic product in market prices* 1,141,747; Net primary incomes received from abroad −98,567; *Gross national income* 1,043,180.

Expenditure on the Gross Domestic Product (million krónur at current prices, 2007, estimates): Government final consumption expenditure 314,433; Private final consumption expenditure 746,582; Increase in stocks 2,952; Gross fixed capital formation 351,613; *Total domestic expenditure* 1,415,579; Exports of goods and services 451,743; *Less* Imports of goods and services 587,943; *Gross domestic product in market prices* 1,279,379.

Gross Domestic Product by Economic Activity (million krónur at current prices, 2005): Agriculture, hunting and forestry 10,859; Fishing 38,830; Mining and quarrying 817; Manufacturing 86,043; Electricity, gas and water supply 33,931; Construction 80,639; Wholesale and retail trade and repair of vehicles and household goods 92,130; Hotels and restaurants 12,649; Transport, storage and communications 53,070; Financial intermediation 83,166; Real estate, renting and business services 146,750; Public administration and compulsory social security 51,531; Education 52,293; Health and social work 85,436; Other community, social and personal services 29,745; Private households with employed persons 572; *Sub-total* 858,461; Correction item, taxes and subsidies on products 5,009; *Gross value added at basic prices* 863,470; Taxes on production and imports 167,532; *Less* Subsidies 9,492; *GDP in market prices* 1,021,510.

Balance of Payments (US $ million, 2006): Exports of goods f.o.b. 3,477; Imports of goods f.o.b. −5,574; *Trade balance* −2,097; Exports of services 1,806; Imports of services −2,587; *Balance on goods and services* −2,878; Other income received 2,336; Other income paid −3,789; *Balance on goods, services and income* −4,330; Current transfers received 8; Current transfers paid −43; *Current balance* −4,365; Capital account (net) −26; Direct investment abroad −4,172; Direct investment from abroad 3,266; Portfolio investment assets −3,471; Portfolio investment liabilities 15,896; Other investment assets −11,371; Other investment liabilities 6,961; Net errors and omissions −1,466; *Overall balance* 1,252. Source: IMF, *International Financial Statistics*.

EXTERNAL TRADE

Principal Commodities (distribution by SITC, million krónur, 2006): *Imports c.i.f.:* Food and live animals 23,754.6; Crude materials, inedible 23,232.1 (Metalliferous ores and metal scrap 16,119.9); Mineral fuels and lubricants 37,381.8 (Petroleum and petroleum products 34,814.3); Chemicals and related products 29,586.7 (Medicinal and pharmaceutical products 8,436.2); Basic manufactures 60,988 (Metal products 19,407.2); Machinery and transport equipment 199,071.3 (Machinery specialized for particular industries 20,796.3; General industrial machinery and equipment 26,284.6; Office machines and computers 9,882.6; Other electrical machinery, apparatus and appliances 30,692.2; Road vehicles 45,951.3; Other transport equipment 45,382.0); Miscellaneous manufactured articles 52,813.1 (Apparel and clothing accessories 10,965.3); Total (incl. others) 432,106.3. *Exports f.o.b.:* Food and live animals 125,315.7 (Fish, crustaceans, molluscs and preparations thereof 114,005.7; Animal feeds, excl. unmilled cereals 10,162.4); Chemicals and related products 6,695.5 (Medicinal and pharmaceutical products 5,728.6); Basic manufactures n.a.; Machinery and transport equipment n.a.; Total (incl. others) 242,740.0.

Principal Trading Partners (million krónur, country of consignment, 2006): *Imports c.i.f.:* Belgium 6,656.0; Canada 1,395.0; China, People's Republic 20,595.9; Denmark (incl. Faroe Islands and Greenland) 27,804.7; Finland 5,928.0; France 16,950.5; Germany 52,306.5; Ireland 8,479.3; Italy 14,089.5; Japan 17,931.1; Netherlands 20,905.5; Norway 30,395.8; Poland, 4,718.7; Russia 1,507.4; Spain 5,805.1; Suriname 3,846.4; Sweden 29,961.1; Switzerland 9,217.1; United Kingdom 22,647.6; USA 55,465.4; Total (incl. others) 422,254.4. *Exports f.o.b.:* Belgium 4,734.7; Denmark (incl. Faroe Islands and Greenland) 11,808.1; France 8,224.5; Germany 36,345.5; Italy 1,829.3; Japan 5,019.2; Netherlands 40,317.7; Nigeria 3,837.4; Norway 9,633.1; Portugal 5,458.3; Poland 1,900.7; Russia 4,653.4; Spain 15,452.2; Sweden 2,201.5; Switzerland 5,879.0; United Kingdom 37,939.3; USA 26,131.3; Total (incl. others) 242,740.0.

TRANSPORT

Road Traffic (registered motor vehicles, 2005): Passenger cars 187,442; Buses and coaches 1,899; Goods vehicles 25,544; Motorcycles 4,183.

Shipping: *Merchant Fleet* (registered vessels, 31 December 2006): Vessels 271; Displacement 184,187 grt (Source: Lloyds-Fairplay, *World Fleet Statistics*). *International Freight Traffic* ('000 metric tons, 2003): Goods loaded 1,800.7; Goods unloaded 3,179.9.

Civil Aviation (scheduled traffic, 2003): Kilometres flown (million) 25; Passengers ('000) 1,134; Passenger-kilometres (million) 2,998; Total ton-kilometres (million) 378. Source: UN, *Statistical Yearbook*.

TOURISM

Overnight Stays by Foreign Visitors in Hotels and Guesthouses, by Country of Origin (2006): Denmark 112,640; France 132,808; Germany 286,728; Italy 69,353; Netherlands 82,525; Norway 80,773; Spain 56,223; Sweden 88,805; Switzerland 50,565; United Kingdom 246,590; USA 154,760; Total (incl. others) 1,719,140.

Receipts from Tourism (US $ million, incl. passenger transport): 486 in 2003; 558 in 2004; 631 in 2005 (Source: World Tourism Organization).

COMMUNICATIONS MEDIA

Radio Receivers (2002): 94,840 licensed.

Television Receivers (2002): 91,952 licensed.

Telephones (2006): 193,700 main lines in use. Source: International Telecommunication Union.

Facsimile Machines (1993): 4,100 in use. Source: UN, *Statistical Yearbook*.

Mobile Cellular Telephones ('000 subscribers, 2006): 328.5. Source: International Telecommunication Union.

Personal Computers ('000 in use, 2005): 142. Source: International Telecommunication Union.

Internet Users ('000, 2006): 194.0. Source: International Telecommunication Union.

Broadband Subscribers ('000, 2006): 87.7. Source: International Telecommunication Union.

Books (production, 2004): 1,499 titles (incl. new editions).

Daily Newspapers (2004): 3 (combined circulation 161,571 copies per issue).

EDUCATION

Institutions (2004 unless otherwise indicated): Pre-primary 267 (2006); Primary and secondary (lower level) 173 (2006); Secondary (higher level) 37; Tertiary (universities and colleges) 17.

Teachers (incl. part-time, 2005 unless otherwise indicated): Pre-primary 5,012; Primary and secondary (lower level) 4,961; Secondary (higher level) 2,358 (2004); Tertiary 2,436 (2004).

Students (2006): Pre-primary 17,216; Primary and Secondary (lower level) 43,875; Secondary (higher level) 24,459; Tertiary 16,738.

Directory

The Constitution

The Constitution came into force on 17 June 1944, when Iceland became an independent Republic. The main provisions of the Constitution, including subsequent amendments, are summarized below:

GOVERNMENT

Legislative power is vested jointly in the President of the Republic and the Althingi (Alþingi). Executive power is vested in the President. The authority vested in the President shall be exercised through the Cabinet. The President appoints the Ministers to the Cabinet under the auspices of the Prime Minister, or the Prime Minister-elect when a new Cabinet is being assembled. The President may be dismissed only if a resolution supported by three-quarters of the Alþingi is approved by a plebiscite.

The President is elected for four years by universal suffrage. All those qualified to vote who have reached the age of 35 years are eligible for the presidency.

The Alþingi is composed of 63 Members, elected by the people by secret ballot on the basis of proportional representation, for four years, in a minimum of six and a maximum of seven multi-member constituencies. The franchise for general elections to the Alþingi is universal above the age of 18. Every national having the right to vote and an unblemished reputation is eligible to be elected to the Alþingi, except for the Justices of the Supreme Court. Seats that fall vacant between legislative elections are filled by substitutes elected at the same time as titular Members.

The Alþingi is convened by the President for a regular session every year on 1 October and continues in session until the same date next year, unless the election period of its Members has elapsed earlier or it has been dissolved. The President may adjourn meetings of the Alþingi, but not for more than two weeks not more than once a year. The President may dissolve the Alþingi. Elections must then be held within two months and the Alþingi must reassemble within eight months. Sessions are held in one chamber and its meetings are public. The Alþingi elects a Speaker, who presides over its proceedings.

ICELAND

Legislative bills are either submitted to the Alþingi by the President through his/her Ministers or by individual Members of the Alþingi. Bills must be given three readings in the Alþingi and be approved by a simple majority before they are submitted to the President. If the President disapproves a bill it nevertheless becomes valid, but must be submitted to a plebiscite.

Each Member of the Alþingi has the right to request, subject to the permission of the Alþingi, information from a Minister or an answer, orally or in writing, regarding a public matter, by tabling a question or requesting a report. Ministers are responsible to the Alþingi and may be impeached by that body, in which case they are tried by the Court of Impeachment.

LOCAL GOVERNMENT

Iceland is divided into 79 municipalities (from 2006), which have definite geographical boundaries and cover the entire island. These municipalities are undergoing a process of amalgamation, which is expected to continue for several years. In each municipality there is a municipal council, elected every four years. All citizens over the age of 18 years are eligible to vote. In larger municipalities councillors are elected by proportional representation and frequently on party political lines. In the smallest rural areas councillors are usually elected on an individual basis. Municipal councils are enacted to set their own property rates and local income taxes, within certain limits determined by law. A municipal executive council (elected every year) is in charge of the chief administration, including municipal finances, budgeting, personnel and legal matters. Executive councils may also take charge of infrastructural investments and public works.

The Government

HEAD OF STATE

President: ÓLAFUR RAGNAR GRÍMSSON (took office 1 August 1996; began a second term in August 2000; re-elected 26 June 2004).

THE CABINET
(March 2008)

A coalition of the Independence Party (IP) and The Alliance (A).

Prime Minister: GEIR H. HAARDE (IP).
Minister of Foreign Affairs: INGIBJÖRG SÓLRÚN GÍSLADÓTTIR (A).
Minister of Justice and Ecclesiastical Affairs: BJÖRN BJARNASON (IP).
Minister of Finance: ÁRNI M. MATHIESEN (IP).
Minister of Social Affairs: JÓHANNA SIGURÐARDÓTTIR (A).
Minister of Education, Science and Culture: ÞORGERÐUR KATRÍN GUNNARSDÓTTIR (IP).
Minister of Industry and Minister for Nordic Co-operation: ÖSSUR SKARPHÉÐINSSON (A).
Minister of Fisheries and of Agriculture: EINAR KRISTINN GUÐFINNSSON (IP).
Minister of the Environment: ÞÓRUNN SVEINBJARNARDÓTTIR (A).
Minister of Communications: KRISTJÁN L. MÖLLER (A).
Minister of Commerce: BJÖRGVIN G. SIGURÐSSON (A).
Minister of Health and Social Security: GUÐLAUGUR ÞÓR ÞÓRÐARSON (IP).

MINISTRIES

Office of the President: Stadastaður, Sóleyjargötu 1, 150 Reykjavík; tel. 5404400; fax 5624802; e-mail president@president.is; internet www.president.is.
Prime Minister's Office: Stjórnarráðshúsinu við Lækjartorg, 150 Reykjavík; tel. 5458400; fax 5624014; e-mail postur@for.stjr.is; internet www.forsaetisraduneyti.is.
Ministry of Agriculture and Fisheries: Skúlagötu 4, 150 Reykjavík; tel. 5458300; fax 5521160; e-mail postur@slr.stjr.is; internet www.sjavarutvegsraduneyti.is.is.
Ministry of Commerce: Sölvhólsgötu 7, 150 Reykjavík; tel. 5458800; fax 5111161; e-mail postur@vrn.stjr.is; internet www.vidskiptaraduneyti.is.
Ministry of Communications: Hafnarhúsinu við Tryggvagötu, 150 Reykjavík; tel. 5458200; fax 5621702; e-mail postur@sam.stjr.is; internet www.samgonguraduneyti.is.
Ministry of Education, Science and Culture: Sölvhólsgötu 4, 150 Reykjavík; tel. 5459500; fax 5623068; e-mail postur@mrn.stjr.is; internet www.menntamalaraduneyti.is.
Ministry of the Environment: Skuggasundi 1, 150 Reykjavík; tel. 5458600; fax 5624566; e-mail postur@environment.is; internet www.environment.is.
Ministry of Finance: Arnarhvoli við Lindargötu, 150 Reykjavík; tel. 5459200; fax 5628280; e-mail postur@fjr.stjr.is; internet www.ministryoffinance.is.
Ministry for Foreign Affairs: Rauðarárstíg 25, 150 Reykjavík; tel. 5459900; fax 5622373; e-mail postur@utn.stjr.is; internet www.utanrikisraduneyti.is.
Ministry of Health and Social Security: Vegmúla 3, 150 Reykjavík; tel. 5458700; fax 5519165; e-mail postur@hbr.stjr.is; internet www.heilbrigdisraduneyti.is.
Ministry of Industry: Arnarhvoli, 150 Reykjavík; tel. 5458500; fax 5621289; e-mail postur@ivr.stjr.is; internet www.idnadarraduneyti.is.
Ministry of Justice and Ecclesiastical Affairs: Skuggasundi, 150 Reykjavík; tel. 5459000; fax 5527340; e-mail postur@dkm.stjr.is; internet www.domsmalaraduneyti.is.
Ministry of Social Affairs: Hafnarhúsinu við Tryggvagötu, 150 Reykjavík; tel. 5458100; fax 5524804; e-mail postur@fel.stjr.is; internet www.felagsmalaraduneyti.is.

President and Legislature

PRESIDENT

Presidential Election, 26 June 2004

	% of votes
Ólafur Ragnar Grímsson	85.6
Baldur Ágústsson	12.3
Ástþór Magnússon	1.9

LEGISLATURE

Althingi
(Alþingi)

v/Austurvöll, 150 Reykjavík; tel. 5630500; fax 5630920; e-mail editor@althingi.is; internet www.althingi.is.

Speaker of the Alþingi: STURLA BÖÐVARSSON (IP).
Secretary-General (Clerk) of the Alþingi: HELGI BERNÓDUSSON.

General Election, 12 May 2007

Party	Votes	% of votes	Seats
Sjálfstæðisflokkurinn (Independence Party)	66,749	36.6	25
Samfylkingin (The Alliance)	48,742	26.8	18
Vinstrihreyfingin—grænt framboð (Left-Green Movement)	26,136	14.3	9
Framsóknarflokkurinn (Progressive Party)	21,349	11.7	7
Frjálslyndi flokkurinn (Liberal Party)	13,233	7.3	4
Íslandshreyfingin (Icelandic Movement)	5,953	3.3	—
Total	**182,162**	**100.0**	**63**

Political Organizations

Framsóknarflokkurinn (Progressive Party—PP): Hverfisgötu 33, POB 453, 101 Reykjavík; tel. 5404300; fax 5404301; e-mail framsokn@framsokn.is; internet www.framsokn.is; f. 1916 with a programme of social liberalism and co-operation; Chair. GUÐNI ÁGÚSTSSON; Parliamentary Leader SIV FRIÐLEIFSDÓTTIR.

Frjálslyndi flokkurinn (Liberal Party): Austurstræti 14, 2nd Floor, 101 Reykjavík; tel. 5522600; e-mail xf@xf.is; internet www.xf.is; f. 1998 by Sverrir Hermannsson, a former IP cabinet minister; incorporated fmr mems of defunct Nýtt Afl (New Force) in 2006; Leader GUÐJÓN ARNAR KRISTJÁNSSON; Parliamentary Leader KRISTINN H. GUNNARSSON.

Íslandshreyfingin—lifandi land (Icelandic Movement—Living Land): Bankastræti 11, 101 Reykjavík; tel. 6942100; e-mail islandshreyfingin@islandshreyfingin.is; internet www.islandshreyfingin.is; f. 2007; environmentalist, liberal; opposed to industrial development in Icelandic highlands; Leader ÓMAR RAGNARSSON.

Samfylkingin (The Alliance): Hallveigarstíg 1, 101 Reykjavík; tel. 4142200; fax 4142201; e-mail samfylking@samfylking.is; internet www.samfylking.is; f. 1999 by merger of Alþýðubandalagið (People's

ICELAND

Alliance, f. 1956), Alþýðuflokkurinn (Social Democratic Party, f. 1916), Samtök um kvennalista (Women's List, f. 1983) and Þjóðvaki—hreyfing fólksins (Awakening of the Nation—People's Movement, f. 1994); Chair. INGIBJÖRG SOLRÚN GÍSLADÓTTIR; Parliamentary Leader LÚÐVÍK BERGVINSSON.

Sjálfstæðisflokkurinn (Independence Party—IP): Háaleitisbraut 1, 105 Reykjavík; tel. 5151700; fax 5151717; e-mail xd@xd.is; internet www.xd.is; f. 1929 by an amalgamation of the Conservative and Liberal Parties; advocates social reform within the framework of private enterprise and the furtherance of national and individual independence; Leader GEIR H. HAARDE; Parliamentary Leader ARNBJÖRG SVEINSDÓTTIR; Sec.-Gen. ANDRI OTTARSSON.

Vinstrihreyfingin—grænt framboð (Left-Green Movement): Suðurgötu 3, POB 175, 101 Reykjavík; tel. 5528872; e-mail vg@vg.is; internet www.vg.is; f. 1999 by dissident mems of the People's Alliance, the Women's List, the Greens and independent left-wingers; around 3,000 mems; Leader STEINGRÍMUR J. SIGFÚSSON; Parliamentary Leader ÖGMUNDUR JÓNASSON; Sec.-Gen. DRIFA SNAEDAL.

Diplomatic Representation

EMBASSIES IN ICELAND

Canada: POB 1510, 121 Reykjavík; Túngata 14, 101 Reykjavík; tel. 5756500; fax 5756501; e-mail rkjvk@international.gc.ca; internet www.canada.is; Ambassador ANNA BLAUVELDT.

China, People's Republic: Víðimelur 29, 107 Reykjavík; tel. 5526751; fax 5626110; e-mail chinaemb_is@mfa.gov.cn; internet is .china-embassy.org; Ambassador ZHANG KEYUAN.

Denmark: Hverfisgata 29, 101 Reykjavík; tel. 5750300; fax 5750310; e-mail rekamb@um.dk; internet www.ambreykjavik.um.dk; Ambassador LASSE REIMANN.

Finland: Túngata 30, 101 Reykjavík; tel. 5100100; fax 5623880; e-mail sanomat.rey@formin.fi; internet www.finland.is; Ambassador KAI GRANHOLM.

France: Túngata 22, 101 Reykjavík; tel. 5759600; fax 5759604; e-mail alain.fortin@diplomatie.gouv.fr; internet www.ambafrance.is; Ambassador OLIVIER MAUVISSEAU.

Germany: Laufásvegur 31, 101 Reykjavík; tel. 5301100; fax 5301101; e-mail info@reykjavik.diplo.de; internet www.reykjavik.diplo.de; Ambassador Dr KARL-ULRICH MÜLLER.

Japan: Laugavegur 182, POB 5380, 105 Reykjavík; tel. 5108600; fax 5108605; e-mail japan@itn.is; Ambassador HISAO YAMAGUCHI (resident in Oslo, Norway).

Norway: Fjólugötu 17, 101 Reykjavík; tel. 5200700; fax 5529553; e-mail emb.reykjavik@mfa.no; internet www.noregur.is; Ambassador MARGIT F. TVEITEN.

Russia: Garðastræti 33, 101 Reykjavík; tel. 5515156; fax 5620633; e-mail russemb@itn.is; internet www.iceland.mid.ru; Ambassador VIKTOR I. TATARINTSEV.

Sweden: POB 8136, 128 Reykjavík; Lágmúla 7, 108 Reykjavík; tel. 5201230; fax 5201235; e-mail embassy.reykjavik@foreign.ministry.se; internet www.swedenabroad.com/reykjavik; Ambassador MADELEINE STRÖJE-WILKENS.

United Kingdom: POB 460, 121 Reykjavík; Laufásvegur 31, 101 Reykjavík; tel. 5505100; fax 5505105; e-mail postmaster@britishembassy.is; internet www.britishembassy.is; Ambassador ALPER (ALP) MEHMET.

USA: Laufásvegur 21, 101 Reykjavík; tel. 5629100; fax 5629110; e-mail reykjavikconsular@state.gov; internet iceland.usembassy.gov; Ambassador CAROL VAN VOORST.

Judicial System

All cases are heard in Ordinary Courts except those specifically within the jurisdiction of Special Courts. The Ordinary Courts include both a lower division of urban and rural district courts presided over by the district magistrates, and the Supreme Court.

Justices of the Supreme Court are appointed by the President and cannot be dismissed except by the decision of a court. The Justices elect the Chief Justice for a period of two years.

Supreme Court

Dómhúsið v. Arnarhól, 150 Reykjavík; tel. 5103030; fax 5623995; e-mail haestirettur@haestirettur.is; internet www.haestirettur.is.

Chief Justice: ÁRNI KOLBEINSSON.

Justices: ÁRNI KOLBEINSSON, GARÐAR GÍSLASON, HJÖRDÍS HÁKONARDÓTTIR, INGIBJÖRG BENEDIKTSDÓTTIR, JÓN STEINAR GUNNLAUGSSON, MARKÚS SIGURBJÖRNSSON, ÓLAFUR BÖRKUR ÞORVALDSSON, PÁLL HREINSSON.

Religion

In 2007 80.7% of the total population were members of the Þjóðkirkja Íslands (Evangelical Lutheran Church of Iceland). The Lutheran Free Churches had a total membership of 4.0% of the population, and 6.3% were members of 25 other recognized and registered religious organizations, including the Roman Catholic Church and the First Baptist Church. A further 6.2% belonged to 'other or unspecified religious organizations' (religions, such as Judaism, which have been practised in the country for years without requesting official recognition), while 2.8% were not part of any religious organization.

CHRISTIANITY

Protestant Churches

Þjóðkirkja Íslands (Evangelical Lutheran Church of Iceland): Biskupsstofa, Laugavegur 31, 150 Reykjavík; tel. 5351500; fax 5513284; e-mail kirkjan@kirkjan.is; internet www.kirkjan.is; the national Church, endowed by the State; Iceland forms one diocese, with two suffragan sees; 280 parishes and 150 pastors; Bishop KARL SIGURBJÖRNSSON.

A further 19 Protestant churches are officially registered, the largest of which are the following:

Fríkirkjusöfnuðurinn í Hafnarfirði (Hafnarfjörður Free Lutheran Church): Linnetsstíg 6-8, 220 Hafnarfjörður; tel. 5653430; e-mail einar@frikirkja.is; internet www.frikirkja.is; 5,024 mems (2007); Head EINAR EYJÓLFSSON.

Fríkirkjusöfnuðurinn í Reykjavík (Reykjavík Free Lutheran Church): POB 1671, 121 Reykjavík; Laufásvegi 13, 101 Reykjavík; tel. 5527270; fax 5527287; e-mail frikirkjan@frikirkjan.is; internet www.frikirkjan.is; f. 1899; Free Lutheran denomination; 7,498 mems (2007); Head HJÖRTUR MAGNI JÓHANNSSON.

Hvítasunnukirkjan á Íslandi (Pentecostal Church): Hátúni 2, 105 Reykjavík; internet www.gospel.is; 1,963 mems (2007); Head JÓN ÞÓR EYJÓLFSSON.

Óháði söfnuðurinn (Independent Congregation): Háteigsvegi 56, 105 Reykjavík; tel. 551099; e-mail afdjoflun@tv.is; internet www.ohadisofnudurinn.is; Free Lutheran denomination; 2,768 mems (2007); Head Rev. PÉTUR ÞORSTEINSSON.

The Roman Catholic Church

Iceland comprises a single diocese, directly responsible to the Holy See. At 31 December 2005 there were an estimated 6,451 adherents in the country (about 2.2% of the total population).

Bishop of Reykjavík: Most Rev. PIERRE BÜRCHER, POB 490, 121 Reykjavík; Biskupsstofa, Hávallagata 14, 101 Reykjavík; tel. 5525388; fax 5623878; e-mail catholica@vortex.is; internet www.vortex.is/catholica/endex.html.

ISLAM

Félag múslima á Íslandi (Muslim Assen of Iceland): Ármúli 38, 3 hæð, 108 Reykjavík; tel. 8245596; e-mail salmann@landspitali.is; f. 1997; 371 mems (2007); Head SALMAN TAMIMI.

BAHÁ'Í FAITH

Bahá'í samfélagið á Íslandi: Öldugötu 2, 101 Reykjavík; tel. 5670344; e-mail nsa@bahai.is; internet www.bahai.is; 399 mems (2007); Sec. INGIBJÖRG DANÍELSDÓTTIR.

BUDDHISM

Búddistafélag Íslands (Buddhist Association of Iceland): Víghólastíg 21, 200 Kópavogur; 758 mems (2007); Head PHAMAHAPRASIT BOONKAM.

Trúfélagið Zen á Íslandi, Nátthagi (Soto Zen Buddhist Assen of Iceland): Grensásvegur 8, 105 Reykjavík; e-mail mikhaelaaron@gmail.com; internet www.zen.is; 68 mems (2007); Head ÓSKAR INGÓLFSSON.

The Press

PRINCIPAL DAILIES

Blaðið: Hádegismóar 2, 110 Reykjavík; tel. 5103700; fax 5103711; e-mail frettir@bladid.net; internet www.bladid.net; f. 2005; distributed free; published by Ar og dagur ehf; Editor ÓLAFUR STEPHENSEN; 76,000 (2006).

ICELAND

DV (Dagblaðið-Vísir): Útgáfufélagið DV ehf, Skaftahlíð 24, POB 5480, 105 Reykjavík; tel. 5127000; e-mail ritstjorn@dv.is; internet www.dv.is; f. 1981; owned by 365 hf; Editor SIGURJÓN M. EGILSSON; circ. 11,810 (2005).

Fréttablaðið (The Newspaper): Útgáfufélagið Frétt ehf, Suðurgata 10, 101 Reykjavík; tel. 5157500; e-mail ristjorn@frettabladid.is; internet www.visir.is; f. 2001; owned by 365 hf; distributed free; Editor KÁRI JÓNASSON; circ. 101,835 (2006).

Morgunblaðið (Morning News): Hádegismóum 2, 110 Reykjavík; tel. 5691100; fax 5691110; e-mail morgunbladid@mbl.is; internet www.mbl.is; f. 1913; independent; Editor-in-Chief STYRMIR GUNNARSSON; circ. 42,300 (2006).

WEEKLIES

Andvari: 101 Reykjavík; tel. 5879189; e-mail andvari@andvari.is; internet www.andvari.is; f. 1874; Editor GUNNAR STEFÁNSSON.

Bæjarins besta (BB): Sólgötu 9, 400 Ísafjörður; tel. 4564560; fax 4564564; e-mail bb@bb.is; internet www.bb.is; f. 1984; local; Editor SIGURJÓN J. SIGURÐSSON.

Fiskifréttir: Skaftahlíð 24, 105 Reykjavík; tel. 5116622; e-mail mottaka@vb.is; f. 1983; weekly; for the fishing industry; Editor GUÐJÓN EINARSSON; circ. 6,000.

Séð & Heyrt: Seljavegur 2, 101 Reykjavík; tel. 5155652; fax 5155599; e-mail bjarni@frodi.is; internet www.dv.is/sedogheyrt; showbusiness and celebrities; Editors BJARNI BRYNJOLFSSON, KRISTJAN THORVALDSSON; circ. 23,000.

Skagablaðið: Skólabraut 21, 300 Akranesi; tel. 4314222; fax 4314122; f. 1984; local newspaper; Editor SIGURÐUR SVERRISSON; circ. 1,500.

Skessuhorn: Bjarnarbraut 8, 310 Borgarnes; tel. 4335500; fax 4335501; e-mail sigrun@skessuhorn.is; internet www.skessuhorn.is; local; Editor SIGRÚN ÓSK KRISTJÁNSDÓTTIR.

Sunnlenska Fréttablaðið: Austurvegi 1, 800 Selfoss; tel. 4823074; fax 4823084; f. 1991; local newspaper; Editor BJARNI HARÐARSON; circ. 6,300.

Suðurnesjafréttir: Hafnargötu 28, 230 Keflavík; tel. 4213800; fax 4213802; f. 1992; local newspaper; Editors EMIL PÁLL JÓNSSON, HALLDÓR LEVI BJÖRNSSON; circ. 6,500.

Vikan: Seljavegur 8, 101 Reykjavík; tel. 5155500; fax 5155592; e-mail johanna@frodi.is; Editors JOHANNA HARDARDOTTIR, HRUND HAUKSDÓTTIR; circ. 13,000–17,000.

Víkurblaðið: Héðinsbraut 1, 640 Húsavík; tel. 4641780; fax 4641399; f. 1979; local newspaper; Editor JÓHANNES SIGURJÓNSSON; circ. 1,300.

Víkurfréttir: Grundarvegur 23, 260 Reykjanesbær; tel. 4214717; fax 4212777; e-mail pket@vf.is; internet www.vf.is; f. 1983; local newspaper; Editor PÁLL KETILSSON; circ. 6,500.

Viðskiptablaðið: Mýrargata 2–8, 101 Reykjavík; tel. 5116622; fax 5116692; e-mail mottaka@vb.is; internet www.vb.is; publ. by Framtíðarsýn hf; business weekly in collaboration with the *Financial Times* (United Kingdom); Editor JÓNAS HARALDSSON.

OTHER PERIODICALS

Atlantica: Borgartún 23, 105 Reykjavík; tel. 5617575; fax 5618646; e-mail heimur@heimur.is; internet www.heimur.is; 6 a year; in-flight magazine of Icelandair; Editor BJARNI BRYNJÓLFSSON.

Bændablaðið: POB 7080, 127 Reykjavík; tel. 5630300; fax 5623058; e-mail ath@bi.bondi.is; f. 1995; fortnightly; organ of the Icelandic farmers' union; Editor ASKELL THÓRISSON; circ. 6,400.

Billinn: Reykjavík; tel. 5526090; fax 5529490; internet www.billinn.is; f. 1982; 3–4 a year; cars and motoring equipment; Editor LEÓ M. JÓNSSON; circ. 4,000.

Bleikt og Blátt: Seljavegur 2, 101 Reykjavík; tel. 5155500; fax 5155599; e-mail bogb@frodi.is; f. 1989; 6 a year; sex education, communication between men and women; Editor RAGNAR PÉTURSSON; circ. 11,000.

Eiðfaxi: Dugguvogur 10, POB 8133, 128 Reykjavík; tel. 5882525; fax 5882528; e-mail eidfaxi@eidfaxi.is; internet www.eidfaxi.is; f. 1977; monthly (Icelandic edn, English and German edns every two months); horse-breeding and horsemanship; Editor and Publisher JÓNAS KRISTJÁNSSON; circ. 7,000.

Fjármálatíðindi: Kalkofnvegur 1, 150 Reykjavík; tel. 5699600; fax 5699608; e-mail sedlabanki@sedlabanki.is; internet www.sedlabanki.is; 2 a year; economic journal published by the Central Bank; circ. 1,600.

Freyr, búnaðarblað: Bændahöllin við Hagatorg, 107 Reykjavík; tel. 5630300; fax 5623058; e-mail me@bondi.is; internet www.bondi.is; monthly; agriculture; Editors ASKELL THORISSON, MATTHIAS EGGERTSSON; circ. 1,600.

Frjáls Verslun (Free Trade): Borgartún 23, 105 Reykjavík; tel. 5617575; fax 5618646; e-mail fv@heimur.is; internet www.heimur.is; f. 1939; 10 a year; business magazine; Editor JÓN G. HAUKSSON; circ. 6,000–9,000.

Gestgjafinn: Héðinshúsið, Seljavegur 2, 101 Reykjavík; tel. 5155506; fax 5155599; e-mail gestgjafinn@frodi.is; f. 1981; 12 a year; food and wine; Editor SÓLVEIG BALDURSDÓTTIR; circ. 13,000–16,000.

Hár og Fegurð (Hair and Beauty Magazine): Skúlagata 54, 105 Reykjavík; tel. and fax 5628141; e-mail pmelsted@vortex.is; internet www.vortex.is/fashion; f. 1980; 3 a year; hair, beauty, fashion; Editor PÉTUR MELSTEÐ.

Heilbrigðismál: 105 Reykjavík; tel. 5621414; fax 5621417; f. 1949; quarterly; public health; Editor JÓNAS RAGNARSSON; circ. 6,000.

Heima er Bezt: 108 Reykjavík; tel. 8971385; fax 5155201; e-mail heb@athjgli.is; f. 1951; monthly; general interest; Editor GUÐJÓN BALDVINSSON; circ. 3,000.

Hús og Híbýli: Seljavegur 2, 101 Reykjavík; tel. 5155500; fax 5155599; e-mail hogh@frodi.is; f. 1978; 12 a year; architecture, family and homes; Editor LÓA ALDÍSARDÓTTIR; circ. 13,000–16,000.

Húsfreyjan (The Housewife): Túngata 14, 101 Reykjavík; tel. 5517044; f. 1950; quarterly; the organ of the Federation of Icelandic Women's Societies; Editor HRAFNHILDUR VALGARÐS; circ. 4,000.

Iceland Business: Borgartún 23, 105 Reykjavík; tel. 5617575; fax 5618646; e-mail icelandreview@icelandreview.com; internet www.icelandreview.com; f. 1994; 3 a year; in English; Editor JON KALDAL.

Iceland Review: Borgartún 23, 105 Reykjavík; tel. 5617575; fax 5618646; e-mail icelandreview@icelandreview.com; internet www.icelandreview.com; f. 1963; quarterly, in English; general; Editor BJARNI BRYNJÓLFSSON.

Lifandi vísindi: Skipholt 17, 105 Reykjavík; tel. 5708300; fax 5703809; e-mail lifandi@vortex.is; popular science.

Lisin að lifa: 108 Reykjavík; tel. 5356000; fax 5681026; e-mail feb@islandia.is; f. 1986; 4 a year; for elderly people; Editor ODDNÝ SV. BJÖRGUINS; circ. 13,000–15,000.

Mannlíf: Seljavegur 2, 101 Reykjavík; tel. 5155500; fax 5155599; e-mail mannlif@frodi.is; f. 1984; 10 a year; general interest; Editor GERDUR KRISTNÝ GUÐJÓNSDÓTTIR; circ. 16,000.

Myndbönd mánaðarins (Videos of the Month): Reykjavík; tel. 5811280; fax 5811286; internet nemendur.khi.is/thorsand/myndböö.htm; f. 1993; monthly; Editor GUÐBERGUR ÍSLEIFSSON; circ. 26,000.

Ný menntamál: Lágmúla 7, 108 Reykjavík; tel. 5531117; e-mail hannes@jsmennt.is; f. 1983; quarterly; educational issues; Editor HANNES ISBERG; circ. 6,500.

NýttLíf: Seljavegur 2, 101 Reykjavík; tel. 5155660; fax 5155599; e-mail nyttlif@frodi.is; f. 1978; 11 a year; fashion; Editor GULLVEIG SÆMUNDSDÓTTIR; circ. 13,000–17,000.

Peningamál: Kalkofnsvegur 1, 150 Reykjavik; tel. 5699600; fax 5699608; e-mail publish@centbk.is; internet www.sedlabanki.is; f. 1999; 3 a year; bulletin published by the Central Bank; circ. 1,600.

The Reykjavík Grapevine: Vesturgata 5, 101 Reykjavík; tel. 5403600; fax 5403609; e-mail grapevine@grapevine.is; internet www.grapevine.is; f. 2003; 18 a year; in English; distributed free of charge; owned by Fröken ehf; Publisher HILMAR STEINN GRÉTARSSON; Editor SVEINN BIRKIR BJÖRNSSON; circ. 30,000.

Skírnir: Síðumúli 21, 108 Reykjavík; tel. 5889060; e-mail hib@islandia.is; internet www.hib.is; f. 1827; Editors YNGVI EGILSSON, SVAVAR HRAFN SVAVARSSON.

Skutull (Harpoon): Fjarðarstræti 2, 400 Isafjörður; tel. 4563948; fax 4565148; e-mail stapi@simnet.is; f. 1923; monthly; organ of the Social Democratic Party; Editor GÍSLI HJARTARSON.

Ský: Borgartún 23, 105 Reykjavík; tel. 5127575; fax 5618646; e-mail tv@heimur.is; internet www.heimur.is; complimentary in-flight magazine of Air Iceland.

Sveitastjórnarmál: Háaleitisbraut 11, 128 Reykjavík; tel. 5813711; fax 5687866; f. 1941; 24 a year; publ. by the Assen of Icelandic Municipalities; Editor UNNAR STEFÁNSSON; circ. 3,400.

Tölvuheimur (PC World Iceland): Borgartún 23, 105 Reykjavík; tel. 5127575; fax 5618646; e-mail tolvuheimur@heimur.is; internet www.heimur.is; in collaboration with International Data Group; computers; Editor OLI KRISTJÁN ARMANNSSON.

Uppeldi: Síðumúli 27, 108 Reykjavík; tel. 5709500; fax 5709501; f. 1988; quarterly; children, parenting and family matters; Editor BERGHILDUR ERLA BERNHARÐSDÓTTIR; Dir STEFANÍA JÓNSDÓTTIR; circ. 7,000.

Veiðimaðurinn (The Angler): Borgartún 23, 105 Reykjavík; tel. 5127575; fax 5618646; e-mail heimur@heimur.is; internet www.heimur.is; f. 1984; 3 a year; angling; Editor BJARNI BRYNJÓLFSSON; circ. 5,000–7,000.

Vera: Laugavegi 59, 101 Reykjavík; tel. 5526310; fax 5527560; e-mail vera@vera.is; internet wwww.vera.is; f. 1982; 6 a year; feminist issues; Editor ELÍSABET THORGEIRSDÓTTIR.

Vikan: Seljavegur 2, 101 Reykjavík; tel. 5155500; fax 5155599; e-mail vikan@frodi.is; internet www.vikan.is; f. 1938; 50 a year; family; Editor ELÍN ALBERTSDÓTTIR; circ. 17,000.

Víkingur (Seaman): Borgartún 18, 105 Reykjavík; 10 a year; Editor SIGURJÓN VALDIMARSSON.

Vinnan (Labour): Sætún 1, 105 Reykjavík; tel. 5355600; fax 5355601; e-mail gra@asi.is; internet www.asi.is; 2 a year; f. 1943; publ. by Icelandic Federation of Labour; Editor Dr GUÐMUNDUR RÚNAR ARNASON; circ. 5,000.

Vísbending: Borgartún 23, 105 Reykjavík; tel. 5127575; fax 5618646; e-mail heimur@heimur.is; internet www.heimur.is; f. 1983; business; Editor EYÞÓR ÍVAR JÓNSSON.

Ægir: Hafnarstræti 82, 600 Akureyri; tel. 4615151; fax 4615159; f. 1905; publ. by the Fisheries Asscn of Iceland in co-operation with Athygli ehf Publishing; monthly; Editor JÓHANN ÓLAFUR HALLDÓRSSON; circ. 2,500.

Publishers

Bifröst: Skjaldborg/Birtingur, bokaklubbur, c/o Reynir Johannsson, Grensasvegi 14, 128 Reykjavík; tel. 5882400; fax 5888994; e-mail skjaldborg@skjaldborg.is; f. 1988; spiritual, self-help, new age; Dir BJORN EIRIKSSON.

Birtíngur útgáfufélag: Lyngháls 5, 110 Reykjavík; tel. 515-5500; fax 515-5599; e-mail birtingur@birtingur.is; internet www.birtingur.is; publ. nine popular magazines: *Gestgjafinn*, *GOLFblaðið*, *Hús & Híbýli*, *Mannlíf*, *Nýtt Líf*, *Sagan Öll*, *Séð & Heyrt*, *Skakki Turninn* and *Vikan*; and two magazines: *Leifur* and *Lifið heil*; Dir ELÍN RAGNARSDÓTTIR.

Bjartur: Bræðraborgarstíg 9, 101 Reykjavík; tel. 5621826; fax 5628360; e-mail bjartur@bjartur.is; internet www.bjartur.is; f. 1989; contemporary fiction, illustrated and children's books; Dir SNÆBJÖRN ARNGRÍMSSON; Editor JÓN KARL HELGASON.

Bókaútgáfan Björk: Birkivöllum 30, 800 Selfoss; tel. 4821394; fax 4823894; e-mail bokbjork@simnet.is; f. 1941; children's; Dir ERLENDUR DANIELSSON.

Bókaútgáfan Æskan ehf: Faxafeni 5, 108 Reykjavík; tel. 5305400; fax 5305401; e-mail karl@aeskanbok.is; internet www.aeskanbok.is; general, children's books; Dir KARL HELGASON.

Edda Publishing: Suðurlandsbraut 12, 108 Reykjavík; tel. 5222000; fax 5222025; e-mail edda@edda.is; internet www.edda.is; imprints: Almenna bókafélagið, Forlagið, Iðunn, Mál og menning, Nýja bókafélagið-Þjóðsaga, Vaka-Helgafell; Icelandic fiction and non-fiction, translated fiction, biography, illustrated books, children's books on Iceland, maps; Man. Dir PÁLL BRAGI KRISTJÓNSSON.

Fjölvi—Vasa: Njörvasundi 15A, 104 Reykjavík; tel. 5688433; fax 5688142; e-mail fjolvi@mmedia.is; f. 1966; general, children's; Dir ÞORSTEINN ÞORARENSEN.

Forlagið: Bræðraborgarstig 7, 101 Reykjavík; tel. 5755600; fax 5755601; e-mail forlagid@forlagid.is; internet www.forlagid.is; general, fiction, biography, reference, illustrated; Dir JÓHANN PÁLL VALDIMARSSON.

Fróði: Höfðabakka 9, 110 Reykjavík; tel. 5155500; fax 5155599; e-mail frodi@frodi.is; internet www.frodi.is; f. 1989; general, magazines; Dir MAGNÚS HREGGVIÐSSON.

Háskólaútgáfan (University of Iceland Press): Háskólabíó v/Hagatorg, 107 Reykjavík; tel. 5254003; fax 5255255; e-mail hu@hi.is; internet www.haskolautgafan.hi.is; f. 1988; non-fiction, science, culture, history; Man. Dir JÖRUNDUR GUÐMUNDSSON.

Hið íslenska bókmenntafélag: Skeifan 3B, 108 Reykjavík; tel. 5889060; fax 5814088; e-mail hib@islandia.is; internet www.hib.is; f. 1816; general; Pres. SIGURÐUR LÍNDAL; Dir SVERRIR KRISTINSSON.

Hið íslenska Fornritafélag: Siðumúli 21, 108 Reykjavík; tel. 5889060; fax 5889095; e-mail hib@islandia.is; internet www.hib.is; f. 1928; Pres. J. NORDAL.

Hólar: Hagasel 14, 109 Reykjavík; tel. 5872619; fax 5871180; e-mail holar@simnet.is; f. 1995; general; Dir GUDJÓN INGI EIRÍKSSON.

Hörpuútgáfan: Kirkjubraut 5, 300 Akranes; tel. 4312860; fax 4313309; e-mail horpuutgafan@horpuutgafan.is; internet www.horpuutgafan.is; f. 1960; fiction, biography, poetry, reference; Dir BRAGI ÞORÐARSON.

Islendingasagnaútgáfan—Muninn: POB 488, 222 Hafnarfjörður; tel. 8985868; fax 5655868; e-mail muninn@isl.is; f. 1945; poetry, fiction, children's, general non-fiction; Dir BENEDIKT KRISTJÁNSSON.

Jentas ehf: Austurströnd 10, 170 Seltjarnarnes; tel. 5687054; fax 5687053; e-mail info@jentas.com; internet www.jentas.com; f. 1997; formerly PP Forlag ehf Ísland; general; Dir SIGRÚN HALLDÓRS.

Krydd í tilveruna: Bakkaseli 10, 109 Reykjavík; tel. 5575444; fax 5575466; e-mail krydd@mi.is; f. 1989; children's, cookery; Dir ANTON ÖRN KJÆRNESTED.

Leiðarljós: Sólbrekku, Hellum, 355 Snæfellsbær; tel. 4356810; fax 4356801; e-mail gulli@hellnar.is; internet www.hellnar.is; f. 1995; self-help, spiritual, non-fiction; Dir GUÐLAUGUR BERGMANN.

Mál og mynd: Bræðraborgarstíg 9, 101 Reykjavík; tel. 5528866; fax 5528870; e-mail malogmynd@centum.is; non-fiction; Dir ÍVAR GISSURARSON.

Myndabókaútgáfan ehf: Vorduberg 18, 221 Hafnarfjörður; tel. 5653690; fax 5659966; e-mail andrea@myndabokautgafan.is; internet www.myndabokautgafan.is; children's; Dir ANDREA ÍSÓLFSDÓTTIR.

Námsgagnastofnun (National Centre for Educational Materials): Laugavegi 166, 105 Reykjavík; tel. 5350400; fax 5350401; e-mail simi@nams.is; internet www.nams.is; f. 1979; state-owned; Man. Dir INGIBJÖRG ÁSGEIRSDÓTTIR.

Ormstunga: Ránargötu 20, 101 Reykjavík; tel. 5610055; fax 5524650; e-mail books@ormstunga.is; internet www.ormstunga.is; f. 1992; Icelandic and foreign fiction and non-fiction; Dir GÍSLI MÁR GÍSLASON.

Pjaxi ehf: Suðurlandsbraut 6, 108 Reykjavík; tel. 5659320; fax 5659325; e-mail pjaxi@pjaxi.is; internet www.pjaxi.is; Dir OMAR SKAPTI GISLASON.

Reykholt: Reykjavík; tel. 5888821; fax 5888380; f. 1987; general; Dir REYNIR JÓHANNSSON.

Salka: Ármúla 20, 108 Reykjavík; tel. 5521122; fax 5528122; e-mail hildur@salkaforlag.is; internet www.salkaforlag.is; books for, by and about women; Dir HILDUR HERMÓÐSDÓTTIR.

Samhjálp: Hverfisgötu 42, 101 Reykjavík; tel. 5611000; fax 5610050; e-mail samhjalp@samhjalp.is; internet www.samhjalp.is; religious, pentecostal; Dir HEIDAR GUÐNASON.

Setberg: Freyjugötu 14, POB 619, 101 Reykjavík; tel. 5517667; fax 5526640; f. 1950; fiction, cookery, juvenile, picture books, activity books and children's books; Dir ÁRNBJÖRN KRISTINSSON.

Skálholtsútgáfan (National Church Publishing): Laugavegi 31, 101 Reykjavík; tel. 5521090; fax 5621595; e-mail skalholtsutgafan@kirkjan.is; f. 1981; non-fiction, religion, children's; Man. Dir EDDA MÖLLER.

Skjaldborg Ltd: Grensásvegi 14, POB 8427, 108 Reykjavík; tel. 5882400; fax 5888994; e-mail skjaldborg@skjaldborg.is; general; Dir BJÖRN EIRÍKSSON.

Skrudda: Eyjarslóð 9, 101 Reykjavík; tel. 5528866; fax 5528870; e-mail skrudda@skrudda.is; internet www.skrudda.is; fiction, non-fiction, translated fiction, biography, children's.

Sögufélagið: Fischersundi 3, 101 Reykjavík; tel. 5514620; f. 1902; non-fiction, history; Dir RAGNHEIÐUR ÞORLÁKSDÓTTIR.

Stofnun Arna Magnussonar í íslenskum fræðum: Arnagarður v/Suðurgotu, 101 Reykjavík; tel. 5254010; fax 5254035; e-mail thorunnr@hi.is; internet www.arnastofnun.is; f. 1972; state-owned; non-fiction; Dir VÉSTEINN ÓLASON.

Útgáfufélagið Heimur: Borgartún 23, 105 Reykjavík; tel. 5127575; fax 5618646; e-mail heimur@heimur.is; internet www.heimur.is; f. 2000; magazines, travel books; Man. Dir BENEDIKT JÓHANNESSON.

PUBLISHERS' ASSOCIATION

Félag íslenskra bókaútgefenda (Icelandic Publishers' Asscn): Barónsstíg 5, 101 Reykjavík; tel. 5118020; fax 5115020; e-mail baekur@mmedia.is; internet www.bokautgafa.is; f. 1889; Pres. SNAEBJORN ARNGRIMSSON; Man. BENEDIKT KRISTJANSSON.

Broadcasting and Communications

TELECOMMUNICATIONS

Post and Telecom Administration: Suðurlandsbraut 4, 108 Reykjavík; tel. 5101500; fax 5101509; e-mail pta@pta.is; internet www.pta.is; supervisory authority; Dir HRAFNKELL V. GÍSLASON.

Síminn hf: Armula 25, 108 Reykjavík; tel. 5506000; fax 5506009; e-mail siminn@siminn.is; internet www.siminn.is; f. 1998 as Iceland Telecom Ltd; present name adopted 2005 following privatization; offers fixed-line telecommunications, digital television services and broadband internet access; Pres. and CEO SÆVAR FREYR ÞRÁINSSON.

Vodafone Iceland: Skútuvogi 2, 104 Reykjavík; tel. 5999000; fax 5999001; internet www.vodafone.is; f. 2003 as Og Vodafone by merger of Tal, Íslandssími and Halló; renamed as above in 2006; provides mobile and fixed-line telecommunications; CEO ÁRNI PÉTUR JÓNSSON.

ICELAND

Directory

BROADCASTING

Ríkisútvarpið (Icelandic National Broadcasting Service—RÚV): Broadcasting Centre, Efstaleiti 1, 150 Reykjavík; tel. 5153000; fax 5153010; e-mail isradio@ruv.is; internet www.ruv.is; f. 1930; Dir-Gen. PÁLL MAGNÚSSON; Dir of Radio SIGRÚN STEFÁNSDÓTTIR; Dir of Television ÞÓRHALLUR GUNNARSSON.

Skjárinn: Skipholt 31, 105 Reykjavík; tel. 5956000; e-mail info@skjarinn.is; internet www.skjarinn.is; f. 2005; multi-channel digital television service; also operates three television channels: *SKJÁR-EINN*, *SKJÁRBÍÓ* and *SKJÁRHEIMUR*; owned by Síminn.

365 miðlar ehf: Skaftahlíð 24, 105 Reykjavík; tel. 5125000; e-mail askrift@stod2.is; internet www.365.is; f. 2005; owns fmr broadcasting assets of Íslenska Sjónvarpsfélagið hf, as well as the dailies *DV* and *Fréttablaðið*; Chair. JÓN ASGEIR JÓHANNESSON.

Radio

Ríkisútvarpið: Radio Division, Efstaleiti 1, 150 Reykjavík; tel. 5153000; fax 5153010; f. 1930; Programmes 1 and 2 are broadcast over a network of 89 transmitters each; Programme 1 is broadcast for 112 hours a week, with the remaining hours simulcast with Programme 2; Programme 2 is broadcast 168 hours a week; two long-wave transmitters broadcast the same programme, alternating between Programme 1 and Programme 2.

Akraneskaupstaður: Stillholt 16–18, 300 Akranes; broadcasts only in Akranes; Dir BJÖRN LÁRUSSON.

Austurbyggot: Hafnargata 12, 750 Fáskrúðsfjörður; e-mail austurbyggot@austurbyggot.is; internet www.austurbyggot.is; formerly Búðarhreppur; broadcasts Fáskrúðsfjörður and Stöðvarfjörður.

Bjarni Jónasson: Brekkugata 1, 900 Vestmannaeyjar; tel. 4811534; fax 4813475; broadcasts only in Vestmannaeyjar; Dir BJARNI JÓNASSON.

Bylgjan: Skaftahlíð 24, 105 Reykjavík; tel. 5671111; fax 5156900; e-mail bylgjan@bylgjan.is; internet www.bylgjan.is; owned by 365 miðlar ehf; Dir AGÚST HEÐINSSON.

Evrópsk Fjölmiðlun: Hlaðbæ 11, 110 Reykjavík; tel. 5676111; Dir EIRÍKUR SIGURBJÖRNSSON.

Fjölbrautarskóli Norðurlands vestra: 550 Sauðárkrókur; broadcasts only in Sauðárkrókur.

FM957: Skaftahlíð 24, 110 Reykjavík; e-mail fm957@fm957.is; internet www.fm957.is; owned by 365 miðlar ehf.

Hallbjörn Hjartarson: Brimnesi, 545 Skagaströnd; tel. 4522960; e-mail hjh@li.is; broadcasts in Skagaströnd, Blönduós and Sauðárkrókur; Dir HALLBJÖRN HJARTARSON.

Kristilega útvarpsstöðin Lindin: Krókháls 4A, 110 Reykjavík; tel. 5671030; e-mail lindin@lindin.is; Dir MICHAEL E. FITZGERALD.

Létt Bylgjan: Skaftahlíð 24, 105 Reykjavík; tel. 5125000; fax 5156830; e-mail lettbylgian@lettbylgian.is; internet www.bylgjan.is; owned by 365 miðlar ehf; Dir AGUST HEÐINSSON.

Útvarp Saga: Suðurlandsbraut 24, 108 Reykjavík; tel. 5333943; fax 5881994; e-mail saga@utvarpsaga.is; internet www.utvarpsaga.is; owned by 365 miðlar ehf; Dir ARNÞRÚÐUR KARLSDÓTTIR.

Útvarp Vestmannaeyjar: Brekkugata 1, 900 Vestmannaeyjar; tel. 4811534; fax 4813475; broadcasts only in Vestmannaeyjar; Dir BJARNI JÓNASSON.

Vila-Árna Útvarp: Skipholt 6, 355 Ólafsvík; tel. 4361334; fax 4361379; Dir VILHELM ÁRNASON.

X 97.7: Skaftahlíð 24, 105 Reykjavík; tel. 5170977; e-mail x977@x977.is; internet www.x977.is; owned by 365 miðlar ehf.

Television

Aksjón ehf: Strandgötu 31, 600 Akureyri; tel. 4611050; fax 4612356; e-mail aksjon@nett.is; broadcasts only in Akureyri; Dir GÍSLI GUNNLAUGSSON.

Almiðlun ehf: Ármúli 36, 108 Reykjavík; tel. 5880101; fax 5651796; Dir HALLDÓR ÁRNI SVEINSSON.

Bíórásin (The Movie Channel): Skaftahlíð 24, 105 Reykjavík; tel. 5125000; owned by 365 miðlar ehf.

Fjölsýn: Strandvegur 47, 900 Vestmannaeyjar; tel. 4811300; fax 4812643; e-mail sigit@eyjar.is; broadcasts only in Vestmannaeyjar; Dir OMAR GUÐMUNDSSON.

Kristniboðskirkjan: Grensásvegur 8, 108 Reykjavík; tel. 5683131; fax 5683741; broadcasts only in the Reykjavík area; religious; Dir EIRÍKUR SIGURBJÖRNSSON.

PoppTíví: Skaftahlíð 24, 105 Reykjavík; tel. 5156000; owned by 365 miðlar ehf; music station.

Stöð 2: Skaftahlíð 24, 105 Reykjavík; tel. 5125000; fax 5125100; e-mail askrift@stod2.is; internet www.stod2.is; f. 1986; owned by 365 miðlar ehf; 'pay-TV' station; Pres. SIGURÐUR G. GUÐJÓNSSON.

Sýn (Vision): Skaftahlíð 24, 105 Reykjavík; tel. 5156000; owned by 365 miðlar ehf.

Villa Video: Skipholt 6, 335 Ólafsvík; tel. 4361563; fax 4361379; broadcasts only in Ólafsvík; Dir VILHELM ÁRNASON.

Finance

(cap. = capital; res = reserves; dep. = deposits; m. = million; amounts in krónur; brs = branches)

BANKING

Iceland's banking and finance system has undergone substantial transformation. In 1989–90 the number of commercial banks was reduced from seven to three, by amalgamating four banks to form Íslandsbanki as the only remaining major commercial bank in private ownership. A further restructuring of the banking sector commenced in 2000 with the merger of Íslandsbanki with the recently privatized investment bank FBA. Íslandsbanki was renamed Glitnir in 2006. By early 2003 the Icelandic Government had withdrawn completely from the country's commercial banking sector, having sold its controlling stakes in the second and third largest retail banks, Bunaðarbanki Íslands and Landsbanki Íslands. Further consolidation of the banking sector was expected. The 17 savings banks operate a commercial bank, Icebank, which functions as a central banking institution.

Central Bank

Seðlabanki Íslands (Central Bank of Iceland): Kalkofnsvegur 1, 150 Reykjavík; tel. 5699600; fax 5699605; e-mail sedlabanki@sedlabanki.is; internet www.sedlabanki.is; f. 1961; cap. and res 48,227m., dep. 256,214m. (Dec. 2006); Chair., Bd of Govs DAVIÐ ODDSSON.

Principal Banks

Glitnir Banki hf: Kirkjusandur, 155 Reykjavík; tel. 4404000; fax 4404001; e-mail glitnir@glitnir.is; internet www.glitnir.is; f. 1990 as Íslandsbanki hf; current name adopted 2006; offices and subsidiaries in Denmark, Finland, Luxembourg, Norway, Russia, Sweden, the USA and the United Kingdom; cap. 14,161m., res 59,351m., dep. 516,848m. (Dec. 2006); Chair. ÞORSTEINN MÁR BALDVINSSON; CEO LÁRUS WELDING; 29 brs.

Icebank hf: Rauðarárstíg 27, POB 5220, 125 Reykjavík; tel. 5404000; fax 5404001; e-mail icebank@icebank.is; internet www.icebank.is; f. 1986 as Sparisjóðabanki Íslands; adopted current name 2006; acts as central bank for Icelandic savings banks, 57.3% owned by them; cap. 691m., res 16,836m., dep. 53,258m. (Dec. 2006); Chair. GEIRMUNDUR KRISTINSSON; CEO AGNAR HANSSON.

Kaupþing Banki hf: Borgartún 19, 105 Reykjavík; tel. 4446000; fax 4446009; e-mail info@kaupthing.is; internet www.kaupthing.is; f. 2003; by merger of Búnaðarbanki and Kaupþing Banki hf; cap. 7,321m., res 181,248m., dep. 861,114m. (Dec. 2006); Chair. SIGURÐUR EINARSSON; Group CEO HREIÐAR MÁR SIGURÐSSON; 35 brs.

Landsbanki Íslands hf (National Bank of Iceland Ltd): Austurstræti 11, 155 Reykjavík; tel. 5606600; fax 5606000; e-mail info@landsbank.is; internet www.landsbanki.is; f. 1885; transferred to the private sector in 2003; cap. 10,581m., res 52,655m., dep. 823,951m. (Dec. 2006); Chair. Bd of Dirs BJÖRGÓLFUR GUÐMUNDSSON; CEO HALLDÓR J. KRISTJÁNSSON, SIGURJÓN Þ. ÁRNASON; 40 brs.

MP Fjárfestingarbanki hf: Skipholti 50D, 105 Reykjavík; tel. 5403200; fax 5403201; e-mail mottaka@mp.is; internet www.mp.is; f. 1999; as a brokerage firm under name MP Verdbref; status changed to investment bank and present name adopted 2003; cap. 1,070m., res 1,265m., dep. 32,644m. (Dec. 2006); Chair. MARGEIR PÉTURSSON; Man. Dir STYRMIR ÞÓR BRAGASON.

STOCK EXCHANGE

NASDAQ OMX Nordic Exchange Iceland: Laugavegur 182, 105 Reykjavík; tel. 5252800; fax 5252888; internet www.nasdaqomx.com; f. 2006 by merger of Kauphöll Íslands and OMX AB (Sweden); part of OMX Nordic Exchange with Copenhagen (Denmark), Helsinki (Finland) and Stockholm (Sweden) exchanges; acquired by NASDAQ Stock Market, Inc (USA) in 2008; Group CEO ROBERT GREIFELD; Group Pres. MAGNUS BÖCKER.

INSURANCE

Tryggingastofnun Ríkisins (Social Insurance Administration): Laugavegi 114, 150 Reykjavík; tel. 5604400; fax 5624535; e-mail tr@tr.is; internet www.tr.is; f. 1936; Man. Dir KARL STEINAR GUÐNASON; Chair. BENEDIKT JOHANNESSON.

ICELAND

Private Insurance Companies

Íslandstrygging hf: Sætúni 8, 105 Reykjavík; tel. 5141000; fax 5141001; f. 2002; Gen. Man. EINAR BALDVINSSON.

Íslensk Endurtrygging hf (Icelandic Reinsurance Co Ltd): Suðurlandsbraut 6, 108 Reykjavík; tel. 5331200; fax 5331201; f. 1939; Gen. Man. BJARNI THORDARSON.

KB líf hf: Sóltúni 26, 105 Reykjavík; tel. 5401400; fax 5401401; e-mail kblif@kblif.is; internet www.kblif.is; f. 1966; formerly Alþjóða líftryggingarfélagið hf; life insurance.

Líftryggingamiðstöin hf: Aðalstræti 6–8, 101 Reykjavík; tel. 5152000; fax 5152020; f. 2002; Gen. Man. OSKAR MAGNUSSON.

Líftryggingafélag Íslands hf: Ármúla 3, 108 Reykjavík; tel. 5605060; fax 5605100; internet www.lif.is.

Sameinaða líftryggingarfélagið hf: Sigtún 42, POB 5180, 125 Reykjavík; tel. 5695400; fax 5815455.

Sjóvá-Almennar tryggingar hf (Marine-General Insurance Co): Kringlan 5, POB 3200, 123 Reykjavík; tel. 5692500; fax 5813718; f. 1988; all branches except life; Chair. BENEDIKT SVEINSSON; Gen. Mans EINAR SVEINSSON, ÓLAFUR B. THORS.

Trygging hf: Aðalstræti 6, 101 Reykjavík; tel. 5152000; fax 5152020.

Tryggingamiðstöðin hf: Aðalstræti 6, 101 Reykjavík; tel. 5152000; fax 5152020; internet www.tmhf.is.

Vátryggingafélag Íslands hf: Ármúla 3, 108 Reykjavík; tel. 5605000; fax 5605100; e-mail info@vis.is; internet www.vis.is; f. 1989; Chair. SIGURÐUR VALTÝSSON; Man. Dir GUÐMUNDUR GUNNARSSON.

Vélbátaábyrgðarfélagið Grótta: Síðumúla 29, 108 Reykjavík; tel. 5536800; fax 5536812.

Viðlagatrygging Íslands: Laugavegi 162, 105 Reykjavík; tel. 5529677; fax 5629675.

Vörður—Vátryggingafélag: Skipagötu 9, 600 Akureyri; tel. 4648000; fax 4648001; e-mail oli@vordur.is.

Supervisory Authority

Fjármálaeftirlitið (FME) (Financial Supervisory Authority): Suðurlandsbraut 32, 108 Reykjavík; tel. 5252700; fax 5252727; e-mail fme@fme.is; internet www.fme.is; f. 1999 by merger of Insurance Supervisory Authority and Bank Inspectorate of the Central Bank of Iceland; Dir Gen. JÓNAS FRIÐRIK JÓNSSON; Deputy Dir Gen. RAGNAR HAFLIÐASON.

Trade and Industry

GOVERNMENT AGENCIES

Orkustofnun (National Energy Authority): Grensásvegur 9, 108 Reykjavík; tel. 5696000; fax 5688896; e-mail os@os.is; internet www.os.is; f. 1967; two main divisions: hydrological research unit and energy administration unit; contracts and supervises energy research projects financed by the national budget, monitors energy consumption and publishes forecasts for energy market; operates United Nations Geothermal Training Programme as independent entity; licenses and monitors exploration for oil and gas in Icelandic waters; Dir-Gen. Prof. GUÐNI A. JÓHANNESSON.

Útflutningsráð Íslands (Trade Council of Iceland): POB 1000, 121 Reykjavík; Borgartún 35, 105 Reykjavík; tel. 5114000; fax 5114040; e-mail icetrade@icetrade.is; internet www.icetrade.is; promotes Icelandic exports; Man. Dir JÓN ÁSBERGSSON.

CHAMBER OF COMMERCE

Viðskiptaráð Íslands (Iceland Chamber of Commerce): Hús verslunarinnar, Kringlunni 7, 7th Floor, 103 Reykjavík; tel. 5107100; fax 5686564; e-mail mottaka@chamber.is; internet www.chamber.is; f. 1917; fmrly Verslunarráð Íslands; Man. Dir FINNUR ODDSSON; 370 mems.

INDUSTRIAL AND TRADE ASSOCIATIONS

Fiskifélag Íslands (Fisheries Asscn of Iceland): Glerárgata 28, POB 145, 602 Akureyri; tel. 5510500; fax 5527969; e-mail fi@fiskifelag.is; internet www.fiskifelag.is; f. 1911; conducts technical and economic research and services for fishing vessels and for fishing industry; Chair. HELGI LAXDAL.

Landssamband Íslenskra Útvegsmanna (Icelandic Fishing Vessel Owners' Federation): Borgartúni 35, 105 Reykjavík; tel. 5910300; fax 5910301; e-mail fridrik@liu.is; internet www.liu.is; f. 1939; Chair. BJÖRGÓLFUR JÓHANNSSON; Man. FRIÐRIK JÓN ARNGRÍMSSON.

Samtök Iðnaðarins (Federation of Icelandic Industries—FII): Borgartúni 35, 105 Reykjavík; tel. 5910100; fax 5910101; e-mail mottaka@si.is; internet www.si.is; f. 1993 by merger of Federation of Icelandic Industries (f. 1933), Federation of Icelandic Crafts and Industries (f. 1932) and four other employers' orgs; Chair. HELGI MAGNUSSON; Gen. Man. JÓN STEINDÓR VALDIMARSSON; 2,500 mems.

EMPLOYERS' ORGANIZATION

Samtök atvinnulífsins (Confederation of Icelandic Employers): Borgartúni 35, 105 Reykjavík; tel. 5910000; fax 5910050; e-mail sa@sa.is; internet www.sa.is; f. 1934; eight mem. asscns; Chair. INGIMUNDUR SIGURPÁLSSON; Man. Dir Dr VILHJÁLMUR EGILSSON.

UTILITIES

Electricity

Hitaveita Suðurnesja hf (Suðurnes Regional Heating Corpn): Brekkustíg 36, POB 225, 260 Reykjanesbær; e-mail hs@hs.is; internet www.hs.is; f. 1974; produces and distributes hot-water heating and electricity for the Suðurnes region; Chair. ÁRNI SIGFÚSSON; Man. Dir JÚLÍUS JÓN JÓNSSON.

Landsvirkjun (National Power Co): Háaleitisbraut 68, 103 Reykjavík; tel. 5159000; fax 5159007; e-mail landsvirkjun@lv.is; internet www.landsvirkjun.com; f. 1965; state-owned; generates and sells electric power wholesale to public distribution systems and industrial enterprises; Chair. PÁLL MAGNÚSSON; Man. Dir FRIDRIK SOPHUSSON.

Orkubú Vestfjarða hf (Vestfjords Power Co): Stakkanesi 1, 400 Ísafjörður; tel. 4503211; fax 4563204; e-mail orkubu@ov.is; internet www.ov.is; f. 1977; produces, distributes and sells electrical energy in the Vestfjords area; state-owned; Chair. GUÐMUNDUR JÓHANNSSON; Man. Dir KRISTJÁN HARALDSSON.

Orkuveita Reykjavíkur (OR) (Reykjavík Energy): Bæjarháls 1, 110 Reykjavík; tel. 5166000; fax 5166709; e-mail or@or.is; internet www.or.is; f. 1999; produces and distributes geothermal hot-water central heating, cold water and electricity for the city of Reykjavík and regions in south-western Iceland; owned by city of Reykjavík and other local authorities; Chair. KJARTAN MAGNÚSSON; CEO HJÖRLEIFUR B. KVARAN.

RARIK ohf (Iceland State Electricity): Bíldshöfða 9, 110 Reykjavík; tel. 5289000; fax 5289009; e-mail rarik@rarik.is; internet www.rarik.is; f. 1947 as Rafmagnsveitur Ríkisins; produces, procures, distributes and sells electrical energy; also provides consultancy services; Chair. HILMAR GUNNLAUGSSON; Man. Dir ÖRLYGUR JÓNASSON.

TRADE UNIONS

Althýðusamband Íslands (ASÍ) (Icelandic Confederation of Labour): Sætún 1, 105 Reykjavík; tel. 5355600; fax 5355601; e-mail asi@asi.is; internet www.asi.is; f. 1916; affiliated to ITUC, ETUC and the Council of Nordic Trade Unions; Chair. GRÉTAR ÞORSTEINSSON; Gen. Sec. GYLFI ARNBJÖRNSSON; c. 108,000 mems.

Bandalag Háskólamanna (BHM) (Asscn of Academics): Borgartún 6, 105 Reykjavík; tel. 5812090; fax 5889239; e-mail bhm@bhm.is; internet www.bhm.is; f. 1958; asscn of 25 trade unions; publishes *BHM-tíðindi* (3 a year); Chair. HALLDÓRA FRIÐJÓNSDÓTTIR; 9,100 mems.

Bandalag Starfsmanna Ríkis og Bæja (BSRB) (Municipal and Government Employees' Asscn): Grettisgötu 89, 105 Reykjavík; tel. 5626688; fax 5629106; e-mail bsrb@tv.is; internet www.brsb.is; f. 1942; Chair. ÖGMUNDUR JÓNASSON; 17,506 mems.

Blaðamannafélag Íslands (Union of Icelandic Journalists): Síðumúla 23, 108 Reykjavík; tel. 5539155; fax 5539177; e-mail bi@press.is; internet www.press.is; f. 1897; Chair. ARNA SCHRAM; 610 mems.

Transport

RAILWAYS

There are no railways in Iceland.

ROADS

Much of the interior is uninhabited and the main road follows the coastline. Regular motor coach services link the main settlements. In 2006 Iceland had 13,038 km of roads, of which 4,230 km were main roads. Approximately one-third of the main roads are paved.

Bifreiðastöð Íslands hf (BSÍ) (Iceland Motor Coach Service): Umferðarmiðstöðinni, Vatnsmýrarveg 10, 101 Reykjavík; tel. 5621011; e-mail bsi@bsi.is; internet www.bsi.is; f. 1936; 45 scheduled bus lines throughout Iceland; also operates sightseeing tours and excursions; Chair. ÓSKAR SIGURJÓNSSON; Man. Dir GUNNAR SVEINSSON.

ICELAND

SHIPPING

Heavy freight is carried by coastal shipping. The principal seaport for international shipping is Reykjavík.

Port Authority

Faxaflóahafnir sf (Associated Icelandic Ports): POB 382, 121 Reykjavík; Harbour Bldg, Tryggvagata 17, 101 Reykjavík; tel. 5258900; fax 5258990; e-mail hofnin@faxaports.is; internet www.faxaports.is; f. 2005 by merger of ports of Akranes, Borgarnes, Grundartangi and Reykjavík; Chair. BJÖRN INGI HRAFNSSON; Dir GISLI GISLASON.

Principal Companies

Atlantsskip ehf: Cuxhavengata 1, 220 Hafnarfjörður; tel. 5913000; fax 5913001; e-mail atlantsskip@atlantsskip.is; internet www.atlantsskip.is; f. 1998; Gen. Man. DAVÍÐ BLÖNDAL.

Eimskip (Iceland Steamship Co Ltd): Korngörðum 2, 104 Reykjavík; tel. 5257000; fax 5257009; e-mail info@eimskip.com; internet www.eimskip.com; f. 1914 as Eimskipafélag Íslands; subsidiary of Avion Group; transportation and logistics services incl. ground operation, warehousing, coastal service, trucking and intermodal transportation between Iceland and the United Kingdom, Scandinavia, the rest of Europe, the USA and Canada; Dirs BALDUR GUÐNASON, HAFÞÓR HAFSTEINSSON, STEINGRÍMUR PÉTURSSON.

Nesskip hf: POB 175, 172 Seltjarnarnes; Nesskip's House, Austurstrond 1, 170 Seltjarnarnes; tel. 5639900; fax 5639919; e-mail nesskip@nesskip.is; internet www.nesskip.is; f. 1974; bulk cargo shipping services to the USA, Canada, Russia, Scandinavia, the Baltic countries and other parts of Europe; agency and chartering for vessels in all Icelandic ports; Chair. Capt. GUÐMUNDUR ÁSGEIRSSON.

Samskip hf: Kjalarvogur, 104 Reykjavík; tel. 4588000; fax 4588100; e-mail samskip@samskip.is; internet www.samskip.is; services to Europe, the USA, South America and the Far East; Exec. Chair ÓLAFUR ÓLAFSSON.

CIVIL AVIATION

Air transport is particularly important to Iceland and is used both for the transport of people and to transport agricultural produce from remote districts. More than 90% of passenger traffic between Iceland and other countries is by air. There are regular air services between Reykjavík and outlying townships. There is an international airport at Keflavík, 47 km from Reykjavík.

Air Atlanta Icelandic: Hlíðasmára 3, 201 Kópavogur; tel. 4584000; fax 4584001; e-mail sales@airatlanta.com; internet www.airatlanta.com; f. 1986; leases cargo and passenger aircraft; Chair. GEIR VALUR ÁGÚSTSSON; Pres. and CEO HANNES HILMARSSON.

Air Iceland: Reykjavík Airport, 101 Reykjavík; tel. 5703030; fax 5703001; e-mail gudnyp@flugfelag.is; internet www.airiceland.is; f. by merger of Icelandair Domestic and Flugfélag Norðurlands; scheduled, regional flights; 96%-owned by Icelandair; Man. Dir ÁRNI GUNNARSSON.

Iceland Express ehf: Grímsbær, Efstaland 26, 108 Reykjavík; tel. 5500650; fax 5500601; e-mail info@icelandexpress.is; internet www.icelandexpress.com; f. 2002; low-cost airline offering daily scheduled flights between Iceland and 13 destinations in Europe; Chair. THORSTEINN ÖRN GUÐMUNDSSON; Man. Dir MATTHÍAS IMSLAND.

Icelandair (Flugleiðir hf): Reykjavík Airport, 101 Reykjavík; tel. 5050300; fax 5050350; e-mail pr@icelandair.is; internet www.icelandair.net; f. 1973 as the holding co for the two principal Icelandic airlines, Flugfélag Íslands (f. 1937) and Loftleiðir (f. 1944); in 1979 all licences, permits and authorizations previously held by Flugfélag Íslands and Loftleiðir were transferred to it; operates flights from Reykjavík to nine domestic airfields and more than 20 destinations in Europe and North America; CEO JÓN KARL ÓLAFSSON.

Tourism

Iceland's main attraction for tourists lies in the rugged beauty of the interior, with its geysers and thermal springs. In 2005 there were 369,000 tourist arrivals and receipts from tourism, including passenger transport, totalled US $631m. Overnight stays by foreign visitors in hotels and guesthouses amounted to 1.7m. in 2006.

Iceland Tourist Board: Lækjargata 3, 101 Reykjavík; tel. 5355500; fax 5355501; e-mail info@icetourist.is; internet www.visiticeland.com; Gen. Dir ÓLÖF ÝRR ATLADÓTTIR.

Höfuðborgarstofa (Visit Reykjavík): Aðalstræti 2, 101 Reykjavík; tel. 5901500; fax 5901501; e-mail info@visitreykjavik.is; internet www.visitreykjavik.is; tourism marketing and events for the city of Reykjavík; Dir, Culture and Tourism SVANHILDUR KONRÁDSDÓTTIR.

INDIA

Introductory Survey

Location, Climate, Language, Religion, Flag, Capital

The Republic of India forms a natural sub-continent, with the Himalaya mountain range to the north. Two sections of the Indian Ocean—the Arabian Sea and the Bay of Bengal—lie to the west and east, respectively. India's neighbours are Tibet (the Xizang Autonomous Region of the People's Republic of China), Bhutan and Nepal to the north, Pakistan to the north-west and Myanmar (formerly Burma) to the north-east, while Bangladesh is surrounded by Indian territory except for a short frontier with Myanmar in the east. Near India's southern tip, across the Palk Strait, is Sri Lanka. India's climate ranges from temperate to tropical, with an average summer temperature on the plains of approximately 27°C (85°F). Annual rainfall varies widely, but the summer monsoon brings heavy rain over much of the country in June and July. The official language is Hindi, spoken by about 30% of the population. English is used as an associate language for many official purposes. The Indian Constitution also recognizes 18 regional languages, of which the most widely spoken are Telugu, Bengali, Marathi, Tamil, Urdu and Gujarati. In addition, many other local languages are used. According to the 2001 census, about 81% of the population are Hindus and 13% Muslims. There are also Christians, Sikhs, Buddhists, Jains and other minorities. The national flag (proportions 2 by 3) has three equal horizontal stripes, of saffron, white and green, with the Dharma Chakra (Wheel of the Law), in blue, in the centre of the white stripe. The capital is New Delhi.

Recent History

After a prolonged struggle against British colonial rule, India became independent, within the Commonwealth, on 15 August 1947. The United Kingdom's Indian Empire was partitioned, broadly on a religious basis, between India and Pakistan. The principal nationalist movement that had opposed British rule was the Indian National Congress (later known as the Congress Party). At independence the Congress leader, Jawaharlal Nehru, became India's first Prime Minister. Sectarian violence, the movement of 12m. refugees, the integration of the former princely states into the Indian federal structure and a territorial dispute with Pakistan over Kashmir presented major problems to the new Government.

India became independent as a dominion, with the British monarch as Head of State, represented by an appointed Governor-General. In November 1949, however, the Constituent Assembly approved a republican Constitution, providing for a president (with mainly ceremonial functions) as head of state. Accordingly, India became a republic on 26 January 1950, although remaining a member of the Commonwealth. France transferred sovereignty of Chandernagore to India in May 1950, and ceded its four remaining Indian settlements in 1954.

The lack of effective opposition to Congress policies expedited industrialization and social reform. In December 1961 Indian forces overran the Portuguese territories of Goa, Daman and Diu, which were immediately annexed by India. Border disputes with the People's Republic of China escalated into a brief military conflict in 1962. Nehru died in May 1964 and was succeeded by Lal Bahadur Shastri. India and Pakistan fought a second war over Kashmir in 1965. Following mediation by the USSR, Shastri and President Ayub Khan of Pakistan signed a joint declaration, aimed at a peaceful settlement of the Kashmir dispute, on 10 January 1966. Shastri died on the following day, however, and Nehru's daughter, Indira Gandhi, became Prime Minister.

Following the presidential election of August 1969, when two factions of Congress supported different candidates, the success of Indira Gandhi's candidate split the party. The Organization (Opposition) Congress, led by Morarji Desai, emerged in November, but at the next general election to the lower house of the legislature, the Lok Sabha (House of the People), held in March 1971, Indira Gandhi's wing of Congress won 350 of the 515 elective seats.

Border incidents led to a 12-day war with Pakistan in December 1971. The Indian army rapidly occupied East Pakistan, which India recognized as the independent state of Bangladesh. Indira Gandhi and President Zulfikar Ali Bhutto of Pakistan held a summit conference at Shimla in June–July 1972, when the two leaders agreed that their respective forces should respect the cease-fire line in Kashmir, and that India and Pakistan should resolve their differences through bilateral negotiations or other peaceful means. In 1975 the former protectorate of Sikkim became the 22nd state of the Indian Union, leading to tensions in India's relations with Nepal.

A general election to the Lok Sabha was held in March 1977, when the number of elective seats was increased to 542. The election resulted in victory for the Janata (People's) Party, chaired by Morarji Desai, who became Prime Minister. The Janata Party and an allied party, the Congress for Democracy, together won 298 of the 540 seats where polling took place. Congress obtained 153 seats. In January 1978 Indira Gandhi became leader of a new breakaway political group, the Congress (Indira) Party, known as Congress (I).

In 1979 the Government's ineffectual approach to domestic problems provoked a wave of defections by Lok Sabha members of the Janata Party. Many joined Raj Narain, who formed a new party, the Lok Dal, the policies of which were based on secularism. Congress (I) lost its position as official opposition party after defections from its ranks to the then official Congress Party by members who objected to Indira Gandhi's perceived authoritarianism. The resignation of Desai's Government in July was followed by the departure from the Janata Party of Charan Singh, who became the leader of the Lok Dal and, shortly afterwards, Prime Minister in a coalition with both Congress parties. When Congress (I) withdrew its support, Singh's 24-day administration collapsed, and Parliament was dissolved. A general election to the Lok Sabha was held in January 1980. Congress (I) received 42.7% of the total votes and won an overwhelming majority (352) of the elective seats. The Janata Party won only 31 seats, while the Lok Dal secured 41 seats. Indira Gandhi was reinstated as Prime Minister. Presidential rule was imposed in nine states, hitherto governed by opposition parties, in February. At elections to state assemblies in June, Congress (I) won majorities in eight of them.

By-elections in June 1981 for the Lok Sabha and state assemblies were notable because of the overwhelming victory that Rajiv Gandhi, the Prime Minister's son, obtained in the former constituency of his late brother (killed in an air crash in 1980) and because of the failure of the fragmented Janata Party to win any seats. In February 1983 Rajiv Gandhi became a General Secretary of Congress (I).

Indira Gandhi's Government faced serious problems, as intercommunal disturbances in several states (particularly Assam and Meghalaya) continued in 1982–83, with violent protests against the presence of Bengali immigrants. Election defeats in Andhra Pradesh, Karnataka and Tripura represented a series of set-backs for Indira Gandhi. Alleged police corruption and the resurgence of caste violence (notably in Bihar and Gujarat) caused further problems for the Government.

There was also unrest in the Sikh community of the Punjab, despite the election to the Indian presidency in July 1982 of Giani Zail Singh, the first Sikh to hold the position. Demands were made for greater religious recognition, for the settlement of grievances over land and water rights, and over the sharing of the state capital at Chandigarh with Haryana; in addition, a minority called for the creation of a separate Sikh state ('Khalistan'). In October 1983 the state was brought under presidential rule. However, the violence continued, and followers of an extremist Sikh leader, Jarnail Singh Bhindranwale, established a terrorist stronghold inside the Golden Temple (the Sikh holy shrine) at Amritsar. The Government sent in troops to dislodge the terrorists and the assault resulted in the death of Bhindranwale and hundreds of his supporters, and serious damage to sacred buildings. A curfew was imposed, and army personnel blockaded Amritsar.

In October 1984 Indira Gandhi was assassinated by militant Sikh members of her personal guard. Her son, Rajiv Gandhi, was immediately sworn in as Prime Minister, despite his lack of ministerial experience. The widespread communal violence that erupted throughout India, resulting in more than 2,000 deaths, was curbed by prompt government action. Congress (I) achieved a decisive victory in elections to the Lok Sabha in December. Including the results of the January 1985 polling, the party received 49.2% of the total votes and won 403 of the 513 contested seats.

In February 1986 there were mass demonstrations and strikes throughout India in protest at government-imposed increases in the prices of basic commodities. The opposition parties united against Rajiv Gandhi's policies, and Congress (I) suffered considerable reversals in the indirect elections to the upper house of the legislature, the Rajya Sabha (Council of States), in March. In April Rajiv Gandhi attempted to purge Congress (I) of critics calling themselves 'Indira Gandhi loyalists', and, in a major government reorganization, he appointed Sikhs to two senior positions. The Prime Minister survived an assassination attempt by three Sikhs in October.

In June 1986 Laldenga, the leader of the Mizo National Front (MNF), signed a peace agreement with Rajiv Gandhi, thus ending Mizoram's 25 years of rebellion. The accord granted Mizoram limited autonomy in the drafting of local laws, independent trade with neighbouring foreign countries and a general amnesty for all Mizo rebels. Laldenga led an interim coalition government until February 1987, when the MNF won an absolute majority at elections to the state assembly. In that month Mizoram and Arunachal Pradesh were officially admitted as the 23rd and 24th states of India, and in May the Union Territory of Goa became India's 25th state.

During 1987 Congress (I) experienced serious political setbacks. It sustained defeats in a number of state elections, and political tensions were intensified by an open dispute between the Prime Minister and the outgoing President, Giani Zail Singh. Public concern was aroused by various accusations of corruption and financial irregularities made against senior figures in the ruling party. Notable among these scandals was the 'Bofors affair', in which large payments were allegedly made to Indian agents by a Swedish company in connection with its sales of munitions to the Indian Government. The Prime Minister denied any involvement, and a committee of inquiry subsequently exonerated him of any impropriety. Several ministers resigned from the Government, among them the Minister of Defence, Vishwanath Pratap (V. P.) Singh, who was also, with three other senior politicians, expelled from Congress (I) in July for 'anti-party activities'. V. P. Singh soon emerged as the leader of the Congress (I) dissidents, and in October formed a new political group, the Jan Morcha (People's Front), advocating more radical social change.

In 1988 a more confrontational style was adopted by the central administration towards non-Congress (I) state governments, and presidential rule was imposed in states suffering political instability. The opposition forces attained a degree of unity when four major centrist parties, the Indian National Congress (S), the Jan Morcha, the Janata Party and the Lok Dal, and three major regional parties formed a coalition National Front (Rashtriya Morcha), to oppose Congress (I) at the next election. Three of the four centrist parties formed a new political grouping, the Janata Dal (People's Party), which was to work in collaboration with the National Front. V. P. Singh, who was widely regarded as Rajiv Gandhi's closest rival, was elected President of the Janata Dal.

At the general election to the Lok Sabha held in November 1989, Congress (I) lost its overall majority. Of the 525 contested seats, it won 193, the Janata Dal and its electoral allies in the National Front won 141 and three, respectively, and the right-wing Hindu nationalist Bharatiya Janata Party (BJP) won 88. In early December, after the National Front had been promised the support of the communist parties and the BJP, V. P. Singh was sworn in as the new Prime Minister. He appointed Devi Lal, the populist Chief Minister of Haryana and President of Lok Dal (B), as Deputy Prime Minister, and a Kashmiri Muslim, Mufti Mohammed Sayeed, as Minister of Home Affairs. This latter appointment was widely seen as a gesture of reconciliation to the country's Muslims and as reaffirmation of the Government's secular stance. A few weeks later V. P. Singh's Government won a vote of confidence in the Lok Sabha, despite the abstention of all the Congress (I) members. In January 1990 the Government ordered the mass resignation of all the state governors; the President then appointed new ones. In February elections were held to 10 state assemblies, all formerly controlled by Congress (I). Congress (I) lost power in eight of the 10 assemblies and there was a notable increase in support for the BJP.

In July 1990 Devi Lal was dismissed from his post as Deputy Prime Minister, for nepotism, disloyalty and for making unsubstantiated accusations of corruption against ministerial colleagues. In August there were violent demonstrations in many northern Indian states against the Government's populist decision to implement the recommendations of the 10-year-old Mandal Commission and to raise the quota of government and public-sector jobs reserved for deprived sections of the population. In October the Supreme Court directed the Government to halt temporarily the implementation of the quota scheme, in an attempt to curb the caste violence.

In October 1990 the BJP withdrew its support for the National Front, following the arrest of its President, Lal Krishna (L. K.) Advani, as he led a controversial procession of Hindu devotees to the holy town of Ayodhya, in Uttar Pradesh, to begin the construction of a Hindu temple on the site of a disused ancient mosque. V. P. Singh accused the BJP leader of deliberately inciting inter-communal hatred by exhorting Hindu extremists to join him in illegally tearing down the mosque. Paramilitary troops were sent to Ayodhya, and thousands of Hindu activists were arrested, in an attempt to prevent a Muslim–Hindu confrontation. However, following repeated clashes between police and crowds, Hindu extremists stormed and slightly damaged the mosque and laid siege to it for several days.

In November 1990 one of the Prime Minister's leading rivals in the Janata Dal, Chandra Shekhar (with the support of Devi Lal), formed his own dissident faction, known as the Janata Dal (Socialist) or Janata Dal (S) (which merged with the Janata Party in April 1991 to become the Samajwadi Party). The Lok Sabha convened for a special session, at which the Government overwhelmingly lost a vote of confidence. V. P. Singh immediately resigned, and the President invited Rajiv Gandhi, as leader of the party holding the largest number of seats in the Lok Sabha, to form a new government. Gandhi refused the offer, in favour of Chandra Shekhar. Although the strength of the Janata Dal (S) in the Lok Sabha comprised only about 60 deputies, Congress (I) had earlier offered it unconditional parliamentary support. On 10 November 1990 Chandra Shekhar was sworn in as Prime Minister. Devi Lal became Deputy Prime Minister and President of the Janata Dal (S). Shekhar won a vote of confidence in the Lok Sabha and a new Council of Ministers was appointed. Although Shekhar succeeded in initiating talks between the two sides in the Ayodhya dispute, violence between Hindus and Muslims increased throughout India in December.

In January 1991 the Prime Minister imposed direct rule in Tamil Nadu, claiming that this was necessitated by the increased activity of Sri Lankan Tamil militants in the state, which had led to the breakdown of law and order. In the resultant riots more than 1,000 arrests were made. The Government suffered a further set-back in February. Five members of the Council of Ministers were forced to resign when they lost their seats in the Lok Sabha for violating India's anti-defection laws: they had left the Janata Dal to join the Janata Dal (S). The fragility of the parliamentary alliance between the Janata Dal (S) and Congress (I) became apparent in March, when the Congress (I) deputies boycotted Parliament, following the revelation that Rajiv Gandhi's house had been kept under police surveillance. In an unexpected counter-move, Chandra Shekhar resigned, but accepted the President's request that he remain as head of an interim Government until the holding of a fresh general election.

As the general election, which was scheduled to take place over three days in late May 1991, approached, it seemed likely that no party would win an outright majority and that the political stalemate would continue. On 21 May, however, after the first day's polling had taken place, Rajiv Gandhi was assassinated, allegedly by members of the Tamil separatist group, the Liberation Tigers of Tamil Eelam (LTTE), while campaigning in Tamil Nadu. Consequently, the remaining elections were postponed until mid-June. The final result gave Congress (I) 227 of the 511 seats contested. The BJP, which almost doubled its share of the vote compared with its performance in the 1989 general election, won 119 seats, and the Janata Dal, the popularity of which had considerably declined, gained only 55 seats. P. V. Narasimha Rao, who had been elected as acting President of Congress (which had gradually shed its (I) suffix) following Rajiv Gandhi's assassination, assumed the premiership and appointed a new Council of Ministers. The new Government's main priority on assuming power was to attempt to solve the country's severe economic crisis, caused by an enormous foreign debt, high inflation, a large deficit on the current account of the balance of payments, and an extreme shortage of foreign-exchange reserves. The new Minister of Finance, Dr Manmohan Singh (an experienced economist and former Governor of the Reserve Bank of India), launched a far-reaching programme of economic liberalization and reform, including the dismantling of bureaucratic regulations and the encouragement of private and foreign investment. In late September the Government announced the adoption of the recommendations of the Mandal Commission that 27% of government jobs and institutional places be reserved for certain lower castes, in addition to the 22.5% already reserved for 'untouchable' castes and tribal people. (In November 1992 the Supreme Court ruled that non-Hindus, such as Christians and Sikhs, who were socially disadvantaged were also entitled to job reservations.)

After a brief reconciliatory period in the latter half of 1991, Narasimha Rao's Government began to be faced with problems, both from opposition agitation and from within its own ranks. In January 1992 the BJP increased communal tension between Hindus and Muslims by hoisting the national flag on Republic Day in Srinagar, the capital of Kashmir (see below). In mid-1992 efforts were also made by the BJP to use the contentious issue of the Ayodhya site (the Ram Janmabhoomi/Babri Masjid—Hindu temple/Muslim mosque—dispute, see above) to embarrass the Government. In May a major financial scandal involving the Bombay Stock Exchange was uncovered. It was alleged that several members of the Council of Ministers were amongst the beneficiaries, allegations that prompted the resignation of the Minister of State for Commerce. In July, however, the Congress candidate, Dr Shankar Dayal Sharma, was elected, with no serious opposition, to the presidency.

Following the collapse of talks in November 1992 between the Vishwa Hindu Parishad (VHP—World Hindu Council) and the All India Babri Masjid Action Committee regarding the Ayodhya dispute, the VHP and the BJP appealed for volunteers to begin the construction of a Hindu temple on the site of the existing mosque in early December. As thousands of Hindu militants assembled in Ayodhya, thousands of paramilitary troops were dispatched to the town in an attempt to avert any violence. Despite the armed presence, however, the temple/mosque complex was stormed by the Hindu volunteers, who proceeded to tear down the remains of the ancient mosque. This highly inflammatory action provoked widespread communal violence throughout India (Bombay, or Mumbai as it was later renamed, being one of the worst-affected areas), which resulted in more than 1,200 deaths, and prompted world-wide condemnation, notably from the neighbouring Islamic states of Pakistan and Bangladesh, where violent anti-Hindu demonstrations were subsequently held. The central Government also strongly condemned the desecration and demolition of the holy building and pledged to rebuild it. The leaders of the BJP, including L. K. Advani and the party's President, Dr Murli Manohar Joshi, and the leaders of the VHP were arrested, the BJP Chief Minister of Uttar Pradesh resigned, the state legislature was dissolved and Uttar Pradesh was placed under President's rule. The security forces took full control of Ayodhya, including the disputed complex, meeting with little resistance. The Government banned five communal organizations, including the VHP and two Muslim groups, on the grounds that they promoted disharmony among different religious communities. Throughout India stringent measures were taken by the security forces to suppress the Hindu–Muslim violence, which lasted for about one week. In mid-December the Government established a commission of inquiry into the events leading to the demolition of the mosque at Ayodhya. In an attempt to avert any further acts of Hindu militancy, the central Government dismissed the BJP administrations in Madhya Pradesh, Rajasthan and Himachal Pradesh and placed these three states under presidential rule. Narasimha Rao's various actions were given implicit approval later that month when a motion of no confidence presented by the BJP against the Government was soundly defeated. In late December the Government announced plans to acquire all the disputed areas in Ayodhya. The acquired land would be made available to two trusts, which would be responsible for the construction of a new Hindu temple and a new mosque and for the planned development of the site.

There was a resurgence of Hindu–Muslim violence in India's commercial centre, Mumbai, and in Ahmedabad in January 1993, however, necessitating the imposition of curfews and the dispatch of thousands of extra paramilitary troops to curb the serious unrest. Despite a government ban on communal rallies, thousands of Hindu militants attempted to converge on the centre of New Delhi to attend a mass rally organized by the BJP in late February. In an effort to prevent the proposed rally taking place, thousands of BJP activists were arrested throughout India and the crowds that did gather in the capital were dispersed by the security forces using batons and tear gas. In March there were a number of bomb explosions in Mumbai, resulting in some 250 casualties. Notorious criminals Dawood Ibrahim and Abu Salem, who fled India after the explosions, were suspected of organizing the bomb attacks in retaliation for the nation-wide communal riots provoked by the destruction of the mosque in Ayodhya.

In July 1993 Narasimha Rao narrowly survived a vote of no confidence, which was proposed in the Lok Sabha by virtually all the opposition parties. However, in November, in the state assembly elections in the four northern states where BJP state administrations had been dismissed by the central Government in December 1992 following the Ayodhya crisis, the BJP regained power in only one state, Rajasthan, while Congress obtained outright majorities in Himachal Pradesh and Madhya Pradesh. These results appeared to highlight a definite decline in the popularity of the BJP. In December 1993 Congress's political standing was strengthened when a small faction of the Janata Dal led by Ajit Singh merged with the ruling party, thus giving the latter a parliamentary majority.

The following year, 1994, was for the most part a period of relative political stability. The extensive economic reforms continued to show positive results and Narasimha Rao's premiership appeared fairly secure, with the opposition suffering from fragmentation (particularly the Janata Dal) and with no serious challenges from within Congress itself. The popularity and strength of the ruling Congress appeared to have declined considerably by the end of 1994, when the party suffered crushing defeats in elections to the state assemblies in its former strongholds of Andhra Pradesh and Karnataka; it was also defeated in state elections in Sikkim. In late December the Government's image was enhanced to some extent when three ministers were finally forced to resign over their alleged roles in corruption scandals (the Prime Minister had earlier been reluctant to dismiss them). Shortly afterwards, the Minister for Human Resource Development, Arjun Singh, who was widely viewed as Narasimha Rao's main rival within Congress, resigned from his post, citing his dissatisfaction and frustration at the Government's perceived incompetence regarding corruption, the Bombay Stock Exchange scandal, the Ayodhya crisis and the investigation into Rajiv Gandhi's assassination. In January 1995, with important state elections rapidly approaching, Narasimha Rao attempted to quell increasing dissent within his Government and party by suspending Arjun Singh from the working committee of Congress for 'anti-party activities'; in the following month the rebel politician was expelled from the party. In May Singh, together with Narain Dutt Tewari, recruited dissident members of Congress in many states and formed a new breakaway party, known as the All India Indira Congress (Tewari); the party merged with Congress, however, in December 1996.

Congress enjoyed mixed results in the state elections held in February–March 1995. In an apparent attempt to bolster his political standing, Narasimha Rao reshuffled and enlarged the Council of Ministers in mid-September. In January 1996, however, accusations of corruption came to the fore in Indian politics when the Central Bureau of Investigation charged seven leading politicians, including L. K. Advani of the BJP, Devi Lal and Arjun Singh, and sought the prosecution of three Union ministers (who subsequently resigned) for allegedly accepting large bribes from a Delhi-based industrialist, Surendra Jain. The sheer scale of the scandal (known as the Hawala—illegal money transfer—case), in terms of the sums involved and the number of people implicated, led to widespread public disillusionment with politicians in general. At the end of January another high-ranking political figure, the President of the Janata Dal, S. R. Bommai, was implicated in the scandal; Bommai subsequently resigned from his post. In February Congress's hopes of retaining power in the forthcoming general election appeared increasingly fragile when three more ministers resigned from the Council of Ministers after their names had been linked to the Hawala case. Meanwhile, the Prime Minister was connected to the prosecution, on charges of cheating and criminal conspiracy, of a flamboyant faith healer and 'godman', Chandraswami, who had been consulted by generations of political leaders, including Narasimha Rao himself.

The results of the general election, which was held over three days at the end of April and early May 1996, gave no party or group an overall majority. The largest party in terms of seats was the BJP, which won 160 seats, and with the support of the Shiv Sena and other smaller allies could count on an overall legislative strength of 194 seats. Congress secured 136 seats. The National Front (comprising the Janata Dal and its allies) and Left Front (representing the two major communist parties) together obtained 179 seats, with the remainder won by minor parties and independents. On 15 May, as soon as the electoral position was clear, the President asked the BJP under its new parliamentary leader, Atal Bihari Vajpayee, to form the new Government and to prove its majority support within two weeks. Given the antagonism felt towards the BJP by the majority of other political parties, the latter task proved impossible, and Vajpayee resigned on 28 May in anticipation of his Government's inevitable defeat in a parliamentary vote of confidence. In the mean time, the National and Left Fronts had merged to form an informal coalition known as the United Front (UF), which comprised a total of 13 parties, with the Janata Dal, the Samajwadi Party, the two communist parties and the regional Dravida Munnetra Kazhagam (DMK) and Telugu Desam as its major components. With Congress prepared to lend external support, the UF was able to form a Government at the end of May. A former Chief Minister of Karnataka, H. D. Deve Gowda, was selected to lead the UF and the new Government.

In September 1996 Narasimha Rao resigned from the leadership of Congress after he was ordered to stand trial for his alleged involvement in the Chandraswami case; the party presidency was assumed by the veteran politician, Sitaram Kesri. Later that month separate charges of forgery and criminal conspiracy (dating back to the former Prime Minister's tenure of the external affairs ministry in the 1980s) were made against the beleaguered Narasimha Rao; he resigned in December 1996 as Congress's parliamentary leader and was replaced in the following month by Kesri.

At the end of March 1997 Deve Gowda was faced with a serious political crisis when Congress threatened to withdraw its parliamentary support for the UF Government. On 11 April the Prime Minister resigned following the defeat of the UF administration in a vote of confidence (by 158 votes to 292). A few days later Inder Kumar Gujral, the Minister of External Affairs in the outgoing Government, was chosen by the UF to replace Deve Gowda as leader of the coalition. On 22 April Gujral was sworn in as Prime Minister and appointed a new Council of Ministers. In May Sonia Gandhi, the widow of the former Prime Minister Rajiv Gandhi, joined Congress as a 'primary member', and in the following month Kesri was re-elected President of the party in Congress's first contested leadership poll since 1977. In June 1997 the ruling coalition was faced with another high-level corruption case when the President of the Janata Dal and Chief Minister of Bihar, Lalu Prasad Yadav, was forced to resign from his posts prior to his arrest on several counts of conspiracy in a corruption scandal involving the supply of animal fodder for non-existent livestock. Yadav subsequently formed a breakaway faction of his party, known as the Rashtriya Janata Dal, and Sharad Yadav was elected as the new President of the Janata Dal. In July Kocheril Raman Narayanan was elected, almost unanimously, as India's new President; this appointment was particularly notable in that Narayanan was the first Indian President to originate from a Dalit (or 'untouchable') background. In September a five-year investigation into the destruction of the mosque at Ayodhya in 1992 led to charges of criminal conspiracy and incitement to riot being filed against senior BJP and religious leaders, including L. K. Advani and the leader of Shiv Sena, Balashaheb 'Bal' Thackeray.

The UF Government looked increasingly insecure in late November 1997 when Congress threatened to withdraw its parliamentary support unless the Tamil Nadu-based DMK, which was alleged to be indirectly implicated in the 1991 assassination of Rajiv Gandhi, was expelled from the coalition. Prime Minister Gujral rejected Congress's demand, and was consequently forced to resign on 28 November when Congress withdrew its support for the Government, as earlier threatened. This constituted the third government collapse in less than two years. In early December President Narayanan dissolved the Lok Sabha following the inability of both Congress and the BJP to form an alternative coalition government. It was announced that Gujral would retain the premiership in an acting capacity pending the holding of a fresh general election in early 1998.

During December 1997 Congress suffered a series of internal splits and defections in at least six states. In an apparent attempt to halt the fragmentation of the ailing party, in late December Sonia Gandhi agreed to campaign on behalf of Congress in the run-up to the general election. After a low-key start Sonia Gandhi gained in confidence and popularity during the campaign and attracted ever-larger crowds; she steadfastly refused, however, to stand for actual parliamentary office. Sonia Gandhi's deceased husband was, once again, in the forefront of political news at the end of January 1998, when 26 Tamil militants implicated in the murder of Rajiv Gandhi were sentenced to death by a court in Chennai (Madras). (In May 1999, however, the Supreme Court in New Delhi acquitted 19 defendants and commuted the sentences of three others.)

In the general election, which was held in February–March 1998, the BJP and its regional allies established themselves as the pre-eminent force in Indian politics. The BJP emerged as the largest party, with 182 of the 545 seats in the Lok Sabha, but failed to win an overall majority. Congress secured 142 seats, and shortly after the election Sonia Gandhi replaced Kesri as the party's President. On 19 March President Narayanan appointed the parliamentary leader of the BJP, Atal Bihari Vajpayee (who had briefly held the premiership in mid-1996), as Prime Minister and asked him to form a stable coalition government and to seek a legislative vote of confidence within the next 10 days. This he did (by 274 votes to 261) on 28 March, with the support of the All-India Anna Dravida Munnetra Kazhagam (AIADMK), the Telugu Desam (which eventually left the UF) and a number of other minor groups. None the less, it was apparent from the very outset that Vajpayee's 14-party coalition Government had a fragile hold on power and that the Prime Minister would be required to use both skill and tact to retain his position.

In May 1998 the Government shocked both India and the rest of the world by ordering the carrying out of a series of underground nuclear test explosions. This provocative action was initially greeted with massive popular enthusiasm, but Pakistan's retaliatory tests and a rapid realization of the negative international consequences (particularly the imposition of economic sanctions by the USA) soon led to a more measured domestic assessment.

In November 1998 Congress showed a strong revival in its popularity at the expense of the BJP when it removed the ruling party from power in state elections to Rajasthan and Delhi (both traditionally BJP strongholds) and unexpectedly retained its majority in the elections to the legislature in Madhya Pradesh. Congress's resurgence was variously ascribed to Sonia Gandhi's rising popularity, a reaction to the BJP's inefficiency and public anger at the soaring prices of basic commodities (notably onions, India's most basic staple after rice).

In early April 1999 Prime Minister Vajpayee rejected demands by the BJP's troublesome coalition partner the AIADMK (whose controversial leader, Jayalalitha Jayaram, was faced with ongoing investigations into corruption allegations) to reinstate the Chief of Staff of the Navy and to dismiss the Minister of Defence, George Fernandes; the following day the two AIADMK ministers resigned from the Government. The President resolved the resultant political stalemate by forcing Vajpayee to seek a parliamentary vote of confidence. The Government narrowly lost the motion (by 270 votes to 269) and the President then invited Sonia Gandhi to assemble a new coalition. Following her failure to do so, the Lok Sabha was dissolved on 26 April and fresh elections were called. Vajpayee and his Government remained in power, in an acting capacity, pending the holding of the polls.

In May 1999 Congress's erstwhile parliamentary leader, Sharad Pawar, who had earlier publicly criticized Sonia Gandhi's foreign (Italian) origins, announced the formation of a breakaway party, entitled the Nationalist Congress Party (NCP); the NCP absorbed the Indian National Congress (S) in the following month. The outbreak of hostilities between Indian and Pakistani troops in the Kargil area of Kashmir in mid-1999 (see below) had a positive effect on the nationalist BJP's standing and, in particular, on that of Vajpayee, who, as acting Prime Minister, was widely perceived to have responded with dignity, firmness and commendable restraint in the face of Pakistani provocation. The fact that India, in effect, emerged victorious from the Kargil crisis (in forcing a Pakistani retreat) had a major impact on the public's perception of the acting Government.

The BJP contested the general election, held in September–October 1999, at the head of a 24-member alliance, known as the National Democratic Alliance (NDA), which comprised numerous and diverse minor regional and national parties with little shared ideology. The NDA won an outright majority in the Lok Sabha, with 299 of the 545 seats, while Congress and its electoral allies obtained 134 seats. Although Sonia Gandhi won both of the seats that she herself contested in Karnataka and Uttar Pradesh, her lack of political experience, her weak grasp of Hindi and her foreign birth all contributed to Congress's worst electoral defeat since India's independence. Following his appointment as leader of the NDA, Vajpayee was sworn in as Prime Minister for a third term at the head of a large coalition Government.

Despite protests organized by Hindu fundamentalists and threats of sabotage, the head of the Roman Catholic Church, Pope John Paul II, conducted a peaceful state visit to India, amid tight security, in early November 1999. During the pontiff's meetings with senior Indian politicians, he broached the subject of a recent upsurge in anti-Christian persecution and called for greater religious tolerance (while asserting the freedom to proselytize).

In February and March 2000 state elections were held. Overall, regional parties fared better than Congress and the BJP. In mid-May the Government introduced three items of legislation in the Lok Sabha to establish the states of Chhattisgarh, Jharkhand and Uttaranchal, and amended versions were finally approved by the Lok Sabha and Rajya Sabha in August. The three new states came into being in November.

In October 2000 the former Prime Minister, P. V. Narasimha Rao, was convicted of corruption and was sentenced to three years' imprisonment, with a fine of Rs 100,000. (In March 2002, however, his conviction was overturned by the High Court in New Delhi.) Also in October 2000 the Central Bureau of Investigation filed charges against three Indian businessmen, the Hinduja brothers, for allegedly accepting bribes in the Bofors affair (see above). In February 2004 the Hinduja brothers were acquitted of the charges of bribery made against them, while Rajiv Gandhi was posthumously cleared of all wrongdoing. In May 2005 the brothers were acquitted of all the remaining charges against them.

In June 2000 violent attacks against Christians resumed. In an attempt to show that the Government was taking the problem seriously, Vajpayee met a delegation of bishops to discuss the renewed violence. Nevertheless, in July Indian Christians protested across South India, demanding protection against the attacks. In October the leader of the fundamentalist Hindu group Rashtriya Swayamsevak Sangh (RSS—National Volunteer Organization) urged the Government to replace 'foreign' churches with a national church and to expel all Christian missionaries. The RSS campaign caused embarrassment for the Government, in particular Vajpayee, who requested the newly appointed BJP President, Bangaru Laxman, to declare that the views of the RSS did not represent those of the BJP.

In early December 2000 communal tension between Hindus and Muslims increased, following Vajpayee's statement that the construction of the Ram Janmabhoomi, the Hindu temple, in Ayodhya was an expression of 'national sentiment that has yet to be realized' and part of the 'unfinished agenda' of his Government. Although the Prime Minister later attempted to downplay his remarks, declaring that he did not support the destruction of the Muslim Babri Masjid mosque, the opposition demanded an immediate apology and forced the abrupt adjournment of the Lok Sabha and Rajya Sabha. Opposition members also called for the resignation of three ministers, including L. K. Advani, who were expected to face charges issued by the Central Bureau of Investigation in a case relating to the demolition of the Babri Masjid. Vajpayee rejected the demand, confirming that the Government would abide by the judgment of the Supreme Court with regard to the three ministers. In February 2001 an Indian high court ruled that around 40 people could be brought to trial in connection with the destruction of the mosque in Ayodhya, and that senior BJP leaders would not be among the defendants, owing to certain technicalities. In January plans for a negotiated settlement over the religious site in Ayodhya suffered a set-back when the All India Babri Masjid Action Committee ruled out negotiations with the VHP. VHP leaders convened a religious parliament, the Dharma Sansad, at the Maha Kumbh Mela (the largest ever Hindu gathering) in January–February. The Dharma Sansad stated that all obstacles impeding the construction of the temple should be removed by the relevant organizations by mid-March 2002.

A new series of political and financial scandals exposed continuing corruption at the highest levels of government and commerce, and further undermined popular confidence in the BJP. In March 2001 an internet news service, tehelka.com, revealed videotaped evidence of senior NDA politicians and army officials accepting bribes from tehelka.com employees posing as facilitators seeking to secure a bogus defence contract. Among those exposed in this way were the President of the BJP, Bangaru Laxman, and the leader of the Samata Party, Jaya Jaitly. Both resigned from their posts following the revelations, as did the Minister of Defence, George Fernandes, who had been implicated in the scandal by Jaitly's use of his official residence as the location for the illicit transaction. (Prime Minister Vajpayee narrowly avoided involvement through implication himself.) The Minister of Railways, Mamata Banerjee of the All India Trinamool Congress, took this opportunity to resign from her government post and withdrew her party from the ruling coalition. Some days later the defence portfolio was assigned to Minister of External Affairs Jaswant Singh, while the railways portfolio was subsequently awarded to the Minister of Agriculture, Nitish Kumar. Although Vajpayee agreed to appoint a commission of inquiry into the affair, his reluctance to agree to the establishment of a joint parliamentary committee to investigate the scandal resulted in (largely successful) opposition attempts to stall proceedings in the lower house during April. In July the chairman of India's largest investment fund (Unit Trust of India—UTI) was arrested on charges of financial misappropriation. Once again, Vajpayee was alleged to have been loosely connected to the affair.

In May 2001 elections to four state assemblies and one union territory assembly resulted in major gains for Congress and its electoral allies (in Kerala and Assam) and significant reversals for the parties of the NDA coalition. At the end of July Vajpayee offered to resign, exasperated by factional tensions within the coalition, but was persuaded to retract the offer on the following day, after an expression of consolidated NDA support for his leadership. At the end of August the All India Trinamool Congress and Pattali Makkal Katchi (which had withdrawn from the NDA in February owing to regional party divisions) rejoined the governing coalition. At the beginning of September Vajpayee expanded and reorganized the Council of Ministers, and in October George Fernandes (now the leader of the Samata Party) was reappointed Minister of Defence.

In the aftermath of the devastating terrorist attacks on the US mainland on 11 September 2001, for which the USA held the al-Qa'ida (Base) organization of the Saudi national Osama bin Laden responsible, the Indian Government sought to emphasize its own uncompromising response to the activities of illegal organizations. In late September national security forces clashed with members of the outlawed Students' Islamic Movement of India (SIMI—which was alleged to be linked to both al-Qa'ida and the militant Hizbul Mujahideen, see below) in Lucknow, Uttar Pradesh. Three SIMI supporters were killed during the altercation, following which some 240 SIMI activists were arrested across the country, together with the organization's president. In late October the Government promulgated the Prevention of Terrorism Act 2001 (POTA), which replaced anti-terrorism legislation dating from 1987. The Government claimed that the new Act, which broadened the definitions of terrorist activity and the preventative and retaliatory powers of the Government (to the evident disapproval of the opposition), was necessary to accommodate the recommendations and resolutions of the UN and the international community since 11 September, and to address the recent increase in domestic terrorist activity in India. The new ordinance proscribed indefinitely 23 organizations engaged in principally separatist activities. Meanwhile, the Indian Government was increasingly frustrated by the conciliatory overtures made to the Pakistani Government by the USA in pursuit of full Pakistani co-operation with its activities in neighbouring Afghanistan.

A series of audacious terrorist attacks perpetrated by Kashmiri separatists and suspected Islamist militants severely tested the resolve of the Government in late 2001 and early 2002 (see below), resulting in an unexpected consolidation of popular and political support for the coalition. Some opponents, however, suggested that the Government's uncompromising approach to foreign policy in particular (which had brought the country to the brink of renewed military conflict with Pakistan in December 2001, see below) amounted to little more than irresponsible 'sabre rattling' designed to attract nationalist support ahead of crucial state elections scheduled for early 2002.

Meanwhile, in mid-October 2000 the Supreme Court approved the continuation of work on the controversial Sardar Sarovar dam, on the Narmada River in Gujarat. Construction had been halted in 1994, when environmental activists representing the tens of thousands of people whom the dam would displace lodged a case against the authorities. The World Bank had withdrawn its funding, citing environmental concerns, in 1993. Campaigners against the project claimed that the authorities had failed to provide an acceptable rehabilitation and resettlement programme. (By late 2006 it was reported that the construction of the dam had almost been completed, but thousands of people had not yet been resettled.) In January 2001 a devastating earthquake occurred in Gujarat. More than 30,000 people were killed and more than 1m. people were made homeless. The central Government and the state government of Gujarat were criticized for their tardy reaction to the disaster, a delay that reportedly led to greater loss of life.

In January 2002 Prime Minister Vajpayee resumed efforts to resolve the dispute over the religious site in Ayodhya. The All India Babri Masjid Action Committee, however, refused to enter negotiations with the uncompromising VHP. In early February the BJP declared in its manifesto for state elections in Uttar Pradesh that it would abide by a court decision or a negotiated settlement between the Hindu and Muslim groups over the disputed site. The BJP had traditionally enjoyed close links with the VHP, but national politics required the governing party to distance itself from the militant Hindu group. As the deadline set by the Dharma Sansad to begin building the temple in mid-March approached (see above), hundreds of Hindu activists assembled in Ayodhya to take part in the illegal construction. Despite warnings by the Government that it would enforce the law, a senior VHP leader announced in late February that the movement of building material to the site would begin on 15 March. In late February communal violence broke out in Gujarat after a train carrying members of the VHP returning from Ayodhya was attacked by a suspected group of Muslims in the town of Godhra. The attack, in which 60 Hindu activists were killed, provoked a cycle of communal violence throughout Gujarat that lasted for several weeks and resulted in the deaths of up to 2,000 people, the majority of whom were Muslims. The Indian army was drafted in to quell the riots. Opposition members demanded the resignation of the Minister of Home Affairs, L. K. Advani, and the Chief Minister of Gujarat, Narendra Modi, for failing to control the riots, amid claims that the Government deliberately prevented the police from controlling the Hindu activists. In late April the European Union's report on the situation in Gujarat, which corroborated a number of other reports published in the same month, concluded that the riots and killings had been, contrary to the official account, not in reaction to the attack on the train, but in fact an organized massacre of Muslims, and that the security forces had been under orders not to intervene. Modi eventually resigned and recommended the dissolution of the state assembly in mid-July; he was requested to continue as leader of an interim administration until state elections were held in December. Meanwhile, in mid-March security forces prevented Hindu nationalists from defying a court order and entering the disputed religious site in Ayodhya. In March 2003 the Allahabad High Court ordered the Archaeological Survey of India to carry out an excavation at the disputed site to ascertain whether an earlier Hindu temple existed beneath the Babri mosque. Meanwhile, the VHP continued its campaign to build a temple at the site.

In the mean time, the BJP fared badly in elections to four state assemblies in late February 2002, while Congress enjoyed two victories (in the Punjab and Uttaranchal). At the end of April the federal Minister of Coal and Mines resigned and withdrew his Lok Jan Shakti party from the NDA in protest against the Government's handling of the situation in Gujarat. Meanwhile, in late March a constitutional review commission, chaired by former Chief Justice M. N. Venkatachaliah, submitted a report of its two-year review of the country's Constitution. The report recommended about 250 changes to the laws relating to political parties, elections, fundamental rights and judicial and executive accountability. The report, however, did not address the issue of whether a person of foreign origin should hold a constitutional post, a question particularly relevant to Italian-born Sonia Gandhi's position. At the end of June, the Minister of Home Affairs, L. K. Advani, was assigned the additional portfolio of Deputy Prime Minister, prompting speculation that he had been nominated as Vajpayee's eventual successor. In early July a government reorganization took place in which Jaswant Singh and Yashwant Sinha, the Ministers of Foreign Affairs and Finance, respectively, exchanged portfolios. At the same time Venkaiah Naidu was designated President of the BJP, replacing Jana Krishnamurthy, who was appointed Minister of Law and Justice. Later that month the Government's candidate, Aavul Pakkiri Jainulabidin Abdul Kalam, a South Indian Muslim who was closely involved in the development of the country's missile and nuclear programme, won a convincing victory in the presidential election. In August the more orthodox Bhairon Singh Shekhawat was elected as Vice-President (his predecessor died two weeks before the scheduled election date).

In mid-August 2002 the Election Commission rejected interim Chief Minister Narendra Modi's request to conduct early elections to the Gujarat state assembly in October, stating that the situation was not stable enough: many people were still displaced as a result of the riots and communal tensions prevailed in the region. In September Modi launched a controversial 4,800-km Hindu nationalist *gaurav rath yatra* (pride march) around the state of Gujarat in an attempt to garner support for the BJP. Although the Election Commission banned Modi from using the incident in Godhra as an election tool, the symbol of a burning train was displayed on election posters across the state. Communal tensions in the region were, not surprisingly, exacerbated by Modi's Hindu nationalist and overtly anti-Muslim election campaign. The elections to the Gujarat state assembly took place on 12 December. The BJP won 51% of the vote, securing 126 of the 182 seats in the state legislature. Congress, criticized for selecting only five Muslim candidates and for attempting to attract the Hindu nationalist vote (albeit at a lesser level than the BJP), despite being a secular party, won only 51 seats. Modi returned to power as Chief Minister. Meanwhile, in late September two armed assailants forced entry into a Hindu temple in Gujarat and shot dead 29 worshippers and injured 74 people; three commandos were also killed. The gunmen were shot dead by security forces, ending a night-long siege of the temple. It was believed that the perpetrators, reportedly members of a relatively unknown militant Islamist group called Tehrik-i-Kasas (Movement of Revenge), carried out the attack in retaliation for the deaths of Gujarati Muslims in the riots earlier in the year. The Indian Government accused the Pakistani Government of orchestrating the attack, an allegation strongly rejected by the latter. Controversy over the 2002 riots continued as communal tensions persisted; complaints were issued about compensation levels for victims of the riots and the failure to prosecute the perpetrators of the violence. In September 2003 the Supreme Court openly challenged the Government of Gujarat's competence and integrity to pursue any case against alleged rioters. Two months later the Court ordered that 10 high-profile trials of people accused of communal violence in Gujarat in 2002 be halted in response to a petition by the National Human Rights Commission to transfer all such trials to courts outside Gujarat because of witness intimidation and inadequate police investigations. Several days later a court in Gujarat convicted 12 Hindus of killing 14 Muslims during the riots in 2002 and sentenced them to life imprisonment.

In January 2003 Vajpayee carried out an extensive government reorganization, promoting several principal economic reformers to senior positions in an attempt to boost the economic liberalization programme. The transfer of senior ministers to leading roles within the BJP was regarded as a move to strengthen the party ahead of state elections scheduled for February and the general election due to take place in 2004. In the weeks leading up to four state elections, Hindu activists representing the BJP and VHP focused on inciting Hindu nationalist sentiment in an attempt to reproduce the victory achieved in Gujarat two months previously. However, the BJP fared badly in all four elections, which were held on 26 February, losing power in Himachal Pradesh to Congress.

In the mean time, in early January 2003 the Government announced that it had established a Nuclear Command Authority to manage India's nuclear weapons, giving sole authority to launch a nuclear strike to the Prime Minister and his advisers. The Government also stated that it would forgo its 'no first use' policy on nuclear weapons if India were the target of a major attack using chemical or biological weapons. A number of bomb explosions occurred in Mumbai in December 2002–January 2003, killing at least two people and injuring almost 90. Another bomb explosion was carried out in the city in March, killing at least 12 people. No group claimed responsibility for any of the attacks. In August two car-bombs exploded in Mumbai, killing 52 people and injuring 150. In June 2004 five people were charged under the POTA in connection with the bombings.

In March 2003 the Supreme Court declared invalid a provision in the Representation of the People (Amendment) Act and restored an earlier order, thus making it mandatory for electoral candidates to disclose criminal records, educational qualifications and assets when filing their nomination papers. The Court criticized the Government for its 'half-hearted' approach to electoral reform. Earlier that month the Chief Minister of Uttar Pradesh and leader of the Bahujan Samaj Party (BSP), Mayawati, was accused of misappropriating state funds. Relations between the BSP and BJP at state level deteriorated and in August Mayawati resigned after the coalition state Government disbanded; the President of the Samajwadi Party, Mulayam Singh Yadav, was appointed as the new Chief Minister. Also in August, the Archaeological Survey of India issued its report on the disputed site in Ayodhya to the Lucknow High Court. The report indicated that there was evidence of a massive temple-like structure existing from the 10th century, supporting claims that a Hindu temple once stood on the site. However, the report was challenged by a group of independent archaeologists and historians, claiming that the Survey had misused or falsified evidence for political reasons, not least because the findings contradicted the Survey's interim report, which was published in June. Meanwhile, in May the Central Bureau of Investigation filed new charges against L. K. Advani and seven other leading politicians in connection with the destruction of the mosque in Ayodhya in December 1992. In September 2003 a special court exonerated L. K. Advani of any role in inciting crowds, provoking the demolition of the mosque and encouraging communal agitation, but sustained the charges against the seven others, including the Minister of Human Resources Development, of Ocean Development and of Science and Technology, Dr Murli Manohar Joshi, who consequently tendered his resignation. In late September, however, a High Court deferred criminal proceedings against Joshi, pending an inquiry into the charges against him; Vajpayee immediately rejected Joshi's resignation.

Assembly elections in the states of Chhattisgarh, Madhya Pradesh, Mizoram and Rajasthan and the National Capital Territory of Delhi took place in November–December 2003. The Mizoram National Front retained power in Mizoram, while the BJP enjoyed notable success in Chhattisgarh, Madhya Pradesh and Rajasthan, at the expense of Congress. The scale of the BJP's victory was attributed to the party's focus on development and governance issues and lack of emphasis on Hindu nationalist themes during its election campaign, and to the anti-incumbency factor. Congress, however, managed to retain power in Delhi, where Sheila Dixit secured a second term as Chief Minister. Encouraged by the BJP's victory at the state elections, and buoyed by a surging economy and an improvement in relations with Pakistan, Vajpayee announced in mid-January 2004 that a general election would be held by the end of April, five months earlier than scheduled. In the mean time, in December 2003 the DMK withdrew its support for the ruling NDA, owing to the BJP's recent support for the AIADMK, the DMK's rival, and to differences over the POTA; the DMK Minister of Environment and Forests, T. R. Baalu, and the DMK Minister of State for Health, A. Raja, consequently resigned. The regional Marumalarchi Dravida Munnetra Kazhagam (MDMK) also withdrew from the NDA; Pattali Makkal Katchi followed suit in January 2004, announcing that it was to form an alliance with the DMK and Congress. The AIADMK, meanwhile, announced that it would form an alliance with the BJP to contest the forthcoming general election. In the same month the NCP split into two factions; the faction led by Sharad Pawar entered into an alliance with Congress, while Purno Shangma's group agreed to support the NDA. The Lok Sabha was dissolved on 6 February in preparation for an early general election.

In April–May 2004 the general election was held. Congress defeated the NDA, securing, together with its allies, a final total of 222 seats (incorporating the results of voting in several constituencies where polling was postponed until later in May) in the 545-member Lok Sabha, compared with 186 for the NDA. Congress alone won 145 seats, while the BJP secured 138. Left Front parties also performed well at the polls, with the Communist Party of India—Marxist (CPI—M) winning 43 seats. Shortly after the election Sonia Gandhi, who had been unanimously endorsed by Congress, its allies and the Left Front (which had offered its support to a Congress-led Government) as a prime ministerial candidate, announced that she did not intend to stand for the office. She would, however, remain President of Congress, and was elected as Chairwoman of the newly formed Congress-led coalition, the United Progressive Alliance (UPA). The respected Sikh economist Dr Manmohan Singh, a former Minister of Finance and member of the Rajya Sabha, was subsequently appointed as India's first non-Hindu Prime Minister by President Kalam on Gandhi's recommendation, assuming office on 22 May. K. Natwar Singh was appointed Minister of External Affairs in the new UPA Government, while P. Chidambaram was allocated the finance portfolio and Shivraj Patil the home affairs portfolio. Following the election, former Prime Minister Vajpayee stood down as parliamentary leader of the BJP; he was replaced by L. K. Advani.

Meanwhile, elections also took place in May 2004 to four state legislative assemblies. Congress secured a dramatic victory in Andhra Pradesh, comprehensively defeating the Telugu Desam, which had previously held a majority in the state.

At the first session of the newly elected Lok Sabha, held in June 2004, the BJP disrupted the meeting by protesting against the UPA's appointment of three ministers—all members of the Bihar-based Rashtriya Janata Dal—who had been charged variously with corruption and attempted murder, most notably the new Minister of Railways, Lalu Prasad Yadav, who continued to face corruption charges related to his tenure as Chief Minister of Bihar in 1997. In the following month the Government dismissed the Governors of Goa, Gujarat, Haryana and Uttar Pradesh, owing to their alleged links to the RSS Hindu fundamentalist group. In September the Council of Ministers approved the repeal of the controversial POTA and stated its intention to amend the Unlawful Activities (Prevention) Act, 1967, by adding another ordinance in order to incorporate legislative provisions against terrorism. The Rajya Sabha gave its assent to the legislation in December.

Meanwhile, in October 2004 state legislative elections took place in Maharashtra, resulting in another victory for Congress. Following the BJP's removal from office in the state, the party's President, Venkaiah Naidu, resigned. L. K. Advani was elected to succeed him. Meanwhile, Congress also secured a majority at legislative elections in the state of Arunachal Pradesh. In December Minister of Railways Lalu Prasad Yadav faced charges of alleged bribery after being filmed handing out money to his supporters during a political rally in Bihar. In April 2005 formal charges were brought against Yadav relating to his alleged involvement in embezzlement during his tenure as Chief Minister of Bihar in the 1990s; further charges were lodged in the following month.

India was one of the countries worst affected by the devastating tsunami generated by a huge earthquake in the Indian Ocean on 26 December 2004. The states of Tamil Nadu, Kerala and Andhra Pradesh and the Union Territory of Pondicherry on the east coast were all affected, together with the Andaman and Nicobar Islands, which were severely damaged. The disaster resulted in the loss of around 16,000 lives and numerous homes and livelihoods. The Government was able to provide aid to those affected in India without requesting any international assistance, and also provided emergency relief to other countries affected by the disaster, notably Sri Lanka and the Maldives.

In June 2005 divisions emerged within the BJP, following comments made by its President, L. K. Advani, during a trip to Pakistan that were perceived to be in praise of Mohammed Ali Jinnah, the founder of Pakistan. Advani's comments attracted harsh criticism from certain elements of his party, which claimed that he had betrayed its *Hindutva* ('Hinduness') ideology. In July charges were brought against Advani (and seven others) in connection with the riots at Ayodhya in 1992, overturning a ruling in September 2003 exonerating him of blame. In September 2005 Advani announced that he would resign from the leadership of the party at the end of the year; his resignation, which took place in December, was believed to be largely a result of pressure from the RSS, which had close links with the BJP. Rajnath Singh, a former Chief Minister of Uttar Pradesh and a federal minister in the Government of Atal Bihari Vajpayee, was subsequently appointed as Advani's successor.

In late 2005 the Government suffered a set-back when the Minister of External Affairs, K. Natwar Singh, was implicated as a beneficiary of corrupt practices following an investigation into the UN's 'oil for food' programme in Iraq. Singh was forced to resign from his post in November, accepting instead the position of Minister without Portfolio; however, he stepped down from the Council of Ministers in the following month after the BJP refused to permit any business to take place in the Lok Sabha until he was removed from the Government. Prime Minister Manmohan Singh subsequently assumed the external affairs portfolio. In August 2006 K. Natwar Singh was suspended from the primary membership of Congress following the release of the official report on the 'oil for food' programme, which found that, although the former minister had not benefited financially, he had been involved to some extent in influencing the corrupt practices; Congress itself was absolved of any involvement. Meanwhile, in

December 2005 a total of 11 legislators (10 from the Lok Sabha and one from the Rajya Sabha) were expelled from Parliament, having been filmed in the process of accepting bribes, apparently in exchange for asking certain questions in the chamber. Six of those expelled were BJP legislators. The expulsion was the largest to have taken place in India since independence.

In January 2006 an extensive reorganization of the Council of Ministers was carried out, as part of which Murli Deora was appointed to the prominent post of Minister of Petroleum and Natural Gas. The Prime Minister retained charge of the external affairs portfolio. In February the BJP assumed a position in government in a southern Indian state for the first time when, in coalition with the Janata Dal (Secular), it came to power in Karnataka. In March Sonia Gandhi resigned as a member of the Lok Sabha and as Chairperson of the National Advisory Council (NAC), following assertions made by her opponents regarding the alleged illegality of her holding both positions simultaneously (the latter was viewed as an 'office of profit' and therefore untenable for a member of parliament). A wider government debate about the issue of such offices ensued, and in May the Parliament (Prevention of Disqualification) Amendment Bill was presented for presidential approval. This piece of legislation categorized 56 posts as non 'office of profit' positions, including the chairmanship of the NAC. In the same month Sonia Gandhi was re-elected to the Lok Sabha in a by-election in Rae Bareilly. In April and May legislative elections were held in four states and in the Union Territory of Pondicherry (now Puducherry). Congress retained power (albeit in alliance with smaller parties) in Assam (Asom) and in Puducherry, but the Congress-led coalition government in Kerala was soundly defeated by a left-wing alliance of parties headed by the CPI—M. The coalition government headed by the CPI—M in West Bengal won a second term in office.

In August 2006 one of Congress's coalition partners, the regional party Telangana Rashtra Samithi (TRS), expressed its dissatisfaction with the Government's apparent lack of commitment to creating an independent Telangana state in Andhra Pradesh, by withdrawing from the UPA; this withdrawal of support entailed the resignation of the leader of the TRS, K. Chandrasekhar Rao, from his post as Minister of Labour and Employment. In October Prime Minister Manmohan Singh instigated a ministerial reorganization, including the allocation of the external affairs portfolio to the erstwhile Minister of Defence, Pranab Mukherjee, and the labour and employment portfolio to Oscar Fernandes. A. K. Antony was appointed as the new Minister of Defence.

In early 2007 state legislative elections were held in Manipur, Punjab and Uttarakhand. Although the Congress coalition secured a victory in Manipur, the party was defeated by an alliance of the Shiromani Akali Dal and the BJP in the Punjab and by the BJP in Uttarakhand. Elections in Uttar Pradesh were carried out in several phases in April and May, and resulted in a clear majority for the BSP; its leader, Mayawati, was subsequently sworn in as Chief Minister for the fourth time. Congress prevailed at elections in Goa in June, retaining a majority through an alliance with the NCP, independent candidates and members of a regional party, although its long-term stability was challenged by a subsequent withdrawal of support. In late 2007 the BJP defeated the incumbent Congress party at elections in Himachal Pradesh, and continued to dominate Gujarati politics with a victory in that state; the latter result in particular was said to bode well for a resurgence of the BJP on a national scale. In response to political instability, direct presidential rule was imposed in Karnataka in October. Nagaland was also brought under presidential rule in January 2008, owing to political uncertainty following the successful passage of a vote of no confidence against the state government. However, legislative elections were held in Nagaland in March, at which the Nagaland People's Front won the largest number of seats and, in alliance with the BJP, NCP and independents, subsequently formed a government. In further state elections in the same month, the ruling CPI—M won a fourth term in office in Tripura after securing a clear majority in the polls, and Congress remained the single largest party in the coalition government in Meghalaya, but without a majority. Without the requisite legislative support, the incumbent Congress Chief Minister of Meghalaya, D. D. Lapang, resigned as Chief Minister ahead of a vote of no confidence and was replaced by Donkupar Roy of the regional United Democratic Party.

The federal Government suffered a set-back in February 2007, when the Samajwadi Party withdrew from the UPA central coalition; this was followed by the withdrawal of the MDMK in March. Later in the year the Government encountered significant opposition to its nuclear agreement with the USA from parties of the Left Front bloc, which, although not a member of the UPA, had traditionally provided parliamentary support to the coalition (see below). In July, upon the expiry of A. P. J. Abdul Kalam's presidential term, the UPA candidate and erstwhile Governor of Rajasthan, Pratibha Patil, was sworn in to succeed him. Although Patil's election as the first woman President of India represented a milestone in the country's history, the UPA's choice of nominee was not without controversy, with critics objecting to a perceived politicization of the office and Patil's reportedly unexceptional record. However, despite a challenge from the incumbent Vice-President, Bhairon Singh Shekhawat, who presented himself as an independent candidate (while having the unofficial support of the NDA), Patil received the larger proportion of votes in Parliament, almost twice as many as Shekhawat. In August Mohammad Hamid Ansari, the UPA nominee, was elected Vice-President. Shortly afterwards, India celebrated its 60th anniversary of independence. In September the rapid rise to political prominence of Rahul Gandhi, the son of Sonia Gandhi and Rajiv Gandhi, continued, with his appointment as a general secretary of Congress.

In 2007 the establishment of Special Economic Zones (SEZs) was a major point of controversy in a number of states, including West Bengal, where activists and local people protested against the forcible seizure of land for industrial development. In March these protests escalated into violence in the Nandigram region of the state, resulting in some 14 fatalities. Land reform became the subject of protests in October, when thousands of rural demonstrators entered Delhi, having marched across the country; among their demands was the formation of a supervisory body. In response, the Government pledged to appoint a panel, including indigenous citizens and representatives of the landless, to assess what action should be taken in the area of land reform. Meanwhile, government plans to introduce larger quotas in higher education for the so-called 'Other Backward Classes' (a category that included numerous under-privileged and low-caste groups) were suspended by the Supreme Court in March, owing to an apparent lack of recent data on the relevant populations. The proposed measures had prompted both praise and criticism, along with large-scale demonstrations.

During 2005–07 there was a series of terrorist attacks against civilian targets in various locations across the country. In late October 2005 a number of bomb attacks in the national capital, New Delhi, resulted in the deaths of more than 60 people. In November police announced that they had arrested a man suspected of having financed and planned the bombings. He was believed to be a member of the Pakistan-based militant group Lashkar-e-Taiba, which had previously denied responsibility for the attacks. In March 2006 a number of bombs exploded at a Hindu temple and a railway station in the holy city of Varanasi in Uttar Pradesh, resulting in the deaths of at least 14 people. Several suspects, allegedly linked to the Bangladesh-based Islamist militant group Harakat-ul-Jihad-i-Islami, were subsequently arrested. On 11 July about 180 people were killed and hundreds more injured in a series of bomb blasts on the Mumbai train network. In October 28 people were charged with involvement in the bombings, including 15 suspects who had not yet been apprehended. Among those charged *in absentia* was Azam Cheema, who was reported to be a member of Lashkar-e-Taiba (although in July Lashkar-e-Taiba had apparently denied responsibility for the attacks). Another series of bomb explosions, at a Muslim cemetery in Malegaon, Maharashtra, killed at least 37 people in September. By the end of November several suspects, with alleged links (according to a police statement) to the banned Students' Islamic Movement of India, had been arrested. In August 2007 two bomb explosions in the southern city of Hyderabad killed some 42 people.

Regional issues continue to play an important role in Indian political affairs. In 1986 the Gurkhas (of Nepalese stock) in West Bengal launched a campaign for a separate autonomous homeland in the Darjiling (Darjeeling) region and the recognition of Nepali as an official language. The violent separatist campaign, led by the Gurkha National Liberation Front (GNLF), was prompted by the eviction of about 10,000 Nepalis from the state of Meghalaya, where the native residents feared that they were becoming outnumbered by immigrants. When violent disturbances and a general strike were organized by the GNLF in June 1987, the central Government agreed to hold tripartite talks with the GNLF's leader, Subhas Ghising, and the Chief Minister of

West Bengal. The Prime Minister rejected the GNLF's demand for an autonomous Gurkha state, but Ghising agreed to the establishment of a semi-autonomous Darjiling Hill Development Council. Under the formal peace agreement, the GNLF was to cease all agitation and to surrender weapons, while the state Government was to release all GNLF detainees. The Government agreed to grant Indian citizenship to all Gurkhas born or domiciled in India. Elections to the Darjiling Hill Development Council were held in November. The GNLF won 26 of the 28 elective seats (the 14 remaining members of the Council were to be nominated) and Ghising was elected Chairman of the Council. However, the GNLF continued to demand the establishment of a fully autonomous Gurkha state. In 1992 a constitutional amendment providing for the recognition of Nepali as an official language was adopted. In September 2006 West Bengal police revealed that a new separatist organization called the United Gurkha Revolution Front had recently been formed. The group, which was led by former GNLF member Ajay Dhahal, was believed to be armed. In February 2008 a splinter group of the GNLF, the Gurkha Liberation Forum, blockaded entry routes into Darjiling to protest against a new autonomy agreement drawn up between the Darjiling Hill Development Council and the state and federal authorities.

In December 1985 an election for the state assembly in Assam was won by the Asom Gana Parishad (AGP—Assam People's Council), a newly formed regional party. This followed the signing, in August, of an agreement between the central Government and two groups of Hindu activists, concluded after five years of sectarian violence, which limited the voting rights of immigrants (mainly Bangladeshis) to Assam. When the accord was announced, Bangladesh stated that it would not take back Bengali immigrants from Assam and denied that it had allowed illegal refugees to cross its borders into Assam. Another disaffected Indian tribal group, the Bodos of Assam, demanded a separate state of Bodoland within India. In February 1989 the Bodos, under the leadership of the All Bodo Students' Union (ABSU), intensified their separatist campaign by organizing strikes, bombings and violent demonstrations. The central Government dispatched armed forces to the state. In August the ABSU held peace talks with the state government and central government officials, agreeing to suspend its violent activities, while the Assam government agreed to suspend emergency security measures. The situation became more complicated in 1989, when a militant Maoist group, the United Liberation Front of Assam (ULFA), re-emerged. The ULFA demanded the outright secession of the whole of Assam from India. In 1990 the ULFA claimed responsibility for about 90 assassinations, abductions and bombings. In November, when the violence began to disrupt the state's tea industry, the central Government placed Assam under direct rule, dispatched troops to the state and outlawed the ULFA. By late December the unrest seemed to have been substantially quelled. In the state elections in 1991 the AGP was defeated, and Congress (I) took power. In September, following the breakdown of prolonged talks with the ULFA, the Government launched a new offensive against the ULFA guerrillas and declared the entire state a disturbed area. Meanwhile, following the suspension of violence by the ABSU, the Bodo Security Force (BSF) assumed the leading role in the violent campaign for a separate state of Bodoland. The BSF was outlawed by the central Government in November 1992. At a tripartite meeting attended by the Minister of State for Home Affairs, the Chief Minister of Assam and the President of the ABSU in Guwahati in February 1993, a memorandum was signed providing for the establishment of a 40-member Bodoland Autonomous Council, which would be responsible for the socio-economic and cultural affairs of the Bodo people. However, attacks leading to substantial loss of life were made by Bodo and ULFA activists in the second half of the 1990s, both on the security forces and on non-tribal groups in the area. In March 2000 the Government and the Bodo Liberation Tigers (BLT—a group that had waged a violent campaign for a separate state for the Bodo people since 1996) agreed to a cease-fire. Peace negotiations were instigated, and in September the cease-fire was extended by one year.

In February 2002 it was reported that the Assam state assembly had passed a resolution granting a degree of autonomy to the Bodo people through the creation of a territorial council for the Bodos of four western districts of the state. One year later, the Union Government, state government and BLT signed a pact formally agreeing upon the introduction of a Bodoland Territorial Council. The Council was established in December 2003 and the Bodo militants surrendered their weapons to mark the formal disbanding of the BLT. However, the ULFA continued its campaign of violence and inter-tribal clashes also occurred in the state. In August 2004 the ULFA was believed to have been responsible for an explosion at a parade held in the town of Dhemaji to commemorate Independence Day, which killed 16 people, many of whom were children. In October a series of violent incidents in Assam and neighbouring Nagaland was attributed to the ULFA and the National Democratic Front of Bodoland (NDFB), one of the militant groups operating in the region. In May 2005 the NDFB signed a cease-fire agreement with both the government of Assam and the Union Government, with all parties pledging to suspend hostile operations for one year. In September the ULFA agreed to conduct peace negotiations with the Union Government, on the condition that the army halted the counter-insurgency operation that it was conducting in the state. Talks between the two sides were held for the first time in February 2006; by September, however, negotiations between the Government and the ULFA-elected People's Consultative Group had collapsed, and the following months witnessed an escalation of violence, with the Government dispatching further troops to the region to deal with the insurgents. There was also an increase in attacks on migrant workers in Assam, allegedly perpetrated by the ULFA, together with the new strategy of targeting Congress officials, the most notable example of which was the murder of a senior regional Congress leader in the eastern district of Golaghat in February 2007, which was blamed on the separatist group. In September a senior military leader of ULFA, Prabal Neog, was reportedly arrested by the Indian security forces.

Elsewhere in north-eastern India, violence, both inter-tribal (particularly against ethnic Bengali settlers) and anti-Government, continued in Tripura, Bihar, Mizoram and Manipur. The Chief Minister of Manipur escaped an assassination attempt by suspected separatists in July 2003. In November the daughter of a Naga state minister in Manipur was kidnapped and killed; no one claimed responsibility. In April 2004 talks between Minister of Home Affairs L. K. Advani and various factions of the militant National Liberation Front of Tripura resulted in the announcement of a six-month cease-fire in Tripura, which, it was hoped, would act as a prelude to further peace negotiations. Meanwhile, however, it was reported that five north-eastern separatist groups, including the ULFA, had rejected an offer by the Prime Minister of unconditional peace talks. In late July 2004 the death of an alleged militant led to a series of violent protests and strikes in Manipur. The protesters demanded the repeal of the Armed Forces Special Powers Act (AFSPA), which they claimed condoned the perpetration of human rights abuses by security forces in the state. In October, in advance of talks between the federal Government and the Apunba Lup, an organization of civil groups leading protests in the state, the Government announced that it was willing to consider lifting the application of the AFSPA in Manipur. In February 2005 the United National Liberation Front (UNLF), another rebel group operating in Manipur, offered to hold peace talks with the Government, stating that it was willing to end conflict in the state if the UN was permitted to mediate in the dispute. However, the condition was rejected by the Government and, in May, fighting was reported to have broken out between the UNLF and another rebel group, the Christian Zomi Revolutionary Army (ZRA). In the following month Naga insurgents imposed a blockade on the main highway into Manipur, which lasted into August, demanding the integration of parts of the state into Nagaland. In October the Indian army launched a widespread offensive against the UNLF, after it rejected a government offer to open peace negotiations. In November the Union Government announced that it would extend its ban on six of the revolutionary groups operating in Manipur, including the UNLF, for a further two years. In May 2006 the Chief Minister of Manipur survived a second assassination attempt carried out by suspected separatist rebels. Statistics released by the federal Ministry of Home Affairs in February 2008 showed an alarming increase in the number of civilian deaths caused by violent unrest in Manipur, Assam and Nagaland.

In June 2001 a decision by the Union Government to extend the duration of a cease-fire arrangement with Nagaland separatists, which encompassed territories beyond the state borders, provoked condemnation and concerns about the expansionist ambitions of the rebels in the neighbouring states of Manipur, Assam and Arunachal Pradesh, where there were known to be bases of the National Socialist Council of Nagaland—Issak

Muivah (NSCN—IM), a rebel organization that had openly advocated the creation of a 'greater Nagaland'. In Manipur, where the collapse of the state government had led to the imposition of President's rule in the previous month, there was consolidated political opposition to the move and fierce popular objection, prompting the dispatch of national paramilitary forces to the region to restore order. In late July the national Government agreed to restrict the cease-fire arrangement to the state of Nagaland, angering local political groups in that state. In November 2002 the central Government lifted its ban on the NSCN—IM and agreed to hold unconditional negotiations on the political status of Nagaland. The move allowed the leaders of the separatist group to travel to India for the first time in 37 years. At the end of talks in January 2003 the Naga leaders declared that the separatist insurgency had ended and both sides declared their commitment to continuing the peace process until a permanent settlement was reached. The issue of a 'greater Nagaland', however, was avoided. In state elections in February, Congress lost power to the Democratic Alliance of Nagaland. In February 2005 the central Government held four rounds of peace talks with the NSCN—IM; further discussions took place in July. In August the Government also held its first formal dialogue with a rival faction of the group, the NSCN—Khaplang (NSCN—K). In January 2006 a delegation from the NSCN—IM met with government officials in Bangkok, Thailand, in order to negotiate a further extension of the ongoing cease-fire, which had continued to be renewed at regular intervals. In July the cease-fire was renewed for a further year, and in August 2007 it was renewed indefinitely.

In September 1985 there was a temporary improvement in the unstable situation in the Punjab when an election for the state assembly was held, following an agreement between the central Government and the main Sikh party, the Shiromani Akali Dal (SAD). The election was peaceful and resulted in a victory for the SAD, which assumed power after two years of presidential rule. Part of the 1985 agreement was the proposed transfer of Chandigarh, since 1966 the joint capital of the Punjab and Haryana, to the Punjab alone. In return, Haryana was to benefit from the completion of the Sutlej-Yamuna canal, to bring irrigation water from the Punjab to the dry south of the state, and the transfer of several Hindi-speaking border villages from the Punjab to Haryana. Four commissions were established to organize the transfer, but all failed, and the transfer subsequently appeared to have been suspended indefinitely. In January 1986 Sikh extremists re-established a stronghold inside the Golden Temple complex at Amritsar and Hindu–Sikh violence continued throughout the year. In mid-1986 the extremists separated from the ruling moderate SAD (Longowal) and formed several militant factions. In 1987 Rajiv Gandhi reimposed President's rule in the Punjab. Despite the resumption of discussions between the Government and the moderate Sikh leaders, the violence continued. In November 1991 more than 50,000 extra troops were deployed in the Punjab (bringing the total number of army, paramilitary and police forces in the state to about 200,000) as part of an intensification of operations against Sikh separatists in the run-up to the state elections and parliamentary by-elections, which were held in mid-February 1992. Congress won 12 of the 13 parliamentary seats in the Punjab and gained an overall majority in the state legislature. The elections, which brought to an end five years of presidential rule, were, however, boycotted by the leading factions of the SAD and attracted an extremely low turn-out. The Congress state government that was formed under the leadership of Beant Singh, therefore, lacked any real credibility. Despite the continuing violence between the separatists and the security forces, the large turn-out in the municipal elections in September (the first in 13 years) afforded some hope that normality was returning to the Punjab. Local council elections, held in January 1993 (the first in 10 years), also attracted a substantial turn-out. The security situation improved steadily in the course of 1993 and political activity revived. In late August 1995, however, violence erupted in the Punjab again when Beant Singh was killed in a car-bomb detonated by suspected Sikh extremists in Chandigarh (in July 2007 two men, including the alleged leader of a Sikh separatist group, were sentenced to death for their involvement in the murder). Fortunately, this appeared to have been an isolated act of terrorism. The national elections in April/May 1996 were conducted smoothly in the Punjab, and gave the mainstream SAD a convincing victory in the state's parliamentary constituencies. The incumbent Congress administration was routed by an SAD/BJP electoral alliance in state elections held in February 1997; in contrast to the 1992 state elections, turn-out was high. In both the 1998 and 1999 parliamentary elections the SAD again established an electoral alliance with the BJP, and was awarded representation in Prime Minister Vajpayee's consecutive administrations.

In June 2004 the recently elected government of Andhra Pradesh agreed a cease-fire with the People's War Group, a faction of the Communist Party of India (Marxist-Leninist), which had been waging a sporadic violent campaign in the state since 1980. The Naxalite rebels demanded the creation of a communist state comprising tribal areas in Andhra Pradesh, Maharashtra, Orissa, Bihar and Chhattisgarh. In July 2004 the 11-year government ban that had been imposed on the organization was removed ahead of planned peace negotiations. In September the People's War Group merged with another militant separatist group, the Maoist Communist Centre, to become the Communist Party of India (Maoist). The first round of peace negotiations was held in Hyderabad in October, and concluded with both sides deciding to continue the dialogue process. However, in January 2005 the rebels announced that they were breaking off peace negotiations in protest at police killings of their members. They accused the state government of failing to observe the cease-fire agreed in June 2004. Violence subsequently escalated, and in August 2005 the state government imposed a fresh ban on the Communist Party of India (Maoist), after rebels murdered nine people in the town of Narayanpet.

In September 2005 an Inter-State Joint Task Force was established following an agreement among the Chief Ministers of 13 states affected by ongoing Naxalite insurgencies. The Force was intended to co-ordinate operations against guerrillas across state borders, and was to have the assistance of the Union Government. In the same month the government of Chhattisgarh outlawed all Naxalite organizations, following a recent increase in insurgent activity in the state. Meanwhile, the Communist Party of India (Maoist) reportedly vowed to co-operate with Maoist insurgents in the neighbouring kingdom of Nepal to promote communism in both countries. In April 2006 Prime Minister Dr Manmohan Singh stated that the Naxalite insurgency posed the 'single biggest internal security challenge' to India, and called for further co-operation between the main affected states. In 2007 insurgents were allegedly involved in the road blockades and attacks on infrastructure staged in protest against the establishment of SEZs in states such as West Bengal (see above). During 2006–07 Naxalite attacks and clashes between rebels and security forces in Chhattisgarh reportedly resulted in several hundred deaths, many of them civilians.

In 1986 India and Bangladesh signed an agreement on measures to prevent 'cross-border terrorism'. In 1988 the two countries established a joint working committee to examine methods of averting the annual devastating floods in the Ganga (Ganges) delta. In 1992 the Indian Government, under the provisions of an accord signed with Bangladesh in 1974, formally leased the Tin Bigha Corridor (a small strip of land covering an area of only 1.5 ha) to Bangladesh for 999 years. India maintained sovereignty over the Corridor, but the lease gave Bangladesh access to its enclaves of Dahagram and Angarpota. The transfer of the Corridor occasioned protests from right-wing quarters in India, who also made an issue over the presence in Delhi and other cities of illegal immigrants from Bangladesh and claimed that the Bangladeshi Government had done little to protect its Hindu minority. In December 1996 India signed an 'historic' treaty with Bangladesh, which was to be in force for 30 years, regarding the sharing of the Ganga waters. The worst fighting between the two countries since 1976 took place in April 2001 on the Bangladeshi border with the Indian state of Meghalaya. Some 16 members of the Indian Border Security Forces and three members of the Bangladesh Rifles were killed. The situation was brought under control and the two sides entered border negotiations in June, as a result of which two joint working groups were established to review the undemarcated section of the border. Relations between India and Bangladesh deteriorated in November 2002 as a result of accusations by India's Deputy Prime Minister and Minister of Home Affairs, L. K. Advani, that al-Qa'ida had increased its activities in Bangladesh since the assumption of power by the coalition headed by the Bangladesh Nationalist Party in October 2001. Advani also claimed that Bangladesh was covertly assisting al-Qa'ida and Pakistan's Inter-Services Intelligence Agency, and was providing refuge for Indian separatist groups. The Bangladeshi Government strongly denied the allegations. In January 2003 the Indian Government announced plans to deport, for reasons of security, some 16m. Bangladeshis who it claimed were working and living in India illegally. The Bangladeshi Government rejected the claim as groundless. In September 2004 senior Indian and Bangladeshi officials held talks in Dhaka concerning security issues and water sharing. While some agreement was reached on water sharing and the two countries agreed to co-ordinate their border patrols, Bangladesh continued to deny the existence of Indian separatists inside its borders. Relations remained strained into 2005, and tensions were exacerbated in February by India's decision not to attend a planned summit of the South Asian Association for Regional Co-operation (SAARC, see p. 384) in Bangladesh in February, citing security concerns; this forced the postponement of the meeting until later that year. Further clashes occurred between the border patrols of the two countries in March and, later in that month, talks were held in an attempt to resolve the ongoing problems, which had been exacerbated by India's continued construction of a fence along the joint border, in contravention of its obligations under a 1974 treaty. The Indian Government claimed that the fence was intended to prevent Bangladeshi insurgents and illegal immigrants from crossing the border. Several further clashes occurred in the following months, as relations remained tense. In October 2007 military officials from Bangladesh and India held talks in Dhaka with the aim of resolving outstanding border issues; the two countries reiterated their commitment to sharing information and co-operating in their fight against militants and criminals in border areas.

Relations between India and Nepal deteriorated in 1989, when India decided not to renew two bilateral treaties determining trade and transit, insisting that a common treaty covering both issues be negotiated. Nepal refused, stressing the importance of keeping the treaties separate on the grounds that Indo-Nepalese trade issues were negotiable, whereas the right of transit was a recognized right of land-locked countries. India responded by closing most of the transit points through which Nepal's trade was conducted. The dispute was aggravated by Nepal's acquisition of Chinese-made military equipment, which, according to India, violated the Treaty of Peace and Friendship of 1950. However, in June 1990 India and Nepal signed an agreement restoring trade relations and reopening the transit points. Chandra Shekhar visited Kathmandu in February 1991 (the first official visit to Nepal by an Indian Prime Minister since 1977), shortly after it was announced that the first free elections in Nepal were to be held in May. In June 1997 the Indian Prime Minister, Inder Kumar Gujral, made a visit to Nepal and announced the opening of a transit route through north-east India between Nepal and Bangladesh. Gujral and the Nepalese Prime Minister, Lokendra Bahadur Chand, also agreed that there should be a review of the 1950 treaty between the two countries. In February 2005 relations with Nepal were seriously affected when the Nepalese king orchestrated a coup, dismissing the Government and declaring a state of emergency in the country. It was feared that a significant number of Maoist rebels from Nepal might infiltrate the country's border with India's fractious north-eastern states, a concern borne out to an extent by a reported decision by the Communist Party of India (Maoist) and Nepalese rebels to co-operate in promoting the spread of communism in both countries. India subsequently ceased provision of all military aid to Nepal and intensified security along the shared border. In July India resumed non-lethal military aid to Nepal. In January 2006 the bilateral transit treaty expired; in order to allow time for a review of the agreement, India subsequently extended the term of the treaty. The bilateral trade treaty expired in March 2007, but was automatically renewed pending its review by the two sides. Meanwhile, in June 2006, following the reinstatement of Parliament, the newly appointed Nepalese Prime Minister, G. P. Koirala, paid an official visit to India, during which India pledged to increase aid to Nepal.

Relations with Pakistan had deteriorated in the late 1970s and early 1980s, owing to Pakistan's potential capability for the development of nuclear weapons and as a result of major US deliveries of armaments to Pakistan. The Indian Government believed that such deliveries would upset the balance of power in the region and precipitate an 'arms race'. Pakistan's President, Gen. Mohammad Zia ul-Haq, visited India in 1985, when he and Rajiv Gandhi announced their mutual commitment not to attack each other's nuclear installations and to negotiate the sovereignty of the disputed Siachen glacier region in Kashmir. Pakistan continued to demand a settlement of the Kashmir problem in accordance with earlier UN resolutions, prescribing a plebiscite under the auspices of the UN in the two parts of the state, now divided between India and Pakistan. India argued that the problem should be settled in accordance with the Shimla Agreement of 1972, which required that all Indo-Pakistani disputes be resolved through bilateral negotiations. The Indian decision to construct a barrage on the River Jhelum in Jammu and Kashmir, in an alleged violation of the 1960 Indus Waters Treaty, also created concern in Pakistan. In December 1988 Rajiv Gandhi visited Islamabad for discussions with Pakistan's Prime Minister, Benazir Bhutto. The resulting agreements included a formal pledge not to attack each other's nuclear installations. Relations reached a crisis in late 1989, when the outlawed Jammu and Kashmir Liberation Front (JKLF) and several other militant Muslim groups intensified their campaigns of civil unrest, strikes and terrorism, demanding an independent Kashmir or unification with Pakistan. The Indian Government dispatched troops to the region and placed the entire Srinagar valley under curfew. Pakistan denied India's claim that the militants were trained and armed in Pakistan-held Kashmir (known as Azad Kashmir). In January 1990 Jammu and Kashmir was placed under Governor's rule, and in July under President's rule. Tension was eased in December, following discussions between the Ministers of External Affairs of both countries. Violence between the Indian security forces and militant groups, however, continued during 1991–92. Throughout 1993 and in early 1994, the Government's approach to the Kashmir crisis was a combination of a tough military policy and generally fruitless attempts to engage in dialogue. In December 1994 Pakistan was successful in securing the passage of a resolution condemning reported human rights abuses by Indian security forces in Kashmir at a summit meeting of the Organization of the Islamic Conference (OIC, see p. 369). (In the same month Pakistan's decision to close down its consulate in Mumbai, amid claims of Indian support for acts of terrorism in Karachi, provided a further indication of the growing rift between the two countries.) By 1996 the total death toll resulting from the conflict in Jammu and Kashmir, including civilians, security force personnel and militants, was estimated at up to 20,000. The situation in Kashmir improved somewhat, however, when elections for the national parliamentary seats were held in the troubled state shortly after the general election in April–May 1996. Following the successful holding of elections to the Lok Sabha, state elections (the first to be held since 1987) were conducted in Jammu and Kashmir in September and attracted a turn-out of more than 50%, despite being boycotted by the majority of the separatist groups and being dismissed as a sham by the Pakistani Government. The moderate Jammu and Kashmir National Conference, led by Dr Farooq Abdullah, won the majority of seats in the state assembly, and, on assuming power, immediately offered to instigate talks with the separatist leaders.

Meanwhile, in June 1994 the Indian army had begun to deploy a new missile, *Prithvi*, which had the capacity to reach most of Pakistan. While the 'arms race' between the two countries continued, with claims on both sides concerning the other's missile programmes, talks (which had been suspended since 1994) were resumed in March 1997, both at official and at ministerial level. Tension increased in September when a large-scale outbreak of artillery exchanges along the Line of Control (LoC) resulted in about 40 civilian deaths. After a hiatus of more than one year (during which time both countries carried out controversial nuclear test explosions—see above), Indo-Pakistani talks at foreign secretary level regarding Kashmir and other issues were resumed in Islamabad in October 1998. In February 1999 relations appeared to improve considerably when Prime Minister Vajpayee made an historic bus journey (inaugurating the first passenger bus service between India and Pakistan) over the border to Lahore. Following his welcome by the Pakistani Prime Minister, Mohammad Nawaz Sharif, the two leaders held a summit meeting (the first to be conducted in Pakistan for 10 years), at which they signed the Lahore Declaration, which, with its pledges regarding peace and nuclear security, sought to allay world-wide fears of a nuclear 'flashpoint' in South Asia, and committed the two sides to working towards better relations and to implementing a range of confidence-building measures. The contentious subject of Jammu and Kashmir was, however, largely avoided.

Despite the apparent *rapprochement* between India and Pakistan, in April 1999 both countries carried out separate tests on their latest missiles, which were capable of carrying nuclear warheads. In early May the situation deteriorated drastically when the Indian army discovered that Islamist guerrilla groups, reinforced by regular Pakistani troops, had occupied strategic positions on the Indian side of the LoC in the Kargil area of Kashmir. Air-strikes launched by the Indian air force at the end of the month failed to dislodge the so-called 'infiltrators', and the army was forced to wage an expensive and lengthy campaign, during which more than 480 Indian soldiers were killed and two Indian military aircraft were shot down. In mid-July, however, Indian military dominance combined with US diplomatic pressure led to a Pakistani withdrawal. In August there was renewed tension when India shot down a Pakistani naval reconnaissance aircraft near Pakistan's border with Gujarat, killing all 16 personnel on board; Pakistan retaliated the following day by opening fire on Indian military aircraft in the same area.

In April 2000 there were indications that the Indian Government was willing to re-establish dialogue with Kashmiri militants. Leaders of the All-Party Hurriyat Conference (APHC), an organization that, to an extent, acted as the political voice for some of the militant groups, were released in April and May. In July one of the main militant groups, the Hizbul Mujahideen, declared a three-month cease-fire. The gesture obtained a quick and positive response from the Indian Government: the Indian Army suspended all offensive operations against the Kashmiri militants for the first time in 11 years. Other militant groups, however, denounced the cessation of hostilities as a betrayal and continued their violent campaign in an attempt to disrupt the peace process. The Hizbul Mujahideen ended the cease-fire at the beginning of August owing to the Indian Government's opposition to instigating tripartite negotiations including representatives of Pakistan. Consequently, Pakistan appeared relatively moderate and India somewhat intransigent. Vajpayee accused Pakistan of orchestrating the events, of encouraging divisions among militant leaders and of turning the Kashmir issue into a pan-Islamic movement.

Following the collapse of the cease-fire, violence in the region intensified. In November 2000 the Chief Minister of Jammu and Kashmir, Dr Farooq Abdullah, announced the instigation of a judicial inquiry into the killing of 36 unarmed Sikhs in March and the killing of five alleged militants a few days later by Indian security forces. In the same month the Indian Government declared the suspension of combat operations against Kashmiri militants during the Muslim holy month of Ramadan. The unilateral cease-fire began at the end of November (and was subsequently extended, at intervals, until the end of May 2001); Indian security forces were authorized to retaliate if fired upon. The majority of national parties and foreign governments supported the cessation of hostilities, although the Pakistani authorities described the cease-fire as 'meaningless' without simultaneous constructive dialogue. The APHC welcomed the development and offered to enter negotiations with Pakistani authorities in order to prepare for tripartite discussions. The Hizbul Mujahideen and other militant groups, however, rejected the offer and continued their campaign of violence, extending their activities as far as the Red Fort in Old Delhi, where three people were shot dead in December 2000. In the same month Pakistan extended an invitation to the APHC to participate in joint preparations for the establishment of tripartite negotiations. Although Abdul Ghani Lone, a leading member of the APHC, was permitted to make a private visit to Islamabad in November, passport applications for a delegation of leaders were subsequently refused. In mid-January 2001 the Indian High Commissioner to Pakistan visited Gen. Musharraf. This meeting constituted the first high-level contact between the two countries since the military coup in Pakistan in 1999. The two officials urged an early resumption of negotiations on the Kashmir question. At the end of May 2001 the Government announced the end of its unilateral cease-fire; more than 1,000 people were estimated to have been killed in violence related to the crisis in the region since the cease-fire was first announced in November 2000.

Relations with Pakistan appeared to improve following the earthquake in Gujarat in January 2001, when Pakistan offered humanitarian relief to India and the leaders of the two countries thus established contact. In May Vajpayee issued an unexpected invitation to Gen. Musharraf to attend bilateral negotiations in Agra in July. However, hopes for a significant breakthrough on the issue of Kashmir were frustrated by the failure of the two leaders to agree to a joint declaration at the conclusion of the dialogue; the divergent views of the two sides on the priority issue in the dispute (cross-border terrorism according to India, and Kashmiri self-determination in the opinion of Pakistan) appeared to be more firmly entrenched than ever. Violence increased in the region following the disappointment engendered by the meeting, and in August the Indian Government extended its official 'disturbed area' designation (invoking the 1990 AFSPA) to cover all districts of the state of Jammu and Kashmir (only Ladakh was unaffected). Tension with Pakistan was heightened considerably following a guerrilla-style attack on the state assembly building in Srinagar on 1 October. An estimated 38 people (including two of the four assailants) were killed and around 70 were wounded in the attack and in the subsequent confrontation with security forces. The Indian Government attributed responsibility for the attack to the Pakistan-based Jaish-e-Mohammed and Lashkar-e-Taiba groups. Tensions were exacerbated later in the month when Gen. Musharraf rejected official Indian requests to ban the activities of the organizations in Pakistan, although he did publicly condemn the attack.

On 13 December 2001 five armed assailants gained access to the grounds of the Union Parliament in New Delhi and attempted to launch an apparent suicide attack on the parliament building. Although no parliamentary deputies were hurt in the attack, 14 people (including the five assailants, a number of policemen, some security officials and a groundsman) were killed and some 25 were injured. The Indian authorities again attributed responsibility for the attack to the Jaish-e-Mohammed and Lashkar-e-Taiba groups, and suggested that the assailants appeared to be of Pakistani origin. Pakistan, which had been among the many countries to express immediate condemnation of the attack (which was popularly described as an assault on democracy), now demanded to see concrete proof to support the allegations made by the Indian Government, while the US Administration urged the Indian authorities to exercise restraint in their response. Tensions between India and Pakistan continued to mount when Mohammed Afzal, a member of Jaish-e-Mohammed arrested in Kashmir on suspicion of complicity in the incident, admitted his involvement and alleged publicly that Pakistani security and intelligence agencies had provided support to those directly responsible for the attack. India recalled its High Commissioner from Islamabad and announced that overground transport services between the two countries would be suspended from 1 January 2002. As positions were reinforced with troops and weapons (including missiles) on both sides of the LoC, there was considerable international concern that such brinkmanship might propel the two countries (each with nuclear capabilities) into renewed armed conflict. Mindful of the potential detriment to security at Pakistan's border with Afghanistan that could result from an escalation in conflict in Kashmir, the USA applied increased pressure on the beleaguered Pakistani Government (already facing vociferous domestic opposition to its accommodation of US activities in Afghanistan) to adopt a more conciliatory attitude towards India's security concerns, and in late December 2001 the Pakistani authorities followed the US Government's lead in 'freezing' the assets of the two groups held responsible for the attack on India. The leaders of the two groups were later detained by the Pakistani authorities (who arrested some 80 suspected militants in the last week of December), but, despite evident satisfaction at this development, the Indian Government continued to dismiss much of the Pakistani response as superficial and demanded that the two leaders be extradited (together with 20 other named Pakistan-based militants) to stand trial in India. However, in December 2002 Pakistan freed one of the leaders, Maulana Masood Azhar, from house arrest. Later that month a special court established under POTA (see above) convicted three Kashmiri Muslims—two of whom were reportedly members of Jaish-e-Mohammed and the third a member of the JKLF—of organizing the attack on the Union Parliament and sentenced them to death. (A High Court ruling, however, overturned the convictions of two of the men following an appeal in October 2003.)

It had been hoped that tensions between the two countries might be defused by renewed dialogue between Vajpayee and Musharraf at a SAARC summit meeting convened in Nepal in the first week of January 2002, but contact between the two men was minimal, and troops on both sides of the LoC continued to exchange gunfire in the days following the conference. However, on 12 January Musharraf yielded to relentless international pressure by publicly condemning the activities of militant extremists based in Pakistan and announcing the introduction of a broad range of measures to combat terrorist activity and religious zealotry, including the proscription of five extremist organizations (among them the Jaish-e-Mohammed and the Lashkar-e-Taiba). Within two days the Pakistani authorities claimed to have closed almost 500 offices used by the five organizations and to have arrested some 1,400 suspected activists, prompting considerable international praise for the initiative. An armed attack by four suspected Islamist militants on a US cultural centre in Kolkata (Calcutta) on 22 January, in which five Indian policeman were killed and more than 20 were injured, placed relations between the two countries under renewed strain when the Indian authorities attempted to link the unidentified assailants (who escaped after the attack) to the Pakistani intelligence services. However, it was hoped that reports published in late January, which indicated that the number of terrorist incidents in Jammu and Kashmir had halved since the introduction of Pakistan's new counter-insurgency measures earlier in the month, would help foster a more substantial improvement in future relations between the two countries. Tensions between the two countries rose again, following a suspected Islamist militant attack on an army camp in Jammu and Kashmir in mid-May, in which 34 people were killed, including 19 civilians. India identified the gunmen as Pakistani nationals and a few days later requested the withdrawal of Pakistan's High Commissioner to India. The two countries appeared to be on the brink of war again as positions were reinforced with troops and weapons on both sides of the LoC and exchanges of gunfire intensified. Indo-Pakistani relations deteriorated further following the assassination of Abdul Ghani Lone, the leader of the APHC, on 21 May, by suspected Islamist militants. As a result of international efforts to ease tensions between the two neighbours, in June India withdrew five naval ships from patrol of the coast of Pakistan and allowed Pakistani civilian aircraft to enter its airspace, in response to Pakistani pledges to halt cross-border infiltration. In mid-October the Minister of Defence stated that India would withdraw a large number of troops from the international border with Pakistan; the number of troops along the LoC would remain unchanged, however. Pakistan responded by withdrawing a portion of its troops.

Meanwhile, the crisis between India and Pakistan and the related militant activity within Kashmir adversely affected the Indian Government's relations with the APHC. In mid-July 2002 the Chief Minister of Jammu and Kashmir announced that scientific tests had shown that five men killed by Indian security forces in March 2000 had been local civilians and not, as maintained at the time, militants responsible for the murder of 36 unarmed Sikhs (see above). In early August 2002 it was announced that state elections would be held in Jammu and Kashmir in four phases, from mid-September. The APHC declared that it would boycott the election, regarding it as meaningless unless a referendum on independence was held first. In September the state Minister of Law and Parliamentary Affairs of Jammu and Kashmir was assassinated by suspected militant Islamists intent on disrupting the election campaign and poll. Violence continued throughout the election period. However, the elections took place in late September–early October; overall, voter turn-out reached 44%. No single party won an outright majority: the Jammu and Kashmir National Conference secured 28 seats, Congress won 20 seats and the regional People's Democratic Party (PDP) won 16 seats. The APHC rejected the result and demanded that a plebiscite be established; the Pakistani Government dismissed the election as a 'sham' and 'farcical'. Violence overshadowed the polls: at least 730 people had reportedly been killed since the announcement of the elections. Congress and the PDP were invited to form a coalition government; however, the national Government had to assume direct control over Jammu and Kashmir after the two parties were unable to come to a power-sharing arrangement by 17 October, the expiry date of the outgoing assembly. Eventually, in late October Congress and the PDP reached a compromise: it was agreed that PDP leader Mufti Mohammed Sayeed would be Chief Minister for the first three years, followed by local Congress president Ghulam Nabi Azad for the next three years. The coalition government was inaugurated in early November. Kashmiri separatists dismissed Sayeed's policy of reconciliation by continuing their violent campaign. Nevertheless, as promised at the end of October, Sayeed authorized the release of several political prisoners charged with 'non-serious' crimes. The release of Yasin Malik, the leader of the JKLF detained under the POTA in March, was the most significant. The state government also pledged to disband the Special Operations Group of the police, which had been accused in the past of serious human rights violations.

Indo-Pakistani relations deteriorated in early 2003. Tensions were exacerbated by India's latest round of 'routine' ballistic-missile tests, the violence in Kashmir and India's new military agreement with Russia (see below). In late January India ordered four officials at Pakistan's High Commission in New Delhi to leave the country for 'indulging in activities incompatible with their official status'—a euphemism for spying. Pakistan reacted by expelling four officials at the Indian High Commission in Islamabad. In early February India expelled Pakistan's acting High Commissioner, Jalil Abbas Jilani, accusing him of funding Kashmiri separatist groups; four other Pakistani officials were charged with spying and expelled. Pakistan retaliated by ordering India's acting High Commissioner, Sudhir Vyas, and four colleagues to leave, for allegedly spying. In March separatist violence in Jammu and Kashmir escalated. The killing of 24 Kashmiri Hindus, including women and children, in a remote village south of Srinagar by suspected Islamists at the end of the month, provoked widespread condemnation and was a set-back to Sayeed's reconciliation programme. Tensions between India and Pakistan, meanwhile, increased after Pakistan responded to India's decision to conduct 'routine' missile tests without advance warning by carrying out a set of its own tests. Nevertheless, in mid-April, during a visit to Jammu and Kashmir, Vajpayee offered to enter dialogue with Pakistan; the Pakistani Prime Minister, Zafarullah Khan Jamali, welcomed the decision and formally invited Vajpayee 10 days later to visit Pakistan. In early May the Indian and Pakistani premiers agreed to restore diplomatic relations and civil aviation links. Two months later the bus service between the Pakistani city of Lahore and New Delhi was restored. India, however, continued to insist on a complete cessation of cross-border infiltration as a precondition for peace talks.

Meanwhile, from July 2003 the security situation worsened: militant activity, including suicide attacks, and the exchange of gunfire across the LoC increased. The assassination of the militant leader Ghazi Baba at the end of August provoked a surge in violence in September. In the same month the APHC openly split after the new leadership of Maulvi Abbas Ansari, the first Shi'a Muslim to chair the Hurriyat Conference, was challenged by a significant faction, which proceeded to elect former Chairman Syed Ali Shah Geelani instead.

In October 2003 the Indian Minister of External Affairs, Yashwant Sinha, announced 12 confidence-building measures to improve and normalize relations with Pakistan, including offers to enter another round of talks to restore civil aviation links, to introduce more transport links (including a bus service between the capitals of the disputed region across the LoC), to resume full sporting contacts and to enter dialogue with separatist politicians in Kashmir. Sinha emphasized, however, that no direct talks on Kashmir between India and Pakistan would take place until the latter ceased cross-border infiltration by Islamist militants. Pakistan issued a cautious welcome to most of the proposals, while declaring that bus travellers in Kashmir would need UN travel documents, but was disappointed that there was no offer of a meeting. On 23 November Pakistani Prime Minister Jamali announced a unilateral cease-fire along the LoC, to begin at midnight two days later (on the Muslim festival of Id). Jamali also responded to Vajpayee's offer to discuss transport links by proposing an additional bus service between the Pakistani city of Lahore and the Indian city of Amritsar. India reciprocated the gesture (but reserved the right to fire at so-called 'infiltrators') and offered to extend the cease-fire across the Actual Ground Position Line in Siachen as well as across the international border. Pakistan agreed to the proposal and at midnight on 25–26 November a cease-fire came into effect. In mid-December the chances of a peace agreement between India and Pakistan improved after President Musharraf declared that Pakistan was prepared to abandon a long-standing demand for a UN-sponsored plebiscite for the Kashmiri people; India welcomed the initiative. At the same time, Indian and Pakistani officials signed a three-year agreement on the restoration from mid-January 2004 of a passenger and freight train service between New Delhi and Lahore. Direct aviation links were resumed on 1 January 2004. In late December 2003 it was reported that, since the implementation of the cease-fire, separatist-related violence in Jammu and Kashmir had declined.

At a ground-breaking SAARC summit meeting in Islamabad in early January 2004, Musharraf assured Vajpayee that he would not permit any territory under Pakistan's control to be used to support terrorism; in return Vajpayee agreed to begin negotiations on all bilateral issues, including Kashmir, in February. A round of 'fruitful' talks between L. K. Advani and a delegation of the APHC took place in New Delhi in January, followed by a second round in March. Meanwhile, however, Islamist militants who were unhappy with what they perceived as a betrayal by Musharraf continued their violent campaign. Indian and Pakistani senior officials opened discussions in Islamabad in mid-February, when a timetable for future dialogue was established. The APHC called for a boycott of the general election, held in April–May, and a series of violent attacks directed at all politicians campaigning in Jammu and Kashmir over the election period resulted in several deaths. Overall electoral turn-out in Kashmir was 35%, although this declined to less than 19% in Srinagar. Following the election the state experienced its worst incidence of violence since April 2003 when a land-mine exploded under a bus carrying Indian soldiers on the Srinagar–Jammu highway, killing at least 33 people. The Hizbul Mujahideen claimed responsibility for the attack. In June 2004 several rounds of discussions took place between Indian and Pakistani officials in New Delhi. In a joint statement issued at the end of the month both sides stressed their renewed commitment to reaching a negotiated final settlement on the Kashmir issue and agreed to restore their diplomatic missions to full strength and, in principle, to reopen their respective consulates in Mumbai and Karachi. An agreement was also reached that each country would, in future, notify the other of any forthcoming missile tests. In September India and Pakistan held their first, official, ministerial-level talks in more than three years in New Delhi. As a result, the two sides agreed to implement a series of confidence-building measures, including the restoration of bilateral transport links.

In November 2004, ahead of his first visit to Kashmir since becoming Prime Minister, Manmohan Singh ordered a 'substantial' reduction in the number of Indian troops deployed in the state, a move welcomed by Pakistan. In January–February 2005 Jammu and Kashmir held its first municipal elections in 27 years. Meanwhile, tensions resurfaced between India and Pakistan in early 2005, with each side accusing the other of violating the ongoing cease-fire along the LoC. However, in February, following talks between the Indian and Pakistani ministers responsible for foreign affairs, the two countries agreed to open a bus service across the LoC, linking Srinagar with Muzaffarabad. Despite militant threats of disruption, and several attacks on the proposed route, the service opened in early April 2005. Plans were also announced to reopen the consulates in Mumbai and Karachi. In mid-April Musharraf travelled to India for the first time since 2001 and met with Manmohan Singh in New Delhi for further peace talks; the two countries subsequently issued a statement referring to the peace process as 'irreversible' and agreeing to improve trade and transport links over the LoC.

In June 2005 a delegation of leaders from the APHC crossed the LoC and travelled to Muzaffarabad, where they held talks with Kashmiri leaders. The visit represented the first time since 1946 that Indian Kashmiri politicians had been permitted to traverse the LoC. In September Manmohan Singh held talks with APHC leaders in New Delhi. In the same month, in a symbolic gesture, the Government began to withdraw paramilitary Border Security Force troops from Srinagar; responsibility for security in the city was subsequently assumed by the Central Reserve Police Force.

In October 2005 the devastating consequences of a massive earthquake centred in Azad Kashmir had implications for the ongoing peace process. In the aftermath of the disaster, which resulted in widespread loss of life and destruction, particularly on the Pakistani side of the LoC, Pakistan accepted an Indian offer of aid. Following a series of negotiations, the two countries subsequently agreed to open a number of crossing points on the LoC, in order to permit the reunification of divided families. The crossing points were finally opened in November. However, continued fears on the part of both countries that the other would take advantage of the situation to conduct military surveillance hampered the prospect of more extensive co-operation. Despite speculation that many militants operating in the area had been killed by the earthquake, sporadic separatist violence continued; in mid-October the state Minister of Education, Ghulam Nabi Lone, was assassinated at his home in Srinagar. In January 2006 a suggestion by Musharraf in a televised interview that India demilitarize three cities in the Kashmir valley in order to advance the peace process was rejected by the Indian Government. In February a second rail link was opened between the two countries, linking the town of Munabao in Rajasthan to the Pakistani town of Khokrapar in Sindh.

Relations between India and Pakistan became strained following the Mumbai bombings in July 2006 (see above). Although President Musharraf condemned the attacks, Prime Minister Singh suggested that those responsible had links to Pakistan. Bilateral peace talks were postponed, and in September the Mumbai police claimed that Lashkar-e-Taiba was responsible for the July bombings and had apparently been aided in the attacks by Pakistan's Inter-Services Intelligence agency (an accusation swiftly denied by the Pakistani authorities). In November, following talks between the foreign secretaries of both countries, India and Pakistan agreed to establish an information-sharing panel to co-operate on anti-terrorism measures. In February 2007, however, explosions on the Samjhauta Express train, which was bound for Lahore, Pakistan, from Delhi, caused a devastating fire on board, killing at least 67 passengers, the majority of whom were Pakistani nationals. The attack was viewed by many as an attempt to hinder the peace process between the two countries. Pakistan immediately called for prompt and decisive action to bring the perpetrators to justice. Later in the month Mukherjee and his Pakistani counterpart, Khurshid Kasuri, signed an agreement designed to prevent inadvertent nuclear conflict between the two countries, and the planning and implementation of other confidence-building measures continued in areas such as trade and transport.

Since 1983 India's relations with Sri Lanka have been dominated by conflicts between the island's Sinhalese and Tamil communities, in which India has sought to arbitrate. In July 1987 Rajiv Gandhi and the Sri Lankan President, Junius Jayewardene, signed an accord aimed at settling the conflict. An Indian Peace-Keeping Force (IPKF) was dispatched to Sri Lanka but encountered considerable resistance from the Tamil separatist guerrillas. Following the gradual implementation of the peace accord, the IPKF troops completed their withdrawal in March 1990. Violence flared up again, however, and the flow of Sri Lankan refugees into Tamil Nadu increased considerably. By late 1991 the number of Sri Lankans living in refugee camps in the southern Indian state was estimated at more than 200,000. The assassination of Rajiv Gandhi in May 1991, allegedly by members of the LTTE, completed India's disenchantment with the latter organization. Measures were subsequently taken by the state government in Tamil Nadu to suppress LTTE activity within the state, and also to begin the process of repatriating refugees. The repatriation programme (allegedly conducted on a voluntary basis) proved a slow and difficult process. In May 1992 the LTTE was officially banned in India. In December 1998 the Indian Prime Minister and Sri Lankan President signed a bilateral free-trade agreement, which finally came into effect in March 2000.

During 1981 there was an improvement in India's relations with the People's Republic of China. Both countries agreed to attempt to find an early solution to their Himalayan border dispute and to seek to normalize relations, and a number of working groups were subsequently established. In February 1991 a major breakthrough occurred when a draft protocol for 1991/92, including the proposed resumption of border trade between the two countries for the first time in three decades, was signed. All six border posts had been closed since the brief border war in 1962. In December 1991 the Chinese Prime Minister, Li Peng, made an official visit to India (the first such visit to India by a Chinese Prime Minister for 31 years), during which a memorandum on the resumption of bilateral border trade was signed. Bilateral border trade was actually resumed between India and China in July 1992. Sino-Indian relations were further strengthened as a result of a three-day visit to India conducted by the Chinese President, Jiang Zemin, in November 1996 (the first visit by a Chinese Head of State to India). Despite the gradual improvement in relations, however, India has frequently indicated that it is unhappy with the nuclear asymmetry between the two countries and with what it perceives as China's willingness to transfer missiles and missile technology to Pakistan. Sino-Indian relations deteriorated following India's 1998 nuclear tests, partly because China believed that India was using a fabricated threat from China to justify its actions. In June 1999 the Indian Minister of External Affairs visited Beijing to restore Sino-Indian dialogue. During border negotiations in November 2000, India and China exchanged detailed maps of the middle sector of the Line of Actual Control: a significant step towards resolving differences. In April 2003 the Indian Minister of Defence paid a week-long visit to Beijing to discuss outstanding bilateral issues, including China's support for Pakistan and Chinese observation posts in the Bay of Bengal. Prime Minister Vajpayee made a state visit to China in June 2003 (the first by an Indian premier in 10 years), during which a number of agreements were signed, the most significant being India's official recognition of Chinese sovereignty over Tibet (the Xizang Autonomous Region). China also agreed to trade with the north-eastern Indian state of Sikkim, thus implicitly acknowledging India's control of that area. The two countries appointed special representatives to discuss the border disputes that had led to the 1962 war. In January 2005 India and China held their first-ever strategic dialogue, in New Delhi, agreeing, *inter alia*, to attempt to resolve their boundary dispute in a fair and mutually satisfactory manner. In April of that year Chinese Premier Wen Jiabao visited India. During his stay he signed a series of agreements with Indian Prime Minister Manmohan Singh; these included plans for the resolution of the boundary dispute and the expansion of bilateral trade. In July 2006 the reopening of the historic border trading post of Nathu La (which was once part of the ancient Silk Road) highlighted the ongoing improvement in Sino-Indian relations, which was further strengthened when the Chinese President, Hu Jintao, paid an official visit to India in November. During his visit the two countries agreed to co-operate in several fields, including nuclear energy, and expressed their mutual aim to double bilateral trade by 2010. Prime Minister Singh reciprocated with a visit to China in January 2008, meeting with President Hu and Premier Wen in order to discuss issues such as trade and defence.

In October 2004 the Chairman of Myanmar's ruling body, the State Peace and Development Council, Field Marshal Than Shwe, paid the first visit to India by a Myanma head of state in 24 years. The visit was illustrative of improving relations between the two countries, deemed necessary if India was to combat successfully the problem of insurgents in north-eastern India establishing bases across the border in Myanmar.

Prior to its disintegration in December 1991, the USSR was a major contributor of economic and military assistance to India. In early 1992 both Russia and Ukraine agreed to maintain arms supplies to India, and in February an Indo-Russian trade and payments protocol was signed. The President of Russia, Boris Yeltsin, made an official visit to India in 1993, during which he signed an Indo-Russian Treaty of Friendship and Co-operation. In October 1996 India and Russia signed a defence co-operation agreement (later extended to 2010), and in December India signed a US $1,800m. contract to purchase 40 fighter aircraft from Russia. In June 1998 Russia defied a Group of Eight (G-8) ban on exporting nuclear technology to India by agreeing to supply the latter with two nuclear reactors. In November 1999 India and Russia signed a defence agreement regarding their joint manufacture of military aircraft and submarines. In October 2000 the newly elected Russian President, Vladimir Putin, visited India. The two countries signed a declaration of 'strategic partnership', which involved co-operation on defence, economic matters and international terrorism issues. India signed a contract to purchase a further 50 fighter aircraft from Russia, with a licence to manufacture around 150 more. The agreement, reportedly worth more than $3,000m., was finalized in December. In February 2001 India agreed to buy 310 Russian tanks, at an estimated cost of $700m. In June the two countries successfully conducted tests of a new, jointly developed supersonic cruise missile; the PJ-10, which was believed to be globally unique. In November it was announced that Russia had been awarded a contract to construct a nuclear power reactor in Tamil Nadu (this was later extended to two reactors). During a visit to India by the Russian President in January 2007, Putin and Prime Minister Singh focused on the key bilateral issues of energy and trade, and announced that Russia was to assist India with the construction of four more nuclear power reactors. In November Singh paid a visit to Russia, during which increased co-operation in the field of military technology was discussed; however, details of the nuclear power reactor construction agreement did not appear to have been finalized.

In mid-1996, in a move that provoked widespread international condemnation, India decided not to be party to the Comprehensive Test Ban Treaty (CTBT), which it had earlier supported, so long as the existing nuclear powers were unwilling to commit themselves to a strict timetable for full nuclear disarmament. In May 1998 India's controversial decision to explode five nuclear test devices and to claim thereby its new status as a nuclear-weapons state led to a rapid escalation in the 'arms race' with Pakistan (which responded with its own series of nuclear tests). The USA, with limited support from other countries, subsequently imposed economic sanctions on both India and Pakistan until such time as they had signed the Nuclear Non-Proliferation Treaty (NPT) and the CTBT and taken steps to reverse their nuclear programmes. Immediately after the tests, India announced a self-imposed moratorium on further testing and launched itself into intense diplomatic activity. During 1998–99 the USA lifted some of the sanctions imposed on India and Pakistan, whilst reiterating its requests that the two countries sign the CTBT and exercise restraint in their respective missile programmes to ensure peace in South Asia. In mid-January 2001 India successfully test-fired its *Agni-II* intermediate ballistic missile for the second time. Prime Minister Vajpayee declared that the test was necessary for India's national security; however, the move was criticized by Pakistan, Japan and the United Kingdom and caused concern in China.

Following the collapse of the USSR, a long-time ally of India, in December 1991, the Indian Government sought to strengthen its ties with the USA. In January 1992 discussions were held between Indian and US officials regarding military co-operation and ambitious joint defence projects. However, the USA remained concerned about the risks of nuclear proliferation in the South Asia region as a whole, and India's ongoing refusal to sign the NPT contributed to the two countries' failure to come to an understanding on the issue, a position not resolved until mid-2005 (see below). In addition, despite India's adoption of a programme of economic liberalization, conflicts over trade and related issues remained. During a visit to India by the US Secretary of Defense in January 1995, a 'landmark' agreement on defence and security co-operation was signed by the two countries.

The US President, Bill Clinton, made an official six-day state visit to India in March 2000 (the first by a US President since 1978), which was widely considered as the start of a new era in bilateral relations. President Clinton appeared to endorse India's opinion that the Kashmir issue was a local matter and did not directly concern the international community. In September Prime Minister Vajpayee visited the USA. He continued to assert that consensus among Indian ministers had to be reached before a decision on the CTBT could be made. In late September 2001 US President George W. Bush announced an end to the military and economic sanctions imposed against India and Pakistan in 1998. The decision followed the renewal of high-level military contacts between the USA and India in April and May and Pakistan's co-operation with US counter-terrorism initiatives against neighbouring Afghanistan in the aftermath of the terrorist attacks carried out on US mainland targets on 11 September. During a visit to India in November, US Secretary of Defense Donald Rumsfeld discussed further defence co-operation possibilities with the Indian authorities and announced that the US Government was prepared to resume the sale of specific defence materials to India. In July 2003 India declined a request by the USA to contribute peace-keeping troops to the US-led forces in Iraq. In September 2004 the USA agreed to ease its export controls on materials intended for India's nuclear and civilian space programmes. The agreement preceded a meeting between US President Bush and Prime Minister Manmohan Singh in New York, USA. In July 2005 Singh visited the USA, where he signed an historic outline agreement with President Bush regarding future nuclear co-operation between the two countries. In return for an Indian pledge to separate its civilian and military nuclear programmes, to allow international monitoring of its civilian nuclear programme, and not to conduct further nuclear weapons tests or to transfer nuclear technology to other countries, the US Government proposed to share civilian nuclear technology with India. The agreement represented a reversal of previous US policy, and reflected the considerable recent improvement in bilateral relations. During negotiations over the proposals, differences arose over plans to separate India's civilian and military nuclear facilities, but the agreement was finalized during a visit to India by President Bush in March 2006. In August 2007, however, the agreement met with opposition not only from the BJP, but from the UPA coalition's allies, the left-wing parties comprising the Left Front, which feared the possibility of US intervention in India's foreign policy and other areas. As the dispute intensified, the future of the agreement appeared increasingly uncertain, while the UPA parliamentary majority itself seemed to be under threat. By early 2008 progress on the implementation of the agreement had almost slowed to a halt, and the Government was faced with the prospect of the withdrawal of support by the Left Front and early elections.

Government

India is a federal republic. Legislative power is vested in Parliament, consisting of the President and two Houses. The Council of States (Rajya Sabha) has 245 members, most of whom are indirectly elected by the state assemblies for six years (one-third retiring every two years), the remainder being nominated by the President for six years. The House of the People (Lok Sabha) has up to 550 elected members, serving for five years (subject to dissolution). A small number of members of the Lok Sabha may be nominated by the President to represent the Anglo-Indian community, while the 550 members are directly elected by universal adult suffrage in single-member constituencies. The President is a constitutional Head of State, elected for five years by an electoral college comprising elected members of both Houses of Parliament and the state legislatures. The President exercises executive power on the advice of the Council of Ministers, which is responsible to Parliament. The President appoints the Prime Minister and, on the latter's recommendation, other ministers.

India contains 28 self-governing states, each with a governor (appointed by the President for five years), a legislature (elected for five years) and a council of ministers headed by the chief minister. Bihar, Jammu and Kashmir, Karnataka, Maharashtra and Uttar Pradesh have bicameral legislatures, the other 23 state legislatures being unicameral. Each state has its own legislative, executive and judicial machinery, corresponding to that of the Indian Union. In the event of the failure of constitutional government in a state, presidential rule can be imposed by the Union. There are also six Union Territories and one National Capital Territory, administered by lieutenant-governors or administrators, all of whom are appointed by the President. The territories of Delhi and Puducherry also have elected chief ministers and state assemblies.

Defence

The total strength of India's armed forces as assessed at November 2007 was 1,288,000: an army of 1,100,000, a navy of 55,000, an air force of 125,000 and a coastguard of 8,000. Active paramilitary forces totalled 1,300,586 men, including the 208,422-strong Border Security Force (based mainly in the troubled state of Jammu and Kashmir). Military service is voluntary, but, under the amended Constitution, it is the fundamental duty of every citizen to perform national service when called upon. The proposed defence budget for 2008/09 was estimated at Rs 1,235,348m. (equivalent to 16.5% of total projected expenditure).

Economic Affairs

In 2006, according to estimates by the World Bank, India's gross national income (GNI), measured at average 2004–06 prices, was US $906,537m., equivalent to $820 per head (or $3,800 per head on an international purchasing-power parity basis). During 1996–2006, it was estimated, the population increased at an average annual rate of 1.6%, while gross domestic product (GDP) per head increased, in real terms, by an average of 4.9% per year. Overall GDP increased, in real terms, at an average annual rate of 6.8% in 1999–2006. According to official sources, the rate of growth was 9.2% in 2005/06 and 9.7% in 2006/07.

Agriculture (including forestry and fishing) contributed 18.3% of GDP in 2006/07. About 57.3% of the economically active population were employed in agriculture in 2005. The principal cash crops are cotton (cotton accounted for 3.1% of total export earnings in 2006/07), tea, rice, spices, sugar cane and groundnuts. Coffee and jute production are also important. The average annual growth rate in the output of the agricultural sector was 2.0% in 1996–2006; agricultural GDP increased by 5.9% in 2005/06 and by 4.0% in 2006/07.

Industry (including mining, manufacturing, power and construction) contributed 29.3% of GDP in 2006/07. According to World Bank estimates, about 12.9% of the working population were employed in the industrial sector in 1995. Industrial GDP increased at an average annual rate of 6.5% in 1996–2006; the rate of growth of the GDP of the industrial sector reached 10.1% in 2005/06 and 11.0% in 2006/07.

Mining contributed 2.7% of GDP in 2006/07, and employed 0.6% of the working population in 1991. Iron ore and cut diamonds are the major mineral exports. Coal, limestone, zinc and lead are also mined. In 2004 India was the third largest coal producer in the world after the People's Republic of China and the USA. Mining GDP increased at an estimated average annual rate of 4.9% during 1999/2000–2000/01. Sectoral GDP increased by 4.9% in 2005/06 and by 5.7% in 2006/07.

Manufacturing contributed 16.3% of GDP in 2006/07, and employed 10.0% of the working population in 1991. The GDP of the manufacturing sector increased at an average annual rate of 6.1% during 1996–2006; manufacturing GDP rose by 9.0% in 2005/06 and by 12.0% in 2006/07.

Production of electricity rose from 617,511m. kWh in 2005/06 to 662,522m. kWh in 2006/07. In 2003/04 thermal plants accounted for an estimated 79.6% of total power generation and hydroelectric plants (often dependent on monsoons) for 17.1%; the remaining 2.8% was contributed by nuclear power. Imports of mineral fuels, lubricants, etc. comprised 33.3% of the cost of total imports in 2006/07.

The services sector, which is dominated by the rapidly expanding data-processing business, the growing number of business call centres and the tourism industry, contributed an estimated 52.4% of GDP in 2006/07, and engaged 20.5% of the economically active population in 1991. The GDP of the services sector increased by an average of 8.7% per year in 1996–2006; the rate of growth reached 10.3% in 2005/06 and 11.1% in 2006/07.

In 2006/07 India reported an estimated trade deficit of US $64,905m. and there was a deficit of $9,609m. on the current account of the balance of payments. In that year the principal source of imports was the People's Republic of China (providing 9.4% of total imports) and the principal market for exports (accounting for 14.9% of total exports) was the USA. Other major trading partners were the United Kingdom, the United Arab Emirates, Belgium, Singapore, Switzerland and Germany. The principal exports in 2006/07 were pearls, precious and semi-precious stones, ready-made garments and mineral fuels and lubricants. The principal imports were mineral fuels and lubricants, pearls, precious and semi-precious stones and nuclear reactors, boilers, machinery and mechanical appliances.

In the financial year ending 31 March 2008 there was a projected budgetary deficit of Rs 1,434,515m., which was equivalent to 3.5% of GDP. In 2003, according to the UN Development Programme (UNDP), India's total official development assistance stood at US $942.2m. India's total external debt was $113,467m. at the end of 2003, of which $92,822m. was long-term public debt. In that year the cost of debt-servicing was equivalent to 18.1% of earnings from the exports of goods and services. The average annual rate of inflation was an estimated 4.9% in 1996/97–2006/07; consumer prices rose by 4.4% in 2005/06 and by 5.4% in 2006/07. In rural India the number of people wholly unemployed comprised about 6% of the potential labour force for adult males in the early 2000s, but the proportion was around 23% when account was taken of underemployment.

India is a member of the ADB, of the UN Economic and Social Commission for Asia and the Pacific (ESCAP, see p. 35), of the South Asian Association for Regional Co-operation (SAARC, see p. 384) and of the Colombo Plan (see p. 411).

The process of wide-ranging economic reform initiated in 1991, including trade and investment liberalization, industrial deregulation, disinvestment by the Government in public enterprises and their gradual privatization, financial and tax reforms, etc., has continued despite several changes in government. By 2006 a variety of sectors—including power, coal, construction, telecommunications, postal services, tourism, car manufacturing, transport (with the exception of the railways) and insurance—had been opened up to private (domestic and foreign) investment. Restrictions on foreign participation in a number of sectors (including the pharmaceuticals industry) were eased or removed in 2001/02 to encourage greater foreign investment. In 2001/02 India recorded a current-account surplus for the first time in 23 years. The economic policies of the new, Congress-led United Progressive Alliance (UPA) Government elected in May 2004, while stressing continued governmental commitment to economic reform, also emphasized increased spending on education and health, public investment in infrastructure and employment creation. In August of that year the Government announced a trade policy intended to encourage exports and double India's share of global trade over the next five years. In November 2004 an Investment Commission was established, which was charged with encouraging investment both from overseas and from within India itself. India's attractiveness as a destination for foreign investment increased markedly in the early 21st century. According to the Ministry of Commerce and Industry, foreign direct investment (FDI) equity inflows for 2006/07 were projected to reach around US $14,000m., compared with $7,700m. in 2005/06. Capital inflows during 2007/08 were extremely high, which facilitated a greater rate of investment and robust growth. Advanced estimates projected an 8.7% expansion in real GDP during 2007/08 and the International Monetary Fund (IMF) expressed optimism that the Indian economy could sustain this momentum. The IMF warned, however, that massive capital inflows could potentially exacerbate inflation and thereby engender further currency appreciation. Increasing volatility on global financial markets and the associated depreciation of the US dollar precipitated a 12.3% rise in the value of the rupee in 2007, which threatened to curtail growth in key export sectors (particularly the textile industry). In late 2007 the Securities and Exchange Board of India introduced measures to stem capital inflows. However, the IMF noted that these restrictions could threaten planned infrastructure developments if employed in the long term.

Ongoing attempts to address India's unwieldy fiscal deficit (traditionally exacerbated by the country's modest tax base and cumbersome local government apparatus) have been largely frustrated by the repeated stalling of the divestment programme and the costs associated with natural disasters and volatile foreign relations and internal security concerns; the deficit remains a major cause of concern to potential foreign investors and international donors. The 2006/07 Union budget envisaged a fiscal deficit equivalent to 3.8% of GDP. Value-added tax (VAT) was introduced at state level in April 2005 and was intended eventually to replace the central sales tax; by January 2007 31 states and union territories had introduced VAT. In 2005–06 the reform agenda of the UPA Government came under increasing pressure from its allies in the Left Front, whose support was necessary if the Government were successfully to implement its economic policies. Several planned divestments were abandoned as a result of Left Front opposition, and in September 2005 employees in the banking and civil-aviation industries staged strike action, in protest at plans to attract foreign investment into the banking sector and the proposed privatization of airports in Mumbai and New Delhi. In April 2006 the Government finalized contracts with private companies to operate and develop the airports as joint ventures. Left Front influence was once again evident in a plan revealed in late 2005 to guarantee 100 days of work annually to every rural family. The increased expenditure upon which this scheme was contingent was expected to hamper efforts to reduce India's mounting fiscal deficit, as was Left Front opposition to government attempts to reduce food subsidies in order to promote budgetary savings. Significant infrastructural development continued to be necessary if the Indian economy was to maintain its rapid rate of expansion. Furthermore, the growing income inequality brought about by the country's swift economic growth generated fears that the widening division between rich and poor might lead to widespread social unrest if its causes were not addressed. The 2007/08 Union budget focused on promoting the expansion of the agricultural sector (with a long-term aim of achieving India's self-sufficiency in food terms) through the provision of affordable credit to farmers and the expansion of the rural job guarantee scheme. The 2008/09 Union budget, which was announced at the end of February 2008, made further provisions for agriculture, including debt relief for small and medium-sized enterprises. There were also notable increases in government expenditure in the education and defence sectors (20% and 10%, respectively).

The late 1990s witnessed India's rapid emergence as a 'software superpower'; in 2000 software exports constituted the country's single largest export item. The rapidly expanding industry presented increasing employment opportunities. Nevertheless, concern grew over the high number of qualified information technology professionals leaving the country for better-paid work elsewhere. By the early 2000s business call centres had become the fastest growing industry in India, expanding by 70% in 2002. An increasing number of multinational companies were transferring their call centre operations to India, largely owing to cheaper labour costs and low long-distance telephone charges. More than 415,000 people were employed in the outsourcing industry in 2005/06. In 2004/05 software exports reached US $17,200m., of which the outsourcing industry provided 30.2% ($5,200m.). The National Association of Software and Service Companies (Nasscom) forecast that the annual revenue from call centres in India would reach $24,000m. by 2008.

Education

Education is primarily the responsibility of the individual state governments. Elementary education for children between the ages of six and 14 years is theoretically compulsory in all states except Nagaland and Himachal Pradesh. There are facilities for free primary education (lower and upper stages) in all the states. In 2004/05 enrolment at primary schools included 88.8% of pupils in the relevant age-group, while enrolment at secondary schools was equivalent to 56.6% of pupils in the relevant age-group. India had a total of 253 universities and institutions with university status in 2001/02, and some 13,150 university and affiliated colleges. University enrolment was 9.2m. in 2002/03. Budgetary expenditure on education and literacy for 2007/08 was forecast at Rs 231,422m. (equivalent to 3.4% of total spending).

Public Holidays

The public holidays observed in India vary locally. The dates given below apply to Delhi.

2008: 1 January (New Year's Day), 10 January* (Muharram, Islamic New Year), 26 January (Republic Day), 6 March (Maha Shivaratri), 20 March (Birth of the Prophet), 14 April (Ram Navami), 18 April (Mahavir Jayanti), 25 April (Good Friday), 19 May (Buddha Purnima), 15 August (Independence Day), 1 October (Id al-Fitr, end of Ramadan), 2 October (Mahatma Gandhi's Birthday), 9 October (Dussehra), 28 October (Diwali), 13 November (Guru Nanak Jayanti), 8 December (Id ul-Zuha, Feast of the Sacrifice), 25 December (Christmas), 29 December* (Muharram, Islamic New Year).

2009: 1 January (New Year's Day), 26 January (Republic Day), 23 February (Maha Shivaratri), 9 March (Birth of the Prophet), 3 April (Ram Navami), 7 April (Mahavir Jayanti), 10 April (Good Friday), 9 May (Buddha Purnima), 15 August (Independence Day), 20 September (Id al-Fitr, end of Ramadan), 28 September (Dussehra), 2 October (Mahatma Gandhi's Birthday), 17 October (Diwali), 2 November (Guru Nanak Jayanti), 27 November (Id ul-Zuha, Feast of the Sacrifice), 18 December (Muharram, Islamic New Year), 25 December (Christmas).

Note: A number of Hindu, Muslim and Buddhist holidays depend on lunar sightings.

*This festival occurs twice (marking the start of the Islamic years AH 1429 and AH 1430) within the same Gregorian year.

Weights and Measures

The metric system has been officially introduced. The imperial system is also still in use, as are traditional Indian weights and measures, including:

    1 tola = 11.66 grams
    1 lakh = (1,00,000) = 100,000
    1 crore = (1,00,00,000) = 10,000,000

Statistical Survey

Source (unless otherwise stated): Central Statistical Organization, Ministry of Statistics and Programme Implementation, Sardar Patel Bhavan, Patel Chowk, New Delhi 110 001; tel. (11) 23742150; fax (11) 23344689; e-mail moscc@bol.net.in; internet mospi.nic.in.

Area and Population

AREA, POPULATION AND DENSITY*

Area (sq km)	3,166,414†
Population (census results)	
1 March 1991‡§	846,302,688
1 March 2001‖	
Males	532,156,772
Females	496,453,556
Total	1,028,610,328
Population (official projected estimates at 1 March)¶	
2006	1,114,202,000
2007	1,131,043,000
2008	1,147,677,000
Density (per sq km) at 1 March 2008	362.5

* Including the Indian-held part of Jammu and Kashmir.
† 1,222,559 sq miles.
‡ Excluding adjustment for underenumeration, estimated at 1.5%.
§ Including estimate for the Indian-held part of Jammu and Kashmir.
‖ Including estimates for certain areas in the states of Gujarat and Himachal Pradesh where the census could not be conducted, owing to recent natural disasters.
¶ Source: Office of the Registrar General and Census Commissioner, *Census of India* (2001).

Source: unless otherwise indicated, Registrar General of India.

STATES AND TERRITORIES
(population at 2001 census)

	Area (sq km)	Population	Density (per sq km)	Capital
States				
Andhra Pradesh	275,069	76,210,007	277	Hyderabad
Arunachal Pradesh*	83,743	1,097,968	13	Itanagar
Assam	78,438	26,655,528	340	Dispur
Bihar†	94,163	82,998,509	881	Patna
Chhattisgarh	135,191	20,833,803	154	Raipur
Goa‡	3,702	1,347,668	364	Panaji
Gujarat	196,022	50,671,017	258	Gandhinagar
Haryana	44,212	21,144,564	478	Chandigarh§
Himachal Pradesh	55,673	6,077,900	109	Shimla
Jammu and Kashmir‖	101,387	10,143,700	100	Srinagar
Jharkhand	79,714	26,945,829	338	Ranchi
Karnataka	191,791	52,850,562	276	Bangalore
Kerala	38,863	31,841,374	819	Thiruvananthapuram (Trivandrum)
Madhya Pradesh†	308,245	60,348,023	196	Bhopal
Maharashtra	307,713	96,878,627	314	Mumbai (Bombay)
Manipur	22,327	2,166,788	97	Imphal
Meghalaya	22,429	2,318,822	103	Shillong
Mizoram¶	21,081	888,573	42	Aizawl
Nagaland	16,579	1,990,036	120	Kohima
Orissa	155,707	36,804,660	236	Bhubaneswar
Punjab	50,362	24,358,999	483	Chandigarh§
Rajasthan	342,239	56,507,188	165	Jaipur
Sikkim	7,096	540,851	76	Gangtok
Tamil Nadu	130,058	62,405,679	479	Chennai (Madras)
Tripura	10,486	3,199,203	305	Agartala
Uttaranchal†	53,483	8,489,349	159	Dehradun
Uttar Pradesh†	240,928	166,197,921	690	Lucknow
West Bengal	88,752	80,176,197	903	Kolkata (Calcutta)
Territories				
Andaman and Nicobar Islands	8,249	356,152	43	Port Blair
Chandigarh§	114	900,635	7,900	Chandigarh
Dadra and Nagar Haveli	491	220,490	449	Silvassa
Daman and Diu‡	112	158,204	1,411	Daman
Delhi	1,483	13,850,507	9,340	Delhi
Lakshadweep	32	60,650	1,895	Kavaratti
Puducherry (Pondicherry)	480	974,345	2,029	Puducherry (Pondicherry)

* Arunachal Pradesh was granted statehood in February 1987.
† Chhattisgarh, Jharkhand and Uttaranchal (formerly parts of Madhya Pradesh, Bihar and Uttar Pradesh, respectively) were granted statehood in November 2000; Uttaranchal was renamed Uttarakhand in 2006.
‡ Goa was granted statehood in May 1987. Daman and Diu remain a Union Territory.
§ Chandigarh forms a separate Union Territory, not within Haryana or the Punjab. As part of a scheme for a transfer of territory between the two states, Chandigarh was due to be incorporated into the Punjab on 26 January 1986, but the transfer was postponed.
‖ Figures refer only to the Indian-held part of the territory.
¶ Mizoram was granted statehood in February 1987.

Source: *Census of India* (2001).

PRINCIPAL TOWNS
(population at 2001 census*)

Greater Mumbai (Bombay)	11,978,450
Delhi	10,181,535
Kolkata (Calcutta)	4,572,876
Chennai (Madras)	4,343,645
Bangalore	4,301,326
Hyderabad	3,612,427
Ahmedabad	3,520,085
Kanpur (Cawnpore)	2,551,337
Pune (Poona)	2,538,473
Surat	2,433,835
Lucknow	2,185,927
Nagpur	2,052,066
Jaipur (Jeypore)	1,870,771
Indore	1,474,968
Bhopal	1,437,354
Ludhiana	1,398,467
Patna	1,366,444
Vadodara (Baroda)	1,306,227
Agra	1,275,134
Thane (Thana)	1,262,551
Kalyan-Dombivli	1,193,512
Varanasi (Banares)	1,091,918
Nashik	1,077,236
Meerut	1,068,772
Faridabad Complex	1,055,938
Pimpri-Chinchwad	1,012,472
Haora (Howrah)	1,007,532
Visakhapatnam (Vizag)	982,904
Allahabad	975,393
Ghaziabad	968,256
Rajkot	967,476
Amritsar	966,862
Jabalpur (Jubbulpore)	932,484
Coimbatore	930,882
Hubli-Dharwad	786,195
Mysore	755,379
Tiruchirapalli	752,066
Thiruvananthapuram (Trivandrum)	744,983
Bareilly	718,395
Jalandhar	706,043
Navi Mumbai	704,002
Salem	696,760
Kota	694,316
Aligarh	669,087
Bhubaneswar	648,032
Moradabad	641,583
Gorakhpur	622,701
Raipur	605,747
Bhiwandi	598,741
Jamshedpur	573,096
Bhilai Nagar	556,366
Amravati	549,510
Cuttack	534,654
Warangal	530,636
Bikaner	529,690
Mira-Bhayandar	520,388
Guntur	514,461
Bhavnagar	511,085
Kochi (Cochin)	504,550
Durgapur	493,405
Kolhapur	493,167
Ajmer	485,575
Asansol	475,439
Ulhasnagar	473,731
Saharanpur	455,754
Jamnagar	443,518
Bhatpara	442,385
Sangli-Miraj-Kupwad	436,781

INDIA

—continued

Madurai	928,869	Kozhikode (Calicut)	436,556
Srinagar	898,440	Nanded-Waghala	430,733
Aurangabad	873,311	Ujjain	430,427
Solapur	872,478	Dehradun	426,674
Vijayawada (Vijayavada)	851,282	Gulbarga	422,569
Jodhpur	851,051	Jaipur	419,778
Ranchi	847,093	Tirunelveli	411,831
Gwalior	827,026	Malegaon	409,403
Guwahati	809,895	Akola	400,520
Chandigarh	808,515		

* Figures refer to the city proper in each case.

Capital: New Delhi, provisional population 294,783 at 2001 census.

Population of principal urban agglomerations at 2001 census: Greater Mumbai 16,434,386; Kolkata 13,205,697; Delhi 12,877,470; Chennai 6,560,242; Hyderabad 5,742,036; Bangalore 5,701,446; Jaipur 5,251,071; Ahmedabad 4,525,013; Pune 3,760,636; Ludhiana 3,032,831; Surat 2,811,614; Kanpur 2,715,555; Lucknow 2,245,509; Faridabad 2,194,586; Nagpur 2,129,500; Patna 1,697,976; Indore 1,516,918; Vadodara 1,491,045; Coimbatore 1,461,139; Bhopal 1,458,416; Kochi 1,355,972; Visakhapatnam 1,345,938; Agra 1,331,339; Varanasi 1,203,961; Madurai 1,203,095; Meerut 1,161,716; Nashik 1,152,326; Jamshedpur 1,104,713; Jabalpur 1,098,000; Asansol 1,067,369; Dhanbad 1,065,327; Allahabad 1,042,229; Vijayawada 1,039,518; Amritsar 1,003,917; Rajkot 1,003,015.

BIRTHS AND DEATHS
(estimates based on Sample Registration Scheme)

	2004	2005	2006
Birth rate (per 1,000)	24.1	23.8	23.5
Death rate (per 1,000)	7.5	7.6	7.5

Expectation of life (years at birth, WHO estimates): 63.0 (males 61.8; females 64.2) in 2005 (Source: WHO, *World Health Statistics*).

ECONOMICALLY ACTIVE POPULATION
(persons aged five years and over, 1991 census, excluding Jammu and Kashmir)

	Males	Females	Total
Agriculture, hunting, forestry and fishing	139,361,719	51,979,110	191,340,829
Mining and quarrying	1,536,919	214,356	1,751,275
Manufacturing	23,969,433	4,702,046	28,671,479
Construction	5,122,468	420,737	5,543,205
Trade and commerce	19,862,725	1,433,612	21,296,337
Transport, storage and communications	7,810,126	207,620	8,017,746
Other services	23,995,194	5,316,428	29,311,622
Total employed	221,658,584	64,273,909	285,932,493
Marginal workers	2,705,223	25,493,654	28,198,877
Total labour force	224,363,807	89,767,563	314,131,370

Unemployment (work applicants at 31 December, '000 persons aged 14 years and over): 41,389 (males 30,636, females 10,752) in 2003; 40,458 (males 29,746, females 10,712) in 2004; 39,348 (males 28,742, females 10,606) in 2005 (Source: ILO).

2001 census: Cultivators 127,312,851 (males 85,416,498, females 41,896,353); Agricultural labourers 106,775,330 (males 57,329,100, females 49,446,230); Household industry workers 16,956,942 (males 8,744,183, females 8,212,759); Other 151,189,601 (males 123,524,695, females 27,664,906); Total employed 402,234,724 (incl. 89,229,741 marginal workers).

Mid-2005 (official estimates in '000): Agriculture, etc. 280,716; Total labour force 489,509 (Source: FAO).

Health and Welfare

KEY INDICATORS

Total fertility rate (children per woman, 2005)	2.9
Under-5 mortality rate (per 1,000 live births, 2005)	74
HIV/AIDS (% of persons aged 15–49, 2005)	0.9
Physicians (per 1,000 head, 2005)	0.60
Hospital beds (per 1,000 head, 2002)	0.70
Health expenditure (2004): US $ per head (PPP)	91.4
Health expenditure (2004): % of GDP	5.0
Health expenditure (2004): public (% of total)	17.3
Access to water (% of persons, 2004)	86
Access to sanitation (% of persons, 2004)	33
Human Development Index (2005): ranking	128
Human Development Index (2005): value	0.619

For sources and definitions, see explanatory note on p. vi.

Agriculture

PRINCIPAL CROPS
('000 metric tons, year ending 30 June)

	2004/05	2005/06	2006/07*
Rice (milled)	83,130	91,790	91,050
Sorghum (Jowar)	7,240	7,630	7,630
Cat-tail millet (Bajra)	7,930	7,680	8,280
Maize	14,170	14,710	13,850
Finger millet (Ragi)	2,430	2,350	1,430
Small millets	480	470	400
Wheat	68,640	69,350	73,700
Barley	1,200	1,220	1,340
Total cereals	185,230	195,220	197,670
Chick-peas (Gram)	5,470	5,600	5,970
Pigeon-peas (Tur)	2,350	2,740	2,510
Dry beans, dry peas, lentils and other pulses	5,310	5,050	5,620
Total food grains	198,360	208,600	211,780
Groundnuts (in shell)	6,770	7,990	4,980
Sesame seed	674	654	561
Rapeseed and mustard	7,590	8,130	6,690
Linseed	170	173	148
Castorseed	793	991	789
Total edible oilseeds (incl. others)	24,354	27,979	23,264
Cotton lint†	16,430	18,500	21,040
Jute and Kenaf‡	10,270	10,840	11,340
Sugar cane: production cane	237,080	281,170	322,940
Tobacco (leaves)	550	550	550
Potatoes	23,060	23,630	23,910

* Estimates at 4 April 2007.
† Production in '000 bales of 170 kg each.
‡ Production in '000 bales of 180 kg each.

Sources: Directorate of Economics and Statistics, Ministry of Agriculture.

Tea (made) ('000 metric tons): 850 in 2004; 831 in 2005; 893 in 2006 (Source: FAO).

INDIA   Statistical Survey

LIVESTOCK
('000 head, year ending September, unrevised data)

	2003	2004	2005
Cattle	187,382	185,500*	185,000*
Sheep	61,789	62,500*	62,500*
Goats	120,097	120,000*	120,000*
Pigs	14,142	14,300*	14,300*
Horses	788	800*	800*
Asses, mules and hinnies*	1,050	1,050	1,050
Buffaloes	96,616	98,175†	98,875†
Camels	635	635*	635*
Chickens	409,000†	425,000	430,000*
Ducks	32,900†	33,000	33,000*

* FAO estimate(s).
† Unofficial figure.

2006 ('000 head, year ending September, FAO estimates): Cattle 180,837; Sheep 62,850; Goats 124,906; Pigs 14,000; Horses 750; Asses, mules and hinnies 800; Buffaloes 98,805; Camels 630; Chickens 475,000; Ducks 30,000.

Source: FAO.

LIVESTOCK PRODUCTS
('000 metric tons)

	2003	2004	2005
Cattle meat*	1,472.9	1,483.2	1,493.5
Buffalo meat*	1,466.7	1,483.1	1,487.6
Sheep meat*	235.8	238.8	238.8
Goat meat*	473	475	475
Pig meat*	490.0	497.0	503.0
Chicken meat†	1,600	1,650	1,900
Duck meat*	65.4	70.4	73.9
Cows' milk†	36,500	37,500	38,500
Buffaloes' milk	50,100†	50,740†	50,740*
Goats' milk†	2,700	2,760	2,700
Hen eggs	2,371.0†	2,486.0*	2,539.0*
Wool: greasy*	51.4	51.4	51.4

* FAO estimate(s).
† Unofficial figure(s).

Source: FAO.

Forestry

ROUNDWOOD REMOVALS
('000 cubic metres, excl. bark)

	2004	2005	2006*
Sawlogs, veneer logs and logs for sleepers	22,014	22,390	22,390
Pulpwood	621	624	624
Other industrial wood	175	178	178
Fuel wood*	303,839	305,485	306,252
Total	326,649	328,677	329,444

* FAO estimate(s).

Source: FAO.

SAWNWOOD PRODUCTION
('000 cubic metres, incl. railway sleepers)

	2003	2004	2005
Coniferous sawnwood	7,990	9,300	9,900
Broadleaved sawnwood	3,890	4,361	4,889
Total	11,880	13,661	14,789

2006: Figures assumed to be unchanged from 2005 (FAO estimates).
Source: FAO.

Fishing
('000 metric tons, live weight)

	2003	2004	2005
Capture	3,720.9	3,391.0	3,481.1
Bombay-duck (Bummalo)	142.6	171.5	188.5
Croakers and drums	265.8	241.2	231.6
Indian oil-sardine (Sardinella)	276.5	273.3	271.8
Giant tiger prawn	108.7	127.8	142.1
Aquaculture	2,313.0	2,794.6	2,837.8
Common carp	442.9	—	—
Roho labeo	437.5	923.2	919.8
Mrigal carp	398.5	221.1	204.2
Catla	421.2	1,010.8	1,086.4
Silver carp	158.6	279.8	348.2
Total catch	6,033.9	6,185.6	6,318.9

Source: FAO.

Mining
('000 metric tons, unless otherwise indicated)

	2003/04	2004/05	2005/06
Coal	361,156	382,615	407,222
Lignite	27,958	30,337	30,049
Iron ore*	122,838	145,942	154,436
Manganese ore*	1,776	2,386	2,003
Bauxite	10,925	11,964	12,335
Chalk (Fireclay)	657	663	486
Kaolin (China clay)	897	934	1,097
Dolomite	4,051	4,339	4,428
Gypsum	2,774	3,685	3,137
Limestone	153,390	165,753	170,378
Crude petroleum	33,373	34,015	32,204
Chromium ore*	2,905	3,621	3,423
Phosphorite	1,436	1,723	1,373
Kyanite	9	8	7
Magnesite	324	384	351
Steatite	726	684	627
Copper ore*	2,903	2,929	2,643
Lead concentrates*	73	82	98
Zinc concentrates*	590	666	893
Mica—crude (metric tons)	1,076	1,276	1,259
Gold (kilograms)	3,457	3,526	3,050
Diamonds (carats)	71,260	78,316	44,170
Natural gas (million cu m)†	30,908	30,820	31,223

* Figures refer to gross weight. The estimated metal content is: Iron 63%; Manganese 40%; Chromium 30%; Copper 1.2%; Lead 70%; Zinc 60%.
† Figures refer to gas utilized.

Source: Indian Bureau of Mines.

Industry

SELECTED PRODUCTS
('000 metric tons, unless otherwise indicated)

	2002/03	2003/04	2004/05
Refined sugar*	19,000	16,000	13,000
Cotton cloth (million sq metres)	12,888	11,876	13,193
Jute manufactures	1,440	1,395	1,447
Paper and paper board	5,239	5,556	5,793
Soda ash	1,610	1,705	2,027
Fertilizers	14,455	14,201	15,326
Petroleum products	119,441	126,817	132,624
Cement	111,778	117,035	125,338
Pig-iron	5,059	5,197	3,982
Finished steel	34,400	39,243	42,326
Aluminium ingots (metric tons)	467,000	601,000	516,000
Diesel engines—stationary (number)	300,545	310,345	298,974
Sewing machines (number)	82,697	74,010	41,188
Television receivers (number)	2,191,000	3,572,000	5,044,000
Electric fans (number)	10,000,000	10,000,000	10,000,000
Passenger cars and multipurpose vehicles	735,941	1,007,993	1,214,540
Commercial vehicles (number)	198,827	275,098	350,032
Motorcycles, mopeds and scooters (number)	5,087,539	5,624,950	6,454,765
Bicycles (number)	11,595,000	12,341,000	8,030,000

* Figures relate to crop year (beginning November) and are in respect of cane sugar only.

Finance

CURRENCY AND EXCHANGE RATES

Monetary Units
100 paise (singular: paisa) = 1 Indian rupee (R).

Sterling, Dollar and Euro Equivalents (31 December 2007)
£1 sterling = Rs 78.954;
US $1 = Rs 39.410;
€1 = Rs 58.015;
1,000 Indian rupees = £12.67 = $25.37 = €17.24.

Average Exchange Rate (rupees per US $)
2005   44.100
2006   45.307
2007   41.349

UNION BUDGET
(Rs million, rounded, year ending 31 March)

Revenue	2006/07	2007/08*	2008/09†
Tax revenue (net)	3,459,710	4,317,730	5,071,500
Customs receipts	818,000	1,007,660	1,189,300
Union excise duties	1,172,660	1,279,470	1,378,740
Corporation tax	1,464,970	1,861,250	2,263,610
Other taxes on income	825,100	1,183,200	1,383,140
Other taxes and duties	397,750	522,520	662,360
Less States' share of tax revenue	1,203,770	1,518,370	1,787,650
Less Surcharge transferred to National Calamity Contingency Fund	15,000	18,000	18,000
Other current revenue	773,600	933,250	957,850
Interest receipts (net)	201,307	174,640	191,350
Dividends and profits	304,383	361,080	432,040
Receipts of Union Territories	7,240	8,200	8,150
External grants	24,690	20,910	17,950
Other receipts (net)	235,980	368,420	308,360
Recoveries of loans (net)	54,500	44,970	44,970
Total	4,287,810	5,295,950	6,074,320

Expenditure	2006/07	2007/08*	2008/09†
Central Ministries/Departments	5,354,120	6,492,602	6,862,886
Agriculture and co-operation (incl. agricultural research and education)	73,440	91,105	102,088
Atomic energy	45,112	39,390	47,970
Defence	1,008,100	1,095,190	1,235,348
Drinking water supply	52,971	74,618	85,019
Economic affairs	1,788,298	1,992,335	2,254,174
External affairs	39,464	47,830	50,620
Fertilizers	263,264	305,820	312,000
Food and public distribution	243,599	320,600	330,950
Health and family welfare	105,679	145,000	169,683
Home affairs	183,740	201,155	240,828
Education and literacy	168,975	231,914	278,500
Petroleum and natural gas	32,960	28,970	29,380
Railways	75,542	81,213	71,000
Road transport and highways	146,615	151,213	160,582
Rural development	242,842	285,235	315,241
Urban development	29,900	45,240	41,288
State plans	436,373	545,809	587,785
Union territories	43,373	55,322	58,164
Total	5,833,866	7,093,733	7,508,835
Current‡	5,146,086	5,885,864	6,581,190
Capital	687,780	1,207,869	927,645

* Estimates.
† Forecasts.
‡ Including interest payments (Rs million): 1,461,920 in 2006/07; 1,719,710 in 2007/08 (estimate); 1,908,070 in 2008/09 (forecast).

Source: Government of India, Union Budget 2008/09.

INTERNATIONAL RESERVES
(US $ million at 31 December)

	2004	2005	2006
Gold (national valuation)	3,808	4,102	5,367
IMF special drawing rights	5	4	1
Reserve position in IMF	1,424	902	550
Foreign exchange	125,164	131,018	170,187
Total	130,401	136,026	176,105

Source: IMF, *International Financial Statistics*.

MONEY SUPPLY
(Rs million, last Friday of year ending 31 March)

	2004/05	2005/06	2006/07
Currency with the public	3,558,630	4,131,430	4,834,710
Demand deposits with banks	2,851,540	4,052,240	4,742,280
Other deposits with Reserve Bank	64,780	68,790	74,960
Total money	6,474,950	8,252,460	9,651,950

Source: Reserve Bank of India.

COST OF LIVING
(Consumer Price Index for Industrial Workers; base: 2000 = 100)

	2004	2005	2006
Food (incl. beverages)	111.5	115.0	125.0
Fuel and light	138.6	136.1	140.0
Clothing (incl. footwear)	108.9	111.4	114.0
Rent	136.4	157.9	137.0
All items (incl. others)	116.6	121.5	127.7

Source: ILO.

INDIA

NATIONAL ACCOUNTS
(Rs '000 million at current prices, year ending 31 March)

National Income and Product

	2004/05	2005/06	2006/07
Domestic factor incomes	25,487.83	28,968.66	33,555.95
Consumption of fixed capital	3,289.23	3,788.04	4,344.68
Gross domestic product at factor cost	28,777.06	32,756.70	37,900.63
Indirect taxes	3,639.67	4,238.99	5,198.21
Less Subsidies	922.61	1,192.25	1,640.74
GDP in purchasers' values	31,494.12	35,803.44	41,458.10
Net factor income from abroad	−223.75	−261.16	−297.78
Gross national product	31,270.37	35,542.28	41,160.32
Less Consumption of fixed capital	3,289.23	3,788.04	4,344.68
National income in market prices	27,981.14	31,754.24	36,815.64

Expenditure on the Gross Domestic Product

	2004/05	2005/06	2006/07
Government final consumption expenditure	3,380.52	3,730.76	4,270.07
Private final consumption expenditure	18,404.06	20,553.87	23,121.05
Increase in stocks	602.15	862.48	961.03
Gross fixed capital formation	8,946.74	11,091.60	13,465.01
Acquisitions, less disposals, of valuables	410.54	413.92	497.09
Total domestic expenditure	31,744.01	36,652.63	42,314.25
Exports of goods and services	5,690.51	7,120.87	9,156.74
Less Imports of goods and services	6,259.45	8,134.66	10,407.97
Statistical discrepancy	319.05	164.60	395.08
GDP in purchasers' values	31,494.12	35,803.44	41,458.10
GDP at constant 1999/2000 prices	26,016.30	28,419.67	31,173.71

Gross Domestic Product by Economic Activity
(at current factor cost)

	2004/05	2005/06	2006/07
Agriculture	5,014.15	5,571.18	6,345.19
Forestry and logging	233.51	258.39	268.55
Fishing	276.56	328.88	340.50
Mining and quarrying	847.76	941.53	1,018.16
Manufacturing	4,536.03	5,193.87	6,179.54
Electricity, gas and water supply	598.92	644.06	705.63
Construction	2,128.12	2,646.16	3,194.97
Trade, hotels and restaurants	4,612.87	5,385.42	6,303.64
Transport, storage and communications	2,447.86	2,771.56	3,191.04
Banking and insurance	1,678.31	1,805.19	2,133.81
Real estate and business services	2,372.50	2,720.74	3,133.74
Public administration and defence	1,734.91	1,948.00	2,188.83
Other services	2,295.56	2,541.72	2,897.03
GDP at factor cost	28,777.06	32,756.70	37,900.63
Indirect taxes	3,639.67	4,238.99	5,198.21
Less Subsidies	922.61	1,192.25	1,640.74
GDP in market prices	31,494.12	35,803.44	41,458.10

BALANCE OF PAYMENTS
(US $ million)

	2004/05	2005/06	2006/07*
Exports of goods f.o.b.	85,206	105,152	127,090
Imports of goods f.o.b.	−118,908	−156,993	−191,995
Trade balance	−33,702	−51,841	−64,905
Services (net)	15,426	23,881	32,727
Balance on goods and services	−18,276	−27,960	−32,178
Other income (net)	−4,979	−5,510	−4,846
Balance on goods, services and income	−23,255	−33,470	−37,024
Current transfers (net)	20,785	24,284	27,415
Current balance	−2,470	−9,186	−9,609
Direct investment abroad	5,987	7,661	19,442
Direct investment from abroad	−2,274	−2,931	−11,005
Portfolio investment assets	9,311	12,494	7,004
Portfolio investment liabilities	−24	—	58
Net loans	10,909	6,113	21,129
Banking capital (net)	3,874	1,373	2,087
Rupee debt service	−417	−572	−162
Other capital (net)	656	−738	6,391
Net errors and omissions	607	838	1,271
Overall balance	26,159	15,052	36,606

* Preliminary figures.

Source: Reserve Bank of India.

OFFICIAL DEVELOPMENT ASSISTANCE
(US $ million)

	1998	1999	2000
Bilateral donors	896.4	826.7	638.7
Multilateral donors	713.2	664.6	848.5
Total	1,609.6	1,491.3	1,487.2
Grants	802.6	772.2	775.3
Loans	807.0	719.1	711.9
Per caput assistance (US $)	1.7	1.5	1.5

Source: UN, *Statistical Yearbook for Asia and the Pacific*.

External Trade

PRINCIPAL COMMODITIES
(Rs million, year ending 31 March)

Imports c.i.f.	2004/05	2005/06	2006/07
Animal and vegetable oils, fats and waxes	113,727	101,517	102,614
Mineral fuels, mineral oils and products of their distillation	1,564,454	2,227,402	2,799,073
Organic chemicals	187,849	227,752	273,297
Natural or cultured pearls, precious and semi-precious stones, precious metals and articles thereof; imitation jewellery; coin	933,873	916,041	1,022,499
Iron and steel	150,774	241,133	277,419
Nuclear reactors, boilers, machinery, mechanical appliances and parts thereof	433,670	616,068	842,283
Electrical machinery and equipment and parts thereof; sound and television apparatus	401,933	526,804	659,248
Aircraft, spacecraft, and parts thereof	71,539	220,456	238,190
Total (incl. others)	5,010,646	6,604,089	8,405,063

INDIA

Statistical Survey

Exports f.o.b.	2004/05	2005/06	2006/07
Cereals	90,226	72,326	76,705
Ores, slag and ash	167,992	197,133	220,595
Mineral fuels, mineral oils and products of their distillation	320,829	525,376	855,420
Organic chemicals	162,674	215,040	259,496
Iron and steel	189,537	168,836	253,371
Articles of iron or steel	103,798	124,614	153,842
Cotton	101,675	132,122	177,555
Articles of apparel and clothing accessories, knitted or crocheted	118,677	141,282	163,717
Articles of apparel and clothing accessories, not knitted or crocheted	176,701	240,649	239,086
Natural or cultured pearls, precious and semi-precious stones, precious metals and articles thereof; imitation jewellery; coin	648,641	702,087	727,842
Nuclear reactors, boilers, machinery, mechanical appliances and parts thereof	148,588	185,398	230,385
Vehicles other than railway or tramway rolling stock, and parts and accessories thereof	110,740	145,805	170,406
Total (incl. others)	3,753,395	4,564,179	5,717,793

Source: Ministry of Commerce and Industry.

PRINCIPAL TRADING PARTNERS
(Rs million, year ending 31 March)

Imports c.i.f.	2004/05	2005/06	2006/07
Australia	171,842	219,061	317,109
Belgium	206,187	209,198	187,416
China, People's Republic	318,923	481,167	790,086
France	85,105	182,110	190,593
Germany	180,416	266,687	341,468
Hong Kong	77,737	97,711	112,393
Indonesia	117,619	133,180	188,649
Italy	61,696	82,155	121,017
Japan	145,359	179,799	207,949
Korea, Republic	157,654	202,058	217,470
Malaysia	103,298	106,947	239,588
Russia	59,433	89,529	109,028
Singapore	119,131	148,483	248,400
South Africa	98,744	109,435	111,841
Switzerland	266,890	290,248	412,832
United Arab Emirates	208,532	192,770	391,749
United Kingdom	160,235	174,008	188,893
USA	314,581	418,595	531,054
Total (incl. others)	5,010,646	6,604,089	8,405,063

Exports f.o.b.	2004/05	2005/06	2006/07
Bangladesh	73,289	73,687	73,660
Belgium	112,765	127,120	157,217
Brazil	30,471	48,285	65,768
Canada	38,947	45,229	50,245
China, People's Republic	252,330	299,249	375,298
France	75,527	92,071	95,060
Germany	126,988	158,770	180,072
Hong Kong	165,879	197,961	211,794
Indonesia	59,876	61,106	91,770
Iran	55,328	52,612	65,648
Israel	45,190	53,194	59,794
Italy	102,713	111,527	162,124
Japan	95,610	109,854	129,536
Korea, Republic	46,804	80,897	113,790
Malaysia	48,708	51,440	59,019
Nepal	33,390	38,074	42,014
Netherlands	72,109	109,567	120,825
Nigeria	28,966	38,696	40,882
Russia	28,364	32,459	40,855
Saudi Arabia	63,446	80,125	117,137

Exports f.o.b.—*continued*	2004/05	2005/06	2006/07
Singapore	179,753	240,197	274,616
South Africa	44,214	67,600	101,653
Spain	62,426	71,088	84,970
Sri Lanka	63,496	89,639	102,064
Taiwan	27,791	27,850	41,335
Thailand	40,501	47,608	65,356
United Arab Emirates	330,151	380,388	544,450
United Kingdom	165,397	223,992	254,213
USA	618,516	768,281	853,685
Total (incl. others)	3,753,395	4,564,179	5,717,793

Source: Ministry of Commerce and Industry.

Transport

RAILWAYS
(million, year ending 31 March)

	2004/05	2005/06	2006/07
Passengers	5,378	5,725	6,219
Passenger-km	575,702	615,614	694,764
Freight (metric tons)	626.2	682.4	744.6
Freight (metric ton-km)	411,280	441,762	483,422

Source: Railway Board, Ministry of Railways and Indian Railways.

ROAD TRAFFIC
('000 motor vehicles in use at 31 March)

	2002	2003	2004*
Private cars, jeeps and taxis	7,613	8,599	9,451
Buses and coaches	635	721	768
Goods vehicles	2,974	3,492	3,749
Motorcycles and scooters	41,581	47,519	51,922
Others	6,121	6,676	6,828
Total	58,924	67,007	72,718

* Provisional figures.

Source: Ministry of Road Transport and Highways.

SHIPPING

Merchant Fleet
(registered at 31 December)

	2004	2005	2006
Vessels	1,066	1,096	1,181
Displacement ('000 grt)	7,517.6	8,056.0	8,381.2

Source: Lloyd's Register-Fairplay, *World Fleet Statistics*.

International Sea-borne Traffic
(year ending 31 March)

	2000/01	2001/02	2002/03*
Vessels ('000 nrt)†:			
entered	55,466	55,981	n.a.
cleared	38,043	41,716	n.a.
Freight ('000 metric tons)‡:			
loaded	135,331	n.a.	115,534
unloaded	233,007	n.a.	182,229

* Provisional figures.
† Excluding minor and intermediate ports.
‡ Including bunkers.

Sources: Transport Research Division, Ministry of Surface Transport; Department of Shipping, Ministry of Shipping, Road Transport and Highways; Directorate General of Commercial Intelligence and Statistics.

CIVIL AVIATION
(all Indian carriers, traffic on scheduled services)

	2003/04	2004/05	2005/06
Kilometres flown (million)	287	n.a.	n.a.
Passengers carried ('000)	20,170	24,771	31,752
Passenger-km (million)	32,673	40,303	51,567
Freight carried (metric tons)	272,031	328,000	335,000
Freight ton-km (million)	590	737	801
Mail carried (metric tons)	23,157	29,000	34,000
Mail ton-km ('000)	32	41	49

Source: Directorate General of Civil Aviation.

Tourism

FOREIGN VISITORS BY COUNTRY OF ORIGIN*

	2004	2005
Australia	81,608	96,258
Canada	135,884	157,643
France	131,824	152,258
Germany	116,679	120,243
Italy	65,561	67,642
Japan	96,851	103,082
Malaysia	84,390	96,276
Nepal	51,534	77,024
Netherlands	51,211	52,755
Singapore	60,710	68,666
Sri Lanka	128,711	136,400
United Kingdom	555,907	651,083
USA	526,120	611,165
Total (incl. others)	3,367,980	3,920,000

*Figures exclude nationals of Bangladesh and Pakistan.

Receipts from tourism (US $ million): 3,533 in 2003; 4,769 in 2004; 5,731 in 2005.

Source: Ministry of Tourism.

Communications Media

	2004	2005	2006
Telephones ('000 main lines in use)	43,960	49,750	40,770
Mobile cellular telephones ('000 subscribers)	47,300	90,000	166,050
Personal computers ('000 in use)	13,030	17,000	n.a.
Internet users ('000)	35,000	60,000	n.a.
Broadband subscribers ('000)	180	1,348	2,300

1997: Radio receivers ('000 in use) 116,000; Facsimile machines ('000 in use, year ending 31 March) 100.

Television receivers ('000 in use): 79,000 in 2000; 85,000 in 2001.

Daily newspapers: 5,364 in 2000; 5,638 in 2001.

Non-daily newspapers and other periodicals: 43,781 in 2000; 46,322 in 2001.

Sources: International Telecommunication Union; UN, *Statistical Yearbook*; Register of Newspapers for India, Ministry of Information and Broadcasting.

Education

(2002/03)

	Institutions	Teachers	Students
Primary	651,382	1,912,931	122,397,715
Middle	245,274	1,581,739	46,845,207
Secondary (high school) / Higher secondary (new pattern) / Intermediate/pre-degree/junior college	137,207	2,033,509	33,214,100

Source: Ministry of Human Resource Development.

Adult literacy rate (2001 census): 61.0% (males 73.4%; females 47.8%) (Source: UNESCO Institute for Statistics).

Directory

The Constitution

The Constitution of India, adopted by the Constituent Assembly on 26 November 1949, was inaugurated on 26 January 1950. The Preamble declares that the People of India solemnly resolve to constitute a Sovereign Democratic Republic and to secure to all its citizens justice, liberty, equality and fraternity. There are 397 articles and nine schedules, which form a comprehensive document.

UNION OF STATES

The Union of India comprises 28 states, six Union Territories and one National Capital Territory. There are provisions for the formation and admission of new states.

The Constitution confers citizenship on a threefold basis of birth, descent, and residence. Provisions are made for refugees who have migrated from Pakistan and for persons of Indian origin residing abroad.

FUNDAMENTAL RIGHTS AND DIRECTIVE PRINCIPLES

The rights of the citizen contained in Part III of the Constitution are declared fundamental and enforceable in law. 'Untouchability' is abolished and its practice in any form is a punishable offence. The Directive Principles of State Policy provide a code intended to ensure promotion of the economic, social and educational welfare of the State in future legislation.

THE PRESIDENT

The President is the head of the Union, exercising all executive powers on the advice of the Council of Ministers responsible to Parliament. He is elected by an electoral college consisting of elected members of both Houses of Parliament and the Legislatures of the States. The President holds office for a term of five years and is eligible for re-election. He may be impeached for violation of the Constitution. The Vice-President is the *ex officio* Chairman of the Rajya Sabha and is elected by a joint sitting of both Houses of Parliament.

THE PARLIAMENT

The Parliament of the Union consists of the President and two Houses: the Rajya Sabha (Council of States) and the Lok Sabha (House of the People). The Rajya Sabha consists of 245 members, of whom a number are nominated by the President. One-third of its members retire every two years. Elections are indirect, each state's legislative quota being elected by the members of the state's legislative assembly. The Lok Sahba has up to 550 members elected by adult franchise; not more than 20 represent the Union Territories and National Capital Territory. Two members are nominated by the President to represent the Anglo-Indian community.

GOVERNMENT OF THE STATES

The governmental machinery of states closely resembles that of the Union. Each of these states has a governor at its head appointed by the President for a term of five years to exercise executive power on the advice of a council of ministers. The states' legislatures consist of the Governor and either one house (legislative assembly) or two houses (legislative assembly and legislative council). The term of the assembly is five years, but the council is not subject to dissolution.

LANGUAGE

The Constitution provides that the official language of the Union shall be Hindi. (The English language will continue to be an associate language for many official purposes.)

LEGISLATION—FEDERAL SYSTEM

The Constitution provides that bills, other than money bills, can be introduced in either House. To become law, they must be passed by both Houses and receive the assent of the President. In financial affairs, the authority of the Lower House is final. The various subjects of legislation are enumerated on three lists in the seventh schedule of the Constitution: the Union List, containing nearly 100 entries, including external affairs, defence, communications and atomic energy; the State List, containing 65 entries, including local government, police, public health and education; and the Concurrent List, with more than 40 entries, including criminal law, marriage and divorce and labour welfare. The Constitution vests residuary authority in the Centre. All matters not enumerated in the Concurrent or State Lists will be deemed to be included in the Union List, and in the event of conflict between Union and State Law on any subject enumerated in the Concurrent List the Union Law will prevail. In time of emergency Parliament may even exercise powers otherwise exclusively vested in the states. Under Article 356, 'If the President on receipt of a report from the government of a state or otherwise is satisfied that a situation has arisen in which the Government of the state cannot be carried on in accordance with the provisions of this Constitution, the President may by Proclamation: (a) assume to himself all or any of the functions of the government of the state and all or any of the powers of the governor or any body or authority in the state other than the Legislature of the state; (b) declare that the powers of the Legislature of the state shall be exercisable by or under the authority of Parliament; (c) make such incidental provisions as appear to the President to be necessary': provided that none of the powers of a High Court shall be assumed by the President or suspended in any way. Unless such a Proclamation is approved by both Houses of Parliament, it ceases to operate after two months. A Proclamation so approved ceases to operate after six months, unless renewed by Parliament. Its renewal cannot be extended beyond a total period of three years. An independent judiciary exists to define and interpret the Constitution and to resolve constitutional disputes arising between states, or between a state and the Government of India.

OTHER PROVISIONS

Other Provisions of the Constitution deal with the administration of tribal areas, relations between the Union and states, inter-state trade and finance.

AMENDMENTS

The Constitution is flexible in character, and a simple process of amendment has been adopted. For amendment of provisions concerning the Supreme Courts and the High Courts, the distribution of legislative powers between the Union and the states, the representation of the states in Parliament, etc., the amendment must be passed by both Houses of Parliament and must further be ratified by the legislatures of not less than half the states. In other cases no reference to the state legislatures is necessary.

Numerous amendments were adopted in August 1975, following the declaration of a state of emergency in June. The Constitution (39th Amendment) Bill laid down that the President's reasons for proclaiming an emergency may not be challenged in any court. Under the Constitution (40th Amendment) Bill, 38 existing laws may not be challenged before any court on the ground of violation of fundamental rights. Thus detainees under the Maintenance of Internal Security Act could not be told the grounds of their detention and were forbidden bail and any claim to liberty through natural or common law. The Constitution (41st Amendment) Bill provided that the President, Prime Minister and state Governors should be immune from criminal prosecution for life and from civil prosecution during their term of office.

In November 1976 a 59-clause Constitution (42nd Amendment) Bill was approved by Parliament and came into force in January 1977. Some of the provisions of the Bill are that the Indian Democratic Republic shall be named a 'Democratic Secular and Socialist Republic'; that the President 'shall act in accordance with' the advice given to him by the Prime Minister and the Council of Ministers, and, acting at the Prime Minister's direction, shall be empowered for two years to amend the Constitution by executive order, in any way beneficial to the enforcement of the whole; that the term of the Lok Sabha and of the state assemblies shall be extended from five to six years; that there shall be no limitation on the constituent power of Parliament to amend the Constitution, and that India's Supreme Court shall be barred from hearing petitions challenging constitutional amendments; that strikes shall be forbidden in the public services and the Union Government has the power to deploy police or other forces under its own superintendence and control in any state. Directive Principles are given precedence over Fundamental Rights: 10 basic duties of citizens are listed, including the duty to 'defend the country and render national service when called upon to do so'.

The Janata Party Government, which came into power in March 1977, promised to amend the Constitution during the year, so as to 'restore the balance between the people and Parliament, Parliament and the judiciary, the judiciary and the executive, the states and the centre, and the citizen and the Government that the founding fathers of the Constitution had worked out'. The Constitution (43rd Amendment) Bill, passed by Parliament in December 1977, the Constitution (44th Amendment) Bill, passed by Parliament in December 1977 and later redesignated the 43rd Amendment, and the Constitution (45th Amendment) Bill, passed by Parliament in December 1978 and later redesignated the 44th Amendment, reversed most of the changes enacted by the Constitution (42nd Amendment) Bill. The 44th Amendment is particularly detailed on emergency provisions: an emergency may not be proclaimed unless 'the security of India or any part of its territory was threatened by war or external aggression or by armed rebellion'. Its introduction must be approved by a two-thirds' majority of Parliament within a month, and after six months the emergency may be continued only with the approval of Parliament. Among the provisions left unchanged after these Bills were a section subordinating Fundamental Rights to Directive Principles and a clause empowering the central Government to deploy armed forces under its control in any state without the state government's consent. In May 1980 the Indian Supreme Court repealed sections 4 and 55 of the 42nd Amendment Act, thus curtailing Parliament's power to enforce directive principles and to amend the Constitution. The death penalty was declared constitutionally valid.

The 53rd Amendment to the Constitution, approved by Parliament in August 1986, granted statehood to the Union Territory of Mizoram; the 55th Amendment, approved in December 1986, granted statehood to the Union Territory of Arunachal Pradesh; and the 57th Amendment, approved in May 1987, granted statehood to the Union Territory of Goa (Daman and Diu remains, however, a Union Territory). The 59th Amendment, approved in March 1988, empowered the Government to impose a state of emergency in the Punjab, on the grounds of internal disturbances. In December 1988 the minimum voting age was lowered from 21 to 18 years. The 69th Amendment, enacted in 1991, declared the Union Territory of Delhi to be the National Capital Territory, and granted it responsible government. The 71st Amendment, approved in August 1992, gave official-language status to Nepali, Konkani and Manipuri. In August 2000 legislation to permit the establishment of three new states, Chhattisgarh, Jharkhand and Uttaranchal (later renamed Uttarakhand), was approved by Parliament. The 93rd amendment, approved in May 2002, ensured free and compulsory education for children from the age of six to 14. The 91st amendment, approved in December 2003, stipulated that the size of the Council of Ministers at the centre and the states should not exceed 15% of the numbers in the Lok Sabha and state legislative assemblies, respectively. The 100th amendment, also approved in December 2003, extended official-language status to Bodo, Santhali, Maithali and Dogri, bringing the total number of official languages in the country to 22.

THE PANCHAYAT RAJ SCHEME

This scheme is designed to decentralize the powers of the Union and state governments. It is based on the Panchayat (Village Council) and the Gram Sabha (Village Parliament) and envisages the gradual transference of local government from state to local authority. Revenue and internal security will remain state responsibilities at present. The 72nd Amendment, approved in late 1992, provided for direct elections to the Panchayats, members of which were to have a tenure of five years.

The Government

President: Pratibha Devisingh Patil (sworn in 25 July 2007).

Vice-President: Mohammad Hamid Ansari (sworn in 12 August 2007).

COUNCIL OF MINISTERS
(April 2008)

A coalition of the Indian National Congress (Congress), the Nationalist Congress Party (NCP), the Rashtriya Janata Dal (RJD), the Lok Jan Shakti Party (LJSP), Dravida Munnetra Kazhagam (DMK), Jharkhand Mukti Morcha (JMM), Pattali Makal Katchi (PMK), Marumalarchi Dravida Munnetra Kazhagam (MDMK), the Rashtriya Lok Dal (RLD), the Muslim League Kerala State Committee (MUL), the Republican Party of India—A (RPI–A), the All India Majlis-e-Ittehadul Muslimeen (AIMIM), the People's Democratic Party (PDP) and Kerala Congress.

Prime Minister and Minister-in-charge of Personnel, Public Grievances and Pensions, of Planning, of Atomic Energy, of Space, of Coal and of Environment and Forests: Dr Manmohan Singh (Congress).

Minister of Defence: A. K. Antony (Congress).

Minister of External Affairs: Pranab Mukherjee (Congress).

Minister of Human Resource Development: Arjun Singh (Congress).

Minister of Agriculture and of Consumer Affairs, Food and Public Distribution: Sharad Pawar (NCP).

Minister of Railways: Lalu Prasad Yadav (RJD).

INDIA
Directory

Minister of Home Affairs: SHIVRAJ V. PATIL (Congress).
Minister of Chemicals and Fertilizers and of Steel: RAM VILAS PASWAN (LJSP).
Minister of Urban Development: S. JAIPAL REDDY (Congress).
Minister of Mines: SISH RAM OLA (Congress).
Minister of Finance: P. CHIDAMBARAM (Congress).
Minister of Micro, Small and Medium Enterprises: MAHAVIR PRASAD (Congress).
Minister of Tribal Affairs: P. R. KYNDIAH (Congress).
Minister of Shipping, Road Transport and Highways: T. R. BAALU (DMK).
Minister of Textiles: SHANKARSINH VAGHELA (Congress).
Minister of Commerce and Industry: KAMAL NATH (Congress).
Minister of Law and Justice: H. R. BHARDWAJ (Congress).
Minister of Rural Development: RAGHUVANSH PRASAD SINGH (RJD).
Minister of Information and Broadcasting: PRIYARANJAN DASMUNSI (Congress).
Minister of Panchayati Raj and of Development of North Eastern Region: MANI SHANKAR AIYAR (Congress).
Minister of Social Justice and Empowerment: MEIRA KUMAR (Congress).
Minister of Communications and Information Technology: A. RAJA.
Minister of Health and Family Welfare: Dr ANBUMANI RAMDOSS (PMK).
Minister of Power: SUSHIL KUMAR SHINDE (Congress).
Minister of Minority Affairs: A. R. ANTULAY (Congress).
Minister of Overseas Indian Affairs and of Parliamentary Affairs: VAYALAR RAVI (Congress).
Minister of Petroleum and Natural Gas: MURLI DEORA (Congress).
Minister of Tourism and of Culture: AMBIKA SONI (Congress).
Minister of Water Resources: Prof. SAIFUDDIN SOZ (Congress).
Minister of Heavy Industries and Public Enterprises: SANTOSH MOHAN DEV (Congress).
Minister of Corporate Affairs: PREM CHAND GUPTA (RJD).
Minister of Science and Technology and of Earth Sciences: KAPIL SIBAL (Congress).

Ministers of State with Independent Charge

Minister of State for Statistics and Programme Implementation: G. K. VASAN (Congress).
Minister of State for Labour and Employment: OSCAR FERNANDES (Congress).
Minister of State for Women and Child Development: RENUKA CHOWDHURY (Congress).
Minister of State for Food Processing Industries: SUBODH KANT SAHAY (Congress).
Minister of State for New and Renewable Energy: VILAS MUTTEMWAR (Congress).
Minister of State for Housing and Urban Poverty Alleviation: KUMARI SELJA (Congress).
Minister of State for Civil Aviation: PRAFUL PATEL (NCP).
Minister of State for Youth Affairs and Sports: Dr M. S. GILL.
There are, in addition, 40 Ministers of State without independent charge.

MINISTRIES

President's Office: Rashtrapati Bhavan, New Delhi 110 004; tel. (11) 23015321; fax (11) 23017290; e-mail presidentofindia@rb.nic.in; internet presidentofindia.nic.in.
Vice-President's Office: 6 Maulana Azad Rd, New Delhi 110 011; tel. (11) 23016344; fax (11) 23018124; e-mail vpindia@nic.in; internet vicepresidentofindia.nic.in.
Prime Minister's Office: South Block, Raisina Hill, New Delhi 110 011; tel. (11) 23012312; fax (11) 23016857; internet www.pmindia.nic.in.
Ministry of Agriculture: Krishi Bhavan, Dr Rajendra Prasad Rd, New Delhi 110 001; tel. (11) 23383370; fax (11) 23384555; e-mail am.krishi@nic.in.
Department of Atomic Energy: Anushakti Bhavan, Chatrapathi Shivaji Maharaj Marg, Mumbai 400 001; tel. (22) 22862500; fax (22) 22048476; e-mail usadmn@dae.gov.in; internet www.dae.gov.in.

Ministry of Chemicals and Fertilizers: Shastri Bhavan, New Delhi 110 001; tel. (11) 23388481; fax (11) 23388116; internet chemicals.gov.in; internet fert.nic.in.
Ministry of Civil Aviation: Rajiv Gandhi Bhavan, Safdarjung Airport, New Delhi 110 023; tel. (11) 24613050; fax (11) 24613054; e-mail web.moca@nic.in; internet www.civilaviation.nic.in.
Ministry of Coal: Shram Shakti Bhavan, Rafi Marg, New Delhi 110 001; tel. (11) 23384884; fax (11) 23381678; e-mail secy.moc@nic.in; internet coal.nic.in.
Ministry of Commerce and Industry: 45c Udyog Bhavan, New Delhi 110 011; tel. (11) 23063086; fax (11) 23019947; e-mail ikeshari@gmail.com; internet commerce.nic.in.
Ministry of Communications and Information Technology: Electronic Niketan, Lodhi Rd, New Delhi 110 003; tel. (11) 24369191; fax (11) 24362333; internet www.mit.gov.in.
Ministry of Consumer Affairs, Food and Public Distribution: Krishi Bhavan, New Delhi 110 001; tel. (11) 23382349; fax (11) 23386052; e-mail secy-food@nic.in; internet www.fcamin.nic.in.
Ministry of Corporate Affairs: 'A' Wing, Shastri Bhavan, Rajendra Prasad Rd, New Delhi 110 001; tel. (11) 23384660; e-mail manoj.arora@mca.gov.in; internet www.mca.gov.in.
Ministry of Culture: Rm 334, 'C' Wing, Shastri Bhavan, Dr Rajendra Prasad Rd, New Delhi 110 001001; tel. (11)23382331; fax (11) 23384867; e-mail js.culture@nic.in; internet indiaculture.nic.in.
Ministry of Defence: 104 South Block, New Delhi 110 011; tel. (11) 23019030; fax (11) 23015403; e-mail ak.antony@sansad.nic.in; internet www.mod.nic.in.
Ministry of Development of North Eastern Region: 233 Vigyan Bhavan Annexe, Maulana Azad Rd, New Delhi 110 011; tel. (11) 23022020; fax (11) 23022024; e-mail secydoner@nic.in; internet northeast.nic.in.
Ministry of Earth Sciences: Block No. 12, CGO Complex, Lodi Rd, New Delhi 110 003; tel. (11) 24360874; fax (11) 24360779; e-mail dodsec-dod@nic.in; internet dod.nic.in.
Ministry of Environment and Forests: Paryavaran Bhavan, CGO Complex Phase II, Lodhi Rd, New Delhi 110 003; tel. (11) 24360721; fax (11) 24362222; e-mail envisect@nic.in; internet www.envfor.nic.in.
Ministry of External Affairs: South Block, Room 144c, New Delhi 110 011; tel. (11) 23011849; fax (11) 23013387; e-mail asppr@mea.gov.in; internet meaindia.nic.in.
Ministry of Finance: North Block, Rm 166-D, 1st Floor, New Delhi 110 001; tel. (11) 23094905; fax (11) 23093422; e-mail mprasad@nic.in; internet www.finmin.nic.in.
Ministry of Food Processing Industries: Panchsheel Bhavan, August Kranti Marg, New Delhi 110 049; tel. (11) 26492475; fax (11) 26493228; e-mail ajitji@nic.in; internet mofpi.nic.in.
Ministry of Health and Family Welfare: Nirman Bhavan, Maulana Azad Rd, New Delhi 110 011; tel. (11) 23018863; fax (11) 23014252; e-mail resp-health@hub.nic.in; internet www.mohfw.nic.in.
Ministry of Heavy Industries and Public Enterprises: Udyog Bhavan, New Delhi 110 011; tel. (11) 23061854; fax (11) 23062633.
Ministry of Home Affairs: North Block, Central Secretariat, New Delhi 110 001; tel. (11) 23092011; fax (11) 23093750; e-mail mhaweb@mhant.delhi.nic.in; internet www.mha.nic.in.
Ministry of Housing and Urban Poverty Alleviation: Nirman Bhavan, Maulana Azad Rd, New Delhi 110 011; tel. (11) 23061444; fax (11) 23061991; e-mail secy-muepa@nic.in; internet mhupa.gov.in.
Ministry of Human Resource Development: Shastri Bhavan, New Delhi 110 001; tel. (11) 23782698; fax (11) 23382365; e-mail hrm@sb.nic.in; internet education.nic.in.
Ministry of Information and Broadcasting: 'A' Wing, Rm 552, Shastri Bhavan, New Delhi 110 001; tel. (11) 23384453; e-mail jsp.onb@nic.in; internet www.mib.nic.in.
Ministry of Labour and Employment: Shram Shakti Bhavan, Rafi Marg, New Delhi 110 001; tel. (11) 23710265; fax (11) 23718730; e-mail laborweb@nic.in; internet www.labour.nic.in.
Ministry of Law and Justice: 'A' Wing, 4th Floor, Shastri Bhavan, Dr Rajendra Prasad Rd, New Delhi 110 001; tel. (11) 23387557; fax (11) 23384241; e-mail vnathan@nic.in; internet lawmin.nic.in.
Ministry of Micro, Small and Medium Enterprises: Udyog Bhavan, Rafi Marg, New Delhi 110 011; tel. (11) 23062107; fax (11) 23063045; e-mail raj.pal@nic.in; internet ssi.nic.in.
Ministry of Mines: 'A' Wing, 3rd Floor, Shastri Bhavan, New Delhi; tel. (11) 23385173; fax (11) 23386402; e-mail secy-mines@nic.in; internet mines.nic.in.

INDIA

Ministry of Minority Affairs: 11th Floor, Paravaran Bhavan, CGO Complex, Lodhi Rd, New Delhi 110 003; tel. (11) 24364271; e-mail sdatta@nic.in; internet minorityaffairs.gov.in.

Ministry of New and Renewable Energy: Block 14, CGO Complex, Lodhi Rd, New Delhi 110 003; tel. (11) 24361027; fax (11) 24367413; e-mail sunilkhatri@nic.in; internet mnes.nic.in.

Ministry of Overseas Indian Affairs: 9th Floor, Akbar Bhavan, Chanakya Puri, New Delhi 110 021; tel. (11) 24197900; fax (11) 24197919; e-mail info@moia.nic.in; internet moia.gov.in.

Ministry of Panchayati Raj: Krishi Bhavan, Dr Rajendra Prasad Rd, New Delhi 110 001; tel. (11) 23389074; fax (11) 23389028; e-mail nicmopr@nic.in; internet panchayat.nic.in.

Ministry of Parliamentary Affairs: 87, Parliament House, New Delhi 110 001; tel. (11) 23017663; fax (11) 23017726; e-mail secympa@nic.in; internet mpa.nic.in.

Ministry of Personnel, Public Grievances and Pensions: North Block, New Delhi 110 001; tel. (11) 23094848; fax (11) 23012432; e-mail secy_mop@nic.in; internet persmin.nic.in.

Ministry of Petroleum and Natural Gas: Shastri Bhavan, New Delhi 110 001; tel. (11) 23382889; fax (11) 23382673; e-mail jse.png@nic.in; internet petroleum.nic.in.

Ministry of Power: Shram Shakti Bhavan, New Delhi 110 001; tel. (11) 23710271; fax (11) 23721487; e-mail razdana@ias.nic.in; internet powermin.nic.in.

Ministry of Railways: Rail Bhavan, Raisina Rd, New Delhi 110 001; tel. (11) 23386645; fax (11) 23387333; e-mail secyrb@rb.railnet.gov.in; internet www.indianrailways.gov.in.

Ministry of Rural Development: Krishi Bhavan, Dr Rajendra Prasad Rd, New Delhi 110 001; tel. (11) 23382230; fax (11) 23382408; e-mail secyrd@nic.in; internet rural.nic.in.

Ministry of Science and Technology: Technology Bhavan, New Mehrauli Rd, New Delhi 110 016; tel. (11) 26567373; fax (11) 26864570; e-mail dstinfo@nic.in; internet dst.gov.in.

Ministry of Shipping, Road Transport and Highways: Ground Floor, Parivahan Bhavan, 1 Parliament St, New Delhi 110 001; tel. (11) 23719955; e-mail ifcmost@nic.in; internet www.morth.nic.in.

Ministry of Social Justice and Empowerment: Shastri Bhavan, Dr Rajendra Prasad Rd, New Delhi 110 001; tel. (11) 23717294; fax (11) 23311802; e-mail secywel@nic.in; internet socialjustice.nic.in.

Ministry of Statistics and Programme Implementation: Sardar Patel Bhavan, Patel Chowk, New Delhi 110 001; tel. (11) 23340884; fax (11) 23340138; e-mail gkvasan@sasnsad.nic.in; internet mospi.nic.in.

Ministry of Steel: Udyog Bhavan, New Delhi 110 011; tel. (11) 23793432; fax (11) 23013236; e-mail fcis@nic.in; internet steel.nic.in.

Ministry of Textiles: Udyog Bhavan, New Delhi 110 011; tel. (11) 23061338; fax (11) 23063711; e-mail secy-ub@nic.in; internet texmin.nic.in.

Ministry of Tourism: Transport Bhavan, Rm 123, 1 Parliament St, New Delhi 110 001; tel. (11) 23715084; e-mail sectour@nic.in; internet tourism.gov.in.

Ministry of Tribal Affairs: Rm 750A, Shastri Bhavan, New Delhi 110 001; tel. (11) 23388482; fax (11) 23381499; e-mail dirit@tribal.nic.in; internet tribal.nic.in.

Ministry of Urban Development: Nirman Bhavan, Maulana Azad Rd, New Delhi 110 011; tel. (11) 23062377; fax (11) 23061459; e-mail secyurban@nic.in; internet urbanindia.nic.in.

Ministry of Water Resources: Shram Shakti Bhavan, Rafi Marg, New Delhi 110 001; tel. and fax (11) 23710343; e-mail jsadm-mowr@nic.in; internet wrmin.nic.in.

Ministry of Women and Child Development: Shastri Bhavan, New Delhi; tel. (11) 23383586; fax (11) 23381495; e-mail secy.wcd@nic.in; internet wcd.nic.in.

Ministry of Youth Affairs and Sports: 501, 'B' Wing, Shastri Bhavan, Dr Rajendra Prasad Rd, New Delhi 110 001; tel. (11) 23383292; fax (11) 23071193; e-mail dsadmn.yas@nic.in; internet yas.nic.in.

Legislature

PARLIAMENT

Rajya Sabha
(Council of States)

Most of the members of the Rajya Sabha are indirectly elected by the State Assemblies for six years, with one-third retiring every two years. The remaining members are nominated by the President.

Chairman: MOHAMMAD HAMID ANSARI.
Deputy Chairman: K. RAHMAN KHAN.

Distribution of Seats, July 2004

Party	Seats
Congress*	70
Communist Party of India (Marxist)	14
Telugu Desam	9
Bharatiya Janata Party	49†
Samajwadi Party	12
Rashtriya Janata Dal	9
Dravida Munnetra Kazhagam	2
Shiromani Akali Dal	2
Biju Janata Dal	5
Nationalist Congress Party	4
Samata Party	1
Muslim League	2
All-India Anna Dravida Munnetra Kazhagam	12
Communist Party of India	2
Jammu and Kashmir National Conference	1
Shiv Sena	4
Bahujan Samaj Party	6
Revolutionary Socialist Party	3
Indian National Lok Dal	4
Independents and others	23
Nominated	9
Vacant	2
Total	**245**

*Formerly known as the Indian National Congress (Indira) or Congress (I); name gradually changed to the Indian National Congress or Congress Party in the early to mid-1990s.
† Including three nominated members.

Lok Sabha
(House of the People)

Speaker: SOMNATH CHATTERJEE.

General Election, 20, 22 and 25 April and 5 and 10 May 2004*

Party	Seats
Congress and allies	222
Congress	145
Rashtriya Janata Dal	24
Dravida Munnetra Kazhagam	16
Nationalist Congress Party	9
Pattali Makkal Katchi	6
Telangana Rashtra Samithi	5
Jharkhand Mukti Morcha	5
Lok Jan Shakti Party	4
Marumalarchi Dravida Munnetra Kazhagam	4
All India Majlis-e-Ittehadul Muslimeen	1
Muslim League Kerala State Committee	1
People's Democratic Party	1
Republican Party of India (A)	1
National Democratic Alliance	186
Bharatiya Janata Party	138
Shiv Sena	12
Biju Janata Dal	11
Shiromani Akali Dal	8
Janata Dal (United)	8
Telugu Desam	5
All India Trinamool Congress	2
Mizo National Front	1
Nagaland People's Front	1
Left Front	59
Communist Party of India (Marxist)	43
Communist Party of India	10
All India Forward Bloc	3
Revolutionary Socialist Party	3
Samajwadi Party	36
Bahujan Samaj Party	19
Janata Dal (Secular)	3
Rashtriya Lok Dal	3
Jammu and Kashmir National Conference	2
Asom Gana Parishad	2
Bharatiya Navshakti Party	1
Kerala Congress	1
Sikkim Democratic Front	1
Independents and others	8
Nominated	2†
Total	**545**

*Includes the results of voting in several constituencies where the elections were postponed until 12–31 May, owing to irregularities and technical error.
† Nominated by the President to represent the Anglo-Indian community.

State Governments
(April 2008)

ANDHRA PRADESH
(Capital—Hyderabad)

Governor: NARAIN DUTT TIWARI.

Chief Minister: Dr Y. S. RAJASEKHARA REDDY (Congress).

Legislative Assembly: 295 seats (Congress 186, Telugu Desam 44, Telangana Rashtra Samithi 26, Communist Party of India—Marxist 9, Communist Party of India 6, All India Majlis-e-Ittehadul Muslimeen 5, Bharatiya Janata Party 2, Bahujan Samaj Party 1, Samata Party 1, independents and others 13, nominated 1, vacant 1).

Legislative Council: revived April 2007; 90 seats (Congress 38, Telugu Desam 13, Telangana Rashtriya Samithi 3, Communist Party of India 2, Communist (CPI—Marxist) 1, All-India Majlis-e-Ittehadul Muslimeen 1, independents 17, nominated 12, vacant 3).

ARUNACHAL PRADESH
(Capital—Itanagar)

Governor: Gen. (retd) JOGINDER JASWANT SINGH.

Chief Minister: DORJEE KHANDU (Congress).

Legislative Assembly: 60 seats (Congress 34, Bharatiya Janata Party 9, Nationalist Congress Party 2, Arunachal Congress 2, independents 13).

ASSAM (ASOM)
(Capital—Dispur)

Governor: Lt-Gen. (retd) AJAY SINGH.

Chief Minister: TARUN GOGOI (Congress).

Legislative Assembly: 126 seats (Congress 53, Asom Gana Parishad 24, Assam United Democratic Front 9, Bharatiya Janata Party 10, Communist Party of India—Marxist 2, independents and others 27, vacant 1).

BIHAR
(Capital—Patna)

Governor: RAMKRISHNAN SURYABHAN GAVAI.

Chief Minister: NITISH KUMAR (Janata Dal—United).

Legislative Assembly: 243 seats (Janata Dal—United 88, Bharatiya Janata Party 55, Rashtriya Janata Dal 54, Lok Jan Shakti 10, Congress 9, Communist Party of India—Marxist-Leninist (Liberation) 5, Bahujan Samaj Party 4, Communist Party of India 3, Samajwadi Party 2, Akhil Jan Vikas Dal 1, Communist Party of India—Marxist 1, Nationalist Congress Party 1, independents 10).

Legislative Council: 54 seats.

CHHATTISGARH
(Capital—Raipur)

Governor: E. S. L. NARASIMHAN.

Chief Minister: Dr RAMAN SINGH (Bharatiya Janata Party).

Legislative Assembly: 91 seats (Bharatiya Janata Party 52, Congress 34, Bahujan Samaj Party 1, Nationalist Congress Party 1, others 1, nominated 1, vacant 1).

GOA
(Capital—Panaji)

Governor: S. C. JAMIR.

Chief Minister: DIGAMBAR KAMAT (Congress).

Legislative Assembly: 40 seats (Congress 15, Bharatiya Janata Party 14, Nationalist Congress Party 3, Maharashtrawadi Gomantak Party 2, Save Goa Front 2, United Goans Democratic Party 1, independents 2, vacant 1).

GUJARAT
(Capital—Gandhinagar)

Governor: NAWAL KISHORE SHARMA.

Chief Minister: NARENDRA DAMODARDAS MODI (Bharatiya Janata Party).

Legislative Assembly: 182 seats (Bharatiya Janata Party 117, Congress 59, Nationalist Congress Party 3, Janata Dal—United 1, independents 2).

HARYANA
(Capital—Chandigarh)

Governor: A. R. KIDWAI.

Chief Minister: BHUPINDER SINGH HOODA (Congress).

Legislative Assembly: 90 seats (Congress 67, Indian National Lok Dal 9, Bharatiya Janata Party 2, Bahujan Samaj Party 1, Nationalist Congress Party 1, independents 10).

HIMACHAL PRADESH
(Capital—Shimla)

Governor: VISHNU SADASHIV KOKJE.

Chief Minister: Prof. PREM KUMAR DHUMAL (Bharatiya Janata Party).

Legislative Assembly: 68 seats (Bharatiya Janata Party 41, Congress 23, Bahujan Samaj Party 1, independents 3).

JAMMU AND KASHMIR
(Capitals—(Summer) Srinagar, (Winter) Jammu)

Governor: Lt-Gen. (retd) S. K. SINHA.

Chief Minister: GHULAM NABI AZAD (Congress).

Legislative Assembly: 87 seats (Jammu and Kashmir National Conference 28, Congress 20, People's Democratic Party 16, Panther's Party 4, Communist Party of India—Marxist 2, Ladakh Union Territory Front 2, independents and others 15).

Legislative Council: 36 seats.

JHARKHAND
(Capital—Ranchi)

Governor: SYED SIBTEY RAZI.

Chief Minister: MADHU KORA (Ind.).

Legislative Assembly: 81 seats (Bharatiya Janata Party 30, Jharkhand Mukti Morcha 17, Congress 9, Rashtriya Janata Dal 7, Janata Dal—United 6, independents and others 12).

KARNATAKA
(Capital—Bangalore)

Governor: RAMESHWAR THAKUR.

Chief Minister: (vacant).

Legislative Assembly: 225 seats (Bharatiya Janata Party 79, Congress 63, Janata Dal—Secular 59, Janata Dal—United 5, Communist Party of India—Marxist 1, Republican Party of India 1, independents and others 16, nominated 1).

Legislative Council: 75 seats.

Direct presidential rule was imposed in Karnataka in early October 2007, lifted in early November and reimposed in late November.

KERALA
(Capital—Thiruvananthapuram)

Governor: R. L. BHATIA.

Chief Minister: V. S. ACHUTHANANDAN (Communist Party of India—Marxist).

Legislative Assembly: 141 seats (Communist Party of India—Marxist 62, Congress 24, CPI 17, Muslim League 7, Kerala Congress (M) 7, Janata Dal—Secular 5, Kerala Congress 4, Revolutionary Socialist Party 3, Kerala Congress (Balakrishna Pillai) 1, Janathipathya Samrakshana Samiti 1, Congress (Secular) 1, Kerala Congress (Secular) 1, independents and others 8).

MADHYA PRADESH
(Capital—Bhopal)

Governor: BALRAM JAKHAR.

Chief Minister: SHIVRAJ SINGH CHAUHAN (Bharatiya Janata Party).

Legislative Assembly: 230 seats (Bharatiya Janata Party 176, Congress 34, Samajwadi Party 7, Gondwana Gantantra Party 3, Bahujan Samaj Party 2, Rashtriya Samata Dal 2, others 6).

MAHARASHTRA
(Capital—Mumbai)

Governor: S. C. JAMIR (acting).

Chief Minister: VILASRAO DESHMUKH (Congress).

Legislative Assembly: 288 seats (Congress 73, Nationalist Congress Party 71, Shiv Sena 58, Bharatiya Janata Party 54, Communist Party of India—Marxist 2, independents and others 32).

Legislative Council: 78 seats.

MANIPUR
(Capital—Imphal)

Governor: SHIVINDAR SINGH SIDHU.

Chief Minister: OKRAM IBOBI SINGH (Congress).

Legislative Assembly: 60 seats (Congress 30, Manipur People's Party 5, Nationalist Congress Party 5, Communist Party of India 4, National People's Party 3, Rashtriya Janata Dal 3, independents 10).

INDIA   *Directory*

MEGHALAYA
(Capital—Shillong)

Governor: SHIVINDAR SINGH SIDHU (acting).
Chief Minister: Dr DONKUPAR ROY (United Democratic Party).
Legislative Assembly: 60 seats (Congress 25, Nationalist Congress Party 15, United Democratic Party 11, Hill State People's Democratic Party 2, independents and others 7).

MIZORAM
(Capital—Aizawl)

Governor: Lt-Gen. (retd) M. M. LAKHERA.
Chief Minister: ZORAMTHANGA (Mizo National Front).
Legislative Assembly: 40 seats (Mizo National Front 22, Congress 11, Mizo People's Conference 3, others 3, independent 1).

NAGALAND
(Capital—Kohima)

Governor: K. SANKARANARAYANAN.
Chief Minister: NEIPHIU RIO (Nagaland People's Front).
Legislative Assembly: 60 seats (Nagaland People's Front 26, Congress 24, Bharatiya Janata Party 2, Nationalist Congress Party 2, independents 6).

ORISSA
(Capital—Bhubaneswar)

Governor: MURLIDHAR CHANDRAKANT BHANDARE.
Chief Minister: NAVEEN PATNAIK (Biju Janata Dal).
Legislative Assembly: 147 seats (Biju Janata Dal 61, Congress 38, Bharatiya Janata Party 32, Jharkhand Mukti Morcha 4, Orissa Gana Parishad 2, Communist Party of India 1, Communist Party of India—Marxist 1, independents 8).

THE PUNJAB
(Capital—Chandigarh)

Governor: Gen. S. F. RODRIGUES (retd).
Chief Minister: PARKASH SINGH BADAL (Shiromani Akali Dal).
Legislative Assembly: 117 seats (Shiromani Akali Dal 49, Congress 44, Bharatiya Janata Party 19, independents 5).

RAJASTHAN
(Capital—Jaipur)

Governor: SHILENDRA KUMAR SINGH.
Chief Minister: VASUNDHARA RAJE SCINDIA (Bharatiya Janata Party).
Legislative Assembly: 200 seats (Bharatiya Janata Party 123, Congress 55, Indian National Lok Dal 3, Janata Dal—United 2, Bahujan Samaj Party 2, Communist Party of India—Marxist 1, independents and others 14).

SIKKIM
(Capital—Gangtok)

Governor: SUDARSHAN AGARWAL.
Chief Minister: PAWAN KUMAR CHAMLING (Sikkim Democratic Front).
Legislative Assembly: 32 seats (Sikkim Democratic Front 31, Congress 1).

TAMIL NADU
(Capital—Chennai)

Governor: SURJIT SINGH BARNALA.
Chief Minister: M. KARUNANIDHI (Dravida Munnetra Kazhagam).
Legislative Assembly: 235 seats, incl. one nominated (Anglo-Indian) mem. (Dravida Munnetra Kazhagam 95, All-India Anna Dravida Munnetra Kazhagam 60, Congress 35, Pattali Makkal Katchi 18, Communist Party of India—Marxist 9, Communist Party of India 6, Marumalarchi Dravida Munnetra Kazhagam 6, Viduthalai Chiruthaigal Katch 2, independents and others 4).

TRIPURA
(Capital—Agartala)

Governor: DINESH NANDAN SAHAYA.
Chief Minister: MANIK SARKAR (Communist Party of India—Marxist).
Legislative Assembly: 60 seats (Communist Party of India—Marxist 46, Congress 10, Revolutionary Socialist Party 2, others 2).

UTTAR PRADESH
(Capital—Lucknow)

Governor: T. V. RAJESHWAR.
Chief Minister: KUMARI MAYAWATI (Bahujan Samaj Party).
Legislative Assembly: 404 seats (Bahujan Samaj Party 206, Samajwadi Party 97, Bharatiya Janata Party 50, Congress 22, Rashtriya Lok Dal 10, Rashtriya Parivartan Dal 2, Akhil Bhartiya Loktantrik Congress 1, Bharatiya Jan Shakti 1, Jan Morcha 1, Janata Dal—United 1, Rashtriya Swabhimaan Party 1, Uttar Pradesh United Democratic Front 1, independents 9, nominated 1, vacant 1).
Legislative Council: 108 seats.

UTTARAKHAND
(Capital—Dehradun)

Governor: B. L. JOSHI.
Chief Minister: BHUVAN CHANDRA KHANDURI (Bharatiya Janata Party).
Legislative Assembly: 70 seats (Bharatiya Janata Party 34, Congress 21, Bahujan Samaj Party 8, Uttarakhand Kranti Dal 3, independents 3, vacant 1).

WEST BENGAL
(Capital—Kolkata)

Governor: GOPALKRISHNA GANDHI.
Chief Minister: BUDDHADEV BHATTACHARYA (Communist Party of India—Marxist).
Legislative Assembly: 294 seats (Communist Party of India—Marxist 176, All India Trinamool Congress 30, All India Forward Bloc 23, Congress 21, Revolutionary Socialist Party 20, Communist Party of India 8, West Bengal Socialist Party 4, Gorakha National Liberation Front 3, independents and others 9).

UNION TERRITORIES

Andaman and Nicobar Islands (Headquarters—Port Blair): Lt-Gov. Lt-Gen. (retd) BHOPINDER SINGH.
Chandigarh (Headquarters—Chandigarh): Administrator Gen. S. F. RODRIGUES (retd).
Chandigarh was to be incorporated into the Punjab state on 26 January 1986, but the transfer was postponed indefinitely.
Dadra and Nagar Haveli (Headquarters—Silvassa): Administrator RAJANI KANT VERMA.
Daman and Diu (Headquarters—Daman): Administrator RAJANI KANT VERMA.
Lakshadweep (Headquarters—Kavaratti): Administrator B. V. SELVARAJ.
Puducherry (Capital—Puducherry): Lt-Gov. Lt-Gen. (retd) BHOPINDER SINGH (acting); Chief Minister N. RANGASAMY (Congress).
Assembly: 30 seats (Congress 10, Dravida Munnetra Kazhagam 7, All-India Anna Dravida Munnetra Kazhagam 3, Puduchcheri Makkal Congress 3, Pattali Makkal Katchi 2, Communist Party of India 1, Marumalarchi Dravida 1, independents 3).

NATIONAL CAPITAL TERRITORY

Delhi (Headquarters—Delhi): Lt-Gov. TEJENDRA KHANNA; Chief Minister SHEILA DIXIT (Congress).
Assembly: 70 seats (Congress 47, Bharatiya Janata Party 20, Janata Dal—Secular 1, Nationalist Congress Party 1, independent 1).

Election Commission

Election Commission of India: Nirvachan Sadan, Ashoka Rd, New Delhi 110 001; tel. (11) 23717391; fax (11) 23713412; e-mail feedback@eci.gov.in; internet www.eci.gov.in; f. 1950; independent; Chief Election Commr N. GOPALASWAMI.

Political Organizations

MAJOR NATIONAL POLITICAL ORGANIZATIONS

Bahujan Samaj Party (Majority Society Party): c/o Lok Sabha, New Delhi; internet www.bahujansamajp.com; promotes the rights of the *Harijans* ('Untouchables') of India; Founder KANSHI RAM; Pres. KUMARI MAYAWATI.

Bharatiya Janata Party (BJP) (Indian People's Party): 11 Ashok Rd, New Delhi 110 001; tel. (11) 23382234; fax (11) 23782163; e-mail bjpco@vsnl.com; internet www.bjp.org; f. 1980 as a breakaway group

INDIA

from Janata Party; right-wing Hindu party; Pres. RAJNATH SINGH; Gen. Secs RAM LAL, GOPINATH MUNDE, ARUN JAITLEY, ANANTH KUMAR, THAWARCHAND GEHLOT, OM PRAKASH MATHUR, VINAY KATIYAR; 10.5m. mems.

Communist Party of India (CPI): 15 Ajoy Bhavan, Kotla Marg, New Delhi 110 002; tel. (11) 23235546; fax (11) 23235543; e-mail cpi@cpofindia.org; internet www.cpindia.org; f. 1925; advocates the establishment of a socialist society led by the working class, and ultimately of a communist society; nine-mem. central secretariat; Leader GURUDA DASGUPTA; Gen. Sec. ARDHENDU BHUSHAN BARDHAN; 486,578 mems (2004).

Communist Party of India—Marxist (CPI—M): A. K. Gopalan Bhavan, 27–29 Bhai Vir Singh Marg, New Delhi 110 001; tel. (11) 23344918; fax (11) 23747483; e-mail cpim@vsnl.com; internet www.cpim.org; f. 1964 as breakaway group from the CPI; maintained an independent position; managed by a central committee of 77 mems and a politburo of 15 mems; Leaders BUDDHADEV BHATTACHARYA, JYOTI BASU, PRAKASH KARAT, SITARAM YECHURY, SOMNATH CHATTERJEE; Gen. Sec. PRAKASH KARAT; 975,799 mems (2006).

Indian National Congress: 24 Akbar Rd, New Delhi 110 011; tel. (11) 23019080; fax (11) 23017047; e-mail aicc@congress.org.in; internet www.congress.org.in; f. 1969 as separate faction under Indira Gandhi; originally known as Indian National Congress (R), then as Indian National Congress (I); name of party gradually changed to Indian National Congress or Congress Party in the early to mid-1990s; Pres. SONIA GANDHI; Gen. Secs MUKUL WASNIK, JANARDAN DWIVEDI, MARGARET ALVA, DIGVIJAY SINGH, ASHOK GEHLOT, B. K. HARIPRASAD, V. NARAYANSWAMY, MOHSINA KIDWAI, RAHUL GANDHI, PRITHVIRAJ CHAVAN, V. KISHORE CHANDRA S. DEO; 35m. mems (1998).

Nationalist Congress Party (NCP): 10 Dr Bishambhar Das Marg, New Delhi 110001; tel. (11) 23359218; fax (11) 23352112; e-mail mail@ncp.org.in; internet www.ncp.org.in; f. 1999 as breakaway faction of Congress; split into two factions in Jan. 2004—one headed by Sharad Pawar and another by Purno Shangma; faction led by Shangma merged with the All India Trinamool Congress; Pres. SHARAD PAWAR; Gen. Secs P. A. SANGMA, TARIQ ANWAR, T. P. PEETHAMBARAN MASTER, Prof. DEVI PRASAD TRIPATHI, Dr AKHTAR HASAN RIZVI, Dr V. RAJESHWARAN.

MAJOR REGIONAL POLITICAL ORGANIZATIONS

Akhil Bharat Hindu Mahasabha: Hindu Mahasabha Bhavan, Mandir Marg, New Delhi 110 001; tel. (11) 23342087; e-mail chakrapani_hms@yahoo.co.in; f. 1915; seeks the establishment of a democratic Hindu state; Pres. SWAMI CHAKRAPANI; Gen. Sec. MUNNA KUMAR SHARMA; 525,000 mems.

All-India Anna Dravida Munnetra Kazhagam (AIADMK) (All-India Anna Dravidian Progressive Asscn): 275 Avvai Shanmugam Salai, Royapet, Chennai 600 014; tel. (44) 28132266; fax (44) 28133510; e-mail aiadmk@vsnl.net; internet aiadmkallindia.org; f. 1972; breakaway group from the DMK; Leader and Gen. Sec. JAYARAM JAYALALITHA.

All India Forward Bloc: 28 Gurudwara Rakabganj Rd, New Delhi 110 001; tel. and fax (11) 23714131; e-mail dbiswas@sansad.nic.in; internet www.forwardbloc.org; f. 1940 by Netaji Subhash Chandra Bose; socialist aims, including nationalization of major industries, land reform and redistribution, and the establishment of a union of socialist republics through revolution; Leader and Gen. Sec. DEBABRATA BISWAS; 900,000 mems (1999).

All India Trinamool Congress: 30B Harish Chatterjee St, Kolkata 700 026; tel. (33) 24540881; fax (33) 24540880; e-mail info@trinamoolcongress.com; internet www.trinamoolcongress.com; merged with the Sangma faction of the Nationalist Congress Party in 2004; Leader MAMATA BANERJEE; Gen. Secs MUKUL ROY, DINESH TRIBEDI.

Asom Gana Parishad (AGP) (Assam People's Council): Gopinath Bordoloi Rd, Guwahati 781 001; f. 1985; draws support from the All-Assam Gana Sangram Parishad and the All-Assam Students' Union (Leader SAMUJJAL KUMAR BHATTACHARYYA; Gen. Sec. TAPAN KUMAR GOGOI); advocates the unity of India in diversity and a united Assam; Pres. BRINDABAN GOSWAMI.

Biju Janata Dal: Naveen Nivas, Aerodrome Gate, Bhubaneswar 751 009; Pres. NAVEEN PATNAIK.

Dravida Munnetra Kazhagam (DMK): Anna Arivalayam, Anna Salai, Chennai 600 018; f. 1949; aims at full autonomy for states (primarily Tamil Nadu) within the Union; Pres. MUTHUVEL KARUNANIDHI; Gen. Sec. K. ANBAZHAGAN; more than 4m. mems.

Indian National Lok Dal: 18 Janpath, New Delhi 110001; tel. (11) 23793409; fmrly mem. of the National Democratic Alliance; Leader OM PRAKASH CHAUTALA; Sec.-Gen. AJAY SINGH CHAUTALA.

Jammu and Kashmir National Conference (JKNC): Mujahid Manzil, Srinagar 190 002; tel. (194) 271500; fmrly All Jammu and Kashmir National Conference; f. 1931; renamed 1939, reactivated 1975; state-based party campaigning for internal autonomy and responsible self-govt; Pres. OMAR ABDULLAH; Gen. Sec. Maulana MASOODI; 1m. mems.

Janata Dal—Secular (People's Party—Secular): 5 Safdarjung Lane, New Delhi 110 003; f. 2000 following split of Janata Dal; Pres. H. D. DEVE GOWDA; Sec.-Gen. KUNWAR DANISH ALI.

Janata Dal—United (People's Party—United): 7 Jantar Mantar Rd, New Delhi 110 001; tel. (11) 23368833; fax (11) 23368138; f. 2000 following split of Janata Dal; merged with Samata Party in 2003; advocates non-alignment, the eradication of poverty, unemployment and wide disparities in wealth, and the protection of minorities; Pres. SHARAD YADAV; State Gen. Sec. OM PRAKASH KHEMKARANI.

Jharkhand Mukti Morcha: Bariatu Rd, Ranchi 834 008; aligned with national ruling coalition, the United Progressive Alliance; Leader SHIBU SOREN.

Lok Jan Shakti Party (LJSP): New Delhi; f. 2000 as breakaway faction of Janata Dal—United; left-wing; Pres. RAM VILAS PASWAN.

Pattali Makkal Katchi: Gounder St, Dharamapuri 636 701; tel. (4342) 263275; Leader Dr ANBUMANI RAMDOSS; Pres. G. K. MANI.

Peasants' and Workers' Party of India: Mahatma Phule Rd, Naigaum, Mumbai 400 014; f. 1949; Gen. Sec. DAJIBA DESAI; c. 10,000 mems.

Rashtriya Janata Dal (RJD) (National People's Party): 13 V. P. House, Rafi Marg, New Delhi 110 011; f. 1997 as a breakaway group from Janata Dal; Leader LALU PRASAD YADAV.

Republican Party of India (RPI): Ensa Hutments, I Block, Azad Maidan, Fort, Mumbai 400 001; tel. (22) 22621888; f. 1952; by 2003 the group had split into 10 factions; the three main factions were led by PRAKASH RAO AMBEDKAR, RAMDAS ATHAVALE and R. S. GAVAI, respectively.

Revolutionary Socialist Party: 17 Feroz Shah Rd, New Delhi 110 001; tel. (11) 23782167; fax (11) 23782342; e-mail abani@sansad.nic.in; Leaders DEBABRATA BANDOPADHYAY, ABANI ROY; Gen. Sec. K. PANKAJAKSHAN.

Samajwadi Party (Socialist Party): 18 Copernicus Lane, New Delhi; e-mail samajwadiparty@gmail.com; f. 1991; Pres. MULAYAM SINGH YADAV; Gen. Sec. AMAR SINGH.

Shiromani Akali Dal: Baradan Shri Darbar Sahib, Amritsar; internet www.shiromaniakalidalbadal.com; f. 1920; Pres. (Shiromani Akali Dal—Badal) PARKASH SINGH BADAL; Sec.-Gen. SUKHDEV SINGH DHINDSA.

Shiv Sena (Army of Shiv): Shiv Sena Bhavan, Ram Ganesh Gadkari Chowk, Dadar, Mumbai 400 028; tel. (22) 24309128; e-mail shivalay@shivsena.org; internet www.shivsena.org; f. 1966; militant Hindu group; labour union, Bharatiya Kamgar Sena (Indian Workers' Army), affiliated to the party; Exec. Pres. BAL THACKERAY.

Sikkim Democratic Front: Upper Deorali, Gangtok, East Sikkim; Pres. Dr PAWAN KUMAR CHAMLING; Gen. Sec. DAWCHU LEPCHA.

Telangana Rashtra Samithi: Karimnagar; f. 2001; Pres. K. CHANDRASEKHAR RAO.

Telugu Desam (Telugu Nation): NTR Bhavan, Rd 2, Banjara Hills, Hyderabad 500 034; tel. (40) 30699999; fax (40) 23542108; e-mail contact@telugudesam.com; internet www.telugudesam.com; f. 1982; state-based party (Andhra Pradesh); Pres. N. CHANDRABABU NAIDU; 8m. mems.

Diplomatic Representation

EMBASSIES AND HIGH COMMISSIONS IN INDIA

Afghanistan: 5/50F Shanti Path, Chanakyapuri, New Delhi 110 021; tel. (11) 2410331; fax (11) 26875439; e-mail afghanspirit@yahoo.com; Ambassador Dr SAYED MAKHDOOM RAHEEN.

Algeria: E-6/5 Vasant Vihar, New Delhi 110 057; tel. (11) 26147036; fax (11) 26147033; internet www.embalgind.com; Ambassador Dr NOUREDDINE BARDAD DAJDJ.

Angola: 5/50F, Nyaya Marg, Chanakyapuri, New Delhi 110 021; tel. (11) 26882680; fax (11) 24673785; e-mail xietuang@del2.vsnl.net.in; internet www.angolaembassyindia.com; Ambassador ANTONIO FWAMINY DACOSTA FERNANDES.

Argentina: A-2/6, Vasant Vihar, New Delhi 110 057; tel. (11) 41661982; fax (11) 41661988; Ambassador ERNESTO CARLOS ALVAREZ.

Armenia: E-1/20, Vasant Vihar, New Delhi 110 057; tel. (11) 24112851; fax (11) 24112853; e-mail armemb@vsnl.com; Ambassador ASHOT KOCHARYAN.

Australia: 1/50-G Shanti Path, Chanakyapuri, New Delhi 110 021; tel. (11) 41399900; fax (11) 41494490; e-mail austhighcom.newdelhi@dfat.gov.au; internet www.ausgovindia.com; High Commissioner JOHN MCCARTHY.

INDIA
Directory

Austria: EP-13 Chandragupta Marg, Chanakyapuri, New Delhi 110 021; tel. (11) 26889037; fax (11) 26886929; e-mail new-delhi-ob@bmeia.gv.at; internet www.aussenministerium.at/newdelhi; Ambassador Dr FERDINAND MAULTASCHL.

Azerbaijan: Vasant Marg, Vasant Vihar E-70, New Delhi; tel. (11) 26152228; fax (11) 26152227; e-mail azembassy@airtelbroadband.in; Ambassador TAMERLAN GARAYEV.

Bahrain: 4 A-4, Palam Marg, Vasant Vihar, New Delhi 110 057; tel. (11) 26154153; fax (11) 26146731; e-mail newdelhi.mission@mofa.gov.bh; Ambassador MOHAMMED GHASSAN SHAIKHO.

Bangladesh: EP-39 Dr S. Radhakrishnan Marg, Chanakyapuri, New Delhi 110 021; tel. (11) 24121389; fax (11) 26878953; e-mail bhcdelhi@mantraonline.com; internet www.bhcdelhi.org; High Commissioner LIAQUAT ALI CHOUDHURY.

Belarus: 163 Jor Bagh, New Delhi 110 003; tel. (11) 24697025; fax (11) 24697029; e-mail india@belembassy.org; Ambassador OLEG LAPTENOK.

Belgium: 50N Shanti Path, Chanakyapuri, New Delhi 110 021; tel. (11) 42428000; fax (11) 42428002; e-mail newdelhi@diplobel.be; internet www.diplomatie.be/newdelhi; Ambassador JEAN M. DEBOUTTE.

Bhutan: Chandragupta Marg, Chanakyapuri, New Delhi 110 021; tel. (11) 26889807; fax (11) 26876710; e-mail bhutan@vsnl.com; Ambassador Lyonpo DAGO TSHERING.

Bosnia and Herzegovina: E-9/11 Vasant Vihar, New Delhi 110 057; tel. (11) 51662481; fax (11) 51662482; e-mail bosher@airtelbroadband.in; Ambassador KEMAL MUFTIĆ.

Brazil: 8 Aurangzeb Rd, New Delhi 110 011; tel. (11) 23017301; fax (11) 23793684; e-mail brasindi@vsnl.com; Ambassador JOSÉ VICENTE DE SA PIMENTEL.

Brunei: 4 Poorvi Marg, Vasant Vihar, New Delhi 110 057; tel. (11) 26148340; fax (11) 26142101; e-mail newdelhi.india@mfa.gov.bn; High Commissioner Dato' Paduka Haji ABDUL GHAFAR BIN Haji ISMAIL.

Bulgaria: 16/17 Chandragupta Marg, Chanakyapuri, New Delhi 110 021; tel. (11) 26115550; fax (11) 26876190; e-mail bulemb@bulgariaembindia.com; internet bulgariaembindia.com; Ambassador DRAGOVEST GORANOV.

Burkina Faso: P 3/1 Vasant Vihar, New Delhi 110 057; tel. (11) 26140641; fax (11) 26140630; e-mail emburnd@bol.net.in; internet www.embassyburkinaindia.com; Chargé d'affaires OUSMAN NACAMBO.

Cambodia: N-14 Panchsheel Park, New Delhi 110 017; tel. (11) 26495092; fax (11) 26495093; e-mail camboemb@bol.net.in; Ambassador CHOEUNG BUNTHENG.

Canada: 7/8 Shanti Path, Chanakyapuri, New Delhi 110 021; tel. (11) 41782000; fax (11) 41782020; e-mail delhi@international.gc.ca; internet www.india.gc.ca; High Commissioner DAVID MALONE.

Chile: 146 Jorbagh, New Delhi 110 003; tel. (11) 24617123; fax (11) 24617102; e-mail embchile@airtelbroadband.in; internet www.echileindia.com; Ambassador OSCAR ALFONSO SILVA.

China, People's Republic: 50D Shanti Path, Chanakyapuri, New Delhi 110 021; tel. (11) 26112345; fax (11) 26885486; e-mail chinaemb_in@mfa.gov.cn; internet www.chinaembassy.org.in; Ambassador ZHANG YAN.

Colombia: 3 Palam Marg, Vasant Vihar, New Delhi 110 057; tel. (11) 51662106; fax (11) 51662108; e-mail edelhi@minrelext.gov.co; Ambassador JUAN ALFREDO PINTO SAAVEDRA.

Congo, Democratic Republic: B-2/6, Vasant Vihar, New Delhi 110 057; tel. (11) 51660976; fax (11) 51663152; e-mail congoembassy@yahoo.co.in; Ambassador BALUMUENE NKUNA FRANCOIS.

Côte d'Ivoire: B-9/6, Vasant Vihar, New Delhi 110 057; tel. (11) 51704234; fax (11) 51704236; e-mail embassy@amb2ci-inde.org; Ambassador GILBERT BLEU-LAINE.

Croatia: A-15 West End, New Delhi 110 021; tel. (11) 41663101; fax (11) 24116873; e-mail croemb.new-delhi@mvpei.hr; Ambassador (vacant).

Cuba: W-124A, Greater Kailash Part I, New Delhi 110 048; tel. (11) 26222467; fax (11) 26222469; e-mail embcuind@del6.vsnl.net.in; Ambassador MIGUEL ANGEL RAMIREZ RAMOS.

Cyprus: 106 Jor Bagh, New Delhi 110 003; tel. (11) 24697503; fax (11) 24462828; e-mail cyprus@del3.vsnl.net.in; High Commissioner ANDREAS G. ZENONOS.

Czech Republic: 50M Niti Marg, Chanakyapuri, New Delhi 110 021; tel. (11) 26110205; fax (11) 26886221; e-mail newdelhi@embassy.mzv.cz; internet www.mfa.cz/newdelhi; Ambassador HYNEK KMONÍČEK.

Denmark: 11 Aurangzeb Rd, New Delhi 110 011; tel. (11) 42090700; fax (11) 23792019; e-mail delamb@um.dk; internet www.ambnewdelhi.um.dk; Ambassador OLE LØNSMANN-POULSEN.

Djibouti: c/o A 2–20 Sarfarjung Enclave, New Delhi 110 029; tel. (11) 41354491; fax (11) 41354490; e-mail info@embassyofdjibouti.org; internet embassyofdjibouti.org/EmbasyNewDelhi.htm; Ambassador YOUSSOUF OMAR DOUALEH.

Dominican Republic: 1st Floor, 4 Munirka Marg, Vasant Vihar, New Delhi 110 057; tel. (11) 46015000; fax (11) 46015004; e-mail info@dr-embassy-india.com; Ambassador FRANK HANS DANNENBERG.

Ecuador: C-156 Second Floor, Defence Colony, New Delhi 110 014; tel. (11) 51555602; fax (11) 51555604; e-mail eecuindia@mmrree.gov.ec; Chargé d'affaires CARLOS ABAD ORTIZ.

Egypt: 1/50M Niti Marg, Chanakyapuri, New Delhi 110 021; tel. (11) 26114096; fax (11) 26885355; e-mail egypt@del2.vsnl.net.in; Ambassador MUHAMMAD ABDUL HAMEED HIJAZI.

Eritrea: C-7/9, Vasant Vihar, New Delhi 110 057; tel. (11) 26146336; fax (11) 26146337; e-mail eriindia@yahoo.co.in; internet www.eritreaembindia.com; Ambassador ALEM TSEHAYE WOLDEMARIAM.

Ethiopia: 7/50G Satya Marg, Chanakyapuri, New Delhi 110 021; tel. (11) 26119513; fax (11) 26875731; e-mail delethem@yahoo.com; Ambassador GENET ZEWDIE.

Fiji: N-87, Panchsheel Park, New Delhi 110 017; tel. (11) 41751092; fax (11) 41751095; e-mail fijihighcommission@yahoo.co.in; High Commissioner SAVENACA KAUNISELA.

Finland: E-3 Nyaya Marg, Chanakyapuri, New Delhi 110 021; tel. (11) 41497500; fax (11) 41497555; e-mail sanomat.NDE@formin.fi; internet www.finland.org.in; Ambassador ASKO NUMMINEM.

France: 2/50E Shanti Path, Chanakyapuri, New Delhi 110 021; tel. (11) 24196100; fax (11) 24196119; e-mail webmaster@france-in-india.org; internet www.france-in-india.org; Ambassador JÉRÔME BONNAFONT.

Germany: 6 Block 50G, Shanti Path, Chanakyapuri, POB 613, New Delhi 110 021; tel. (11) 44199199; fax (11) 26873117; internet www.new-delhi.diplo.de; Ambassador BERND MÜTZELBURG.

Ghana: 50-N Satya Marg, Chanakyapuri, New Delhi 110 021; tel. (11) 26883298; fax (11) 26883202; High Commissioner (vacant).

Greece: EP-32, Dr S. Radhakrishnan Marg, Chanakyapuri, New Delhi 110 021; tel. (11) 26880700; fax (11) 26888010; e-mail gremb@bol.net.in; internet www.greeceinindia.com; Ambassador STAVROS LYKIDIS.

Guyana: F-8/22, Vasant Vihar, New Delhi 110 057; tel. (11) 41669717; fax (11) 41669714; e-mail hcommguy.del@gmail.com; High Commissioner J. RONALD GAJRAJ.

Holy See: 50C Niti Marg, Chanakyapuri, New Delhi 110 021 (Apostolic Nunciature); tel. (11) 26889184; fax (11) 26874286; e-mail nuntius@apostolicnunciatureindia.com; internet www.apostolicnunciatureindia.com; Nuncio Most Rev. PEDRO LÓPEZ QUINTANA (Titular Archbishop of Agropoli).

Hungary: Plot 2, 50M Niti Marg, Chanakyapuri, New Delhi 110 021; tel. (11) 26114737; fax (11) 26886742; e-mail mission.del@kum.hu; Ambassador Dr IVÁN NÉMETH.

Iceland: 11 Aurangzeb Rd, New Delhi 110 011; tel. (11) 43530300; fax (11) 42403001; e-mail newdelhi@mfa.is; internet www.iceland.org/in; Ambassador Dr GUNNAR PÁLSSON.

Indonesia: 50A Kautilya Marg, Chanakyapuri, New Delhi 110 021; tel. (11) 26118642; fax (11) 26874402; e-mail iembassy@giasdl01.vsnl.net.in; internet www.indonesianembassy.org.in; Chargé d'affaires a.i. RIZALI W. INDRAKESUMA.

Iran: 5 Barakhamba Road, New Delhi 110 001; tel. (11) 23329600; fax (11) 23325493; e-mail info@iran-embassy.org.in; internet www.iran-embassy.org.in; Ambassador SAYED MAHDI NABIZADEH.

Iraq: B-5/8, Vasant Vihar, New Delhi 110 057; tel. (11) 26149085; fax (11) 26149076; e-mail dlhemb@iraqmofamail.net; Chargé d'affaires a.i. MUAYAD HUSSAIN.

Ireland: 230 Jor Bagh, New Delhi 110 003; tel. (11) 24626733; fax (11) 24697053; e-mail ireland@ndf.vsnl.net.in; internet www.irelandinindia.com; Ambassador KIERAN DOWLING.

Israel: 3 Aurangzeb Rd, New Delhi 110 011; tel. (11) 23013238; fax (11) 23014298; e-mail newdelhi.mfa@mfa.gov.il; internet delhi.mfa.gov.il; Ambassador MARK SOFER.

Italy: 50E Chandragupta Marg, Chanakyapuri, New Delhi 110 021; tel. (11) 26114355; fax (11) 26873889; e-mail ambasciata.newdelhi@esteri.it; internet www.ambnewdelhi.esteri.it; Ambassador ANTONIO ARMELLINI.

Japan: Plots 4–5, 50G Shanti Path, Chanakyapuri, New Delhi 110 021; tel. (11) 26876581; fax (11) 26885587; e-mail jpembjic@bol.net.in; internet www.in.emb-japan.go.jp; Ambassador HIDEAKI DOMICHI.

Jordan: 30 Golf Links, New Delhi 110 003; tel. (11) 24653318; fax (11) 24653353; e-mail jordan@jordanembassyindia.org; internet www.jordanembassyindia.org; Ambassador MOHAMMAD ALI DAHER.

Kazakhstan: 61 Poorvi Marg, Vasant Vihar, New Delhi 110 057; tel. (11) 46007700; fax (11) 46007701; e-mail embassy@kazind.com; internet www.kazind.com; Ambassador KAIRAT UMAROV.

INDIA

Kenya: 34 Paschimi Marg, New Delhi 110 057; tel. (11) 26146537; fax (11) 26146550; e-mail info@kenyamission-delhi.com; internet www.kenyamission-delhi.com; High Commissioner Prof. FESTUS KABERIA.

Korea, Democratic People's Republic: D-14 Maharani Bagh, New Delhi 110 065; tel. (11) 26829644; fax (11) 26829645; e-mail dprk194899@yahoo.com; Ambassador HAN CHANG ON.

Korea, Republic: 9 Chandragupta Marg, Chanakyapuri, POB 5416, New Delhi 110 021; tel. (11) 26885412; fax (11) 26884840; e-mail kobe@mail.mofat.go.kr; internet ind.mofat.go.kr; Ambassador PAEK YUNG-SUN.

Kuwait: 11 Olof Palme Marg, Vasant Vihar, New Delhi 110 057; tel. (11) 26150124; fax (11) 26873516; e-mail kuinfo@kuwait-info.com.com; internet www.kuwait-info.com; Ambassador KHALAF ABBAS KHALAF AL-FOUDARI.

Kyrgyzstan: C-93 Anand Niketan, New Delhi 110 021; tel. (11) 24108008; fax (11) 24108009; e-mail alatoo@starith.net; Ambassador IRINA A. OROLBAYEVA.

Laos: A-104/7 Parmanand Estate, Maharani Bagh, New Delhi 110 065; tel. (11) 26933319; fax (11) 26323048; Ambassador LY BUN KHAM.

Lebanon: H-1, Anand Niketan, New Delhi 110 021; tel. (11) 24111415; fax (11) 24110818; e-mail lebemb@bol.net.in; Ambassador KHALED SALMAN.

Libya: 22 Golf Links, New Delhi 110 003; tel. (11) 24697717; fax (11) 24633005; e-mail libya@bol.net.in; Chargé d'affaires MAHFUD R. M. RAHIAM.

Luxembourg: 730 Gadaipur Rd, Branch Post Office, Gadaipur, New Delhi 110 030; tel. (11) 26801966; fax (11) 26801971; e-mail vm.bharathi@mae.etat.lu; internet www.luxembourgindia.org; Ambassador MARC COURTE.

Malaysia: 50M Satya Marg, Chanakyapuri, New Delhi 110 021; tel. (11) 26111291; fax (11) 26881538; e-mail maldelhi@kln.gov.my; internet www.kln.gov.my/perwakilan/newdelhi; High Commissioner Datuk TAN SENG SUNG.

Maldives: B-2, Anand Niketan, New Delhi 110 021; tel. (11) 41435701; fax (11) 41435709; e-mail admin@maldiveshighcom.co.in; internet www.maldiveshighcom.co.in; High Commissioner Lt-Gen. (retd) ABDUL SATTAR ADAM.

Malta: D70 East of Kailash, New Delhi 110 065; tel. (11) 26439090; fax (11) 41659090; e-mail malta@kathpalia.in; High Commissioner WILFRED KENNELY.

Mauritius: 41 Jesus and Mary Marg, Chanakyapuri, New Delhi 110 021; tel. (11) 24102161; fax (11) 24102194; e-mail mhcnd@bol.net.in; High Commissioner M. CHOONEE.

Mexico: C-8 Anand Niketan, New Delhi 110 021; tel. (11) 24107182; fax (11) 24117193; e-mail embamexindia@airtelbroadband.in; internet www.sre.gob.mx/india; Ambassador ROGELIO GRANGUILLHOME MORFIN.

Mongolia: 34 Archbishop Makarios Marg, New Delhi 110 003; tel. (11) 24631728; fax (11) 24633240; e-mail mongemb@vsnl.net; internet www.mongemb.com; Ambassador VIKTORYN ENKHBOLD.

Morocco: 33 Golf Links, New Delhi 110 003; tel. (11) 24636920; fax (11) 24636925; e-mail sifamand@giasdl01.vsnl.net.in; internet www.moroccoembindia.com; Ambassador LARBI MOUKHARIQ.

Mozambique: B-3/24, Vasant Vihar, New Delhi 110 057; tel. (11) 26156663; fax (11) 26156665; e-mail salvaro64@hotmail.com; High Commissioner CARLOS A. DO ROSARIO.

Myanmar: 3/50F Nyaya Marg, Chanakyapuri, New Delhi 110 021; tel. (11) 26889007; fax (11) 26877942; e-mail myandeli@nda.vsnl.net.in; Ambassador U KYI THEIN.

Namibia: E-2/6, Poorvi Marg, Vasant Vihar, New Delhi 110 057; tel. (11) 26140389; fax (11) 26146120; e-mail nhcdelhi@del2.vsnl.net.in; High Commissioner MARTEN KAPEWASHA.

Nepal: Barakhamba Rd, New Delhi 110 001; tel. (11) 23329218; fax (11) 23326857; e-mail nepembassydelhi@bol.net.in; Ambassador Dr DURGESH MAN SINGH.

Netherlands: 6/50F Shanti Path, Chanakyapuri, New Delhi 110 021; tel. (11) 24197600; fax (11) 24197710; e-mail nde@minbuza.nl; internet www.holland-in-india.org; Ambassador BOB H. HIENSCH.

New Zealand: Sir Edmund Hillary Marg, Chanakyapuri, New Delhi 110 021; tel. (11) 26883170; fax (11) 26883165; e-mail nzhc@ndf.vsnl.net.in; internet www.nzembassy.com/home.cfm?c=26; High Commissioner RUPERT HOLBOROW.

Nigeria: Plot No. 4, Chandragupta Marg, Chanakyapuri, New Delhi 110 021; tel. (11) 24122142; fax (11) 24122138; e-mail nhcnder@vsnl.com; High Commissioner ABUBAKAR GARBA ABDULLAHI.

Norway: 50C Shanti Path, Chanakyapuri, New Delhi 110 021; tel. (11) 41779200; fax (11) 41680145; e-mail emb.newdelhi@mfa.no; internet www.norwayemb.org.in; Ambassador ANN OLLESTAD.

Oman: EP-10/11, Chandragupta Marg, Chankyapuri, New Delhi 110 021; tel. (11) 26885622; fax (11) 26885621; e-mail omandelhi@vsnl.com; Ambassador MOHAMMED BIN YOUSUF SHALWANI.

Pakistan: 2/50G Shanti Path, Chanakyapuri, New Delhi 110 021; tel. (11) 26110601; fax (11) 26872339; e-mail pakhc@nda.vsnl.net.in; High Commissioner SHAHID MALIK.

Panama: 3-D, Palam Marg, Vasant Vihar, New Delhi 110 057; tel. (11) 26148268; fax (11) 26148261; e-mail panaind@bol.net.in; Ambassador ALBERTO J. PINZÓN.

Peru: G-15 Maharani Bagh, New Delhi 110 065; tel. (11) 26312610; fax (11) 26312557; e-mail info@embaperuindia.com; internet www.embaperuindia.com; Ambassador LUIS HERNANDEZ.

Philippines: 50N Nyaya Marg, Chanakyapuri, New Delhi 110 021; tel. (11) 26889091; fax (11) 26876401; e-mail newdelhipe@bol.net.in; Ambassador TERESITA V. BERNER.

Poland: 50M Shanti Path, Chanakyapuri, New Delhi 110 021; tel. (11) 41496900; fax (11) 26871914; e-mail polemb@airtelbroadband.in; internet www.newdelhi.polemb.net; Ambassador Dr KRZYSZTOF MAJKA.

Portugal: 8 Olof Palme Marg, Vasant Vihar, New Delhi 110 057; tel. (11) 26142215; fax (11) 26152837; e-mail embportin@ndf.vsnl.net.in; internet www.embportindia.com; Ambassador JOAQUIM JOSÉ L. F. MARQUES CURTO.

Qatar: EP-31A, Chandragupta Marg, Chanakyapuri, New Delhi 110 021; tel. (11) 26117988; fax (11) 26886080; e-mail newdelhi@mofa.gov.qa; Ambassador HUSSAN MOHAMMED RAFEH ALEMADI.

Romania: A-47 Vasant Marg, Vasant Vihar, New Delhi 110 057; tel. (11) 26140447; fax (11) 26140611; e-mail embrom@touchtelindia.net; Ambassador VASILE SOFINETI.

Russia: Shanti Path, Chanakyapuri, New Delhi 110 021; tel. (11) 26873799; fax (11) 26876823; e-mail indrusem@del2.vsnl.net.in; internet www.india.mid.ru; Ambassador VYACHESLAV TRUBNIKOV.

Rwanda: 41 Paschimi Marg, Vasant Vihar, New Delhi 110 057; tel. (11) 51661604; fax (11) 51661605; e-mail ambadelhi@minaffet.gov.rw; Ambassador Lt-Gen. KAYUMBA NYAMWASA.

Saudi Arabia: 2 Paschimi Marg, Vasant Vihar, New Delhi 110 057; tel. (11) 26144102; fax (11) 26144244; Ambassador SALEH M. AL-GHAMDI.

Senegal: C-6/11, Vasant Vihar, New Delhi 110 057; tel. (11) 26147687; fax (11) 41662673; e-mail embassy@senindia.org; Ambassador AMADOU BOCOUM.

Serbia: 3/50G Niti Marg, Chanakyapuri, New Delhi 110 021; tel. (11) 26873661; fax (11) 26885535; e-mail office@embassyofserbiadelhi.net.in; internet www.embassyofserbiadelhi.net.in; Ambassador VUK ZUGIĆ.

Singapore: N-88 Panchsheel Park, New Delhi 110 017; tel. (11) 41019801; fax (11) 41019805; e-mail singhc_del@sgmfa.gov.sg; internet www.mfa.gov.sg/newdelhi; High Commissioner CALVIN EU MUN HOO.

Slovakia: 50M Niti Marg, Chanakyapuri, New Delhi 110 021; tel. (11) 26889071; fax (11) 26877941; e-mail skdelhi@giasdl01.vsnl.net.in; Ambassador ALEXANDER ILASCIK.

Slovenia: 46 Poorvi Marg, Vasant Vihar, New Delhi 110 057; tel. (11) 51662891; fax (11) 51662895; e-mail vnd@mzz-dkp.gov.si; Chargé d'affaires MIKLAVZ BORŠTNIK.

Somalia: A-7, Defence Colony, New Delhi 110 024; tel. (11) 24335026; e-mail mosman65@yahoo.com; Ambassador EBYAN MAHAMED SALAH.

South Africa: B-18 Vasant Marg, Vasant Vihar, New Delhi 110 057; tel. (11) 26149411; fax (11) 26143605; e-mail highcommissioner@sahc-india.com; internet www.sahc-india.com; High Commissioner SEHLOHO FRANCIS MOLOI.

Spain: 16 Sunder Nagar, New Delhi 110 003; tel. (11) 24359004; fax (11) 24359040; e-mail embspain@ndb.vsnl.net.in; Ambassador Don RAFAEL CONDE DE SARO.

Sri Lanka: 27 Kautilya Marg, Chanakyapuri, New Delhi 110 021; tel. (11) 23010201; fax (11) 23793604; e-mail lankacom@del2.vsnl.net.in; High Commissioner C. ROMESH JAYASINGHE.

Sudan: Plot No. 3, Shanti Path, Chanakyapuri, New Delhi 110 021; tel. (11) 26873785; fax (11) 26883758; e-mail sudandel@del3.vsnl.net.in; internet www.embassysudanindia.org; Ambassador ABDEL RAHMAN MOHAMED BAKHIET.

Suriname: C-15 Malcha Marg, New Delhi 110 021; tel. (11) 26888543; fax (11) 26888450; e-mail embsurnd@vsnl.net; internet www.embsurnd.com; Ambassador K. BAJNATH.

Sweden: Nyaya Marg, Chanakyapuri, New Delhi 110 021; tel. (11) 24197100; fax (11) 26885401; e-mail ambassaden.new-delhi@foreign.ministry.se; internet www.swedenabroad.se/pages/start_21488.asp; Ambassador LARS-OLOF LINDGREN.

INDIA
Directory

Switzerland: Nyaya Marg, Chanakyapuri, New Delhi 110 021; tel. (11) 26878372; fax (11) 26873093; e-mail ndh.vertretung@eda.admin.ch; Ambassador Dominique Dreyer.

Syria: D-5/8, Vasant Vihar, New Delhi 110 057; tel. (11) 26140233; fax (11) 26143107; Ambassador Fahd Salim.

Tajikistan: D-1/13, Vasant Vihar, New Delhi 110 057; tel. and fax (11) 26154282; e-mail tajembindia@yahoo.com; Ambassador Salohoddin Nasriddinov.

Tanzania: 10/1 Sav Priya Vihar, New Delhi 110 016; tel. (11) 26153148; fax (11) 26153289; e-mail tanzrep@del1.vsnl.net.in; High Commissioner Eva Lilian Nzaro.

Thailand: 56n Nyaya Marg, Chanakyapuri, New Delhi 110 021; tel. (11) 26118103; fax (11) 26872029; e-mail thaidel@mfa.go.th; internet www.thaiemb.org.in; Ambassador Chirasak Thanesnant.

Trinidad and Tobago: 6/25 Shanti Niketan, New Delhi 110 021; tel. (11) 24118427; fax (11) 24118463; e-mail admin@hctt.org; High Commissioner Pundit Manideo Persad.

Tunisia: A-42 Vasant Marg, Vasant Vihar, New Delhi 110 057; tel. (11) 26145346; fax (11) 26145301; e-mail embtundelhi@dishnetdsl.net; Ambassador Raouf Chatti.

Turkey: 50n Nyaya Marg, Chanakyapuri, New Delhi 110 021; tel. (11) 26889054; fax (11) 26881409; e-mail tembdelhi@mantraonline.com; Ambassador Hasan Gogus.

Turkmenistan: C-11, West End Colony, New Delhi 110 021; tel. (11) 24676526; fax (11) 24676527; e-mail turkmind@starith.net; Ambassador Parahat Hommadovich Durdyev.

Uganda: B-3/26, Vasant Vihar, New Delhi 110 057; tel. (11) 26144413; fax (11) 26144405; e-mail ughcom@ndb.vsnl.net.in; High Commissioner Nimisha Madhvani.

Ukraine: E-1/8 Vasant Vihar, New Delhi 110 057; tel. (11) 26146041; fax (11) 26146043; e-mail embassy@bol.net.in; internet www.ukraineembassyindia.org; Chargé d'affaires a.i. Mischuk Mykola.

United Arab Emirates: EP-12 Chandragupta Marg, New Delhi 110 021; tel. (11) 26872937; fax (11) 26873272; e-mail embassyabudhabi@bol.net.in; Chargé d'affaires Abdulla Jassim Kashwani.

United Kingdom: Shantipath, Chanakyapuri, New Delhi 110 021; tel. (11) 26872161; fax (11) 26870065; e-mail postmaster.nedel@fco.gov.uk; internet www.ukinindia.com; High Commissioner Sir Richard Stagg.

USA: Shanti Path, Chanakyapuri, New Delhi 110 021; tel. (11) 24198000; fax (11) 241900170; e-mail ndcentral@state.gov; internet newdelhi.usembassy.gov; Ambassador David Campbell Mulford.

Uruguay: A-16/2 Vasant Vihar, New Delhi 110 057; tel. (11) 26151991; fax (11) 26144306; e-mail uruind@del3.vsnl.net.in; Ambassador William Ehlers.

Uzbekistan: EP-40 Dr S. Radhakrishnan Marg, Chanakyapuri, New Delhi 110 021; tel. (11) 24670774; fax (11) 24670773; e-mail uzembind@vsnl.com; internet www.uzbekembassy.in; Ambassador Prof. Saydakmal Saydakhmedovitch Saydaminov.

Venezuela: E-106 Malcha Marg, Chanakyapuri, New Delhi 110 021; tel. (11) 41680218; fax (11) 41750743; e-mail embavene@del2.vsnl.net.in; Ambassador Milena Santana-Ramírez.

Viet Nam: 17 Kautilya Marg, Chanakyapuri, New Delhi 110 021; tel. (11) 23012123; fax (11) 23017714; e-mail sqdelhi@del3.vsnl.net.in; Ambassador Vu Quang Diem.

Yemen: B-3/61, Safdarjung Enclave, New Delhi 110 029; tel. (11) 26179612; fax (11) 26179614; e-mail yemenembnd@yahoo.com; Ambassador Mustafa Nuaman.

Zambia: D/54 Vasant Vihar, New Delhi 110 057; tel. (11) 26145883; fax (11) 26145764; e-mail zambiand@sify.com; High Commissioner S. K. Walubita.

Zimbabwe: E 12/7, Vasant Vihar, New Delhi 110 057; tel. (11) 26140430; fax (11) 26154316; e-mail ambassador@zimdelhi.com; internet www.zimdelhi.com; Ambassador Jonathan Wutawunashe.

Judicial System

THE SUPREME COURT

The Supreme Court, consisting of a Chief Justice and not more than 25 judges appointed by the President, exercises exclusive jurisdiction in any dispute between the Union and the states (although there are certain restrictions where an acceding state is involved). It has appellate jurisdiction over any judgment, decree or order of the High Court where that Court certifies that either a substantial question of law or the interpretation of the Constitution is involved. The Supreme Court can enforce fundamental rights and issue writs covering habeas corpus, mandamus, prohibition, quo warranto and certiorari. The Supreme Court is a court of record and has the power to punish for its contempt.

Provision is made for the appointment by the Chief Justice of India of judges of High Courts as ad hoc judges at sittings of the Supreme Court for specified periods, and for the attendance of retired judges at sittings of the Supreme Court. The Supreme Court has advisory jurisdiction in respect of questions which may be referred to it by the President for opinion. The Supreme Court is also empowered to hear appeals against a sentence of death passed by a State High Court in reversal of an order of acquittal by a lower court, and in a case in which a High Court has granted a certificate of fitness.

The Supreme Court also hears appeals which are certified by High Courts to be fit to be heard, subject to rules made by the Court. Parliament may, by law, confer on the Supreme Court any further powers of appeal.

The judges hold office until the age of 65 years.

Supreme Court: Tilak Marg, New Delhi 110 001; tel. (11) 23388942; fax (11) 23383792; e-mail supremecourt@nic.in; internet supremecourtofindia.nic.in.

Chief Justice of India: K. G. Balakrishnan.

Judges of the Supreme Court: A. K. Mathur, Ashok Bhan, C. K. Thakker, Hotoi Khetoho Sema, Bishwanath Agarwal, Sarosh Homi Kapadia, S. B. Sinha, Govind Prasad Mathur, Arijit Passayat, Prakash P. Naolekar, Tarun Chatterjee, P. K. Balasubramanyam, Altamas Kabir, Raju Varadarajulu Raveendran, Dalveer Bhandari, Lokeshwar Singh Panta, D. K. Jain, Markandey Katju, H. S. Bedi, V. S. Sirpurkar, B. Sudershan Reddy, P. Sathasivam, G. S. Singhvi, Aftab Alam, J. M. Panchal.

Attorney-General: Milon Banerjee.

HIGH COURTS

The High Courts are the Courts of Appeal from the lower courts, and their decisions are final except in cases where appeal lies with the Supreme Court.

LOWER COURTS

Provision is made in the Code of Criminal Procedure for the constitution of lower criminal courts called Courts of Session and Courts of Magistrates. The Courts of Session are competent to try all persons duly committed for trial, and inflict any punishment authorized by the law. The President and the local government concerned exercise the prerogative of mercy.

The constitution of inferior civil courts is determined by regulations within each state.

Religion

BUDDHISM

The Buddhists in Ladakh (Jammu and Kashmir) are followers of the Dalai Lama. Head Lama of Ladakh: Kaushak Sakula, Dalgate, Srinagar (Jammu and Kashmir). The Buddhists in Sikkim are also followers of Mahayana Buddhism. In 2001 there were 8.0m. Buddhists in India, representing 0.8% of the population.

Mahabodhi Society of India: 4-A, Bankim Chatterjee St, Kolkata 700 073; tel. and fax (33) 22415214; internet www.mahabodhiindia.com; 11 centres in India, five centres world-wide; Pres. Dr Bhupendra Kumar Modi; Gen. Sec. Dr D. Rewatha Thero.

HINDUISM

In 2001 there were 827.6m. Hindus in India, representing 80.5% of the population.

Rashtriya Swayamsevak Sangh (RSS) (National Volunteer Organization): Keshav Kunj, Jhandewala, D. B. Gupta Marg, New Delhi 110 055; tel. (11) 23611372; fax (11) 23611385; e-mail rss@rss.org; internet www.rss.org; f. 1925; 934,000 service centres in tribal, rural and urban slum areas; 58,000 working centres; Pres. K. S. Sudarshan; Gen. Sec. Mohan Bhagwat.

Sarvadeshik Arya Pratinidhi Sabha: 3/5 Asaf Ali Rd, Near Ram Lila Maidan, New Delhi 110 002; tel. (11) 23274771; e-mail sanjayyogi1@rediffmail.com; f. 1875 by Maharishi Dayanand Saraswati; the international body for Arya Samaj temples propagating reforms in all fields on the basis of Vedic principles; Pres. Capt. Dev Ratna Arya; Sec. Vimal Wadhawan.

Vishwa Hindu Parishad (VHP) (World Hindu Council): Sankat Mochan Ashram, Ramakrishna Puram VI, New Delhi 110 022; tel. (11) 26178992; fax (11) 26195527; e-mail vishwahindu@gmail.com; internet www.vhp.org; f. 1964, banned in Dec. 1992–June 1993 for its role in the destruction of the Babri mosque in Ayodhya; Pres. Ashok Singhal; Gen. Sec. Dr Praveen Togadiya.

ISLAM

Muslims are divided into two main sects, Shi'as and Sunnis. Most of the Indian Muslims are Sunnis. At the 2001 census Islam had 138.2m. adherents (13.4% of the population).

Jamiat Ulama-i-Hind (Assembly of Muslim Religious Leaders of India): 1 Bahadur Shah Zafar Marg, New Delhi 110 002; tel. (11) 23311455; fax (11) 23316173; e-mail jamiat@vsnl.com; internet jamiatulama.org; f. 1919; Pres. ASAD MADANI; Gen. Sec. Maulana MAHMOOD MADANI.

SIKHISM

In 2001 there were 19.2m. Sikhs (comprising 1.9% of the population), the majority living in the Punjab.

Shiromani Gurdwara Parbandhak Committee: Darbar Sahab, Amritsar 143 001; tel. (183) 2553956; fax (183) 2553919; e-mail info@sgpc.net; internet www.sgpc.net; f. 1925; highest authority in Sikhism; Pres. Jathedar AVTAR SINGH; Jathedar Shri Akal Takht Saheb JOGINDER SINGH VEDANTI.

CHRISTIANITY

According to the 2001 census, Christians represented 2.3% of the population in India.

National Council of Churches in India: Christian Council Lodge, Civil Lines, POB 205, Nagpur 440 001; tel. (712) 2531312; fax (712) 2520554; e-mail nccindia_ngp@sancharnet.in; internet www.nccindia.in; f. 1914; mems: 29 protestant and orthodox churches, 17 regional Christian councils, 16 All-India ecumenical orgs and seven related agencies; represents c. 13m. mems; Pres. Rt Rev. S. JEYAPAUL DAVID; Gen. Sec. Bishop D. K. SAHU.

Orthodox Churches

Malankara Orthodox Syrian Church: Devalokam, Kottayam 686 038; tel. (481) 2578500; fax (481) 2570569; e-mail orthodox@md4.vsnl.net.in; c. 2.5m. mems (1995); 22 bishops, 21 dioceses, 1,340 parishes; Catholicos of the East and Malankara Metropolitan HH BASELIUS MARTHOMA MATHEWS II; Asscn Sec. A. K. THOMAS.

Mar Thoma Syrian Church of Malabar: Mar Thoma Sabha Office, Poolatheen, Tiruvalla 689 101; tel. (473) 2630449; fax (473) 2630327; e-mail sabhaoffice@marthoma.in; internet www.marthomasyrianchurch.org; c. 1m. mems (2001); Valia Metropolitan Most Rev. Dr PHILIPOSE MAR CHRYSOSTOM MAR THOMA; Sec. Rev. Dr CHERIAN THOMAS.

The Malankara Jacobite Syrian Orthodox Church is also represented.

Protestant Churches

Church of North India (CNI): CNI Bhavan, 16 Pandit Pant Marg, New Delhi 110 001; tel. (11) 23731079; fax (11) 23716901; e-mail gscni@ndb.vsnl.net.in; internet www.cnisynod.com; f. 1970 by merger of the Church of India (fmrly known as the Church of India, Pakistan, Burma and Ceylon), the Council of the Baptist Churches in Northern India, the Methodist Church (British and Australasian Conferences), the United Church of Northern India (a union of Presbyterians and Congregationalists, f. 1924), the Church of the Brethren in India, and the Disciples of Christ; comprises 26 dioceses; c. 1.2m. mems (1999); Moderator Most Rev. JOEL V. MAL (Bishop of Chandigarh); Gen. Sec. Rev. Dr ENOS DAS PRADHAN.

Church of South India (CSI): CSI Centre, 5 Whites Rd, Chennai 600 014; tel. (44) 28521566; fax (44) 28523528; e-mail csi@vsnl.com; internet www.csisynod.com; f. 1947 by merger of the Weslyan Methodist Church in South India, the South India United Church (itself a union of churches in the Congregational and Presbyterian/Reformed traditions) and the four southern dioceses of the (Anglican) Church of India; comprises 22 dioceses (incl. one in Sri Lanka); c. 3m. mems (2003); Moderator Most Rev. Dr B. P. SUGANDHAR (Bishop of Medak); Gen. Sec. Dr PAULINE SATHIAMURTHY.

Methodist Church in India: Methodist Centre, 21 YMCA Rd, Mumbai 400 008; tel. (22) 23094316; fax (22) 23074137; e-mail gensecmci@vsnl.com; f. 1856 as the Methodist Church in Southern Asia; 648,000 mems (2005); Gen. Sec. Rev. Dr ELIA PRADEEP SAMUEL.

Samavesam of Telugu Baptist Churches: A. B. M. Compound, Kavali 524 201; tel. (8626) 241201; fax (8626) 241847; f. 1962; comprises 856 independent Baptist churches; 578,295 mems (1995); Functional Adviser Dr G. DEVADANAM.

United Evangelical Lutheran Church in India: Martin Luther Bhavan, 95 Purasawalkam High Rd, Kilpauk, Chennai 600 010; tel. (44) 26421575; fax (44) 26431144; e-mail uelci@vsnl.net; internet www.uelci-india.org; f. 1975; 11 constituent denominations: Andhra Evangelical Lutheran Church, Arcot Lutheran Church, Evangelical Lutheran Church in Madhya Pradesh, Evangelical Lutheran Church in the Himalayan States, Gossner Evangelical Lutheran Church in Chotanagpur and Assam (Asom), India Evangelical Lutheran Church, Jeypore Evangelical Lutheran Church, Northern Evangelical Lutheran Church, South Andhra Lutheran Church, Good Samaritan Evangelical Lutheran Church and Tamil Evangelical Lutheran Church; more than 1.5m. mems; Pres. Rt Rev. Dr GIDEON DEVANESAN; Exec. Sec. Rev. Dr AUGUSTINE JEYAKUMAR.

Other denominations active in the country include the Assembly of the Presbyterian Church in North East India, the Bengal-Orissa-Bihar Baptist Convention (6,000 mems), the Chaldean Syrian Church of the East, the Convention of the Baptist Churches of Northern Circars, the Council of Baptist Churches of North East India, the Council of Baptist Churches of Northern India, the Hindustani Convent Church and the Mennonite Church in India.

The Roman Catholic Church

India comprises 30 archdioceses and 128 dioceses. These include five archdioceses and 10 dioceses of the Syro-Malabar rite, and two archdioceses and three dioceses of the Syro-Malankara rite. The archdiocese of Goa and Daman is also the seat of the Patriarch of the East Indies. The remaining archdioceses are metropolitan sees. In December 2005 there were an estimated 29.4m. adherents of the Roman Catholic faith in the country.

Catholic Bishops' Conference of India (CBCI): CBCI Centre, 1 Ashok Place, nr Gole Dakkhana, New Delhi 110 001; tel. (11) 23344470; fax (11) 23364615; e-mail cbci@vsnl.com; internet www.cbcisite.com; f. 1944; Pres. Cardinal TELESPHORE P. TOPPO (Archbishop of Ranchi); Sec.-Gen. Most Rev. STANISLAUS FERNANDES (Archbishop of Gandhinagar).

Latin Rite

Conference of Catholic Bishops of India (CCBI): CCBI Centre, 2nd Cross, Hutchins Rd, POB 8490, Bangalore 560 084; tel. (80) 25498282; fax (80) 25498180; e-mail ccbi@airtelbroadband.in; internet www.ccbi.in; f. 1994; Pres. Cardinal TELESPHORO P. TOPPO (Archbishop of Ranchi).

Syro-Malabar Rite

Major Archbishop of Ernakulam-Angamaly: Cardinal MAR VARKEY VITHAYATHIL, Major Archbishop's House, Thrikkakara, POB 2580, Kochi 682 031; tel. (484) 2352629; fax (484) 2355010; e-mail secretary@ernakulamarchdiocese.org; internet www.ernakulamarchdiocese.org.

Archbishop of Kottayam: Most Rev. MATHEW MOOLAKKATTU, Archbishop's House, POB 71, Kottayam 686 001; tel. (481) 2563527; fax (481) 2563327; e-mail cbhktym@hotmail.com; internet www.kottayamad.org.

Archbishop of Changanasserry: Most Rev. JOSEPH MAR POWATHIL, Archbishop's House, POB 20, Changanasserry 686 101; tel. (481) 2420040; fax (481) 2422540; e-mail abpchry@sancharnet.in; internet www.archdiocesechanganacherry.org.

Archbishop of Tellicherry: Most Rev. GEORGE VALIAMATTAM, Archbishop's House, POB 70, Tellicherry 670 101; tel. (490) 2341058; fax (49) 2341412; e-mail diocese@eth.net; internet www.archdioceseoftellicherry.org.

Archbishop of Trichur: Most Rev. MAR ANDREWS THAZHATH, Archbishop's House, Trichur 680 005; tel. (487) 2333325; fax (487) 2338204; e-mail carbit@md4.vsnl.net.in; internet www.trichurarchdiocese.org.

Syro-Malankara Rite

Archbishop of Trivandrum: Most Rev. Dr THOMAS MAR KOORILOS, Archbishop's House, Pattom, Thiruvananthapuram 695 004; tel. (471) 2541643; fax (471) 2541635; e-mail marcleemis@hotmail.com; internet www.malankara.net.

BAHÁ'Í FAITH

National Spiritual Assembly: Bahá'í House, 6 Shrimant Madhavrao Scindia Rd, POB 19, New Delhi 110 001; tel. (11) 23389326; fax (11) 23782178; e-mail nsaindia@bahaindia.org; internet www.bahaindia.org; f. 1923; c. 2m. mems; Sec.-Gen. Dr A. K. MERCHANT.

OTHER FAITHS

Jainism: 4.2m. adherents (2001 census), 0.4% of the population.

Zoroastrianism: In 2001 69,601 Parsis practised the Zoroastrian religion, compared with 76,382 in 1991.

The Press

Freedom of the Press was guaranteed under the 1950 Constitution. In 1979 a Press Council was established (its predecessor was abolished in 1975), the function of which was to uphold the freedom of the press and maintain and improve journalistic standards.

The growth of a thriving press has been inhibited by cultural barriers caused by religious, social and linguistic differences. Consequently the English-language press, with its appeal to the educated middle-class urban readership throughout the states, has retained its dominance. The English-language metropolitan dailies are some of the widest circulating and most influential newspapers. The main Indian language dailies, by paying attention to rural affairs, cater for the increasingly literate non-anglophone provincial population. Most Indian-language papers have a relatively small circulation.

The majority of publications in India are under individual ownership (75% in 2002/03), and they claim a large part of the total circulation (60% in 1999). The most powerful groups, owned by joint stock companies, publish most of the large English dailies and frequently have considerable private commercial and industrial holdings. Four of the major groups are as follows:

Times of India Group: controlled by family of the late ASHOK JAIN; dailies: *The Times of India* (published in 11 regional centres), *Economic Times*, the Hindi *Navbharat Times* and *Sandhya Times*, the Marathi *Maharashtra Times* (Mumbai); periodicals: the English fortnightly *Femina* and monthly *Filmfare*.

Indian Express Group: controlled by the family of the late RAMNATH GOENKA; publishes nine dailies including the *Indian Express*, the Marathi *Lokasatta*, the Tamil *Dinamani*, the Telugu *Andhra Prabha*, the Kannada *Kannada Prabha* and the English *Financial Express*; six periodicals including the English weeklies the *Indian Express* (Sunday edition), *Screen*, the Telugu *Andhra Prabha Illustrated Weekly* and the Tamil *Dinamani Kadir* (weekly).

Hindustan Times Group: controlled by the K. K. BIRLA family; dailies: the *Hindustan Times* (published from 10 regional centres), *Pradeep* (Patna) and the Hindi *Hindustan* (Delhi, Lucknow, Patna and Ranchi); periodicals: the weekly *Overseas Hindustan Times* and the Hindi monthly *Nandan* and *Kadambini* (New Delhi).

Ananda Bazar Patrika Group: controlled by AVEEK SARKAR and family; dailies: the *Ananda Bazar Patrika* (Kolkata) and the English *The Telegraph* (Guwahati, Kolkata and Siliguri); periodicals include: *Business World*, Bengali weekly *Anandamela*, Bengali fortnightly *Desh*, Bengali monthly *Anandalok* and the Bengali monthly *Sananda*.

PRINCIPAL DAILIES

Delhi (incl. New Delhi)

The Asian Age: S-7, Green Park, Main Market, New Delhi 110 016; tel. (11) 26530001; fax (11) 26530027; e-mail marketing@asianage.com; internet www.asianage.com; f. 1994; morning; English; also publ. from Ahmedabad, Bangalore, Kolkata, Mumbai and London; Editor-in-Chief M. J. AKBAR.

Business Standard: Pratap Bhavan, 5 Bahadur Shah Zafar Marg, New Delhi 110 002; tel. (11) 23720202; fax (11) 23720201; e-mail editor@business-standard.com; internet www.business-standard.com; morning; English; also publ. from Kolkata, Ahmedabad, Bangalore, Chennai, Hyderabad and Mumbai; Editor T. N. NINAN; combined circ. 61,700.

Daily Milap: 8A Bahadur Shah Zafar Marg, New Delhi 110 002; tel. (11) 23317651; fax (11) 23319166; e-mail info@milap.com; internet www.milap.com; f. 1923; Urdu; nationalist; Man. Editor PUNAM SURI; Chief Editor NAVIN SURI; circ. 37,057.

Daily Pratap: Pratap Bhawan, 5 Bahadur Shah Zafar Marg, New Delhi 110 002; tel. (11) 23317938; fax (11) 41509555; e-mail news@dailypratap.com; internet www.dailypratap.com; f. 1919; Urdu; Chief Editor K. NARENDRA; CEO S. M. AFIF AHSEN; circ. 47,962.

Delhi Mid Day: World Trade Tower, Barakhamba Lane, New Delhi 110 001; tel. (11) 23414224; fax (11) 23412491; e-mail editordelhi@mid-day.com; f. 1989; Editor ANIL SHARMA (acting).

The Economic Times: 7 Bahadur Shah Zafar Marg, New Delhi 110 002; tel. (11) 23492234; fax (11) 23491248; internet www.economictimes.com; f. 1961; English; also publ. from Kolkata, Ahmedabad, Bangalore, Hyderabad, Chennai and Mumbai; Editor (Delhi) RAHUL JOSHI; combined circ. 461,900, circ. (Delhi) 125,800.

Financial Express: The Indian Express Online Media (Pvt) Ltd, B14/A Qutab Institutional Area, New Delhi 110 016; tel. (11) 23702167; fax (11) 26530114; e-mail editor@financialexpress.com; internet www.financialexpress.com; f. 1961; morning; English; also publ. from Ahmedabad (in Gujarati), Mumbai, Bangalore, Kolkata and Chennai; Editor MYTHILI BHUSNURMATH; combined circ. 50,000.

The Hindu: INS Bldg, Rafi Marg, New Delhi 110 001; tel. (11) 23715426; fax (11) 23718158; e-mail thehindu@vsnl.com; internet www.hinduonnet.com; f. 1878; morning; English; also publ. from 11 other regional centres; Editor-in-Chief N. RAM; combined circ. 1,180,000.

Hindustan: 18–20 Kasturba Gandhi Marg, New Delhi 110 001; tel. (11) 23361234; fax (11) 23704600; internet www.hindustandainik.com; f. 1936; morning; Hindi; also publ. from Lucknow, Muzaffarpur, Ranchi, Bhagalpur, Varanasi and Patna; Group Editor MRINAL PANDE; combined circ. 753,500.

Hindustan Times: 18–20 Kasturba Gandhi Marg, New Delhi 110 001; tel. (11) 23361254; fax (11) 23704600; e-mail feedback@hindustantimes.com; internet www.hindustantimes.com; f. 1923; morning; English; also publ. from nine regional centres; Editor-in-Chief CHAITANYA KALBAG; combined circ. 1,142,600.

Indian Express: Bahadur Shah Zafar Marg, New Delhi 110 002; tel. (11) 26511015; fax (11) 26511615; e-mail editor@expressindia.com; internet www.indianexpress.com; f. 1953; English; also publ. from seven other towns; Man. Editor VIVEK GOENKA; Editor-in-Chief SHEKHAR GUPTA; combined circ. 688,878, circ. 138,100 (New Delhi, Jammu and Chandigarh).

Janasatta: 9/10 Bahadur Shah Zafar Marg, New Delhi 110 002; tel. (11) 23702100; fax (11) 23702141; e-mail jansatta@expressindia.com; f. 1983; Hindi; also publ. from Kolkata and Raipur; Editor OM THANVI.

National Herald: Herald House, 5A Bahadur Shah Zafar Marg, New Delhi 110 002; tel. (11) 23313815; fax (11) 23313458; e-mail nationalheralddelhi@rediffmail.com; f. 1938; English; nationalist; Editor T. V. VENKITACHALAM; circ. 33,000.

Navbharat Times: 7 Bahadur Shah Zafar Marg, New Delhi 110 002; tel. (11) 23492041; fax (11) 23492168; f. 1947; Hindi; also publ. from Mumbai; Editor MADHUSUDAN ANAND; combined circ. 398,300, circ. 248,400 (Delhi).

The Pioneer: Link House, 3 Bahadur Shah Zafar Marg, New Delhi 110 002; tel. (11) 23755271; fax (11) 23755275; e-mail feedback@dailypioneer.com; internet www.dailypioneer.com; f. 1865; also publ. from Lucknow; Editor CHANDAN MITRA; combined circ. 154,000, circ. 78,000 (Delhi).

Punjab Kesari: Romesh Bhavan, 2 Printing Press Complex, nr Wazirpur DTC Depot, Ring Rd, Delhi 110 035; tel. (11) 27194459; fax (11) 27194470; e-mail ashwanik@nda.vsnl.net.in; internet www.punjabkesari.com; f. 1983; Hindi; also publ. from Jalandhar and Ambala; circulated in Haryana, Rajasthan, Uttar Pradesh, Uttarakhand, Madhya Pradesh, Punjab, Himachal Pradesh, Maharashtra, Bihar and Gujarat; Resident Editor ASHWINI KUMAR; circ. 333,031 (Delhi), Sunday circ. 448,519 (2007).

Rashtriya Sahara: Amba Deep, Kasturba Gandhi Marg, New Delhi 110 001; tel. (11) 23704193; fax (11) 23704113; morning; Hindi; also publ. from Lucknow and Gorakhpur; Resident Editor NISHIT JOSHI; circ. 81,900 (New Delhi), 42,300 (Lucknow), 30,600 (Gorakhpur).

Sandhya Times: 7 Bahadur Shah Zafar Marg, New Delhi 110 002; tel. (11) 23492162; fax (11) 23492047; f. 1979; Hindi; evening; Editor SAT SONI; circ. 44,400.

The Statesman: Statesman House, 148 Barakhamba Rd, New Delhi 110 001; tel. (11) 23315911; fax (11) 23315295; e-mail thestatesman@vsnl.com; internet www.thestatesman.net; f. 1875; English; also publ. from Bhubaneswar, Kolkata and Siliguri; Editor and Man. Dir RAVINDRA KUMAR; combined circ. 180,000.

The Times of India: 7 Bahadur Shah Zafar Marg, New Delhi 110 002; tel. (11) 23492049; fax (11) 23351606; internet www.timesofindia.com; f. 1838; English; also publ. from 10 other towns; Resident Editor ARINDAM SENGUPTA; combined circ. 2,214,700.

Andhra Pradesh

Hyderabad

Deccan Chronicle: 36 Sarojini Devi Rd, Hyderabad 500 003; tel. (40) 27803930; fax (40) 27805256; f. 1938; English; also publ. from six other regional centres; Editor-in-Chief M. J. AKBAR; Editor A. T. JAYANTI; circ. 342,100.

Eenadu: Somajiguda, Hyderabad 500 082; tel. (40) 23318181; fax (40) 23318555; e-mail feedback@eenadu.net; internet www.eenadu.net; f. 1974; Telugu; also publ. from 22 other towns; Chief Editor RAMOJI RAO; circ. 1,010,300 (weekdays), 1,145,000 (Sunday).

Rahnuma-e-Deccan: 12-2-837/A/3, Asif Nagar, Hyderabad 500 028; tel. (40) 23534943; fax (40) 23534945; e-mail rahnumadeccan@email.com; f. 1949; morning; Urdu; independent; Chief Editor SYED VICARUDDIN; circ. 25,000.

Siasat Daily: Jawaharlal Nehru Rd, Hyderabad 500 001; tel. (40) 24744109; fax (40) 24603188; e-mail info@siasat.com; internet www.siasat.com; f. 1949; morning; Urdu; Editor ZAHID ALI KHAN; circ. 41,600.

Vijayawada

Andhra Jyoti: Andhra Jyoti Bldg, POB 712, Vijayawada 520 010; tel. (866) 2474532; f. 1960; Telugu; also publ. from 13 other regional centres; Editor K. RAMACHANDRA MURTHY; combined circ. 162,400.

Andhra Prabha: 16-1-28, Kolandareddy Rd, Poornanandampet, Vijayawada 520 003; tel. (866) 2571351; e-mail info@andhraprabha.com; internet www.andhraprabha.com; f. 1935; Telugu; also publ. from Bangalore, Hyderabad, Chennai and Visakhapatnam; Editor M. SATISH CHANDRA; combined circ. 24,500.

New Indian Express: 16-1-28, Kolandareddy Rd, Poornanandampet, Vijayawada 520 003; tel. (866) 2571351; English; also publ. from Bangalore, Belgaum, Kochi, Kozhikode, Thiruvananthapuram,

Madurai, Chennai, Hyderabad, Visakhapatnam, Coimbatore and Bhubaneswar; Man. Editor MANOJ KUMAR SONTHALIA; Editor (Andhra Pradesh) P. S. SUNDARAM; combined circ. 197,400.

Assam (Asom)
Guwahati

Amar Asom: G. S. Rd, Ulubari, Guwahati 781 007; tel. (361) 2544356; fax (361) 2540664; e-mail glpl@sancharnet.in; f. 1997; Assamese; also publ. from Jorhat; Editor HOMEN BORGOHAIN; circ. 76,500.

Asomiya Pratidin: Maniram Dewan Rd, Guwahati 781 003; tel. (361) 2660420; fax (361) 2666377; e-mail pratidinedi@vsnl.net; morning; Assamese; also published from Dibrugarh, Lakhimpur and Bongaigaon; circ. 121,800.

Assam Tribune: Tribune Bldgs, Maniram Dewan Rd, Chandmari, Guwahati 781 003; tel. (361) 2661357; fax (361) 2666398; e-mail webmaster@assamtribune.com; internet www.assamtribune.com; f. 1939; English; Man. Dir and Editor P. G. BARUAH; circ. 59,200.

Dainik Agradoot: Agradoot Bhavan, Dispur, Guwahati 781 006; tel. (361) 2261923; fax (361) 2260655; e-mail agradoot@sify.com; internet www.dainikagradoot.com; f. 1995; Assamese; Editor K. S. DEKA; circ. 70,973.

Dainik Assam: Tribune Bldgs, Maniram Dewan Rd, Chandmari, Guwahati 781 003; tel. (361) 2541360; fax (361) 2516356; e-mail webmaster@assamtribune.com; internet www.assamtribune.com; f. 1965; Assamese; Editor DHIRENDRA NATH CHAKRAVARTTY; circ. 16,700.

Dainik Jugasankha: Jugasankha Bldg, Green Path, G. S. Rd, Guwahati 781 007; tel. (361) 2547444; fax (361) 2544971; e-mail dainikjugasankha@yahoo.com; f. 1950; Bengali; also publ. from Silchar; Editor-in-Chief BIJOY KRISHNA NATH; Editor SANTANU GHOSH; circ. 52,900.

The North East Daily: Maniram Dewan Rd, Chandmari, Guwahati 781 003; tel. (361) 2524594; fax (361) 2524634; e-mail protidin@gw1.vsnl.net.in; Assamese; circ. 34,891.

The Sentinel: G. S. Rd, Guwahati 781 005; tel. (361) 2529237; fax (361) 2529624; e-mail sentinelghy@sancharnet.in; internet www.sentinelassam.com; f. 1983; English; Editor INDIRA RAJKHEWA; circ. 44,900.

Jorhat

Dainik Janmabhumi: Nehru Park Rd, Jorhat 785 001; tel. (376) 23320033; fax (376) 23321713; e-mail clarionl@sancharnet.in; f. 1972; Assamese; also published from Guwahati; Editor DEVA KR. BORAH; circ. 32,000.

Bihar
Patna

Aryavarta: Mazharul Haque Path, Patna 800 001; tel. (612) 2230716; fax (612) 2222350; e-mail aryavart@dte.vsnl.net.in; morning; Hindi; Editor BHAKTISHWAR JHA.

Hindustan Times: Buddha Marg, Patna 800 001; tel. (612) 2223434; fax (612) 2226120; f. 1918; morning; English; also publ. from nine regional centres; Editor SHEKHAR BHATIA; combined circ. 1,142,600.

Indian Nation: Mazharul Haque Path, Patna 800 001; tel. (612) 2237780; fax (612) 2222350; e-mail aryavart@dte.vsnl.net.in; morning; English; Editor BHAKTISHWAR JHA.

The Times of India: Times House, Fraser Rd, Patna 800 001; tel. (612) 2226301; fax (612) 2233525; internet www.timesofindia.com; also publ. from New Delhi, Mumbai, Ahmedabad, Bangalore and Lucknow; Exec. Editor ARINDAM SENGUPTA; combined circ. 2,214,700.

Chhattisgarh
Raipur

Dainik Bhaskar: Press Complex, Rajbandha Mandan, G. E. Rd, Raipur 492 001; tel. (771) 2535277; fax (771) 2535255; Hindi; morning; also publ. from 18 other regional centres; Editor R. C. AGRAWAL; circ. 109,300.

Deshbandhu: Deshbandhu Complex, Ramsagar Para, Raipur 492 001; tel. (771) 2292011; fax (771) 2534955; e-mail deshbandhu@mantrafreenet.com; internet www.dailydeshbandhu.com; f. 1959; Hindi; also publ. from Jabalpur, Satna, Bilaspur and Bhopal; Chief Editor LALIT SURJAN; circ. 84,357 (Raipur), 24,289 (Satna), 46,785 (Bhopal), 50,468 (Jabalpur), 59,013 (Bilaspur).

Highway Channel: Deshbandhu Complex, Ramsagar Para, Raipur 492 001; tel. (771) 2292011; fax (771) 2534955; e-mail deshbandhu@mantrafreenet.com; internet www.dailydeshbandhu.com; f. 1997; evening; Hindi; also publ. from Bilaspur and Jagdalpur; Chief Editor LALIT SURJAN; Editor PRABHAKAR CHOUBEY; combined circ. 49,468.

Nava Bharat: Nava Bharat Bhavan Press Complex, G. E. Rd, Raipur 492 001; tel. (771) 2535544; fax (771) 2534936; Hindi; also publ. from six other regional centres; Editor PRAKASH MAHESHWARI; circ. 177,600 (Raipur and Bilaspur).

Goa
Panaji

Gomantak: Gomantak Bhavan, St Inez, Panaji, Goa 403 001; tel. (832) 2422700; fax (832) 2422701; f. 1962; morning; Marathi and English edns; Editor LAXMAN T. JOSHI; circ. 20,700 (Marathi), 6,200 (English).

Navhind Times: Navhind Bhavan, Rua Ismail Gracias, POB 161, Panaji, Goa 403001; tel. (832) 6651111; fax (832) 2224258; e-mail advt@navhindtimes.com; internet www.navhindtimes.com; f. 1963; morning; English; Editor ARUN SINHA; circ. 37,204.

Panjim

O Heraldo: Herald Publications Pvt Ltd, Rua St, Tome, Panjim 403 001; tel. (832) 2224202; fax (832) 2225622; e-mail hppltd@goatelecom.com; internet www.oherald.com; f. 1900; English; Editor RAJAN NARAYAN; circ. 36,100.

Gujarat
Ahmedabad

Gujarat Samachar: Gujarat Samachar Bhavan, Khanpur, Ahmedabad 380 001; tel. (79) 5504010; fax (79) 5502000; e-mail editor@gujaratsamachar.com; f. 1930; morning; Gujarati; also publ. from Surat, Rajkot, Vadodara, Mumbai, London and New York; Editor SHANTIBHAI SHAH; combined circ. 1,051,000.

Indian Express: 5th Floor, Sanidhya Bldg, Ashram Rd, Ahmedabad 380 009; tel. (79) 26583023; fax (79) 26575826; e-mail praman@express2.indexp.co.in; f. 1968; English; also publ. in 10 other towns; Man. Editor VIVEK GOENKA; Chief Editor SHEKHAR GUPTA; circ. (Ahmedabad and Vadodara) 28,200.

Lokasatta—Janasatta: Mirzapur Rd, POB 188, Ahmedabad 380 001; tel. (79) 25507307; fax (79) 25507708; f. 1953; morning; Gujarati; also publ. from Rajkot and Vadodara; Man. Editor VIVEK GOENKA; circ. (Ahmedabad) 48,000.

Sandesh: Sandesh Bhavan, Lad Society Rd, Ahmedabad 380 054; tel. (79) 40004000; fax (79) 40004121; e-mail advt@sandesh.com; internet www.sandesh.com; f. 1923; Gujarati; also publ. from Bhavnagar, Vadodara, Rajkot and Surat; Editor FALGUNBHAI C. PATEL; combined circ. 743,200.

The Times of India: 139 Ashram Rd, POB 4046, Ahmedabad 380 009; tel. (79) 26553300; fax (79) 26583758; f. 1968; English; also publ. from Mumbai, Delhi, Bangalore, Patna, Kolkata, Chandigarh, Pune, Mangalore and Lucknow; Resident Editor BHARAT DESAI; circ. (Ahmedabad) 129,100.

Western Times: Western House, Sudama Resort Bldg, Pritamnagar's First Slope, Ashram Rd, Ahmedabad 380 006; tel. (79) 26576738; fax (79) 26577421; e-mail western@icenet.net; internet www.westerntimes.co.in; f. 1967; English and Gujarati edns; also publ. (in Gujarati) from eight other towns; Man. Editor NIKUNJ PATEL; Editor RAMU PATEL; circ. (Ahmedabad) 30,728 (English), 45,736 (Gujarati).

Bhuj

Kutchmitra: Kutchmitra Bhavan, nr Indirabai Park, Bhuj 370 001; tel. (2832) 252090; fax (2832) 250271; e-mail kutchmitra@yahoo.com; f. 1947; Gujarati; Propr Saurashtra Trust; Editor KIRTI J. KHATRI; circ. 41,241.

Rajkot

Jai Hind: Jai Hind Press Bldg, Babubhai Shah Rd, POB 59, Rajkot 360 001; tel. (281) 3048684; fax (281) 2448677; e-mail info@jaihinddaily.com; internet www.jaihinddaily.com; f. 1948; morning and evening (in Rajkot as Sanj Samachar); Gujarati; also publ. from Ahmedabad; Editor Y. N. SHAH; combined circ. 107,300.

Phulchhab: Phulchhab Bhavan, Phulchhab Chowk, Rajkot 360 001; tel. (281) 2444611; fax (281) 2448751; f. 1950; morning; Gujarati; Propr Saurashtra Trust; Editor DINESH RAJA; circ. 84,500.

Surat

Gujaratmitra and Gujaratdarpan: Gujaratmitra Bhavan, nr Old Civil Hospital, Sonifalia, Surat 395 003; tel. (261) 2599992; fax (261) 2595400; e-mail gujaratmitra@satyam.net.in; f. 1863; morning; Gujarati; Editor B. P. RESHAMWALA; circ. 91,000.

Haryana
Rohtak

Bharat Janani: Sonipat Rd, Rohtak; tel. and fax (1262) 427191; f. 1971; Hindi; morning; Editor Dr R. S. Santoshi.

Himachal Pradesh
Shimla

Dainik Himachal Sewa: Hans Kutir, Khalini, Shimla 171 002; tel. (177) 2224119; fax (177) 2260187; f. 1986; Hindi; Editor-in-Chief Dr R. S. Santoshi.

Himachal Times: Himachal Times Complex, 64–66, The Mall, Shimla 171 001; tel. (177) 2201057; f. 1949; English; Chief Editor Vijay Pandhi.

Jammu and Kashmir
Jammu

Daily Excelsior: Excelsior House, Excelsior Lane, Janipura, Jammu Tawi 180 007; tel. (191) 2537055; fax (191) 2537831; e-mail editor@dailyexcelsior.com; internet www.dailyexcelsior.com; f. 1965; English; Editor S. D. Rohmetra.

Kashmir Times: Residency Rd, Jammu 180 001; tel. (191) 2543676; fax (191) 2542028; e-mail kashmirtimes@rediffmail.com; internet www.kashmirtimes.com; f. 1955; morning; English and Hindi; Editor Prabodh Jamwal.

Srinagar

Greater Kashmir: 6 Pratap Park, Residency Rd, Srinagar 190 001; tel. (194) 2474339; fax (194) 2477782; e-mail editor@greaterkashmir.com; internet www.greaterkashmir.com; f. 1993; English; Chief Editor Fayaz Ahmed Kaloo.

Jharkhand
Ranchi

Aj: Main Rd, Ranchi 834 001; tel. (651) 2311416; fax (651) 2306224; Hindi; morning; also publ. from eight other cities; Editor Shardul V. Gupta; circ. 43,800; combined circ. 930,200.

Hindustan: Circular Court, Circular Rd, Ranchi 834 001; tel. (651) 2205811; Hindi; morning; also publ. from Patna, Delhi, Bhagalpur, Lucknow, Varanasi and Muzaffarpur; Editor Mrinal Pande; combined circ. 753,500.

Prabhat Khabar: 15-P, Kokar Industrial Area, Kokar, Ranchi 834 001; tel. (651) 2544002; fax (651) 254405; e-mail pkhabar@ushamartin.co.in; internet www.prabhatkhabar.com; f. 1984; Hindi; also publ. from Dhanbad, Kolkata, Jamshedpur and Patna; Chief Editor H. B. N. Singh; circ. 123,100 (Ranchi).

Ranchi Express: 55 Baralal St, Ranchi 834 001; tel. (651) 2206320; fax (651) 2203466; e-mail rexpress@dte.vsnl.net.in; internet www.ranchiexpress.com; f. 1963; Hindi; morning; Editor Ajay Maroo; circ. 72,400.

Karnataka
Bangalore

Deccan Herald: 75 Mahatma Gandhi Rd, Bangalore 560 001; tel. (80) 25588000; fax (80) 25580523; e-mail ads@deccanherald.co.in; internet www.deccanherald.com; f. 1948; morning; English; also publ. from Hubli-Dharwar, Mangalore and Gulbarga; Editor-in-Chief K. N. Shanth Kumar; combined circ. 154,600.

Kannada Prabha: Express Bldgs, 1 Queen's Rd, Bangalore 560 001; tel. (80) 22866893; fax (80) 22866617; e-mail bexpress@bgl.vsnl.net.in; internet www.kannadaprabha.com; f. 1967; morning; Kannada; also publ. from Belgaum and Shimoga; Editor Y. N. Krishnamurthy; circ. 60,700.

New Indian Express: 1 Queen's Rd, Bangalore 560 001; tel. (80) 22256998; fax (80) 22256617; f. 1965; English; also publ. from Kochi, Hyderabad, Chennai, Madurai, Vijayawada and Vizianagaram; Man. Editor Manoj Kumar Sonthalia; combined circ. 197,400.

Prajavani: 75 Mahatma Gandhi Rd, Bangalore 560 001; tel. (80) 25588999; fax (80) 25586443; e-mail ads@deccanherald.co.in; internet www.prajavani.net; f. 1948; morning; Kannada; also publ. from Hubli-Dharwar and Gulbarga; Editor-in-Chief K. N. Shanth Kumar; combined circ. 309,500.

Hubli-Dharwar

Samyukta Karnataka: Koppikar Rd, Hubli 580 020; tel. (836) 2364303; fax (836) 2362760; e-mail skhubli@gmail.com; internet www.samyuktakarnataka.com; f. 1933; Kannada; also publ. from Bangalore, Davangere, Gulburga and Mangalore; Editor Manoj Patil; combined circ. 130,823.

Vijay Karnataka: Giriraj Annexe, Circuit House Rd, Hubli 580 029; tel. (836) 2237556; fax (836) 2253630; e-mail hubli@vkmktg.com; f. 1999; Kannada; also publ. from Bangalore, Gangavati, Gulbarga, Mangalore, Mysore, Bagalkot, Chitradurga and Shimoga; Printer and Publr Vijay Sankeshwar; combined circ. 576,071.

Manipal

Udayavani: Udayavani Bldg, Press Corner, Manipal 576 104; tel. (820) 2570845; fax (820) 2570563; e-mail udayavani@manipalpress.com; internet www.udayavani.com; f. 1970; Kannada; also publ. from Manipal-Udupi and Mumbai; Editor T. Satish U. Pai; Regional Editors N. Guraj (Manipal), R. Poornima (Bangalore), T. Satish (Mumbai); circ. 198,233.

Kerala
Kottayam

Deepika: POB 7, Kottayam 686 001; tel. (481) 2566706; fax (481) 2567947; e-mail deepika@deepika.com; internet www.deepika.com; f. 1887; Malayalam; independent; also publ. from Kannur, Kochi, Kozhikode, Thiruvananthapuram and Thrissur; Man. Dir Jose T. Pattara; Chief Editor Jose Panthaplamthottiyil; combined circ. 251,000.

Malayala Manorama: K. K. Rd, POB 26, Kottayam 686 001; tel. (481) 2563646; fax (481) 2562479; e-mail editor@malayalamanorama.com; internet www.manoramaonline.com; f. 1890; Malayalam; also publ. from 12 other regional centres; morning; Man. Dir and Editor Mammen Mathew; Chief Editor K. M. Mathew; combined circ. 1,296,400.

Kozhikode

Deshabhimani: 11/127 Convent Rd, Kozhikode 673 032; tel. (495) 2365286; fax (495) 2365883; f. 1946; Malayalam; morning; publ. by the CPI—M; also publ. from Kochi, Kottayam, Thrissur and Thiruvananthapuram; Chief Editor S. Ramachandran Pillai; combined circ. 266,400.

Mathrubhumi: Mathrubhumi Bldgs, K. P. Kesava Menon Rd, POB 46, Kozhikode 673 001; tel. (495) 2366655; fax (495) 2366656; e-mail mathrelt@md2.vsnl.net.in; internet www.mathrubhumi.com; f. 1923; Malayalam; also publ. from Thiruvananthapuram, Kannur, Thrissur, Kollam, Malappuram, Kottayam, Kochi, Bangalore, Chennai and Mumbai; Editor R. Gopalakrishnan; combined circ. 910,000.

Thiruvananthapuram

Kerala Kaumudi: POB 77, Pettah, Thiruvananthapuram 695 024; tel. (471) 2461010; fax (471) 2461985; e-mail editor@kaumudi.com; internet www.keralakaumudi.com; f. 1911; Malayalam; also publ. from Kollam, Alappuzha, Kochi, Kannur, Kozhikode and Bangalore; Editor-in-Chief M. S. Mani; Man. Editor Deepu Ravi; combined circ. 147,126.

Vikshanam: Thiruvananthapuram; f. 2005; Malayalam; publ. by Kerala Congress.

Madhya Pradesh
Bhopal

Dainik Bhaskar: 6 Press Complex, M. P. Nagar, Bhopal; tel. (755) 39888840; fax (755) 5270333; e-mail editor@bhaskar.com; internet www.bhaskar.com; f. 1958; morning; Hindi; also publ. from 18 other regional centres; Chief Editor R. C. Agarwal; combined circ. 1,549,800.

Indore

Naidunia: 60/1 Babu Labhchand Chhajlani Marg, Indore 452 009; tel. (731) 2763111; fax (731) 2763120; e-mail editor@naidunia.com; internet www.naidunia.com; f. 1947; morning; Hindi; Editor Abhay Chhajlani; circ. 145,600.

Maharashtra
Kolhapur

Pudhari: 2318, 'C' Ward, Kolhapur 416 002; tel. (231) 222251; fax (231) 222256; internet www.pudhari.com; f. 1974; Marathi; Editor P. G. Jadhav; circ. 211,200.

Mumbai (Bombay)

Afternoon Courier: 6 Nanabhai Lane, Fort, Mumbai 400 001; tel. (22) 22871616; fax (22) 22870371; e-mail aftnet@bom2.vsnl.net.in; internet www.cybernoon.com; evening; English; Editor Mark Manuel Hubert; circ. 65,800.

Bombay Samachar: Red House, Syed Abdulla Brelvi Rd, Fort, Mumbai 400 001; tel. (22) 22045501; fax (22) 22046642; e-mail samachar@vsnl.com; f. 1822; morning and Sunday; Gujarati; political, social and commercial; Editor PINKY DALAL (acting); circ. 107,300.

Daily News and Analysis (DNA): Lower Parel, Mumbai; f. 2005; English; also publ. from Delhi, Chennai, Bangalore, Hyderabad and Kolkata; Chief Editor GAUTAM ADHIKARI.

Dainik Saamana: Sadguru Darshan, Nagu Sayaji Wadi, Dainik Saamana Marg, Prabhadevi, Mumbai 400 028; tel. (22) 24370591; fax (22) 24316590; f. 1989; Marathi; Exec. Editor SANJAY RAUT; circ. 102,900.

The Economic Times: Times of India Bldg, Dr Dadabhai Naoroji Rd, Mumbai 400 001; tel. (22) 22733535; fax (22) 22731344; e-mail etbom@timesgroup.com; internet www.economictimes.com; f. 1961; also publ. from New Delhi, Kolkata, Ahmedabad, Hyderabad, Chennai and Bangalore; English; Editor (Mumbai) SUDESHNA SEN; combined circ. 461,900, circ. (Mumbai) 140,200.

Financial Express: Express Towers, Nariman Point, Mumbai 400 021; tel. (22) 22022627; fax (22) 22022139; e-mail iemumbai@express.indexp.co.in; internet www.financialexpress.com; f. 1961; morning; English; also publ. from New Delhi, Bangalore, Kolkata, Coimbatore, Kochi, Ahmedabad (Gujarati) and Chennai; Man. Editor VIVEK GOENKA; Editor MYTHILI BHUSNURMATH; combined circ. (English) 50,000.

The Free Press Journal: Free Press House, 215 Free Press Journal Rd, Nariman Point, Mumbai 400 021; tel. (22) 22874566; fax (22) 22874688; e-mail fpj@vsnl.com; f. 1930; English; also publ. from Indore; Man. Editor G. L. LAKHOTIA; combined circ. 87,000.

Hindustan Times: 220–230, Mhatre Pen Building Complex, 'B' Wing, 2nd Floor, Senapati Bapat Marg, Dadar (W), Mumbai 400 028; tel. (22) 24368012; fax (22) 24303625; e-mail feedback@hindustantimes.com; internet www.hindustantimes.com/mumbai; f. 1923; also publ. from Delhi, Lucknow, Bhopal and Chandigarh; Editor SHEKHAR BHATIA; combined circ. 1,142,600.

Indian Express: 3/50, Lalbaug Industrial Estate, Dr B. Ambedkar Marg, Lalbaug, Mumbai 400 012; tel. (22) 24717600; fax (22) 24717636; f. 1940; English; also publ. from Pune and Nagpur; Man. Editor VIVEK GOENKA; Chief Editor SHEKHAR GUPTA; combined circ. 191,900.

Inquilab: 156 D. J. Dadajee Rd, Tardeo, Mumbai 400 034; tel. (22) 24942586; fax (22) 24936571; e-mail azizk@mid-day.mailserve.net; internet www.inquilab.com; f. 1938; morning; Urdu; Editor FUZAIL JAFFEREY; circ. 35,600.

Janmabhoomi: Janmabhoomi Bhavan, Janmabhoomi Marg, Fort, POB 62, Mumbai 400 001; tel. (22) 22870831; fax (22) 22874097; e-mail bhoomi@bom3.vsnl.net.in; f. 1934; evening; Gujarati; Propr Saurashtra Trust; Editor KUNDAN VYAS; circ. 55,395.

Lokasatta: 3/50, Lalbaug Industrial Estate, Dr B. Ambedkar, Lalbaug, Mumbai 400 012; tel. (22) 24717677; fax (22) 24717654; internet www.loksatta.com; f. 1948; morning (incl. Sunday); Marathi; also publ. from Pune, Nagpur and Ahmednagar; Editor KUMAR KETKAR; combined circ. 369,400.

Maharashtra Times: Dr Dadabhai Naoroji Rd, POB 213, Mumbai 400 001; tel. (22) 22353535; fax (22) 22731175; f. 1962; Marathi; Editor BHARAT KUMAR RAUT; circ. 247,100.

Mid-Day: 64 Sitaram Mills Compound, N. M. Joshi Marg, Lower Parel, Mumbai 400 011; tel. (22) 23054545; fax (22) 23054861; e-mail mid-day@giasbm01.vsnl.net.in; internet www.mid-day.com; f. 1979; daily and Sunday; English; Editor AKAR PATEL; circ. 136,000.

Mumbai Mirror: Mumbai; tel. (22) 26005555; e-mail mumbai.mirror@timesgroup.com; internet www.mumbaimirror.com; f. 2005; English; Editor MEENAL BAGHEL.

Navakal: 13 Shenviwadi, Khadilkar Rd, Girgaun, Mumbai 400 004; tel. (22) 23860978; fax (22) 23860989; f. 1923; Marathi; Editor N. Y. KHADILKAR; circ. 139,800.

Navbharat Times: Dr Dadabhai Naoroji Rd, Mumbai 400 001; tel. (22) 22733535; fax (22) 22731144; f. 1950; Hindi; also publ. from New Delhi, Jaipur, Patna and Lucknow; Chief Editor VISHWANATH SACHDEV; circ. (Mumbai) 142,100.

Navshakti: Free Press House, 215 Nariman Point, Mumbai 400 021; tel. (22) 22874566; fax (22) 22874688; f. 1932; Marathi; Chief Editor PRAKASH KULKARNI; circ. 65,000.

Sakal: Sakal Bhavan, Plot No. 42-B, Sector No. 11, CBD Belapur, Navi Mumbai 400 614; tel. (22) 27572916; fax (22) 27574280; e-mail sakal@vsnl.in; f. 1970; Marathi; also publ. from Pune, Aurangabad, Nasik, Kolhapur and Solapur; Chief Editor SANJEEV LATKAR; combined circ. 667,500.

The Times of India: The Times of India Bldg, Dr Dadabhai Naoroji Rd, Mumbai 400 001; tel. (22) 56353535; fax (22) 22731444; e-mail toieditorial@timesgroup.com; internet www.timesofindia.com; f. 1838; morning; English; also publ. from 10 regional centres; Exec. Editor ARINDAM SENGUPTA; circ. (Mumbai) 545,600, combined circ. 2,214,700.

Nagpur

The Hitavada: Pandit Jawaharlal Nehru Marg, POB 201, Nagpur 440 012; tel. (712) 2523155; fax (712) 2535093; e-mail hitavada_ngp@sancharnet.in; f. 1911; morning; English; also publ. from Raipur and Jabalpur; Man. Editor BANWARILAL PUROHIT; Editor V. PHANSHIKAR; circ. 60,700.

Lokmat: Lokmat Bhavan, Wardha Rd, Nagpur 440 012; tel. (712) 2523527; fax (712) 2526923; internet onlinenews.lokmat.com; also publ. from Jalgaon, Pune and Nasik; Marathi; Lokmat Samachar (Hindi) publ. from Nagpur, Akola and Aurangabad; Lokmat Times (English) publ. from Nagpur and Aurangabad; Editor VIJAY DARDA; combined circ. (Marathi) 436,800, (Hindi) 62,300.

Nava Bharat: Nava Bharat Bhavan, Cotton Market, Nagpur 440 018; tel. (712) 2726677; fax (712) 2723444; f. 1938; morning; Hindi; also publ. from 10 other cities; Editor-in-Chief R. G. MAHESWARI; combined circ. 640,400.

Tarun Bharat: 28 Farmland, Ramdaspeth, Nagpur 440 010; tel. (712) 2525052; fax (712) 2531758; e-mail ibharat_ngp@sancharnet.in; internet www.tarunbharat.net; f. 1941; Marathi; independent; also publ. from Belgaum; Man. Editor ANIL DANDEKAR; Chief Editor SUDHIR PATHAK; circ. (Nagpur) 58,200.

Pune

Kesari: 568 Narayan Peth, Pune 411 030; tel. (20) 4459250; fax (20) 4451677; f. 1881; Marathi; also publ. from Solapur, Chiplun, Ahmednagar and Sangli; Editor ARVIND VYANKATESH GOKHALE; circ. (Pune) 42,600.

Sakal: 595 Budhawar Peth, Pune 411 002; tel. (20) 24455500; fax (20) 24450583; e-mail sakal@giaspn01.vsnl.net.in; internet www.esakal.com; f. 1932; daily; Marathi; also publ. from 10 other regional centres; Editor YAMAJI MALKAR (Pune); Man. Editor PRATAP PAWAR; combined circ. 830,654.

Meghalaya

Shillong

The Shillong Times: Rilbong, Shillong 793 004; tel. (364) 2223488; fax (364) 2229488; e-mail shillongtimes@yahoo.com; f. 1945; English; Editor MANAS CHAUDHURI; circ. 28,700.

Orissa

Bhubaneswar

Dharitri: B-26, Industrial Estate, Bhubaneswar 751 010; tel. (674) 2580101; fax (674) 2580795; e-mail advt@dharitri.com; internet www.dharitri.com; evening and morning; Oriya; Editor TATHAGATA SATPATHY; circ. 175,100.

Pragativadi: 178-B, Mancheswar Industrial Estate, Bhubaneswar 751 010; tel. (674) 2588297; fax (674) 2582709; e-mail pragativadi@yahoo.com; internet www.pragativadi.com; f. 1973; Exec. Editor SAMAHIT BAL; circ. 152,453.

The Samaya: Plot No. 44 and 54, Sector A, Zone D, Mancheswar Industrial Estate, Bhubaneswar 751 017; tel. (674) 2583690; fax (674) 2582565; e-mail samayabbsr@usanet.com; internet www.thesamaya.com; f. 1966; Oriya; Editor SATAKADI HOTA; circ. 134,400.

Sambad: Eastern Media Ltd, A-62, Nayapalli, Bhubaneswar 751 003; tel. (674) 2561198; fax (674) 2562914; e-mail sambad00@rediffmail.com; internet www.orissasambad.com; f. 1984; Oriya; also publ. from seven other regional centres; Editor S. R. PATNAIK; combined circ. 213,600.

Cuttack

Prajatantra: Prajatantra Bldg, Behari Bag, Cuttack 753 002; tel. (671) 2608071; fax (671) 2607111; f. 1947; Oriya; Editor GOVINDA DAS; circ. 113,824.

Samaja: Gopabandhu Bhavan, Buxibazar, Cuttack 753 001; tel. (671) 2301598; fax (671) 2301384; e-mail samajactc@hotmail.com; internet www.thesamaja.com; f. 1919; Oriya; also publ. from Sambalpur, Vizag, Bhubaneswar, Rourkela and Kolkata; Editor MANORAMA MAHAPATRA; circ. 170,700.

The Punjab

Chandigarh

The Tribune: Sector 29C, Chandigarh 160 020; tel. (172) 2655066; fax (172) 2651293; e-mail tribunet@ch1.dot.net.in; internet www.tribuneindia.com; f. 1881 (English edn), f. 1978 (Hindi and Punjabi edns); Editor-in-Chief H. K. DUA; Editor (Hindi edn) VIJAY SAIGHAL; Editor (Punjabi edn) G. S. BHULLAR; circ. 220,500 (English), 40,300 (Hindi), 66,200 (Punjabi).

INDIA   *Directory*

Jalandhar

Ajit: Ajit Bhavan, Nehru Garden Rd, Jalandhar 144 001; tel. (181) 22800960; f. 1955; Punjabi; Man. Editor S. BARJINDER SINGH; CEO SARVINDER KAUR; circ. 369,474.

Hind Samachar: Civil Lines, Jalandhar 144 001; tel. (181) 2280115; fax (181) 2280113; e-mail punjabkesari@vsnl.com; f. 1948; morning; Hindi; also publ. from Ambala Cantt; Editor-in-Chief VIJAY KUMAR CHOPRA; Jt Editor AVINASH CHOPRA; combined circ. 34,664.

Jag Bani: Civil Lines, Jalandhar 144 001; tel. (181) 2280115; fax (181) 2280113; e-mail punjabkesari@vsnl.com; f. 1978; morning; Punjabi; Editor-in-Chief VIJAY KUMAR CHOPRA; Jt Editor AVINASH CHOPRA; circ. 269,744.

Punjab Kesari: Civil Lines, Jalandhar 144 001; tel. (181) 2280115; fax (181) 2280113; e-mail punjabkesari@vsnl.com; internet www.punjabkesari.com; f. 1965; morning; Hindi; also publ. from Delhi and Ambala; Editor-in-Chief VIJAY KUMAR CHOPRA; Jt Editor AVINASH CHOPRA; combined circ. 864,095.

Rajasthan

Jaipur

Rajasthan Patrika: Kesargarh, Jawaharlal Nehru Marg, Jaipur 302 004; tel. (141) 2561582; fax (141) 2566011; e-mail info@rajasthanpatrika.com; internet www.rajasthanpatrika.com; f. 1956; Hindi edn also publ. from 17 other towns; Chief Editor GULAB KOTHARI; combined circ. 732,860 (Hindi).

Rashtradoot: M.I. Rd, POB 30, Jaipur 302 001; tel. (141) 2372634; fax (141) 2373513; f. 1951; Hindi; also publ. from Kota, Udaipur, Ajmer, Bikaner and Jalore; CEO SOMESH SHARMA; Chief Editor RAJESH SHARMA; circ. 200,672 (Jaipur), 90,936 (Kota), 49,402 (Bikaner), 62,375 (Udaipur), 53,851 (Ajmer), 62,547 (Jalore).

Tamil Nadu

Chennai (Madras)

Daily Thanthi: 86 E.V.K. Sampath Rd, POB 467, Chennai 600 007; tel. (44) 26618661; fax (44) 26618676; f. 1942; Tamil; also publ. from 13 other regional centres; Gen. Man. R. CHANDRASEKARAN; Editor V. SUNDARESON; combined circ. 817,194.

Dinakaran: 229 Kutchery Rd, Mylapore, POB 358, Chennai 600 004; tel. (44) 24641006; fax (44) 24951008; e-mail murasu@dishdsl.net; internet www.dinakaran.com; f. 1977; Tamil; also publ. from Madurai, Tiruchirapalli, Vellore, Tirunelveli, Salem, Coimbatore and Puducherry (Pondicherry); Man. Dir KALANIDHI MARAN; Editor R. M. R. RAMESH; combined circ. 351,872.

Dinamalar: 8 Casa Major Rd, Egmore, Chennai 600 008; tel. (44) 28195000; fax (44) 28195003; e-mail demregr@dinamalar.com; internet www.dinamalar.com; f. 1951; Tamil; also publ. from 10 other towns; Editor Dr R. KRISHNAMURTHY; combined circ. 582,958.

Dinamani: Express Estates, Mount Rd, Chennai 600 002; tel. (44) 8520751; fax (44) 8524500; e-mail express@giasmd01.vsnl.net.in; internet www.dinamani.com; f. 1934; morning; Tamil; also publ. from Madurai, Coimbatore and Bangalore; Editor T. SAMBANDAM; combined circ. 136,300.

Financial Express: Vasanthi Medical Center, 30/20 Pycrofts Garden Rd, Chennai 600 006; tel. (44) 28231112; fax (44) 28231489; internet www.financialexpress.com; f. 1961; morning; English; also publ. from Mumbai, Ahmedabad (in Gujarati), Bangalore, Kochi, Kolkata and New Delhi; Man. Editor VIVEK GOENKA; combined circ. 32,594.

The Hindu: Kasturi Bldgs, 859/860 Anna Salai, Chennai 600 002; tel. (44) 28413344; fax (44) 28415325; e-mail wsvcs@thehindu.co.in; internet www.hinduonnet.com; f. 1878; morning; English; independent; also publ. from 11 other regional centres; Editor-in-Chief N. RAM; combined circ. 981,600.

The Hindu Business Line: Kasturi Bldgs, 859/860 Anna Salai, Chennai 600 002; tel. (44) 28589060; fax (44) 28545703; e-mail bleditor@thehindu.co.in; internet www.blonnet.com; f. 1994; morning; English; also publ. from 11 other regional centres; Editor-in-Chief N. RAM; combined circ. 56,100.

Murasoli: 93 Kodambakkam High Rd, Chennai 600 034; tel. (44) 28270044; fax (44) 28217515; f. 1960; organ of the DMK; Tamil; Editor S. SELVAM; circ. 54,000.

New Indian Express: Club House Rd, Chennai 600 002; tel. (44) 28461260; fax (44) 28461829; e-mail newexpress@vsnl.com; internet www.newindpress.com; f. 1932 as Indian Express; morning; English; also publ. from 11 other cities; Chair. and Man. Dir MANOJ KUMAR SONTHALIA; combined circ. 197,400.

Tripura

Agartala

Dainik Sambad: 11 Jagannath Bari Rd, POB 2, Agartala 799 001; tel. (381) 2326676; fax (381) 2324845; e-mail dainik2@sanchar.net.in; f. 1966; Bengali; morning; Editor BHUPENDRA CHANDRA DATTA BHAUMIK; circ. 49,000.

Uttarakhand

Dehradun

Amar Ujala: Shed 2, Patel Nagar Industrial Estate, Dehradun 248 003; tel. (135) 2720378; fax (135) 2721776; internet www.amarujala.com; Hindi; morning; also publ. from 10 other cities; Editor AJAY K. AGRAWAL; combined circ. 630,100.

Uttar Pradesh

Agra

Amar Ujala: Sikandra Rd, Agra 282 007; tel. (562) 2321600; fax (562) 2322181; e-mail amarujal@nde.vsnl.net.in; internet www.amarujala.com; f. 1948; Hindi; also publ. from Bareilly, Allahabad, Jhansi, Kanpur, Moradabad, Chandigarh and Meerut; Editor AJAY K. AGRAWAL; combined circ. 630,100.

Allahabad

Amrita Prabhat: 10 Tashkent Marg, Allahabad 211 001; tel. (532) 2600654; fax (532) 2605394; f. 1977; Hindi; CEO S. S. BAGGA; circ. 44,000.

Northern India Patrika: 10 Edmonstone Rd, Allahabad 211 001; tel. (532) 2600654; fax (532) 2605394; f. 1959; English; CEO S. S. BAGGA; circ. 46,000.

Kanpur

Dainik Jagran: Jagran Bldg, 2 Sarvodaya Nagar, Kanpur 208 005; tel. (512) 2216161; fax (512) 2216972; e-mail jpl@jagran.com; internet www.jagran.com; f. 1942; Hindi; also publ. from 25 other cities; Man. Editor MAHENDRA MOHAN GUPTA; Editor SANJAY GUPTA; combined circ. 2,600,000.

Lucknow

National Herald: Lucknow; f. 1938 Lucknow, 1968 Delhi; English; Editor-in-Chief D. V. VENKITACHALAM.

The Pioneer: Sahara Shopping Centre, Faizabad Rd, Lucknow 226 016; tel. (522) 2346444; fax (522) 2345582; f. 1865; English; also publ. from New Delhi; Editor CHANDAN MITRA; combined circ. 136,000.

Swatantra Bharat: 1st Floor, Suraj Deep Complex, 1 Jopling Rd, Lucknow 226 001; tel. (522) 2204306; fax (522) 2208701; e-mail sbharats@satyam.net.in; f. 1947; Hindi; also publ. from Kanpur; Editor K. K. SRIVASTAVA; circ. 80,700 (Lucknow), 65,157 (Kanpur).

Varanasi

Aj: Aj Bhavan, Sant Kabir Rd, Kabirchaura, Varanasi 221 001; tel. (542) 2393981; fax (542) 2393989; f. 1920; Hindi; also publ. from Gorakhpur, Patna, Allahabad, Ranchi, Agra, Bareilly, Lucknow, Jamshedpur, Dhanbad and Kanpur; Editor SHARDUL VIKRAM GUPTA; combined circ. 930,200.

West Bengal

Kolkata (Calcutta)

Aajkaal: 96 Raja Rammohan Sarani, Kolkata 700 009; tel. (33) 23509803; fax (33) 23500877; e-mail aajkaal@cal.vsnl.net.in; f. 1981; morning; Bengali; also publ. from Agartala and Siliguri; Chief Editor PRATAP K. ROY; circ. 140,100.

Ananda Bazar Patrika: 6 Prafulla Sarkar St, Kolkata 700 001; tel. (33) 22374880; fax (33) 22253241; internet www.anandabazar.com; f. 1922; morning; Bengali; also publ. from Baharampore and Siliguri; Editor AVEEK SARKAR; circ. 950,400.

Bartaman: 76A A. J. C. Bose Rd, Kolkata 700 014; tel. (33) 22443907; fax (33) 22441215; internet www.bartamanpatrika.com; f. 1984; also publ. from Barddhaman and Siliguri; Editor BARUN SENGUPTA; circ. 427,100.

Business Standard: 4/1 Red Cross Place, Kolkata 700 001; tel. (33) 22101314; fax (33) 22101599; f. 1975; morning; also publ. from New Delhi, Ahmedabad, Hyderabad, Bangalore, Chennai and Mumbai; English; Editor T. N. NINAN; combined circ. 60,000.

The Economic Times: 105/7A, S. N. Banerjee Rd, Kolkata 700 014; tel. (33) 22444243; fax (33) 22453018; English; also publ. from Ahmedabad, Delhi, Bangalore, Chennai, Hyderabad and Mumbai; circ. (Kolkata) 54,300.

Financial Express: 83 B. K. Pal Ave, Kolkata 700 005; morning; English; also publ. from Mumbai, Ahmedabad, Bangalore, Coimba-

INDIA   *Directory*

tore, Kochi, Chennai and New Delhi; Man. Editor VIVEK GOENKA; combined circ. 30,800.

Ganashakti: 74A A. J. C. Bose Rd, Kolkata 700 016; tel. (33) 22278950; fax (33) 2278090; e-mail mail@ganashakti.co.in; internet www.ganashakti.com; f. 1967; owned by Communist Party of India (Marxist), West Bengal State Cttee; morning; Bengali; also publ. from Durgapur and Siliguri; Editor NARAYAN DATTA; circ. 167,320.

Sandhya Aajkaal: 96 Raja Rammohan Sarani, Kolkata 700 009; tel. (33) 23509803; fax (33) 23500877; evening; Bengali; Chief Editor PRATAP K. ROY; circ. 17,400.

Sangbad Pratidin: 20 Prafulla Sarkar St, Kolkata 700 072; tel. (33) 22128400; fax (33) 22126031; e-mail pratidin@cal2.vsnl.net.in; internet www.sangbadpratidin.com; morning; Bengali; also publ. from Ranchi and Siliguri; Editor SWAPAN SADHAN BASU; circ. 278,700.

Sanmarg: 160B Chittaranjan Ave, Kolkata 700 007; tel. (33) 22414800; fax (33) 22415087; e-mail sanmarg@satyam.net.in; f. 1948; Hindi; Editor RAMAWATAR GUPTA; circ. 107,700.

The Statesman: Statesman House, 4 Chowringhee Sq., Kolkata 700 001; tel. (33) 22127070; fax (33) 22370054; e-mail thestatesman@vsnl .com; internet www.statesman.net; f. 1875; morning; English; independent; also publ. from New Delhi, Siliguri and Bhubaneswar; Editor-in-Chief C. R. IRANI; combined circ. 166,300.

The Telegraph: 6 Prafulla Sarkar St, Kolkata 700 001; tel. (33) 22374800; fax (33) 22253240; e-mail thetelegraphindia@newscom .com; f. 1982; English; also publ. from Guwahati, Jamshedpur and Siliguri; Editor AVEEK SARKAR; circ. 325,100.

Uttar Banga Sambad: 7 Old Court House St, Kolkata 700 001; tel. (33) 22435663; fax (33) 22435618; e-mail uttarmail@sify.com; internet www.uttarbangasambad.com; f. 1980; Bengali; Editor S. C. TALUKDAR; circ. 134,209.

Vishwamitra: 74 Lenin Sarani, Kolkata 700 013; tel. (33) 22441139; fax (33) 22446393; e-mail vismtra@cal2.vsnl.net.in; f. 1915; morning; Hindi; commercial; Editor PRAKASH CHANDRA AGRAWALLA; circ. 92,533.

SELECTED PERIODICALS

Delhi and New Delhi

Alive: Delhi Press Bldg, E-3 Jhandewala Estate, Rani Jhansi Rd, New Delhi 110 055; tel. (11) 41398888; fax (11) 41540714; e-mail editorial@delhipressgroup.com; internet www.grihsobaindia.com; f. 1940 as Caravan; monthly; English; men's interests; Editor, Publr and Printer PARESH NATH; circ. 10,000.

Bal Bharati: Patiala House, Publications Division, Ministry of Information and Broadcasting, New Delhi; tel. (11) 2387038; f. 1948; monthly; Hindi; for children; Editor SHIV KUMAR; circ. 30,000.

Biswin Sadi: B-1, Nizamuddin West, New Delhi 110 013; tel. (11) 24626556; f. 1937; monthly; Urdu; Editor Z. REHMAN NAYYAR; circ. 32,000.

Business Today: Videocon Towers, E-1 Jhandelwalan Extn, New Delhi 110 055; tel. (11) 23684893; fax (11) 23684819; e-mail btoday@ giasdl01.vsnl.net.in; internet www.business-today.com; fortnightly; English; Editor SANJAY NARAYAN; circ. 124,600.

Catholic India: CBCI Centre, 1 Ashok Place, Goldakkhana, New Delhi 110 001; tel. (11) 23344470; fax (11) 23364615; e-mail cbci@vsnl .com; internet www.cbcisite.com; quarterly.

Champak: Delhi Press Bldg, E-3 Jhandewala Estate, Rani Jhansi Rd, New Delhi 110 055; tel. (11) 41398888; fax (11) 41540714; e-mail editorial@delhipressgroup.com; internet www.grihsobaindia.com; f. 1968; fortnightly (Hindi, English, Gujarati, Tamil, Telugu, Malayalam, Marathi and Kannada edns); children's; Editor, Publr and Printer PARESH NATH; circ. 77,000 (Hindi), 32,089 (English), 17,000 (Marathi), 20,000 (Gujarati), 10,000 (Malayalam), 3,664 (Telugu), 2,153 (Tamil), 10,000 (Kannada).

Children's World: Nehru House, 4 Bahadur Shah Zafar Marg, New Delhi 110 002; tel. (11) 23316970; fax (11) 23721090; e-mail cbtnd@ vsnl.com; internet www.childrensbooktrust.com; f. 1968; monthly; English; Editor NAVIN MENON; circ. 25,000.

Competition Refresher: 2767, Bright House, Daryaganj, New Delhi 110 002; tel. (11) 23282226; fax (11) 23269227; e-mail psbright@ndf.vsnl.net.in; internet www.brightcareers.com; f. 1984; monthly; English; Chief Editor, Publr and Man. Dir PRITAM SINGH BRIGHT; circ. 175,000.

Competition Success Review: 604 Prabhat Kiran Bldg, Rajendra Place, Delhi 110 008; tel. (11) 25712898; fax (11) 25754647; e-mail csrindia@mantraonline.com; monthly; English; f. 1964; Editor S. K. SACHDEVA; circ. 247,400.

Computers Today: Marina Arcade, G-59 Connaught Circus, New Delhi 110 001; tel. (11) 23736233; fax (11) 23725506; e-mail ctoday@ india-today.com; f. 1984; Editor J. SRIHARI RAJU; circ. 46,300.

Cosmopolitan: 5th Floor, Videocon Tower, E-1 Jhandewalan Extn, New Delhi 110 055; tel. (11) 23684800; e-mail cathy.cosmo@intoday .com; monthly; English; women's lifestyle; Editor PAYAL KOHLI.

Cricket Samrat: L-1, Kanchan House, Najafgarh Rd, Commercial Complex, nr Milan Cinema, New Delhi 110 015; tel. (11) 25191175; fax (11) 25469581; f. 1978; monthly; Hindi; Editor ANAND DEWAN; circ. 64,000.

Employment News: Government of India, East Block IV, Level 5, R. K. Puram, New Delhi 110 066; tel. (11) 26174975; fax (11) 26105875; e-mail empnews@bol.net.in; f. 1976; weekly; Hindi, Urdu and English edns; Gen. Man. and Chief Editor VISHWANATH RAMESH; Editor RANJANA DEV SARMAH; combined circ. 550,000.

Filmi Duniya: 16 Darya Ganj, New Delhi 110 002; tel. (11) 23278087; fax (11) 23279341; f. 1958; monthly; Hindi; Chief Editor NARENDRA KUMAR; circ. 132,100.

Filmi Kaliyan: 4675-B/21 Ansari Rd, New Delhi 110 002; tel. (11) 23272080; f. 1969; monthly; Hindi; cinema; Editor-in-Chief V. S. DEWAN; circ. 82,400.

Global Travel Express: 26F Rajiv Gandhi Chowk (Connaught Place), New Delhi 110 001; tel. (11) 23312329; fax (11) 24621636; e-mail indian_observer@hotmail.com; f. 1993; monthly; English; travel and tourism; Chief Editor HARBHAJAN SINGH; Editor GURINDER SINGH; circ. 28,902.

Grihshobha: Delhi Press Bldg, E-3 Jhandewala Estate, Rani Jhansi Rd, New Delhi 110 055; tel. (11) 41398888; fax (11) 41540714; e-mail editorial@delhipressgroup.com; internet www.grihsobaindia.com; f. 1979; fortnightly Hindi and Bangla edns; monthly Tamil, Telugu, Kannada, Marathi, Malayalam and Gujarati edns; women's interests; Editor, Publr and Printer PARESH NATH; circ. 78,000 (Kannada), 46,355 (Gujarati), 105,096 (Marathi), 364,096 (Hindi), 28,000 (Telugu), 32,000 (Tamil), 35,000 (Malayalam), 10,000 (Bangla).

India Perspectives: Room 149B, 'A' Wing, Shastri Bhavan, New Delhi 110 001; tel. (11) 23389471; f. 1988; Editor BHARAT BHUSHAN.

India Today: F-14/15, Connaught Place, New Delhi 110 001; tel. (11) 23315801; fax (11) 23316180; e-mail ratnam@intoday.com; internet www.india-today.com; f. 1975; English, Tamil, Telugu, Malayalam and Hindi; weekly; Editor PRABHU CHAWLA; Editor-in-Chief AROON PURIE; circ. 463,800 (English), 353,700 (Hindi), 65,300 (Tamil), 42,900 (Malayalam), 56,800 (Telugu).

Indian Railways: 411 Rail Bhavan, Raisina Rd, New Delhi 110 001; tel. (11) 23383540; fax (11) 23384481; e-mail editorir@rb.railnet.gov .in; f. 1956; monthly; English; publ. by the Ministry of Railways (Railway Board); Editor M. R. KALYANI; circ. 12,000.

Journal of Industry and Trade: Ministry of Commerce, Delhi 110 011; tel. (11) 23016664; f. 1952; monthly; English; Man. Dir A. C. BANERJEE; circ. 2,000.

Junior Science Refresher: 2769, Bright House, Daryaganj, New Delhi 110 002; tel. (11) 23282226; fax (11) 23269227; e-mail psbright@ndf.vsnl.net.in; internet www.brightcareers.com; f. 1987; monthly; English; Chief Editor, Publr and Man. Dir PRITAM SINGH BRIGHT; circ. 118,000.

Kadambini: Hindustan Times House, Kasturba Gandhi Marg, New Delhi 110 001; tel. and fax (11) 55561605; e-mail vnagar@ hindustantimes.com; f. 1960; monthly; Hindi; Editor MRINAL PANDE; Exec. Editor VISHNU NAGAR; circ. 120,000.

Krishak Samachar: Bharat Krishak Samaj, Dr Panjabrao Deshmukh Krishak Bhavan, A-1 Nizamuddin West, New Delhi 110 013; tel. (11) 24619508; e-mail ffi@mantraonline.com; f. 1957; monthly; English and Hindi edns; agriculture; Editor Dr KRISHAN BIR CHAUDHARY; circ. 6,000 (English), 17,000 (Hindi).

Kurukshetra: Ministry of Rural Development, Room No. 655/661, 'A' Wing, Nirman Bhavan, New Delhi 110 011; tel. (11) 23015014; fax (11) 23386879; monthly; English; rural development; Editor KAPIL KUMAR; circ. 19,000.

Mainstream: 145/1D Shahpur Jat, 1st Floor, nr Asiad Village, New Delhi 110 049; tel. (11) 26497188; fax (11) 26569352; e-mail mnstrm@ nda.vsnl.net.in; internet www.mainstreamweekly.com; English; weekly; politics and current affairs; Editor SUMIT CHAKRAVARTTY.

Maxim India: Media Transasia (India) Ltd, K-35, Green Park, New Delhi 110 016; tel. (11) 26862687; fax (11) 26867641; e-mail circulation@mediatransasia.com; f. 2005; monthly; English; men's lifestyle; CEO PIYUSH SHARMA; Editor SUNIL MEHRA.

Mayapuri: A-5, Mayapuri Phase 1, New Delhi 110 064; tel. (11) 28116120; fax (11) 25133120; e-mail mayapuri@hotmail.com; f. 1974; weekly; Hindi; cinema; Editor A. P. BAJAJ; circ. 146,144.

Mukta: Delhi Press Bldg, E-3 Jhandewala Estate, Rani Jhansi Rd, New Delhi 110 055; tel. (11) 41398888; fax (11) 41540714; e-mail editorial@delhipressgroup.com; internet www.grihsobaindia .com; f. 1961; monthly; Hindi; youth; Editor, Publr and Printer PARESH NATH; circ. 13,000.

Nandan: Hindustan Times House, Kasturba Gandhi Marg, New Delhi 110 001; tel. (11) 23704562; fax (11) 23704600; e-mail jbharti@

hindustantimes.com; f. 1963; monthly; Hindi; Editor Jai Prakash Bharti; circ. 58,400.

New Age Weekly: Ajoy Bhavan, 15 Comrade Indrajeet Gupta Marg, Delhi 110 002; tel. (11) 23230762; fax (11) 23235543; e-mail cpindia@del2.vsnl.net.in; f. 1953; main organ of the Communist Party of India; weekly; English; Editor Shameem Faizee; circ. 215,000.

Organiser: Sanskriti Bhavan, D. B. Gupta Rd, Jhandewalan, New Delhi 110 055; tel. (11) 23626977; fax (11) 23516635; e-mail editor@organiserweekly.com; internet www.organiser.org; f. 1947; weekly; English; Editor R. Balashankar; circ. 44,100.

Outlook: AB-10 Safdarjung Enclave, New Delhi 110 029; tel. (11) 51651471; fax (11) 51651472; e-mail outlook@outlookindia.com; internet www.outlookindia.com; f. 1995; weekly; Hindi and English edns; Editor-in-Chief Vinod Mehta; circ. 256,300.

Panchjanya: Sanskriti Bhavan, Deshbandhu Gupta Marg, Jhandewala, New Delhi 110 055; tel. (11) 23514244; fax (11) 23558613; e-mail panch@nde.vsnl.net.in; f. 1947; weekly; Hindi; general interest; nationalist; Chair. S. N. Bansal; Editor Tarun Vijay; circ. 59,300.

Punjabi Digest: 209 Hemkunt House, 6 Rajendra Place, POB 2549, New Delhi 110 008; tel. (11) 25715225; fax (11) 25761053; f. 1971; literary monthly; Gurmukhi; Chief Editor Sardar S. B. Singh; circ. 48,600.

Sainik Samachar: Block L-1, Church Rd, New Delhi 110 001; tel. (11) 23094668; f. 1909; pictorial fortnightly for India's armed forces; English, Hindi, Urdu, Tamil, Punjabi, Telugu, Marathi, Kannada, Gorkhali, Malayalam, Bengali, Assamese and Oriya edns; Editor P. K. Pattanayak; circ. 20,000.

Saras Salil: Delhi Press Bldg, E-3 Jhandewala Estate, Rani Jhansi Rd, New Delhi 110 055; tel. (11) 41398888; fax (11) 41540714; e-mail editorial@delhipressgroup.com; internet www.grihshobhaindia.com; f. 1993; fortnightly; Hindi, Telugu, Tamil, Gujarati and Marathi edns; Editor, Publr and Printer Paresh Nath; circ. 1,051,279 (Hindi), 10,059 (Telugu), 8,223 (Tamil), 5,388 (Gujarati), 20,000 (Marathi).

Sarita: Delhi Press Bldg, E-3 Jhandewala Estate, Rani Jhansi Rd, New Delhi 110 055; tel. (11) 41398888; fax (11) 41540714; e-mail editorial@delhipressgroup.com; internet www.grihshobhaindia.com; f. 1945; fortnightly; Hindi; family magazine; Editor, Publr and Printer Paresh Nath; circ. 110,001.

Shama: 13/14 Asaf Ali Rd, New Delhi 110 002; tel. (11) 23232674; fax (11) 23235167; f. 1939; monthly; Urdu; art and literature; Editors M. Yunus Dehlvi, Idrees Dehlvi, Ilyas Dehlvi; circ. 58,000.

Suman Saurabh: Delhi Press Bldg, E-3 Jhandewala Estate, Rani Jhansi Rd, New Delhi 110 055; tel. (11) 41398888; fax (11) 41540714; e-mail editorial@delhipressgroup.com; internet www.grihshobhaindia.com; f. 1983; monthly; Hindi; youth; Editor, Publr and Printer Paresh Nath; circ. 39,477.

Sushama: 13/14 Asaf Ali Rd, New Delhi 110 002; tel. (11) 23232674; fax (11) 23235167; f. 1959; monthly; Hindi; art and literature; Editors Idrees Dehlvi, Ilyas Dehlvi, Yunus Dehlvi; circ. 30,000.

Vigyan Pragati: NISCAIR (CSIR), Dr K. S. Krishnan Marg, New Delhi 110 012; tel. (11) 25846301; fax (11) 25847062; e-mail vp@niscair.res.in; f. 1952; monthly; Hindi; popular science; Editor Pradeep Sharma; circ. 40,000.

Woman's Era: Delhi Press Bldg, E-3 Jhandewala Estate, Rani Jhansi Rd, New Delhi 110 055; tel. (11) 41398888; fax (11) 41540714; e-mail editorial@delhipressgroup.com; internet www.grihshobhaindia.com; f. 1973; fortnightly; English; women's interests; Editor, Publr and Printer Paresh Nath; circ. 83,655.

Yojana: Yojana Bhavan, Sansad Marg, New Delhi 110 001; tel. (11)23717910; e-mail yojana@techpilgrim.com; f. 1957; monthly; English, Tamil, Bengali, Marathi, Gujarati, Assamese, Malayalam, Telugu, Kannada, Punjabi, Urdu, Oriya and Hindi edns; Chief Editor Subhash Setia; circ. 72,000.

Andhra Pradesh

Hyderabad

Andhra Prabha Illustrated Weekly: 591 Lower Tank Bund Rd, Express Centre, Domalaguda, Hyderabad 500 029; tel. (40) 2233586; f. 1952; weekly; Telugu; Editor Potturi Venkateswara Rao; circ. 21,800.

Secunderabad

Andhra Bhoomi Sachitra Masa Patrika: 36 Sarojini Devi Rd, Secunderabad 500 003; tel. (842) 27802346; fax (842) 27805256; f. 1977; fortnightly; Telugu; Editor T. Venkatram Reddy; circ. 25,600.

Vijayawada

Andhra Jyoti Sachitra Vara Patrika: Vijayawada 520 010; tel. (866) 2474532; f. 1967; weekly; Telugu; Editor Puranam Subramanya Sarma; circ. 59,000.

Bala Jyoti: Labbipet, Vijayawada 520 010; tel. (866) 2474532; f. 1980; monthly; Telugu; Assoc. Editor A. Sasikant Satakarni; circ. 12,500.

Jyoti Chitra: Andhra Jyoti Bldgs, Vijayawada 520 010; tel. (866) 2474532; f. 1977; weekly; Telugu; Editor T. Kutumba Rao; circ. 20,100.

Swati Saparivara Patrika: Anil Bldgs, Suryaraopet, POB 339, Vijayawada 520 002; tel. (866) 2431862; fax (866) 2430433; e-mail advt_swati@sify.com; f. 1984; weekly; Telugu; Editor Vemuri Balaram; circ. 252,100.

Vanita Jyoti: Labbipet, POB 712, Vijayawada 520 010; tel. (866) 2474532; f. 1978; monthly; Telugu; Asst Editor J. Satyanarayana; circ. 13,100.

Assam (Asom)

Guwahati

Agradoot: Agradoot Bhavan, Dispur, Guwahati 781 006; tel. (361) 2261923; fax (361) 2260655; e-mail agradoot@sify.com; f. 1971; bi-weekly; Assamese; Editor K. S. Deka; circ. 29,463.

Asam Bani: Tribune Bldg, Guwahati 781 003; tel. (361) 2661356; fax (361) 2660594; e-mail dileepchandan@yahoo.com; internet www.assamtribune.com; f. 1955; weekly; Assamese; Editor Dileep Chandan; circ. 14,000.

Sadin: Maniram Dewan Rd, Chandmari, Guwahati 781 003; tel. (361) 2524594; fax (361) 2524634; e-mail protidin@gw1.vsnl.net.in; weekly; Assamese; circ. 39,500.

Bihar

Patna

Anand Digest: Govind Mitra Rd, Patna 800 004; tel. (612) 2656557; fax (612) 2225192; f. 1981; monthly; Hindi; family magazine; Editor Dr S. S. Singh; circ. 44,500.

Balak: Govind Mitra Rd, POB 5, Patna 800 004; tel. (612) 2650341; f. 1926; monthly; Hindi; children's; Editor S. R. Saran; circ. 32,000.

Chhattisgarh

Raipur

Krishak Jagat: A-23, Sector 1, Shankar Nagar, Raipur 492 001; tel. (771) 2420449; e-mail krishjag@sancharnet.in; internet www.krishakjagatindia.com; weekly; Hindi; Chief Editor Vijay Kumar Bondriya; circ. 35,000.

Gujarat

Ahmedabad

Akhand Anand: Anand Bhavan, Relief Rd, POB 123, Ahmedabad 380 001; tel. (79) 2357482; e-mail innitadi@sancharnet.in; f. 1947; monthly; Gujarati; Pres. Anand Amin; Editor Dr Dilavarsinh Jadeja; circ. 10,000.

Chitralok: Gujarat Samachar Bhavan, Khanpur, POB 254, Ahmedabad 380 001; tel. (79) 5504010; fax (79) 5502000; f. 1952; weekly; Gujarati; films; Man. Editor Shreyans S. Shah; circ. 20,000.

Sakhi: Sakhi Publications, Jai Hind Press Bldg, nr Gujarat Chamber, Ashram Rd, Navrangpura, Ahmedabad 380 009; tel. (79) 26581734; fax (79) 26587681; f. 1984; fortnightly; Gujarati; women's; Man. Editor Nita Y. Shah; Editor Y. N. Shah; circ. 10,000.

Shree: Gujarat Samachar Bhavan, Khanpur, Ahmedabad 380 001; tel. (79) 5504010; fax (79) 5502000; f. 1964; weekly; Gujarati; women's; Editor Smrutiben Shah; circ. 20,000.

Stree: Sandesh Bhavan, Lad Society Rd, Ahmedabad 380 054; tel. (79) 26765480; fax (79) 26753587; e-mail stree@sandesh.com; internet www.sandesh.com; f. 1962; weekly; Gujarati; Editor Ritaben Patel; circ. 42,000.

Zagmag: Gujarat Samachar Bhavan, Khanpur, Ahmedabad 380 001; tel. (79) 5508001; f. 1952; weekly; Gujarati; for children; Editor Bahubali S. Shah; circ. 38,000.

Rajkot

Amruta: Jai Hind Publications, Jai Hind Press Bldg, Babubhai Shah Marg, Rajkot 360 001; tel. (281) 2440513; fax (281) 2448677; e-mail info@jaihinddaily.com; f. 1967; weekly; Gujarati; films; Editor Y. N. Shah; circ. 12,500.

Niranjan: Jai Hind Publications, Jai Hind Press Bldg, Babubhai Shah Marg, Rajkot 360 001; tel. (281) 2440517; fax (281) 2448677;

e-mail info@jaihinddaily.com; f. 1972; fortnightly; Gujarati; children's; Editor N. R. Shah; circ. 10,500.

Parmarth: Jai Hind Publications, Jai Hind Press Bldg, Babubhai Shah Marg, Rajkot 360 001; tel. (281) 2440511; fax (281) 2448677; e-mail info@jaihinddaily.com; monthly; Gujarati; philosophy and religion; Editor Y. N. Shah; circ. 8,000.

Phulwadi: Jai Hind Publications, Jai Hind Press Bldg, Babubhai Shah Marg, Rajkot 360 001; tel. (281) 2440513; fax (281) 2448677; e-mail info@jaihinddaily.com; f. 1967; weekly; Gujarati; for children; Editor Y. N. Shah; circ. 10,000.

Karnataka
Bangalore

Mayura: 75 Mahatma Gandhi Rd, Bangalore 560 001; tel. (80) 25588999; fax (80) 25587179; e-mail ads@deccanherald.co.in; f. 1968; monthly; Kannada; Editor-in-Chief K. N. Shanth Kumar; circ. 28,600.

Sudha: 75 Mahatma Gandhi Rd, Bangalore 560 001; tel. (80) 25588999; fax (80) 25587179; e-mail ads@deccanherald.co.in; f. 1965; weekly; Kannada; Editor-in-Chief K. N. Hari Kumar; circ. 67,400.

Manipal

Taranga: Udayavani Bldg, Press Corner, Manipal 576 104; tel. (820) 2570845; fax (820) 2570563; e-mail taranga@manipalpress.com; internet www.udayavani.com; f. 1983; weekly; Kannada; Editor-in-Chief Sandhya S. Pai; circ. 85,400.

Kerala
Kochi

The Week: Malayala Manorama Buildings, POB 4278, Kochi 682 036; tel. (484) 2316285; fax (484) 2315745; e-mail editor@theweek.com; internet week.manoramaonline.com; f. 1982; weekly; English; current affairs; Chief Editor Mammen Mathew; Editor Philip Mathew; circ. 202,000.

Kottayam

Balarama: MM Publications Ltd, POB 226, Kottayam 686 001; tel. (481) 2563721; fax (481) 2564393; e-mail childrensdivision@mmpublications.com; f. 1972; children's weekly; Malayalam; Chief Editor Bina Mathew; Senior Gen. Man. V. Sajeev George; circ. 295,288.

Malayala Manorama: K. K. Rd, POB 26, Kottayam 686 001; tel. (481) 2563646; fax (481) 2562479; e-mail editor@malayalamanorama.com; internet www.malayalamanorama.com; f. 1937; weekly; Malayalam; also publ. from Kozhikode; Man. Dir and Editor Mammen Mathew; Chief Editor Mammen Varghese; combined circ. 982,419.

Vanitha: MM Publications Ltd, POB 226, Kottayam 686 001; tel. (481) 2563721; fax (481) 2564393; e-mail vanitha@mmp.in; f. 1975; women's fortnightly; Malayalam (monthly) and Hindi editions; Chief Editor Prema Mammen Mathew, Mariam Mammen Mathew; Gen. Man. V. Sajeev George; circ. 479,452 (Malayalam), 145,060 (Hindi).

Kozhikode

Arogya Masika: Mathrubhumi Bldgs, K. P. Kesava Menon Rd, Kozhikode 673 001; tel. (495) 2765381; fax (495) 2760138; e-mail arogyamasika@mpp.co.in; owned by Mathrubhumi Printing and Publishing Co Ltd; monthly; Malayalam; health; Man. Editor P. V. Chandran; circ. 198,367.

Balabhumi: Matrabhumi Bldgs, K. P. Kesava Menon Rd, Kozhikode 673 001; tel. (495) 2366655; fax (495) 2366656; e-mail balabhumi@mpp.co.in; internet www.mathrabhumi.com; f. 1996; weekly; Malayalam; children's; Editor K. K. Sreedharan Nair; circ. 95,500.

Chithrabhumi: Mathrubhumi Bldgs, K. P. Kesava Menon Rd, Kozhikode 673 001; tel. (495) 2366655; fax (495) 2366656; e-mail cinema@mpp.co.in; internet www.mathrubhumi.com; f. 1982; weekly; Malayalam; films; Editor K. K. Sreedharan Nair; circ. 33,241.

Grihalakshmi: Mathrubhumi Bldgs, K. P. Kesava Menon Rd, POB 46, Kozhikode 673 001; tel. (495) 2366655; fax (495) 2366656; e-mail mathrclt@md2.vsnl.net.in; internet www.mathrubhumi.com; f. 1979; monthly; Malayalam; women's; Editor K. K. Sreedharan Nair; circ. 167,800.

Mathrubhumi Illustrated Weekly: Mathrubhumi Bldgs, K. P. Kesava Menon Rd, POB 46, Kozhikode 673 001; tel. (495) 2366655; fax (495) 2356656; f. 1923; weekly; Malayalam; Editor K. K. Sreedharan Nair; circ. 38,300.

Sports Masika: Mathrubhumi Bldgs, K. P. Kesava Menon Rd, Kozhikode 673 001; tel. (495) 366655; fax (495) 366656; e-mail sports@mpp.co.in; internet www.mathrubhumi.com; monthly; Malayalam; sport; Editor K. K. Sreedharan Nair; circ. 67,900.

Thozhilvartha: Mathrubhumi Bldgs, K. P. Kesava Menon Rd, Kozhikode 673 001; tel. (495) 2366655; fax (495) 2366656; e-mail mathrclt@md2.vsnl.net.in; internet www.mathrubhumi.com; f. 1992; weekly; Malayalam; employment; Editor K. K. Sreedharan Nair; circ. 172,200.

Quilon

Kerala Sabdam: Thevally, Quilon 691 009; tel. (474) 272403; fax (474) 2740710; f. 1962; weekly; Malayalam; Man. Editor B. A. Rajakrishnan; circ. 66,600.

Thiruvananthapuram

Kalakaumudi: Kaumudi Bldgs, Pettah, Thiruvananthapuram 695 024; tel. (471) 2443531; fax (471) 2442895; e-mail kalakaumudi@vsnl.com; f. 1975; weekly; Malayalam; Chief Editor M. S. Mani; Editor N. R. S. Babu; circ. 73,000.

Vellinakshatram: Kaumudi Bldgs, Pettah, Thiruvananthapuram 695 024; tel. (471) 2443531; fax (471) 2442895; e-mail kalakaumudi@vsnl.com; internet www.vellinakshatram.com; f. 1987; film weekly; Malayalam; Editor Prasad Lakshmanan; Man. Editor Sukumaran Mani; circ. 55,000.

Madhya Pradesh
Bhopal

Krishak Jagat: 14 Indira Press Complex, M. P. Nagar, POB 37, Bhopal 462 011; tel. (755) 2768452; fax (755) 2760449; e-mail krishjag@sancharnet.in; internet www.krishakjagat.com; f. 1946; weekly; Hindi; agriculture; also published in Jaipur and Raipur; Chief Editor Vijay Kumar Bondriya; Editor Sunil Gangrade; combined circ. 150,000.

Maharashtra
Mumbai (Bombay)

Abhiyaan: Sambhaav Media Ltd, 4 AB, Government Industrial Estate, Charkop, Kandivli (W), Mumbai 400 067; tel. (22) 28687515; fax (22) 28680991; e-mail rajeshpathak@sambhaav.com; f. 1986; weekly; Gujarati; Chief Man. Dir Kiran Vadodaria; Group Editor Deepal Trevedie; circ. 99,300.

Arogya Sanjeevani: C-14 Royal Industrial Estate, 5-B Naigaum Cross Rd, Wadala, Mumbai 400 031; tel. (22) 24138723; fax (22) 24133610; e-mail woman17@zediffmail.com; f. 1990; quarterly; Hindi; Editor Ram Krishna Shukla; circ. 56,472.

Auto India: Nirmal, Nariman Point, Mumbai 400 021; tel. (22) 22883946; fax (22) 22883940; e-mail editor@auto-india.com; f. 1994; monthly; Editor Raj Warrior; circ. 44,500.

Bhavan's Journal: Kulapati Dr K. M. Munshi Marg, Chowpatty, Mumbai 400 007; tel. (22) 23631261; fax (22) 23630058; e-mail brbhavan@bom7.vsnl.net.in; f. 1954; fortnightly; English; literary; Man. Editor J. H. Dave; Editor V. N. Narayanan; circ. 25,000.

Bombay Samachar: Red House, Sayed Abdulla Brelvi Rd, Mumbai 400 001; tel. (22) 22045531; fax (22) 22046642; e-mail samachar@vsnl.com; f. 1822; weekly; Gujarati; Editor P. D. Dalal (acting); circ. 118,213.

Business India: Nirmal, 14th Floor, Nariman Point, Mumbai 400 021; tel. (22) 22883943; fax (22) 22883940; f. 1978; fortnightly; English; Publr Ashok Advani; circ. 75,700.

Business World: 25–28 Atlanta, 2nd Floor, Nariman Point, Mumbai 400 021; tel. (22) 22851352; fax (22) 22870310; f. 1980; weekly; English; Editor Tony Joseph; circ. 146,500.

Chitralekha: 62 Vaju Kotak Marg, Fort, Mumbai 400 001; tel. (22) 22614730; fax (22) 22615895; e-mail advertise@chitralekha.com; internet www.chitralekha.com; f. 1950 (Gujarati), f. 1989 (Marathi); weekly; Gujarati and Marathi; Editors Bharat Ghelani, Gyanesh Maharao; circ. 240,300 (Gujarati), 95,300 (Marathi).

Cine Blitz Film Monthly: Rifa Publications Pvt Ltd, A/3, Sangam Bhavan, Ground Floor, Brahma Kumaris Rd, nr Strand Cinema, Colaba, Mumbai 400 005; tel. (22) 22830668; fax (22) 22830672; e-mail cbedit@sify.com; f. 1974; English; Editor Nishi Prem; circ. 184,100.

Debonair: Mumbai; e-mail maurya@debonairindia.com; f. 1972; monthly; English; Publr Chaitanya Prabhu; CEO Joseph Mascarenhas; circ. 110,000.

Economic and Political Weekly: Hitkari House, 284 Shahid Bhagatsingh Rd, Mumbai 400 001; tel. (22) 22696073; fax (22) 22696072; e-mail epw@vsnl.com; internet www.epw.org.in; f. 1966; English; Editor C. Rammanohar Reddy; circ. 132,800.

Femina: Times of India Bldg, Dr Dadabhai Naoroji Rd, Mumbai 400 001; tel. and fax (22) 22731385; e-mail femina@timesgroup.com;

internet www.feminaindia.com; f. 1959; fortnightly; English; Editor AMY FERNANDES; circ. 122,200.

Filmfare: 4th Floor, Times of India Bldg, Dr Dadabhai Naoroji Rd, Mumbai 400 001; tel. (22) 22731187; fax (22) 22731585; e-mail shashi.baliga@wwm.co.in; internet www.filmfare.com; f. 1952; monthly; English; Exec. Editor SHASHI BALIGA; circ. 147,000.

G: 62 Vaju Kotak Marg, Fort, Mumbai 400 001; tel. (22) 22614730; fax (22) 22615895; e-mail advertise@chitralekha.com; internet www.gmagazine.com; f. 1989; monthly; English; Editor MAULIK KOTAK; circ. 65,000.

Gentleman: B-201, Teritex Business Service Centre, Saki Vihar, Mumbai 400 072; tel. (22) 28571490; fax (22) 28572447; e-mail gentleman@vsnl.com; f. 1980; monthly; English; Editor PREMNATH NAIR (acting).

Hi Blitz: Rifa Publications Pvt Ltd, A/3, Sangam Bhavan, Ground Floor, Brahma Kumaris Rd, nr Strand Cinema, Colaba, Mumbai 400 005; tel. (22) 22830668; fax (22) 22830672; e-mail cbedit@sify.com; f. 2002; English; lifestyle; Editor SHALINI SHARMA; 65,000.

Indian PEN: Theosophy Hall, 40 New Marine Lines, Mumbai 400 020; tel. (22) 22032175; e-mail ambika.sirkar@gems.vsnl.net.in; f. 1934; quarterly; organ of Indian Centre of the International PEN; Editor RANJIT HOSKOTE.

Janmabhoomi-Pravasi: Janmabhoomi Bhavan, Janmabhoomi Marg, Fort, POB 62, Mumbai 400 001; tel. (22) 22870831; fax (22) 22874097; e-mail bhoomi@bom3.vsnl.net.in; f. 1939; weekly; Gujarati; Propr Saurashtra Trust; Editor KUNDAN VYAS; circ. 94,100.

JEE: 62 Vaju Kotak Marg, Fort, Mumbai 400 001; tel. (22) 22614730; fax (22) 22615895; e-mail advertise@chitralekha.com; fortnightly; Gujarati and Marathi; Editor MADHURI KOTAK; circ. 92,160 (Gujarati), 30,150 (Marathi).

Meri Saheli: C-14 Royal Industrial Estate, 5-B Naigaum Cross Rd, Wadala, Mumbai 400 031; tel. (22) 24138723; fax (22) 24133610; e-mail woman17@zediffmail.com; f. 1987; monthly; Hindi; Editor HEMA MALINI; circ. 352,362.

Movie: Mahalaxmi Chambers, 5th Floor, 22 Bhulabhai Desai Rd, Mumbai 400 026; tel. (22) 24935636; fax (22) 24938406; f. 1981; monthly; English; Editor DINESH RAHEJA; circ. 70,700.

New Woman: C-14 Royal Industrial Estate, 5-B Naigaum Cross Rd, Wadala, Mumbai 400 031; tel. (22) 24138723; fax (22) 24133610; e-mail newwomanmag@gmail.com; f. 1996; monthly; English; Editor HEMA MALINI; circ. 71,677.

Onlooker: Free Press House, 215 Free Press Journal Marg, Nariman Point, Mumbai 400 021; tel. (22) 22874566; f. 1939; fortnightly; English; news magazine; Exec. Editor K. SRINIVASAN; circ. 61,000.

Reader's Digest: 45 Vaju Kotak Marg, Ballard Estate, Mumbai 400 001; tel. (22) 22617292; fax (22) 22613347; e-mail ashok.mahadevan@intoday.com; internet www.rd-india.com; f. 1954; monthly; English; Publr and Editor ASHOK MAHADEVAN; circ. 389,378.

Savvy: Magna Publishing Co Ltd, Magna House, 100/E Old Prabhadevi Rd, Prabhadevi, Mumbai 400 025; tel. (22) 24362270; fax (22) 24306523; e-mail savvy@magnamags.com; internet www.magnamags.com; f. 1984; monthly; English; Editor SAIRA MENEZES; circ. 99,500.

Screen: Express Tower, Nariman Point, Mumbai 400 021; tel. (22) 22022627; fax (22) 22022139; e-mail iemumbai@expressindia.co.in; internet www.screenindia.com; f. 1950; film weekly; English; Editor BHAVNA SOMAYA; circ. 90,000.

Society: Magna Publishing Co Ltd, Magna House, 100/E Old Prabhadevi Rd, Prabhadevi, Mumbai 400 025; tel. (22) 24362270; fax (22) 24306523; e-mail society@magnamags.com; internet www.magnamags.com; f. 1979; monthly; English; Editorial Dir ASHWIN VARDE; circ. 67,200.

Stardust: Magna Publishing Co Ltd, Magna House, 100/E Old Prabhadevi Rd, Prabhadevi, Mumbai 400 025; tel. (22) 24362270; fax (22) 24306523; e-mail magnapub@vsnl.com; internet www.stardustindia.com; f. 1985; monthly; English; Editor ASHWIN VARDE; circ. 308,000.

Vyapar: Janmabhoomi Bhavan, Janmabhoomi Marg, POB 62, Fort, Mumbai 400 001; tel. (22) 22870831; fax (22) 22874097; e-mail rajeshbhayani@hotmail.com; f. 1949; (Gujarati), 1987 (Hindi); Gujarati (2 a week) and Hindi (weekly); commerce; Propr Saurashtra Trust; Editor RAJESH M. BHAYANI; circ. 27,900 (Gujarati), 12,800 (Hindi).

Nagpur

All India Reporter: AIR Ltd, Congress Nagar, POB 209, Nagpur 440 012; tel. (712) 2534321; fax (712) 2526283; e-mail air@allindiareporter.com; internet www.allindiareporter.com; f. 1914; weekly and monthly; English; law journals; Chief Editor V. R. MANOHAR; circ. 55,500.

Rajasthan
Jaipur

Balhans: Kesargarh, Jawahar Lal Nehru Marg, Jaipur 302 004; tel. (141) 2561582; fax (141) 2566011; e-mail info@rajasthanpatrika.com; internet www.rajasthanpatrika.com; fortnightly; Hindi; circ. 26,700.

Itwari Patrika: Kesargarh, Jawahar Lal Nehru Marg, Jaipur 302 004; tel. (141) 2561582; fax (141) 2566011; weekly; Hindi; circ. 12,000.

Krishak Jagat: F-47, Ghiya Marg, Bani Park, Jaipur 302 016; tel. (141) 2207680; e-mail krishjag@sancharnet.in; internet www.krishakjagatindia.com; Hindi; weekly; Chief Editor VIJAY KUMAR BONDRIYA; circ. 32,000.

Rashtradoot Saptahik: M.I. Rd, POB 30, Jaipur 302 001; tel. (141) 2372634; fax (141) 2373513; f. 1983; Hindi; also publ. from Kota and Bikaner; Chief Editor and Man. Editor RAJESH SHARMA; CEO SOMESH SHARMA; combined circ. 324,721.

Tamil Nadu
Chennai (Madras)

Ambulimama: 82 Defence Officers Colony, Ekkatuthangal, Chennai 600 097; tel. (44) 22313637; e-mail chandamama@vsnl.com; f. 1947; children's monthly; Tamil; Editor B. VISWANATHA REDDI; circ. 65,000.

Ambuli Ammavan: 82 Defence Officers Colony, Ekkatuthangal, Chennai 600 097; tel. (44) 22313637; e-mail chandamama@vsnl.com; f. 1970; children's monthly; Malayalam; Editor B. VISWANATHA REDDI; circ. 12,000.

Ananda Vikatan: 757 Anna Salai, Chennai 600 002; tel. (44) 28524054; fax (44) 28523819; e-mail editor@vikatan.com; internet www.vikatan.com; f. 1924; weekly; Tamil; Editor and Man. Dir S. BALASUBRAMANIAN; circ. 316,000.

Aval Vikatan: 757 Anna Salai, Chennai 600 002; tel. (44) 28524054; fax (44) 28523819; e-mail editor@vikatan.com; internet www.vikatan.com; f. 1998; fortnightly; Tamil; Editor B. SRINIVASAN; circ. 100,000.

Chandamama: 82 Defence Officers Colony, Ekkatuthangal, Chennai 600 097; tel. (44) 22313637; e-mail chandamama@vsnl.com; f. 1947; children's monthly; Hindi, Gujarati, Telugu, Kannada, English, Sanskrit, Bengali, Assamese; Editor B. VISWANATHA REDDI; combined circ. 420,000.

Chandoba: 82 Defence Officers Colony, Ekkatuthangal, Chennai 600 097; tel. (44) 22313637; e-mail chandamama@vsnl.com; f. 1952; children's monthly; Marathi; Editor B. VISWANATHA REDDI; circ. 93,000.

Chutti Vikatan: 757 Anna Salai, Chennai 600 002; tel. (44) 28524054; fax (44) 28523819; e-mail editor@vikatan.com; internet www.chuttivikatan.com; f. 1999; fortnightly; children's; Tamil; Editor B. SRINIVASAN; Man. Dir S. BALASUBRAMANIAN; circ. 100,000.

Devi: 727 Anna Salai, Chennai 600 006; tel. (44) 28521428; f. 1979; weekly; Tamil; Editor B. RAMACHANDRA ADITYAN; circ. 64,800.

Dinamani Kadir: Express Estate, Mount Rd, Chennai 600 002; tel. (44) 28520751; fax (44) 28524500; weekly; Editor G. KASTURI RANGAN (acting); circ. 55,000.

Frontline: Kasturi Bldgs, 859/860 Anna Salai, Chennai 600 002; tel. (44) 28413344; fax (44) 28415325; e-mail subs@thehindu.co.in; internet www.flonnet.com; f. 1984; fortnightly; English; current affairs; independent; Publr S. RANGARAJAN; Editor N. RAM; circ. 62,700.

The Hindu International Edition: Kasturi Bldgs, 859/860 Anna Salai, Chennai 600 002; tel. (44) 28413344; fax (44) 28415325; e-mail subs@thehindu.co.in; f. 1975; weekly; English; independent; Publr S. RANGARAJAN; Editor N. RAVI; circ. 1,590.

Jahnamamu (Oriya): 82 Defence Officers Colony, Ekkatuthangal, Chennai 600 097; tel. (44) 22313637; e-mail chandamama@vsnl.com; f. 1972; children's monthly; Editor B. VISWANATHA REDDI; circ. 111,000.

Junior Vikatan: 757 Anna Salai, Chennai 600 002; tel. (44) 28524054; fax (44) 28523819; e-mail editor@vikatan.com; internet www.vikatan.com; f. 1983; twice a week; Tamil; Editor and Man. Dir S. BALASUBRAMANIAN; circ. 190,300.

Kalai Magal: POB 604, Chennai 600 004; tel. (44) 24983099; f. 1932; monthly; Tamil; literary and cultural; Editor R. NARAYANASWAMY; circ. 10,200.

Kalki: Kalki Bldgs, 47-NP Jawaharlal Nehru Rd, Ekkatuthangal, Chennai 600 097; tel. (44) 22345622; fax (44) 22345621; e-mail kalki@kalkiweekly.com; internet www.kalkionline.com; f. 1941; weekly; Tamil; literary and cultural; Editor SEETHA RAVI; circ. 42,700.

Kumudam: 151 Purasawalkam High Rd, Chennai 600 010; tel. (44) 26422146; fax (44) 26425041; e-mail kumudam@hotmail.com;

INDIA

internet www.kumudam.com; f. 1947; weekly; Tamil; Editor Dr S. A. P. Jawahar Palaniappan; circ. 385,900.

Kungumam: 93A Kodambakkam High Rd, Chennai 600 034; tel. (44) 28268177; f. 1978; weekly; Tamil; Editor Parasakthi; circ. 63,700.

Malaimathi: Chennai; f. 1958; weekly; Tamil; Editor P. S. Elango; circ. 48,100.

Muththaram: 93A Kogambakkam High Rd, Chennai 600 034; tel. (44) 2476306; f. 1980; weekly; Tamil; Editor Parasakthi; circ. 11,800.

Rani Muthu: 86 Periyar E.V.R. High Rd, Chennai 600 007; tel. (44) 25324771; fax (44) 26426884; e-mail raniweekly@vsnl.net; f. 1969; fortnightly; Tamil; Editor Ragupathy Baskaran; circ. 38,180.

Rani Weekly: 86 Periyar E.V.R. High Rd, Chennai 600 007; tel. (44) 25324771; fax (44) 26426884; e-mail raniweekly@vsnl.net; f. 1962; Tamil; Editor Ragupathy Baskaran; circ. 141,911.

Sportstar: Kasturi Bldgs, 859/860 Anna Salai, Chennai 600 002; tel. (44) 28413344; fax (44) 28415325; e-mail wsvcs@thehindu.co.in; internet www.tssonnet.com; f. 1978; weekly; English; independent; Publr S. Rangarajan; Editor N. Ram; circ. 48,900.

Thuglak: 46 Greenways Rd, Chennai 600 028; tel. (44) 24936913; fax (44) 24936915; f. 1970; weekly; Tamil; Editor Cho S. Ramaswamy; circ. 78,130.

Uttar Pradesh

Allahabad

Manohar Kahaniyan: 1A, Tagore Town, Hashimpur Rd, Allahabad 211 002; tel. (532) 2415549; fax (532) 2415533; e-mail mayapressalld@rediffmail.com; f. 1940; monthly; Hindi; Editor Ashok Mitra.

Nutan Kahaniyan: 15 Sheo Charan Lal Rd, Allahabad 211 003; tel. (532) 2400612; f. 1975; Hindi; monthly; Chief Editor K. K. Bhargava; circ. 167,500.

Satya Katha: 1A, Tagore Town, Hashimpur Rd, Allahabad 211 002; e-mail mayapressalld@rediffmail.com; f. 1974; monthly; Hindi; Editor Ashok Mitra.

West Bengal

Kolkata (Calcutta)

All India Appointment Gazette: 7 Old Court House St, Kolkata 700 001; tel. (33) 22435663; fax (33) 22435618; e-mail sambadmail@sify.com; f. 1973; weekly; English; Editor S.C. Talukdar; circ. 37,469.

Anandalok: 6 Prafulla Sarkar St, Kolkata 700 001; tel. (33) 22374880; fax (33) 22253240; f. 1975; fortnightly; Bengali; film; Editor Dulendra Bhowmik; circ. 98,600.

Anandamela: 6 Prafulla Sarkar St, Kolkata 700 001; tel. (33) 22216600; fax (33) 22253240; f. 1975; weekly; Bengali; for children; Editor Debashis Bandopadhyay; circ. 41,800.

Contemporary Tea Time: 1/2 Old Court House Corner, POB 14, Kolkata 700 001; tel. (33) 22200099; fax (33) 22435753; e-mail calcutta@ctl.co.in; internet www.ctl.co.in; f. 1988; quarterly; English; tea industry; Exec. Editor Gita Narayani; circ. 5,000.

Desh: 6 Prafulla Sarkar St, Kolkata 700 001; tel. (33) 22374880; fax (33) 22253240; f. 1933; fortnightly; Bengali; literary; Editor Harsha Datta; circ. 100,000.

Khela: 96 Raja Rammohan Sarani, Kolkata 700 009; tel. (33) 23509803; f. 1981; weekly; Bengali; sports; Editor Asoke Dasgupta; circ. 7,800.

Naba Kallol: 11 Jhamapookur Lane, Kolkata 700 009; tel. (33) 23504294; e-mail devsahityer@caltiger.com; f. 1960; monthly; Bengali; Editor P. K. Mazumdar; circ. 37,000.

Prabuddha Bharata (Awakened India): 5 Dehi Entally Rd, Kolkata 700 014; tel. (33) 22440898; e-mail advaita@vsnl.com; internet www.advaitaonline.com; f. 1896; monthly; art, culture, religion and philosophy; Publr Swami Bodhasarananda; Editor Swami Satyaswarupananda; circ. 7,500.

Sananda: 6 Prafulla Sarkar St, Kolkata 700 001; tel. (33) 22374880; fax (33) 22253241; f. 1986; monthly; Bengali; Editor Aparna Sen; circ. 172,500.

Saptahik Bartaman: 76A J. C. Bose Rd, Kolkata 700 014; tel. (33) 22448208; fax (33) 22441215; f. 1988; weekly; Bengali; Editor Barun Sengupta; circ. 111,900.

The Statesman: Statesman House, 4 Chowringhee Sq., Kolkata 700 001; tel. (33) 22127070; fax (33) 22120054; e-mail thestatesman@vsnl.com; internet www.thestatesman.net; f. 1875; overseas weekly; English; Editor-in-Chief C. R. Irani.

Suktara: 11 Jhamapooker Lane, Kolkata 700 009; tel. (33) 23504294; e-mail devsahityer@caltiger.com; f. 1948; monthly; Bengali; juvenile; Editor M. Majumdar; circ. 44,300.

NEWS AGENCIES

Press Trust of India Ltd: PTI Bldg, 4 Parliament St, New Delhi 110 001; tel. (11) 23716621; fax (11) 23718714; e-mail trans@pti.in; internet www.ptinews.com; f. 1947; re-established 1978; Chair. Dr R. Lakshmipathy; Editor-in-Chief and CEO M. K. Razdan.

United News of India (UNI): 9 Rafi Marg, New Delhi 110 001; tel. (11) 23710522; fax (11) 23355841; e-mail uninet@uniindia.com; internet www.uniindia.com; f. 1959; national and international news service in English, Hindi (UNIVARTA) and Urdu; photograph and graphics service; brs in 72 centres in India; Chair. Manoj Kumar Sonthalia; Gen. Man. Mahinder Kumar Laul.

CO-ORDINATING BODIES

Press Information Bureau: Shastri Bhavan, Dr Rajendra Prasad Rd, New Delhi 110 001; tel. (11) 23383643; fax (11) 23383203; e-mail pib@alpha.nic.in; internet www.pib.nic.in; f. 1946 to co-ordinate press affairs for the govt; represents newspaper managements, journalists, news agencies, parliament; has power to examine journalists under oath and may censor objectionable material; Prin. Information Officer Deepak Sandhu.

Registrar of Newspapers for India: Ministry of Information and Broadcasting, West Block 8, Wing 2, Ramakrishna Puram, New Delhi 110 066; tel. (11) 26107504; fax (11) 26189801; e-mail rni.hub@nic.in; internet rni.nic.in; f. 1956 as a statutory body to collect press statistics; maintains a register of all Indian newspapers; Press Registrar Amitabha Chakrabarti.

PRESS ASSOCIATIONS

All-India Newspaper Editors' Conference: 36–37 Northend Complex, Rama Krishna Ashram Marg, New Delhi 110 001; tel. (11) 23364519; fax (11) 23317499; f. 1940; c. 370 mems; Pres. Vishwa Bandhu Gupta; Sec.-Gen. Bishamber Newer.

All India Small and Medium Newspapers' Federation: 26-F Rajiv Gandhi Chowk (Connaught Place), New Delhi 110 001; tel. (11) 23326000; fax (11) 24621636; e-mail indian_observer@hotmail.com; c. 9,000 mems; Pres. Harbhajan Singh; Gen. Secs B. C. Gupta, B. M. Sharma.

The Foreign Correspondents' Club of South Asia: AB-19 Mathura Rd, opp. Pragati Maidan Gate 3, New Delhi 110 001; tel. (11) 23385118; fax (11) 23385517; e-mail fcc@fccsouthasia.org; internet www.fccsouthasia.com; f. 1992; 450 mems; Pres. Dr Waiel S. H. Awwad; Man. Kiran Kapur.

Indian Federation of Working Journalists: A-4/199 Basant Lane, nr Connaught Pl., New Delhi 110 055; tel. (11) 23348871; fax (11) 23348871; e-mail ifwj.media@gmail.com; internet www.ifwj.in; f. 1950; 30,000 mems; Pres. K. Vikram Rao; Sec.-Gen. Parmanand Pandey.

Indian Journalists' Association: New Delhi; Pres. Vijay Dutt; Gen. Sec. A. K. Dhar.

Indian Languages Newspapers' Association: Janmabhoomi Bhavan, Janmabhoomi Marg, POB 10029, Fort, Mumbai 400 001; tel. (22) 22870537; f. 1941; 320 mems; Pres. Vijay Kumar Bondriya; Hon. Gen. Secs Pradeep G. Deshpande, Krishna Shewdikar, Lalit Shrimal.

Indian Newspaper Society: INS Bldg, Rafi Marg, New Delhi 110 001; tel. (11) 23715401; fax (11) 23723800; e-mail indnews@nde.vsnl.net.in; f. 1939; 685 mems; Pres. M. P. Veerendrakumar; Sec.-Gen. Deepak S. Raja.

National Union of Journalists (India): 7 Jantar Mantar Rd, 2nd Floor, New Delhi 110 001; tel. (11) 23368610; e-mail nujindia@ndf.vsnl.in; internet www.education.vsnl.com/nujindia; f. 1972; 12,000 mems; Pres. A. N. Mishra; Sec.-Gen. M. D. Gangwar.

Press Club of India: 1 Raisina Rd, New Delhi 110 001; tel. (11) 23719844; fax (11) 23357048; f. 1948; 4,500 mems.

Press Council of India: Soochna Bhavan, 8 C. G. O. Complex, Ground Floor, Lodhi Rd, New Delhi 110 003; tel. (11) 24366746; e-mail pcids@vsnl.net; internet www.presscouncil.nic.in; established under an Act of Parliament to preserve the freedom of the press and maintain and improve the standards of newspapers and news agencies in India; 28 mems; Chair. Justice Ganendra Narayan Ray; Sec. Vibha Bhargaval.

Press Institute of India: Administrative Block, Jamia Millia Islamia, Jamia Nagar, New Delhi 110 025; tel. (11) 26985156; fax (11) 26985159; e-mail arunchacko@pressinstitute.org; internet www.pressinstitute.org; f. 1963; 32 mem. newspapers and other orgs; Chair. N. Murali; Dir Arun Chacko.

INDIA   Directory

Publishers

DELHI AND NEW DELHI

Affiliated East-West Press (Pvt) Ltd: G-1/16 Ansari Rd, Daryaganj, New Delhi 110 002; tel. (11) 23264180; fax (11) 23260538; e-mail affiliat@vsnl.com; internet www.aewpress.com; textbooks and reference books; also represents scientific societies; Dirs SUNNY MALIK, KAMAL MALIK.

Allied Publishers (Pvt) Ltd: 13–14 Asaf Ali Rd, New Delhi 110 002; tel. (11) 23239001; fax (11) 23235967; e-mail alliedpublishers@eth.net; internet alliedpublishers.com; academic and general; Man. Dir SUNIL SACHDEV.

All India Publishers & Distributors: 4380/4B, Ansari Rd, Kaushalya Bldg, Daryaganj, New Delhi 110 002; tel. (11) 22324429; fax (11) 22467613; e-mail aipdraj@vsnl.com; CEO ARYA RAJENDER.

Amerind Publishing Co (Pvt) Ltd: c/o Mohan Primlani, A-61, Mayfair Gardens, New Delhi 110 016; tel. (11) 23324578; fax (11) 23710090; e-mail mohanprimlani@hotmail.com; f. 1970; offices at Kolkata, Mumbai and New York; scientific and technical; Dirs MOHAN PRIMLANI, GULAB PRIMLANI.

Arnold Heinman Publishers (India) Pvt Ltd: New Delhi; f. 1969 as Arnold Publishers (India) Pvt Ltd; literature and general; Man. Dir G. A. VAZIRANI.

Atma Ram and Sons: 1376 Kashmere Gate, POB 1429, Delhi 110 006; tel. (11) 23946466; fax (11) 23973082; e-mail atmaram_books@hotmail.com; f. 1909; scientific, technical, humanities, medical; Man. Dir S. PURI; Dir Y. PURI.

B. I. Publications Pvt Ltd: B. I. House, 54 Janpath, New Delhi 110 001; tel. (11) 23325313; fax (11) 23323138; e-mail bipgroup@vsnl.com; internet www.biindia.in/publication.htm; f. 1959; academic, general and professional; Man. Dir SHASHANK BHAGAT.

Book Circle: 19A Ansari Rd, Daryaganj, New Delhi 110 002; tel. (11) 23264444; fax (11) 23263050; e-mail bookcircle@vsnl.net; f. 2001; social sciences, art and architecture, technical, medical, scientific; Propr and Dir HIMANSHU CHAWLA.

S. Chand and Co Ltd: 7361 Ram Nagar, Qutab Rd, nr New Delhi Railway Station, New Delhi 110 055; tel. (11) 23672080; fax (11) 23677446; e-mail schand@vsnl.com; internet www.schandgroup.com; f. 1917; educational and general in English and Hindi; also book exports and imports; Man. Dir RAVINDRA KUMAR GUPTA.

Children's Book House: A-4 Ring Rd, South Extension Part I, POB 3854, New Delhi 110 049; tel. (11) 24636030; fax (11) 24636011; e-mail info@neetaprakashan.com; internet www.neetaprakashan.com; f. 1952; educational and general; Dir R. S. GUPTA.

Children's Book Trust: Nehru House, 4 Bahadur Shah Zafar Marg, New Delhi 110 002; tel. (11) 23316970; fax (11) 23721090; e-mail cbtnd@vsnl.com; internet www.childrensbooktrust.com; f. 1957; children's books in English and other Indian languages; Editor C. G. R. KURUP; Gen. Man. RAVI SHANKAR.

Concept Publishing Co: A/15-16, Commercial Block, Mohan Garden, New Delhi 110 059; tel. (11) 25351794; fax (11) 25357103; e-mail publishing@conceptpub.com; f. 1975; agriculture and rural development, Ayurveda, health sciences, communication, mass media, journalism, education, psychology, community development, management; Man. Dir ASHOK KUMAR MITTAL; CEO NITIN MITTAL.

Frank Bros & Co (Publishers) Ltd: 4675A Ansari Rd, 21 Daryaganj, New Delhi 110 002; tel. (11) 23263393; fax (11) 23269032; e-mail connect@frankbros.com; f. 1930; children's, educational and management; Chair. and Man. Dir R. C. GOVIL.

Heritage Publishers: 19A Ansari Rd, Daryaganj, New Delhi 110 002; tel. (11) 23266633; fax (11) 23263050; e-mail heritage@nda.vsnl.net.in; internet www.meditechbooks.com; f. 1973; social sciences, art and architecture, technical, medical, scientific; Propr and Dir B. R. CHAWLA.

Hindustan Publishing Corpn (India): 4805/24 Bharat Ram Rd, Suite 102, Daryaganj, New Delhi 110 002; tel. (11) 26520784; fax (11) 26520784; e-mail hpcedu@rediffmail.com; archaeology, anthropology, business management, demography and population dynamics, economics, pure and applied sciences, geology, mathematics, physics, sociology; publ. *Demography India* and *Journal of Economic Geology and Georesource Management*; exporter of Indian journals and periodicals, Indian and foreign books; Man. Partner B. B. JAIN.

Kali for Women: K-36 Hauz Khas Enclave, New Delhi 110 016; tel. (11) 26964947; fax (11) 26496597; e-mail womenunltd@vsnl.net; women's studies, social sciences, humanities, general non-fiction, fiction, etc.; Heads of Organization URVASHI BUTALIA, RITU MENON.

Lalit Kala Akademi: Rabindra Bhavan, New Delhi 110 001; tel. (11) 23387241; fax (11) 23782485; e-mail lka@lalitkala.org.in; internet www.lalitkala.gov.in; books on Indian art; CEO Dr SUDHAKAR SHARMA.

Lancers Books: POB 4236, New Delhi 110 048; tel. (11) 26241617; fax (11) 26992063; e-mail lancersbooks@hotmail.com; f. 1977; politics (with special emphasis on north-east India), defence; Propr S. KUMAR.

Motilal Banarsidass Publishers (Pvt) Ltd: 41 U.A. Bungalow Rd, Jawahar Nagar, Delhi 110 007; tel. (11) 23851985; fax (11) 25797221; e-mail mlbd@vsnl.com; internet www.mlbd.com; f. 1903; religion, philosophy, astrology, yoga, linguistic, history, art, architecture, literature, music and dance, alternative medicine, in English and Sanskrit; offices in Bangalore, Chennai, Kolkata, Mumbai, Patna, Pune and Varanasi; Man. Dir N. P. JAIN.

Munshiram Manoharlal Publishers Pvt Ltd: 54 Rani Jhansi Rd, POB 5715, New Delhi 110 055; tel. (11) 23673650; fax (11) 23612745; e-mail mrml@mrmlbooks.com; internet www.mrmlbooks.com; f. 1952; Indian art, architecture, archaeology, religion, music, law, medicine, dance, dictionaries, travel, history, politics, numismatics, Buddhism, philosophy, sociology, etc.; Dirs PANKAJ JAIN, VIKRAM JAIN.

National Book Trust: A-5 Green Park, New Delhi 110 016; tel. (11) 26518607; fax (11) 26851795; e-mail nbtindia@ndb.vsnl.net.in; internet www.nbtindia.org.in; f. 1957; autonomous organization established by the Ministry of Human Resources Development to produce and encourage the production of good literary works; Chair. Prof. BIPAN CHANDRA; Dir NUZHAT HASSAN.

National Council of Educational Research and Training (NCERT): Sri Aurobindo Marg, New Delhi 110 016; tel. (11) 26560620; fax (11) 26868419; e-mail directorncert@vsnl.com; internet www.ncert.nic.in; f. 1961; school textbooks, teachers' guides, research monographs, journals, etc.; Dir Prof. KRISHNA KUMAR.

Neeta Prakashan: A-4 Ring Rd, South Extension Part I, POB 3853, New Delhi 110 049; tel. (11) 24636010; fax (11) 24636011; e-mail neetabooks@vsnl.com; internet www.neetaprakashan.com; f. 1960; educational, children's, general; Dir RAJESH GUPTA.

New Age International Pvt Ltd: 4835/24 Ansari Rd, Daryaganj, New Delhi 110 002; tel. (11) 23276802; fax (11) 23267437; e-mail saumya.gupta@newagepublishers.com; internet www.newagepublishers.com; f. 1966; science, engineering, technology, management, humanities, social science; Man. Dir SAUMYA GUPTA.

Oxford and IBH Publishing Co (Pvt) Ltd: 66 Janpath, New Delhi 110 001; tel. (11) 23415896; fax (11) 51517599; e-mail oxford@vsnl.com; f. 1964; science, technology and reference in English; Man. Dir MOHAN PRIMLANI.

Oxford University Press: YMCA Library Bldg, 1st Floor, 1 Jai Singh Rd, POB 43, New Delhi 110 001; tel. (11) 23747124; fax (11) 23360897; e-mail manzar.khan@oup.com; internet www.oup.com/in; f. 1912; educational, scientific, medical, general, humanities and social science, dictionaries and reference; Man. Dir MANZAR KHAN.

Penguin Books India (Pvt) Ltd: 11 Community Centre, Panchsheel Park, New Delhi 110 017; tel. (11) 26494401; fax (11) 26494403; e-mail penguin@del2.vsnl.net.in; internet www.penguinbooksindia.com; f. 1987; Indian literature and general non-fiction in English; Chair. JOHN MAKINSON; Pres. THOMAS ABRAHAM.

People's Publishing House (Pvt) Ltd: 5E Rani Jhansi Rd, New Delhi 110 055; tel. (11) 27524701; f. 1947; Marxism, Leninism, peasant movt; Dir SHAMEEM FAIZEE.

Pitambar Publishing Co Pvt Ltd: 888 East Park Rd, Karol Bagh, New Delhi 110 005; tel. (11) 23676058; fax (11) 23676058; e-mail pitambar@bol.net.in; internet www.pitambarbooks.com; academic, children's books, textbooks and general; Man. Dir ANAND BHUSHAN; five brs.

Prentice-Hall of India (Pvt) Ltd: M-97 Connaught Circus, New Delhi 110 001; tel. (11) 22143344; fax (11) 23417179; e-mail phi@phindia.com; internet www.phindia.com; f. 1963; university-level text and reference books; Man. Dir A. K. GHOSH.

Pustak Mahal: J-3/16 Daryaganj, New Delhi 110 002; tel. (11) 23272783; fax (11) 23260518; e-mail pustakmahal@vsnl.net.in; internet www.pustakmahal.com; children's, general, computers, religious, encyclopaedias; Chair. T. R. GUPTA; Man. Dir RAM AVTAR GUPTA.

Rajkamal Prakashan (Pvt) Ltd: 1B Netaji Subhas Marg, Daryaganj, New Delhi 110 002; tel. (11) 23274463; fax (11) 23278144; e-mail info@rajkamalprakashan.com; internet www.rajkamalprakashan.com; f. 1947; Hindi; literary; also literary journal and monthly trade journal; Man. Dir ASHOK KUMAR MAHESHWARI.

Rajpal and Sons: 1590 Madrasa Rd, Kashmere Gate, Delhi 110 006; tel. (11) 23865483; fax (11) 23867791; e-mail orienpbk@ndb.vsnl.net.in; f. 1891; humanities, social sciences, art, juvenile; Hindi; Chair. VISHWANATH MALHOTRA.

Research and Information System for Developing Countries: Zone IV-B, 4th Floor, India Habitat Centre, Lodhi Rd, New Delhi 100 003; tel. (11) 24682177; fax (11) 24682173; e-mail dgoffice@ris.org.in; internet www.ris.org.in; f. 1983; trade and development issues; Dir-Gen. Dr NAGESH KUMAR.

Rupa & Co: 7/16 Ansari Rd, Daryaganj, POB 7017, New Delhi 110 002; tel. (11) 23278586; fax (11) 23277294; e-mail rupa@ndb.vsnl.net.in; internet www.rupapublications.com; f. 1936; Chief Exec. R. K. MEHRA.

Sage Publications India Pvt Ltd: B-42, Panchsheel Enclave, POB 4109, New Delhi 110 017; tel. and fax (11) 26491290; e-mail journalsubs@indiasage.com; internet www.indiasage.com; f. 1981; social science, development studies, business and management studies; Man. Dir TEJESHWAR SINGH.

Sahitya Akademi: Rabindra Bhavan, 35 Ferozeshah Rd, New Delhi 110 001; tel. (11) 23386626; fax (11) 23364207; e-mail secy@ndb.vsnl.net.in; internet www.sahitya-akademi.gov.in; f. 1956; bibliographies, translations, monographs, encyclopaedias, literary classics, etc.; Pres. Prof. GOPICHAND NARANG; Sec. A. KRISHNA MURTHY.

Scholar Publishing House (P) Ltd: 85 Model Basti, New Delhi 110 005; tel. (11) 23541299; fax (11) 23676565; e-mail scholar@vsnl.com; internet www.scholargroup.com; f. 1968; educational; Man. Dir RAMESH RANADE.

Shiksha Bharati: 1590 Madrasa Rd, Kashmere Gate, Delhi 110 006; tel. (11) 23869812; fax (11) 23867791; e-mail orientpbk@vsnl.com; f. 1955; textbooks, creative literature, popular science and juvenile in Hindi and English; Editor MEERA JOHRI.

Sterling Publishers (Pvt) Ltd: A-59 Okhla Industrial Area, Phase II, New Delhi 110 020; tel. (11) 26387070; fax (11) 26383788; e-mail sterlingpublishers@airtelbroadband.in; internet www.sterlingpublishers.com; f. 1965; academic books on the humanities and social sciences, children's books, trade paperbacks; Chair. and Man. Dir S. K. GHAI; Dirs VIKAS GHAI, GAURAV GHAI.

Tata McGraw-Hill Publishing Co Ltd: 7 West Patel Nagar, New Delhi 110 008; tel. (11) 25882743; fax (11) 25885154; e-mail info_india@mcgraw-hill.com; internet www.tatamcgrawhill.com; f. 1970; engineering, computers, sciences, medicine, management, humanities, social sciences; Chair. Dr F. A. MEHTA; Man. Dir Dr N. SUBRAHMANYAM.

Vikas Publishing House (Pvt) Ltd: 576 Masjid Rd, Jangpura, New Delhi 110 014; tel. (11) 24376605; fax (11) 24370879; e-mail helpline@vikaspublishing.com; f. 1969; computers, management, commerce, sciences, engineering textbooks; Dir PIYUSH CHAWLA.

A. H. Wheeler & Co Ltd: 411 Surya Kiran Bldg, 19 K. G. Marg, New Delhi 110 001; tel. (11) 23312629; fax (11) 23357798; e-mail wheelerpub@mantraonline.com; f. 1958; textbooks, reference books, computer science and information technology, electronics, management, telecommunications, social sciences, etc.; Exec. Pres. ALOK BANERJEE.

CHENNAI (MADRAS)

Emerald Publishers: 15A Casa Major Rd, 1st Floor, Egmore, Chennai 600 008; tel. (44) 28193206; fax (44) 28192380; e-mail emeraldpublishers@touchtelindia.net; internet www.emeraldpublishers.com; self-help and general, college and university textbooks in English; CEO G. OLIVANNAN.

Eswar Press: Archana Arcade, 27 Natesan St, T. Nagar, Chennai 600 017; tel. (44) 52030431; fax (44) 24339590; e-mail gempeyes@md3.vsnl.net.in; science and technology; CEO M. PERIYASAMY.

Higginbothams Ltd: 814 Anna Salai, POB 311, Chennai 600 002; tel. (44) 28520640; fax (44) 28528101; e-mail higginbothams@vsnl.com; f. 1844; general; Dir S. CHANDRASEKHAR.

Minerva Publications: 6 Pycrofts Rd, 1st Floor, Triplicane, Chennai 600 005; tel. (44) 28445674; fax (44) 28445674; e-mail minerva@hathway.com; internet www.minervaa.com; children's books and dictionaries; CEO T. NAZIBUDEEN.

Premier Publishing (Pvt) Ltd: 47 Noor Veerasamy St, Nungambakkam, Chennai 600 034; tel. (44) 28222566; e-mail manahabi2002@hotmail.com; internet www.sambooks.com; business and management, health, religion, culture, etc.; Man. Dir S. HABIBULLAH.

Scitech Publications (India) (Pvt) Ltd: 7/3-C Madley Rd, T. Nagar, Chennai 600 017; tel. (44) 24328737; e-mail scitech@md5.vsnl.net.in; internet www.scitechpublications.com; science, technology, management, reference, etc.; Man. Dir M. R. PURUSHOTHAMAN.

Sura Books (Pvt) Ltd: 1620 J Block, 16th Main Rd, Anna Nagar, Chennai 600 040; tel. (44) 26161099; fax (44) 26162173; e-mail surabooks@eth.net; internet www.surabooks.com; children's books, dictionaries, examinations guides, tourist guides, Indology, etc.; Man. Dir V. K. SUBBURAJ.

T. R. Publications Pvt Ltd: PMG Complex, 2nd Floor, 57 South Usman Rd, T. Nagar, Chennai 600 017; tel. (44) 24340765; fax (44) 24348837; e-mail trpubs@md5.vsnl.net.in; internet www.trpublications.com; Chief Exec. S. GEETHA.

JAIPUR

Aavishkar Publishers, Distributors: 807 Vyas Bldg, Chaura Rasta, Jaipur 302 003; tel. (141) 2708286; fax (141) 2578159; e-mail aavishkarbooks@hotmail.com; internet www.pointerpublishers.com; f. 1984; general and reference books on humanities, arts, science, agriculture, environmental science, commerce; CEO PREM C. BAKLIWAL.

Mangal Deep Publications: Duggar Bldg, M. I. Rd, Jaipur 302 001; tel. (141) 2365086; fax (141) 5102022; e-mail mdpbk@sancharnet.net; humanities, social sciences, science, technology; Propr B. K. MANGAL.

Pointer Publishers: 807 Vyas Bldg, Chaura Rasta, Jaipur 302 003; tel. and fax (141) 2578159; e-mail pointerpub@hotmail.com; internet www.pointerpublishers.com; f. 1986; sciences, commerce, economics, education, literature, history, journalism, law, philosophy, psychology, sociology, tourism; in English and Hindi; Contact VIPIN JAIN.

Publication Scheme: C 12/13, 1st Floor, Ganga Mandir, Sansar Chandra Rd, Jaipur 302 001; tel. (141) 5104038; fax (141) 2376922; e-mail parampsj@datainfosys.net; internet www.pubscheme.com; social sciences, humanities, Ayurveda, Indology; Propr S. S. NATANI.

Rajasthan Hindi Granth Akademi: Plot No. 1, Jhalana Sansthani Shetra, Jaipur 302 004; tel. (141) 2711129; fax (141) 2710341; e-mail hindigranth@vsnl.net; internet www.rajhga.org; engineering, agriculture, science, social sciences, law, journalism; Dir SHAILENDRA JOSHI.

Shyam Prakashan: Film Colony, Chaura Rasta, Jaipur 302 003; tel. (141) 2317659; fax (141) 2326554; Propr OM PRAKASH AGARWAL.

University Book House (Pvt) Ltd: 79 Chaura Rasta, Jaipur 302 003; tel. (141) 2311466; fax (141) 2313382; e-mail uni_bookhouse@yahoo.com; commerce, management, home science, history, political science, public administration; Man. Dir CHETAN K. JAIN.

KOLKATA (CALCUTTA)

Academic Publishers: 12/1A Bankim Chatterjee St, POB 12341, Kolkata 700 073; tel. (33) 22414857; fax (33) 22413702; e-mail acabooks@cal.vsnl.net.in; f. 1958; textbooks, management, medical, technical; Man. Partner B. K. DHUR.

Advaita Ashrama: 5 Dehi Entally Rd, Kolkata 700 014; tel. (33) 22164000; e-mail advaita@vsnl.com; internet www.advaitaonline.com; f. 1899; religion, philosophy, spiritualism, Vedanta; publication centre of Ramakrishna Math and Ramakrishna Mission; Publication Man. Swami BODHASARANANDA.

Allied Book Agency: 18A Shyama Charan De St, Kolkata 700 073; general and academic; Dir B. SARKAR.

Ananda Publishers (Pvt) Ltd: 45 Beniatola Lane, Kolkata 700 009; tel. (33) 22414352; fax (33) 22193856; e-mail ananda@cal3.vsnl.net.in; internet www.anandapub.com; literature, general; Man. Dir S. MITRA.

Assam Review Publishing Co: 27A Waterloo St, 1st Floor, Kolkata 700 069; tel. (33) 22482251; fax (33) 22482251; e-mail assamrev@yahoo.co.in; f. 1926; publrs of The Assam Review and Tea News (monthly) and The Assam Directory and Tea Areas Handbook (annually); Chief Exec. GOBINDALAL BANERJEE.

Dev Sahitya Kutir: 21 Jhamapukur Lane, Kolkata 700 009; tel. (33) 22417406; children's, general; Dir PRABIR KUMAR MAJUMDAR.

Dey's Publishing: 13 Bankim Chatterjee St, Kolkata 700 073; tel. (33) 22412330; fax (33) 22192041; e-mail deyspublishing@hotmail.com; academic books, religion, philosophy, general; Dir SUDHANGSHU KUMAR DEY.

Eastern Law House (Pvt) Ltd: 54 Ganesh Chunder Ave, Kolkata 700 013; tel. (33) 22151989; fax (33) 22150491; e-mail elh@cal.vsnl.net.in; internet www.easternlawhouse.com; f. 1918; legal, commercial and accountancy; Dir ASOK DE; br. in New Delhi.

Firma KLM Private Ltd: 257B B. B. Ganguly St, Kolkata 700 012; tel. (33) 22374391; fax (33) 22217294; e-mail fklm@satyam.net.in; f. 1950; Indology, scholarly in English, Bengali, Sanskrit and Hindi, alternative medicine; Man. Dir S. MUKHERJI.

Indian Museum: 27 Jawaharlal Nehru Rd, Kolkata 700 016; tel. (33) 22499902; fax (33) 22495696; e-mail imbot@cal12.vsnl.net.in; internet www.indianmuseum-calcutta; social sciences and humanities; Dir S. K. CHAKRAVARTI.

Intertrade Publications (India) (Pvt) Ltd: 55 Gariahat Rd, POB 10210, Kolkata 700 019; f. 1954; economics, medicine, law, history and trade directories; Man. Dir Dr K. K. ROY.

A. Mukherjee and Co (Pvt) Ltd: 2 Bankim Chatterjee St, Kolkata 700 073; tel. (33) 22417406; fax (33) 27448172; f. 1940; educational and general in Bengali and English; Man. Dir RAJEEV NEOGI.

Naya Udyog: 206 Bidhan Sarani, Kolkata 700 006; tel. (33) 22413540; e-mail navudyog@vsnl.net; f. 1992; books in English and Bengali; agriculture, horticulture, social science, history,

INDIA

botany; distributes Naya Prokash publications; Man. Dir PARTHA SANKAR BASU.

New Age Publishers (Pvt) Ltd: 12B Bankim Chatterjee St, Kolkata 700 073; tel. (33) 22418509; e-mail newagepub@vsnl.net; literature, art, philosophy, history, social and cultural studies; Propr SHILADITYA.

Patra's Publication: 2 Shyamacharan Dey St, Kolkata 700 073; tel. (33) 22197297; e-mail manaspatra@vsnl.net; f. 1975; fiction, general; Propr PRAFULLA KUMAR PATRA.

Punthi Pustak: 136/4B Bidhan Sarani, Kolkata 700 004; tel. and fax (33) 25555573; e-mail info@punthipustak.com; f. 1956; religion, history, philosophy; Propr P. K. BHATTACHARYA.

Renaissance Publishers (Pvt) Ltd: 15 Bankim Chatterjee St, Kolkata 700 012; f. 1949; politics, philosophy, history; Man. Dir J. C. GOSWAMI.

Sahitya Sansad: 33 Acharya Prafulla Chandra Rd, Kolkata 700 009; tel. (33) 23507669; fax (33) 23603508; e-mail samsad@cal3.vsnl.net.in; children's, reference, science, literature, philosophy; Man. Dir DEBAJYOTI DUTTA.

Samya: 16 Southern Ave, Kolkata 700 026; tel. (33) 24660812; fax (33) 24644614; e-mail stree@cal2.vsnl.net.in; internet www.samyabooks.com; f. 1996; owned by joint partnership, Bhatkal and Sen; social change, culture and Dalit issues; Dir MANDIRA SEN.

Saraswati Library: 206 Bidhan Sarani, Kolkata 700 006; f. 1914; history, philosophy, religion, literature; Man. Partner B. BHATTACHARJEE.

M. C. Sarkar and Sons (Pvt) Ltd: 14 Bankim Chatterjee St, Kolkata 700 073; f. 1910; reference; Dir SAMIT SARKAR.

Seagull Books (Pvt) Ltd: 26 Circus Ave, Kolkata 700 017; tel. (33) 22403636; fax (33) 22805143; e-mail seagullfoundation@vsnl.com; internet www.seagullindia.com; academic, literary, general; CEO NAVIN KISHORE.

Stree-Samya: 16 Southern Ave, Kolkata 700 026; tel. (33) 24660812; fax (33) 24644614; e-mail stree@cal2.vsnl.net.in; internet www.streebooks.com; f. 1990 (Stree); 1996 (Samya); imprints publ. by joint venture of Harsha Bhatkal, Popular Prakashan and Mandira Sen; women's issues and writings in English and Bengali; Dir MANDIRA SEN.

Visva-Bharati: 6 Acharya Jagadish Bose Rd, Kolkata 700 017; tel. (33) 22479868; f. 1923; literature; Dir ASHOKE MUKHOPADHYAY.

MUMBAI (BOMBAY)

Bharatiya Vidya Bhavan: Munshi Sadan, Kulapati K. M. Munshi Marg, Mumbai 400 007; tel. (22) 24950916; fax (22) 23630058; e-mail brbhavan@bom7.vsnl.net.in; internet www.bhavans.info; f. 1938; art, literature, culture, education, philosophy, religion, history of India; various periodicals in English, Hindi, Sanskrit and other Indian languages; Pres. PRAVINCHANDRA V. GANDHI; Dir-Gen. DHIRU MEHTA.

Himalaya Publishing House: Dr Bhalerao Marg (Kelewadi), Girgaon, Mumbai 400 004; tel. (22) 23860170; fax (22) 23877178; e-mail himpub@vsnl.com; internet www.himpub.com; f. 1976; textbooks and research work; Publr MEENA PANDEY.

India Book House (Pvt) Ltd: 412 Tulsiani Chambers, Nariman Point, Mumbai 400 021; tel. (22) 22840165; fax (22) 22835099; e-mail info@ibhworld.com; internet www.ibhworld.com; Man. Dir DEEPAK MIRCHANDANI.

International Book House (Pvt) Ltd: Indian Mercantile Mansions (Extension), Madame Cama Rd, Mumbai 400 039; tel. (22) 22021634; fax (22) 22851109; e-mail ibh@vsnl.com; internet www.intbh.com; f. 1941; children's, general, educational, scientific, technical, engineering, social sciences, humanities and law; Dir ROHIT GUPTA; Dir SANJEEV GUPTA.

Jaico Publishing House: 127 Mahatma Gandhi Rd, opp. Mumbai University, Mumbai 400 023; tel. (22) 22676702; fax (22) 22656412; e-mail jaicowbd@vsnl.com; internet www.jaicobooks.com; f. 1947; general paperbacks, management, computer and engineering books, etc.; imports scientific, medical, technical and educational books; Man. Dir ASHWIN J. SHAH.

Popular Prakashan (Pvt) Ltd: 35C Pandit Madan Mohan Malaviya Marg, Tardeo, opp. Crossroads, Mumbai 400 034; tel. (22) 23265245; fax (22) 24945294; e-mail infor@popularprakashan.com; internet www.popularprakashan.com; f. 1968; sociology, biographies, religion, philosophy, fiction, arts, music, current affairs, medicine, history, politics and administration in English and Marathi; CEO HARSHA BHATKAL.

Sheth Publishing House: G-12 Suyog Industrial Estate, nr LBS Marg, Vikhroli (W), Mumbai 400 083; tel. (22) 25773707; fax (22) 25774200; e-mail no.sph@bom5.vsnl.net.in; educational, children's; Propr NILESH M. SHETH.

Somaiya Publications (Pvt) Ltd: 172 Mumbai Marathi Granthasangrahalaya Marg, Dadar, Mumbai 400 014; tel. (22) 24130230; fax (22) 22047297; e-mail somaiyabooks@rediffmail.com; internet www.somaiya.com; f. 1967; economics, sociology, history, politics, mathematics, sciences, language, literature, education, psychology, religion, philosophy, logic; Chair. Dr S. K. SOMAIYA.

Taraporevala, Sons and Co (Pvt) Ltd D.B.: 210 Dr Dadabhai Naoroji Rd, Fort, Mumbai 400 001; tel. (22) 22071433; f. 1864; Indian art, culture, history, sociology, scientific, technical and general in English; Chief Exec. R. J. TARAPOREVALA.

N. M. Tripathi (Pvt) Ltd: 164 Shamaldas Gandhi Marg, Mumbai 400 002; tel. (22) 22013651; e-mail mistertripathi@rediffmail.com; f. 1888; general in English and Gujarati; Chair. A. S. PANDYA; Man. Dir KARTIK R. TRIPATHI.

K. M. Varghese Co: Hind Rajasthan Bldg, Dada Saheb Phalke Rd, Dadar, Mumbai 400 014; tel. (22) 24149074; fax (22) 24146904; e-mail km@varghese.net; internet www.varghese.net; f. 1960; medicine, pharmacy, nursing, physiotherapy; Propr K. M. VARGHESE.

Vora Medical Publications: 6 Princess Bldg, E. R. Rd, Mumbai 400 003; tel. (22) 23754161; fax (22) 23704053; e-mail voramedpub@yahoo.co.in; medicine, nursing, management, spiritualism, general knowledge; Propr R. K. VORA.

OTHER TOWNS

Anada Prakashan (Pvt) Ltd: 1756 Gandhi Rd, Ahmedabad 380 001; tel. (79) 2169956; fax (79) 2139900; e-mail anadaad1@sancharnet.in; internet www.anada.com; children's, educational, dictionaries; Man. Dir B. R. ANADA.

Bharati Bhawan: Thakurbari Rd, Kadamkuan, Patna 800 003; tel. (612) 2671356; fax (612) 2670010; e-mail bbpdpat@sancharnet.in; f. 1942; educational and juvenile; Man. Partner TARIT KUMAR BOSE.

Bishen Singh Mahendra Pal Singh: 23A New Connaught Place, POB 137, Dehradun 248 001; tel. (135) 2715748; fax (135) 2715107; e-mail bsmps@vsnl.com; f. 1957; botany, forestry, agriculture; Dirs GAJENDRA SINGH GAHLOT, ABHIMANYU GAHLOT.

Books for Change: 139 Richmond Rd, Bangalore 560 025; tel. (80) 25321747; fax (80) 25586284; e-mail shoba.ram@actionaid.org; internet www.booksforchange.net; f. 1997; operated by ActionAid Karnataka Projects; pblr and distributor of books and other media relating to social issues; Publr and Chief Editor SHOBA RAMACHANDRAN.

Catholic Press: Ranchi 834 001; f. 1928; books and periodicals; Dir WILLIAM TIGGA.

DC Books: POB 214, DC Kizhakemuri Edam, Good Shepherd St, Kottayam 686 001; tel. (481) 2563114; fax (481) 2564758; e-mail ceo@dcbooks.com; internet www.dcbooks.com; f. 1974; fiction, general and reference books in Malayalam; CEO RAVI DEECEE.

Hind Pocket Books (Pvt) Ltd: B-13, Sector 81, Phase II, Noida 201305; tel. (120) 3093992; fax (120) 2563983; e-mail gbp@del2.vsnl.net.in; f. 1958; fiction and non-fiction paperbacks in English, Hindi, Punjabi, Malayalam and Urdu; Chair DINA NATH MALHOTRA; Man. Dir SHEKHAR MALHOTRA.

Indica Books: D-40/18 Godowlia, Varanasi 221 001; tel. (542) 3094999; fax (542) 2452258; e-mail indicabooks@satyam.net.in; internet www.indicabooks.com; Indology, philosophy, religion, culture; Propr DILIP KUMAR JAISWAL.

Jnan Bichitra: Jogendranagar, Vidyasagar Chowmuhani, Agartala, West Tripura 799 001; tel. (381) 2323781; e-mail jnanbichitra@rediffmail.com; f. 1976; general, science; Propr DEBANANDA DAM.

Kalyani Publishers: 1/1 Rajinder Nagar, Civil Lines, Ludhiana 141 008; tel. (161) 2745756; fax (161) 2745872; textbooks; Dir RAJ KUMAR.

Krishna Prakashan Media (P) Ltd: (Unit) Goel Publishing House, 11 Shivaji Rd, Meerut 250 001; tel. (121) 2644766; fax (121) 2645855; e-mail sk_kpm@yahoo.com; textbooks; Man. Dir SATYENDRA KUMAR RASTOGI; Dir ANITA RASTOGI.

Law Publishers: Sardar Patel Marg, Civil Lines, POB 1004, Allahabad 211 001; tel. (532) 2622758; fax (532) 2622781; e-mail lawpub@vsnl.com; internet www.law-publishers.com; f. 1929; legal texts in English; Dir NARESH SAGAR.

Macmillan India Ltd: 315/316 Raheja Chambers, 12 Museum Rd, Bangalore 560 001; tel. (80) 25594120; fax (80) 25588713; e-mail rberi@bgl.vsnl.net.in; internet www.macmillanindia.com; school and university books in English; general; Pres. and Man. Dir RAJIV BERI; Dir (Technical) DEBASHISH BANERJEE.

Madhuban Educational Books: A-22, Sector 4, Noida 201 301; tel. (120) 4078900; fax (120) 4078999; e-mail info@madhubunbooks.com; f. 1969; school books, children's books; Dir SAJILI SHIRODKAR.

Mapin Publishing (Pvt) Ltd: 10B Vidyanagar Society Part I, Usmanpura, Ahmedabad 380 014; tel. (79) 27545390; fax (79) 27545392; e-mail mapin@mapinpub.com; internet www.mapinpub.com; Indian art, architecture, archaeology, crafts and performing arts; Chair. MALLIKA SARABHAI.

Navajivan Publishing House: PO Navajivan, Ahmedabad 380 014; tel. (79) 7540635; f. 1919; Gandhiana and related social science; in English, Hindi and Gujarati; Man. Trustee JITENDRA DESAI; Sales Man. KAPIL RAWAL.

Neelkamal Publications (Pvt) Ltd: NN Complex, Hyderabad 500 095; tel. (40) 24757140; fax (40) 24757951; e-mail suresh@neelkamalpub.com; internet www.neelkamalpub.com; education, psychology, dictionaries, encyclopaedias; Man. Dir SURESH CHANDRA SHARMA.

Orient Longman (Pvt) Ltd: 3-6-752 Himayat Nagar, Hyderabad 500 029; tel. (40) 27665466; fax (40) 27645046; e-mail hyd2_orlongco@sancharnet.in; f. 1948; educational, technical, general and children's in English and almost all Indian languages; Chair. SHANTA RAMESHWAR RAO; Dirs Dr NANDINI RAO, J. KRISHNADEV RAO.

Parikalpana Prakashan: D-68 Nirala Nagar, Lucknow 226 010; tel. (522) 2786782; fax (11) 27296559; e-mail janchetna@rediffmail.com; f. 1996; fiction, poetry, literary criticism, history, political sciences, philosophy; Hindi and English; CEO KATYAYANI.

Pilgrims Publishing: Pilgrims Book House, B27/98-A-8 Nawabganj Rd, Durga Kund, Varanasi 221 001; tel. (542) 2314060; fax (542) 2314059; e-mail pilgrims@satyam.net.in; internet www.pilgrimsbooks.com; f. 1986; first edition and reprint books on Nepal, Tibet, India and the Himalayas; also operates Pilgrims Book House; Man. Editor CHRISTOPHER N. BURCHETT.

Publication Bureau: Panjab University, Chandigarh 160 014; tel. (172) 2541782; f. 1948; textbooks, academic and general; CEO DARSHAN SINGH; Man. H. R. GROVER.

Publication Bureau: Punjabi University, Patiala 147 002; tel. (175) 3046093; fax (175) 2283073; internet www.universitypunjabi.org; f. 1966; university-level text and reference books, and other general interest books; Punjabi, English and other languages; CEO Dr B. S. MANGAT.

Ram Prasad and Sons: Hospital Rd, Agra 282 003; tel. (562) 2461904; fax (562) 2460920; e-mail rpsons@sancharnet.in; f. 1905; agricultural, arts, history, commerce, education, general, computing, engineering, pure and applied science, economics, sociology; Dirs R. N, B. N, Y. N, RAVI AGARWAL; Man. S. N. AGARWAL; br. in Bhopal.

Sahitya Bhandar: 50 Chahchand Zero Rd, Allahabad 211 001; tel. (532) 2400787; Hindi literature, children's, science, literary criticism, etc.; Propr SATISH CHANDRA AGGARWAL.

Sahitya Bhawan Publications: Hospital Rd, Agra 282 003; tel. (562) 2151665; fax (562) 2151568; e-mail info@sbpagra.com; internet www.sbpagra.com; social sciences, humanities; Propr RAHUL BANSAL.

Sahitya Sangam: New 100, Lukerganj, Allahabad 211 001; Hindi literature, communication, journalism, political science, art, history, etc.; Propr ALOK CHATURVEDI.

Samvad Prakashan: I-499 Shastri Nagar, Meerut 250 004; tel. (121) 2764866; e-mail samvadindia@vsnl.net; Hindi translations of world literature; biographies, autobiographies, fiction, cinema; Propr NAMITA SRIVASTAVA.

Universities Press (India) (Pvt) Ltd: 3-6-752 Himayat Nagar, Hyderabad 500 029; tel. (40) 27662849; fax (40) 27645046; e-mail info@universitiespress.com; internet www.universitiespress.com; academic and educational books on science, technology, management; Man. Dir MADHU REDDY.

Vishwavidyalaya Prakashan: Vishalakshi Bldg, POB 1149, Chowk, Varanasi 221 001, Uttar Pradesh; tel. (542) 2413741; fax (542) 2413082; e-mail vvp@vsnl.com; internet www.vvpbooks.com; f. 1950; Hindu and Sanskrit literature, Indology, history, art and culture, spiritualism, religion, philosophy, education, sociology, psychology, music, journalism, mass communication, science and social science; Partner ANURAG KUMAR.

GOVERNMENT PUBLISHING HOUSE

Publications Division: Ministry of Information and Broadcasting, Govt of India, Patiala House, New Delhi 110 001; tel. and fax (11) 24366670; e-mail dpd@sb.nic.in; internet publicationsdivision.nic.in; f. 1941; culture, art, literature, planning and development, general; also 21 periodicals in English and 13 Indian languages; Dir VEENA JAIN.

PUBLISHERS' ASSOCIATIONS

Bombay Booksellers' and Publishers' Association: No. 25, 6th Floor, Bldg No. 3, Navjivan Commercial Premises Co-op Society Ltd, Dr Bhadkamkar Marg, Mumbai 400 008; tel. (22) 23088691; e-mail bbpassn@yahoo.co.in; f. 1961; 400 mems; Pres. K. M. VARGHESE; Hon. Gen. Sec. B. S. FERNANDES.

Delhi State Booksellers' and Publishers' Association: 3026/7-H Shiv Chowk, (South Patel Nagar) Ranjit Nagar, New Delhi 110 008; tel. (11) 25847377; fax (11) 25842605; e-mail rpnbooks@indiatimes.com; f. 1941; 400 mems; Pres. Dr S. K. BHATIA; Sec. K. K. SAXENA.

Federation of Educational Publishers in India: X-39, Institutional Area, Karkardoma, New Delhi 110 092; tel. (11) 22377017; f. 1987; 14 affiliated asscns; 150 life mems; 45 annual mems; Pres. R. K. GUPTA; Sec.-Gen. KAMAL ARORA.

Federation of Indian Publishers: Federation House, 18/1-C Institutional Area, nr JNU, New Delhi 110 067; tel. (11) 26964847; fax (11) 26864054; e-mail fipl@satyam.net.in; internet www.fiponweb.com; 18 affiliated asscns; 190 mems; Pres. ANAND BHUSHAN; Hon. Gen. Sec. SHAKTI MALIK.

Akhil Bharatiya Hindi Prakashak Sangh: 139, Purani Anarkali, Gali No. 4, Delhi 110 051; f. 1954; 400 mems; Pres. KRISHNAN DEV SHARMA; Gen. Sec. ARUN KUMAR SHARMA.

Akhil Bharatiya Marathi Prakashak Sangha: c/o Dilipraj Prakashan (Pvt) Ltd, 251-C, Shaniwar Peth, Pune 411 030; Pres. SHARAD GOGATE.

All Assam Publishers' and Booksellers' Association: Chancellor Bldg, H. B. Rd, Panbazar, Guwahati 781 001; tel. (361) 2634790; fax (361) 2513886; e-mail devchowdhurygp@rediffmail.com; Pres. GIRIPADA DEV CHOWDHURY; Sec. BIDYUT GUHA.

All India Urdu Publishers' and Booksellers' Association: 3243 Kuchatarachand, Daryaganj, New Delhi 110 002; tel. (11) 23257189; fax (11) 23265480; e-mail aakif@del3.vsnl.net.in; internet www.indiamart.com/aakifbooks; f. 1988; 175 mems; Pres. Dr KHALIQ ANJUM; Gen. Sec. S. M. ZAFAR ALI.

All Kerala Publishers' and Booksellers' Association: D. C. Kizhakemuri Edam, Good Shepherd St, Kottayam 686 001; tel. (481) 2563114; fax (481) 2564758; e-mail info@dcbooks.com; Pres. E. N. NANTHAKUMAR.

Booksellers' and Publishers' Association of South India: 8, 2nd Floor, Sun Plaza, G. N. Chetty Rd, Chennai 600 006; 251 mems; Pres. GANDHI KANNADASAN; Sec. R. S. SHANMUGAM.

Gujarati Publishers' Association: Navajivan Trust, PO Navajivan, Ahmedabad 380 014; tel. (79) 7540635; 125 mems; Pres. JITENDRA DESAI; Sec. K. N. MADRASI.

Karnataka Publishers' Association: c/o Ankita Pustaka, 53 Sham Singh Complex, Gandhi Bazar Main Rd, Bangalore 560 004; tel. (80) 26617100; Pres. Dr RAMAKANT JOSHI.

Orissa Publishers' and Booksellers' Association: Binodbihari, Cuttack 753 002; tel. (671) 2620637; f. 1973–74; 280 mems; Pres. PITAMBAR MISHRA; Sec. SUBHENDU SEKHAR RATHA.

Paschimbanga Prakasak Sabha: 206 Bidhan Sarani, Kolkata 700 006; tel. (33) 23506720; fax (33) 22413852; Pres. BIPLAB BHOWAL; Gen. Sec. SOMENATH MUKHERJEE.

Publishers' Association of West Bengal: 6-B, Ramanath Mazumder St, Kolkata 700 009; tel. (33) 2325580; 164 mems; Pres. MOHIT KUMAR BASU; Gen. Sec. SHANKARI BHUSAN NAYAK.

Publishers' and Booksellers' Association of Bengal: 93 Mahatma Gandhi Rd, Kolkata 700 007; tel. (33) 22411993; f. 1912; 4,500 mems; Pres. KHIMANGSHU BANDYOPADHYAY; Gen. Sec. CHITTA SINGHA ROY.

Punjabi Publishers' Association: Bazar Mai Sewan, Amritsar 143 006; tel. (183) 2545787; fax (183) 2543965; Pres. KULWANT SINGH SURI; Gen. Sec. PARAMJIT SINGH.

Vijayawada Publishers' Association: 27-1-68, Karl Marx Rd, Vijayawada 520 002; tel. (866) 2433353; fax (866) 2426348; 41 mems; Pres. DUPATI VIJAY KUMAR; Sec. U. N. YOGI.

Federation of Publishers' and Booksellers' Associations in India: 2nd Floor, 84 Daryaganj, New Delhi 110 002; tel. (11) 23272845; fax (11) 23281227; e-mail fpbai@vsnl.net; internet www.fpbai.org; f. 1955; 12 affiliated asscns; 507 mems; Pres. A. S. CHOWDHRY; Hon. Sec. BALDEV VERMA.

Publishers' and Booksellers' Guild: Guild House, 2B Jhamapukur Lane, Kolkata 700 009; tel. (33) 23544417; fax (33) 23604566; e-mail guild@cal2.vsnl.net.in; internet www.kolkatabookfaironline.com; f. 1975; 35 mems; organizes annual internationally recognized Kolkata Book Fair; Pres. JAYANT MANAKTALA; Hon. Gen. Sec. TRIDIB KR. CHATTERJEE.

UP Publishers' Association: Bharati Bhavan, Western Kutchery Rd, Meerut 250 001; Pres. RAJENDRA AGARWAL.

Broadcasting and Communications

TELECOMMUNICATIONS

Telecom Regulatory Authority of India (TRAI): Mahanagar Doorsanchar Bhavan (next to Zakir Hussain College), Jawaharlal Nehru Marg (Old Minto Rd), New Delhi 110 002; tel. (11) 23211934; fax (11) 23213294; e-mail trai@del2.vsnl.net.in; internet www.trai

INDIA
Directory

.gov.in; f. 1998; Chair. NRIPENDRA MISRA; Vice-Chair. BAL KRISHAN ZUTSHI.

Bharat Sanchar Nigam Ltd (BSNL): Statesman House, B-148, Barakhamba Rd, New Delhi 110 001; fax (11) 23765296; internet www.bsnl.co.in; f. 2000; fmrly Dept of Telecom Operations; state-owned; Chair. and Man. Dir ANIL K. SINHA.

Bharti Airtel Ltd: Quatab Ambience, H-5/12, Mehrauli Rd, New Delhi 110 030; tel. (11) 51666000; fax (11) 51666011; e-mail gupta_n@bhartient.com; internet www.bhartiairtel.in; f. 1998; India's first privately owned telephone network; Chair. and Man. Dir SUNIL BHARTI MITTAL.

Ericsson India Pvt Ltd: Ericsson Forum, DLF Cyberciti, Sector 25A, 60 Mtr. Sector Rd, Gurgaon 122 002; tel. (124) 2560808; fax (124) 2565454; e-mail marketing-int.communications@eci.ericsson.se; internet www.ericsson.co.in; Man. Dir JAN CAMPBELL.

Hutchison Essar Ltd (Hutch): Hutch House, Peninsula Corporate Park, Ganpatrao Kadam Marg, Lower Parel, Mumbai 400 013; tel. (22) 66645000; fax (22) 66661222; e-mail isaac.d@hutch.in; internet www.hutch.in; f. 1994; Vodafone (United Kingdom) acquired controlling 67% share from Hutchison Telecommunications International (Hong Kong) in Feb. 2007, 33 % owned by Essar Group; CEO ARUN SARIN.

Idea Cellular: Sharada Centre, 11/1, Erandwane, off Karve Rd, Pune 411 004; tel. (20) 24123123; fax (20) 24123999; e-mail carson.dalton@ideacellular.com; internet www.ideacellular.com; f. 2001; provides mobile telephony services in seven states; CEO VIKRAM MEHMI.

ITI (Indian Telephone Industries) Ltd: F29 Ground Floor, Doorvaninagar, Bangalore 560 016; tel. (80) 255660527; fax (80) 25660521; e-mail dgm_swr@itiltd.co.in; internet www.itiltd-india.com; f. 1948; mfrs of all types of telecommunication equipment, incl. telephones, automatic exchanges and long-distance transmission equipment; also produces optical fibre equipment and microwave equipment; will manufacture all ground communication equipment for the 22 earth stations of the Indian National Satellite; in conjunction with the Post and Telegraph Department, a newly designed 2,000-line exchange has been completed; Chair. and Man. Dir Y. K. PANDEY.

Mahanagar Telephone Nigam Ltd (MTNL): Jeevan Bharati Tower 1, 124 Connaught Circus, New Delhi 110 001; tel. (11) 23742212; fax (11) 23314243; e-mail cmd@bol.net.in; internet www.mtnl.net.in; f. 1986; 56% state-owned; owns and operates telecommunications and information technology services in Mumbai and Delhi; Chair. and Man. Dir R. S. P. SINHA.

Reliance Infocomm Ltd: Dhirunhai Ambani Knowledge City, Navi Mumbai 400 709; tel. (22) 30373333; e-mail customercare@relianceinfo.com; internet www.relianceinfo.com; f. 1999; provides mobile and fixed-line telephony services throughout India; Chair. and Man. Dir ANIL D. AMBANI.

Tata Teleservices Ltd: Ispat House, B. G. Kher Marg, Worli, Mumbai 400 018; tel. (22) 56615445; fax (22) 4605517; internet www.tataindicom.com; f. 1996; privately owned telecommunications services provider; Chair. RATAN N. TATA; CEO DARRYL GREEN.

Videsh Sanchar Nigam Ltd (VSNL): Lok Manya Videsh Sanchar Bhawan, Kasinath Dhuru Marg, Prabhadevi, Mumbai 400 028; tel. (22) 66578765; fax (22) 24365689; e-mail helpdesk@giaspn01.vsnl.net.in; internet www.vsnl.com; f. 1986; 26% state-owned; 45% owned by the Tata Group; Chair. SUBODH BHARGAVA.

BROADCASTING

Prasar Bharati (Broadcasting Corpn of India): 2nd Floor, PTI Bldg, Sansad Marg, New Delhi 110 001; tel. (11) 23737603; fax (11) 23352549; e-mail kssarma@prasarbharati.org.in; f. 1997; autonomous body; oversees operations of state-owned radio and television services; Chair. M. V. KAMATH; CEO K. S. SARMA.

Radio

All India Radio (AIR): Akashvani Bhavan, Parliament St, New Delhi 110 001; tel. (11) 23710300; fax (11) 23421956; e-mail dgair@air.org.in; internet allindiaradio.org; broadcasting is controlled by the Ministry of Information and Broadcasting and is primarily govt-financed; operates a network of 208 stations and 332 transmitters (grouped into four zones—north, south, east and west), covering almost the entire population and over 90% of the total area of the country; Dir-Gen. BRIJESHWAR SINGH.

The News Services Division of AIR, centralized in New Delhi, is one of the largest news organizations in the world. It has 45 regional news units, which broadcast 364 bulletins daily in 24 languages and 38 dialects. Eighty-four bulletins in 19 languages are broadcast in the Home Services, 187 regional bulletins in 65 languages and dialects, and 64 bulletins in 25 languages in the External Services.

Television

Doordarshan India (Television India): Mandi House, Doordarshan Bhavan, Copernicus Marg, New Delhi 110 001; tel. (11) 23385958; fax (11) 23386507; e-mail webadmin@dd.nic.in; internet www.ddindia.gov.in; f. 1976; broadcasting is controlled by the Ministry of Information and Broadcasting and is govt-financed; programmes: 280 hours weekly; 5 all-India channels, 11 regional language satellite channels, 5 state networks and 1 international channel; Dir-Gen. NAVEEN KUMAR.

By March 2005 78% of the country's area and 90% of the population were covered by the television network. There were 1,314 transmitters in operation, and 56 studio centres and 23 satellite channels had been established.

Finance

(cap. = capital; p.u. = paid up; res = reserves; dep. = deposits;
m. = million; brs = branches; amounts in rupees unless otherwise stated)

BANKING

State Banks

Reserve Bank of India: Central Office Bldg, Shahid Bhagat Singh Rd, POB 10007, Mumbai 400 001; tel. (22) 22661602; fax (22) 22658269; e-mail helpprd@rbi.org.in; internet www.rbi.org.in; f. 1934; nationalized 1949; sole bank of issue; cap. 50m., res 65,000m., dep. 1,883,189m. (June 2006); Gov. Y. VENUGOPAL REDDY; Dep. Govs Dr RAKESH MOHAN, V. LEELADHAR, SHYAMALA GOPINATH, USHA THORAT; 4 offices and 14 brs.

State Bank of India: Corporate Centre, Madame Cama Rd, POB 10121, Mumbai 400 021; tel. (22) 22022426; fax (22) 22851391; e-mail gm.gbu@sbi.co.in; internet www.statebankofindia.com; f. 1955; cap. p.u. 5,263.0m., res 307,719.2m., dep. 4,752,244.2m. (March 2007); 7 associates, 7 domestic subsidiaries/affiliates, 3 foreign subsidiaries, 4 jt ventures abroad; Chair. O. P. BHATT; Man. Dirs T. S. BHATTACHARYA, S. K. BHATTACHARYYA; 9,593 brs (incl. 52 overseas brs and rep. offices in 34 countries).

State-owned Commercial Banks

Fourteen of India's major commercial banks were nationalized in 1969 and a further six in 1980. They are managed by 15-member boards of directors (two directors to be appointed by the central Government, one employee director, one representing employees who are not workmen, one representing depositors, three representing farmers, workers, artisans, etc., five representing persons with special knowledge or experience, one Reserve Bank of India official and one Government of India official). The Department of Banking of the Ministry of Finance controls all banking operations.

There were 66,644 branches of public-sector and other commercial banks in June 2003.

Aggregate deposits of all scheduled commercial banks amounted to an estimated Rs 19,406,940m. in December 2005.

Allahabad Bank: 2 Netaji Subhas Rd, Kolkata 700 001; tel. (33) 22208668; fax (33) 22488323; e-mail cmd@allahabadbank.co.in; internet www.allahabadbank.com; f. 1865; nationalized 1969; cap. p.u. 4,467.0m., res 39,276.3m., dep. 598,008.1m. (March 2007); Chair. and Man. Dir AVINASH CHANDER MAHAJAN; Exec. Dir SUBODH KUMAR GOEL; 1,935 brs.

Andhra Bank: Andhra Bank Bldgs, Saifabad, 5-9-11 Secretariat Rd, Hyderabad 500 004; tel. (40) 23230001; fax (40) 23211050; e-mail customerser@andhrabank.co.in; internet www.andhrabank.in; f. 1923; nationalized 1980; cap. 4,850.0m., res 23,327.5m., dep. 346,930.1m. (March 2006); Chair. and Man. Dir Dr K. RAMAKRISHNAN; Exec. Dir KALYAN MUKHERJEE; 1,100 brs and 113 extension counters.

Bank of Baroda: Baroda Corporate Centre, C-26, G Block, Bandra-Kurla Complex, Bandra (East), Mumbai 400 054; tel. (22) 26985000; fax (22) 22610341; e-mail secbob@bol.net.in; internet www.bankofbaroda.com; f. 1908; nationalized 1969; merged with Benares State Bank in 2002; cap. 3,655.3m., surplus and res 82,844.1m., dep. 1,249,159.8m. (March 2007); Chair. and Man. Dir ANIL K. KHANDELWAL; Exec. Dir A. C. MAHJAN; 2,641 brs in India, 38 brs overseas.

Bank of India: Star House, C-5, G Block, 3rd Floor, Bandra-Kurla Complex, Bandra (East), Mumbai 400 051; tel. (22) 66684444; fax (22) 56684558; e-mail hocsd@bankofindia.co.in; internet www.bankofindia.com; f. 1906; nationalized 1969; cap. 4,881.4m., res 48,654.7m., dep. 1,265,025.6m. (March 2007); Chair. and Man. Dir T. S. NARAYANASAMI; 2,562 brs in India, 19 brs overseas.

Bank of Maharashtra: 'Lokmangal', 1501 Shivajinagar, Pune 411 005; tel. (20) 25532731; fax (20) 25533246; e-mail bomcocmd@vsnl.com; internet www.maharashtrabank.com; f. 1935; nationalized

1969; cap. 4,305.2m., surplus and res 13,113.7m., dep. 339,193.4m. (March 2007); Chair. and Man. Dir S. C. BASU; 1,291 brs.

Canara Bank: 112 Jayachamarajendra Rd, POB 6648, Bangalore 560 002; tel. (80) 22223118; fax (80) 22223168; e-mail canbank@blr.vsnl.net.in; internet www.canbankindia.com; f. 1906; nationalized 1969; cap. 4,100.0m., res and surplus 99,439.9m., dep. 1,439,558.0m. (March 2007); Chair. and Man. Dir M. B. N. RAO; Exec. Dir ALOK KUMAR MISRA; 2,512 brs.

Central Bank of India: Chandermukhi, Nariman Point, Mumbai 400 021; tel. (22) 66387777; fax (22) 22044336; e-mail cbicpp@b01.net.in; internet www.centralbankofindia.co.in; f. 1911; nationalized 1969; cap. 11,241.4m., res and surplus 23,178.2m., dep. 664,826.5m. (March 2006); Chair. and Man. Dir HOMAI A. DARUWALLA; 3,130 brs.

Corporation Bank: Mangaladevi Temple Rd, POB 88, Mangalore 575 001; tel. (824) 2426416; fax (824) 2444617; e-mail corpho@corpbank.com; internet www.corpbank.com; f. 1906; nationalized 1980; cap. 1,434.4m., res 22,267.6m., dep. 231,909.3m. (March 2004); Chair. and Man. Dir B. SAMBAMURTHY; Exec. Dir P. K. GUPTA; 617 brs.

Dena Bank: C-10, G Block, Bandra-Kurla Complex, Bandra (East), Mumbai 400 051; tel. (22) 26545607; fax (22) 26545605; e-mail akk@denabank.co.in; internet www.denabank.com; f. 1938 as Devkaran Nanjee Banking Co Ltd; nationalized 1969; cap. 2,868.2m., res and surplus 12,095.8m., dep. 276,899.1m. (March 2007); Chair. and Man. Dir P. L. GAIROLA; Exec. Dir U. S. KOHLI; 1,122 brs.

Indian Bank: 31 Rajaji Salai, POB 1866, Chennai 600 001; tel. (44) 25233231; fax (44) 25231278; e-mail indianbank@vsnl.com; internet www.indian-bank.com; f. 1907; nationalized 1969; cap. 7,438.2m., res and surplus 17,475.8m., dep. 408,055.0m. (March 2006); Chair. and Man. Dir M. S. SUNDARA RAJAN; 1,376 brs.

Indian Overseas Bank: 763 Anna Salai, POB 3765, Chennai 600 002; tel. (44) 28524212; fax (44) 28523595; e-mail iobmail@vsnl.com; internet www.iob.com; f. 1937; nationalized 1969; cap. 5,448.0m., res and surplus 34,455.7m., dep. 716,366.4m. (March 2007); Chair. and Man. Dir T. S. NARAYANASAMI; Exec. Dir A. V. DUGADE; 1,496 brs.

Oriental Bank of Commerce: Harsha Bhavan, E Block, Connaught Place, POB 329, New Delhi 110 001; tel. (11) 23323444; fax (11) 23321514; e-mail bdncmd@obcindia.com; internet www.obcindia.co.in; f. 1943; nationalized 1980; cap. 2,505.4m., res 59,493.6m., dep. 639,959.7m. (March 2007); Chair. and Man. Dir K. N. PRITHVIRAJ; Exec. Dir ALLEN C. A. PEREIRA; 1,130 brs.

Punjab and Sind Bank: Bank House, 21 Rajendra Place, New Delhi 110 008; tel. (11) 25768831; fax (11) 25752501; internet www.psbindia.com; f. 1908; nationalized 1980; cap. 7,430.6m., res and surplus 6,626.3m., dep. 195,238.3m. (March 2007); Chair. and Man. Dir R. P. SINGH; Exec. Dir G. S. MATTA; 866 brs.

Punjab National Bank: 7 Bhikaiji Cama Place, Africa Ave, New Delhi 110 066; tel. (11) 26102303; fax (11) 26196456; e-mail cmd@pnb.co.in; internet www.pnbindia.com; f. 1895; nationalized 1969; merged with New Bank of India in 1993; cap. 3,153.0m., res 101,046.4m., dep. 1,418,085.3m. (March 2007); Chair. and Man. Dir K. C. CHAKRABARTY; Exec. Dirs K. RAGHURAMAN, J. M. GARG; 4,487 brs.

Syndicate Bank: POB 1, Manipal 576 119; tel. (825) 2571181; fax (825) 2570266; e-mail idcb@syndicatebank.com; internet www.syndicatebank.com; f. 1925 as Canara Industrial and Banking Syndicate Ltd; name changed as above 1964; nationalized 1969; cap. 5,219.7m., res 23,116.5m., dep. 539,674.5m. (March 2006); Chair. C. P. SWARNKAR; Exec. Dir GEORGE JOSEPH; 1,963 brs.

UCO Bank: 10 Biplabi Trailokya Maharaj Sarani (Brabourne Rd), POB 2455, Kolkata 700 001; tel. (33) 22254120; fax (33) 22253986; e-mail ucobank@vsnl.net; internet www.ucobank.com; f. 1943 as United Commercial Bank Ltd; nationalized 1969; name changed as above 1985; cap. 7,993.6m., res 14,574.6m., dep. 673,258.7m. (March 2007); Chair. and Man. Dir S. K. GOEL; Exec. Dir V. K. DHINGRA; 1,849 brs.

Union Bank of India: Union Bank Bhavan, 239 Vidhan Bhavan Marg, Nariman Point, Mumbai 400 021; tel. (22) 22024647; fax (22) 22025238; e-mail ibd@unionbankofindia.com; internet www.unionbankofindia.co.in; f. 1919; nationalized 1969; cap. 5,051.2m., res 46,842.7m., dep. 893,957.5m. (March 2007); Chair. and Man. Dir M. V. NAIR; 2,023 brs.

United Bank of India: 16 Old Court House St, Kolkata 700 001; tel. (33) 2487471; fax (33) 2485852; e-mail homail@unitedbank.co.in; internet www.unitedbankofindia.com; f. 1950; nationalized 1969; cap. 15,324.3m., res and surplus 8,828.6m., dep. 375,663.8m. (March 2007); Chair. and Man. Dir P. K. GUPTA; Exec. Dir T. M. BHASIN; 1,354 brs.

Vijaya Bank: 41/2 Mahatma Gandhi Rd, Bangalore 560 001; tel. (80) 25584066; fax (80) 25598040; e-mail ibd@vijayabank.co.in; internet www.vijayabank.com; f. 1931; nationalized 1980; cap. 4,335.2m., res and surplus 12,356.3m., dep. 282,251.1m. (March 2006); Chair. and Man. Dir PRAKASH P. MALLYA; Exec. Dir T. VALLIAPPAN; 932 brs.

Principal Private Banks

The Bank of Rajasthan Ltd: C-3 Sardar Patel Marg, Jaipur 302 001; tel. (141) 2381222; fax (141) 2381123; e-mail p&d@rajbank.com; internet www.bankofrajasthan.com; f. 1943; cap. 1,075.7m., res and surplus 2,550.8m., dep. 89,023.3m. (March 2006); Chair. PRAVIN KUMAR TAYAL; Man. Dir and CEO B. M. SHARMA; 430 brs.

Bharat Overseas Bank Ltd: Habeeb Towers, 196 Anna Salai, Chennai 600 002; tel. (44) 28522983; fax (44) 28524700; e-mail help@bharatoverseasbank.com; internet www.boblonline.com; f. 1973; cap. 157.5m., res 1,826.4m., dep. 27,492.4m. (March 2005); Chair. and CEO G. KRISHNA MURTHY; Gen. Man. G. CHANDRAN; 77 brs.

Bombay Mercantile Co-operative Bank Ltd: 78 Mohammed Ali Rd, Mumbai 400 003; tel. (22) 23425961; fax (22) 23433385; e-mail bmcb@bom5.vsnl.net.in; f. 1939; cap. 213.8m., res 3,365.6m., dep. 16,889.4m. (March 2006); Chair. M. RAHMAN; Man. Dir S. U. PATHAN; 52 brs.

The Catholic Syrian Bank Ltd: St Mary's College Rd, POB 502, Trichur 680 020; tel. (487) 2333020; fax (487) 2333435; e-mail chairman@csb.co.in; internet www.csb.co.in; f. 1920; cap. 107.1m., res 2,048.6m., dep. 42,891.6m. (March 2006); Chair. and CEO R. VENKATARAMAN; Gen. Man. V. P. ISWARDAS; 297 brs.

Centurion Bank of Punjab Ltd: 1201 Raheja Centre, Free Press Journal Marg, Nariman Point, Mumbai 400 021; tel. (22) 22047234; fax (22) 22845860; e-mail cblho@bom3.vsnl.net.in; internet www.centurionbop.co.in; f. 1995; fmrly Centurion Bank Ltd; name changed as above following merger with Bank of Punjab in 2005; cap. 1,566.9m., res and surplus 12,149.0m., dep. 157,946.1m. (March 2007); Chair. RANA TALWAR; Man. Dir and CEO SHAILENDRA BHANDARI.

City Union Bank Ltd: 149 TSR (Big) St, Kumbakonam 612 001; tel. (435) 2432322; fax (435) 2431746; e-mail cubco_kmb@sancharnet.in; internet www.cityunionbank.com; f. 1904; cap. 252.0m., res 3,404.4m., dep. 47,192.2m. (March 2007); Chair. S. BALASUBRAMANIAN; Exec. Dir N. KAMAKODI; 125 brs.

The Federal Bank Ltd: Federal Towers, POB 103, Alwaye 683 101; tel. (484) 2623620; fax (484) 2621687; e-mail fbl@federalbank.co.in; internet www.federal-bank.com; f. 1931; cap. 856.0m., res 11,509.2m., dep. 184,892.3m. (March 2006); Chair. M. VENUGOPALAN; 520 brs.

HDFC Bank: HDFC Bank House, Senapati Bapat Marg, Lower Parel, Mumbai, 400 013; tel. (22) 66521185; fax (22) 24960696; internet www.hdfcbank.com; announced plans to merge with Centurion Bank of Punjab in Feb. 2008; cap. 3,193.9m., res and surplus 61,137.6m., dep. 682,979.4m. (March 2007); Man. Dir ADITYA PURI; 744 brs.

ICICI Bank Ltd: ICICI Towers, 4th Floor, South Tower, Bandra-Kurla Complex, Bandra (East), Mumbai 400 051; tel. (22) 26531414; fax (22) 26531167; e-mail info@icicibank.com; internet www.icicibank.com; f. 1994; cap. 12,398.3m., res 210,227.2m., dep. 1,650,831.7m. (March 2006); Man. Dir K. V. KAMATH; Chair. N. VAGHUL; 348 brs.

IndusInd Bank Ltd: IndusInd House, 425 Dadasaheb Bhadkamkar Marg, Lamington Rd, nr Opera House, Mumbai 400 004; tel. (22) 23859901; fax (22) 23859913; e-mail glob@indusind; internet www.indusind.com; f. 1994; cap. 2,905.1m., res 3,896.6m., dep. 155,412.5m. (March 2006); Chair. R. J. SAHANEY; Man. Dir BHASKAR GHOSE; 77 brs.

ING Vysya Bank Ltd: 22 M. G. Rd, Bangalore 560 001; tel. (80) 25005000; fax (80) 22272220; e-mail ingvysyabank@ingvysyabank.com; internet www.ingvysyabank.com; f. 1930; cap. 909.0m., res 9,939.5m., dep. 162,621.4m. (March 2007); Man. Dir and CEO VAUGHN NIGEL RICTOR; 404 brs.

Jammu and Kashmir Bank Ltd: Corporate Headquarters, M. A. Rd, Srinagar 190 001; tel. (194) 2481930; fax (194) 2481923; e-mail jkbcosgr@jkbmail.com; internet jkbank.net; f. 1938; cap. p.u. 484.9m., res and surplus 19,602.4m., dep. 258,144.8m. (March 2007); Chair. Dr HASEEB A. DRABU; Exec. Dir ABDUL RAUF FAZILI; 462 brs.

The Karnataka Bank Ltd: POB 716, Kodialbail, Mangalore 575 003; tel. (824) 2228222; fax (824) 2225588; e-mail info@ktkbank.com; internet www.ktkbankltd.com; f. 1924; cap. 1,213.5m., res 11,172.5m., dep. 140,374.4m. (March 2007); Chair. and CEO ANANTHAKRISHNA; 370 brs.

The Karur Vysya Bank Ltd: Erode Rd, POB 21, Karur 639 002; tel. (4324) 226520; fax (4324) 225700; e-mail kvbcopdd@sancharnet.in; internet www.kvb.co.in; f. 1916; cap. 494.9m., res 10,123.3m., dep. 95,688.2m. (March 2007); Chair. P. T. KUPPUSWAMY; 222 brs.

Lakshmi Vilas Bank Ltd: Kathaparai, Salem Rd, POB 2, Karur 639 006; tel. (4324) 220051; fax (4324) 220068; e-mail info@lvbank.com; internet www.lvbank.com; f. 1926; cap. 195.3m., res 2,711.5m., dep. 43,416.8m. (March 2006); Chair. and CEO R. M. NAYAK; 234 brs.

The Sangli Bank Ltd: Rajwada Chowk, POB 158, Sangli 416 416; tel. (233) 2623611; fax (233) 2620666; e-mail san_sanbank@sancharnet.in; internet www.sangli-bank.com; f. 1916; cap. p.u. 204.1m., res 560m., dep. 16,777.6m. (March 2003); Chair. and CEO A. R. BORDE; Gen. Man. S. R. GODBOLE; 178 brs.

The South Indian Bank Ltd: SIB House, Mission Quarters, Thrissur 680 001; tel. (487) 2420020; fax (487) 2442021; e-mail sib@vsnl.com; internet www.southindianbank.com; f. 1929; cap. 704.1m., res 5,639.7m., dep. 95,793.8m. (March 2006); Man. Dir and CEO V. S. REDDY; 450 brs.

Tamilnad Mercantile Bank Ltd: 57 Victoria Extension Rd, Tuticorin 628 002; tel. (461) 2321932; fax (461) 2322994; e-mail ttn_tmbankhi@sancharnet.in; internet www.tmb.in; f. 1921 as Nadar Bank; name changed as above 1962; cap. 2.8m., surplus res 6,565.0m., dep. 52,260.1m. (March 2006); Chair. M. G. M MARAN; 173 brs.

Banking Organizations

Indian Banks' Association: Unit Nos 1, 2 and 4, 6th Floor, Centre I Bldg, World Trade Centre Complex, Cuffe Parade, Mumbai 400 005; tel. (22) 22844999; fax (22) 22835638; e-mail webmaster@iba.org.in; internet www.iba.org.in; 156 mems; Chair. V. P. SHETTY; Chief Exec. H. N. SINOR.

Indian Institute of Banking and Finance: 'The Arcade', World Trade Centre Complex, 2nd Floor, East Wing, Cuffe Parade, Mumbai 400 005; tel. (22) 22187003; fax (22) 22185147; e-mail iibgen@bom5.vsnl.net.in; internet www.iibf.org.in; f. 1928; 343,202 mems; Pres. K. CHERIAN VARGHESE; CEO R. BHASKARAN; four zonal offices.

National Institute of Bank Management: NIBM Post Office, Kondhwe Khurd, Pune 411 048; tel. (20) 26833080; fax (20) 26834478; e-mail director@nibmindia.org; internet www.nibmindia.org; f. 1969; Chair. Dr Y. V. REDDY; Dir Dr ASHISH SAHA.

DEVELOPMENT FINANCE ORGANIZATIONS

Agricultural Finance Corporation Ltd: Dhanraj Mahal, 1st Floor, Chhatrapati Shivaji Maharaj Marg, Mumbai 400 001; tel. (22) 22028924; fax (22) 22028966; e-mail afcl@vsnl.com; internet www.afcindia.com; f. 1968 by a consortium of 45 public- and private-sector commercial banks including development finance institutions to help increase the flow of investment and credit into agriculture and rural development projects; provides project consultancy services to commercial banks, Union and state govts, public-sector corpns, the World Bank, the ADB, FAO, the International Fund for Agricultural Development and other institutions and to individuals; undertakes techno-economic and investment surveys in agriculture and agro-industries etc.; publishes quarterly journal Financing Agriculture; three regional offices and nine br. offices; cap. p.u. 150m., res and surplus 20.5m. (March 2001); Chair. Y. C. NANDA; Man. Dir A. K. GARG.

Export-Import Bank of India: Centre One Bldg, Floor 21, World Trade Centre Complex, Cuffe Parade, Mumbai 400 005; tel. (22) 22185272; fax (22) 22182572; e-mail eximcord@vsnl.com; internet www.eximbankindia.com; f. 1982; cap. 8,499.9m., res 16,625.0m., dep. 22,023.1m. (March 2005); Chair. and Man. Dir T. C. VENKAT SUBRAMANIAN; Exec. Dirs R. M. V. RAMAN, S. SRIDHAR; 14 offices worldwide.

Housing Development Finance Corpn Ltd (HDFC): Ramon House, 169 Backbay Reclamation, Churchgate, Mumbai 400 020; tel. (22) 22836255; fax (22) 22046758; e-mail info@hdfc.com; internet www.hdfc.com; f. 1977; provides loans to individuals and corporate bodies; cap. p.u. 2,466.1m., res 36,471.8m., dep. 93,376.5m. (March 2004); Chair. DEEPAK S. PAREKH; Man. Dir KEKI M. MISTRY; 173 brs (incl. one overseas br).

Industrial Development Bank of India (IDBI): IDBI Tower, World Trade Centre Complex, Cuffe Parade, Mumbai 400 005; tel. (22) 56553355; fax (22) 22181294; internet www.idbi.com; f. 1964; reorg. 1976; 72.1% govt-owned; merged with The United Western Bank Ltd in 2006; provides direct finance, refinance of industrial loans and bills, finance to large- and medium-sized industries, extends financial services, such as merchant banking and forex services, to the corporate sector; cap. 7,238m., res and surplus 56,744m., dep. 26,009m. (March 2006); Chair. and Man. Dir V. P. SHETTY; five zonal offices and 36 br. offices.

  Small Industries Development Bank of India: 10/10 Madan Mohan Malviya Marg, Lucknow 226 001; tel. (522) 2209517; fax (522) 2209514; e-mail snairan@sidbi.com; internet www.sidbi.com; f. 1990; wholly owned subsidiary of Industrial Development Bank of India; promotes, finances and develops small-scale industries; cap. p.u. 4,500m., res 24,240m. (March 2000); Chair. and Man. Dir N. BALASUBRAMANIAN; 39 offices.

Industrial Finance Corpn of India Ltd: IFCI Tower, 61 Nehru Place, New Delhi 110 020; tel. (11) 26384909; fax (11) 26384907; e-mail helpdesk@ifciltd.com; internet www.ifciltd.com; f. 1948 to provide medium- and long-term finance to cos and co-operative socs in India, engaged in manufacture, preservation or processing of goods, shipping, mining, hotels and power generation and distribution; promotes industrialization of less developed areas, and sponsors training in management techniques and development banking; cap. p.u. 10,679.5m., res 4,697m. (March 2003); Chair. M. B. MUTHU; CEO R. M. MALLA; 11 regional offices and six other offices.

Industrial Investment Bank of India: 19 Netaji Subhas Rd, Kolkata 700 001; tel. (33) 22209941; fax (33) 22208049; e-mail iibiho@vsnl.com; internet www.iibiltd.com; Chair. and Man. Dir Dr B. SAMAL (acting).

National Bank for Agriculture and Rural Development: Plot no. C-24, G Block, Bandra-Kurla Complex, Bandra (East), Mumbai 400 051; tel. (22) 26539060; fax (22) 26539399; e-mail nabrmd@vsnl.net; internet www.nabard.org; f. 1982 to provide credit for agricultural and rural development through commercial, co-operative and regional rural banks; cap. p.u. 20,000m., res 52,910m. (March 2004); held 50% each by the cen. Govt and the Reserve Bank; Man. Dir Y. S. P. THORAT; Chair. RANJANA KUMAR; 28 regional offices, 10 sub-office and six training establishments.

STOCK EXCHANGES

There are 23 stock exchanges (with a total of more than 9,985 listed companies) in India, including:

National Stock Exchange of India Ltd: Exchange Plaza, Bandra-Kurla Complex, Bandra (East), Mumbai 400 051; tel. (22) 26598100; fax (22) 26598120; e-mail cc_nse@nse.co.in; internet www.nseindia.com; f. 1994; New York Stock Exchange, Goldman Sachs, General Atlantic (all of the USA) and SoftBank Asian Infrastructure Fund (Hong Kong) each acquired a 5% share in Jan. 2007; Chair. S. B. MATHUR; Man. Dir RAVI NARAIN.

Ahmedabad Stock Exchange: Kamdhenu Complex, opp. Sahajanand College, Panjarapole, Ambawadi, Ahmedabad 380 015; tel. (79) 26307971; fax (79) 26308877; e-mail cosec@aseindia.org; internet www.aseindia.org; f. 1894; 2,000 mems; Administrator P. K. GHOSH; Exec. Dir V. V. RAO.

Bangalore Stock Exchange Ltd: 51 Stock Exchange Towers, 1st Cross, J. C. Rd, Bangalore 560 027; tel. (80) 22995234; fax (80) 22995242; e-mail edbgse@giasbg01.vsnl.net.in; 234 mems; Pres. JAGDISH V. AHUJA; Exec. Dir K. KAMALA.

Bombay Stock Exchange: Phiroze Jeejeebhoy Towers, 25th Floor, Dalal St, Fort, Mumbai 400 001; tel. (22) 22721233; fax (22) 22721919; e-mail info@bseindia.com; internet www.bseindia.com; f. 1875; 4,482 listed cos; Chair. JAGDISH CAPOOR; Man. Dir. and CEO RAJNIKANT PATEL; Sec. VISHVESH BHAGAT.

Calcutta Stock Exchange Association Ltd: 7 Lyons Range, Kolkata 700 001; tel. (33) 22104470; fax (33) 22104486; e-mail secretary@cse.india.com; internet www.cse-india.com; f. 1908; 917 mems; Sec. P. K. RAY.

Delhi Stock Exchange Association Ltd: DSE House, 3/1 Asaf Ali Rd, New Delhi 110 002; tel. (11) 23292182; fax (11) 23292174; e-mail admin@dseindia.org.in; internet www.dseindia.org.in; f. 1947; some 3,000 listed cos (March 2007); Exec. Dir P. K. SINGHAL.

Ludhiana Stock Exchange Association Ltd: Firoze Gandhi Market, Ludhiana 141 001; tel. (161) 2412318; fax (161) 2401645; e-mail lse@satyam.net.in; internet lse.co.in; f. 1981; 292 mems; Chair. DINA RATH SHARMA; Gen. Man. H. S. SIDHU.

Madras Stock Exchange Ltd: Exchange Bldg, 30 Second Line Beach, POB 183, Chennai 600 001; tel. (44) 25228951; fax (44) 25244897; e-mail mseed@vsnl.com; f. 1760; 158 mems; Exec. Dir R. K. PILLAI.

Mangalore Stock Exchange: Rama Bhavan Complex, 4th Floor, Kodialbail, Mangalore 575 003; tel. (824) 2440581; fax (824) 2440736; 146 mems; Pres. RAMESH RAI; Exec. Dir UMESH P. MASKERI.

Thiruvananthapuram Stock Exchange: Thiruvananthapuram; Dir JOSE JOHN.

Uttar Pradesh Stock Exchange Association Ltd: Padam Towers, 14/113 Civil Lines, Kanpur 208 001; tel. (512) 2293115; fax (512) 2293175; e-mail upse@vsnl.net.in; 540 mems; Pres. R. K. AGARWAL; Exec. Dir Dr J. N. GUPTA.

The other recognized stock exchanges are: Hyderabad, Madhya Pradesh (Indore), Kochi, Pune, Guwahati, Jaipur, Bhubaneswar (Orissa), Coimbatore, Saurashtra, Meerut, Vadodara and Magadh (Patna).

INSURANCE

In January 1973 all Indian and foreign insurance companies were nationalized. The general insurance business in India is now transacted by only four companies, subsidiaries of the General Insurance Corpn of India, formed under the 1972 General Insurance Business Nationalisation Act. The Insurance Regulatory Development Authority Bill, approved by the legislature in December 1999, established a regulatory authority for the insurance sector and henceforth permitted up to 26% investment by foreign companies in new domestic, private-sector insurance companies.

General Insurance Corpn of India (GIC): 'Suraksha', 170 J. Tata Rd, Churchgate, Mumbai 400 020; tel. (22) 22833046; fax (22) 22855423; e-mail pcghosh@gicofindia.com; internet www.gicofindia.com; f. 1973 by the reorg. of 107 private non-life insurance cos (incl. brs of foreign cos operating in the country) as the four subsidiaries listed below; Chair. R. K. JOSHI; Man. Dir P. B. RAMANUJAN.

National Insurance Co Ltd: 3 Middleton St, Kolkata 700 071; tel. (33) 22831705; fax (33) 22831740; e-mail website .administrator@nic.co.in; internet www.nationalinsuranceindia.com; Chair. and Man. Dir V. RAMASAAMY; 19 regional offices, 254 divisional offices and 690 branch offices.

New India Assurance Co Ltd: New India Assurance Bldg, 87 Mahatma Gandhi Rd, Fort, Mumbai 400 001; tel. (22) 22674617; fax (22) 22652811; e-mail cmd.nia@newindia.co.in; internet www.newindia.co.in; f. 1919; 26 regional offices, 393 divisional offices, 703 branch offices and 37 overseas offices; Chair. and Man. Dir B. CHAKRABARTI.

The Oriental Insurance Co Ltd: Oriental House, A-25/27 Asaf Ali Rd, New Delhi 110 002; tel. (11) 23279221; fax (11) 23263175; e-mail slmohan@oriental.nic.in; internet www.orientalinsurance.nic.in; Chair. and Man. Dir RAMADASS.

United India Insurance Co Ltd: 24 Whites Rd, Chennai 600 014; tel. (44) 28520161; fax (44) 28525280; e-mail knb@united.nic.in; internet www.united.nic.in; Chair. and Man. Dir MAHINDER KUMAR GARG.

Life Insurance Corpn of India (LIC): 'Yogakshema', Jeevan Bima Marg, Mumbai 400 021; tel. (22) 22021645; fax (22) 22810680; e-mail chairman@licindia.com; internet www.licindia.com; f. 1956; controls all life insurance business; Chair. A. K. SHUKLA; Man. Dirs T. S. VIJAYAN, D. K. MEHROTRA; 100 divisional offices, 2,048 brs and three overseas offices.

Trade and Industry

GOVERNMENT AGENCIES AND DEVELOPMENT ORGANIZATIONS

Coal India Ltd: 10 Netaji Subhas Rd, Kolkata 700 001; tel. (33) 22488099; fax (33) 22435316; e-mail cil@wb.nic.in; internet www.coalindia.nic.in; cen. govt holding co with eight subsidiaries; responsible for almost total (more than 90%) exploration for, planning and production of coal mines; owns 467 coal mines throughout India; marketing of coal and its products; cap. p.u. Rs 72,205.4m., res and surplus Rs 21,324.9m. (March 2002), sales Rs 258,029m. (2004/05); Chair. PARTHA S. BHATTACHARYYA; 462,000 employees (2005).

Cotton Corpn of India Ltd: Plot No. 3A, Sector No. 10, CBD Belapur, Navi Mumbai 400 614; tel. (22) 27579217; fax (22) 27576030; e-mail headoffice@cotcorp.com; internet www.cotcorp.gov.in; f. 1970 as an agency in the public sector for the purchase, sale and distribution of home-produced cotton and imported cotton staple fibre; exports long staple cotton; cap. p.u. Rs 250m., res and surplus Rs 2,159.7m. (March 2002), sales Rs 14,627.7m. (2004/05); Chair. and Man. Dir SUBHASH C. GROVER.

Export Credit Guarantee Corpn of India Ltd: Express Towers, 10th Floor, Nariman Point, Mumbai 400 021; tel. (22) 22845471; fax (22) 22045253; e-mail webmaster@ecgcindia.com; internet www.ecgcindia.com; f. 1957 to insure for risks involved in exports on credit terms and to supplement credit facilities by issuing guarantees, etc.; cap. Rs 3,900m., res Rs 4,079.3m. (March 2002); Chair. and Man. Dir P. K. DASH; 29 brs.

Fertilizer Corpn of India Ltd: PDIL Bhavan, A-14, 5th Floor, Sector 1, Noida 201 301, Uttar Pradesh; tel. (120) 2530023; fax (120) 2537612; e-mail fci@fci.hub.nic.in; internet fertcorpindia.nic.in; f. 1961; fertilizer factories at Sindri (Jharkhand), Gorakhpur (Uttar Pradesh), Talcher (Orissa) and Ramagundam (Andhra Pradesh), producing nitrogenous and some industrial products; production suspended at all factories since 2002; cap. Rs 7,547.3m., sales Rs 1,262m. (March 2002); Gen. Man. K. L. RAO.

Food Corpn of India: DDA Complex, Ground Floor, Rajendra Pl., Rajendra Bhavan, New Delhi 110 008; tel. (11) 25710962; fax (11) 25750670; e-mail rgm@fcidelhiro.in; internet www.fciweb.nic.in; f. 1965 to undertake trading in food grains on a commercial scale but within the framework of an overall govt policy; to provide farmers an assured price for their produce; to supply food grains to the consumer at reasonable prices; also purchases, stores, distributes and sells food grains and other foodstuffs and arranges imports and handling of food grains and fertilizers at the ports; distributes sugar in a number of states and has set up rice mills; cap. p.u. Rs 23,245m., sales Rs 315,562.2m. (March 2002); Man. Dir Dr P. C. RAM; 59,800 employees (2002).

Handicrafts and Handlooms Exports Corpn of India Ltd: Jawahar Vyapar Bhavan Annexe, 5th Floor, 1 Tolstoy Marg, New Delhi 110 001; tel. (11) 23701086; fax (11) 23701051; e-mail hhecnd@eth.net; internet www.hhecworld.com; f. 1958; govt undertaking dealing in export of handicrafts, handloom goods, ready-to-wear clothes, carpets, jute, leather and precious jewellery, and import of bullion and raw silk; promotes exports and trade development; cap. p.u. Rs 138.2m., res and surplus Rs 91.8m., sales Rs 3,339.4m. (March 2002); Chair. and Man. Dir K. K. SINHA.

Housing and Urban Development Corpn Ltd: HUDCO Bhavan, India Habitat Centre, Lodhi Rd, New Delhi 110 003; tel. (11) 24649610; fax (11) 24625308; e-mail hudco@hudco.org; internet www.hudco.org; f. 1970 to finance and undertake housing and urban development programmes including the establishment of new or satellite towns and building material industries; cap. p.u. Rs 20,019.0m., res Rs 17,735.0m., sales Rs 37,359.9m. (Jan. 2007); 21 brs; Chair. and Man. Dir T. PRABAKARAN; Sec. M. K. GUPTA.

India Trade Promotion Organisation (ITPO): Pragati Bhavan, Pragati Maidan, Lal Bahadur Shastri Marg, New Delhi 110 001; tel. (11) 23371540; fax (11) 23371492; e-mail info@itpo-online.com; internet www.indiatradefair.com; f. 1992 following merger; promotes selective development of exports of high quality products; arranges investment in export-orientated ventures undertaken by India with foreign collaboration; organizes trade fairs; operates Trade Information Centre; cap. p.u. Rs 2.5m., res and surplus Rs 2,311.8m., sales Rs 818.4m. (March 2002); regional offices in Bangalore, Mumbai, Kolkata and Chennai, and international offices in Frankfurt, New York, Moscow, São Paulo and Tokyo; Chair. and Man. Dir N. N. KHANNA; Exec. Dir RAJIV YADAV.

Jute Corpn of India Ltd: 15-N, Nellie Sengupta Sarani, 7th Floor, Kolkata 700 087; tel. (33) 22166770; fax (33) 22166771; e-mail feedback@jutecorp.com; internet www.jutecorp.com; f. 1971; objects: (i) to undertake price support operations in respect of raw jute; (ii) to ensure remunerative prices to producers through efficient marketing; (iii) to operate a buffer stock to stabilize raw jute prices; (iv) to handle the import and export of raw jute; (v) to promote the export of jute goods; cap. p.u. Rs 50m., sales Rs 576.0m. (March 2002); Chair. and Man. Dir R. C. TEWARI.

Minerals and Metals Trading Corpn of India Ltd (MMTC): Scope Complex, Core-1, 7 Institutional Areas, Lodhi Rd, New Delhi 110 003; tel. (11) 24362200; fax (11) 24360724; e-mail cpmr@mmtclimited.com; internet www.mmtclimited.com; f. 1963; export of iron and manganese ore, ferro-manganese, finished stainless steel products, engineering, agricultural and marine products, textiles, leather items, chemicals and pharmaceuticals, mica, coal and other minor minerals; import of steel, non-ferrous metals, rough diamonds, fertilizers, etc. for supply to industrial units in the country; cap. p.u. Rs 500m., sales Rs 62,546.8m. (March 2003); res Rs 6,348.0m. (March 2004); 13 regional offices in India; foreign offices in Japan, the Republic of Korea, Jordan and Romania; Chair. and Man. Dir SANJIV BATRA; 2,378 employees (2002).

National Co-operative Development Corpn: 4 Siri Institutional Area, Hauz Khas, New Delhi 110 016; tel. (11) 26569246; fax (11) 26962370; e-mail editor@ncdc.stpn.soft.net; f. 1963 to plan, promote and finance country-wide programmes through co-operative societies for the production, processing, marketing, storage, export and import of agricultural produce, foodstuffs and notified commodities and minor forest produce; also programmes for the development of poultry, dairy, fish products, coir, handlooms, distribution of consumer articles in rural areas, industrial and service co-operatives, water conservation work, irrigation, micro-irrigation, animal care, health, disease prevention, agricultural insurance and credit, rural sanitation etc.; 18 regional directorates; Pres. SHARAD PAWAR; Man. Dir P. UMA SHANKAR.

National Industrial Development Corpn Ltd: Chanakya Bhavan, Africa Ave, New Delhi 110 021; tel. (11) 24670153; fax (11) 26876166; e-mail nidc123@del2.vsnl.net.in; f. 1954; consultative engineering, management and infrastructure services to cen. and state govts, public and private sector enterprises, the UN and overseas investors; cap. p.u. Rs 18.7m. (March 2002); Chair. and Man. Dir PRANAB GHOSH.

National Mineral Development Corpn Ltd: Khanij Bhavan, 10-3-311/A Castle Hills, Masab Tank, POB 1352, Hyderabad 500 028; tel. (40) 23538713; fax (40) 23538711; e-mail hois@nmdc.co.in; internet www.nmdc.co.in; f. 1958; cen. govt undertaking; to exploit minerals (excluding coal, atomic minerals, lignite, petroleum and natural gas) in public sector; may buy, take on lease or otherwise acquire mines for prospecting, development and exploitation; iron ore mines at Bailadila-11C, Bailadila-14 and Bailadila-5 in Madhya Pradesh, and at Donimalai in Karnataka State; new 5m. metric ton iron ore mine under construction at Bailadila-10/11A; diamond mines at Panna in Madhya Pradesh; research and development laboratories and consultancy services covering all aspects of mineral

INDIA

Directory

exploitation at Hyderabad; investigates mineral projects; cap. p.u. Rs 1,321.6m., res and surplus Rs 18,932m., sales Rs 14,536.9m. (March 2004); Chair. and Man. Dir B. RAMESH KUMAR.

National Productivity Council: Utpadakta Bhavan, 5–6 Institutional Area, Lodhi Rd, New Delhi 110 003; tel. (11) 24690331; fax (11) 24615002; e-mail info@npcindia.org; internet www.npcindia.org; f. 1958 to increase productivity and to improve quality by improved techniques which aim at efficient and proper utilization of available resources; autonomous body representing national orgs of employers and labour, govt ministries, professional orgs, local productivity councils, small-scale industries and other interests; 13 regional professional management groups, one training institute; 75 mems; Chair. Dr AJAY DUA; Dir-Gen. N. A. VISWANATHAN.

National Research Development Corpn: 20–22 Zamroodpur Community Centre, Kailash Colony Extension, New Delhi 110 048; tel. (11) 29240401; fax (11) 29240409; e-mail write2@nrdcindia.com; internet www.nrdcindia.com; f. 1953 to stimulate development and commercial exploitation of new inventions with financial and technical aid; finances development projects to set up demonstration units in collaboration with industry; exports technology; cap. p.u. Rs 44.2m., res and surplus Rs 47.6m. (March 2002); Chair. and Man. Dir SOMENATH GHOSH.

National Seeds Corpn Ltd: Beej Bhavan, Pusa, New Delhi 110 012; tel. (11) 25846292; fax (11) 25846462; e-mail nsc@vsnl.com; internet www.indiaseeds.com; f. 1963 to improve and develop the seed industry; cap. p.u. Rs 206.2m., res and surplus Rs 216.1m., sales Rs 658.5m. (March 2002); Chair. and Man. Dir R. S. PANDEY.

National Small Industries Corpn Ltd: NSIC Bhavan, Okhla Industrial Estate, New Delhi 110 020; tel. (11) 26926275; fax (11) 26926820; e-mail pro@nsic.co.in; internet www.nsic.co.in; f. 1955 to aid, advise, finance and promote the interests of small industries; establishes and supplies machinery for small industries in other developing countries on turn-key basis; cap. p.u. Rs 1,679.9m., res and surplus Rs 87.2m., sales Rs 1,851m. (March 2002); all shares held by the Govt; Chair. and Man. Dir H. P. KUMAR.

PEC Ltd: 'Hansalaya', 15 Barakhamba Rd, New Delhi 110 001; tel. (11) 23314723; fax (11) 23314797; e-mail pec@peclimited.com; internet www.peclimited.com; f. 1971; export of engineering, industrial and railway equipment; undertakes turn-key and other projects and management consultancy abroad; countertrade, trading in agrocommodities, construction materials (steel, cement, clinkers, etc.) and fertilizers; cap. p.u. Rs 15m., res and surplus Rs 245.6m., sales Rs 22,499.9m. (March 2002); sales Rs 58,500.0m. (March 2004); Chair. and Man. Dir A. K. SRIVASTAVA.

Rehabilitation Industries Corpn Ltd: Kolkata; tel. (33) 22441185; fax (33) 22451055; f. 1959 to create employment opportunities through multi-product industries, ranging from consumer goods to engineering products and services, for refugees from Bangladesh and migrants from Pakistan, repatriates from Myanmar and Sri Lanka, and other immigrants of Indian extraction; cap. p.u. Rs 47.6m. (March 2000); Chair. and Man. Dir ASHOK BASU.

State Farms Corpn of India Ltd: Farm Bhavan, 14–15 Nehru Place, New Delhi 110 019; tel. (11) 26446903; fax (11) 26226898; e-mail sfci@vsnl.net; internet sfci.nic.in; f. 1969 to administer the central state farms; activities include the production of quality seeds of high-yielding varieties of wheat, paddy, maize, bajra and jowar; advises on soil conservation, reclamation and development of waste and forest land; consultancy services on farm mechanization; auth. cap. Rs 241.9m., res and surplus Rs 371.0m., sales Rs 465.4m. (March 2002); Chair. and Man. Dir Brig. S. P. MEHLA.

State Trading Corpn of India Ltd: Jawahar Vyapar Bhavan, Tolstoy Marg, New Delhi 110 001; tel. (11) 23701100; fax (11) 23701123; e-mail co.stc@nic.in; internet stc.gov.in; f. 1956; govt undertaking dealing in exports and imports; cap. p.u. Rs 300m., res and surplus Rs 2,628m., sales Rs 83,487.5m. (March 2004); sales Rs 71,240.0m. (March 2006); 10 regional brs, five sub-brs and one office overseas; Chair. and Man. Dir Dr ARVIND PANDALAI; 1,069 employees (2002).

Steel Authority of India Ltd (SAIL): Ispat Bhavan, Lodhi Rd, POB 3049, New Delhi 110 003; tel. (11) 24367481; fax (11) 24367015; e-mail sail.co@vsnl.com; internet www.sail.co.in; f. 1973 to provide co-ordinated development of the steel industry in the public sector; integrated steel plants at Bhilai, Bokaro, Durgapur, Rourkela; stainless and alloy steel plants at Chhattisgarh, West Bengal, Orissa, Jharkhand, Tamil Nadu and Karnataka; subsidiary co Maharashtra Elektrosmelt Ltd (Maharashtra); five jt venture power and steel-related cos, with sixth proposed at mid-2007; subsidiaries: Bhilai Oxygen Ltd (Chhattisgarh), Indian Iron and Steel Co (West Bengal)86% govt-ownedMaharashtra Elektrosmelt Ltd; combined crude steel capacity is 12m. metric tons annually; equity cap. Rs 41,304m., res and surplus Rs 9,072.7m., sales Rs 248,773.1m. (March 2004); Chair. S. K. ROONGTA; 131,910 employees (March 2004).

Tea Board of India: 14 B. T. M. Sarani (Brabourne Rd), POB 2172, Kolkata 700 001; tel. (33) 2251411; fax (33) 2251417; provides financial assistance to tea research stations; sponsors and finances independent research projects in universities and tech. institutions to supplement the work of tea research establishments; also promotes tea production and export; Chair. N. K. DAS.

CHAMBERS OF COMMERCE

Associated Chambers of Commerce and Industry of India (ASSOCHAM): 1 Community Centre, Zamrudpur Kailash Colony, New Delhi 110 048; tel. (11) 46550555; fax (11) 46536481; e-mail assocham@nic.in; internet www.assocham.org; f. 1920; central org. of 350 chambers of commerce and industry and industrial asscns representing more than 100,000 cos throughout India; five promoter chambers, 115 ordinary mems, 45 patron mems and 500 corporate associates; Pres. VENUGOPAL N. DHOOT; Sec.-Gen. D. S. RAWAT.

Federation of Indian Chambers of Commerce and Industry (FICCI): Federation House, Tansen Marg, New Delhi 110 001; tel. (11) 23738760; fax (11) 23320714; e-mail ficci@ficci.com; internet www.ficci.com; f. 1927; more than 1,500 corporate mems, 500 chamber of commerce and business asscn mems; Pres. HABIL KHORAKIWALA; Sec.-Gen. Dr AMIT MITRA.

ICC India: Federation House, Tansen Marg, New Delhi 110 001; tel. (11) 23322472; fax (11) 23320714; e-mail iccindia@iccindiaonline.org; internet www.iccindiaonline.org; f. 1929; 43 org. mems, 375 corporate mems, eight patron mems, 130 cttee mems; Pres. SAROJ KUMAR PODDAR; Exec. Dir ASHOK UMMAT.

Associated Chambers of Commerce and Industry of Uttar Pradesh: 2/210 Vikas Khand, Gomti Nagar, POB 17, Lucknow 226 010; tel. (522) 2301957; fax (522) 2301958; e-mail asochmup@yahoo.com; internet www.asochamup.org; 405 mems; Pres. IRSHAD MIRZA; Sec.-Gen. S. B. AGRAWAL.

Bengal Chamber of Commerce and Industry: 6 Netaji Subhas Rd, Kolkata 700 001; tel. (33) 22203733; fax (33) 22301289; e-mail bencham@bengalchamber.com; internet www.bengalchamber.com; f. 1853; more than 220 mems; Pres. S. RADHAKRISHNAN; Vice-Pres. SUPRIYA DAS GUPTA.

Bengal National Chamber of Commerce and Industry: BNCCI House, 23 Sir R. N. Mukherjee Rd, Kolkata 700 001; tel. (33) 22482951; fax (33) 22487058; e-mail bncci@bncci.com; internet www.bncci.com; f. 1887; 500 mems, 35 affiliated industrial and trading asscns; Pres. SHANTA GHOSH; Sec. D. P. NAG.

Bharat Chamber of Commerce: 9 Park Mansions, 2nd Floor, 57-A Park Street, Kolkata, 700 016; tel. (33) 22299591; fax (33) 22294947; e-mail bcc@cal2.vsnl.net.in; internet www.bharatcham.com; f. 1900; c. 500 mems. Pres. P. R. AGARWALA; Sec. K. SARMA.

Bihar Chamber of Commerce: Khem Chand Chaudhary Marg, POB 71, Patna 800 001; tel. (612) 2670535; fax (612) 2689505; e-mail bcc_chamber@rediffmail.com; f. 1926; 552 ordinary mems; Pres. S. K. CHOUDHARY; Sec.-Gen. RAJA BABU GUPTA.

Bombay Chamber of Commerce and Industry: Mackinnon Mackenzie Bldg, 4 Shoorji Vallabhdas Rd, Ballard Estate, POB 473, Mumbai 400 001; tel. (22) 22614681; fax (22) 22621213; e-mail bcci@bombaychamber.com; internet www.bombaychamber.com; f. 1836; 935 ordinary mems, 650 assoc. mems, 75 hon. mems; Pres. ASHOK WADHWA; Exec. Dir L. A. D'SOUZA.

Calcutta Chamber of Commerce: 18H Park St, Stephen Court, Kolkata 700 071; tel. (33) 22298236; fax (33) 22298961; e-mail calchamb@cal3.vsnl.net.in; internet www.calcuttachamber.com; 300 mems; Pres. H. V. PATODIA; Vice-Pres. ALKA BANGUR.

Chamber of Commerce and Industry (Regd): OB 31, Rail Head Complex, Jammu 180 012; tel. (191) 2472266; fax (191) 2472255; 1,069 mems; Pres. RAM SAHAI; Sec.-Gen. RAJENDRA MOTIAL.

Cochin Chamber of Commerce and Industry: Bristow Rd, Willingdon Island, POB 503, Kochi 682 003; tel. (484) 2668349; fax (484) 2668651; e-mail cochinchamber@eth.net; internet www.cochinchamber.org; f. 1857; 206 mems; Pres. JOSE DOMINIC; Sec. EAPEN KALAPURAKAL.

Federation of Andhra Pradesh Chambers of Commerce and Industry: Federation House, 11-6-841, Red Hills, POB 14, Hyderabad 500 004; tel. (40) 23393658; fax (40) 23393712; e-mail info@fapcci.in; internet www.fapcci.in; f. 1917; 2,674 mems; Pres. ATLURI SUBBA RAO; Sec. G. HEMALATA.

Federation of Karnataka Chambers of Commerce and Industry: Federation House, Dempegowda Rd, POB 9996, Bangalore 560 009; tel. (80) 22262355; fax (80) 22251826; e-mail fkcci@blr.vsnl.net.in; internet www.fkcci.org; f. 1916; 2,100 mems; Pres. R. C. PUROHIT; Sec. C. MANOHAR.

Federation of Madhya Pradesh Chambers of Commerce and Industry: Udyog Bhavan, 129A Malviya Nagar, Bhopal 462 003; tel. (755) 2573612; fax (755) 2551451; e-mail fmcci@bom6.vsnl.net.in; f. 1975; 500 ordinary mems, 58 asscn mems; Pres. PRAFULLA K. MAHESHWARI.

INDIA

Goa Chamber of Commerce and Industry: Narayan Rajaram Bandekar Bhavan, Rua de Ormuz, POB 59, Panaji 403 001; tel. (832) 2422635; fax (832) 2425560; e-mail goachamber@gmail.com; internet www.goachamber.org; f. 1908 as Associacao Commercial da India Portuguesa; more than 500 mems; Pres. NITIN KUNKOLIENKER; Dir-Gen. Air Cmmdre (retd) P. K. PINTO.

Gujarat Chamber of Commerce and Industry: Shri Ambica Mills, Gujarat Chamber Bldg, Ashram Rd, POB 4045, Ahmedabad 380 009; tel. (79) 26582301; fax (79) 26587992; e-mail gcci@gujaratchamber.org; internet www.gujaratchamber.org; f. 1949; 7,713 mems; Pres. PARU M. JAYAKRISHNA; Sr Vice-Pres. KAUSHIK D. SHAH.

Indian Chamber of Commerce: ICC Towers, 4 India Exchange Place, Kolkata 700 001; tel. (33) 22203242; fax (33) 22213377; e-mail info@indianchamber.org; internet www.indianchamber.org; f. 1925; 500 corporate group mems, more than 1,200 mem. cos; Pres. S. K. BANGUR; Sec.-Gen. Dr RAJEEV SINGH.

Indian Chamber of Commerce and Industry: 49 Community Centre, New Friends Colony, New Delhi 110 065; tel. (11) 26836468; fax (11) 26840775; e-mail iccind@yahoo.co.in; internet www.iccinewdelhi.com; f. 1987; Pres. LALIT K. MODI; Sec.-Gen. R. P. SWAMI.

Indian Merchants' Chamber: IMC Bldg, IMC Marg, Churchgate, Mumbai 400 020; tel. (22) 22046633; fax (22) 22048508; e-mail imc@imcnet.org; internet www.imcnet.org; f. 1907; 185 asscn mems, 2,915 mem. firms; Pres. NIRAJ BAJAJ; Sec.-Gen. P. N. MOGRE.

Karnataka Chamber of Commerce and Industry: G. Mahadevappa Karnataka Chamber Bldg, Jayachamaraj Nagar, Hubli 580 020; tel. (836) 2218234; fax (836) 2360933; e-mail kccihble@sify.net; internet www.kccihubli.org; f. 1928; 2,500 mems; Pres. SHANKARANNA I. MUNAVALLI; Hon. Sec. MAHENDRA LADHAD.

Madhya Pradesh Chamber of Commerce and Industry: Chamber Bhavan, Sanatan Dharam Mandir Marg, Gwalior 474 009; tel. (751) 2332916; fax (751) 2323844; e-mail info@mpcci.com; internet www.mpcci.com; f. 1906; 1,705 mems; Pres. G. D. LADHA; Hon. Sec. VIJAY GOYAL.

Madras Chamber of Commerce and Industry: Karumuttu Centre, 634 Anna Salai, Chennai 600 035; tel. (44) 24349452; fax (44) 24349164; e-mail mascham@md3.vsnl.net.in; internet www.mascham.com; f. 1836; 375 mem. firms, 20 affiliated, 10 hon., three others; Pres. ARUN BEWOOR; Sec.-Gen. R. SUBRAMANIAN.

Maharashtra Chamber of Commerce, Industry and Agriculture: Oricon House, 6th Floor, 12 K. Dubhash Marg, Fort, Mumbai 400 001; tel. (22) 22855859; fax (22) 22855861; e-mail maharashtrachamber@vsnl.com; internet www.maccia.org.in; f. 1927; more than 3,500 mems; more than 800 affiliated trade asscns and professional bodies; Pres. HEMANT RATHI; Sec.-Gen. SHRIKANT SARDESHPANDE.

Mahratta Chamber of Commerce, Industries and Agriculture: MCCIA Trade Tower, 505, A-Wing, ICC Complex, 403 Senapati Pabat Rd, Pune 411 016; tel. (20) 24440371; fax (20) 24447902; e-mail info@mcciapune.com; internet www.mcciapune.com; f. 1934; more than 2,000 mems; Pres. MADHUR BAJAJ; Additional Dir-Gen. Cdre SUBODH PUROHIT.

Merchants' Chamber of Commerce: 15B Hemanta Basu Sarani, Kolkata 700 001; tel. (33) 22483123; fax (33) 22488657; e-mail mercham@cal.vsnl.net.in; internet www.mercham.org; f. 1901; 600 mems; Pres. ADITYA VARDHAN AGARWAL; Dir-Gen. R. K. SEN.

Merchants' Chamber of Uttar Pradesh: 14/76 Civil Lines, Kanpur 208 001; tel. and fax (512) 2530877; fax (512) 2531306; e-mail info@merchantschamber-up.com; internet www.merchantschamber-up.com; f. 1932; 200 mems; Pres. JWALA PRASAD AGRAWAL; Sec. A. K. SINHA.

North India Chamber of Commerce and Industry: 9 Gandhi Rd, Dehra Dun; tel. (935) 223479; f. 1967; 105 ordinary mems, 29 asscn mems, seven mem. firms, 91 assoc. mems; Pres. DEV PANDHI; Hon. Sec. ASHOK K. NARANG.

Oriental Chamber of Commerce: 6A Dr Rajendra Prasad Sarani (Clive Row), Kolkata 700 001; tel. (33) 22302120; fax (33) 22303609; e-mail orientchamb@vsnl.net; f. 1932; 245 ordinary mems, three assoc. mems; Pres. SAMAR MOHAN SAHA; Sec. Kazi ABU ZOBER.

PHD Chamber of Commerce and Industry (PHDCCI): PHD House, 4/2 Siri Institutional Area, August Kranti Marg, New Delhi 110 016; tel. (11) 26863801; fax (11) 26863135; e-mail phdcci@phdcci.in; internet www.phdcci.in; f. 1905; 1,760 mems, 150 asscn mems; Pres. SANJAY BHATIA; Sec.-Gen. KRISHAN KALRA.

Rajasthan Chamber of Commerce and Industry: Rajasthan Chamber Bhavan, M. I. Rd, Jaipur 302 003; tel. (141) 2565163; fax (141) 2561419; e-mail info@rajchamber.com; internet www.rajchamber.com; 575 mems; Pres. MAHENDRA S. DAGA; Hon. Sec.-Gen. Dr K. L. JAIN.

Southern India Chamber of Commerce and Industry: Indian Chamber Bldgs, 6 Esplanade, POB 1208, Chennai 600 108; tel. (44) 25342228; fax (44) 25341876; e-mail sicci@md3.vsnl.net.in; f. 1909; 1,000 mems; Pres. R. VEERAMANI; Sec. S. RAGHAVAN.

Upper India Chamber of Commerce: 113/47, Swaroop Nagar, POB 63, Kanpur 208 002; tel. (512) 2543905; fax (512) 2531684; f. 1888; 52 mems; Pres. DILIP BHARGAVA; Sec. S. P. SRIVASTAVA.

Utkal Chamber of Commerce and Industry Ltd: N/6, IRC Village, Nayapalli, Bhubaneswar 751 015; tel. (674) 3296035; fax (674) 25575981; e-mail contact@utkalchamber.com; internet utkalchamber.com; f. 1964; 250 mems; Pres. M. V. RAO; Hon. Sec. JAYANTA KUMAR SAHOO.

Uttar Pradesh Chamber of Commerce: 15/197 Civil Lines, Kanpur 208 001; tel. 2211696; f. 1914; 200 mems; Pres. Dr B. K. MODI; Sec. AFTAB SAMI.

INDUSTRIAL AND TRADE ASSOCIATIONS

Ahmedabad Textile Mills' Association: Ashram Rd, Navrangpura, POB 4056, Ahmedabad 380 009; tel. (79) 26582273; fax (79) 26588574; e-mail sec_gen@atmaahd.com; f. 1891; 21 mems; Pres. CHINTAN N. PARIKH; Sec.-Gen. ABHINAVA SHUKLA.

All India Federation of Master Printers: 605 Madhuban, 55 Nehru Place, New Delhi 110 019; tel. (11) 26451742; fax (11) 26451743; e-mail aifmp@vsnl.com; internet www.aifmp.net; f. 1953; 51 affiliates, 800 mems; Pres. MANOJ B. MEHTA; Hon. Gen. Sec. B. L. SRINIVAASA.

All India Manufacturers' Organization (AIMO): Jeevan Sahakar, 4th Floor, Sir P.M. Rd, Fort, Mumbai 400 001; tel. (22) 22661016; fax (22) 22660838; e-mail aimoindia@mtnl.net.in; internet www.aimoindia.com; f. 1941; 800 mems; Pres. AMIT KUMAR SEN; Sr Vice-Pres. JAGDISH P. TODI.

All India Plastics Manufacturers' Association: AIPMA House, A-52, St No. 1, MIDC, Andheri (East), Mumbai 400 093; tel. (22) 28217324; fax (22) 28216390; e-mail aipma@bom2.vsnl.net.in; internet www.aipma.net; f. 1947; 1,800 mems; Chair. SURESH J. ATRE; Hon. Sec. AJAY DESAI.

All India Shippers' Council: Federation House, Tansen Marg, New Delhi 110 001; tel. (11) 23738760; fax (11) 23320714; e-mail ficci.bisnet@gems.vsnl.net.in; f. 1967; 82 mems; Chair. RAMU S. DEORA; Sec. M. Y. REDDY.

Association of Man-made Fibre Industry of India: Resham Bhavan, 78 Veer Nariman Rd, Mumbai 400 020; tel. (22) 22040009; fax (22) 22049172; e-mail amfiirayon@hotmail.com; internet www.viscoserayonindia.com; f. 1954; seven mems; Pres. K. K. MAHESHWARI; Sec. M. P. JOSEPH.

Automotive Component Manufacturers' Association of India: 6th Floor, The Capital Court, Olof Parme Marg, Munirka, New Delhi 110 067; tel. (11) 26160315; fax (11) 26160317; e-mail acma@vsnl.com; internet www.acmainfo.com; 485 mems; Pres. RAGHU MODY; Exec. Dir VISHNU MATHUR.

Automotive Tyre Manufacturers' Association: PHD House, opp. Asian Games Village, Siri Fort Institutional Area, New Delhi 110 016; tel. (11) 26851187; fax (11) 26864799; e-mail atma@vsnl.in; internet www.atmaindia.org; 10 mems; Chair. RAGHUPATI SINGHANIA; Dir-Gen. D. RAVINDRAN.

Bharat Krishak Samaj (Farmers' Forum, India): Dr Panjabrao Deshmukh Krishak Bhavan, A-1 Nizamuddin West, New Delhi 110 013; tel. (11) 24359508; fax (11) 24359509; e-mail ffi@mantraonline.com; f. 1954; national farmers' org.; 5m. ordinary mems, 75,000 life mems; Chair. Dr BAL RAM JAKHAR; Exec. Chair. and Gen. Sec. Dr KRISHAN BIR CHAUDHARY.

Bombay Metal Exchange Ltd: 88/90 Kika St, 1st Floor, Gulalwadi, Mumbai 400 004; tel. (22) 22421964; fax (22) 22422640; e-mail bme@bom8.vsnl.net.in; f. 1950; promotes trade and industry in non-ferrous metals; 460 mems; Pres. ROHIT V. SHAH; Sec. T. S. B. IYER.

Bombay Shroffs Association: 233 Sheikh Memon St, Mumbai 400 002; tel. (22) 23425588; f. 1910; 325 mems; Pres. PRANLAL R. SHETH; Hon. Secs MOHANBHAI M. PATEL, DHIRAJ S. KOTHARI.

Calcutta Flour Mills Association: 25/B Shakespeare Sarani, Kolkata 700 017; tel. (33) 22876723; fax (33) 22875944; e-mail swaika@vsnl.com; f. 1932; 28 mems; Chair. NAVNEET SWAIKA; Hon. Sec. RAVI BHAGAT.

Calcutta Tea Traders' Association: 6 Netaji Subhas Rd, Kolkata 700 001; tel. (33) 22301574; fax (33) 22301289; e-mail ctta@cal3.vsnl.net.in; internet www.cttacal.org; f. 1886; 1,300 mems; Chair. AZAM MONEM; Sec. J. KALYANA SUNDARAM.

Cement Manufacturers' Association: CMA Tower, A-2E, Sector 24, Noida 201 301; tel. (95120) 2411955; fax (95120) 2411956; e-mail cmand@vsnl.com; internet cmaindia.org; 54 mems; 126 major cement plants; Pres. N. SRINIVASAN; Sec.-Gen. E. N. MURPHY.

Confederation of Indian Industry (CII): 23 Institutional Area, Lodhi Rd, New Delhi 110 003; tel. (11) 24629992; fax (11) 24626149; e-mail cii@ciionline.org; internet www.ciionline.org; f. 1974; 3,800 mem. cos; Pres. SUNIL KANT MUNJAL; Dir-Gen. N. SRINIVASAN.

Consumer Electronics and Appliances Manufacturers' Association (CEAMA): J-13, 1st Floor, Jangpura Extension, New Delhi 110 014; tel. (11) 24327777; fax (11) 24321616; e-mail ceama@vsnl.net; internet www.cetmaindia.org; f. 1978; 98 mems; Pres. ANOOP KUMAR; Sec.-Gen. SURESH KHANNA.

East India Cotton Association: Cotton Exchange Bldg, 2nd Floor, Cotton Green, Mumbai 400 033; tel. (22) 23704401; fax (22) 23700337; e-mail eica@bom8.vsnl.net.in; internet www.eicaindia.org; f. 1921; 415 mems; Pres. K. F. JHUNJHUNWALA; Exec. Dir and Sec.-Gen. S. M. JOSHI.

Electronic Component Industries Association (ELCINA): ELCINA House, 422 Okhla Industrial Estate, New Delhi 110 020; tel. (11) 26928053; fax (11) 26923440; e-mail elcina@vsnl.com; internet www.elcina.com; f. 1967; 255 mems; Pres. R. G. DESHPANDE; Sec.-Gen. RAJOO GOEL.

Federation of Automobile Dealers Associations: 805 Surya Kiran, 19 Kasturba Gandhi Marg, New Delhi 110 001; tel. (11) 23320046; fax (11) 23320093; e-mail fadadelhi@vsnl.net; internet www.fadaweb.com; f. 1964; Pres. JAYENDRA KACHALIA; Sec.-Gen. GULSHAN AHUJA; 1,072 mems.

Federation of Gujarat Industries: Sidcup Tower, 4th Floor, Race Course, Vadodara 390 007; tel. (265) 2311101; fax (265) 2339054; e-mail info@fgibaroda.org; internet www.fgibaroda.org; f. 1918; 350 mems; Pres. YOGENDRA GANGWAL; Sec. Dr PARESH RAVAL.

Federation of Hotel and Restaurant Associations of India: B-82 Himalaya House, 23 K. G. Marg, New Delhi 110 001; tel. (11) 23322634; fax (11) 23322645; e-mail fhrai@vsnl.com; internet www.fhrai.com; f. 1955; 2,572 mems; Pres. S. K. KHULLAR; Sec.-Gen. KAMAL SHARMA.

Federation of Indian Export Organisations: PHD House, 3rd Floor, Siri Institutional Area, Hauz Khas, New Delhi 110 016; tel. (11) 26851310; fax (11) 26863087; e-mail fieo@nda.vsnl.net.in; internet www.fieo.org; f. 1965; 8,000 mems; Pres. O. P. GARG; Dir-Gen. G. BALACHANDHRAN.

Federation of Indian Mineral Industries (FIMI): 301 Bakshi House, 40–41 Nehru Place, New Delhi 110 019; tel. (11) 26410786; fax (11) 26217004; e-mail fimi@fedmin.com; internet www.fedmin.com; f. 1966; 350 mems; Pres. H. A. WAHAB.

The Fertiliser Association of India: 10 Shaheed Jit Singh Marg, New Delhi 110 067; tel. (11) 26567144; fax (11) 26960052; internet www.faidelhi.org; f. 1955; 1,414 mems; Chair. H. C. GROVER; Dir-Gen. B. K. SAHA; Sec. DEEPAK BHANDARI.

Grain, Rice and Oilseeds Merchants' Association: 14-C, Groma House, 2nd Floor, Sector 19, Vashi, Navi Mumbai 400 703; tel. (22) 27897454; fax (22) 27897458; e-mail groma@vsnl.com; f. 1899; 1,200 mems; Pres. SHARADKUMAR D. MARU.

Indian Drug Manufacturers' Association: 102B Poonam Chambers, Dr A. B. Rd, Worli, Mumbai 400 018; tel. (22) 24944624; fax (22) 24950723; e-mail idma@idmaindia.com; internet www.idma-assn.org; 600 mems; Pres. SURESH KARE; Sec.-Gen. DAARAB PATEL.

Indian Electrical and Electronics Manufacturers' Association (IEEMA): 501 Kakad Chambers, 132 Dr Annie Besant Rd, Worli, Mumbai 400 018; tel. (22) 24936528; fax (22) 24932705; e-mail mumbai@ieema.org; internet www.ieema.org; f. 1948; 400 mems; Pres. P. KRISHNAKUMAR; Sec.-Gen. SUNIL P. MORE.

Indian Jute Mills Association: Royal Exchange, 6 Netaji Subhas Rd, Kolkata 700 001; tel. (33) 22300742; fax (33) 22305643; e-mail ijma@cal2.vsnl.net.in; sponsors and operates export promotion, research and product development; regulates labour relations; 36 mems; Chair. A. K. BAJORIA; Exec. Vice-Chair. S. K. BHATTACHARYA.

Indian Leather Products Association: Suite 6, Chatterjee International Centre, 14th Floor, 33-A, Jawaharlal Nehru Rd, Kolkata 700 071; tel. (33) 22267102; fax (33) 22468339; e-mail ilpa@cal2.vsnl.net.in; 120 mems; Pres. M. V. KULKARNI; Exec. Dir Dr P. K. DEY.

Indian Machine Tool Manufacturers' Association: Plot 249F, Phase IV, Udyog Vihar, Sector 18, Gurgaon 122 015; tel. (124) 4014101; fax (124) 4014108; e-mail imtma@del2.vsnl.net.in; internet www.imtma.org; 400 mems; Pres. C. P. RANGACHAR; Sec. and Exec. Dir V. ANBU.

Indian Mining Association: 6 Netaji Subhas Rd, Kolkata 700 001; tel. (33) 22203733; f. 1892; 50 mems; Sec. K. MUKERJEE.

Indian Motion Picture Producers' Association: IMPPA House, Dr Ambedkar Rd, Bandra (West), Mumbai 400 050; tel. (22) 26486344; fax (22) 26480757; e-mail indiafilm@gmail.com; f. 1938; 10,200 mems; Pres. T. P. AGGARWAL; Sec. ANIL NAGRATH.

Indian National Shipowners' Association: 22 Maker Tower F, Cuffe Parade, Mumbai 400 005; tel. (22) 22182103; fax (22) 22182104; e-mail secygen@insa.org.in; internet www.insa.org.in; f. 1929; 35 mems; Pres. YUDHISHTHIR D. KHATAU; Sec.-Gen. S. S. KULKARNI.

Indian Oilseeds & Produce Exporters' Association (IOPEA): 78/79 Bajaj Bhavan, Nariman Point, Mumbai 400 021; tel. (22) 22023225; fax (22) 22029236; e-mail info@iopea.org; internet www.iopea.org; f. 1956; export promotion council; 350 mems; Chair. SANJIV SAWLA; Sec. A. N. SUBRAMANIAN.

Indian Refractory Makers' Association: 5 Lala Lajpat Rai Sarani, 4th Floor, Kolkata 700 020; tel. (33) 22810868; fax (33) 22814357; e-mail irma@vsnl.com; internet www.irmaindia.org; 85 mems; Chair. U. C. DEVESHWAR; Exec. Dir P. DAS GUPTA.

Indian Soap and Toiletries Makers' Association: 614 Raheja Centre, 6th Floor, Free Press Journal Marg, Nariman Point, Mumbai 400 021; tel. (22) 22824115; fax (22) 22853649; e-mail istma@bom3.vsnl.net.in; 26 mems; Pres. K. V. VAIDYANATHAN; Sec.-Gen. R. HARIHARAN.

Indian Sugar Mills' Association: Ansal Plaza, C-Block, 2nd Floor, Andrews Ganj, New Delhi 110 049; tel. (11) 26262294; fax (11) 26263231; e-mail sugarmil@nda.vsnl.net.in; internet www.indiansugar.com; f. 1932; 181 mems; Pres. VIVEK M. PITTIE; Dir-Gen. S. L. JAIN.

Indian Tea Association: Royal Exchange, 6 Netaji Subhas Rd, Kolkata 700 001; tel. (33) 22102474; fax (33) 22434301; e-mail ita@indiatea.org; internet www.indiatea.org; f. 1881; 210 mem. cos; 420 tea estates; Chair. C. K. DHANUKA; Sec.-Gen. D. CHAKRABARTI.

Indian Woollen Mills' Federation: Churchgate Chambers, 7th Floor, 5 New Marine Lines, Mumbai 400 020; tel. (22) 22624372; fax (22) 22624675; e-mail iwmf@vsnl.com; f. 1963; 50 mems; Chair. V. K. BHARTIA; Sec.-Gen. MAHESH N. SANIL.

Industries and Commerce Association: ICO Association Rd, POB 70, Dhanbad 826 001; tel. (326) 2303147; fax (326) 2303787; f. 1933; 70 mems; Pres. B. N. SINGH; Sec. PRADEEP CHATTERJEE.

Jute Balers' Association: 12 India Exchange Place, Kolkata 700 001; tel. (33) 22201491; f. 1909; 300 mems; Chair. NIRMAL KUMAR BHUTORIA; Sec. SUJIT CHOUDHURY.

Maharashtra Motor Parts Dealers' Association: 13 Kala Bhavan, 3 Mathew Rd, Mumbai 400 004; tel. (22) 23614468; 375 mems; Pres. J. C. UNADKAT; Sec. J. R. CHANDAWALLA.

Millowners' Association, Mumbai: Elphinstone Bldg, 10 Veer Nariman Rd, Fort, Mumbai 400 001; tel. (22) 22040411; fax (22) 22832611; f. 1875; 23 mem. cos; Chair. R. K. DALMIA; Sec.-Gen. V. Y. TAMHANE.

Mumbai Motor Merchants' Association Ltd: 304 Sukh Sagar, N. S. Patkar Marg, Mumbai 400 007; tel. (22) 28112769; 409 mems; Pres. S. TARLOCHAN SINGH ANAND; Gen. Sec. S. BHUPINDER SINGH SETHI.

Mumbai Textile Merchants' Mahajan: 250 Sheikh Memon St, Mumbai 400 002; tel. (22) 22411686; fax (22) 22400311; f. 1879; 1,900 mems; Pres. SURENDRA TULSIDAS SAVAI; Hon. Secs DHIRAJ S. KOTHARI, RAJESH B. PATEL.

National Association of Software and Service Companies (NASSCOM): International Youth Centre, Uma Shankar Dixit Marg, Chanakyapuri, New Delhi 110 021; tel. (11) 23010199; fax (11) 23015452; e-mail nasscom@nasscom.org; internet www.nasscom.org; 860 mems; Pres. KIRAN KARNIK; Chair. JERRY RAO.

Organisation of Pharmaceutical Producers of India (OPPI): Peninsular Corporate Park, Peninsular Chambers, Ground Floor, Ganpatrao Kadam Marg, Lower Parel, Mumbai 400 013; tel. (22) 24918123; fax (22) 24915168; e-mail indiaoppi@vsnl.com; internet www.indiaoppi.com; 74 mems; Pres. RANJIT SHAHANI; Dir-Gen. Dr AJIT DANGI.

Society of Indian Automobile Manufacturers: Core 4B, 5th Floor, India Habitat Centre, Lodhi Rd, New Delhi 110 003; tel. (11) 24647810; fax (11) 24648222; e-mail siam@vsnl.com; f. 1960; 36 mems; Pres. JAGDISH KHATTER; Dir-Gen. DILIP CHENOY.

Southern India Mills' Association: 41 Race Course, Coimbatore 641 018; tel. (422) 2211391; fax (422) 2217160; e-mail simacbe@vsnl.com; internet www.simamills.com; f. 1933; 303 mems; Chair. VIJAY VENKATASWAMY; Sec. P. R. SUBRAMANIAN.

Surgical Manufacturers and Traders' Association: 60 Darya Ganj, New Delhi 110 002; tel. (11) 23271027; fax (11) 23258576; e-mail raviawasthi@hotmail.com; Pres. RAKESH SAWHNEY; Sec. RAVI AWASTHI.

Synthetic and Art Silk Mills' Association Ltd: Sasmira Bldg, 3rd Floor, Sasmira Marg, Worli, Mumbai 400 030; tel. (22) 24945372; fax (22) 24938350; e-mail sasma_100@pacific.net.in; f. 1939; 150 mems; Chair. V. S. CHALKE; Sec.-Gen. K. A. SAMUEL.

Telecom Equipment Manufacturers' Association of India (TEMA): PHD House, 4th Floor, Khel Gaon Marg, Hauz Khas, New Delhi 110 016; tel. (11) 26859621; fax (11) 26859620; e-mail tema@eth.net; internet www.tematelecom.net; Pres. P. S. RAMESH; Sec.-Gen. RAKESH MALIK.

Travel Agents' Association of India: 2D Lawrence and Mayo House, 276 Dr D. N. Rd, Mumbai 400 001; tel. (22) 22074022; fax (22) 22074559; e-mail taai@hathway.com; internet www.taainet.com; 1,692 mems; Pres. S. THOMAS; Hon. Sec.-Gen. BHAGWAN KANUGA.

INDIA   *Directory*

United Planters' Association of Southern India (UPASI): Glenview, POB 11, Coonoor 643 101; tel. (423) 2230270; fax (423) 2232030; e-mail upasi@sancharnet.in; internet www.upasi.org; f. 1893; 850 mems; Pres. J. K. THOMAS; Sec.-Gen. ULLAS MENON.

EMPLOYERS' ORGANIZATIONS

Council of Indian Employers: Federation House, Tansen Marg, New Delhi 110 001; tel. (11) 23316121; fax (11) 23320714; e-mail aioe@del3.vsnl.net.in; f. 1956; comprises:

All India Organisation of Employers (AIOE): Federation House, Tansen Marg, New Delhi 110 001; tel. (11) 23316121; fax (11) 23320714; e-mail aioe@del3.vsnl.net.in; f. 1932; 115 mems; Pres. SAROJ KUMAR PODDAR; Sec.-Gen. Dr AMIT MITRA.

Employers' Federation of India (EFI): Army and Navy Bldg, 148 Mahatma Gandhi Rd, Mumbai 400 001; tel. (22) 22844232; fax (22) 22843028; e-mail efisolar@vsnl.com; f. 1933; 28 asscn mems, 182 ordinary mems, 18 hon. mems; Pres. Dr RAM S. TARNEJA; Sec.-Gen. SHARAD S. PATIL.

Standing Conference of Public Enterprises (SCOPE): SCOPE Complex, 1st Floor, Core No. 8, 7 Lodhi Rd, New Delhi 110 003; tel. (11) 24360101; fax (11) 24361371; e-mail scope@nicsco.delhi.nic.in; internet www.scopeonline.in; f. 1973; representative body of all central public enterprises in India; advises the Govt and public enterprises on matters of major policy and co-ordination; trade enquiries, regarding imports and exports of commodities, carried out on behalf of mems; 200 mems; Chair. C. P. JAIN; Sec.-Gen. Dr S. M. DEWAN.

Employers' Association of Northern India: 14/113 Civil Lines, POB 344, Kanpur 208 001; tel. (512) 2210513; f. 1937; 190 mems; Chair. RAJIV KEHR; Sec.-Gen. P. DUBEY.

Employers' Federation of Southern India: Karumuttu Centre, 1st Floor, 634 Anna Salai, Chennai 600 035; tel. (44) 24349452; fax (44) 24349164; e-mail efsi@vsnl.net; internet www.efsi.org.in; f. 1920; 520 mems; Pres. SHAJI VARGHESE; Sec. T. M. JAWAHARLAL.

UTILITIES

Electricity

Central Electricity Authority (CEA): Sewa Bhavan, R. K. Puram, New Delhi 110 066; tel. (11) 26108476; fax (11) 26105619; e-mail cea-edp@hub.nic.in; internet www.cea.nic.in; responsible for technical co-ordination and supervision of electricity programmes; advises Ministry of Power on all technical, financial and economic issues; Chair. RAKESH NATH.

Bangalore Electricity Supply Co Ltd: K. R. Circle, 4th Floor, Bangalore 560 001; tel. (80) 22354939; internet www.bescom.org.

Calcutta Electricity Supply Corpn Ltd (CESC): CESC House, Chouringhee Sq., Kolkata 700 001; tel. (33) 22256040; fax (33) 22256334; internet cesc.co.in; f. 1978; generation and supply of electricity; Chair. R. P. GOENKA; Man. Dir SUMANTRA BANERJEE.

Chattisgarh Electricity Co Ltd: Industrial Growth Centre, Siltara, Raipur 493 111; tel. (771) 5093925; Dir P. K. JAIN.

Damodar Valley Corpn: DVC Towers, VIP Rd, Kolkata 700 054; tel. (33) 23551935; fax (33) 23551937; e-mail dvchq@wb.nic.in; internet www.dvcindia.org; f. 1948 to administer the first multipurpose river valley project in India, the Damodar Valley Project, which aims at unified development of irrigation, flood control and power generation in West Bengal and Jharkhand; operates nine power stations, incl. thermal, hydel and gas turbine; power generating capacity 2,761.5 MW (1999); Chair. AJAY SHANKAR.

Essar Power Ltd: Essar House, 11 Keshavrao Khadye Marg, Mahalaxmi, Mumbai 400 034; tel. (22) 56601100; fax (22) 24954787; e-mail essarpower@essar.com; internet www.essar.com/power; Chair. S. N. RUIA; Man. Dir A. K. SRIVASTAVA.

Jaipur Vidyut Vitran Nigam Ltd: Old Power House Premises, Banipark, Jaipur 302 006; tel. (141) 2208098; fax (141) 2202025.

National Hydroelectric Power Corporation: Sector 33, Faridabad 121 003; tel. (129) 2278421; fax (129) 2277941; e-mail webmaster@nhpc.nic.in; internet www.nhpcindia.com; f. 1975; Chair and Man. Dir S. K. GARG.

National Thermal Power Corporation Ltd: Core-7, SCOPE Complex, Lodhi Rd, New Delhi 110 003; tel. (11) 24360100; fax (11) 24361018; e-mail info@ntpc.co.in; internet www.ntpc.co.in; f. 1975; operates 11 coal-fired and five gas-fired power stations throughout India; Chair. and Man. Dir T. SANKARALINGAM; 24,000 employees.

Noida Power Co Ltd: Commercial Complex, H Block, Alpha Sector II, Greater Noida 201 308; tel. (95120) 4326559; fax (95120) 4326448; e-mail npcl@noidapower.com; internet www.noidapower.com; f. 1922; distribution of electricity; Chair. and Man. Dir USHA CHATRATH; CEO P. NEOGI.

Nuclear Power Corporation of India Ltd: Commerce Center-1, World Trade Centre, Cuffe Parade, Mumbai 400 005; tel. (22) 22182171; fax (22) 22180109; e-mail cswtc@vsnl.com; internet www.npcil.org; Chair. and Man. Dir SHREYANS KUMAR JAIN.

Power Grid Corporation of India Ltd: Saudamani, Plot No. 2, Sector 29, Gurgaon 122 001; tel. (124) 2571700; fax (124) 2571760; internet www.powergridindia.com; f. 1989; responsible for formation of national power grid; Chair. and Man. Dir R. P. SINGH.

Ratnagiri Gas and Power Pvt Ltd: NTPC Bhavan, SCOPE Complex, 7 Institutional Area, Lodi Rd, New Delhi 110 003; tel. (11) 24367089; fax (11) 24361003; internet www.rgppl.com; f. 2005 to take over assets and revive operations of Dabhol Power Co; 28% owned by National Thermal Power Corpn Ltd, 28% by Gas Authority of India Ltd, 15% by the Maharashtra State Electricity Board (MSEB) and 29% by Indian banking institutions; operates plant with three units with a total combined power-generating capacity of 2,150 MW; Chair. R. K. GOEL; Man. Dir A. K. AHUJA.

Reliance Energy: Reliance Energy Centre, Santacruz (East), Mumbai 400 055; tel. (22) 30099999; fax (22) 30099536; e-mail rel.website@rel.co.in; internet www.rel.co.in; f. 1929 as Bombay Suburban Electric Supply Ltd, merged with the Reliance Group in Jan. 2003; generates, transmits and distributes power in Maharashtra, Goa and Andhra Pradesh; Chair. and Man. Dir ANIL AMBANI.

Rural Electrification Corpn Ltd: Core-4, SCOPE Complex, 7 Lodhi Rd, New Delhi 110 003; tel. (11) 24365161; fax (11) 24360644; e-mail recorp@recl.nic.in; internet www.recindia.com; Chair. and Man. Dir M. N. PRASAD.

Tata Power Co Ltd: Bombay House, 24 Homi Mody St, Mumbai 400 001; tel. (22) 56658282; fax (22) 56658801; internet www.tatapower.com; generation, transmission and distribution of electrical energy; Chair. RATAN N. TATA; Man. Dir FIRDOSE VANDREWALA.

Thana Electric Supply Co Ltd: Asian Bldg, 1st Floor, 17 Ramji Kamani Marg, Ballard Estate, Mumbai 400 001; tel. (22) 22615444; fax (22) 22611069; e-mail thanaele@bom2.vsnl.net.in; f. 1927; Man. Dir SURESH S. HEMMADY.

Torrent Power Ltd (TPL): Torrent House, off Ashram Road, Ahmedabad 380 009; tel. (79) 26583060; fax (79) 26589581; e-mail tpld@torrentpower.com; internet www.torrentpower.com; generation and distribution of electricity; f. 1996; Exec. Chair. SUDHIR MEHTA.

Gas

Gas Authority of India Ltd: 16 Bhikaji Cama Place, R. K. Puram, Delhi 110 066; tel. (11) 26172580; fax (11) 26185941; internet gail.nic.in; f. 1984; 80% state-owned; transports, processes and markets natural gas; constructing gas-based petrochemical complex; Chair. and Man. Dir MOHAN R. HINGNIKAR; 1,513 employees.

Gujarat Gas Co Ltd: 2 Shantisadan Society, Ellis Bridge, Ahmedabad 380 006; Chair. HASMUKH SHAH; Man. Dir B. S. SHANTHARAJU.

Indraprastha Gas Ltd: Dr Gopal Das Bhawan, 14th–15th Floors, 28 Barakhamba Rd, New Delhi 110 001.

Water

Brihanmumbai Municipal Corporation (Hydraulic Engineers' Department): Municipal Corporation Head Offices, Ground Floor, Annex Bldg, Mahapalika Marg, Mumbai 400 001; tel. (22) 22620251; fax (22) 22634329; Head Eng. R. R. HASINAME.

Calcutta Municipal Corporation (Water Supply Department): 5 S. N. Banerjee Rd, Kolkata 700 013; tel. (33) 22444518; fax (33) 22442578; f. 1870; Chief Municipal Eng. DIBYENDU ROY CHOWDHURY.

Chennai Metropolitan Water Supply and Sewerage Board: No. 1 Pumping Station Rd, Chintadripet, Chennai 600 002; tel. (44) 28525717; f. 1978; Chair. and Man. Dir SANTHA SHEELA NAIR.

Delhi Jal Board: Varunalaya Phase II, Karol Bagh, New Delhi 110 005; tel. and fax (11) 23678380; e-mail prodjb@bol.net.in; internet www.delhijalboard.nic.in; f. 1957 as Delhi Water Supply and Sewage Disposal Undertaking, reconstituted as above in 1998; part of the Delhi Municipal Corporation; production and distribution of potable water and treatment and disposal of waste water in Delhi; Chair. SHEILA DIXIT.

Karnataka Rural Water Supply and Sanitation Agency: 2nd Floor, E Block, KHB Complex, Cauvery Bhavan, K. G. Rd, Bangalore 560 009; tel. (80) 22246508; fax (80) 22240509; e-mail jalnirmal@vsnl.net; internet www.jalnirmal.org.

Karnataka Urban Water Supply and Drainage Board: Sir M. Visvesvaraya Rd, D. C. Compound, Dharwad 580 001; tel. (836) 2447090; fax (836) 2446890; internet www.kuwsdb.org.

TRADE UNIONS

Indian National Trade Union Congress (INTUC): 4 Bhai Veer Singh Marg, New Delhi 110 001; tel. (11) 23747767; fax (11)

23364244; e-mail info@intuc.net; internet www.intuc.net; f. 1947; 4,411 affiliated unions with a total membership of 7.93m.; affiliated to ICFTU; 32 state brs and 29 nat. feds; Pres. G. SANJEEVA REDDY; Gen. Sec. RAJENDRA PRASAD SINGH.

Major affiliated unions:

Indian National Cement Workers' Federation: Mazdoor Karyalaya, Congress House, Mumbai 400 004; tel. (22) 23870804; fax (22) 2622299; e-mail nanjappanintuc@dataone.in; 35,000 mems; 42 affiliated unions; Pres. Dr G. SANJEEVA REDDY; Gen. Sec. N. NANJAPPAN.

Indian National Chemical Workers' Federation: Tel Rasayan Bhavan, Tilak Rd, Dadar, Mumbai 400 014; tel. (22) 24121742; fax (22) 24130950; 35,000 mems; Pres. RAJA KULKARNI; Gen. Sec. R. D. BHARADWAJ.

Indian National Electricity Workers' Federation: 392 Sector 21-B, 452 Kotwaliward, Jabalpur 482 002; tel. (129) 2215089; fax (129) 2215868; e-mail inef@ndf.vsnl.net.in; f. 1950; 187,641 mems; 146 affiliated unions; Pres. G. SANJEEVA REDDY; Sec.-Gen. D. P. PATHAK.

Indian National Metal Workers' Federation: Shramik Kendra, 4 Bhai Veer Singh Marg, New Dehli 110 001; tel. (661) 24646611; Pres. G. SANJEEVA REDDY; Gen. Sec. RAJSEKHAR MANTRI.

Indian National Mineworkers' Federation: CJ 49 Salt Lake, Kolkata 700 091; tel. and fax (33) 23372158; e-mail imme@vsnl.com; f. 1949; 351,454 mems in 139 affiliated unions; Pres. RAJENDRA P. SINGH; Sec.-Gen. S. Q. ZAMA.

Indian National Paper Mill Workers' Federation: 6/B, LIGH, Barkatpura, Hyderabad 500 027; tel. (40) 27564706; Pres. G. SANJEEVA REDDY; Gen. Sec. R. CHANDRASEKHARAN.

Indian National Port and Dock Workers' Federation: 15 Coal Dock Rd, Kolkata 700 043; tel. (33) 22455929; f. 1954; 18 affiliated unions; 81,000 mems; Pres. P. K. SAMANTRAY; Gen. Sec. G. KALAN.

Indian National Sugar Mills Workers' Federation: A-176, Darulsafa Marg, Lucknow 226 001; tel. (522) 2282719; 100 affiliated unions; 40,000 mems; Pres. ASHOK KUMAR SINGH; Gen. Sec. P. K. SHARMA.

Indian National Textile Workers' Federation: 27 Burjorji Bharucha Marg, Fort, Mumbai 400 023; tel. (22) 22671577; f. 1948; 400 affiliated unions; 363,790 mems; Pres. SACHINBHAU AHIR; Gen. Sec. P. L. SUBHAIH.

Indian National Transport Workers' Federation: Bus Mazdoor Karyalaya, L/1, Hathital Colony, Jabalpur 482 001; tel. (761) 2429210; 365 affiliated unions; 412,275 mems; Pres. G. SANJEEVA REDDY; Gen. Sec. K. S. VERMA.

National Federation of Petroleum Workers: Tel Rasayan Bhavan, Tilak Rd, Dadar, Mumbai 400 014; tel. (22) 24181742; fax (22) 24130950; f. 1959; 22,340 mems; Pres. RAJA KULKARNI; Gen. Sec. N. A. KHANVILKAR.

Bharatiya Mazdoor Sangh: Ram Naresh Bhavan, Tilak Gali, Pahar Ganj, New Delhi 110 055; tel. (11) 23562654; fax (11) 23582648; e-mail ho@bms.org.in; internet www.bms.org.in; f. 1955; 4,700 affiliated unions with a total membership of 8.5m.; 27 state brs; 34 nat. feds; Pres. GIRISH AWASTHI; Gen. Sec. UDAY RAO PATWARDHAN.

Major affiliated unions:

Bharatiya Jute Mazdoor Sangh: 10 Kiran Shankar Roy Rd, Kolkata 700 001; tel. (33) 22489210; Pres. RAGHUNATH SINGH; Gen. Sec. TARUN KANTI GHOSE.

Bharatiya Paribahan Mazdoor Mahasangh (Transport Workers' Union): 542 Dr Munje Marg, Congress Nagar, Nagpur 440 012; tel. (712) 2534464; Pres. WAMAN RAO KHEDKAR; Gen. Sec. CHETAN KUMAR DESAI.

Kendriya Karmachari Mahasangh: Ram Naresh Bhawan, Tilak Gali, Paharganj, New Delhi 110 055; tel. (11) 23620654; Pres. K. K. PODDAR; Gen. Sec. CHANDRA MOHAN.

National Organisation of Bank Workers: 542 Dr Munje Marg, Congress Nagar, Nagpur 440 012; tel. (712) 2560808; fax (712) 2542442; Pres. V. B. INDURKAR; Gen. Sec. K. R. POONJA.

National Organisation of Insurance Workers: 3-AB, Hashim Bldg, 40 Veer Nariman Rd, Mumbai 400 023; tel. (22) 22040958; Pres. M. P PATWARDHAN; Gen. Sec. ATUL DESHPANDE.

Centre of Indian Trade Unions: BTR Bhavan, 13-A Rouse Ave, New Delhi 110 002; tel. (11) 23221288; fax (11) 23221284; e-mail citu@bol.net.in; internet www.citu.org.in; f. 1970; 3.37m. mems; 24 state and union territory brs; 4,300 affiliated unions, 12 nat. federations; Pres. M. K. PANDHE; Gen. Sec. MOHAMMED AMIN.

Major affiliated unions:

All India Coal Workers' Federation: Koyla Shramik Bhavan, N. S. B. Rd, Raniganj 713 347; Pres. M. K. PANDHE.

All India Road Transport Workers' Federation: 53 A. J. C. Bose Rd, Kolkata 700 016; Pres. SHYAMAL CHAKRABORTY.

Steel Workers' Federation of India: 1 Vidyasagar Ave, Durgapur 713 205; Pres. ARDHENDU DHAKI.

Water Transport Workers' Federation of India: 16 Birsa Munda Sarani, Kolkata 700 043; Pres. T. NARENDRA RAO.

Assam Chah Karmachari Sangha: POB 13, Dibrugarh 786 001; tel. 20870; 13,553 mems; 20 brs; Pres. G. C. SARMAH; Gen. Sec. A. K. BHATTACHARYA.

All-India Trade Union Congress (AITUC): 24 Canning Lane, New Delhi 110 001; tel. (11) 23387320; fax (11) 23386427; e-mail aitucong@bol.net.in; f. 1920; affiliated to WFTU; 4.6m. mems, 2,272 affiliated unions; 28 state brs, 21 national federations; Pres. J. CHITHARANJAN; Gen. Sec. GURUDAS DASGUPTA.

Major affiliated unions:

Annamalai Plantation Workers' Union: Valparai, Via Pollachi, Tamil Nadu; over 21,000 mems.

Zilla Cha Bagan Workers' Union: Mal, Jalpaiguri, West Bengal; 15,000 mems; Pres. NEHAR MUKHERJEE; Gen. Sec. BIMAL DAS GUPTA.

United Trades Union Congress (UTUC): 1st Floor, 249 Bipin Behari Ganguly St, Kolkata 700 012; tel. (33) 22259234; fax (33) 22375609; f. 1949; 1.2m. mems from 387 affiliated unions; 12 state brs and six nat. feds; Pres. SHANKARAN NAIR; Gen. Sec. ABANI ROY.

Major affiliated unions:

Bengal Provincial Chatkal Mazdoor Union: Kolkata; textile workers; 28,330 mems.

Dooars Cha Bagan Union: Jalpaiguri; tel. (3564) 255220; 94,532 mems; Pres. SURESH TALUKDAR; Gen. Sec. MANOHAR TIRKEY.

Hind Mazdoor Sabha (HMS): 120 Babar Rd, New Delhi 110 011; tel. (11) 23413519; fax (11) 23411037; e-mail hms@nde.vsnl.net.in; internet www.mkiindia.org; f. 1948; affiliated to ICFTU; 4.8m. mems from 2,800 affiliated unions; 25 state councils; 18 nat. industrial feds; Pres. MANOHAR KOTWAL; Gen. Sec. UMRAOMAL PUROHIT.

Major affiliated unions:

Colliery Mazdoor Congress (Coalminers' Union): Bengal Hotel, 2nd Md Hussain St, Asansol 713 301; tel. (341) 202342; fax (341) 201336; 45,188 mems; Pres. MADHU DANDAVATE; Gen. Sec. JAYANTA PODDER.

Mumbai Port Trust Dock and General Employees' Union: Port Trust Kamgar Sadan, Nawab Tank Rd, Mazgaon, Mumbai 400 010; tel. (22) 23776320; fax (22) 23754794; e-mail mbptdgeu@vsnl.net; 7,448 mems; Pres. Dr SHANTI PATEL; Gen. Sec. S. K. SHETYE.

South Central Railway Mazdoor Union: 7C Railway Bldg, Accounts Office Compound, Secunderabad 500 371; tel. (40) 27821351; fax (40) 27821351; e-mail scrmu@hotmail.com; internet www.scrmu.org; f. 1966; 88,900 mems; Pres. C. SANKARA RAO; Gen. Sec. C. H. SANKARRAO; 135 brs.

Transport and Dock Workers' Union: P. D. Mello Bhavan, P. D. Mello Rd, Carnec Bunder, Mumbai 400 038; tel. (22) 22616951; fax (22) 22659087; 25,979 mems; Pres. S. R. KULKARNI.

West Bengal Cha Mazdoor Sabha: Cha Shramik Bhavan, Jalpaiguri 735 101, West Bengal; tel. (3561) 231140; fax (3561) 230349; f. 1947; 55,000 mems; Pres. Prof. SUSHIL ROY; Gen. Sec. SAMIR ROY.

Western Railway Employees' Union: Grant Road Railway Station Bldg, Grant Rd (East), Mumbai 400 007; tel. (22) 23088102; fax (22) 23003185; 150,000 mems; Pres. UMRAOMAL PUROHIT; Gen. Sec. C. S. MENON.

Confederation of Central Government Employees and Workers: 4B/6 Ganga Ram Hospital Marg, New Delhi 110 060; tel. (11) 22587804; 1.2m. mems; Pres. S. MADHUSUDAN; Sec.-Gen. S. K. VYAS.

Affiliated union:

National Federation of Postal Employees (NFPE): D-7, North Ave Post Office Bldg, 1st Floor, New Delhi 110 001; tel. and fax (11) 23092771; e-mail nfpe_hq@hotmail.com; f. 1954 as National Federation of Post and Telegraph Employees, reconstituted as above in 1986; 400,000 mems from seven affiliated unions; Pres. R. N. CHAUDHARY; Sec.-Gen. C. CHANDRAN PILLAI.

All India Bank Employees' Association (AIBEA): Prabhat Nivas, Singapore Plaza, 164 Linghi Chetty St, Chennai 600 001; tel. (44) 25351522; fax (44) 25358853; e-mail aibeahq@gmail.com; internet bankunionaibea.org; 32 state units, 710 affiliated unions, 525,000 mems; Pres. RAJEN NAGAR; Gen. Sec. C. H. VENKATACHALAM.

All India Defence Employees' Federation (AIDEF): Survey No. 81, Elphinstone Rd, Khadki, Pune 411 003; tel. (20) 25818761; 358 affiliated unions; 200,000 mems; Pres. S. N. PATHAK; Gen. Secs S. BHATTACHARYA, C. SRIKUMAR.

INDIA

All India Port and Dock Workers' Federation: 9 Second Line Beach, Chennai 600 001; tel. (44) 25224222; fax (44) 25225983; f. 1948; 100,000 mems in 34 affiliated unions; Pres. S. R. KULKARNI; Gen. Sec. S. C. C. ANTHONY PILLAI.

All India Railwaymen's Federation (AIRF): 4 State Entry Rd, New Delhi 110 055; tel. (11) 23343493; fax (11) 23363167; e-mail airf@ndb.vsnl.net.in; f. 1924; 1,034,747 mems (2005); 24 affiliated unions; Pres. UMRAOMAL PUROHIT; Gen. Sec. J. P. CHAUBEY.

National Federation of Indian Railwaymen (NFIR): 3 Chelmsford Rd, New Delhi 110 055; tel. (11) 23343305; fax (11) 23744013; e-mail nfir@satyam.net.in; f. 1952; 26 affiliated unions; 925,500 mems (2003); Pres. GUMAN SINGH; Gen. Sec. M. RAGHAVAIAH.

Transport

RAILWAYS

India's railway system is the largest in Asia and the fourth largest in the world. In March 2003 the total length of Indian railways exceeded 63,140 route-km. The network carried 14m. passengers and more than 1m. metric tons of freight traffic per day. The Government exercises direct or indirect control over all railways through the Railway Board. India's largest railway construction project of the 20th century, the 760-km Konkan railway line (which took seven years and almost US $1,000m. to build), was officially opened in January 1998.

A 16.45-km underground railway, which carries more than 1m. people daily, was completed in Kolkata in 1995. The first phase of a partially underground new metro system in New Delhi was completed in late 2004; the final phase was expected to be completed in 2010.

Ministry of Railways (Railway Board): Rail Bhavan, Raisina Rd, New Delhi 110 001; tel. (11) 23384010; fax (11) 23384481; e-mail crb@del2.vsnl.net.in; internet www.indianrailways.gov.in; Chair. KALYAN COOMAR JENA.

Zonal Railways

The railways are grouped into 16 zones:

Central: Chhatrapati Shivaji Terminus (Victoria Terminus), Mumbai 400 001; tel. (22) 22621230; fax (22) 22612354; e-mail gmcr@bom2.vsnl.net.in; internet www.centralrailwayonline.com; Gen. Man. SOWMYA RAGHAVAN.

East Central: Hajipur 844 101; tel. (6224) 274728; fax (6224) 274738; f. 1996; Gen. Man. R. S. VARSHNEYA.

East Coast: Rail Vihar, Chandrasekhar Pur, Bhubaneswar 751 023; tel. (674) 230073; fax (674) 2300196; internet www.eastcoastrailway.gov.in; f. 1996; Gen. Man. A. K. GOYAL.

Eastern: 17 Netaji Subhas Rd, Kolkata 700 001; tel. (33) 22207596; fax (33) 22480370; internet www.easternrailway.gov.in; Gen. Man. N. K. GOEL.

North Central: Allahabad 211 001; tel. (532) 2603551; fax (532) 2603900; e-mail secyncr@hotmail.com; f. 1996; Gen Man. BUDH PRAKASH.

North Eastern: Gorakhpur 273 012; tel. (551) 2201041; fax (551) 2201299; e-mail gm@ner.railnet.gov.in; internet www.ner.railnet.gov.in; Gen. Man. OM PRAKASH.

North Western: Ganpati Nagar, opp. Railway Hospital, Loco Colony Rd, Jaipur 302 006; tel. (141) 2222695; fax (141) 2222936; e-mail itnwr@yahoo.com; internet www.northwesternrailway.gov.in; Gen. Man. S. S. BHATTACHARYA.

Northeast Frontier: Maligaon, Guwahati 781 011; tel. (361) 2570422; fax (361) 2570580; e-mail gm@nfr.railnet.gov.in; internet www.nfr.railnet.gov.in; f. 1958; Gen. Man. ASHUTOSH SWAMI.

Northern: Baroda House, Kasturba Gandhi Marg, New Delhi 110 001; tel. (11) 23747084; fax (11) 23363469; e-mail cpro@nr.railnet.gov.in; internet www.nr.indianrail.gov.in; Gen. Man. Shri PRAKASH.

South Central: Rm 312, 3rd Floor, Rail Nilayam, Secunderabad 500 071; tel. (40) 27822874; fax (40) 27833203; internet www.scrailway.gov.in; Gen. Man. H. K. PADHEE.

South East Central Railway: R. E. Complex, Bilaspur 495 004; tel. (7752) 47102; e-mail webmaster@secr.railnet.gov.in; internet www.secr.gov.in; Gen. Man. PRADEEP KUMAR.

South Eastern: 11 Garden Reach Rd, Kolkata 700 043; tel. (33) 24393532; fax (33) 24397831; e-mail gm@ser.railnet.gov.in; internet www.serailway.gov.in; Gen. Man. A. K. JAIN.

South Western: Club Road, Keshwapur, Hubli 580 023; tel. (836) 2360888; fax (836) 2365209; e-mail gm@southwesternrailway.in; internet www.southwesternrailway.in; f. 1996; Gen. Man. PRAVEEN KUMAR.

Directory

Southern: Park Town, Chennai 600 003; tel. (44) 25353455; fax (44) 25354950; e-mail srailway@gmail.com; internet www.southernrailway.org; Gen. Man. RAKESH CHOPRA.

West Central: Jabalpur 482 001; tel. (761) 2627444; fax (761) 2607555; e-mail osdwcr@yahoo.com; internet www.westcentralrailway.com; f. 1996; Gen. Man. MAHEEP KAPUR.

Western: Churchgate, Mumbai 400 020; tel. (22) 22005670; fax (22) 22068545; e-mail secygm@wr.railnet.gov.in; internet www.wr.indianrail.gov.in; Gen. Man. M. Z. ANSARI.

ROADS

In December 2002 there were an estimated 3.3m. km of roads in India, 58,112 km of which were national highways. About 50% of the total road network was paved. In March 2004 there were an estimated 65,569 km of national highways. In January 1999 the Government launched the ambitious Rs 500,000m. National Highways Development project, which included plans to build an east–west corridor linking Silchar with Porbandar and a north–south corridor linking Kashmir with Kanyakumari, as well as a circuit of roads linking the four main cities of Mumbai, Chennai, Kolkata and New Delhi. A further phase of the project, the widening and upgrading of an estimated 65,000 km of national highways, was implemented in 2005. In May 2007 the Government pledged Rs 480,000m. for the upgrade of India's rural road network by 2009 with the stated aim of connecting 66,000 villages; the allocation represented part of a four-year initiative (at an estimated cost of Rs 1,740,000m.) to enhance infrastructure and rural incomes by increasing connectivity with roads, telecommunications and drinking water.

Ministry of Shipping, Road Transport and Highways: Parivahan Bhavan, 1 Sansad Marg, New Delhi 110 001; tel. (11) 23710121; fax (11) 23719023; internet morth.nic.in; responsible for the construction and maintenance of India's system of national highways, with a total length of 65,569 km in March 2004, connecting the state capitals and major ports and linking with the highway systems of neighbouring countries. This system includes 172 national highways which constitute the main trunk roads of the country.

Border Roads Organisation: Seema Sadak Bhavan, Ring Road Naraina, Delhi 110 010; e-mail bro-jdedp@nic.in; internet www.bro.nic.in; f. 1960 to accelerate the economic development of the north and north-eastern border areas; it has constructed 31,061 km and improved 37,077 km of roads, and built permanent bridges totalling a length of 19,544 m in the border areas.

National Highways Authority of India: G-5 and 6, Sector 10, Dwarka, New Delhi 110 075; tel. (11) 25074100; fax (11) 25093507; e-mail scjindal@nhai.org; internet www.nhai.org; f. 1995; planning, designing, construction and maintenance of national highways; under Ministry of Shipping, Road Transport and Highways; Chair. N. GOKULRAM.

INLAND WATERWAYS

About 14,500 km of rivers are navigable by power-driven craft, and 3,700 km by large country boats. Services are mainly on the Ganga and Brahmaputra and their tributaries, the Godavari, the Mahanadi, the Narmada, the Tapti and the Krishna.

Central Inland Water Transport Corpn Ltd: 4 Fairlie Place, Kolkata 700 001; tel. (33) 22202321; fax (33) 22436164; e-mail ciwtc@cal3.vsnl.net.in; internet www.ciwtcltd.com; f. 1967; inland water transport services in Bangladesh and the east and north-east Indian states; also shipbuilding and repairing, general engineering, lightering of ships and barge services; Chair. and Man. Dir PRAFUL TAYAL.

SHIPPING

In March 2002 India was 15th in terms of dwt and 19th in terms of gwt on the list of principal merchant fleets of the world. In December 2005 the total fleet had 1,096 ships, with a total displacement of 8.06m. grt. There were some 102 shipping companies operating in India in January 2000. The major ports are Chennai, Haldia, Jawaharlal Nehru (at Nhava Sheva near Mumbai), Kandla, Kochi, Kolkata, Mormugao, Mumbai, New Mangalore, Paradip (Paradeep), Tuticorin and Visakhapatnam.

Chennai (Madras)

South India Shipping Corpn Ltd: Chennai; Chair. J. H. TARAPORE; Man. Dir F. G. DASTUR.

Kolkata (Calcutta)

India Steamship Co Ltd: 44 Park St, Kolkata 700 016; tel. (33) 22481171; fax (33) 22488133; e-mail india.steamship@gems.vsnl.net.in; f. 1928; cargo services; Chair. K. K. BIRLA; Man. Dir ASHOK KAK; br in Delhi.

Surrendra Overseas Ltd: Apeejay House, 15 Park St, Kolkata 700 016; tel. (33) 22172372; fax (33) 22179596; e-mail solcal@

apeejaygroup.com; internet www.apeejaygroup.com; shipowners; Chair. JIT PAUL.

Mumbai (Bombay)

Century Shipping Ltd: Mumbai; tel. (22) 22022734; fax (22) 22027274; Chair. B. K. BIRLA; Pres. N. M. JAIN.

Chowgule Brothers (Pvt) Ltd: Malhotra House, 3rd Floor, Mumbai 400 001.; tel. (22) 22616301; fax (22) 22610659; e-mail mumbai.cb@chowgule.co.in; internet www.chowgulebros.com.

Essar Shipping Ltd: Essar House, 11 Keshavrao Khadye Marg, Mahalaxmi, Mumbai 400 034; tel. (22) 24950606; fax (22) 24954312; e-mail contactshipping@essar.com; internet www.essar.com/shipping.htm; f. 1975; Chair. S. N. RUIA; Man. Dir SANJAY MEHTA.

The Great Eastern Shipping Co Ltd: Ocean House, 134/A Dr Annie Besant Rd, Worli, Mumbai 400 018; tel. (22) 66613000; fax (22) 24925900; e-mail corp_comm@greatship.com; internet www.greatship.com; f. 1948; shipping; Exec. Chair. K. M. SHETH; Dep. Chair. and Man. Dir BHARAT SHETH; br. in New Delhi.

Shipping Corpn of India Ltd: Shipping House, 245 Madame Cama Rd, Mumbai 400 021; tel. (22) 22026666; fax (22) 22026905; e-mail mail@sci.co.in; internet www.shipindia.com; f. 1961 as a govt undertaking; Chair. and Man. Dir S. HAJARA; brs in Kolkata, New Delhi, Chennai and London.

Tolani Shipping Co Ltd: 10A Bakhtawar, Nariman Point, Mumbai 400 021; tel. (22) 56568989; fax (22) 22870697; e-mail ops@tolanigroup.com; Chair. and Man. Dir Dr N. P. TOLANI.

Varun Shipping Co Ltd: Laxmi Bldg, 3rd Floor, 6 Shoorji Vallabhdas Marg, Ballard Estate, Mumbai 400 001; tel. (22) 66350100; fax (22) 66350274; e-mail systems@varunship.com; internet www.varunship.com; f. 1971; Chair. DILIP D. KHATAU.

CIVIL AVIATION

There are 11 designated international airports, 85 domestic airports and 28 civil enclaves. By 2004 10 airports (in Ahmedabad, Amritsar, Goa, Guwahati, Jaipur, Lucknow, Mangalore, Madurai, Thiruvananthapuram and Udaipur) had been identified for the second round of modernization and restructuring. The process of long-term leasing of Mumbai, Delhi, Chennai and Kolkata airports was under way in 2006.

Airports Authority of India: Rajiv Gandhi Bhavan, Safdarjung Airport, New Delhi 110 003; tel. (11) 24632950; fax (11) 24641088; e-mail aaichmn@vsnl.com; internet www.aai.aero; manages 124 international and domestic airports; Chair. K. RAMALINGAM; Gen. Man. PRAM NATH.

Air Deccan: 214/33, 7th Cross, Vasanthnagar, Bangalore 560 052; tel. (80) 51148190; fax (80) 22352645; internet www.airdeccan.net; f. 2003; unit of Deccan Aviation Pvt Ltd; low-cost domestic passenger service; Man. Dir Capt. G. R. GOPINATH.

Air-India: Air-India Bldg, 218 Backbay Reclamation, Nariman Point, Mumbai 400 021; tel. (22) 22024142; fax (22) 22023686; e-mail hqpsai@bom3.vsnl.net.in; internet www.airindia.com; f. 1932 as Tata Airlines; renamed Air-India in 1946; in 1953 became a state corpn responsible for international flights; merged with Indian Airlines in Aug. 2007 to form the National Aviation Company of India, operating as Air-India; services to 46 online stations (incl. two cargo stations) and 84 offline offices throughout the world; Chair. and Man. Dir V. THULASIDAS.

Air Sahara: Dr Gopaldas Bhawan, 3rd Floor, 28 Barakhamba Rd, New Delhi 110 001; tel. (11) 23326851; fax (11) 23755510; internet www.airsahara.net; f. 1991 as Sahara India Airlines; commenced operations 1993; acquired by Jet Airways (India) Ltd in April 2007; private co; scheduled passenger and cargo services to domestic and regional destinations; Man. GARRY KINGSHOTT.

Airline Allied Services Ltd: Domestic Arrival Terminal, 1st Floor, Indira Gandhi International Airport, Palam, New Delhi 110 037; tel. (11) 25672729; fax (11) 25672006; e-mail aaslmd@del2.net.in; internet www.allianceair-india.com/; f. 1996; 100% owned by Indian Airlines; scheduled passenger services to regional destinations; Man. Dir MANET PAES.

Archana Airways: 41A Friends Colony (East), Mathura Rd, New Delhi 110 065; tel. (11) 26842001; fax (11) 26847762; f. 1991; commenced operations 1993; scheduled and charter passenger services to domestic destinations; Dir/Chair. A. K. BHARTIYA; Man. Dir N. K. BHARTIYA.

Blue Dart Express: 88–89 Old International Terminal, Meenambakkam Airport, Chennai 600027; tel. (44) 22334995; fax (44) 22349067; e-mail bdal@md2.vsnl.net.in; internet www.bluedart.com; f. 1983 as Blue Dart Courier Services; name changed as above in 1990; air express transport co; Chair. TUSHAR K. JANI; Chief Exec. NITEEN GUPTE.

Go Air: Paper Box House, off Mahakali Caves Rd, Andheri (East), Mumbai 400 093; e-mail feedback@goair.in; internet www.goair.in; f. 2005; passenger services to domestic destinations; Man. Dir JEHANGIR 'JEH' WADIA.

Gujarat Airways Ltd: Sapana Shopping Centre, 1st Floor, 20 Vishwas Colony, Alkapuri, Vadodara 390 005; tel. (265) 2330864; fax (265) 2339628; e-mail info@gujaratairways.com; f. 1994; commenced operations 1995; scheduled services to domestic destinations; Chair. G. N. PATEL; Man. Dir R. C. SHARMA.

Indigo Airlines: internet www.flyindigo.com; f. 2005; private co; passenger services to domestic destinations; Man. Dir RAHUL BHATIA; CEO BRUCE ASHBY.

Jagson Airlines: Vandana Bldg, 3rd Floor, 11 Tolstoy Marg, New Delhi 110 001; tel. (11) 23721594; fax (11) 23324693; e-mail jagson-id@eth.net; internet www.jagsonairline.com; f. 1991; scheduled and charter passenger services to domestic destinations; Chair. JAGDISH GUPTA; Man. Dir PRADEEP GUPTA.

Jet Airways (India) Ltd: S. M. Centre, 1st Floor, Andheri-Kurla Rd, Andheri (East), Mumbai 400 059; tel. (22) 40191000; fax (22) 29201313; internet www.jetairways.com; f. 1992; commenced operations 1993; acquired Air Sahara in April 2007; private co; scheduled passenger services to domestic and regional destinations; operates flights to 50 domestic and international destinations; Chair. and Man. Dir NARESH GOYAL; CEO WOLFGANG PROCK-SCHAUER.

Kingfisher Airlines: Bhagwati House, 2nd Floor, A/19, off Veera Desai Rd, Fun Republic Theatre Rd, Andheri (West), Mumbai 400 053; tel. (22) 55031091; fax (22) 55031095; e-mail info@flykingfisher.com; internet www.flykingfisher.com; f. 2005; 100% owned by UB Group; low-cost domestic passenger service; Chair. and Man. Dir VIJAY MALLYA.

Paramount Airways: Rajanarayan Towers, 70 Race Course, Coimbatore 641 018; fax (422) 5394441; e-mail feedback@paramountairways.com; internet www.paramountairways.com; f. 2005; scheduled flights to domestic destinations; Man. Dir M. THIAGARAJAN.

SpiceJet: Cargo Complex, Terminal 1-B, Indira Gandhi International Airport, Domestic Terminal, New Delhi 110 037; e-mail corpoffice@spicejet.com; internet www.spicejet.com; f. 2005; low-cost domestic passenger service; Chair. SIDDHANTA SHARMA; CEO MARK WINDERS.

Trans Bharat Aviation Ltd: 212–213, Somdutt Chamber I, 2nd Floor, Bhikaji Cama Place, Delhi 110 066; tel. (11) 26181824; fax (11) 26160146; e-mail qcmtba@rediffmail.com; internet www.transbharataviation.com; f. 1990; commenced operations 1991; charter services throughout India.

UP Airways Ltd: Roopali House, A-2 Defence Colony, New Delhi 110 024; tel. (11) 24646290; fax (11) 24646292; e-mail sgsimpex@del3.vsnl.net.in; private co; charter services to domestic destinations; Chair. and Man. Dir SUBHASH GULATI; Chief Exec. Capt. H. S. BEDI.

Tourism

The tourist attractions of India include its scenery, its historic forts, palaces and temples, and its rich variety of wildlife. Tourist infrastructure has recently been expanded by the provision of more luxury hotels and improved means of transport. In 2006 there were about 4.4m. foreign visitors to India, and revenue from tourism totalled an estimated US $6,569.3m.

Ministry of Tourism: Transport Bhavan, Rm 123, 1 Parliament St, New Delhi 110 001; tel. and fax (11) 23715084; e-mail sectour@nic.in; internet tourism.gov.in; formulates and administers govt policy for promotion of tourism; plans the organization and development of tourist facilities; operates tourist information offices in India and overseas; Sec. SHILABHADRA BANERJEE.

India Tourism Development Corpn Ltd: SCOPE Complex, Core 8, 6th Floor, 7 Lodhi Rd, New Delhi 110 003; tel. (11) 24360182; fax (11) 24360185; e-mail cmditdc@theashokgroup.com; internet www.theashokgroup.com; f. 1966; operates Ashok Group of hotels (largest hotel chain owner), resort accommodation, tourist transport services, duty-free shops and a travel agency and provides consultancy and management services; Chair. and Man. Dir PARVEZ DEVAN.

INDONESIA

Introductory Survey

Location, Climate, Language, Religion, Flag, Capital

The Republic of Indonesia consists of a group of about 18,108 islands (including rocks, reefs, sandbanks, etc.), lying between the mainland of South-East Asia and Australia. The archipelago is the largest in the world, and it stretches from the Malay peninsula to New Guinea. The principal islands are Java, Sumatra, Kalimantan (comprising more than two-thirds of the island of Borneo), Sulawesi (Celebes), Papua (formerly Irian Jaya, comprising the western part of the island of New Guinea), Maluku (the Moluccas) and West Timor (comprising part of the island of Timor). Indonesia's only land frontiers are with Papua New Guinea, to the east of Papua, with the Malaysian states of Sarawak and Sabah, which occupy northern Borneo, and with Timor-Leste (formerly East Timor), to the east of West Timor. The climate is tropical, with an average annual temperature of 26°C (79°F) and heavy rainfall during most seasons. Rainfall averages 706 mm (28 ins) annually in Indonesia, although there are large variations throughout the archipelago; the heaviest annual rainfall (2,286 mm or 90 ins) is along the equatorial rain belt, which passes through Sumatra, Borneo and Sulawesi. The official language is Bahasa Indonesia (a form of Malay); there are an estimated 583 other languages and dialects spoken in the archipelago, including Javanese, Sundanese, Arabic and Chinese. An estimated 88% of the inhabitants profess adherence to Islam. About 10% of the population are Christians, while most of the remainder are either Hindus or Buddhists. The national flag (proportions 2 by 3) has two equal horizontal stripes, of red and white. The capital is Jakarta, on the island of Java.

Recent History

Indonesia was formerly the Netherlands East Indies (except for the former Portuguese colony of Timor-Leste, see below). Dutch occupation began in the 17th century and gradually extended over the whole archipelago. Nationalist opposition to colonial rule began in the early 20th century. During the Second World War the territory was occupied by Japanese forces from March 1942. On 17 August 1945, three days after the Japanese surrender, a group of nationalists proclaimed the independence of Indonesia. The first President of the self-proclaimed republic was Dr Sukarno, a leader of the nationalist movement since the 1920s. The declaration of independence was not recognized by the Netherlands, which attempted to restore its pre-war control of the islands. After four years of intermittent warfare and negotiations between the Dutch authorities and the nationalists, agreement was reached on a formal transfer of power. On 27 December 1949 the United States of Indonesia became legally independent, with Sukarno continuing as President. Initially, the country had a federal Constitution which gave limited self-government to the 16 constituent regions. In August 1950, however, the federation was dissolved, and the country became the unitary Republic of Indonesia. The 1949 independence agreement excluded West New Guinea (subsequently Irian Jaya and known as Papua from 1 January 2002), which remained under Dutch control until October 1962; following a brief period of UN administration, however, it was transferred to Indonesia in May 1963.

Sukarno followed a policy of extreme nationalism, and his regime became increasingly dictatorial. His foreign policy was sympathetic to the People's Republic of China but, under his rule, Indonesia also played a leading role in the Non-aligned Movement (see p. 424). Inflation and widespread corruption eventually provoked opposition to Sukarno's regime; in September–October 1965 there was an abortive military coup, in which the Partai Komunis Indonesia (PKI—Indonesian Communist Party) was strongly implicated. A mass slaughter of alleged PKI members and supporters ensued. In March 1966 Sukarno was forced to transfer emergency executive powers to military commanders, led by Gen. Suharto, Chief of Staff of the Army, who outlawed the PKI. In February 1967 Sukarno transferred full power to Suharto. In March the Majelis Permusyawaratan Rakyat (MPR—People's Consultative Assembly) removed Sukarno from office and named Suharto acting President. He became Prime Minister in October 1967 and, following his election by the MPR, he was inaugurated as President in March 1968. In July 1971, in the first general election since 1955, the government-sponsored Sekretariat Bersama Golongan Karya (Joint Secretariat of Functional Groups), known as Golkar, won a majority of seats in the Dewan Perwakilan Rakyat (DPR—House of Representatives). Suharto was re-elected to the presidency in March 1973.

Under Suharto's 'New Order', real power passed from the legislature and the Cabinet to a small group of army officers and to the Operation Command for the Restoration of Order and Security (Kopkamtib), the internal security organization. Left-wing movements were suppressed, and a liberal economic policy adopted. A general election in May 1977 gave Golkar a majority in the legislature, and Suharto was re-elected President (unopposed) in March 1978. Despite criticism of the Government, Golkar won an increased majority in the elections in May 1982. In March 1983 Suharto was re-elected, again unopposed, as President.

During 1984 Suharto's attempt to introduce legislation requiring all political, social and religious organizations to adopt *Pancasila*, the five-point state philosophy (belief in a supreme being; humanitarianism; national unity; democracy by consensus; social justice), as their only ideology encountered violent opposition, allegedly instigated by Muslim opponents of the proposed legislation; many Muslims were tried and sentenced to long terms of imprisonment. All the political parties had accepted *Pancasila* by July 1985. At the April 1987 general election, despite persistent international allegations of corruption and of abuses of human rights, Golkar won 299 of the 500 seats in the DPR. Moreover, for the first time, the party achieved an overall majority of seats in each of Indonesia's 27 provinces.

In February 1988 new legislation reaffirmed the *dwifungsi*, or 'dual (i.e. military and socio-economic) function', of the Indonesian Armed Forces (ABRI). In March Suharto was again re-elected unopposed as President. At the subsequent vice-presidential election, in a departure from previous procedure, Suharto did not recommend a candidate, but encouraged the MPR to choose one. However, Lt-Gen. (retd) Sudharmono, the Chairman of Golkar, and Dr Jailani Naro, the leader of the Partai Persatuan Pembangunan (PPP—United Development Party), were both nominated for the post, and Gen. Suharto was obliged to indicate his preference for Sudharmono. ABRI disapproved of Sudharmono's appointment as, under his chairmanship of Golkar, there had been a shift away from military dominance in the grouping. In October Sudharmono resigned as Chairman of Golkar and was replaced by Gen. (retd) Wahono.

In early 1989 tension arising from land disputes produced social unrest in three areas of Java and on the island of Sumbawa (east of Bali and Lombok), in Nusa Tenggara. The first student demonstrations since 1978 were held to protest against the Government's expropriation of land without sufficient indemnification for those subject to relocation. Meanwhile, speculation over Suharto's successor had begun. In May 1989, however, Suharto warned officials to dismiss the topic of the succession and in September, when the Partai Demokrasi Indonesia (PDI—Indonesian Democratic Party) announced that it would support his candidacy, it appeared likely that he would seek election for a sixth term. In August 1990 a group of 58 prominent Indonesians issued a public demand to Suharto to retire from the presidency at the end of his current term of office.

During 1991, in response to the growing demand for political openness, several new organizations were formed to promote freedom of expression and other democratic values. As labour unrest grew, arrests and the alleged intimidation of political activists were instrumental in curbing expressions of dissent; political campaigns were banned on university campuses. In September Suharto removed several of the most outspoken members of Golkar from the list of candidates to contest the legislative elections, scheduled to take place in June 1992.

The Government had, for some time, been seeking to win the support of the Muslim electorate in preparation for the presidential elections in 1993. In 1989 Suharto promoted legislation whereby decisions by Islamic courts no longer required confirmation by civil courts, and in December 1990 the President opened the symposium of the newly formed Association of Indonesian Muslim Intellectuals (ICMI), an organization that united a broad spectrum of Islamic interests. In 1991 Suharto made his first pilgrimage to Mecca. ABRI was opposed to the establishment of ICMI because it regarded the polarization of politics by religion as a threat to stability.

During the strictly monitored four-week campaign period leading to elections for the DPR, for local government bodies and for district councils, political parties were prohibited from addressing religious issues, the question of the dominant role of the ethnic Chinese community in the economy, or any subject that might present a threat to national unity. The opposition parties did, however, exploit the increasing public resentment about the rapidly expanding businesses of Suharto's children (some of whom had been awarded monopoly rights). On 9 June 1992 90.4% of the electorate participated in the election to the DPR, which resulted in a further victory for Golkar, which secured 282 of the 400 elective seats; 62 seats were won by the PPP (a gain of one seat compared with its 1987 election result) and 56 seats (compared with 40) by the PDI, which had recently mobilized almost 3m. supporters at a rally in Jakarta.

In October 1992 Suharto accepted nominations by Golkar, the PPP, the PDI and ABRI for a sixth term of office as President. His victory in the forthcoming presidential election was thus assured. Attention then focused on the vice-presidency. Owing to increasing public debate over ABRI's active involvement in political affairs and, in particular, concern over whether the appointment of 100 members of ABRI to the DPR remained justifiable, it was deemed important that ABRI consolidate its position through the election to the vice-presidency of its own principal candidate, Sutrisno. Suharto, however, was rumoured to support the prospective candidacy of the Minister of State for Research and Technology, Prof. Dr Ir Bucharuddin Jusuf (B. J.) Habibie, an influential Muslim leader and the then Chairman of ICMI. Sutrisno was subsequently endorsed as a vice-presidential candidate by the PDI, the PPP, ABRI and, finally, Golkar. In March 1993 the DPR duly elected Suharto and Sutrisno to the posts of President and Vice-President respectively. Suharto's new 41-member Cabinet comprised 22 new appointees. ABRI representation was reduced from 11 to eight members. Those primarily responsible for the country's economic policy since 1988, Prof. Dr Johannes B. Sumarlin, Adrianus Mooy and Radius Prawiro (all western-educated Christians) were replaced, leaving only three Christians in the Cabinet; several members of ICMI were included in the new list, thus advancing the faction led by Habibie, who was unpopular with ABRI.

In October 1993, at the party Congress, the Minister of Information, Harmoko, became the first civilian to be elected to the chairmanship of Golkar. In an unprecedented move, Suharto had openly endorsed Harmoko's candidacy. Also at the Congress, Suharto's family entered active national politics; his son, Bambang Trihatmodjo, and daughter, Siti Hardijanti Rukmana (known as Mbak Tutut), who had both been appointed to the MPR in 1992, were elected to positions of responsibility within Golkar.

In July 1993 the incumbent Chairman of the PDI, Soerjadi, was re-elected to the post at a fractious party Congress. The Government invalidated the election of Soerjadi, who had incurred Suharto's displeasure by campaigning during the 1992 elections for a limited presidential term of office, and appointed a 23-member 'caretaker board' pending new elections. An extraordinary Congress of the PDI ended inconclusively in December owing to the unexpected candidacy for the chairmanship of Megawati Sukarnoputri, the daughter of former President Sukarno. Despite government pressure to elect Budi Hardjono, a senior party official, Megawati received overwhelming support from the participants of the Congress, and the 'caretaker board' prevented a vote from taking place. The Government then ordered the holding of a new PDI Congress, at which Megawati was elected Chairman.

In June 1993 the USA imposed a deadline of February 1994 for Indonesia to improve workers' rights or lose trade privileges under the Generalized System of Preferences. The Government adopted reforms to the only officially recognized trade union, the Serikat Pekerja Seluruh Indonesia (All Indonesia Workers' Union), introduced a substantial increase in the minimum wage and revoked the controversial 1986 Labour Law, which allowed the intervention of the armed forces in labour disputes. Workers subsequently went on strike, accusing employers of failing to pay the new minimum wage and demanding improved working conditions. In February 1994 the independent Serikat Buruh Sejahtera Indonesia (SBSI—Indonesian Prosperous Labour Union), which had had its application for registration formally rejected in June 1993, appealed for a one-hour national work stoppage. The General Secretary of the SBSI, Muchtar Pakpahan, was charged with inciting hatred against the Government and temporarily detained. In April 1994 riots broke out in Medan, Sumatra, over workers' demands for improved factory conditions and the implementation of the new minimum wage, and rapidly degenerated into attacks on ethnic Chinese property and business executives, who were widely perceived to have benefited disproportionately from the country's rapid economic growth. Three members of the SBSI surrendered to the authorities in May and admitted to having organized the protest. Further strikes took place in other parts of northern Sumatra. In August Pakpahan was rearrested. He was given a three-year prison sentence in November for inciting labour unrest (which was later extended to four years).

In January 1995 it was announced by the armed forces that 300 members of the PDI were to be investigated for links to the 1965 coup attempt, following allegations that many members had relatives or contacts in the banned PKI. This apparent attempt to discredit the opposition grouping was followed in May by a ban on the presence of Megawati at the commemoration, in June, of the 25th anniversary of the death of her father, Sukarno. The authorities attempted to ascribe social unrest to communist subversion. In September the Chief of Staff of the Armed Forces named several prominent dissidents, including Muchtar Pakpahan (whose conviction for incitement had been rescinded by the Supreme Court in that month), as members of 'formless organizations', which, he claimed, had infiltrated pressure groups to promote the revival of communism. In November 300 alleged subversives were arrested in Java.

In July 1995, in response to widespread condemnation of Indonesia's human rights violations, Suharto announced that three prisoners detained for their complicity in the 1965 coup attempt would be released to coincide with the 50th anniversary of independence in August. The administration also subsequently announced that the code ET (which stood for *Eks Tahanan Politik*—former political prisoner) was to be removed from identity papers following the anniversary. The measure affected about 1.3m. citizens, most of whom had been arrested following the 1965 coup attempt, but released without trial; ET status had subjected them to certain restrictions (for example, in employment) and to widespread discrimination. In October 1995 30 members of an extreme right-wing group, the Islamic State of Indonesia, were arrested in western Java for attempting to overthrow 'the unitary state of Indonesia'. In January 1996 in Bandung, West Java, thousands took part in demonstrations against the disproportionately wealthy ethnic Chinese.

In December 1995 Suharto implemented an unprecedented mid-term cabinet reorganization, in which Prof. Dr Satrio Budiardjo Yudono was dismissed and the Ministry of Trade, over which he had presided, was merged with the Ministry of Industry. This dismissal of one of Habibie's protégés, the day before Habibie's re-election to the chairmanship of the increasingly powerful ICMI, was widely interpreted as a signal from Suharto for Habibie to restrain his political ambitions. In January 1996 the Government abolished permit requirements for political meetings (police permission was still necessary for public gatherings and demonstrations). In March a group of political activists established an Independent Election Monitoring Committee, which was immediately declared unconstitutional by the Government. In April the Government restored voting rights to 1,157,820 people who had been associated with the PKI, leaving a further 20,706 still ineligible to vote. The Government's increasing concern over potential opposition to Golkar in the 1997 elections, however, resulted in a return to more authoritarian practices. In May 1996 Sri Bintang Pamungkas, an outspoken member of the PPP expelled from the DPR in March 1995, received a custodial sentence of 34 months for insulting Suharto; he remained free, however, pending an appeal. In the same month Pamungkas formed a new political organization, the Partai Uni Demokrasi Indonesia (PUDI—United Democratic Party of Indonesia), which ABRI and the Government refused to recognize. In December the High Court upheld the verdict against Pamungkas.

In June 1996 the Government responded to the increasing popularity of Megawati's leadership of the PDI, and consequent potential threat to Golkar: government supporters within the

PDI organized a party congress in the northern Sumatran town of Medan, which removed Megawati as leader of the party, and installed a former Chairman, Soerjadi. PDI members loyal to Megawati organized demonstrations in her support throughout the country during July, and occupied the PDI headquarters in Jakarta. At the end of July members of Soerjadi's PDI faction and the armed forces acted to remove Megawati and her supporters forcibly from the PDI headquarters, prompting violence in which five people were killed. The Government declared the minor, Marxist-influenced Partai Rakyat Demokrasi (PRD) to be responsible for the rioting, and renewed its campaign against communism, claiming that the PRD was the PKI's successor. In September the Government disbanded the PRD, declaring it to be a proscribed organization. In the same month Megawati's new party headquarters in eastern Jakarta were closed.

In October 1996 Suharto ordered ABRI to suppress all political dissent. The Government's continued lack of commitment to its stated policy of political openness was demonstrated when, in November, it declared that it would take action against non-governmental organizations (NGOs) that violated Indonesian law and the *Pancasila* ideology. In December the DPR ratified legislation granting the Government extensive powers to revoke the broadcasting permits of private television and radio stations. In the same month a government decree banned mass rallies during campaigning for the forthcoming legislative election. In February 1997 the Government announced that all proposed campaign speeches were to be examined to ensure their adherence to the *Pancasila*. In April thousands of supporters of Megawati rallied outside the DPR to protest against the exclusion from the final list of candidates nominated by her faction.

Prior to the election, which was held on 29 May 1997, the Government permitted a campaign period of 25 days during which no two parties were permitted to campaign simultaneously in the same region. Despite this, there was extensive localized pre-election violence. In the worst incident 125 people were killed when a shopping centre was set alight during clashes between supporters of Golkar and the PPP in the provincial capital of Kalimantan, Banjarmasin; more than 150 others were killed in various other incidents across the country. Following the election, riots in Madura, as a result of PPP claims that ballots had not been counted, resulted in an unprecedented repeat of voting at 86 polling stations on 4 June. The final results of the election, which continued to attract allegations of fraud, revealed that Golkar had secured 74.3% of the vote (compared with 68.1% in 1992) giving it control of 325 seats, the PPP had won 89 seats, while Soerjadi's PDI had secured only 11 seats (compared with 56 in 1992).

Widespread social unrest continued throughout 1997, as a result of religious tension, income disparity between social and ethnic groups and the repercussions of the transmigration programme initiated in 1971. The worst violence began in West Kalimantan in December 1996 as indigenous Dayak tribesmen massacred hundreds of Madurese transmigrants following an attack by Muslim youths on local schoolgirls. Thousands were displaced by the unrest.

In August 1997 the two principal Muslim leaders, Abdurrahman Wahid and Amien Rais, the leader of the second largest Islamic grouping, Muhammadiyah, were excluded from the list of 500 civilian and military appointees to the MPR. Amien Rais had been forced to resign from a board of experts in ICMI in February for publicly criticizing the controversial Freeport mine in Irian Jaya (now Papua, see below).

Following a massive decline in the value of the Indonesian currency between August and October 1997, President Suharto was forced to accept a rescue programme from the IMF. However, Suharto subsequently failed to implement the requisite reforms, fearing that they would provoke social and political unrest and adversely affect the business interests of his family and friends. At the end of October an unprecedented gathering of Muslim leaders and intellectuals took place, including members of ICMI; the participants rejected Suharto's leadership and rallied around Amien Rais, who had already offered himself as a presidential candidate. Wahid subsequently joined Amien Rais and Megawati (who had entered an informal alliance) in demanding Suharto's resignation. In a largely symbolic gesture, Megawati also presented herself as a presidential candidate. Despite opposition to his candidacy, Suharto declared his acceptance of Golkar's nomination for the presidency (announced in October), thus assuring his victory in the forthcoming election. He indicated that of the 13 contenders for the vice-presidency he would support Habibie's candidacy.

At the presidential election held on 10 March 1998 Suharto was re-elected unopposed. He then endorsed the nomination of Habibie as the new Vice-President. Suharto announced the appointment of a new, 36-member Cabinet, which included a number of members of his immediate circle of friends and family. (Prior to his re-election, Suharto had also appointed his son-in-law, Lt-Gen. Prabowo Subianto, as Commander of Kostrad—the Indonesian army's strategic reserve.) Suharto's appointment of such a Cabinet defied the recommendations of the IMF. Student protests in support of demands for the President's resignation and for fundamental political and economic reforms increased. In May riots erupted in Jakarta, precipitated by the announcement of a 70% increase in the price of fuel. Six students were shot dead by military snipers during a protest at Trisakti University in Jakarta. It was initially estimated that 500 people had been killed in the unrest in the capital, while a further 700 perished elsewhere; however, a report published by Indonesia's leading human rights group in early June stated that at least 1,188 people had died in Jakarta alone. Indonesia's ethnic-Chinese minority was the target for much of the violence: an uncertain number of Chinese were murdered, numerous Chinese women were raped, and Chinese homes and businesses were looted and burned. On 21 May, following sustained popular and political pressure to step down (including an unprecedented demand for his resignation by Harmoko, and the resignation of the 14 economic ministers in the Cabinet), Suharto announced his resignation as President. Vice-President Habibie was sworn in immediately as Suharto's successor, and subsequently appointed a new 'reform Cabinet', which, however, included some ministers from the previous administration. The new President also announced the release of a number of political prisoners (including Muchtar Pakpahan and Sri Bintang Pamungkas), encouraged government departments to sever links with enterprises owned by Suharto's family, and supported Gen. Wiranto in his dismissal of Suharto's son-in-law, Lt-Gen. Prabowo, from his position in Kostrad (it was subsequently announced that Prabowo had been formally dismissed from the army following an investigation into his conduct as Commander of the unit, and was also to face a court martial). Habibie also announced that elections would be held in 1999; new political parties began to be formed in anticipation of fresh electoral laws. At the beginning of June 1998 an investigation into the assets of former President Suharto and other government officials was announced, and later the same month Habibie expelled 41 members of the MPR, including several close associates of Suharto, on account of alleged corruption, nepotism and collusion. (Seven members of Suharto's family were removed from their seats in the MPR the following month.) Nevertheless, Habibie was considered by many to be under the control of Suharto, and there were repeated demands from student groups and other opposition organizations for Habibie to relinquish the presidency and for a transitional government to be installed.

Discontent and rioting continued across the archipelago throughout the latter half of 1998, exacerbated by dissatisfaction at the pace of change under the new administration and by severe food shortages, as well as by increasing ethnic and religious tension. A four-day special session of the MPR was convened in Jakarta in November, and at least 16 people were killed and more than 400 injured when students and civilians clashed with soldiers outside the building where the MPR session was being held. At least another 14 people died during clashes between Muslims and Catholics in further riots. In the same month a report was published containing the findings of a panel appointed by the Government to investigate the riots in May. The panel found that elements of the military had acted as provocateurs during the riots (with particular suspicion falling on a unit led by Lt-Gen. Prabowo), concluding that the riots had been 'created as part of a political struggle at the level of the élite', and recommended that further investigations be carried out. In December former President Suharto faced questioning at the Higher Prosecutor's Office over allegations of corruption.

In December 1998 it was announced that a legislative election would be held on 7 June 1999; it was further announced that the MPR (including 200 additional delegates) would convene on 29 August to elect a new President. In early 1999 a new electoral system was announced: combining both district and proportional voting, seats in the DPR were to be allocated proportionally, but only parties presenting candidates in a substantial number of districts would be permitted to contest the election. It was also announced that civil servants were no longer to be obliged to support Golkar, that the number of seats in the DPR allocated to the military was to be reduced from 75 to 38 and that the membership of the MPR was to be reduced from 1,000 to 700 (500 of whom would comprise the members of the DPR while, of the remainder, 135 were to be elected by the provincial assemblies and 65 appointed by the Komite Pemilihan Umum—General Election Committee).

Violent unrest continued across the archipelago in early 1999: at least 159 people were killed during clashes between Muslims and Christians on the island of Ambon, in the province of Maluku. The Habibie Government continued to pursue an extensive programme of reform. Several new laws benefited the provinces, including one providing for the election of district heads (*bupati*) by the district assemblies. In April the Subversion Law, introduced in 1963 and previously applied in the suppression of political dissidents, was repealed by the MPR (although some of the prohibitions covered by the law were retained). In May a presidential decree removed a ban on the use and teaching of the Mandarin Chinese language and also outlawed discrimination on the grounds of ethnic origin. Two significant changes also took place in the armed forces in the first half of 1999: following a reorganization of military personnel in January, in April the police force—part of the Indonesian military since 1962—was formally separated from the armed forces (although it remained under the control of the Ministry of Defence); and the armed forces resumed their revolutionary-era name, Tentara Nasional Indonesia (TNI—the Indonesian National Defence Forces), in place of the name of ABRI (the Armed Forces of the Republic of Indonesia).

President Habibie was nominated as the sole presidential candidate of the Golkar party in May 1999, despite concerns expressed by some elements of the party regarding Habibie's close association with former President Suharto. The three leading opposition parties—Megawati's Partai Demokrasi Indonesia Perjuangan (PDI—P, Indonesian Democratic Struggle Party), Abdurrahman Wahid's Partai Kebangkitan Bangsa (PKB—National Awakening Party), and Amien Rais's Partai Amanat Nasional (PAN—National Mandate Party)—agreed to form an informal electoral alliance against Golkar; however, the alliance exhibited instability from an early stage. The election campaign proceeded with only minimal incidents of violent disruption, as 48 parties competed for a share of the votes. The election was held as scheduled on 7 June; approximately 118m. people voted (a turn-out of 91%). As expected, Megawati's PDI—P led the polls, winning 34% of the votes cast (securing 154 seats); the second largest share of the vote was unexpectedly won by Golkar, which received 20% of votes cast (120 seats), performing poorly in the cities but achieving a strong result in the outer islands. Abdurrahman Wahid's PKB secured 59 seats, while Amien Rais's PAN won just 7% of the vote (35 seats). Some 14 other smaller parties also won seats in the MPR. Despite allegations of irregularities, the results were finally endorsed by President Habibie in early August. Megawati and Habibie thus emerged initially as the main candidates for the presidency, which was originally scheduled to be decided in November. In October, however, following the rejection of his presidential record by the MPR in a secret ballot, Habibie withdrew his candidacy shortly before the rescheduled vote was due to be held. Expectations that Megawati would be elected President increased immediately; however, she failed to win the contest, receiving 313 votes compared with the 373 secured by Abdurrahman Wahid, the only other serious candidate, who had received the endorsement of a number of Islamic parties, as well as the support of the Golkar party following the withdrawal of Habibie. The announcement of Wahid's victory provoked outrage among Megawati's supporters, and violent protests ensued in Jakarta and elsewhere on Java, as well as on the island of Bali. The MPR voted to appoint Megawati as Vice-President. The new Cabinet reflected the conciliatory and inclusive approach of the incoming President: it incorporated both Islamist and nationalist representatives, as well as representatives of non-Javanese groups. Gen. Wiranto, who was appointed Co-ordinating Minister for Political, Legal and Security Affairs, was replaced as Minister of Defence by the former Minister of Education and Culture, Juwono Sudarsono, the first civilian to hold the post. Wiranto was replaced as Commander-in-Chief of the TNI by Adm. Widodo Adi Sutjipto.

The newly appointed Attorney-General, Marzuki Darusman, announced that the investigation into the allegations of corruption made against former President Suharto was to be reopened. The apparent commitment of the new administration to addressing the issue of corruption was further emphasized in November 1999, when Wahid urged the investigation of three government ministers. One of the ministers reportedly implicated, the Co-ordinating Minister for People's Welfare and leader of the PPP, Hamzah Haz, subsequently resigned from the Cabinet.

In the months following Wahid's election to the presidency, there was further unrest across the archipelago. Particularly serious ethnic violence continued on the island of Ambon in Maluku province where, according to official estimates in December 1999, more than 750 people had died and many thousands more had fled the region, since the renewal of violent clashes between Muslims and Christians in the region in January of that year. (Aid agencies, however, estimated the total number of dead to be much higher.) In mid-December President Wahid and Vice-President Megawati (who was subject to harsh criticism for her failure to address the crisis, despite having been charged by Wahid with special responsibility for Maluku) visited the region and appealed for an end to the conflict. Hundreds of additional troops were sent to Ambon to supplement the 2,500 already deployed in Maluku, following the occurrence of dozens more deaths. Although the predominantly Muslim northern districts of Maluku were formally separated as the new province of North Maluku in late 1999, at least 265 people were believed to have been killed in clashes between Christians and Muslims on the island of Halmahera at the end of December, with violence also reported on other islands.

At the end of January 2000 Indonesia's National Human Rights Commission released the results of its investigation into the role of the Indonesian armed forces in human rights abuses in the former Indonesian province of Timor-Leste (see below). Thirty-three military officers, including the former Commander-in-Chief of the armed forces, Gen. Wiranto, were implicated. In response to the Commission's report, President Wahid demanded Wiranto's resignation from his post of Co-ordinating Minister for Political, Legal and Security Affairs; Wiranto, however, openly defied Wahid's demands. In mid-February Wahid suspended Wiranto from his position; Wiranto was to retain his ministerial rank, although his portfolio was allocated to the Minister of Home Affairs, Gen. (retd) Suryadi Sudirja, pending further investigation. Wiranto resigned in mid-May. In January, meanwhile, a reorganization took place within the TNI, in which officers loyal to Wiranto were apparently removed from positions of influence. A second reorganization of senior military personnel was announced in February, in which Maj.-Gen. Agus Wirahadikusumah, who was reportedly committed to Wahid's policy of disengaging the military from Indonesian politics, was appointed as the head of Kostrad. In August doubts concerning the commitment of the Indonesian Government to the trial of military personnel suspected of involvement in gross human rights violations in Timor-Leste (see below) were provoked when the MPR introduced a constitutional amendment that excluded military personnel from prosecution for crimes committed prior to the enactment of the relevant legislation. Doubts regarding the likelihood of the prosecution of those members of the Indonesian military believed to be responsible for human rights abuses were compounded in early September, when Wiranto's name was not included on a list, announced by the Attorney-General's office, of 19 suspects.

In April 2000 President Wahid dismissed from the Cabinet the Minister of State for Investment and Development of State Enterprises, Laksamana Sukardi of the PDI—P, and the Minister of Trade and Industry, Yusuf Kalla of the pro-Habibie wing of Golkar; Wahid subsequently suggested that both Ministers were guilty of corruption. In July Wahid faced fierce criticism from the DPR when he refused to explain the reasons for his dismissal of the two Ministers. Meanwhile, general misgivings about Wahid's style of government also increased. In August Wahid announced that he was to delegate the daily administration of the Government to Vice-President Megawati, although the President was to retain overall control. It was speculated by many observers that Wahid's announcement had been intended to safeguard his own position during the 12-day session of the MPR held in August. Amendments to the Constitution approved by the MPR included articles defining explicitly the authority of the DPR, particularly in relation to the body's questioning and investigating of government activities; legislation was also enacted to extend military representation in the MPR until 2009, four years after the date at which the military had been scheduled to lose its remaining 38 seats in the chamber. President Wahid announced the formation of a new 26-member Cabinet. The incoming Cabinet included considerably fewer representatives of Megawati's PDI—P, and two of the most influential cabinet posts were allocated to Wahid loyalists: Gen. (retd) Susilo Bambang Yudhoyono was appointed Co-ordinating Minister for Political, Legal and Security Affairs, while Rizal Ramli was designated Co-ordinating Minister for Economic Affairs.

In August 2000 former President Suharto was formally charged with corruption. In September, however, the charges against him were dismissed after an independent team of doctors declared that he was mentally and physically unfit to stand trial, thereby provoking violent protests on the streets of Jakarta. (In May 2006 criminal charges against the former President were formally abandoned on account of his deteriorating health, but a civil case was subsequently instigated—see below.) President Wahid announced that he had ordered the arrest of Suharto's youngest son, Hutomo Mandala Putra (also known as Tommy Suharto), in connection with a series of bomb threats and explosions in Jakarta in August and September. In one such attack at least 15 people were killed in September 2000 when a bomb exploded at the Jakarta Stock Exchange. Hutomo Mandala Putra was sentenced to 18 months' imprisonment after being convicted on an unrelated charge of fraudulent activity; however, he subsequently evaded arrest and went into hiding.

In July 2001 Justice Syafiuddin Kartasasmita, the judge who had upheld the sentence passed on Hutomo Mandala Putra, was shot dead. Two suspects confessed to the murder, but admitted in custody that Suharto's son had financed them and supplied the weapons used in the attack. Meanwhile, two men were convicted of the bombing of the Jakarta Stock Exchange and sentenced to 20 years' imprisonment each. In October the corruption charge on which Hutomo Mandala Putra had initially been convicted was rejected by the Supreme Court. However, he remained in hiding owing to his suspected involvement in several other cases. In November police arrested the fugitive, and in December the Supreme Court announced that Hutomo Mandala Putra would serve at least 11 months in prison for evading arrest, despite the fact that his original conviction had been overruled. Suharto's son claimed that in October 2000 he had given a sum of money to two men close to President Wahid on the understanding that this would secure for him a presidential pardon. (Wahid denied all knowledge of this when questioned early in 2002.) In March 2002, following the conclusion of the police investigation, Hutomo Mandala Putra was charged with murder, illegal possession of weapons and fleeing from justice; his trial began in the same month. Meanwhile, the two defendants alleged to have assassinated Justice Syafiuddin were found guilty of murder and sentenced to life imprisonment. A third man was sentenced to a four-year prison term in a separate trial for his involvement in planning the assassination. In July Hutomo Mandala Putra was found guilty of murder and sentenced to a 15-year prison term. However, in October 2006 he was granted conditional early release, provoking anger from human rights campaigners.

In September 2000 the DPR appointed a committee to investigate two financial scandals with which President Wahid had been linked. The first of the two scandals involved the irregular diversion of US $4.1m. from the funds of the Badan Urusan Logistic (BULOG—the National Logistics Agency), allegedly to finance the Golkar party election campaign in 1999, whilst the second concerned a donation of $2m. made by Sultan Hassanal Bolkiah of Brunei. The President's refusal to be questioned on either matter provoked intense frustration among legislators. In January 2001 the commission concluded that Wahid 'could be suspected of playing a role' in the theft of BULOG funds by his personal masseur and that the President had been deliberately inconsistent in his explanations of how the donation from Sultan Hassanal Bolkiah (originally intended for social welfare) had been spent; however, the commission was unable to present clear evidence that Wahid had personally benefited from either situation. In early February the DPR voted by 393 votes to four for the formal censure of Wahid over his alleged involvement in the scandals. Wahid was given three months in which to provide a satisfactory explanation of his actions to the DPR. The President continued to deny any wrongdoing and stated his intention to complete his term of presidential office. Tens of thousands of pro-Wahid demonstrators took to the streets in Surabaya and elsewhere in East Java (President Wahid's home province), and protesters set fire to the regional offices of Golkar, which had supported the vote to censure Wahid. Later in the same month Wahid offered himself for questioning by police investigating the two scandals.

In March 2001 more than 12,000 students held a demonstration in Jakarta to demand the President's resignation. In view of Wahid's unsatisfactory reply to his first censure, at the end of April the DPR voted overwhelmingly to issue a second censure and requested that the MPR convene a special session to begin impeachment proceedings. Violent pro-Wahid demonstrations took place in East Java. However, in late May the DPR voted by a huge majority to instruct the MPR to instigate an impeachment hearing. In response, at the beginning of June the President reorganized his Cabinet, dismissing the Co-ordinating Minister for Political, Legal and Security Affairs, Susilo Bambang Yudhoyono. The Chief of Police, Gen. Surojo Bimantoro, was suspended. The President then initiated a further reallocation of ministerial portfolios. In July the President threatened to declare a state of emergency if no compromise had been reached, and effected another reorganization of the Cabinet. He also appointed a new Chief of Police without the support of the legislature. A special session of the MPR was convened to which the President was summoned to give an account of his 21 months in power. President Wahid deemed the session illegal and refused to attend. He suspended the legislature, declaring a state of civil emergency, and urged that new elections be held in one year's time. However, the military refused to support the declaration, and the MPR stated that the President did not have the constitutional authority to dissolve it.

On 23 July 2001 Abdurrahman Wahid was deposed as President following an impeachment hearing. He was replaced by Vice-President Megawati Sukarnoputri, in a peaceful transition of power. Legislators elected the leader of the PPP, Hamzah Haz, to act as the new President's deputy, and in August Megawati announced the composition of her first Cabinet. Of its 32 members, only four were former military men, in sharp contrast to previous practice. Most of the principal posts were allocated to non-political professionals, including the appointment of Dorodjatun Kuntjoro-Jakti as Co-ordinating Minister for Economic Affairs. Susilo Bambang Yudhoyono was reinstated as Co-ordinating Minister for Political, Legal and Security Affairs.

In October 2001 President Megawati gave her assent to a prosecution request to question the Speaker of the DPR, Akbar Tandjung, over the alleged misappropriation of BULOG funds. Tandjung admitted that he had handled the money on the orders of President Habibie, but had passed it on to an Islamic charity to fund food supplies for the poor. However, Attorney-General Muhammad Abdul Rachman claimed that investigations showed that such contributions had never taken place. In December state prosecutors questioned former President Habibie, and in January 2002 Akbar Tandjung was formally declared to be a suspect. In March approximately 1,500 protesters gathered outside the DPR building to demand Tandjung's resignation and the establishment of an independent inquiry; his trial on charges of corruption began later in the month. In September Tandjung was convicted of the charges against him and sentenced to a three-year prison term; despite the failure of his first appeal, in February 2004 the Supreme Court overruled his conviction, prompting demonstrations in several cities.

In August 2002 a series of constitutional amendments was approved at the annual session of the MPR. These provided for the direct election of both the President and Vice-President at the next national poll, scheduled to be held in 2004, and for the abolition of all seats held by non-elected representatives, effectively terminating military involvement in the legislature five years earlier than originally intended. The legislation also provided for a bicameral legislature through the creation of the Dewan Perwakilan Daerah (DPD—House of Representatives of the Regions), which, together with the DPR, would form the MPR. A total of 14 amendments received legislative assent; these constituted the 'Fourth Amendment' to the Constitution. The DPR ratified the amendments in 2003.

An increasing challenge facing the Indonesian Government was the threat posed by terrorist activity, at both a domestic and regional level. In October 2002 the Government's response to this threat was tested when two bombs exploded in the tourist resort of Kuta, on the island of Bali. An explosion outside a night-club resulted in the deaths of 202 people, many of whom were tourists, mainly Australians. In its first admission that Islamist fundamentalists were operative within Indonesia, the Government initially attributed the attack to the international network of al-Qa'ida, which it believed to have collaborated with local terrorists. The DPR authorized two emergency decrees, bringing into effect several previously delayed anti-terrorism measures, including a law permitting suspects to be detained for up to seven days without charge. The Muslim cleric Abu Bakar Bashir, commander of the Majelis Mujahidin Indonesia (MMI—Indonesian Mujahideen Council) and alleged to be the spiritual head of the regional Islamist organization Jemaah Islamiah (JI), was detained in connection with the attacks. (He had been questioned by police in January over alleged links to al-Qa'ida but had been released without charge.) The USA and the UN announced that they had designated JI a terrorist entity and 'frozen' its financial assets. The police made several further arrests as the investigation into the bombings proceeded and in November 2002 one of the suspects, Amrozi bin Nurhasyim, confessed to his involvement and to having strong links to JI, as well as implicating several others in the attack. Later in the same month Imam Samudra was arrested on suspicion of having organized the attacks. He confessed to being a member of JI and to having planned earlier attacks, including the bombing of churches across the archipelago in December 2000 (see below), together with the operational leader of the organization, Riduan Isamuddin, also known as Hambali. In December 2002 Ali Gufron, also known as Mukhlas, who apparently had succeeded Hambali as the operational leader of JI, was also arrested and confessed to having helped to plan the Bali attack. The trials of those involved began in Denpasar in May 2003; a total of 34 people had been detained on suspicion of involvement in the bombings. In July it was reported that another suspect, Idris, also known as Jhoni Hendrawan, had been arrested in the previous month, and in August the Thai authorities announced that they had finally captured Hambali, who was subsequently taken into custody by the USA.

In March 2003 the DPR gave its assent to legislation specifically designating terrorism as a crime and providing for detention without trial for terrorist suspects. The legislation was enacted retrospectively in order to cover the Bali bombing. In April the trial of Abu Bakar Bashir on charges of subversion, immigration violations, providing false documents and statements to the police and involvement in several terrorist attacks, including the bombings carried out on churches in late 2000, began in Jakarta. In August 2003 more than 3,000 Islamist militants attended a demonstration organized by the MMI in the capital to signal their support for Bashir. In the following month Bashir was convicted of the subversion charges against him but, owing to insufficient evidence, was acquitted both of any involvement in terrorist attacks and of the charge that he was the spiritual leader of JI. He was sentenced to a four-year prison term, which on appeal was later reduced to three years, although the remaining charges against him were upheld. Bashir's sentence was further reduced to 18 months by the Supreme Court in March 2004. In the following month, immediately after his release from prison, Bashir was rearrested on suspicion of terrorism. Meanwhile, in August 2003 Amrozi became the first person to be convicted in connection with the bombings in Bali; his appeal against the death sentence was subsequently rejected. In the following month Imam Samudra was also convicted and sentenced to death. A further suspect, Ali Imron, was sentenced to life imprisonment, having expressed some remorse for his actions. In October Ali Gufron, generally believed to have been responsible for planning the attacks, was also found guilty of the charges against him and sentenced to death. A further 13 suspects had been sentenced to prison terms for having played minor parts in the bombings. In July 2004 the Constitutional Court declared that the counter-terrorism legislation approved in 2003 and used to convict a number of those responsible for the Bali bombings should not have been applied retroactively. The Minister of Justice and Human Rights Affairs stated that the ruling did not rescind the convictions already secured, but made it impossible to continue using the law in future cases for crimes committed before its enactment.

In April 2003 a bomb exploded at the Sukarno-Hatta International Airport, injuring 11 people, and in July an explosion outside the DPR building caused minor damage. In August an explosive device detonated by a suicide bomber outside the Marriott Hotel in Jakarta resulted in the deaths of 12 people. The police apprehended a number of suspects, all of whom were believed to be members of JI, and the first trial in connection with the Marriott bombing began in January 2004. In February Sardono Siliwangi was convicted of involvement in the bombing; he was sentenced to a 10-year prison term. A second suspect, Mohammed Rais, was convicted in May and sentenced to seven years in prison. In June two alleged Acehnese separatists were sentenced to prison terms for the bombing of the DPR building in July 2003. In August 2004 Idris was sentenced to 10 years' imprisonment for his part in the hotel bombing, but charges against him in connection with the Bali bombings were withdrawn, owing to the Constitutional Court's July ruling, despite an earlier confession of his involvement.

A bomb exploded outside the Australian embassy in Jakarta in September 2004, killing nine people, mostly Indonesians, and injuring more than 180 others. JI was held responsible for the attack, and a number of suspects were subsequently detained. In October at least nine people were injured when a bomb exploded outside the Indonesian embassy in Paris, France; no group claimed responsibility. In the same month the trial of Bashir on charges of conspiring and inciting acts of terrorism, including the Bali and Marriott bombings, commenced in Jakarta. In addition, he was again accused of being the spiritual leader of JI. In relation to the Bali attacks, Bashir was to be tried under the criminal code. In February 2005, testifying at his ongoing trial, Bashir formally denied any involvement in the Bali and Marriott bombings and any connection with JI. In March, however, while being cleared of charges relating to the bombing of the Marriott Hotel, Bashir was found guilty of conspiracy over the Bali attacks and sentenced to a prison term of two-and-a-half years. Australia and the USA immediately expressed their disappointment at the leniency of the sentence. Bashir appealed against the verdict, but the appeal was rejected by the Supreme Court in August and the original sentence was upheld. However, Bashir's sentence was reduced as part of Indonesia's 60th independence celebrations, and he was released from prison in June 2006. He again appealed against the original verdict, and in January 2007 his conviction was overruled by the Supreme Court on the grounds of insufficient evidence. In July 2005 the first suspect to be tried in connection with the bombing of the Australian embassy in September 2004, the Islamist militant Irun Hidayat, was convicted of being an accessory to the attack and was sentenced to three-and-a-half years' imprisonment. In September three men, Iwan 'Rois' Darmawan, Ahmad Hasan and Syaiful Bahri, were found guilty of helping to organize the attack; Darmawan and Hasan both received the death penalty, while Bahri was sentenced to 10 years' imprisonment.

In early October 2005 Bali was again seriously affected by terrorist activity. Three bombs were detonated at tourist locations on the island, killing 23 people, including the bombers, and injuring more than 100 others. JI was thought to have been responsible for the attack. Later that month, on the third anniversary of the 2002 Bali bombings, protesters attempted forcibly to enter Kerobokan prison in Denpasar, where they believed that Amrozi, Imam Samudra and Mukhlas remained, awaiting execution following their convictions in connection with the bombings. The demonstrators demanded the immediate execution of the three men, who had in fact been transferred to another prison on the previous day. During 2007 the Supreme Court rejected the three prisoners' final appeals against the death sentence, and they awaited execution in early 2008.

In November 2005 one of JI's senior leaders, the Malaysian bomb-maker Azahari Husin, who was suspected of organizing the 2005 Bali bombings with fellow-Malaysian Noordin Mohammad Top, was killed during a raid on a property in Batu, near Malang, in East Java. Acting upon information received, Indonesian police officers surrounded the house in which Azahari and two other suspected militants were hiding. The three men barricaded themselves inside the building, where they then detonated a series of devices, culminating in the explosion of a suicide bomb that killed all three men. In January 2006 Noordin Mohammad Top released a statement claiming responsibility for the Bali attacks of 2005. In his message, Noordin also claimed to have formed a new South-East Asian Islamist militant organization, namely Tanzam Qaedat-al Jihad (Organization for the Basis of Jihad). In the same month six people were arrested in relation to the 2005 Bali bombings. In September four suspects were convicted of involvement in the attacks and were sentenced to between eight and 18 years' imprisonment. In November eight members of JI were found guilty of carrying out and supporting terrorist activity; they received prison terms of between six years and life. In March 2007 police arrested several suspected JI members in the Javanese city of Yogyakarta. The militants were believed to have links to Abu Dujana, who according to some reports had become the commander of JI's military operations. In June Abu Dujana was one of eight suspects apprehended by the authorities in central Java. In a separate police operation conducted on the same day, Zarkasih (also known as Nuaim or Mbah, among other aliases), who was believed to have acted as the head of JI since 2004, was also arrested. Both members of JI admitted their involvement with the organization. The trial of Abu Dujana, on charges of plotting terrorist activities and of sheltering other militants, and also of Zarkasih, who was accused of conspiring to commit terrorism and of supplying weapons and training to JI members, concluded in April 2008. Each defendant was sentenced to 15 years' imprisonment.

Meanwhile, in early 2004 preparations were under way for legislative and local elections, scheduled to take place on 5 April, as well as the country's first direct presidential and vice-presidential elections, which were to be held on 5 July. A total of 24 parties had registered to contest the elections. The success of Akbar Tandjung's appeal against his corruption conviction rendered him eligible for the Golkar presidential nomination, which was also being contested by, amongst others, Gen. (retd) Wiranto. The Co-ordinating Minister for Political, Legal and Security Affairs, Gen. (retd) Susilo Bambang Yudhoyono, resigned from the Cabinet in March in advance of declaring his candidacy for the presidential election as the representative of the Partai Demokrat (PD—Democratic Party). The legislative and local elections took place, as planned, on 5 April. The Golkar party secured 128 of the 550 seats in the expanded DPR, while the PDI—P won 109 seats in the legislature. The former thus replaced the PDI—P as the largest parliamentary grouping. Of the smaller parties, the PPP won 58 seats, the PD 57, and the PAN and the PKB each secured 52 seats. An estimated 84% of registered voters participated in the polls. In mid-April the Co-ordinating Minister for People's Welfare, Yusuf Kalla, announced his resignation from the Cabinet to be Yudhoyono's vice-presidential candidate. A few days later Golkar nominated Wiranto as its presidential candidate at its National Convention. In May President Megawati announced that her vice-presidential candidate was to be Ahmad Hasyim, head of the country's largest Muslim organization, Nahdlatul Ulama (NU).

Yudhoyono secured the largest share of the vote in the presidential election on 5 July 2004, receiving 33.6% of the votes cast, followed by Megawati, with 26.6%, and Wiranto, with 22.2%. Amien Rais and Vice-President Hamzah Haz also contested the election on behalf of their respective parties, the PAN and the PPP. As no candidate won more than 50% of the votes, Yudhoyono and Megawati proceeded to a second round of voting, which was held on 20 September. Despite Golkar's declared support for the incumbent, this second poll resulted in a clear victory for Yudhoyono, who secured 60.6% of the votes cast. Estimated voter turn-out in the second round was 75%, compared with 78% in the first. Yudhoyono's election campaign had focused on pledges to stimulate the economy and to combat corruption and terrorism. The new President was inaugurated on 20 October, and on the following day announced the composition of his new Cabinet, which included representatives of several political organizations. Notable new appointees included Adm. (retd) Widodo Adi Sutjipto, a former Commander-in-Chief of the TNI, as Co-ordinating Minister for Political, Legal and Security Affairs, and Aburizal Bakrie, of Golkar, as Co-ordinating Minister for Economic Affairs, while Hassan Wirajuda, the Minister of Foreign Affairs, was one of five ministers retained from Megawati's administration.

In September 2004 the DPR approved the proposed creation of a 21-member truth and reconciliation commission to resolve all cases of human rights abuses perpetrated since independence in 1945. The commission was originally expected to be established by March 2005, but in December 2006 the Constitutional Court rescinded the 2004 law approving the establishment of the commission, deeming it to be unconstitutional.

Vice-President Yusuf Kalla was elected as Chairman of Golkar in mid-December 2004, defeating the incumbent, Akbar Tandjung. As a result, it was anticipated that Golkar would henceforth broadly support the Government, enabling Yudhoyono to secure legislative approval for his policies. In late December Abdullah Puteh, the Governor of Aceh, became the first person to be prosecuted by the recently formed Corruption Eradication Commission. Puteh, who was suspended from office by Yudhoyono, was charged with corruption in relation to the purchase of a Russian helicopter in 2002. He was convicted in April 2005 and was sentenced to 10 years' imprisonment; he was also ordered to repay the 3,600m. rupiah that he was deemed to have embezzled from state funds and was fined an additional 500m. rupiah.

In November 2004 it emerged that Munir Said Thalib, a leading Indonesian human rights activist who had died during a flight to the Netherlands in September, had been poisoned with arsenic. The Indonesian police launched an investigation into Munir's death, and in December President Yudhoyono authorized the formation of an independent team to monitor and assist the police inquiry. In March 2005 Pollycarpus Priyanto, a pilot of Garuda Indonesia, the state-owned airline, was arrested and charged with the murder of Munir. It was alleged that Pollycarpus, who had been off duty and had disembarked in Singapore, had administered arsenic to Munir. Independent investigators subsequently purported to have revealed links between Pollycarpus and the country's State Intelligence Agency. Notwithstanding this alleged connection, the pilot was convicted of Munir's murder and was sentenced to 14 years' imprisonment in December. However, in September 2006 Pollycarpus was acquitted on appeal by the Supreme Court, and it was subsequently announced by the Attorney-General's office that this verdict foreclosed any further judicial proceedings. Nevertheless, in an attempt to reverse the Supreme Court's decision, prosecutors argued that Indra Setiawan, the former president of Garuda, had played a significant part in the murder of Munir by allowing the off-duty pilot the opportunity to carry out the poisoning. The case was reopened, and in January 2008 Pollycarpus was found guilty of pre-meditated murder and forgery. The former pilot was sentenced to 20 years' imprisonment. Indra Setiawan and Rohainil Aini, a flight operations officer, were found guilty of assisting in Munir's murder.

Indonesia, in particular the province of Aceh, was devastated by a series of tsunamis caused by a massive earthquake in the Indian Ocean on 26 December 2004. The provincial capital, Banda Aceh, was severely damaged, while the town of Meulaboh, 150 km from the epicentre of the earthquake, was completely destroyed. UN agencies and other organizations commenced operations to distribute food, medical supplies and shelter to survivors. Aceh had been under emergency rule prior to the disaster and largely closed to foreign agencies and the international media. In January 2005 an emergency summit meeting of world leaders was convened in Jakarta. Most official estimates subsequently concurred that in Aceh alone as many as 170,000 had died; more than 400,000 were made homeless. In March a massive after-shock precipitated by the original earthquake in December struck off the Sumatran coast, killing approximately 300 people, while an estimated 2,000 were reported missing.

In July 2005 the Indonesian Ulama Council (Majelis Ulama Indonesia—MUI) issued 11 *fatwa* (religious edicts), the most controversial of which outlawed secularism, pluralism and liberal Islamic teachings. The issue of the *fatwa* was thought to be in response to the activities of two moderate, progressive Islamic organizations: the Liberal Islam Network (Jaringan Islam Liberal—JIL) and the Muhammadiyah Youth Intellectuals Network. Meanwhile, criticism of the Ahmadiyah sect continued; although deemed an heretical group, the sect was believed to have attracted 200,000 followers. In July 2005 thousands of members of the so-called Indonesian Muslim Solidarity group attacked the Ahmadiyah compound in Jakarta, damaging buildings and setting fire to the women's dormitory. The assailants cited an edict issued in 1980 by the MUI, which had declared members of Ahmadiyah to be deviants. The edict was renewed in August 2005. Ahmadiyah followers in Bandung and other Javanese cities were also targeted. In April 2008, after a government panel recommended that the group be banned, a large protest was held in Jakarta; demonstrators demanded the expulsion from Indonesia of Ahmadiyah followers. Later in the month a mosque in western Java belonging to the minority sect was set on fire. Meanwhile, in October 2007 the leader of another controversial sect, al-Qidayah al-Islamiyah, was questioned by police in Jakarta, along with several followers.

In mid-2005 Indonesia's first human fatalities from avian influenza ('bird flu') were confirmed, following the deaths from the virus of a man and his two daughters in Tangerang, on the outskirts of Jakarta. Amid escalating fears that the virus might mutate into a form readily transmissible between humans, the Government introduced a series of measures, including the power of forced admission to hospital of any person suspected to be suffering from the disease. Unlike other governments in the region, the Indonesian administration opted for a programme of mass vaccination, rather than mass culling, of poultry; the decision was believed to have been influenced by the prospective expense of compensating farmers for losses of stock. By January 2008, despite government efforts to restrict the individual ownership of 'backyard poultry', the number of confirmed cases of 'bird flu' within Indonesia had reached 124, of which 100 had proved fatal.

Meanwhile, in early December 2005 President Yudhoyono effected a long-anticipated cabinet reorganization, which focused predominantly on economic personnel. Co-ordinating Minister for Economic Affairs, Aburizal Bakrie, who had attracted much criticism in previous months for his failure to halt the rapid decline in the value of the rupiah, was transferred to the position of Co-ordinating Minister for People's Welfare; Bakrie was replaced by Boediono, former Minister of Finance during the presidency of Megawati Sukarnoputri. Minister of State for National Development Planning Sri Mulyani Indrawati was transferred to the finance portfolio, in place of Jusuf Anwar, who was not retained by Yudhoyono. Various ministerial portfolios were reallocated in May 2007. Changes included the appointment of a new Attorney-General, Hendarman Supandji, who immediately announced his intention to pursue allegations of corruption against two outgoing ministers. The Minister of Justice and Human Rights Affairs, Hamid Awaluddin, and State Secretary Yusril Ihza Mahendra were dismissed as a result of their alleged involvement in the illegal transfer of the sum of US $10m. to Hutomo Mandala Putra, son of former President Suharto, from a bank account located in the United Kingdom.

In July 2007 a civil case was filed against former President Suharto, in the hope of recovering some US $440m. that prosecutors claimed he had misappropriated from funds ostensibly allocated to an educational foundation; the Government was also seeking damages of $1,100m. In January 2008, however, Suharto died.

Jakarta's first ever direct gubernatorial election took place in August 2007. The election was won by the incumbent Deputy Governor, Fauzi Bowo, who received nearly 58% of the votes cast, there being only one other candidate. The level of participation reached 65% of those eligible to vote.

From 2000 a major challenge facing successive governments was the escalation of communal violence across the archipelago, together with separatist tensions in individual regions such as Aceh and Irian Jaya (now Papua—see below). In that year some of the worst such violence again occurred in the provinces of Maluku and North Maluku, arising from the ongoing conflict between the region's Christian and Muslim populations. By mid-2000 more than 4,000 people were reported to have been killed and some 300,000 displaced. In June President Wahid declared a state of civil emergency in the provinces of Maluku and North Maluku. Later the same month it was announced that around 1,400 of the 10,200 members of the armed forces in the region were to be replaced because they had become involved in the conflict. In the case of at least one outbreak of serious violence it was reported that evidence had emerged of the military's collusion with elements of the militant Muslim paramilitary organization, Laskar Jihad, which had travelled to the region to participate in the campaign of violence, thus supporting the view of many observers that the Indonesian military was allowing Muslim attacks on Christians to take place. In December 18 people were reported to have been killed and more than 80 others injured in a series of bombings of Christian churches in nine towns and cities across Indonesia, including Jakarta, on Christmas Eve. Initially, no group claimed responsibility for the explosions, which were condemned by President Wahid. (In June 2002 an Iraqi citizen, Omar al-Faruq, who claimed to be the South-East Asian representative of al-Qa'ida, was arrested and allegedly confessed to having participated in carrying out the bombings. Following the bombings in Bali, a senior operative of JI also confessed to involvement in the attacks. In a television broadcast in April 2004 four Malaysians detained in Indonesia admitted involvement in the church bombings and membership of JI. However, human rights groups claimed that the statements of the four had been obtained through coercion.) In February 2001 violence also broke out in the province of Central Kalimantan, where fierce resentment of Madurese transmigrants remained rife among the indigenous Dayak tribespeople. At least 428 Madurese were murdered by native Dayaks, and many of the victims were beheaded in accordance with traditional Dayak practices; many thousands more fled their homes. The failure of the armed forces to control the violence—the legacy of a resettlement programme begun under the Suharto Government in the 1970s—and to protect Madurese refugees in their care led to further allegations of the military's complicity in ethnic violence.

In February 2002, following negotiations between the warring Muslim and Christian factions in Maluku and North Maluku, a peace treaty—the 'Malino II Agreement'—was signed in an attempt to bring an end to the violence endemic in the region. The agreement urged the expulsion of external groups such as Laskar Jihad from the area. When a series of bombs exploded in the city of Ambon, the Government condemned the attacks but insisted that they did not signify the failure of the peace agreement. In early April a further bombing took place in Ambon and the residence of the Governor was set alight. Another outbreak of violence occurred in the same month, following which Alex Manuputty, the leader of the Christian separatist organization the Maluku Sovereignty Front, was arrested and charged with treason for planning to raise a flag to commemorate the 52nd anniversary of the proclamation of the South Maluku Republic. On 25 April the Maluku Sovereignty Front raised flags in Ambon in remembrance of the anniversary, provoking Muslims in the area and prompting the leader of Laskar Jihad, Ja'far Umar Thalib, to urge all Muslims in the region to renew their war against the Christian community. Shortly afterwards violence broke out again in Ambon, resulting in the deaths of 14 Christians. In May Ja'far Umar Thalib was arrested for allegedly inciting the violence that had led to the massacre of the Christians. During his detention Thalib was visited by Vice-President Hamzah Haz. In August the trial of Alex Manuputty and another Christian leader, Samuel Waileruny, for subversion began; meanwhile, Thalib also went on trial on charges of inciting hatred and rebellion and of defaming the President and Vice-President. In October, following the Bali bombings, Laskar Jihad reportedly disbanded and left the region; Ja'far Umar Thalib claimed that the decision had been taken owing to the group's increasing political involvement and denied that it had any connection to events in Bali. In the same month 14 members of the Maluku Sovereignty Front were sentenced to terms of imprisonment for raising separatist flags in the province in April. In late January 2003 Alex Manuputty and Samuel Waileruny were found guilty of subversion and sentenced in absentia to three-year prison terms, later increased to four years. Ja'far Umar Thalib was, however, acquitted of the charges against him. In late 2003, following the rejection of his appeal against his conviction by the Supreme Court, Manuputty fled to the USA; it was reported later that the Government had requested his deportation to Indonesia.

In April 2003 supporters of the separatist movement in Maluku were again alleged to have flown flags in commemoration of the anniversary of the South Maluku Republic. An estimated 129 such supporters were arrested, and in the following month it was announced that they were to be prosecuted on charges of subversion. However, owing to the relative peace that had been maintained in the province since the signing of the Malino II Agreement, in September it was reported that the Government had revoked the state of civil emergency in Maluku; several battalions of peace-keeping troops would continue to be stationed in the province. The civil emergency status in North Maluku had been revoked in the previous year. In January 2004 nine men were sentenced to prison terms of up to 15 years for membership of the Maluku Sovereignty Front. At least 40 people were killed and around 150 injured in violent clashes in Ambon in late April, following a rally by a predominantly Christian separatist group on the island. More than 1,000 police officers and troops were dispatched to Ambon in an attempt to quell the unrest. Observers thus questioned the long-term success of the peace treaty, and in late May one person was killed and at least 22 others injured in a series of bomb explosions on Ambon. In late November Moses Tuanakotta, a leader of the Maluku Sovereignty Front, was convicted of subversion and sentenced to nine years in prison for instigating the rally in April.

In late 2001 violence also broke out in the province of Sulawesi, where ongoing religious tensions had caused approximately 1,000 deaths in the previous two years. In the first week of December at least seven people were killed and thousands left homeless following clashes between armed Muslim groups and Christians. The violence was believed to have been precipitated by the recent arrival of members of Laskar Jihad on the island, and more than 2,000 police and troop reinforcements were sent to the area. In late December, following two days of negotiations, a peace agreement was concluded between the parties involved, but explosions at four churches in the provincial capital, Palu, during New Year celebrations highlighted the continuing political instability in the province. Sporadic violence continued to occur in Sulawesi. In June 2002 a bomb exploded on a bus travelling towards Poso, Central Sulawesi, killing four people. In December the Government announced that it intended to maintain the existing level of troops in the area, determined for one year under the terms of the peace agreement, for a further six months. Also in December, two bombs exploded in Makassar, the capital of South Sulawesi, resulting in the deaths of three people.

In October 2003 an estimated 11 people died as a result of an outbreak of sectarian violence in Poso. There was speculation that the renewal of violence in the province had been co-ordinated by JI to coincide with the anniversary of the bombings in Bali. In the following month three more people died following an outbreak of anti-Christian violence in the city. Further rioting occurred later in that month, resulting in at least one death. In January 2004 a bomb exploded in the town of Palopo, South Sulawesi, killing four people. In October the new province of West Sulawesi, formed from five former regencies of South Sulawesi, was inaugurated. A bomb exploded on a bus in Poso in November, killing six people. The bombing followed a series of other attacks in Central Sulawesi, including the shooting of a Christian bus driver in Poso earlier that month. In May 2005 two bombs exploded in a busy market in the predominantly Christian town of Tentena, in Central Sulawesi, killing 21 people and injuring dozens more; the town's only mosque was stoned by angry Christian demonstrators. In July a total of 24 alleged members of JI were arrested in connection with these attacks, as well as with the Bali bombings of 2002. In October 2005 religious tensions were further exacerbated in Central Sulawesi by the brutal killing of three Christian schoolgirls, allegedly by Islamist militants; the girls were beheaded after being ambushed while on their way to a Christian school near Poso. In September 2006 three Christian men were executed following their convictions on charges of inciting an attack on an Islamic school in Poso, in which approximately 200 people had been killed in May 2000. The executions led to angry demonstrations, during which rioters stormed a prison in Atambua, West Timor (the home town of one of the executed men), and reportedly released approximately 200 inmates. In the following month a Christian priest, well-known locally for leading protests against the executions, was shot dead in Palu. Sporadic violence continued in subsequent months, with many Christians maintaining that responsibility for the bloodshed had been wrongly attributed to the three men. In November three suspected Islamist militants went on trial, charged with the beheading of the three Christian schoolgirls in 2005. Hasanuddin, one of the three defendants, admitted to involvement in the murders, although he denied having organized the attack. In March 2007 Hasanuddin was found guilty and sentenced to 20 years' imprisonment, and two of his accomplices received sentences of 14 years. In December three further convictions were made in connection with the beheadings of the Christian girls: Rahman Kalale received a 19-year prison sentence and Yudi Heryanto a 14-year sentence, with another defendant being sentenced to a term of 10 years. Kalale and Heryanto were also found guilty of injuring two other schoolgirls in a subsequent shooting incident in Poso. Also in late 2007 several other Muslim militants were convicted of carrying out attacks in Central Sulawesi. Abdul Muis was sentenced to 19 years' imprisonment, having been found guilty of the murder of the Christian priest in Palu in October 2006 and also of a bomb attack on a market selling pork in 2005, in which eight people had been killed. Syaiful Anam (alias Brekele) was found guilty of organizing the Tentena bomb attacks and was sentenced to 18 years' imprisonment. Amril Niode was also convicted of involvement in that attack, again receiving a long prison sentence. Ardin Djanatu, suspected of planting one of the bombs in Tentena, was being tried separately.

On 1 January 2001 new legislation took effect devolving increased financial and administrative control to Indonesia's regional governments. (The central Government was, meanwhile, to retain control over justice, defence, foreign affairs and monetary policy.) The day after the introduction of the new legislation, the Minister of State for State Administrative Reforms, Ryaas Rasyid, resigned from his post, reportedly because of his frustration at the inadequacy of the Government's preparations for the implementation of the new decentralization policy, which was intended to defuse separatist tensions across the archipelago; he was later replaced by Feisal Tamin.

During 1974, meanwhile, several parties emerged within the small Portuguese colony of East Timor (which became known as Timor-Leste following its accession to independence on 20 May 2002), with aims ranging from full independence to integration with Indonesia or Australia. Indonesia, which had never presented a claim to East Timor, initially showed little interest in the territory. In 1975 Portuguese forces withdrew from the colony, and the territory's capital, Dili, was occupied by the forces of the left-wing Frente Revolucionária do Timor Leste Independente (Fretilin), which advocated independence for East Timor. To prevent Fretilin from gaining full control of the territory, Indonesian troops intervened and established a provincial government. (In December 2001 the declassification of US state papers relating to the Indonesian occupation revealed that the US Government had endorsed the invasion in the belief that it would curb the spread of communism in the region.) In July 1976 East Timor was declared the 27th province of Indonesia. Human rights organizations subsequently claimed that as many as 200,000 people, from a total population of 650,000, might have been killed by the Indonesian armed forces during the annexation. The UN continued officially to recognize Portugal as the administrative power in East Timor. In February 1983 the UN Commission on Human Rights adopted a resolution affirming East Timor's right to independence and self-determination. In November 1990 the Indonesian Government rejected proposals by the military commander of Fretilin, José Alexandre (Xanana) Gusmão, for unconditional peace negotiations aimed at ending the armed struggle in East Timor. In August 1992 the UN General Assembly adopted its first resolution condemning Indonesia's violations of human rights in East Timor.

The downfall of President Suharto in May 1998 and the subsequent accession to the presidency of Habibie raised hopes that independence for the territory might be granted in the near future. In August it was announced that Indonesia and Portugal had agreed to hold discussions on the possibility of 'wide-ranging' autonomy for East Timor. In January 1999, however, the Indonesian Government unexpectedly announced that, if the East Timorese were to vote to reject Indonesia's proposals for autonomy, it would consider granting independence to the province. Although the Government was initially opposed to a referendum on the issue of independence for East Timor, it signed an agreement with Portugal in May, giving its assent to a process of 'popular consultation' to take the form of a UN-supervised poll. The referendum proceeded on 30 August, and resulted in an overwhelming rejection by 78.5% of voters of the Indonesian Government's proposals for autonomy and in an endorsement of independence for East Timor. The announcement of the result of the referendum led to a rapid deterioration in the territory's security situation in East Timor. In late September Indonesia and Portugal reiterated their agreement for the transfer of authority in East Timor to the UN. Also in late September the Indonesian armed forces formally relinquished responsibility for security in the territory to the UN peace-keeping force, the International Force for East Timor (Interfet); the last Indonesian troops left East Timor in late October. In October the result of the referendum was ratified by the Indonesian MPR, thus permitting East Timor's accession to independence to proceed. (See the chapter on Timor-Leste.) In September 2000 Indonesia faced outrage from the UN and the international community following the murder of three UN aid workers by pro-Jakarta militias in West Timor. The Indonesian Government came under strong criticism for its failure to control the militia groups, which were believed by many to be receiving the support of the Indonesian military. In December 2001 10 members of a pro-Indonesia militia became the first individuals to be convicted of crimes against humanity in connection with the violence of 1999. However, the Indonesian Government continued to obstruct efforts to bring all those culpable to justice, blocking attempts to extradite an 11th suspect, a special forces officer, to face trial.

In January 2002 the Government established a special court in Jakarta to try those suspected of contravening human rights, in East Timor and elsewhere. In February 17 pro-Jakarta militiamen and Indonesian soldiers were indicted by international prosecutors for alleged crimes against humanity in East Timor in 1999. Seven people, including the former Governor of East Timor, Abílio Soares, the chief of police, Brig.-Gen. Timbul Silaen, and the former district head, Herman Sedyono, were formally charged with crimes against humanity. Their cases were the first to be submitted to the newly established human rights tribunal in Jakarta; the trials began in March. In June the trial of militia leader Eurico Guterres, head of the youth wing of President Megawati's PDI—P, began. In August Abílio Soares was found guilty of two charges of 'gross rights violations' for his failure to prevent violence involving those subordinate to him and was sentenced to a three-year prison term. The human rights tribunal acquitted Brig.-Gen. Timbul Silaen of charges of failing to control his subordinates; five other police and army officers were also found not guilty. The verdicts provoked widespread international condemnation and led to calls for the UN to establish an international tribunal on Timor-Leste. In November 2002 the tribunal found Eurico Guterres guilty of crimes against humanity; he received a 10-year prison sentence. However, a further four defendants were then acquitted by the tribunal, prompting renewed criticism from human rights activists and legal experts, who claimed that the court was deliberately sparing Indonesian police and military officers; both those convicted thus far were ethnic East Timorese civilians. In late December Lt-Col Soejarwo, Indonesia's military commander in Dili in 1999, became the first Indonesian officer to be found guilty of the charges against him; he was sentenced to a five-year prison term. However, international criticism was reinforced when another Indonesian army officer was acquitted of the charges against him in the same month. In January 2003 Hulman Gultom, a former Indonesian police chief, was found guilty and sentenced to a three-year prison term. In March of that year Brig.-Gen. Noer Muis was sentenced to five years in prison, having been convicted of failing to prevent massacres in the territory in 1999. However, in May 2003 the commander of Indonesian troops in East Timor, Brig.-Gen. Tono Suratman, was acquitted of the charges against him. In August of that year, the most senior military officer to have been charged in relation to the violence, Maj.-Gen. Adam Damiri, was found guilty of having committed crimes against humanity and sentenced to a three-year prison term. His sentence was the final one to be handed down by the tribunal, which continued to draw widespread international criticism for having passed only six guilty verdicts. Meanwhile, in February 2003 a UN-sponsored Special Panel for Serious Crimes (SPSC) that had been established in Dili indicted Gen. (retd) Wiranto, Abílio Soares and six other Indonesian generals for crimes committed in East Timor and, later in the same month, a further 50 indictments were issued; the Indonesian Government continued to refuse to hand over any of those indicted for trial. The SPSC issued an arrest warrant for Wiranto in May 2004. In July Abílio Soares became the first person convicted by the human rights tribunal in Jakarta to be imprisoned, after the failure of an appeal. In August a court in Jakarta overruled the convictions of Lt-Col Soejarwo, Hulman Gultom, Brig.-Gen. Noer Muis and Maj.-Gen. Adam Damiri, and halved the sentence of Eurico Guterres, who remained free pending an appeal against his conviction. In November Abílio Soares was also cleared of the charges against him by Indonesia's Supreme Court, leaving only the conviction of Guterres standing. In December Indonesia and Timor-Leste announced the establishment of a joint Commission of Truth and Friendship (CTF) to investigate human rights violations during the violence in East Timor in 1999. In the previous month the UN Security Council had expressed concern at Indonesia's failure to punish those responsible. Meanwhile, in August 2004 the human rights tribunal acquitted the head of the Kopassus special forces regiment, Maj.-Gen. Sriyanto Muntrasan, who had been accused of human rights violations in connection with the shooting of several Muslim activists near Jakarta's Tanjung Priok port in 1984, despite sentencing Sriyanto's immediate superior, Maj.-Gen. (retd) Rudolf Butar-Butar, to 10 years' imprisonment in April for failing to prevent the shooting; later in August 11 soldiers received prison terms, having been found guilty in the same case of systematic attacks against civilians. However, in July 2005 the convictions of Butar-Butar and the 11 soldiers were overruled on appeal by the High Court, which deemed the shooting to have been accidental. The first hearing of the CTF opened on Bali in February 2007. Its 10 members were drawn from both Indonesia and Timor-Leste and included experts in the fields of law and human rights. The final session of the CTF took place in Dili in September 2007.

In the mid-1970s dissent re-emerged in Aceh, which, at the end of the war of independence, had held the status of a full province of the Republic of Indonesia but which had subsequently had this status removed before being made a special territory (Daerah Istimewa) with considerable autonomy in religious and educational affairs. The dissent was provoked by the central Government's exploitation of Aceh's natural resources and the subsequent lack of benefits from these operations received by the region itself. A sense of the erosion of Aceh's autonomy was heightened by the migration and transmigration of other Indonesians into the region and by the increasing power of the central Government, and in 1976 the Gerakan Aceh Merdeka (GAM—Free Aceh Movement) was formed by Hasan di Tiro, who declared independence in 1977. This small rebellion was swiftly suppressed by the armed forces; however, Tiro later established a government-in-exile in Sweden.

In 1989 opposition to the central Government rose again, this time led by the National Liberation Front Acheh Sumatra. The region was made a 'military operations zone' in 1990, thus allowing the armed forces far greater freedom to counter the uprising. By mid-1991 the rebellion had been largely suppressed; however, it was estimated that about 1,000 Acehnese had been killed in the process, as a result of the use of excessive and indiscriminate force by the military. The number of deaths continued to rise in subsequent years, and in 1993 Amnesty International estimated that about 2,000 Acehnese had been killed since 1989, with hundreds of others having 'disappeared'.

Aceh's status as a 'military operations zone' was revoked in June 1998, following the downfall of President Suharto in May, and an apology for past military excesses was made by Gen. Wiranto. The subsequent intended withdrawal of Indonesian troops from the province was suspended, however, following rioting in Aceh in September. Decentralization measures introduced by President Habibie failed to defuse resentment in the province, and public opinion in Aceh became increasingly sympathetic towards the notion of independence. In 1999 the discovery of several mass graves of people killed by the armed forces during security operations further exacerbated tension in the province. Violence continued to escalate following the legislative elections of 9 June as GAM guerrillas intensified their campaign for independence for Aceh.

In early November 1999, following the rejection by legislators in the provincial assembly of demands for the holding of a referendum on self-determination for Aceh, a provincial government building in western Aceh was set on fire during a demonstration by 5,000 protesters. While much of the ongoing widespread violence in the province was attributed to the separatist movement, it was believed by observers that some unrest was initiated by so-called 'provocateurs' acting to destabilize the province and undermine the separatist movement. In November the newly appointed President of Indonesia, Abdurrahman Wahid, confirmed an unexpected statement that the holding of a referendum in Aceh was a possibility. In late November, however, Wahid made it clear that the suggested poll would not include the option of independence, but would instead offer Aceh a broad degree of autonomy. Wahid's proposals angered the TNI, which, following the vote in favour of independence in East Timor in August, reportedly feared that, unless brought under control, the separatist movement in Aceh could potentially incite rebellion across the archipelago and contribute to national disintegration. The offer of increased autonomy, rather than independence, also failed to satisfy Acehnese separatists. In May 2000 the Indonesian Government and Acehnese rebel negotiators agreed upon a cease-fire, which took effect from 2 June and was subsequently extended for an indefinite period. Violence continued throughout the province, however, and it was estimated by Acehnese human rights groups that more than 1,000 civilians had died in clashes between the Indonesian military and Acehnese rebels during 2000. In December thousands of Acehnese protesters rallied peacefully in Banda Aceh, demanding independence for the province. However, it was reported that at least 34 (and possibly as many as 200, according to human rights groups) unarmed civilians had been killed in the days preceding the rally as the result of military action to target Acehnese en route to the demonstration. Acehnese separatists withdrew from peace talks with the Indonesian Government, stating that they would resume negotiations only when the military ceased killing Acehnese civilians. In January 2001 peace talks between the Indonesian Government and Acehnese separatists recommenced.

In March 2001, following talks between GAM and the security forces, 'peace zones' were established in two Aceh districts. These proved to be of limited effectiveness, however, and in April President Wahid signed a decree authorizing the security forces to assist the military in restoring law and order in the province by targeting armed separatist organizations. This brought an end to the uneasy truce prevailing in the region. In July one of President Megawati's first official actions was to sign into law a special autonomy plan for Aceh intended to assuage separatism. However, while generous in its scope, the legislation was criticized for failing to address the problems posed by the continued military presence in the area. Critics' concerns were borne out when an estimated 30 civilians were massacred on an Aceh palm oil plantation in August 2001. According to GAM, the military was responsible, having carried out the attack as retribution for a previous assault on a military post that had left several soldiers dead. In September President Megawati visited the region in an attempt to defuse the tensions there. On 4 December 2001 Acehnese separatists marked the 25th anniversary of their struggle for independence. Security forces tore down over 100 separatist flags, and there were reports of some clashes between GAM members and the military.

In January 2002 the commander of GAM, Abdullah Syafei, was killed during a gun battle with security forces on Sumatra; six other GAM members also died. In February talks took place between GAM and government representatives in Geneva, Switzerland, despite an earlier declaration by GAM that it intended to boycott negotiations while mourning the death of Syafei. However, renewed fighting prompted the Government to resume a separate military command for Aceh, a decision denounced by both GAM and human rights groups. In the following month fighting between separatists and government troops in the province resulted in the deaths of at least 23 people. In May, following further talks in Geneva, the Government and GAM agreed to work towards a cease-fire, signing an agreement that was to act as a mandate for future negotiations. However, the violence continued, with a GAM commander alleging later in the same month that the armed forces had killed 43 civilians in North Aceh in the preceding 10 days alone. At the end of June GAM issued a statement in support of the ongoing peace negotiations taking place in Geneva and in July it released 18 hostages whom it had been holding since the previous month, including nine crewmen who had been kidnapped while servicing the offshore petroleum industry near North Aceh. Meanwhile, following a trip to Aceh, the Co-ordinating Minister for Political, Legal and Security Affairs, Susilo Bambang Yudhoyono, declared his support for the regional military commander's request to increase the military presence in the area if GAM did not accept the conditions that had been outlined following the talks that had been held in May. Aceh's Legal Aid Institute reportedly claimed that, during the first six months of 2002, 771 people had been killed as a result of the conflict in the region.

In November 2002 GAM announced that it was willing to sign a short-term peace accord with the Government to bring to an end the armed conflict in the region. GAM announced a unilateral truce during the period of the Islamic religious festival of Ramadan, but the truce broke down almost immediately as five people died during an exchange of gunfire in North Aceh. Meanwhile, government troops besieged a suspected GAM base in the industrial centre of Lhokseumawe. In December government and GAM representatives finally signed a peace agreement in Geneva. As well as establishing an immediate cease-fire, the deal provided for free elections (to be held in 2004), which would establish an autonomous, although not independent, government. The new provincial government would retain 70% of all fuel revenues. In return all rebels in the province would disarm in designated areas. Following the signing of the peace accord, international peace monitors arrived in the region.

In February 2003 GAM rebels began surrendering their weapons in compliance with the terms of the peace accord. However, by April of that year the agreement had come close to collapse. Offices occupied by the international monitors for the Joint Security Committee had been attacked and, in one instance, burned down. In May peace talks were held in Tokyo, Japan, with the support of the host country, the European Union (EU) and the USA. However, GAM negotiators were unable to accept the Government's demands that it abandon its goal of independence, accept a special autonomy agreement and immediately begin to disarm its forces. President Megawati immediately authorized the imposition of martial law in Aceh, initially for a six-month period, and the commencement of military action against GAM. Owing to the restrictions placed on media-reporting of the conflict, little independent information was available as to its progress throughout the succeeding months. However, in June three government soldiers were sentenced to brief prison terms, having been found guilty of committing human rights violations during the military campaign. In November the Government announced that it would extend its military operations in Aceh indefinitely, prompting international criticism. In December a bomb exploded at a market in the eastern town of Pereulak, killing 10 people. The Government downgraded the status of martial law in Aceh to a state of civil emergency in May 2004, restoring power to the civilian Governor. The security forces, which were to remain in the province, claimed to have killed some 2,000 suspected GAM rebels and arrested a further 3,000 since commencing the military offensive against the separatist movement a year earlier. Human rights groups alleged that at least 300 of those killed had been civilians. In June Indonesia welcomed Sweden's decision to arrest two senior GAM leaders who were in exile in that country; GAM's founder, Hasan di Tiro, escaped arrest because of ill health. They were later released, however, owing to insufficient evidence, although investigations were to continue. In November President Yudhoyono extended the state of civil emergency in Aceh by up to six months and, during a visit to the province, offered an amnesty to all GAM rebels who surrendered their weapons.

Following the tsunami disaster that devastated Aceh in December 2004 (see above), GAM and the Government agreed to an informal cease-fire to facilitate relief efforts. In mid-January 2005, however, the Chief of Staff of the Army, Gen. Ryamizard Ryacudu, announced that in the previous two weeks the security forces had killed 120 GAM rebels who had been stealing aid intended for victims of the tsunamis; GAM dismissed these claims. None the less, the natural disaster in the province appeared to have provided a new impetus for GAM and the Indonesian Government to seek a resolution to their conflict, and in late January formal talks between the two sides were held in Helsinki, Finland. At the end of January the Government rejected an offer by GAM to suspend demands for independence in exchange for a referendum on Aceh's future. In early February the army claimed to have killed at least seven GAM rebels. Notwithstanding these set-backs, after several rounds of negotiations, brokered by former Finnish President Martti Ahtisaari, the two sides reached agreement in July upon the terms of a draft accord, which was formally signed on 15 August. GAM agreed to discard its long-standing claims for independence and the Indonesian Government was to allow GAM to operate as an official political party, a concession that would require constitutional change (current laws decreed that all political parties be based in Jakarta and that branches be maintained in at least half of the country's 33 provinces) which was to be effected by 31 March 2006. Furthermore, the province of Aceh was to be allocated as much as 70% of the revenues arising from the exploitation of its natural resources. In late August the Indonesian authorities released approximately 200 Acehnese detainees, including four senior GAM members; GAM effected a process of complete disarmament within three months of the signing of the agreement; and the Indonesian Government began a phased withdrawal from the province of its 24,000 troops based there; by the end of 2005 almost 10,000 troops had departed. In January 2006 the Indonesian Government submitted a draft law to the country's legislature that would grant Aceh partial autonomy and allow for the formation of political parties in the province; however, the legislature failed to approve the proposed law by the stipulated deadline of 31 March, but it was finally enacted in July. Although GAM agreed to its terms, critics argued that the law was strongly biased in favour of the central Government, which was to monitor all the affairs of the Acehnese administration. Furthermore, Aceh's demand that it be granted full control over its own natural resources was not met, with the law stipulating that management of oil and gas in Aceh was to be conducted jointly by the provincial administration (which was to control 70% of production revenues) and the central Government.

In December 2006 the province of Aceh held its first-ever direct gubernatorial and district elections, formally marking the culmination of the peace process. The polls passed without incident. Irwandi Yusuf, an independent candidate and former GAM spokesman, secured the position of provincial Governor, attracting 38.2% of the total votes cast along with his deputy gubernatorial candidate, Muhammad Nazar. Ahmad Humam Hamid, the candidate of the PPP and supported by the veteran GAM leadership, was placed second, he and Hasbi Abdullah, candidate for the post of Deputy Governor, having received a total of 16.6% of the votes. The level of participation in the polls was good, at approximately 85% of the total electorate. In the same month the Indonesian Government finalized draft regulation providing for the establishment of local political parties in Aceh, although candidates would only be allowed to stand for seats within the House of Representatives in Jakarta if they secured the support of national parties and would be required to relinquish membership of their local party once nominated. At his inauguration ceremony in February 2007, the new Governor of Aceh declared his intention to focus on the economic recovery of the province.

In May 1977 a rebellion in the province of Irian Jaya (annexed to Indonesia in 1963—see above) was said to have been organized by the Organisasi Papua Merdeka (OPM—Free Papua Movement), which sought unification with Papua New Guinea. Fighting continued until December 1979, when Indonesia and Papua

New Guinea finalized a new border administrative agreement. Frequent border incidents followed, however, and in early 1984 fighting broke out in Jayapura, the capital of Irian Jaya. As a result, about 10,000 refugees fled over the border into Papua New Guinea. In October 1984 Indonesia and Papua New Guinea signed a five-year agreement establishing a joint border security committee; by the end of 1985 Indonesians were continuing to cross into Papua New Guinea, but a limited number of repatriations took place in 1986. There was also concern among native Irian Jayans (who are of Melanesian origin) at the introduction of large numbers of Javanese into the province, under the central Government's transmigration scheme. This was interpreted as an attempt to reduce the Melanesians to a minority and thus to stifle opposition. In 1986 it was announced that the Government intended to resettle 65m. people over a 20-year period, in spite of protests from human rights and conservation groups. Relations with Papua New Guinea improved when the Prime Minister, Paias Wingti, visited Suharto in January 1988. However, a series of cross-border raids by the Indonesian armed forces in October and November, in an attempt to capture Melanesian separatists operating on the border, led to renewed tension between the two countries. In October 1990 the Governments of Indonesia and Papua New Guinea renewed the basic accord on border arrangements, which included an agreement on the formation of a joint defence committee and a formal commitment to share border intelligence. In September 1992 the two countries agreed to facilitate the passage of border trade, and in the following month an Indonesian consulate was established in Vanimo.

In April 1995 the Australian Council for Overseas Aid (ACFOA) alleged that 37 Irian Jayans had been killed by security forces near the Freeport copper and gold mine between June 1994 and February 1995. In August the ACFOA's claims were reiterated by NGOs, which lodged a complaint with the National Commission on Human Rights in Jakarta about summary executions, arbitrary detentions and torture in the province between mid-1994 and mid-1995. In November 1995 four members of ABRI were arrested in an investigation into the killing in May of 11 unarmed civilians at a prayer meeting. Also in November the Overseas Private Investment Corporation (a US government agency) cancelled political risk insurance valued at US $100m. for Freeport (a subsidiary of a US enterprise), citing environmental concerns. Freeport's perceived responsibility for the situation in Irian Jaya arose from its role as civil administrator in the area of the mine and also because the indigenous inhabitants' campaigns against Freeport's indiscriminate exploitation of natural resources in the area often resulted in their being killed by security forces as suspected members of the OPM.

In December 1995 clashes between Indonesian forces and the OPM intensified, forcing hundreds of refugees to cross into Papua New Guinea. Four people were killed in riots in Jayapura in March 1996. Riots near the Grasberg mine in the same month were the result of problems similar to those experienced by residents in the Freeport area (relating principally to the lack of any benefit from the mining project to the local community and to the potential impact of the project on the local environment). There were also tensions among the local Irianese, Indonesians from other provinces and commercial operators. In April Freeport agreed to allocate 1% of revenue over a period of 10 years to community development programmes for tribal groups living around the mine, and to improve environmental safeguards.

In July 1998 troops clashed with pro-independence demonstrators in Jayapura. Two people were reported to have been killed in the violence, and a further five were reportedly killed during an outbreak of violence on the island of Biak in July. In early October the Government revoked the status of Irian Jaya as a 'military operations zone' following the conclusion of a cease-fire agreement with the OPM in late September; however, the move was not followed by the withdrawal of troops from the region. In February 1999 Irian Jayan tribal leaders raised the issue of independence for the province at a meeting with President Habibie. (A referendum on self-determination for the province had been promised by the Indonesian Government prior to the territory's annexation in 1963; however, whilst a vote was eventually held in 1969, only tribal chiefs selected by Jakarta were allowed to participate and the result was widely discredited.) The independence movement in the province continued to strengthen throughout 1999, and was encouraged by the achievements of the East Timorese independence movement (see above). In December independence demonstrations took place throughout Irian Jaya. A delegation from the DPR visited the province and announced that the administration of the newly elected President Abdurrahman Wahid had agreed to the popular demand that the province's name be changed from Irian Jaya to West Papua, although it was emphasized that this decision should not be construed as implying the Government's approval of any moves towards the province's secession from Indonesia. (It was subsequently reported, however, that the proposed change had failed to receive the requisite approval of the Indonesian legislature.)

In mid-2000 the Papuan People's Congress was held in Jayapura. The Congress concluded with the adoption of a five-point resolution reinstating a declaration of independence for West Papua originally made in 1961, before the province's annexation to Indonesia. The declaration was, however, immediately rebuffed by the Indonesian Government. In early October between 30 and 40 people were killed and many others injured in clashes between police and West Papuan separatists in the town of Wamena when police attempted to remove a Morning Star independence flag being flown by the separatists. Although President Wahid had previously decreed that the flying of the Morning Star flag was allowed, provided that the flag was flown alongside, and slightly lower than, the Indonesian flag, following the violence the Government introduced a ban on the flying of the flag. In November and early December the Indonesian military took severe action against separatists; seven people were shot dead by the armed forces in an outbreak of violence in the town of Merauke, and dozens of separatist sympathizers, including the pro-independence leader, Theys Eluay, were arrested. On 1 December pro-independence supporters rallied in the province to mark the 39th anniversary of the first unilateral declaration of West Papua's independence.

In March 2001 five West Papuan separatist leaders, including Theys Eluay, the leader of the Presidium Dewan Papua (PDP—Papua Presidium Council), were released on bail to await trial on charges of treason. In October the DPR gave its assent to legislation giving greater autonomy to the province, in an effort to defuse the separatist tensions that had given rise to more than 40 years of sporadic violence. As well as giving Irian Jaya more autonomy and a larger share of tax revenues, the so-called Special Autonomy Law for Papua also proposed that the region be officially known as Papua and made provision for a bicameral Papuan People's Council, intended to safeguard indigenous interests. However, the separatist PDP swiftly rejected the deal as it failed to grant Irian Jaya complete independence. In November 2001 Theys Eluay was found dead in his car. He was believed to have been assassinated; some military involvement was suspected. In late December hundreds of students occupied the parliament building in Jayapura to demand a referendum on independence and to express their anger at the authorities' failure to find the killer of Theys Eluay. The protest came days before the autonomy reforms came into force on 1 January 2002, when the province officially became known as Papua.

In late August 2002 two US citizens and an Indonesian were killed following an ambush near the Freeport mine. In November it was alleged by police that Kopassus soldiers had been involved in the attack. (In June 2004 the US authorities indicted *in absentia* Anthonius Wamang, an Indonesian, for murdering the two US citizens, describing him as an operational commander for the OPM, although human rights groups reportedly claimed that Wamang had close links to the Kopassus special forces.) In April 2003 four Kopassus officers and three soldiers were convicted of the abduction, torture and murder of Theys Eluay and were sentenced to brief prison terms. However, the trial was criticized both for the leniency of the verdicts and for its failure to investigate the reasons for the murder of Eluay. Meanwhile, the central Government gave its approval in January 2003 to an initiative that would lead to the division of Papua into three smaller provinces—Central Papua, East Papua (or Papua) and West Papua (known initially as West Irian Jaya, but formally renamed in April 2007). The proposal angered local leaders, who claimed that such action would threaten the region's autonomy. Following reports that six people had died during fighting in Timika, the designated capital of Central Papua, since the inauguration of the new province in August of that year, the creation of Central Papua was postponed. However, the appointment of a Governor for West Papua was approved in November. In the same month the Government announced provisional plans for the creation of two further provinces in Papua. Meanwhile, it was reported that 10 members of the OPM had been killed in clashes with government troops in East Papua. In December the appointment of Brig.-Gen. Timbul

Silaen to the post of regional police commander was criticized by the USA, owing to Silaen's indictment for crimes against humanity in East Timor (see above). In March 2004 it was reported that Leo Warisman, a leader of the OPM, had been killed in a gunfight with security forces in Papua. Another OPM leader, Yance Hembring, was sentenced to 10 years' imprisonment by a court in Jayapura in August for advocating Papua's independence. In December at least five people were injured and 18 arrested during violent clashes between protesters and police at a pro-independence rally in Jayapura.

In October 2005 the Papuan People's Council (Majelis Rakyat Papua—MRP) was formally established; it was charged primarily with the issue of the partition of Papua and with the forthcoming gubernatorial elections. Originally scheduled to be held in November, the elections were postponed until mid-February 2006, owing to a lack of preparedness. They were subsequently postponed a second time, again because of poor administrative planning, but finally proceeded on 11 March. Barnabas Suebu and his co-candidate, Alex Hessegem, were subsequently pronounced Governor and Deputy Governor, respectively, of Papua; however, in early April the nearest rival candidates, Lukas Enembe and Arobi Aituarauwm, filed a lawsuit with the Jayapura High Court, alleging that Suebu and Hessegem had manipulated the vote.

In January 2006 more than 200 demonstrators forced their way into the local legislative building in protest at the continued presence of Indonesian troops within Papua; the protesters demanded the immediate withdrawal of all Indonesian military personnel from the province. In February the Minister of Defence, Juwono Sudarsono, conceded that some members of the Indonesian military and police force had been committing human rights abuses, including incidents of torture and rape, against local residents in Papua. In the same month the Constitutional Court officially reaffirmed the legitimacy of West Irian Jaya's status as a province, maintaining that the 2001 Special Autonomy Law for Papua could not be applied retroactively. In February 2006 protests by unlicensed miners operating in the area resulted in a temporary suspension of production at the Freeport mine, which continued to be regarded locally as a symbol of oppression. In the following month five members of the security forces were killed in Jayapura by demonstrators reiterating demands for the closure of the mine, and in April four people, including two soldiers, were killed in an assault on an army post in the province.

In February 2007 Human Rights Watch, a widely respected international organization based in the USA, drew attention to the continued imprisonment of 18 Papuan activists, who were reported to have received substantial sentences following their peaceful protests in support of self-determination for the province. Human Rights Watch urged the Indonesian Government to release these prisoners and also to abandon charges against other political detainees who had yet to be brought to trial. In July, furthermore, Human Rights Watch accused the Papuan police force of perpetrating, with apparent impunity, extra-judicial killings and other serious abuses. In October a number of people were killed and dozens injured during several days of fighting between rival tribal groups near the Freeport mine.

Indonesia's foreign policy has focused on its leading role in the regional grouping of the Association of South East Asian Nations (ASEAN, see p. 185), which it founded, together with Malaysia, the Philippines, Singapore and Thailand, in 1967. Indonesia supported the organization's opposition to Viet Nam's military presence in Cambodia and played a prominent role in attempts to find a political solution to the situation in Cambodia (q.v.). The Indonesian Minister of Foreign Affairs and his French counterpart were appointed Co-Chairmen of the Paris International Conference on Cambodia, which first met in August 1989. In 1997, following Second Prime Minister Hun Sen's assumption of sole power in Cambodia, Indonesia led ASEAN attempts to resolve the crisis. In August 2001 President Megawati Sukarnoputri embarked on a tour of all ASEAN member states on her first overseas trip since assuming the presidency.

In July 1985 Indonesia and the People's Republic of China signed a memorandum of understanding (MoU) on the resumption of direct trade links, which had been suspended since 1967. In April 1988 the Indonesian Government indicated its readiness to re-establish full diplomatic relations with China, subject to an assurance that the latter would not seek to interfere in Indonesia's internal affairs; previously, Suharto had insisted that China acknowledge its alleged complicity in the 1965 attempted coup. Diplomatic relations were finally restored in August 1990, following an Indonesian undertaking to settle financial debts incurred with China by the Sukarno regime. In November Suharto visited China and Viet Nam (the first Indonesian leader to do so since 1964 and 1975 respectively). In 1995 China extended claims to territorial waters within Indonesia's exclusive economic zone, consequently threatening Indonesia's natural gas resources, in particular those situated in the region of the Natuna Islands.

Bilateral relations between Indonesia and China suffered a reverse in 1998 following the violence perpetrated against ethnic Chinese Indonesians at the time of the removal of President Suharto in May. China issued a strong diplomatic protest. President Habibie publicly expressed his sympathy for the plight of the ethnic Chinese victims of violence. Subsequently, in May 1999, as part of a programme of general reform, Habibie removed a ban that had existed on the use and teaching of the Mandarin Chinese language within Indonesia. In early December President Abdurrahman Wahid made an official visit to China. In November 2001 new President Megawati held discussions with Chinese Premier Zhu Rongji during his visit to the region.

In December 1989 Indonesia and Australia concluded a temporary agreement providing for joint exploration for petroleum and gas in the Timor Gap, which had been a disputed area since 1978. However, no permanent sea boundary was approved. The validity of the Timor Gap agreement was challenged by Portugal, which instituted proceedings at the International Court of Justice (ICJ), on the grounds that the agreement infringed Portuguese sovereignty and interests; however, in June 1995 the ICJ rejected the case on the grounds that it would affect a country that was not represented, as Indonesia did not recognize the ICJ's jurisdiction. In June 1993 the East Timorese resistance began proceedings in the High Court of Australia to overrule legislation confirming the Timor Gap agreement on the grounds that Australia was bound by international law, which did not recognize Indonesia's annexation of East Timor. In April 1990 Indonesia and Australia restored defence co-operation links, following a four-year disruption. In September 1994 Vice-President Sutrisno became the first high-ranking Indonesian official to visit Australia since Suharto's last visit in 1975.

In July 1995 Indonesia withdrew the nomination of Lt-Gen. Herman Mantiri, a former Chief of the General Staff, as ambassador to Australia, owing to widespread protests there concerning his defence of the actions of the Indonesian armed forces in the 1991 Dili massacre of unarmed civilians (see the chapter on Timor-Leste). Relations with Australia were also strained by Australia's decision to allow 18 East Timorese refugees to remain in the country following their arrival by boat in May (although they were not granted political asylum), by several incidents involving the burning of the Indonesian flag in Australian cities in protest at Indonesia's occupation of East Timor, and by Australia's decision to investigate claims of new evidence about the killing of six Australia-based journalists during the annexation of East Timor in 1975. The Indonesian Government claimed that the journalists had died in cross-fire. In June 1996 an Australian government report concluded that the journalists had been killed by the Indonesian army. A report published by the International Commission of Jurists, a human rights organization based in Switzerland, in 1998 similarly concluded that Indonesian troops had killed the journalists in order to conceal Indonesia's invasion of East Timor, and in October of that year it was announced that Australia was to reopen a judicial inquiry into the killings. In late 2000 newly declassified documents provided conclusive evidence that Australian officials had been aware of Indonesia's plans to invade East Timor. In November 2007 the Deputy State Coroner of New South Wales ruled that five of the Australia-based journalists (the 'Balibo five') had been deliberately killed by Indonesian special forces, declaring that there was sufficient evidence to constitute the case for a war crime.

Meanwhile, in December 1995 Indonesia signed a treaty with Australia to enhance defence links, committing the two countries to consultation in the event of a threat to security. In October 1996 the Australia-Indonesia Development Area was created to develop economic links between the two countries and in March 1997 Indonesia and Australia signed a treaty defining permanent maritime boundaries between the two countries, whilst retaining the Timor Gap agreement. (Indonesia later ceased to be a party to the Timor Gap agreement when it relinquished control of the territory in October 1999.) Following the downfall of Suharto in May 1998, relations between Indonesia and Australia continued to be affected by the issue of East Timor.

In January 1999 the Indonesian Government expressed its 'deep regret' at Australia's announcement earlier that month that it was to change its policy on East Timor and actively promote 'self-determination' in the territory. Following the vote in favour of independence held in East Timor in August 1999, Australia committed 4,500 peace-keeping troops to Interfet, which was formed by the UN to restore order in the territory following the violence perpetrated by pro-Jakarta militias after the announcement of the result of the poll. A military co-operation agreement between Indonesia and Australia, which had been signed four years previously, was reported in October to have been cancelled as a result of the Indonesian Government's displeasure at Australia's leading involvement in the peace-keeping operation. In November 2000 the Australian ambassador to Indonesia, John McCarthy, was physically attacked by a pro-Jakarta mob in Makassar, Sulawesi. The Australian Government accepted the Indonesian Government's apology for the incident.

In June 2001, following several postponements, President Wahid paid an official visit to Australia, the first by an Indonesian head of state for 26 years. The Australian Prime Minister, John Howard, became the first foreign leader to make an official visit to Indonesia following President Megawati's assumption of power when he arrived in Jakarta in August. However, later in the same month relations were strained once again when a cargo ship carrying hundreds of mainly Afghan asylum-seekers became stranded in the international waters between the two countries. Neither country agreed to accept responsibility for the refugees. In early September the Australian Minister for Foreign Affairs, Alexander Downer, arrived in Jakarta for talks with Indonesian Ministers on the problems raised by illegal trafficking of immigrants. In October more than 350 refugees, believed to be heading for Australia, drowned when their boat sank off the Indonesian coast, and in the same month a missing boat carrying approximately 170 Iraqi and Afghan asylum-seekers was found on the Indonesian island of Wera. In February 2002 Australia co-hosted a regional conference on people-smuggling. Also in February, John Howard revisited Indonesia. Both the Speaker of the DPR and the Speaker of the MPR cancelled scheduled meetings with the Australian Prime Minister, and during his stay protests were mounted in response to allegations that Australia was providing funding for separatist groups in Aceh and Papua. Howard denied such charges and signed an agreement with President Megawati concerning counter-terrorism measures. Australia participated in a trilateral dialogue with Indonesia and East Timor regarding future co-operation issues. In May, following an initiative proposed during Prime Minister Howard's visit, the inaugural Australia-Indonesia dialogue was held in Bogor, where Minister of Foreign Affairs Hassan Wirajuda met with his Australian counterpart, Alexander Downer.

In October 2002 Indonesia's relations with Australia were seriously affected by the bomb attacks on the island of Bali, a popular destination for Australian tourists, which resulted in the deaths of almost 90 Australian citizens. While the Australian Government immediately offered assistance to Indonesia, a subsequent series of raids on the homes of Indonesian Muslims resident in Australia prompted Vice-President Hamzah Haz to warn that such an offensive could damage bilateral relations. In late November 2002 Howard appeared to jeopardize Australia's relations with several South-East Asian countries, including Indonesia, when the Prime Minister stated that Australia was prepared to launch pre-emptive attacks against perceived terrorist threats in other Asian countries. In February 2003 Howard visited Indonesia again and, in April, Australia co-hosted a second conference on people-smuggling. In February 2004 Australia and Indonesia co-hosted a counter-terrorism conference held on Bali, at which it was announced that a regional counter-terrorism centre would be established in Jakarta. In August, however, the Indonesian Government expressed concern at Australia's stated intention to arm its fighter aircraft with a cruise missile system, and in December relations were further strained by the Australian Government's announcement that it was to create a coastal security zone extending five times as far as its territorial waters.

Relations with Australia fluctuated considerably during the course of 2005. Following the tsunami disaster of late December 2004, Australia dispatched some 1,000 troops to assist with relief operations in the province of Aceh and pledged US $773m. in aid to the Indonesian Government, to be disbursed over a five-year period. Prime Minister John Howard visited Aceh in February. In the same month, however, the leniency of Abu Bakar Bashir's sentence for his role in the 2002 Bali bombings (see above) provoked much criticism from the Australian Government. In April President Yudhoyono visited Australia to meet with Prime Minister Howard; the two leaders signed a Comprehensive Partnership Agreement, which addressed economic, trade, security and reconstruction issues. Within the space of a week in June two hoax terrorist threats at the Indonesian embassy in Canberra (involving suspect packages containing white powder, which caused the building to be evacuated on both occasions) exacerbated recent tensions between the two countries. These tensions had been increased in the previous month following the imposition by an Indonesian court of a 20-year prison sentence on an Australian woman who had been arrested in Bali on drug-smuggling charges. In July the Australian Minister for Education, Science and Training, Dr Brendan Nelson, visited Jakarta, where he was received by Indonesian Minister of National Education Bambang Soedibyo and Minister of State for Research and Technology Kusmayanto Kadiman. An MoU aimed at promoting confidence and understanding in the areas of science, research and technology was signed, as well as a bilateral agreement to encourage Indonesian scientific agencies to enter into new partnerships within Australia.

Events in early 2006 had a negative impact on Indonesia's relations with Australia. In January the trials of the 'Bali nine' attracted much media attention. This group of eight men and one woman from Australia had been arrested by the Indonesian authorities in April 2005 for attempting to smuggle a large quantity of heroin into Australia from the island of Bali. Upon their conviction in February 2006, the two ring-leaders of the group were sentenced to death by firing squad; the other seven were all sentenced to life imprisonment. Prime Minister Howard stressed his country's opposition to capital punishment and stated the intention of the Australian Government to appeal to the Indonesian authorities for clemency on behalf of the two men sentenced to death. Although the terms of three of the seven sentenced to life imprisonment were subsequently reduced to 20 years, in September the Supreme Court ruled that this decision had been misguided in its leniency and that the death penalty should be imposed on all three, together with a fourth member of the group. In October 2007 the three defendants lost their appeal against the death penalty when the Indonesian Constitutional Court rejected a challenge from their lawyers.

In January 2006 a dispute arose over the case of 43 Papuans who had fled to Australia by boat in search of asylum from alleged human rights abuses; the refugees claimed that they had been tortured whilst imprisoned without charge, and that they had witnessed the shooting of friends and relatives. The Indonesian ambassador in Canberra, Mohammad Hamzah Thayeb, stated that if Australia, which officially supported the 'territorial integrity' of Indonesia and hence was opposed to Papuan claims for independence, were to grant asylum to the Papuan refugees, bilateral relations would become 'strained'. In March, however, the Australian Government announced that all but one of the asylum-seekers were to be granted temporary visas. On the following day Indonesia recalled Thayeb from his post in Canberra, accusing Australia of giving tacit support to the Papuan separatist movement. However, Thayeb returned to Australia in June, prior to Prime Minister Howard's visit to the Indonesian island of Batam to meet with President Yudhoyono, and in July the remaining detainee was finally granted a temporary visa. In November Indonesian Minister of Foreign Affairs Hassan Wirajuda and his Australian counterpart, Alexander Downer, signed a security pact, which it was hoped would promote co-operation in law enforcement and counter-terrorism.

In October 1996 Indonesia and Malaysia agreed to submit disputed claims to the islands of Ligitan and Sipadan to the ICJ, and in August 1997 the two countries agreed to postpone talks on the issue of the islands, pending a ruling by the Court. In December 2002 the ICJ awarded the islands to Malaysia; both countries had earlier stated that they would abide by the Court's decision, thus bringing an end to the dispute. The forced repatriation in early 1998 of thousands of Indonesian workers from Malaysia as a result of the regional economic crisis placed a strain on relations between the two countries. Relations were further strained in October when the Indonesian Government condemned the treatment received in custody by the former Malaysian Deputy Prime Minister and Minister of Finance, Anwar Ibrahim (see the chapter on Malaysia), breaking with a tradition amongst ASEAN countries of non-interference in the internal affairs of other member countries. In May 2002 Indonesia signed a trilateral security pact with Malaysia and the Philippines, enabling the signatories to exchange intelligence and launch joint police operations in an attempt to combat terrorism in the region; Cambodia and Thailand later also acceded to the agreement. In November 2006 Indonesia and the Philippines signed an additional security treaty, which was intended further to increase co-operation in addressing transnational crime and terrorism. Indonesia also concluded agreements relating to extradition and defence co-operation with Singapore in April 2007.

Meanwhile, in August 2002 relations with Malaysia were further affected by that country's introduction of stringent anti-immigration laws, which resulted in the forced deportation of many illegal immigrants, most of whom were Indonesian, and provoked protests outside the Malaysian embassy in Jakarta. In February 2004 Indonesia urged a global boycott of Malaysian timber products, following reports that protected trees from Indonesia were being smuggled across the border to Malaysia and re-exported. In July Indonesia, Malaysia and Singapore commenced co-ordinated patrols of the Strait of Melaka (Malacca), a critical maritime trade route through which 50% of the world's oil passes, in an attempt to curb piracy. At the beginning of February 2005 Malaysia extended an amnesty for illegal immigrants to leave the country before facing legal action in response to a written request from President Susilo Bambang Yudhoyono. In the same month President Yudhoyono visited both Malaysia and Singapore to meet with Malaysian Prime Minister Abdullah Badawi and Singaporean Prime Minister Lee Hsien Loong; this was the first visit to Singapore by an Indonesian head of state since 1974. In February 2006 President Yudhoyono embarked upon a four-day tour of Brunei, Cambodia and Myanmar, in an attempt to consolidate relations with the three countries.

Meanwhile, in May 2002 President Megawati Sukarnoputri attracted criticism when she attended celebrations in Timor-Leste to mark the territory's official accession to nation status; in February Indonesia and East Timor had agreed to establish full diplomatic relations following independence. In July the newly appointed President of Timor-Leste, Xanana Gusmão, visited Indonesia; during his stay he met with President Megawati, and the two leaders discussed the possibility of compensation for Indonesian assets remaining in Timor-Leste and the extent of Indonesian assistance with which the new country would be provided. In October the first meeting of the Indonesia-Timor-Leste Joint Ministerial Commission for Bilateral Co-operation took place in Jakarta. In April 2005, during an official visit to Timor-Leste, President Yudhoyono met with President Gusmão; the two heads of state signed a border agreement resolving the demarcation of approximately 96% of the land borders between the two countries. Yudhoyono also visited the cemetery in which the bodies of victims of the Dili massacre in 1991 were buried. In May the UN-sponsored three-member Commission of Experts opened its investigation into human rights abuses allegedly perpetrated by Indonesian troops during the period of the Timorese vote for independence in 1999.

In March 1996 the USA ended a ban on military training for members of ABRI, which had been imposed after the Dili massacre. In early June 1997, however, it was announced that President Suharto had cancelled Indonesia's participation in US military training programmes in response to the recent condemnation by the US House of Representatives of abuses of human rights committed by Indonesian armed forces in East Timor; the planned purchase by Indonesia of a number of US military aircraft was also cancelled. In November 1999 the newly appointed President of Indonesia, Abdurrahman Wahid, made an official visit to the USA. In October 2000, however, relations between Indonesia and the USA deteriorated markedly as the result of a combination of factors, including the perceived 'interference' in Indonesian domestic political affairs of the recently appointed US ambassador to Indonesia, Robert Gelbard, US criticism of Indonesia's failure to control pro-Jakarta militias in West Timor following the murder of three UN workers by militia members in September, and Indonesian perceptions of US bias towards Israel in the Middle East conflict. In late October and early November Muslim groups rallied outside the US embassy in Jakarta, calling for *jihad*; threats were made against US citizens in Indonesia; US companies in the country were attacked; and it was reported that the Indonesian Government had requested Gelbard's immediate removal and replacement. In late October the USA closed its embassy in Jakarta for two weeks, and in early November the US Government warned citizens to defer all non-essential travel to the archipelago.

Following the terrorist attacks of 11 September 2001 on the USA, in the same month President Megawati became the first leader of a predominantly Muslim country to meet with President George W. Bush. However, following the commencement of air strikes against the Taliban regime in Afghanistan in October, fundamentalist Muslims threatened violence if the Indonesian Government did not sever diplomatic relations with the USA. In October the Front Pembela Islam (FPI—Islamic Defenders' Front) warned that if British and US citizens did not leave the country immediately their safety could not be guaranteed. President Megawati, under pressure from Muslim groups and Vice-President Hamzah Haz, indirectly condemned the US attacks in Afghanistan for the first time.

In April 2002 Indonesia and the USA held sensitive security talks, during which measures to combat terrorism and to strengthen civilian control over the armed forces were discussed. In July the US Congress approved legislation awarding US $16m. to the Indonesian police forces; this included $12m. for the establishment of a dedicated anti-terrorism unit and followed a vote by the Senate Appropriations Committee to remove all remaining restrictions on the provision of military training to Indonesia (the vote awaited approval by Congress). The proposed legislation for the resumption of military assistance did, however, include human rights conditions. In August, during a two-day visit to Indonesia, US Secretary of State Colin Powell guaranteed substantial financial aid to the country to combat the terrorist threat within its borders. Powell also announced the resumption of a training programme for Indonesian army officers at US military schools and $50m. of funding for Indonesia's police and counter-terrorism units over a three-year period. The bombings in Bali in October were widely perceived to constitute a further justification for the strengthening of military links with the USA. In early 2003, however, the USA placed Indonesia on a list of countries of which citizens were required to register with the US immigration authorities if they visited the country. In October President George W. Bush visited Indonesia and announced plans for a $157m. programme to improve education in the country in an attempt to create a system that would discourage the development of Islamist extremism. However, the US Senate approved amendments proposing that funding be withdrawn for the enrolment of Indonesians in US military training programmes and that the restoration of normal military links between the two countries be suspended until the Indonesian Government co-operated fully with the investigation into the murder of two US citizens in Papua in August 2002 (see above).

The USA took an active part in relief operations in Indonesia following the tsunamis of December 2004, notably deploying some 13,000 military personnel in the region and providing an aircraft carrier to dispatch helicopters to the province of Aceh. In January 2005 US Secretary of State Colin Powell visited Aceh. The brevity of the 30-month prison sentence given to Abu Bakar Bashir in February, following his conviction on charges pertaining to the Bali bombings of 2002, attracted much US criticism. In the same month the USA resumed International Military Education and Training (IMET) for Indonesia, which had been restricted as a result of the 'insufficient co-operation' on the part of the Indonesian military in investigating the murders in August 2002 of two US citizens in Papua. In May 2005 President Yudhoyono made an official visit to the USA, during which he met with President Bush. In a joint communiqué, the two heads of state stressed their common commitment to work towards the establishment of normal military relations; to improve economic co-operation and trade relations; and to strengthen co-operation and investment in the fields of counter-terrorism, energy and education. President Bush reiterated the US Administration's support for Indonesia's territorial integrity and its opposition to secessionist movements within the archipelago. In November the USA resumed Foreign Military Financing for Indonesia with a view to modernizing the Indonesian military and supporting joint objectives. During a visit to Indonesia in June 2006, US Secretary of Defense Donald Rumsfeld avowed that the Bush Administration did intend fully to restore normal military relations with Indonesia but that this was not yet possible owing to resistance within the US Congress.

In September 1994 a 220-strong medical detachment from the Indonesian army joined the UN Protection Force in Bosnia and Herzegovina (UNPROFOR), in the first mission of its kind to Europe. Indonesia's international standing was further enhanced when, in January 1995, it replaced Pakistan as the non-permanent Asian representative on the UN Security Council for a period of two years. In October 1994 Indonesia underscored its pivotal regional role through hosting its fifth informal meeting to resolve peacefully the dispute over the conflicting claims of six Asian countries to sovereignty over parts of the South China Sea, particularly the Spratly Islands. Moreover, in November the Asia-Pacific Economic Co-operation (APEC, see p. 176) summit meeting took place in Bogor. Indonesia had been one of the founding members of APEC, which had been established in 1989.

In August 1995 Queen Beatrix of the Netherlands, the former colonial power in Indonesia, visited Indonesia (the first Dutch monarch to do so for 24 years) and spoke of her regret for the suffering caused to Indonesians by Dutch rule. In December 1999, with the issue of the status of East Timor resolved following the vote in favour of independence at a referendum in August, Indonesia and Portugal formally re-established full diplomatic relations.

In mid-2000 it was reported that President Wahid had expressed his desire to develop Indonesia's relations with Iraq and other Muslim countries. In June of the same year President Wahid made an official visit to Iran, and in October Indonesia and Pakistan signed an MoU relating to the promotion of bilateral links. In January 2001 the Prime Minister of India made a four-day visit to Indonesia, following a visit to India by President Wahid in February 2000. In October 2005 King Abdullah of Jordan made a state visit to Jakarta and held discussions with President Yudhoyono on bilateral relations and issues pertaining to the international Islamic community. In the following month President Yudhoyono paid an official visit to Pakistan, during which he signed a framework agreement on bilateral economic co-operation with his Pakistani counterpart, Pervez Musharraf. The two Presidents also held discussions regarding the challenge of countering tendencies to associate Islam with terrorism. In April–May 2006 President Yudhoyono conducted a 10-day tour of the Middle East, visiting Jordan, Kuwait, Qatar, Saudi Arabia and the United Arab Emirates. During the five-nation trip Yudhoyono reached preliminary energy and investment agreements, worth many millions of dollars, with his various counterparts and expressed Indonesia's support for the creation of an independent Palestinian state. In July demonstrations were held outside the US embassy in Jakarta in protest at Israel's ongoing military activity against the Palestinians in Gaza, while Muslim protesters accused the US Administration of bias towards Israel. Despite this support for Palestinian independence, it was unexpectedly announced in October that Indonesia was to buy four unmanned aerial vehicles (UAVs) from Israel. In response to the resultant controversy, the Commander-in-Chief of the Armed Forces, Air Chief Marshal Djoko Suyanto, asserted that the decision to purchase UAVs from Israel had been based purely on military considerations.

Relations with Denmark were severely strained in February 2006, following the publication in a Danish newspaper of cartoons depicting the Prophet Muhammad, which provoked international outrage among Muslim communities. Later that month, despite security assurances from the Indonesian authorities, the Danish ambassador and embassy staff temporarily withdrew from Jakarta amid mounting concerns for their safety. Danish nationals resident in Indonesia were advised to leave the country following statements from extremists based therein, threatening to target those of Danish origin. The publication of the cartoons also provoked considerable ill-feeling against the USA, which many Indonesian Muslims accused of having exacerbated the controversy. In mid-February hundreds of demonstrators attacked the US embassy in Jakarta.

Indonesia signed an important free trade agreement with Japan in August 2007 during a state visit by Prime Minister Shinzo Abe to Jakarta. The agreement envisaged the eventual removal of most bilateral import taxes (with the notable exception of Japanese imports of rice). Indonesia also confirmed its supplies of liquefied natural gas (LNG) to Japan.

During a visit to Moscow in April 2003 President Megawati signed an agreement to buy Russian defence equipment to the value of US $197m., which was to be partly financed by the bartering of Indonesian palm oil. In September 2007 President Vladimir Putin of Russia visited Jakarta, where he concluded an agreement with President Yudhoyono providing for further purchases of Russian armaments. This arrangement was to be financed by a 10-year loan of $1,000m. from Russia, the defence equipment including helicopters, submarines, tanks and *Sukhoi* jet fighter aircraft. Various other agreements, relating to co-operation in the areas of economic relations, counter-terrorism measures and environmental protection, were also signed.

Government

The highest authority of the State is the Majelis Permusyawaratan Rakyat (MPR—People's Consultative Assembly), which, following a constitutional amendment in 2002 (see below), from 2004 comprised 678 members (reduced from 700) serving for five years. The MPR includes all 550 members of the Dewan Perwakilan Rakyat (DPR—House of Representatives), the country's legislative organ. Executive power rests with the President, elected for five years by the MPR. He or she governs with the assistance of an appointed Cabinet, which is responsible to the President. In August 2002 the MPR approved a series of amendments to the Constitution. These provided for: the direct election of the President and Vice-President; the termination of all non-elected representation in the DPR and MPR; and the creation of the Dewan Perwakilan Daerah (DPD—House of Representatives of the Regions), which, together with the DPR, would comprise the MPR. The changes took effect at the country's next national elections, held in 2004.

There are 33 provinces, and local government is through a three-tier system of provincial, regency and village assemblies. Each province is headed by a Governor, who is elected to a five-year term of office by the Provincial Assembly. Provincial Governors must be confirmed by the President. The Governor of Jakarta, which is designated as a 'special district' (as are Aceh and Yogyakarta), was chosen by direct election for the first time in August 2007.

Defence

As assessed at November 2007, the total strength of the armed forces was 302,000 men: army an estimated 233,000, navy 45,000 and air force 24,000. There were also some 280,000 paramilitary forces, including a police 'mobile brigade' of 14,000 and an estimated 40,000 trainees of KAMRA (People's Security). Military service is selective and lasts for two years. Defence expenditure for 2007 was budgeted at an estimated Rp. 32,600,000m.

Economic Affairs

In 2006, according to estimates by the World Bank, Indonesia's gross national income (GNI), measured at average 2004–06 prices, was US $315,759m., equivalent to US $1,420 per head (or $3,950 per head on an international purchasing-power parity basis). During 1996–2006, it was estimated, the population increased at an average annual rate of 1.3%, while gross domestic product (GDP) per head increased, in real terms, by an average of 1.1% per year. Overall GDP increased, in real terms, by an average of 2.5% per year in 1996–2006. GDP increased by 5.5% in 2006 and expanded by 6.3% in 2007, according to the Asian Development Bank (ADB).

Agriculture, forestry and fishing contributed 12.9% of GDP in 2006, and engaged 43.7% of the employed labour force in 2007. Principal crops for domestic consumption include rice, cassava and maize. Although Indonesia remains a major exporter of rubber and palm oil, the respective contributions to the country's total export earnings has declined. Other important cash crops are coffee, spices, tea, cocoa, tobacco, bananas, coconuts and sugar cane. In 2000 an estimated 58% of Indonesia's land area was covered by tropical rain forests. However, illegal logging practices have been widespread, leading to serious environmental damage. During 1996–2006, according to the World Bank, agricultural GDP increased by an estimated average of 2.4% per year. According to the ADB, the GDP of the agricultural sector expanded by 3.5% in 2007.

In 2007 industry (including mining, manufacturing, construction and utilities) engaged 18.2% of the employed labour force. The sector provided 47.0% of GDP in 2006. During 1996–2006, according to the World Bank, industrial GDP increased by an average of 2.3% per year. According to the ADB, the GDP of the sector increased by 4.7% in 2007.

Mining engaged 1.0% of the employed labour force in 2007, but contributed 10.6% of GDP in 2006. Indonesia's principal mineral resource is petroleum, and the country is a leading exporter of liquefied natural gas. At the end of 2006 proven reserves of petroleum amounted to 4,300m. barrels, sufficient to sustain production at that year's rate for about 10 years. At March 2007 Indonesia's agreed quota for petroleum production within the Organization of the Petroleum Exporting Countries (OPEC) was 1,396,000 b/d. In 2006 natural gas production was 74,000m. cu m, from proven reserves amounting to 263,000m. cu m. In 2006 coal production reached 119.9m. metric tons (oil equivalent). Indonesia is one of the world's largest producers of tin, with output of ore reaching 80,933 metric tons in 2006. Bauxite, nickel, copper, gold, silver and coal are also mined. During 2000–2006, according to figures from the ADB, mining GDP increased by an annual average of only 0.1%. The GDP of the sector increased by 2.2% in 2006.

Manufacturing contributed 28.0% of GDP in 2006, and engaged 12.4% of the employed labour force in 2007. Apart from petroleum refineries, the main branches of the sector include food products, textiles, clothing and footwear, transport equipment, electrical machinery and electronic equipment. According to the World Bank, manufacturing GDP increased by an estimated average of 3.0% per year in 1996–2005. According to figures from the ADB, manufacturing GDP increased by 4.6% in 2006.

From the 1980s Indonesia broadened the base of its energy supplies to include gas, coal, hydroelectricity and geothermal energy, in addition to the traditional dependence on petroleum. In 2004, of the total electricity produced, coal accounted for 40.1%, petroleum for 30.2%, natural gas for 16.1% and hydroelectricity for 8.1%. In 2005 imports of petroleum and its products comprised 30.6% of the total value of merchandise imports. A tender for the construction of Indonesia's first nuclear power plant, suspended in 1997 and to be located on Muria peninsula, Java, was expected to be issued in 2008, with the revised aim of producing electricity by 2017.

Services (including trade, transport and communications, finance and tourism) provided an estimated 40.1% of GDP in 2006, and engaged 38.1% of the employed labour force in 2007. Tourism is normally a major source of foreign exchange. Revenue from tourism (including passenger transport) reached US $5,092m. in 2005. The number of tourists arrivals totalled an estimated 4.8m. in 2006. According to the World Bank, the GDP of the services sector expanded by an estimated average of 2.8% per year in 1996–2006. According to the ADB, the sector's GDP increased by 8.9% in 2007.

In 2006 Indonesia recorded a visible trade surplus of US $29,646m. In the same year a surplus of $9,937m. was recorded on the current account of the balance of payments. In 2006 the principal sources of imports were Singapore (which supplied 30.5% of the total), the People's Republic of China (11.6%) and Japan (8.9%). Other major suppliers were Malaysia, Thailand, the Republic of Korea and the USA. Japan was the principal market for exports in that year (purchasing 19.4%). Other major purchasers were Singapore, the USA, the Republic of Korea and China. The principal exports in 2006 included petroleum and its products, machinery, mechanical appliances and electronic equipment, shrimps and coffee. The principal imports were machinery, mechanical appliances and electrical equipment, base metals, mineral and chemical products and transport equipment.

The budget for 2008 envisaged revenue of Rp. 781,400,000m. (including grants) and expenditure of Rp. 854,700,000m.; the resultant deficit of Rp. 73,300,000m. was originally projected to be the equivalent of 1.7% of GDP. Indonesia's total external debt stood at US $138,300m. at the end of 2005, of which $72,335m. was long-term public debt. In 2007, according to the ADB, the cost of debt-servicing was equivalent to 19.2% of revenue from exports of goods and services. The annual rate of inflation averaged 14.0% in 1996–2006. Consumer prices were estimated by the ADB to have risen by 6.4% in 2007. The average rate of unemployment in 2007 was estimated at 9.1% of the labour force. The level of underemployment also remained very high, at almost 28% according to one estimate.

Indonesia is a member of the UN Economic and Social Commission for Asia and the Pacific (ESCAP, see p. 35), the Association of South East Asian Nations (ASEAN, see p. 185), the Asian Development Bank (ADB, see p. 182), the Asia-Pacific Economic Co-operation (APEC, see p. 176) forum, the Colombo Plan (see p. 411) and the Organization of the Petroleum Exporting Countries (OPEC, see p. 373). As a member of ASEAN, Indonesia signed an accord in January 1992, pledging to establish a free trade zone, to be known as the ASEAN Free Trade Area (AFTA), within 15 years (subsequently reduced to 10 years), beginning in January 1993. AFTA was formally established on 1 January 2002.

Following Indonesia's recovery from the regional financial crisis of the late 1990s, the country's economic progress was disrupted by the tsunami disaster of December 2004. A four-year recovery plan was drafted for the devastated province of Aceh, in northern Sumatra. In January 2005 the Consultative Group for Indonesia (CGI—a donor grouping chaired by the World Bank and incorporating IMF representatives) convened in Jakarta and pledged a total of US $5,100m., of which $1,700m. was to be allocated to the tsunami relief efforts. In 2007 GDP growth reached its highest level since 1996, supported by the strength of private consumption, rising investment and an increase in the value of exports. The easing of inflationary pressures during 2007 and the central bank's reduction in interest rates to 8.0% in December combined to stimulate consumer spending. Foreign direct investment increased from an estimated $4,914m. in 2006 to $5,571m. in 2007. Export growth remained strong in 2007, partly owing to the sharp rises in international commodity prices, although the increase in revenue from Indonesia's oil and gas sector was constrained by production difficulties. Merchandise exports expanded by 14% in 2007 to reach an estimated $118,000m., although imports were reported to have increased by 15%. The 2008 budget emphasized the reduction of the incidence of poverty, with an increasing focus on infrastructural improvements as well as on the provision of social assistance to vulnerable members of society. The ADB forecast GDP growth of 6.0% in 2008. In March of that year, in view of global economic conditions, notably the deceleration of the US economy, Indonesia's anticipated budget deficit was revised upwards to a projected 2.1% of GDP. Furthermore, the Government's decision in early 2008 to implement substantial increases in its energy and food subsidies, to reflect rising costs of international commodities, was expected to have a major impact on the economy, and in April the Government imposed restrictions on the export of rice.

Education

Education is mainly under the control of the Ministry of National Education, but the Ministry of Religious Affairs is in charge of Islamic religious schools at the primary level. In 1987 primary education, beginning at seven years of age and lasting for six years, was made compulsory. In 1993 it was announced that compulsory education was to be expanded to nine years. Secondary education begins at 13 years of age and lasts for six years, comprising two cycles of three years each. In 2004/05 enrolment at pre-primary schools was equivalent to 33% of pupils in the relevant age group (males 33%; females 34%). Primary enrolment in the same year included 95% of pupils in the relevant age group (males 96%; females 93%), while enrolment at secondary level included 57% of pupils in the relevant age group (males 58%; females 57%). In the same year there were 50,083 pre-primary institutions, 147,793 primary schools, 31,173 general secondary schools and 5,665 vocational secondary schools. In 2004/05 enrolment at tertiary level was equivalent to 17% of the relevant population (males 19%; females 15%). In 2004/05 there were 2,516 tertiary institutions. The Government's budget for 2007 allocated Rp. 43,500,000m., representing 5.7% of total expenditure, to education.

Public Holidays

2008: 1 January (New Year's Day), 10 January*† (Muharram, Islamic New Year), 7 February (Chinese New Year), 20 March* (Mouloud, Prophet Muhammad's Birthday), 21 March (Good Friday), 24 March (Easter Monday), 1 May (Ascension Day), 20 May (Waisak Day), 17 August (Independence Day), 30 July* (Ascension of the Prophet Muhammad), 1 October* (Id al-Fitr, end of Ramadan), 8 December (Id al-Adha, Feast of the Sacrifice), 25 December (Christmas Day), 29 December*† (Muharram, Islamic New Year).

2009: 1 January (New Year's Day), 26 January (Chinese New Year), 9 March* (Mouloud, Prophet Muhammad's Birthday), 10 April (Good Friday), 21 May (Ascension Day), May/June (Waisak Day), 20 July* (Ascension of the Prophet Muhammad), 17 August (Independence Day), 21 September* (Id al-Fitr, end of Ramadan), 28 November* (Id al-Adha, Feast of the Sacrifice), 18 December* (Muharram, Islamic New Year), 25 December (Christmas Day).

* These holidays are dependent on the Islamic lunar calendar and may vary by one or two days from the dates given.

† This festival occurs twice (marking the start of the Islamic years AH 1429 and 1430) within the same Gregorian year.

Weights and Measures

The metric system is in force.

INDONESIA

Statistical Survey

Source (unless otherwise stated): Badan Pusat Statistik (Central Bureau of Statistics/Statistics Indonesia), Jalan Dr Sutomo 6–8, Jakarta 10710; tel. (21) 3507057; fax (21) 3857046; e-mail bpshq@bps.go.id; internet www.bps.go.id.

Note: Unless otherwise stated, figures for East Timor (now Timor-Leste, occupied by Indonesia between July 1976 and October 1999) are not included in the tables.

Area and Population

AREA, POPULATION AND DENSITY

Area (sq km)	1,922,570*
Population (census results)	
31 October 1990	178,631,196
30 June 2000†	
Males	103,417,180
Females	102,847,415
Total	206,264,595
Population (UN estimates at mid-year)‡	
2005	226,063,000
2006	228,864,000
2007	231,627,000
Density (per sq km) at mid-2007	120.5

* 742,308 sq miles.
† Includes non-permanent residents (421,399), estimates for areas where the census could not be carried out (2,317,216), and adjustment for under-enumeration (2,283,981).
‡ Source: UN, World Population Prospects: The 2006 Revision.

ISLANDS
(population at 2000 census, including adjustment)*

	Area (sq km)	Population	Density (per sq km)
Jawa (Java) and Madura	127,499	121,352,608	951.8
Sumatera (Sumatra)	482,393	43,309,707	89.8
Sulawesi (Celebes)	191,800	14,946,488	77.9
Kalimantan	547,891	11,331,558	20.7
Nusa Tenggara†	67,502	7,961,540	117.9
Bali	5,633	3,151,162	559.4
Maluku (Moluccas)	77,871	1,990,598	25.6
Papua‡	421,981	2,220,934	5.3
Total	1,922,570	206,264,595	107.3

* Figures refer to provincial divisions, each based on a large island or group of islands but also including adjacent small islands.
† Comprising most of the Lesser Sunda Islands, principally Flores, Lombok, Sumba, Sumbawa and part of Timor.
‡ Formerly Irian Jaya (West Papua).

PRINCIPAL TOWNS
(estimated population at 31 December 1996)

Jakarta (capital)	9,341,400	Malang	775,900
Surabaya	2,743,400	Padang	739,500
Bandung	2,429,000	Banjarmasin	544,700
Medan	1,942,000	Surakarta	518,600
Palembang	1,394,300	Pontianak	459,100
Semarang	1,366,500	Yogyakarta (Jogjakarta)	421,000
Ujung Pandang (Makassar)	1,121,300		

Mid-2007 ('000, incl. suburbs, UN estimates): Jakarta 9,125; Surabaya 2,845; Bandung 2,394; Medan 2,115; Palembang 1,749; Ujung Pandang 1,262 (Source: UN, World Urbanization Prospects: The 2007 Revision).

BIRTHS AND DEATHS
(annual averages, UN estimates)

	1990–95	1995–2000	2000–05
Birth rate (per 1,000)	24.3	22.0	20.7
Death rate (per 1,000)	8.2	7.2	6.6

Source: UN, World Population Prospects: The 2006 Revision.

Birth rate (per 1,000): 22.9 in 1997; 22.8 in 1998; 22.4 in 1999 (Source: UN, Statistical Yearbook for Asia and the Pacific).

Death rate (per 1,000): 7.5 in 1997; 7.7 in 1998; 7.5 in 1999 (Source: UN, Statistical Yearbook for Asia and the Pacific).

Expectation of life (years at birth, WHO estimates): 67.3 (males 65.9; females 68.7) in 2005 (Source: WHO, World Health Statistics).

ECONOMICALLY ACTIVE POPULATION
(persons aged 15 years and over, at February)

	2005	2006	2007
Agriculture, hunting, forestry and fishing	41,814,197	42,323,190	42,608,760
Mining and quarrying	808,842	947,097	1,020,807
Manufacturing	11,652,406	11,578,141	12,094,067
Electricity, gas and water	186,801	207,102	247,059
Construction	4,417,087	4,373,950	4,397,132
Trade, restaurants and hotels	18,896,902	18,555,057	19,425,270
Transport, storage and communications	5,552,525	5,467,308	5,575,499
Financing, insurance, real estate and business services	1,042,786	1,153,292	1,252,195
Public services	10,576,572	10,571,965	10,962,352
Total employed	94,948,118	95,177,102	97,583,141
Unemployed	10,854,254	11,104,693	10,547,917
Total labour force	105,802,372	106,281,795	108,131,058

Health and Welfare

KEY INDICATORS

Total fertility rate (children per woman, 2005)	2.3
Under-5 mortality rate (per 1,000 live births, 2005)	36
HIV/AIDS (% of persons aged 15–49, 2005)	0.1
Physicians (per 1,000 head, 2003)	0.13
Hospital beds (per 1,000 head, 1998)	0.60
Health expenditure (2004): US $ per head (PPP)	118.2
Health expenditure (2004): % of GDP	2.8
Health expenditure (2004): public (% of total)	34.2
Access to water (% of persons, 2004)	77
Access to sanitation (% of persons, 2004)	55
Human Development Index (2005): ranking	107
Human Development Index (2005): value	0.728

For sources and definitions, see explanatory note on p. vi.

Agriculture

PRINCIPAL CROPS
('000 metric tons, incl. East Timor)

	2004	2005	2006
Rice (paddy)	54,088	53,985	54,400*
Maize	11,225	12,524	11,611
Potatoes	1,072	1,010	1,010†
Sweet potatoes	1,902	1,857	1,852
Cassava (Manioc)	19,425	19,321	19,928
Sugar cane*	26,750	29,300	30,150
Dry beans	321	316	327

INDONESIA

—continued

	2004	2005	2006
Cashew nuts	120	122†	122†
Soybeans (Soya beans)	723	808	749
Groundnuts (in shell)	1,469	14,670	14,700
Coconuts*	16,285	18,250	16,375
Oil palm fruit†	60,426	64,255	64,255
Cabbages	1,433	1,293	1,203†
Tomatoes	627	588	588†
Pumpkins, squash and gourds	180	196	196†
Cucumbers and gherkins	478	553	553†
Aubergines (Eggplants)	312	252	252†
Chillies and green peppers	1,101	871	871†
Dry onions	757	809	809†
Leeks and other alliaceous vegetables	476	501	501†
Green beans	830	830†	830†
Carrots and turnips	424	440	440†
Oranges	2,071	2,214	2,214†
Avocados	222	228	228†
Mangoes and guavas	1,438	1,413	1,413†
Pineapples	710	925	925†
Bananas	4,874	5,178	5,178†
Papayas	733	549	549†
Coffee (green)	700	640	653
Cocoa beans	601	610*	580*
Tea (made)	165	171	171†
Cinnamon†	62	64	64
Cloves	111	111†	111†
Ginger†	155	159	159
Tobacco (leaves)	141*	141†	141†
Natural rubber	2,066	2,128	2,350*

* Unofficial figure(s).
† FAO estimate(s).

Aggregate production ('000 metric tons, may include official, semi-official or estimated data): Total cereals 65,313.7 in 2004, 66,508.5 in 2005, 66,010.6 in 2006; Total roots and tubers 22,748.6 in 2004, 22,537.8 in 2005, 23,139.0 in 2006; Total vegetables (incl. melons) 7,609.4 in 2004, 7,395.5 in 2005, 7,408.0 in 2006; Total fruits (excl. melons) 14,747.5 in 2004, 15,405.8 in 2005, 15,405.8 in 2006.

Source: FAO.

LIVESTOCK
('000 head)

	2004	2005	2006
Cattle	11,108	10,943	11,218
Sheep	8,075	8,307	8,543
Goats	12,781	13,409	14,512
Pigs	5,980	6,801	7,087
Horses	397	387	399
Buffaloes	2,403	2,428	2,428†
Chickens	1,149,374	1,174,933	1,366,132
Ducks	32,572	32,405	34,612

* FAO estimate.
Source: FAO.

LIVESTOCK PRODUCTS
('000 metric tons)

	2004	2005	2006
Cattle meat	447.6	358.7	389.3
Buffalo meat	40.2	38.1	39.5
Sheep meat	66.1	47.3	51.9
Goat meat	57.1	50.6	53.3
Pig meat*	566.5	594.6	594.6
Chicken meat	1,213.1	1,125.7	1,332.8
Cows' milk	596.3	536.0	577.6
Goats' milk*	220	220	215
Hen eggs	857.4	856.6	932.1
Other poultry eggs	173.2	195.0	201.7
Wool: greasy*	24.4	24.4	24.4

* FAO estimates.

Note: Figures for meat refer to inspected production only, i.e. from animals slaughtered under government supervision.

Source: FAO.

Forestry

ROUNDWOOD REMOVALS
('000 cubic metres, excl. bark)

	2004	2005	2006
Sawlogs, veneer logs and logs for sleepers	26,000	24,223	21,602
Pulpwood*†	3,248	3,248	3,248
Other industrial wood*†	3,249	3,249	3,249
Fuel wood*	76,564	73,720	70,719
Total	109,061	104,440	98,818

* FAO estimates.
† Output assumed to be unchanged since 1999.
Source: FAO.

SAWNWOOD PRODUCTION
('000 cubic metres, incl. railway sleepers)

	2004	2005	2006
Total (all broadleaved)	4,330	1,472	1,472*

* FAO estimate.
Source: FAO.

Fishing

('000 metric tons, live weight)

	2003	2004	2005
Capture	4,627.2*	4,642.4	4,381.3
Scads	297.9	325.2	314.3
Goldstripe sardinella	153.8	145.4	137.7
'Stolephorus' anchovies	161.1	154.8	144.9
Skipjack tuna	196.9	232.4	235.1
Indian mackerels	n.a.	10.6	10.1
Aquaculture	996.7	1,045.1	1,197.1
Common carp	220.3	192.5	216.9
Milkfish	226.1	241.4	254.1
Total catch	5,623.8*	5,687.4	5,578.4

* FAO estimate.

Note: Figures exclude aquatic plants ('000 metric tons): 296.5 (capture 64.6, aquaculture 231.9) in 2003; 419.3 (capture 8.7, aquaculture 410.6) in 2004; 918.3 (capture 7.7, aquaculture 910.6). Also excluded are crocodiles, recorded by number rather than by weight. The number of crocodiles caught was: 11,558 in 2003; 14,467 in 2004; 18,302 in 2005.

Source: FAO.

Mining

('000 metric tons, unless otherwise indicated)

	2004	2005	2006
Crude petroleum (million barrels)*	362.0	352.0	340.0
Natural gas (million cubic metres)	83,740	85,830	86,000
Bauxite	1,331	1,082	1,502
Coal (bituminous)	131,530	142,920	153,400
Nickel†	136.0	135.0	140.0
Copper†	840.3	1,064.2	793.0
Tin ore (metric tons)†	65,772	78,404	80,933
Gold (kg)‡	91,710	130,620	164,400
Silver (kg)‡	261,960	328,749	327,557

* Including condensate.
† Figures refer to the metal content of ores and concentrates.
‡ Including gold and silver in copper concentrate.

Source: US Geological Survey.

INDONESIA

Statistical Survey

Industry

SELECTED PRODUCTS
('000 metric tons, unless otherwise indicated)

	2001	2002	2003
Raw sugar (centrifugal)[1]	2,025	1,902	1,730
Refined sugar[1,2]	2,023	1,750	2,431
Palm oil[1]	8,080[3]	9,350	10,530
Veneer sheets ('000 cubic metres)[1]	94	45[2]	289
Plywood ('000 cubic metres)[1]	7,300	7,550	6,111
Jackets (men's and boys', '000)	55,849	32,777	n.a.
Trousers (men's and boys', '000)	42,403	45,168	n.a.
Shirts (men's and boys', '000)	18,069	76,897	n.a.
Underwear (men's and boys', '000)	76,232	48,154	n.a.
Underwear (women's and girls', '000)	55,769	145,284	n.a.
Blouses (women's and girls', '000)	25,259	22,540	n.a.
Footwear ('000 pairs, excl. rubber)	325,169	306,761	n.a.
Newsprint	1,022	1,022	1,022
Other printing and writing paper[2]	5,394	5,394	5,394
Other paper and paperboard	3,620	3,612	3,612
Nitrogenous fertilizers[1,4]	2,549	n.a.	n.a.
Jet fuel	1,087	1,216	1,186
Motor spirit (petrol)	7,617	8,344	8,306
Naphthas	1,435	1,399	1,790
Kerosene	7,564	7,263	7,451
Gas-diesel oil	14,075	13,724	14,432
Residual fuel oils	12,009	11,951	11,755
Lubricating oils	375	315	349
Liquefied petroleum gas	1,684	1,833	2,316
Rubber tyres ('000)[5]	20,500[2]	n.a.	n.a.
Cement (hydraulic)[6]	n.a.	34,640	35,000
Aluminium (unwrought)[2,6,7]	209	160	200
Tin (unwrought, metric tons)[6,7]	53,470	67,455	65,000
Passenger motor cars ('000)[8]	74	n.a.	n.a.
Television receivers (colour, '000)	21,519	23,680	n.a.
Electric accumulators (for motor vehicles, '000)	49,496	22,510	n.a.
Batteries and cells (primary, millions)	14,059	14,800	n.a.
Electric energy (million kWh)	95,097	113,245	101,381
Gas from gasworks (terajoules)	30,400	30,000[2]	n.a.

2004 ('000 metric tons unless otherwise stated): Palm oil 12,080[1,3]; Veneer sheets ('000 cubic metres) 155[1]; Plywood ('000 cubic metres) 4,514; Cement (hydraulic) 33,230[2,6]; Aluminium (unwrought) 247[6]; Tin (unwrought, metric tons) 49,872[6]; Gas-diesel oil 14,623; Residual fuel oils 10,995; Jet fuels 1,486; Motor spirit (petrol) 9,398; Naphthas 1,424; Lubricating oils 420; Kerosene 7,341; Electric energy (million kWh) 103,536.

2005 ('000 metric tons unless otherwise stated): Palm oil 14,070[1,3]; Veneer sheets ('000 cubic metres) 101[1,2]; Plywood ('000 cubic metres) 4,534[1]; Cement (hydraulic) 33,917[6]; Aluminium (unwrought) 252[6]; Tin (unwrought) 65[6].

2006 ('000 metric tons unless otherwise stated): Palm oil 15,900[1,3]; Veneer sheets ('000 cubic metres) 101[1,2]; Plywood ('000 cubic metres) 3,812[1]; Cement (hydraulic) 34,000[6]; Aluminium (unwrought) 250[6]; Tin (unwrought) 63[6].

Cigarettes (million): 254,276 in 1999.

[1] Source: FAO.
[2] Provisional or estimated production.
[3] Unofficial figure.
[4] Production in terms of nitrogen.
[5] For road motor vehicles, excluding bicycles and motorcycles.
[6] Source: US Geological Survey.
[7] Primary metal production only.
[8] Vehicles assembled from imported parts.

Source (unless otherwise indicated): UN, *Industrial Commodity Statistics Yearbook*.

Finance

CURRENCY AND EXCHANGE RATES

Monetary Units
100 sen = 1 rupiah (Rp.).

Sterling, Dollar and Euro Equivalents (31 December 2007)
£1 sterling = 18,870.041 rupiah;
US $1 = 9,419.000 rupiah;
€1 = 13,865.703 rupiah;
100,000 rupiah = £5.30 = $10.62 = €7.21.

Average Exchange Rate (rupiah per US $)
2005 9,704.74
2006 9,159.32
2007 9,143.36

GOVERNMENT FINANCE
(central government operations, '000 million rupiah)

Summary of Balances

	2005	2006*	2007*
Revenue and grants	495,444	637,799	723,058
Less Expenditure and net lending	509,419	669,880	763,571
Overall balance	–13,975	–32,081	–40,513

Revenue and Grants

	2005	2006*	2007*
Tax revenue	346,834	409,020	509,462
Income tax	175,380	208,834	261,698
Value added tax (VAT) on goods and services, and tax on sales of luxury goods	16,184	20,684	21,267
Tax of rights in land and building	3,429	3,179	5,390
Excise duties	33,256	37,772	42,035
Import duties	14,921	12,142	14,417
Export taxes	318	1,094	453
Other taxes	2,051	2,287	3,158
Non-tax revenue	147,314	226,906	210,927
Grants	1,296	1,873	2,669
Total	495,444	637,799	723,058

Expenditure and Net Lending

	2005	2006*	2007*
Central government expenditure	358,903	443,509	504,776
Personnel expenditure	55,589	72,238	101,202
Material expenditure	33,060	46,944	72,186
Interest payments	57,651	78,910	
Domestic interest	43,496	54,778	85,087
External interest	14,155	24,132	
Subsidies	120,708	107,463	102,924
Oil subsidies	95,661	64,212	61,838
Non-oil subsidies	25,047	43,251	41,086
Social expenditure	24,247	43,254	51,409
Capital expenditure	36,854	59,605	73,130
Other expenditure	30,794	35,095	18,838
Regional expenditure	150,516	226,371	258,795
Balance funds	143,301	222,322	250,343
Specific autonomous fund	7,215	4,049	8,452
Total	509,419	669,880	763,571

* Preliminary figures.

INTERNATIONAL RESERVES
(US $ million at 31 December)

	2004	2005	2006
Gold (market prices)	1,351	1,590	1,485
IMF special drawing rights	2	7	18
Reserve position in IMF	226	208	219
Foreign exchange	34,724	32,774	50,697
Total	36,303	34,579	52,419

Source: IMF, *International Financial Statistics*.

INDONESIA

MONEY SUPPLY
('000 million rupiah at 31 December)

	2004	2005	2006
Currency outside banks	109,028	123,991	150,671
Demand deposits at deposit money banks	136,422	146,768	196,268
Total money (incl. others)	245,675	270,825	346,971

Source: IMF, *International Financial Statistics*.

COST OF LIVING
(Consumer Price Index; base: 2000 = 100)

	2004	2005	2006
Food	128.3	140.3	161.9
Clothing	125.9	n.a.	n.a.
All items (incl. others)	141.3	156.0	176.5

Source: ILO.

NATIONAL ACCOUNTS
('000 million rupiah at current prices)
Expenditure on the Gross Domestic Product

	2004	2005	2006
Government final consumption expenditure	191,056	224,981	288,080
Private final consumption expenditure	1,532,888	1,785,596	2,092,656
Increase in stocks	36,911	27,685	19,552
Gross fixed capital formation	515,381	657,625	800,084
Total domestic expenditure	2,276,236	2,695,887	3,200,372
Exports of goods and services	739,639	935,960	1,030,779
Less Imports of goods and services	632,376	816,406	870,090
Statistical discrepancy	−87,673	−30,480	−22,863
GDP in purchasers' values	2,295,826	2,784,960	3,338,196
GDP at constant 2000 prices	1,656,517	1,750,656	1,846,655

Source: Asian Development Bank, *Key Indicators of Developing Asian and Pacific Countries*.

Gross Domestic Product by Economic Activity

	2004	2005	2006
Agriculture, forestry and fishing	329,125	363,929	430,494
Mining and quarrying	205,252	308,339	354,627
Manufacturing	644,343	771,724	936,362
Electricity, gas and water	23,730	26,694	30,399
Construction	151,248	195,776	249,128
Trade, hotels and restaurants	368,556	430,154	496,336
Transport, storage and communications	142,292	180,969	230,922
Finance, insurance, real estate and business services	194,411	230,587	271,543
Public administration	121,129	135,133	167,800
Other services	115,741	141,656	170,586
Total	2,295,826	2,784,960	3,338,196

Source: Asian Development Bank, *Key Indicators of Developing Asian and Pacific Countries*.

BALANCE OF PAYMENTS
(US $ million)

	2004	2005	2006
Exports of goods f.o.b.	70,767	86,995	103,514
Imports of goods f.o.b.	−50,615	−69,462	−73,868
Trade balance	20,152	17,534	29,646
Exports of services	12,045	12,926	11,518
Imports of services	−20,856	−22,049	−21,625
Balance on goods and services	11,341	8,411	19,539
Other income received	1,995	2,338	2,577
Other income paid	−12,912	−15,264	−17,042
Balance on goods, services and income	424	−4,515	5,074
Current transfers received	2,433	5,993	6,079
Current transfers paid	−1,294	−1,200	−1,216

—continued	2004	2005	2006
Current balance	1,563	278	9,937
Capital account (net)	—	334	350
Direct investment abroad	−3,408	−3,065	−2,703
Direct investment from abroad	1,896	8,336	5,580
Portfolio investment assets	353	−1,080	−1,933
Portfolio investment liabilities	4,056	5,270	6,058
Other investment assets	985	−8,646	−2,588
Other investment liabilities	−4,549	−3,401	−5,792
Net errors and omissions	−3,094	−136	2,460
Overall balance	−2,198	−2,111	11,370

Source: IMF, *International Financial Statistics*.

External Trade

PRINCIPAL COMMODITIES
(distribution by SITC, US $ million)

Imports c.i.f.	2002	2003	2004
Food and live animals	2,852.4	3,121.1	3,786.3
Cereals and cereal preparations	1,194.6	1,151.6	1,205.0
Crude materials (inedible) except fuels	2,668.3	2,595.7	3,505.6
Textile fibres and waste	924.2	839.4	957.2
Mineral fuels, lubricants, etc.	6,558.5	7,664.4	8,220.6
Crude petroleum oils, etc.	3,216.9	4,027.4	3,537.0
Refined petroleum products	3,279.8	3,528.9	4,549.9
Chemicals and related products	5,276.4	5,316.3	7,613.4
Organic chemicals	2,005.2	2,078.9	3,166.1
Hydrocarbons and derivatives thereof	897.0	984.1	1,603.2
Xylenes, pure	456.0	383.1	627.6
Plastics in primary forms	869.6	907.8	1,284.5
Basic manufactures	4,242.7	4,158.5	6,203.5
Textile yarn, fabrics, etc.	878.1	662.8	738.8
Iron and steel	1,403.2	1,447.1	2,788.5
Machinery and transport equipment	8,605.8	8,566.9	12,175.4
Machinery specialized for particular industries	1,490.2	1,294.1	2,032.0
General industrial machinery, equipment and parts	1,799.3	1,673.7	2,479.0
Telecommunications, sound recording and reproducing equipment	531.1	703.7	1,215.4
Other electrical machinery, apparatus, appliances and parts	1,182.1	1,258.4	1,796.2
Road vehicles and parts*	1,639.0	1,879.0	2,395.4
Total (incl. others)	31,288.8	32,550.6	42,947.7

Exports f.o.b.	2002	2003	2004
Food and live animals	3,606.3	3,666.0	3,968.4
Fish, crustaceans and molluscs	1,487.0	1,546.7	1,700.6
Coffee, tea, cocoa, spices and manufactures thereof	1,238.3	1,190.6	1,144.1
Crude materials (inedible) except fuels	4,522.1	5,317.2	6,432.6
Crude rubber (incl. synthetic and reclaimed)	1,059.2	1,520.2	2,212.7
Natural rubber (other than latex)	1,031.6	1,482.5	2,166.5
Technically specified natural rubber (TSNR)	970.4	1,407.5	1,979.1
Metalliferous ore and metal scrap	1,930.7	2,186.6	2,724.9
Mineral fuels, lubricants, etc.	13,909.5	15,709.8	11,462.2
Coal, coke and briquettes	1,770.8	2,009.8	2,758.3
Coal, lignite and peat	1,762.4	1,980.1	2,748.8
Petroleum, petroleum products, etc.	6,561.9	7,223.1	6,490.6
Crude petroleum oils, etc.	5,227.6	5,621.0	4,678.7
Gas, natural and manufactured	5,577.6	6,476.7	2,213.3
Natural gas, liquefied	5,277.8	6,145.6	1,753.1

INDONESIA   Statistical Survey

Exports f.o.b.—continued	2002	2003	2004
Animal and vegetable oils, fats and waxes	2,657.0	3,013.8	4,492.8
Fixed vegetable oils, fluid or solid, crude, refined or purified	2,525.6	2,884.6	4,216.3
Palm oil	2,092.4	2,454.6	3,441.8
Chemicals and related products	2,969.2	3,386.6	4,015.9
Organic chemicals	1,124.0	1,283.8	1,620.2
Basic manufactures	10,926.0	11,175.4	12,866.5
Wood and cork manufactures (excl. furniture)	2,853.2	2,720.9	2,801.0
Veneers, plywood, etc.	2,067.5	1,945.2	1,954.9
Plywood of wood sheets	1,567.3	1,506.8	1,403.1
Paper, paperboard, etc.	2,074.1	1,968.7	2,181.7
Textile yarn, fabrics, etc.	2,895.8	2,922.7	3,151.9
Textile yarn	1,229.9	1,238.1	1,480.9
Machinery and transport equipment	9,788.7	9,772.6	11,522.7
Office machines and automatic data-processing machines	2,226.4	1,867.6	2,729.1
Telecommunications and sound equipment	3,359.4	2,984.3	3,078.8
Video recording or reproducing apparatus	1,314.4	872.6	1,278.6
Other electrical machinery, apparatus, appliances and parts	2,386.7	2,805.2	3,193.4
Miscellaneous manufactured articles	8,193.0	8,484.7	9,196.0
Furniture and parts thereof	1,512.0	1,569.6	1,669.3
Clothing and accessories (excl. footwear)	3,945.0	4,105.3	4,454.2
Footwear	1,148.1	1,182.2	1,320.5
Total (incl. others)	57,158.8	61,058.2	64,483.5

* Excluding tyres, engines and electrical parts.

Source: UN, *International Trade Statistics Yearbook*.

2005 (US $ million): *Imports:* Prepared foodstuffs 2,059; Mineral products 18,129; Chemical products 6,689; Plastics and rubber 2,360; Textiles and textile articles 1,606; Base metals and articles thereof 6,090; Machinery, mechanical appliances, and electrical equipment 11,416; Transportation equipment 3,887; Total (incl. others) 57,701. *Exports:* Animal or vegetable fats 4,951; Prepared foodstuffs 1,986; Mineral products 27,422; Chemical products 3,522; Plastics and rubber 5,142; Wood and wood products 3,176; Wood pulp products 3,257; Textiles and textile articles 8,604; Base metals and articles thereof 5,227; Machinery, mechanical appliances, and electrical equipment 11,889; Miscellaneous manufactured articles 2,248; Total (incl. others) 85,660 (Source: Asian Development Bank, *Key Indicators of Developing Asian and Pacific Countries*).

2006 (US $ million): *Imports:* Prepared foodstuffs 2,166; Mineral products 19,687; Chemical products 7,258; Plastics and rubber 2,554; Textiles and textile articles 1,714; Base metals and articles thereof 5,770; Machinery, mechanical appliances, and electrical equipment 10,522; Transportation equipment 4,958; Total (incl. others) 61,078. *Exports:* Animal or vegetable fats 6,070; Prepared foodstuffs 2,316; Mineral products 32,939; Chemical products 4,071; Plastics and rubber 7,267; Wood and wood products 3,426; Wood pulp products 3,983; Textiles and textile articles 9,446; Base metals and articles thereof 7,262; Machinery, mechanical appliances, and electrical equipment 11,654; Miscellaneous manufactured articles 2,331; Total (incl. others) 100,690 (Source: Asian Development Bank, *Key Indicators of Developing Asian and Pacific Countries*).

PRINCIPAL TRADING PARTNERS
(US $ million)*

Imports c.i.f.	2003	2004	2005
Australia	1,648.4	2,214.9	2,567.1
Canada	321.8	551.8	698.0
China, People's Republic	2,957.5	4,101.3	5,842.9
France	453.2	544.2	706.6
Germany	1,181.2	1,734.0	1,780.8
Hong Kong	222.2	266.7	291.1
Italy	323.7	473.3	568.9
Japan	4,228.3	6,081.6	6,906.3
Korea, Republic	1,527.9	1,942.6	2,869.1
Malaysia	1,138.2	1,681.9	2,148.5
Netherlands	369.6	474.6	369.1
Singapore	4,155.1	6,082.8	9,470.7
Taiwan	877.1	1,240.3	1,338.1
Thailand	1,701.7	2,771.6	3,447.0
United Kingdom	463.7	703.2	645.3
USA	2,694.8	3,225.4	3,878.9
Total (incl. others)	32,550.7	46,524.5	57,700.9

Exports f.o.b.	2003	2004	2005
Australia	1,791.6	1,887.4	2,227.6
Belgium/Luxembourg	912.2	926.1	n.a.
China, People's Republic	3,802.5	4,604.7	6,662.4
France	652.8	659.8	624.0
Germany	1,416.8	1,654.6	1,781.6
Hong Kong	1,183.3	1,387.5	n.a.
Italy	843.9	922.6	1,007.2
Japan	13,603.5	15,962.1	18,049.1
Korea, Republic	4,328.8	4,830.2	7,085.6
Malaysia	2,363.8	3,016.0	3,431.3
Netherlands	1,401.5	1,767.5	2,233.5
Philippines	944.7	1,237.6	n.a.
Singapore	5,399.7	6,001.2	7,836.6
Spain	1,022.4	837.5	n.a.
Taiwan	2,233.1	2,854.3	2,475.0
Thailand	1,392.6	1,976.2	n.a.
United Kingdom	1,135.8	1,295.3	1,291.5
USA	7,373.8	8,767.3	9,868.5
Total (incl. others)	61,058.2	71,584.6	85,660.0

* Imports by country of production, exports by country of consumption; figures include trade in gold.

2006 (US $ million): *Imports:* Australia 3,619; China, People's Republic 10,403; Germany 2,018; Japan 7,971; Korea, Republic 3,542; Malaysia 4,481; Saudi Arabia 2,944; Singapore 27,391; Thailand 3,671; USA 3,386; Total (incl. others) 89,697. *Exports:* Australia 3,036; China, People's Republic 8,746; India 3,619; Japan 21,972; Korea, Republic 8,908; Malaysia 4,502; Netherlands 2,413; Singapore 13,415; USA 13,038; Total (incl. others) 113,209 (Source: Asian Development Bank, *Key Indicators of Developing Asian and Pacific Countries*).

Transport

RAILWAYS
(traffic)

	2003	2004	2005
Passengers embarked (million)	155	150	152
Freight loaded ('000 tons)	16,293	17,146	17,340

Source: Indonesian State Railways.

ROAD TRAFFIC
(motor vehicles registered at 31 December)

	2003	2004	2005
Passenger cars	3,885,228	4,464,281	5,494,034
Lorries and trucks	2,047,022	2,315,779	2,920,828
Buses and coaches	798,079	933,199	1,184,918
Motorcycles	19,976,376	23,055,834	28,556,498

Source: State Police of Indonesia.

INDONESIA

SHIPPING

Merchant Fleet
(registered at 31 December)

	2004	2005	2006
Number of vessels	2,826	3,214	4,271
Displacement ('000 grt)	4,072.1	4,330.4	5,287.1

Source: Lloyd's Register-Fairplay, *World Fleet Statistics*.

Sea-borne Freight Traffic
('000 metric tons)

	1999	2000	2001*
International:			
goods loaded	139,340	141,528	143,750
goods unloaded	43,477	45,040	46,659
Domestic:			
goods loaded	113,633	127,740	163,685
goods unloaded	122,368	137,512	138,667

* Preliminary figures.

CIVIL AVIATION
(traffic on scheduled services)

	2001	2002	2003
Kilometres flown (million)	150	159	211
Passengers carried ('000)	10,397	12,113	20,358
Passenger-km (million)	16,169	18,419	21,274
Total ton-km (million)	1,978	1,879	2,164

Source: UN, *Statistical Yearbook*.

Tourism

FOREIGN TOURIST ARRIVALS

Country of residence	2004	2005	2006
Australia	406,389	391,862	226,981
Germany	134,625	156,414	106,629
Japan	615,720	517,879	419,213
Korea, Republic	228,408	251,971	295,514
Malaysia	622,541	591,358	769,988
Netherlands	92,152	114,687	110,272
Singapore	1,644,717	1,417,803	1,401,804
Taiwan	384,226	247,037	236,384
United Kingdom	113,578	163,898	110,412
USA	153,268	157,936	130,963
Total (incl. others)	5,321,165	5,002,101	4,871,351

Receipts from tourism (US $ million, incl. passenger transport): 4,461 in 2003; 5,226 in 2004; 5,092 in 2005 (Source: World Tourism Organization).

Communications Media

	2004	2005	2006
Telephones ('000 main lines in use)	9,990.0	12,772.3	14,820.7
Mobile cellular telephones ('000 subscribers)	30,000	46,910	63,803
Personal computers ('000 in use)	3,022	3,022	n.a.
Internet users ('000)	11,226	16,000	16,000
Broadband subscribers ('000)	84.9	108.2	108.2

Facsimile machines (estimated number in use): 185,000 in 1997.

Television receivers ('000 in use): 31,700 in 2000 (Source: UN, *Statistical Yearbook*).

Radio receivers ('000 in use): 31,500 in 1997 (Source: UN, *Statistical Yearbook*).

Daily newspapers: 225 (average circulation 4,782,000) in 1999 (Source: UN, *Statistical Yearbook*).

Non-daily newspapers: 433 (average circulation 7,838,000) in 1998 (Source: UN, *Statistical Yearbook*).

Book Production: 6,000 titles in 2003.

Source (unless otherwise indicated): mostly International Telecommunication Union.

Education

(2004/05)

	Institutions	Teachers	Pupils and Students
Kindergarten	50,083	178,727	2,178,875
Primary schools	147,793	1,335,086	25,997,445
General junior secondary schools	22,274	542,591	7,553,086
General senior secondary schools	8,899	253,574	3,402,615
Vocational senior secondary schools	5,665	181,892	2,164,068
Tertiary institutions	2,516	168,236	2,790,391

Source: Ministry of National Education.

Adult literacy rate (UNESCO estimates): 90.4% (males 94.0%; females 86.8%) in 2004 (Source: UNESCO Institute for Statistics).

Directory

The Constitution

Indonesia had three provisional Constitutions: in August 1945, February 1950 and August 1950. In July 1959 the Constitution of 1945 was re-enacted by presidential decree. The General Elections Law of 1969 supplemented the 1945 Constitution, which has been adopted permanently by the Majelis Permusyawaratan Rakyat (MPR—People's Consultative Assembly). Amendments made to the Constitution in 2001 and 2002 took effect in 2004, when Indonesia held its next general election. The following is a summary of the Constitution's main provisions, with subsequent amendments:

GENERAL PRINCIPLES

The 1945 Constitution consists of 37 articles, four transitional clauses and two additional provisions, and is preceded by a preamble. The preamble contains an indictment of all forms of colonialism, an account of Indonesia's struggle for independence, the declaration of that independence and a statement of fundamental aims and principles. Indonesia's National Independence, according to the text of the preamble, has the state form of a Republic, with sovereignty residing in the People, and is based upon five fundamental principles, the *Pancasila*:

1. Belief in the One Supreme God.
2. Just and Civilized Humanity.
3. The Unity of Indonesia.
4. Democracy led by the wisdom of deliberations (*musyawarah*) and consensus among representatives.
5. Social Justice for all the people of Indonesia.

STATE ORGANS

Majelis Permusyawaratan Rakyat—MPR (People's Consultative Assembly)

Sovereignty is in the hands of the People and is exercised in full by the MPR as the embodiment of the whole Indonesian People. The MPR is the highest authority of the State, and is to be distinguished from the legislative body proper (Dewan Perwakilan Rakyat—DPR, see below), which is incorporated within the MPR. The bicameral MPR, with a total of 678 members (reduced from 700 in 2004), is composed of the 550 members of the DPR and the members of the Dewan Perwakilan Daerah—DPD (see below). Elections to the MPR are held every five years. The MPR sits at least once every five years, and its primary competence is to determine the Constitution and the broad lines of the policy of the State and the Government. It also inaugurates the President and Vice-President, who are responsible for implementing that policy. All decisions are taken unanimously in keeping with the traditions of *musyawarah*.

The President

The highest executive of the Government, the President, holds office for a term of five years and may be re-elected once. As Mandatory of the MPR he/she must execute the policy of the State according to the Decrees determined by the MPR during its Fourth General and Special Sessions. In conducting the administration of the State, authority and responsibility are concentrated in the President. The Ministers of the State are his/her assistants and are responsible only to him/her. The President and Vice-President are to be directly elected on a single ticket (until November 2001 the MPR had exercised the power to elect them). If no candidate succeeds in obtaining more than one-half of the votes cast in a presidential election, a second round of voting shall be held. The President and Vice-President may be dismissed by the MPR on the proposal of the DPR if it is proven that he/she has either violated the law or no longer meets the requirements of his/her office. The President may not freeze or dissolve the Dewan.

Dewan Perwakilan Rakyat—DPR (House of Representatives)

The legislative branch of the State, the Dewan Perwakilan Rakyat, sits at least once a year. Its members are all directly elected. Every statute requires the approval of the Dewan. Members of the Dewan have the right to submit draft bills, which require ratification by the President, who has the right of veto. In times of emergency the President may enact ordinances, which have the force of law, but such Ordinances must be ratified by the Dewan during the following session or be revoked.

Dewan Perwakilan Daerah—DPD (House of Representatives of the Regions)

The Dewan Perwakilan Daerah is the second chamber of the MPR. Its members are directly elected from every province. Each province has an equal number of members and total membership of the DPD is no more than one-third of the total membership of the DPR. The DPD sits at least once a year. It may propose to the DPR bills relating to regional autonomy, the relationship between central and local government, the formation, expansion and merger of regions, the management of natural and other economic resources, and the financial balance between the centre and the localities. It may also participate in the discussion of such bills and oversee the implementation of regional laws, as well as the state budget, taxation, education and religion.

Dewan Pertimbangan Agung—DPA (Supreme Advisory Council)

The DPA is an advisory body assisting the President, who chooses its members from political parties, functional groups and groups of prominent persons.

Mahkamah Agung (Supreme Court)

The judicial branch of the State, the Supreme Court and the other courts of law (public courts, religious courts, military tribunals, administrative courts and a Constitutional Court) are independent of the Executive in exercising their judicial powers. There is an independent Judicial Commission, which is authorized to propose candidates for appointment as justices of the Supreme Court and to ensure the good behaviour of judges. Its members are appointed and dismissed by the President with the approval of the DPR.

Badan Pemeriksa Keuangan (Supreme Audit Board)

Controls the accountability of public finance, enjoys investigatory powers and is independent of the Executive. Its findings are presented to the Dewan.

The Government

HEAD OF STATE

President: Susilo Bambang Yudhoyono (inaugurated 20 October 2004).
Vice-President: Yusuf Kalla.

CABINET
(April 2008)

Co-ordinating Minister for Political, Legal and Security Affairs: Adm. (retd) Widodo Adi Sutjipto.
Co-ordinating Minister for Economic Affairs: Dr Boediono.
Co-ordinating Minister for People's Welfare: Aburizal Bakrie.
Minister of Home Affairs and Regional Autonomy: Mardiyanto.
Minister of Foreign Affairs: Hassan Wirajuda.
Minister of Defence: Juwono Sudarsono.
Minister of Justice and Human Rights Affairs: Andi Mattalata.
Minister of Finance and State Enterprises Development: Dr Sri Mulyani Indrawati.
Minister of Energy and Mineral Resources: Dr Ir Purnomo Yusgiantoro.
Minister of Industry: Fahmi Idris.
Minister of Trade: Mari Elka Pangestu.
Minister of Agriculture: Anton Apriyantono.
Minister of Forestry: M. S. Ka'ban.
Minister of Transportation and Telecommunication: Jusman Syafii Djamal.
Minister of Marine Affairs and Fisheries: Freddy Numberi.
Minister of Manpower and Transmigration: Erman Suparno.
Minister of Public Works: Joko Kirmanto.
Minister of Health: Siti Fadila Supari.
Minister of National Education: Bambang Soedibyo.
Minister of Social Affairs: Bachtiar Chamsyah.
Minister of Religious Affairs: M. Maftuh Basyuni.
Minister of Culture and Tourism: Jero Watjik.
Minister of Communications and Information Technology: Muhammad Nuh.
Minister of State for Research and Technology: Kusmayanto Kadiman.
Minister of State for Co-operatives and Small and Medium-Sized Businesses: Suryadarma Ali.
Minister of State for the Environment: Rachmat Witoelar.
Minister of State for Women's Empowerment: Meutia Hatta.
Minister of State for Administrative Reform: Taufik Effendi.
Minister of State for State Enterprises: Dr Sofyan A. Djalil.
Minister of State for Acceleration of Development in Backwards Regions: Lukman Edy.
Minister of State for National Development Planning: Paskah Suzetta.
Minister of State for Public Housing: M. Jusuf Anshari.
Minister of State for Youth and Sports Affairs: Adyaksa Dault.
Officials with the rank of Minister of State:
Attorney-General: Hendarman Supandji.
State Secretary: Hatta Radjasa.
Cabinet Secretary: Sudi Silalahi.

MINISTRIES

Office of the President: Istana Merdeka, Jakarta 10110; tel. (21) 3840946.
Office of the Vice-President: Jalan Merdeka Selatan 6, Jakarta; tel. (21) 363539.
Office of the Attorney-General: Jalan Sultan Hasanuddin 1, Kebayoran Baru, Jakarta; tel. (21) 7221377; fax (21) 7392576; e-mail postmaster@kejaksaan.go.id; internet www.kejaksaan.go.id.
Office of the Cabinet Secretary: Jalan Veteran 18, 4th Floor, Jakarta Pusat 10110; tel. (21) 3846463; fax (21) 3866579; e-mail itcp@setkab.go.id; internet www.setkab.go.id.
Office of the Co-ordinating Minister for Economic Affairs: Gedung Utama, Lantai 4, Jalan Lapangan Banteng Timur 2–4, Jakarta; tel. (21) 3521835; fax (21) 3511643; internet www.ekon.go.id.
Office of the Co-ordinating Minister for People's Welfare: Jalan Merdeka Barat 3, Jakarta Pusat; tel. (21) 34832544; fax (21) 3453289; internet www.menkokesra.go.id.

INDONESIA

Office of the Co-ordinating Minister for Political, Legal and Security Affairs: Jalan Medan Merdeka Barat 15, Jakarta 10110; tel. (21) 3849453; fax (21) 3450918; e-mail dkpt@polkam.go.id; internet www.polkam.go.id.

Office of the State Secretary: Jalan Veteran 18, Jakarta 10110; tel. (21) 3849043; fax (21) 3452685; e-mail webmaster@setneg.go.id; internet www.setneg.ri.go.id.

Ministry of Agriculture: Jalan Harsono R. M. 3, Gedung D, Lantai 4, Ragunan, Pasar Minggu, Jakarta Selatan 12550; tel. (21) 7822803; fax (21) 7816385; e-mail harisno@deptan.go.id; internet www.deptan.go.id.

Ministry of Communication and Information Technology: Jalan Medan Merdeka Barat 9, Jakarta Pusat; e-mail info@depkominfo.go.id; internet www.depkominfo.go.id.

Ministry of Culture and Tourism: Sapta Pesona Bldg, Jalan Medan Merdeka Barat 17, Jakarta Pusat 10110; tel. (21) 3838167; fax (21) 3849715; e-mail pusdatin@budpar.go.id; internet www.budpar.go.id.

Ministry of Defence: Jalan Medan Merdeka Barat 13–14, Jakarta Pusat 10200; tel. (21) 3456184; fax (21) 3440023; e-mail postmaster@dephan.go.id; internet www.dephan.go.id.

Ministry of Energy and Mineral Resources: Jalan Medan Merdeka Selatan 18, Jakarta 10110; tel. (21) 3519882; fax (21) 3450846; internet www.esdm.go.id.

Ministry of Finance and State Enterprises Development: Jalan Lapangan Banteng Timur 2–4, Jakarta 10710; tel. (21) 3814324; fax (21) 353710; internet www.depkeu.go.id.

Ministry of Foreign Affairs: Jalan Taman Pejambon 6, 10th Floor, Jakarta Pusat 10110; tel. (21) 3813453; fax (21) 3857316; e-mail infomed@deplu.go.id; internet www.deplu.go.id.

Ministry of Forestry: Gedung Manggala Wanabakti, Jalan Jenderal Gatot Subroto, Senayan, Jakarta 10270; tel. (21) 5730212; fax (21) 5720216; e-mail pusdata@dephut.go.id; internet www.dephut.go.id.

Ministry of Health and Social Welfare: Jalan H. R. Rasuna Said, Block X5, Kav. 4–9, Jakarta 12950; tel. (21) 5201587; fax (21) 5203874; e-mail webadmin@depkes.go.id; internet www.depkes.go.id.

Ministry of Home Affairs and Regional Autonomy: Jalan Medan Merdeka Utara 7, Gedung Utama Lt. 4, Jakarta Pusat 10110; tel. and fax (21) 3811120; e-mail pusdatinkomtel@depdagri.go.id; internet www.depdagri.go.id.

Ministry of Industry and Trade: Jalan Jenderal Gatot Subroto, Kav. 52–53, 2nd Floor, Jakarta Selatan 12950; tel. (21) 5252194; fax (21) 5261086; e-mail karomas@dprin.go.id; internet www.dprin.go.id.

Ministry of Justice and Human Rights Affairs: Jalan H. R. Rasuna Said, Kav. 6–7, Kuningan, Jakarta Selatan; tel. (21) 5253004; fax (21) 5253095; internet www.depkumham.go.id.

Ministry of Manpower and Transmigration: Jalan T. M. P Kalibata 17, Jakarta Selatan; tel. (21) 5255683; fax (21) 515669; e-mail redaksi_balitfo@nakertrans.go.id; internet www.nakertrans.go.id.

Ministry of Marine Affairs and Fisheries: Jalan Harsono R. M. 3, Rangunan, Jakarta 12550; tel. (21) 3522515; fax (21) 3519070; internet www.dkp.go.id.

Ministry of National Education: Jalan Jenderal Sudirman, Senayan, Jakarta Pusat; tel. (21) 5731618; fax (21) 5736870; e-mail pusdatin@depdiknas.go.id; internet www.depdiknas.go.id.

Ministry of Public Works: Jalan Pattimura 20, Kebayoran Baru, Jakarta Selatan 12110; tel. (21) 7392262; fax (21) 7200793; e-mail dkirmanto@pu.go.id; internet www.pu.go.id.

Ministry of Religious Affairs: Jalan Lapangan Banteng Barat 3–4, Jakarta Pusat 10710; tel. (21) 3843005; fax (21) 3812306; e-mail pikmas@depag.go.id; internet www.depag.go.id.

Ministry of Social Affairs: Jalan Salemba Raya 28, Jakarta; tel. (21) 3103612; fax (21) 3103613; e-mail pusdatin@depsos.go.id; internet www.depsos.go.id.

Ministry of Transportation: Jalan Medan Merdeka Barat 8, Jakarta 10110; tel. (21) 3456703; fax (21) 3862371; e-mail pusdatin@dephub.go.id; internet www.dephub.go.id.

Office of the Minister of State for Co-operatives and Small and Medium-Sized Businesses: Jalan H. R. Rasuna Said, Kav. 3–5, POB 177, Jakarta Selatan 12940; tel. (21) 52992777; fax (21) 5204378; e-mail datin@depkop.go.id; internet www.depkop.go.id.

Office of the Minister of State for the Environment: Bldg A, 6th Floor, Jalan D. I. Panjaitan, Kav. 24, Kebon Nanas Lt. II, Jakarta 13410; tel. and fax (21) 8517184; e-mail edukom@menlh.go.id; internet www.menlh.go.id.

Office of the Minister of State for Research and Technology: BPP Teknologi II Bldg, Lt. 6, Jalan M. H. Thamrin 8, Jakarta Pusat 10340; tel. (21) 3169166; fax (21) 3101952; e-mail webmstr@ristek.go.id; internet www.ristek.go.id.

Office of the Minister of State for State Enterprises: Gedung Keuangan Enambelas Lantai, Lt. 10, Jalan Dr Wahidin Raya 2, Jakarta 10710; e-mail sekretariat@bumn-ri.com; internet www.bumn-ri.com.

Office of the Minister of State for Women's Empowerment: Jalan Medan Merdeka Barat 15, Jakarta 10110; tel. (21) 3805563; fax (21) 3805562; e-mail biroren@menegpp.go.id; internet www.menegpp.go.id.

Office of the Minister of State for Youth and Sports Affairs: Jakarta.

OTHER GOVERNMENT BODY

Badan Pemeriksa Keuangan (BPK) (Supreme Audit Board): Jalan Gatot Subroto 31, Jakarta 10210; tel. (21) 5704395; e-mail webmaster@bpk.go.id; internet www.bpk.go.id; Chair. Dr ANWAR NASUTION; Vice-Chair. ABDULLAH ZAINIE.

President and Legislature

PRESIDENT

Presidential Election, First Ballot, 5 July 2004

Candidate	Votes	% of votes
Gen. (retd) Susilo Bambang Yudhoyono (PD)	39,838,184	33.57
Megawati Sukarnoputri (PDI—P)	31,569,104	26.61
Gen. (retd) Wiranto (Golkar)	26,286,788	22.15
Amien Rais (PAN)	17,392,931	14.66
Hamzah Haz (PPP)	3,569,861	3.01
Total	118,656,868	100.00

Presidential Election, Second Ballot, 20 September 2004

Candidate	Votes	% of votes
Gen. (retd) Susilo Bambang Yudhoyono (PD)	69,266,350	60.62
Megawati Sukarnoputri (PDI—P)	44,990,704	39.38
Total	114,257,054	100.00

LEGISLATURE

Majelis Permusyawaratan Rakyat (MPR)
(People's Consultative Assembly)

Jalan Jendral Gatot Subroto 6, Jakarta 10270; tel. (21) 5715773; fax (21) 5734526; e-mail kotaksurat@mpr.go.id; internet www.mpr.go.id.

In late 2002 the Constitution was amended to provide for the direct election of all members of the Majelis Permusyawaratan Rakyat (MPR—People's Consultative Assembly) at the next general election, held in 2004. The MPR thus became a bicameral institution comprising the Dewan Perwakilan Daerah (DPD—House of Representatives of the Regions) and the Dewan Perwakilan Rakyat (DPR—House of Representatives). The MPR consists of the 550 members of the DPR and 128 regional delegates (subject to confirmation).

Speaker: HIDAYAT NUR WAHID.

	Seats
Members of the Dewan Perwakilan Rakyat	550
Regional representatives	128
Total	678

Dewan Perwakilan Rakyat (DPR)
(House of Representatives)

Jalan Gatot Subroto 16, Jakarta; tel. (21) 586833; e-mail humas@dpr.go.id; internet www.dpr.go.id.

Speaker: AGUNG LAKSONO.

INDONESIA

General Election, 5 April 2004

	Seats
Partai Golongan Karya (Golkar)	128
Partai Demokrasi Indonesia Perjuangan (PDI—P)	109
Partai Persatuan Pembangunan (PPP)	58
Partai Demokrat (DP)	57
Partai Amanat Nasional (PAN)	52
Partai Kebangkitan Bangsa (PKB)	52
Partai Keadilan Sejahtera (PKS)	45
Partai Bintang Reformasi (PBR)	13
Partai Damai Sejahtera (PDS)	12
Partai Bulan Bintang (PBB)	11
Partai Persatuan Demokrasi Kebangsaan (PPDK)	5
Partai Karya Peduli Bangsa (PKPB)	2
Partai Keadilan dan Persatuan Indonesia (PKPI)	1
Others	5
Total	**550**

Election Commission

Komisi Pemilihan Umum (KPU): Jalan Imam Bonjol 29, Jakarta 10310; tel. (21) 31937223; fax (21) 3157759; e-mail redaktur@kpu.go.id; internet www.kpu.go.id; f. 1999; govt body.

Political Organizations

Prior to 1998, electoral legislation permitted only three organizations (Golkar, the PDI and PPP) to contest elections. Following the replacement of President Suharto in May 1998, political restrictions were relaxed and new parties were allowed to form (with the only condition being that all parties must adhere to the *pancasila* and reject communism). A total of 24 parties registered to contest the legislative elections of April 2004.

Barisan Nasional (National Front): Jakarta; f. 1998; committed to ensuring that Indonesia remains a secular state; Sec.-Gen. RACHMAT WITOELAR.

Koalisi Kebangsaan (Nationhood Coalition): Jakarta; f. 2004; coalition formed to contest the presidential election of 2004 in support of Megawati Sukarnoputri, comprising Golkar, Partai Demokrasi Indonesia Perjuangan (PDI—P), Partai Persatuan Pembangunan (PPP), Partai Demokrasi Indonesia (PDS) and Partai Kebangkitan Bangsa (PKB); PPP defected to Koalisi Kerakyatan following the election.

Koalisi Kerakyatan (People's Coalition): Jakarta; f. 2004; coalition formed in support of Susilo Bambang Yudhoyono to contest the presidential election of 2004, centred around Partai Demokrat (PD), Partai Amanat Nasional (PAN) and Partai Keadilan Sejahtera (PKS); Partai Persatuan Pembangunan (PPP) joined after defecting from Koalisi Kebangsaan following the election.

Partai Amanat Nasional (PAN) (National Mandate Party): Jalan H. Nawi 15, Jakarta Selatan 12420; tel. (21) 72794535; fax (21) 7268695; internet www.geocities.com/CapitolHill/Congress/6678; f. 1998; aims to achieve democracy, progress and social justice, to limit the length of the presidential term of office and to increase autonomy in the provinces; Gen. Chair. Dr AMIEN RAIS; Sec.-Gen. FAISAL BASRI.

Partai Bhinneka Tunggal Ika (PBI): c/o Dewan Perwakilan Rakyat, Jalan Gatot Subroto 16, Jakarta.

Partai Bintang Reformasi (PBR) (Reform Star Party): Jalan Radio IV 5, Kramat Pela, Kebayoran Baru, Jakarta; tel. (21) 7211132; fax (21) 7209734; f. 2002 by fmr members of the Partai Persatuan Pembangunan (PPP); Islamic party; Chair. ZAENUDDIN; Sec.-Gen. DJA'FAR BADJEBER.

Partai Bulan Bintang (PBB) (Crescent Moon and Star Party): Jalan Raya Pasar Minggu 1B, Km 18, Jakarta Selatan; tel. (21) 3106739; internet www.pbb-online.org; f. 1998; Leader M. S. KABAN; Sec.-Gen. SAHAR HASSAN.

Partai Buruh Sosial Demokrat (PBSD) (Socialist Democratic Labour Party): Jalan Kramat Raya 91A, Jakarta Pusat; tel. (21) 3154092; fax (21) 3909834; f. 2002; Chair. MUCHTAR PAKPAHAN; Sec.-Gen. DIAH INDRIASTUTI.

Partai Damai Sejahtera (PDS) (Prosperous Peace Party): Tirtayasa 20, Kebayoran Baru, Jakarta Selatan 12410; tel. (21) 7220725; fax (21) 7250953; e-mail berita@partaidamaisejahtera.com; internet www.partaidamaisejahtera.com; f. 2001; Chair. RUYANDI MUSTIKA HUTASOIT; Sec.-Gen. MAGIT LES DENNY TEWU.

Partai Demokrasi Indonesia (PDI) (Indonesian Democratic Party): Jalan Diponegoro 58, Jakarta 10310; tel. (21) 336331; fax (21) 5201630; f. 1973 by merger of five nationalist and Christian parties; Chair. SOERJADI (installed to replace Megawati Sukarnoputri as leader of the party following govt action of 1996).

Partai Demokrasi Indonesia Perjuangan (PDI—P) (Indonesian Democratic Struggle Party): Jalan Raya Pasar Minggu, Lenteng Agung, Jakarta; established by Megawati Sukarnoputri, fmr leader of the Partai Demokrasi Indonesia (PDI—see above), following her removal from the leadership of the PDI by Govt in 1996; Chair. MEGAWATI SUKARNOPUTRI; Sec.-Gen. PRAMONO ANUNG WIBOWO.

Partai Demokrasi Kasih Bangsa Indonesia (PDKB) (The Nation Compassion Democratic Party of Indonesia): Kompleks Widuri Indah Blok A-4, Jalan Palmerah Barat 353, Jakarta Selatan 12210; tel. and fax (21) 5330973; e-mail info@kasihbangsa.net.

Partai Demokrat (PD): Jalan Pemuda 712A, Jakarta Timur; tel. (21) 4755146; fax (21) 4757957; internet www.demokrat.or.id; f. 2001; Chair. HADI UTOMO; Sec.-Gen. H. MARZUKI ALIE.

Partai Golongan Karya (Golkar) (Party of Functional Groups): Jalan Anggrek Nellimurni, Jakarta 11480; tel. (21) 5302222; fax (21) 5303380; e-mail info@golkar.or.id; internet www.golkar.or.id; f. 1964; reorg. 1971; 23m. mems (1999); Pres. and Chair. YUSUF KALLA; Sec.-Gen. Lt-Gen. (retd) SOEMARSONO.

Partai Karya Peduli Bangsa (PKPB) (Concern for the Nation Functional Party): Jalan Cimandiri 30, Raden Saleh Cikini, Jakarta Pusat 13033; tel. (21) 31927421; fax (21) 31937417; f. 2002; Chair. R. HARTONO; Sec.-Gen. H. ARY MARDJONO.

Partai Keadilan dan Persatuan Indonesia (PKPI) (Justice and Unity Party): Villa Pejaten Mas Blok F-3, No. 3, Jakarta Selatan; tel. (21) 7802758; f. 2002; Chair. EDI SUDRADJAT; Sec.-Gen. HAYONO ISMAN.

Partai Keadilan Sejahtera (PKS) (Prosperous Justice Party): Jalan Mampang Prapatan Raya 98 D–E–F, Jakarta Selatan; tel. (21) 7995425; fax (21) 7995433; e-mail partai@pks.or.id; internet www.pk-sejahtera.org; f. 2002; Islamic party; Chair. TIFATUL SEMBIRING (acting); Sec.-Gen. ANIS MATTA.

Partai Kebangkitan Bangsa (PKB) (National Awakening Party): Jalan Kalibata Timur 12, Jakarta Selatan 12740; tel. (21) 7974353; fax (21) 7974263; e-mail dpp@dpp-pkb.org; internet www.dpp-pkb.org; nationalist Islamic party; f. 1998; Chair. MUHAIMIN ISKANDAR; Sec.-Gen. YENNY ZANUBA WAHID.

Partai Kebangkitan Umat (PKU) (Islamic Awakening Party): c/o Dewan Perwakilan Rakyat, Jalan Gatot Subroto 16, Jakarta; f. 1998; by clerics and members of the Nahdlatul Ulama (NU), with the aim of promoting the adoption of Islamic law in Indonesia.

Partai Merdeka (Freedom Party): Jalan Majapahit, Kav. 26, Jakarta Pusat; tel. (21) 3861464; fax (21) 3861465; e-mail info@partaimerdeka.or.id; internet www.partaimerdeka.or.id; f. 2002; Chair. ADI SASONO; Sec.-Gen. DHARMA SETIAWAN.

Partai Nahdlatul Ummah Indonesia (PNUI) (Indonesian Nahdlatul Community Party): Jalan Cipinang Cempedak 4, 1 Jatinegara, Jakarta Timur 13340; tel. and fax (21) 8571736; f. 2003; Islamic party; Chair. SYUKRON MA'MUN; Sec.-Gen. ACHMAD SJATARI.

Partai Nasional Banteng Kemerdekaan (PNBK) (Freedom Bull National Party): Jalan Penjernihan I 50, Jakarta Utara; tel. (21) 5739550; fax (21) 5739519; f. 2002; Chair. EROS DJAROT; Sec.-Gen. SOEHARDI SOEDIRO.

Partai Nasional Indonesia Marhaenisme (PNI Marhaenisme): Jalan Cikoko 15, Pancoran, Jakarta 12770; tel. (21) 8971241; fax (21) 7900489; f. 2002; Chair. SUKMAWATI SUKARNOPUTRI; Sec.-Gen. ACHMAD MARHAEN.

Partai Patriot Pancasila (Pancasila Patriot Party): Gedung Tri Tangguh, 3rd Floor, Jalan Haji Samali 31, Kalibata, Jakarta Selatan; tel. (21) 79198510; fax (21) 79198520; f. 2001; Chair. YAPTO SULISTIO SOERJOSOEMARNO; Sec.-Gen. SOPHAR MARU.

Partai Pelopor (Pioneer Party): Jalan K. H. Syafei A22, Gudang Peluru, Tebet, Jakarta Selatan; tel. (21) 8299112; fax (21) 8301569; f. 2002; Chair. RACHMAWATI SUKARNOPUTRI; Sec.-Gen. EKO SURYO SANTJOJO.

Partai Penegak Demokrasi Indonesia (PPDI) (Indonesian Democratic Vanguard Party): Jalan R. E. Martadinata, Kompleks Rukan Permata, Blok E-1, Ancol, Jakarta Utara; tel. (21) 6456215; fax (21) 6456216; f. 2003; Chair. DIMMY HARYANTO; Sec.-Gen. JOSEPH WILLIEM LEA.

Partai Perhimpunan Indonesia Baru (PIB) (New Indonesia Alliance Party): Jalan Teuku Cik Ditiro 31, Jakarta; tel. (21) 3108057; internet www.partai-pib.or.id; f. 2002; Chair. Dr SYAHRIR; Sec.-Gen. AMIR KARAMOY.

Partai Persatuan Daerah (Regional United Party): Jalan Dr Satrio C-4 18, Jakarta Selatan 12940; tel. (21) 5205764; fax (21) 5273249; f. 2002; Chair. OESMAN SAPTA; Sec.-Gen. H. RONGGO SOENARSO.

Partai Persatuan Demokrasi Kebangsaan (PPDK) (National Democratic Unity Party): Jalan Ampera Raya 99, Jakarta Selatan

INDONESIA

12560; tel. (21) 7807432; fax (21) 7817341; f. 2002; Chair. Dr RYAAS RASYID; Sec.-Gen. RIVAI PULUNGAN.

Partai Persatuan Pembangunan (PPP) (United Development Party): Jalan Diponegoro 60, Jakarta Pusat 10310; tel. (21) 31936338; fax (21) 3142558; e-mail dpp@ppp.or.id; internet www.ppp.or.id; f. 1973 by the merger of four Islamic parties; Leader SURYADHARMA ALI; Sec.-Gen. YUNUS YOSFIAH.

Partai Rakyat Demokratik (PRD) (People's Democratic Party): Jalan Tebet Barat Dalam VIII Nomor 4, Jakarta Selatan 12820; tel. and fax (21) 8296467; e-mail prd@centrin.net.id; internet www.prd.4-all.org; f. 1996; Chair. BUDIMAN SUDJATMIKO.

Partai Reformasi Tionghoa Indonesia (Chinese Indonesian Reform Party): Jakarta; e-mail parti_id@usa.net; f. 1998; Chinese.

Partai Sarikat Indonesia (PSI) (Indonesia Unity Party): Jalan Ampera Raya 65, Cilandak, Jakarta Selatan; tel. (21) 78847138; fax (21) 7800106; e-mail dpppsi@indosat.net.id; f. 2002; Chair. RAHARDJO TJAKRANINGRAT; Sec.-Gen. MUHAMMAD JUMHUR HIDAYAT.

Partai Uni Demokrasi Indonesia (PUDI) (Democratic Union Party of Indonesia): Jalan Raya Tanjung Barat 81, Jakarta 12530; tel. (21) 7817565; fax (21) 7814765; e-mail pudi@pudi.or.id; f. 1996; Chair. Sri BINTANG PAMUNGKAS; Sec.-Gen. ESA HARUMAN.

Other groups with political influence include:

Ikatan Cendekiawan Muslim Indonesia (ICMI) (Association of Indonesian Muslim Intellectuals): Gedung BPPT, Jalan M. H. Thamrin 8, Jakarta; tel. (21) 3410382; internet www.icmi.or.id; f. 1990 with govt support; Chair. MARWAH DAUD IBRAHIM; Sec.-Gen. AGUS SALIM DASUKI.

Masyumi Baru: Jalan Pangkalan Asem 12, Cempaka Putih Ba, Jakarta Pusat; tel. (21) 4225774; fax (21) 7353077; Sec.-Gen. RIDWAN SAIDI.

Muhammadiyah: Jalan Menteng Raya 62, Jakarta Pusat 10340; tel. (21) 3903021; fax (21) 3903024; e-mail redaksi@muhammadiyah.or.id; internet www.muhammadiyah.or.id; second largest Muslim organization; f. 1912; 28m. mems; Chair. Dr DIN SYAMSUDDIN; Sec.-Gen. Drs H. A. ROSYAD SHOLEH.

Nahdlatul Ulama (NU) (Council of Scholars): Jalan Kramat Raya 164, Jakarta 10430; tel. (21) 3914014; fax (21) 3914013; internet www.nu.or.id; largest Muslim organization; 30m. mems; Chair. HASYIM MUZADI.

Partai Syarikat Islam Indonesia 1905: Jalan Prof. Dr Latumenten, Brt 16, Jakarta; tel. (21) 5659790.

The following groups are, or have been, in conflict with the Government:

Gerakan Aceh Merdeka (GAM) (Free Aceh Movement): based in Aceh; e-mail info@asnlf.net; internet www.asnlf.net; f. 1976; signed a peace deal with the Indonesian Govt in July 2005, under the terms of which GAM agreed to relinquish its claims for independence and the Govt agreed to facilitate the establishment of Aceh-based political parties; Leader HASAN DI TIRO; Military Commdr MUZZAKIR MANAF.

Organisasi Papua Merdeka (OPM) (Free Papua Movement): based in Papua; e-mail opmpapua@yahoo.com; internet www.geocities.com/opm-irja; f. 1963; seeks unification with Papua New Guinea; Chair. MOZES WEROR; Leader KELLY KWALIK.

Presidium Dewan Papua (PDP) (Papua Presidium Council): based in Papua; e-mail pdp@westpapua.net; internet www.melanesianews.org/pdp/org; seeks independence from Indonesia; Chair. TOM BEANAL.

Diplomatic Representation

EMBASSIES IN INDONESIA

Afghanistan: Jalan Dr Kusuma Atmaja 15, Jakarta Pusat 10310; tel. (21) 3143169; fax (21) 31935390; e-mail afghanembassy_jkk@yahoo.com; Ambassador BESMULLAH BESMEL.

Algeria: Jalan H. R. Rasuna Said, Kav. 10-1, Kuningan, Jakarta 12950; tel. (21) 5254719; fax (21) 5254654; e-mail ambaljak@rad.net.id; internet www.algeria-id.org; Ambassador HAMZA YAHIA-CHERIF.

Argentina: Menara Thamrin, Suite 1602, 16th Floor, Jalan M. H. Thamrin, Kav. 3, Jakarta; tel. (21) 2303061; fax (21) 2303962; e-mail embargen@cbn.net.id; Ambassador JAVIER A. SANZ DE URQUIZA.

Australia: Jalan H. R. Rasuna Said, Kav. C15–16, Kuningan, Jakarta 12940; tel. (21) 25505555; fax (21) 25505467; e-mail public-affairs-jakt@dfat.gov.au; internet www.austembjak.or.id; Ambassador BILL FARMER.

Austria: Jalan Terusan Denpasar Raya, Kuningan, Jakarta 12950; tel. (21) 2593037; fax (21) 52920651; e-mail jakarta-ob@bmeia.gv.at; internet www.austrian-embassy.or.id; Ambassador Dr KLAUS WÖLFER.

Azerbaijan: Jalan Mas Putih D, Persil 29, Grogol Utara Kebayoran Lama, Jakarta Selatan 12210; tel. (21) 5491939; fax (21) 5491745; e-mail azerbembjkt@u.net.id; internet www.azembassy.or.id; Ambassador IBRAHIM HAJIYEV.

Bangladesh: Jalan Denpasar Raya 3, Block A-13, Kav. 10, Kuningan, Jakarta 12950; tel. (21) 5221574; fax (21) 5261807; Ambassador SALMA KHAN.

Belgium: Deutsche Bank Bldg, 16th Floor, Jalan Imam Bonjol 80, Jakarta 10310; tel. (21) 3162030; fax (21) 3162035; e-mail jakarta@diplobel.org; internet www.diplomatie.be/jakarta; Ambassador MARC TRENTESEAU.

Bosnia and Herzegovina: Menara Imperium, 11th Floor, Suite D-2, Metropolitan Kuningan Super Blok, Kav. 1, Jalan H. R. Rasuna Said, Jakarta 12980; tel. (21) 83703022; fax (21) 83703029; Chargé d'affaires a.i. DINKO TOMAC.

Brazil: Menara Mulia, Suite 1602, Jalan Jenderal Gatot Subroto, Kav. 9–11, Jakarta 12390; tel. (21) 5265656; fax (21) 5265659; internet www.brazilembassy.or.id; Ambassador EDMUNDO SUSSUMU FUJITA.

Brunei: Jalan Tanjung Karang 7, Jakarta Pusat 10230; tel. (21) 31906080; fax (21) 31905070; Ambassador Dato' Paduka Seri Haji HUSIN AHMAD.

Bulgaria: Jalan Imam Bonjol 34–36, Menteng, Jakarta Pusat 10310; tel. (21) 3904048; fax (21) 3904049; e-mail bgemb.jkt@centrin.net.id; Ambassador BOYKO MIRCHEV.

Cambodia: Jalan T. B. Simatupang, Kav. 13, Jakarta Selatan 12520; tel. (21) 7812523; fax (21) 7812524; e-mail recjkt@cabi.net.id; Ambassador KHEM BUNNEANG.

Canada: World Trade Center, 6th Floor, Jalan Jenderal Sudirman, Kav. 29–31, POB 8324/JKS.MP, Jakarta 12920; tel. (21) 25507800; fax (21) 25507811; e-mail canadianembassy.jkrta@international.gc.ca; internet www.international.gc.ca/asia/jakarta/; Ambassador JOHN T. HOLMES.

Chile: Bina Mulia Bldg, 7th Floor, Jalan H. R. Rasuna Said, Kav. 10, Kuningan, Jakarta 12950; tel. (21) 5201131; fax (21) 5201955; e-mail emchijak@indosat.net.id; Ambassador ROLANDO DRAGO RODRÍGUEZ.

China, People's Republic: Jalan Mega Kuningan 2, Karet Kuningan, Jakarta 12950; tel. (21) 5761038; fax (21) 5761034; e-mail enbsychn@cbn.net.id; internet id.china-embassy.org/eng/; Ambassador LAN LIJUN.

Croatia: Menara Mulia, Suite 2101, Jalan Gatot Subroto, Kav. 9–11, Jakarta 12930; tel. (21) 5257822; fax (21) 5204073; e-mail embassy@croatemb.or.id; internet www.croatemb.or.id; Ambassador ALEKSANDAR BROZ.

Cuba: Taman Puri, Jalan Opal, Blok K-1, Permata Hijau, Jakarta 12210; tel. (21) 5304293; fax (21) 53676906; e-mail cubaindo@cbn.net.id; Ambassador JORGE LEÓN.

Czech Republic: Jalan Gereja Theresia 20, Menteng, Jakarta Pusat 10350; tel. (21) 3904075; fax (21) 3904078; e-mail jakarta@embassy.mzv.cz; internet www.mfa.cz/jakarta; Ambassador PAVEL REZÁČ.

Denmark: Menara Rajawali, 25th Floor, Jalan Mega Kuningan, Lot 5.1, Jakarta 12950; tel. (21) 5761478; fax (21) 5761535; e-mail jktamb@um.dk; internet www.ambjakarta.um.dk/en; Ambassador NIELS ERIK ANDERSEN.

Ecuador: World Trade Center, 17th Floor, Jalan Jenderal Sudirman, Kav. 31, Jakarta 12920; tel. (21) 5211484; fax (21) 5226954; e-mail ecuadorinindonesia@gmail.com; Ambassador RODRIGO YÉPEZ ENRÍQUEZ.

Egypt: Jalan Denpasar Raya, Blok A12, No. 1, Kuningan Timur, Setiabudi, Jakarta Selatan 12950; tel. (21) 5204359; fax (21) 5204792; e-mail egypt@indosat.net.id; internet www.mfa.gov.eg/missions/indonesia/jakarta/embassy/en-gb/; Ambassador MOHAMED EL SAYED TAHA.

Finland: Menara Rajawali, 9th Floor, Lot 5.1, Jalan Mega Kuningan, Kawasan Mega Kuningan, Jakarta 12950; tel. (21) 5761650; fax (21) 5761631; e-mail sanomat.jak@formin.fi; internet www.finland.or.id; Ambassador ANTTI KOISTINEN.

France: Jalan M. H. Thamrin 20, Jakarta Pusat 10350; tel. (21) 23557601; fax (21) 23557600; e-mail ambassade@ambafrance-id.org; internet www.ambafrance-id.org; Ambassador CATHERINE BOIVINEAU.

Germany: Jalan M. H. Thamrin 1, Jakarta 10310; tel. (21) 39855000; fax (21) 3901757; e-mail germany@rad.net.id; internet www.jakarta.diplo.de; Ambassador PAUL FREIHERR VON MALTZAHN.

Greece: Plaza 89, 12th Floor, Suite 1203, Jalan H. R. Rasuna Said, Kav. X-7 No. 6, Kuningan, Jakarta 12940; tel. (21) 5207776; fax (21) 5207753; e-mail grembas@cbn.net.id; internet www.greekembassy.or.id; Ambassador CHARALAMBOS CHRISTOPOULOS.

Holy See: Jalan Merdeka Timur 18, POB 4227, Jakarta Pusat (Apostolic Nunciature); tel. (21) 3841142; fax (21) 3841143; e-mail

INDONESIA

vatjak@cbn.net.id; Apostolic Nuncio Most Rev. LEOPOLDO GIRELLI (Titular Archbishop of Capri).

Hungary: 36 Jalan H. R. Rasuna Said, Kav. X/3, Kuningan, Jakarta 12950; tel. (21) 5203459; fax (21) 5203461; e-mail huembjkt@telkom.net; internet www.huembjkt.or.id; Ambassador MIHÁLY ILLÉS.

India: Jalan H. R. Rasuna Said, Kav. S/1, Kuningan, Jakarta 12950; tel. (21) 5204150; fax (21) 5204160; e-mail eoijakarta@indo.net.id; internet www.embassyofindiajakarta.org; Ambassador NAVREKHA SHARMA.

Iran: Jalan Hos Cokroaminoto 110, Menteng, Jakarta Pusat 10310; tel. (21) 31931378; fax (21) 3107860; e-mail irembjkt@indo.net.id; internet www.iranembassy.or.id; Ambassador BEHROUZ KAMALVANDI.

Iraq: Jalan Teuku Umar 38, Jakarta 10350; tel. (21) 3904067; fax (21) 3904066; Chargé d'affaires a.i. FALIH ABDULKADIR AL-HAYALI.

Italy: Jalan Diponegoro 45, Menteng, Jakarta Pusat 10310; tel. (21) 31937445; fax (21) 31937422; e-mail embitaly@italambjkt.or.id; internet www.ambjakarta.esteri.it; Ambassador ROBERTO PALMIERI.

Japan: Menara Thamrin, 7th–10th Floors, Jalan M. H. Thamrin 24, Kav. 3, Jakarta Pusat 10350; tel. (21) 31924308; fax (21) 31925460; internet www.id.emb-japan.go.jp; Ambassador SHIN EBIHARA.

Jordan: Artha Graha Tower, 9th Floor, Sudirman Central Business District, Jalan Jenderal Sudirman, Kav. 52–53, Jakarta 12190; tel. (21) 5153483; fax (21) 5153482; e-mail jordanem@cbn.net.id; internet www.jordanembassy.or.id; Ambassador MOHAMMAD HASSAN DAWODIEH.

Korea, Democratic People's Republic: Jalan Teluk Betung 1–2, Jakarta Pusat 12050; tel. (21) 31908425; fax (21) 31908427; e-mail dprkorea@rad.net.id; Ambassador JONG CHUN GUN.

Korea, Republic: Jalan Jenderal Gatot Subroto 57, Jakarta Selatan; tel. (21) 5201915; fax (21) 5254159; e-mail koemb@indo.net.id; Ambassador LEE SUN-JIN.

Kuwait: Jalan Teuku Umar 51, Menteng, Jakarta 10310; tel. (21) 3919916; fax (21) 3912285; e-mail ami@Kuwait-toplist.com; Ambassador MOHAMMED FADEL KHALAF.

Laos: Jalan Patra Kuningan XIV 1-A, Kuningan, Jakarta 12950; tel. (21) 5229602; fax (21) 5229601; e-mail laoemjktof@hotmail.com; Chargé d'affaires a.i. OUKHAM SENGKEOMIXAY.

Lebanon: Jalan YBR V 82, Kuningan, Jakarta 12950; tel. (21) 5253074; fax (21) 5207121; e-mail lebanon_embassy_jkt@yahoo.com; Ambassador VICTOR ZMETER.

Libya: Jalan Pekalongan 24, Jakarta Pusat 10310; tel. (21) 31935308; fax (21) 31935726; Ambassasdor SALAHEDDIN MOHAMED EL BISHARI.

Malaysia: Jalan H. R. Rasuna Said, Kav. X/6, 1–3 Kuningan, Jakarta 12950; tel. (21) 5224947; fax (21) 5224974; e-mail maljakarta@kln.gov.my; internet www.kln.gov.my/perwakilan/jakarta; Ambassador Dato' ZAINAL ABIDIN MOHAMAD ZAIN.

Marshall Islands: Jalan Pangeran Jayakarta 115, Blok A-11, Jakarta Pusat 10730; tel. (21) 7248565; fax (21) 7248566; e-mail marshall@idola.net.id; Ambassador CARL L. HEINE.

Mexico: Menara Mulia, Suite 2306, Jalan Jenderal Gatot Subroto, Kav. 9–11, Jakarta Selatan 12930; tel. (21) 5203980; fax (21) 5203978; Ambassador PEDRO GONZÁLEZ-RUBIO SÁNCHEZ.

Morocco: Menara Mulia, 19th Floor, Suite 1901, Kav. 9–11, Jakarta 12930; tel. (21) 5200773; fax (21) 5200586; e-mail sifamaind@telkomvision.com; Ambassador M. ABDERRAHMANE DRISSI ALAMI.

Mozambique: Wisma GKBI, 37th Floor, Suite 3709, Jalan Jenderal Sudirman 28, Jakarta 10210; tel. (21) 5740901; fax (21) 5740907; e-mail embamoc@cbn.net.id; Ambassador GERALDO ANTONIO CHIRINZA.

Myanmar: Jalan Haji Agus Salim 109, Jakarta Selatan; tel. (21) 327684; fax (21) 327204; e-mail myanmar@cbn.net.id; Ambassador U KHIN ZAW WIN.

Netherlands: Jalan H. R. Rasuna Said, Kav. S/3, Kuningan, Jakarta 12950; tel. (21) 5248200; fax (21) 5700734; e-mail jak@minbuza.nl; internet indonesia.nlembassy.org; Ambassador Dr NIKOLAOS VAN DAM.

New Zealand: BRI II Bldg, 23rd Floor, Jalan Jenderal Sudirman, Kav. 44–46, Jakarta; tel. (21) 5709460; fax (21) 5709457; e-mail nzembjak@cbn.net.id; internet www.nzembassy.com/home.cfm?c=41; Ambassador PHILLIP GIBSON.

Nigeria: Jalan Taman Patra XIV/11–11A, Kuningan Timur, POB 3649, Jakarta Selatan 12950; tel. (21) 5260922; fax (21) 5260924; e-mail embnig@centrin.net.id; Ambassador MUHAMMED BUBA AHMED.

Norway: Menara Rajawali, 25th Floor, Kawasan Mega Kuningan, Jakarta 12950; tel. (21) 5761523; fax (21) 5761537; e-mail emb.jakarta@mfa.no; internet www.norway.or.id/info/embassy.htm; Ambassador BJØRN BLOKHUS.

Pakistan: Jalan Lembang 10, Menteng, Jakarta; tel. (21) 3144008; fax (21) 3103945; e-mail parepjakarta@link.net.id; Ambassador Maj.-Gen. (retd) ALI BAZ KHAN.

Panama: World Trade Center, 8th Floor, Jalan Jenderal Sudirman, Kav. 29–31, Jakarta 12920; tel. (21) 5711867; fax (21) 5711933; Ambassador RAÚL ANTONIO ENKILDSEN ARIAS.

Papua New Guinea: Panin Bank Centre, 6th Floor, Jalan Jenderal Sudirman 1, Jakarta 10270; tel. (21) 7251218; fax (21) 7201012; e-mail kdujkt@cbn.net.id; Ambassador CHRISTOPHER MERO.

Peru: Menara Rajawali, 12th Floor, Jalan Mega Kuningan, Lot 5.1, Kawasan Mega Kuningan, Jakarta 12950; tel. (21) 5761820; fax (21) 5761825; e-mail embaperu@cbn.net.id; Ambassador JUAN JOSÉ ALVAREZ VITA.

Philippines: Jalan Imam Bonjol 6–8, Jakarta Pusat 10310; tel. (21) 3100334; fax (21) 3151167; e-mail phjkt@indo.net.id; Ambassador VIDAL E. QUEROL.

Poland: Jalan H. R. Rasuna Said, Kav. X, Blok IV/3, Jakarta Selatan 12950; tel. (21) 2525938; fax (21) 2525958; e-mail consular@polandembjak.org; internet www.jakarta.polemb.net; Ambassador TOMASZ ŁUKASZUK.

Portugal: Jalan Indramayu 2A, Menteng, Jakarta 10310; tel. (21) 31908030; fax (21) 31908031; e-mail embassyportugaljakarta@cbn.net.id; internet www.embassyportugaljakarta.or.id; Ambassador JOSÉ MANUEL SANTOS BRAGA.

Qatar: Jalan Mega Kuningan Barat I, No. 7, Kawasan Mega Kuningan, Jakarta 12950; tel. (21) 2510751; fax (21) 2510754; e-mail qataremj@indosat.net.id; Ambassador YOUSEF KHALIFA AL-SADA.

Romania: Jalan Teuku Cik Di Tiro, No. 42A, Menteng, Jakarta Pusat; tel. (21) 3900489; fax (21) 3106241; e-mail romind@cbn.net.id; Ambassador GHEORGHE VÎLCU.

Russia: Jalan H. R. Rasuna Said, Kav. X-6, Jakarta; tel. (21) 5222912; e-mail rusembjkt@uninet.net.id; internet www.indonesia.mid.ru; Ambassador ALEXANDER A. IVANOV.

Saudi Arabia: Jalan M. T. Haryono, Kav. 27, Cawang Atas, Jakarta Timur; tel. (21) 8011533; fax (21) 3905864; e-mail idemb@mofa.gov.sa; Ambassador ABDULLAH BIN ABDULRAHMAN A'ALIM AL-KHAYYAT.

Serbia: Jalan Hos Cokroaminoto 109, Jakarta 10310; tel. (21) 3143560; fax (21) 3143613; Ambassador ZORAN KAZAZOVIĆ.

Singapore: Jalan H. R. Rasuna Said, Blok X/4, Kav. 2, Kuningan, Jakarta 12950; tel. (21) 5201489; fax (21) 5201486; e-mail singemb_jkt@sgmfa.gov.sg; internet www.mfa.gov.sg/jkt; Ambassador ASHOK MIRPURI.

Slovakia: Jalan Prof. Mohammed Yamin 29, POB 1368, Menteng, Jakarta Pusat 10310; tel. (21) 3101068; fax (21) 3101180; e-mail slovemby@indo.net.id; Ambassador PETER HOLASEK.

Somalia: Jalan Permata Hijau Raya Block T, No. 8, Kebayoran Lama, Jakarta Selatan 12210; tel. (21) 5321920; fax (21) 5494730; e-mail somalirep_jkt@yahoo.com; internet somaliembassyjkt.com; Ambassador MOHAMUD OLOW BAROW.

South Africa: Suite 705, Wisma GKBI, Jalan Jenderal Sudirman 28, Jakarta 10210; tel. (21) 5740660; fax (21) 5740661; e-mail saembhom@centrin.net.id; internet www.southafricanembassy-jakarta.or.id; Ambassador GRIFFITHS MEMELA.

Spain: Jalan H. Agus Salim 61, Jakarta 10350; tel. (21) 3142355; fax (21) 31935134; e-mail emb.yakarta@mae.es; Ambassador AURORA BERNÁLDEZ.

Sri Lanka: Jalan Diponegoro 70, Jakarta 10320; tel. (21) 3161886; fax (21) 3107962; e-mail lankaemb@rad.net.id; Ambassador Maj.-Gen. (retd) NANDA MALLAWAARACHCHI.

Sudan: Mayapada Tower, 7th Floor, Suite 01, Jalan Jenderal Sudirman, Kav. 28, Jakarta 12920; tel. (21) 3908234; fax (21) 3908235; e-mail sudanind@cbn.net.id; Ambassador ABDEL G. A. RAHMAN HASSAN.

Suriname: Jalan Padalarang No. 9, Menteng, Jakarta Pusat 10310; tel. (21) 3154437; fax (21) 3154556; e-mail suramjkt@cbn.net.id; Ambassador ANGELIC C. ALIHUSAIN-DEL CASTILHO.

Sweden: Menara Rajawali, 9th Floor, Jalan Mega Kuningan, Lot 5.1, Kawasan Mega Kuningan, Jakarta Selatan 12950; tel. (21) 55535900; fax (21) 5762691; e-mail ambassaden.jakarta@foreign.ministry.se; internet www.swedenabroad.com/jakarta; Ambassador ANN MARIE BOLIN PENNEGÅRD.

Switzerland: Jalan H. R. Rasuna Said, Kav. X-3/2, Kuningan, Jakarta Selatan 12950; tel. (21) 5256061; fax (21) 5202289; e-mail vertretung@jak.rep.admin.ch; internet www.eda.admin.ch/jakarta; Ambassador BERNARDINO REGAZZONI.

Syria: Jalan Karang Asem I/8, Jakarta 12950; tel. (21) 5255991; fax (21) 5202511; Ambassador MOHAMAD DARWISH BALADI.

INDONESIA

Thailand: Jalan Imam Bonjol 74, Jakarta 10310; tel. (21) 3904052; fax (21) 3107469; e-mail thaijkt@indo.net.id; internet www.thaiembassy.org/jakarta; Ambassador AKRASID AMATAYAKUL.

Timor-Leste: Gedung Surya, 11th Floor, Jalan M. H. Thamrin, Kav. 9, Jakarta; tel. (21) 3902678; fax (21) 3902660; Ambassador OLIVIO DE JESUS AMARAL.

Tunisia: Wisma Dharmala Sakti, 11th Floor, Jalan Jenderal Sudirman 32, Jakarta 10220; tel. (21) 5703432; fax (21) 5700016; e-mail atjkt@uninet.net.id; Ambassador FAYCAL GOUIA.

Turkey: Jalan H. R. Rasuna Said, Kav. 1, Kuningan, Jakarta 12950; tel. (21) 5256250; fax (21) 5226056; e-mail cakartabe@telkom.net; Ambassador FERYAL ÇOTUR.

Ukraine: World Trade Center, 8th Floor, Jalan Jenderal Sudirman, Kav. 29–31, Jakarta 12920; tel. (21) 5211700; fax (21) 5211710; e-mail uaembas@indo.net.id; Chargé d'affaires a.i. VALERIY KRAVCENKO.

United Arab Emirates: Jalan Prof. Dr Satrio, Kav. 16–17, Jakarta 12950; tel. (21) 5206518; fax (21) 5206526; e-mail uaeemb@rad.net.id; Ambassador YOUSIF RASHID ALSHRAM.

United Kingdom: Jalan M. H. Thamrin 75, Jakarta 10310; tel. (21) 3156264; fax (21) 3926263; e-mail commercial@dnet.net.id; internet www.britishembassy.gov.uk/indonesia; Ambassador CHARLES HUMFREY.

USA: Jalan Merdeka Selatan 4–5, Jakarta 10110; tel. (21) 34359000; fax (21) 34359922; e-mail jakconsul@state.gov; internet jakarta.usembassy.gov; Ambassador CAMERON R. HUME.

Uzbekistan: Menara Mulia, 24th Floor, Suite 2401, Jalan Jenderal Gatot Subroto, Kav. 9–11, Jakarta Selatan 12930; tel. (21) 5222581; fax (21) 5222582; e-mail registan@indo.net.id; Ambassador (vacant).

Venezuela: Menara Mulia, 20th Floor, Suite 2005, Jalan Jenderal Gatot Subroto, Kav. 9–11, Jakarta Selatan 12930; tel. (21) 5227547; fax (21) 5227549; e-mail evenjakt@indo.net.id; Chargé d'affaires a.i. MARÍA VIRGINIA MENZONES LICCIONI.

Viet Nam: Jalan Teuku Umar 25, Jakarta; tel. (21) 3100358; fax (21) 3100359; e-mail embvnam@uninet.net.id; internet www.vietnamembassy-indonesia.org; Ambassador NGUYEN HUU DZUNG.

Yemen: Jalan Yusuf Adiwinata 29, Menteng, Jakarta Pusat 10310; tel. (21) 3108029; fax (21) 3904946; e-mail yememb@rad.net.id; Ambassador ABDURAHMAN MOHAMED HASSAN AL-HOTHI.

Judicial System

There is one codified criminal law for the whole of Indonesia. In December 1989 the Islamic Judicature Bill, giving wider powers to Shari'a courts, was approved by the Dewan Perwakilan Rakyat (House of Representatives). The new law gave Muslim courts authority over civil matters, such as marriage. Muslims may still choose to appear before a secular court. Europeans are subject to the Code of Civil Law published in the State Gazette in 1847. Alien orientals (i.e. Arabs, Indians, etc.) and Chinese are subject to certain parts of the Code of Civil Law and the Code of Commerce. The work of codifying this law has started, but, in view of the great complexity and diversity of customary law, it may be expected to take a considerable time to achieve. In June 2005 a judicial commission was established; the seven-member body, appointed by the House of Representatives, was charged with reforming the judiciary and for nominating Supreme Court justices, including the Chief Justice. In February 2006 there were 49 Supreme Court justices. In that month the Judicial Commission announced that it was drafting a government regulation in lieu of law urging the re-evaluation of all justices as part of a wider process of judicial reform intended to address the issue of corruption within the legal system.

Supreme Court
(Mahkamah Agung)

Jalan Merdeka Utara 9–13, Jakarta 10110; tel. (21) 3843348; fax (21) 3811057; e-mail info@ma-ri.go.id; internet www.mahkamahagung.go.id.

The Supreme Court is the final court of appeal.

Chief Justice: Prof. BAGIR MANAN.

Deputy Chief Justices: MARIANNA SUTADI, Dr HARIFIN TUMPA.

High Courts in Jakarta, Surabaya, Medan, Makassar, Banda Aceh, Padang, Palembang, Bandung, Semarang, Banjarmasin, Menado, Denpasar, Ambon and Jayapura deal with appeals from the District Courts. District Courts deal with marriage, divorce and reconciliation.

Religion

All citizens are required to state their religion. The Ministry of Religion accords official status to six religions—Islam, Protestantism, Catholicism, Hinduism, Buddhism and Confucianism. According to a survey in 2000, 88.2% of the population were Muslims, while 5.9% were Protestant, 3.1% were Roman Catholic, 1.8% were Hindus, 0.8% were Buddhists and 0.2% professed adherence to other religions, such as other Christian denominations and Judaism, which remains unrecognized.

National religious councils—representing the official religious traditions—were established to serve as liaison bodies between religious adherents and the Government and to advise the Government on the application of religious principles to various elements of national life.

ISLAM

Indonesia has the world's largest Muslim population.

Majelis Ulama Indonesia (MUI) (Indonesian Ulama Council): Komp. Masjid Istiqlal, Jalan Taman Wijaya Kusuma, Jakarta 10710; tel. (21) 3455471; fax (21) 3855412; e-mail mui-online@mui.or.id; internet www.mui.or.id; central Muslim organization; Chair. SAHAL MAHFUDZ; Sec.-Gen. DIEN SYAMSUDDIN.

CHRISTIANITY

Persekutuan Gereja-Gereja di Indonesia (Communion of Churches in Indonesia): Jalan Salemba Raya 10, Jakarta Pusat 10430; tel. (21) 3150451; fax (21) 3150457; e-mail pgi@bit.net.id; internet www.pgi.or.id; f. 1950; 81 mem. churches; Chair. Rev. Dr A. A. YEWANGOE; Gen. Sec. Rev. Dr RICHARD M. DAULAY.

The Roman Catholic Church

Indonesia comprises 10 archdioceses and 27 dioceses. At 31 December 2005 there were an estimated 6,542,234 adherents in Indonesia, representing 3.1% of the population.

Bishops' Conference

Konferensi Waligereja Indonesia (KWI), Jalan Cut Meutia 10, POB 3044, Jakarta 10340; tel. (21) 336422; fax (21) 3918527; e-mail kwi@parokinet.org.

f. 1973; Pres. Cardinal JULIUS RIYADI DARMAATMADJA (Archbishop of Jakarta).

Archbishop of Ende: Most Rev. ABDON LONGINUS DA CUNHA, Keuskupan Agung, POB 210, Jalan Katedral 5, Ndona-Ende 86312, Flores; tel. (381) 21176; fax (381) 21606; e-mail uskup@ende.parokinet.org.

Archbishop of Jakarta: Cardinal JULIUS RIYADI DARMAATMADJA, Keuskupan Agung, Jalan Katedral 7, Jakarta 10710; tel. (21) 3813345; fax (21) 3855681.

Archbishop of Kupang: Most Rev. PETER TURANG, Keuskupan Agung Kupang, Jalan Thamrin, Oepoi, Kupang 85111, Timor NTT; tel. (380) 826199; fax (380) 833331.

Archbishop of Makassar: Most Rev. JOHANNES LIKU ADA', Keuskupan Agung, Jalan Thamrin 5–7, Makassar 90111, Sulawesi Selatan; tel. (411) 315744; fax (411) 326674; e-mail sekr_kams@yahoo.com.

Archbishop of Medan: Most Rev. ALFRED GONTI PIUS DATUBARA, Jalan Imam Bonjol 39, POB 1191, Medan 20152, Sumatra Utara; tel. (61) 4519768; fax (61) 4145745; e-mail sekrkam@hotmail.com.

Archbishop of Merauke: Most Rev. NICOLAUS ADI SEPTURA, Keuskupan Agung, Jalan Mandala 30, Merauke 99602, Papua; tel. (971) 321011; fax (971) 326574.

Archbishop of Palembang: Most Rev. ALOYSIUS SUDARSO, Keuskupan Agung, Jalan Tasik 18, Palembang 30135; tel. (711) 350417; fax (711) 314776; e-mail alva@mdp.net.id.

Archbishop of Pontianak: Most Rev. HIERONYMUS HERCULANUS BUMBUN, Keuskupan Agung, Jalan A. R. Hakin 92A, POB 1119, Pontianak 78011, Kalimantan Barat; tel. (561) 732382; fax (561) 738785; e-mail kap@pontianak.wasantara.net.id.

Archbishop of Samarinda: Most Rev. FLORENTINUS SULUI HAJANG HAU, Keuskupan Agung, POB 1062, Jalan Gunung Merbabu 41, Samarinda 75010; tel. (541) 741193; fax (541) 203120.

Archbishop of Semarang: Most Rev. IGNATIUS SUHARYO HARDJOATMODJO, Keuskupan Agung, Jalan Pandanaran 13, Semarang 50244; tel. (24) 8312276; fax (24) 8414741; e-mail uskup@semarang.parokinet.org.

Other Christian Churches

Protestant Church in Indonesia (Gereja Protestan di Indonesia): Jalan Medan Merdeka Timur 10, Jakarta 10110; tel. (21) 3519003; fax (21) 34830224; consists of 10 churches of Calvinistic tradition;

INDONESIA

2,789,155 mems, 3,841 congregations, 1,965 pastors (1998); Chair. Rev. Dr D. J. LUMENTA.

Numerous other Protestant communities exist throughout Indonesia, mainly organized on a local basis. The largest of these are: the Batak Protestant Christian Church; the Christian Church in Central Sulawesi; the Christian Evangelical Church in Minahasa; the Christian Protestant Church in Indonesia; the East Java Christian Church; the Evangelical Christian Church in Irian Jaya; the Evangelical Christian Church of Sangir-Talaud; the Indonesian Christian Church/Huria Kristen Indonesia; the Javanese Christian Churches; the Kalimantan Evangelical Church; the Karo Batak Protestant Church; the Nias Protestant Christian Church; the Protestant Church in the Moluccas; the Simalungun Protestant Christian Church; and the Toraja Church.

BUDDHISM

All-Indonesia Buddhist Association: Jakarta.
Indonesian Buddhist Council: Jakarta.

HINDUISM

Hindu Dharma Council: Jakarta.

The Press

PRINCIPAL DAILIES

Bali

Harian Pagi Umum (Bali Post): Jalan Kepudang 67A, Denpasar 80232; e-mail balipost@indo.net.id; internet www.balipost.co.id; f. 1948; daily (Indonesian edn), weekly (English edn); Editor K. NADHA; circ. 25,000.

Java

Angkatan Bersenjata: Jalan Kramat Raya 94, Jakarta Pusat; tel. (21) 46071; fax (21) 366870; armed forces newspaper.

Bandung Post: Jalan Lodaya 38A, Bandung 40264; tel. (22) 305124; fax (22) 302882; f. 1979; Chief Editor AHMAD SAELAN; Dir AHMAD JUSACC.

Berita Buana: Jalan Tahah Abang Dua 33–35, Jakarta 10110; tel. (21) 5487175; fax (21) 5491555; f. 1970; relaunched 1990; Indonesian; circ. 150,000.

Berita Yudha: Jalan Letjenderal Haryono MT22, Jakarta; tel. (21) 8298331; f. 1971; Indonesian; Editor SUNARDI; circ. 50,000.

Bisnis Indonesia: Wisma Bisnis Indonesia, Jalan K. H. Mas Mansyur 12A, Karet, Jakarta 10220; tel. (21) 57901023; fax (21) 57901025; e-mail redaksi@bisnis.co.id; internet www.bisnis.com; f. 1985; available online; Indonesian; Editor SUKAMDANI S. GITOSARDJONO; circ. 60,000.

Harian Indonesia (Indonesia Rze Pao): Jalan Toko Tiga Seberang 21, POB 4755, Jakarta 11120; tel. (21) 6295948; fax (21) 6297830; e-mail info@harian-indonesia.com; internet www.harian-indonesia.com; f. 1966; Chinese; Editor W. D. SUKISMAN; Dir HADI WIBOWO; circ. 42,000.

Harian Terbit: Jalan Pulogadung 15, Kawasan Industri Pulogadung, Jakarta 13920; tel. (21) 4602953; fax (21) 4602950; e-mail terbit@harianterbit.com; internet www.harianterbit.com; f. 1972; Indonesian; Editor-in-Chief TARMAN AZZAM; circ. 125,000.

Harian Umum AB: CTC Bldg, 2nd Floor, Kramat Raya 94, Jakarta Pusat; f. 1965; official armed forces journal; Dir GOENARSO; Editor-in-Chief N. SOEPANGAT; circ. 80,000.

The Indonesia Times: Jalan Pulo Lentut 12, Jakarta Timur; tel. (21) 4611280; fax (21) 375012; e-mail info@webpacific.com; f. 1974; English; Editor TRIBUANA SAID; circ. 35,000.

Jakarta Post: Jalan Palmerah Selatan 15, Jakarta 10270; tel. (21) 5300476; fax (21) 5492685; e-mail editorial@thejakartapost.com; internet www.thejakartapost.com; f. 1983; English; Chief Editor ENDY M. BAYUNI; circ. 50,000.

Jawa Pos: Graha Pena Bldg, 4th Floor, Achmad Yani 88, Surabaya 60234; tel. (31) 8202216; fax (31) 8285555; e-mail editor@jawapos.co.id; internet www.jawapos.co.id; f. 1949; Indonesian; CEO DAHLAN ISKAN; circ. 120,000.

Kedaulatan Rakyat: Jalan P. Mangkubumi 40–44, Yogyakarta; tel. (274) 565685; fax (274) 563125; internet www.kr.co.id; f. 1945; Indonesian; independent; Editor IMAN SUTRISNO; circ. 50,000.

Kompas: Jalan Palmerah Selatan 26–28, Jakarta 10270; tel. (21) 5347710; fax (21) 5486085; e-mail kompas@kompas.com; internet www.kompas.com; f. 1965; Indonesian; Editor NINOK LEKSONO; circ. 523,453.

Koran Tempo: Gedung Tempo, Jalan H. R. Rasuna Said, Kav. C-17, Kuningan, Jakarta 10270; tel. (21) 5201022; fax (21) 5200092; internet www.korantempo.com; f. 2001; Indonesian; Editor-in-Chief BAMBANG HARYMURTI.

Media Indonesia Daily: Jalan Pilar Mas Raya, Kav. A–D, Kedoya Selatan, Kebon Jeruk, Jakarta 11520; tel. (21) 5812088; fax (21) 5812105; e-mail miol@mediaindonesia.co.id; internet www.mediaindo.co.id; f. 1989; fmrly Prioritas; Indonesian; Publr SURYA PALOH; Editor DJAFAR H. ASSEGAFF; circ. 2,000.

Neraca: Jalan Jambrut 2–4, Jakarta; tel. (21) 323969; fax (21) 3101873.

Pelita (Torch): Jalan Jenderal Sudirman 65, Jakarta; f. 1974; Indonesian; Muslim; Editor AKBAR TANDJUNG; circ. 80,000.

Pewarta Surabaya: Jalan Karet 23, POB 85, Surabaya; f. 1905; Indonesian; Editor RADEN DJAROT SOEBIANTORO; circ. 10,000.

Pikiran Rakyat: Jalan Asia-Afrika 77, Bandung 40111; tel. (22) 51216; e-mail pdr@pikiran-rakyat.com; internet www.pikiran-rakyat.com; f. 1950; Indonesian; independent; Editor BRAM M. DARMAPRAWIRA; circ. 150,000.

Pos Kota: Yayasan Antar Kota, Jalan Gajah Mada 100, Jakarta 10130; tel. and fax (21) 5652603; e-mail redaksi@poskota.co.id; internet www.poskota.co.id; f. 1970; Indonesian; Editor H. SOFYAN LUBIS; circ. 500,000.

Rakyat Merdeka: Graha Pena, 9th Floor, Jalan Raya Kebayoran Lama 12, Jakarta Selatan 12210; tel. (21) 5556059; fax (21) 5556063; e-mail redaksi@rakyatmerdeka.co.id; internet www.rakyatmerdeka.co.id; f. 1945; Indonesian; independent; Chief Editor TEGUH SANTOSA; circ. 130,000.

Republika: Jalan Warung Buncit Raya 37, Jakarta Selatan 12510; tel. (21) 7803747; fax (21) 7983623; e-mail sekretariat@republika.co.id; internet www.republika.co.id; f. 1993; organ of the Asscn of Indonesian Muslim Intellectuals (ICMI); Chief Editor IKHWANUL KIRAM MASHURI.

Sinar Pagi: Jalan Letjenderal Haryono MT22, Jakarta Selatan.

Suara Karya: Jalan Bangka Raya 2, Kebayoran Baru, Jakarta Selatan 12720; tel. (21) 7192656; fax (21) 71790746; e-mail redaksi@suarakarya-online.com; internet www.suarakarya-online.com; f. 1971; Indonesian; Chief Editor RICKY RACHMADI; circ. 100,000.

Suara Merdeka: Jalan Pandanaran 30, Semarang 50242; tel. (24) 8412600; fax (24) 8411116; e-mail rep@suaramerdeka.com; internet www.suaramerdeka.com; f. 1950; Indonesian; Publr Ir H. TOMMY HETAMI; Editor-in-Chief AULIA A. MUHAMMAD; circ. 200,000.

Suara Pembaruan: Jalan Dewi Sartika 136/D, Cawang, Jakarta 13630; tel. (21) 8013208; fax (21) 8007262; e-mail koransp@suarapembaruan.com; internet www.suarapembaruan.com; f. 1987; licence revoked in 1986 as Sinar Harapan (Ray of Hope); Publr Dr ALBERT HASIBUAN.

Surabaya Post: Jalan Bukit Darmo Golf 31–32, Surabaya 60226; tel. (31) 7382800; fax (31) 7382700; e-mail redaksi@surabayapost.info; internet www.surabayapost.info; f. 1953; independent; Publr TUTY AZIS; Editor ABDURRAHMAN J. BAWAZIER; circ. 115,000.

Kalimantan

Banjarmasin Post: Gedung HJ Djok Mentaya, Jalan AS Musyaffa 16, Banjarmasin 70111; tel. (511) 3354370; fax (511) 4366123; internet www.banjarmasinpost.co.id; f. 1971; Indonesian; Editor-in-Chief H. PRAMONO; circ. 50,000.

Gawi Manuntung: Jalan Pangeran Samudra 97B, Banjarmasin; f. 1972; Indonesian; Editor M. ALI SRI INDRADJAYA; circ. 5,000.

Harian Umum Akcaya: Pontianak Post Group, Jalan Gajah Mada 2–4, Pontianak 78121; tel. (561) 735071; fax (561) 736607; e-mail redaksi@pontianakpost.com; internet www.pontianakpost.com; Editor B. SALMAN.

Kaltim Post: Jalan Jenderal Sudirman RT XVI 82, Balikpapan 76144; tel. (542) 35359; internet www.kaltimpost.web.id; f. 1988; fmrly *Manuntung*; Editor-in-Chief H. BADRUL MUNIR.

Lampung Post: Jalan Pangkal Pinang, Lampung; internet www.lampungpost.com.

Maluku

Ambon Ekspres: Ambon.

Pos Maluku: Jalan Raya Pattimura 19, Ambon; tel. (911) 44614.

Suara Maluku: Komplek Perdagangan Mardikas, Blok D3/11A, Ternate; tel. (911) 44590.

Nusa Tenggara

Pos Kupang: Jalan Kenari 1, Kupang; tel. (380) 833820; fax (380) 831801; internet www.indomedia.com/poskup; Chief Editor DION D. B. PUTRA.

Papua

Berita Karya: Jayapura.

INDONESIA

Cenderawasih Post: Jalan Cenderawasih No. 10, Kelapa II, Entrop, Jayapura 99013; tel. (967) 532417; fax (967) 532418; e-mail cepos_jpr@yahoo.com; internet www.cenderawasihpos.com; Editor-in-Chief DAUD SONY.

Teropong: Jalan Halmahera, Jayapura.

Riau

Batam Pos: Gedung Graha Pena Batam, Lt. 6–7, Batam 29432; tel. (778) 462110; fax (778) 462162; e-mail redaksi@batampos.co.id; internet www.harianbatampos.com; Editor-in-Chief CANDRA IBRAHIM.

Riau Pos: Jalan H. R. Subrantas, KM 10.5, Pekanbaru, Riau 28294; tel. (761) 64633; fax (761) 64640; e-mail redaksi@riaupos.com; internet www.riaupos.com; Editor-in-Chief KAZZAINI KS; circ. 40,000.

Sulawesi

Bulletin Sulut: Jalan Korengkeng 38, Lt. II, Manado, 95114, Sulawesi Utara.

Cahaya Siang: Jalan Kembang II 2, Manado, 95114, Sulawesi Utara; tel. (431) 61054; fax (431) 63393.

Fajar (Dawn): Jalan Racing Centre 101, Makassar; tel. (411) 441441; fax (411) 441224; e-mail redaksi@fajar.co.id; internet www.fajar.co.id; Editor-in-Chief ALWI HAMU; circ. 35,000.

Manado Post: Manado Post Centre, Jalan Babe Palar 54, Manado; tel. (431) 853393; fax (431) 860398; e-mail editor@mdopost.com; internet www.mdopost.com; Editor-in-Chief SUHENDRO BOROMA.

Pedoman Rakyat: Jalan H. A. Mappanyukki 28, Makassar; f. 1947; independent; Editor M. BASIR; circ. 30,000.

Suluh Merdeka: Jalan R. W. Mongsidi 4/96, POB 1105, Manado, 95110; tel. and fax (431) 866150.

Tegas: Jalan Mappanyukki 28, Makassar; tel. (411) 3960.

Sumatra

Harian Analisa: Jalan Jenderal A. Yani 37–43, Medan; tel. (61) 326655; fax (61) 514031; internet www.analisadaily.com; f. 1972; Indonesian; Editor H. ALI SOEKARDI; circ. 75,000.

Harian Berita Sore: Jalan Brigjenderal Katamso, Medan; tel. (61) 4158787; fax (61) 4150383; internet www.beritasore.com; Indonesian; Publr MOHAMMAD SAID; Editor-in-Chief H. TERUNA JASA SAID.

Harian Haluan: Jalan Damar 59 C/F, Padang; f. 1948; Editor-in-Chief Drs ASRIL KASOEMA; circ. 40,000.

Harian Umum Nasional Waspada: Jalan Brigjenderal 1 Katamso, Medan 20151; tel. (61) 4150858; fax (61) 4510025; e-mail waspada@indosat.net.id; internet www.waspada.co.id; f. 1947; Indonesian; Editor-in-Chief H. PRABUDI SAID.

Mimbar Umum: Merah, Medan; tel. (61) 517807; f. 1947; Indonesian; independent; Editor MOHD LUD LUBIS; circ. 55,000.

Serambi Indonesia: Jalan Raya Lambaro, Km 4.5, Tanjung Permai, Manyang PA, Banda Aceh; tel. (651) 635544; fax (651) 637180; e-mail redaksi@serambinews.com; internet www.serambinews.com; Editor-in-Chief MAWARDI IBRAHIM.

Sinar Indonesia Baru: Jalan Brigjenderal Katamso 66, Medan 20151; tel. (61) 4512530; fax (61) 4538150; e-mail redaksi@hariansib.com; internet www.hariansib.com; f. 1970; Indonesian; Chief Editor G. M. PANGGABEAN; circ. 150,000.

Sriwijaya Post: Jalan Jenderal Basuki Rahmat 1608 B-C-D, Palembang; tel. (711) 310088; fax (711) 312888; e-mail sriwijayapost@yahoo.com; internet www.sripo-online.com; f. 2002; Editor-in-Chief HADI PRAYOGO.

Suara Rakyat Semesta: Jalan K. H. Ashari 52, Palembang; Indonesian; Editor DJADIL ABDULLAH; circ. 10,000.

Waspada: Jalan Letjen Suprapto, cnr Jalan Brigjen Katamso 1, Medan 20151; tel. (61) 4150868; fax (61) 4510025; e-mail waspada@waspada.co.id; internet www.waspada.co.id; f. 1947; Indonesian; Chief Editors ANI IDRUS, PRABUDI SAID; circ. 60,000 (daily), 55,000 (Sun.).

PRINCIPAL PERIODICALS

Amanah: Jalan Garuda 69, Kemayoran, Jakarta; tel. (21) 410254; fortnightly; Muslim current affairs; Indonesian; Man. Dir MASKUN ISKANDAR; circ. 180,000.

Ayahbunda: Jalan H. R. Rasuna Said, Blok B, Kav. 32–33, Jakarta 12910; tel. (21) 5209370; fax (21) 5209366; e-mail info@ayahbunda-online.com; internet www.ayahbunda-online.com; fortnightly; family magazine.

Berita Negara: Jalan Pertjetakan Negara 21, Kotakpos 2111, Jakarta; tel. and fax (21) 4207251; f. 1951; 2 a week; official gazette.

Bobo (PT Penerbitan Sarana Bobo): Gramedia Magazine Bldg, 2nd Fl., Jalan Panjang 8A, Kebon Jeruk, Jakarta 11530; tel. (21) 5330150; fax (21) 5320681; f. 1973; subsidiary of Gramedia Group; weekly; children's magazine; Editor KOES SABANDIYAH; circ. 206,000.

Bola: Tunas Bola, Jalan Palmerah Barat 33–37, Jakarta 10270; tel. (21) 53677835; fax (21) 5301952; e-mail info@bolanews.com; internet www.bolanews.com; 2 a week; Tue. and Fri.; sports magazine; Indonesian; Chief Editor IAN SITUMORANG; circ. 715,000.

Buana Minggu: Jalan Tanah Abang Dua 33, Jakarta Pusat 10110; tel. (21) 364190; weekly; Sunday; Indonesian; Editor WINOTO PARARTHO; circ. 193,450.

Business News: Jalan H. Abdul Muis 70, Jakarta 10160; tel. (21) 3848207; fax (21) 3454280; f. 1956; 3 a week (Indonesian edn), 2 a week (English edn); Chief Editor SANJOTO SASTROMIHARDJO; circ. 15,000.

Cita Cinta: Jalan H. R. Rasuna Said, Blok B, Kav. 32–33, Jakarta 12910; tel. (21) 5254206; fax (21) 5262131; e-mail citacinta@feminagroup.com; internet www.citacinta.com; f. 2000; teenage lifestyle magazine.

Citra: Gramedia Bldg, Unit 11, 5th Floor, Jalan Palmerah Selatan 24–26, Jakarta 10270; tel. (21) 5483008; fax (21) 5494035; e-mail citra@gramedia-majalah.com; f. 1990; weekly; TV and film programmes, music trends and celebrity news; Chief Editor H. MAMAN SUHERMAN; circ. 239,000.

Depthnews Indonesia: Jalan Jatinegara Barat III/6, Jakarta 13310; tel. (21) 8194994; fax (21) 8195501; f. 1972; weekly; publ. by Press Foundation of Indonesia; Editor SUMONO MUSTOFFA.

Dunia Wanita: Jalan Brigjenderal, Katamso 1, Medan; tel. (61) 4150858; fax (61) 4510025; e-mail waspada@indosat.net.id; internet www.dunia-indonesia.com; f. 1949; fortnightly; Indonesian; women's tabloid; Chief Editor Dr RAYATI SYAFRIN; circ. 10,000.

Economic Review: Bank BNI, Strategic Planning Division, Gedung Bank BNI, Jalan Jenderal Sudirman, Kav. 1, POB 2955, Jakarta 10220; tel. (21) 5728692; fax (21) 5728456; e-mail renkek01@bni.co.id; internet www.bni.co.id; f. 1946; 3 a year; English; economic and business research and analysis; Editor-in-Chief DARWIN SUZANDI.

Ekonomi Indonesia: Jalan Merdeka, Timur 11–12, Jakarta; tel. (21) 494458; monthly; English; economic journal; Editor Z. ACHMAD; circ. 20,000.

Eksekutif: Jalan R. S. Fatmawati 20, Jakarta 12430; tel. (21) 7659218; fax (21) 7504018; internet www.pacific.net.id/eksekutif.

Femina: Jalan H. R. Rasuna Said, Blok B, Kav. 32–33, Jakarta Selatan 12910; tel. (21) 5209370; fax (21) 5209366; e-mail redaksi@feminagroup.com; internet www.femina-online.com; f. 1972; weekly; women's magazine; Publr SVIDA ALISJAHBANA; Editor PETTY S. FATIMAH; circ. 130,000.

Forum: Kebayoran Centre, 12A–14, Jalan Kebayoran Baru, Welbak, Jakarta 12240; tel. (21) 7255625; fax (21) 7255645; internet www.forum.co.id.

Gadis: Jalan H. R. Rasuna Said, Blok B, Kav. 32–33, Jakarta 12910; tel. (21) 5253816; fax (21) 5262131; e-mail gadis@indosat.net.id; internet www.gadis-online.com; f. 1973; every 10 days; Indonesian; teenage lifestyle magazine; Editor-in-Chief PETTY S. F.; circ. 100,000.

Gatra: Gedung Gatra, Jalan Kalibata Timur IV/15, Jakarta 12740; tel. (21) 7973535; fax (21) 79196941; e-mail admin@gatra.com; internet www.gatra.com; f. 1994; by fmr employees of Tempo (banned 1994–98); Gen. Man. BENY SUHARSONO; Editor-in-Chief IWAN QODAR HIMAWAN.

Gugat (Accuse): Surabaya; politics, law and crime; weekly; circ. 250,000.

Hai: Gramedia, Jalan Palmerah Selatan 22, Jakarta 10270; tel. (21) 5483008; fax (21) 6390080; f. 1973; weekly; youth magazine; Editor ARSWENDO ATMOWILOTO; circ. 70,000.

Indonesia Business News: Wisma Bisnis Indonesia, 7th Floor, Jalan K. H. Mas Mansyur 12A, Karet, Jakarta 10220; tel. (21) 57901023; fax (21) 57901025; e-mail redaksi@bisnis.co.id; internet www.bisnis.co.id; Indonesian and English.

Indonesia Business Weekly: Wisma Bisnis Indonesia, Jalan Letjenderal S. Parman, Kav. 12, Slipi, Jakarta 11410; tel. (21) 5304016; fax (21) 5305868; English; Editor TAUFIK DARUSMAN.

Indonesia Magazine: 20 Jalan Merdeka Barat, Jakarta; tel. (21) 352015; f. 1969; monthly; English; Chair. G. DWIPAYANA; Editor-in-Chief HADELY HASIBUAN; circ. 15,000.

Intisari (Digest): Jalan Palmerah Selatan 24–26, Gedung Unit II, 5th Floor, Jakarta 10270; tel. (21) 5483008; fax (21) 53696525; e-mail intisari@gramedia-majalah.com; internet www.intisari-online.com; f. 1963; monthly; Indonesian; popular science, health, technology, crime and general interest; Editors AL. HERU KUSTARA, IRAWATI; circ. 141,000.

Jakarta Jakarta: Gramedia Bldg, Unit II, 5th Floor, Jalan Palmerah Selatan No. 24–26, Jakarta 10270; tel. (21) 5483008; fax (21)

INDONESIA

5494035; f. 1985; weekly; food, fun, fashion and celebrity news; circ. 70,000.

Jurnal Indonesia: Jalan Hos Cokroaminoto 49A, Jakarta 10350; tel. (21) 31901774; fax (21) 3916471; e-mail jurnal@cbn.net.id; monthly; political, economic and business analysis.

Keluarga: Jalan Sangaji 11, Jakarta; fortnightly; women's and family magazine; Editor S. DAHONO.

Kontan: Jalan Kebayoran Lama 1119, Jakarta 12210; tel. (21) 5357636; fax (21) 5357633; e-mail red@kontan-online.com; internet www.kontan-online.com; weekly; Indonesian; business newspaper; Editor-in-Chief YOPIE HIDAYAT.

Majalah Ekonomis: POB 4195, Jakarta; monthly; English; business; Chief Editor S. ARIFIN HUTABARAT; circ. 20,000.

Majalah Kedokteran Indonesia (Journal of the Indonesian Medical Asscn): Jalan Kesehatan 111/29, Jakarta 11/16; internet www.mkionline.net; f. 1951; monthly; Indonesian, English.

Manglé: Jalan Lodaya 19–21, 40262 Bandung; tel. (22) 411438; f. 1957; weekly; Sundanese; Chief Editor Drs OEJANG DARAJATOEN; circ. 74,000.

Matra: Grafity Pers, Kompleks Buncit Raya Permai, Kav. 1, Jalan Warung, POB 3476, Jakarta; tel. (21) 515952; f. 1986; monthly; men's magazine; general interest and current affairs; Editor-in-Chief SRI RUSDY; circ. 100,000.

Mimbar Kabinet Pembangunan: Jalan Merdeka Barat 7, Jakarta; f. 1966; monthly; Indonesian; publ. by Dept of Information.

Mutiara: Jalan Dewi Sartika 136D, Cawang, Jakarta Timur; general interest; Publr H. G. RORIMPANDEY.

Nova: PT Gramedia, Gedung Unit II, Lantai V, Jalan Palmerah Selatan No. 24–26, Jakarta 10270; tel. (21) 5483008; fax (21) 5483146; e-mail nova@gramedia-majalah.com; internet www.tabloidnova.com; weekly; Wed.; women's interest; Indonesian; Editor KOES SABANDIYAH; circ. 618,267.

Oposisi: Jakarta; weekly; politics; circ. 400,000.

Otomotif: Gramedia Bldg, Unit II, 5th Floor, Jalan Palmerah Selatan 24–26, Jakarta 10270; tel. (21) 5490666; fax (21) 5494035; e-mail iklanmjl@ub.net.id; internet www.otomotif-online.com; f. 1990; weekly; automotive specialist tabloid; circ. 215,763.

PC Magazine Indonesia: Jalan H. R. Rasuna Said, Blok B, Kav. 32–33, Jakarta 12910; tel. (21) 5209370; fax (21) 5209366; internet www.pcmag.co.id; computers; Editor-in-Chief SVIDA ALISJAHBANA.

Peraba: Bintaran Kidul 5, Yogyakarta; weekly; Indonesian and Javanese; Roman Catholic; Editor W. KARTOSOEHARSONO.

Pertani PT: Jalan Pasar Minggu, Kalibata, POB 247/KBY, Jakarta Selatan; tel. (21) 793108; f. 1974; monthly; Indonesian; agricultural; Pres. Dir Ir RUSLI YAHYA.

Petisi: Surabaya; weekly; Editor CHOIRUL ANAM.

Rajawali: Jakarta; monthly; Indonesian; civil aviation and tourism; Dir R. A. J. LUMENTA; Man. Editor KARYONO ADHY.

Selecta: Kebon Kacang 29/4, Jakarta; fortnightly; illustrated; Editor SAMSUDIN LUBIS; circ. 80,000.

Simponi: Jakarta; f. 1994; est. by fmr employees of DeTik (banned 1994–98).

Sinar Jaya: Jakarta Selatan; fortnightly; agricultural; Chief Editor Ir SURYONO PROJOPRANOTO.

Swasembada: Jalan Tanah Abang, III/23, Jakarta 10610; tel. (21) 3523839; internet www.swa.co.id; Editor-in-Chief KEMAL EFFENDI GANI.

Tempo: Kebayoran Center Blok A11–A15, Jalan Kebayoran Baru Majestik, Jakarta 12440; tel. (21) 7255625; fax (21) 7255645; e-mail interaktif@tempo.co.id; internet www.tempointeractive.com; f. 1971; weekly; Editor-in-Chief BAMBANG HARYMURTI.

Tiara: Gramedia Bldg, Unit 11, 5th Floor, Jalan Palmerah Selatan 24–26, Jakarta 10270; tel. (21) 5483008; fax (21) 5494035; f. 1990; fortnightly; lifestyles, features and celebrity news; circ. 47,000.

Ummat: Jakarta; Islamic; sponsored by ICMI.

Wenang Post: Jalan R. W. Mongsidi 4/96, POB 1105, Manado 95115; tel. and fax (431) 866150; weekly.

NEWS AGENCIES

Antara (Indonesian National News Agency): Wisma Antara, 3rd, 19th and 20th Floors, 17 Jalan Merdeka Selatan, POB 1257, Jakarta 10012; tel. (21) 3802383; fax (21) 3840907; e-mail newsroom@antara.co.id; internet www.antara.co.id; f. 1937; 20 radio, seven television, 96 newspaper, eight foreign newspaper, seven tabloid, seven magazine, two news agency, nine embassy and seven dotcom subscribers in 2001; 26 brs in Indonesia, five overseas brs; four bulletins in Indonesian and one in English; monitoring service of stock exchanges world-wide; photo service; Exec. Editor HERU PURWANTO; Man. Dir MOHAMAD SOBARY.

Kantorberita Nasional Indonesia (KNI News Service): Jalan Jatinegara Barat III/6, Jakarta Timur 13310; tel. (21) 811003; fax (21) 8195501; f. 1966; independent national news agency; foreign and domestic news in Indonesian; Dir and Editor-in-Chief Drs SUMONO MUSTOFFA; Exec. Editor HARIM NURROCHADI.

PRESS ASSOCIATIONS

Aliansi Jurnalis Independen (AJI) (Alliance of Independent Journalists): Jalan Danau Poso 29, Blok D1, Jakarta 10210; tel. (21) 57900489; fax (21) 5734581; e-mail ajioffice@aji-indonesia.or.id; internet ajiindonesia.org; f. 1994; unofficial; aims to promote freedom of the press; Pres. HERU HENDRATMOKO; Sec.-Gen. ABDUL MANAN.

Jakarta Foreign Correspondents' Club: Suite 1401, Deutsche Bank Bldg, Jalan Imam Bonjol 80, Jakarta 10310; tel. (21) 39831474; fax (21) 39831473; e-mail jfcc@cbn.net.id; internet www.expat.or.id/orgs/jfcc.html; Pres. JOHN AGLIONBY.

Persatuan Wartawan Indonesia (Indonesian Journalists' Asscn): Gedung Dewan Pers, 4th Floor, Jalan Kebon Sirih 34, Jakarta 10110; tel. (21) 353131; fax (21) 353175; f. 1946; govt-controlled; 5,041 mems (April 1991); Chair. TARMAN AZZAM; Gen. Sec. H. SOFJAN LUBIS.

Serikat Penerbit Suratkabar (SPS) (Indonesian Newspaper Publishers' Asscn): Gedung Dewan Pers, 6th Floor, Jalan Kebon Sirih 34, Jakarta 10110; tel. (21) 3459671; fax (21) 3862373; e-mail spspusat@spsindonesia.or.id; internet www.spsindonesia.or.id; f. 1946; Exec. Chair. DAHLAN IKSAN; Sec.-Gen. SUKARDI DARMAWAN.

Yayasan Pembina Pers Indonesia (Press Foundation of Indonesia): Jalan Jatinegara Barat III/6, Jakarta 13310; tel. (21) 8194994; f. 1967; Chair. SUGIARSO SUROYO, MOCHTAR LUBIS.

Publishers

JAKARTA

Aries Lima/New Aqua Press PT: Jalan Rawagelan II/4, Jakarta Timur; tel. (21) 4897566; general and children's; Pres. TUTI SUNDARI AZMI.

Aya Media Pustaka PT: Wijaya Grand Centre C/2, Jalan Dharmawangsa III, Jakarta 12160; tel. (21) 7206903; fax (21) 7201401; f. 1985; children's; Dir Drs ARIANTO TUGIYO.

PT Balai Pustaka Peraga: Jalan Gunung Sahari Raya 4, Gedung Balai Pustaka, 7th Floor, Jakarta 10710; tel. (21) 3451616; fax (21) 3846809; e-mail con_bpustaka@bumn-ri.com; internet members.bumn-ri.com/balaipustaka; f. 1917; children's, school textbooks, literary, scientific pubs and periodicals; Dir R. SISWADI.

Bhratara Niaga Media PT: Jalan Cipinang Bali 17, Jakarta Timur 13420; tel. (21) 8520319; fax (21) 8191858; f. 1986; fmrly Bhratara Karya Aksara; university and educational textbooks; Man. Dir ROBINSON RUSDI.

Bina Rena Pariwara PT: Jalan Pejaten Raya 5-E, Pasar Minggu, Jakarta 12510; tel. (21) 7901931; fax (21) 7901939; e-mail hasanbas@softhome.net; f. 1988; financial, social science, economic, Islamic, children's; Dir Drs HASAN BASRI.

Bulan Bintang PT: Jalan Kramat Kwitang I/8, Jakarta 10420; tel. (21) 3901651; fax (21) 3901652; e-mail bulanbintang@indosat.net.id; internet www.bulanbintang.co.id; f. 1954; Islamic, social science, natural and applied sciences, art; Man. Dir FAUZI AMELZ.

Bumi Aksara PT: Jalan Sawo Raya 18, Rawamangu, Jakarta 13220; tel. (21) 4717049; fax (21) 4700989; f. 1990; university textbooks; Dir H. AMIR HAMZAH.

Cakrawala Cinta PT: Jalan Minyak I/12B, Duren Tiga, Jakarta 12760; tel. (21) 7990725; fax (21) 7974076; f. 1984; science; Dir Drs M. TORSINA.

Centre for Strategic and International Studies (CSIS): Jalan Tanah Abang III/23–27, Jakarta 10160; tel. (21) 3865532; fax (21) 3809641; e-mail csis@csis.or.id; internet www.csis.or.id; f. 1971; political and social sciences; Exec. Dir HADI SOESASTRO.

Cipta Adi Pustaka: Graha Compaka Mas Blok C 22, Jalan Cempaka Putih Raya, Jakarta Pusat; tel. (21) 4213821; fax (21) 4269315; f. 1986; encyclopedias; Dir BUDI SANTOSO.

Dian Rakyat PT: Jalan Rawagelas I/4, Kaw. Industri Pulo Gadung, Jakarta; tel. (21) 4604444; fax (21) 4609115; f. 1966; general; Dir MARIO ALISJAHBANA.

Djambatan PT: Jalan Wijaya I/39, Jakarta 12170; tel. (21) 7203199; fax (21) 7227989; f. 1954; children's, textbooks, social sciences, fiction; Dir SJARIFUDIN SJAMSUDIN.

Dunia Pustaka Jaya: Jalan Kramat Raya 5K, Komp. Maya Indah, Jakarta 10450; tel. (21) 3909322; fax (21) 3909284; f. 1971; fiction, religion, essays, poetry, drama, criticism, art, philosophy and children's; Man. A. RIVAI.

EGC Medical Publishers: Jalan Agung Timur 4, No. 39 Blok 0–1, Jakarta 14350; tel. (21) 65306283; fax (21) 6510840; e-mail contact@

INDONESIA

egc-arcan.com; f. 1978; medical and public health, nursing, dentistry; Dir IMELDA DHARMA.

PT Elex Media Komputindo: Gedung Kompas Gramedia, 6th Floor, Jalan Palmerah Selatan 22, Jakarta 10270; tel. (21) 5483008; fax (21) 5326219; e-mail langganan@elexmedia.co.id; internet www.elexmedia.co.id; f. 1985; management, computing, software, children's, parenting, self-development and fiction; Dir AL. ADHI MARDHIYONO.

Erlangga PT: Kami Melayani II, Pengetahuan, Jalan H. Baping 100, Ciracas, Jakarta 13740; tel. (21) 8717006; fax (21) 8717011; f. 1952; secondary school and university textbooks; Man. Dir GUNAWAN HUTAURUK.

Gaya Favorit Press: Jalan Rawagelam II/4, Kawasan Industri Pulo Gadung, Jakarta 13930; tel. (21) 46821321; fax (21) 46821419; f. 1971; fiction, popular science, lifestyle and children's; Vice-Pres. MIRTA KARTOHADIPRODJO; Man. Dir WIDARTI GUNAWAN.

Gema Insani Press: Jalan Kalibata Utara II/84, Jakarta 12740; tel. (21) 7984391; fax (21) 7984388; e-mail gemainsani@gemainsani.co.id; internet www.gemainsani.co.id; f. 1986; Islamic; Dir UMAR BASYARAHIL.

Ghalia Indonesia: Jalan Pramuka Raya 4, Jakarta 13140; tel. (21) 8584330; fax (21) 8502334; f. 1972; children's and general science, textbooks; Man. Dir LUKMAN SAAD.

Gramedia Widyasarana Indonesia: Jalan Palmerah Selatan 22, Lantai IV, POB 615, Jakarta 10270; tel. (21) 5483008; fax (21) 5300545; f. 1973; university textbooks, general non-fiction, children's and magazines; Gen. Man. ALFONS TARYADI.

Gunung Mulia PT: Jalan Kwitang 22–23, Jakarta 10420; tel. (21) 3901208; fax (21) 3901633; e-mail corp.off@bpkgm.com; internet www.bpkgm.com; f. 1946; general, children's, Christian; Chair. IWAN ARKADY; Pres. Dir STEPHEN Z. SATYAHADI.

Hidakarya Agung PT: Jalan Kebon Kosong F/74, Kemayoran, Jakarta Pusat; tel. (21) 4241074; Dir MAHDIARTI MACHMUD.

Ichtiar: Jalan Majapahit 6, Jakarta Pusat; tel. (21) 3841226; f. 1957; textbooks, law, social sciences, economics; Dir JOHN SEMERU.

Indira PT: Jalan Borobudur 20, Jakarta 10320; tel. (21) 3148868; fax (21) 3921079; e-mail editorial@indira-book.com; internet www.indira-book.com; f. 1953; general science, general trade and children's; Dir BAMBANG P. WAHYUDI.

Kinta CV: Jalan Kemanggisan Ilir V/110, Pal Merah, Jakarta Barat; tel. (21) 5494751; f. 1950; textbooks, social science, general; Man. Drs MOHAMAD SALEH.

Midas Surya Grafindo PT: Jalan Kesehatan 54, Cijantung, Jakarta 13760; tel. (21) 8400414; fax (21) 8400270; f. 1984; children's; Dir Drs FRANS HENDRAWAN.

Mutiara Sumber Widya PT: Jalan Kramat II 55, Jakarta; tel. (21) 3926043; fax (21) 3160313; f. 1951; textbooks, Islamic, social sciences, general and children's; Pres. FADJRAA OEMAR.

Penebar Swadya PT: Jalan Gunung Sahari III/7, Jakarta Pusat; tel. (21) 4204402; fax (21) 4214821; agriculture, animal husbandry, fisheries; Dir Drs ANTHONIUS RIYANTO.

Penerbit Universitas Indonesia: Jalan Salemba Raya 4, Jakarta; tel. (21) 335373; f. 1969; science; Man. S. E. LEGOWO.

Pradnya Paramita PT: Jalan Bunga 8–8A, Matraman, Jakarta 13140; tel. (21) 8504944; e-mail pradnya@centrin.net.id; f. 1973; children's, general, educational, technical and social science; Pres. Dir KONDAR SINAGA.

Pustaka Antara PT: Jalan Taman Kebon Sirih III/13, Jakarta Pusat 10250; tel. (21) 3156994; fax (21) 322745; e-mail nacelod@cbn.net.id; f. 1952; textbooks, political, Islamic, children's and general; Man. Dir AIDA JOESOEF AHMAD.

Pustaka Binaman Pressindo: Bina Manajemen Bldg, Jalan Menteng Raya 9–15, Jakarta 10340; tel. (21) 2300313; fax (21) 2302047; e-mail pustaka@bit.net.id; f. 1981; management; Dir Ir MAKFUDIN WIRYA ATMAJA.

Pustaka LP3ES Indonesia: Jalan Letjen. S. Parman 81, Jakarta 11420; tel. (21) 5663527; fax (21) 56964691; e-mail puslp3es@indo.net.id; f. 1971; general; Dir M. D. MARUTO.

Pustaka Sinar Harapan PT: Jalan Dewi Sartika 136D, Jakarta 13630; tel. (21) 8093208; fax (21) 8091652; f. 1981; general science, fiction, comics, children's; Dir W. M. NAIDEN.

Pustaka Utma Grafiti PT: Jalan Wahid Hasyim Nomor 166A, Jakarta 10250; tel. (21) 31902906; fax (21) 31902435; f. 1981; social sciences, humanities and children's books; Dir ZULKIFLY LUBIS.

Rajagrafindo Persada PT: Jalan Pelepah Hijau IV TN-1 14–15, Kelapa Gading Permai, Jakarta 14240; tel. (21) 4529409; fax (21) 4520951; f. 1980; general science and religion; Dir Drs ZUBAIDI.

Rineka Cipta PT: Blok B/5, Jalan Jenderal Sudirman, Kav. 36A, Bendungan Hilir, Jakarta 10210; tel. (21) 5737646; fax (21) 5711985; f. 1990 by merger of Aksara Baru (f. 1972) and Bina Aksara; general science and university texts; Dir Dr H. SUARDI.

Rosda Jayaputra PT: Jalan Kembang 4, Jakarta 10420; tel. (21) 3904984; fax (21) 3901703; f. 1981; general science; Dir H. ROZALI USMAN.

Sastra Hudaya: Jalan Kalasan 1, Jakarta Pusat; tel. (21) 882321; f. 1967; religious, textbooks, children's and general; Man. ADAM SALEH.

Tintamas Indonesia: Jalan Kramat Raya 60, Jakarta 10420; tel. and fax (21) 3911459; f. 1947; history, modern science and culture, especially Islamic; Man. MARHAMAH DJAMBEK.

Tira Pustaka: Jalan Cemara Raya 1, Kav. 10D, Jaka Permai, Jaka Sampurna, Bekasi 17145; tel. (21) 8841277; fax (21) 8842736; e-mail Tirapus@cbn.net.id; f. 1977; translations, children's; Dir ROBERT B. WIDJAJA.

Toko Buku Walisongo PT: Gedung Idayu, Jalan Kwitang 13, Jakarta 10420; tel. (21) 3154890; fax (21) 3154889; e-mail edp@tokowalisongo.com; f. 1986; fmrly Masagung Group; general, Islamic, textbooks, science; Pres. H. KETUT ABDURRAHMAN MASAGUNG.

Widjaya: Jalan Pecenongan 48C, Jakarta Pusat; tel. (21) 3813446; f. 1950; textbooks, children's, religious and general; Man. DIDI LUTHAN.

Yasaguna: Jalan Minangkabau 44, POB 422, Jakarta Selatan; tel. (21) 8290422; f. 1964; agricultural, children's, handicrafts; Dir HILMAN MADEWA.

Bandung

Alma'arif: Jalan Tamblong 48–50, Bandung; tel. (22) 4264454; fax (22) 4239194; f. 1949; textbooks, religious and general; Man. H. M. BAHARTHAH.

Alumni PT: Jalan Bukit Pakar Timur II/109, Bandung 40197; tel. (22) 2501251; fax (22) 2503044; f. 1968; university and school textbooks; Dir EDDY DAMIAN.

Angkasa: Jalan Merdeka 6, POB 1353 BD, Bandung 40111; tel. (22) 4204795; fax (22) 439183; Dir H. FACHRI SAID.

Armico: Jalan Madurasa Utara 10, Cigereleng, Bandung 40253; tel. (22) 5202234; fax (22) 5201972; f. 1980; school textbooks; Dir Ir ARSIL TANJUNG.

Citra Aditya Bakti PT: Jalan Geusanulun 17, Bandung 40115; tel. (22) 438251; fax (22) 438635; f. 1985; general science; Dir Ir IWAN TANUATMADJA.

Diponegoro Publishing House: Jalan Mohammad Toha 44–46, Bandung 40252; tel. and fax (22) 5201215; fax (22) 5201815; e-mail dpnegoro@indosat.net.id; internet www.penerbitdiponegoro.com; f. 1963; Islamic, textbooks, fiction, non-fiction, general; Dir HADIDJAH DAHLAN.

Epsilon Group: Jalan Marga Asri 3, Margacinta, Bandung 40287; tel. (22) 7567826; f. 1985; school textbooks; Dir Drs BAHRUDIN.

Eresco PT: Jalan Megger Girang 98, Bandung 40254; tel. (22) 5205985; fax (22) 5205984; f. 1957; scientific and general; Man. Drs ARFAN ROZALI.

Ganeca Exact Bandung: Jalan Kiaracondong 167, Pagauban, Bandung 40283; tel. (22) 701519; fax (22) 775329; f. 1982; school textbooks; Dir Ir KETUT SUARDHARA LINGGIH.

Mizan Pustaka PT: Jalan Cinambo 135, Bandung 40294; tel. (22) 7834310; fax (22) 7834311; e-mail info@mizan.com; internet www.mizan.com; f. 1983; Islamic and general books; Pres. Dir HAIDAR BAGIR.

Penerbit ITB: Jalan Ganesa 10, Bandung 40132; tel. and fax (22) 2504257; e-mail itbpress@bdg.centrin.net.id; f. 1971; academic books; Dir EMMY SUPARKA; Chief Editor SOFIA MANSOOR-NIKSOLIHIN.

Putra A. Bardin: Jalan Ganesa 4, Bandung; tel. (22) 2504319; f. 1998; textbooks, scientific and general; Dir NAI A. BARDIN.

Remaja Rosdakarya PT: Jalan Ciateul 34–36, POB 284, Bandung 40252; tel. (22) 5200287; fax (22) 5202529; textbooks and children's fiction; Pres. ROZALI USMAN.

Sarana Panca Karyam PT: Jalan Kopo 633 KM 13/4, Bandung 40014; f. 1986; general; Dir WIMPY S. IBRAHIM.

Tarsito PT: Jalan Guntur 20, Bandung 40262; tel. (22) 304915; fax (22) 314630; academic; Dir T. SITORUS.

Flores

Nusa Indah: Jalan El Tari, Ende 86318, Flores; tel. (0381) 21502; fax (0381) 23974; e-mail namkahu@yahoo.com; f. 1970; religious and general; Dir LUKAS BATMOMOLIN.

Kudus

Menara Kudus: Jalan Menara 4, Kudus 59315; tel. (291) 371143; fax (291) 36474; f. 1958; Islamic; Man. CHILMAN NAJIB.

INDONESIA

Medan

Hasmar: Jalan Letjenderal Haryono M. T. 1, POB 446, Medan 20231; tel. (61) 24181; f. 1962; primary school textbooks; Dir FAUZI LUBIS; Man. AMRAN SAID RANGKUTI.

Impola: Jalan H. M. Joni 46, Medan 20217; tel. (61) 711415; f. 1984; school textbooks; Dir PAMILANG M. SITUMORANG.

Madju Medan Cipta PT: Jalan Amaliun 37, Medan 20215; tel. (61) 7361990; fax (61) 7367753; e-mail koboi@indosat.net; f. 1950; textbooks, children's and general; Pres. H. MOHAMED ARBIE; Man. Dir Drs DINO IRSAN ARBIE.

Masco: Jalan Sisingamangaraja 191, Medan 20218; tel. (61) 713375; f. 1992; school textbooks; Dir P. M. SITUMORANG.

Monora: Jalan Letjenderal Jamin Ginting 583, Medan 20156; tel. (61) 8212667; fax (61) 8212669; e-mail monora_cv@plasa.com; f. 1962; school textbooks; Dir CHAIRIL ANWAR.

Semarang

Aneka Ilmu: Jalan Raya Semarang Demak Km 8.5, Sayung, Demak; tel. (24) 6580335; fax (24) 6582903; e-mail pemasaran@anekailmu.com; internet www.anekailmu.com; f. 1983; general and school textbooks; Dir H. SUWANTO.

Effhar COY PT: Jalan Dorang 7, Semarang 50173; tel. (24) 3511172; fax (24) 3551540; e-mail effhar_dahara@yahoo.com; f. 1976; general books; Dir H. DARADJAT HARAHAP.

Intan Pariwara: Jalan Beringin, Klaten Utara, Kotak Pos III, Kotif Klaten, Jawa-Tengah; tel. (272) 322441; fax (272) 322607; e-mail intan@intanpariwara.co.id; internet www.intanpariwara.co.id; school textbooks; Pres. CHRIS HARJANTO.

Mandira PT: Jalan Letjenderal M. T. Haryono 501, Semarang 50241; tel. (24) 316150; fax (24) 415092; f. 1962; Dir Ir A. HARIYANTO.

Mandira Jaya Abadi PT: Jalan Letjenderal M. T. Haryono 501, Semarang 50241; tel. (24) 519547; fax (24) 542189; e-mail mjabadi@indosat.net.id; f. 1981; Dir Ir A. HARIYANTO.

Solo

Pabelan PT: Jalan Raya Pajang, Kertasura KM 8, Solo 57162; tel. (271) 743975; fax (271) 714775; f. 1983; school textbooks; Dir AGUNG SASONGKO.

Tiga Serangkai PT: Jalan Dr Supomo 23, Solo; tel. (271) 714344; fax (271) 713607; f. 1977; school textbooks; Dir ABDULLAH.

Surabaya

Airlangga University Press: Kampus C, Jalan Mulyorejo, Surabaya 60115; tel. (31) 5992246; fax (31) 5992248; e-mail aupsby@rad.net.id; academic; Dir Dr ARIFAAN RAZAK.

Bina Ilmu PT: Jalan Tunjungan 53E, Surabaya 60275; tel. (31) 5323214; fax (31) 5315421; f. 1973; school textbooks, Islamic; Pres. ARIEFIN NOOR.

Bintang: Jalan Potroagung III/41C, Surabaya; tel. (31) 3770687; fax (31) 3715941; school textbooks; Dir AGUS WINARNO.

Grip PT: Jalan Rungkut Permai II/C–11, Surabaya; tel. (31) 22564; f. 1958; textbooks and general; Man. SURIPTO.

Jaya Baya: Jalan Embong Malang 69H, POB 250, Surabaya 60001; tel. (31) 41169; f. 1945; religion, philosophy and ethics; Man. TADJIB ERMADI.

Sinar Wijaya: Jalan Raya Sawo VII/58, Bringin-Lakarsantri, Surabaya; tel. (31) 706615; general; Dir DULRADJAK.

Yogyakarta

Andi Publishers: Jalan Beo 38–40, Yogyakarta 55281; tel. (274) 561881; fax (274) 588282; e-mail andi_pub@indo.net.id; f. 1980; Christian, computing, business, management and technical; Dir J. H. GONDOWIJOYO.

BPFE PT: Jalan Gambiran 37, Yogyakarta 55161; tel. (274) 373760; fax (274) 380819; f. 1984; university textbooks; Dir Drs INDRIYO GITOSUDARMO.

Centhini Yayasan: Gg. Bekisar UH V/716 E–1, Yogyakarta 55161; tel. (274) 383148; f. 1984; Javanese culture; Chair. H. KARKONO KAMAJAYA.

Gadjah Mada University Press: Jalan Grafika 1, Kampus UGM, Bulaksumur, Yogyakarta 55281; tel. and fax (274) 561037; e-mail gmupress@ugm.ac.id; internet www.gmup.ugm.ac.id; f. 1971; university textbooks; Dir BAMBANG PURWONO.

Indonesia UP: Gg. Bekisar UH V/716 E–1, Yogyakarta 55161; tel. (274) 383148; f. 1950; general science; Dir H. KARKONO KAMAJAYA.

Kanisius Printing and Publishing: Jalan Cempaka 9, Deresan, Yogyakarta 55281; tel. (274) 588783; fax (274) 563349; e-mail office@kanisiusmedia.com; internet www.kanisiusmedia.com; f. 1922; philosophy, children's, textbooks, Christian and general; Pres. Dir S. J. SARWANTO.

Kedaulatan Rakyat PT: Jalan P. Mangkubumi 40–42, Yogyakarta; tel. (274) 2163; Dir DRONO HARDJUSUWONGSO.

Penerbit Tiara Wacana Yogya: Jalan Kaliurang KM 7, 8 Kopen 16, Banteng, Yogyakarta 55581; tel. and fax (274) 880683; f. 1986; university textbooks and general science; Dir SITORESMI PRABUNINGRAT.

Government Publishing House

Balai Pustaka PT (Persero) (State Publishing and Printing House): Jalan Gunung Sahari Raya 4, Gedung Balai Pustaka, 7th Floor, Jakarta Pusat 10710; tel. (21) 3447003; fax (21) 3446555; e-mail mail@balaiperaga.com; history, anthropology, politics, philosophy, medical, arts and literature; Pres. Dir H. R. SISWADI IDRIS.

PUBLISHERS' ASSOCIATION

Ikatan Penerbit Indonesia (IKAPI) (Asscn of Indonesian Book Publishers): Jalan Kalipasir 32, Jakarta Pusat 10330; tel. (21) 3141907; fax (21) 3146050; e-mail sekretariat@ikapi.or.id; f. 1950; 689 mems (July 2005); Pres. MAKFUDIN WIRYA ATMAJA; Sec.-Gen. ROBINSON RUSDI.

Broadcasting and Communications

TELECOMMUNICATIONS

Directorate-General of Posts and Telecommunications (Postel): Gedung Sapta Pesona, Jalan Medan Merdeka Barat 17, Jakarta 10110; tel. (21) 3835955; fax (21) 3860754; e-mail admin@postel.go.id; internet www.postel.go.id; Dir-Gen. BASUKI YUSUF ISKANDAR.

PT Excelcomindo Pratama Tbk (Excelcom): Jalan Mega Kuningan Lot E4-7 1, Kawasan Mega Kuningan, Jakarta 12950; tel. (21) 5761881; fax (21) 57959036; e-mail corpcomm@xl.co.id; internet www.xl.co.id; f. 1996; fixed-line and cellular telephone network provider; Pres. Dir CHRISTIAN M. DE FARIA.

PT Hutchison CP Telecommunications (HCPT): Wisma Barito Pacific, Tower II, 2nd Floor, Jalan Letjenderal S. Parman, Kav. 62–63, Slipi, Jakarta 11410; tel. (21) 53650000; fax (21) 53660000; internet www.three.co.id; f. 2003, as PT Cyber Access Communications; name changed as above in 2005; 60% stake owned by Hutchison Telecom International Ltd (Hong Kong), 40% stake owned by Charoen Pokphand Group (Thailand); cellular telephone network operator providing GSM 1800 and third-generation (3G) video services; CEO LAURENTIUS BULTERS.

PT Indonesian Satellite Corporation Tbk (INDOSAT): Jalan Medan Merdeka Barat 21, POB 2905, Jakarta 10110; tel. (21) 30003001; fax (21) 3804045; e-mail icare@indosat.com; internet www.indosat.com; f. 1967; telecommunications; partially privatized in 1994; 41.94% stake sold to Singapore Technologies Telemedia in 2002; Pres. Dir JOHNY SWANDI SJAM; Pres. Commr PETER SEAH LIM HUAT.

PT Mobile-8 Telecom (Tbk): Menara Kebon Sirih, 18th Floor, Jalan Kebon Sirih, Kav. 17–19, Jakarta 10340; tel. (21) 3920218; fax (21) 3920129; e-mail recruitment@mobile-8.com; internet www.mobile-8.com; 2m. subscribers (2007); Pres. Dir HIDAJAT TJANDRADJAJA.

PT Natrindo Telepon Seluler (Lippo Telecom): Jalan Pemuda 24, Surabaya; tel. (31) 5343988; e-mail careline@lippotel.com; internet www.lippotel.com/en/default.asp; f. 2001; cellular telephone network operator; provides GSM 1800 and 3G video services; Pres. Commr Dato' JAMALUDIN BIN IBRAHIM; Pres. Dir and CEO KUSNADI SUKARJA.

PT Satelit Palapa Indonesia (SATELINDO): Jalan Daan Mogot Km 11, Jakarta 11710; tel. (21) 5455121; fax (21) 5418548; e-mail palapa-c@satelindo.co.id; internet satelindo.boleh.com; f. 1993; owned by INDOSAT; telecommunications and satellite services; Pres. Dir DJOKO PRAJITNO.

PT Telekomunikasi Indonesia Tbk (TELKOM): Corporate Office, Jalan Japati No. 1, Bandung 40133; tel. (22) 4521405; fax (22) 7206757; internet www.telkom.co.id; domestic telecommunications; 24.2% of share capital was transferred to the private sector in 1995; Pres. Commr TANRI ABENG; CEO RINALDI FIRMANSYAH.

PT Telekomunikasi Selular (TELKOMSEL): Gedung Atrium Mulia, Jalan H.R. Rasuna Said, Kav. B10–11, Kuningan, Jakarta 12920; tel. (21) 52919811; fax (21) 5222080; internet www.telkomsel.com; f. 1995; provides domestic cellular services with international roaming available through 356 network partners; jt venture between PT Telekomunikasi Indonesia Tbk (65%) and Singapore Telecommunications Ltd (35%); Pres. Commr RINALDI FIRMANSYAH; Pres. Dir KISKENDA SURIAHARDJA.

INDONESIA

BROADCASTING

Regulatory Authority

Directorate-General of Radio, Television and Film: Jalan Merdeka Barat 9, Jakarta 10110; tel. (21) 3846740; fax (21) 3813170; Dir-Gen. DEWABRATA KOBARSJIH.

Radio

Radio Republik Indonesia (RRI): Jalan Medan Merdeka Barat 4–5, Jakarta 10110; tel. (21) 3846817; fax (21) 3457134; e-mail rri@rri-online.com; internet www.rri-online.com; f. 1945; 49 stations; Dir PARNI HADI.

Voice of Indonesia: Jalan Medan Merdeka Barat 4–5, POB 1157, Jakarta; tel. (21) 3456811; fax (21) 3500990; e-mail voi@rri-online.com; international service provided by Radio Republik Indonesia; daily broadcasts in Arabic, English, French, German, Bahasa Indonesia, Japanese, Bahasa Malaysia, Mandarin, Spanish and Thai.

Television

In March 1989 Indonesia's first private commercial television station began broadcasting to the Jakarta area. In 2008 there were 10 privately owned television stations in operation.

PT Cakrawala Andalas Televisi (ANTEVE): Gedung Sentra Mulia, 18th Floor, Jalan H. R. Rasuna Said, Kav. X-6 No. 8, Jakarta Selatan 12940; tel. (21) 5222086; fax (21) 5277068; e-mail humas@an.tv; internet www.an.tv; f. 1993; private channel; broadcasting to 10 cities; Pres. Commr PAUL FRANCIS AIELLO; Pres. Dir ANINDYA N. BAKRIE.

PT CIPTA TPI: Jalan Pintu II—Taman Mini Indonesia Indah, Pondok Gede, Jakarta Timur 13810; tel. (21) 8412473; fax (21) 8412470; e-mail info@tpi.tv; internet www.tpi.tv; f. 1991; private channel funded by commercial advertising; Pres. Commr DANDY NUGROHO RUKMANA; Pres. Dir SANG NYOMAN SUWISMA.

PT Rajawali Citra Televisi Indonesia (RCTI): Jalan Raya Pejuangan 3, Kebon Jeruk, Jakarta 11000; tel. (21) 5303540; fax (21) 5493852; e-mail webmaster@rcti.tv; internet www.rcti.tv; f. 1989; first private channel; 20-year licence; Pres. Dir M. TACHRIL SAPTIE; Vice-Pres. Commr BAMBANG RUDIJANTO TANOESOEDIBJO.

PT Surya Citra Televisi (SCTV): GRHA SCTV, 2nd Floor, Jalan Gatot Subroto, Kav. 21, Jakarta 12930; tel. (21) 5225555; fax (21) 5224777; e-mail pr@sctv.co.id; internet www.sctv.co.id; f. 1990; private channel broadcasting nationally; Pres. Dir FOFO SARIAATMADJA.

Televisi Republik Indonesia (TVRI): TVRI Senayan, Jalan Gerbang Pemuda, Senayan, Jakarta 10270; tel. (21) 5704720; fax (21) 5731973; e-mail support@tvri.co.id; internet www.tvri.co.id; f. 1962; fmrly state-controlled; became independent in 2003; Pres. Dir Maj.-Gen. (retd) I GDE NYOMAN ARSANA.

Finance

(cap. = capital; p.u. = paid up; res = reserves; dep. = deposits; m. = million; brs = branches; amounts in rupiah)

BANKING

Central Bank

Bank Indonesia (BI): Jalan M. H. Thamrin 2, Jakarta Pusat 10350; tel. (21) 3817187; fax (21) 3501867; e-mail humasbi@bi.go.id; internet www.bi.go.id; f. 1828; nationalized as central bank in 1953; cap. 2,948,029m., res 94,214,866m., dep. 402,286,316m. (Dec. 2006); Gov. BOEDIONO; 42 brs.

State Banks

PT Bank Ekspor Indonesia (Persero) (BEI): Gedung Bursa Efek, Menara II, Lt. 8, Jalan Jenderal Sudirman, Kav. 52–53, Jakarta; tel. (21) 5154638; fax (21) 5154639; e-mail webmaster@bexi.co.id; internet www.bexi.co.id; cap. 3,000,000m., dep. 2,140,066m., res 731,148m. (Dec. 2006); Pres. Commr MUKHLIS RASYID; Pres. Dir ARIFIN INDRA SULISTYANTO.

PT Bank Mandiri (Persero): Plaza Mandiri, Jalan Jenderal Gatot Subroto, Kav. 36–38, Jakarta 12190; tel. (21) 52997777; fax (21) 52997735; internet www.bankmandiri.co.id; f. 1998; est. following merger of four state-owned banks—PT Bank Bumi Daya, PT Bank Dagang Negara, PT Bank Ekspor Impor Indonesia and PT Bank Pembangunan Indonesia; cap. 10,315,609m., res 9,911,971m., dep. 216,528,790m. (Dec. 2006); Chair. EDWIN GERUNGAN; Pres. Dir and CEO AGUS MARTOWARDOJO; 909 local brs; 6 overseas brs.

PT Bank Negara Indonesia (Persero) Tbk: Jalan Jenderal Sudirman, Kav. 1, Jakarta 10220; tel. (21) 2511946; fax (21) 2511221; e-mail hin@bni.co.id; internet www.bni.co.id; f. 1946; commercial bank; specializes in credits to the industrial sector; cap. 7,042,194m., res 5,012,064m., dep. 140,328,329m. (Dec. 2006); Pres. Commr ERY RIYANA HARDJAPAMEKAS; Pres. Dir GATOT MUDIANTORO SUWONDO; 585 local brs, 5 overseas brs.

PT Bank Rakyat Indonesia (Persero): Jalan Jenderal Sudirman, Kav. 44–46, POB 94, Jakarta 10210; tel. (21) 2510244; fax (21) 2500077; internet www.bri.co.id; f. 1895; present name since 1946; commercial and foreign exchange bank; specializes in agricultural smallholdings and rural devt; cap. 6,143,211m., res 3,296,417m., dep. 128,820,268m. (Dec. 2006); Pres. Dir SOFYAN BASIR; 326 brs.

PT Bank Tabungan Negara (Persero): 10th Floor, Bank BTN Tower, Jalan Gajah Mada 1, Jakarta 10130; tel. (21) 6336789; fax (21) 6336704; e-mail webadmin@btn.co.id; internet www.btn.co.id; f. 1964; commercial bank; state-owned; cap. 1,250,000m., res 14,231,094m., dep. 19,841,506m. (Dec. 2005); Pres. Commr DONO ISKANDAR DJOJOSUBROTO; Pres. Dir KODRADI; 44 brs.

PT BPD Jawa Timur (Bank Jatim): Jalan Basuki Rachmad 98–104, Surabaya; tel. (31) 5310090; fax (31) 5312226; f. 1961; cap. 321,636m., res 113,788m., dep. 6,643,440m. (Dec. 2003); Chair. NANIK KUSMINI; Pres. AGUS SULAKSONO.

Commercial Banks

PT ANZ Panin Bank: Panin Bank Centre, Ground Floor, Jalan Jenderal Sudirman (Senayan), Jakarta 10270; tel. (21) 5750300; fax (21) 5727447; e-mail products@anz.com; internet www.anz.com/indonesia; f. 1990; est. as Westpac Panin Bank; name changed as above in 1993; 85% owned by the Australia and New Zealand Banking Group Ltd; cap. 50,000m., res. 10,000m., dep. 3,725,520m. (Dec. 2006); Pres. Dir JOHN M. COLLINS.

PT Bank Artha Graha: Bank Artha Graha Tower, 5th Floor, Jalan Jenderal Sudirman, Kav. 52–53, Jakarta 12190; tel. (21) 5152168; fax (21) 5152162; e-mail agraha@rad.net.id; f. 1967; est. as PT Bank Bandung; merged with PT Bank Arta Pratama in 1999; cap. 558,840m., res 422,710m., dep. 9,226,191m. (Dec. 2006); Pres. and Dir FRANCISCUS THE F. K.; Chair. LETJEN; 78 brs.

PT Bank Bumiputera Indonesia Tbk: Wisma Bumiputra, 14th Floor, Jalan Jenderal Sudirman, Kav. 75, Jakarta 12910; tel. (21) 5701626; fax (21) 5701635; e-mail bank@bumiputera.co.id; internet www.bumiputera.co.id; f. 1989; cap. 500,000m., res 7,845.7m., dep. 4,814,196m. (Dec. 2006); Pres. Commr Tan Sri Dr HADENAN A. JALIL; Pres. Dir PALANIAPPAN MURUGAPPA CHETTIAR.

PT Bank Central Asia Tbk (BCA): Wisma BCA, 5th Floor, Jalan Jenderal Sudirman, Kav. 22–23, Jakarta 12920; tel. (21) 52999888; fax (21) 5701865; e-mail humas@bca.co.id; internet www.klikbca.com; f. 1957; placed under the supervision of the Indonesian Bank Restructuring Agency (IBRA) in May 1998; 51% share sold to Farallon Capital Management (USA) in March 2002; cap. 1,540,938m., res 4,969,948m., dep. 155,214,787m. (Dec. 2006); Pres. Commr EUGENE KEITH GALBRAITH; Pres. Dir DJOHAN EMIR SETIJOSO; 760 local brs.

PT Bank Chinatrust Indonesia: 16th and 17th Floors, Wisma Tamara, Jalan Jenderal Sudirman, Kav. 24, Jakarta 12920; tel. (21) 5207878; fax (21) 5206767; e-mail ctcbjak@rad.net.id; f. 1995; cap. 150,000m., dep. 2,815,141m. (Dec. 2006); Pres. Dir JOHN TENG; Chair. JEFFREY L. S. KOO.

PT Bank Danamon Indonesia Tbk: Menara Danamon, Jalan Prof. Dr Satrio 6, Kav. E/4, Mega Kuningan, Jakarta 12930; tel. (21) 34358888; fax (21) 57991008; e-mail danamon.access@danamon.co.id; internet www.danamon.co.id; f. 1956; placed under the supervision of the IBRA in April 1998; merged with PT Bank Tiara Asia, PT Tamara Bank, PT Bank Duta and PT Bank Nusa Nasional in 2000; 51% share sold to consortium led by Singapore's Temasek Holdings in May 2003; cap. 3,569,247m., res 67,945m., dep. 51,309,597m. (Dec. 2005); Pres. Commr NG KEE CHOE; Pres. Dir SEBASTIAN PAREDES; 737 brs.

PT Bank Internasional Indonesia Tbk (BII): Plaza BII, Jalan M. H. Thamrin 51, Kav. 22, Jakarta 10350; tel. (21) 3183888; fax (21) 2301494; e-mail cs@bii.co.id; internet www.bii.co.id; cap. 3,226,627m., res 363,558m., dep. 40,537,574m. (Dec. 2006); Pres. Commr PETER SEAH LIM HUAT; Pres. Dir HENRY HO HON CHEONG; 246 local brs; 3 overseas brs.

PT Bank KEB Indonesia: Suite 1201, 12th Floor, Wisma GKBI, Jalan Jenderal Sudirman, Kav. 28, Selatan, Jakarta; tel. (21) 5741030; fax (21) 5741032; e-mail compliance@kebi.co.id; internet www.keb.co.kr; owned by KEB Seoul (99%) and PT Clemont Finance Indonesia (1%); f. 1990; fmrly PT Korea Exchange Bank Danamon; cap. 150,000m., dep. 953,781m. (Dec. 2005); Pres. CHONG SOO CHO; Chair. HO SUN YUN.

PT Bank Mayapada Internasional Tbk: Gedung Mayapada Tower, Jalan Jenderal Sudirman, Kav. 28, Jakarta 12920; tel. (21) 5212288; fax (21) 5211985; e-mail mayapada@bankmayapada.com; internet www.bankmayapada.com; f. 1989; cap. 284,129m., res 16,440m., dep. 3,069,375m. (Dec. 2006); Chair. TAHIR; Pres. Dir Ir HENDRA MULYONO; 28 brs.

INDONESIA

PT Bank Mizuho Indonesia: Plaza B11, 24th Floor, Menara 2, Jalan M. H. Thamrin 51, Jakarta 10350; tel. (21) 3925222; fax (21) 3926354; f. f. 1989; fmrly PT Bank Fuji International Indonesia; name changed as above in 2001; cap. 396,250m., res 11,121m., dep. 4,603,212m. (Dec. 2005); Pres. Dir ATSUSHI HITANO.

PT Bank Muamalat Indonesia (BMI): Gedung Arthaloka, Jalan Jenderal Sudirman 2, Jakarta 10220; tel. (21) 2511414; fax (21) 2511453; internet www.muamalatbank.com; Indonesia's first Islamic bank; cap. 165,593m. (July 2000); Pres. Dir A. RIAWAN AMIN; Chair. SAHAL MAHFUDH.

PT Bank Niaga Tbk: Graha Niaga, Jalan Jenderal Sudirman, Kav. 58, Jakarta 12190; tel. (21) 2505252; fax (21) 2505205; e-mail caniaga@attglobal.net; internet www.bankniaga.com; f. 1955; cap. 958,880m., res 2,343,570m., dep. 39,306,400m. (Dec. 2006); Pres. Commr Dato' HALIM BIN MUHAMAT; Pres. Dir PETER B. STOK; 168 brs.

PT Bank NISP Tbk: Jalan Taman Cibeunying Selatan 31, Jakarta 40114; tel. (22) 7234123; fax (22) 7100466; e-mail nisp@banknisp.com; internet www.banknisp.com; f. 1941; cap. 616,996m., res 521,643m., dep. 16,716,922m. (Dec. 2005); Pres. Commr KAMAKA SURJAUDAJA; Pres. Dir PRAMUKTI SURJAUDAJA; 168 brs.

PT Bank Permata Tbk: PermataBank Tower I, 17th Floor, Jalan Jenderal Sudirman, Kav. 27, Jakarta 12920; tel. (21) 5237899; fax (21) 5237253; e-mail isaptono@permatabank.co.id; internet www.permatabank.com; f. 1954; est. as Bank Persatuan Dagang Indonesia; became PT Bank Bali in 1971 and PT Bank Bali Tbk in 1990; name changed as above Sept. 2002 following merger with PT Bank Prima Express, PT Bank Universal Tbk, PT Arthamedia Bank and PT Bank Patriot; cap. 1,300,534m., res 6,686,532m., dep. 31,608,121m. (Dec. 2006); Pres. Commr Dr MULIA P. NASUTION; Pres. Dir and Chair. STEWART D. HALL; 307 brs.

PT Bank Rabobank International Indonesia: Plaza 89, 9th Floor, Jalan H. R. Rasuna Said, Kav. X-7 No. 6, Jakarta 12940; tel. (21) 2520876; fax (21) 2520875; e-mail indonesia@rabobank.com; internet www.rabobank.com; f. 1990; est. as PT Rabobank Duta Indonesia; name changed as above in 2001 when Rabobank Nederland secured sole ownership; cap. 600,000m., res 2,741m., dep. 1,568,685m. (Dec. 2006); Pres. Commr HUMAYUNBOSHA; Pres. Dir ANTONIO DA SILVA COSTA.

PT Bank Sumitomo Mitsui Indonesia: Gedung Summitmas II, 10th Floor, Jalan Jenderal Sudirman, Kav. 61–62, Jakarta 12190; tel. (21) 5227011; fax (21) 5227022; internet www.smbc-jkt.co.id; f. 1989; fmrly PT Bank Sumitomo Indonesia, merged with PT Bank Sakura Swadharma in April 2001; cap. 1,502,441m., res −517,642m., dep. 3,271,792m. (Dec. 2006); Pres. Commr HIROSHI MINOURA; Pres. Dir SHINICHI SHIMURA; 1 br.

PT Bank UOB Buana Tbk: Jalan Asemka 32–36, Jakarta 11110; tel. (21) 2601015; fax (21) 2601013; e-mail cir@bankbuanaina.co.id; internet www.bankbuana.com; f. 1956; fmrly PT Bank Buana Indonesia Tbk; cap. 1,663,339m., res 920,424m., dep. 12,995,568m. (Dec. 2006); Pres. Commr WEE CHO YAW; Pres. Dir ARMAND B. ARIEF; 31 brs.

PT Bank UOB Indonesia: Sona Topas Tower, 1st–3rd Floors, Jalan Jenderal Sudirman, Kav. 26, Jakarta 12920; tel. (21) 2506330; fax (21) 2506331; e-mail uob.jakarta@uobgroup.com; internet www.uobgroup.com; 99%-owned by United Overseas Bank Ltd, Singapore; cap. 520,000m., res 10,841m., dep. 3,706,109m. (Dec. 2006); Chair. WEE CHO YAW; Pres. Dir CHUA KIM HAY; 9 brs.

PT Hagabank: Jalan Abdul Muis 28, Jakarta 10160; tel. (21) 2312021; fax (21) 2312250; e-mail info@hagabank.com; internet www.hagabank.com; f. 1989; cap. 65,000m., res 41,897m., dep. 3,813,329m. (Dec. 2006); Pres. Dir DANNY HARTONO; Chair. TIMOTY E. MARNANDUS; 48 brs.

PT Lippo Bank Tbk: Gedung Menara Asia, 20th Floor, Jalan Raya Diponegoro 101, Lippo Karawaci, Tangerang 15810; tel. (21) 5460555; fax (21) 5460816; e-mail info_crc@lippobank.co.id; internet www.lippobank.co.id; f. 1948; est. as NV Bank Perniagaan; name changed as above in 1998; cap. 811,494m., res 10,526,683m., dep. 27,259,675m. (Dec. 2006); Pres. Commr ALI DEWAL; Pres. Dir Dr JOS LUHUKAY; 397 brs, 21 sub-brs.

PT Pan Indonesia Tbk (Panin Bank): Panin Bank Centre, 11th Floor, Jalan Jenderal Sudirman, Senayan, Jakarta 10270; tel. (21) 2700545; fax (21) 2700340; e-mail panin@panin.co.id; internet www.panin.co.id; f. 1971; est. as a result of the merger of three private national banks; cap. 2,008,179m., res 2,987,694m., dep. 28,680,210m. (Dec. 2006); Pres. Commr JOHNNY N. WIRAATMADJA; Pres. Dir Drs H. ROSTIAN SJAMSUDIN; 138 local brs, 2 overseas brs.

PT Woori Bank Indonesia: Jakarta Stock Exchange Bldg, Jalan Jenderal Sudirman, Kav. 52–53, Jakarta 12190; tel. (21) 5151919; fax (21) 5151477; e-mail wooridealingroom@yahoo.com; fmrly PT Hanvit Bank Indonesia; cap. 170,000m., dep. 1,503,277m. (Dec. 2005); Pres. IN CHUL PARK; Chair. A. T. PRASTOWO.

Banking Association

The Association of Indonesian National Private Commercial Banks (Perhimpunan Bank-Bank Umum Nasional Swasta—PERBANAS): Jalan Perbanas, Karet Kuningan, Setiabudi, Jakarta 12940; tel. (21) 5223038; fax (21) 5223037; e-mail secretariat@perbanas.org; internet www.perbanas.org; f. 1952; 94 mems; Chair. SIGIT PRAMONO; Sec.-Gen. TIMOTY E. MARNANDUS.

STOCK EXCHANGE

Indonesia Stock Exchange (ISX): Indonesia Stock Exchange Bldg, Jalan Jenderal Sudirman, Kav. 52–53, Jakarta 12190; tel. (21) 5150515; fax (21) 5150330; e-mail webmaster@jsx.co.id; internet www.isx.co.id; fmrly Jakarta Stock Exchange; name changed as above upon merger with Surabaya Stock Exchange in 2007; 128 securities houses constitute the members and the shareholders of the exchange, each company owning one share; Pres. Dir ERRY FIRMANSYAH.

Regulatory Authority

Badan Pengawas Pasar Modal (BAPEPAM) (Capital Market Supervisory Agency): Gedung Baru Depkeu RI, Lt. 4, Jalan Dr Wahidin Raya, Jakarta 10710; tel. (21) 3858001; fax (21) 3857917; e-mail bapepam@bapepam.go.id; internet www.bapepam.go.id; Chair. A. FAUD RAHMANY; Exec. Sec. NGALIM SAWEGA.

INSURANCE

In August 2006 there were 157 insurance companies, including 97 non-life companies, 51 life companies, four reinsurance companies and two social insurance companies.

Insurance Supervisory Authority of Indonesia: Directorate of Financial Institutions, Jalan Dr Wahidin, Jakarta 10710; tel. (21) 3451210; fax (21) 3849504; wing of the Ministry of Finance; Dir H. FIRDAUS DJAELANI.

Selected Life Insurance Companies

PT Asuransi AIA Indonesia: Gedung Bank Panin Senayan, 7th and 8th Floors, Jalan Jenderal Sudirman, Senayan, Jakarta 10270; tel. (21) 5721388; fax (21) 5721389; e-mail aiai.customer-service@aig.com; internet www.aia.co.id; f. 1975; Pres. Dir HARRY HARMAIN DIAH.

PT Asuransi Allianz Life Indonesia: Gedung Summitmas II, 20th Floor, Jalan Jenderal Sudirman, Kav. 61–62, Jakarta 12190; tel. (21) 52998888; fax (21) 2526953; e-mail general@allianz.co.id; internet www.allianz.co.id; f. 1996; Pres. Dir Dr JENS REISCH.

Asuransi Jiwa Bersama Bumiputera 1912: Wisma Bumiputera, 17th–21st Floors, Jalan Jenderal Sudirman, Kav. 75, Jakarta 12910; tel. (21) 2512154; fax (21) 2512172; e-mail humas@bumiputera.com; internet www.bumiputera.com; Chair. Prof. Dr Ir H. SOLEH SOLAHUDDIN; Pres. Dir SOESENO HARIO SAPUTRO.

PT Asuransi Jiwa Central Asia Raya: Blue Dot Center Blok A-C, Jalan Gelong Baru Utara 5–8, Jakarta Barat 11440; tel. (21) 56961929; fax (21) 56961939; e-mail lancar@car.co.id; internet www.car.co.id; Chair. SOEDONO SALIM.

PT Asuransi Jiwa 'Panin Putra': Jalan Pintu Besar Selatan 52A, Jakarta 11110; tel. (21) 672586; fax (21) 676354; f. 1974; Pres. Dir SUJONO SOEPENO; Chair. NUGROHO TJOKROWIRONO.

PT Asuransi Jiwasraya (Persero): Jalan H. Juanda 34, Jakarta 10120; tel. (21) 3845031; fax (21) 3862344; e-mail asuransi@jiwasraya.co.id; internet www.jiwasraya.co.id; f. 1959; Chief Commr MINTO WIDODO.

PT Asuransi Panin Life: Panin Bank Plaza, 5th Floor, Jalan Palmerah Utara 52, Jakarta 11480; tel. (21) 5484870; fax (21) 5484570; e-mail customer.service@paninlife.co.id; internet www.paninlife.co.id; Pres. MU'MIN ALI GUNAWAN; Dir FADJAR GUNAWAN.

Bumi Asih Jaya Life Insurance Co Ltd: Jalan Matraman Raya 165–167, Jakarta 13140; tel. (21) 2800700; fax (21) 8509669; e-mail baj@bajlife.com; internet www.bajlife.co.id; f. 1967; Chair. P. SITOMPUL; Pres. VIRGO HUTAGALUNG.

Selected Non-Life Insurance Companies

PT Asuransi Bina Dana Arta Tbk: Plaza ABDA, 27th Floor, Jalan Jenderal Sudirman, Kav. 59, Jakarta 122190; tel. (21) 51401688; fax (21) 51401698; internet www.abdainsurance.co.id; Chair. TJAN SOEN ENG; Pres. ROBERT SUTANTO.

PT Asuransi Bintang Tbk: Jalan R. S. Fatmawati 32, Jakarta Selatan 12430; tel. (21) 75902777; fax (21) 7506197; e-mail asuransibintang@asuransibintang.com; internet www.asuransibintang.com; f. 1955; general insurance; Chair. AMIR ABADI JUSUF; Pres. Dir MUHAIMIN IQBAL.

PT Asuransi Buana Independen: Jalan Pintu Besar Selatan 78, Jakarta 11110; tel. (21) 6904331; fax (21) 6263005; e-mail abipst99@indosat.net.id; Exec. Vice-Pres. SUSANTY PURNAMA.

INDONESIA

PT Asuransi Central Asia: Wisma Asia, 12th–15th Floors, Jalan Letjen S. Parman, Kav. 79, Slipi, Jakarta Barat 11420; tel. (21) 5637933; fax (21) 5638029; e-mail cust-aca@aca.co.id; internet www.aca.co.id; Pres. Commr ANTHONY SALIM; Pres. Dir TEDDY HAILAMSAH.

PT Asuransi Danamon: Gedung Danamon Asuransi, Jalan H. R. Rasuna Said, Kav. C10, Jakarta 12920; tel. (21) 516512; fax (21) 516832; Chair. USMAN ADMADJAJA; Pres. Dir OTIS WUISAN.

PT Asuransi Dayin Mitra: Jalan Raden Saleh Raya, Kav. 1 B–1D, Jakarta 10430; tel. (21) 3153577; fax (21) 3912902; e-mail nuning@dayinmitra.co.id; internet www.dayinmitra.co.id; f. 1982; general insurance; Man. Dir LARSOEN HAKER.

PT Asuransi Indrapura: Jakarta; tel. (21) 5703729; fax (21) 5705000; f. 1954; Pres. Dir ROBERT TEGUH.

PT Asuransi Jasa Indonesia: Jalan Letjenderal M. T. Haryono, Kav. 61, Jakarta 12041; tel. (21) 7994508; fax (21) 7995364; e-mail jasindo@jasindo.co.id; internet www.jasindo.co.id; Pres. Commr MOELYADI; Pres. Dir Drs EKO BUDIWIYONO.

PT Asuransi Jasa Tania: Wisma Jasa Tania, Lt. 3–4, Jalan Teuku Cik Ditiro 14, Jakarta 10350; tel. (21) 3101912; fax (21) 323089; e-mail ajstania@jasatania.co.id; internet www.jasatania.co.id; Pres. Drs DUDUH SADARACHMAT; Dir H. HARYANTO.

PT Asuransi Parolamas: Komplek Golden Plaza, Blok G 39–42, Jalan R. S. Farmawati 15, Jakarta 12420; tel. (21) 7508983; fax (21) 7506339; internet www.parolamas.co.id; Chief Commr TJUT ROEKMA RAFFLI; Pres. Dir Drs SYARIFUDDIN HARAHAP.

PT Asuransi Ramayana: Jalan Kebon Sirih 49, Jakarta 10340; tel. (21) 31937148; fax (21) 31934825; f. 1965; Chair. R. G. DOERIAT; Pres. Dir Dr A. WINOTO DOERIAT.

PT Asuransi Tri Pakarta: Jalan Paletehan I/18, Jakarta 12160; tel. (21) 711850; fax (21) 7394748; internet www.tripakarta.co.id; Chair. Drs SRI HARYANTO; Pres. SURANTO W. H.

PT Asuransi Wahana Tata: Jalan H. R. Rasuna Said, Kav. C-4, Jakarta 12920; tel. (21) 5202665; fax (21) 5203149; e-mail aswata@aswata.co.id; internet www.aswata.co.id; Chair. RUDY WANANDI; Pres. Dir ROBERT JEREMIA.

PT Berdikari Insurance: Jalan Merdeka Barat 1, Jakarta 10002; tel. (21) 3440266; fax (21) 3440586; e-mail ho@berdikari-insurance.com; internet www.berdikari-insurance.com; Pres. HOTBONAR SINAGA.

PT Asuransi Maipark Indonesia: Setiabudi Atrium Bldg, 4th Floor, Suite 408, Jalan H. R. Rasuna Said, Kav. 62, Jakarta 12920; tel. (21) 5210803; fax (21) 510738; e-mail maipark@maipark.com; internet www.maipark.com; fmrly PT Maskapai Asuransi Indonesia; Chair. FRANS Y. SAHUSILAWANE; Pres. Dir WERNER G. BUGL.

PT Tugu Pratama Indonesia: Wisma Tugu I, Jalan H. R. Rasuna Said, Kav. C8–9, Kuningan, Jakarta Selatan 12940; tel. (21) 52961777; fax (21) 52961555; e-mail tpi@tugu.com; internet www.tugu.com; f. 1981; general insurance; Chair. ACHMAD FAISAL; Pres. Dir M. AFDAL BAHAUDIN.

Joint Ventures

PT Asuransi AIG Life: Matahari AIG Lippo Cyber Tower, 5th-7th Floors, Jalan Bulevar Palem Raya 7, Lippo Karawaci 1200, Tangerang 15811; tel. (21) 54218888; fax (21) 5475415; e-mail contact@aig-lippo.com; internet www.aig-lippo.com; jt venture between American International Group, Inc, and PT Asuransi Lippo Life; life insurance; Dep. Pres. Dir S. BUDISUHARTO.

PT Asuransi AIU Indonesia: The Indonesia Stock Exchange Bldg, Tower II, Floor 3A, Jalan Jenderal Sudirman, Kav. 52–53, Jakarta 12190; tel. (21) 52914888; fax (21) 52914889; e-mail aiu.indonesia@aig.com; Pres. Dir PETER MEYER; Vice-Pres. Dir SWANDI KENDY; Dir GUNAWAN TJIU.

PT Asuransi Allianz Utama Indonesia: Gedung Summitmas II, 9th Floor, Jalan Jenderal Sudirman, Kav. 61–62, Jakarta Selatan 12190; tel. (21) 2522470; fax (21) 2523246; e-mail general@allianz.co.id; internet www.allianz.co.id; f. 1989; non-life insurance; Chair. EDI SUBEKTI; Pres. Dir VICTOR SANDJAJA.

PT Asuransi Jiwa Manulife Indonesia: Jalan Pegangsaan Timur 1A, Jakarta 10320; tel. (21) 23559966; fax (21) 23559900; e-mail communication_id@manulife.com; internet www.manulife-indonesia.com; f. 1985; life insurance; Pres. Dir DAVID BEYNON.

PT Asuransi Jiwa Sinarmas: Wisma EKA Jiwa, 9th Floor, Jalan Mangga Dua Raya, Jakarta 10730; tel. (21) 6257808; fax (21) 6257837; e-mail cs@sinarmaslife.co.id; internet www.sinarmaslife.com; fmrly PT Asuransi Jiwa EKA Life.

PT Asuransi Mitsui Sumitomo Indonesia (MSI): Summitmas II Bldg, 15th Floor, Jalan Jenderal Sudirman, Kav. 61–62, Jakarta 12190; tel. (21) 2523110; fax (21) 2524307; e-mail msi@ms-ins.co.id; internet www.ms-ins.co.id; f. 1975 under the name PT Asuransi Mitsui Marine Indonesia; name changed as above in 2003 following merger with PT Asuransi Sumitomo Marine and Pool; Chair. RUDY WANANDI; Pres. Dir TADASHI MAEKAWA.

PT Asuransi Tokio Marine Indonesia: Sentral Senayan I, 4th Floor, Jalan Asia Afrika, No. 8, Jakarta 10270; tel. (21) 5725772; fax (21) 5724005; e-mail cp@tokiomarine.co.id; internet www.tokiomarine.co.id; jt venture between Tokio Marine Asia Pte Ltd and PT Asuransi Jasa Indonesia.

Insurance Associations

Asosiasi Asuransi Jiwa Indonesia (Indonesia Life Insurance Association): Grand International Trade Center, Complex Permata Hijau, Block Diamond G, No. 17, Jakarta 12210; tel. (21) 53664164; fax (21) 52664135; internet www.aaji.or.id; f. 2002; Co-Chairs JOHN HARRISON, ROBERT W. BUSH.

Asosiasi Asuransi Umum Indonesia (General Insurance Association of Indonesia): Jalan Majapahit 34, Blok V/29, Jakarta 10160; tel. (21) 3454387; fax (21) 3454307; e-mail aaui@aaui.or.id; internet www.aaui.or.id; f. 1957 as Dewan Asuransi Indonesia (Insurance Council of Indonesia); name changed as above 2003; Chair. FRANS SAHUSILAWANE; Exec. Dir ADRIAN J. K.

Trade and Industry

GOVERNMENT AGENCIES

Badan Pelaksana Kegiatan Usaha Hulu Minyak dan Gas Bumi (BP Migas): Gedung Patra Jasa, Lantai 1,2,13,14,16,21,22, Jalan Gatot Subroto, Kav. 32–34, Jakarta Selatan; tel. (21) 52900245; fax (21) 52900132; e-mail helpdesk@bpmigas.com; internet www.bpmigas.com; f. 2002; regulates upstream petroleum and natural gas industry; Chair. KARDAYA WARNIKA.

Badan Pengatur Hilir Minyak dan Gas Bumi (BPH Migas): Jalan Jenderal Gatot Subroto, Kav. 49, Jakarta 12950; tel. (21) 5254269; fax (21) 5207568; internet www.bphmigas.go.id; f. 2002; regulates downstream petroleum and gas industry; Chair. TUBAGUS HARYONO.

Badan Pengembangan Industri Strategis (BPIS) (Agency for Strategic Industries): Gedung Arthaloka, 3rd Floor, Jalan Jenderal Sudirman 2, Jakarta 10220; tel. (21) 5705335; fax (21) 3292516; f. 1989; co-ordinates production of capital goods.

Badan Pengkajian dan Penerapan Teknologi (BPPT) (Agency for the Assessment and Application of Technology): Jalan M. H. Thamrin 8, Jakarta 10340; tel. (21) 3168200; fax (21) 3904537; internet www.bppt.go.id; Chair. Prof. Ir SAID DJAIHARSYAH JENIE.

Badan Tenaga Nuklir Nasional (BATAN) (National Nuclear Energy Agency): Jalan Kuningan Barat, Mampang Prapatan, Jakarta 12710; tel. (21) 5251109; fax (21) 5251110; e-mail humas@batan.go.id; internet www.batan.go.id; Chair. Dr SOEDYARTOMO.

Badan Urusan Logistik (BULOG) (National Logistics Agency): Jalan Jenderal Gatot Subroto, Kav. 49, Jakarta 12950; tel. and fax (21) 5256482; e-mail rotu03@bulog.co.id; internet www.bulog.co.id; Chair. MUSTAFA ABUBAKAR.

National Agency for Export Development (NAFED): Jalan Kramat Raya 172, Jakarta 10430; tel. (21) 3100569; fax (21) 31904914; e-mail nafed@nafed.go.id; internet www.nafed.go.id; Chair. HATANTO REKSODIPOETRO (acting).

National Economic Council: Jakarta; f. 1999; 13-member council formed to advise the President on economic policy; Chair. EMIL SALIM; Sec.-Gen. Sri MULYANI INDRAWATI.

DEVELOPMENT ORGANIZATIONS

Badan Koordinasi Penanaman Modal (BKPM) (Investment Co-ordinating Board): Jalan Jenderal Gatot Subroto 44, POB 3186, Jakarta 12190; tel. (21) 5252008; fax (21) 5254945; e-mail sysadm@bkpm.go.id; internet www.bkpm.go.id; f. 1976; Chair. MUHAMMAD LUTFI.

Badan Perencanaan Pembangunan Nasional (Bappenas) (National Planning Development Board): Jalan Taman Suropati 2, Jakarta 10310; tel. (21) 3905650; fax (21) 3145374; e-mail admin@bappenas.go.id; internet www.bappenas.go.id; formulates Indonesia's economic devt plans; Chair. H. PASKAH SUZETTA.

CHAMBER OF COMMERCE

Kamar Dagang dan Industri Indonesia (KADIN) (Indonesian Chamber of Commerce and Industry): Menara Kadin Indonesia, Lantai 29, Jalan H. R. Rasuna Said X5, Kav. 2–3, Jakarta 12950; tel. (21) 5274484; fax (21) 5274331; e-mail kadin@kadin-indonesia.or.id; internet www.kadin-indonesia.or.id; f. 1969; 27 regional offices throughout Indonesia; Chair. MOHAMAD S. HIDAYAT; Sec.-Gen. Ir IMAN SUCIPTO UMAR.

INDUSTRIAL AND TRADE ASSOCIATIONS

Association of Indonesian Automotive Industries (GAIKINDO): Jalan H. O. S. Cokroaminoto 6, Jakarta Pusat 10350; tel. (21) 3157178; fax (21) 3142100; e-mail gaikindo@cbn.net.id; internet www.gaikindo.org; Chair. BAMBANG TRISULO.

Association of Indonesian Beverage Industries (ASRIM): Wisma GKBI, Jalan Jenderal Sudirman 28, Jakarta 10210; tel. (21) 5723838; fax (21) 5740817; 12 mems; Chair. MUGIJANTO; Sec.-Gen. SUROSO NATAKUSUMA.

Association of Indonesian Coffee Exporters (AIKE): Jalan R. P. Soeroso 20, Jakarta 10350; tel. (21) 3106768; fax (21) 3144115; e-mail aeki@indonesia.net.id; 800 mems; Chair. HASSAN WIDJAYA; Sec.-Gen. RACHIM KARTABRATA.

Association of State-Owned Companies: CTC Bldg, Jalan Kramat Raya 94–96, Jakarta; tel. (21) 346071; co-ordinates the activities of state-owned enterprises; Pres. ODANG.

Electric and Electronic Appliance Manufacturers' Association: Jalan Pangeran, Blok 20/A-1D, Jakarta; tel. (21) 6480059.

Importers' Association of Indonesia (GINSI): Wisma Kosgoro Bldg, 8th Floor, Jalan M. H. Thamrin 53, Jakarta 10350; tel. (21) 39832510; fax (21) 39832540; f. 1956; 2,921 mems (1996); Chair. AMIRUDIN SAUD; Sec.-Gen. DEDDY BINTANG.

Indonesian Cement Association (ICA): Graha Irama Bldg, 11th Floor, Suite 11G, Jalan H. R. Rasuna Said, Blok X-1, Kav. 1–2, Jakarta Selatan 12950; tel. (21) 5261174; fax (21) 5261176; e-mail info@asi.or.id; internet www.asi.or.id; f. 1969.

Indonesian Coal Mining Association (APBI-ICMA): Menara Kuningan Lt. 1, Jalan H. R. Rasuna Said, Blok X-7, Kav. 5, Jakarta 12940; tel. (21) 30015935; fax (21) 30015936; e-mail apbi-icma@indo.net.id; internet www.apbi-icma.com; 47 mems; Chair. JEFFREY MOLYONO; Sec.-Gen. Ir SOEDJOKO.

Indonesian Cocoa Association (ASKINDO): AEKI Bldg, Jalan R. P. Suroso, No. 20, Jakarta 10330; tel. (21) 3925053; fax (21) 3925024; internet www.askindo.org.

Indonesian Exporters' Federation: Menara Sudirman, 8th Floor, Jalan Jenderal Sudirman, Kav. 60, Jakarta 12190; tel. (21) 5226522; fax (21) 5203303; Chair. HAMID IBRAHIM GANIE.

Indonesian Food and Beverages Association (GAPMMI): Kantor Pusat Departemen Pertanian, Ground Floor, Lot 2, Jalan Harsono, Room No. 3, No. 224A Ragunan, Pasarminggu, Jakarta 12550; tel. (21) 70322627; fax (21) 7804347; e-mail gapmmi@cbn.net.id; internet www.gapmmi.or.id; f. 1976; 260 mems.

Indonesian Footwear Association (APRISINDO): Gedung Adis Dimension Footwear, Jalan Tanah Abang III/18, Jakarta Pusat 10160; tel. (21) 3447575; fax (21) 3447572; e-mail aprisindo@vision.net.id; internet www.aprisindo.info; 95 mems; Chair. EDDY WIJANARKO; Sec.-Gen. YUDHI KOMARUDIN.

Indonesian Furniture Industry and Handicraft Association (ASMINDO): Jalan Pegambiran 5A, 3rd Floor, Rawamangun Jakarta 13220; tel. (21) 47864028; fax (21) 47864031; e-mail asmindo@indo.net.id; internet furniturecraft.org; Chair. AMBAR TJAHYONO; Sec.-Gen. TANANGGA KARIM.

Indonesian National Board of Arbitration (BANI): Wahana Graha, 2nd Floor, Jalan Mampang Prapatan 2, Jakarta 12760; tel. (21) 7940542; fax (21) 7940543; e-mail bani-arb@indo.net.id; internet www.bani-arb.org; f. 1977; resolves business disputes; Chair. Prof. H. PRIYATNA ABDURRASYID.

Indonesian Nutmeg Exporters' Association: c/o PT Berdirari (Persero) Trading Division, Jalan Yos Sudarso 1, Jakarta; tel. (21) 4301625; e-mail bnuina@indosat.net.id.

Indonesian Palm Oil Producers' Association (GAPKI): Jalan Murai II, No. 40, Komplek Tomang Elok, Medan 20122; tel. (61) 8473331; fax (61) 8473332; e-mail sekretariat@gapki.org; internet www.gapki.org; Chair. Ir DEROM BANGUN.

Indonesian Precious Metals Association: Galva Bldg, 5th Floor, Jakarta Pusat, Jakarta 10120; tel. (21) 3451202; fax (21) 3812713.

Indonesian Pulp and Paper Association: Jalan Cimandiri 6, Jakarta 10330; tel. (21) 326084; fax (21) 3140168.

Indonesian Tea Association (ATI): Jalan Polombangkeng 15, Kebayoran Baru, Jakarta; tel. (21) 7260772; fax (21) 7205810; e-mail insyaf@hotmail.com; internet www.indotea.org; Chair. SUGIAT; Gen. Sec. ATIK DHARMADI.

Indonesian Textile Association (API): Panin Bank Centre, 3rd Floor, Jalan Jenderal Sudirman 1, Jakarta Pusat 10270; tel. (21) 7396094; fax (21) 7396341; f. 1974; Sec.-Gen. DANANG D. JOEDONAGORO.

Indonesian Tobacco Association: Jalan H. Agus Salim 85, Jakarta 10350; tel. (21) 3140627; fax (21) 325181; Pres. H. A. ISMAIL.

Masyarakat Perhutanan Indonesia (MPI) (Indonesian Forestry Community): Gedung Manggala Wanabakti, 9th Floor, Wing B/Blok IV, Jalan Jenderal Gatot Subroto, Jakarta Pusat 10270; tel. (21) 5733010; fax (21) 5732564; f. 1974; nine mems; Pres. M. HASAN.

Rubber Association of Indonesia (Gapkindo): Jalan Cideng Barat 62A, Jakarta 10150; tel. (21) 3501510; fax (21) 3500368; e-mail karetind@indosat.net.id; internet www.gapkindo.or.id; Chair. Ir DAUD HUSNI BASTARI; Exec. Dir SUHARTO HONGGOKUSUMO.

Shippers' Council of Indonesia: Jalan Kramat Raya 4–6, Jakarta; Pres. R. S. PARTOKUSUMO.

UTILITIES

Electricity

PT Perusahaan Listrik Negara (Persero) (PLN): Jalan Trunojoyo, Blok M1/135, Kebayoran Baru, Jakarta Selatan 12160; tel. (21) 7251234; fax (21) 7204929; e-mail pengelolaweb@pln.co.id; internet www.pln.co.id; state-owned electricity co; Pres. EDDIE WIDIONO.

Gas

PT Perusahaan Pertambangan Minyak dan Gas Bumi Negara (PERTAMINA): Jalan Medan Merdeka Timur 1A, Jakarta 10110; tel. (21) 3815111; fax (21) 3846865; e-mail wpurnama@pertamina.com; internet www.pertamina.com; f. 1968; state-owned petroleum and natural gas mining enterprise; Pres. Dir and CEO ARI H. SOEMARNO.

Perusahaan Gas Negara (PGN) (Public Gas Corporation): Jalan K. H. Zainul Arifin 20, Jakarta 11140; tel. (21) 6334838; fax (21) 6333080; e-mail investor_relation-pgn-group@pgn.co.id; internet www.pgn.co.id; monopoly of domestic gas distribution; Pres. Dir W. M. P. SIMANDJUNTAK.

Water

PDAM DKI Jakarta (PAM JAYA): Jalan Penjernihan 11, Pejompongan, Jakarta 10210; tel. (21) 5704250; fax (21) 5711796; f. 1977; responsible for the water supply systems of Jakarta; Pres. Dir Ir H. MUZAHIEM MOKHTAR.

PDAM Kodya Dati II Bandung: Jalan Badaksinga 10, Bandung 40132; tel. (22) 2509030; fax (22) 2508063; e-mail pdambdg@elga.net.id; f. 1974; responsible for the water supply and sewerage systems of Bandung; Pres. Dir Ir SOENITIYOSO HADI PRATIKTO.

PDAM Tirtanadi Medan: Jalan Sisingamangaraja 1, Medan 20212; tel. (61) 571666; fax (61) 572771; f. 1979; manages the water supply of Medan and nearby towns and cities; Man. Dir Ir KUMALA SIREGAR.

CO-OPERATIVES

In 1996 there were 48,391 primary and secondary co-operatives in Indonesia; membership of primary co-operatives was 27,006,000 in the same year.

Dewan Koperasi Indonesia (DEKOPIN) (Indonesian Co-operative Council): Graha Induk KUD, Lt. 2, Jalan Warung Buncit Raya Kav. 18–20, Jakarta Selatan; tel. (21) 79195712; fax (21) 79195718; e-mail info@dekopin.coop; internet www.dekopin.coop; Chair. ADI SASONO.

TRADE UNIONS

Konfederasi Serikat Pekerja Seluruh Indonesia (KSPSI) (Confederation of All Indonesian Trades Unions): Jalan Raya Pasar Minggu Km 17 No. 9, Jakarta Selatan 12740; tel. (21) 7974359; fax (21) 7974361; f. 1973; renamed 2001; sole officially recognized National Industrial Union; 5.1m. mems in June 2005; Gen. Chair. JACOB NUWA WEA; Gen. Sec. LATIEF NASUTION.

Konfederasi Serikat Buruh Sejahtera Indonesia (KSBSI) (Confederation of Indonesia Prosperity Trade Union): Jalan Cipinang Muara Raya, No. 33, Jatinegara, Jakarta Timur, Jakarta 13420; tel. (21) 70984671; fax (21) 8577646; e-mail sbsi@pacific.net.id; internet www.ksbsi.or.id; f. 1998; application for official registration rejected in May 1998; 1,228,875 mems in 168 branches in 27 provinces throughout Indonesia; Pres. REKSON SILABAN; Sec.-Gen. IDIN ROSIDIN.

Transport

Directorate General of Land Transport and Inland Waterways: Ministry of Transportation, Jalan Medan Merdeka Barat 8, Jakarta 10110; tel. (21) 3502971; fax (21) 3503013; e-mail hubdat@hubdat.web.id; internet www.hubdat.web.id; Dir-Gen. ISKANDAR ABUBAKAR.

RAILWAYS

There are railways on Java, Madura and Sumatra, totalling 6,458 km in 1996, of which 125 km were electrified.

INDONESIA

Directory

In 1995 a memorandum of understanding was signed by a consortium of European, Japanese and Indonesian companies for the construction of a 15-km Mass Rapid Transport (MRT) rail system in Jakarta, part of which would be underground. In 2006 the Japanese Government agreed to provide a US $741m. loan to finance the project, and in the following year the Ministry of Transportation announced that construction of the system would commence in 2010, with completion scheduled for 2014.

Directorate General of Railways: Ministry of Transportation, Jalan Medan Merdeka Barat 8, Jakarta 10110; internet perkeretaapian.dephub.go.id; Head Ir NUGROHO INDRIO.

PT Kereta Api (Persero) (PERUMKA): Jalan Perintis Kermedekaan 1, Bandung 40117; tel. (22) 4230031; fax (22) 4241370; e-mail info@kereta-api.com; internet www.kereta-api.com; six regional offices; transferred to the private sector in 1991; Chief Commr BUDHI MULYAWAN SUYITNO; Chief Dir RONNY WAHYUDI.

ROADS

There is an adequate road network on Java, Sumatra, Sulawesi, Kalimantan, Bali and Madura, but on most of the other islands traffic is by jungle track or river boat. In 2004 Indonesia had a total road length of 372,929 km, of which less than 55% was asphalted.

SHIPPING

The four main ports are Tanjung Priok (near Jakarta), Tanjung Perak (near Surabaya), Belawan (near Medan) and Makassar (formerly Ujung Pandang, in South Sulawesi); these have been designated gateway ports for nearly all international shipping to deal with Indonesia's exports, and are supported by 15 collector ports. More than 100 of Indonesia's ports and harbours are classified as capable of handling ocean-going shipping.

Directorate General of Sea Communications: Ministry of Transportation, Jalan Medan Merdeka Barat 8, Jakarta 10110; tel. (21) 3456332; internet www.dephub.go.id/ditlaut; Dir-Gen. SOENTORO.

Indonesian National Ship Owners' Association (INSA): Jalan Gunung Sahari 79, Jakarta Pusat; tel. (21) 414908; fax (21) 416388; Chair. OENTORO SURYA.

Shipping Companies

Indonesian Oriental Lines, PT Perusahaan Pelayaran Nusantara: Jalan Raya Pelabuhan Nusantara, POB 2062, Jakarta 10001; tel. (21) 494344; Pres. Dir A. J. SINGH.

PT Admiral Lines: POB 1476, Jakarta 10014; tel. (21) 4247908; fax (21) 4206267; e-mail admiral@uninet.net.id; internet www.admirallines.com; f. 1966; fmrly PT Pelayaran Samudera Admiral Lines; Pres. Commr DAUHAN SYAMSURI; Pres. Dir MOCHAMAD SOEGIARTO.

PT Djakarta Lloyd: Jalan Senen Raya, No. 44, Jakarta 10410; tel. (21) 3456208; fax (21) 3441401; internet www.dlloyd.co.id; f. 1950; services to USA, Europe, Japan, Australia and the Middle East; Pres. Dir BRAVO M. H. KARLIO.

PT Karana Line: 12-13/F, Jalan M. T. Haryono, Wisma Kalimanis, Kav. 33, Jakarta 12770; tel. (21) 7985914; fax (21) 7985913; internet www.karana.co.id; Pres. Dir BAMBANG EDIYANTO.

PT Pelayaran Bahtera Adhiguna (Persero): Jalan Kalibesar Timur 10–12, POB 4313, Jakarta 11043; tel. (21) 6912613; fax (21) 6901450; e-mail pelba@bahteradhiguna.co.id; internet www.bahteradhiguna.co.id; f. 1971; Pres. Commr HASUDUNGAN ARITONANG; Pres. Dir DJOKO TAHONO.

PT Pelayaran Nasional Indonesia (PELNI): Jalan Gajah Mada 14, Jakarta 10130; tel. (21) 63857747; fax (21) 63854130; e-mail humas@pelni.co.id; internet www.pelni.co.id; state-owned; national shipping co; Pres. Commr Ir TJUK SUKARDIMAN; Pres. Dir ISNOOR HARYANTO.

PT Pertamina (Persero): Downstream Directorate for Shipping, Jalan Yos Sudarso 32–34, POB 14020, Tanjung Priok, Jakarta Utara 14320; tel. (21) 4301086; fax (21) 43932628; e-mail marketing@pertaminashipping.com; internet www.pertaminashipping.com; f. 1959; state-owned; maritime business services; Pres. and Chair. Dr IBNU SUTOWO; Senior Vice-Pres. DEDENG WAHYU EDI.

PT Perusahaan Pelayaran Gesuri Lloyd: Gesuri Lloyd Bldg, Jalan Tiang Bendera IV 45, Jakarta 11230; tel. (21) 6904000; fax (21) 6925987; e-mail operation_agency@gesuri.co.id; internet www.gesuri.co.id; f. 1963; Pres. FRANKIE NURIMBA.

PT Perusahaan Pelayaran Samudera 'Samudera Indonesia': Jalan Kali Besar Barat 43, POB 1244, Jakarta; tel. (21) 671093; fax (21) 674242; Chair. and Dir SOEDARPO SASTROSATOMO; Exec. Dir RANDY EFFENDI.

PT Perusahaan Pelayaran Samudera Trikora Lloyd: Graha Satria, 4th Floor, Jalan R. S. Fatmawati, No. 5, Jakarta Selatan, Jakarta 12430; tel. (21) 75915381; fax (21) 75915385; internet www.boedihardjogroup.com/shipping/trikora_lloyd.htm; e-mail tkldir@cbn.net.id; f. 1964; Pres. Dir GANESHA SOEGIHARTO; Man. Dir P. R. S. VAN HEEREN.

CIVIL AVIATION

The first stage of a new international airport, the Sukarno-Hatta Airport, at Cengkareng, near Jakarta, was opened in 1985, to complement Halim Perdanakusuma Airport, which was to handle charter and general flights only. A new terminal was opened at Sukarno-Hatta in 1991, vastly enlarging airport capacity. Construction of an international passenger terminal at the Frans Kaisepo Airport, in Papua (then Irian Jaya), was completed in 1988. Other international airports include Ngurah Rai Airport at Denpasar (Bali), Polonia Airport in Medan (North Sumatra), Juanda Airport, near Surabaya (East Java), Sam Ratulangi Airport in Manado (North Sulawesi) and Hasanuddin Airport, near Makassar (formerly Ujung Pandang, South Sulawesi). There are a total of 179 commercial airports, 61 of which are capable of accommodating wide-bodied aircraft. Domestic air services link the major cities.

In 2000 the Government announced a policy of liberalization for the airline industry. This led to a dramatic increase in the number of airlines operating in Indonesia; by January 2005 Indonesia had 29 domestic airlines, compared with only five in 2000.

Directorate-General of Civil Aviation: Jalan Medan Merdeka Barat 8, Jakarta Pusat 10110; tel. (21) 3505133; fax (21) 3505139; e-mail hubud@dephub.go.id; internet hubud.dephub.go.id; Dir-Gen. CUCUK SURYO SUPROJO.

PT Adam SkyConnection Airlines (Adam Air): Jalan Gedong Panjang Raya 28, Jakarta 11240; tel. (21) 6917540; fax (21) 6927071; e-mail general@adamair.co.id; internet www.flyadamair.com; f. 2003; privately owned carrier offering scheduled flights to 15 domestic and regional destinations; operations suspended March 2008; Pres. Dir ADAM ADHITYA SUHERMAN; Chair. AGUNG LAKSONO.

PT Batavia Airlines: Jalan Ir H. Juanda 15, Jakarta Pusat 10120; tel. (21) 3864308; fax (21) 3864486; internet www.batavia-air.co.id; f. 2002; scheduled domestic and regional services; Pres. YUDIAWAN TANSARI.

Citilink: Jakarta; internet www.citilink.co.id; f. 2001; subsidiary of PT Garuda Indonesia; low-cost carrier providing shuttle services between 7 domestic destinations.

Deraya Air Taxi (DRY): Terminal Bldg, 1st Floor, Rm 150/HT, Halim Perdanakusuma Airport, Jakarta 13610; tel. (21) 8093627; fax (21) 8095770; e-mail admderaya@deraya.co.id; internet www.deraya.co.id; f. 1967; scheduled and charter passenger and cargo services to domestic and regional destinations; Pres. Dir SITI RAHAYU SUMADI.

Dirgantara Air Service (DAS): POB 6154, Terminal Bldg, Halim Perdanakusuma Airport, Rm 231, Jakarta 13610; tel. (21) 8093372; fax (21) 8094348; charter services from Jakarta, Barjarmas and Pontianak to destinations in West Kalimantan; Pres. MAKKI PERDANAKUSUMA.

PT Garuda Indonesia: Garuda Indonesia Bldg, Jalan Merdeka Selatan 13, Jakarta 10110; tel. (21) 2311801; fax (21) 2311679; internet www.garuda-indonesia.com; f. 1949; state airline; operates scheduled domestic, regional and international services to destinations in Europe, the USA, the Middle East, Australasia and the Far East; Pres. and CEO EMIRSYAH SATAR; Chair. HADIYANTO.

Lion Mentari Airlines: Lion Air Tower, Jaland Gajah Mada 7, Jakarta Pusat; tel. (21) 6326039; fax (21) 6348744; e-mail contact.us@lionair.co.id; internet www.lionair.co.id; f. 1999; budget carrier providing domestic and international services; Pres. Dir RUSDI KILANA.

PT Mandala Airlines: Jalan Tomang Raya, Kav. 33–37, Jakarta 11440; tel. (21) 5665434; fax (21) 5663788; e-mail widya@mandalaair.com; internet www.mandalaair.com; f. 1969; privately owned; scheduled regional and domestic passenger and cargo services; Pres. Commr HADI WALUYO; CEO WARWICK BRADY.

PT Merpati Nusantara Airlines: Jalan Angkasa, Blok B-15, Kav. 2–3, Jakarta 10720; tel. (21) 6548888; fax (21) 6540620; e-mail pr@merpati.co.id; internet www.merpati.co.id; f. 1962; subsidiary of PT Garuda Indonesia; domestic and regional services to Australia and Malaysia; Chair. GUNAWAN KOSWARA; Pres. Dir HOTASI NABABAN.

Pelita Air Service: Jalan Abdul Muls 52–56A, Jakarta 10160; tel. (21) 2312030; fax (21) 2312216; internet www.pelita-air.com; f. 1970; subsidiary of the state oil co, Pertamina; domestic scheduled and charter passenger and cargo services; Pres. Dir SOERATMAN.

Sriwijaya Air: No. 68, Blok C, 15–16, Jalan Pangeran Jayakarta, Jakarta; tel. (21) 6396006; internet www.sriwijayaair-online.com; f. 2003; domestic services; Dir CHANDRA LIE.

Wings Abadi Airlines (Wings Air): Lion Air Tower, Jalan Gajah Mada 7, Jakarta Pusat; tel. (21) 6326039; fax (21) 6348744; f. 2003; subsidiary co of Lion Air; budget carrier providing scheduled domestic passenger services.

Tourism

Indonesia's tourist industry is based mainly on the islands of Java, famous for its volcanic scenery and religious temples, and Bali, renowned for its scenery and Hindu-Buddhist temples and religious festivals. Lombok, Sumatra and Sulawesi are also increasingly popular. Domestic tourism within Indonesia has also increased significantly. Revenue from tourism (including passenger transport) was US $5,092m. in 2005. The number of tourists arrivals totalled an estimated 4.8m. in 2006, compared with 5.0m. in 2002.

Indonesia Tourism Promotion Board: Wisma Nugra Santana, 9th Floor, Jalan Jenderal Sudirman 8, Jakarta 10220; tel. (21) 5704879; fax (21) 5704855; e-mail itpb@cbn.net.id; private body; promotes national and international tourism; Chair. PONTJO SUTOWO; CEO GATOT SOEMARTONO.

IRAN

Introductory Survey

Location, Climate, Language, Religion, Flag, Capital

The Islamic Republic of Iran lies in western Asia, bordered by Azerbaijan and Turkmenistan to the north, by Turkey and Iraq to the west, by the Persian (Arabian) Gulf and the Gulf of Oman to the south, and by Pakistan and Afghanistan to the east. The climate is one of great extremes. Summer temperatures of more than 55°C (131°F) have been recorded, but in the winter the great altitude of much of the country results in temperatures of −18°C (0°F) and below. The principal language is Farsi (Persian), spoken by about 50% of the population. Turkic-speaking Azerbaijanis form about 27% of the population, and Kurds, Arabs, Balochis and Turkomans form less than 25%. The great majority of Persians and Azerbaijanis are Shi'ite Muslims, while the other ethnic groups are mainly Sunni Muslims. There are also small minorities of Christians (mainly Armenians), Jews and Zoroastrians. The Bahá'í faith, which originated in Iran, has been severely persecuted, being denied rights given to other recognized religious minorities. The national flag (proportions 4 by 7) comprises three unequal horizontal stripes, of green, white and red, with the emblem of the Islamic Republic of Iran (the stylized word Allah) centrally positioned in red, and the inscription 'Allaho Akbar' ('God is Great') written 11 times each in white Kufic script on the red and green stripes. The capital is Tehran.

Recent History

Iran, called Persia until 1935, was formerly a monarchy, ruled by a Shah (Emperor). In 1927 Reza Khan, a Cossack officer, seized power in a military coup, and was subsequently elected Shah, adopting the title Reza Shah Pahlavi. In 1941 British and Soviet forces occupied Iran, and the Shah (who favoured Nazi Germany) was forced to abdicate in favour of his son, Muhammad Reza Pahlavi. British and US forces left Iran in 1945, but Soviet forces remained in the north-west of the country (Azerbaijan province) until 1946. The United Kingdom retained considerable influence through the Anglo-Iranian Oil Co, which controlled much of Iran's extensive petroleum reserves. In March 1951, however, the Majlis (National Consultative Assembly) approved the nationalization of the petroleum industry, despite British and other Western opposition. The leading advocate of nationalization, Dr Muhammad Mussadeq, who became Prime Minister in May 1951, was deposed in August 1953 in a military *coup d'état*, engineered by the US and British intelligence services.

The Shah gradually increased his personal control of government following the coup, assuming dictatorial powers in 1963 with the so-called 'White Revolution'. Large estates were redistributed to small farmers, and women were granted the right to vote in elections, provoking opposition from landlords and the conservative Muslim clergy. In 1965 Prime Minister Hassan Ali Mansur was assassinated, reportedly by a follower of Ayatollah Ruhollah Khomeini, a fundamentalist Shi'ite Muslim leader strongly opposed to the Shah. (Khomeini had been deported in 1964 for his opposition activities, and was living in exile in Iraq.) Amir Abbas Hoveida held the office of Prime Minister until 1977.

Between 1965 and 1977 Iran enjoyed political stability and considerable economic growth, based on substantial petroleum revenues which funded a high level of expenditure on defence equipment and infrastructure projects. From late 1977, however, public opposition to the regime increased dramatically, largely in response to a declining economy and the repressive nature of the Shah's rule. By the end of 1978 anti-Government protests were widespread, involving both left-wing and liberal opponents of the Shah, as well as Islamist activists. The most effective opposition came from supporters of Ayatollah Khomeini, who was now based in France. The growing unrest forced the Shah to leave Iran in January 1979. Khomeini arrived in Tehran on 1 February and effectively assumed power 10 days later. A 15-member Islamic Revolutionary Council was formed to govern the country, in co-operation with a Provisional Government, and on 1 April Iran was declared an Islamic republic. Supreme authority was vested in the Wali Faqih, a religious leader (initially Khomeini) appointed by the Shi'ite clergy. Executive power was to be vested in a President, to which post Abolhasan Bani-Sadr was elected in January 1980. Elections to a 270-member Majlis (renamed the Islamic Consultative Assembly) took place in two rounds in March and May. The Islamic Republican Party (IRP), which was identified with Khomeini and traditionalist Muslims, won some 60 seats, but subsequently increased its support base.

In November 1979 Iranian students seized 63 hostages at the US embassy in Tehran. The original purpose of the siege was to force the USA (where the Shah was undergoing medical treatment) to return the former monarch to Iran to face trial. The Shah died in Egypt in July 1980, by which time Iran had made other demands, notably for a US undertaking not to interfere in its affairs. Intense diplomatic activity led to the release of the 52 remaining hostages in January 1981, but not before a failed rescue operation by the US military in April 1980 resulted in the deaths of eight US servicemen.

The hostage crisis had forced the resignation of the moderate Provisional Government, and during 1980 it became clear that a rift was developing between President Bani-Sadr and his modernist allies on the one hand, and the IRP and traditionalist elements on the other. In June 1981 clashes between supporters of the two groups escalated into sustained fighting between members of the Mujahidin-e-Khalq (an Islamist guerrilla group which supported Bani-Sadr) and troops of the Revolutionary Guard Corps. The Majlis voted to impeach the President, who was subsequently dismissed by Khomeini. Bani-Sadr fled to France, as did the leader of the Mujahidin, Massoud Rajavi. A presidential election in July resulted in victory for the Prime Minister, Muhammad Ali Rajani, who was himself replaced by Muhammad Javar Bahonar. Meanwhile, conflict between the Mujahidin-e-Khalq and government forces intensified. In August both the President and Prime Minister were killed in a bomb attack attributed to the Mujahidin. A further presidential election, held in October, was won by Hojatoleslam Ali Khamenei. Mir Hussein Moussavi was appointed Prime Minister.

The resignation or dismissal of five ministers, all 'bazaaris' (members of the merchant class), in August 1983 characterized opposition to the policies of nationalization and land reform advocated by technocrats in the Government. Moussavi's attempts to implement such economic reforms were continually obstructed by the predominantly 'conservative', clerical Majlis. Elections to the second Majlis in April and May 1984 resulted in a clear win for the IRP. The elections were boycotted by the sole opposition party to have a degree of official recognition, Nehzat-e Azadi-ye Iran (Liberation Movement of Iran), led by Dr Mehdi Bazargan (Prime Minister of the Provisional Government during February–November 1979), in protest at the allegedly undemocratic conditions prevailing in Iran.

Three candidates, including the incumbent, contested the August 1985 presidential election. The Council of Guardians (responsible for the supervision of elections) had rejected almost 50 others, among them Bazargan, who opposed the continuation of the war with Iraq (see below). Khamenei was elected President for a second four-year term, with 85.7% of the votes cast. Despite some opposition in the Majlis, Hussein Moussavi was reconfirmed as Prime Minister in October.

For most of the 1980s Iran's domestic and foreign policy was dominated by the war with Iraq. In September 1980, ostensibly to assert a claim of sovereignty over the disputed Shatt al-Arab waterway, Iraqi forces invaded Iran along a 500-km front, apparently anticipating a rapid military victory. The Iranian military offered strong resistance, and began a counter-offensive in early 1982; by June Iraq had been forced to withdraw from Iranian territory, and Iranian troops subsequently entered Iraq. A conflict of attrition thus developed, characterized by mutual offensives and the targeting of each other's petroleum reserves, installations and transhipment facilities. From 1984 Iraq began attacking tankers using Iran's Kharg Island oil terminal, in the Persian (Arabian) Gulf, and Iran retaliated by targeting Saudi Arabian and Kuwaiti tankers in the Gulf. Despite subsequent efforts by the UN to establish a basis for peace negotiations, Iran's conditions for peace were the removal from power of the

Iraqi President, Saddam Hussain, in conjunction with agreement by Iraq to pay war reparations.

The war had left Iran in virtual diplomatic isolation; however, in late 1986 it emerged that the USA, in contradiction to its active discouragement of arms sales to Iran by other countries, had begun secret negotiations with the country in 1985 and had made shipments of weapons, allegedly in exchange for Iranian assistance in securing the release of US hostages held by Shi'ite groups in Lebanon, and an Iranian undertaking to relinquish involvement in international terrorism. Meanwhile, Iran was attacking Kuwaiti shipping, and neutral vessels using Kuwait, in retaliation for Kuwait's support for Iraq. In mid-1987 the USA agreed to re-register 11 Kuwaiti tankers under its own flag, thus entitling them to US naval protection. The United Kingdom, France, the Netherlands, Belgium and Italy subsequently dispatched minesweepers to the Gulf region.

In April 1988 Iraq recaptured the Faw peninsula (which Iran had taken in 1986), forcing the Iranian military to withdraw across the Shatt al-Arab. In June Iraq also retook Majnoun Island and the surrounding area (which had been captured by Iran in 1984). In July an IranAir passenger flight, allegedly mistaken for an attacking fighter jet, was shot down by a US aircraft carrier in the Strait of Hormuz; all 290 passengers and crew were killed. In that month Iraqi troops crossed into Iranian territory for the first time since 1986, and the last Iranian troops on Iraqi territory were dislodged. On 18 July 1988 Iran unexpectedly announced its unconditional acceptance of UN Security Council Resolution 598, adopted one year earlier. This urged an immediate cease-fire, the withdrawal of military forces to international boundaries and the co-operation of Iran and Iraq in mediation efforts to achieve a peace settlement. More than 1m. people were estimated to have died in the eight-year conflict. A cease-fire came into effect on 20 August, and UN-sponsored peace negotiations began shortly afterwards in Geneva, Switzerland. In the same month a UN Iran-Iraq Military Observer Group (UNIIMOG) was deployed in the region. However, the negotiations soon became deadlocked in disputes regarding the sovereignty of the Shatt al-Arab, the exchange of prisoners of war and the withdrawal of armed forces to within international boundaries. Hopes of a comprehensive peace settlement were raised by a meeting of the Iranian and Iraqi Ministers of Foreign Affairs in Geneva in July 1990, but were swiftly overshadowed by Iraq's invasion of Kuwait at the beginning of August. Saddam Hussain sought an immediate, formal peace with Iran, accepting all the claims that Iran had pursued since the declaration of a cease-fire (including the reinstatement of the Algiers Agreement of 1975, dividing the Shatt al-Arab waterway), and Iraq immediately began to redeploy troops from its border with Iran to Kuwait. Prisoner exchanges took place, and in September 1990 Iran and Iraq restored diplomatic relations. In February 1991 the withdrawal of all armed forces to internationally recognized boundaries was confirmed by UNIIMOG, whose mandate was terminated shortly afterwards.

Iran denounced Iraq's invasion of Kuwait, and observed the economic sanctions imposed by the UN on Iraq. However, it was unequivocal in its condemnation of the deployment of the US-led multinational force in the Gulf region. Relations between Iran and Iraq deteriorated after the liberation of Kuwait in February 1991. Iran protested strongly against the Baathist regime's suppression of the Shi'a-led rebellion in southern and central Iraq, and the accompanying destruction of Shi'a shrines, and renewed its demand for the resignation of Saddam Hussain. Iraq, in turn, accused Iran of supporting the rebellion. Thus, there was little further progress in implementing the terms of Resolution 598 until late 1993, when high-level bilateral talks recommenced on the exchange of remaining prisoners of war. (See below for further details of Iran's relations with Iraq.)

Elections to the Majlis in April and May 1988 apparently provided a stimulus to 'reformist' elements in the Government (identified with Ali Akbar Hashemi Rafsanjani, since 1980 the Speaker of the Majlis, and Prime Minister Moussavi) by producing an assembly strongly representative of their views. (The elections were the Islamic Republic's first not to be contested by the IRP, which had been dissolved in 1987.) In June 1988 Rafsanjani was re-elected as Speaker and Moussavi was overwhelmingly endorsed as Prime Minister. In February 1989, however, Ayatollah Khomeini referred explicitly to a division in the Iranian leadership between 'reformers' (who sought a degree of Western participation in Iran's post-war reconstruction) and 'conservatives' (who opposed such involvement), and declared that he would never permit the 'reformers' to prevail.

His intervention was reportedly prompted by Rafsanjani's decision to contest the presidential election scheduled for mid-1989. A number of prominent 'reformers', among them Ayatollah Ali Hossein Montazeri (who had been designated as successor to Khomeini by the Council of Experts in 1985), subsequently resigned from the Iranian leadership.

Ayatollah Khomeini died on 3 June 1989. In an emergency session on 4 June the Council of Experts elected President Khamenei to succeed Khomeini as Iran's spiritual leader (Wali Faqih). The presidential election, scheduled for mid-August, was brought forward to 28 July, to be held simultaneously with a referendum on proposed amendments to the Constitution. Both 'conservatives' and 'reformers' within the leadership apparently united in support of Rafsanjani's candidacy for the presidency, and Rafsanjani (opposed only by a 'token' candidate) secured an overwhelming victory, with 95.9% of the votes cast. A similar proportion of voters approved the constitutional amendments, the most important of which was the abolition of the post of Prime Minister (and a consequent increase in power for the President).

President Rafsanjani appointed a Government balancing 'conservatives', 'reformers' and technocrats, and its endorsement by the Majlis, in August 1989, was viewed as a mandate for Rafsanjani to conduct a more conciliatory policy towards the West, despite the opposition of certain 'conservative' elements. Large-scale protests against food shortages and high prices in early 1990 demonstrated the urgent need for economic reform. In October, with the co-operation of Ayatollah Khamenei, Rafsanjani was able to prevent the election of many powerful 'conservatives' to the Council of Experts. An estimated 70% of deputies elected to the fourth Majlis in April and May 1992 were, broadly speaking, pro-Rafsanjani. However, economic reform was lowering the living standards of the traditional constituency of the Islamic regime, the urban lower classes, leading to serious rioting in several cities. The extent to which President Rafsanjani had lost popular support became clear when he stood for re-election in June 1993: competing against three ostensibly 'token' candidates, Rafsanjani received 63.2% of the votes. In May 1994 the Government indicated that it would proceed more cautiously with a plan to reduce economic subsidies applied to basic commodities. Meanwhile, in August 1995 it was reported that political parties, associations and groups were free to conduct political activities in Iran on condition that they honoured the country's Constitution, although Nehzat-e Azadi was subsequently refused formal registration as a political party.

Elections to the fifth Majlis in March and April 1996 provided an important measure of the shifting balance of power between 'reformers', or 'liberals', and 'conservatives' in Iranian politics. The first round of voting produced results in some 140 of the total 270 seats. Candidates of the Servants of Iran's Construction, a new pro-Rafsanjani faction, were reported to have won some 70% of the seats. However, the 'conservative' Society of Combatant Clergy, with the unofficial patronage of Ayatollah Khamenei, claimed that its candidates had achieved an equally conclusive victory. After the second round of voting, unofficial sources suggested that the Society of Combatant Clergy would command the loyalty of 110–120 deputies in the new Majlis, and the Servants of Iran's Construction that of 90–100 deputies.

In March 1997 Rafsanjani was appointed Chairman of the Council to Determine the Expediency of the Islamic Order (which arbitrates in disputes between the Majlis and the Council of Guardians) for a further five-year term, indicating that he would continue to play an influential role in political life upon the imminent expiry of his presidential mandate. (Rafsanjani was reappointed as head of the Expediency Council in March 2002 and February 2007.) In early May the Council of Guardians approved four candidatures for that month's presidential election, rejecting 234. It had been widely predicted that Ali Akbar Nateq Nouri, the Majlis Speaker favoured by the Society of Combatant Clergy, would secure an easy victory, but Sayed Muhammad Khatami (a presidential adviser and former Minister of Culture and Islamic Guidance) emerged as a strong contender immediately prior to the election. Regarded as a 'liberal', Khatami—supported by the Servants of Iran's Construction as well as by intellectuals, professionals, women's and youth groups—took some 69.1% of the total votes cast, ahead of Nateq Nouri, with 24.9%. (Nateq Nouri was re-elected Speaker of the Majlis in June.)

Taking office in August 1997, President Khatami emphasized his commitment to fostering sustained and balanced growth in the political, economic, cultural and educational spheres. In foreign affairs, the President undertook to promote the principle of mutual respect, but pledged that Iran would stand up to any power seeking to subjugate Iranian sovereignty. Notable among the 'liberal' or 'moderate' appointees in Khatami's first Council of Ministers were Ata'ollah Mohajerani (a former Vice-President) as Minister of Culture and Islamic Guidance, and Abdollah Nuri as Minister of the Interior (a post he had previously held in 1989–93). Dr Massoumeh Ebtekar, as Vice-President and Head of the Organization for the Protection of the Environment, was the first woman to be appointed to such a senior government post since the Islamic Revolution.

In the months following his election, President Khatami appeared conciliatory towards the West, and also urged toleration of dissent in Islamic societies among groups who remained 'within the framework of law and order'. Khamenei, meanwhile, continued to denounce the West's military and cultural ambitions, particularly those of the USA and Israel. Although Iranian officials denounced reports by Western commentators of tensions within the regime as Western propaganda, the cases of two leading politicians seemed to illustrate this apparent divergence between the 'moderate' and 'conservative' factions. In April 1998 Gholamhossein Karbaschi, the mayor of Tehran and a popular 'moderate', was arrested on charges of corruption. Karbaschi's detention led to clashes between 'moderate' and 'conservative' students during a rally by his supporters at the University of Tehran, resulting in about 100 arrests. In May the Ministry of the Interior authorized the registration of the Servants of Iran's Construction as a political party (styled the Servants of Construction Party—Hezb-e Kargozaran-e Sazandegi), with Karbaschi as its Secretary-General. However, following a televised trial, Karbaschi was sentenced in July to five years' imprisonment and fined IR 1,000m., having been convicted of embezzlement, squandering state property and mismanagement (but acquitted of bribery charges). The custodial sentence was reduced on appeal to two years, and although Karbaschi began his prison term in May 1999, he eventually received a presidential pardon and was released in January 2000. Meanwhile, in June 1998 the Majlis voted to dismiss Abdollah Nuri as Minister of the Interior, a group of 'conservative' deputies having initiated impeachment on the grounds that he had made provocative statements and was a supporter of Karbaschi. They further maintained that Nuri had permitted dissident rallies and had also failed to counter unrest involving supporters of Ayatollah Montazeri in late 1997. Khatami appointed Abdolvahed Musavi-Lari (also regarded as a relative 'moderate') to the Ministry of the Interior, and later named Nuri as Vice-President in charge of Development and Social Affairs.

During 1998 the Khatami administration moved to formalize its support base, primarily through the registration or establishment of 'reformist' parties such as the Servants of Construction, the Islamic Iran Solidarity Party (Hezb-e Hambastegi-ye Iran-e Islami) and the Islamic Iran Participation Front (Jebbeh-ye Mosharekat-e Iran-e Islami—which counted Vice-President Massoumeh Ebtekar among its leaders). However, at elections to the Council of Experts in October, 'conservatives' retained overwhelming control of the assembly, with an estimated 60% of the 86 seats being won by candidates of the 'radical' right wing; candidates of a 'centrist' grouping apparently associated with ex-President Rafsanjani took about 10% of the seats. Khatami's Government suffered a further setback in February 1999 with the resignation of Qorbanali Dorri Najafabadi, the Minister of Information, after it was admitted that agents of his ministry had (allegedly without his knowledge) been responsible for the murders of several intellectuals and dissident writers (among them Dariush Foruhar, leader of the unauthorized but officially tolerated Iranian People's Party) in late 1998. His successor, Ali Yunesi, had led an investigative commission into the murders.

Iran's first local government elections since the Islamic Revolution took place in February 1999, when some 60% of the electorate voted to elect representatives in 200,000 council seats. The elections resulted in considerable success for 'reformist' candidates, notably in Tehran, Shiraz and Esfahan, while 'conservatives' secured control of councils in their traditional strongholds of Qom and Mashad. In subsequent weeks 'conservative' elements challenged the election of many 'reformist' councillors: among those whose victories were overturned was former Minister of the Interior Abdollah Nuri. In April the Mujahidin-e-Khalq claimed responsibility for the assassination, in Tehran, of the Deputy Chief of Staff of the Armed Forces, Lt-Gen. Ali Sayyad Shirazi. Meanwhile, Mohsen Kadivar, a prominent 'reformist' cleric, was sentenced to 18 months' imprisonment by the Special Clerical Court, having been found guilty of disseminating false information about the Islamic regime.

The issue of press censorship had increasingly become a focus of the political rivalries between 'conservatives' and 'reformists'. During 1998 several prominent journals had been closed, and their journalists prosecuted, and Ayatollah Khamenei had personally sought action against publications that he perceived as abusing freedom of speech to weaken Islamic beliefs. Legislation adopted by the Majlis in June 1999 further curbed the activities of 'liberal' publications. In July the closure of *Salam*, a 'reformist' newspaper with close links to President Khatami, triggered a small demonstration by students at the University of Tehran, which was dispersed with considerable violence by police. This action, in conjuction with a raid on student dormitories by security forces, aided by militant vigilantes of the Ansar-e Hezbollah (in which at least one student was killed), provoked five days of rioting in Tehran and other cities, resulting in some 1,400 arrests. Within a year both the national and the Tehran chiefs of police had been dismissed, while as many as 100 police officers had been arrested for their role in the campus raid. In July 2000 the former Tehran chief of police and 17 co-defendants were acquitted on charges arising from the police invasion of student dormitories, but two police officers received custodial sentences, having been convicted on relatively minor charges. Of the student demonstrators tried for alleged crimes relating to the unrest, four suspected leaders had their initial death sentences commuted to 15 years' imprisonment in April 2000, 45 were given custodial terms, and another 20 were acquitted.

Meanwhile, in August 1999 the ban on *Salam* was extended to five years, and the journal's publisher (who had in July been convicted on charges including defamation and publication of a classified document) was given a suspended 42-month prison sentence, and also fined and banned from publishing for three years. Abdollah Nuri was brought before the Special Clerical Court in October, accused in his capacity as editor of the 'liberal' *Khordad* daily of insulting Islamic sanctities, publishing reports contrary to religious fundamentals and refuting the values of Ayatollah Khomeini. Many observers regarded the charges against Nuri as a clear attempt to prevent his standing in the forthcoming elections to the Majlis, where, if elected, he was likely to be a strong contender for the post of Speaker. In November Nuri was convicted on 15 charges and sentenced to five years' imprisonment; he was also fined IR 15m., and the closure of *Khordad* was ordered. An appeal lodged with the Supreme Court was rejected in January 2000. However, it was reported in November 2002 that Nuri had been pardoned by Ayatollah Khamenei following the sudden death of his brother, Ali Reza Nuri, a 'reformist' deputy who had achieved success in the 2000 general election (see below).

The process of scrutinizing candidates by the Council of Guardians, in preparation for elections to the Majlis scheduled for February 2000, resulted in the disqualification of many known 'reformist' candidates, on the grounds principally of disloyalty to Islam, to Iran's Constitution or to its spiritual leader. ('Conservative' deputies had in late 1999 introduced legislation giving the Council extensive powers to vet election candidates.) Nevertheless, while there were indications, as lesser-known 'reformist' candidates were approved by the Guardians, that the sixth Majlis might include sufficient numbers of 'liberals' and 'moderates' to present the first real challenge to the 'conservative' majority, the extent of the success achieved by candidates of the Islamic Iran Participation Front and the Servants of Construction was not widely predicted. An estimated 80% of Iran's registered electorate participated in the poll on 18 February 2000, at which the number of seats in the Majlis had been increased from 270 to 290. Among those who secured notable victories were Muhammad Reza Khatami (brother of the President and head of the Participation Front's political bureau), Jamileh Kadivar (the wife of Ata'ollah Mohajerani and sister of dissident cleric Mohsen Kadivar) and Ali Reza Nuri. 'Conservative' candidates, meanwhile, were overwhelmingly defeated in Mashad, Esfahan, Shiraz and Tabriz. There was a marked increase in the proportion of Majlis seats won by women, while the number of clerics in the new assembly declined. The Council of Guardians ordered the recount of almost one-third of the votes cast in Tehran, following allegations of irregularities; however, Ayatollah Khamenei intervened to prevent a complete recount of ballots for all 30 of the capital's seats. Principal among those whose election was initially in doubt was former President Rafsanjani; however, Rafsanjani resigned his Tehran seat in late May, thereby relinquishing his ambition to become the new

Speaker of the Majlis. Meanwhile, a second round of voting, for 66 undecided seats, proceeded on 5 May. At the end of May the incoming Majlis elected Mahdi Karrubi, the candidate of the Servants of Construction, as Speaker, a post that he had previously held in 1989–92. By mid-2000 'reformist' or 'liberal' deputies were believed to hold some 200 seats in the new Majlis, with the remaining 90 occupied by 'conservatives'. (By-elections were to take place in mid-2001—concurrently with the scheduled presidential election—for 18 seats where the results of earlier voting had been annulled.) 'Reformist' deputies acted swiftly to draft legislation to replace a restrictive new press law, endorsed by the outgoing, 'conservative'-controlled Majlis, which made criticism of the Constitution illegal and increased judicial powers to close newspapers.

In August 2000 Ayatollah Khamenei issued a decree instructing the new Majlis not to debate proposed amendments to the press law (which would make it more difficult for the judiciary to imprison journalists), on the grounds that such reforms would endanger state security and religious faith. This intervention appeared to sanction a more vigorous campaign against 'liberal' interests in subsequent months. At the end of August a police officer was killed, and around 100 people were injured, in four days of violent clashes between 'pro-reform' students and Ansar-e Hezbollah militants in the western town of Khorramabad. The confrontations occurred as two 'reformists', including the dissident cleric Mohsen Kadivar, were prevented by the militants from addressing an annual student congress. (Kadivar had been released from prison in July, although he had been informed of the possibility of indictment on further, as yet unknown, political charges.) In late 2000 it was reported that about 30 'pro-reform' publications had been closed down by the authorities since April, some of which had subsequently reopened under new names.

In November 2000 the trial opened in Tehran of a group of prominent 'reformists', accused of 'acting against national security and propagandizing against the regime' through their attendance at a conference on Iranian political reform, held in Berlin, Germany, in April. The severity of the sentences, pronounced in January 2001, against seven of the defendants, who were given custodial terms of between four and 10 years, was denounced by 'reformist' politicians within Iran. The renowned investigative journalist Akbar Ganji received the maximum prison term, followed by five years' internal exile, having been found guilty of harming national security, propagandizing against the regime, possessing secret documents and committing offences against senior officials. In July an appeal found Ganji guilty of having threatened national security, and he was given a six-year custodial sentence; Ganji was released from detention in March 2006. A further five of those convicted had their sentences dramatically reduced by a court of appeal in December 2001. Meanwhile, in October 2001 it was reported that a dissident cleric, Hassan Yousefi Eshkevari, had been sentenced to seven years' imprisonment resulting from his participation in the Berlin conference; however, he too was released in February 2005. A focus of Ganji's investigations had been the deaths of dissident intellectuals in late 1998 (see above), which he claimed involved senior 'conservatives', but which the authorities maintained had been instigated by 'rogue' agents of the Ministry of Information. The trial of 18 people, including senior intelligence officers, accused of involvement in the murders began, in camera, before a military court in Tehran in December 2000. (The court had recently announced that former Minister of Information Najafabadi had no case to answer.) In January 2001 three intelligence agents were condemned to death, having been convicted of perpetrating the killings; five received life sentences, and seven others custodial terms of up to 10 years (the other defendants were acquitted). However, after a retrial was ordered by the Supreme Court, in January 2003 at least two of the agents had their death sentences commuted to terms of life imprisonment; of those given life sentences, two now received prison terms of 10 years, while seven of the agents were given gaol terms of between two and 10 years. The remaining agents were to have their cases reviewed.

As had been widely predicted, on 8 June 2001 Khatami was re-elected as President, winning some 76.9% of the total votes cast, compared with 15.6% for his closest rival, Ahmed Tavakkoli, a former Minister of Labour and Social Affairs. (The Council of Guardians had endorsed the candidatures of 10 people, several of whom were independent 'conservatives'.) Khatami became the first Iranian President to win a greater number of votes for his second term than for his first, although the rate of participation by voters (at around 67%) was considerably lower than the 88% recorded in 1997. Khatami's victory was seen as a public endorsement of his programme of political and economic reforms; nevertheless, it soon became apparent that the 'ultra-conservatives' were unwilling to cede control of the Council of Guardians to 'reformist' supporters of Khatami. On 5 August Khatami's scheduled inauguration was postponed after the 'reformist' Majlis refused to approve two of the judiciary's 'conservative' nominees to the Council of Guardians. Ayatollah Khamenei requested, to strenuous 'reformist' opposition, that the dispute be resolved by the 'conservative'-dominated Council to Determine the Expediency of the Islamic Order. Two days later, however, the Majlis finally endorsed the two candidates, following a ruling that candidates did not require the support of a majority of deputies in order to be elected to the Council of Guardians. Khatami was duly sworn in for a second presidential term on 8 August. In mid-August he presented his 20-member Council of Ministers to the Majlis, which approved the list later in the month. The composition of the new Government was criticized both by 'conservatives' for being too liberal and by 'reformists' for not being sufficiently bold.

The judiciary's campaign against 'pro-reform' activists intensified following Khatami's re-election, including mass arrests, public floggings and even public executions, ordered ostensibly to reduce crime and encourage greater morality. In September 2001 Hossein Loqmanian, a 'reformist' deputy in the Majlis, lost his appeal against a custodial sentence imposed in October 2000 after he had condemned in a parliamentary speech the closure by the press court of several 'pro-reform' publications. Sentenced to 10 months' custody, Loqmanian became the first serving member of the Majlis to be imprisoned since 1979; his imprisonment in December 2001 provoked strong protests from his constituents in the western city of Hamedan and, in January 2002, a brief boycott of the Majlis by 'liberal' deputies. Apparently as a result of the parliamentary boycott, Loqmanian was swiftly pardoned by Ayatollah Khamenei and duly released.

In November 2001 trial proceedings, held in camera, began of more than 30 members of the Nehzat-e Azadi movement who had been arrested on charges including acting against national security and plotting to overthrow the Islamic regime. Among the defendants—in what was reported to be the largest political trial in Iran since 1979—were two former ministers and a former mayor of Tehran. Custodial sentences of up to 10 years were handed down to 33 of the activists by the Revolutionary Court in July 2002, and Nehzat-e Azadi was formally banned. Meanwhile, in late November 2001 the Council to Determine the Expediency of the Islamic Order rejected a bill to amend the electoral law that proposed a reduction in the power of the Council of Guardians to vet and disqualify electoral candidates. The new legislation had been proposed by 'reformist' deputies after the Council rejected about 60 of their candidates in the approach to by-elections due to be held in the province of Golestan.

Iran's Deputy Foreign Minister for Education and Research, Sadegh Kharrazi, was forced to resign in April 2002, amid speculation that he had made contact with US officials. There was a renewed clampdown on the 'reformist' movement by the judiciary in May, with the closure of two 'liberal' newspapers and a warning from the Tehran judiciary to journalists that publication of any article advocating dialogue between Iranian and US representatives would be regarded as a criminal offence. In July the authorities declared a ban on any rallies and protests organized to commemorate the third anniversary of the violent clashes between students and the security forces in 1999. However, several hundred protesters were reported to have defied the ban in Tehran, resulting in sporadic clashes between protesters demanding political reform on the one side and security forces and 'right-wing' elements on the other. In late July 2002 Mohsen Mirdamadi, a Majlis deputy and publisher of the Participation Front's *Norouz*, Iran's main 'pro-reform' newspaper, had a six-month gaol term handed down in May for propagandizing against the Islamic regime confirmed by a court of appeal. Mirdamadi was also fined and banned from involvement in press activities for four years, and his publication was closed down for six months. (He had alleged in an article published in *Norouz* to have information that Iran had held secret talks with the USA.) More than 30 other 'reformists' were also imprisoned during July, and in subsequent weeks at least three 'pro-reform' newspapers were banned by the authorities.

During September 2002 President Khatami presented draft legislation to the Majlis which was aimed at reducing the powers of Iran's 'ultra-conservative' establishment in order to accelerate his reform programme. The first bill envisaged transferring the rights of the Council of Guardians to approve or disqualify electoral candidates to the Ministry of the Interior. The second bill proposed granting Khatami wider powers to enforce adherence to the terms of the Constitution by the judiciary and other government departments. Both bills required approval by the Majlis and the Council of Guardians prior to becoming law. However, the 'pro-reform' movement suffered a setback in October when Behrouz Geranpayeh, director of a research institute affiliated to the 'reformist'-led Ministry of Culture and Islamic Guidance, was arrested on charges including publishing 'inappropriate' information, acting against national security and passing information to foreign intelligence agencies, and the institute was closed down by the authorities. The action came after a recent poll commissioned by the Majlis and published by Geranpayeh's research institute showed that a large majority of Iranians favoured the resumption of political dialogue with the USA. In November another such organization was closed and its directors were arrested; they included Abbas Abdi, a journalist and leading member of the Islamic Iran Participation Front. Trial proceedings began in Tehran against Geranpayeh, Abdi and another polling institute official in the following month; the defendants were accused of espionage and of fabricating opinion polls. Abdi was sentenced to eight years' imprisonment in February 2003, having been found guilty of selling information to a US polling institute, while the other researcher received a nine-year term; Geranpayeh awaited a verdict. Abdi was released from prison in May 2005, after the charges against the dissident were dismissed by the Supreme Court.

In early November 2002 President Khatami's two reform bills, concerning the vetting of electoral candidates and violations of the Constitution, received preliminary approval by the Majlis. However, at the same time a prominent 'reformist' academic, writer and close ally of the President, Hashem Aghajari, was handed down a death sentence by a court in the western city of Hamedan, having been found guilty of apostasy for a speech he had made to a university audience in June, in which he questioned the divine authority of the Islamic clergy and advocated reform within the religious establishment. (On other charges, Aghajari was sentenced to eight years in prison and 74 lashes, as well as receiving a 10-year teaching ban.) Aghajari had been tried in camera, and the severity of the sentence was widely condemned by academics, 'liberals' and even moderate 'conservatives'; it led to several weeks of student protests—the largest witnessed in Iran since 1999. In mid-November 2002 Ayatollah Khamenei intervened in the worsening crisis by requesting that the judiciary initiate an urgent review of the case. However, this did not prevent further protests by students in Tehran, which resulted in clashes with members of a 'hardline' militia who were calling for Aghajari's execution. In late November four students who had instigated the recent protests were arrested on charges of acting against national security. In early December Aghajari's lawyers filed an appeal against his conviction, while further demonstrations were staged in Tehran by students demanding the release of the academic, some of whom also sought the resignation of the Head of the Judiciary; a number of arrests were made. Later in the month Hussain Mir-Muhammad Sadeghi, the official spokesman for the judiciary, resigned his post, reportedly citing dissatisfaction over the 'politicization' of the judiciary and Aghajari's death sentence. In February 2003 the Supreme Court commuted the death sentence against Aghajari to a prison term of less than four years; however, he was ordered to face a retrial by the court in Hamedan that had issued the initial verdict (see below). Meanwhile, in January the dissident cleric Ayatollah Montazeri was released from house arrest, following reports that a 'conservative' daily newspaper, *Resalat*, had joined the 'pro-reform' lobby in demanding his release.

Official results of voting in Iran's second local government elections since the Islamic Revolution, held in February 2003, indicated a heavy defeat for President Khatami's Islamic Iran Participation Front by candidates of the 'conservative' wing. Electoral turn-out was reported to have been extremely low (at some 39%), as some 'moderate' voters appeared to have boycotted the poll in protest at Khatami's failure to secure vital political reforms. 'Conservative' candidates were said to have secured all 15 seats on the council in Tehran. Inevitably, however, the results of these elections were overshadowed by events in neighbouring Iraq.

Iran officially opposed the US-led military intervention in Iraq, which commenced in March 2003, despite the not unwelcome removal from power of Saddam Hussain and his Baathist regime. This opposition manifested itself in public statements by 'hardline' figures such as Ahmad Jannati, Chairman of the Council of Guardians, and Yahya Rahim-Safavi, Commander of the Revolutionary Guards, as well as in several demonstrations outside the British embassy in Tehran, which became a focal point for protests against the conflict. On several occasions during 2003 the embassy was the target of small arms fire and, in the most serious incident, in March, a fuel-laden truck was driven into the embassy gates, killing the driver. However, Kamal Kharrazi, the Minister of Foreign Affairs, described this last incident as an 'accident'. Moreover, there was a suspicion that three shooting incidents at the British embassy in September might be more closely related to the arrest of the former Iranian ambassador to Argentina by the British authorities (see below) than to events in Iraq.

On the domestic front, there remained significant divisions between 'conservatives' and 'reformists'. Prompted by the refusal of the Council of Guardians to ratify two of President Khatami's reform bills, which had been approved by the Majlis in late 2002, in May 2003 127 'reformist' deputies wrote to Khatami urging him to intervene in the blocked reform process. In July a group of Sunni Muslim deputies sent an 'open letter' to the Government complaining about official treatment of the country's Sunni minority.

In August 2003 an independent judge, Javad Esmaili, was appointed to lead an investigation into the death in police custody of an Iranian-born Canadian photojournalist, Zahra Kazemi, in July, following her arrest in the previous month for taking photographs at the notorious Evin prison in Tehran. Kazemi had apparently died as a result of injuries sustained during the police interrogation, and although the Iranian authorities initially claimed that her death was accidental, both Kazemi's family and the Canadian Government exerted pressure on the Iranian authorities to open an investigation into her death. An interrogator from the Ministry of Intelligence and Security was charged with the journalist's 'quasi-intentional murder', but all charges against him were dismissed in July 2004 because of what was stated to be lack of sufficient evidence, and Kazemi's death was termed an 'accident'. In August 2003, meanwhile, the Council of Guardians rejected a Majlis-approved bill on women's rights and also a motion condemning the use of torture in interrogation, stating that both cases contradicted Islamic law. In October the human rights lawyer Shirin Ebadi was awarded the Nobel Peace Prize, becoming both the first Iranian and the first Muslim woman to receive a Nobel prize. (Ebadi was subsequently appointed by the family of Zahra Kazemi to represent them at the trial of the intelligence agent accused of her murder.)

A Ministry of Welfare and Social Security was established in December 2003 as part of new legislation to reform the country's social security provisions. However, the almost complete destruction of the historic city of Bam on 26 December, as a result of a powerful earthquake, dominated the domestic agenda into early 2004. According to official figures released in March of that year, 26,271 people lost their lives in the earthquake. The international community immediately sent emergency teams to assist in the rescue effort, while the USA announced a temporary easing of sanctions to facilitate the transfer of financial aid and essential equipment to Bam.

Meanwhile, a new political crisis was unfolding in early 2004. With elections to the seventh Majlis scheduled for late February, the Council of Guardians announced in early January that, from a preliminary list of around 8,200 candidates, more than 2,000 candidates would be barred from standing in the polls, including 80 current Majlis deputies. ('Reformists' insisted that at least one-half of the proposed candidates would effectively be disqualified.) President Khatami's brother and the Secretary-General of the Islamic Iran Participation Front, Muhammad Reza Khatami, was perhaps the most notable of these 'reformist' candidates, along with two other leaders of the party. President Khatami and several of his ministers threatened to resign in protest at the ban, as did all of the country's 27 regional governors, and about 100 deputies staged a 'sit-in' at the Majlis. Although, as a result of two direct interventions by Ayatollah Khamenei, the Council of Guardians reversed its decision in relation to a small number of the barred candidates, in late January the Council vetoed emergency legislation that had been adopted by the Majlis with the intention of weakening the former's control over the election process and thereby reversing the bans on all of the candidates. At the elections to the Majlis, held on 20 February, turn-out by voters was estimated to be as low as 51% (with a recorded rate of only 28% in Tehran); 229 candidates received enough votes to be elected directly to the Majlis, with the remainder of the 290 seats to be filled at a second round of voting, held on 7 May. The 'reformist' Speaker of the outgoing Majlis, Mahdi Karrubi, withdrew his candidacy after failing to secure re-election at the first round. As had been widely predicted, 'conservatives' were confirmed as having secured a majority in the legislature, and following the second round of voting were estimated to have secured 195 seats in the Majlis and the 'reformists' fewer than 50, with the remainder being held by 'independents'.

In early May 2004 a law banning the use of torture in Iran was approved by the Council of Guardians. Later that month the new Majlis took office and nominated Gholam-Ali Haddad-Adel as the first non-cleric Speaker since the Islamic Revolution; Haddad-Adel was elected to the post in June. In the same month the death sentence imposed on the academic, Hashem Aghajari, for apostasy (see above), which had been reinstated in May, was revoked by the Supreme Court. In July he was sentenced to a five-year gaol term, two years of which were suspended, and in early August he was released on bail. In October the Majlis impeached the Minister of Roads and Transport, Ahmad Khorram, for corruption and mismanagement. Muhammad Ramati was appointed as his successor in February 2005. Also in October 2004 the Vice-President in charge of Legal and Parliamentary Affairs, Muhammad Ali Abtahi, resigned, citing his frustration with 'conservatives' who were impeding his ability to perform his duties. Majid Ansari was subsequently appointed to the post.

It was announced in January 2005 that the vote to elect President Khatami's successor was to take place on 17 June, simultaneously with by-elections in eight parliamentary constituencies where results of the February 2004 elections were overturned by the Council of Guardians and in the earthquake-devastated city of Bam; one undecided seat in the Tehran constituency was also to be filled. In May 2005 the Council of Guardians disqualified all but six out of 1,014 candidacies submitted for the presidential election, including prominent 'reformist' candidates Moustafa Moin and Mohsen Mehr-Alizadeh. Under the threat of a boycott by 'reformist' supporters, however, these two candidates were allowed to stand, after Ayatollah Khamenei reportedly intervened to instruct the Council to accept their candidacies. The six other eligible candidates included former President Hashemi Rafsanjani, who attempted to place himself in the middle ground between 'reformers' and 'hardliners' and was broadly considered the favourite to win in advance of the election (although his candidacy was thought to be opposed by Khamenei). Among the candidates regarded as 'hardline' were Muhammad Baqir Qalibaf, a former national chief of police, Mohsen Rezai, ex-commander of the Revolutionary Guards, Ali Ardeshir Larijani, former head of the state broadcasting agency, and Mahmoud Ahmadinejad, the mayor of Tehran. The final candidate, Mahdi Karrubi, a former Speaker of the Majlis (see above), was considered to be a moderate 'reformist'. Two days before the first round of voting, however, Rezai withdrew his candidacy.

The first round of voting in the 2005 presidential election, held on 17 June, did not result in any of the seven candidates receiving 50% or more of the total vote, thereby ensuring that a second round of voting would be held—an unprecedented event in a presidential election in the Islamic Republic. As had been widely predicted, Rafsanjani received the most votes, with 21.0%; more unexpected, however, was the success of Ahmadinejad, who finished in second place, with 19.5% of votes cast, to secure a place in the second round. Ahmadinejad's campaign promised greater economic equality, reduced corruption and a return to the values of the 1979 Islamic Revolution, and was thought to be strongly supported by poorer Iranians. Several allegations of electoral fraud were made regarding the poll, most notably by defeated candidate Mahdi Karrubi, who wrote an open letter to the Supreme Leader alleging that Revolutionary Guards and Basij forces had interfered in the election, and resigning from his official posts. The Council of Guardians, however, announced following a partial recount that no evidence of electoral fraud had been uncovered, and that the second stage of voting could therefore proceed. At the second round, held on 24 June 2005, Ahmadinejad secured 61.7% of the vote, thereby defeating Rafsanjani to be elected the sixth President of the Islamic Republic of Iran. Turn-out at this stage was recorded at 59.6%.

The election of Ahmadinejad led to a major overhaul of political personnel. The President was inaugurated on 6 August 2005, and on 14 August he presented his list of ministerial nominees to the Majlis for approval. The list was widely described by commentators as both 'hardline' and inexperienced, and included only one member of the outgoing cabinet. Among the more prominent nominations were Manouchehr Mottaki as Minister of Foreign Affairs, Moustafa Pour-Muhammadi as Minister of the Interior, Gholam Hossein Mohseni Ejeie as Minister of Information and Muhammad Hossein Saffar-Harandi as Minister of Culture and Islamic Guidance. The Majlis approved 17 of Ahmadinejad's 21 nominations, but rejected his candidates for the portfolios of Co-operatives, Education, Welfare and Social Security, and Oil. Three of the four vacant posts were subsequently filled when the Majlis approved Ahmadinejad's new nominations in early November, but the appointment of a new Minister of Oil—a key ministerial post, in view of the high proportion of government revenue generated by petroleum and gas sales—proved more contentious. Eventually, Ahmadinejad's fourth nominee for the post, Sayed Kazem Vaziri Hamaneh, who had been caretaker of the Ministry since August, was accepted by the Majlis in December. Subsequently, in January 2006 Vaziri Hamaneh announced new managerial appointments at all the major state-owned hydrocarbons companies. The protracted opposition demonstrated by the (predominantly 'conservative') Majlis over the oil portfolio was one prominent example of resistance within the political establishment to Ahmadinejad's attempts to impose his authority by appointing supporters and sympathizers to positions of influence. In November 2005, meanwhile, the newly appointed Minister of Foreign Affairs, Manouchehr Mottaki, announced significant changes in Iran's diplomatic service, with some 40 ambassadors expected to be recalled by March 2006.

There were notable instances of violent tension in ethnic minority-dominated regions of Iran in 2005. In April riots broke out in the town of Ahvaz, in the largely Arab-populated province of Khuzestan, leading to clashes with police in which between three and 20 people died, according to various reports. The unrest was apparently connected to a letter, attributed to former Vice-President in charge of Legal and Parliamentary Affairs Muhammad Ali Abtahi, which appeared to describe a deliberate government policy to 'Persianize' this oil-rich south-eastern province by forcibly relocating much of its historically Arab population. (Abtahi strongly denied the authenticity of the letter.) In June, shortly before the first round of the presidential election, several bombs exploded in Ahvaz, resulting in the deaths of some eight people, while an explosion also occurred in Tehran, killing one person. No group claimed responsibility for the attacks, although government spokesmen blamed Arab separatists acting in conjunction with the Mujahidin-e-Khalq and former members of the Baath Party of deposed Iraqi President Saddam Hussain, while also suggesting the involvement of the United Kingdom and the USA. Further bombings occurred in Ahvaz in October, killing at least six people; on this occasion official sources alleged that the British forces occupying southern Iraq had been involved in the attacks. Meanwhile, in August 2005 troops were reportedly deployed in the Kurdish regions of north-western Iran in order to suppress weeks of protests and riots, apparently initiated by the death of a Kurdish separatist in police custody and the posting by his family on the internet of pictures purporting to show his tortured body. Up to 20 people were thought to have died in the unrest, which commentators linked to long-standing dissatisfaction among Kurds at their treatment within the Iranian state, this being aggravated by the relative autonomy and influence recently gained by the Kurds of neighbouring Iraq.

Ethnic unrest continued in 2006, with two bombs exploding in Ahvaz in January, causing nine deaths. The Iranian Government immediately accused the United Kingdom of involvement in the attacks, and claimed that the bombers had enjoyed the co-operation of British armed forces and had used their military facilities in Basra, Iraq. British officials strenuously denied the accusations. In February a court in Ahvaz sentenced at least 11 Iranians to death for their alleged involvement in bomb attacks in Khuzestan (two of whom were subjected to public hanging in the following month), although the use of one-day secret trials and forced televised confessions drew the condemnation of international human rights observers. A further three of the accused were executed in December, and reportedly another eight during January and February 2007. The authorities again accused both the United Kingdom and the USA of attempting to provoke ethnic unrest in Iran during March 2006 when armed rebels in the south-eastern province of Sistan and Baluchestan ambushed a convoy of government and provincial officials and killed 22 of them. All of the victims were members of the Shi'a community, whom the province's Baluchi Sunni population had long accused of religious discrimination. The governor of Zahedan, the provinial capital, was among seven officials who were shot and wounded during the incident. In February 2007 11 people were believed to have died in an explosion on a bus carrying members of the Revolutionary Guards in Zahedan.

In January 2006 President Ahmadinejad launched his first crackdown on the media since taking office, closing the daily financial newspaper *Asia* and preventing a new publication for female readers, *Nour-e-Banovan*, from being launched. No official reasons were given for the closures, although reports suggested that *Nour-e-Banovan* had received warnings concerning the publication of images of women deemed to be dressed inappropriately. A second series of repressive measures was taken in September, when the Press Supervisory Board closed four publications, including the popular 'reformist' daily *Shargh*, which had printed a cartoon appearing to liken Ahmadinejad to a donkey. (The newspaper resumed publication in May 2007, but in August a further ban was imposed.)

The issue of human rights in Iran came under renewed scrutiny in July 2006, when a prominent dissident and former student leader, Akbar Muhammadi, died after going on hunger strike at Evin prison in Tehran. Muhammadi had been condemned to death for his involvement in the student protests during 1999, although his sentence had later been commuted to 15 years in gaol. In a further setback for human rights campaigners, in August 2006 the Government banned the Centre for Defence of Human Rights, on the grounds that it was an 'illegal' organization since it had failed to apply for a permit. Under the presidency of Nobel Peace Prize winner Shirin Ebadi, the Centre provided free legal advice to dissidents and other activists who had been detained for protesting against the authorities or criticizing government policies. Ebadi vowed to continue the group's activities, despite the threat of arrest. In the following month Ahmadinejad was reported to have urged students to demand that their 'liberal' and secular university lecturers be removed from their posts. According to a report issued by the US-based Human Rights Watch in late 2006, the Iranian judiciary had sentenced 35 students to prison terms as a result of their political activities, while suspending or banning 15 student associations. Student activists, meanwhile, alleged that 47 student publications had been closed down by the authorities and 28 student organizations banned in 2006. In December an address by President Ahmadinejad at Amirkabir University of Technology in Tehran was interrupted by students angered by the administration's attempts to restrict their freedom of expression.

Meanwhile, the country began to prepare for two important polls to be held on 15 December 2006, to elect members of the Council of Experts and more than 113,000 municipal councillors, including members of the 15-seat Tehran council. Both the Council of Experts and Tehran municipal council were dominated by political 'hardliners', and the composition of the former was especially crucial as it is charged with electing the country's Supreme Leader. In September 2006 Ahmadinejad appointed Mojtaba Samare, described by many as the President's closest aide, as deputy of political affairs at the Ministry of the Interior and thus the official responsible for monitoring the elections. Although in October reports indicated that some 500 candidates had registered for membership of the Council of Experts, by the following month more than two-thirds of these had been disqualified. According to the Council of Guardians, 100 prospective candidates had withdrawn their applications, while all the female candidates had reportedly failed the exam concerning religious interpretation. As a result, it was clear that in some constituencies there would only be one person running for office. None the less, the results of the municipal election on 15 December demonstrated an unexpected victory for the 'moderates', the President's allies having failed to win control of any municipal council. Associates of Ahmadinejad secured only two seats on the 15-member council in Tehran, while allies of the 'hardline' mayor Muhammad Baqir Qalibaf won eight seats, 'reformists' four and an independent one seat. A significant majority of municipal seats were secured by 'reformists', independents, 'moderate conservatives' and other opponents of the President. Turn-out for the elections was estimated at 60%, significantly higher than the figure recorded for municipal polls in 2003. Particularly notable among those elected to the Council of Experts was former President Hashemi Rafsanjani (who was also elected as Speaker of the Council in early September 2007, following the death of Ayatollah Ali Akbar Meshkini in July).

Further weaknesses in President Ahmadinejad's control over the domestic agenda became apparent in early 2007. In January 50 legislators were reported to have signed a document demanding that the President answer questions in the Majlis with regard to his increasingly aggressive stance on the nuclear issue (see below). The 'reformist' Islamic Iran Participation Front was quoted in several news sources as having rejected Ahmadinejad's isolationist stance, instead asking that the country suspend its programme to enrich uranium. Even 'conservative' newspapers, which tended to be closely allied with Ahmadinejad, began to voice criticism of his policies, and media speculation suggested that Ayatollah Khamenei was growing so disillusioned with the President that he had occasionally refused to meet him. In a separate development, 150 Majlis deputies were reported to have signed a letter blaming Ahmadinejad for the country's high levels of inflation and unemployment, and condemning him for failing to deliver the state budget on time. Significantly, a number of the President's former allies were among the letter's signatories. Ahmadinejad also received strong criticism from the dissident cleric Ayatollah Montazeri, who warned that the use of provocative language would serve only to exacerbate the crisis with the West over Iran's nuclear programme, although the Ayatollah maintained that Iran did reserve the right to produce nuclear energy.

In May 2007 the Government raised the price of petrol and, in the following month, with very little advanced warning, introduced petrol rationing in order to reduce the fuel subsidies that were contributing to Iran's considerable state budget deficit. The measures resulted in attacks being carried out by angry protesters against a number of petrol stations and other state buildings in Tehran and elsewhere. Several Iranian newspapers reported that President Ahmadinejad had dismissed two prominent members of the Council of Ministers in mid-August; the state news agency, however, insisted that the two men had resigned their posts. Minister of Industries and Mines Ali Reza Tahmasbi was replaced by Ali Akbar Mehrabian, and Minister of Petroleum Sayed Kazem Vaziri Hamaneh by Gholamhossein Nozari (head of the National Iranian Oil Co), both in an acting capacity until mid-November, when the Majlis endorsed their permanent appointment. Vaziri Hamaneh was said to have been appointed as a special adviser to the President on oil and gas affairs. No official explanation for the ministerial changes appeared to have been given, and certain senior members of the regime, including the Head of the Judiciary, Ayatollah Sayed Mahmoud Hashemi Shahrudi, were reported to have criticized President Ahmadinejad's alleged role in ordering the reshuffle. In September Brig.-Gen. Muhammad Ali Jafari was named as the new Chief of Staff of the Revolutionary Guards in place of Maj.-Gen. Yahya Rahim-Safavi. The Minister of Education, Mahmoud Farshidi, resigned in early December, and was succeeded on an interim basis by Ali Reza Ali Ahmadi, who was confirmed in the post in mid-February 2008. In a further change to the Council of Ministers in late April, Hossein Samsami replaced Davoud Danesh-Ja'afari as the Minister of Economic Affairs and Finance, in an acting capacity.

Press reports in January 2008 suggested that, in advance of the eighth elections to the Majlis scheduled to be held in March, almost one-half of the 7,168 candidates who had registered for the polls (the majority of these being 'reformists') had been disqualified by either the Ministry of the Interior or the Council of Guardians. It was again evident at this time that the popularity of President Ahmadinejad was waning, as the public became increasingly frustrated by the persistent problems of high unemployment and inflation, and at the tightening of restrictive measures by the authorities in many aspects of their lives. For example, 'reformist' students at Tehran University had demonstrated against Ahmadinejad in October 2007, with some describing him as a 'dictator'; such direct protests against the President are extremely rare in Iran. Ahmadinejad's authority was further questioned in late January 2008, when Ayatollah Khamenei overruled his decision not to supply subsidized gas to Iranians in rural areas who were suffering shortages owing to the extreme weather conditions. In early March it was reported that 'conservatives' had split into two separate lists to contest the forthcoming polls: the United Principlist Front was formed by traditionalists who supported President Ahmadinejad's policies, while the Broad Principlist Coalition consisted of those who were more critical of the President's foreign and economic policies (including so-called 'revisionists' Ali Larijani, Mohsen Rezai and Muhammad Baqir Qalibaf).

Although no official results were issued at this stage, it appeared that just over 200 of the 290 seats had been filled at the first legislative ballot, held on 14 March 2008. Several sources indicated that the Majlis would be dominated by 'conservatives', who already controlled an estimated 132 seats in the legislature (with a reported 90 of these being supporters of President Ahmadinejad). However, 'reformists', who won some 31 seats at the first round, asserted that the election had been neither free nor fair, owing to the disqualification by the authorities of at least 1,700 of their candidates in advance of the poll (some of those disqualified in early 2008 were subsequently reinstated). Opposition politicians also remarked that Iran's state-controlled media had been noticeably biased in favour of the President's supporters during electoral campaigning. US and EU officials were strongly critical of the conduct of the election. 'Conservatives' secured 19 of the 30 seats in Tehran, with the remainder to be decided at the run-off election. According to the Ministry of the Interior, almost 60% of eligible voters had participated in the first ballot. A second round of voting for the 82 undecided Majlis seats was held on 25 April. However, three seats remained vacant following both rounds, after election officials had annulled the results for unspecified reasons; by-elections for these seats were to be held at a later date. According to official reports, 'conservatives' had consolidated their control of the legislature, with an estimated 198–200 seats; 'reformists' secured around 46–50 seats, and the remainder were held by 'independents'. Only one of the 11 contested seats in Tehran went to a 'reformist' candidate at the second round; thus 29 of the 30 seats in the capital would be controlled by 'conservatives'. However, despite 'conservative' factions having consolidated their control of the Majlis, some of these were members of the Broad Principlist Coalition. It was, therefore, generally assumed that President Ahmadinejad would experience greater levels of opposition among Majlis deputies than had been the case in the previous parliament, especially in the run-up to the presidential polls scheduled for 2009.

Relations with the USA since the end of the Iran–Iraq War have continued to be characterized by mutual suspicion. The USA, alleging that Iran is pursuing a programme of military expansion, has expressed particular concern over the nature of nuclear co-operation between the People's Republic of China, Russia and Iran, and has sought to persuade Iran's Western allies to reduce economic and technical assistance to, and direct investment in, the country. Iran maintains that it is not engaged in the development of weapons of mass destruction (asserting that its nuclear programme is required to meet domestic energy demands rather than for military purposes), while the Chinese and Russian Governments have strenuously denied involvement in non-civilian nuclear projects in Iran. In July 1994 the USA accused Iran of being responsible for bomb attacks against Jewish targets in the United Kingdom and Argentina in an attempt to disrupt the Middle East peace process. (A former Iranian intelligence agent alleged in July 2002 that Iranian agents had plotted and carried out the bombing in Buenos Aires in 1994 with the backing of the Iranian Government, although Iranian officials have persistently denied the claims. In October 2006 Argentine prosecutors brought formal charges against eight former Iranian officials, including Ali Akbar Hashemi Rafsanjani, who had been President at the time of the bomb attack.)

In April 1995 US efforts to isolate Iran internationally culminated in the announcement that all US companies and their overseas subsidiaries would be banned from investing in, or trading with, Iran (with the subsequent exception of US oil companies in the Caucasus and Central Asia involved in marketing petroleum from the countries of the former USSR). Russia refused to support the embargo, but announced in May that it would henceforth separate the civilian and military components of an agreement to supply Iran with a nuclear reactor, to be constructed at Bushehr, in south-western Iran. In mid-1996 the US Congress approved legislation (termed the Iran-Libya Sanctions Act—ILSA) to penalize companies operating in US markets that were investing US $40m. (subsequently amended to $20m.) or more in energy projects in prescribed countries deemed to be sponsoring terrorism. However, these so-called secondary economic sanctions received little international support. In December Iran and Russia concluded an extensive co-operation agreement. In September 1997, furthermore, a consortium comprising French, Malaysian and Russian energy companies signed a contract with the Iranian National Oil Company to invest some $2,000m. in the development of natural gas reserves in Iranian waters of the Persian Gulf. Threats of sanctions were effectively averted in May 1998, when the US Administration agreed to waive penalties for which the Secretary of State deemed the companies involved to be liable. This decision apparently facilitated further foreign investment in Iran, most notably in hydrocarbons projects.

Khatami's election to the Iranian presidency in mid-1997 prompted speculation regarding prospects for an improvement in relations with the USA and other Western countries. A notable development was the designation by the USA, in October, of the opposition Mujahidin-e-Khalq as one of 30 proscribed terrorist organizations. (The Mujahidin-e-Khalq's parent organization, the National Council of Resistance, also based in France, was proscribed by the USA in October 1999.) In December 1997 Khatami expressed his desire to engage in a 'thoughtful dialogue' with the American people. In what was interpreted as a major concession, US President Bill Clinton stated subsequently that the USA would not require Iran (or any other Islamic state) to modify its attitude towards the Middle East peace process. The cautious rapprochement continued in January 1998, when Khatami made a widely publicized address, via a US television news network, emphasizing the need for Iran to develop closer cultural links with the USA.

The announcement, in July 1998, that Iran had successfully test-fired a new ballistic missile, the *Shahab-3*, capable of striking targets at a distance of 1,300 km, caused renewed tensions. (The missile could potentially target Israel and also US forces in the Gulf.) US concerns regarding what it perceived as Iran's efforts to acquire weapons of mass destruction remained a principal cause of mutual suspicion, and there was continuing evidence of efforts by the Clinton Administration to block trading agreements deemed to assist Iran's military programme. Nevertheless, earlier in that year Russia, stating that the Bushehr plant conformed with standards prescribed by the International Atomic Energy Agency (IAEA) for the prevention of nuclear weapons proliferation, declared its willingness to provide equipment for the reactor. In September 1999 the US House of Representatives approved non-proliferation legislation requiring the imposition of sanctions against any country aiding Iran in the development of weapons of mass destruction.

Addressing the American-Iranian Council in Washington, DC, in March 2000, US Secretary of State Madeleine Albright announced an end to restrictions on imports from Iran of several non-hydrocarbons items. This substantive step towards the normalization of relations was in recognition of what the US Administration regarded as trends towards democracy under President Khatami. Albright furthermore offered what amounted to an apology for the role played by the USA in the *coup d'état* of 1953, as well as for US support for Iraq in the Iran–Iraq War. Such concessions were, however, accompanied by the assertion that Iran had done little to modify its support for what Albright termed international terrorism and its efforts to develop nuclear weaponry. Hopes of a further rapprochement were encouraged by open meetings and other contacts involving Iranian and US officials at the UN Millennium Summit in New York in September 2000. However, relations between Iran and the USA deteriorated in June 2001 after 14 men (13 Saudi Arabians and one Lebanese) were indicted *in absentia* by the US Government, having been charged in connection with the bomb attack at al-Khobar in 1996 (see below). Although no Iranians were among the accused, US officials reiterated allegations that members of the Iranian Government were behind the bombing. In August 2001 the new Administration of President George W. Bush, inaugurated in January, confirmed that ILSA was to be extended for a further five years. Iran's 20th application to enter negotiations regarding membership of the World Trade Organization (WTO, see p. 396) was vetoed by the USA in December 2004. However, in March 2005 President Bush announced a series of economic incentives, including the removal of the ban on Iran's membership of the WTO, provided that Iran agreed permanently to suspend its nuclear energy programme. Subsequently, with Iran still at that time maintaining the suspension of its nuclear activities (see below), the USA abandoned its objection to Iran's WTO application, enabling membership talks to begin in May.

President Khatami was swift to offer his condolences to the American nation following the suicide bombings in New York and Washington, DC, on 11 September 2001. Although Ayatollah Khamenei also condemned the terrorist attacks, he and Iran's 'conservative' press warned against any large-scale US military offensive targeting the Taliban regime and militants of the al-Qa'ida (Base) network—led by the principal suspect for the attacks, the radical Islamist Osama bin Laden—in Afghanistan. Iranians strongly condemned the commencement of hostilities in October, but details subsequently emerged of a secret agreement between Iran and the USA whereby Iran would offer assistance to any US military personnel either shot down or forced to land within its borders, provided that the USA respect Iran's territorial integrity. Iranian and US officials held UN-sponsored talks in Geneva in that month to discuss the composition of a future Afghan government.

In 2002 the Iranian administration denied accusations by the USA that it was permitting fleeing al-Qa'ida and Taliban fighters to cross the Afghan border into Iran. Relations deteriorated abruptly in January, when, in his annual State of the Union address, the US President referred to Iran as forming (together with Iraq and the Democratic People's Republic of Korea—North Korea) an 'axis of evil', explicitly accusing Iran of aggressively pursuing the development of weapons of mass destruction and of 'exporting terror'. Bush's remarks were denounced in the strongest terms by the Iranian leadership, with President Khatami accusing his US counterpart of 'warmongering'. In May Khatami urged 'reformist' deputies in the Majlis not to attempt to hold discussions with US officials. Meanwhile, the US Department of State again designated Iran as the world's 'most active' sponsor of terrorism (as the country was also termed during 2003–08), and US officials reiterated their claims that Russia was assisting Iran in the manufacture of nuclear weapons. In July the US Administration was angered by Russia's conclusion of a development and co-operation accord with Iran, which reportedly involved the construction of additional reactors at the Bushehr nuclear plant. President Khatami, for his part, openly condemned US plans to use military force to bring about 'regime change' in Iraq, warning that such action posed a serious risk to regional stability. In October the Minister of Foreign Affairs, Kamal Kharrazi, declared that, in the event of US-led military action leading to a change of regime in Iraq, Iran strongly opposed any post-war Iraqi government being imposed by the USA. The announcement made by Iranian officials in early February 2003 that the country was to extract recently discovered deposits of uranium in order to produce nuclear fuel heightened fears within the US Administration that Iran was secretly involved in the manufacture of nuclear weapons. Inspectors from the IAEA began an assessment of Iran's nuclear programme later in the month (see below), although the dialogue on Iran's nuclear capabilities was temporarily interrupted by the conflict in neighbouring Iraq in early 2003.

Iran had been host to many Iraqi groups-in-exile, most notably the Shi'ite-dominated Supreme Council for the Islamic Revolution in Iraq (renamed the Supreme Islamic Iraqi Council in 2007) and its military wing, the Badr Brigade (subsequently renamed Badr Organization). Therefore, following the removal from power of Saddam Hussain by the US-led coalition in April 2003, the US Administration warned Tehran not to get involved in Iraqi affairs, fearing that the Iranian leadership sought a political settlement that would favour the Shi'a Muslim majority and lead to the formation of a Shi'ite bloc in the Middle East antipathetic to US interests. However, in May it became necessary for the USA and Iran to instigate talks in Geneva, under the auspices of the UN, to discuss the return of Iraqi exiles and refugees in Iran, as well as the presence in Iraq of the Mujahidin-e-Khalq and its military wing, the National Liberation Army (NLA—see below). The talks collapsed after Ayatollah Khamenei described them as 'tantamount to surrender', and when US officials accused Iran of interfering in Iraqi internal affairs and of sheltering al-Qa'ida militants suspected of masterminding suicide bombings at expatriate compounds in Riyadh, Saudi Arabia, earlier that month. (Iranian officials subsequently admitted that a group of al-Qa'ida suspects were in Iranian detention and were to stand trial.) After the earthquake at Bam in December (see above), it appeared that the USA and Iran might be embarking on a process of 'earthquake diplomacy', with the US Administration agreeing to ease financial sanctions and restrictions on the export of technical apparatus to Iran in order to facilitate the reconstruction process. However, at the beginning of 2004 President Bush denied that offers of humanitarian aid to Iran would in any way influence US policy towards Iran. In April Iranian officials refuted suggestions that the USA had asked Iran for assistance in its struggle to defeat the insurgency in Iraq or that any Iranian element was supporting the radical Shi'ite movement led by Hojatoleslam Muqtada as-Sadr. An Iranian diplomatic mission, supposedly dispatched upon the request of the United Kingdom to mediate between US troops and as-Sadr's forces around the Iraqi city of Najaf, was withdrawn following the assassination of the first secretary of the Iranian embassy in Baghdad. In July a further rift in Iranian–US relations developed when the USA declared a group of 3,800 members of the Mujahidin-e-Khalq interned in Iraq to be protected persons under the Geneva Convention. Iran criticized the USA for supporting 'terrorists', but US officials emphasized that they would not protect any individuals suspected of carrying out terrorist attacks.

The introduction to the US Senate in August of the Iran Freedom and Support Act of 2004, which was designed to promote 'regime change' in Tehran and to provide US $10m. in support of pro-democracy opposition groups in Iran, was seen as further evidence of the desire of the Bush Administration to use military force against Iran. (A US investigative journalist claimed in January 2005 that US special forces had been conducting surveillance operations in Iran for several months, in preparation for military strikes; however, a spokesman for the US Administration described the allegations as being 'riddled with inaccuracies'.) Meanwhile, despite its vehement opposition to the US-led invasion and occupation of Iraq, it seemed increasingly likely that the Iranian regime would in fact prove to be one of the main beneficiaries of the ousting of Saddam Hussain, following the success of Shi'a religio-political parties in the elections to Iraq's new permanent legislature in December 2005. In November of that year President Jalal Talabani became the first Iraqi head of state for over 30 years to visit Iran.

Following President Khatami's announcement in February 2003 regarding the discovery and successful extraction of uranium (see above), the USA urged the IAEA to declare Iran to be in violation of the nuclear non-proliferation treaty (NPT), and appealed for Russia to end its collaboration with Iran on the Bushehr plant. In June the Director-General of the IAEA, Dr Muhammad el-Baradei, presented his report concerning Iran's nuclear capabilities to the IAEA board, in which he called on Iran to open its nuclear programme to a more rigorous system of inspections. Iran responded that it would only comply with this request if it were given access to the nuclear technology it required, thereby increasing the likelihood of censure by the UN and the possible imposition of sanctions. In July it was revealed that Iran had finally brought into service the *Shahab-3* ballistic missile (see above), causing concern in the USA and Israel. Although in August President Khatami stated that Iran's nuclear programmes were 'entirely peaceful', the USA insisted that Iran was in breach of its nuclear safeguards obligations, and the IAEA (with US support) adopted a resolution on 12 September giving Iran until 31 October to disclose full details of its nuclear programme and to show evidence that it was not developing nuclear weapons. This followed the discovery of enriched uranium at a processing plant south of Tehran. In October IAEA officials travelled to Iran in order to re-engage Iran in the nuclear inspections process, as did the foreign ministers of France, Germany and the United Kingdom. On 21 October it was announced that Iran would accept a more rigorous system of inspections at its nuclear facilities, and in November the IAEA produced a report indicating that there was no evidence that Iran was producing nuclear weapons.

In February 2004, however, the IAEA reported that it had found evidence of undeclared facilities that could be used for the enrichment of uranium. In March the IAEA adopted a resolution condemning Iran for the secrecy of its nuclear activities, which resulted in the temporary suspension by Iranian officials of inspections. The two sides were reported to have agreed a new timetable for further monitoring of Iran's nuclear facilities in April, and it was announced that Iran would suspend voluntarily all centrifuge construction. However, after the IAEA, on 18 June, adopted a resolution criticizing Iran for failing to co-operate with the inspections process, in late June the Iranian leadership announced that, although it would adhere to its pledge to suspend actual uranium enrichment, it would resume manufacturing parts for centrifuges and would also recommence the testing and assembly of centrifuges. Moreover, Iran criticized the United Kingdom, France and Germany for not supplying it with the technology and trade they had promised in October 2003 in return for Iran's pledge to freeze its uranium enrichment programme. In October 2004 Russia and Iran completed the construction of the Bushehr nuclear plant. Russian officials pressed the Islamic regime to cease its uranium enrichment programme, apparently fearing that sanctions imposed by the UN Security Council would threaten the Bushehr deal. Iran also tested a long-range satellite-launching rocket, the *Shahab-4*, asserting that it would only use its missiles in self-defence. In early November, rejecting UN demands that Iran end all uranium enrichment activities, the Majlis approved a motion urging the Government to continue with efforts to develop a nuclear energy programme. In mid-November, following further talks with French, German and British officials in Paris, France, Iran complied with IAEA demands to suspend temporarily its uranium enrichment programme, averting the possibility of such activities being reported to the UN and the subsequent imposition of sanctions. Iran insisted that the suspension was voluntary and was not a legal obligation, and asserted its right to nuclear technologies, emphasizing in late November that the suspension would last for 'months, not years'.

In March 2005 the US Administration announced a series of economic incentives to Iran (see above) to persuade the country to suspend permanently its uranium enrichment programme, while the United Kingdom, France and Germany agreed to refer Iran to the UN Security Council if the programme was not suspended; Iran dismissed the offer as insignificant. Following an Iranian announcement in May that the conversion of uranium to gas (the stage before enrichment) would soon recommence at the Esfahan conversion facility, negotiations between Iran and the United Kingdom, France and Germany began in Geneva. Later that month, in an apparently provocative gesture, Iran's Ministry of Defence and Armed Forces Logistics announced that it had successfully tested a new motor for the *Shahab-3* missile that increased the weapon's accuracy. Meanwhile, the news in July that the US Administration had decided to grant recognition of nuclear status to India—a country that, unlike Iran, had never signed the NPT—prompted accusations of 'double standards' from Iranian officials.

The election of the 'ultra-conservative' Mahmoud Ahmadinejad to the Iranian presidency in June 2005 (see above) caused concern in US political circles. Rumours circulated in the US media that Ahmadinejad had, as a student, been involved in the taking of hostages at the US embassy in Tehran shortly after the Iranian Revolution in 1979 (see above); the Iranian Government denied the allegations. In early August 2005 Iran resumed the conversion of uranium at the Esfahan plant, having previously rejected as 'worthless' a set of compensatory proposals put forward by the United Kingdom, France and Germany in exchange for the abandonment of its enrichment programme. The IAEA subsequently adopted a resolution on 11 August expressing 'serious concern' at the resumption of nuclear activities at Esfahan, and urging Iran to revert to suspension. Also in August President Ahmadinejad appointed defeated presidential candidate Ali Larijani (believed to be a close ally of Ayatollah Khamenei) as Secretary of the Supreme Council for National Security and chief nuclear negotiator, replacing the more moderate Hassan Rohani. A further IAEA resolution on 24 September found Iran guilty of 'non-compliance' and asserted that it should increase the transparency of its nuclear programme and reinstate suspension.

However, Iran announced on 10 January 2006 that it had reopened its uranium enrichment research facility at Natanz, south of Tehran, after a moratorium of two years. On 4 February the Board of Governors of the IAEA voted to report Iran to the UN Security Council. The Governments of the USA and Israel, meanwhile, stated that they could not rule out the possibility of taking military action in order to halt the progress of Iran's nuclear programme. Iran confirmed on 14 February that small-scale uranium enrichment work had recommenced at the Natanz plant. On 8 March the Director-General of the IAEA, Muhammad el-Baradei, transmitted his report on Iran's nuclear programme to the Security Council, which, on 29 March, unanimously approved a statement calling on Iran to suspend all uranium enrichment activities within 30 days. On 11 April President Ahmadinejad responded to this demand by announcing that, two days previously, Iran had successfully enriched uranium for the first time. Despite Ahmadinejad's insistence that his country had no intention of developing nuclear weapons, this announcement precipitated serious concern among the international community. The US Administration revealed at this time that it was allocating US $75m. to fund Iranian dissident groups.

On 28 April 2006 el-Baradei delivered a report to the UN Security Council which concluded that Iran had failed to comply with the 30-day deadline imposed by the Council to halt its uranium enrichment activities, and affirmed that since Tehran had failed fully to co-operate with the IAEA, there could be no guarantee that the Islamic Republic's nuclear activities were purely peaceful. In response, the US ambassador to the UN, John Bolton, called on the Security Council to invoke Chapter VII of the UN Charter, which contained provision for the use of military action—a demand that was immediately rejected by China and Russia. Earlier in April the US investigative journalist Seymour Hersh claimed in an article published in *The New Yorker* that the Bush Administration was planning military strikes against Iran and had not completely rejected the use of tactical nuclear weapons against the country in the event that it continued to flout international demands for the cessation of uranium enrichment. President Bush dismissed the allegations as 'wild speculation'. In a surprise development in early May, President Ahmadinejad sent an 18-page letter to Bush, proposing 'new solutions' for the two states to settle their differences. The letter was reported to be the first direct communication between an Iranian President and his US counterpart since the 1979 Islamic Revolution. The US response to the letter, which was received as Secretary of State Condoleezza Rice was meeting members of the UN Security Council in New York to formulate a common response to the Iranian regime, was dismissive. Meanwhile, Tehran threatened to withdraw from the nuclear NPT if Western pressure over its nuclear programme intensified.

Meeting in Brussels, Belgium, in mid-May 2006, EU ministers responsible for foreign affairs attempted to find a way out of the impasse by proposing a 'bold' package of trade and technical incentives for Tehran to halt its nuclear programme. Offering the Iranian authorities what they deemed to be 'the most sophisticated technology', the EU representatives stated that they would be prepared to assist Iran as long as the technology was used for peaceful, rather than military, activities. However, the offer was firmly rejected by the Iranian leadership. At the end of May Rice declared that Washington would be prepared to hold direct talks with Tehran as soon as the regime suspended its uranium enrichment activities and co-operated with UN inspectors. Further economic incentives for Iran to renounce uranium enrichment were offered by the EU's High Representative for Common Foreign and Security Policy, Javier Solana, in June, following an agreement reached by the five permanent members of the Security Council, together with Germany, concerning new proposals to encourage Tehran to end the programme. These included an offer of nuclear technical assistance, the removal of certain US economic sanctions and the possible opening of direct discussions between Iran and the USA. Iran's chief nuclear negotiator, Ali Larijani, responded by declaring that the package contained some 'positive steps', while also containing unspecified 'ambiguities' that needed to be resolved.

However, on 31 July 2006 the UN Security Council approved a resolution (No. 1696), which expressed 'serious concern' regarding Iran's refusal to co-operate with the IAEA and warned that the country could face possible sanctions unless it halted its uranium enrichment programme by 31 August. Significantly, however, the text of Resolution 1696 fell short of mentioning specific sanctions (at the request of China and Russia), instead referring to 'appropriate measures' being adopted. On 22 August Larijani presented a formal response to the package of economic incentives offered by the permanent members of the Security Council plus Germany in June. Despite indicating that Iran was prepared to begin serious negotiations with the international community, Larijani gave no indication that Tehran was prepared to suspend its enrichment activities, which he described as an 'inalienable right'. The IAEA reported to the UN Security Council on 31 August that Iran had failed to meet its requirement to cease uranium enrichment and that Iranian officials had not co-operated with the agency's investigators. In an attempt to defuse the nuclear crisis, UN Secretary-General Kofi Annan travelled to Tehran in early September to hold talks with President Ahmadinejad and other senior Iranian leaders. Ahmadinejad reaffirmed Iran's preparedness to hold discussions with Western nations, but insisted that the country would not suspend its nuclear enrichment activities prior to the convening of any talks. Meanwhile, the US Administration blacklisted Iran's state-owned Bank Saderat, following accusations that the bank was involved in the transfer of money to terrorist organizations.

The five permanent members of the UN Security Council, together with Germany, agreed at a meeting in London, United Kingdom, in early October 2006 that they would begin discussing the possible imposition of sanctions against Iran. While the USA and the United Kingdom were reported to be in favour of immediate and punitive sanctions, they were expected to pursue a more gradual approach to mollify critics of such a move in Russia and China, with initial, limited sanctions possibly including an embargo on the supply of nuclear technology that could have a military use, followed by the freezing of assets and travel bans on Iranian officials. Larijani responded by threatening that if sanctions were imposed, Iran might ban IAEA inspectors from entering its nuclear sites. There was evidence in late October that Iran was in fact expanding its uranium enrichment programme. Although talks were held between the five permanent members of the Security Council plus Germany in early December, they ended in stalemate. The United Kingdom, France and Germany drafted a resolution proposing sanctions aimed at hampering Iran's nuclear programme; however, both China and Russia continued to press for further dialogue.

On 23 December 2006 the UN Security Council adopted Resolution 1737, which imposed a serious of limited sanctions on the Iranian regime owing to its lack of compliance with the terms of Resolution 1696. The sanctions banned the import and export of nuclear-related technology and materials, and froze the assets of leading individuals and companies involved in the nuclear programme. The threat of further non-military sanctions was also outlined in the resolution. Iran was granted 60 days in which to cease all enrichment activities and thus avoid the imposition of sanctions. Both Russia and China, which had sought to ensure that the original EU sanctions proposal was considerably weakened, voted in favour of the resolution, which was to be binding. However, the Iranian leadership rejected the terms of Resolution 1737, with President Ahmadinejad declaring that the Security Council would come to regret its actions and insisting that his country would press ahead with its nuclear ambitions. This resolve was clearly demonstrated when, in late December, the Majlis adopted legislation that required the Iranian Government to review its co-operation with the IAEA and urged an acceleration of Iran's nuclear energy programme.

Iran's Revolutionary Guard Corps conducted a series of military exercises to the south-east of Tehran in January 2007. The missile tests were apparently launched following a decision by the USA to send a second warship to the region, fuelling concerns in Iran that the Bush Administration was preparing to launch a military strike against the Islamic regime. At the same time Iran announced that it was barring 38 IAEA inspectors from the country, in retaliation for the imposition of sanctions. However, Iranian officials denied reports that they had commenced the installation of 3,000 new centrifuges at the Natanz nuclear facility. Renewed tension erupted between Iran and the USA in that month, when US troops detained five Iranians during a raid on an Iranian liaison office in the northern Iraqi town of Irbil (Arbil). The USA accused the officials of being linked to the Revolutionary Guards, whom they alleged to be training insurgents within Iraq. The Iranian Government, for its part, accused the US of having made illegal arrests, stating that, since the liaison office was in the process of being registered as a consulate, the officials enjoyed diplomatic immunity. Also in January the US Administration froze the assets of Iran's Bank Sepah, accusing the bank of acting as the conduit for an agreement with a North Korean organization that allegedly provided missile technology to Iran.

In February 2007 a leading British security correspondent claimed to have evidence that the US Administration had formulated detailed plans for widespread military strikes against Iran, in the event that Iran was discovered to have been directly involved in insurgent attacks against US forces in Iraq or that it was confirmed to have been developing nuclear weapons. In his report to the IAEA on 22 February, el-Baradei affirmed that Iran had failed to meet the deadline of the previous day to cease uranium enrichment and that the Islamic regime had actually expanded the programme from 'research-scale' to 'industrial-scale' enrichment. This refusal to halt uranium enrichment resulted in renewed efforts by the five permanent members of the UN Security Council to agree tougher sanctions against Iran. Indeed, on 24 March the Security Council adopted Resolution 1747, which again required Iran to suspend all uranium enrichment-related and reprocessing activities and to agree to grant IAEA inspectors full access to its nuclear sites. Resolution 1747 imposed, *inter alia*, an embargo on the sale of arms to and from Iran, and a ban on the transfer of funds to Iran by state and international financial institutions except where these were intended for humanitarian or development aid. The UN granted Iran 60 days to comply with the measures or face 'further appropriate measures'. The Iranian Minister of Foreign Affairs, Manouchehr Mottaki, rejected the resolution as being 'illegitimate' and reiterated Iran's assertions that its nuclear programme was entirely for peaceful purposes.

Indeed, Iran's continued defiance with regard to the UN measures was evident in early April 2007, when President Ahmadinejad confirmed that the country had begun the enrichment of uranium on an 'industrial scale' at the Natanz plant, and boasted that Iran had joined the 'nuclear club of nations'. Following an inspection of the facility in that month, IAEA inspectors agreed that Iran had commenced this process, but asserted that they were uncertain as to whether all of the 1,300 centrifuges at Natanz were actually in operation. The Iranian authorities, meanwhile, continued to deny that the country was seeking to enrich uranium in order to develop nuclear weapons, maintaining that the programme was intended for civilian purposes alone. The day before the UN Security Council's deadline for Iranian compliance of 24 May (according to the terms of UN Resolution 1747), the IAEA issued a report claiming that Iran remained in defiance of the demands of the international community to suspend its enrichment programme and open its nuclear facilities fully to agency inspectors. El-Baradei subsequently declared that he believed Iran to possess the capability to build a nuclear weapon in between three to eight years. However, the IAEA Director-General asserted that he did not have evidence to support the claim that Iran was seeking to produce such weapons of mass destruction.

Despite the considerable tension in Iranian–US relations during mid-2007, exacerbated by the nuclear crisis, by military exercises being carried out by US naval forces in the Gulf and by US accusations that Iran was assisting Iraqi militants in their insurgency against US-led forces, two rounds of direct talks concerning the sectarian conflict in Iraq were held by the US and Iranian ambassadors to Baghdad at the end of May and late July. In the latter month Iran made what were deemed to be significant concessions in the ongoing dispute with the international community regarding its nuclear programme. Following a meeting between Iranian and IAEA officials in Vienna, Austria, Iran agreed to provide information about previous nuclear experiments, to allow inspectors to visit a plutonium-producing reactor being built at Arak and to decelerate its uranium enrichment progamme at Natanz. In August news reports stated that the US Administration was shortly to add the Iranian Revolutionary Guard Corps to its list of foreign terrorist organizations, owing to the organization's alleged support for Shi'a militias in Iraq. At the end of the month el-Baradei presented his latest report on Iran to the IAEA Board, in which he concluded that the country's programme of uranium enrichment was not progressing as fast as had previously been expected. The report brought into question President Ahmadinejad's recent claim that the enrichment had now reached an 'industrial' level, since the number of centrifuges had apparently only risen from 1,300 to around 2,000. (Ahmadinejad announced in early November that the country now possessed 3,000 centrifuges capable of enriching uranium at Natanz.)

El-Baradei was reported at the end of August 2007 to have agreed a 'work plan' with Iranian officials, whereby Iran was given a three-month deadline by which to end any technical ambiguities concerning its nuclear programme. However, the US Administration continued to demand a complete and immediate cessation of uranium enrichment. President Sarkozy of France also indicated that his country was henceforth to adopt a tougher approach to Iranian non-compliance with UN resolutions. In late October Iran's Deputy Foreign Minister for European and American Affairs, Saeed Jalili, was chosen to replace Larijani as Secretary of the Supreme Council for National Security and principal negotiator on the nuclear issue, after Larijani had tendered his resignation. It was widely reported that the appointment of Jalili, who was closely affiliated with President Ahmadinejad, would result in Iran taking a firmer stance in the ongoing negotiations with the IAEA and international community regarding its nuclear capabilities. Towards the end of October the USA imposed further unilateral sanctions against Iran, with Secretary of State Condoleezza Rice stating that the Administration's intention was 'to confront the threatening behaviour of the Iranians'. The sanctions principally targeted Iranian state-owned banks, organizations and agencies deemed to be involved in a clandestine nuclear programme or to sponsor terrorism abroad, and in particular named affiliates of the Revolutionary Guards Corps and its élite Qods Force.

In early November 2007 details emerged of a plan recently put forward by members of the Co-operation Council for the Arab

States of the Gulf (Gulf Co-operation Council—GCC, see p. 219), which would enable Iran to pursue its programme of uranium enrichment as part of a joint consortium with its neighbouring Gulf states in a neutral country such as Switzerland. The Iranian leadership did not immediately respond to the proposal. In mid-November el-Baradei informed the IAEA that, although there had been improvements as far as transparency in the programme was concerned (as recently agreed under the terms of the 'work plan'), the Iranian authorities were continuing to restrict inspectors' access to nuclear plants. The IAEA chief emphasized that such inspections were vital in order to ensure that no enrichment was being carried out for military purposes, and confirmed that Iran now had an estimated 3,000 centrifuges in operation. The US Administration insisted in early December that a joint report (entitled the National Intelligence Estimate—NIE) published by the 16 US intelligence agencies, in which they disclosed their findings that Iran had in fact suspended its nuclear weapons development programme in 2003, would not lead his country to re-evaluate its policy towards the Islamic republic. This report contradicted an earlier NIE report released in 2005 which assessed that Tehran was 'determined' to build nuclear weapons. Although President Ahmadinejad hailed the findings of the report, he reiterated his assertion that Iran had never sought to develop a clandestine nuclear weapons programme.

During discussions between Iranian and IAEA representatives in mid-January 2008, Iran promised to answer outstanding questions concerning its alleged clandestine nuclear activities within one month. In a report issued in late February the IAEA commended Iran for having improved access to its nuclear sites, but revealed that it could provide no 'credible assurances' that the regime was not seeking to produce atomic weapons; there was also said to be some evidence that Iran had in fact continued with its programme to develop such weapons after 2003. After lengthy discussions among member states, on 3 March the UN Security Council adopted Resolution 1803, which tightened the sanctions already imposed on Iran with regard to the financial assets and ability to travel of officials and institutions allegedly involved in nuclear activities.

Amid the continuing international disquiet over the country's nuclear ambitions in recent years, Iran has fuelled further outrage by its frequent statements about Israel and the Holocaust. Remarks by President Ahmadinejad in October 2005, in which he reiterated the demand of Ayatollah Khomeini that Israel be 'wiped off the map', provoked an international outcry and were condemned in a statement by the UN Security Council. Subsequent public statements by Ahmadinejad in December, to the effect that the Holocaust was a 'fabrication' and that the Jewish state should be moved outside the Middle East, were similarly condemned by Israel, the USA and the EU as illustrating the dangers of allowing Iran to develop military nuclear capabilities. Hostility between Iran and Israel was exacerbated by the victory of the Islamic Resistance Movement (Hamas) in the Palestinian legislative elections of January 2006 and Iran's subsequent offer of financial support to the Hamas-led administration. In April, just days after announcing that Iranian nuclear scientists had succeeded for the first time in enriching uranium (see above), Ahmadinejad described the Israeli Government as a 'dried tree that will be eliminated by one storm', a phrase that was widely interpreted in the Western media as referring to a nuclear Armageddon. The Holocaust also formed the subject, in August, of an international cartoon competition launched in Tehran by the *Hamshahri* daily newspaper, which was aimed at highlighting what many Iranians deemed to be the West's hypocrisy with regard to its alleged commitment to free speech. (In February 2006 Iran had been the scene of mass protests after Iranians reacted angrily to a cartoon published in a Danish newspaper that was deemed to be extremely offensive to Muslims.) Iran was viewed as having played a leading role in the conflict between Israel and the militant Lebanese organization Hezbollah in July–August; however, while the Iranian leadership admitted its support for Hezbollah, it denied that Iran was providing the group with military assistance. In November a spokesman from the Iranian Ministry of Foreign Affairs warned that any pre-emptive military strikes launched by Israel against Iran's nuclear facilities would be met with a swift and powerful military response.

The European Union (EU, see p. 244) pursued a policy of 'critical dialogue' with Iran during the 1990s, despite US pressure as well as tensions between Iran and certain EU states. Notably, a lengthy period of strained relations with the United Kingdom developed after Ayatollah Khomeini issued a *fatwa* (edict) in February 1989, imposing a death penalty against a British writer, Salman Rushdie, for material deemed offensive to Islam in his novel *The Satanic Verses*. 'Critical dialogue' was suspended in April 1997, after a German court ruled that the Iranian authorities had ordered the assassination of four prominent members of the dissident Democratic Party of Iranian Kurdistan in Berlin in September 1992. Germany announced the withdrawal of its ambassador to Tehran and expelled four Iranian diplomats, while other EU members similarly withdrew their representatives. In November 1997, following the inauguration of President Khatami and the formation of a new Council of Ministers, a compromise arrangement was finally reached allowing the readmission of all EU ambassadors, and in February 1998 EU ministers responsible for foreign affairs agreed to resume senior-level ministerial contacts with Iran. Despite assurances given to the British Secretary of State for Foreign and Commonwealth Affairs, Robin Cook, in September by the Iranian Minister of Foreign Affairs that the Iranian Government had no intention of threatening the life of Rushdie or anyone associated with his work, 'conservative' clerics maintained that the *fatwa* issued by Ayatollah Khomeini was irrevocable, and the Qom-based 15 Khordad Foundation subsequently increased its financial reward offered for the writer's murder. President Khatami became the first Iranian head of state to visit the West since the Islamic Revolution when, in March 1999, he travelled to Italy and the Vatican; in September President Thomas Klestil of Austria made the first visit to Iran by an EU head of state since 1979. Following the suicide attacks on the USA in September 2001, Cook's successor, Jack Straw, visited Tehran, primarily to request Iran's support for a US-led military campaign in Afghanistan (see above). In that month the most high-level discussions since 1979 were held between Iranian and EU representatives in Brussels and later Tehran.

In December 2002 the EU commenced negotiations with Iran regarding a trade and co-operation agreement, with the stipulation that the accord be linked with consideration of political issues (notably human rights and terrorism). In May 2003, following the US-led campaign to oust the regime of Saddam Hussain in Iraq, British Prime Minister Tony Blair echoed statements made by the US Administration that Iran should desist from 'interfering' in Iraq's affairs. Diplomatic relations between Iran and the United Kingdom deteriorated again in early September, following the refusal of a British court to grant bail to Hadi Soleimanpour, a former Iranian ambassador to Argentina, who had been detained in the United Kingdom in August on charges relating to the bombing of a Jewish cultural centre in Buenos Aires in 1994. Iran recalled its ambassador to London, but Soleimanpour was eventually granted bail in mid-September 2003. In June 2004 a crisis erupted in relations with the United Kingdom when Iran captured three British patrol craft and detained eight Royal Navy personnel on the Shatt al-Arab waterway dividing Iran from Iraq. Iran asserted that the vessels had entered Iranian territorial waters, but the sailors, who were released four days later, alleged that they had been 'forcibly escorted' into Iranian waters. The relationship between Iran and the United Kingdom was dominated in 2005 by the prominent role played by Jack Straw in negotiations with Iran over its nuclear programme (see above). Existing tension resulting from these negotiations was exacerbated in October, when British officials accused the Iranians of supplying explosives to and running training camps for Iraqi Shi'a insurgents operating in the British-controlled region of southern Iraq. Conversely, Iran accused the United Kingdom of involvement in two bomb attacks in October in the town of Ahvaz, in the Arab-dominated south-eastern Khuzestan province, and later made similar accusations after further explosions occurred in the region in early 2006 (see above).

In late March 2007 15 British Royal Navy and Royal Marines personnel were captured and detained by Iranian Revolutionary Guards while patrolling the Shatt al-Arab waterway. As in 2004, Iran claimed that the sailors had trespassed into Iranian territorial waters; however, British naval officials insisted that the two crews were operating in Iraqi waters at the time of their arrest. The sailors were subsequently transferred to Tehran, where they were denied contact with consular officials; Iranian television broadcast footage of them apparently admitting to their 'intrusion' into Iranian territory. Following high-level discussions between Iranian and British officials in early April 2007 (in which the Secretary of the Supreme Council for National Security, Ali Larijani, was reported to have played an influential role), the 15 sailors were finally released from detention 13 days after their capture. President Ahmadinejad stated that he had granted them a pardon as a 'gift to the British people', while the British Government denied that a deal had been agreed with Iran to secure the sailors' release. However, several commentators noted that shortly before the pardon five diplomats who had been seized by US forces at the Iranian consulate in Arbil, Iraq, in January 2007 (see above) had been granted consular access; moreover, a senior diplomat at the Iranian embassy in Baghdad, who had been abducted by gunmen in February, had also recently been released. Relations between Iran and the United Kingdom deteriorated further when Tony Blair accused 'elements' of the Iranian regime of direct involvement in the deaths of four British soldiers in a roadside ambush in the Iraqi city of Basra, which occurred on the same day as the sailors' release.

Relations between Iran and Saudi Arabia were frequently strained after the Islamic Revolution of 1979. A period of particularly hostile relations, following the deaths of 275 Iranian pilgrims as a result of fierce clashes with Saudi security forces in the Islamic holy city of Mecca during the *Hajj* (annual pilgrimage) in July 1987, culminated in the suspension of diplomatic relations in April 1988. Links were restored in March 1991. Allegations of Iranian involvement in the bombing of a US military housing complex at al-Khobar, Saudi Arabia, in June 1996 again strained relations for several months. However, the installation of a new Iranian Government in August 1997 facilitated further rapprochement, perhaps reflecting the desire of the two countries, as the region's principal petroleum producers, to co-operate in maintaining world oil prices and in efforts to curtail over-production by members of the Organization of the Petroleum Exporting Countries (OPEC, see p. 373). An Iranian delegation led by former President Rafsanjani began a 10-day visit to Saudi Arabia in February 1998, at the end of which the formation of a joint ministerial committee for bilateral relations was announced, and several co-operation agreements were signed following a visit to Iran by the Saudi Minister of State for Foreign Affairs in May. The signing of a Saudi-Iranian security agreement was announced in April 2001. During the latter part of 2003 Iran countered US accusations that certain suspected al-Qa'ida militants who remained in Iranian custody had been involved in plotting suicide attacks against expatriate compounds in Riyadh in May of that year. In March 2007 President Ahmadinejad undertook his first state visit to Saudi Arabia, where he held discussions with King Abdullah; the meeting was believed to represent an attempt by the two leaders to demonstrate that perceived differences between their countries as a result of recent sectarian tensions in Iraq and Lebanon had been exaggerated and that they were seeking closer diplomatic relations.

The Khatami administration has also sought improved relations with Saudi Arabia's fellow members of the GCC, although a long-standing territorial dispute with the United Arab Emirates (UAE) remains unresolved. In March 1992 Iran occupied those parts of the Abu Musa islands and the Greater and Lesser Tunbs that had remained under the control of the emirate of Sharjah since the original occupation in 1971. In December 1994 the UAE announced its intention to refer the dispute to the International Court of Justice in The Hague, Netherlands. In early 1995 Iran was reported to have deployed air defence systems on Abu Musa and the Greater and Lesser Tunbs, prompting the USA to warn of a potential threat to shipping. In November talks between Iran and the UAE aimed at facilitating ministerial-level negotiations on the disputed islands ended in failure. Relations deteriorated further in the first half of 1996, after Iran opened an airport on Abu Musa and a power station on Greater Tunb. In 1997 the UAE protested that Iran was repeatedly violating the emirates' territorial waters, and in June complained to the UN about Iran's construction of a pier on Greater Tunb. Following a meeting with the UAE's Minister of Foreign Affairs during the eighth conference of the Organization of the Islamic Conference (OIC, see p. 369), held in Tehran in December 1997, President Khatami emphasized his willingness to discuss bilateral issues directly with President Zayed bin Sultan an-Nayhan of the UAE. Although the latter was said to be cautious about Iran's attempts at rapprochement, in the following month UAE officials expressed willingness to enter into negotiations. By the mid-2000s the UAE remained an important trading partner of Iran and, although both countries continued to assert their sovereignty over the three disputed areas, political relations were generally improving.

Iran hosts one of the largest refugee populations in the world. At the end of 2003, according to data published by the office of the UN High Commissioner for Refugees (UNHCR), the number of refugees in the country was 984,896, of whom 834,699 were from Afghanistan and 150,196 from Iraq. By the end of 2006 the UNHCR estimated that the total number of refugees in Iran had declined marginally, to 968,370. Those fleeing Afghanistan now accounted for a larger proportion of the total refugee population—at 914,260—while the number of Iraqi refugees had declined to 54,024. All of the refugees were reported to be receiving UNHCR assistance.

Victories achieved by the Sunni fundamentalist Taliban in the Afghan civil war in September 1996 prompted Iran, which supported the Government of President Burhanuddin Rabbani, to express fears for its national security, and to accuse the USA of interference in Afghanistan's internal affairs. In June 1997 the Taliban accused Iran of espionage and ordered the closure of the Iranian embassy in Kabul and the withdrawal of all Iranian diplomats. Iran retaliated by halting all trade across its land border with Afghanistan, prompting Taliban protests that the ban violated international law. In September 1998, as it emerged that nine Iranian diplomats missing since August had been murdered by Taliban militia as they stormed the city of Mazar-i-Sharif, 500,000 Iranian troops were reportedly placed on full military alert in readiness for open conflict with Afghanistan. In an attempt to defuse the crisis, in October the Taliban agreed to free all Iranian prisoners being held in Afghanistan and to punish those responsible for the killing of the nine Iranian diplomats. Following the terrorist attacks on the USA in September 2001, as the USA began preparations for military action against al-Qa'ida and its Taliban hosts, Iran closed its eastern border with Afghanistan and sent a large contingent of troops there in order to prevent a further influx of Afghan refugees. In the following month, however, when the US-led military action began, Iran reportedly agreed to the establishment of eight refugee camps within its borders to provide shelter for some 250,000 Afghan refugees. Although Iran refused to give military assistance to the US-led coalition, it actively supported the Western-backed opposition forces, collectively known as the United National Islamic Front for the Salvation of Afghanistan (the Northern Alliance), and welcomed their swift victory over the Taliban. A programme allowing for voluntary repatriations of Afghan refugees under UNHCR auspices was inaugurated by the Iranian and Afghan authorities in April 2002, although UNHCR put the number of 'spontaneous' repatriations prior to that date at 57,000. (More than 1.5m. Afghan refugees in Iran were estimated by UNHCR to have returned to Afghanistan by November 2005.) In August 2002 President Khatami became the first Iranian head of state to visit Afghanistan for 40 years. Meanwhile, it was reported that Iran had, in June, extradited 16 Saudis believed to be al-Qa'ida militants who had fled the Afghan conflict. In November, moreover, Iranian officials declared that the authorities had arrested and extradited some 250 people suspected of having links with al-Qa'ida.

In September 1997 Iraq opened a border crossing with Iran, thereby permitting, for the first time since the Iran–Iraq War, Iranian pilgrims to visit Shi'ite Muslim shrines on its territory. At the end of the month, however, Iranian aircraft violated the air exclusion zone over southern Iraq in order to bomb two bases of the Mujahidin-e-Khalq (prompting Iraqi aircraft also to enter the zone). Vice-President Taha Yassin Ramadan of Iraq, attending December's OIC conference in Tehran, was the most senior Iraqi official to visit Iran since 1979. President Khatami subsequently expressed the hope that problems between the two countries could be resolved 'through negotiation and understanding'. During a visit to Iran by Iraq's Minister of Foreign Affairs in January 1998, it was agreed to establish joint committees with the aim of expediting prisoner exchanges, facilitating pilgrimages for Iranians to Shi'a shrines in Iraq, and addressing other contentious issues. Exchanges of prisoners of war and the remains of troops killed in the 1980–88 conflict were reported at intervals in 1998–2003, despite periodic mutual accusations of failure to comply with obligations in this respect. In October 2000 Kharrazi became the first Iranian Minister of Foreign Affairs to visit Iraq for a decade, and the two countries agreed to reactivate a 1975 border and security agreement that had been in abeyance since 1980.

Tensions between the two sides increased in April 2001, however, when Iran launched a heavy missile attack against Iraqi military bases used by the Mujahidin-e-Khalq, apparently in response to repeated attacks by that group on Iranian targets.

By early 2002 a general thaw in bilateral relations was evident, despite a protest lodged with the UN by Iraq in June stating that Iran was continuing to violate agreements reached at the end of the Iran–Iraq war. It was reported in September that Iran had made preparations for the provision of humanitarian assistance to Iraqi refugees along their joint border in the event of a US-led military campaign to remove the regime of Saddam Hussain. Discussions held between the Iraqi Minister of Foreign Affairs, Naji Sabri, and Kharrazi in Tehran in February 2003 resulted in demands by several Iranian deputies for the impeachment of Kharrazi; the deputies claimed that many issues of contention between the two sides remained unresolved. Despite gloomy predictions, there was no refugee crisis in Iran during the US-led intervention in Iraq in early 2003; indeed, the movement of refugees was in the other direction as Iraqis-in-exile returned to Iraq following the removal from power of Saddam Hussain's regime. (UNHCR estimated that, by December 2004, an estimated 107,000 Iraqi refugees—more than one-half of the pre-conflict total in Iran—had returned to their homeland; a further 56,000 returned to Iraq in 2005.) On the other hand, Tehran was concerned about the status of the armed opposition group, the Mujahidin-e-Khalq, which had been based in Iraq since 1986. After US-led coalition aircraft had launched attacks against training camps of the NLA, in April 2003 the Mujahidin and its military wing agreed a cease-fire with the occupying forces in Iraq, a move that was condemned by Iran. (For further details regarding Iran and Iraq in the aftermath of the conflict, see above.)

Closer relations were developed with Turkey during the 1990s, despite periodic tensions arising particularly from Turkish allegations of Iranian support for the Kurdish separatist Kurdistan Workers' Party (Partiya Karkeren Kurdistan—PKK) in its conflict with the armed forces in south-eastern Turkey (q.v.). In 1997 Iran was a founder member of the Istanbul-based Developing Eight (D-8, see p. 412) group of Islamic countries. In May 2004 Tehran's Imam Khomeini International Airport, which the Turkish-led consortium Tepe-Akfen-Vie (TAV) was contracted to operate, was closed by the Islamic Revolutionary Guards Corps after only one flight had landed because it was seen as a danger to national security, and apparently owing to Iran's hostility towards Turkey for its links with Israel and the USA. The airport only reopened in May 2005, following complex negotiations that reportedly resulted in TAV rescinding control of operations to IranAir. Meanwhile, considerable political and economic advantage has been perceived arising from Iran's potential as a transit route for hydrocarbons from the former Soviet republics of Central Asia, and since the early 1990s Iran has sought to strengthen its position in Central Asia through bilateral economic, security and cultural agreements as well as institutions such as the Tehran-based Economic Co-operation Organization (see p. 238). Relations between Iran and Azerbaijan—already tense owing to disagreement over a contested section of the Caspian Basin—deteriorated in July 2001, when Iran ordered a military patrol boat into the disputed waters in order to prevent foreign companies from undertaking oil exploration there. Subsequent meetings of the five littoral states (Iran, Russia, Azerbaijan, Kazakhstan and Turkmenistan) failed to resolve the dispute regarding the legal status of the Caspian. An improvement in relations between Iran and Azerbaijan was evident during the early 2000s, and moves towards the imposition of wider economic sanctions against Iran in the second half of the decade (see above) was of concern to Azerbaijan, owing to Iran's large ethnic Azeri population, as well as the energy agreements in place between the two countries.

In March 2001 Russia pledged to assist Iran with the completion of the nuclear plant at Bushehr (see above), and in May Russian officials reportedly agreed to supply Iran with advanced ship-borne cruise missiles. The two countries signed a military co-operation pact in October, believed to amount to annual sales to Iran of Russian weapons worth some US $300m. In July 2002 Russia and Iran concluded a draft 10-year development and co-operation accord, which was reported to include the construction of a further three nuclear reactors at Bushehr. In mid-2003 the USA failed to persuade Russia to withdraw its assistance from the development of the nuclear facility, particularly the export to Iran of nuclear fuel. Construction of the Bushehr plant was completed in October 2004, and in February 2005 Russia agreed to supply Iran with fuel for the plant; however, following international pressure, the deal required that Iran return to Russia spent nuclear fuel rods, which could be used to produce nuclear weapons, from the site. As the diplomatic crisis over Iran's nuclear programme intensified during that year (see above), Russia developed an alternative proposal whereby the sensitive elements of Iran's nuclear programme, such as uranium enrichment, could be conducted on Russian territory, thereby allowing the Iranians to maintain their nuclear programme while satisfying the concerns of the IAEA, the USA and EU member states that their nuclear activities would not lead to the development of a bomb. However, this proposal was rejected by the Iranian administration in early 2006.

It was reported in January 2007 that Russia had, at the end of 2006, sold some 30 air defence missile systems to Iran, in a contract that was estimated to be worth US $700m. Russia sought to assure concerned US and Israeli officials that the missile systems were intended purely for defensive purposes. In March 2007 the Russian Government rejected a deadline by which it was to deliver nuclear fuel to the Bushehr plant, claiming that Iran had failed to make the requisite payments; Russia also warned Iran that it would continue to withhold the provision of fuel until Iran agreed to suspend uranium enrichment, as demanded by the UN Security Council (see above). President Vladimir Putin attended a summit meeting of the five littoral states of the Caspian Sea in Tehran in October, at which the Russian leader expressed his opposition to any US-led military strike against Iran's nuclear facilities and all parties asserted Iran's right to develop nuclear energy for peaceful purposes. The first shipment of Russian nuclear fuel to the Bushehr reactor arrived in December, after Russia and Iran had finally agreed on a timetable for completion of the project; it was thought that the plant would be fully operational by the latter part of 2008.

Iran's relations with South and Central America grew in importance during 2006, not least owing to the election of new leaders in that region who shared President Ahmadinejad's hostility towards the US Administration under President Bush. In January 2007, amid increasing domestic political pressure (see above), Ahmadinejad embarked on a four-day tour of Venezuela—whose President, Lt-Col (retd) Hugo Rafael Chávez Frías, had consistently supported Ahmadinejad's insistence on Iran's right to nuclear energy—together with Nicaragua, Ecuador and Bolivia. During Ahmadinejad's visit the Iranian delegation signed 11 bilateral agreements with its Venezuelan counterpart, with the aim of increasing the price of petroleum and furthering co-operation on energy, trade, industry and construction. Presidents Ahmadinejad and Chávez also agreed to expedite the creation of a US $2,000m. fund to invest in countries joining their anti-US alliance. In July President Chávez was reported to have offered the sale of petrol to Iran after the Iranian Government had introduced fuel rationing (see above). A number of bilateral trade accords were signed with Nicaragua in August.

Government

Legislative power is vested in the Islamic Consultative Assembly (Majlis-e-Shura-e Islami), with 290 members. The chief executive of the administration is the President. The Majlis and the President are both elected by universal adult suffrage for a term of four years. A 12-member Council of Guardians supervises elections and ensures that legislation is in accordance with the Constitution and with Islamic precepts. The Council to Determine the Expediency of the Islamic Order, created in February 1988 and formally incorporated into the Constitution in July 1989, rules on legal and theological disputes between the Majlis and the Council of Guardians. The executive, legislative and judicial wings of state power are subject to the authority of the Wali Faqih (supreme religious leader). Iran is divided into 30 provinces, each with an appointed Governor.

Defence

As assessed at November 2007, Iran's regular armed forces totalled an estimated 420,000: army 350,000 (incl. 220,000 conscripts), navy 18,000, air force around 52,000. There were some 350,000 army reserves. The Islamic Revolutionary Guard Corps (Pasdaran Inquilab) were thought to total at least 125,000, and possessed the ability to mobilize up to an estimated 1m. volunteers of the Basij Resistance Force if required. There were also some 40,000 paramilitary forces under the command of the Ministry of the Interior. There is an 18-month period of compulsory military service. Defence expenditure for the Iranian year ending 20 March 2008 was budgeted at an estimated IR 78,000,000m.

Economic Affairs

In 2006, according to estimates by the World Bank, Iran's gross national income (GNI), measured at average 2004–06 prices, was US $207,643m., equivalent to $3,000 per head (or $8,490 per head on an international purchasing-power parity basis). During 1996–2006, it was estimated, the population increased at an average annual rate of 1.5%, while gross domestic product (GDP) per head increased, in real terms, by an average of 3.2% per year. Overall GDP increased, in real terms, at an average annual rate of 4.75% in 1996–2006; according to official estimates, growth was 5.8% in 2006/07 (Iranian year to March).

Agriculture (including forestry and fishing) contributed 10.1% of GDP in 2006/07, according to provisional figures. About 24.9% of the employed labour force were engaged in agriculture in 2005. The principal cash crops are fresh and dried fruit and nuts, which accounted for a provisional 12.1% of non-petroleum export earnings in 2006/07. Wheat, rice, barley, sugar cane and sugar beet are the main subsistence crops. Imports of cereals comprised some 2.3% of the value of total imports in 2005/06. Production of fruit and vegetables is also significant. Agricultural GDP increased by an average of 3.6% per year in 1996–2006; according to official figures, the sector's GDP grew by an estimated 4.7% in 2006/07.

Industry (including mining, manufacturing, construction and power) contributed 42.5% of GDP in 2006/07, according to provisional figures, and engaged some 30.4% of the employed labour force in 2005. During 1996–2006 industrial GDP increased by an average of 5.1% per year; growth was recorded at 6.9% in 2006/07, according to official estimates.

Mining (including petroleum refining) contributed 26.5% of GDP in 2006/07, according to provisional figures, although the sector engaged only an estimated 0.6% of the working population in 2005. Metal ores are the major non-hydrocarbon mineral exports, and coal, magnesite and gypsum are also mined. The sector is dominated by the hydrocarbons sector, which contributed some 26.5% of GDP in 2006/07. At the end of 2006 Iran's proven reserves of petroleum were estimated at 137,500m. barrels, sufficient to maintain the 2006/07 rate of production—estimated at 4.1m. barrels per day (b/d)—for almost 87 years. As a member of the Organization of the Petroleum Exporting Countries (OPEC, see p. 373), Iran is subject to production quotas agreed by the Organization's Conference. Iran's proven reserves of natural gas (28,130,000m. cu m at the end of 2006) are the second largest in the world, after those of Russia. The GDP of the mining sector increased by an average of 4.2% per year in 2002/03–2006/07; according to official figures, mining GDP expanded by an estimated 3.8% in 2006/07.

Manufacturing (excluding petroleum refining) contributed 10.6% of GDP in 2006/07, according to provisional figures, and engaged about 18.4% of the employed labour force in 2005. The most important sectors, in terms of value added, are textiles, food processing and transport equipment. The sector's GDP increased by an average of 8.1% per year in 1996–2006, with official estimates recording growth of 9.5% in 2006/07.

Principal sources of energy are natural gas (providing around 76.2% of total electricity production in 2004) and petroleum (some 17.3% in the same year). Imports of mineral fuels and lubricants comprised 9.7% of the value of total imports in 2005. The first phase of Iran's South Pars offshore gasfield (an extension of Qatar's North Field) was brought on stream in 2004. Gas reserves in the South Pars field are estimated at more than 14,000,000m. cu m, with production of about 25m. cu m of natural gas a day at the end of 2004. In December 2007 a Malaysian company secured the rights to develop the Golshan and Ferdows gasfields in southern Iran, in an agreement valued at US $16,000m. In February 2008 reports indicated that a long-delayed investment proposal submitted by the China National Offshore Oil Corpn, also worth $16,000m., had been finalized; the proposal concerned the development of natural gas facilities in the North Pars field.

The services sector contributed 47.5% of GDP in 2006/07, according to provisional figures, and engaged an estimated 44.7% of the employed labour force in 2005. During 1996–2006 the GDP of the services sector increased by an average of 4.5% per year; according to official figures, growth in the sector was about 6.5% in 2006/07.

According to preliminary figures, in the year ending March 2006 Iran recorded a visible trade surplus of US $19,044m., and there was a surplus of $14,038m. on the current account of the balance of payments. In 2005/06 the principal source of imports was the United Arab Emirates (which supplied 19.7% of total imports); other major suppliers included Germany, France, Italy and China. The principal market for exports in 2005/06 was Japan (which took 16.9% of total exports); China, Italy and Turkey were also important markets for Iranian exports. Other than petroleum and natural gas, Iran's principal exports in 2006/07 were chemical products, iron and steel, fruit and nuts, and carpets. Exports of petroleum and gas comprised 82.8% of the value of total exports in that year, according to provisional figures. The principal imports in 2005/06 were machinery and transport equipment, basic manufactures, chemicals, and food and live animals.

For the financial year ending March 2006 Iran recorded a budget surplus estimated at IR 19,433m., equivalent to 1.0% of GDP. Iran's total external debt was US $21,260m. at the end of 2005, of which $10,493m. was long-term public debt. In 2003 the cost of debt-servicing was equivalent to 3.9% of the value of exports of goods and services. The annual rate of inflation averaged 14.1% in 2002/03–2006/07; according to official figures, consumer prices increased by an average of 13.6% in 2006/07. According to the Central Bank, the rate of unemployment was 9.9% in mid-2007. It was suggested in some quarters, however, that actual rates of inflation and unemployment might be considerably higher.

Iran is a member of OPEC, of the Economic Co-operation Organization (ECO, see p. 238), of the Developing Eight (D-8, see p. 412) group of Islamic countries, and was admitted to the Group of 15 developing countries (G-15) in mid-2000. A working party was established in May 2005 to examine Iran's application to join the World Trade Organization (WTO, see p. 396); however, accession negotiations had not begun by early 2008.

Notable weaknesses in the Iranian economy include the Government's dependence on revenue from the petroleum sector, high rates of inflation and unemployment, and disparities in the distribution of income. Additional strain has been placed on domestic resources by the presence of large numbers of refugees from Afghanistan and Iraq. The Third Five-Year Development Plan (2000–05) allowed for the private ownership of banks for the first time since the Revolution. The Fourth Five-Year Development Plan (FoFYDP), which took effect in March 2005 under former President Muhammad Khatami, emphasized job creation, privatization and the encouragement of competition and foreign investment. 'Conservatives' attacked the 'reformist' FoFYDP as being hostile to the constitutional goals of social justice and national independence, asserting that it would lead to wealth concentration among certain interest groups, although in October 2004 the Expediency Council had revoked articles in the Constitution advocating a state monopoly of the economy. The future of the economic policies embodied by the FoFYDP was rendered uncertain by the election to the presidency in June 2005 of 'hardliner' Mahmoud Ahmadinejad, whose campaign had focused on wealth distribution and greater state control over the economy; nevertheless, the new Government emphasized its commitment to implementing the FoFYDP. Iranian budgets have since included considerable increases in public spending, despite concerns that this could aggravate Iran's already high rate of inflation. During 2006–07 there was evidence of growing dissatisfaction with the administration's management of the economy: the introduction of a new minimum wage in 2006 had resulted in a large number of redundancies and significant levels of industrial unrest, while it was claimed that many of the President's pre-election pledges had not been met. It was hoped that the introduction in March 2008 of the 'justice shares' scheme—according to which low-income households were to be allocated stocks in Iran's state-owned companies—would redistribute wealth and reduce levels of poverty. The crisis in Iran's relations with many Western nations as a result of its ongoing nuclear programme—which during 2006–08 resulted in the imposition by the UN of steadily tighter economic and technological sanctions (see Recent History)—had the effect of drastically reducing foreign investment and removing many sources of financing for vital petroleum projects. The hydrocarbons sector remains the crucial element in the Iranian economy, and the fact that the country maintains high domestic fuel subsidies severely restricts its capacity to use oil revenue to promote growth. Furthermore, the country's refining capacity is considerably lower than production levels, consequently more than one-half of the petrol used by Iranian motorists is imported. In mid-2007 the Government raised petrol prices and introduced petrol rationing in an effort to reduce fuel subsidies and thereby lower its substantial budget deficit. A pipeline enabling Iran to export natural gas to Armenia was inaugurated in March 2007, and a preliminary agreement concerning a proposed pipeline to transport gas from Iran's South Pars field to India via Pakistan was reached in January of that year. In December 2006, as the USA continued to exert financial pressure on Iran, the Government announced the decision henceforth to conduct all overseas transactions in euros rather than US dollars, and to calculate its national budget in euros as well as Iranian rials. According to the Central Bank, real GDP increased by 4.7% in 2005/06 and by an estimated 5.8% in 2006/07.

Education

Primary education is officially compulsory, and is provided free of charge for five years between six and 10 years of age, although this has not been fully implemented in rural areas. Secondary education, from the age of 11, lasts for up to seven years, comprising a first cycle of three years and a second of four years. According to UNESCO estimates, in 2004/05 primary enrolment included 95.2% of children in the relevant age-group, while enrolment at secondary schools included 77.0% of the appropriate age-group. There are 37 universities, including 16 in Tehran. According to official sources, there were some 1,191,048 students enrolled at Iran's public colleges and universities in 2005/06, in addition to the 1,197,521 students enrolled at the Islamic Azad University. Budgetary expenditure on education by the central Government in the financial year 2004/05 was IR 31,518,000m. (8.2% of total spending).

Public Holidays

The Iranian year 1387 runs from 20 March 2008 to 20 March 2009, and the year 1388 from 21 March 2009 to 20 March 2010.

2008: 19 January* (Ashoura), 11 February (Victory of the Islamic Revolution), 28 February* (Arbain), 8 March* (Martyrdom of Imam Reza), 19 March (Day of Oil Industry Nationalization), 20–23 March† (Norouz, Iranian New Year), 25 March (Birth of Prophet Muhammad and Birth of Imam Jafar Sadegh), 31 March (Islamic Republic Day), 1 April (Sizdah-bedar, Nature Day—13th Day of Nowrooz), 3 June (Death of Imam Khomeini), 4 June (1963 Uprising), 7 June (Martyrdom of Hazrat Fatemeh), 16 July* (Birth of Imam Ali), 30 July* (Prophet Muhammad receives his calling), 17 August* (Birth of Imam Mahdi), 22 September* (Martyrdom of Imam Ali), 1 October* (Eid-e Fitr, end of Ramadan), 25 October* (Martyrdom of Imam Jafar Sadeq), 9 December* (Qorban, Feast of the Sacrifice), 17 December* (Eid-e Ghadir Khom).

2009: 7 January*‡ (Ashoura), 8 January* (Tassoua), 10 February (Victory of the Islamic Revolution), 16 February* (Arbain), 25 February* (Demise of Prophet Muhammad), 26 February (Martyrdom of Imam Reza*), 15 March (Birth of Prophet Muhammad and Birth of Imam Jafar Sadegh), 19 March (Day of Oil Industry Nationalization), 21–24 March† (Norouz, Iranian New Year), 1 April (Islamic Republic Day), 2 April (Sizdah-bedar, Nature Day—13th Day of Nowrooz), 28 May (Martyrdom of Hazrat Fatemeh), 4 June (Death of Imam Khomeini), 5 June (1963 Uprising), 6 July* (Birth of Imam Ali), 19 July* (Prophet Muhammad receives his calling), 7 August* (Birth of Imam Mahdi), 12 September* (Martyrdom of Imam Ali), 20 September* (Eid-e Fitr, end of Ramadan), 15 October* (Martyrdom of Imam Jafar Sadeq), 27 November* (Qorban, Feast of the Sacrifice), 7 December* (Eid-e Ghadir Khom), 27 December*‡ (Ashoura).

* These holidays are dependent on the Islamic lunar calendar and may vary by one or two days from the dates given.
† This festival begins on the date of the Spring Equinox.
‡ This festival occurs twice (in the Iranian years 1387 and 1388) within the same Gregorian year.

Weights and Measures

The metric system is in force, but some traditional units are still in general use.

Statistical Survey

The Iranian year runs from approximately 21 March to 20 March

Sources (except where otherwise stated): Statistical Centre of Iran, POB 14155-6133, Dr Fatemi Ave, Tehran 14144; tel. (21) 88965061; fax (21) 88963451; e-mail sci@sci.org.ir; internet www.sci.org.ir; Bank Markazi Jomhouri Islami Iran (Central Bank), POB 15875-7177, 144 Mirdamad Blvd, Tehran; tel. (21) 29951; fax (21) 3115674; e-mail g.secdept@cbi.ir; internet www.cbi.ir.

Area and Population

AREA, POPULATION AND DENSITY

Area (sq km)	1,648,195*
Population (census results)†	
25 October 1996	60,055,488
28 October 2006 (preliminary)	
Males	35,866,362
Females	34,629,420
Total	70,495,782
Density (per sq km) at 2006 census	42.8

* 636,372 sq miles.
† Excluding adjustment for underenumeration.

PROVINCES

(estimated averages for year ending 20 March 2006)*

Province (Ostan)	Area (sq km)†	Population (estimates)	Density (per sq km)	Provincial capital
Tehran (Teheran)	18,814	12,150,742	645.8	Tehran (Teheran)
Markazi (Central)	29,130	1,361,394	46.7	Arak
Gilan	14,042	2,410,523	171.7	Rasht
Mazandaran	23,701	2,818,831	118.9	Sari
Azarbayejan-e-Sharqi (East Azerbaijan)	45,650	3,500,183	76.7	Tabriz
Azarbayejan-e-Gharbi (West Azerbaijan)	37,437	2,949,426	78.8	Orumiyeh
Bakhtaran (Kermanshah)	24,998	1,938,060	77.5	Bakhtaran
Khuzestan	64,055	4,345,607	67.8	Ahvaz
Fars	122,608	4,385,869	35.8	Shiraz
Kerman	180,836	2,432,927	13.5	Kerman
North Khorasan	28,434	786,918	27.7	Bojnurd
South Khorasan	69,555	510,218	7.3	Birjand
Razavi Khorasan	144,681	5,202,770	36.0	Mashhad
Esfahan	107,029	4,454,595	41.6	Esfahan
Sistan and Baluchestan	181,785	2,290,076	12.6	Zahedan
Kordestan (Kurdistan)	29,137	1,574,118	54.0	Sanandaj
Hamadan	19,368	1,738,772	89.8	Hamadan
Chaharmahal and Bakhtiyari	16,332	842,002	51.6	Shahr-e-Kord

Province (Ostan)—continued	Area (sq km)†	Population (estimates)	Density (per sq km)	Provincial capital
Lorestan	28,294	1,758,628	62.2	Khorramabad
Ilam	20,133	545,093	27.1	Ilam
Kohgiluyeh and Boyerahmad	15,504	695,099	44.8	Yasuj
Bushehr	22,743	816,115	35.9	Bushehr
Zanjan	21,773	970,946	44.6	Zanjan
Semnan	97,491	589,512	6.0	Semnan
Yazd	129,285	958,318	7.4	Yazd
Hormozgan	70,669	1,314,667	18.6	Bandar Abbas
Ardebil	17,800	1,257,624	70.7	Ardebil
Qom	11,526	1,064,456	92.4	Qom
Qazvin	15,549	1,166,861	75.0	Qazvin
Golestan	20,195	1,637,063	81.1	Gorgan
Total	1,628,554	68,467,413	42.0	—

* In January 1997 the legislature approved a law creating a new province, Qazvin (with its capital in the city of Qazvin), by dividing the existing province of Zanjan. In June of that year the Council of Ministers approved draft legislation to establish another new province, Golestan (with its capital in the city of Gorgan), by dividing the existing province of Mazandaran. In September 2004 legislation was enacted whereby the province of Khorasan was divided into three new provinces: North Khorasan, South Khorasan and Razavi Khorasan (with their respective capitals in the cities of Bojnurd, Birjand and Mashhad).

† Excluding inland water; densities are calculated on basis of land area only.

PRINCIPAL TOWNS
(population at 1996 census)

Tehran (Teheran, the capital)	6,758,845	Hamadan	401,281
Mashad (Meshed)	1,887,405	Kerman	384,991
Esfahan (Isfahan)	1,266,072	Arak	380,755
Tabriz	1,191,043	Ardabil (Ardebil)	340,386
Shiraz	1,053,025	Yazd	326,776
Karaj	940,968*	Qazvin	291,117
Ahvaz	804,980	Zanjan	286,295
Qom	777,677	Sanandaj	277,808
Bakhtaran (Kermanshah)	692,986	Bandar-e-Abbas	273,578
Orumiyeh	435,200	Khorramabad	272,815
Zahedan	419,518	Eslamshahr (Islam Shahr)	265,450
Rasht	417,748		

* Including towns of Rajayishahr and Mehrshahr. Estimated population of Mehrshahr at 1 October 1994 was 413,299 (Source: UN, *Demographic Yearbook*).

Mid-2007 ('000, incl. suburbs, UN estimates): Tehran 7,873; Mashad 2,469; Esfahan 1,628; Karaj 1,423; Tabriz 1,413; Shiraz 1,240; Ahvaz 996; Qom 973; Bakhtaran 802 (Source: UN, *World Urbanization Prospects: The 2007 Revision*).

BIRTHS, MARRIAGES AND DEATHS
(annual averages, UN estimates)

	1990–95	1995–2000	2000–05
Birth rate (per 1,000)	30.6	19.5	19.0
Death rate (per 1,000)	6.7	5.6	5.5

Source: UN, *World Population Prospects: The 2006 Revision*.

Births ('000): 1,172 in 2003/04; 1,154 in 2004/05; 1,234 in 2005/06; 1,254 in 2006/07 (preliminary).

Marriages ('000): 681 in 2003/04; 724 in 2004/05; 788 in 2005/06; 778 in 2006/07 (preliminary).

Deaths ('000): 369 in 2003/04; 355 in 2004/05; 361 in 2005/06; 409 in 2006/07 (preliminary).

Expectation of life (years at birth, WHO estimates): 70.5 (males 68.3; females 72.9) in 2005 (Source: WHO, *World Health Statistics*).

ECONOMICALLY ACTIVE POPULATION
('000 persons aged 10 years and over, excl. armed forces, 2005)

	Males	Females	Total
Agriculture, hunting and forestry	3,565	1,298	4,863
Fishing	66	1	66
Mining and quarrying	115	7	122
Manufacturing	2,586	1,046	3,632
Electricity, gas and water supply	181	8	189
Construction	2,043	17	2,061
Wholesale and retail trade; repair of motor vehicles, motorcycles and personal and household goods	2,647	169	2,816
Hotels and restaurants	163	11	174
Transport, storage and communications	1,703	37	1,740
Financial intermediation	214	34	248
Real estate, renting and business activities	336	61	397
Public administration and defence; compulsory social security	1,156	103	1,259
Education	658	643	1,301
Health and social work	242	200	441
Other community, social and personal service activities	267	144	412
Private households with employed persons	7	20	27
Extra-territorial organizations and bodies	7	1	9
Activities not adequately defined	3	1	4
Total employed	15,959	3,801	19,760
Unemployed	1,780	776	2,556
Total labour force	17,740	4,577	22,317

Source: ILO.

Health and Welfare

KEY INDICATORS

Total fertility rate (children per woman, 2005)	2.1
Under-5 mortality rate (per 1,000 live births, 2005)	36
HIV/AIDS (% of persons aged 15–49, 2005)	0.2
Physicians (per 1,000 head, 2004)	0.87
Hospital beds (per 1,000 head, 2005)	1.7
Health expenditure (2004): US $ per head (PPP)	603.7
Health expenditure (2004): % of GDP	6.6
Health expenditure (2004): public (% of total)	47.8
Access to water (% of persons, 2004)	94
Access to sanitation (% of persons, 2002)	84
Human Development Index (2005): ranking	94
Human Development Index (2005): value	0.759

For sources and definitions, see explanatory note on p. vi.

Agriculture

PRINCIPAL CROPS
('000 metric tons)

	2004	2005	2006
Wheat	14,568.5	14,308.0	14,500.0*
Rice (paddy)	2,542.4	2,736.8	3,600.0*
Barley	2,940.3	2,856.7	3,000.0*
Maize	1,926.1	1,995.3	1,700.0
Potatoes	4,453.8	4,830.1	4,830.1*
Sugar cane	5,911.0	5,530.4	5,530.4*
Sugar beet	4,916.3	4,902.4	5,000.0*
Dry beans	225.7	216.1	216.1*
Chick-peas*	296.8	292.8	292.8
Lentils	110.8	113.2	113.2*
Almonds (with shell)	70.0	108.7	108.7*
Walnuts (with shell)	168.3	150.0*	150.0
Pistachios	184.9	229.7	229.7*
Soybeans (Soya beans)†	198	210	240
Cottonseed†	252	218	145
Cabbages and other brassicas*	297.5	318.2	318.2

IRAN

Statistical Survey

—continued	2004	2005	2006
Lettuce and chicory*	111.6	125.5	125.5
Tomatoes*	4,022.9	4,781.0	4,781.0
Pumpkins, squash and gourds*	558.7	591.5	591.5
Cucumbers and gherkins*	1,715.0	1,720.7	1,721.0
Aubergines (Eggplants)*	104.4	93.9	93.9
Chillies and green peppers*	118.2	128.0	128.0
Dry onions	1,626.9	1,685.5	1,685.5*
Garlic	34.9*	27.9*	27.9
Watermelons	2,526.4	3,259.4	3,259.4*
Cantaloupes and other melons*	1,144.0	1,125.7	1,125.7
Oranges	2,129.5	2,253.2	2,253.2*
Tangerines, mandarins, clementines and satsumas	755.4	701.9	701.9*
Lemons and limes	564.7	615.1	615.1*
Apples	2,178.6	2,661.9	2,661.9*
Pears	154.7	166.3	166.3*
Apricots	166.4	275.6	275.6*
Sweet cherries	174.6	224.9	224.9*
Peaches and nectarines*	428.6	456.3	456.3
Plums*	147.7	146.1	146.1
Grapes	2,795.9	2,963.8	2,963.8*
Figs	80.8	87.5	87.5*
Dates	989.6	996.8	996.8*
Cotton (lint)†	134.0	120.0	114.0
Tea (made)	40.3	59.2	59.2*

* FAO estimate(s).
† Unofficial figures.
Source: FAO.

LIVESTOCK
('000 head)

	2004	2005	2006*
Horses*	140	140	140
Asses, mules and hinnies*	1,775	1,775	1,775
Cattle*	9,190	n.a.	9,378
Buffaloes*	560	n.a.	580
Camels*	146	146	146
Sheep	52,215	52,219	52,219
Goats	25,756	25,807	25,807
Ducks*	1,600	1,600	1,600
Geese and guinea fowls*	1,000	1,000	1,000
Turkeys*	2,000	2,000	2,000

* FAO estimates.
Source: FAO.

Chickens ('000 head raised by traditional methods, year ending March 2003): 24,783.

LIVESTOCK PRODUCTS
('000 metric tons)

	2004	2005	2006*
Cattle meat	336.8	n.a.	341.8
Buffalo meat*	13.4	n.a.	13.9
Sheep meat*	348.0	388.9	388.9
Goat meat*	105	105	105
Chicken meat	1,171.0	1,152.9*	1,152.9
Turkey meat*	16.3	16.9	16.9
Cows' milk	5,843.0	6,242.4	6,242.4
Buffaloes' milk	217.6	232.4	232.4
Goats' milk*	365	365	365
Hen eggs	645	n.a.	685
Honey*	35	36	36
Wool (greasy)*	75	75	75

* FAO estimate(s).
Source: FAO.

Forestry

ROUNDWOOD REMOVALS
('000 cubic metres, excl. bark)

	2004	2005	2006
Sawlogs, veneer logs and logs for sleepers	274	250	285
Pulpwood	240	246	235
Other industrial wood	229	206	209
Fuel wood	77	72	65
Total	820	774	794

Source: FAO.

SAWNWOOD PRODUCTION
('000 cubic metres, incl. railway sleepers)

	2004	2005	2006
Total (all broadleaved)	68	68	50

Source: FAO.

Fishing

('000 metric tons, live weight)

	2003	2004	2005
Capture	350.1	370.0	410.6
Caspian shads	15.5	19.6	22.6
Indian oil sardine	14.2	18.4	15.7
Kawakawa	14.1	11.6	11.8
Skipjack tuna	36.0	53.6	80.7
Longtail tuna	30.3	19.5	18.5
Yellowfin tuna	37.7	51.6	43.6
Aquaculture	91.7	104.3	117.4
Silver carp	37.9	36.0	40.4
Total catch	441.8	474.3	527.9

Source: FAO.

Production of caviar (metric tons, year ending 20 March): 53 in 2003/04; 40 in 2004/05; 34 in 2005/06.

Mining

CRUDE PETROLEUM
('000 barrels per day, year ending 20 March)

	2004/05	2005/06	2006/07
Total production	3,918	4,106	4,051

NATURAL GAS
(excluding reinjection gas; million cu metres, year ending 20 March)*

	2004/05	2005/06	2006/07
Consumption (domestic)†	97,700	106,700	121,200
Flared	14,700	15,800	15,100
Regional uses and wastes	9,400	7,400	5,000
Gas for export	3,500	4,800	5,700
Total production	119,400	130,600	143,200

* Discrepancy in sum of components and total production is due to imports. Figures for previous years not adjusted owing to lack of data.
† Includes gas for household, industrial, generator and refinery consumption.

Gas injection (year ending 20 March, million cu metres): 28,430 in 2003/04; 29,298 in 2004/05; 28,163 in 2005/06.

IRAN

OTHER MINERALS
('000 metric tons, unless otherwise indicated, year ending 20 March)

	2002/03	2003/04	2004/05*
Iron ore: gross weight	18,287	18,205	19,000
Iron ore: metal content†	9,000	8,900	9,000
Copper concentrates‡†	130	150	208
Bauxite	364	366	365
Lead concentrates‡†	20	22	22
Zinc concentrates‡†	110	121	125
Manganese ore§	116	129	125
Chromium concentrates‖	97	139	224
Molybdenum concentrates (metric tons)‡†	2,200	1,800	2,000
Silver (metric tons)‡	23	25	25
Gold (kilograms)‡	203	195	200
Bentonite	141	193	200
Kaolin	485	531	500
Other clays	389	579	550
Magnesite	88	88	88
Fluorspar (Fluorite)	48	54	54
Feldspar	243	253	250
Barite (Barytes)	196	276	280
Salt (unrefined)	2,003	1,791	2,000
Gypsum (crude)	13,828	12,594	13,000
Pumice and related materials	1,228	1,536	1,500
Mica (metric tons)	5,500	7,032	7,000
Talc	66	187	190
Turquoise (kilograms)†	20,000	20,000	20,000
Coal	1,902	2,498	2,500

* Preliminary estimates.
† Estimated figures.
‡ Figures refer to the metal content of ores and concentrates.
§ Figures refer to gross weight. The estimated metal content (in '000 metric tons) was: 38 in 2002/03; 43 in 2003/04; 42 in 2004/05.
‖ Figures refer to gross weight. The estimated chromic oxide content (in '000 metric tons) was: 48 in 2002/03; 68 in 2003/04; 110 in 2004/05.

Source: US Geological Survey.

Industry

PETROLEUM PRODUCTS
(average cu m per day, year ending 20 March)

	2003/04	2004/05	2005/06
Liquefied petroleum gas	8,608	8,427	8,204
Motor spirit (petrol)	39,872	40,155	41,332
Burning oil (for electricity)	24,745	22,965	20,269
Jet fuel	3,000	2,739	2,929
Gas-diesel (distillate fuel) oil	73,154	77,037	79,214
Residual fuel oils	77,073	74,762	76,136
Lubricating oils	96	—	—
Petroleum bitumen (asphalt)	7,138	8,090	672

OTHER PRODUCTS
(year ending 20 March)

	2002/03	2003/04	2004/05
Refined sugar ('000 metric tons)	1,275	1,495	1,375
Soft drinks (million bottles)	4,816	4,976	5,084
Malt liquor (million bottles)	98	112	123
Cigarettes (million)	13,580	13,873	21,117
Threads ('000 metric tons)	286	293	368
Finished fabrics (million metres)	364	396	382
Machine-made carpets ('000 sq m)	61,455	41,195	56,600
Hand-woven carpets (moquette—'000 sq m)	55,478	81,286	67,961
Paper ('000 metric tons)	327	390	414
Detergent powder ('000 metric tons)	306	360	398
Soap (metric tons)	48,613	60,607	62,375
Cement ('000 metric tons)	23,670	28,241	31,105
Washing machines ('000)	260	447	346
Radio receivers ('000)	275	400	351
Television receivers ('000)	894	858	849
Water metres ('000)	859	832	796
Electricity meters ('000)	990	1,190	1,211
Passenger cars and jeeps ('000)	465	663	793
Electric energy (million kWh)	140,655	153,877	167,052

Electric energy (million kWh): 180,390 in 2005/06 (preliminary).

Finance

CURRENCY AND EXCHANGE RATES

Monetary Units
100 dinars = 1 Iranian rial (IR).

Sterling, Dollar and Euro Equivalents (31 December 2007)
£1 sterling = 18,595.575 rials;
US $1 = 9,282.000 rials;
€1 = 13,664.026 rials;
100,000 Iranian rials = £5.38 = $10.77 = €7.32.

Average Exchange Rate (rials per US $)
2005 8,963.96
2006 9,170.94
2007 9,281.15

Note: In March 1993 the former multiple exchange rate system was unified, and since then the exchange rate of the rial has been market-determined. The foregoing information on average exchange rates refers to the base rate, applicable to receipts from exports of petroleum and gas, payments for imports of essential goods and services, debt-servicing costs and imports related to large national projects. There was also an export rate, set at a mid-point of US $1 = 3,007.5 rials in May 1995, which applied to receipts from non-petroleum exports and to all other official current account transactions not effected at the base rate. In addition, a market rate was determined by transactions on the Tehran Stock Exchange: at 31 January 2002 it was US $1 = 7,924 rials. The weighted average of all exchange rates (rials per US $, year ending 20 December) was: 3,206 in 1997/98; 4,172 in 1998/99; 5,731 in 1999/2000. A new unified exchange rate, based on the market rate, took effect from 21 March 2002.

BUDGET
(consolidated accounts of central government and Oil Stabilization Fund—OSF, '000 million rials, year ending 20 March)

Revenue	2003/04	2004/05	2005/06*
Oil and gas revenue	185,748	237,663	361,866
Budget revenue	184,261	214,165	316,277
Transfers from OSF	56,107	63,752	69,383
Revenues transferred to OSF	1,487	23,498	45,589
Non-oil budgetary revenue	78,837	103,587	139,823
Tax revenue	65,099	84,422	102,705
Taxes on income, profits and capital gains	32,034	41,897	52,161
Domestic taxes on goods and services	10,664	9,437	14,950
Taxes on international trade and transactions	22,401	33,088	35,954
Non-tax revenue	13,738	19,166	37,118
Non-oil OSF revenues	2,056	1,578	2,076
Total	266,641	342,828	503,765

Expenditure	2003/04	2004/05	2005/06*
Central government expenditures	251,178	303,230	447,570
Current expenditure	178,255	231,923	330,884
Wages and salaries	78,264	93,656	137,180
Social contributions	13,151	18,550	16,040
Interest payments	3,341	2,752	4,264
Subsidies	33,615	42,463	53,192
Goods and services	24,478	30,837	41,637
Grants	7,048	4,855	2,168
Social benefits	2,945	3,613	7,142
Gasoline imports	0	0	35,748
Other expenses	15,413	35,198	33,513
Capital expenditure	72,923	71,307	116,687
OSF expenditures	555	16,060	36,762
Total	251,733	319,290	484,332

* Preliminary.

Source: IMF, *Islamic Republic of Iran: Statistical Appendix* (March 2007).

IRAN

INTERNATIONAL RESERVES
(US $ million at 31 December)*

	1993	1994	1995
Gold (national valuation)	229.1	242.2	251.9
IMF special drawing rights	144.0	142.9	133.6
Total	373.1	385.1	385.5

* Excluding reserves of foreign exchange, for which no figures have been available since 1982 (when the value of reserves was US $5,287m.).

IMF special drawing rights (US $ million at 31 December): 425 in 2004; 393 in 2005; 415 in 2006.

Source: IMF, *International Financial Statistics*.

MONEY SUPPLY
('000 million rials at 20 December)

	2004	2005	2006
Currency outside banks	34,247	39,232	49,774
Non-financial public enterprises' deposits at Central Bank	8,611	10,915	12,091
Demand deposits at commercial banks	169,348	210,510	266,196
Total money	212,205	260,656	328,061

Source: IMF, *International Financial Statistics*.

COST OF LIVING
(Consumer Price Index in urban areas, year ending 20 March; base: 1997/98 = 100)

	2004/05	2005/06	2006/07
Food, beverages and tobacco	281.0	310.3	353.9
Clothing	156.3	171.0	186.6
Housing	332.8	381.7	442.7
Fuel and light	419.2	432.7	440.0
All items (incl. others)	274.5	307.6	349.5

NATIONAL ACCOUNTS
('000 million rials at current prices, year ending 20 March)

National Income and Product

	2001/02	2002/03	2003/04
Compensation of employees	153,562	213,021	265,739
Operating surplus	492,014	612,063	760,461
Domestic factor incomes	645,576	825,084	1,026,200
Consumption of fixed capital	89,281	127,306	150,549
Gross domestic product (GDP) at factor cost	734,857	952,390	1,176,749
Taxes on production and imports	31,605	38,507	51,562
Less Subsidies	13,463	15,179	23,646
GDP in purchasers' values	752,999	975,718	1,204,665
Net factor income from abroad	1,455	−15,932	−22,667
Gross national product (GNP)	754,454	959,786	1,181,998
Less Consumption of fixed capital	89,281	127,306	150,549
National income in market prices	665,173	832,480	1,031,450

Expenditure on the Gross Domestic Product*

	2004/05	2005/06	2006/07
Final consumption expenditure	800,483	990,021	1,214,295
Private	640,266	765,501	924,562
Public	160,218	224,520	289,733
Changes in inventories	104,666	98,198†	126,749†
Gross fixed capital formation	401,765	464,532	538,720
Total domestic expenditure	1,306,914	1,552,751	1,879,764
Exports of goods and services	408,414	568,975	663,301
Less Imports of goods and services	364,559	424,421	499,040
Statistical discrepancy	55,262	—	—
GDP at market prices	1,406,031	1,697,306	2,044,024
GDP at constant 1997/98 prices	404,334	423,208	447,961

* Provisional.
† Includes statistical discrepancy.

Gross Domestic Product by Economic Activity*

	2004/05	2005/06	2006/07
Hydrocarbon GDP	346,673	471,520	540,091
Non-hydrocarbon GDP	1,038,145	1,216,385	1,498,341
Agriculture	155,471	171,982	211,275
Industry	245,140	283,098	349,446
Mining	8,114	10,375	15,327
Manufacturing	156,076	181,343	221,487
Construction	60,739	69,220	88,408
Electricity, gas and water	20,211	22,160	24,224
Services	667,251	800,915	994,632
Transport and communication	101,195	121,804	149,777
Banking and insurance	49,419	66,230	93,212
Trade, restaurants and hotels	160,862	188,552	226,542
Ownership and dwellings	174,145	206,305	257,392
Public services	143,809	173,242	212,696
Private services	37,821	44,782	55,013
Less Imputed bank service charge	29,716	39,611	57,012
GDP at factor prices	1,384,819	1,687,905	2,038,432
Net indirect taxes	21,212	9,400	5,592
GDP at market prices	1,406,031	1,697,305	2,044,024

* Provisional.

BALANCE OF PAYMENTS
(US $ million, year ending 20 March)

	2003/04	2004/05	2005/06*
Exports of goods f.o.b.	33,991	44,364	60,013
Petroleum and gas	27,355	36,827	48,824
Non-petroleum and gas exports	6,636	7,537	11,189
Imports of goods f.o.b.	−29,561	−38,199	−40,969
Trade balance	4,430	6,165	19,044
Exports of services and other income received	6,249	6,905	7,612
Imports of services and other income paid	−10,784	−11,917	−13,506
Balance on goods, services and income	−105	1,153	13,150
Transfers (net)	921	799	888
Current balance	816	1,952	14,038
Medium and long-term capital	−360	586	258
Short-term capital	2,714	5,462	247
Other capital	−285	295	−1,254
Foreign direct investment and portfolio equity	2,407	1,073	776
Net errors and omissions	−2003	−819	−1,033
Overall balance	3,289	8,548	13,032

* Preliminary.

Source: IMF, *Islamic Republic of Iran: Statistical Appendix* (March 2007).

IRAN

Statistical Survey

External Trade

PRINCIPAL COMMODITIES
(US $ million, year ending 20 March)

Imports c.i.f. (distribution by SITC)	2003/04	2004/05	2005/06
Food and live animals	1,419	1,733	1,791
Cereals and cereal preparations	785	875	909
Crude materials (inedible) except fuels	1,081	1,494	1,289
Animal and vegetable oils and fats	675	618	646
Vegetable oils and fats	668	613	638
Chemicals and related products	3,391	4,208	4,191
Chemical elements and compounds	835	944	921
Plastic, cellulose and artificial resins	992	1,317	1,361
Basic manufactures	5,445	7,182	8,266
Iron and steel	3,315	4,609	5,412
Machinery and transport equipment	12,005	15,825	17,217
Non-electric machinery	6,346	8,565	9,228
Electrical machinery, apparatus, etc.	2,373	2,936	2,876
Transport equipment	3,285	4,324	5,113
Miscellaneous manufactured articles	900	913	1,142
Total (incl. others)	26,598	35,389	39,248

Exports f.o.b.*	2003/04	2004/05	2005/06
Agricultural and traditional goods	2,104	1,952	2,682
Carpets	539	490	467
Fruits (fresh and dried)	991	893	1,336
Industrial manufactures	3,823	4,799	7,623
Chemical products	1,389	1,732	3,133
Iron and steel	299	926	1,122
Total (incl. others)	5,972	6,848	10,474

*Excluding exports of crude petroleum and associated gas (US $ million): 27,355 in 2003/04; 36,315 in 2004/05; 53,820 in 2005/06.

Note: Imports include registration fee, but exclude defence-related imports and imports of refined oil products.

Source: mostly IMF, *Islamic Republic of Iran: Statistical Appendix* (March 2007).

Non-oil exports (US $ million, year ending 20 March 2007, provisional): Agricultural and traditional goods 3,012 (Carpets 413; Fresh and dried fruits 1,571); Industrial manufactures 9,550 (Chemical products 3,783; Iron and steel 1,327) 9,550; Total (incl. others) 12,997.

Oil and gas exports (US $ million, year ending 20 March 2007, provisional): Total 62,458.

PRINCIPAL TRADING PARTNERS
(US $ million, year ending 20 March)

Imports c.i.f.	2003/04	2004/05	2005/06
Austria	345	648	710
Belgium	517	724	710
Brazil	833	729	818
China, People's Republic	1,541	2,062	2,157
France	2,262	2,585	2,648
Germany	3,042	4,481	5,147
India	883	1,221	1,114
Italy	1,677	2,432	2,358
Japan	997	951	1,310
Korea, Republic	1,315	1,871	2,100
Russia	1,098	868	1,034
Singapore	443	600	462
Spain	340	353	365
Sweden	674	1,046	1,016
Switzerland	866	1,441	1,273
Turkey	518	724	867
United Arab Emirates	3,536	6,093	7,673
United Kingdom	888	1,030	982
Total (incl. others)	26,598	35,389	39,009

Exports f.o.b.*	2003/04	2004/05	2005/06
China, People's Republic	3,177	4,066	7,108
France	1,178	1,776	2,501
Greece	980	1,350	1,913
Italy	1,941	2,691	3,375
Japan	6,820	7,788	10,073
Korea, Republic	1,783	2,421	3,401
Netherlands	1,149	1,844	2,890
Philippines	487	791	1,112
Singapore	658	936	1,279
South Africa	1,564	2,226	2,375
Spain	960	1,144	1,778
Taiwan	1,630	1,994	2,375
Turkey	1,654	1,999	3,478
Total (incl. others)	33,002	43,622	59,622

*Data based on direction of trade reporting by recipient nations.

Source: IMF, *Islamic Republic of Iran: Statistical Appendix* (March 2007).

Transport

RAILWAYS
(traffic, year ending 20 March)

	2003/04	2004/05	2005/06
Passengers carried ('000)	16,112	17,397	19,400
Passenger-km (million)	9,314	10,012	11,149
Freight carried ('000 metric tons)	28,797	29,453	30,278
Freight ton-km (million)	18,048	18,182	19,127

ROAD TRAFFIC
(registered motor vehicles, year ending 20 March)

	2003/04	2004/05	2005/06
Passenger cars*	634,482	801,112	831,829
Pick-ups and light trucks	75,212	76,436	126,857
Motorcycles	1,206,494	1,363,543	1,062,811
Total (incl. others)	1,926,449	2,273,505	2,054,322

*Including ambulances.

SHIPPING

Merchant Fleet
(registered at 31 December)

	2004	2005	2006
Number of vessels	430	453	475
Displacement ('000 grt)	5,324.3	5,270.6	5,207.3

Source: Lloyd's Register-Fairplay, *World Fleet Statistics*.

International Sea-borne Freight Traffic
(year ending 20 March, '000 metric tons)*

	2003/04	2004/05	2005/06
Goods loaded	28,605	30,941	31,651
Crude petroleum and petroleum products	18,106	17,793	15,439
Goods unloaded	53,078	56,900	59,759
Petroleum products	22,845	25,324	26,818

* Cargo loaded onto and from vessels with a capacity of 1,000 metric tons or greater only.

CIVIL AVIATION
(year ending 20 March)

	2003/04	2004/05	2005/06
Passengers ('000):			
domestic flights	8,942	9,355	10,508
international arrivals	2,169	2,403	2,523
international departures	2,168	2,406	2,583
Freight (excl. mail, metric tons):			
domestic flights	27,937	22,611	24,975
international arrivals	44,151	42,859	69,667
international departures	20,081	33,024	23,725
Mail (metric tons):			
domestic flights	2,218	2,702	3,706
international arrivals	1,345	2,652	3,667
international departures	1,154	1,504	1,398

Tourism

FOREIGN TOURIST ARRIVALS
(year ending 20 March)

Country of nationality	1997/98	1998/99	1999/2000
Afghanistan	69,793	125,189	146,322
Azerbaijan	302,574	383,123	447,797
Kuwait	19,642	26,472	30,941
Pakistan	100,427	115,431	134,916
Russia	16,466*	10,191*	11,911
Saudi Arabia	17,406	21,093	24,654
Turkey	93,105	160,959	188,130
Total (incl. others)	764,092	1,007,597	1,320,905

* Including Belarus.

Total arrivals (year ending 20 March): 1,341,762 in 2000/01; 1,402,160 in 2001/02; 1,584,922 in 2002/03; 1,500,439 in 2003/04; 1,659,479 in 2004/05.

Tourism receipts (US $ million, excl. passenger transport): 1,266 in 2003; 1,305 in 2004; 1,329 in 2005 (Source: World Tourism Organization).

Communications Media

	2004	2005	2006
Telephones ('000 main lines in use)	16,342.0	18,985.7	21,980.9
Mobile cellular telephones ('000 subscribers)	4,271.0	7,222.5	13,659.1
Internet users ('000)	6,600	7,600	18,000
Broadband subscribers ('000)	19.2	20.8	465.1
Book production*:			
titles	40,920	52,627	n.a.
copies ('000)	175,306	223,638	n.a.
Newspapers and periodicals (number of titles)*:			
daily	177	198	n.a.
other	3,608	4,278	n.a.

* Twelve months beginning 21 March of year stated.

Personal computers ('000 in use): 7,347 in 2004.

Television receivers ('000 in use, year ending 20 March): 11,040 in 2001/02.

Radio receivers ('000 in use, year ending 20 March): 17,400 in 1998/99.

Facsimile machines (number in use, year ending 20 March): 30,000 in 1994/95.

Sources: partly International Telecommunication Union; UN, *Statistical Yearbook*.

Education
(2005/06)

	Institutions	Teachers	Males	Females	Total
Special	1,284	11,099	40.8	26.6	67.4
Pre-primary	19,912	16,047	262.3	278.1	540.4
Primary	65,507	274,922	3,108.9	2,897.7	6,006.7
Lower secondary:					
mainstream	31,908	185,758	2,214.7	1,931.4	4,146.1
adult	447		16.7	23.3	40.0
Upper secondary:					
mainstream	21,475	188,777	1,917.2	1,845.9	3,763.0
adult	2,462		202.0	118.8	320.8
Pre-university:					
mainstream	5,915	n.a.	153.8	265.1	418.9
adult	1,889		55.7	63.2	118.8
Teacher training	90	n.a.	5.0	4.7	9.8
Islamic Azad University	n.a.	43,933	622.7	574.8	1,197.5
Other higher	n.a.	78,135	534.2	656.8	1,191.0

Adult literacy rate (UNESCO estimates): 82.4% (males 88.0%; females 76.8%) in 2005 (Source: UNESCO Institute for Statistics).

Directory

The Constitution

A draft constitution for the Islamic Republic of Iran was published on 18 June 1979. It was submitted to a 'Council of Experts', elected by popular vote on 3 August, to debate the various clauses and to propose amendments. The amended Constitution was approved by a referendum on 2–3 December 1979. A further 45 amendments to the Constitution were approved by a referendum on 28 July 1989.

The Constitution states that the form of government of Iran is that of an Islamic Republic, and that the spirituality and ethics of Islam are to be the basis for political, social and economic relations. Persians, Turks, Kurds, Arabs, Balochis, Turkomans and others will enjoy completely equal rights.

The Constitution provides for a President to act as Chief Executive. The President is elected by universal adult suffrage for a term of four years. Legislative power is held by the Majlis (Islamic Consultative Assembly), with 290 members (effective from the 2000 election) who are similarly elected for a four-year term. Provision is made for the representation of Zoroastrians, Jews and Christians.

All legislation passed by the Islamic Consultative Assembly must be sent to the Council for the Protection of the Constitution (Article 94), which will ensure that it is in accordance with the Constitution and Islamic legislation. The Council for the Protection of the Constitution consists of six religious lawyers appointed by the Wali Faqih (see below) and six lawyers appointed by the High Council of the Judiciary and approved by the Islamic Consultative Assembly. Articles 19–42 deal with the basic rights of individuals, and provide for equality of men and women before the law and for equal human, political, economic, social and cultural rights for both sexes.

The press is free, except in matters that are contrary to public morality or insult religious belief. The formation of religious, political and professional parties, associations and societies is free, provided they do not negate the principles of independence, freedom, sovereignty and national unity, or the basis of Islam.

The Constitution provides for a Wali Faqih (religious leader) who, in the absence of the Imam Mehdi (the hidden Twelfth Imam), carries the burden of leadership. The amendments to the Constitution that were approved in July 1989 increased the powers of the Presidency by abolishing the post of Prime Minister, formerly the Chief Executive of the Government.

The Government

SUPREME RELIGIOUS LEADER

Wali Faqih: Ayatollah SAYED ALI KHAMENEI.

HEAD OF STATE

President: MAHMOUD AHMADINEJAD (assumed office 6 August 2005).
First Vice-President: PARVIZ DAVOUDI.
Vice-President in charge of Legal and Parliamentary Affairs: (vacant).
Vice-President and Head of the Iranian Atomic Energy Organization: GHOLAMREZA AGHAZADEH.
Vice-President and Head of the Organization for the Protection of the Environment: FATEMEH JAVADI.
Vice-President for Strategic Planning and Supervision Affairs: AMIR MANSOUR BORQEI.
Vice-President and Head of the National Youth Organization: MUHAMMAD JAVAR ALI AKBARI.
Vice-President and Head of the Martyrs' and Self-Sacrificers' Affairs Foundation: HOSSEIN DEHGHAAN.
Vice-President and Head of the Cultural Heritage, Handicrafts and Tourism Organization: ESFANDIAR RAHIM MASHAI.
Vice-President for Physical Training and Head of the Physical Education Organization: MUHAMMAD ALIABADI.
Vice-President in charge of Executive Affairs: ALI SAIDLOO.

COUNCIL OF MINISTERS
(April 2008)

Minister of Education: ALI REZA ALI AHMADI.
Minister of Information and Communications Technology: MUHAMMAD SOLEYMANI.
Minister of Intelligence and Security: GHOLAM HOSSEIN MOHSENI EJEIE.
Acting Minister of Economic Affairs and Finance: HOSSEIN SAMSAMI.
Minister of Foreign Affairs: MANOUCHEHR MOTTAKI.
Minister of Commerce: MASOUD MIR-KAZEMI.
Minister of Health and Medical Education: KAMRAN BAQERI LANKARANI.
Minister of Co-operatives: MUHAMMAD ABBASI.
Minister of Agricultural Jihad: MUHAMMAD REZA ESKANDARI.
Minister of Justice: GHOLAM HOSSEIN ELHAM.
Minister of Defence and Armed Forces Logistics: MOUSTAFA MUHAMMAD-NAJAR.
Minister of Roads and Transport: MUHAMMAD RAHMATI.
Minister of Welfare and Social Security: ABDOLREZA MESRI.
Minister of Industries and Mines: ALI AKBAR MEHRABIAN.
Minister of Science, Research and Technology: MUHAMMAD MAHDI ZAHEDI.
Minister of Culture and Islamic Guidance: MUHAMMAD HOSSEIN SAFFAR-HARANDI.
Minister of Labour and Social Affairs: MUHAMMAD JAHROMI.
Minister of the Interior: MOUSTAFA POUR-MUHAMMADI.
Minister of Housing and Urban Development: MUHAMMAD SAEEDI-KIA.
Minister of Petroleum: GHOLAMHOSSEIN NOZARI.
Minister of Energy: PARVIZ FATTAH.

MINISTRIES

Office of the President: POB 1423-13185, Pasteur Ave, Tehran 13168-43311; tel. (21) 64451; e-mail webmaster@president.ir; internet www.president.ir.

Ministry of Agricultural Jihad: 20 Malaei Ave, Vali-e-Asr Sq., Tehran; tel. (21) 81363301; fax (21) 81363345; e-mail pr@maj.ir; internet www.maj.ir.

Ministry of Commerce: POB 14155-6399, Vali-e-Asr Ave, Tehran; tel. (21) 88893620; fax (21) 88901601; e-mail minister@moc.gov.ir; internet www.moc.gov.ir.

Ministry of Co-operatives: 16 Bozorgmehr St, Vali-e-Asr Ave, Tehran 14169; tel. (21) 66400938; fax (21) 66498440; e-mail info@icm.gov.ir; internet www.icm.gov.ir.

Ministry of Culture and Islamic Guidance: Baharestan Sq., Tehran; tel. (21) 32411; fax (21) 33117535; e-mail info@ershad.gov.ir; internet www.ershad.gov.ir.

Ministry of Defence and Armed Forces Logistics: Shahid Yousuf Kaboli St, Sayed Khandan Area, Tehran; tel. (21) 21401; fax (21) 864008; e-mail info@mod.ir; internet www.mod.ir.

Ministry of Economic Affairs and Finance: Sour Esrafil Ave, Nasser Khosrou St, Tehran 11149-43661; tel. (21) 22553401; fax (21) 22581933; e-mail info@mefa.gov.ir; internet mefa.gov.ir.

Ministry of Education: Si-e-Tir St, Emam Khomeini Sq., Tehran; tel. (21) 32421; fax (21) 675503; e-mail info@medu.ir; internet www.medu.ir.

Ministry of Energy: North Palestine St, Tehran; tel. (21) 8890001; fax (21) 88801995; e-mail webmaster@moe.org.ir; internet www.moe.org.ir.

Ministry of Foreign Affairs: Shahid Abd al-Hamid Mesri St, Ferdowsi Ave, Tehran; tel. (21) 61151; fax (21) 66743149; e-mail matbuat@mfa.gov.ir; internet www.mfa.gov.ir.

Ministry of Health and Medical Education: POB 310, Tehran 11344; tel. (21) 66700017; fax (21) 3853947; e-mail webmaster@mohme.gov.ir; internet www.mohme.gov.ir.

Ministry of Housing and Urban Development: Shahid Khoddami St, Vanak Sq., Tehran; tel. (21) 877711; fax (21) 88776634; internet www.mhud.gov.ir.

Ministry of Industries and Mines: POB 1416, 248 West Somayeh St, Tehran 15996; tel. (21) 88877588; fax (21) 88807817; e-mail mimwebmaster@mim.gov.ir; internet www.mim.gov.ir.

Ministry of Information and Communications Technology: POB 15875-4415, Shariati St, Tehran 16314; tel. (21) 88469000; fax (21) 88467673; e-mail khajeh@ict.gov.ir; internet www.ict.gov.ir.

Ministry of Intelligence and Security: POB 16765-1947, Tehran; tel. (21) 233031; fax (21) 23305.

Ministry of the Interior: Jahad Sq., Fatemi St, Tehran; tel. (21) 88967866; fax (21) 88964678; e-mail entekhabat@moi.gov.ir; internet www.moi.ir.

Ministry of Justice: Panzdah-e-Khordad Sq., Tehran; tel. (21) 3904331; fax (21) 3904986; e-mail ijpr@iranjudiciary.org; internet www.iranjudiciary.org.

Ministry of Labour and Social Affairs: 209 Fatemi Ave, Tehran; tel. (21) 88977415; fax (21) 88951536; e-mail rezaaeifars@yahoo.com; internet www.irimlsa.ir.

Ministry of Petroleum: Hafez Crossing, Taleghani Ave, Tehran; tel. (21) 66152606; fax (21) 66154977; e-mail public-relations@mop.ir; internet www.nioc.ir.

Ministry of Roads and Transport: Shahid Dadman Bldg, Africa Ave, Argentina Sq., Tehran; tel. (21) 88878031; fax (21) 88878059; e-mail webmaster@mrt.ir; internet www.mrt.ir.

Ministry of Science, Research and Technology: POB 15875-4375, Central Bldg, Ostad Nejatollahi Ave, Tehran; tel. (21) 88891065; fax (21) 88827234; e-mail hashemi@msrt.ir; internet www.msrt.ir.

Ministry of Welfare and Social Security: Tehran.

President and Legislature

PRESIDENT

Presidential Election, First Ballot, 17 June 2005

Candidates	Votes	%
Ali Akbar Hashemi Rafsanjani	6,159,453	21.0
Mahmoud Ahmadinejad	5,710,354	19.5
Mahdi Karrubi	5,066,316	17.3
Muhammad Baqir Qalibaf	4,075,189	13.9
Moustafa Moin	4,054,304	13.8
Ali Ardeshir Larijani	1,740,163	5.9
Mohsen Mehr-Alizadeh	1,289,323	4.4
Total*	29,317,042	100.0

* Including 1,221,940 invalid votes (4.2% of total votes cast).

IRAN

Presidential Election, Second Ballot, 24 June 2005

Candidate	Votes	%
Mahmoud Ahmadinejad	17,248,782	61.7
Ali Akbar Hashemi Rafsanjani	10,046,701	35.9
Total*	27,959,253	100.0

* Including 663,770 invalid votes (2.4% of total votes cast).

MAJLIS-E-SHURA-E ISLAMI—ISLAMIC CONSULTATIVE ASSEMBLY

Elections to the eighth Majlis took place in early 2008. Prior to the elections the Council of Guardians and the Ministry of the Interior barred at least 1,700 of the 7,168 registered candidates from standing, including a number of current Majlis deputies. The majority of the barred candidates were recognized as being 'reformists'. At the first round of voting, held on 14 March, 208 deputies received a sufficient number of votes to be elected directly to the Majlis; at the second round, on 25 April, a further 79 deputies were elected. Three seats remained vacant following both rounds, after election officials had annulled the results for unspecified reasons; by-elections for these seats were to be held at a later date. According to official reports, 'conservatives' controlled the eighth Majlis, with an estimated 198–200 seats; 'reformists' secured around 46–50 seats, and some 40–43 seats were held by 'independents'. A reported 29 of the 30 seats in Tehran would be controlled by 'conservatives', with only one seat being secured by a 'reformist'. However, despite the 'conservatives' having consolidated their control of the Majlis, some of the successful candidates were reported to be critical of the policies of President Mahmoud Ahmadinejad.

Speaker: GHOLAM-ALI HADDAD-ADEL.
First Deputy Speaker: MUHAMMAD REZA BAHONAR.
Second Deputy Speaker: MUHAMMAD HASSAN ABU TURABI.

SHURA-YE ALI-YE AMNIYYAT-E MELLI—SUPREME COUNCIL FOR NATIONAL SECURITY

Formed in July 1989 to co-ordinate defence and national security policies, the political programme and intelligence reports, and social, cultural and economic activities related to defence and security. The Council is chaired by the President and includes a representative of the Wali Faqih, the Minister of the Interior, the Speaker of the Majlis, the Head of the Judiciary, the Chief of the Supreme Command Council of the Armed Forces, the Minister of Foreign Affairs, the Head of the Management and Planning Organization and the Minister of Intelligence and Security.

Secretary: SAEED JALILI.

MAJLIS-E KHOBREGAN—COUNCIL OF EXPERTS

Elections were held on 10 December 1982 to appoint a Council of Experts which was to choose an eventual successor to the Wali Faqih (then Ayatollah Khomeini) after his death. The Constitution provides for a three- or five-man body to assume the leadership of the country if there is no recognized successor on the death of the Wali Faqih. The Council comprises 86 clerics, who are elected to serve an eight-year term. Elections to a fourth term of the Council were held on 15 December 2006.

Speaker: Hojatoleslam ALI AKBAR HASHEMI RAFSANJANI.
First Deputy Speaker: Ayatollah MUHAMMAD MO'MEN.
Second Deputy Speaker: Ayatollah MUHAMMAD TAQI MESBAH-YAZDI.
Secretaries: Ayatollah AHMAD KHATAMI, Ayatollah QORBANALI DORRI NAJAFABADI.

SHURA-E-NIGAHBAN—COUNCIL OF GUARDIANS

The Council of Guardians, composed of six qualified Muslim jurists appointed by Ayatollah Khomeini and six lay Muslim lawyers, appointed by the Majlis from among candidates nominated by the Head of the Judiciary, was established in 1980 to supervise elections and to examine legislation adopted by the Majlis, ensuring that it accords with the Constitution and with Islamic precepts.

Chairman: Ayatollah AHMAD JANNATI.

SHURA-YE TASHKHIS-E MASLAHAT-E NEZAM— COUNCIL TO DETERMINE THE EXPEDIENCY OF THE ISLAMIC ORDER

Formed in February 1988, by order of Ayatollah Khomeini, to arbitrate on legal and theological questions in legislation passed by the Majlis, in the event of a dispute between the latter and the supervisory Council of Guardians. Its permanent members, defined in March 1997, are Heads of the Legislative, Judiciary and Executive Powers, the jurist members of the Council of Guardians and the Minister or head of organization concerned with the pertinent arbitration. Four new members were appointed to the Expediency Council in February 2007, when Rafsanjani was reappointed as Chairman; the term of the Council is five years.

Chairman: Hojatoleslam ALI AKBAR HASHEMI RAFSANJANI.
Secretary: MOHSEN REZAI.

HEY'AT-E PEYGIRI-YE QANUN ASASI VA NEZARAT BAR AN—COMMITTEE FOR ENSURING AND SUPERVISING THE IMPLEMENTATION OF THE CONSTITUTION

Formed by former President Khatami in November 1997; members are appointed for a four-year term. Two new members were appointed to the Committee in April 2002.

Members: Dr GUDARZ EFTEKHAR-JAHROMI, MUHAMMAD ISMAIL SHOUSHTARI, HASHEM HASHEMZADEH HERISI, Dr HOSSEIN MEHRPUR, Dr MUHAMMAD HOSSEIN HASHEMI, MUHAMMAD ALI ABTAHI.

Political Organizations

Numerous political organizations were registered in the late 1990s, following the election of former President Khatami, and have tended to be regarded as either 'conservative' or 'reformist', the principal factions in the legislature. Under the Iranian electoral system, political parties do not field candidates *per se* at elections, but instead back lists of candidates, who are allowed to be members of more than one party. In the mid-2000s there were estimated to be more than 100 registered political organizations. The following organizations contested elections to the seventh Majlis in 2004:

Association of Technocrats: f. 2003; Sec.-Gen. KHOSRAU NASSIRI-RAD.

Etelaf-e Abadgaran-e Iran-e Islami (Islamic Iran Developers' Council): e-mail info@abadgaran.ir; internet www.abadgaran.ir; f. 2003 to contest that year's municipal elections; conservative; includes mems of Jame'e-ye Eslaami-e Mohandesin (Islamic Society of Engineers); Leader GHOLAM-ALI HADDAD-ADEL.

Hezb-e Etedal va Toseh (Moderation and Development Party): first congress held 2002; conservative; Sec.-Gen. MUHAMMAD BAQIR NOBAKHT.

Hezb-e Iran-e Sarfaraz (Proud Iran Party): reformist; Sec.-Gen. RUZBEH MESHKIN.

Hezb-e Islami-ye Kar (Islamic Labour Party): f. 1999 as splinter group of Khaneh-ye Kargar (Workers' House); reformist; Sec.-Gen. ABOLQASEM SARHADIZADEH.

Hezb-e Kargozaran-e Sazandegi (Servants of Construction Party): f. 1996 as Servants of Iran's Construction; authorized as political party in 1998; reformist; Sec.-Gen. GHOLAMHOSSEIN KARBASCHI.

Jam'iyat-e Motalefeh-e Islami (Islamic Coalition Party): f. 1963; conservative; Sec.-Gen. MOHAMMAD NABI HABIBI.

Khaneh-ye Kargar (Workers' House): reformist, leftist; Sec.-Gen. ALIREZA MAHJUB.

Majma'-e Niruha-ye Khat-e Imam (Assembly of the Followers of the Imam's Line): Sec.-Gen. HADI KHAMENEI.

Majma'-e Ruhaniyun-e Mobarez (Militant Clergy Association): f. 1988 as splinter group of the Jam'-ye Ruhaniyat-e Mobarez-i Tehran (Tehran Militant Clergy Association); reformist; Sec.-Gen. Hojatoleslam MUHAMMAD ASQAR MUSAVI-KHOENIHA.

Most of the following are either registered political parties which boycotted the elections to the Majlis in early 2004, or are unregistered organizations or guerrilla groups:

Ansar-e Hezbollah (Helpers of the Party of God): internet www.ansarehezbollah.org; f. 1995; militant, ultra-conservative youth movement; pledges allegiance to the Wali Faqih (supreme religious leader).

Daftar-e Tahkim-e Vahdat (Office for Strengthening Unity): Tehran; national organization of Islamist university students who supported Khatami in the presidential election of 1997 and reformist candidates in the Majlis elections of 2000; Spokesman ALI NIKUNESBATI.

Democratic Party of Iranian Kurdistan: POB 102, Paris 75623, France; e-mail pdkiran@club-internet.fr; internet www.pdki.org; f. 1945; seeks a federal system of government in Iran, in order to secure the national rights of the Kurdish people; mem. of the Socialist International; 95,000 mems; Sec.-Gen. MUSTAFA HIJRI.

Fedayin-e-Khalq (Organization of the Iranian People's Fedayeen—Majority): Postfach 260268, 50515 Köln, Germany; e-mail info@fadai.org; internet www.fadai.org; f. 1971; Marxist; Sec. of Int. Dept FARROKH NEGAHDAR.

IRAN

Fraksion-e Hezbollah: f. 1996 by deputies in the Majlis who had contested the 1996 legislative elections as a loose coalition known as the Society of Combatant Clergy; Leader ALI AKBAR HOSSAINI.

Hezb-e Etemad-e Melli (National Confidence Party—NCP): Tehran; tel. (21) 88373305; fax (21) 88373306; e-mail Ravabet_Omomi@Etemademelli.ir; internet etemademelli.ir; f. 2005 by Mahdi Karrubi, fmrly of the Militant Clergy Association, shortly after his defeat in the presidential election of June; reformist, centrist; Sec.-Gen. MAHDI KARRUBI.

Hezb-e Hambastegi-ye Iran-e Islami (Islamic Iran Solidarity Party): f. 1998; reformist; Sec.-Gen. EBRAHIM ASHGARZADEH.

Hezb-e-Komunist Iran (Communist Party of Iran): POB 70445, 107 25 Stockholm, Sweden; e-mail cpi@cpiran.org; internet www.cpiran.org; f. 1979 by dissident mems of Tudeh Party; Sec.-Gen. 'AZARYUN'.

Jame'e-ye Eslaami-e Mohandesin (Islamic Society of Engineers): f. 1988; mems incl. President Mahmoud Ahmadinejad; Sec.-Gen. MUHAMMAD REZA BAHONAR.

Jebbeh-ye Mosharekat-e Iran-e Islami (Islamic Iran Participation Front): e-mail mail.emrooz@gmail.com; internet www.mosharekat.com; f. 1998; reformist, left-wing; Sec.-Gen. MOHSEN MIRDAMADI.

Komala Party of Iranian Kurdistan: e-mail webmaster@komala.org; internet www.komala.org; f. 1969; Kurdish wing of the Communist Party of Iran; Marxist-Leninist; Sec.-Gen. ABDULLAH MOHTADI.

Marze Por Gohar (Glorious Frontiers Party): 1351 Westwood Blvd, Suite 111, Los Angeles, CA 90024, USA; tel. (310) 473-4763; fax (310) 477-8484; e-mail info@marzeporgohar.org; internet www.marzeporgohar.org; f. 1998 in Tehran; nationalist party advocating a secular republic in Iran; Chair. ROOZBEH FARAHANIPOUR.

Mujahidin-e-Khalq (Holy Warriors of the People): e-mail mojahed@mojahedin.org; internet www.mojahedin.org; Marxist-Islamist guerrilla group opposed to clerical regime; since June 1987 comprising the National Liberation Army; mem. of the National Council of Resistance; based in Paris 1981–86 and in Baghdad, Iraq, 1986–2003; whereabouts of Massoud Rajavi uncertain since US-led occupation of Iraq in 2003; Leaders MARYAM RAJAVI, MASSOUD RAJAVI.

National Democratic Front: f. March 1979; Leader HEDAYATOLLAH MATINE-DAFTARI (based in Paris, Jan. 1982–).

National Front (Union of National Front Forces): comprises Iran Nationalist Party, Iranian Party and Society of Iranian Students; Leader Dr KARIM SANJABI (based in Paris, Aug. 1978–).

Nehzat-e Azadi-ye Iran (Liberation Movement of Iran): e-mail info@nehzateazadi.info; internet www.nehzateazadi.org; f. 1961; emphasis on basic human rights as defined by Islam; Sec.-Gen. Dr IBRAHIM YAZDI.

Pan-Iranist Party: POB 31535-1679, Karaj; internet www.paniranist.com; calls for a Greater Persia; Leader Dr SOHRAB AZAM ZANGANEH.

Sazeman-e Mujahidin-e Enqelab-e Islami (Organization of the Mujahidin of the Islamic Revolution): reformist; Sec.-Gen. MUHAMMAD SALAMATI.

Sazmane Peykar dar Rahe Azadieh Tabaqe Kargar (Organization Struggling for the Freedom of the Working Class): Marxist-Leninist.

Tudeh Party (Party of the Masses): POB 100644, 10566 Berlin, Germany; tel. (30) 3241627; e-mail mardom@tudehpartyiran.org; internet www.tudehpartyiran.org; f. 1941; declared illegal 1949; came into open 1979; banned again April 1983; First Sec. Cen. Cttee ALI KHAVARI.

The National Council of Resistance (NCR) was formed in Paris, France, in October 1981 by former President Abolhasan Bani-Sadr and Massoud Rajavi, the leader of the Mujahidin-e-Khalq in Iran. In 1984 the Council comprised 15 opposition groups, operating either clandestinely in Iran or from exile abroad. Bani-Sadr left the Council in that year because of his objection to Rajavi's growing links with the Iraqi Government. The French Government asked Rajavi to leave Paris in June 1986 and he moved his base of operations to Baghdad. In June 1987 Rajavi, Secretary of the NCR, announced the formation of a 10,000–15,000-strong National Liberation Army as the military wing of the Mujahidin-e-Khalq. However, the status of the Mujahidin was initially uncertain following the invasion of Iraq by the US-led coalition in March 2003 (see the chapter on Iraq) and firmer measures being taken against the activities of the organization by the authorities in Paris in mid-2003. In July 2004 the USA declared a group of 3,800 members of the Mujahidin-e-Khalq interned in Iraq to have 'protected status' under the Geneva Convention. There is also a National Movement of Iranian Resistance, based in Paris.

Diplomatic Representation

EMBASSIES IN IRAN

Afghanistan: Dr Beheshti Ave, Cnr of 4th St, Pakistan St, Tehran; tel. (21) 88737050; fax (21) 88735600; e-mail afghaembassytehran@hotmail.com; Ambassador YAHYA MAROUFI.

Algeria: Tehran; tel. (21) 22420017; fax (21) 22420015; e-mail ambalg_teheran@yahoo.fr; Ambassador MUHAMMAD AMIN DRAGI.

Argentina: POB 15875-4335, 11 Ghoo Alley, Yar Moh., Darrous, Tehran; tel. (21) 22577433; fax (21) 22577432; e-mail eiran@mrecic.gov.ar; Chargé d'affaires MARIO QUINTEROS.

Armenia: 1 Ostad Shahriar St, Razi St, Jomhouri Islami Ave, Tehran 11337; tel. (21) 66704833; fax (21) 66700657; e-mail emarteh@yahoo.com; Ambassador KAREN NAZARIAN.

Australia: POB 15875-4334, No. 13, 23rd St, Intifada Ave, Tehran 15138; tel. (21) 88724456; fax (21) 88720484; e-mail dfat-tehran@dfat.gov.au; internet www.iran.embassy.gov.au; Ambassador GREG MORIARTY.

Austria: 3rd Floor, 78 Argentine Sq., Tehran; tel. (21) 88710753; fax (21) 88710778; e-mail teheran-ob@bmaa.gv.at; Ambassador MICHAEL POSTL.

Azerbaijan: 10 Akdsihi St, Tehran; tel. (21) 22215191; fax (21) 22217504; e-mail info@azembassy.ir; internet www.azembassy.ir; Ambassador ABBASALI K. HASANOV.

Bahrain: Intifada Ave, 31st St, No. 16, Tehran; tel. (21) 88773383; fax (21) 88779112; e-mail bahmanama@neda.net; Ambassador RASHID BIN SAAD AD-DOSARI.

Bangladesh: POB 11365-3711, Gandhi Ave, 5th St, Bldg No. 14, Tehran; tel. (21) 88772979; fax (21) 88778295; e-mail banglaemb@irtp.com; Ambassador SHAMEEM ASHAN.

Belarus: 1 Azar St, Aban St, Shahid Taheri St, Zafaranieyeh Ave, Tehran 19887; tel. (21) 22708829; fax (21) 22718682; e-mail iran@belembassy.org; Ambassador LEONID V. RACHKOV.

Belgium: POB 11365-115, 155–157 Shahid Fayyaz Bakhsh Ave, Shemiran, Elahieh, Tehran 16778; tel. (21) 22041617; fax (21) 22044608; e-mail teheran@diplobel.be; internet www.diplomatie.be/tehran; Ambassador HERVÉ GOYENS.

Bosnia and Herzegovina: No. 485, Aban Alley, 4th St, Iran Zamin Ave, Shahrak-e-Ghods, Tehran; tel. (21) 88086929; fax (21) 88092120; e-mail ba-emb-ir-teh@kavosh.net; Ambassador SENAHID BRISTRIĆ.

Brazil: POB 19886-3854, 26 Yekta St, Zafaranieh, Tehran; tel. (21) 22743996; fax (21) 22744009; e-mail emb_brazil@yahoo.com; internet www.braziliran.com; Ambassador LUIZ ANTÔNIO FECHINI GOMEZ.

Brunei: 6/1, Mina Blvd, Africa Ave, Tehran; tel. (21) 88797946; fax (21) 88770162; e-mail bruneiran@hotmail.com; Ambassador Pengiran Haji SAHARI Pengiran Haji SALEH.

Bulgaria: POB 11365-7451, Vali-e-Asr Ave, Dr Abbaspour Ave, 82 Nezami-e-Ganjavi St, Tehran; tel. (21) 88775662; fax (21) 88779680; e-mail bulgr.tehr@neda.net; Ambassador PLAMEN GEORGIEV SHUKYURLIEV.

Canada: POB 11365-4647, 57 Shahid Sarafraz St, Ostad Motahari Ave, Tehran 15868; tel. (21) 81520000; fax (21) 81523900; e-mail teran@international.gc.ca; internet www.iran.gc.ca; Chargé d'affaires JAMES CARRICK.

China, People's Republic: 13 Narenjestan 7th, Pasdaran Ave, Tehran; tel. (21) 22291242; fax (21) 22291243; e-mail chinaemb_ir@mfa.gov.cn; internet www.chinaembassy.ir; Ambassador XIE XIAOYAN.

Colombia: 5 Faryar St, Hedayat St, Darrous, Tehran; tel. (21) 22541981; e-mail emteh@apadana.com; Ambassador PEDRO PUBLO BRUT GOUR.

Croatia: No. 25, 1st Behestan, Pasdaran St, Tehran; tel. (21) 22589923; fax (21) 22549199; e-mail vrh.teheran@mvp.hr; Ambassador ESAD PROHIĆ.

Cuba: Africa Ave, Shahid Azafi Sharqi St, No. 21, Tehran; tel. (21) 22257809; fax (21) 22222989; e-mail embacuba-iran@apadana.com; Ambassador FERNANDO NÉSTOR GARCÍA RICARDO.

Cyprus: 328 Shahid Karimi, Dezashib, Tajrish, Tehran; tel. (21) 22219842; fax (21) 22219843; Ambassador GEORGE LIKOURGUS.

Czech Republic: POB 11365-4457, No. 199, Lavasani Ave, Cnr of Yas St, Tehran 195376-4358; tel. (21) 22288149; fax (21) 22802079; e-mail teheran@embassy.mzy.cz; internet www.mfa.cz/tehran; Chargé d'affaires a.i. MICHAL ČERNÝ.

Denmark: POB 19395-5358, 18 Dashti St, Dr Shariati Ave, Tehran 19148; tel. (21) 22640009; fax (21) 22640007; e-mail thramb@um.dk; internet www.ambteheran.um.dk; Ambassador SØREN HASLUND.

IRAN

Finland: No. 4, Shirin Alley, Agha Bozorgi St, Elahiyeh, Tehran; tel. (21) 22230979; fax (21) 22210948; e-mail finlandiran@hotmail.com; Ambassador HEIKKI PUURUNEN.

France: 85 Neauphle-le-Château Ave, Tehran; tel. (21) 66706005; fax (21) 66706543; e-mail consulaire@ambafrance-ir.org; internet www.ambafrance-ir.org; Ambassador BERNARD POLETTI.

Georgia: POB 19575-379, Elahiyeh, Tehran; tel. (21) 22211470; fax (21) 22206848; e-mail georgia@apadana.com; Ambassador LEVAN ASATIANI.

Germany: POB 11365-179, 320–324 Ferdowsi Ave, Tehran; tel. (21) 39990000; fax (21) 39991899; e-mail info@tehe.diplo.de; internet www.teheran.diplo.de; Ambassador HERBERT HONSOWITZ.

Greece: POB 11365-8151, Africa Ave, Esfandiar St, No. 43, Tehran; tel. (21) 22050533; fax (21) 22057431; e-mail embgreece@parsonline.net; Ambassador MARCARIOUS KARAFOTIAS.

Guinea: POB 11365-4716, Dr Shariati Ave, Malek St, No. 10, Tehran; tel. (21) 77535744; fax (21) 77535743; e-mail ambaguinee_thr@hotmail.com; Ambassador OLIA KAMARA.

Holy See: Apostolic Nunciature, POB 11365-178, Razi Ave, 97 Neauphle-le-Château Ave, Tehran; tel. (21) 66403574; fax (21) 66419442; e-mail apnun-thr@parsonline.net; Apostolic Nuncio Most Rev. JEAN-PAUL GOBEL (Titular Archbishop of Galazia in Campania).

Hungary: POB 6363-19395, Darrous, Hedayat Sq., Shadloo St, No. 16, Tehran; tel. (21) 22550460; fax (21) 22550503; e-mail huembthr@neda.net; Ambassador GIORGY BOUSTIN.

Iceland: 30–32 Fayazi St (Fereshteh), Vali-e-Asr Ave, Tehran; tel. (21) 22039990; fax (21) 22040640; e-mail info@consulate-of-iceland-tehran.com; Ambassador STEFAN SKJALDARSON.

India: POB 15875-4118, 46 Mir-Emad St, Cnr of 9th St, Dr Beheshti Ave, Tehran; tel. (21) 88755103; fax (21) 88755973; e-mail indemteh@dpimail.net; internet www.indianembassy-tehran.com; Ambassador MANBIR SINGH.

Indonesia: POB 11365-4564, Ghaem Magham Farahani Ave, No. 210, Tehran; tel. (21) 88716865; fax (21) 88718822; e-mail kbritehran@safineh.net; internet www.indonesian-embassy.ir; Chargé d'affaires a.i. SUGENG WAHONO.

Iraq: Karamian Alley, No. 17, Pol-e-Roomi, Dr Shariati Ave, Tehran; tel. (21) 22210672; fax (21) 22233902; e-mail tehemb@iraqmofamail.net; Ambassador MUHAMMAD MAJID ABBAS ASH-SHEIKH.

Ireland: Bonbast Nahid St, North Kamranieh Ave, No. 9, Tehran 19369; tel. (21) 22803835; fax (21) 22286933; e-mail irelembteh@padisar.net; Ambassador JOHN DEADY.

Italy: POB 11365-7863, 81 Neauphle-le-Château Ave, Tehran; tel. (21) 66726955; fax (21) 66726961; e-mail segreteria.teheran@esteri.it; internet www.ambteheran.esteri.it; Ambassador ROBERTO TOSCANO.

Japan: POB 11365-814, Bucharest Ave, Cnr of 5th St, Tehran; tel. (21) 88713396; fax (21) 88713515; internet www.ir.emb-japan.go.jp; Ambassador AKIO SHIROTA.

Jordan: POB 14665-835, Shahrak-e-Ghods, Faz 4, Khayaban Flamk, Khayaban 8, Block 1647, Tehran 009821; tel. (21) 88088356; fax (21) 88080496; e-mail jordanemb-teh@hotmail.com; Ambassador AHMAD JALAL AL-MEFLAH.

Kazakhstan: 4 North Hedayet St, Cnr of Masjed Alley, Darrus, Tehran; tel. (21) 22565933; fax (21) 22546400; e-mail kazembir@apadana.com; internet www.kazembassy-iran.org; Ambassador ERIK M. UTEMBAYEV.

Kenya: POB 19395-4566, 46 Gulshar St, Africa Ave, Tehran; tel. (21) 22059154; fax (21) 22053372; e-mail kenemteh@irtp.com; Ambassador ALI ABBAS ALI.

Korea, Democratic People's Republic: 349 Shahid Dastjerdi Ave, Africa Ave, Tehran; tel. (21) 88783341; Ambassador KIM CHANG RYONG.

Korea, Republic: No. 37, Ahmad Ghasir Ave, Tehran; tel. (21) 88711125; fax (21) 88737917; e-mail korth@dpi.net.ir; Ambassador KIM YOUNG-MOKE.

Kuwait: Africa Ave, Mahiyar St, No. 15, Tehran; tel. (21) 88785997; Ambassador MAJDI ADH-DHUFAIRI.

Kyrgyzstan: POB 19579-3511, Bldg 12, 5th Naranjestan Alley, Pasdaran St; tel. (21) 22830354; fax (21) 22281720; e-mail krembiri@mydatak.net; Ambassador MEDETKAN SH. SHERIMKULOV.

Lebanon: No. 31, Shahid Kalantari St, Gharani Ave, Tehran; tel. (21) 88908451; fax (21) 88907345; Ambassador ZAIN EL-MUSAWI.

Libya: No. 163, Ostad Motahari Ave, Shahid Muftahi Ave, Tehran; tel. (21) 88742572; Ambassador ALI MARIA.

Macedonia, former Yugoslav republic: No. 7, 4th Alley, Intifada Ave, Tehran; tel. and fax (21) 88720810.

Malaysia: POB 11365-8518, No. 6, Shahid Akhgan St, Fereshteh Ave, Tehran; tel. (21) 22010016; fax (21) 22010477; e-mail mwtehran@parsonline.net; internet myperwakilan.mfa.gov.my/me/tehran; Ambassador Dato SYED MUNSHE AFDZARUDDIN BIN SYED HASSAN.

Mali: 3/F, 10 Maleck Ave, Tehran; tel. (21) 77500074; e-mail ambmali_teheran@yahoo.fr; Ambassador AMADOU MODY DIALL.

Mexico: No. 41, Golfam St, Africa Ave, Tehran POB 19156-74741; tel. (21) 22057586; fax (21) 22057589; e-mail embiran@sre.gob.mx; Ambassador ÁNGEL LUIS ORTIZ MONASTERIO CASTELLANOS.

Morocco: 5 Lavasani Ave, Davoud Barati, Tehran; tel. (21) 22206731; fax (21) 22210162; e-mail sifamateh@sefaratmaghreb.com; internet www.sefaratmaghreb.com; Ambassador MUHAMMAD LOUFA.

Netherlands: POB 11365-138, Darrous, Shahrzad Blvd, Kamasaie St, 1st East Lane, No. 33, Tehran 19498; tel. (21) 22567005; fax (21) 22566990; e-mail teh@minbuza.nl; internet www.mfa.nl/teh; Ambassador RADINK VAN VOLLENHOVEN.

New Zealand: POB 15875-4313, 34 North Golestan Complex, Cnr of 2nd Park Alley and Sosan St, Aghdasiyeh St, Niavaran, Tehran 11365; tel. (21) 22800289; fax (21) 22831673; e-mail newzealand@mavara.com; internet www.nzembassy.com/iran; Ambassador HAMISH MACMASTER.

Nigeria: No. 9, Intifada Ave, 31st St, Tehran; tel. (21) 88774936; e-mail ngrembtehran@yahoo.com; Ambassador IBRAHIM GANYANA ABUBAKAR.

Norway: POB 19395-5398, Lavasani Ave 201, Tehran; tel. (21) 22291333; fax (21) 22292776; e-mail emb.tehran@mfa.no; internet www.norway-iran.org; Ambassador ROALD NÆSS.

Oman: No. 12, Tandis Alley, Africa Ave, Tehran; tel. (21) 22056831; fax (21) 22044672; Ambassador Sheikh YAHYA BIN ABDULLAH.

Pakistan: No. 1, Ahmed Eitmadzadeh Ave, Jamshidabad Shomali, Dr Fatemi Ave, Tehran 14118; tel. (21) 66941388; fax (21) 66944898; e-mail pareptehran@yahoo.com; Ambassador IQBAL SHAFKAT SAEED.

Philippines: POB 19395-4797, 5 Khayyam St, Vali-e-Asr Ave, Tehran; tel. (21) 22668774; fax (21) 22668990; e-mail tehranpe@yahoo.com; internet www.philippine-embassy.ir; Ambassador ALADIN VILLACORTE.

Poland: POB 11365-3489, Africa Ave, Piruz St, No. 1/3, Tehran; tel. (21) 88787262; fax (21) 88788774; e-mail info@embpoltehran.com; internet www.embpoltehran.com; Ambassador WITOLD SMIDOWSKI.

Portugal: No. 13, Rouzbeh Alley, Darrous, Hedayat St, Tehran; tel. (21) 22543237; fax (21) 22552668; e-mail portugal@myrlatak.com; Ambassador Dr JOSÉ FERNANDO MOREIRA DA CUNHA.

Qatar: POB 11365-1631, Africa Ave, Golazin Ave, Parke Davar, No. 4, Tehran; tel. (21) 22051255; fax (21) 22056023; e-mail tehran@mofa.gov.qa; Ambassador Dr SALEH IBRAHIM AL-KAWARI.

Romania: 12 Fakhrabad Ave, Baharestan Ave, Tehran; tel. (21) 77539041; fax (21) 77535291; e-mail ambrotehran@parsonline.net; Chargé d'affaires a.i. MIRCEA HAS.

Russia: 39 Neauphle-le-Château Ave, Tehran; tel. (21) 66701161; fax (21) 66701652; e-mail rusembiran@parsonline.net; internet www.iran.mid.ru; Ambassador ALEKSANDR ALEXEYEVICH SADOVNIKOV.

Saudi Arabia: No. 1, Niloufar St, Boustan St, Pasdaran Ave, Tehran; tel. (21) 22288543; fax (21) 22294691; e-mail iremb@mofa.gov.sa; Ambassador OSAMA BIN AHMAD AS-SANOUSI.

Senegal: POB 19395-4743, 76 Sepand West St, Nejatollahi Ave, Tehran; tel. (21) 88881123; fax (21) 88805676.

Serbia: POB 11365-118, Velenjak Ave, 9th St, No. 12, Tehran 19858; tel. (21) 22412569; fax (21) 22402869; e-mail scgambateh@neda.net; Chargé d'affaires a.i. FAHRUDIN MEKIĆ.

Sierra Leone: No. 10, Malek St, off Dr Shariati Ave, Tehran; tel. (21) 77502819; fax (21) 77529515; e-mail leone@nasim.net; Ambassador Haja ALARI COLE.

Slovakia: POB 19395-6341, 38 Sarlashgar Fallahi St, Tehran 19887; tel. (21) 22411164; fax (21) 22409719; e-mail svkemb@parsonline.sk; internet www.tehran.mfa.sk; Ambassador ANTON HAJDUK.

Slovenia: POB 19575-459, 30 Narenjestan 8th Alley, Pasdaran Ave, Tehran 19576; tel. (21) 22802223; fax (21) 22282131; e-mail vte@mzz-dkp.sigov.si; Chargé d'affaires a.i. MILJAN MAJHEN.

Somalia: 1 Hadaiyan St, Mirzapour St, Dr Shariati Ave, Tehran; tel. and fax (21) 22245146; e-mail safarian@hotmail.com; Chargé d'affaires a.i. KHALIFA AHMED SAHAL.

South Africa: POB 11365-7476, 5 Yekta St, Bagh-e-Ferdows, Vali-e-Asr Ave, Tehran; tel. (21) 22702866; fax (21) 22719516; e-mail saemb@neda.net; Ambassador YUSUF SALOOJEE.

Spain: 76 Sarv St, Africa Ave, Tehran 19689; tel. (21) 88714575; fax (21) 88727082; e-mail embespir@mail.mae.es; Ambassador ANTONIO PÉREZ-HERNÁNDEZ Y TORRA.

IRAN

Sri Lanka: 28 Golazin St, Africa Ave, Tehran; tel. (21) 22052688; fax (21) 22052149; e-mail emblanka@afranet.com; Ambassador MOHAMED MOHAMED ZUHAIR.

Sudan: No. 17, Africa Ave, Zafar St, Kuchahi Nur, Tehran; tel. (21) 88781183; fax (21) 88792331; e-mail abdallasaahilmi@yahoo.com; internet www.sudanembassyir.com; Ambassador ABD AL-MAHMOUD ABD AL-HALIM.

Sweden: POB 19575-458, 2 Nastaran Ave, Pasdaran Ave, Tehran; tel. (21) 22296802; fax (21) 22296451; e-mail ambassaden.teheran@foreign.ministry.se; internet www.swedenabroad.com/tehran; Ambassador MAGNUS WERNSTEDT.

Switzerland: POB 19395-4683, 13 Yasaman St, Cnr of Sharifi Manesh Ave, Elahieh, Tehran 19649; tel. (21) 22008333; fax (21) 22006002; e-mail vertretung@teh.rep.admin.ch; internet www.eda.admin.ch/tehran_emb; Ambassador PHILIPPE WELTI.

Syria: 19 Iraj St, Africa Ave, Tehran; tel. (21) 22052780; fax (21) 22059409; e-mail syrambir@mail.dci.co.ir; Ambassador Dr HAMED HASSAN.

Tajikistan: 10 3rd Alley, Shahid Zeynali St, Tehran; tel. (21) 22299584; fax (21) 22291607; e-mail tajemb-iran@mail.ru; Ambassador RAMAZAN MIRZOYEV.

Thailand: POB 11495-111, 4 Esteghlal Alley, Baharestan Ave, Tehran; tel. (21) 77531433; fax (21) 77532022; e-mail info@thaiembassy-tehran.org; internet www.thaiembassy-tehran.org; Ambassador SUWIT SAICHEUA.

Tunisia: No. 12, Shahid Dr Lavasani, Tehran; tel. (21) 22704161; e-mail at-teheran@safineh.net; Ambassador HATEM ESSAYEM.

Turkey: POB 11365-8758, 314 Ferdowsi Ave, Africa Ave, Tehran; tel. (21) 33118997; fax (21) 33117928; e-mail tctahranbe@parsonline.net; Ambassador SELIM KANAOSMANOĞLU.

Turkmenistan: No. 9, 5th Golestan St, Pasdaran Ave, Tehran; tel. (21) 22542178; fax (21) 22580432; e-mail tmnteh@afranet.com; Ambassador MURAT NAZAROV.

Uganda: 3/F, 10 Malek St, Shariati Ave, Tehran; tel. (21) 77643335; fax (21) 77643337; e-mail uganda_teh@yahoo.com; Ambassador Dr MOHAMMAD AHMAD KISSULE.

Ukraine: 101 Vanak St, Vanak Sq., Tehran; tel. (21) 88034119; fax (21) 88007130; e-mail ir@mfa.gov.ua; Ambassador IHOR LOHINOV.

United Arab Emirates: POB 19395-4616, No. 355, Vahid Dastjerdi Ave, Vali-e-Asr Ave, Tehran; tel. (21) 88781333; fax (21) 88789084; e-mail uae_emb_thr@universalmail.com; Ambassador KHALIFA SHAHEEN AL-MERREE.

United Kingdom: POB 11365-4474, 198 Ferdowsi Ave, Tehran 11344; tel. (21) 64052000; fax (21) 64052289; e-mail britishembassytehran@fco.gov.uk; internet www.britishembassy.gov.uk/iran; Ambassador GEOFFREY ADAMS.

Uruguay: 45 Shabnam Alley, Shahid Atefi Shargi St, Africa Ave, Tehran; tel. (21) 22052030; fax (21) 22053322; e-mail uruter@yahoo.com; Ambassador JOSÉ LUIS REMEDI ZUNINI.

Uzbekistan: No. 6, Nastaran Alley, Boustan St, Pasdaran Ave; tel. and fax (21) 22299780; fax (21) 22299158; Ambassador ILHAM SOLIEVICH AKRAMOV.

Venezuela: POB 19395-7137, No. 26, Tandis St, Africa Ave, Tehran; tel. (21) 88715185; fax (21) 22053677; e-mail embajadavenezuela@emveniran.gob.ve; internet www.iran.gob.ve; Ambassador ARTURO ANIBAL GALLEGOS RAMÍREZ.

Viet Nam: 6 East Ordibehesht, Mardani Sharestan, 8th St, Pey Syan St, M. Ardabili Vali-e-Asr Ave, Tehran; tel. (21) 22411670; fax (21) 22416045; e-mail dinh@mail.dci.co.ir; Ambassador NGUYEN VAN HAI.

Yemen: Africa Ave, Golestan St, No. 15, Tehran; tel. (21) 22042701; e-mail yem.emb.ir@neda.net; Ambassador JAMAL ABDULLAH AS-SOLAL.

Zimbabwe: 24 Shad Avar St, Mogghadas Ardabili, Tehran; tel. (21) 22027553; fax (21) 22041109; e-mail zimbabwe@neda.net; Ambassador STEPHEN CLETUS CHIKETA.

Judicial System

In August 1982 the Supreme Court revoked all laws dating from the previous regime which did not conform with Islam; in October all courts set up prior to the Islamic Revolution were abolished. In June 1987 Ayatollah Khomeini ordered the creation of clerical courts to try members of the clergy opposed to government policy. A new system of *qisas* (retribution) was established, placing the emphasis on swift justice. Islamic codes of correction were introduced in 1983, including the dismembering of a hand for theft, flogging for fornication and violations of the strict code of dress for women, and stoning for adultery. The Supreme Court has 33 branches, each of which is presided over by two judges.

Head of the Judiciary: Ayatollah SAYED MAHMOUD HASHEMI SHAHRUDI.

SUPREME COURT

Chief Justice: Ayatollah HUSSEIN MOFID.

Prosecutor-General: Ayatollah QORBANALI DORRI NAJAFABADI.

Religion

According to the 1979 Constitution, the official religion is Islam of the Ja'fari sect (Shi'ite), but other Islamic sects, including Zeydi, Hanafi, Maleki, Shafe'i and Hanbali, are valid and will be respected. Zoroastrians, Jews and Christians will be recognized as official religious minorities. According to the 1996 census, there were 59,788,791 Muslims, 78,745 Christians (mainly Armenian), 27,920 Zoroastrians and 12,737 Jews in Iran.

ISLAM

The great majority of the Iranian people are Shi'a Muslims, but there is a minority of Sunni Muslims. Persians and Azerbaijanis are mainly Shi'ite, while the other ethnic groups are mainly Sunni.

CHRISTIANITY

The Roman Catholic Church

At 31 December 2005 there were an estimated 24,550 adherents in Iran, comprising 10,000 of the Armenian Rite, 10,000 of the Latin Rite and 4,550 of the Chaldean Rite.

Armenian Rite

Bishop of Esfahan: (vacant), Armenian Catholic Bishopric, POB 11318, Khiaban Ghazzali 65, Tehran; tel. (21) 66707204; fax (21) 66727533; e-mail arcaveso@yahoo.com.

Chaldean Rite

Archbishop of Ahvaz: HANNA ZORA, Archbishop's House, 334 Suleiman Farsi St, Ahvaz; tel. (61) 2224980.

Archbishop of Tehran: RAMZI GARMOU, Archevêché, Enghelab St, Sayed Abbas Moussavi Ave 91, Tehran 15819; tel. (21) 88823549; fax (21) 88308714.

Archbishop of Urmia (Rezayeh) and Bishop of Salmas (Shahpour): THOMAS MERAM, Khalifagari Kaldani Katholiq, POB 338, 7 Mirzaian St, Orumiyeh 57135; tel. (441) 2222739; fax (441) 2236031; e-mail thmeram@yahoo.com.

Latin Rite

Archbishop of Esfahan: IGNAZIO BEDINI, Consolata Church, POB 11365-445, 73 Neauphle-le-Château Ave, Tehran; tel. (21) 66703210; fax (21) 66724749; e-mail latin_diocese@parsonline.net.

The Anglican Communion

Anglicans in Iran are adherents of the Episcopal Church in Jerusalem and the Middle East, formally inaugurated in January 1976. The Bishop in Cyprus and the Gulf is resident in Cyprus.

Bishop in Iran: Right Rev. AZAD MARSHALL, POB 135, 81465 Esfahan; tel. (21) 88801383; fax (21) 88906908; internet dioceseofiran.org; diocese founded 1912.

Presbyterian Church

Synod of the Evangelical (Presbyterian) Church in Iran: POB 14395-569, Assyrian Evangelical Church, Khiaban-i Hanifnejad, Khiaban-i Aramanch, Tehran; tel. (21) 88006135; Moderator Rev. ADEL NAKHOSTEEN.

ZOROASTRIANS

There are an estimated 28,000 Zoroastrians, a remnant of a once widespread sect.

OTHER COMMUNITIES

Communities of Armenians, and somewhat smaller numbers of Jews, Assyrians, Greek Orthodox Christians, Uniates and Latin Christians are also found as officially recognized faiths. The Bahá'í faith, which originated in Iran, has about 300,000 Iranian adherents, although at least 10,000 are believed to have fled since 1979 in order to escape persecution. The Government banned all Bahá'í institutions in August 1983.

The Press

Tehran dominates the media, as many of the daily papers are published there, and the bi-weekly, weekly and less frequent publications in the provinces generally depend on the major metropolitan dailies as a source of news. A press law announced in August 1979 required all newspapers and magazines to be licensed and imposed penalties of imprisonment for insulting senior religious figures. Offences against the Act will be tried in the criminal courts. Under the Constitution the press is free, except in matters that are contrary to public morality, insult religious belief or slander the honour and reputation of individuals. From the late 1990s the press has been the target of an intense judicial campaign to curb its freedoms: some sources estimate that more than 100 publications have been closed down.

PRINCIPAL DAILIES

Aftab-e-Yazd (Sun of Yazd): POB 13145-1134, Tehran; tel. (21) 66495833; fax (21) 66495835; internet www.aftabyazd.ir; f. 2000; Farsi; pro-reform; Chief Editor Sayed Mojtaba Vahedi; circ. 100,000.

Alik: POB 11365-953, Jomhouri Islami Ave, Alik Alley, Tehran 11357; tel. (21) 88768567; fax (21) 88760994; e-mail alikmail@hyenet.ir; internet www.alikonline.com; f. 1931; afternoon; Armenian; political, literary, cultural, social, sport; Propr A. Ajemian; circ. over 4,500.

Donya-e-Eqtesad (Economic World): Tehran; fax 88986834; e-mail info@donya-e-eqtesad.com; internet www.donya-e-eqtesad.com; Farsi.

Entekhab (Choice): 12 Noorbakhsh Ave, Vali-e-Asr Ave, Tehran; tel. (21) 88893954; fax (21) 88893951; e-mail info@tiknews.net; internet www.tiknews.net; online only; Farsi; Man. Dir Dr Taha Hashemi.

Etemaad (Confidence): e-mail info@etemaad.com; internet www.etemaad.com; Farsi; pro-reform; Man. Dir Elias Hazrati.

Etemaad Melli (National Confidence): Etemaad Melli Bldg, Karimkhan Ave, Tehran; e-mail info@roozna.com; internet www.roozna.com; f. 2006; Farsi; pro-reform; publ. by the Hezb-e Etemaad-e Melli (National Confidence Party); Pres. Mahdi Karrubi; Man. Dir Muhammad Javad Hagh Shenas.

Ettela'at (Information): Ettela'at Bldg, Mirdamad Ave, South Naft St, Tehran 15499; tel. and fax (21) 29999; fax (21) 22258022; e-mail ettelaat@ettelaat.com; internet www.ettelaat.com; f. 1925; evening; Farsi; political and literary; operates under the direct supervision of *wilayat-e-faqih* (religious jurisprudence); Editor Sayed Mahmoud Do'ayi; circ. 500,000.

Hambastegi Daily (Solidarity): Tehran; e-mail info@hambastegi-news.com; internet www.hambastegidaily.com; Farsi; Editor Saleh Abadi.

Ham-Mihan (Compatriot): Tehran; internet www.ham-mihan.org; f. 2000; Farsi; independent, pro-reform; suspended in July 2007; Founder and Man. Dir Gholamhossein Karbaschi; Chair. of Bd Muhammad Atrianfar.

Hamshahri (Citizen): POB 19395-5446, Tehran; tel. (21) 22059386; fax (21) 22058811; e-mail Editorial@Hamshahri.Org; internet hamshahri.org; Farsi; conservative; economics, society and culture; owned by the Municipality of Tehran; Man. Dir Morteza Alviri; Editor-in-Chief Muhammad Reza Zaeri; circ. 400,000.

Hayat-e No (New Life): 50 North Sohrvardi Ave, Tehran; tel. (21) 88747437; fax (21) 88766373; e-mail info@hayateno.org; internet www.hayateno.org; f. 2000; Farsi; pro-reform; Man. Dir Sayed Hadi Khamenei; publ. temporarily suspended in 2003.

Iran: tel. (21) 88761720; fax (21) 88761254; e-mail iran-newspaper@iran-newspaper.com; internet www.iran-newspaper.com; Farsi; conservative; connected to the Islamic Republic News Agency; publ. suspended between May and Oct. 2006; Man. Dir Hossein Ziyaei; Editor-in-Chief Bijan Moghaddam.

Iran Daily: tel. (21) 88755761; fax (21) 88761869; e-mail iran-daily@iran-daily.com; internet www.iran-daily.com; publ. by the Islamic Republic News Agency; English; Exec. Editor Amin Sabooni.

Iran News: POB 15875-8551, 41 Lida St, Vali-e-Asr Ave, North of Vanak Sq., Tehran 19697-33814; tel. (21) 88880231; fax (21) 88786475; e-mail info@irannewsdaily.com; internet www.irannewsdaily.com; f. 1994; English; Man. Dir Payman Jalali; circ. 35,000.

Jam-e Jam: Tehran; tel. (21) 22222315; fax (21) 22226252; e-mail info@jamejamonline.ir; internet www.jamejamonline.ir; online only; Farsi, English and French; conservative; linked to Islamic Republic of Iran Broadcasting; Man. Dir Hossein Entezami.

Jomhouri-e-Eslami (Islamic Republic): tel. (21) 33916111; fax (21) 33117552; e-mail info@jomhourieslami.com; internet www.jomhourieslami.com; Farsi; conservative; Man. Dir Masih Mohajeri.

Kayhan (Universe): POB 11365-3631, Ferdowsi Ave, Tehran 11444; tel. (21) 33110251; fax (21) 33111120; e-mail kayhan@kayhannews.ir; internet www.kayhannews.ir; f. 1941; evening; Farsi; political; also publishes Kayhan International (f. 1959; daily; English; Editor Hamid Najafi), Kayhan Arabic (f. 1980; daily; Arabic), Kayhan Persian (f. 1942; daily; Farsi), Zan-e-Ruz (Woman Today; f. 1964; weekly; Farsi), Kayhan Varzeshi (World of Sport; f. 1955; daily and weekly; Farsi), Kayhan Bacheha (Children's World; f. 1956; weekly; Farsi), Kayhan Farhangi (World of Culture; f. 1984; monthly; Farsi); owned and managed by Mostazafin Foundation from October 1979 until January 1987, when it was placed under the direct supervision of *wilayat-e-faqih* (religious jurisprudence); Man. Dir Hossein Shariatmadari; circ. 350,000.

Khorasan: Mashad; Head Office: Khorasan Daily Newspapers, 14 Zohre St, Mobarezan Ave, Tehran; tel. (511) 7634000; fax (511) 7624395; e-mail info@khorasannews.com; internet www.khorasannews.com; f. 1948; Farsi; Propr Muhammad Sadegh Teheranian; Editor Hossein Ghazali; circ. 40,000.

Neshat: Tehran; f. 1998; Farsi; pro-reform; Publr Latif Safari; Editor Mashallah Shamsolvaezin.

Quds Daily: POB 91735-577, Khayyam Sq., Sajjad Blvd, Mashad; tel. (51) 7685011; fax (511) 7684004; e-mail info@qudsdaily.com; internet www.qudsdaily.com; f. 1987; Farsi; owned by Astan Quds Razavi, the org. that oversees the shrine of Imam Reza at Mashad; also publ. in Tehran; Man. Dir Gholamreza Ghalandarian; Editor-in-Chief Muhammad Hadi Zahedi.

Resallat (The Message): POB 11365-777, 53 Ostad Nejatollahi Ave, Tehran; tel. (21) 88902642; fax (21) 88900587; e-mail info@resalat-news.com; internet www.resalat-news.com; f. 1985; organ of right-wing group of the same name; Farsi; conservative; political, economic, social; Propr Ressallat Foundation; Man. Dir Sayed Morteza Nabavi; circ. 100,000.

Sarmayeh (Capital): Tehran; tel. (21) 88842448; e-mail info@sarmayeh.net; internet www.sarmayeh.net; Farsi; pro-reform; economic and financial news.

Shargh (East): Tehran; e-mail info@sharghnewspaper.com; internet www.sharghnewspaper.com; f. 2003; Farsi; reformist; publ. suspended in Sept. 2006, allowed to resume in May 2007, then closed again in August; Man. Dir Mehdi Rahmanian; Editor Ahmad Gholami.

Tehran Times: POB 14155-4843, 32 Bimeh Alley, Ostad Nejatollahi Ave, Tehran; tel. (21) 88800293; fax (21) 88808214; e-mail info@tehrantimes.com; internet www.tehrantimes.com; f. 1979; English; independent; Man. Dir Parviz Esmaeili; Editor-in-Chief Hassan Lasjerdi.

PRINCIPAL PERIODICALS

Acta Medica Iranica: Bldg No. 8, Faculty of Medicine, Tehran Medical Sciences Univ., Poursina St, Tehran 14174; tel. and fax (21) 88962510; e-mail acta@tums.ac.ir; internet diglib.tums.ac.ir/pub/journals.asp; f. 1956; bi-monthly; English; Editors-in-Chief A. R. Dehpour, M. Samini; circ. 2,000.

Ashur (Assyria): Ostad Motahari Ave, 11–21 Kuhe Nour Ave, Tehran; tel. (21) 622117; f. 1969; Assyrian; monthly; Founder and Editor Dr Wilson Bet-Mansour; circ. 8,000.

Bulletin of the National Film Archive of Iran: POB 11155, Baharestan Sq., Tehran 11499-43381; tel. (21) 38512583; fax (21) 38512710; e-mail khoshnevis_nfai@yahoo.com; f. 1989; English; Editor M. H. Khoshnevis.

Bukhara: POB 15655-166, Tehran; tel. and fax (21) 88707132; e-mail dehbashi@bukharamagazine.com; internet www.bukharamagazine.com; bi-monthly; Farsi; arts, culture and humanities; Editor Ali Dehbashi.

Daneshmand (Scientist): POB 15875-3649, 1st Floor, No. 106, Ostad Nejatollahi, Somayyeh Crossroads, Tehran; tel. (21) 88908757; fax (21) 88908720; e-mail info@daneshmandonline.ir; internet www.daneshmandonline.ir; f. 1963; monthly; Farsi; owned by Mostazafari Foundation; science and technology in Iran and abroad; CEO Yaghoub Moshfegh; Editor-in-Chief Ali A. Ghazvini.

Daneshkadeh Pezeshki: Faculty of Medicine, Tehran Medical Sciences Univ.; tel. (21) 66112743; fax (21) 66404377; f. 1947; 10 a year; Farsi; medical magazine; Propr Dr Hassan Arefi; circ. 1,500.

Donyaye Varzesh (World of Sports): Tehran; tel. (21) 3281; fax (21) 33115530; weekly; sport; Editor G. H. Shabani; circ. 200,000.

The Echo of Iran: POB 14155-1168, 4 Hourtab Alley, Hafez Ave, Tehran; tel. (21) 22930477; e-mail info@iranalmanac.com; internet www.iranalmanac.com; f. 1952; monthly; English; news, politics and economics; Man. Farjam Behnam; Editor Jahangir Behrouz.

Echo of Islam: POB 14155-3899, Tehran; tel. (21) 88897663; fax (21) 88902725; e-mail echoofislam@itf.org.ir; internet www.itf.org.ir; quarterly; English; publ. by the Islamic Thought Foundation; Man. Dir Ali Akbar Ziaie; Editor-in-Chief Hamid Tehrani.

IRAN *Directory*

Economic Echo: POB 14155-1168, 4 Hourtab Alley, Hafez Ave, Tehran; tel. (21) 22930477; e-mail info@iranalmanac.com; internet www.iranalmanac.com; f. 1998; English; Man. FARJAM BEHNAM.

Ettela'at Haftegi: 11 Khayyam Ave, Tehran; tel. (21) 311238; fax (21) 33115530; f. 1941; general weekly; Farsi; Editor F. JAVADI; circ. 150,000.

Ettela'at Javanan: POB 15499-51199, Ettela'at Bldg, Mirdamad Ave, South Naft St, Tehran; tel. (21) 29999; fax (21) 22258022; f. 1966; weekly; Farsi; youth; Editor M. J. RAFIZADEH; circ. 120,000.

Farhang-e-Iran Zamin: POB 19575-583, Niyavaran, Tehran; tel. (21) 283254; annual; Farsi; Iranian studies; Editor Prof. IRAJ AFSHAR.

Film International, Iranian Film Quarterly: POB 11365-875, Tehran; tel. (21) 66709374; fax (21) 66719971; e-mail filmmag@apadana.com; internet www.massoudmehrabi.com; f. 1993; quarterly; English and Farsi; Editor-in-Chief MASSOUD MEHRABI; circ. 15,000.

Iran Almanac: POB 14155-1168, 4 Hourtab Alley, Hafez Ave, Tehran; tel. and fax (932) 9139201; e-mail behnam.f@iranalmanac.com; internet www.iranalmanac.com; f. 2000; English; reference; history, politics, trade and industry, tourism, art, culture and society; Researcher and Editor FARJAM BEHNAM.

Iran Tribune: POB 111244, Tehran; e-mail matlab@iran-tribune.com; internet www.iran-tribune.com; monthly; English; socio-political and cultural.

Iran Who's Who: POB 14155-1168, 4 Hourtab Alley, Hafez Ave, Tehran; tel. (21) 66468114; fax (21) 66464790; e-mail info@iranalmanac.com; internet www.iranalmanac.com; annual; English; Editor KARAN BEHROUZ.

Iranian Cinema: POB 11155, Baharestan Sq., Tehran 11499-43381; tel. (21) 35812583; fax (21) 35812710; e-mail khoshnevis-nfai@yahoo.com; f. 1985; annual; English.

JIDA: 94 West Piroozi St, Nasr Place, Tehran 14477; tel. (21) 88269591; fax 88269592; e-mail info@idaweb.org; internet www.idaweb.org; f. 1963; four a year; journal of the Iranian Dental Assen; Editor-in-Chief Dr MUHAMMAD MOSHREF.

Kayhan Bacheha (Children's World): Institute Kayhan, Shahid Shahcheraghi Alley, Ferdowsi Ave, Tehran 11444; tel. (21) 33110251; fax (21) 33111120; f. 1956; weekly; illustrated magazine for children; Editor AMIR HOSSEIN FARDI; circ. 150,000.

Kayhan Varzeshi (World of Sport): Institute Kayhan, Shahid Shahcheraghi Alley, Ferdowsi Ave, Tehran 11444; tel. (21) 33110246; fax (21) 33114228; e-mail info@kayhanvarzeshi.com; internet www.kayhanvarzeshi.com; f. 1955; weekly; Farsi; Dir MAHMAD MONSETI; circ. 125,000.

Mahjubah: POB 14155-3899, Tehran; tel. (21) 88000067; fax (21) 88001453; e-mail mahjubah@iran-itf.com; internet www.itf.org.ir; Islamic family magazine; publ. by the Islamic Thought Foundation; Editor-in-Chief TURAN JAMSHIDIAN.

Salamate Fekr: M.20, Kharg St, Tehran; tel. (21) 223034; f. 1958; monthly; organ of the Mental Health Society; Editors Prof. E. TCHEHRAZI, ALI REZA SHAFAI.

Soroush: POB 15875-1163, Soroush Bldg, Motahari Ave, Mofatteh Crossroads, Tehran; tel. and fax (21) 88847602; e-mail cultural@soroushpress.com; internet www.soroushpress.com; f. 1972; one weekly magazine; four monthly magazines, one for women, two for adolescents and one for children; one quarterly review of philosophy; all in Farsi; Editor-in-Chief ALI AKBAR ASHARI.

Tavoos: POB 19395-6434, 6 Asgarian St, East Farmanieh Ave, Tehran 19546-44755; tel. (21) 22817700; fax (21) 22813851; e-mail info@tavoosmag.com; internet www.tavoosmag.com; quarterly; Farsi and English; arts; currently suspended; Man. Dir MANIJEH MIREMADI; circ. 5,000.

Tchissta: POB 13145-593, Tehran; tel. (21) 678581; e-mail tchissta@tchissta.com; internet tchissta.com; Farsi; politics, society, science and literature; Editor-in-Chief PARVIZ SHAHRIARI.

Vaqt: weekly; Farsi; pro-reform; Editor SHAHRAM MUHAMMADI-NEID; publ. suspended in Sept. 2002.

ZamZam: POB 14155-3899, Tehran; internet www.itf.org.ir; children's magazine; English; publ. by the Islamic Thought Foundation; Editor-in-Chief MARYAM TAMHIDI.

Zan-e-Ruz (Woman Today): Institute Kayhan, Shahid Shahcheraghi Alley, Ferdowsi Ave, Tehran; tel. (21) 33911575; fax (21) 33911569; e-mail kayhan@istn.irost.com; f. 1964; weekly; women's; circ. over 60,000; closure ordered April 1999.

PRESS ASSOCIATION

Association of Iranian Journalists: No. 87, 7th Alley, Shahid Kabkanian St, Keshavarz Blvd, Tehran; tel. (21) 88954796; fax (21) 88963539; e-mail secretary@aoij.org; internet www.aoij.org; Pres. MAZROOEI RAJABALI; Sec. MOFIDI BADRALSADAT.

NEWS AGENCIES

Fars News Agency: Tehran; e-mail Info@Farsnews.ir; internet www.farsnews.ir; f. 2003; independent; news in Farsi and English; MEHDI FAZAELI.

Iranian Quran News Agency (IQNA): 97 Bozorgmehr St, Qods Ave, Tehran; tel. (21) 66485657; fax (21) 66970769; e-mail info@iqna.ir; internet www.iqna.ir; f. 2003; general news and news on Quranic activities.

Islamic Republic News Agency (IRNA): POB 764, 873 Vali-e-Asr Ave, Tehran; tel. (21) 88902050; fax (21) 88905068; e-mail irna@irna.com; internet www.irna.com; f. 1936; state-controlled; Man. Dir JALAL FAYYAZI.

Mehr News Agency: 32, Bimeh Alley, Nejatollahi St, Tehran; tel. (21) 88809500; fax (21) 88805801; e-mail director@mehrnews.com; internet www.mehrnews.com; f. 2003; news in Farsi, English and Arabic; Man. Dir PARVIZ ESMAEILI.

Publishers

Amir Kabir Book Publishing and Distribution Co: POB 11365-4191, Jomhouri Islami Ave, Esteghlal Sq., Tehran; tel. (21) 33900751; fax (21) 33903747; e-mail info@amirkabir.net; internet www.amirkabir.net; f. 1948; historical, philosophical, social, literary and children's books; Dir AHMAD NESARI.

Avayenoor Publications: 31 Roshan Alley, Vali-e-Asr Ave, Tehran; tel. (21) 88899001; fax (21) 88907452; e-mail info@avayenoor.com; internet www.avayenoor.com; f. 1988; sociology, politics and economics; Editor-in-Chief Sayed MUHAMMAD MIRHOSSEINI.

Caravan Books Publishing House: POB 186-14145, 18 Salehi St, Sartip Fakouri Ave, Northern Karegar Ave, Tehran 14136; tel. (21) 88007421; fax (21) 88029486; e-mail info@caravan.ir; internet caravan.ir; f. 1997; fiction and non-fiction.

Ebn-e-Sina: No. 2P, Shahid Ekhtari, South Dabirstan St, Hashimi, Tehran; f. 1957; educational publishers and booksellers; Dir EBRAHIM RAMAZANI.

Echo Publishers & Printers: POB 14155-1168, 4 Hourtab Alley, Hafez Ave, Tehran; tel. and fax (21) 22930477; e-mail info@iranalmanac.com; internet www.iranalmanac.com; f. 2000; politics, economics and current affairs; Dir and Man. FARJAM BEHNAM.

Eghbal Printing & Publishing Organization: 15 Booshehr St, Dr Shariati Ave, Tehran; tel. (21) 768113; f. 1903; Man. Dir DJAVAD EGHBAL.

Farhang Moaser: 43 Khiaban Daneshgah, Tehran 13147; tel. (21) 66402728; fax (21) 66317018; e-mail info@farhangmoaser.com; internet www.farhangmoaser.com; dict.

Gooya Publications: 139 Karimkhan-e Zand Ave, Tehran 15856; tel. (21) 8838453; fax (21) 8842987; e-mail info@goyabooks.com; internet www.goyabooks.com; f. 1981; art; Dir NASER MIR BAGHERI.

Iran Chap Co: Ettela'at Bldg, Mirdamad Ave, South Naft St, Tehran; tel. (21) 29999; fax (21) 22258022; e-mail ettelaat@ettelaat.com; internet www.ettelaat.com; f. 1966; newspapers, books, magazines, book-binding and colour printing; Man. Dir M. DOAEI.

Iran Exports Publication Co Ltd: POB 14335-746, 27 Eftekhar St, Vali-e-Asr Ave, Tehran 15956; tel. (21) 88801800; fax (21) 88900547; e-mail info@iranexportsmagazine.com; internet www.iranexportsmagazine.com; f. 1987; business and trade.

Ketab Sara Co: POB 15117-3695, Tehran; tel. (21) 88711321; fax (21) 88717819; e-mail rashti@ketabsara.org; f. 1980; Man. Dir SADEGH SAMII.

Khayyam: 31 Ishteyani, Daneshgahi, Enghelab St, Tehran; tel. (21) 44394004; Dir MUHAMMAD ALI TARAGHI.

Kowkab Publishers: POB 19575-511, Tehran; tel. (21) 22583723; fax (21) 22949834; e-mail info@kkme.com; internet www.kkme.com; engineering, science, medicine, humanities, reference; Exec. Man. Dr AHMAD GHANDI.

The Library, Museum and Documentation Center of the Islamic Consultative Assembly (Ketab-Khane, Muze va Markaz-e Asnad-e Majles-e-Shora-ye Eslami): POB 11365-866, Ketab-Khane Majlis-e-Shora-ye Eslami No. 2, Baharestan Sq., Tehran; tel. (21) 33130919; fax (21) 33124339; e-mail frelations@majlislib.com; internet www.majlislib.com; f. 1912 as Majlis Library; renamed as above in 1996; arts, humanities, social sciences, politics, Iranian and Islamic studies; Dir SAYED MOHAMMAD ALI AHMADI ABHARI.

Ofoq Publishers: 181 Nazari St, 12 Farvardine St, Tehran 13146-75351; tel. (21) 66413367; fax (21) 66414285; e-mail info@ofoqco.com; internet www.ofoqco.com; art and children's books; Dir REZA HASHEMINEJAD.

Qoqnoos Publishing House: 215 Shohadaye Jandarmeri St, Enghelab Ave, Tehran; tel. (21) 66460099; fax (21) 66413933;

IRAN

e-mail qoqnoos@morva.net; internet www.qoqnoos.ir; f. 1977; society, history, cultural studies, philosophy; privately owned; Gen. Man. AMIR HOSSEINZADEGAN; Editor-in-Chief ARSALAN FASIHI.

Sahab Geographic and Drafting Institute: POB 11365-617, 30 Somayeh St, Hoquqi Crossroads, Dr Ali Shariati Ave, Tehran 16517; tel. (21) 77535651; fax (21) 77535876; internet www.sahabmap.com; f. 1936; maps, atlases, and books on geography, science, history and Islamic art; Man. Dir MUHAMMAD REZA SAHAB.

Scientific and Cultural Publications Co: Ministry of Science, Research and Technology, Tehran; tel. (21) 88048037; f. 1974; Iranian and Islamic studies and scientific and cultural books; Pres. SAYED JAVAD AZHARS.

Soroush Press: POB 15875-1163, Soroush Bldg, Motahari Ave, Mofatteh Crossroads, Tehran; tel. and fax (21) 88847602; e-mail cultural@soroushpress.com; internet www.soroushpress.com; part of Soroush Publication Group, the pubs dept of Islamic Republic of Iran Broadcasting; publishes books, magazines and multimedia products on a wide range of subjects; Man. Dir ALI AKBAR ASHARI.

Tehran University Press: 16th St, North Karegar St, Tehran; tel. (21) 88012076; fax (21) 88012077; e-mail press@ut.ac.ir; internet press.ut.ac.ir; f. 1944; univ. textbooks; Man. Dir Dr MUHAMMAD SHEKARCIZADEH.

Broadcasting and Communications

TELECOMMUNICATIONS

In April 2003, as a first step towards the liberalization of the telecommunications sector, the appointment of an independent regulator was announced, with a view to establishing a board initially to oversee the issue of Iran's second GSM licence. The licence was awarded to Irancell, a consortium led by Turkcell (Turkey), in February 2004. However, the contract was subsequently revised by the Majlis and the Council of Guardians to require that domestic firms hold a majority stake in the consortium, and Turkcell was replaced as the foreign partner by the second-placed bidder, the South African company MTN. The licence award was eventually signed in November 2005, and initial services commenced in October 2006.

Telecommunications Regulator: Deputy Minister for Telecommunications MASSOUD DAVARI-NEJAD.

Telecommunications Company of Iran (TCI): POB 3316-17, Dr Ali Shariati Ave, Tehran; tel. (21) 88429595; fax (21) 88405055; e-mail info@irantelecom.ir; internet www.irantelecom.ir; scheduled for partial privatization; Chair. VAFA GHAFFARIAN; Man. Dir SABER FAYAZI.

   Mobile Communications Company of Iran (MCCI): Tehran; f. 2004; wholly owned subsidiary of TCI; some 11m. subscribers (Dec. 2006); CEO VAHID SADOUGHI.

MTN Irancell: internet www.irancell.ir; f. 2004 as Irancell, name changed as above 2005; mobile telecommunications; consortium of Iran Electronic Devt Co (51%) and MTN (South Africa—49%); some 2m. subscribers (June 2006); Chair. Dr IBRAHIM MAHMOUDZADEH; Man. Dir ALIREZA GHALAMBOR DEZFOULI.

BROADCASTING

Islamic Republic of Iran Broadcasting (IRIB): POB 19395-3333, Vali-e-Asr Ave, Jame Jam St, Tehran; tel. (21) 22041093; fax (21) 22014802; e-mail info@iribnews.ir; internet www.irib.com; semi-autonomous authority, affiliated with the Ministry of Culture and Islamic Guidance; non-commercial; operates seven national and 26 local television stations, and nine national radio networks; 30 provincial centres, 18 foreign bureaux; broadcasts world-wide in 27 languages; Pres. SAYED EZZATOLLAH ZARGHAMI.

Radio

Radio Network 1 (Voice of the Islamic Republic of Iran): There are three national radio channels: Radio Networks 1 and 2 and Radio Quran, which broadcasts recitals of the Quran (Koran) and other related programmes; covers whole of Iran and also reaches Europe, Asia, Africa and part of the USA; medium-wave regional broadcasts in local languages; Arabic, Armenian, Assyrian, Azerbaijani, Balochi, Bandari, Dari, Farsi, Kurdish, Mazandarani, Pashtu, Turkoman, Turkish and Urdu; external broadcasts in English, French, German, Spanish, Turkish, Arabic, Kurdish, Urdu, Pashtu, Armenian, Bengali, Russian and special overseas programme in Farsi; Hebrew service introduced in 2002; 53 transmitters.

Television

Television (Vision of the Islamic Republic of Iran): 625-line, System B; Secam colour; two production centres in Tehran producing for two networks and 28 local television stations.

Finance

(cap. = capital; res = reserves; dep. = deposits; brs = branches; m. = million; amounts in rials)

BANKING

Banks were nationalized in June 1979 and a revised commercial banking system was introduced consisting of nine banks (subsequently expanded to 10). Three banks were reorganized, two (Bank Tejarat and Bank Mellat) resulted from mergers of 22 existing small banks, three specialize in industry and agriculture, and one, the Islamic Bank of Iran (now Islamic Economy Organization), set up in May 1979, was exempt from nationalization. The 10th bank, the Export Development Bank, specializes in the promotion of exports. A change-over to an Islamic banking system, with interest (forbidden under Islamic law) being replaced by a 4% commission on loans, began on 21 March 1984. All short- and medium-term private deposits and all bank loans and advances are subject to Islamic rules. A partial liberalization of the banking sector was implemented by the administration of former President Khatami during 1997–2005, beginning with the establishment of four private banks after 2001. Two further private banks were granted licences to commence operations in 2005/06. Notable banks included in the current Government's privatization programme are Mellat, Refah, Saderat and Tejarat.

Although the number of foreign banks operating in Iran has fallen dramatically since the Revolution, some 21 are still represented, in the form of representative offices. However, it was announced in 2007 that legislation to enable foreign banks to establish actual branches in Iran was to be presented to the Majlis.

Central Bank

Bank Markazi Jomhouri Islami Iran (Central Bank): POB 15875-7177, 144 Mirdamad Blvd, Tehran; tel. (21) 229951; fax (21) 66735674; e-mail g.secdept@cbi.ir; internet www.cbi.ir; f. 1960; Bank Markazi Iran until Dec. 1983; issuing bank, govt banking; cap. 1,200,000m., res 50,069,940m., dep. 288,856,253m. (March 2005); Gov. Dr TAHMASB MAZAHERI; Gen. Sec. Dr MAHMOUD BAHMANI.

Commercial Banks

Bank Keshavarzi (Agricultural Bank): POB 14155-6395, 129 Patrice Lumumba Ave, Jalal al-Ahmad Expressway, Tehran 14454; tel. (21) 88250135; fax (21) 88262313; e-mail info@agri-bank.com; internet www.agri-bank.com; f. 1980 by merger of Agricultural Co-operative Bank of Iran and Agricultural Development Bank of Iran; state-owned; cap. 8,021,118m., res 632,599m., dep. 99,488,663m. (March 2006); Chair. and Man. Dir SAYED HASSAN NOORBAKHSH; 1,834 brs.

Bank Mellat (Nation's Bank): Head Office Bldg, 327 Taleghani Ave, Tehran 15817; tel. (21) 82962043; fax (21) 88834417; e-mail info@bankmellat.ir; internet www.bankmellat.ir; f. 1980 by merger of 10 fmr private banks; state-owned; cap. 13,100,000m., res 1,766,502m., dep. 188,449,109m. (March 2005); Chair. and Man. Dir Dr ALI DIVANDARI; 1,943 brs in Iran, 6 abroad.

Bank Melli Iran (The National Bank of Iran): POB 11365-171, Ferdowsi Ave, Tehran; tel. (21) 3231; fax (21) 33912813; e-mail intlrel@bankmelli-iran.com; internet www.bankmelli-iran.com; f. 1928; present name since 1943; state-owned; cap. 2,260,000m., res 6,038,297m., dep. 188,713,048m. (March 2004); Man. Dir ALI SEDGHI; 3,061 brs in Iran, 16 abroad.

Bank Pasargad: 300 Mirdamad Ave, Tehran; tel. (21) 88649502; fax 88649501; e-mail info@bankpasargad.com; internet fa.bpi.ir; f. 2005; cap. 3,500,000m., res 32,836m., dep. 888,717m. (March 2006); Pres. Dr MAJID GHASEMI; Chair. SAYED KAZEM MIRVALAD; 70 brs.

Bank Refah (Workers' Welfare Bank): POB 15815, 40 Northern Shiraz Ave, Molla Sadra Ave, Tehran 19917; tel. (21) 88042926; fax (21) 88041394; e-mail info@bankrefah.ir; internet www.bankrefah.ir; f. 1960 as Bank Refah Kargaran; name changed as above 1999; state-owned; cap. 895,000m., res 214,658m., dep. 36,278,981m. (March 2006); Chair. and Man. Dir Dr PEYMAN NOORI BROJERDI; 1,324 brs.

Bank Saderat Iran (The Export Bank of Iran): POB 15745-631, Bank Saderat Tower, 43 Somayeh Ave, Tehran; tel. (21) 88302699; fax (21) 88839539; e-mail foreign.dept@saderbank.com; internet www.saderbank.com; f. 1952; state-owned; cap. 16,803,000m., res 6,875,000m., dep. 203,129,000m. (March 2006); Chair. and Man. Dir Dr HAMID BORHANI; 3,255 brs in Iran, 21 abroad.

Bank Sepah: POB 9569, Imam Khomeini Sq., Tehran 11364; tel. (21) 66743761; fax (21) 66743282; e-mail info@banksepah.ir; internet www.banksepah.ir; f. 1925; nationalized in June 1979; cap. 7,821,522m., res 1,524,320m., dep. 101,695,822m. (March 2006); Chair. and Man. Dir AHMAD DERAKHSHANDEH; 1,691 brs in Iran, 3 abroad.

Bank Tejarat (Commercial Bank): POB 11365-5416, 130 Taleghani Ave, Nejatoullahie, Tehran 15994; tel. (21) 81041; fax (21) 88828215; internet tejaratbank.ir; f. 1979 by merger of 12 banks; state-owned; cap. 10,437,384m., res 2,159,811m., dep. 132,042,054m. (March 2006); Chair. and Man. Dir Dr Reza Raei; 2,010 brs in Iran, 5 abroad.

Eghtesad Novin Bank (EN Bank): 28 Esfandiar Blvd, Vali-e-Asr Ave, Tehran 196865-5944; tel. (21) 88788960; fax (21) 88880166; e-mail info@enbank.ir; internet www.enbank.net; private bank; granted operating licence in 2001; cap. 1,000,000m., res 103,080m., dep. 12,848,139m. (March 2006); Chair. Muhammad Sadr Hashemi Nejad; CEO Jalal Rasoulof; 47 brs.

Islamic Economy Organization: Ferdowsi Ave, Tehran; f. 1980 as the Islamic Bank of Iran; cap. 2,000m.; provides interest-free loans and investment in small industry; 1,200 funds under its supervision.

Karafarin Bank: POB 15875-4659, No. 6, Ahmad Ghasir Ave, Tehran 15137; tel. (21) 88550316; fax (21) 88550291; e-mail info@karafinbank.com; internet www.karafarinbank.com; f. 1999 as Karafarin Credit Institute; converted into private bank in 2001; cap. 700,000m., res 117,440m., dep. 11,386,905m. (March 2006); Chair. Mohsen Khalili-Araghi; Man. Dir Parviz Aghili-Kermani; 10 brs.

Parsian Bank: 65 Keshavarz Blvd, Tehran; tel. (21) 88979333; fax (21) 88979344; e-mail info@parsian-bank.net; internet www.parsian-bank.com; f. 2002; private bank; cap. 5,000,000m., res 550,000m., dep. 67,310,000m. (March 2006); Man. Dir Ali Soleimani Shayesteh; Chair. of Bd Bahram Fathali; 149 brs.

Saman Bank Corpn: 118 Mirdamad St, Tehran; tel. (21) 22902001; fax (21) 22275881; e-mail info@sb24.ir; internet www.sb24.com; f. 2001; private bank; cap. 900,000m., res 120,777m., dep. 22,766,359m. (March 2006); Chair. Muhammad Zarrabieh; Man. Dir Allahverdi Rajaie Salmassi.

Development Banks

Bank of Industry and Mine: POB 15875-4456, Firouzeh Tower, 1655 Vali-e-Asr Ave (above Chamran Crossroads), Tehran; tel. (21) 22029811; fax (21) 22029894; e-mail bim@bim.ir; internet w3.bim.ir; f. 1979 as merger of the following: Industrial Credit Bank, Industrial and Mining Development Bank of Iran, Development and Investment Bank of Iran and Iranian Bankers Investment Co; cap. 5,672,000m., total assets 18,824,000m. (2004); Man. Dir Mehdi Razavi; 31 brs.

Export Development Bank of Iran: POB 151674-7913, 4 Gandhi Ave, Tehran 15167; tel. (21) 88798213; fax (21) 88798259; e-mail info@edbi.ir; internet www.edbi.ir; f. 1991; cap. 3,068,554m., res 982,440m., dep. 6,157,529m. (March 2006); Chair. and Man. Dir Dr Kouroush Parvizian; 26 brs.

Housing Bank

Bank Maskan (Housing Bank): POB 11365-3499, 247 Cross Sakhaei St, Ferdowsi Ave, Tehran; tel. (21) 66706742; fax (21) 66709667; e-mail intl_div@bank-maskan.org; internet www.bank-maskan.org; f. 1979; state-owned; cap. 5,848,157m., res 2,195,318m., dep. 74,431,824m. (March 2006); provides mortgage and housing finance; 630 brs; Chair. and Man. Dir Hassan Kari.

Regulatory Authority

Supreme Council of Banks: Tehran; comprises two bankers and five ministerial appointees; regulates internal affairs of all Iranian banks; Chair. Dr Hossein Nemazi.

STOCK EXCHANGE

Tehran Stock Exchange: 228 Hafez Ave, Tehran 11355; tel. (21) 66708385; fax (21) 66702124; e-mail info@tse.ir; internet www.irbourse.com; f. 1966; Chair. Moustafa Omid Ghaemi; Man. Dir Dr Ali Rahmani.

INSURANCE

The nationalization of insurance companies was announced in June 1979. However, as part of the reforms to the financial sector undertaken by the former Khatami administration, a private insurance firm was established in February 2003; a number of other private insurance companies were subsequently registered.

Bimeh Alborz (Alborz Insurance Co): POB 4489-15875, Alborz Bldg, 234 Sepahboad Garani Ave, Tehran; tel. (21) 88803776; fax (21) 88803771; e-mail info@alborz-insurance.com; internet www.alborz-insurance.com; f. 1959; state-owned; all types of insurance; Chair. and Man. Dir Amin Muhammad Ebrahim; 39 brs.

Bimeh Asia (Asia Insurance Co): POB 15815-1885, Asia Insurance Bldg, 299 Taleghani Ave, Tehran; tel. (21) 88800951; fax (21) 88898113; e-mail info@bimehasia.ir; internet www.bimehasia.com; f.1959; state-owned; all types of insurance; Man. Dir Masoum Zamiri; 90 brs.

Bimeh Dana (Dana Insurance Co): 25 Fifteenth St, Ghandi Ave, Tehran 151789-5511; tel. (21) 88770971; fax (21) 88792997; e-mail info@dana-insurance.com; internet www.dana-insurance.com; f. 1988; state-owned; life, personal accident and health insurance; Chair. Abdorreza Ghasemi.

Bimeh Day (Day Insurance Co): 241 Mirdamad Blvd, Tehran; tel. (21) 22900551; fax (21) 22900516; e-mail info@dayins.com; internet www.dayins.com; privately owned; all types of insurance.

Bimeh Iran (Iran Insurance Co): POB 14155-6363, 107 Dr Fatemi Ave, Tehran; tel. (21) 88954712; e-mail info@iraninsurance.ir; internet www.iraninsurance.ir; f. 1935; state-owned; all types of insurance; Chair. and Man. Dir Dr Sayed Muhammad Asoudeh; 246 brs in Iran, 12 brs abroad.

Bimeh Karafarin (Karafarin Insurance Co): POB 15875-8475, No. 9, 17th St, Ahmad Ghasir Ave, Argentina Sq., Tehran; tel. (21) 88723830; fax (21) 88723840; e-mail karafarin@karafarin-insurance.com; internet www.karafarininsurance.com; f. 2003; privately owned; all types of insurance; 13 brs.

Bimeh Novin (Novin Insurance Co): POB 15179-9611, No.19, 21st St, Gandi St, Tehran; tel. (21) 88772393; fax (21) 88789923; e-mail info@novininsurance.com; internet www.novininsurance.com; f. 2006; privately owned; all types of insurance; Chair. Dr Sayed Muhammad Abbas Zadegan.

Mellat Insurance Co: 4 Chehelsotoon St, Fatemi Sq., Tehran; tel. (21) 88971786; fax (21) 88971787; e-mail info@mellatinsurance.com; internet www.mellatinsurance.com; privately owned; property, life, engineering, aviation and marine insurance; Chair. Abdolhossein Sabet; Man. Dir Masoud Hajjarian.

Regulatory Authority

Bimeh Markazi Iran (Central Insurance of Iran): POB 19395-5588, 72 Africa Ave, Tehran 19157; tel. (21) 22050001; fax (21) 22054099; e-mail pr@centinsur.ir; internet www.centinsur.ir; f. 1971; regulates and supervises the insurance market and tariffs for new types of insurance cover; the sole state reinsurer for domestic insurance cos, which are obliged to reinsure 50% of their direct business in life insurance and 25% of business in non-life insurance with Bimeh Markazi Iran; Pres. Dr Norouz Kohzadi.

Trade and Industry

CHAMBER OF COMMERCE

Iran Chamber of Commerce, Industries and Mines: 254 Taleghani Ave, Tehran 15875-4671; tel. (21) 88308331; fax (21) 88825111; e-mail info@iccim.org; internet www.iccim.org; supervises the affiliated 30 chambers in the provinces; Pres. Dr Muhammad Nahavandian.

INDUSTRIAL AND TRADE ASSOCIATIONS

National Iranian Industries Organization (NIIO): POB 15875-1331, No. 11, 13th Alley, Miremad St, Tehran; tel. (21) 88744198; fax (21) 88757126; f. 1979; owns 400 factories in Iran; Man. Dir Ali Toosi.

National Iranian Industries Organization Export Co (NECO): No. 8, 2nd Alley, Bucharest Ave, Tehran; tel. (21) 44162384; fax (21) 212429.

STATE HYDROCARBONS COMPANIES

The following are subsidiary companies of the Ministry of Petroleum:

National Iranian Gas Co (NIGC): POB 6394-4533, 7th Floor, No. 401, Saghitaman, Taleghani Ave, Tehran; tel. (21) 88133347; fax (21) 88133456; e-mail webmaster@nigc.org; internet www.nigc.ir; f. 1965; Man. Dir Reza Kassaiezadeh.

National Iranian Oil Co (NIOC): POB 1863, Taleghani Ave, Tehran 15875-1863; tel. (21) 66154975; fax (21) 66154977; e-mail public-relations@nioc.com; internet www.nioc.com; f. 1948; state org. controlling all 'upstream' activities in the petroleum and natural gas industries; incorporated April 1951 on nationalization of petroleum industry to engage in all phases of petroleum operations; in Feb. 1979 it was announced that, in future, Iran would sell petroleum direct to the petroleum companies, and in Sept. 1979 the Ministry of Petroleum assumed control of the NIOC; Man. Dir Seifollah Jashnsaz.

   Iranian Offshore Oil Co (IOOC): POB 5591, 38 Tooraj St, Vali-e-Asr Ave, Tehran 19395; tel. (21) 22024725; fax (21) 22024733; e-mail A.Hassani@iooc.co.ir; internet www.iooc.co.ir; wholly owned subsidiary of NIOC; f. 1980; devt, exploitation and production of crude petroleum, natural gas and other hydrocarbons in all offshore areas of Iran in the Persian (Arabian) Gulf and the Caspian Sea; Man. Dir Mahmoud Zirakchian Zadeh.

   Pars Oil and Gas Co (POGC): POB 14141-73111, 133 Parvin Etesami Alley, Dr Fatemi Ave, Tehran; tel. (21) 88966031; fax (21)

88989273; e-mail info@pogc.ir; internet www.pogc.ir; f. 1994; a subsidiary of NIOC; Man. Dir ALI VAKILI.

National Iranian Oil Refining and Distribution Co (NIORDC): POB 15815-3499, NIORDC Bldg, 140 Ostad Nejatollahi Ave, Tehran 15989; tel. (21) 88801001; fax (21) 66152138; e-mail info@niordc.ws; f. 1992 to assume responsibility for refining, pipeline distribution, engineering, construction and research in the petroleum industry from NIOC; Chair. and Man. Dir MUHAMMAD REZA NEMATZADEH.

National Petrochemical Company (NPC): POB 19395-6896, North Sheikh Bahaei St, Tehran; tel. (21) 88059760; fax (21) 88059701; e-mail webmaster@nipc.net; internet www.nipc.net; f. 1964; oversees the devt and operation of Iran's petrochemical sector; directs activities of over 50 subsidiaries; Pres. and Vice-Chair. GHOLAMHOSSEIN NEJABAT.

CO-OPERATIVES

Ministry of Co-operatives: 16 Bozorgmehr St, Vali-e-Asr Ave, Tehran 14169; tel. (21) 66400938; fax (21) 66498440; e-mail info@icm.gov.ir; internet www.icm.gov.ir; f. 1993; 15m. mems in 70,000 co-operative societies.

Central Union of Rural and Agricultural Co-operatives of Iran: POB 14155-6413, 78 North Palestine St, Opposite Ministry of Energy, Tehran; tel. (21) 88978150; fax (21) 88964166; e-mail info@keshavarzonline.com; internet www.keshavarzonline.com; f. 1963; educational, technical, commercial and credit assistance to rural co-operative societies and unions; Chair. and Man. Dir SAYED MUHAMMAD MIRMUHAMMADI.

UTILITIES

Electricity

Iran Power Generation, Transmission and Distribution Co (Tavanir): POB 19988-36111, Tavanir Blvd, Rashid Yasami St, Vali-e-Asr Ave, Tehran; tel. (21) 88774088; fax (21) 88778437; e-mail ceo@tavanir.org.ir; internet www.tavanir.org.ir; f. 1979; state-owned; operates a network of 16 regional electricity cos, 27 generating cos and 42 distribution cos; also responsible for electricity transmission; Man. Dir MUHAMMAD ALI VAHDATI.

Transport

RAILWAYS

Iranian Islamic Republic Railways: POB 13185-1498, Shahid Kalantari Bldg, Railway Sq., Tehran 13165; tel. (21) 55641600; fax (21) 55650532; e-mail webmaster@rai.ir; internet www.rai.ir; f. 1934; affiliated to Ministry of Roads and Transport; Pres. Dr HASSAN ZIARI.

Raja Passenger Trains Co: POB 15875-1363, 1 Sanaie St, Karimkhan Zand Ave, Tehran; tel. (21) 88310880; fax (21) 88834340; e-mail info@raja.ir; internet www.raja.ir; f. 1996; state-owned; affiliated with Iranian Islamic Republic Railways; Man. Dir MAHMOUD JAFARI.

In 2005 the Iranian railway network system was estimated to comprise 8,108 km of mainline track, of which 7,866 km was 1,435 mm standard gauge, 148 km was electrified and 94 km was wide 1,676 mm gauge. The Government planned to expand the rail network to 28,000 km by 2020, although it remained doubtful whether foreign companies would finance the necessary loans. The system includes the following main routes:

Trans-Iranian Railway: runs 1,392 km from Bandar Turkman on the Caspian Sea in the north, through Tehran, and south to Bandar Imam Khomeini on the Persian (Arabian) Gulf.

Southern Line: links Tehran to Khorramshahr via Qom, Arak, Dorood, Andimeshk and Ahvaz; 937 km.

Northern Line: links Tehran to Gorgan via Garmsar, Firooz Kooh and Sari; 499 km.

Tehran–Kerman Line: via Kashan, Yazd and Zarand; 1,106 km.

Tehran–Tabriz Line: linking with the Azerbaijan Railway; 736 km.

Tabriz–Djulfa Electric Line: 146 km.

Garmsar–Mashad Line: connects Tehran with Mashad via Semnan, Damghan, Shahrud and Nishabur; 812 km. Two further lines link Mashad with Sarakhs on the Turkmen border, and Mashad with Bafq.

Qom–Zahedan Line: when completed, will be an intercontinental line linking Europe and Turkey, through Iran, with India. Zahedan is situated 91.7 km west of the Baluchistan frontier, and is the end of the Pakistani broad gauge railway. The section at present links Qom to Kerman via Kashan, Sistan, Yazd, Bafq and Zarand; 1,005 km. A branch line from Sistan was opened in 1971 via Esfahan to the steel mill at Zarrin Shahr; 112 km. A broad-gauge (1,976-mm) track connects Zahedan and Mirjaveh, on the border with Pakistan; 94 km.

Zahedan–Quetta (Pakistan) Line: 685 km; not linked to national network.

Ahvaz–Bandar Khomeini Line: connects Bandar Khomeini with the Trans-Iranian railway at Ahvaz; this line is due to be double-tracked; 112 km.

Azerbaijan Railway: extends from Tabriz to Djulfa (146.5 km), meeting the Caucasian railways at the Azerbaijani frontier. Electrification works for this section have been completed and the electrified line was opened in April 1982. A standard gauge railway line (139 km) extends from Tabriz (via Sharaf–Khaneh) to the Turkish frontier at Razi.

Bandar Abbas–Bafq: construction of a 730-km double-track line to link Bandar Abbas and Bafq commenced in 1982. The first phase, linking Bafq to Sirjan (260 km), was opened in May 1990, and the second phase was opened in March 1995. The line provides access to the copper mines at Sarcheshmeh and the iron ore mines at Gole-Gohar.

Bafq–Chadormalou: a 130-km line connecting Bafq to the Chadormalou iron-ore mines is under construction.

Bafq–Mashad: an 800-km line connecting Bafq to Mashad was completed in 2005, reducing the distance between Central Asia and the Gulf.

Chadormalou–Tabas: a 220-km line is under construction.

Underground Railway

In May 1995 the Tehran Urban and Suburban Railway Co concluded agreements with three Chinese companies for the completion of the Tehran underground railway, on which work had originally commenced in 1977. By 2003 the system consisted of three lines: Line 1, a 32-km line linking north and south Tehran, an extension to which was opened in 2002 and a further extension to which (reaching Imam Khomeini International Airport) was scheduled for construction from 2006–08; Line 2, a 23-km line running east–west across the city, the first 9.3 km of which were opened in 2000 and extended in 2001; and Line 5, a 31-km suburban line, linking Tehran with the satellite city of Karaj, which was inaugurated in February 1999 and extended by 10 km westward to Golshahr in 2005. Several new underground lines were being planned in the mid-2000s.

Tehran Urban and Suburban Railway Co (Tehranmetro) (TUSRC): 37 Mir Emad St, Tehran 15878-13113; tel. (21) 88740110; fax (21) 88740114; e-mail info@tehranmetro.com; internet www.tehranmetro.com; f. 1976; Chair. and Man. Dir MOHSEN HASHEMI.

ROADS

In 2003 there were an estimated 179,388 km of roads, including 878 km of motorways, 29,244 km of highways, main or national roads, and 149,266 km of secondary or regional roads; some 67.4% of the road network was paved. There is a paved highway (A1, 2,089 km) from Bazargan on the Turkish border to the Afghanistan border. The A2 highway runs 2,473 km from the Iraqi border to Mir Javeh on the Pakistan border. A new highway linking the eastern city of Dogharun to Herat in Afghanistan was opened in January 2005.

Ministry of Roads and Transport: see The Government (Ministries), above.

INLAND WATERWAYS

Principal waterways:

Lake Rezaiyeh (Lake Urmia): 80 km west of Tabriz in north-western Iran; and Karun river flowing south through the oilfields into the Shatt al-Arab, thence to the head of the Persian (Arabian) Gulf near Abadan.

Lake Rezaiyeh: From Sharafkhaneh to Golmankhaneh there is a twice-weekly service of tugs and barges for transport of passengers and goods.

Karun River: Regular cargo service, as well as daily motor boat services for passengers and goods.

SHIPPING

Persian (Arabian) Gulf: The main oil terminal is at Kharg Island. The principal commercial non-oil ports are Bandar Shahid Rajai (which was officially inaugurated in 1983 and handles a significant proportion of the cargo passing annually through Iran's Gulf ports), Bandar Khomeini, Bushehr, Bandar Abbas and Chah Bahar. A project to develop Bandar Abbas port, which predates the Islamic Revolution and was originally to cost 1,900,000m. rials, is now in progress. Khorramshahr, Iran's biggest port, was disabled in the war with Iraq, but has since been repaired. The ports at Bushehr and Bandar Khomeini also sustained war damage, which has restricted their use. In August 1988 it was announced that Iran was to spend US $200m. on the construction of six 'multi-purpose' ports on the Arabian and Caspian Seas, while ports which had been damaged in the war were to be repaired.

Caspian Sea: Principal ports at Bandar Anzali (formerly Bandar Pahlavi) and Bandar Nowshahr.

Ports and Shipping Organization: 751 Enghelab Ave, Tehran; tel. (21) 88809280; fax (21) 88804100; e-mail porsan@pso.ir; internet www.pso.ir; affiliated to Ministry of Roads and Transport; Man. Dir ALI TAHERI.

Principal Shipping Companies

Bonyad Shipping Co (BOSCO): 1st Floor, 24 Ghandi St, Tehran; tel. (21) 88795211; fax (21) 88795211; e-mail master@bosco-ir.com; internet www.bosco-ir.com; Man. Dir ALI SAFARALI.

Iran Marine Services: 151 Mirdamad Blvd, Tehran 19116; tel. (21) 22222249; fax (21) 22223380; e-mail info@imsiran.com; f. 1981; Chair. and Man. Dir MUHAMMAD HASSAN ASHRAFIAN LAK.

Irano–Hind Shipping Co (IHSC): POB 15875-4647, 18 Sedaghat St, Vali-e-Asr Ave, Tehran; tel. (21) 22058095; fax (21) 22057739; e-mail admin@iranohind.com; internet www.iranohind.com; f. 1974; jt venture between the Islamic Republic of Iran and the Shipping Corpn of India; Chair. MUHAMMAD HOSSEIN DAJMAR; Man. Dir Capt. C. P. ATHAIDE.

Islamic Republic of Iran Shipping Lines (IRISL): POB 19395-1311, 37 Asseman Tower, Sayyad Shirazee Sq., Pasdaran Ave, Tehran; tel. (21) 20100369; fax (21) 20100367; e-mail e-pr@irisl.net; internet www.irisl.net; f. 1967; Chair. and Man. Dir MUHAMMAD HOSSEIN.

National Iranian Tanker Co (NITC): POB 19395-4833, 67–68 Atefis St, Africa Ave, Tehran; tel. (21) 23801; fax (21) 22223011; e-mail souri@nitc.co.ir; internet www.nitc.co.ir; Chair. and Man. Dir MUHAMMAD SOURI.

CIVIL AVIATION

The two main international airports are Mehrabad (Tehran) and Abadan. An international airport was opened at Esfahan in July 1984 and the first international flight took place in March 1986. Construction of a new international airport, 40 km south of Tehran, was abandoned in 1979 but resumed in the mid-1980s, and work on three others, at Tabas, Ardebil and Ilam was under way by 1990. The airports at Urumiyeh, Ahvaz, Bakhtaran, Sanandaz, Abadan, Hamadan and Shiraz were to be modernized and smaller ones constructed at Lar, Lamard, Rajsanjan, Barm, Kashan, Maragheh, Khoy, Sirjan and Abadeh. Construction of the Imam Khomeini International Airport (IKIA) in Tehran, anticipated to be one of the largest airports in the world, began in the late 1990s. The first phase of the project was completed in early 2001, and the first flights landed in February 2003. However, the airport was closed by the Revolutionary Guards Corps in May 2004, amid security concerns owing to the fact that it was to be operated by a Turkish-led consortium, Tepe-Akfen-Vie. The IKIA finally reopened in May 2005, and had taken over all international flights from Mehrabad airport by mid-2006.

Civil Aviation Organization (CAO): POB 13445-1798, Taleghani Ave, Tehran; tel. (21) 66025131; fax (21) 64665496; e-mail info@cao.ir; internet www.cao.ir; affiliated to Ministry of Roads and Transport; Pres. HASSAN HAJALIFARD.

Caspian Airlines: Tehran; tel. (21) 44940428; fax (21) 44860252; e-mail admin@caspian-air.com; internet www.caspian-air.com; f. 1992; operates more than 50 flights per week from Tehran to other cities in Iran, as well as scheduled flights to the United Arab Emirates, Syria and several European destinations; rep. offices abroad; Gen. Dir Capt. ASGAR RAZZAGHI.

IranAir (Airline of the Islamic Republic of Iran): POB 13185-755, IranAir Bldg, Mehrabad Airport, Tehran; tel. (21) 466222; fax (21) 46662907; e-mail pr@iranair.com; internet www.iranair.com; f. 1962; serves the Middle East and Persian (Arabian) Gulf area, Europe, Asia and the Far East; scheduled for privatization in 2008; Chair. and CEO SAEED HESAMI.

Iran Airtours: 187 Motahari Ave, Mofatteh Crossroads, Tehran 15879-97811; tel. (21) 88755535; fax (21) 88755884; e-mail info@iranairtours.com; internet iranairtours.ir; f. 1992; low-cost subsidiary of Iran Air, offering flights from Tehran and Mashad; serves domestic routes and the wider Middle East; Chair. ABBAS POUR-MUHAMMADI; Man. Dir SAYED MAHDI SADEGHI.

Iran Aseman Airlines: POB 141748, Mehrabad Airport, Tehran 13145-1476; tel. (21) 66484198; fax (21) 66404318; e-mail mostafavee@iaa.ir; internet www.iaa.ir; f. 1980 as result of merger of Air Taxi Co (f. 1958), Pars Air (f. 1969), Air Service Co (f. 1962) and Hoor Asseman; domestic routes and charter services to destinations in Central Asia and the Middle East; Chair. and CEO ALI ABEDZADEH.

Kish Air: POB 19395-4639, 215 Africa Ave, Tehran 19697; tel. (21) 44665639; fax (21) 44665221; e-mail info@kishairline.com; internet www.kishairline.com; f. 1989, under the auspices of the Kish Development Organization; serves Persian (Arabian) Gulf area and several European countries; Pres. Capt. YADOLLAH KHALILI.

Mahan Air: POB 14515-411, Mahan Tower, 21 Azadegan St, Tehran; tel. (21) 44076081; fax (21) 44070404; e-mail international@mahanairlines.com; internet www.mahan.aero; f. 1991; domestic routes and charter services between Europe and the Middle East; Man. Dir HAMID ARABNEJAD.

Qeshm Air: 17 Ghandi Ave, Tehran; tel. (21) 88776012; fax (21) 88786252; e-mail qeshmair@farazqeshm.com; operates regular flights from Qeshm Island to the Iranian mainland and the United Arab Emirates.

Saha Airline: POB 13445-956, Karadj Old Rd, Tehran 13873; tel. (21) 66696200; fax (21) 66698016; e-mail saha2@iran-net.com; f. 1990; operates passenger and cargo charter domestic flights and services to Europe, Asia and Africa; Man. Dir Capt. MANSOUR NIKUKAR.

Tourism

Tourism was adversely affected by political upheaval following the Islamic Revolution. Iran's principal attraction for tourists is its wealth of historical sites, notably Esfahan, Rasht, Tabriz, Susa and Persepolis. Some 1,659,479 international tourist arrivals were recorded in 2004/05 (year ending 20 March), compared with 326,048 in 1994. Receipts from tourism in 2005 totalled US $1,329m. Tourism centres are currently administered by the state, through the Ministry of Culture and Islamic Guidance, although in the late 1990s the ministry indicated its intention to transfer all tourism affairs to the private sector. In 2006 it was announced that Iran was seeking to attract tourists from neighbouring Muslim coutries by developing the tourism industry on Kish island, declared a free trade zone in 1992. Projects include the 'Flowers of the East' development, scheduled to be completed by 2010, which was to feature one seven-star and two five-star hotels, sports facilities, shops and a marina. The Government plans to attract 20m. foreign tourists each year to Iran by 2018.

Iran Cultural Heritage, Handicrafts and Tourism Organization (ICHTO): POB 13445-719, Zanyan Crossroads, Azadi Ave, Tehran; tel. (21) 66059015; fax (21) 66013524; e-mail administator@iranmiras.org; internet www.iranmiras.ir; f. 1985; Pres. ESFANDIAR RAHIM MASHAI; Vice-Pres. SAYED MUHAMMAD BEHESHTI.

IRAQ

Introductory Survey

Location, Climate, Language, Religion, Flag, Capital

The Republic of Iraq is an almost land-locked state in western Asia, with a narrow outlet to the sea on the Persian (Arabian) Gulf. Its neighbours are Iran to the east, Turkey to the north, Syria and Jordan to the west, and Saudi Arabia and Kuwait to the south. The climate is extreme, with hot, dry summers, when temperatures may exceed 43°C (109°F), and cold winters, especially in the highlands. Summers are humid near the Persian Gulf. The official language is Arabic, spoken by about 80% of the population; about 15% speak Kurdish, while there is a small Turkoman-speaking minority. Some 95% of the population are Muslims, of whom about 60% belong to the Shi'i sect. However, the Baath regime that was in power during 1968–2003 was dominated by members of the Sunni sect. In January 2008 the Council of Representatives approved the design of a new, temporary national flag, which was to be replaced by a permanent one within one year. The temporary flag (proportions 2 by 3) has three equal horizontal stripes, of red, white and black, and the inscription 'Allahu Akbar' ('God is Great') on the central white stripe. The capital is Baghdad.

Recent History

Iraq was formerly part of Turkey's Ottoman Empire. During the First World War (1914–18), when Turkey was allied with Germany, the territory was captured by British forces. In 1920 Iraq was placed under a League of Nations mandate, administered by the United Kingdom. In 1921 Amir Faisal ibn Hussain, a member of the Hashimi (Hashemite) dynasty of Arabia, was proclaimed King of Iraq, and his brother, Abdullah, was proclaimed Amir (Emir) of neighbouring Transjordan (later renamed Jordan), also administered by the United Kingdom under a League of Nations mandate. The two new monarchs were sons of Hussain (Hussein) ibn Ali, the Sharif of Mecca, who had proclaimed himself King of the Hedjaz (now part of Saudi Arabia) in 1916. The British decision to nominate Hashemite princes to be rulers of Iraq and Transjordan was a reward for Hussain's co-operation in the wartime campaign against Turkey. After prolonged negotiations, a 25-year Anglo-Iraqi Treaty of Alliance was signed in 1930. The British mandate ended on 3 October 1932, when Iraq became fully independent.

During its early years the new kingdom was faced with Kurdish revolts (1922–32) and with border disputes in the south. The leading personality in Iraqi political life under the monarchy was Gen. Nuri as-Said, who became Prime Minister in 1930 and held the office for seven terms over a period of 28 years. He strongly supported Iraq's close links with the United Kingdom and with the West in general. After the death of King Faisal I in 1933, the Iraqi monarchy remained pro-British in outlook, and in 1955 Iraq signed the Baghdad Pact, a British-inspired agreement on collective regional security. However, following the overthrow of King Faisal II (the grandson of Faisal I) during a military revolution on 14 July 1958, which brought to power a left-wing nationalist regime headed by Brig. (later Lt-Gen.) Abd al-Karim Kassem, the 1925 Constitution was abolished, the legislature was dissolved, and in March 1959 Iraq withdrew from the Baghdad Pact. Kassem, who had maintained a precarious and increasingly isolated position, opposed by pan-Arabists, Kurds and other groups, was assassinated in February 1963 in a coup by members of the armed forces. The new Government of Col (later Field Marshal) Abd as-Salem Muhammad Aref was more pan-Arab in outlook, and sought closer relations with the United Arab Republic (Egypt). Following his death in March 1966, President Aref was succeeded by his brother, Maj.-Gen. Abd ar-Rahman Muhammad Aref, who was ousted on 17 July 1968 by members of the Arab Renaissance (Baath) Socialist Party. Maj.-Gen. (later Field Marshal) Ahmad Hassan al-Bakr, a former Prime Minister, became President and Prime Minister, and supreme authority was vested in the Revolutionary Command Council (RCC), of which President al-Bakr was also Chairman.

On 16 July 1979 the Vice-Chairman of the RCC, Saddam Hussain, who had long exercised real power in Iraq, replaced al-Bakr as RCC Chairman and as President of Iraq. Shortly afterwards several members of the RCC were executed for their alleged role in a coup plot. The suspicion of Syrian involvement in the attempted putsch, exacerbated by the rivalry between the Baathist movements of both countries, resulted in the suspension of discussions concerning political and economic union between Iraq and Syria. During 1979 the Iraqi Communist Party (ICP) broke away from the National Progressive Front (NPF), an alliance of Baathists, Kurdish groups and Communists, claiming that the Baathists were conducting a 'reign of terror'. In February 1980 Saddam Hussain announced a National Charter, reaffirming the principles of non-alignment. In June elections took place (the first since the 1958 revolution) for a 250-member legislative National Assembly; these were followed in September by the first elections to a 50-member Kurdish Legislative Council in the Kurdish Autonomous Region (which had been established in 1970).

In 1982 Saddam Hussain consolidated his positions as Chairman of the RCC and Regional Secretary of the Baath Party by conducting a purge throughout the administration. Kurdish rebels became active in northern Iraq, occasionally supporting Iranian forces in the war with Iraq (see below). Another threat was posed by the Supreme Council for the Islamic Revolution in Iraq (SCIRI), formed in the Iranian capital, Tehran, in November 1982 by the exiled Shi'ite leader Hojatoleslam Muhammad Baqir al-Hakim. None the less, the majority of Iraq's Shi'ite community was not attracted by the fundamentalist Shi'ite doctrine of Ayatollah Khomeini of Iran, remaining loyal to Iraq and its Sunni President, while Iranian-backed militant groups (such as the predominantly Shi'ite Islamic Dawa Party—Hizb ad-Da'wa al-Islamiya, which made numerous attempts to assassinate Saddam Hussain) were ineffective.

Relations with Iran, precarious for many years, descended into full-scale war in September 1980. Iraq had become increasingly dissatisfied with the 1975 Algiers Agreement, which had defined the southern border between Iran and Iraq as the mid-point of the Shatt al-Arab waterway, and also sought the withdrawal of Iranian forces from Abu Musa and the Tunb islands, which Iran had occupied in 1971. The Iranian Revolution of 1979 exacerbated these grievances, and conflict soon developed as Iran accused Iraq of encouraging Arab demands for autonomy in Iran's Khuzestan ('Arabistan') region. Tehran's support for SCIRI and other Iraqi opposition groups increased the fears among Iraq's Sunni leadership that Iran under Ayatollah Khomenei sought to interfere in its internal affairs. In September 1980, following clashes on the border, Iraq abrogated the Algiers Agreement and its forces advanced into Iran. Fierce Iranian resistance led to military deadlock until mid-1982, when Iranian counter-offensives led to the retaking of the port of Khorramshahr and the withdrawal of Iraqi troops from territory occupied in 1980. In July 1982 the Iranian army crossed into Iraq. However, the balance of military power in the war moved in Iraq's favour in 1984, and its financial position improved as the USA and the USSR provided aid. (Diplomatic relations between the USA and Iraq were restored in November 1984, having been suspended since the Arab–Israeli War of 1967). By early 1988 Iraqi forces had begun to recapture land occupied by Iran, and in July they crossed into Iran for the first time since 1986. In that month Iran announced its unconditional acceptance of UN Security Council Resolution 598, and by August a UN-monitored cease-fire was in force. However, negotiations on the full implementation of the resolution had made little progress by the time of Iraq's invasion of Kuwait in August 1990 (see below), at which point Saddam Hussain abruptly sought a formal peace agreement with Iran—accepting all the claims that Iran had pursued since the cease-fire, including the reinstatement of the Algiers Agreement of 1975. (For a fuller account of the 1980–88 Iran-Iraq War and of subsequent bilateral relations, see the chapter on Iran.)

In the second half of the 1980s Saddam Hussain consolidated his control over the country and secured the loyalty of Iraq's Shi'ite community. In 1988, as a reward for its role in the war against Iran, the President announced political reforms, including the introduction of a multi-party system, and in January

1989 declared that these would be incorporated into a new permanent constitution. In April 1989 elections took place to the 250-seat National Assembly, in which one-quarter of the candidates were members of the Baath Party and the remainder either independent or members of the NPF. More than 50% of the newly elected deputies were reported to be Baathists. In July the National Assembly approved a new draft Constitution, under the terms of which a 50-member Consultative Assembly was to be established; both institutions would assume the duties of the RCC, which was to be abolished after a presidential election.

During the 1980s representatives of Iraq's 2.5m.–3m. Kurds demanded greater autonomy. Resources were repeatedly diverted from the war with Iran to control Kurdish insurgency in the north-east of the country. Saddam Hussain sought an accommodation with the Kurds, and a series of discussions began in December 1983, after a cease-fire had been agreed with Jalal Talabani, the leader of the Patriotic Union of Kurdistan (PUK). The talks did not, however, include the other main Kurdish group, the Kurdistan Democratic Party (KDP), led by Masoud Barzani. Negotiations collapsed in May 1984, and armed conflict resumed in Kurdistan in January 1985 between PUK guerrillas and government troops, with Kurdish and Iranian forces repeatedly collaborating in raids against Iraqi military and industrial targets. In February 1988 KDP and PUK guerrillas (assisted by Iranian forces) made inroads into government-controlled territory in Iraqi Kurdistan. In March the Iraqi Government retaliated by using chemical weapons against the Kurdish town of Halabja. In May the KDP and the PUK announced the formation of a coalition of six organizations to continue the struggle for Kurdish self-determination and to co-operate militarily with Iran. The cease-fire in the Iran–Iraq War in August allowed Iraq to launch a new offensive to overrun guerrilla bases near the borders with Iran and Turkey, again allegedly employing chemical weapons. Kurdish civilians and fighters fled across the borders, and by September there were reported to be more than 200,000 Kurdish refugees in Iran and Turkey. In that month, with the army effectively in control of the border with Turkey, the Iraqi Government offered a full amnesty to all Iraqi Kurds inside and outside the country, excluding only Jalal Talabani. It also began to evacuate inhabitants of the Kurdish Autonomous Region to the interior of Iraq, as part of a plan to create a 30-km uninhabited 'security zone' along the whole of Iraq's border with Iran and Turkey. By October 1989, despite international censure of the evacuation programme, the 'security zone' was reported to be in place, prompting the PUK to announce a nation-wide urban guerrilla campaign against the Government. In September elections had proceeded to the legislative council of the Kurdish Autonomous Region.

In mid-1990 the Iraqi Government criticized countries (principally Kuwait and the United Arab Emirates—UAE) that had persistently produced petroleum in excess of the quotas imposed by the Organization of the Petroleum Exporting Countries (OPEC, see p. 373). Iraq also accused Kuwait of violating the Iraqi border in order to secure petroleum resources, and demanded that Kuwait waive Iraq's debt repayments. Direct negotiations between Iraq and Kuwait, with the aim of resolving their disputes over territory and Iraq's war debt, failed, and on 2 August Iraqi forces invaded Kuwait, taking control of the country and establishing a provisional 'free government'. On 8 August Iraq announced its formal annexation of Kuwait. The UN Security Council unanimously adopted, on the day of the invasion, Resolution 660, demanding the immediate and unconditional withdrawal of Iraqi forces from Kuwait. Subsequent resolutions imposed mandatory economic sanctions against Iraq and occupied Kuwait (No. 661), and declared Iraq's annexation of Kuwait null and void (No. 662). On 7 August the US Government dispatched troops and aircraft to Saudi Arabia, at the request of King Fahd, in order to secure the country's border with Kuwait against a possible Iraqi attack; other countries quickly lent their support to what was designated 'Operation Desert Shield', and a multinational force was formed to defend Saudi Arabia. At a meeting of the League of Arab States (the Arab League, see p. 332) on the day after the invasion, 14 of the 21 members condemned the invasion and demanded an unconditional withdrawal by Iraq; one week later 12 member states voted to send an Arab deterrent force to the region of the Persian (Arabian) Gulf.

Diplomatic efforts to achieve a peaceful solution to the Gulf crisis all foundered on Iraq's refusal to withdraw its forces from Kuwait. In November 1990 the UN Security Council adopted Resolution 678, authorizing member states to use 'all necessary means' to enforce the withdrawal of Iraqi forces from Kuwait if they had not left by 15 January 1991. 'Operation Desert Storm'—in effect, war with Iraq—began on the night of 16–17 January, with air attacks on Baghdad by the multinational force, and by the end of January the allied force had achieved air supremacy. Although Iraq managed to launch *Scud* missiles against Saudi Arabia and Israel, the latter's refusal to retaliate against this attack by an Arab state was the result of considerable diplomatic pressure aimed at ensuring Arab unity in the coalition. In February Iraq formally severed diplomatic relations with Egypt, France, Italy, Saudi Arabia, Syria, the United Kingdom and the USA. During the night of 23–24 February the multinational force began a ground offensive for the liberation of Kuwait: Iraqi troops were quickly defeated and surrendered in large numbers. A cease-fire was declared by the US Government on 28 February. Iraq agreed to renounce its claim to Kuwait, to release prisoners of war and to comply with all pertinent UN Security Council resolutions. Resolution 687, adopted in April, provided for the establishment of a commission to demarcate the border between Iraq and Kuwait. The resolution also linked the removal of sanctions imposed on Iraq following its invasion of Kuwait to the elimination of non-conventional weaponry, to be certified by a UN Special Commission (UNSCOM), and also required that Iraq accept proposals for the establishment of a war reparation fund to be derived from Iraqi petroleum reserves. Later that month the UN Security Council approved Resolution 689, which established a demilitarized zone between the two countries, to be monitored by the UN Iraq-Kuwait Observation Mission (UNIKOM).

Within Iraq, the war was followed by domestic unrest: in March 1991 rebel forces, including Shi'ite Muslims and disaffected soldiers, were reported to have taken control of Al-Basrah (Basra) and other southern cities, although the rebellion was soon crushed by troops loyal to Saddam Hussain. In the north, Kurdish separatists overran a large area of Kurdistan. The various Kurdish factions, allied since 1988 in the Kurdistan Iraqi Front (KIF), claimed that the objective of the northern insurrection was the full implementation of a 15-article peace plan concluded between Kurdish leaders and the Iraqi Government in 1970. Lacking military support from the multinational force, the Kurdish guerrillas were unable to resist the onslaught of the Iraqi armed forces, which were redeployed northwards as soon as they had crushed the uprising in southern Iraq, and an estimated 1m.–2m. Kurds fled before the Iraqi army across the northern mountains into Turkey and Iran. UN Security Council Resolution 688, adopted in April 1991, condemned the repression of Iraqi civilians and provided for the establishment of an international repatriation and relief effort—co-ordinated by a multinational task force, designated 'Operation Provide Comfort', and based in south-east Turkey to provide relief to displaced persons and to secure designated 'safe havens' on Iraqi territory north of latitude 36°N.

A second air exclusion zone, south of latitude 32°N, was established by France, Russia, the United Kingdom and the USA in August 1992, with the aim of protecting the southern Iraqi Shi'ite communities, including the semi-nomadic Ma'dan (Marsh Arabs). Subsequent Iraqi military excursions into the northern and southern exclusion zones were repelled by Western aircraft. In July 1993 Iraqi armed forces were reported to have renewed the Government's offensive against the inhabitants of the marshlands of southern Iraq. In May 1996 government forces launched a major offensive against the Shi'a opposition and tribes in Basra governorate, which led to armed clashes between Iraqi security forces and the Shi'a opposition throughout the southern regions. In April 1998 SCIRI claimed that a renewed offensive against the Shi'a in southern Iraq had resulted in the execution of some 60 people during March.

Meanwhile, in April 1991 the PUK leader, Jalal Talabani, announced that President Saddam Hussain had agreed in principle to implement the provisions of the Kurdish peace plan of 1970. However, negotiations subsequently became deadlocked over the Kurdish demand for the inclusion of Kirkuk in the Kurdish Autonomous Region. Therefore, in October the Iraqi Government withdrew all services from the region, effectively subjecting the Kurds to an economic blockade. The KIF proceeded to organize elections, in May 1992, to a 105-member Iraqi Kurdistan National Assembly, and for a paramount Kurdish leader. The outcome of voting, in which virtually the entire electorate (of some 1.1m.) participated, was that the KDP and the PUK were entitled to an almost equal number of seats in the new assembly. None of the smaller Kurdish parties achieved representation, and the KDP and the PUK subsequently agreed to share equally the seats. The election for an overall Kurdish leader was deemed inconclusive, with Masoud Barzani, the leader of the KDP, receiving 47.5% of the votes cast, and Jalal Talabani 44.9%.

In December 1993 armed conflict broke out between militants of the PUK and the Islamic League of Kurdistan (or Islamic Movement of Iraqi Kurdistan—IMIK). Following mediation by the Iraqi National Congress (INC—a broad coalition of largely foreign-based opposition groups), the two parties signed a peace agreement in February 1994. However, more serious armed conflict between partisans of the PUK and the KDP led, in May, to the division of the northern Kurdish-controlled enclave into two zones. In June 1995 the IMIK withdrew from the INC, and in July there was renewed fighting between PUK and KDP forces, as a result of which scheduled elections to the Iraqi Kurdistan National Assembly were postponed. Peace negotiations under US auspices began in Dublin, Ireland, in August 1995 but collapsed in the following month. Subsequent discussions in the Iranian capital in October led to the signing of an agreement by the KDP and the PUK to hold elections to the Iraqi Kurdistan National Assembly in May 1996.

In early and mid-1995 Turkish armed forces attacked bases of the Kurdistan Workers' Party (Partiya Karkeren Kurdistan—PKK) in the Kurdish enclave of northern Iraq. Turkey's continued support for the KDP in its efforts to expel PKK fighters from the enclave was believed by some observers to have encouraged the PUK to seek support from Iran. The USA and Turkey were concerned at reports in late 1995 that the armed wing of SCIRI had begun to deploy inside the Kurdish enclave. None the less, in February 1996 Turkey and NATO agreed to continue 'Operation Provide Comfort', which had become controversial in Turkey owing to the presence of PKK bases in the enclave.

In early 1996 the PUK leader, Jalal Talabani, offered to participate in peace negotiations with the KDP, and to take part in new elections to the Iraqi Kurdistan National Assembly. However, hostilities escalated in August, as the PUK contested the KDP's monopoly of duties levied on Turkish traders. At the end of the month Iraqi military support for the KDP in the recapture of the PUK-held towns of Irbil (Arbil) and As-Sulaimaniya (Sulaimaniya) in the Kurdish area of northern Iraq provoked a new international crisis. In September the USA unilaterally launched retaliatory 'limited' air-strikes on air defence and communications targets in southern Iraq, and extended the southern air exclusion zone from latitude 32°N to latitude 33°N (thereby incorporating some southern suburbs of Baghdad). Turkey, which had refused to allow the use of its air bases for the US operation, deployed some 20,000 troops to reinforce its border with Iraq. Also in September the KDP gained control of all three Kurdish provinces. The Iraqi Government subsequently announced the restoration of Iraqi sovereignty over Kurdistan, and offered an amnesty to its Kurdish opponents. In late September the KDP formed a KDP-led coalition administration comprising, among others, the IMIK, the Kurdistan Communist Party and representatives of the northern Assyrian and Turkoman communities. In October PUK fighters were reported to have recaptured much of the territory they had ceded to the KDP, having regained control of Sulaimaniya and Halabja. Concern that Iran's alleged involvement in the conflict would provoke direct Iraqi intervention in the north prompted renewed diplomatic efforts on the part of the USA and Turkey, and US-sponsored peace talks in Ankara, Turkey, in late October resulted in a truce agreement. Following the termination of 'Operation Provide Comfort', a new air surveillance programme, 'Northern Watch', began in January 1997; the new operation, based in south-east Turkey, was to be conducted by British, Turkish and US forces.

In March 1997 the KDP withdrew from the US-sponsored peace negotiations, and in May as many as 50,000 Turkish troops entered northern Iraq, where, apparently in co-operation with the KDP, they launched a major offensive against PKK bases. As Turkey began to withdraw its armed forces in October, the PUK launched a massive military offensive against the KDP, targeting several strategic points along the 1996 cease-fire line. The KDP (which subsequently claimed to have regained most of the territory recently lost to the PUK) alleged that the assault had been co-ordinated by Iran and supported by the PKK. By mid-1998 a fragile cease-fire between the PUK and the KDP appeared to be enduring, and the two organizations agreed to exchange prisoners and to seek to co-operate in other areas. In September the USA brokered a formal peace agreement: the accord, signed in Washington, DC, by Masoud Barzani on behalf of the KDP and Jalal Talabani for the PUK, provided for Kurdish legislative elections in 1999 (although these did not take place), a unified regional administration, the sharing of local revenues, an end to hostilities and co-operation in implementing the 'oil-for-food' programme (see below) to benefit the Kurdish population. A new Kurdish coalition government was appointed by the Iraqi Kurdistan National Assembly in December 1999.

Since Iraq's defeat by the US-led coalition forces in 1991, Saddam Hussain had strengthened his control over the country by placing family members and close supporters in the most important government positions. In September Saddam Hussain was re-elected Secretary-General of the Baath Party's powerful Regional Command at its 10th Congress, and in May 1994 he personally assumed the post of Prime Minister. Unsuccessful *coups d'état* reportedly took place in January and March 1995; the latter was instigated by the former head of Iraqi military intelligence and supported by Kurdish insurgents in the north and Shi'ite rebels in the south. In an apparent attempt to re-establish domestic and international recognition of Saddam Hussain's mandate, in September the RCC approved an interim amendment of the Constitution whereby the elected Chairman of the RCC would automatically assume the Presidency of the Republic, subject to the approval by the National Assembly and endorsement by national plebiscite. Saddam Hussain's candidature was duly approved by the Assembly, and the referendum proceeded on 15 October, at which 99.96% of the votes cast endorsed the President's continuing in office. The result was declared null and void in a statement issued by nine Iraqi opposition groups.

The first elections to the Iraqi National Assembly since 1989 took place in March 1996, when 689 candidates (all of whom had received the prior approval of a government selection committee) contested 220 of the Assembly's 250 seats: the remaining 30 seats were reserved for representatives of the Autonomous Regions of Arbil, D'hok and Sulaimaniya, and were filled by presidential decree. The elections were denounced by the INC, based in London, United Kingdom, and other groups opposed to the Government.

Following reports in late 1997 that Saddam Hussain had ordered the execution of a number of senior military officers, Baath Party members and prisoners, internal unrest continued during 1998. The Special Rapporteur of the UN Commission on Human Rights, Max van der Stoel, denounced the assassination of two senior Shi'a religious leaders, Ayatollah Murtada al-Burujirdi and Grand Ayatollah Mirza Ali al-Gharawi, and expressed fears that the murders were part of a systematic attack on the independent leadership of Iraq's Shi'a community. In February 1999 the killing of Iraq's Shi'a leader, Grand Ayatollah Muhammad Sadiq as-Sadr, provoked demonstrations in Baghdad and other cities. Despite claims by the INC that the unrest marked the beginning of an uprising against the Iraqi regime, it was reported that the demonstrations had been brutally suppressed by units of the Sunni-dominated Iraqi Special Republican Guard.

In October 1998 the US Congress had approved the Iraq Liberation Act, permitting the US President to provide up to US $97m. in military assistance to Iraqi opposition groups in exile. In April 1999 11 opposition groups gathered in London, where they undertook to reform the moribund INC and to prepare by July a plan of campaign against Saddam Hussain's regime. Although representatives of the two main Kurdish factions, the KDP and the PUK, attended the meeting, SCIRI and the ICP did not participate. In November delegates to a national assembly of the INC, held in New York, USA, elected a 65-member central council and a new, seven-member collegiate leadership. Several INC leaders meanwhile relocated to the USA, with a view to lobbying US support for the Iraqi opposition movement. The USA continued to support Iraqi opposition groups in the build-up to the US-led coalition's military intervention in early 2003 (see below); however, in May 2004 the USA announced that it had ceased payments to the INC, apparently to facilitate the granting of sovereignty to the Iraqi people.

In April 1999, meanwhile, the Iraqi authorities announced that four men had been executed for the murder of Grand Ayatollah as-Sadr. Several Western-based Arabic newspapers reported in early 2000 that the Iraqi authorities had foiled a coup attempt, with some sources claiming that about 40 officers of the Republican Guard had been executed for their part in an attempt to assassinate Saddam Hussain. In May SCIRI claimed to have perpetrated a rocket attack on presidential offices in Baghdad, where Saddam Hussain had reportedly been scheduled to meet with his sons. In July 2001 SCIRI again claimed to have launched rocket assaults against a number of official targets in Baghdad, in reprisal for attacks on Shi'a religious leaders: most recently, a leading Shi'a cleric, Grand Ayatollah Sayed Hussain Bahr al-'Ulum, had died in apparently suspicious circumstances in An-Najaf (Najaf).

Elections took place on 27 March 2000 for 220 seats in the National Assembly. Official results stated that 165 seats had been won by members of the Baath Party, and the remaining 55 elective seats by independent candidates; a further 30 independents were nominated by the Government to fill the seats reserved for representatives of the Kurdish areas of the north, where the Iraqi authorities stated it was impossible to organize elections since the region remained 'occupied' by the USA. Saddam Hussain's elder son, Uday, was elected to the legislature for the first time, having reportedly received the highest number of votes of any candidate. In May 2001 Saddam Hussain was re-elected Secretary-General of the Baath Party Command at the organization's 12th Regional Congress, while speculation that the Iraqi leader's younger son, Qusay, was being prepared as his successor was further fuelled by his election to the party Command and by his subsequent appointment as a deputy commander of the party's military section. Significant changes to the Council of Ministers were made from April, when Deputy Prime Minister Tareq Aziz assumed the foreign affairs portfolio on an interim basis: the outgoing Minister of Foreign Affairs, Muhammad Saeed as-Sahaf, became Minister of Information. Naji Sabri, formerly Iraq's ambassador to Austria, was appointed to the new position of Minister of State for Foreign Affairs, and was formally promoted to the post of Minister of Foreign Affairs in August.

In August 2002 the National Assembly unanimously endorsed the nomination of President Saddam Hussain to face a national referendum on his remaining in office for a further seven-year term. The referendum was duly held on 15 October, at which the President was officially reported to have received 100% of the votes. A general amnesty for prisoners held in Iraqi gaols was subsequently announced by the authorities; however, opposition groups maintained that there were still thousands of political prisoners in Iraq. This proved to be the last major internal political development under the Baath regime prior to the US-led coalition's military campaign of early 2003, which led to the removal of Saddam Hussain's Government, and which was the de facto culmination of more than a decade of international diplomatic manouevring on the issues of 'oil-for-food' and banned weapons programmes.

Issues of the maintenance of sanctions originally imposed under UN Security Council Resolution 661 and of Iraqi non-compliance with its obligations under Resolution 687 with regard to its weapons capabilities remained inextricably linked in the decade following the Gulf conflict. Security Council Resolution 692, adopted in May 1991, provided for the establishment of the UN Compensation Commission (UNCC) for victims of Iraqi aggression (both governments and individuals), to be financed by a levy (subsequently fixed at 30%) on Iraqi petroleum revenues. In August the Security Council adopted Resolution 706 (subsequently approved in Resolution 712 in September), proposing that Iraq should be allowed to sell petroleum worth up to US $1,600m. over a six-month period, the revenue from which would be paid into an escrow account controlled by the UN. Part of the sum thus realized was to be made available to Iraq for the purchase of food, medicines and supplies for essential civilian needs. Iraq rejected the terms proposed by the UN for the resumption of exports of petroleum, and in February 1992 withdrew from further negotiations, but in October UN Security Council Resolution 778 permitted the confiscation of oil-related Iraqi assets to the value of up to $500m.

UN Security Council Resolution 707, adopted in August 1991, condemned Iraq's failure to comply with UN weapons inspectors, and demanded that Iraq: disclose details of all non-conventional weaponry; allow members of UNSCOM and of the International Atomic Energy Agency (IAEA) unrestricted access to necessary areas and records; and halt all nuclear activities. Resolution 715, adopted in October, established the terms under which UNSCOM was to inspect Iraq's weapons capabilities. Although by November Iraq had accepted the provisions for long-term weapons-monitoring, neither the Security Council nor the US Administration were willing to allow even a partial easing of sanctions until Iraq had demonstrated a sustained commitment to the dismantling of its weapons systems. In February 1994 it was reported that Iraq had agreed to co-operate with UN weapons inspectors under Resolution 715. Thereafter, the Iraqi Government engaged in a campaign of diplomacy to obtain the removal of economic sanctions, and in July the first signs emerged of a division within the UN Security Council regarding their continuation. Russia, France and the People's Republic of China favoured acknowledging Iraq's increased co-operation with UN agencies, but were unable to obtain the agreement of the other permanent members of the Council—the USA and the United Kingdom. Following a military stand-off between Iraq and the US and British military, prompted by the movement of Iraqi forces towards the south of the country near the border with Kuwait, the Iraqi National Assembly voted in November to recognize Kuwait within the border defined by the UN in April 1992.

Economic sanctions imposed on Iraq were renewed on a 60-day basis in 1995 (and thereafter). In April the Iraqi Government rejected as a violation of its sovereignty a revised UN proposal (contained in Security Council Resolution 986) for the partial resumption of exports of Iraqi petroleum to generate funds for humanitarian supplies under what was designated an 'oil-for-food' programme. However, in May 1996 Iraq accepted the UN's terms governing a resumption of crude petroleum sales. At the insistence of the USA and the United Kingdom, it was stipulated that Iraq should not be involved in the distribution to the Kurdish governorates of humanitarian aid purchased with funds realized. The memorandum of understanding signed by Iraq and the UN permitted Iraq to sell some 700,000 barrels per day (b/d) of petroleum over a period of six months, after which the UN would review the situation. Of every US $1,000m. realized through the sales, $300m. would be paid into the UN reparations fund; $30m.–$50m. would contribute to the costs of UN operations in Iraq; and $130m.–$150m. would go towards funding UN humanitarian operations in Iraq's Kurdish governorates. Remaining revenues would be used for the purchase and distribution, under close UN supervision, of humanitarian goods in Iraq. Iraqi officials heralded the memorandum of understanding as the beginning of the dismantling of the sanctions regime, while the UN emphasized that the embargo on sales of Iraqi petroleum would not be fully revoked until all the country's weapons of mass destruction had been accounted for and destroyed.

In October 1996 UNSCOM rejected Iraq's 'full, final and complete disclosures on its weapons programmes'. The USA was said to have granted its approval for the opening of an escrow account with the New York branch of the Banque Nationale de Paris, but the implementation of Resolution 986 (which had been postponed in September, in response to the deployment of Iraqi forces inside the Kurdish 'safe haven' in northern Iraq—see above) was now dependent on stability in northern Iraq and the approval by the UN sanctions committee of a formula fixing the value of Iraqi crude petroleum to be sold. In April 1997 the head of UNSCOM, Rolf Ekeus, reiterated concerns that Iraq was not fully co-operating with UNSCOM weapons inspectors. The UN reported renewed co-operation by Iraq in July, following the inauguration of Richard Butler as the new head of UNSCOM. In October, however, Butler's initial report to the UN Security Council asserted that although some progress had been made in inspecting Iraqi missiles, Iraq had failed to produce a credible account of its biological, chemical and nuclear warfare programmes and was continuing to hinder UNSCOM's work. Subsequently, within the UN Security Council, the USA and the United Kingdom proposed a resolution to prohibit Iraqi officials considered to be responsible for obstructing weapons inspections from leaving the country. France and Russia objected to the draft resolution but approved a revised version whereby a travel ban would be imposed on Iraqi officials in April 1998 should non-co-operation with UNSCOM continue. Meanwhile, Iraq's RCC criticized the high proportion of UNSCOM personnel supplied by the USA, demanding that these should leave the country by 5 November 1997; the deadline was subsequently extended by one week, in order to allow a UN mission to travel to Baghdad to attempt to resolve the dispute. When negotiations failed, the Security Council unanimously adopted a resolution (No. 1137) that immediately activated the travel ban on Iraqi officials.

The confrontation over weapons inspections deepened in January 1998, when Iraq prohibited inspections by an UNSCOM team led by a former US marine officer, Scott Ritter, claiming that Ritter was spying for the US Central Intelligence Agency. The UN Security Council issued a statement deploring Iraq's failure to provide UNSCOM with 'full, unconditional and immediate access to all sites'. However, the Security Council was essentially divided on the issue of weapons inspections: the USA, supported by the United Kingdom, indicated that it was prepared to respond militarily to Iraq's continued non-co-operation, while China, France and Russia opposed the use of force. Moreover, Kuwait was the only country in the region to announce its approval of force if diplomatic efforts should fail; Saudi Arabia and Bahrain refused to authorize military attacks from their territories, while Egypt and Syria notably signalled their disapproval of such a response. In February the five permanent members of the UN Security Council approved a compromise formula whereby a group of diplomats, specially appointed by the UN Secretary-General, Kofi Annan, in consultation with experts from UNSCOM and the IAEA, would be allowed unconditional and unrestricted access to the eight so-called presidential sites. The compromise was accepted by Iraq following a meeting between Annan and Saddam Hussain; a new memorandum of understanding governing inspections was subsequently signed by the Deputy Prime Minister, Tareq Aziz, and Annan, thus averting the immediate threat of military action. In March the UN Security Council unanimously approved a resolution (No. 1154) endorsing the memorandum of understanding and warning of 'extreme consequences' should Iraq renege on the agreement. Inspection teams returned to Iraq shortly afterwards, and members of the special group began visiting the presidential sites later in the month. In April, in his six-monthly report to the Security Council, the head of UNSCOM concluded that there had been no progress in the disarmament verification process since October 1997, and that the destruction of Iraq's chemical and biological weapons was incomplete. Iraq, however, insisted that all such weapons had been destroyed, and urged the complete and comprehensive removal of sanctions. US and British opposition frustrated Russian attempts to secure a vote on a draft resolution proposing an end to weapons inspections, in view of an IAEA report concluding that it had failed to uncover evidence of a nuclear weapons programme in Iraq, and in April 1998 the UN Security Council, in response to Butler's report, voted not to review the sanctions in force against Iraq. The USA began in May to withdraw military reinforcements deployed in the region at the height of the inspections crisis.

Richard Butler visited Baghdad in June 1998, where during talks with Tareq Aziz significant progress was reportedly made on plans for the verification of Iraqi disarmament and the eventual removal of sanctions. Later in the month the UNSCOM head was said to have informed the UN Security Council that US military tests on weaponry dismantled as part of the inspection process had shown that Iraq had loaded missile warheads with a chemical weapon component prior to the Gulf conflict. The IAEA again reported in July that it had no evidence that Iraq was concealing nuclear weapons, but considered that Iraq lacked 'full transparency' in its disclosures to inspectors. In August negotiations between Butler and Aziz collapsed, Iraq suspended arms inspections, and Saddam Hussain announced new terms and conditions for their resumption, including the establishment of a new executive bureau to supervise UNSCOM's operations. The UN Security Council voted later in August to renew the sanctions regime for a further 60 days, but in September unanimously adopted a resolution (No. 1194) condemning Iraq's action of the previous month, demanding that Iraq co-operate fully with UNSCOM and suspending indefinitely the review of the sanctions regime. This prompted the Iraqi Government to halt all co-operation with UNSCOM indefinitely. Reporting to the Security Council in October, Richard Butler asserted that while Iraq was close to fulfilling its obligations with regard to missiles and chemical weapons programmes, UNSCOM remained concerned about the country's capacity for biological warfare. In early November the Security Council unanimously adopted a British-drafted resolution (No. 1205) demanding that Iraq immediately and unconditionally resume co-operation with UNSCOM. US and British military enforcements were again dispatched to the Gulf region to prepare for possible air-strikes against Iraqi targets. Egypt, Saudi Arabia and Syria, while they opposed the threat of force, urged Iraq to resume co-operation. In mid-November Iraq declared that UNSCOM would be permitted unconditionally to resume the weapons inspection programme, and inspectors subsequently returned to Iraq.

However, Iraq's relations with UNSCOM deteriorated once again in early December 1998, after a weapons inspection team conducting a new series of what were termed 'surprise' or 'challenge' inspections was denied access to the Baath Party headquarters in Baghdad. On the night of 16–17 December, following the withdrawal from Iraq of UNSCOM and IAEA personnel, the USA and the United Kingdom commenced a campaign of air-strikes against Iraqi targets; the operation, designated 'Desert Fox' was terminated on 20 December, with US and British forces claiming to have caused significant damage to Iraqi military installations. France, Russia and China contended that the military action had been undertaken without UN Security Council authorization; however, the USA and the United Kingdom maintained that Resolution 1154, adopted in March, provided sufficient legitimacy. In January 1999 US and Iraqi fighter aircraft clashed in the air exclusion zone over southern Iraq, while ground-launched attacks on US aircraft engaged in policing the zone apparently indicated that Iraq was pursuing a more confrontational policy of refusing to recognize the exclusion zone.

The new US Administration of George W. Bush, which assumed office in January 2001, swiftly adopted an uncompromising stance with regard to Iraq. In February US and British fighter aircraft launched their first attack since Operation Desert Fox on air defence targets near Baghdad, in what the US President described as a 'routine mission' to enforce the northern and southern air exclusion zones. Iraq protested that the air-strikes had targeted residential areas of Baghdad, while there were Western media reports that three people had been killed in the initial attacks. In June 2001 Iraq reported that 23 people had been killed by a bomb dropped on a football field outside Al-Mawsil (Mosul—within the northern exclusion zone); the USA and the United Kingdom denied involvement, asserting that any deaths had been caused by Iraqi anti-aircraft shells. US and British military aircraft launched air-strikes against Iraqi air defence installations in the northern and southern exclusion zones during late 2001 and in September 2002, in response to what they claimed were continuing Iraqi attacks on allied aircraft patrolling the zones; Iraqi officials reported that a number of civilians had died in the raids.

Meanwhile, the campaign of air-strikes conducted against Iraqi targets in December 1998 was regarded as marking the collapse of UNSCOM's mission. Diplomatic initiatives undertaken by the Netherlands and the United Kingdom from early 1999 with the aim of drafting a proposal—acceptable to all the permanent members of the Security Council—to establish a successor body to UNSCOM culminated, in December, in the adoption by the Security Council of a resolution (No. 1284) that modified the regime in force for monitoring Iraqi weapons systems. Under the new resolution UNSCOM was to be replaced by a UN Monitoring, Verification and Inspection Commission (UNMOVIC). The resolution provided for the suspension of the economic sanctions in force against Iraq for renewable 120-day periods, provided that Iraq co-operated fully with the new weapons inspectorate and the IAEA throughout such periods. The resolution also effectively removed restrictions on the maximum amount of petroleum that Iraq was permitted to sell under the oil-for-food programme. Resolution 1284 was not approved unanimously, with China, France and Russia, together with Malaysia (a non-permanent member) abstaining. Iraq immediately responded that it would not co-operate with UNMOVIC—although it was notable that the Government did not categorically reject the resolution. In January 2000 the Security Council unanimously endorsed the appointment of Hans Blix, a former Director-General of the IAEA, as head of UNMOVIC. Meanwhile, IAEA personnel undertook the first routine inspection of Iraqi facilities since their withdrawal in December 1998. In his first report to the UN Security Council in March 2000, Blix emphasized that, should Iraq permit the return of weapons inspectors, UNMOVIC would resume 'challenge' inspections of Iraqi sites. In the same month Iraq's Deputy Prime Minister, Tareq Aziz, decisively rejected the terms of Resolution 1284. In March 2001 it was reported that a recent UNMOVIC assessment had concluded that Iraq might still have the ability to build and use biological and chemical weapons, and might possess stocks of mustard gas, biological weapons and anthrax, as well as having the capability to deliver *Scud* missiles.

Exports of Iraqi crude petroleum, under the terms of Resolution 986, had recommenced in December 1996, and continued until immediately prior to the US-led military intervention to oust the regime of Saddam Hussain in March 2003 (see below). The first supplies of food purchased with the revenues from these exports arrived in Iraq in March 1997. In February 1998 the UN Security Council raised the maximum permitted revenue from exports of petroleum to US $5,200m. in the six months to the end of July, of which Iraq would be permitted to spend some $3,550m.

on humanitarian goods. The remainder would be used to finance reparations and UN operations. However, a revised agreement was approved by the UN Secretary-General in May, after Iraq stated that without the rehabilitation of its oil sector it would be unable to export more than $4,000m.-worth of oil every six months. UN technicians also assessed that Iraq was only able to export oil to the value of $3,000m., and that it would need to import essential spare parts in order to maintain this level. Accordingly, the UN Secretary-General requested the Security Council to allow Iraq to divert $300m. of oil revenues in order to carry out repairs to oil production facilities. The new plan provided for oil sales worth $4,500m. over the following six months, of which $3,100m. was to be allocated for humanitarian supplies and urgent infrastructural repairs, while the remainder would finance war reparations. In June the UN Security Council approved a resolution allowing Iraq to purchase spare parts to the value of $300m. for the oil sector. The Security Council renewed the oil-for-food agreement in November, allowing Iraq to sell $5,200m.-worth of oil over six months. In October 1999 the Security Council adopted a resolution permitting Iraq to sell $3,040m.-worth of oil in addition to the quota agreed in May, to compensate for a severe shortfall in oil revenues in the two previous sale periods. In November Iraq rejected a proposal by the Security Council that the oil-for-food programme should be extended for a further two weeks, pending the revision of the programme's terms of reference. Iraq then temporarily suspended its exports of oil, causing world prices to rise to their highest levels since 1990. Nevertheless, the Security Council continued to vote in favour of extending the oil-for-food programme, and under the ninth phase of the programme from December 2000 Iraq was allocated a maximum of $525m. for the local costs of maintaining the oil industry.

In February 2000 both the UN Humanitarian Co-ordinator in Iraq (responsible for the oil-for-food programme), Hans von Sponeck, and the head of World Food Programme operations in the country, Jutta Burghardt, resigned in protest at the hardship inflicted on the Iraqi people by the continuing sanctions regime. (The previous oil-for-food co-ordinator, Denis Halliday, had resigned in 1998 after similarly denouncing the failure of the sanctions policy.) Tun Myat, who became UN Humanitarian Co-ordinator in Baghdad in April 2000, rejected criticism of the oil-for-food programme but undertook to seek to improve its management. In August a rail link between Baghdad and Aleppo, Syria, was reopened after an interval of some 20 years. Furthermore, in November Iraq began to transport crude petroleum to Syria, via a pipeline not used since the early 1980s (the oil-for-food agreement permitted oil exports only via two designated outlets).

In September 2000 the UN Security Council approved the payment to Kuwait of US $15,900m. in compensation for lost production and sales of petroleum as a result of the 1990–91 occupation. However, it was agreed to reduce the levy on Iraq's petroleum revenues destined for reparations under the oil-for-food programme from 30% to 25%.

While Saddam Hussain insisted that the sanctions regime was beginning to disintegrate, and the Iraqi leader appeared to be deriving considerable political capital from the increasing international concern at the evident humanitarian suffering that had resulted from more than a decade of sanctions, in early 2001 the new US Administration under President George W. Bush emphasized its commitment to ensuring the maintenance of the sanctions regime pending the full implementation of Resolution 1284. The new US Secretary of State, Colin Powell, swiftly undertook to secure implementation of a revised sanctions regime, with a view to resolving humanitarian concerns, by means of allowing the direct sale or supply to Iraq of most consumer goods without prior UN approval, while at the same time maintaining strict controls on the supply to Iraq of goods with potential military applications. Supporters of so-called 'smart' sanctions considered that these would have the effect of countering smuggling (of oil out of, and goods into, Iraq), as well as the divisions within the Security Council and delays in approving import contracts at the UN that had severely undermined the credibility of the oil-for-food programme in recent years. The ninth phase of the programme was extended for a further month from June 2001, to allow further consideration of a British-drafted initiative on 'smart' sanctions, which had US approval but was opposed by China, France and Russia. In protest at the scheme, Iraq swiftly suspended exports under oil-for-food, and urged other OPEC members not to increase production to compensate for the shortfall in supply. Intensive diplomatic activity in subsequent weeks resulted in the endorsement by China and France of a compromise list of items that Iraq would be unable to import under the new system. However, Russia maintained its threat to veto the British resolution, after its counter-initiative to defer a decision on 'smart' sanctions for a further six months—whereby Resolution 1284 would be revised to allow a suspension of sanctions if Iraq agreed to readmit UN weapons inspectors—was rejected by other Security Council members. Thus, the United Kingdom withdrew its resolution, and in July the Security Council unanimously adopted Resolution 1360, extending the oil-for-food regime for a further five months. Iraq resumed oil exports under the UN programme one week later.

In late November 2001, shortly before the end of the 10th phase, Minister of Foreign Affairs Naji Sabri emphasized that Iraq would end participation in oil-for-food if 'smart' sanctions revisions were adopted; he also reiterated that weapons inspectors would not be permitted to return to Iraq. Implementation of 'smart' sanctions was effectively deferred for a further six-month period when, at the end of November, the UN Security Council unanimously approved Resolution 1382—essentially a compromise whereby Russia agreed to adopt an annexed list of embargoed items with military and civilian purposes before the expiry of the new (11th) phase, while the USA consented to review Resolution 1284. In May 2002 the Security Council adopted Resolution 1409, extending the oil-for-food programme for a further six months (the 12th phase) while implementing a mechanism to accelerate the processing of contracts not subject to inclusion on the Goods Review List. In late November the Security Council approved Resolution 1443, which extended the 12th phase of the oil-for-food programme for a further nine days, amid disagreement concerning the issue of the Goods Review List. Resolution 1447 of early December extended the programme for a further six months (the 13th phase), while Resolution 1454, approved at the end of that month, expanded the list of goods subject to review to include certain items with a potential military use. In mid-March 2003, immediately prior to the start of the US-led military campaign in Iraq (see below), the UN announced a temporary suspension of the oil-for-food programme. However, amid a sharp deterioration in the living conditions of Iraqi citizens following the outbreak of hostilities, at the end of March the UN Security Council adopted Resolution 1472, granting the Secretary-General, Kofi Annan, the authority to implement existing contracts and to facilitate the delivery of aid for an initial 45-day period. The Security Council voted in late April to extend the Secretary-General's mandate until the beginning of June. On 22 May the UN Security Council passed Resolution 1483, which removed sanctions against Iraq; the oil-for-food programme was formally discontinued on 21 November.

After the defeat of the Taliban regime in Afghanistan (q.v.) in late 2001, there was considerable speculation that the USA would seek 'regime change' in Iraq as part of its declared 'war on terror'. Iraq had strenuously denied any involvement in the suicide attacks of September 2001 against New York and Washington, DC, and the majority of analysts highlighted the incompatible nature of Iraq's secular regime with the militant Islamism espoused by Osama bin Laden, the Saudia Arabian-born dissident whose al-Qa'ida (Base) network was held responsible for the attacks. In response to demands by George W. Bush that Iraq readmit UN inspectors to prove that it was not developing weapons of mass destruction, or otherwise be 'held accountable', the Iraqi authorities reiterated that UN sanctions should first be ended and the air exclusion zones revoked. Tensions were heightened in January 2002 when, in his State of the Union address, President Bush assessed Iraq as forming what he termed an 'axis of evil' (with Iran and the Democratic People's Republic of Korea) seeking to develop weapons of mass destruction, specifically accusing Iraq of plotting to develop anthrax, nerve gas and nuclear weapons. The USA reacted with extreme caution to the announcement in February that the Secretary-General of the Arab League had conveyed to Kofi Annan a message from Saddam Hussain stating Iraq's willingness to resume talks at the UN 'without preconditions', after a one-year hiatus. It was subsequently confirmed that Annan was to meet with Naji Sabri in New York in March (with the head of UNMOVIC, Hans Blix, also in attendance), for talks focusing on implementation of pertinent Security Council resolutions adopted since 1990, including the return to Iraq of weapons inspectors. The day before the meeting the USA presented new evidence to a committee of the Security Council purportedly showing that Iraq was violating UN sanctions and developing weapons capabilities.

In August 2002 the UN Security Council declined an offer by the Iraqi Government to resume negotiations on the return of weapons inspectors, stating that Iraq should not impose any preconditions on the resumption of inspections. At the same time the USA continued to give clear signals that it intended to intervene to bring about 'regime change' in Baghdad, pursuing attempts to secure a UN resolution that would authorize military action, while indicating that the USA would be prepared to act unilaterally. Both US and British officials greeted with scepticism Iraq's declaration, made in mid-September, of its willingness to readmit weapons inspectors 'without conditions'. In late September the British Government published a dossier outlining its case against the regime of Saddam Hussain and the perceived threat posed by Iraq's 'illicit weapons programmes' to the security of both the West and the Middle East. Shortly afterwards the US Secretary of Defense, Donald Rumsfeld, reiterated US claims that Iraq had provided assistance in the training of al-Qa'ida militants. In early October Hans Blix stated that Iraq had agreed to allow inspectors 'unconditional and unrestricted access' to all relevant sites, but that no new agreement had been reached concerning access to Iraq's presidential palaces. (The memorandum of understanding signed by the UN and Iraq in February 1998 placed restrictions on such inspections.) The USA and the United Kingdom were keen for the Security Council to approve a new resolution that would strengthen the mandate under which the UN inspectors were to operate. China, France and Russia all maintained that—in the event of Iraq's failure to comply with the terms of a future resolution concerning Iraqi disarmament—a second UN resolution should be passed prior to any military action being taken against the Iraqi regime. The UN Secretary-General, Kofi Annan, was also said to favour a 'two-step' approach.

In mid-October 2002 President Bush signed a resolution adopted by the US Congress authorizing the use of force, if necessary unilaterally, to disarm Saddam Hussain's regime. On 8 November, after a compromise had been reached between the five permanent members, the UN Security Council unanimously adopted Resolution 1441, which demanded, *inter alia*, that Iraq permit weapons inspectors from UNMOVIC and the IAEA unrestricted access to sites suspected of holding illegal weapons (including the presidential palaces) and required the Iraqi leadership to make a full declaration of its chemical, biological, nuclear and ballistic weapons, as well as related materials used in civilian industries, within 30 days. The resolution warned that this represented a 'final opportunity' for Baghdad to comply with its disarmament obligations under previous UN resolutions, affirming that Iraq would face 'serious consequences' in the event of non-compliance with the UN inspectors or of any 'false statements and omissions' in its weapons declaration. Despite an initial rejection of Resolution 1441 by the Iraqi National Assembly on 12 November, on the following day the RCC announced its formal and unconditional acceptance of the terms of the resolution. Iraqi officials, however, repeatedly stated that they did not possess any weapons of mass destruction. Personnel from UNSCOM and the IAEA resumed weapons inspections in Iraq in late November.

Iraq presented UNMOVIC officials with a 12,000-page declaration of its weapons programmes in early December 2002. In mid-December, however, the USA stated that Iraq was in 'material breach' of UN Resolution 1441 since it had failed to give a complete account of its weapons capabilities, citing in particular Iraq's failure to account for stocks of biological weapons such as anthrax. Meanwhile, both Hans Blix and the IAEA head, Dr Muhammad el-Baradei, affirmed to the UN Security Council that their inspectors required a greater level of co-operation from Iraqi officials. In January 2003 UNMOVIC personnel to the south of Baghdad reported the discovery of several empty chemical warheads, which had reportedly not been included in Iraq's recent declaration. Meanwhile, it was reported that some Arab states (including Saudi Arabia and Egypt) were attempting to persuade Saddam Hussain either to stand down or go into exile—suggestions that were immediately dismissed by Iraqi officials. At an emergency summit meeting of the Arab League in Cairo, Egypt, at the beginning of March, the UAE was reported to have presented a plan for the Iraqi President to stand down, and later in the month the King of Bahrain was said to have offered asylum to Saddam Hussain in order to avert an imminent war.

During January 2003 the USA and the United Kingdom ordered a massive deployment of troops to the Gulf region, while asserting that a conflict was not inevitable if Iraq complied with the UN's disarmament terms. Both the French and German Governments, meanwhile, were vociferous in their opposition to military action and advocated an extension of the UN inspectors' mandate. In late January the ministers responsible for foreign affairs of Turkey, Syria, Iran, Jordan, Egypt and Saudi Arabia attended a conference in Istanbul, Turkey, at the end of which they issued a joint communiqué urging Iraq to co-operate fully with UN inspectors in order to avoid a new conflict in the region. On 27 January, 60 days after the resumption of UN weapons inspections in Iraq (as stipulated under Resolution 1441), Hans Blix and Muhammad el-Baradei briefed the UN Security Council on the progress of inspections. El-Baradei stated that IAEA inspectors had found no evidence that Iraq had restarted its nuclear weapons programme, but requested more time for the organization to complete its research. Hans Blix, for his part, claimed that there was no evidence that Iraq had destroyed known stocks of illegal chemical and long-range ballistic weapons, and announced that he was sceptical about Baghdad's willingness to disarm. Following the briefing, the British Secretary of State for Foreign and Commonwealth Affairs, Jack Straw, declared Iraq to be in 'material breach' of Resolution 1441.

As the likelihood of a US-led military response to the crisis increased, at the end of January 2003 eight European countries (including the United Kingdom, Italy and Spain) signed a joint statement expressing support for the USA's stance with regard to Iraq. In February the British Prime Minister, Tony Blair, accelerated his efforts to secure a second UN Security Council resolution authorizing a US-led campaign in Iraq should inspectors from UNMOVIC continue to report Baghdad's non-compliance. President Bush asserted that, although he favoured the adoption of a second resolution, Resolution 1441 had given the USA the authority to disarm Iraq, if necessary by military means. The US Secretary of State, Colin Powell, had, on 5 February, presented to the Security Council what the USA claimed to be overwhelming evidence of Iraq's possession of weapons of mass destruction, its attempts to conceal such weapons from the UN inspectorate and its links with international terrorism, including the al-Qa'ida network. Despite signs of progress being reported by Hans Blix in his report on UNMOVIC's inspections to the Security Council on 14 February—Iraqi officials had submitted new documents relating to banned materials, had announced an easing of restrictions governing the questioning by UN inspectors of Iraqi scientists, and had agreed to allow aerial reconnaissance flights over Iraq—the UNMOVIC chief stated that the inspections should continue, in order to determine whether Iraq did possess undeclared weapons of mass destruction.

On 24 February 2003 the USA, the United Kingdom and Spain presented a draft resolution to the UN Security Council effectively authorizing a US-led military campaign against Saddam Hussain's regime, in response to Baghdad's failure to disarm peacefully. The resolution stated that a deadline of 17 March would be set, by which time Iraq should prove that it was disarming; however, no specific mention was made of consequent military action in the event of the deadline not being met, apparently in an effort by the US-led coalition to persuade France, Russia and China not to exercise their right of veto. Officials from France, Russia and Germany responded to the draft resolution by presenting an alternative proposal involving an extended timetable of weapons inspections in order to avert a war. At the beginning of March Turkey's Grand National Assembly voted to allow US military aircraft to use Turkish airspace in the event of a campaign being waged against the Iraqi regime; however, the parliament rejected a plan for US forces to use Turkey's military bases, even for refuelling their aircraft. Shortly afterwards France and Russia pledged to veto a second UN resolution authorizing the use of force to disarm Saddam Hussain. On 12 March Tony Blair proposed six new conditions that Iraq must meet in order to prove its intention to disarm: this was seen as an attempt at a compromise that might encourage wavering countries in the Security Council to support an amended resolution. The British proposals came a day after President Bush had rejected a suggested 45-day postponement of any decision to go to war by six countries which had the power to influence the Security Council vote. On 15 March, in anticipation of a probable US-led invasion, Iraq's RCC issued a decree dividing the country into four military commands, under the overall leadership of Saddam Hussain. On the following day a summit meeting was held in the Azores, Portugal, between Bush, Blair and the Spanish Prime Minister, José María Aznar. Several commentators described the Azores summit as a 'council of war'. On 17 March the USA, the United Kingdom and Spain withdrew their draft resolution from the UN, demonstrating that the resolution's co-sponsors had realized the unlikelihood of winning UN support for military action; they stated that they reserved the right to take their own action to ensure Iraqi disarmament. On the same day President Bush issued an ultimatum giving Saddam Hussain and his two sons 48 hours to leave Baghdad or face military action. The Iraqi National Assembly rejected the ultimatum. UN weapons inspectors, humanitarian aid workers and UNIKOM observers along the Kuwait–Iraq border were subsequently withdrawn from Iraq.

Shortly after the expiry of President Bush's 48-hour deadline, in the early hours of 20 March 2003 US and British armed forces launched a 'broad and concerted campaign' (code-named 'Operation Iraqi Freedom') to oust the regime of Saddam Hussain. An initial wave of air-strikes against sites in the suburbs of Baghdad, apparently aimed at leading members of the Iraqi regime, failed to achieve their principal targets. Meanwhile, US-led coalition forces crossed into Iraq from Kuwait and began a steady advance towards the capital. At the same time a concerted campaign of massive air-strikes was launched against the key symbols of the Iraqi regime in and around Baghdad, including selected military bases, communications sites, government buildings and broadcasting headquarters. US and British forces adopted a simultaneous campaign of distributing leaflets and broadcasting radio messages, in an effort to persuade Iraqi citizens to abandon their support for the Baath regime: their declared intention was that Operation Iraqi Freedom would precipitate the disintegration of the regime 'from within'. British troops were principally engaged in securing towns in southern Iraq, including Iraq's second city of Basra, after the US-led coalition had seized control of the key southern port of Umm Qasr and the Al-Faw Peninsula. It was their intention that the Shi'a Muslim population of Basra would quickly initiate an uprising against the regime of Saddam Hussain, as had occurred following the Gulf War in 1991. Although fighting between US-led troops and Iraqi armed forces was often intense, resistance from the Iraqi army and from a number of *fedayeen* (martyrs) and volunteers from other Arab countries was generally lighter than had been anticipated by the allies. Moreover, there were widespread reports of Iraqi soldiers surrendering to the advancing forces. Shortly after the commencement of Operation Iraqi Freedom, in late March 2003 US forces had opened a second front in the Kurdish-controlled regions of northern Iraq, where Kurdish forces joined US troops in targeting bases of Ansar al-Islam. Fears that Turkey might exploit the situation to stage a mass deployment of its forces proved to be unfounded.

At an emergency summit meeting of Arab League states in Cairo on 24 March 2003, representatives of the 17 member states in attendance (except Kuwait) issued a resolution condemning the US-led invasion of Iraq and demanding the withdrawal of all foreign forces from Iraqi territory. Although the USA and the United Kingdom persistently maintained that they were seeking to avoid targeting civilian infrastructure, there was considerable anger in the Arab world and elsewhere at the reports of high numbers of civilian casualties. By 7 April US armed forces had entered central Baghdad, including its presidential palaces. The expected strong resistance from Saddam Hussain's élite Republican Guard did not materialize, and the disintegration of the Baath regime appeared to be complete on 9 April when crowds of Iraqis staged street demonstrations denouncing Saddam Hussain and destroying images and statues of the Iraqi President. Kurdish *peshmerga* fighters gained control of the northern town of Kirkuk on 10 April, while the town of Mosul was seized by Kurdish and US forces on the following day. Also on 11 April the USA issued a 'most wanted' list of 55 members of the deposed regime whom it sought to arrest: one of the most high-profile of these, former Deputy Prime Minister Tareq Aziz, surrendered to US forces two weeks later. The seizure by US troops of Saddam Hussain's birthplace and power base, Tikrit (to the north of Baghdad), on 14 April was widely viewed as the last strategic battle of the US-led campaign to remove the Baathist regime. On 1 May President Bush officially declared an end to 'major combat operations' in Iraq.

The US-led coalition initially acted swiftly to fill the political and administrative vacuum that emerged in the aftermath of the removal of the former Baathist regime. On 15 April 2003 a US-sponsored meeting of various Iraqi opposition groups took place in An-Nasiriyah (Nasiriya) in southern Iraq. However, while the participants produced a 13-point resolution detailing proposals for Iraq's future political development, emphasizing their desire for democratic, sovereign government, it became clear that in the interim period the practical day-to-day responsibilities of repairing, rebuilding and maintaining the material infrastructure of Iraq, as well as combating guerrilla supporters of the ousted regime and emerging 'resistance' groups, would fall to the US-led coalition. Retired US army general Jay Garner, Director of the USA's Office of Reconstruction and Humanitarian Assistance (ORHA), arrived in the country on 21 April to manage the restoration of basic services to the Iraqi population and to enforce law and order. However, after the ORHA was deemed to have failed in this task, it was subsequently replaced by the Coalition Provisional Authorty (CPA), headed by US diplomat L. Paul Bremer, III. Bremer assumed his responsibilities on 12 May, his first act being to outlaw the Baath Party and related organizations, and to demobilize the Iraqi armed forces and security apparatus. The Ministries of Defence, of Information and of Military Affairs were all dissolved.

UN Security Council Resolution 1483, passed on 22 May 2003, recognized the CPA as the legal occupying power in Iraq, and mandated the CPA to establish a temporary Iraqi governing authority. On 13 July the inaugural meeting of the 25-member Iraqi Governing Council was held in Baghdad; members of the Governing Council were appointed by the CPA in direct proportion to the principal ethnic and religious groups in Iraq: 13 Shi'ite Muslims, five Sunni Muslims, five Kurds, one Assyrian Christian and one Turkoman. They were mostly drawn from the main parties who had been in opposition to the former regime of Saddam Hussain, notably Ahmad Chalabi of the INC, Dr Ayad Allawi of the Iraqi National Accord (INA), Jalal Talabani of the PUK, Masoud Barzani of the KDP and Abd al-Aziz al-Hakim of SCIRI. The Governing Council had no executive powers, but could appoint ministers and diplomatic representatives, set a date for the holding of free elections and formulate a new constitution. At the end of July the Governing Council adopted a system of rotating presidency, based on the EU model, in which nine members would share the presidency, each serving for one month beginning in September. Under this system Ibrahim al-Ja'fari, previously a spokesman for the predominantly Shi'ite Islamic Dawa Party, was chosen as Iraq's first President of the post-Baathist era. In mid-August the UN Security Council passed a resolution 'welcoming', but not formally recognizing, the establishment of the Iraqi Governing Council. On 1 September the Governing Council announced the formation of a 25-member interim Cabinet, also appointed along the same ethnic and religious lines, which was to administer the country until the holding of legislative elections. Finally, on 15 November a timetable for the transition of power to an elected, sovereign government was published by the CPA and the Governing Council. The plan was threefold: these two authorities were to be dissolved and replaced by an Iraqi Transitional National Assembly by 30 June 2004; a constitutional convention was to take place by mid-2005, after which a popular referendum would be held on the new constitution; and, by the end of 2005, national elections were to be held to select a new Iraqi government. This process of democratic development was subject, however, to the extremely volatile security situation in Iraq since the declared end of major combat operations.

The *Fedayeen Saddam*, regarded as the most fanatical of the Baathist partisans, were blamed for many of the early attacks against the US-led coalition forces in the aftermath of the war. However, it soon became clear that the arrest or elimination of the main figures of the old regime was not diminishing the level of armed resistance to coalition forces. By early September 2003 a reported 139 US troops had been killed since the end of combat operations was announced on 1 May, exceeding the number killed during the conflict itself. The attacks were not restricted to the occupying forces: the UN, diplomatic missions, Shi'ite clergy, members of the interim Cabinet and NGOs were also targeted. In early August the Jordanian embassy in Baghdad was severely damaged by a car bomb, which killed a reported 17 people. The militant Islamist group Ansar al-Islam, suspected of having links with al-Qa'ida, was initially held to be responsible. (In November 2007 a military court in Jordan sentenced to death a Jordanian national found to have plotted the embassy bombing on the orders of al-Qa'ida in Iraq.) The UN Special Representative for Iraq, Sergio Vieira de Mello, and some 20 others were killed in late August 2003, when a truck laden with explosives was detonated in front of the UN compound in Baghdad. A previously unknown Islamist group, the Armed Vanguards of the Second Muhammad Army, claimed responsibility for the explosion, which resulted in most of the UN's foreign personnel being withdrawn from Iraq. On 29 August a car bomb exploded in the holy city of Najaf, killing Hojatoleslam Muhammad Baqir al-Hakim and up to 125 of his followers after Friday prayers at which the Shi'ite cleric had presided. The murdered cleric (who had returned to Iraq from exile in mid-2003) was succeeded as leader of SCIRI by his brother Abd al-Aziz al-Hakim, a member of the Governing Council. Evident Shi'ite discord had already given rise to the suspicion that the various Shi'ite factions might be attacking each other in order to establish a dominant position among Iraq's majority Shi'ite population. In September Aquila al-Hashimi, one of only three female members of the Governing Council, was attacked in Baghdad by unidentified gunmen, and died of her wounds a few days later.

The US-led coalition had initially been unable to apprehend Saddam Hussain and his immediate family after the removal from power of his regime. However, in July 2003, acting on information received from an Iraqi citizen, US special forces shot dead Hussain's two sons, Uday and Qusay, at a house in Mosul where they had apparently been hiding. Finally, in December Saddam Hussain was captured by US special forces in the village of Ad-Dawr near the former President's hometown of Tikrit; they were also believed to have acted as the result of information provided by an informant. Saddam Hussain's identity was formally confirmed by DNA testing and by members of the Governing Council; he was accorded prisoner-of-war status and detained in US military custody. In July 2004 Hussain, along with 11 co-defendants, appeared in front of a special US-appointed court in Baghdad to face seven charges, including the use of chemical weapons against Kurds in Halabja in 1988 and the invasion of Kuwait in 1990. The former Iraqi leader, declaring the proceedings to be illegal, refused to sign the list of charges. In October 2004 US investigators seeking evidence as part of preparations for war crime trials against Saddam Hussain and former senior Iraqi officials found a mass grave in Hatra, near the ancient city of Nineveh, in which they uncovered the bodies of hundreds of Kurds apparently killed in late 1987 or early 1988, when the Iraqi regime was waging a war against the Kurdish resistance movement.

Meanwhile, there appeared to be little sign of the chemical, biological and nuclear weapons which had been the *raison d'être* for the US-led campaign; as early as July 2003 David Kay, the head of the Iraq Survey Group (ISG)—comprising more than 1,000 experts appointed by the US-led coalition in May to find these banned weapons—told US congressmen that only 'bits of evidence' had been found. In September 2004 a report issued by the ISG following its 15-month search for weapons of mass destruction concluded that the Baathist regime's involvement with chemical or biological agents prior to the 2003 invasion had been restricted to small quantities of poisons, probably for use in assassinations. According to the report, while no illegal stockpiles of weapons had been found, and there was no evidence of any attempts to recommence Iraq's nuclear weapons programme (the last Iraqi factory capable of producing weapons of mass destruction having been destroyed in 1996), there was evidence to suggest that the regime under Saddam Hussain intended to reintroduce its illegal weapons programmes if the UN lifted sanctions against the country. However, subsequent to the release of the report, the IAEA, whose monitors the USA had not allowed into Iraq after the war began in March 2003, announced that buildings used during Iraq's nuclear programme prior to the Gulf War in 1991 had been dismantled, and that specialized equipment and material inside them that could be utilized to produce nuclear weapons had disappeared. The US Administration officially announced an end to the search for weapons of mass destruction in January 2005.

By January 2004 US-led forces had apprehended or killed 42 of the 55 'most wanted' former Baathists (with only 10 of these believed to remain at liberty in 2007). However, during the final weekend of the month some 105 people, mostly Kurds, were killed in suicide bomb attacks directed against the offices of the principal Kurdish parties—the KDP and the PUK—in Arbil. Iraq's most senior Shi'ite cleric, Ayatollah Ali as-Sistani, escaped an assassination attempt in early February 2004, and a few days later nearly 100 Iraqis were killed in two separate attacks against the Iraqi police and army in Iskandariya and Baghdad, respectively. The identity of the assailants was unclear, but it now appeared that the insurgents regarded as legitimate targets those Iraqis working with or directly for the coalition forces.

Fears that the insurgents sought to provoke sectarian violence in Iraq appeared to be realized in early March when a series of bombs exploded among crowds of Shi'ites who had gathered in Baghdad and Karbala to celebrate the festival of Ashoura. More than 180 people were killed and a further 550 injured in the blasts, and although al-Qa'ida purportedly issued a statement denying involvement, the CPA claimed that a Jordanian national, Abu Musab az-Zarqawi, believed to have ties with al-Qa'ida, was responsible for the bombings and was also the mastermind behind the majority of attacks on coalition and civilian targets in Iraq. The bombings had the additional effect of delaying the signing of the interim constitution.

According to the timetable outlining the transferral of power published on 15 November 2003, the Governing Council had been scheduled to agree on an interim constitution (to take effect from 30 June 2004) by 28 February 2004. However, delays in producing the draft constitution were largely ascribed to objections from Shi'ite members of the Governing Council, who argued that Islam should be the only source of law and who were opposed to Kurdish being recognized as an official language. Negotiations on the proposed interim constitution were postponed due to the Ashoura bombings, and after meeting Ayatollah as-Sistani on 7 March the Shi'ite members dropped their opposition to the document. The Transitional Administrative Law (TAL) was signed by the Governing Council on 8 March; most notably, it outlined a new timetable for the establishment of a permanent legislature and sovereign government (see Government, below), which superseded that previously outlined by the agreement of 15 November 2003. This development was interpreted as evidence of as-Sistani's growing influence on the political process: in particular, plans to elect a transitional national assembly by regional caucuses were abandoned and replaced by proposals to hold national elections to an interim legislature, probably leading to a political settlement that would favour Iraq's Shi'ite majority.

In May 2004 the Independent Electoral Commission of Iraq (IECI) was formed by the CPA to organize elections to a 275-member Transitional National Assembly (TNA), to be held by 31 January 2005. Voter registration for the polls began in November 2004, when the election date of 30 January 2005 was announced. Seats within the TNA were to be allocated on the basis of proportional representation. Key functions of the TNA were to be to draft, by 15 August 2005, a permanent constitution, to be submitted to a popular referendum by 15 October; and to elect a President and two Vice-Presidents, together constituting a state Presidency Council, responsible for appointing a Prime Minister and cabinet. Under the timetable for Iraq's political transition, constitutionally elected organs of government were to be installed by 15 December 2005. Voting for the TNA was to be held simultaneously with elections to 18 provincial assemblies and to a new Iraqi Kurdistan National Assembly. A group of 15 primarily Sunni and secular Iraqi political parties, along with the two principal Kurdish factions, the PUK and the KDP, subsequently signed a manifesto demanding that the Interim Government hold the elections at least six months later than scheduled, in order to ensure that they would take place in a secure environment. In early December 2004 the two main Kurdish parties further attempted to increase their chances of success in the ballot, when they announced that they had agreed to contest the polls, and to operate in the interim legislature, on a joint list, the Kurdistan Alliance List. Subsequently, major Shi'ite groups, backed by as-Sistani, announced that they too would be campaigning on a shared list of 228 candidates, to be known as the United Iraqi Alliance (UIA). In late December, after failing to secure a delay in the holding of the ballot, the Sunni Iraqi Islamic Party (IIP—al-Hizb al-Islami al-'Iraqi) withdrew from the campaign, advocating, together with various Sunni clerics and groups, a boycott of the polls.

In March 2004 Bremer announced the re-establishment of the Ministry of Defence. Meanwhile, the CPA closed down the Baghdad newspaper *Al-Hawza an-Natiqa* for allegedly inciting violence against the US-led coalition. The newspaper was closely associated with Hojatoleslam Muqtada as-Sadr, a Shi'ite cleric whose father had been assassinated by the previous regime in February 1999 (see above), and who, a suspect in the murder of a moderate Shi'ite cleric in Najaf in 2003, had become the coalition's most vocal opponent. Several of the cleric's supporters had formed a militia known as the 'Mahdi Army', and protests outside the newspaper offices were the precursor to a nation-wide upsurge in violence against coalition forces. After four US private security contractors were killed in an ambush in the

Sunni-dominated town of Fallujah, to the west of Baghdad in Al-Anbar (Anbar) province, in early April 2004, US forces surrounded and effectively blockaded the town; around 450 Iraqis (including many civilians) and 40 US soldiers died in the ensuing violence. Two members of the interim Cabinet, Minister of Human Rights Abd al-Basit Turki and Minister of the Interior Nuri al-Badran, resigned in protest against the coalition's response to the militant violence. In mid-April a senior Iranian diplomat was killed by unidentified gunmen in Baghdad, while a series of bombings later in that month resulted in a large number of civilian deaths in Basra.

Meanwhile, in late April 2004 the UN Security Council adopted Resolution 1538, beginning an investigation into allegations by the US General Accounting Office that Saddam Hussain had obtained US $4,400m. in bribes and $5,700m. in petroleum smuggled through neighbouring countries during the now discontinued UN oil-for-food programme (see above). In January 2005 an independent investigation commission appointed by the UN Secretary-General estimated the total amount of money involved to be $21,300m. In February the commission reported that Benon Sevan, the Executive Director of the programme, had negotiated undisclosed oil contracts with Saddam Hussain's regime, failed to tell the truth to investigators and had given no explanation for large cash payments to his personal account. The report also accused the former UN Secretary-General, Boutros Boutros-Ghali, of disregarding UN rules in order to guarantee that a French bank won the contract to oversee oil sales.

Another scandal developed in late April 2004, when photographs taken by US guards of US soldiers coercing Iraqi prisoners into performing degrading sexual acts and other humiliating activities were broadcast world-wide. One soldier received a 10-year gaol sentence in mid-January 2005 in connection with the abuse of prisoners at the Abu Ghraib prison, west of Baghdad, while other officers received lesser sentences for their involvement. Meanwhile, three British soldiers were accused of abusing Iraqi prisoners (who had been detained for alleged looting offences in Basra in May 2003) when a collection of 22 photographs purportedly constituting evidence of the mistreatment was released. One soldier who had taken the photographs received an 18-month gaol sentence later in January 2005, while in February, at a separate trial, the soldiers accused of the abuse were discharged from the army and sentenced to prison terms of between five months and two years.

In mid-May 2004 Sunni insurgents in central Baghdad assassinated the President of the Governing Council, Izzadine Salim, who was replaced by the Sunni Sheikh Ghazi Mashal Ajil al-Yawar. The INA Secretary-General, Dr Ayad Allawi, was appointed interim Prime Minister of Iraq in late May, and in early June it was announced that Ghazi al-Yawar had been appointed President in the Interim Government, to which power was to be transferred from the CPA on 30 June. On 8 June the UN Security Council unanimously approved Resolution 1546, which formally recognized the forthcoming transfer of sovereignty from the CPA to the Interim Government. However, following an increase in the number of insurgent attacks, and the kidnapping and killing of foreign workers, the date for the granting of sovereignty to the Interim Government was secretly moved forward to 28 June, in order to prevent a major insurgent assault. A low-key ceremony was held in Baghdad, and hours later Paul Bremer left Iraq; the CPA and the Governing Council were both dissolved. Around 140,000 US soldiers remained in Iraq following the handover of power. In August delegates to a national conference in Baghdad declared the appointment of a 100-member transitional national council that was to govern Iraq in conjunction with the Interim Government until the January 2005 elections. The transitional council was given the authority to veto proposed legislation, appoint a new President or Prime Minister in the event of either position becoming vacant, and approve the 2005 budget.

The US military had, in April 2004, arranged for an Iraqi security force, led by one of Saddam Hussain's ex-generals, to replace the US Marine Corps in Fallujah; this initially resulted in a significant decrease in the level of fighting. The CPA's decision to re-employ members of the former Baathist security forces was an important development. However, in May coalition forces launched major assaults against Muqtada as-Sadr's Mahdi Army, and particularly heavy fighting was reported in Sadr City (a predominantly Shi'a suburb of Baghdad previously known as Saddam City), Karbala, Najaf, and in Kufa, to the east of Najaf. In June nine of Iraq's leading political factions reached agreement with Dr Allawi to disband their militias by January 2005. According to the agreement, some 100,000 fighters (but excluding members of the Mahdi Army) would join the security forces or return to civilian life. Meanwhile, US forces reached an accommodation with as-Sadr to end his insurgency, without pressuring him to reduce his military, and in July 2004 the ban on the newspaper Al-Hawza an-Natiqa was lifted. However, a Sunni uprising in Najaf, where the Mahdi Army seized the Imam Ali Mosque, and in other southern cities from early August, led to renewed fighting, with almost 80 people reported killed in a single 24-hour period in late August. Ayatollah as-Sistani ordered Iraqi Shi'ites to descend upon Najaf to end the fighting there. Thousands of people accompanied him as he entered the city, where he negotiated a cease-fire with as-Sadr, including an end to the siege of the mosque. It was reported the same day that almost 100 people had died in a 24-hour period in Najaf and in Kufa, where some 27 Iraqis preparing to march on Najaf were killed. Although the plan stipulated that US troops were to withdraw from both cities, which were to be designated weapons-free zones, the local and national authorities requested that US forces stay in Najaf. A cease-fire in Sadr City lasted only a week after talks with interim Prime Minister Ayad Allawi failed to negotiate a permanent agreement. Meanwhile, Abu Musab az-Zarqawi had declared that he had managed a spate of co-ordinated attacks across Iraq in June, including five car bomb explosions in Mosul which had killed about 100 people. In July the Interim Government introduced new legislation granting it wider powers to control the insurgency by enabling the Prime Minister to declare a state of emergency for periods of up to 60 days. The death penalty was reintroduced for certain crimes in August, having been suspended by the CPA following the US-led invasion.

As-Sadr's Mahdi Army announced a cease-fire in October 2004 and stated that they would begin to disarm, provided that the Interim Government released all the army's prisoners, and agreed not to arrest or harm any of its supporters. An incident of particular concern for the security of coalition forces in Iraq was the penetration of and attack on Baghdad's 'Green Zone'—a complex with about 10,000 residents where a high level of security is maintained, and which contains the headquarters of the Interim Government and the US and British embassies—in mid-October; at least 10 people, including four US civilians, were killed by two suicide bombers. Az-Zarqawi's group, which had recently named itself Tanzim Qa'idat al-Jihad fi Bilad ar-Rafidain (Base of Holy War in Mesopotamia, also known as al-Qa'ida in Iraq), asserted that it had been the mastermind behind the attack, and also claimed responsibility for the killing in late October of 49 unarmed National Guard soldiers in Diala province, near the Iranian border. It was estimated later in the month that 100,000 Iraqi civilians had died in the period since the US-led invasion, principally as a result of air-strikes by coalition forces.

Allawi declared a 60-day state of emergency in early November 2004, closing Baghdad airport and imposing martial law across most of the country as an estimated 15,000 US troops and 3,000 Iraqi troops descended upon Fallujah, which was still dominated by insurgents. Rebels killed at least 37 people across the country as forces prepared for the military assault. Meanwhile, in Samarra co-ordinated bomb and mortar attacks killed at least 30 people, many of them police officers, and there was also a marked increase in insurgent attacks in mid-November in Mosul, where as many as 50 rebels captured 10 police stations in the city centre and police officers were reported to have supported the insurgents; US and Iraqi forces entered the city and took control of the police stations, but Mosul continued to experience insurgent attacks. By mid-November US troops claimed to be in absolute control of Fallujah, having killed an estimated 1,200 insurgents, with losses of a reported 38 US and six Iraqi military. (In November 2005 the US Administration admitted that white phosphorus, a substance classified by some as a chemical weapon, had been used in the assault on Fallujah, further damaging the public image of US forces in Iraq.) In early December around 30 people were killed in Baghdad when rebels raided a police station and bombed a Shi'a mosque; az-Zarqawi's group declared that it had carried out the attacks. It was reported at this time that 1,000 US soldiers had been killed in action in Iraq since the March 2003 invasion. On 15 December 2004, the first day of campaigning for the elections scheduled for January 2005, seven people were killed and 30 people, including a senior aide to as-Sistani, were injured in Karbala in an assassination attempt on the cleric. Four days later suicide car bomb attacks killed at least 62 people in Karbala and Najaf. In late December 22 soldiers were killed at a US military base near Mosul, and around 50 people, about one-half of whom were police officers, were killed in a spate of attacks in Sunni areas around Baghdad.

In early January 2005 insurgents killed 18 Iraqi national guardsmen and one civilian in a suicide car bomb attack in Balad. Two days later the Governor of Baghdad province was assassinated. The number of insurgents at this time was estimated at 200,000, greater than the number of coalition troops and many more than had previously been estimated, and the state of emergency imposed in November 2004 was extended for another month. Suicide bombers killed 25 people at a Baghdad mosque and at a Shi'ite wedding party in mid-January 2005, ending a week in which almost 100 people had died. In response to the growing violence, and, specifically, to a militant group's murder of 15 Iraqi soldiers that it had been holding hostage, the Interim Government again closed Baghdad airport and imposed a strict curfew in advance of the legislative elections scheduled for later that month. Az-Zarqawi, who had castigated Shi'ites for assisting the occupying forces, vowed in the week before the poll to launch a violent battle against the elections. Meanwhile, fighters opposed to both the US-led occupation and the elections killed a senior judge and his son, as well as several police officers, and attacked polling stations and the offices of political organizations. Five days before the scheduled ballot 37 US troops were killed—the highest single death toll for US forces since March 2003. In advance of the elections more than 100,000 Iraqi police and soldiers provided tight security in an attempt to forestall insurgent attacks, and the Interim Government closed Iraq's borders and imposed a vehicle curfew.

Yet despite appeals for a boycott by some, especially Sunni, political groups, insurgents' threats to attack citizens intending to vote, and the general acceptance that some areas of the country were too dangerous for secure polls to be held, legislative elections took place as scheduled on 30 January 2005. At least 44 people died in opposition attacks across the country, although the level of violence was in fact lower than had been widely predicted. In the elections to the TNA, the UIA took 47.6% of the total votes, winning 140 of the 275 seats, the Kurdistan Alliance List won 75 seats (with 25.4% of the votes) and the Iraqi List, a bloc led by Dr Allawi, came third, securing 40 seats (with 13.6% of the votes); nine other parties achieved representation in the interim legislature. The rate of participation was put at some 58% of the registered electorate. Voting for the TNA was held simultaneously with elections to 18 provincial assemblies and to a new Iraqi Kurdistan National Assembly, where the Kurdistan Democratic List won 104 of the 111 seats.

In early February 2005 a prominent grouping of Iraqi Sunni clerics, the Association of Muslim Scholars (Hayat al-Ulama al-Muslimin), which had urged a Sunni boycott of the elections, declared the results of the polls illegitimate, asserting that the elected Iraqi transitional government would not represent the will of the people owing to the boycott of the ballot by a number of different sects and political parties, and that the group would therefore consider the government's authority, including its power to draft a constitution, to be restricted. Meanwhile, in what was widely conceived to be an attempt to further aggravate the division between Shi'ite and Sunni communities, militants killed over 30 people as Shi'ites celebrated one of their holy days, Ashoura, in mid-February. At the end of the month some 125 people died as the result of a massive suicide bombing in Hillah.

The legislative elections were followed by protracted negotiations over the formation of the transitional government. Eventually, on 6 April 2005 the TNA voted to appoint Jalal Talabani, the leader of the PUK, to the post of President. A Sunni, Ghazi al-Yawar (previously the President of the Interim Government), and a Shi'a, Adil Abd al-Mahdi (the Minister of Finance in the interim administration), were appointed Vice-Presidents. The three, together constituting a state Presidency Council, were sworn in on 7 April, whereupon they appointed Ibrahim al-Ja'fari (a leading member of the Islamic Dawa Party, and a Vice-President in the Interim Government) to the post of Prime Minister. On 28 April the TNA overwhelmingly approved al-Ja'fari's proposed new Council of Ministers, members of which were sworn in on 3 May. However, in large part owing to disagreements regarding the level of ministerial representation for Sunnis, seven posts remained unallocated, including those of defence (which was to be assumed on an interim basis by al-Ja'fari), oil (temporarily allocated to Deputy Prime Minister Ahmad Chalabi) and human rights (to be adopted by the Minister of the Environment, Narmin Othman Hassan, on an acting basis). Six of the seven vacancies were filled later in May, when Saadoun ad-Dulaimi, a Sunni Arab, was appointed Minister of Defence, while the important oil portfolio was awarded to Dr Ibrahim Bahr al-Ulum, a Shi'a. However, the nominee to the post of Minister of Human Rights, Hashim ash-Shible, declined to accept the post, which was retained temporarily by Othman Hassan. On 12 June the Iraqi Kurdistan National Assembly voted unanimously to appoint Masoud Barzani, leader of the KDP, to the post of President of the Kurdish Autonomous Region.

The incidence of violent attacks in Iraq increased in tandem with the formation of the new Transitional Government. In mid-April 2005 insurgents executed 19 Iraqi soldiers at a stadium in Haditha, west of Baghdad, while 57 bodies, believed to be those of hostages, were recovered from the Tigris river. On 27 April a female member of the TNA, Lame'a Abed Khadawi, was assassinated. On 29 April, the day after the Council of Ministers had been approved by the TNA, at least 50 people were killed in bomb attacks across the country, while on 4 May a suicide bomb attack in a queue at a police recruitment centre in Arbil killed a further 50 people. In the fortnight following the approval of the new Government, at least 370 people were thought to have been killed in various insurgent attacks across the country, while estimates for May put the number of casualties close to 700. In June the US military launched a major offensive centred on the town of Karabila, near the Syrian border, with the intention of disrupting the flow of fighters, supplies and money to the insurgency from across the border. Meanwhile, fears of sectarian tension were exacerbated when az-Zarqawi announced that he would form a special unit, the Omar Brigade, specifically in order to target the Badr Organization, the armed faction of SCIRI, which had been founded in Tehran in 1983 as the Badr Brigade but was renamed upon its relocation to Iraq following the overthrow of the Baathist regime. In a major suicide bomb attack in July 2005, some 98 people were killed at a marketplace in Musayyib, south of Baghdad. It appeared increasingly that large areas of the country were beyond the control of the central Government and coalition forces. One prominent example was the western town of Haditha, reportedly administered by Sunni insurgents according to strict Islamic law, where 14 US marines were killed by a roadside bomb in early August. On 31 August almost 1,000 people were estimated to have died in a stampede on a bridge in Baghdad during a Shi'ite religious festival. The stampede was thought to have started after rumours of the presence of suicide bombers spread through the crowd of pilgrims walking to the Qadimiya Mosque.

Meanwhile, the transitional administration was engaged in negotiations to draw up an Iraqi constitution. Under the schedule outlined by the TAL, a draft document was to be agreed by a constitutional committee and submitted to the TNA for approval by 15 August 2005, in order to be put to a nation-wide referendum by 15 October. Although their boycott of the January 2005 elections proportionally gave the Sunnis a very minor representation on the constitutional committee, this was increased in an attempt to reach an agreeable consensus. Significant points of disagreement included: the degree of federalism to be incorporated into the new state; the distribution of oil revenue; the question of 'de-Baathification' of the official sphere; and the role of Islam as a source of legislation. The agreed deadline was twice missed, largely because of Sunni objections on these key issues, before a final text could be submitted to the TNA for approval on 28 August. Violence was reported in late August between the Mahdi Army and the Badr Organization, apparently reflecting disagreement among Shi'ites over the federalist provisions in the proposed Constitution. The text was subsequently submitted to the UN on 14 September. That same day a series of car bombings in Baghdad caused the deaths of some 150 people. Az-Zarqawi's al-Qa'ida in Iraq organization claimed responsibility for the attacks, describing them as revenge for a joint US-Iraqi assault on Sunni fighters in the northern town of Tal Afar and announcing a 'declaration of war' against Iraq's Shi'ite population. In the run-up to the scheduled referendum on the Constitution, some Sunni groups, including the Association of Muslim Scholars, campaigned for a rejection of the text. The IIP, however, urged Sunnis to vote in favour of ratification, after negotiating a late change to the text enabling further amendments to be made once a permanent government had been formed. Ayatollah Ali as-Sistani, meanwhile, encouraged Shi'ites to support the Constitution. Under the TAL, the text was to be rejected if two-thirds of voters in three or more provinces voted against it: in the event, in the vote on 15 October the two-thirds' threshold was surpassed in only two provinces—Salah ad-Din and al-Anbar—and consequently the Constitution was ratified with the support of 78.6% of votes cast.

The trial of former Iraqi President Saddam Hussain began on 19 October 2005, and was conducted by the new Supreme Iraqi Criminal Tribunal—the body that replaced the Iraqi Special Tribune established by the CPA in December 2003 to adjudicate crimes against humanity committed under the Baathist regime. Together with his seven co-defendants, Hussain was charged with organizing the killing of 148 Shi'ites in the town of Ad-Dujail, where he had survived an assassination attempt in 1982. All eight defendants pleaded not guilty to the charges. After a day's proceedings the trial was adjourned until late November 2005, by which time two defence lawyers had been killed. In January 2006 the appointment of a Kurd from Halabja (where chemical weapons had been employed against the population by Saddam Hussain's Government in 1988—see above) as the new presiding judge compounded the objections of the defence team that the trial was incapable of impartiality. (For further details regarding the Dujail trial, see below.)

In October 2005 the toll of fatalities suffered by the US military since the invasion of Iraq passed 2,000. In November US troops discovered more than 170 prisoners, many malnourished and showing signs of torture, in the basement of the Shi'ite-dominated Ministry of the Interior. The IIP, with the support of the USA, demanded an inquiry into the practices of the Ministry's officials. In January 2006 some 28 people were killed in a suicide bomb attack on the Ministry of the Interior, which al-Qa'ida in Iraq announced it had carried out in revenge for the maltreatment of Sunni prisoners.

Following the approval of the Constitution, several Sunni groups that had boycotted the elections of January 2005 decided that it would be in their interests to participate in the elections to the first permanent Council of Representatives, which were now scheduled to be held on 15 December 2005. Three major Sunni groups—the IIP, the General Council for the People of Iraq and the Iraqi National Dialogue Council—formed the Iraqi Accord Front (IAF—Jabhat at-Tawafuq al-Iraqiya) in October 2005, in a bid to engage the Sunni population in the political process. Another Sunni coalition, the Iraqi Front for National Dialogue (Hewar National Iraqi Front), was formed from parties that declined to join the IAF in protest at the IIP's acceptance of the Constitution. Meanwhile, the UIA announced a 17-party list dominated once more by Shi'ites, including supporters of as-Sadr alongside the Islamic Dawa Party, SCIRI and other groups. However, the INC, which had been transformed since the removal of Saddam Hussain's regime from a multi-party coalition into a political party headed by Ahmad Chalabi, declined to run on the UIA list, creating instead a coalition of its own, the National Congress Coalition. In contrast to his support of the UIA in January, Ayatollah as-Sistani indicated his neutrality in the elections, encouraging Shi'ites to participate but to follow their own judgement. Former Prime Minister Ayad Allawi established a secular coalition, the Iraqi National List (INL), including his own INA, the Iraqis party of Ghazi al-Yawar and the ICP, while the PUK and the KDP maintained their co-operation at the centre of the Kurdistan Alliance List. Voting occurred as scheduled on 15 December, with minor disruptions from violence; turn-out was evaluated at around 70% of the electorate. The publication of the final results of the election was delayed while the IECI investigated several complaints of electoral fraud, none of which were, in the event, deemed significant enough to affect the outcome. The final results, released on 10 February 2006, gave the UIA 41.2% of votes cast and 128 of the Council's 275 seats, slightly less than an overall majority. The Kurdistan Alliance List secured 53 seats with 21.7% of votes cast, while the IAF won 15.1% of the vote and 44 seats. Allawi's INL won 25 seats, and 11 seats were allocated to the Iraqi Front for National Dialogue. (Chalabi's coalition failed to win a seat.)

In January 2006 a tripling of petroleum prices, caused by the reduction of government subsidies, led to sporadically violent demonstrations and the temporary resignation of the Minister of Oil, Dr al-Ulum, who was replaced for a short period by Chalabi. On 22 February, while negotiations were ongoing over the composition of the new government, two bombs were exploded inside the al-Askari Mosque (or Golden Mosque) in Samarra, destroying the dome of one of the holiest Shi'ite shrines in Iraq. The attack on the mosque caused a sharp increase in sectarian violence across the country, which resulted in the deaths of at least 300 people within a week, according to official sources, although independent media reports suggested that more than 1,000 had died. Sunni mosques were destroyed or damaged in retaliatory attacks, while curfews were extended in Baghdad and elsewhere. Following the upsurge in violence, Kurdish, Sunni and secular factions increased their opposition to the continued premiership of al-Ja'fari, who had narrowly won the nomination of the UIA to the post of Prime Minister in the new government in February. Sunnis criticized the administration's failure to control the violence, while Kurds, including President Talabani, voiced their disapproval concerning al-Ja'fari's decision to visit Turkey in late February without consulting other members of the administration. Over 60 people were killed in a series of bomb attacks in Sadr City on 12 March, while some 85 bodies were reportedly discovered the following day by Iraqi police in various parts of Baghdad, apparently the victims of increasingly common execution-style killings by sectarian 'death squads'. The Council of Representatives eventually convened for the first time in Baghdad's 'Green Zone' on 16 March. On the same day US and Iraqi forces launched a major offensive targeting villages north of Samarra, involving reportedly the largest single deployment of air power since the US-led invasion of Iraq in March 2003.

By April 2006 many Arab politicians—including the Egyptian President and the Saudi Minister of Foreign Affairs—were warning that civil war in Iraq was, if not already occurring, at the least imminent. On 7 April three suicide bombers detonated their explosives in an important Shi'ite mosque owned by SCIRI in northern Baghdad. Although reports of the number of deaths varied, it was believed that at least 71 people were killed. Seeking to resolve the impasse in negotiations over the new government, on 20 April al-Ja'fari withdrew his candidacy for the post of Prime Minister. The following day the UIA nominated Nuri Kamal (Jawad) al-Maliki, another prominent member of the Islamic Dawa Party, as their replacement candidate, a compromise apparently accepted by Sunni and Kurdish factions. At the second session of the Council of Representatives on 22 April President Talabani was elected for a second term; two Vice-Presidents, Tareq al-Hashimi of the IIP and incumbent Adil Abd al-Mahdi, were also appointed, and Mahmoud al-Mashhadani was chosen as the chamber's Speaker. Talabani subsequently invited al-Maliki to form a permanent government within 30 days. Meanwhile, a new Kurdish regional government, led by the President of the Kurdish Autonomous Region and KDP leader, Masoud Barzani, assumed office on 7 May; the new administration represented the Kurdish region's first unified Cabinet.

The various parties continued to wrangle over the formation of the new Iraqi administration during May 2006, with each pressing for their own ethnic and sectarian interests. On 12 May the Islamic Virtue Party (one of the smaller parties in the Shi'a alliance) announced that it was withdrawing from the negotiations altogether. However, finally on 20 May the Council of Representatives approved a list of ministerial nominees submitted by Prime Minister-designate al-Maliki and the Council of Ministers was sworn into office. This Government of national unity represented the first permanent Iraqi Government to hold office since the removal of the regime of Saddam Hussain in 2003, and it constituted the first administration since that date to include the principal Sunni factions. However, the portfolios of the interior and defence, each the subject of particular dispute during the protracted negotiations, remained unfilled; Prime Minister al-Maliki assumed the interior portfolio on an interim basis, while Deputy Prime Minister Salam az-Zubaie was to serve as acting Minister of Defence. The appointment of a permanent Minister of State for National Security Affairs was also deferred, the position being filled temporarily by the Deputy Prime Minister, Dr Barham Salih, hitherto Minister of Planning and Development Co-operation. Four other members of the outgoing Transitional Government—including Minister of Foreign Affairs Hoshyar az-Zibari and Minister of the Environment Narmin Uthman—remained in post, while former Minister of the Interior Baqir Sulagh (Bayan) Jabr az-Zubeidi was transferred to the Ministry of Finance. Dr Hussain ash-Shahristani (an independent Shi'a member of the UIA) became Minister of Oil. In all, the new Council of Ministers included 20 Shi'a, eight Kurds, eight Sunni Arabs and one Christian; four of its 37 members were women. Of the 275 seats in the Council of Representatives, the Government—composed principally of the UIA, the Kurdish Alliance, the IAF and the INL—plus three smaller parties, controlled 240. On 8 June 2006 the Council of Representatives approved al-Maliki's nominations for three key positions: Lt-Gen. Abd al-Qadir Muhammad Jasim Obeidi, a

Sunni who had served as a general in Saddam Hussain's armed forces, was appointed Minister of Defence; Jawad al-Bulani, a Shi'a, became Minister of the Interior; and Shirwan al-Waili, also a Shi'a, was named as Minister of State for National Security Affairs.

The security situation, however, remained a serious concern. At the end of May 2006 al-Maliki imposed a month-long state of emergency in Basra, in an effort to prevent a continuation of the violence perpetrated by militants and criminal gangs that had seen at least 100 people killed in that month alone. The new Government appeared initially to have been strengthened by reports on 7 June that Abu Musab az-Zarqawi, the leader of al-Qa'ida in Iraq, had been killed during a US air-strike close to the town of Baquba. None the less, fears remained that the death of such a prominent figure could lead to reprisals, and a curfew was imposed on Baghdad. It was claimed by the Ministry of Health the day before az-Zarqawi's death that almost 1,400 civilians had been killed in Baghdad the previous month. However, neither the curfew nor a massive security operation involving thousands of extra troops, imposed by al-Maliki's administration on 14 June, appeared to lessen the violence. The new strategy, code-named 'Operation Together Forward', was a joint offensive by Iraqi and US forces. Meanwhile, it was claimed that Abu Ayyub al-Masri, also known as Abu Hamza al-Muhajir, had been appointed to succeed az-Zarqawi as the leader of al-Qa'ida in Iraq. Al-Maliki also called for a dialogue with Sunni insurgents, and on 25 June announced a 'national reconciliation plan' offering an amnesty to members of certain militant groups who renounced violence and outlining plans to disarm the country's various militias.

Despite the new security measures, the violence perpetrated by both Sunni insurgents and Shi'a militias continued relentlessly. In early July 2006 a bomb in Sadr City killed at least 66 people, while eight days later Shi'a gunmen shot dead up to 50 people in a predominantly Sunni district of the capital. As the death toll continued to mount at a dramatic rate, al-Maliki admitted that he was dealing with a 'sectarian issue', but insisted that his country would not descend into civil war. By August President Talabani was vowing that Iraqi security forces would be in a position to take full control by the end of the year, and that his country would defeat terrorism. This view did not appear to be shared by the international community, however. A confidential memo to Prime Minister Tony Blair by the outgoing British ambassador to Iraq, William Patey, predicted the break-up of Iraq along ethnic lines, while the most senior US commander in the Middle East, Gen. John Abizaid, warned that Iraq could slide into civil war if the violence was not stemmed. To counter the influence of the predominantly Shi'a militias, Vice-President Tareq al-Hashimi was reported to be setting up his own unit of the National Guard, which would effectively act as his personal bodyguard and a Sunni militia.

Meanwhile, US armed forces on the streets of Baghdad, as part of a security plan to station up to 7,000 extra US troops in the capital, conducted street-by-street searches for insurgents. According to initial reports from both US and Iraqi officials, the new security initiative showed positive results, leading to a dramatic reduction in the number of killings in the capital. However, in September 2006 a more sombre assessment was provided by the Ministry of Health, which noted that more than 1,500 people had been killed in Baghdad during the previous month—almost three times the level that the Ministry had estimated the previous week. As the violence worsened, Ayatollah as-Sistani announced that he would no longer act as a political leader, warning his aides that he was powerless to prevent civil war. The continuing bloodshed was not enough, however, to prevent the formal handover of control of Iraq's armed forces from the US-led coalition to the Government of Prime Minister al-Maliki on 7 September (five days later than scheduled). First to be transferred to Iraqi control were the small air and naval forces, and one of Iraq's 10 army divisions, while other units were to be transferred during the coming months.

Also in September 2006 the Council of Representatives began to debate the controversial issue of federal devolution, which certain pessimistic analysts claimed might eventually lead to the dissolution of Iraq along ethnic lines. In the previous month Vice-President Adil Abd al-Mahdi had vowed to bring the issue of a federal Shi'a state before the legislature within two months, leading growing calls for Shi'a autonomy. The UIA, which submitted a draft federalism law to the Council of Representatives, stated that it favoured the division of Iraq into autonomous regions, thereby permitting the oil-rich Shi'a south to rule as an autonomous region along the lines of the Kurdish north. While Sunni politicians had previously opposed the move, fearing that it would leave them only with the resource-poor centre and west of the country, they now hinted that they might support the 'administrative application of federalism' so long as a strong central Government remained in place. By late September a compromise had emerged: a parliamentary committee was to be set up immediately to draft constitutional amendments to ensure that national oil revenues were shared fairly and to limit the potential of regions to secede from the central state. Moreover, the Council of Representatives agreed that any legislation on federalism could only be implemented after an 18-month delay. On 26 September both Kurdish and Shi'a legislators tabled federalism bills. The Kurdish bill (which showed the disputed, oil-rich city of Kirkuk as belonging to the Kurdish Autonomous Region) was rejected, but the Shi'a-proposed draft was given a first reading. The draft made provisions for Iraq's 18 provinces to hold referendums on whether they wanted to merge with neighbouring areas, thus forming larger areas with powers of self-rule. Legislators were given until 22 October to resolve the issue. In the event, a law was adopted by the Council of Representatives on 11 October; while the vote was unanimous, only 138 of the 275 legislators attended the session, the two largest Sunni blocs and two factions making up the Shi'a alliance having refused to attend.

In an effort to stem the continuing violence, in mid-September 2006 the Ministry of the Interior had announced plans to dig trenches around Baghdad and to surround the capital with checkpoints. A UN report issued later in the month showed that almost 3,600 civilians had been killed across the country in July, and 3,000 in August. According to the UN Assistance Mission for Iraq, the inability of the Government to reduce the violence and bring the perpetrators to justice risked fuelling the sectarian conflict. In late September British and Iraqi forces operating in Basra initiated a campaign, 'Operation Sinbad', which was aimed at preventing the infiltration of some of the city's police units by Shi'a militants. In early October al-Maliki announced a further plan, the main provision of which was the establishment of local security committees to monitor the violence in their respective areas. Reports, however, suggested that the violence was worsening, with Sunni leaders from Anbar province, west of Baghdad, forming their own security forces. Many Iraqis were fleeing their homes and seeking refuge either in other parts of the country or in neighbouring states (see below). In late October Iraqi clerics from across the sectarian divide met in Mecca, Saudi Arabia, where they issued a *fatwa* (religious edict) describing the shedding of Muslim blood—whether Sunni or Shi'a—as forbidden. Days later a dispute emerged between al-Maliki and the US Administration: the Prime Minister vowed to tackle the militias, but insisted that he was not working to a timetable imposed by Washington. (Al-Maliki's reputation had recently been damaged by accusations that he was unwilling to confront Shi'a militias such as the Mahdi Army.)

The trial of Saddam Hussain and seven co-defendants accused of involvement in the murder of 148 Iraqi Shi'a in Dujail in 1982 (see above) continued in 2006, albeit marred by numerous setbacks. In January the former Iraqi President staged a boycott of the trial in protest against the removal from the court of one of his defence lawyers; however, having been returned forcibly to the hearings, in March he commenced his formal defence. In June one of Saddam Hussain's lawyers was murdered, becoming the third defence lawyer to be killed since the start of trial proceedings. In response to what they claimed was inadequate security for his legal team, in early July the deposed Iraqi leader and three co-defendants began a hunger strike and boycotted the proceedings, but Hussain was again returned to the courtroom later that month. On 5 November Saddam Hussain and two of his co-defendants—Awad Hamed al-Bandar (former head of the Revolutionary Court under the Baathist regime) and Barzan Ibrahim at-Tikriti (half-brother of the former President)—were found guilty of crimes against humanity in connection with the killing of the 148 Shi'a, and were sentenced to death. Former Vice-President Taha Yassin Ramadan was sentenced to life imprisonment, while three others received 15-year custodial sentences; one defendant was acquitted owing to a lack of evidence. The verdict provoked a combination of rage and jubilation in Iraq, with thousands defying a curfew to express publicly either their support for Hussain or to celebrate the verdict. Nevertheless, many commentators questioned the impartiality of the trial, with the US-based Human Rights Watch warning that it had been so flawed that the verdict should be considered unsound. After Saddam Hussain's lawyers complained that he had been prevented from filing the necessary papers, an appeal against the verdict was eventually lodged in December, just two days before the expiry of the month-long deadline.

In mid-November 2006 at least 100 employees were reportedly abducted from a research institute owned by the Ministry of Higher Education and Scientific Research in central Baghdad. News reports suggested that the kidnappings had been carried out by militias wearing uniforms designed for police commandos; however, the reports disagreed as to whether those captured were both Sunni and Shi'a, or were in fact exclusively Sunni. Although many of the hostages were believed to have been freed quickly, the Minister of Higher Education and Scientific Research, Dr Abd ad-Dhiab Ajili, voiced concerns that some had been tortured and killed, and announced that he would suspend co-operation with the Government until all those abducted were released. A few days later Ajili claimed that some 70 captives had been released, but that they had been seriously beaten. In late November a series of apparently co-ordinated car bombs and mortar rounds exploded in Sadr City; these were followed by mortar attacks on Sunni areas of the capital. At least 215 people were reported to have died in what was described as one of the worst terrorist attacks since the US-led invasion. Prime Minister al-Maliki, who was scheduled to meet US President Bush in Jordan to discuss the security situation in Iraq, imposed an indefinite curfew in the capital, while urging all sides to exercise restraint. However, the killings continued, prompting a group led by Shi'a cleric Muqtada as-Sadr to threaten withdrawal from the unity Government, in which his followers held six cabinet posts. This threat was carried out when al-Maliki flew to the Jordanian capital, Amman, for discussions with President Bush, a move that as-Sadr's group described as 'a provocation to the Iraqi people and a violation of their constitutional rights'. The talks took place against a backdrop of reports that the US cross-party Iraq Study Group was preparing to recommend a withdrawal of US troops from Iraq and direct discussions with both Syria and Iran. UN Secretary-General Kofi Annan, meanwhile, conceded publicly that Iraq was 'on the brink of civil war'.

The publication of the Iraq Study Group report on 6 December 2006 appeared to herald a change in US policy towards Iraq. This was precipitated partly by the resounding defeat of the Republican Party in US mid-term elections held the previous month, and the subsequent resignation of Donald Rumsfeld as Secretary of Defense. In its report, the panel demanded 'urgent action', warning that Iraq was sliding towards chaos. Rather than conducting a combat mission, the report recommended, US troops should be used to train Iraqis; it also rejected the idea of a massive increase in troop numbers. The report, which was welcomed by many within the Iraqi Government (although not by President Talabani or the leaders of Iraqi Kurdistan), also called for direct dialogue on Iraq's future with Syria and Iran. President Bush's reaction to the report, however, was cautious; while he promised to 'seriously consider' the report's recommendation, he appeared to rule out unconditional dialogue with Iraq's neighbours and phasing out the US combat role in Iraq.

A double suicide bomb attack in Baghdad on 12 December 2006 resulted in at least 71 deaths. This latest attack came at a time when Iraqi politicians were reportedly attempting to isolate as-Sadr, whose Mahdi Army Sunni politicians continued to accuse of perpertrating much of the sectarian violence. News reports in December suggested that a number of Shi'a, Kurdish and Sunni politicians were hoping to form a new alliance, although Prime Minister al-Maliki was said to be undecided as to whether or not he would join the bloc, believing that isolating as-Sadr could be counter-productive. A report published by the US Department of Defense in that month named the Mahdi Army as the single largest threat to Iraq's security, while also pointing to an increase in violence, with an average of 959 attacks each week on troops and civilians between August and November. This continued violence was highlighted on 18 December when militia forces kidnapped up to 30 Red Crescent officials from the aid organization's offices in Baghdad, prompting the Red Crescent to suspend its operations in the Iraqi capital. Meanwhile, al-Maliki issued a call to former members of Saddam Hussain's Baathist armed forces to return, in an apparent effort to appease members of the Sunni community.

Saddam Hussain was executed by hanging on 30 December 2006, following the rejection, on 26 December, of his appeal against the death sentence imposed by the Supreme Iraqi Criminal Tribunal in November. The execution provoked a mixed reaction, with condemnation from some unexpected quarters. Most contentious was the manner of his killing: news reports apparently revealed that the former Iraqi President had been taunted by onlookers as he approached the gallows, and that his execution had been filmed on a mobile telephone, resulting in footage of the event soon appearing on the internet. Fearing a rise in sectarian violence as a result of this development, the Iraqi Government immediately launched an investigation into the circumstances of Saddam Hussain's execution. While some in Iraq celebrated the death of the deposed leader, Baathist loyalists vowed revenge. Many Sunnis described Saddam Hussain as a martyr and protested against the hanging in Baghdad, Samarra and his hometown of Tikrit. A statement issued by the Baath Party at the start of January 2007 named Deputy Secretary-General Izzat Ibrahim ad-Douri as its new Secretary-General. In mid-January Saddam Hussain's two aides, al-Bandar and at-Tikriti, were also hanged, including his half-brother Barzan at-Tikriti, who was accidentally decapitated. The hangings came despite protests from the UN and appeals from President Talabani for the executions to be delayed. In March former Vice-President Ramadan was also executed, after the Court of Appeal had decided that his sentence of life imprisonment was too lenient and recommended that the death sentence be imposed.

At the time of Saddam Hussain's death, trial proceedings (initiated in August 2006) were ongoing against the former President and six co-defendants on charges of genocide and crimes against humanity in relation to an offensive in the Anfal region (code-named 'Operation Anfal') during 1987–88 in which, according to the prosecution, more than 180,000 Iraqi Kurds were killed. Following the passage of the death sentence against Saddam Hussain, it had initially been hoped that a verdict on these charges could be reached prior to his expected execution; however, when this trial resumed in early January 2007 the charges against the former Iraqi leader were abandoned. (As with the first trial, the Anfal trial was beset by difficulties, and in September 2006 the chief judge was replaced after having reportedly dismissed the allegation that Saddam Hussain had been a dictator.) In late June 2007 Gen. Ali Hassan al-Majid, a cousin of Saddam Hussain, was sentenced to death by the Supreme Iraqi Criminal Tribunal, having been convicted of genocide, war crimes and crimes against humanity for his role in 'Operation Anfal', when he was a regional commander of the Baath Party. Two of al-Majid's co-defendants, Gen. Sultan Hashim Ahmad al-Jabouri at-Tai and Hussein Rashid at-Tikriti, were handed down the same sentence, while a further two were sentenced to life imprisonment; the sixth defendant was acquitted owing to a lack of evidence. The three death sentences were upheld by an appeals court in early September; however, amid a legal dispute in the Iraqi leadership concerning who should sign the execution orders, the three men remained in US military detention in early 2008. The execution of al-Majid was finally approved by the Presidency Council at the end of February, but had not been carried out by late April, at which time al-Majid was reportedly hospitalized. In late August 2007, meanwhile, al-Majid was one of 15 former members of the Baathist regime to go on trial in relation to charges of involvement in the violent suppression of thousands of Shi'a rebels in southern Iraq following the Gulf conflict of 1990–91.

In 2007 there were growing fears concerning the large exodus of Iraqi citizens, both to neighbouring states and through displacement from one region of the country to another. According to UNHCR estimates, by September between 2.1m. and 2.5m. Iraqis had become refugees in neighbouring countries, notably Syria (1.2m.–1.4m.) and Jordan (500,000–750,000), while around 2.3m. Iraqis were displaced internally. (An estimated 1m. of these had been displaced before the 2003 conflict, and although a reported 300,000 Iraqis did return to their homes from Iran, Jordan, Lebanon and Saudi Arabia, among other countries, an increasing number were choosing to flee the violence.) UNHCR estimated in September 2007 that the number of internally displaced people (IDPs) had increased markedly in the aftermath of the sectarian violence precipitated by the bombing of the al-Askari Mosque in Samarra in February 2006; more than 1,043,900 new IDPs had been reported during that period. Moreover, displacement of Iraqis was thought to be continuing at a rate of up to 60,000 a month, with Syria, Jordan, Egypt and Lebanon hosting most of the refugees. Aid agencies, meanwhile, warned that neighbouring countries were closing their doors to Iraqis, with many countries imposing severe limitations on the number of refugees allowed to enter (see below). UNHCR also expressed concern in September 2007 regarding the estimated 13,000 Palestinian refugees who were believed to remain in Iraq, as well as the Christian and other minority communities.

About 50 suspected Sunni insurgents were said to have been killed on 9 January 2007 in the area of Baghdad's Haifa Street, which was attacked by US and Iraqi forces supported by helicopters and fighter jets. The battle took place just hours after Prime Minister al-Maliki had announced a new security plan for the capital, centred on the deployment of additional Iraqi forces, including Kurdish troops, with US backing. Sunni leaders denounced the plan as unconstitutional, noting that it had not been referred to the Council of Representatives for debate. The following day US President Bush confirmed that the USA would send an additional 21,000 troops to Iraq, while warning the Iraqi Government that it would be required to adhere to previously set benchmarks on controlling sectarian violence. Bush's new so-called 'surge' strategy also included the following provisions: the Iraqi Government was to appoint a new military commander for Baghdad; there was to be accelerated training of Iraqi security forces, leading to them being brought under Iraqi control by November 2007; provincial elections were to be held later that year; and increased diplomacy was to be sought with Iraq's neighbours, excluding Iran and Syria.

On 16 January 2007 Baghdad experienced more serious violence, when at least 70 people—most of them female students—were killed in a double bomb attack at the capital's Mustansiriyah University. Six days later more than 130 people were killed in and around Baghdad, including some 88 who were killed in a car bombing at a second-hand clothes market. None the less, the ending of the two-month political boycott by followers of as-Sadr (see above), appeared to suggest a greater unity among Iraq's Shi'a factions. The announcement that the boycott was to end came just a day before security forces claimed to have captured 600 members of as-Sadr's reportedly 60,000-strong Mahdi Army. In late January officials announced that some 300 militants had been killed in battles near Najaf. The insurgents were said to have been from a previously unknown group, calling themselves the Army of Heaven. Some news reports, however, disputed these claims, and asserted that those killed were innocent Shi'a pilgrims. In early February Iraq experienced its most deadly single bombing since the US-led invasion, with at least 130 people killed in a lorry bombing in a central Baghdad marketplace. It was thought that the attack was deliberately timed to coincide with the launch of the new Iraqi-US security initiative in the capital, known as 'Operation Law and Order' (or the Baghdad Security Plan). In the second week of February the first anniversary of the bombing of the Samarra shrine saw insurgents again launch a series of explosions in Baghdad, with at least 70 people being killed in Shorja market alone. Muqtada as-Sadr and several commanders of the Mahdi Army were reported at this time to have fled Iraq for the Iranian capital, in advance of the USA imposing tighter security measures in the country; however, supporters of the cleric denied such claims. The Iraqi authorities declared in mid-February that the borders with Iran and Syria were to be closed for a 72-hour period in an attempt to stem the alleged flow of insurgents from these neighbouring states. However, amid a series of bomb attacks across the country during March, in the first week more than 110 Shi'a pilgrims on their approach to Karbala were killed by insurgents in central Iraq. In late March the recently appointed UN Secretary-General, Ban Ki-Moon, was the apparent target of a mortar or rocket attack at the press conference he was attending in Baghdad; the Secretary-General was unhurt in the attack.

It was reported at the end of March 2007 that the Minister of Justice, Hashim ash-Shebli, had resigned, citing dissatisfaction over the manner in which the Government was being run and also differences with his party, the INL. (These were believed to concern the future status of Kirkuk, which the party does not wish to join the Kurdish Autonomous Region.) Ash-Shebli became the first cabinet minister to tender his resignation since the formation of the administration under Prime Minister al-Maliki in May 2006. However, in mid-April 2007 the six representatives of Muqtada as-Sadr's faction in the Council of Ministers also resigned their posts, in protest against al-Maliki's failure to agree a timetable for the withdrawal of coalition forces from Iraq. Four days prior to the resignations at least one Iraqi legislator was killed in a suicide bombing which exploded at a cafeteria inside the Council of Representatives building, adjacent to the heavily fortified 'Green Zone' in the centre of Baghdad. On the same day a further bombing by insurgents resulted in the deaths of at least 10 people, when one of the most strategically important bridges across the Tigris river in the Iraqi capital was destroyed.

An international conference to discuss reconstruction and security in Iraq was convened in the Egyptian resort of Sharm esh-Sheikh in early May 2007. At the conference, which was attended by the UN Secretary-General, a five-year framework for the country's future development, known as the International Compact with Iraq, was launched by Prime Minister al-Maliki (see Economic Affairs). In early June it was reported that a number of people had been killed as serious fighting broke out between rival Sunni insurgent groups in a western suburb of Baghdad. Indeed, by June it appeared that 'Operation Law and Order' was not achieving significant results in curbing sectarian violence in the capital. In mid-June suspected Sunni insurgents again targeted the al-Askari Mosque in Samarra, bombings against which had, in February 2006, precipitated the dramatic increase in Sunni–Shi'a violence; in this latest attack two minarets of the Shi'a shrine were destroyed by the militants. During July 2007 it was apparent that violence was intensifying in the north of the country, particularly in Kirkuk and the surrounding area, where vehicle bomb attacks resulted in a large number of fatalities. In one incident, the headquarters of the PUK were targeted, causing extensive damage to the building. While such bombings were clearly designed to influence any future decision regarding the status of Kirkuk (where tensions between the ethnic Kurdish, Arab and Turkmen communities were growing in advance of a proposed referendum—initially scheduled to be held by the end of 2007, but subsequently postponed for six months), many commentators noted that the recent tightening of security by joint Iraqi-US forces in Baghdad had led some insurgents to disperse to other parts of the country. Meanwhile, on 29 June 2007 the UN Security Council adopted Resolution 1762, which, *inter alia*, ended the mandate of UNMOVIC, on the grounds that Iraq's known weapons of mass destruction had now been rendered harmless and that the new Iraqi Government had declared itself to be in favour of non-proliferation.

The perilous state of the Iraqi administration was demonstrated on 1 August 2007, when the IAF withdrew its six ministers from the national unity Government, resulting in an even weaker participation by Sunni politicians in the country's decision-making processes. (One of the six, the Minister of Planning and Development Co-operation, Ali Baban, returned to the Council of Ministers in early September and was immediately dismissed by the party.) Moderate Kurdish and Shi'a political parties responded to this announcement by establishing a new alliance aimed at assisting the Prime Minister in pushing forward important legislation; this new grouping included the PUK and the KDP, together with al-Maliki's Islamic Dawa Party and SCIRI (which had recently been renamed the Supreme Islamic Iraqi Council). On 5 August cabinet ministers representing the INL had also announced that they were to boycott meetings of the Council of Ministers since the Prime Minister had not met certain of their key demands as far as reforms were concerned; the ministers were to continue to administer their portfolios, however.

The UN Security Council voted on 10 August 2007 to expand the organization's operations in Iraq, describing this greater role as to 'advise, support and assist the government and people of Iraq on advancing their inclusive, political dialogue and national reconciliation'. (The UN had played a minimal role in Iraq's political affairs following the attack against its Baghdad headquarters in August 2003.) On 14 August 2007 an estimated 400–500 people from the minority (primarily Kurdish) Yazidi community in northern Iraq were killed as the result of co-ordinated suicide bombings carried out by militants. US military officials asserted that al-Qa'ida in Iraq had been responsible for the blasts. Muqtada as-Sadr, meanwhile, declared at the end of the month that his Mahdi Army was to suspend its campaign against rival militias and US-led forces for a six-month period. (In mid-July as-Sadr's bloc in the Council of Representatives had chosen to end a boycott of legislative proceedings that it had commenced following the bombing of the al-Askari Mosque in the previous month. The Mahdi Army's truce was extended for a further six months in late February 2008.) By the end of November 2007 new Ministers of Agriculture and of Health had been sworn in, thereby filling two of the portfolios left vacant by the departure of as-Sadr's Shi'a faction in April.

British armed forces withdrew from their remaining base in the city of Basra on 3 September 2007, transferring military control of the city centre to Iraqi troops and police. The formal handover of security from British to Iraqi forces in the remainder of Basra province took place on 16 December; this represented the transfer to Iraqi authority of the last of the four southern provinces controlled by the British military since 2003. However, some 40 people in the southern town of Amara died in a triple car bombing days prior to the British withdrawal. It was reported in late 2007 that independent assessments of the number of casualties among civilians and security forces in Iraq were all showing a marked decline; US officials were keen to attribute this apparent outcome to the effectiveness of the Bush Administration's 'surge' strategy in Baghdad. It was also noted that the US military's preparedness to support certain Sunni militias who were now prepared to fight against al-Qa'ida in Iraq was likely to have reduced levels of violence in areas such as Anbar province. In early November Prime Minister al-Maliki added to this positive message by announcing that sectarian Sunni–Shi'a violence and 'terrorist acts' such as suicide and car bombings had all fallen notably since the previous year's levels. Moreover, it was revealed that large numbers of Iraqi refugees were returning to the country, notably from neighbouring countries such as Syria. This did appear to demonstrate an improvement in the security situation, particularly in Baghdad; yet other factors were also relevant, such as Syria's tightening of visa regulations for fleeing Iraqis in late November. In early December the UN Secretary-General's Special Representative for Iraq, Staffan de Mistura, launched a plan worth US $11,400m. to provide assistance to thousands of refugees and internally displaced families who had chosen to return home.

Nevertheless, insurgent groups pledged to continue their campaign against the US-led occupation of Iraq, and it was reported in early October 2007 that 22 such groups had agreed to establish a new coalition, the Supreme Command for Jihad and Liberation, to be led by the Baath Party's Izzat Ibrahim ad-Douri. In early 2008 an independent monitoring group, Iraq Body Count, estimated that between 22,586 and 24,159 civilians had died as a result of violence during 2007—the second highest annual death toll since the start of the conflict in 2003. However, the group did observe a significant decrease in the number of fatalities in Baghdad, possibly owing to the 'surge' in US troop numbers. As of 1 January 2008, Iraq Body Count assessed the number of violent civilian deaths during the entire period since the US-led invasion to be between 81,174 and 88,585. This contrasted dramatically with figures released jointly by WHO and the Iraqi Ministry of Health, based on the results of a household survey, which estimated that around 151,000 civilians had died as a result of the conflict between 2003 and June 2006 (although, allowing for misreporting, the total could have been anywhere between 104,000 and 223,000). A survey published by US researchers in *The Lancet* medical journal in October 2006 had assessed the number of Iraqi civilians killed as the result of the conflict as being as high as 601,027—a finding that was widely disputed.

On 12 January 2008 the Council of Representatives appoved a law permitting former middle- and low-ranking members of the Baath Party who had not been charged with crimes to reclaim positions of public office. The Accountability and Justice Law effectively overturned the de-Baathification legislation adopted by the CPA in the immediate aftermath of the overthrow of Saddam Hussain's regime in 2003, which resulted in the dismissal of many thousand Baathist officials. It was hoped that the reform, which was ratified by the Presidential Council on 3 February, would assist in national reconciliation efforts, since many Sunnis had protested that the de-Baathification order 'collectively punished' their community. However, some Sunnis expressed their reservations about the new law (partly because they claimed it would result in the forced retirement of members of Saddam Hussain's former intelligence and police services, and partly because reinstated Baathist officials might be targets of retaliatory attacks by Shi'as), while a number of Shi'a groups were strongly opposed to the change.

The period of relatively less violence being experienced in Baghdad came to a dramatic end on 1 February 2008, when two massive suicide bomb attacks were carried out in two crowded markets in the capital, resulting in the deaths of an estimated 100 people. Local residents and international observers expressed particular outrage at the fact that those who had planned the attacks—widely believed to be al-Qa'ida operatives—had recruited two disabled women to detonate the remote-controlled explosives. On 13 February it was announced that the Council of Representatives had passed three important pieces of legislation: one relating to the 2008 state budget; an amnesty law allowing for the possible release of thousands of suspected insurgents being held without charge in US military and Iraqi detention; and a law determining the relationship between the central and provincial authorities in Iraq, and stipulating that provincial elections should be held by the end of the year. (These elections, which were originally supposed to have been held by the end of 2007, were subsequently scheduled for 1 October 2008.)

A general improvement was perceived in Iraq's relations with other Arab states from late 2000, although in September Iraq reiterated allegations that Kuwait was stealing Iraqi petroleum by drilling in an area near the Iraq–Kuwait border. Iraq also accused both Kuwait and Saudi Arabia of inflicting (through the maintenance of the sanctions regime) suffering on the Iraqi population, and alleged that Saudi Arabia was appropriating Iraqi petroleum transported under the oil-for-food programme. In October Iraq was represented at a summit meeting of the Arab League for the first time since the 1990–91 Gulf crisis, as RCC Vice-President Izzat Ibrahim ad-Douri attended the emergency session convened in Cairo, Egypt, to discuss the Israeli–Palestinian crisis that had erupted in September 2000. Saddam Hussain (to whom an invitation had been issued for the first time since 1990) was represented by senior officials of the Iraqi Government at the Arab League summit held in Amman in March 2001. The summit was considered as having made the most comprehensive effort hitherto in addressing divisions arising from the Gulf conflict. None the less, a draft resolution presented by the Iraqi delegation urging an end to UN sanctions and a resumption of civilian flights failed to secure adoption, owing to Iraq's unwillingness to accede to a requirement of a specific guarantee that Iraq would not repeat the invasion of 1990: Iraq contended that it had already done sufficient to make clear its recognition of Kuwait's territorial integrity.

In the context of a long-standing commitment to establish a regional common market under the auspices of the Council of Arab Economic Unity (see p. 222), plans for a quadripartite free trade zone encompassing Iraq, Egypt, Libya and Syria were advanced following a meeting of the Council held in Baghdad in June 2001. In the previous month Iraq had participated with Jordanian, Moroccan and Tunisian representatives at a meeting in Agadir, Morocco, at which the four countries agreed to establish a free trade zone. In August the Syrian Prime Minister, Muhammad Mustafa Mero, leading a ministerial and commercial delegation, became the most senior Syrian official to visit Iraq for two decades.

The extent of Iraq's rehabilitation among the majority of Arab states was particularly evident as, from the latter part of 2001, speculation increased regarding potential US-led military action against Iraq. Leaders of influential Arab states, among them Egypt, Jordan and Syria, all expressed particular concern at the likely consequences should the Bush Administration's campaign be directed against any Arab state, warning against exacerbating tensions in a region under great strain because of the Israeli–Palestinian crisis. During talks with a senior representative of the Qatari ruling family in January 2002, Saddam Hussain issued an appeal to Arab states to set aside their differences, referring specifically to the need to improve relations with Kuwait and Saudi Arabia; later in the month Iraq reportedly announced its preparedness to allow a delegation from Kuwait to visit Iraq to verify that no Kuwaiti prisoners of war were being held (Kuwait continued to assert that Iraq was detaining at least 90 Kuwaiti nationals). At the Arab League summit held in Beirut, Lebanon, in March it was announced that Kuwait and Iraq had reached agreement on the resolution of outstanding differences (see the chapter on Kuwait). In May Iraq notified the UN of its intention to return to Kuwait the official documents and archives removed during the 1990–91 occupation. Iraq's relations with Kuwait were significantly affected by the US-led campaign to oust the Baathist regime in March 2003, especially since the coalition forces launched their ground assault from Kuwait. The mandate of UNIKOM (see above) was declared to have been completed in October, and in June 2004, when sovereignty was transferred to the Iraqi Interim Government, Kuwait announced the resumption of diplomatic relations with Iraq. The two countries were thus to begin the process of exchanging diplomatic staff.

In September 2003 the new Iraqi Minister of Oil, Ibrahim Bahr al-Ulum, was invited to take Iraq's seat at an OPEC meeting in Vienna, Austria. Iraq also attended a summit meeting of the Organization of the Islamic Conference (OIC) in Malaysia during October as a full member. In June 2005 Egypt became the first Arab state to nominate an ambassador to Baghdad since the US-led invasion, with others expected to follow; however, this trend was halted by the abduction and murder of Egypt's ambassador, Ihab ash-Sherif, in July. Al-Qa'ida in Iraq claimed responsibility for the killing of ash-Sharif, together with the subsequent abduction and killing of two Algerian diplomats later in July. The ambassador of Pakistan and the head of Bahrain's mission in Baghdad were also attacked in that month, while the diplomatic staff of the countries in question were withdrawn in reaction to the attacks.

From its inauguration, the Iraqi Interim Government repeatedly accused Iran and Syria of supporting insurgents in Iraq, claims that were rejected by both countries. Nevertheless, the Iranian Government undoubtedly increased its influence in Iraq through the rise to power of Shi'ites in the administration formed in mid-2006 (see above). Iraq and Iran resumed diplomatic relations in September 2004, although many issues relating to the 1980–88 War remained unresolved. Prime Minister al-Ja'fari visited Iran in July 2005, followed by President Talabani in November—the first visit to Tehran by an Iraqi head of state in over 30 years. Also in November an Iraqi passenger flight landed in Tehran for the first time since the outbreak of war in 1980. In February 2005, meanwhile, it was reported that Syria had captured and handed over to Iraqi security forces Sabawi Ibrahim al-Hassan, a half-brother of Saddam Hussain, as a gesture of 'goodwill'; al-Hassan was accused of involvement in the insurgency against coalition forces.

A breakthrough in Iraq's relations with Syria occurred in November 2006, when the two countries declared that they would restore diplomatic ties that had been severed in 1982. The announcement, made during a visit to Baghdad by the Syrian Minister of Foreign Affairs, Walid Mouallem, came as some Western countries began to accept the idea of including Iran and Syria in regional security talks concerning Iraq. Iraqi officials hoped that the resumption in relations with Syria would assist in stemming the flow of insurgents across their joint border (a US spokesman had earlier claimed that between 70 and 100 foreign fighters opposed to the presence of coalition troops were entering Iraq from Syria each month). In December Iraq and Syria formally opened embassies in each other's capitals, and in January 2007 President Talabani became the first Iraqi President to pay an official visit to Syria for nearly three decades. However, bilateral relations became strained in the following month, when Iraq accused Syria of harbouring fugitive militants and refusing refuge for genuine Iraqi refugees.

Iran, meanwhile, offered to host security talks on Iraq; these took place in November 2006 when President Talabani made his second official visit to Tehran. According to Iranian television, Talabani spoke of Iraq's 'dire need of Iran's help in establishing security and stability', while also urging the two sides to raise the profile of bilateral economic, political, security and cultural relations. Although the Iranian leadership pledged to assist Iraq by any possible means, it warned that the restoration of security was dependent on the withdrawal of US troops. In March 2007 the most significant international conference to be held in Baghdad since the Arab League summit meeting of 1990 was attended by representatives from Iraq's neighbouring states, as well as other leading regional powers, the Arab League, the UN and the OIC. The aim of the conference was to seek to find a means of reducing the violence in Iraq and accelerating the handover of the country to full Iraqi control. Two sessions of direct discussions took place between the US and Iranian ambassadors to Baghdad in May and July 2007. The two sides pledged to co-operate in an effort to end the sectarian violence in Iraq, and the first meeting of their newly established joint subcommittee was held in the Iraqi capital in early August. The Iranian President, Mahmoud Ahmadinejad, undertook an official two-day visit to Baghdad in early March 2008, where he held cordial discussions with his Iraqi counterpart.

In late September 2007 Turkey and Iraq signed a security co-operation pact intended to curb the military activities of the Kurdish separatist organization, the PKK. However, although the pact did not include Turkey's principal demand that its military be permitted to enter Iraqi territory in pursuit of Kurdish fighters, in mid-December Turkish troops began an offensive against PKK bases in Iraq's northern region, in response to a series of cross-border raids by armed separatists to carry out bomb attacks against Turkish soldiers in south-eastern Turkey. (The Turkish Grand National Assembly had voted in mid-October to authorize its military to carry out cross-border military operations in Iraq.) The Iraqi Government protested to its Turkish counterpart that it had not been consulted over the military action, while the President of the Kurdish Autonomous Region, Masoud Barzani, described Turkey's actions as a violation of Iraqi sovereignty. In late February 2008 it was initially reported that up to 10,000 Turkish troops had entered northern Iraq, in what appeared to be a much larger incursion than that of the previous December, and with the additional launching of air-strikes against PKK militant bases; however, it was reported at the end of February that only several hundred forces had participated in the military campaign. Nevertheless, dozens of PKK militants were killed in the week-long offensive, together with several Turkish soldiers. (The Turkish military claimed by this time to have killed at least 230 PKK fighters, and to have lost 27 of its soldiers; however, PKK sources alleged that around 90 Turkish soldiers had died in the recent incursion.)

Government

Prior to the ousting of Saddam Hussain's regime by the US-led coalition in April 2003, Iraq was divided into 18 governorates (including three Autonomous Regions). In the immediate aftermath of the war, a US-led Coalition Provisional Authority (CPA) was established to govern the country in the absence of an elected sovereign government. UN Security Council Resolution 1483 of 22 May gave legitimacy to the occupying powers in this task. On 13 July a 25-member interim Governing Council was formed, whose members were selected by the CPA in proportion to Iraq's main ethnic and religious groups. It had no executive power, but could appoint ministers and diplomatic representatives, draw up a new constitution and set a date for free elections. The Governing Council decided upon a rotating presidency, commencing in September, with nine members of the council each serving for one month. In the same month 25 ministers were appointed to serve in an interim Cabinet, also chosen according to ethnicity and creed. On 15 November the CPA and Governing Council jointly published a plan for the creation of a democratically elected, sovereign government and constitution by the end of 2005. However, this plan was superseded by the Transitional Administrative Law (TAL) signed on 8 March 2004. Under the terms of the TAL, an Iraqi Interim Government assumed power on 28 June 2004 (two days earlier than was stipulated), and the CPA and Governing Council were dissolved. The Interim Government was replaced by an Iraqi Transitional Government, consisting of a state Presidency Council (comprising a President and two Vice-Presidents) and a Prime Minister and Cabinet to be appointed by the Council, in April 2005, following elections to the 275-member Transitional National Assembly (TNA), which took place on 30 January. Members of the TNA were required to produce a draft constitution by 15 August 2005, to be approved by national referendum by 15 October 2005. In the event, disagreements over key issues delayed the submission of the draft Constitution to the TNA until 28 August, and a further amended text was presented to the UN on 14 September. The draft Constitution was then submitted to the Iraqi people in a national referendum on 15 October, which resulted in its ratification (with the endorsement of 78.6% of votes cast). National elections for a permanent legislature, the Council of Representatives, took place on 15 December.

Defence

The US-led Coalition Provisional Authority (CPA) dissolved the armed forces and security organizations in place under Saddam Hussain in May 2003, following the ousting of the regime in the previous month. In August the CPA promulgated the establishment of the New Iraqi Army, to which an estimated ID 34,800m. was allocated in the full-year budget for 2004. As assessed at November 2007, Iraq's armed forces numbered an estimated 360,100. Those serving in the army, including the Iraqi National Guard (which replaced the Iraqi Civil Defence Corps), numbered some 163,500, and those in the navy an estimated 1,100, while 1,200 were serving in the air force, the Iraqi Air Wing. In addition, there were estimated to be 33,000 members of the Ministry of Interior Forces, 135,000 members of the Iraqi Police Service and about 26,300 members of the National Police. There were also a number of foreign armed forces operating in the country, principally those of the USA and the United Kingdom (for further details, see Recent History).

Economic Affairs

In 2006, according to estimates by the IMF, Iraq's gross domestic product (GDP), measured in current prices, was US $49,527m. (equivalent to $1,723 per head). During 1997–2007, according to estimates by the UN, the population increased at an average annual rate of 2.3%. According to the World Bank, overall GDP increased, in real terms, at an average annual rate of 2.5% during 1997–2004; real GDP declined by an estimated 41.3% in 2003, following the US-led invasion, but increased by 46.5% in 2004. Real GDP growth was estimated by the IMF to have contracted again, by 0.7%, in 2005, before increasing by 6.2% in 2006.

Agriculture (including forestry and fishing) contributed 5.3% of GDP in 2006, according to the IMF. FAO estimated that 7.9% of the labour force were employed in agriculture in mid-2005. Dates are the principal cash crop. Other crops include wheat, barley, potatoes, tomatoes, cucumbers, aubergines and melons. Production of eggs, milk and poultry meat is also important. During 1997–2003, according to World Bank data, the real GDP of the agricultural sector declined by an average of 1.2% per year; agricultural GDP decreased by an estimated 29.1% in 2003.

Industry (including mining, manufacturing, construction and power) provided 67.6% of GDP in 2006, according to IMF data. During 1997–2003 industrial GDP increased by an average of 1.0% per year; however, the GDP of the sector decreased by an estimated 37.7% in 2003.

The mining sector accounted for 64.7% of GDP in 2006, according to the IMF, with crude oil contributing 64.6%. Iraq had proven reserves of 115,000m. barrels of petroleum at the end of 2006 (the third largest in the world, after Saudi Arabia and Iran), as well as 3,170,000m. cu m of natural gas. In addition, Iraq is believed to possess undiscovered petroleum reserves of considerable magnitude. According to oil industry data, the rate of petroleum production in 2006 was 1.99m. barrels per day (b/d), well below the 2.58m. b/d produced in 2000; however, the reopening of a pipeline to Turkey in August 2006 was reported to have increased oil output again to an average of some 2.5m. b/d. Continuing insurgent attacks on Iraq's petroleum facilities have undermined official projections for future output. Reserves of phosphates, sulphur, gypsum and salt are also exploited.

Manufacturing contributed 1.7% of GDP in 2006, according to the IMF. During 1997–2003 manufacturing GDP declined at an annual average rate of 6.2%; sectoral GDP decreased by some 28.5% in 2003. Since the outbreak of the current conflict in Iraq, the development of the manufacturing sector and the likelihood of increased capacity being achieved in the near future have been hindered by issues such as fuel shortages, damaged and outdated equipment, poor security and communication problems.

Energy is derived principally from petroleum, which accounted for an estimated 98.5% of total electricity generation in 2004. Since 2003 power shortages and rationing have been a persistent feature in Iraq, particularly in Baghdad and the northern region. The Ministry of Electricity estimated actual electricity generating capacity at 4,500 MW in early 2006, although Iraq, in theory, had an installed capacity of some 7,000 MW; the shortfall was the result of various factors, such as outdated technology, insurgent attacks on power stations and disruptions in fuel supplies. Required capacity, estimated at 8,700 MW in 2006, was forecast to increase to 12,000 MW by the end of 2007.

The services sector contributed 27.0% of GDP in 2006, according to IMF data. During 1997–2003 the real GDP of the sector decreased by an annual average of 7.5%; services GDP declined by an estimated 23.7% in 2003.

In 2006, according to IMF estimates, Iraq recorded a trade surplus of US $7,787m., and there was a surplus of $4,589m. on the current account of the balance of payments. Crude petroleum was by far the most important export prior to the imposition of international economic sanctions in 1990. According to the Central Bank, mineral fuels and lubricants constituted 99.2% of Iraqi exports in 2006. The principal imports in that year were machinery and transport equipment, miscellaneous manufactured articles, mineral fuels and lubricants, and basic manufactures.

Budget proposals for 2008 forecast expenditure of ID 64,318,000m. and revenue of ID 57,222,000m. According to IMF estimates, Iraq's total external debt was US $98,100m., equivalent to 198% of GDP, at the end of 2006, with projections anticipating a decline towards 162% of GDP in 2007. According to the Central Bank, the annual average rate of inflation was 27.0% in 2004, 37.0% in 2005 and 53.2% in 2006. Estimates concerning the rate of unemployment in Iraq vary considerably; however, many sources suggest that the rate could have reached 60%–70% by 2007.

Iraq is a member of the Arab Fund for Economic and Social Development (see p. 174), the Council of Arab Economic Unity (see p. 222), the Organization of Arab Petroleum Exporting Countries (see p. 366) and the Organization of the Petroleum Exporting Countries (see p. 373). Iraq was granted observer status at the World Trade Organization (WTO, see p. 396) in February 2004, and working party discussions to negotiate the country's eventual membership of the WTO began in May 2007.

The International Compact with Iraq, inaugurated in May 2007, was intended to provide a framework for Iraq's economic revival, transformation, and regional and international integration, together with its political and social development, over a five-year period. A critical determinant of the success of the programme, initiated by the Iraqi Government in co-operation with institutions of the UN and other international financial organizations, would be the success of efforts to restore stability and security. The common emphasis of assessments of the Iraqi economy four years after the overthrow of the Baathist regime was that among the principal factors impeding recovery, stabilization and infrastructural development was the grave security situation. Iraq's difficulties were compounded by the effects of many years of chronic underinvestment and rigid state control in key sectors under Saddam Hussain. Lack of investment and a consequent decline in capacity had been much exacerbated by the international sanctions regime operated following Iraq's invasion of Kuwait in 1990. A severe deterioration (despite the institution of the UN-administered 'oil-for-food' programme from 1996) in health, welfare and educational provision had not been reversed after 2003. Moreover, production in the oil sector had by early 2007 not yet recovered to pre-2003 levels. Iraq was obliged to offset through imports severe shortages of motor fuel, kerosene and cooking gas, while frequent power shortages were impeding the expansion of capacity in manufacturing and other sectors.

A significant development was the agreement by the Government, in February 2007, of the terms of its draft hydrocarbons law, whereby the oil and gas sector would be opened to foreign investment, in joint venture with Iraqi interests. Regional authorities would be permitted to award contracts for exploration and exploitation, in accordance with procedures and guidelines established by a Federal Oil and Gas Council; agreements previously negotiated by regional authorities would be required to be redefined as necessary to conform with the new legislation. Associated legislation provided for the proceeds of the exploitation of Iraq's hydrocarbons reserves to be pooled and redistributed across the country's regions according to population. The Iraq National Oil Co was to be restructured as an independent holding company, with affiliated regional operating companies. The legislation was subject to approval by the Council of Representatives, but its passage through parliament was expected to be slow owing to its complex and politically sensitive nature. Following the adoption by the Kurdish regional government of its own oil law in August, the central Government threatened to prevent any foreign company that signed a production-sharing agreement with the Kurdish authorities from doing business in, and exporting oil from, Iraq (although several foreign firms did agree deals). The first petroleum to be pumped by a foreign company for more than 35 years was extracted in mid-2007, when DNO of Norway produced a small amount from Iraqi Kurdistan. During a visit to Turkey by the Iraqi President in March 2008, plans were revealed for the construction of a second pipeline to transport oil from Kirkuk to southern Turkey. Meanwhile, in March 2007 the IMF, in its assessment of economic performance under the programme supported by the stand-by arrangement (of SDR 475.4m.) approved in December 2005 (at the review, the 15-month arrangement was extended to September 2007), drew attention to what it considered positive measures taken by the Iraqi authorities, including the maintenance of fiscal discipline, the tightening of monetary policy, the liberalization of fuel imports and the appreciation of the national currency. Despite agreements on debt reduction signed with official creditors of the 'Paris Club' and with private lenders, further progress was needed in the conclusion of arrangements for debt-relief with non-'Paris Club' members, including the Gulf states. GDP growth was estimated at 1.3% in 2007, although the IMF suggested that this was a conservative figure, and forecast growth of 7.1% in 2008 (amid a predicted recovery in the oil sector). Inflation had been a key concern in Iraq up to 2006, primarily due to fuel shortages together with increased security costs; however, the performance of the economy under the first stand-by arrangement was described by the IMF as being very impressive, with inflation declining from 53.2% in 2006 to just 4.7% by the end of 2007, and international reserves increasing to some US $27,000m.

Education

Education is provided free of charge, and primary education, beginning at six years of age and lasting for six years, has been made compulsory in an effort to reduce illiteracy. Enrolment at primary schools of children in the relevant age-group reached 100% in 1978, fell to 76% by 1995, but reportedly rose again, to 91%, in 2000/01. According to UNESCO estimates, in 2004/05 enrolment at primary schools included 87.7% of pupils in the relevant age-group. Secondary education begins at 12 years of age and lasts for up to six years, divided into two cycles of three years each. Enrolment at secondary schools in 2004/05 included some 37.8% of children in the appropriate age-group, according to UNESCO. There are 43 technical institutes and colleges, two postgraduate commissions and 20 universities. In the 2002/03 academic year there were an estimated 240,000 undergraduates enrolled in courses of higher education. Following the change of regime in Iraq in April 2003, a comprehensive reform of the country's education system was implemented; however, it was reported in late 2006 that a significant number of pupils were failing to attend school or university as a result of the worsening security situation in many parts of the country. The combined forecast budgetary expenditure of the Ministries of Education and of Higher Education and Scientific Research in 2005 was ID 1,014,800m. (equivalent to some 3.5% of total spending).

Public Holidays

2008: 1 January (New Year's Day), 10 January*† (Islamic New Year), 20 March* (Mouloud, Birth of Muhammad), 9 April (National Holiday, commemorating overthrow of the Baath regime in 2003), 14 July (National Holiday, commemorating overthrow of the Hashemite monarchy in 1958), 30 July* (Leilat al-Meiraj, ascension of Muhammad), 1 October* (Id al-Fitr, end of Ramadan), 9 December* (Id al-Adha, Feast of the Sacrifice), 29 December*† (Islamic New Year).

2009: 1 January (New Year's Day), 7 January*‡ (Ashoura), 9 March* (Mouloud, Birth of Muhammad), 9 April (National Holiday, commemorating overthrow of the Baath regime in 2003), 14 July (National Holiday, commemorating overthrow of the Hashemite monarchy in 1958), 19 July* (Leilat al-Meiraj, ascension of Muhammad), 20 September* (Id al-Fitr, end of Ramadan), 27 November* (Id al-Adha, Feast of the Sacrifice), 18 December* (Islamic New Year), 27 December*‡ (Ashoura).

* These holidays are dependent on the Islamic lunar calendar and may vary by one or two days from the dates given.

† This festival occurs twice (marking the start of the Islamic years AH 1429 and 1430) within the same Gregorian year.

‡ This festival occurs twice (in the Islamic years AH 1430 and 1431) within the same Gregorian year.

Weights and Measures

The metric system is in force. Local measurements are also used, e.g. 1 meshara or dunum = 2,500 sq m (0.62 acre).

Statistical Survey

Sources (unless otherwise indicated): Central Statistical Organization, Ministry of Planning and Development Co-operation, 929/29/6 Arrasat al-Hindiya, Baghdad; tel. and fax (1) 885-3653; e-mail ministry@mopdc-iraq.org; Central Bank of Iraq, POB 64, Ar-Rashid St, Baghdad; tel. (1) 816-5170; fax (1) 816-6802; e-mail cbi@cbiraq.org; internet www.cbiraq.org.

Area and Population

AREA, POPULATION AND DENSITY*

Area (sq km)	438,317†
Population (census results)	
17 October 1987	16,335,199
17 October 1997	
Males	10,940,764
Females	11,077,219
Total	22,017,983
Population (UN estimates at mid-year)‡	
2005	27,996,000
2006	28,506,000
2007	28,993,000
Density (per sq km) at mid-2007	66.1

* No account has been taken of the reduction in the area of Iraq as a result of the adjustment to the border with Kuwait that came into force on 15 January 1993.

† 169,235 sq miles. This figure includes 924 sq km (357 sq miles) of territorial waters but excludes the Neutral Zone, of which Iraq's share is 3,522 sq km (1,360 sq miles). The Zone lies between Iraq and Saudi Arabia, and is administered jointly by the two countries. Nomads move freely through it, but there are no permanent inhabitants.

‡ Source: UN, *World Population Prospects: The 2006 Revision*.

GOVERNORATES
(population at 1987 census)

	Area (sq km)*	Population	Density (per sq km)
Nineveh	37,698	1,479,430	39.2
Salah ad-Din	29,004	726,138	25.0
At-Ta'meem	10,391	601,219	57.9
Diala	19,292	961,073	49.8
Baghdad	5,159	3,841,268	744.6
Al-Anbar	137,723	820,690	6.0
Babylon	5,258	1,109,574	211.0
Karbala	5,034	469,282	93.2
An-Najaf (Najaf)	27,844	590,078	21.2
Al-Qadisiya	8,507	559,805	65.8
Al-Muthanna	51,029	315,816	6.2
Thi-Qar	13,626	921,066	67.6
Wasit	17,308	564,670	32.6
Maysan	14,103	487,448	34.6
Al-Basrah (Basra)	19,070	872,176	45.7
Autonomous Regions:			
D'hok	6,120	293,304	47.9
Irbil (Arbil)	14,471	770,439	53.2
As-Sulaimaniya (Sulaimaniya)	15,756	951,723	60.4
Total	437,393	16,335,199	37.3

* Excluding territorial waters (924 sq km).

IRAQ

PRINCIPAL TOWNS
(population at 1987 census)

Baghdad (capital)	3,841,268	As-Sulaimaniya (Sulaimaniya)		364,096
Al-Mawsil (Mosul)	664,221	An-Najaf (Najaf)		309,010
Irbil (Arbil)	485,968	Karbala		296,705
Kirkuk	418,624	Al-Hillah (Hilla)		268,834
Al-Basrah (Basra)	406,296	An-Nasiriyah (Nasiriya)		265,937

Source: UN, *Demographic Yearbook*.

Mid-2007 ('000, incl. suburbs, UN estimates): Baghdad 5,054; Mosul 1,316; Arbil 926; Basra 870 (Source: UN, *World Urbanization Prospects: The 2007 Revision*).

BIRTHS AND DEATHS
(annual averages, UN estimates)

	1990–95	1995–2000	2000–05
Birth rate (per 1,000)	39.0	38.3	35.6
Death rate (per 1,000)	9.6	10.0	10.6

Source: UN, *World Population Prospects: The 2006 Revision*.

Expectation of life (years at birth, WHO estimates): 55 (males 51; females 61) in 2004 (Source: WHO, *World Health Report*).

ECONOMICALLY ACTIVE POPULATION*
(persons aged 7 years and over, 1987 census)

	Males	Females	Total
Agriculture, forestry and fishing	422,265	70,741	493,006
Mining and quarrying	40,439	4,698	45,137
Manufacturing	228,242	38,719	266,961
Electricity, gas and water	31,786	4,450	36,236
Construction	332,645	8,541	341,186
Trade, restaurants and hotels	191,116	24,489	215,605
Transport, storage and communications	212,116	12,155	224,271
Financing, insurance, real estate and business services	16,204	10,811	27,015
Community, social and personal services	1,721,748	233,068	1,954,816
Activities not adequately defined	146,616	18,232	167,848
Total labour force	**3,346,177**	**425,904**	**3,772,081**

* Figures exclude persons seeking work for the first time, totalling 184,264 (males 149,938, females 34,326), but include other unemployed persons.

Source: ILO, *Yearbook of Labour Statistics*.

Mid-2005 (estimates in '000): Agriculture, etc. 651; Total labour force 8,189 (Source: FAO).

Health and Welfare

KEY INDICATORS

Total fertility rate (children per woman, 2005)	4.5
Under-5 mortality rate (per 1,000 live births, 2004)	125
HIV/AIDS (% of persons aged 15–49, 2003)	<0.1
Physicians (per 1,000 head, 2004)	0.66
Hospital beds (per 1,000 head, 2005)	1.30
Health expenditure (2004): US $ per head (PPP)	135.3
Health expenditure (2004): % of GDP	5.3
Health expenditure (2004): public (% of total)	78.5
Access to water (% of persons, 2004)	81
Access to sanitation (% of persons, 2004)	79
Human Development Index (2000): value	0.567*

* Based on incomplete information.

For sources and definitions, see explanatory note on p. vi.

Agriculture

PRINCIPAL CROPS
('000 metric tons)

	2003	2004	2005
Wheat	2,329	1,832	2,228
Rice (paddy)	90	250	309
Barley	861	805	754
Maize	233	416	401
Potatoes	872	630	808
Sugar cane*	65	65	65
Chick-peas	104†	100*	95†
Tomatoes	234	988	939
Cauliflower	27	26	30
Pumpkins, squash and gourds*	30	32	32
Cucumbers and gherkins	369	433	526
Aubergines (Eggplants)	274	399	439
Dry onions	116	115	162
Watermelons	190	200*	200*
Canteloupes and other melons	190	240	243
Grapes	335	330*	330*
Oranges	200†	270	270*
Tangerines, mandarins, clementines and satsumas	28†	33*	33*
Apples	64	29	25
Apricots*	20	22	22
Peaches and nectarines*	18	20	20
Plums*	25	27	27
Dates	868	875	404

* FAO estimate(s).
† Unofficial figure.

2006 ('000 metric tons, FAO estimates): Barley 600; Rice paddy 230; Sesame seed 23; Sunflower oil 27.

Aggregate production ('000 metric tons, may include official, semi-official or estimated data): Total cereals 3,516 in 2003, 3,308 in 2004, 3,701 in 2005; Total roots and tubers 872 in 2003, 630 in 2004, 81 in 2005; Total vegetables (incl. melons) 1,868 in 2003, 2,925 in 2004, 3,058 in 2005; Total fruits (excl. melons) 1,641 in 2003, 1,685 in 2004, 1,209 in 2005.

Source: FAO.

LIVESTOCK
('000 head, year ending September, FAO estimates)

	2003	2004	2005
Horses	48	48	48
Asses, mules and hinnies	391	391	391
Cattle	1,500	1,500	1,500
Buffaloes	120	120	120
Camels	10	10	10
Sheep	6,200	6,200	6,200
Goats	1,650	1,650	1,650
Poultry	33,000	33,000	33,000

2006: No data were available.

Source: FAO.

LIVESTOCK PRODUCTS
('000 metric tons, FAO estimates)

	2002	2003	2004
Cattle meat	49.9	49.9	49.9
Buffalo meat	3.9	3.7	3.7
Sheep meat	20	20	20
Goat meat	8.0	8.3	8.3
Chicken meat	95	97	97
Cows' milk	440	450	450
Buffaloes' milk	27.6	27.6	27.6
Sheep's milk	157.5	157.5	157.5
Goats' milk	54	54	54
Hen eggs	53	55	55
Wool: greasy	13	13	13
Cattle and buffalo hides	6	6	6

2005: Figures assumed to be unchanged from 2004 (FAO estimates).
2006: No data were available.

Source: FAO.

Forestry

ROUNDWOOD REMOVALS
('000 cubic metres, excl. bark, FAO estimates)

	2004	2005	2006
Sawlogs, veneer logs and logs for sleepers	25.0	25.0	25.0
Other industrial wood	34.0	34.0	34.0
Fuel wood	55.4	56.4	57.4
Total	114.4	115.4	116.4

Source: FAO.

SAWNWOOD PRODUCTION
('000 cu m, incl. railway sleepers)

	1996	1997	1998
Total (all broadleaved)	8	8	12

1999–2006: Annual production as in 1998 (FAO estimates).
Source: FAO.

Fishing

('000 metric tons, live weight)

	2003	2004	2005
Capture	17.2	14.7	20.1
Cyprinids (incl. Common carp)*	7.5	7.6	9.7
Freshwater siluroids*	0.7	0.5	4.8
Other freshwater fishes*	5.0	2.4	n.a.
Marine fishes	4.0	0.6	n.a.
Aquaculture	2.0*	12.2	12.9
Common carp	2.0*	8.7	8.4
Total catch	19.2	26.9	33.0

* FAO estimate(s).
Source: FAO.

Mining

('000 metric tons, unless otherwise indicated)

	2004	2005	2006
Crude petroleum (barrels per day)	737,940	660,000	730,000
Natural gas (million cu m)*	9,600	9,000	10,000
Ammonia (nitrogen content)	30	30	10
Sulphur†	20	30	30
Salt (unrefined)	50	25	25

* Figures refer to gross production.
† Figures refer to native production and byproducts of petroleum and natural gas processing.
Source: US Geological Survey.

Industry

SELECTED PRODUCTS
('000 metric tons, unless otherwise indicated)

	2002	2003	2004
Naphtha	571	511	540
Motor spirit (petrol)	3,460	3,097	3,278
Kerosene	1,189	1,064	1,127
Jet fuel	640	573	607
Gas-diesel (distillate fuel) oil	6,884	6,610	4,906
Residual fuel oils	8,221	7,404	8,257
Lubricating oils	259	232	246
Paraffin wax	102	91	96
Petroleum bitumen (asphalt)	533	477	505
Liquefied petroleum gas:			
from natural gas plants	1,357	679	824
from petroleum refineries	189	169	114
Cement*	6,834	1,901	2,500
Electric energy (million kWh)	34,978	29,455	33,410

* Source: US Geological Survey.
Source (unless otherwise indicated): UN, *Industrial Commodity Statistics Yearbook*.

Finance

CURRENCY AND EXCHANGE RATES

Monetary Units
1,000 fils = 20 dirhams = 1 new Iraqi dinar (ID).

Sterling, Dollar and Euro Equivalents (31 December 2007)
£1 sterling = 2,450.160 Iraqi dinars;
US $1 = 1,223.000 Iraqi dinars;
€1 = 1,800.377 Iraqi dinars;
10,000 Iraqi dinars = £4.08 = $8.18 = €5.55.

Average Exchange rate (Iraqi dinars per US $)
2004   1,453.42
2005   1,472.00
2006   1,467.42

Note: Following the overthrow of the regime of Saddam Hussain in 2003, the new Coalition Provisional Authority established an exchange rate of US $1 = 1,400 dinars. A new dinar currency, known as the new Iraqi dinar (ID) was introduced on 15 October to replace both the 'Swiss' dinar (at ID 1 = 150 'Swiss' dinars), the currency in use in the Kurdish autonomous regions of northern Iraq since 1991, and the 'Saddam' dinar (at par), the official currency of the rest of Iraq. The new currency was to be fully convertible.

BUDGET
(ID '000 million)

Revenue	2003	2004*	2005†
Oil revenues	4,096.5	21,262.9	27,750.0
Reconstruction levy	—	172.5	525.0
Personal income tax	—	7.5	45.0
Civil service pension contributions	—	101.4	—
Corporate income tax	—	—	75.0
Interest	76.5	15.0	—
Transfers from state enterprises	337.5	—	142.5
Central bank	—	—	90.0
Agricultural supplies company	135.0	—	7.5
Ar-Rashid Hotel	7.5	—	22.5
Fees and charges	85.5	96.3	132.5
Prescription charges	—	30.0	37.5
Court fees	3.0	7.5	7.5
Vehicle registration	—	30.0	45.0
Fees from emergency services	—	7.5	15.0
Flight overpass charges for commercial airlines	7.5	15.0	15.0
Other taxes	—	73.5	105.0
Excise tax	—	3.0	15.0
Hotel and restaurant service tax	—	7.5	7.5
Land tax	—	10.5	30.0
Total	4,596.0	21,729.1	28,775.0

IRAQ

Statistical Survey

Expenditure by department‡	2003	2004*	2005†
Ministry of Agriculture	29.1	64.2	117.2
Ministry of Awqaf (Religious Endowments) and Religious Affairs	5.9	27.5	2.3
Board of Supreme Audit	0.5	36.5	3.8
Central Organization of Standards	0.3	204.6	1.7
Ministry of Communications	131.4	3.3	231.3
Ministry of Culture	38.4	20.1	31.8
Ministry of Displacement and Migration	0.5	10.4	8.4
Ministry of Education	14.6	1,429.4	836.2
Electricity Commission	447.5	1,033.9	2,252.2
Office of the Environment	0.5	12.2	30.9
Ministry of Finance	6,395.6	21,615.7	17,681.4
Ministry of Foreign Affairs	26.3	69.4	71.9
Governing Council	6.3	10.1	12.0
Ministry of Health	317.4	1,540.7	1,742.9
Ministry of Higher Education and Scientific Research	55.2	288.6	178.6
Ministry of Housing and Construction	35.4	406.8	496.7
Ministry of Human Rights	0.5	19.7	8.4
Ministry of Industry and Minerals	3.8	12.9	10.5
Ministry of the Interior	208.4	717.7	350.0
Iraqi Media Network	—	148.3	2.2
Ministry of Justice	49.8	213.0	284.4
Ministry of Labour and Social Affairs	3.9	76.5	59.7
Ministry of Municipalities, Utilities and Public Works	264.3	487.8	812.0
New Iraqi Army	187.5	150.4	109.8
Ministry of Oil	519.5	528.8	1,501.9
Ministry of Planning	72.9	95.9	54.9
Ministry of Science and Technology	17.9	45.3	46.0
Ministry of Trade	6.0	17.0	6.3
Ministry of Transport	113.9	354.5	758.1
Ministry of Water Resources	51.6	225.6	779.3
Ministry of Youth and Sport	8.1	24.2	93.2
Unallocated expenditure	219.8	—	180.0
Total	**9,232.2**	**29,890.9**	**28,755.7**

* Preliminary figures.
† Forecasts.
‡ Names of departments may have been altered since the publication of the budget proposals in October 2003.

Sources: Ministries of Finance and of Planning; Coalition Provisional Authority.

2006 (ID '000 million, preliminary): *Revenues and grants:* Revenues 49,430 (Crude oil export revenues 43,736); Grants 9,065; Total 58,495. *Expenditures:* Current 40,187 (Salaries and pensions 10,959; Non-oil goods and services 12,191; Oil sector goods and services 6,560; Transfers 7,928); Capital 9,463 (Non-oil 7,702, Oil 1,761); Contingency 104; Total 49,754 (Source: IMF, *Iraq: Request for Stand-By Arrangement and Cancellation of Current Arrangement—Staff Report; Staff Supplement; Press Release on the Executive Board Discussion; and Statement by the Executive Director for Iraq*—January 2008).

2007 (ID '000 million, projected): *Revenues and grants:* Revenues 48,448 (Crude oil export revenues 41,725); Grants 2,304; Total 50,753. *Expenditures:* Current 38,774 (Salaries and pensions 14,098; Non-oil goods and services 8,709; Oil sector goods and services 4,005; Transfers 9,336); Capital 9,655 (Non-oil 7,773, Oil 1,882); Contingency 1,137; Total 49,566 (Source: IMF, *Iraq: Request for Stand-By Arrangement and Cancellation of Current Arrangement—Staff Report; Staff Supplement; Press Release on the Executive Board Discussion; and Statement by the Executive Director for Iraq*—January 2008).

2008 (ID '000 million, budget forecasts): *Revenues and grants:* Revenues 55,520 (Crude oil export revenues 42,442); Grants 1,701; Total 57,222. *Expenditures:* Current 44,073 (Salaries and pensions 16,324; Non-oil goods and services 8,613; Oil sector goods and services 5,105; Transfers 11,148); Capital 20,071 (Non-oil 17,623, Oil 2,403, Other 45); Contingency 175; Total 64,318 (Source: IMF, *Iraq: Request for Stand-By Arrangement and Cancellation of Current Arrangement—Staff Report; Staff Supplement; Press Release on the Executive Board Discussion; and Statement by the Executive Director for Iraq*—January 2008).

CENTRAL BANK RESERVES
(US $ million at 31 December)

	2004	2005	2006
Gold (national valuation)	79.0	96.8	119.9
IMF special drawing rights	459.9	419.6	438.8
Reserve position in IMF	265.7	244.5	257.4
Foreign exchange	7,098.5	11,439.9	18,839.2
Total	**7,903.1**	**12,200.8**	**19,655.3**

Source: IMF, *International Financial Statistics*.

MONEY SUPPLY
(ID '000 million at 31 December)

	2004	2005	2006
Currency outside banks	7,163	9,113	10,965
Bank reserves	5,056	4,682	6,556
Broad money	**12,219**	**13,795**	**17,521**

COST OF LIVING
(Consumer Price Index; base: 1993 = 100)

	2004	2005	2006
Food	4,544	5,558	7,218
Fuel and light	32,227	64,161	183,515
Clothing and fabrics	3,132	3,428	4,164
Rent	34,336	48,912	66,075
All items (incl. others)	**8,816**	**12,074**	**18,501**

NATIONAL ACCOUNTS

National Income and Product
(ID million at current prices, UN estimates)

	2000	2001	2002
Compensation of employees	1,340,001	1,507,349	1,661,849
Operating surplus	3,150,521	3,478,128	3,837,770
Domestic factor incomes	**4,490,522**	**4,985,477**	**5,499,619**
Consumption of fixed capital	555,974	613,786	677,252
Gross domestic product (GDP) at factor cost	**5,046,496**	**5,599,264**	**6,176,871**
Indirect taxes	−172,336	−237,687	−252,329
GDP in purchasers' values	**4,874,160**	**5,361,576**	**5,924,542**

Source: UN Economic and Social Commission for Western Asia, *National Accounts Studies of the ESCWA Region* (2001).

Gross Domestic Product (US $ million at current prices, estimates): 31,379 in 2005; 49,527 in 2006; 62,574 in 2007 (projection) (Source: IMF, *Iraq: Request for Stand-By Arrangement and Cancellation of Current Arrangement—Staff Report; Staff Supplement; Press Release on the Executive Board Discussion; and Statement by the Executive Director for Iraq*—January 2008).

EXPENDITURE ON THE GROSS DOMESTIC PRODUCT
(ID million at current prices, UN estimates)

	2000	2001	2002
Government final consumption expenditure	1,043,685	1,150,957	1,273,690
Private final consumption expenditure	3,560,338	3,921,066	4,301,897
Increase in stocks	−131,256	−143,658	−158,023
Gross fixed capital formation	421,318	472,068	543,280
Total domestic expenditure	**4,894,085**	**5,400,433**	**5,960,844**
Exports of goods and services	753,482	878,881	1,048,376
Less Imports of goods and services	773,407	917,738	1,084,678
GDP in purchasers' values	**4,874,160**	**5,361,576**	**5,924,542**
GDP at constant 1995 prices	**2,909,277**	**3,171,112**	**3,393,090**

Source: UN Economic and Social Commission for Western Asia, *National Accounts Studies of the ESCWA Region* (2001).

IRAQ

Gross Domestic Product by Economic Activity
(ID '000 million at current prices)

	2004	2005	2006
Agriculture, hunting, forestry and fishing	3,539	4,249	4,133
Mining and quarrying	30,543	39,366	50,302
Crude oil	30,496	39,316	50,240
Manufacturing	771	1,221	1,288
Electricity, gas and water	263	393	367
Construction	468	2,932	616
Trade, restaurants and hotels	3,071	4,084	4,630
Transport, storage and communications	3,688	4,911	5,562
Finance, insurance and real estate	663	931	840
Government, community, social and personal services	5,200	6,140	9,983
Statistical discrepancy	—	—	3
Sub-total	48,207	64,228	77,724
Less Imputed bank service charge	248	227	357
GDP at factor cost	47,959	64,000	77,367
Indirect taxes	246	777	1,260
Less Subsidies	11,155	14,786	16,781
GDP in market prices	37,049	49,991	61,845

Source: IMF, *Iraq: Statistical Appendix* (August 2007).

BALANCE OF PAYMENTS
(US $ million)

	2005*	2006*	2007†
Exports of goods	19,772	28,412	34,134
Imports of goods	−18,749	−20,625	−26,464
Trade balance	1,024	7,787	7,671
Services (net)	−5,740	−5,164	−4,198
Balance on goods and services	−4,716	2,623	3,473
Other income (net)	−4,420	−3,428	−3,200
Balance on goods, services and income	−9,136	−805	273
Current transfers received	8,749	6,178	1,838
Current transfers paid	−959	−1,385	−1,664
Private transfers (net)	500	600	790
Current balance	−845	4,589	1,237
Financial account (net)	3,106	380	2,687
Net errors and omissions	23	3,023	2,278
Statistical discrepancy	—	110	—
Overall balance	2,283	8,102	6,202

* Estimates.
† Projected figures.

Source: IMF, *Iraq: Request for Stand-By Arrangement and Cancellation of Current Arrangement—Staff Report; Staff Supplement; Press Release on the Executive Board Discussion; and Statement by the Executive Director for Iraq*—January 2008.

External Trade

PRINCIPAL COMMODITIES
(US $ million)

Imports c.i.f.	2005	2006
Food and live animals	807	716
Beverages and tobacco	308	274
Crude materials (inedible) except fuels	414	368
Mineral fuels, lubricants, etc.	2,320	2,060
Animal and vegetable oils and fats	1,504	1,335
Chemicals	1,582	1,404
Basic manufactures	1,967	1,747
Machinery and transport equipment	10,234	9,086
Miscellaneous manufactured articles	3,725	3,307
Total (incl. others)	24,203	21,487

Exports c.i.f.	2005	2006
Food and live animals	60	86
Crude materials (inedible) except fuels	44	46
Mineral fuels, lubricants, etc.	23,578	30,298
Chemicals	—	2
Basic manufactures	15	16
Machinery and transport equipment	—	72
Total (incl. others)	23,697	30,536

PRINCIPAL TRADING PARTNERS
(US $ million)

Imports c.i.f.	1988	1989	1990
Australia	153.4	196.2	108.7
Austria	n.a.	1.1	50.9
Belgium-Luxembourg	57.6	68.2	68.3
Brazil	346.0	416.4	139.5
Canada	169.9	225.1	150.4
China, People's Republic	99.2	148.0	157.9
France	278.0	410.4	278.3
Germany	322.3	459.6	389.4
India	32.3	65.2	57.5
Indonesia	38.9	122.7	104.9
Ireland	150.4	144.9	31.6
Italy	129.6	285.1	194.0
Japan	533.0	621.1	397.2
Jordan	164.3	210.0	220.3
Korea, Republic	98.5	123.9	149.4
Netherlands	111.6	102.6	93.8
Romania	113.3	91.1	30.1
Saudi Arabia	37.2	96.5	62.5
Spain	43.4	129.0	40.5
Sri Lanka	50.1	33.5	52.3
Sweden	63.0	40.6	64.8
Switzerland	65.7	94.4	126.6
Thailand	22.3	59.2	68.9
Turkey	874.7	408.9	196.0
USSR	70.7	75.7	77.9
United Kingdom	394.6	448.5	322.1
USA	979.3	1,001.7	658.4
Yugoslavia	154.5	182.0	123.1
Total (incl. others)	5,960.0	6,956.2	4,833.9

Exports f.o.b.	1988	1989	1990*
Belgium-Luxembourg	147.5	249.6	n.a.
Brazil	1,002.8	1,197.2	n.a.
France	517.4	623.9	0.8
Germany	122.0	76.9	1.7
Greece	192.5	189.4	0.3
India	293.0	438.8	14.7
Italy	687.1	549.7	10.6
Japan	712.1	117.1	0.1
Jordan	28.4	25.2	101.6
Netherlands	152.9	532.3	0.2
Portugal	120.8	125.8	n.a.
Spain	370.0	575.7	0.7
Turkey	1,052.6	1,331.0	83.5
USSR	835.7	1,331.7	8.9
United Kingdom	293.1	167.0	4.4
USA	1,458.9	2,290.8	0.2
Yugoslavia	425.4	342.0	10.4
Total (incl. others)	10,268.3	12,333.7	392.0

* Excluding exports of most petroleum products.

Source: UN, *International Trade Statistics Yearbook*.

2005 (US $ million): *Imports by region:* Arab nations 7,198; North and South America 3,546; EU 2,685; Other Europe 6,975; Asia 2,530; Other countries 598; Total imports 23,532. *Exports by region:* Arab nations 763; North and South America 13,185; EU 6,277; Other Europe 393; Asia 2,292; Other countries 787; Total exports 23,697.

2006 (US $ million): *Imports by region:* Arab nations 7,855; North and South America 1,650; EU 2,946; Other Europe 6,226; Asia 2,194; Other countries 21; Total imports 20,892. *Exports by region:* Arab nations 946; North and South America 17,035; EU 6,808; Other Europe 611; Asia 5,098; Other countries 30; Total exports 30,528.

Transport

RAILWAYS
(traffic)

	1995*	1996†	1997†
Passenger-km (million)	2,198	1,169	1,169
Freight ton-km (million)	1,120	931	956

* Source: UN, *Statistical Yearbook*.
† Source: Railway Gazette International, *Railway Directory*.

ROAD TRAFFIC
(estimates, '000 motor vehicles in use)

	1995	1996
Passenger cars	770.1	773.0
Buses and coaches	50.9	51.4
Lorries and vans	269.9	272.5
Road tractors	37.2	37.2

Source: IRF, *World Road Statistics*.

SHIPPING
Merchant Fleet
(registered at 31 December)

	2004	2005	2006
Number of vessels	86	86	86
Total displacement ('000 grt)	163.1	142.2	142.2

Source: Lloyd's Register-Fairplay, *World Fleet Statistics*.

CIVIL AVIATION
(revenue traffic on scheduled services)

	1991	1992	1994*
Kilometres flown (million)	0	0	0
Passengers carried ('000)	28	53	31
Passenger-km (million)	17	35	20
Freight ton-km (million)	0	3	2

* Figures for 1993 unavailable.
Source: UN, *Statistical Yearbook*.

Tourism

ARRIVALS AT FRONTIERS OF VISITORS FROM ABROAD*

Country of nationality	1999	2000	2001
India	4,893	3,092	3,714
Iran	20,849	69,155	117,368
Lebanon	780	8	6
Pakistan	2,063	2,985	2,377
Total (incl. others)	30,328	78,457	126,654

* Including same-day visitors.
Tourism receipts (US $ million): 13 in 1998.
Source: World Tourism Organization.

Communications Media

	1997	1998	1999
Radio receivers ('000 in use)	4,850	n.a.	n.a.
Television receivers ('000 in use)	1,750	1,800	1,850
Telephones ('000 main lines in use)	651	650	675*

* Estimate.

2006: Telephones ('000 main lines in use) 1,034.2; Mobile cellular telephones ('000 subscribers) 574; Internet users ('000) 36.

Sources: UN, *Statistical Yearbook*; International Telecommunication Union.

Education

(2003/04, unless otherwise indicated)

	Institutions	Teachers	Students
Pre-primary	631	2,993	53,499
Primary	11,066	206,953	4,280,602
Secondary:			
academic	2,968	74,681	1,454,775
vocational	158	4,693	62,842
Teacher training	101	2,984	66,139
Higher*	65	14,700	240,000†

* 2002/03.
† Figure for undergraduates only.
Sources: Ministries of Education and Higher Education.

Adult literacy rate (UNESCO estimates): 74.1% (males 84.1%; females 62.4%) in 2001 (Source: UNESCO Institute for Statistics).

Directory

As a result of the US-led military campaign to oust the regime of Saddam Hussain in early 2003, and the ensuing insurgency, buildings occupied by a number of government ministries and other institutions were reported to have been damaged or destroyed.

The Constitution

On 15 November 2003 the Coalition Provisional Authority, established following the overthrow of the regime of Saddam Hussain that April, and the Governing Council, inaugurated in July, agreed on a timetable for the restoration of full Iraqi sovereignty, the drafting of a permanent constitution and the holding of free national elections. The Governing Council signed a Transitional Administrative Law (TAL) on 8 March 2004, which outlined a new timetable for the establishment of sovereign, elected organs of government. The basic tenets of the TAL were to: define the structures of a transitional government and procedures for electing members of the Transitional National Assembly (TNA); guarantee basic rights for all Iraqis, including freedom of speech and the press; and respect the Islamic identity of the Iraqi majority and guarantee religious plurality. The TAL was to expire once a permanent, constitutionally elected government had been established.

Following national elections to the 275-member TNA, held on 30 January 2005, the elected members of this transitional legislature approved the text of a draft Constitution, which was ratified by the Iraqi people in a national referendum on 15 October (with the endorsement of 78.6% of votes cast). National elections for a permanent legislature, the Council of Representatives, took place on 15 December, with members to serve a four-year term. (For further details regarding the text of the new Constitution, see Recent History.)

The Government

HEAD OF STATE

President: JALAL TALABANI (assumed office 7 April 2005, re-elected by the Council of Representatives 22 April 2006).
Vice-Presidents: TAREQ AL-HASHIMI, Dr ADIL ABD AL-MAHDI.

COUNCIL OF MINISTERS
(March 2008)

The radical Shi'a cleric Muqtada as-Sadr ordered the six ministers from his faction to withdraw from the Council of Ministers on 16 April 2007. This was followed, on 1 August, by the resignation from the Government of six members of the Sunni Iraqi Accord Front. Eight of the 12 ministerial portfolios affected by these withdrawals remained vacant in early 2008.

Prime Minister: NURI KAMAL (JAWAD) AL-MALIKI.
Deputy Prime Minister: Dr BARHAM SALIH.
Minister of Agriculture: Dr ALI AL-BAHADILI.
Minister of Communications: MUHAMMAD TAWFIQ ALLAWI.
Minister of Construction and Housing: BAYAN DAZEE.
Minister of Culture: (vacant).
Minister of Defence: Lt-Gen. ABD AL-QADIR MUHAMMAD JASIM OBEIDI.
Minister of Displacement and Migration: Dr ABD AS-SAMAD RAHMAN SULTAN.
Minister of Education: KHUDAYER AL-KHUZAIE.
Minister of Electricity: KARIM WAHID HASSAN.
Minister of the Environment: NARMIN OTHMAN HASSAN.
Minister of Finance: BAQIR SULAGH (BAYAN) JABR AZ-ZUBEIDI.
Minister of Foreign Affairs: HOSHYAR AZ-ZIBARI.
Minister of Health: Dr SALIH AL-HASNAWI.
Minister of Higher Education and Scientific Research: (vacant).
Minister of Human Rights: WIJDAN MIKHA'IL.
Minister of Industry and Minerals: FAWZI AL-HARIRI.
Minister of the Interior: JAWAD AL-BULANI.
Minister of Justice: (vacant).
Minister of Labour and Social Affairs: MAHMOUD MUHAMMAD AR-RADI.
Minister of Municipalities and Public Works: RIYAD GHARIB.
Minister of National Dialogue and Reconciliation: Dr AKRAM AL-HAKIM.
Minister of Oil: Dr HUSSAIN ASH-SHAHRISTANI.
Minister of Planning and Development Co-operation: ALI GHALIB BABAN.
Minister of Science and Technology: RA'ID FAHMI JAHID.
Minister of Trade: ABD AL-FALAH HASSAN AS-SUDANI.
Minister of Transport: (vacant).
Minister of Water Resources: Dr ABD AL-LATIF JAMAL RASHID.
Minister of Youth and Sports: JASIM MUHAMMAD JA'FAR.
Minister of State for Civil Society Affairs: (vacant).
Minister of State for Council of Representatives Affairs: SAFA AD-DIN MUHAMMAD AS-SAFI.
Minister of State for Foreign Affairs: (vacant).
Minister of State for National Security Affairs: SHIRWAN AL-WAILI.
Minister of State for Provincial Affairs: (vacant).
Acting Minister of State for Tourism and Archaeology Affairs: MUHAMMAD ABBAS AL-OREIBI.
Minister of State for Women's Affairs: (vacant).
Ministers of State: ALI MUHAMMAD AHMAD, HASSAN RADI KAZIM AS-SARI.

MINISTRIES

Ministry of Agriculture: Khulafa St, Khullani Sq., Baghdad; tel. (1) 887-3251; e-mail minis_of_agr@moagr.org; internet www.moagr.com.
Ministry of Communications: Baghdad; tel. (1) 717-9440; e-mail iraqimoc@iraqimoc.net; internet www.iraqimoc.net.
Ministry of Construction and Housing: Baghdad; e-mail mochiraqi@yahoo.com; internet www.uruklink.net/moch/english/eindex.htm.
Ministry of Culture: POB 624, Qaba bin Nafi Sq., Sadoun St, Baghdad; tel. (1) 538-3171.
Ministry of Defence: Baghdad; e-mail webmaster@mod.iraqiaf.org; internet www.iraqmod.org.
Ministry of Displacement and Migration: Baghdad; tel. (1) 537-0842; fax (1) 537-2497.
Ministry of Education: Saad State Enterprises Bldg, nr the Convention Centre, Baghdad; tel. (1) 883-2571.
Ministry of Electricity: Baghdad; e-mail infocen@moelc.gov.iq; internet www.moelc.gov.iq.
Ministry of the Environment: POB 10026, Baghdad.
Ministry of Finance: Khulafa St, nr ar-Russafi Sq., Baghdad; tel. (1) 887-4871.
Ministry of Foreign Affairs: opp. State Org. for Roads and Bridges, Karradat Mariam, Baghdad; tel. (1) 537-0091; e-mail press@iraqmofa.net; internet www.mofa.gov.iq.
Ministry of Health: Baghdad.
Ministry of Higher Education and Scientific Research: Baghdad; tel. and fax (1) 280-6315; e-mail ministry@moheiraq.org; internet www.moheiraq.org.
Ministry of Human Rights: Baghdad.
Ministry of Industry and Minerals: POB 13, Baghdad; tel. (1) 822-7136; e-mail admin@industry.gov.iq; internet www.industry.gov.iq.
Ministry of the Interior: Baghdad.
Ministry of Justice: Baghdad; fax (964) 537-2269; e-mail minister@iraqi-justice.org; internet www.iraqi-justice.org.
Ministry of Labour and Social Affairs: Baghdad; e-mail info@iraqi-molsa.org; internet www.iraqi-molsa.org.
Ministry of Municipalities and Public Works: Baghdad.
Ministry of National Dialogue and Reconciliation: Baghdad.
Ministry of National Security Affairs: North Gate, Baghdad; tel. (1) 888-9071.
Ministry of Oil: Oil Complex Bldg, Port Said St, Baghdad; tel. (1) 817-7000; fax (1) 886-9432; e-mail oilminoffice@oil.gov.iq; internet www.oil.gov.iq.
Ministry of Planning and Development Co-operation: 929/29/6 Arrasat al-Hindiya, Baghdad; tel. and fax (1) 885-3653; e-mail ministry@mopdc-iraq.org; internet www.mop-iraq.org.
Ministry of Science and Technology: Baghdad.
Ministry of Trade: POB 5833, Khullani Sq., Baghdad; tel. (1) 887-2681; fax (1) 790-1907; e-mail motcenter@motiraq.org; internet www.motiraq.org.
Ministry of Transport: nr Martyr's Monument, Karradat Dakhil, Baghdad; tel. (1) 776-6041; e-mail iraqitransport@yahoo.com; internet www.transportiraq.org.
Ministry of Water Resources: Palestine St, Baghdad; tel. (1) 772-0240; fax (1) 774-0672; e-mail waterresmin@yahoo.co.uk; internet iraq-mowr.org.
Ministry of Youth and Sports: Baghdad; e-mail info@iraqmoys.com; internet www.iraqimoys.com.

Legislature

COUNCIL OF REPRESENTATIVES

Speaker: MAHMOUD AL-MASHHADANI.
Election, 15 December 2005

	Valid votes cast	% of valid votes	Seats
United Iraqi Alliance	5,021,137	41.19	128
Kurdistan Alliance List	2,642,172	21.67	53
Iraqi Accord Front	1,840,216	15.09	44
Iraqi National List	977,325	8.02	25
Iraqi Front for National Dialogue	499,963	4.10	11
Kurdistan Islamic Union	157,688	1.29	5
Reconciliation and Liberation Bloc	129,847	1.07	3
Risaliyun	145,028	1.19	2
Iraqi Turkmen Front	87,993	0.72	1
National Rafidain List	47,263	0.39	1
Mithal al-Aloosi List for Iraqi Nation	32,245	0.26	1
Al-Ezediah Movement for Progress and Reform	21,908	0.18	1
Others	588,348	4.83	—
Total	**12,191,133***	**100.00**	**275**

* Excluding 139,656 invalid votes and 62,836 blank votes cast at polling stations in Iraq, and 1,912 invalid votes and 1,094 blank votes cast by eligible Iraqi voters abroad. Of the total, 11,895,756 valid votes were cast in Iraq, and 295,377 valid votes were cast abroad.

Kurdish Autonomous Regions

A 15-article accord signed by the Iraqi Government and Kurdish leaders in 1970 provided for: the creation of a unified autonomous area for the Kurdish population, comprising the administrative departments of As-Sulaimaniya (Sulaimaniya), D'hok and Irbil (Arbil), and the Kurdish sector of the city of Kirkuk; and the establishment of a 50-member Kurdish Legislative Council. Following the recapture of Kuwait from Iraqi forces by a multinational military coalition in early 1991, a designated 'safe haven' north of latitude 36°N (encompassing much of the Kurdish-inhabited regions) was imposed by the coalition partners. Renewed negotiations between the Iraqi Government (under Saddam Hussain) and Kurdish groups stalled over the status of Kirkuk, and in October 1991 the Government effectively severed all economic and administrative support to the region. In May 1992 the Kurdish Iraqi Front (KIF), an alliance of several Kurdish factions—including the two largest, the Patriotic Union of Kurdistan (PUK) and the Kurdistan Democratic Party (KDP)—established in 1988, organized elections to a new 105-member Iraqi Kurdistan National Assembly (see below). After bitter factional disputes had led to the effective disintegration of the KIF, in September 1996 the Government announced the restoration of full Iraqi sovereignty over the Kurdish areas, but the KDP, which, under Masoud Barzani, had established the predominant influence in the region, announced the composition of a coalition administration for the territories (excluding the PUK, with which it was still in open conflict), to be based in Arbil, later that month. In September 1998 the USA brokered a formal peace agreement between representatives of the PUK and the KDP in Washington, DC, which provided for a unified regional administration, the sharing of local revenues and co-operation in implementing the UN-sponsored 'oil-for-food' programme. Legislative elections, scheduled to take place in 1999 under the terms of the Washington agreement, were subsequently postponed. In December 1999 the KDP announced the composition of a new 25-member coalition administration (comprising the KDP, the Iraqi Communist Party, the Assyrian Movement, the Independent Workers' Party of Kurdistan, the Islamic Union and independents) for the areas under its control, principally the departments of Arbil and D'hok. Municipal elections (to select 571 officials) were conducted in the KDP-administered region in May 2001; according to official KDP sources, KDP candidates received 81% of votes cast. Negotiations between representatives of the KDP and the PUK for the full implementation of the Washington accord were held during 2002, and resulted in the resumption of a transitional joint session of the Iraqi Kurdistan National Assembly in October (see below). The autonomous regions retained their status following the removal of the regime of Saddam Hussain in early 2003, but the status of Kirkuk remained highly controversial (see Recent History).

IRAQI KURDISTAN NATIONAL ASSEMBLY

In May 1992, negotiations with the Iraqi Government over the full implementation of the 1970 accord on Kurdish regional autonomy having stalled, the KIF unilaterally organized elections to a 105-member Iraqi Kurdistan National Assembly, in which almost the entire electorate of 1.1m. participated. The KDP and the PUK were the only parties to achieve representation in the new Assembly and subsequently agreed to share seats equally (50 seats each—five having been reserved for two Assyrian Christian parties). The subsequent disintegration of the KIF and prolonged armed conflict between elements of the KDP and the PUK prevented the Assembly from becoming properly instituted, although the KDP attempted to incorporate the legislature into the administration of the territories under its control in the late 1990s and early 2000s, retaining the name of the Assembly and continuing to appoint officials. Relations between the KDP and the PUK were generally improved following the Washington agreement of September 1998, and on 8 September 2002 representatives of the two parties signed an agreement providing for the inauguration of a transitional joint parliamentary session (with representation based on the results of the May 1992 elections) before the end of the year. On 4 October 2002 a joint session of the Iraqi Kurdistan National Assembly was convened for the first time since 1996. Following the removal of the regime of Saddam Hussain by US-led forces in early 2003, elections to a new Iraqi Kurdistan National Assembly took place on 30 January 2005, concurrently with elections to the Transitional National Assembly. The Kurdistan Democratic List won 104 of the 111 seats, the Islamic Group of Kurdistan six and the Kurdistan Toilers Party one. On 12 June the new Kurdish legislature voted unanimously to appoint Masoud Barzani, leader of the KDP, to the post of President of the Kurdish Autonomous Region. (Barzani's election was widely considered to be part of a power-sharing arrangement reached with PUK leader Jalal Talabani, who had been appointed President of Iraq in April.) The current Kurdish government, led by Barzani, assumed office on 7 May 2006, and represented the region's first unified Cabinet. Prior to a unification agreement signed in January 2006, Sulaimaniya had been governed by the PUK, while Arbil and D'hok were administered by the KDP. One of the key objectives of the new Arbil-based government is for Kirkuk to be included in the Kurdish Autonomous Region.

Election Commission

Independent Electoral Commission of Iraq (IECI): Baghdad; tel. (1) 743-2519; e-mail public@ieciraq.org; internet www.ieciraq.org; f. 2004 by former Coalition Provisional Authority; independent; Chair. IZZADIN AL-MUHAMMADI.

Political Organizations

Following the removal from power of the Baathist regime, restrictions were effectively lifted on opposition political organizations that were either previously declared illegal, forced to operate clandestinely within Iraq or were based abroad. A total of 307 political parties and 19 coalitions registered with the Independent Electoral Commission of Iraq for the elections to a permanent Council of Representatives in December 2005.

Arab Baath Socialist Party: revolutionary Arab socialist movement founded in Damascus, Syria, in 1947; governed Iraq during 1968–2003 as principal constituent of ruling coalition, the National Progressive Front (NPF); the NPF was removed from power by US-led forces in May 2003, whereupon membership of the Baath Party was declared illegal and former party mems were barred from government and military posts; subsequently thought to be involved in insurgent activities in Iraq; in Feb. 2008 new legislation was ratified permitting certain former Baathists to be reinstated to official posts; in Jan. 2007, following the execution of former Iraqi President Saddam Hussain, former Vice-President IZZAT IBRAHIM AD-DOURI was named as the party's new leader.

Assyrian Democratic Movement (Zowaa Dimuqrataya Aturaya—Zowaa): e-mail info@zowaa.org; internet www.zowaa.org; f. 1979; seeks recognition of Assyrian rights within framework of democratic national government; Sec.-Gen. YOUNADAM YOUSUF KANNA.

Assyrian Socialist Party: Baghdad; e-mail gaboatouraya@yahoo.co.uk; internet asp2.no.sapo.pt; f. 2002 (refounded); calls for the establishment of an Assyrian nation.

Bet-Nahrain Democratic Party (BNDP): POB 4354, Modesto, CA 95352, USA; fax (425) 696-4984; e-mail info@bndp.net; internet www.bndp.net; f. 1976; seeks the establishment of an autonomous state for Assyrians in Bet-Nahrain (Iraq); Sec. YOUASH JON YOUASH.

Al-Ezediah Movement for Progress and Reform: Yazidi grouping; Leader AMIN FARHAN JEJO.

Free Officers and Civilians Movement: Baghdad; f. 1996; fmrly Free Officers' Movement; Founder and Leader Brig.-Gen. NAGIB AS-SALIHI.

General Council for the People of Iraq: Sunni; contested Dec. 2005 legislative elections as part of the Iraqi Accord Front (IAF); Leader ADNAN AD-DULAIMI.

Independent Democratic Movement (IDM) (Democratic Centrist Tendency): f. 2003; seeks a secular and democratic government of Iraq; Founder ADNAN PACHACHI (returned from exile in the United Arab Emirates in 2003).

Iraqi Accord Front (IAF) (Jabhat at-Tawafuq al-Iraqiya): f. 2005; Sunni; coalition of the Iraqi Islamic Party (IIP), the General Council for the People of Iraq and the Iraqi National Dialogue Council; formed to encourage Sunni voters to participate in the Dec. 2005 legislative elections; Leaders ADNAN AD-DULAIMI, TAREQ AL-HASHIMI.

Iraqi Communist Party (ICP): Baghdad; e-mail iraq@iraqcp.org; internet www.iraqcp.org; f. 1934; became legally recognized in July 1973 on formation of NPF; left NPF March 1979; contested elections of Dec. 2005 as mem. of the Iraqi National List (INL); First Sec. HAMID MAJID MOUSSA.

Iraqi Constitutional Monarchy (ICM): Baghdad; tel. (1) 778-2897; fax (1) 778-0199; e-mail webmaster@iraqcmm.org; internet www.iraqcmm.org; f. 1993; fmrly Constitutional Monarchy Movement; supports the claim to the Iraqi throne of Sharif ALI BIN AL-HUSSAIN, cousin to the late King FAISAL II, as constitutional monarch with an elected government.

Iraqi Front for National Dialogue (Hewar National Iraqi Front): f. 2005; coalition of minor Sunni parties; declined to join the IAF prior to the Dec. 2005 elections owing to its objection to the (constituent mem.) IIP's acceptance of the Constitution; Founder and Leader SALEH AL-MUTLAQ.

Iraqi Islamic Party (IIP) (al-Hizb al-Islami al-'Iraqi): e-mail info@iraqiparty.com; internet www.iraqiparty.com; f. 1960; Sunni; branch of the Muslim Brotherhood; boycotted elections of Jan. 2005, but participated in the Dec. 2005 elections as part of the IAF; Leader Dr MOHSEN ABD AL-HAMID; Sec.-Gen. TAREQ AL-HASHIMI.

Iraqi National Accord (INA): e-mail wifaq_ina@hotmail.com; internet www.wifaq.com; f. 1990; contested Dec. 2005 legislative elections as mem. of INL; Founder and Sec.-Gen. Dr AYAD ALLAWI.

Iraqi National Alliance (INA) (at-Tahaluf al-Watani al-Iraqi): f. 1992; fmrly based in Syria; supports constitutional multi-party government; publishes bi-weekly online journal *Nida'a Al-Muqawamah (The Call to Resistance)*, advocating armed resistance to the presence of US-led coalition forces in Iraq; Leader ABD AL-JABBAR AL-QUBAYSI.

Iraqi National Congress (INC): e-mail info@inciraq.com; internet inciraq.com; f. 1992 in London, United Kingdom, as a multi-party coalition supported by the US Government; following the removal of the regime of Saddam Hussain, the INC moved to Baghdad and was transformed into a distinct political party; contested Jan. 2005 elections as part of the United Iraqi Alliance (UIA), but split to form National Congress Coalition for Dec. 2005 legislative elections, at which it failed to win any seats; Leader AHMAD CHALABI.

Iraqi National Dialogue Council: Sunni; participated in Dec. 2005 elections as mem. of IAF; Leader KHALAF AL-ULAYYAN.

Iraqi National Foundation Congress (INFC): Baghdad; f. 2004; multi-party coalition incl. Nasserites, pre-Saddam Hussain era Baathists, Kurds, Christians, Sunnis and Shi'ites; seeks secular government of national unity; opposed to presence of US-led coalition in Iraq, and consequently boycotted the electoral process initiated by the coalition; led by 25-mem. secretariat; Gen. Sec. Sheikh JAWAD AL-KHALISI.

Iraqi National List (INL): secular electoral list formed prior to the Dec. 2005 elections, consisting of a number of political orgs, incl. the INA, Iraqis, IDM and ICP; Leader Dr AYAD ALLAWI.

Iraqis (Iraqiyun): f. 2004; moderate; includes both Sunnis and Shi'ites; joined INL to contest Dec. 2005 legislative elections; Leader Sheikh GHAZI MASHAL AJIL AL-YAWAR.

Iraqi Turkmen Front (Irak Türkmen Cephesi): Arbil; internet www.kerkuk.net; f. 1995; coalition of Turkmen groups; seeks autonomy for Turkmen areas in Iraq and recognition of Turkmen as one of main ethnic groups in Iraq, and supports establishment of multi-party democratic system in Iraq; contests status of Kirkuk with Kurds; Leader SADETTIN ERGEÇ; Sec.-Gen. YUNUS BAYRAKTAR.

Islamic Action Organization (Munazzamat al-Amal al-Islami): Karbala; f. 1961; also known as Islamic Task Organization; Shi'ite; contested Jan. 2005 elections as mem. of UIA; Leaders Sheikh MUHAMMAD TAQI AL-MUDARRISI, HASSAN SHIRAZI, MUHAMMAD HUSSAIN SHIRAZI.

Islamic Dawa Party (Hizb ad-Da'wa al-Islamiya): Baghdad; e-mail info@islamicdawaparty.org; internet www.islamicdawaparty.org; f. 1957 in Najaf; banned 1980; fmrly based in Tehran, Iran, and London, re-established in Baghdad 2003; contested Jan. and Dec. 2005 elections as part of UIA coalition; predominantly Shi'ite, but with Sunni mems; advocates government centred on the principles of Islam; Gen. Sec. NURI KAMAL (JAWAD) AL-MALIKI.

Islamic Group of Kurdistan (Komaleh Islami): Khurmal; f. 2001; splinter group of IMIK; moderate Islamist, aligned with the PUK; Founder and Leader Mullah ALI BAPIR.

Islamic Movement in Iraqi Kurdistan (IMIK): Halabja; e-mail info@bzotnawa.net; internet www.bzotnawa.net; f. 1987; Islamist movement seeking to obtain greater legal rights for Iraqi Kurds; Founder and Leader Sheikh UTHMAN ABD AL-AZIZ.

Islamic Virtue Party (Hizb al-Fadhila al-Islamiya—IVP): Basra; Shi'ite; an offshoot of the Sadrist movement; follows the spiritual leadership of Ayatollah as-Sayyid Muhammad al-Ya'qubi; joined UIA for Jan. and Dec. 2005 elections, but withdrew from alliance in March 2007; Sec.-Gen. ABD AR-RAHIM AHMAD ALI AL-HASINI.

Jund al-Imam (Soldiers of the [Twelfth] Imam): f. 1969; Shi'ite; mem. of SIIC; Leader SA'D JAWAD QANDIL.

Kurdistan Alliance List: f. 2004 to contest Jan. 2005 legislative elections; participated in Dec. 2005 elections as a coalition of largely Kurdish parties, incl. the PUK, the KDP, the Kurdistan Toilers Party and the Kurdistan Communist Party.

Kurdistan Communist Party: e-mail regay_kurdistan@yahoo.com; internet www.kurdistancp.org; f. 1993; branch of the Iraqi Communist Party; Leader KAMAL SHAKIR.

Kurdistan Democratic List: coalition list of seven parties formed to contest the elections to the Iraqi Kurdistan National Assembly in Jan. 2005; includes the KDP, the BNDP and the Assyrian Patriotic Party.

Kurdistan Democratic Party (KDP): European Office (Germany), 10749 Berlin, POB 301516; tel. (30) 79743741; fax (30) 79743746; e-mail party@kdp.se; internet www.kdp.se; f. 1946; seeks to protect Kurdish rights and promote Kurdish culture and interests through regional political and legislative autonomy, as part of a federative republic; see also Kurdistan Alliance List and Kurdistan Democratic List; Pres. MASOUD BARZANI; Vice-Pres. ALI ABDULLAH.

Kurdistan Islamic Union (Yakgrtui Islami Kurdistan): internet kurdiu.org; f. 1991; seeks establishment of Islamic state in Iraq which recognizes the rights of Kurds; branch of the Muslim Brotherhood; withdrew from Kurdistan Alliance List to run independently in the Dec. 2005 elections; Sec.-Gen. SALAHEDDIN MUHAMMAD BAHAEDDIN.

Kurdistan Socialist Democratic Party (KSDP): Sulaimaniya; f. 1994; splinter group of the KDP, aligned with the PUK; joined Kurdistan Alliance List for Dec. 2005 legislative elections; Leader MUHAMMAD HAJI MAHMUD.

Kurdistan Toilers Party (Hizbi Zahmatkeshani Kurdistan): f. 1985; advocates a federal Iraq; closely associated with the KSDP; contested Jan. and Dec. 2005 elections as part of Kurdistan Alliance List; Leader QADIR AZIZ.

Mithal al-Aloosi List for Iraqi Nation: nationalist secular Sunni grouping formed for Dec. 2005 elections, comprising the Iraqi Federalist Gathering and the Iraqi Ummah Party; Leader MITHAL AL-ALOOSI.

National Democratic Party (NDP) (al-Hizb al-Watani ad-Dimuqrati): f. 1946; ceased political activities on occasion of Baathist coup in 1963; resumed activities following overthrow of Baathist regime in 2003; Leaders NASSER KAMAL AL-CHADERCHI, HUDAYB AL-HAJJ MAHMOUD.

National Rafidain List: f. 2004; Assyrian-Christian list headed by the Assyrian Democratic Movement; Leader YOUNADAM KANA.

Patriotic Union of Kurdistan (PUK): European Office (Germany), 10502 Berlin, POB 210213; tel. (30) 34097850; fax (30) 34097849; e-mail puk@puk.org; internet www.puk.org; f. 1975; seeks to protect and promote Kurdish rights and interests through self-determination; see also Kurdistan Alliance List; Pres. JALAL TALABANI.

Reconciliation and Liberation Bloc (Kutla al-Musalaha wa't-Tahrir): Mosul; f. 1995 in Jordan as Iraqi Homeland Party (Hizb al-Watan al-Iraqi); moved to Damascus, Syria, and to Mosul in 2003; liberal, secular Sunni; advocates withdrawal of coalition troops and partial rehabilitation of mems of the former Baathist regime; publishes newspaper *al-Ittijah al-Akhar*; Leader MISH'AN AL-JUBURI.

Risaliyun (Upholders of the Message): Shi'ite, Sadrist.

Sadr II Movement (Jamaat as-Sadr ath-Thani): Najaf; f. 2003; Shi'ite; opposes presence of US-led coalition in Iraq; mems of the Movement participated in Dec. 2005 elections within the UIA, under the registered title of As-Sadriah Advertising; military wing is Imam al-Mahdi army; Leader Hojatoleslam MUQTADA AS-SADR.

Socialist Nasserite Party (Hizb al-Ishtiraqi an-Nasiri): f. 2003; merger of Iraqi Socialist Party, Vanguard Socialist Nasserite Party, Unity Socialist Party and one other party; Leader MUBDIR AL-WAYYIS.

Supreme Islamic Iraqi Council (SIIC): Najaf; internet www.almejlis.org; f. 1982 as the Supreme Council for the Islamic Revolution in Iraq; name changed as above in 2007; Shi'ite; seeks government based on principle of *wilayat-e-faqih* (guardianship of the jurisprudent); armed faction, the Badr Organization (fmrly Badr Brigade), assisted coalition forces in Iraq after the removal of Saddam Hussain's regime; contested Jan. and Dec. 2005 elections on UIA list; Leader ABD AL-AZIZ AL-HAKIM.

Turkmen People's Party (Turkmen Halk Partisi): e-mail halk@turkmenhalk.zzn.com; internet www.angelfire.com/tn/halk; Leader IRFAN KIRKUKLI.

United Iraqi Alliance (UIA): list of mainly Shi'ite parties, dominated by the Islamic Dawa Party and the SIIC, which contested the Jan. and Dec. 2005 legislative elections as a single coalition; Leader ABD AL-AZIZ HAKIM.

United Iraqi Scholars' Group: f. 2004; pan-Iraqi coalition of 35 parties; opposed to presence of US-led coalition in Iraq; Leader Sheikh JAWAD AL-KHALISI.

Worker Communist Party of Iraq (IWCP): Sulaimaniya; e-mail wpiraq_leader@yahoo.com; internet www.wpiraq.net; f. 1993; opposes presence of US-led coalition in Iraq; Leader REBWAR AHMAD.

Other political, regional, ethnic and military groups based in Iraq, or based abroad and active in Iraq, include: **Action Party for the Independence of Kurdistan** (based in Arbil; splinter group of Iraqi Communist Party; Leader YOUSUF HANNA YOUSUF); **Assyrian Patriotic Party** (internet www.atranaya.org; f. 1973; active in northern Iraq; Leaders ALBERT YELDA, NIMRUD BAITO); **Free Democratic Homeland Party** (f. 2003 by merger of three political groups: the National Independence Party, the Arab National Democratic Movement and the Iraqi National Coalition); **Free Iraq Council** (f. 1991, following dissolution of the Umma—Nation—Party; London-based; Leader SA'D SALIH JABR); **Free Iraqi Society Party** (f. 2003; supports the return of a constitutional monarchy; Leader ABD AL-

MUHSIN SHALASH); **Grouping of Free Iraqis** (f. 1978; re-emerged 2003; supports the return of monarchy, but is not opposed to a republican system of governance; Leader FARIS KAHRDI); **Higher Council for National Salvation** (f. 2002; founded by fmr head of Iraqi Military Intelligence WAFIQ HAMUD AS-SAMARRA'I; has offered logistical support to US-led coalition); **Iraqi Arab Socialist Movement** (f. 2005, with the aim of promoting national unity; **Iraqi Democratic Party** (f. 1993; supports religious and political freedom; active in the exile movement in the 1990s; Leader ABD AL-AZIZ HAMAD AL-ALAYAN); **Iraqi Islamic Forces Union** (f. 2002; splinter group of SIIC); **Iraqi Justice and Development Party** (f. 2003; calls for Islam to be the basic source of legislation); **Iraqi National Movement** (INM; f. 2001; split from the INC, mainly Sunni military officers; Leader HATEM MUKHLIS); **Iraqi National Unity Grouping** (calls for national reconciliation among ethnic and political groups; Leader NIHRU MUHAMMAD ABD AL-KARIM AL-KASANZAN AL-HUSAYNI); **Iraqi Turkoman Birth Party** (f. 1999; aims to defend the rights of Turkomans in Iraq; Leader MUWAFFAQ MUHAMMAD CEVHER KURYALI); **Iraqi Turkoman Democratic Party** (f. 2002; supports federal Iraq; Leader AHMET GUNES); **Iraqi Turkoman National Party** (formed through the consolidation of five Turkmen parties; Dep. Leader JAMAL SHAN); **Islamic Democratic Current Party** (f. 2003; the party claims some 40,000 Shi'ite, Sunni and Christian members; Leader MUHAMMAD ABD AL-JABER SHABBUT); **Kurdistan National Democratic Union** (YNDK; e-mail midya@yndk.com; internet www.yndk.com; f. 1996; split between factions aligned with either the KDP or the PUK; Leader GHAFUR MAKHMURI); **Kurdistan Turkoman Democratic Party** (Leader DILSHAD CHAWUSHLI); **National Front for Unified National Action** (Sec.-Gen. ABD AR-RAHMAN NASRALLAH); **Turkoman Islamic Union** (f. 1991; Leader ABBAS AL-BAYATI); **Unified National Movement** (Sunni; linked to Muslim Brotherhood; Leader AHMAD AL-KUBAYSI).

Major militant groups which have launched attacks against Iraqis and the US-led coalition include: **Fedayeen Saddam** (Saddam's Martyrs; f. 1995 by members of the former Baathist regime; paramilitary group); **Ansar al-Islam** (f. 1998; splinter group of IMIK; Islamist; suspected of having links with al-Qa'ida); **Hezbollah** (Shi'ite Marsh Arab; Leader ABD AL-KARIM MAHMOUD MOHAMMEDAWI—'ABU HATEM'); **Ansar as-Sunnah** (f. 2003 by members of Ansar al-Islam; Islamist); **Imam al-Mahdi Army** (armed wing of the Sadr II Movement—Jamaat as-Sadr ath-Thani); **Base of Holy War in Mesopotamia** (Tanzim Qa'idat al-Jihad fi Bilad ar-Rafidain; Sunni insurgent network, also known as al-Qa'ida in Iraq; Leader ABU AYYUB AL-MASRI, also known as ABU HAMZA AL-MUHAJIR).

Diplomatic Representation

EMBASSIES IN IRAQ

Algeria: 13/14/613 Hay ad-Daoudi, Baghdad; tel. (1) 543-4137; fax (1) 542-5829; Ambassador (vacant).

Australia: International Zone, Baghdad; tel. (1) 538-2103; e-mail austemb.baghdad@dfat.gov.au; internet www.iraq.embassy.gov.au; Ambassador MARC INNES-BROWN.

Austria: 929/30/38 Hay Babel, Baghdad; tel. (1) 719-9049; fax (1) 718-2427; Chargé d'affaires GUDRUN HARRER.

Bahrain: 41/6/605 Hay al-Mutanabi, Baghdad; tel. (1) 541-0841; fax (1) 541-2027; Chargé d'affaires HASSAN AL-ANSARI.

Bangladesh: 6/14/929 Hay Babel, Baghdad; tel. (1) 719-0068; fax (1) 718-6045; Ambassador MUHAMMAD FAZLUR RAHMA.

Bulgaria: 12/25/624 al-Ameriya, Baghdad; tel. (1) 556-8197; fax (1) 556-4182; e-mail bulgemb@uruklink.net; Ambassador NIKOLAY GEORGIEV NICOLOV.

China, People's Republic: POB 15097, 624 New Embassy Area, Hitteen Quarter, Baghdad; tel. (1) 556-2741; fax (1) 556-9721; e-mail chinaemb_iq@mfa.gov.cn; Ambassador CHEN YIAU DONG.

Czech Republic: POB 27124, 37/11/601 Hay al-Mansour, Baghdad; tel. (1) 542-4868; fax (1) 214-2621; e-mail baghdad@embassy.mzv.cz; Ambassador PETER VOZNICA.

Denmark: Al-Jana'a Quarter, Hay at-Tashriya, Baghdad; tel. (1) 778-8440; e-mail bgwamb@um.dk; internet www.ambbagdad.um.dk; Ambassador BO ERIC WEBER.

Egypt: 103/11/601 Hay al-Mansour, Baghdad; tel. (1) 543-0572; fax (1) 242-5839; e-mail egypt@uruklink.net; Ambassador (vacant).

Finland: POB 2041, 86/25/925 Hay Babel, Baghdad; tel. (1) 776-6271; fax (1) 778-0488; e-mail fin-emb@yahoo.com.

France: POB 118, 7/55/102 Abu Nawas, Baghdad; tel. (1) 790-6061; fax (1) 718-1975; Ambassador JEAN FRANÇOIS GIRAULT.

Germany: POB 2036, Hay al-Mansour, Baghdad; tel. (1) 543-1470; fax (1) 541-5840; e-mail info@bagdad.diplo.de; internet www.bagdad.diplo.de; Ambassador Dr HANNS SCHUMACHER.

Greece: 63/13/913 Hay Babel, Baghdad; tel. (1) 718-2433; fax (1) 718-8729; e-mail greekembirq@hotmail.com; Ambassador PANAYOTIS MAKRIS.

Holy See: POB 2090, Saadoun St, 904/2/46, Baghdad; tel. (1) 719-5183; e-mail nuntiusiraq@yahoo.com; Apostolic Nuncio Most Rev. FRANCIS ASSISI CHULLIKATT (Titular Archbishop of Ostra).

Hungary: POB 2065, 43/4/609 al-Mansour, Hay al-Mutanabi, Baghdad; tel. (1) 543-2956; fax (1) 541-4766; e-mail huembbgd@hotmail.com; Chargé d'affaires ANDRÁS NAGY.

India: 6/25/306 Hay al-Maghrib, Baghdad; tel. (1) 422-2014; fax (1) 422-9549; Ambassador R. DAYAKAR.

Iran: POB 39095, Salehiya, Karadeh Maryam, Baghdad; tel. (1) 884-3033; fax (1) 537-5636; Ambassador HASSAN KAZEMI QOMI.

Italy: 33/7/15 Hay al-Maghrib, Mahala 304, Baghdad; tel. (1) 425-0720; e-mail ambasciata.baghdad@esteri.it; internet www.italian-embassy.org.ae/ambasciata_baghdad; Ambassador MAURIZIO MELANI.

Japan: 50/21/929 Hay Babel, Baghdad; tel. (1) 776-6791; e-mail azza_fh@yahoo.com; Ambassador KENJIRO MONJI.

Jordan: POB 6314, 145/49/617 Hay al-Andalus, Baghdad; tel. (1) 541-2892; fax (1) 541-2009; e-mail jordan@uruklink.net; Ambassador AHMAD AL-LOZI.

Korea, Republic: Baghdad; e-mail kembiraq@mofat.go.kr; Ambassador HA CHAN-HO.

Lebanon: 51/116, Askari St, Al-Liwadiat, Baghdad; tel. (1) 416-7850; fax (1) 416-8092; Chargé d'affaires HASSAN HUJAZI.

Morocco: POB 6039, 27/11/601 Hay al-Mansour, Baghdad; tel. (1) 542-1779; fax (1) 542-3030; Chargé d'affaires ESSADEK ABDELKRIM.

Netherlands: Park as-Sadoun, 10/38/103, Hay an-Nidhal, Baghdad; tel. (1) 7782571; e-mail bad@minbuza.nl; internet www.mfa.nl/bag; Ambassador ROBERT KABRELSEH.

Nigeria: 43/11/601 Hay al-Mansour, Baghdad; tel. (1) 541-3133; fax (1) 543-4513; Ambassador IBRAHIM MOHAMMED.

Pakistan: 14/7/609 Hay al-Mansour, Baghdad; tel. (1) 542-5343; fax (1) 542-8707; e-mail pakembbag@yahoo.com; Ambassador (vacant).

Philippines: POB 3236, 4/22/915 al-Jadriyah, Hay al-Jamiyah, Baghdad; tel. (1) 776-2696; fax (1) 719-3228; e-mail baghdadpe@dfa.gov.ph; Chargé d'affaires a.i. WILFREDO R. CUYUGAN.

Poland: 22–24/60/904 Hay al-Wihda, Baghdad; tel. (1) 719-0297; fax (1) 719-0296; e-mail ambaspol@tlen.pl; Ambassador EDWARD PIETRZYK.

Portugal: POB 2123, Alwiya, Baghdad; tel. (1) 541-3376; fax (1) 542-0845; Ambassador FRANCISCO DOMINGOS GARCIA FALÇÃO MACHADO.

Romania: POB 2571, Arassat al-Hindia St, 452A/31/929 Hay Babel, Baghdad; tel. (1) 776-2860; fax (1) 776-7553; e-mail ambrobagd@yahoo.com; Ambassador MIHAI STUPARU.

Russia: 4/5/605 Hay al-Mutanabi, Baghdad; tel. (1) 541-4749; fax (1) 543-4462; e-mail russian_embassy_in_iraq@land.ru; Ambassador VLADIMIR CHAMOV.

Serbia: 16/35/923 Hay Babel, Baghdad; tel. (1) 776-7887; fax (1) 717-1069; e-mail embscgb@warkaa.net; Ambassador NINO MALJEVIĆ.

Slovakia: 94/28/923 Hay Babel, Baghdad; tel. (1) 776-7367; fax (1) 776-7368; Ambassador JOZEF MARÉFKA.

Spain: POB 2072, 50/1/609 al-Mansour, Baghdad; tel. (1) 542-4851; fax (1) 541-9857; Ambassador IGNACIO RUPÉREZ RUBIO.

Switzerland: 41/5/929, Masbah House, Alwiya, Baghdad; tel. (1) 719-3091; e-mail vertretung@bag.rep.admin.ch; Ambassador MARTIN AESCHBACHER.

Syria: Baghdad.

Tunisia: 1/49/617 Hay al-Andalus, Baghdad; tel. (1) 542-0602; fax (1) 542-8585; Ambassador (vacant).

Turkey: 2/8 al-Waziriyah, Baghdad; tel. (1) 422-0022; fax (1) 422-8353; Ambassador DERYA KAMBAY.

Ukraine: POB 15192, 20/1/609 al-Mansour, al-Yarmouk, Baghdad; tel. (1) 542-6677; e-mail emb_iq@mfa.gov.ua; Ambassador (vacant).

United Arab Emirates: 81/34/611 Hay al-Andalus (ad-Daoudi), Baghdad; tel. (1) 543-9174; fax (1) 543-9093; Chargé d'affaires AHMAD ABDULLAH BIN SAID.

United Kingdom: c/o Iraq Policy Unit, Foreign and Commonwealth Office, London, SW1A 2AH, United Kingdom; tel. (20) 7008-1500; fax (20) 7008-4119; e-mail britembBaghdad@fco.gov.uk; internet www.britishembassy.gov.uk/iraq; Ambassador CHRISTOPHER PRENTICE.

USA: APO AE 09316, Baghdad; e-mail BaghdadPressOffice@state.gov; internet iraq.usembassy.gov; Ambassador RYAN C. CROCKER.

Viet Nam: POB 15054, 71/34/611 Hay al-Mansour, Baghdad; tel. (1) 541-3409; fax (1) 541-1388; e-mail vietnam@uruklink.net; Ambassador NGUYEN QUANG KHAI.

Yemen: 4/36/904 Hay al-Wahada, Baghdad; tel. (1) 718-6682; fax (1) 717-2318.

Judicial System

Following the ousting of the Baath regime, the judicial system was subject to a process of review and de-Baathification. In June 2003 the former Coalition Provisional Authority (CPA) established a **Judicial Review Committee**, whose task was to review and repair the material status of the courts and to assess personnel. In December the Governing Council created the **Iraqi Special Tribunal**, in order to bring to trial those senior members of the former regime accused of war crimes, crimes against humanity and genocide. The statute of the Tribunal was amended by the former Transitional National Assembly in October 2005, when it was renamed the **Supreme Iraqi Criminal Tribunal**.

In the interim period, a new judicial system was formed. The **Central Criminal Court of Iraq**, consisting of an **Investigative Court** and a **Trial Court**, was created by the CPA in July 2003 as the senior court in Iraq, with jurisdiction over all crimes committed in the country since 19 March 2003. With a few exceptions, the application of justice was to be based upon the 1969 Penal Code of Iraq and the 1971 Criminal Proceedings Code of Iraq.

Religion

ISLAM

About 95% of the population are Muslims, some 60% of whom are of the Shi'ite sect. The Arabs of northern Iraq, the Bedouins, the Kurds, the Turkomans and some of the inhabitants of Baghdad and Basra are mainly of the Sunni sect, while the remaining Arabs south of the Diyali are Shi'a.

CHRISTIANITY

There are Christian communities in all the principal towns of Iraq, but their main villages lie mostly in the Mosul district. The Christians of Iraq comprise three groups: (a) the free Churches, including the Nestorian, Gregorian and Syrian Orthodox; (b) the churches known as Uniate, since they are in union with the Roman Catholic Church, including the Armenian Uniates, Syrian Uniates and Chaldeans; (c) mixed bodies of Protestant converts, New Chaldeans and Orthodox Armenians. There are estimated to be 500,000–700,000 Christians of various denominations in Iraq; however, there has been an exodus to neighbouring countries in the mid-2000s, as a result of the ongoing sectarian conflict.

The Assyrian Church

Assyrian Christians, an ancient sect having sympathies with Nestorian beliefs, were forced to leave their mountainous homeland in northern Kurdistan in the early part of the 20th century. The estimated 550,000 members of the Apostolic Catholic Assyrian Church of the East are now exiles, mainly in Iraq (about 50,000 adherents), Syria, Lebanon and the USA. Their leader is the Catholicos Patriarch, His Holiness MAR DINKHA IV.

The Orthodox Churches

Armenian Apostolic Church: Diocese of the Armenian Diocese of Iraq, POB 2280, Jadriyah, Tayaran Sq., Baghdad; tel. (1) 815-1853; fax (1) 815-1857; e-mail iraqitem@yahoo.com; Primate Archbishop AVAK ASADOURIAN; 12 churches (four in Baghdad); 1,639 adherents in Baghdad, 1,375 in Mosul, 1,222 in Basra.

Syrian Orthodox Church: Archbishop of Baghdad and Basra SEVERIUS HAWA; 12,000 adherents in Iraq.

The Greek Orthodox Church is also represented in Iraq.

The Roman Catholic Church

Armenian Rite

At 31 December 2005 the archdiocese of Baghdad contained an estimated 2,000 adherents.

Archbishop of Baghdad: (vacant), 27/903 Archevêché Arménien Catholique, POB 2344, Karrada Sharkiya, Baghdad; tel. (1) 719-4034; e-mail derandon1@hotmail.com.

Chaldean Rite

Iraq comprises the patriarchate of Babylon, five archdioceses (including the patriarchal see of Baghdad) and five dioceses (all of which are suffragan to the patriarchate). Altogether, the Patriarch has jurisdiction over 21 archdioceses and dioceses in Iraq, Egypt, Iran, Lebanon, Syria, Turkey and the USA, and the Patriarchal Vicariate of Jerusalem. At 31 December 2005 there were an estimated 222,718 Chaldean Catholics in Iraq (including 145,000 in the archdiocese of Baghdad).

Patriarch of Babylon of the Chaldeans: Cardinal EMMANUEL III DELLY, POB 6112, Patriarcat Chaldéen Catholique, Al-Mansour, Baghdad; tel. (1) 537-9164; fax (1) 537-8556.

Archbishop of Arbil: (vacant), Archevêché Catholique Chaldéen, Ainkawa, Arbil; tel. (665) 225-0009.

Archbishop of Baghdad: the Patriarch of Babylon (see above).

Archbishop of Basra: (vacant), Archevêché Chaldéen, POB 217, Ashar-Basra; tel. (40) 613427.

Archbishop of Kirkuk: Most Rev. LOUIS SAKO, Archevêché Chaldéen, POB 490, Kirkuk; tel. (50) 220525; fax (50) 213978; e-mail bish_Luissako@yahoo.com.

Archbishop of Mosul: (vacant), Archevêché Chaldéen, POB 757, Mayassa, Mosul; tel. (60) 815831; fax (60) 816742; e-mail archdioceseofmossul@yahoo.com.

Latin Rite

The archdiocese of Baghdad, directly responsible to the Holy See, contained an estimated 2,500 adherents at 31 December 2005.

Archbishop of Baghdad: Most Rev. JEAN BENJAMIN SLEIMAN, Archevêché Latin, POB 35130, Hay al-Wahda—Mahallat 904, rue 8, Immeuble 44, 12906 Baghdad; tel. (1) 719-9537; fax (1) 717-2471; e-mail jbsleiman@yahoo.com.

Melkite Rite

The Greek-Melkite Patriarch of Antioch (GRÉGOIRE III LAHAM) is resident in Damascus, Syria.

Patriarchal Exarchate of Iraq: Exarchat Patriarchal Grec-Melkite, Karradat IN 903/10/50, Baghdad; tel. (1) 719-1082; 100 adherents (2005); Exarch Patriarchal (vacant).

Syrian Rite

Iraq comprises two archdioceses and the Patriarchal Exarchate of Basra; there were an estimated 62,000 adherents at 31 December 2005.

Archbishop of Baghdad: Most Rev. ATHANASE MATTI SHABA MATOKA, Archevêché Syrien Catholique, 903/2/1 Baghdad; tel. (1) 719-1850; fax (1) 719-0166; e-mail mattishaba@yahoo.com.

Archbishop of Mosul: Most Rev. BASILE GEORGES CASMOUSSA, Archevêché Syrien Catholique, Hosh al-Khan, Mosul; tel. (60) 762160; fax (60) 771439; e-mail syrcam2003@yahoo.com.

The Anglican Communion

Within the Episcopal Church in Jerusalem and the Middle East, Iraq forms part of the diocese of Cyprus and the Gulf. Expatriate congregations in Iraq meet at St George's Church, Baghdad. The Bishop in Cyprus and the Gulf is resident in Cyprus.

JUDAISM

A tiny Jewish community, numbering only an estimated eight people at mid-2007, remains in Baghdad.

OTHERS

About 550,000 Yazidis and a smaller number of Sabians and Shebeks reside in Iraq.

Sabian Community: An-Nasiriyah (Nasiriya); 20,000 adherents; Mandeans, mostly in Nasiriya; Head Sheikh DAKHIL.

Yazidis: Ainsifni; Leader TASHIN SAID ALI.

The Press

Since the overthrow of the regime of Saddam Hussain by US-led coalition forces in early 2003, the number of publications has proliferated: by the end of 2003 an estimated 250 newspapers and periodicals were in circulation, although only some 100 of these were reportedly still being published in mid-2005. Most newspapers are affiliated with political or religious organizations; however, the daily *As-Sabah* is controlled by the Iraqi Government, with coalition backing. Security issues have resulted in severe distribution problems, and some newspaper offices have either relocated or chosen to publish online-only editions following threats being issued against journalists by militant groups, militias and security forces. A selection of publications is given below.

DAILIES

Baghdad: Az-Zeitoun St, Al-Harthiya, Baghdad; e-mail baghdadwifaq@yahoo.com; f. 1991; organ of the Iraqi National Accord; Publr AYAD ALLAWI.

Al-Bayan (The Manifesto): Baghdad; f. 2003; Arabic; organ of Islamic Dawa Party; Man. Editor SADIQ AR-RIKABI.

Ad-Dustur (The Constitution): Baghdad; f. 2003; Arabic; politics; independent; publ. by Ad-Dustur Press, Publishing and Distribution House; Chair. BASIM ASH-SHEIKH; Editor-in-Chief ALI ASH-SHARQI.

Al-Jaridah (The Newspaper): Baghdad; Arabic; organ of the Iraqi Arab Socialist Movement; Editor Prof. QAYS AL-AZZAWI.

Kul al-Iraq (All Iraq): Baghdad; e-mail info@kululiraq.com; internet www.kululiraq.com; f. 2003; Arabic; independent; Editor-in-Chief Dr ABBAS AS-SIRAF.

Al-Mada: 41/1 Abu Nuwas St, Baghdad; e-mail fakhri_kareem@almadapaper.com; internet www.almadapaper.com; f. 2004; Arabic; independent; publ. by Al-Mada Institution for Media, Culture and Arts; Dir FAKHRI KARIM.

Al-Mannarah (Minarets): Basra; tel. (40) 315758; e-mail almannarah@almannarah.com; internet www.almannarah.com; Arabic; publ. by South Press & Publishing; Editor-in-Chief Dr KHALAF ALMANSHADI.

Al-Mashriq: Baghdad; internet www.al-mashriq.net; f. 2004; Arabic; independent; publ. by Al-Mashriq Institution for Media and Cultural Investments; circ. 25,000.

Al-Mutamar (Congress): Baghdad; e-mail almutamer@yahoo.com; internet www.inciraq.com/index_paper.php; f. 1993; Arabic; publ. by the Iraqi National Congress; Editor-in-Chief LUAY Baldawi.

As-Sabah (Morning): Baghdad; internet www.alsabaah.com; f. 2003; Arabic and English; state-controlled; publ. by the Iraqi Media Network; Exec. Editor FALAH AL-MISHAAL.

As-Sabah al-Jadid (New Morning): Baghdad; f. 2004; Arabic; independent; Editor-in-Chief ISMAIL ZAYER.

At-Taakhi (Brotherhood): internet www.taakhinews.org; f. 2003; Kurdish and Arabic; organ of the Kurdistan Democratic Party (KDP); Editor FALAKEDDIN KAKA'IE; circ. 20,000 (Baghdad).

Tariq ash-Sha'ab (People's Path): as-Sa'adoun St, Baghdad; internet www.tareekalshaab.com; f. 1974; Arabic and English; organ of the Iraqi Communist Party; Editor ABD AR-RAZZAK AS-SAFI.

Xebat: Arbil; e-mail info@xebat.net; internet www.xebat.net; f. 1959; Arabic and Kurdish; organ of the KDP; Editor-in-Chief NAZHAD AZIZ SURME.

Az-Zaman (Time): Baghdad; e-mail postmaster@azzaman.com; internet www.azzaman.com; f. 1997 in the United Kingdom, f. 2003 in Baghdad; Arabic, with some news translated into English; Editor-in-Chief SAAD AL-BAZZAZ.

WEEKLIES

Al-Adala (Justice): Baghdad; f. 2004; twice weekly; Arabic; organ of the Supreme Islamic Iraqi Council; Owner Dr ADIL ABD AL-MAHDI.

Al-Ahali (The People): Baghdad; e-mail info@ahali-iraq.net; internet www.ahali-iraq.net; Arabic; politics; Editor HAVAL ZAKHOUBI.

Alif Baa al-Iraq: Baghdad; Arabic and English; general, social and political affairs; Editor-in-Chief (vacant).

Habazbuz fi Zaman al-Awlamah (Habazbuz in the Age of Globalization): Baghdad; f. 2003; Arabic; satirical; Editor ISHTAR AL-YASIRI.

Hawlati: e-mail hawlati@hawlati.com; internet www.hawlati.com; f. 2001; Kurdish, Arabic and English; mainly Kurdish politics.

Iraq Today: Baghdad; f. 2003; English; current affairs; Founder and Editor-in-Chief HUSSAIN SINJARI.

Al-Iraq al-Yawm (Iraq Today): Baghdad; e-mail iraqtoday@iraqtoday.net; Arabic; Editor ISRA SHAKIR.

Al-Ittihad (Union): Sulaimaniya and Baghdad; internet www.alitthad.com; Arabic and Kurdish; publ. by the Patriotic Union of Kurdistan; Editor ABD AL-HADI; circ. 30,000 (Baghdad).

Al-Ittijah al-Akhar (The Other Direction): Baghdad; tel. (1) 776-3334; fax (1) 776-3332; e-mail alitijahalakhar@yahoo.com; internet www.alitijahalakhar.com; Arabic; organ of Reconciliation and Liberation Bloc; Chair. and Editor MISHAAN AL-JUBOURI.

Majallati: POB 8041, Children's Culture House, Baghdad; Arabic; children's newspaper; Editor-in-Chief Dr SHAFIQ AL-MAHDI.

Al-Muajaha (The Witness): 6/41/901, Karrada Dakhil, Baghdad; e-mail almuajaha@riseup.net; f. 2003; Arabic and English; current affairs; independent; Editor RAMZI MAJID JARRAR.

An-Nahda (Renaissance): Basra; f. 2003; Arabic; organ of the Independent Democratic Movement; Publr ADNAN PACHACHI.

Ar-Rasid (The Register): Baghdad; Arabic; general.

Regay Kurdistan: Arbil; internet www.iraqcp.org/regay; Arabic and Kurdish; organ of the Iraqi and Kurdistan Communist Parties.

As-Sina'i (The Industrialist): Baghdad; Arabic; general; publ. by National Industrialist Coalition; Editor-in-Chief Dr ZAYD ABD AL-MAJID BILAL.

Al-Waqai al-Iraqiya (Official Gazette of the Republic of Iraq): Ministry of Justice, Baghdad; tel. (1) 537-2023; e-mail Hashim_Jaffar_alsaieg@yahoo.com; f. 1922; Arabic and English; publ. by the Ministry of Justice; Dir HASHIM N. JAFFAR; circ. 5,000.

PERIODICALS

Majallat al-Majma' al-'Ilmi al-Iraqi (Journal of the Academy of Sciences): POB 4023, Waziriya, Baghdad; tel. (1) 422-4202; fax (1) 422-2066; e-mail iraqacademy@yahoo.com; internet www.iraqacademy.org; f. 1950; quarterly; Arabic; scholarly magazine on Arabic Islamic culture; Editor-in-Chief Prof. Dr AHMAD MATLOUB.

As-Sa'ah (The Hour): Baghdad; twice weekly; Arabic; organ of the Iraqi Unified National Movement; Publr AHMAD AL-KUBAYSI; Editor NI'MA ABD AR-RAZZAQ.

Sawt at-Talaba (Voice of the Students): Baghdad; fortnightly; Arabic; publ. by New Iraq Youth and Students' Organization; Editor MUSTAFA AL-HAYIM.

PRESS ORGANIZATION

Iraqi Union for Journalists: POB 14101, Baghdad; tel. (1) 537-0762; Chair. (vacant).

NEWS AGENCIES

Aswat al-Iraq (Voices of Iraq): e-mail webmaster@aswataliraq.info; internet www.aswataliraq.info; f. 2004; Arabic, English and Kurdish; independent news agency with contributions from Iraqi correspondents and three Iraqi newspapers; Editor-in-Chief ZUHAIR AL-JEZAIRY.

National Iraqi News Agency: Baghdad; tel. (1) 719-3459; e-mail news@ninanews.com; internet www.ninanews.com; f. 2005; Arabic and English; independent; Chair. Dr FARID AYAR.

Publishers

Afaq Arabiya Publishing House: POB 4032, Adamiya, Baghdad; tel. (1) 443-6044; fax (1) 444-8760; publr of literary monthlies, periodicals and cultural books; Chair. Dr MOHSIN AL-MUSAWI.

Dar al-Ma'mun for Translation and Publishing: POB 24015, Karradat Mariam, Baghdad; tel. (1) 538-3171; publr of newspapers and magazines.

Al-Hurriyah Printing Establishment: Karantina, Sarrafiya, Baghdad; f. 1970.

Al-Jamaheer Press House: POB 491, Sarrafiya, Baghdad; tel. (1) 416-9341; fax (1) 416-1875; f. 1963; publr of a number of newspapers and magazines; Pres. SAAD QASSEM HAMMOUDI.

Kurdish Culture Publishing House: Baghdad; f. 1976.

Al-Ma'arif Ltd: Mutanabi St, Baghdad; f. 1929; publishes periodicals and books in Arabic, Kurdish, Turkish, French and English.

Al-Muthanna Library: Mutanabi St, Baghdad; f. 1936; booksellers and publrs of books in Arabic and oriental languages; Man. ANAS K. AR-RAJAB.

An-Nahdah: Mutanabi St, Baghdad; tel. (1) 416-2689; e-mail yehya_azawy@yahoo.com; politics, Arab affairs.

National House for Publishing, Distribution and Advertising: POB 624, al-Jumhuriya St, Baghdad; tel. (1) 425-1846; f. 1972; publishes books on politics, economics, education, agriculture, sociology, commerce and science in Arabic and other Middle Eastern languages; Dir-Gen. M. A. ASKAR.

Ath-Thawra Printing and Publishing House: POB 2009, Aqaba bin Nafi's Sq., Baghdad; tel. (1) 719-6161; f. 1970; Chair. (vacant).

Thnayan Printing House: Baghdad.

Broadcasting and Communications

REGULATORY AUTHORITY

Iraqi National Communications and Media Commission (NCMC): Media Development and Regulation, 3rd Floor, Convention Centre, Baghdad; tel. (1) 718-0009; f. 2004 by fmr Coalition Provisional Authority; independent telecoms and media regulator; responsibilities include the award and management of telecommunications licences, broadcasting, media and information services, as well as spectrum allocation and management; CEO SIYAMEND ZAID OTHMAN.

TELECOMMUNICATIONS

Under the former Baathist regime, the Iraqi Telecommunications and Posts Co was the sole provider of telecommunications and postal services. Following the removal from power of Saddam Hussain, in 2003 the Coalition Provisional Authority issued three short-term licences for the provision of mobile telephone services to stimulate competition in the sector. Asiacell, led by the Iraqi Kurdish Asiacell Co for Telecommunication Ltd, was awarded the licence for the northern region; the licence for Baghdad and the central region was

IRAQ

Directory

won by Orascom Telecom Iraq Corpn (Iraqna), led by Orascom Telecom of Egypt; and Atheer Telecom Iraq (MTC Atheer), led by the Mobile Telecommunications Co of Kuwait, won the licence for Basra and the southern region. In August 2007 Asiacell, Korek Telecom Ltd and MTC Atheer (which subsequently acquired 100% of Iraqna shares) won the auction launched by the Government for three new national licences to provide mobile telephone services over a 15-year period; Iraqna withdrew from the bidding process.

Asiacell: Headquarters Bldg, Sulaimaniya; tel. 7701-100-111; e-mail customercare@asiacell.com; internet www.asiacell.com; f. 1999; 51% owned by Asiacell Co for Telecommunication Ltd, 40% by Wataniya Telecom (Kuwait) and 9% owned by United Gulf Bank (Bahrain); 3.7m. subscribers (Dec. 2007); Chair. of Bd FAROUK MUSTAFA RASOUL.

Iraqi Telecommunications and Posts Co (ITPC): POB 2450, Abu Nuwas St, Baghdad; tel. (1) 718-0400; fax (1) 718-2125; state-owned, but privatization pending in 2008; Dir-Gen. UDAY A. ABED AL-AMEER.

Korek Telecom Ltd: Kurdistan St, Pirmam, Arbil; e-mail info@korektel.com; internet korektel.com; f. 2001; 730,000 subscribers (2007); Chair. and CEO SIRWAN S. MUSTAFA.

Zain: Basra; e-mail info@iq.zain.com; internet www.zain.com; f. 2003 as MTC Atheer, a subsidiary of Mobile Telecommunications Co (Kuwait); acquired Iraqna Co for Mobile Phone Services Ltd (operated by Orascom Telecom Holding—Egypt) in Dec. 2007; name changed to above in Jan. 2008; 7m. subscribers (2007); Pres. and Gen. Man. ALI AD-DAHWI.

BROADCASTING

The **Iraqi Media Network (IMN)** was established by the former Coalition Provisional Authority (CPA) to replace the Ministry of Information following the ousting of the former regime. The IMN established new television and both FM and AM radio stations. In January 2004 the CPA announced that a consortium led by the US-based Harris Corpn had been awarded the contract to take over from the IMN the control of 18 television channels, two radio stations and the As-Sabah daily newspaper.

Iraqi Media Network (IMN): Baghdad; e-mail info@iraqimedianet .net; internet www.iraqimedianet.net; f. 2003.

Al-Iraqiya Television: Baghdad; internet www.iraqimedianet .net/tv.

Iraq Media Network—Southern Region: internet www.imnsr .com.

Republic of Iraq Radio: Baghdad; e-mail rir.info@iraqimedianet.net; internet www.iraqimedianet.net/radio.

Radio

Radio Dijla: House 3, Hay al-Jamia Zone 635/52, Baghdad; tel. (1) 555-8787; e-mail post@radiodijla.com; internet www.radiodijla.com; f. 2004; first talk radio station to be established in post-invasion Iraq; Founder Dr AHMAD AR-RIKABI.

Television

Ash-Sharqiya: 10/13/52 Karrada Kharj, Baghdad; tel. (88216) 6775-1380 (satellite); e-mail alsharqiya@alsharqiya.com; internet www.alsharqiya.com; f. 2004; privately owned, independent; broadcasts news and entertainment programming 24 hours a day via satellite; Founder SAAD AL-BAZZAZ; Dir ALAA AD-DAHAN.

Finance

(cap. = capital; dep. = deposits; res = reserves; brs = branches; m. = million; amounts in Iraqi dinars, unless otherwise stated)

All banks and insurance companies in Iraq, including all foreign companies, were nationalized in July 1964. The assets of foreign companies were taken over by the state. In May 1991 the Government announced its decision to end the state's monopoly in banking, and during 1992–2000 17 private banks were established; however, they were prohibited by the former regime from conducting international transactions. Following the establishment of the Coalition Provisional Authority in 2003, efforts were made to reform the state-owned Rafidain and Rashid Banks, and in October the Central Bank allowed private banks to begin processing international transactions. In January 2004 the Central Bank of Iraq announced that three foreign banks—HSBC and Standard Chartered (both of the United Kingdom), and the National Bank of Kuwait—had been awarded licences to operate in Iraq, the first such licences awarded for 40 years. A further five foreign banks had also been granted licences by mid-2005. There were six public sector banks and 23 private sector banks operating in Iraq at the end of 2006.

BANKING

Central Bank

Central Bank of Iraq: POB 64, Ar-Rashid St, Baghdad; tel. (1) 816-5170; fax (1) 816-6802; e-mail cbi@cbiraq.org; internet www.cbiraq .org; f. 1947 as National Bank of Iraq; name changed as above 1956; has the sole right of note issue; cap. and res –480,371m. (Dec. 2004); Gov. Dr SINAN MUHAMMAD RIDA ASH-SHIBIBI; brs in Mosul and Basra.

Nationalized Commercial Banks

Rafidain Bank: POB 11360, General Administration, Baghdad; tel. (1) 816-0287; fax (1) 816-5035; e-mail emailcenter9@yahoo.com; internet www.rafidain-bank.org; f. 1941; cap. 4,000m., res 9,649.0m., dep. 453,678m. (Dec. 2001); total assets US $1,030m. (2003); Pres. ABD AL-HUSSAIN A. AL-YASIRY; 153 brs in Iraq, 9 brs abroad.

Rashid Bank: Ar-Rashid St, Baghdad; tel. (1) 885-3411; fax (1) 882-6201; e-mail natbank@uruklink.net; f. 1988; cap. 2,000m., res 6,023.8m., dep. 815,521.5m. (Dec. 2001); total assets US $750m. (2003); Chair. and Gen. Man. ABD AL-HADI S. ABD AL-MAHDI; 170 brs.

Private Commercial Banks

Babylon Bank: Al-Amara St, Baghdad; tel. (1) 717-3686; e-mail info@babylonbank-iq.com; internet www.babylonbank-iq.com; f. 1999; cap. 30,000m., total assets 74,829m. (Dec. 2005); Chair. ABD AR-RAZZAQ MANSOUR; Gen. Man. TARIQ ABD AL-BAKI ABOUD; 6 brs.

Bank of Baghdad: POB 3192, Al-Karada St, Alwiya, Baghdad; tel. (1) 717-5007; fax (1) 717-5006; e-mail info@bankofbaghdad.net; f. 1992; cap. 5,280m., res 3,355m., total assets 11,970m. (2004); Chair. Dr MUNIB K. AS-SIKOUTI; CEO MUWAFAQ H. MAHMOUD; 5 brs.

Commercial Bank of Iraq SA: POB 5639, 13/14/904 Al-Wahda St, Baghdad; tel. (1) 717-0057; fax (1) 718-4312; e-mail commerce_iraq@hotmail.com; f. 1992; cap. 10,000.0m., res 2,807.5m., dep. 32,891.5m. (Dec. 2004); Chair. MUHAMMAD H. DRAGH; Gen. Man. HUSSEIN AZ-ZAHRI; 32 brs.

Credit Bank of Iraq: POB 3420, Alwiya Bldg, Saadoun St, Alwiya, Baghdad; tel. (1) 718-2198; fax (1) 717-5997; e-mail creditbiq@yahoo .com; 1998; cap. 1,250m., res 528m., dep. 16,376.9m. (Dec. 2002); Chair. HIKMET H. KUBBA; Man. Dir FOUAD M. MUSTAFA; 10 brs.

Gulf Commercial Bank: POB 3101, Nr Baghdad Hotel, Saadoun St, Alwiya, Baghdad; tel. (1) 776-0170; fax (1) 778-8251; e-mail gulfbank1@yahoo.com; f. 2000; Gen. Man. MUDHER M. AL-HILLAWI; 8 brs.

National Bank of Iraq (al-Ahli al-Iraqi Bank): POB 2568, Saadoun St, Baghdad; tel. (1) 717-7735; fax (6) 569-5942; e-mail Info@nbirq .com; internet www.nbirq.com; f. 1995; Chair. TALAL FANAR AL-FAISAL; 4 brs.

Sumer Commercial Bank: POB 3476, 13/6 Khalid bin al-Waleed St, Hay al-Wahda 908, Alwiya, Baghdad; tel. (1) 719-6472; fax (1) 719-3557; e-mail sumerbank99@hotmail.com; cap. 10,200m., res 531m., dep. 7,500m. (Aug. 2005); Chair. KHALIL KHAIRALLAH S. AL-JUMAILI; Man. Dir MAKKI H. OBEIDA; 6 brs.

Specialized Banks

Agricultural Co-operative Bank of Iraq: POB 2421, Ar-Rashid St, Baghdad; tel. (1) 886-4768; fax (1) 886-5047; f. 1936; state-owned; Dir-Gen. HDIYA H. AL-KHAYOUN; 32 brs.

Al-Baraka Bank for Investment and Financing: POB 3445, 904/14/50, Hay al-Wehda, Baghdad; tel. (1) 717-3201; fax (1) 718-3766; e-mail albaraka@uruklink.net.

Basra National Bank for Investment: Watani St, Ashar, Basra; tel. (40) 616955; e-mail info@basrahbank.com; internet www .basrahbank.com; cap. 50,000m. (2004); GHALIB ABD AL-HUSSEIN KUBBA; 11 brs.

Dar es-Salaam Investment Bank: 39/1 23/101, Tunis St, Baghdad; e-mail info@daressalam.net; f. 1999; 70.1% share acquired by HSBC (United Kingdom) in 2005; total assets 35,562m. (Aug. 2005); 14 brs.

Economy Bank for Investment and Financing: POB 55432, 108/54 Al-Khulfa St, Shurgah, Baghdad; tel. (1) 817-6202; fax (1) 885-0018.

Industrial Bank of Iraq: POB 5825, as-Sinak, Baghdad; tel. (1) 887-2181; fax (1) 888-3047; e-mail bank2004@maktoob.com; f. 1940; state-owned; total assets US $34.7m. (2003); Dir-Gen. BASSIMA ABD AL-HADDI ADH-DHAHIR; 9 brs.

Investment Bank of Iraq: POB 3724, 902/2/27 Hay al-Wahda, Alwiya, Baghdad; tel. (1) 718-0996; fax (1) 719-8505; e-mail investmentiraq@yahoo.com; internet www.ibi-bankiraq.com; f. 1993; cap. 25,000m.; total assets 138,578m. (Dec. 2005); Chair. THAMIR RESOUKI ABD AL-WAHAB ASH-SHEIKHLY; Gen. Man. ABBAS HADI ALI AL-BAYATTI; 19 brs.

Iraqi Islamic Bank for Investment and Development: POB 940, Muathem Al-Kahiay Bldg, Baghdad; tel. (1) 416-4939; fax (1) 414-0697.

Iraqi Middle East Investment Bank: POB 10379, Bldg 65, Hay Babel, 929 Arasat al-Hindiya, Baghdad; tel. (1) 719-2336; e-mail cendep@iraqimdlestbank.com; internet www.iraqinet.net/com/3/mdlestbank.htm; f. 1993; cap. and res 15,992m., dep. 85,265m., total assets 167,850m. (June 2005); Man. Dir M. F. AL-ALOOSI; Exec. Man. SUDAD A. AZIZ; 10 brs.

Kurdistan International Bank for Investment and Development: 70 Abd as-Salam Barzani St, Arbil; e-mail info@kibid.com; internet www.kibid.com; private bank; Chair. SALAR MUSTAFA HAKIM.

Mosul Bank for Development and Investment: POB 1292, Senter St, Mosul.

Real Estate Bank of Iraq: POB 8118, 29/222 Haifa St, Baghdad; tel. (1) 885-3212; fax (1) 884-0980; f. 1949; state-owned; gives loans to assist the building industry; acquired the Co-operative Bank in 1970; total assets US $10m. (2003); Dir-Gen. ABD AR-RAZZAQ AZIZ; 25 brs.

United Investment Bank: POB 24211, Banks St, Baghdad; tel. (1) 888-112; e-mail united@uruklink.net.

Warka Bank for Investment and Finance: POB 3559, 902/14/50, Hay al-Wehda, Baghdad; tel. (1) 717-4970; fax (1) 717-9555; internet www.warka-bank.com; f. 1999; private bank; cap. 24,000m. (2006); Chair. of Bd SAAD SAADOUN AL-BUNNIA; 30 brs.

Trade Bank

Trade Bank of Iraq (TBI): 20 St 1, al-Yarmouk District 608, Baghdad; tel. (1) 543-3561; fax (1) 543-3560; e-mail info@tbiraq.com; internet www.tbiraq.com; f. 2003 by the former Coalition Provisional Authority; facilitates export and imports of goods and services; independent of Central Bank of Iraq; cap. US $96.1m., dep. $35.4m., total assets $414.1m. (Dec. 2004); Chair. HUSSAIN AL-UZRI; Sec. ABD AL-KHALIK MUHAMMAD ASH-SHABOOT.

INSURANCE

Al-Hamra'a Insurance Co: POB 10491, Karrada, Baghdad; tel. (1) 717-7573; fax (1) 717-7574; e-mail info@alhamraains.com; internet www.alhamraains.com; f. 2001; private co; general and life insurance.

Iraq Insurance Co: POB 989, Khaled bin al-Walid St, Aqaba bin Nafi Sq., Baghdad; tel. (1) 719-2185; fax (1) (1) 719-2606; state-owned; life, fire, accident and marine insurance.

Iraq Reinsurance Co: POB 297, Aqaba bin Nafi Sq., Khalid bin al-Waleed St, Baghdad; tel. (1) 719-5131; fax (1) 719-1497; e-mail iraqre@yahoo.com; f. 1960; state-owned; transacts reinsurance business on the international market; Chair. and Gen. Man. SAID ABBAS M. A. MIRZA.

National Insurance Co: POB 248, National Insurance Co Bldg, Al-Khullani St, Baghdad; tel. (1) 885-3026; fax (1) 886-1486; f. 1950; state-owned; cap. 20m.; all types of general and life insurance, reinsurance and investment; Chair. and Gen. Man. MUHAMMAD HUSSAIN JAAFAR ABBAS.

STOCK EXCHANGE

Iraq Stock Exchange (ISX): Baghdad; tel. (1) 717-4484; fax (1) 717-4461; e-mail Info-isx@isx-iq.net; internet www.isx-iq.net; following the closure of the former Baghdad Stock Exchange by the Coalition Provisional Authority in March 2003, the ISX recommenced trading in June 2004; some 93 cos listed in Aug. 2006; Chair. TALIB AT-TABATABIE.

Trade and Industry

DEVELOPMENT ORGANIZATION

Iraq Foreign Investment Board: e-mail info@ishtargate.org; internet www.ishtargate.org; seeks to attract inward private sector investment into Iraq and to stimulate domestic capital resources for growth and innovation, as well as promote Iraqi businesses; Senior Advisor WILLIAM C. DAHM.

CHAMBERS OF COMMERCE

Baghdad Chamber of Commerce: POB 5015, As-Sanal, Baghdad; tel. (1) 880-220; fax (1) 816-3347; e-mail mhkazzaz@uruklink.net; internet www.baghdadchamber.com; f. 1926; Pres. MUHAMMAD HASSAN AL-KAZZAZ.

Basra Chamber of Commerce: Manawi Pasha, Ashar, Basra; tel. (40) 614630; e-mail info@bcoc-iraq.net; internet www.bcoc-iraq.net; f. 1926; Chair. JABBAR SHAGHAITH MANSOUR.

Federation of Iraqi Chambers of Commerce: POB 3388, Sa'adoun St, Al-Elwiyah, Baghdad; tel. (1) 717-1798; fax (1) 719-2479; e-mail ficcbaghdad@hotmail.com; f. 1969; all 18 Iraqi chambers of commerce are affiliated to the Federation; Chair. ABOUD M. J. AT-TUFAILY; Sec.-Gen. ABD HAFIDH A. S. KADER.

Sulaimaniya Chamber of Commerce: Sulaimaniya; e-mail info@sule-chamber.org; internet www.sule-chamber.org; Chair. TALIB ALI AHMAD.

EMPLOYERS' ORGANIZATION

Iraqi Federation of Industries: 191/22/915 Az-Zaweya, Karada, Baghdad; tel. (1) 778-3502; fax (1) 776-3041; e-mail fed.und.irg@warkaa.net; f. 1956; 35,000 mems; Pres. KAIS KAZIM AL-KHAFAJI; Dir-Gen. KARIM AL-AHMAD.

PETROLEUM AND GAS

Ministry of Oil: Oil Complex Bldg, Port Said St, Baghdad; tel. (1) 817-7000; fax (1) 886-9432; e-mail oilcompo@uruklink.net; internet www.oil.gov.iq; merged with INOC in 1987; affiliated cos: Oil Marketing Co, Oil Projects Co, Midland Refineries Co, Oil Exploration Co, Oil Products Distribution Co, Gas Filling Co, Pipelines Co, Iraqi Drilling Co, South Oil Co, South Refineries Co, North Oil Co, North Refineries Co, North Gas Co, South Gas Co, Iraqi Oil Tankers Co.

Iraq National Oil Co (INOC): POB 476, al-Khullani Sq., Baghdad; tel. (1) 887-1115; f. in 1964 to operate the petroleum industry at home and abroad; when Iraq nationalized its petroleum industry, structural changes took place in INOC, and it became solely responsible for exploration, production, transportation and marketing of Iraqi crude petroleum and petroleum products. INOC was merged with the Ministry of Oil in 1987, and the functions of some of the organizations under its control were transferred to newly created ministerial departments or to companies responsible to the ministry. Following the start of US-led military action in March 2003, the INOC remained under the authority of the Ministry of Oil. However, it was reported that the INOC might become an independent company as part of plans for the regeneration of Iraq's economy.

UTILITIES

Electricity

Electricity production in Iraq has been greatly diminished as a result of the US-led military campaign in 2003, subsequent looting and sabotage by Baathist loyalists, and disruptions in fuel supplies to power stations. Power outages are common, especially in Baghdad and the surrounding area, and the Government has resorted to rationing. With ongoing reconstruction of the means of generation, transmission and distribution, the Ministry of Electricity expected to achieve peak production levels of 9,000 MW by early 2005; however, available generating capacity was reported not to have exceeded some 4,500 MW by early 2006. In that year the Ministry of Electricity forecast that Iraq would require 12,000 MW of capacity by the end of 2007.

State Enterprise for Generation and Transmission of Electricity: POB 1098, 4/356 Al-Masbah Bldg, Baghdad; f. 1987 from State Org. for Major Electrical Projects.

TRADE UNIONS

General Federation of Iraqi Workers (GFIW): POB 3049, Tahrir Sq., Ar-Rashid St, Baghdad; e-mail abdullahmuhsin@iraqitradeunions.org; internet www.iraqitradeunions.org; f. 2006 by merger of three trade unions, incl. the General Federation of Trade Unions of Iraq and the Iraqi Federation of Workers' Trade Unions; Vice-Pres. IBRAHIM AL-MASHHADANI; Gen. Sec. RASEM AL-AWADI.

Iraqi Teachers' Union (ITU): Al-Mansour, Baghdad; f. 2003; Pres. MAHDI ALI LAFTA.

There are also unions of doctors, pharmacologists, jurists, writers, journalists, artists, engineers, electricity and railway workers.

Transport

RAILWAYS

Iraq's railway lines extend over some 2,339 km. A line covers the length of the country, from Rabia, on the Syrian border, via Mosul, to Baghdad (534 km), and from Baghdad to Basra and Umm Qasr (608 km), on the Persian (Arabian) Gulf. A 404-km line links Baghdad, via Radi and Haditha, to Husaibah, near the Iraqi–Syrian frontier. Baghdad is linked with Arbil, via Khanaqin and Kirkuk, and a 252-km line (designed to serve industrial projects along its route) runs from Kirkuk to Haditha, via Baiji (though this was out of service in mid-2006, as a result of bombing by US forces). A 638-km

IRAQ

line runs from Baghdad, via al-Qaim (on the Syrian border), to Akashat (with a 150-km line linking the Akashat phosphate mines and the fertilizer complex at al-Qaim). As well as the internal service, there is a regular international service between Baghdad and Istanbul, Turkey (although this was suspended in early 2006, owing to security concerns). Passenger rail services between Mosul and Aleppo, Syria, resumed in August 2000 after an interruption of almost 20 years, but were closed again in 2004 after repeated insurgent attacks. The railway system was due to be repaired and upgraded as part of the reconstruction of Iraq following the removal from power of Saddam Hussain's regime in 2003. Eventually, it was planned that the system would be divided, with the infrastructure being kept as a state asset, while operations were to be privatized. It was reported in 2006 that the Ministry of Transport hoped to add an additional 2,300 km to the existing rail network, although concerns remained over funding.

Iraqi Republic Railways Co (IRRC): West Station, Baghdad; tel. (1) 537-0011; Dir (Baghdad) MUHAMMAD ALI HASHIM.

New Railways Implementation Authority: POB 17040, al-Hurriya, Baghdad; tel. (1) 537-0021; responsible for devt of railway network; Sec.-Gen. R. A. AL-UMARI.

ROADS

At the end of 1999, according to estimates by the International Road Federation, Iraq's road network extended over 45,550 km, of which approximately 38,400 km were paved.

The most important roads are: Baghdad–Mosul–Tel Kotchuk (Syrian border), 521 km; Baghdad–Kirkuk–Arbil–Mosul–Zakho (border with Turkey), 544 km; Kirkuk–Sulaimaniya, 160 km; Baghdad–Hilla–Diwaniya–Nasiriya–Basra, 586 km; Baghdad–Kut–Nasiriya, 186 km; Baghdad–Ramadi–Rurba (border with Syria), 555 km; Baghdad–Kut–Umara–Basra–Safwan (border with Kuwait), 660 km; Baghdad–Baqaba–Kanikien (border with Iran). Most sections of the six-lane 1,264-km international Express Highway, linking Safwan (on the Kuwaiti border) with the Jordanian and Syrian borders, had been completed by June 1990. Studies have been completed for a second, 525-km Express Highway, linking Baghdad and Zakho on the Turkish border. A complex network of roads was constructed behind the war front with Iran in order to facilitate the movement of troops and supplies during the 1980–88 conflict. The road network was included in the US-led coalition's programme of reconstruction following the ousting of the Baathist regime in 2003.

Iraqi Land Transport Co: Baghdad; f. 1988 to replace State Organization for Land Transport; fleet of more than 1,000 large trucks; Dir-Gen. AYSAR AS-SAFI.

Iraqi-Jordanian Land Transport Co: Baghdad; e-mail ijltco@hotmail.com; f. 1980; jt venture between Iraq and Jordan; operates a fleet of some 200 trucks.

State Enterprise for Roads and Bridges: POB 917, Karradat Mariam, Karkh, Baghdad; tel. (1) 32141; responsible for road and bridge construction projects under the Ministry of Construction and Housing.

SHIPPING

The ports of Basra and Umm Qasr are usually the commercial gateway of Iraq. They are connected by various ocean routes with all parts of the world, and constitute the natural distributing centre for overseas supplies. The Iraqi State Enterprise for Maritime Transport maintains a regular service between Basra, the Persian (Arabian) Gulf and north European ports. There is also a port at Khor az-Zubair, which came into use in 1979.

At Basra there is accommodation for 12 vessels at the Maqal Wharves and accommodation for seven vessels at the buoys. There is one silo berth and two berths for petroleum products at Muftia and one berth for fertilizer products at Abu Flus. There is room for eight vessels at Umm Qasr. There are deep-water tanker terminals at Khor al-Amaya and Faw for three and four vessels, respectively. The latter port, however, was abandoned during the early part of the Iran–Iraq War.

For the inland waterways, which are now under the control of the General Establishment for Iraqi Ports, there are 1,036 registered river craft, 48 motor vessels and 105 motor boats.

The port at Umm Qasr was heavily damaged during the early part of the US-led coalition's campaign to oust Saddam Hussain. The contract for subsequent repair work to Umm Qasr was awarded to the US company SSA Marine, Inc. In 2007 a large-scale project to redevelop the port was experiencing severe delays, owing to disagreement between central and local government authorities regarding the distribution of future revenues.

Iraqi Port Authority (IPA): Basra; e-mail dg@iraqports.com; internet www.iraqports.com; Dir-Gen. MAHMOUD SALEH.

State Enterprise for Iraqi Water Transport: POB 23016, Airport St, al-Furat Quarter, Baghdad; f. 1987, when State Org. for Iraqi Water Transport was abolished; responsible for the planning, supervision and control of six nat. water transportation enterprises, incl.:

State Enterprise for Maritime Transport (Iraqi Line): POB 13038, al-Jadiriya al-Hurriya Ave, Baghdad; Basra office: POB 766, 14 July St, Basra; tel. (1) 776-3201; f. 1952; Dir-Gen. JABER Q. HASSAN; Operations Man. M. A. ALI.

Shipping Company

Arab Bridge Maritime Navigation Co: Aqaba, Jordan; tel. (3) 2092000; fax (3) 2092001; f. 1987; jt venture by Egypt, Iraq and Jordan to improve economic co-operation; an expansion of the company that established a ferry link between the ports of Aqaba, Jordan, and Nuweibeh, Egypt, in 1985; four vessels; cap. US $40m. (2007); Chair. Eng. ALAA ARIF BATAYNEH; Man. Dir Adm. NABIL LUFTI.

Gulf Shipping Co: POB 471, Basra; tel. (40) 776-1945; fax (40) 776-0715; f. 1988; imports and exports goods to and from Iraq.

CIVIL AVIATION

There are international airports at Baghdad, Basra and Mosul. Baghdad's airport, previously named Saddam International Airport, reopened in August 2000, after refurbishment necessitated by damage sustained during the war with the multinational force in 1991. However, international air links were virtually halted by the UN embargo imposed in 1990. Internal flights, connecting Baghdad to Basra and Mosul, recommenced in November 2000. In April 2003 the capital's airport was renamed Baghdad International Airport by US forces during their military campaign to oust the regime of Saddam Hussain. Following a programme of reconstruction, the airports at Baghdad and Basra were reopened to commercial flights from late 2003. The expansion of Arbil International Airport (including the construction of a new passenger terminal and runway) was in progress in 2007.

National Co for Civil Aviation Services: al-Mansour, Baghdad; tel. (1) 551-9443; f. 1987 following the abolition of the State Organization for Civil Aviation; responsible for the provision of aircraft, and for airport and passenger services.

Iraqi Airways Co: Baghdad International Airport; tel. (1) 537-2002; e-mail Info@IraqiAirways.co.uk; internet www.iraqiairways.co.uk; f. 1948; partial privatization pending; Dir-Gen. Capt. KIFAH HUSSEIN JABBAR.

Tourism

In 2001 (the last year for which statistics are available) some 126,654 tourists visited Iraq. Tourist receipts in 1998 were estimated at US $13m. Since the outbreak of conflict in 2003, the site housing the ruins of the ancient civilization of Babylon has become part of a US military base; several other places of interest have become military or refugee camps. In August 2006 the Kurdish Autonomous Region launched a tourism campaign, with advertisements broadcast on US television.

Iraq Tourism Board: POB 7783, Baghdad; Chair AHMAD AL-JABOURI; 2,474 employees (Dec. 2004).

IRELAND

Introductory Survey

Location, Climate, Language, Religion, Flag, Capital

Ireland consists of 26 of the 32 historic counties that comprise the island of Ireland. The remaining six counties, in the north-east, form Northern Ireland, which is part of the United Kingdom. Ireland lies in the Atlantic Ocean, about 80 km (50 miles) west of Great Britain. The climate is mild and equable, with temperatures generally between 0°C (32°F) and 21°C (70°F). Irish (Gaeilge) is the official first language, but its use as a vernacular is now restricted to certain areas, collectively known as the Gaeltacht, mainly in the west of Ireland. English is universally spoken. Official documents are printed in English and Irish. The vast majority of the inhabitants profess Christianity: about 87% of the population are Roman Catholics. The national flag (proportions 1 by 2) consists of three equal vertical stripes, of green, white and orange. The capital is Dublin.

Recent History

The whole of Ireland was formerly part of the United Kingdom. In 1920 the island was partitioned, the six north-eastern counties remaining part of the United Kingdom, with their own government. In 1922 the 26 southern counties achieved dominion status, under the British Crown, as the Irish Free State. The dissolution of all remaining links with Great Britain culminated in 1937 in the adoption of a new Constitution, which gave the Irish Free State full sovereignty within the Commonwealth. Formal ties with the Commonwealth were ended in 1949, when the 26 southern counties became a republic. The partition of Ireland remained a contentious issue, and in 1969 a clandestine organization, calling itself the Provisional Irish Republican Army (IRA—see United Kingdom), initiated a violent campaign to achieve reunification.

In the general election of February 1973, the Fianna Fáil party, which had held office, with only two interruptions, since 1932, was defeated. Jack Lynch, who had been Prime Minister (Taoiseach) since 1966, resigned, and Liam Cosgrave formed a coalition between his own party, Fine Gael, and the Labour Party. The Irish Government remained committed to power-sharing in the six counties, but opposed any British military withdrawal from Northern Ireland. Following the assassination of the British Ambassador to Ireland by the Provisional IRA in July 1976, the Irish Government introduced stronger measures against terrorism. Fianna Fáil won the general election of June 1977 and Lynch again became Prime Minister. Following his resignation in December 1979, he was succeeded by Charles Haughey. In June 1981, following an early general election, Dr Garret FitzGerald of Fine Gael became Prime Minister in a coalition Government between his own party and the Labour Party. However, the rejection by the Dáil (the lower house of the legislature) of the coalition's budget proposals precipitated a further general election in February 1982, in which Haughey was returned to power. The worsening economic situation, however, made the Fianna Fáil Government increasingly unpopular, and in November Haughey lost the support of two independent deputies, precipitating an early general election, at which Fianna Fáil failed to gain an overall majority. In December FitzGerald took office as Prime Minister in a Fine Gael-Labour Party coalition.

During 1986 FitzGerald's coalition lost support, partly due to the formation of a new party, the Progressive Democrats (PD), by disaffected members of Fianna Fáil. In June a controversial government proposal to end a constitutional ban on divorce was defeated by national referendum. Shortly afterwards, as a result of a series of defections, the coalition lost its parliamentary majority. In January 1987 the Labour Party refused to support Fine Gael's budget proposals and the coalition collapsed. Fianna Fáil, led by Haughey, won 81 of the 166 seats in the Dáil at a general election held in February, forming a minority Government that introduced a programme of unprecedented economic austerity.

Prior to the general election of June 1989 Fine Gael and the PD concluded an electoral pact to oppose Fianna Fáil. Although the Haughey administration had achieved significant economic improvements, severe reductions in public expenditure and continuing problems of unemployment and emigration adversely affected Fianna Fáil's electoral support, and it obtained only 77 of the 166 seats in the Dáil, while Fine Gael won 55 seats and the PD six seats. Following nearly four weeks of negotiations, a Fianna Fáil-PD coalition Government, led by Haughey, was formed.

In October 1991 the Government narrowly defeated a motion of 'no confidence', which had been introduced following a series of financial scandals involving public officials. In November, however, a group of Fianna Fáil deputies proposed a motion demanding Haughey's removal as leader of the party. Albert Reynolds, the Minister for Finance and a former close associate of Haughey, and Pádraig Flynn, the Minister for the Environment, announced their intention to support the motion, and were immediately dismissed from office. The attempt to depose Haughey was defeated by a substantial majority of the Fianna Fáil parliamentary grouping.

In January 1992 allegations arose that, contrary to his previous denials, Haughey had been aware of the secret monitoring, in 1982, of the telephone conversations of two journalists perceived to be critical of the Government. The PD made their continued support of the Government conditional on Haughey's resignation. In February 1992 Reynolds replaced Haughey as leader of Fianna Fáil and assumed the premiership. Reynolds extensively reshuffled the Cabinet, but retained the two representatives of the PD, in an attempt to preserve the coalition Government.

In June 1992 the leader of the PD, Desmond O'Malley, criticized Reynolds' conduct as Minister for Industry and Commerce in a parliamentary inquiry, which had been established in June 1991 to investigate allegations of fraud and political favouritism during 1987–88. In October 1992, in his testimony to the inquiry, the Prime Minister accused O'Malley of dishonesty. Following Reynolds' refusal to withdraw the allegations, in early November the PD left the coalition, and the Government was defeated on the following day in a motion of 'no confidence', proposed by the Labour Party. It was subsequently announced that a general election was to take place on 25 November, concurrent with three constitutional referendums on abortion. Fianna Fáil suffered a substantial loss of support, securing only 68 of the 166 seats in the Dáil and Fine Gael also obtained a reduced number of seats, taking only 45. In contrast, the Labour Party attracted substantial support, more than doubling its number of seats, to 33, while the PD increased their representation to 10 seats. In the referendums on abortion two of the proposals (on the right to seek an abortion in another member state of the European Community (EC, now European Union—EU, see p. 244) and the right to information on abortion services abroad) were approved by about two-thirds of the votes cast. The third proposal—on the substantive issue of abortion, permitting the operation only in cases where the life (not merely the health) of the mother was threatened—was rejected, also by a two-thirds' majority.

Following prolonged negotiations, in January 1993 Fianna Fáil and the Labour Party agreed to form a coalition Government. Reynolds retained the premiership, while Dick Spring, the leader of the Labour Party, was allocated the foreign affairs portfolio, as well as the post of Deputy Prime Minister (Tánaiste).

In November 1994 serious differences arose within the coalition Government over the insistence by Fianna Fáil that the Attorney-General, Harry Whelehan, be appointed to a senior vacancy that had arisen in the High Court. Although such promotions accorded with past precedent, Whelehan's conservative record on social issues was unacceptable to the Labour Party. However, Reynolds and the Fianna Fáil members of the Cabinet approved the appointment in the absence of the Labour Party ministers. The Labour Party subsequently withdrew from the coalition, and the Government resigned. Reynolds, while remaining as Prime Minister of a 'caretaker' Government, relinquished the Fianna Fáil leadership on 19 November and was succeeded by the Minister for Finance, Bertie Ahern. Whelehan, meanwhile, resigned as President of the High Court.

The desire of all the major political parties to avoid an immediate general election led to protracted efforts to form a new coalition administration. Discussions between Spring and Ahern, however, failed to produce an agreement. Following extensive negotiations, a new coalition of the Labour Party, Fine Gael, and a small party, the Democratic Left, took office on 15 December 1994. John Bruton, who had assumed the leadership of Fine Gael in late 1990, became Prime Minister; Spring was again appointed Minister for Foreign Affairs and Deputy Prime Minister.

In November 1995 a referendum on the constitutional ban on divorce resulted in a narrow majority (50.3% to 49.7%) in favour of legalizing the dissolution of marriage. The first divorce under the revised constitutional arrangements was granted in January 1997.

In November 1996 the Minister for Transport, Energy and Communications, Michael Lowry, resigned following allegations that he had received personal financial gifts from an Irish business executive, Ben Dunne. During 1997 an inquiry into other political donations by Dunne, chaired by Justice Brian McCracken, revealed that payments totalling some IR£1.3m. had been made to Haughey during his premiership. Haughey later admitted the allegations, although he insisted that he had no knowledge of the donations until he resigned from office; however, McCracken's report, published in August, condemned Haughey's earlier misleading evidence given to the tribunal and recommended further legal investigation. The Government, at that time led by Ahern following a general election (see below), endorsed the results of the inquiry and agreed to establish a new tribunal to investigate further payments made to politicians and the sources of specific 'offshore' bank accounts that had been used by Haughey. In December 1998 it was revealed that a tax liability on some IR£2m. of personal financial gifts received by Haughey, including those made by Dunne, had been cancelled by the Revenue Commission. Opposition criticism of the decision intensified following the disclosure that the tax appeals commissioner responsible for the concession was Ahern's brother-in-law.

In a general election held on 6 June 1997 none of the main political parties secured an overall majority in the Dáil. Fine Gael increased its representation to 54 seats, while Fianna Fáil secured 77 seats. Support for the Labour Party declined substantially and the party won just 17 seats. Sinn Féin won its first ever seat in the Dáil at the election. After Bruton conceded that he could not form a majority coalition administration, Ahern undertook to form a new Fianna Fáil-led government, in alliance with the PD, who had won four parliamentary seats, and with the support of independents. A new administration, with Ahern as Prime Minister and the leader of the PD, Mary Harney, as his deputy, was formally approved in the Dáil in late June.

In September 1997 the President, Mary Robinson, who had been elected in November 1990 as an independent candidate, resigned her position in order to assume her new functions as the United Nations High Commissioner for Human Rights. In the ensuing election, conducted on 30 October 1997, the Fianna Fáil candidate, Dr Mary McAleese, was elected as president, receiving 45.2% of the first-preference votes cast. McAleese was inaugurated on 11 November; she was the country's first President from Northern Ireland. In early November Ruairí Quinn succeeded Spring as leader of the Labour Party.

During 2000 independent judicial inquiries investigating corruption among politicians implicated many senior political figures. In mid-April Frank Dunlop, a political lobbyist and former government press secretary, admitted to an inquiry into planning irregularities in Dublin, headed by Justice Feargus Flood, that in 1991 he had paid a total of IR£112,000 to 15 Dublin county councillors on behalf of a property developer in order to ensure a favourable decision. Dunlop also testified that the Fine Gael leader, Bruton, was aware that a member of Fine Gael had demanded IR£250,000 from Dunlop to secure that member's vote in favour of the decision. Furthermore, Bruton was also accused by Liam Lawlor, a Fianna Fáil deputy, who himself had received payments from Dunlop, of benefiting from the decision. Bruton vehemently denied both accusations against him. In late January 2001 Fine Gael deputies passed a motion of 'no confidence' in Bruton, who resigned as leader of the party with immediate effect. He was replaced the following month by Michael Noonan, a former Minister for Health and Children.

Meanwhile, in late May 2000 a tribunal chaired by Justice Michael Moriarty (which was continuing the work of the McCracken inquiry) heard that between 1979 and 1996 Haughey had received payments totalling IR£8.5m., a much larger figure than had previously been acknowledged, and it was announced that Haughey would appear before the tribunal as a witness. Haughey appeared before the tribunal in July and continued to give evidence during late 2000 despite fears regarding his health. In early June Lawlor, who had resigned from the Dáil's Members' Interests Committee in April, resigned from Fianna Fáil following the publication of a report by the party's Standards in Public Life Committee, which described him as 'unco-operative and contradictory' in his dealings with its investigation. In mid-January 2001 Lawlor served seven days of a three-month prison sentence imposed following his failure to comply with a High Court order to give evidence regarding the use of his credit cards to the Flood tribunal.

In late March 2001 it was revealed that Lawlor had still not complied fully with the High Court order, and was again sentenced to seven days' imprisonment. Lawlor was also informed that he was required to make a full disclosure of his financial affairs to the Flood tribunal by early September or face further punishment. Lawlor subsequently launched an appeal against the sentence in the Supreme Court; however, in mid-December the Supreme Court upheld the High Court's verdict and Lawlor was ordered to serve the seven-day prison term. In late January 2002 lawyers for the Flood tribunal informed the High Court of Lawlor's failure to meet his obligations to the tribunal, and in early February Lawlor was sentenced to one month's imprisonment and also fined €12,500.

Also in March 2001 investigations by the Flood tribunal into the financial conduct of Ray Burke, who had resigned as Minister for Foreign Affairs in October 1997, revealed that Burke had held money in offshore accounts during the 1980s while a minister, and had transferred money to and from bank accounts held abroad without requesting permission from the Central Bank (as the law stipulated). He also admitted to misleading the Dáil regarding his financial affairs. Furthermore, in mid-May 2001 the tribunal heard that Burke made representations to the Chairman of the Revenue Commissioners on behalf of a construction company while he was Minister for Industry and Commerce in 1989. The hearing was adjourned in November, and in February 2002 it was announced that it was unlikely that the tribunal would produce any findings before the general election, which was scheduled to be held in May. In September Justice Flood issued the second interim report into the tribunal's findings thus far in which, most notably, he stated that Burke had received several 'corrupt payments' totalling up to IR£200,000 between 1974 and 1989. A number of prominent figures implicated in the proceedings were criticized for failing to co-operate fully with the tribunal and it was anticipated that criminal proceedings against 15 people, including Burke, would be instigated in 2003. Ahern came under intense political pressure regarding his appointment of Burke as Minister for Foreign Affairs.

The tribunal recommenced hearings in November 2002, when Dunlop alleged that nine Dublin county councillors had received payments totalling IR£25,000 in order to secure planning permission via the favourable rezoning (reclassification) of land owned by Jackson Way, a British property company in which Lawlor had a significant stake. All those implicated in the scandal denied any wrongdoing, and in December Jackson Way announced that it would no longer co-operate with the tribunal.

In mid-March 2001 Haughey finished giving evidence to the Moriarty tribunal; however, shortly afterwards he was admitted to hospital having suffered a heart attack. It was subsequently announced that it was unlikely he would give any further evidence to the inquiry. In March 2003 Haughey agreed to pay the Irish Revenue Commissioners €5m. in settlement of his outstanding tax liabilities resulting from undisclosed payments made to him between 1979 and 1996. In mid-December 2006 Justice Moriarty issued the first report, which detailed the tribunal's findings regarding payments made to Haughey, who died in June 2006. Most notably, Moriarty stated that, between 1979 and 1996, funds totalling IR£9.1m. had been made available for Haughey's personal use. In early 2007 hearings regarding the financial affairs of Lowry were ongoing; a second report into the tribunal's findings was due to be issued by the end of that year.

In May 2003 the Government was reported to be investigating ways of closing down or reforming the nine tribunals currently proceeding, the total costs of which were predicted to amount to more than €500m. by the time of their conclusions. Indeed, it was claimed that the Flood tribunal would continue for another 15 years at its current rate of progress. In June Justice Flood informed the Government that he wished to resign as Chairman of the tribunal, which, by that month, had incurred costs totalling some €26m.; later that month Justice Alan Mahon replaced Flood as the Chairman of the inquiry. In December Burke was formally charged with making false tax returns. In September 2004 Mahon rejected Burke's application for assistance with legal costs, estimated to amount to €10m., and in January 2005 Burke was sentenced to six months' imprisonment.

Meanwhile, in 2004 Ahern was implicated in the alleged tax evasion and corruption of another former minister, Pádraig Flynn. In February a British property developer, Tom Gilmartin, revealed that in 1989, while seeking approval for the construction of two shopping complexes in Dublin, he had given IR£50,000 to Flynn as a donation to Fianna Fáil. However, it was revealed that Flynn had, in fact, personally invested the money in an offshore bank account, allegedly with assistance from his daughter, Beverley Cooper Flynn, a Fianna Fáil deputy. Cooper Flynn dismissed the claims and Ahern (then Minister for Labour) denied any knowledge of the transaction before it became public knowledge. The tribunal commenced hearings in March 2004 to fully investigate Gilmartin's allegations. Again Ahern stated he knew nothing of the events that took place in 1989 and initially denied having attended a meeting between Gilmartin and several other ministers to discuss Gilmartin's intended property developments. However, in April 2004 Ahern conceded that there was a possibility that he had attended this meeting. In May Cooper Flynn was expelled from the party for her part in the affair.

Despite the death of Lawlor in November 2005, the tribunal continued. In December Gilmartin alleged that, in 1994, a former business partner, Owen O'Callaghan, had paid Ahern (then Minister for Finance) two separate sums of IR£50,000 and IR£30,000 for his role in blocking a proposed favourable tax designation for a shopping centre development that rivalled another being developed by Gilmartin and O'Callaghan. Ahern denied the allegation, insisting that the matter of tax designation had not been raised in his 1994 meeting with O'Callaghan.

In February 2006 the leader of the Labour Party, Pat Rabbitte, confirmed to the Mahon tribunal that in 1992, whilst a Dublin county councillor and member of the Democratic Left (which merged into the Labour Party in 1999), he had received IR£2,000 for election expenses from Dunlop. Dunlop claimed the amount was IR£3,000, and that it had been donated following Rabbitte's support of a controversial planning proposal, against the advice of council experts. Rabbitte told the tribunal that he had never discussed the proposal with Dunlop and that the donation had later been repaid in full. Dunlop confirmed that IR£2,000 had been returned to him. Rabbitte was questioned about why he had previously failed to divulge this information either to the Mahon tribunal or to a Garda inquiry into planning corruption.

Meanwhile, in early June 2001 the removal of all references to the death penalty from the Constitution along with the prohibition of any future legislation allowing capital punishment, and the ratification of the Rome Statute, which provided for the establishment of an International Criminal Court for crimes against humanity, were approved at separate referendums, by 62.1% and 64.2% of the electorate, respectively. However, at a third concurrently held referendum on the ratification of the Treaty of Nice, which proposed changes to the future size of the European Commission and the European Parliament as well as changes in the number of votes allocated to each member state prior to the enlargement of the EU from 2003, 53.9% of those who voted rejected the endorsement of the treaty, resulting in an embarrassing reverse for the Government, which had campaigned in favour of the treaty. The referendum was also marred by a voter participation rate of just 34.8%. The defeat was attributed to fears that ratification of the treaty would result in Irish participation in the EU's proposed rapid reaction force, thus undermining Ireland's neutrality, and concerns that Ireland would receive reduced funding and assistance from the EU.

The Government suffered a further reverse when, at a referendum on abortion held in early March 2002, 50.4% of the electorate voted against proposed changes, which would have removed the constitutional protection accorded by the Supreme Court to the lives of suicidal pregnant women wishing to terminate their pregnancies, and would have made abortion a criminal offence, punishable by 12 years' imprisonment. The rate of voter participation remained low, however, at just 42.9%.

At the general election held on 17 May 2002 Fianna Fáil won 41.5% of the first-preference votes cast, increasing its parliamentary representation to 81 seats, and thus only narrowly failing to achieve an overall majority in the Dáil. Fine Gael suffered a significant loss of support, winning just 31 seats and 22.5% of the votes. The PD and Sinn Féin increased their representation to eight seats and five seats, respectively, while the ecologist Green Party obtained six seats. The official rate of participation, at 63.0%, was the lowest to be recorded at an Irish general election. Following Fine Gael's poor performance at the election, Michael Noonan resigned as party leader and in early June he was succeeded by Enda Kenny. Also in early June Fianna Fáil and the PD successfully concluded their discussions on the formation of a new coalition Government. Ahern was duly re-elected Prime Minister, with Harney continuing as his deputy.

In June 2002 the Irish Government won support at an EU summit meeting held in Seville, Spain, for a declaration that formally stated that Ireland's participation in the EU rapid reaction force would be limited to those operations with a UN mandate, approved by the Government and sanctioned by the Dáil. For their part, Ireland's EU partners issued a complementary declaration reiterating that neither the Treaty of Nice nor previous EU treaties compromised Ireland's traditional neutrality and that no member state envisaged the rapid reaction force as a future European Army. In September the Irish Government announced that a second constitutional referendum which, as well as providing for the final ratification of the Treaty of Nice, would now explicitly prohibit Irish participation in any future common European defence force, would take place on 19 October. At the referendum, 62.9% of those who voted approved the treaty's ratification, with voter turn-out recorded at 49.5%.

In January 2003 the Irish Supreme Court issued a ruling, declaring that non-national parents of Irish-born children and their non-national siblings were not entitled to live in Ireland by virtue of having an Irish-born child. The ruling was passed after appeals were launched by Nigerian and Czech nationals who had been issued with deportation orders, despite having given birth to children in Ireland. The Minister for Justice swiftly allayed fears that this would lead to mass deportations of non-EU immigrant parents of children born in the country; it was officially estimated that some 11,000 applications for residency on the basis of having given birth to a child in Ireland were outstanding. By early 2004 only three families had been deported as a result of the ruling. A referendum was subsequently scheduled for June, to coincide with the elections to the European Parliament, to amend the Constitution so that children born in Ireland would not automatically be entitled to Irish citizenship. The constitutional amendment, which the Government hoped would deter immigrants from exploiting the current position to gain entitlement for their child to residence in any EU state (since Ireland was the only EU country with an automatic right to citizenship at birth), was approved by 79.2% of voters; turn-out was registered at nearly 60%.

Meanwhile, in March 2003 a government-supported motion to continue to allow US armed forces, which were engaged in military action against the regime of Saddam Hussain in Iraq, to use Shannon Airport and Irish airspace was approved by 77 votes to 60 in the Dáil. A number of deputies, in particular the Fine Gael leader, Kenny, had voiced their vehement opposition to the motion as they feared that Ireland's traditional neutrality would be compromised as a result.

In September 2004 Ahern effected a major cabinet reorganization, following the appointment of the Minister for Finance, Charlie McCreevy, as a member of the European Commission. Three new ministers were appointed, while eight existing ministers assumed new roles; McCreevy was succeeded as Minister of Finance by Brian Cowen. On 1 October 2004, as the sole nominee for the post, two other candidates having failed to secure the support of the 20 members of parliament or four local authorities required to stand for election, Dr Mary McAleese was deemed to be duly re-elected as President.

In November 2005 Ahern stated that objections to Sinn Féin's economic policies would preclude a coalition or any form of arrangement in the Dáil between that party and Fianna Fáil after the next general election, scheduled for May 2007, and noted that the mere inclusion of Sinn Féin in any government would be likely to cause a significant loss of investment confidence. The comments followed earlier declarations by Sinn Féin that it would consider participation in a coalition government with either Fianna Fáil or Fine Gael after the general election. Throughout 2006 reports persisted of a rift between Harney and the Minister for Justice, Equality and Law Reform,

Michael McDowell, regarding the leadership of the PD. The PD denied the claims, reiterating the party's commitment to the coalition Government. In early September Harney resigned as party leader and Deputy Prime Minister, but retained the role of Minister for Health and Children. McDowell subsequently replaced her as leader of the PD and was also appointed to the role of Deputy Prime Minister. In early October the unity of the coalition partners appeared in doubt after McDowell responded equivocally to allegations of financial impropriety against Ahern. However, later that month the controversy dissipated following discussions between the coalition partners on future legislation regarding the acceptance of gifts by ministers (see above).

From mid-2006 the main parties began to position themselves for the 2007 general election. Fine Gael and the Labour Party agreed to present a joint electoral programme and invited the Green Party to form part of a future coalition government. However, the Labour Party refused to rule out a coalition agreement with Fianna Fáil after the election. Following the election, held on 24 May, Fianna Fáil remained the largest party in the Dáil, with its representation declining slightly, to 78 seats, despite having marginally increased its share of the first-preference votes to 41.6%. Fine Gael obtained 27.3% of the votes cast and increased its representation substantially, obtaining 51 deputies. The Labour Party received 20 deputies, one fewer than it held in the outgoing legislature, while the Green Party's representation remained unchanged, with six deputies. Despite widespread expectations, in advance of the poll, that Sinn Féin would benefit from increased support, its faction in the Dáil declined from five to four deputies. More significantly, the representation of the PD was reduced from eight deputies to only two, and their share declined from 4.0% to 2.7%. Five independent deputies were also elected. Having failed to obtain re-election, McDowell was obliged (by the terms of the PD's Constitution) to resign as Leader of the PD. He was replaced, initially in an interim capacity, by Harney.

Following the general election, negotiations on the formation of a coalition administration that would enjoy a working majority in the Dáil commenced between Fianna Fáil, the PD and (despite an undertaking before the election by the party leader, Trevor Sargent, not to join an administration with Fianna Fáil) the Green Party. Three of the five independent deputies were also to support the administration. In mid-June 2007 a coalition agreement was signed; this was formalized one day later, following a vote in support of the party's participation in the Government by Green Party members. Sargent duly resigned as party leader. A new Government was formed on 14 June, again headed by Ahern, and in which many senior appointments remained unchanged from the outgoing administration. Cowen retained his post as Minister of Finance, being concurrently appointed as Deputy Prime Minister. Harney was reappointed as Minister for Health and Children, as the sole PD minister, while two ministers from the Green Party were appointed: John Gormley as Minister for the Environment, Heritage and Local Government; and Eamon Ryan as Minister for Communications, Energy and Natural Resources. The only new minister appointed from Fianna Fáil was Brian Lenihan, as Minister for Justice, Equality and Law. Despite the inclusion of the Green Party in the new administration, it had been agreed that several policies to which the party had expressed opposition—notably the construction of several major roadways, the granting of permission for UN-mandated US military flights bound for Iraq to use Shannon Airport, and the 'co-location' of private hospitals in the grounds of publicly funded hospitals—would remain unaltered.

In mid-July 2007 Gormley was elected as leader of the Green Party. In mid-August Rabbitte resigned as leader of the Labour Party; in the following month he was succeeded by Eamon Gilmore, who stated that the party would not enter into alliance with any other party in the Dáil. On 25 September a vote of 'no confidence' in Ahern, brought by Fine Gael and the Labour Party in response to concerns about the veracity of evidence he had presented to the Mahon tribunal (see below) was defeated. In late November a further vote of 'no confidence' in Harney, in her capacity of Minister of Health and Children, was also defeated; the vote, presented by Labour Party deputies, had been brought in relation to cases of misreporting of the results of tests for breast cancer.

Meanwhile, in September 2006 it was reported that the Mahon tribunal was investigating the personal finances of Ahern. It was alleged that, in 1993, Ahern (then Minister for Finance) had received a loan of £IR50,000 that had since remained unpaid. Furthermore, four of the individuals to whom the loan was owed had been appointed by Ahern to state bodies. Ahern denied any impropriety on his part. However, on 27 September he admitted during a television interview that he had received a loan from 12 friends, including a number of prominent business executives, but that it had been intended solely to help him during a time of difficulty in his personal life. On the following day Ahern revealed in the Dáil that he had also received a payment of IR£8,000 for a lecture given in his capacity as Minister for Finance in 1994. In October Ahern revealed that the 1993 loan had been repaid in full. It subsequently emerged that Ahern was to be questioned by the tribunal on several further matters, including several payments to a bank account that had been made in his name and in that of his then partner, Celia Larkin, in 1993–95, and foreign exchange transactions that had preceded each payment. The payments appeared to be connected with the renovation of a property that Ahern and Larkin were renting, and subsequently purchased, from a British-based business executive, Michael Wall, who was also being investigated by the tribunal. One particular payment in December 1994, which Ahern stated had constituted £28,772.90 (pounds sterling), was under investigation because banking records suggested that this sum constituted more than 14 times the amount of British currency received by the branch of the bank in question on that day. The tribunal was investigating allegations that the sum paid had originated from a transaction in US dollars (which should have been subject to taxation), an allegation that Ahern denied, although bank records suggested that the sum paid was exactly equivalent, in Irish currency, to the amount that a customer depositing US $45,000, using one of the rates of exchange in operation on that day, would have received. Ahern gave evidence to the Mahon tribunal over four days in mid-September 2007, in matters pertaining to various other apparently incongruous or seemingly undocumented banking transactions. Ahern stated that he had received donations from some 39 business executives, but denied that he had granted favours in return for donations, and stated that he could not recall the identity of many of the donors; he also amended his account to the tribunal of several financial transactions, admitting that he had not presented the tribunal with the complete information that it sought.

Ahern was subject to further questioning by the Mahon tribunal in mid-December 2007, when it emerged that he had not operated any bank accounts in 1987–93, during which time he had maintained his personal funds in two safes, located in his ministerial office and his constituency office. (It also emerged that Ahern had failed to pay taxes resulting from his having resided free of charge in his constituency office during the period that he was Minister of Finance.) In January 2008 Ahern criticized the tribunal, alleging that it had not given him a fair hearing and that it had permitted the release of confidential information. Later that month Kenny and Gilmore, as leaders of the two principal opposition parties, both called for Ahern's resignation from the post of Prime Minister, while the two parties governing in coalition with Fianna Fáil, the PD and the Green Party, expressed their support for the tribunal.

In early April 2008 Ahern announced that he was to resign from the positions of Prime Minister and leader of Fianna Fáil with effect from 6 May. On 9 April the Deputy Prime Minister and Minister of Finance, Cowen, was elected unopposed to succeed Ahern as leader of Fianna Fáil and, consequently, as Prime Minister; he was duly elected as Prime Minister by the Dáil on 7 May.

Consultations between the United Kingdom and Ireland on the future of Northern Ireland resulted in November 1985 in the signing of the Anglo-Irish Agreement, which provided for regular participation in Northern Ireland affairs by the Irish Government on political, legal, security and cross-border matters. The Agreement maintained that no change in the status of Northern Ireland would be made without the assent of the majority of its population. The terms of the Agreement were approved by both the Irish and the British Parliaments. Under the provisions of the Agreement, the Irish Government pledged co-operation in enhanced cross-border security, in order to suppress IRA operations. Despite underlying tensions, the ensuing co-ordination between the Garda Síochána (Irish police force) and the Northern Ireland police force, the Royal Ulster Constabulary (RUC), was broadly successful. In February 1989 a permanent joint consultative assembly, comprising 25 British MPs and 25 Irish deputies, was established. The representatives were selected in October. The assembly's meetings, the first of which began in

February 1990, were to take place twice a year, alternately in Dublin and London.

In January 1990 the British Secretary of State for Northern Ireland, Peter Brooke, launched an initiative to convene meetings between representatives from the major political parties in Northern Ireland, and the British and Irish Governments, to discuss the restoration of devolution to Northern Ireland, which had been abandoned in 1974. In May the unionists agreed to hold direct discussions with the Irish Government, an unprecedented concession. Following extensive negotiations, discussions between the Northern Ireland parties, which were a prelude to the inclusion of the Irish Government, commenced in June 1991. They were suspended several times but did reach the inclusion of the Irish Government in April and September 1992. The principal point of contention was the unionists' demand that Ireland hold a referendum on Articles 2 and 3 of its Constitution, which lay claim to the territory of Northern Ireland. Ireland was unwilling to make such a concession except as part of an overall settlement. The negotiations formally ended in November.

In October 1993 the new Irish Prime Minister, Reynolds, and his British counterpart, John Major, issued a joint statement setting out the principles on which future negotiations were to be based, including, notably, that Sinn Féin permanently renounce violence before being admitted to the negotiations. In December the Prime Ministers issued a joint declaration, known as the 'Downing Street Declaration', which referred to the possibility of a united Ireland and accepted the legitimacy of self-determination, but insisted on majority consent within Northern Ireland. While Sinn Féin and the unionist parties considered their response to the Declaration, Reynolds received both groups' conditional support for his proposal to establish a 'Forum for Peace and Reconciliation', which was to encourage both sides to end violent action. In August 1994 the IRA announced that it had ceased all military operations; this was followed in October by a similar suspension on the part of loyalist organizations.

Intergovernmental talks were maintained, resulting in the publication, in February 1995, of a 'Joint Framework' discussion document, in which the Irish Government undertook to support its constitutional claim to jurisdiction over Northern Ireland, while providing for cross-border institutions and economic programmes that would operate on an all-island basis.

An international panel, under the chairmanship of George Mitchell (a former US Senator), began work in December 1995 to consider the merits of decommissioning of arms in Northern Ireland. Its findings, announced in January 1996, recommended that the decommissioning of arms should take place in parallel with all-party talks, and that their destruction should be monitored by an independent commission. The British and Irish Governments accepted those recommendations, but the Irish Government deemed unacceptable proposals put forward by the British Government for elections to be held to a Northern Ireland assembly, which would provide the framework for all-party negotiations. In February 1996, following a bomb explosion in London, marking the termination of the IRA's cease-fire, the British and Irish Governments suspended official contacts with Sinn Féin.

In May 1997 a meeting of the Irish Prime Minister, Bruton, with the newly elected British premier, Tony Blair, and the new Secretary of State for Northern Ireland, Dr Marjorie (Mo) Mowlam, generated speculation that significant progress could be achieved in furthering a political agreement. In June the two Governments announced a new initiative to proceed with weapons decommissioning, while simultaneously pursuing negotiations for a constitutional settlement. In early July the newly elected Irish Prime Minister, Ahern, confirmed his commitment to the peace initiative during a meeting with Blair in London. On 19 July the IRA announced a restoration of its cease-fire. A few days later the Irish and British Governments issued a joint statement that all-party negotiations would commence in mid-September with the participation of Sinn Féin. At the end of July the Irish Government restored official contacts with Sinn Féin and resumed the policy of considering convicted IRA activists for early release from prison.

In September 1997 Sinn Féin announced that it would accept the outcome of the peace process and would renounce violence as a means of punishment or resolving problems, providing for the party's participation in all-party talks when they resumed in the middle of that month. A procedural agreement to pursue negotiations in parallel with the decommissioning of weapons (which was to be undertaken by an Independent International Commission on Decommissioning—IICD, led by Gen. John de Chastelain of Canada) was signed by all the main parties later in September.

On 10 April 1998 the two Governments and eight political parties involved in the talks signed the Good Friday (or Belfast) Agreement at Stormont Castle. Immediately thereafter the two Governments signed a new British-Irish Agreement, replacing the Anglo-Irish Agreement, committing them to enact the provisions of the multi-party agreement, subject to approval of the Good Friday Agreement by referendums to be held in Ireland and Northern Ireland in May. The peace settlement provided for changes to the Irish Constitution (notably Articles 2 and 3) and to British constitutional legislation to enshrine the principle that a united Ireland could be achieved only with the consent of the majority of the people of both Ireland and Northern Ireland. Under the terms of the Good Friday Agreement the new Northern Ireland Assembly was to have legislative powers over areas of social and economic policy, while security, justice, taxation and foreign policy were to remain under the authority of the British Government. Executive authority was to be discharged by an Executive Committee, comprising a First Minister, Deputy First Minister and as many as 10 ministers. The Assembly, which was to be elected in June, was initially to operate without legislative or executive powers, until the establishment of the North/South and British-Irish institutions. In addition, provision was made for the release of paramilitary prisoners affiliated to organizations that established a complete and unequivocal cease-fire. The decommissioning of paramilitary weapons was to be completed within two years of the approval by referendum of the Good Friday Agreement. On 22 April the Dáil overwhelmingly approved the peace agreement. On 22 May, at referendums held simultaneously in Ireland and Northern Ireland, 94.4% and 71.1% voted in favour of the Good Friday Agreement, respectively.

Elections to the 108-member Assembly were conducted on 25 June 1998; the Assembly convened for the first time in July and elected the leader of the Ulster Unionist Party (UUP), David Trimble, as Northern Ireland's First Minister. The peace process was threatened with disruption by sectarian violence in July and by the detonation of an explosive device in August in Omagh, Northern Ireland; the device was planted by a republican splinter group, the Real IRA, and caused 29 deaths, more than had been killed in any other single incident since the beginning of unrest related to Northern Ireland. In August 2003 the leader of the Real IRA, Kevin McKevitt, was sentenced to 20 years' imprisonment by the Special Criminal Court in Dublin for directing a terrorist organization.

Meanwhile, progress in the peace process continued to be obstructed by a dispute between unionists and Sinn Féin concerning weapons decommissioning. As a result of the dispute the deadlines for the formation both of the Executive Committee and the North/South body, and for the devolution of powers to the new Northern Ireland institutions were not met. An 'absolute' deadline for the devolution of powers was set for 30 June 1999. On 25 June the two Prime Ministers presented a compromise plan that envisaged the immediate establishment of the Executive Committee prior to the surrender of paramilitary weapons, with the condition that Sinn Féin guarantee that the IRA complete decommissioning by May 2000. Negotiations effectively collapsed in July 1999 and a review of the peace process, headed by George Mitchell, began in September. In November Mitchell succeeded in producing an agreement providing for the devolution of powers to the Executive Committee, after the IRA issued a statement announcing that it would appoint a representative to enter discussions with the IICD. On 29 November the Assembly convened to appoint the 10-member Executive Committee. On 2 December power was officially transferred from Westminster to the new Northern Ireland Executive. On the same day, in accordance with the Good Friday Agreement, the Irish Government removed from the Constitution the state's territorial claim over Northern Ireland.

In December 1999 the Irish Cabinet attended the inaugural meeting, in Armagh, of the North/South Ministerial Council. The British-Irish Council met for the first time later that month. With the failure of the IRA to undertake disarmament threatening to result in the collapse of the peace process the British and Irish Governments engaged in intensive negotiations. On 1 February the IRA released a statement giving assurances that its cease-fire would not be broken. However, on 11 February legislation came into effect returning Northern Ireland to direct rule. The IRA subsequently announced its withdrawal from discussions with the IICD.

Direct talks between the Irish and British Governments and the principal parties resumed in May 2000 with the British Government pledging to restore the Northern Ireland institutions on 22 May and postpone the deadline for decommissioning until June 2001 subject to a commitment by the IRA on the arms issue. On 6 May 2000 the IRA responded by offering to 'initiate a process that will completely and verifiably put arms beyond use'. On 30 May power was again transferred from Westminster to the new Northern Ireland institutions.

The issue of IRA weapons decommissioning continued to threaten the peace process during 2001. Prior to the general election held in the United Kingdom in June, Trimble had announced his intention to resign as First Minister on 1 July, thus precipitating the collapse of the Northern Ireland institutions, if there was no independently confirmed decommissioning of weapons by the IRA by that date. On 1 July Trimble duly stood down; Sir Reg Empey, the Minister of Enterprise, Trade and Investment, assumed the role of acting First Minister. In August Ahern and Blair announced that they would formulate a package of non-negotiable proposals to be tabled to the pro-Agreement parties. The ensuing proposals did not meet with the approval of the major political parties, and on 10 August the British Government suspended the Assembly for 24 hours in order to delay the necessity to appoint a new First Minister for a further six weeks. Following the temporary suspension the IRA retracted its earlier offer to put arms 'beyond use'.

The Assembly was again suspended on 22 September 2001 as the deadlock continued, and in October the three UUP ministers and two Democratic Unionist Party (DUP) ministers resigned. Later in the month, however, the IRA announced that it had begun a process of 'putting arms beyond use'; later that day the IICD revealed that it had witnessed the 'significant' disposal of IRA weapons. The UUP and DUP ministers therefore reassumed their posts. Trimble subsequently reassumed the position of First Minister and was finally re-elected, with Mark Durkan (who replaced John Hume as leader of the Social and Democratic Labour Party—SDLP in November) as his deputy. In September 2002 the ruling council of the UUP, the Ulster Unionist Council (UUC) announced that it would withdraw UUP ministers from the Northern Ireland Executive on 18 January 2003 if the IRA and Sinn Féin had not demonstrated a complete transition to democracy and non-violence. In October 2002 Sinn Féin's offices at the Assembly were raided by police, who suspected that the IRA had infiltrated the Northern Ireland Office and gained access to large numbers of confidential documents. Among a number of people detained by the police was Sinn Féin's Head of Administration, Denis Donaldson, who was charged with possession of documents likely to be of assistance to terrorist organizations. (It subsequently emerged that Donaldson had been an informer working for the British security services for some 20 years; his body was found in Co. Donegal in April 2006, and dissident republicans were suspected of his murder.)

On 14 October 2002 the British Secretary of State for Northern Ireland, Dr John Reid, returned Northern Ireland to direct rule. In a joint statement, Blair and Ahern announced that the devolved institutions would only be restored if Sinn Féin ended its link with paramilitary organizations and Blair subsequently called on the IRA to disband itself. Later that month the IRA announced that it had suspended all contact with the IICD.

Talks aimed at resolving the impasse continued between the major parties during late 2002 and early 2003; however, relations between unionists and nationalists remained strained. In March 2003 Ahern and Blair announced that the elections to the Assembly would be postponed until 29 May. In April the US President, George W. Bush, held talks with Ahern and the pro-Agreement parties at which he urged their leaders to 'seize the opportunity for peace'. Despite these efforts, the IRA failed to respond to the British Government's demand for a definitive cessation of paramilitary activities, and in May Blair postponed the elections until an unspecified date. Also in May the British and Irish Governments published a Joint Declaration containing their proposals for reinstating the Northern Ireland institutions and Blair and Ahern met in Dublin to discuss their implementation. The Declaration called for a full and permanent cessation of all paramilitary activity. Both Prime Ministers stressed that political talks would continue to address the impasse over the holding of elections and pledged that aspects of the Joint Declaration not conditional upon IRA acts of complete disarmament would be implemented.

Talks between the British and Irish Governments and the major Northern Ireland political parties continued during late 2003, and in September the four members of the International Monitoring Commission (IMC) were appointed. Trimble and Adams met with Ahern and Blair in London in mid-October, and on 21 October it was announced that elections to the Assembly would take place on 26 November. However, later on 21 October Trimble issued a statement in which he maintained that the acts of decommissioning of IRA weapons witnessed by de Chastelain earlier that day had been lacking in the transparency that the UUP required to be convinced of the IRA's desire to commit to peace. A statement issued by the IRA on 29 October maintained that it had honoured its commitments and that there would be no more acts of weapons decommissioning until the UUP agreed to support the restoration of power-sharing.

At elections to the Assembly, held on 26 November 2003, the anti-Good Friday Agreement DUP secured 30 of the 108 seats, thus becoming the largest party. The election result increased the pressure on Trimble from anti-Agreement factions of the UUP, who again called for him to resign. Furthermore, the DUP demanded a full renegotiation of the Good Friday Agreement. However, both Ahern and Blair reiterated that the principles and values incorporated in the Agreement would not be changed.

In talks with Ahern in January 2004 the leader of the DUP, Rev. Ian Paisley, remained insistent that his party would not conduct direct talks with Sinn Féin until the IRA had disbanded. The review of the Good Friday Agreement commenced in February; however, in March Trimble left the talks in protest at the alleged IRA involvement in the kidnapping of a dissident republican in Belfast. In April the IMC issued its first report in which it highlighted the levels of ongoing paramilitary activity in Northern Ireland. Blair and Ahern announced in May, following a meeting in Dublin, that they had agreed the basis of a 'roadmap' to restore the suspended Northern Ireland Assembly and Executive by October.

In September 2004 Blair and Ahern hosted a three-day meeting at Leeds Castle, England, in a further attempt to restore the suspended devolved institutions. Blair increased the political pressure on the participants by suggesting that if no agreement on power-sharing could be reached in September 'an alternative way' would have to be found. Although progress was apparently made towards the complete disbandment and disarmament of the IRA, the talks became deadlocked, following a DUP demand for changes to the functioning of the Assembly and the Executive before it would enter a government with Sinn Féin. In October Paisley met Ahern in Dublin, his first formal political meeting with the Irish Prime Minister, to try to break the impasse. In early November, however, the IMC's second report on paramilitary violence reported that the IRA was still recruiting volunteers and gathering intelligence. Later that month the British and Irish Governments passed their proposals for restoring the power-sharing Executive to the DUP and Sinn Féin for consultation.

In December 2004 Blair and Ahern met in Belfast to reveal their final proposals to restore devolution, although neither the DUP nor Sinn Féin had agreed to the terms. The following day an IRA statement was released, rejecting a demand made by Paisley for photographic proof of decommissioning and stating that, although the IRA was committed to the peace process, it would not be subjected to humiliation. In January 2005 the Northern Ireland Chief Constable placed the blame for a raid on the Belfast headquarters of the Northern Bank in December 2004, in which £26.5m. was stolen, on the IRA. Furthermore, following the murder in Belfast of Robert McCartney in January 2005, allegedly carried out by members of the IRA, allegations surfaced that Sinn Féin members had been involved in covering up the killing. In February McDowell accused three senior Sinn Féin officials of holding membership of the IRA army council. Adams, Martin McGuinness, Sinn Féin's chief negotiator, and Martin Ferris, a member of the Dáil, all denied the allegations. Also in February Ahern and Blair warned the IRA that its failure to demilitarize was the only obstacle to reaching an agreement on power-sharing; the following day the IRA withdrew its commitment to decommissioning. However, on 28 July the IRA announced the end of its armed campaign, and renewed its commitment to decommissioning. The British and Irish Governments welcomed the announcement, although the DUP and others remained sceptical regarding its veracity. In September the IICD confirmed that the IRA's weapons had been fully decommissioned. In late December the British Secretary of State for Northern Ireland, Peter Hain, warned Sinn Féin and the DUP that the Assembly elections, scheduled for 2007, would be cancelled if they did not reach an agreement on power-sharing in 2006. Hain and the Irish Minister for Foreign Affairs, Dermot Ahern, chaired talks with the Northern Ireland parties in February 2006, while Blair and Bertie Ahern met to discuss plans for the restoration of the institutions in March. The IMC published its ninth report into paramilitary activity in that month, in which it reported that, although no longer a threat to security, the IRA continued to gather intelligence. The report also noted continuing loyalist and republican involvement in criminal activity. Dermot Ahern subsequently announced that if attempts to restore the institutions of Northern Ireland in accordance with the Good Friday Agreement failed, then the British and Irish Governments would adopt an intergovernmental approach.

In April 2006 Bertie Ahern and Blair issued a joint statement clarifying the development of the peace process in that year, following a meeting held in Armagh. On 15 May the Assembly was restored; however, no further progress was made regarding the nomination of candidates for the roles of First Minister and Deputy First Minister. The IMC's 12th report, published in early October, stated that the IRA was no longer engaged in terrorist activity and was committed to the peace process but noted that members both of loyalist and republican paramilitary groups continued to engage in criminal activity. Despite the positive overall tone of the IMC report, the DUP remained sceptical concerning the progress of the disbandment of the IRA. On 13 October, following talks in St Andrews, Scotland, Bertie Ahern and Blair announced an agreement (the St Andrews Agreement) that was intended to precipitate the restoration of a power-sharing Executive, and set a deadline of 10 November by which the Northern Ireland main parties were to agree to adhere to its provisions, which included support by all parties for the Police Force of Northern Ireland (PSNI) and the Northern Ireland Policing Board, and the formation of a North-South Inter-parliamentary Forum, including an equal number of representatives from both the Assembly and the Irish Parliament. Devolution was to be restored on 24 November, when the DUP and Sinn Féin would nominate candidates for the posts of First Minister and Deputy First Minister, respectively. The Assembly duly convened on 24 November where Paisley refused to accept his nomination as First Minister, while hinting that he would assume the role after elections to the Assembly, scheduled to be held in early March 2007, should Sinn Féin formally signal its support for the PSNI and the Policing Board. Following a long period of consultation among Sinn Féin members, in late January 2007 the party leadership convened a special conference in Dublin, at which some 90% of delegates voted in favour of a proposal to support the policing institutions. The result was welcomed by both Governments. The DUP, for its part, stated that, while it recognized the significance of the decision, tangible evidence of Sinn Féin's commitment was required before power-sharing could be restored. Nevertheless, the two Governments insisted that the deadline of 26 March was binding and that, in the absence of an agreement, the Assembly would be dissolved.

In elections to the Assembly, held on 7 March 2007, the DUP secured 36 seats and Sinn Féin 28 seats, thereby confirming their status as the main parties in Northern Ireland. As the deadline approached, the Irish Government and Hain indicated that the deadline could be flexible, should the two parties agree an alternative arrangement. On 26 March Paisley and Adams held their first ever direct meeting, during which an agreement was reached for a power-sharing Executive, which was duly installed on 8 May. In early April Bertie Ahern had met Paisley in Dublin to discuss arrangements for future co-operation between the Executive and the Irish Government. In July Dermot Ahern, who had been reappointed as Minister of Foreign Affairs in the Irish Government formed in the previous month, participated in two rounds of discussions, hosted in Northern Ireland, concerned with the eventual establishment of further cross-border institutions. In December Bertie Ahern announced that two branches of Fianna Fáil at the two principal universities in Northern Ireland had been registered, and that the party was considering organizing further in the territory.

Ireland became a member of the EC (now the EU) in 1973. In May 1987 the country affirmed its commitment to the EC when, in a referendum, 69.9% of Irish voters supported adherence to the Single European Act, which provided for closer economic and political co-operation between EC member-states (including the creation of a single market by 1993). In December 1991 Ireland agreed to the far-reaching Treaty on European Union (the Maastricht Treaty). Ireland secured a special provision within the Treaty (which was signed by all parties in February 1992), guaranteeing that Ireland's constitutional position on abortion would be unaffected by any future EC legislation. Despite opposition, from both pro- and anti-abortion campaigners, to the special provision within the Treaty and the threat to Ireland's neutrality inherent in the document's proposals for a common defence policy, ratification of the Treaty was endorsed by 68.7% of the votes cast at a referendum held in June 1992 (57.3% of the electorate participated). In a referendum conducted in May 1998 some 62% of those who voted endorsed the Amsterdam Treaty, which had been signed by EU ministers in October 1997, amending the Maastricht Treaty. In October 2002 the Treaty of Nice, which provided for the impending enlargement of the EU, was approved by 62.9% of those who voted in a national referendum, despite having been rejected in an earlier referendum held in 2001 (see above). In January 2004 Ireland assumed the rotating six-month Presidency of the EU. Ahern, in his capacity as President of the Council of the European Union, led intense negotiations and proposed a compromise on voting rights in the Council that enabled the leaders of all 25 member states to approve a draft constitutional treaty for the organization on 18 June 2004. The constitutional treaty was formally signed in October 2004 but required ratification by all 25 member states either by parliamentary vote or referendum. However, following the treaty's rejection in national referendums in France and the Netherlands in mid-2005, further referendums in EU countries yet to ratify the treaty, including Ireland, were postponed indefinitely. On 1 January 2007 Irish became an official and working language of the EU. Following the signature, in December, of the Lisbon Treaty, which further amended the Maastricht Treaty and replaced the proposed constitutional treaty, a referendum was to be held in order to permit Ireland's ratification of the treaty; in March 2008 it was announced that this plebiscite would be conducted in June. Ireland was the sole EU member state to require the ratification of the treaty by referendum.

In February 2006 the Minister for Defence, Willie O'Dea, announced that Ireland would participate in EU battle groups (13 of which were to be established by 2007 for deployment to international crisis areas), reversing a decision made in 2005. In July 2006 an amendment to previous defence legislation was promulgated following a vote in the Dáil. Under the amended legislation, Irish troops could join EU battle groups in emergency humanitarian, reconnaissance and training missions prior to receiving a UN mandate or approval from the Dáil, thus circumventing the so-called 'triple-lock' that required any deployment of Irish troops abroad to be mandated by the UN and approved by the Irish Government and Parliament. However, if either or both decline to approve such a mission, troops would be withdrawn.

Government

Legislative power is vested in the bicameral National Parliament (Oireachtas), comprising the Senate (with restricted powers) and the House of Representatives. The Senate (Seanad Éireann) has 60 members, including 11 nominated by the Prime Minister (Taoiseach) and 49 indirectly elected for five years. The House of Representatives (Dáil Éireann) has 166 members (Teachtaí Dála), elected by universal adult suffrage for five years (subject to dissolution) by means of the single transferable vote, a form of proportional representation.

The President (Uachtarán) is the constitutional Head of State, elected by direct popular vote for seven years. Executive power is effectively held by the Cabinet, led by the Prime Minister, who is appointed by the President on the nomination of the Dáil. The President appoints other Ministers on the nomination of the Prime Minister with the previous approval of the Dáil. The Cabinet is responsible to the Dáil.

Defence

As assessed at November 2007 the regular armed forces totalled an estimated 10,460. The army comprised 8,500, the navy 1,110 and the air force 850. There was also a reserve of 14,875. Defence was allocated €791.1m. in the 2007 budget (2.1% of total expenditure). Military service is voluntary. In November 2004 the European Union (EU, see p. 244) ministers responsible for defence agreed to create 13 'battlegroups' (each numbering about 1,500 men), which could be deployed at short notice to crisis areas around the world. The EU battlegroups, two of which were to be ready for deployment at any one time, following a rotational schedule, reached full operational capacity from 1 January 2007. Ireland contributed to the Nordic battlegroup, which was com-

IRELAND

manded by Sweden, with the participation of Finland, Norway and Estonia.

Economic Affairs

In 2006, according to estimates by the World Bank, Ireland's gross national income (GNI), measured at average 2004–06 prices, was US $191,887.4m., equivalent to $45,580 per head (or $35,900 on an international purchasing-power parity basis). During 1996–2006, it was estimated, the population increased at an average annual rate of 1.5%, while gross domestic product (GDP) per head increased, in real terms, by an average of 5.7% per year. Overall GDP increased, in real terms, at an average annual rate of 7.3% in 1996–2006; in 2006 it grew by 6.0%.

Agriculture (including forestry and fishing) contributed 2.6% of GDP in 2006. An estimated 5.5% of the working population were employed in the sector in 2007. Beef and dairy production dominate Irish agriculture. Principal crops include sugar beet, barley, wheat and potatoes. Agricultural GDP increased by an average of 0.6% per year during 1996–2006; however, this sector contracted by 6.8% in 2006.

Industry (comprising mining, manufacturing, construction and utilities) provided an estimated 34.6% of GDP in 2006, and employed an estimated 27.3% of the working population in 2007. Industrial GDP increased by an average of 8.1% per year during 1996–2006; it grew by an estimated 4.6% in 2006.

Mining (including quarrying and turf production) provided employment to 0.4% of the working population in 2006. Ireland possesses substantial deposits of lead-zinc ore and recoverable peat, both of which are exploited. Natural gas is produced from the Kinsale field off the south coast of Ireland (although production here is declining) and from the Seven Heads field that came on stream in 2003. Further gas supplies were discovered at the Corrib field situated off the west coast of Ireland; production was expected to begin in 2008. Small quantities of coal are also extracted. Offshore reserves of petroleum have also been located and several licences awarded to foreign-owned enterprises to undertake further exploration.

Manufacturing was estimated to employ 20.3% of the working population in 1997. The manufacturing sector comprises many high-technology, largely foreign-owned, capital-intensive enterprises. In 2005 manufacturing production increased by 3.1%.

Electricity is derived principally from natural gas, which provided 51.1% of total requirements in 2004, while coal provided 30.6% and petroleum 12.7%. There was potential for the further development of wind-generated energy, which was increasing in importance. The merger of island-wide distributive operations, agreement on which was finalized in late 2007, was expected to result in a substantial increase in demand for electricity and promote further the development of renewable energy sources. In 2005 imports of mineral fuels were 7.7% (by value) of total merchandise imports.

Service industries (including commerce, finance, transport and communications and public administration) contributed an estimated 62.9% of GDP in 2006, and employed an estimated 67.2% of the working population in 2007. The financial sector is of increasing importance to Ireland. An International Financial Services Centre in Dublin was opened in 1990; in 2007 more than 430 companies were participating in the Centre, many of which were foreign concerns attracted by tax concessions offered by the Irish Government. Tourism is one of the principal sources of foreign exchange. Revenue from the tourism and travel sector amounted to an estimated US $6,772m. in 2005. The GDP of the services sector increased by an average of 6.7% per year during 1996–2006, and by an estimated 6.8% in 2006.

In 2006, according to IMF statistics, Ireland recorded a visible trade surplus of US $31,888m. while there was a deficit of $9,095m. on the current account of the balance of payments. In 2005 the principal source of imports was the United Kingdom (30.7%); other major sources were the USA (13.9%) and Germany (7.5%). The USA was the principal market for exports (18.6%); other major purchasers were the United Kingdom (17.3%), Belgium (15.0%), Germany (7.4%) and France (6.4%). In 2006 principal imports included office equipment and other electrical machinery, chemical products, road vehicles and parts, and other manufactured items. Principal exports included chemicals, office equipment and food and live animals.

A budgetary deficit of €1,845m. (equivalent to 0.9% of GDP) was forecast for 2008; Ireland's total national debt was estimated to be €38,182m. in 2005. The annual rate of inflation averaged 3.3% in 1996–2006. The rate increased to 4.0% in 2006. Unemployment stood at 4.5% of the labour force in May 2007.

Ireland is a member of the European Union (EU, see p. 244), and of the EU Exchange Rate Mechanism (ERM, see p. 288).

In the late 1990s the Irish economy enjoyed an unprecedentedly high rate of growth, which was attributed to prudent fiscal and monetary management, low levels of corporate taxation, an expanding, well-qualified and English-speaking labour force and social partnership agreements between the Government, businesses and trade unions, providing for guaranteed pay rises in return for productivity and 'no strike' agreements. Government policies offering financial incentives to foreign-owned enterprises resulted in a substantial increase in direct foreign investment and expansion in the financial services and electronic manufacturing industries. Continuing high levels of growth (though lower than in the 1990s) were sustained in 2004–06 by rapid growth in the construction sector and high levels of consumer spending, in large part due to migrant workers entering the work-force, including several hundred thousand migrant workers from the states of Central and Eastern Europe that acceded to EU membership in 2004. Investment in infrastructure has hitherto failed to accommodate Ireland's rapid economic growth. In particular, attempts under the National Development Plan (NDP) 2000–06 to address road congestion, low levels of broadband internet penetration and a shortage of housing, exacerbated by sharp rises in house prices, largely failed to meet their targets. In January 2007 the Government published an NDP for 2007–13, which envisaged further substantial investment in the local authority housing sector, the national road network and public transport infrastructure. For the first time, the NDP allocated funds for improvements to the infrastructure in Northern Ireland, in an attempt both to encourage the growth of economic ties on an all-island basis. Economic growth slowed to an estimated 4.7% in 2007, compared with 6.0% the previous year. The 2008 budget included a substantial decrease in stamp duty on mid-range properties and broadened the scope of mortgage interest relief for first time buyers. The Government hoped these measures would temper the decline in house prices that had constrained economic growth in 2007. The slowing housing market engendered an associated decrease in construction activities towards the end of 2007, which resulted in an increase in unemployment. Moreover, decreasing asset prices inhibited the growth of household incomes and adversely affected consumer expenditure. The slowing of demand was, however, likely to moderate the inflationary pressures that had increased consumer prices to above the EU average in 2007. While Ireland remained one of the fastest growing economies in the EU, GDP growth was expected to slow further in 2008–09.

Education

The state in Ireland has constitutional responsibility for the national education system. An aided system is in operation: Irish schools are funded by the state, but owned and run (with a few minor exceptions) by community bodies, usually religious groups. Education in Ireland is compulsory for nine years between six and 15 years of age. Primary education may begin at the age of six and lasts for six years. Aided primary schools account for the education of 99.0% of children in the primary sector. Post-primary education begins at 12 years of age and lasts for up to six years, comprising a junior cycle of three years and a senior cycle of two or three years. The Junior Certificate examination is taken after three years in post-primary (second-level) education. The Leaving Certificate examination is taken after a further two to three years and is a necessary qualification for entry into university education. By 2003/04 some 95.7% of 16-year-olds were participating in full-time, post-compulsory education. There are four universities: the University of Dublin (Trinity College); the National University of Ireland (comprising the University Colleges of Cork, Dublin and Galway); Dublin City University; and the University of Limerick (former National Institutes of Higher Education, which obtained university status in 1989). In addition, there are 16 technical colleges providing a range of craft, technical, professional and other courses.

In the 2007 budget €7,898m. (equivalent to 21.2% of total expenditure) was allocated to education.

Public Holidays

2008: 1 January (New Year), 17 March (St Patrick's Day), 24 March (Easter Monday), 5 May (May Day Holiday), 2 June (June Bank Holiday), 4 August (August Bank Holiday), 27 October (October Bank Holiday), 25 December (Christmas), 26 December (St Stephen's Day).

IRELAND

2009: 1 January (New Year), 17 March (St Patrick's Day), 13 April (Easter Monday), 4 May (May Bank Holiday), 1 June (June Bank Holiday), 3 August (August Bank Holiday), 26 October (October Bank Holiday), 25 December (Christmas Day), 26 December (St Stephen's Day).

Weights and Measures

The metric system of weights and measures is the primary system in force, but the imperial system is still used in a number of limited activities.

Statistical Survey

Source (unless otherwise stated): Central Statistics Office, Skehard Rd, Cork; tel. (21) 4535000; fax (21) 4535555; e-mail information@cso.ie; internet www.cso.ie.

Area and Population

AREA, POPULATION AND DENSITY

Area (sq km)	70,182*
Population (census results)	
28 April 2002	3,917,203
23 April 2006	
Males	2,121,171
Females	2,118,677
Total	4,239,848
Density (per sq km) at April 2006	60.4

* 27,097 sq miles.

ADMINISTRATIVE DIVISIONS
(2006 census)

Province/County	Area (sq km)	Population	Density (per sq km)
Connaught	17,713	504,121	28.5
Galway	6,151	231,670	37.7
Galway City	51	72,414	1,419.9
Galway County	6,010	159,256	26.5
Leitrim	1,589	28,950	18.2
Mayo	5,588	123,839	22.2
Roscommon	2,548	58,768	23.1
Sligo	1,837	60,894	33.1
Leinster	19,774	2,295,123	116.1
Carlow	898	50,349	56.1
Dublin	921	1,187,176	1,289.0
Dublin City	118	506,211	4,289.9
Dún Laoghaire-Rathdown	127	194,038	1,527.9
Fingal	453	239,992	529.8
South Dublin	223	246,935	1,107.3
Kildare	1,694	186,335	110.0
Kilkenny	2,072	87,558	42.3
Laoighis	1,719	67,059	39.0
Longford	1,091	34,391	31.5
Louth	832	111,267	133.7
Meath	2,335	162,831	69.7
Offaly	1,990	70,868	35.6
Westmeath	1,825	79,346	43.5
Wexford	2,365	131,749	55.7
Wicklow	2,033	126,194	62.1
Munster	24,608	1,173,340	47.7
Clare	3,442	110,950	32.2
Cork	7,508	481,295	64.1
Cork City	40	119,418	2,985.5
Cork County	7,468	361,877	48.5
Kerry	4,735	139,835	29.5
Limerick	2,760	184,055	66.7
Limerick City	20	52,539	2,627.0
Limerick County	2,740	131,516	48.0
Tipperary	4,304	149,244	34.8
Tipperary North	2,046	66,023	32.3
Tipperary South	2,258	83,221	36.9
Waterford	1,859	107,961	58.1
Waterford City	42	45,748	1,089.2
Waterford County	1,817	62,213	34.2
Ulster (part)	8,087	267,264	33.0
Cavan	1,932	64,003	33.1
Donegal	4,860	147,264	30.3
Monaghan	1,296	55,997	43.2
Total	**70,182**	**4,239,848**	**60.4**

PRINCIPAL TOWNS
(population at 2006 census)

Dublin (capital)	506,211	Limerick	52,539	
Cork	119,418	Waterford	45,748	
Galway	72,414			

BIRTHS, MARRIAGES AND DEATHS

	Registered live births		Registered marriages		Registered deaths	
	Number	Rate (per 1,000)	Number	Rate (per 1,000)	Number	Rate (per 1,000)
1999	53,924	14.4	18,526	5.0	32,608	8.7
2000	54,789	14.5	19,168	5.1	31,391	8.3
2001	57,854	15.0	19,246	5.0	30,212	7.9
2002	60,503	15.4	20,556	5.2	29,683	7.6
2003	61,529	15.5	20,302	5.1	29,074	7.3
2004	61,684	15.3	20,619	5.1	28,151	7.0
2005	61,042	14.8	21,355	5.2	27,441	6.6
2006	64,237	15.2	21,841	5.1	27,479	6.5

Expectation of life (years at birth, WHO estimates): 79.2 (males 76.9; females 81.3) in 2005 (Source: WHO, *World Health Statistics*).

IMMIGRATION AND EMIGRATION
('000, year ending April, official preliminary estimates)

Immigrants

Country of origin	2003/04	2004/05	2005/06
United Kingdom	13.0	13.8	15.5
Other EU*	12.6	35.1	48.1
USA	4.8	4.3	3.5
Rest of the world	19.7	16.8	19.8
Total	**50.1**	**70.0**	**86.9**

Emigrants

Country of destination	2003/04	2004/05	2005/06
United Kingdom	4.9	4.1	4.4
Other EU*	3.4	3.4	3.9
USA	2.8	1.7	1.4
Rest of the world	7.4	7.4	7.3
Total	**18.5**	**16.6**	**17.0**

* From 2004/05, figures include data for the 10 new member states that acceded to the European Union on 1 May 2004.

IRELAND

ECONOMICALLY ACTIVE POPULATION
('000 persons, quarterly (March–May) labour force survey, estimates)

	2005	2006	2007
Agriculture, forestry and fishing	113.7	114.5	114.7
Mining and quarrying			
Manufacturing	294.2	288.5	291.5
Electricity, gas and water			
Construction	242.2	262.7	280.3
Wholesale and retail trade	266.9	284.4	293.5
Hotels and restaurants	111.0	116.3	124.8
Transport, storage and communications	118.2	120.7	122.4
Financial and other business services	257.1	267.3	287.6
Public administration and defence	98.2	105.1	104.6
Education	123.1	135.6	141.5
Health	188.0	201.2	213.0
Other services	116.4	120.6	121.6
Total employed	1,929.2	2,017.0	2,095.4
Males	1,110.1	1,162.0	1,195.9
Females	819.1	855.0	899.4
Total unemployed	85.6	91.4	98.8
Total labour force	2,014.8	2,108.3	2,194.1

Health and Welfare

KEY INDICATORS

Total fertility rate (children per woman, 2005)	2.0
Under-5 mortality rate (per 1,000 live births, 2005)	5
HIV/AIDS (% of persons aged 15–49, 2005)	0.2
Physicians (per 1,000 head, 2004)	2.8
Hospital beds (per 1,000 head, 2004)	3.5
Health expenditure (2004): US $ per head (PPP)	2,617.8
Health expenditure (2004): % of GDP	7.2
Health expenditure (2004): public (% of total)	79.5
Human Development Index (2005): ranking	5
Human Development Index (2005): value	0.959

For sources and definitions, see explanatory note on p. vi.

Agriculture

PRINCIPAL CROPS
('000 metric tons)

	2004	2005	2006
Wheat	1,019.2	802.7	767.7
Oats	155.2	112.8	153.4
Barley	1,326.6	1,024.4	1,096.4
Potatoes	552.2	409.2	409.2*
Sugar beet	1,861.4	1,395.0	1,450.0*
Carrots and turnips*	18.9	16.4	16.4
Cabbages and other brassicas	42.6	39.6	39.6

* FAO estimate(s).
Source: FAO.

LIVESTOCK
('000 head at June)

	2004	2005	2006
Cattle	7,015.6	6,982.6	6,876.7
Sheep	6,777.2	6,392.2	5,969.6
Pigs	1,653.1	1,687.7	1,643.2
Chickens*	12,800	12,700	12,700

* FAO estimates.
Source: FAO.

LIVESTOCK PRODUCTS
('000 metric tons)

	2004	2005	2006
Cattle meat	563.5	546.0	572.2
Sheep meat	71.8	73.1	70.3
Pig meat	204.3	205.3	209.1
Chicken meat*	95.0	98.5	98.5
Cows' milk	5,500.0†	5,500.0*	5,500.0*
Hen eggs	31.9	32.0*	32.0*

* FAO estimate(s).
† Unofficial figure.
Source: FAO.

Forestry

ROUNDWOOD REMOVALS
('000 cubic metres, excluding bark)

	2004	2005	2006
Sawlogs, veneer logs and logs for sleepers	1,723	1,763	1,788
Pulpwood	722	759	760
Other industrial wood	98	107	107
Fuel wood	20	19	16
Total	2,562	2,648	2,671

Source: FAO.

SAWNWOOD PRODUCTION
('000 cubic metres, including railway sleepers)

	2004	2005	2006
Coniferous (softwood)	937	1,014	1,091
Broadleaved (hardwood)	2	1	3
Total	939	1,015	1,094

Source: FAO.

Fishing

('000 metric tons, live weight)

	2003	2004	2005
Capture*	301,226	310,628	292,032
Blue whiting	22,586	58,426	69,650
Atlantic herring	28,839	26,234	29,341
Sardinellas	20,764	19,651	24,084
European pilchard	9,153	12,997	8,223
Atlantic horse mackerel	35,854	26,432	33,295
Atlantic mackerel	73,341	61,557	45,303
Edible crab	11,462	13,690	5,690
Aquaculture	62,516	58,359	60,050
Atlantic salmon	16,347	14,067	13,764
Blue mussel	39,289	37,315	38,265
Total catch	363,742	368,987	352,082

* FAO estimates.
Source: FAO.

IRELAND

Mining

('000 metric tons, unless otherwise indicated)

	2003	2004*	2005*
Natural gas (million cu m)*	2,500	2,500	2,500
Lead†	50.3	65.9	63.8
Zinc†	419.0	444.1	428.6
Peat‡	3,190	5,600	5,450

* Estimates.
† Figures refer to the metal content of ores mined.
‡ Excluding peat for horticultural use ('000 metric tons): 451 in 2003; 400 in 2004 (estimate); 450 in 2005 (estimate).

Source: US Geological Survey.

Industry

SELECTED PRODUCTS
('000 metric tons unless otherwise indicated)

	2002	2003	2004
Cigarettes (million)	6,599	n.a.	n.a.
Motor spirit (gasoline)	660	639	552
Gas-diesel oil (distillate fuel oil)	955	988	964
Mazout (residual fuel oil)	1,047	1,005	966
Electric energy (million kWh)	25,170	25,235	25,627

Margarine ('000 metric tons): 33 in 1998.

Woven woollen fabrics ('000 sq m): 800 in 1998.

Flour ('000 metric tons): 190 in 2001 (FAO estimate).

Sources: FAO; UN, *Industrial Commodity Statistics Yearbook*; US Geological Survey.

Finance

CURRENCY AND EXCHANGE RATES

Monetary Units
100 cent = 1 euro (€).

Sterling and Dollar Equivalents (31 December 2007)
£1 sterling = €1.3609;
US $1 = €0.6793;
€10 = £7.35 = $14.72.

Average Exchange Rate (euros per US $)
2005 0.8041
2006 0.7971
2007 0.7306

Note: The national currency was formerly the Irish pound (or punt). From the introduction of the euro, with Irish participation, on 1 January 1999, a fixed exchange rate of €1 = 78.7564 pence was in operation. Euro notes and coins were introduced on 1 January 2002. The euro and local currency circulated alongside each other until 9 February, after which the euro became the sole legal tender.

BUDGET
(€ million)

Revenue*	2006	2007†	2008‡
Current revenue	56,984	60,557	63,031
Taxes on income and wealth	19,910	21,012	21,725
Social insurance and health contributions	8,162	9,036	9,629
Taxes on expenditure	24,607	25,626	26,528
Gross trading and investment income	1,794	2,011	2,292
Current transfers from rest of the world	158	427	381
Miscellaneous receipts	2,330	2,445	2,475
Capital revenue	5,097	5,370	5,426
Taxes on capital	3,437	3,581	3,626
Total	**62,081**	**65,927**	**68,457**

Expenditure§	2006	2007†	2008‡
Current expenditure	48,615	54,791	58,985
National debt interest	1,781	1,688	1,923
Current transfer payments to residents	18,239	21,095	22,045
Current transfer payments to rest of the world	2,011	2,241	2,480
Current expenditure on goods and services (excluding depreciation)	20,477	22,990	25,443
Current expenditure on goods and services by local authorities	5,195	5,541	5,742
Capital expenditure	8,359	10,237	11,317
Gross fixed capital formation	6,496	7,355	8,159
Total	**56,974**	**65,027**	**70,302**

* Excluding loan repayments and equity sales (€ million): 1,030 in 2006; 850 in 2007 (provisional); 860 in 2008 (forecast). Also excluding borrowing (€ million): –4,802 in 2006; –420 in 2007 (provisional); 2,333 in 2008 (forecast).
† Provisional.
‡ Forecast.
§ Excluding debt redemption (€ million): 614 in 2006; 610 in 2007 (provisional); 633 in 2008 (forecast). Also excluding loans and purchase of share capital (€ million): 721 in 2006; 721 in 2007 (provisional); 721 in 2008 (forecast).

Source: Department of Finance.

INTERNATIONAL RESERVES
(US $ million at 31 December)

	2004	2005	2006
Gold (Eurosystem valuation)	77	90	112
IMF special drawing rights	89	88	95
Reserve position in IMF	418	176	131
Foreign exchange	2,324	514	494
Total	**2,908**	**869**	**832**

Source: IMF, *International Financial Statistics*.

MONEY SUPPLY
(€ million at 31 December)

	2004	2005	2006
Currency issued*	6,437	7,247	8,021
Demand deposits at banking institutions	55,371	65,794	79,101

* Total currency put into circulation by the Central Bank of Ireland was: €11,491m. in 2004; €14,180m. in 2005; €17,409m. in 2006.

Source: IMF, *International Financial Statistics*.

COST OF LIVING
(Consumer Price Index; base: December 2001 = 100)

	2005	2006	2007
Food and non-alcoholic beverages	102.1	103.5	106.5
Alcoholic beverages and tobacco	118.7	120.0	126.5
Clothing and footwear	84.8	83.1	80.4
Housing, water, electricity, gas and other fuel	118.7	137.8	165.8
Furnishings, household equipment and routine household maintenance	95.6	94.4	92.7
Health	127.7	133.3	137.3
Transport	114.6	118.5	121.0
Communications	104.8	104.3	104.8
Recreation and culture	108.2	109.6	111.2
Education	127.2	133.3	140.2
Restaurants and hotels	119.5	124.2	129.4
Miscellaneous goods and services	108.3	110.0	111.1
All items	**111.3**	**115.7**	**121.3**

IRELAND

NATIONAL ACCOUNTS
(€ million at current prices)

National Income and Product

	2004	2005	2006
Gross domestic product in market prices	148,502	161,498	174,705
Net factor income from abroad	−23,215	−25,775	−25,575
Gross national product in market prices	125,286	135,723	149,130
Subsidies paid by the EU	1,788	2,239	1,778
Less Taxes paid to the EU	−324	−432	−421
Gross national income in market prices	126,750	137,529	150,487
Net current transfers from abroad (excl. EU subsidies and taxes)	−1,071	−1,542	−1,822
Gross national disposable income	125,679	135,988	148,665

Expenditure on the Gross Domestic Product

	2004	2005	2006
Government final consumption expenditure	20,896	22,870	24,939
Private final consumption expenditure	70,075	76,435	82,483
Increase in stocks	325	162	1,476
Gross fixed capital formation	35,108	42,079	46,027
Total domestic expenditure	126,404	141,546	154,925
Exports of goods and services	124,793	132,098	139,766
Less Imports of goods and services	−102,468	−112,279	−120,997
Statistical discrepancy	−226	132	1,011
GDP in market prices	148,502	161,498	174,705
GDP in constant 2005 prices	152,467	161,498	170,760

Gross Domestic Product by Economic Activity

	2004	2005	2006
Agriculture, forestry and fishing	3,569	4,097	3,918
Mining and quarrying; Manufacturing; Electricity, gas and water supply; Construction	48,198	50,465	53,043
Wholesale and retail trade, repair and hotels and restaurants; Transport, storage and communications	20,211	21,759	23,075
Public administration and defence	4,845	5,127	5,485
Other services	54,358	61,098	67,856
Statistical discrepancy	226	−132	−1,011
Gross value added at factor cost	131,409	142,413	152,367
Taxes (excl. taxes on products)	1,398	1,550	1,678
Less Subsidies (excl. subsidies on products)	−488	−1,476	−1,471
Gross value added in basic prices	132,319	142,486	152,574
Taxes on products	18,252	20,655	23,350
Less Subsidies on products	−2,068	−1,643	−1,220
GDP in market prices	148,502	161,498	174,705

BALANCE OF PAYMENTS
(US $ million)

	2004	2005	2006
Exports of goods f.o.b.	100,116	102,825	104,667
Imports of goods f.o.b.	−61,102	−67,730	−72,779
Trade balance	39,014	35,096	31,888
Exports of services	52,718	59,920	69,191
Imports of services	−65,384	−71,437	−78,528
Balance on goods and services	26,348	23,579	22,550
Other income received	43,457	53,862	75,321
Other income paid	−71,388	−84,876	−106,422
Balance on goods, services and income	−1,583	−7,434	−8,551
Current transfers received	6,626	6,963	6,648
Current transfers paid	−6,123	−6,679	−7,192
Current balance	−1,081	−7,150	−9,095
Capital account (net)	368	323	283
Direct investment abroad	−18,107	−14,491	−14,708
Direct investment from abroad	−10,994	−30,334	−882
Portfolio investment assets	−168,940	−151,139	−269,093
Portfolio investment liabilities	186,471	215,056	251,426
Financial derivatives assets	−1,903	−5,347	4,239
Financial derivatives liabilities	2,945	−2,694	−2,190
Other investment assets	−57,406	−133,298	−126,184
Other investment liabilities	71,236	119,746	168,124
Net errors and omissions	−4,023	7,552	−2,032
Overall balance	−1,435	−1,776	−112

Source: IMF, *International Financial Statistics*.

External Trade

PRINCIPAL COMMODITIES
(distribution by SITC, € million)

Imports c.i.f.	2004	2005	2006
Food and live animals	3,273.1	3,681.2	4,090.9
Mineral fuels, lubricants, etc.	2,813.5	4,020.3	4,698.6
Petroleum and petroleum products	2,255.1	3,315.2	3,830.2
Chemicals and related products	7,139.6	7,419.0	7,963.6
Organic chemicals	2,209.2	2,117.3	2,082.8
Medicinal and pharmaceutical products	1,969.6	1,995.2	2,234.6
Basic manufactures	4,619.8	4,947.2	5,565.1
Machinery and transport equipment	21,963.6	25,001.9	25,542.6
Office machines and automatic data-processing equipment	7,854.5	9,194.8	10,460.2
Telecommunications and sound equipment	1,677.6	2,026.3	2,128.0
Other electrical machinery, apparatus, etc.	4,721.2	4,353.1	3,810.6
Road vehicles and parts (excl. tyres, engines and electrical parts)	3,291.6	3,797.0	4,070.5
Miscellaneous manufactured articles	6,331.6	7,086.4	7,356.0
Total (incl. others)*	51,105.4	57,464.9	60,804.5

*Including transactions not classified by commodity.

IRELAND

Statistical Survey

Exports f.o.b.	2004	2005	2006
Food and live animals	6,063.0	6,379.8	7,030.0
Chemicals and related products	37,491.8	40,420.8	39,687.8
Organic chemicals	14,650.8	17,757.2	17,049.0
Medicinal and pharmaceutical products	15,154.8	14,531.1	14,249.0
Essential oils, perfume materials and toilet and cleansing preparations	4,761.9	5,216.5	5,327.9
Machinery and transport equipment	22,935.0	22,709.6	23,200.9
Office machines and automatic data-processing equipment	13,383.0	13,980.1	14,061.9
Telecommunications and sound equipment	1,495.9	1,459.5	1,382.0
Electrical machinery, apparatus, etc.	5,527.8	4,911.1	5,152.0
Miscellaneous manufactured articles	9,910.0	9,066.0	8,646.7
Professional, scientific and controlling apparatus	3,796.1	2,703.3	2,308.2
Total (incl. others)*	84,409.5	86,732.3	86,777.1

* Including transactions not classified by commodity.

PRINCIPAL TRADING PARTNERS
(€ million)*

Imports c.i.f.	2003	2004	2005
Belgium	751.2	945.4	1,055.8
Canada	452.4	270.8	284.0
China, People's Republic	2,215.5	2,776.7	3,710.9
Denmark	815.2	763.2	752.1
Finland	264.3	255.1	271.0
France	1,913.6	2,343.7	1,918.5
Germany	3,498.2	3,850.1	4,306.4
Italy	1,072.0	1,125.1	1,223.9
Japan	2,296.4	2,174.8	2,099.0
Netherlands	1,679.2	1,944.0	2,252.4
Spain	666.5	679.7	829.7
Sweden	435.1	521.2	511.4
Switzerland	487.5	537.3	543.4
United Kingdom	14,704.4	16,034.7	17,628.1
USA	7,416.4	6,984.5	7,985.0
Total (incl. others)	47,864.6	51,105.4	57,346.5

Exports f.o.b.	2003	2004	2005
Belgium	10,334.5	12,321.8	13,373.7
China, People's Republic	585.0	639.2	906.3
France	5,010.5	5,041.1	5,658.4
Germany	6,845.4	6,552.7	6,618.0
Italy	3,748.6	3,812.5	3,625.1
Japan	2,109.4	2,332.6	2,334.9
Netherlands	4,184.4	3,864.6	4,254.0
Spain	2,359.6	2,447.5	2,949.3
Sweden	1,163.3	988.2	1,070.0
Switzerland	2,603.3	2,761.4	3,205.7
United Kingdom	14,843.0	15,198.7	15,424.8
USA	16,939.2	16,555.6	16,545.4
Total (incl. others)	82,076.1	84,409.5	88,917.9

* Imports by country of origin; exports by country of final destination.

2006: *Imports* (€ million): United Kingdom (incl. Northern Ireland) 19,400.8; Other EU countries 17,164.2; USA and Canada 7,203.9; Total (incl. others) 60,804.5. *Exports* (€ million): United Kingdom (incl. Northern Ireland) 15,550.0; Other EU countries 39,340.5; USA and Canada 16,570.1; Total (incl. others) 86,777.1.

Sources: Central Statistics Office, and Department of Finance.

Transport

RAILWAYS
(traffic, '000)

	2004	2005	2006
Passengers carried	34,550	37,655	43,352
Freight tonnage	2,140	1,820	1,245

ROAD TRAFFIC
(licensed motor vehicles at 31 December)

	2001	2002	2003
Passenger cars	1,384,704	1,447,908	1,526,962
Lorries and vans	219,510	233,069	251,130
Buses and coaches	23,631	25,342	n.a.
Motorcycles and mopeds	32,913	33,147	35,094

SHIPPING
Merchant Fleet
(registered at 31 December)

	2004	2005	2006
Number of vessels	253	246	238
Total displacement (grt)	496,775	309,846	193,350

Source: Lloyd's Register-Fairplay, *World Fleet Statistics*.

Sea-borne Freight Traffic
('000 metric tons)*

	2004	2005	2006
Goods loaded	13,017	14,492	14,763
Goods unloaded	34,703	37,654	38,555

* Figures refer to vessels engaged in both international and coastal trade.

CIVIL AVIATION*

	2002	2003	2004
Passengers carried ('000)	19,313	20,439	21,788
Freight (incl. mail) carried (tons)	177,685	195,064	n.a.
Total aircraft movements	263,653	269,689	271,137
Scheduled	177,656	186,028	186,770
Non-scheduled	25,723	26,292	27,472
Cargo	13,447	12,730	11,308

* Figures refer to traffic at Dublin, Cork and Shannon airports.

Tourism

FOREIGN TOURIST ARRIVALS BY ORIGIN
('000)

	2003	2004	2005
United Kingdom*	4,139	4,095	4,210
France	321	297	310
Germany	302	298	402
Netherlands	146	151	157
Other continental Europe	715	836	1,034
USA	809	867	854
Canada	84	89	83
Other areas	248	320	284
Total	6,764	6,953	7,334

* Including residents of Northern Ireland.

Tourism receipts (US $ million, incl. passenger transport): 5,206 in 2003; 6,075 in 2004; 6,772 in 2005.

Source: World Tourism Organization.

Communications Media

	2004	2005	2006
Telephone lines ('000 in use)	2,015	2,033	2,097
Mobile cellular telephones ('000 subscribers)	3,860	4,270	4,690
Personal computers ('000 in use)	2,011	n.a.	n.a.
Internet users ('000)	1,198.0	1,400.0	1,437.0
Broadband subscribers ('000)	152.1	322.5	517.3

1997 (estimates): Radio receivers 2,550,000 in domestic use; Television receivers 1,470,000 in domestic use; Facsimile machines 100,000 (in use).

2004: Daily newspapers 7 (average circulation 742,000); Non-daily newspapers 63 (average circulation 2,117,000).

Source: UNESCO, *Statistical Yearbook*, and International Telecommunication Union.

Education

(2005/06, unless otherwise indicated)

	Institutions	Teachers (full-time)	Students (full-time)
National schools*	3,284	27,515	457,889
Secondary schools	398	11,553†	183,766
Vocational schools	247	5,994†	96,903
Community and comprehensive schools	90	3,487†	51,738
Teacher (primary and home economics) training colleges	5	127‡	1,158§
Technology colleges|	16	3,347‡	53,386
Universities and other Higher Education Authority Institutions	11	3,507‡	80,801
Other aided institutions[1]	2	71‡	2,492†

* National schools are state-aided primary schools. Includes Special National Schools (numbering 124 in 2005/06).
† 2004/05.
‡ 2000/01.
§ 2001/02.
\| Comprising 14 Institutes of Technology, Tipperary Institute, and the Hotel Training and Catering College, Killybegs, Co Donegal.
[1] Refers to the National College of Ireland and the Pontifical College, Maynooth, Co Kildare.

Sources: Central Statistics Office, and Department of Education and Science.

Directory

The Constitution

The Constitution took effect on 29 December 1937. Ireland became a republic on 18 April 1949. The following is a summary of the Constitution's main provisions:

TITLE OF THE STATE

The title of the State is Éire or, in the English language, Ireland.

NATIONAL STATUS

The Constitution declares that Ireland is a sovereign, independent, democratic State. It affirms the inalienable, indefeasible and sovereign right of the Irish nation to choose its own form of government, to determine its relations with other nations, and to develop its life, political, economic and cultural, in accordance with its own genius and traditions.

The Constitution applies to the whole of Ireland, but, pending the reintegration of the national territory, the laws enacted by the Parliament established by the Constitution have the same area and extent of application as those of the Irish Free State.

Note: Under the terms of the Good Friday Agreement, signed in April 1998 and approved by referendum in May, provision was made for a change to the Constitution to enshrine the principle that a united Ireland could be achieved only with the agreement and consent of the majority of the people of both Ireland and Northern Ireland. Accordingly, Articles 2 and 3 of the Constitution, which lay claim to the territory of Northern Ireland, were removed on 2 December 1999.

THE PRESIDENT

At the head of the State is the President, elected by direct suffrage, who holds office for a period of seven years. The President, on the advice of the Government or its head, summons and dissolves Parliament, signs and promulgates laws and appoints judges; on the nomination of the Dáil, the President appoints the Prime Minister (Taoiseach) and, on the nomination of the Prime Minister with the previous approval of the Dáil, the President appoints the other members of the Government. The supreme command of the Defence Forces is vested in the President, its exercise being regulated by law.

In addition, the President has the power to refer certain Bills to the Supreme Court for decision on the question of their constitutionality; and also, at the instance of a prescribed proportion of the members of both Houses of Parliament, to refer certain Bills to the people for decision at a referendum.

The President, in the exercise and performance of certain of his or her constitutional powers and functions, has the aid and advice of a Council of State.

PARLIAMENT

The Oireachtas, or National Parliament, consists of the President and two Houses, viz. a House of Representatives, called Dáil Éireann, and a Senate, called Seanad Éireann. The Dáil consists of 166 members, who are elected for a five-year term by adult suffrage on the system of proportional representation by means of the single transferable vote. Of the 60 members of the Senate, 11 are nominated by the Prime Minister, six are elected by the universities, and 43 are elected from five panels of candidates established on a vocational basis, representing: national language and culture, literature, art, education and such professional interests as may be defined by law for the purpose of this panel; agriculture and allied interests, and fisheries; labour, whether organized or unorganized; industry and commerce, including banking, finance, accountancy, engineering and architecture; and public administration and social services, including voluntary social activities.

A maximum period of 90 days is afforded to the Senate for the consideration or amendment of Bills sent to that House by the Dáil, but the Senate has no power to veto legislation.

EXECUTIVE

The Executive Power of the State is exercised by the Government, which is responsible to the Dáil and consists of not fewer than seven and not more than 15 members. The head of the Government is the Prime Minister.

FUNDAMENTAL RIGHTS

The State recognizes the family as the natural, primary and fundamental unit group of Society, possessing inalienable and imprescriptible rights antecedent and superior to all positive law. It acknowledges the right to life of the unborn and, with due regard to the equal right to life of the mother, guarantees in its laws to defend and vindicate that right. It acknowledges the right and duty of parents to provide for the education of their children, and, with due regard to that right, undertakes to provide free education. It pledges itself also to guard with special care the institution of marriage.

The Constitution contains special provision for the recognition and protection of the fundamental rights of citizens, such as personal liberty, free expression of opinion, peaceable assembly, and the formation of associations and unions.

IRELAND

Freedom of conscience and the free practice and profession of religion are, subject to public order and morality, guaranteed to every citizen. No religion may be endowed or subjected to discriminatory disability. Since December 1972, when a referendum was taken on the issue, the Roman Catholic Church has no longer enjoyed a special, privileged position.

SOCIAL POLICY

Certain principles of social policy intended for the general guidance of Parliament, but not cognizable by the courts, are set forth in the Constitution. Among their objects are the direction of the policy of the State towards securing the distribution of property so as to subserve the common good, the regulation of credit so as to serve the welfare of the people as a whole, the establishment of families in economic security on the land, and the right to an adequate means of livelihood for all citizens.

The State pledges itself to safeguard the interests, and to contribute where necessary to the support, of the infirm, the widow, the orphan and the aged, and shall endeavour to ensure that citizens shall not be forced by economic necessity to enter occupations unsuited to their sex, age or strength.

AMENDMENT OF THE CONSTITUTION

No amendment to the Constitution can be effected except by the decision of the people given at a referendum.

The Government

HEAD OF STATE

Uachtarán (President): Dr MARY MCALEESE (assumed office 11 November 1997; re-elected unopposed 1 October 2004, inaugurated for second term in office 11 November 2004).

THE CABINET
(May 2008)

A coalition of Fianna Fáil (FF), Green Party/Comhaontas Glas (GP) and the Progressive Democrats (PD).

Taoiseach (Prime Minister): BRIAN COWEN (FF).
Tánaiste (Deputy Prime Minister) and Minister for Enterprise, Trade and Employment: MARY COUGHLAN (FF).
Minister for Health and Children: MARY HARNEY (PD).
Minister for Transport: NOEL DEMPSEY (FF).
Minister for Finance: BRIAN LENIHAN (FF).
Minister for Foreign Affairs: MICHEÁL MARTIN (FF).
Minister for Arts, Sport and Tourism: MARTIN CULLEN (FF).
Minister for Social and Family Affairs: MARY HANAFIN (FF).
Minister for Community, Rural and Gaeltacht Affairs: ÉAMON Ó CUÍV (FF).
Minister for Agriculture, Fisheries and Food: BRENDAN SMITH (FF).
Minister for Education and Science: BATT O'KEEFE (FF).
Minister for Defence: WILLIE O'DEA (FF).
Minister for Justice, Equality and Law Reform: DERMOT AHERN (FF).
Minister for the Environment, Heritage and Local Government: JOHN GORMLEY (GP).
Minister for Communications, Energy and Natural Resources: EAMON RYAN (GP).

MINISTRIES

Office of the President: Áras an Uachtaráin, Phoenix Park, Dublin 8; tel. (1) 6171000; fax (1) 6171001; e-mail webmaster@president.ie; internet www.president.ie.

Department of the Taoiseach: Government Bldgs, Upper Merrion St, Dublin 2; tel. (1) 6194000; fax (1) 6194297; e-mail webmaster@taoiseach.gov.ie; internet www.taoiseach.gov.ie.

Department of Agriculture, Fisheries and Food: Agriculture House, Kildare St, Dublin 2; tel. (1) 6072000; fax (1) 6616263; e-mail info@agriculture.gov.ie; internet www.agriculture.gov.ie.

Department of Arts, Sport and Tourism: 23 Kildare St, Dublin 2; tel. (1) 6313800; fax (1) 6611201; e-mail seamusbrennan@dast.gov.ie; internet www.dast.gov.ie.

Department of Communications, Energy and Natural Resources: 29–31 Adelaide Road, Dublin 2; tel. (1) 6782000; fax (1) 6782441; e-mail minister.ryan@dcmnr.gov.ie; internet www.dcmnr.gov.ie.

Department of Community, Rural and Gaeltacht Affairs: Dún Aimhirgin, 43–49 Mespil Rd, Dublin 4; tel. (1) 6473000; fax (1) 6473051; e-mail aire@pobail.ie; internet www.pobail.ie.

Department of Defence: Parkgate, Infirmary Rd, Dublin 7; tel. (1) 8042000; fax (1) 8045000; e-mail info@defence.irlgov.ie; internet www.defence.ie.

Department of Education and Science: Marlborough St, Dublin 1; tel. (1) 8892162; fax (1) 8892367; e-mail minister_hanafin@education.gov.ie; internet www.education.ie.

Department of Enterprise, Trade and Employment: 23 Kildare St, Dublin 2; tel. (1) 6312121; fax (1) 6312827; e-mail minister_martin@entemp.ie; internet www.entemp.ie.

Department of the Environment, Heritage and Local Government: Custom House, Dublin 1; tel. (1) 8882000; fax (1) 8882888; e-mail minister@environ.ie; internet www.environ.ie.

Department of Finance: Government Bldgs, Upper Merrion St, Dublin 2; tel. (1) 6767571; fax (1) 6789936; e-mail minister@finance.gov.ie; internet www.finance.gov.ie.

Department of Foreign Affairs: 80 St Stephen's Green, Dublin 2; tel. (1) 4780822; fax (1) 4781484; e-mail minister@dfa.ie; internet www.dfa.ie.

Department of Health and Children: Hawkins House, Hawkins St, Dublin 2; tel. (1) 6354000; fax (1) 6354001; e-mail minister's_office@health.irlgov.ie; internet www.dohc.ie.

Department of Justice, Equality and Law Reform: 94 St Stephen's Green, Dublin 2; tel. (1) 6028202; fax (1) 6615461; e-mail info@justice.ie; internet www.justice.ie.

Department of Social and Family Affairs: Áras Mhic Dhiarmada, Store St, Dublin 1; tel. (1) 7043000; fax (1) 7043870; e-mail minister@welfare.ie; internet www.welfare.ie.

Department of Transport: 44 Kildare St, Dublin 2; tel. (1) 6707444; fax (1) 6041185; e-mail minister@transport.ie; internet www.transport.ie.

Legislature

OIREACHTAS (NATIONAL PARLIAMENT)

Parliament comprises two Houses: Dáil Éireann (House of Representatives), with 166 members (Teachtaí Dála), elected for a five-year term by universal adult suffrage; and Seanad Éireann (Senate), with 60 members serving a five-year term, of whom 11 are nominated by the Taoiseach (Prime Minister) and 49 elected (six by the universities and 43 from specially constituted panels).

Dáil Éireann

Leinster House, Dublin 2; tel. (1) 6183000; fax (1) 6184118; e-mail kieran.coughlan@Oireachtas.ie; internet www.oireachtas.ie.

Ceann Comhairle (Chairman): JOHN O'DONOGHUE (Fianna Fáil).
Leas-Cheann Comhairle (Deputy Chairman): BRENDAN HOWLIN (Labour).

General Election, 24 May 2007

Party	Votes*	% of votes*	Seats
Fianna Fáil	858,565	41.56	78†
Fine Gael	564,428	27.32	51
Labour Party	209,175	10.13	20
Green Party	96,936	4.69	6
Sinn Féin	143,410	6.94	4
Progressive Democrats	56,396	2.73	2
Others	136,900	6.63	5
Total	2,065,810	100.00	166

*The election was conducted by means of the single transferable vote. Figures refer to first-preference votes.
† Including the Ceann Comhairle (Chairman).

Seanad Éireann

Leinster House, Dublin 2; tel. (1) 6183000; fax (1) 6184118; e-mail kieran.coughlan@Oireachtas.ie; internet www.oireachtas.ie.

Cathaoirleach (Chairman): PAT MOYLAN (Fianna Fáil).
Leas-Chathaoirleach (Deputy Chairman): PADDY BURKE (Fine Gael).

Elections were held to the Seanad Éireann in July 2007, with the closing date for the receipt of votes from the members of five vocational panels (Administrative, Agricultural, Cultural and Educational, Industrial and Commercial, and Labour) being 23 July, and

IRELAND

that for the two university panels (National University of Ireland, and University of Dublin) being 24 July. Following the nomination of 11 members by the Taoiseach (Prime Minister) on 3 August, the strength of the parties was as follows:

Party	Elected	Appointed	Total seats
Fianna Fáil	22	6	28
Fine Gael	14	—	14
Labour Party	6	—	6
Progressive Democrats	—	2	2
Green Party	—	2	2
Sinn Féin	1	—	1
Independents	6	1	7
Total	49	11	60

Political Organizations

Christian Solidarity Party (An Comhar Críostaí): 14 North Frederick St, Dublin 1; tel. (1) 8783529; e-mail comharcriostai@eircom.net; conservative; Chair. CATHAL LOFTUS; Nat. Sec. MICHAEL F. MAGUIRE.

Communist Party of Ireland (Páirtí Cumannach na hÉireann): James Connolly House, 43 East Essex St, Dublin 2; tel. and fax (1) 6711943; e-mail cpoi@eircom.net; internet www.communistpartyofireland.ie; f. 1933; advocates a united, socialist, independent Ireland; Chair. LYNDA WALKER; Gen. Sec. EUGENE MCCARTAN.

Fianna Fáil (The Republican Party) (Soldiers of Destiny): 65–66 Lower Mount St, Dublin 2; tel. (1) 6761551; fax (1) 6785690; e-mail info@fiannafail.ie; internet www.fiannafail.ie; f. 1926; centrist; Pres. and Leader BRIAN COWEN; Gen. Sec. SEÁN DORGAN.

Fine Gael (United Ireland Party) (Family of the Irish): 51 Upper Mount St, Dublin 2; tel. (1) 6198444; fax (1) 6625046; e-mail finegael@finegael.com; internet www.finegael.ie; f. 1933; centrist; Pres. and Leader ENDA KENNY; Gen. Sec. TOM CURRAN.

Green Party (Comhaontas Glas): 16–17 Suffolk St, Dublin 2; tel. (1) 6790012; fax (1) 6797168; e-mail info@greenparty.ie; internet www.greenparty.ie; f. 1981 as the Ecology Party of Ireland; name changed as above in 1983; advocates a humane, ecological society, freedom of information and political decentralization; Leader JOHN GORMLEY; Chair. DAN BOYLE; Gen. Sec. COLM O CAOMHÁNAIGH.

The Labour Party: 17 Ely Place, Dublin 2; tel. (1) 6784700; fax (1) 6612640; e-mail head_office@labour.ie; internet www.labour.ie; f. 1912; merged with Democratic Left (f. 1992) in 1999; democratic socialist party; affiliated to the Party of European Socialists; Leader EAMON GILMORE; Pres. MICHAEL D. HIGGINS; Gen. Sec. MIKE ALLEN.

Progressive Democrats (An Páirtí Daonlathach): 25 South Frederick St, Dublin 2; tel. (1) 6794399; fax (1) 6794757; e-mail gensec@progressivedemocrats.ie; internet www.progressivedemocrats.ie; f. 1985 by fmr mems of Fianna Fáil; affiliated to the Liberal parties of Europe; Pres. (vacant); Leader MARY HARNEY; Gen. Sec. (vacant).

Sinn Féin (We Ourselves): 44 Parnell Sq., Dublin 1; tel. (1) 8726100; fax (1) 8733441; e-mail sfadmin@eircom.net; internet www.sinnfein.ie; f. 1905; advocates the termination of British rule in Northern Ireland; seeks a mandate to establish a democratic socialist republic in a reunified Ireland; Pres. GERRY ADAMS; Chair. MARY LOU MCDONALD; Gen. Sec. RITA O'HARE.

The Workers' Party: 23 Hill St, Dublin 1; tel. (1) 8740716; fax (1) 8748707; e-mail wpi@indigo.ie; internet www.workerspartyireland.net; f. 1905; fmrly Sinn Féin The Workers' Party; name changed as above in 1982; aims to establish a unitary socialist state on the island of Ireland; Pres. SEÁN GARLAND; Gen. Sec. JOHN LOWRY.

Diplomatic Representation

EMBASSIES IN IRELAND

Argentina: 15 Ailesbury Dr., Dublin 4; tel. (1) 2691546; fax (1) 2600404; e-mail embassyofargentina@eircom.net; Chargé d'affaires a.i. ANA C. PISANO.

Australia: Fitzwilton House, 7th Floor, Wilton Terrace, Dublin 2; tel. (1) 6645300; fax (1) 6785185; e-mail austremb.dublin@dfat.gov.au; internet www.ireland.embassy.gov.au; Ambassador ANNE PLUNKETT.

Austria: 15 Ailesbury Court, 93 Ailesbury Rd, Dublin 4; tel. (1) 2694577; fax (1) 2830860; e-mail dublin-ob@bmeia.gv.at; Ambassador Dr WALTER HAGG.

Belgium: 2 Shrewsbury Rd, Dublin 4; tel. (1) 2057100; fax (1) 2057106; e-mail dublin@diplobel.org; internet www.diplomatie.be/dublin; Ambassador LEOPOLD CARREWYN.

Brazil: HSBC House, 5th Floor, 41–54 Harcourt St, Dublin 2; tel. (1) 4756000; fax (1) 4751341; e-mail brasembdublin@brazil-ie.org; internet www.brazil.ie; Ambassador STÉLIO MARCOS AMARANTE.

Bulgaria: 22 Burlington Rd, Dublin 4; tel. (1) 6603293; fax (1) 6603915; e-mail bulgarianembassydublin@eircom.net; internet www.mfa.bg/dublin; Ambassador EMIL SAVOV YALNAZOV.

Canada: 7–8 Wilton Terrace, 3rd Floor, Dublin 2; tel. (1) 2344000; fax (1) 2344001; e-mail dubln@international.gc.ca; internet www.canada.ie; Ambassador PATRICK G. BINNS.

Chile: 44 Wellington Rd, Dublin 4; tel. (1) 6675094; fax (1) 6675156; e-mail echile@eircom.net; internet www.embachile-irlanda.ie; Ambassador ALBERTO YOACHAM SOFFIA.

China, People's Republic: 40 Ailesbury Rd, Dublin 4; tel. (1) 2691707; fax (1) 2839938; e-mail chinaemb_ie@mfa.gov.cn; internet ie.china-embassy.org; Ambassador LIU BIWEI.

Croatia: Adelaide Chambers, Peter St, Dublin 8; tel. (1) 4767181; fax (1) 4767183; e-mail croatianembassy@eircom.net; internet ie.mfa.hr; Ambassador VESELKO GRUBIŠIĆ.

Cuba: 2 Adelaide Court, Adelaide Rd, Dublin 2; tel. (1) 4752999; fax (1) 4763674; e-mail carillo@eircom.net; Ambassador PEDRO NOEL CARRILLO ALFONSO.

Cyprus: 71 Lower Leeson St, Dublin 2; tel. (1) 6763060; fax (1) 6763099; e-mail dublinembassy@mfa.gov.cy; internet www.mfa.gov.cy/embassydublin; Ambassador SOTOS A. LIASSIDES.

Czech Republic: 57 Northumberland Rd, Dublin 4; tel. (1) 6681135; fax (1) 6681660; e-mail dublin@embassy.mzv.cz; internet www.mfa.cz/dublin; Ambassador JOSEF HAVLAS.

Denmark: 7th Floor, Block E, Iveagh Court, Harcourt Rd, Dublin 2; tel. (1) 4756404; fax (1) 4784536; e-mail dubamb@um.dk; internet www.ambdublin.um.dk; Ambassador HENRIK RÉE IVERSEN.

Egypt: 12 Clyde Rd, Dublin 4; tel. (1) 6606566; fax (1) 6683745; e-mail info@embegyptireland.ie; internet www.embegyptireland.ie; Ambassador AMR MOSTAFA HELMY.

Estonia: Riversdale House, St Ann's, Ailesbury Rd, Dublin 4; tel. (1) 2196730; fax (1) 2196731; e-mail embassy.dublin@mfa.ee; internet www.estemb.ie; Ambassador ANDRE PUNG.

Ethiopia: 1–3 Merrion House, Fitzwilliam St Lower, Dublin 2; tel. (1) 6787062; fax (1) 6787065; e-mail info@ethiopianembassy.ie; Ambassador ATO ZERIHUN RETTA.

Finland: Russell House, Stokes Place, St Stephen's Green, Dublin 2; tel. (1) 4781344; fax (1) 4783727; e-mail sanomat.dub@formin.fi; internet www.finland.ie; Ambassador SEPPO KAUPPILA.

France: 36 Ailesbury Rd, Dublin 4; tel. (1) 2775000; fax (1) 2775001; e-mail chancellerie@ambafrance.ie; internet www.ambafrance-ie.org; Ambassador YVON ROÉ D'ALBERT.

Germany: 31 Trimleston Ave, Booterstown, Blackrock, Co Dublin; tel. (1) 2693011; fax (1) 2693946; e-mail info@dublin.diplo.de; internet www.dublin.diplo.de; Ambassador CHRISTIAN PAULS.

Greece: 1 Upper Pembroke St, Dublin 2; tel. (1) 6767254; fax (1) 6618892; e-mail embgr@eircom.net; Ambassador GEORGIOS-ALEXANDROS VALLINDAS.

Holy See: 183 Navan Rd, Dublin 7; tel. (1) 8380577; fax (1) 8380276; e-mail nuncioirl@eircom.net; Apostolic Nuncio Most Rev. GIUSEPPE LEANZA (Titular Archbishop of Lilybaeum).

Hungary: 2 Fitzwilliam Place, Dublin 2; tel. (1) 6612902; fax (1) 6612880; e-mail mission.dub@kum.hu; internet www.mfa.gov.hu/kulkepviselet/ie; Ambassador FERENC JÁRI.

India: 6 Leeson Park, Dublin 6; tel. (1) 4966792; fax (1) 4978074; e-mail indembassy@eircom.net; internet indianembassy.ie; Ambassador P. S. RAGHAVAN.

Iran: 72 Mount Merrion Ave, Blackrock, Co Dublin; tel. (1) 2880252; fax (1) 2834246; e-mail iranemb@indigo.ie; Ambassador EBRAHIM RAHIMPOUR.

Israel: Carrisbrook House, 122 Pembroke Rd, Dublin 4; tel. (1) 2309400; fax (1) 2309446; e-mail info@dublin.mfa.gov.il; internet dublin.mfa.gov.il; Ambassador ZION EVRONY.

Italy: 63–65 Northumberland Rd, Dublin 4; tel. (1) 6601744; fax (1) 6682759; e-mail ambasciata.dublino@esteri.it; internet www.ambdublino.esteri.it; Ambassador Dr LUCIO ALBERTO SAVOIA.

Japan: Nutley Bldg, Merrion Centre, Nutley Lane, Dublin 4; tel. (1) 2028300; fax (1) 2838726; e-mail protocol@embip.ie; internet www.ie.emb-japan.go.jp; Ambassador TOSHINAO URABE.

Kenya: Dublin; Ambassador CATHERIN MUIGAI MWANGI.

Korea, Republic: Clyde House, 15 Clyde Rd, POB 2101, Dublin 4; tel. (1) 6608800; fax (1) 6608716; e-mail irekoremb@mofat.go.kr; Ambassador TAE-YONG CHO.

IRELAND

Latvia: 92 St Stephen's Green, Dublin 2; tel. (1) 4283320; fax (1) 4283311; e-mail embassy.ireland@mfa.gov.lv; internet www.am.gov.lv/en/ireland; Ambassador INDULIS ĀBELIS.

Lesotho: 2 Clanwilliam Sq., Grand Canal Quay, Dublin 2; tel. (1) 6762233; fax (1) 6762258; e-mail lesothodublin@eircom.net; Ambassador MANNETE MALETHOLE RAMAILI.

Lithuania: 90 Merrion Rd, Dublin 4; tel. (1) 6688292; fax (1) 6680004; e-mail amb.ie@urm.lt; internet ie.mfa.lt; Ambassador IZOLDA BRIČKOVSKIENĖ.

Malaysia: Level 3A–5A Shelbourne House, Shelbourne Rd, Dublin 4; tel. (1) 6677280; fax (1) 6677283; e-mail mwdublin@mwdublin.ie; Ambassador Dato' SIDDIQ FIRDAUSE HAJI MOHD ALI.

Malta: 17 Earlsfort Terrace, Dublin 2; tel. (1) 6762340; fax (1) 6766066; e-mail maltaembassy.dublin@gov.mt; Chargé d'affaires RUTH FARRUGIA.

Mexico: 19 Raglan Rd, Dublin 4; tel. (1) 6673105; fax (1) 6641013; e-mail info@embamex.ie; internet www.sre.gob.mx/irlanda; Ambassador CECILIA JABER BRECEDA.

Morocco: 39 Raglan Rd, Dublin 4; tel. (1) 6609449; fax (1) 6609468; e-mail sifamdub@indigo.ie; Chargé d'affaires MINA TOUNSI.

Netherlands: 160 Merrion Rd, Dublin 4; tel. (1) 2693444; fax (1) 2839690; e-mail info@netherlandsembassy.ie; internet www.netherlandsembassy.ie; Ambassador (vacant).

Nigeria: 56 Leeson Park, Dublin 6; tel. (1) 6604366; fax (1) 6604092; e-mail enquiries@nigerianembassy.ie; internet www.nigerianembassy.ie; Chargé d'affaires ONOCHIE B. AMOBI.

Norway: 34 Molesworth St, Dublin 2; tel. (1) 6621800; fax (1) 6621890; e-mail emb.dublin@mfa.no; internet www.norway.ie; Ambassador TRULS HANEVOLD.

Pakistan: Ailesbury Villa, 1B Ailesbury Rd, Dublin 4; tel. (1) 2613032; fax (1) 2613007; e-mail parepdbn@yahoo.com; internet www.pakembassydublin.com; Ambassador NAGHMANA A. HASHMI.

Poland: 5 Ailesbury Rd, Ballsbridge, Dublin 4; tel. (1) 2830855; fax (1) 2698309; e-mail info@dublin.polemb.net; internet www.dublin.polemb.net; Ambassador TADEUSZ SZUMOWSKI.

Portugal: 15 Leeson Park, Foxrock, Dublin 6; tel. (1) 4127040; fax (1) 4970299; e-mail embport@dublin.dgaccp.pt; Ambassador PAULO GUILHERME PIRES DE LIMA DE CASTILHO.

Romania: 26 Waterloo Rd, Dublin 4; tel. (1) 6681085; fax (1) 6681761; e-mail ambrom@eircom.net; internet dublin.mae.ro; Ambassador SILVIA STANCU DAVIDOIU.

Russia: 184–186 Orwell Rd, Dublin 14; tel. (1) 4922048; fax (1) 4923525; e-mail russiane@indigo.ie; internet www.ireland.mid.ru; Ambassador MIKHAIL YE. TIMOSHKIN.

Slovakia: 20 Clyde Rd, Ballsbridge, Dublin 4; tel. (1) 6600012; fax (1) 6600014; e-mail slovak@iol.ie; Ambassador JÁN GÁBOR.

Slovenia: Morrison Chambers, 2nd Floor, 32 Nassau St, Dublin 2; tel. (1) 6705240; fax (1) 6705243; e-mail vdb@gov.si; internet dublin.veleposlanistvo.si; Ambassador FRANC MIKŠA.

South Africa: Alexandra House, 2nd Floor, Earlsfort Centre, Earlsfort Terrace, Dublin 2; tel. (1) 6615553; fax (1) 6615590; e-mail information@saedublin.com; Ambassador DEVIKARANI PRISCILLA SEWPAL JANA.

Spain: 17A Merlyn Park, Dublin 4; tel. (1) 2691640; fax (1) 2691854; e-mail emb.dublin.inf@maec.es; Ambassador DON JOSÉ DE CARVAJAL SALIDO.

Sweden: Iveagh Court, Block E, 3rd Floor, Harcourt Rd, Dublin 2; tel. (1) 4744400; fax (1) 4744450; e-mail ambassaden.dublin@foreign.ministry.se; internet www.swedenabroad.com/dublin; Ambassador CLAES LJUNGDAHL.

Switzerland: 6 Ailesbury Rd, Dublin 4; tel. (1) 2186382; fax (1) 2830344; e-mail dubvertretung@eda.admin.ch; internet www.eda.admin.ch/dublin; Ambassador JOSEF DOSWALD.

Turkey: 11 Clyde Rd, Dublin 4; tel. (1) 6685240; fax (1) 6685014; e-mail turkembassy@eircom.net; Ambassador TURAN MORALI.

Ukraine: 16 Elgin Rd, Dublin 4; tel. (1) 6685189; fax (1) 6697917; e-mail ukrembassy@eircom.net; internet www.mfa.gov.ua/ireland; Ambassador BORYS M. BAZYLEVSKIY.

United Kingdom: 29 Merrion Rd, Ballsbridge, Dublin 4; tel. (1) 2053700; fax (1) 2053885; e-mail chancery.dublx@fco.gov.uk; internet www.britishembassy.ie; Ambassador DAVID NORMAN REDDAWAY.

USA: 42 Elgin Rd, Ballsbridge, Dublin 4; tel. (1) 6688777; fax (1) 6689946; e-mail webmasterireland@state.gov; internet dublin.usembassy.gov; Ambassador THOMAS C. FOLEY.

Judicial System

Justice is administered in public by judges appointed by the President on the advice of the Government. The judges of all courts are completely independent in the exercise of their judicial functions. The jurisdiction and organization of the courts are dealt with in the Courts (Establishment and Constitution) Act, 1961, and the Courts (Supplemental Provisions) Acts, 1961 to 1981.

Attorney-General: PAUL GALLAGHER.

SUPREME COURT

An Chúirt Uachtarach
(The Supreme Court)

Four Courts, Dublin 7; tel. (1) 8886569; fax (1) 8732332; e-mail supremecourt@courts.ie; internet www.courts.ie.

Consisting of the Chief Justice and seven other judges, has appellate jurisdiction from all decisions of the High Court. The President of Ireland may, after consultation with the Council of State, refer a bill that has been passed by both Houses of the Oireachtas (other than a money bill or certain others), to the Supreme Court to establish whether it or any other provisions thereof are repugnant to the Constitution. The President of the High Court is ex officio a member of the Supreme Court.

Chief Justice: JOHN L. MURRAY.

Judges: SUSAN DENHAM, ADRIAN HARDIMAN, HUGH GEOGHEGAN, NIAL FENNELLY, NICHOLAS KEARNS, FIDELMA MACKEN, JOSEPH FINNEGAN.

COURT OF CRIMINAL APPEAL

The Court of Criminal Appeal, consisting of the Chief Justice or an ordinary judge of the Supreme Court and two judges of the High Court, deals with appeals by persons convicted on indictment, where leave to appeal has been granted. The Court has jurisdiction to review a conviction or sentence on the basis of an alleged miscarriage of justice. The Director of Public Prosecutions may appeal against an unduly lenient sentence. The decision of the Court of Criminal Appeal is final unless the Court or Attorney-General or the Director of Public Prosecutions certifies that a point of law involved should, in the public interest, be taken to the Supreme Court.

HIGH COURT

An Ard-Chúirt
(The High Court)

Four Courts, Dublin 7; tel. (1) 8886505; fax (1) 8725669; e-mail highcourtcentraloffice@courts.ie; internet www.courts.ie.

Consists of the President of the High Court and 35 ordinary judges, has full original jurisdiction in, and power to determine, all matters and questions whether of law or fact, civil or criminal. The High Court on circuit acts as an appeal court from the Circuit Court. The Central Criminal Court sits as directed by the President of the High Court to try criminal cases outside the jurisdiction of the Circuit Court. The duty of acting as the Central Criminal Court is assigned to a judge, or judges, of the High Court. The Chief Justice and the President of the Circuit Court are ex officio additional Judges of the High Court.

President: RICHARD JOHNSON.

Judges: VIVIAN LAVAN, PAUL J. P. CARNEY, DECLAN BUDD, MARY LAFFOY, MICHAEL MORIARTY, PETER KELLY, THOMAS C. SMYTH, KEVIN C. O'HIGGINS, JOHN QUIRKE, IARFHLAITH O'NEILL, RODERICK MURPHY, DANIEL HERBERT, PAUL BUTLER, LIAM MCKECHNIE, HENRY ABBOTT, EAMON DE VALERA, MARY FINLAY GEOGHEGAN, MICHAEL PEART, BARRY WHITE, PAUL GILLIGAN, SEAN RYAN, ELIZABETH DUNNE, MICHAEL HANNA, JOHN MACMENAMIN, FRANK CLARKE, KEVIN HAUGH, KEVIN FEENEY, BRIAN MCGOVERN, PETER CHARLETON, MAUREEN CLARK, JOHN HEDIGAN, BRYAN MACMAHON, GEORGE BIRMINGHAM, MARY C. IRVINE, JOHN A. EDWARDS, PATRICK J. MCCARTHY, GARRETT SHEEHAN.

Master of the High Court: EDMUND HONOHAN.

CIRCUIT AND DISTRICT COURTS

The civil jurisdiction of the Circuit Court is limited to €38,092.14 in contract and tort and in actions founded on hire-purchase and credit-sale agreements and to a rateable value of €252.95 in equity, and in probate and administration, but where the parties consent the jurisdiction is unlimited. In criminal matters the Court has jurisdiction in all cases except murder, rape, treason, piracy and allied offences. One circuit court judge is permanently assigned to each of the circuits outside Dublin with the exception of Cork, which has three judges. Dublin has 10 permanent judges. In addition there are eight permanently unassigned judges. The President of the District Court is ex officio an additional Judge of the Circuit Court. The Circuit Court acts as an appeal court from the District Court, which has a summary jurisdiction in a large number of criminal cases where the offence is not of a serious nature. In civil matters the District Court has jurisdiction in contract and tort (except slander, libel, seduction, slander of title, malicious prosecution and false imprisonment) where the claim does not exceed €6,348.69 and in actions founded on hire-purchase and credit-sale agreements.

All criminal cases, except those dealt with summarily by a judge in the District Court, are tried by a judge and a jury of 12 members. Juries are also used in some civil cases in the High Court. In a criminal case 10 members of the jury may, in certain circumstances, agree on a verdict, and in a civil case the agreement of nine members is sufficient.

President of An Chúirt Chuarda (the Circuit Court): MATTHEW DEERY.

President of the District Court (An Chúirt Dúiche): MIRIAM MALONE.

Religion

CHRISTIANITY

The organization of the churches takes no account of the partition of Ireland into two separate political entities; both the Republic of Ireland and Northern Ireland are subject to a unified ecclesiastical jurisdiction. The Roman Catholic Primate of All Ireland and the Church of Ireland (Protestant Episcopalian) Primate of All Ireland have their seats in Northern Ireland, at Armagh, and the headquarters of the Presbyterian Church in Ireland is at Belfast, Northern Ireland.

Adherents of the Roman Catholic Church were enumerated at 3,681,446 in the 2006 census, representing some 87% of the population. In 2006 there were some 23,546 adherents of the Presbyterian Church and 12,160 of the Methodist Church. In 2006 there were some 125,585 adherents of the Church of Ireland.

Irish Council of Churches: Inter-Church Centre, 48 Elmwood Ave, Belfast, BT9 6AZ, Northern Ireland; tel. (28) 9066-3145; fax (28) 9066-4160; e-mail irish.churches@btconnect.com; internet www.irishchurches.org; f. 1922; present name adopted 1966; 15 mem. churches; Pres. GILLIAN KINGSTON; Gen. Sec. MICHAEL EARLE.

The Roman Catholic Church

Ireland (including Northern Ireland) comprises four archdioceses and 22 dioceses.

Irish Episcopal Conference: Ara Coeli, Cathedral Rd, Armagh, BT61 7QY, Northern Ireland; tel. (28) 3752-2045; fax (28) 3752-6182; e-mail admin@aracoeli.com; f. 1999; Pres. Cardinal SEÁN B. BRADY (Archbishop of Armagh).

Archbishop of Armagh and Primate of All Ireland: Cardinal SEÁN B. BRADY, Ara Coeli, Cathedral Rd, Armagh, BT61 7QY, Northern Ireland; tel. (28) 3752-2045; fax (28) 3752-6182; e-mail admin@aracoeli.com; internet www.armagharchdiocese.org.

Archbishop of Cashel and Emly: Most Rev. DERMOT CLIFFORD, Archbishop's House, Thurles, Co Tipperary; tel. (504) 21512; fax (504) 22680; e-mail office@cashel-emly.ie; internet www.cashel-emly.ie.

Archbishop of Dublin and Primate of Ireland: Most Rev. Dr DIARMUID MARTIN, Archbishop's House, Drumcondra, Dublin 9; tel. (1) 8373732; fax (1) 8369796; e-mail communications@dublindiocese.ie; internet www.dublindiocese.ie.

Archbishop of Tuam: Most Rev. MICHAEL NEARY, Archbishop's House, St Jarlath's, Tuam, Co Galway; tel. (93) 24166; fax (93) 28070; e-mail archdiocesetuam@eircom.net; internet www.tuamarchdiocese.org.

Numerous Roman Catholic religious orders are strongly established in the country. These play an important role, particularly in the spheres of education, health and social welfare.

Church of Ireland
(The Anglican Communion)

Ireland (including Northern Ireland) comprises two archdioceses and 10 dioceses.

The Representative Body of the Church of Ireland

Church of Ireland House, Church Ave, Rathmines, Dublin 6; tel. (1) 4978422; fax (1) 4978821; e-mail office@rcbdub.org; internet rcb.ireland.anglican.org; Chief Officer and Sec. DENIS REARDON.

Archbishop of Armagh and Primate of All Ireland and Metropolitan: Most Rev. ALAN HARPER, The See House, Cathedral Close, Armagh, BT61 7EE, Northern Ireland; tel. (28) 37527144; fax (28) 37527823; e-mail archbishop@armagh.anglican.org; internet www.ireland.anglican.org.

Archbishop of Dublin and Bishop of Glendalough, Primate of Ireland and Metropolitan: Most Rev. Dr JOHN R. W. NEILL, The See House, 17 Temple Rd, Milltown, Dublin 6; tel. (1) 4977849; fax (1) 4976355; e-mail archbishop@dublin.anglican.org; internet www.dublin.anglican.org.

Orthodox Churches

Greek Orthodox Church in Ireland: Sacred Church of the Annunciation, 46 Arbour Hill, Dublin 7; tel. and fax (1) 6779020; Pres. Very Rev. Dr IRENEU IOAN CRACIUN.

Russian Orthodox Church (Moscow Patriarchate) in Ireland: Harold's Cross Rd, Dublin 6; tel. (1) 4969038; fax (1) 4640976; e-mail rvgeorge@utvinternet.com; internet www.stpeterstpaul.net; f. 2001; Parish Priest Very Rev. Fr MICHAEL GOGOLEFF.

Other Christian Churches

Association of Baptist Churches in Ireland: The Baptist Centre, 19 Hillsborough Rd, Moira, BT67 0HG, Northern Ireland; tel. (28) 9261-9267; e-mail abc@thebaptistcentre.org; internet www.baptistireland.org; Pres. D. BAXTER.

Lutheran Church in Ireland: Lutherhaus, 24 Adelaide Rd, Dublin 2; tel. and fax (1) 6766548; e-mail info@lutheranireland.org; Pres. Pastors Dr JOACHIM DIESTELKAMP, CORINNA DIESTELKAMP.

Methodist Church in Ireland: 71B Brighton Rd, Rathgar, Dublin 6; tel. (1) 4907855; e-mail president@irishmethodist.org; internet www.irishmethodist.org; Pres. Rev. ROBERT COOPER.

Presbyterian Church in Ireland: Church House, Fisherwick Place, Belfast, BT1 6DW, Northern Ireland; tel. (28) 9032-2284; fax (28) 9041-7301; e-mail info@presbyterianireland.org; internet www.presbyterianireland.org; Moderator of Gen. Assembly Rev. Dr JOHN FINLAY; Clerk of Assembly and Gen. Sec. Rev. Dr DONALD WATTS.

The Religious Society of Friends (Quakers) in Ireland: Quaker House, Stocking Lane, Rathfarnham, Dublin 16; tel. (1) 4956888; fax (1) 4956889; e-mail office@quakers-in-ireland.ie; internet www.quakers-in-ireland.org; 19 meetings in Rep. of Ireland and 13 in Northern Ireland; Registrar ROSEMARY CASTAGNER.

ISLAM

The Muslim population of the Republic of Ireland stood at 32,539 at the 2006 census.

Irish Council of Imams: 19 Roebuck Rd, Clonskeagh, Dublin 14; tel. (1) 2195454; e-mail aliselim_2000@yahoo.com; f. 2006; comprises 14 imams from across Ireland; Chair. Imam Sheikh HUSSEIN HALAWA; Gen. Sec. ALI SELIM.

Islamic Cultural Centre of Ireland: 19 Roebuck Rd, Clonskeagh, Dublin 14; tel. (1) 2080000; fax (1) 2080001; e-mail info@islamireland.ie; internet www.islamireland.ie; f. 1996; CEO Dr NOOH AL-KADDO; Imam Sheikh HUSSEIN HALAWA.

Islamic Foundation of Ireland: 163 South Circular Rd, Dublin 8; tel. (1) 4533242; fax (1) 4532785; e-mail info@islamireland.com; internet www.islaminireland.com; f. 1959; religious, cultural, educational and social org.; Imam YAHYA MUHAMMAD AL-HUSSEIN.

Supreme Muslim Council of Ireland: Dublin; e-mail irishmuslimcouncil@gmail.com; internet www.irishmuslims.org; f. 2003; seeks to co-operate with educational institutions and state bodies; Chair. Sheikh Dr SHAHEED SATARDIEN.

JUDAISM

At the 2006 census, the Jewish community numbered 1,930. In 2004 there were a total of four synagogues operating, of which three were Orthodox and one was progressive.

Chief Rabbi: Dr YAAKOV PEARLMAN, Herzog House, Zion Rd, Rathgar, Dublin 6; tel. (1) 4923751; fax (1) 4924680; e-mail irishcom@iol.ie; internet www.jewishireland.org.

The Press

A significant feature of the Irish press is the number of weekly and twice-weekly newspapers published in provincial centres.

DAILIES
(Average net circulation figures, including Ireland and the United Kingdom, as at December 2007, unless otherwise stated)

Cork

Evening Echo: City Quarter, Lapps Quay, Cork; tel. (21) 4272722; fax (21) 4275112; e-mail maurice.gubbins@eecho.ie; internet www.eecho.ie; f. 1892; Chief Exec. DAN LINEHAN; Editor MAURICE GUBBINS; circ. 25,904.

Irish Examiner: City Quarter, Lapps Quay, Cork; tel. (21) 4272722; fax (21) 4273846; e-mail editor@examiner.ie; internet www.irishexaminer.com; f. 1841; Editor TIM VAUGHAN; circ. 55,948.

IRELAND

Dublin

Evening Herald: Independent House, 27–32 Talbot St, Dublin 1; tel. (1) 7055416; fax (1) 7055497; e-mail herald.news@independent.ie; internet www.independent.ie; f. 1891; Editor STEPHEN RAE; circ. 82,084.

Irish Daily Mail: 3rd Floor, Embassy House, Herbert Park Lane, Dublin 4; tel. (1) 6375800; fax (1) 6375880; internet www.dailymail.co.uk; Propr Associated Newspapers (United Kingdom); Editor-in-Chief TED VERITY; circ. 56,449 (Ireland only, July 2007).

Irish Daily Star: Star House, 62A Terenure Rd North, Dublin 6; tel. (1) 4901228; fax (1) 4902193; e-mail info@thestar.ie; internet www.thestar.ie; Editor GERARD COLLERAN; circ. 98,006 (Ireland only).

Irish Independent: 27–32 Talbot St, Dublin 1; tel. (1) 7055333; fax (1) 8720304; internet www.independent.ie; f. 1905; Editor GERRY O'REGAN; circ. 160,854.

The Irish Times: Irish Times Bldg, 24–28 Tara St, Dublin 2; tel. (1) 6758000; fax (1) 6758035; e-mail editor@irish-times.ie; internet www.ireland.com; f. 1859; Editor GERALDINE KENNEDY; circ. 119,051.

OTHER NEWSPAPERS

(Average net circulation figures, including Ireland and the United Kingdom, as at December 2006, unless otherwise stated)

An Phoblacht/Republican News: 58 Parnell Sq., Dublin 1; tel. (1) 8733611; fax (1) 8733074; e-mail editor@anphoblacht.com; internet www.anphoblacht.com; f. 1970; Editor SÉAN BRADY; circ. 15,000 (2007).

Anglo-Celt: Station House, Drumnavanagh, Cavan; tel. (49) 4331100; fax (49) 4332280; e-mail tom@anglocelt.net; internet www.anglocelt.ie; f. 1846; Fri.; Editor JOHNNY O'HANLON; circ. 14,713.

Argus: Partnership Court, Park St, Dundalk, Co Louth; tel. (42) 9334632; fax (42) 9331643; e-mail editorial@argus.ie; internet www.argus.ie; f. 1835; Thurs.; Editor KEVIN MULLIGAN; circ. 11,507.

Clare Champion: Barrack St, Ennis, Co Clare; tel. (65) 6828105; fax (65) 6820374; e-mail editor@clarechampion.ie; internet www.clarechampion.ie; f. 1903; Thurs.; Editor AUSTIN HOBBS; circ. 19,539.

Connacht Tribune: 15 Market St, Galway; tel. (91) 536222; fax (91) 567970; e-mail news@ctribune.ie; internet www.ctribune.ie; f. 1909; Fri.; Editor JOHN CUNNINGHAM; circ. 24,598.

Connaught Telegraph: Cavendish Lane, Castlebar, Co Mayo; tel. (94) 9021711; fax (94) 9024007; e-mail info@con-telegraph.ie; internet www.con-telegraph.ie; f. 1828; Wed.; Editor TOM GILLESPIE; circ. 18,500 (2007).

Donegal Democrat: Pier 1, Quay St, Donegal, Co Donegal; tel. (7497) 40160; fax (7497) 40161; e-mail editorial@donegaldemocrat.com; internet www.donegaldemocrat.com; f. 1919; Tues. and Thurs.; Editor MICHAEL DALY; circ. 9,580 (Tues.); 13,060 (Thurs.).

Drogheda Independent: 9 Shop St, Drogheda, Co Louth; tel. (41) 9876800; fax (41) 9834271; e-mail editorial@drogheda-independent.ie; internet www.drogheda-independent.ie; f. 1884; Thurs.; Group Editor MARIE KIERANS; circ. 10,328.

Dundalk Democrat: 7 Crowe St, Dundalk, Co Louth; tel. (42) 9334058; fax (42) 9331399; e-mail editor@dundalkdemocrat.ie; internet www.dundalkdemocrat.ie; f. 1849; Sat.; Editor DOLAN O'HAGAN; circ. 16,000 (2007).

Dungarvan Observer: Shandon, Dungarvan, Co Waterford; tel. (58) 41205; fax (58) 41559; e-mail news@dungarvanobserver.com; f. 1912; Editor JAMES A. LYNCH.

The Echo: Mill Park Rd, Enniscorthy, Co Wexford; tel. (54) 33231; fax (54) 33506; e-mail production@theecho.ie; internet www.theecho.ie; f. 1902; Wed.; edns for Enniscorthy, Gorey, New Ross and Wexford; Editor TOM MOONEY.

Iris Oifigiúil (Official Irish Gazette): 51 St Stephen's Green, Dublin 2; tel. (1) 6476867; fax (1) 6476843; e-mail irisoifigiuil@opw.ie; internet www.irisoifigiuil.ie; f. 1922; twice weekly (Tues. and Fri.); Editor MICK DUNNE.

Irish Mail on Sunday: 3rd Floor, Embassy House, Herbert Park Lane, Dublin 4; tel. (1) 6375800; fax (1) 4179830; Propr Associated Newspapers (United Kingdom); fmrly Ireland on Sunday; name changed as above in 2006; Editor-in-Chief TED VERITY; circ. 101,870 (July 2007).

The Kerryman: Clash, Tralee, Co Kerry; tel. (66) 7145500; fax (66) 7145572; e-mail dmalone@kerryman.ie; internet www.kerryman.ie; f. 1904; Thurs.; Editor DECLAN MALONE; circ. 26,392.

Kilkenny People: 34 High St, Kilkenny; tel. (56) 7721015; fax (56) 7721414; e-mail editor@kilkennypeople.ie; internet www.kilkennypeople.ie; f. 1892; weekly; Editor THOMAS MOLLOY; circ. 16,113.

Leinster Express: Dublin Rd, Portlaoise, Co Laois; tel. (57) 8621666; fax (57) 8620491; e-mail editor@leinsterexpress.ie; internet www.laoistoday.ie; f. 1831; weekly; Editor BRIAN KEYES; circ. 15,318 (incl. Offaly Express).

Leinster Leader: 19 South Main St, Naas, Co Kildare; tel. (45) 897302; fax (45) 897647; e-mail editor@leinsterleader.ie; internet www.leinsterleader.ie; f. 1880; Wed.; Editor MICHAEL SHEERAN; circ. 12,100.

Limerick Chronicle: 54 O'Connell St, Limerick; tel. (61) 315233; fax (61) 314804; f. 1766; Tues.; Editor BRENDAN HALLIGAN.

Limerick Leader: 54 O'Connell St, Limerick; tel. (61) 214500; fax (61) 314804; e-mail admin@limerick-leader.ie; internet www.limerick-leader.ie; f. 1889; 4 a week; Editor BRENDAN HALLIGAN; circ. 21,619 (weekend edn).

Limerick Post: Town Hall Centre, Rutland St, Limerick; tel. (61) 413322; fax (61) 417684; e-mail news@limerickpost.ie; internet www.limerickpost.ie; f. 1986; distributed free of charge; Thurs.; Editor BILLY RYAN; circ. 48,124.

Mayo News: The Fairgreen, Westport, Co Mayo; tel. (98) 25311; fax (98) 26108; e-mail info@mayonews.ie; internet www.mayonews.ie; f. 1892; Wed.; Editor DENISE HORAN; circ. 10,569.

Meath Chronicle and Cavan and Westmeath Herald: 12 Market Sq., Navan, Co Meath; tel. (46) 9079600; fax (46) 9023565; e-mail ken@meathchronicle.ie; internet www.meathchronicle.ie; f. 1897; Sat.; Editor KEN DAVIS; circ. 16,010.

Midland Tribune: Emmet St, Birr, Co Offaly; tel. (509) 20003; fax (509) 20588; e-mail midtrib@iol.ie; f. 1881; Wed.; Editor JOHN O'CALLAGHAN; circ. 10,105.

The Munster Express: 37 The Quay, Waterford; tel. (51) 872141; e-mail newscopy@munster-express.ie; internet www.munster-express.ie; f. 1859; Wed. and Fri.; Editor JOHN O'CONNOR; circ. 10,849.

The Nationalist: Hill Crest, Hanover, Carlow; tel. (59) 9170100; fax (59) 9130301; e-mail news@carlow-nationalist.ie; internet www.carlow-nationalist.ie; f. 1883; owned by Thomas Crosbie Holdings; Editor EDDIE COFFEY.

The Northern Standard: The Diamond, Monaghan; tel. (47) 81867; fax (47) 72257; e-mail garysmyth@eircom.net; f. 1839; Fri.; Editor MARTIN SMYTH.

Offaly Express: Bridge St, Tullamore, Co Offaly; tel. (57) 9321744; fax (57) 9351930; e-mail lexpress@indigo.ie; internet www.offalyexpress.ie; weekly; Editor JOHN WHELAN; circ. 15,318 (incl. Leinster Express).

Sligo Champion: Finisklin Rd., Sligo; tel. (71) 9169222; fax (71) 9169040; e-mail editor@sligochampion.ie; internet www.sligochampion.ie; f. 1836; Wed.; Editor SEAMUS FINN; circ. 12,574 (2007).

The Southern Star: Ilen St, Skibbereen, Co Cork; tel. (28) 21200; fax (28) 21071; e-mail info@southernstar.ie; internet www.southernstar.ie; f. 1889; Sat.; Editor LIAM O'REGAN.

Sunday Business Post: 80 Harcourt St, Dublin 2; tel. (1) 6026000; fax (1) 6796498; e-mail sbpost@iol.ie; internet www.sbpost.ie; Editor CLIFF TAYLOR; circ. 53,581.

Sunday Independent: Independent House, 90 Middle Abbey St, Dublin 1; tel. (1) 7055333; fax (1) 7055779; e-mail sunday.letters@unison.independent.ie; internet www.independent.ie; f. 1905; Editor AENGUS FANNING; circ. 282,459.

Sunday Tribune: 15 Lower Baggot St, Dublin 2; tel. (1) 6314300; fax (1) 6615302; e-mail newsdesk@tribune.ie; internet www.tribune.ie; f. 1980; Editor NOIRIN HEGARTY; circ. 70,058.

Sunday World: Independent House, 27–32 Talbot St, Dublin 1; tel. (1) 8849000; fax (1) 8849002; e-mail news@sundayworld.com; internet www.sundayworld.com; f. 1973; Editor COLM MACGINTY; circ. 283,801.

Tipperary Star: Friar St, Thurles, Co Tipperary; tel. (504) 21122; e-mail info@tipperarystar.ie; internet www.tipperarystar.ie; f. 1909; Wed.; Editor MICHAEL DUNDON; circ. 9,223.

Tuam Herald: Dublin Rd, Tuam, Co Galway; tel. (93) 24183; fax (93) 24478; e-mail editor@tuamherald.ie; internet www.tuamherald.ie; f. 1837; Wed.; Editor DAVID BURKE; circ. 9,580.

Tullamore Tribune: Church St, Tullamore, Co Offaly; tel. (506) 21152; e-mail editor@tullamoretribune.ie; internet www.tullamoretribune.ie; f. 1978; Wed.; Editor GER SCULLY.

Waterford News & Star: 25 Michael St, Waterford; tel. (51) 874951; fax (51) 855281; e-mail editor@waterford-news.ie; internet www.waterford-news.ie; f. 1848; Thurs.; Editor P. DOYLE.

Western People: Kevin Barry St, Ballina, Co Mayo; tel. (96) 60999; fax (96) 70208; e-mail info@westernpeople.ie; internet www.westernpeople.ie; f. 1883; Tues.; Editor JAMES LAFFEY; circ. 19,289.

Westmeath Examiner: Blackhall Pl., Mullingar, Co Westmeath; tel. (44) 9346764; fax (44) 9330765; e-mail editor@westmeathexaminer.ie; internet www.westmeathexaminer.ie; f. 1882; weekly; Editor EILÍS RYAN; circ. 9,273.

IRELAND

Wicklow People: Channing House, Upper Row St, Co Wexford; tel. (53) 9140100; fax (53) 9140192; e-mail front.office@peoplenews.ie; internet www.wicklowpeople.ie; weekly; circ. 13,122.

SELECTED PERIODICALS

Auto Ireland: 2 Clanwilliam Court, Lower Mount St, Dublin 2; tel. (1) 2405300; fax (1) 6671598; e-mail automags@harmonia.ie; internet www.harmonia.ie; Editor BRIAN FOLEY; circ. 40,361 (Dec. 2006).

Banking Ireland: 1 North Wall Quay, Dublin 1; tel. (1) 6116500; fax (1) 6116565; e-mail info@bankers.ie; internet www.instbankers.com/bi/index.html; f. 1898; quarterly; journal of the Inst. of Bankers in Ireland; Editor GERRY LAWLOR; circ. 15,500 (Dec. 2006).

Books Ireland: 11 Newgrove Ave, Dublin 4; tel. (1) 2692185; e-mail booksi@eircom.net; f. 1976; 9 a year; reviews Irish-interest books; Editor JEREMY ADDIS; circ. 2,350 (Dec. 2006).

Business & Finance: 1–4 Swift's Alley, Francis St, Dublin 8; tel. (1) 4167800; fax (1) 4167899; e-mail info@businessandfinance.ie; internet www.businessandfinance.ie; f. 1964; weekly; Editor Dr CONSTANTIN GURDGIEV; circ. 13,060.

Food & Wine: 2 Clanwilliam Court, Lower Mount St, Dublin 2; tel. (1) 2405300; fax (1) 6671598; e-mail aboase@harmonia.ie; internet www.harmonia.ie; f. 1997; published by Harmonia Ltd; Editor ERNIE WHALLEY; circ. 8,672.

History Ireland: POB 69, Bray, Co Wicklow; tel. (1) 2765221; fax (1) 2765207; e-mail info@historyireland.com; internet www.historyireland.com; quarterly; Editor TOMMY GRAHAM.

Hot Press: 13 Trinity St, Dublin 2; tel. (1) 2411500; fax (1) 2411538; e-mail info@hotpress.com; internet www.hotpress.com; fortnightly; music, leisure, current affairs; Editor NIALL STOKES; circ. 19,215.

Ireland Afloat: 2 Lower Glenageary Rd, Dún Laoghaire, Co Dublin; tel. (1) 2846161; fax (1) 2846162; e-mail info@afloat.ie; monthly; sailing and boating; Man. Editor DAVID O'BRIEN.

Ireland's Own: Channing House, Rowe St, Wexford; tel. (53) 40140; fax (53) 40192; e-mail irelands.own@peoplenews.ie; f. 1902; weekly; family interest; Editors PHILIP MURPHY, SEAN NOLAN; circ. 40,305.

The Irish Catholic: Irish Farm Centre, Bluebell, Dublin 12; tel. (1) 8555619; fax (1) 8364805; e-mail news@irishcatholic.ie; internet www.irishcatholic.ie; published by The Agricultural Trust; weekly; Editor GARY O'SULLIVAN; circ. 32,000 (2006).

Irish Computer: Media House, South County Business Park, Leopardstown, Dublin 18; tel. (1) 2947772; fax (1) 2947799; e-mail cliff.hutton@mediateam.ie; internet www.techcentral.ie; f. 1977; monthly; Editor CLIFF HUTTON; circ. 9,000 (+1,500 to Irish Computer Society members).

Irish Farmers' Journal: Irish Farm Centre, Bluebell, Dublin 12; tel. (1) 4199530; fax (1) 4520876; e-mail editdept@farmersjournal.ie; internet www.farmersjournal.ie; f. 1948; weekly; Editor MATTHEW DEMPSEY; circ. 68,486.

The Irish Field: Irish Farm Centre, Bluebell, Dublin 12; tel. (1) 4051100; fax (1) 4554008; e-mail info@irishfield.ie; internet www.irishfield.ie; f. 1870; published by the Agricultural Trust; weekly; horse racing, breeding and equine leisure; Man. Editor LEO POWELL; circ. 15,923.

Irish Historical Studies: c/o Dept of Modern History, Trinity College, Dublin 2; tel. (1) 6081020; e-mail wvaughan@tcd.ie; 2 a year; Editors Dr DAVID HAYTON, Dr JOHN MCCAFFERTY.

Irish Journal of Medical Science: Royal Academy of Medicine in Ireland, Frederick House, 19 South Frederick St, Dublin 2; tel. (1) 6334820; fax (1) 6334918; e-mail journal@rami.ie; internet www.ijms.ie; f. 1832; quarterly; organ of the Royal Academy of Medicine; Editor DAVID BOUCHIER-HAYES.

Irish Law Times: Round Hall Sweet & Maxwell, 43 Fitzwilliam Pl., Dublin 2; tel. (1) 6625301; fax (1) 6625302; e-mail terri.mcdonnell@roundhall.ie; f. 1983; 20 a year; Editor DAVID BOYLE.

Irish Medical Journal: 10 Fitzwilliam Pl., Dublin 2; tel. (1) 6767273; fax (1) 6612758; e-mail imj@imj.ie; internet www.imj.ie; 10 a year; journal of the Irish Medical Org; Editor Dr JOHN MURPHY.

The Irish Skipper: Taney Hall, Eglinton Terrace, Dublin 14; tel. (1) 2960000; fax (1) 2960383; e-mail skippereditor@iol.ie; internet www.irishskipper.net; f. 1964; monthly; journal of the commercial fishing and aquaculture industries; Editor CORMAC BURKE.

Irish Tatler: 2 Clanwilliam Court, Lower Mount St, Dublin 2; tel. (1) 2405300; fax (1) 6619757; internet www.harmonia.ie/ratecard/it/index.html; f. 1890; monthly; Editor ELAINE PRENDEVILLE; circ. 26,427.

Irish University Review: Rm J211, School of English Drama and Film, University College Dublin, Belfield, Dublin 4; tel. (1) 7168159; fax (1) 7161174; e-mail anne.fogarty@ucd.ie; internet www.irishuniversityreview.ie; f. 1970; 2 a year; literature, history, fine arts, politics, cultural studies; Editor Prof. ANNE FOGARTY.

Magill: 1–4 Swift's Alley, Francis St, Dublin 8; tel. (1) 4167800; e-mail editor@magill.ie; internet www.magill.ie; published by The Business and Finance Group; monthly; politics and current affairs; Editor EAMON DELANEY; circ. 14,985 (Dec. 2006).

Motoring Life: 48 North Great George's St, Dublin 1; tel. (1) 8780444; fax (1) 8787740; e-mail info@motoringlife.ie; internet www.motoringlife.ie; f. 1946; bi-monthly; Editor GERALDINE HERBERT.

PC Live!: Prospect House, 3 Prospect Rd, Glasnevin, Dublin 9; tel. (1) 8824444; fax (1) 8300888; e-mail info@scope.ie; internet www.techcentral.ie; f. 1994; monthly; computers and the internet; Editor STEPHEN CAWLEY.

The Phoenix: 44 Lower Baggot St, Dublin 2; tel. (1) 6611062; fax (1) 6624532; e-mail editor@phoenix-magazine.com; internet www.phoenix-magazine.com; f. 1983; every two weeks; news and comment, satirical; Editor PADDY PRENDIVILLE; circ. 18,268.

Poetry Ireland Review (Éigse Éireann): 2 Proud's Lane, Dublin 2; tel. (1) 4789974; fax (1) 4780205; e-mail poetry@iol.ie; Editor EILÉAN NÍ CHUILLEANÁIN.

Prudence: 99 South Circular Rd, Dublin 8; tel. (1) 4167990; fax (1) 4167901; e-mail editor@prudence.ie; internet www.prudence.ie; f. 2005; monthly; lifestyle magazine for women; Editor ALANNA GALLAGHER; circ. 9,539.

RTÉ Guide: Radio Telefís Éireann, Donnybrook, Dublin 4; tel. (1) 2082666; fax (1) 2082092; internet www.rteguide.ie; weekly; programmes of the Irish broadcasting service; Editor RAY WALSH; circ. 113,033 (2006).

Studies: An Irish Quarterly Review: 35 Lower Leeson St, Dublin 2; tel. (1) 6766785; fax (1) 6762984; e-mail studies@jesuit.ie; internet www.studiesirishreview.com; f. 1912; published by the Jesuits In Ireland; quarterly review of letters, history, religious and social questions; Editor Fr FERGUS O'DONOGHUE.

U Magazine: 2 Clanwilliam Court, Lower Mount St, Dublin 2; tel. (1) 2405300; fax (1) 6619757; internet www.harmonia.ie/ratecard/u/index.html; f. 1979; every two weeks; for women aged 18–27; Editor JENNIFER STEVENS; circ. 34,103.

Village Magazine: 44 Westland Row, Dublin 2; tel. (1) 6425050; fax (1) 6425001; e-mail news@villagemagazine.ie; internet www.villagemagazine.ie; f. 2004; monthly; current affairs; Editor VINCENT BROWNE.

Woman's Way: 2 Clanwilliam Court, Lower Mount St, Dublin 2; tel. (1) 6623158; fax (1) 6628719; e-mail ltaylor@smurfit-comms.ie; internet www.harmonia.ie/ratecard/ww/index.html; f. 1963; weekly; Editor SIMONE KENNY; circ. 26,576.

The Word: Divine Word Missionaries, Maynooth, Co Kildare; tel. (1) 5054467; fax (1) 6289184; e-mail wordeditor@eircom.net; internet www.theword.ie; f. 1953; monthly; Roman Catholic general interest; Editor-in-Chief VINCENT TWOMEY.

NEWS AGENCY

Ireland International News Agency: 51 Wellington Quay, Dublin 2; tel. (1) 6712442; fax (1) 6796586; e-mail iina@eircom.net; Man. Dir DIARMAID MACDERMOTT.

PRESS ORGANIZATIONS

National Newspapers of Ireland: Clyde Lodge, 15 Clyde Rd, Dublin 4; tel. (1) 6689099; fax (1) 6689872; e-mail nni@cullencommunications.ie; internet www.nni.ie; f. 1985; 19 mems; Chair. MAEVE DONOVAN; Co-ordinating Dir FRANK CULLEN.

Regional Newspapers Association and Printers of Ireland: Sheridan House, 33 Parkgate St, Dublin 8; tel. (1) 6779112; fax (1) 6779144; e-mail neville@rnan.ie; f. 1917; 50 mems; Pres. FRANK MULRENNAN; CEO NEVILLE GALLOWAY.

Publishers

Anvil Books: 45 Palmerston Rd, Dublin 6; tel. (1) 4973628; e-mail dardisanvil@eircom.net; f. 1964; Irish history and biography, folklore; Dirs R. DARDIS, M. DARDIS.

Attic Press: Crawford Business Park, Crosses Green, Cork; tel. (21) 4321725; fax (21) 4315329; e-mail corkunip@ucc.ie; internet www.corkuniversitypress.com; imprint of Cork University Press; Dir Prof. DES CLARKE.

BookConsult: 68 Mountjoy Sq, Dublin 1; tel. (1) 8740354; e-mail cprojectsltd@eircom.net; internet www.bookconsult.com; f. 2001; publishing and author consultancy; Consultant and Publisher SEAMUS CASHMAN.

Boole Press: 19 Silchester Rd, Glenageary, Co Dublin; e-mail info@boolepress.com; internet www.boolepress.com; f. 1979; scientific, technical, medical, scholarly; Man. Dir Dr J. MILLER.

IRELAND

Comhairle Bhéaloideas Éireann (Folklore of Ireland Council): c/o Dept of Irish Folklore, University College, Belfield, Dublin 4; tel. (1) 7168216; e-mail cumann@ucd.ie; Editor Prof. SÉAMAS Ó CATHÁIN.

Cork University Press: Youngline Industrial Estate, Pouladuff Road, Togher, Cork; tel. (21) 4902980; fax (21) 4315329; e-mail corkuniversitypress@ucc.ie; internet www.corkuniversitypress .com; f. 1925; owned by University College Cork; academic, art, architecture, music; imprints include Attic Press and Atrium; Publications Dir MIKE COLLINS.

Dominican Publications: 42 Parnell Sq., Dublin 1; tel. (1) 8731355; fax (1) 8731760; e-mail sales@dominicanpublications .com; internet www.dominicanpublications.com; f. 1897; religious affairs in Ireland and the developing world, pastoral-liturgical aids; Man. Rev. BERNARD TREACY.

Dundalgan Press: The Industrial Estate, Coe's Road, Dundalk, Co Louth; tel. (42) 9334013; fax (42) 9332351; e-mail info@dundalgan.ie; f. 1859; history and biography; Man. Dir GERARD GORMLEY.

CJ Fallon: Ground Floor, Block B, Liffey Valley Office Campus, Dublin 22; tel. (1) 6166400; fax (1) 6166499; e-mail editorial@cjfallon .ie; internet www.cjfallon.ie; f. 1927; educational; Man. Dir H. J. MCNICHOLAS.

Four Courts Press: 7 Malpas St, Dublin 8; tel. (1) 4534668; fax (1) 4534672; e-mail info@fourcourtspress.ie; internet www .fourcourtspress.ie; f. 1970; philosophy, theology, Celtic and Medieval studies, art, literature, modern history; Dirs MICHAEL ADAMS, MARTIN HEALY, GERARD O'FLAHERTY.

Gallery Press: Loughcrew, Oldcastle, Co Meath; tel. and fax (49) 8541779; e-mail contactus@gallerypress.com; internet www .gallerypress.com; f. 1970; poetry, plays, prose by Irish authors; Editor PETER FALLON.

Gill and Macmillan: Hume Ave, Park West, Dublin 12; tel. (1) 5009500; fax (1) 5009597; e-mail sales@gillmacmillan.ie; internet www.gillmacmillan.ie; f. 1968; literature, biography, history, social sciences, current affairs and textbooks; Man. Dir M. D. O'DWYER.

Goldsmith Press: Newbridge, Co Kildare; tel. (45) 433613; fax (45) 434648; f. 1972; poetry, Irish art, plays, foreign language, general; Dirs DESMOND EGAN, VIVIENNE ABBOTT.

Irish Academic Press: 44 Northumberland Rd, Dublin 4; tel. (1) 6688244; fax (1) 6686769; e-mail info@iap.ie; internet www.iap.ie; f. 1974; academic, mainly history and Irish studies; Dir STEWART CASS; Man. Editor RACHEL MILOTTE.

LexisNexis Butterworths Ireland: 24–26 Upper Ormond Quay, Dublin 7; tel. (1) 8731555; fax (1) 8745036; e-mail customer.services@ lexisnexis.ie; internet www.lexisnexis.ie; subsidiary of Reed Elsevier United Kingdom; taxation and law; Chair. H. MUMFORD.

Liberties Press: Guinness Enterprise Centre, Taylor's Lane, Dublin 8; tel. (1) 4151224; e-mail info@libertiespress.com; internet www.libertiespress.com; f. 2003; sport, health, food, music, history, religion and politics; Editorial Dir SEAN O'KEEFFE.

Lilliput Press: 62/63 Sitric Rd, Arbour Hill, Dublin 7; tel. (1) 6711647; fax (1) 6711233; e-mail info@lilliputpress.ie; internet www.lilliputpress.ie; f. 1985; ecology and environment, literary criticism, biography, memoirs, fiction, Irish history, general; Publr ANTONY FARRELL.

Mentor Books: 43 Furze Rd, Sandyford Industrial Estate, Dublin 18; tel. (1) 2952112; fax (1) 2952114; e-mail all@mentorbooks.ie; internet www.mentorbooks.ie; adult and children's fiction and non-fiction, educational; Man. Dir DANIEL MCCARTHY.

Mercier Press Ltd: Douglas Village, Cork; tel. (21) 4899858; fax (21) 4899887; e-mail info@mercierpress.ie; internet www .mercierpress.ie; f. 1944; folklore, history, biography, current affairs, fiction, politics, humour, religious; Man. Dir CLODAGH FEEHAN.

O'Brien Press Ltd: 12 Terenure Rd East, Rathgar, Dublin 6; tel. (1) 4923333; fax (1) 4922777; e-mail books@obrien.ie; internet www .obrien.ie; f. 1974; biography, history, sport, Celtic, politics, travel, crime, children's; Man. Dir IVAN O'BRIEN; Publr MICHAEL O'BRIEN.

Poolbeg Press: 123 Baldoyle Industrial Estate, Dublin 13; tel. (1) 8321477; fax (1) 8321430; e-mail info@poolbeg.com; internet www .poolbeg.com; f. 1976; general, poetry, politics, children's; Man. Dir PHILIP MACDERMOTT.

Royal Irish Academy (Acadamh Ríoga na hÉireann): 19 Dawson St, Dublin 2; tel. (1) 6762570; fax (1) 6762346; e-mail admin@ria.ie; internet www.ria.ie; f. 1785; humanities and sciences; Pres. NICHOLAS P. CANNY; Exec. Sec. PATRICK BUCKLEY.

Sáirséal–Ó Marcaigh: 13 Bóthar Chríoch Mhór, Dublin 11; tel. and fax (1) 8378914; e-mail tearman@gofree.indigo.ie; f. 1981; publishers of books in Irish, particularly fiction, poetry, history and autobiography; Dirs AINGEAL Ó MARCAIGH, CAOIMHÍN Ó MARCAIGH.

Thomson Round Hall: 43 Fitzwilliam Pl., Dublin 2; tel. (1) 6625301; fax (1) 6625302; e-mail brendan.reid@thomson.com; internet www.roundhall.thomson.com; f. 1980 as The Round Hall Press; law books and journals; subsidiary of Sweet & Maxwell (United Kingdom); Publr CATHERINE DOLAN.

Veritas Publications: 7–8 Lower Abbey St, Dublin 1; tel. (1) 8788177; fax (1) 8786507; e-mail publications@veritas.ie; internet www.veritas.ie; f. 1969; Roman Catholic, religious and educational, mariology, homiletics; Dir MAURA HYLAND.

GOVERNMENT PUBLISHING HOUSE

Oifig an tSoláthair/Stationery Office: Government Publications, 51 St Stephen's Green, Dublin 2; tel. (1) 6476849; fax (1) 6476843.

PUBLISHERS' ASSOCIATION

CLÉ—Irish Book Publishers' Association/Cumann Leabharfhoilsitheoirí Éireann: 25 Denzille Lane, Dublin 2; tel. (1) 6394868; e-mail info@publishingireland.com; internet www .publishingireland.com; f. 1970; 80 mem. publishers; Pres. SEÁN Ó CEARNAIGH.

Broadcasting and Communications

TELECOMMUNICATIONS

Commission for Communications Regulation (ComReg): Block DEF, Abbey Court, Irish Life Centre, Lower Abbey St, Dublin 1; tel. (1) 8049600; fax (1) 8049680; e-mail info@comreg.ie; internet www.comreg.ie; f. 2002; regulatory authority for Ireland's postal and telecommunications sectors; issues licences to service providers; manages the interconnection of telecommunications networks; approves equipment and oversees national telephone numbering; Chair. JOHN DOHERTY.

Cable and Wireless: 1 Airton Rd, Tallaght, Dublin 24; tel. (1) 4040333; fax (1) 4040339; e-mail enquiries.ireland@cw.com; internet www.cw.com/ie; independent telecommunications services provider; Man. Dir NOREEN O'HARE.

eircom: 114 St Stephen's Green West, Dublin 2; tel. (1) 6714444; fax (1) 6716916; e-mail press-office@eircom.ie; internet www.eircom.ie; f. 1984; fmrly Telecom Éireann; responsible for the provision of national and international telecommunications services, including mobile services; partially privatized in 1999, acquired by Valentia Telecommunications Ltd in September 2001, purchased by BCM Ireland Holdings Ltd in August 2006; Exec. Chair. PIERRE DANON; CEO REX COMB.

Hutchison 3G Ireland Limited (3 Ireland): Kildress House, Pembroke Row, Lower Baggot St, Dublin 2; tel. (1) 4773412; internet www.3ireland.ie; f. 2002; wholly owned by Hong Kong-based Hutchison Whampoa; Man. Dir ROBERT FINNEGAN.

Meteor: 4030 Kingswood Ave, Citywest Business Park, Naas Rd, Dublin 24; tel. (1) 4307000; fax (1) 4307013; e-mail info@meteor.ie; internet www.meteor.ie; f. 2001; wholly owned by eircom; 900,000 subscribers (Sept. 2007); CEO ROBERT HAULBROOK.

O$_2$ Communications (Ireland): 28–29 Sir John Rogerson's Quay, Dublin 2; tel. (1) 6095000; e-mail customercare@o2.ie; internet www .o2.ie; f. 1997; wholly owned subsidiary of Telefónica (Spain); present name adopted 2002; CEO DANUTA GRAY.

Vodafone Ireland: Mountainview, Leopardstown, Dublin 18; tel. (1) 2037777; fax (1) 2037778; e-mail custcare@vodafone.ie; internet www.vodafone.ie; subsidiary of Vodafone Group PLC (United Kingdom); Chair. BRIAN PATTERSON; Chief Exec. CHARLES BUTTERWORTH.

BROADCASTING

The Radio and Television Act of 1988 provided for the establishment of an independent television station, an independent national radio service and a series of local radio stations (see below).

Broadcasting Commission of Ireland (BCI): 2–5 Warrington Pl., Dublin 2; tel. (1) 6441200; fax (1) 6441299; e-mail info@bci.ie; internet www.bci.ie; f. 1988 as the Independent Radio and Television Commission; ; renamed as above in 2001 following the introduction of the 2001 Broadcasting Act; established by the Govt to ensure the creation, licensing, development and monitoring of independent broadcasting in Ireland; also responsible for the licensing of new digital, cable, multi-mode digital and satellite television services, as well as the development of codes of programming and advertising standards for television and radio services and the provision of a secretariat to the Broadcasting Complaints Commission; operations are financed by levies paid by franchised stations; Chair. CONOR J. MAGUIRE; CEO MICHAEL O'KEEFFE.

Broadcasting Complaints Commission: 2–5 Warrington Pl., Dublin 2; tel. (1) 6761097; fax (1) 6760948; e-mail info@bcc.ie; internet www.bcc.ie; f. 1977; responsible for acting upon complaints relating to material broadcast by RTE and independent broadcasting stations; Chair. MICHAEL MACGRATH; Dir ANNE O'BRIEN.

IRELAND	*Directory*

Radio

Radio Telefís Éireann (RTÉ): Donnybrook, Dublin 4; tel. (1) 2083111; fax (1) 2083080; e-mail info@rte.ie; internet www.rte.ie; national public-service broadcasting corpn; f. 1960; financed by net licence revenue and sale of advertising time; governed by Authority of nine mems; operates four radio networks, RTÉ Radio 1 (news, music, drama and variety shows), RTÉ 2FM (popular music), RTÉ Lyric FM (music, arts and culture) and RTÉ Raidió na Gaeltachta (see below); Chair. of Authority MARY FINAN; Dir-Gen. CATHAL GOAN; Man. Dir of Radio ADRIAN MOYNES; Man. Dir of Television NOEL CURRAN; Man. Dir of News ED MULHALL; Dir of Communications BRIDE ROSNEY.

   RTÉ Raidió na Gaeltachta: Casla, Connemara, Co Galway; tel. (91) 506677; fax (91) 506666; e-mail rnag@rte.ie; internet www.rte.ie/rnag; f. 1972; broadcasts in Irish language; financed by RTÉ; Controller TOMAS MAC CON IOMAIRE.

100-102 Today FM: Today FM House, 124 Upper Abbey St, Dublin 1; tel. (1) 8049000; fax (1) 8049099; e-mail 100-102@todayfm.com; internet www.todayfm.com; f. 1998; national, independent station; acquired by Communicorp Group in July 2007; Chair. JOHN MCCOLGAN; CEO WILLIE O'REILLY.

Dublin's 98 FM: South Block, The Malt House, Grand Canal Quay, Dublin 2; tel. (1) 4398800; fax (1) 6708969; e-mail info@98fm.ie; internet www.98fm.ie; provides news service to independent local radio stations under contract from the BCI; Propr Communicorp Group; CEO CIARAN DAVIS; Head of News TEENA GATES.

NewsTalk 106–108 FM: 3rd Floor, Warrington House, Mount St Crescent, Dublin 2; tel. (1) 6445100; fax (1) 6611602; e-mail info@newstalk.ie; internet www.newstalk.ie; f. 2002; began broadcasting news and talk programmes to most of Ireland in 2006; Propr Communicorp Group; Chair. DENIS O'BRIEN; Chief Exec. ELAINE GERAGHTY.

There are also local radio stations operating under the supervision of the Independent Radio and Television Commission.

Television

Radio Telefís Éireann (RTÉ): see above; operates two television channels: RTÉ 1 and RTÉ 2; Dir-Gen. CATHAL GOAN; Man. Dir of Television NOEL CURRAN; Man. Dir of News ED MULHALL.

TG4 (Teilifís na Gaeilge): Baile na hAbhann, Connemara, Co Galway; tel. (91) 505050; fax (91) 505021; e-mail eolas@tg4.ie; internet www.tg4.ie; f. 1996; national public-service Irish-language broadcaster; frmly operated under RTÉ, became an independent statutory authority in April 2007; financed by the Govt and sales of commercial airtime; Chief Exec. PÓL Ó GALLCHÓIR; Dir of Television ALAN ESSLEMONT.

TV3: Westgate Business Park, Ballymount, Dublin 24; tel. (1) 4193333; fax (1) 4193300; e-mail info@tv3; internet www.tv3.ie; f. 1998; first national, commercial, independent television network; Chair. (vacant); CEO DAVID MCREDMOND; Dir of Programming BEN FROW; Dir of News ANDREW HANLON.

Finance

(cap. = capital; p.u. = paid up; res = reserves; dep. = deposits; m. = million; brs = branches; amounts in euros (€), unless otherwise indicated)

BANKING

Central Bank

Bank Ceannais agus Údarás Serbhísi Airgeadais na hÉireann (Central Bank and Financial Services Authority of Ireland): POB 559, Dame St, Dublin 2; tel. (1) 4344000; fax (1) 6716561; e-mail enquiries@centralbank.ie; internet www.centralbank.ie; f. 1942; bank of issue; cap. and res 1,155.0m., dep. 30,320.7m. (Dec. 2006); Gov. JOHN HURLEY; Dir-Gen. LIAM BARRON.

Principal Banks

AIB Capital Markets PLC: AIB International Centre, IFSC, Dublin 1; tel. (1) 8740222; fax (1) 6642124; e-mail grouppa@iol.ie; internet www.aibcm.com; f. 1966; merchant banking and investment management; Man. Dir COLM E. DOHERTY; 7 brs.

AIB Group (Allied Irish Banks PLC): POB 452, Bankcentre, Dublin 4; tel. (1) 6600311; fax (1) 6604715; e-mail aibtoday@aib.ie; internet www.aib.ie; f. 1966; cap. 294m., res 2,733m., dep. 139,561m. (Dec. 2006); Chair. DERMOT GLEESON; CEO EUGENE SHEEHY; over 800 brs and offices.

Anglo Irish Bank Corpn PLC: Stephen Court, 18–21 St Stephen's Green, Dublin 2; tel. (1) 6162000; fax (1) 6162481; e-mail enquiries@angloirishbank.ie; internet www.angloirishbank.com; f. 1964; cap. 115m., res 604m., dep. 66,077m. (Sept. 2006); Chair. SEAN FITZPATRICK; CEO DAVID DRUMM; 9 brs.

Bank of Ireland Asset Management: 40 Mespil Rd, Dublin 4; tel. (1) 6378000; fax (1) 6378100; e-mail biaminfo@biam.boi.ie; internet www.biam.ie; f. 1966; investment management; CEO MICK SWEENEY.

Bank of Ireland Group: Lower Baggot St, Dublin 2; tel. (1) 6615933; fax (1) 6615193; e-mail careline@boimail.com; internet www.bankofireland.ie; f. 1783; cap. 663m., res 1,389m., dep. 162,119m. (March 2007); Gov. RICHARD BURROWS; CEO BRIAN GOGGIN; 357 brs.

Bank of Scotland (Ireland) Ltd: Bank of Scotland House, 124–127 St Stephen's Green, Dublin 2; tel. (1) 2674000; fax (1) 2674010; e-mail info@bankofscotland.ie; internet www.bankofscotland.ie; f. 1965 as Equity Bank Ltd; present name adopted 2000; provides consumer banking services under the Halifax brand; owned by HBOS PLC (United Kingdom); cap. 65.9m., res 74.2m., total assets 23,565.5m. (Dec. 2005); Chair. MAURICE PRATT; Chief Exec. MARK DUFFY; 26 brs.

Bear Stearns Bank PLC: Block 8, Harcourt Centre, Charlotte Way, Dublin 2; tel. (1) 4026200; fax (1) 4026237; e-mail lmacnamara@bear.com; internet www.bearstearns.com; f. 1996; cap. US $1.0m., res US $260.0m., dep. US $12,738.7m. (Nov. 2005); Chair. PASCAL LAMBERT; Chief Execs NIAMH WALSH, LIAM MACNAMARA.

DEPFA Bank Europe PLC: 1 Commons St, Dublin 1; tel. (1) 6071600; fax (1) 8290213; e-mail info@depfa.com; internet www.depfa.com; wholly owned subsidiary of Hypo Real Estate Holding AG (Germany) since Oct. 2007; cap. 106m., res 1,269m., dep. 217,661m. (Dec. 2006); Co-CEOs PAUL LEATHERDALE, ANDREW T. READINGER.

DZ BANK Ireland PLC: Guild House, Guild St, IFSC, Dublin 1; tel. (1) 6700715; fax (1) 8290298; e-mail info@dzbank.ie; internet www.dzbank.ie; f. 1994; present name adopted 2001; wholly owned subsidiary of DZ BANK AG Deutsche Zentral-Genossenschaftsbank, (Germany); cap. 203.4m., res 4.0m., dep. 6,193.1m. (Dec. 2006); Man. Dirs Dr TILMANN GERHARDS, MARK JACOB.

First Active PLC: First Active House, Central Park, Dublin 18; tel. (1) 2075000; fax (1) 2074900; e-mail info@firstactive.com; internet www.firstactive.com; f. 1861; present name adopted 1998; wholly owned by Ulster Bank Group; mem. of Royal Bank of Scotland Group (United Kingdom); cap. 47.6m., res 17.6m., dep. 9,255.9m. (Dec. 2004); Chair. Prof. NIAMH BRENNAN; Man. Dir COLM FURLONG.

IIB Bank PLC: Sandwith St, Dublin 2; tel. (1) 6646000; fax (1) 6785034; e-mail info@iibbank.ie; internet www.iibbank.ie; f. 1973; present name adopted 2006; wholly owned subsidiary of KBC Bank NV (Belgium); cap. 347.0m., res 515.1m., dep. 20,665.2m. (Dec. 2006); Chair. GUIDO SEGERS; CEO EDWARD A. MARAH; 1 br.

Intesa Bank Ireland PLC: KBC House, 4 St George's Dock, IFSC, Dublin 1; tel. (1) 6726720; fax (1) 6276727; e-mail mail@intesabank.ie; f. 1994; present name adopted 2003; subsidiary of Intesa Sanpaolo (Italy); cap. 8m., res 346.7m., dep. 8,412.2m. (Dec. 2006); Chair. JOHN BROUGHAN; Gen. Man. RICHARD BARKLEY.

Intesa Sanpaolo Bank Ireland PLC: 3rd Floor. KBC House, 4 St George's Dock, IFSC, Dublin 1; tel. (1) 6726720; fax (1) 6726727; f. 1987; present name adopted 2007; frmly Sanpaolo IMI Bank Ireland PLC; wholly owned subsidiary of Intesa Sanpaolo (Italy); cap. 7.5m., res 505.7m., dep. 11,202.7m. (Dec. 2006); Chair. STEFANO DEL PUNTA; Man Dir PIER CARLO ARENA.

Irish Life & Permanent PLC (permanent tsb): Lower Abbey St, Dublin 1; tel. (1) 7042000; fax (1) 7041908; internet www.irishlifepermanent.ie; f. 1884; present name adopted 1999; cap. 88m., res 393m., dep. 66,821m. (Dec. 2006); CEO DENIS CASEY; 104 brs.

LBBW Bank Ireland PLC: POB 4566, 6 George's Dock, Dublin 1; tel. (1) 8244500; fax (1) 6701817; e-mail info@lbbwie.com; internet www.lbbwie.com; f. 1994; wholly owned subsidiary of Landesbank Baden–Württemberg (Germany); cap. 6.7m., res 330.1m., dep. 7,204.0m. (Dec. 2005); Chair. HANS-JOACHIM STRÜDER; Man. Dir LIAM MILEY.

JP Morgan Bank (Ireland) PLC: JP Morgan House, IFSC, Dublin 1; tel. (1) 6123000; fax (1) 6123123; internet www.chase.com; f. 1968 as Chase and Bank of Ireland (International) Ltd; 100% owned by Chase Morgan International Finance Ltd (NJ, USA); cap. US $33.3m., res US $208.5m., dep. US $543.7m. (Dec. 2006); Chair. M. GARVIN; 1 br.

Pfizer International Bank Europe: La Touche House, IFSC, Dublin 1; tel. (1) 4484600; fax (1) 4484698; f. 1985; subsidiary of Pfizer Inc. (USA); cap. US $1.1m., dep. US $4.2m., total assets US $1,416.5m. (Nov. 2005); Man. Dir CAMILLA UDEN; Financial Dir SUSAN WEBB.

Rabobank Ireland PLC: George's Dock House, IFSC, Dublin 1; tel. (1) 6076100; fax (1) 6701724; e-mail justin.sheridan@rabobank.com; internet www.rabobank.ie; f. 1994; corporate and investment banking; owned by Rabobank International Holding, BV (Netherlands); cap. 7.1m., res 355.4m., dep. 23,453.9m. (Dec. 2006); Chair. R. SCHELLENS; Man. Dir ROB HARTOG.

Ulster Bank Ireland Ltd: 33 College Green, Dublin 2; tel. (1) 6777623; fax (1) 6775035; internet www.ulsterbank.com; wholly owned by Royal Bank of Scotland Group (United Kingdom); Chair. Prof. NIAMH BRENNAN; Chief Exec. CORMAC MCCARTHY.

UniCredito Italiano Bank (Ireland) PLC: La Touche House, IFSC, Dublin 1; tel. (1) 6702000; fax (1) 6702100; e-mail enquiry@unicredito.ie; internet www.unicredito.ie; f. 1995; present name adopted 1999; wholly owned subsidiary of UniCredito Italiano SpA (Italy); cap. 1,388.9m., res 996.8m., dep. 24,977.7m. (Dec. 2006); Man. Dir and CEO STEFANO VAIANI.

WestLB Covered Bond Bank PLC: IFSC House, Dublin 1; tel. (1) 8290040; fax (1) 8290037; e-mail bond@westlb.ie; internet www.westlbcbb.com; f. 2002; public sector finance; wholly owned by WestLB AG (Germany); cap. 6.4m., res 227.9m., dep. 15,301.7m. (Dec. 2006); Chair. NEIL COLVERD; Man. Dir MICHAEL DOHERTY.

WestLB Ireland PLC: IFSC House, IFSC, Dublin 1; tel. (1) 6127199; fax (1) 6127107; e-mail info@westlb.ie; internet www.westlb.ie; f. 1978; present name adopted 2002; wholly owned by WestLB AG (Germany); cap. 17.7m., res 277.3m., dep. 2,134.5m. (Dec. 2006); Chair. NEIL COLVERD; Man. Dir MICHAEL DOHERTY.

Banking Associations

The Institute of Bankers in Ireland: 1 North Wall Quay, Dublin 1; tel. (1) 6116500; fax (1) 6116565; e-mail info@bankers.ie; internet www.bankers.ie; f. 1898; over 22,000 mems; Pres. JOHN TRETHOWAN; CEO ANTHONY WALSH.

Irish Banking Federation: Nassau House, Nassau St, Dublin 2; tel. (1) 6715311; fax (1) 6796680; e-mail ibf@ibf.ie; internet www.ibf.ie; more than 60 mems; CEO PAT FARRELL; Pres. MIKE RYAN.

STOCK EXCHANGE

The Irish Stock Exchange: 28 Anglesea St, Dublin 2; tel. (1) 6174200; fax (1) 6776045; e-mail info@ise.ie; internet www.ise.ie; f. 1799 as the Dublin Stock Exchange; amalgamated in 1973 with the United Kingdom stock exchanges to form The International Stock Exchange of the United Kingdom and the Republic of Ireland; separated from The International Stock Exchange in 1995; operates independently under the supervision of the Irish Financial Services Regulatory Authority; Chair. DAVID KINGSTON; CEO DEIRDRE SOMERS; 69 listed cos.

SUPERVISORY BODY

The Irish Financial Services Regulatory Authority (IFSRA), established in 2003, is responsible for the regulation of banking practices and other financial services and oversees consumer protection. The Government has also approved the establishment of the Irish Monetary Authority, which will handle the implementation of monetary policy and will report to the European Central Bank.

Financial Regulator (Rialtóir Airgeadais): POB 9138, College Green, Dublin 2; tel. (1) 4104000; fax (1) 4104900; e-mail consumerinfo@financialregulator.ie; internet www.ifsra.ie; f. 2003; regulates all financial services firms in Ireland and assists consumers to make informed financial decisions; Chair. BRIAN PATTERSON; Chief Exec. PATRICK NEARY.

INSURANCE
Principal Companies

Allianz Ireland PLC: Burlington House, Burlington Rd, Dublin 4; tel. (1) 6133000; fax (1) 6134444; internet www.allianz.ie; f. 1998; 66.4% owned by Allianz AG (Germany), 30.4% by Irish Life and Permanent PLC; Chief Exec. BRENDAN MURPHY.

AXA Insurance Ltd: Wolfe Tone House, Wolfe Tone St, Dublin 1; tel. (1) 8726444; fax (1) 8729703; e-mail axa.dublincity@axa.ie; internet www.axa.ie; f. 1967; Chief Exec. JOHN O'NEILL.

Bank of Ireland Life: Grattan House, Lower Baggot St, Dublin 2; tel. (1) 7039537; fax (1) 6620811; e-mail info@bankofirelandlife.ie; internet www.bankofirelandlife.ie; f. 1987; present name adopted 2002; Chair. JAMES P. GALLIVAN; Man. Dir BRIAN FORRESTER.

Canada Life Assurance (Ireland) Ltd: Canada Life House, Temple Rd, Blackrock, Co Dublin; tel. (1) 2102000; fax (1) 2102020; e-mail customerservices@canadalife.ie; internet www.canadalife.ie; f. 1903; Man. Dir TOM BARRY.

Eagle Star Insurance: Eagle Star House, Ballsbridge Park, Dublin 2; tel. (1) 6770666; fax (1) 6670644; e-mail info@eaglestar.ie; internet www.eaglestar.ie; f. 1919; mem. of the Zürich Financial Services Group (Switzerland); Man. Dir BOB RHEEL.

Eagle Star Life Assurance Co (Ireland) Ltd: Eagle Star House, Frascati Rd, Blackrock, Co Dublin; tel. (1) 2831301; fax (1) 2831578; e-mail customerservices@eaglestarlife.ie; internet www.eaglestarlife.ie; f. 1950; mem. of the Zürich Financial Services Group (Switzerland); Man. Dir MICHAEL J. BRENNAN.

Hibernian Group PLC: Haddington Court, Haddington Rd, Dublin 4; tel. (1) 6078000; fax (1) 6078112; internet www.hibernian.ie; f. 1908; wholly owned subsidiary of Aviva PLC, United Kingdom; life and non-life; Chair. DÓNAL BYRNE.

Irish Life & Permanent PLC: see Banking.

New Ireland Assurance Co PLC: 11–12 Dawson St, Dublin 2; tel. (1) 6172000; fax (1) 6172800; e-mail info@newireland.ie; internet www.newireland.ie; f. 1924; wholly owned subsidiary of Bank of Ireland Group; Man. Dir BRIAN FORRESTER.

Quinn-direct Insurance Ltd: Dublin Rd, Cavan, Co Cavan; tel. (1) 8500845; fax (49) 4368101; e-mail info@quinn-direct.com; internet www.quinn-direct.com; f. 1996; property, motor; Chief Exec. SEAN QUINN.

Royal & SunAlliance: 13–17 Dawson St, Dublin 2; tel. (1) 6771851; fax (1) 6717625; e-mail talktous@royalsunalliance.ie; internet www.royalsunalliance.ie; Gen. Man. PHILIP SMITH.

Standard Life Assurance Co: 90 St Stephen's Green, Dublin 2; tel. (1) 6397000; fax (1) 6397909; e-mail marketing@standardlife.ie; internet www.standardlife.ie; f. 1834; life assurance, pensions, investments and annuities; Chief Exec. MICHAEL LEAHY.

Zurich Insurance Co: Eagle Star House, Ballsbridge Park, Ballsbridge, Dublin 4; tel. (1) 6670666; fax (1) 6670644; internet www.zurich.com; property, liability, motor; CEO IAN STUART.

Insurance Associations

Insurance Institute of Ireland: 39 Molesworth St, Dublin 2; tel. (1) 6772582; fax (1) 6772621; e-mail info@insurance-institute.ie; internet www.insurance-institute.ie; f. 1885; Pres. AIDAN CASSELLS; CEO DENIS HEVEY; around 6,000 mems.

Irish Brokers' Association: 87 Merrion Sq., Dublin 2; tel. (1) 6613067; fax (1) 6619955; e-mail info@irishbrokers.ie; internet www.irishbrokers.com; f. 1990; Pres. (2007–08) INEZ CONNOLLY; 700 mems.

Irish Insurance Federation: Insurance House, 39 Molesworth St, Dublin 2; tel. (1) 6761820; fax (1) 6761943; e-mail fed@iif.ie; internet www.iif.ie; f. 1986; Pres. JOHN O'NEILL; CEO MICHAEL KEMP; 62 mems.

Professional Insurance Brokers' Association (PIBA): Unit 14B, Cashel Business Centre, Cashel Rd, Crumlin, Dublin 12; tel. (1) 4922202; fax (1) 4991569; e-mail info@piba.ie; internet www.piba.ie; f. 1995; Chair. LIAM CARBERRY; CEO DIARMUID KELLY; 870 mems.

Trade and Industry
GOVERNMENT AGENCIES

An Post (The Post Office): General Post Office, O'Connell St, Dublin 1; tel. (1) 7057000; fax (1) 8723553; e-mail press-office@anpost.ie; internet www.anpost.ie; f. 1984; provides national postal, savings and agency services through c. 1,400 outlets; Chair. MARGARET MCGINLEY; CEO DONAL CONNELL.

FÁS—Foras Áiseanna Saothair (State Training and Employment Authority): 27–33 Upper Baggot St, Dublin 4; tel. (1) 6070500; fax (1) 6070600; e-mail info@fas.ie; internet www.fas.ie; f. 1988; responsible for the provision of specific skills training, apprenticeships and traineeships, employment programmes provided by a network of 70 nation-wide, local and regional centres; supports co-operative and community enterprise; offers an industrial advisory service; public recruitment service at all levels of occupations; Chair. PETER MCLOONE; Dir-Gen. RODY MOLLOY.

Food Safety Authority of Ireland: Abbey Court, Lower Abbey Street, Dublin 1; tel. (1) 8171300; fax (1) 8171301; e-mail info@fsai.ie; internet www.fsai.ie; f. 1998; takes all reasonable steps to ensure that food produced, distributed or marketed in Ireland meets the highest standards of food safety and hygiene reasonably available and to ensure that food complies with legal requirements, or, where appropriate, with recognized codes of good practice; Chair. EAMONN RYAN; Chief Exec. Dr JOHN O'BRIEN.

Forfás: Wilton Park House, Wilton Pl., Dublin 2; tel. (1) 6073000; fax (1) 6073030; e-mail info@forfas.ie; internet www.forfas.ie; f. 1993; the national policy advisory board for enterprise, trade, science, technology and innovation; Chair. EOIN O'DRISCOLL; Chief Exec. MARTIN CRONIN.

National Economic and Social Council (NESC): 16 Parnell Sq., Dublin 1; tel. (1) 8146300; fax (1) 8146301; e-mail info@nesc.ie; internet www.nesc.ie; f. 1973; analyses and reports on strategic issues relating to the efficient development of the economy and the achievement of social justice; Chair. DERMOT MCCARTHY; Dir Dr RORY O'DONNELL.

IRELAND   *Directory*

DEVELOPMENT ORGANIZATIONS

Enterprise Ireland: Glasnevin, Dublin 9; tel. (1) 8082000; fax (1) 8082020; e-mail client.service@enterprise-ireland.com; internet www.enterprise-ireland.com; f. 1998; combines the activities of the fmr An Bord Tráchtála, Forbairt and the in-company training activities of FÁS (q.v.); Chair. PATRICK J. MOLLOY; Chief Exec. FRANK RYAN.

IDA Ireland: Wilton Park House, Wilton Pl., Dublin 2; tel. (1) 6034000; fax (1) 6034040; e-mail idaireland@ida.ie; internet www.idaireland.com; f. 1993; govt agency with national responsibility for securing new investment from overseas in manufacturing and international services and for encouraging existing foreign enterprises in Ireland to expand their businesses; Chair. JOHN DUNNE; CEO BARRY O'LEARY.

Irish Productivity Centre: 4B–5 Blanchardstown Corporate Park, Dublin 15; tel. (1) 8227125; fax (1) 8227116; e-mail ipc@ipc.ie; internet www.ipc.ie; aims to increase industrial productivity in Ireland; its council is composed of representatives from the Irish Business and Employers' Confed. and the Irish Congress of Trade Unions in equal numbers; offers consultancy services and practical assistance to Irish cos; CEO TOM MCGUINNESS.

Sustainable Energy Ireland: Glasnevin, Dublin 9; tel. (1) 8369080; fax (1) 8372848; e-mail info@sei.ie; internet www.sei.ie; promotes and assists environmentally and economically sustainable production, supply and use of energy, in support of govt policy, across all sectors of the economy; CEO DAVID TAYLOR.

Teagasc (Agriculture and Food Development Authority): Oak Park, Carlow; tel. (59) 9170200; fax (59) 9182097; e-mail info@hq.teagasc.ie; internet www.teagasc.ie; f. 1988; provides research, educational and training services to agri-food sector and rural communities; Chair. Dr TOM O'DWYER; Nat. Dir Prof. GERRY BOYLE.

CHAMBERS OF COMMERCE

Chambers of Commerce of Ireland (CCI): 17 Merrion Sq., Dublin 2; tel. (1) 6612888; fax (1) 6612811; e-mail info@chambersireland.ie; internet www.chambersireland.ie; f. 1923; represents over 12,000 businesses nation-wide, with 59 chamber mems; Pres. ROBIN O'SULLIVAN; Chief Exec. JOHN DUNNE.

Cork Chamber: Fitzgerald House, Summerhill North, Cork; tel. (21) 4509044; fax (21) 4508568; e-mail info@corkchamber.ie; internet www.corkchamber.ie; f. 1819; Pres. JOE GANTLY; Chief Exec. CONOR HEALY.

Dublin Chamber of Commerce: 7 Clare St, Dublin 2; tel. (1) 6647200; fax (1) 6766043; e-mail info@dubchamber.ie; internet www.dubchamber.ie; f. 1783; Pres. RONAN KING; Chief Exec. GINA QUIN.

INDUSTRIAL AND TRADE ASSOCIATIONS

Construction Industry Federation: Construction House, Canal Rd, Dublin 6; tel. (1) 4066000; fax (1) 4966953; e-mail cif@cif.ie; internet www.cif.ie; 37 asscns representing 3,000 mems; Pres. GERALD PURCELL; Dir-Gen. TOM PARLON.

Irish Creamery Milk Suppliers' Association (ICMSA): John Feely House, Dublin Rd, Castletroy, Limerick; tel. (61) 314677; fax (61) 315737; e-mail info@icmsa.ie; internet www.icmsa.ie; f. 1950; Pres. PAT O'ROURKE; Gen. Sec. CIARAN DOLAN.

Irish Farmers' Association (IFA): Irish Farm Centre, Bluebell, Dublin 12; tel. (1) 4500266; fax (1) 4551043; e-mail postmaster@ifa.ie; internet www.ifa.ie; Pres. PÁDRAIG WALSHE; Gen. Sec. MICHAEL BERKEREY.

Irish Fishermen's Organisation Ltd: Cumberland House, Fenian St, Dublin 2; tel. (1) 6612400; fax (1) 6612424; e-mail irishfish@eircom.net; f. 1974; representative body for Irish commercial fishermen; Chair. J. V. MADDOCK; Sec.-Gen. J. F. DOYLE.

Irish Grain and Feed Association: 18 Herbert St, Dublin 2; tel. (1) 6760680; fax (1) 6616774; e-mail igfa@cereal.iol.ie; Pres. M. MURPHY; Dir S. A. FUNGE.

EMPLOYERS' ORGANIZATIONS

Irish Business and Employers Confederation (IBEC): Confederation House, 84–86 Lower Baggot St, Dublin 2; tel. (1) 6051500; fax (1) 6381500; e-mail info@ibec.ie; internet www.ibec.ie; f. 1993; represents c. 7,000 cos and orgs; Pres. MAURICE HEALY; Dir-Gen. TURLOUGH O'SULLIVAN.

Irish Exporters' Association: 28 Merrion Sq., Dublin 2; tel. (1) 6612182; fax (1) 6612315; e-mail iea@irishexporters.ie; internet www.irishexporters.ie; f. 1951; Pres. JOSEPH LYNCH; CEO JOHN WHELAN.

UTILITIES

Electricity

An Coimisiún um Rialáil Fuinnimh/Commission for Electricity Regulation (CER): Plaza House, Belgard Rd, Tallaght, Dublin 24; tel. (1) 4000800; fax (1) 4000850; e-mail info@cer.ie; internet www.cer.ie; f. 1999 under the Electricity Regulation Act of 1999; responsible for licensing and regulating the generation and supply of electricity and authorizing construction of new generating plants; Chair. TOM REEVES.

Airtricity: Airtricity House, Ravenscourt Office Park, Sandyford, Dublin 18; tel. (1) 2130400; fax (1) 2130444; e-mail info@airtricity.com; internet www.airtricity.com; f. 1999; supplier of renewable energy; CEO PAUL DOWLING.

Bord Gáis Éireann (BGÉ) (Irish Gas Board): see Gas.

EirGrid PLC: 27 Lower Fitzwilliam St, Dublin 2; tel. (1) 6771700; fax (1) 6615375; e-mail info@eirgrid.com; internet www.eirgrid.com; f. 2006; state-owned; manages transmission of Ireland's electricity; Chair. BERNIE GRAY; CEO DERMOT BYRNE.

Electricity Supply Board (ESB): 27 Lower Fitzwilliam St, Dublin 2; tel. (1) 6765831; fax (1) 6760727; e-mail service@esb.ie; internet www.esb.ie; f. 1927; reorg. 1988; state-owned; supplier of electricity and operator of 19 generating stations; Chair. LOCHLAN QUINN; CEO PADRAIG MCMANUS.

Energia: Mill House, Ashtowngate, Navan Rd, Dublin 15; tel. (1) 850363744; fax (1) 8692050; e-mail sales@energia.ie; internet www.energia.ie; f. 1999; wholly owned subsidiary of Viridian Group PLC; CEO HARRY MCCRACKEN.

Gas

Bord Gáis Éireann (BGÉ) (The Irish Gas Board): POB 51, Gasworks Rd, Cork, Co Cork; tel. (21) 4534000; fax (21) 4534001; internet www.bordgais.ie; f. 1976; natural gas transmission and distribution, gas and electricity supply, electricity generation; Chair. ED O'CONNELL; CEO JOHN MULLINS.

Water

Dept of the Environment, Heritage and Local Government: Custom House, Dublin 1; tel. (1) 8882479; fax (1) 8882576; e-mail press-office@environ.irlgov.ie; internet www.environ.ie; responsible for water supply.

CO-OPERATIVES

Irish Co-operative Organisation Society (ICOS): 84 Merrion Sq., Dublin 2; tel. (1) 6764783; fax (1) 6624502; e-mail info@icos.ie; internet www.icos.ie; f. 1894; three operating divisions; offices in Dublin, Cork and Brussels (Belgium); Pres. PADRAIG GIBBONS; Dir-Gen. JOHN TYRRELL; over 150 mem. co-operatives representing c. 150,000 farmers.

Irish Dairy Board: Grattan House, Lower Mount St, Dublin 2; tel. (1) 6619599; fax (1) 6612778; e-mail idb@idb.ie; internet www.idb.ie; f. 1961; reorg. 1973 as a farmers' co-operative; principal exporter of Irish dairy products; Chair. MICHAEL CRONIN; Chief Exec. NOEL COAKLEY.

TRADE UNIONS

Central Organization

Irish Congress of Trade Unions (ICTU): 31–32 Parnell Sq., Dublin 1; tel. (1) 8897777; fax (1) 8872012; e-mail congress@ictu.ie; internet www.ictu.ie; f. 1894; represents some 770,000 workers in 56 affiliated unions in the Republic and Northern Ireland (2005); Pres. PATRICIA MCKEOWN; Gen. Sec. DAVID BEGG.

Principal Trade Unions Affiliated to the ICTU

Amalgamated Transport and General Workers' Union: 55–56 Middle Abbey St, Dublin 1; tel. (1) 8734577; fax (1) 8734602; e-mail tgwu@tgwu.org.uk; internet www.tgwu.org.uk/ireland; head office based in London, United Kingdom; Irish Regional Sec. JIMMY KELLY; 46,750 mems (2002, incl. Northern Ireland).

Association of Higher Civil and Public Servants: Fleming's Hall, 12 Fleming's Place, Dublin 4; tel. (1) 6686077; fax (1) 6686380; e-mail info@ahcps.ie; internet www.ahcps.ie; Chair. CIARAN ROHAN; Gen. Sec. DAVE THOMAS; 3,200 mems (2004).

Building and Allied Trades' Union: Arus Hibernia, 13 Blessington St, Dublin 7; tel. (1) 8301911; fax (1) 8304869; e-mail union@batu.ie; internet www.batu.ie; Pres. MICHAEL MCNALLY; Gen. Sec. PATRICK O'SHAUGHNESSY; 10,020 mems (2002).

Civil, Public & Services Union: 19–20 Adelaide Rd, Dublin 2; tel. (1) 6765394; fax (1) 6762918; e-mail headoffice@cpsu.ie; internet www.cpsu.ie; f. 1922; Pres. BETTY TYRRELL-COLLARD; Gen. Sec. BLAIR HORAN; 13,810 mems (2004).

IRELAND

Communications Workers' Union: Áras Ghaibréil, 575 North Circular Rd, Dublin 1; tel. (1) 8663000; fax (1) 8663099; e-mail cwu@cwu.ie; internet www.cwu.ie; f. 1922; Gen. Sec. STEVE FITZPATRICK; 19,600 mems (2003).

Electricity Supply Board Officers' Association: 43 East James's Pl., Baggot St, Dublin 2; tel. (1) 6767444; fax (1) 6789226; e-mail info@esboa.ie; internet www.esboa.ie; f. 1959; Pres. DAVE BYRNE; Gen. Sec. FRAN O'NEILL; c. 2,000 mems.

Irish Bank Officials' Association: IBOA House, Upper Stephen Street, Dublin 8; tel. (1) 4755908; fax (1) 4780567; e-mail info@iboa.ie; internet www.iboa.ie; Pres. BRIAN DEASY; Gen. Sec. LARRY BRODERICK; over 20,000 mems.

Irish Federation of University Teachers: 11 Merrion Sq., Dublin 2; tel. (1) 6610910; fax (1) 6610909; e-mail ifut@eircom.net; internet www.ifut.ie; f. 1965; Pres. JOE BRADY; Gen. Sec. MIKE JENNINGS; 1,715 mems (2007).

Irish Medical Organization: IMO House, 10 Fitzwilliam Pl., Dublin 2; tel. (1) 6767273; fax (1) 6612758; e-mail imo@imo.ie; internet www.imo.ie; Pres. Dr PAULA GILVARRY; CEO GEORGE McNEICE; 5,700 mems (2004).

Irish Municipal, Public and Civil Trade Union (IMPACT): Nerney's Court, Dublin 1; tel. (1) 8171500; fax (1) 8171501; internet www.impact.ie; f. 1991; Pres. STEPHEN LYONS; Gen. Sec. PETER McLOONE; over 55,000 mems.

Irish National Teachers' Organization: 35 Parnell Sq., Dublin 1; tel. (1) 8047700; fax (1) 8722462; e-mail info@into.ie; internet www.into.ie; f. 1868; Pres. ANGELA DUNNE; Gen. Sec. JOHN CARR; 34,124 mems (Dec. 2006, including 6,149 mems in Northern Ireland).

Irish Nurses' Organization: The Whitworth Bldg, North Brunswick St, Dublin 7; tel. (1) 6640600; fax (1) 6610466; e-mail ino@ino.ie; internet www.ino.ie; Pres. MADELINE SPIERS; Gen. Sec. LIAM DORAN; over 40,000 mems.

Mandate Trade Union: 9 Cavendish Row, Dublin 1; tel. (1) 8746321; fax (1) 8729581; e-mail mandate@mandate.ie; internet www.mandate.ie; f. 1994 by merger of Irish National Union of Vintners', Grocers' & Allied Trades' Assistants and Irish Distributive and Administrative Union; Gen. Sec. JOHN DOUGLAS; 45,000 mems (2006).

Public Service Executive Union: 30 Merrion Sq., Dublin 2; tel. (1) 6767271; fax (1) 6615777; e-mail info@pseu.ie; internet www.pseu.ie; f. 1890; Pres. SEAN BEADES; Gen. Sec. DAN MURPHY; over 10,000 mems.

Services, Industrial, Professional and Technical Union (SIPTU): Liberty Hall, Dublin 1; tel. (1) 8586300; fax (1) 8749466; e-mail info@siptu.ie; internet www.siptu.ie; f. 1990; Gen. Pres. JACK O'CONNOR; Gen. Sec. JOE O'FLYNN; 200,000 mems (2008).

Teachers' Union of Ireland: 73 Orwell Rd, Rathgar, Dublin 6; tel. (1) 4922588; fax (1) 4922953; e-mail tui@tui.ie; internet www.tui.ie; f. 1955; Pres. TIM O'MEARA; Gen. Sec. PETER MACMENAMIN; 13,027 mems (2006).

Technical, Engineering and Electrical Union: 5 Cavendish Row, Dublin 1; tel. (1) 8747047; fax (1) 8747048; e-mail info@teeu.ie; internet www.teeu.ie; f. 1992; Gen. Sec. OWEN WILLS; 35,012 mems (2004).

Union of Construction, Allied Trades and Technicians: 56 Parnell Sq. West, Dublin 1; tel. (1) 8731599; fax (1) 8731403; e-mail info@ucatt.ie; internet www.ucatt.ie; head office based in London, United Kingdom; Regional Sec. JIM MOORE; over 15,000 mems.

Unions not Affiliated to the ICTU

Association of Secondary Teachers, Ireland (ASTI): ASTI House, Winetavern St, Dublin 8; tel. (1) 6040160; fax (1) 6719280; e-mail info@asti.ie; internet www.asti.ie; Pres. PATRICIA WROE; Gen. Sec. JOHN WHITE; 16,500 mems (2005).

National Bus and Rail Union: 54 Parnell Sq., Dublin 1; tel. (1) 8730411; fax (1) 8730137; e-mail nbru@eircom.net; internet www.nbru.ie; Gen. Sec. MICHAEL FAHERTY; 3,500 mems.

Transport

Córas Iompair Éireann (CIÉ) (The Irish Transport Co): Heuston Station, Dublin 8; tel. (1) 6771871; fax (1) 7032276; internet www.cie.ie; f. 1945; state corpn operating rail and road transport services; three operating cos: Iarnród Éireann (Irish Rail), Bus Éireann (Irish Bus) and Bus Átha Cliath (Dublin Bus); Chair. Dr JOHN LYNCH.

RAILWAYS

In 2002 there were 1,919 km of track. Railway services are operated by Iarnród Éireann.

Iarnród Éireann (Irish Rail): Connolly Station, Dublin 1; tel. (1) 8363333; fax (1) 8364760; e-mail info@irishrail.ie; internet www.irishrail.ie; f. 1987; division of CIÉ; Chair. Dr JOHN LYNCH; Man. Dir DICK FEARN.

INLAND WATERWAYS

The Grand and Royal Canals and the canal link into the Barrow Navigation system are controlled by CIÉ. The Grand Canal and Barrow are open to navigation by pleasure craft, and the rehabilitation and restoration of the Royal Canal is proceeding. The River Shannon, which is navigable from Limerick to Lough Allen, includes stretches of the Boyle, Suck, Camlin, and Inny Rivers, the Erne Navigation, and the Shannon-Erne Waterway. The total length of Irish navigable waterways is about 700 km.

ROADS

At 31 December 2003 there were an estimated 96,602 km of roads, of which 200 km were motorways, 5,310 km were national primary roads and 11,654 km were national secondary roads. The National Development Plan (NDP) 2000–2006 envisaged expenditure of €6,000m. on new or improved roads from Dublin to most major regional centres by 2006 and to Waterford by 2007. However, the targets were not met; these roads are now expected to be completed by 2010 at a cost of €20,000m. The NDP 2007–13, published in 2007, envisaged expenditure of €13,300m. on national roads and €4,300m. on non-national roads.

National Roads Authority: St Martin's House, Waterloo Rd, Dublin 4; tel. (1) 6602511; fax (1) 6680009; e-mail info@nra.ie; internet www.nra.ie; f. 1994; responsible for the planning, supervision and maintenance of nat. road network; Chair. PETER MALONE; Chief Exec. FRED BARRY.

Bus Éireann (Irish Buses): Heuston Station, Dublin 8; internet www.buseireann.ie; f. 1987; provides bus and coach services across Ireland, except Dublin area; subsidiary of CIÉ; Chair. Dr JOHN LYNCH; Chief Exec. TIM HAYES.

Dublin Bus (Bus Átha Cliath): 59 Upper O'Connell St., Dublin 1; tel. (1) 8734222; internet www.dublinbus.ie; f. 1987; provides bus services in Dublin area; subsidiary of CIÉ; Chair. Dr JOHN LYNCH; Chief Exec. JOE MEAGHER.

SHIPPING

The principal sea ports are Dublin, Dún Laoghaire, Cork, Waterford, Rosslare, Limerick, Foynes, Galway, New Ross, Drogheda, Dundalk, Fenit and Whiddy Island.

Arklow Shipping: North Quay, Arklow, Co Wicklow; tel. (402) 39901; fax (402) 39902; e-mail chartering@asl.ie; internet www.asl.ie; f. 1966; Man. Dir JAMES S. TYRRELL; 37 carriers.

Irish Continental Group PLC: Ferryport, Alexandra Rd, Dublin 1; tel. (1) 6075628; fax (1) 8552268; e-mail info@icg.ie; internet www.icg.ie; f. 1972; controls Irish Ferries, operating passenger vehicle and roll-on/roll-off freight ferry services between Ireland, the United Kingdom and continental Europe; Chair. JOHN B. MCGUCKIAN; Man. Dir EAMONN ROTHWELL.

Irish Ferries: Ferryport, Alexandra Rd, POB 19, Dublin 1; tel. (81) 8552222; fax (1) 8552272; e-mail info@irishferries.com; internet www.irishferries.com; drive-on/drive-off car ferry and roll-on/roll-off freight services between Ireland, the United Kingdom and continental Europe, operating up to 109 sailings weekly; Group Man. Dir EAMONN ROTHWELL.

Stena Line: Ferry Terminal, Dún Laoghaire Harbour, Co Dublin; tel. (1) 2047700; fax (1) 2047620; e-mail info.ie@stenaline.com; internet www.stenaline.ie; services between Dún Laoghaire and Dublin Port—Holyhead (Wales, United Kingdom) including high-speed catamaran, Rosslare–Fishguard (Wales, United Kingdom), Belfast (Northern Ireland) and Stranraer (Scotland, United Kingdom), Larne–Fleetwood (England, United Kingdom), passengers, drive-on/drive-off car ferry, roll-on/roll-off freight services; Man. Dir GUNNAR BLOMDAHL.

Associations

Irish Chamber of Shipping: Port Centre, Alexandra Rd, Dublin Port, Dublin 1; tel. (1) 8559011; fax (1) 8559022; e-mail bks@iol.ie; Pres. Capt. S. HICKEY; Dir B. W. KERR.

Irish Ship Agents' Association: Ormonde House, 26 Harbour Row, Cobh, Co Cork; tel. (21) 4813180; fax (21) 4811849; e-mail info@irishshipagents.com; internet www.irishshipagents.com; Pres. PAT COONEY.

CIVIL AVIATION

There are international airports at Shannon, Dublin, Cork and Knock (Ireland West Airport). In 2006 Dublin Airport handled 21.2m. passengers, while Shannon and Cork Airports handled 3.6m. and 3.0m., respectively.

Dublin Airport Authority PLC: Dublin Airport, Dublin; tel. (1) 8141111; fax (1) 8415386; internet www.dublinairportauthority.com; state-controlled; responsible for the management of Dublin, Shannon and Cork airports; Chair. GARY MCGANN; Chief Exec. DECLAN COLLIER.

Commission for Aviation Regulation: 3rd Floor, Alexandra House, Earlsfort Terrace, Dublin 2; tel. (1) 6611700; fax (1) 6611269; e-mail info@aviationreg.ie; internet www.aviationreg.ie; f. 2001; responsible for licensing the travel trade in Ireland as well as airlines; approves providers of ground handling services under EU regulations; Commissioner CATHAL GUIOMARD.

Irish Aviation Authority: Aviation House, Hawkins St, Dublin 2; tel. (1) 6718655; fax (1) 6792934; e-mail info@iaa.ie; internet www.iaa.ie; f. 1994; provides air traffic management, engineering and communications in airspace controlled by Ireland and related air traffic technological infrastructure; also regulates aircraft airworthiness certification and registration; the licensing of personnel and orgs involved in the maintenance of aircraft, as well as the licensing of pilots and aerodromes; Chair. JERRY LISTON; Chief Exec. EAMONN BRENNAN.

Airlines

Aer Arann: 1 Northwood Ave, Santry, Dublin 9; tel. (1) 8447700; fax (1) 8447701; e-mail info@aerarann.com; internet www.aerarann.ie; f. 1970; operates flights serving eight domestic, 13 UK (incl. Belfast, Northern Ireland) and eight continental European destinations; Exec. Chair. PADRAIG O'CEIDIGH; Man. Dir GARRY CULLEN.

Aer Lingus Group PLC: Dublin Airport, Dublin; tel. (1) 8868844; fax (1) 8863832; internet www.aerlingus.com; f. 1936; reorg. 1993; 28% owned by Ryanair, 25.4% Govt-owned; domestic and international scheduled services; Chair. JOHN SHARMAN; CEO DERMOT MANNION.

CityJet: Swords Business Campus, Balheary Rd, Swords, Co Dublin; tel. (1) 8700100; fax (1) 8700115; e-mail info@cityjet.com; internet www.cityjet.com; f. 1994; operates chartered and scheduled passenger routes between Dublin and Belfast (Northern Ireland), London (United Kingdom) and destinations in continental Western Europe; 100%-owned by Air France; CEO GEOFFREY O'BYRNE WHITE.

Ryanair: Dublin Airport, Dublin; tel. (1) 8121212; fax (1) 8121213; internet www.ryanair.com; f. 1985; scheduled and charter passenger services to European and North African destinations; Chair. DAVID BONDERMAN; CEO MICHAEL O'LEARY.

Tourism

Intensive marketing campaigns have been undertaken in recent years to develop new markets for Irish tourism. In addition to many sites of historic and cultural interest, the country has numerous areas of natural beauty, notably the Killarney Lakes and the west coast. In 2005 a total of 7.33m. foreign tourists (including residents of Northern Ireland) visited the Republic. Receipts from tourism (including passenger transport) totalled US $6,772m. in that year.

Dublin Regional Tourism Authority Ltd: Suffolk St, Dublin 2; tel. (1) 6057700; fax (1) 6057757; e-mail reservations@dublintourism.ie; internet www.visitdublin.com; Chair. MICHAEL FLOOD; CEO FRANK MAGEE.

Fáilte Ireland (National Tourism Development Authority): 88–95 Amiens St, Dublin 1; tel. (1) 8847700; fax (1) 8556821; e-mail info@failteireland.ie; internet www.failteireland.ie; f. 1955; Chair. GILLIAN BOWLER; Chief Exec. SHAUN QUINN.

Irish Tourist Industry Confederation: 17 Longford Terrace, Monkstown, Co Dublin; tel. (1) 2844222; fax (1) 2804218; e-mail itic@eircom.net; internet www.itic.ie; Chair. RICHARD BOURKE.

Tourism Ireland: 5th Floor, Bishop's Sq., Redmond's Hill, Dublin 2; tel. (1) 4763400; fax (1) 4763666; e-mail corporate.admin@tourismireland.com; internet www.tourismireland.com; f. 2001; promotes jointly the Republic of Ireland and Northern Ireland as a tourist destination; Chair. ANDREW COPPEL; Chief Exec. PAUL O'TOOLE.

ISRAEL

Introductory Survey

Location, Climate, Language, Religion, Flag, Capital

The State of Israel lies in western Asia, occupying a narrow strip of territory on the eastern shore of the Mediterranean Sea. The country also has a narrow outlet to the Red Sea at the northern tip of the Gulf of Aqaba. All of Israel's land frontiers are with Arab countries, the longest being with Egypt to the west and with Jordan to the east. Lebanon lies to the north, and Syria to the north-east. The climate is Mediterranean, with hot, dry summers, when the maximum temperature in Jerusalem is generally between 30°C and 35°C (86°F to 95°F), and mild, rainy winters, with a minimum temperature in the city of about 5°C (41°F). The climate is sub-tropical on the coast but more extreme in the Negev Desert, in the south, and near the shores of the Dead Sea (a lake on the Israeli–Jordanian frontier), where the summer temperature may exceed 50°C (122°F). The official languages are Hebrew and Arabic. Hebrew is spoken by about two-thirds of the population, including most Jews. About 15% of Israeli residents, including Muslim Arabs, speak Arabic (which is also the language spoken by the inhabitants of the Occupied Territories and the Palestinian Autonomous Areas), while many European languages are also spoken. Some 75.8% of the population profess adherence to Judaism, the officially recognized religion of Israel, while 16.5% are Muslims. The national flag (proportions 8 by 11) has a white background, with a six-pointed blue star composed of two overlapping triangles (the 'Shield of David') between two horizontal blue stripes near the upper and lower edges. Although the Israeli Government has designated the city of Jerusalem (part of which is Jordanian territory annexed by Israel in 1967) as the country's capital, this is not recognized by the UN, and most foreign governments maintain their embassies in Tel-Aviv.

Recent History

The Zionist movement emerged in Europe in the 19th century in response to the growing sense of insecurity felt by Jewish minorities in many European countries as a result of the racial and religious persecution known as anti-semitism. The primary objective of Zionism was defined in 1897 at the Basle Congress, when Dr Theodor Herzl stated that Zionism sought 'to create for the Jewish people a home in Palestine secured by public law'. Zionists aimed to re-establish an autonomous community of Jews in what was their historical homeland.

Palestine was almost entirely populated by Arabs and had become part of the Turkish Ottoman Empire in the early 16th century. During the First World War the empire's Arab subjects launched the so-called Arab Revolt and, following the withdrawal of the Turks, in 1917–18 British troops occupied Palestine. In November 1917 the British Foreign Secretary, Arthur Balfour, declared British support for the establishment of a Jewish national home in Palestine, on condition that the rights of 'the existing non-Jewish communities' were safeguarded; this became known as the Balfour Declaration and was confirmed by the governments of other countries then at war with Turkey. The British occupation of Palestine continued after the war under the terms of a League of Nations mandate, which also incorporated the Balfour Declaration. (In 1920 Palestine had been formally placed under British administration.) British rule in Palestine was hampered by the conflict between the declared obligations to the Jews and the rival claims of the indigenous Arab majority. In accordance with the mandate, Jewish settlers were admitted to Palestine only on the basis of limited annual quotas. There was serious anti-Jewish rioting by Arabs in 1921 and again in 1929. However, attempts to restrict immigration led to Jewish-sponsored riots in 1933. The extreme persecution of Jews by Nazi Germany caused an increase in the flow of Jewish immigrants, both legal and illegal, which intensified the unrest in Palestine. In 1937 a British proposal to establish separate Jewish and Arab states, while retaining a British-mandated area, was accepted by most Zionists but rejected by the Arabs, and by the end of that year hostilities between the two communities had descended into open conflict. A British scheme offering eventual independence for a bi-communal Palestinian state was postponed because of the Second World War, during which the Nazis caused the deaths of an estimated 6m. Jews in central and eastern Europe (more than one-third of the world's total Jewish population). The enormity of the Holocaust greatly increased international sympathy for Jewish claims to a homeland in Palestine.

After the war there was strong opposition by Palestinian Jews to continued British occupation. Numerous terrorist attacks were made by Jewish groups against British targets. In November 1947 the UN approved a plan for the partition of Palestine into two states, one Jewish (covering about 56% of the area) and one Arab. The plan was, however, rejected by Arab states and by Palestinian Arab leaders. Meanwhile, the conflict between the two communities in Palestine escalated into full-scale war.

On 14 May 1948 the United Kingdom terminated its Palestine mandate, and Jewish leaders immediately proclaimed the State of Israel, with David Ben-Gurion as Prime Minister. Despite the absence of recognized borders, the new state quickly received international recognition. Neighbouring Arab countries attempted to conquer Israel by military force, and fighting continued until January 1949, when cease-fire agreements left Israel in control of 75% of Palestine, including West Jerusalem. The de facto territory of Israel was thus nearly one-third greater than the area assigned to the Jewish State under the original UN partition plan. Jordanian forces controlled most of the remainder of Palestine, the area eventually known as the West Bank (or, to Israelis, as Judea and Samaria) and which was fully incorporated into Jordan in April 1950.

By the end of the British mandate the Jewish population of Palestine was about 650,000 (or 40% of the total). The new State of Israel encouraged further Jewish immigration: the Law of Return, adopted in July 1950, established a right of immigration for all Jews, and resulted in a rapid influx of Jewish settlers. Many former Arab residents of Palestine, meanwhile, had become refugees in neighbouring countries, mainly Jordan and Lebanon. About 400,000 Arabs had evacuated their homes prior to May 1948, and a similar number fled subsequently. In 1964 exiled Palestinian Arabs formed the Palestine Liberation Organization (PLO), with the aim, at that time, of overthrowing Israel.

Israel, together with the United Kingdom and France, launched an attack on Egypt in October 1956 following the nationalization of the Suez Canal by President Nasser; Israel seized the Gaza Strip (part of Palestine occupied by Egypt since 1949) and the Sinai Peninsula. After pressure from the UN and the USA, Israeli forces evacuated these areas in 1957, when a UN Emergency Force (UNEF) was established in Sinai. In 1967 the United Arab Republic (Egypt) secured the withdrawal of UNEF from its territory. Egyptian forces immediately reoccupied the garrison at Sharm esh-Sheikh, near the southern tip of Sinai, and closed the Straits of Tiran to Israeli shipping, effectively (as in 1956) blockading the Israeli port of Eilat. In retaliation, Israeli forces attacked Egypt, Jordan and Syria, swiftly making substantial territorial gains. The so-called Six-Day War left Israel in possession of all Jerusalem, the West Bank area of Jordan, the Sinai Peninsula in Egypt, the Gaza Strip and the Golan Heights in Syria. East Jerusalem was almost immediately integrated into the State of Israel, while the other conquered areas were regarded as Occupied Territories. In November 1967 the UN Security Council passed Resolution 242, calling on Israel to withdraw from all the recently occupied Arab territories.

Ben-Gurion resigned in June 1963 and was succeeded by Levi Eshkol. Three of the parties in the ruling coalition merged to form the Israel Labour Party in 1968. On the death of Eshkol in 1969, Golda Meir was elected Prime Minister. A cease-fire between Egypt and Israel was arranged in August 1970, but other Arab states and Palestinian guerrilla (mainly PLO) groups continued hostilities. Another Arab–Israeli war began on 6 October 1973, as Arab forces invaded Israeli-held territory on Yom Kippur (the Day of Atonement), the holiest day of the Jewish year. Egyptian forces crossed the Suez Canal and reoccupied part of Sinai, while Syrian troops launched an offensive on the Golan Heights. Having successfully repelled these advances, Israel made cease-fire agreements with Egypt and Syria on 24 October.

The UN Security Council passed another resolution (No. 338) in that month, urging a cease-fire and reaffirming the principles of Resolution 242. Gen. Itzhak Rabin succeeded Meir as Prime Minister of a Labour Alignment coalition in 1974. In May 1977 the Labour Alignment was defeated in a general election, and the Likud (Consolidation) bloc, led by Menachem Begin of the Herut (Freedom) Party, formed a Government with the support of minority parties.

In November 1977 the Egyptian President, Anwar Sadat, visited Israel, indicating tacit recognition of the Jewish State. In September 1978 President Jimmy Carter of the USA, President Sadat and Prime Minister Begin met at the US presidential retreat at Camp David, Maryland, and concluded two agreements: a 'framework for peace in the Middle East', providing for autonomy for the West Bank and Gaza Strip after a transitional period of five years; and a 'framework for the conclusion of a peace treaty between Egypt and Israel'. In February 1980 Egypt became the first Arab country to grant diplomatic recognition to Israel. However, approval by the Israeli Knesset (parliament) in that year of legislation stating explicitly that Jerusalem should be forever the undivided capital of Israel, and Israel's formal annexation of the Golan Heights in 1981, subsequently impeded prospects of agreement on Palestinian autonomy.

Israel's phased withdrawal from Sinai was completed in April 1982. In June Israeli forces, under 'Operation Peace for Galilee', advanced through Lebanon and surrounded west Beirut, trapping 6,000 PLO fighters. Egypt withdrew its ambassador from Tel-Aviv in protest. Diplomatic efforts resulted in the evacuation of 14,000–15,000 PLO and Syrian fighters from Beirut to various Arab countries. In September Lebanese Phalangists massacred Palestinian refugees in the Sabra and Chatila camps in Beirut (see the chapter on Lebanon); an official Israeli inquiry found the Israeli leadership to be indirectly responsible through negligence and forced the resignation of Gen. Ariel Sharon as Minister of Defence. In May 1983 Israel and Lebanon concluded a peace agreement, declaring an end to hostilities and envisaging the withdrawal of all foreign forces from Lebanon within three months. Syria's refusal, however, to withdraw some 30,000 troops, and the continued presence of some 7,000 PLO fighters in the Beka'a valley and northern Lebanon, delayed the Israeli withdrawal, although by the end of 1983 only 10,000 Israeli troops (of the original 30,000) remained in Lebanon.

The Government's prestige had been damaged by the Beirut massacre and by a capitulation to wage demands by Israeli doctors. In August 1983 Itzhak Shamir succeeded Begin as leader of the Likud bloc and Prime Minister. However, economic difficulties further undermined the Government, and the Labour Party forced a general election in July 1984. Neither the Labour Alignment nor Likud could form a viable coalition, so President Chaim Herzog invited the Labour leader, Shimon Peres, to form a government of national unity with Likud.

Israel's forces finally completed their withdrawal from Lebanon in June 1985, leaving responsibility for policing the occupied southern area of Lebanon to the Israeli-controlled 'South Lebanon Army' (SLA). During 1986 rocket attacks on settlements in northern Israel were resumed by Palestinian guerrillas. Israel responded with air assaults on Palestinian targets in southern Lebanon. Meanwhile, the Shi'ite fundamentalist Hezbollah intensified attacks on SLA positions within the southern buffer zone. The conflict escalated following the abduction, in July 1989, of a local Shi'a Muslim leader by Israeli agents; and again in February 1992, after the assassination by the Israeli air force of the Hezbollah Secretary-General, Sheikh Abbas Moussawi.

In July 1988 King Hussein abrogated Jordan's legal and administrative responsibilities in the West Bank, and declared that he would no longer represent the Palestinians in any international conference on the Palestinian question, which from 1984 had come to dominate the political landscape of the Middle East. King Hussein's decision strengthened the PLO's negotiating position as the sole legitimate representative of the Palestinian people. Since December 1987 international attention had been focused on the Palestinian cause after the outbreak of an *intifada* (uprising) against Israeli rule in the Occupied Territories and Israeli attempts to suppress the rebellion. In November 1988 the PLO declared an independent Palestinian State (notionally the West Bank and Gaza Strip), and endorsed UN Security Council Resolution 242, thereby implicitly granting recognition to Israel. The USA refused to accept PLO proposals for a two-state solution put forward by the Chairman of the PLO, Yasser Arafat, in December, but it did open a dialogue with the organization. However, Prime Minister Itzhak Shamir (the Likud leader had assumed the Israeli premiership in October 1986, in accordance with the 1984 coalition agreement) would not negotiate, distrusting the PLO's undertaking to abandon violence. Instead, he appeared to favour the introduction of limited self-rule for the Palestinians of the West Bank and Gaza, as outlined in the 1978 Camp David accords. At the general election in November 1988 neither Likud nor Labour secured enough seats in the Knesset to form a viable coalition, leading to another Government of national unity being formed under Shamir, with Shimon Peres as Deputy Prime Minister and Minister of Finance.

In April 1989 Shamir presented a peace proposal that would include a reaffirmation by Egypt, Israel and the USA of the Camp David accords, and plans for the holding of free democratic elections in the West Bank and Gaza for Palestinian delegates who could negotiate self-rule under Israeli authority. The proposals, precluding direct talks with the PLO, were unacceptable to the PLO, which did not consider that elections could establish the basis for a political settlement. In September, none the less, President Hosni Mubarak of Egypt invited clarification of Shamir's plans and offered to convene an Israeli-Palestinian meeting in Cairo. This was rejected by Likud ministers, on the grounds that it would entail direct contact with PLO delegates. In November Israel provisionally accepted a proposal by the US Secretary of State, James Baker, for a preliminary meeting to discuss the holding of elections in the West Bank and Gaza, on condition that Israel would not be required to negotiate with the PLO and that the talks would concern only Israel's election proposals. However, the PLO continued to demand a direct role, and the Baker initiative foundered.

The fragile Likud-Labour coalition was endangered in early 1990 by disputes and dismissals, and in March the Knesset adopted a motion of no confidence in Prime Minister Shamir. Shimon Peres was unable to form a new coalition, and in June, after several weeks of political bargaining, Shamir formed a new Government—a narrow, right-wing coalition of Likud and five small parties, with three independent members of the Knesset. In a policy document Shamir emphasized the right of Jews to settle in all parts of 'Greater Israel', his opposition to the creation of an independent Palestinian state and his refusal to negotiate with the PLO—or with any Palestinians other than those resident in the Occupied Territories (excluding East Jerusalem).

In March 1990 US President George Bush opposed the granting to Israel of a loan of some US $400m. for the housing of Soviet Jewish immigrants, since Israel would not guarantee to refrain from constructing new settlements in the Occupied Territories. Violence erupted throughout Israel and the Occupied Territories in May. The PLO's refusal to condemn the violence caused the USA to suspend its dialogue with the organization and to veto a UN Security Council resolution urging that international observers be dispatched to the Occupied Territories. In June Shamir invited President Hafiz al-Assad of Syria to enter into peace negotiations; however, Shamir rejected US proposals for direct talks between Israeli and Palestinian delegations.

Iraq's invasion of Kuwait in August 1990 brought about an improvement in US-Israeli relations: it was imperative, if a coalition of Western and Arab powers opposed to Iraq was to be maintained, that Israel should not become actively involved in the conflict. In October some 17 Palestinians were shot dead by Israeli police, following clashes with Jewish worshippers. International outrage at the shootings resulted in a UN Security Council vote to send an investigative mission, although Israel agreed only to receive a UN emissary. Iraqi missile attacks on Israel in January 1991, shortly after the US-led multinational force had begun its offensive against Iraq, threatened the cohesion of the force. US diplomatic efforts, and the installation in Israel of US air defence systems, averted an immediate Israeli response. Meanwhile, widespread support for Iraq among Palestinians increased the Israeli Government's insistence that Shamir's 1989 peace plan could be the only basis for dialogue.

In March 1991 President Bush identified the resolution of the Arab–Israeli conflict as a priority of his Administration. By August intensive diplomacy by Baker had secured the agreement of the Israeli, Syrian, Egyptian, Jordanian and Lebanese Governments, and of Palestinian representatives, to attend a regional peace conference, the terms of reference for which would be a comprehensive peace settlement based on UN Security Council Resolutions 242 and 338. An initial, 'symbolic' session was held in Madrid, Spain, in October. However, subsequent talks soon became deadlocked over procedural issues. Israel repeatedly questioned the status of the Palestinian-Jordanian delegation and the right of the Palestinian component to participate separately in negotiations; furthermore, Israel's refusal to end construction of new settlements in the Occupied Territories continually jeopardized the peace process. In February 1992, immediately prior to the fourth session of peace talks, to be held in Washington, DC, Baker demanded a complete halt to Israel's settlement-building programme as a precondition for the granting of loan guarantees to the value of US $10,000m. for the housing of Jewish immigrants from the former USSR.

A fifth round of negotiations was held in Washington in April 1992. Procedural issues were resolved, and, during talks with the Palestinian component of the Palestinian-Jordanian delegation, Israeli representatives presented proposals for the holding of municipal elections in the West Bank and Gaza, and for the transfer of control of health care provision there to Palestinian authorities. The Palestinian delegation did not reject the proposals outright, although they fell far short of the Palestinians' aim of full legislative control of the Occupied Territories. In May the first multilateral negotiations between the parties to the Middle East peace conference commenced; however, the sessions were boycotted by Syria and Lebanon, considering them futile until progress had been made in the bilateral negotiations. Various combinations of delegations in several cities attended discussions concerning regional economic co-operation, arms control, water resources, environmental issues and Palestinian refugees. Israel boycotted the meetings on Palestinian refugees and regional economic development after the USA approved Palestinian proposals to allow exiles (i.e. non-residents of the Occupied Territories) to be included in the Palestinian delegations to these two sessions.

A general election was held in June 1992, following the collapse of Itzhak Shamir's coalition Government in January. The Labour Party won 44 of the 120 seats in the Knesset, and Likud 32. Meretz—an alliance of Ratz, Shinui and the United Workers' Party, which had won 12 seats—confirmed its willingness to form a coalition administration with Labour. However, even with the support of the two Arab parties—the Democratic Arab Party and Hadash—which together held five seats in the Knesset, such a coalition would have a majority of only two votes over the so-called 'right bloc' (Likud, Tzomet, Moledet and Tehiya) and the religious parties which had allied themselves with Likud in the previous legislature. The new Chairman of the Labour Party, Itzhak Rabin, was accordingly obliged to solicit support among the religious parties. His Government, presented to the Knesset in July, was an alliance of Labour, Meretz and the ultra-Orthodox Shas; the coalition held a total of 62 Knesset seats, and also commanded the unofficial support of the two Arab parties. Most international observers regarded the installation of the Labour-led coalition as having improved the prospects for peace in the Middle East. However, the sixth and seventh rounds of bilateral negotiations between Israeli, Syrian, Lebanese and Palestinian-Jordanian delegations in September–November 1992 failed to achieve any progress.

An eighth round of bilateral negotiations between Israeli and Arab delegations commenced in Washington in December 1992, but were soon overshadowed by events in the Occupied Territories (where there had been violent confrontations between Palestinians and the Israeli security forces), which led to the withdrawal of the Arab participants. In mid-December, in response to the deaths in the Territories of five members of the Israeli security forces, and to the abduction and murder by the Islamic Resistance Movement (Hamas) of an Israeli policeman, the Government ordered the deportation to Lebanon of 413 alleged Palestinian supporters of Hamas. The expulsions provoked international outrage, while the UN Security Council approved Resolution 799 condemning the deportations and demanding the return of the deportees to Israel. Despite threats by the Palestinian delegation to boycott future talks until all of the deportees had been readmitted, in February 1993 the Israeli Government insisted that the majority of the deportees would have to serve a period of exile. Consequently, the ninth round of bilateral negotiations was formally suspended; although the Security Council welcomed the Israeli Government's decision to permit the return of 100 deportees, Palestinian delegates insisted on full implementation of Resolution 799 as a precondition for resumed discussions. In March, amid a sharp escalation in violence between Palestinians and Israeli security forces in the West Bank and Gaza, Israel sealed off the territories indefinitely.

The suspended ninth round of bilateral negotiations in the Middle East peace process resumed in Washington in April 1993. The Palestinian delegation apparently agreed to attend the sessions following pressure by Arab governments, and after Israel had agreed to allow Faisal Husseini, the nominal leader of the Palestinian delegation and a resident of East Jerusalem, to participate. Israel was also reported to have undertaken to halt punitive deportations, and, with the USA, to have reaffirmed its commitment to Resolutions 242 and 338 as the terms of reference for the peace process. In May Ezer Weizman was inaugurated as Israeli President; Weizman, leader of the Yahad party, had been elected by the Knesset in March. Also in March Binyamin Netanyahu was chosen to replace Shamir as the Likud leader.

At the 10th round of bilateral negotiations, convened in Washington in June 1993, the participants agreed to establish a committee charged with the drafting of a statement of principles concerning Palestinian self-rule in the Occupied Territories—now regarded as the key element in the Middle East peace process. In July Israeli armed forces mounted the most intensive air and artillery attacks on targets in Lebanon since 'Operation Peace for Galilee' in 1982, in retaliation for attacks by Hezbollah fighters on settlements in northern Israel.

On 13 September 1993 Israel and the PLO signed a Declaration of Principles on Palestinian Self-Rule in the Occupied Territories. The agreement, which entailed mutual recognition by Israel and the PLO, had been elaborated during a series of secret negotiations mediated by Norwegian diplomacy (and therefore became known as the Oslo accords). The Declaration of Principles established a detailed timetable for Israel's disengagement from the Occupied Territories, and stipulated that a permanent settlement of the Palestinian question should be in place by December 1998. From 13 October 1993 Palestinian authorities were to assume responsibility for education and culture, health, social welfare, direct taxation and tourism in the Gaza Strip and the Jericho area of the West Bank, and a transitional period of Palestinian self-rule was to begin on 13 December. Although Prime Minister Rabin secured ratification of the Declaration of Principles, and of Israel's recognition of the PLO, by the Knesset on 23 September 1993, there was widespread opposition to it from right-wing Israelis. The PLO Central Council, meeting in the Tunisian capital, approved the accord on 11 October. However, the conclusion of the agreement aggravated divisions in the Palestinian liberation movement, while the reaction by the other Arab states engaged in peace negotiations with Israel was mixed.

Also in September 1993 the resignation of Shas leader Aryeh Der'i as Minister of the Interior, following allegations of corruption, provoked the withdrawal from the Government of other Shas ministers, thus reducing the coalition to an alliance between the Labour Party and Meretz (and the Government's majority in the Knesset to only two). Protracted negotiations failed to achieve the return of Shas to the Government and, in July 1994, were superseded by a coalition agreement signed with Yi'ud, a breakaway group from the Tzomet Party.

Itzhak Rabin and Yasser Arafat held their first meeting in the context of the Declaration of Principles in Cairo on 6 October 1993. A joint PLO-Israeli liaison committee subsequently met on 13 October, with delegations headed, respectively, by Mahmud Abbas (Abu Mazen) and Shimon Peres; the committee was to meet frequently to monitor the implementation of the accord. A technical committee also held three meetings during October in the Egyptian resort of Taba: its task was to define the precise details of Israel's military withdrawal from the Gaza Strip and Jericho, scheduled to take place between 13 December 1993 and 13 April 1994. However, it proved impossible satisfactorily to negotiate the details of Israel's withdrawal by December 1993, largely because of a failure to agree on security arrangements for border crossings between the Gaza Strip and Jericho, and Jordan and Egypt.

Following meetings in Damascus between US Secretary of State Warren Christopher and Syria's President Assad and Minister of Foreign Affairs, Farouk ash-Shara', in December 1993, Syria announced its willingness to resume bilateral talks with Israel. In January 1994 Israel appeared to indicate, tentatively, that it might be prepared to execute a full withdrawal from the Golan Heights in return for a comprehensive peace agreement with Syria. Bilateral negotiations between Israeli and Syrian delegations resumed in Washington later that month.

In February 1994 Israel and the PLO reached an agreement to share control of the two future international border crossings.

Security arrangements for Jewish settlers in the Gaza Strip had also reportedly been decided, whereby three access routes to settlements were to remain under Israeli control. Talks followed regarding the implementation of the first stage of Palestinian autonomy in the Gaza Strip and Jericho; the size, structure and jurisdiction of a future Palestinian police force; control of sea and airspace; and the delineation of the Jericho enclave. Meeting in Cairo, on 4 May the two parties signed an accord detailing arrangements for Palestinian self-rule in the Gaza Strip and Jericho. The accord provided for Israel's military withdrawal from these areas, and for the deployment there of a 9,000-strong Palestinian police force. A nominated Palestinian (National) Authority (PA) was to assume the responsibilities of the Israeli military administration in Gaza and Jericho, although Israeli authorities were to retain control in matters of external security and foreign affairs. Elections for a Palestinian Council, which, under the terms of the Oslo accords, were to have taken place in Gaza and the West Bank in July, were now postponed until October. Israel's military withdrawal from Gaza and Jericho was completed on 13 May, and on 17 May the PLO formally assumed control of the Israeli Civil Administration's departments there. On 26–28 May the PA held its inaugural meeting in Tunis, defining a political programme and distributing ministerial portfolios. Arafat made a symbolic return to Gaza City on 1 July—his first visit for 25 years—and the PA was formally inaugurated in Jericho on 5 July. In August Israel and the PLO signed an agreement extending the authority of the PA to include education, health, tourism, social welfare and taxation.

On 25 July 1994 Israel and Jordan signed a joint declaration formally ending the state of war between them and further defining arrangements for future bilateral negotiations. In September Itzhak Rabin announced details of a plan for a partial withdrawal of Israeli armed forces from the occupied Golan Heights, after which a three-year trial period of Israeli-Syrian 'normalization' would ensue. The proposals were rejected by President Assad; however, the Syrian leader did state his willingness to work towards peace with Israel. In late September Rabin and King Hussein held talks in Aqaba, Jordan, with the aim of devising a timetable for a full Israeli-Jordanian peace treaty. Also in that month Morocco, closely followed by Tunisia, became the second and third Arab states to establish diplomatic ties with Israel, and the six members of the Co-operation Council for the Arab States of the Gulf (the Gulf Co-operation Council, see p. 219) also decided to revoke the subsidiary elements of the Arab economic boycott of Israel. On 26 October Israel and Jordan signed a formal peace treaty, defining their common border and providing for a normalization of relations. The peace treaty was denounced by the Syrian Government, all elements of Palestinian opinion and by some Islamists in Jordan.

Meeting in Oslo, Norway, in September 1994, Arafat and Peres negotiated a 15-point agreement aimed at accelerating economic aid to the PA. Later in September Arafat and Rabin met at the Erez crossing-point between Gaza and Israel to discuss the future Palestinian elections in the West Bank and Gaza Strip. Israel rejected Arafat's proposal for elections on 1 November as unrealistic, although it was agreed to meet again in October to negotiate a compromise. At the same time, Arafat pledged to 'take all measures' to prevent attacks on Israeli targets by opponents of the Oslo process. In late September, however, Rabin approved a plan to build some 1,000 new housing units at a Jewish settlement just inside the West Bank, in an apparent reversal of the moratorium he had imposed on construction in 1992. The PLO claimed that this contravened the Declaration of Principles. In early October 1994 an Israeli soldier was abducted by Hamas fighters near Tel-Aviv, who subsequently demanded that Israel release the detained Hamas spiritual leader, Sheikh Ahmad Yassin, and other Palestinian prisoners in exchange for his life. Despite Palestinian action to detain some 300 Hamas members in the Gaza Strip, the kidnapped soldier was killed in the West Bank in mid-October. Shortly afterwards an attack by a Hamas suicide bomber in Tel-Aviv, in which 22 people died, prompted Israel to close its borders with the Palestinian territories.

In November 1994 a member of another militant Palestinian organization, Islamic Jihad, was killed in a car bomb attack in Gaza. The attack was blamed on the Israeli security forces by many Palestinians opposed to the Oslo accords. Three Israeli soldiers were subsequently killed in a suicide bombing in the Gaza Strip, for which Islamic Jihad claimed responsibility. It became clear that Israel's security concerns would continue to delay the redeployment of its armed forces in the West Bank and the holding of Palestinian elections, since Rabin stated, in December, that the elections would either have to take place in the continued presence of Israeli forces or be postponed for a year. In January 1995 a suicide bombing (responsibility for which was again claimed by Islamic Jihad) at Beit Lid, in which 21 Israeli soldiers and civilians died, seriously jeopardized the peace process. The Government again closed Israel's borders with the West Bank and Gaza, and postponed the planned release of some 5,500 Palestinian prisoners. An emergency meeting of the leaders of Egypt, Israel, Jordan and the PLO was convened in Cairo early the following month; the summit's final communiqué condemned acts of terror and violence, and expressed support for the Declaration of Principles and the wider peace process. On 9 February, meanwhile, Israeli armed forces completed their withdrawal from Jordanian territories, in accordance with the bilateral peace treaty concluded in October 1994.

In March 1995 it was announced that Israel and Syria had agreed to resume peace negotiations for the first time since February 1994. In May 1995 the two countries were reported to have concluded a 'framework understanding on security arrangements', intended to facilitate discussions on security issues. Peres subsequently indicated that Israel had proposed that its forces should withdraw from the Golan Heights over a four-year period; Syria, however, had insisted that the withdrawal be effected over 18 months.

Despite intensive negotiations, it proved impossible to conclude an agreement on the expansion of Palestinian self-rule in the West Bank by the target date of 1 July 1995. The principal obstacles remained the question of precisely to where Israeli troops in the West Bank would redeploy, and the exact nature of security arrangements for some 130,000 Jewish settlers who were to remain there. On 28 September the Israeli-Palestinian Interim Agreement on the West Bank and the Gaza Strip was finally signed by Israel and the PLO. Its main provisions were the withdrawal of Israeli armed forces from a further six West Bank towns (Nablus, Ramallah, Jenin, Tulkaram, Qalqilya and Bethlehem) and a partial redeployment from the town of Hebron; national Palestinian legislative elections to an 82-member Palestinian Council and for a Palestinian Executive President; and the release, in three phases, of Palestinians detained by Israel. In anticipation of a violent reaction against the Interim Agreement by so-called 'rejectionist' groups within the Occupied Territories, Israel immediately sealed its borders with the West Bank and Gaza. Meanwhile, right-wing elements within Israel also denounced the agreement.

On 4 November 1995 Itzhak Rabin was assassinated in Tel-Aviv by a Jewish student opposed to the peace process, in particular the Israeli withdrawal from the West Bank. The assassination caused a further marginalization of those on the extreme right wing of Israeli politics who had advocated violence as a means of halting the Oslo process, and provoked criticism of the opposition Likud, which, it was widely felt, had not sufficiently distanced itself from such extremist elements. The Minister of Foreign Affairs, Shimon Peres, was, with the agreement of Likud, invited to form a new government. The members of the outgoing administration—Labour, Meretz and Yi'ud—subsequently signed a new coalition agreement, and the Cabinet was formally approved by the Knesset in late November. In February 1996 Peres announced that elections to the Knesset and, for the first time, the direct election of the Prime Minister would take place in May 1996.

In spite of Rabin's assassination, Israeli armed forces completed their withdrawal from the West Bank town of Jenin on 13 November 1995, and in December they withdrew from Tulkaram, Nablus, Qalqilya, Bethlehem and Ramallah. With regard to Hebron, Israel and the PA signed an agreement transferring jurisdiction in some 17 areas of civilian affairs from Israel to the PA. At talks with Arafat at Erez in December, Peres confirmed that Israel would release some 1,000 Palestinian prisoners before the impending Palestinian elections.

Peace negotiations between Israel and Syria resumed in December 1995 in Maryland, USA, followed by a second round in January 1996. Also in January King Hussein made a public visit to Tel-Aviv, during which Israel and Jordan signed a number of agreements relating to the normalization of economic and cultural relations.

Palestinian legislative and presidential elections were held in late January 1996, leading in principle to the final stage of the peace process, when Palestinian and Israeli negotiators would address such issues as Jerusalem, the rights of Palestinian refugees and the status of Jewish settlements in the Palestinian territories. In February and March, however, more than 50 Israelis died as a result of suicide bomb attacks in Jerusalem, Ashkelon and Tel-Aviv, and talks were suspended. Israel again ordered the indefinite closure of its borders with the Palestinian territories, and demanded that the PA suppress the activities of Hamas and Islamic Jihad in the areas under its control. A hitherto unknown group, the 'Yahya Ayyash Units', claimed responsibility for the attacks, to avenge the assassination—allegedly by Israeli agents—of Ayyash, a leading Hamas activist, in January 1996. Yasser Arafat, now the elected Palestinian President, condemned the bombings, and in late February more than 200 members of Hamas were detained by Palestinian security forces. Following the attacks, Israel asserted the right of its armed forces to enter PA-controlled areas when Israeli security was at stake. Furthermore, an agreement to redeploy troops from Hebron by 20 March was rescinded.

The suicide bombings also undermined the talks taking place between Israeli and Syrian representatives in the USA, and in March 1996 the Israeli negotiators returned home. Syria and Lebanon both declined an invitation to attend the so-called 'Summit of Peacemakers', held at the Egyptian resort of Sharm esh-Sheikh in that month, at which some 27 heads of state expressed their support for the Middle East peace process and pledged to redouble their efforts to combat terrorism. In April Israel and Turkey signed a number of military co-operation agreements, a development condemned by Syria as a threat to its own security and to that of all Arab and Islamic countries.

In April 1996 Israeli armed forces began a sustained campaign of intense air and artillery attacks on alleged Hezbollah positions in southern Lebanon and the southern suburbs of Beirut. The declared aim of the Israeli operation (code-named 'Grapes of Wrath') was to achieve the complete cessation of rocket attacks by Hezbollah on settlements in northern Israel. Some 400,000 Lebanese were displaced northwards, after the Israeli military authorities warned that they would be endangered by the offensive against Hezbollah. Moreover, the shelling by Israeli forces of a base of the UN peace-keeping force at Qana resulted in the deaths of more than 100 Lebanese civilians who had been sheltering there, and of four UN peace-keepers. A cease-fire 'understanding' took effect in late April; this was effectively a compromise confining the conflict to the area of the security zone in southern Lebanon, recognizing both Hezbollah's right to resist Israeli occupation and Israel's right to self-defence; the 'understanding' also envisaged the establishment of an Israel-Lebanon Monitoring Group (ILMG), comprising Israel, Lebanon, Syria, France and the USA, to supervise the cease-fire.

Israel welcomed the decision of the Palestine National Council (PNC) in late April 1996 to amend the Palestinian National Charter (or PLO Covenant), removing all clauses demanding the destruction of Israel: the Israeli Government had demanded that the Covenant be amended as a precondition for participation in the final stage of peace negotiations with the PLO.

No party gained an outright majority of the 120 seats in the elections to the Knesset, held on 19 May 1996, but the Likud leader, Binyamin Netanyahu, achieved a marginal victory over Peres in the direct election for the Prime Minister. Prior to the legislative election a formal alliance between Likud, the Tzomet Party and Gesher had been announced. This alliance secured 32 seats, and Labour 34. The success of the ultra-Orthodox Shas and the National Religious Party (NRP), with 10 seats and nine, respectively, was the key factor in determining that the new Government would be formed by Likud. Netanyahu proceeded to sign agreements between the Likud alliance and Shas, the NRP, Israel B'Aliyah, United Torah Judaism and the Third Way, to form a coalition that would command the support of 66 deputies in the Knesset. The new Government's statement of policy excluded the possibility of granting Palestinian statehood or, with regard to Syria, of relinquishing de facto sovereignty of the occupied Golan Heights. Moreover, Netanyahu reportedly postponed further discussion of the withdrawal of Israeli armed forces from the West Bank town of Hebron—where they provided security for some 400 Jewish settlers—and refused to meet the Palestinian President. In late June a summit meeting of all Arab leaders (with the exception of Iraq) was convened in Cairo. The meeting's final communiqué reiterated Israel's withdrawal from all occupied territories (including East Jerusalem) as a basic requirement for a comprehensive Middle East peace settlement. However, in July the likely stance of the new Government was underlined by the incorporation into the Cabinet, as Minister of Infrastructure, of Ariel Sharon—who had played a leading role in the creation and expansion of Jewish settlements in the West Bank. Netanyahu and Arafat did in fact meet in September, at the Erez crossing-point, when they confirmed their commitment to the implementation of the Interim Agreement.

In September 1996 it was announced that Israel's Ministry of Defence had approved plans to construct some 1,800 new homes at existing Jewish settlements in the West Bank, causing many observers to conclude that the new Israeli Government had effectively halted the peace process by either abandoning or postponing many of the commitments inherited from its predecessor. Violent confrontations erupted between Palestinian security forces and civilians and the Israeli armed forces, in which at least 50 Palestinians and 18 Israelis were killed. The direct cause of the disturbances was attributed to the decision of the Israeli Government to open the north end of the Hasmonean tunnel running beneath the al-Aqsa Mosque in Jerusalem, although it appeared to be the inevitable culmination of Palestinian frustration at Israel's failure to implement agreements previously signed with the PA. The Israeli military authorities declared a state of emergency in the Gaza Strip and the West Bank. A special session of the UN Security Council was convened, and intense international diplomacy facilitated a crisis summit in Washington hosted by US President Bill Clinton and attended by Netanyahu, Arafat and King Hussein of Jordan. In October Israel agreed to resume negotiations on the partial withdrawal of its armed forces from Hebron. Netanyahu subsequently stated that once this issue had been settled Israel would reopen its borders with the West Bank and Gaza—which had remained closed since February—and move quickly towards seeking a final settlement with the Palestinians.

In January 1997 Israel and the PA finally concluded an agreement on the withdrawal of Israeli armed forces from Hebron. The principal terms of the accord were that Israeli forces should withdraw from 80% of the town within 10 days, and that the first of three subsequent redeployments from the West Bank should take place six weeks after the signing of the agreement, and the remaining two by August 1998. The 'final status' negotiations on borders, the Jerusalem issue, Jewish settlements and Palestinian refugees were to commence within two months. As guarantor of the Hebron agreement, the USA undertook to obtain the release of Palestinian prisoners, and to ensure that Israel continued to engage in negotiations for a Palestinian airport in the Gaza Strip and on safe passage for Palestinians between the West Bank and Gaza. The USA also undertook to ensure that the PA would continue to combat terrorism, complete the revision of the Palestinian National Charter and consider Israeli requests to extradite Palestinians suspected of involvement in attacks in Israel.

Progress achieved through the agreement on Hebron was severely undermined in February 1997, when Israel announced that it was to proceed with the construction of 6,500 housing units at Har Homa (Jabal Abu Ghunaim in Arabic) in East Jerusalem. Tensions escalated in the following month, after Israel decided unilaterally to withdraw its armed forces from only 9% of the West Bank. Arafat denounced the decision and King Hussein accused Netanyahu of intentionally destroying the peace process. Increasing anti-Israeli sentiment reportedly motivated a Jordanian soldier to murder seven Israeli schoolgirls in Nayarim, an enclave between Israel and Jordan. Israeli intransigence over the Har Homa settlement prompted Palestinians to abandon the 'final status' talks, scheduled to begin on 17 March, and on the following day construction at the site began. Riots among Palestinians erupted immediately, and shortly afterwards Hamas carried out a bomb attack in Tel-Aviv, killing four people. In late March the League of Arab States (the Arab League, see p. 332) voted to resume its economic boycott of Israel, suspend moves to establish diplomatic relations and withdraw from multilateral peace talks. (Jordan, the PA and Egypt were excluded from the resolution, owing to their binding bilateral agreements with Israel.)

In June 1997 the US House of Representatives voted in favour of recognizing Jerusalem as the undivided capital of Israel and of transferring the US embassy there, from Tel-Aviv. The decision coincided with violent clashes between Palestinian civilians and Israeli troops in both Gaza and Hebron. In the same month Ehud Barak, a former government minister and army chief of staff, was elected to replace Peres as Labour Party Chairman.

In July 1997 the USA brokered an agreement between Israel and the PA to resume peace talks the following month. At the end of July, however, on the eve of a planned visit to Israel by the USA's chief Middle East negotiator, Dennis Ross, two Hamas suicide bombers killed 14 civilians in Jerusalem. Ross cancelled his visit and Israel suspended payment of tax revenues to the PA and again closed off the Gaza Strip and the West Bank. Further suicide bombings in West Jerusalem in early September resulted in eight deaths. Following a visit by US Secretary of State Madeleine Albright in mid-September, Israel released further Palestinian assets (one-third of tax revenues owed to the PA had been released in August), while the Palestinians announced the closure of 17 institutions affiliated to Hamas. In October Israel announced plans to release further dues to the PA and to reopen the sealed borders. However, Netanyahu stated that further redeployments would not take place until Palestinians made further efforts to combat terrorism.

Renewed hostilities erupted in northern Israel in August 1997 after Hezbollah launched a rocket attack on civilians in Kiryat Shmona. The attack, made in retaliation for raids by Israeli commandos in which five Hezbollah members were killed, prompted further air-strikes by Israel in southern Lebanon. Violence escalated, with the shelling by the SLA of the Lebanese port of Sidon resulting in at least six deaths. Domestic pressure for an Israeli withdrawal from southern Lebanon increased after 12 Israeli marines, allegedly on a mission to assassinate Shi'ite leaders, were killed south of Sidon in September. Meanwhile, relations between Jordan and Israel deteriorated, after members of the Israeli intelligence force, Mossad, attempted to assassinate Hamas's political leader, Khalid Meshaal, in Amman. Following intensive negotiations between Netanyahu, Crown Prince Hassan of Jordan and US officials, several agreements regarding the release of prisoners ensued: in October Israel freed the Hamas spiritual leader, Sheikh Ahmad Yassin, in return for the release by Jordan of two Mossad agents arrested in connection with the attack on Meshaal; a further 12 Mossad agents were expelled by the Jordanian authorities following the release of 23 Jordanian and 50 Palestinian prisoners by Israel.

Bilateral negotiations between Israel and the PA resumed in November 1997. Israel offered to decelerate its construction of Jewish settlements in return for Palestinian approval of a plan to delay further redeployments of Israeli troops from the West Bank. At the same time, the Israeli Government announced plans to build 900 new housing units in the area. This prompted several Arab states to boycott the Middle East and North Africa economic conference, held in Doha, Qatar, in mid-November, which an Israeli delegation was scheduled to attend. At the end of November the Israeli Cabinet agreed in principle to a partial withdrawal from the West Bank, but specified neither its timing nor its scale. Conflicting opinions within the Cabinet meant that Netanyahu failed to produce a conclusive redeployment plan to present at talks with Albright in Paris in December. Divisions within the coalition Government in late 1997 obliged Netanyahu to grant concessions to right-wing members of the coalition. In January 1998 David Levy, the Gesher leader, withdrew from the Government, citing dissatisfaction with the budget and with the slow rate of progress in the peace talks. Gesher's departure reduced Netanyahu's majority to only two votes, although the budget secured the approval of the Knesset, and Netanyahu subsequently survived a vote of no confidence. Meanwhile, Netanyahu announced that he would not make any further decisions regarding the peace process until the Palestinians had demonstrated further efforts to combat terrorism, reduced their security forces from 40,000 to 24,000 and amended their National Charter to recognize Israel's right to exist. The Israeli premier again failed to present a plan of redeployment in talks with President Clinton in Washington. Netanyahu did express interest in a US proposal to withdraw troops from at least 10% of the land in several stages, but this was decisively rejected by Arafat. In February Arafat also rejected Netanyahu's appeals for a peace summit, stating that he would hold talks only after Israel had agreed to further redeployment and had fully implemented existing agreements.

Addressing the Knesset in March 1998, UN Secretary-General Kofi Annan urged Israel to end 'provocative acts' towards the Palestinians, including the building of Jewish settlements. Meanwhile, Dennis Ross visited the region, briefing Netanyahu, Arafat and Egypt's President Mubarak on a US peace proposal whereby Israel would redeploy from 13.1% of the West Bank over a 12-week period in exchange for specific security guarantees from the Palestinians. (Israel, however, reportedly agreed only to a phased redeployment from 9% of the territory.) In April Netanyahu and President Mubarak held their first meeting (in Cairo) since May 1997, during which President Mubarak reportedly advised Netanyahu to 'respond positively' to the US peace initiative. However, the Israeli Prime Minister rejected the proposal, which was publicly accepted by Arafat the following day. In May 1998 US Secretary of State Albright conducted separate rounds of talks with Netanyahu and Arafat in London, United Kingdom, and later in Washington, with the aim of reviving negotiations on redeployments; the talks failed to achieve a breakthrough. Meanwhile, celebrations to commemorate the 50th anniversary of the founding of the State of Israel provoked widespread rioting in the Occupied Territories.

Details of the US peace plan were published in the Israeli newspaper *Ha'aretz* in June 1998. Although several Jewish settler groups threatened a campaign of civil disobedience in protest at any further redeployments from the West Bank, it became apparent that Netanyahu was under increasing pressure to accept the US initiative. In late June President Weizman (who had been elected for a second presidential term in March) angered Netanyahu by publicly demanding the dissolution of the Knesset and early elections so that Israelis might choose the future direction of peace talks. Meanwhile, further controversy arose when the Cabinet approved Netanyahu's draft plan whereby the municipal boundaries of Jerusalem would be extended to incorporate seven West Bank Jewish settlements—to create a 'Greater Jerusalem' covering six times the current area of the city. Arab leaders accused Netanyahu of seeking formally to annex parts of the West Bank, and the UN Security Council urged Israel to abandon the proposals.

On 23 October 1998, after nine days of intensive talks with President Clinton at the Wye Plantation, Maryland, Netanyahu and Arafat signed an agreement (the Wye River Memorandum) that outlined a three-month timetable for the implementation of the 1995 Interim Agreement and signalled the commencement of 'final status' talks, which should have begun in May 1996. With the mediation of Clinton and King Hussein of Jordan, Israel agreed to redeploy its troops from 13.1% of the West Bank, while the PA agreed to intensify measures to prevent terrorism and to rewrite the Palestinian National Charter. On 11 November 1998, after the postponement of four scheduled meetings (due to a bombing by Islamic Jihad in Jerusalem and Israeli fears of further terrorist attacks), the Israeli Cabinet approved the Wye Memorandum by a majority of eight votes to four. Netanyahu subsequently reiterated that a number of conditions would first have to be met by the Palestinians, and threatened effective Israeli annexation of areas of the West Bank if a Palestinian state were to be declared on 4 May 1999. (Arafat continued to reassert his right to declare a Palestinian state on the expiry date of the interim stage defined in Oslo, an act Netanyahu claimed would fundamentally violate the Oslo accords.) On 17 November 1998 the Knesset ratified the Wye Memorandum by 75 votes to 19. Three days later the Israeli Government implemented the first stage of renewed redeployment from the West Bank, also releasing 250 Palestinian prisoners and signing a protocol allowing for the opening of an international airport at Gaza.

During December 1998 it became increasingly evident that divisions within Netanyahu's coalition over implementation of the Wye Memorandum were making government untenable. The administration effectively collapsed when the Minister of Finance, Yaacov Ne'eman, announced his resignation. Shortly afterwards the Knesset voted to hold elections to the legislature and premiership in the spring of 1999. In January 1999 Netanyahu dismissed Itzhak Mordechai as Minister of Defence, appointing Moshe Arens in his place. Speculation that Mordechai had been intending to leave Likud was apparently confirmed when he launched the new Centre Party.

In December 1998 President Clinton attended a session of the PNC, at which the removal from the Palestinian National Charter of all clauses seeking Israel's destruction was reaffirmed. Following a meeting between Clinton, Arafat and Netanyahu at the Erez checkpoint, Netanyahu reiterated accusations that the Palestinians had not adequately addressed their security commitments and announced that he would not release Palestinian prisoners considered to have 'blood on their hands'. Netanyahu announced that the second phase of Israeli troop deployment envisaged by the Wye Memorandum, scheduled for 18 December, would not be undertaken. The Knesset subsequently voted to suspend implementation of the Wye Memorandum, thereby effectively suspending the peace process. In late December Arafat freed the Hamas spiritual leader, Sheikh Ahmad Yassin, from house arrest, prompting further Israeli claims that agreed anti-terrorism measures were not being implemented. In January 1999 it was reported that the US Secretary of State would refuse to meet Ariel Sharon (redesignated the Minister of Foreign Affairs and National Infrastructure in October 1998) during a visit to the USA, owing to US frustration with Israel's freezing of peace negotiations. The US Administration threatened to withhold US $1,200m. promised to Israel to fund its redeployment in the West Bank unless it complied with the terms of the Wye Memorandum. For several months President Clinton refused to hold a private meeting with Netanyahu, while agreeing to meet Arafat in March to discuss his threatened unilateral declaration of statehood on 4 May; following intense international pressure, the declaration was postponed at the end of April.

In 1998 the conclusion of several bilateral trade agreements indicated an improvement in Israeli-Jordanian relations. In April King Hussein and the Israeli Prime Minister met for the first time since the assassination attempt which had strained relations in 1997. In December 1998 Israel agreed to allow foreign airlines en route to Jordan to use Israeli airspace. There was widespread apprehension about the future of Israel's relations with Jordan following the death, in February 1999, of King Hussein (whose funeral was attended by Netanyahu). Nevertheless, the Israeli Government expected 'continuity' in bilateral relations under Jordan's new King Abdullah, and in September Israel commended the Jordanian authorities for their arrest of Khalid Meshaal and two other Hamas leaders.

Hostilities between Israeli forces and Hezbollah in southern Lebanon persisted throughout 1998. In that year some 23 Israeli soldiers were killed, and there was increasing pressure on Netanyahu, even from some Likud ministers, for a unilateral withdrawal from the territory. On 1 April the Israeli Security Cabinet voted unanimously to adopt UN Resolution 425 (which called for an immediate withdrawal of Israeli troops from all Lebanese territory), provided that the Lebanese army gave security guarantees. However, both Lebanon and Syria demanded an unconditional withdrawal. In June the first Israeli-Lebanese exchange of prisoners and bodies since July 1996 took place. Fighting escalated when, in August 1998, Hezbollah launched rocket attacks on northern Israel in retaliation for an Israeli helicopter attack in which a senior Lebanese military official died. Seven Israeli soldiers died in two attacks in November, leading Netanyahu to curtail a European tour in order to hold an emergency cabinet meeting on a possible withdrawal. In December an Israeli air attack in which eight Lebanese civilians were killed provoked condemnation from the ILMG, which declared it to be a violation of the cease-fire 'understanding' reached in April 1996. Following several Hezbollah attacks, in January 1999 Netanyahu reiterated previous warnings that in the event of further attacks, Israeli troops would target Lebanese infrastructure. In February the commander of the Israeli army unit for liaison with the SLA became the most senior Israeli officer to be killed in southern Lebanon since 1982. Israel responded with its heaviest air raids against Lebanon since the 1996 'Grapes of Wrath' operation, prompting fears of another major conflict.

By the time of the general election, held on 17 May 1999, Netanyahu and Ehud Barak were the only remaining candidates for the premiership. Barak was elected Prime Minister with 56.1% of the total votes cast. In the elections to the Knesset, Barak's One Israel alliance (including Gesher and the moderate Meimad) secured 26 seats, while Likud's strength declined from 32 seats to 19. Shas, meanwhile, increased its representation to 17 seats. The new Knesset contained an unprecedented 15 factions. Netanyahu subsequently resigned from both the Knesset and the Likud leadership, and in September Ariel Sharon was elected as Likud's new Chairman. Although Barak had received a clear mandate to form a government that would attempt to revive the stalled Middle East peace process, Israel's Prime Minister-elect committed himself only to seek a formula for regional peace. Barak stated that he would observe four 'security red lines' concerning negotiations with the Palestinians: Jerusalem would remain under Israeli sovereignty; there would be no return to the pre-1967 borders; most West Bank settlers would remain in settlements under Israeli sovereignty; and no 'foreign armies' would be based west of the Jordan river. Following complex negotiations, Barak forged a broad coalition of the Centre Party, Shas, Meretz, Israel B'Aliyah and the NRP, which was endorsed by the Knesset in early July 1999. Barak himself took the defence portfolio, while David Levy became the Minister of Foreign Affairs and Shimon Peres the Minister of Regional Co-operation. In the same month the Speaker of the Palestinian Legislative Council (PLC) became the first senior Palestinian official to address the Knesset.

In early September 1999, during a visit to the region by US Secretary of State Albright, Barak and Arafat travelled to Egypt for talks at Sharm esh-Sheikh. On 4 September the two leaders signed the Sharm esh-Sheikh Memorandum (or Wye Two accords), which outlined a revised timetable for implementation of the outstanding provisions of the original Wye Memorandum in order to facilitate the resumption of 'final status' talks: a new target date—13 September 2000—was set for the conclusion of a comprehensive 'final status' settlement, with a framework agreement to be in place by 13 February. (One important change was the reduction, to 350, of the number of Palestinian prisoners to be released by Israel.) On 8 September the Knesset ratified the Wye Two accords; the following day Israel released some 200 Palestinian prisoners, and on 10 September a further 7% of the West Bank was transferred to Palestinian civilian control. A ceremony marking the launch of 'final status' negotiations between Israel and the PA was held at the Erez checkpoint on 13 September, and a few days later it was reported that Barak and Arafat had held a secret meeting to discuss an agenda for such talks. Meanwhile, Israel signed an agreement with the USA to purchase 50 F-16 fighter aircraft. A further 151 Palestinian prisoners were released from Israeli custody in mid-October. On 25 October a southern 'safe passage' for Palestinians travelling between Gaza and Hebron was finally opened, under the terms of the Wye Memorandum. In late 1999 Barak encountered severe criticism by left-wing groups and Palestinians over his Government's apparent intention to continue to approve the expansion of Jewish settlements in the West Bank. (Since coming to power, the Government had issued tenders for some 2,600 new homes in such settlements.) Barak subsequently angered settler groups with a ruling that several of the 42 'outpost settlements' established in the West Bank under the Likud Government had been built illegally; 12 of the 'outposts' were dismantled in October.

Mauritania became the third member of the Arab League (after Egypt and Jordan) to establish full diplomatic relations with Israel in October 1999. Representatives of Israel and the PA commenced talks on 'final status' issues on 8 November in the West Bank city of Ramallah, and further rounds of discussions were held during November and December. The redeployment of Israeli armed forces from a further 5% of the West Bank (due on 15 November) was delayed owing to a dispute over which areas were to be transferred. In December Barak and Arafat met on Palestinian territory for the first time. At the end of the month Israel released some 26 Palestinian 'security' prisoners as a 'goodwill' gesture.

On 6–7 January 2000 Israeli troops withdrew from a further 5% of the West Bank. However, Israel subsequently announced the postponement of a third redeployment, agreed under Wye Two (and scheduled for 20 January), until Barak had returned from talks with Syrian representatives in the USA (see below). In early February PA officials suspended peace negotiations with Israel, following the decision by the Israeli Cabinet to withdraw its armed forces from a sparsely populated 6.1% of the West Bank. The redeployment from a further 6.1% of the West Bank took place on 21 March (Israel had on the previous day released 15 Palestinian prisoners), facilitating an official resumption of 'final status' talks. In that month a ruling by Israel's Supreme Court that the allocation of state-owned land on the basis of religion, nationality or ethnicity was illegal allowed Israeli Arabs to purchase land for the first time.

Meanwhile, in May 1999 senior Israeli commanders in southern Lebanon for the first time urged an immediate Israeli withdrawal. (Prime Minister-elect Barak had made a pre-election pledge to recall Israeli troops from Lebanon by July 2000.) In June 1999 the SLA completed a unilateral withdrawal from the Jezzine enclave. Later that month Barak was reportedly angered when the outgoing Netanyahu administration launched a series of air attacks on Beirut, destroying Beirut's main power station and other infrastructure, in response to Hezbollah rocket attacks on northern Israel. Barak confirmed in July that he would propose to his Cabinet a unilateral withdrawal from Lebanon if no peace accord had been reached (in the context of an agreement with Syria over the Golan Heights) within one year. In December Israel and Syria reached an 'understanding in principle' to limit the fighting in southern Lebanon; the informal cease-fire did not endure, however, and in January 2000 a senior SLA commander became the first Israeli soldier to be killed there for five months. At the end of January the deaths of another three of its soldiers led Israel to declare that peace talks with Syria would not resume until Syria took action to restrain Hezbollah, but attacks by the militant Shi'ite group continued, and in

February Israel retaliated with a massive series of bombing raids on Lebanese infrastructure. Israel announced a unilateral withdrawal from the 1996 'cease-fire' agreement, and there were renewed fears of a major conflict. Following the killing of three Israeli soldiers by Hezbollah in the same month, the Israeli Security Cabinet approved wide powers for the Prime Minister to order immediate retaliatory bombing raids into Lebanon.

Two senior political figures were embroiled in scandal in early 2000. In April the Israeli President, Ezer Weizman, was informed that, owing to insufficient evidence, he would not be prosecuted for accepting some US $450,000 in undeclared donations from a French businessman while serving as a member of the Knesset. However, the police investigation failed completely to exonerate him, and he stated in May that he would resign on 10 July. Meanwhile, in May Itzhak Mordechai, the Deputy Prime Minister and Minister of Transport, was arraigned on three charges of sexual harassment, leading to his resignation as leader of the Centre Party. In March 2001 he was found guilty of committing indecent assault against two women and was awarded an 18-month suspended sentence.

A third round of 'final status' discussions opened in Eilat on 30 April 2000, but maps presented by Israeli officials to the PA in early May, defining Barak's interpretation of a future Palestinian state, were firmly rejected by the Palestinians. Two days later Barak and Arafat held a crisis meeting in Ramallah, at which Barak proposed that Israel transfer to full PA control three Arab villages situated close to Jerusalem, on condition that the third West Bank redeployment (scheduled for June) was postponed until after the conclusion of a final peace settlement. The Knesset approved the transfer in mid-May. However, Barak later announced that an Israeli withdrawal from the Arab villages would not be implemented until the PA took appropriate measures to curb unrest in the West Bank, where Palestinians had been protesting in support of gaoled Palestinians on hunger strike.

In June 2000 the right-wing Shas, One Israel's largest coalition partner, threatened to withdraw from the Government unless its demands regarding the peace process and the funding of its religious schools were met. After Barak capitulated to most of the party's demands, the four Shas ministers withdrew their resignations, thereby averting the collapse of the coalition; however, the return of Shas to the Government led to the departure of the two Meretz ministers, who were both strong supporters of the Oslo peace process. In early July, in advance of a US-brokered summit aimed at reaching a framework agreement for a final settlement, the three right-wing parties (Israel B'Aliyah, the NRP and Shas) withdrew from the coalition in protest at what they perceived to be Barak's willingness to concede to PA territorial claims. Yet despite the loss of six ministers, Barak survived a motion of no confidence in the Knesset.

President Clinton opened the Camp David talks on 11 July 2000, and, although no accord had been reached by their scheduled close on 19 July, he persuaded Israeli and Palestinian negotiators to remain at Camp David. However, despite intensive mediation efforts, the summit ended on 25 July without agreement. Progess had reportedly been made on the issues of the borders of a future Palestinian entity (to comprise all of the Gaza Strip and at least 90% of the West Bank) and the status of Palestinian refugees, but the two sides were unable to reach a compromise regarding the future status of Jerusalem. Barak had apparently offered the PA municipal authority over certain parts of East Jerusalem and access to Islamic holy sites in the Old City, although Israel would retain full sovereignty. Arafat, meanwhile, had continued to demand a Palestinian state with East Jerusalem as its capital and sovereignty over the Islamic holy sites. In the summit's final communiqué both sides vowed to continue the pursuit of a 'final status' settlement and to avoid 'unilateral actions'—thereby implying that Arafat would not declare a Palestinian state on 13 September. (Shortly before that date the Palestinian legislature voted to delay such a declaration for an indefinite period.)

In the presidential election held on 31 July 2000, the little-known Moshe Katsav of Likud unexpectedly secured a narrow defeat over Barak's nominee, Shimon Peres. Katsav was duly sworn in as the eighth President of Israel on 1 August, to serve an exceptional seven-year term. Immediately after the election Barak survived another no confidence motion. However, in early August the Minister of Foreign Affairs, David Levy, announced his resignation, citing disagreements with Barak over the peace process. The Minister of Public Security, Shlomo Ben-Ami, was subsequently appointed acting Minister of Foreign Affairs, and was confirmed in the post in November.

In late September 2000 Barak and Arafat met, at the Israeli premier's home, for the first time since the Camp David summit. Yet the resumption of contacts was swiftly overshadowed by the escalation of what became known as the al-Aqsa *intifada*, a renewed uprising by Palestinians against Israeli occupation which resulted in the suspension of the Middle East peace process. On 28 September Likud leader Ariel Sharon made a highly controversial visit to the Temple Mount/Haram ash-Sharif compound in Jerusalem (the site of the Dome of the Rock and the al-Aqsa Mosque), provoking protests by stone-throwing Palestinians which in turn triggered violent unrest throughout the Palestinian territories. For the first time Israeli Arabs clashed with security forces within Israel, and the uncompromising response of the Israeli security forces to the uprising attracted international criticism. On 7 October the UN Security Council issued a resolution condemning the 'excessive use of force' employed by Israeli security forces against Palestinian demonstrators. Israel closed the borders of the Palestinian territories and Gaza airport, and Barak emphasized to Arafat his intention to suspend the peace process if the Palestinian unrest continued, demanding that Arafat re-arrest about 60 militant Islamists who had recently been freed from Palestinian detention. Arafat, for his part, demanded an international inquiry into the causes of the violence.

The crisis escalated in mid-October 2000 after Israeli forces launched rocket attacks on the headquarters of Arafat's Fatah movement in Ramallah and other PA offices, in response to the murders of two Israeli army reservists by a Palestinian crowd. On 16–17 October an emergency summit meeting between Barak and Arafat was convened by President Clinton and hosted by President Mubarak at Sharm esh-Sheikh, at which the Israelis and Palestinians agreed what the US President termed 'immediate concrete measures' to end the fighting (including the formation of an international fact-finding commission to investigate the causes of the conflict). However, violence intensified, and on 22 October Barak announced that Israel was to take a 'time-out' from the peace process. This declaration came as Barak undertook discussions with Likud on the formation of a national unity government prior to the reconvening of the Knesset for the new parliamentary term; but no compromise was reached, reportedly owing to Ariel Sharon's demand for a veto on all decisions relating to national security. Barak's decision formally to suspend Israel's participation in the peace process was precipitated by the final communiqué issued by Arab leaders after an emergency summit of the Arab League held in Cairo on 21–22 October, declaring that Israel bore full responsibility for the recent violence. Morocco, Tunisia and Oman announced that they had severed diplomatic relations with Israel, and Qatar broke off ties in November.

A suicide bomb attack perpetrated by Islamic Jihad on an Israeli military target in Gaza at the end of October 2000 apparently signalled a new campaign of violence by militant Palestinian organizations, and led the Israeli army to declare a new strategy of targeting for assassination the leaders of such groups, as well as senior Fatah commanders, whom it held responsible for 'terrorist' actions. (Israeli officials referred to this new policy as 'initiated attacks' or 'targeted killings'.) In early November the Israeli Minister of Regional Co-operation, Shimon Peres, held crisis talks with Arafat in Gaza, at which the two sides agreed a fragile 'cease-fire' based on the provisions agreed the previous month at Sharm esh-Sheikh. The truce was broken almost immediately, however, when a car bomb planted by Islamic Jihad exploded in Jerusalem, killing two Israelis; Barak held the PA responsible for the attack through the recent release of dozens of Islamist militants. Arafat, meanwhile, requested US support in his appeal to the UN to provide an international peace-keeping force to protect Palestinians in the Occupied Territories. In mid-November Israel effectively imposed a complete economic blockade of the Palestinian areas, in an effort to overcome increasing concerns over its national security. Later in the month the explosion of a bomb close to a bus carrying Israeli schoolchildren (as a result of which two people died and several children were injured) provoked public outrage and led Israel to launch further air raids against Fatah targets in Gaza. Egypt responded by announcing that it was recalling its ambassador from Tel-Aviv, and in April 2002 suspended all direct contact with the Israeli Government other than for negotiations aimed at restoring peace in the region. (Egypt did not return an ambassador to Israel until March 2005.)

Meanwhile, in early December 2000 a US-led investigative committee—the Sharm esh-Sheikh Fact-Finding Committee or Mitchell Committee (its Chairman was a former US senator, George Mitchell)—began conducting its research into the Israeli–Palestinian violence, which by now increasingly involved fighting between Jewish settlers and Palestinians in the West Bank and Gaza. It was reported at the end of November that the PA had rejected a partial peace plan put forward by Barak, whereby Israel would effect further troop redeployments from the West Bank in exchange for a postponement of discussions concerning the remaining 'final status' issues.

At the end of November 2000 Barak had unexpectedly called early prime ministerial elections for 2001, in an apparent attempt to secure his increasingly beleaguered Government. The Likud leader, Ariel Sharon, immediately declared his candidacy for the premiership, as did Netanyahu (although he later withdrew his candidacy). The premiership election, held on 6 February 2001, resulted in an overwhelming victory for Sharon, with 62.4% of the votes cast; the rate of participation was 62.3% of registered voters. Barak had lost the Israeli Arab vote—as the Arab parties had urged their supporters to boycott or abstain in the poll—and his defeat was interpreted as a decisive rejection of the Oslo peace process by the majority of Israelis. Sharon, whose principal election pledge had been the restoration of domestic and regional stability, immediately sought the formation of a broadly based government of national unity, essentially in an effort to secure a political base in the Knesset (where Likud held only 19 of the 120 seats). Following his defeat, Barak had announced his resignation as Labour leader, leaving the party in disarray. Barak later declared that he would not enter a government under Sharon and was to withdraw from political life 'for some time'. In late February Labour's Central Committee voted to join a coalition administration, despite objections from prominent members of the party. This enabled Sharon to conclude coalition agreements principally with the religious and right-wing parties, and the national unity Government was approved by the Knesset in early March. The 26-member Cabinet (reportedly the largest in Israel's history) included the ultra-Orthodox Shas (whose leader, Eliyahu Yishai, became Deputy Prime Minister and Minister of the Interior), Israel B'Aliyah (Natan Sharansky was named as Deputy Prime Minister and Minister of Construction and Housing) and the extreme right-wing National Union-Israel Beytenu bloc.

While Israel's new Minister of Defence, Binyamin Ben-Eliezer of the Labour Party, was known for his uncompromising stance, the appointment of Shimon Peres as Deputy Prime Minister and Minister of Foreign Affairs was a cause for cautious optimism for those who wished to see a revival of the Middle East peace process. However, there was considerable uncertainty regarding the prospects for a continuation of the Oslo process under Ariel Sharon, and without the active involvement of the Administration of Bill Clinton (whose term of office as US President had come to an end in January 2001): the new US Administration under George W. Bush chose initially to disengage itself from Arab–Israeli affairs in terms of its Middle East policy. Following his election victory, Sharon affirmed that he was not prepared to resume negotiations with the PA from their point of suspension in January, and rejected an appeal by the new US Secretary of State, Colin Powell, for Israel to end its blockade on the West Bank and Gaza Strip and to deliver overdue tax transfers to the PA. In March Sharon travelled to Washington for discussions with President Bush, while Arab League heads of state, meeting in the Jordanian capital, resolved, *inter alia*, to reinstate the 'secondary' economic boycott of Israel.

It was announced in early April 2001 that the Israeli Government had issued tenders for the construction of a further 708 Jewish housing units in the West Bank. The al-Aqsa *intifada* intensified in that month when Israel took unprecedented action in response to a Palestinian mortar attack on the Israeli town of Sderot. Israeli armed forces imposed road blockades which effectively divided the Gaza Strip into three sections, and sent tanks and bulldozers into the Gazan town of Beit Hanoun; this was Israel's first armed incursion into territory that it had transferred to PA control under the terms of the Oslo accords. Amid heavy pressure from the US Administration, Israel withdrew its forces less than 24 hours later. Hopes of an end to the Israeli–Palestinian conflict and a resumption of the Oslo peace talks were raised in mid-April amid a revival of the so-called 'Egyptian-Jordanian initiative' or Taba plan. The initiative, based on the fragile understanding reached at Sharm esh-Sheikh in October 2000, required that the situation on the ground be restored to that prior to the start of the al-Aqsa *intifada*. It also stipulated that negotiations be resumed from the point at which they stalled in January 2001, and that Israel agree to halt its settlement programme in the Occupied Territories. Sharon stated in late April that Israel would endorse the Taba plan provided that the PA end its demand for a complete freeze on the construction of Jewish settlements, and that all Palestinian violence should cease prior to the resumption of peace talks.

Israeli officials admitted in mid-May 2001 that the killing of five Palestinian police officers in the West Bank had been 'accidental'. A few days later, following a Hamas suicide bombing in Netanya in which five Israelis died, Israel deployed US-made F-16 fighter aircraft to shell security targets in the West Bank towns of Nablus and Ramallah, killing a number of Palestinians. In late May the Arab League and the Organization of the Islamic Conference (OIC, see p. 369) both urged member states to suspend all 'political' contacts with Israel. Meanwhile, the Sharm esh-Sheikh Fact-Finding Committee published its recommendations relating to the causes of the Israeli–Palestinian clashes. The so-called Mitchell Report referred to the visit of Ariel Sharon to the Islamic holy sites in September 2000 as 'provocative', but declined to single out for blame either Sharon or the PA leadership (which Israeli officials had accused of having orchestrated the violence). The Mitchell Report also demanded that Arafat undertake further measures to curb Palestinian 'terrorist' attacks, and called on Israel to end its economic blockade of the West Bank and Gaza Strip and to halt its settlement expansion programme. At the beginning of June 21 Israelis were killed, and more than 100 injured, in an attack by a Palestinian suicide bomber at a Tel-Aviv discothèque. As part of diplomatic efforts by the US Administration to revive the Israeli-Palestinian dialogue, the Director of the US Central Intelligence Agency, George Tenet, was dispatched to the region by President Bush. On 12 June proposals for a comprehensive cease-fire, brokered by Tenet, were approved by Israel and the PA; however, although Israel began to implement provisions made under the terms of the cease-fire to pull back troops from PA-controlled towns and to ease the economic blockade, the murder of two West Bank settlers by Palestinian gunmen and the killing of two Israeli soldiers in a suicide bombing in the Gaza Strip again hindered moves towards peace. During discussions in Washington with Bush at the end of June, Sharon reportedly demanded 10 days of 'total calm' before Israel would implement the provisions of the Tenet plan. However, the PA rejected the terms of the US initiative, stating that the agreement favoured Israel.

In early July 2001 Israel's 'inner' Security Cabinet voted to accelerate its strategy of 'targeted killings' of leading Palestinians alleged to have orchestrated 'terrorist' acts against Israeli citizens; some right-wing members of the Sharon Government had even reportedly advocated the assassination of Yasser Arafat. In mid-July the USA indicated for the first time that it would support the deployment of an international peace-keeping force in the Palestinian territories, although Israel continued to oppose such a move. On several occasions during late 2001 Israel ordered its forces into PA-controlled towns—among them Hebron, Bethlehem, Jenin and Beit Jala—where violent clashes between Israelis and Palestinians were taking place. At the end of July, meanwhile, two leading Hamas members, alleged by Israel to have been involved in the Tel-Aviv nightclub bombing, were killed during an air raid on Hamas media offices in Nablus, prompting the militant Islamist group to threaten the assassination of senior Israeli politicians. In early August the Israeli administration published a 'most wanted' list of seven Palestinians whom it alleged to be prominent in the preparation of 'terrorist' attacks. Only days later at least 15 Israelis (including six children) were killed, and up to 100 injured, by a Palestinian suicide bomber at a Jerusalem restaurant. The Israeli Government responded to the bombing by taking temporary control of Orient House, the de facto headquarters of the PA in East Jerusalem. At the end of August Abu Ali Moustafa, leader of the Popular Front for the Liberation of Palestine (PFLP), was killed by Israeli security forces at the party's offices in Ramallah. In September the PFLP claimed responsibility for four bomb attacks in Jerusalem.

However, international attention was abruptly distracted from events in Israel and the Palestinian territories following the massive suicide attacks apparently perpetrated by members of the al-Qa'ida (Base) network against New York and Washington, DC, on 11 September 2001. The attacks on the USA accelerated US and European Union (EU, see p. 244) efforts to urge Israel and the PA to effect a lasting cease-fire; however, Sharon demanded that he would not meet Arafat until the Palestinian leader could bring about 48 hours of 'complete quiet'. By the time of the first anniversary of the outbreak of the al-Aqsa *intifada* on 28 September, the Israeli–Palestinian violence had led to the deaths of at least 600 Palestinians and more than 160 Israelis. In early October two young Jewish settlers were killed by Hamas militants in Gaza. Israel responded by launching military strikes against Palestinian targets in Gaza City and sending troops into PA-controlled areas of Gaza and the West Bank; moreover, Israeli forces were granted the requisite powers to resume 'initiated attacks' against Palestinians deemed to be involved in 'terrorist' actions. Following further attacks by Palestinian militants within Israel, crisis talks were convened between Deputy Prime Minister and Minister of Foreign Affairs Shimon Peres and two senior PA officials, Saeb Erakat and Ahmad Quray (Abu Ala).

In mid-October 2001 the right-wing National Union-Israel Beytenu bloc withdrew from the governing coalition in protest at the Sharon administration's decision to pull back Israeli armed forces from the West Bank town of Hebron; two ministers thus resigned. Two days later one of these ministers, the hardline Minister of Tourism, Rechavam Ze'evi, was assassinated at a hotel in Arab East Jerusalem by a PFLP militant, in apparent retaliation for the recent assassination of the group's leader. Following the murder of Ze'evi—who was the first Israeli cabinet minister to be assassinated by an Arab militant—the National Union-Israel Beytenu bloc maintained its presence in the Government, with the other minister who had resigned, Minister of National Infrastructure Avigdor Lieberman, retaining his post and Rabbi Binyamin Elon subsequently being named as Ze'evi's successor. Sharon held Arafat personally responsible for the minister's death and suspended all contact with the PA. The Israeli Government also decided to reverse its recent moves to ease the economic restrictions on Palestinians in the West Bank and Gaza, and demanded that the PA immediately extradite the PFLP militants implicated in the assassination. Israeli armed forces entered six Palestinian towns in the West Bank (including Ramallah, Jenin, Nablus and Bethlehem) and killed a leading member of Arafat's Fatah movement. US and European leaders urged restraint from Sharon as the Israeli–Palestinian conflict escalated, and in late October US officials pressed Israel to pull back its troops from PA-controlled areas. Discussions took place between Israeli, Palestinian and US security officials at the end of the month, during which the Israeli representatives declared their terms for a staged withdrawal of troops from the six West Bank towns. Israeli forces duly withdrew from Bethlehem and Beit Jala; however, Sharon announced that the withdrawal from the remaining four towns would not take place until the PA arrested more Islamist militants.

Meanwhile, on the domestic front, in November 2001 Sharon was obliged to repay what had been found to be an illegal donation received by his campaign team in the approach to the premiership election. In December the Minister of Defence, Binyamin Ben-Eliezer, was elected as the new Labour Party leader.

The Israeli–Palestinian crisis escalated in early December 2001 when Palestinian militants launched suicide attacks in Haifa and Jerusalem, in retaliation for the 'targeted killing' of a Hamas leader: in one weekend some 25 Israelis were killed, and scores wounded. Sharon cut short his official visit to the USA, and Israel launched heavy military strikes against Palestinian security targets. Israel escalated its military operations in the Palestinian territories in mid-December after 10 Israelis had died in a bomb attack in the West Bank. The Government demanded 'concrete action' from the PA, despite a recent speech in which Arafat had ordered the Palestinian militant groups to end their armed campaign against Israel. Israeli armed forces staged a 'tactical' withdrawal from areas around Nablus and Ramallah to permit Arafat's security forces to arrest wanted Palestinian militants. However, Arafat remained confined to his headquarters in Ramallah after Israel imposed a travel ban on the Palestinian leader.

US special envoy to the Middle East Anthony Zinni returned to the region in early January 2002, immediately after the Israeli administration had ordered the partial withdrawal of its forces from some West Bank towns and the easing of certain restrictions against Palestinians there. Meanwhile, it was announced that Israeli forces in the Red Sea had intercepted a freighter ship, the *Karine-A*, which Israel claimed was carrying a large consignment of Iranian-made heavy weaponry destined for the Gaza Strip. Israeli and US officials claimed to have evidence of the PA's involvement in the trafficking of arms into the Occupied Territories, leading Arafat to institute an internal inquiry into the *Karine-A* affair, although he denied any knowledge of the shipment. In mid-January Israeli forces assassinated a leader of the Fatah-affiliated Al-Aqsa Martyrs' Brigades, provoking retaliatory attacks by that organization in Hadera and Jerusalem in which six Israelis died. Israeli forces proceeded to tighten the blockade around Arafat's Ramallah offices. At the end of the month Sharon approved a security plan involving the physical 'separation' of Jerusalem from the West Bank, in order to prevent attacks by Palestinian Islamist groups on Israeli territory.

In early March 2002 the UN Security Council adopted Resolution 1397, affirming its 'vision' of both Israeli and Palestinian states 'within secure and recognized borders'. Israel rejected a peace initiative put forward by Crown Prince Abdullah of Saudi Arabia at the Arab League summit held in Beirut in late March, due to its objection to the proposal that Israel withdraw from all Arab lands occupied since 1967 in exchange for full recognition of the State of Israel by the Arab states. Towards the end of March 2002 a Hamas suicide bombing at a Passover celebration in Netanya resulted in the deaths of 30 Israelis, while some 140 were injured in the attack. The so-called 'Passover massacre' led the Israeli Government, on 29 March, to initiate a massive campaign of military incursions into West Bank towns—codenamed 'Operation Defensive Shield'—with the declared aim of dismantling the Palestinian 'terrorist infrastructure'. Yasser Arafat's presidential compound at Ramallah was surrounded by Israeli troops, leaving the Palestinian leader isolated. (A Hamas leader was convicted in September 2005 of having masterminded the bombing, as well as a further attack in Netanya that killed five people; he received 35 life sentences.) At the end of March 2002 an emergency session of the UN Security Council produced Resolution 1402 expressing 'grave concern' at the escalation of violence in Israel and the Palestinian territories.

During the first two weeks of April 2002 intense fighting between the Israeli army and Palestinian militias occurred in the Jenin refugee camp—considered by Israel to be a base for Palestinian militants opposed to the Oslo accords. Some 23 Israeli soldiers were reportedly killed in ambushes and gun battles at the Jenin camp, while Palestinian sources claimed that over 100 Palestinians had died in the fighting. Despite subsequent attempts by a UN fact-finding mission to investigate Palestinian allegations of 'war crimes' committed by the Israeli army at Jenin, Israel refused to recognize the composition and mandate of the UN team. In mid-April US Secretary of State Powell arrived in Israel in an attempt to negotiate an Israeli-Palestinian cease-fire, and the Bush Administration repeated demands for Israel to withdraw from PA-controlled towns. There was a subsequent redeployment of Israeli forces from areas of the West Bank, but Israeli troops continued to encircle Arafat's presidential compound in Ramallah, as well as part of Bethlehem. Sharon insisted that the siege in Ramallah would continue until the PA handed over five men suspected of involvement in the assassination of Rechavam Ze'evi, as well as a militant believed to have plotted the shipment of weapons to Gaza aboard the *Karine-A* freighter ship. Arafat was freed by the Israeli authorities at the beginning of May, after the PA agreed to hand over the prisoners: four of the men were convicted of direct involvement in Ze'evi's murder by an ad hoc Palestinian court inside the Ramallah compound and sentenced to various terms of imprisonment. (For further details of events in the West Bank and Gaza Strip in March–May 2002, see the chapter on the Palestinian Autonomous Areas.)

The right-wing National Union-Israel Beytenu bloc withdrew from the governing coalition in March 2002, in protest against recent concessions made towards the Palestinians. However, the Government was strengthened a month later by the appointment of David Levy of Gesher and two ministers from the NRP as ministers without portfolio. The Central Committee of Likud voted in May to categorically reject the creation of a Palestinian state; this was interpreted as a reversal for Ariel Sharon, who publicly accepted the possibility of Palestinian independence. In mid-June Israel commenced the construction of a 'security fence', to extend the entire length of its border with the West Bank, with a view to preventing Palestinian militants from infiltrating Israeli territory and perpetrating further attacks. (The barrier was to be constructed using sections of barbed wire, electrified metal and concrete wall.) Despite international diplomatic efforts aimed at securing a new round of peace talks between Israel and the PA, and reports of a potential US initiative involving the creation of an 'interim' Palestinian state, there was a marked increase in violence at this time: Israel launched a new offensive, code-named 'Operation Determined Path', ordering troops into several West Bank and Gaza towns, in retaliation for another series of suicide attacks by Palestinian militants. Once again, Arafat's headquarters in Ramallah were blockaded by the Israeli military. At the end of June there were reports that a senior commander of Hamas's military wing had been killed by Israeli troops in Nablus; Israel alleged that he was a prominent bomb-maker, who had been responsible for attacks such as the Passover bombing in Netanya. Senior-level talks were resumed between Israel and the PA, while the Quartet group (comprising the USA, Russia, the UN and EU) held discussions in London in a bid to reactivate the Oslo peace process.

As new peace talks were being convened by the Quartet, several Israelis died in an attack on a bus near a Jewish settlement in the West Bank in mid-July 2002, for which three Palestinian militant groups all claimed responsibility. The Israeli response to the latest assaults included freezing plans to ease some of the restrictions imposed on Palestinians living in the Territories. Human rights organizations criticized plans by Israel to deport a number of relatives of suspected Palestinian militants to the Gaza Strip; however, a ruling by the Israeli Supreme Court in September declared the expulsions to be legitimate. Meanwhile, tensions increased between Israelis and Palestinians in late July, when an Israeli air-strike on a residential building in Gaza City resulted in the deaths of up to 15 Palestinians (including several children) in addition to their intended target, a leader of Hamas's military wing. Following international (and especially US) pressure, Israel moved to ease the restrictions in the West Bank and Gaza, and Sharon pledged to release some of the tax revenues owed to the PA. The Gaza air-strike precipitated a new round of violence, however, with four Jewish settlers being killed near Hebron. Israel responded by ordering tanks into the Gaza Strip. At the end of July at least seven Israelis were killed in a suicide bomb attack at the Hebrew University in Jerusalem; Hamas claimed responsibility for the blast. Following at least 15 further Israeli fatalities in early August as a result of Palestinian militant attacks, the Israeli Government ordered a total ban on freedom of movement for Palestinians in most West Bank cities, and targeted a number of leading militants in the Gaza Strip. Israel and the PA agreed at this time to implement a security plan (termed the 'Gaza, Bethlehem First' plan) whereby Israel would withdraw from the Gaza Strip and Bethlehem, in return for Palestinian security guarantees and a crackdown on militants. Israel began to withdraw its forces from Bethlehem on the following day; however, violence continued and further talks were cancelled. In early September the Israeli Ministry of the Interior took the unprecedented step of revoking the citizenship of an Arab Israeli who was accused of assisting Palestinian militants in plotting suicide attacks against Israelis. Two suicide bombings in Um al-Fahm and Tel-Aviv in mid-September caused the situation to deteriorate further. Israeli forces began to demolish buildings in Arafat's Ramallah compound, claiming that some 20 Palestinian militants were being sheltered there.

Elections to the Knesset were held on 28 January 2003, a few months earlier than scheduled. In October 2002 the Labour Party had withdrawn from Sharon's governing coalition in opposition to provisions in the 2003 budget which allocated funds to Jewish settlements in the West Bank. Sharon and his Likud party won a resounding victory over the left-wing parties at the polls, securing 38 seats in the Knesset; however, the electoral turn-out (at under 68%) was reportedly the lowest in Israel's history. Following lengthy discussions (during which Sharon attempted to persuade the Labour leader, Amram Mitzna, to join a new government of national unity with Likud), a new coalition Government was announced on 28 February 2003. The Cabinet was composed of Likud, the secularist Shinui party, and the right-wing and religious NRP, National Union and Israel B'Aliyah parties. (Mitzna had declared that Labour would only join the Government on the condition that Sharon agreed to close Jewish settlements in the Gaza Strip and to resume peace talks with the PA.) The former Likud premier, Binyamin Netanyahu, was named as Minister of Finance, while the Shinui and NRP leaders were both appointed as Deputy Prime Ministers. Reuven Rivlin became the new Speaker of the Knesset. In May Amram Mitzna resigned as Labour leader and was subsequently replaced, in an acting capacity, by Shimon Peres.

President Bush announced in mid-April 2003 that he would publish the Quartet-sponsored 'roadmap' for achieving peace in the Middle East once the new Palestinian Prime Minister, Mahmud Abbas—who had been appointed in March—had announced a new Cabinet. On 29 April, the same day that the Palestinian legislature endorsed the new Palestinian administration, two Britons carried out a suicide bombing at a café in Tel-Aviv, killing five people. Nevertheless, on 30 April the USA presented both the Israeli and Palestinian Prime Ministers with copies of the 'roadmap'. This latest peace initiative envisaged the creation of a sovereign Palestinian state by 2005–06 in a process comprising three phases. The first phase dealt largely with Palestinian issues, namely the cessation of militant operations against Israel and the establishment of a civilian and government infrastructure. Israel would be required to withdraw from areas it had occupied since 2000 and to dismantle Jewish settlements constructed since 2001. In phase two, Israel would hold peace talks with Lebanon and Syria regarding Palestinian borders; and the third and final phase would deal with the issues of Jerusalem and refugees. The roadmap emphasized the importance of UN Security Council Resolutions 242, 338 and 1397 in establishing a two-state settlement, and also reiterated that the Arab states must recognize Israel's right to exist. On 25 May the Israeli Cabinet accepted the terms of the roadmap, and at the end of the month Sharon made the unprecedented admission that Israel was in occupation of the Palestinian areas.

In early June 2003 Ariel Sharon, Mahmud Abbas and President Bush met in Aqaba, Jordan, to discuss the implementation of the roadmap, particularly the contentious issue of Jewish settlements. On 9 June Israeli troops commenced the dismantlement of settlements in the West Bank, but the nascent peace process was subsumed by a resumption of violence. On 10 June Israel attempted to kill a prominent Hamas leader, Abd al-Aziz ar-Rantisi, prompting a retaliatory suicide attack against a bus in Jerusalem, in which 16 people died. Israeli helicopter gunships were subsequently ordered to attack targets in Gaza. In all, 26 people were killed in the renewed hostilities, and the USA condemned Israel's attempt to assassinate ar-Rantisi. However, Israel continued to dismantle the settlements as well as to instigate troop withdrawals from the West Bank and Gaza Strip and release a number of Palestinian prisoners. Though the release of Palestinian prisoners was not a condition of the roadmap, it was regarded as an important expression of support for Abbas. By mid-August more than 400 prisoners had been released, including members of Hamas and Islamic Jihad who had not been involved in planning or executing attacks against Israeli targets. These two militant groups, along with Arafat's Fatah movement, had declared a three-month cease-fire at the end of June. Following these positive first steps, however, the roadmap was threatened by growing international concerns over Israel's construction of a 'security fence' in the West Bank, as well as by a resumption of Israeli–Palestinian hostilities in late August.

Israel had begun construction of the West Bank 'security fence' in mid-2002 (see above). It was initially intended to prevent Palestinian militants from covertly crossing into Israel to carry out attacks, but by mid-2003 Israel was being accused of using the barrier to annex Palestinian territory, and it was feared that it would become a permanent border in any future peace settlement. President Bush urged Sharon to remove the 'security fence' when the two leaders met at the end of July, and the US Administration further threatened to withhold nearly US $10,000m. of essential loan guarantees unless construction ceased. Despite international pressure, Israel continued to erect the barrier as well as to maintain its policy of 'targeted attacks' against senior Palestinian militants. On 14 August Israeli forces killed a senior commander of Islamic Jihad in Hebron, and on 19 August a suicide bomber killed 20 Israelis on a bus in Jerusalem, an attack for which both Hamas and Islamic Jihad claimed responsibility. In retaliation, on 22 August Israel reimposed road-blocks on the main north–south highway in the Gaza Strip, reversing one of the earliest roadmap initiatives.

At the beginning of September 2003 a lengthy Israeli judicial inquiry, led by Justice Theodore Or, released its report on the deaths of 14 Israeli Arabs during protests in October 2000. The report severely criticized the use of 'excessive force' by Israeli security forces during the early days of the al-Aqsa *intifada*, and recommended that neither Shlomo Ben-Avi nor Yehuda Wilk, respectively the Minister of Public Security and the Commissioner of Police at the time of the deaths, should again be allowed to take responsibility for security affairs. Former Prime Minister Ehud Barak was also criticized in the report. In October 2003 the Cabinet approved the next phase of the 'security fence'; although this was not contiguous to sections of the barrier already built, it was completely to enclose settlements in the West Bank. Additionally, a tender was issued for the construction of 550 new homes in a Jewish settlement close to Jerusalem.

The USA announced in November 2003 that it was cutting US $290m. from a loan package guarantee for Israel as a penalty for renewed settlement construction in the West Bank and Gaza. The issue of the settlements was one raised by the authors of a new peace plan, launched by senior Palestinian and Israeli political figures in Geneva, Switzerland, on 1 December. The Geneva Accords, which did not have the official approval of either the Israeli or Palestinian administrations, outlined a two-state solution to the Israeli–Palestinian issue, including proposals that Palestinians would receive compensation for giving up the right of return; that most settlements in the West Bank and Gaza (except those neighbouring Jerusalem) would be dismantled; and that Jerusalem (to become the capital of two states) would be divided administratively rather than physically. On 8 December the UN General Assembly passed a resolution asking the International Court of Justice (ICJ) in The Hague, Netherlands, to issue a (non-binding) ruling on the legality of Israel's 'security fence'; the hearings began in February 2004.

Meanwhile, Ariel Sharon was becoming increasingly embroiled in the investigation, details of which had first prior to the general election in January 2003, into allegations that he had received US $1.5m. in illegal campaign contributions. Israel's Supreme Court ordered the Prime Minister's son Gilad to hand over documents relating to a loan from a family friend and South African businessman to repay allegedly illegal donations during the campaign for the Likud leadership. A secondary matter was the circumstances under which Gilad Sharon had been employed as a consultant on an Israeli-backed development in Greece. Ariel Sharon was able to distract attention from his legal problems when he issued an ultimatum to the Palestinian leadership in mid-December 2003, demanding that unless the PA started disarming and disbanding Palestinian militant groups, Israel would adopt a 'disengagement plan', which would effectively consist of accelerating the construction of the 'security fence' in the West Bank and physically separating Israel from the Palestinian territories. Yet Sharon's speech attracted criticism from right-wing and ultra-Orthodox settler groups when it became clear that the disengagement plan would involve the evacuation of 17 settlements in the Gaza Strip, considered beyond the reach of the 'security fence'. Under the terms of the roadmap, which Sharon stated he was willing to implement if the Palestinians also carried out their obligations, at least 60 settlements in the West Bank and Gaza would have to be dismantled.

In January 2004 an Israeli businessman, David Appel, was formally charged with offering bribes to both Ariel and Gilad Sharon, as well as to Deputy Prime Minister Ehud Olmert. In the late 1990s Appel had allegedly offered US $700,000 to Ariel Sharon, who was then Minister of Foreign Affairs, to exert pressure on the Greek authorities to approve the development of an island holiday resort and casino in which Appel had business interests. Although Sharon was not charged, he faced a police investigation in relation to the claims, while the Labour Party tabled a parliamentary motion of no confidence against the Prime Minister. However, in June 2004 the Attorney-General, Menachem Mazuz, dismissed the corruption charges against Ariel and Gilad Sharon relating to the development in Greece (despite the fact that the state prosecutor had presented evidence allegedly proving the premier's guilt), and, in February 2005, dropped the charges against Ariel Sharon relating to the laundering of illegal funds for his 1999 campaign for the leadership of Likud (see above), citing insufficient evidence in both cases. Ariel Sharon's son Omri still faced charges, and investigations continued into allegations that Omri and Gilad Sharon had used a loan from a family friend and South African businessman to repay illegal donations during the leadership campaign. However, the state prosecution submitted a revised indictment against Appel in April 2005, in which it dismissed the bribery charges. In November Omri pleaded guilty to the falsification of documents, perjury and violating election law: according to the indictment, he had raised more than seven times the amount of campaign funds permitted under Israeli election law. Omri resigned his seat in the Knesset in January 2006, and was sentenced to nine months' imprisonment and fined $64,000 in February. (His prison sentence was first postponed until mid-2007, owing to the stroke suffered by his father in January 2006—see below—and as the result of an appeal; the length of Omri's sentence was later reduced to seven months, and he entered prison in February 2008.)

Ariel Sharon announced in an interview published in the Ha'aretz newspaper in early February 2004 that he had drawn up a plan to evacuate all Jewish settlements in the Gaza Strip. The evacuation would reportedly affect 7,500 settlers in 17 settlements (although details of the plan were subsequently amended—see below). This news was welcomed by the recently appointed Palestinian Prime Minister, Ahmad Quray, and in late February Sharon met officials from the US Administration to discuss his proposed evacuation of the Gaza settlements. However, the proposed disengagement was overshadowed in late March by Israel's most high profile 'targeted killing', namely that of Sheikh Ahmed Yassin, the founder and spiritual leader of Hamas. The decision to kill Yassin was reportedly made by Prime Minister Sharon and his 'inner' Security Cabinet following a double suicide bombing at the southern port of Ashdod on 14 March, in which 10 Israelis died; responsibility for the bombings was claimed jointly by Hamas and the Al-Aqsa Martyrs' Brigades. The 'targeted killing' of the Hamas leader by Israeli helicopter gunships on 22 March, which provoked international condemnation, apparently indicated the start of a campaign by the Israeli Government to eliminate the entire leadership of Hamas. On 26 March the USA vetoed a UN Security Council resolution condemning the Israeli action, reportedly due to the fact that the resolution failed to refer to Hamas as a 'terrorist' organization. Abd al-Aziz ar-Rantisi was appointed leader of Hamas in Gaza after Yassin's death, but his tenure was short-lived as on 17 April he was also killed in a rocket attack by Israeli helicopter gunships. In the aftermath of ar-Rantisi's death, Hamas kept secret the identity of his successor and reportedly adopted a policy of 'collective leadership' in order to prevent future leaders of the organization from being similarly targeted.

In mid-April 2004 Sharon travelled to the USA to discuss the roadmap with President Bush; however, the outcome of the meeting was the endorsement by Bush of Sharon's proposals to 'disengage' from Gaza, which also involved the consolidation of six Jewish settlements in the West Bank. This was regarded as a major diplomatic coup for Sharon, but one which was inimical to the spirit of the roadmap. Sharon suffered a setback in early May, when members of his own Likud party overwhelmingly rejected the disengagement plan at a party ballot. Determined that the plan be approved, Sharon drew up a slightly modified version of the proposals, and in early June removed Minister of Transport Avigdor Lieberman and Minister of Tourism Binyamin Elon, both from the far-right National Union party and both opposed to an Israeli disengagement from Gaza. A few days later the NRP Minister of Construction and Housing, Efraim Eitam, resigned after Sharon's broad proposals were approved in principle by a cabinet vote. However, Sharon lost his Knesset majority when National Union's six deputies resigned, and he entered into negotiations with the Labour Party. In mid-June Sharon narrowly survived a parliamentary vote of no confidence prompted by opposition to his disengagement plan.

Meanwhile, as attacks by Palestinian militants against Israeli soldiers in the Gaza Strip intensified, with a number of fatalities being reported, in mid-May 2004 Israel launched one of its largest military operations in Gaza for decades. The aims of the offensive, code-named 'Operation Rainbow', were to locate and dismantle tunnels in the Rafah refugee camps through which militants were able to smuggle weapons from Egypt for use in attacks against Israelis, and to arrest Palestinians wanted for involvement in such attacks. A reported 40 Palestinians, whom Israel claimed to be terrorists, were killed during the operation. In late June, after a petition had been filed by several Palestinian councils, the Israeli Supreme Court ordered the Government to alter the route of part of the 'security fence', including a 30-km section in a Palestinian village, Beit Sourik. In early July the ICJ gave its advisory opinion that the barrier contravened international law and effectively constituted the annexation of Palestinian land, and disrupted thousands of civilians' lives, frustrating Palestinian attempts to achieve self-determination. The ICJ urged Israel to remove parts of the fence and pay compensation to affected Palestinians. Sharon rejected the ruling, which he asserted was politically motivated and detrimental to the 'war on terror'. In late July the UN

General Assembly voted to demand that Israel comply with the ICJ ruling and take down the barrier (the USA voted against the resolution). In mid-August, at a special convention of Sharon's Likud party, members voted against the Prime Minister's proposals to form a coalition with any Zionist party or Labour. Sharon dismissed the resolutions and vowed to pursue his plans for a coalition government to secure a parliamentary majority for his plan to disengage from Gaza, and to avoid having to call early general elections. He also approved the construction of 1,000 new Jewish homes in the West Bank.

In October 2004 the Knesset voted to accept Sharon's proposal to dismantle all 21 settlements in Gaza, and four in the northern West Bank. However, the Israeli premier carried out a threat made prior to the vote to discharge any cabinet members who voted against the plan, dismissing Uzi Landau, a Likud minister without portfolio, and a deputy minister. In November the Cabinet approved a plan to compensate Jewish settlers due to be evacuated from Gaza, and to imprison settlers who resisted evacuation. The NRP's six parliamentary members withdrew from the coalition Government in opposition to Sharon's proposals for the Gaza Strip. In early December Sharon dismissed Shinui's five ministers when they voted against the first reading of the 2005 budget because it pledged US $98m. in subsidies to projects backed by United Torah Judaism. The Prime Minister's Likud party was left with only 40 out of the Knesset's 120 seats. After a period of negotiations, Labour agreed in mid-December 2004 to form a coalition with Likud. It was reported at the end of the month that Sharon had agreed a deal with the Labour leader, Shimon Peres, whereby Peres would become his 'senior deputy', assuming a new title of Vice-Premier. In January 2005 the Knesset narrowly approved the new coalition Government, to be composed principally of Likud, Labour and United Torah Judaism, thereby restoring Sharon's parliamentary majority. (United Torah Judaism, which subsequently split into its constituent parties of Agudat Israel and Degel Hatorah, was only represented at the deputy ministerial level.)

Meanwhile, in early October 2004 34 people, most of whom were Israelis, were killed by bomb blasts in three resorts in Egypt's Sinai Peninsula; Egypt later blamed the blasts on a Palestinian and three Sinai Bedouins. In mid-October the Israeli army ended a 16-day assault, code-named 'Operation Days of Penitence', in northern and southern Gaza that left 135 Palestinians dead and destroyed an estimated 95 homes, according to UN figures. The operation had been prompted by a Hamas rocket that killed two children in Sderot, close to the Gaza Strip. Egypt pledged to provide 750 border guards to replace Israeli troops along the Egypt–Gaza frontier to attempt to prevent Palestinian arms-smuggling and to stop Hamas and other Palestinian factions from firing rockets into Israel in the event of Israel carrying out its Disengagement Plan. Israel accepted Egypt's offer in early December, and later in the month Israel released 159 Palestinian prisoners as a gesture of 'goodwill' to Egypt's President Mubarak, after Mubarak had agreed to release an Arab Israeli, Azzam Azzam, who had been serving a sentence in Egypt for espionage. The prisoner release was also interpreted as a 'goodwill' gesture to the newly elected Executive President of the PA, Mahmud Abbas, following the death of Yasser Arafat in November 2004 (for further details, see the chapter on the Palestinian Autonomous Areas). In January 2005, despite initial hopes of negotiations with Abbas, Sharon announced that he refused to meet the new Palestinian leader until he adopted measures to combat Palestinian militant activity. The announcement followed a Palestinian attack that killed six Israelis at the Karni cargo crossing between Gaza and Israel.

In early February 2005 the Israeli Cabinet approved the withdrawal of Israeli forces from five West Bank towns as well as the release of 500 Palestinian prisoners immediately following a summit meeting that was to be held in Egypt; a further 400 prisoners were to be freed after a three-month period. The summit was duly convened between Sharon, Mahmud Abbas, President Mubarak and King Abdullah of Jordan in Sharm esh-Sheikh on 8 February, amid hopes of a breakthrough in the Middle East peace process following the election of a new Palestinian leadership. Sharon and Abbas shook hands and issued verbal declarations to end hostilities between their two peoples; however, no formal cease-fire was agreed, and the militant groups Hamas and Islamic Jihad refused to be bound by the declaration. Israel also agreed to hand over to PA security control the towns of Jericho, Tulkaram, Bethlehem, Qalqilya and Ramallah in the coming weeks; Israeli forces duly withdrew from Jericho and Tulkaram in March. Moreover, shortly after the Sharm esh-Sheikh summit, Israel allowed 56 deported Palestinians to return to the West Bank, and also transferred the bodies of 15 Palestinian bombers to the PA. In late February Israel began the release of 500 Palestinian prisoners as a 'goodwill' gesture. At this time the Israeli Cabinet gave its final approval to the Government's planned disengagement from all settlements in the Gaza Strip and four in the West Bank. Amid hopes for an improvement in Israeli–Arab relations, Jordan returned an ambassador to Israel. However, towards the end of the month a suicide bombing in Tel-Aviv, subsequently claimed by Islamic Jihad, killed four Israelis. Palestinians, meanwhile, were angered by reports that Israel was planning to construct a further 6,391 homes in existing West Bank settlements during 2005. In mid-March 13 armed Palestinian factions, including Hamas and Islamic Jihad, declared a cease-fire until the end of the year, on the condition that Israel refrained from attacks and released 8,000 Palestinian prisoners. The Knesset voted in late March to reject a bill that would require a national referendum to be held prior to any implementation of Sharon's Disengagement Plan, and approved the 2005 budget, thus avoiding the need to call general elections and preventing a delay to the Israeli withdrawal from the Gaza Strip and the four settlements in the West Bank. Following a series of rocket attacks on settlements in Gaza and communities in southern Israel in May, Sharon announced that the country was delaying the redeployment of Israeli forces from West Bank towns and the release of the 400 Palestinian prisoners due to be freed under the agreements made at Sharm esh-Sheikh in February, demanding that the PA be more effective in reining in militants; however, Israel released the prisoners in June. Meanwhile, Natan Sharansky, the Minister without Portfolio, responsible for Jerusalem, Social and Diaspora Affairs, announced his resignation in May, asserting that the proposed disengagement would create a 'rift' in the Israeli nation and was a threat to the country's security.

In July 2005 Israeli and Palestinian officials were reported to have agreed in principle to the establishment of a 'safe passage' between the West Bank and the Gaza Strip following the implementation of Israel's Disengagement Plan. In early August an Israeli army deserter shot dead four Arabs on a bus in the Arab Israeli town of Shfaram, apparently in an attempt to stall the disengagement process by creating unrest; Arab passengers responded by beating him to death. On 7 August, shortly before the Cabinet voted to implement the first stage of the Disengagement Plan, Minister of Finance Binyamin Netanyahu announced his resignation. Like Sharansky, he denounced the disengagement as a threat to the security of the country and the unity of the nation, and criticized the unilateral nature of the withdrawal. Sharon appointed Vice-Prime Minister and Minister of Industry, Trade and Labour Ehud Olmert to the vacated portfolio in an acting capacity. Despite public protests and the need to forcefully evacuate settlers who refused to leave the territories after the deadline of 17 August, the disengagement was completed ahead of schedule, on 12 September, when the last Israeli forces left Gaza. Israel had approved the deployment of 750 Egyptians troops along Egypt's border with the Gaza Strip in late August. Although Israel had announced soon after the disengagement had been completed that the Rafah border crossing between Egypt and the Gaza Strip would not be reopened for six months, in November, following US intervention, Israeli and Egyptian officials agreed to reopen the crossing, which was to be managed by the PA with the assistance of European monitors. Meanwhile, on 22 September 2005 Israeli forces completed their withdrawal from the northern West Bank.

Soon after the completion of the withdrawal, in response to a series of rocket attacks on Israel by Hamas militants from Gaza, Israel carried out air-strikes on the Gaza Strip in which it targeted militant leaders. (Israel had resumed its policy of 'targeted killings' in June 2005, following a series of attacks perpetrated largely by Islamic Jihad.) Although Hamas announced the cessation of attacks, Israel continued to target premises in Gaza associated with arms storage or production and carried out a series of arrests of suspected militants. Following the murder of three Israeli settlers in the West Bank in mid-October 2005, Israel announced the suspension of security contacts with the PA. Later in the month Israel responded to a suicide bombing in Hadera that killed five Israelis with a series of missile strikes on Gaza, killing seven Palestinians, including four members of Islamic Jihad. A planned meeting between Sharon and Abbas was delayed. In early November, following the 'targeted killing' of a Hamas leader by Israeli forces in Gaza, the militant organization announced that it would not renew its cease-fire, which was to expire at the end of the year. Sharon continued to assert that Israeli operations against militants would not cease until Abbas disarmed militants and destroyed the 'terrorist infrastructure'.

Meanwhile, the Supreme Court voted in September 2005 to reject the non-binding ICJ ruling of July 2004 that the 'security fence' contravened international law (see above), criticizing the verdict for not taking into account Israel's security needs. The Government had approved a controversial plan for the final route of its 'security fence' in July 2005, which was to result in four Arab areas of Jerusalem being separated from local schools and hospitals. However, new amenities were apparently to be built on the Palestinian side, and transport and crossing-points were to be provided. Despite the Supreme Court's decision to reject the ICJ's verdict, justices ordered that a section of the barrier around the Jewish village of Alfei Menashe in the West Bank be removed, asserting that due consideration for the rights of Palestinians living in the area had not been taken during its construction. Moreover, following complaints from residents of Palestinian villages near Qalqilya that the 'security fence' isolated them from the rest of the West Bank, the Supreme Court ordered a review of the route of the barrier.

Vice-Prime Minister Ehud Olmert, who already held the Industry, Trade and Labour portfolio, formally assumed the finance portfolio in early November 2005. Following his defeat of Vice-Premier Shimon Peres in an internal ballot for the leadership of the Labour Party in mid-November, the Chairman of the Histadrut trade union confederation, Amir Peretz, announced his decision to seek approval for the withdrawal of his party from the Government. The new Labour leader wished to force early legislative elections (scheduled for November 2006), and cited the need to address social problems, which he criticized the current Likud-dominated Government for having neglected, as well as the need to advance the peace process. Peretz and Sharon subsequently agreed to hold elections in early 2006. Eight Labour-Meimad ministers resigned their posts on 21 November 2005, after Peretz's proposal had apparently won the support of an absolute majority of Labour members at a party conference. The ministers, whose resignation came into effect two days later, included Peres, Minister of National Infrastructure Binyamin Ben-Eliezer and Minister of the Interior Ophir Pines-Paz. Sharon adopted the vacated portfolios on an interim basis, and additionally assumed Peres's responsibilities as Vice-Premier.

Sharon also announced on 21 November 2005 that he was leaving Likud to establish a breakaway faction, Kadima (Forward), explaining that he believed his former party could not achieve what he considered to be national objectives owing to the constant distraction of political struggles, and emphasized his wish to prioritize the good of the nation over personal interests. The new party, he declared, would aim to pursue a peace agreement with the Palestinians in accordance with the roadmap, and to combat economic and social problems. (The premier was legally permitted to form Kadima as he managed to secure the agreement of more than one-third of Likud members of the Knesset to join the faction.) In addition to one Labour Party Minister without Portfolio, a total of 14 Knesset members from Likud joined the new grouping, including six ministers and six deputy ministers, most notably Vice-Prime Minister Olmert and Minister of Immigrant Absorption and of Justice Tzipi Livni. (A second former Labour-Meimad minister, Dalia Itzik, announced her decision to join Kadima later in the month; Itzik had formerly held the communications portfolio.) Sharon did not invite Peres to join the new party. On the same day the Prime Minister submitted a request to President Katsav for permission to dissolve the Knesset, announcing that the majority of its members were opposed to the current Government. Katsav accepted the request and issued a decree dissolving the legislature on 23 November: the decree was to come into effect on 8 December, and legislative elections were to be held on 28 March 2006. On 30 November 2005 Peres announced his decision to leave the Labour Party in order to campaign for Kadima in the forthcoming elections, without stating whether he would actually join the new party. Acting Chairman of Likud and Minister without Portfolio Tzachi Hanegbi announced his decision to join Kadima in early December, while Minister of Defence Lt-Gen. Shaul Mofaz also joined later in the month. Netanyahu was confirmed as the new Likud Chairman in mid-December, following an internal ballot, and announced plans to withdraw his party from the Government.

Prime Minister Ariel Sharon was hospitalized in mid-December 2005, following a minor stroke. Although Sharon was discharged from hospital two days later, on 4 January 2006 he suffered a second stroke, which left him in a coma from which he had not emerged by early 2008. Vice-Prime Minister and Minister of Finance Ehud Olmert took over as acting Prime Minister following Sharon's incapacitation. Minister of Foreign Affairs Silvan Shalom resigned his post on 13 January 2006, after Netanyahu had asked ministers to withdraw from the Government in protest at its policies and in order to prepare the party list for the forthcoming elections. Shalom was the last representative of Likud (and indeed of any party excluding Kadima) in the Cabinet, since the other three Likud ministers had tendered their resignations the previous day. Netanyahu apparently reneged on a promise to support the three former ministers in elections to the Likud Knesset list, and, after they received relatively low positions in the list, they vowed to remove him from the party chairmanship if the party did not win the legislative elections. All four Likud ministers had initially been reluctant to resign their posts, arguing that the party's representation in the Cabinet would increase its popularity at the election. Netanyahu, however, had apparently become even more determined to withdraw his party from the Government after it had become increasingly likely that the Cabinet would decide to allow Arab residents of East Jerusalem to vote in the elections to the PLC scheduled for 25 January (see below). The party leader saw this expected decision as a precursor to the division of Jerusalem as part of a 'final status' agreement with the Palestinians. The Cabinet approved the appointment of three new ministers and the reallocation of various portfolios among existing government members on 18 January 2006. Acting Prime Minister Ehud Olmert adopted the interior portfolio (he additionally held those of industry, trade and labour, finance, and social affairs), while the Minister of Immigrant Absorption and of Justice, Tzipi Livni, replaced Shalom as Minister of Foreign Affairs. Olmert was appointed acting leader of Kadima on the same day.

On 15 January 2006, 10 days prior to the elections to the PLC, the Israeli Cabinet voted unanimously to permit Arabs in East Jerusalem to participate in the poll. However, members of Hamas (which was prohibited from directly contesting the elections) were to be banned from campaigning there. In the event, Hamas, which was contesting the polls as the Change and Reform list in order to circumvent the prohibition, secured a decisive majority in the new legislature, with 74 of the 132 seats, while President Abbas's Fatah movement retained 45 seats. Abbas subsequently confirmed that he would ask the militant group to form a new cabinet to succeed the administration led by Fatah, which announced that it would not join Hamas in government.

Following the announcement of preliminary results of the poll, Olmert declared that Israel would not deal with what he termed an 'armed terror organization that calls for Israel's destruction', while Livni urged the EU to oppose the creation of a militant-led government. The Quartet group appealed to Hamas to reject violence and recognize Israel, and President Bush declared that the USA would not negotiate with a Hamas-led administration unless the organization renounced its call to destroy the Jewish State. However, in early February 2006 Russian President Vladimir Putin announced his intention to invite cabinet representatives of Hamas, which Russia did not consider to be a terrorist organization, to visit the Russian capital, Moscow, for talks. Israel described the move as undermining prospects for peace. Meanwhile, Khalid Meshaal, the head of Hamas's political bureau, declared that his organization would not renounce violence, asserting that it was a legitimate form of resistance to Israeli occupation. Hamas was willing to negotiate a long-term truce only if Israel agreed to certain conditions, including a return to the pre-1967 borders. In an interview on Israeli television, Olmert pledged to separate Israel from the Palestinians within permanent borders, and to preserve a Jewish majority in Israel, should Kadima win the general election: Israel would retain the whole of Jerusalem and the main West Bank settlement blocs of Ma'aleh Adumim, Ariel and Gush Etzion, in addition to the Jordan Valley, but would be willing to relinquish parts of the West Bank where the majority of the population were Palestinian. Olmert later announced that Israel's permanent borders would be established by 2010. He added that Israel would attempt to secure an internationally backed peace plan with Hamas, and would only pursue a unilateral solution should such attempts fail, and after giving the militant group time to reform and disarm and observe past interim peace agreements. Meshaal called Olmert's proposals 'a war declaration', asserting that they were intended only to meet Israel's security requirements and would not help to achieve peace. He dismissed the so-called Convergence Plan as allowing Israel to: illegally retain its possession of the largest section of the West Bank and its 'security fence'; reject concessions on the status of Jerusalem; and thwart the 'right of return' of Palestinian refugees.

Following the inauguration of the new PLC on 18 February 2006, Israel approved a series of measures designed to weaken the future Hamas-led administration, including withholding monthly tax payments to the PA and a ban on the transfer of equipment to Palestinian security forces, but promised not to prevent humanitarian aid from reaching Palestinians. The EU, meanwhile, was reported to be considering plans to withhold funds to the PA. In early March, on its scheduled visit to Moscow, Hamas announced that it would never accept Israel's right to exist, asserting that doing so would negate Palestinian rights, including the right to 'their property' of Jerusalem and the holy sites, and the 'right to return' of Palestinian refugees. However, the militant group pledged to extend the cease-fire it had agreed with Israel in March 2005 for another year, on the condition that Israel refrained from the use of force throughout the period. The new Palestinian administration was sworn in on 28 March 2006.

In the event, Kadima obtained the largest share of the votes cast (22.0% of valid votes) in the elections to the Knesset on 28 March 2006, thereby securing 29 of the 120 seats. As at the previous election, Labour-Meimad obtained the second highest proportion of votes (15.1%), and again secured 19 seats. Shas won 12 seats, Likud only 12 and Israel Beytenu 11; the Pensioners' Party, which stood for pensioners' rights, took seven seats. At some 63.2% of the eligible electorate, the rate of participation was the lowest in the country's history. The new Knesset was sworn in on 17 April, and Dalia Itzik was appointed Speaker on 4 May. Meanwhile, on 11 April 2006 the Government voted to change the status of Acting Prime Minister Ehud Olmert to Interim Prime Minister: Israeli legislation stipulates that an interim Prime Minister must be appointed from the governing faction if the Prime Minister is unable to discharge the duties of his office for 100 days. The Cabinet's decision came into effect on 14 April.

President Katsav had asked Olmert to form a new administration in early April 2006, and Olmert entered into negotiations with various parties on the formation of a new coalition government. Likud, which strongly opposed Olmert's plans for Israel to withdraw from large areas of the West Bank, ruled out the possibility of its joining the cabinet. Labour-Meimad, however, supported Olmert's plans in principle, and in late April signed an agreement with Kadima to join the future administration. A coalition agreement with Shas and the Pensioners' Party was signed in early May, giving Olmert and his party a 67-seat majority in the legislature. The Knesset voted to approve the new Government on 4 May. Olmert was to serve as Prime Minister and Minister of Social Affairs. Other notable appointees from Kadima included Shimon Peres as Vice-Premier and Minister for the Development of the Negev and Galilee, Tzipi Livni as Vice-Prime Minister and Minister of Foreign Affairs, and Abraham Hirchson as Minister of Finance; the Labour leader, Amir Peretz, was appointed Deputy Prime Minister and Minister of Defence. Meanwhile, on 17 April 2006—the day that the new Knesset was sworn in—a suicide bomber launched an attack in Tel-Aviv, killing himself and nine others. Hamas justified the attack (for which Islamic Jihad claimed responsibility) as an act of self-defence by the Palestinian people, while President Abbas condemned it, asserting that it was harmful to Palestinian interests.

Olmert spent the initial months of his premiership attempting to secure diplomatic support for his unilateralist Convergence Plan, visiting a number of international leaders to explain his strategy. However, the likely success of such a plan was severely challenged amid the violence that broke out in the Gaza Strip in late June 2006, following the kidnapping of an Israeli soldier, Corporal Gilad Shalit, in a cross-border raid by Hamas militants; two other soldiers were killed during the raid (see the chapter on the Palestinian Autonomous Areas). The following day Palestinian militant groups issued a statement demanding that Israel release all female Palestinian prisoners and all Palestinian prisoners under 18 years of age in exchange for Shalit. Israel responded by launching air-strikes on Gaza and entering the southern part of the Strip, while Israeli security forces arrested dozens of Hamas officials, including cabinet ministers and parliamentarians, for questioning in relation to their alleged involvement in attacks against Israeli targets. Israel's military operation (code-named 'Summer Rains') to seek to secure the release of Corporal Shalit in the Gaza Strip continued despite the conflict that began between Israel and Hezbollah in July.

On 12 July 2006 Hezbollah militants kidnapped two Israeli soldiers and killed three others in a raid across Lebanon's border with northern Israel, simultaneously firing rockets at Israeli communities and military posts. A further five Israeli soldiers were killed when troops crossed into Lebanon in an attempt to rescue the kidnapped soldiers. Hezbollah declared that it would free the abducted soldiers in exchange for the release of Lebanese prisoners in Israeli gaols. On the same day Olmert secured the approval of his Cabinet, which held the Lebanese Government responsible for the cross-border raid, to pursue a military campaign against Hezbollah targets and Lebanese infrastructure with the aim of securing the release of the soldiers and forcing the disarmament of Hezbollah and the deployment of the Lebanese army in southern Lebanon. During the course of the month-long conflict Hezbollah launched thousands of rockets into Israeli territory, having declared 'open war' on Israel on 14 July; two days later at least eight Israelis were killed in a Hezbollah rocket attack against Haifa. Israel, meanwhile, systematically targeted Lebanese infrastructure, blockading seaports, destroying numerous roads and bridges, and bombing important strategic targets such as Beirut International Airport. When at least 28 Lebanese (many of them children) died in a bombing raid on an apartment building in Qana on 30 July, Prime Minister Olmert expressed his 'deep sorrow'. Israeli military chiefs, however, asserted that Hezbollah had been using the building in order to launch missile attacks against Israel. In early August the Israeli Cabinet approved a plan to send ground troops further into Lebanon, as far as the Litani river—some 30 km north of the Israeli border. (For further details regarding the conflict, see the chapter on Lebanon.)

Finally, on 11 August 2006 the UN Security Council adopted Resolution 1701, which, *inter alia*, called for: an immediate and full cessation of hostilities; the extension of the Lebanese Government's authority over the whole country; and the delineation of Lebanon's international boundaries, with particular regard to disputed areas such as Shebaa Farms. Although the Lebanese Government endorsed the resolution on 12 August, and Hezbollah stated that it would honour the calls for a cease-fire, 24 Israeli soldiers were killed on that day. Similarly, despite Israel's Cabinet approving Resolution 1701 on 13 August, on the following day Israeli troops launched an attack on a refugee camp in Sidon, killing an UNRWA staff member approximately one hour before the cease-fire was scheduled to take effect. Nevertheless, the cease-fire between Israel and Hezbollah did commence, as stipulated, on 14 August. Lebanese government forces and an enhanced UNIFIL contingent were to be deployed in southern Lebanon, while Israel was simultaneously to withdraw its forces from the territory. In line with former UN resolutions, Resolution 1701 also required that all armed groups in Lebanon disarm in order that the Government extend its sovereignty over the whole state. The resolution called on the parties involved to address the underlying causes of the conflict, including making efforts towards settling the issue of Lebanese prisoners in Israeli gaols, and pressed Hezbollah to release unconditionally the kidnapped Israeli soldiers. By the time that the cease-fire came into effect, 43 Israeli civilians and 119 soldiers had been killed in the conflict, and more than 1,000 Lebanese civilians had lost their lives; the number of Hezbollah militants killed was unknown. As international forces began controlling positions at Lebanon's seaports and airports, Israel lifted its naval blockade of Lebanon on 8 September, the day after it had removed restrictions on air travel to and from that country. The last Israeli ground forces were withdrawn from Lebanon on 1 October, in accordance with the terms of the cease-fire.

In mid-August 2006 Israel's Deputy Prime Minister and Minister of Defence, Amir Peretz, appointed a committee of inquiry to investigate Israel's military capabilities and performance before and during the conflict with Hezbollah. However, Prime Minister Olmert refused to order a full judicial inquiry into the war (as demanded by many Israelis), but instead suggested forming two commissions—one political and the other military—to examine how both administrations had acted. In the event, the Cabinet voted in mid-September to establish a joint committee under the chairmanship of a retired judge, Dr Eliyahu Winograd. The Winograd Commission published the initial results of its investigation into Israel's military campaign in

Lebanon on 30 April 2007. In this interim report, which covered the period between Israel's withdrawal from southern Lebanon in 2000 to mid-July 2006, the Commission found Olmert and other senior Israeli officials to have demonstrated 'very serious failings' in their handling of the war with Hezbollah, and to have neglected to devise a comprehensive plan before deciding to launch the military campaign. The Prime Minister was said to have shown 'a serious failure in exercising judgement, responsibility and prudence' during the early stages of the conflict. The investigative panel also found that the declared aims of the Israeli military—i.e. the defeat of Hezbollah—were 'overly ambitious and impossible to achieve'. Although no specific resignations were recommended by the Winograd Commission, it did single out Peretz and former Chief of Staff Lt-Gen. Dan Halutz as being responsible for Israel's military failures (see below for details regarding Halutz's resignation). Following the publication of the Commission's initial findings, Eitan Cabel, a Minister responsible for the Israel Broadcasting Authority in Olmert's Government, tendered his resignation on 1 May 2007, stating that he could no longer serve under Olmert. During subsequent days mass protests were held by Israelis demanding the resignation of the Prime Minister and his administration; although Olmert survived three votes of no confidence in the Knesset in early May, doubts remained over the long-term viability of his governing coalition.

Meanwhile, following the resignation a few days previously of the Minister of Justice, Haim Ramon, who was facing charges of sexual harassment, in August 2006 the Minister of Construction and Housing, Meir Sheetrit, assumed temporary responsibility for the justice portfolio. Trial proceedings were initiated against Ramon in October, while a former Minister of the Environment, Tzahi Hanegbi, also faced charges in relation to allegations of election bribery, fraud and perjury. Significantly, police also recommended that President Katsav be charged with a number of serious offences, including rape and sexual harassment, fraud, bribery and obstruction of justice. On 25 January 2007 the Knesset voted to declare Katsav 'temporarily incapacitated' for a three-month period while he was contesting the charges. (This followed the President's formal request to take a leave of absence.) The Speaker, Dalia Itzik, was named as acting President for this period. Attorney-General Menachem Mazuz declared in early April that Katsav was to face a second rape charge; the President awaited a hearing with Mazuz in May to discover whether or not he would be indicted. In mid-April the Knesset granted Katsav the request that his period of 'temporary incapacity' be extended until after the Attorney-General had ruled on whether he could return to office: Katsav was to extend his leave of absence by a further three months, or until his presidential term was scheduled to end in July. Itzik thus continued as acting President. Ramon, Hanegbi and Katsav all persistently denied the charges against them.

In October 2006 the Labour Minister of Science, Culture and Sport, Ophir Pines-Paz, had resigned from the Government, shortly after the Cabinet approved the appointment of ultra-nationalist Avigdor Lieberman of Israel Beiteinu as Deputy Prime Minister and Minister of Strategic Affairs. Pines-Paz declared that he intended to stand for the leadership of the Labour Party in May 2007. In early November 2006 Minister of Education Yuli Tamir was additionally named as acting Minister of Science, Culture and Sport. Later that month the Vice-Prime Minister and Minister of Foreign Affairs, Tzipi Livni, also assumed responsibility for the justice portfolio, replacing Sheetrit in that post. In late January 2007 the Israeli Cabinet endorsed the appointment of an Arab Israeli member of the Knesset, Rajeb Majadele, as a Minister without Portolio; he was assigned the science, culture and sport porfolio in March. However, Majadele's appointment to the Cabinet was strongly opposed by members of Israel's right-wing parties. In early February Prof. Daniel Friedmann was named as Minister of Justice. Lt-Gen. Gabi Ashkenazi assumed the position of Chief of Staff of the Armed Forces in the middle of that month, following the resignation, in mid-January, of Lt-Gen. Dan Halutz at the conclusion of military investigations into the conduct of the Israeli armed forces during its conflict with Hezbollah in mid-2006. (Although Halutz's management of the armed forces was sharply criticized in a report presented to the Knesset's Defense and Foreign Affairs Committee in January 2007, none of the investigations specifically concluded that Halutz should leave office.)

Meanwhile, Israel intensified Operation Summer Rains in October 2006, asserting that the actions of its armed forces in the Gaza Strip were intended to prevent Palestinian militant groups from launching rockets against Israeli targets and to disrupt the supply of weapons from Egypt. Much of the military action in November focused on the town of Beit Hanoun, in northern Gaza, which was reported to have become a base for militants who were launching rocket attacks on Israeli communities living close to the border. However, towards the end of November—by which time hundreds of Palestinians had been killed in the military campaign—President Abbas brokered a cease-fire between Palestinian fighters and Israeli forces, resulting in an Israeli withdrawal from Gaza. Shortly afterwards Olmert made it clear that he now favoured the resumption of Middle East peace discussions with a view to the eventual creation of a Palestinian state, rather than any further unilateral Israeli withdrawals from the West Bank, and indicated in a speech that Israel was prepared to free a significant number of Palestinian prisoners, in exchange for the release of Corporal Gilad Shalit unharmed. Three Israelis died in January 2007 when a Palestinian suicide bomber attacked the resort of Eilat; responsibility for the assault—the first Palestinian suicide attack in Israel since April 2006—was claimed by both Islamic Jihad and the Al-Aqsa Martyrs' Brigades. In March 2007 members of the Arab League held a summit meeting in the Saudi capital, Riyadh, at which they urged Israel to accept the terms of the Arab peace initiative first unveiled in Beirut in 2002 (see above). In mid-April 2007 Abbas and Olmert held discussions regarding a future Palestinian state and a possible prisoner exchange, in what was intended to be the first of a series of regular fortnightly meetings between the two leaders. However, later in the month militants from Hamas declared that the cease-fire brokered in November 2006 was ended, and launched a series of rockets into Israel from the Gaza Strip. Israel responded in May 2007 by conducting a series of air-strikes against alleged militant targets in Gaza; a number of Hamas legislators, ministers and local government officials were also detained by Israeli security forces.

In mid-January 2007 police began investigations into the role played by Ehud Olmert in the privatization of Bank Leumi in 2005, when the Prime Minister held the finance portfolio in the Government of Ariel Sharon; it was alleged that Olmert had promoted the interests of two foreign businessmen in the sale of a controlling stake in the bank. Meanwhile, Haim Ramon was found guilty of sexual harassment at the end of January 2007 and was sentenced to 120 hours of community service at the end of March. In late April the Minister of Finance, Abraham Hirchson, declared that he was taking a temporary leave of absence as a result of police investigations into his failure to report an embezzlement of funds by a former employee; Olmert assumed the finance portfolio in an acting capacity. A few days later the State Comptroller recommended that the Prime Minister face a criminal investigation into allegations that he arranged investment opportunities for an associate when he served as Minister of Industry, Trade and Labour; a decision by the Attorney-General was pending. Olmert faced a new police investigation into his personal dealings in late September: it was alleged that, while serving as mayor of Jerusalem, Olmert had acquired a property in the city at a price significantly below its market value, in exchange for the accelerated provision of building permits to the property developer involved. The Prime Minister's Office strenuously denied the claims. At the end of November the police recommended that there was insufficient evidence to launch criminal proceedings against Olmert in the case concerning the privatization of Bank Leumi.

Following an agreement signed between representatives of Hamas and Fatah in Mecca, Saudi Arabia, in February 2007 to form a Palestinian administration of national unity, Israeli officials maintained that they would refuse to have contact with any cabinet that failed to recognize Israel's right to exist, renounce violence and respect existing agreements between Israel and the PA—the conditions demanded by the international Quartet group in order for the Palestinian administration to secure a resumption of international financial assistance. The new Palestinian Cabinet appointed in March was a coalition of ministers from Hamas and Fatah, together with independents and representatives from two smaller Palestinian parties (for further details, see the chapter on the Palestinian Autonomous Areas). Although Israel persisted with its boycott of the Palestinian administration, the USA and some EU governments revealed that they would initiate contacts with non-Hamas ministers. However, on 14 June Hamas militants seized control of the Gaza Strip, leading President Abbas to dissolve the national unity Cabinet under the premiership of Ismail Haniya of Hamas and to appoint an independent, Dr Salam Fayyad, as

Prime Minister. An Emergency Cabinet, consisting principally of independents and technocrats, as well as one Fatah representative, was sworn in by Abbas on 17 June. Although Israel was swift to recognize the Fayyad administration, the fact that governance of the Palestinian territories was now effectively divided between a Cabinet backed by President Abbas of Fatah in the West Bank and a Hamas-led administration in Gaza made the likelihood of a resumption of bilateral peace negotiations more remote. The Israeli Government moved quickly to show its support for Abbas by agreeing to transfer tax revenues to the PA that it had withdrawn following Hamas's election victory of January 2006. A meeting was also held in Sharm esh-Sheikh on 25 June 2007 between Olmert, Abbas President Mubarak of Egypt and King Abdullah of Jordan, with the Israeli premier declaring that Israel was to free 250 Fatah activists from gaol as a gesture of 'goodwill' to the Palestinian President; this was agreed by Israel's Cabinet on 8 July, and a final total of 255 (mainly Fatah) security prisoners were released on 20 July. Upon the expiry of the 30-day state of emergency, on 13 July the Palestinian President had appointed three new ministers to a reshuffled Cabinet, which was to function as a caretaker administration under Prime Minister Fayyad. Hamas again refused to recognize the legitimacy of this interim administration.

Former Prime Minister Ehud Barak won the second round of elections to the Labour Party leadership on 12 June 2007, defeating his rival candidate, Ayi Ayalon. (Labour's former leader, Amir Peretz, had been defeated at the first round of voting in late May.) On 18 June Barak assumed the post of Deputy Prime Minister and Minister of Defence, although he asserted that he believed Olmert should resign as premier prior to the publication of the final findings of the Winograd Commission's inquiry into the 2006 military campaign against Hezbollah in Lebanon (see below). Meanwhile, on 13 June 2007 Shimon Peres was elected by the Knesset as President of Israel, in succession to Moshe Katsav. Peres had defeated Reuben Rivlin of Likud and Colette Avital of Labour to assume the post; he was officially inaugurated as President on 15 July. On 28 June 2007 Katsav was reported to have agreed the terms of a plea bargain, according to which the rape charges against him were to be withdrawn in exchange for him admitting to charges for the lesser sexual offences involving two female employees; he was to receive a suspended prison sentence and pay a fine of NIS 50,000. Katsav duly tendered his resignation, which entered effect on 2 July. (The Supreme Court upheld the plea bargain in late February 2008; however, in early April Katsav decided that he would prefer to contest all the charges in court.) As part of a government reorganization on 4 July 2007, the former Minister of Justice, Haim Ramon, was returned to the Cabinet as Vice-Premier. Abraham Hirchson was succeeded as Minister of Finance by Ronnie Bar-On, whose post as Minister of the Interior was given to Meir Sheetrit.

Olmert and Abbas held discussions in the West Bank town of Jericho on 6 August 2007—the first talks to be convened between Israeli and Palestinian leaders in Palestinian territory since May 2000. The Israeli Prime Minister was reported to have expressed his hopes that bilateral negotiations concerning the establishment of a Palestinian state could commence in the near future. The two leaders held further talks on 'fundamental issues' later in August 2007 and again in early September. On 16 August Israel and the USA signed a memorandum of understanding concerning the provision to the Jewish state of some US $30,000m. of military assistance during the period of 2008–18. On 5 September 2007 Israel's Supreme Court issued a ruling that the route of a further section of the 'security fence' along Israel's boundary with the West Bank should be altered in order to improve the living conditions of Palestinians residing at that location. Israel released another 57 Palestinian prisoners to the West Bank and 29 to the Gaza Strip at the start of October. Towards the end of that month the Israeli Government responded to the launching of rockets into northern Israel by Palestinian militants from the Gaza Strip by confirming a policy of reducing fuel and electricity supplies to Gaza, which it now classified as a 'hostile entity'. (An intervention by the Supreme Court prevented the authorities from phasing out electricity supplies until they could prove that this would not impede vital services such as hospitals and sanitation provision, although the fuel sanctions were permitted.) The Israeli Government had been petitioned by several of the country's most influential novelists in late September to open a dialogue with Hamas, in an effort to bring an end to the rocket attacks against Israel and the frequent military incursions into, and air-strikes against, Gaza.

Following a series of preparatory meetings between US officials and Israeli and Palestinian delegations in the preceding weeks, an international peace meeting intended officially to relaunch the Middle East peace process was held under US auspices in Annapolis, Maryland, USA, on 27 November 2007. Members of the international Quartet group and the Arab League attended the talks, and Syria notably sent a low-level delegation. At the close of the meeting US President Bush read a statement of 'joint understanding' between Olmert and Abbas, who both expressed their commitment to achieving a final settlement of the outstanding issues of contention between Israelis and Palestinians by the end of 2008. In order to succeed in this effort finally to effect a two-state solution to the Israeli–Palestinian conflict, it was revealed that: an Israeli-Palestinian steering committee would oversee 'vigorous, ongoing and continuous' negotiations between the two sides; the Israeli and Palestinian leaders would continue to meet on a fortnightly basis; and both Israel and the PA would comply with their obligations as agreed under the terms of the roadmap signed in 2003. However, Palestinians were angered in early December 2007 when an Israeli ministry issued tenders for more than 300 new housing units at the Har Homa settlement in East Jerusalem. The US Secretary of State, Condoleezza Rice, had warned Israel that expanding Jewish settlements on the West Bank threatened to undermine recent progress in the peace process. Moreover, Olmert appeared to indicate that Israel would not be required to conclude a peace treaty with the PA by the end of 2008 if it considered that the Palestinians had not met their security obligations.

A spokesman for Hamas's de facto Prime Minister in the Gaza Strip, Ismail Haniya, reportedly responded to the Annapolis meeting by pledging that Palestinian 'resistance' to Israeli occupation would continue. Nevertheless, the Israeli authorities released a further 429 Palestinian prisoners (none of whom had been involved in attacks against Israelis) at this time as a renewed 'goodwill' gesture to President Abbas. Also in early December 2007 a court in Jerusalem sentenced a PLFP militant to a term of life imprisonment, after he was convicted of having assassinated the Minister of Tourism, Rechavam Ze'evi, in Jerusalem in October 2001, as well as involvement in other attacks against Israeli citizens. (The detainee had been serving a sentence for the crime at a West Bank prison; however, when Western supervisors withdrew from the Jericho gaol and Israeli forces entered it in 2006, he was handed over to the Israeli legal system.) In the second week of December 2007 Israeli forces conducted a series of air-strikes against militants in the Gaza Strip, as well as sending tanks into the southern part of the Strip in an attempt to prevent the continuing rocket fire against Sderot in northern Israel; a number of Palestinian militants (mostly from Islamic Jihad) were reported to have died.

Following a Palestinian rocket assault against Ashkelon (in which no one was injured) in early January 2008, Israel intensified its military offensive in the Gaza Strip, killing at least nine people on one day; further Palestinian lives were lost in that month as the Gaza campaign continued. Israeli officials claimed that militants were deliberately firing on Israeli troops from civilian areas. Israeli forces also conducted house-to-house searches in the West Bank city of Nablus, and a number of arrests of suspected militants were reported. In the second week of January US President Bush undertook a three-day visit to Israel and the West Bank, where he held discussions with both Olmert and Abbas. Bush assured Israelis that he understood their security concerns, but he also asserted that a future Palestinian state should be contiguous territory and not a 'Swiss cheese' of separate cantons. The US leader again urged Israel to cease the expansion of existing Jewish settlements in the West Bank and to remove illegal outposts, while he stated that the PA must ensure that militant groups be dismantled. Bush also surprised some commentators by issuing a firm statement urging Israel to withdraw from Arab territory that its forces had occupied in 1967. In mid-January 2008 Israel imposed virtually a complete blockade on the Gaza Strip, which prompted vehement international criticism: the Israeli response to Palestinian violence targeted at its citizens was widely viewed as 'collective punishment' of the people of Gaza for the actions of a small number of militants. The blockade resulted in disruption to Gaza's electricity supply and serious international concerns that the territory would suffer a humanitarian crisis. (Olmert did subsequently agree to allow food, medicine and necessary fuel to be supplied to Palestinians in Gaza.)

Also in mid-January 2008 Olmert's governing coalition suffered a serious reverse, when the Deputy Prime Minister and Minister of Strategic Affairs, Avigdor Lieberman, announced that his party, the right-wing Israeli Beytenu, was to withdraw its members, in protest at the Prime Minister's policy of engaging in peace negotiations with the PA. This left Olmert with a reduced majority in the Knesset and resulted in the resignation of Lieberman and of the Minister of Tourism, Yitzhak Aharonovitch, from the Cabinet; the Prime Minister subsequently assumed temporary responsibility for the tourism portfolio.

The long-awaited final report of the Winograd Commission was issued on 30 January 2008. Although the Commission described Israel's ground offensive in Lebanon in mid-2006 as a 'serious failure' in both military and political terms—noting the lack of any clear strategy prior to initiating the 34-day campaign against Hezbollah—it assessed Prime Minister Olmert to have acted 'in the sincere interest of Israel' in ordering the military action. Many observers expressed intense surprise at the lack of any serious personal criticism aimed at Olmert, particularly after he had ordered Israeli armed forces to undertake a large-scale ground offensive in southern Lebanon only hours before an agreed cease-fire was scheduled to take effect; 33 Israeli soldiers had died during this final stage of the war. It was notable that the Winograd Commission acknowledged Israel's failure to secure an obvious military victory as a result of its conflict with Hezbollah. Thus, although Olmert initially survived the aftermath of the report's publication, it was widely acknowledged that he had been weakened by the Commission's findings, especially at a time when he was already under investigation for alleged corrupt practices.

Meanwhile, in the third week of January 2008 thousands of Palestinians entered Egypt from Gaza in search of food and other essential supplies, after Hamas militants had breached the border separating the two territories. When, in early February, an Israeli woman died in a suicide bombing in the southern town of Dimona, the Government implied that the Gazan perpetrator of the attack must have entered Israel via Egypt as a direct result of the border having been breached. A representative of the Al-Aqsa Martyrs' Brigades initially claimed responsibility for the suicide bombing—the first in Israel for more than a year—although there was some confusion about this claim after Hamas stated that militants of its organization had carried out the attack from Hebron in the West Bank. Amid an obvious stalling of bilateral peace negotiations as Israeli officials even threatened a full-scale military invasion of Gaza, the Israeli Prime Minister announced that, in his view, the status of Jerusalem would be the final 'core issue' to be negotiated by the two parties. A number of Palestinian politicians asserted that the issue of how to divide the city could not be postponed until the end of the peace process.

Israeli–Palestinian relations witnessed a new low-point in early March 2008. Eight students died, and several others were wounded, in a shooting at a Jewish religious college in Jerusalem believed to have been perpetrated by a Palestinian resident of East Jerusalem; the gunman was immediately shot dead by an off-duty Israeli soldier. Once again, the issue of whether ultimate responsibility for the shooting could be attributed to Hamas was unclear: a spokesman for the militant group appeared to claim, and later deny, its involvement in the attack, which represented the worst such incident to take place in Jerusalem since 2004. The Israeli Government affirmed that it would pursue peace negotiations with its Palestinian counterpart, despite the sudden upsurge in violence. However, the likelihood of a swift breakthrough in the peace process was again impeded when, shortly after the Jerusalem shooting, Olmert approved a controversial plan to construct a further 330 homes for Jewish settlers in the West Bank. Moreover, in mid-March 2008 the Israeli premier insisted that his Government would continue with its policy of settlement expansion in East Jerusalem.

In March 2000 the Israeli Cabinet voted unanimously to withdraw its forces from southern Lebanon by 7 July, even in the absence of a peace agreement with Syria. The Lebanese Government responded by demanding that Israel also depart from a small area on the Syrian border known as Shebaa Farms. (Shebaa Farms has been designated by the UN as being part of Syria, and thus subject to the Syrian track of the peace process; Hezbollah, however, considers it to be part of southern Lebanon.) In April Israel released 13 Lebanese prisoners who had been detained without trial for more than a decade, apparently as 'bargaining chips' for Israeli soldiers missing in Lebanon. Fighting between Israeli troops and Hezbollah intensified in May, and there were fears that further violence might follow an Israeli withdrawal after it was announced that Israel would not disarm the SLA. On 23 May Israel's Security Cabinet voted to accelerate the withdrawal of its remaining troops from southern Lebanon. By this date Hezbollah had taken control of about one-third of the territory following the evacuation by the SLA of outposts transferred to its control by the Israeli army; moreover, mass defections from the SLA were reported. Meanwhile, Lebanese citizens stormed the al-Khiam prison in the security zone and freed 144 inmates. The rapid departure of all Israeli forces from southern Lebanon was completed on 24 May, nearly six weeks before Barak's original July deadline. Israeli public opinion generally welcomed an end to the occupation, since about 900 Israelis had been killed in southern Lebanon since 1978. After the withdrawal several thousand SLA members and their families fled across the border into northern Israel. In June 2000 the UN Security Council confirmed that Israel had completed its withdrawal from Lebanon in compliance with UN Resolution 425. UNIFIL's mandate was extended for a six-month period in July, by which time UNIFIL personnel were patrolling the area vacated by Israeli forces, monitoring the line of withdrawal and providing humanitarian assistance. Further extensions of UNIFIL's mandate were announced at six-monthly intervals.

Hezbollah reaffirmed in mid-2000 that it would pursue its armed campaign against Israel until Shebaa Farms was returned to Lebanese control. The al-Aqsa *intifada*, which erupted in late September (see above), precipitated renewed operations by Hezbollah against the Israeli army. In early October three Israeli soldiers were kidnapped on the border with Lebanon by Hezbollah militants demanding the release of Arab prisoners held in Israel. One week later an Israeli businessman and army reservist, Elhanan Tannenbaum, was also captured by Hezbollah. Tensions escalated in November when an Israeli soldier was killed by a Hezbollah bomb in Shebaa Farms; Israel responded by launching air raids on suspected Hezbollah targets. In April 2001 Israeli helicopter gunships attacked a Syrian radar base in central Lebanon (in which at least one Syrian soldier died), in retaliation for the recent killing by Hezbollah of another Israeli soldier in Shebaa Farms. Israeli military officials declared in October that the three soldiers kidnapped by Hezbollah in late 2000 were 'almost certainly' dead. In November 2003 the Israeli Cabinet agreed to release more than 400 Palestinian and Lebanese prisoners in exchange for the remains of the three kidnapped soldiers, as well as the return of Tannenbaum. Germany, which had acted as mediator during four years of negotiations between Israel and Hezbollah, agreed to oversee the exchange, and in January 2004 the first 30 Lebanese and other Arab prisoners to be released by Israel were flown to the airport at Cologne, where they were exchanged for Tannenbaum and the remains of the Israeli soldiers. The remainder of the Palestinian prisoners, and the remains of 59 Lebanese militants held by Israel, were later released at Israeli border posts.

Syria had welcomed the election of Ehud Barak to the Israeli premiership in May 1999. In July Barak undertook to negotiate a bilateral peace with Syria, based on UN Resolutions 242 and 338: this was interpreted as a signal of his intention to return most of the occupied Golan Heights in exchange for peace and normalized relations. On 20 July Syria ordered a 'cease-fire' with Israel. However, it was not until December that the two sides agreed to a resumption of negotiations from the point at which they had broken off in 1996, reportedly as a result of diplomatic efforts by US President Clinton and secret meetings between Israeli and Syrian officials. The Knesset subsequently approved the decision to resume talks, while Barak reasserted that any agreement concluded with Syria would be put to a national referendum. Clinton inaugurated peace negotiations between Barak and the Syrian Minister of Foreign Affairs, Farouk ash-Shara', in Washington, DC, on 15 December 1999. The talks commenced amid rising tensions in southern Lebanon, and resulted only in an agreement to resume discussions in January 2000. Barak, meanwhile, was encountering growing opposition in Israel to a possible return of the Golan Heights to Syria. In late December 1999 Israel and Syria agreed an informal 'cease-fire' to curb hostilities in Lebanon. Barak and ash-Shara' attended further discussions (in which President Clinton played an active role) on 3–10 January 2000 in Shepherdstown, West Virginia. As a preliminary to the talks it was agreed that four committees would be established to discuss simultaneously the issues of borders, security, normalization of relations and water sharing.

As further discussions proved inconclusive, the US Administration presented a 'draft working document' to both sides as the basis for a framework agreement. However, Syria announced that it required a commitment from Israel to withdraw from the Golan Heights before negotiations could resume. Israel, meanwhile, demanded the personal involvement of President Hafiz al-Assad in the peace process. In early January a huge demonstration was held in Tel-Aviv by Israelis opposed to any withdrawal from the Golan Heights, while Israel B'Aliyah and the NRP threatened to leave Barak's coalition in any such event. On 17 January talks between Israel and Syria, which had been scheduled to reconvene two days later, were postponed indefinitely. Despite the intensification of the conflict in southern Lebanon (see above), and a Knesset vote in early March to change the majority required in the event of a referendum on an Israeli withdrawal from the Golan Heights from 50% of participants to 50% of the registered electorate, hopes of an imminent breakthrough in the Syrian track of the peace process were raised by the announcement, later in March, that Presidents Clinton and Assad were to meet in Geneva, Switzerland. However, the talks, on 26 March, broke down after only three hours, when it became apparent that the US President had no new Israeli proposals to offer to Syria regarding its demand for a full and unconditional withdrawal from the Golan Heights. In April Barak declared that the Israeli Government would resume the construction of Jewish settlements in the Golan Heights (following a declared suspension prior to the December 1999 talks).

The prospect of further peace-making initiatives between Israel and Syria was further distanced by the death of President Assad in June 2000, although Assad's second son, Bashar—who assumed the Syrian presidency in July—promised a continuation of his father's policies towards Israel. The Israeli-Syrian track remained deadlocked following the election of Ariel Sharon as Israel's premier. Despite reports in January 2002 that the Israeli Minister of Defence, Binyamin Ben-Eliezer, had informed the Syrian leadership that Israel would be willing to resume peace negotiations provided that there were no preconditions, by early 2003 the possibility of a swift resumption of talks appeared remote (especially as the USA increasingly referred to Syria as a possible target in President Bush's 'war on terror'). In October Israel launched an air-strike against an alleged training camp for Palestinian militants in Syria. The attack on the Ein Saheb camp, near Damascus, was prompted by a suicide bombing in Haifa a few days previously which killed 19 Israelis. Syria sought a UN Security Council resolution condemning the attack, while both the PFLP and Islamic Jihad denied having used the training camp.

In late 2003 and early 2004 the Israeli President, Moshe Katsav, issued a proposition to President Bashar al-Assad for Syria to start direct negotiations with Israel 'without preconditions'. However, the Syrian leadership dismissed the Israeli offer as being 'not serious'. In February 2005 Israeli officials stated that they would not resume negotiations with Syria regarding the Golan Heights until Syria had implemented a complete withdrawal of its forces from Lebanon (for further details, see the chapters on Lebanon and Syria). No agreement on the resumption of talks had been reached between Israel and Syria by early 2008. However, it was alleged by Israel's *Ha'aretz* newspaper in January 2007 that secret discussions had taken place between Israeli and Syrian representatives between September 2004 and the start of the conflict between Israel and Hezbollah in July 2006, reportedly leading to important mutual understandings having been reached with regard to the Golan Heights and other contentious issues. Although officials from both countries denied the claim, in March 2007 President Assad was reported to have confirmed that secret talks had taken place between 'non-official' channels. Tensions between Israel and Syria worsened in early September, after Israel carried out an air-strike on a military installation 'deep within' Syrian territory. The reason for the military strike was not immediately evident, although there was speculation in the Israeli media that the target had been a shipment of Iranian-supplied weapons en route to Lebanon for use by Hezbollah fighters. In early April 2008 US intelligence claimed to have evidence that the target of the Israeli air-strike was in fact a nuclear facility that was being constructed with assistance from the Democratic People's Republic of Korea (North Korea).

In January 2004 Israel and India signed an agreement involving the sale to India of three Phalcon early-warning radar systems worth US $1,100m. Israel also agreed to sell military technology to Turkey in exchange for 50m. cu m of fresh water per year over a 20-year period. In May the Chairman of the Knesset Foreign Affairs and Defence Committee, Yuval Steinitz, expressed concern that Egypt was building up its store of weapons, many of which were supplied by the USA, asserting that Egypt was simulating a war with Israel. Israel pressed the USA to continue to maintain Israeli military qualitative superiority in the Middle East. In July, during a visit by the UN's International Atomic Energy Agency (IAEA), Israel maintained its policy of 'strategic ambiguity' by not commenting on whether or not it possessed nuclear weapons; however, international experts reported that Israel might have as many as 200 nuclear warheads. Prime Minister Ariel Sharon announced his support for the idea of a Middle East free from nuclear weapons, and urged the IAEA Director-General, Muhammad el-Baradei, to exert more pressure on Iran over its suspected uranium enrichment programme. In September the USA agreed to sell Israel $20m.-worth of heavy weaponry, which was apparently intended to serve Israel against a possible military threat from Iran, and which analysts noted could be used to launch strikes against Iran's nuclear facilities. Further concern was expressed at Iran's intentions towards Israel following an announcement by President Mahmoud Ahmadinejad in October 2005 that he wished to see Israel 'wiped off the map'. The comment provoked international condemnation, and Israel demanded an emergency meeting of the UN Security Council, at which all 15 members approved a motion condemning Ahmadinejad's declaration. However, later in the month the Iranian Ministry of Foreign Affairs rejected the Security Council's verdict and declared that the country had no intention of attacking Israel, while the President asserted that he had merely expressed the will of his people. Amid the continuing international disquiet over Iran's nuclear ambitions in 2006, Iran provoked further outrage by its frequent statements about Israel and the Holocaust. Moreover, Iran was viewed as having played a leading role in the conflict between Israel and Hezbollah in July–August; however, while the Iranian leadership admitted its support for Hezbollah, it denied claims that it was providing the group with military assistance. In November a spokesman from the Iranian Ministry of Foreign Affairs warned that any pre-emptive military strikes launched by Israel against Iran's nuclear facilities would be met with a swift and powerful response.

Government

Supreme authority in Israel rests with the Knesset (Assembly), with 120 members elected by universal suffrage for four years (subject to dissolution), on the basis of proportional representation. The President, a constitutional Head of State, is elected by the Knesset for five years. (Moshe Katsav, who assumed the presidency in August 2000, was exceptionally elected for a seven-year term.) Executive power lies with the Cabinet, led by a Prime Minister. The Cabinet takes office after receiving a vote of confidence in the Knesset, to which it is responsible. Ministers are usually members of the Knesset, but non-members may be appointed.

The country is divided into six administrative districts. Local authorities are elected at the same time as elections to the Knesset. There are 31 municipalities (including two Arab towns), 115 local councils (46 Arab and Druze) and 49 regional councils (one Arab) comprising representatives of 700 villages.

Defence

The Israel Defence Forces consist of a small nucleus of commissioned and non-commissioned regular officers, a contingent enlisted for national service and a large reserve. Men are enlisted for 36 months of military service (excluding officers, who serve for 48 months), and women for 24 months. Military service is compulsory for Jews and Druzes, but voluntary for Christians, Circassians and Muslims. Total regular armed forces, as assessed at November 2007, numbered an estimated 176,500 (including 107,000 conscripts), comprising an army of 133,000, a navy of 9,500 and an air force of 34,000; full mobilization to 741,500 can be quickly achieved with reserves of 565,000. There were also an estimated 8,050 paramilitary troops. The budget for 2007 allocated NIS 47,892m. to defence.

Economic Affairs

In 2005, according to estimates by the World Bank, Israel's gross national income (GNI), measured at average 2003–05 prices, was US $128,667m., equivalent to $18,580 per head (or $25,480 per head on an international purchasing-power parity basis). During 1996–2006, it was estimated, the population increased at an average annual rate of 2.1%, while gross domestic product (GDP) per head increased, in real terms, by an average of 0.8% per year in 1996–2005. Overall GDP increased, in real terms, at an average annual rate of 3.5% in 1996–2006; growth of 5.3% was recorded in 2007, according to preliminary official figures.

Agriculture (including hunting, forestry and fishing) contributed a preliminary 1.9% of GDP in 2007, and in the same year engaged 1.6% of the employed labour force. Most agricultural workers live in large co-operatives (*kibbutzim*), of which there were 267 at December 2006, or co-operative smallholder villages (*moshavim*), of which there were 441. Israel is largely self-sufficient in foodstuffs. Citrus fruits constitute the main export crop. Other important crops are vegetables (particularly potatoes, tomatoes, chillies and green peppers), wheat, melons and apples. The export of exotic fruits, winter vegetables and flowers has increased significantly in recent years. Poultry, livestock and fish production are also important. According to FAO data, agricultural output increased at an average annual rate of 1.8% in 1990–2006; production increased by 1.4% in 2006.

Industry (comprising mining, manufacturing, construction and power) contributed a preliminary 21.5% of GDP in 2007, and engaged 22.1% of the employed labour force in that year. The State plays a major role in all sectors of industry, and there is a significant co-operative sector.

The mining and manufacturing sectors together contributed a preliminary 14.5% of GDP in 2007, and engaged 15.9% of the employed labour force in the same year; mining and quarrying employed about 0.2% of the working population in 1997. Israel has small proven reserves of petroleum (of some 3.9m. barrels), from which less than 500 barrels per day are currently produced; however, in 1999 potential new reserves were discovered in central Israel and off the southern coast. (Israel's Petroleum Commission has estimated that the country could possess up to 5,000m. barrels of oil reserves, most likely located underneath gas reserves, and that offshore gas could supply its short-term energy needs.) Some natural gas is also produced, and significant offshore gas discoveries were made in the south in 1999 and 2000. Phosphates, potash, bromides, magnesium and other salts are mined, and Israel is the world's largest exporter of bromine.

Manufacturing employed 19.3% of the working population in 1997. The principal branches of manufacturing, measured by gross revenue, are: food products, beverages and tobacco; chemical, petroleum and coal products; electrical machinery; metal products; scientific, photographic, optical equipment, etc.; paper, publishing and printing; textiles and clothing; non-metallic mineral manufactures; rubber and plastic products; and non-electrical machinery.

Energy is derived principally from coal (accounting for 75.3% of total electricity output in 2004) and imported petroleum (15.8%); however, it is intended that natural gas should eventually become Israel's principal energy source. Energy derived from natural gas contributed 8.8% of total electricity output in 2004, up from just 0.1% in 2003. Imports of mineral fuels comprised 13.9% of the total value of imports in 2006.

Services contributed a preliminary 76.6% of GDP in 2007, and engaged 76.2% of the employed labour force in the same year. Tourism is an important source of revenue, although the sector has been severely damaged by regional instability and a series of bomb attacks carried out by militant Islamist groups in recent years. The significant upsurge in violence from September 2000 once again deterred many foreign visitors, resulting in hotel closures, redundancies and a reduction in air travel. However, a decline in the number of militant attacks in the second half of the decade has resulted in an increase in tourist numbers: in 2007 some 2.3m. tourists visited Israel (up from 1.8m. in 2006), and receipts from tourism totalled US $3,414m. in 2005. Financial services are also important: banking, insurance, real estate and business services together contributed a preliminary 25.9% of GDP in 2007, and employed 17.7% of the working population in the same year.

In 2006 Israel recorded a visible trade deficit of US $3,233m.; however, there was a surplus of $7,990m. on the current account of the balance of payments. Excluding trade with the West Bank and Gaza Strip, in 2007 the principal source of imports was the USA, which supplied 13.9% of imports to Israel; other major suppliers were the Belgo-Luxembourg Economic Union (BLEU), Germany, the People's Republic of China and Switzerland-Liechtenstein. The USA was also the principal market for exports, taking 34.9% of Israeli exports in that year; other important purchasers were the BLEU and Hong Kong. Israel is the world's largest supplier of polished diamonds. The principal exports in 2006 were basic manufactures (chiefly non-metallic mineral manufactures), machinery and transport equipment, chemicals and related products, and miscellaneous manufactured articles. The principal imports in that year were basic manufactures (mainly non-metallic mineral manufactures), machinery and transport equipment, mineral fuels and lubricants, chemicals and related products, and miscellaneous manufactured articles.

In 2001 the overall budgetary deficit (excluding net allocation of credit) rose from the planned NIS 8,400m. (equivalent to some 1.7% of GDP) to NIS 21,300m. (equivalent to about 4.6% of GDP). This was mainly due to increased spending on security provisions prompted by the al-Aqsa *intifada*. Government revenue each year normally includes some US $3,000m. in economic and military aid from the USA. In 2006 there was a budgetary deficit of NIS 24,571m. (equivalent to 3.9% of GDP). The planned budget deficit for 2007 was NIS 15,813m. At 31 December 2006 Israel's gross foreign debt amounted to $83,258m. Government debt amounted to $31,190m. at the end of 2005. During 1990–2006 consumer prices rose at an average annual rate of 6.5%; annual inflation averaged 2.2% in 2006. The unemployment rate was reported to be 7.3% in 2007. A report by the National Insurance Institute of Israel issued in early 2006 indicated that 1.6m. Israelis (nearly one-quarter of the population) were living in poverty in 2004–05. Impoverished people were defined as those earning less than $358 per month (one-half of the national average salary in 2004). The number had apparently increased by 45% over five years, and more Arab citizens than Jewish citizens were reported to be affected by poverty.

The most significant factor affecting the Israeli economy in the 1990s was the mass influx of Jews from the former USSR, which led to a substantial increase in the population, additional flexibility in the labour market and growth in construction. In 1996, however, a period of economic slowdown began, reflecting an end to the demand boom and reduced tourism revenues following an increase in Islamist violence. After the Middle East peace process was revived under the administration of Ehud Barak in 1999, the economy entered a period of recovery, with a significant improvement in business activity and increased foreign investment. The strong rate of economic growth in 2000 was led by the success of Israel's high-technology sector. However, in the fourth quarter of 2000 the economic boom ended as a new *intifada* by Palestinians in the West Bank and Gaza dramatically reduced foreign investment and tourism revenues, while the global economic downturn had a particularly detrimental effect on high-tech companies. The negative growth in the Israeli economy in 2001–02 was reported to have been the first contraction since 1953, and in March 2003 the IMF described the Israeli economy as being 'in the midst of a deep recession'. Following the deregulation of the domestic telecommunications market and the privatization of Bank Hapoalim in 2000, the new Government of Ariel Sharon initiated its own privatization programme in May 2001, although structural reforms have often proceeded slowly. Nevertheless, GDP growth was again recorded during 2003–05. Despite the month-long conflict between the Lebanese militant group Hezbollah and Israeli armed forces (now under the premiership of Ehud Olmert) in mid-2006 and continuing Israeli–Palestinian violence, the Israeli economy grew by 5.1% in that year. A preliminary growth rate of 5.3% was recorded in 2007. Meanwhile, the Government has maintained its commitment to energy reform: it was reported in January 2008 that it had commissioned automotive manufacturers to mass-produce electric cars in order drastically to reduce oil imports. In late 2007 the Government also signalled its intention to purchase around 1,500m. cu m–1,800m. cu m of natural gas per year over a period of 12–14 years from 2010 for the same purpose. In early 2008 the IMF reported favourably on Israel's economic progress in 2007, pointing to strong budgetary and interest rate policies in particular. The tourism sector performed especially well, largely owing to improved security and the weakness of the US dollar. However, the IMF also expressed concern regarding Israel's high levels of public debt, and urged the Government to pursue a programme of debt reduction. The potential for Israeli economic growth in the long term will undoubtedly be dependent upon progress towards a comprehensive and enduring regional peace settlement.

Education

Israel has high standards of literacy and advanced educational services. Free, compulsory education is provided for all children between five and 15 years of age; in 1999 legislation was passed allowing for the introduction of free education for pre-primary children. Primary education is provided for all those between five

ISRAEL

and 10 years of age. There is also secondary, vocational and agricultural education. Post-primary education comprises two cycles of three years. According to UNESCO estimates, enrolment at primary schools in 2004/05 included 97.4% of pupils in the relevant age group, while 88.8% of pupils in the appropriate age group were enrolled at secondary schools. There are six universities, one institute of technology (the Technion) and one institute of science (the Weizmann Institute), which incorporates a graduate school of science. In 2007 budgetary expenditure on education by the central Government was forecast at NIS 31,928m. (some 10.9% of total spending).

Public Holidays

The Sabbath starts at sunset on Friday and ends at nightfall on Saturday. The Jewish year 5769 begins on 29 September 2008, and the year 5770 on 18 September 2009.

2008: 19–25 April (Pesach, Passover—public holidays on first and last days of festival), 7 May (Yom Ha'atzmaut, Independence Day), 8 June (Shavuot, Feast of Weeks), 29–30 September (Rosh Hashanah, Jewish New Year), 8 October (Yom Kippur, Day of Atonement), 13–19 October (Succot, Feast of the Tabernacles).

2009: 8–14 April (Pesach, Passover—see 2008), 28 April (Yom Ha'atzmaut, Independence Day), 28 May (Shavuot, Feast of Weeks), 18–19 September (Rosh Hashanah, Jewish New Year), 27 September (Yom Kippur, Day of Atonement), 2–8 October (Succot, Feast of the Tabernacles).

(The Jewish festivals and fast days commence in the evening of the dates given.)

Islamic holidays are observed by Muslim Arabs, and Christian holidays by the Christian Arab community.

Weights and Measures

The metric system is in force.
1 dunum = 1,000 sq metres.

Statistical Survey

Source (unless otherwise indicated): Central Bureau of Statistics, POB 13015, Hakirya, Romema, Jerusalem 91130; tel. 2-6592037; fax 2-6521340; e-mail yael@cbs.gov.il; internet www.cbs.gov.il.

Area and Population

AREA, POPULATION AND DENSITY

Area (sq km)	
Land	21,643
Inland water	429
Total	22,072*
Population (*de jure*; census results)†	
4 June 1983	4,037,620
4 November 1995	
Males	2,738,175
Females	2,810,348
Total	5,548,523
Population (*de jure*; official estimates at 31 December)†	
2005	6,990,700
2006	7,116,700
2007‡	7,243,700
Density (per sq km) at 31 December 2007†‡	334.7§

* 8,522 sq miles. Area includes East Jerusalem, annexed by Israel in June 1967, and the Golan sub-district (1,154 sq km), annexed by Israel in December 1981.
† Including the population of East Jerusalem and Israeli residents in certain other areas under Israeli military occupation since June 1967. Beginning in 1981, figures also include non-Jews in the Golan sub-district, an Israeli-occupied area of Syrian territory. Census results exclude adjustment for underenumeration.
‡ Provisional figure.
§ Land area only.

POPULATION BY RELIGION
(31 December 2006)

	Number	%
Jews	5,393,400	75.8
Muslims	1,173,100	16.5
Christians	149,100	2.1
Druze	117,500	1.7
Unclassified	280,900	3.9
Total*	**7,116,700**	**100.0**

* Including Lebanese not classified by religion (2,700 at 31 December 2006).

DISTRICTS
(31 December 2006)

	Area (sq km)*	Population (rounded)†	Density (per sq km)
Jerusalem‡	653	870,100	1,332.5
Northern§	4,473	1,203,300	269.0
Haifa	866	864,200	997.9
Central	1,294	1,690,800	1,306.6
Tel-Aviv	172	1,203,500	6,997.1
Southern	14,185	1,020,900	72.0
Total	**21,643**	**7,116,700**	**328.8**

* Excluding lakes, with a total area of 474 sq km.
† Components exclude, but total includes, Israelis residing in Jewish localities in the West Bank totalling some 261,600 at 31 December 2006. Also included in the total, but excluded from the components, are an estimated 2,300 former residents of Gaza with no known relocation residence following the 2005 Disengagement Plan Law.
‡ Including East Jerusalem, annexed by Israel in June 1967.
§ Including the Golan sub-district (area 1,154 sq km, population an estimated 39,800 at 31 December 2006), annexed by Israel in December 1981.

PRINCIPAL TOWNS
(population at 31 December 2006)

Jerusalem (capital)*	733,300	Petach-Tikva	184,200
Tel-Aviv—Jaffa	384,400	Netanya	173,800
Haifa	266,300	Holon	167,100
Rishon LeZiyyon	222,000	Bene Beraq	147,900
Ashdod	204,200	Ramat-Gan	129,700
Beersheba	185,400	Bat Yam	129,400

* The Israeli Government has designated the city of Jerusalem (including East Jerusalem, annexed by Israel in June 1967) as the country's capital, although this is not recognized by the UN.

ISRAEL

BIRTHS, MARRIAGES AND DEATHS*

	Registered live births Number	Rate (per 1,000)	Registered marriages Number	Rate (per 1,000)	Registered deaths Number	Rate (per 1,000)
1999	131,936	21.5	40,236	6.6	37,291	6.1
2000	136,390	21.7	38,894	6.4	37,688	6.0
2001	136,638	21.2	38,924	6.3	37,187	5.8
2002	139,535	21.3	39,718	6.2	38,409†	5.8†
2003	144,936	21.7	39,154	6.1	38,499†	5.7†
2004	145,207	21.3	39,855	5.9	37,939†	5.6†
2005	143,913	20.8	41,029	5.9	39,026†	5.6†‡
2006	148,170	21.0	n.a.	n.a.	38,666†	5.5†‡

* Including East Jerusalem.
† Including deaths abroad of Israelis residing outside of Israel less than one year.
‡ Provisional figures.

Expectation of life (years at birth, WHO estimates): 80.2 (males 78.1; females 82.2) in 2005 (Source: WHO, *World Health Statistics*).

IMMIGRATION*

	2004	2005	2006
Immigrants:			
on immigrant visas	18,367	18,979	16,841
on tourist visas†	2,530	2,199	2,428
Potential immigrants on tourist visas†	—	1	2
Total	20,898	21,180	19,269

* Excluding immigrating citizens (3,253 in 2004; 3,579 in 2005; 3,051 in 2006–preliminary) and Israeli residents returning from abroad.
† Figures refer to tourists who changed their status to immigrants or potential immigrants.

2007: Total 18,075.

ECONOMICALLY ACTIVE POPULATION

(sample surveys, '000 persons aged 15 years and over, excluding armed forces)*

	2005	2006	2007
Agriculture, hunting, forestry and fishing	50.0	45.1	43.3
Industry†	391.7	401.9	421.6
Electricity, gas and water supply	21.3	18.1	16.8
Construction	127.1	134.4	150.2
Wholesale and retail trade; repair of motor vehicles, motorcycles and personal and household goods	337.2	336.7	358.2
Hotels and restaurants	115.1	122.1	122.1
Transport, storage and communications	162.6	171.5	171.2
Financial intermediation	82.1	87.4	95.0
Real estate, renting and business activities	335.3	354.4	375.3
Public administration and defence; compulsory social security	116.0	115.6	120.3
Education	314.1	325.9	344.4
Health and social work	265.6	263.7	267.0
Other community, social and personal service activities	116.8	128.2	124.2
Private households with employed persons	40.5	45.8	49.0
Extra-territorial organizations and bodies	2.0	1.9	1.3
Not classifiable by economic activity	16.4	20.8	22.1
Total employed	2,493.6	2,573.6	2,682.0
Unemployed	246.0	236.1	211.8
Total labour force	2,740.1	2,809.7	2,893.8
Males	1,465.0	1,502.2	1,546.7
Females	1,275.0	1,307.6	1,347.1

* Figures are estimated independently, so the totals may not be the sum of the component parts.
† Comprising mining and quarrying, and manufacturing.

Health and Welfare

KEY INDICATORS

Total fertility rate (children per woman, 2005)	2.8
Under-5 mortality rate (per 1,000 live births, 2005)	5
HIV/AIDS (% of persons aged 15–49, 2005)	0.1
Physicians (per 1,000 head, 2003)	3.82
Hospital beds (per 1,000 head, 2005)	6.3
Health expenditure (2004): US $ per head (PPP)	1,971.6
Health expenditure (2004): % of GDP	8.7
Health expenditure (2004): public (% of total)	70.0
Human Development Index (2005): ranking	23
Human Development Index (2005): value	0.932

For sources and definitions, see explanatory note on p. vi.

Agriculture

PRINCIPAL CROPS
('000 metric tons)

	2004	2005	2006
Wheat	154	201	131
Maize	71	60	70
Potatoes	600	594	544
Olives	62	29	40
Cottonseed	39	29	34
Cabbages and other brassicas	60	59	56
Lettuce and chicory	39	37	36
Tomatoes	514	433	387
Cucumbers and gherkins	145	127	133
Aubergines (Eggplants)	49	45	48
Chillies and green peppers	129	135	151
Dry onions	97	100	84
Carrots and turnips	97	103	128
Watermelons	317	143	125
Cantaloupes and other melons	49	50	46
Bananas	129	118	122
Oranges	123	188	147
Tangerines, mandarins, clementines and satsumas	93	133	133
Grapefruit and pomelos	236	264	266
Apples	150	140	122
Peaches and nectarines	89	69	54
Grapes	140	126	133
Avocados	73	86	78

Aggregate production ('000 metric tons, may include official, semi-official or estimated data): Total cereals 273 in 2004, 307 in 2005, 237 in 2006; Total roots and tubers 622 in 2004, 616 in 2005, 569 in 2006; Total vegetables (incl. melons) 1,821 in 2004, 1,508 in 2005, 1,462 in 2006; Total fruits (excl. melons) 1,346 in 2004, 1,468 in 2005, 1,322 in 2006.

Source: FAO.

LIVESTOCK
('000 head, year ending September, FAO estimates)

	2004	2005	2006
Cattle	350	357	398
Pigs	190	205	205
Sheep	420	435	445
Goats	75	83	87
Chickens	30,060	30,828	37,055
Geese*	1,000	1,400	1,400
Turkeys	4,141	4,195	4,080
Ducks*	200	200	200

* FAO estimates.
Source: FAO.

ISRAEL

LIVESTOCK PRODUCTS
('000 metric tons)

	2004	2005	2006
Cattle meat	83.0	89.9	108.3
Sheep meat*	5.1	5.1	5.1
Pig meat	18.0	18.7	17.5
Chicken meat	350.0	370.0	390.0
Goose meat	3.4	3.4	3.4*
Turkey meat	115.0	113.3	105.0
Cows' milk	1,168.1	1,178.7	1,150.0
Sheep's milk	23.0	21.0	21.0
Goats' milk	17.0	16.6	17.2
Hen eggs	90.7	92.4	93.5
Honey	3.6	3.2	3.3

* FAO estimate(s).
Source: FAO.

Forestry

ROUNDWOOD REMOVALS
('000 cubic metres, excl. bark)

	1999*	2000†	2001†
Sawlogs, veneer logs and logs for sleepers	36	28	11
Pulpwood	32	22	7
Other industrial wood	32	22	7
Fuel wood	13	8	2
Total	113	81	27

* FAO estimates.
† Unofficial figures.

2002–06: Figures assumed to be unchanged from 2001 (FAO estimates).
Source: FAO.

Fishing

('000 metric tons, live weight)

	2003	2004	2005
Capture	4,055	3,340	4,151
Carps, barbels, etc.	801	640	802
Aquaculture	20,776	22,303	22,404
Common carp	7,339	5,765	6,413
Tilapias	6,826	9,270	7,404
Gilthead seabream	2,546	2,860	3,366
Flathead grey mullet	1,705	1,792	2,108
Total catch	24,831	25,643	26,555

Source: FAO.

Mining

('000 metric tons unless otherwise indicated, estimates)

	2003	2004	2005
Crude petroleum ('000 barrels)	27.4	23.1	22.8
Natural gas (million cu m)	8	1,193	1,655
Phosphate rock*	3,300	2,900	3,000
Potash salts†	1,990	2,170	2,260
Salt (unrefined, marketed)	376	385	406
Gypsum	141	125	107
Bromine (elemental)	176	202	207

* Figures refer to beneficiated production; the phosphoric acid content (in '000 metric tons) was: 900 in 2003; 800 in 2004; 800 in 2005.
† Figures refer to K_2O content.

Source: US Geological Survey.

Industry

SELECTED PRODUCTS
('000 metric tons, unless otherwise indicated)

	1992	1993	1994
Refined vegetable oils (metric tons)	56,463	57,558	45,447
Margarine	35.1	33.8	24.7
Wine ('000 litres)	12,373	12,733	n.a.
Beer ('000 litres)	51,078	58,681	50,750
Cigarettes (metric tons)	5,742	5,525	5,638
Newsprint (metric tons)	0	247	0
Writing and printing paper (metric tons)	66,334	65,426	65,790
Other paper (metric tons)	32,368	30,446	28,985
Cardboard (metric tons)	92,072	95,108	103,142
Rubber tyres ('000)	892	854	966
Ammonia	41	41	46
Ammonium sulphate (metric tons)	12,444	n.a.	n.a.
Sulphuric acid	138	n.a.	n.a.
Chlorine (metric tons)	33,912	35,241	37,555
Caustic soda (metric tons)	29,459	29,851	32,765
Polyethylene (metric tons)	128,739	144,147	126,979
Paints (metric tons)	58,963	57,429	53,260
Cement	3,960	4,536	4,800
Commercial vehicles (number)	852	836	1,260
Electricity (million kWh)	24,731	26,042	28,327

1996 ('000 metric tons, unless otherwise indicated): Margarine 35; Cigarettes (metric tons) 4,793; Ammonia 65 (Source: US Geological Survey); Chlorine 35; Caustic soda 41; Paints 58.0 (Source: mainly UN, *Industrial Commodity Statistics Yearbook*).

1997 ('000 metric tons, unless otherwise indicated): Rubber tyres ('000) 792; Ammonia 57 (Source: US Geological Survey) (Source: mainly UN, *Monthly Bulletin of Statistics*).

2000 ('000 metric tons, unless otherwise indicated): Margarine 29.8 (Source: FAO); Wine ('000 litres) 7,500 (FAO estimate); Beer ('000 litres) 65,000 (unofficial estimate—Source: FAO); Sulphuric acid (sulphuric content) 613 (Source: US Geological Survey); Cement 5,703 (Source: US Geological Survey); Writing and printing paper 95 (FAO estimate); Commercial vehicles (number) 373 (Source: International Road Federation, *World Road Statistics*); Electricity (total production, million kWh) 42,958.

2001 ('000 metric tons, unless otherwise indicated): Margarine 29.8 (Source: FAO); Wine ('000 litres) 5,000 (FAO estimate); Beer ('000 litres) 52,000 (unofficial estimate—Source: FAO); Writing and printing paper 95 (FAO estimate); Sulphuric acid (sulphuric content) 621 (Source: US Geological Survey); Caustic soda 47 (estimate—Source: US Geological Survey); Cement 4,700 (estimate—Source: US Geological Survey); Electricity (total production, million kWh) 43,838.

2002 ('000 metric tons, unless otherwise indicated): Margarine 31.0 (FAO estimate); Wine ('000 litres) 5,700 (FAO estimate); Beer ('000 litres) 55,000 (FAO estimate); Electricity (total production, million kWh) 45,428; Writing and printing paper 95 (FAO estimate); Sulphuric acid (sulphuric content) 639 (Source: US Geological Survey); Caustic soda 54 (estimate—Source: US Geological Survey); Cement 4,584 (estimate—Source: US Geological Survey); Electricity (total production, million kWh) 39,920.

2003 ('000 metric tons, unless otherwise indicated): Margarine 32.0 (FAO estimate); Wine ('000 litres) 5,700 (FAO estimate); Beer ('000 litres) 72,200 (Unofficial—Source: FAO); Writing and printing paper 95 (FAO estimate); Sulphuric acid (sulphuric content) 619 (Source: US Geological Survey); Caustic soda 57 (estimate—Source: US Geological Survey); Cement 4,632 (estimate—Source: US Geological Survey); Electricity (total production, million kWh) 41,721.

2004 ('000 metric tons, unless otherwise indicated): Margarine 33.0 (FAO estimate); Wine ('000 litres) 6,500 (FAO estimate); Beer ('000 litres) 72,200; Writing and printing paper 95 (FAO estimate); Sulphuric acid (sulphuric content) 581 (Source: US Geological Survey); Caustic soda 64 (estimate—Source: US Geological Survey); Cement 4,494 (Source: US Geological Survey); Electricity (total production, million kWh) 42,933.

2005 ('000 metric tons, unless otherwise indicated): Wine ('000 litres) 6,500 (FAO estimate); Beer ('000 litres) 58,000 (FAO estimate); Writing and printing paper 95 (FAO estimate); Sulphuric acid (sulphuric content) 550 (Source: US Geological Survey); Caustic soda 64 (estimate—Source: US Geological Survey); Cement 5,093 (Source: US Geological Survey); Electricity (total production, million kWh) 44,309.

2006 ('000 metric tons, unless otherwise indicated): Wine ('000 litres) 6,500 (FAO estimate); Beer ('000 litres) 58,000 (FAO estimate); Writing and printing paper 95 (FAO estimate); Electricity (total production, million kWh) 46,175.

ISRAEL

Statistical Survey

Finance

CURRENCY AND EXCHANGE RATES

Monetary Units
100 agorot (singular: agora) = 1 new sheqel (plural: sheqalim) or shekel (NIS).

Sterling, Dollar and Euro Equivalents (31 December 2007)
£1 sterling = NIS 7.705;
US $1 = NIS 3.846;
€1 = NIS 5.662;
NIS 100 = £12.98 = $26.00 = €17.66.

Average Exchange Rate (NIS per US $)
2005   4.4877
2006   4.4558
2007   4.1081

STATE BUDGET*
(NIS million)

Revenue and grants†	2005	2006‡	2007§
Taxes and compulsory payments	163,123	169,200	180,756
Income and property taxes	87,469	88,600	99,100
Taxes on expenditure	75,654	80,600	81,656
Interest, royalties, etc.	7,217	4,936	4,344
Other income	38,833	36,414	35,029
Total	201,956	205,614	215,785

Expenditure‖	2005	2006‡	2007§
Consumption and investment	105,414	103,881	111,025
Domestic	103,570	93,481	101,521
Transfer and support payments	72,263	77,316	81,880
Interest payments and credit subsidies	33,193	35,531	35,555
Domestic	26,651	28,171	28,424
Other expenditure	7,784	11,936	11,506
Total	218,653	228,666	239,966

* Excluding Bank of Israel.
† Revenue excludes grants received from abroad (NIS million): 11,480 in 2005; 11,592 in 2006 (preliminary); 10,964 in 2007 (forecast).
‡ Preliminary data.
§ Forecasts.
‖ Expenditure excludes the central Government's credit issuance (NIS million): 3,017 in 2005; 3,111 in 2006 (preliminary); 2,596 in 2007 (forecast).

Source: Ministry of Finance, Budget Division.

INTERNATIONAL RESERVES
(US $ million at 31 December, excluding gold)

	2004	2005	2006
IMF special drawing rights	15.2	18.6	19.2
Reserve position in IMF	463.2	201.8	123.0
Foreign exchange	26,616.0	27,839.0	29,011.0
Total	27,094.4	28,059.4	29,153.2

Source: IMF, *International Financial Statistics*.

MONEY SUPPLY
(NIS million at 31 December)

	2004	2005	2006
Currency outside banks	17,758	20,957	21,655
Demand deposits at deposit money banks	35,012	39,942	43,140
Total money (incl. others)	52,931	61,077	64,965

Source: IMF, *International Financial Statistics*.

COST OF LIVING
(Consumer Price Index, annual averages; base: 2002 = 100)

	2004	2005	2006
Food (excl. fruit and vegetables)	104.0	105.5	110.2
Fruit and vegetables	96.5	99.2	105.1
Housing	92.6	91.6	92.7
Clothing (incl. footwear)	90.8	85.3	84.4
All items (incl. others)	100.3	101.6	103.8

NATIONAL ACCOUNTS
(NIS million at current prices)

National Income and Product

	2005	2006	2007*
Gross domestic product in market prices	588,970	633,057	665,463
Net income paid abroad	−7,163	−2,507	331
Gross national income (GNI)	581,807	630,550	665,794
Less Consumption of fixed capital	78,804	82,644	85,612
Net national income	503,003	547,906	580,182

*Preliminary.

Expenditure on the Gross Domestic Product

	2005	2006	2007*
Final consumption expenditure	477,204	508,290	540,728
Private	322,298	343,999	371,063
General government	154,906	164,291	169,665
Gross capital formation	111,877	119,791	135,980
Total domestic expenditure	589,081	628,081	676,708
Exports of goods and services	258,328	280,339	290,423
Less Imports of goods and services	258,439	275,363	301,668
GDP in market prices	588,970	633,057	665,463
GDP at constant 2005 prices	588,969	619,657	652,639

*Preliminary.

Gross Domestic Product by Economic Activity

	2005	2006	2007*
Agriculture, hunting, forestry and fishing	10,959	11,038	11,377
Manufacturing, mining and quarrying	77,091	86,888	86,676
Electricity, gas and water supply	11,070	11,175	11,674
Construction	25,107	28,158	30,356
Wholesale, retail trade, repair of motor vehicles, motorcycles and personal and household goods; hotels and restaurants	60,561	66,021	69,686
Transport, storage and communications	41,609	44,340	47,887
Financial intermediation; real estate, renting and business activities	134,291	141,280	155,198
Public administration and community services†	96,660	102,177	105,450
Housing services	63,347	65,312	66,042
Other community, social and personal services	12,427	13,367	14,906
Sub-total	533,122	569,756	599,252
Less Imputed bank service charge	15,461	14,164	16,968
Net taxes on products	68,438	71,316	78,076
Net errors and omissions	2,870	6,150	5,104
GDP in market prices	588,970	633,057	665,463

*Preliminary.
† Including non-profit institutions serving households.

ISRAEL

Statistical Survey

BALANCE OF PAYMENTS
(US $ million)

	2004	2005	2006
Exports of goods f.o.b.	36,658	40,101	43,725
Imports of goods f.o.b.	−39,488	−43,868	−46,958
Trade balance	**−2,830**	**−3,768**	**−3,233**
Exports of services	16,029	17,447	19,267
Imports of services	−12,825	−13,711	−14,934
Balance on goods and services	**374**	**−31**	**1,100**
Other income received	2,999	5,579	7,921
Other income paid	−6,670	−7,187	−8,497
Balance on goods, services and income	**−3,298**	**−1,638**	**524**
Current transfers received	7,358	7,010	8,577
Current transfers paid	−1,081	−1,038	−1,111
Current balance	**2,980**	**4,334**	**7,990**
Capital account (net)	667	727	904
Direct investment abroad	−4,544	−2,930	−14,399
Direct investment from abroad	2,041	4,792	14,302
Portfolio investment assets	−2,381	−8,244	−8,956
Portfolio investment liabilities	3,571	3,875	3,269
Financial derivatives (net)	−26	29	−21
Other investment assets	−6,218	−5,144	−10,112
Other investment liabilities	166	541	2,729
Net errors and omissions	724	3,730	−140
Overall balance	**−3,020**	**1,710**	**−4,435**

Source: IMF, *International Financial Statistics*.

External Trade

PRINCIPAL COMMODITIES
(US $ million)

Imports c.i.f.	2005	2006
Food and live animals	1,914.6	2,182.8
Mineral fuels, lubricants, etc.	5,920.1	6,664.0
Petroleum, petroleum products, etc.	5,840.4	6,563.2
Chemicals and related products	4,632.2	5,401.0
Basic manufactures	14,329.0	14,264.5
Non-metallic mineral manufactures	9,559.2	10,096.9
Machinery and transport equipment	12,454.0	13,188.6
General industrial machinery, equipment and parts	1,275.3	1,469.3
Office machines and automatic data-processing machines	1,646.1	1,693.2
Telecommunications and sound equipment	1,565.0	1,644.3
Other electrical machinery, apparatus, etc.	3,403.5	3,264.9
Road vehicles and parts	2,500.2	2,679.9
Other transport equipment and parts	585.0	624.7
Miscellaneous manufactured articles	3,503.4	3,911.7
Total (incl. others)	45,034.5	47,840.6

Exports f.o.b.	2005	2006
Chemicals and related products	7,725.6	9,191.9
Organic chemicals	1,181.4	1,239.6
Medical and pharmaceutical products	2,067.5	3,163.6
Basic manufactures	18,700.3	19,238.3
Non-metallic mineral manufactures	16,276.1	16,470.2
Machinery and transport equipment	10,526.2	12,015.1
Telecommunications and sound equipment	3,114.4	3,580.5
Other electrical machinery, apparatus, etc.	3,220.4	3,772.2
Road vehicles and other transport equipment and parts	1,190.0	1,303.9
Miscellaneous manufactured articles	3,663.8	4,137.0
Professional, scientific and controlling instruments, etc.	1,443.8	1,804.9
Total (incl. others)	42,770.5	46,789.4

PRINCIPAL TRADING PARTNERS
(US $ million)*

Imports (excl. military goods) c.i.f.	2005	2006	2007
Belgium-Luxembourg	4,588.2	3,983.4	4,546.8
Canada	320.4	369.1	433.8
China, People's Republic	1,888.3	2,427.7	3,477.1
France	1,203.8	1,301.5	1,480.7
Germany	2,896.0	3,201.4	3,484.1
Hong Kong	1,277.7	1,527.5	1,747.6
India	1,276.2	1,433.7	1,688.8
Italy	1,733.7	1,839.4	2,302.1
Japan	1,238.1	1,292.3	1,881.5
Korea, Republic	852.7	893.6	945.4
Netherlands	1,626.7	1,786.8	2,090.3
Russia	1,055.7	1,141.6	1,398.8
South Africa	183.3	119.1	158.7
Spain	613.7	749.0	811.8
Sweden	365.1	443.4	556.0
Switzerland-Liechtenstein	2,464.7	2,805.9	2,882.4
Taiwan	553.4	617.0	708.5
Turkey	1,221.1	1,272.7	1,606.9
United Kingdom	2,552.1	2,458.6	2,681.2
USA	6,042.1	5,919.5	7,848.4
Total (incl. others)	45,034.5	47,840.6	56,621.4

Exports	2005	2006	2007
Australia	423.1	446.0	517.8
Belgium-Luxembourg	3,690.5	3,077.2	4,085.9
Brazil	467.3	465.7	662.7
Canada	482.7	577.9	715.3
China, People's Republic	747.9	958.8	1,024.3
France	882.6	1,092.2	1,328.1
Germany	1,345.9	1,757.9	1,920.5
Hong Kong	2,373.6	2,776.1	3,115.6
India	1,222.8	1,289.4	1,606.7
Italy	897.8	1,072.7	1,316.0
Japan	799.1	792.8	775.6
Korea, Republic	449.8	650.0	748.2
Malaysia	130.7	68.1	70.0
Netherlands	1,259.7	1,312.2	1,617.1
Philippines	154.1	140.5	199.8
Singapore	354.2	412.6	414.6
Spain	687.8	903.0	1,081.1
Switzerland-Liechtenstein	900.3	809.0	1,036.3
Taiwan	602.3	589.8	564.2
Thailand	449.2	427.2	451.8
Turkey	903.2	821.2	1,221.9
United Kingdom	1,649.9	1,601.7	1,954.3
USA	15,500.1	17,846.5	18,892.9
Total (incl. others)	42,770.4	46,789.4	54,065.2

* Imports by country of purchase; exports by country of destination.

Transport

RAILWAYS
(traffic)

	2004	2005	2006
Passengers carried ('000 journeys)	22,898	26,767	28,351
Passenger-km (million)	1,423	1,618	1,609
Freight carried ('000 metric tons)	7,920	7,492	7,642
Freight ton-km (million)	1,173	1,149	1,123

ROAD TRAFFIC
(motor vehicles in use at 31 December)

	2004	2005	2006
Private passenger cars	1,567,021	1,626,388	1,684,694
Taxis	17,204	17,423	18,420
Minibuses	16,449	16,082	15,957
Buses and coaches	11,415	11,779	12,549
Lorries, vans and road tractors	344,573	351,136	354,472
Special service vehicles	4,012	3,706	3,773
Motorcycles and mopeds	77,041	80,804	85,651

ISRAEL

SHIPPING

Merchant Fleet
(registered at 31 December)

	2004	2005	2006
Number of vessels	51	51	51
Displacement ('000 grt)	740.0	741.4	763.5

Source: Lloyd's Register of Shipping, *World Fleet Statistics*.

International Sea-borne Freight Traffic
('000 metric tons)

	2004	2005	2006
Goods loaded	15,924	16,635	15,898
Goods unloaded*	33,462	33,223	32,226

* Including traffic between Israeli ports.

CIVIL AVIATION
(traffic on scheduled services)

	2001	2002	2003
Kilometres flown (million)	83	90	89
Passengers carried ('000)	3,989	3,708	3,678
Passenger-km (million)	13,514	12,234	12,465
Total ton-km (million)	2,083	2,437	2,535

Source: UN, *Statistical Yearbook*.

Tourism

TOURIST ARRIVALS
('000)*

Country of residence	2005	2006	2007
Canada	50.8	51.4	59.3
France	311.4	252.2	246.0
Germany	105.2	89.6	101.1
Italy	72.9	58.1	81.8
Jordan	8.3	15.1	11.5
Netherlands	49.8	43.0	41.7
Russia	68.0	73.6	193.4
Spain	51.9	30.7	47.1
Ukraine	28.3	30.6	n.a.
United Kingdom	156.7	161.2	171.9
USA	457.5	494.0	541.6
Total (incl. others)	1,902.7	1,825.2	2,267.9

* Excluding arrivals of Israeli nationals residing abroad.

Tourism receipts (US $ million, incl. passenger transport): 2,401 in 2003; 2,813 in 2004; 3,414 in 2005 (Source: World Tourism Organization).

Communications Media

	2004	2005	2006
Telephones ('000 main lines in use)	2,896.0	2,936.3	3,004.7
Mobile cellular telephones ('000 subscribers)	7,222.0	7,757.0	8,403.8
Internet users ('000)	1,496.6	1,685.9	1,899.1
Broadband subscribers ('000)	980.0	1,229.6	1,421.0

Television receivers ('000 in use): 2,100 in 2000; 2,150 in 2001.

Radio receivers (1997): 3,070,000 in use.

Facsimile machines (1995): 140,000 in use.

Book production (1998): 1,969 titles.

Daily newspapers (1996): 34 titles (estimated circulation 1,650,000 copies).

Non-daily newspapers (1988): 80 titles.

Other periodicals (1985): 807 titles.

Personal computers ('000 in use): 5,037 in 2004.

Sources: International Telecommunication Union; UNESCO, *Statistical Yearbook*; UN, *Statistical Yearbook*; UNESCO Institute for Statistics.

Education

(2006/07*)

	Schools	Pupils	Teachers
Hebrew			
Kindergarten	n.a.	315,000	9,487
Primary schools	1,799	588,900	50,726
Special needs	202	8,902	n.a.
Intermediate schools	501	186,201	19,524
Secondary schools	1,176	282,098	33,423
Vocational schools	112	90,288	n.a.
Agricultural schools	2	3,128	n.a.
Teacher training colleges	55	30,557	5,359
Arab			
Kindergarten	n.a.	93,000	2,377
Primary schools	446	228,313	17,296
Special needs	47	2,333	n.a.
Intermediate schools	139	69,029	5,257
Secondary schools	215	72,341	5,797
Vocational schools	24	26,585	n.a.
Agricultural schools	n.a.	558	n.a.
Teacher training colleges	4	3,664	491

* Provisional figures.

Adult literacy rate (UNESCO estimates): 96.9% (males 98.3%; females 95.6%) in 2003 (Source: UN Development Programme, *Human Development Report*).

Directory

The Constitution

There is no written constitution. In June 1950 the Knesset voted to adopt a state constitution by evolution over an unspecified period. A number of laws, including the Law of Return (1950), the Nationality Law (1952), the State President (Tenure) Law 1952), the Education Law (1953) and the 'Yad-va-Shem' Memorial Law (1953), are considered as incorporated into the state Constitution. Other constitutional laws are: the Law and Administration Ordinance (1948), the Knesset Election Law (1951), the Law of Equal Rights for Women (1951), the Judges Act (1953), the National Service and National Insurance Acts (1953), and the Basic Law (the Knesset—1958). The provisions of constitutional legislation that affect the main organs of government are summarized below:

THE PRESIDENT

The President is elected by the Knesset for a maximum of one seven-year term.

Ten or more Knesset members may propose a candidate for the Presidency.

Voting will be by secret ballot.

The President may not leave the country without the consent of the Government.

The President may resign by submitting his resignation in writing to the Speaker.

The President may be relieved of his duties by the Knesset for misdemeanour.

The Knesset is entitled to decide by a two-thirds' majority that the President is too incapacitated owing to ill health to fulfil his duties permanently.

The Speaker of the Knesset will act for the President when the President leaves the country, or when he cannot perform his duties owing to ill health.

THE KNESSET

The Knesset is the parliament of the state. There are 120 members.

ISRAEL

It is elected by general, national, direct, equal, secret and proportional elections.

Every Israeli national of 18 years or over shall have the right to vote in elections to the Knesset unless a court has deprived him of that right by virtue of any law.

Every Israeli national of 21 and over shall have the right to be elected to the Knesset unless a court has deprived him of that right by virtue of any law.

The following shall not be candidates: the President of the State; the two Chief Rabbis; a judge (shofet) in office; a judge (dayan) of a religious court; the State Comptroller; the Chief of the General Staff of the Defence Army of Israel; rabbis and ministers of other religions in office; senior state employees and senior army officers of such ranks and in such functions as shall be determined by law.

The term of office of the Knesset shall be four years.

The elections to the Knesset shall take place on the third Tuesday of the month of Marcheshvan in the year in which the tenure of the outgoing Knesset ends.

Election day shall be a day of rest, but transport and other public services shall function normally.

Results of the elections shall be published within 14 days.

The Knesset shall elect from among its members a Chairman (Speaker) and Vice-Chairman.

The Knesset shall elect from among its members permanent committees, and may elect committees for specific matters.

The Knesset may appoint commissions of inquiry to investigate matters designated by the Knesset.

The Knesset shall hold two sessions a year; one of them shall open within four weeks after the Feast of the Tabernacles, the other within four weeks after Independence Day; the aggregate duration of the two sessions shall not be less than eight months.

The outgoing Knesset shall continue to hold office until the convening of the incoming Knesset.

The members of the Knesset shall receive a remuneration as provided by law.

THE GOVERNMENT

The Government shall tender its resignation to the President immediately after his election, but shall continue with its duties until the formation of a new government. After consultation with representatives of the parties in the Knesset, the President shall charge one of the members with the formation of a government. The Government shall be composed of a Prime Minister (elected on a party basis from 2003) and a number of ministers from among the Knesset members or from outside the Knesset. After it has been chosen, the Government shall appear before the Knesset and shall be considered as formed after having received a vote of confidence. Within seven days of receiving a vote of confidence, the Prime Minister and the other ministers shall swear allegiance to the State of Israel and its Laws and undertake to carry out the decisions of the Knesset.

The Government

HEAD OF STATE

President: SHIMON PERES (took office 15 July 2007).

THE CABINET
(March 2008)

A coalition of Kadima, Labour-Meimad, Shas and the Pensioners' Party.

Prime Minister and Acting Minister of Tourism: EHUD OLMERT (Kadima).
Vice-Prime Minister and Minister of Foreign Affairs: TZIPI LIVNI (Kadima).
Vice-Premier: HAIM RAMON (Kadima).
Deputy Prime Minister and Minister of Industry, Trade and Labour: ELIYAHU YISHAI (Shas).
Deputy Prime Minister and Minister of Transport and Road Safety: SHAUL MOFAZ (Kadima).
Deputy Prime Minister and Minister of Defence: EHUD BARAK (Labour).
Minister of Finance: RONNIE BAR-ON (Kadima).
Minister of Communications: ARIEL ATIAS (Shas).
Minister of the Interior: MEIR SHEETRIT (Kadima).
Minister of Health: YACOV BEN YIZRI (Pensioners' Party).
Minister of National Infrastructure: BINYAMIN BEN-ELIEZER (Labour-Meimad).
Minister of Immigrant Absorption and Minister for the Development of the Negev and Galilee: YA'AKOV EDERY (Kadima).
Minister of Public Security: ABRAHAM DICTER (Kadima).
Minister of Environmental Protection: GIDEON EZRA (Kadima).
Minister of Justice: Prof. DANIEL FRIEDMANN.
Minister of Construction and Housing: ZE'EV BOIM (Kadima).
Minister of Social Affairs and Social Services, and Minister of the Diaspora, Society and Fight Against Anti-Semitism: ISAAC HERZOG (Labour-Meimad).
Minister of Pensioner Affairs: RAFI EITAN (Pensioners' Party).
Minister of Agriculture and Rural Development: SHALOM SIMHON (Labour-Meimad).
Minister of Science, Culture and Sport: RALEB MAJADELE (Labour-Meimad).
Minister of Education: YULI TAMIR (Labour-Meimad).
Minister without Portfolio, responsible for Religious Councils: YITZHAK COHEN (Shas).
Minister without Portfolio, responsible for liaison with the Knesset: RUHAMA AVRAHAM (Kadima).
Minister without Porfolio: AMI AYALON (Labour-Meimad).
Minister in the Ministry of Finance, responsible for Education and Social Affairs: MESHULAM NAHARI (Shas).

MINISTRIES

Office of the President: 3 Hanassi St, Jerusalem 92188; tel. 2-6707211; fax 2-5611033; e-mail president@president.gov.il; internet www.president.gov.il.

Office of the Prime Minister: POB 187, 3 Kaplan St, Kiryat Ben-Gurion, Jerusalem 91919; tel. 2-6705511; fax 2-6512631; e-mail webmaster@pmo.gov.il; internet www.pmo.gov.il.

Ministry of Agriculture and Rural Development: POB 50200, Agricultural Centre, Beit Dagan 50250; tel. 3-9485555; fax 3-9485858; e-mail pniot@moag.gov.il; internet www.moag.gov.il.

Ministry of Communications: 23 Jaffa St, Jerusalem 91999; tel. 2-6706320; fax 2-6706372; internet www.moc.gov.il.

Ministry of Construction and Housing: POB 18110, Kiryat Hamemshala (East), Jerusalem 91180; tel. 2-5847211; fax 2-5811904; e-mail pniot@moch.gov.il; internet www.moch.gov.il.

Ministry of Defence: Kaplan St, Hakirya, Tel-Aviv 67659; tel. 3-5692010; fax 3-6916940; e-mail public@mod.gov.il; internet www.mod.gov.il.

Ministry for the Development of the Negev and Galilee: 8 Shaul Hamelech Blvd, Tel-Aviv 64733; tel. 3-6060700; fax 3-6958414; internet www.vpmo.gov.il.

Ministry of Education: POB 292, 34 Shivtei Israel St, Jerusalem 91911; tel. 2-5602222; fax 2-5602223; e-mail info@education.gov.il; internet www.education.gov.il.

Ministry of Environmental Protection: POB 34033, 5 Kanfei Nesharim St, Givat Shaul, Jerusalem 95464; tel. 2-6495803; fax 2-6495892; e-mail pniot@environment.gov.il; internet www.environment.gov.il.

Ministry of Finance: POB 13195, 1 Kaplan St, Kiryat Ben-Gurion, Jerusalem 91008; tel. 2-5317111; fax 2-5637891; e-mail webmaster@mof.gov.il; internet www.mof.gov.il.

Ministry of Foreign Affairs: 9 Yitzhak Rabin Blvd, Kiryat Ben-Gurion, Jerusalem 91035; tel. 2-5303111; fax 2-5303367; e-mail feedback@mfa.gov.il; internet www.mfa.gov.il.

Ministry of Health: POB 1176, 2 Ben-Tabai St, Jerusalem 91010; tel. 2-6705705; fax 2-6796267; e-mail pniot@moh.health.gov.il; internet www.health.gov.il.

Ministry of Immigrant Absorption: 2 Kaplan St, Kiryat Ben-Gurion, Jerusalem 91950; tel. 2-6752691; fax 2-5669244; e-mail info@moia.gov.il; internet www.moia.gov.il.

Ministry of Industry, Trade and Labour: POB 299, 30 Rehov Agron, Jerusalem 94190; tel. 2-6220661; fax 2-6222412; e-mail dover@moit.gov.il; internet www.tamas.gov.il.

Ministry of the Interior: POB 6158, 2 Kaplan St, Kiryat Ben-Gurion, Jerusalem 91008; tel. 2-6701411; fax 2-6701628; e-mail pniot@moin.gov.il; internet www.moin.gov.il.

Ministry of Justice: POB 49029, 29 Rehov Salahadin, Jerusalem 91490; tel. 2-6466666; fax 2-6466357; e-mail pniot@justice.gov.il; internet www.justice.gov.il.

Ministry of National Infrastructure: POB 36148, 216 Jaffa St, Jerusalem 91360; tel. and fax 2-8644024; e-mail pniot@mmi.gov.il; internet www.mni.gov.il; also responsible for:

Israel Lands Administration: POB 2600, 6 Shamai St, Jerusalem 94631; tel. 2-6208422; fax 2-6241286; e-mail pniot@mmi.gov.il; internet www.mmi.gov.il.

Ministry of Public Security: POB 18182, Bldg 3, Kiryat Hamemshala (East), Jerusalem 91181; tel. 2-5309999; fax 2-5847872; e-mail dover@mops.gov.il; internet www.mops.gov.il.

Ministry of Science, Culture and Sport: POB 49100, Kiryat Hamemshala, Hamizrachit, Bldg 3, Jerusalem 91490; tel. 2-5411115; fax 2-5323497; e-mail meirae@most.gov.il; internet www.most.gov.il.

Ministry of Social Affairs and Social Services: POB 915, 2 Kaplan St, Kiryat Ben-Gurion, Jerusalem 91008; tel. 2-6752311; fax 2-6752803; e-mail sar@molsa.gov.il; internet www.molsa.gov.il.

Ministry of Tourism: POB 1018, 5 Bank of Israel St, Jerusalem 91009; tel. 2-6664200; fax 2-6664450; e-mail webmaster@tourism.gov.il; internet www.tourism.gov.il.

Ministry of Transport and Road Safety: POB 867, Government Complex, 5 Bank of Israel St, Jerusalem 91008; tel. 2-6663190; fax 2-6663195; e-mail dover@mot.gov.il; internet www.mot.gov.il.

GOVERNMENT AGENCY

The Jewish Agency for Israel

POB 92, 45 King George St, Jerusalem 91000; tel. 2-6202222; fax 2-6202303; e-mail yardenv@jafi.org; internet www.jewishagency.org. f. 1929; reconstituted in 1971 as a partnership between the World Zionist Organization and the fund-raising bodies United Israel Appeal, Inc (USA) and Keren Hayesod.

Organization: The governing bodies are: the Assembly, which determines basic policy; the Board of Governors, which sets policy for the Agency between Assembly meetings; and the Executive, responsible for the day-to-day running of the Agency.

Chairman of Executive: ZEEV BIELSKI.
Chairman of Board of Governors: RICHARD L. PEARLSTONE.
Director-General: MOSHE VIGDOR.
Treasurer: HAGAI MEIROM.

Functions: According to the Agreement of 1971, the Jewish Agency undertakes the immigration and absorption of immigrants in Israel, including: absorption in agricultural settlement and immigrant housing; social welfare and health services in connection with immigrants; education, youth care and training; and neighbourhood rehabilitation through project renewal.

Legislature

KNESSET

Speaker: DALIA ITZIK.
General Election, 28 March 2006

Party	Valid votes cast	% of valid votes	Seats
Kadima	690,901	22.02	29
Labour-Meimad	472,366	15.06	19
Shas	299,054	9.53	12
Likud	281,996	8.99	12
Israel Beytenu	281,880	8.99	11
National Union-National Religious Party	224,083	7.14	9
Pensioners' Party	185,759	5.92	7
United Torah Judaism	147,091	4.69	6
Meretz	118,302	3.77	5
United Arab List-Arab Movement for Renewal	94,786	3.02	4
Hadash	86,092	2.74	3
Balad	72,066	2.30	3
Total (incl. others)	3,137,064*	100.00	120

* Excluding 49,675 invalid votes.

Election Commission

Central Elections Committee: Knesset, Kiryat Ben-Gurion, Jerusalem 91950; tel. 2-6753407; e-mail doverd@knesset.gov.il; internet knesset.gov.il/elections17/eng/cec/CecIndex_eng.htm; independent; Supreme Court elects a Justice as Chair; each parliamentary group nominates representatives to the Cttee in proportion to the group's level of representation in the Knesset; Chair. Justice DORIT BEINISCH; Dir-Gen. TAMAR EDRI.

Political Organizations

Agudat Israel (Union of Israel): POB 513, Jerusalem; tel. 2-385251; fax 2-385145; f. 1912; mainly Ashkenazi ultra-Orthodox Hasidic Jews; stands for introduction of laws and institutions based on Jewish religious law (the Torah).

Agudat Israel World Organization (AIWO): POB 326, Hacherut Sq., Jerusalem 91002; tel. 2-5384357; fax 2-5383634; f. 1912 at Congress of Orthodox Jewry, Kattowitz, Germany (now Katowice, Poland), to help solve the problems facing Jewish people world-wide; more than 500,000 mems in 25 countries; Chair. Rabbi J. M. ABRAMOWITZ (Jerusalem); Secs Rabbi MOSHE GEWIRTZ, Rabbi CHAIM WEINSTOCK.

Arab Movement for Renewal (Tnua'a Aravit le'Hitkadshut—Ta'al): Jerusalem; tel. (2) 6753333; fax (2) 6753927; e-mail atibi@knesset.gov.il; f. 1996 following split from Balad; contested March 2006 legislative elections on a joint list with United Arab List; Leader Dr AHMAD TIBI.

Balad (National Democratic Assembly): POB 2248, Nazareth Industrial Zone, Nazareth 16000; tel. 4-6455070; fax 4-6463457; e-mail info@tajamoa.org; internet tajamoa.org; f. 1999; united Arab party; Leader Dr AZMI BISHARA.

Communist Party of Israel (Maki—Miflagah Kommonistit Yisraelit): POB 26205, 5 Hess St, Tel-Aviv 61261; tel. 3-6293944; fax 3-6297263; e-mail info@maki.org.il; internet www.maki.org.il; f. 1948; Jewish-Arab party descended from the Socialist Workers' Party of Palestine (f. 1919); renamed Communist Party of Palestine 1921, Jewish and Arab sections split 1945, reunited as Communist Party of Israel (Maki) 1948; further split 1965: pro-Soviet predominantly Arab anti-Zionist group formed New Communist Party of Israel (Rakah) 1965, while predominantly Jewish bloc retained name Maki; Rakah joined with other leftist orgs as Hadash 1977; name changed to Maki 1989, as the dominant component of Hadash (q.v.); Gen. Sec. ISSAM MAKHOUL.

Council for Peace and Security: POB 1320, Ramat HaSharon 47112; e-mail givoli99@zahav.net.il; internet www.peace-security.org.il; f. 1988; composed of former senior army officers and officials in the Israeli security and diplomatic establishment; seeks peace with Israel's Arab neighbours based on territorial concessions and grounded in the country's security needs; 1,200 mems; Founder Maj.-Gen. (retd) AHARON YARIV; Pres. Maj.-Gen. (retd) DANNY ROTHSCHILD.

Degel Hatorah (Flag of the Torah): 103 Rehov Beit Vegan, Jerusalem; tel. 2-6438106; fax 2-6418967; f. 1988 by Lithuanian Jews as breakaway faction from Agudat Israel; mainly Ashkenazi ultra-Orthodox Jews.

Hadash (Hachazit Hademokratit Leshalom Uleshivyon—Democratic Front for Peace and Equality): POB 26205, Tel-Aviv 61261; tel. 3-6293944; fax 3-6297263; e-mail info@hadash.org.il; internet www.hadash.org.il; f. 1977 by merger of the New Communist Party of Israel (Rakah) with other leftist groups; party list, the principal component of which is the Communist Party of Israel (q.v.); Jewish-Arab membership; aims for a socialist system in Israel, a lasting peace between Israel and the Arab countries and the Palestinian Arab people, favours full implementation of UN Security Council Resolutions 242 and 338, Israeli withdrawal from all Arab territories occupied since 1967, formation of a Palestinian Arab state in the West Bank and Gaza Strip (with East Jerusalem as its capital), recognition of national rights of State of Israel and Palestinian people, democratic rights and defence of working-class interests, and demands an end to discrimination against Arab minority in Israel and against oriental Jewish communities; Chair. MUHAMMAD BARAKEH.

Herut (Freedom): 55 Hamasger St, Tel-Aviv; tel. 3-5621521; fax 3-5618699; e-mail herut@herut.org.il; internet www.herut.org.il; f. 1948; reconstituted 1999; right-wing nationalist party; opposed to further Israeli withdrawal from the Occupied Territories; Leader MICHAEL KLEINER.

Israel Beytenu (Israel Is Our Home) (Nash dom Izrail): 78 Yirmeyahu St, Jerusalem 94467; tel. 2-5012999; fax 2-5377188; e-mail gdv7191@hotmail.com; internet www.beytenu.org.il; f. 1999; right-wing immigrant party; joined National Union in 2000, but contested March 2006 legislative elections alone; seeks resolution of the Israeli–Palestinian conflict through the exchange of territory and population with the Palestinians, incl. the transfer of Arab Israelis to territory under Palestinian control; membership largely drawn from former USSR; 18,000 mems (2006); Leader AVIGDOR LIEBERMAN.

Israel Labour Party (Mifleget HaAvoda HaYisraelit): POB 62033, Tel-Aviv 61620; tel. 3-6899444; fax 3-6899420; e-mail inter@havoda.org.il; internet www.aavoda.co.il; f. 1968 as a merger of the three Labour groups, Mapai, Rafi and Achdut Ha'avoda; Am Ehad (One Nation) merged with Labour in 2004; a Zionist democratic socialist party; Chair. EHUD BARAK.

Kadima (Forward): Petach Tikva, Tel-Aviv; tel. 3-9788000; fax 3-9788020; internet www.kadima.org.il; f. 2005; liberal party formed as a breakaway faction from Likud by former party Chairman Ariel Sharon; aims to pursue a peace agreement with the Palestinians in accordance with the 'roadmap' peace plan, and to establish Israel's permanent borders, if necessary unilaterally; seeks to combat economic and social problems; Leader EHUD OLMERT.

Likud (Consolidation): 38 Rehov King George, Tel-Aviv 61231; tel. 3-5630666; fax 3-5282901; e-mail likud@likud.org.il; internet www.likud.org.il; f. Sept. 1973; fmrly a parliamentary bloc of Herut (f. 1948), the Liberal Party of Israel (f. 1961), Laam (For the Nation—f. 1976), Ahdut, Tami (f. 1981; joined Likud in June 1987) and an independent faction led by Itzhak Modai (f. 1990), which formed the nucleus of a new Party for the Advancement of the Zionist Idea; Herut and the Liberal Party formally merged in Aug. 1988 to form the Likud-National Liberal Movement; Israel B'Aliyah merged with Likud in 2003; former Prime Minister and Likud Chair. Ariel Sharon established a breakaway faction, Kadima, in 2005; aims: territorial integrity (advocates retention of all the territory of post-1922 mandatory Palestine); absorption of newcomers; a social order based on freedom and justice, elimination of poverty and want; development of an economy that will ensure a decent standard of living; improvement of the environment and the quality of life; Chair. BINYAMIN NETANYAHU.

Meimad: POB 53139, 19 Yad Harutzim St, Jerusalem 91533; tel. 2-6725134; fax 2-6725051; e-mail info@meimad.org.il; internet www.meimad.org.il; f. 1988; moderate democratic Jewish party; Founder and Chair. Rabbi YEHUDA AMITAL.

Meretz–Yahad (Vitality–Together–Social Democratic Party of Israel): Beit Amot Mishpat, 8th Shaul Hamelech Blvd, Tel-Aviv 64733; tel. 3-6098998; fax 3-6961728; e-mail dror@myparty.org.il; internet www.myparty.org.il; f. 2003 as Yahad (Together—Social Democratic Israel) from a merger of Meretz (f. 1992; an alliance of Ratz, Shinui and the United Workers' Party) and Shahar (f. 2002; a breakaway faction of the Israel Labour Party); name changed to above in 2005; Jewish-Arab social democratic party; stands for: civil rights; welfarism; Palestinian self-determination and a return to the 1967 borders, with minor adjustments; a divided Jerusalem, but no right of return for Palestinian refugees to Israel; separation of religion from the state; Chair. HAIM ORON.

Moledet (Homeland): 14 Rehov Yehuda Halevi, Tel-Aviv; tel. 3-654580; e-mail moledet@moledet.org.il; internet www.moledet.org.il; f. 1988; right-wing nationalist party; aims: the expulsion ('transfer') of Palestinians living in the West Bank and Gaza Strip; united with Tehiya—Zionist Revival Movement in June 1994 as the Moledet—the Eretz Israel Faithful and the Tehiya; Leader Rabbi BINYAMIN (BENNY) ELON.

National Religious Party (NRP) (Mafdal): POB 1022, Jerusalem 91009; tel. 2-6232103; fax 2-6232236; e-mail mafdal1@beqeqint.net; internet www.mafdal.org.il; f. 1902 as the Mizrachi Organization within the Zionist Movement; present name adopted in 1956; believes in a 'Greater Israel'; opposed to further withdrawals from the Occupied Territories; stands for strict adherence to Jewish religion and tradition, and strives to achieve the application of religious precepts of Judaism in everyday life, incl. in education; it also endeavours to establish a constitution for Israel based on Jewish religious law (the Torah); contested March 2006 legislative elections as joint list with National Union, led by National Union Chair. Rabbi Binyamin (Benny) Elon; stated aim of joint list was the creation of an Israeli society based on the spiritual and social values of Judaism; retention of an undivided Israel; 126,000 mems; Chair. ZEVULUN ORLEV.

National Union (Haichud Haleumi): e-mail info@leumi.org.il; internet www.leumi.org.il; f. 1999 as right-wing coalition comprising Herut, Moledet and Tekuma parties; Israel Beytenu joined following withdrawal of Herut in 2000, but contested March 2006 legislative elections alone; believes in a 'Greater Israel'; opposed to further withdrawals from the Occupied Territories; contested March 2006 legislative elections on joint list with National Religious Party, led by Rabbi Binyamin (Benny) Elon; stated aim of joint list was the creation of an Israeli society based on the spiritual and social values of Judaism; retention of an undivided Israel; Leader Rabbi BINYAMIN (BENNY) ELON.

Pensioners' Party (Gil—Gimla'ey Yisrael LaKneset) (Age—Pensioners of Israel to the Knesset): Tel-Aviv; internet www.gil.org.il; stands for pensioners' rights; Leader RAFI EITAN.

Poale Agudat Israel: f. 1924; working-class Orthodox Judaist party; Leader Dr KALMAN KAHANE.

Progressive List for Peace: 5 Simtat Lane, Nes Tziona, Tel-Aviv; tel. 3-662457; fax 3-659474; f. 1984; Jewish-Arab; advocates recognition of the Palestine Liberation Organization and the establishment of a Palestinian state in the West Bank and Gaza Strip; Leader MUHAMMAD MI'ARI.

Shas (Sephardic Torah Guardians): Beit Abodi, Rehov Hahida, Bene Beraq; tel. 3-579776; internet www.shasnet.org.il; f. 1984 by splinter groups from Agudat Israel; ultra-Orthodox Sephardic party; Spiritual Leader Rabbi OVADIA YOSEF; Chair. ELIYAHU YISHAI.

Shinui (Change): POB 20533, 100 Rehov Ha' Hashmonaim, Tel-Aviv 61200; tel. 3-5620118; fax 3-5620139; e-mail shinui@shinui.org.il; internet www.shinui.org.il; f. 1974 as a new liberal party; combines an anti-religious coercion policy and secularism with a free-market economic philosophy; Leader RON LEVENTHAL.

Social Justice (Tzedek Hevrati—Za'am): f. 2007; aims to remove Govt of Ehud Olmert from power, through the promotion of democratic values, freedoms and social equality; Leader ARCADI ALEXANDROVICH GAYDAMAK.

United Arab List (Reshima Aravit Me'uchedet—Ra'am): Jerusalem; tel. (2) 6753333; fax (2) 6753927; e-mail telsana@knesset.gov.il; f. 1996 by merger of the Arab Democratic Party and individuals from the Islamic Movement and National Unity Front (left-wing Arab parties); supports establishment of a Palestinian state, with East Jerusalem as its capital, and equality for all Israeli citizens; contested March 2006 legislative elections on a joint list with Arab Movement for Renewal; Chair. TALAB ES-SANA.

United Torah Judaism (Yahadut Hatorah): internet www.gimel2006.com; f. prior to 1992 election; electoral list of four minor ultra-Orthodox parties (Moria, Degel Hatorah, Poale Agudat Israel and Agudat Israel) established to overcome the increase in election threshold from 1% to 1.5% and to seek to counter the rising influence of the secular Russian vote; contested 2003 election composed of Degel Hatorah and Agudat Israel, into which constituent parties it split in early 2005; two parties reunited in late 2005 and contested 2006 elections together; represents Ashkenazi ultra-Orthodox Jews and advocates the application of religious precepts in all areas of life and government.

Diplomatic Representation

EMBASSIES IN ISRAEL

Albania: 54/26 Pinkas St, Tel-Aviv 62261; tel. 3-5465866; fax 3-5444545; e-mail alb_emb@netvision.net.il; Ambassador TONIN GJURAJ.

Angola: 8 Shaul Hamelech Blvd, Tel-Aviv 64733; tel. 3-6912093; fax 3-6912094; e-mail embangi@zahav.net.il; Ambassador JOSÉ JOÃO MANUEL.

Argentina: Apt 3, Medinat Hayeudim 85, Herzliya Business Park, Herzliya Pitauch 46120; tel. 9-9702740; fax 9-9702747; e-mail embarg@netvision.net.il; Ambassador ATILIO NORBERTO MOLTENI.

Australia: Europe House, 4th Floor, 37 Shaul Hamelech Blvd, Tel-Aviv 64928; tel. 3-6935000; fax 3-6935002; e-mail info@australianembassy.org.il; internet www.australianembassy.org.il; Ambassador JAMES LARSEN.

Austria: Beit Crystal, 12 Hahilazon, Ramat-Gan 52522; tel. 3-6120924; fax 3-7510716; e-mail tel-aviv-ob@bmaa.gv.at; internet www.austrian-embassy.org.il; Ambassador MICHAEL RENDI.

Belarus: POB 11129, 3 Reines St, Tel-Aviv 64381; tel. 3-5231069; fax 3-5231273; e-mail press@belembassy.co.il; internet www.belembassy.co.il; Ambassador IGOR LESHCHENYA.

Belgium: 12 Hahilazon St, Ramat-Gan 52522; tel. 3-6138130; fax 3-6138160; e-mail telaviv@diplobel.org; internet www.diplomatie.be/telaviv; Ambassador DANIELLE DEL MARMOL.

Bolivia: Toyota Bldg, 13th Floor, 65 Yigal Alon St, Tel-Aviv 67443; tel. 3-5621992; fax 3-5621990; e-mail embolivia-telaviv@emb.co.il; Ambassador Gen. REYNALDO CACERES QUIROGA.

Bosnia and Herzegovina: 13th Floor, 7 Menachim Begin Rd, Ramat-Gan 52681; tel. 3-6124499; fax 3-6124488; Ambassador NEDELJKO MASLEŠKA.

Brazil: 2 Beit Yachin, 8th Floor, Kaplan St, Tel-Aviv 64734; tel. 3-6919292; fax 3-6916060; e-mail embrisra@netvision.net.il; Ambassador SERGIO MOREIRA LIMA.

Bulgaria: 21 Leonardo da Vinci St, Tel-Aviv 64733; tel. 3-6961361; fax 3-6961430; e-mail bgemtlv@netvision.net.il; Chargé d'affaires a.i. SERGEI TASSEV.

Cameroon: 28 Moshe Sharet St, Ramat-Gan 52425; tel. 3-5298401; fax 3-5270352; Ambassador HENRI ETOUNDI ESSOMBA.

Canada: POB 9442, 3/5 Nirim St, Tel-Aviv 67060; tel. 3-6363300; fax 3-6363380; e-mail taviv@international.gc.ca; internet www.international.gc.ca/telaviv; Ambassador JON ALLEN.

Chile: Beit Sharbat, 8th Floor, 4 Kaufman St, Tel-Aviv 68012; tel. 3-5102751; fax 3-5100102; e-mail echileil@inter.net.il; Ambassador IRENE FAIVOVICH BRONFMAN.

China, People's Republic: POB 6067, 222 Ben Yehuda St, Tel-Aviv 61060; tel. 3-5467277; fax 3-5467311; e-mail chnemb@isdn.net.il; internet www.chinaembassy.org.il; Ambassador CHEN YONGLONG.

Colombia: Shekel Bldg, 8th Floor, 111 Arlozovov St, Tel-Aviv 62068; tel. 3-6953416; fax 3-6957847; e-mail emcolis@netvision.net.il; Ambassador JUAN HURTADO.

ISRAEL

Congo, Democratic Republic: Rehov Rachel 1/2, Tel-Aviv 64584; tel. 3-5248306; fax 3-5292623; Chargé d'affaires a.i. KIMBOKO MA MAKENGO.

Congo, Republic: POB 12504, 9 Maskit St, Herzliya Pitauch 46120; tel. 9-9577130; fax 9-9577216; Chargé d'affaires a.i. DAVID MADOUKA.

Costa Rica: 14 Abba Hillel St, 15th Floor, Ramat-Gan 52506; tel. 3-6135061; fax 3-6134779; e-mail emcri@netvision.net.il; Ambassador NOEMÍ JUDITH BARUCH GOLDBERG.

Côte d'Ivoire: South Africa Bldg, 12 Menachim Begin St, Ramat-Gan 52521; tel. 3-6126677; fax 3-6126688; e-mail ambacita@netvision.net.il; Ambassador LÉON H. KACOU ADOM.

Croatia: 40 Einstein St, Canion Ramat Aviv, 40 Einstein St, Tel-Aviv 69101; tel. 3-6438654; fax 3-6438503; e-mail croemb.israel@mvpei.hr; Ambassador IVAN DEL VECHIO.

Cyprus: Top Tower, 14th Floor, Dizengoff Centre, 50 Dizengoff St, Tel-Aviv 64322; tel. 3-5250212; fax 3-6290535; e-mail cyprus@netvision.net.il; Ambassador GEORGE ZODIATES.

Czech Republic: POB 16361, 23 Zeitlin St, Tel-Aviv; tel. 3-6918282; fax 3-6918286; e-mail telaviv@embassy.mzv.cz; internet www.mfa.cz/telaviv; Ambassador MICHAEL ŽANTOVSKÝ.

Denmark: POB 21080, Museum Tower, 4 Berkowitz St, Tel-Aviv 61210; tel. 3-6085850; fax 3-6085851; e-mail tlvamb@um.dk; internet www.ambtelaviv.um.dk; Ambassador A. CARSTEN DAMSGAARD.

Dominican Republic: 19/1 Soutine St, Tel-Aviv 64884; tel. 3-5277073; fax 3-5277074; e-mail embajdom@netvision.net.il; Ambassador LEONARDO COHEN.

Ecuador: Asia House, 4 Rehov Weizman, Tel-Aviv 64239; tel. 3-6958764; fax 3-6913604; e-mail mecuaisr@infolink.net.il; Ambassador FRANCISCO RIOFRÍO MALDONADO.

Egypt: 54 Rehov Bazel, Tel-Aviv 62744; tel. 3-5464151; fax 3-5441615; e-mail egypem.ta@zahav.net.il; Ambassador MUHAMMAD ASIM IBRAHIM.

El Salvador: 6 Hamada St, Herzliya Pituach; tel. 9-9556342; fax 9-9556603; e-mail embassy@el-salvador.org.il; internet www.el-salvador.org.il; Ambassador SUZANA GUN DE HASENSON.

Eritrea: 33 Jabotinsky St, Ramat-Gan 52511; tel. 3-6120039; fax 3-5750133; Ambassador TESFAMARIAM TEKESTE.

Ethiopia: Bldg B, Floor 8B, 48 Darech Menachem Begin, Tel-Aviv 66184; tel. 3-6397831; fax 3-6397837; e-mail ethembis@netvision.net.il; internet www.ethioemb.org.il; Ambassador FESSEHA ASGHEDOM TESSEMA.

Finland: Canion Ramat Aviv, 40 Einstein St, Tel-Aviv 69101; tel. 3-7456600; fax 3-7440314; e-mail sanomat.tel@formin.fi; internet www.finland.org.il; Ambassador KARI VEIJALAINEN.

France: 112 Tayelet Herbert Samuel, Tel-Aviv 63572; tel. 3-5208300; fax 3-5208342; e-mail diplomatie@ambafrance-il.org; internet www.ambafrance-il.org; Ambassador JEAN-MICHEL CASA.

Georgia: 3 Daniel Frisch St, Tel-Aviv; tel. 3-6093206; fax 3-6093205; e-mail geoemba@netvision.net.il; Ambassador LASHA ZHVANIA.

Germany: POB 16038, 19th Floor, 3 Daniel Frisch St, Tel-Aviv 64731; tel. 3-6931313; fax 3-6969217; e-mail ger_emb@netvision.net.il; internet www.tel-aviv.diplo.de; Ambassador Dr HARALD KINDERMANN.

Ghana: 3rd Floor, 12 Hahilazon St, Ramat-Gan 52522; tel. 3-7520834; fax 3-7520827; e-mail chancery@ghanaemb.co.il; Ambassador Lt-Col LAWRENCE KPABITEY KODJIKU.

Greece: 3 Daniel Frisch St, Tel-Aviv 64731; tel. 3-6953060; fax 3-6951329; e-mail gremb.tlv@mfa.gr; Ambassador MICHAIL SPINELIS.

Guatemala: 103 Medinat Hayehudim St, Herzliya Pitauch 46766; tel. 9-9577335; fax 9-9518506; e-mail embguate@netvision.net.il; Ambassador MOISÉS RUSS TOPOLSKY.

Holy See: 1 Netiv Hamazalot, Old Jaffa 68037; tel. 2-6835658; fax 2-6835659; e-mail vatge@netvision.net.il; Apostolic Nuncio Most Rev. ANTONIO FRANCO (Titular Archbishop of Gallese).

Honduras: Zohar Tal St 1, Herzliya Pituach 46766; tel. 9-9577686; fax 9-9577457; e-mail honduras@netvision.net.il; Chargé d'affaires DENNIS WEIZENBLUT.

Hungary: POB 21095, 18 Pinkas St, Tel-Aviv 62661; tel. 3-5466985; fax 3-5467018; e-mail huembtlv@bezeqint.net; internet www.hungaryemb.org.il; Ambassador Dr ANDRÁS GYENGE.

India: POB 3368, 140 Hayarkon St, Tel-Aviv 61033; tel. 3-5291999; fax 3-5291953; e-mail indemtel@indembassy.co.il; internet www.indembassy.co.il; Ambassador ARUN KUMAR SINGH.

Ireland: The Tower, 17th Floor, 3 Daniel Frisch St, Tel-Aviv 64731; tel. 3-6964166; fax 3-6964160; e-mail telavivembassy@dfa.ie; Ambassador MICHAEL FORBES.

Italy: Trade Tower Bldg, 25 Hamered St, Tel-Aviv 68125; tel. 3-5104004; fax 3-5100235; e-mail info@telaviv.esteri.it; internet www.ambtelaviv.esteri.it; Ambassador SANDRO DE BERNARDIN.

Japan: 4 Berkowitz St, Museum Tower, Tel-Aviv 64238; tel. 3-6957292; fax 3-6910516; e-mail embjpcul@netvision.net.il; internet www.israel.emb-japan.go.jp; Ambassador YOSHINORI KATORI.

Jordan: 14 Abba Hillel, Ramat-Gan 52506; tel. 3-7517722; fax 3-7517712; Ambassador ALI HAMDAN ABD AL-QADER AL-AYED.

Kazakhstan: 52A Rehov Hayarkon, Tel-Aviv 63432; tel. 3-5163411; fax 3-5163437; e-mail kzisrael@netvision.net.il; internet www.kazakhemb.org.il; Ambassador VADIM P. ZVERKOV.

Kenya: 15 Aba Hillel Silver St, Ramat-Gan 52136; tel. 3-5754633; fax 3-5754788; e-mail info@kenyaembassytlv.org; internet www.kenyaembassyisrael.org; Ambassador FELISTAS VUNORO KHAYUMBI.

Korea, Republic: 38 Sderot Chen, Tel-Aviv 64166; tel. 3-6963244; fax 3-6963243; e-mail israel@mofat.go.kr; Ambassador KAK SOO SHIN.

Latvia: Europe Israel Tower, 15th Floor, Rehov Weizman, Tel-Aviv 64239; tel. 3-7775800; fax 3-6953101; e-mail embassy.israel@mfa.gov.lv; Ambassador KĀRLIS EIHENBAUMS.

Liberia: 74 Derech Menachim Begin, Tel-Aviv 67215; tel. 3-5611068; fax 3-5610896.

Lithuania: 8 Shaul Ha Meleh, Tel-Aviv 64733; tel. 3-6958685; fax 3-6958691; e-mail lrambizr@netvision.net.il; internet lt.mfa.lt; Ambassador ASTA SKAISGIRYTE-LIAUSKIENE.

Mauritania: Rehov Arlosoroff 111, Tel-Aviv 62098; tel. 3-6916820; fax 3-6957046; Ambassador AHMAD OULD TEGUEDDI.

Mexico: Trade Tower, 5th Floor, 25 Hamered St, Tel-Aviv 68125; tel. 3-5163938; fax 3-5163711; e-mail embamex@netvision.net.il; internet portal.sre.gob.mx/israel; Ambassador CARLOS RICO-FERRAT.

Moldova: 38 Rembrandt St, Tel-Aviv 64045; tel. 3-5231000; fax 3-5233000; Ambassador LARISA MICULET.

Myanmar: Textile Centre Bldg, 12th Floor, 2 Kaufman St, Tel-Aviv 68012; tel. 3-5170760; fax 3-5163512; e-mail teltaman@zahav.net.il; Ambassador U MYINT SWE.

Netherlands: Beit Oz, 14 Abba Hillel St, Ramat-Gan 52506; tel. 3-7540777; fax 3-7540748; e-mail nlgovtel@012.net.il; internet www.netherlands-embassy.co.il; Ambassador MICHIEL DEN HOND.

Nigeria: 34 Gordon St, Tel-Aviv 63414; tel. 3-5222144; fax 3-5237886; Ambassador SAM AZUBUIKE DADA OLISA.

Norway: POB 17575, 13th Floor, Canion Ramat Aviv, 40 Einstein St, Tel-Aviv 69101; tel. 3-7441490; fax 3-7441498; e-mail emb.telaviv@mfa.no; internet www.norway.org.il; Ambassador JAKKEN BIØRN LIAN.

Panama: 10 Rehov Hei Be'Iyar, Kikar Hamedina, Tel-Aviv 62998; tel. 3-6960849; fax 3-6910045; Ambassador MANUEL BARLETTA MILLAN.

Peru: Rehov Medinat Hayehudim 60, Entrance A, 2nd Floor, Herzliya Pituach 46766; tel. 9-9578835; fax 9-9568495; e-mail emperu@012.net.il; Ambassador LUIS MENDIVIL.

Philippines: Textile Centre Bldg, 13th Floor, 2 Kaufman St, Tel-Aviv 68012; tel. 3-5175263; fax 3-5102229; e-mail filembis@netvision.net.il; Ambassador ANTONIO C. MODENA.

Poland: 16 Soutine St, Tel-Aviv 64684; tel. 3-7253111; fax 3-5237806; e-mail embpol@netvision.net.il; internet www.telaviv.polemb.net; Ambassador AGNIESZKA MAGDZIAK-MISZEWSKA.

Portugal: 12th Floor, 3 Daniel Frisch St, Tel-Aviv 64731; tel. 3-6956373; fax 3-6956366; e-mail eptel@012.net.il; Ambassador JOSEFINA REIS CARVALHO.

Romania: 24 Rehov Adam Hacohen, Tel-Aviv 64585; tel. 3-5230066; fax 3-5247379; e-mail rouembil@netvision.net.il; Ambassador VALERIA MARIANA STOICA.

Russia: 120 Rehov Hayarkon, Tel-Aviv 63573; tel. 3-5226736; fax 3-5226713; e-mail amb_ru@mail.netvision.net.il; internet www.russianembassy.org.il; Ambassador GENNADII PAVLOVICH TARASOV.

Serbia: 10 Bodenheimer St, Tel-Aviv 62008; tel. 3-6045535; fax 3-6049456; e-mail yuamb@netvision.net.il; internet www.embserbmont.co.il; Ambassador MIODRAG ISAKOV.

Slovakia: POB 6459, 37 Jabotinsky St, Tel-Aviv 62287; tel. 3-5449119; fax 3-5449144; e-mail slovemb1@barak.net.il; Ambassador MILAN DUBČEK.

Slovenia: Top Tower, 50 Dizengoff St, POB 23245, Tel-Aviv 61231; tel. 3-6293563; fax 3-5282214; e-mail vta@mzz-dkp.gov.si; Chargé d'affaires a.i. TATJANA MISKOVA.

South Africa: POB 7138, Top Tower, 16th Floor, 50 Dizengoff St, Tel-Aviv 61071; tel. 3-5252566; fax 3-5253230; e-mail admin@saemb.org.il; internet www.safis.co.il; Ambassador Maj.-Gen. FUMANEKILE GQIBA.

Spain: Dubnov Tower, 18th Floor, 3 Daniel Frisch St, Tel-Aviv 64731; tel. 3-6958671; fax 3-6965217; e-mail embespil@mae.es; Ambassador EUDALDO MIRAPEIX Y MARTÍNEZ (Baron of Abella).

Sri Lanka: 4 Jean Jaures St, Tel-Aviv 63412; tel. 3-5277635; fax 3-5277634; Ambassador TISSA WIJERATNE.

ISRAEL

Sweden: Asia House, 4 Rehov Weizman, Tel-Aviv 64239; tel. 3-6958111; fax 3-6958116; e-mail ambassaden.tel-aviv@foreign.ministry.se; internet www.swedenabroad.com/telaviv; Ambassador ELISABET BORSIIN BONNIER.

Switzerland: POB 6068, 228 Rehov Hayarkon, Tel-Aviv 61060; tel. 3-5464455; fax 3-5464408; e-mail vertretung@tel.rep.admin.ch; internet www.eda.admin.ch/telaviv; Ambassador WALTER HAFFNER.

Thailand: 21 Shaul Hamelech Blvd, Tel-Aviv 64367; tel. 3-6958980; fax 3-6958991; e-mail thaisr@netvision.co.il; internet www.mfa.go.th/web/1315.php?depid=210; Ambassador KASIVAT PARUGGAMANONT.

Turkey: 202 Rehov Hayarkon, Tel-Aviv 63405; tel. 3-5171731; fax 3-5176157; e-mail turqua2@netvision.net.il; Ambassador FERIDUN SINIRLIOĞLU.

Ukraine: 50 Yirmiyagu, Tel-Aviv 62594; tel. 3-6040242; fax 3-6042512; e-mail embukr@netvision.net.il; internet www.ukraine-embassy.co.il; Ambassador IHOR V. TIMOFEYEV.

United Kingdom: 192 Rehov Hayarkon, Tel-Aviv 63405; tel. 3-7251222; fax 3-5278574; e-mail webmaster.telaviv@fco.gov.uk; internet www.britemb.org.il; Ambassador TOM R. V. PHILLIPS.

USA: 71 Hayarkon St, Tel-Aviv 63903; tel. 3-5197575; e-mail ac5@bezeqint.net; internet telaviv.usembassy.gov; Ambassador RICHARD H. JONES.

Uruguay: POB 12244, G.R.A.P. Bldg, 1st Floor, 4 Shenkar St, Industrial Zone, Herzliya Pitauch 46733; tel. 9-9569611; fax 9-9515881; e-mail emrou@netvision.net.il; Ambassador ALFREDO E. CAZES ALVAREZ.

Uzbekistan: 35 Dvora Ha'Nevia St, Tel-Aviv 69350; tel. 3-6447746; fax 3-6447748; e-mail uzecon@barak-online.net; Ambassador FARHOD HAKIMOV.

Venezuela: POB 2058, Beit Grap, 3rd Floor, 4 Rehov Shenkar, Herzliya Pituach 46120; tel. 9-9573363; fax 9-9580292; e-mail emven@netvision.net.il; Ambassador HÉCTOR QUINTERO (withdrawn in Aug. 2006).

Judicial System

The law of Israel is composed of the enactments of the Knesset and, to a lesser extent, of the acts, orders-in-council and ordinances that remain from the period of the British Mandate in Palestine (1922–48). The pre-1948 law has largely been replaced, amended or reorganized, in the interests of codification, by Israeli legislation. This legislation generally follows a very similar pattern to that operating in England and the USA. However, there is no jury system.

Attorney-General: MENACHEM MAZUZ.

CIVIL COURTS

The Supreme Court

Sha'arei Mishpat St, Kiryat David Ben-Gurion, Jerusalem 91950; tel. 2-6759666; fax 2-6759648; e-mail marcia@supreme.court.gov.il; internet www.court.gov.il.

This is the highest judicial authority in the state. It has jurisdiction as an Appellate Court over appeals from the District Courts in all matters, both civil and criminal (sitting as a Court of Civil Appeal or as a Court of Criminal Appeal). In addition it is a Court of First Instance (sitting as the High Court of Justice) in actions against governmental authorities, and in matters in which it considers it necessary to grant relief in the interests of justice and which are not within the jurisdiction of any other court or tribunal. The High Court's exclusive power to issue orders in the nature of *habeas corpus, mandamus*, prohibition and *certiorari* enables the court to review the legality of and redress grievances against acts of administrative authorities of all kinds.

President of the Supreme Court: DORIT BEINISCH.

Deputy President of the Supreme Court: ELIEZER RIVLIN.

Justices of the Supreme Court: ASHER D. GRUNIS, MIRIAM NAOR, ELIEZER RIVLIN, EDMOND E. LEVY, AYALA PROCACCIA, EDNA ARBEL, ESTHER HAYUT, ELYAKIM RUBINSTEIN, SALIM JOUBRAN.

Registrars: Judge YIGAL MERSEL, Judge SHOSHANA LEIBOVIC.

District Courts: There are five District Courts (Jerusalem, Tel-Aviv, Haifa, Beersheba, Nazareth). They have residual jurisdiction as Courts of First Instance over all civil and criminal matters not within the jurisdiction of a Magistrates' Court (e.g. civil claims exceeding NIS 1m.), all matters not within the exclusive jurisdiction of any other tribunal, and matters within the concurrent jurisdiction of any other tribunal so long as such tribunal does not deal with them. In addition, the District Courts have appellate jurisdiction over appeals from judgments and decisions of Magistrates' Courts and judgments of Municipal Courts and various administrative tribunals.

Magistrates' Courts: There are 29 Magistrates' Courts, having criminal jurisdiction to try contraventions, misdemeanours and certain felonies, and civil jurisdiction to try actions concerning possession or use of immovable property, or the partition thereof whatever may be the value of the subject matter of the action, and other civil claims not exceeding NIS 1m.

Labour Courts: Established in 1969. Regional Labour Courts in Jerusalem, Tel-Aviv, Haifa, Beersheba and Nazareth, composed of judges and representatives of the public. A National Labour Court in Jerusalem. The Courts have jurisdiction over all matters arising out of the relationship between employer and employee or parties to a collective labour agreement, and matters concerning the National Insurance Law and the Labour Law and Rules.

RELIGIOUS COURTS

The Religious Courts are the courts of the recognized religious communities. They have jurisdiction over certain defined matters of personal status concerning members of their respective communities. Where any action of personal status involves persons of different religious communities the President of the Supreme Court decides which Court will decide the matter. Whenever a question arises as to whether or not a case is one of personal status within the exclusive jurisdiction of a Religious Court, the matter must be referred to a Special Tribunal composed of two Justices of the Supreme Court and the President of the highest court of the religious community concerned in Israel. The judgments of the Religious Courts are executed by the process and offices of the Civil Courts. Neither these Courts nor the Civil Courts have jurisdiction to dissolve the marriage of a foreign subject.

Jewish Rabbinical Courts: These Courts have exclusive jurisdiction over matters of marriage and divorce of Jews in Israel who are Israeli citizens or residents. In all other matters of personal status they have concurrent jurisdiction with the District Courts.

Muslim Religious Courts: These Courts have exclusive jurisdiction over matters of marriage and divorce of Muslims who are not foreigners, or who are foreigners subject by their national law to the jurisdiction of Muslim Religious Courts in such matters. In all other matters of personal status they have concurrent jurisdiction with the District Courts.

Christian Religious Courts: The Courts of the recognized Christian communities have exclusive jurisdiction over matters of marriage and divorce of members of their communities who are not foreigners. In all other matters of personal status they have concurrent jurisdiction with the District Courts.

Druze Courts: These Courts, established in 1963, have exclusive jurisdiction over matters of marriage and divorce of Druze in Israel, who are Israeli citizens or residents, and concurrent jurisdiction with the District Courts over all other matters of personal status of Druze.

Religion

JUDAISM

Judaism, the religion of the Jews, is the faith of the majority of Israel's inhabitants. On 31 December 2006 Judaism's adherents totalled 5,393,400, equivalent to 75.8% of the country's population. Its basis is a belief in an ethical monotheism.

There are two main Jewish communities: the Ashkenazim and the Sephardim. The former are the Jews from Eastern, Central or Northern Europe, while the latter originate from the Balkan countries, North Africa and the Middle East.

There is also a community of about 10,000 Falashas (Ethiopian Jews) who have been airlifted to Israel at various times since the fall of Emperor Haile Selassie in 1974.

The supreme religious authority is vested in the Chief Rabbinate, which consists of the Ashkenazi and Sephardi Chief Rabbis and the Supreme Rabbinical Council. It makes decisions on interpretation of the Jewish law, and supervises the Rabbinical Courts. There are eight regional Rabbinical Courts, and a Rabbinical Court of Appeal presided over by the two Chief Rabbis.

According to the Rabbinical Courts Jurisdiction Law of 1953, marriage and divorce among Jews in Israel are exclusively within the jurisdiction of the Rabbinical Courts. Provided that all the parties concerned agree, other matters of personal status can also be decided by the Rabbinical Courts.

There are over 170 Religious Councils, which maintain religious services and supply religious needs, and about 400 religious committees with similar functions in smaller settlements. Their expenses are borne jointly by the state and the local authorities. The Religious Councils are under the administrative control of the Ministry of Religious Affairs. In all matters of religion, the Religious Councils are subject to the authority of the Chief Rabbinate. There are 365 officially appointed rabbis. The total number of synagogues is

ISRAEL

about 7,000, most of which are organized within the framework of the Union of Israel Synagogues.

Head of the Ashkenazi Community: The Chief Rabbi YONA METZGER.

Head of the Sephardic Community: The Chief Rabbi SHLOMO AMAR, Jerusalem; tel. 2-5313131.

Two Jewish sects still loyal to their distinctive customs are:

The Karaites: a sect which recognizes only the Jewish written law and not the oral law of the Mishna and Talmud. The community of about 12,000, many of whom live in or near Ramla, has been augmented by immigration from Egypt.

The Samaritans: an ancient sect mentioned in 2 Kings xvii, 24. They recognize only the Torah. The community in Israel numbers about 500; about one-half of this number live in Holon, where a Samaritan synagogue has been built, and the remainder, including the High Priest, live in Nablus, near Mt Gerazim, which is sacred to the Samaritans.

ISLAM

The Muslims in Israel belong principally to the Sunni sect of Islam, and are divided among the four rites: the Shafe'i, the Hanbali, the Hanafi and the Maliki. Before June 1967 they numbered approx. 175,000; in 1971, approx. 343,900. On 31 December 2006 the total Muslim population of Israel was 1,173,100, equivalent to 16.5% of the country's population.

Mufti of Jerusalem: POB 19859, Jerusalem; tel. 2-283528; Sheikh IKRIMAH SABRI (also Chair. Supreme Muslim Council for Jerusalem); appointed by the Palestinian (National) Authority (PA).

There was also a total of 117,500 Druzes in Israel at 31 December 2006. The official spiritual leader of the Druze community in Israel is Sheikh MUWAFAK TARIF, but his leadership is not widely recognized.

CHRISTIANITY

The total Christian population of Israel (including East Jerusalem) at 31 December 2006 was 149,100.

United Christian Council in Israel: POB 116, Jerusalem 91000; tel. and fax 2-6259012; e-mail ucci@ucci.net; internet www.ucci.net; f. 1956; member of World Evangelical Alliance; over 30 mems (evangelical churches and social and educational insts); Chair. CHARLES KOPP.

The Roman Catholic Church

Armenian Rite

The Armenian Catholic Patriarch of Cilicia is resident in Beirut, Lebanon.

Patriarchal Exarchate of Jerusalem and Amman: POB 19546, 36 Via Dolorosa, Jerusalem 91190; tel. 2-6284262; fax 2-6272123; e-mail acpejerusalem@yahoo.com; f. 1885; about 800 adherents (31 December 2005); Exarch Patriarchal (vacant).

Chaldean Rite

The Chaldean Patriarch of Babylon is resident in Baghdad, Iraq.

Patriarchal Exarchate of Jerusalem: Chaldean Patriarchal Vicariate, POB 20108, 7 Chaldean St, Saad and Said Quarter, Jerusalem 91200; tel. 2-6844519; fax 2-6274614; e-mail kolin-p@zahav.net.il; Exarch Patriarchal Mgr PAUL COLLIN.

Latin Rite

The Patriarchate of Jerusalem covers Palestine, Jordan and Cyprus. At 31 December 2005 there were an estimated 78,215 adherents.

Bishops' Conference: Conférence des Evêques Latins dans les Régions Arabes, Notre Dame of Jerusalem Center, POB 20531, Jerusalem 91204; tel. 2-6288554; fax 2-6288555; e-mail evcat@palnet.com; f. 1967; Pres. His Beatitude MICHEL SABBAH (Patriarch of Jerusalem).

Patriarchate of Jerusalem: Latin Patriarchate of Jerusalem, POB 14152, Jerusalem 91141; tel. 2-6282323; fax 2-6271652; e-mail chancellery@latinpat.org; internet www.lpj.org; Patriarch His Beatitude MICHEL SABBAH; Archbishop Coadjutor FOUAD TWAL; Vicar-General for Jerusalem KAMAL HANNA BATHISH (Titular Bishop of Jericho); Vicar-General for Israel GIACINTO-BOULOS MARCUZZO (Titular Bishop of Emmaus Nicopolis); Vicariat Patriarcal Latin, Street 6191/3, Nazareth 16100; tel. 4-6554075; fax 4-6452416; e-mail latinpat@rannet.com.

Maronite Rite

The Maronite community, under the jurisdiction of the Maronite Patriarch of Antioch (resident in Lebanon), has about 7,000 members.

Patriarchal Exarchate of Jerusalem: Maronite Patriarchal Exarchate, POB 14219, 25 Maronite Convent St, Jaffa Gate, Jerusalem 91141; tel. 2-6282158; fax 2-6272821; e-mail fmm@maronitejerusalem.org; about 504 adherents (31 December 2005); Exarch Patriarchal Mgr PAUL NABIL SAYAH (also the Maronite Archbishop of Haifa).

Melkite Rite

The Greek-Melkite Patriarch of Antioch and all the East, of Alexandria and of Jerusalem (GRÉGOIRE III LAHAM) is resident in Damascus, Syria.

Patriarchal Vicariate of Jerusalem
Patriarcat Grec-Melkite Catholique, POB 14130, Porte de Jaffa, Jerusalem 91141; tel. 2-6282023; fax 2-6289606; e-mail gcpjer@p-ol.com; about 3,300 adherents (31 December 2005); Protosyncellus Archim. Archbishop GEORGES MICHEL BAKAR.

Archbishop of Akka (Acre): ELIAS CHACOUR, Archevêché Grec-Catholique, POB 279, 33 Hagefen St, 31002 Haifa; tel. 4-8523114; fax 4-8520798; 80,000 adherents at 31 December 2006.

Syrian Rite

The Syrian Catholic Patriarch of Antioch is resident in Beirut, Lebanon.

Patriarchal Exarchate of Jerusalem: Vicariat Patriarcal Syrien Catholique, POB 19787, 6 Chaldean St, Jerusalem 91191; tel. 2-6282657; fax 2-6284217; e-mail st_thomas@bezeqint.net; about 1,550 adherents (31 December 2006); Exarch Patriarchal Mgr GRÉGOIRE PIERRE MELKI.

The Armenian Apostolic (Orthodox) Church

Patriarch of Jerusalem: Archbishop TORKOM MANOOGIAN, Armenian Patriarchate of St James, POB 14235, Jerusalem; tel. 2-6264853; fax 2-6264862; e-mail webmaster@armenian-patriarchate.org; internet www.armenian-patriarchate.org.

The Greek Orthodox Church

The Patriarchate of Jerusalem contains an estimated 260,000 adherents in Israel, the Occupied Territories, Jordan, Kuwait, Saudi Arabia and the United Arab Emirates.

Patriarch of Jerusalem: THEOPHILOS III, POB 19632-633, Greek Orthodox Patriarchate St, Old City, Jerusalem; tel. 2-6274941; fax 2-6282048; internet www.jerusalem-patriarchate.info.

The Anglican Communion

Episcopal Diocese of Jerusalem and the Middle East: POB 19122, St George's Cathedral Close, Jerusalem 91191; tel. 2-6271670; fax 2-6273847; e-mail bishop@j-diocese.org; internet www.j-diocese.com; Bishop The Rt Rev. SUHEIL DAWANI (Anglican Bishop in Jerusalem).

Other Christian Churches

Other denominations include the Coptic Orthodox Church (700 members), the Russian Orthodox Church, the Ethiopian Orthodox Church, the Romanian Orthodox Church, the Baptist Church, the Lutheran Church and the Church of Scotland.

The Press

Tel-Aviv is the main publishing centre. Largely for economic reasons, no local press has developed away from the main cities; hence all papers regard themselves as national. Friday editions, issued on Sabbath eve, are increased to as much as twice the normal size by special weekend supplements, and experience a considerable rise in circulation. No newspapers appear on Saturday.

Most of the daily papers are in Hebrew, and others appear in Arabic, English, French, Polish, Yiddish, Hungarian, Russian and German. The total daily circulation is 500,000–600,000 copies, or 21 papers per hundred people, although most citizens read more than one daily paper.

Most Hebrew morning dailies have strong political or religious affiliations. Hatzofeh, for example, is affiliated to the National Religious Party. Most newspapers depend on subsidies from political parties, religious organizations or public funds. The limiting effect on freedom of commentary entailed by this party press system has provoked repeated criticism. There are around 400 other newspapers and magazines including some 50 weekly and 150 fortnightly; over 250 of them are in Hebrew, the remainder in 11 other languages.

The most influential and respected daily, for both quality of news coverage and commentary, is Ha'aretz. This is the most widely read of the morning papers, exceeded only by the popular afternoon press, Ma'ariv and Yedioth Aharonoth. The Jerusalem Post gives detailed and sound news coverage in English.

ISRAEL

DAILIES

Al Anba (The News): Jerusalem Publications Ltd, POB 428, 37 Hillel St, Jerusalem; f. 1968; Arabic; circ. 10,000.

Globes: POB 5126, Rishon le Zion 75150; tel. 3-9538611; fax 3-9525971; e-mail mailbox@globes.co.il; internet www.globes.co.il; f. 1983; evening; Hebrew; business and economics; CEO EITAN MADMON; Editor-in-Chief HAGGAI GOLAN; circ. 45,000.

Ha'aretz (The Land): 21 Schocken St, Tel-Aviv 61001; tel. 3-5121212; fax 3-6810012; e-mail contact@haaretz.co.il; internet www.haaretz.co.il; f. 1919; morning (excl. Sat); Hebrew; liberal; independent; 25% stake acquired by M. DuMont Schauberg (Germany) in 2006; Man. Dir YOSSI WARSHAVSKI; Editor-in-Chief DAVID LANDAU; circ. 75,000 (weekdays), 95,000 (Fri.).

Hamodia (The Informer): POB 1306, 5 Yehudah Hamacabi St, Jerusalem 91012; tel. 2-5389255; fax 2-5003384; e-mail english@hamodia.co.il; internet www.hamodia.com; f. 1950; morning; Hebrew and English dailies, and French weekly; Orthodox; organ of Agudat Israel; Editor HAIM MOSHE KNOPF; circ. 100,000.

Hatzofeh (The Watchman): POB 2045, 66 Hamasger St, Tel-Aviv; tel. 3-5622951; fax 3-5621502; e-mail hazofe@zahav.net.il; internet www.hazofe.co.il; f. 1938; morning; Hebrew; organ of the National Religious Party; Editor GONEN GINAT; circ. 60,000.

Israel Nachrichten (News of Israel): POB 28397, Tel-Aviv 61283; tel. 3-5372059; fax 3-5376166; e-mail info@israelnachrichten.de; f. 1974; morning; German; Editor HELGA MÜLLER-GAZMAWE; circ. 20,000.

Al-Itihad (Unity): POB 104, Haifa; tel. 4-511296; fax 4-511297; f. 1944; Arabic; organ of Hadash; Editor AHMAD SA'AD; circ. 60,000.

The Jerusalem Post: POB 81, The Jerusalem Post Bldg, Romema, Jerusalem 91000; tel. 2-5315666; fax 2-5389527; e-mail feedback@jpost.com; internet www.jpost.com; f. 1932; morning; English; independent; CEO RONIT HASIN-HOCHMAN; Editor-in-Chief DAVID HOROVITZ; circ. 15,000 (weekdays), 40,000 (weekend edn); there is also a weekly international edn, circ. 40,000.

Ma'ariv (Evening Prayer): 2 Carlebach St, Tel-Aviv 61200; tel. 3-5632111; fax 3-5610614; internet www.nrg.co.il/online/HP_0.html; f. 1948; mid-morning; Hebrew; independent; publ. by Modiin Publishing House; Editor AMNON DANKNER; circ. 150,000 (weekdays), 250,000 (weekends).

Mabat: 8 Toshia St, Tel-Aviv 67218; tel. 3-5627711; fax 3-5627719; f. 1971; morning; Hebrew; economic and social; Editor S. YARKONI; circ. 7,000.

Nasha Strana (Our Country): 52 Harakeret St, Tel-Aviv 67770; tel. 3-370011; fax 3-5371921; f. 1970; morning; Russian; Editor S. HIMMELFARB; circ. 35,000.

Novosti nedeli (Week's News): 15 Ha-Ahim Mi-Slavita St, Tel-Aviv; tel. 3-6242225; fax 3-6242227; Russian; Editor-in-Chief DMITRII LODYZHENSKII.

Al-Quds (Jerusalem): POB 19788, Jerusalem; tel. 2-6272663; fax 2-6272657; e-mail info@alquds.com; internet www.alquds.com; f. 1968; Arabic; Founder and Publr MAHMOUD ABU ZALAF; Gen. Man. Dr MARWAN ABU ZALAF; circ. 55,000.

Ash-Shaab (The People): POB 20077, Jerusalem; tel. 2-289881; Arabic.

Shearim (The Gates): POB 11044, 64 Frishman St, Tel-Aviv; tel. 3-242126; Hebrew; organ of the Poale Agudat Israel party.

Viata Noastra: 49 Tchlenor St, Tel-Aviv 61351; tel. 3-5372059; fax 3-6877142; e-mail erancourt@shani.co.il; f. 1950; morning; Romanian; Editor GEORGE EDRI; circ. 30,000.

Yated Ne'eman: POB 328, Bnei Brak; tel. 3-6170800; fax 3-6170801; e-mail let-edit@yatedneman.co.il; f. 1986; morning; Hebrew; religious; Editors Y. ROTH, N. GROSSMAN; circ. 25,000.

Yedioth Ahronoth (The Latest News): 2 Yehuda and Noah Mozes St, Tel-Aviv 61000; tel. and fax 3-6082222; e-mail service@y-i.co.il; internet www.ynet.co.il; f. 1939; evening; Hebrew; independent; Editor-in-Chief MOSHE VARDI; circ. 350,000, Fri. 600,000.

WEEKLIES AND FORTNIGHTLIES

Akhbar an-Naqab (News of the Negev): POB 426, Rahat 85357; tel. 8-9919202; fax 8-9917070; e-mail akhbar@akhbarna.com; internet www.akhbarna.com; f. 1988; weekly; Arabic; educational and social issues concerning the Negev Bedouins; Editor-in-Chief MUHAMMAD YOUNIS.

Aurora: Aurora Ltd, POB 18066, Tel-Aviv 61180; tel. 3-5625216; fax 3-5625082; e-mail aurora@aurora-israel.co.il; internet www.aurora-israel.co.il; f. 1963; weekly; Spanish; Editor-in-Chief ARIE AVIDOR; Director MARIO WAINSTEIN; circ. 20,000.

Bama'alah: 120 Kibbutz Gabuyot St, Tel-Aviv; tel. 3-6814488; fax 3-6816852; Hebrew; journal of the young Histadrut Movement; Editor ODED BAR-MEIR.

Bamahane (In the Camp): Military POB 1013, Tel-Aviv; f. 1948; military, illustrated weekly of the Israel Defence Forces; Hebrew; Editor-in-Chief YOSSEF ESHKOL; circ. 70,000.

Etgar (The Challenge): POB 35252, Tel-Aviv 61351; tel. 3-5373268; fax 3-5373269; e-mail info@etgar.info; internet www.etgar.info; twice weekly; Hebrew; publ. by Hanitzotz Publishing House; Editor NATHAN YALIN-MOR.

InformationWeek: POB 1161, 13 Yad Harutzim St, Tel-Aviv 61116; tel. 3-6385858; fax 3-6889207; e-mail world@pc.co.il; internet www.pc.co.il; weekly; Hebrew and English; Man. Dirs DAHLIA PELED, PELI PELED; Editor-in-Chief PELI PELED.

The Israeli Tourist Guide Magazine: Tourist Guide Communications Ltd, POB 53333, Tel-Aviv 61533; tel. 3-5168282; fax 3-5168284; e-mail ishchori@touristguide.co.il; internet www.touristguide.org.il; f. 1994; weekly; Hebrew and English; Publr and Editor ILAN SHCHORI; circ. 10,000.

The Jerusalem Post International Edition: POB 81, Romema, Jerusalem 91000; tel. 2-5315666; fax 2-5389527; e-mail liat@jpost.com; internet www.jpost.co.il; f. 1959; weekly; English; overseas edn of The Jerusalem Post (q.v.); circ. 70,000 to 106 countries; Editor LIAT COLLINS.

Jerusalem Report: POB 1805, Jerusalem 91017; tel. 2-5315440; fax 2-5379489; e-mail jrep@jreport.co.il; internet www.jrep.com; f. 1990; bi-weekly; English; Editor-in-Chief EETTA PRINCE-GIBSON; publ. by Jerusalem Report Publications Ltd.

Kol Ha'am (Voice of the People): Tel-Aviv; f. 1947; Hebrew; organ of the Communist Party of Israel; Editor BERL BALTI.

Laisha (For Women): POB 28122, 35 Bnei Brak St, Tel-Aviv 66021; tel. 3-6386977; fax 3-6386933; e-mail laisha@laisha.co.il; f. 1949; Hebrew; women's magazine; Editor-in-Chief MIRIAM NOFECH-MOSES; circ. 100,000.

Ma'ariv Lanoar: POB 20020, 2 Carlebach St, Tel-Aviv 67132; tel. 3-5632525; fax 3-5632030; e-mail maariv_lanoar@maariv.co.il; f. 1957; weekly for teenagers; Hebrew; Editor DANA BEN-NAFTALI; circ. 100,000.

Otiot: Jerusalem; tel. 2-895097; fax 2-895196; f. 1987; weekly for children; English; Editor URI AUERBACH.

Reshumot: Ministry of Justice, POB 1087, 29 Rehov Salahadin, Jerusalem 91010; f. 1948; Hebrew, Arabic and English; official govt gazette.

Russkii izrailtyanin (Russian Israeli): 93 Allenby St, Tel-Aviv 65134; tel. 3-5606456; fax 3-5606474; internet isratop.com/ri.asp; weekly; Russian; Editor VADIM KORSH.

As-Sabar: POB 2647, Nazareth 16126; tel. 4-6462156; fax 4-6462152; e-mail alsabar.mag@gmail.com; internet www.alsabar-mag.com; publ. by the Organization for Democratic Action; Arabic; political and cultural Israeli-Palestinian affairs.

Sada at-Tarbia (The Echo of Education): publ. by the Histadrut and Teachers' Assn, POB 2306, Rehovot; f. 1952; fortnightly; Arabic; educational; Editor TUVIA SHAMOSH.

As-Sennara: Nazareth; e-mail varia@n-adv.com; for Christian and Muslim Arabs in the region; weekly; Arabic; Founder LUFTI MASHOUR; Editor-in-Chief VIDA MASHOUR.

Vesti (News): 2 Homa U'Migdal, Tel-Aviv 67771; tel. 3-6383444; fax 3-6383440; f. 1992; publ. Sun.–Thur; Russian; Thur. edn includes supplements; Editor-in-Chief SERGEI PODRAZHANSKII.

OTHER PERIODICALS

Asakim Vekalkala (Business and Economics): POB 20027, 84 Ha' Hashmonaim St, Tel-Aviv 61200; tel. 3-5631010; fax 3-5612614; monthly newsletter of the Federation of Israeli Chambers of Commerce; Hebrew; Editor YOSEF SHOSTAK; circ. 5,000.

Bitaon Heyl Ha'avir (Israel Air Force Magazine): Military POB 01560, Zahal; tel. 3-5694153; fax 3-5695806; e-mail iaf@inter.net.il; internet www.iaf.org.il; f. 1948; bi-monthly; Hebrew and English; Dep. Editor U. ETSION; Editor-in-Chief MERAV HALPERIN; circ. 30,000.

Al-Bushra (Good News): POB 6228, Haifa 31061; tel. 4-8385002; fax 4-8371612; f. 1935; monthly; Arabic; organ of the Ahmadiyya movement; Editor MUSA ASA'AD O'DEH.

Business Diary: Haifa; f. 1947; weekly; English and Hebrew; information such as shipping movements, import licences, stock exchange listings and business failures; Editor G. ALON.

Challenge: POB 35252, Tel-Aviv 61351; tel. 3-5373268; fax 3-5373269; e-mail oda@netvision.net.il; internet www.challenge-mag.com; f. 1989; magazine on the Israeli–Palestinian conflict, publ. by Hanitzotz Publishing House; bi-monthly; English; Editor-in-Chief RONI BEN EFRAT; Editor LIZ LEYH LEVAC; circ. 1,000.

Diamond Intelligence Briefs: POB 3441, Ramat-Gan 52133; tel. 3-5750196; fax 3-5754829; e-mail office@tacy.co.il; internet www.diamondintelligence.com; f. 1985; English; Publr CHAIM EVEN-ZOHAR.

ISRAEL

Eastern Mediterranean Tourism/Travel: Israel Travel News Ltd, POB 3251, Tel-Aviv 61032; tel. 3-5251646; fax 3-5251605; e-mail travel01@netvision.net.il; internet www.itn.co.il; f. 1979; monthly; English; Editor GERRY AROHOW; circ. 19,515.

Hamizrah Hehadash (The New East): Israel Oriental Society, The Hebrew University, Mount Scopus, Jerusalem 91905; tel. 2-5883633; e-mail ios49@hotmail.com; f. 1949; annual of the Israel Oriental Society; Middle Eastern, Asian and African Affairs; Hebrew with English summary; Editors HAIM GERBER, ELIE PODEH; circ. 1,500–2,000.

Hapraklit (Law): POB 14152, 8 Wilson St, Tel-Aviv 61141; tel. 3-5614695; fax 3-561476; f. 1943; quarterly; Hebrew; publ. by the Israel Bar Asscn; Editor-in-Chief A. POLONSKI; Editor ARNAN GAVRIELI; circ. 7,000.

Harefuah (Medicine): POB 3566, 2 Twin Towers, 35 Jabotinsky St, Ramat-Gan 52136; tel. 3-6100444; fax 3-5753303; e-mail tguvot@ima.org.il; internet www.ima.org.il/harefuah; f. 1920; monthly journal of the Israel Medical Asscn; Hebrew with English summaries; also publishes Israel Medical Asscn Journal; Editor Prof. YEHUDA SHOENFELD; circ. 16,000.

Hassadeh: POB 40044, 8 Shaul Hamelech Blvd, Tel-Aviv 61400; tel. 3-6929018; fax 3-6929979; f. 1920; monthly; English and Hebrew; review of Israeli agriculture; Publr GUY KING; Editor NAAMA DOTAN; circ. 13,000.

Hed Hachinuch (Echoes of Education): 2 Tashach St, Tel-Aviv 62093; tel. 3-6091819; fax 3-6094521; e-mail hed@itu.org.il; internet www.itu.org.il; f. 1926; monthly; Hebrew; also publishes Arabic edn; educational; publ. by the Israeli Teachers Union; Editor DALIA LACHMAN; circ. 40,000.

Hed Hagan (Echoes of Kindergarten): 8 Ben Saruk St, Tel-Aviv 62969; tel. 3-6922958; e-mail hed@itu.org.il; internet www.itu.org.il; f. 1935; quarterly; Hebrew; early education issues; publ. by the Israel Teachers Union; Editor ILANA MALCHI; circ. 9,000.

Historia: POB 4179, Jerusalem 91041; tel. 2-5650444; fax 2-6712388; e-mail shazar@shazar.org.il; internet www.shazar.org.il/historia.htm; f. 1998; bi-annual; Hebrew, with English summaries; general history; publ. by the Historical Society of Israel; Editors Prof. YITZHAK HEN, Prof. ISRAEL SHATZMAN, Prof. SHULAMIT VOLKOV; circ. 1,000.

Israel Agritechnology Focus: 8 Twersky St, Tel-Aviv 61574; tel. 3-5628511; fax 3-5628512; f. 1993; quarterly; English; farming technology, agricultural company and investment news; Editor NICKY BLACKMAN.

Israel Environment Bulletin: Ministry of the Environment, POB 34033, Jerusalem 95464; tel. 2-6553777; fax 2-6535934; e-mail shoshana@environment.gov.il; internet www.environment.gov.il; f. 1973; bi-annual; English; Editor SHOSHANA GABBAY; circ. 3,500.

Israel Exploration Journal: POB 7041, 5 Avida St, Jerusalem 91070; tel. 2-6257991; fax 2-6247772; e-mail ies@vms.huji.ac.il; internet israelexplorationsociety.huji.ac.il/iej.htm; f. 1950; bi-annual; English; general and biblical archaeology, ancient history and historical geography of Israel and the Holy Land; Editors S. AHITUV, MIRIAM TADMOR; circ. 2,500.

Israel Export News: POB 50084, 29 Hamered St, Tel-Aviv 68125; tel. 3-5142830; fax 3-5142902; internet www.export.gov.il; f. 1949; bi-monthly; English; commercial and economic; publ. by Israel Export Institute; Dir of Media Dept DANI BLOCH.

Israel Journal of Chemistry: POB 34299, Jerusalem 91341; tel. 2-6522226; fax 2-6522277; e-mail info@israelsciencejournals.com; internet www.sciencefromisrael.com; f. 1951; quarterly; English; publ. by Science from Israel; Editor Prof. H. LEVANON.

Israel Journal of Earth Sciences: POB 34299, Jerusalem 91341; tel. 2-6522226; fax 2-6522277; e-mail info@israelsciencejournals.com; internet www.sciencefromisrael.com; f. 1951; quarterly; English; publ. by Science from Israel; Editors Prof. YOSSI MART, Dr AHUUA ALMOGI.

Israel Journal of Ecology and Evolution: POB 34299, Jerusalem 91341; tel. 2-6522226; fax 2-6522277; e-mail info@israelsciencejournals.com; internet www.sciencefromisrael.com; f. 1951 as Israel Journal of Zoology; name changed in 2006; quarterly; English; publ. by Science from Israel; Editors Prof. ALAN DEGEN, Dr MICHA ILAN.

Israel Journal of Mathematics: The Hebrew University Magnes Press, POB 39099, Jerusalem 91390; tel. 2-6586656; fax 2-5633370; e-mail iton@math.huji.ac.il; internet www.ma.huji.ac.il/~ijmath; f. 1951; bi-monthly; English; Editor-in-Chief AVINOAM MANN.

Israel Journal of Plant Sciences: POB 34299, Jerusalem 91341; tel. 2-6522226; fax 2-6522277; e-mail info@israelsciencejournals.com; internet www.sciencefromisrael.com; f. 1951 as Israel Journal of Botany; quarterly; English; publ. by Science from Israel; Editor Dr DANIEL JOEL.

Israel Journal of Psychiatry and Related Sciences: Gefen Publishing House Ltd, 6 Hatzvi St, Jerusalem 94386; tel. 2-5380247; fax 2-5388423; e-mail ijp@gefenpublishing.com; internet www.psychiatry.org.il/journal; f. 1963; quarterly; English; Editor-in-Chief Dr DAVID GREENBERG.

Israel Journal of Veterinary Medicine: POB 22, Ra'nana 43100; tel. 9-7419929; fax 9-7431778; e-mail ivma@zahav.net.il; internet www.isrvma.org/journal.htm; f. 1943; fmrly Refuah Veterinarith; quarterly of the Israel Veterinary Medical Asscn; English; Editor Z. TRAININ.

Israel Law Review: Israel Law Review Asscn, Faculty of Law, Hebrew University of Jerusalem, Mt Scopus, Jerusalem 91905; tel. 2-5882535; fax 2-5882565; e-mail ilr@savion.huji.ac.il; internet law.huji.ac.il/eng/pirsumim.asp; f. 1966; 3 a year; English; Editors-in-Chief MARGIT COHN, BARAK MEDINA.

Israel Medical Asscn Journal (IMAJ): POB 3604, 11th Floor, 2 Twin Towers, 35 Jabotinsky St, Ramat-Gan 52136; tel. 3-6100475; fax 3-5751616; e-mail imaj@ima.org.il; internet www.ima.org.il/imaj; f. 1999; monthly English-language journal of the Israel Medical Asscn; also publ. Harefuah; Editor Prof. YEHUDA SHOENFELD.

Israel Press Service (IPS): POB 33188, Jerusalem 91330; tel. 2-5332825; fax 2-2345433; e-mail junes@netvision.net.il; internet www.israel-press-service.co.il; fmrly the World Zionist Press Service; English; Zionist; Israeli society, culture, economics, education, business, science, sport, tourism and Jewish holidays; Editor and Publr JUNE SPITZER.

Israels Aussenhandel: Tel-Aviv; tel. 3-5280215; f. 1967; monthly; German; commercial; publ. by Israel Periodicals Co Ltd; Editor PELTZ NOEMI; Man. Dir ZALMAN PELTZ.

Al-Jadid (The New): POB 104, Haifa; f. 1951; literary monthly; Arabic; Editor SALEM JUBRAN; circ. 5,000.

Journal d'Analyse Mathématique: The Hebrew University Magnes Press, POB 39099, Jerusalem 91390; tel. 2-6586656; fax 2-5633370; e-mail magnes@vms.huji.ac.il; internet www.ma.huji.ac.il/jdm; f. 1955; bi-annual; French; Exec. Editor EVA GOLDMAN.

Leshonenu: Academy of the Hebrew Language, Givat Ram Campus, Jerusalem 91904; tel. 2-6493555; fax 2-5617065; e-mail acad2u@vms.huji.ac.il; internet hebrew-academy.huji.ac.il; f. 1929; quarterly; Hebrew; for the study of the Hebrew language and cognate subjects; Editor MOSHE BAR-ASHER.

Leshonenu La'am: Academy of the Hebrew Language, Givat Ram Campus, Jerusalem 91904; tel. 2-6493555; fax 2-5617065; e-mail acad2u@vms.huji.ac.il; internet hebrew-academy.huji.ac.il; f. 1945; quarterly; Hebrew; popular Hebrew philology; Editors MOSHE FLORENTIN, DAVID TALSHIR, YOSEF OFER.

Lilac: Nazareth; e-mail editor@lilac-m.net; internet www.lilac-m.com; f. 2000 for Christian and Muslim Arab women in the region; monthly; Arabic; Israel's first magazine for Arab women; Founder and Editor-in-Chief YARA MASHOUR.

Ma'arachot (Campaigns): Military POB 02432, Israel Defence Forces; tel. 3-5694345; fax 3-5694343; e-mail maarachotp@gmail.com; f. 1939; military and political bi-monthly; Hebrew; periodical of Israel Defence Force; Editor-in-Chief HAGGAI GOLAN; circ. 20,000.

MB-Yakinton (Yakinton): POB 1480, Tel-Aviv 61014; tel. 3-5164461; fax 3-5164435; e-mail irgunmb@netvision.net.il; internet www.irgun-jeckes.org; f. 1932; monthly journal of the Irgun Jotsei Merkaz Europa(Asscn of Israelis of Central European Origin); Hebrew and German; Editor MICHA LIMOR.

M'Lakha V'ta Asiya (Israel Industry): POB 11587, 40 Rembrandt St, Tel-Aviv; monthly; Hebrew; publ. by Israel Publications Corpn Ltd; circ. 8,500.

Moznaim (Balance): POB 7098, Tel-Aviv; tel. 3-6953256; fax 3-6919681; f. 1929; monthly; Hebrew; literature and culture; publ. by Hebrew Writers Asscn; Editors ASHER REICH, AZRIEL KAUFMAN; circ. 2,500.

New Outlook: 9 Gordon St, Tel-Aviv 63458; tel. 3-5236496; fax 3-5232252; f. 1957; bi-monthly; English; Israeli and Middle Eastern Affairs; dedicated to the quest for Arab-Israeli peace; Editor-in-Chief CHAIM SHUR; Senior Editor DAN LEON; circ. 10,000.

News from Within: POB 31417, Jerusalem 91313; tel. 2-6241159; fax 2-6253151; e-mail bryan@alt-info.org; internet www.alternativenews.org; monthly; joint Israeli-Palestinian publ; political, economic, social and cultural; publ. by the Alternative Information Centre.

PC Plus: PC Media, POB 11438, 13 Yad Harutzim St, Tel-Aviv 61114; tel. 3-6385810; fax 3-6889207; e-mail editor@pc.co.il; internet www.pc.co.il; f. 1992; monthly; Hebrew; information on personal computers; CEO and Man. Editor DAHLIA PELED; CEO and Editor-in-Chief PELI PELED; circ. 23,000.

Proche-Orient Chrétien: St Anne's Church, POB 19079, Jerusalem 91190; tel. 2-6281992; fax 2-6280764; e-mail mafrpoc@steanne

ISRAEL

.org; f. 1951; quarterly on churches and religion in the Middle East; French; circ. 1,000.

Publish Israel: Tel-Aviv; tel. 3-5622744; fax 3-5621808; e-mail olamot@inter.net.il; f. 1998; six times a year; magazine for printers and publrs; Gen. Man. DAN SHEKEL; circ. 12,000.

Shituf (Co-operation): POB 7151, 24 Ha'arba St, Tel-Aviv; f. 1948; bi-monthly; Hebrew; economic, social and co-operative problems in Israel; publ. by the Central Union of Industrial, Transport and Service Co-operative Societies; Editor L. LOSH; circ. 12,000.

Shivuk (Marketing): POB 20027, Tel-Aviv 61200; tel. 3-5631010; fax 3-5612614; monthly; Hebrew; publ. by Federation of Israeli Chambers of Commerce; Editor SARA LIPKIN.

Sinai: POB 642, Jerusalem 91006; tel. 2-6526231; fax 2-6526968; e-mail mosad-haravkook@neto.bezeqint.net; f. 1937; Hebrew; Torah science and literature; Editor Rabbi YOSEF MOVSHOVITZ.

As-Sindibad: POB 28049, Tel-Aviv; tel. 3-371438; f. 1970; children's monthly; Arabic; Man. JOSEPH ELIAHOU; Editor WALID HUSSEIN; circ. 8,000.

Terra Santa: POB 14038, Jaffa Gate, Jerusalem 91142; tel. 2-6272692; fax 2-6286417; e-mail cicts@netmedia.net.il; f. 1973; bi-monthly; publ. by the Christian Information Centre, which is sponsored by the Custody of the Holy Land (the official custodians of the Holy Shrines); Italian, Spanish, French, English and Arabic edns publ. in Jerusalem by the Franciscan Printing Press, German edn in Munich, Maltese edn in Valletta; Dir Fr ATHANASIUS MACORA.

WIZO Review: Women's International Zionist Organization, 38 Sderot David Hamelech Blvd, Tel-Aviv 64237; tel. 3-6923805; fax 3-6923801; e-mail wreview@wizo.org; internet www.wizo.org; f. 1947; English (3 a year) and Spanish (internet version); Chair. HILLEL SCHENKER; Editor INGRID ROCKBERGER; circ. 20,000.

Zion: POB 4179, Jerusalem 91041; tel. 2-5650444; fax 2-6712388; e-mail shazar@shazar.org.il; f. 1935; quarterly; publ. by the Historical Society of Israel; Hebrew, with English summaries; research in Jewish history; Editors I. ETKES, Prof. A. BAUMGARTEN, Y. KAPLAN; circ. 1,000.

PRESS ASSOCIATIONS

Daily Newspaper Publishers' Asscn of Israel: POB 51202, 74 Petach Tikva Rd, Tel-Aviv 61200; fax 3-5617938; safeguards professional interests and maintains standards, supplies newsprint to dailies; negotiates with trade unions; mems all daily papers; affiliated to International Federation of Newspaper Publishers; Pres. SHABTAI HIMMELFARB; Gen. Sec. BETZALEL EYAL.

Foreign Press Asscn: Beit Sokolov, 4 Kaplan St, Tel-Aviv 64734; tel. 3-6916143; fax 3-6961548; e-mail fpa@netvision.net.il; internet www.fpa.org.il; f. 1957; represents journalists employed by international news orgs who report from Israel, the West Bank and the Gaza Strip; private, non-profit org.; almost 500 mems from 30 countries; Chair. SIMON MCGREGOR-WOOD.

Israel Association of the Periodical Press (IAPP): 17 Keilat Venezia St, Tel-Aviv 69400; tel. 3-6449851; fax 3-6449852; e-mail iapp@zahav.net.il; internet www.iapp.co.il; f. 1962; Chair. JOSEPH FRENKEL.

Israel Journalists' Asscn: 4 Kaplan St, Tel-Aviv 64734; tel. 3-6956141; Man. Dir TUVIA SAAR.

Israel Press Council: Beit Sokolov, 4 Kaplan St, Tel-Aviv; tel. 3-6951437; fax 3-6951145; e-mail moaza@m-i.org.il; internet www.m-i.org.il; f. 1963; deals with matters of common interest to the Press such as drafting the code of professional ethics, which is binding on all journalists; Chair. ORNA LIN; Gen. Sec. AVI WEINBERG.

NEWS AGENCIES

Jerusalem Media and Communication Centre: POB 25047, 7 Nablus Rd, Sheikh Jarrah, Jerusalem; tel. 2-5819777; fax 2-5829534; e-mail jmcc@jmcc.org; internet www.jmcc.org; f. 1988 as the Palestine Press Service.

Jewish Telegraphic Agency (JTA): Mideast Bureau, Jerusalem Post Bldg, Romema, Jerusalem 91000; tel. 2-610579; fax 2-536635; e-mail info@jta.org; internet www.jta.org; Correspondents LESLIE SUSSER (diplomatic affairs), DINA KRAFT (news and features).

Publishers

Achiasaf Publishing House Ltd: POB 8414, 4 Tzoran St, Poleg Industrial Zone, Netanya 42504; tel. 9-8851390; fax 9-8851391; e-mail info@achiasaf.co.il; internet www.achiasaf.co.il; f. 1937; general; Pres. MATAN ACHIASAF.

Am Oved Publishers Ltd: 22 Mazeh St, Tel-Aviv 65213; tel. 3-6288500; fax 3-6298911; e-mail info@am-oved.co.il; internet www.am-oved.co.il; f. 1942; fiction, non-fiction, reference books, school and university textbooks, children's books, poetry, classics, science fiction; Man. Dir YARON SADAN.

Amihai Publishing House Ltd: POB 8448, 19 Yad Harutzim St, Netanya Darom 42505; tel. 9-8859099; fax 9-8853464; e-mail ami1000@bezeqint.net; internet www.amichaibooks.co.il; f. 1948; fiction, general science, linguistics, languages, arts; Dir ITZHAK ORON.

Arabic Publishing House: 93 Arlozorof St, Tel-Aviv; tel. 3-6921674; f. 1960; established by the Histadrut; periodicals and books; Gen. Man. GHASSAN MUKLASHI.

Ariel Publishing House: POB 3328, Jerusalem 91033; tel. 2-6434540; fax 2-6436164; e-mail elysch@netvision.net.il; internet www.arielpublishinghouse.com; f. 1976; history, archaeology, religion, geography, folklore; CEO ELY SCHILLER.

Astrolog Publishing House: POB 1231, Hod Hasharon 45111; tel. 3-9190957; fax 3-9190958; e-mail abooks@netvision.net.il; f. 1994; general non-fiction, religion, alternative medicine; Man. Dir SARA BEN-MORDECHAI.

Carta, The Israel Map and Publishing Co Ltd: POB 2500, 18 Ha'uman St, Industrial Area, Talpiot, Jerusalem 91024; tel. 2-6783355; fax 2-6782373; e-mail carta@carta.co.il; internet www.holyland-jerusalem.com; f. 1958; the principal cartographic publr; Pres. and CEO SHAY HAUSMAN.

Rodney Franklin Agency: POB 37727, 53 Mazeh St, Tel-Aviv 65789; tel. 3-5600724; fax 3-5600479; e-mail rodneyf@netvision.net.il; internet www.rodneyagency.com; f. 1974; exclusive representative of various British, other European and US publrs; e-marketing services for academic and professional journal publrs in 15 countries; Dir RODNEY FRANKLIN.

Gefen Publishing House Ltd: 6 Hatzvi St, Jerusalem 94386; tel. 2-5380247; fax 2-5388423; e-mail info@gefenpublishing.com; internet www.israelbooks.com; f. 1981; largest publr of English-language books in Israel; also publishes wide range of fiction and non-fiction; CEO ILAN GREENFIELD.

Globes Publishers: POB 5126, Rishon le Zion 75150; tel. 3-9538611; fax 3-9525971; e-mail mailbox@globes.co.il; internet www.globes.co.il; business, finance, technology, law, marketing; CEO EITAN MADMON; Editor-in-Chief HAGGAI GOLAN.

Gvanim: POB 11138, 29 Bar-Kochba St, Tel-Aviv 61111; tel. 3-5281044; fax 3-5283648; e-mail traklinm@zahav.net.il; f. 1992; poetry, belles lettres, fiction; Man. Dir MARITZA ROSMAN.

Hakibbutz Hameuchad—Sifriat Poalim Publishing Group: POB 1432, Bnei Brak, Tel-Aviv 51114; tel. 3-5785810; fax 3-5785811; e-mail bruria@kibutz-poalim.co.il; internet www.kibutz-poalim.co.il; f. 1939 as Hakibbutz Hameuchad Publishing House Ltd; subsequently merged with Sifriat Poalim; general; Gen. Dir UZI SHAVIT.

Hanitzotz Publishing House: POB 35252, Tel-Aviv 61351; tel. 3-5373268; fax 3-5373269; e-mail oda@netvision.net.il; internet www.hanitzotz.com; f. 1985; 'progressive' booklets and publications, incl. the periodicals Challenge (in English), Etgar (Hebrew), and As-Sabar (Arabic); also produces documentary films on human and workers' rights; Contact RONI BEN EFRAT.

Hed Arzi (Ma'ariv) Publishing Ltd: 3A Yoni Netanyahu St, Or-Yehuda, Tel-Aviv 60376; tel. 3-5383333; fax 3-6343205; e-mail shimoni@hed-arzi.co.il; f. 1954 as Sifriat-Ma'ariv Ltd; later known as Ma'ariv Book Guild Ltd; general; Man. Dir ELI SHIMONI.

Hod-Ami—Computer Books Ltd: POB 6108, Herzliya 46160; tel. 9-9564716; fax 9-9571582; e-mail info@hod-ami.co.il; internet www.hod-ami.co.il; f. 1984; information technology, management; translations from English into Hebrew and Arabic; CEO ITZHAK AMIHUD.

Intermedia Publishing Enterprises Ltd (IPE): POB 2121, 23 Hataas St, Kefar-Sava 44641; tel. 9-5608501; fax 9-5608513; e-mail freed@inter.net.il; f. 1993; business, education, English as a second language, journalism, health, nutrition, mathematics, medicine, philosophy, self-help; Man. Dir ARIE FRIED.

Israeli Music Publications Ltd: POB 7681, Jerusalem 94188; tel. 2-6251370; fax 2-6241378; e-mail khanukaev@pop.isracom.net.il; f. 1949; music, dance, musical works; Dir of Music Publications SERGEI KHANUKAEV.

Jerusalem Center for Public Affairs: 13 Tel Hai St, Jerusalem 92107; tel. 2-5619281; fax 2-5619112; e-mail jcpa@netvision.net.il; internet www.jcpa.org; f. 1976; Jewish political tradition; publishes the Jewish Political Studies Review; Pres. DORE GOLD; Chair. Dr MANFRED GERSTENFELD.

The Jerusalem Publishing House: Beit Hashenhav, 12 Beit Hadefus St, Jerusalem 95483; tel. 2-6537966; fax 2-6537988; e-mail info@jerpub.com; internet jerpub.com; f. 1966; biblical research, history, encyclopaedias, archaeology, arts of the Holy Land, cookbooks, guidebooks, economics, politics; Dir SHLOMO S. GAFNI; Man. Editor RACHEL GILON.

ISRAEL *Directory*

The Jewish Agency—Department of Jewish Zionist Education: POB 10615, Jerusalem 91104; tel. 2-6202629; fax 2-6204122; e-mail bookshop@jazo.org.il; f. 1945; education, Jewish philosophy, studies in the Bible, children's books publ. in Hebrew, English, French, Spanish, German, Swedish and Portuguese, Hebrew teaching material; Dir of Publication Division IDA REINMAN.

Jewish History Publications (Israel 1961) Ltd: POB 1232, 29 Jabotinsky St, Jerusalem 92141; tel. 2-5632310; f. 1961; encyclopaedias, World History of the Jewish People series.

Keter Publishing House Ltd: POB 7145, Givat Shaul B, Jerusalem 91071; tel. 2-6557822; fax 2-6536811; e-mail info@keter-books.co.il; internet www.keter-books.co.il; f. 1959; original and translated works of fiction, encyclopaedias, non-fiction, guidebooks and children's books; publishing imprints: Israel Program for Scientific Translations, Keter Books, Domino, Shikmona, Encyclopedia Judaica; Man. Dir YIPHTACH DEKEL.

Kinneret Zmora Dvir Publishing House: 10 Hataasiya St, Or-Yehuda 60212; tel. 3-6344977; fax 3-6340953; e-mail kinneret-zmora.co.il; f. 2002 following merger between Kinneret and Zmora Bitan-Dvir publishing houses; child devt and care, cookery, dance, educational, humour, non-fiction, music, home-care, psychology, psychiatry, travel; Man. Dir YORAM ROS; Editor-in-Chief DOV ALFON.

Kiryat Sefer: Tel-Aviv 65812; tel. 3-5660188; fax 3-5100227; f. 1933; concordances, dictionaries, textbooks, maps, scientific books; Dir AVRAHAM SIVAN.

Magnes Press: The Hebrew University, The Sherman Bldg for Research Management, POB 39099, Givat Ram, Jerusalem 91390; tel. 2-6586656; e-mail info@magnespress.co.il; internet www.magnespress.co.il; f. 1929; academic books and journals on many subjects, incl. biblical, classical and Jewish studies, social sciences, language, literature, art, history and geography; Dir HAI TSABAR.

MAP-Mapping and Publishing Ltd (Tel-Aviv Books): POB 56024, 17 Tchernikhovski St, Tel-Aviv 61560; tel. 3-6210500; fax 3-5257725; e-mail info@mapa.co.il; internet www.mapa.co.il; f. 1985; maps, atlases, travel guides, textbooks, reference books; Man. Dir DANI TRACZ; Editor-in-Chief MOULI MELTZER.

Rubin Mass Ltd: POB 990, 7 Ha-Ayin-Het St, Jerusalem 91009; tel. 2-6277863; fax 2-6277864; e-mail rmass@barak.net.il; internet www.rubin-mass.com; f. 1927; Hebraica, Judaica, export of all Israeli books and periodicals; Man. OREN MASS.

Ministry of Defence Publishing House: POB 916, Yaakov Dori Rd, Kiryat Ono 55108; tel. 3-7380738; fax 3-7380645; e-mail minuy@inter.net.il; internet ecom.gov.il/Mod/; f. 1958; military literature, Judaism, history and geography of Israel; Dir JOSEPH PERLOVITZ.

M. Mizrachi Publishing House Ltd: 67 Levinsky St, Tel-Aviv 66855; tel. 3-6870936; fax 3-6888185; e-mail mizrahi.co@jmail.com; f. 1960; children's books, fiction, history, medicine, science; Dirs MEIR MIZRACHI, ISRAEL MIZRACHI.

Mosad Harav Kook: POB 642, 1 Maimon St, Jerusalem 91006; tel. 2-6526231; fax 2-6526968; e-mail mosad-haravkook@neto.bezeqint.net; f. 1937; editions of classical works, Torah and Jewish studies; Dir Rabbi YOSEF MOVSHOVITZ.

Otsar Hamoreh: c/o Israel Teachers Union, 8 Ben Saruk, Tel-Aviv 62969; tel. 3-6922983; fax 3-6922988; f. 1951; educational; Man. Dir JOSEPH SALOMAN.

Alexander Peli Jerusalem Publishing Co Ltd: 29 Jabotinsky St, Jerusalem 92141; tel. 2-5632310; f. 1961; encyclopaedias such as the Standard Jewish Encyclopedia, history, the arts, educational material.

People and Computers Ltd: POB 11438, 53 Derech Asholom St, Givatayim 53454; tel. 3-7330733; fax 3-7330703; e-mail info@pc.co.il; internet www.pc.co.il; information technology; Pres. and CEO PELI PELED; Publr and CEO DAHLIA PELED.

Schocken Publishing House Ltd: POB 2316, 24 Nathan Yelin Mor St, Tel-Aviv 67015; tel. 3-5610130; fax 3-5622668; e-mail find@schocken.co.il; f. 1938; general; Dir RACHELI EDELMAN.

Science from Israel—A Division of LPP Ltd: POB 34299, Merkaz Sapir 6/36, Givat Shaul, Jerusalem 91341; tel. 2-6522226; fax 2-6522277; e-mail laserpages@netmedia.net.il; internet www.sciencefromisrael.com; fmrly Laser Pages Publishing Ltd; scientific journals.

Shalem Press: POB 8787, 13 Yehoshua Bin-Nun St, Jerusalem 93102; tel. 2-5605555; fax 2-5605565; e-mail shalempress@shalem.org.il; internet www.shalem.org.il; f. 1994; economics, political science, history, philosophy, cultural issues; Pres. DANIEL POLISAR.

Sinai Publishing: 72 Allenby St, Tel-Aviv 65812; tel. 3-5163672; fax 3-5176783; f. 1853; Hebrew books and religious articles; Dir MOSHE SCHLESINGER.

Steinhart-Katzir: POB 8333, Netanya 42505; tel. 9-8854770; fax 9-8854771; e-mail mail@haolam.co.il; internet www.haolam.co.il; f. 1991; travel; Man. Dir OHAD SHARAV.

Tcherikover Publishers Ltd: 12 Hasharon St, Tel-Aviv 66185; tel. 3-6396099; fax 3-6874729; e-mail barkay@inter.net.il; education, psychology, economics, psychiatry, literature, literary criticism, essays, history geography, criminology, art, languages, management; Man. Editor S. TCHERIKOVER.

Yachdav United Publishers Co Ltd: POB 20123, 29 Carlebach St, Tel-Aviv 67132; tel. 3-5614121; fax 3-5611996; e-mail info@tbpai.co.il; f. 1960; educational; Chair. EPHRAIM BEN-DOR; Exec. Dir AMNON BEN-SHMUEL.

Yavneh Publishing House Ltd: 4 Mazeh St, Tel-Aviv 65213; tel. 3-6297856; fax 3-6293638; e-mail publishing@yavneh.co.il; internet www.dbook2.co.il; f. 1932; general; Man. Dir NIRA PREISKEL.

Yedioth Ahronoth Books: POB 53494, 10 Kehilat Venezia, Tel-Aviv 61534; tel. 3-7683333; fax 3-7683300; e-mail info@ybook.co.il; internet www.ybook.co.il; f. 1952; non-fiction, politics, Judaism, health, music, dance, fiction, education; Man. Dir DOV EICHENWALD; Editor-in-Chief DOV ELBOIM.

S. Zack: 31 Beit Hadfus St, Jerusalem 95483; tel. 2-6537760; fax 2-6514005; e-mail zackmt@bezeqint.net; internet www.zack.co.il; f. 1935; fiction, science, philosophy, Judaism, children's books, educational and reference books, dictionaries, languages; Dir MICHAEL ZACK.

PUBLISHERS' ASSOCIATION

The Book Publishers' Association of Israel: POB 20123, 29 Carlebach St, Tel-Aviv 67132; tel. 3-5614121; fax 3-5611996; e-mail info@tbpai.co.il; internet www.tbpai.co.il; f. 1939; mems: 84 publishing firms; Chair. RACHELI EDELMAN; Man. Dir AMNON BEN-SHMUEL.

Broadcasting and Communications

TELECOMMUNICATIONS

Barak I.T.C.: Cibel Industrial Park, 15 Hamelacha St, Rosh Ha'ayin 48091; tel. 3-9001900; fax 3-9001800; e-mail service@013barak.net.il; internet www.barak.net.il; f. 1997; Chair. AMOS SAPIR (acting).

Bezeq—The Israel Telecommunication Corpn Ltd: POB 1088, 15 Hazvi St, Jerusalem 91010; tel. 2-5395503; fax 2-5000410; e-mail bzqspk@bezeq.com; internet www.bezeq.co.il; f. 1984; privatized in May 2005; launched own cellular network, Pelephone Communications Ltd, in 1986; total assets US $3,674m. (July 2004); Chair. SHLOMO RODAV; CEO AVI GABAI.

Pelephone Communications Ltd: 33 Hagvura St, Givatayim, Tel-Aviv 53483; tel. 3-5728881; fax 3-5728111; internet www.pelephone.co.il; f. 1986; 2.2m. subscribers (2006); Chair. BENNY VAKNIN; CEO GIL SHARON.

Cellcom Israel: POB 4060, 10 Hagavish St, Netanya 42140; tel. 9-9989755; fax 9-9599700; e-mail investors@cellcom.co.il; internet www.cellcom.co.il; f. 1994; mobile telecommunications operator; Chair. AMI EREL; Pres. and CEO AMOS SHAPIRA.

ECI Telecom Ltd: POB 3038, 30 Hasivim St, Petach Tikva, Tel-Aviv 49133; tel. 3-9266555; fax 3-9266500; e-mail sandra.welfeld@ecitele.com; internet www.ecitele.com; f. 1961; Pres. and CEO RAFI MAOR.

Partner Communications Co Ltd: POB 435, 8 Amal St, Afeq Industrial Park, Rosh Ha'ayin 48103; tel. 54-7814888; fax 54-7814999; e-mail dan.eldar@orange.co.il; internet www.orange.co.il; f. 1999; provides mobile telecommunications and wire-free applications services under the Orange brand name; represents about one-third of the mobile-cellular market in Israel; Chair. CANNING FOK; CEO DAVID AVNER; 2.6m. subscribers (Dec. 2005).

Vocal Tec Communications Ltd (Vocal Tec): POB 4041, 60 Medinat Hayehudim St, Herzliya 46140; tel. 9-9703888; fax 9-9558175; e-mail info@vocaltec.com; internet www.vocaltec.com; carrier services and telecommunications infrastructure; revenues US $7.3m. (2006); Chair. ILAN ROSEN; Pres. and CEO JOSEPH (YOSI) ALBAGLI.

BROADCASTING

In 1986 the Government approved the establishment of a commercial radio and television network to be run in competition with the state system.

Radio

Israel Broadcasting Authority (IBA) (Radio): POB 28080, 161 Jaffa Rd, Jerusalem 94342; tel. 2-5015555; e-mail dover@iba.org.il; internet www.iba.org.il; f. 1948; state-owned station in Jerusalem with additional studios in Tel-Aviv and Haifa. IBA broadcasts six programmes for local and overseas listeners on medium, shortwave and VHF/FM in 16 languages: Hebrew, Arabic, English, Yiddish, Ladino, Romanian, Hungarian, Moghrabi, Farsi, French, Russian, Bukharian, Georgian, Portuguese, Spanish and Amharic; Chair.

MICHA YINON; Dir-Gen. (vacant); Dir of Radio (vacant); Dir External Services VICTOR GRAJEWSKY.

Galei Zahal: MPOB, Zahal; tel. 3-5126666; fax 3-5126760; e-mail glz@galatz.co.il; internet www.glz.co.il; f. 1950; Israel Defence Force broadcasting station, Tel-Aviv, with studios in Jerusalem; broadcasts 24-hour news, current affairs, music and cultural programmes in Hebrew on FM, medium and short waves; Dir ITZHAK TUNIK.

Kol Israel (The Voice of Israel): POB 1082, 21 Heleni Hamalka, Jerusalem 91010; tel. 1-53013201; e-mail Allegraa@iba.org.il; internet kolisrael.iba.org.il; broadcasts music, news and multilingual programmes within Israel and overseas on short wave, AM and FM stereo, in 15 languages, incl. Hebrew, Arabic, French, English, Spanish, Ladino, Russian, Yiddish, Romanian, Hungarian, Amharic and Georgian; Dir SHMUEL BEN-ZVI; Gen. Dir YONI BEN-MENACHEM.

Television

Israel Broadcasting Authority (IBA) (Television): 161 Jaffa Rd, Jerusalem; tel. 2-5301333; fax 2-292944; internet www.iba.org.il; broadcasts began in 1968; station in Jerusalem with additional studios in Tel-Aviv; one colour network (VHF with UHF available in all areas); one satellite channel; broadcasts in Hebrew, Arabic and English; Dir-Gen. URI PORAT; Dir of Television YAIR STERN; Dir of Engineering RAFI YEOSHUA.

The Council of Cable TV and Satellite Broadcasting: 23 Jaffa Rd, Jerusalem 91999; tel. 2-6702210; fax 2-6702273; e-mail inbard@moc.gov.il; f. 1982; Chair. YORAM MOKADY.

Israel Educational Television: Ministry of Education, 14 Klausner St, Tel-Aviv 69011; tel. 3-646227; fax 3-6466164; e-mail webmaster@ietv.gov.il; internet www.ietv.gov.il; f. 1966 by Hanadiv (Rothschild Memorial Group) as Instructional Television Trust; began transmission in 1966; school programmes form an integral part of the syllabus in a wide range of subjects; also adult education; Gen. Man. AHUVA FAINMESSE; Dir of Engineering S. KASIF.

Second Authority for Television and Radio: 5 Kanfi Nesharim St, POB 3445, Jerusalem 95464; tel. 2-6556222; fax 2-6556287; e-mail rashut@rashut2.org.il; internet www.rashut2.org.il; f. 1991; responsible for providing broadcasts through two principal television channels, Channel 2 and Channel 10, and some 14 radio stations; Chair. NURIT DABUSH.

Finance

(cap. = capital; res = reserves; dep. = deposits; m. = million; brs = branches; amounts in shekels)

BANKING

Central Bank

Bank of Israel: POB 780, Bank of Israel Bldg, Kiryat Ben-Gurion, Jerusalem 91007; tel. 2-6552211; fax 2-6528805; e-mail webmaster@bankisrael.gov.il; internet www.bankisrael.gov.il; f. 1954 as the Central Bank of the State of Israel; cap. 60m., res –13,592m., dep. 106,438m. (Dec. 2004); Gov. Prof. STANLEY FISCHER; 1 br.

Principal Commercial Banks

Arab-Israel Bank Ltd: POB 207, 48 Bar Yehuda St, Tel Hanan, Nesher 36601; tel. 4-8205222; fax 4-8205250; e-mail aravi@bll.co.il; internet www.bank-aravi-israeli.co.il; dep. 3,062m., total assets 3,431m. (Dec. 2005); subsidiary of Bank Leumi le-Israel BM; Chair. S. ZUSMAN; Gen. Man. ITZHAK EYAL.

Bank Hapoalim: 50 Rothschild Blvd, Tel-Aviv 66883; tel. 3-5673333; fax 3-5607028; e-mail international@bnhp.co.il; internet www.bankhapoalim.co.il; f. 1921 as the Workers' Bank; name changed as above 1961; mergers into the above: American-Israel Bank in 1999, Maritime Bank of Israel in 2003, Mishkan-Hapoalim Mortgage Bank and Israel Continental Bank in 2004; privatized in June 2000; dep. 223,679m., total assets 273,265m. (Dec. 2005); Chair. DANNY DANKNER; Pres. and CEO ZVI ZIV; 325 brs in Israel and 8 brs abroad.

Bank of Jerusalem Ltd: POB 2255, 2 Herbert Samuel St, Jerusalem 91022; tel. 2-6706018; fax 2-6234043; e-mail webmaster@bankjerusalem.co.il; internet www.bankjerusalem.co.il; private bank; dep. 7,556.6m., total assets 8,399.3m. (Dec. 2006); Chair. JONATHAN IRONI; Man. Dir and Gen. Man. DAVID BARUCH; 14 brs.

Bank Leumi le-Israel BM: 34 Yehuda Halevi St, Tel-Aviv 65546; tel. 3-5148111; fax 3-5148656; e-mail pniot@bll.co.il; internet www.bankleumi.co.il; f. 1902 as Anglo-Palestine Co; renamed Anglo-Palestine Bank 1930; reincorporated as above 1951; 34.78% state-owned; dep. 228,400m., total assets 272,824m. (Dec. 2005); Chair. EITAN RAFF; Pres. and CEO GALIA MAOR; 229 brs in Israel and abroad.

Bank Otsar Ha-Hayal Ltd: POB 52136, 11 Menachem Begin St, Ramat-Gan 52521; tel. 3-7556000; fax 3-7556007; e-mail ozfrndep@netvision.net.il; internet www.bankotsar.co.il; f. 1946; 68% owned by First International Bank of Israel, 24% by Hever Veterans & Pensions Ltd, 8% by Provident Fund of the Employees of IAILTD; dep. 8,937.0m., total assets 10,324.5m. (Dec. 2005); Chair. ZEEV GUTMAN; Gen. Man. ISRAEL TRAU.

First International Bank of Israel Ltd: Shalom Mayer Tower, 9 Ahad Ha'am St, Tel-Aviv 62251; tel. 3-5196111; fax 3-5100316; e-mail zucker.d@fibi.co.il; internet www.fibi.co.il; f. 1972 by merger between Foreign Trade Bank Ltd and Export Bank Ltd; dep. 62,707m., total assets 71,924m. (Dec. 2005); Chair. JACK ELAAD; CEO SMADAR BARBER-TSADIK; 140 brs in Israel and abroad.

Industrial Development Bank of Israel Ltd: POB 33580, 82 Menachem Begin Rd, Tel-Aviv 67138; tel. 3-6972727; fax 3-6272700; internet www.idbi.co.il; f. 1957; 65% state-owned; dep. 8,110m., total assets 8,721m. (Dec. 2005); Chair. Dr RA'ANAN COHEN; Gen. Man. URI GALILI.

Israel Discount Bank Ltd: POB 456, 27–31 Yehuda Halevi St, Tel-Aviv 61003; tel. 3-5145555; fax 3-5146954; e-mail contact@discountbank.net; internet www.discountbank.net; f. 1935; name changed as above in 1957; 25% state-owned; cap. 98m. (June 2003), dep. 138,735m., total assets 162,538m. (Dec. 2006); Chair. SHLOMO ZOHAR; Pres. and CEO GIORA OFFER; 124 brs in Israel.

Mercantile Discount Bank Ltd: POB 1292, 103 Allenby Rd, Tel-Aviv 61012; tel. 3-710550; fax 3-7105532; e-mail fec@mdb.co.il; internet www.mercantile.co.il; f. Oct. 1971 as Barclays Discount Bank Ltd, to take over as from Jan. 1972 the Israel brs of Barclays Bank International Ltd; Barclays Bank PLC, one of the joint owners, sold its total shareholding to the remaining owner, Israel Discount Bank Ltd, in Feb. 1993, and name changed as above that April; Mercantile Bank of Israel Ltd became branch of the above in March 1997; cap. 51m., res 136m., dep. 14,522m. (Dec. 2005); Chair. SHLOMO ZOHAR; Gen. Man. JACOB TENNENBAUM; 66 brs.

Mizrahi Tefahot Bank Ltd: POB 3450, 7 Jabotinsky St, Ramat-Gan 52136; tel. 3-7559468; fax 3-7559940; e-mail lernerh@umtb.co.il; internet www.mizrahi-tefahot.co.il; f. 1923 as Mizrahi Bank Ltd; mergers into the above: Hapoel Hamizrahi Bank Ltd, as United Mizrahi Bank Ltd; Finance and Trade Bank Ltd in 1990; Tefahot Israel Mortgage Bank Ltd in 2005, when name changed as above; cap. 4,676m. (Dec. 2005), dep. 76,867, total assets 90,711m. (Dec. 2006); Chair. JACOB PERRY; Pres. and CEO ELIEZER YONES; 120 brs.

UBank Ltd: POB 677, 38 Rothschild Blvd, Tel-Aviv 61006; tel. 3-5645353; fax 3-5645285; e-mail gsteiger@u-bank.net; internet www.u-bank.net; f. 1934 as Palestine Credit Utility Bank Ltd; renamed Israel General Bank Ltd 1964; ownership transferred to Investec Bank Ltd (South Africa) 1996; name changed to Investec Clali Bank Ltd 1999, and to Investec Bank (Israel) Ltd 2001; control of bank transferred to First International Bank of Israel 2004 and name changed as above 2005; dep. 6,177.5m., total assets 6,739.7m. (Dec. 2005); Chair. JACK ELAAD; CEO ILAN RAVIV; 2 brs.

Union Bank of Israel Ltd: 6–8 Ahuzat Bayit St, Tel-Aviv 65143; tel. 3-5191111; fax 3-5191274; tel. riggs@ubi.co.il; internet www.ubi.co.il; f. 1951; dep. 25,700m., total assets 29,400m. (Dec. 2006); Chair. ZEEV ABELES; CEO and Gen. Man. HAIM FREILICHMAN; 26 brs in Israel and abroad.

Mortgage Banks

Discount Mortgage Bank Ltd: POB 2844, 16–18 Simtat Beit Hashoeva, Tel-Aviv 61027; tel. 3-5643311; fax 3-5661704; e-mail contact@discountbank.net; internet www.discountbank.net; f. 1959; subsidiary of Israel Discount Bank Ltd; total assets 10,355m. (Dec. 2005); Chair. SHLOMO ZOHAR; Pres. and CEO GIORA OFFER; 3 brs.

First International Mortgage Bank Ltd: 39 Montefiore St, Tel-Aviv 65201; tel. 3-7102233; fax 3-5643321; internet www.fibi-mashkanta.co.il; f. 1922 as the Mortgage and Savings Bank; name changed as above 1996; subsidiary of First International Bank of Israel Ltd; Chair. SHLOMO PIOTRKOWSKY; Man. Dir P. HAMO; 50 brs.

Leumi Mortgage Bank Ltd: POB 69, 31–37 Montefiore St, Tel-Aviv 65201; tel. 3-5648444; fax 3-5648334; f. 1921 as General Mortgage Bank Ltd; subsidiary of Bank Leumi le-Israel BM; dep. 28,731m., total assets 33,090m. (Dec. 2005); Chair. AVI ZELDMAN; Gen. Man. R. ZABAG; 9 brs.

STOCK EXCHANGE

The Tel-Aviv Stock Exchange: 54 Ahad Ha'am St, Tel-Aviv 65202; tel. 3-5677411; fax 3-5105379; e-mail info@tase.co.il; internet www.tase.co.il; f. 1953; Chair. SAUL BRONFELD; CEO ESTER LEVANON.

INSURANCE

The Israel Insurance Asscn lists 15 member companies; a selection of these are listed below, as are some non-members.

Aryeh Insurance Co of Israel Ltd: 9 Ahad Ha'am St, Tel-Aviv 65251; tel. 3-5141777; fax 3-5179339; e-mail rubens@aryeh-ins.co.il;

f. 1948; subsidiary of Clal Insurance Enterprise Holdings; Pres. RUBEN SHARONI.

Clal Insurance Co Ltd: POB 326, 46 Petach Tikva Rd, Tel-Aviv 66184; tel. 3-6387777; fax 3-6387676; e-mail avigdork@clal-ins.co.il; internet www.clalbit.co.il; f. 1962; subsidiary of Clal Insurance Enterprises Holdings Ltd; Chair. ELIAHU COHEN.

Dikla Insurance Co Ltd: 1 Ben Gurion Rd, BSR-2 Tower, Bnei Brak 51201; tel. 3-6145555; fax 3-6145566; internet www.dikla.co.il; f. 1976; health and long-term care insurance.

Eliahu Insurance Co Ltd: 2 Ibn Gvirol St, Tel-Aviv 64077; tel. 3-6920911; fax 3-6956995; e-mail gad.nussbaum@eliahu.com; internet www.eliahu.co.il; Gen. Man. OFER ELIAHU.

Harel Insurance Investments Ltd: Tel-Aviv; tel. 3-7547000; e-mail infonet@harel-group.co.il; internet www.harel-group.co.il; f. 1935 as Hamishmar Insurance Service; Harel established 1975, became Harel Hamishmar Investment Ltd 1982 and current name adopted 1998; Chair. GIDEON HAMBURGER.

Israel Phoenix Assurance Co Ltd: 30 Levontin St, Tel-Aviv 61020; tel. 3-7332222; fax 3-5735151; e-mail info@phoenix.co.il; internet www.phoenix.co.il; f. 1949; CEO BAR-KOCHVA BEN-GERA; Chair. of Bd JOSEPH D. HACKMEY.

Menorah Insurance Co Ltd: Menorah House, 15 Allenby St, Tel-Aviv 65786; tel. 3-7107777; fax 3-7107402; e-mail anat-by@bezeqint.net; f. 1935; Chair. MENACHEM GUREWITZ; Gen. Man. SHABTAI ENGEL.

Migdal Insurance Co Ltd: POB 37633, 26 Sa'adiya Ga'on St, Tel-Aviv 67135; tel. 3-5637637; fax 3-9295189; e-mail marketing@migdal-group.co.il; internet www.migdal.co.il; part of Bank Leumi Group; f. 1934; Chair. AHARON FOGEL; CEO IZZY COHEN.

Trade and Industry

CHAMBERS OF COMMERCE

Beersheba Chamber of Commerce: POB 5278, 7 Hamuktar St, Beersheba 84152; tel. 08-6234222; fax 08-6234899; e-mail chamber7@zahav.net.il; internet www.negev-chamber.org.il.

Israel Federation of Bi-National Chambers of Commerce and Industry with and in Israel: POB 50196, 29 Hamered St, Tel-Aviv 61500; tel. 3-5177737; fax 3-5142881; e-mail felixk@export.gov.il; Chair. AMNON DOTAN; Man. Dir FELIX KIPPER.

Federation of Israeli Chambers of Commerce: POB 20027, 84 Ha' Hashmonaim St, Tel-Aviv 67132; tel. 3-5631020; fax 3-5619027; e-mail chamber@chamber.org.il; internet www.chamber.org.il; co-ordinates the Tel-Aviv, Jerusalem, Haifa, Nazareth and Beersheba Chambers of Commerce; Pres. URIEL LYNN.

Chamber of Commerce and Industry of Haifa and the North: POB 33176, 53 Ha'atzmaut Rd, Haifa 31331; tel. 4-8626364; fax 4-8645428; e-mail main@haifachamber.org.il; internet www.haifachamber.com; f. 1921; 850 mems; Pres. O. FELLER; Man. Dir DOV MAROM.

Israel-British Chamber of Commerce: POB 50321, 13th Floor, Industry House, 29 Hamered St, Tel-Aviv 61502; tel. 3-5109424; fax 3-5109540; e-mail info@ibcc.co.il; internet www.ibcc.co.il; f. 1951; 350 mems; annual bilateral trade of more than US $3,000m.; Chair. LEN JUDES; Exec. Dir FELIX KIPPER.

Jerusalem Chamber of Commerce: POB 2083, Jerusalem 91020; tel. 2-6254333; fax 2-6254335; e-mail jerccom@inter.net.il; f. 1908; 200 mems; Pres. RAMI MANDEL.

INDUSTRIAL AND TRADE ASSOCIATIONS

Agricultural Export Co (AGREXCO): POB 2061, 121 Ha'Hashmonaim St, Tel-Aviv 61206; tel. 3-5630900; fax 3-5630814; e-mail info@agrexco.com; internet www.agrexco.co.il; state-owned agricultural marketing org.; CEO SHLOMO TIROSH.

The Agricultural Union: Tel-Aviv; consists of more than 50 agricultural settlements and is connected with marketing and supplying orgs, and Bahan Ltd, controllers and auditors.

The Centre for International Agricultural Development Cooperation (CINADCO): POB 30, Beit Dagan 50250; tel. 3-9485760; fax 3-9485761; e-mail cinadco@moag.gov.il; internet www.cinadco.moag.gov.il; shares agricultural experience through the integration of research and project devt; runs specialized training courses, advisory missions and feasibility projects in Israel and abroad, incl. those in co-operation with developing countries; Dir of Training ZVI A. HERMAN.

Citrus Marketing Board of Israel: POB 54, Beit Dagan 50280; tel. 3-9595654; fax 3-9501495; e-mail info@jaffa.co.il; internet www.jaffa.co.il; f. 1941; central co-ordinating body of citrus growers and exporters in Israel; represents the citrus industry in international orgs; licenses private exporters; controls the quality of fruit; has responsibility for Jaffa trademarks; mounts advertising and promotion campaigns for Jaffa citrus fruit world-wide; carries out research and devt of new varieties of citrus and 'environmentally friendly' fruit; Chair. M. KEDMON; Gen. Man. TAL AMIT.

Farmers' Union of Israel: POB 209, 8 Kaplan St, Tel-Aviv; tel. 3-69502227; fax 3-6918228; f. 1913; membership of 7,000 independent farmers, citrus and winegrape growers; Pres. PESACH GRUPPER; Dir-Gen. SHLOMO REISMAN.

Fruit Board of Israel: POB 20117, 119 Rehov Ha 'Hashmonaim, Tel-Aviv 61200; tel. 3-5632929; fax 3-5614672; e-mail fruits@fruit.org.il; internet www.fruit.org.il; Dir-Gen. DANY BRUNER.

General Asscn of Merchants in Israel: Tel-Aviv; retail traders org.; has a membership of 30,000 in 60 brs.

Israel Dairy Board: POB 15578, 46 Derech Ha'macabim, Rishon le Zion 75054; tel. 3-9564750; fax 3-9564766; e-mail office@is-d-b.co.il; internet www.israeldairy.com; regulates dairy farming and the dairy industry; implements govt policy on the planning of milk production and marketing.

Israel Diamond Exchange Ltd: POB 3222, Ramat-Gan; tel. 3-5760211; fax 3-5750652; e-mail yuval@isde.co.il; internet www.isde.co.il; f. 1937; production, export, import and finance facilities; exports: polished diamonds US $6,610m., rough diamonds $2,701m. (2006); Pres. AVI PAZ; Man. Dir YAIR COHEN-PRIVA.

Israel Export and International Co-operation Institute: POB 50084, 29 Hamered St, Tel-Aviv 68125; tel. 3-5142830; fax 3-5142902; e-mail library@export.gov.il; internet www.export.gov.il; f. 1958; jt venture between the state and private sectors; Dir-Gen. YECHIEL ASSIA.

The Israeli Cotton Board: POB 384, Herzlia B 46103; tel. 9-9604003; fax 9-9604010; e-mail mali@cotton.co.il; internet www.cotton.co.il; f. 1956 as the Israel Cotton Production and Marketing Board.

Kibbutz Industries' Asscn: POB 40012, 13 Leonardo da Vinci St, Tel-Aviv 61400; tel. 3-6955413; fax 3-6951464; e-mail kia@kia.co.il; internet www.kia.co.il; liaison office for marketing and export of the goods produced by Israel's kibbutzim; Chair. JONATHAN MELAMED; Man. Dir AMOS RABIN.

Manufacturers' Asscn of Israel: POB 50022, Industry House, 29 Hamered St, Tel-Aviv 61500; tel. 3-5198814; fax 3-5198770; e-mail trade@industry.org.il; internet www.industry.org.il; 1,700 mem. enterprises employing nearly 85% of industrial workers in Israel; Man. Dir YEHUDA SEGEV; Pres. SHRAGA BROSH.

National Federation of Israeli Journalists: POB 585, Beit Agron, 37 Hillet St, Jerusalem 91004; tel. 2-6254351; fax 3-6254353; e-mail office@jaj.org.il; Chair. ARIE SHAKED.

Plants Production and Marketing Board: 46 Derech Ha'macabim, Rishon le Zion 75359; tel. 3-9595666; fax 3-9596610; e-mail webmaster@plants.org.il; internet www.plants.org.il.

UTILITIES

Israel Electric Corporation Ltd (IEC): POB 8810, 2 Ha 'Haganah St, Haifa 31086; tel. 4-6348807; e-mail Tinfo@iec.co.il; internet www.iec.co.il; state-owned; total assets US $16,000m. (Dec. 2006); Chair. MOTI FRIEDMAN; CEO MOSHE BACHAR.

Mekorot (Israel National Water Co): POB 20128, 9 Lincoln St, Tel-Aviv 61201; tel. 3-6348807; e-mail m-doveret@mekorot.co.il; internet www.mekorot.co.il; f. 1937; state-owned; sales more than US $700m. (2006); Chair. ELI RONEN; CEO RONEN WOLFMAN.

The Histadrut

Histadrut (General Federation of Labour in Israel): 93 Arlozorof St, Tel-Aviv 62098; tel. 3-6921513; fax 3-6921512; e-mail histint@netvision.net.il; internet www.histadrut.org.il; f. 1920.

The Histadrut is the largest labour organization in Israel. It strives to ensure the social security, welfare and rights of workers, and to assist in their professional advancement, while endeavouring to reduce the divisions in Israeli society. Membership of the Histadrut is voluntary, and open to all men and women of 18 years of age and above who live on the earnings of their own labour without exploiting the work of others. These include the self-employed and professionals, as well as housewives, students, pensioners and the unemployed. Workers' interests are protected through a number of occupational and professional unions affiliated to the Histadrut (see below). The organization operates courses for trade unionists and new immigrants, as well as apprenticeship classes. It maintains an Institute for Social and Economic Issues and the International Institute, one of the largest centres of leadership training in Israel, for students from Africa, Asia, Latin America and Eastern Europe, which includes the Levinson Centre for Adult Education and the Jewish-Arab Institute for Regional Co-operation. Attached to the Histadrut is Na'amat, a women's organization which promotes changes in legislation, oper-

ISRAEL

ates a network of legal service bureaux and vocational training courses, and runs counselling centres for the treatment and prevention of domestic violence; women joining the Histadrut automatically become members of Na'amat.

Chair.: OFER EINI.

ORGANIZATION

In 2006 the Histadrut had a membership of 700,000. In addition, over 100,000 young people under 18 years of age belong to the Organization of Working and Student Youth, HaNoar HaOved VeHalomed, a direct affiliate of the Histadrut.

All members take part in elections to the Histadrut Convention (Veida), which elects the General Council (Moetsa) and the Executive Committee (Vaad Hapoel). The latter elects the 41-member Executive Bureau (Vaada Merakezet), which is responsible for day-to-day implementation of policy. The Executive Committee also elects the Secretary-General, who acts as its chairman as well as head of the organization as a whole and chairman of the Executive Bureau. Nearly all political parties are represented on the Histadrut Executive Committee.

The Executive Committee has the following departments: Trade Union, Organization and Labour Councils, Education and Culture, Social Security, Industrial Democracy, Students, Youth and Sports, Consumer Protection, Administration, Finance and International.

TRADE UNION ACTIVITIES

Collective agreements with employers fix wage scales, which are linked with the retail price index; provide for social benefits, including paid sick leave and employers' contributions to sick and pension and provident funds; and regulate dismissals. Dismissal compensation is regulated by law. The Histadrut actively promotes productivity through labour management boards and the National Productivity Institute, and supports incentive pay schemes.

There are unions for the following groups: clerical workers, building workers, teachers, engineers, agricultural workers, technicians, textile workers, printing workers, diamond workers, metal workers, food and bakery workers, wood workers, government employees, seamen, nurses, civilian employees of the armed forces, actors, musicians and variety artists, social workers, watchmen, cinema technicians, institutional and school staffs, pharmacy employees, medical laboratory workers, X-ray technicians, physiotherapists, social scientists, microbiologists, psychologists, salaried lawyers, pharmacists, physicians, occupational therapists, truck and taxi drivers, hotel and restaurant workers, workers in Histadrut-owned industry, garment, shoe and leather workers, plastic and rubber workers, editors of periodicals, painters and sculptors and industrial workers.

Histadrut Trade Union Department: Dir SHLOMO SHANI.

OTHER TRADE UNIONS

Histadrut Haovdim Haleumit (National Labour Federation): 23 Sprintzak St, Tel-Aviv 64738; tel. 3-6958351; fax 3-6961753; e-mail nol@netvision.net.il; f. 1934; 220,000 mems.

Histadrut Hapoel Hamizrachi (National Religious Workers' Party): 166 Ibn Gvirol St, Tel-Aviv 62023; tel. 3-5442151; fax 3-5468942; 150,000 mems in 85 settlements and 15 kibbutzim.

Histadrut Poale Agudat Israel (Agudat Israel Workers' Organization): POB 11044, 64 Frishman St, Tel-Aviv; tel. 3-5242126; fax 3-5230689; has 33,000 mems in 16 settlements and 8 educational insts.

Transport

RAILWAYS

Freight traffic consists mainly of grain, phosphates, potash, containers, petroleum and building materials. A rail route serves Haifa and Ashdod ports on the Mediterranean Sea, while a combined rail-road service extends to Eilat port on the Red Sea. Passenger services operate between the main towns: Nahariya, Haifa, Tel-Aviv and Jerusalem. In 1988 the Israel Ports Authority assumed responsibility for the rail system, creating the Ports and Railways Authority. However, it was decided in 1996 that Israel Railways should become a separate state concern. The first line of a light railway network intended to ease traffic congestion in Jerusalem was expected to begin operating in 2010.

Israel Railways (IR): POB 18085, Central Station, Tel-Aviv 61180; tel. 3-5774000; fax 3-6937443; e-mail ayariv@rail.org.il; internet www.israrail.org.il; in 2006 the total length of railway line was 905 km; Dir-Gen. OFER LINCZEWSKI.

Underground Railway

Haifa Underground Funicular Railway: 122 Hanassi Ave, Haifa 34633; tel. 4-8376861; fax 4-8376875; opened 1959; 2 km in operation.

ROADS

In 2006 there were 17,686 km of paved roads, of which 9,832 km were urban roads, 6,260 km were non-urban roads and 1,594 km were access roads.

Ministry of Transport and Road Safety: POB 867, Government Complex, 5 Bank of Israel St, Jerusalem 91008; tel. 2-6663190; fax 2-6663195; e-mail dover@mot.gov.il; internet www.mot.gov.il.

SHIPPING

At 31 December 2006 Israel's merchant fleet consisted of 51 vessels, with a combined aggregate displacement of 763,538 grt.

Haifa and Ashdod are the main ports in Israel. The former is a natural harbour, enclosed by two main breakwaters and dredged to 45 ft below mean sea level. In 1965 the deep water port at Ashdod was completed, providing a capacity of about 8.6m. tons in 1988.

The port of Eilat is Israel's gateway to the Red Sea. It is a natural harbour, operated from a wharf. Another port, to the south of the original one, started operating in 1965.

Israel Ports Development and Assets Co (IPC): POB 20121, 74 Menachem Begin Rd, Tel-Aviv 61201; tel. 3-5657060; fax 3-5622281; e-mail dovf@israports.co.il; internet www.israports.co.il; f. 1961 as the Israel Ports Authority (PRA); the IPC was established by legislation in 2005 as part of the Israeli Port Reform Program, whereby the PRA was abolished and replaced by four govt-owned cos: the IPC as owner and develper of port and infrastructure and three port-operating cos responsible for handling cargo in each of Israel's three commercial seaports; responsible for devt and management of Israel's port infrastructure on behalf of the Govt; Chair. YIFTACH RON-TAL; CEO SHLOMO BRIEMAN (acting).

Ofer (Ships Holding) Ltd: POB 15090, 9 Andre Saharov St, Matam Park, Haifa 31905; tel. 4-8610610; fax 4-8501515; e-mail mail@oferb.co.il; internet www.oferb.co.il; f. 1957; runs cargo and container services; operates some 30 vessels; Chair. Y. OFER; CEO E. ANGEL.

ZIM Integrated Shipping Services Ltd: POB 1723, 9 Andrei Sakharov St, Matam Park, Haifa 31016; tel. 4-8652111; fax 4-8652956; e-mail shats.avner@il.zim.com; internet www.zim.co.il; f. 1945; 100% owned by the Israel Corpn; international integrated transportation system providing door-to-door services around the world; operates about 100 vessels; estimated 2m. TEUs of cargo carried in 2006; Chair. of Bd IDAN OFER; Pres. and CEO DORON GODER.

CIVIL AVIATION

Israir Airports Authority: Ben-Gurion International Airport, Tel-Aviv; tel. 3-9752002; fax 3-9752010; e-mail janets@iaa.gov.il; internet www.ben-gurion-airport.co.il; f. 1977; Chair. ELI OVADIA; Dir-Gen. GABRIEL (GABI) OFIR.

El Al Israel Airlines Ltd: POB 41, Ben-Gurion International Airport, Tel-Aviv 70100; tel. 3-9716111; fax 3-9716040; e-mail customer@elal.co.il; internet www.elal.co.il; f. 1948; over 40% owned by Knafaim-Arkia Holdings Ltd; about 31% state-owned; daily services to most capitals of Europe; over 20 flights weekly to New York; services to the USA, Canada, China, Egypt, India, Kenya, South Africa, Thailand and Turkey; Chair. of Bd Prof. ISRAEL BOROVICH; Pres. HAIM ROMANO.

Arkia Israeli Airlines Ltd: POB 39301, Dov Airport, Tel-Aviv 61392; tel. 3-6903760; e-mail hilar@arkia.co.il; internet www.arkia.co.il; f. 1980 by merger of Kanaf-Arkia Airlines and Aviation Services; scheduled passenger services linking Tel-Aviv, Jerusalem, Haifa, Eilat, Rosh Pina, Kiryat Shmona and Yotveta; charter services to European destinations, Turkey and Jordan; Chair. YIGAL ARNON; Pres. and CEO Prof. ISRAEL BOROVICH.

Israir Airlines: POB 26444, 23 Ben Yehuda St, Tel-Aviv 63806; tel. 3-7955888; fax 3-7955830; e-mail Isranet@Israir.co.il; internet www.israir.co.il; f. 1996; domestic flights between Tel-Aviv and Eilat, and international flights to destinations in Europe and the USA; Pres. and CEO ZOHAR ENDELMAN.

Tourism

Israel possesses a wealth of antiquities and cultural attractions, in particular the historic and religious sites of Jerusalem. The country has a varied landscape, with a Mediterranean coastline, as well as desert and mountain terrain. The Red Sea resort of Eilat has become an important centre for diving holidays, while many tourists visit the treatment spas of the Dead Sea. In 2007 an estimated 2,267,900 tourists visited Israel, compared with some 1,825,200 in 2006. Tourism receipts, including passenger transport, in 2005 totalled US $3,414m.

Ministry of Tourism: See The Government—Ministries; Dir-Gen. SHAUL TZEMACH.

OCCUPIED TERRITORIES

THE GOLAN HEIGHTS

LOCATION AND CLIMATE

The Golan Heights, a mountainous plateau that formed most of Syria's Quneitra Province (1,710 sq km) and parts of Dera'a Province, was occupied by Israel after the Arab–Israeli War of June 1967. Following the Disengagement Agreement of 1974, Israel continued to occupy some 70% of the territory (1,176 sq km), valued for its strategic position and abundant water resources (the headwaters of the Jordan river have their source on the slopes of Mount Hermon). The average height of the Golan is approximately 1,200 m above sea level in the northern region and about 300 m above sea level in the southern region, near Lake Tiberias (the Sea of Galilee). Rainfall ranges from about 1,000 mm per year in the north to less than 600 mm per year in the southern region.

ADMINISTRATION

Prior to the Israeli occupation, the Golan Heights were incorporated by Syria into a provincial administration of which the city of Quneitra, with a population at the time of 27,378, was capital. The Disengagement Agreement that was mediated by US Secretary of State Henry Kissinger in 1974 (after the 1973 Arab–Israeli War) provided for the withdrawal of Israeli forces from Quneitra. Before they withdrew, however, Israeli army engineers destroyed the city. In December 1981 the Israeli Knesset enacted the Golan Annexation Law, whereby Israeli civilian legislation was extended to the territory of Golan, now under the administrative jurisdiction of the Commissioner for the Northern District of Israel. The Arab-Druze community of the Golan responded immediately by declaring a strike and appealed to the UN Secretary-General to force Israel to rescind the annexation decision. At the seventh round of multilateral talks between Israeli and Arab delegations in Washington, DC, USA, in August 1992, the Israeli Government of Itzhak Rabin for the first time accepted that UN Security Council Resolution 242, adopted in 1967, applied to the Golan Heights. In January 1999 the Knesset passed legislation stating that any transfer of land under Israeli sovereignty (referring to the Golan Heights and East Jerusalem) was conditional on the approval of at least 61 of the 120 Knesset members and of the Israeli electorate in a subsequent national referendum. Following the election of Ehud Barak as Israel's Prime Minister in May 1999, peace negotiations between Israel and Syria were resumed in December. However, in January 2000 the talks were postponed indefinitely after Syria demanded a written commitment from Israel to withdraw from the Golan Heights. In July 2001 Israel's recently elected premier, Ariel Sharon, stated that he would be prepared to resume peace talks with Syria, but Sharon also declared that the Israeli occupation of the Golan was 'irreversible'. The withdrawal of Israel from the disputed territory is one of Syria's primary objectives in any future peace agreement with Israel. Following his appointment in April 2006, Sharon's successor to the Israeli premiership, Ehud Olmert, expressed his willingness to resume direct peace negotiations with Syria; however, the Israeli Government demanded that the Syrian leadership first end its support for militant Islamist groups in the Palestinian territories and Lebanon. Syrian officials, for their part, continued to insist that Israel commit to a complete withdrawal from the Golan Heights in advance of any resumption of bilateral negotiations, a demand persistently rejected by the Israeli Government. Peace negotiations between Israel and Syria had not resumed by early 2008, although Syrian President Bashar al-Assad claimed in March 2007 that Syrian representatives had been conducting secret, unofficial discussions with Israeli officials during recent years. Olmert refuted that any such talks had taken place. However, in July a spokesman for the Israeli Ministry of Foreign Affairs confirmed that messages had been relayed between Israel and Syria by third parties for some time.

DEMOGRAPHY AND ECONOMIC AFFAIRS

As a consequence of the Israeli occupation, an estimated 93% of the ethnically diverse Syrian population of 147,613, distributed across 163 villages and towns and 108 individual farms, was expelled. The majority were Arab Sunni Muslims, but the population also included Alawite and Druze minorities and some Circassians, Turcomen, Armenians and Kurds. Approximately 9,000 Palestinian refugees from the 1948 Arab–Israeli War also inhabited the area. At the time of the occupation, the Golan was a predominantly agricultural province, 64% of the labour force being employed in agriculture. Only one-fifth of the population resided in the administrative centres. By 1991 the Golan Heights had a Jewish population of about 12,000 living in 21 Jewish settlements (four new settlements had been created by the end of 1992), and a predominantly Druze population of some 16,000 living in the only six remaining villages, of which Majd ash-Shams is by far the largest. According to official figures, at the end of 2006 the Golan Heights had a total population of 39,800 (comprising Jews, Druze and Muslims). The Golan Heights have remained largely an agricultural area, and although many Druze now work in Israeli industry in Eilat, Tel-Aviv and Jerusalem, the indigenous economy relies almost solely on the cultivation of apples, for which the area is famous. The apple orchards benefit from a unique combination of fertile soils, abundance of water and a conducive climate.

EAST JERUSALEM

LOCATION

Greater Jerusalem includes Israeli West Jerusalem (99% Jewish), the Old City and Mount of Olives, East Jerusalem (the Palestinian residential and commercial centre), Arab villages declared to be part of Jerusalem by Israel in 1967 and Jewish neighbourhoods constructed since 1967, either on land expropriated from Arab villages or in areas requisitioned as 'government land'. Although the area of the Greater Jerusalem district is 627 sq km, the Old City of Jerusalem covers just 1 sq km.

ADMINISTRATION

Until the 1967 Arab–Israeli War, Jerusalem had been divided into the new city of West Jerusalem—captured by Jewish forces in 1948—and the old city, East Jerusalem, which was part of Jordan. Israel's victory in 1967, however, reunited the city under Israeli control. Two weeks after the fighting had ended, on 28 June, Israeli law was applied to East Jerusalem and the municipal boundaries were extended by 45 km (28 miles). Jerusalem had effectively been annexed. Israeli officials, however, still refer to the 'reunification' of Jerusalem.

DEMOGRAPHY AND ECONOMIC AFFAIRS

In June 1993 the Deputy Mayor of Jerusalem, Avraham Kahila, declared that the city now had 'a majority of Jews', based on population forecasts that estimated the Jewish population at 158,000 and the Arab population at 155,000. For the Israeli administration this signified the achievement of a long-term objective. Immediately prior to the 1967 Arab–Israeli War, East Jerusalem and its Arab environs had an Arab population of approximately 70,000, and a small Jewish population in the old Jewish quarter of the city. By contrast, Israeli West Jerusalem had a Jewish population of 196,000. As a result of this imbalance, in the Greater Jerusalem district as a whole the Jewish population was in the majority even prior to the occupation of the whole city in 1967. Israeli policy following the occupation of East Jerusalem and the West Bank consisted of encircling the eastern sector of the city with Jewish settlements. In contrast to the more politically sensitive siting of Jewish settlements in the old Arab quarter of Jerusalem, the Government of Itzhak Rabin concentrated on the outer circle of settlement building. Official statistics for the end of 2006 reported that Greater Jerusalem had a total population of 733,300, of whom 469,900 (64.1%) were Jews and 263,400 Arabs. The Jerusalem Institute for Israel Studies (JIIS) estimated in August 2007 that the growth rate for the Arab population of Greater Jerusalem was almost double that of the Jewish population. According to the JIIS, if this trend continued, the city's population would have a Jewish-Arab ratio of 60:40 by 2020, and of 50:50 by 2035. In May 2007 the mayor of Jerusalem, Uri Lupolianski, suggested easing the restrictions on family reunification for the estimated 10,000 Christian Arabs in Jerusalem, in order to prevent a further decline in their number.

The Old City, within the walls of which are found the ancient quarters of the Jews, Christians, Muslims and Armenians, is predominantly Arab. In 2003 the Old City was reported to have a population of 31,405 Arabs and 3,965 Jews. In addition, there are some 800 recent Jewish settlers living in the Arab quarter.

Many imaginative plans have been submitted with the aim of finding a solution to the problem of sharing Jerusalem between Arabs and Jews, including the proposal that the city be placed under international trusteeship, under UN auspices. However, to make the implementation of such plans an administrative as well as a political quagmire, the Israeli administration, after occupying the whole city in June 1967, began creating 'facts on the ground'. Immediately following the occupation, all electricity, water and telephone grids in West Jerusalem were extended to the east. Roads were widened and cleared, and the Arab population immediately in front of the 'Wailing Wall' was forcibly evicted. Arabs living in East Jerusalem became 'permanent residents' and could apply for Israeli citizenship if they wished (in contrast to Arabs in the West Bank and Gaza Strip). However, few chose to do so. None the less, issued with identity cards (excluding the estimated 25,000 Arabs from the West Bank and Gaza living illegally in the city), the Arab residents were taxed by the Israeli authorities, and their businesses and banks became subject to Israeli laws and business regulations. Now controlling approximately one-half of all land in East Jerusalem and the surrounding Palestinian villages (previously communally, or privately, owned by Palestinians), the Israeli authorities allowed Arabs to construct buildings on only 10%–15% of the land in the city; and East Jerusalem's commercial district has been limited to three streets.

Since the 1993 signing of the Declaration of Principles on Palestinian Self-Rule, the future status of Jerusalem and the continuing expansion of Jewish settlements in East Jerusalem have emerged as two of the most crucial issues affecting the peace process. In May 1999 the Israeli Government announced its refusal to grant Israeli citizenship to several hundred Arabs living in East Jerusalem, regardless of their compliance with the conditions stipulated under the Citizenship Law. In October, however, Israel ended its policy of revoking the right of Palestinians to reside in Jerusalem if they had spent more than seven years outside the city. Moreover, the Israeli Government announced in March 2000 that Palestinian residents of Jerusalem who had had their identity cards revoked could apply for their restoration.

At the Camp David talks held between Israel and the Palestinian (National) Authority (PA) in July 2000, the issue of who would have sovereignty over East Jerusalem in a future 'permanent status' agreement proved to be the principal obstacle to the achievement of a peace deal. It was reported that the Israeli Government had offered the PA municipal autonomy over certain areas of East Jerusalem (including access to the Islamic holy sites), although sovereignty would remain in Israeli hands; the proposals were rejected by Palestinian President Yasser Arafat. In September the holy sites of East Jerusalem were the initial focal point of a renewed uprising by Palestinians against the Israeli authorities, which became known as the al-Aqsa *intifada* (after Jerusalem's al-Aqsa Mosque) and which had not been declared officially ended by early 2008. Although the publication of the internationally sponsored 'roadmap' peace plan in April 2003 offered directions for talks on the Jerusalem issue, the resumption of attacks by Palestinian militants against Israeli citizens in mid-2003 and Israeli counter-strikes against Palestinian targets, made any such discussions untenable at that time.

Following a lengthy period during which all negotiations between Israel and the PA were effectively stalled, owing to the continued Israeli–Palestinian violence as well as political instability in the Palestinian territories, some optimism was expressed in August 2007 when the Israeli Prime Minister, Ehud Olmert, held direct talks with the Palestinian President, Mahmud Abbas, in the West Bank town of Jericho in preparation for an international Middle East peace conference, which was convened in Annapolis, Maryland, USA, in November. During the conference Olmert and Abbas agreed to hold regular bilateral meetings in 2008, with a view to negotiating the terms of a permanent Israeli-Palestinian settlement. The US Administration of President George W. Bush declared its intention that such a deal, including the establishment of a Palestinian state, could be reached by the end of the year. However, an increase in attacks being perpetrated by Palestinian militants from the Gaza Strip into northern Israel from January 2008, and a consequent military campaign by Israeli forces in Gaza, resulted in a stalling of negotiations. In February the Israeli Prime Minister angered Palestinians by declaring that talks concerning the final status of Jerusalem, and the key Palestinian demand that East Jerusalem become their capital, would be the last 'core issue' on the agenda to be negotiated by the two parties. Moreover, the Israeli Government continued to issue tenders for hundreds of new housing units at Jewish settlements in East Jerusalem and the West Bank, thereby contravening its obligations under the terms of the roadmap.

ITALY

Introductory Survey

Location, Climate, Language, Religion, Flag, Capital

The Italian Republic comprises a peninsula, extending from southern Europe into the Mediterranean Sea, and a number of adjacent islands. The two principal islands are Sicily, to the south-west, and Sardinia, to the west. The Alps form a natural boundary to the north, where the bordering countries are France to the north-west, Switzerland and Austria to the north and Slovenia to the north-east. The climate is temperate in the north and Mediterranean in the south, with mild winters and long, dry summers. The average temperature in Rome is 7.4°C (45.3°F) in January and 25.7°C (78.3°F) in July. The principal language is Italian. German and Ladin are spoken in the Alto Adige region on the Austrian border, and French in the Valle d'Aosta region (bordering France and Switzerland), while in southern Italy there are Greek-speaking and Albanian minorities. A dialect of Catalan is spoken in north-western Sardinia. Almost all of the inhabitants profess Christianity: more than 90% are adherents of the Roman Catholic Church. The national flag (proportions 2 by 3) has three equal vertical stripes, of green, white and red. The capital is Rome.

Recent History

The Kingdom of Italy, under the House of Savoy, was proclaimed in 1861 and the country was unified in 1870. Italy subsequently acquired an overseas empire, comprising the African colonies of Eritrea, Italian Somaliland and Libya. Benito Mussolini, leader of the Fascist Party, became President of the Council (Prime Minister) in October 1922 and assumed dictatorial powers in 1925–26. Relations between the Italian State and the Roman Catholic Church, a subject of bitter controversy since Italy's unification, were codified in 1929 by a series of agreements, including the Lateran Pact, which recognized the sovereignty of the State of the Vatican City (q.v.), a small enclave within the city of Rome, under the jurisdiction of the Pope. Under Mussolini, Italian forces occupied Ethiopia in 1935–36 and Albania in 1939. Italy supported the fascist forces in the Spanish Civil War of 1936–39, and from June 1940 supported Nazi Germany in the Second World War. In 1943, however, as forces from the allied powers invaded Italy, the fascist regime collapsed. In July of that year King Victor Emmanuel III dismissed Mussolini, and the Fascist Party was dissolved.

In April 1945 German forces in Italy surrendered and Mussolini was killed. In June 1946, following a referendum, the monarchy was abolished and Italy became a republic. Until 1963 the Partito della Democrazia Cristiana (DC—Christian Democratic Party) held power unchallenged, while industry expanded rapidly, supported by capital from the USA. By the early 1960s, however, public discontent was increasing, largely owing to low wage rates and a lack of social reform. In the general election of 1963 the Partito Comunista Italiano (PCI—Italian Communist Party), together with other parties of the extreme right and left, made considerable gains at the expense of the DC. During the next decade there was a rapid succession of mainly coalition Governments, involving the DC and one or more of the other major non-communist parties.

Aldo Moro's coalition Government of the DC and the Partito Repubblicano Italiano (PRI—Italian Republican Party), formed in 1974, resigned in 1976, following the withdrawal of support by the Partito Socialista Italiano (PSI—Italian Socialist Party). After the failure of a minority DC administration, the PCI won 228 seats at elections to the 630-member Camera dei Deputati (Chamber of Deputies). The DC remained the largest party, but could no longer govern against PCI opposition in the legislature. However, the DC continued to insist on excluding the PCI from power, and in July formed a minority Government, with Giulio Andreotti as premier. He relied on the continuing abstention of PCI deputies to introduce severe austerity measures in response to the economic crisis. In January 1978 the minority Government was forced to resign under pressure from the PCI, which wanted more active participation in government (the PCI had for several months been allowed to participate in policy-making but had no direct role in government), although Andreotti subsequently formed a new, almost identical Government, with PCI support. In May of the same year Moro was murdered by the extreme left-wing Brigate Rosse (Red Brigades). In July Alessandro Pertini was inaugurated as Italy's first socialist head of state.

The Andreotti administration collapsed in January 1979, when the PCI withdrew from the official parliamentary majority. A new coalition Government, formed by Andreotti in March, lasted only 10 days before being defeated on a vote of 'no confidence'. Following elections in June, at which its representation in the Camera dei Deputati declined to 201 seats, the PCI returned to opposition. In August Francesco Cossiga, a former Minister of the Interior, formed a minority Government, composed of the DC, the Partito Liberale Italiano (PLI—Italian Liberal Party) and the Partito Socialista Democratico Italiano (PSDI—Italian Social Democratic Party). However, the new Government was continually thwarted by obstructionism in Parliament. In April 1980 Cossiga formed a majority coalition, comprising members of the DC, the PRI and the PSI. In September, however, the Government resigned after losing a vote on its economic programme. A four-party coalition Government assembled by Arnaldo Forlani, the Chairman of the DC, was beset with allegations of corruption, and in turn was forced to resign in May 1981 after it became known that more than 1,000 of Italy's foremost establishment figures belonged to a secret masonic lodge, P-2 ('Propaganda Due'), which had extensive criminal connections both in Italy and abroad. The lodge was linked with many political and financial scandals and with right-wing terrorism, culminating in 1982 with the collapse of one of Italy's leading banks, Banco Ambrosiano, and the death of its President, Roberto Calvi.

In June 1981 Senator Giovanni Spadolini, leader of the PRI, formed a coalition Government, thus becoming the first non-DC Prime Minister since 1946. Spadolini resigned in November 1982. Amintore Fanfani, a former DC Prime Minister, formed a new coalition in December which lasted until the PSI withdrew its support in April 1983. A general election was held in June, at which the DC lost considerable support, winning only 32.9% of the votes for the Camera dei Deputati. The PSI increased its share of the votes to 11.4%, and its leader, Bettino Craxi, was subsequently appointed Italy's first socialist Prime Minister, at the head of a coalition. His Government lost a vote of confidence in the Camera dei Deputati in June 1986, bringing to an end Italy's longest administration (1,060 days) since the Second World War. Craxi resigned, and Cossiga—who had succeeded Pertini as President in July 1985—nominated the former DC Prime Minister, Andreotti, to attempt to form a new government. However, the refusal of other parties to support Andreotti led to Craxi's return to power in July, on condition that he transfer the premiership to a DC member in March 1987. Craxi accordingly submitted his resignation, and that of his Government, at that time. After several unsuccessful attempts to form a coalition, a general election was held in June, at which the DC won 34.3% of the votes cast and the PSI obtained 14.3%. The PCI suffered its worst post-war electoral result, winning 26.6% of the votes. Giovanni Goria, a DC member and the former Minister of the Treasury, became Prime Minister of a coalition Government. By the end of the year, however, the Government had lost considerable support. Goria offered his resignation in November and again in February 1988, but it was rejected both times by President Cossiga; Goria finally resigned in March. Ciriaco De Mita, the Secretary-General of the DC, formed a coalition with the same five parties that had served in Goria's administration.

Severe criticism by Craxi of De Mita's premiership led to the collapse of the coalition Government in May 1989. In June President Cossiga nominated De Mita to form a new government, but he was unsuccessful and it was not until late July that the coalition partners of the outgoing Government agreed to form a new administration, with Andreotti as Prime Minister. Andreotti resigned the premiership in March 1991, accused by the PSI of failing to implement effectively policies on key issues. The President none the less nominated Andreotti to form a new government (Italy's 50th since 1945), which comprised the same coalition partners as the outgoing administration, other than the

PRI, whose members had rejected the portfolios they had been allocated.

From late 1989, meanwhile, the PCI, began a process of transforming itself from a communist into a social democratic party. In early 1991 the party was renamed the Partito Democratico della Sinistra (PDS—Democratic Party of the Left). A minority of members of the former PCI refused to join the PDS, and in May they formed the Partito della Rifondazione Comunista (PRC—Party of Communist Refoundation).

In September 1991, apparently in response to widespread nationalist fervour in parts of Eastern Europe, German-speaking separatists from the Alto Adige region made demands for greater autonomy from Italy. In the same month the Union Valdôtaine, the nationalist party governing the Aosta Valley on the borders of France and Switzerland, announced that it was planning a referendum on secession. In January 1992 the Italian Government, in an attempt to end a long-standing dispute with Austria over the Alto Adige area, agreed to grant further autonomy to the region.

In February 1992 Cossiga dissolved the legislature and announced that a general election would take place on 5 April. The election campaign was marred by the murder of Salvatore Lima, an associate of Andreotti (see below). At the election, support for the DC declined to less than 30% of votes cast. The PDS won 16.1% of votes cast for the Camera dei Deputati, while the PSI received 13.6%. The Lega Nord (Northern League), a grouping of regionalist parties led by Umberto Bossi, performed well in northern Italy, as did a new anti-Mafia political party, La Rete per il Partito Democratico (Democratic Network Party), in the south. Andreotti announced his resignation following the election, as did Cossiga, who was succeeded in May by Oscar Luigi Scalfaro. In the following month Giuliano Amato, of the PSI, was appointed Prime Minister.

The uncovering of a corruption scandal in Milan in 1992, in a series of events that became known as 'Mani pulite' (Clean Hands), subsequently assumed wider implications. It was alleged that politicians (mainly of the PSI and DC) and government officials had accepted bribes in exchange for the awarding of large public contracts. Among those accused of corruption was the former PSI Minister of Foreign Affairs, Gianni De Michelis. The Amato Government's credibility was seriously undermined in February 1993 when the Minister of Justice, Claudio Martelli of the PSI, was obliged to resign, having being placed under formal investigation for alleged complicity in the collapse of Banco Ambrosiano. Shortly afterwards Craxi resigned as Secretary-General of the PSI, although he continued to deny accusations of fraud. The Prime Minister's difficulties were compounded by the resignation of four senior ministers in February and March 1993. Also in March, five DC politicians, including Andreotti, were placed under investigation over their alleged links with the Mafia.

Nation-wide referendums proceeded in April 1993 on a number of proposed changes to the Constitution, including an amendment providing for the election by majority vote of 75% of the 315 elective seats in the upper legislative chamber, the Senato della Repubblica (Senate), while the remainder would be elected under a system of proportional representation, and the end of state funding of political parties. These amendments, intended to prevent electoral malpractice and, in particular, interference by organized crime, were overwhelmingly approved. (In August Parliament approved a similar system for elections to the Camera dei Deputati.)

Amato resigned as Prime Minister shortly after the referendums, and Carlo Azeglio Ciampi was invited by President Scalfaro to form a new government. Ciampi, hitherto Governor of the Banca d'Italia (the central bank), was the first non-parliamentarian to be appointed to the premiership. His proposed coalition comprised the four parties of the outgoing administration, but also included the PDS, the PRI and the Federazione dei Verdi (Green Party). The PDS and the Federazione dei Verdi immediately withdrew their ministers from the coalition, in protest at the new administration's refusal to revoke Craxi's parliamentary immunity from prosecution, although both continued to support Ciampi's Government. In May 1993 the Camera dei Deputati voted overwhelmingly to abolish parliamentary immunity in cases of corruption and serious crime; while the Senato approved the removal of Andreotti's parliamentary immunity, to allow investigations into his alleged association with the Mafia, although his arrest remained prohibited. Meanwhile, investigations began in April into the activities of former DC Prime Minister Forlani. The investigations were subsequently extended to encompass politicians of the PDS and PRI, as arrests of leading political and business figures multiplied. In August the Camera dei Deputati voted to allow Craxi to be investigated by magistrates on four charges of corruption. In the following month Diego Curto, head of Milan's commercial court, became the first member of the judiciary to be investigated in connection with the corruption scandals. At the end of the month Andreotti was charged with having provided the Sicilian Mafia with political protection in exchange for votes in Sicily, and with complicity in the murder of an investigative journalist, Mario Francese, who had allegedly discovered evidence linking Andreotti with the Mafia (see below).

Ciampi resigned in January 1994, in response to parliamentary divisions over the timing of a general election. Scalfaro dissolved the legislature, but requested that Ciampi remain in office until the forthcoming elections in March. In January Silvio Berlusconi, the principal shareholder in and former manager of the media-based Fininvest, Italy's third largest private business group, announced the formation of a right-wing organization, Forza Italia (Come on, Italy!), to contest the elections. The liberal wing of the DC, whose mainstream was now discredited by corruption scandals, relaunched itself as the centrist Partito Popolare Italiano (PPI—Italian People's Party). In subsequent weeks, parties of the left, right and centre sought to form alliances capable of securing a majority in the Camera dei Deputati. Seven parties—including the PDS, the PRC, the Federazione dei Verdi and La Rete—formed I Progressisti (the Progressives); the Polo delle Libertà e del Buon Governo (hereafter referred to as the Polo delle Libertà—the Freedom Alliance), under the leadership of Berlusconi, was formed by the Lega Nord, Forza Italia and the Alleanza Nazionale (AN—National Alliance, a new party led by Gianfranco Fini and incorporating members of the neo-fascist Movimento Sociale Italiano-Destra Nazionale—MSI-DN—Italian Social Movement-National Right); and the centre-right Patto per l'Italia (Pact for Italy) comprised Mario Segni's Patto Segni and the PPI. The election campaign intensified against a background of judicial investigations and mutual accusations of media bias and malpractice, while Berlusconi's popularity increased markedly, despite the arrest of a number of senior Fininvest executives on suspicion of corruption. The Polo delle Libertà won an outright majority in the Camera dei Deputati, with 366 of the 630 seats, and was only three seats short of an outright majority in the Senato. In spite of the success of the alliance, major differences divided its constituent parties. Berlusconi selected his own candidates for the usually non-partisan posts of President of the Camera dei Deputati and President of the Senato. In April President Scalfaro invited Berlusconi to form a government. The new Council of Ministers, announced in May, included five members of the AN, including Roberto Maroni of the Lega Nord as Minister of the Interior and two members of the MSI-DN.

In July 1994 Craxi and the former Deputy Prime Minister and Minister of Justice, Martelli, were both sentenced for fraudulent bankruptcy in relation to the collapse of Banco Ambrosiano. Craxi, who claimed to be too ill to return from his residence in Tunisia, was sentenced *in absentia*. In July 1995 was formally declared a fugitive from justice. Also in July 1994 two Fininvest employees were arrested on charges of bribing the finance police (Guardi di Finanza). In November Berlusconi was placed under investigation for bribery. In the following month Antonio Di Pietro, a high-profile magistrate in Milan, resigned in protest at increasing government interference in the work of the Milanese judiciary. The failure of the Prime Minister to resolve his conflict of business and political interests, together with the growing tension between the Government and the judiciary, undermined the integrity of the Government and precipitated the disintegration of the coalition and Berlusconi's resignation. In January 1995 Lamberto Dini, the Minister of the Treasury, was invited to form an interim government. Dini appointed a Council of Ministers comprised of technocrats, and pledged to hold elections once he had implemented a programme to improve public finances, reform the state pension system, introduce new regional electoral laws, and establish controls on media ownership and its use during electoral campaigns. In March it was announced that Berlusconi was to be subject to further investigation on charges of financial irregularities. Moreover, his Polo delle Libertà was defeated by the centre-left parties in nine of the 15 regional elections held in April.

New political alliances emerged during 1995 in preparation for legislative elections. In January the MSI-DN was officially disbanded and most of its members were absorbed in the AN.

The AN leader, Fini, distanced the party from its neo-fascist past in an attempt to widen support. The PSI had been dissolved in November 1994 and reformed as the Socialisti Italiani (Italian Socialists). In the same month Romano Prodi, a business executive, offered to lead the centre-left parties to challenge Berlusconi in the forthcoming elections. In March the PPI rejected a proposed alliance with Berlusconi, deposing its leader, Rocco Buttiglione, who subsequently founded a new centre-right party, the Cristiani Democratici Uniti (CDU—United Christian Democrats). In July the PDS formally endorsed Prodi as leader of the centre-left electoral alliance, subsequently named L'Ulivo (The Olive Tree).

In June 1995 12 referendums were held on issues including media ownership, trade union and electoral reform and crime. Significantly, the majority of the voters who participated in the referendums on media ownership approved the retention of laws permitting an individual to own more than one commercial television channel and preserving the existing monopoly on television advertising. Furthermore, the majority of voters supported the partial privatization of the state broadcasting company, Radiotelevisione Italiana (RAI), control of which had become increasingly contentious since the resignation of its directorate in mid-1994 in protest at increased government control over appointments. Another outcome was the endorsement of greater restrictions on trade unions' powers of representation.

In October 1995 the Minister of Justice, Filippo Mancuso, refused to resign from the Council of Ministers despite a successful motion of 'no confidence' in him, which had been prompted by his alleged vendetta against anti-corruption magistrates in Milan. Scalfaro revoked Mancuso's mandate, appointing Dini as interim Minister of Justice. Dini's administration remained precarious, however, and shortly afterwards Berlusconi allied himself with Mancuso and proposed a motion of 'no confidence' in the Government, claiming the support of the PRC. The Government narrowly defeated the motion, having forged an agreement whereby PRC deputies abstained from the vote on condition that Dini resign as premier by the end of the year. Dini's resignation, submitted in late December, was, however, rejected by President Scalfaro, pending a parliamentary debate to resolve the political crisis. In January 1996 the AN tabled a resolution demanding Dini's resignation, which it was expected to win with the support of parties of the extreme left. Scalfaro was thus obliged to accept Dini's resignation, which he submitted prior to the vote. In February Scalfaro dissolved Parliament and asked Dini to remain as interim Prime Minister until a general election in April. In October 1995, meanwhile, all 22 defendants were convicted in a trial concerning illegal funding of political parties. Among those convicted were former Prime Ministers Craxi, who was sentenced *in absentia* to four years' imprisonment, and Forlani, sentenced to 28 months' custody; Bossi received a suspended sentence.

At the legislative elections, held in April 1996, L'Ulivo (dominated by the PDS, but also including the PPI and Dini's newly formed, centrist Rinnovamento Italiano, RI—Italian Renewal) narrowly defeated the Polo per le Libertà (as the Polo delle Libertà had been renamed), securing 284 of the 630 seats in the Camera dei Deputati and 157 of the 315 elective seats in the Senato. President Scalfaro invited Prodi to form a government; Prodi announced his intention to introduce educational and constitutional reforms, reduce unemployment, address the contentious issue of media ownership and to implement a policy of economic austerity.

In May 1996 Bossi of the Lega Nord announced the formation of an 11-member 'Government of the Independent Republic of Padania' (a territory comprising the regions of Liguria, Emilia-Romagna, Lombardy, Piedmont and the Veneto). The Lega Nord fared relatively poorly in key northern cities at local elections in June, however, and a rally in Venice to mark what was described as 'the formal independence of Padania' was poorly attended.

Meanwhile, former magistrate Di Pietro was alleged to have abused his position within the judiciary to extort favours and to have attempted to discredit Berlusconi to further his own political ambitions. In March 1996, after a court in Brescia dismissed charges against Di Pietro, Berlusconi's brother, Paolo, and Cesare Previti, a former Minister of Defence and a lawyer for Fininvest, were placed under investigation for allegedly attempting to discredit him. Although Di Pietro was appointed Minister of Public Works in May, in November he resigned from the post, in protest at renewed investigations into his affairs. In December the Court of Review ruled that raids on Di Pietro's home and offices by the finance police (suspected of seeking vengeance on Di Pietro for his earlier investigations into their affairs) were 'unjustified and illegitimate'. Paolo Berlusconi and Previti were acquitted in January 1997. In November 1996 Prodi was himself placed under investigation for alleged abuse of office while head of the state holding company Istituto per la Ricostruzione Industriale (Iri) during 1993–94; the Prime Minister dismissed the allegations and pledged to co-operate fully with the inquiry.

In July 1996 the Government had presented draft legislation on media reform that would allow Berlusconi's Mediaset organization to convert one of its three television channels to cable or satellite (or else reduce its share of the terrestrial audience) rather than to divest it. The draft legislation also envisaged the establishment of a telecommunications and media regulator, while the RAI broadcasting group would be obliged to convert one of its channels to a regional network. However, the reforms failed to receive parliamentary approval prior to the deadline set by the Constitutional Court, and the Court ruled that its recommendation to reduce the maximum proportion of television companies permitted to be owned by any one group from 25% to 20% would take effect. It consequently announced that it would block the transmission of one of Mediaset's channels with effect from 22 December. In early December the Secretary-General of the PDS, Massimo D'Alema, secured the postponement of the Constitutional Court's decision to enforce its ruling on broadcasting and indicated that the Government might support the introduction of judicial reforms that could permit extensive plea-bargaining in corruption cases—thereby taking advantage of Berlusconi's vulnerability with regard both to media legislation and judicial investigations into his business affairs (see below). In return, Berlusconi agreed to co-operate with the Government and support the rapid conversion of numerous decrees into law. In January 1997 the co-operation of the Polo per le Libertà enabled the Senato to approve the creation of a bicameral commission on constitutional reform. In June the commission presented its recommendations, including a directly elected presidency, a reduction in the size of the Camera dei Deputati and the Senato, and greater regional financial autonomy.

In December 1997 Berlusconi and four associates were convicted on charges of false accounting with regard to the purchase of a film group in 1988. Later in December 1997 Berlusconi and Previti were ordered to stand trial on charges relating to allegations that they had accumulated funds with the intention of bribing judges. In two separate trials in July 1998 Berlusconi was convicted of bribing tax inspectors involved in Fininvest audits and of making illicit payments to Craxi and the PSI in 1991. The prescribed custodial sentences were not, however, to be enforced as the former Prime Minister (who was awaiting trial on several further charges) was protected by parliamentary immunity. Further allegations against Berlusconi emerged in August when a witness in an unrelated corruption trial accused him of money-laundering on behalf of the Mafia; Berlusconi strenuously denied the charge.

In May 1997 the Lega Nord organized a 'referendum' to determine the level of popular support for 'Padania'. Despite media reports that participation levels had been low, Bossi claimed that 5m. people had voted, of whom 99% supported an independent 'Republic of Padania'. In local elections in April the Lega Nord had suffered a sharp decline in support. In October elections to a 200-seat constituent assembly in the 'Republic of Padania', organized by the Lega Nord, were contested by 63 parties. In January 1998 Bossi received a one-year suspended prison sentence for inciting criminal acts during a Lega Nord meeting in 1995; in July 1998 he received a second sentence, of seven months, for resistance to authority and offensive behaviour.

In June 1998 the Camera dei Deputati approved legislation endorsing the admission to the North Atlantic Treaty Organization (NATO, see p. 340) of Hungary, Poland and the Czech Republic. The vote, which had become an issue of confidence in the Prodi Government as the PRC (on which the coalition relied in parliamentary votes) opposed the eastward expansion of the alliance and thus withdrew its support, was carried with the support of the new, centrist Unione Democratica per la Repubblica (UDR—Democratic Union for the Republic, led by former President Cossiga) and with the abstention of Forza Italia. Inter-party talks on the proposed constitutional reforms had collapsed earlier that month, the principal area of contention being the issue of presidential powers. Berlusconi, in particular, opposed any alteration of the presidential mandate and demanded greater reform of the judiciary, including a curb on the power of the magistrates. There was a further political crisis in October, when the PRC again withdrew its support for the Government on the issue of the 1999 budget. The Government lost an ensuing confidence motion by one vote, and Prodi was forced to resign. D'Alema, of the Democratici di Sinistra (DS—Democrats of the Left—as the PDS had been renamed), was asked to assume the premiership. The new Government comprised members of the DS, the Federazione dei Verdi, the Partito dei Comunisti Italiani, the UDR, the PPI, the Socialisti Democratici Italiani (SDI—Italian Democratic Socialists) and RI.

In March 1999 Berlusconi was acquitted on charges of tax fraud; his 1998 conviction for making illicit payments to Craxi and the PSI was overturned in October 1999. In the following month, however, Berlusconi was ordered to stand trial in two cases involving charges of bribery and false accounting; in one of the cases the former Minister of Defence, Previti, was also to stand trial on a charge of perverting the course of justice. Meanwhile, in June a new trial had been ordered against Craxi on charges of illegal party financing; however, in January 2000 Craxi died in exile in Tunisia.

In May 1999 the former Prime Minister, Ciampi, was elected to succeed Scalfaro as President of the Republic. In that month, Massimo D'Antona, an adviser to the Minister of Employment and Social Welfare, was shot dead. Responsibility was claimed by the Brigate Rosse, which had until then been believed to have been inactive since the late 1980s. Municipal and provincial elections in June resulted in a number of defeats for the governing coalition, most notably in Bologna, where a right-wing candidate was elected Mayor for the first time since 1945; elections to the European Parliament also showed increased support for right-wing parties.

D'Alema tendered his resignation as Prime Minister in December 1999, following the withdrawal of support by an alliance of parties including the SDI and the UDR. President Ciampi asked D'Alema to form a new government; D'Alema forged a new coalition of parties of the left and centre, including I Democratici per l'Ulivo (The Democrats for the Olive Tree), founded earlier in that year by Prodi, and the Unione Democratici per l'Europa (UDEUR—Union of Democrats for Europe). At regional elections held in April 2000, however, the new centre-left coalition was defeated by a centre-right alliance composed of Forza Italia and Lega Nord. In an attempt to avert a general election, which would follow his predicted defeat in a parliamentary confidence motion, D'Alema resigned. The Minister of Treasury and the Budget, former premier Amato, was appointed in his stead, and in late April a new, eight-party centre-left coalition Government was sworn in.

In May 2000, at a first appeal, Berlusconi was acquitted of one charge of bribing tax inspectors involved in Fininvest audits on which he had been convicted in 1998; the appeals court also invoked the statute of limitations to overturn his convictions on three similar counts. In June 2000 Berlusconi was further acquitted at a pre-trial hearing of bribery charges relating to his acquisition of the Mondadori publishing company in 1991.

At the general election held on 13 May 2001, Berlusconi's Casa delle Libertà (House of Freedoms) alliance—the successor to the Polo per le Libertà—won a decisive victory over L'Ulivo alliance led by the former Mayor of Rome, Francesco Rutelli, securing majorities in both legislative chambers. The Casa delle Libertà won 177 seats in the Senato (compared with 128 held by L'Ulivo), and 368 in the Camera dei Deputati (compared with 242 for L'Ulivo). Following his nomination as premier by Ciampini, in June Berlusconi formed a coalition Government composed of Forza Italia, the AN, the Lega Nord, the CDU, the Centro Cristiano Democratico (CDD—Christian Democratic Centre) and independents. The AN leader, Fini, became Deputy Prime Minister, while the Government included three members of Lega Nord: Bossi as Minister without Portfolio, with responsibility for Reforms and Devolution; Roberto Castelli as Minister of Justice; and Maroni as Minister of Labour and Welfare.

The issue of apparent conflict of interest between Berlusconi's political role and business interests was heightened by the general election. Berlusconi's new position as Prime Minister placed him in effective control of the state broadcasting company, RAI, and this, coupled with his ownership of the media company Fininvest (which operates Italy's principal private television concern, Mediaset), potentially gave him control over the majority of the Italian television network. Prior to the election Berlusconi had apparently contradicted earlier indications that, should he become premier, he would relinquish a significant proportion of his media interests—stating that he had no intention of selling any part of Fininvest but that he would introduce legislation addressing conflicts of interest.

In August 2001 legislation to decriminalize fraud associated with false accounting was approved by the Camera dei Deputati. Furthermore, in October legislation was adopted by the Senato which altered regulations governing the use of evidence in criminal cases. Opposition parties protested that Berlusconi would directly benefit from the new regulations, which were likely to invalidate legal proceedings against himself and Previti in respect of allegations that they had bribed judges in return for a favourable court judgment over the sale of a state-owned food company, SME Meridionale. Prior to the trial's commencement, in January 2002, an attempt by the Minister of Justice to remove one of the three judges on the case caused public and judicial consternation. In October 2001 Italy's Supreme Court of Appeal overturned Berlusconi's 1998 conviction on charges of bribing tax inspectors in exchange for favourable audits of Fininvest.

The resignation of the Minister of Foreign Affairs, Renato Ruggiero, in January 2002 exposed severe divisions within the Government over European policy. Ruggiero's resignation was prompted by comments made by three other ministers expressing their disapproval of the new European currency. Berlusconi subsequently assumed the foreign affairs portfolio, initially on an interim basis, reiterating Italy's commitment to full participation in Economic and Monetary Union (EMU). In February Berlusconi announced his intention to transfer to private ownership two of the three state-owned RAI television channels. The planned privatization was heavily criticized by opposition members as well as by the outgoing President of RAI. In April a 'conflict of interest' bill was passed in the Camera dei Deputati, after all of the L'Ulivo deputies absented themselves from the chamber. The legislation prohibited a figure in public office from active involvement in running a company, but did not forbid ownership, thus permitting Berlusconi's continued possession of Mediaset. (The bill finally became law in July 2004.)

In March 2002 Marco Biagi, an adviser to the Minister of Labour and Welfare was shot dead. Responsibility for the assassination was claimed by a faction of the Brigate Rosse. Nation-wide protests against the proposed legislation, which would ease employers' restrictions on the employment and dismissal of workers, led to a general strike in April. An agreement was signed in July by the Government and two major trade unions, the Confederazione Italiana Sindacati Lavoratori (CISL) and the Unione Italiana del Lavoro (UIL), which allowed for increased flexibility in the labour market while reintroducing consultation with workers. The accord, however, caused a split in the trade union movement (and consequently the affiliations of the political left), through the exclusion of the Confederazione Generale Italiana del Lavoro (CGIL), Italy's largest trade union.

Meanwhile, prior to local elections in mid-2002 the PPI, RI and I Democratici per l'Ulivo merged into a single electoral coalition within L'Ulivo, entitled Democrazia è Libertà—La Margherita (Democracy is Freedom—The Daisy), without UDEUR. The first round of local elections in May seemed to confirm the strength of the centre-right coalition, comprising Forza Italia, the AN, the Lega Nord and Marco Follini's Unione dei Democratici Cristiani e di Centro (UDC—Christian Democratic and Centrist Union, a coalition of the CDU and the CCD). However, at the second round of voting, held in early June, the coalition was defeated unexpectedly in nine major cities, following a concerted effort by L'Ulivo, in alliance with Fausto Bertinotti's PRC and Di Pietro's Italia dei Valori (IDV—Italy of Values).

Following the rejection of an appeal by Berlusconi in May 2002 to have his bribery trial moved from Milan (where, he alleged, the judicial system was dominated by Communists), several bills proposing judicial reform provoked controversy in the legislature and the judiciary. A Trial Bill, which would allow proceedings to be rescheduled and relocated if there was 'legitimate suspicion' of prosecutorial bias on the part of the judge, aroused concern that Berlusconi would make use of the new legislation in the corruption trial involving himself and Previti. Nevertheless, the bill was passed by the Senato in August as opposition members again absented themselves from the chamber, while members of the centre-right coalition were alleged to have voted electronically for absent colleagues, which elicited large-scale street protests in September against Berlusconi's judicial policies. The bill was subsequently passed by the Camera dei Deputati in November, also amid widespread opposition protest.

Further concerns about Berlusconi's influence over the news media were engendered in August 2002 by the dismissal of a television journalist at RAI who had been accused of bias by the Prime Minister; this followed an attempt in May to pass legislation forcing four television programmes off the air. Berlusconi's actions aroused anger from the opposition and journalists' organizations, who accused him of threatening freedom of speech and of acting with political motivation. Berlusconi's problems were compounded by the resignation in November of three RAI directors in protest at government interference, followed in March 2003 by the resignation of the company's President.

During November 2002 Bossi presented a draft bill that provided for the devolution of powers to the regions in matters of education, the health service and the police. Although the opposition tabled 1,600 amendments in an effort to hinder the progress of the bill, Berlusconi threatened a vote of confidence if the bill was not approved. Bossi created splits in the ruling coalition, however, when he attacked President Ciampi for seeking assurances that the bill would not threaten national unity. Bossi's determination to withdraw the Lega Nord from the coalition if the bill was blocked coincided with a similar threat from the UDC, which cited its lack of influence within the alliance. The devolution bill was passed in December.

In November 2002 an appeals court in Palermo overturned the acquittal of Andreotti on charges of conspiracy to murder a journalist in 1979, and sentenced the former Prime Minister to 24 years' imprisonment; the sentence aroused condemnation of the judicial system by politicians, including Berlusconi. The Court of Cassation overturned this ruling, acquitting Andreotti of the murder in October 2003. In May an appeal court upheld a 1999 ruling exonerating Andreotti of charges of association with the Mafia; the judicial report, published in July 2003, observed that although Andreotti's relations with the Mafia were close until 1980, the legislation proscribing association with the Mafia did not come into effect until 1982. In October 2004 Andreotti was acquitted by the Supreme Court of Cassation of collusion with the Mafia while in office.

In January 2003, after a further bid to relocate his bribery trial was rejected by the Supreme Court, Berlusconi announced the possible reintroduction of immunity from prosecution for members of Parliament (removed after the corruption scandal of 1992), arousing opposition protest. He also confirmed that he would complete his mandate as Prime Minister even if found guilty. In that month a UN report accused Berlusconi of attempting to undermine the judiciary. In April Berlusconi's trial opened in Milan. Later that month Previti was sentenced to 11 years' imprisonment for bribing judges to influence two corporate takeovers in the 1990s. In May it was announced that Berlusconi would be tried separately from his co-defendants. However, in June the trial was halted, following the adoption of a bill granting immunity while in office to Italy's five most senior politicians (the President, the Prime Minister, the head of the Constitutional Court and the leaders of the two chambers of Parliament). This legislation removed the possibility of the potential conviction of Berlusconi during Italy's presidency of the European Union (EU, see p. 244), which was to begin on 1 July, but also rendered unlikely the probability of the trial reaching its conclusion, as Berlusconi's term of office extended until 2006, by which time the statute of limitations would prevent the resumption of legal proceedings against him on the grounds that too much time had elapsed since the perpetration of the crimes. The Constitutional Court announced in January 2004 that the legislation was illegal, thus paving the way for the resumption in April of Berlusconi's trial on charges of corruption. Berlusconi was acquitted on one charge in December; the court ruled that the statute of limitations had expired on the second charge.

In the local elections of May–June 2003 the centre-left made significant gains against the centre-right, partly because of the failure of the latter to present a united front; owing to its coalition partners' lack of support for devolution, the Lega Nord presented its candidates separately in several northern cities. The poor electoral performance of the ruling coalition heightened tension between Bossi and Berlusconi, with Bossi demanding the enactment of legislation on devolution and immigration. Later in June the Lega Nord threatened to leave the coalition if no further progress was achieved.

In October 2003 a police operation led to the arrest of six members of Brigate Rosse, who were thought to be implicated in the murders of D'Antona in 1999 and Biagi in 2002; information leading to the arrests had emerged during the interrogation of another member of the organization, Nadia Lioce, who had been arrested in March, following an armed struggle in which a further suspect and a police officer were killed. Lioce's intelligence also led to the arrests in January 2004 of Maurizio and Fabio Viscido, and of Rita Algranati, who had previously been convicted *in absentia* of the murder of former Prime Minister Moro in 1978. In July 2005 the trial for D'Antona's murder was concluded, with life sentences being awarded to three members of the Brigate Rosse, including Lioce.

In December 2003 President Ciampi refused to sign legislation designed to reduce restrictions on media ownership, which had been adopted by the two chambers of Parliament earlier in the month. The bill would overturn the High Court's decision requiring Berlusconi to convert one of his three terrestrial television channels (Rete 4) to a satellite channel by 1 January 2004 and would also lift a ban on a single company owning licences to both broadcast television and to publish a newspaper. Opponents of the bill maintained that it would allow Berlusconi to expand his media holdings and thereby reduce further the freedom of the press. Through his indirect influence on the state broadcaster RAI (four of the five board members were associated with the ruling coalition), and his own company, Mediaset, Berlusconi already controlled more than 90% of Italy's television media. Ciampi returned the bill to Parliament for further consideration, and published his opinion that the bill was contrary to constitutional court rulings regarding the plurality of the media. In late December the Government issued an emergency decree allowing Rete 4 to continue broadcasting as a terrestrial channel until May 2004. Following a temporary suspension of discussions in the lower house, the bill was approved by the Camera dei Deputati in February 2004, as the Government linked the vote to a motion of confidence, a method that had been used to gain approval for the 2004 budget in October 2003. The bill received final approval in the Senato in April 2004 and President Ciampi was constitutionally obliged to sign it into law in early May. The President of RAI consequently resigned.

In July 2004, following poor results in regional and local elections the previous month, divisions began to appear within the governing coalition. The AN, which did not support Berlusconi's plan to reduce income tax, threatened to leave the coalition unless Giulio Tremonti resigned as Minister of Economy and Finance, in protest at the 2005 budget plans. Tremonti resigned in early July, and his portfolio was temporarily assumed by Berlusconi until the appointment later that month of Domenico Siniscalco, a non-aligned technocrat. In mid-July Bossi resigned from the Government, citing its failure to introduce devolution. Bossi announced his intention to take up his seat in the European Parliament, which he had won in elections the previous month. Forza Italia had performed poorly in the European elections of 13 June, placing further strain on the coalition as the other members of the coalition had increased their share of the vote. The UDC, which opposed the constitutional reform advocated by the Lega Nord and had supported the AN's position regarding the budget, also threatened to leave the coalition, and in mid-July voted with the opposition to dismiss the board of RAI. However, the UDC subsequently withdrew its opposition to a devolution reform bill later in the month. Also in July controversial legislation regulating conflicts of interests was approved by the Camera dei Deputati, having already been endorsed by the Senato, and legislation concerning pension reform was passed by the Camera dei Deputati in a vote of confidence in the Government. The proposed legislation had precipitated a series of strikes beginning in October 2003, which had led to a compromise agreement with the three main unions in February.

Prodi, who had served as President of the European Commission since 1999, completed his term in October 2004 and returned to domestic politics. Earlier in 2004 he had declared that he would lead the L'Ulivo coalition in the 2006 election. He subsequently announced the creation of a broad left-wing alliance, the Grande Alleanza Democratica, later restyled L'Unione, incorporating members of L'Ulivo and the PRC.

In November 2004 Berlusconi nominated Buttiglione, the leader of the UDC, as European Commissioner for Justice, Freedom and Security. Buttiglione was forced to withdraw from the proposed Commission after controversy arose over his views on homosexuality. The Minister of Foreign Affairs, Franco Frattini, was subsequently appointed as Italy's nominee to the Commission. Gianfranco Fini replaced Frattini as Minister of Foreign Affairs, while retaining his post as Deputy Prime Minister. The AN and the CDU, however, continued to disagree with Berlusconi over proposed tax reductions amounting to

€6,500m., which were to be included in the 2005 budget. The EU expressed concern over the proposed cuts, stating that they might result in Italy's budget deficit rising above the threshold of 3% of gross domestic product demanded of members of the euro area. Berlusconi threatened to call an early general election if the tax reductions were not approved by the Government, and in late November the ruling coalition finally agreed to reductions of €6,000m. in income tax (although, as a concession, Berlusconi agreed that the cuts would not be implemented until 2006). In the same month a general strike marked the culmination of protests against proposed reductions in public expenditure.

In late November 2004 employees in the legal profession organized a strike to protest against planned judicial reform which, it was claimed, would reduce the independence of the judiciary, increase the power of the Ministry of Justice, and reduce the power of the legal professionals to prosecute politicians for corruption. Although it was passed by both houses of Parliament, on 16 December President Ciampi refused to sign the legislation (for the second time in two years) and returned it to Parliament, stating that it was unconstitutional. On the same day the Camera dei Deputati passed a bill reducing the statute of limitations for business-related crimes, including fraud and corruption. The bill was criticized as being intended to halt the prosecution of Cesare Previti.

At regional elections held on 3–4 April 2005 the ruling coalition won control of only two of the 13 regions contested, while the centre-left won 11; the Government had previously controlled eight of the regions. The centre-left retained a further region in elections held later in the month, giving it control of 16 of the 20 regions. The poor electoral performance of the coalition, and most notably of Forza Italia, was widely attributed to popular discontent with the Government's economic policies and its continued support for the US-led war in Iraq. The UDC subsequently withdrew from the governing coalition and the AN threatened to do likewise. Berlusconi resigned on 20 April in order to form a new Government, which was duly inaugurated on 23 April. The new Government comprised representatives of the four parties in the previous Government, the PRI, the Nuovo Partito Socialista Italiano (Nuovo PSI—New Italian Socialist Party) and independents. Although responsibility for the principal portfolios remained unchanged, new ministers were appointed to oversee industry and communications and the AN and the UDC each gained an additional portfolio, health and culture, respectively; Marco Follini, the Secretary-General of the UDC and Deputy Prime Minister from December 2004, declined to rejoin the Government. The former Minister of Economy and Finance, Tremonti, rejoined the Council of Ministers as a Deputy Prime Minister.

The Minister of Economy and Finance, Domenico Siniscalco, resigned in September 2005 in protest at his isolation over proposed spending cuts in the budget and the Government's failure to remove the Governor of the Banca d'Italia, Antonio Fazio, from his post. Fazio had been widely criticized for favouring the Italian Banca Popolare Italiana over the Dutch ABN AMRO during a takeover battle for the Banca Antonveneta, Italy's ninth largest bank. However, Fazio, whose appointment to the independent central bank was for life and who could only be dismissed by other officials at the bank, ignored calls for his resignation. Tremonti, who had resigned from the economy and finance portfolio in July 2004, was reappointed to the post in Siniscalco's place. Following increasing governmental and international pressure, Fazio eventually resigned in December 2005, and in the same month legislation was passed which, among other measures, limited the tenure of the governor of the Banca d'Italia to two six-year terms.

Legislation providing for a return to total proportional representation prior to the elections in 2006 and setting a threshold for the percentage of votes a party was required to win to be eligible for seats in Parliament was approved by the Camera dei Deputati in October 2005. The opposition abstained from voting, claiming that the legislation was designed to reduce the representation of L'Unione (which was made up of nine parties) in the next parliament. The legislation was approved by the Senato in December. In November the Government agreed a controversial decree reforming the pension system, which would enable the transfer of funds from employers to private pension funds; the decree would come into effect in 2008. In the same month a general strike—the fifth since Berlusconi took office in 2001—was held to protest against proposed reductions in government expenditure in the 2006 budget.

In October 2005 Berlusconi announced that legislative elections would take place on 9 April 2006. Earlier in the year Berlusconi had mooted the idea of the formation of one rightwing party to contest the 2006 elections, but this had not commanded the support of Forza Italia's coalition partners. Berlusconi's position had been strengthened, however, earlier in October, when Follini resigned as leader of the UDC, having failed to convince his party to support an alternative primeministerial candidate to Berlusconi for the forthcoming elections. In the same month L'Unione held its first primary election to choose a prime-ministerial candidate. The election was widely seen as an attempt to preclude any opposition to the candidacy of Prodi, who won 74.1% of the vote.

In November 2005 the two chambers of Parliament approved legislation reducing the statute of limitations for corruption and similar crimes and lengthening it for Mafia-related crimes. The bill had attracted criticism not only because of the perception that it was designed to protect Previti from a prison sentence (although the bill was subsequently amended to exclude current cases), but also because other legislation had been delayed while it was being debated. Lawyers staged a three-day strike in protest at the legislation in January 2006. Also in January President Ciampi refused to sign legislation, approved earlier in the month by Parliament, that abolished the right of prosecutors to appeal against an acquittal, claiming that it was unconstitutional. The legislation was widely regarded as designed to exempt Berlusconi from further prosecution since a court in Milan was due to begin hearing an appeal of a case in which Berlusconi was acquitted on four charges of bribing judges; the appeal was rejected in April 2007.

In mid-February 2006, following growing anger in the Islamic world over a number of cartoons—first published in Denmark, but widely reprinted in the European press—depicting the founder of the Islamic religion, Muhammad, Roberto Calderoli, the Minister without Portfolio for Institutional Reforms and Devolution and a member of the Lega Nord, was asked by Berlusconi to resign. Riots in Libya had resulted in the deaths of at least 10 people, following Calderoli's appearance on television wearing an item of clothing depicting one of the cartoons.

In March 2006 Berlusconi went on trial in Milan, along with 13 other defendants, on charges of fraud relating to the purchase of television rights by Mediaset in the 1990s. Later that year a separate trial opened involving Berlusconi and his former lawyer, David Mills (the estranged husband of British Government minister Tessa Jowell), in which the former was accused of paying Mills at least US $600,000 after Mills gave favourable testimony in a corruption trial involving Berlusconi, also in the 1990s. It was considered unlikely that either trial would end in a conviction, as proceedings were not likely to be concluded until after 2008, by which time 10 years would have elapsed since the alleged crimes and the trials would thus be invalid under Italian law.

In the general election, which was held on 9–10 April 2006, Prodi's L'Unione coalition won a narrow victory in both the Senato and the Camera dei Deputati. In the upper house L'Unione obtained 158 seats, while the Casa delle Libertà took 156 seats. New legislation, which automatically awarded 55% of the seats in the lower house to the party or group with the largest number of votes, meant that L'Unione obtained 348 seats in the Camera dei Deputati, while Berlusconi's coalition won 281 seats. It was reported that the turn-out at the elections was more than 80% of the electorate. Berlusconi contested the results, claiming that thousands of the ballots were disputed; these allegations were rejected, however, by the Supreme Court of Appeal. In late April the new Parliament convened, and Franco Marini of La Margherita and Bertinotti of the PRC were elected Presidents of the Senato and Camera dei Deputati, respectively. In May Giorgio Napolitano, a left-wing politician who had served as President of the Camera dei Deputati and as Minister for Internal Affairs in 1992–94, was elected to succeed Ciampi as President of the Republic; Ciampi had rejected an appeal from the centre-right to stand for a second term. The election of a President allowed Prodi to form a new Government, which included two former Prime Ministers: D'Alema as Minister of Foreign Affairs and Amato as Minister of Internal Affairs. Tommaso Padoa-Schioppa, an economist with no party affiliation who had previously served on the executive board of the European Central Bank, was appointed Minister of Economy and Finance.

In June 2006 a referendum was held over controversial constitutional reforms, introduced by the previous administration and approved by Parliament in November 2005, that would have granted greater autonomy to Italy's regions and extended the powers of the Prime Minister. The reforms were rejected by the electorate, with 61.7% of votes against the proposal, from a relatively high turn-out of 52%. President Ciampi and the opposition had been severely critical of the reforms, claiming that the power of the legislature would be diminished and that the devolution of power to the regions, promoted by the Lega Nord, favoured the more affluent northern regions at the expense of their southern counterparts. In the referendum the greatest opposition to the reform was in Calabria, the poorest region of Italy, where 82% voted against. The referendum result was viewed as a significant indication of support for the new Government, following its narrow victory in the elections two months previously.

Prodi's majority in the Senato was reduced to just one seat in September 2006, when an IDV member left that party and the L'Unione coalition to sit as an independent. The defection came at a time when Prodi was struggling to maintain control over his coalition in order to ensure the passage through Parliament of a controversial budget. The budget, which sought to reduce the country's large economic deficit, had been criticized by parties on the left of the coalition because of the envisaged reduction in public spending and by centrists for its tax increases. The budget was approved by the Camera dei Deputati and the Senato in December, but the Government had to resort to the increasingly common tactic of turning the bill into a vote of confidence in both chambers of Parliament in order to win the support of its coalition partners.

In February 2007 the Government was defeated in the Senato by two votes on the continued presence of troops in Afghanistan (see below) and the expansion of a US military base near Vicenza, actions which were opposed by far-left and pacifist members of the ruling coalition. (The Government had also lost the support of life Senator Andreotti, who opposed a controversial bill granting rights to unmarried and homosexual couples that was concurrently being considered by the Senato.) Although the vote was not tied to a motion of confidence, it caused Prodi to submit his resignation to the President; however, this was not accepted by Napolitano, who asked him to test his authority by calling confidence votes in Parliament. Prodi went on to win the votes in the Senato in February and the Camera dei Deputati in early March, after persuading all parties in the coalition to agree to a 12-point programme that included support for the peace-keeping mission in Afghanistan, as well as measures to liberalize the economy. In a subsequent vote in late March the Senato approved continued funding for all Italian missions abroad, including Afghanistan.

In an attempt to consolidate support for the main left-wing parties and to promote a more centrist agenda, in April 2007 it was announced that the DS and La Margherita were to merge later that year, as the Partito Democratico (PD—Democratic Party). Nevertheless, at local elections held in May, the centre-right parties took control of 13 provincial city councils, compared with six for the parties of the governing coalition. At a referendum held in early October, 82% of voters approved a welfare reform package that had been agreed by the Government and the trade unions in July 2007, under which the minimum age for retirement was to be raised, from 57 years to 61, by 2013. Following the vote, the measures were approved by the Government, despite the opposition of some far-left members of the coalition. On 14 October 2007 some 3.6m. people nation-wide participated in an open primary election, at which the Mayor of Rome, the former Deputy Prime Minister Walter Veltroni, was elected as National Secretary of the PD, with 75.8% of the votes cast. On 27 October, at a special conference in Milan, the DS and La Margherita completed a formal merger, as the PD; Veltroni was confirmed as the party's leader.

Meanwhile, attempts by the main parties to consolidate support continued in mid-October 2007, when Berlusconi announced his intention to form a new, centre-right party, under his leadership. Berlusconi urged his former coalition partners to join the new formation, which was named the Popolo della Libertà (PdL—People of Freedom) in early December. However, both the AN and the Lega Nord opposed the creation of a single organization. In late October the Supreme Court of Appeal upheld the decision of a court in Milan to acquit Berlusconi on four charges of making illegal payments to judges (see above).

On 6 December 2007 the Government narrowly defeated a vote of 'no confidence' in the Senato, by 160 votes to 156. The vote followed the adoption in November of a controversial decree that allowed local authorities to order the removal from Italy of citizens of other EU member states suspected of threatening public security. The decree had been adopted in response to a public outcry following the murder earlier that month of an Italian woman in Rome and the subsequent arrest of a Romanian man on suspicion of perpetrating the crime. Some senators belonging to the governing coalition had voted against the Government, accusing it of xenophobia, while opposition parties claimed that the measures were not sufficiently robust. The decree also prompted criticism from the Romanian Government, following comments by the Minister of the Interior, Amato, regarding the large number of Romanians who had entered Italy since Romania's accession to the EU in January 2007. Moreover, Prodi's increasing reliance on votes of confidence to ensure approval for government policies reflected the Prime Minister's continued difficulty in maintaining control over the coalition, and prompted further speculation over the prospect of its collapse.

The ongoing struggle to maintain stability within L'Unione culminated on 17 January 2008 with the resignation of the Minister of Justice, Clemente Mastella, following the arrest of his wife on charges of corruption. (Prodi additionally assumed the justice portfolio on an interim basis.) Immediately after his resignation, Mastella pledged his support for the Government. Days later, however, he announced the withdrawal from the governing coalition of his UDEUR party, thereby removing the Government's narrow majority in the upper house. On 24 January the Government lost a vote of confidence in the Senato, by 161 votes to 156, which had been prompted by its response to an ongoing refuse collection crisis in Naples. Immediately after the vote, Prodi submitted the Government's resignation, which was accepted by President Napolitano, who, nevertheless, requested that Prodi remain in office on an interim basis pending the appointment of a new Council of Ministers. Later that month Napolitano asked the President of the Senato, Franco Marini, to lead discussions over the formation of a cross-party interim administration with a mandate to pursue electoral reform. However, the main opposition parties refused to agree such measures, which would have reversed reforms implemented during Berlusconi's second term as Prime Minister, and urged Napolitano to call an early general election, at which, opinion polls suggested, the centre-right parties were likely to emerge victorious. By early February it became clear that an agreement was not possible and, consequently, the talks collapsed. On 6 February Napolitano dissolved the two chambers of parliament and called a general election for 13–14 April. In February Berlusconi and Fini announced that Forza Italia and the AN were to present a joint list of candidates at the general election as the PdL, a coalition that was subsequently joined by numerous smaller parties. While ruling out a formal merger, the Lega Nord and the Movimento per l'Autonomia agreed to form an alliance with the PdL. The UDC, however, was to contest the election as part of a new coalition, the Unione di Centro (UdC), which it had formed with other centrist, Christian-democratic parties in late December 2007. In late February 2008 Luigi Scotti, an independent and former magistrate, who hitherto had been a junior minister in the Prodi Government, was appointed Minister of Justice.

Meanwhile, in late January 2008 a court in Milan acquitted Berlusconi on charges of false accounting, on the grounds that, since reforms promulgated in 2001 under Berlusconi's premiership (see above), it was no longer a criminal offence. In late February a court in Milan upheld a defence request to suspended the two ongoing trials in which Berlusconi was a defendant, to allow him to campaign as a candidate at the forthcoming general election.

At the general election, conducted on 13 and 14 April 2008, the number of parties represented in Parliament was greatly reduced, partly owing to the consolidation of the main, centrist alliances. Berlusconi's PdL and its allies won a majority in both the Camera dei Deputati and the Senato. In the lower house the PdL won 276 seats, while its allies the Lega Nord and the Movimento per l'Autonomia won 60 and eight seats, respectively, compared with 217 seats for the PD. Meanwhile, in the upper house, the PdL won 147 seats, while the Lega Nord and the Movimento per l'Autonomia won 25 and two seats, respectively; the PD won 118 seats. The UdC, Italia dei Valori (and a number of small parties also gained representation in both houses. However, the left-wing La Sinistra—L'Arcobaleno (The Left—The Rainbow) alliance, which had been formed in December 2007 by the Federazione dei Verdi, the PRC, the PCI and Sinistra

Democratica, failed to gain representation in either chamber. A high voter turn-out of 81% was recorded.

Despite mass trials of Mafia suspects in the late 1980s, the Italian Government continued to experience problems in dealing with organized crime. In 1992 the murders of Salvatore Lima, a Sicilian politician and member of the European Parliament, Giovanni Falcone, a prominent anti-Mafia judge, and Paolo Borsellino, a colleague of Falcone, provoked renewed public outrage, and later that year, following an increase in the powers of the police and the judiciary, hundreds of suspects were detained. In January 1993 the capture of Salvatore Riina, the alleged head of the Sicilian Mafia, was regarded as a significant success in the Government's campaign against organized crime. In 1993 the judiciary mounted a campaign to seize Mafia funds, and in the course of the year several suspects, alleged to be leading figures in the world of organized crime, were arrested. In September 1997 24 influential members of the Mafia, including Riina, were sentenced to life imprisonment for their part in the murder of Falcone. The following July Riina received another conviction, along with 17 others, for complicity in the murder of Salvatore Lima in 1992; this constituted Riina's 13th sentence of life imprisonment. In April 1999 an official of the treasury ministry was arrested on charges of external complicity with the Mafia; he was the first serving government member to be taken into preventive detention. In December 17 Mafia members were sentenced to life imprisonment for the murder of Borsellino. Emergency measures were decreed in November 2000 in an attempt to prevent the early release from prison of those accused of Mafia-related crimes. The laws followed the discharge, on technical grounds, of 10 detainees accused of involvement in murders attributed to the Mafia. Magistrates were granted greater powers in determining the length of preventive detention for suspects and a ban on plea-bargaining was introduced. Benedetto Spera, reputedly the closest colleague of the head of the Sicilian Mafia, Bernardo Provenzano, had also been arrested at the end of January; Spera had been convicted *in absentia* for his role in the murders of Falcone and Borsellino. In April 2001 Riina, along with six others, was sentenced to 30 years' imprisonment for the murder, in 1979, of Mario Francese (see above).

Organized crime continued to be problematic during Berlusconi's second term as Prime Minister. Although a murder charge against Berlusconi was dropped in May 2002, the trial of his close friend Marcello Dell'Utri, one of the founders of Forza Italia, on charges of Mafia collusion resulted in the imposition of a nine-year prison sentence in December 2004. Further allegations about Berlusconi's links with the Mafia emerged during Dell'Utri's trial in January 2003, when it was alleged by a Mafia informer that the Mafia had transferred its allegiance in the 1990s from the DC to Berlusconi's Forza Italia. Provenzano's closest accomplice, Antonino Giuffrè, was arrested in April 2002 near Palermo. In December Giuffrè directly implicated Berlusconi in the bribing of the Mafia for votes in Sicily in 1993. In September 2004 an investigation into the President of Sicily, Salvatore Cuffaro of the UDC, concluded that he had indirectly aided the Mafia by transmitting sensitive information. In mid-January 2008 Cuffaro was convicted and sentenced to five years' imprisonment; nevertheless, he continued to protest his innocence. Later that month Cuffaro was forced to resign as President of Sicily, despite having refused to do so in the aftermath of his conviction. In February it was announced that Cuffaro was to head the list of UDC candidates in Sicily at elections to the Senato scheduled for 13 and 14 April. Meanwhile, in April 2006 Provenzano himself, who had been in hiding since 1963, was arrested in Sicily.

Italy's foreign policy has traditionally been governed by its firm commitment to Europe, notably through its membership of the European Community (now EU) and NATO. Under the premiership of Berlusconi in 2001–05 enthusiasm for European integration was more muted and increasing emphasis was put on promoting national interests; this was accompanied by a repositioning of Italy in foreign policy terms, as Berlusconi allied himself with the USA, the United Kingdom and Spain in his political support for the US-led campaign to remove the regime of Saddam Hussain in Iraq, rather than with Italy's traditional allies, France and Germany. After Prodi, a former President of the European Commission, took office he declared his intention to restore good relations with other EU member states and criticized British and US policy in Iraq. However, Italy has continued to align itself with the USA in other areas of policy in the Middle East.

The deployment of some 2,700 Italian troops to assist military efforts as part of the US-led 'campaign against terror', following the September 2001 suicide attacks on New York and Washington, DC, was approved by the Italian Parliament in November. An investigation into the existence of terrorist cells possibly connected with the al-Qa'ida (Base) organization headed by the Saudi-born dissident Osama bin Laden led to a number of arrests in Italy in 2002–03. Berlusconi's increasing political allegiance with the so-called 'coalition of the willing' (the group of powers, including the USA, the United Kingdom and Spain, which was in favour of military action against the regime of Saddam Hussain in Iraq), gave rise to massive nation-wide protests in February 2003. Because of the level of popular dissent, the Italian Government did not at this stage agree to supply troops for the US-led military campaign in Iraq; it did, however, offer the USA the use of Italy's bases and airspace for logistical purposes. At the onset of armed conflict in Iraq in March, the anti-war movement in Italy gained momentum, with the trade unions organizing a general strike and protests in Rome continuing on a daily basis. Following a request by the US authorities, Italy was the first EU country to expel a number of Iraqi diplomatic staff. In April the Government approved the provision of humanitarian support for Iraq; however, by November Italy had approximately 2,400 troops stationed in the country. In that month a suicide bombing took place at an Italian base in Nasiriyah, Iraq, killing 19 Italian soldiers; this led to renewed calls from the centre-left for Italy to withdraw. Pressure for the withdrawal of troops from Iraq increased following the kidnapping and murder of an Italian journalist, Enzo Baldoni, in August 2004. Relations with the USA were strained by the countries' different findings in separate investigations into the accidental killing in March 2005 of an Italian intelligence officer, Nicola Calipari, by a US soldier, during the release of another Italian hostage. In what was generally regarded as an attempt to win popular support for the forthcoming legislative elections, in October 2005 Berlusconi stated in a television interview that he had attempted to persuade the US President, George W. Bush, not to invade Iraq. In January 2006 the Italian Government announced that all 3,000 Italian troops then stationed in Iraq (the fourth largest contingent) would be withdrawn by the end of the year; this timetable was confirmed in June by Prodi, who had promised to bring home the troops in Iraq as part of his campaign for the April elections. The last Italian troops left Iraq in early December.

Relations with the USA were also adversely affected by the actions of a court in Milan, which in June 2005 issued arrest warrants for 26 US citizens, most of them intelligence agents. The suspects were believed to have abducted the Egyptian cleric Hassan Mustafa Osama Nasr, known as Abu Omar, from Milan in 2003 and transported him for interrogation in Egypt, where he was allegedly tortured. In February 2007 the court ordered the suspects to stand trial; the Italian Government subsequently attempted to have the case blocked by the Constitutional Court on the grounds that the prosecutors had breached state secrets. Relations between the two countries deteriorated further in April, after the trial *in absentia* of Mario Lozano, a US soldier accused of unlawfully killing Nicola Calipari in Iraq in March 2005, commenced in Rome. However, in October 2007 judges ruled the case to be inadmissible under Italian law.

Following the conflict in Lebanon between Israeli forces and the militant group Hezbollah in July–August 2006, Italy sent some 2,500 peace-keeping troops to form part of the UN Interim Force in Lebanon. In February 2007 Italy assumed command of the 12,000-strong multinational force, of which Italian troops formed the largest component. Italy also had around 1,800 troops stationed in Afghanistan as part of the NATO-led peace-keeping force. In March Parliament voted by a narrow margin to maintain the Italian presence in Afghanistan, after it had prompted a crisis of confidence in the Government the previous month by opposing the motion.

The heads of state and of government of the EU formally approved the Treaty establishing a Constitution for Europe in October 2004, which required ratification by all 25 member states. Italy ratified the constitutional treaty by parliamentary vote in April 2005. However, the process of ratification was stalled, following the treaty's rejection in national referendums in France and the Netherlands in May and June, respectively. In late June 2007, however, EU leaders reached a preliminary agreement over a reform treaty, which was to replace the constitutional treaty rejected by French and Dutch voters in 2005. The reform treaty was signed by EU heads of state and of government, including Prodi, at a summit meeting in Lisbon,

Portugal, on 13 December 2007. By April 2008, seven of the 27 member states had ratified the treaty; the Italian Parliament was due to ratify the treaty by the end of 2008.

Italy's extended coastline and geographical position attracts many illegal immigrants from South-Eastern Europe and North Africa. Following Italy's accession to the EU's Schengen Agreement on cross-border travel in late October 1997, large numbers of refugees, mainly Turkish and Iraqi Kurds, began arriving in southern Italy, provoking concern from Italy's EU partners. These concerns were partially alleviated by the initial approval, in November, of a bill designed to facilitate the deportation of illegal immigrants. However, the concerns resurfaced in January 1998, following comments by President Scalfaro that Italy had an 'open arms' policy towards refugees. On 1 April 1998 the Schengen Agreement, which had previously only been applicable to air travel between Italy and the other EU member states, was fully implemented, opening the borders with Austria and France. In order to comply with the terms of the agreement, a new law had been promulgated in February, providing for the detention, prior to forcible repatriation, of illegal immigrants; previously they had been given unenforced expulsion orders and released. In August the discovery of ambiguities in the new immigration law led to renewed fears of excessive immigration. In February 1999 legislation was approved allowing for the detention of illegal immigrants arriving in Italy without making an asylum application. In March 2002 a state of emergency was declared following the arrival of 1,000 Kurdish refugees in Sicily. Berlusconi expressed concern over the rise in the level of immigration into Italy, and in early June legislation was passed allowing for the fingerprinting of non-EU nationals and requiring residence permits to be renewed every two years. Further increases in arrivals of immigrants prompted a government decree in June 2003 enabling the Italian navy to board ships carrying illegal immigrants and divert them away from the Italian coast. In August 2004 an agreement was reached with Libya on controlling immigration through that country, and in early October the Italian Government commenced returning would-be immigrants to Libya by aircraft. In September 2006 a human rights organization accused the Italian and Libyan Governments of abusing the human rights of African migrants through thousands of forced repatriations. The continuing influx of immigrants prompted Italy and Spain to campaign for a common EU policy on immigration.

Government

Under the 1948 Constitution, legislative power was held by the bicameral Parliament, elected by universal suffrage for five years (subject to dissolution) on the basis of proportional representation. A referendum held in April 1993 supported the amendment of the Constitution to provide for the election of 75% of the members of the Senato della Repubblica (Senate of the Republic) by a simple plurality and the remainder under a system of proportional representation, and provided for further electoral reform. In August the Parlamento (Parliament) approved a similar system for elections to the Camera dei Deputati (Chamber of Deputies). In December 2005 new legislation providing for the return to full proportional representation was signed into law. The Senato has 315 elected members (seats allocated on a regional basis) and seven life Senators. The Camera dei Deputati has 630 members. The minimum voting age is 25 years for the Senato and 18 years for the Camera dei Deputati. The two houses have equal power.

The President of the Republic is a constitutional Head of State elected for seven years by an electoral college comprising both Houses of Parliament and 58 regional representatives. Executive power is exercised by the Council of Ministers. The Head of State appoints the President of the Council (Prime Minister) and, on the latter's recommendation, other ministers. The Council is responsible to Parliament.

The country is divided into 20 regions, of which five (Sicily, Sardinia, Trentino-Alto Adige, Friuli-Venezia Giulia and Valle d'Aosta) enjoy a special status. There is a large degree of regional autonomy. Each region has a Regional Council elected every five years by universal suffrage and a Giunta Regionale responsible to the regional council. The Regional Council is a legislative assembly, while the Giunta holds executive power. The regions are subdivided into a total of 95 provinces.

Defence

Italy has been a member of the North Atlantic Treaty Organization (NATO, see p. 340) since 1949. As assessed at November 2007 it maintained armed forces totalling 186,049, comprising an army of 108,000, a navy of 34,000 and an air force of 44,049. There were also paramilitary forces numbering 254,300 (including 111,367 Carabinieri). Conscription was phased out by December 2004. In 2006 expenditure on defence was €21,222m., accounting for 2.8% of total government expenditure.

Economic Affairs

In 2006, according to estimates by the World Bank, Italy's gross national income (GNI), measured at average 2004–06 prices, was US $1,875,640.8m., equivalent to $32,020 per head (or $30,550 per head on an international purchasing-power parity basis). During 1996–2006, it was estimated that the population increased by 0.3%, while Italy's gross domestic product (GDP) per head increased, in real terms, by an average of 1.1% per year. Overall GDP increased, in real terms, at an average annual rate of 1.4% in 1996–2006; GDP growth in 2006 was 1.9%.

Agriculture (including forestry and fishing) contributed 2.0% of GDP in 2006 and engaged 4.1% of the employed labour force in 2006. The principal crops are sugar beet, maize, grapes, wheat and tomatoes. Italy is a leading producer and exporter of wine. According to the World Bank, during 1996–2005 the real GDP of the agricultural sector increased at an average rate of 0.9% per year. Real agricultural GDP increased by 13.5% in 2004, before declining some 2.3% in 2005.

Industry (including mining, manufacturing, construction and power) contributed 27.0% of GDP in 2007 and engaged 28.4% of the employed labour force in 2006. In 1996–2005 industrial GDP increased, in real terms, at an average annual rate of 0.3% per year. Real industrial GDP increased by 1.6% in 2004, before declining by 1.7% in 2005.

The mining sector contributed just 0.4% of GDP in 2006 and engaged 0.2% of the employed labour force in that year. The major product of the mining sector is petroleum, followed by talc, feldspar, rock salt and gypsum. Italy also has reserves of lignite, lead and zinc. Reserves of epithermal gold in Sardinia were discovered in 1996. Average annual growth in the GDP of the mining sector was negligible in 1990–2000; mining GDP increased by 0.6% in 2003, but decreased by 3.1% in 2004.

Manufacturing contributed 20.8% of GDP in 2007 and engaged 20.2% of the employed labour force in 2006. In 2001 the most important branches of manufacturing, measured by production value at factor cost, were metals and metal products (12.1% of total industrial output), non-electric machinery (10.7%), food (9.1%), electric machinery (7.7%), and chemical products (7.2%). In 1996–2005 the GDP of the manufacturing sector increased, in real terms, at an average annual rate of 0.2%, according to the World Bank. Manufacturing GDP increased by 0.8% in 2004, before declining by 2.1% in 2005.

More than 80% of energy requirements are imported. According to World Bank figures, in 2004 natural gas-fired stations provided 44.3% of electricity production, coal-fired electricity generating stations provided 17.4%, petroleum provided 15.7% and hydroelectric power stations provided 13.5%. In 1987 Italy's four nuclear power stations ceased production following a referendum on the use of nuclear power. In October 2004 Libya began delivering natural gas to Sicily through a pipeline financed by Ente Nazionale Idrocarburi (Eni), the main—formerly wholly state-owned—gas provider, and its Libyan counterpart. In 2005, according to the World Bank, fuel imports accounted for 11.9% of the value of total merchandise imports.

Services accounted for 70.9% of GDP in 2007 and engaged 67.5% of the employed labour force in 2006. Tourism is an important source of income, and in 2005 an estimated 38.1m. foreigners visited Italy. Tourism receipts totalled an estimated €38,264m. in 2005. The combined GDP of the services sector increased, in real terms, at an estimated average rate of 1.7% per year in 1996–2005. Services GDP increased by 0.8% in 2005.

In 2006 Italy recorded a visible trade deficit of US $11,690m., and a deficit of $47,312m. on the current account of the balance of payments, equivalent to 3.2% of GDP. In 2005 the principal source of imports (17.2%) was Germany; other major suppliers were France (9.9%), the People's Republic of China (4.6%), Spain (4.2%) and the United Kingdom (4.0%). Germany was also the principal market for exports (13.1%); other major purchasers in that year were France (12.2%), the USA (8.1%), Spain (7.4%) and the United Kingdom (6.4%). In 2005 Italy's fellow members of the European Union (EU, see p. 244) were the source for 59.9% of Italy's imports and purchased 59.3% of its exports. The principal exports in 2006 were machinery and mechanical equipment, transport equipment, chemicals and artificial fibres, metal and metal products and textile products. The principal imports were transport equipment, chemicals and artificial fibres, electrical and precision equipment, minerals for fuel and metal and metal products.

The budgetary deficit for 2007 was €29,179m., equivalent to 1.9% of annual GDP. At the end of 2006 Italy's total accumulated government debt was equivalent to 107% of annual GDP, compared with the EU target of 60%. The average annual rate of inflation in 1996–2006 was 2.2%. Consumer prices increased by an annual average of 2.0% in 2006. The number of people registered as unemployed stood at 1.4m. as of the end of September 2007, representing 5.6% of the total labour force.

Italy is a member of the EU, the Organisation for Economic Co-operation and Development (OECD, see p. 347) and the Central European Initiative (see p. 423).

Italy's economy is the fourth largest in Europe. The country suffers from significant structural problems, including an economic disparity between the more industrialized, prosperous north and the impoverished south. Economic growth in Italy was weak or negligible in 2001–2005, contributing to a further deterioration in public finances. In July 2005 the European Commission launched an excessive deficit procedure against Italy, since its budget deficit was expected to exceed the limit of 3% of GDP imposed under the EU's Stability and Growth Pact for the third consecutive year. The Commission subsequently agreed to allow Italy further time to comply with the rules and Italy pledged to reduce the deficit from 4.3% of GDP in 2005, to 3.5% in 2006 and 2.8% in 2007. The Government of Silvio Berlusconi, which assumed power in June 2001, achieved little in the way of much-needed structural reform. The exceptions included a limited reform of the labour market, in the form of contract liberalization, where many new jobs were exempted from rules requiring most work to be permanent and full-time. This resulted in the rapid creation of many new part-time jobs. However, poor productivity growth and escalating wages caused unit labour costs to increase more rapidly than in other member states in the euro area. In the decade to 2007 the Italian economy performed poorly in comparison with the rest of the euro area. Decrees in July 2006 and January 2007 implementing limited measures to increase competition and reduce regulation were aimed at increasing relatively low levels of productivity and employment, although more radical reform was still urgently required. An ageing population, low fertility, an early average retirement age and increasing life expectancy all contributed to the continuing pressure to reform the pensions system. Under the Berlusconi Government legislation had been passed in July 2004, under which the state retirement age was extended from 57 years to 60 from January 2008. Under amended legislation introduced by the subsequent administration of Romano Prodi, the increase of the state retirement age was to be introduced in a series of stages, with the threshold increased to 58 years in 2008, and to 61 by 2010. Despite achieving one of the lowest unemployment rates in the euro area at around 6.0%, in some southern regions the rate of unemployment is as high as 20%. The European Central Bank suggested in March 2008 that Italy was unlikely to achieve its goal of a balanced budget by 2010, due to low economic growth concomitant with insufficient measures to curb public spending. Although the fiscal deficit fell to 1.9% of GDP in 2007, it was anticipated to rise towards the Stability and Growth Pact's 3% ceiling within the following two years. GDP growth was projected to decline from 1.5% in 2007, to just 0.8% in 2008. However, the Government revised this growth forecast to just 0.6% in March 2008, with the employers' organization Confindustria stating a risk that growth would decline to zero due to high oil prices and the strength of the euro. Italian exports have experienced a dramatic decline as the currency appreciated, although structural factors have also had a detrimental impact upon trade. While remaining high, government debt did reduce by a larger than anticipated amount in 2007, representing 104% of GDP, compared with 106.5% in the previous year.

Education

Education is free and compulsory between the ages of six and 15 years, comprising five years of primary education, three years of lower secondary education and one year of higher secondary education. The curricula of all Italian schools are standardized by the Ministry of Education. After elementary school (scuola elementare), for children aged six to 11 years, the pupil enters the first level of secondary school (scuola media inferiore). An examination at the end of three years leads to a lower secondary school certificate (Diploma di Licenza della Scuola Media), which gives access to higher secondary school (scuola secondaria superiore), of which only the first year is compulsory. Pupils wishing to enter a classical lycée (liceo classico) must also pass an examination in Latin.

Higher secondary education consists of three-, four- or five-year courses and is provided by classical (including linguistic, scientific and historico-social), artistic, technical and professional lycées and institutes. After five years at a lycée, the student sits an examination for the higher secondary school certificate (Diploma di Esame di Stato), which allows automatic entry into any university or non-university institute of higher education. Special four-year courses are provided at the teachers' training schools and the diploma obtained permits entry to a special university faculty of education, the magistero, and a few other faculties. The technical institutes provide practical courses that prepare students for a specialized university faculty.

In 2005/06 the total enrolment at primary schools was 99% of all children in the relevant age-group, while the comparable ratio for secondary enrolment, according to UNESCO estimates, was 92%. In 2005/06 2.5m. children were enrolled in primary education, and 4.2m. were enrolled in secondary education.

In 2001 70.0% of students taking school-leaving examinations enrolled at university. In 2005/06 there were 1.8m. students in higher education in Italy; the largest universities were La Sapienza in Rome (with around 170,000 students) and Bologna (more than 100,000 students). In 2005/06 there were 74 institutes of higher education. Following the introduction of university reforms, courses last for a three-year cycle, followed by a two-year specialized cycle. Study allowances are awarded to students according to their means and merit; however, 90% of parents pay fees. In 2006 public expenditure on education totalled €65,746m. (equivalent to 8.8% of total spending).

Public Holidays

2008: 1 January (New Year's Day), 6 January (Epiphany), 24 March (Easter Monday), 25 April (Liberation Day), 1 May (Labour Day), 2 June (Republic Day), 15 August (Assumption), 1 November (All Saints' Day), 8 December (Immaculate Conception), 25 December (Christmas Day), 26 December (St Stephen's Day).

2009: 1 January (New Year's Day), 6 January (Epiphany), 13 April (Easter Monday), 25 April (Liberation Day), 1 May (Labour Day), 2 June (Republic Day), 15 August (Assumption), 1 November (All Saints' Day), 8 December (Immaculate Conception), 25 December (Christmas Day), 26 December (St Stephen's Day).

There are also numerous local public holidays, held on the feast day of the patron saint of each town.

Weights and Measures

The metric system is in force.

ITALY   Statistical Survey

Statistical Survey

Source (unless otherwise stated): Istituto Nazionale di Statistica, Via Cesare Balbo 16, 00184 Roma; tel. (06) 46731; fax (06) 467313101; e-mail info@istat.it; internet www.istat.it.

Area and Population

AREA, POPULATION AND DENSITY

Area (sq km)	301,338*
Population (census results)†	
20 October 1991	56,778,031
21 October 2001	
Males	27,586,982
Females	29,408,762
Total	56,995,744
Population (official projected estimates of resident population at 1 January)†	
2005	58,462,375
2006	58,751,711
2007	59,131,287
Density (per sq km) at 1 January 2007	196.2

* 116,346 sq miles.
† Census figures are *de jure*, the de facto population in 2001 was 57,110,144 (males 27,617,335, females 29,492,809).

REGIONS
(estimated population at 1 January 2007*)

Region	Area (sq km)	Population	Density (per sq km)	Regional capital(s)
Abruzzo	10,798	1,309,797	121.3	L'Aquila
Basilicata	9,992	591,338	59.2	Potenza
Calabria	15,080	1,998,052	132.5	Catanzaro
Campania	13,595	5,790,187	425.9	Napoli (Naples)
Emilia-Romagna	22,124	4,223,264	190.9	Bologna
Friuli-Venezia Giulia	7,855	1,212,602	154.4	Trieste
Lazio	17,207	5,493,308	319.2	Roma (Rome)
Liguria	5,421	1,607,878	296.6	Genova (Genoa)
Lombardia (Lombardy)	23,861	9,545,441	400.0	Milano (Milan)
Marche	9,694	1,536,098	158.5	Ancona
Molise	4,438	320,074	72.1	Campobasso
Piemonte (Piedmont)	25,399	4,352,828	171.4	Torino (Turin)
Puglia	19,362	4,069,869	210.2	Bari
Sardegna (Sardinia)	24,090	1,659,443	68.9	Cagliari
Sicilia (Sicily)	25,708	5,016,861	195.1	Palermo
Toscana (Tuscany)	22,997	3,638,211	158.2	Firenze (Florence)
Trentino-Alto Adige	13,607	994,703	73.1	Bolzano (Bozen), Trento (Trent, Trient)†
Umbria	8,456	872,967	103.2	Perugia
Valle d'Aosta	3,263	124,812	38.3	Aosta
Veneto	18,392	4,773,554	259.5	Venezia (Venice)
Total	301,338	59,131,287	196.2	—

* Population is *de jure*.
† Joint regional capitals.

PRINCIPAL TOWNS
(estimated population at 31 December 2005, measured by *comune*)*

Roma (Rome, the capital)	2,547,677	Livorno (Leghorn)	160,534
Milano (Milan)	1,308,735	Cagliari	160,391
Napoli (Naples)	984,242	Reggio nell'Emilia	157,388
Torino (Turin)	900,608	Foggia	153,650
Palermo	670,820	Ravenna	149,084
Genova (Genoa)	620,316	Rimini	135,682
Bologna	373,743	Salerno	134,820
Firenze (Florence)	366,901	Ferrara	132,471
Bari	326,915	Sassari	127,893
Catania	304,144	Siracusa (Syracuse)	122,972
Venezia (Venice)	269,780	Pescara	122,457
Verona	259,380	Monza	121,961
Messina	246,323	Bergamo	116,197
Padova (Padua)	210,985	Vicenza	114,232
Trieste	206,058	Latina	112,943
Taranto	197,582	Forlí	112,477
Brescia	191,059	Trento (Trent, Trient)	111,044
Reggio di Calabria	184,369	Terni	109,569
Prato	183,823	Giugliano in Campania	108,772
Modena	180,469	Novara	102,817
Parma	175,789	Ancona	101,862
Perugia	161,390		

* Population is *de jure*.

BIRTHS, MARRIAGES AND DEATHS

	Registered live births		Registered marriages		Registered deaths	
	Number	Rate (per 1,000)	Number	Rate (per 1,000)	Number	Rate (per 1,000)
1999	523,463	9.1	275,250	4.9	565,838	9.8
2000	538,999	9.3	280,488	4.9	560,121	9.7
2001	531,880	9.2	264,026	4.6	555,247	9.6
2002	538,198	9.4	270,093	4.7	557,393	9.8
2003	544,063	9.4	264,097	4.6	586,468	10.2
2004	562,599	9.7	248,969	4.3	546,658	9.4
2005	554,022	9.7	247,740	4.2	567,304	9.8
2006	560,010	9.6	n.a.	n.a.	557,892	9.5

Expectation of life (years at birth, WHO estimates): 80.9 (males 77.9; females 83.8) in 2005 (Source: WHO, *World Health Statistics*).

ITALY

IMMIGRATION AND EMIGRATION

Immigrants by country of last residence	1998	1999	2000
European Union (EU)	24,140	24,088	25,955
France	4,160	3,892	4,328
Germany	9,435	9,608	10,054
United Kingdom	3,587	3,604	3,844
Other European countries	49,585	69,650	86,477
Albania	19,973	28,838	32,181
Poland	3,012	3,165	5,086
Romania	7,119	10,986	19,710
Switzerland	5,027	5,507	5,687
former Yugoslavia	7,813	11,926	11,991
Africa	30,930	41,967	48,925
Morocco	12,984	19,526	20,344
Senegal	2,167	3,458	4,681
Middle East and Asia	30,406	25,362	36,513
China, People's Republic	7,224	6,119	9,451
India	3,162	3,607	4,759
Philippines	9,089	4,898	7,003
Sri Lanka	3,463	2,942	4,243
Americas	21,287	23,491	28,485
Peru	4,893	3,935	5,279
USA	3,619	3,631	4,055
Oceania	537	494	613
Total	156,885	185,052	226,968

Emigrants by country of destination	1998	1999	2000
European Union (EU)	19,844	28,595	24,493
France	2,848	4,052	3,394
Germany	9,128	13,372	11,413
United Kingdom	3,187	4,535	3,919
Other European countries	9,881	13,677	12,245
Switzerland	6,127	8,850	7,416
former Yugoslavia	1,102	1,163	1,310
Africa	3,185	4,441	4,149
Middle East and Asia	2,849	3,613	3,423
Americas	9,677	13,912	11,740
Argentina	2,141	3,188	2,685
Brazil	953	1,349	1,168
USA	3,555	4,973	4,156
Oceania	453	635	551
Total	45,889	64,873	56,601

Total immigrants: 444,566 in 2004; 326,673 in 2005; 297,640 in 2006.

Total emigrants: 64,849 in 2004; 65,029 in 2005; 75,230 in 2006.

EMPLOYMENT
('000)

	2004	2005	2006
Agriculture, hunting and forestry	965.9	943.2	955.2
Fishing	56.6	57.1	59.4
Mining and quarrying	41.0	40.9	39.6
Manufacturing	5,026.4	4,940.6	5,001.5
Electricity, gas and water	129.6	126.7	126.0
Construction	1,786.7	1,853.5	1,861.7
Wholesale and retail trade; repair of motor vehicles, motorcycles and personal and household goods	3,575.8	3,567.3	3,628.3
Restaurants and hotels	1,114.0	1,134.8	1,196.8
Transport and communications	1,211.5	1,213.1	1,219.7
Financial intermediation	605.3	609.2	622.6
Real estate, renting and business activities	2,813.6	2,889.1	2,973.5
Public administration and defence; compulsory social security	1,409.3	1,389.0	1,385.9
Education	1,606.1	1,605.8	1,634.7
Health and social work	1,551.0	1,572.9	1,603.4
Other community, social and personal service activities	1,007.0	1,023.4	1,099.7
Private households with employed persons	1,356.3	1,366.0	1,346.3
Total	24,256.1	24,332.6	24,754.3

Unemployed (July–September, '000 persons aged 15 years and over): 1,800 in 2004; 1,726 in 2005; 1,673 in 2006.

Health and Welfare

KEY INDICATORS

Total fertility rate (children per woman, 2005)	1.3
Under-5 mortality rate (per 1,000 live births, 2005)	4
HIV/AIDS (% of persons aged 15–49, 2005)	0.5
Physicians (per 1,000 head, 2004)	4.20
Hospital beds (per 1,000 head, 2004)	4.0
Health expenditure (2004): US $ per head (PPP)	2,414.4
Health expenditure (2004): % of GDP	8.7
Health expenditure (2004): public (% of total)	75.1
Human Development Index (2005): ranking	20
Human Development Index (2005): value	0.941

For sources and definitions, see explanatory note on p. vi.

Agriculture

PRINCIPAL CROPS
('000 metric tons)

	2004	2005	2006
Wheat	8,639	7,717	7,092
Rice (paddy)	1,523	1,413	1,448
Barley	1,169	1,214	1,282
Maize	11,368	10,428	9,671
Oats	338	429	395
Sorghum	215	185	222
Potatoes	1,822	1,754	1,783
Sugar beet	8,473	14,156	10,641
Almonds (in the shell)	105	118	113
Hazelnuts (Filberts)	143	89	142
Soybeans (Soya beans)	518	553	551
Olives	4,534	3,715	3,424
Sunflower seed	274	289	308
Cabbages	274	479	326
Artichokes	489	470	469
Lettuce	993	1,011	965
Tomatoes	7,683	7,187	6,351
Cauliflowers	461	431	438
Pumpkins, squash and gourds	495	488	512
Aubergines (Eggplants)	362	339	338
Chillies and green peppers	364	363	345
Dry onions	403	359	378
Green beans	207	219	191
Carrots	607	595	615
Watermelons	563	519	490
Cantaloupes and other melons	580	612	625
Oranges	2,105	2,261	2,356
Tangerines, mandarins, clementines and satsumas	611	586	590
Lemons and limes	583	579	583
Apples	2,136	2,192	2,113
Pears	877	926	907
Apricots	213	233	222
Sweet cherries	95	101	111
Peaches and nectarines	1,710	1,698	1,665
Plums	179	185	180
Strawberries	168	147	131
Grapes	8,692	8,554	8,326
Kiwi fruit	429	415	422
Tobacco	118	110*	120*

* FAO estimate.

Aggregate production ('000 metric tons, may include official, semi-official or estimated data): Total cereals 23,283 in 2004, 21,423 in 2005, 20,145 in 2006; Total roots and tubers 1,844 in 2004, 1,774 in 2005, 1,803 in 2006; Total vegetables (incl. melons) 16,351 in 2004, 15,994 in 2005, 15,132 in 2006; Total fruits (excl. melons) 18,001 in 2004, 18,134 in 2005, 17,812 in 2006.

Source: FAO.

ITALY

LIVESTOCK
('000 head, year ending September)

	2004	2005	2006
Horses	278	300*	300*
Asses, mules or hinnies	29	33*	33*
Cattle	6,504	6,304	6,255
Buffaloes	223	210	205
Pigs	9,157	8,972	9,200
Sheep	7,952	8,106	7,954
Goats	961	978	945
Chickens*	100,000	100,000	100,000
Turkeys*	25,000	26,000	26,000
Rabbits*	67,000	68,000	68,000

* FAO estimate(s).
Source: FAO.

LIVESTOCK PRODUCTS
('000 metric tons)

	2004	2005	2006
Cattle meat	1,145	1,102	1,109
Buffalo meat	3	6	1
Sheep meat	59	59	59
Pig meat	1,590	1,515	1,559
Horse meat	48	33	41
Chicken meat	704	695	628
Turkey meat	279	300	274
Rabbit meat*	222	225	225
Cows' milk	10,728	11,013	11,013
Buffaloes' milk	184	215	215*
Sheep's milk	612	554	554*
Goats' milk	42	49	49*
Hen eggs*	705	700	700

* FAO estimate(s).
Source: FAO.

Forestry

ROUNDWOOD REMOVALS
('000 cubic metres, excl. bark)

	2004	2005	2006
Sawlogs, veneer logs and logs for sleepers	1,448	1,340	1,246
Pulpwood	533	767	819
Other industrial wood	902	911	948
Fuel wood	5,814	5,673	5,606
Total	8,697	8,691	8,619

SAWNWOOD PRODUCTION
('000 cubic metres, incl. railway sleepers)

	2004	2005	2006
Coniferous (softwood)	753	790	948
Broadleaved (hardwood)	827	800	800
Total	1,580	1,590	1,748

Source: FAO.

Fishing
('000 metric tons, live weight)

	2003	2004	2005
Capture*	295.7	287.0	298.4
European anchovy	44.3	58.3	63.4
Mediterranean mussel	42.7	35.1	10.0*
Striped venus	41.8	37.4	14.9
Aquaculture	191.7	117.8	180.9
Rainbow trout	38.0	30.2	30.6
Mediterranean mussel	100.0	42.6	63.6
Clams	25.0	27.7	65.9
Total catch*	487.4	404.9	479.3

* FAO estimate(s).
Note: Figures exclude aquatic plants (FAO estimates, all capture, '000 metric tons): 2.0 in 2003; 1.9 in 2004; 1.6 in 2005.
Source: FAO.

Mining
('000 metric tons, unless otherwise indicated)

	2002	2003	2004
Crude petroleum	5,394.2	5,529.9	5,406.7
Natural methane gas (million cu m)	14,941.5	13,735.1	12,915.1
Manganese (metric tons)	867	763	714
Lead (metric tons)*	4,709	4,017	1,226
Gold (kilograms)*†	600	500	100
Fluorspar (Fluorite)	53.3	26.4	17.9
Barite (Barytes)	10.2	12.2	9.6
Feldspar	3,159.6	2,972.2	2,941.3
Bentonite	463.2	474.5	437.7
Kaolin	175.0	224.8	246.6
Salt: Marine†‡	600	600	600
Salt (rock)	3,343.0	2,922.3	2,876.5
Loam (rock)	13,561.3	14,090.5	13,821.1
Gypsum	1,531.5	1,783.9	1,615.3
Pumice†§	600	600	600
Pozzolan†	4,000	4,000	4,000
Talc and steatite	125.0	122.8	138.4

* Metal content of ores and concentrates.
† Source: US Geological Survey.
‡ Excluding production from Sardinia and Sicily, estimated at 200,000 metric tons per year.
§ Including pumiceous lapilli.

2005 ('000 metric tons, unless otherwise indicated): Natural methane gas (million cu m) 13,000; Gold (kilograms) 100; Marine salt 600; Pumice 600; Pozzolan 4,000 (Source: US Geological Survey).

ITALY

Industry

SELECTED PRODUCTS
('000 metric tons, unless otherwise indicated)

	2002	2003	2004
Wine (thousand hectolitres)*	44,604.1	44,086.1	53,135.2
Cotton yarn	231.8	212.0	193.9
Cotton woven fabrics	209.8	197.1	186.9
Wood pulp, mechanical	309.2	341.4	364.8
Newsprint†	175.1	182.0	193.0
Magazine print	780.0	830.0	945.1
Other printing and writing paper	2,104.5	2,091.2	2,164.7
Washing powders and detergents	1,982.0	2,123.8	2,174.5
Jet fuels	2,458.8	2,626.8	2,550.9
Benzene	20,999.1	20,759.4	n.a.
Motor gasoline	37,297.0	38,349.5	38,025.0
Naphthas	3,243.3	4,287.7	3,938.8
Gas-diesel oil	12,286.3	12,166.5	13,278.2
Bitumen	2,942.3	3,274.8	3,496.3
Coke	3,973.9	3,663.1	3,964.6
Tyres for road motor vehicles	258.6	265.4	278.9
Glass bottles and other containers of common glass	2,939.8	3,139.5	3,171.1
Cement	41,722.3	43,580.0	45,342.9
Steel	26,301.4	26,832.1	28,385.4
Rolled iron	24,165.6	25,608.6	28,710.6
Other iron and steel-finished manufactures	3,260.2	3,133.9	3,164.8
Refrigerators for household use ('000 units)	7,088.8	6,715.3	6,444.1
Washing machines for household use ('000 units)	8,884.0	9,666.8	9,679.9
Passenger motor cars ('000 units)	1,125.8	1,026.5	839.2
Lorries (Trucks) ('000 units)	266.4	267.4	283.9
Motorcycles, scooters, etc. ('000 units)	588.9	572.5	622.3
Bicycles ('000 units)	597.7	581.6	501.5
Hydroelectric power (million kWh)‡	47,262	44,277	n.a.
Thermoelectric power (million kWh)‡	231,069	242,784	n.a.
Other electric power (million kWh)‡	6,066	6,799	n.a.

* Provisional data.
† Source: FAO.
‡ Net production.

2005 ('000 metric tons): Newsprint 191.2; Mechanical wood pulp 376.5; Other printing and writing paper 3,289 (Source: FAO); Crude steel 28,913; Cement 38,000 (Source: US Geological Survey).

Finance

CURRENCY AND EXCHANGE RATES

Monetary Units
100 cent = 1 euro (€).

Sterling, Dollar and Euro Equivalents (31 December 2007)
£1 sterling = 1.3069 euros;
US $1 = 0.6793 euros;
€10 = £7.35 = $14.72.

Average Exchange Rate (euros per US $)
2005   0.8041
2006   0.7971
2007   0.7306

Note: The national currency was formerly the Italian lira (plural: lire). From the introduction of the euro, with Italian participation, on 1 January 1999, a fixed exchange rate of €1 = 1,936.27 lire was in operation. Euro notes and coins were introduced on 1 January 2002. The euro and local currency circulated alongside each other until 28 February, after which the euro became the sole legal tender.

STATE BUDGET
(€ million, consolidated account)

Revenue	2002	2003	2004
Direct taxation	178,964	178,098	184,175
Indirect taxation	185,116	187,345	195,207
Social security contributions	161,241	168,899	174,756
Other current revenue*	40,613	40,617	44,055
Capital revenue	5,586	23,481	13,007
Total	**571,520**	**598,440**	**611,200**

Expenditure	2002	2003	2004
Public services	238,921	253,035	260,063
General administration	29,277	31,795	30,862
Defence	13,611	16,411	16,435
Public order and safety	23,487	24,511	23,394
Economic affairs	15,947	16,991	17,977
Environmental protection	3,418	3,820	4,160
Housing and community amenities	3,103	3,365	3,622
Health	77,959	81,194	87,369
Recreation, culture and religion	5,260	5,429	5,767
Education	56,872	60,299	60,148
Social protection	9,982	10,220	10,329
Social security and assistance contributions	214,035	224,445	234,181
Other current expenditure	31,829	35,020	36,612
Capital expenditure	48,651	58,420	55,562
Total†	**533,436**	**570,920**	**586,418**

* Including foreign aid (€ million): 546 in 2002; 1,146 in 2003; 1,803 in 2004.
† Excluding interest payments (€ million): 72,547 in 2002; 69,275 in 2003; 68,434 in 2004.

Revised totals (€ million): *2003:* Revenue 601,852; Expenditure 579,374 (excl. interest payments 68,515). *2004:* Revenue 619,024; Expenditure 600,923 (excl. interest payments 65,753).

2005: *Revenue:* Total current revenue 625,695 (Taxes 392,603); Total capital revenue 5,849; Total revenue 631,544. *Expenditure:* Total current expenditure 633,038; Other (capital account) expenditure 58,029; Total expenditure 691,067.

2006: *Revenue:* Total current revenue 675,582 (Taxes 431,914); Total capital revenue 4,472; Total revenue 680,054. *Expenditure:* Total current expenditure 656,577; Other (capital account) expenditure 88,981; Total expenditure 745,558.

2007: *Revenue:* Total current revenue 719,632 (Taxes 459,588); Total capital revenue 4,614; Total revenue 724,246. *Expenditure:* Total current expenditure 684,932; Other (capital account) expenditure 68,493; Total expenditure 753,425.

INTERNATIONAL RESERVES
(US $ million at 31 December)

	2004	2005	2006
Gold*	34,527	40,439	50,112
IMF special drawing rights	145	229	272
Reserve position in IMF	3,703	1,758	977
Foreign exchange	24,011	23,528	24,413
Total	**62,386**	**65,954**	**75,774**

* Valued at market-related prices.

Source: IMF, *International Financial Statistics*.

ITALY

MONEY SUPPLY
(€ '000 million at 31 December)

	2004	2005	2006
Currency issued*	86.79	97.89	108.70
Demand deposits at banking institutions	549.46	593.89	633.14

* Currency put into circulation by the Banca d'Italia was (€ '000 million): 86.79 in 2004; 97.89 in 2005; 108.70 in 2006.

Source: IMF, *International Financial Statistics*.

COST OF LIVING
(Consumer Price Index; base: 1995 = 100)

	2003	2004	2005
Food (incl. non-alcoholic beverages)	119.6	122.2	122.2
Alcohol and tobacco	133.8	144.5	154.4
Rent and utilities	127.1	129.6	136.0
Clothing (incl. footwear)	124.4	127.2	129.2
Household goods	118.3	120.6	122.7
Health services	121.7	123.2	122.1
Transport	121.4	125.2	130.8
Communications	90.8	85.0	81.1
Recreation, entertainment and culture	115.9	117.9	119.0
Education	122.9	125.7	130.1
Hotels, restaurants and public services	131.8	136.0	139.2
All items (incl. others)	122.0	124.7	127.1

All items (base: 2000 = 100): 110.5 in 2004; 112.4 in 2005; 114.7 in 2006 (Source: ILO).

NATIONAL ACCOUNTS
(€ million at current prices)

National Income and Product

	2004	2005	2006
Compensation of employees	555,481	581,122	607,699
Operating surplus and mixed income (net)	443,413	431,729	432,561
Domestic factor incomes	998,894	1,012,851	1,040,260
Consumption of fixed capital	211,912	222,223	231,672
Gross domestic product (GDP) at factor cost	1,121,806	1,235,074	1,271,932
Taxes on production and imports	199,129	206,272	222,251
Less Subsidies	19,396	18,298	18,782
GDP in market prices	1,390,539	1,423,048	1,475,401
Net primary income received from abroad	−8,021	−6,210	−4,017
Gross national product	1,382,518	1,416,838	1,471,384
Less Consumption of fixed capital	211,912	222,223	231,672
Net national income	1,170,606	1,194,615	1,239,712
Net current transfers from abroad	−9,006	−9,881	−13,198
Net national disposable income	1,161,600	1,184,734	1,226,515

Expenditure on the Gross Domestic Product

	2005	2006	2007
Government final consumption expenditure	296,027	305,272	303,950
Private final consumption expenditure	834,264	869,209	906,331
Changes in inventories	−1,191	3,672	4,485
Acquisitions, less disposals, of valuables	2,377	2,754	2,199
Gross fixed capital formation	292,621	306,605	323,281
Total domestic expenditure	1,424,098	1,487,512	1,540,246
Exports of goods and services	370,731	410,732	448,291
Less Imports of goods and services	371,780	422,843	452,996
GDP in market prices	1,423,048	1,475,401	1,535,540
GDP at constant 2000 prices	1,232,773	1,255,848	1,284,919

Gross Domestic Product by Economic Activity

	2004	2005	2006
Agriculture, hunting and forestry	30,937	28,712	28,728
Fishing	1,507	1,507	1,588
Mining and quarrying	4,500	5,014	4,805
Manufacturing	227,095	223,315	229,372
Electricity, gas and water supply	24,044	24,267	25,166
Construction	70,831	74,396	77,254
Wholesale and retail trade; repair of motor vehicles, motorcycles and personal and household goods	145,306	146,460	146,595
Hotels and restaurants	45,460	47,368	49,316
Transport and communications	93,528	95,401	98,127
Financial intermediation	55,867	57,189	59,743
Real estate, renting and business activities	263,617	272,578	281,618
Public administration and defence; compulsory social security	77,069	80,318	84,208
Education	57,849	60,383	61,612
Health and social work	66,836	70,211	74,142
Other community, social and personal service activities	35,040	36,002	37,354
Private households with employed persons	11,319	11,954	12,304
Sub-total	1,210,806	1,235,074	1,271,931
Net taxes on products	179,733	187,974	203,469
GDP in market prices	1,390,539	1,423,048	1,475,401

2007 (€ million): Agriculture, hunting, forestry and fishing 27,926; Industry 370,806; Services 973,102; *Sub-total* 1,371,833; Net taxes on products 163,707; *GDP in market prices* 1,535,540.

ITALY

BALANCE OF PAYMENTS
(US $ million)

	2004	2005	2006
Exports of goods f.o.b.	352,171	372,378	417,054
Imports of goods f.o.b.	−341,278	−371,814	−428,744
Trade balance	10,893	564	−11,690
Exports of services	84,524	89,204	98,581
Imports of services	−83,246	−90,046	−100,409
Balance on goods and services	12,172	−277	−13,519
Other income received	53,118	61,288	72,350
Other income paid	−71,457	−78,423	−89,468
Balance on goods, services and income	−6,168	−17,413	−30,637
Current transfers received	21,833	24,017	22,021
Current transfers paid	−32,120	−36,044	−38,696
Current balance	−16,456	−29,441	−47,312
Capital account (net)	2,172	1,239	2,393
Direct investment abroad	−19,143	−40,714	−42,407
Direct investment from abroad	16,772	19,587	38,884
Portfolio investment assets	−26,393	−108,077	−48,503
Portfolio investment liabilities	58,553	164,399	115,307
Financial derivatives liabilities	2,286	3,129	−591
Other investment assets	−47,937	−100,109	−142,315
Other investment liabilities	24,288	86,834	123,223
Net errors and omissions	3,014	2,123	754
Overall balance	−2,844	−1,030	−567

Source: IMF, *International Financial Statistics*.

External Trade

Note: Figures refer to the trade of Italy, San Marino and the Vatican City.

PRINCIPAL COMMODITIES
(distribution by SITC, US $ million)

Imports c.i.f.	2002	2003	2004
Food and live animals	17,912	22,449	26,249
Crude materials (inedible) except fuels	12,101	13,658	16,326
Mineral fuels, lubricants, etc.	21,956	26,698	33,725
Petroleum, petroleum products, etc.	18,553	22,694	28,443
Crude petroleum oils, etc.	14,351	18,103	23,590
Chemicals and related products	31,875	38,869	47,328
Medicinal and pharmaceutical products	8,754	10,822	13,013
Basic manufactures	36,219	42,772	56,211
Iron and steel	8,146	10,750	16,164
Machinery and transport equipment	82,101	96,151	114,749
General industrial machinery, equipment and parts	8,915	11,000	13,621
Office machines and automatic data-processing equipment	7,682	8,470	9,648
Telecommunications and sound equipment	7,570	9,072	13,137
Other electrical machinery, apparatus, etc.	11,030	13,045	14,962
Road vehicles and parts*	29,836	36,527	42,444
Passenger motor cars (excl. buses)	20,720	26,042	30,112
Miscellaneous manufactured articles	26,799	32,327	38,728
Clothing and accessories (excl. footwear)	7,570	9,430	11,394
Total (incl. others)	246,843	297,462	355,225

Exports f.o.b.	2002	2003	2004
Food and live animals	12,124	14,509	16,535
Chemicals and related products	26,349	30,710	36,081
Medicinal and pharmaceutical products	8,968	10,254	11,272
Basic manufactures	51,309	59,640	74,700
Textile yarn, fabrics, etc.	12,134	13,817	15,526
Non-metallic mineral manufactures	8,308	9,390	10,926
Iron and steel	6,967	8,637	13,684
Machinery and transport equipment	95,184	111,099	134,359
Machinery specialized for particular industries	16,313	19,370	22,401
General industrial machinery and equipment	22,138	27,372	33,256
Electrical machinery, apparatus, etc. (excl. office machines and telecommunications equipment)	14,921	17,404	20,685
Road vehicles and parts*	19,450	24,053	27,874
Motor vehicle parts and accessories*	7,603	9,819	11,949
Miscellaneous manufactured articles	53,222	60,249	68,603
Furniture and parts	8,810	9,896	11,379
Clothing and accessories (excl. footwear)	14,647	16,632	18,670
Total (incl. others)	254,501	299,510	353,492

* Data on parts exclude tyres, engines and electrical parts.

Source: UN, *International Trade Statistics Yearbook*.

2005 (€ million): *Imports*: Agriculture and fishing 9,321; Energy-producing minerals 43,693; Food, beverages and tobacco 20,569; Textiles and clothing 15,305; Leather and leather products 6,544; Wood and wood products 3,578; Paper and paper products, printing and publishing 6,664; Refined oil products 5,593; Chemicals and man-made fibres 41,142; Rubber and plastics 6,353; No-metal mineral ore products 3,182; Metals and metal products 31,938; Machinery and mechanical equipment 21,690; Electric and precision instruments 38,389; Transportation means 41,149; Other manufactured products 5,133; Electricity, gas and water 2,175; Other products 6,875; Total 309,292. *Exports*: Agriculture and fishing 4,130; Energy-producing minerals 1,003; Food, beverages and tobacco 16,497; Textiles and clothing 26,161; Leather and leather products 12,696; Wood and wood products 1,364; Paper and paper products, printing and publishing 6,399; Refined oil products 9,772; Chemicals and man-made fibres 30,278; Rubber and plastics 11,207; No-metal mineral ore products 8,874; Metals and metal products 30,195; Machinery and mechanical equipment 59,690; Electric and precision instruments 27,571; Transportation means 32,433; Other manufactured products 15,118; Electricity, gas and water 63; Other products 6,475; Total 299,923.

2006 (€ million): *Imports*: Agriculture and fishing 9,689; Energy-producing minerals 55,250; Food, beverages and tobacco 21,886; Textiles and clothing 17,204; Leather and leather products 7,445; Wood and wood products 3,960; Paper and paper products, printing and publishing 6,937; Refined oil products 6,892; Chemicals and man-made fibres 44,400; Rubber and plastics 6,857; No-metal mineral ore products 3,361; Metals and metal products 43,068; Machinery and mechanical equipment 23,452; Electric and precision instruments 39,941; Transportation means 43,173; Other manufactured products 5,671; Electricity, gas and water 2,168; Other products 6,976; Total 348,348. *Exports*: Agriculture and fishing 4,312; Energy-producing minerals 1,083; Food, beverages and tobacco 17,672; Textiles and clothing 27,184; Leather and leather products 13,472; Wood and wood products 1,480; Paper and paper products, printing and publishing 6,644; Refined oil products 10,800; Chemicals and man-made fibres 32,509; Rubber and plastics 11,959; No-metal mineral ore products 9,467; Metals and metal products 37,382; Machinery and mechanical equipment 66,223; Electric and precision instruments 29,701; Transportation means 35,162; Other manufactured products 15,878; Electricity, gas and water 149; Other products 5,915; Total 326,992.

ITALY

PRINCIPAL TRADING PARTNERS
(€ million)*

Imports c.i.f.	2003	2004	2005†
China, People's Republic	9,553	11,828	14,131
France	29,951	31,278	30,309
Germany	47,521	51,319	52,516
Japan	5,281	5,520	4,976
Russia	8,230	9,716	11,789
Spain	12,729	13,317	12,721
United Kingdom	12,708	12,294	12,141
USA	10,272	9,991	10,716
Total (incl. others)	262,998	285,634	305,686

Exports f.o.b.	2003	2004	2005†
China, People's Republic	3,850	4,448	4,065
France	33,033	35,230	36,188
Germany	37,233	38,761	38,768
Japan	4,333	4,333	4,541
Russia	3,847	4,963	6,064
Spain	18,911	20,727	21,936
United Kingdom	18,686	20,153	19,032
USA	21,970	22,368	23,940
Total (incl. others)	264,616	284,413	295,739

* Imports by country of production; exports by country of consignment.
† Provisional figures.

Transport

STATE RAILWAYS
(traffic)

	2003	2004	2005
Passenger journeys (million)	497.9	504.4	516.8
Passenger-km (million)	45,222	45,577	46,144
Freight carried ('000 metric tons)	82,107	83,087	n.a.
Freight ton-km (million)	22,458	23,271	n.a.

ROAD TRAFFIC
(vehicles in use at 31 December)

	2002	2003	2004
Passenger motor cars	33,706,153	34,310,446	33,973,147
Buses and coaches	91,716	92,701	92,874
Trucks (lorries)	3,751,699	3,933,930	4,015,612
Tractors	132,622	139,402	142,413
Motorcycles (incl. sidecars)	4,405,867	4,746,698	4,917,383

SHIPPING
Merchant Fleet
(registered at 31 December)

	2004	2005	2006
Number of vessels	1,516	1,539	1,566
Displacement ('000 grt)	10,956	11,616	12,571

Source: Lloyd's Register-Fairplay, *World Fleet Statistics*.

International Sea-borne Traffic

	2002	2003	2004
Goods loaded ('000 metric tons)	73,402	74,479	79,222
Goods unloaded ('000 metric tons)	260,986	266,914	270,811
Passengers embarked ('000)	2,841	2,863	3,041
Passengers disembarked ('000)	2,873	2,831	3,187

Source: Ministry of Transport.

CIVIL AVIATION
(traffic on scheduled and charter services)

	2002	2003	2004
Passengers carried ('000):			
domestic	45,221	49,145	49,026
international	45,777	50,587	57,963
Freight carried ('000 metric tons):*			
domestic	165.5	164.4	135.5
international	570.2	598.8	684.6

* Includes mail.
Source: Ministry of Transport.

Tourism

TOURIST ARRIVALS BY COUNTRY OF ORIGIN
(arrivals in registered accommodation establishments)

	2003	2004	2005
Austria	1,718,364	1,731,915	1,697,571
Belgium	811,911	814,680	833,335
France	2,746,459	2,915,678	2,936,714
Germany	8,693,108	8,586,149	8,504,489
Japan	1,603,479	1,656,214	1,657,688
Netherlands	1,329,544	1,342,951	1,444,923
Spain	1,242,349	1,483,202	1,606,237
Switzerland-Liechtenstein	1,533,932	1,550,648	1,611,946
United Kingdom	2,781,776	2,933,131	3,184,908
USA	3,289,349	4,072,949	4,334,644
Total (incl. others)	35,006,124	36,715,739	38,126,691

Tourism receipts (US $ million, incl. passenger transport): 32,592 in 2003; 37,872 in 2004; 38,264 in 2005 (Source: World Tourism Organization).

Communications Media

	2004	2005	2006
Telephones ('000 main lines in use)	25,957	25,049	25,049
Mobile cellular telephones ('000 in use)	62,750	71,500	71,500
Personal computers ('000 in use)	18,150	18,040	n.a.
Internet users ('000)	27,170	28,000	28,855
Broadband subscribers ('000)	4,725	6,822	8,639

Book production (number of titles, first editions): 34,496 in 2003.

Facsimile machines ('000 in use): 1,800 in 1997.

Television receivers ('000 in use): 28,300 in 2000.

Radio receivers ('000 in use): 50,500 in 1997.

Daily newspapers (2004): Titles 96; Average circulation 8,017,000.

Non-daily newspapers (1995): Titles 274; Average circulation 2,132,000.

Sources: mainly UNESCO Institute for Statistics; UN, *Statistical Yearbook*; International Telecommunication Union.

Education

(state education, 2005/06, unless otherwise indicated)

	Schools	Teachers	Students
Pre-primary	13,614	84,130	979,301
Primary	16,100	248,028	2,545,491
Secondary:			
Scuola Media	7,055	171,045	1,668,184
Scuola Secondaria Superiore	5,039	233,161	2,521,581
of which:			
Technical	1,776	83,967	892,534*
Professional	1,418	46,103	536,845*
Art Licei and institutes	262	9,727	96,996*
Classical, linguistic and scientific Licei	1,583	68,375	952,862*
Higher†	74	57,402	1,820,221‡

* 2004/05 figures.
† Includes private institutions.
‡ Undergraduates only.

Source: Ufficio di Statistica, Ministero dell'Istruzione, dell'Università e della Ricerca.

Adult literacy rate (UNESCO estimates): 98.4% (males 98.8%; females 98.0%) in 2001 (Source: UNESCO Institute for Statistics).

Directory

The Constitution

The Constitution of the Italian Republic was approved by the Constituent Assembly on 22 December 1947 and came into force on 1 January 1948 (and was subsequently amended on numerous occasions). The fundamental principles are declared in Articles 1–12, as follows:

Italy is a democratic republic based on the labour of the people.

The Republic recognizes and guarantees as inviolable the rights of its citizens, either as individuals or in a community, and it expects, in return, the fulfilment of political, economic and social obligations.

All citizens shall enjoy equal status and shall be regarded as equal before the law.

It shall be the function of the Republic to remove the economic and social inequalities which, by restricting the liberty of the individual, impede the full development of the human personality, thereby reducing the effective participation of the citizen in the political, economic and social life of the country.

The Republic, while remaining one and indivisible, shall recognize and promote local autonomy, fostering the greatest possible decentralization in those services which are administered by the State.

The State and the Catholic Church shall be sovereign and independent, each in its own sphere. Their relations shall be governed by the Lateran Pact, and any modification in the pact agreed upon by both parties shall not necessitate any revision of the Constitution.

All religious denominations shall have equal liberty before the law.

The judicial system of the Italian Republic shall be in conformity with the generally recognized practice of international law. The legal rights of foreigners in the country shall be regulated by law in accordance with international practice.

Italy repudiates war as a means of resolving international disputes. Italy accepts the limitations of sovereignty necessary for the preservation of peace and justice between nations. To that end, it will support and promote international organizations.

The Constitution is further divided into Parts I and II, in which are set forth respectively the rights and responsibilities of the citizen and the administration of the Republic.

PART I

Civic Clauses

Section I (Articles 13–28). The liberty of the individual is inviolable and no form of detention, restriction or inspection is permitted unless it be for juridical purposes and in accordance with the provisions of the law. The domicile of a person is likewise inviolable, except according to the provisions of the law. Furthermore, all citizens shall enjoy freedom of movement, and to leave and to return to the country. Right of public meeting, if peaceful and without arms, is guaranteed. Secret organizations pursuing, either directly or indirectly, political aims through military organizations are, however, prohibited.

Freedom in the practice of religious faith is guaranteed.

The Constitution further guarantees complete freedom of thought, speech and writing, and lays down that the Press shall be entirely free from all control or censorship.

The death penalty is prohibited. The accused shall be considered 'not guilty' until otherwise proven.

Ethical and Social Clauses

Section II (Articles 29–34). The Republic regards the family as the fundamental basis of society. The Republic shall provide economic assistance for the family, with special regard to large families, and shall make provision for maternity, infancy and youth, subject always to the liberty and freedom of choice of the individuals.

Education, the arts and science shall be free, the function of the State being merely to indicate the general lines of instruction. Private entities and individuals shall have the right to conduct educational institutions without assistance from the State. Institutions of higher culture, universities and academies shall be autonomous within the limitations prescribed by the law.

Education is available freely to all and is obligatory for at least eight years. Higher education for students of proven merit shall be aided by scholarships and other allowances made by the Republic.

Economic Clauses

Section III (Articles 35–47). The Republic shall safeguard the right to work, and shall promote agreement and co-operation with international organizations in matters pertaining to the regulation of labour and the rights of workers. The rights of Italian workers abroad shall be protected.

All workers shall be entitled to remuneration proportionate to the quantity and quality of their work, and in any case shall be ensured of sufficient to provide freedom and a dignified standard of life for themselves and their families.

Women shall have the same rights and, for equal work, the same remuneration as men.

All citizens have the right to sickness, unemployment and disability maintenance.

Liberty to organize in trade unions is guaranteed, provided they are organized on a democratic basis. The right to strike is admitted within the limitations of the relevant legislation.

Private enterprise is permitted in so far as it does not run counter to the well-being of society nor constitute a danger to security, freedom and human dignity.

Ownership of private property is permitted and guaranteed within the limitations laid down by the law regarding the acquisition, extent

ITALY *Directory*

and enjoyment of private property. Inheritance and testamentary bequests shall be regulated by law.

Limitation is placed by law on private ownership of land and on its use, with a view to its best exploitation for the benefit of the community.

The Republic recognizes the value of mutual co-operation and the right of the workers to participate in management.

Political Clauses

Section IV (Articles 48–54). The electorate comprises all citizens, who have attained their majority. Voting is free, equal and secret, and its exercise is a civic duty. All citizens have the right to associate freely together in political parties, and may also petition Parliament to legislate as may be deemed necessary.

Defence of one's country is a sacred duty of the citizen, and military service is obligatory within the limits prescribed by law. The organization of the armed forces shall be imbued with the spirit of democracy.

All citizens must contribute to the public expenditure, in proportion to their capacity.

All citizens must be loyal to the Republic and observe the terms of the law and the Constitution.

PART II

Sections I, II and III (Articles 55–100). These sections are devoted to a detailed exposition of the Legislature and legislative procedure of the Republic.

Parliament shall comprise two Chambers: the Camera dei Deputati (Chamber of Deputies); and the Senato della Repubblica (Senate of the Republic).

The 630 deputies of the Camera dei Deputati are elected by direct universal suffrage, and the seats are allocated by proportional representation.

The 315 elective members of the Senato are elected on a regional basis. The seats are allocated by proportional representation.

Both Chambers are elected for five years.

The term of each House cannot be extended except by law and only in the case of war.

The President of the Republic must be a citizen of at least 50 years of age and in full enjoyment of all civic and political rights. The person shall be elected for a period of seven years.

The Government shall consist of the President of the Council and the Ministers (Consiglio dei Ministri) who themselves shall form the Council. The President of the Council, or Prime Minister, shall be nominated by the President of the Republic, who shall also appoint the ministers on the recommendation of the Prime Minister.

Section IV (Articles 101–113). Sets forth the judicial system and procedure.

Section V (Articles 114–133). Deals with the division of the Republic into regions, provinces and communes, and sets forth the limits and extent of autonomy enjoyed by the regions. Under Article 131 the regions are enumerated as follows: Piemonte (Piedmont); Valle d'Aosta; Lombardia (Lombardy); Trentino-Alto Adige; Veneto; Friuli-Venezia Giulia; Liguria; Emilia-Romagna; Toscana (Tuscany); Umbria; Marche; Lazio; Abruzzo; Molise; Campania; Puglia; Basilicata; Calabria; Sicilia (Sicily); and Sardegna (Sardinia).

Each region shall be administered by a Regional Council, in which is vested the legislative power and which may make suggestions for legislation to the Chambers, and the Giunta regionale, which holds the executive power

The regions of Trentino-Alto Adige, Sicilia, Friuli-Venezia Giulia, Sardegna and Valle d'Aosta have a wider form of autonomy, based on constitutional legislation specially adapted to their regional characteristics.

The final articles provide for the establishment of the Corte Costituzionale to deal with constitutional questions and any revisions that may be found necessary after the Constitution has come into operation.

The Government

HEAD OF STATE

President of the Republic: GIORGIO NAPOLITANO (took office 15 May 2006).

COUNCIL OF MINISTERS
(March 2008)

On 24 January 2008 the Prime Minister, Romano Prodi, announced the resignation of his Government, following its defeat in a vote of confidence in the Senato della Repubblica. Prodi agreed to remain in office until a new government could be formed. Following the collapse, in early February, of talks over the formation of a cross-party interim administration, President Giorgio Napolitano dissolved the two houses of Parliament and called a general election. At the election, conducted on 13 and 14 April 2008, the right-wing Popolo della Libertà (PdL) and its allies, the Lega Nord and the Movimento per l'Autonomia, won a majority of seats in both houses. The leader of the PdL, the former Prime Minister Silvio Berlusconi, was to form a new Government, which was expected to take office in early May.

Prime Minister: ROMANO PRODI.

Deputy Prime Minister and Minister of Foreign Affairs: MASSIMO D'ALEMA (DS).

Deputy Prime Minister and Minister of Cultural Assets and Activities: FRANCESCO RUTELLI (DL).

Minister of Internal Affairs: GIULIANO AMATO (Ind.).

Minister of Justice: LUIGI SCOTTI (Ind.).

Minister of the Economy and Finance: TOMMASO PADOA-SCHIOPPA (Ind.).

Minister of Economic Development: PIERLUIGI BERSANI (DS).

Minister of Universities and Research: FABIO MUSSI (DS).

Minister of Education: BEPPE FIORONI (DL).

Minister of International Trade and Minister without Portfolio for European Policies: EMMA BONINO (La Rosa nel Pugno).

Minister of Labour and Social Security: CESARE DAMIANO (DS).

Minister of Social Solidarity: PAOLO FERRERO (PRC).

Minister of Defence: ARTURO PARISI (DL).

Minister of Agriculture Policies, Food and Forestry: PAOLO DE CASTRO (Ind.).

Minister of the Environment and Land Management: ALFONSO PECORARO SCANIO (I Verdi).

Minister of Infrastructure: ANTONIO DI PIETRO (Italia dei Valori).

Minister of Transport: ALESSANDRO BIANCHI (PdCI).

Minister of Health: LIVIA TURCO (DS).

Minister of Communications: PAOLO GENTILONI (DL).

Minister without Portfolio for Reform and Innovation within Public Administration: LUIGI NICOLAIS (DS).

Minister without Portfolio for Implementation of Government Programmes: GIULIO SANTAGATA (DL).

Minister without Portfolio for the Family: ROSY BINDI (DL).

Minister without Portfolio for Regional Affairs and Local Autonomy: LINDA LANZILLOTTA (DL).

Minister without Portfolio for Rights and Equal Opportunities: BARBARA POLLASTRINI (DS).

Minister without Portfolio for Youth and Sport: GIOVANNA MELANDRI (DS).

Minister without Portfolio for Relations with Parliament and Institutional Reform: VANNINO CHITI (DS).

MINISTRIES

Office of the President: Palazzo del Quirinale, 00187 Roma; tel. (06) 46991; fax (06) 46993125; internet www.quirinale.it.

Office of the Prime Minister: Palazzo Chigi, Piazza Colonna 370, 00187 Roma; tel. (06) 67791; e-mail redazione.web@governo.it; internet www.governo.it.

Ministry of Agriculture Policies, Food and Forestry: Via XX Settembre 20, 00187 Roma; tel. (06) 46651; fax (06) 4742314; e-mail stampa@politicheagricole.it; internet www.politicheagricole.it.

Ministry of Communications: Viale America 201, 00144 Roma; tel. (06) 54442100; fax (06) 54440014; e-mail urpcom@comunicazioni.it; internet www.comunicazioni.it.

Ministry of Cultural Assets and Activities: Via del Collegio Romano 27, 00186 Roma; tel. (06) 67231; fax (06) 6798441; e-mail urp@beniculturali.it; internet www.beniculturali.it.

Ministry of Defence: Palazzo Baracchini, Via XX Settembre 8, 00187 Roma; tel. (06) 46911; e-mail pi@smd.difesa.it; internet www.difesa.it.

Ministry of Economic Development: Via Veneto 33, 00187 Roma; tel. (06) 420434000; fax (06) 47887964; e-mail segreteria.ministro@attivitaproduttive.gov.it; internet www.sviluppoeconomico.gov.it.

Ministry of the Economy and Finance: Via XX Settembre 97, 00187 Roma; tel. (06) 476111; fax (06) 5910993; e-mail pubblicazione.sito@tesoro.it; internet www.mef.gov.it.

Ministry of Education: Viale Trastevere 76A, 00153 Roma; tel. (06) 58491; fax (06) 5803381; e-mail uffstampa@istruzione.it; internet www.istruzione.it.

Ministry of the Environment and Land Management: Via Cristoforo Colombo 44, 00147 Roma; tel. (06) 57221; fax (06) 5728513; e-mail segr.ufficiostampa@minambiente.it; internet www.minambiente.it.

ITALY

Ministry of Foreign Affairs: Piazzale della Farnesina 1, 00194 Roma; tel. (06) 36911; fax (06) 36918899; e-mail relazioni.pubblico@esteri.it; internet www.esteri.it.

Ministry of Health: Lungotevere Ripa 1, 00153 Roma; tel. (06) 59941; fax (06) 59945320; e-mail ufficiostampa@sanita.it; internet www.ministerosalute.it.

Ministry of Infrastructure: Piazzale Porta Pia 1, 00198 Roma; tel. (06) 44121; fax (06) 8415693; e-mail ufficio.stampa@infrastrutturetrasporti.it; internet www.infrastrutturetrasporti.it.

Ministry of Internal Affairs: Piazzale del Viminale, Via Agostino Depretis 7, 00184 Roma; tel. (06) 4651; internet www.interno.it.

Ministry of International Trade: Viale Boston 25, 00144 Roma; tel. (06) 59931; e-mail urp@mincomes.it; internet www.mincomes.it.

Ministry of Justice: Via Arenula 71, 00186 Roma; tel. (06) 68851; fax (06) 68897342; e-mail ufficio.stampa@giustizia.it; internet www.giustizia.it.

Ministry of Labour and Social Security: Via Veneto 56, 00187 Roma; tel. (06) 481611; e-mail centrodicontatto@lavoro.gov.it; internet www.lavoro.gov.it.

Ministry of Social Solidarity: Via Fornova 8, 00192 Roma; tel. (06) 36754600; e-mail stampa@solidarietasociale.gov.it; internet www.solidarietasociale.gov.it.

Ministry of Transport: Piazzale della Croce Rossa 1, 00187 Roma; tel. (06) 59083000; fax (06) 44267135; e-mail segreteria.bianchi@trasporti.it; internet www.trasporti.it.

Ministry of Universities and Research: Piazzale Kennedy 20, 00144 Roma; tel. (06) 58491; e-mail ufficio.stampa@miur.it; internet www.miur.it.

President

The President of the Republic is elected by the members of both parliamentary chambers, in addition to representations (Grand Electors) of each administrative region, and is required to receive the support of at least two-thirds of votes cast in the first three rounds of voting, or a simple majority thereafter. GIORGIO NAPOLITANO was elected President in a fourth round of voting conducted on 10 May 2006, receiving 543 votes (from 1,000 voters present at the session).

Legislature

PARLAMENTO
(Parliament)

Camera dei Deputati
(Chamber of Deputies)

Palazzo di Montecitorio, Roma; tel. (06) 67603316; e-mail dlwebmast@camera.it; internet www.camera.it.

President: GIANFRANCO FINI (PdL).

General Election, 13 and 14 April 2008

Parties/Alliances	Total seats
Popolo della Libertà*	276
Partito Democratico†	217
Lega Nord*	60
Unione di Centro (UdC)	36
Italia dei Valori—Lista Di Pietro†	29
Movimento per l'Autonomia*	8
Südtiroler Volkspartei	2
Autonomie Liberté Démocratie	1
Movimento Associativo Italiani all'Estero	1
Total	**630**

*The Popolo della Libertà, Lega Nord and the Movimento per l'Autonomia contested the election in alliance.
†The Partito Democratico and Italia dei Valori—Lista Di Pietro contested the election in alliance.

Senato
(Senate)

Piazza Madama, 00186 Roma; tel. (06) 67061; e-mail infopoint@senato.it; internet www.senato.it.

President: RENATO SCHIFANI (PdL).

General Election, 13 and 14 April 2008

Parties/Alliances	Elective seats
Popolo della Libertà*	147
Partito Democratico†	118
Lega Nord*	25
Italia dei Valori—Lista Di Pietro†	14
Unione di Centro (UdC)	3
Movimento per l'Autonomia*	2
Südtiroler Volkspartei (SVP)	2
SVP—Insieme per le Autonomie	2
Vallée d'Aoste	1
Movimento Associativo Italiani all'Estero	1
Total‡	**315**

*The Popolo della Libertà, the Lega Nord and the Movimento per l'Autonomia contested the election in alliance.
†The Partito Democratico and Italia dei Valori—Lista Di Pietro contested the election in alliance.
‡In addition to the 315 elected members, there are seven life members.

Political Organizations

PRINCIPAL COALITIONS

Popolo della Libertà (PdL) (People of Freedom): Roma; e-mail tuonome@popoladellaliberta.net; internet www.popolodellaliberta.it; f. 2007; successor to Casa delle Libertà; centre-right coalition; mem. orgs include Forza Italia, Alleanza Nazionale, Nuovo Partito Socialista Italiano, Partito Repubblicano Italiano, Democrazia Cristiana per le Autonomie and Partito Pensionati; contested April 2008 general election in alliance with the Lega Nord and the Movimento per l'Autonomia; Leader SILVIO BERLUSCONI.

La Sinistra—L'Arcobaleno (The Left—The Rainbow): Via Veneto 54B, Roma; tel. (06) 42016329; fax (06) 42020316; e-mail info@sinistrarcobaleno.it; internet www.sinistrarcobaleno.it; f. 2007; left-wing coalition; mem. orgs include Federazione dei Verdi, Partito della Rifondazione Comunista, Partito dei Comunisti Italiani and Sinistra Democratica; Leader FAUSTO BERTINOTTI.

Unione di Centro (UdC) (Union of the Centre): Roma; internet www.unionedicentro.it; f. 2008; coalition includes Unione dei Democratici Cristiani e di Centro and Rosa Bianca; Leader PIER FERDINAND CASINI.

NATIONAL PARTIES

Alleanza Nazionale (AN) (National Alliance): Via della Scrofa 39, 00186 Roma; tel. (06) 68817300; fax (06) 6892953; e-mail internet@alleanzanazionale.it; internet www.alleanzanazionale.it; f. 1994; in early 1995 absorbed the neo-fascist Movimento Sociale Italiano-Destra Nazionale (MSI-DN, f. 1946); mem. of Popolo della Libertà; Sec.-Gen. GIANFRANCO FINI; 400,000 mems.

Azione Sociale: Viale Regina Margherita 239, 00198 Roma; tel. (06) 44251916; fax (06) 45442757; e-mail info@azionesociale.it; internet www.azionesociale.net; f. 2003 as Libertà di Azione following split from the Alleanza Nazionale; Nat. Sec. ALESSANDRA MUSSOLINI.

Decidere! (Decide!): Roma; tel. (06) 98264450; fax (06) 98264451; internet www.decidere.net; f. 2007; mem. of the Popolo della Libertà; Pres. DANIEL CAPEZZONE.

Democrazia Cristiana per le Autonomie (DC): Piazza del Gesù 46, 00186 Roma; tel. (06) 6793662; e-mail info@lademocraziacristiana.it; internet www.lademocraziacristiana.it; the DC was disbanded in 1994, following a period of dominance in Italian politics since 1946; refounded 2005 by former mems of UDC; mem. of Popolo della Libertà; Sec. GIANFRANCO ROTONDI.

Federazione dei Liberali Italiani (Federation of Italian Liberals): Via Laurina 20, 00187 Roma; tel. and fax (06) 32110200; e-mail info@liberali.it; internet www.liberali.it; Pres. RAFAELLO MORELLI.

Federazione dei Verdi (I Verdi) (Green Party): Via Antonio Salandra 6, 00187 Roma; tel. (06) 4203061; fax (06) 42004600; e-mail federazione@verdi.it; internet www.verdi.it; f. 1986; mem. of La Sinistra—L'Arcobaleno; advocates environmentalist and anti-nuclear policies; branch of the European Green movement; Pres. ALFONSO PECORARO SCANIO.

orza Italia (FI) (Come on, Italy!): Via dell'Umiltà 36, 00187 Roma; tel. (06) 67311; fax (06) 6788255; e-mail lettere@forza-italia.it; internet www.forza-italia.it; f. 1993; mem. of Popolo della Libertà; advocates principles of market economy; Pres. SILVIO BERLUSCONI.

Italia dei Valori—Lista Di Pietro (IDV) (Italy of Values—Di Pietro List): Via dei Prefetti 17, 00186 Roma; tel. (06) 6840721; fax (06) 68132711; e-mail italiadeivalori@antoniodipietro.it; internet www.italiadeivalori.it; anti-corruption; Pres. ANTONIO DI PIETRO.

Liberaldemocratici (LD) (Liberal Democrats): Roma; internet www.liberaldemocratici.org; f. 2007; liberal centrist; mem. of Popolo della Libertà; Leader LAMBERTO DINI.

Lista Consumatori: Via Tagliamento 3, Ardea, 00040 Roma; tel. (06) 452214426; fax (06) 23328286; e-mail info@listaconsumatori.it; internet www.listaconsumatori.it; f. 2004; Pres. RENATO CAMPIGLIA; Nat. Sec. DAVID BADINI.

Movimento Associativo Italiani all'Estero (MAIE) (Associative Movement Italians Abroad): represents Italian voters living in South America; Leaders MIRELLA GIAI, RICARDO ANTONIO MERLO.

Movimento Cristiano-Sociali (Christian-Social Movement): Piazza Adriana 5, 00193 Roma; tel. (06) 68300537; fax (06) 68300539; e-mail info@cristianosociali.it; internet www.cristianosociali.it; f. 1983; Pres. DOMENICO LUCÀ; Nat. Co-ordinator MIMMO LUCÀ.

Movimento Federalista Europeo (MFE) (European Federalist Movement): Via Poloni 9, 37122 Verona; tel. and fax (045) 8032194; e-mail mfe@mfe.it; internet www.mfe.it; f. 1943; Sec.-Gen. GIORGIO ANSELMI.

Movimento Repubblicani Europei (MRE): Via IV Novembre 107, 00187 Roma; tel. (06) 45423036; fax (06) 45423051; e-mail nazionale@repubblicanieuropei.org; internet www.repubblicanieuropei.org; Sec.-Gen. LUCIANA SBARBATI.

Movimento Sociale—Fiamma Tricolore (Tricolour Flame): Circonvallazione Clodia, 145/a, 00195 Roma; tel. (06) 37501046; fax (06) 37517492; e-mail info@fiammatricolore.net; internet www.fiammatricolore.net; f. 1996; electoral alliance incorporating fmr mems of neo-fascist Movimento Sociale Italiano-Destra Nazionale; Nat. Sec. LUCA ROMAGNOLI.

Nuovo Partito Socialista Italiano (Nuovo PSI) (New Italian Socialist Party): Via di Torre Argentina 47, 00186 Roma; tel. (06) 68892583; fax (06) 6892000; e-mail segreteria@nuovopsi.com; internet www.nuovopsi.com; f. 1994 following dissolution of the Partito Socialista Italiano (PSI); mem. of Popola della Libertà; Pres. GIANNI DE MICHELIS; Sec. MAURO DEL BUE.

Partito dei Comunisti Italiani (PdCI) (Party of Italian Communists): Piazza Augusto Imperatore 31, 00186 Roma; tel. (06) 686271; fax (06) 68627230; e-mail direzionenazionale@comunisti-italiani.org; internet www.comunisti-italiani.it; f. 1998; mem. of La Sinistra—L'Arcobaleno; Chair. ARMANDO COSSUTTA; Gen. Sec. OLIVIERO DILIBERRO.

Partito Democratico: Piazza Saint'Anastasia 7, 00186 Roma; tel. (06) 675471; fax (06) 67547319; e-mail info@partitodemocratico.it; internet www.partitodemocratico.it; f. 2007; centre-left; formed by a merger of Democratici di Sinistra, Democrazia è Libertà—La Margherita and other left-wing and centrist parties that had formed part of L'Unione; Pres. ROMANO PRODI; National Sec. WALTER VELTRONI.

Partito Liberale Italiano (PLI) (Italian Liberal Party): Via del Corso 117, 00187 Roma; tel. (06) 90283125; fax (06) 90283126; e-mail info@partitoliberale.info; internet www.partitoliberale.it; Pres. Prof. CARLA MARTINO; Sec. STEFANO DE LUCA.

Partito Pensionati (Pensioners' Party): Piazza Risorgimento 14, 24128 Bergamo; tel. (035) 253487; fax (035) 4326799; internet www.partitopensionati.it; f. 1987; mem. of Popolo della Libertà; Pres. GIACINTO BOLDRINI; Nat. Sec. CARLO FATUZZO.

Partito Repubblicano Italiano (PRI) (Italian Republican Party): Corso Vittorio Emanuele 326, 00186 Roma; tel. (06) 6865044; fax (06) 6893002; e-mail nucarapri@libero.it; internet www.pri.it; f. 1897; mem. of Popolo della Libertà; followers of the principles of Mazzini (social justice in a modern free society) and modern liberalism; Pres. GIORGIO LA MALFA; Nat. Sec. FRANCESCO NUCARA; 110,000 mems.

Partito della Rifondazione Comunista (PRC) (Party of Communist Refoundation): Viale del Policlinico 131, 00161 Roma; tel. (06) 441821; fax (06) 44182286; e-mail esteri.prc@rifondazione.it; internet www.rifondazione.it; f. 1991 by former members of the Partito Comunista Italiano (Italian Communist Party); mem. of La Sinistra—L'Arcobaleno; Nat. Sec. FRANCO GIORDANO.

Partito Socialista (SDI) (Socialist Party): Piazza S. Lorenzo in Lucina 26, 00186 Roma; tel. (06) 6878688; fax (06) 68307659; e-mail info@partitosocialista.it; internet www.sdionline.it; f. 2007 by fmr leadership of Socialisti Democratici Italiani; Sec. ENRICO BOSELLI.

Patto—Partito dei Liberaldemocratici (The Pact—Liberal Democratic Party): Via Vittorio Veneto 169, 00187 Roma; tel. and fax (06) 4744916; e-mail info@ilpatto.it; internet www.ilpatto.it; f. 1993 as Patto Segni; liberal party, advocating institutional reform; Leader MARIO SEGNI.

Popolari—UDEUR (Alleanza Popolare—Unione Democratici per l'Europa) (Union of Democrats for Europe): Largo Arenula 34, 00186 Roma; tel. (06) 684241; fax (06) 68210615; e-mail info@popolariudeur.it; internet www.popolariudeur.it; f. 1999; Sec. CLEMENTE MASTELLA.

Radicali Italiani: Via di Torre Argentina 76, 00186 Roma; tel. (06) 689791; fax (06) 68805396; e-mail segreteria.roma@radicali.it; internet www.radicali.it; f. 2001 as Partito Radicale; mem. of La Rosa nel Pugno; Pres. MARIA ANTONIETTA FARINA COSCIONI; Gen. Sec. RITA BERNARDINI.

Rosa Bianca (White Rose): Roma; internet www.rosabianca.net; f. 2008 by fmr mems of the Unione dei Democratici Cristiani e di Centro; mem. of Unione di Centro; Leader BRUNO TABACCI.

La Rosa nel Pugno (Rose In The Fist): Via Germanico 12, 00182 Roma; internet www.rosanelpugno.it; f. 2005; coalition of Radicali Italiani, Socialisti Democratici Italiani, Associazione Luca Coscioni and Federazione dei Giovani Socialisti; Secs EMMA BONINO, ENRICO BOSELLI.

Sinistra Democratica (Democratic Left): Via Merulana 272, 00185 Roma; tel. (06) 4620701; fax (06) 462070219; e-mail info@sinistra-democratica.it; internet www.sinistra-democratica.it; f. 2007 by members of Democratici di Sinistra opposed to foundation of the Partito Democratico; mem. of La Sinistra—L'Arcobaleno; Leader FABIO MUSSI.

Unione dei Democratici Cristiani e di Centro (UDC) (Union of Christian and Centre Democrats): Via dei Due Macelli 66, 00182 Roma; tel. (06) 69791001; fax (06) 6791574; e-mail info@udc-italia.it; internet www.udc-italia.it; f. 2002 from merger of Centro Cristiano Democratico (f. 1994) and Cristiani Democratici Uniti (f. 1995 after split from Partito Popolare Italiano); mem. of Unione di Centro; Leader PIER FERDINANDO CASINI.

Political organizations for Italians abroad include the Associazioni Italiane in Sud America, Alternativa Indipendente Italiani all'Estero (AIIE), the Partito degli Italiani nel Mondo and the Unione Sudamericana Emigranti Italiani.

REGIONAL PARTIES

Autonomie Liberté Démocratie (ALD) (Autonomy Liberty Democracy): f. 2006; coalition of parties active in the Aosta valley.

Lega Nord per l'Indipendenza della Padania (Northern League for the Independence of Padania): Via C. Bellerio 41, 20161 Milano; tel. (02) 66234236; fax (02) 66234402; e-mail webmaster@leganord.org; internet www.leganord.org; f. 1991; advocates federalism and transfer of control of resources to regional govts; in 1996 declared the 'Independent Republic of Padania'; opposes immigration; contested April 2008 general election in alliance with the Popolo della Libertà; Pres. ANGELO ALESSANDRI; Sec. UMBERTO BOSSI.

Liga Veneta Repubblica (Venetian Republic League): Via Catania 11, 37138 Verona; tel. and fax (045) 566433; e-mail info@ligafronteveneto.org; internet www.ligavenetarepubblica.org; f. 2001 by merger of Liga Veneta Repubblica—Veneti d'Europa and Fronte Marco Polo; advocates independence for Veneto region; Gen. Sec. FABRIZIO COMENCINI.

Movimento per l'Autonomia (MPA) (Autonomy Movement): Via dell'Oca 27, Roma; tel. and fax (06) 3220836; fax (06) 32647632; e-mail info@mpa-italia.it; internet www.mpa-italia.it; pro-regional autonomy in the South; contested April 2008 general election in alliance with the Popolo della Libertà; Fed. Sec. RAFFAELE LOMBARDO.

Partito Autonomista Trentino Tirolese (PATT) (Autonomist Party of Trento and the Tyrol): Corso 3 Novembre, 72/A, 38100 Trento; tel. (0461) 391399; fax (0461) 394940; e-mail info@patt.tn.it; internet www.patt.tn.it; advocates autonomy for Tyrol region; Pres. WALTER KASWALDER; Pol Sec. UGO ROSSI.

Partitu Sardu—Partito Sardo d'Azione (Sardinian Action Party): Piazza Repubblica 18, 09125 Cagliari; tel. (070) 3481434; fax (070) 3481434; e-mail info@psdaz-fedca.it; internet www.psdaz-fedca.it; Pres. SILVANO CADONI; Sec. GIACOMO SANNA.

Südtiroler Volkspartei (SVP) (South Tyrol People's Party): Brennerstrasse 7A, 39100 Bozen/Bolzano; tel. (0471) 304040; fax (0471) 981473; e-mail info@svpartei.org; internet www.svpartei.org; regional party of the German and Ladin-speaking people in the South Tyrol; Pres. ELMAR PICHLER ROLLE; Gen. Sec. ALEXANDER MITTERMAIR.

Union Autonomista Ladina (Autonomist Ladin Movement): Via Pilat 8, 38039 Vigo di Fassa; tel. and fax (0462) 763666; Pres. GINO FONTANA; Sec. GIUSEPPE DETOMAS.

Union Valdôtaine (Aosta Valley Union): Ave des Maquisards 27/29, 11100 Aosta; tel. (0165) 235181; fax (0165) 364289; internet www.unionvaldotaine.org; f. 1945; promotes interests of the Aosta Valley; Pres. GUIDO CESAL.

Other regional parties and coalitions include the **Alleanza Lombarda**, the **Alleanza Siciliana**, **Die Freiheitlichen** (South Tyrol), **IRS—Indipendentzia Repruburica de Sardigna**, the **Movimento Democraticao Siciliana-Noi Siciliani**, the **Movimento Triveneto**, **Nuova Sicilia**, **Per il Sud**, **Progetto Nordest** and **Sardigna Natzione**.

ITALY

Diplomatic Representation

EMBASSIES IN ITALY

Afghanistan: Via Nomentana 120, 00161 Roma; tel. (06) 8611009; fax (06) 86322939; e-mail afghanembassy.rome@flashnet.it; Ambassador MUHAMMAD MUSA MAROOFI.

Albania: Via Asmara 3–5, 00199 Roma; tel. (06) 86224110; fax (06) 86224120; e-mail embassy.rome@mfa.gov.al; internet www.ambalbania.it; Ambassador LLESH KOLA.

Algeria: Via Bartolomeo Eustachio 12, 00161 Roma; tel. (06) 44202533; fax (06) 44292744; Ambassador RACHID MARIF.

Angola: Via Druso 39, 00184 Roma; tel. (06) 7726951; fax (06) 77590009; e-mail ambasciata@ambasciatangola.it; internet www.ambasciatangola.com; Ambassador MANUEL PEDRO PACAVIRA.

Argentina: Piazza dell'Esquilino 2, 2°, 00185 Roma; tel. (06) 48073300; fax (06) 4819787; e-mail ambasciata.argentina@ambargentina.mysam.it; Ambassador VICTORIO MARÍA JOSÉ TACCETTI.

Armenia: Via dei Colli della Farnesina 174, 00194 Roma; tel. (06) 3296638; fax (06) 3297763; e-mail ambarmit@tin.it; Ambassador ROUBEN SHUGARIAN.

Australia: Via A. Bosio 5, 00161 Roma; tel. (06) 852721; fax (06) 85272300; e-mail info-rome@dfat.gov.au; internet www.italy.embassy.gov.au; Ambassador AMANDA VANSTONE.

Austria: Via G. B. Pergolesi 3, 00198 Roma; tel. (06) 8440141; fax (06) 8543286; e-mail rom-ob@bmaa.gv.at; internet www.austria.it; Ambassador CHRISTIAN BERLAKOVITS.

Azerbaijan: Via Regina Margherita 1, Piano 2, 00198 Roma; tel. (06) 85305557; fax (06) 85231448; e-mail azerb.roma@azembassy.it; internet www.azembassy.it; Ambassador EMIL ZULFGAR OĞLU KARIMOV.

Bangladesh: Via Antonio Bertoloni 14, 00197 Roma; tel. (06) 8078541; fax (06) 8084853; e-mail embangrm@mclink.it; Ambassador KARIM FAZLUL.

Belarus: Via delle Alpi Apuane 16, 00141 Roma; tel. (06) 8208141; fax (06) 82002509; e-mail italy@belembassy.org; internet www.belembassy.it; Ambassador ALEKSEI SKRIPKO.

Belgium: Via dei Monti Parioli 49, 00197 Roma; tel. (06) 3609511; fax (06) 3226935; e-mail ambelrom@tin.it; internet www.diplomatie.be/romeit; Ambassador JEAN DE RUYT.

Belize: Piazza di Spagna 81, 00187 Roma; tel. (06) 69190776; fax (06) 69925794; Ambassador NUNZIO ALFREDO D'ANGIERI.

Bolivia: Via Brenta 2A, int. 18, 00198 Roma; tel. and fax (06) 8841001; e-mail embolivia-roma@rree.gov.bo; Ambassador ESTEBAN ELMER CATARINA MAMANI.

Bosnia and Herzegovina: Piazzale Clodio 12, int. 17/18, 00195 Roma; tel. (06) 39742817; fax (06) 39030567; e-mail ambasciata@ambih.191.it; Ambassador MIDHAT HARACIC.

Brazil: Palazzo Pamphili, Piazza Navona 14, 00186 Roma; tel. (06) 683981; fax (06) 6867858; e-mail info@ambrasile.it; internet www.ambasciatadelbrasile.it; Ambassador ADHEMAR GABRIEL BAHADIAN.

Bulgaria: Via Pietro Paolo Rubens 21, 00197 Roma; tel. (06) 3224640; fax (06) 3226122; e-mail embassy@bulemb.it; internet www.bulemb.it; Ambassador ATANAS MLADENOV.

Burkina Faso: Via XX Settembre 86, 00187 Roma; tel. (06) 42010611; fax (06) 48903514; e-mail ambabf.roma@tin.it; Ambassador MAMADOU SISSOKO.

Burundi: Corso Francia 221, 00919 Roma; tel. (06) 36381786; fax (06) 36381511; Ambassador LEOPOLD NDAYISABA.

Cameroon: Via Siracusa 4–6, 00161 Roma; tel. (06) 44291285; fax (06) 44291323; internet www.cameroonembassy.it; Ambassador MICHAEL TABONG KIMA.

Canada: Via Salaria 243, 00199 Roma; tel. (06) 854441; fax (06) 854443915; e-mail rome@international.gc.ca; internet www.canada.it; Ambassador ALEXANDER HIMMELFARB.

Cape Verde: Via Giosuè Carducci 4, 1°, 00187 Roma; tel. (06) 4744678; fax (06) 4744643; Ambassador JOSÉ EDUARDO DANTAS FERREIRA BARBOSA.

Chile: Via Po 23, 00198 Roma; tel. (06) 844091; fax (06) 8841452; e-mail echileit@flashnet.it; internet www.chileit.it; Ambassador GABRIEL VALDES SUBERCASEAUX.

China, People's Republic: Via Bruxelles 56, 00198 Roma; tel. (06) 8413458; fax (06) 85352891; e-mail chinaemb_it@mfa.gov.cn; internet it.china-embassy.org; Ambassador SUN YUXI.

Colombia: Via Giuseppe Pisanelli 4, 00196 Roma; tel. (06) 3612131; fax (06) 3225798; e-mail info@embajadadecolombia.it; internet www.ambasciatadicolombia.it; Ambassador SABAS EDUARDO PRETELT DE LA VEGA.

Congo, Democratic Republic: Via Barberini 3, 00187 Roma; tel. and fax (06) 42010779; Ambassador ALBERT TSHISELEKA FEHLA.

Congo, Republic: Via Ombrone 8–10, 00198 Roma; tel. and fax (06) 8417422; Ambassador MAMADOU DEKAMO KAMARA.

Costa Rica: Viale Liegi 2, int. 8, 00198 Roma; tel. (06) 84242853; fax (06) 85355956; e-mail embcosta@tiscalinet.it; internet www.ambasciatacostarica.org; Ambassador (vacant).

Côte d'Ivoire: Via Guglielmo Saliceto 6–10, 00161 Roma; tel. (06) 44231129; fax (06) 44292531; Ambassador RICHARD GBAKA ZADY.

Croatia: Via Luigi Bodio 74–76, 00191 Roma; tel. (06) 36307650; fax (06) 36303405; e-mail vhrim@mvpei.hr; internet it.mfa.hr; Ambassador TOMISLAV VIDOŠEVÍC.

Cuba: Via Licinia 7, 00153 Roma; tel. (06) 5717241; fax (06) 5745445; e-mail embajada@ecuitalia.it; internet www.ambasciatacuba.com; Ambassador RODNEY ALEJANDRO LÓPEZ CLEMENTE.

Cyprus: Via Francesco Denza 15, 00197 Roma; tel. (06) 8088365; fax (06) 8088338; e-mail ciproamb@tin.it; Ambassador ATHENA K. MAVRONICOLA.

Czech Republic: Via dei Gracchi 322, 00192 Roma; tel. (06) 36309571; fax (06) 3244466; e-mail rome@embassy.mzv.cz; internet www.mzv.cz/rome; Ambassador VLADIMÍR ZAVÁZAL.

Denmark: Via dei Monti Parioli 50, 00197 Roma; tel. (06) 9774831; fax (06) 97748399; e-mail romamb@um.dk; internet www.ambrom.um.dk; Ambassador GUNNAR ORTMANN.

Dominican Republic: Via Giuseppe Pisanelli 1, int. 8, 00196 Roma; tel. (06) 36004377; fax (06) 36004380; e-mail embajadadominicana@yahoo.it; Chargé d'affaires a.i. IGNACIO MANUEL GONZÁLEZ FRANCO.

Ecuador: Via Antonio Bertoloni 8, 00197 Roma; tel. (06) 45439007; fax (06) 8076271; e-mail mecuroma@flashnet.it; Ambassador GEOCONDA GALÁN CASTELO.

Egypt: Villa Savoia, Via Salaria 267, 00199 Roma; tel. (06) 84401976; fax (06) 8554424; e-mail amb.egi@pronet.it; internet www.mfa.gov.eg/missions/italy/rome/embassy/en-gb; Ambassador MUHAMMAD ASHRAF GAML ELDIN RASHED.

El Salvador: Via G. Castellini 13, 00197 Roma; tel. (06) 8076605; fax (06) 8079726; e-mail embasalvaroma@iol.it; internet www.embasalvaroma.com; Ambassador JOSÉ ROBERTO ANDINO SALAZAR.

Eritrea: Via Boncompagni 16, int. 6, 00187 Roma; tel. (06) 42741293; fax (06) 42741514; e-mail segretaria@embassyoferitrea.it; Ambassador ZEMEDE TEKLE WOLDETATIOS.

Estonia: Viale Liegi 28, int. 5, 00198 Roma; tel. (06) 84407510; fax (06) 84407519; e-mail embassy.rome@mfa.ee; internet www.estemb.it; Ambassador ANDRES TOMASBERG.

Ethiopia: Via Andrea Vesalio 16–18, 00161 Roma; tel. (06) 4416161; fax (06) 4403676; Ambassador GRUM ABAY TESHOME.

Finland: Via Lisbona 3, 00198 Roma; tel. (06) 852231; fax (06) 8540362; e-mail sanomat.roo@formin.fi; internet www.finland.it; Ambassador PAULI ANTERO MÄKELÄ.

France: Piazza Farnese 67, 00186 Roma; tel. (06) 686011; fax (06) 68601418; e-mail fatima.madjer@diplomatie.gouv.fr; internet www.ambafrance-it.org; Ambassador JEAN-MARC DE LA SABLIÈRE.

Gabon: Via San Marino 36A, 00198 Roma; tel. (06) 85358970; fax (06) 8417278; e-mail ambagabon@tiscali.net; Ambassador NOEL BAIOT.

Georgia: Corso Vittorio Emanuele II 21, III piano, 00186 Roma; tel. (06) 69925809; fax (06) 69941942; e-mail amgeorgia@libero.it; internet www.italy.mfa.gov.ge; Ambassador ZAAL GOGSADZE.

Germany: Via San Martino della Battaglia 4, 00185 Roma; tel. (06) 492131; fax (06) 49213319; e-mail info@rom.diplo.de; internet www.rom.diplo.de; Ambassador MICHAEL STEINER.

Ghana: Via Ostriana 4, 00199 Roma; tel. (06) 86217191; fax (06) 86325762; e-mail ghembrom@rdn.it; Ambassador CHARLES AGYEI AMOAMA.

Greece: Viale G. Rossini 4, 00198 Roma; tel. (06) 8537551; fax (06) 85375503; e-mail gremroma@tin.it; internet www.greekembassy.it; Ambassador CHARALAMBOS ROCANAS.

Guatemala: Via dei Colli della Farnesina 128, 00194 Roma; tel. (06) 36381143; fax (06) 3291639; e-mail embaguate.italia@tin.it; Ambassador FRANCISCO EDUARDO BONIFAZ RODRÍGUEZ.

Guinea: Via Adelaide Ristori, 9B 13, 00197 Roma; tel. (06) 8078989; fax (06) 8077588; e-mail ambaguineerome1@virgilio.it; Ambassador El Hadj THIERNO MAMADOU CELLOU DIALLO.

Haiti: Via di Villa Patrizi 7/7A, 00161 Roma; tel. (06) 44254106; fax (06) 44254208; e-mail amb.haiti@tiscali.it; Ambassador YVON SIMEON.

Holy See: Via Po 27–29, 00198 Roma; tel. (06) 8546287; fax (06) 8549725; e-mail nunzio@nunziatura.it; Apostolic Nuncio Most Rev. GIUSEPPE BERTELLO (Titular Archbishop of Urbisaglia).

Honduras: Via Giambattista Vico 40, int. 8, 00197 Roma; tel. (06) 3207236; fax (06) 3207973; e-mail embhon@fastwebnet.it; Ambassador ROBERTO OCHOA MADRID.

ITALY

Hungary: Via dei Villini 12–16, 00161 Roma; tel. (06) 4402032; fax (06) 4403270; e-mail mission.rom@kum.hu; internet www.huembit.it; Ambassador MIKLÓS MERÉNYI.

Iceland: Via di San Saba 12, int 7, 00153 Roma; tel. (06) 57250509; fax (06) 5758012; e-mail gudni@mfa.is; internet www.iceland.org/it; Chargé d'affaires GUÐNI BRAGASON.

India: Via XX Settembre 5, 00187 Roma; tel. (06) 4884642; fax (06) 4819539; e-mail gen.email@indianembassy.it; internet www.indianembassy.it; Ambassador RAJIV DOGRA.

Indonesia: Via Campania 55, 00187 Roma; tel. (06) 4200911; fax (06) 4880280; e-mail indorom@uni.net; internet www.indonesianembassy.it; Ambassador SUSANTO SUTOYO.

Iran: Via Nomentana 361, 00162 Roma; tel. (06) 86328485; fax (06) 86328492; e-mail info@iranembassy.it; internet www.iranembassy.it; Ambassador ABOLFAZL ZOHREVAND.

Iraq: Via della Camilluccia, 355, 00135 Roma; tel. (06) 3014508; fax (06) 3014445; e-mail romemb@iraqmofamail.net; Ambassador MUHAMMAD MAHMOUD AL-AMILI.

Ireland: Piazza di Campitelli 3, 00186 Roma; tel. (06) 6979121; fax (06) 6792354; e-mail romeembassy@dfa.ie; internet www.ambasciata-irlanda.it; Ambassador SEÁN Ó HUIGINN.

Israel: Via Michele Mercati 12, 00197 Roma; tel. (06) 36198500; fax (06) 36198555; e-mail adm-sec@roma.mfa.gov.il; internet roma.mfa.gov.il; Ambassador GIDEON MEIR.

Japan: Via Quintino Sella 60, 00187 Roma; tel. (06) 487991; fax (06) 4873316; internet www.it.emb-japan.go.jp; Ambassador YUKI NAKAMURA.

Jordan: Via G. Marchi 1B, 00161 Roma; tel. (06) 86205303; fax (06) 8606122; e-mail embroma@jordanembassy.it; Ambassador HRH Princess WIJDAN BINT FAWAZ AL-HASHIMI.

Kazakhstan: Via della Camilluccia 693, 00135 Roma; tel. (06) 36301130; fax (06) 36292675; e-mail kazakstan.emb@agora.it; internet www.embkaz.it; Ambassador ALMAZ N. KHAMZAYEV.

Kenya: Via Archimede 164, 00197 Roma; tel. (06) 8082717; fax (06) 8082707; e-mail info@embassyofkenya.it; internet www.embassyofkenya.it; Ambassador ANN BELINDA NYIKULI.

Korea, Democratic People's Republic: Via dell'Esperanto 26, 00144 Roma; tel. (06) 54220749; fax (06) 54210090; e-mail permerepun@hotmail.com; Ambassador HAN TAE SONG.

Korea, Republic: Via Barnaba Oriani 30, 00197 Roma; tel. (06) 802461; fax (06) 802462259; Ambassador YOUNG JAE CHO.

Kuwait: Via Archimede 124–126, 00197 Roma; tel. (06) 8078415; fax (06) 8076651; Chargé d'affaires a.i. AHMAD SALEH AHMAD AS-SALEM AL-WEHAIB.

Latvia: Viale Liegi 42, 00198 Roma; tel. (06) 8841227; fax (06) 8841239; e-mail embassy.italy@mfa.gov.lv; internet www.mfa.gov.lv/rome; Ambassador ASTRA KURME.

Lebanon: Via Giacomo Carissimi 38, 00198 Roma; tel. (06) 8537211; fax (06) 8411794; e-mail liban@tiscali.it; internet www.liban.it; Ambassador MELHEM NASRI MISTOU.

Lesotho: Via Serchio 8, 00198 Roma; tel. (06) 8542496; fax (06) 8542527; e-mail les.rome@flashnet.it; Ambassador JONAS SPONKIE MALEWA.

Liberia: Piazzale delle Medaglie d'Oro 7, 00136 Roma; tel. (06) 35453399; fax (06) 35344729; e-mail info@liberiaembassy.it; internet www.liberiaembassy.it; Chargé d'affaires a.i. MUSU JATU RUHLE.

Libya: Via Nomentana 365, 00162 Roma; tel. (06) 86320951; fax (06) 86205473; Ambassador ABD AL-HAFID GADDUR.

Lithuania: Viale di Villa Grazioli 9, 00198 Roma; tel. (06) 8559052; fax (06) 8559053; e-mail amb.it@urm.lt; internet it.mfa.lt; Ambassador ŠARŪNAS ADOMAVIČIUS.

Luxembourg: Via Santa Croce in Gerusalemme 90, 00185 Roma; tel. (06) 77201177; fax (06) 77201055; e-mail rome.amb@mae.etat.lu; internet www.ambasciatalussemburgo.it; Ambassador JEAN FALTZ.

Macedonia, former Yugoslav republic: Viale Bruxelles 73–75, 00198 Roma; tel. (06) 84241109; fax (06) 84241131; e-mail rome@mfa.gov.mk; Ambassador LJUPCO TOZIJA.

Madagascar: Via Riccardo Zandonai 84A, 00194 Roma; tel. (06) 36307797; fax (06) 3294306; e-mail ambamad@hotmail.com; Ambassador AUGUSTE RICHARD PARAINA.

Malaysia: Via Nomentana 297, 00162 Roma; tel. (06) 8415764; fax (06) 8555040; e-mail mw.rome@embassymalaysia.it; Ambassador Dato' LILY ZACHARIAH.

Mali: Via Antonio Bosio 2, 00161 Roma; tel. (06) 44254068; fax (06) 44254029; e-mail amb.malirome@tiscalinet.it; Ambassador IBRAHIM BOCAR DAGA.

Malta: Lungotevere Marzio 12, 00186 Roma; tel. (06) 6879990; fax (06) 6892687; e-mail maltaembassy.rome@gov.mt; Ambassador WALTER BALZAN.

Mauritania: Via Giovanni Paisiello 26, 00198 Roma; tel. (06) 85351530; fax (06) 85351441; Ambassador YAHYA NGAM.

Mexico: Via Lazzaro Spallanzani 16, 00161 Roma; tel. (06) 44115204; fax (06) 4403876; e-mail ofna.embajador@emexitalia.it; internet www.sre.gob.mx/italia; Ambassador JORGE EDUARDO CHEN CHARPENTIER.

Moldova: Via Montebello 8, 00185 Roma; tel. (06) 4740210; fax (06) 47881092; e-mail roma@mfa.md; internet www.ambmoldova.it; Ambassador NICOLAE DUDĂU.

Monaco: Via Antonio Bertoloni 36, 00197 Roma; tel. (06) 8083361; fax (06) 8077692; e-mail monaco@ambasciatadimonaco.it; Ambassador PHILIPPE BLANCHI.

Montenegro: Via Antonio Gramsci 9, 00197 Roma; tel. (06) 45471660; fax (06) 45443800; e-mail montenegro-roma@libero.it; Ambassador DARKO USKOKOVIĆ.

Morocco: Via Lazzaro Spallanzani 8, 00161 Roma; tel. (06) 4402524; fax (06) 4402695; e-mail sifaroma@ambasciatadelmarocco.it; internet www.ambasciatadelmarocco.it; Ambassador TAJEDDINE BADDOU.

Mozambique: Via Filippo Corridoni 14, 00195 Roma; tel. (06) 37514852; fax (06) 37514699; e-mail segretaria@ambasciatamozambico.it; Chargé d'affaires a.i. LAURINDA FERNANDO SAIDE BANZE.

Myanmar: Viale Gioacchino Rossini 18, int. 2, I piano, 00198 Roma; tel. (06) 8543974; fax (06) 8413167; e-mail meroma@tiscali.it; Ambassador U KHIN MAUNG AYE.

Netherlands: Via della Camilluccia 701–3, 00135 Roma; tel. (06) 367671; fax (06) 36767256; e-mail rom-az@minbuza.nl; internet www.olanda.it; Ambassador EGBERT FREDERIK JACOBS.

New Zealand: Via Zara 28, 00198 Roma; tel. (06) 4417171; fax (06) 4402984; e-mail nzemb.rom@flashnet.it; internet www.nzembassy.com/italy; Ambassador LAWRENCE MARKES.

Nicaragua: Via Brescia 16, 00198 Roma; tel. (06) 8413471; fax (06) 85304079; e-mail embanicitalia@hotmail.com; Ambassador PIERO COEN MONTEALEGRE.

Niger: Via Antonio Baiamonti 10, 00195 Roma; tel. (06) 3720164; fax (06) 3729013; Ambassador FATOUMA MIREILLE AUSSEIL.

Nigeria: Via Orazio 14–18, 00193 Roma; tel. (06) 6896243; fax (06) 6832528; e-mail embassy@nigerian.it; Chargé d'affaires EDWARD DOLAPO OSUNMAKINDE.

Norway: Via delle Terme Deciane 7, 00153 Roma; tel. (06) 5717031; fax (06) 57170326; e-mail emb.rome@mfa.no; internet www.amb-norvegia.it; Ambassador EINAR MARENTIUS BULL.

Oman: Via della Camilluccia 625, 00135 Roma; tel. (06) 36300517; fax (06) 3296802; e-mail embassyoman@virgilio.it; Ambassador SAID NASSER MANSOUR AS-SINAWI AL-HARTHY.

Pakistan: Via della Camilluccia 682, 00135 Roma; tel. (06) 36301775; fax (06) 36301936; e-mail pacepromec@linet.it; Ambassador TASNIM ASLAM.

Panama: Viale Regina Margherita 239, 00198 Roma; tel. (06) 44252173; fax (06) 44252237; Ambassador EUDORO JAEN ESQUIVEL.

Paraguay: Via Firenze 43, Scala A int. 17, 00187 Roma; tel. (06) 4741715; fax (06) 4745473; e-mail ambaparoman@tiscali.it; Ambassador JORGE FIGUEREDO FRATTA.

Peru: Via Francesco Siacci 2B, 00197 Roma; tel. (06) 80691510; fax (06) 80691777; e-mail emb.peru@aambasciataperu2.191.it; tel. www.ambasciataperu.it; Ambassador CARLOS ROCA CÁCERES.

Philippines: Viale delle Medaglie d'Oro 112–114, 00136 Roma; tel. (06) 39746621; fax (06) 39740872; e-mail philrepfao@libero.it; Ambassador PHILIPPE J. LHUILLIER.

Poland: Via Pietro Paolo Rubens 20, 00197 Roma; tel. (06) 36204200; fax (06) 3217895; e-mail ufficio.stampa@ambasciatapolonia.it; internet www.rzym.polemb.net; Ambassador JERZY CHMIELEWSKI.

Portugal: Viale Liegi 21–23, 00198 Roma; tel. (06) 844801; fax (06) 8417404; e-mail embport@embportroma.it; internet www.embportroma.it; Ambassador VASCO TAVEIRA DA CUNHA VALENTE.

Qatar: Via Antonio Bosio 14, 00161 Roma; tel. (06) 44249450; fax (06) 44245273; e-mail info@qatarembassy.it; internet www.qatarembassy.it; Ambassador SOLTAN SAAD AL-MORAIKHI.

Romania: Via Nicolo Tartaglia 36, 00197 Roma; tel. (06) 8084529; fax (06) 8084995; e-mail secretariat.ambasada@roembit.org; internet www.roembit.org; Ambassador RĂZVAN VICTOR RUSU.

Russia: Via Gaeta 5, 00185 Roma; tel. (06) 4941680; fax (06) 491031; e-mail ambrus@ambrussia.it; internet www.ambrussia.com; Ambassador ALEXEI YU. MESHKOV.

San Marino: Via Eleonora Duse 35, 00197 Roma; tel. (06) 8072511; fax (06) 8070072; e-mail asmarino@ambrsm.it; Ambassador BARBARA PARA.

Saudi Arabia: Via G. B. Pergolesi 9, 00198 Roma; tel. (06) 844851; fax (06) 8551781; e-mail ambasciata@arabia-saudita.it; internet

ITALY

www.arabia-saudita.it; Ambassador MUHAMMAD IBRAHIM AL-JARALLAH.

Senegal: Via Giulia 66, 00186 Roma; tel. (06) 6872381; fax (06) 68219294; e-mail ambasenequiri@tiscali.it; Ambassador PAPA CHEIKH SAADIBOU FALL.

Serbia: Via dei Monti Parioli 20, 00197 Roma; tel. (06) 3200805; fax (06) 3200868; e-mail info@ambroma.com; Ambassador SANDA RAŠKOVIĆ-IVIĆ.

Slovakia: Via dei Colli della Farnesina 144, 00194 Roma; tel. (06) 36715201; fax (06) 36715265; e-mail embassy@rome.mfa.sk; internet www.rome.mfa.sk; Ambassador STANISLAV VALLO.

Slovenia: Via Leonardo Pisano 10, 00197 Roma; tel. (06) 80914310; fax (06) 8081471; e-mail vri@gov.si; Ambassador ANDREJ CAPUDER.

Somalia: Via dei Villini 9, 00161 Roma; Chargé d'affaires ABSCIR OSMAN HUSSEIN.

South Africa: Via Tanaro 14, 00198 Roma; tel. (06) 852541; fax (06) 85254301; e-mail sae2@sudafrica.it; internet www.sudafrica.it; Ambassador LENIN MAGIGWANE SHOPE.

Spain: Palazzo Borghese, Largo Fontanella Borghese 19, 00186 Roma; tel. (06) 6840401; fax (06) 6872256; e-mail ambespit@mail.mae.es; Ambassador D. LUIS CALVO MERINO.

Sri Lanka: Via Adige 2, 00198 Roma; tel. (06) 8554560; fax (06) 84241670; e-mail slembassy@tiscali.it; Ambassador E. RODNEY M. PERERA.

Sudan: Via Prati della Farnesina 57, 00194 Roma; tel. (06) 33222138; fax (06) 3340841; Ambassador RABIE HASSAN AHMED.

Sweden: Piazza Rio de Janeiro 3, 00161 Roma; tel. (06) 441941; fax (06) 44194760; e-mail ambassaden.rom@foreign.ministry.se; internet www.swedenabroad.com/rome; Ambassador ANDERS BJURNER.

Switzerland: Via Barnaba Oriani 61, 00197 Roma; tel. (06) 809571; fax (06) 8088510; e-mail amsuisse@rom.rep.admin.ch; internet www.eda.admin.ch/roma; Ambassador BRUNO MAX SPINNER.

Syria: Piazza dell'Ara Coeli, 00186 Roma; tel. (06) 6749801; fax (06) 6794989; e-mail uffstampasyem@hotmail.it; Ambassador SAMIR NASER AL QASIR.

Tanzania: Viale Cortina d'Ampezzo 185, 00135 Roma; tel. (06) 33485801; fax (06) 33485828; e-mail info@tanzania-gov.it; internet www.tanzania-gov.it; Ambassador ALI ABEID AMAN KARUME.

Thailand: Via Nomentana 132, 00162 Roma; tel. (06) 86202051; fax (06) 86220555; e-mail thai.em.rome@wind.it.net; internet www.thaiembassy.org/rome; Ambassador PRADAP PIBULSONGGRAM.

Tunisia: Via Asmara 7, 00199 Roma; tel. (06) 8603060; fax (06) 86218204; e-mail at.roma@tiscali.it; Ambassador HABIB MANSOUR.

Turkey: Palazzo Gamberini, Via Palestro 28, 00185 Roma; tel. (06) 445941; fax (06) 4941526; e-mail roma.be@libero.it; internet www.ambasciataditurchia.it; Ambassador SITKI UGUR ZIYAL.

Uganda: Lungotevere dei Mellini 44, 1°, Scala Valadier int. B, 00193 Roma; tel. (06) 3225220; fax (06) 3213688; Ambassador DEO K. RWABITA.

Ukraine: Via Guido d'Arezzo 9, 00198 Roma; tel. (06) 8413345; fax (06) 8547539; e-mail segretaria@amb-ucraina.com; internet www.amb-ucraina.com; Ambassador HEORHIY V. CHERNYAVSKY.

United Arab Emirates: Via della Camilluccia 492, 00135 Roma; tel. (06) 36306100; fax (06) 36306155; e-mail uaeroma@tin.it; Ambassador ABD AL-HAMID ABD AL-FATTAH KAZIM.

United Kingdom: Via XX Settembre 80A, 00187 Roma; tel. (06) 42200001; fax (06) 42202333; e-mail romepoliticalsection@fco.gov.uk; internet www.britain.it; Ambassador EDWARD CHAPLIN.

USA: Palazzo Margherita, Via Vittorio Veneto 119A, 00187 Roma; tel. (06) 46741; fax (06) 46742217; internet italy.usembassy.gov; Ambassador RONALD P. SPOGLI.

Uruguay: Via Vittorio Veneto 183, 00187 Roma; tel. (06) 4821776; fax (06) 4823695; e-mail uruit@ambasciatauruguay.it; Ambassador RAMÓN CARLOS ABIN DE MARÍA.

Uzbekistan: Via Tolmino 12, 00198 Roma; tel. (06) 8542456; fax (06) 8541020; e-mail uzbembass@libero.it; Ambassador ZHAHONGIR D. GANIYEV.

Venezuela: Via Nicolò Tartaglia 11, 00197 Roma; tel. (06) 8079797; fax (06) 8084410; e-mail embaveit@iol.it; internet www.ambasciatadelvenezuela.it; Ambassador RAFAEL ALEJANDRO LACAVA EVANGELISTA.

Viet Nam: Via di Bravetta 156–58, 00164 Roma; tel. (06) 66160726; fax (06) 66157520; e-mail vnemb.it@mofa.gov.vn; internet www.vnembassy.it; Ambassador NGUYEN VAN NAM.

Yemen: Via Antonio Bosio 10, 00161 Roma; tel. (06) 44231679; fax (06) 44234763; e-mail info@yemenembassy.it; internet www.yemenembassy.it; Ambassador Dr SHAYA MOHSIN MUHAMMAD ZINDANI.

Zambia: Via Ennio Quirino Visconti 8, 00193 Roma; tel. (06) 36003590; fax (06) 97613035; Ambassador LUCY M. MUNGOMA.

Zimbabwe: Via Virgilio 8, 00193 Roma; tel. (06) 68308265; fax (06) 68308324; e-mail zimrome-wolit@tiscali.it; Ambassador MARY MARGARET MUCHADA.

Judicial System

The Constitutional Court was established in 1956 and is an autonomous constitutional body, standing apart from the judicial system. Its most important function is to pronounce on the constitutionality of legislation both subsequent and prior to the present Constitution of 1948. It also judges accusations brought against the President of the Republic or ministers.

At the base of the system of penal jurisdiction are the Preture (District Courts), where offences carrying a sentence of up to four years' imprisonment are tried. Above the Preture are the Tribunali (Tribunals) and the Corti di Assise presso i Tribunali (Assize Courts attached to the Tribunals), where graver offences are dealt with. From these courts appeal lies to the Corti d'Appello (Courts of Appeal) and the parallel Corti di Assise d'Appello (Assize Courts of Appeal). Final appeal may be made, on juridical grounds only, to the Corte Suprema di Cassazione.

Civil cases may be taken in the first instance to the Giudici Conciliatori (Justices of the Peace), Preture or Tribunali, according to the economic value of the case. Appeal from the Giudici Conciliatori lies to the Preture, from the Preture to the Tribunali, from the Tribunali to the Corti d'Appello, and finally, as in penal justice, to the Corte Suprema di Cassazione on juridical grounds only.

Special divisions for cases concerning labour relations are attached to civil courts. Cases concerned with the public service and its employees are tried by Tribunali Amministrativi Regionali and the Consiglio di Stato. Juvenile courts have criminal and civil jurisdiction.

A new penal code was introduced in late 1989.

CONSTITUTIONAL COURT

Corte Costituzionale

Palazzo della Consulta, Piazza del Quirinale 41, 00187 Roma; tel. (06) 46981; fax (06) 4698916; e-mail ccost@cortecostituzionale.it; internet www.cortecostituzionale.it.

Consists of 15 judges, one-third appointed by the President of the Republic, one-third elected by Parliament in joint session, and one-third by the ordinary and administrative supreme courts.

President: Prof. FRANCO BILE.

ADMINISTRATIVE COURTS

Consiglio di Stato

Palazzo Spada, Piazza Capo di Ferro 13, 00186 Roma; tel. (06) 68272339; fax (06) 68272336; e-mail webmaster@giustizia-amministrativa.it; internet www.giustizia-amministrativa.it.

Established in accordance with Article 10 of the Constitution; has both consultative and judicial functions.

President: MARIO EGIDIO SCHINAIA.

Corte dei Conti

Via Giuseppe Mazzini 105, 00195 Roma; tel. (06) 38761; fax (06) 38763477; e-mail urp@corteconti.it; internet www.corteconti.it.

Functions as the court of public auditors for the State.

President: TULLIO LAZZARO.

SUPREME COURT OF APPEAL

Corte Suprema di Cassazione

Palazzo di Giustizia, Piazza Cavour, 00193 Roma; tel. (06) 68832423; e-mail cassazione@giustizia.it; internet www.cortedicassazione.it.

Supreme court of civil and criminal appeal.

First President: Dott. VINCENZO CARBONE.

SUPERVISORY BODY

Consiglio Superiore della Magistratura (CSM): Piazza dell'Indipendenza 6, 00185 Roma; tel. (06) 444911; fax (06) 4457175; e-mail seg-seggen@cosmag.it; internet www.csm.it; f. 1958; 27 mems; Pres. GIORGIO NAPOLITANO (President of the Republic); Vice-Pres. NICOLA MANCINO.

ITALY								Directory

Religion

More than 90% of the population of Italy are adherents of the Roman Catholic Church. Under the terms of the Concordat formally ratified in June 1985, Roman Catholicism was no longer to be the state religion, compulsory religious instruction in schools was abolished and state financial contributions reduced. The Vatican City's sovereign rights as an independent state, under the terms of the Lateran Pact of 1929, were not affected.

Several Protestant churches also exist in Italy, with a total membership of about 50,000. There is a small Jewish community, and in 1987 an agreement recognized certain rights for the Jewish community, including the right to observe religious festivals on Saturdays by not attending school or work. There is also a substantial Islamic population.

CHRISTIANITY

The Roman Catholic Church

For ecclesiastical purposes, Italy comprises the Papal See of Rome, the Patriarchate of Venice, 60 archdioceses (including three directly responsible to the Holy See), two eparchies, 153 dioceses (including seven within the jurisdiction of the Pope, as Archbishop of the Roman Province, and 11 directly responsible to the Holy See), two territorial prelatures and seven territorial abbacies (including four directly responsible to the Holy See). Almost all adherents follow the Latin rite, but there are two dioceses and one abbacy (all directly responsible to the Holy See) for Catholics of the Italo-Albanian (Byzantine) rite.

Bishops' Conference

Conferenza Episcopale Italiana, Circonvallazione Aurelia 50, 00165 Roma; tel. (06) 663981; fax (06) 6623037; e-mail segrgen@chiesacattolica.it; internet www.chiesacattolica.it.
f. 1965; Pres. Cardinal ANGELO BAGNASCO (Archbishop of Genova); Sec.-Gen. Mgr GIUSEPPE BETORI.

Primate of Italy, Archbishop and Metropolitan of the Roman Province and Bishop of Rome: His Holiness Pope BENEDICT XVI.

Patriarch of Venice: Cardinal ANGELO SCOLA.

Archbishops

Acerenza: Most Rev. GIOVANNI RICCHIUTI.
Agrigento: Most Rev. CARMELO FERRARO.
Amalfi-Cava de' Tirreni: Most Rev. ORAZIO SORICELLI.
Ancona-Osimo: Most Rev. EDOARDO MENICHELLI.
Bari-Bitonto: Most Rev. FRANCESCO CACUCCI.
Benevento: Most Rev. ANDREA MUGIONE.
Bologna: Cardinal CARLO CAFFARRA.
Brindisi-Otsuni: Most Rev. ROCCO TALUCCI.
Cagliari: Most Rev. GIUSEPPE MANI.
Camerino-San Severino Marche: Most Rev. ANGELO FAGIANI.
Campobasso-Boiano: Most Rev. GIANCARLO MARIA BREGANTINI.
Capua: Most Rev. BRUNO SCHETTINO.
Catania: Most Rev. SALVATORE GRISTINA.
Catanzaro-Squillace: Most Rev. ANTONIO CILIBERTI.
Chieti-Vasto: Most Rev. BRUNO FORTE.
Cosenza-Bisignano: Most Rev. SALVATORE NUNNARI.
Crotone-Santa Severina: DOMENICO GRAZIANI.
Fermo: Most Rev. LUIGI CONTI.
Ferrara-Comacchio: Most Rev. PAOLO RABITTI.
Firenze (Florence): Cardinal EMILIO ANTONELLI.
Foggia-Bovino: Most Rev. FRANCESCO PIO TAMBURRINO.
Gaeta: Most Rev. PIER LUIGI MAZZONI.
Genova (Genoa): Cardinal ANGELO BAGNASCO.
Gorizia: Most Rev. DINO DE ANTONI.
Lanciano-Ortona: Most Rev. CARLO GHIDELLI.
L'Aquila: Most Rev. GIUSEPPE MOLINARI.
Lecce: Most Rev. COSMO FRANCESCO RUPPI.
Lucca: Most Rev. BENVENUTO ITALO CASTELLANI.
Manfredonia-Vieste-San Giovanni Rotondo: Most Rev. DOMENICO UMBERTO D'AMBROSIO.
Matera-Irsina: Most Rev. SALVATORE LIGORIO.
Messina-Lipari-Sant Lucia del Mela: Most Rev. CALOGERO LA PIANA.
Milano (Milan): Cardinal DIONIGI TETTAMANZI.
Modena-Nonantola: Most Rev. BENITO COCCHI.
Monreale: Most Rev. SALVATORE DI CRISTINA.
Napoli (Naples): Cardinal CRESCENZIO SEPE.
Oristano: Most Rev. IGNAZIO SANNA.
Otranto: Most Rev. DONATO NEGRO.
Palermo: Most Rev. PAOLO ROMEO.
Perugia-Città della Pieve: Most Rev. GIUSEPPE CHIARETTI.
Pesaro: Most Rev. PIERO COCCIA.
Pescara-Penne: Most Rev. TOMMASO VALENTINETTI.
Pisa: Most Rev. GIOVANNI PAOLO BENOTTO.
Potenza-Muro Lucano-Marsico Nuovo: Most Rev. AGOSTINO SUPERBO.
Ravenna-Cervia: Most Rev. GIUSEPPE VERUCCHI.
Reggio Calabria-Bova: Most Rev. VITTORIO LUIGI MONDELLO.
Rossano-Cariati: Most Rev. SANTO MARCHIANÒ.
Salerno-Campagna-Acerno: Most Rev. GERARDO PIERRO.
Sant'Angelo dei Lombardi-Conza-Nusco-Bisaccia: Most Rev. FRANCESCO ALFANO.
Sassari: Most Rev. PAOLO MARIO VIRGILIO ATZEI.
Siena-Colle di Val d'Elsa-Montalcino: Most Rev. ANTONIO BUONCRISTIANI.
Siracusa (Syracuse): Most Rev. GIUSEPPE COSTANZO.
Sorrento-Castellamare di Stabia: Most Rev. FELICE CECE.
Spoleto-Norcia: Most Rev. RICCARDO FONTANA.
Taranto: Most Rev. BENIGNO LUIGI PAPA.
Torino (Turin): Cardinal SEVERINO POLETTO.
Trani-Barletta-Bisceglie: Most Rev. GIOVANNI BATTISTA PICHIERRI.
Trento: Most Rev. LUIGI BRESSAN.
Udine: Most Rev. PIETRO BROLLO.
Urbino-Urbania-Sant'Angelo in Vado: Most Rev. FRANCESCO MARINELLI.
Vercelli: Most Rev. ENRICO MASSERONI.

Protestant Churches

Federazione delle Chiese Evangeliche in Italia (Federation of the Protestant Churches in Italy): Via Firenze 38, 00184 Roma; tel. (06) 4825120; fax (06) 4828728; e-mail fcei@fcei.it; internet www.fcei.it; f. 1967; total mems 65,000; Pres. DOMENICO MASELLI; 10 mem. churches, incl. the following:

Chiesa Evangelica Luterana in Italia (Lutheran Church): Via Aurelia Antica 391, 00165 Roma; tel. (06) 66030104; fax (06) 66017993; e-mail decanato@elki-celi.org; internet www.elki-celi.org; Dean HOLGER MILKAU; 7,000 mems.

Chiesa Evangelica Valdese (Unione delle Chiese Metodiste e Valdesi) (Waldensian Evangelical Church): Via Firenze 38, 00184 Roma; tel. (06) 4743695; fax (06) 47885308; e-mail info@chiesavaldese.org; internet www.chiesavaldese.org; in 2002 the Tavola Valdese merged with the Chiese Evangeliche Metodiste in Italia (Methodists); Moderator GIANNI GENRE; Sec.-Treas. ROSELLA PANZIRONI; 27,465 mems.

ISLAM

Associazione Musulmani Italiani (AMI) (Italian Muslim Association): CP 7167, Roma; tel. and fax (06) 44360619; e-mail info@amimuslims.org; internet www.amimuslims.org; f. 1982; Pres. OMAR DANILO SPERANZA.

Unione delle Comunità ed Organizazioni Islamiche in Italia (UCOII): tel. (0183) 767601; fax (0183) 764735; e-mail ucoii@uno.it; internet www.islam-ucoii.it; f. 1990; Pres. MOHAMED NOUR DACHAN; Sec. HAMZA PICCARDO.

JUDAISM

Unione delle Comunità Ebraiche Italiane (UCEI) (Union of Italian Jewish Communities): Lungotevere Sanzio 9, 00153 Roma; tel. (06) 5803667; fax (06) 5899569; e-mail amministrazione@ucei.it; internet www.ucei.it; f. 1930; represents 21 Jewish communities in Italy; Pres. RENZO GATTEGNA; Chief Rabbi of Rome Dott. RICCARDO DI SEGNI.

The Press

Relative to the size of Italy's population, the number of daily newspapers is rather small. Rome and Milan are the main press centres. The most important national dailies are *Corriere della Sera* in Milan and Rome and *La Repubblica* in Rome, followed by Turin's *La Stampa* and Milan's *Il Sole 24 Ore*, the economic and financial newspaper with the highest circulation in Europe. Among the

ITALY

most widely read newspapers are *La Gazzetta dello Sport* and *Il Corriere dello Sport—Stadio*, both of which exclusively cover sports news.

PRINCIPAL DAILIES

Ancona

Il Corriere Adriatico: Via Berti 20, 60126 Ancona; tel. (071) 4581; fax (071) 42980; e-mail info@corriereadriaticonline.it; internet www.corriereadriatico.it; f. 1860; Editorial Dir PAOLO TRAINI; circ. 29,349.

Bari

La Gazzetta del Mezzogiorno: Viale Scipione l'Africano 264, 70124 Bari; tel. (080) 5470200; fax (080) 5502130; e-mail direzione.politica@gazzettamezzogiorno.it; internet www.lagazzettadelmezzogiorno.it; f. 1887; independent; Editor LINO PATRUNO; circ. 54,997.

Il Quotidiano di Bari: Piazza Aldo Moro 31, 70121 Bari; tel. (080) 5240473; fax (080) 5245486; e-mail redazione@quotidianodibari.it; internet www.quotidianodibari.it; Dir LUCIANO VENTURA.

Bergamo

L'Eco di Bergamo: Viale Papa Giovanni XXIII 118, 24121 Bergamo; tel. (035) 386111; fax (035) 386217; e-mail redazione@eco.bg.it; internet www.eco.bg.it; f. 1880; Catholic; Man. Dott. ETTORE ONGIS; circ. 55,919.

Bologna

Il Resto del Carlino: Via Enrico Mattei 106, 40138 Bologna; tel. (051) 6006111; fax (051) 536111; e-mail segreteria@ilrestodelcarlino.it; internet www.ilrestodelcarlino.it; f. 1885; publr Poligrafici Editoriale, SpA; Dir GIANCARLO MAZZUCA; circ. 169,774.

Bolzano/Bozen

Alto Adige: Via Volta 10, 39100 Bozen; tel. (0471) 904111; fax (0471) 9042663; e-mail bolzano@altoadige.it; internet www.altoadige.it; f. 1945; publr Gruppo Editoriale L'Espresso, SpA; Dir TIZIANO MARSON; circ. 36,567.

Dolomiten: Weinbergweg 7, 39100 Bozen; tel. (0471) 925111; fax (0471) 925440; e-mail dolomiten@athesia.it; internet www.dolomiten.it; f. 1882; independent; German language; Dir Dr TONI EBNER; circ. 56,623.

Brescia

Il Giornale di Brescia: Via Solferino 22, 25121 Brescia; tel. (030) 37901; fax (030) 292226; internet www.giornaledibrescia.it; f. 1945; Dir GIACOMO SCANZI; circ. 49,929.

Cagliari

L'Unione Sarda: Viale Regina Elena 12, 9100 Cagliari; tel. (070) 60131; fax (070) 6013306; e-mail unione@unionesarda.it; internet www.unionesarda.it; f. 1889; independent; Editor-in-Chief PAOLO FIGUS; circ. 81,000 (2006).

Catania

La Sicilia: Viale Odorico da Pordenone 50, 95126 Catania; tel. (095) 330544; fax (095) 336466; e-mail segreteria@lasicilia.it; internet www.lasicilia.it; f. 1945; independent; Man. Dott. MARIO CIANCIO SANFILIPPO; circ. 64,600.

Como

La Provincia di Como: Via Pasquale Paoli 21, 22100 Como; tel. (031) 582211; fax (031) 526450; e-mail laprovincia@laprovincia.it; internet www.laprovinciadicomo.it; f. 1892; independent; Dir MICHELE BRAMBILLA; circ. 56,000.

Firenze
(Florence)

La Nazione: Viale Giovase Italia 17, 50121 Firenze; tel. (055) 249511; fax (055) 2478207; e-mail segreteria@lanazione.it; internet www.lanazione.it; f. 1859; publr Poligrafici Editoriale, SpA; Dir FRANCESCO CARRASI; circ. 138,175.

Foggia

Quotidiano di Foggia: Via Gramsci 73A, 71100 Foggia; tel. (0881) 686967; fax (0881) 632247; internet www.quotidianodifoggia.it; Dir MATTEO TATTARELLA; circ. 25,000 (2007).

Genova
(Genoa)

Corriere Mercantile: Via Archimede 169/R, 16142 Genova; tel. (010) 53691; fax (010) 504148; f. 1824; political and financial; independent; Editor MIMMO ANGELI; circ. 16,000.

Il Secolo XIX: Piazza Piccapietra 21, 16121 Genova; tel. (010) 53881; fax (010) 5388388; e-mail marketing@ilsecoloxix.it; internet www.ilsecoloXIX.it; f. 1886; independent; Dir LANFRANCO VACCARI; circ. 179,360.

Lecce

Nuovo Quotidiano di Puglia: Via dei Mocenigo 29, 73100 Lecce; tel. (0832) 3382000; fax (0832) 338244; e-mail quotidiano@caltanet.it; f. 1979 as *Il Quotidiano di Lecce*; 3 local edns covering Lecce, Brindisi and Taranto; Dir GIANCARLO MINICUCCI; circ. 19,671.

Livorno

Il Tirreno: Viale Alfieri 9, 57124 Livorno; tel. (0586) 220111; fax (0586) 402066; e-mail redazione.li@iltirreno.it; internet iltirreno.repubblica.it; f. 1978; publr Gruppo Editoriale L'Espresso, SpA; Dir BRUNO MANFELLOTTO; circ. 83,294.

Mantova
(Mantua)

Gazzetta di Mantova: Via Fratelli Bandiera 32, 46100 Mantova; tel. (0376) 3031; fax (0376) 303263; e-mail redazione.mn@gazzettadimantova.it; internet www.gazzettadimantova.it; f. 1664; publr Gruppo Editoriale L'Espresso, SpA; Dir ENRICO GRAZIOLE; circ. 34,556.

Messina

Gazzetta del Sud: Uberto Bonino 15C, 98124 Messina; tel. (090) 2261; fax (090) 2936359; internet www.gazzettadelsud.it; f. 1952; independent; Dir NINO CALARCO; circ. 52,578.

Milano
(Milan)

Avvenire: Piazza Carbonari 3, 20125 Milano; tel. (02) 67801; fax (02) 6780208; internet www.avvenire.it; f. 1968; Catholic; Man. Dir DINO BOFFO; circ. 148,000.

Corriere della Sera: Via Solferino 28, 20121 Milano; tel. (02) 6339; fax (02) 29009668; internet www.corriere.it; f. 1876; independent; contains weekly supplement, Sette; Dir PAOLO MIELI; circ. 672,000 (2005).

Il Foglio Quotidiano: Largo Corsia dei Servi 3, 20122 Milano; tel. (02) 7712951; fax (02) 781378; e-mail lettere@ilfoglio.it; internet www.ilfoglio.it; Dir GIULIANO FERRARA.

La Gazzetta dello Sport: RCS Editoriale Quotidiani, SpA, Via Solferino 28, 20121 Milano; tel. (02) 6339; e-mail segretgaz@rcs.it; internet www.gazzetta.it; f. 1896; sport; Dir CARLO VERDELLI; circ. 426,000.

Il Giornale: Via Gaetano Negri 4, 20123 Milano; tel. (02) 85661; fax (02) 72023880; e-mail segreteria@ilgiornale.it; internet www.ilgiornale.it; f. 1974; Editor MARIO GIORDANO; circ. 215,796.

Il Giorno: Via Stradivari 4, 20123 Milano; tel. (02) 277991; fax (02) 27799537; e-mail ilgiorno@ilgiorno.it; internet www.ilgiorno.it; f. 1956; publr Poligrafici Editoriale, SpA; Dir GIOVANNI MORANDI; circ. 74,284.

Italia Oggi: Class Editori, Via M. Burigozzo 5, 20122 Milano; tel. (02) 58219256; e-mail italiaoggi@class.it; internet www.italiaoggi.it; f. 1991; economic daily; circ. 88,538; Dir FRANCO BECHIS.

Libero: Viale L. Majno 42, 20129 Milano; tel. (02) 99966300; fax (02) 99966305; e-mail redazione@libero-news.eu; internet www.libero-news.it; f. 2000; Dir VITTORIO FELTRI; circ. 133,885.

MF (Milano Finanza): Class Editori, Via M. Burigozzo 5, 20122 Milano; tel. (02) 582191; internet www.milanofinanza.it; f. 1989; economic daily; Dir ENRICO ROMAGNA MANOJA.

Il Sole 24 Ore: Via Monte Rosa 91, 20149 Milano; tel. (02) 30221; fax (02) 312055; internet www.ilsole24ore.com; f. 1865; financial, political, economic; Dir FERRUCCIO DE BORTOLI; circ. 348,702.

Napoli
(Naples)

Corriere del Mezzogiorno: Vico II San Nicola alla Dogana 9, 80133 Napoli; tel. (081) 7602001; fax (081) 5802779; e-mail m.demarco@corrieredelmezzogiorno.it; internet www.corrieredelmezzogiorno.it; f. 1997; publr RCS MediaGroup; Dir MARCO DEMARCO.

Il Denaro: Piazza dei Martiri 58, 80121 Napoli; tel. (081) 421900; fax (081) 422212; e-mail denaro@denaro.it; internet www.denaro.it; economic daily; Dir ALFONSO RUFFO.

ITALY

Il Mattino: Via Chiatamone 65, 80121 Napoli; tel. (081) 7947111; fax (081) 7947288; e-mail posta@ilmattino.it; internet www.ilmattino.it; f. 1892; reformed 1950; independent; Dir Gen. MASSIMO GARZILLI; Editor MARIO ORFEO; circ. 84,184.

Padova
(Padua)

Il Mattino di Padova: Via N. Tommaseo, 65B, 35131 Padova; tel. (049) 8083411; fax (049) 8070067; e-mail mattino@mattinopadova.it; internet www.mattinopadova.it; f. 1978; publr Gruppo Editoriale L'Espresso, SpA; Dir OMAR MONESTIER; circ. 30,461.

Palermo

Giornale di Sicilia: Via Lincoln 21, 90122 Palermo; tel. (091) 6627111; fax (091) 6627280; e-mail gds@gestelnet.it; internet www.gds.it; f. 1860; independent; Dir ANTONIO ARDIZZONE; circ. 87,189.

Parma

Gazzetta di Parma: Via Mantova 68, 43100 Parma; tel. (0521) 2251; fax (0521) 225522; e-mail gazzetta@gazzettadiparma.net; internet www.gazzettadiparma.it; f. 1735; Dir GIULIANO MOLOSSI; circ. 56,000.

Perugia

Corriere dell'Umbria: Via Pievaiola Km 5700, 06100 Perugia; tel. (075) 52731; fax (075) 5273259; internet umbria.corr.it; f. 1983; independent; Editor FEDERICO FIORAVANTI; circ. 23,000.

Pescara

Il Centro: Via Michelangelo 18, 65122 Pescara; tel. (085) 20521; fax (085) 4212460; e-mail lettere@ilcentro.it; internet www.ilcentro.it; f. 1986; publr Gruppo Editoriale L'Espresso, SpA; Dir LUIGI VICINANZA; circ. 23,217.

Piacenza

Libertà: Via Benedettine 68, 29100 Piacenza; tel. (0523) 393939; fax (0523) 321723; e-mail prestampa@liberta.it; internet www.liberta.it; f. 1883; Dir GAETANO RIZZUTO; circ. 40,000.

Rimini

Corriere di Romagna: Piazza Tre Martiri 43A, 47900 Rimini; tel. (0541) 354111; fax (0541) 351499; e-mail lega@corriereromagna.it; internet www.corriereromagna.it; also distributed in San Marino; Dir STEFANO TAMBURINI.

Roma
(Rome)

Conquiste del Lavoro: Via Po 21, 00198 Roma; tel. (06) 84731; fax (06) 8413782; e-mail conquiste_lavoro@cisl.it; internet www.conquistedellavoro.it; owned by Confederazione Italiana Sindacati Lavoratori (CISL); circ. 50,000.

Il Corriere dello Sport—Stadio: Piazza Indipendenza 11B, 00185 Roma; tel. (06) 49921; fax (06) 4992690; internet www.corsport.it; f. 1924; Editor MARIO SCONCERTI; circ. 239,249.

Europa Quotidiano: Via di Ripetta 142, 00186 Roma; tel. (06) 45401010; fax (06) 45401041; e-mail segr.redazione@europaquotidiano.it; internet www.europaquotidiano.it; f. 2003; organ of the Margherita coalition; Dir STEFANO MENICHINI.

Il Giornale d'Italia: Società Editrice Esedra Srl, Via Parigli 11, 00185 Roma; tel. (06) 474901; fax (06) 4883435; e-mail g.italia@tiscalinet.it; f. 1901; Man. PAOLO FRAIOLI; Editor MATTIAS MAINIERO; circ. 70,000.

Liberazione: Viale del Policlinico 131, 00161 Roma; tel. (06) 441831; fax (06) 44183247; e-mail posta@liberazione.it; internet www.liberazione.it; organ of the Partito della Rifondazione Comunista; Dir ALESSANDRO CURZI; circ. 41,897.

Il Manifesto: Via Tomacelli 146, 00186 Roma; tel. (06) 687191; fax (06) 68719573; e-mail redazione@ilmanifesto.it; internet www.ilmanifesto.it; f. 1971; splinter communist; Dir RICCARDO BARENGHI; circ. 29,885.

Il Messaggero: Via del Tritone 152, 00187 Roma; tel. (06) 47201; fax (06) 4720300; e-mail posta@ilmessaggero.it; internet www.ilmessaggero.it; f. 1878; independent; Pres. FRANCO G. CALTAGIRONE; Editor ROBERTO NAPOLETANO; circ. 235,000 (2005).

E Polis: Piazza Farnese 58, 00186 Roma; tel. (06) 42883523; e-mail roma@epolisroma.it; internet www.epolis.sm; f. 2004; free; 17 local edns: *E Polis Roma*, *E Polis Milano*, *Il Bari*, *Il Bergamo*, *Il Bologna*, *Il Brescia*, *Il Firenze*, *Il Mestre*, *Il Napoli*, *Il Padova*, *Il Sardegna (nord)*, *Il Sardegna (sud)*, *Il Treviso*, *Il Venezia*, *Il Verona* and *Il Vicenza*; Dir ANTONIO CIPRIANI; circ. 337,237.

La Repubblica: Via Cristoforo Colombo 149, 00147 Roma; tel. (06) 49821; fax (06) 49822923; e-mail larepubblica@repubblica.it; internet www.repubblica.it; f. 1976; publr Gruppo Editoriale L'Espresso, SpA; left-wing; Editor EZIO MAURO; circ. 625,090.

Il Riformista: Piazza Barberini 52, 00187, Roma; tel. (06) 427481; e-mail redazione@ilriformista.it; internet www.ilriformista.it; political; Dir PAOLO FRANCHI.

Secolo d'Italia: Via della Scrofa 43, 00186 Roma; tel. (06) 68899221; fax (06) 6861598; e-mail segreteria@secoloditalia.it; internet www.alleanzanazionale.it/secoloditalia.aspx; f. 1951; organ of the AN; Editor-in-Chief LUCIANO LANNA.

Il Tempo: L'Editrice Romana, SpA, Piazza Colonna 366, 00187 Roma; tel. (06) 675881; fax (06) 6758869; internet www.iltempo.it; f. 1944; independent; right-wing; Editor GIUSEPPE SANZOTTA; circ. 51,948.

L'Unità: Via Francesco Benaglia 25, 00153 Roma; tel. (06) 585571; fax (06) 58557219; e-mail unitaonline@unita.it; internet www.unita.it; f. 1924; Dir ANTONIO PADELLARO; circ. 55,961 (2007).

Salerno

La Città: Corso Garibaldi 215, 84100 Salerno; tel. (089) 245111; fax (089) 245236; internet www.lacittadisalerno.it; Dir MAURIZIO DE LUCA.

Sassari

La Nuova Sardegna: Strada 30–31, Predda Niedda, 07100 Sassari; tel. (079) 222400; fax (079) 200144; e-mail redazione@lanuovasardegna.it; internet lanuovasardegna.repubblica.it; f. 1891; publr Gruppo Editoriale L'Espresso, SpA; Dir STEFANO DEL RE; circ. 58,643.

Torino
(Turin)

La Stampa: Via Marenco 32, 10126 Torino; tel. (011) 656811; fax (011) 655306; e-mail lettere@lastampa.it; internet www.lastampa.it; f. 1867; independent; Dir GIULIO ANSELMI; circ. 410,000.

Trento

L'Adige: Via Missioni Africane 17, 38100 Trento; tel. (0461) 886111; fax (0461) 886264; e-mail p.giovanetti@ladige.it; internet www.ladige.it; f. 1946; independent; Dir Dott. PIERANGELO GIOVANETTI; circ. 30,308.

Trieste

Il Piccolo: Via Guido Reni 1, 34123 Trieste; tel. (040) 3733111; fax (040) 3733262; e-mail ufficio.centrale@ilpiccolo.it; internet ilpiccolo.repubblica.it; f. 1881; publr Gruppo Editoriale L'Espresso, SpA; Dir SERGIO BARALDI; circ. 42,241.

Primorski Dnevnik: Via dei Montecchi 6, 34137 Trieste; tel. (040) 7786300; fax (040) 772418; e-mail redakcija@primorski.it; internet www.primorski.it; f. 1945; Slovene; Editor-in-Chief BOJAN BREZIGAR; circ. 11,282.

Udine

Il Messaggero Veneto: Viale Palmanova 290, 33100 Udine; tel. (0432) 5271; fax (0432) 523072; e-mail redazione@messaggeroveneto.it; internet www.messaggeroveneto.it; f. 1946; publr Gruppo Editoriale L'Espresso, SpA; Dir ANDREA FILIPPI; circ. 51,684.

Varese

La Prealpina: Viale Tamagno 13, 21100 Varese; tel. (0332) 275700; fax (0332) 275701; e-mail direttore@prealpina.it; internet www.prealpina.it; f. 1888; Dir ROBERTO FERRARIO; circ. 40,000.

Venezia
(Venice)

Il Gazzettino: Via Torino 110, 30172 Venezia-Mestre; tel. (041) 665111; fax (041) 665413; e-mail segredazione@gazzettino.it; internet www.gazzettino.it; f. 1887; independent; Dir ROBERTO PAPETTI; circ. 95,545.

Verona

L'Arena: Viale del Lavoro 11, 37036, San Martino Buon Albergo, Verona; tel. (045) 8094899; fax (045) 597966; e-mail redazione@larena.it; internet www.larena.it; f. 1866; independent; Editor-in-Chief MAURIZIO CATTANEO; Man. Dir Ing. ALESSANDRO ZELGER; circ. 68,000.

Vicenza

Il Giornale di Vicenza: Viale S. Lazzaro 89, 36100 Vicenza; tel. (0444) 396311; fax (0444) 396333; internet www.ilgiornaledivicenza.it; f. 1945; Dir GIULIO ANTONACCI; circ. 42,425.

SELECTED PERIODICALS

Art, Architecture and Design

Abitare: Via Ventura 5, 20134 Milano; tel. (02) 210581; fax (02) 21058316; e-mail redazione@abitare.it; internet www.abitare.it; f. 1962; monthly; architecture and design; in Italian and English; Editor RENATO MINETTO; Dir ITALO LUPI.

Casabella: Via Trentacoste 7, 20134 Milano; tel. (02) 215631; fax (02) 21563260; e-mail casabella@mondadori.it; f. 1928; 10 a year; architecture and interior design; Editor FRANCESCO DAL CO; circ. 43,000.

Domus: Via Gianni Mazzocchi 1/3, 20089 Rozzano, Milano; tel. (02) 824721; fax (02) 82472386; e-mail redazione@domusweb.it; internet www.domusweb.it; f. 1928; 11 a year; architecture, interior design and art; Editor G. MAZZOCCHI; circ. 53,000.

Graphicus: Alberto Greco Editore, Via Salvator Rosa 14, 20156 Milano; tel. (02) 300391; fax (02) 30039300; e-mail graphicus.age@gruppodg.com; internet www.eurographicus.com; f. 1911; 10 a year; printing and graphic arts; circ. 7,200.

Interni: Via D. Trentacoste 7, 20134 Milano; tel. (02) 215631; fax (02) 26410847; e-mail interni@mondadori.it; internet www.interimagazine.it; monthly; interior decoration and design; Editor GILDA BOJARDI; circ. 50,000.

Lotus International: Via Santa Marta 19A, 20123 Milano; tel. (02) 45475745; fax (02) 45475746; e-mail lotus@editorialelotus.it; internet www.editorialelotus.it; f. 1963; quarterly; architecture, town-planning; Editor PIERLUIGI NICOLIN.

Storia dell'Arte: CAM Editrice, Srl, Via Capodiferro 4, 00186 Roma; tel. and fax (06) 68300889; e-mail info@cameditrice.com; internet www.cameditrice.com; f. 1968; quarterly; art history; Dir MAURIZIO CALVESI; circ. 2,500.

Education

Cooperazione Educativa: Edizioni Erickson, Via dei Piceni 16, 00185 Roma; tel. (06) 4457228; fax (06) 4460386; e-mail mceroma@tin.it; f. 1952; 3 a year; education; Dir MIRELLA GRIECO.

Il Maestro: Clivo di Monte del Gallo 48, 00165 Roma; tel. (06) 634651; fax (06) 39375903; e-mail a.i.m.c@flashnet.it; internet www.aimc.it; f. 1945; monthly; Catholic teachers' magazine; Dir GIUSEPPE DESIDERI; circ. 40,000.

Scuola e Didattica: Via Luigi Cadorna 11, 25124 Brescia; tel. (030) 2993245; e-mail sdid@lascuola.it; internet www.lascuola.it; f. 1955; 18 a year; education; Editor PIERPAOLO TRIANI; circ. 40,000.

General, Political and Economic

Economy: Arnoldo Mondadori Editore, SpA, Via Mondadori 1, 20090 Segrate (Milano); tel. (02) 75421; fax (02) 75422302; e-mail economy@mondadori.it; f. 2003; weekly; economics and finance; Dir SERGIO LUCIANO; circ. 85,000.

L'Espresso: Via Cristoforo Colombo 90, 00147 Roma; tel. (06) 84781; fax (06) 84787220; e-mail espresso@espressoedit.it; internet espresso.repubblica.it; weekly; independent left; political; Editor DANIELA HAMAUI; circ. 390,000.

Famiglia Cristiana: Via Giotto 36, 20145 Milano; tel. (02) 48071; fax (02) 48008247; e-mail famigliacristiana@stpauls.it; internet www.sanpaolo.org/fc; f. 1931; weekly; Catholic; illustrated; Dir ANTONIO SCIORTINO; circ. 697,265.

Gazzetta del Lunedì: Via Archimede 169/R, 16142 Genova; tel. (010) 53691; fax (010) 504148; f. 1946; Monday edn of *Corriere Mercantile*; political; Dir GEROLAMO ANGELI; circ. 15,588.

Gente: Viale Sarca 235, 20126 Milano; tel. (02) 27751; f. 1957; weekly; illustrated current events and general interest; circ. 443,469.

Il Mulino: Strada Maggiore 37, 40125 Bologna; tel. (051) 222419; fax (051) 6486014; e-mail ilmulino@mulino.it; internet www.mulino.it/ilmulino; f. 1951; every 2 months; culture and politics; Dir EDMONDO BERCELLI; Editor-in-Chief BRUNO SIMILI.

Oggi: Via San Marco 21, 20121 Milano; tel. (02) 25841; fax (02) 27201485; f. 1945; weekly; current affairs, culture, family life; illustrated; Dir PINO BELLERI; circ. 663,540.

Panorama: Arnoldo Mondadori Editore, SpA, Via Marconi 27, 20090 Segrate, Milano; tel. (02) 75421; fax (02) 75422769; e-mail panorama@mondadori.it; internet www.panorama.it; f. 1962; weekly; current affairs; Dir MAURIZIO BELPIETRO; circ. 501,111.

Selezione dal Reader's Digest: Via Lorenzini 4, 20139 Milano; tel. (02) 53584761; fax (02) 61293497; e-mail info@selezionerd.it; internet www.selezionerd.it; monthly; circ. 521,432.

Visto: Via Rizzoli 4, 20132 Milano; tel. (02) 25843961; fax (02) 25843907; f. 1989; weekly; entertainment, celebrities, current events; Editor-in-Chief LUCIANA FRATTESI; circ. 193,235.

Zett—Die Zeitung am Sonntag: Weinberggweg 7, 39100 Bozen; tel. (0471) 925500; fax (0471) 200462; e-mail zett@athesia.it; f. 1989; Sundays; German language; circ. 34,000.

History, Literature and Music

Belfagor: Leo S. Olschki, Viuzzo del Pozzetto, 50126 Firenze; tel. (055) 6530684; fax (055) 6530214; e-mail celso@olschki.it; internet www.olschki.it/riviste/belfagor.htm; f. 1946; every 2 months; historical and literary criticism; Editor CARLO FERDINANDO RUSSO; circ. 2,500.

Giornale della Libreria: Corso di Porta Romana 108, 20122 Milano; tel. (02) 89280802; fax (02) 89280862; e-mail redazione@giornaledellalibreria.it; internet www.giornaledellalibreria.it; f. 1888; monthly; organ of the Associazione Italiana Editori; bibliographical; Editor FEDERICO MOTTA; circ. 5,000.

Lettere Italiane: Leo S. Olschki, CP 66, 50123 Firenze; tel. (055) 6530684; fax (055) 6530214; e-mail pizzamig@unive.it; internet www.olschki.it/riviste/lettital.htm; f. 1949; quarterly; literary; Dirs CARLO OSSOLA, CARLO DELCORNO.

Il Pensiero Politico: Leo S. Olschki, Viuzzo del Pozzetto, 50126 Firenze; tel. (055) 6530684; fax (055) 6530214; e-mail penspol@unipg.it; internet www.olschki.it/riviste/penspol.htm; f. 1968; every 4 months; political and social history; Editor VITTOR IVO COMPARATO.

Rivista di Storia della Filosofia: Viale Monza 106, 20127 Milano; tel. (02) 28371454; fax (02) 26141958; e-mail riviste@francoangeli.it; internet www.francoangeli.it/riviste/sommario.asp?IDRivista=45; f. 1946; quarterly; philosophy; Editor ENRICO I. RAMBALDI.

Leisure and Sport

Ciak: Arnoldo Mondadori Editore, SpA, Via Mondadori 1, 20090 Segrate, Milano; tel. (02) 75421; fax (02) 75422302; e-mail ciak@mondadori.it; f. 1985; monthly; cinema; Dir PIERA DETASSIS; circ. 102,022.

Cucina Moderna: Arnoldo Mondadori Editore SpA, Via Mondadori 1, 20090 Segrate, Milano; tel. (02) 75421; fax (02) 75422302; f. 1996; monthly; cookery; Dir GIOVANNA CAMOZZI; circ. 299,866.

Dove: Via Angelo Rizzoli 2, 20132 Milano; e-mail marina.poggi@rcs.it; internet viaggi.corriere.it; f. 1991; monthly; lifestyle and travel; Dir CARLO MONTANARO; circ. 123,395.

Gambero Rosso: GRH, SpA, Via E. Fermi 161, 00146 Roma; tel. (06) 551121; fax (06) 55112260; e-mail gambero@gamberorosso.it; internet www.gamberorosso.it; f. 1986; monthly; food and wine; Dir STEFANO BONILLI.

Max: Via Angelo Rizzoli 2, 20132 Milano; e-mail max@rcs.it; internet max.corriere.it; f. 1985; monthly; men's lifestyle; Dir ANDREA MONTI; circ. 132,412.

Motor: Piazza Antonio Mancini 4G, 00196 Roma; tel. (06) 3233195; fax (06) 3233309; e-mail motor@rivistamotor.com; internet www.rivistamotor.com; f. 1940; monthly; cars; Dir SERGIO FAVIA DEL CORE; circ. 35,500.

OK: RCS MediaGroup, Via San Marco 21, 20121 Milan; e-mail redazione@ok.rcs.it; internet ok.corriere.it; monthly; health; Editor ELIANA LIOTTA; circ. 277,931.

Quattroruote: Via Gianni Mazzocchi 1/3, 20089 Rozzano, Milano; tel. (02) 824721; fax (02) 57500416; e-mail redazione@quattroruote.it; internet www.quattroruote.it; f. 1956; motoring; monthly; Editor MAURO TEDESCHINI; circ. 650,000.

Starbene: Arnoldo Mondadori Editore SpA, Via Mondadori 1, 20090 Segrate, Milano; tel. (02) 75421; e-mail starbene@mondadori.it; internet www.starbene.it; f. 1978; monthly; health and beauty; Dir CRISTINA MERLINO; 395,050.

Telesette: Corso di Porta Nuova 3A, 20121 Milano; tel. (02) 63675415; fax (02) 63675524; e-mail segreteria@casaeditriceuniverso.com; f. 1978; weekly; television; Editor NICOLA DE FEO; circ. 485,389.

TV Sorrisi e Canzoni: Corso Europa 5–7, 20122 Milano; tel. (02) 77941; fax (02) 77947363; e-mail sorrisi@mondadori.it; internet www.sorrisi.com; f. 1952; weekly; television, entertainment; Dir UMBERTO BRINDANI; circ. 1.1m.

Vita in Campagna: Via Bencivenga/Biondani 16, 37133 Verona; tel. (045) 8057511; fax (045) 8009240; e-mail vitaincampagna@vitaincampagna.it; internet www.vitaincampagna.it; publr Editoriale L'Informatore Agrario, SpA; f. 1983; 11 a year; horticulture and smallholding; Editor ALBERTO RIZZOTTI; circ. 96,725.

Religion

Città di Vita: Piazza Santa Croce 16, 50122 Firenze; tel. and fax (055) 242783; e-mail info@cittadivita.org; internet www.cittadivita

.org; f. 1946; every 2 months; cultural review, theology, art and science; Dir MASSIMILIANO G. ROSITO; circ. 2,000.

La Civiltà Cattolica: Via di Porta Pinciana 1, 00187 Roma; tel. (06) 6979201; fax (06) 69792022; e-mail civcatt@laciviltacattolica.it; internet www.laciviltacattolica.it; f. 1850; fortnightly; Catholic; Editor GIAN PAOLO SALVINI; circ. 17,000.

Humanitas: Via G. Rosa 71, 25121 Brescia; tel. (030) 46451; fax (030) 2400605; e-mail redazione@morcelliana.it; internet www.morcelliana.it; f. 1946; every 2 months; religion, philosophy, science, politics, history, sociology, literature, etc.; Dir ILARIO BERTOLETTI.

Protestantesimo: Via Pietro Cossa 42, 00193 Roma; tel. (06) 3207055; fax (06) 3201040; e-mail protestantesimo@facoltavaldese.org; internet www.facoltavaldese.org; f. 1946; quarterly; Waldensian review; Dir Prof. FULVIO FERRARIO.

Rivista di Storia della Chiesa in Italia: Piazza San Giovanni in Laterano 4, 00184 Roma; tel. and fax (06) 69886176; e-mail rsci@pul.it; internet www.vitaepensiero.it; f. 1947; twice a year; Editor AGOSTINO PARAVICINI BAGLIANI.

Science, Technology and Medicine

Alberi e Territorio: Via Goito 13, 40126 Bologna; tel. (051) 65751; e-mail redazione.edagricole@ilsole24ore.com; internet www.edagricole.it; f. 2004 as successor to *Monti e Boschi* (f. 1949); 6 a year; ecology and forestry; Editor ELIA ZAMBONI; circ. 4,500.

Focus: Arnoldo Mondadori Editore SpA, Via Mondadori 1, 20090 Segrate, Milano; e-mail redazione@focus.it; internet www.focus.it; f. 1992; monthly; popular science and sociology; Dir SANDRO BOERI; circ. 606,563.

Il Nuovo Medico d'Italia: Via Monte Oliveto 2, 00141 Roma; tel. and fax (06) 87185017; e-mail numedi@tiscalinet.it; internet www.numedionline.it; monthly; medical science; Editor-in-Chief Dott. MARIO BERNARDINI.

Newton: Via Vitruvio 43, 20124 Milano; tel. (02) 675781; e-mail newton@rcs.it; internet newton.corriere.it; f. 1997; monthly; popular science; Dir GIORGIO RIVIECCIO; circ. 91,124.

Rivista Geografica Italiana: Via S. Gallo 10, 50129 Firenze; tel. and fax (055) 2757956; e-mail info@societastudigeografici.it; f. 1894; quarterly geographical review; Editor BRUNO VECCHIO.

Women's Interest

Amica: Via Angelo Rizzoli 2, 20132 Milano; tel. (02) 2588; f. 1962; monthly; Dir DANIELA BIANCHINI; circ. 175,663.

Anna: Via San Marco 21, 20121 Milano; tel. (02) 25843213; f. 1933; weekly; Editor MARIA LATELLA; circ. 219,294.

Chi: Arnoldo Mondadori Editore SpA, Via Mondadori 1, 20090 Segrate, Milano; e-mail chi@mondadori.it; f. 1995; weekly; celebrities, fashion; Dir ALFONSO SIGNORINI; 528,880.

Confidenze: Arnoldo Mondadori Editore, SpA, Via Mondadori 1, 20090 Segrate, Milano; tel. (02) 75421; fax (02) 75422806; e-mail braccif@mondadori.it; f. 1946; weekly; Dir CHRISTINA MAGNASCHI; circ. 229,825.

Cosmopolitan: Arnoldo Mondadori Editore, SpA, Via Marconi 27, 20090 Segrate, Milano; e-mail cosmopolitan@mondadori.it; internet www.cosmopolitan.it; f. 2000; monthly; Dir SIMONA MOVILIA; circ. 232,106.

Donna Moderna: Arnoldo Mondadori Editore, SpA, Via Mondadori 1, 20090 Segrate, Milano; e-mail donnamoderna@mondadori.it; internet www.donnamoderna.com; weekly; Dir PATRIZIA AVOLEDO.

Gioia: Viale Sarca 235, 20126 Milano; tel. (02) 66191; fax (02) 66192717; e-mail gioia@rusconi.it; f. 1937; weekly; Dir VERA MONTANARI; circ. 215,189.

Grazia: Arnoldo Mondadori Editore, SpA, Via Mondadori 1, 20090 Segrate, Milano; tel. (02) 75422390; fax (02) 75422515; e-mail grazia@mondadori.it; f. 1938; weekly; Dir CARLA VANNI; circ. 379,820.

Intimità: Piazza Aspromonte 13, 20131 Milano; tel. (02) 706421; fax (02) 70642306; e-mail intimita@quadratum.it; internet www.quadratum.it; weekly; Dir ANNA GIUSTI; circ. 275,579.

Vogue Italia: Piazza Castello 27, 20121 Milano; tel. (02) 85611; fax (02) 8055716; internet www.vogue.it; monthly; Editor FRANCA SOZZANI; circ. 106,187.

NEWS AGENCIES

AdnKronos: Palazzo dell'Informazione, Piazza Mastai 9, 00153 Roma; tel. (06) 58017; fax (06) 5807807; e-mail segreteria.redazione@adnkronos.com; internet www.adnkronos.it; Dir-Gen. MARIA ROSARIA BELLIZZI DE MARCO.

Agenzia Giornalistica Italia (AGI): Via Cristoforo Colombo 98, 00147 Roma; tel. (06) 519961; fax (06) 51996362; e-mail info@agenziaitalia.it; internet www.agi.it; f. 1950; Gen. Man. GIULIANO DE RISI.

Agenzia Nazionale Stampa Associata (ANSA): Via della Dataria 94, 00187 Roma; tel. (06) 67741; fax (06) 6774638; e-mail redazione.internet@ansa.it; internet www.ansa.it; f. 1945; co-operative, owned by 36 Italian newspapers; 22 regional offices in Italy and 81 brs internationally; service in Italian, Spanish, French, English; Pres. BORIS BIANCHERI; Dir-Gen. MARIO ROSSO.

APCOM (Telecom Media News, SpA): Via del Gesù 62, 00186 Roma; tel. (06) 695391; fax (06) 69539522; e-mail redazione@apcom.it; internet www.apcom.it; f. 2001; owned by Telecom Italia Media; partner of Associated Press (USA); operates in Italy and Switzerland.

Asca (Agenzia Stampa Quotidiana Nazionale): Via Ennio Quirino Visconti 8, 00193 Roma; tel. (06) 361484; e-mail agenzia@asca.it; internet www.asca.it; f. 1969; Dir CLAUDIO SONZOGNO.

Documentazioni Informazioni Resoconti (Dire): Via Guiseppe Marchi 4, 00161 Roma; tel. (06) 45499500; fax (06) 45499609; e-mail segr.direzione@dire.it; internet www.dire.it; Dir GIUSEPPE PACE.

Inter Press Service International Association (IPS): Via Panisperna 207, 00184 Roma; tel. (06) 485692; fax (06) 4817877; e-mail headquarters@ips.org; internet www.ips.org; f. 1964; non-profit co-operative; international daily news agency; 7 bureaux world-wide; Dir-Gen. MARIO LUBETKIN.

PRESS ASSOCIATIONS

Associazione della Stampa Estera in Italia: Via della Umiltà 83C, 00187 Roma; tel. (06) 6759191; fax (06) 67591262; e-mail segreteria@stampa-estera.it; internet www.stampa-estera.it; foreign correspondents' asscn; Pres. TOBIAS PILLER; Sec. MIRIAM MURPHY.

Federazione Italiana Editori Giornali (FIEG): Via Piemonte 64, 00187 Roma; tel. (06) 4881683; fax (06) 4871109; e-mail info@fieg.it; internet www.fieg.it; f. 1950; asscn of newspaper publishers; Pres. BORIS BIANCHERI; 268 mems.

Federazione Nazionale della Stampa Italiana (FNSI): Corso Vittorio Emanuele II 349, 00186 Roma; tel. (06) 6833879; fax (06) 6871444; e-mail segrefnsi1@tin.it; internet www.fnsi.it; f. 1908; 19 affiliated unions; Pres. FRANCO SIDDI; Sec.-Gen. PAOLO SERVENTI LONGHI; 16,000 mems.

Unione Stampa Periodica Italiana (USPI): Viale Bardanzellu 95, 00155 Roma; tel. (06) 4071388; fax (06) 4066859; e-mail uspi@uspi.it; internet www.uspi.it; Pres. ANTONIO BARBIERATO; Gen. Sec. FRANCESCO SAVERIO VETERE; 4,500 mems.

Publishers

There are more than 300 major publishing houses and many smaller ones.

Adelphi Edizioni, SpA: Via S. Giovanni sul Muro 14, 20121 Milano; tel. (02) 725731; fax (02) 89010337; e-mail info@adelphi.it; internet www.adelphi.it; f. 1962; classics, philosophy, biography, music, art, psychology, religion and fiction; Pres. ROBERTO CALASSO.

Alfieri Edizioni d'Arte: San Marco 1991, 30124 Venezia; tel. (041) 23323; f. 1939; modern and Venetian art, architecture, periodicals; Chair. GIORGIO FANTONI; Gen. Man. MASSIMO VITTA ZELMAN.

Franco Angeli Editore Srl: Viale Monza 106, 20127 Milano; tel. (02) 2837141; fax (02) 26144793; e-mail redazione@francoangeli.it; internet www.francoangeli.it; f. 1955; academic and general non-fiction; Man. Dir (vacant).

Armando Armando Srl: Viale Trastevere 236, 00153 Roma; tel. (06) 5806420; fax (06) 5818564; e-mail segreteria@armando.it; internet www.armando.it; f. 1950; philosophy, psychology, social sciences, languages, ecology, education; Man. Dir ENRICO JACOMETTI.

Bollati Boringhieri Editore: Corso Vittorio Emanuele II 86, 10121 Torino; tel. (011) 5591711; fax (011) 543024; e-mail info@bollatiboringhieri.it; internet www.bollatiboringhieri.it; f. 1957; history, economics, natural sciences, psychology, social and human sciences, fiction and literary criticism; Chair. ROMILDA BOLLATI; Editorial Dir FRANCESCO M. CATALUCCIO.

Bramante Editrice: Viale Bianca Maria 19, 20122 Milano; tel. (02) 760759; fax (02) 780904; f. 1958; art, history, encyclopaedias, natural sciences, interior decoration, arms and armour, music; Chair. Dott. GUIDO CERIOTTI.

Bulzoni Editore: Via dei Liburni 14, 00185 Roma; tel. (06) 4455207; fax (06) 4450355; e-mail bulzoni@bulzoni.it; internet www.bulzoni.it; f. 1969; science, arts, fiction, textbooks; Man. Dir IVANA BULZONI.

Caltagirone Editore, SpA: Via Barberini 28, 00187 Roma; tel. (06) 45412200; fax (06) 45412288; e-mail investor.relations@caltagironeeditore.com; internet www.caltagironeeditore.it; f. 1999; news publisher; Pres. FRANCESCO GAETANO CALTAGIRONE.

Cappelli Editore: Via Farini 14, 40124 Bologna; tel. (051) 239060; fax (051) 239286; e-mail info@cappellieditore.com; internet www

ITALY

.cappellieditore.com; f. 1880; medical science, history, politics, literature, textbooks; Chair. and Man. Dir MARIO MUSSO.

Casa Editrice Bonechi: Via dei Cairoli 18B, 50131 Firenze; tel. (055) 576841; fax (055) 5000766; e-mail informazioni@bonechi.it; internet www.bonechi.com; f. 1973; art, travel, cooking, CD-Roms; Pres. GIAMPAOLO BONECHI.

Casa Editrice Clueb Scarl (Cooperativa Libraria Universitaria Editrice Bologna): Via Marsala 31, 40126 Bologna; tel. (051) 220736; fax (051) 237758; e-mail info@clueb.com; internet www.clueb.com; f. 1959; university education, arts, business, history, literature; Man. Dir LUIGI GUARDIGLI.

Casa Editrice Edumond-Le Monnier, SpA: Via A. Meucci 2, 50015 Grassina, Firenze; tel. (055) 64910; fax (055) 6491310; e-mail informazioni.lemonnier@lemonnier.it; internet www.lemonnier.it; f. 1837; from 1999, part of Gruppo Mondadori; academic and cultural books, textbooks, dictionaries; Pres. GIUSEPPE DE RITA.

Casa Editrice Leo S. Olschki: CP 66, 50123 Firenze; tel. (055) 6530684; fax (055) 6530214; e-mail celso@olschki.it; internet www.olschki.it; f. 1886; reference, periodicals, textbooks, humanities; Man. ALESSANDRO OLSCHKI.

Casa Editrice Luigi Trevisini Srl: Via Tito Livio 12, 20137 Milano; tel. (02) 5450704; fax (02) 55195782; e-mail trevisini@trevisini.it; internet www.trevisini.it; f. 1859; school textbooks; Dirs LUIGI TREVISINI, GIUSEPPINA TREVISINI.

Casa Editrice Marietti, SpA: Via Donizetti 41, 20122 Milano; tel. (02) 778899; fax (02) 76003491; e-mail mariettieditore@mariettieditore.it; internet www.mariettieditore.it; f. 1820; liturgy, theology, fiction, history, politics, literature, philosophy, art, children's books; Editor GIOVANNI UNGARELLI.

Casa Ricordi, SpA: Via Berchet 2, 20121 Milano; tel. (02) 88811; fax (02) 88812212; e-mail promozione.ricordi@bmg.com; internet www.ricordi.it; f. 1808; academic, art, sheet music; Chair. GIANNI BABINI; Man. Dir Dott. TINO GENNAMO.

CEDAM, SpA: Via Jappelli 5/6, 35121 Padova; tel. (049) 8239111; fax (049) 8752900; e-mail info@cedam.com; internet www.cedam.com; f. 1903; law, economics, political and social sciences, engineering, science, medicine, literature, philosophy, textbooks; Dirs ANTONIO MILANI, CARLO PORTA, FRANCESCO GIORDANO.

Cremonese: Borgo Santa Croce 17, 50122 Firenze; tel. (055) 2476371; fax (055) 2476372; e-mail cremonese@ed-cremonese.it; internet www.ed-cremonese.it; f. 1929; history, reference, engineering, science, textbooks, architecture, mathematics, aviation; Chair. ALBERTO STIANTI.

De Agostini Editore: Via Giovanni da Verrazano 15, 28100 Novara; tel. (0321) 4241; fax (0321) 471286; e-mail ufficio.stampa@deagostini.it; internet www.deagostini.it; f. 1901; geography, maps, encyclopaedias, dictionaries, art, literature, textbooks, science; CEO STEFANO BELLA.

Editori Laterza: Via di Villa Sacchetti 17, 00197 Roma; tel. (06) 45465311; fax (06) 3223853; e-mail laterza@laterza.it; internet www.laterza.it; f. 1885; belles-lettres, biography, reference, religion, art, classics, history, economics, philosophy, social science; Editorial Dirs ALESSANDRO LATERZA, GIUSEPPE LATERZA.

Editrice Ancora: Via G. B. Niccolini 8, 20154 Milano; tel. (02) 3456081; fax (02) 34560866; e-mail editrice@ancoralibri.it; internet www.ancoralibri.it; f. 1934; religious, educational; Dir GILBERTO ZINI.

Editrice Ave (Anonima Veritas Editrice): Via Aurelia 481, 00165 Roma; tel. (06) 6631545; fax (06) 6620207; e-mail info@editriceave.it; internet www.editriceave.it; f. 1935; theology, sociology, pedagogy, psychology, essays, learned journals, religious textbooks; Pres. ARMANDO OBERTI.

Editrice Ciranna: Via G. Besio 143, 90145 Palermo; tel. (091) 224499; fax (091) 311064; e-mail info@ciranna.it; internet www.ciranna.it; f. 1950; school textbooks; Man. Dir LIDIA FABIANO.

Editrice La Scuola, SpA: Via Cadorna 11, 25124 Brescia; tel. (030) 29931; fax (030) 2993299; e-mail direzione@tin.it; internet www.lascuola.it; f. 1904; educational magazines, educational textbooks, audiovisual aids and toys; Chairs Dott. Ing. LUCIANO SILVERI, Dott. Ing. GIORGIO RACCIS; Man. Dir Rag. GIUSEPPE COVONE.

Edizioni Borla Srl: Via delle Fornaci 50, 00165 Roma; tel. (06) 39376728; fax (06) 39376620; e-mail borla@edizioni-borla.it; internet www.edizioni-borla.it; f. 1863; religion, philosophy, psychoanalysis, ethnology, literature; Man. Dir VINCENZO D'AGOSTINO.

Edizioni Lavoro: Via G. M. Lancisi 25, 00161 Roma; tel. (06) 44251174; fax (06) 44251177; e-mail info@edizionilavoro.it; internet www.edizionilavoro.it; f. 1982; history, politics, political philosophy, sociology, religion, Islamic, African, Arab and Caribbean literature; Chair. and Man. Dir PIETRO GELARDI.

Edizioni Mediterranee Srl: Via Flaminia 109, 00196 Roma; tel. (06) 32235433; fax (06) 3236277; e-mail press@edizionimediterranee.it; internet www.edizionimediterranee.it; f. 1953; alchemy, astrology, esoterism, meditation, natural medicine, parapsychology, hobbies, martial arts, zen.

Edizioni Minerva Medica: Corso Bramante 83–85, 10126 Torino; tel. (011) 678282; fax (011) 674502; e-mail minervamedica@minervamedica.it; internet www.minervamedica.it; medical books and journals; Pres. ALBERTO OLIARO.

Edizioni Rosminiane Sodalitas Sas: Centro Internazionale di Studi Rosminiani, Corso Umberto I 15, 28838 Stresa; tel. (0323) 30091; fax (0323) 31623; e-mail edizioni@rosmini.it; internet www.rosmini.it; f. 1925; philosophy, theology, Rivista Rosminiana (quarterly); Dir Prof. PIER PAOLO OTTONELLO.

Edizioni San Paolo: Piazza Soncino 5, 20092 Cinisello Balsamo—Milano; tel. (02) 660751; fax (02) 66075211; e-mail sanpaoloedizioni@stpauls.it; internet www.edizionisanpaolo.it; f. 1914; Catholic; Gen. Man. VINCENZO SANTARCANGELO.

Edizioni Scientifiche Italiane, SpA (ESI): Via Chiatamone 7, 80121 Napoli; tel. (081) 7645443; fax (081) 7646477; e-mail info@edizioniesi.it; internet www.edizioniesi.it; f. 1945; law, economics, literature, arts, history, science; Pres. PIETRO PERLINGIERI.

Edizioni Studium: Via Cassiodoro 14, 00193 Roma; tel. (06) 6865846; fax (06) 6875456; e-mail info@edizionistudium.it; internet www.edizionistudium.it; f. 1927; philosophy, literature, sociology, pedagogy, religion, economics, law, science, history, psychology; Pres. VINCENZO CAPPELLATTI.

Giulio Einaudi Editore, SpA: Via Umberto Biancamano 2, 10121 Torino; tel. (011) 56561; fax (011) 542903; e-mail einaudi@einaudi.it; internet www.einaudi.it; f. 1933; fiction, classics, general; Chair. ROBERTO CERATI; CEO ENRICO SELVA CODDÈ.

Giangiacomo Feltrinelli Editore, SpA: Via Andegari 6, 20121 Milano; tel. (02) 725721; fax (02) 72572500; e-mail ufficio.stampa@feltrinelli.it; internet www.feltrinelli.it; f. 1954; fiction, juvenile, science, technology, history, literature, political science, philosophy; Chair. INGE FELTRINELLI; Publr CARLO FELTRINELLI.

Garzanti Libri, SpA: Via Gasparotto 1, 20124 Milano; tel. (02) 674171; fax (02) 67417260; e-mail info@garzantilibri.it; internet www.garzantilibri.it; f. 1938; literature, poetry, science, art, history, politics, encyclopaedias; Chair. STEFANO MAURI; Gen. Dir RENZO GUIDIERI.

Ghisetti e Corvi Editori: Corso Concordia 7, 20129 Milano; tel. (02) 76006232; fax (02) 76009468; e-mail sedes.spa@gpa.it; internet www.sedes.gpa.it; f. 1937; educational textbooks.

G. Giappichelli Editore Srl: Via Po 21, 10124 Torino; tel. (011) 8153511; fax (011) 8125100; e-mail spedizioni@giappichelli.com; internet www.giappichelli.it; f. 1921; university publications on law, economics, politics and sociology.

Giunti Editore SpA: Via Bolognese 165, 50139 Firenze; tel. (055) 5062231; fax (055) 5062298; e-mail segrgen@giunti.it; internet www.giunti.it; f. 1841; art, psychology, literature, science, law; CEO MARTINO MONTANARINI.

Guida Monaci, SpA: Via Salaria 1319, 00138 Roma; tel. (06) 8887777; fax (06) 8889996; e-mail infoitaly@italybygm.it; internet www.italybygm.it; f. 1870; commercial and industrial, financial, administrative and medical directories; Dir Ing. GIANCARLO ZAPPONINI.

Gruppo Editoriale il Saggiatore: Via Melzo 9, 20129 Milano; tel. (02) 201301; fax (02) 29513061; e-mail commerciale@saggiatore.it; internet www.saggiatore.it; f. 1958; art, fiction, social sciences, history, travel, current affairs, popular science; Pres. LUCA FORMENTON.

Gruppo Ugo Mursia Editore, SpA: Via Melchiorre Gioia 45, 20124 Milano; tel. (02) 67378500; fax (02) 67378605; e-mail info@mursia.com; internet www.mursia.com; f. 1955; general fiction and non-fiction, reference, art, history, nautical books, philosophy, biography, sports, children's books; Gen. Man. FIORENZA MURSIA.

Hachette Rusconi, SpA: Viale Sarca 235, 20126 Milano; tel. (02) 66191; fax (02) 66192758; e-mail info@rusconi.it; internet www.rusconi.it; f. 1969 as Rusconi Libri Srl; magazines; Pres. ALBERTO RUSCONI.

Idelson Gnocchi Editore Srl: Via Michele Pietrasalle 85, 80131 Napoli; tel. (081) 5453443; fax (081) 5464991; e-mail info@idelson-gnocchi.com; internet www.idelson-gnocchi.com; f. 1908; medical and scientific; CEO GUIDO GNOCCHI.

Jandi Sapi Editori Srl: Via Crescenzio 62, 00193 Roma; tel. (06) 68805515; fax (06) 68218203; e-mail info@jandisapi.com; internet www.jandisapi.com; f. 1941; industrial and legal publications, art books.

S. Lattes e C. Editori, SpA: Via Confienza 6, 10121 Torino; tel. (011) 5625335; fax (011) 5625070; e-mail info@latteseditori.it; internet www.latteseditori.it; f. 1893; technical, textbooks; Pres. CATERINA BOTTARI LATTES; Man. Dir RENATA LATTES.

Levrotto e Bella, Libreria Editrice Universitaria: Via Pigafetta Antonio 2E, 10129 Torino; tel. (011) 5097367; fax (011) 504025; e-mail

ITALY

info@levrotto-bella.net; internet shop.levrotto-bella.net; f. 1911; university textbooks; Man. Dir Dott. ELISABETTA GUALINI.

Libreria Editrice Gregoriana: Via Roma 82, 35122 Padova; tel. (049) 661033; fax (049) 663640; e-mail l.gregoriana@mclink.it; f. 1922; Lexicon Totius Latinitatis, religion, philosophy, psychology, social studies; Dir GIANCARLO MINOZZI.

Liguori Editore Srl: Via Posillipo 394, 80123 Napoli; tel. (081) 7206111; fax (081) 7206244; e-mail info@liguori.it; internet www.liguori.it; f. 1949; linguistics, mathematics, engineering, economics, law, history, philosophy, sociology; Man. Dir Dott. GUIDO LIGUORI.

Loescher Editore: Via Vittorio Amedeo II 18, 10121 Torino; tel. (011) 5654111; fax (011) 5625822; e-mail mail@loescher.it; internet www.loescher.it; f. 1867; school textbooks, general literature, academic books; Chair. LORENZO ENRIQUES.

Longanesi e C., SpA: Via Gherardini 10, 20145 Milano; tel. (02) 34597620; fax (02) 34597212; e-mail info@longanesi.it; internet www.longanesi.it; f. 1946; art, archaeology, culture, history, philosophy, fiction; Pres. STEFANO PASSIGLI; Man. Dir STEFANO MAORI.

Arnoldo Mondadori Editore, SpA: Via Mondadori 1, 20090 Segrate, Milano; tel. (02) 75421; fax (02) 75422302; e-mail rapportistampa@mondadori.it; internet www.mondadori.it; f. 1907; books, magazines, printing, DVDs, radio, advertising; Pres. MARINA BERLUSCONI; CEO MAURIZIO COSTA.

Neri Pozza Editore, SpA: Contrà Oratorio dei Servi 21, 36100 Vicenza; tel. (0444) 320787; fax (0444) 324613; e-mail info@neripozza.it; internet www.neripozza.it; f. 1946; art, fiction, history, politics; Pres. VITTORIO MINCATO; Dir GIUSEPPE RUSSO.

Palombi & Partner Srl: Via Timavo 12, 00195 Roma; tel. (06) 3214150; fax (06) 3214752; e-mail info@palombieditori.it; internet www.palombieditori.it; f. 1914; history, art, etc. of Rome; Man. Dir Dott. FRANCESCO PALOMBI.

Paravia Bruno Mondadori Editori (PBM Editori): Via Archimede 23, 20129 Milano; tel. (02) 748231; fax (02) 74823278; internet www.pbmeditori.it; f. 1946; 80% owned by Pearson, UK; school and university textbooks.

Petrini Editore: Strada del Portone 179, 10095 Grugliasco, Torino; tel. (011) 2098741; fax (011) 2098765; e-mail redazione@petrini.it; internet www.petrini.it; f. 1872; school textbooks.

Piccin Nuova Libraria, SpA: Via Altinate 107, 35121 Padova; tel. (049) 655566; fax (049) 8750693; e-mail info@piccinonline.com; internet www.piccinonline.com; f. 1980; scientific and medical textbooks and journals; Man. Dir Dott. MASSIMO PICCIN.

RCS Libri, SpA: Via Mecenate 91, 20138 Milano; tel. (02) 50951; fax (02) 50952647; internet www.rcslibri.it; f. 1947; imprints include Rosellina Archinto Editore, Bompiani, BUR (Biblioteca Universale Rizzoli), Etas Srl, Fabbri, Marsilio Editore, La Nuova Editrice, SpA, Rizzoli, Sansoni, Sonzogno; fiction, juveniles, education, textbooks, reference, literature, art books; Chair. NICOLÒ NEFRI; CEO FERRUCCIO DE BORTOLI; Gen. Man. GIULIO LATTANZI.

Rosenberg & Sellier: Via Andrea Doria 14, 10123 Torino; tel. (011) 8127820; fax (011) 8127808; e-mail info@rosenbergesellier.it; internet www.rosenbergesellier.it; f. 1883; economics, history, gender studies, social sciences, philosophy, linguistics, Latin, dictionaries, scientific journals; Chair. and Man. Dir UGO GIANNI ROSENBERG.

Adriano Salani Editore Srl: Via Gherardini 10, 20145 Milano; tel. (02) 34597624; fax (02) 34597206; e-mail info@salani.it; internet www.salani.it; f. 1988; fiction, children's books; Editor MARIAGRAZIA MAZZITELLI.

Selezione dal Reader's Digest: Camuzzi Editoriale SpA, Via Lorenzini 4, 20139 Milano; fax (02) 57372760; e-mail readerd@tin.it; internet www.selezionerd.it; f. 1948; Reader's Digest, educational, reference, general interest; Man. Dir CHARLES J. LOBKOWICZ.

Skira Editore: Palazzo Casati Stampa, Via Torino 61, 20123 Milano; tel. (02) 724441; fax (02) 72444211; e-mail skira@skira.net; internet www.skira.net; f. 1928; arts and literature; Pres. MASSIMO VITTA ZELMAN.

Società Editrice Dante Alighieri Srl: Via Timavo 3, 00195 Roma; tel. (06) 3725870; fax (06) 37514807; e-mail nuovarivistastorica@danteaighierisrl.191.it; internet www.nuovarivistastorica.it; f. 1917; school textbooks, science and general culture; Dir GIGLIOLA SOLDI RONDININI.

Società Editrice Internazionale, SpA (SEI): Corso Regina Margherita 176, 10152 Torino; tel. (011) 52271; fax (011) 5211320; e-mail sei@seieditrice.com; internet www.seieditrice.com; f. 1908; textbooks, religion, history, education, multimedia; Head of Editorial Dept ULISSE JACOMUZZI.

Società Editrice Il Mulino: Strada Maggiore 37, 40125 Bologna; tel. (051) 222419; fax (051) 6486014; e-mail segreteria.associazione@mulino.it; internet www.mulino.it; f. 1965; politics, history, philosophy, social sciences, linguistics, literary criticism, law, psychology, economics, journals; Pres. ALESSANDRO CAVALLI.

Il Sole 24 Ore Edagricole: Via Goito 13, 40126 Bologna; tel. (051) 65751; fax (051) 6575800; e-mail commerciale@gce.it; internet www.edagricole.it; group includes Calderini (f. 1960; art, sport, electronics, mechanics, university and school textbooks, travel guides, nursing, architecture) and Edagricole (f. 1935; agriculture, veterinary science, gardening, biology, textbooks); Pres. Prof. GIORGIO AMADEI; Man. Dir GIOVANNA VILLANI PERDISA.

Sugarco Edizioni Srl: Via don Gnocchi 4, 20148 Milano; tel. (02) 4078370; fax (02) 4078493; e-mail info@sugarcoedizioni.it; f. 1957; fiction, biography, history, philosophy, Italian classics; Gen. Man. ATTILIO TRENTINI.

Ulrico Hoepli Casa Editrice Libraria, SpA: Via Hoepli 5, 20121 Milano; tel. (02) 864871; fax (02) 864322; e-mail libreria@hoepli.it; internet www.hoepli.it; f. 1870; grammars, art, technical, scientific and school books, encyclopaedias; Chair. Dott. ULRICO HOEPLI; Man. Dir GIANNI HOEPLI.

Unione Tipografico-Editrice Torinese (UTET): Corso Raffaello 28, 10125 Torino; tel. (011) 2099111; fax (011) 2099394; e-mail assistenza@utet.it; internet www.utet.it; f. 1791; part of Gruppo De Agostini; university and specialized editions on history, geography, art, literature, economics, sciences, encyclopaedias, dictionaries, etc.; Pres. ANTONIO BELLONI.

Vallecchi Editore, SpA: Via Maragliano 6 int., 50144 Firenze; tel. (055) 324761; e-mail dire@vallecchi.it; internet www.vallecchi.it; f. 1903; art, fiction, literature, essays, media; Editor-in-Chief LAURA CATTANEO.

Vita e Pensiero: Largo A. Gemelli 1, 20123 Milano; tel. (02) 72342335; fax (02) 72342260; e-mail editrice.vp@unicatt.it; internet www.vitaepensiero.it; f. 1918; publisher of the Catholic University of the Sacred Heart, Milan; philosophy, literature, social science, theology, history; Dir AURELIO MOTTOLA.

Zanichelli Editore, SpA: Via Irnerio 34, 40126 Bologna; tel. (051) 293111; fax (051) 249782; e-mail zanichelli@zanichelli.com; internet www.zanichelli.it; f. 1859; educational, history, literature, philosophy, mathematics, science, technical books, law, psychology, architecture, reference books, dictionaries, atlases, earth sciences, linguistics, medicine, economics, etc.; Chair. and Gen. Man. FEDERICO ENRIQUES; Vice-Chair. and Man. Dir LORENZO ENRIQUES.

GOVERNMENT PUBLISHING HOUSE

Istituto Poligrafico e Zecca dello Stato (IPZS): Piazza Verdi 10, 00198 Roma; tel. (06) 85081; fax (06) 85082517; e-mail informazioni@ipzs.it; internet www.ipzs.it; f. 1928; art, literary, scientific, technical books and reproductions; Chair. Dott. MICHELE TEDESCHI; Man. Dir Dott. LAMBERTO GABRIELLI.

PUBLISHERS' ASSOCIATION

Associazione Italiana Editori (AIE): Via delle Erbe 2, 20121 Milano; tel. (02) 86463091; fax (02) 89010863; e-mail aie@aie.it; internet www.aie.it; f. 1869; Pres. FEDERICO MOTTA; Dir IVAN CECCHINI.

Broadcasting and Communications

REGULATORY AUTHORITY

Autorità per le Garanzie nelle Communicazioni (AGCOM): Centro Direzionale, Isola B5, Torre Francesco, 80143 Napoli; tel. (081) 7507111; fax (081) 7507616; e-mail info@agcom.it; internet www.agcom.it; regulatory authority with responsibility for telecommunications, broadcasting and publishing; Pres. CORRADO CALABRÒ; Sec.-Gen. ALESSANDRO BOTTO.

TELECOMMUNICATIONS

3 Italia: Via Leonardo da Vinci 1, 20090 Trezzano sul Naviglio, Milano; tel. (02) 44581; fax (02) 445812713; internet www.tre.it; f. 2003; owned by Hutchison Whampoa Ltd (Hong Kong); mobile operator; Man. Dir VINCENZO NOVARI.

Telecom Italia: Piazza Affari 2, 20123 Milano; tel. (02) 85951; e-mail investitori.individuali@telecomitalia.it; internet www.telecomitalia.it; Italy's leading telecommunications operator; controlling stake owned by Telco, a consortium of Telefónica (Spain) and four Italian companies, in 2007; Chair. GABRIELE GALATERI DI GENOLA; Man. Dir FRANCO BERNABÈ.

TIM (Telecom Italia Mobile): Via Luigi Rizzo 22, 00136 Roma; tel. (06) 39001; internet www.tim.it; f. 1995; owned by Telecom Italia; mobile cellular telecommunications; Gen. Man. LUCA LUCIANI.

Tiscali Italia: Ioc. Sa Illetta, SS 195 Km 2300, 09122 Cagliari; tel. (070) 46011; fax (070) 4601296; e-mail info@tiscali.com; internet www.tiscali.it; f. 1998; internet service provider; Chair. VITTORIO SERAFINO; CEO TOMMASO POMPEI.

ITALY

Vodafone Italia: Via Caboto 15, 20094 Milano; tel. (02) 41431; internet www.vodafone.it; f. 1995; operates mobile network; CEO Pietro Guindani.

WIND Telecomunicazioni: Via Cesare Giulio Viola 48, 00148 Roma; tel. (06) 83111; internet www.windgroup.it; f. 1997; brands include WIND (mobile services) and Infostrada (fixed-line and broadband internet services); Pres. Naguib Onsi Naguib Sawiris; Man. Dir Luigi Gubitosi.

BROADCASTING

Radio

Rai—Radiotelevisione Italiana: Viale Mazzini 14, 00195 Roma; tel. (06) 38781; fax (06) 3725680; e-mail radio@rai.it; internet www.radio.rai.it; f. 1924; a public share capital co; programmes comprise Radio Uno (general), Radio Due (recreational), Radio Tre (cultural); there are also regional programmes in Italian and in the languages of minority ethnic groups, and a foreign service, Rai International; Pres. Claudio Petruccioli; Dir-Gen. Claudo Cappon.

Independent Stations

Radio Deejay: CP 314, Milano; tel. (02) 342522; e-mail diretta@deejay.it; internet www.deejay.it; f. 1982; propr Gruppo Editoriale L'Espresso, SpA; popular music; Dir Guido Quintino Mariotti.

Radio Italia Solo Musica Italiana: Viale Europa 49, 20093 Cologno Monzese, Milano; tel. (02) 254441; fax (02) 25444220; e-mail franco.nisi@radioitalia.it; internet www.radioitalia.it; f. 1982.

Radio Maria: Via F. Turati 7, 22036 Erba, Como; tel. (031) 610610; e-mail info.ita@radiomaria.org; internet www.radiomaria.it; f. 1987; Roman Catholic; founder mem. of World Family of Radio Maria, comprising 40 national asscns; Dir Fr Livio Fanzaga.

RDS Radio Dimensione Suono: Viale G. Mazzini 119, 00195 Roma; tel. (06) 377051; e-mail customercare@rds.it; internet www.rds.it; f. 1978.

RTL 102.5: Via Piemonte 61/63, 20093 Cologno Monzese, Milano; tel. (02) 251515; fax (02) 25096201; e-mail ufficiostampa@rtl.it; internet www.rtl.it; Pres. Lorenzo Suraci.

Rundfunk Anstalt Südtirol (RAS): Europaallee 164A, 39100 Bozen; tel. (0471) 546666; fax (0471) 200378; e-mail info@ras.bz.it; internet www.ras.bz.it; f. 1975; relays television and radio broadcasts from Germany, Austria and Switzerland to the population of South Tyrol; Pres. Helmuth Hendrich; Dir Georg Plattner.

Television

Rai—Radiotelevisione Italiana: Viale Mazzini 14, 00195 Roma; tel. (06) 38781; fax (06) 3725680; e-mail rai-tv@rai.it; internet www.rai.it; f. 1924; operates three terrestrial channels, RAI Uno, RAI Due and RAI Tre; satellite and digital channels include Rai News 24, Rai Sport and Rai Utile; also broadcasts local programmes in Italian and in German for the South Tyrol; Pres. Claudio Petruccioli; Dir-Gen. Claudio Cappon.

Independent Television Companies

Gruppo Mediaset: Piazza SS Giovanni e Paolo 8, 00184 Roma; tel. (06) 77081; e-mail mediaset@mediaset.it; internet www.gruppomediaset.it; f. 1993; operates Canale 5, Italia 1 and Retequattro; owned by Fininvest; Pres. Fedele Confalonieri; Vice-Pres. Pier Silvio Berlusconi; Man. Dir Giuliano Adreani.

Rundfunk Anstalt Südtirol (RAS): see Radio.

Sky Italia: CP 13057, 20130 Milano; tel. (02) 70027300; e-mail info@sky.it; internet www.sky.it; f. 2003; owned by News Corporation (USA); broadcasts digital satellite channels; Man. Dir Tom Mockridge.

Telecom Italia Media: Via della Pineta Sacchetti 229, 00168 Roma; tel. (06) 355841; e-mail carlo.demartino@telecomitalia.it; internet www.telecomitaliamedia.it; subsidiary of Telecom Italia, SpA; digital terrestrial broadcaster; operates two channels, La7 and MTV Italia; also operates APCOM (see News Agencies); Pres. Enrico Parazzini; Man. Dir Antonio Campo Dall'Orto.

Finance

(cap. = capital; res = reserves; dep. = deposits; m. = million; amounts in euros; brs = branches)

The number of Italian banks fell during the 1990s, from 1,156 in 1990 to 784 in 2005, owing to an increasing number of mergers. In 1990 a programme of privatization of state-controlled banks was initiated and in November 1999 the last state-controlled bank was divested. In 2005, of the 784 banks in existence, 243 were private banks, 439 were co-operative banks, 36 were banche popolari (a form of savings bank), and 66 were branches of foreign banks. In that year 85 banking groups were operating in Italy.

BANKING

Central Bank

Banca d'Italia: Via Nazionale 91, 00184 Roma; tel. (06) 47921; fax (06) 47922983; internet www.bancaditalia.it; f. 1893; cap. 0.2m., res 16,770.9m., dep. 40,092.6m. (Dec. 2006); Gov. Mario Draghi; Dir-Gen. Fabrizio Saccomanni; 83 brs.

Major Commercial Banks

Banca Agricola Mantovana, SpA: Corso Vittorio Emanuele 30, 46100 Mantova; tel. (0376) 3111; fax (0376) 313566; e-mail intl.rel@bam.it; internet www.bam.it; f. 1871; cap. 787.8m., res 33.1m., dep. 10,946.5m. (Dec. 2006); Chair. Emilio Tonini; Gen. Man. Claudio Pieri; 287 brs.

Banca Antonveneta, SpA: Piazzetta Turati 2, 35131 Padova; tel. (049) 6991111; fax (049) 6991605; e-mail servizio.estero.pd@antonveneta.it; internet www.antonveneta.it; f. 1893 as Antoniana; merged with Banca Popolare di Veneta Scarl in July 1996; cap. 926.3m., res 2,398.8m., dep. 37,205.9m. (Dec. 2006); CEO Piero Montani; 993 brs.

Banca Carige, SpA (Cassa di Risparmio di Genova e Imperia): Via Cassa di Risparmio 15, 16123 Genova; tel. (010) 5791; fax (010) 5794000; e-mail carige@carige.it; internet www.gruppocarige.it; f. 1846; cap. 1,374.5m., res 1,227.2m., dep. 15,898.1m. (Dec. 2006); Chair. Dott. Giovanni Berneschi; Gen. Man. Dott. Alfredo Sanguinetto.

Banca Carime, SpA: Viale Crati, 87100 Cosenza; tel. (0984) 8011; fax (0984) 806988; internet www.carime.it; f. 1998 as a result of merger of Carical, Carisal and Caripuglia savings banks; cap. 1,468.2m., res 73.9m., dep. 7,433.5m. (Dec. 2006); Chair. Andrea Pisani Massamormile; Gen. Man. Riccardo Sora; 344 brs.

Banca CR Firenze, SpA: Via Bufalini 4/6, 50122 Firenze; tel. (055) 26121; fax (055) 2613872; e-mail estero@carifirenze.it; internet www.carfirenze.it; f. 1829; cap. 827.3m., res 398.9m., dep. 13,276.5m. (Dec. 2006); Chair. and Pres. Aureliano Benedetti; Gen. Man. and CEO Lino Moscatelli; 317 brs and agencies.

Banca Fideuram: Piazzale Giulio Douhet 31, 00143 Milano; tel. (06) 59021; fax (06) 59022634; internet www.fideuram.it; f. 1913; cap. 131.8m., res 404.1m., dep. 8,310.5m. (Dec. 2006); Chair. Mario Prati; Gen. Man. Ugo Ruffolo; 53 brs.

Banca d'Intermediazione Mobiliare IMI, SpA: Corso Matteotti 6, 20121 Milano; tel. (02) 77511; fax (02) 77512030; e-mail bancaimi@bancaimi.it; internet www.bancaimi.it; f. 1974 as Imisigeco Sim, SpA; cap. 180.0m., res 282.4m., dep. 31,253.2m. (Dec. 2006); Chair. Pietro Modiano; Man. Dir Massimo Mattera.

Banca delle Marche, SpA: Via Alessandro Ghislieri 6, 60035 Jesi; tel. (0731) 5391; fax (0731) 539695; e-mail info@bancamarche.it; internet www.bancamarche.it; f. 1994; cap. 386,4m., res 405,8m., dep. 14,385.9m. (Dec. 2006); Chair. Lauro Costa; Gen. Man. Massimo Bianconi; 216 brs.

Banca Monte dei Paschi di Siena, SpA (Mps): Piazza Salimbeni 3, 53100 Siena; tel. (0577) 294111; fax (0577) 294313; e-mail international@banca.mps.it; internet www.mps.it; f. 1472; jt stock co; cap. 1,984.8m., res 4,821.9m., dep. 95,251.2m. (Dec. 2006); Chair. and CEO Giuseppi Mussari; 1,172 brs.

Banca Nazionale del Lavoro, SpA: Via Vittorio Veneto 119, 00187 Roma; tel. (06) 47021; fax (06) 47026646; e-mail webmaster.bnl@bnl.it; internet www.bnl.it; f. 1913; cap. 2,224.9m., res 2,252.3m., dep. 76,940.8m. (Dec. 2006); Chair. Dott. Luigi Abete; Gen. Man. Mario Girotti; 701 brs.

Banca Popolare Commercio e Industria, SpA: CP 10167, Via della Moscova 33, 20121 Milano; tel. (02) 62755; fax (02) 62755640; e-mail intbkg@bpci.it; internet www.bpci.it; f. 1888; cap. 682.5m., res 43.3m., dep. 9,493.5m. (Dec. 2006); Chair. Antonio Bulgheroni; Gen. Man. Domenico Guidi; 225 brs.

Banca Popolare di Bergamo: Piazza Vittorio Veneto 8, 24122 Bergamo; tel. (035) 392111; fax (035) 392910; e-mail info@bpb.it; internet www.bpb.it; f. 1869; co-operative bank; cap. 1,256.3m., res 79.6m., dep. 22,363.8m. (Dec. 2006); Chair. Emilio Zanetti; Man. Dir Guido Lupini; 377 brs.

Banca Popolare dell'Emilia Romagna Società Cooperativa: Via San Carlo 8/20, 41100 Modena; tel. (059) 2021111; fax (059) 220537; e-mail relest@bper.it; internet www.bper.it; f. 1867; cap. 714.6m., res 1,597.8m., dep. 19,768.3m. (Dec. 2006); Chair. Prof. Giovanni Marani; Gen. Man. Ettore Caselli; 297 brs.

Banca Popolare di Milano Scarl: Piazza F. Meda 4, 20121 Milano; tel. (02) 77001; fax (02) 77002993; e-mail bipiemme@bpm.it; internet www.bpm.it; f. 1865; cap. 1,245.1m., res 1,544.0m., dep. 28,235.8m. (Dec. 2006); Pres. Dott. Roberto Mazzotta; Gen. Man. Dott. Fabrizio Viola; 495 brs.

ITALY

Banca Popolare di Sondrio Società Cooperativa per Azioni: Piazza Garibaldi 16, 23100 Sondrio; tel. (0342) 528111; fax (0342) 528204; internet www.popso.it; f. 1871; cap. 660.3m., res 617.1m., dep. 14,096.9m. (Dec. 2006); Chair. and CEO PIERO MELAZZINI; Gen. Man. MARIO ALBERTO PEDRANZINI; 232 brs.

Banca Popolare di Vicenza SCPA: Via Battaglione Framarin 18, 36100 Vicenza; tel. (0444) 339111; fax (0444) 329364; e-mail info@popvi.it; internet www.popolarevicenza.it; f. 1866; cap. 230.9m., res 1,996.9m., dep. 14,716.2m. (Dec. 2006); Chair. GIANNI ZONIN; Gen. Man. LUCIANO COLOMBINI; 352 brs.

Banco Popolare Soc Coop: Piazza Nogara 2, 37121 Verona; internet www.bancopopolare.it; f. 2007 by merger of Banca Popolare Italiana and Banco Popolare di Verona e Novara; Chair. CARLO FRATTA PASINI; Gen. Man. VITTORIO CODA.

Banca Regionale Europea Spa: Via Monte di Pietà 7, 20121 Milano; tel. (02) 721211; fax (02) 865413; e-mail banca.regionale .europea@bancalombarda.it; internet www.brebanca.it; cap. 442.0m., res 466.5m., dep. 8,004.8m. (Dec. 2006); Chair. PIERO BERTOLOTTO; Gen. Man. ARGANTE DEL MONTE; 289 brs.

Banca di Roma SpA: Viale Umberto Tupini 180, 00144 Roma; tel. (06) 54451; fax (06) 54453154; e-mail webmaster@bancaroma.it; internet www.bancaroma.it; f. 2002 as result of reorganization of Capitalia; cap. 2,335.6m., res 2,242.9m., dep. 53,827.7m. (Dec. 2006); Chair. BERARDINO LIBONATI; CEO FABIO GALLIA; 1,123 brs.

Banca Toscana, SpA: Via Leone Pancaldo 4, 50127 Firenze; tel. (055) 43911; fax (055) 4360061; e-mail international.dept@bancatoscana.it; internet www.bancatoscana.it; f. 1904; cap. 1,010.0m., 86.6m., dep. 14,562.1m. (Dec. 2006); Chair. ALDIGHIERO FINI; Gen. Man. and CEO GIORGIO OLIVATO; 415 brs.

Banco di Brescia San Paolo Cab, SpA: Corso Martiri della Libertà 13, 25171 Brescia; tel. (030) 29921; fax (030) 2992470; e-mail info@bancodibrescia.com; internet www.bancodibrescia .com; f. 1999; cap. 593.3m., res 275.0m., dep. 14,610.7m. (Dec. 2006); Chair. FRANCO POLOTTI; Gen. Man. COSTANTINO VITALI; 374 brs.

Banco di Sardegna, SpA: Viale Umberto 36, 07100 Sassari; tel. (079) 226000; fax (079) 226015; internet www.bancosardegna.it; f. 1953; cap. 147.4m., 832.3m., dep. 10,208.5m. (Dec. 2006); Chair. FRANCO FARINA; Gen. Man. NATALINO OGGIANO; 391 brs.

Banco di Sicilia, SpA: Via Generale Magliocco 1, 90141 Palermo; tel. (091) 6081111; fax (091) 6085124; internet www.bancodisicilia.it; f. 1860; owned by Capitalia SpA; cap. 739.3m., res 351.6m., dep. 21,552.7m. (Dec. 2006); Pres. FRANCESCO CARBONETTI; Man. Dir BENIAMINO ANSELMI; 507 brs.

Bipop Carire, SpA: Via Sorbanella 26, 25125 Brescia; tel. (030) 35591; fax (030) 3559876; e-mail info@bipop.it; internet www.bipop .it; f. 1999 by merger of Banca Popolare di Brescia and Cassa di Risparmio di Reggio Emilia; owned by Capitalia, SpA; cap. 915.8m., res 11.5m., dep. 9,740.3m. (Dec. 2006); Chair. FRANCESCO SPINELLI; Gen. Man. ENRICO DE CECCO; 69 brs.

Cassa di Risparmio di Padova e Rovigo, SpA: CP 1088, Corso Garibaldi 22/26, 35122 Padova; tel. (049) 8368111; fax (049) 8368540; e-mail direzione.generale@cariparo.it; internet www.cariparo.it; f. 1822; cap. 628.9m., res 243.6m., dep. 13,544.6m. (Dec. 2006); Pres. ORAZIO ROSSI; Man. Dir PIO BUSSOLOTTO; 272 brs.

Cassa di Risparmio di Parma e Piacenza, SpA (CARIPARMA SpA): Via Università 1, 43100 Parma; tel. (0521) 912111; fax (0521) 912976; e-mail crprpc@cariparma.it; internet www.cariparma.it; f. 1860; cap. 500.0m., res 449.9m., dep. 14,218.8m. (Dec. 2006); Chair. ARIBERTO FASSATI; Man. Dir. GUIDO CORRADI; 300 brs.

Cassa di Risparmio di Venezia SpA: San Marco 4216, Venezia 30124; tel. (041) 5291111; fax (041) 5292336; internet www.carive.it; f. 1822; cap. 219.0m., res 119.7m., dep. 4,580.0m. (Dec. 2005); Chair. GIOVANNI SAMMARTINI; Gen. Man. MASSIMO MAZZEGA.

Cassa di Risparmio in Bologna, SpA (CARISBO): Via Farini 22, 40124 Bologna; tel. (051) 6454111; fax (051) 6454366; internet www .carisbo.it; f. 1837; cap. 586.9m., res 156.7m., dep. 9,016.1m. (Dec. 2006); Pres. and Chair. FILIPPO CAVAZUTTI; Gen. Man. GIUSEPPE FELIZIANI; 204 brs.

Credito Bergamasco, SpA: Largo Porta Nuova 2, 24122 Bergamo; tel. (035) 393111; fax (035) 393144; e-mail ufficio.estero@creberg.it; internet www.creberg.it; f. 1891; cap. 185.2m., res 669.4m., dep. 10,571.1m. (Dec. 2005); Pres. CESARE ZONCA; Gen. Man. FRANCO MENINI; 235 brs.

Credito Emiliano, SpA (CREDEM): Via Emilia S. Pietro 4, 42100 Reggio-Emilia; tel. (0522) 582111; fax (0522) 433969; internet www .credem.it; f. 1910; cap. 281.5m., res 675.0m., dep. 17,792.8m. (Dec. 2006); Pres. GIORGIO FERRARI; CEO ADOLFO BIZZOCCHI; 437 brs.

Credito Valtellinese Soc Coop: Piazza Quadrivio 8, 23100 Sondrio; tel. (0342) 522111; fax (0342) 522700; e-mail creval@creval.it; internet www.creval.it; f. 1908; present name adopted 2005; cap. 272.2m., res 550.2m., dep. 5,839.7m. (Dec. 2006); Chair. GIOVANNI DE CENSI; Man. Dir RENATO BARTESAGHI; 107 brs.

Intesa Sanpaolo SpA: Piazza San Carlo 156, 10121 Torino; tel. (011) 5551; fax (011) 5552989; e-mail investor.relations@ intesasanpaolo.com; internet www.intesasanpaolo.com; f. 2006 by merger of Sanpaolo IMI, SpA with Banca Intesa, SpA; cap. 6,616.0m., res 64,124.0m., dep. 471,631.0m. (Dec. 2006); Man. Dir. and CEO CORRADO PASSERA; 5,500 brs.

MCC, SpA: Via Piemonte 51, 00187 Roma; tel. (06) 47911; fax (06) 47912219; e-mail mcc@mcc.it; internet www.mcc.it; f. 1952 as Mediocredito Centrale; changed name as above in 2002; owned by Capitalia banking group; cap. 475.1m., res 193.7m., dep. 6,554.6m. (Dec. 2005); Chair. FRANCO CARRARO; CEO CESARE CALETTI.

UniCredito Italiano, SpA: Piazza Cordusio, 20123 Milano; tel. (02) 88621; fax (02) 88623034; e-mail info@unicredito.it; internet www .unicredito.it; f. 1870; cap. 4,856.9m., res 28,325.1m., dep. 750,356.7m. (Dec. 2006); Chair. DIETER RAMPL; CEO ALESSANDRO PROFUMO; 973 brs.

Unione di Banche Italiane Scpa: Piazza Vittorio Veneto 8, 24122 Bergamo; tel. (035) 392111; fax (02) 62755640; internet www .unibanca.it; f. 2003 as Banche Popolari Unite; present name adopted 2007, following merger with Banca Lombarda e Piemontese; cap. and res 10,149.8m., dep. 96,945.6m. (Dec. 2006, pro forma figures); Chair. Dott. EMILIO ZANETTI; Gen. Man. VICTOR MASSIAH.

FINANCIAL INSTITUTIONS

CENTROBANCA—Banca di Credito Finanziario e Mobiliare, SpA: Corso Europa 16, 20122 Milano; tel. (02) 77811; fax (02) 77814509; e-mail comunica@centrobanca.it; internet www .centrobanca.it; f. 1946; central org. for medium- and long-term operations of Banche Popolari (co-operative banks) throughout Italy; cap. 336.0m., res 199.7m., dep. 8,276.5m. (Dec. 2006); Chair. MARIO BOSELLI; Gen. Man. VALERIANO D'URBANO.

Dexia Crediop, SpA: Via Venti Settembre 30, 00187 Roma; tel. (06) 47711; fax (06) 47715952; e-mail contact@dexia-crediop.it; internet www.dexia-crediop.it; f. 1919; incorporated 1996; cap. 450.2m., res 533.3m., dep. 45,117.0m. (Dec. 2006); Pres. MAURO CICCHINÉ; Gen. Man. MARC BRUGIÈRE GARDE.

EFIBANCA, SpA (Ente Finanziario Interbancario SpA): Via Boncompagni 71, 00187 Roma; tel. (06) 422981; fax (06) 42298923; internet www.efibancaspa.it; f. 1939; Chair. DIVO GRONCHI; CEO ENRICO MARIA LUIGI FAGIOLI MARZOCCHI; 6 brs.

ICCREA Banca (Istituto Centrale del Credito Cooperativo): Via Lucrezia Romana 41, 00178 Roma; tel. (06) 72071; fax (06) 72077706; e-mail info@iccrea.bcc.it; internet www.iccrea.it; f. 1963; cap. 216.9m., res 92.1m., dep. 8,345.4m. (Dec. 2006); Chair. AUGUSTO DELL'ERBA; Gen. Man. LUCIANO GIORGIO GORNATI; 6 brs.

INTERBANCA, SpA: Corso Venezia 56, 20121 Milano; tel. (02) 77311; fax (02) 784321; internet www.interbanca.it; f. 1961; cap. 180.9m., res 406.6m., dep. 7,770.7m. (Dec. 2006); Chair. FRANCESCO SPINELLI; Man. Dir GIORGIO CIRLA; 11 brs.

Mediobanca—Banca di Credito Finanziario, SpA: Piazzetta Enrico Cuccia 1, 20121 Milano; tel. (02) 88291; fax (02) 8829367; e-mail info@mediobanca.it; internet www.mediobanca.it; f. 1946; cap. 406.0m., res 3,488.4m., dep. 28,049.1m. (Dec. 2006); Chair. GABRIELE GALATERI DI GENOLA; Gen. Man. ALBERT NAGEL; 1 br.

BANKERS' ORGANIZATIONS

Associazione Bancaria Italiana: Palazzo Altieri, Piazza del Gesù 49, 00186 Roma; tel. (06) 67671; fax (06) 6767457; e-mail abi@abi.it; internet www.abi.it; f. 1919; advocates the common interests of the banking industry; Pres. GIOVANNI DE CENSI; Dir-Gen. Dott. CAMILLO VENESIO; membership (1,003 mems) is composed of the following institutions: banks authorized to gather savings from the general public and exercise credit business as well as to perform other financial activities; brs and representative offices of foreign banks; asscns of banks or financial intermediaries; financial intermediaries engaging in one or more of the activities subject to mutual recognition under the Second Banking Directive or other financial activities subject to public prudential supervision.

Associazione di Fondazioni e di Casse di Risparmio, SpA (ACRI): Piazza Mattei 10, 00186 Roma; tel. (06) 681841; fax (06) 68184269; e-mail info@acri.it; internet www.acri.it; f. 1912; Chair. Avv. GIUSEPPE GUZZETTI; Gen. Man. Dott. STEFANO MARCHETTINI.

Associazione dell'Industria del Risparmio Gestito (Assogestioni): Via in Lucina 17, 00186 Roma; tel. (06) 6840591; fax (06) 6893262; e-mail info@assogestioni.it; internet www.assogestioni.it; f. 1984; 219 assoc. cos; Pres. Prof. GUIDO CAMMARANO; Sec.-Gen. FABIO GALLI.

Associazione Italiana per il Factoring: Via Cerva 9, 20122 Milano; tel. (02) 76020127; fax (02) 76020159; e-mail assifact@ assifact.it; internet www.assifact.it; Pres. GIORGIO BONDIOLI; Sec.-Gen. Prof. ALESSANDRO CARRETTA.

Associazione Italiana Leasing (ASSILEA): Piazzale Ezio Tarantelli 100, 00144 Roma; tel. (06) 9970361; fax (06) 45440739; e-mail

ITALY

info@assilea.it; internet www.assilea.it; Pres. Dott. Rosario Corso; Dir-Gen. Ing. Fabrizio Marafini.

Associazione Nazionale fra le Banche Popolari: Piazza Venezia 11, 00187 Roma; tel. (06) 695351; internet www.assopopolari.it; Pres. Carlo Fratta Pasini; Sec.-Gen. Dott. Giuseppe De Lucia Lumeno.

Associazione Nazionale Banche Private (ASSBANK): Via Cosimo del Fante 7, 20122 Milano; tel. (02) 5821261; fax (02) 58212650; e-mail assbank@assbank.it; internet www.assbank.it; Pres. Camillo Venesio.

STOCK EXCHANGES

Commissione Nazionale per le Società e la Borsa (CONSOB) (Commission for Companies and the Stock Exchange): Via G. B. Martini 3, 00198 Roma; tel. (06) 84771; fax (06) 8417707; e-mail consob@consob.it; internet www.consob.it; f. 1974; regulatory control over cos quoted on stock exchanges, convertible bonds, unlisted securities, insider trading, all forms of public saving except bank deposits and mutual funds; Dir-Gen. Massimo Tezzon; the following is a list of the most important stock exchanges:

Borsa Italiana (Italian Stock Exchange): Piazza degli Affari 6, 20123 Milano; tel. (02) 724261; fax (02) 72004333; e-mail info@borsaitalia.it; internet www.borsaitalia.it; Chair. Angelo Tantazzi; Pres. and CEO Massimo Capuano; 331 listed cos (July 2007).

Borsa Valori di Genova: Via G. Boccardo 1, Genova; tel. (010) 590920; f. 1855; Pres. Luciano Gambarotta.

Borsa Valori di Napoli: Piazza Bovio, Napoli; tel. (081) 269151; Pres. Giorgio Focas.

Borsa Valori di Roma: Via dei Burro 147, 00186 Roma; tel. (06) 6792701; f. 1821; Pres. Alberto Borti.

INSURANCE

In 2005 there were 183 insurance and reinsurance companies operating in Italy, of which 174 were Italian.

Alleanza Assicurazioni, SpA: Viale Luigi Sturzo 35, 20154 Milano; tel. (02) 62961; fax (02) 659545; e-mail comunicazione@alleanza.it; internet www.alleanzaassicurazioni.it; f. 1898; life insurance; subsidiary of Gruppo Generali; Pres. Amato Luigi Molinari.

Allianz Subalpina, SpA: Via Alfieri 22, 10121 Torino; tel. (011) 5161111; fax (011) 5161255; e-mail info@azs.it; internet www.allianzsubalpina.it; f. 1928; part of Gruppo Ras; net profit 55.6m. (2004); CEO Alessandro Santoliquido.

Assicuratrice Edile, SpA: Via A. De Togni 2, 20123 Milano; tel. (02) 480411; fax (02) 48041292; e-mail cauzioni@assedile.it; internet www.assedile.it; f. 1960; net profit 29.6m. (2005); Chair. Christian Huot; Man. Dir Antoine Ninu.

Assicurazioni Generali, SpA: Piazza Duca degli Abruzzi 2, 34132 Trieste; tel. (040) 671111; fax (040) 671600; internet www.generali.com; f. 1831; subsidiary of Gruppo Generali; Chair. Antoine Bernheim.

Le Assicurazioni d'Italia, SpA (ASSITALIA): Corso d'Italia 33, 00198 Roma; tel. (06) 84831; fax (06) 84833898; internet www.assitalia-assicurazioni.it; f. 1923; subsidiary of Gruppo Generali; cap. 91m. (2005); Pres. Francesco Procaccini; CEO Fabio Buscarini.

Atradius Credit Insurance, NV, Rappresentanza Generale per l'Italia: Via Crescenzio 12, 00193 Roma; tel. (06) 688121; fax (06) 6874418; e-mail info.it@atradius.com; internet www.atradius.com; Legal Representative Arnold van den Esschert.

Aurora Assicurazioni, SpA: Via della Unione Europea 3/B, 20097 San Donato Milanese; tel. (02) 51815181; fax (02) 51815252; internet www.auroraassicurazioni.it; cap. 150,000m.; f. 2004; Pres. Pierluigi Stefanini.

Axa Assicurazioni: Via Leopardi 15, 20123 Milano; tel. (02) 480841; fax (02) 48084331; internet www.axa-italia.it; f. 1956; Chair. and Man. Dir Massimo Michaud.

Carige Assicurazioni: Viale Certosa 222, 20156 Milano; tel. (02) 30761; fax (02) 3086125; e-mail info@carigeassicurazioni.it; internet www.carigeassicurazioni.it; f. 1963; Pres. Dott. Giovanni Berneschi; Man. Dir Ferdinando Menconi.

FATA Assicurazioni, SpA (Fondo Assicurativo Tra Agricoltori): Via Urbana 169A, 00184 Roma; tel. (06) 47651; fax (06) 4871187; e-mail info@fata-assicurazioni.it; internet www.fata-assicurazioni.it; f. 1927; subsidiary of Gruppo Generali; Pres. Giuseppe Perissinotto; CEO Giuseppe Vecchione.

Fondiaria—Sai, SpA: Piazza della Libertà 6, 50129 Firenze; tel. (055) 4794308; fax (055) 4792006; e-mail fondiaria-sai@fondiaria-sai.it; internet www.fondiaria-sai.it; f. 1879; owned by Gruppo Fondiaria-Sai; Pres. Jonella Ligresti; CEO Fausto Marchionni.

HDI Assicurazioni, SpA: Via Abruzzi 10, 00187 Roma; tel. (06) 421031; fax (06) 42103500; e-mail hdi.assicurazioni@hdia.it; internet www.hdia.it; f. 1927.

Istituto Nazionale delle Assicurazioni, SpA (INA): Via Sallustiana 51, 00187 Roma; tel. (06) 47221; fax (06) 47224559; internet www.gruppoina.it; f. 1912; subsidiary of Gruppo Generali; Chair. Dott. Sergio Siglienti; Man. Dir Lino Benassi.

Italiana Assicurazioni, SpA: Via Marco Ulpio Traiano 18, 20149 Milano; tel. (02) 397161; fax (02) 3271270; internet www.italiana.it; f. 1898.

ITAS (Istituto Trentino-Alto Adige per Assicurazioni, Società Mutua di Assicurazioni): Via Mantova 67, 38100 Trento; tel. (0461) 891702; fax (0461) 980297; e-mail itas.direzione@gruppoitas.it; internet www.gruppoitas.it; f. 1821; cap. 60m. (May 2006); Chair. Dott. Edo Benedetti; Gen. Man. Dott. Ettore Lombardo.

Lloyd Adriatico, SpA: Largo Ugo Irneri 1, 34123 Trieste; tel. (040) 77811; fax (040) 7781311; e-mail info@lloydadriatico.it; internet www.lloydadriatico.it; f. 1936; part of Allianz Group; Pres. and Man. Dir Dott. Enrico Tomaso Cucchiani.

Mediolanum Vita, SpA: Palazzo Meucci, Via Francesco Sforza 15, 20080 Basiglio, Milano; tel. (02) 90491; fax (02) 90492427; e-mail info@mediolanum.it; internet www.mediolanumvita.it; f. 1972; Pres. and CEO Dott. Alfredo Messina.

Milano Assicurazioni (Compagnia di Assicurazioni di Milano, SpA): Via Senigallia 18, 20161 Milano; tel. (02) 64021; fax (02) 64025389; e-mail milass@milass.it; internet www.milass.it; f. 1825; owned by Gruppo Fondiaria-Sai; Pres. and CEO Fausto Marchionni.

MMI Assicurazioni, SpA: Via Egidio Galbani 68, 00156 Roma; tel. (06) 682801; fax (06) 82004163; e-mail posta@mmaweb.it; internet www.mmiweb.it; f. 1962; owned by Mutuelles du Mans Assurances (France); cap. 25m. (2005); Pres. Pascal Guenoit; Dir-Gen. Salvatore Passaro.

Nuova Tirrena, SpA: Via Massimi 158, 00136 Roma; tel. (06) 30181; fax (06) 30183382; internet www.nuovatirrena.it; f. 1929; subsidiary of Gruppo Toro; Pres. Francesco Torri; Dir-Gen. Dott. Luciano Becchio.

Ras, SpA (Riunione Adriatica di Sicurtà): Corso Italia 23, 20122 Milano; tel. (02) 72161; fax (02) 72169145; e-mail info@rasnet.it; internet www.ras.it; f. 1838; 55.51% owned by Allianz; cap. 403.4m. (2005); Chair. Dott. Giuseppe Vita; Man. Dir Paolo Vagnone.

SARA Assicurazioni, SpA: Via Po 20, 00198 Roma; tel. (06) 84751; fax (06) 8475223; internet www.sara.it; f. 1924; net profit 33.5m. (2005); Chair. Rosario Alessi; Gen. Man. Dott. Marco Rocca.

Società Cattolica di Assicurazione—Società Cooperativa: Lungadige Cangrande 16, 37126 Verona; tel. (045) 8391111; fax (045) 8391112; e-mail investor.relations@cattolicaassicurazioni.it; internet www.cattolicaassicurazioni.it; f. 1896; total premiums 4,617m. (Dec. 2004); Gen. Man. Dott. Ezio Paolo Reggia.

Società Reale Mutua di Assicurazioni: Via Corte d'Appello 11, 10122 Torino; tel. (011) 4311111; fax (011) 4350966; e-mail buongiornoreale@realmutua.it; internet www.realemutua.it; f. 1828; net profit 267.8m. (2006); Chair. Dott. Iti Mihalich; Gen. Man. Ing. Luigi Lana.

Swiss Re Italia, SpA: Via dei Giuochi Istmici 40, 00194 Roma; tel. (06) 323931; fax (06) 36303398; e-mail srit-communicazione@swissre.com; internet www.swissre.com; f. 1922; cap. 100m. (Dec. 2001); CEO Antonio Solari.

Toro Assicurazioni, SpA: Via Mazzini 53, 10123 Torino; tel. (011) 0029111; fax (011) 837554; e-mail toro@toroassicurazioni.it; internet www.toroassicurazioni.it; f. 1833; net profit 334m. (Dec. 2005); CEO Sandro Salvati.

Unipol Assicurazioni, SpA: Via Stalingrado 45, 40128 Bologna; tel. (051) 6097111; fax (051) 375349; internet www.unipolonline.it; f. 1963; part of Grupo Unipol; Pres. Pierluigi Stefanini; CEO Carlo Salvatori.

Vittoria Assicurazioni, SpA: Via Caldera 21, 20153 Milano; tel. (02) 482191; fax (02) 48203693; e-mail servizioclienti@vittoriaassicurazioni.it; internet www.vittoriaassicurazioni.com; f. 1921; cap. 30m. (Dec. 2003); Chair. Prof. Luigi Guatri; CEO Roberto Guarena.

Regulatory Authority

Istituto per la Vigilanza sulle Assicurazioni Private e di Interesse Collettivo (ISVAP): Palazzo Volpi, Via del Quirinale 21, 00187 Roma; tel. (06) 421331; fax (06) 42133206; e-mail scrivi@isvap.it; internet www.isvap.it; f. 1982; supervises insurance cos; Pres. and Dir-Gen. Giancarlo Giannini.

Insurance Association

Associazione Nazionale fra le Imprese Assicuratrici (ANIA): Piazza S. Babila 1, 20122 Milano; tel. (02) 7764256; fax (02)

ITALY

77005303; e-mail info@ania.it; internet www.ania.it; f. 1944; Pres. Dott. FABIO CERCHIAI; Dir-Gen. Dott. GIAMPAOLO GALLI; 210 mems.

Trade and Industry

GOVERNMENT AGENCIES

Autorità Garante della Concorrenza e del Mercato (AGCM) (Regulatory Authority for Competition and Markets): Piazza Verdi 6 A, 00198 Roma; tel. (06) 858211; fax (06) 85821256; e-mail antitrust@agcm.it; internet www.agcm.it; Pres. ANTONIO CATRICALÀ; Sec.-Gen. FABIO CINTIOLI.

Cassa depositi e prestiti SpA (CDP): Via Goito 4, 00185 Roma; tel. (06) 42211; fax (06) 42214026; internet www.cassaddpp.it; f. 1850; provides loans to public bodies and local govt; 70% owned by Ministry of the Economy and Finance, 30% by banking foundations; Chair. ALFONSO IOZZO; Gen. Man. ANTONINO TURICCHI.

Istituto Nazionale per il Commercio Estero (ICE) (National Institute for Foreign Trade): Via Liszt 21, 00144 Roma; tel. (06) 59921; fax (06) 59926899; e-mail ice@ice.it; internet www.ice.it; f. 1919; govt agency for the promotion of foreign trade; Pres. UMBERTO VATTANI; Dir-Gen. UGO CALZONI.

Società Italiana per le Imprese All'Estero, SpA (SIMEST) (Italian Company for Businesses Abroad): Corso Vittorio Emanuele II 323, 00186 Roma; tel. (06) 686351; fax (06) 68635220; e-mail info@simest.it; internet www.simest.it; Pres. GIANCARLO LANNA.

CHAMBER OF COMMERCE

Unioncamere (Union of Chambers of Commerce, Industry, Crafts and Agriculture): Piazza Sallustio 21, 00187 Roma; tel. (06) 47041; fax (06) 4704240; e-mail segretaria.generale@unioncamere.it; internet www.unioncamere.it; f. 1954; frmly Unione Italiana delle Camere di Commercio, Industria, Artigianato e Agricoltura (Italian Union of Chambers of Commerce, Industry, Crafts and Agriculture); Pres. CARLO SANGALLI; Sec.-Gen. GIUSEPPE TRIPOLI.

INDUSTRIAL AND TRADE ASSOCIATIONS

Confederazione Generale dell'Industria Italiana (Confindustria) (General Confederation of Italian Industry): Viale dell'Astronomia 30, 00144 Roma; tel. (06) 59031; fax (06) 5919615; e-mail confindustria@confindustria.it; internet www.confindustria.it; f. 1910; re-established 1944; mems: 107 categorized asscns, 105 territorial asscns, 18 regional confeds, 15 sectoral feds and 259 associated orgs, totalling 117,000 firms and 4.25m. employees; Pres. EMMA MARCEGAGLIA; Dir-Gen. MAURIZIO BERETTA.

Principal Organizations Affiliated to Confindustria

Associazione delle Imprese del Farmaco (FARMINDUSTRIA) (Pharmaceutical Industry): Largo del Nazareno 3/8, 00187 Roma; tel. (06) 675801; fax (06) 6786494; e-mail farmindustria@farmindustria.it; internet www.farmindustria.it; f. 1978; Pres. Dott. SERGIO DOMPÉ; 214 mem. firms (2007).

Associazione Industrie per l'Aerospazio, i Sistemi e la Difesa (AIAD) (Aerospace, Systems and Defence Industries): Via Nazionale 54, 00184 Roma; tel. (06) 4880247; fax (06) 4827476; e-mail aiad@aiad.it; internet www.aiad.it; f. 1947; Pres. Dott. GIORGIO ZAPPA; Sec.-Gen. CARLO FESTUCCI.

Associazione Italiana Tecnico Economica del Cemento (AITEC) (Cement): Piazza G. Marconi 25, 00144 Roma; tel. (06) 54210237; fax (06) 5915408; e-mail aitec@aitecweb.com; internet www.aitecweb.com; f. 1959; Pres. GIACOMO MARAZZI; Dir Dott. Ing. FRANCESCO CURCIO.

Associazione Mineraria Italiana (ASSOMINERARIA) (Oil and Mining Industry): Via delle Tre Madonne 20, 00197 Roma; tel. (06) 8073045; fax (06) 8073385; e-mail info@assomineraria.org; internet www.assomineraria.org; f. 1944; Pres. Dott. CLAUDIO DESCALZI; Dir-Gen. Dott. ANDREA KETOFF; 100 mems.

Associazione Nazionale Costruttori Edili (ANCE) (Construction): Via Guattani 16, 00161 Roma; tel. (06) 845671; fax (06) 84567550; e-mail info@ance.it; internet www.ance.it; f. 1946; Pres. Dott. Ing. CLAUDIO DE ALBERTIS; Dir-Gen. CARLO FERRONI; mems: 19,000 firms in 101 provincial and 20 regional asscns.

Associazione Nazionale delle Imprese Elettriche (ASSOELETTRICA) (Electricity Generators and Distributors): Via Benozzo Gozzoli 24, 00142 Roma; tel. (06) 8537281; fax (06) 85356431; e-mail info@assoelettrica.it; internet www.assoelettrica.it; f. 1946; Pres. ENZO GATTA; Dir-Gen. FRANCESCO DE LUCA; 150 mem. cos.

Associazione Nazionale fra Industrie Automobilistiche (ANFIA) (Motor Vehicle Industries): Corso Galileo Ferraris 61, 10128 Torino; tel. (011) 5546511; fax (011) 545986; e-mail anfia@anfia.it; internet www.anfia.it; f. 1912; Pres. Dott. CARLO SINCERI; 260 mems.

Associazione Nazionale Italiana Industrie Grafiche, Cartotecniche e Trasformatrici (ASSOGRAFICI) (Printing and Paper-Processing Industries): Piazza Conciliazione 1, 20123 Milano; tel. (02) 4981051; fax (02) 4816947; e-mail assografici@assografici.it; internet www.assografici.it; f. 1946; Pres. MARCO SPADA; Gen. Dir Dott. CLAUDIO COVINI; 1,200 mems.

Confindustria Servizi Innovativi e Tecnologici (FITA) (Online Media, Market Research, Information Technology, etc.): Via Barberini 11, 00187 Roma; tel. (06) 421401; fax (06) 42140444; internet www.confindustriasi.it; Pres. ALBERTO TRIPI; 46 associated orgs and 60 regional sections.

Federazione delle Associazioni Nazionali di Categorie Industriali Varie (FEDERVARIE) (Miscellaneous Industries): Via Marco Antonio Colonna 46, 20149 Milano; tel. (02) 32672234; fax (02) 32672299; e-mail segreteriafedervarie@betam.it; Pres. Dott. DINO FENZI.

Federazione delle Associazioni Nazionali dell'Industria Meccanica Varia ed Affine (ANIMA) (Mechanical and Engineering Industries): Via Scarsellini 13, 20161 Milano; tel. (02) 45418500; fax (02) 45418545; e-mail anima@anima-it.com; internet www.anima-it.com; f. 1945; Pres. Dott. Ing. SAVINO RIZZIO; Sec.-Gen. Dott. Ing. ENRICO MALCOVATI; 1,500 mems.

Federazione delle Imprese delle Comunicazioni e dell'Informatica (FEDERCOMIN) (Information and Communications Technologies): Via Barberini 11, 00187 Roma; tel. (06) 421401; fax (06) 42140444; e-mail info@federcomin.it; Pres. ALBERTO TRIPI; Dir-Gen. PIETRO VARALDO.

Federazione Industrie Prodotti Impianti e Servizi per le Costruzioni (FINCO) (Construction Services and Systems): Via A. Torlonia 15, 00161 Roma; tel. (06) 44291533; fax (06) 44237930; e-mail info@fincoweb.org; f. 1994; Pres. ROSSELLA RODELLI GIAVARINI; Sec.-Gen. FABRIZIO PIERMATTEI.

Federazione Italiana dell'Accessorio Moda e Persona (FIAMP) (Personal and Fashion Accessories): Piazza M. Buonarroti 32, 20149 Milano; tel. (02) 4815364; fax (02) 4815118; e-mail segreteria@fiamp.it; internet www.fiamp.it; f. 2004; Pres. ALESSANDRO BIFFI.

Federazione Italiana dell'Industria Alimentare (FEDERALIMENTARE) (Food Industry): Viale Pasteur 10, 00144 Roma; e-mail direzione@federalimentare.it; internet www.federalimentare.it; Pres. LUIGI ROSSI DI MONTELERA; 19 mem. asscns.

Federazione Italiana delle Industrie del Legno, del Sughero, del Mobile e dell'Arredamento (FEDERLEGNO-ARREDO) (Wood, Cork, Furniture and Interior Design): Foro Bonaparte 65, 20121 Milano; tel. (02) 806041; fax (02) 80604392; e-mail fla@federlegno.it; internet www.federlegno.it; Dir-Gen. PAOLO LOMBARDI; 2,200 mems.

Federazione Italiana Industriali Produttori Esportatori ed Importatori di Vini, Acquaviti, Liquori, Sciroppi, Aceti ed Affini (FEDERVINI) (Producers, Importers and Exporters of Wines, Brandies, Liqueurs, Syrups, Vinegars, etc.): Via Mentana 2B, 00185 Roma; tel. (06) 4941630; fax (06) 4941566; e-mail federvini@federvini.it; internet www.federvini.it; f. 1917; Pres. PIERO MASTROBERARDINO; Dir-Gen. OTTAVIO CAGIANO DE AZEVEDO.

Confindustria Servizi Innovativi e Tecnologici (FITA) (Online Media, Market Research, Information Technology, etc.): Via Barberini 11, 00187 Roma; tel. (06) 421401; fax (06) 42140444; internet www.confindustriasi.it; Pres. ALBERTO TRIPI; 46 associated orgs and 60 regional sections.

Federazione Nazionale delle Associazioni dei Produttori di Beni Strumentali destinati allo Svolgimento di Processi Manifatturieri dell'Industria e dell'Artigianato (FEDERMACCHINE) (Machine-manufacture): Viale Fulvio Testi 128, 20092 Cinisello Balsamo, MI; tel. (02) 26255288; fax (02) 26255880; e-mail federmacchine@federmacchine.it; internet www.federmacchine.it; Pres. Dott. ALBERTO SACCHI; Sec.-Gen. Dott. ALFREDO MARIOTTI.

Federazione Nazionale Fonderie (ASSOFOND) (Foundries): Via Copernico 54, 20090 Trezzano Sul Naviglio (Milano); tel. (02) 48400967; fax (02) 48401282; e-mail info@assofond.it; internet www.assofond.it; f. 1948; Pres. EMILIO CREMONA; Dir PAOLO PONZINI.

Federazione Nazionale Imprese Elettrotecniche ed Elettroniche (ANIE) (Electric and Electronic Sectors): Via Gattamelata 34, 20149 Milano; tel. (02) 32641; fax (02) 3264212; e-mail info@anie.it; internet www.anie.it; Pres. GIAN FRANCESCO IMPERIALI; Dir ROBERTO TARANTO.

Federazione Nazionale dell'Industria Chimica (FEDERCHIMICA) (Chemical Industry): Via Giovanni da Procida 11, 20149 Milano; tel. (02) 345651; fax (02) 34565310; e-mail federchimica@federchimica.it; internet www.federchimica.it; f. 1945; Pres. DIANA BRACCO; Dir Dott. CLAUDIO BENEDETTI.

Federazione Nazionale Industria dei Viaggi e del Turismo (FEDERTURISMO) (Tourism and Travel): Viale Pasteur 10, 00144

ITALY

Roma; tel. (06) 5911758; fax (06) 5910390; e-mail federturismo@federturismo.it; internet www.federturismo.it; Dir-Gen. Dott. FULVIO NANNELLI.

Federazione Nazionale dei Sistemi e delle Modalità di Trasporto e delle Attività Connesse (FEDERTRASPORTO): Viale Pasteur 10, 00144 Roma; tel. (06) 97279400; fax (06) 97279408; e-mail borghese@federtrasporto.it; f. 1993; Pres. GIAN MARIA GROSPIETRO; Dir LUIGI CICCARELLI; 10 mem. asscns.

Federazione Sindacale dell'Industria Metalmeccanica Italiana (FEDERMECCANICA) (Mechanics): Piazzale B. Juarez 14, 00144 Roma; tel. (06) 5925446; fax (06) 5911913; e-mail mail.roma@federmeccanica.it; internet www.federmeccanica.it; f. 1971; 102 mem. asscns; Dir ROBERTO SANTARELLI.

Unione Industriali Pastai Italiani (UNIPI) (Pasta Manufacturers): Via Po 102, 00198 Roma; tel. (06) 8543291; fax (06) 8415132; e-mail unipi@unipi-pasta.it; internet www.unipi-pasta.it; f. 1968; Pres. Dott. MARIO RUMMO; Dir Gen. RAFFAELLO RAGAGLINI.

Unione Nazionale Cantieri e Industrie Nautiche ed Affini (UCINA) (Marine Industry): Piazzale Kennedy 1, 16129 Genova; tel. (010) 5769811; fax (010) 5531104; e-mail ucina@ucina.it; internet www.ucina.it; Pres. Dott. PAOLO VITELLI; Sec.-Gen. Dott. Ing. LORENZO POLLICARDO.

Unione Petrolifera (Petroleum Industries): Via Giorgione 129, 00147 Roma; tel. (06) 5423651; fax (06) 59602925; e-mail info@unionepetrolifera.it; internet www.unionepetrolifera.it; f. 1948; Pres. Dott. PASQUALE DE VITA; Dir-Gen. Dott. PIETRO DE SIMONE; 30 mem. cos.

Other Industrial and Trade Organizations

Associazione fra le Società Italiane per Azioni (ASSONIME) (Limited Cos): Piazza Venezia 11, 00187 Roma; tel. (06) 695291; fax (06) 6790487; e-mail assonime@assonime.it; internet www.assonime.it; f. 1911; Pres. Dott. VITTORIO MERLONI; Dir-Gen. Prof. STEFANO MICOSSI.

Confederazione Generale della Agricoltura Italiana (CONFAGRICOLTURA) (Agriculture): Corso Vittorio Emanuele II 101, 00186 Roma; tel. (06) 68521; fax (06) 68308578; e-mail info@confagricoltura.it; internet www.confagricoltura.it; f. 1945; Pres. Dott. AUGUSTO BOCCHINI; Dir-Gen. VITO BIANCO.

Confederazione Generale Italiana del Commercio, del Turismo, dei Servizi e delle Piccole e Medie Industrie (PMI) (CONFCOMMERCIO) (Commerce, Tourism, Services and Small and Medium-sized Industries): Piazza G.G. Belli 2, 00153 Roma; tel. (06) 58661; fax (06) 5809425; e-mail confcommercio@confcommercio.it; internet www.confcommercio.it; f. 1946; Pres. Dott. SERGIO BILLÈ; Dir-Gen. LUIGI TARANTO.

Confederazione Italiana della Piccola e Media Industria Privata (CONFAPI) (Small and Medium-sized Private Industry): Via della Colonna Antonina 52, 00186 Roma; tel. (06) 690151; fax (06) 6791488; e-mail mail@confapi.org; internet www.confapi.org; f. 1947; Pres. Dott. PAOLO GALASSI; Dir-Gen. Dott. SANDRO NACCARELLI; 55,000 mems.

Confederazione Italiana della Proprietà Edilizia (CONFEDILIZIA) (Real Estate): Via Borgognona 47, 00187 Roma; tel. (06) 6793489; fax (06) 6793447; e-mail roma@confedilizia.it; internet www.confedilizia.it; Pres. Avv. CORRADO SFORZA FOGLIANI; Sec.-Gen. GIORGIO SPAZIANI TESTA.

Federazione delle Associazioni Italiane Alberghi e Turismo (FEDERALBERGHI) (Hotels and Tourism): Via Toscana 1, 00187 Roma; tel. (06) 42741151; fax (06) 42871197; internet www.federalberghi.it; f. 1950; Pres. BERNABO BOCCA; Gen. Man. ALESSANDRO CIANELLA; 30,000 mems.

UTILITIES

In 2004 there were 550 local power companies in Italy.

Autorità per l'Energia Elettrica e il Gas (AEEG) (Electric Energy and Gas Authority): Piazza Cavour 5, 20121 Milano; tel. (02) 655651; fax (02) 65565266; e-mail segretariatogenerale@autorita.energia.it; internet www.autorita.energia.it; regulatory authority; Pres. ALESSANDRO ORTIS.

Electricity

A2A, SpA: Via Lamarmora 230, 25124 Brescia; tel. (030) 2977900; fax (030) 2977928; e-mail infobs@a2a.eu; internet www.a2a.eu; f. 2007 by merger of AEM, AMSA and ASM; electricity and gas manufacture and distribution; Chair. of Bd RENZO CAPRA.

Acea, SpA: Piazzale Ostiense 2, 00154 Roma; tel. (06) 57991; fax (06) 5758095; e-mail info@aceaspa.it; internet www.aceaspa.it; produces and distributes electricity in Rome area; also engaged in water provision; Chair. FABIANO FABIANI; CEO ANDREA MANGONI.

Edison, SpA: Foro Buonaparte 31, 20121 Milano; tel. (02) 62221; fax (02) 62227379; e-mail infoweb@edison.it; internet www.edison.it; f. 1884 as Società Generale Italiana di Elettricità Sistema Edison; electricity and natural gas; 71.2% owned by Transalpina di energia Srl; Chair. GIULIANO ZUCCOLI; CEO UMBERTO QUADRINO.

Enel, SpA: Via le Regina Margherita 137, 00198 Roma; tel. (06) 85091; fax (06) 85092162; internet www.enel.it; f. 1962; 21.4% directly state-owned; partially privatized; generates and distributes electricity and gas; Chair. PIERO GNUDI; CEO FULVIO CONTI.

Gestore del sistema eletrico, SpA (GRTN): Viale Maresciallo Pilsudski 92, 00197 Roma; tel. (06) 80111; fax (06) 80114392; e-mail info@grtn.it; internet www.grtn.it; f. 2000; owned by the Ministry of the Economy and Finance; manages electricity transmission and co-ordinates the power network; Chair. CARLO ANDREA BOLLINO; CEO NANDO PASQUALI.

Terna, SpA—Rete Elettrica Nazionale: Via Arno 64, 00198 Roma; tel. (06) 83138111; e-mail info@terna.it; internet www.terna.it; f. 1999; electricity transmission co; owns over 97% of electricity transmission grid; Pres. LUIGI ROTH; CEO FLAVIO CATTANEO.

Gas

In 2002 the Government's stake in the gas sector was sold in order to comply with European Union regulations. See the section on Electricity for companies that are involved in the supply of both gas and electricity.

Eni, SpA: Piazzale Mattei 1, 00144 Roma; tel. (06) 59821; fax (06) 59822141; e-mail segreteriasocietaria.azionisti@eni.it; internet www.eni.it; f. 1953; frmly Ente Nazionale Idrocarburi; natural gas exploration, oil and gas power; 20.3% owned by Ministry of the Economy and Finance; Pres. ROBERTO POLI; CEO PAOLO SCARONI.

Eni Power: Piazza Vanoni 1, 20097 San Donato Milanese; tel. (02) 5201; fax (02) 5203180; internet www.enipower.eni.it; owned by Eni, SpA (q.v.); power generation and sale; Pres. FRANCESCO ZOFREA; CEO ENRICO GRIGESI.

Gruppo Hera, SpA: Viale C. Berti Pichat 2, 40127 Bologna; tel. (051) 287111; fax (051) 2814036; internet www.gruppohera.it; f. 2002; distributes gas; also engaged in water provision; Chair. TOMASO TOMMASI DI VIGNANO; Man. Dir MAURIZIO CHIARINI.

Italgas, SpA: Via XX Settembre 41, 10121 Torino; tel. (01) 123941; fax (01) 12394499; internet www.italgas.it; gas distribution; owned by Eni, SpA (q.v.); Pres. PAOLO CAROPRESO; CEO GIOVANNI LOCANTO.

Linde Gas Italia, Srl: Via Guido Rossa 3, 20010 Arluno, Milano; tel. (02) 903731; fax (02) 90373500; internet www.linde-gas.it.

Plurigas: Corso di Porta Vittoria 4, 20122 Milano; tel. (02) 77203033; fax (02) 77203255; e-mail info@plurigas.it; internet www.plurigas.it; f. 2001; gas distribution; 40% owned by AEM Milano; Chair. ROBERTO BAZZANO; CEO RENZO CAPRA.

Snam Rete Gas: Piazza Santa Barbara 7, 20097 San Donato Milanese; tel. (02) 5201; fax (02) 52038227; e-mail postmaster@snamretegas.it; internet www.snamretegas.it; f. 1941 as Società Nazionale Metanodotti (Snam); adopted current name 2001; owned by Eni, SpA (q.v.); transports natural gas; Chair. ALBERTO MEOMARTINI; CEO CARLO MALACAME.

TRADE UNIONS

There are three main federations of Italian trade unions, the Confederazione Generale Italiana del Lavoro (CGIL), the Confederazione Italiana Sindacati Lavoratori (CISL) and the Unione Italiana del Lavoro (UIL), all of which have close ties with political parties. The CGIL was formerly dominated by the Partito Comunista Italiano (Italian Communist Party, now the Democratici di Sinistra—Democrats of the Left), the CISL has links with the Christian Democrats, and the UIL is associated with the socialists.

National Federations

Confederazione Autonoma Italiana del Lavoro (CONFAIL): Viale Abruzzi 38, 20131 Milano; tel. (02) 29404554; fax (02) 29525692; e-mail info@confail.org; Gen. Sec. EVANGELISTA ZACCARIA.

Confederazione Autonoma Sindacati Artigiani (CASARTIGIANI): Via Flaminio Ponzio 2, 00153 Roma; tel. (06) 5758081; fax (06) 5755036; e-mail casartigiani@tiscalinet.it; internet www.casartigiani.org; f. 1958; federation of artisans' unions and regional and provincial asscns; Pres. GIACOMO BASSO.

Confederazione Generale Italiana dell'Artigianato (CONFARTIGIANATO) (Artisans): Via di S. Giovanni in Laterano 152, 00184 Roma; tel. (06) 703741; fax (06) 70452188; e-mail confartigianato@confartigianato.it; internet www.confartigianato.it; f. 1945; independent; 20 regional feds, 121 provincial asscns; 521,000 associate enterprises; Pres. LUCIANO PETRACCHI.

Confederazione Generale Italiana del Lavoro (CGIL) (Italian General Confederation of Labour): Corso d'Italia 25, 00198 Roma; tel. (06) 84761; fax (06) 8476321; e-mail info@mail.cgil.it; internet www.cgil.it; f. 1906 as Confederazione Generale del Lavoro; refounded

ITALY

1944; confederation of 13 feds; Sec.-Gen. GUGLIELMO EPIFANI; 5,402,408 mems.

Confederazione Generale dei Sindacati Autonomi dei Lavoratori (CONFSAL): Viale Trasevere 60, 00153 Roma; tel. (06) 5852071; fax (06) 5818218; e-mail info@confsal.it; internet www.confsal.it; f. 1979; Sec.-Gen. Prof. MARCO PAOLO NIGI.

Confederazione Italiana Dirigenti e Alte Professionalità (CIDA): Via Nazionale 75, 00184 Roma; tel. (06) 4888241; fax (06) 48882452; e-mail dirigenti@cida.it; internet www.cida.it; federation of eight managers' unions; Pres. Prof. GIORGIO REMBADO; Sec.-Gen. Dott. GIOVANNI CARDEGNA.

Confederazione Italiana Lavoratori Liberi (CONFIL): Via di Campo Marzio 46, 00186 Roma; tel. (06) 6872508; fax (06) 6872509; Gen. Sec. FRANCESCO BRUNETTI.

Confederazione Italiana Sindacati Addetti ai Servizi (CISAS): Via Sapri 6, 00185 Roma; tel. (06) 4466618; fax (06) 4466617; internet www.cisas.org; Gen. Sec. ONOFRIO DANIELLO.

Confederazione Italiana Sindacati Lavoratori (CISL): Via Po 21, 00198 Roma; tel. (06) 84731; fax (06) 8413782; e-mail cisl@cisl.it; internet www.cisl.it; f. 1950; affiliated to the International Confederation of Free Trade Unions and the European Trade Union Confederation; fed. of 14 unions; publishes *Conquiste del Lavoro* (see Press); Sec.-Gen. SAVINO PEZZOTTA; 4,200,000 mems.

Confederazione Nazionale dell'Artigianato e delle Piccole Imprese (CNA) (National Confederation of Italian SMEs and Handicrafts): Via G. A. Guattani 13, 00161 Roma; tel. (06) 441881; fax (06) 44249513; e-mail cna@cna.it; internet www.cna.it; provincial asscns; Pres. IVAN MALAVASI; Gen. Sec. Dott. GIAN CARLO SANGALLI.

Confederazione Generale dei Sindacati Autonomi dei Lavoratori (CONFSAL): Viale Trasevere 60, 00153 Roma; tel. (06) 5852071; fax (06) 5818218; e-mail info@confsal.it; internet www.confsal.it; f. 1979; Sec.-Gen. Prof. MARCO PAOLO NIGI.

Confederazione Unitaria Quadri (CUQ): Via XX Settembre 58, 10121 Torino; tel. (011) 5612042; fax (011) 5620362; e-mail confquadri@tin.it; f. 1995; Pres. MARIO VIGNA.

Confederazione Unitaria Sindacati Autonomi Lavoratori (CUSAL): Via di Campo Marzio 46, 00186 Roma; tel. (06) 6872508; fax (06) 6872509; Pres. DOMENICO MANNO; Gen. Sec. FRANCESCO BRUNETTI.

Sindacato Nazionale dei Funzionari Direttivi, Dirigenti e delle Alte Professionalità della Pubblica Amministrazione (DIRSTAT): Via Ezio 12, 00192 Roma; tel. (06) 3211535; fax (06) 3212690; e-mail dirstat@dirstat.it; internet www.dirstat.it; f. 1948; fed. of 33 unions and asscns of civil-service executives and officers; Sec.-Gen. ARCANGELO D'AMBROSIO; Treas. Dott. SERGIO DI DONNA.

Unione Generale del Lavoro (UGL): Via Margutta 19, 00187 Roma; tel. (06) 324821; fax (06) 324820; e-mail ugl@ugl.it; internet www.ugl.it; f. 1950 as CISNAL; name changed as above 1995; upholds traditions of national syndicalism; fed. of 64 unions, 77 provincial unions; Gen. Sec. STEFANO CETICA; 2,137,979 mems.

Unione Italiana del Lavoro (UIL): Via Lucullo 6, 00187 Roma; tel. (06) 4753210; fax (06) 4753295; e-mail segretariagenerale@uil.it; internet www.uil.it; f. 1950; socialist, social democrat and republican; affiliated to the International Confederation of Free Trade Unions and European Trade Union Confederation; 18 national trade union feds and 108 provincial union councils; Gen. Sec. LUIGI ANGELETTI; 1,758,729 mems.

Principal Unions

Banking and Insurance

Federazione Autonoma Bancari Italiana (FABI) (Bank, Tax and Finance Workers): Via Tevere 46, 00198 Roma; tel. (06) 8415751; fax (06) 8559220; internet www.fabi.it; f. 1948; independent; Pres. ENZO SCOLA; Sec.-Gen. CARLO GIORGETTI; 69,000 mems.

Federazione Autonoma Lavoratori del Credito e del Risparmio Italiani (FALCRI) (Savings Banks Workers): Viale Liegi 48B, 00198 Roma; tel. (06) 8416336; fax (06) 8416343; e-mail segretaria@falcri.it; internet www.falcri.it; f. 1950; Sec.-Gen. MARIA FRANCESCA FURFARO.

Federazione Italiana Bancari e Assicuratori (FIBA): Via Modena 5, 00184 Roma; tel. (06) 4741245; fax (06) 4746136; e-mail fiba@fiba.it; internet www.fiba.it; affiliated to the CISL; Sec.-Gen. GIUSEPPE GALLO; 58,980 mems.

Federazione Italiana Sindacale Lavoratori Assicurazioni Credito (Employees of Credit Institutions): Via Vicenza 5A, 00184 Roma; tel. (06) 448841; fax (06) 4457356; e-mail fisac@fisac.it; internet www.fisac.it; affiliated to the CGIL; Sec.-Gen. MARCELLO TOCCO; 60,000 mems.

Federazione Nazionale Assicuratori (FNA) (Insurance Workers): Via Vincenzo Monti 25, 20123 Milano; Via Montebello 104, 00185 Roma; e-mail fnami@fnaitalia.org; internet www.fnaitalia.org; f. 1946; independent; Pres. LUIGI PERAZZI; Sec.-Gen. TEODORO SYLOS CARLÓ.

Unione Italiana Lavoratori Credito, Esattorie e Assicurazioni (UILCA) (Credit and Assurance Workers and Tax Collectors): Via Lombardia 30, 00187 Roma; tel. (06) 4872132; fax (06) 484704; internet www.uilca.it; affiliated to the UIL; Sec.-Gen. ELIO PORINO; 37,453 mems.

Building and Building Materials

Federazione Autonoma Italiana Lavoratori Edili e Affini (FAILEA) (Workers in Construction and Allied Trades): Via della Rosa 91, 00171 Roma; affiliated to the CISL; Sec. RAUL VIOZZI.

Federazione Italiana Lavoratori Costruzioni e Affini (FILCA) (Building Industries' Workers): Via del Viminale 43, 00184 Roma; tel. (06) 4870634; fax (06) 4818884; e-mail federazione_filca@cisl.it; internet www.filca.cisl.it; f. 1955; affiliated to the CISL; Sec.-Gen. DOMENICO PESENTI; 215,990 mems.

Federazione Italiana Lavoratori del Legno, dell'Edilizia, delle Industrie Affini (FILLEA) (Wood-workers, Construction Workers and Allied Trades): Via G. B. Morgagni 27, 00161 Roma; tel. (06) 441141; fax (06) 44235849; e-mail fillea@mail.cgil.it; internet www.filleacgil.it; affiliated to the CGIL; Sec.-Gen. FRANCO MARTINI; 434,154 mems.

Federazione Nazionale Costruzioni (Construction): Lungotevere Sanzio 5, Roma; tel. (06) 585511; fax (06) 5815184; affiliated to the UGL; Sec. EGIDIO SANGUE.

Federazione Nazionale Lavoratori Edili Affini e del Legno (FENEAL) (Builders and Woodworkers): Via Alessandria 171, 00198 Roma; tel. (06) 8547393; fax (06) 8547423; e-mail fineal-uil@feneal-uil.it; internet www.feneal-uil.it; f. 1951; affiliated to the UIL; Sec.-Gen. FRANCESCO MARABOTTINI; 106,698 mems.

Chemical, Mining and Allied Industries

Federazione Energia, Moda, Chimica e Settori Affini (FEMCA) (Energy, Fashion, Chemicals and Allied Workers): Via Bolzano 16, 00198 Roma; tel. (06) 83034422; fax (06) 83034414; e-mail femca.nazionale@cisl.it; internet www.femcacisl.it; affiliated to the CISL; Sec.-Gen. SERGIO GIGLI.

Federazione Italiana Lavoratori Chimica, Energia e Manifatture (FILCEM-CGIL) (Chemicals, Energy and Manufacturing): Via Piemonte 32, 00187 Roma; tel. (06) 4620091; fax (06) 4824246; e-mail nazionale@filcemcgil.it; internet www.filcemcgil.it; f. 2006 by merger of FILCEA (chemicals) and FNLE (energy); affiliated to the CGIL; Sec.-Gen. ALBERTO MORSELLI; 164,000 mems.

Federazione Nazionale Chimici (Chemicals): Via Daniele Manin 53, Roma; tel. (06) 4818313; fax (06) 4820554; e-mail uglchimicnazionale@tiscali.net; internet www.ugl.it/confederazione/chimici/index.htm; affiliated to the UGL; Sec. DOMENICO SCOPELLITI.

Unione Italiana Lavoratori Chimici, Energia e Manufatturiero (UILCEM) (Chemicals, Energy and Manufacturing Workers): Via Bolzano 16, 00198 Roma; tel. (06) 83034305; fax (06) 83034307; e-mail segretara@uilcem-nazionale.it; internet www.uilcem.it; affiliated to the UIL; Pres. ROMANO BELLISSIMA; Sec.-Gen. AUGUSTO PASCUCCI; 84,649 mems.

Clothing and Textiles

Federazione Italiana Lavoratori Tessili, Abbigliamento, Cuoio e Calzature (FILTEA) (Textile, Clothing, Leather and Footwear Workers): Via Leopoldo Serra 31, 00153 Roma; tel. (06) 5836828; fax (06) 5803182; e-mail filtea@mail.cgil.it; internet www.filtea.cgil.it; f. 1966; affiliated to the CGIL; Gen. Sec. VALERIA FEDELI; 150,000 mems.

Unione Italiana Lavoratori Tessili e Abbigliamento (UILTA): Via del Viminale 43, 00184 Roma; tel. (06) 4883486; fax (06) 4819421; e-mail uilta.roma@libero.it; internet www.uil.it/uilta/; affiliated to the UIL; Sec.-Gen. PASQUALE ROSSETTI.

Engineering and Metallurgy

Federazione Impiegati Operai Metallurgici (FIOM-CGIL) (Metalworkers): Corso Trieste 36, 00198 Roma; tel. (06) 852621; fax (06) 85303079; e-mail organizzazione@fiom.cgil.it; internet www.fiom.cgil.it; f. 1901; affiliated to the CGIL; Sec. GIANNI RINALDINI; 400,000 mems.

Federazione Italiana Metalmeccanici (FIM-CISL) (Metal Mechanic Workers): Corso Trieste 36, 00198 Roma; tel. (06) 852621; fax (06) 85262464; internet www.cisl.it/fim; f. 1951; affiliated to the CISL; Sec.-Gen. GIORGIO CAPRIOLI; 190,000 mems.

Federazione Nazionale Metalmeccanici: Via Amadeo 23, Roma; tel. (06) 4741808; fax (06) 4881236; affiliated to the UGL; Sec. DOMENICO FRESILLI.

ITALY

Sindacato Nazionale Ingegneri Liberi Professionisti Italiana (SNILPI) (Liberal Professionals-Engineers): Via Salaria 292, 00199 Roma; tel. (06) 8549796; fax (06) 85830308; e-mail info@snilpi.it; internet www.snilpi.it; Pres. Dott. Ing. LUIGI LUCHERINI; Sec.-Gen. Dott. Ing. GIUSEPPE MILONE.

Unione Italiana Lavoratori Metalmeccanici (UILM) (Metalworkers): Corso Trieste 36, 00198 Roma; tel. (06) 85262201; fax (06) 85262203; e-mail uilm@uil.it; internet www.uil.it/uilm; f. 1950; affiliated to the UIL; Sec.-Gen. ANTONINO REGAZZI; 100,534 mems.

Food and Agriculture

Confederazione Italiana Agricoltori (CIA) (Farmers): Via Mariano Fortuny 20, 00196 Roma; tel. (06) 32687502; fax (06) 3204924; e-mail segreteriapresidente@cia.it; internet www.cia.it; independent; Pres. GIUSEPPE POLITI; Vice-Pres. ENZO PIERANGIOLI.

Confederazione Italiana Dirigenti, Quadri e Impiegati dell' Agricoltura (CONFEDERDIA): Viale Beethoven 48, 00144 Roma; tel. (06) 5912808; fax (06) 5915014; e-mail confederdia@confederdia.it; internet www.confederdia.it; Pres. LUCIANO BOZZATO; Gen. Sec. TOMMASO BRANDONI.

Confederazione Nazionale Coltivatori Diretti (COLDIRETTI) (Small-holders): Via XXIV Maggio 43, 00187 Roma; tel. (06) 46821; fax (06) 4682305; e-mail coldiretti@coldiretti.it; internet www.coldiretti.it; independent; Pres. PAOLO BEDONI; Sec.-Gen. Dott. FRANCO PASQUALI; mems: 18 regional federations, 98 provincial federations.

Federazione Agricola Alimentare Ambientale Industriale (FAI-CISL) (Agriculture, Food and Environment Workers' Federation): Via Tevere 20, 00198 Roma; tel. (06) 845691; fax (06) 8840652; e-mail federazione.fai@cisl.it; internet www.fai.cisl.it; f. 1997 by merger of FISBA and FAT.

Federazione Lavoratori Agro Industria (FLAI-CGIL) (Workers in Agro-industry): Via Leopoldo Serra 31, 00153 Roma; tel. (06) 585611; fax (06) 58561334; e-mail flai-nazionale@flai.it; internet www.flai.it; f. 1988; affiliated to the CGIL; Sec.-Gen. FRANCO CHIRIACO; 309,524 mems.

Unione Coltivatori Italiana (UCI) (Farmers): Via in Lucina 10, 00186 Roma; tel. (06) 6871043; Pres. VINCENZO PANDOVINO.

Unione Generale Coltivatori (UGC): Via Tevere 44, 00198 Roma; tel. (06) 8552383; fax (06) 8553891; affiliated to the CISL; Pres. GAVINO DERUDA; 151,625 mems.

Unione Italiana Lavoratori Agroalimentari (UILA-UIL) (Food Workers): Via Savoia 80, 00198 Roma; tel. (06) 85301610; fax (06) 85303253; e-mail uilanazionale@uila.it; internet www.uila.it; affiliated to the UIL; Sec. STEFANO MANTEGAZZA.

Unione Italiana Mezzadri e Coltivatori Diretti (UIMEC) (Land Workers): Via Reno 30, 00198 Roma; tel. (06) 85305458; fax (06) 85344469; e-mail uimecuil@uimecuil.it; affiliated to the UIL; Pres. GIOVANBATTISTA AIUTO; 100,000 mems.

Medical

Confederazione Unitaria Medici Italiani—Associazione dei Medici Specialisti e Specializzandi (CUMI—AISS) (Doctors—Association of Medical Specialists): Via Livorno 36, 00162 Roma; tel. (06) 44254168; fax (06) 44254160; e-mail info@cumiaiss.it; internet www.cumiaiss.it; f. 2000 by fusion of CUMI and AISS; Pres. COSMO DE MATTEIS; Sec.-Gen. SALVO CALÌ.

Federazione Italiana Servizi Territoriali (FIST) (Hospital and Regional Municipal Workers' Unions): Via Lancisi 25, 00161 Roma; tel. (06) 4425981; fax (06) 44230114; e-mail fist@cisl.it; internet www.mclink.it/com/fist; affiliated to the CISL; Sec.-Gen. ERMENEGILDO BONFANTI; 250,000 mems.

Federazione Nazionale Medici (Doctors): Via Amendola 7, Roma; tel. (06) 4870444; fax (06) 4874323; e-mail federmed@flashnet.it; affiliated to the UGL; Sec.-Gen. GIOVANNI PALOMBI.

Public Services

Confederazione dei Quadri Direttivi e Dirigenti della Funzione Pubblica (CONFEDIR) (Public Office Managers): Largo dell'Amba Aradam 1, 00184 Roma; tel. (06) 77204826; fax (06) 77077029; e-mail confedir@confedir.org; internet www.confedir.org; Gen. Sec. ROBERTO CONFALONIERI.

Federazione Italiana Lavoratori Organi Costituzionali (Employees of Constitutional Bodies): Via del Parlamento 9, 00187 Roma; tel. (06) 67609118; fax (06) 67604890; e-mail uiloocc@uil.it; internet www.uilorganicostituzionali.it; affiliated to the UIL; Sec.-Gen. Dott. SILVANO SGREVI.

Federazione Lavoratori Aziende Elettriche Italiane (FLAEI) (Workers in Italian Electrical Undertakings): Via Salaria 83, 00198 Roma; tel. (06) 8440421; fax (06) 8548458; e-mail nazionale@flaei.org; internet www.flaei.org; f. 1948; affiliated to the CISL; Sec. ARSENIO CAROSI; 32,000 mems.

Directory

Federazione Lavoratori Pubblici e dei Servizi (FPI) (Public Sector and Services Workers): Via Lancisi 25, 00161 Roma; tel. (06) 440071; fax (06) 44007512; e-mail fps@cisl.it; internet www.fps.cisl.it; affiliated to the CISL.

Federazione Nazionale Dipendenti Enti Pubblici UGL (UGL-FEDEP) (Public Employees): Via del Corea 13, Roma; tel. (06) 3233363; fax (06) 3226052; e-mail info@uglfedep.org; internet www.uglfedep.org; f. 1962; affiliated to the UGL; Gen. Sec. GIUSEPPE MARO.

Federazione Nazionale Energia (Energy): Via Filiberto 125, Roma; tel. (06) 7005935; fax (06) 7003451; affiliated to the UGL; Sec. LUIGI DE NARDIS.

Federazione Nazionale Enti Locali (Employees of Local Authorities): Via Amendola 5, 00185 Roma; tel. (06) 4743418; fax (06) 4743853; e-mail quesiti@uglentilocali.it; internet www.uglentilocali.it; affiliated to the UGL; Sec. GIUSEPPE VIGLIANESI.

Federazione Nazionale Lavoratori Funzione Pubblica: Via Leopoldo Serra 31, 00153 Roma; tel. (06) 585441; fax (06) 5836970; e-mail posta@fpcgil.it; internet www.fpcgil.it; f. 1980; affiliated to the CGIL, Public Services International, and European Public Services Union (EPSU); Gen. Sec. CARLO PODDA; 390,000 mems.

Federazione Nazionale Sanità (Sanitary Workers): Via Farini 16, Roma; tel. (06) 4814678; fax (06) 4814651; affiliated to the UGL; Sec. SALVATORE GALIZIA.

Unione Italiana Lavoratori Federazione Poteri Locali (UILFPL) (Local Authority Employees): Via di Tor Fiorenza 35, 00199 Roma; tel. (06) 865081; fax (06) 86508235; e-mail info@uilfpl.it; internet www.uilfpl.it; affiliated to the UIL; Gen. Sec. CARLO FIORDALISO; 89,179 mems.

Unione Italiana Lavoratori Pubblico Amministrazione (UILPA) (Public Office Workers): Via Emilio Lepido 46, 00175 Roma; tel. (06) 71588888; fax (06) 71582046; e-mail uilpa@uilpa.it; internet www.uilpa.it; affiliated to the UIL; Sec.-Gen. SALVATORE BOSCO; 67,702 mems.

Unione Italiana Lavoratori Sanità (UIL Sanità) (Sanitary Workers): Via di Tor Fiorenza 35, 00199 Roma; tel. (06) 865081; fax (06) 86508235; e-mail info@uilfpl.it; internet www.uilfpl.it; affiliated to the UIL; Sec.-Gen. CARLO FIORDALISO; 98,669 mems.

Teachers

Cisl-Scuola (School Teachers): Via Bargoni 8, 00153 Roma; tel. (06) 58311913; fax (06) 5881713; internet www.cislscuola.it; f. 1997; affiliated to the CISL; Sec.-Gen. FRANCESCO SCRIMA; 208,000 mems.

Cisl-Università (University Teachers): Via Rovereto 11, 00198 Roma; tel. (06) 8840772; fax (06) 8844977; e-mail info@cisluniversita.it; internet www.cisluniversita.it; affiliated to the CISL; Sec.-Gen. ANTONIO MARSILIA.

Sindacato Nazionale Scuola (School Teachers): Via Leopoldo Serra 31, Roma; tel. (06) 585480; e-mail mail@cgilscuola.it; internet www.cgilscuola.it; affiliated to the CGIL; 97,149 mems (1997).

Sindacato Nazionale Università Ricerca (SNUR-CGIL): Via Leopoldo Serra 31, 00153 Roma; tel. (06) 5883383; fax (06) 5883926; e-mail comren@snur-cgil.it; internet www.snur-cgil.it.

UGL-Federazione Nazionale Università (University Teachers): Lungotevere Rio Sanzio 5, Roma; tel. (06) 58551; fax (06) 58551223; e-mail ugluniversita@mclink.it; internet www.ugl.it/confederazione/newuniversita/index.htm; affiliated to the UGL; Dir CLARA VALLI.

Unione Italiana Lavoratori Scuola (UIL Scuola) (School Workers): Via Marino Laziale 44, 00179 Roma; tel. (06) 7846941; fax (06) 7842858; e-mail uilscuola@uil.it; internet www.uil.it/uilscuola; affiliated to the UIL; Sec.-Gen. MASSIMO DI MENNA; 59,402 mems.

Tourism and Entertainment

Federazione Informazione Spettacolo e Telecomunicazioni (FISTEL) (Actors, Artists and Media Workers): Via Palestro 30, 00185 Roma; tel. (06) 492171; fax (06) 4457330; affiliated to the CISL; Sec.-Gen. FULVIO GIACOMASSI; 43,388 mems.

Federazione Italiana Lavoratori Commercio, Turismo e Servizi (FILCAMS) (Hotel and Catering Workers): Via Leopoldo Serra 31, 00153 Roma; tel. (06) 5885102; fax (06) 5885323; e-mail post@filcams.cgil.it; internet www.filcams.cgil.it; f. 1960; affiliated to the CGIL; Sec.-Gen. IVANO CORRAINI; 189,000 mems.

Federazione Italiana Sindacati Addetti Servizi Commerciali Affini e del Turismo (FISASCAT-CISL) (Commercial and Tourist Unions): Via Livenza 7, 00198 Roma; tel. (06) 8541042; fax (06) 8558057; internet www.fisascat.it; Sec.-Gen. GIANNI BARATTA; 153,900 mems.

Federazione Nazionale Informazione e Spettacolo (Actors, Artists and Media Workers): Via Margutta 19, Roma; tel. (06) 324821; fax (06) 323420; affiliated to the UGL; Sec. GIANNI IMPROTA.

ITALY

Sindacato Attori Italiano (SAI) (Actors): Via Ofanto 18, 00198 Roma; tel. (06) 8411288; fax (06) 8546780; e-mail sai-slc@cgil.it; internet www.cgil.it/sai-slc; affiliated to the CGIL; Pres. MASSIMO GHINI; Sec.-Gen. MAURIZIO FERIAUD.

Unione Italiana Lavoratori Turismo Commercio e Servizi (UILTuCS): Via Nizza 154, 00198 Roma; tel. (06) 84242268; fax (06) 84242292; e-mail info@uiltucs.it; internet www.uiltucs.it; f. 1977; affiliated to the UIL; Gen. Sec. BRUNO BOCO; 75,042 mems.

Transport and Telecommunications

Federazione Italiana Lavoratori Postelegrafonici (Filpt) (Postal, Telegraph and Telephone Workers): Piazza Verdi 5, Ferrara; tel. (05) 32783111; affiliated to the CGIL; division of Sindicato Lavoratori Comunicazione; Sec. GIUSEPPE MASTRACCHI; 35,000 mems.

Federazione Italiana Lavoratori dei Trasporti (FILT-CGIL): Via G. B. Morgagni 27, 00161 Roma; tel. (06) 442961; fax (06) 44293313; e-mail filt@mail.cgil.it; affiliated to the CGIL; Sec. GUIDO ABBADESSA.

Federazione Italiana Trasporti (FIT-CISL): Via A. Musa 4, 00161 Roma; tel. (06) 442861; fax (06) 44266336; e-mail federazione_fit@cisl.it; internet www.fit.cisl.it; f. 1950; affiliated to the CISL; Sec.-Gen. CLAUDIO CLAUDIANI; 40,000 mems.

Federazione Nazionale Comunicazioni (UGL-Comunicazioni) (Communications): Via Volturno 40, Roma; tel. (06) 4464649; fax (06) 49384693; e-mail comunicazione@ugl.it; internet www.ugl.it/confederazione/fedcomun/nuovahome.htm; f. 1997; affiliated to the UGL; Sec. SERAFINO CABRAS.

Federazione Nazionale Trasporti (Transport): Via Margutta 19, Roma; tel. (06) 324821; fax (06) 3232420; affiliated to the UGL; Sec. PAOLO SEGARELLI.

Sindacato Lavoratori Communicazione (SLC) (Communications Workers): Piazza Sallustio 24, 00187 Roma; tel. (06) 42048201; fax (06) 4824325; e-mail segreteria.nazionale@slc.cgil.it; internet www.cgil.it/slc; affiliated to the CGIL; Gen. Sec. EMILIO MICELI.

SLP—Federazione Lavoratori Poste e Appalti (Postal Workers): Via dell'Esquilino 38, 00185 Roma; internet www.slp-cisl.it; affiliated to the CISL; Sec.-Gen. ANTONINO SORGI.

Unione Italiana Lavoratori della Comunicazione (UILCOM) (Media and Telecommunications): Via Belisario 7, 00187 Roma; tel. (06) 4204021; fax (06) 42744897; e-mail uilcom@uilcom.it; internet www.uilcom.it; affiliated to the UIL; Sec.-Gen. BRUNO DI COLA.

Unione Italiana Lavoratori Postelegrafonici (UIL Post) (Post, Telegraph and Telephone Workers): Via Eroi di Cefalonia 135, 00128 Roma; tel. (06) 64531601; fax (06) 64530400; e-mail info@uilpost.net; internet www.uilpost.net; f. 1950; affiliated to the UIL; Sec.-Gen. CIRO AMICONE; 30,853 mems.

Unione Italiana Lavoratori Trasporti (UILTRASPORTI) (Transport Workers): Via di Priscilla 101, 00199 Roma; tel. (06) 862671; fax (06) 86208396; e-mail segreteriagenerale@uiltrasporti.it; internet www.uiltrasporti.it; affiliated to the UIL; Sec.-Gen GIUSEPPE CARONIA; 103,687 mems.

Miscellaneous

Federazione Nazionale Pensionati (FNP) (Pensioners): Via Castelfidardo 47, 00185 Roma; tel. (06) 448811; fax (06) 4452608; e-mail andrea.pellicari@fnp.cisl.it; internet fnp.cisl.it; f. 1952; affiliated to the CISL; Sec. CARMELO MUSCOLIMO; 1,180,000 mems.

Federazione Nazionale Pensionati dell'Unione Generale del Lavoro (Pensioners): Via Principe Amadeo 23, 00185 Roma; tel. (06) 48904445; fax (06) 48930972; e-mail pensionati@ugl.it; internet www.pensionatiugl.it; affiliated to the UGL; Sec. CORRADO MANNUCCI.

Federazione Nazionale Terziario (Service Sector Workers): Via Farini 62, 00185 Roma; tel. (06) 4820754; fax (06) 4820702; affiliated to the UGL; Sec. MARIO GAETANI.

Sindacato Pensionati Italiani SPI-Cgil (Pensioners): Via Frentani 4A, 00185 Roma; tel. (06) 444811; fax (06) 4440941; e-mail spi@mail.cgil.it; f. 1948; affiliated to the CGIL; Sec.-Gen. ELISABETTA LEONE; 2,757,010 mems.

Unione Italiana Lavoratori Pensionati (UILP) (Pensioners): Via Po 162, 00198 Roma; tel. (06) 852591; fax (06) 8548632; e-mail segreteria@uilpensionati.it; internet www.uilpensionati.it; affiliated to the UIL; Sec.-Gen. SILVANO MINIATI; 682,000 mems.

Co-operative Unions

Associazione Generale delle Cooperative Italiane (AGCI): Via A. Bargoni, 00153 Roma; tel. (06) 583271; fax (06) 58327210; e-mail info@agci.it; internet www.agci.it; f. 1952; Pres. MAURIZIO ZAFFI.

Confederazione Cooperative Italiane (CONFCOOPERATIVE): Borgo S. Spirito 78, 00193 Roma; tel. (06) 680001; fax (06) 68134236; e-mail confcooperative@confcooperative.it; internet www.confcooperative.it; f. 1919; confederation of co-operative unions; Pres. LUIGI MARINO; Dir GUISEPPE MAGGI; Sec.-Gen. VINCENZO MANNINO.

Lega Nazionale delle Cooperative e Mutue (National League of Co-operative and Friendly Societies): Via Guattani 9, 00161 Roma; tel. (06) 84439391; fax (06) 84439370; e-mail presidenza@legacoop.it; internet www.legacoop.it; f. 1886; nine affiliated unions; Pres. IVANO BARBERINI.

Unione Nazionale Cooperative Italiane (UNCI): Via San Sotero 32, 00165 Roma; tel. (06) 39367752; fax (06) 39375080; e-mail info@unci.org; internet www.unci.org; Pres. LUCIANO D'ULIZIA.

Transport

RAILWAYS

The majority of Italian lines are controlled by an independent state-owned corporation. In 2004 the total length of the network was 16,200 km, of which two-thirds were electrified. Apart from the state railway system there are 24 local and municipal railway companies, many of whose lines are narrow gauge. There are metro systems in Rome, Milan, Naples and Turin.

Ferrovie dello Stato, SpA (FS): Piazza della Croce Rossa 1, 00161 Roma; tel. (06) 44101; e-mail redazioneweb@ferroviedellostato.it; internet www.ferroviedellostato.it; controls nine subsidiaries; Pres. INNOCENZO CIPOLLETTA; CEO Ing. MAURO MORETTI.

ROADS

In 2003 there were an estimated 484,668 km of roads in Italy, including 6,621 km of motorway, 46,009 km of major roads and 119,909 km of secondary roads. All the *autostrade* (motorways) are toll roads except for that between Salerno and Reggio Calabria and those in Sicily.

ANAS, SpA: Via Monzambano 10, 00185 Roma; tel. (06) 44462223; fax (06) 44464442; e-mail uff.stampa@stradeanas.it; internet www.stradeanas.it; f. 1928 as Azienda Autonoma Statale della Strada (AASS); responsible for the administration of state roads and their improvement and extension; Pres. Dott. PIETRO CIUCCI.

Autostrade, SpA: Via Alberto Berganini 50, 00159 Roma; tel. (06) 43631; fax (06) 43634090; e-mail info@autostrade.it; internet www.autostrade.it; maintenance and management of motorway network; Pres. Prof. GIAN MARIA GROS-PIETRO; CEO Ing. GIOVANNI CASTELLUCCI.

SHIPPING

In 2006 the Italian merchant fleet (1,566 vessels) had a combined aggregate displacement of 12.6m. grt. In 2006 there were 66 ports in Italy.

Genoa

Costa Crociere, SpA: Via XII Ottobre 2, 16121 Genova; tel. (010) 54831; fax (010) 5483290; e-mail info@costa.it; internet www.costa.it; passenger and cargo service; Mediterranean, Northern Europe, Central and South America; Caribbean cruises; Chair. NICOLA COSTA.

'Garibaldi' Società Cooperativa di Navigazione Srl: Piazza Dante 8, 16121 Genova; tel. (010) 581635; fax (010) 5702386; f. 1918; tanker and cargo services; Pres. GIAN FRANCO VIALE.

Grandi Navi Veloci SpA: Via Fieschi 17/17A, 16121 Genova; tel. (010) 55091; fax (010) 5509333; internet www1.gnv.it; f. 1947; passenger, cargo, containers and tramp to Europe; Dirs M. GRIMALDI, A. GRIMALDI.

Messina, Ignazio and C., SpA: Via G. d'Annunzio 91, 16121 Genova; tel. (010) 53961; fax (010) 5396264; e-mail info@messinaline.it; internet www.messinaline.it; services to Arabian Gulf, India, Pakistan, Nigeria, North, East, South and West Africa, Libya and Near East, Red Sea, Malta, Europe; Chair. GIANFRANCO MESSINA.

Naples

Tirrenia di Navigazione, SpA: Head Office: Palazzo Sirignano, Rione Sirignano 2, 80121 Napoli; tel. (081) 7201111; fax (081) 7201441; internet www.tirrenia.it; ferry services to Sardinia, Sicily, North Africa; part of Gruppo Tirrenia di Navigazione; Man. Dir and Dir-Gen. FRANCO PECORINI.

Palermo

Sicilia Regionale Marittima, SpA (SIREMAR): Calata Marinai d'Italia, Porto di Palermo, 90139 Palermo; tel. (091) 7493111; fax (091) 582267; internet www.siremar.it; owned by Gruppo Tirrenia di Navigazione; ferry services; Pres. Dott. GIUSEPPE RAVERA; Man. Dir PIERO GIGLIO.

ITALY *Directory*

Sicula Oceanicas SA (SIOSA): Via dei Cartari 18, 90139 Palermo; tel. (091) 217939; f. 1941; cruises, passenger and cargo; Italy to North Europe, South, Central, North America; Dir G. GRIMALDI.

Rome

D'Amico Fratelli, SpA: Via Liguria 36, 00187 Roma; tel. (06) 4671; fax (06) 4871914; e-mail damiship@damicofratelli.it; internet www.damicofratelli.it; dry cargo and tankers; Pres. GIUSEPPE D'AMICO; Gen. Man. CARLO CAMELI.

Trieste

Fratelli Cosulich, SpA: Piazza S. Antonio 4, 34122 Trieste; tel. (040) 6797111; fax (040) 6797777; internet www.cosulich.it; f. 1854; shipowners and shipping agents; domestic network and cargo to Near East, Red Sea, Hong Kong, Singapore, New York and Zürich; Chair. and Man. Dir GEROLIMICH COSULICH.

Lloyd Triestino di Navigazione, SpA: Palazzo della Marineria, Passeggio S. Andrea 4, 34123 Trieste; tel. (040) 3180388; fax (040) 3180296; e-mail headoffice@ts.lloydtriestino.it; internet www.lloydtriestino.it; f. 1836; cargo services by container to South Africa, Australasia and Far East, plus trans-Pacific and -Atlantic services; privatized 1998; Pres. PIER LUIGI MANESCHI; Vice-Pres. and Man. Dir REN-GUNG SHYU; Dir-Gen. MAURIZIO SALCE.

Navigazione Montanari, SpA: Corso Italia 31, 34122 Trieste; fax (0721) 830430; e-mail giovannip@navmont.com; internet www.navmont.com; f. 1889; cargo services to Mediterranean, Northern Europe, USA and Far East.

Venice

Adriatica di Navigazione, SpA: Zattere 1411, CP 705, 30123 Venezia; tel. (041) 781861; fax (041) 781818; e-mail adrnav@interbusiness.it; internet www.adriatica.it; f. 1937; owned by Gruppo Tirrenia di Navigazione; passenger services from Italy, Albania, Croatia and Montenegro; Pres. GIORGIO GROSSO; Man. Dir ANTONIO CACUCCI.

Shipping Association

Confederazione Italiana Armatori (CONFITARMA): Piazza SS. Apostoli 66, 00187 Roma; tel. (06) 674811; fax (06) 69783730; e-mail confitarma@confitarma.it; internet www.confitarma.it; f. 1901; shipowners' asscn; Pres. NICOLA COCCIA; Dir-Gen. GENNARO FIORE; 230 mems.

CIVIL AVIATION

In 2005 there were 50 commercial airports in Italy.

Civil Aviation Authority

Ente Nazionale per l'Aviazione Civile (ENAC) (Italian Civil Aviation Authority): Viale del Castro Pretorio 118, 00185 Roma; tel. (06) 445961; internet www.enac-italia.it; Pres. VITO RIGGIO; Dir-Gen. SILVANO MANERA.

National Airline

Alitalia (Linee Aeree Italiane): Viale Alessandro Marchetti 111, 00148 Roma; tel. (06) 2222; fax (06) 7093065; internet www.alitalia.com; f. 1946; state-owned; domestic and international services throughout Europe and to Africa, North and South America, the Middle East, the Far East and Australia; Chair. Prof. ARISTIDE POLICE.

Other Airlines

Air Dolomiti: Via Paolo Bembo 70, 37062 Dossobuono VR; tel. (045) 8605211; fax (045) 8605229; internet www.airdolomiti.it; f. 1989; operates domestic flights and services between Italy and Austria, France and Germany; Pres. and CEO MICHAEL KRAUS.

Air Europe: Via Carlo Noè 3, 21013 Gallarate, Varese; tel. (0331) 713111; fax (0331) 713850; e-mail marketing@aireurope.it; internet www.aireurope.it; f. 1988; international charter flights from Rome (Fiumicino) and Milan (Malpensa) to Cuba, Jamaica, Maldives, Mauritius, Mexico and Sri Lanka; Chair. LUPO RATTAZZI; Man. Dir ISABELLA ANTONELLO.

Air One: Via Sardegna 14, 00187 Roma; tel. (06) 478761; fax (06) 4820399; internet www.flyairone.it; f. 1983 as Aliadriatica; adopted current name in 1995; private co; domestic flights; Chair. GIOVANNI SEBASTIANI; Pres. CARLO TOTO.

Meridiana, SpA: Aeroporto Costa Smeralda, Olbia, 07026 Sardinia; tel. (0789) 52821; fax (0789) 52972; internet www.meridiana.it; f. 1963 as Alisarda, renamed 1991; scheduled and charter services throughout Italy and Europe, and on a limited number of intercontinental services; Chair. FRANCO TRIVI; CEO GIOVANNI SEBASTIANI.

Myair.com: Via Brescia 31, CP 122, 36040 Torri di Quartesolo; e-mail info@myair.com; internet www.myair.com; owned by My Way Airlines; low cost airline; domestic and international flights; Pres. CARLO BERNINI.

Volare, SpA: Milano; e-mail info@volareweb.com; internet www.volareweb.com; low-cost airline operating flights within Italy and to other European destinations.

Tourism

A great number of tourists are attracted to Italy by its Alpine and Mediterranean scenery, sunny climate, Roman archaeological remains, medieval and Baroque churches, Renaissance towns and palaces, paintings and sculpture and famous opera houses. Each of the 95 provinces has a Board of Tourism; there are also about 300 Aziende Autonome di Cura, Soggiorno e Turismo, with information about tourist accommodation and health treatment, and about 2,000 Pro Loco Associations concerned with local amenities. In 2008 there were 41 UNESCO World Heritage Sites in Italy. In 2005 an estimated 38.1m. foreign visitors (including excursionists) arrived in Italy; tourism receipts totalled an estimated €38,264m. in that year.

Dipartimento per lo Sviluppo e la Competitività del Turismo: Via della Ferratella in Laterano 51, 00184 Roma; tel. (06) 7732432; fax (06) 77209808; e-mail a.balducci@governo.it; part of the Presidency of the Council of Ministers; Head of Dept ANGELO BALDUCCI.

Ente Nazionale Italiano per il Turismo (ENIT) (Italian State Tourist Board): Via Marghera 2, 00185 Roma; tel. (06) 49711; fax (06) 4463379; e-mail sedecentrale@cert.enit.it; internet www.enit.it; f. 1919; Chair. AMEDEO OTTAVIANI; Dir-Gen. EUGENIO MAGNANI.

JAMAICA

Introductory Survey

Location, Climate, Language, Religion, Flag, Capital

Jamaica is the third largest island in the Caribbean Sea, lying 145 km (90 miles) to the south of Cuba and 160 km (100 miles) to the south-west of Haiti. The climate varies with altitude, being tropical at sea-level and temperate in the mountain areas. The average annual temperature is 27°C (80°F) and mean annual rainfall is 198 cm (78 ins). The official language is English, although a local patois is widely spoken. The majority of the population belong to Christian denominations, the Church of God being the most numerous. The national flag (proportions 1 by 2) consists of a diagonal yellow cross on a background of black (hoist and fly) and green (above and below). The capital is Kingston.

Recent History

Jamaica, a British colony from 1655, was granted internal self-government in 1959, and full independence, within the Commonwealth, was achieved on 6 August 1962. Jamaica formed part of the West Indies Federation between 1958 and 1961, when it seceded, following a referendum. The Federation was dissolved in May 1962. The two dominant political figures after the Second World War were the late Sir Alexander Bustamante, leader of the Jamaica Labour Party (JLP), who retired as Prime Minister in 1967, and Norman Manley, a former Premier and leader of the People's National Party (PNP), who died in 1969. The JLP won the elections of 1962 and 1967 but, under the premiership of Hugh Shearer, it lost the elections of February 1972 to the PNP, led by Michael Manley, the son of Norman Manley. Michael Manley advocated democratic socialism and his Government put great emphasis on social reform and economic independence.

The early 1970s were marked by escalating street violence and crime, with gang warfare rife in the deprived areas of Kingston. More than 160 people were killed in the first half of 1976, and in June the Government declared a state of emergency (which remained in force until June 1977). Despite the unrest, high unemployment and severe economic stagnation, the PNP was returned to power in December 1976 with an increased majority. By January 1979, however, there was widespread political unrest, and violent demonstrations signalled growing discontent with the Manley administration. In February 1980, in the context of a worsening economic crisis, Manley rejected the stipulation of the IMF, as a condition of its making further loans to Jamaica, that economic austerity measures be undertaken. He called a general election to seek support for his economic policies and his decision to end dependence on the IMF. The electoral campaign was one of the most violent in Jamaica's history. In the October election the JLP received about 57% of the total votes and won 51 of the 60 seats in the House of Representatives. Edward Seaga, the leader of the JLP, became Prime Minister; he supported closer political and economic links with the USA and the promotion of free enterprise. Seaga severed diplomatic relations with Cuba in October 1981, and secured valuable US financial support for the economy. Negotiations on IMF assistance were resumed.

In November 1983, before the completion of a new electoral roll, Seaga announced that an election would take place in mid-December. Only four days were allowed for the nomination of candidates, and the PNP, unable to present candidates at such short notice, refused to participate and declared the elections void. The JLP, opposed in only six constituencies (by independent candidates), won all 60 seats in the House of Representatives and formed a one-party legislature.

Devaluations of the Jamaican dollar and the withdrawal of food subsidies provoked demonstrations and sporadic violence in 1984, as the prices of foodstuffs and energy increased by between 50% and 100%. Despite government attempts to offset the effects of these economic austerity measures, imposed at the instigation of the IMF, unemployment, together with the consequences of illicit trading in drugs, contributed to a rise in the incidence of crime and violence, especially in Kingston. In 1985 another increase in fuel prices precipitated further violent demonstrations in the capital and industrial unrest in the public sector.

After a brief, and relatively peaceful, campaign, a general election took place in February 1989, in which the PNP secured an absolute majority of seats in the House of Representatives. Manley, who had developed a more moderate image during his years in opposition, again became Prime Minister. The Government conceded the necessity for a devaluation of the Jamaican dollar, which was announced in October. Unusually for Jamaican politics, the two main parties achieved a limited consensus on the pursuit of an economic policy of austerity, despite its unpopularity. There was also agreement that further action should be taken against the drugs trade. The Government was particularly anxious to prevent the use of Jamaican shipping and aviation for the smuggling of illegal drugs, and demanded increased security measures, despite the consequent impediment to normal trade movements.

In December 1991 controversy surrounding the waiving of taxes worth some US $30m. that were owed to Jamaica by an international company, Shell, resulted in the resignation of Horace Clarke, the Minister of Mining and Energy, and Percival Patterson, the Deputy Prime Minister, amid opposition allegations of corruption and misconduct. In March 1992 Manley announced his resignation, owing to ill health, from the premiership and from the presidency of the PNP. Patterson was elected as Manley's successor by members of the PNP, and was appointed Prime Minister at the end of the month.

At a general election in March 1993 Patterson's PNP secured 52 of the 60 seats in the House of Representatives, while the JLP won the remaining eight seats. The scale of the PNP victory was widely attributed to the success of Patterson's populist overtures to the island's majority population of African origin, and a perceived shift in political influence away from the capital, traditionally a power base of the JLP (which won the remaining eight seats). In April Patterson announced plans to reform and modernize the electoral system. However, allegations of electoral malpractice and demands by the JLP for an official inquiry into suspected procedural abuses were rejected by the PNP, prompting the JLP to boycott the official opening of Parliament later in the month. By February 1994 attempts at electoral reform had been undermined by the resignation of the Chairman of the Electoral Advisory Committee (EAC), and by the failure of the EAC to appoint a new Director of Elections. Demands for constitutional and electoral reform continued, and the JLP repeatedly accused the Government of seeking to delay progress towards any such reforms. Proposals drafted in late 1994 recommended the establishment of a permanent electoral commission to supervise elections, the publication of a revised register of voters every six months, and rules governing political campaigning and the nomination of candidates. An electronic voter registration system was installed in 1996 and new electoral rolls were completed in late 1997. (Local elections, which had been repeatedly postponed since 1993, finally took place in September 1998.)

Industrial relations deteriorated in 1994, and there was further industrial unrest in 1995, as workers in both the public and private sectors argued for large pay increases to compensate for high rates of inflation. Meanwhile, the country's poor economic performance (particularly its high inflation rate and increasing trade deficit) and an increase in violent crime in Kingston compounded widespread dissatisfaction with the Government.

In an effort to stabilize the economy, and, in particular, to address the problem of continuing industrial unrest, in 1996 the Government sought the agreement of a 'social contract' with trade unions and the private sector. In return for a commitment to increase its efforts to reduce inflation, the Government hoped to secure an undertaking from the labour organizations to moderate their wage demands. In July the Government implemented a 60% increase in the minimum wage. However, efforts to establish a 'social contract' were frustrated during 1997 owing to trade union intransigence concerning demands for salary increases.

A general election was held in December 1997, at which the PNP won 50 of the 60 seats in the House of Representatives. The

JLP obtained 10 seats, but the National Democratic Movement (NDM, formed in 1995 by Bruce Golding), failed to gain parliamentary representation. Patterson, who was subsequently sworn in as Prime Minister for a third consecutive term, appointed a new Cabinet in January 1998 and announced plans for Jamaica to become a republic within five years.

In 1998 and 1999 there were many public protests against police actions and the deepening economic crisis, several of which resulted in riots. There was further unrest in April 1999 following the announcement made in the 1999/2000 budget proposals of a significant increase in the price of diesel. The JLP and NDM, while initially helping to organize the protests, dissociated themselves from the subsequent violence, in which eight people were killed and many businesses were set alight or looted. The Government later agreed to reduce the proposed increase. In July the authorities announced that army personnel were to be deployed on patrols in greater Kingston in an attempt to combat the high incidence of criminal activity, the majority of which was reportedly related to drugs-trafficking. In October the British Government announced that it would grant £2.9m. in assistance towards the reform and modernization of the Jamaican police force. In the same month an investigation was initiated in response to widespread allegations of corruption in the police force.

Despite the measures implemented by the Government in the previous year, confrontations between the police and various sectors of the community continued in 2001. In March the killing of seven young men in the Kingston suburb of Braeton during a police raid provoked accusations of excessive brutality by the police force. The human rights organization Amnesty International claimed that the Jamaican police force had the one of the highest records for the execution of its own citizens in the world. In 2000 the police had shot dead 140 suspected criminals. Furthermore, in July conflict broke out between police and rival PNP and JLP factions in Kingston, reportedly caused by an exchange of gunfire between police and a group of civilians during a weapons patrol. Following three days of fighting, in which 25 people were reported to have been killed, units of the Jamaica Defence Force were deployed to restore order.

A Commission of Inquiry into the July disturbances opened in September 2001, chaired by a Canadian former chief justice, Julius Alexander Isaac. Seaga and the JLP's team of lawyers refused to co-operate with the investigation on several occasions. Meanwhile, sporadic outbreaks of violence in the Kingston suburbs continued: in October 2001 the Government was forced to deploy army, air and coastguard units to suppress unrest. In January 2002 seven people were shot dead by as many as 30 gunmen in a suburb known to be a traditional stronghold of the PNP, leading to accusations that the killings were politically motivated. In July the Commission of Inquiry cleared the security forces of the use of excessive brutality.

The social unrest and the perceived decline in popularity of the PNP prompted the Prime Minister to reorganize the Government in October 2001. K. D. Knight, Minister of National Security and Justice for the previous 13 years, was appointed Minister of Foreign Affairs and Foreign Trade, while Dr Peter Phillips, hitherto Minister of Transportation and Works, was appointed Minister of National Security. Phillips introduced legislation that gave the police the power to intercept the telephone calls of individuals thought to be involved in the illegal trafficking of drugs and weapons and extended the death penalty to crimes that involved drugs-trafficking.

In February 2002, in an attempt to improve the transparency of the financial sector, the Government amended the 1964 Money Laundering Act to include money transfer and remittance companies in the clause relating to financial institutions. Henceforth, financial institutions would be required to report all suspicious transactions exceeding US $50,000.

Parliament was dissolved in September 2002, in advance of legislative elections scheduled for 16 October. Although the two main parties vowed to work together to halt the rise in violence, some 11 murders were committed during the months preceding the ballot. The PNP was re-elected for a fourth consecutive term but its majority in the House of Representatives was reduced, by 14 seats, to 34. The JLP won the remaining 26 seats

At his inauguration, on 23 October 2002, Patterson became the first Jamaican Prime Minister to swear allegiance to the people and Constitution of Jamaica, rather than to the British monarch, in accordance with new legislation introduced in August. He subsequently formed a new Cabinet, retaining most of the members of the previous administration. At a subsequent meeting with Patterson, Seaga outlined a number of proposals for reform, including the appointment of an independent Governor-General for Jamaica and a restructuring of the police force.

In December 2002 the armed forces and police began a joint offensive on crime. The Government also revived a previously debated proposal to extend capital punishment to drugs-related crimes and to replace the Privy Council in London with a Caribbean Court of Justice (CCJ, see below) as the final court of appeal, thereby removing the Privy Council's ability to commute death sentences to life imprisonment. More than 1,000 murders were reported in 2002 and extended use of capital punishment gained increasing popular support. However, the Crime Management Unit (CMU), established in 2000 in response to the rising rate of violent crime, had been repeatedly criticized for its excessive use of force. In June 2003, following the shooting of four people during a police raid, the CMU was disbanded and replaced by an Organised Crime Investigation Division. Nevertheless, the crime rate continued to increase. In 2003 the number of murders totalled 975, and in 2004 the rate reached a record 1,445 homicides; this rise was largely attributed to gang-related conflicts.

In October 2003 the police force was further criticized after two elderly men were accidentally shot during a confrontation between police and an armed gang. The killings prompted a protest, involving some 2,000 people, against alleged police and army tactics. In the same month a report on purported extra-judicial executions by the Jamaican police force was published by the UN Special Rapporteur. The report condemned the Government and state security forces for the misuse of force and for failing properly to investigate those accused of extra-judicial executions. In its 2004 annual report, Amnesty International asserted that at least 114 people had been killed by police in Jamaica in 2003, many in circumstances suggesting extra-judicial executions. The degree of impunity enjoyed by the police was highlighted by the dismissal of a case in early 2004 against an officer charged with killing a 13-year-old girl in April 2000, after evidence for the prosecution went missing. In mid-2004 the Prime Minister announced the launch of a National Investigative Authority to pursue allegations against the police. In April of that year the former head of the CMU, Renato Adams, and five former colleagues were charged with murder in connection with the deaths of the four people during the 2003 raid; in December 2005 all six were acquitted of murder.

In July 2004 the Privy Council abolished Jamaica's mandatory death sentence for convicted murderers. Legislative amendments to this effect were approved by the Senate in November. However, at the same time, amendments were also passed increasing the minimum period a convicted murderer must serve before being granted parole from seven to 20 years. In October the armed forces and the police launched 'Operation Kingfish', an intelligence-based task force intended to reduce the ever-rising crime rate. The initiative was particularly targeted at dismantling the estimated 13 major criminal networks on the island, which were thought to be responsible for much of the crime. By October 2007 more than 2,000 operations had been mounted, leading to 567 arrests and the recovery of nearly 300 firearms.

In January 2005, after more than 30 years in the post, Seaga retired as leader of the JLP and as a member of Parliament. He was succeeded as party leader in the following month by Bruce Golding, following a bitterly fought leadership contest with Pearnel Charles. In February 2006 Patterson was succeeded as leader of the PNP by Portia Simpson-Miller, Minister of Local Development, Community Development and Sport. Upon assuming office at the end of March, Simpson-Miller, Jamaica's first female Prime Minister, pledged to eradicate violent crime, protect human rights and create employment.

Addressing violent and drugs-related crime became an increasingly urgent concern of the Government in 2007 following reports that the murder rate had not declined appreciably in 2006 (when 1,340 murders were recorded, including that of former Ambassador for Trade, Peter King, from a total of 1,674 in 2005). More than 128 murders were reported in January 2007 alone, with St James being identified as a particularly vulnerable parish; the rising incidence of violent crime in Montego Bay, largely perpetrated by organized criminal gangs, provoked the Government to pledge further resources to developing corrective strategies. The police force did meet with some successes, none the less; in January a substantial seizure of marijuana products was made in Kingston and Clarendon. (Drugs with an estimated street value exceeding J $2,000m. were discovered in a residential district of Kingston in the same month.) In February the Senate commenced discussions on the proposed Proceeds of Crime Act, passed by the House of Representatives in the previous month. The opposition had expressed concerns that provisions contained within the new Act—awarding courts greater power to order the surrender of assets and property in the absence of a criminal conviction—might impinge upon citizens' fundamental rights. A Trafficking in Persons Act was also ratified and became effective from 1 March, providing a legal framework to combat human-trafficking, for which no legislation had previously existed. These developments were regarded as fundamental to the country's anti-crime preparations ahead of the Cricket World Cup in March–April when international scrutiny of Jamaica, one of the host countries, would intensify. However, the country attracted negative publicity during that tournament after the coach of the Pakistani team, Bob Woolmer, was found dead in suspicious circumstances in his hotel room in Kingston in mid-March. Detectives from the United Kingdom and a forensics expert from the International Criminal Police Organization (INTERPOL) were seconded to the island to assist in what was the Jamaican police force's most high-profile murder inquiry. However, three independent pathologists from Britain, South Africa and Canada concluded that Woolmer had died of natural causes, leading the Jamaican police to revoke their initial conclusion. An inquest was opened in October to determine the cause of death; it returned an open verdict the following month, and the Jamaican police subsequently closed their investigation.

Prime Minister Simpson-Miller's administration suffered its first significant challenge in early October 2006 when it emerged that the PNP had accepted some US $31m. from the Dutch trading company Trafigura Beheer BV. Allegations levelled by the opposition leader, Bruce Golding, that the money was being used to finance the PNP's political campaign ahead of the general election—constitutionally due by October 2007—provoked the resignation of Colin Campbell, Minister of Information and Development, who conceded that he had approached the company in August requesting a contribution to the governing party's election campaign. The Prime Minister refuted the accusations of corruption but ordered that the monies be returned to Trafigura. The Dutch company initially asserted that such a donation was not prohibited under Jamaican law, but prompted further controversy when it issued a subsequent claim that the transaction was part of a commercial agreement with CCOC Associates for the development of its business interests in Jamaica: it later transpired that CCOC Associates was a government fund-raising account, prompting the JLP's General Secretary, Karl Samuda, to demand the Government's resignation. An opposition motion of no confidence was defeated in mid-October, but the Government's credibility was severely compromised. The scandal's repercussions continued into 2007, with the JLP in March demanding full disclosure of the process by which the funds were returned to Trafigura and continuing to insist that the Government had behaved unethically. The office of the Dutch Public Prosecutor launched an investigation into the allegations in the same year, and in November the Jamaican Parliament adopted a resolution to allow the investigators to conduct enquiries on the island. The process was ongoing in early 2008, when it was expected that a number of members of the PNP would be questioned.

In January 2007 the Attorney-General, Arnold J. Nicholson, marked the bicentenary of the abolition of the trans-Atlantic slave trade by proposing several constitutional reforms that would effectively eliminate the remaining vestiges of the country's former colonial status. The proposals included the amalgamation of a series of reports and recommendations, discussed by successive constitutional reform committees since 1992, to culminate in the consideration of Jamaica's transformation to a republic. An indigenous President would replace the British monarch as head of state. This post would not be vested with legislative or executive powers, but would be designated an independent arbiter of selected state appointments. Furthermore, a new Charter of Rights, the subject of extensive deliberations, was to be instituted and all constitutional amendments would be ratified through an act of the Jamaican legislature, subject to approval in a plebiscite. It was also proposed that subscription to the CCJ's appellate jurisdiction, denied on several occasions by the Privy Council (see below), again be sought. Approval for the substitution of the CCJ as Jamaica's highest appellate body could only be elicited from the Privy Council if representatives of the opposition endorsed the reform; the JLP had previously indicated that its support was contingent upon the entrenchment of the Court within Jamaica's Constitution and the assurance that a national referendum be held on the issue.

Meanwhile, in November 2006 the Government commissioned a Jamaican Justice System Reform Task Force to conduct a comprehensive review of the country's judicial system, with the assistance of representatives from the Canadian Bar Association. The Government announced, in an expansion of its initial budgetary estimates for 2006/07, that the Ministry of Justice would receive an increased allocation of J $552.7m., to reflect the extensive developments to be effected. The final report was presented to the Minister of Justice in May 2007. The main problems identified were delays in the justice system, poor infrastructure, underfunding, and a lack of consistency in the enforcement of laws.

The general election of 2007, originally scheduled for 27 August, was postponed until 3 September due to the widespread disruption caused by 'Hurricane Dean', in which three people were killed and much of the country's infrastructure damaged, leading Simpson-Miller to impose a state of emergency. The Prime Minister was criticized for her slow response to the situation, which was believed to have had a negative effect on her ratings ahead of the election. The JLP won a narrow victory, securing 50.1% of the votes cast and 32 of the legislative seats, while the PNP won 49.8% of the votes and the remaining 28 seats. Some 60.5% of the registered electorate participated in the ballot. According to reports, at least 17 people were killed in political violence during the election campaign, in which the JLP focused on the high levels of crime in the country and the large fiscal deficit. Bruce Golding was sworn in as Prime Minister on 11 September, and announced his Cabinet the following day. Notable appointments included Audley Shaw as the new Minister of Finance and the Public Service, and Dorothy Lightbourne, who became the country's first female Attorney-General as well as Minister of Justice. Golding assumed the portfolios for planning and development, and defence. The JLP's position was strengthened in local elections held on 5 December, in which it won nine of the 13 contested parishes.

In his inaugural speech Golding stated that anti-corruption measures and justice system reform would be priorities of the new Government. In November 2007 the Cabinet approved the drafting of legislation to create an Office of the Special Prosecutor, which would investigate high-level acts of corruption in the public and private sectors, and an independent commission to examine allegations of excessive use of force and of abuse by members of the security forces. Lightbourne announced in February 2008 that the recommendations of the Jamaican Justice Reform Task Force would be incorporated into a national development plan, Vision 2030, which would include the building of new courthouses and the creation of a court agency service, in which the Chief Justice would be responsible for the administration of the courts. Golding had declared his commitment to a referendum on the issue of the CCJ in September 2007 but had not announced a date for the ballot by early 2008.

The high level of violent crime continued to be a significant matter of concern for the Government in 2008. In total, 1,574 murders were committed the previous year, an increase of 16% from 2006. In November 2007 the Cabinet approved the use of J $280m. to increase the capability of the police service by repairing police stations damaged by recent hurricanes, purchasing motor vehicles, and acquiring protective equipment. The Minister of National Security, Derrick Smith, also declared the Government's intention to resume the hanging of convicted murderers, a practice that had not been employed in Jamaica since 1988. Further measures to reduce the crime level included a compulsory national identification system, which Golding announced would be introduced in the 2008/09 fiscal year.

In January 1998 Jamaica withdrew from a UN treaty that had hitherto allowed prisoners sentenced to death to appeal for a review by the UN Commission on Human Rights; later that year it also withdrew from the Inter-American Court of Human Rights (see p. 361) of the Organization of American States. In February 2001, following legislative approval in November 2000, Patterson and 10 other Caribbean leaders signed an agreement to establish a CCJ, to be based in Trinidad and Tobago. The Court was to replace the Privy Council in the United Kingdom as the final court of appeal for the Jamaican legal system, and would allow for the executions of convicted criminals. (The Privy Council generally commuted death sentences to life imprisonment on appeal.) The JLP opposed the move, and demanded that a referendum be held on the issue. Despite opposition from the

JAMAICA

JLP and from the Jamaica Bar Association, in late July 2004 Parliament approved legislation replacing the Privy Council with the CCJ as Jamaica's final court of appeal. The Jamaican Bar Association and opposition groupings appealed to the Privy Council itself that the legislation should be annulled because it had been passed without the approval of the electorate in a referendum. In February 2005 the Privy Council upheld the appeal. In total, the Privy Council annulled three such bills to confer trading and appellate jurisdiction on to the CCJ. Nevertheless, on 15 April the House of Representatives ratified membership of the CCJ, but only as a court of original jurisdiction on trade matters. The CCJ was inaugurated the following day in Port of Spain, Trinidad and Tobago.

Relations between Jamaica and the USA have been hampered by persistent demands by the USA for the eradication of Jamaica's marijuana crop. In May 1997, after months of negotiation, the two countries concluded a counter-narcotics agreement, permitting officials of the US Drug Enforcement Agency to pursue suspected drugs-traffickers in Jamaican airspace and territorial waters. In August 1999 a Jamaican delegation visited the USA to discuss the prospect of increasing US assistance in measures aimed at combating crime.

Government

The Head of State is the British monarch, who is represented locally by the Governor-General, appointed on the recommendation of the Prime Minister in consultation with the Leader of the Opposition. The Governor-General acts, in almost all matters, on the advice of the Cabinet.

Legislative power is vested in the bicameral Parliament: the Senate, with 21 appointed members, and the House of Representatives, with 60 elected members. Thirteen members of the Senate are appointed by the Governor-General on the advice of the Prime Minister and eight on the advice of the Leader of the Opposition. Members of the House are elected by universal adult suffrage for five years (subject to dissolution). Executive power lies with the Cabinet. The Prime Minister is appointed from the House of Representatives by the Governor-General, and is the leader of the party that holds the majority of seats in the House of Representatives. The Cabinet is responsible to Parliament. Jamaica is divided into 13 parishes.

Defence

As assessed at November 2007, the total strength of the Jamaica Defence Force was 2,830, including an army of 2,500, a coastguard of 190 and an air wing of 140 members on active service. A Jamaica Military Aviation School was opened in December 2006 pursuant to a bilateral agreement between the Canadian and Jamaican Governments. There are reserves of some 953 personnel. The defence budget for 2006 was J $7,500m. (US $105m.).

Economic Affairs

In 2006, according to estimates by the World Bank, Jamaica's gross national income (GNI), measured at average 2004–06 prices, was US $9,260.9m., equivalent to US $3,480 per head (or US $4,030 per head on an international purchasing-power parity basis). During 1996–2006, it was estimated, the population increased at an average rate of 0.6% per year, while gross domestic product (GDP) per head remained constant. Overall GDP increased, in real terms, at an average annual rate of 1.1% in 1996–2006; growth was 2.7% in 2006.

Agriculture (including forestry and fishing) contributed an estimated 5.4% of GDP and engaged an estimated 18.3% of the economically active population in 2006. The principal cash crops are sugar cane (sugar accounted for an estimated 5.0% of total export earnings in 2005), bananas, coffee, citrus fruit and cocoa. The cultivation of vegetables, fruit and rice is being encouraged, in an attempt to reduce imports and diversify agricultural exports. The illegal production of hemp (marijuana) is also believed to generate significant export revenue. Agricultural GDP declined at an average annual rate of 3.3% in 1996–2006; the sector decreased by 8.0% in 2006.

Industry (including mining, manufacturing, public utilities and construction) contributed an estimated 30.9% of GDP and engaged an estimated 16.3% of the economically active population in 2006. Industrial GDP increased at an average rate of 1.0% during 1996–2006; the sector grew by 4.0% in 2006.

Mining and quarrying contributed an estimated 3.8% of GDP, but engaged only 0.6% of the active labour force in 2006. Mining is the principal productive sector of the economy, and in 2005 bauxite and its derivative, alumina (aluminium oxide), accounted for an estimated 66.5% of total export earnings.

Introductory Survey

Bauxite, of which Jamaica is one of the world's leading producers, is the major mineral mined, but there are also reserves of marble, gypsum, limestone, silica and clay. The mining of gold began in March 2001; however, in December 2003 the depletion of reserves, as well as industrial unrest, resulted in the closure of Jamaica's only gold mine.

Manufacturing contributed an estimated 12.8% of GDP and engaged some 6.0% of the active labour force in 2006. Much of the activity in the sector is dependent upon the processing of sugar and bauxite. Manufacturing GDP decreased at an average annual rate of 0.6% during 1996–2006; the sector decreased by 2.5% in 2006.

Energy is derived almost entirely from imported hydrocarbon fuels. In 2006 imports of mineral fuels and lubricants accounted for 31.1% of the total value of merchandise imports.

The services sector contributed an estimated 63.7% of GDP and engaged some 58.8% of the active labour force in 2006. Tourism is the principal source of foreign exchange earnings. Visitor arrivals (excluding cruise-ship passengers) stood at an estimated 1.7m. in 2007. The largest proportion of tourists is from the USA (71.7% in 2005). Tourism revenue totalled some US $1,783m. in 2005. The GDP of the services sector increased at an average annual rate of 2.9% in 1996–2006; the sector increased by 17.3% in 2006.

In 2006 Jamaica recorded a visible trade deficit of US $2,943.5m., and there was a deficit of US $1,170.3m. on the current account of the balance of payments. In 2006 the principal source of imports (37.3%) was the USA. Other major suppliers were the United Kingdom and members of the Caribbean Community and Common Market (CARICOM, see p. 196). In the same year the USA was also the principal market for exports (27.2%). Canada and the United Kingdom were among other important purchasers. The principal exports in 2006 were bauxite and alumina. Foodstuffs, including sugar and bananas, were also important export commodities. The principal imports in 2006 were mineral fuels and lubricants, and machinery and transport equipment.

In the financial year ending 31 March 2006 Jamaica recorded a budget surplus of J $5,125m. Total external debt in 2005 was US $6,511m., of which US $5,508m. was long-term public debt. In that year the cost of debt-servicing was equivalent to 16.3% of earnings from exports of goods and services. The average annual rate of inflation was 10.1% in 2000–06; consumer prices increased by an annual average of 16.8% in 2007. Some 9.6% of the labour force were unemployed in 2006.

Jamaica is a founding member of the CARICOM and of the Inter-American Development Bank (IDB, see p. 308). Jamaica was also one of the six founder members of CARICOM's Caribbean Single Market and Economy (CSME), which was inaugurated on 1 January 2006. The CSME is intended to facilitate the free movement of goods, services and labour throughout the CARICOM region.

The Jamaican economy has been impeded in recent years by persistent fiscal imbalances and a high rate of inflation. Bauxite and alumina production have increased significantly, although the sector's vulnerability to international market prices has at times meant that improved productivity has not generated increased revenue. The sugar and coffee industries have been affected by aberrant climatic conditions and a lack of investment. Furthermore, measures implemented from mid-2006 by the European Union (see p. 244) to reform its sugar import regime, including the removal of trade preferences, were a cause of considerable concern for the Jamaican sugar sector. The Government subsequently announced plans to restructure the sugar sector to concentrate on the production for the domestic market, as well as production of molasses for distilling rum, and of ethanol as a petroleum substitute. In 2003 a 10-year development plan for the tourism sector was implemented, and from May 2005 Jamaica introduced a US $10 charge on tourists who arrived by air, in an attempt to raise capital for tourism projects. Although the sector was boosted in 2007 by the region's hosting of the Cricket World Cup, a decline in tourist arrivals from the important US market caused concern during that year. The Government aimed to take advantage of the growing market for religious-orientated tourism with a new convention centre anticipated for completion by 2009. Meanwhile, in 2006 the IMF recommended that the national airline, Air Jamaica, following a decade of poor performance, be either privatized again or closed. In the same year the Government failed to sell its 20% stake in The Jamaica Public Service Company. The new Jamaica Labour Party Government, which took office in September 2007, announced its intention to achieve a GDP growth rate of 3%–4% in the 2008/09 fiscal year. The IMF, which estimated growth at 1.3% in 2007, commended the new administration's stated priorities of addressing the problems of low growth and high indebtedness, and considered that its intention to balance the budget over a three-year period would contribute substantially to reducing public debt, which would, in turn, encourage investment and improve growth. In the longer term the Government planned to simplify investment procedures, increase efficiency in the public sector, and reform the tax system.

Education

Primary education is compulsory in certain districts, and free education is ensured. The education system (which begins at six years of age) consists of a primary cycle of six years, followed by two secondary cycles of three and four years, respectively. In 2004/05 enrolment at primary schools included 89.9% of pupils in the relevant age-group, while enrolment at secondary schools included 78.5% of children in the appropriate age-group. Higher education is provided by technical colleges and by the University of the West Indies, which has five faculties situated at its Mona campus in Kingston. In April 2005 the Government announced plans to upgrade 200 schools and to create an additional 2,400 places at high schools. Government expenditure on education during the financial year 2005/06 was estimated to be some J $34,000m., representing 9.8% of total budgetary expenditure.

Public Holidays

2008: 1 January (New Year's Day), 6 February (Ash Wednesday), 21 March (Good Friday), 24 March (Easter Monday), 23 May (Labour Day), 1 August (Emancipation Day), 6 August (Independence Day), 20 October (National Heroes' Day), 25 December (Christmas Day), 26 December (Boxing Day).

2009: 1 January (New Year's Day), 25 February (Ash Wednesday), 10 April (Good Friday), 13 April (Easter Monday), 23 May (Labour Day), 1 August (Emancipation Day), 6 August (Independence Day), 19 October (National Heroes Day), 25 December (Christmas Day), 26 December (Boxing Day).

Weights and Measures

Both the imperial and the metric systems are in use.

Statistical Survey

Sources (unless otherwise stated): Statistical Institute of Jamaica, 7 Cecelio Ave, Kingston 10; tel. 926-5311; fax 926-1138; e-mail info@statinja.com; internet www.statinja.com; Jamaica Information Service, 58A Half Way Tree Rd, POB 2222, Kingston 10; tel. 926-3740; fax 926-6715; e-mail jis@jis.gov.jm; internet www.jis.gov.jm; Bank of Jamaica, Nethersole Pl., POB 621, Kingston; tel. 922-0752; fax 922-0854; e-mail info@boj.org.jm; internet www.boj.org.jm.

Area and Population

AREA, POPULATION AND DENSITY

Area (sq km)	10,991*
Population (census results)	
7 April 1991	2,314,479
10 September 2001	
Males	1,283,547
Females	1,324,085
Total	2,607,632
Population (official estimates at 31 December)	
2004	2,648,200
2005	2,660,600
2006	2,673,800
Density (per sq km) at 31 December 2006	243.3

* 4,243.6 sq miles.

PARISHES

	Area (sq km)	Population (census of 2001)	Capitals (with population*)
Kingston and St Andrew	453†	651,880	Kingston M.A. (587,798)
St Thomas	743	91,604	Morant Bay (9,185)
Portland	814	80,205	Port Antonio (13,246)
St Mary	611	111,466	Port Maria (7,651)
St Ann	1,213	166,762	St Ann's Bay (10,518)
Trelawny	875	73,066	Falmouth (7,245)
St James	595	175,127	Montego Bay (83,446)
Hanover	450	67,037	Lucea (6,002)
Westmoreland	807	138,947	Savanna La Mar (16,553)
St Elizabeth	1,212	146,404	Black River (3,675)
Manchester	830	185,801	Mandeville (39,430)
Clarendon	1,196	237,024	May Pen (46,785)
St Catherine	1,192	482,308	Spanish Town (92,383)
Total	**10,991**	**2,607,632**	—

* Population at 1991 census.
† Kingston 22 sq km, St Andrew 431 sq km.

PRINCIPAL TOWNS
(population at census of 7 April 1991)

Kingston (capital)	587,798	Montego Bay		83,446
Spanish Town	92,383	May Pen		46,785
Portmore	90,138	Mandeville		39,430

Source: Thomas Brinkhoff, *City Population* (internet www.citypopulation.de).

Mid-2007 ('000, incl. suburbs, UN estimate): Kingston 580 (Source: UN, *World Urbanization Prospects: The 2007 Revision*).

BIRTHS, MARRIAGES AND DEATHS*

	Registered live births†		Registered marriages		Registered deaths
	Number	Rate (per 1,000)	Number	Rate (per 1,000)	Number (estimates)
1999	48,987	19.0	29,155	11.3	16,294
2000	48,717	18.8	27,028	10.4	15,248
2001	48,065	18.5	22,308	8.6	14,473
2002	44,331	16.9	23,070	8.8	15,711
2003	43,407	16.5	22,476	8.6	15,581
2004	42,448	16.2	21,670	8.2	15,389
2005	41,836	15.7	n.a.	n.a.	15,523
2006	45,436	17.0	n.a.	n.a.	15,180

* Data are tabulated by year of registration rather than by year of occurrence.
† Including births to non-resident mothers.

Sources: UN, *Demographic Yearbook* and *Population and Vital Statistics Report*.

Expectation of life (years at birth, WHO estimates): 72.4 (males 70.3; females 74.5) in 2005 (Source: WHO, *World Health Statistics*).

JAMAICA

ECONOMICALLY ACTIVE POPULATION
('000 persons aged 14 years and over)

	2004	2005	2006
Agriculture, forestry and fishing	195.6	197.2	206.1
Mining and quarrying	5.3	4.8	6.4
Manufacturing	72.3	73.2	73.6
Electricity, gas and water	6.5	5.4	7.1
Construction	109.2	110.1	113.1
Trade, restaurants and hotels	248.6	260.8	272.4
Transport, storage and communications	77.2	78.4	79.3
Financing, insurance, real estate and business services	58.3	55.7	59.3
Community, social and personal services	285.3	303.4	310.4
Activities not adequately defined	0.4	2.7	1.8
Total employed	1,058.7	1,091.7	1,129.5
Unemployed	136.8	133.3	119.6
Total labour force	1,195.5	1,225.0	1,249.1
Males	667.9	661.1	697.8
Females	527.6	563.9	551.3

Source: ILO.

Health and Welfare

KEY INDICATORS

Total fertility rate (children per woman, 2005)	2.4
Under-5 mortality rate (per 1,000 live births, 2005)	20
HIV/AIDS (% of persons aged 15–49, 2005)	1.5
Physicians (per 1,000 head, 2004)	0.85
Hospital beds (per 1,000 head, 2005)	1.7
Health expenditure (2004): US $ per head (PPP)	223.4
Health expenditure (2004): % of GDP	5.2
Health expenditure (2004): public (% of total)	54.3
Access to water (% of persons, 2004)	93
Access to sanitation (% of persons, 2004)	80
Human Development Index (2005): ranking	101
Human Development Index (2005): value	0.736

For sources and definitions, see explanatory note on p. vi.

Agriculture

PRINCIPAL CROPS
('000 metric tons, FAO estimates)

	2004	2005	2006
Sweet potatoes	25	25	25
Yams	156	157	157
Sugar cane	2,100	1,900	1,900
Coconuts	189	199	199
Cabbages	27	27	27
Tomatoes	22	23	23
Pumpkins, squash and gourds	38	39	39
Carrots and turnips	21	22	22
Bananas	108	106	106
Plantains	21	20	20
Oranges	160	172	172
Lemons and limes	24	24	24
Grapefruit and pomelos	42	43	43
Pineapples	23	24	24
Pimento, allspice	10	10	n.a.

Aggregate production ('000 metric tons, may include official, semi-official or estimated data): Total cereals 1.4 in 2004, 1.4 in 2005, 2.0 in 2006; Total roots and tubers 225.7 in 2004, 227.0 in 2005, 227.0 in 2006; Total vegetables (incl. melons) 206.2 in 2004, 212.6 in 2005, 213.6 in 2006; Total fruits (excl. melons) 472.4 in 2004, 485.5 in 2005, 485.5 in 2006.

Source: FAO.

LIVESTOCK
('000 head, year ending September, FAO estimates)

	2001	2002	2003
Horses	4	4	4
Mules	10	10	10
Asses	23	23	23
Cattle	400	400	430
Pigs	180	150	180
Sheep	1	1	1
Goats	440	440	440
Poultry	13,000	13,000	11,000

2004–06: Figures assumed to be unchanged from 2003 (FAO estimates).
Source: FAO.

LIVESTOCK PRODUCTS
('000 metric tons, FAO estimates)

	2003	2004	2005
Cattle meat	13.6	13.2	13.2
Goat meat	1.6	1.6	1.6
Pig meat	5.5	5.8	5.9
Chicken meat	81.3	85.6	88.3
Cows' milk	28.5	21.7	18.0
Hen eggs	5.8	7.0	7.3
Honey	1	1	1

2006: Figures assumed to be unchanged from 2005 (FAO estimates).
Source: FAO.

Forestry

ROUNDWOOD REMOVALS
('000 cubic metres, excl. bark, FAO estimates)

	2004	2005	2006
Sawlogs, veneer logs and logs for sleepers	132	128	128
Other industrial wood	150	150	150
Fuel wood	570	563	559
Total	852	841	837

Source: FAO.

SAWNWOOD PRODUCTION
('000 cubic metres, incl. railway sleepers)

	1996	1997	1998
Coniferous (softwood)	3	3	3
Broadleaved (hardwood)	61	62	63
Total	64	65	66

1999–2006: Annual production as in 1998 (FAO estimates).
Source: FAO.

Fishing

('000 metric tons, live weight)

	2003	2004	2005
Capture*	8.7	13.5	13.1
Marine fishes	7.6	8.6	7.2
Freshwater fishes*	0.4	0.4	0.4
Aquaculture	3.0	4.5	5.7
Nile tilapia	2.5	4.2	4.8
Total catch*	11.7	18.0	18.8

* FAO estimates.
Source: FAO.

JAMAICA

Mining

('000 metric tons)

	2003	2004	2005
Bauxite*	13,445	13,297	14,118
Alumina	3,844	4,021	4,086
Crude gypsum	249	283	302
Salt	19.0	19.0	19.0†

* Dried equivalent of crude ore.
† Estimate.
Source: US Geological Survey.

Industry

SELECTED PRODUCTS

	2004	2005	2006
Sugar (metric tons)	181,042	127,001	143,806
Molasses (metric tons)	78,884	60,927	73,426
Rum ('000 litres)	24,777	24,674	24,468
Beer and stout ('000 litres)	76,522	83,241	86,955
Fuel oil ('000 litres)	674,747	257,301	625,211
Gasoline (petrol) ('000 litres)	109,109	107,292	178,736
Kerosene, turbo and jet fuel ('000 litres)	72,055	52,042	81,762
Auto diesel oil ('000 litres)	144,782	100,103	257,422
Cement ('000 metric tons)	807,869	848,365	762,912
Concrete ('000 cu metres)	194,375	212,900	250,835

Electrical energy (million kWh): 7,146 in 2003; 7,217 in 2004 (Source: UN, *Industrial Commodity Statistics Yearbook*).

Finance

CURRENCY AND EXCHANGE RATES

Monetary Units
100 cents = 1 Jamaican dollar (J $).

Sterling, US Dollar and Euro Equivalents (31 November 2007)
£1 sterling = J $147.136;
US $1 = J $71,204;
€1 = J $105.104;
J $1,000 = £6.80 = US $14.04 = €9.51.

Average Exchange Rate (J $ per US $)
2004   61.197
2005   62.281
2006   65.744

GOVERNMENT FINANCE
(budgetary central government, cash basis, J $ million, year ending 31 March)

Summary of Balances

	2003	2004	2005
Revenue	151,434	172,798	186,684
Less Expense	173,248	188,382	192,250
Net cash inflow from operating activities	−21,813	−15,584	−5,566
Less Purchases of non-financial assets	6,754	2,592	15,474
Cash surplus/deficit	−28,567	−18,175	−21,040

Revenue

	2003	2004	2005
Tax revenue	133,208	152,961	165,700
Taxes on income, profits and capital gains	26,814	27,530	31,940
Taxes on goods and services	57,007	65,017	70,226
Grants	586	4,220	717
Other revenue	17,641	15,618	20,267
Total	151,434	172,798	186,684

Expense/Outlays

Expense by economic type	2003	2004	2005
Compensation of employees	60,463	63,517	63,108
Use of goods and services	24,615	32,081	40,846
Interest	88,170	92,784	88,296
Total	173,248	188,382	192,250

Outlays by functions of government*	2003	2004	2005
General public services	107,590	115,901	107,806
Defence	3,244	3,369	3,804
Public order and safety	13,776	14,517	17,425
Economic affairs	8,857	12,059	15,751
Environmental protection	368	575	385
Housing and community amenities	3,460	4,565	4,318
Health	11,763	15,875	14,281
Recreation, culture and religion	—	3,240	2,368
Education	29,184	30,267	36,718
Social protection	4,589	2,359	2,735
Statistical discrepancy	−2,829	−11,753	2,134
Total	180,002	190,974	207,724

* Including purchases of non-financial assets.

2006 (budgetary central government, cash basis, J $ million, year ending 31 March): Total revenue 260,101; Total expenditure 254,976.

Source: IMF, *Government Finance Statistics Yearbook*.

INTERNATIONAL RESERVES
(US $ million at 31 December, excluding gold)

	2004	2005	2006
IMF special drawing rights	0.1	0.0	0.3
Foreign exchange	1,846.4	2,169.8	2,317.9
Total	1,846.5	2,169.8	2,318.2

Source: IMF, *International Financial Statistics*.

MONEY SUPPLY
(J $ million at 31 December)

	2004	2005	2006
Currency outside banks	25,750	28,705	34,745
Demand deposits at commercial banks	31,409	36,781	45,632
Total money (incl. others)	61,424	73,581	90,912

Source: IMF, *International Financial Statistics*.

COST OF LIVING
(Consumer Price Index; base: January 1988 = 100)

	2004	2005	2006
Food (incl. beverages)	1,711.0	1,987.9	2,218.2
Fuel and power	1,795.6	2,131.3	2,395.5
Clothing and footwear	1,490.9	1,551.0	1,659.1
Rent and housing	1,813.6	2,034.1	2,435.2
Transport	1,994.2	2,051.9	2,623.6
All items (incl. others)	1,801.8	2,032.8	2,295.7

JAMAICA

Statistical Survey

NATIONAL ACCOUNTS
(J $ million at current prices)

Expenditure on the Gross Domestic Product

	2003	2004	2005
Government final consumption expenditure	72,888	77,507	91,755
Private final consumption expenditure	343,226	391,675	440,755
Increase in stocks	861	558	60
Gross fixed capital formation	140,438	165,458	192,042
Total domestic expenditure	557,413	635,198	724,612
Exports of goods and services	192,129	231,324	248,628
Less Imports of goods and services	276,624	325,714	368,210
GDP in purchasers' values	472,918	540,808	605,030
GDP at constant 1996 prices	235,190	237,475	240,864

Source: IMF, *International Financial Statistics*.

Gross Domestic Product by Economic Activity

	2004	2005	2006
Agriculture, forestry and fishing	27,706.5	31,814.0	35,520.6
Mining and quarrying	22,716.9	23,837.6	24,660.3
Manufacturing	68,489.7	76,158.7	84,030.4
Electricity and water	18,584.4	24,084.1	28,096.3
Construction	53,289.2	61,078.4	65,984.8
Wholesale and retail trade	105,139.4	120,279.4	133,822.9
Transport, storage and communication	62,054.4	67,917.0	78,196.0
Finance and insurance services	34,671.0	38,217.5	42,498.9
Real estate and business services	31,293.5	35,862.9	40,719.8
Producers of government services	61,611.9	64,968.0	74,732.5
Household and private non-profit services	2,554.9	39,129.9	45,167.5
Other services	35,732.4	3,031.0	3,380.6
Sub-total	523,844.2	586,378.5	656,810.6
Value-added tax	41,395.4	45,499.8	55,889.1
Less Imputed bank service charge	24,431.0	26,848.0	30,772.2
GDP in purchasers' values	540,808.6	605,030.3	681,927.5

BALANCE OF PAYMENTS
(US $ million)

	2004	2005	2006
Exports of goods f.o.b.	1,601.6	1,664.3	2,133.6
Imports of goods f.o.b.	−3,546.1	−4,245.5	−5,077.1
Trade balance	−1,944.5	−2,581.2	−2,943.5
Exports of services	2,297.1	2,329.7	2,648.7
Imports of services	−1,725.4	−1,722.2	−2,021.0
Balance on goods and services	−1,372.8	−1,973.7	−2,315.8
Other income received	269.6	327.9	378.4
Other income paid	−852.1	−1,004.1	−981.4
Balance on goods, services and income	−1,955.4	−2,649.9	−2,918.8
Current transfers received	1,892.1	1,935.5	2,088.5
Current transfers paid	−445.9	−357.0	−339.9
Current balance	−509.1	−1,071.5	−1,170.3
Capital account (net)	2.2	−2.7	−0.1
Direct investment abroad	−60.0	−101.0	−85.4
Direct investment from abroad	601.6	682.5	882.2
Portfolio investment assets	−1,132.8	−1,406.4	−506.4
Portfolio investment liabilities	1,228.8	1,280.4	377.9
Other investment assets	−127.4	−290.8	−269.0
Other investment liabilities	705.6	1,093.2	981.5
Net errors and omissions	−14.2	46.2	19.9
Overall balance	694.7	229.9	230.3

Source: IMF, *International Financial Statistics*.

External Trade

PRINCIPAL COMMODITIES
(J $ million)

Imports c.i.f.	2004	2005	2006*
Foods	31,874.3	37,641.2	40,540.8
Beverages and tobacco	2,666.7	3,491.2	4,498.6
Crude materials (excl. fuels)	4,141.9	4,933.9	5,418.9
Mineral fuels and lubricants	59,615.1	84,849.5	115,612.8
Animal and vegetable oils and fats	1,928.8	1,724.1	1,655.4
Chemicals	26,107.8	34,613.6	44,706.3
Manufactured goods	33,651.7	39,735.1	45,767.9
Machinery and transport equipment	52,053.0	54,211.8	74,177.2
Miscellaneous manufactured articles	24,360.5	29,771.8	33,589.5
Total (incl. others)	241,156.5	295,567.7	371,360.1

Exports f.o.b.	2004	2005	2006*
Foods	15,103.5	11,971.0	15,478.3
Beverages and tobacco	3,793.8	4,907.2	5,920.9
Crude materials (excl. fuels)	56,411.1	64,697.0	82,708.0
Mineral fuels and lubricants	2,051.3	7,011.9	17,570.9
Chemicals	4,735.4	3,541.9	4,862.3
Machinery and transport equipment	1,487.5	1,123.8	1,445.0
Miscellaneous manufactured articles	1,343.7	1,326.1	1,261.9
Total (incl. others)	85,784.1	95,275.1	130,176.2

* Preliminary.

PRINCIPAL TRADING PARTNERS
(US $ million)

Imports c.i.f.	2004	2005	2006
Canada	103.7	109.6	123.7
CARICOM*	562.7	752.2	857.3
Latin America	560.2	652.9	939.6
United Kingdom	93.2	112.4	1,333.1
Other European Union	223.7	237.2	344.8
USA	1,605.8	1,939.3	2,165.0
Total (incl. others)	3,927.2	4,739.4	5,801.4

Exports f.o.b.	2004	2005	2006
Canada	273.5	295.0	308.3
CARICOM*	51.9	50.0	53.0
Latin America	9.5	14.5	13.5
United Kingdom	149.6	163.4	204.3
Other European Union	304.7	294.1	342.5
Norway	49.9	98.2	90.4
USA	302.1	395.0	579.4
Total (incl. others)	1,404.5	1,531.5	2,133.6

* Caribbean Community and Common Market.

Transport

RAILWAYS
(traffic)

	1988	1989	1990
Passenger-km ('000)	36,146	37,995	n.a.
Freight ton-km ('000)	115,076	28,609	1,931

Source: Jamaica Railway Corporation.

JAMAICA

ROAD TRAFFIC
(motor vehicles in use)

	2003	2004
Passenger cars	316,182	357,660
Commercial vehicles	113,482	128,239
Motorcycles	23,420	26,969

Source: IRF, *World Road Statistics*.

SHIPPING

Merchant Fleet
(registered at 31 December)

	2004	2005	2006
Number of vessels	23	29	31
Total displacement ('000 grt)	131.2	139.0	121.0

Source: Lloyd's Register-Fairplay, *World Fleet Statistics*.

International Sea-borne Freight Traffic
(estimates, '000 metric tons)

	1989	1990	1991
Goods loaded	7,711	8,354	8,802
Goods unloaded	5,167	5,380	5,285

Source: Port Authority of Jamaica.

CIVIL AVIATION
(traffic on scheduled services)

	2001	2002	2003
Kilometres flown (million)	46	41	48
Passengers carried ('000)	1,946	2,016	1,838
Passenger-km (million)	4,412	4,912	5,005
Total ton-km (million)	471	589	484

Source: UN, *Statistical Yearbook*.

Tourism

VISITOR ARRIVALS BY COUNTRY OF ORIGIN

	2003	2004	2005
Canada	95,265	105,623	116,862
Cayman Islands	11,966	15,036	15,822
Germany	16,290	18,090	19,860
United Kingdom	149,714	161,606	152,483
USA	969,699	997,621	1,059,640
Total (incl. others)	1,350,285	1,414,786	1,478,663

Total visitor arrivals: 1,678,905 in 2006.

Tourism revenue (US $ million, incl. passenger transport): 1,621 in 2003; 1,733 in 2004; 1,783 in 2005.

Source: partly World Tourism Organization.

Communications Media

	2004	2005	2006
Telephones ('000 main lines in use)	500	319	319
Mobile cellular telephones ('000 subscribers)	2,200	2,804	2,804
Personal computers ('000 in use)	153	166	n.a.
Internet users ('000)	1,067	1,232	1,232
Broadband subscribers ('000)	27	45	45

Radio receivers ('000 in use): 1,215 in 1997.
Television receivers ('000 in use): 510 in 2001.
Facsimile machines (number in use): 1,567 in 1992*.
Daily newspapers: 3 in 1996 (circulation 158,000).

*Year ending 1 April.

Sources: International Telecommunication Union; UN, *Statistical Yearbook*; UNESCO, *Statistical Yearbook*.

Education

(2003/04 unless otherwise indicated)

	Institutions*	Teachers	Students
Pre-primary	2,137†	7,066‡	152,404‡
Primary	355	11,793‡	326,411‡
Secondary	161	13,336‡	246,332‡
Tertiary	15	1,051	11,600

* Excludes 349 all-age schools and 88 primary and junior high schools.
† Includes 2,008 community-operated basic schools.
‡ 2004/05 data.

Source: partly Ministry of Education and Youth.

Adult literacy rate (UNESCO estimates): 79.9% (males 74.1%; females 85.9%) in 1999 (Source: UNESCO Institute for Statistics).

Directory

The Constitution

The Constitution came into force at the independence of Jamaica on 6 August 1962. Amendments to the Constitution are enacted by Parliament, but certain entrenched provisions require ratification by a two-thirds' majority in both chambers of the legislature, and some (such as a change of the head of state) require the additional approval of a national referendum.

HEAD OF STATE

The Head of State is the British monarch, who is locally represented by a Governor-General, appointed by the British monarch, on the recommendation of the Jamaican Prime Minister in consultation with the Leader of the Opposition party.

THE LEGISLATURE

The Senate or Upper House consists of 21 Senators, of whom 13 will be appointed by the Governor-General on the advice of the Prime Minister and eight by the Governor-General on the advice of the Leader of the Opposition. (Legislation enacted in 1984 provided for eight independent Senators to be appointed, after consultations with the Prime Minister, in the eventuality of there being no Leader of the Opposition.)

The House of Representatives or Lower House consists of 60 elected members called Members of Parliament.

A person is qualified for appointment to the Senate or for election to the House of Representatives if he or she is a citizen of Jamaica or other Commonwealth country, of the age of 21 or more and has been ordinarily resident in Jamaica for the immediately preceding 12 months.

THE PRIVY COUNCIL

The Privy Council consists of six members appointed by the Governor-General after consultation with the Prime Minister, of whom at least two are persons who hold or who have held public office. The functions of the Council are to advise the Governor-General on the exercise of the Prerogative of Mercy and on appeals on disciplinary matters from the three Service Commissions.

THE EXECUTIVE

The Prime Minister is appointed from the House of Representatives by the Governor-General, and is the leader of the party that holds the majority of seats in the House of Representatives. The Leader of the party is voted in by the members of that party. The Leader of the Opposition is voted in by the members of the Opposition party.

The Cabinet consists of the Prime Minister and not fewer than 11 other ministers, not more than four of whom may sit in the Senate. The members of the Cabinet are appointed by the Governor-General on the advice of the Prime Minister.

THE JUDICATURE

The Judicature consists of a Supreme Court, a Court of Appeal and minor courts. Judicial matters, notably advice to the Governor-General on appointments, are considered by a Judicial Service Commission, the Chairman of which is the Chief Justice, members being the President of the Court of Appeal, the Chairman of the Public Service Commission and three others.

CITIZENSHIP

All persons born in Jamaica after independence automatically acquire Jamaican citizenship and there is also provision for the acquisition of citizenship by persons born outside Jamaica of Jamaican parents. Persons born in Jamaica (or persons born outside Jamaica of Jamaican parents) before independence who immediately prior to independence were citizens of the United Kingdom and colonies also automatically become citizens of Jamaica.

Appropriate provision is made which permits persons who do not automatically become citizens of Jamaica to be registered as such.

FUNDAMENTAL RIGHTS AND FREEDOMS

The Constitution includes provisions safeguarding the fundamental freedoms of the individual, irrespective of race, place of origin, political opinions, colour, creed or sex, subject only to respect for the rights and freedoms of others and for the public interest. The fundamental freedoms include the rights of life, liberty, security of the person and protection from arbitrary arrest or restriction of movement, the enjoyment of property and the protection of the law, freedom of conscience, of expression and of peaceful assembly and association, and respect for private and family life.

The Government

HEAD OF STATE

Monarch: HM Queen ELIZABETH II (succeeded to the throne 6 February 1952).

Governor-General: Prof. KENNETH OCTAVIUS HALL (appointed 15 February 2006).

PRIVY COUNCIL OF JAMAICA

KENNETH SMITH, DONALD MILLS, DENNIS LALOR, JAMES KERR, ELSA LEO RHYNIE, HEADLEY CUNNINGHAM.

CABINET
(March 2008)

Prime Minister and Minister of Planning and Development and of Defence: BRUCE GOLDING.
Deputy Prime Minister and Minister of Foreign Affairs and Foreign Trade: Dr KENNETH BAUGH.
Minister of Finance and the Public Service: AUDLEY SHAW.
Minister of National Security: DERRICK SMITH.
Attorney-General and Minister of Justice: DOROTHY LIGHTBOURNE.
Minister of Education: ANDREW HOLNESS.
Minister of Industry, Commerce and Investment: KARL SAMUDA.
Minister of Tourism: EDMUND BARTLETT.
Minister of Agriculture: Dr CHRISTOPHER TUFTON.
Minister of Energy, Mining and Telecommunications: CLIVE MULLINGS.
Minister of Water and Housing: Dr HORACE CHANG.
Minister of Labour and Social Security: PEARNEL CHARLES.
Minister of Health and Environment: RUDYARD SPENCER.
Minister of Information, Culture, Youth and Sports: OLIVIA GRANGE.
Minister of Transport and Works: MICHAEL HENRY.
Minister without Portfolio in the Office of the Prime Minister: JAMES ROBERTSON.
Minister without Portfolio in the Ministry of Finance and the Public Service: DON WEHBY.
Minister without Portfolio in the Ministry of Finance and the Public Service: DWIGHT NELSON.

MINISTRIES

Office of the Governor-General: King's House, Hope Rd, Kingston 10; tel. 927-9941; fax 929-0005; e-mail hpm@opm.gov.jm; internet www.kingshousejamaica.gov.jm.
Office of the Prime Minister: Jamaica House, 1 Devon Rd, POB 272, Kingston 10; tel. 927-9941; fax 927-4101; e-mail pmo@opm.gov.jm.
Ministry of Agriculture: Hope Gardens, POB 480, Kingston 6; tel. 927-1731; fax 927-1904; e-mail psoffice@moa.gov.jm; internet www.moa.gov.jm.
Ministry of Education: 2 National Heroes Circle, Kingston 4; tel. 922-1400; fax 948-7755; e-mail maria.jones@moey.gov.jm; internet www.moey.gov.jm.
Ministry of Energy, Mining and Telecommunications: 36 Trafalgar Road, Kingston 10; tel. 929-8990; fax 929-8103; e-mail jdixon@mct.gov.jm; internet www.mct.gov.jm.
Ministry of Finance and the Public Service: 30 National Heroes Circle, Kingston 4; tel. 922-8600; fax 922-7097; e-mail info@mof.gov.jm; internet www.mof.gov.jm.
Ministry of Foreign Affairs and Foreign Trade: 21 Dominica Dr., POB 624, Kingston 5; tel. 926-4220; fax 929-5112; e-mail mfaftjam@cwjamaica.com; internet www.mfaft.gov.jm.
Ministry of Health and Environment: Oceana Hotel Complex, 2–4 King St, Kingston; tel. 967-1101; fax 967-7293; e-mail blairs@moh.gov.jm; internet www.moh.gov.jm.
Ministry of Industry, Commerce and Investment (MITEC): PCJ Bldg, 36 Trafalgar Rd, Kingston 10; tel. 929-8990; fax 960-1623; e-mail communications@mct.gov.jm; internet www.mct.gov.jm.
Ministry of Information, Culture, Youth and Sports: Jamaica House, Kingston 6; tel. 927-9941; e-mail maria.jones@moey.gov.jm.
Ministry of Justice and Attorney-General's Department: Mutual Life Bldg North Tower and NCB Towers, 2 Oxford Rd, Kingston 5; tel. 906-4923; fax 922-4983; e-mail psec1@moj.gov.jm; internet www.moj.gov.jm.
Ministry of Labour and Social Security: 1F North St, POB 10, Kingston; tel. 922-9500; fax 922-6902; e-mail mlss_perm_sect@yahoo.com; internet www.mlss.gov.jm.
Ministry of National Security: Mutual Life Bldg, North Tower, 2 Oxford Rd, Kingston 5; tel. 906-4908; fax 906-1724; e-mail information@mns.gov.jm; internet www.mns.gov.jm.
Ministry of Tourism: 64 Knutsford Blvd, Kingston 5; tel. 920-4924; fax 920-4944; e-mail mts@cwjamaica.com; internet www.visitjamaica.com.
Ministry of Transport and Works: 138H Maxfield Ave, Kingston 10; tel. 754-1900; e-mail ps@mtw.gov.jm; internet www.mtw.gov.jm.
Ministry of Water and Housing: 25 Dominica Drive, Kingston 5; tel. 754-2584; fax 960-2886; e-mail nwhinfo@cwjamica.com; internet www.mhtww.gov.jm.

Legislature

PARLIAMENT

Houses of Parliament: Gordon House, 81 Duke St, POB 636, Kingston; tel. 922-0202; fax 967-0064; Clerk HEATHER COOKE.

Senate

President: SYRINGA A. MARSHALL-BURNETT.
Deputy-President: NAVEL FOSTER CLARKE.
The Senate has 19 other members.

JAMAICA

House of Representatives
Speaker: DELROY CHUCK.
Deputy Speaker: MARISA DALRYMPLE-PHILIBERT.
General Election, 3 September 2007

	% of votes cast	Seats
Jamaica Labour Party (JLP)	50.1	32
People's National Party (PNP)	49.8	28
Total (incl. others)	100.0	60

Election Commission

Electoral Office of Jamaica (EOJ): 43 Duke St, Kingston; tel. 922-0425-9; fax 967-0728; e-mail eojinfo@eoj.com.jm; internet www.eoj.com.jm; f. 1943; Dir DANVILLE WALKER.

Political Organizations

Jamaica Labour Party (JLP): 20 Belmont Rd, Kingston 5; tel. 929-0987; e-mail join@jamaicalabourparty.com; internet www.jlpteam.com; f. 1943; supports free enterprise in a mixed economy and close co-operation with the USA; Leader ORRETT BRUCE GOLDING; Chair. KEN BAUGH; Gen. Sec. KARL SAMUDA.

Jamaica Alliance Movement (JAM): Flamingo Beach, Falmouth, Trelawny, Kingston; tel. 861-5233; e-mail jamovement@yahoo.com; f. 2001; Rastafarian; Pres. ASTOR BLACK.

National Democratic Movement (NDM): 72 Half Way Tree Rd, Kingston 10; tel. 909-8316; e-mail ndmjamaica@yahoo.com; internet www.ndm4jamaica.org; f. 1995; advocates a clear separation of powers between the central executive and elected representatives; supports private investment and a market economy; mem. of the New Jamaica Alliance; Chair. HUGH THOMPSON; Pres. EARLE DELISSER.

People's National Party (PNP): 89 Old Hope Rd, Kingston 6; tel. 978-1337; fax 927-4389; e-mail information@pnpjamaica.com; internet www.pnpjamaica.com; f. 1938; socialist principles; affiliated with the National Workers' Union; Pres. PORTIA SIMPSON-MILLER; Gen. Sec. PETER BUNTING; Vice-Pres. Dr PETER PHILLIPS.

Diplomatic Representation

EMBASSIES AND HIGH COMMISSIONS IN JAMAICA

Argentina: Dyoll Life Bldg, 6th Floor, 40 Knutsford Blvd, Kingston 5; tel. 926-5588; fax 926-0580; e-mail embargen@cwjamaica.com; Ambassador MARIO JOSÉ PINO.

Brazil: Pan Caribbean Bldg, 10th Floor, 60 Knutsford Blvd, Kingston 5; tel. 929-8607; fax 968-5897; Ambassador (vacant).

Canada: 3 West Kings House Rd, POB 1500, Kingston 10; tel. 926-1500; fax 511-3493; e-mail kngtn@international.gc.ca; internet www.kingston.gc.ca; High Commissioner DENIS KINGSLEY.

Chile: Island Life Centre, 5th Floor, South Sixth St, Lucia Ave, Kingston 5; tel. 968-0260; fax 968-0265; e-mail chilejam@cwjamaica.com; Ambassador PEDRO GARCÍA CASTELBLANCO.

China, People's Republic: 8 Seaview Ave, POB 232, Kingston 10; tel. 927-3871; fax 927-6920; e-mail chinaemb_jm@mfa.gov.cn; internet jm.chineseembassy.org/eng; Ambassador CHEN JINGHUA.

Colombia: Victoria Mutual Bldg, 3rd Floor, 53 Knutsford Blvd, Kingston 5; tel. 929-1701; fax 968-0577; e-mail ekingston@cancilleria.gov.co; Ambassador VENTURA EMILIO DIAZ MEJÍA.

Costa Rica: Belvedere House, Beverly Dr., Hopedale, Old Hope Rd, Kingston 6; tel. 927-5988; fax 978-3946; e-mail cr_emb_jam14@hotmail.com; Ambassador NIDIA LORENA SANDOVAL ARCE.

Cuba: 9 Trafalgar Rd, Kingston 10; tel. 978-0931; fax 978-5372; e-mail embacubajam@cwjamaica.com; Ambassador GISELA BEATRIZ GARCÍA RIVERA.

Dominican Republic: 32 Earls Court, Kingston 8; tel. 755-4155; fax 755-4156; e-mail domemb@cwjamaica.com; Ambassador FILOMENA ALTAGRACIA NAVARRO TAVAREZ.

France: 13 Hillcrest Ave, POB 93, Kingston 6; tel. 978-0210; fax 927-4998; e-mail frenchembassy@cwjamaica.com; internet www.ambafrance-jm-bm.org; Ambassador FRANCIS HURTUT.

Germany: 10 Waterloo Rd, POB 444, Kingston 10; tel. 926-6728; fax 929-8282; e-mail germanembassa.kingston@gmail.com; internet www.kingston.diplo.de; Ambassador JÜRGEN ENGEL.

Haiti: 2 Munroe Rd, Kingston 6; tel. 927-7595; fax 978-7638; Ambassador JEAN-GABRIEL AUGUSTIN.

Honduras: 7 Lady Kay Dr., Norbrook, Kingston 8; tel. 941-1790; fax 941-6470; e-mail eduardonorris@hotmail.com; Ambassador JOSÉ EDUARDO NORRIS MADRID.

India: 4 Retreat Ave, POB 446, Kingston 6; tel. 927-4480; fax 978-2801; e-mail hicomindkin@cwjamaica.com; High Commissioner M.S. GROVER.

Japan: Mutual Life Centre, North Tower, 6th Floor, 2 Oxford Rd, POB 8104, Kingston 5; tel. 929-3338; fax 968-1373; internet www.jamaica.emb-japan.go.jp; Ambassador MASAHIRO OBATA.

Mexico: PCJ Bldg, 36 Trafalgar Rd, Kingston 10; tel. 926-4242; fax 929-7995; e-mail embamexj@cwjamaica.com; Ambassador ROSAURA LEONORA RUEDA GUTIÉRREZ.

Nigeria: 5 Waterloo Rd, POB 94, Kingston 10; tel. 926-6400; fax 968-7371; High Commissioner F. A. UKONGA.

Panama: 1 St Lucia Ave, Spanish Court, Suite 26, Kingston 5; tel. 968-2928; fax 960-1618; Ambassador RICARDO MORENO.

Peru: 23 Barbados Ave, Kingston 5; tel. 920-5027; fax 920-4360; e-mail embaperu-kingston@rree.gob.pe; Ambassador LUIS SÁNDIGA CABRERA.

Russia: 22 Norbrook Dr., Kingston 8; tel. 924-1048; fax 925-8290; e-mail rusembja@colis.com; Ambassador EDUARD MALAYAN.

Saint Christopher and Nevis: 11A Opal Ave, Golden Acres, Red Hills, St Andrew; tel. 944-3861; fax 945-0105; High Commissioner CEDRIC HARPER.

South Africa: 15 Hillcrest Ave, Kingston 6; tel. 978-3160; fax 978-0339; e-mail sahc-jamaica@cwjamaica.com; High Commissioner FAITH DOREEN RADEBE.

Spain: Island Life Centre, 6th Floor, 8 St Lucia Ave, Kingston 5; tel. 929-5555; fax 929-8965; e-mail emb.kingston@mae.es; Ambassador JESÚS SILVA FERNÁNDEZ.

Trinidad and Tobago: First Life Bldg, 3rd Floor, 60 Knutsford Blvd, Kingston 5; tel. 926-5730; fax 926-5801; High Commissioner YVONNE GITTENS-JOSEPH.

United Kingdom: 28 Trafalgar Rd, POB 575, Kingston 10; tel. 510-0700; fax 510-0737; e-mail bhc.kingston@fco.gov.uk; internet www.britishhighcommission.gov.uk/jamaica; High Commissioner JEREMY M. CRESSWELL.

USA: 142 Old Hope Rd, Kingston 6; tel. 702-6000; e-mail opakgn@state.gov; internet kingston.usembassy.gov; Ambassador BRENDA LAGRANGE JOHNSON.

Venezuela: PCJ Bldg, 3rd Floor, 36 Trafalgar Rd, POB 26, Kingston 10; tel. 926-5510; fax 926-7442; e-mail embavene@n5.com.jm; Ambassador NOEL ENRIQUE MARTÍNEZ OCHOA.

Judicial System

The judicial system is based on English common law and practice. Final appeal is to the Judicial Committee of the Privy Council in the United Kingdom, although in 2001 the Jamaican Government signed an agreement to establish a Caribbean Court of Justice to fulfil this function.

Justice is administered by the Privy Council, Court of Appeal, Supreme Court (which includes the Revenue Court, the Gun Court and, since 2001, the Commercial Court), Resident Magistrates' Court (which includes the Traffic Court), two Family Courts and the Courts of Petty Sessions.

Judicial Service Commission: Office of the Services Commissions, 63–67 Knutsford Blvd, Kingston 5; advises the Governor-General on judicial appointments, etc.; chaired by the Chief Justice.

SUPREME COURT
(Public Bldg E, 134 Tower St, POB 491, Kingston; tel. 922-8300; fax 967-0669; e-mail webmaster@sc.gov.jm; internet www.sc.gov.jm)

Chief Justice: ZAILA MCCALLA.
Senior Puisne Judge: MARVA MCINTOSH.
Master: AUDRE LINDO.
Registrar: NICOLE SIMMONS.

COURT OF APPEAL
(POB 629, Kingston; tel. 922-8300)

President: SEYMOUR PANTON.
Registrar: G. P. LEVERS.

Religion

CHRISTIANITY

There are more than 100 Christian denominations active in Jamaica. According to the 2001 census, the largest religious bodies were the Church of God (whose members represented 24% of the population), Seventh-day Adventists (11% of the population), Pentecostalist (10%), Baptists (7%) and Anglicans (4%). Other denominations include Jehovah's Witnesses, the Methodist and Congregational Churches, United Church, the Church of the Brethren, the Ethiopian Orthodox Church, the Disciples of Christ, the Moravian Church, the Salvation Army and the Society of Friends (Quakers).

Jamaica Council of Churches: 14 South Ave, Kingston 10; tel. and fax 926-0974; e-mail jchurch@cwjamaica.com; f. 1941; 10 mem. churches and three agencies; Gen. Sec. GARY HARRIOT.

The Anglican Communion

Anglicans in Jamaica are adherents of the Church in the Province of the West Indies, comprising eight dioceses. The Archbishop of the Province is the Bishop of the North East Caribbean and Aruba. The Bishop of Jamaica, whose jurisdiction also includes Grand Cayman (in the Cayman Islands), is assisted by three suffragan Bishops (of Kingston, Mandeville and Montego Bay). The 2001 census recorded that some 4% of the population were Anglicans.

Bishop of Jamaica: Rt Rev. ALFRED C. REID, Church House, 2 Caledonia Ave, Kingston 5; tel. 952-4963; fax 952-2933; e-mail info@anglicandiocese.com; internet anglicandiocese.dthost.com.

The Roman Catholic Church

Jamaica comprises the archdiocese of Kingston in Jamaica (also including the Cayman Islands), and the dioceses of Montego Bay and Mandeville. At 31 December 2005 the estimated total of adherents in Jamaica was 72,945, representing about 3% of the total population. The Archbishop and Bishops participate in the Antilles Episcopal Conference (currently based in Port of Spain, Trinidad and Tobago).

Archbishop of Kingston in Jamaica: Most Rev. LAWRENCE ALOYSIUS BURKE, Archbishop's Residence, 21 Hopefield Ave, POB 43, Kingston 6; tel. 927-9915; fax 927-4487; e-mail rcabkgn@cwjamaica.com; internet www.archdioceseofkingston.org.

Other Christian Churches

Assembly of God: Evangel Temple, 3 Friendship Park Rd, Kingston 3; tel. 928-2995; Sec. Pastor WILSON.

Baptist Union: 2B Washington Blvd, Kingston 20; tel. 969-2223; fax 924-6296; e-mail info@jbu.org.jm; internet www.jbu.org.jm; 40,000 mems; Pres. Rev. KARL E. HENLIN; Gen. Sec. Rev. KARL JOHNSON.

First Church of Christ, Scientist: 17 National Heroes Circle, Kingston 4; tel. 967-3814.

Methodist Church (Jamaica District): 143 Constant Spring Rd, POB 892, Kingston 8; tel. 925-6768; fax 924-2560; e-mail jamaicamethodist@cwjamaica.com; internet www.jamaicamethodist.org; f. 1789; 15,820 mems; Pres. Rev. Dr BYRON CHAMBERS; Synod Sec. Rev. EVERALD GALBRAITH.

Moravian Church in Jamaica: 3 Hector St, POB 8369, Kingston 5; tel. 928-1861; fax 928-8336; e-mail moravianchurch@cwjamaica.com; internet www.jamaicamoravian.com; f. 1754; 30,000 mems.

New Testament Church of God in Jamaica: New Testament Church of God Convention Centre, Rodons Pen, Old Harbour, St Catherine; 87,965 mems of 337 churches; Overseer Rev. Dr DENNIS MCQUIRE.

United Church in Jamaica and the Cayman Islands: 12 Carlton Cres., POB 359, Kingston 10; tel. 926-6059; fax 929-0826; e-mail churchunited@hotmail.com; internet www.ucjci.netfirms.com; f. 1965 by merger of the Congregational Union of Jamaica (f. 1877) and the Presbyterian Church of Jamaica and Grand Cayman to become United Church of Jamaica and Grand Cayman; merged with Disciples of Christ in Jamaica in 1992 when name changed as above; 20,000 mems; Moderator RODERICK HEWITT; Gen. Sec. Rev. COLLIN COWAN.

West Indies Union Conference of Seventh-day Adventists: 125 Manchester Rd, Mandeville; tel. 962-2284; fax 962-3417; e-mail president@wiunion.org; internet www.wiunion.org; f. 1903; 205,000 mems; Pres. Dr PATRICK ALLEN.

RASTAFARIANISM

Rastafarianism is an important influence in Jamaican culture. The cult is derived from Christianity and a belief in the divinity of Ras (Prince) Tafari Makonnen (later Emperor Haile Selassie) of Ethiopia. It advocates racial equality and non-violence, but causes controversy in its use of 'ganja' (marijuana) as a sacrament. The 2001 census recorded 24,020 Rastafarians (0.9% of the total population).

Although the religion is largely unorganized, there are some denominations.

Haile Selassie Rastafari Royal Ethiopian Judah Coptic Church: 11 Welcome Ave, Kingston 11; tel. 970-4171; e-mail drmatt@anbell.net; not officially incorporated; Leader Abuna BONGO BLACKART; Pres. Dr MATT O. MYRIE.

BAHÁ'Í FAITH

National Spiritual Assembly: 208 Mountain View Ave, Kingston 6; tel. 927-7051; fax 978-2344; incorporated in 1970; Chair. DOROTHY WHYTE.

ISLAM

At the 2001 census there were an estimated 5,000 Muslims.

JUDAISM

The 2001 census recorded some 350 Jews.

United Congregation of Israelites: K. K. Shaare Shalom Synagogue, 92 Duke St, Kingston 6; tel. and fax 922-5931; e-mail shaareshalom@cwjamaica.com; internet www.ucija.org; f. 1655; 250 mems; Pres. MICHAEL MATALON.

The Press

DAILIES

Daily Gleaner: 7 North St, POB 40, Kingston; tel. 922-3400; fax 922-6223; e-mail feedback@jamaica-gleaner.com; internet www.jamaica-gleaner.com; f. 1834; morning; independent; Chair. and Man. Dir OLIVER CLARKE; Editor-in-Chief GARFIELD GRANDISON; circ. 50,000.

Daily Star: 7 North St, POB 40, Kingston; tel. 922-3400; fax 922-6223; e-mail feedback@jamaica-gleaner.com; internet www.jamaica-gleaner.com; f. 1951; evening; Editor-in-Chief GARFIELD GRANDISON; Editor DWAYNE GORDON; circ. 45,000.

Jamaica Observer: 40 Beechwood Ave, Kingston 5; tel. 920-8136; fax 926-7655; e-mail feedback@jamaicaobserver.com; internet www.jamaicaobserver.com; f. 1993; Chair. GORDON 'BUTCH' STEWART.

PERIODICALS

Catholic Opinion: Roman Catholic Chancery Office, 21 Hopefield Ave, POB 43, Kingston 6; tel. 927-9915; fax 927-4487; e-mail rcabkgn@cwjamaica.com; internet www.archdioceseofkingston.org; 6 a year; religious; circulated in the Sunday Gleaner; Editor Very Rev. Fr MICHAEL LEWIS; circ. 100,000.

Children's Own: 7 North St, POB 40, Kingston; tel. 922-3400; fax 922-6223; e-mail feedback@jamaica-gleaner.com; internet www.jamaica-gleaner.com; weekly during term time; Editor-in-Chief GARFIELD GRANDISON; circ. 120,000.

Jamaica Churchman: 2 Caledonia Ave, Kingston 5; tel. 926-6608; quarterly; circ. 7,000.

Jamaica Journal: 10–16 East St, Kingston; tel. 922-0620; fax 922-1147; e-mail ioj.jam@mail.infochan.com; internet www.instituteofjamaica.org.jm; f. 1967; 3 a year; literary, historical and cultural review; publ. by Institute of Jamaica; Chair. of Editorial Cttee KIM ROBINSON.

Mandeville Weekly: 31 Ward Ave, Mandeville, Manchester; tel. 961-0118; fax 961-0119; internet www.eyegrid.com/mandevilleweekly; Chief Editor ANTHONY FRECKLETON; Man. WENDY HENRY.

North Coast Times: 130 Main St, Ocho Rios; tel. 795-4201; fax 974-9306; internet www.northcoasttimes.com; weekly; Publr FRANKLIN MCKNIGHT; Gen. Man. DESRINE PRICE.

Sunday Gleaner: 7 North St, POB 40, Kingston; tel. 922-3400; fax 922-6223; e-mail feedback@jamaica-gleaner.com; internet www.jamaica-gleaner.com; weekly; Editor-in-Chief GARFIELD GRANDISON; circ. 100,000.

Sunday Herald: 17 Norwood Ave, Kingston 5; tel. 906-7572; fax 908-4044; e-mail sunherald@cwjamaica.com; internet www.sunheraldja.com; f. 1997; weekly; Man. Editor DESMOND RICHARDS; Exec. Editor R. CHRISTENE KING.

Sunday Observer: 40 Beechwood Ave, Kingston 5; tel. 920-8136; fax 926-7655; internet www.jamaicaobserver.com; weekly; Chair. GORDON 'BUTCH' STEWART.

The Visitor Vacation Guide: 4 Cottage Rd, POB 1258, Montego Bay; tel. 952-5256; fax 952-6513; Editor LLOYD B. SMITH.

Weekend Star: 7 North St, POB 40, Kingston; tel. 922-3400; fax 922-6223; e-mail feedback@jamaica-gleaner.com; internet www.jamaica-gleaner.com; f. 1951; weekly; Editor-in-Chief GARFIELD GRANDISON; Editor DWAYNE GORDON; circ. 80,000.

JAMAICA   Directory

Western News: 40 Beechwood Ave, Kingston 5; tel. 920-8136; fax 926-7655; e-mail feedback@jamaicaobserver.com; internet www.jamaicaobserver.com; Chair. GORDON 'BUTCH' STEWART; circ. 20,000.

West Indian Medical Journal: Faculty of Medical Sciences, University of the West Indies, Kingston 7; tel. 927-1214; fax 927-1846; e-mail wimj@uwimona.edu.jm; internet www.mona.uwi.edu/fms/wimj; f. 1951; quarterly; Editor EVERARD N. BARTON; circ. 2,000.

X-News Jamaica: 86 Hagley Park Rd, Kingston 10; tel. 937-7304; fax 901-7667; e-mail comments@xnewsjamaica.com; internet www.xnewsjamaica.com; f. 1993; weekly; Assistant Editor CECELIA CAMPBELL-LIVINGSTON.

PRESS ASSOCIATION

Press Association of Jamaica (PAJ): Kingston 8; tel. 925-7836; f. 1943; Pres. DESMOND RICHARDS.

Foreign Bureaux

Associated Press (USA), Caribbean Media Corpn and Inter Press Service (Italy) are represented in Jamaica.

Publishers

Jamaica Publishing House Ltd: 97B Church St, Kingston; tel. 967-3866; fax 922-5412; e-mail jph@cwjamaica.com; f. 1969; wholly owned subsidiary of Jamaica Teachers' Asscn; educational, English language and literature, mathematics, history, geography, social sciences, music; Chair. WOODBURN MILLER; Man. ELAINE R. STENNETT.

LMH Publishing Ltd: 7 Norman Rd, Suite 10, LOJ Industrial Complex, Kingston CSO; tel. 938-0005; fax 759-8752; e-mail lmhbookpublishing@cwjamaica.com; internet www.lmhpublishing.com; f. 1970; educational textbooks, general, travel, fiction, non-fiction, children's books; Chair. L. MICHAEL HENRY; Man. Dir DAWN CHAMBERS-HENRY.

Ian Randle Publishers (IRP): 11 Cunningham Ave, POB 686, Kingston 6; tel. 978-0745; fax 978-1156; e-mail ian@ianrandlepublishers.com; internet www.ianrandlepublishers.com; f. 1991; history, gender studies, politics, sociology, law, cooking and music; Chair. IAN RANDLE; Man. Dir CHRISTINE RANDLE.

University of the West Indies Press (UWI Press): 7A Gibraltar Hall Rd, Mona, Kingston 7; tel. 977-2659; fax 977-2660; e-mail cuserv@cwjamaica.com; f. 1992; Caribbean history, culture and literature, gender studies, education and political science; Man. Editor SHIVAUN HEARNE; Gen. Man. LINDA SPETH.

Western Publishers Ltd: 4 Cottage Rd, POB 1258, Montego Bay; tel. 952-5253; fax 952-6513; e-mail westernmirror@mail.infochan.com; f. 1980; Man. Dir and Editor-in-Chief LLOYD B. SMITH.

GOVERNMENT PUBLISHING HOUSE

Jamaica Printing Services: 77 1/2 Duke St, Kingston; tel. 967-2250; fax 967-2225; e-mail jps_1992@yahoo.com; internet jps1992.org; Gen. Man. RALPH BELL.

Broadcasting and Communications

TELECOMMUNICATIONS

The telecommunications sector became fully liberalized in 2003. The sector was regulated by the Office of Utilities Regulation (see Utilities).

Cable & Wireless Jamaica Ltd: 7 Cecilio Ave, Kingston 10; tel. 926-9450; fax 929-9530; internet home.cwjamaica.com; f. 1989; name changed as above in 1995, following merger with Jamaica Telephone Co Ltd and Jamaica International Telecommunications Ltd; 79% owned by Cable & Wireless (United Kingdom); Pres. RODNEY DAVIS.

Digicel Jamaica: 10–16 Grenada Way, Kingston 5; tel. 960-2696; fax 920-0948; internet www.digiceljamaica.com; mobile cellular telephone operator; owned by Irish consortium, Mossel (Jamaica) Ltd; f. 2001; Chair. DENIS O'BRIEN; CEO (Jamaica) DAVID HALL.

Oceanic Digital Jamaica (MiPhone): 30–36 Knutsford Blvd, Kingston 5; tel. 621-1000; fax 906-3486; e-mail info@miphone.com; internet www.miphone.com; mobile cellular telephone operator; fmrly Centennial Digital; Oceanic Digital, 49% stockholder, bought remaining 51% in Aug. 2002; Pres. CRAIG G. MCBURNETT; 100,000 subscribers.

BROADCASTING
Radio

Independent Radio: 6 Bradley Ave, Kingston 10; tel. 968-4880; fax 968-9165; commercial; broadcasts 24 hrs a day on FM; Gen. Man. NEWTON JAMES.

Music 99 FM: 6 Bradley Ave, Kingston 10.

Power 106: 6 Bradley Ave, Kingston 10; tel. 968-4880; fax 968-9165; e-mail power106@cwjamaica.com; internet www.go-jamaica.com/power; f. 1992; talk and sports programmes.

IRIE FM: 1B Derrymore Rd, Kingston 10; tel. 968-5023; fax 968-8332; e-mail iriefmmarket@cwjamaica.com; internet www.iriefm.net; f. 1991; commercial radio station owned by Grove Broadcasting Co; plays only reggae music; Man. BRIAN SCHMIDT.

Island Broadcasting Services Ltd: 41B Half Way Tree Rd, Kingston 5; tel. 968-8115; fax 929-1345; commercial; broadcasts 24 hrs a day on FM; Exec. Chair. NEVILLE JAMES.

KLAS-FM 89: 81 Knutsford Blvd, Kingston 5; tel. 929-1344; f. 1991; sports broadcasting.

Love FM: 81 Hagley Park Rd, Kingston 10; tel. 968-9596; e-mail webmaster@love101.org; internet www.love101.org; f. 1997; commercial radio station, broadcasts religious programming on FM; owned by Religious Media Ltd; Gen. Man. WINSTON RIDGARD.

Radio Jamaica Ltd (RJR): Broadcasting House, 32 Lyndhurst Rd, POB 23, Kingston 5; tel. 926-1100; fax 929-7467; e-mail rjr@radiojamaica.com; internet www.radiojamaica.com; f. 1947; commercial, public service; 3 channels; Man. Dir LESTER SPAULDING.

FAME 95 FM: internet www.famefm.fm; broadcasts on FM, island-wide 24 hrs a day; Exec. Producer FRANCOIS ST JUSTE.

Hitz 92 FM: internet www.hitz92fm.com; broadcasts on FM, island-wide 24 hrs a day; youth station.

RJR 94 FM: internet www.rjr94fm.com; broadcasts on AM and FM, island-wide 24 hrs a day; Exec. Producer NORMA BROWN-BELL.

ZIP 103 FM: 1B Derrymore Rd, Kingston 10, Jamaica; tel. 819-7699; fax 929-6233; e-mail zip103fm@cwjamaica.com; internet www.ZIPFM.net; f. 2002; commercial radio station; Dir D'ADRA WILLIAMS.

Other stations broadcasting include Hot 102 FM, Kool 97 FMRoots FM and TBC FM.

Television

Creative TV (CTV): Kingston; tel. 967-4482; fax 924-9432; internet www.creativetvjamaica.com; operated by Creative Production & Training Centre Ltd (CPTC); local cable channel; regional cultural, educational and historical programming; CEO Dr HOPETON DUNN.

CVM Television: 69 Constant Sprint Rd, Kingston 10; tel. 931-9400; fax 931-9417; e-mail wsmith@cvmtv.com; internet www.cvmtv.com; Pres. and CEO DAVID MCBEAN.

Love Television: Kingston; internet www.love101.org; f. 1997; religious programming; owned by National Religious Media Ltd.

Television Jamaica Limited (TVJ): 32 Lyndhurst Rd, Kingston 5; tel. 926-1100; fax 929-1029; e-mail tvjadmin@cwjamaica.com; internet www.televisionjamaica.com; f. 1959 as Jamaica Broadcasting Corpn; privatized 1997, name changed as above; subsidiary of RJR Communications Group; island-wide VHF transmission 24 hrs a day.

Finance

(cap. = capital; res = reserves; dep. = deposits; m. = million; brs = branches; amounts in Jamaican dollars)

BANKING
Central Bank

Bank of Jamaica: Nethersole Pl., POB 621, Kingston; tel. 922-0750; fax 922-0854; e-mail info@boj.org.jm; internet www.boj.org.jm; f. 1960; cap. 4.0m., res 3,004.2m., dep. 187,526.2m. (Dec. 2005); Gov. DERICK MILTON LATIBEAUDIÈRE.

Commercial Banks

Bank of Nova Scotia Jamaica Ltd (Canada): Scotiabank Centre Bldg, cnr Duke and Port Royal Sts, POB 709, Kingston; tel. 922-1000; fax 924-9294; internet www.scotiabank.com.jm; f. 1967; cap. 2,927.2m., res 9,509.7m., dep. 120,490.1m. (Oct. 2006); Chair. R. H. PITFIELD; Man. Dir WILLIAM E. CLARKE; 35 brs.

Citimerchant Bank Ltd: 63–67 Knutsford Blvd, POB 286, Kingston 5; tel. 926-3270; fax 929-3745; internet www.citibank.com/jamaica; owned by Citifinance Ltd; cap. 25.7m., res 128.4m., dep. 87.2m. (Dec. 2003); Vice-Pres EVA LEWIS, PETER MOSES.

FirstCaribbean International Bank (Jamaica) Ltd (Canada): 78 Halfway Tree Rd, POB 762, Kingston 10; tel. 929-9310; fax 926-

JAMAICA

7751; internet www.firstcaribbeanbank.com; 91.5% owned by CIBC Investments (Cayman) Ltd (CICL—Cayman Islands-based subsidiary of CIBC, Canada) (Barbados); cap. and res 4,144.4m., dep. 27,028.8m. (Oct. 2006); Chair. MICHAEL MANSOOR; Man. RAYMOND CAMPBELL; 12 brs.

National Commercial Bank Jamaica Ltd: 'The Atrium', 32 Trafalgar Rd, POB 88, Kingston 10; tel. 929-9050; fax 929-8399; internet www.jncb.com; f. 1977; merged with Mutual Security Bank in 1996; cap. 2,466.8m., res 13,167.5m., dep. 182,710.4m. (Sept. 2006); Chair. MICHAEL LEE-CHIN; Man. Dir PATRICK HYLTON; 37 brs.

RBTT Bank Jamaica Ltd: 17 Dominica Dr., Kingston 5; tel. 960-2340; fax 960-2332; e-mail rbtt@cwjamaica.com; internet www.rbtt.com; f. 1993 as Jamaica Citizens Bank Ltd; name changed to Union Bank of Jamaica Ltd; acquired by Royal Bank of Trinidad and Tobago in 2001 and name changed as above; Chair. Dr OWEN JEFFERSON; Man. Dir MICHAEL E. A. WRIGHT; 23 brs.

Development Banks

Development Bank of Jamaica Ltd: 11A–15 Oxford Rd, POB 466, Kingston 5; tel. 929-6124-7; fax 929-6055; e-mail dbank@cwjamaica.com; f. 2000 following merger of Agricultural Credit Bank of Jamaica Ltd and the National Devt Bank of Jamaica Ltd; provides funds for medium- and long-term devt-orientated projects in the agricultural, tourism, industrial, manufacturing and services sectors through financial intermediaries; Man. Dir MILVERTON REYNOLDS.

Jamaica Mortgage Bank: 33 Tobago Ave, POB 950, Kingston 5; tel. 929-6350; fax 968-5428; e-mail jmb@cwjamaica.com; internet www.jamaicamortgagebank.com; f. 1971 by the Jamaican Govt and the US Agency for Int. Devt; govt-owned statutory org. since 1973; intended to function primarily as a secondary market facility for home mortgages and to mobilize long-term funds for housing devts in Jamaica; also insures home mortgage loans made by approved financial institutions, thus transferring risk of default on a loan to the Govt; Chair. GEORGE THOMAS; Gen. Man. PATRICK THELWALL.

Pan Caribbean Financial Services: 60 Knutsford Blvd, Kingston 5; tel. 929-5583; fax 926-4385; e-mail options@gopancaribbean.com; internet www.gopancaribbean.com; fmrly Trafalgar Development Bank, name changed as above in Dec. 2002; Chair. RICHARD O. BYLES; Pres. DONOVAN H. PERKINS.

Other Banks

National Export-Import Bank of Jamaica Ltd: 11 Oxford Rd, Kingston 5; tel. 922-9690; fax 960-5956; e-mail info@eximbankjacom; internet www.eximbankja.com; f. 1986; govt-owned; replaced Jamaica Export Credit Insurance Corpn; finances import and export of goods and services; Chair. GARY CRAIG 'BUTCH' HENDRICKSON; Man. Dir PAMELLA McLEAN.

National Investment Bank of Jamaica Ltd: 11 Oxford Rd, POB 889, Kingston 5; tel. 960-9691; fax 920-0379; e-mail info@nibj.com; internet www.nibj.com; Chair. AUBYN HILL; Sec. JENNIFER CAMPBELL.

Banking Association

Jamaica Bankers' Association: PSOJ Bldg, 39 Hope Rd, POB 1079, Kingston 10; tel. 927-6238; fax 927-5137; e-mail jbainfo@jba.org.jm; internet www.jba.org.jm; f. 1973; Pres. PATRICK HYLTON.

STOCK EXCHANGE

Jamaica Stock Exchange Ltd: 40 Harbour St, POB 1084, Kingston; tel. 967-3271; fax 922-6966; internet www.jamstockex.com; f. 1968; 55 listed cos (2008); Chair. CURTIS MARTIN; Gen. Man. MARLENE STREET-FORREST.

INSURANCE

Financial Services Commission: 39–43 Barbados Ave, Kingston 5; tel. 906-3010; fax 906-3018; e-mail inquiry@fscjamaica.org; internet www.fscjamaica.org; f. 2001; succeeded the Office of the Superintendent of Insurance; regulatory body; Exec. Dir BRIAN WYNTER.

Jamaica Association of General Insurance Companies: 3–3A Richmond Ave, Kingston 10; tel. 929-8404; e-mail jagic@cwjamaica.com; internet www.jagiconline.com/index.htm; Man. GLORIA M. GRANT; Chair. LESLIE CHUNG.

Principal Companies

British Caribbean Insurance Co Ltd: 36 Duke St, POB 170, Kingston; tel. 922-1260; fax 922-4475; e-mail bricar@cwjamaica.com; internet www.bcionline.com; f. 1962; general insurance; Man. Dir LESLIE W. CHUNG.

General Accident Insurance Co Jamaica Ltd: 58 Half Way Tree Rd, Kingston 10; tel. 929-8451; fax 929-1074; e-mail genac@cwjamaica.com; internet www.genac.com; f. 1981; Gen. Man. SHARON E. DONALDSON.

Directory

Globe Insurance Co of Jamaica Ltd: 19 Dominica Dr., POB 401, Kingston 5; tel. 926-3720; fax 929-2727; e-mail info@globeins.com; internet www.globeins.com; f. 1963; subsidiary of Lascelles deMercado Group; Man. Dir EVAN THWAITES.

Guardian Life: 12 Trafalgar Rd, Kingston 5; tel. 978-8815; fax 978-4225; e-mail guardian@ghl.com.jm; internet www.guardianlife.com.jm; subsidiary of Guardian Holdings (Trinidad and Tobago); pension and life policies; Pres. and CEO EARL MOORE.

Insurance Co of the West Indies Ltd (ICWI): 2 St Lucia Ave, POB 306, Kingston 5; tel. 926-9040; fax 929-6641; e-mail direct@icwi.net; internet www.icwi.net; Chair. and CEO DENNIS LALOR.

Jamaica General Insurance Co Ltd: 9 Duke St, POB 408, Kingston; tel. 922-6420; fax 922-2073; acquired by Lascelles deMercado Group in 2003.

Life of Jamaica Ltd: 28–48 Barbados Ave, Kingston 5; tel. 960-8920; fax 960-1927; internet www.life-of-ja.com; f. 1970; 76% owned by Sagicor Group (Barbados—fmrly Barbados Mutual Life Assurance Co); merged with Island Life Insurance Co Ltd in 2001; Chair. DODRIDGE D. MILLER; Pres. and CEO RICHARD O. BYLES.

NEM Insurance Co (Jamaica) Ltd: NEM House, 9 King St, Kingston; tel. 922-1460; fax 922-4045; e-mail info@nemjam.com; internet www.nemjam.com; fmrly the National Employers' Mutual General Insurance Asscn; Chair. GEORGE MAGNUS.

Trade and Industry

GOVERNMENT AGENCY

Jamaica Information Service (JIS): 58A Half Way Tree Rd, POB 2222, Kingston 10; tel. 926-3740; fax 929-6727; e-mail edit@jis.gov.jm; internet www.jis.gov.jm; f. 1963; information agency for govt policies and programmes, ministries and public-sector agencies; CEO HUNTLEY MEDLEY.

DEVELOPMENT ORGANIZATIONS

Agricultural Development Corpn (ADC) Group of Companies: Mais House, Hope Rd, POB 552, Kingston; tel. 977-4412; fax 977-4411; f. 1989; manages and develops breeds of cattle, provides warehousing, cold storage, offices and information for exporters and distributors of non-traditional crops and ensures the proper utilization of agricultural lands under its control; Chair. DONOVAN STANBERRY (acting); Gen. Man. LENNIE MORGAN.

Jamaica Promotions Corpn (JAMPRO): 18 Trafalgar Rd, Kingston 10; tel. 978-7755; fax 946-0090; e-mail jampro@investjamaica.com; internet www.investjamaica.com; f. 1988 by merger of Jamaica Industrial Development Corpn, Jamaica National Export Corpn and Jamaica Investment Promotion Ltd; trade and investment promotion agency; Pres. SANCIA BENNETT-TEMPLER (acting); Chair. PETER BUNTING.

Planning Institute of Jamaica: 10–16 Grenada Way, Kingston 5; tel. 906-4463; fax 906-5011; e-mail doccen@mail.colis.com; internet www.pioj.gov.jm; f. 1955 as the Central Planning Unit; adopted current name in 1984; formulates policy on and monitors performance in the fields of the economy and social, environmental and trade issues; publishing and analysis of social and economic performance data; Dir-Gen. Dr WESLEY HUGHES.

Urban Development Corpn: The Office Centre, 8th Floor, 12 Ocean Blvd, Kingston; tel. 922-8310; fax 922-9326; e-mail info@udcja.com; internet www.udcja.com; f. 1968; responsibility for urban renewal and devt within designated areas; Chair. LOUIS WILLIAMS; Gen. Man. JOY DOUGLAS.

CHAMBERS OF COMMERCE

American Chamber of Commerce of Jamaica: The Jamaica Pegasus, 81 Knutsford Blvd, Kingston 5; tel. 929-7866; fax 929-8597; e-mail amcham@cwjamaica.com; internet www.amchamjamaica.org; f. 1986; affiliated to the Chamber of Commerce of the USA; Exec. Dir BECKY STOCKHAUSEN.

Jamaica Chamber of Commerce: UDC Bldg, Shops 13–15, 12 Ocean Blvd, Kingston 10; tel. 922-0150-1; fax 924-9056; e-mail jamcham@cwjamaica.com; internet www.jamaicachamber.org.jm; f. 1779; Pres. FRANCIS KENNEDY (acting); 450 mems.

INDUSTRIAL AND TRADE ASSOCIATIONS

Cocoa Industry Board: Marcus Garvey Dr., POB 1039, Kingston 15; tel. 923-6411; fax 923-5837; e-mail cocoajam@cwjamaica.com; f. 1957; has statutory powers to regulate and develop the industry; owns and operates 4 central fermentaries; Chair. JOSEPH SUAH; Man. and Sec. NAUBURN NELSON.

Coconut Industry Board: 18 Waterloo Rd, Kingston 10; tel. 926-1770; fax 968-1360; e-mail cocindbrd@cwjamaica.com; internet www

JAMAICA

.j-cib.gov.jm; f. 1945; 9 mems; Chair. Dr RICHARD JONES; Research Dir BASIL BEEN.

Coffee Industry Board: Marcus Garvey Dr., POB 508, Kingston 15; tel. 923-5850; fax 923-7587; e-mail coffeeboard@jamaicancoffee.gov.jm; internet www.jamaicancoffee.gov.jm; f. 1950; 9 mems; has wide statutory powers to regulate and develop the industry; Chair. RICHARD DOWNER.

Jamaica Bauxite Institute: Hope Gardens, POB 355, Kingston 6; tel. 927-2073; fax 927-1159; f. 1975; adviser to the Govt in the negotiation of agreements, consultancy services to clients in the bauxite/alumina and related industries, laboratory services for mineral and soil-related services, Pilot Plant services for materials and equipment testing, research and devt; Chair. CARLTON DAVIS; Gen. Man. PARRIS LYEW-AYEE.

Jamaica Export Trading Co Ltd (JETCO): 188 Spanish Town Rd, AMC Complex, Kingston 11; tel. 937-1798; fax 937-6547; e-mail jetcoja@mail.infochan.com; internet www.exportjamaica.org/jetco; f. 1977; export trading in non-traditional products, incl. spices, fresh produce, furniture, garments, processed foods, minerals, etc.; Man. Dir HERNAL L. HAMILTON.

Sugar Industry Authority: 5 Trevennion Park Rd, POB 127, Kingston 5; tel. 926-5930; fax 926-6149; e-mail sia@cwjamaica.com; internet www.jamaicasugar.org; f. 1970; statutory body under portfolio of Ministry of Agriculture and Land; responsible for regulation and control of sugar industry and sugar marketing; conducts research through Sugar Industry Research Institute; Exec. Chair. DERICK HEAVEN.

Trade Board: 107 Constant Spring Rd, Kingston 10; tel. 969-3228; fax 925-6513; e-mail tboard@cwjamaica.com; internet www.tradeboard.gov.jm; Trade Admin. JEAN MORGAN.

EMPLOYERS' ORGANIZATIONS

All-Island Banana Growers' Association Ltd: Banana Industry Bldg, 10 South Ave, Kingston 4; tel. 922-5492; fax 922-5497; f. 1946; 1,500 mems (1997); Chair. A. A. POTTINGER; Sec. I. CHANG.

All-Island Jamaica Cane Farmers' Association (AIJCFA): 4 North Ave, Kingston Gardens, Kingston 4; tel. 922-3010; fax 922-2077; e-mail allcane@cwjamaica.com; f. 1941; registered cane farmers; 27,000 mems; Pres. ALAN RICKARDS; Gen. Man. KARL JAMES.

Banana Export Co (BECO): 1A Braemar Ave, Kingston 10; tel. 978-8762; fax 978-6096; e-mail beco@cwjamaica.com; f. 1985 to replace Banana Co of Jamaica; oversees the devt of the banana industry; Chair. Dr MARSHALL MCGOWAN HALL; Man. KEDRICK RANDAL.

Citrus Growers' Association Ltd: Bog Walk, Linstead; tel. 922-8230; f. 1944; 13,000 mems; Chair. C. L. BENT.

Jamaica Association of Sugar Technologists: c/o Sugar Industry Research Institute, Kendal Rd, Mandeville; tel. 962-2241; fax 962-1288; f. 1936; 275 mems; Chair. KARL JAMES; Pres. GILBERT THORNE.

Jamaica Exporters' Association (JEA): 39 Hope Rd, Kingston 10; tel. 927-6238; fax 927-5137; e-mail infojea@exportja.org; internet www.exportjamaica.org; Pres. Dr ANDRÉ GORDON; Exec. Dir PAULINE GRAY.

Jamaica Gasoline Retailers' Association (JGRA): 38C Spring Rd, Kingston 11; tel. 926-4463; Pres. TREVOR HEAVEN.

Jamaica Livestock Association: Newport East, POB 36, Kingston; tel. 922-7130; fax 922-8934; e-mail jlapurch@cwjamaica.com; internet www.jlaltd.com; f. 1941; 7,584 mems; Chair. Dr JOHN MASTERTON; Man. Dir and CEO HENRY J. RAINFORD.

Jamaica Manufacturers' Association Ltd: 85A Duke St, Kingston; tel. 922-8880; fax 922-9205; e-mail jma@cwjamaica.com; internet www.jma.com.jm; f. 1947; 400 mems; Pres. OMAR AZAN.

Jamaica Producers' Group Ltd: 6A Oxford Rd, POB 237, Kingston 5; tel. 926-3503; fax 929-3636; e-mail cosecretary@jpjamaica.com; internet www.jpjamaica.com; f. 1929; fmrly Jamaica Banana Producers' Asscn; Chair. C. H. JOHNSTON; Man. Dir Dr MARSHALL HALL.

Private Sector Organization of Jamaica (PSOJ): 39 Hope Rd, POB 236, Kingston 10; tel. 927-6238; fax 927-5137; e-mail psojinfo@psoj.org; internet www.psoj.org; federative body of private business individuals, cos and asscns; Pres. CHRIS ZACCA.

Shipping Association of Jamaica: see Transport—Shipping.

Small Businesses' Association of Jamaica (SBAJ): 2 Trafalgar Rd, Kingston 5; tel. 927-7071; fax 978-2738; e-mail sbaj@anbell.net; internet www.sbaj.org.jm; Chair. ADOLPH BROWN; Man. ALBERT HUIE.

Sugar Manufacturing Corpn of Jamaica Ltd: 5 Trevennion Park Rd, Kingston 5; tel. 926-5930; fax 926-6149; est. to represent the sugar manufacturers in Jamaica; deals with all aspects of the sugar industry and its by-products; provides liaison between the Govt, the Sugar Industry Authority and the All-Island Jamaica Cane Farmers' Asscn; 9 mems; Gen. Man. DERYCK T. BROWN.

UTILITIES

Regulatory Authority

Office of Utilities Regulation (OUR): PCJ Resource Centre, 3rd Floor, 36 Trafalgar Rd, Kingston 10; tel. 929-6672; fax 929-3635; e-mail office@our.org.jm; internet www.our.org.jm; f. 1995; regulates provision of services in the following sectors: water, electricity, telecommunications, public passenger transportation, sewerage; Dir-Gen. J. PAUL MORGAN.

Electricity

Jamaica Energy Partners (JEP): Old Harbour, St Catherine; bought by Basic Energy (Dominican Republic) in 2008; sells electricity to JPSCo; Gen. Man. WAYNE MCKENZIE.

Jamaica Public Service Co (JPSCo): Dominion Life Bldg, 6 Knutsford Blvd, POB 54, Kingston 5; tel. 926-3190; fax 968-5341; e-mail media@jpsco.com; internet www.jpsco.com; responsible for the generation and supply of electricity to the island; 80% sold to Mirant Corpn (USA) in March 2001; Marubeni (Japan) acquired Mirant Corpn's 80% stake in JPSCo in July 2007; the JPSCo operating licence was subsequently extended by six years, to expire in 2027; Pres. and CEO DAMIAN OBIGLIO.

Water

National Water Commission: LOJ Centre, 28–48 Barbados Ave, Kingston 5; tel. 929-5430; fax 929-1329; e-mail pr@nwc.com.jm; internet www.nwcjamaica.com; f. 1980; statutory body; provides potable water and waste water services; Chair. RICHARD O. BYLES.

Water Resources Authority: Hope Gardens, POB 91, Kingston 7; tel. 927-0077; fax 977-0179; e-mail commander@cwjamaica.com; internet www.wra-ja.org; f. 1996; manages, protects and controls allocation and use of water supplies; Man. Dir BASIL FERNANDEZ.

TRADE UNIONS

Bustamante Industrial Trade Union (BITU): 98 Duke St, Kingston; tel. 922-2443; fax 967-0120; e-mail bitu@cwjamaica.com; f. 1938; Pres. RUDY SPENCER; Gen. Sec. GEORGE FYFFE; 60,000 mems.

Jamaica Confederation of Trade Unions (JCTU): 1A Hope Blvd, Kingston 6; tel. 977-5170; fax 977-4575; e-mail jctu@cwjamaica.com; Pres. DWIGHT NELSON; Sec.-Gen. LLOYD GOODLEIGH; Exec. Dir LILIETH HARRIS.

National Workers' Union of Jamaica (NWU): 130–132 East St, POB 344, Kingston 16; tel. 922-1150; e-mail nwyou@toj.com; f. 1952; affiliated to the International Trade Union Confederation; Pres. CLIVE DOBSON; Gen. Sec. LLOYD GOODLEIGH; 10,000 mems.

Trades Union Congress of Jamaica: 25 Sutton St, POB 19, Kingston; tel. 922-5313; fax 922-5468; affiliated to the Caribbean Congress of Labour and the International Trade Union Confederation; Pres. EDWARD SMITH; Gen. Sec. HOPETON CRAVEN; 20,000 mems.

Principal Independent Unions

Caribbean Union of Teachers: 97 Church St, Kingston; tel. 922-1385; fax 922-3257; e-mail jta@cwjamaica.com; Pres. BYRON FARQUHARSON; Gen. Sec. Dr ADOLPH CAMERON.

Jamaica Association of Local Government Officers: 15A Old Hope Rd, Kingston 5; tel. 929-5123; fax 960-4403; e-mail jalgo@cwjamaica.com; Pres. STANLEY THOMAS; Gen. Sec. HELENE DAVIS-WHITE.

Jamaica Civil Service Association: 10 Caledonia Ave, Kingston 5; tel. 968-7087; fax 926-2042; e-mail jacisera@cwjamaica.com; Pres. WAYNE JONES; Sec. DENHAM WHILBY.

Jamaica Federation of Musicians and Affiliated Artistes Union: 5 Balmoral Ave, Kingston 10; tel. 926-8029; fax 929-0485; e-mail jafedmusic@cwjamaica.com; internet jafedmusic.tripod.com; f. 1958; Pres. DESMOND YOUNG; Sec. CHARMAINE BOWMAN; 1,500 mems.

Jamaica Teachers' Association: 97B Church St, Kingston; tel. 922-1385-7; fax 922-3257; e-mail jta@cwjamaica.com; internet www.jamaicateachers.org.jm; Pres. HOPETON HENRY; Sec.-Gen. Dr ADOLPH CAMERON.

Jamaica Union of Public Officers and Public Employees: 4 Northend Pl., Kingston 10; tel. 929-1354; Pres. FITZROY BRYAN; Gen. Sec. NICKELLOH MARTIN.

Jamaica Workers' Union: 3 West Ave, Kingston 4; tel. 922-3222; fax 967-3128; Pres. CLIFTON BROWN; Gen. Sec. MICHAEL NEWTON.

Union of Schools, Agricultural and Allied Workers (USAAW): 2 Wildman St, Kingston; tel. 967-2970; f. 1978; Pres. DEVON BROWN; Gen. Sec. KEITH COMRIE.

JAMAICA

Union of Technical, Administrative and Supervisory Personnel: 108 Church St, Kingston; tel. 922-2086; Pres. ANTHONY DAWKINS; Gen. Sec. REG ENNIS.

United Portworkers' and Seamen's Union (UPWU): Kingston.

United Union of Jamaica: 35A Lynhurst Rd, Kingston; tel. 960-4206; Pres. JAMES FRANCIS; Gen. Sec. WILLIAM HASFAL.

University and Allied Workers' Union (UAWU): 50 Lady Musgrave Rd, Kingston; tel. 927-7968; fax 927-9931; e-mail jacisera@cwjamaica.com; affiliated to the WPJ; Pres. Prof. TREVOR MUNROE; Gen. Sec. LAMBERT BROWN.

There are also some 30 associations registered as trade unions.

Transport

RAILWAYS

There are about 339 km of railway, all standard gauge, in Jamaica. The government-subsidized Jamaica Railway Corpn operated 207 km of the track until freight and passenger services were suspended in 1992, as falling revenues failed to meet maintenance costs. Negotiations towards the privatization of the Jamaica Railway Corpn between the Government and the Indian/Canadian consortium Railtech broke down in late 2003. In early 2005 the Government signed a memorandum of understanding with China National Machinery and Equipment Corpn for the possible reconstruction of the railway system between Kingston, Spanish Town and May Pen, including the provision of passengers coaches and engines.

Jamaica Railway Corpn (JRC): 142 Barry St, POB 489, Kingston; tel. 922-6443; fax 922-4539; internet www.mtw.gov.jm/dep_agencies/ja_rail.aspx; f. 1845 as Jamaica Railway Co, the earliest British colonial railway; transferred to JRC in 1960; govt-owned, but autonomous, statutory corpn until 1990, when it was partly leased to Alcan Jamaica Co Ltd (subsequently West Indies Alumina Co) as the first stage of a privatization scheme; 215 km of railway; Gen. Man. OWEN CROOKS.

Jamalco (Alcoa Minerals of Jamaica): May Pen PO; tel. 986-2561; fax 986-2026; internet www.alcoa.com/jamaica/en/home.asp; 43 km of standard-gauge railway; transport of bauxite; CEO ALAIN BELDA; Man. DAHLIA ALERT (Railroad Operations and Maintenance).

ROADS

Jamaica has a good network of tar-surfaced and metalled motoring roads. According to statistics published by the Ministry of Housing, Water, Transport and Works in 2006, there were 20,963 km of roads in Jamaica. In 2004 an estimated 70.1% of roads were paved, according to the International Road Federation. In 2001 a consortium of two British companies, Kier International and Mabey & Johnson, was awarded a contract to supply the materials for and construct six road bridges in Kingston and Montego Bay, and a further 20 bridges in rural areas. In the same year the Inter-American Development Bank approved a US $24.5m. loan to improve road maintenance.

Transport Authority: 119 Maxfield Ave, Kingston 10; tel. 929-4642; e-mail transauth@infochan.com; internet www.mhtw.gov.jm/dep_agencies/transport_authority.aspx; regulatory body; administers the licensing of public and commercial vehicles; assumed functions formerly executed by the Licensing Authority and Public Passenger Transport (Corporate and Rural areas) Boards of Control in 1987; Chair. HENSLEY WILLIAMS; Man. Dir JOAN FLETCHER.

SHIPPING

The principal ports are Kingston, Montego Bay and Port Antonio. The port at Kingston has four container berths, and is a major transhipment terminal for the Caribbean area. Jamaica has interests in the multinational shipping line WISCO (West Indies Shipping Corpn—based in Trinidad and Tobago). Services are also provided by most major foreign lines serving the region. In January 2004 a US $35m. plan to expand Kingston's container-handling capacity by 25% was announced; the fifth phase of development, at an estimated cost of US $240m., was approaching completion in early 2008 and would more than double the port's handling capacity. Further plans for the expansion of Jamaica's port facilities, to include the construction of three additional berths and a second terminal at Montego Bay, were scheduled for completion by August 2009.

Port Authority of Jamaica: 15–17 Duke St, Kingston; tel. 922-0290; fax 924-9437; e-mail paj@portjam.com; internet www.portjam.com; f. 1966; Govt's principal maritime agency; responsible for monitoring and regulating the navigation of all vessels berthing at Jamaican ports, for regulating the tariffs on public wharves, and for the devt of industrial free zones in Jamaica; Pres. and Chair. NOEL A. HYLTON.

Kingston Free Zone Co Ltd: 27 Shannon Dr., POB 1025, Kingston 15; tel. 923-6021; fax 923-6023; e-mail blee@portjam.com; internet www.pajfz.com; f. 1976; subsidiary of Port Authority of Jamaica; management and promotion of an export-orientated industrial free trade zone for cos from various countries; Gen. Man. KARLA HUIE.

Montego Bay Free Zone: POB 1377, Montego Bay; tel. 979-8696-8; fax 979-8088; e-mail clients-mbfz@jadigiport.com; internet www.pajfz.com; Gen. Man. GLORIA HENRY.

Shipping Association of Jamaica: 4 Fourth Ave, Newport West, POB 1050, Kingston 15; tel. 923-3491; fax 923-3421; e-mail saj@jamports.com; internet www.jamports.com; f. 1939; 73 mems; regulates the supply and management of stevedoring labour in Kingston; represents mems in negotiations with govt and trade bodies; Pres. MICHAEL GEORGE BERNARD; Gen. Man. TREVOR RILEY.

Principal Shipping Company

Jamaica Freight and Shipping Co Ltd (JFS): 80–82 Second St, Port Bustamante, POB 167, Kingston 13; tel. 923-9271; fax 923-4091; e-mail jfs@jashipco.com; internet www.jashipco.com; f. 1976; liner and port agents, stevedoring services; Exec. Chair. CHARLES JOHNSTON; Man. Dir MICHAEL BERNARD.

CIVIL AVIATION

There are two international airports linking Jamaica with North America, Europe, and other Caribbean islands. The Norman Manley International Airport is situated 22.5 km outside Kingston. The Donald Sangster International Airport is 5 km from Montego Bay. A J $800m. programme to expand and improve the latter was well advanced by early 2007, the second phase having commenced ahead of schedule in December 2005, with completion anticipated by mid-2008.

Airports Authority of Jamaica: Norman Manley International Airport, Palisadoes; tel. 924-8452; fax 924-8419; e-mail aaj@cwjamaica.com; internet www.aaj.com.jm; Chair. DENNIS E. MORRISON; Pres. EARL A. RICHARDS.

Civil Aviation Authority: 4 Winchester Rd, POB 8998, Kingston 10; tel. 960-3948; fax 920-0194; e-mail jcivav@jcaa.gov.jm; internet www.jcaa.gov.jm; f. 1996; Dir-Gen. Col TORRANCE LEWIS.

Air Jamaica Ltd: 72–76 Harbour St, Kingston; tel. 922-3460; fax 967-3125; internet www.airjamaica.com; f. 1968; privatized in 1994, reacquired by Govt in 2004; plans for reprivatization by 2009 announced in Nov. 2007; services within the Caribbean and to Canada (in asscn with Air Canada), the USA and the United Kingdom; scheduled to withdraw services to the United Kingdom in Oct. 2007 following transferral of market share to Virgin Atlantic; Chair. SHIRLEY WILLIAMS; Pres. and CEO WILLIAM B. RODGERS (acting).

Air Negril: Montego Bay; tel. 940-7747; fax 940-6491; e-mail negriljeff@yahoo.com; internet caribbean-travel.com/airnegril; domestic charter services.

Spirit Airlines: Kingston; internet www.spiritair.com; daily flights to the USA, the Bahamas, and other Caribbean destinations, from Kingston and Montego Bay; Pres. and CEO BEN BALDANZA; Sr Vice-Pres. BARRY BIFFLE.

Tourism

Tourists, mainly from the USA, visit Jamaica for its beaches, mountains, historic buildings and cultural heritage. In 2007 there were 1,700,785 visitors (excluding cruise-ship passengers). In that year there were some 27,231 rooms in all forms of tourist accommodation. In 2005 tourism receipts were estimated to be US $1,783m.

Jamaica Hotel and Tourist Association (JHTA): 2 Ardenne Rd, Kingston 10; tel. 926-3635-6; fax 929-1054; e-mail info@jhta.org; internet www.jhta.org; f. 1961; trade asscn for hoteliers and other cos involved in Jamaican tourism; Pres. WAYNE CUMMINGS; Exec. Dir CAMILLE NEEDHAM.

Jamaica Tourist Board (JTB): 64 Knutsford Blvd, Kingston 5; tel. 929-9200; fax 929-9375; e-mail info@visitjamaica.com; internet www.visitjamaica.com; f. 1955; a statutory body set up by the Govt to promote all aspects of the tourism industry; Chair. JOHN LYNCH; Dir of Tourism BASIL H. SMITH.

JAPAN

Introductory Survey

Location, Climate, Language, Religion, Flag, Capital

Japan lies in eastern Asia and comprises a curved chain of more than 3,000 islands. Four large islands, named (from north to south) Hokkaido, Honshu, Shikoku and Kyushu, account for about 98% of the land area. Hokkaido lies just to the south of Sakhalin, a large Russian island, and about 1,300 km (800 miles) east of Russia's mainland port of Vladivostok. Southern Japan is about 150 km (93 miles) east of the Republic of Korea (South Korea). Although summers are temperate everywhere, the climate in winter varies sharply from cold in the north to mild in the south. Temperatures in Tokyo range from −6°C (21°F) to 30°C (86°F). Typhoons and heavy rains are common in summer. The language is Japanese. The major religions are Shintoism and Buddhism, and there is a Christian minority. The national flag (proportions 7 by 10) is white, with a red disc (a sun without rays) in the centre. The capital is Tokyo.

Recent History

Following Japan's defeat in the Second World War, Japanese forces surrendered in August 1945. Japan signed an armistice in September, and the country was placed under US military occupation. A new democratic Constitution, which took effect from May 1947, renounced war and abandoned the doctrine of the Emperor's divinity. Following the peace treaty of September 1951, Japan regained its independence on 28 April 1952, although it was not until 1972 that the last of the US-administered outer islands were returned to Japanese sovereignty.

In November 1955 rival conservative groups merged to form the Liberal-Democratic Party (LDP). Nobusuke Kishi, who became Prime Minister in February 1957, was succeeded by Hayato Ikeda in July 1960. Ikeda was replaced by Eisaku Sato in November 1964. Sato remained in office until July 1972, when he was succeeded by Kakuei Tanaka.

Tanaka's premiership was beset by problems, leading to his replacement by Takeo Miki in December 1974. Tanaka was subsequently accused of accepting bribes from the Marubeni Corporation, and he was arrested in July 1976. The LDP lost its overall majority in the House of Representatives (the lower house of the Diet) at a general election held in December 1976. Miki resigned and was succeeded by Takeo Fukuda. However, Masayoshi Ohira defeated Fukuda in the LDP presidential election of November 1978, and replaced him as Prime Minister in December. Ohira was unable to win a majority in the lower house at elections in October 1979. In May 1980 the Government was defeated in a motion of no confidence, forcing the dissolution of the lower house. Ohira died before the elections in June, when the LDP won 284 of the 511 seats. In July Zenko Suzuki, a compromise candidate, was elected President of the LDP, and subsequently appointed Prime Minister. The growing factionalism of the LDP and the worsening economic crisis prompted Suzuki's resignation as Prime Minister and LDP President in October 1982. He was succeeded by Yasuhiro Nakasone.

At elections in June 1983 for one-half of the seats in the House of Councillors (the upper house of the Diet), a new electoral system was used. Of the 126 contested seats, 50 were filled on the basis of proportional representation. As a result, two small parties entered the House of Councillors for the first time. The LDP increased its strength from 134 to 137 members in the 252-seat chamber. This result was seen as an endorsement of Nakasone's policies of increased expenditure on defence, closer ties with the USA and greater Japanese involvement in international affairs.

In October 1983 former Prime Minister Tanaka was found guilty of accepting bribes. However, Tanaka's refusal to relinquish his parliamentary seat prompted an opposition-led boycott of the Diet, forcing Nakasone to call a premature general election in December 1983. The Komeito (Clean Government Party), the Democratic Socialist Party (DSP) and the Japan Socialist Party (JSP) gained seats, at the expense of the Communists and the New Liberal Club (NLC). The LDP, which had performed badly in the election, formed a coalition with the NLC (which had split from the LDP over the Tanaka affair in 1976) and several independents.

Nakasone called another premature general election for July 1986, which coincided with elections for one-half of the seats in the House of Councillors. In the election to the House of Representatives, the LDP won a record 304 of the 512 seats. The increased majority enabled the LDP to dispense with its coalition partner, the NLC (which disbanded in August and rejoined the LDP). In September the leaders of the LDP agreed to alter by-laws to allow party presidents one-year extensions beyond the normal limit of two terms of two years each. Nakasone was thus able to retain the posts of President of the LDP and Prime Minister until October 1987.

In July 1987 the Secretary-General of the LDP, Noboru Takeshita, left the Tanaka faction, with 113 other members, and announced the formation of a major new grouping within the ruling party. In the same month Tanaka's political influence was further weakened when the Tokyo High Court upheld the decision, taken in 1983, declaring him guilty of accepting bribes. (In February 1995 this ruling was upheld by the Supreme Court.)

In October 1987 Nakasone nominated Takeshita as his successor. The Diet was convened and Takeshita was formally elected as Prime Minister in November. In the new Cabinet Takeshita maintained a balance among the five major factions of the LDP, retaining only two members of Nakasone's previous Cabinet, but appointing four members of the Nakasone faction to senior ministerial posts (including Nakasone's staunch ally, Sosuke Uno, as Minister of Foreign Affairs).

The implementation of a programme of tax reforms was one of the most important issues confronting Takeshita's Government. In June 1988 the proposed introduction of a new indirect tax (a general consumption tax, or a form of value-added tax) aroused widespread opposition. In the same month the Prime Minister and the LDP suffered a serious set-back when several leading figures in the party, including Nakasone, Kiichi Miyazawa and Takeshita himself, were alleged to have been indirectly involved in share-trading irregularities with the Recruit Cosmos Company. In November the House of Representatives approved proposals for tax reform (which constituted the most wide-ranging revision of the tax system for 40 years). Three cabinet ministers and the Chairman of the DSP were subsequently forced to resign, owing to their alleged involvement in the Recruit affair.

In January 1989 Emperor Hirohito, who had reigned since 1926, died after a long illness, thus ending the Showa era. He was succeeded by his son, Akihito, and the new era was named Heisei ('achievement of universal peace').

In April 1989, as the allegations against politicians widened to include charges of bribery and malpractice, Takeshita announced his resignation. He was subsequently found to have accepted donations worth more than 150m. yen from the Recruit organization. Takeshita nominated Sosuke Uno as his successor. Uno was elected Prime Minister by the Diet on 2 June; a new Cabinet was appointed on the same day. Uno thus became the first Japanese Prime Minister since the foundation of the LDP not to command his own political faction. In May, following an eight-month investigation into the Recruit affair undertaken by an LDP special committee, public prosecutors indicted 13 people. Nakasone resigned from the LDP, assuming responsibility for the scandal, but did not relinquish his seat in the Diet.

Within a few days of Uno's assumption of office, a Japanese magazine published allegations of sexual impropriety involving the Prime Minister, which precipitated demands for his resignation. Serious losses suffered by the LDP in Tokyo's municipal elections in July 1989 further discredited Uno. As a result of a considerable increase in support for the JSP, led by Takako Doi, the LDP lost its majority in the upper house for the first time in its history. Uno's offer to resign was accepted by the LDP, which in August chose the relatively unknown Toshiki Kaifu, a former Minister of Education, to be the party's President and the new Prime Minister. Although the House of Councillors' ballot rejected Kaifu as the new Prime Minister in favour of Takako Doi, the decision of the lower house was adopted, in accordance with stipulations embodied in the Constitution. This was the first time in 41 years that the two Houses of the Diet had disagreed over the choice of Prime Minister. In October Kaifu was re-elected as President of the LDP for a further two-year term.

At a general election held in February 1990, the LDP was returned to power with an unexpectedly large measure of support, securing 275 of the 512 seats in the lower house. In January 1991 the JSP changed its English name to the Social Democratic Party of Japan (SDPJ) and Makato Tanabe later replaced Takako Doi as Chairman of the party. In September senior LDP officials forced Kaifu to abandon proposals for electoral reform and the Takeshita faction of the LDP subsequently withdrew its support for the Prime Minister. Sponsored by the faction, the former Minister of Finance, Kiichi Miyazawa, was elected President of the LDP in October, and in November the Diet endorsed his appointment as Prime Minister. New allegations of involvement in the Recruit affair, publicized by the SDPJ in December 1991, seriously undermined Miyazawa's position.

In early 1992 public disgust at official corruption was registered at two prefectural by-elections to the upper house, when the LDP lost seats, which had previously been considered secure, to Rengo-no-kai (the political arm of RENGO, the trade union confederation). However, the anti-Government alliance that had supported Rengo-no-kai disintegrated in May over the issue of the authorization of Japanese involvement in UN peace-keeping operations. Members of the SDPJ attempted to obstruct the vote in the lower house by submitting their resignations *en masse*. The Speaker, however, ruled that these could not be accepted during the current Diet session. The successful passage through the Diet of the legislation on international peace-keeping improved the Government's standing, and in elections to the upper house in July the LDP won 69 of the 127 seats contested. The SDPJ, by contrast, lost 25 of its 46 seats; the Komeito increased its total strength from 20 to 24 seats, but Rengo-no-kai failed to win any seats, owing to the dissolution of the informal coalition it had facilitated between the SDPJ and the DSP. The Japan New Party (JNP), founded only two months prior to the election by LDP dissidents, secured four seats. A formal split within the Takeshita faction took place in December 1992. The new faction was to be led nominally by Tsutomu Hata, the Minister of Finance, although it was widely recognized that Ichiro Ozawa held the real power in the grouping.

Electoral reform was a major political issue in the first half of 1993. While the LDP favoured a single-member constituency system, the opposition parties proposed various forms of proportional representation. In June the lower house adopted a motion of no confidence against the Government, after the LDP refused to modify its reform proposals to meet opposition demands. Numerous LDP members opposed the Government or abstained. The Ozawa-Hata group, comprising 44 former LDP members, immediately established a new party, the Shinseito (Japan Renewal Party, JRP), in order to contest the forthcoming general election. Another new party, the New Party Sakigake, was also formed by LDP Diet members. In the election to the House of Representatives, held in July, the LDP won 223 of the 511 seats, and was thus 33 seats short of a majority. Miyazawa resigned as Prime Minister and a coalition Government was formed. On 6 August Morihiro Hosokawa, the leader of the JNP, was elected Prime Minister, defeating the new President of the LDP, Yohei Kono.

In November 1993 four items of electoral reform legislation were passed by a majority of 270 to 226 votes in the House of Representatives (they were opposed by the LDP). Although the reform bills were defeated in the upper house in January 2004, Hosokawa subsequently reached agreement with the LDP on modifications to the reform bills (see below).

Hosokawa resigned as Prime Minister in April 1994. Tsutomu Hata was subsequently appointed Prime Minister, at the head of a minority Government that excluded the SDPJ and the New Party Sakigake. Hata was obliged to resign in June, however, owing to his continued failure to command a viable majority in the Diet, and a new coalition of the SDPJ, the LDP and the New Party Sakigake took office. Tomiichi Murayama, the leader of the SDPJ, became Prime Minister, and Kono was appointed Deputy Prime Minister and Minister of Foreign Affairs.

In July 1994 Murayama recognized the constitutional right to the existence of Japan's Self-Defence Forces (SDF, the armed forces), thereby effectively contradicting official SDPJ policy on the issue. (The SDPJ amended its policy to accord with Murayama's statement in September.) In December nine opposition parties, including the JNP, the JRP, the DSP and the Komeito, amalgamated to form a new political party, the Shinshinto (New Frontier Party, NFP). A faction of Komeito remained outside the new party and was renamed Komei. Kaifu, the former LDP Prime Minister, was elected leader of the NFP; Ozawa was appointed Secretary-General.

The creation of the NFP was widely perceived to be a response to the approval by the Diet in November 1994 of the electoral reform bills first proposed in 1993, which appeared to favour larger political parties. Under the terms of the new law, the House of Representatives was to be reduced to 500 seats, comprising 300 single-seat constituencies and 200 seats determined by proportional representation; the proportional-representation base was to be divided into 11 regions, and a party would qualify for a proportional-representation seat if it received a minimum of 2% of the vote; donations amounting to 500,000 yen annually per private sector corporation to individual politicians were permitted, but this was to be phased out after five years; restrictions on corporate donations would be subsidized by the State; door-to-door campaigning was to be permitted and an independent body would draw up new electoral boundaries. In June 1995 the first distribution of public money to political parties took place.

In January 1995 a massive earthquake in the Kobe region caused thousands of deaths and serious infrastructural damage. The Government was severely criticized for the poor co-ordination of the relief operation. In March a poisonous gas, sarin, was released into the Tokyo underground railway system, killing 12 people and injuring more than 5,000. A religious sect, Aum Shinrikyo, was accused of perpetrating the attack. Following a further gas attack in Yokohama in April, a number of sect members were detained by the authorities. In June Shoko Asahara, the leader of Aum Shinrikyo, was indicted on a charge of murder. The trial of Asahara opened in April 1996. In September Asahara and two other members of the sect were instructed to pay some US \$7.3m. in compensation to victims of the Tokyo incident.

Participation in the elections to the House of Councillors, held in July 1995, was low. With one-half of the 252 seats being contested, the LDP won only 49 seats, the SDPJ 16 and the New Party Sakigake three, whereas the NFP, benefiting from the support of the Soka Gakkai religious organization, won 40 seats. In September Ryutaro Hashimoto, the Minister of International Trade and Industry, was elected leader of the LDP, after Yohei Kono announced that he would not seek re-election.

Conflict in the Diet escalated in 1995 over government plans to issue a resolution to commemorate the 50th anniversary of the ending of the Second World War. The resolution was to constitute an apology to countries whose citizens had suffered from the actions of the Japanese army during the war. The New Party Sakigake threatened to withdraw from the coalition if an apology were not made, while a group of 160 LDP Diet members objected to the definition of Japan as an aggressor. A resolution was finally passed in June, despite a boycott of the vote by the NFP.

In December 1995 Toshiki Kaifu was succeeded by Ichiro Ozawa as leader of the NFP. In January 1996 Tomiichi Murayama resigned as Prime Minister; he was, however, re-elected Chairman of the SDPJ. The LDP leader, Ryutaro Hashimoto, was elected Prime Minister on 11 January. A coalition Cabinet, largely dominated by the LDP, was formed.

In August 1996 Shoichi Ide and Hiroyuki Sonoda were elected Leader and Secretary-General, respectively, of the New Party Sakigake following the resignations of Masayoshi Takemura and Yukio Hatoyama. Hatoyama left the party and founded the Democratic Party of Japan (DPJ), with other dissident members of the New Party Sakigake and individual members of the SDPJ and NFP.

A general election was held in October 1996. The LDP won 239 of the 500 seats in the House of Representatives, while the NFP secured 156, the DPJ 52, the Japan Communist Party (JCP) 26, the SDPJ 15, and the New Party Sakigake two seats. In November Ryutaro Hashimoto was re-elected Prime Minister, and formed the first single-party Cabinet since 1993.

Soon after the election several government ministers and party leaders were implicated in various official corruption scandals. In December 1996 former Prime Minister Hata left the NFP and formed a new party, Taiyoto (Sun Party), together with 12 other dissident NFP members. In late December Takako Doi was formally appointed Chairwoman of the SDPJ (she had been acting Chairwoman since the dissolution of the House of Representatives in September).

In mid-1997 Hosokawa resigned from the NFP, reportedly owing to dissatisfaction with Ozawa's leadership. (In December Hosokawa formed a new party—From Five.) In addition, the NFP lost all of its seats in elections to the Tokyo Metropolitan Assembly, held in July. The LDP and the JCP, by contrast, increased their representation in the Assembly. By September the LDP had regained its majority in the House of Representatives, following a series of defections by members of the NFP. In December a much-reduced NFP was dissolved. Six new parties were founded by former NFP members, Ozawa and his supporters forming the Liberal Party (LP), and a significant political realignment thus took place. In January 1998 six opposition parties, including the DPJ, formed a parliamentary group, Minyuren, which constituted the largest opposition bloc in the Diet. In March the parties comprising Minyuren agreed on their integration into the DPJ, formally establishing a new DPJ, with Naoto Kan as its President, in the following month.

Meanwhile, during 1997 various circumstances, including continuing financial corruption, an increase in the rate of the unpopular consumption tax, a decrease in public expenditure and the collapse of several prominent financial institutions, together with the threat of further bankruptcies, contributed to the development of an economic crisis. The Government announced a series of measures designed to encourage economic growth, including a reduction in taxes and, in a major reversal of policy, the use of public funds to support the banking system. In January 1998 two senior officials from the Ministry of Finance were arrested on suspicion of accepting bribes from banks. The Minister of Finance, Hiroshi Mitsuzuka, resigned, accepting full moral responsibility for the affair. As more banks and other financial institutions became implicated in the bribery scandal, the central bank initiated an internal investigation into its own operations. In March the Governor resigned after a senior bank executive was arrested amid further allegations of bribery. Trials of those implicated in the financial scandals took place in 1998 and 1999. A number of financial deregulation measures took effect on 1 April 1998, as part of Japan's 'Big Bang' reform process. The economy continued to stagnate, however, and Hashimoto's administration was widely criticized for its slow reaction to the crisis. In June the SDPJ and the New Party Sakigake withdrew from their alliance with the ruling LDP.

The LDP performed poorly in elections for one-half of the seats in the House of Councillors in July 1998, retaining only 44 of its 61 seats contested, while the DPJ won 27 seats, increasing its representation to 47 seats, and the JCP became the third largest party in the upper house, taking 15 seats. Hashimoto resigned as Prime Minister and President of the LDP and was succeeded by Keizo Obuchi, hitherto Minister for Foreign Affairs. Obuchi was elected Prime Minister on 30 July.

Although Obuchi's Government was designated an 'economic reconstruction' Cabinet, doubts arose about its commitment to comprehensive reform. Kiichi Miyazawa, the former Prime Minister, was appointed Minister of Finance. In his inaugural policy speech, Obuchi announced the establishment of an Economic Strategy Council and promised substantial tax cuts. As Japan's economic situation worsened, political disputes over banking reform dominated the following months, with the Government reluctant to commit itself to the closure of failing banks. Following weeks of negotiations, in October 1998 the Diet approved banking legislation that included provisions for the nationalization of failing banks, as demanded by the opposition. Shinto Heiwa and Komei merged in November 1998 to form New Komeito, which thus became the second largest opposition party. Also in that month Fukushiro Nukaga, the Director-General of the Defence Agency, resigned from the Government to assume responsibility for a procurement scandal involving his agency. In mid-November the LDP and the LP reached a basic accord on the formation of a coalition, which would still remain short of a majority in the upper house. The Cabinet was reorganized in January 1999 to include the LP, the leader of which, Ichiro Ozawa, had refused a cabinet position. At the end of January the Government adopted an administrative reform plan, which aimed to reduce further the number of cabinet ministers and public servants and to establish an economic and fiscal policy committee.

At local elections in April 1999, 11 of the 12 governorships contested were won by the incumbents, all standing as independents. At the gubernatorial election for Tokyo, the convincing victory of Shintaro Ishihara, a nationalist writer and a former Minister of Transport under the LDP (although now unaffiliated), was regarded as an embarrassment for the ruling party. Ishihara immediately provoked controversy, making inflammatory comments about the 1937 Nanjing massacre (in which more than 300,000 Chinese citizens had been killed by Japanese soldiers) and criticizing the Chinese Government, which responded angrily, prompting the Japanese Government to distance itself publicly from the new Governor's remarks. In November the Chinese Government also expressed its concern regarding an unofficial visit by Ishihara to Taiwan, which had recently suffered a major earthquake. Ishihara also angered the People's Republic of China by visiting Taiwan in May 2000 for the inauguration of the latter's new President, Chen Shui-bian, despite having refused an invitation to visit China as part of celebrations to mark the anniversary of the establishment of relations between Beijing and Tokyo.

In June 1999 the Government voted to grant official legal status to the de facto national flag (*Hinomaru*) and anthem (*Kimigayo*), despite considerable opposition owing to their association with Japan's militaristic past. The necessary legislation became effective in August, following approval by the Diet. Meanwhile, in July New Komeito agreed to join the ruling LDP-LP coalition, giving the Government a new majority in the upper house and expanding its control in the lower house to more than 70% of the seats. Negotiations on policy initiatives proved difficult, however, owing to differences over issues such as constitutional revision and New Komeito's opposition to a reduction in the number of seats in the lower house, as favoured by the LP. Obuchi was re-elected President of the LDP in September. Naoto Kan was replaced as President of the DPJ by Yukio Hatoyama, hitherto Secretary-General of the party.

A new Cabinet was appointed in October 1999. Notably, Michio Ochi was appointed Chairman of the Financial Reconstruction Commission. The LP and New Komeito each received one cabinet post. A basic accord on coalition policy included an agreement to seek a reduction in the number of seats in the House of Representatives, initially by 20 and subsequently by a further 30. A Vice-Minister at the Defence Agency resigned shortly after being appointed, following widespread criticism of his suggestion that Japan should arm itself with nuclear weapons. Obuchi, whose judgement in the affair was questioned, subsequently apologized to the nation in a speech to the Diet.

Trials continued in 1997–99 of members of Aum Shinrikyo, the cult accused of perpetrating the sarin gas attack on the Tokyo underground railway system in March 1995. In September 1999 Masato Yokoyama became the first of those accused to receive the death sentence. In an apparent attempt to avert any restriction on the cult or seizure of its assets, the leaders of Aum Shinrikyo announced a suspension of all external activities from October, and in December acknowledged its culpability for a number of crimes, including the 1995 gas attack. Moreover, in January 2000 the cult announced that it was changing its name to Aleph and renouncing its leader, Shoko Asahara, who was still being tried for his part in the gas attack.

In December 1999 a political crisis was averted when Ozawa was persuaded not to withdraw the LP from the ruling coalition, as he had threatened, over a delay in the proposal of legislation to reduce the number of seats in the lower house. The ruling parties had earlier agreed also to postpone the consideration of a proposal to expand Japan's participation in UN peace-keeping activities. In early 2000 the Diet approved the controversial legislation on the reduction in seats, despite an opposition boycott. Multi-party committees were established in both houses in January, which were to review the Constitution over a period of five years. In February Michio Ochi was forced to resign from the Cabinet over remarks that suggested he would be lenient on banking reform.

Discord within the coalition increased, and in April 2000 the LP withdrew from the Government; 26 members of the LP formed the New Conservative Party—NCP (Hoshuto). Keizo Obuchi, however, suffered a stroke and went into a coma from which he never regained consciousness. The Government was criticized for not releasing the news of Obuchi's condition (it was not reported in the media for at least 24 hours) even though the country had effectively been without a premier. The LDP elected Yoshiro Mori, the Secretary-General, as party President, and he was subsequently elected Prime Minister by both Houses of the Diet. Mori immediately affirmed his commitment to the economic and political reform initiatives of his predecessor and formed a coalition with New Komeito and the NCP. All ministers from the Obuchi administration were retained. Noboru Takeshita, the former Prime Minister, announced his retirement from politics and from the LDP; he died shortly afterwards. Former

Prime Minister Ryutaro Hashimoto was appointed head of the Takeshita faction of the LDP, which had been led by Obuchi.

Following his appointment as Prime Minister, Mori made a number of controversial public statements, expressing imperialist views. Although forced to issue apologies, he did not retract his remarks. In the general election held on 25 June 2000 the number of seats in the House of Representatives was reduced from 500 to 480. The LDP won the most seats, although its representation was reduced to 233 and many of its key political figures, including current and former cabinet ministers, lost their seats, particularly in metropolitan areas. The DPJ increased its representation to 127 seats, New Komeito won 31 seats, the LP 22 seats, the NCP 20 seats and the SDPJ 19 seats. The participation rate was 62.5%. Although remaining in power, the LDP faced serious problems, among the most prominent of which related to the suitability of its leadership, Mori having made numerous political gaffes and public errors of protocol. Nevertheless, Mori was returned as Prime Minister and announced the composition of his new Cabinet in July.

In October 2000 an amendment to the voting system, under which electors would choose to vote either for a party or for an individual candidate, was proposed by the governing coalition. The opposition strongly criticized the proposed changes and, following the Government's insistence that they be passed through the Diet, commenced a boycott of proceedings. The bill was approved in the House of Representatives despite the boycott, which lasted 18 days and ended following an agreement between the Government and the opposition to debate the proposed legislation in the House of Representatives. It was enacted in late October.

Corruption was a major issue throughout 2000, particularly the taking of bribes, revelations of which resulted in several resignations. Among the most serious incidents was a 'cash for questions' scandal involving an insurance company. One LDP member resigned and another was arrested in connection with the affair in November, and in January 2001 Fukushiro Nukaga, the Minister of State for Economy, Industry and Information Technology, resigned, having earlier admitted that he had accepted bribes from the firm. An LDP ally of Yoshiro Mori, Masakuni Murakami, was implicated in the case and arrested in March. In October 2000 Hidenao Nakagawa, Minister of State, Chief Cabinet Secretary, Director-General of the Okinawa Development Agency and Minister in Charge of Information Technology, resigned after it was alleged, *inter alia*, that he had links to a right-wing activist. In the following month the former Minister of Construction, Eiichi Nakao, acknowledged in court that he had taken bribes in 1996 in exchange for the allocation of public works contracts.

The high incidence of corruption further undermined Mori, and during October 2000 the Prime Minister came under increasing pressure to resign after it was alleged in a magazine that some years previously he had been arrested for violation of an anti-prostitution law. Mori denied the allegation and sued the publication for libel. Later that month, during a meeting with Tony Blair, the British Prime Minister, Mori reportedly suggested that the Democratic People's Republic of Korea (DPRK—North Korea) could release Japanese hostages (see below) to a third country in order to avoid any admission of their existence. Harsh criticism ensued, and subsequent attempts to mitigate the situation, by claiming that the remarks referred to an episode from the past, proved unsuccessful. In November the opposition launched a motion of no confidence in the Prime Minister. Furthermore, LDP member Koichi Kato publicly criticized Mori and declared himself ready to form a government. However, the Prime Minister survived the vote, following threats by the party leadership that rebels voting against Mori would be expelled from the LDP. In December Mori suffered a set-back when Hiromu Nonaka, a strong ally, resigned as Secretary-General of the LDP and retired from politics. His nominated successor, Makoto Koga, subsequently assumed the role.

Meanwhile, in November 2000 Fusako Shigenobu, the founder of the extremist left-wing Japanese Red Army, which had been responsible for a number of terrorist attacks during the 1970s, was arrested in Osaka. She was detained on suspicion of the seizure of the French embassy in The Hague, Netherlands, in 1974 and subsequently indicted on various related charges. A number of other members had been repatriated from several countries since 1995 to be tried for terrorism. (Shigenobu was sentenced to 20 years' imprisonment in February 2006 for her involvement in the seizure of the embassy.)

A major cabinet reorganization was effected in December 2000, and substantial changes were made to the government structure. The number of ministries was reduced from 23 to 13, mainly through mergers, and various state agencies were absorbed into the newly created Cabinet Office. The new structure was not fully implemented until January 2001, following an administrative reform. Notable appointments to the new Cabinet included the leader of the largest LDP faction and former Prime Minister, Ryutaro Hashimoto, and Hakuo Yanagisawa, the former Director-General of the Financial Reconstruction Commission. The former was appointed Minister of State for the Development of Okinawa and the Settlement of the Northern Territories, and the latter became Minister of State for Financial Affairs. Both men were well-respected and enjoyed considerable political support, and their appointment was seen as an attempt by Mori to strengthen his position. During December 2000, however, photographs showing the Prime Minister in the company of an alleged gangster and convicted murderer were published. Mori won another vote of confidence in March 2001, but in early April announced his intention to resign.

In late April 2001 Junichiro Koizumi, a former Minister of Health and Welfare, unexpectedly defeated Ryutaro Hashimoto and one other candidate to secure the presidency of the ruling LDP and thus the post of Prime Minister. Koizumi's victory was due to a change in party election rules that allowed a greater influence of local and ordinary party members in selecting the President. He subsequently reorganized the Cabinet, largely disregarding LDP factional politics, and appointed a number of reformists, including Makiko Tanaka, daughter of former Prime Minister Kakuei Tanaka, as Japan's first female Minister of Foreign Affairs; Heizo Takenaka, an economics professor, as Minister of State for Economy, Industry and Information Technology; and Nobuteru Ishihara as Minister of State for Administrative Reform. At the same time Koizumi also reorganized the LDP's senior leadership, appointing his ally Taku Yamasaki as Secretary-General, and Taro Aso as Chairman of the Policy Research Council. In addition to according priority to economic reform, Koizumi also sought to introduce direct elections for the post of Prime Minister and to upgrade the status of the SDF into that of a full army, a move that would involve changing Article 9 of the Constitution, whereby Japan renounces the use of war. This led to fears in neighbouring countries of a growth of nationalism in Japan.

In June 2001 the Government finally announced an economic reform programme, consisting of the privatization of special public institutions, a review of regulatory economic laws, the strengthening of insurance functions, improving human resources, including assistance to business entrepreneurs, revitalizing urban areas, promoting regional autonomy and a reduction of public works projects. Despite his warnings of economic hardship ahead, Koizumi's high popularity was a major factor in the LDP's gains in the Tokyo assembly elections in late June. However, veteran members of the LDP, particularly the Hashimoto faction, remained opposed to Koizumi's reforms.

Elections to the House of Councillors were held on 29 July 2001, and Koizumi's personal popularity once more enabled the LDP to make gains. Of the 121 seats being contested, the LDP won 64, bringing its total in the upper chamber to 110, a net gain of eight seats. The opposition DPJ won 26 seats, raising its strength to 60 seats, a net gain of 13 seats, while New Komeito won 23 seats, thus gaining one additional seat. The elections were widely seen as a test for Koizumi's reformist agenda and as a victory for the LDP after years of declining popularity. Koizumi was re-elected unopposed for a further two-year term as LDP President in early August.

Koizumi aroused controversy in mid-August 2001 when he made an official visit to the Yasukuni Shrine to honour Japan's war dead. He sought to diminish the controversy by visiting two days before the anniversary of Japan's surrender in the Second World War, but nevertheless drew both domestic and international criticism. Left-wingers opposed the visit on principle, while right-wingers denounced Koizumi for bringing forward his visit to placate critics.

In September 2001 the terrorist attacks on the USA again raised the subject of the role of Japan's military, with Koizumi apparently using the USA's war against the Taliban regime of Afghanistan to expand the role of the SDF. The Diet in October approved new legislation for the overseas deployment of the SDF in a non-combat support role, and in November Japan dispatched warships to the Indian Ocean, in the biggest such deployment since the Second World War (see below). The Japanese people strongly supported logistical assistance to the USA, but there remained considerable public opposition to any amendment to Article 9. Amid the worsening economic situation, meanwhile, the Government introduced emergency stimulus measures in September to counter rising unemployment, the deteriorating situation in the corporate sector and the banking crisis.

By November 2001 Koizumi was in dispute with Minister of Foreign Affairs Tanaka over bureaucratic reform in her ministry, her occasional failure to meet visiting foreign dignitaries and her absence from two major international forums. Koizumi had meanwhile formed a new 'foreign policy taskforce' to deal more efficiently with international affairs. There was increasing speculation about a cabinet reorganization, with members of the LDP's Hashimoto faction keen to modify reforms and regain ministerial posts. Koizumi had in previous months indicated his willingness to work with the opposition DPJ if the LDP continued to block his reforms; later in the month more than 50 LDP legislators formed a group aimed at obstructing them.

Also in November 2001, hundreds of people filed lawsuits against Koizumi over his visit to the Yasukuni Shrine, claiming that he had violated the constitutional separation of religion and state. In December Princess Masako, wife of Crown Prince Naruhito, gave birth to her first child, Princess Aiko. However, the Constitution forbade females from succeeding to the 'Chrysanthemum Throne', leading to calls for an amendment to the rules at a future date, a suggestion that was strongly supported by the public. The last female ruler had been Empress Gosakuramachi in the late 1700s.

In mid-December 2001 the Government agreed to abolish 17 public corporations and transfer 45 others (of a total of 163) to the private sector; it also showed signs of addressing the problems of the banking sector. However, Koizumi's major reform of privatizing the postal savings system was further delayed. Meanwhile, the opposition DPJ itself experienced divisions, between those who favoured co-operation with Koizumi and his reforms (including the President of the DPJ, Yukio Hatoyama) and those who favoured greater co-operation with other opposition parties. The latter group was led by DPJ Deputy President Takahiro Yokomichi, who in late November held meetings with the LP leader, Ichiro Ozawa, and the SDPJ leader, Takako Doi. The DPJ had failed to make a significant impact against the LDP during the ongoing economic crisis.

By the beginning of 2002 Koizumi had failed to deliver tangible economic results. Shizuka Kamei, a senior LDP official, accused Koizumi of damaging the economy in order to implement his reform agenda, highlighting the strong resistance within the LDP. In the first week of January Koizumi appointed two members of the Hashimoto faction as vice-ministers, in a bid to placate his main opponents. At the end of the month Koizumi dismissed his Minister of Foreign Affairs, Makiko Tanaka, following months of disputes over reform within the ministry, which had delayed the passage of a supplementary budget through the Diet. The dismissal of the popular Tanaka was regarded as a victory for LDP veterans and as a set-back for reform. She was replaced by Yoriko Kawaguchi, hitherto Minister of the Environment. In March the LDP suffered a reverse as one Diet member was accused of exerting undue influence upon officials in the Ministry of Foreign Affairs, and another was arrested on suspicion of tax evasion. Both subsequently resigned from the party.

The LDP suffered further set-backs in April 2002 when its candidates lost the election for the mayoralty of Yokohama and a by-election in Niigata Prefecture. The electoral defeats, and Koizumi's unscheduled visit to the Yasukuni Shrine in late April, led to renewed criticism of the Prime Minister. In June 2002 the LDP suspended Makiko Tanaka from the party for a two-year period owing to her failure to co-operate with an investigation into the misuse of state funds at the Ministry of Foreign Affairs. Tanaka relinquished her seat in the Diet in August. Meanwhile, the sitting session of the Diet was extended until July in order to enable Koizumi to draft legislation for reforms to Japan Post, as well as the health service and defence and security sectors, which were opposed by considerable elements within the LDP. In July Koizumi was forced to accept a compromise with anti-reformist LDP elements over his plans to reform postal services. Meanwhile, the Governor of Nagano Prefecture, Yasuo Tanaka, was ousted by the prefectural assembly owing to his policy of reducing major public works projects, which were often used by local politicians as a means of generating support. Tanaka, a former novelist, was one of an increasing number of independent, reformist candidates who had been elected to prefectural governorships as a protest against traditional political parties. However, he was overwhelmingly re-elected to the post of Governor in September, in what was seen as a victory for reformist forces.

In late September 2002 Koizumi implemented a long-expected cabinet reorganization, dismissing the Minister of State for the Financial Services Agency, Hakuo Yanagisawa, and appointing the Minister of State for Economic and Fiscal Policy, Heizo Takenaka, concurrently to hold that post. The ministers responsible for agriculture, defence, disaster management, environment, food safety, and Okinawa and the Northern Territories, were also replaced. It was widely believed that the reallocation of portfolios was related to a plan by the Governor of the Bank of Japan, Masaru Hayami, to support the ailing banking sector by buying poorly performing shares owned by commercial banks—a proposal opposed by Yanagisawa. Plans to reform the banking sector also created tensions between the LDP and its two coalition partners, New Komeito and the NCP. At the end of October a tripartite committee of the ruling coalition published a banking-sector reform plan that was far less radical than that sought by Takenaka, who had urged the nationalization of major banks to prevent their collapse. The disagreements over how to revive Japan's economy and reform the banking system continued throughout the remainder of 2002. Despite these political tensions, the LDP in late October won five out of seven by-elections, strengthening the reputation of Prime Minister Koizumi following his visit to the DPRK in September. At the same time Japan witnessed its first political assassination since 1960, when a member of the DPJ, Koki Ishii, a known campaigner against corruption, was stabbed to death. (In June 2004 Hakusui Ito, a right-wing extremist, was sentenced to life imprisonment for the murder.)

In December 2002 the opposition DPJ elected Naoto Kan as its President, replacing Yukio Hatoyama, who had himself been re-elected to a third term as party President in September. Hatoyama was forced to resign after the failure of secret attempts to merge the party with the smaller opposition LP, led by Ichiro Ozawa. Katsuya Okada, Kan's main rival for the DPJ presidency, was appointed Secretary-General. Kan had previously led the DPJ during 1997–99. Four DPJ members of the Diet, led by former party Vice-President Hiroshi Kumagai, resigned from the party in December and joined the ruling coalition's NCP; the President of that party, Takeshi Noda, resigned in favour of Kumagai.

In January 2003 Junichiro Koizumi visited the Yasukuni Shrine for the third time since becoming Prime Minister, once again prompting criticism within Japan as well as in the region. In early March the Governor of Tokyo, Shintaro Ishihara, announced that he would seek re-election in April, ending months of speculation that he might form a new political party in order to challenge Koizumi. Ishihara's announcement was welcomed by Koizumi, since the Governor had been seen as the Prime Minister's most serious rival, and had been holding discussions with Shizuka Kamei, an LDP faction leader who was Koizumi's main opponent within the party. However, the LDP was, in early March, embarrassed by the arrest of one of its Diet members over the illicit management of political donations. At the end of the month the Minister of Agriculture, Forestry and Fisheries, Tadamori Oshima, resigned over a series of financial scandals concerning his aides. Oshima was the first minister in Koizumi's Cabinet to resign over a funding scandal. He was replaced by Yoshiyuki Kamei.

The 15th unified quadrennial local elections, comprising gubernatorial elections in 11 prefectures (including Tokyo), one city mayoral election, and local assembly elections in 44 prefectures and 12 cities, were held in mid-April 2003. In Tokyo, Governor Ishihara was overwhelmingly re-elected, and pledged to use his position to campaign for reform in the country as a whole. Three other incumbent governors were also re-elected, and it was noted that independent candidates performed strongly or won posts in several prefectures, at the expense of traditional political parties. Turn-out in the gubernatorial elections was a record low of 52.6%, however. The LDP won 1,309 of 2,634 local seats contested, an improvement on the 1,288 seats it had won four years earlier. By-elections for three seats in the House of Representatives and one seat in the House of Councillors were held in late April; the LDP won three seats and the DPJ one seat.

In April 2003 the LDP announced that it aimed to amend the Constitution explicitly to state the legitimacy of the SDF and to expand its role in international peace-keeping and collective self-defence. In May the House of Representatives approved new legislation granting the Government and the SDF greater powers to act in the event of an attack on Japan. In June the new legislation, outlining the circumstances in which the Government would be able to authorize military action by the SDF, was approved by the House of Councillors. The legislation was supported by the DPJ as well as by the ruling coalition. However, the SDP, the JCP and the LP opposed the legislation on the grounds that it violated the pacifist principle of Japan's Constitution.

In July 2003 the House of Councillors approved, by 136 votes to 102, proposals to send peace-keeping forces to Iraq, thereby allowing the largest deployment of Japanese troops abroad since the Second World War. Opposition to the proposals was vehement, involving physical violence among parliamentary representatives. Although troops were to engage in humanitarian work only, critics argued that the deployment would violate the Constitution, as in practice troops would be unable to avoid conflict areas.

In September 2003 Koizumi was re-elected as leader of the LDP, defeating the three rival candidates (Shizuka Kamei, Masahiko Koumura and Takao Fujii) for the leadership. Koizumi then made appointments to a new Cabinet, which included the reappointment of Heizo Takenaka as Minister of State responsible for the Financial Services Agency, despite criticism of his banking reform policies (see above). Also in September, a merger agreement between the DPJ and the LP, originally reached in July, was signed, with the aim of creating an opposition movement capable of presenting a strong challenge to the LDP at the forthcoming general election. In October the House of Representatives was dissolved. Also in October, the House of Councillors voted to extend legislation, first approved in 2001, allowing the Japanese SDF to provide logistical support to the USA in its 'war on terror' (see below).

At the general election, held on 9 November 2003, the LDP won 237 seats, thus losing 10 of its previous 247 seats in the House of Representatives. The party's strength increased to 245 following the recruitment of four independent candidates and the absorption of the New Conservative Party, one of the LDP's two coalition partners, which had won four seats. The LDP's other coalition partner, the New Komeito party, secured 34 seats. Naoto Kan's DPJ (incorporating the former LP) won 177 seats, thereby increasing its number of seats by 40 and representing a serious challenge to the LDP's hold on power. A further potential threat to the LDP was the success of the former Minister of Foreign Affairs, Makiko Tanaka, in securing a seat as an independent candidate. Tanaka had been suspended from the LDP in 2002 following allegations of misappropriation of funds (see above), but was able to stand in the 2003 election after the charges against her were abandoned. Tanaka, who had become increasingly critical of the Koizumi administration, subsequently joined a DPJ-led Diet group.

In December 2003 plans were announced for an SDF deployment to Iraq, following the approval of the requisite legislation on the issue in July (see above). The plans were strongly criticized by DPJ leader Naoto Kan, and popular protests against the Iraq mission took place in mid-December. Opposition within Japan to the deployment had been strengthened by the deaths of two Japanese diplomats in Iraq in November. Also in December, the Government outlined proposals to expand Japan's defence capacity with the development of a ballistic missile defence system in co-operation with the USA. In January 2004 the first Japanese troops departed for Iraq, amid further popular protests in Tokyo. In the same month it was announced that legislation on the reform of Japan's Constitution, including an amendment to Article 9, would be submitted in 2005. Also in January 2004 Koizumi made a fourth visit to the Yasukuni Shrine, again prompting criticism. In February Shoko Asahara, leader of the Aum Shinrikyo sect, which had released poisonous gas into the Tokyo underground system in 1995, was sentenced to death for his role in the attack. Public support for Koizumi was tested in April, when three Japanese civilians were taken hostage in Iraq. Their captors threatened to kill them by burning them alive if Japanese troops were not withdrawn. Despite the Government's steadfast refusal to comply with the Iraqi militants' demands, the hostages were released unharmed a week later.

In May 2004 a scandal over pension contributions prompted resignations by senior officials from the LDP as well as the opposition DPJ. Chief Cabinet Secretary Yasuo Fukuda of the LDP resigned after admitting that he had not made the required payments to the compulsory state pension scheme. DPJ Chairman Naoto Kan resigned shortly afterwards on similar grounds. Kan was replaced by Katsuya Okada, hitherto General Secretary of the DPJ. In the same month a government proposal for pension reform, involving increased premiums and reduced benefits, was approved by the House of Representatives. The reform plan was approved by the House of Councillors in June, despite strong opposition from the DPJ. In July 2004 nation-wide voting took place to elect one-half of the members of the House of Councillors. Of the 121 seats contested, the LDP won 49, while the DPJ won 50 (thus increasing its overall representation in the chamber from 60 seats to 82). Although the LDP and its coalition partner New Komeito, with a combined total of 139 seats, retained a majority in the 242-member House, the outcome was generally interpreted as reflecting a decline in the popularity of Koizumi's administration. In September Koizumi effected a major reorganization of cabinet portfolios. Among notable new appointments was that of Nobutaka Machimura as Minister of Foreign Affairs. The Minister of Economic and Fiscal Policy, Heizo Takenaka, was given responsibility for a portfolio for privatization of the postal services, while Sadakazu Tanigaki remained Minister of Finance. From October 2004 there were renewed protests against Japanese support for military operations in Iraq following the beheading of a Japanese tourist who had been taken hostage by a militant group. None the less, in December the LDP announced that the term of the SDF mission in Iraq was to be extended by one year. In the same month a revision of Japanese defence policy was announced. While reaffirming Japan's commitment not to engage in offensive military action against other nations, the new policy eased some restrictions on weapons exports.

In August 2005 Prime Minister Koizumi's important postal reform bill, which had been narrowly approved by the House of Representatives in the previous month, was defeated in the House of Councillors. A total of 37 LDP members from both houses rebelled against the party leadership and voted against the proposed legislation. Koizumi responded to the defeat by dissolving the House of Representatives and calling an election for 11 September. Prohibited from standing as party members, several LDP 'rebels' formed separate parties—including the People's New Party (Kokumin Shinto), led by Tamisuke Watanuki, and the New Party Nippon (Shinto Nippon), led by Yasuo Tanaka—while others chose to stand as independent candidates. In the event, the election resulted in unequivocal victory for Kozumi and, by implication, an endorsement of his reform programme by the electorate. The LDP increased its representation in the House to 296 of the 480 seats (its first overall majority since 1990 and the largest number of seats won by a single party since the end of the Second World War), thereby creating, with its ally New Komeito, a ruling coalition bloc of 327 seats and thus securing more than two-thirds of the chamber. The DPJ's share of seats, meanwhile, was reduced by 64 to 113, prompting the resignation of Chairman Katsuya Okada. The subsequent DPJ leadership election was won by Seiji Maehara, who narrowly defeated former leader Naoto Kan. In October Koizumi reorganized his Cabinet. The new Government was widely considered to be have been formulated so as to strengthen the positions of potential successors to Koizumi, who maintained that he would stand down as LDP President (and consequently as Prime Minister) in 2006 upon the expiry of his term. Shinzo Abe, who was appointed Chief Cabinet Secretary, Taro Aso, who became Minister of Foreign Affairs, and Sadakazu Tanigaki, who was retained as Minister of Finance, were regarded as particularly prominent candidates for the leadership. The postal reform bill was resubmitted to the legislature, and in mid-October passed successfully through both Houses of the Diet. Also in October Koizumi visited the Yasukuni Shrine for the fifth time since becoming Prime Minister. In December it was announced that the SDF troops stationed in Iraq were to remain there for another year.

During 2005 Japan's traditional corporate culture was unsettled by the attempted takeover of Nippon Broadcasting System Inc by Livedoor, an internet service provider headed by a prominent young entrepreneur, Takafumi Horie. In January 2006 Livedoor's offices were searched by prosecutors; Horie and three other executives were subsequently indicted on charges of violating securities law. In March, furthermore, after only six months in office, Seiji Maehara was obliged to resign from the presidency of the DPJ following the revelation of a scandal connected to Livedoor. On the basis of a purported e-mail, a DPJ legislator had claimed in the House of Representatives that the son of the LDP Secretary-General had financial links with

Horie. The e-mail in question proved to be a forgery, and the DPJ issued an apology for having made a false allegation against the ruling party. Maehara was replaced in April by veteran politician Ichiro Ozawa, a former Secretary-General of the LDP and latterly leader of the NFP and the LP, who had joined the DPJ upon its merger with the LP in 2003. At the conclusion of his trial in March 2007, Takafumi Horie was found guilty of fraud, whereupon he received a prison sentence of two years and six months. A second executive of Livedoor was similarly convicted later in the month.

Following a government panel's conclusion in October 2005 that the imperial succession law should be changed to allow a female to ascend the 'Chrysanthemum Throne', speculation that the rules might be amended was moderated in February 2006 by the news that Princess Kiko, wife of the Emperor's second son, Prince Akishino, was expecting another child. The amendment had initially been supported by Koizumi, who in January had vowed to secure the passage of the new law before the end of the parliamentary session in June. Following the birth to the Princess of a son in September, however, the proposed legislation was not pursued.

The contentious issue of the Yasukuni Shrine remained dominant during 2006, as did the quest for a successor to Koizumi, whose term of office was due to expire in September. Largely owing to the clear support that he received from the Prime Minister, Chief Cabinet Secretary Shinzo Abe emerged as the leading candidate. By mid-August two other legislators had formally declared their candidacies: the Minister of Finance, Sadakazu Tanigaki, and the Minister of Foreign Affairs, Taro Aso. Abe, however, appeared to have the firm support of key factions within the LDP, and in September the party duly elected him to succeed Koizumi as its President; Abe received 464 of 703 votes. Having proceeded to secure the support of 339 of 476 members of the House of Representatives and 136 of 240 votes in the House of Councillors, at the end of the month Abe formally took office as Prime Minister. Only one incumbent minister of the Koizumi administration, namely the Minister of Foreign Affairs, Taro Aso, retained his position in the new Cabinet. Koji Omi was appointed Minister of Finance. Many believed that Abe had appointed predominantly those LDP members who had supported him during his campaign for the leadership.

Shinzo Abe, who was regarded as a forthright politician, immediately announced an ambitious policy agenda. Just days after assuming office the new Prime Minister arranged discussions with China and the Republic of Korea, relations with both of which had been strained by his predecessor's visits to the Yasukuni Shrine (see below). Abe envisaged the pursuit of an assertive foreign policy, stating that Japan should continue to seek a permanent seat on the UN Security Council and making clear his commitment to an uncompromising stance against the DPRK. This assertiveness also included, more controversially, an undertaking to revise the country's pacifist Constitution to permit the Japanese military a greater role abroad. (Abe's position on the issue, and his reported decision to pay a clandestine visit to the Yasukuni Shrine in April 2006, was possibly influenced by the fact that his grandfather had been imprisoned, although never tried, as a 'Class A' war criminal—convicted at the most serious level of crimes against peace.) Similarly, he advocated educational reforms that would include the stipulation that Japanese schoolchildren be actively taught to love their country (and in November legislation, boycotted by the opposition, was approved by the lower house encouraging teachers to instil patriotism and respect for tradition in their students). In terms of economic strategy, Abe pledged to pursue the reformist policies of his predecessor, setting a growth target of no less than 3% a year, to be achieved predominantly through reductions in expenditure and tax concessions for technological innovation. However, in an acknowledgement of the growing income disparities in Japanese society, he also launched an initiative known as 'rechallenge society', which was aimed at helping the unemployed and failed entrepreneurs.

Prime Minister Abe suffered his first political embarrassment in December 2006 when an official investigation found that during the tenure of his predecessor the Government had paid members of the public to ask specific questions of ministers at local meetings and that government officials had masqueraded as ordinary citizens. Abe had been in charge of these public meetings, which had been promoted as an open forum for debate. To take responsibility for the affair, Abe pledged to work without pay for the next 90 days. Meanwhile, Abe's credentials were brought sharply into focus by the passage through the upper house in December 2006 of legislation to upgrade the Defence Agency, as well as a bill requiring schools to teach patriotism. While the former was approved by a majority and received support from the opposition (the Defence Agency was officially upgraded to become a full ministry in January 2007), the latter proved more contentious. Four groups, including the DPJ, filed a motion of no confidence against Abe in a desperate attempt to halt the education bill, but the motion was rejected by the House of Representatives. (The lower house also rejected a similar motion against Minister of Foreign Affairs Taro Aso, resulting from his comments on the necessity for a debate on the issue of nuclear weapons.)

Abe drew further criticism in December 2006 following the resignation of the official he had appointed to head a government tax panel, Masaaki Homma (who was alleged to have been living with his mistress in a state-subsidized apartment). A week later the Minister of State responsible for the regulatory and administrative reform portfolio, Genichiro Sata, resigned over accusations of funding irregularities by his political support group. The Minister of Health, Labour and Welfare, Hakuo Yanagisawa, also came under intense pressure to resign at the end of January 2007, after he likened women to 'birth-giving machines' while commenting on Japan's declining birth rate. Despite a week-long boycott of the Diet by opposition parties in protest at Yanagisawa's remarks, the minister remained in his post.

Local elections were held in two stages in April 2007. The DPJ performed well in elections to 44 prefectural assemblies held on 8 April, winning 375 of the 2,544 seats contested, an increase of 145 compared with the 2003 elections, while the LDP took 1,212 seats (compared with 1,309 in 2003). On the same day 13 gubernatorial, 15 city assembly and four city mayoral elections were held. Governor Ishihara was re-elected in Tokyo for a third consecutive term, with the (unsolicited) support of the ruling coalition, while eight other incumbent governors also secured re-election. On 22 April mayoral and local assembly elections took place in 77 cities, 96 towns and villages and 13 wards of Tokyo. In Nagasaki, Tomihisa Taue was elected Mayor, defeating Makoto Yokko, the son-in-law of the former Mayor, Itcho Ito, who had been assassinated five days before polling, allegedly by a member of an organized crime group. Two vacant seats in the House of Councillors were won by the LDP and the DPJ in by-elections held concurrently with the second round of local voting.

Following his assumption of office, Prime Minister Abe had confirmed his intention to proceed with constitutional changes, notably to ease the limits on military action by Japanese forces. In April 2007 the House of Representatives approved legislation setting out procedures for national referendums on constitutional reform. Although the 1947 Constitution stipulated that amendments required the approval of at least two-thirds of the members of both houses of the Diet, followed by endorsement in a national referendum, the legal framework for such a referendum had never been established. The new law provided for the participation of all citizens over the age of 18 (compared with a voting age of 20 for elections), but failed to impose a minimum turn-out rate for the validity of the referendum. The House of Councillors adopted the legislation in mid-May, but it was not scheduled to enter into force until 2010. Meanwhile, rallies were held nation-wide both for and against constitutional revision.

It emerged in early May 2007 that, in an apparent compromise designed to appease both his more nationalistic supporters and neighbouring countries, Prime Minister Abe had sent an offering to the Yasukuni Shrine in the previous month, but had refrained from visiting the Shrine himself. Similarly, he chose not to visit the Shrine on the anniversary of Japan's surrender in the Second World War in August, instead attending a commemoration ceremony in Tokyo.

Financial scandals continued to damage the Government in mid-2007. The Minister of Agriculture, Forestry and Fisheries, Toshikatsu Matsuoka, committed suicide in late May, shortly before he was due to appear before a committee of the Diet that was investigating allegations that he had claimed false office expenses. Matsuoka had also been accused of accepting political donations from companies awarded contracts for public works projects by an agency affiliated to his ministry. By June public support for Abe had declined significantly, according to opinion polls, amid widespread anger over the loss of some 50m. pension records by the Social Insurance Agency. The term of the current parliamentary session was extended for 12 days in mid-June to allow the passage of several pieces of legislation. The Diet approved bills providing for the disbandment of the Social Insurance Agency; the abolition of the five-year statute of limitations on pension claims; the reform of the controversial *amakudari* practice (in which senior civil servants retired to well-paid positions, often with organizations linked to the government ministry or agency where they were formerly employed); and measures aimed at enhancing the transparency of the management of political funds.

Despite its efforts to address public concerns regarding the pension crisis and official corruption, the Government suffered a further reverse in early July 2007 when the Minister of Defence, Fumio Kyuma, was forced to resign after provoking an outcry with his suggestion that the US nuclear attacks on the Japanese cities of Hiroshima and Nagasaki in 1945, towards the end of the Second World War, had been inevitable. Yuriko Koike, hitherto Abe's special adviser on national security affairs, was appointed to replace Kyuma, thus becoming Japan's first female Minister of Defence. A major earthquake in mid-July killed at least 10 people and caused a fire and a leak of water contaminated with radioactive material at the Kashiwazaki-Kariwa nuclear power plant in Niigata prefecture. Operations at the plant were halted pending the satisfactory completion of safety inspections, and it remained closed in early 2008.

The ruling LDP-New Komeito coalition lost its overall majority in the House of Councillors as a result of partial elections that were held on 29 July 2007, having been postponed by one week owing to the extension of the Diet session. Of the 121 seats contested, the LDP secured only 37 and New Komeito a further nine, leaving the coalition with a total of 103 of the upper house's 242 seats. By contrast, the DPJ made significant gains, particularly in rural constituencies, winning 60 seats and, with 109 seats overall, control of the House of Councillors. A turn-out of 58.6% was recorded. The DPJ's Satsuki Eda subsequently became the first opposition politician to be elected Speaker of the upper house. Despite the ruling coalition's overwhelming defeat in the elections, Abe insisted that he intended to remain in office, although Hidenao Nakagawa relinquished the post of Secretary-General of the LDP. At the beginning of August Norihiko Akagi, Matsuoka's successor as Minister of Agriculture, Forestry and Fisheries, was forced to resign from the Government over allegations that he, too, had submitted inaccurate claims for office expenses. Abe was criticized for not dismissing Akagi earlier. The Minister of Justice, Jinen Nagase, was also accused of financial impropriety when it was revealed that he had accepted 500,000 yen from a company he had advised on visa applications for its Chinese workers. Nagase denied any wrongdoing, maintaining that the money had been a legitimate political donation.

The Prime Minister reorganized his Cabinet in late August 2007 in an attempt to restore confidence in his administration. Several veteran members of the LDP were appointed to the Government, including faction leaders Nobutaka Machimura and Masahiko Koumura as Minister for Foreign Affairs and Minister of Defence, respectively, and Fukushiro Nukaga as Minister of Finance. Taro Aso became Secretary-General of the LDP. Only a week later, however, the new Minister of Agriculture, Forestry and Fisheries, Takehiko Endo, resigned, causing further embarrassment for Abe, after admitting that a private farming group he headed had misappropriated state funds. In mid-September Abe himself resigned as Prime Minister and President of the LDP, acknowledging that he had lost the support and trust of the public. The timing of his resignation surprised observers, as it was announced just two days after he had outlined his future legislative programme.

Two candidates contested the election to replace Abe as LDP leader: Taro Aso and Yasuo Fukuda, a moderate politician who had served as Chief Cabinet Secretary under Koizumi. Although Aso was initially considered to be the leading contender, he was regarded by many as being too closely associated with Abe, and Fukuda soon gained the support of eight of the party's nine factions. Fukuda was duly elected as LDP President in late September 2007, receiving 330 of the 527 valid votes cast, and subsequently took office as Prime Minister, having secured the approval of 338 members of the House of Representatives. In the opposition-controlled House of Councillors, Fukuda won only 106 votes to the 133 cast in favour of Ichiro Ozawa, the President of the DPJ, but the decision of the lower house took precedence, in accordance with the Constitution. Fukuda retained most of the ministers from his predecessor's Cabinet. Koumura, who became Minister for Foreign Affairs, was replaced at the Ministry of Defence by one of the few new appointees, Shigeru Ishiba (who had also held the defence portfolio in Koizumi's Government), while Machimura was appointed Chief Cabinet Secretary and Minister of State for the Abduction Issue. Nukaga, who had withdrawn from the LDP leadership election in favour of Fukuda, remained Minister of Finance. Aso, who had declined a post in the new administration, was replaced as LDP Secretary-General by Bunmei Ibuki, hitherto Minister of Education, Culture, Sports, Science and Technology.

The son of a former Prime Minister, Fukuda advocated seeking closer relations with neighbouring Asian countries (pledging not to visit the controversial Yasukuni Shrine), while maintaining a strong alliance with the USA, and promised to continue to pursue economic structural reforms. The new Prime Minister's first challenge was to secure approval for the extension of legislation that enabled the Maritime Self-Defence Force to provide logistical support in the Indian Ocean to ships involved in US-led counter-terrorism operations in Afghanistan. The renewal of the legislation, which had first been adopted in 2001 and, following successive extensions, was scheduled to expire at the beginning of November 2007, was opposed by the DPJ on the grounds that the US-led operations had not been sanctioned by the UN and that Japan's involvement violated its pacifist Constitution. Following the failure of efforts to reach a political consensus, in mid-October the Cabinet approved draft legislation that would extend the mission but, in a concession to its critics, would limit its role to supplying fuel and water to ships on anti-terrorism patrols rather than those involved in military operations. Yearly renewal of the proposed legislation would also be required. However, the Government's case was damaged by revelations that the Ministry of Defence had misled politicians over the quantity of fuel supplied in the past. The Diet remained in deadlock over the issue at the end of October, leading to the suspension of the support mission.

During private talks with Ozawa in early November 2007 Fukuda proposed the inclusion of the DPJ in a 'grand coalition' Government. Ozawa subsequently offered his resignation as President of the DPJ after he was criticized by the party for not immediately rejecting the suggestion, but was persuaded to remain in the post by party officials. None the less, opinion polls indicated that the episode, which had underlined the divisions within the DPJ, had prompted a decline in support for the main opposition party. A few days later the Diet's current session was extended by five weeks, until mid-December, in order to continue consideration of the proposed legislation renewing the naval deployment in the Indian Ocean. The House of Representatives approved the legislation in mid-November, shortly before Fukuda was due to visit the USA, which had been exerting strong pressure on Japan to resume its support for US counter-terrorism activities. In late November Takemasa Moriya, who had served as Vice-Minister of Defence until August, was arrested on suspicion of having accepted bribes from companies in return for providing them with contracts to supply defence equipment. Fukuda subsequently initiated a reform of the Ministry of Defence, which had been searched for evidence relating to the case. Meanwhile, Minister of Finance Fukushiro Nukaga, who had been Director-General of the then Defence Agency in 2005–06, was summoned to the House of Councillors to respond to questions about the bribery allegations. The House of Councillors began debating the proposed resumption of the Japanese naval deployment in the Indian Ocean in early December 2007, but the DPJ continued to refuse to approve the necessary legislation and the Diet's session was extended for a further month in mid-December. In mid-January 2008 the Government forced through the passage of the legislation, using its majority in the House of Representatives to override another vote against it by the House of Councillors (the first time this power had been used since 1951). Two Japanese vessels were dispatched to assist US forces in the Indian Ocean later that month.

Japan's bilateral security arrangements with the USA, concluded by treaty in 1951, together with trade issues, continued to be the focus of Japanese-US relations. The treaty granted the use of military bases in Japan to the USA, in return for a US commitment to provide military support to Japan in the event of external aggression. From 1982 Japan remained under pressure from the USA to increase its defence expenditure and to assume greater responsibility for security in the Western Pacific area. In December 1990 the Government announced a new five-year programme to develop the country's defence capability. The new programme also envisaged that Japan would assume a greater share of the cost of maintaining the US troops stationed in Japan. In January 1992 the 'Tokyo declaration on the US-Japan global partnership' was issued, whereby the two countries undertook to co-operate in promoting international security and prosperity. In February 1993 Japan and the USA reaffirmed their security relationship, with the USA agreeing to protect Japan from the threat posed by potential nuclear proliferation around the world. In November 1995 the Cabinet approved a new national defence programme, which envisaged a 20% reduction in troops and confirmed Japan's security co-operation with the USA. In September 1997 revised Guidelines for Japan-US Defense Co-operation (first compiled in 1978) were issued. The Guidelines envisaged enhanced military co-operation between the USA and Japan, not only on Japanese territory, but also in situations in unspecified areas around Japan. In April 1998 the LDP Government approved legislation on the implementation of the revised Guidelines, which was enacted in May 1999, prompting criticism from China and Russia. Its approval was ensured by an agreement concluded by the LDP, the LP and New Komeito to exclude a clause that would have allowed the inspection of unidentified foreign ships by the SDF, with the aim of enforcing economic sanctions. In August 1999 the Japanese Government formally approved a memorandum of understanding with the USA stipulating details of joint technical research on the development of a theatre missile defence system, which aims to detect and shoot down incoming ballistic missiles within a 3,000-km radius.

From the mid-1990s Japan's growing trade surplus with the USA became a matter of increasing concern for the US authorities. In October 1994 trade agreements in three of the four main areas under bilateral discussion were signed. Negotiations concerning the automobile trade resulted in the signing of an agreement with the USA in June 1995. However, an increase in the export of Japanese vehicles to the USA in 1997, and a concomitant rise in the US trade deficit with Japan, caused growing tension between the two countries. In September an agreement to reform Japanese port operations was concluded shortly after the USA imposed large fines on Japanese companies for employing restrictive harbour practices. Negotiations on increased access to airline routes were successfully concluded in January 1998. However, relations were again strained by trade disputes in 1998, with Japan's high tariffs on rice, in the forestry and fisheries sectors, and low-priced steel exports being of particular concern to the USA. Tension also arose over the USA's repeated criticism that Japan was not doing enough to stimulate its own economy and alleviate the Asian economic crisis. During a visit to Japan in November 1998, President Bill Clinton urged the Government rapidly to implement measures to encourage domestic demand, reform the banking sector and liberalize its markets. Meanwhile, Japan's trade surplus with the USA continued to increase, and in 1998 reached its highest level since 1987. In May 1999, during a visit by Prime Minister Obuchi to the USA (the first such official state visit in 12 years), Clinton praised Obuchi's efforts to promote economic recovery and welcomed Japanese plans for further deregulation in several sectors.

The presence of US forces in Japan continued to provoke much debate. In November 1995 three US servicemen were arrested and subsequently imprisoned for the rape of a schoolgirl on Okinawa. Considerable civil unrest ensued and legal proceedings were initiated against the Governor of Okinawa, Masahide Ota, following his refusal to renew the leases for US military installations in the region. Protracted negotiations between the two countries resulted in the USA agreeing, in December 1996, to release 21% of the land used for US military purposes on Okinawa, and to build a floating offshore helicopter base to replace the air base at Futenma. In April 1997 it was proposed to relocate several of the US bases to other prefectures. In December, in a non-binding referendum held in Nago, Okinawa, to assess public opinion concerning the construction of the offshore helicopter base, the majority of voters rejected the proposal, prompting the resignation of the Mayor of Nago. Governor Ota stated his opposition to the proposed base, a position also adopted by the new Mayor, elected in February 1998. In November 1998 Keiichi Inamine defeated Ota in the Okinawa gubernatorial elections. Inamine, who had been supported by the LDP, presented an alternative solution, proposing that a military-commercial airport be built in northern Okinawa and leased to the USA for a period of 15 years. In December 1998 a US military site was the first of the 11 bases to be returned under the 1996 agreement. In December 1999 Inamine's proposal for the relocation of the Futenma air base was approved by both the local authorities and the Japanese Government, with the Henoko district of Nago chosen as the site for the new airport; at the same time funding was allocated for a 10-year development plan for northern Okinawa. Negotiations with the US Government, which opposed any time limit on its use of the airport, took place in October 2000; no progress was made.

In November 2000 the Japanese House of Representatives approved a five-year agreement, to commence in April 2001, to reduce host nation spending for US forces stationed in Japan. Although the Administration of US President George W. Bush favoured stronger links with Japan than its predecessor, relations between Japan and the USA briefly deteriorated in February 2001 when a Japanese trawler sank, killing the entire crew, following a collision with a US submarine, the *Greenville*, off Hawaii. The revelation that a civilian had been at the controls of the submarine at the time caused fury in Japan, as did reports that Yoshiro Mori had insisted on finishing a game of golf before dealing with the situation. In April Japan banned US nuclear submarines from visiting its ports after the US Navy failed to give prior notification of such a visit, as required. The Japanese victims of the submarine collision, and their relatives, accepted US $13m. in compensation from the US Navy in November 2002.

Following the terrorist attacks on the USA in September 2001, Japan immediately pledged co-operation with the USA's 'war on terror', including military support within the framework of Japan's Constitution. Koizumi visited Washington, DC, later that month and announced that Japan would assist in the gathering of intelligence, the delivery of supplies and of medical and humanitarian relief. The requisite legislation was approved by the Diet, and in November Japan deployed several warships and 1,500 personnel to the Indian Ocean in this capacity; however, Japanese forces were still forbidden to participate in combat activities. At this time, several Japanese companies signed a deal with a US firm to build air-defence systems for Japan's military.

President Bush visited Japan in February 2002 and praised Koizumi, urging him to reform the country's economy. Disagreements remained, however, over the USA's description of North Korea as part of an 'axis of evil' and over measures to reduce global warming. Japan pursued a policy of engagement with the DPRK, while the USA adopted a more sceptical attitude to that country. None the less, Japan, along with the Republic of Korea, sought to encourage the USA to support Koizumi's visit to the North in September (see below). However, the USA adopted a harder line towards the DPRK after it allegedly admitted to pursuing a secret nuclear weapons programme in October. In November Keiichi Inamine was re-elected Governor of Okinawa, having strongly campaigned in preceding months for a significant reduction in US troops stationed on the island.

In December 2002 Japan and the USA held a meeting of ministers of defence and foreign affairs in Tokyo on outstanding security issues. In addition to seeking an early resolution of the crisis over the North Korean nuclear weapons programme, the two countries moved closer to agreement on the deployment of a joint missile shield (see below). In February 2003 the Japanese Government stated that the two countries would conduct joint training of ballistic missile interception off the coast of Hawaii for a period of two years, beginning in 2004. In March 2003 Japan launched its first spy satellites, aiming to improve its independent intelligence-gathering capabilities.

Koizumi gave President Bush his full support for the USA's military offensive against Iraq, which commenced in late March 2003, despite strong opposition from the Japanese public. However, Japan refused to close the Iraqi embassy in Tokyo, despite requests from the USA. Following the approval of legislation to permit the dispatch of Japanese troops to Iraq in a peace-keeping capacity, in early 2004 the first Japanese soldiers were deployed. Meanwhile, in December 2003 plans were announced by the Japanese Government for the development of a ballistic missile defence system in co-operation with the USA, reportedly intended to protect Japan in the event of an attack by the DPRK.

In 2004 there was renewed public resentment at the US military presence on Okinawa following the crash of a US military helicopter in the grounds of a university in August. At a meeting in December it was agreed that Japan would resume air traffic control over Okinawa within three years. Following a meeting of Japanese and US defence officials in February 2005, Japan and the USA issued a joint statement claiming that security in the Taiwan Straits was a 'common strategic objective'. In October it was reported that the US Government had agreed to transfer its forces from the base at Futenma in the south of Okinawa to Camp Schwab in the less residential northern area of the island, in reaction to tensions between the troops and the local population. Later that month the announcement that a nuclear-powered US aircraft carrier was to be stationed in Japanese waters provoked controversy. It was also announced, however, that the number of US soldiers based on Okinawa was to be halved. Some 8,000 troops were to be relocated to the US Pacific Territory of Guam. A final agreement on the transfer to Camp Schwab and the relocation of troops to Guam was concluded on 1 May 2006. None the less, the local residents of Okinawa remained sceptical of the plans, and in November elected a new governor, Hirokazu Nakaima, supported by the ruling coalition. While pledging to negotiate on the issue of the US presence in Okinawa, Nakaima rejected his rival's demands for the complete removal of the bases from Japan. Meanwhile, in June Koizumi paid his last official visit as Prime Minister to the USA, where a summit meeting with President George W. Bush resulted in little progress in the area of bilateral agreements but clearly demonstrated the close personal rapport between the two leaders. Official discussions focused on the issue of North Korea, which had announced plans to test a long-range missile (see below). The decision by Japan to withdraw its troops from Iraq (see below) just days before the visit did not appear to affect the relationship with the USA. In December Japan approved a military budget for the fiscal year beginning in April 2007 that would provide for a 30.5% rise in the nation's spending on the joint Japanese-US missile shield; this was largely in response to the North Korean nuclear test in October (see below). Upon taking office in September 2006, Prime Minister Shinzo Abe first sought to improve relations with China and the Republic of Korea, visiting both countries in the following month, and it was not until April 2007 that he travelled to the USA. None the less, Abe and President Bush both reaffirmed their commitment to strong US-Japanese relations following their talks, which focused on North Korea's nuclear weapons programme, climate change and trade issues (notably Japanese restrictions on imports of US beef), as well as other matters of bilateral concern.

In early November 2007 the USA expressed disappointment at the withdrawal of Japan's Maritime Self-Defence Force from the Indian Ocean, where it had been supporting US-led counter-terrorism operations since 2001 (see above), following the failure to secure approval for an extension of the mission in the Japanese Diet. Prime Minister Yusuo Fukuda held talks with President Bush in the USA later that month during his first overseas visit since taking office in September. Fukuda promised to continue in his efforts to secure authorization for a renewal of the Indian Ocean mission and urged Bush not to remove the DPRK from the USA's list of states accused of sponsoring terrorism. In partnership with the US Missile Defense Agency, Japan tested its ballistic missile defence system for the first time in mid-December, when a Japanese warship stationed off Hawaii successfully intercepted and destroyed a mock target some 160 km above the Pacific Ocean. The eventual deployment of the missile defence system on four destroyers was envisaged. Meanwhile, land-based missile defence systems had already been installed at two bases in Japan, with an expansion to a total of 11 sites planned by 2011. Japan resumed its naval mission in support of US forces in the Indian Ocean in January 2008, after the Government forced the necessary legislation through the Diet (see above).

The alleged rape of a 14-year-old Japanese girl by a US serviceman on Okinawa in February 2008 prompted the prefectural assembly to adopt a resolution of protest against the incident and a petition demanding, *inter alia*, a reduction in US forces and the enforcement of stricter discipline by US military leaders. The assembly cited the assault of a Japanese woman by a relative of a US soldier in October 2007 and the robbery of a taxi driver by two US servicemen in January 2008 as further evidence that such measures were required. In response, US military leaders initiated a review of existing programmes designed to prevent sexual harassment and assaults, and subsequently imposed a curfew restricting the movements of US troops on Okinawa.

Despite the signing of a treaty of peace and friendship with the People's Republic of China in 1978, relations deteriorated in the late 1980s after China expressed concern at Japan's increased defence expenditure and its more assertive military stance. Japanese aid to China was suspended in June 1989, following the Tiananmen Square massacre in Beijing, and was not resumed until November 1990. Relations between the two countries were strengthened by the visits to China by Emperor Akihito in October 1992, the first-ever Japanese imperial visit to China, and by Prime Minister Hosokawa in March 1994. However, in August of that year Japan announced the suspension of economic aid to China, following renewed nuclear testing by the Chinese Government. The provision of economic aid was resumed in early 1997, following the declaration of a moratorium on Chinese nuclear testing.

In July 1996 Japan's relations with both China and Taiwan were strained when a group of nationalists, the Japan Youth Federation, constructed a lighthouse and war memorial on the Senkaku Islands (or Diaoyu Islands in Chinese), a group of uninhabited islands situated in the East China Sea, to which China, Japan and Taiwan all laid claim. In October a flotilla of small boats, operated by activists from Taiwan, Hong Kong and Macao, raised the flags of China and Taiwan on the disputed islands. The Japanese Government sought to defuse tensions with China and Taiwan by withholding official recognition of the lighthouse; it did not, however, condemn those who had constructed the controversial buildings. In May 1997 China expressed serious concern when a member of the Japanese Diet landed on one of the disputed islands. The Japanese Government distanced itself from the action.

In September 1997 Hashimoto visited China to commemorate the 25th anniversary of the normalization of relations between the two countries. China expressed concern at the revised US-Japanese security arrangements, following a statement by a senior Japanese minister that the area around Taiwan might be covered under the new guidelines. Procedures for the removal of chemical weapons, deployed in China by Japanese forces during the Second World War, were also discussed. During a visit to Japan by the Chinese Premier, Li Peng, in November, a bilateral fisheries agreement was signed. In November 1998, during a six-day state visit by President Jiang Zemin, Obuchi and Jiang issued (but declined to sign) a joint declaration on friendship and co-operation, in which Japan expressed deep remorse for past aggression against China. China, however, was reported to be displeased by the lack of a written apology. A subsequent US-Japanese agreement to initiate joint technical research on the development of a theatre missile defence system, followed by the Japanese Diet's approval, in May 1999, of legislation on the implementation of the revised US-Japanese defence guidelines (see above), provoked severe criticism from China, despite Japan's insistence that military co-operation with the USA was purely defensive. In July a meeting in Beijing between Obuchi and the Chinese Premier, Zhu Rongji, resulted in the formalization of a bilateral agreement on China's entry to the World Trade Organization (WTO), following several months of intense negotiations on the liberalization of trade in services. In August 2000 China withdrew permission for the Japanese Minister of Transport, Hajime Morita, to visit the People's Republic in September, owing to scheduling difficulties with Chinese officials. The Japanese media, however, attributed the Chinese change of attitude to a recent visit by Morita to a shrine honouring Japan's war dead, including those convicted of war crimes. Zhu Rongji visited Japan in October, and admitted that his failure to demand an apology for the host country's wartime conduct had attracted criticism in China.

In April 2001 a trade dispute broke out between China and Japan after the latter, seeking to protect its domestic producers, imposed tariffs on imports of Chinese mushrooms, leeks and rushes. China responded by introducing tariffs on Japanese consumer goods, leading to further disputes, which persisted throughout the rest of 2001. China was further angered by Japan's decision to allow former Taiwanese President Lee Teng-hui to visit the country in May. These disagreements led to a postponement of a visit to Japan by former Chinese Premier Li Peng. Meanwhile, China reacted angrily to Koizumi's visit to the Yasukuni Shrine, and a senior official of the Chinese Ministry of Foreign Affairs urged Japan to take 'visible action' to renounce its militaristic past. Koizumi travelled to China in October, when he visited the Marco Polo Bridge (the site of a clash between China and Japan that led to full-scale war in 1937) and apologized for Japan's past crimes in China. The visit was also aimed at reassuring China about Japan's support for the USA's 'war on terror', and bilateral relations subsequently improved, although Chinese concerns about Japan's military deployment remained. In November China and Japan, along with the Republic of Korea, agreed to hold regular meetings of their ministers of finance and of foreign affairs in order to foster closer co-operation.

In March 2002 Makiko Tanaka, the former Minister of Foreign Affairs, visited China to mark 30 years of diplomatic relations between the two countries. (Her father, Kakuei Tanaka, had overseen the restoration of relations in 1972.) Li Peng visited Japan in early April, stating that he was optimistic about improving bilateral relations. However, Koizumi's second visit to the Yasukuni Shrine in late April was condemned by China, as was a third visit to the shrine in January 2003. In April 2002 the leader of the opposition LP, Ichiro Ozawa, warned that Japan was capable of developing thousands of nuclear warheads in response to China's military build-up, if necessary. In May Japan strongly protested against the entry by Chinese security forces into the Japanese consulate in Shenyang, China, to remove several North Koreans who had sought refuge there. China responded that Japanese officials had consented to the move. The dispute was resolved when both sides allowed the North Koreans to travel to the Republic of Korea via a third country. The confrontation raised mutual suspicions, although in June China allowed Japan to salvage an alleged North Korean spy vessel from its territorial waters.

Although China had, in October 2001, invited Japanese Crown Prince Naruhito and Crown Princess Masako to visit China to mark the occasion of the 30th anniversary, in September 2002, of the establishment of diplomatic relations, the royal couple did not attend the ceremonies. None the less, in late 2002 Japan and China were increasingly seeking to forge a tripartite free trade agreement with the Republic of Korea, and Koizumi held discussions with Jiang Zemin in Mexico at the summit meeting of Asia-Pacific Economic Co-operation (APEC, see p. 176) in October. In February 2003 China agreed to allow a Japanese escapee from the DPRK to travel to Japan after she sought asylum at the Japanese consulate in Shenyang. Several other such cases were subsequently reported.

In May 2003 a Japanese court rejected compensation claims from five residents of China's Heilongjiang Province who had been injured by chemical weapons left in China by the Japanese army at the end of the Second World War. However, in August the Japanese Government apologized to China following a similar incident in which 29 people were injured by weapons abandoned by the Japanese army. In September a Tokyo court ordered the Japanese Government to pay compensation to 13 Chinese people injured by dumped Japanese weapons. There were tensions between China and Japan over the disputed Senkaku Islands in June 2003, when a boat carrying Chinese activists entered Japanese waters in the vicinity of the islands. Despite these problems, China and Japan, with the Republic of Korea, agreed to increase co-operation in various areas, including security and technology, on the occasion of a summit meeting of the Association of South East Asian Nations (ASEAN, see p. 185) on the Indonesian island of Bali in October (see below). However, no agreement was reached on the establishment of a free trade area.

In early 2004 there were renewed disputes over the Senkaku Islands, with two Chinese boats being sighted in Japanese waters in January, and the arrest in March by Japanese police of seven Chinese activists who had landed on one of the islands. In January there was a fourth visit by Prime Minister Koizumi to the Yasukuni Shrine. In March, in an unprecedented ruling, a Japanese District Court required the Government to pay compensation to former Chinese slave labourers who had been forced to work in a Japanese harbour transport company during the Second World War. Sino-Japanese relations deteriorated further in late 2004 following a reported intrusion by a Chinese submarine into Japanese waters in early November. Later in the month Prime Minister Koizumi and Chinese President Hu Jintao held talks at an APEC summit meeting in Chile. Koizumi admonished Hu over the submarine intrusion, whereas Hu expressed China's strong opposition to Koizumi's repeated visits to the Yasukuni Shrine. In December China was further incensed when a revision of Japanese defence policy identified China as a potential security threat. Despite political tensions, observers noted that the growth in Japanese exports to China had been a major factor in promoting Japan's economic recovery during 2003–04.

China was angered in February 2005 by the joint statement made by Japan and the USA on Taiwan (see above). In April violent anti-Japanese protests took place across China, following Japan's approval of school textbooks that reportedly omitted any references to Japanese war crimes in China. The subsequent attacks on Japanese embassies and boycotts of Japanese products and companies were also thought to be partially motivated by Japan's ongoing campaign to acquire a permanent seat on the UN Security Council (see below), a move that China, a long-standing permanent member, vehemently opposed. In May Chinese Vice-Premier Wu Yi cancelled a scheduled meeting with Prime Minister Koizumi while visiting Japan, a decision considered by some to have been motivated by comments made by Koizumi denying the political significance of his Yasukuni visits. A dispute between the two countries over the status of the Okinotori Shima coral reef chain in the Pacific Ocean to the south of Japan continued in 2005: Japan claimed that the chain constituted islands and thus, under international maritime law, Japanese sovereignty over them gave it the right to an exclusive economic zone in the surrounding waters, while China insisted that Okinotori Shima merely constituted 'rocks', lacking the sustainable economic activity required to engender an exclusive zone. Other factors influencing the Sino-Japanese relationship included competition over an oil pipeline project with Russia (see below) and competing claims to petroleum exploration fields in the East China Sea. In July the Chinese Government protested against its Japanese counterpart's granting of drilling rights in disputed waters to Teikoku Oil Co, and in October Japanese officials asserted that their reconnaissance information showed that Chinese platforms were operating in a contested region. Also in October Koizumi visited the Yasukuni Shrine for the fifth time since becoming Prime Minister, prompting the Chinese Government to cancel a scheduled visit by the Japanese Minister of Foreign Affairs. Subsequently, in December an annual trilateral meeting to have been attended by Japan, China and the Republic of Korea and to have been held during the course of the inaugural East Asia Summit in Kuala Lumpur, Malaysia, was cancelled. Chinese and Korean officials cited Koizumi's visits to the Yasukuni Shrine as the motive for their cancellation. Further Chinese (and Korean) anger was incurred in January 2006 when the recently appointed Minister of Foreign Affairs, Taro Aso, apparently suggested that Emperor Akihito should visit the Yasukuni Shrine. Neither Akihito nor his father Hirohito had visited the shrine since 1978 when 14 Class A war criminals had been enshrined there. Aso subsequently moderated his proposal; however, in February 2006 he once again offended Chinese opinion with comments to the effect that the high quality of Taiwan's education system was a consequence of Japan's colonial occupation of the island. Relations between the two countries appeared to be improving when, in May, Aso held discussions with his Chinese counterpart, Li Zhaoxing, during the course of a meeting of APEC convened in Doha, Qatar. While the two ministers failed to reach any agreement on the controversial shrine visits, they pledged to conduct further discussions on scientific, economic and other forms of co-operation, stressing the supreme importance of the Sino-Japanese relationship. They also agreed to accelerate negotiations on the development of disputed gas exploration in the East China Sea. The improvement continued in June when the Japanese Government agreed to remove its moratorium on a programme of low-interest loans to China, which had earlier been suspended. By August, however, the relationship had once more deteriorated, following the publication of a Japanese defence policy document that was perceived to have exaggerated the Chinese military threat. On 15 August, furthermore, Koizumi fulfilled a pledge made five years previously to visit the Yasukuni Shrine on the anniversary of Japan's surrender in the Second World War. While the Japanese Prime Minister insisted that the visit was not an attempt to justify the war, the Chinese Ministry of Foreign Affairs issued a statement warning that the visit would undermine the two countries' relations.

The appointment of Shinzo Abe as Prime Minister in late September 2006, however, raised hopes of a significant improvement in Sino-Japanese relations. Just days after taking office, the new Prime Minister confirmed that he had arranged a visit to Beijing, in what would be the first bilateral summit meeting between Chinese and Japanese leaders for five years. Despite Abe's reported visit to the Yasukuni Shrine in April and his refusal to state whether or not he would continue to visit the shrine as Prime Minister (see above), the Chinese Government appeared more willing to engage with Abe than with his predecessor, and Prime Minister Wen Jiabao of China made reference to a 'relentless effort' to improve bilateral relations. Meeting Abe in Beijing in October, President Hu described the visit as a turning point in Sino-Japanese relations and commended Abe for choosing China as the first destination for an official overseas trip, during which the two nations pledged to expand relations in the areas of trade, investment and technology. Also, Abe acknowledged that Japan had inflicted suffering on Asian people in the past, and with regard to the issue of Taiwan he confirmed that the Japanese Government would adhere firmly to its 'one China' policy.

In December 2006 Japan made further overtures towards China when Prime Minister Abe issued a formal invitation to President Hu Jintao and Prime Minister Wen Jiabao to visit Japan. Also in December, 10 academics from each nation met in Beijing to begin a project aimed at resolving disputes over the two countries' historical issues. The project, which received support from the Ministers of Foreign Affairs of both nations, was expected to continue for more than a year. The Chinese Minister of Foreign Affairs travelled to Tokyo for discussions in February 2007, in advance of Prime Minister Wen's visit to Japan, which took place in April. In his address to the Japanese Diet, the first ever by a Chinese Prime Minister, Wen urged a spirit of reconciliation. Wen and Abe agreed to increase bilateral co-operation in a wide range of areas. Meanwhile, in March Abe's questioning of the degree of compulsion used by Japan in engaging women for sexual purposes during the Second World War (see below) had provoked much criticism in China and elsewhere, following which the Prime Minister was obliged to issue an apology for his remarks. In April the Japanese Supreme Court dismissed two appeals for compensation by Chinese nationals over their treatment by the Japanese during the war (see below) on the grounds that China had renounced all claims for reparation from Japan in a communiqué signed by the two countries in 1972. Further similar appeals to the Court were also rejected in the following months.

It was anticipated that the improvement in Sino-Japanese relations experienced under Abe's premiership of Japan would continue under Prime Minister Yusuo Fukuda, who, upon taking office in September 2007, expressed his intention to develop closer links with China and other neighbouring Asian countries. Fukuda and Wen held amicable talks in Singapore in November while attending the annual summit meeting of ASEAN, with both leaders emphasizing their commitment to strengthening bilateral relations. They agreed to accelerate efforts to resolve the dispute over gas exploration in the East China Sea, which remained outstanding, despite 11 rounds of consultations on the issue. A goodwill visit to Japan by a Chinese warship later that month, the first since 1934, was a further sign of improving relations, as was the first high-level dialogue on closer economic co-operation, which was held in Beijing at the beginning of December with the participation of senior government ministers from both countries. In late December Fukuda made his first visit to China as Prime Minister. Discussions between Fukuda and Wen resulted in agreement to enhance co-operation in various areas, including the environment, energy, and science and technology, and to promote youth exchanges between their countries. President Hu was expected to visit Japan during the first half of 2008.

In January 1993, meanwhile, Prime Minister Miyazawa toured four member countries of ASEAN, during which he advocated an expansion of political and economic co-operation in the region. A visit by Prime Minister Hashimoto to ASEAN countries in January 1997 aimed to strengthen economic and security relations with the member countries. During 1998 Japan was widely criticized for its slow response to the Asian economic crisis. The weakness of the Japanese currency adversely affected financial markets throughout Asia, undermining efforts to stimulate regional economic recovery. As a result of increasing international pressure, in October the Japanese Government announced a US $30,000m. aid 'package' for Asian countries. In November the USA and Japan presented a joint initiative for growth and economic recovery in Asia, and in the following month Japan pledged further aid, to be disbursed over a three-year period. In January 2000 Prime Minister Obuchi visited Cambodia, Laos and Thailand. In May Japan provided Myanmar with a substantial aid programme, aimed at building closer bilateral ties. Also in May, Singapore agreed to allow Japan to use its military bases for evacuating its citizens from crisis locations, and for regional peace-keeping missions, the first agreement of its kind between Japan and another country. In April 2001 Japan provided another aid programme for Myanmar, despite a de facto international moratorium on such aid owing to the repressive nature of the country's ruling military junta. In October Japan reached a comprehensive free trade agreement with Singapore, and in January 2002 Prime Minister Koizumi visited Indonesia, Malaysia, the Philippines, Singapore and Thailand. Japan's influence in South-East Asia largely depended on its aid and investment programmes, both of which were being curtailed owing to Japan's economic problems.

In April 2002 Koizumi also visited Viet Nam, East Timor (now Timor-Leste), Australia and New Zealand, and in November he attended the ASEAN summit meeting in Phnom-Penh, Cambodia, where he signed an agreement to develop a comprehensive economic partnership with ASEAN members within 10 years—including the possible formation of a Japan-ASEAN free trade area. In November Japan's free trade agreement with Singapore took effect. In February 2003 the Secretary-General of ASEAN urged Japan to develop political, security, and cultural co-operation with the organization. In June 2003 Japan announced that financial aid to Myanmar would be suspended in protest at the detention of the country's opposition leader, Aung San Suu Kyi. In December Japan hosted an ASEAN summit meeting at which Japan offered US $3,000m. in financial aid to ASEAN countries. At the Tokyo summit meeting it was also announced that Japan would begin negotiations on free trade agreements with Thailand, Malaysia and the Philippines. These developments followed agreement between China and ASEAN in November 2002 to establish a China-ASEAN free trade area by 2010. Japan participated in the inaugural East Asia Summit meeting, convened in Malaysia in December 2005, which was attended by the 'ASEAN + 3' countries (the member nations of ASEAN, plus China, Japan and the Republic of Korea), along with Australia, New Zealand and India.

In July 2006 a free trade agreement between Japan and Malaysia took effect, and a similar agreement with the Philippines was approved by the Japanese legislature in December. Japanese Prime Minister Shinzo Abe and his Thai counterpart, Gen. (retd) Surayud Chulanont, signed a free trade agreement at a bilateral summit meeting in April 2007; the agreement entered into force in November. Similar accords were signed with Brunei in June and with Indonesia, which was to provide Japan with a stable supply of liquefied natural gas, in August, while several rounds of talks on a free trade agreement with Viet Nam were also held during 2007. Negotiations on a comprehensive free trade agreement between Japan and ASEAN were concluded in November. Once signed and implemented, the agreement was to result in the immediate elimination of tariffs on some 70 categories of goods (mainly from the agricultural, fisheries and chemical sectors), accounting for more than 90% of the products subject to free trade arrangements, with tariffs on the remaining goods covered by the accord to be abolished gradually over a five-year period. In January 2008 Prime Minister Yusuo Fukuda held a meeting in Tokyo with the ministers responsible for foreign affairs of Cambodia, Laos, Myanmar, Thailand and Viet Nam, offering increased economic aid to the five countries, while encouraging them to make more progress on human rights issues and democratization.

Attempts to establish full diplomatic relations with the DPRK in early 1991 were hindered by North Korean demands for financial reparations for the Japanese colonization of the country during 1910–45 and by the DPRK's refusal to allow International Atomic Energy Agency inspectors access to its nuclear facilities. Relations improved in 1995 and 1996 after Japan provided emergency aid to the DPRK when serious food shortages were reported. Concerns that the DPRK had developed a missile capable of reaching Japanese territory resulted in the suspension of food aid in mid-1996, but, following bilateral negotiations in August 1997, at which it was agreed to reopen discussions aimed at restoring full diplomatic relations, provision of food aid resumed in October. Agreement was also reached concerning the issue of visits to relatives in Japan by the estimated 1,800 Japanese nationals resident in the DPRK. The first such visits took place in November. However, food aid and normalization talks were suspended in mid-1998, following the testing by the DPRK of a suspected missile over Japanese territory. Tensions were exacerbated in March 1999, when two suspected North Korean spy ships, which had infiltrated Japanese waters, were pursued and fired on by Japanese naval forces. In mid-1999 it was reported that Japanese components had been used by the DPRK for the construction of weapons and other military equipment. Relations improved following the DPRK's agreement with the USA, in September, to suspend its reported plans to test a new long-range missile. In October, following unofficial talks between Japanese and North Korean government officials in Singapore, Japan lifted a ban on charter flights to the DPRK. In December the Japanese Government announced that it would resume the provision of food aid. Later that month intergovernmental preparatory talks on re-establishing diplomatic relations were held in Beijing, after Japanese and North Korean Red Cross officials reached an agreement on humanitarian issues. Most notably, the Red Cross organization of the DPRK promised to urge its Government to co-operate in an investigation into the fate of some 10 missing Japanese nationals, believed by the Japanese Government to have been abducted by North Korean agents in the 1970s and 1980s. Full negotiations on the establishment of diplomatic relations were held in April 2000, and several further rounds of talks took place during the year, despite an announcement by Japan in September that normal bilateral relations would not be restored until the cases of Japanese citizens allegedly abducted by North Korean agents had been solved. Meanwhile, in September the long-delayed third series of visits to their homeland by the Japanese wives of North Korean men took place. In February 2001 the North Korean Government again reiterated the need for compensation from Japan. In May Japan expelled Kim Jong Nam, the son of North Korean leader Kim Jong Il, and Jong Nam's wife, son and a second woman, when they attempted to enter the country on false passports. The DPRK was one of several Asian countries that condemned Junichiro Koizumi's visit to the Yasukuni Shrine in August.

In December 2001 Japan's coastguard sank a suspected North Korean spy vessel after it had been expelled from Japan's exclusive economic zone. The DPRK condemned the incident, but denied any involvement. Japanese coastguard forces searched the sunken vessel in May 2002, and raised it in September of that year. Japan's concerns had been heightened in early 2002 when US President Bush referred to North Korea as one of three countries forming an 'axis of evil', comments that Japan viewed as inconsistent with aims of reducing regional tensions.

In an unexpected diplomatic move, Junichiro Koizumi visited Pyongyang in mid-September 2002, becoming the first incumbent Japanese Prime Minister to do so. His one-day visit, during which he held discussions with Kim Jong Il, was dominated by the latter's admission that North Korean agents had abducted 12 Japanese citizens in the 1970s and 1980s, of whom five were still alive. The remainder were said to have died of natural causes, although suspicions remained that they might have been executed, after Pyongyang failed to locate their graves. Kim apologized for the incidents, but attributed them to rogue elements within the security services. The admission led to a hardening of attitudes against the DPRK among the Japanese public, with some sources indicating that the total number of Japanese abductees might be as high as 100. The surviving captives were temporarily allowed to return to Japan in mid-October, although they had to leave behind any spouses or children. The Japanese authorities, however, refused to allow them to return to the DPRK after the visit. Despite this, representatives from the two countries held the first round of resumed discussions on the restoration of normal diplomatic relations in Malaysia at the end of October, but failed to make any progress.

Japan became alarmed in October 2002 after North Korean representatives allegedly admitted to visiting US officials that the DPRK was pursuing a secret nuclear weapons programme. Koizumi announced that Japan would halt further economic co-operation with the DPRK until the issues of the abducted Japanese citizens and the nuclear programme were resolved. North Korea's admission led to increased co-operation between Japan and the USA over how to resolve the crisis, with Japan moving closer to participating in a missile shield with the USA (see above). The North Korean Government warned Japan that it would abandon its moratorium on missile-testing if normalization talks failed to make any progress. In separate incidents in late February and early March 2003 the DPRK test-launched two short-range ground-to-ship missiles in the Sea of Japan, and in early April tested a third missile in the Yellow Sea. However, it refrained from testing longer-range ballistic missiles, which Japan considered a threat to its security. The director-general of Japan's Defence Agency warned the DPRK that Japan could conduct a pre-emptive strike on North Korean missile facilities if necessary. In June 2003 Japan detained two North Korean cargo ships on safety grounds, following US pressure to increase inspections of North Korean shipping; the DPRK denounced the detentions as sanctions. Japan was one of the six countries to participate in the talks on the DPRK's nuclear programme, hosted by China, the first round of which commenced in Beijing in August (see the chapter on the DPRK for further details).

In January 2004 the House of Representatives approved legislation allowing Japan to impose economic sanctions on the DPRK. In April the House of Councillors approved legislation requiring all ships entering Japanese ports from March 2005 to be insured against oil damage. This in practice amounted to a ban on entry by North Korean ships. Following a further visit by Koizumi to Pyongyang in May 2004, five children of the abductees who had returned to Japan in 2002 (see above) were permitted to fly to Tokyo. Their release had been secured in return for pledges of food aid and medical supplies. However, suspicions remained over the fate of other missing Japanese nationals. In November the DPRK handed over human remains which it claimed were those of Megumi Yokota, who had been kidnapped by the DPRK in 1977. The North Korean Government claimed that she had committed suicide. However, subsequent DNA tests indicated that the remains were not those of Yokota. The Government of the DPRK joined South Korea and China in condemning the approval of a controversial history textbook for use in Japanese schools in 2005, as well as Prime Minister Koizumi's repeated visits to the controversial Yasukuni Shrine. The first round of bilateral talks between Japan and the DPRK since 2002, aimed at the restoration of normal diplomatic relations, was held in Beijing in February 2006. However, the discussions concluded without significant progress on the crucial issues of abducted Japanese citizens (Japan claiming that some abductees had yet to be accounted for), compensation for Japanese military aggression, or the resumption of the stalled six-party talks on the North's nuclear programme (see above).

The issue of abducted Japanese citizens came to the fore again in June 2006, when the Diet approved the North Korean Human Rights Act, which warned that economic sanctions would be imposed on the DPRK unless it worked to resolve human rights issues, including the question of the abductees. Relations deteriorated further in the following month when the DPRK conducted missile tests over the Sea of Japan, including the test of a *Taepo Dong 2* intercontinental ballistic missile. Japan reacted immediately by banning a North Korean trading ferry from its ports and by imposing a moratorium on charter flights from Pyongyang. In September the Japanese Government announced the unilateral imposition of more comprehensive sanctions, which included 'freezing' the assets of North Korean officials suspected of having links to their country's nuclear weapons programme.

Following Shinzo Abe's appointment as Prime Minister in September 2006, Japan adopted a more aggressive policy towards the DPRK. Long known for his uncompromising stance on the North Korean issue, Abe made a point of meeting the families of abductees just three days after taking office. Signalling the seriousness with which he regarded the issue, the new Prime Minister also appointed a special adviser, former cabinet secretary councillor Kyoko Nakayama, on North Korean abductions, and established a cabinet panel to deal with the affair. The DPRK's announcement on 9 October that it had tested a nuclear device greatly increased tensions. Clearly alarmed by the possibility of a nuclear power within the immediate region, Japan not only gave strong support to the UN Security Council's sanctions but also imposed its own additional restrictions, including a ban on all North Korean imports and on the entry of North Korean ships into Japanese waters. The DPRK's apparent willingness to return to six-party talks on its nuclear programme in late October did little to placate the Japanese Government, which insisted that it would maintain the pressure on the DPRK and would disregard North Korean demands for it to be excluded from the negotiating process. In November, in a development that angered Japan's opposition politicians and human rights activists, the Government stated that it would order public broadcaster NHK to focus on the North Korean abduction issue in its international transmissions. It also announced a ban on the export of luxury goods to the DPRK, a measure that it hoped would inconvenience the country's ruling élite.

In February 2007 the six-party talks resulted in an agreement aimed at curbing North Korea's nuclear activities, beginning with the closure of its Yongbyon nuclear site in return for substantial amounts of fuel aid from the other five participating countries. However, Japan insisted that it would only provide aid once progress had been made on the question of the abducted Japanese nationals. As a result of the agreement, Japan and the DPRK held their first bilateral talks for more than a year in March, with the ultimate aim of restoring normal relations, although no apparent progress was made. After Yongbyon was officially declared closed in July (after a delay of several months), the DPRK accused Japan of attempting to obstruct the talks on the restoration of normal relations and to disrupt the six-party process with its refusal to provide energy aid and its insistence on the resolution of the abduction issue, which the DPRK claimed had already been settled. A second round of bilateral negotiations took place in early September. Yasuo Fukuda, who took office as Japanese Prime Minister later that month, favoured a more conciliatory approach to the DPRK than his predecessor. Nevertheless, in October Japan announced that it would not resume aid to the DPRK and extended sanctions for a further six months, despite the latter's recent commitment to disabling fully its Yongbyon facilities and declaring details of all its nuclear programmes by the end of the year (a deadline that, in the event, was missed), citing a continued lack of progress in the dispute over the abductees. The sanctions were further renewed in April 2008.

During 1996–98 Japan's relations with the Republic of Korea were strained for various reasons, principally concerning territorial and fishing disputes. Relations improved, however, during a four-day state visit by the South Korean President, Kim Dae-Jung, to Japan in October 1998, when a joint declaration was signed, in which Japan apologized for the suffering inflicted on the Korean people during Japanese colonial rule. Japan also pledged substantial aid to the Republic of Korea to stimulate economic recovery. In November the two countries concluded negotiations on the renewal of their bilateral fisheries agreement, which came into effect in January 1999. An agreement to modify some of the terms of the accord was reached in March 1999, following a series of differences over its implementation. Increased co-operation was emphasized during a visit by Obuchi to the Republic of Korea later that month, when both countries agreed to strengthen bilateral economic relations, and Japan pledged further aid. In August Japan and the Republic of Korea held their first joint military exercises since the Second World War, in the Tsushima Straits. Prime Minister Mori visited Seoul in May 2000, where he advocated closer bilateral ties and pledged support for the inter-Korean summit meeting held in June.

Relations with the Republic of Korea deteriorated in 2001, however, following Japan's official endorsement of a new history school textbook, which minimized the suffering of Chinese and Koreans during Japanese occupation. In April the Republic of Korea recalled its ambassador, cancelled planned exchanges in protest and demanded 35 revisions to the text. In July Japan stated that there would be no revisions, further inflaming public opinion in Korea. This anger was exacerbated in August when Prime Minister Koizumi visited the Yasukuni Shrine, leading to many protests. In October Koizumi visited Seoul and apologized for past crimes and suffering under Japanese rule; however, he was forced to cancel a visit to the National Assembly, owing to hostility against him there. In November Japan and the Republic of Korea, along with China, agreed to establish regular contacts between their ministers of finance and foreign affairs. In March 2002 Koizumi again visited the Republic of Korea and discussed the possibility of establishing a free trade pact, as well as Japan's policy towards the DPRK.

Along with China and the DPRK, the Republic of Korea condemned Koizumi's visits to the Yasukuni Shrine in April 2002 and January 2003. However, in March 2002 Koizumi and Kim Dae-Jung agreed to begin discussions on a possible bilateral free trade agreement, and at the end of May Koizumi attended the opening ceremony of the 2002 football World Cup, which was hosted jointly by Japan, in Seoul. Also in attendance was Prince Takamado (who died in November) and his wife, who were making the first official visit to the Republic of Korea by a member of the Imperial family. The football tournament, a major source of prestige to both countries, passed by without incident. Any remaining mutual hostility between the two countries was overshadowed in 2002 by the need for co-operation in engaging with the North. In December Koizumi and South Korean President-elect Roh Moo-Hyun agreed to form a united front when dealing with the North. Koizumi subsequently attended Roh's inauguration in February 2003. In June President Roh made his first state visit to Japan, in the course of which he held talks with Koizumi on the issue of the DPRK's nuclear weapons programme. Although both leaders agreed that North Korean nuclear proliferation should not be tolerated, Koizumi advocated strict policies towards the DPRK, such as inspections and blockades of goods transport, whereas Roh stressed the need for dialogue with Pyongyang. On the occasion of an ASEAN summit meeting in Bali in October 2003, the Republic of Korea and Japan agreed, with China, to increased co-operation in various spheres. Negotiations towards a free trade agreement between Japan and the Republic of Korea commenced in December 2003, but faltered in late 2004, reportedly owing to disagreement over the liberalization of trade in agricultural and fisheries products. Meanwhile, in January 2004 the Republic of Korea criticized a fourth visit by Prime Minister Koizumi to the Yasukuni Shrine.

A long-standing dispute between Japan and the Republic of Korea concerned sovereignty over a group of islands, called 'Takeshima' in Japanese or 'Dokdo' in Korean, situated in the Sea of Japan. The South Korean Government claimed that the islands were historically part of Korea, while the Japanese Government maintained that they had been incorporated into Japan at the beginning of the 20th century. This issue came to the fore again in 2005 (the 40th anniversary of the establishment of diplomatic links between the two countries), when the administration of Shimane Prefecture in Japan (of which the islands, in the Japanese view, formed a part) declared 22 February to be 'Takeshima Day', prompting official and public protest in the Republic of Korea. Meanwhile, the approval in April 2005 of Japanese history textbooks considered misleading with regard to Japan's wartime aggression once more drew condemnation from the Government of the Republic of Korea, together with public anti-Japanese demonstrations in that country. Prime Minister Koizumi's visit to the Yasukuni Shrine in October aroused similar condemnation and prompted South Korean President Roh Moo-Hyun to cancel a visit to Japan scheduled for December. Also in December, an annual trilateral meeting due to have been attended in Kuala Lumpur by Japan, the Republic of Korea and China was cancelled (see above).

Anti-Japanese sentiment re-emerged in the Republic of Korea in April 2006 when Japan announced plans to conduct a maritime survey around the Takeshima islands. While the Republic of Korea warned of a major confrontation and dispatched 20 patrol boats to the area, supported by helicopters and reconnaissance aircraft, Japan remained defiant. Later in the month, however, the two countries agreed to hold discussions on the issue. In what was perceived to be at best a precarious compromise, Japanese officials emerged from the talks having agreed to cancel the survey, in exchange for a South Korean pledge to abandon plans to register new names for trenches and ridges on the sea-bed. None the less, in a televised address South Korean President Roh Moo-Hyun reiterated his country's determination to retain control of the islands. In the following month the South Korean Government provoked fury in Japan by announcing a five-year plan for the disputed islands, which included the development of island facilities and the exploration of marine and mineral resources. In July the Republic of Korea announced that it was sending its own maritime survey to the islands.

The issue of the Yasukuni Shrine also continued to dominate relations between Japan and the Republic of Korea throughout 2006, with the latter making repeated requests for no further visits to proceed. However, these requests did little to influence Prime Minister Koizumi, who on 15 August (Liberation Day in Korea) performed what was regarded in Seoul as an openly defiant gesture when he visited the contoversial shrine for a sixth time (see above). The South Korean Minister of Foreign Affairs, Ban Ki-Moon (who had visited Tokyo just days before the visit to attend the funeral of former Prime Minister Ryutaro Hashimoto, and to protest against the shrine visits), described the visit as 'a total disrespect for the Korean Government and people' and expressed his 'deep disappointment'. In the following month negotiators from the two nations held discussions in Seoul aimed at resolving the Takeshima issue, but failed to reach an agreement.

The appointment of Shinzo Abe as Prime Minister in September 2006, however, marked the return of a more conciliatory stance by Japan towards the Republic of Korea. Immediately after assuming office, Abe telephoned South Korean President Roh Moo-Hyun, and the two leaders agreed to meet for discussions over the coming months. Abe flew to Seoul in early October, but his visit was inevitably overshadowed by the DPRK's announcement that it had tested a nuclear device (see above). The two sides emphasized their condemnation of the nuclear test, while agreeing to continue collaborating on the abduction issue. However, in March 2007 Abe's comments doubting whether coercion had been used to engage women for sexual purposes during the Second World War (see below) were criticized by the South Korean Minister of Foreign Affairs and Trade. Abe's successor as Prime Minister, Yasuo Fukuda, who took office in September, declared his intention to strengthen relations with the Republic of Korea and other neighbouring Asian countries, notably pledging not to visit the controversial Yasukuni Shrine. In January 2008, in a gesture of reconciliation, the relatives of 101 South Koreans who were forced to fight for the Japanese army during the Second World War were invited to a memorial service in Tokyo to mark the return of their remains. Japan had relinquished more than 1,000 sets of remains to South Korean diplomats since 2004, but this was the first time that the families of the dead had participated in events. The Japanese Senior Vice-Minister for Foreign Affairs apologized at the ceremony for the suffering inflicted by Japan on Koreans.

The actions of the Japanese army in the Second World War proved to be a contentious issue from the mid-1990s, both domestically and in Japan's relations with neighbouring Asian countries, in the context of the 50th anniversary, in August 1995, of the surrender of Japanese forces. In November 1994 an international ruling that Asian women used for sexual purposes by the Japanese army during the Second World War ('comfort women') should receive compensation was rejected by the Japanese Government, which insisted that the issue of reparation payments to individuals had been fully covered under the terms of the peace treaty of 1951. Japan also applied this policy to claims for compensation made by former prisoners of war belonging to the Allied forces. In February 1995 Prime Minister Murayama publicly acknowledged that Japan was responsible, in part, for the post-war division of the Korean peninsula. He was forced to retract the statement, however, following bitter controversy in the Diet. In June a resolution was passed apologizing for Japanese actions in the war, despite considerable disagreement in the Diet. However, countries whose citizens had been prisoners of the Japanese army criticized the resolution as being insufficiently explicit. In August 1996 the first compensation payments, accompanied by a letter of apology from Prime Minister Hashimoto, were made from a private fund to four Philippine victims, who had been used as 'comfort women' during the war. The majority of groups representing South Korean victims refused to accept payment from the fund, demanding that compensation be forthcoming from official, rather than private, sources. In April 1998, however, a Japanese district court ordered the Government to pay compensation to three former 'comfort women' from the Republic of Korea. Another group of South Korean 'comfort women' was refused the right to compensation by the Japanese High Court in November 2000.

In late 1999 a lawsuit was filed in the US state of California against several large Japanese corporations on behalf of former prisoners of war and civilians from various countries, who alleged that the companies had profited from their forced labour during the Second World War. In November 2000 one of these corporations agreed to pay compensation to Chinese forced labourers used during the war. The Japanese Government's endorsement of high school textbooks that minimized Japan's atrocities in Asia during the 1930s and 1940s, combined with Prime Minister Koizumi's regular visits to the Yasukuni Shrine from 2001, raised regional fears (especially in China and the Koreas—see above) of the development of a more nationalistic stance on the part of Japan. In July 2002 Koizumi and his Cabinet agreed to donate 10% of their annual salary to a fund designed to compensate former 'comfort women'. In August a Tokyo court rejected a compensation claim by 180 Chinese for damages inflicted in biological warfare during the 1930s and 1940s, but acknowledged that Japan had, in fact, waged such warfare in China at that time. This was corroborated by a former member of Japan's biological warfare division, who testified to such crimes at the trial. Historians estimated that 300,000 Chinese had been killed by Japanese biological warfare schemes. In September 2003 compensation was granted to 13 Chinese people injured by Second World War weapons left behind by the Japanese army, and in March 2004 former Chinese slave labourers were granted compensation from the Japanese Government (see above). Koizumi stated in early 2005 that he would not visit the Yasukuni Shrine during the New Year period, as he had done in 2004. In July 2005 Japan commemorated the 60th anniversary of the end of the Second World War. Prime Minister Koizumi admitted in a speech that the wartime conduct of Japan had caused 'tremendous suffering and damage' and reiterated the country's commitment to peaceful co-existence with its neighbours. However, in October he made his fifth visit to the Yasukuni Shrine since becoming Prime Minister, once more drawing condemnation from the countries occupied by Japan during the war (see above).

Prime Minister Shinzo Abe provoked considerable anger in March 2007, particularly in China and South Korea, when he claimed that there was no evidence that coercion had been used to recruit 'comfort women' during the Second World War. His comments followed the introduction of a resolution in the US House of Representatives (which was approved in July) urging the Japanese Prime Minister formally to apologize and accept responsibility 'in a clear and unequivocal manner' for the treatment of 'comfort women'. Abe apologized for his remarks before the Japanese House of Councillors later in March. The private fund established in 1995 to compensate former 'comfort women' ceased its activities at the end of that month, having made payments to 285 women from the Republic of Korea, Taiwan and the Philippines. In April, in two landmark judgments, the Supreme Court upheld a Tokyo High Court ruling rejecting claims for reparation by two Chinese 'comfort women' and rescinded a Hiroshima High Court ruling awarding compensation to a group of Chinese labourers who had been forced to work for a Japanese construction company during the war. The Supreme Court ruled that China had renounced all claims for reparation from Japan in a communiqué signed by the two countries in 1972, dismissing the plaintiffs' argument that no reference had been made in the document to individual rights. Similarly, in May and June the Supreme Court dismissed appeals for compensation by 198 Chinese victims of biological warfare during the 1930s and 1940s and by a further group of Chinese nationals who had been forced to work in Japan during the war.

Japan's relations with Russia have been dominated by the issue of the Northern Territories, four small islands situated close to Hokkaido, which were annexed in 1945 by the USSR. Both countries claim sovereignty over the islands, and there has been no substantial progress towards resolving the situation since 1956, when Japan and the USSR resumed diplomatic relations. In February 1992 a joint Japanese-Russian working group began discussions about a prospective peace treaty (formally ending the Second World War), and meetings on the issue took place in 1992 and 1993. However, relations between the two countries deteriorated, following the disposal of nuclear waste in Japanese waters by Russian ships in November, and Russia's decision, in August 1994, to open fire on Japanese vessels that were alleged to have been fishing in Russian waters. Bilateral negotiations over the status of the disputed territory opened in March 1995. In November 1996 Japan indicated that it was prepared to resume the disbursement of an aid 'package', withheld since 1991, and in May 1997 the Japanese Government abandoned its opposition to Russia's proposed membership of the Group of Seven industrialized nations (G-7). Russian plans for joint development of the mineral and fishing resources of the disputed territory were followed, in July, by an outline agreement on the jurisdiction of the islands. Later in that month a new diplomatic policy was forged, based on 'trust, mutual benefit and long-term prospects'. At an informal summit meeting in November, the two parties agreed to work towards the conclusion of a formal peace treaty by the year 2000. Negotiations resulted in the conclusion of a framework fisheries agreement in December 1997. The Japanese Government offered considerable financial aid to Russia during a visit by President Yeltsin to Japan in April 1998, and agreement was reached on the expansion of economic co-operation. In November Prime Minister Obuchi and Yeltsin signed a joint declaration on bilateral relations in Moscow. During Obuchi's visit Yeltsin reportedly submitted proposals on the resolution of the territorial dispute, in response to suggestions made by Hashimoto in April. Although it had been agreed that the contents of the proposals should not be made public, it was widely reported that both countries still claimed sovereignty over the islands, with Japan advocating a transitional period of Russian administrative control. Agreement was reached on the establishment of subcommissions to examine issues of border delimitation and joint economic activity on the disputed islands. In September 1999 Japan agreed to resume lending to Russia, which had been suspended since the Russian Government had effectively devalued the rouble and defaulted on some of its debts in mid-1998. At the same time an accord was concluded on improved access to the disputed islands for former Japanese inhabitants. Negotiations achieved little progress during 2000, a major obstacle being the issue of how many of the islands should be returned. Despite Russian President Vladimir Putin's repudiation of Japan's claim to any of the islands during his first official visit to Tokyo in September, Russia subsequently offered to abide by a 1956 declaration that it would relinquish two of the islands after the signature of a peace treaty, but Japan initially rejected this partial solution.

In March 2001 Prime Minister Mori met President Putin in Irkutsk, Russia, and discussed the future of the islands; however, no new agreements were reached. Nevertheless, in April Japanese and Russian military leaders agreed to improve bilateral military co-operation. In May Prime Minister Koizumi adopted a harder stance than his predecessor, and demanded that all four islands be relinquished, a position rejected by Russia. Prime Minister Koizumi met Putin at the Group of Eight (G-8) summit meeting in July, amid Japanese anger that Russia had permitted South Korean vessels to fish off the islands. The ongoing disputes meant that no agreement was reached on developing a Japan-Russia-Europe transport corridor, and in August Koizumi warned of serious damage to relations with Russia if the fishing dispute were not resolved. Japanese officials met their Russian counterparts on the margins of the G-8 summit meeting and the Asian security summit in Brunei in mid-2002, and both sides expressed a willingness to expand relations in all fields.

By late 2002 Koizumi was increasingly seeking Russia's assistance in persuading the DPRK to abandon its nuclear weapons programme. In January 2003 Koizumi visited Moscow and held a summit meeting with Putin, during which the two agreed to engage the DPRK. Koizumi also visited the Russian Far East, where he met regional leaders. Both Japan and Russia were keen to build a pipeline that would transport petroleum from Angarsk, in Siberia, to Nakhodka on Russia's Pacific coast, from where it could be shipped to Japan. The cost, estimated at US $5,000m., was considered a prohibitive factor, but the scheme would reduce Japan's dependency on Middle Eastern supplies (see Economic Affairs). Talks on the pipeline took place amid competition from China, which was negotiating for the pipeline to be built to the Chinese city of Daqing instead. By April 2006, when construction work on the first stage of the 4,130-km pipeline commenced, the planned route appeared to be from Taishet in eastern Siberia to Perevoznaya (near Nakhodka), via Kazachinskoe and Skovorodino, with an extension to Daqing to be built from Skovorodino. The 2,694-km first section of the pipeline, to Skovorodino and Daqing, was scheduled to be completed by the end of 2008. It seemed, therefore, that China would benefit from deliveries from the new line before Japan. Meanwhile, Japan and Russia both attended three rounds of six-party talks in Beijing on the North Korean nuclear weapons programme in 2003 and 2004 (see above). Tensions over the disputed Northern Territories islands (see above) were exacerbated in September 2004 when Prime Minister Koizumi embarked on a boat trip within sight of the islands. Hopes for 'two-track' negotiations (dealing with two of the four islands separately from the other two) were in doubt following a statement by Japan in November that it would be not be satisfied with the return of only two of the four disputed islands. A visit to Japan by President Putin in November 2005 resulted in little progress on the issue of the islands.

Tensions were renewed in August 2006 when, in the first such incident for 50 years, a Japanese fisherman was shot dead by a Russian patrol boat near the Northern Territories; three other fishermen were detained. While the Russian coastguard insisted that the fishing vessel had defied orders to halt, the Japanese Government disputed this claim and demanded that the three men be released immediately. Japan accused Russia of acting with excessive force, while Russian officials countered by implicating the three fishermen in poaching and illegal border crossing. By late August Japan had sent 39 fishing boats to the area around the islands, a move that Russia viewed as deliberate provocation. None the less, at the end of August Russia released two of the men, while continuing to detain the captain (who was fined by a Russian court in the following month). After the incident, Russia was reported to have intensified its patrols in the area, and in January 2007 a further Japanese boat, with six crew on board, was believed to have been detained by Russian officials. Bilateral tensions were raised in early June following the seizure of another Japanese fishing boat, and its crew of 17, by a Russian patrol boat and a visit to the disputed islands by the Russian Minister of Foreign Affairs, Sergei Lavrov. Prime Minister Abe and President Putin discussed the territorial issue while attending the G-8 summit meeting held in Germany that month, but no specific progress was made. In February 2008 Japan accused Russia of violating its airspace over the Izu islands in the Pacific, lodging an official protest with the Russian embassy in Tokyo.

The Japanese Government criticized India and Pakistan for conducting nuclear tests in mid-1998, and in response suspended grants of non-humanitarian aid and loans to both countries. A series of missile tests carried out by India and Pakistan in April 1999 again provoked criticism from Japan. Following a visit to India by the Japanese Prime Minister in August 2000, differences over nuclear testing were set aside in favour of enhanced security, defence and research co-operation between Japan and India, which continued during 2001. The Indian Prime Minister, Atal Bihari Vajpayee, visited Japan in December, the first such visit since 1992. In addition to security issues, the two countries discussed closer co-operation in their software and computer industries. In December 2006 Indian Prime Minister Manmohan Singh visited Japan, where the two countries agreed to commence negotiations on a bilateral economic partnership agreement aimed at reducing the high tariffs hitherto imposed on Japanese automobiles and electronics; these negotiations were ongoing in early 2008.

In November 2000 the Peruvian President, Alberto Fujimori, arrived in Tokyo from where he submitted his resignation by fax, following increasing allegations of domestic corruption. In December Japan announced that Fujimori possessed dual nationality as his father had been a Japanese citizen, and that he was therefore entitled to remain indefinitely in the country. In March 2001, however, the Peruvian authorities charged Fujimori with criminal abuse of power and requested his extradition. Japan refused, despite Peruvian warnings of serious consequences if the former President did not return. Fujimori remained in Japan throughout 2002, refusing to co-operate with members of a Peruvian Truth and Reconciliation Commission who visited Japan. In March 2003 Japan refused to extradite Fujimori, despite Interpol's issue of a warrant for his arrest. In August the Peruvian ambassador to Japan, Luis Macchiavello, issued a formal request for Fujimori's extradition; however, the Japanese Ministry of Foreign Affairs indicated that Japan was likely to reject the request. In November 2005 Fujimori left Japan and travelled to Chile, where he was detained by the authorities. In the same month Macchiavello was recalled to Peru in protest at the conduct of the Japanese Government in the Fujimori case. While still under house arrest in Chile, Fujimori contested the elections to the Japanese House of Councillors in July 2007 as a candidate of the New People's Party. It was speculated that Fujimori hoped to secure immunity from extradition or prosecution as an elected official if successful, but he failed to win a seat and, in September, was extradited from Chile to stand trial in Peru.

Japan's urgent need for new oil supplies prompted the visit to the country in October 2000 of the Iranian President, Muhammad Khatami, the first by an Iranian Head of State since the revolution of 1979. The trip culminated in Japan's acquisition of negotiation rights over the world's largest undeveloped oilfield, Azadegan field, in Iran. In July 2001 the Minister of Economy, Trade and Industry visited Iran, Kuwait, Saudi Arabia and the United Arab Emirates, in order to promote Japan's oil interests in the Middle East. In February 2004 an agreement was signed granting Japan exploitation rights in Iran's Azadegan oilfield, despite US concerns relating to development of nuclear weapons in Iran. The USA continued to put pressure on Japan with regard to the oilfield throughout 2005 and 2006. In late 2006 Japan lost its controlling stake in the Azadegan project, owing to Iranian dissatisfaction with Japan's lack of progress.

In January 2002 Japan hosted an international conference on the reconstruction of Afghanistan, and emerged as the largest single donor, pledging some US $500m. over two-and-a-half years. During 2002 and early 2003 Japan also sought to bring a lasting peace settlement to Sri Lanka, and pledged to continue overseas development assistance to the war-ravaged island. However, in January 2008 the Japanese peace envoy to Sri Lanka suggested that the Sri Lankan Government's decision to end a six-year cease-fire with rebels might necessitate a review of Japanese aid to Sri Lanka.

In September 1990, meanwhile, Japan contributed to the international effort to force an unconditional Iraqi withdrawal from Kuwait. A controversial LDP-sponsored Peace Co-operation Bill, which provided for the dispatch to the Persian (Arabian) Gulf area of some 2,000 non-combatant personnel, was withdrawn in November after it encountered severe political opposition. In January 1991, following repeated US demands for a greater financial commitment to the resolution of the Gulf crisis (and a swifter disbursement of moneys already pledged), the Japanese Government announced plans substantially to increase its contribution and to provide aircraft for the transport of refugees in the region. Opposition to the proposal was again vociferous. The Government secured the support of several centrist parties, by pledging that any financial aid from Japan would be employed in a 'non-lethal' capacity, and legislation to approve the new contribution was adopted by the Diet in March. In June 1992 controversial legislation to permit the SDF to participate in UN peace-keeping operations was approved. Their role, however, was to be confined to logistical and humanitarian tasks, unless a special dispensation from the Diet were granted. In September members of the SDF were dispatched to serve in the UN Transitional Authority in Cambodia (UNTAC). Japanese troops participated in further UN peace-keeping operations in Mozambique, in 1993, and, under Japanese command, on the Rwandan–Zairean border, in 1994. Legislation was approved in November 1994 to enable Japanese forces to be deployed overseas if the Government believed the lives of Japanese citizens to be at risk. In September Japan reiterated its desire to be a permanent member of the UN Security Council, particularly in view of its status as the world's largest donor of development aid and the second largest contributor (after the USA) to the UN budget. In October 1996 the UN General Assembly voted to allocate to Japan a non-permanent seat on the Security Council, to be held for a two-year period from January 1997. In the late 1990s and early 2000s the Japanese Government continued its campaign to obtain a permanent seat on the UN Security Council. In a speech to the UN General Assembly in September 2004 Koizumi stated that Japan's role in supporting reconstruction in Afghanistan and Iraq, as well as the Japanese contributions to negotiations with the DPRK on its nuclear programme, entitled Japan to a permanent seat. Japanese frustration at the perceived inequity between the country's financial contribution to the UN and its exclusion from the Security Council continued in 2005. Japan's bid for a permanent seat was believed to have the support of the USA. However, the prospect of Japan gaining permanent representation in the UN's highest forum provoked strong objections from China and the Republic of Korea, as victims of past Japanese military aggression, and the issue was regarded as one factor in the anti-Japanese demonstrations in those countries in April 2005.

In November 2001 Japan announced plans to send 700 SDF members to East Timor as part of the international peace-keeping force. The force consisted mostly of engineers, and the first contingent arrived in March 2002. In February 2002 the Japanese Government planned to revise the 1992 law on peace-keeping missions, in order to allow the dispatch of the SDF without the consent of those in conflict, following a UN request. SDF personnel were also to be equipped with more powerful weapons, rather than purely defensive ones.

Following the commencement of US military action in Iraq in March 2003, the House of Councillors approved legislation to allow SDF forces to be dispatched to Iraq in a peace-keeping capacity. There was also increasing suggestion from 2003 of a revision of Japan's Constitution to give the SDF the status of a conventional army (see above). In mid-January 2004 an advance group of 30 SDF troops was dispatched, and by mid-April there were some 550 Japanese troops stationed in Iraq. In June 2004 Koizumi informed US President George W. Bush that Japanese troops would remain in Iraq after the transfer of sovereignty to an interim government at the end of that month. In December 2004 it was announced that the term of SDF involvement in Iraq would be extended by one year to aid reconstruction of the country. In December 2005 the Japanese Government announced that the SDF forces deployed in Iraq would remain there for a further year. None the less, there were indications of an early withdrawal, and in June 2006 the Government officially announced that Japanese forces would leave Iraq as soon as British and Australian troops in Samawa, in southern Iraq, were able to transfer responsibilities for security to Iraqi forces. The withdrawal of Japanese troops from Iraq commenced at the end of that month and was completed in July. However, a small contingent from the Japanese Air Self-Defence Force remained in a minor support role, transporting materials and personnel between Iraq and Kuwait. In mid-2007 the mission was extended for a further two years.

In January 2007 Prime Minister Abe visited four European capital cities, including Brussels, Belgium, where he met leaders of the North Atlantic Treaty Organization (NATO) to discuss closer co-operation between Japan and the military alliance. In March the Australian Prime Minister, John Howard, visited Tokyo for discussions with his Japanese counterpart. The two heads of government signed a new security agreement, to encompass peace-keeping and counter-terrorism operations, as well as issues of maritime and aviation security. The conclusion of this agreement, the first such bilateral accord since Japan's signing of the security treaty with the USA in 1951, was regarded as a clear manifestation of Japan's changing position with regard to international affairs. In April 2007 Japan and Australia commenced negotiations on a bilateral economic partnership agreement. Abe conducted a tour of five Middle Eastern countries in late April and early May, holding discussions with his counterparts on issues such as energy supplies for Japan, the Middle East peace process and Japanese reconstruction assistance for Iraq. Talks on a free trade agreement between Japan and the six member states of the Gulf Co-operation Council (Bahrain, Kuwait, Oman, Qatar, Saudi Arabia and the United Arab Emirates) had been initiated in September 2006.

Government

Under the Constitution of 1947, the Emperor is Head of State but has no governing power. Legislative power is vested in the bicameral Diet, comprising the House of Representatives (lower house), whose members are elected for a four-year term, and the House of Councillors (upper house), members of which are elected for six years, one-half being elected every three years. The House of Representatives comprises 480 seats—300 single-seat constituencies and 180 determined by proportional representation—and there are 242 seats in the House of Councillors. The number of seats in the House of Representatives was reduced from 500 for the 2000 elections; the reduction was in the number of seats determined by proportional representation. There is universal suffrage for all adults from 20 years of age. Executive power is vested in the Cabinet, which is responsible to the Diet. The Emperor appoints the Prime Minister (on designation by the Diet), who appoints the other Ministers in the Cabinet.

Japan has 47 prefectures, each administered by an elected Governor.

Defence

Although the Constitution renounces war and the use of force, the right of self-defence is not excluded, and in January 2007 the Defence Agency was upgraded to become the Ministry of Defence. Japan maintains ground, maritime and air self-defence forces. Military service is voluntary. According to Western estimates, the total strength of the Japanese Self-Defence Forces as assessed at November 2007 was some 240,400: army 148,300, navy 44,500, air force 45,900 and central staff 1,700. The USA has provided equipment and training staff and maintains bases in Japan. US forces stationed in Japan included 2,417 army and 13,164 airforce personnel, as assessed at November 2007. The projected defence budget for 2007/08 was 4,779,600m. yen.

Economic Affairs

In 2006, according to estimates by the World Bank, Japan's gross national income (GNI), measured at average 2004–06 prices, was US $4,899,966m., equivalent to $38,410 per head (or $33,150 per head on an international purchasing-power parity basis). During 1996–2006, it was estimated, the population increased at an average annual rate of 0.1%, while gross domestic product (GDP) per head increased, in real terms, by an average of 1.0% per year. According to World Bank figures, overall GDP increased, in real terms, at an average annual rate of 1.2% in 1996–2006. Compared with the previous year, GDP increased by 2.2% in 2006.

Agriculture (including forestry and fishing) contributed 1.4% of GDP in 2006 and engaged 4.3% of the employed labour force in 2007. The principal crops are rice, sugar beets, potatoes, cabbages and citrus fruits. During 1996–2006, according to official sources, agricultural GDP declined, in real terms, at an average rate of 0.7% annually. Compared with the previous year, the sector's GDP declined by 2.8% in 2006.

Industry (including mining, manufacturing, construction and utilities) contributed 29.1% of GDP in 2006, and engaged 27.7% of the employed labour force in 2007. During 1996–2006, according to official sources, industrial GDP increased at an average annual rate of 0.9%. In 2006 the industrial sector's GDP increased by 4.1%.

Mining and quarrying contributed 0.1% of GDP in 2006 and engaged less than 0.1% of the employed labour force in 2007. While the domestic output of limestone and sulphur is sufficient to meet domestic demand, all of Japan's requirements of bauxite, crude petroleum and iron ore, and a high percentage of its requirements of copper ore and coking coal, are met by imports.

In 2006 manufacturing contributed 20.7% of GDP, and 18.4% of the employed labour force were engaged in the sector in 2007. Manufacturing GDP increased by an average of 1.8% per year in 1996–2006. Manufacturing GDP increased by 5.7% in 2006, compared with the previous year. The most important branches of manufacturing are machinery and transport equipment, electrical and electronic equipment, and iron and steel.

Japan imports most of its energy requirements, with imports of crude and partly refined petroleum comprising 17.1% of the value of total imports in 2006. Nuclear power accounted for 26.4% of electricity output in 2004, coal for 27.5%, natural gas for 22.8%, petroleum for 9.2% and hydropower for 8.8%.

The services sector contributed 69.5% of GDP in 2006 and engaged 68.0% of the employed labour force in 2007. The GDP of the services sector increased by an average of 1.3% annually in 1996–2006, expanding by just 0.4% in 2006 compared with the previous year. Tourist receipts, totalling US $15,555m. in 2005, are an important source of revenue. In comparison with the previous year, the number of tourist arrivals increased by 13.8% in 2007 to reach 8.3m.

In 2006 Japan recorded a visible trade surplus of US $81,300m., and there was a surplus of $170,520m. on the current account of the balance of payments. In 2006 the principal market for exports was the USA (22.5%), which was also a major source of imports (11.7%). The principal source of imports in that year was the People's Republic of China (20.5%), which was also a major market for exports (14.3%). Other major suppliers in 2006 were Saudi Arabia, the United Arab Emirates, Australia, the Republic of Korea and Indonesia, and other leading purchasers of Japanese exports were the Republic of Korea, Taiwan, Hong Kong, Thailand and Germany. The principal exports in 2006 were machinery and transport equipment. The principal imports were mineral fuels and lubricants.

The budget for the financial year ending March 2009 projected expenditure of 83,061,000m. yen, compared with 82,909,000m. yen in the previous year. The allocation for social security remained the largest single category of government expenditure, mainly as a consequence of the need to support the ageing population. Although Japan has no external debt, the level of public debt reached the equivalent of about 180% of GDP in 2007. The annual rate of deflation averaged 0.05% in 1996–2006. According to official figures, an inflation rate of 0.3% was recorded in 2006, but in 2007 consumer prices remained unchanged. The average rate of unemployment declined for the fifth consecutive year in 2007, to reach 3.9% of the labour force.

Japan is a member of the UN Economic and Social Commission for Asia and the Pacific (ESCAP, see p. 35), the Asia-Pacific Economic Co-operation (APEC, see p. 176) forum, the Asian Development Bank (ADB, see p. 182), the Organisation for Economic Co-operation and Development (OECD, see p. 347), the Colombo Plan (see p. 411) and the World Trade Organization (WTO, see p. 396). Japan became an observer member of the South Asian Association for Regional Co-operation (SAARC, see p. 384) in 2005.

As part of a programme of major economic reforms initiated in 2001 and scheduled for completion by 2017, the reorganization of Japan Post was to involve the restructuring of post office services into four separate companies: postal savings, postal life insurance, mail delivery and post office management. The transfer of the postal savings system to the private sector was approved in October 2005, and the Japan Post Bank commenced operations in October 2007. Following a prolonged period of economic stagnation, from 2004 the Japanese economy recorded stronger rates of growth. However, the IMF anticipated that Japan's GDP growth would decline from an estimated 2.1% in 2007 to 1.4% in 2008. The Nikkei 225 Stock Average rose to exceed 17,000 points at the end of 2006, but in 2007 the stock market lost more than 11% of its value, with the index decreasing to close at 15,308 points at the end of December. The stock market was subject to much volatility in early 2008. In July 2006 the Bank of Japan raised its key interest rate from 0% to 0.25%, the first such rise in nearly six years. A further increase, to 0.5%, was implemented in February 2007 and, despite expectations to the contrary, this interest rate remained unchanged in early 2008. Meanwhile, the current account surplus continued to increase throughout 2007, in spite of the deceleration of the US economy and the global credit crisis. The strength of the yen in relation to the US dollar, which in early 2008 was trading at less than 100 yen, was expected to depress exports and thus reduce Japan's current account surplus in 2008. Meanwhile, the country's consistently low birth rate had become a cause for concern. A natural decrease in the Japanese population, the first since records began in 1899, was registered in 2005 and again in 2006. Moreover, the population was also steadily ageing, thus raising the question of the ability of the declining labour force to support an increasing number of elderly dependants. Following his appointment as Prime Minister in September 2007, Yasuo Fukuda pledged to implement radical changes to the tax system; in particular, he raised the possibility of an increase in consumption tax.

Education

A kindergarten (*yochien*) system provides education for children aged between three and five years of age, although the majority of kindergartens are privately controlled. Education is compulsory between the ages of six and 15. Elementary education, which begins at six years of age, lasts for six years. Lower secondary education lasts for a further three years. In 2004/05 enrolment at pre-primary school included 85% of pupils in the relevant age-group, while enrolment at primary and secondary school level included 100% of pupils in the relevant age-group. In 2005 some 10.8m. children aged six to 15 were enrolled in compulsory education, while some 3.6m. of those aged 15 to 18 received upper secondary education. Upper secondary schools provide a three-year course in general topics, or a vocational course in subjects such as agriculture, commerce, fine art and technical studies. There are four types of institution for higher education. Universities (*daigaku*) offer a four-year degree course, as well as postgraduate courses. In 2005 there were 726 universities in Japan. Junior colleges (*tanki-daigaku*) provide less specialized two- to three-year courses. In 2005 there were 488 junior colleges in Japan. Both universities and junior colleges offer facilities for teacher-training. Colleges of technology (*koto-senmon-gakko*), of which there were 63 in 2005, offer a five-year specialized training. Since 1991 colleges of technology have been able to offer short-term advanced courses. Special training colleges (*senshu-gakko*) offer advanced courses in technical and vocational subjects, lasting for at least one year. In 2005 there were 3,439 special training colleges in Japan. Fiscal expenditure on education in 2005 was equivalent to 9.3% of total government spending.

Public Holidays

2008: 1 January (New Year's Day), 14 January (Coming of Age Day), 11 February (National Foundation Day), 20 March (Vernal Equinox Day), 29 April (Showa Day), 3 May (Constitution Memorial Day), 5 May (Children's Day), 6 May (Greenery Day), 20 July (Marine Day), 15 September (Respect for the Aged Day), 23 September (Autumnal Equinox), 13 October (Sports Day), 3 November (Culture Day), 24 November (Labour Thanksgiving Day), 23 December (Emperor's Birthday).

2009: 1 January (New Year's Day), 12 January (Coming of Age Day), 11 February (National Foundation Day), 20 March (Vernal Equinox Day), 29 April (Showa Day), 3 May (Constitution Memorial Day), 4 May (Greenery Day), 5 May (Children's Day), 20 July (Marine Day), 21 September (Respect for the Aged Day), 23 September (Autumnal Equinox), 12 October (Sports Day), 3 November (Culture Day), 23 November (Labour Thanksgiving Day), 23 December (Emperor's Birthday).

Weights and Measures

The metric system is in force.

Statistical Survey

Source (unless otherwise stated): Statistics Bureau and Statistics Center, Ministry of Public Management, Home Affairs, Posts and Telecommunications, 2-1-2, Kasumigaseki, Chiyoda-ku, Tokyo 100-8926; tel. (3) 5253-5111; fax (3) 3504-0265; e-mail webmaster@stat.go.jp; internet www.stat.go.jp.

Area and Population

AREA, POPULATION AND DENSITY

Area (sq km)	377,923*
Hokkaido district	83,456
Honshu district	231,105
Shikoku district	18,790
Kyushu district	42,178
Okinawa district	2,275
Population (census results)†	
1 October 2000	126,925,843
1 October 2005‡	
Males	62,349,000
Females	65,419,000
Total	127,768,000
Population (official provisional estimate at 1 February) 2007	127,760,000
Density (per sq km) at 1 February 2008	338.1

* 145,917 sq miles; total includes 118 sq km (45.6 sq miles) within Honshu and Shikoku districts yet to be demarcated fully.
† Excluding foreign military and diplomatic personnel and their dependants.
‡ Provisional.

PREFECTURES
(2006, estimates)

Prefecture	Area (sq km)	Population ('000)	Density (per sq km)
Aichi	5,115	7,308	1,428.7
Akita	11,434	1,134	99.2
Aomori	8,918	1,423	159.6
Chiba	5,082	6,074	1,195.2
Ehime	5,677	1,460	257.2
Fukui	4,189	819	195.5
Fukuoka	4,844	5,054	1,043.4
Fukushima	13,783	2,080	150.9
Gifu	9,768	2,105	215.5
Gumma	6,363	2,021	317.6
Hiroshima	8,479	2,875	339.1
Hokkaido	83,456	5,601	67.1
Hyogo	8,395	5,590	665.9
Ibaraki	6,096	2,972	487.5
Ishikawa	4,185	1,172	280.0
Iwate	15,279	1,375	90.0
Kagawa	1,862	1,009	541.9
Kagoshima	9,043	1,743	192.7
Kanagawa	2,416	8,830	3,654.8
Kochi	7,105	789	111.0
Kumamoto	6,403	1,836	286.7
Kyoto	4,613	2,643	52.7
Mie	5,761	1,873	325.1
Miyagi	6,862	2,355	343.2
Miyazaki	6,346	1,148	180.9
Nagano	13,105	2,189	167.0
Nagasaki	4,095	1,466	358.0
Nara	3,691	1,416	383.6
Niigata	10,789	2,418	224.1
Oita	5,099	1,206	236.5
Okayama	7,009	1,955	278.9
Okinawa	2,275	1,368	601.3
Osaka	1,897	8,815	4,646.8
Saga	2,440	863	353.7
Saitama	3,767	7,071	1,877.1
Shiga	3,794	1,389	366.1
Shimane	6,708	737	109.9
Shizuoka	7,329	3,797	518.1
Tochigi	6,408	2,015	314.5
Tokushima	4,146	805	194.2
Tokyo-to	2,103	12,659	6,019.5
Tottori	3,507	604	172.2
Toyama	2,046	1,110	542.5
Wakayama	4,726	1,028	217.5
Yamagata	6,652	1,208	181.6
Yamaguchi	6,112	1,483	242.6
Yamanashi	4,201	880	209.5
Total	**377,923***	**127,770**	**338.1**

* Total includes 14,547 sq km of area straddling more than one prefecture or not fully demarcated.

PRINCIPAL CITIES
(2005 census results)*

Tokyo (capital)†	8,489,653		Oita	462,317
Yokohama	3,579,628		Utsunomiya	457,673
Osaka	2,628,811		Kanazawa	454,607
Nagoya	2,215,062		Nagasaki	442,699
Sapporo	1,880,863		Yokosuka	426,178
Kobe	1,525,393		Toyama	421,239
Kyoto	1,474,811		Fukuyama	418,509
Fukuoka	1,401,279		Toyota	412,141
Kawasaki	1,327,011		Machida	405,534
Saitama	1,176,314		Hirakata	404,044
Hiroshima	1,154,391		Gifu	399,931
Sendai	1,025,098		Fujisawa	396,014
Kitakyushu‡	993,525		Toyonaka	386,623
Chiba	924,319		Kashiwa	380,963
Sakai	830,966		Nagano	378,512
Hamamatsu	804,032		Wakayama	375,591
Niigata	785,134		Toyohashi	372,479
Shizuoka	700,886		Nara	370,102
Okayama	674,746		Asahikawa	355,004
Kumamoto	669,603		Okazaki	354,704
Sagamihara	628,698		Iwaki	354,492
Kagoshima	604,367		Suita	353,885
Funabashi	569,835		Takatsuki	351,826
Hachioji	560,012		Koriyama	338,834
Matsuyama	514,937		Takamatsu	337,902
Higashiosaka	513,821		Tokorozawa	336,100
Himeji	482,304		Kawagoe	333,795
Kawaguchi	480,079		Kochi	333,484
Matsudo	472,579		Akita	333,109
Kurashiki	469,377		Maebashi	318,584
Ichikawa	466,608		Koshigaya	315,792
Nishinomiyai	465,337		Naha	312,393
Amagasaki	462,647		Aomori	311,508

* With the exception of Tokyo the data for each city refer to an urban county (*shi*), an administrative division which may include some scattered or rural population as well as an urban centre.
† The figure refers to the 23 wards (*ku*) of the old city. The population of Tokyo-to (Tokyo Prefecture) was 12,577,000 at the census of 1 October 2005.
‡ Including Kokura, Moji, Tobata, Wakamatsu and Yahata (Yawata).

2006 ('000 persons): Chiba 930; Fukuoka 1,414; Hiroshima 1,158; Kawasaki 1,342; Kitakyushu 991; Kobe 1,529; Kyoto 1,473; Nagoya 2,223; Osaka 2,635; Saitama 1,192; Sakai 832; Sapporo 1,889; Sendai 1,027; Shizuoka 712; Tokyo 8,568.

2007 ('000 persons): Chiba 937; Fukuoka 1,427; Hamamatsu 811; Hiroshima 1,162; Kawasaki 1,369; Kitakyushu 987; Kobe 1,530; Kyoto 1,469; Nagoya 2,237; Niigata 813; Osaka 2,644; Saitama 1,200; Sakai 835; Sapporo 1,894; Sendai 1,029; Shizuoka 711; Tokyo 8,653.

JAPAN

Statistical Survey

BIRTHS, MARRIAGES AND DEATHS*

	Registered live births		Registered marriages†		Registered deaths	
	Number	Rate (per 1,000)	Number	Rate (per 1,000)	Number	Rate (per 1,000)
1999	1,177,669	9.4	762,011	6.1	982,031	7.8
2000	1,190,547	9.5	798,138	6.4	961,653	7.7
2001	1,170,662	9.3	799,999	6.4	970,331	7.7
2002	1,153,855	9.2	757,331	6.0	982,379	7.8
2003	1,123,610	8.9	740,191	5.9	1,014,951	8.0
2004	1,110,721	8.8	720,417	5.7	1,028,602	8.2
2005	1,062,530	8.4	714,265	5.7	1,083,796	8.6
2006	1,092,674	8.7	730,971	5.8	1,084,450	8.6

* Figures relate only to Japanese nationals in Japan.
† Data are tabulated by year of registration rather than by year of occurrence.

Source: Ministry of Health, Labour and Welfare, Tokyo.

Expectation of life (years at birth, WHO estimates): 82.2 (males 78.7; females 85.5) in 2005 (Source: WHO, *World Health Statistics*).

ECONOMICALLY ACTIVE POPULATION*
(annual averages, '000 persons aged 15 years and over)

	2005	2006	2007
Agriculture and forestry	2,590	2,500	2,510
Fishing and aquaculture	230	220	210
Mining and quarrying	30	30	40
Manufacturing	11,420	11,610	11,650
Electricity, gas and water	350	360	330
Construction	5,680	5,590	5,520
Wholesale and retail trade	11,220	11,130	11,130
Restaurants and hotels	3,430	3,370	3,420
Transport, information and communications	4,930	5,050	5,200
Financing, insurance, real estate and business services	2,320	2,340	2,400
Health and welfare	5,530	5,710	5,790
Education	2,860	2,870	2,840
Government	2,290	2,220	2,260
Other services and activities not elsewhere classified	9,920	10,130	10,050
Activities not adequately defined	760	690	770
Total employed	**63,560**	**63,820**	**64,120**
Unemployed	2,940	2,750	2,570
Total labour force	**66,500**	**66,570**	**66,690**
Males	39,010	38,980	39,070
Females	27,500	27,590	27,620

* Figures are rounded to the nearest 10,000 persons.

Health and Welfare

KEY INDICATORS

Total fertility rate (children per woman, 2005)	1.3
Under-5 mortality rate (per 1,000 live births, 2005)	4
HIV/AIDS (% of persons aged 15–49, 2005)	<0.1
Physicians (per 1,000 head, 2002)	1.98
Hospital beds (per 1,000 head, 2001)	13
Health expenditure (2004): US $ per head (PPP)	2,292.6
Health expenditure (2004): % of GDP	7.8
Health expenditure (2004): public (% of total)	81.3
Human Development Index (2005): ranking	8
Human Development Index (2005): value	0.953

For sources and definitions, see explanatory note on p. vi.

Agriculture

PRINCIPAL CROPS
('000 metric tons)

	2004	2005	2006
Wheat	860.3	874.7	837.2
Rice (paddy)	10,912.0	11,342.0	10,695.0
Barley	198.6	183.4	174.2
Potatoes	2,888.0	2,752.0	2,598.0
Sweet potatoes	1,009.0	1,053.0	988.9
Taro (Coco yam)	184.8	184.6	184.6*
Yams	197.9	204.1	204.1*
Sugar cane	1,187.0	1,214.0	1,250.0†
Sugar beets	4,656.0	4,201.0	3,923.0
Dry beans	117.8	104.6	83.0
Soybeans (Soya beans)	163.2	225.0	229.2
Cabbages and other brassicas	2,166.0	2,286.8	2,286.8*
Lettuce and chicory	509.3	551.6	551.6*
Spinach	288.6	297.9	297.9*
Tomatoes	754.9	759.2	726.3
Cauliflowers and broccoli	117.0	130.6	130.6*
Pumpkins, squash and gourds	225.5	234.1	233.0
Cucumbers and gherkins	672.9	674.7	628.3
Aubergines (Eggplants)	390.2	395.7	372.4
Chillies and green peppers	153.4	154.0	146.9
Green onions and shallots	547.1	554.0	554.0*
Dry onions	1,128.0	1,087.0	1,158.0
Carrots and turnips	783.5	762.1	762.1*
Green corn	265.6	250.9	233.0
Mushrooms and truffles	66.2	64.0	64.0*
Watermelons	454.1	450.2	418.7
Cantaloupes and other melons	248.6	241.2	216.6
Grapes	205.6	219.9	209.8
Apples	754.6	818.9	831.8
Pears	351.9	394.7	319.1
Peaches and nectarines	151.9	174.0	146.3
Plums and sloes	27.1	26.8	21.4
Oranges	88.1	74.7	63.0
Tangerines, mandarins, clementines and satsumas	1,060.0	1,132.0	841.9
Persimmons	232.5	285.9	232.7
Strawberries	198.2	196.2	190.6
Tea (made)	100.7	100.0	91.8
Tobacco (leaves)	52.7	47.0	47.0*

* FAO estimate.
† Unofficial figure.

Aggregate production ('000 metric tons, may include official, semi-official or estimated data): Total cereals 11,993.5 in 2004, 12,433.4 in 2005, 11,741.5 in 2006; Total roots and tubers 4,340.4 in 2004, 4,257.9 in 2005, 4,039.8 in 2006; Total vegetables (incl. melons) 11,564.1 in 2004, 11,745.4 in 2005, 11,623.8 in 2006; Total fruits (excl. melons) 3,460.8 in 2004, 7,255.4 in 2005, 5,122.6 in 2006.

Source: FAO.

LIVESTOCK
('000 head at 30 September)

	2004	2005	2006
Horses*	25	25	25
Cattle	4,478	4,402	4,391
Pigs	9,724	9,600†	9,620
Sheep*	11	11	11
Goats*	34	34	34
Chickens	279,500	265,200	280,642

* FAO estimates.
† Unofficial figure.

Source: FAO.

JAPAN

LIVESTOCK PRODUCTS
('000 metric tons)

	2004	2005	2006
Cattle meat	513.6	499.5	496.7
Pig meat	1,262.6	1,245.0	1,247.0
Chicken meat	1,242.0	1,273.1	1,336.5
Cows' milk	8,329.0	8,285.2	8,133.9
Hen eggs	2,480.8	2,482.6	2,496.7

Source: FAO.

Forestry

ROUNDWOOD REMOVALS
('000 cubic metres, excl. bark)

	2004	2005	2006
Sawlogs, veneer logs and logs for sleepers	12,015	12,434	12,789
Pulpwood	3,600	3,732	3,820
Other industrial wood	0	0	0
Fuel wood*	114	110	105
Total*	15,729	16,276	16,714

*FAO estimates.
Source: FAO.

SAWNWOOD PRODUCTION
('000 cubic metres, incl. railway sleepers)

	2004	2005	2006
Coniferous (softwood)	13,263	12,517	12,228
Broadleaved (hardwood)	340	308	326
Total	13,603	12,825	12,554

Source: FAO.

Fishing

('000 metric tons, live weight)

	2003	2004	2005
Capture	4,670.5	4,311.8	4,072.9*
Chum salmon (Keta or Dog salmon)	275.8	261.6	242.5
Alaska (Walleye) pollock	219.7	239.4	194.0
Atka mackerel	168.0	175.5	140.5
Pacific saury (Skipper)	264.8	204.4	234.5
Japanese jack mackerel	241.9	254.3	191.3
Japanese anchovy	534.9	495.8	348.6
Skipjack tuna (Oceanic skipjack)	335.5	273.2	293.1
Chub mackerel	329.3	338.1	620.4
Yesso scallop	344.2	313.8	287.5
Japanese flying squid	253.8	234.6	222.4
Aquaculture	823.9	776.4	746.2
Pacific cupped oyster	224.9	234.1	218.9
Yesso scallop	258.3	215.2	203.4
Total catch	5,494.3	5,088.2	4,819.1*

*FAO estimate.

Note: Figures exclude aquatic plants ('000 metric tons): 579.2 (capture 111.5, aquaculture 467.7) in 2003; 598.2 (113.8 capture, 484.4 aquaculture) in 2004; 612.6 (capture 104.9, aquaculture 507.7) in 2005. Also excluded are aquatic mammals (generally recorded by number rather than by weight), pearls, corals and sponges. The number of whales caught was: 830 in 2003; 1,018 in 2004; 945 in 2005. The number of dolphins and porpoises caught was: 16,881 in 2003; 15,156 in 2004; 0 in 2005. The catch of other aquatic mammals (in '000 metric tons) was: 1.8 in 2003; 2.0 in 2004; 1.7 in 2005. For the remaining categories, catches (in metric tons) were: Pearls 31.6 in 2003; 29.3 in 2004; 29.0 in 2005. Corals 2.8 in 2003; 4.8 in 2004; 4.2 in 2005.

Source: FAO.

Mining

('000 metric tons, unless otherwise indicated)

	2003	2004	2005*
Hard coal	1,338	1,339	1,146
Zinc ore†	45	48	41
Iron ore (gross weight)	0.7	n.a.	n.a.
Iron ore (metal content)	0.2‡	n.a.	n.a.
Quartzite stone	12,838	12,218	11,900‡
Limestone	163,565	161,858	165,240
Lead ore (metric tons)†	5,660	5,512	3,437
Gold ore (kg)†	8,143	8,021	8,318
Crude petroleum ('000 barrels)	5,161	5,247	5,774
Natural gas (million cu m)§	2,844	2,883	3,120

* Preliminary figures.
† Figures refer to the metal content of ores.
‡ Estimate.
§ Includes output from gas wells and coal mines.

Source: US Geological Survey.

Industry

SELECTED PRODUCTS
('000 metric tons, unless otherwise indicated)

	2001	2002	2003
Refined sugar	2,257*	2,225	2,215
Cotton yarn—pure[1]	125.8	111.4	97.6
Cotton yarn—mixed	13.7	10.7	9.9
Woven cotton fabrics—pure and mixed (million sq m)	603	541	507
Flax, ramie and hemp yarn	0.5	0.9	0.8
Linen fabrics (million sq m)	3.2	3.2	3.3
Woven silk fabrics—pure and mixed ('000 sq m)	30,837	27,873	24,658
Wool yarn—pure and mixed	29.6	25.7	20.1
Woven woollen fabrics—pure and mixed (million sq m)	94.9	88.1	78.1
Woven fabrics of cellulosic fibres—pure and mixed (million sq m)[3]	241.3	211.5	200.7
Woven fabrics of non-cellulosic fibres (million sq m)	1,484.5	1,293.1	1,217.8
Leather footwear ('000 pairs)	34,667	29,657	27,478
Mechanical wood pulp	1,394	1,258	1,236
Chemical wood pulp[4]	9,245	9,258	9,215
Newsprint	3,464	3,597	3,552
Other printing and writing paper	11,163	11,217	11,168
Other paper and paperboard	16,090	15,872	15,737
Synthetic rubber	1,465.5	1,521.9	1,577.4
Road motor vehicle tyres ('000)	165,063	170,023	172,270
Rubber footwear ('000 pairs)	10,999	7,753	6,153
Ethylene—Ethene	7,361	7,152	7,367
Propylene—Propene	5,342	5,309	5,610
Benzene—Benzol	4,261	4,313	4,551
Toluene—Toluol	1,423	1,548	1,584
Xylenes—Xylol	4,798	4,900	5,213
Sulphuric acid—100%	6,727	6,763	6,534
Caustic soda—Sodium hydroxide	4,291	4,271	4,369
Soda ash—Sodium carbonate	680	690	n.a.
Ammonia	1,604	1,450	1,291
Phosphate fertilizers	334	364	n.a.
Liquefied petroleum gas	5,016	4,902	4,525
Naphtha	12,902	13,442	14,071
Motor spirit—gasoline[5]	42,836	42,599	43,073
Kerosene	22,299	22,866	22,031
Jet fuel	8,149	8,188	7,671
Gas–diesel oil	58,969	57,948	57,402
Residual fuel oil	31,325	32,943	34,037
Lubricating oil	2,329	2,375	n.a.
Petroleum bitumen—Asphalt	5,425	5,248	5,529
Coke-oven coke	44,140	45,354	46,075
Cement	76,550	71,828	68,766
Pig-iron	78,836	80,979	82,091
Ferro-alloys[6]	1,056	1,037	n.a.
Crude steel	102,866	107,745	110,510
Aluminium—unwrought[7]	1,171	1,239	1,261
Refined copper—unwrought	1,426	1,401	1,430

JAPAN

Statistical Survey

—continued	2001	2002	2003
Electrolytic, distilled and rectified zinc—unwrought	644.4	639.9	651.2
Air-conditioning machines ('000)	24,019	21,879	21,126
Calculating machines ('000)	1,301	683	378
Photographic cameras ('000)	1,274	610	409
Video cameras ('000)	9,097	10,015	n.a.
Digital cameras ('000)	12,785	16,909	n.a.
DVD players ('000)	2,832	2,338	n.a.
Television receivers ('000)	2,862	3,130	3,051
Cellular telephones ('000)	53,652	46,072	n.a.
Personal computers ('000)	11,465	9,448[8]	n.a.
Passenger motor cars ('000)	8,118	8,618	8,478
Lorries and trucks ('000)	1,596	1,566	1,735
Motorcycles, scooters and mopeds ('000)	2,328	2,115	1,831
Bicycles ('000)	4,184	3,076	2,520
Watches	515,302	528,608	523,545
Construction: new dwellings started ('000)	1,174	1,151	n.a.
Electric energy (million kWh)*	1,044,930	1,064,101	1,051,104

* Twelve months beginning 1 April of the year stated.
[1] Including condenser cotton yarn.
[2] Including finished fabrics and blanketing made of synthetic fibres.
[3] Fabrics of continuous and discontinuous rayon and acetate fibres, including pile and chenille fabrics at loom stage.
[4] Including pulp prepared by semi-chemical processes.
[5] Not including aviation gasoline.
[6] Including silico-chromium.
[7] Including alloys.
[8] Not directly comparable to figures for previous years owing to change in method of calculation.

Source: mostly UN, *Industrial Commodity Statistics Yearbook*.

2004 ('000 metric tons, unless otherwise indicated): Liquefied petroleum gas 4,448; Naphtha 14,552; Motor spirit—gasoline 42,647; Kerosene 22,014; Jet fuel 7,902; Gas–diesel oil 57,059; Residual fuel oil 31,004; Petroleum bitumen—Asphalt 5,671; Coke-oven coke 46,237; Electric energy (million kWh) 1,080,124; Mechanical wood pulp 1,237; Chemical wood pulp 9,349; Newsprint 3,695; Other printing and writing paper 9,734; Other paper and paperboard 15,824; Crude steel 112,718; Aluminium—unwrought 1,015; Refined copper—unwrought 1,380 (Source: UN, *Industrial Commodity Statistics Yearbook*; FAO; US Geological Survey).

2005 ('000 metric tons): Mechanical wood pulp 1,203; Chemical wood pulp 9,490; Newsprint 3,720; Other printing and writing paper 9,841; Other paper and paperboard 15,734; Crude steel 112,471; Aluminium—unwrought 1,035; Refined copper—unwrought 1,395 (Sources: FAO; US Geological Survey).

2006 ('000 metric tons): Mechanical wood pulp 1,166; Chemical wood pulp 9,572; Newsprint 3,771; Other printing and writing paper 9,919; Other paper and paperboard 15,783 (Sources: FAO).

Finance

CURRENCY AND EXCHANGE RATES

Monetary Units
100 sen = 1 yen.

Sterling, Dollar and Euro Equivalents (31 December 2007)
£1 sterling = 228.388 yen;
US $1 = 114.000 yen;
€1 = 167.819 yen;
1,000 yen = £4.38 = $8.77 = €5.96.

Average Exchange Rate (yen per US $)
2005   110.218
2006   116.299
2007   117.754

BUDGET
('000 million yen, year ending 31 March)*

Revenue†	2006/07	2007/08	2008/09
Tax and stamp revenues	45,878	53,467	53,554
Government bond issues	29,973	25,432	25,348
Total (incl. others)	79,686	82,909	83,061

Expenditure†	2006/07	2007/08	2008/09
Defence	4,814	4,801	4,780
Social security	20,574	21,141	21,782
Public works	7,201	6,947	6,735
Servicing of national debt‡	18,762	20,999	20,163
Transfer of local allocation tax to local governments	14,558	14,932	15,614
Total (incl. others)	79,686	82,909	83,061

* Figures refer only to the operations of the General Account budget. Data exclude transactions of other accounts controlled by the central Government: two mutual aid associations and four special accounts (including other social security funds).
† Initial forecasts.
‡ Including the repayment of debt principal and administrative costs.

Source: Ministry of Finance, Tokyo.

INTERNATIONAL RESERVES
(US $ million at 31 December)

	2004	2005	2006
Gold (national valuation)	1,337	1,231	1,295
IMF special drawing rights	2,839	2,584	2,812
Reserve position in IMF	6,789	2,877	1,934
Foreign exchange	824,264	828,813	874,936
Total	835,228	835,506	880,977

Source: IMF, *International Financial Statistics*.

MONEY SUPPLY
('000 million yen at 31 December)

	2004	2005	2006
Currency outside banks	72,851	74,859	76,157
Demand deposits at deposit money banks	339,561	361,426	362,935
Total money (incl. others)	414,082	438,771	439,723

Source: IMF, *International Financial Statistics*.

COST OF LIVING
(Consumer Price Index; average of monthly figures; base: 2005 = 100)

	2004	2006	2007
Food (incl. beverages)	100.9	100.5	100.8
Housing	100.1	100.0	99.8
Rent	100.0	100.0	99.8
Fuel, light and water charges	99.2	103.6	104.4
Clothing and footwear	99.3	101.3	101.7
Miscellaneous	99.7	100.9	101.7
All items	100.3	100.3	100.3

NATIONAL ACCOUNTS
('000 million yen at current prices, year ending 31 December)

National Income and Product

	2004	2005	2006
Compensation of employees	256,353.7	258,451.8	262,617.2
Operating surplus and mixed income	94,425.5	98,170.0	93,493.1
Domestic primary incomes	350,779.2	356,621.8	356,110.3
Consumption of fixed capital	105,132.2	104,356.1	105,971.1
Statistical discrepancy	4,826.5	1,902.1	6,375.8
Gross domestic product (GDP) at factor cost	460,737.8	462,879.9	468,457.3
Indirect taxes	41,604.4	42,406.3	43,645.8
Less Subsidies	4,013.8	3,551.8	3,178.0
GDP in purchasers' values	498,328.4	501,734.4	508,925.1
Primary incomes received from abroad	14,082.6	17,619.9	21,758.1
Less Primary incomes paid abroad	4,462.7	5,771.1	7,339.7
Gross national income (GNI)	507,948.3	513,583.2	523,343.5

JAPAN

Expenditure on the Gross Domestic Product

	2004	2005	2006
Government final consumption expenditure	89,468.0	90,601.8	89,958.0
Private final consumption expenditure	284,428.4	285,935.6	290,719.0
Changes in stocks	1,647.4	1,356.1	2,484.4
Gross fixed capital formation	113,158.6	116,884.9	119,415.1
Total domestic expenditure	488,702.4	494,778.4	502,576.6
Exports of goods and services	66,286.3	71,912.7	81,756.3
Less Imports of goods and services	56,660.3	64,956.7	75,407.8
GDP in purchasers' values	498,328.4	501,734.4	508,925.1
GDP at constant 1995 prices	529,807.5	542,249.0	556,734.2

Source: IMF, *International Financial Statistics*.

Gross Domestic Product by Economic Activity

	2004	2005	2006
Agriculture, hunting, forestry and fishing	8,052.6	7,628.3	7,437.7
Mining and quarrying	481.2	488.2	504.5
Manufacturing	105,410.1	107,876.5	108,602.8
Electricity, gas and water	12,726.5	12,051.4	11,433.2
Construction	32,953.8	31,861.4	32,148.0
Wholesale and retail trade	67,734.3	69,065.2	68,722.0
Transport, storage and communications	34,277.0	33,611.5	33,419.3
Finance and insurance	33,647.7	34,939.9	35,218.4
Real estate*	59,841.2	60,099.7	60,460.0
Public administration	28,389.4	28,432.6	28,611.2
Other government services	18,592.2	18,617.0	18,558.7
Other business, community, social and personal services	105,134.7	107,733.4	108,760.1
Private non-profit services to households	9,740.8	10,089.3	10,694.3
Sub-total	516,981.3	522,494.5	524,570.3
Import duties	4,279.1	4,769.1	5,407.5
Less Imputed bank service charge	24,598.1	24,341.6	24,130.6
Less Consumption taxes for gross capital formation	3,160.4	3,089.7	3,297.9
Statistical discrepancy	4,826.5	1,902.1	6,375.8
GDP in purchasers' values	498,328.4	501,734.4	508,925.1

* Including imputed rents of owner-occupied dwellings.
Source: Economic and Social Research Institute, Tokyo.

BALANCE OF PAYMENTS
(US $ million)*

	2004	2005	2006
Exports of goods f.o.b.	539,000	567,570	615,810
Imports of goods f.o.b.	−406,870	−473,610	−534,510
Trade balance	132,130	93,960	81,300
Exports of services	97,610	110,210	117,300
Imports of services	−135,510	−134,260	−135,560
Balance on goods and services	94,230	69,910	63,050
Other income received	113,330	141,060	165,800
Other income paid	−27,630	−37,620	−47,650
Balance on goods, services and income	179,930	173,360	181,200
Current transfers received	6,910	9,740	6,180
Current transfers paid	−14,780	−17,310	−16,870
Current balance	172,060	165,780	170,520
Capital account (net)	−4,790	−4,880	−4,760
Direct investment abroad	−30,960	−45,440	−50,170
Direct investment from abroad	7,800	3,210	−6,780
Portfolio investment assets	−173,770	−196,400	−71,040
Portfolio investment liabilities	196,720	183,130	198,560
Financial derivatives assets	56,440	230,590	143,480
Financial derivatives liabilities	−54,040	−237,120	−141,030
Other investment assets	−48,010	−106,600	−86,240
Other investment liabilities	68,310	45,940	−89,120
Net errors and omissions	−28,920	−15,900	−31,440
Overall balance	160,850	22,330	31,980

* Figures are rounded to the nearest US $10m.
Source: IMF, *International Financial Statistics*.

JAPANESE DEVELOPMENT ASSISTANCE
(net disbursement basis, US $ million)

	2002	2003	2004
Official flows	4,018	5,213	6,009
Bilateral assistance	6,726	6,014	5,954
Grants	4,473	4,544	7,235
Grant assistance	1,718	1,699	4,326
Technical assistance	2,754	2,845	2,909
Loans	2,253	1,469	−1,281
Contributions to multilateral institutions	2,633	2,624	3,048
Other official flows	−5,341	−3,425	−2,993
Export credits	−469	−127	−156
Equities and other bilateral assets, etc.	−2,360	−3,682	−2,471
Transfers to multilateral institutions	−2,512	384	−366
Private flows	4,813	−4,541	9,734
Export credits	−1,078	4,753	1,074
Direct investment and others	12,108	8,765	13,955
Bilateral investment in securities, etc.	−3,413	−18,430	−2,275
Transfers to multilateral institutions	−2,804	371	−3,020
Grants from private voluntary agencies	152	335	425
Total	8,983	1,007	16,167

External Trade

PRINCIPAL COMMODITIES
('000 million yen)

Imports c.i.f.	2004	2005	2006
Food and live animals	5,302	5,559	5,710
Fish and fish preparations*	1,539	1,562	1,573
Crude materials (inedible) except fuels	3,079	3,505	4,733
Mineral fuels, lubricants, etc.	10,671	14,560	18,657
Crude and partly refined petroleum	6,065	8,823	11,535
Liquefied natural gas	1,650	1,985	4,321
Chemicals	3,816	4,321	4,909
Manufactured goods	4,863	5,417	6,554
Non-electrical machinery	5,171	5,661	6,240
Electrical machinery	6,851	7,402	8,645
Transport equipment	1,926	2,063	2,259
Other	7,539	8,463	9,637
Clothing and clothing accessories	2,230	2,469	2,754
Total (incl. others)†	49,217	56,949	67,344

* Including crustacea and molluscs.
† Including re-imports not classified according to kind.

Exports f.o.b.	2004	2005	2006
Chemicals	5,221	5,848	6,794
Manufactured goods	6,537	7,397	8,674
Iron and steel	2,519	3,037	3,485
Machinery and transport equipment	41,087	43,098	49,120
Non-electrical machinery	12,607	13,352	14,800
Power-generating machinery	1,920	2,186	2,320
Electrical machinery, apparatus, etc.	14,373	14,549	16,076
Thermionic valves, tubes, etc.	4,395	4,402	4,855
Transport equipment	14,107	15,197	18,244
Road motor vehicles	9,214	9,929	12,300
Road motor vehicle parts	2,562	2,801	3,023
Other	7,176	7,779	8,757
Scientific instruments and optical equipment	2,499	2,478	2,469
Total (incl. others)*	61,170	65,657	75,246

* Including re-exports not classified according to kind.

JAPAN

Statistical Survey

PRINCIPAL TRADING PARTNERS
('000 million yen)*

Imports c.i.f.	2004	2005	2006
Australia	2,103	2,706	3,248
Canada	910	985	1,118
China, People's Republic	10,199	11,975	13,784
France	902	941	1,044
Germany	1,846	1,968	2,146
Indonesia	2,022	2,298	2,807
Iran	893	1,139	1,293
Ireland	411	415	406
Italy	746	758	818
Korea, Republic	2,383	2,695	3,178
Kuwait	621	843	1,058
Malaysia	1,526	1,619	1,801
Philippines	892	850	926
Qatar	852	1,178	1,721
Russia	617	683	774
Saudi Arabia	1,996	3,171	4,325
Singapore	680	739	870
Switzerland	520	557	594
Taiwan	1,805	1,994	2,365
Thailand	1,525	1,718	1,964
United Arab Emirates	1,982	2,795	3,672
United Kingdom	720	740	781
USA	6,763	7,074	7,911
Total (incl. others)	49,217	56,949	67,344

Exports f.o.b.	2004	2005	2006
Australia	1,277	1,370	1,453
Belgium	780	786	832
Canada	826	927	1,158
China, People's Republic	7,994	8,873	10,794
France	903	856	887
Germany	2,050	2,058	2,376
Hong Kong	3,831	3,969	4,239
Indonesia	982	1,017	858
Italy	698	632	748
Korea, Republic	4,785	5,146	5,849
Malaysia	1,359	1,383	1,537
Mexico	561	765	1,079
Netherlands	1,447	1,448	1,714
Panama	656	813	942
Philippines	1,038	1,000	1,048
Singapore	1,945	2,035	2,250
Taiwan	4,542	4,809	5,131
Thailand	2,192	2,478	2,665
United Kingdom	1,619	1,663	1,770
USA	13,731	14,805	16,934
Total (incl. others)	61,170	65,657	75,246

* Imports by country of production; exports by country of last consignment.

Transport

RAILWAYS
(traffic, year ending 31 March)

	2003	2004	2005
Japan Railways Group:			
Passengers (million)	8,642	8,618	8,683
Passenger-km (million)	241,160	241,977	245,996
Freight ('000 tons)	37,552	36,789	36,864
Freight ton-km (million)	22,565	22,264	22,601
Other private railways:			
Passengers (million)	13,116	13,068	13,280
Passenger-km (million)	144	143	145
Freight ('000 tons)	16,050	15,430	15,609
Freight ton-km (million)	229	212	n.a.
Total:			
Passengers (million)	21,758	21,686	21,963
Passenger-km (million)	384,958	385,163	391,228
Freight ('000 tons)	53,602	52,219	52,473
Freight ton-km (million)	22,794	22,476	22,813

ROAD TRAFFIC
('000 motor vehicles owned, year ending 31 March)

	2003	2004	2005
Passenger cars	42,624	42,776	42,747
Buses and coaches	232	232	232
Trucks, incl. trailers	7,414	7,280	7,160
Special use vehicles	1,350	1,318	1,293
Heavy special vehicles	324	325	325
Light two-wheeled vehicles	1,370	1,397	1,428
Light motor vehicles	24,075	24,950	25,807
Total	77,390	78,279	78,992

SHIPPING

Merchant Fleet
(registered at 31 December)

	2004	2005	2006
Number of vessels	6,937	6,842	6,731
Total displacement ('000 grt)	13,180	12,752	12,798

Source: Lloyd's Register-Fairplay, *World Fleet Statistics*.

International Sea-borne Traffic
('000 metric tons)

	2003	2004	2005
Exports	38,869	41,971	45,403
Imports	554,937	547,602	529,239
Cross transport	178,251	186,526	203,225
Total	772,057	776,099	777,867

CIVIL AVIATION
(traffic on scheduled services)

	2003	2004	2005
Kilometres flown (million)	950	974	996
Passengers carried (million)	111,278	111,471	112,329
Passenger-km (million)	157,124	164,976	169,190
Total ton-km (million)	7,958	8,502	8,630

Tourism

FOREIGN VISITOR ARRIVALS
(excl. Japanese nationals resident abroad)

Country of nationality	2003	2004	2005
Australia	172,134	194,276	154,571
Canada	126,065	142,091	107,591
China, People's Republic	448,782	616,009	652,820
Germany	93,571	106,297	118,429
Hong Kong	260,214	300,246	292,810
Korea, Republic	1,459,333	1,588,472	1,747,171
Philippines	137,584	154,588	139,572
Taiwan	785,379	1,080,590	1,274,612
United Kingdom	200,543	215,704	221,535
USA	655,821	759,753	822,033
Total (incl. others)	5,211,725	6,137,905	6,727,926

Source: Japan National Tourist Organization.

Receipts from tourism (US $ million, incl. passenger transport): 11,475 in 2003; 14,343 in 2004; 15,555 in 2005.

Source: World Tourism Organization.

Communications Media

	2004	2005	2006
Telephones ('000 main lines in use)	59,608	58,053	55,155
Mobile telephones ('000 subscribers)	91,474	96,484	101,698
Personal computers ('000 in use)	69,200	69,200	n.a.
Internet users ('000)	79,480	85,290	87,540
Broadband subscribers ('000)	19,557	22,375	25,755
Book production:			
titles	74,587	76,528	77,722
copies (million)	749	739	755
Daily newspapers:			
number	120	120	121
circulation ('000 copies)	53,022	52,568	52,310

Television receivers ('000 in use): 92,000 in 2000.

Radio receivers ('000 in use): 120,500 in 1997.

Facsimile machines ('000 in use): 16,000 in 1997.

Sources: The Japan Newspaper Publishers and Editors Association; Foreign Press Center, *Facts and Figures of Japan*; UNESCO, *Statistical Yearbook*; UN, *Statistical Yearbook*; International Telecommunication Union.

Education

(2005)

	Institutions	Teachers*	Students
Kindergartens	13,949	110,393	1,738,766
Elementary schools	23,123	416,833	7,197,458
Lower secondary schools	11,035	248,694	3,626,415
Upper secondary schools	5,418	251,408	3,605,242
Schools for the blind	71	3,383	3,809
Schools for the deaf	106	4,974	6,639
Other special needs schools	825	55,275	91,164
Colleges of technology	63	4,469	59,160
Junior colleges	488	11,960	219,355
Universities	726	161,690	2,865,051
Special training schools	3,439	41,776	783,783
Miscellaneous vocational schools	1,830	11,045	163,667

*Figures refer to full-time teachers only.

Source: Ministry of Education, Culture, Sports, Science and Technology, Tokyo.

Directory

The Constitution

The Constitution of Japan was promulgated on 3 November 1946 and came into force on 3 May 1947. The following is a summary of its major provisions, with subsequent amendments:

THE EMPEROR

Articles 1–8. The Emperor derives his position from the will of the people. In the performance of any state act as defined in the Constitution, he must seek the advice and approval of the Cabinet, though he may delegate the exercise of his functions, which include: (i) the appointment of the Prime Minister and the Chief Justice of the Supreme Court; (ii) promulgation of laws, cabinet orders, treaties and constitutional amendments; (iii) the convocation of the Diet, dissolution of the House of Representatives and proclamation of elections to the Diet; (iv) the appointment and dismissal of Ministers of State, the granting of amnesties, reprieves and pardons, and the ratification of treaties, conventions or protocols; (v) the awarding of honours and performance of ceremonial functions.

RENUNCIATION OF WAR

Article 9. Japan renounces for ever the use of war as a means of settling international disputes.

Articles 10–40 refer to the legal and human rights of individuals guaranteed by the Constitution.

THE DIET

Articles 41–64. The Diet is convened once a year, is the highest organ of state power and has exclusive legislative authority. It comprises the House of Representatives (480 seats—300 single-seat constituencies and 180 determined by proportional representation) and the House of Councillors (242 seats). The members of the former are elected for four years whilst those of the latter are elected for six years and election for approximately one-half of the members takes place every three years. If the House of Representatives is dissolved, a general election must take place within 40 days and the Diet must be convoked within 30 days of the date of the election. Extraordinary sessions of the Diet may be convened by the Cabinet when one-quarter or more of the members of either House request it. Emergency sessions of the House of Councillors may also be held. A quorum of at least one-third of the Diet members is needed to carry out parliamentary business. Any decision arising therefrom must be passed by a majority vote of those present. A bill becomes law having passed both Houses, except as provided by the Constitution. If the House of Councillors either vetoes or fails to take action within 60 days upon a bill already passed by the House of Representatives, the bill becomes law when passed a second time by the House of Representatives, by at least a two-thirds' majority of those members present.

The Budget must first be submitted to the House of Representatives. If, when it is approved by the House of Representatives, the House of Councillors votes against it or fails to take action on it within 30 days, or failing agreement being reached by a joint committee of both Houses, a decision of the House of Representatives shall be the decision of the Diet. The above procedure also applies in respect of the conclusion of treaties.

THE EXECUTIVE

Articles 65–75. Executive power is vested in the Cabinet, consisting of a Prime Minister and such other Ministers as may be appointed. The Cabinet is collectively responsible to the Diet. The Prime Minister is designated from among members of the Diet by a resolution thereof.

If the House of Representatives and the House of Councillors disagree on the designation of the Prime Minister, and if no agreement can be reached even through a joint committee of both Houses, provided for by law, or if the House of Councillors fails to make designation within 10 days, exclusive of the period of recess, after the House of Representatives has made designation, the decision of the House of Representatives shall be the decision of the Diet.

The Prime Minister appoints and may remove other Ministers, a majority of whom must be from the Diet. If the House of Representatives passes a no-confidence motion or rejects a confidence motion, the whole Cabinet resigns, unless the House of Representatives is dissolved within 10 days. When there is a vacancy in the post of Prime Minister, or upon the first convocation of the Diet after a general election of members of the House of Representatives, the whole Cabinet resigns.

The Prime Minister submits bills, reports on national affairs and foreign relations to the Diet. He exercises control and supervision over various administrative branches of the Government. The Cabinet's primary functions (in addition to administrative ones) are to: (a) administer the law faithfully; (b) conduct State affairs; (c) conclude treaties subject to prior (or subsequent) Diet approval; (d) administer the civil service in accordance with law; (e) prepare and present the budget to the Diet; (f) enact Cabinet orders in order to make effective legal and constitutional provisions; (g) decide on amnesties, reprieves or pardons. All laws and Cabinet orders are signed by the competent Minister of State and countersigned by the Prime Minister. The Ministers of State, during their tenure of office, are not subject to legal action without the consent of the Prime Minister. However, the right to take that action is not impaired.

Articles 76–95. Relate to the Judiciary, Finance and Local Government.

AMENDMENTS

Article 96. Amendments to the Constitution are initiated by the Diet, through a concurring vote of two-thirds or more of all the members of each House, and are submitted to the people for ratification, which requires the affirmative vote of a majority of all votes cast at a special referendum or at such election as the Diet may specify.

Amendments when so ratified must immediately be promulgated by the Emperor in the name of the people, as an integral part of the Constitution.

Articles 97–99 outline the Supreme Law, while Articles 100–103 consist of Supplementary Provisions.

The Government

HEAD OF STATE

His Imperial Majesty AKIHITO, Emperor of Japan (succeeded to the throne 7 January 1989).

THE CABINET
(April 2008)

A coalition of the Liberal-Democratic Party (LDP) and New Komeito.

Prime Minister: YASUO FUKUDA.
Minister of Internal Affairs and Communications and Minister of State for Decentralization Reform, Regional Revitalization, Regional Government and Privatization of the Postal Services: HIROYA MASUDA.
Minister of Justice: KUNIO HATOYAMA.
Minister for Foreign Affairs: MASAHIKO KOUMURA.
Minister of Finance: FUKUSHIRO NUKAGA.
Minister of Education, Culture, Sports, Science and Technology: KISABURO TOKAI.
Minister of Health, Labour and Welfare: YOICHI MASUZOE.
Minister of Agriculture, Forestry and Fisheries: MASATOSHI WAKABAYASHI.
Minister of Economy, Trade and Industry: AKIRA AMARI.
Minister of Land, Infrastructure and Transport and of Ocean Policy: TETSUZO FUYUSHIBA.
Minister of the Environment and Minister in Charge of Global Environmental Problems: ICHIRO KAMOSHITA.
Minister of Defence: SHIGERU ISHIBA.
Chief Cabinet Secretary and Minister of State for the Abduction Issue: NOBUTAKA MACHIMURA.
Chairman of the National Public Safety Commission and Minister of State for Disaster Management and Food Safety: SHINYA IZUMI.
Minister of State for Okinawa and Northern Territories Affairs, Minister of State for Science and Technology Policy, Quality of Life Policy and Regulatory Reform: FUMIO KISHIDA.
Minister of State for Financial Services and Administrative Reform: YOSHIMI WATANABE.
Minister of State for Economic and Fiscal Policy: HIROKO OTA.
Minister of State for Gender Equality and Social Affairs: YOKO KAMIKAWA.

MINISTRIES

Imperial Household Agency: 1-1, Chiyoda, Chiyoda-ku, Tokyo 100-8111; tel. (3) 3213-1111; fax (3) 3282-1407; e-mail information@kunaicho.go.jp; internet www.kunaicho.go.jp.
Prime Minister's Office: 1-6-1, Nagata-cho, Chiyoda-ku, Tokyo 100-8968; tel. (3) 3581-2361; fax (3) 3581-1910; internet www.kantei.go.jp.
Cabinet Office: 1-6-1, Nagata-cho, Chiyoda-ku, Tokyo 100-8914; tel. (3) 5253-2111; internet www.cao.go.jp.
Ministry of Agriculture, Forestry and Fisheries: 1-2-1, Kasumigaseki, Chiyoda-ku, Tokyo 100-8950; tel. (3) 3502-8111; fax (3) 3592-7697; internet www.maff.go.jp.
Ministry of Defence: 5-1, Ichigaya, Honmura-cho, Shinjuku-ku, Tokyo 162-8801; tel. (3) 3268-3111; e-mail infomod@mod.go.jp; internet www.mod.go.jp.
Ministry of Economy, Trade and Industry: 1-3-1, Kasumigaseki, Chiyoda-ku, Tokyo 100-8901; tel. (3) 3501-1511; fax (3) 3501-6942; e-mail webmail@meti.go.jp; internet www.meti.go.jp.
Ministry of Education, Culture, Sports, Science and Technology: 3-2-2, Kasumigaseki, Chiyoda-ku, Tokyo 100-8959; tel. (3) 5253-4111; fax (3) 3595-2017; internet www.mext.go.jp.
Ministry of the Environment: 1-2-2, Kasumigaseki, Chiyoda-ku, Tokyo 100-8975; tel. (3) 3581-3351; fax (3) 3502-0308; e-mail moe@eanet.go.jp; internet www.env.go.jp.
Ministry of Finance: 3-1-1, Kasumigaseki, Chiyoda-ku, Tokyo 100-8940; tel. (3) 3581-4111; fax (3) 5251-2667; e-mail info@mof.go.jp; internet www.mof.go.jp.
Ministry of Foreign Affairs: 2-11-1, Shiba-Koen, Minato-ku, Tokyo 105-8519; tel. (3) 3580-3311; fax (3) 3581-2667; e-mail webmaster@mofa.go.jp; internet www.mofa.go.jp.
Ministry of Health, Labour and Welfare: 1-2-2, Kasumigaseki, Chiyoda-ku, Tokyo 100-8916; tel. (3) 5253-1111; fax (3) 3501-2532; internet www.mhlw.go.jp.
Ministry of Internal Affairs and Communications: 2-1-2, Kasumigaseki, Chiyoda-ku, Tokyo 100-8926; tel. (3) 5253-5111; fax (3) 3504-0265; internet www.soumu.go.jp.
Ministry of Justice: 1-1-1, Kasumigaseki, Chiyoda-ku, Tokyo 100-8977; tel. (3) 3580-4111; fax (3) 3592-7011; e-mail webmaster@moj.go.jp; internet www.moj.go.jp.
Ministry of Land, Infrastructure and Transport: 2-1-3, Kasumigaseki, Chiyoda-ku, Tokyo 100-8918; tel. (3) 5253-8111; fax (3) 3580-7982; e-mail webmaster@mlit.go.jp; internet www.mlit.go.jp.
Financial Services Agency: 3-1-1, Kasumigaseki, Chiyoda-ku, Tokyo 100-8967; tel. (3) 3506-6000; internet www.fsa.go.jp.
National Public Safety Commission: 2-1-2, Kasumigaseki, Chiyoda-ku, Tokyo 100-8974; tel. (3) 3581-0141; internet www.npsc.go.jp.

Legislature

KOKKAI
(Diet)

The Diet consists of two Chambers: the House of Councillors (upper house) and the House of Representatives (lower house). The members of the House of Representatives are elected for a period of four years (subject to dissolution). Following the enactment of reform legislation in December 1994, the number of members in the House of Representatives was reduced to 500 (from 511) at the general election of October 1996. Further legislation was enacted in February 2000, reducing the number of members in the House of Representatives to 480, comprising 300 single-seat constituencies and 180 seats determined by proportional representation. For the House of Councillors, which has 242 members (reduced from 247 at the 2004 election), the term of office is six years, with approximately one-half of the members elected every three years.

House of Councillors

Speaker: SATSUKI EDA.

Party	Seats after elections* 11 July 2004	29 July 2007
Democratic Party of Japan	82	109
Liberal-Democratic Party	115	83
New Komeito	24	20
Japanese Communist Party	9	7
Social Democratic Party of Japan	5	5
People's New Party†	—	4
New Party Nippon†	—	1
Independents	7	12
Other parties	—	1
Total	**242**	**242**

* Approximately one-half of the seats are renewable every three years. At the 2004 and 2007 elections 48 of the 121 seats were allocated on the basis of proportional representation.
† Formed in August 2005.

House of Representatives

Speaker: YOHEI KONO.
General Election, 11 September 2005

Party	Seats
Liberal-Democratic Party*	296
Democratic Party of Japan	113
New Komeito*	31
Japanese Communist Party	9
Social Democratic Party of Japan	7
Independents and others†	24
Total	**480**

* Following the election, New Komeito renewed its alliance with the Liberal-Democratic Party, thus creating a ruling coalition bloc of 327 seats.
† Among these were three small parties created following the dissolution of the House of Representatives in the previous month: the People's New Party and the New Party Nippon, both formed by rebels from the Liberal-Democratic Party, won four seats and one seat, respectively, while the New Party Daichi, a Hokkaido regional grouping, took one seat.

JAPAN

Election Commission

Central Election Management Council: 2nd Bldg of Central Common Government Office, 2-1-2, Kasumigaseki, Chiyoda-ku, Tokyo 100-8926; tel. (3) 5253-5111; fax (3) 5253-5575; mems nominated by Diet and approved by Cabinet; regulates proportional representation electoral elements for both Houses of the Diet; single-constituency elections for both chambers are supervised by an Election Control Committee established by each prefectural government; Chair. AKIRA ISHIHARA.

Political Organizations

The Political Funds Regulation Law provides that any organization wishing to support a candidate for an elective public office must be registered as a political party. There are more than 10,000 registered parties in the country, mostly of local or regional significance.

Dai-Niin Club: Rm 531, Sangiin Kaikan, 2-1-1, Nagata-cho, Chiyoda-ku, Tokyo 100-0014; tel. (3) 3508-8531; fax (3) 3560-6792; e-mail info@niinkurabu.gr.jp; internet www.niinkurabu.gr.jp; successor to the Green Wind Club (Ryukufukai), which originated in the House of Councillors in 1946–47.

Democratic Party of Japan (DPJ): 1-11-1, Nagata-cho, Chiyoda-ku, Tokyo 100-0014; tel. (3) 3595-9960; fax (3) 3595-7318; e-mail dpjenews@dpj.or.jp; internet www.dpj.or.jp; f. 1998 by the integration into the original DPJ (f. 1996) of the Democratic Reform League, Minseito and Shinto Yuai; advocates a cabinet formed and controlled by the people; absorbed Party Sakigake in March 2001; absorbed Liberal Party in Sept. 2003; Pres. ICHIRO OZAWA; Sec.-Gen. YUKIO HATOYAMA.

Japanese Communist Party (JCP): 4-26-7, Sendagaya, Shibuya-ku, Tokyo 151-8586; tel. (3) 3403-6111; fax (3) 3746-0767; e-mail intl@jcp.jp; internet www.jcp.or.jp; f. 1922; 400,000 mems (2007); Chair. of Exec. Cttee KAZUO SHII; Sec.-Gen. TADAYOSHI ICHIDA.

Liberal-Democratic Party—LDP (Jiyu-Minshuto): 1-11-23, Nagata-cho, Chiyoda-ku, Tokyo 100-8910; tel. (3) 3581-6211; e-mail koho@ldp.jimin.or.jp; internet www.jimin.jp; f. 1955; advocates the establishment of a welfare state, the promotion of industrial devt, the improvement of educational and cultural facilities and constitutional reform as needed; absorbed New Conservative Party in Nov. 2003; 2,369,252 mems (2001); Pres. YASUO FUKUDA; Sec.-Gen. BUNMEI IBUKI; Chair. of Gen. Council TOSHIHIRO NIKAI.

New Komeito: 17, Minami-Motomachi, Shinjuku-ku, Tokyo 160-0012; tel. (3) 3353-0111; internet www.komei.or.jp; f. 1964 as Komeito; renamed Komei 1994 following defection of a number of mems to the New Frontier Party (Shinshinto, dissolved Dec. 1997); absorbed Reimei Club Jan. 1998; renamed as above Nov. 1998 following merger of Komei and Shinto Heiwa; advocates political moderation, humanism and globalism, and policies respecting 'dignity of human life'; 400,000 mems (2003); Chief Representative AKIHIRO OTA; Sec.-Gen. KAZUO KITAGAWA.

New Party Daichi (Shinto Daichi): Sapporo 060-0061; tel. (11) 251-5351; internet www.muneo.gr.jp; f. 2005; regional grouping based in Hokkaido; Leader MUNEO SUZUKI.

New Party Nippon (Shinto Nippon): Tokyo 102-0093; tel. (3) 5213-0333; fax (3) 5213-0888; internet www.love-nippon.com; f. 2005; founding members included LDP rebels opposed to the postal reforms of Prime Minister Koizumi; Leader YASUO TANAKA.

New Socialist Party: Sanken Bldg, 6th Floor, 4-3-7, Hatchobori, Chuo-ku, Tokyo 104-0032; tel. (3) 3551-3980; e-mail honbu@sinsyakai.or.jp; internet www.sinsyakai.or.jp; f. 1996 by left-wing defectors from SDPJ; opposed to US military bases on Okinawa and introduction in 1996 of new electoral system; seeks to establish an ecological socio-economic system; Chair. TATSUKUNI KOMORI; Sec.-Gen. KENICHI UENO.

People's New Party (Kokumin Shinto): Tokyo 102-0093; tel. (3) 5275-2671; fax (3) 5275-2675; e-mail info@kokumin.or.jp; internet www.kokumin.or.jp; f. 2005 by rebels from LDP opposed to the postal reform proposals of Prime Minister Koizumi; Leader TAMISUKE WATANUKI.

Social Democratic Party of Japan—SDPJ (Shakai Minshuto): 1-8-1, Nagata-cho, Chiyoda-ku, Tokyo 100-0014; tel. (3) 3580-1171; fax (3) 3580-0691; e-mail kokusai@sdp.or.jp; internet www.sdp.or.jp; f. 1945 as the Japan Socialist Party (JSP); adopted present name in 1996; seeks the establishment of collective non-aggression and a mutual security system, including Japan, the USA, the CIS and the People's Republic of China; 115,000 mems (1994); Chair. MIZUHO FUKUSHIMA; Sec.-Gen. SEJI MATAICHI.

Diplomatic Representation

EMBASSIES IN JAPAN

Afghanistan: Matsumoto International House (MIH), 3-37-8, Nishihara, Shibuya-ku, Tokyo 151-0066; tel. (3) 5465-1219; fax (3) 5465-1229; e-mail info@afghanembassyjp.com; internet www.afghanembassyjp.com; Ambassador HARON AMIN.

Albania: 4/F Hokkoku Shimbun Bldg, 6-4-8, Tsukiji, Chuo-ku, Tokyo 104-0045; tel. (3) 3543-6861; fax (3) 3543-6862; e-mail embassy.tokyo@mfa.gov.al; Chargé d'affaires a.i. FATOS KERCIKU.

Algeria: 2-10-67, Mita, Meguro-ku, Tokyo 153-0062; tel. (3) 3711-2661; fax (3) 3710-6534; Ambassador SID ALI KETRANDJI.

Angola: 2-10-24, Daizawa, Setagaya-ku, Tokyo 155-0032; tel. (3) 5430-7879; fax (3) 5712-7481; e-mail embassy@angola.or.jp; internet www.angola.or.jp; Ambassador ALBINO MALUNGO.

Argentina: 2-14-14, Moto Azabu, Minato-ku, Tokyo 106-0046; tel. (3) 5420-7101; fax (3) 5420-7173; e-mail ejapo@mb.rosenet.ne.jp; internet www.embargentina.or.jp; Ambassador DANIEL ADÁN DZIEWEZO POLSKI.

Australia: 2-1-14, Mita, Minato-ku, Tokyo 108-8361; tel. (3) 5232-4111; fax (3) 5232-4149; internet www.australia.or.jp; Ambassador ALISTAIR MURRAY MCLEAN.

Austria: 1-1-20, Moto Azabu, Minato-ku, Tokyo 106-0046; tel. (3) 3451-8281; fax (3) 3451-8283; e-mail tokio-ob@bmaa.gv.at; internet www.bmeia.gv.at/tokio; Ambassador Dr JUTTA STEFAN-BASTL.

Azerbaijan: 1-19-15, Higashigaoka, Meguro-ku, Tokyo; tel. (3) 5486-4744; fax (3) 5486-7374; e-mail info@azerbembassy.jp; Ambassador AZER HUSEYN.

Bahrain: Residence Viscountess 720, 1-11-36, Akasaka, Minato-ku, Tokyo 107-0052; tel. (3) 3584-8001; e-mail info@bahrain-embassy.or.jp; internet www.bahrain-embassy.or.jp; Ambassador Dr KHALIL HASSAN.

Bangladesh: 4-15-15, Meguro, Meguro-ku, Tokyo 153-0063; tel. (3) 5704-0216; fax (3) 5704-1696; e-mail bdootjp@gol.com; internet www.bdembjp.com; Ambassador ASHRAF UD-DOULA.

Belarus: 4-14-12, Shirogane K House, Shirogane, Minato-ku, Tokyo 108-0072; tel. (3) 3448-1623; fax (3) 3448-1624; e-mail japan@belembassy.org; internet www.belarus.jp; Chargé d'affaires a.i. LEONID I. BATYANOVSKY.

Belgium: Shiba Daimon Front Bldg, 1-7-13, Shiba Koen, Minato-ku, Tokyo 105-0011; tel. (3) 3262-0191; fax (3) 3262-0651; e-mail tokyo@diplobel.be; internet www.diplomatie.be/tokyo; Ambassador JOHAN MARICOU.

Benin: Shokokusha Bldg 6/F, 2-16-9, Hirakawachu, Chiyoda-ku, Tokyo 102-0093; tel. (3) 3556-2562; fax (3) 3556-2563; e-mail abenintyo@mist.ocn.ne.jp; Ambassador ALLASSANE YASSO.

Bolivia: Kowa Bldg, No. 38, Room 804, 4-12-24, Nishi Azabu, Minato-ku, Tokyo 106-0031; tel. (3) 3499-5441; fax (3) 3499-5443; e-mail emboltk1@ad.il24.net; Ambassador MASAKATSU JAIME ASHIMINE OSHIRO.

Bosnia and Herzegovina: 3-4, Rokuban-cho, Chiyoda-ku, Tokyo 102-0085; tel. (3) 3556-4151; fax (3) 3556-4152; e-mail bih8emb@gol.com; Chargé d'affaires a.i. MITHAT PAŠIĆ.

Botswana: 6F Kearny Place, 4-5-10, Shiba, Minato-ku, Tokyo 108-0014; tel. (3) 5440-5676; fax (3) 5765-7581; e-mail botjap@sepia.ocn.ne.jp; internet www.botswanaembassy.or.jp; Ambassador OSCAR MOTSWAGAE.

Brazil: 2-11-12, Kita Aoyama, Minato-ku, Tokyo 107-8633; tel. (3) 3404-5211; fax (3) 3405-5846; e-mail brasemb@brasemb.or.jp; internet www.brasemb.or.jp; Ambassador ANDRÉ MATTOSO MAIA AMADO.

Brunei: 6-5-2, Kita Shinagawa, Shinagawa-ku, Tokyo 141-0001; tel. (3) 3447-7997; fax (3) 3447-9260; e-mail contact@bruemb.jp; internet www.bruemb.jp; Ambassador Dato'Paduka Haji ADNAN BUNTAR.

Bulgaria: 5-36-3, Yoyogi, Shibuya-ku, Tokyo 151-0053; tel. (3) 3465-1021; fax (3) 3465-1031; e-mail bulemb@gol.com; internet www.mfa.bg/tokyo; Ambassador Prof. BLAGOVEST SENDOV.

Burkina Faso: Apt 301, Hiroo Glisten Hills, 3-1-17, Hiroo, Shibuya-ku, Tokyo 150-0012; tel. (3) 3400-7919; fax (3) 3400-6945; e-mail faso-amb@khaki.plala.or.jp; internet www.embassy-avenue.jp/burkina; Chargé d'affaires a.i. PATRICE KAFANDO.

Cambodia: 8-6-9, Akasaka, Minato-ku, Tokyo 107-0052; tel. (3) 5412-8521; fax (3) 5412-8526; e-mail aap33850@hkg.odn.ne.jp; internet www.cambodianembassy.jp; Ambassador POU SOTHIREAK.

Cameroon: 3-27-16, Nozawa, Setagaya-ku, Tokyo 154-0003; tel. (3) 5430-4381; fax (3) 5430-6489; e-mail ambacamtokyo@gol.com; Chargé d'affaires a.i. APOLLINAIRE ESSOMBA.

Canada: 7-3-38, Akasaka, Minato-ku, Tokyo 107-8503; tel. (3) 5412-6200; fax (3) 5412-6249; internet www.canadanet.or.jp; Ambassador JOSEPH CARON.

JAPAN

Chile: Nihon Seimei Akabanebashi Bldg, 8th Floor, 3-1-14, Shiba, Minato-ku, Tokyo 105-0014; tel. (3) 3452-7561; fax (3) 3452-4457; e-mail embajada@chile.or.jp; internet www.chile.or.jp; Ambassador Daniel Carvallo.

China, People's Republic: 3-4-33, Moto Azabu, Minato-ku, Tokyo 106-0046; tel. (3) 3403-3380; fax (3) 3403-3345; e-mail lsb@china-embassy.or.jp; internet www.china-embassy.or.jp; Ambassador Cui Tiankai.

Colombia: 3-10-53, Kami Osaki, Shinagawa-ku, Tokyo 141-0021; tel. (3) 3440-6451; fax (3) 3440-6724; e-mail embajada@emcoltokyo.or.jp; internet www.colombiaembassy.org; Ambassador Patricia Cárdenas.

Congo, Democratic Republic: Harajuku Green Heights, Room 701, 3-53-17, Sendagaya, Shibuya-ku, Tokyo 151-0051; tel. (3) 3423-3981; fax (3) 3423-3984; Ambassador Marcel Mulumba Tshidimba.

Costa Rica: Kowa Bldg, No. 38, Room 901, 4-12-24, Nishi Azabu, Minato-ku, Tokyo 106-0031; tel. (3) 3486-1812; fax (3) 3486-1813; e-mail ecrj@tky3.web3.ne.jp; Ambassador Mario Fernández Silva.

Côte d'Ivoire: 2-19-12, Uehara, Shibuya-ku, Tokyo 151-0064; tel. (3) 5454-1401; fax (3) 5454-1405; e-mail ambacijn@yahoo.fr; internet www.ahibo.com/ambaci-jp; Chargé d'affaires a.i. Tui Digbe.

Croatia: 3-3-10, Hiroo, Shibuya-ku, Tokyo 150-0012; tel. (3) 5469-3014; fax (3) 5469-3015; e-mail croemb.tokyo@mvpei.hr; Ambassador Drago Stambuk.

Cuba: 1-28-4, Higashi-Azabu, Minato-ku, Tokyo 106-0044; tel. (3) 5570-3182; fax (3) 5570-8566; e-mail embajada@ecujapon.jp; internet embacuba.cubaminrex.cu/japon; Ambassador José Fernández de Cossio.

Czech Republic: 2-16-14, Hiroo, Shibuya-ku, Tokyo 150-0012; tel. (3) 3400-8122; fax (3) 3400-8124; e-mail tokyo@embassy.mzv.cz; internet www.mzv.cz/tokyo; Ambassador Jaromir Novotny.

Denmark: 29-6, Sarugaku-cho, Shibuya-ku, Tokyo 150-0033; tel. (3) 3496-3001; fax (3) 3496-3440; e-mail tyoamb@um.dk; internet www.ambtokyo.um.dk; Ambassador Freddy Svane.

Djibouti: 5-18-10, Shimo Meguro, Meguro-ku, Tokyo 153-0064; tel. (3) 5704-0682; fax (3) 5725-8305; internet www.angelfire.com/de3/djibouti-embassy-tok; Ambassador Ahmed Araita Ali.

Dominican Republic: Kowa Bldg, No. 38, Room 904, 4-12-24, Nishi Azabu, Minato-ku, Tokyo 106-0031; tel. (3) 3499-6020; fax (3) 3499-2627; e-mail embdomjapon@serex.gov.do; Ambassador José Ureña.

Ecuador: Kowa Bldg, No. 38, Room 806, 4-12-24, Nishi Azabu, Minato-ku, Tokyo 106-0031; tel. (3) 3499-2800; fax (3) 3499-4400; e-mail ecujapon@alto.ocn.ne.jp; internet www.ecuador-embassy.or.jp; Chargé d'affaires a.i. Juan Larrea Miño.

Egypt: 1-5-4, Aobadai, Meguro-ku, Tokyo 153-0042; tel. (3) 3770-8022; fax (3) 3770-8021; e-mail egyptemb@mc.kcom.ne.jp; internet www.embassy-avenue.jp/egypt/index.htm; Ambassador Walid Abdelnasser.

El Salvador: Kowa Bldg, No. 38, 8th Floor, 4-12-24, Nishi Azabu, Minato-ku, Tokyo 106-0031; tel. (3) 3499-4461; fax (3) 3486-7022; e-mail embesaltokio@gol.com; Ambassador José Ricardo Paredes-Osorio.

Eritrea: Shirokanedai ST Bldg, Room 401, 4-7-4, Shirokanedai, Minato-ku, Tokyo, 108-0071; tel. (3) 5791-1815; fax (3) 5791-1816; e-mail eritrea-embassy@excite.co.jp; internet www.embassy-avenue.jp/eritrea; Ambassador Estifanos Afeworki.

Estonia: 2-6-15, Jingu-mae, Shibuya-ku 150-0001; tel. (3) 5412-7281; fax (3) 5412-7282; e-mail embassy.tokyo@mfa.ee; internet www.estemb.or.jp; Ambassador Peeter Miller.

Ethiopia: 2F Takanawa Kaisei Bldg, 3-4-1, Takanawa, Minato-ku, Tokyo 108-0074; tel. (3) 5420-6860; fax (3) 5420-6866; e-mail info@ethiopia-emb.or.jp; internet www.ethiopia-emb.or.jp; Ambassador Abdirashid Dulane.

Fiji: Noa Bldg, 14th Floor, 2-3-5, Azabudai, Minato-ku, Tokyo 106-0041; tel. (3) 3587-2038; fax (3) 3587-2563; e-mail info@fijiembassy.jp; internet www.fijiembassy.jp; Ambassador Ratu Inoke Kubuabola.

Finland: 3-5-39, Minami Azabu, Minato-ku, Tokyo 106-8561; tel. (3) 5447-6000; fax (3) 5447-6042; e-mail sanomat.tok@formin.fi; internet www.finland.or.jp; Ambassador Jorma Kari Johannes Julin.

France: 4-11-44, Minami Azabu, Minato-ku, Tokyo 106-8514; tel. (3) 5420-8800; fax (3) 5420-8847; e-mail ambafrance.tokyo@diplomatie.fr; internet www.ambafrance-jp.org; Ambassador Philippe Faure.

Gabon: 1-34-11, Higashigaoka, Meguro-ku, Tokyo 152-0021; tel. (3) 5430-9171; fax (3) 5430-9175; e-mail info@gabonembassy-tokyo.org; internet www.geocities.jp/gabontky; Ambassador Jean-Christian Obame.

Georgia: 2/F, Nanbu Bldg, 3-3, Kioi-cho, Chiyoda-ku, Tokyo 102-0094; tel. (3) 5226-5011; fax (3) 5226-5014; e-mail tokio.emb@mfa.gov.ge; Ambassador Ivane Machavariani.

Germany: 4-5-10, Minami Azabu, Minato-ku, Tokyo 106-0047; tel. (3) 5791-7700; fax (3) 3473-4243; e-mail germtoky@ma.rosenet.ne.jp; internet www.tokyo.diplo.de; Ambassador Hans-Joachim Daerr.

Ghana: 1-5-21, Nishi Azabu, Minato-ku, Tokyo 106-0031; tel. (3) 5410-8631; fax (3) 5410-8635; e-mail mission@ghanaembassy.or.jp; internet www.ghanaembassy.or.jp; Ambassador Dr Barfuor Adjei-Barwuah.

Greece: 3-16-30, Nishi Azabu, Minato-ku, Tokyo 106-0031; tel. (3) 3403-0871; fax (3) 3402-4642; e-mail gremb.tok@mfa.gr; internet www.greekemb.jp; Ambassador Ioannos Vavvas.

Guatemala: Kowa Bldg, No. 38, Room 905, 4-12-24, Nishi Azabu, Minato-ku, Tokyo 106-0031; tel. (3) 3400-1830; fax (3) 3400-1820; e-mail embguate@vega.ocn.ne.jp; internet www.embassy-avenue.jp/guatemala; Ambassador Arturo Duarte.

Guinea: 12-9, Hachiyama-cho, Shibuya-ku, Tokyo 150-0035; tel. (3) 3770-4640; fax (3) 3770-4643; e-mail ambagui-tokyo@gol.com; Ambassador Ousmane Tolo Thiam.

Haiti: Kowa Bldg, No. 38, Room 906, 4-12-24, Nishi Azabu, Minato-ku, Tokyo 106-0031; tel. (3) 3486-7096; fax (3) 3486-7070; Chargé d'affaires a.i. Jean-Claude Bordes.

Holy See: Apostolic Nunciature, 9-2, Sanban-cho, Chiyoda-ku, Tokyo 102-0075; tel. (3) 3263-6851; fax (3) 3263-6060; Apostolic Nuncio Most Rev. Alberto Bottari de Castello (Titular Archbishop of Oderzo).

Honduras: Kowa Bldg, No. 38, Room 802, 8/F, 4-12-24, Nishi Azabu, Minato-ku, Tokyo 106-0031; tel. (3) 3409-1150; fax (3) 3409-0305; e-mail honduras@interlink.or.jp; Ambassador Nadina Joyce Lefebvre Labro.

Hungary: 2-17-14, Mita, Minato-ku, Tokyo 108-0073; tel. (3) 3798-8801; fax (3) 3798-8812; e-mail huembtio@gol.com; internet www.mfa.gov.hu/kulkepviselet/JP/HU; Ambassador Gyula Dabrónaki.

Iceland: 4-18-26, Takanawa, Minato-ku, Tokyo 108-0074; tel. (3) 3447-1944; fax (3) 3447-1945; e-mail icemb.tokyo@utn.stjr.is; internet www.iceland.org/jp; Ambassador Thordur Aegir Oskarsson.

India: 2-2-11, Kudan Minami, Chiyoda-ku, Tokyo 102-0074; tel. (3) 3262-2391; fax (3) 3234-4866; e-mail indembjp@gol.com; internet www.embassyofindiajapan.org; Ambassador Hemant Krisham Singh.

Indonesia: 5-2-9, Higashi Gotanda, Shinagawa-ku, Tokyo 141-0022; tel. (3) 3441-4201; fax (3) 3447-1697; e-mail info@indonesian-embassy.or.jp; internet www.indonesian-embassy.or.jp; Ambassador Jusuf Anwar.

Iran: 3-13-9, Minami Azabu, Minato-ku, Tokyo 106-0047; tel. (3) 3446-8011; fax (3) 3446-9002; e-mail sjei@gol.com; internet www.iranembassyjp.com; Ambassador Abbas Araqchi.

Iraq: 2-16-11, Takanawa, Minato-ku, Tokyo 108-0074; tel. (3) 5449-3231; fax (3) 5449-7719; e-mail tokemb@iraqmofamail.net; internet www.iraqi-japan.com; Ambassador Ghanim Alwan al-Jumaily.

Ireland: Ireland House, 2-10-7, Kojimachi, Chiyoda-ku, Tokyo 102-0083; tel. (3) 3263-0695; fax (3) 3265-2275; e-mail irljapan@gol.com; internet www.irishembassy.jp; Ambassador Brendan Scannell.

Israel: 3, Niban-cho, Chiyoda-ku, Tokyo 102-0084; tel. (3) 3264-0911; fax (3) 3264-0791; e-mail consular@tky.mfa.gov.il; internet tokyo.mfa.gov.il; Ambassador Nissim Ben Sheetrit.

Italy: 2-5-4, Mita, Minato-ku, Tokyo 108-8302; tel. (3) 3453-5291; fax (3) 3456-2319; e-mail ambasciata.tokyo@esteri.it; internet www.ambtokyo.esteri.it/ambasciata_tokyo; Ambassador Mario Bova.

Jamaica: Toranomon Yatsuka Bldg, 2nd Floor, 1-1-11, Atago, Minato-ku, Tokyo 105-0002; tel. (3) 3435-1861; fax (3) 3435-1864; e-mail mail@jamaicaemb.jp; internet www.jamaicaemb.jp; Ambassador (vacant).

Jordan: Chiyoda House, 4th Floor, 2-17-8, Nagata-cho, Chiyoda-ku, Tokyo 100-0014; tel. (3) 3580-5856; fax (3) 3593-9385; e-mail jor-emb@mc.kcom.ne.jp; internet www18.ocn.ne.jp/~jor-emb; Ambassador Samir Naouri.

Kazakhstan: 5-9-8, Himonya, Meguro-ku, Tokyo 152-0003; tel. (3) 3791-5273; fax (3) 3791-5279; e-mail embkazjp@gol.com; internet www.embkazjp.org; Ambassador Akylbek Kamaldinov.

Kenya: 3-24-3, Yakumo, Meguro-ku, Tokyo 152-0023; tel. (3) 3723-4006; fax (3) 3723-4488; e-mail info@kenrep-jp.com; internet www.kenyarep-jp.com; Ambassador Dennis N.O. Awori.

Korea, Republic: 1-2-5, Minami Azabu, Minato-ku, Tokyo 106-0047; tel. (3) 3452-7611; fax (3) 5232-6911; internet jpn-tokyo.mofat.go.kr; Ambassador Yu Myung-Hwan.

Kuwait: 4-13-12, Mita, Minato-ku, Tokyo 108-0073; tel. (3) 3455-0361; fax (3) 3456-6290; e-mail ask.kwt@kuwait-embassy.or.jp; internet kuwait-embassy.or.jp; Ambassador Sheikh Abdul Rahman al-Otaibi.

JAPAN

Kyrgyzstan: 5-6-16, Shimomeguro, Meguro-ku, Tokyo 153-0064; tel. (3) 3719-0828; fax (3) 3719-0868; e-mail chancery@kyrgyzemb.jp; internet www.kyrgyzemb.jp; Ambassador ASKAR KUTANOV.

Laos: 3-3-22, Nishi Azabu, Minato-ku, Tokyo 106-0031; tel. (3) 5411-2291; fax (3) 5411-2293; Ambassador SITHONG CHITNHOTHINH.

Latvia: 37-11, Kamiyama-cho, Shibuya-ku, Tokyo 150-0047; tel. and fax (3) 3467-6888; e-mail embassy.jp@mfa.gov.lv; Ambassador PĒTERIS VAIVARS.

Lebanon: Chiyoda House, 5th Floor, 2-17-8, Nagata-cho, Chiyoda-ku, Tokyo 100-0014; tel. (3) 3580-1227; fax (3) 3580-2281; e-mail ambaliba@cronos.ocn.ne.jp; Ambassador MOHAMMED HARAKE.

Lesotho: U & M Akasaka Bldg, 3/F, 7-5-47, Akasaka, Minato-ku, Tokyo 107-0052; tel. (3) 3584-7455; Ambassador MOKHELE LIKATE.

Liberia: Sugi Terrace 201, 3-13-11, Okusawa, Setagaya-ku, Tokyo 158; tel. (3) 3726-5711; fax (3) 3726-5712; Chargé d'affaires a.i. ADAM BILITY.

Libya: 10-14, Daikanyama-cho, Shibuya-ku, Tokyo 150-0034; tel. (3) 3477-0701; fax (3) 3464-0420; Secretary of the People's Bureau MUFTAH M. H. FAITOURI.

Lithuania: 3-7-18, Moto Azabu, Minato-ku, Tokyo 106-0046; tel. (3) 3408-5091; fax (3) 3408-5092; e-mail linfo@lithemb.or.jp; internet www.lithemb.or.jp; Ambassador DAINIUS PETRAS KAMAITIS.

Luxembourg: 1/F Luxembourg House, 1st Floor, 8–9, Yonban-cho, Chiyoda-ku, 102-0081; tel. (3) 3265-9621; fax (3) 3265-9624; internet www.luxembourg.or.jp; Ambassador PAUL STEINMETZ.

Madagascar: 2-3-23, Moto Azabu, Minato-ku, Tokyo 106-0046; tel. (3) 3446-7252; fax (3) 3446-7078; Ambassador JIMMY RAMIANDRISOA.

Malawi: Takanawa-Kaisei Bldg, 7th Floor, 3-4-1, Takanawa, Minato-ku, Tokyo 108-0074; tel. (3) 3449-3010; fax (3) 3449-3220; e-mail malawi@luck.ocn.ne.jp; internet www.malawiembassy.org; Ambassador ROOSEVELT LASTON GONDWE.

Maldives: Iikura MINT Bldg, 8/F, 1-9-10, Azabudai, Minato-ku, Tokyo 106-0041; tel. 6234-4315; fax 6234-4316; e-mail info@maldivesembassy.jp; internet www.maldivesembassy.jp; Ambassador ABDUL HAMEED ZAKARIYYA.

Malaysia: 20-16, Nanpeidai-cho, Shibuya-ku, Tokyo 150-0036; tel. (3) 3476-3840; fax (3) 3476-4971; e-mail maltokyo@kln.gov.my; Ambassador Dato' MOHD RADZI ABDUL RAHMAN.

Mali: 3-12-9, Kamiosaki, Shinagawa-ku, Tokyo 141-0021; tel. (3) 3705-3437; fax (3) 3705-3489; e-mail info@ambamali-jp.org; internet www.ambamali-jp.org; Ambassador GUISSE MAÏMOUNA DIAL.

Marshall Islands: Meiji Park Heights 101, 9-9, Minamimotomachi, Shinjuku-ku, Tokyo 106; tel. (3) 5379-1701; fax (3) 5379-1810; e-mail ambassador@rmiembassyjp.org; Ambassador PHILLIP KABUA.

Mauritania: 5-17-5, Kita Shinagawa, Shinagawa-ku, Tokyo 141-0001; tel. (3) 3449-3810; fax (3) 3449-3822; e-mail ambarim@seagreen.ocn.ne.jp; internet www.amba-mauritania.jp; Ambassador MUHAMMAD MAHMOUD OULD JAAFAR.

Mexico: 2-15-1, Nagata-cho, Chiyoda-ku, Tokyo 100-0014; tel. (3) 3581-1131; fax (3) 3581-4058; e-mail embamex@mexicoembassy.jp; internet www.sre.gob.mx/japon; Ambassador MIGUEL RUIZ-CABAÑAS IZQUIERDO.

Micronesia, Federated States: Reinanzaka Bldg, 2nd Floor, 1-14-2, Akasaka, Minato-ku, Tokyo 107-0052; tel. (3) 3585-5456; fax (3) 3585-5348; e-mail fsmemb@fsmemb.or.jp; Ambassador JOHN FRITZ.

Mongolia: Pine Crest Mansion, 21-4, Kamiyama-cho, Shibuya-ku, Tokyo 150-0047; tel. (3) 3469-2088; fax (3) 3469-2216; e-mail embmong@gol.com; Ambassador RENTSENDOOGIIN JIGJID.

Morocco: 5-4-30, Minami Aoyama, Minato-Ku, Tokyo 107-0062; tel. (3) 5485-7171; fax (3) 5485-7173; e-mail sifamato@circus.ocn.ne.jp; internet www.morocco-emba.jp; Ambassador ABDELKADER LECHEHEB.

Mozambique: Shiba Amerex Bldg, 6th Floor, 3-12-17 Mita, Minato-ku, Tokyo 108-0073; tel. (3) 5419-0973; fax (3) 5442-0556; e-mail mozambiq@tkk.att.ne.jp; internet www.embamoc.jp; Ambassador DANIEL ANTÓNIO.

Myanmar: 4-8-26, Kita Shinagawa, Shinagawa-ku, Tokyo 140-0001; tel. (3) 3441-9291; fax (3) 3447-7394; e-mail contact@myanmar-embassy-tokyo.net; internet www.myanmar-embassy-tokyo.net; Ambassador U HLA MYINT.

Nepal: 7-14-9, Todoroki, Setagaya-ku, Tokyo 158-0082; tel. (3) 3705-5558; fax (3) 3705-8264; e-mail nepembjp@big.or.jp; internet www.nepal.co.jp/embassy; Ambassador GANESH YONZAN TAMANG.

Netherlands: 3-6-3, Shiba Koen, Minato-ku, Tokyo 105-0011; tel. (3) 5401-0411; fax (3) 5401-0420; e-mail nlgovtok@oranda.or.jp; internet www.oranda.or.jp; Ambassador ALPHONS HAMER.

New Zealand: 20-40, Kamiyama-cho, Shibuya-ku, Tokyo 150-0047; tel. (3) 3467-2271; fax (3) 3467-2278; e-mail nzemb.tky@mail.com; internet www.nzembassy.com/japan; Ambassador IAN KENNEDY.

Nicaragua: Kowa Bldg, No. 38, Room 903, 9th Floor, 4-12-24, Nishi Azabu, Minato-ku, Tokyo 106; tel. (3) 3499-0400; fax (3) 3710-2028; e-mail nicjapan@gol.com; Ambassador SAÚL ARANA CASTELLÓN.

Nigeria: 5-11-17, Shimo-Meguro, Meguro-ku, Tokyo 153-0064; tel. (3) 5721-5391; fax (3) 5721-5342; internet www.nigeriaembassy.jp; Ambassador YAHAYA TABARI ZARIA.

Norway: 5-12-2, Minami Azabu, Minato-ku, Tokyo 106-0047; tel. (3) 3440-2611; fax (3) 3440-2620; e-mail emb.tokyo@mfa.no; internet www.norway.or.jp; Ambassador ÅGE BERNHARD GRUTLE.

Oman: 2-28-11, Sendagaya, Shibuya-ku, Tokyo 151-0051; tel. (3) 3402-0877; fax (3) 3404-1334; e-mail omanemb@gol.com; Ambassador KHALID BIN HASHIL BIN MOHAMMED AL-MUSLAHI.

Pakistan: 2-14-9, Moto Azabu, Minato-ku, Tokyo 106-0046; tel. (3) 3454-4861; fax (3) 3457-0341; e-mail info@pakistanembassyjapan.com; internet www.pakistanembassyjapan.com; Ambassador KAMRAN NIAZ.

Palau: Rm 201, 1-1, Katamachi, Shinjuku-ku, Tokyo 160-0001; tel. (3) 3354-5500; Ambassador DAIZIRO NAKAMURA.

Panama: Kowa Bldg, No. 38, Room 902, 4-12-24, Nishi Azabu, Minato-ku, Tokyo 106-0031; tel. (3) 3499-3741; fax (3) 5485-3548; e-mail panaemb@gol.com; internet www.embassyofpanamainjapan.org; Ambassador ALFREDO MARTIZ.

Papua New Guinea: Mita Kokusai Bldg, Room 313, 3rd Floor, 1-4-28, Mita, Minato-ku, Tokyo 108; tel. (3) 3454-7801; fax (3) 3454-7275; e-mail png-tyo@nifty.ne.jp; Ambassador MICHAEL MAUE.

Paraguay: 3-12-9, Kami-Osaki, Shinagawa-ku, Tokyo 141-0021; tel. (3) 5485-3101; fax (3) 5485-3103; e-mail embapar@gol.com; internet www.embapar.jp; Ambassador ISAO TAOKA.

Peru: 4-100-1, Higashi, Shibuya-ku, Tokyo 150-0011; tel. (3) 3406-4243; fax (3) 3409-7589; e-mail embperutokyo@embperujapan.org; Ambassador HUGO PALMA.

Philippines: 5-15-5, Roppongi, Minato-ku, Tokyo 106-8537; tel. (3) 5562-1600; fax (3) 5562-1603; e-mail info@tokyope.org; internet www.tokyope.org; Ambassador DOMINGO L. SIAZON, Jr.

Poland: 2-13-5, Mita, Meguro-ku, Tokyo 153-0062; tel. (3) 5794-7020; fax (3) 5794-7024; e-mail polamb@poland.or.jp; internet www.tokio.polemb.net; Ambassador MARCIN RYBICKI.

Portugal: Kamiura-Kojimachi Bldg, 5th Floor, 3-10-3, Kojimachi, Chiyoda-ku, Tokyo 102-0083; tel. (3) 5212-7322; fax (3) 5226-0616; e-mail tokyo.delegation@portugal.or.jp; internet www.portugal.or.jp; Ambassador JOÃO PEDRO ZANATTI.

Qatar: 2-3-28, Moto Azabu, Minato-ku, Tokyo 106-0046; tel. (3) 5475-0611; fax (3) 5475-0617; e-mail tokyo@mofa.gov.qa; Ambassador REYAD ALI AL-ANSARI.

Romania: 3-16-19, Nishi Azabu, Minato-ku, Tokyo 106-0031; tel. (3) 3479-0311; fax (3) 3479-0312; e-mail office@ambrom.jp; internet www.ambrom.jp; Ambassador AURELIAN NEAGU.

Russia: 2-1-1, Azabu-dai, Minato-ku, Tokyo 106-0041; tel. (3) 3583-4224; fax (3) 3505-0593; e-mail rosconsl@ma.kcom.ne.jp; internet www.russia-emb.jp; Ambassador MIKHAIL M. BELY.

Rwanda: Kowa Bldg, No. 38, 4-12-24, Nishi Azabu, Minato-ku, Tokyo 106; tel. (3) 3486-7801; fax (3) 3409-2334; Ambassador EMILE RWAMASIRABO.

San Marino: 3-5-1, Moto Azabu, Minato-ku, Tokyo 106-0046; tel. (3) 5414-7745; fax (3) 3405-6789; e-mail sanmarinoemb@tiscali.it; Ambassador MANLIO CADELO.

Saudi Arabia: 1-8-4, Roppongi, Minato-ku, Tokyo 106-0032; tel. (3) 3589-5241; fax (3) 3589-5200; e-mail info@saudiembassy.or.jp; internet www.saudiembassy.or.jp; Ambassador FAISAL HASSAN TRAD.

Senegal: 1-3-4, Aobadai, Meguro-ku, Tokyo 153-0042; tel. (3) 3464-8451; fax (3) 3464-8452; e-mail senegal@senegal.jp; Ambassador GABRIEL ALEXANDRE SAR.

Serbia: 4-7-24, Kita-Shinagawa, Shinagawa-ku, Tokyo 140-0001; tel. (3) 3447-3571; fax (3) 3447-3573; e-mail embassy@serbianembassy.jp; internet www.serbianembassy.jp; Ambassador IVAN MRKIC.

Singapore: 5-12-3, Roppongi, Minato-ku, Tokyo 106-0032; tel. (3) 3586-9111; fax (3) 3582-1085; e-mail singemb@gol.com; internet www.mfa.gov.sg/tokyo; Ambassador TAN CHIN TIONG.

Slovakia: POB 35, 2-16-14, Hiroo, Shibuya-ku, Tokyo 150-8691; tel. (3) 3400-8122; fax (3) 3406-6215; e-mail information@slovak-embassy.jp; internet www.embassy-avenue.jp/slovakia; Ambassador PETER VRŠANSKÝ.

Slovenia: 7-5-15, Akasaka, Minato-ku, Tokyo 107-0052; tel. (3) 5570-6275; fax (3) 5570-6075; e-mail vto@mzz-dkp.gov.si; Ambassador MIRAN ČUPKOVIČ SKENDER.

South Africa: Oriken Hirakawa Bldg, 2-1-1, Hirakawa-cho, Chiyoda-ku, Tokyo 102-0093; tel. (3) 3265-3366; fax (3) 3265-1108; e-mail rsatk-info@rsatk.org; internet www.rsatk.org; Ambassador Dr BALDWIN SIPHO NGUBANE.

JAPAN

Spain: 1-3-29, Roppongi, Minato-ku, Tokyo 106-0032; tel. (3) 3583-8531; fax (3) 3582-8627; e-mail embspjp@mail.mae.es; internet www2.gol.com/users/esptokio; Ambassador MIGUEL ANGEL CARRIEDO MOMPÍN.

Sri Lanka: 2-1-54, Takanawa, Minato-ku, Tokyo 108-0074; tel. (3) 3440-6911; fax (3) 3440-6914; e-mail tokyojp@lankaembassy.jp; internet www.lankaembassy.jp; Ambassador RANJITH UYANGODA.

Sudan: Chiyoda House, 7th Floor, 2-17-8, Nagata-cho, Chiyoda-ku, Tokyo 100-0014; tel. (3) 3506-7801; fax (3) 3506-7804; e-mail info@sudanembassy.jp; internet www.sudanembassy.jp; Ambassador STEVEN KILIONA WONDU.

Sweden: 1-10-3-100, Roppongi, Minato-ku, Tokyo 106-0032; tel. (3) 5562-5050; fax (3) 5562-9095; e-mail info@sweden.or.jp; internet www.sweden.or.jp; Ambassador STEFAN NOREÉN.

Switzerland: 5-9-12, Minami Azabu, Minato-ku, Tokyo 106-8589; tel. (3) 5449-8400; fax (3) 3473-6090; e-mail vertretung@tok.rep.admin.ch; internet www.eda.admin.ch/tokyo; Ambassador PAUL FIVAT.

Syria: Homat Jade, 6-19-45, Akasaka, Minato-ku, Tokyo 107-0052; tel. (3) 3586-8977; fax (3) 3586-8979; Chargé d'affaires a.i. RANIA AL-HAJ ALI.

Tanzania: 4-21-9, Kami Yoga, Setagaya-ku, Tokyo 158-0098; tel. (3) 3425-4531; fax (3) 3425-7844; e-mail tzrepjp@tanzaniaembassy.or.jp; internet www.tanzaniaembassy.or.jp; Ambassador ELLY E. E. MTANGO.

Thailand: 3-14-6, Kami Osaki, Shinagawa-ku, Tokyo 141-0021; tel. (3) 3447-2247; fax (3) 3442-6750; e-mail sathana@thaiembassy.jp; internet www.thaiembassy.jp; Ambassador SUVIDHYA SIMASKUL.

Timor-Leste: Rokuban-cho House, 1/F, 3-4, Rokuban-cho, Chiyoda-ku, Tokyo 102-0085; tel. (3) 3238-0210; Ambassador DOMINGOS SARMENTO ALVES.

Tunisia: 3-6-6, Kudan-Minami, Chiyoda-ku, Tokyo 102-0074; tel. (3) 3511-6622; fax (3) 3511-6600; internet www.tunisia.or.jp; Ambassador NOUREDDINE HACHED.

Turkey: 2-33-6, Jingumae, Shibuya-ku, Tokyo 150-0001; tel. (3) 3470-5131; fax (3) 3470-5136; e-mail embassy@turkey.jp; internet www.turkey.jp; Ambassador SERMET ATACANLI.

Uganda: 9-23 Hachiyamacho Shibuya-ku, Tokyo 150-0035; tel. (3) 3462-7107; fax (3) 3462-7108; e-mail ugabassy@hpo.net; internet www.uganda-embassy.jp; Ambassador WASSWA BIRIGGWA.

Ukraine: 3-15-6, Nishi Azabu, Minato-ku, Tokyo 106-0046; tel. (3) 5474-9770; fax (3) 5474-9772; e-mail ukremb@rose.ocn.ne.jp; internet ukremb-japan.gov.ua; Ambassador MYKOLA KULINICH.

United Arab Emirates: 9-10, Nanpeidai-cho, Shibuya-ku, Tokyo 150-0036; tel. (3) 5489-0804; fax (3) 5489-0813; e-mail info@uaeembassy.jp; internet www.uaeembassy.jp; Ambassador SAEED ALI AL-NOWAIS.

United Kingdom: 1, Ichiban-cho, Chiyoda-ku, Tokyo 102-8381; tel. (3) 5211-1100; fax (3) 5275-3164; e-mail embassy.tokyo@fco.gov.uk; internet www.uknow.or.jp; Ambassador GRAHAM FRY.

USA: 1-10-5, Akasaka, Minato-ku, Tokyo 107-8420; tel. (3) 3224-5000; fax (3) 3505-1862; internet tokyo.usembassy.gov; Ambassador THOMAS SCHIEFFER.

Uruguay: Kowa Bldg, No. 38, Room 908, 4-12-24, Nishi Azabu, Minato-ku, Tokyo 106-0031; tel. (3) 3486-1888; fax (3) 3486-9872; e-mail urujap@luck.ocn.ne.jp; Ambassador ANA MARÍA ESTÉVEZ MERCADER.

Uzbekistan: 5-11-8, Shimo-Meguro, Meguro-ku, Tokyo 153-0064; tel. (3) 3760-5625; fax (3) 3760-5950; Ambassador Dr MIRSOBIT FOZILOVICH OCHILOV.

Venezuela: Kowa Bldg, No. 38, Room 703, 4-12-24, Nishi Azabu, Minato-ku, Tokyo 106-0031; tel. (3) 3409-1501; fax (3) 3409-1505; e-mail embavene@interlink.or.jp; Ambassador SEIKO LUIS ISHIKAWA KOBAYASHI.

Viet Nam: 50-11, Moto Yoyogi-cho, Shibuya-ku, Tokyo 151-0062; tel. (3) 3466-3313; fax (3) 3466-3391; e-mail vnembasy@blue.ocn.ne.jp; internet www.vietnamembassy.jp; Ambassador NGUYEN PHU BINH.

Yemen: Kowa Bldg, No. 38, Room 807, 4-12-24, Nishi Azabu, Minato-ku, Tokyo 106-0031; tel. (3) 3499-7151; fax (3) 3499-4577; Ambassador MARWAN ABDULLA ABDULWAHAB NOMAN.

Zambia: 1-10-2, Ebara, Shinagawa-ku, Tokyo 142-0063; tel. (3) 3491-0121; fax (3) 3491-0123; e-mail emb@zambia.or.jp; internet www.zambia.or.jp; Ambassador GODFREY S. SIMASIKU.

Zimbabwe: 5-9-10, Shiroganedai, Minato-ku, Tokyo 108-0071; tel. (3) 3280-0331; fax (3) 3280-0466; e-mail zimtokyo@chive.ocn.ne.jp; Ambassador STUART H. COMBERBACH.

Judicial System

The basic principles of the legal system are set forth in the Constitution, which lays down that judicial power is vested in the Supreme Court and in such inferior courts as are established by law, and enunciates the principle that no organ or agency of the Executive shall be given final judicial power. Judges are to be independent in the exercise of their conscience, and may not be removed except by public impeachment, unless judicially declared mentally or physically incompetent to perform official duties. The justices of the Supreme Court are appointed by the Cabinet, the sole exception being the Chief Justice, who is appointed by the Emperor after designation by the Cabinet.

The Court Organization Law, which came into force on 3 May 1947, decreed the constitution of the Supreme Court and the establishment of four types of lower court—High, District, Family (established 1 January 1949) and Summary Courts. The constitution and functions of the courts are as follows:

Supreme Court

4-2, Hayabusa-cho, Chiyoda-ku, Tokyo 102-8651; tel. (3) 3264-8111; fax (3) 3221-8975; internet www.courts.go.jp.

This court is the highest legal authority in the land, and consists of a Chief Justice and 14 associate justices. It has jurisdiction over Jokoku (Jokoku appeals) and Kokoku (Kokoku appeals), prescribed in codes of procedure. It conducts its hearings and renders decisions through a Grand Bench or three Petty Benches. Both are collegiate bodies, the former consisting of all justices of the Court, and the latter of five justices. A Supreme Court Rule prescribes which cases are to be handled by the respective Benches. It is, however, laid down by law that the Petty Bench cannot make decisions as to the constitutionality of a statute, ordinance, regulation, or disposition, or as to cases in which an opinion concerning the interpretation and application of the Constitution, or of any laws or ordinances, is at variance with a previous decision of the Supreme Court.

Chief Justice: NIRO SHIMADA.

Secretary-General: HIRONOBU TAKESAKI.

LOWER COURTS

High Court

A High Court conducts its hearings and renders decisions through a collegiate body, consisting of three judges, though for cases of insurrection the number of judges must be five. The Court has jurisdiction over the following matters:

Koso appeals from judgments in the first instance rendered by District Courts, from judgments rendered by Family Courts, and from judgments concerning criminal cases rendered by Summary Courts.

Kokoku appeals against rulings and orders rendered by District Courts and Family Courts, and against rulings and orders concerning criminal cases rendered by Summary Courts, except those coming within the jurisdiction of the Supreme Court.

Jokoku appeals from judgments in the second instance rendered by District Courts and from judgments rendered by Summary Courts, except those concerning criminal cases.

Actions in the first instance relating to cases of insurrection.

Presidents: TOKUJI IZUMI (Tokyo), YOSHIO OKADA (Osaka), REISUKE SHIMADA (Nagoya), TOYOZO UEDA (Hiroshima), TOSHIMARO KOJO (Fukuoka), FUMIYA SATO (Sendai), KAZUO KATO (Sapporo), FUMIO ARAI (Takamatsu).

District Court

A District Court conducts hearings and renders decisions through a single judge or, for certain types of cases, through a collegiate body of three judges. It has jurisdiction over the following matters:

Actions in the first instance, except offences relating to insurrection, claims where the subject matter of the action does not exceed 900,000 yen, and offences liable to a fine or lesser penalty.

Koso appeals from judgments rendered by Summary Courts, except those concerning criminal cases.

Kokoku appeals against rulings and orders rendered by Summary Courts, except those coming within the jurisdiction of the Supreme Court and High Courts.

Family Court

A Family Court handles cases through a single judge in case of rendering judgments or decisions. However, in accordance with the provisions of other statutes, it conducts its hearings and renders decisions through a collegiate body of three judges. A conciliation is effected through a collegiate body consisting of a judge and two or more members of the conciliation committee selected from among citizens.

It has jurisdiction over the following matters:

JAPAN

Judgment and conciliation with regard to cases relating to family as provided for by the Law for Adjudgment of Domestic Relations.

Judgment with regard to the matters of protection of juveniles as provided for by the Juvenile Law.

Actions in the first instance relating to adult criminal cases of violation of the Labour Standard Law, the Law for Prohibiting Liquors to Minors, or other laws especially enacted for protection of juveniles.

Summary Court

A Summary Court handles cases through a single judge, and has jurisdiction in the first instance over the following matters:

Claims where the value of the subject matter does not exceed a certain sum (excluding claims for cancellation or change of administrative dispositions).

Actions that relate to offences liable to a fine or lesser penalty, offences liable to a fine as an optional penalty, and certain specified offences such as habitual gambling and larceny.

A Summary Court cannot impose imprisonment or a graver penalty. When it deems proper the imposition of a sentence of imprisonment or a graver penalty, it must transfer such cases to a District Court, but it can impose imprisonment with labour not exceeding three years for certain specified offences.

Religion

The traditional religions of Japan are Shintoism and Buddhism. Neither is exclusive, and many Japanese subscribe at least nominally to both. Since 1945 a number of new religions (Shinko Shukyo) have evolved, based on a fusion of Shinto, Buddhist, Daoist, Confucian and Christian beliefs. In 1995 there were some 184,000 religious organizations registered in Japan, according to the Ministry of Education.

SHINTOISM

Shintoism is an indigenous religious system embracing the worship of ancestors and of nature. It is divided into two cults: national Shintoism, which is represented by the shrines; and sectarian Shintoism, which developed during the second half of the 19th century. In 1868 Shinto was designated a national religion and all Shinto shrines acquired the privileged status of a national institution. Complete freedom of religion was introduced in 1947, and state support of Shinto was prohibited. In the mid-1990s there were 81,307 shrines, 90,309 priests and 106.6m. adherents.

BUDDHISM

World Buddhist Fellowship: Hozenji Buddhist Temple, 3-24-2, Akabane-dai, Kita-ku, Tokyo; Head Rev. FUJI NAKAYAMA.

CHRISTIANITY

In 1993 the Christian population was estimated at 1,050,938.

National Christian Council in Japan: Japan Christian Centre, 2-3-18-24, Nishi Waseda, Shinjuku-ku, Tokyo 169-0051; tel. (3) 3203-0372; fax (3) 3204-9495; e-mail general@ncc-j.org; internet www.jca.apc.org/ncc-j; f. 1923; 14 mems (churches and other bodies), 18 assoc. mems; Chair. ISAMU KOSHIISHI; Gen. Sec. Rev. TOSHIMASA YAMAMOTO.

The Anglican Communion

Anglican Church in Japan (Nippon Sei Ko Kai): 65, Yarai-cho, Shinjuku-ku, Tokyo 162-0805; tel. (3) 5228-3171; fax (3) 5228-3175; e-mail general-sec.po@nskk.org; internet www.nskk.org; f. 1887; 11 dioceses; Primate of Japan Rt Rev. JAMES TORU UNO (Bishop of Osaka); Gen. Sec. LAURENCE Y. MINABE; 57,003 mems (2004).

The Orthodox Church

Japanese Orthodox Church (Nippon Haristosu Seikyoukai): Holy Resurrection Cathedral (Nicolai-Do), 4-1-3, Kanda Surugadai, Chiyoda-ku, Tokyo 101; tel. (3) 3291-1885; fax (3) 3291-1886; e-mail ocj@gol.com; three dioceses; Archbishop of Tokyo, Primate and Metropolitan of All Japan Most Rev. DANIEL; 24,821 mems.

Protestant Church

United Church of Christ in Japan (Nihon Kirisuto Kyodan): Japan Christian Centre, Room 31, 2-3-18, Nishi Waseda, Shinjuku-ku, Tokyo 169-0051; tel. (3) 3202-0541; fax (3) 3207-3918; e-mail ecumeni-c@uccj.org; f. 1941; union of 34 Congregational, Methodist, Presbyterian, Reformed and other Protestant denominations; Moderator Rev. NOBUHISHA YAMAKITA; Gen. Sec. Rev. NOBORU TAKEMAE; 196,044 mems (2002).

The Roman Catholic Church

Japan comprises three archdioceses and 13 dioceses, and the Apostolic Prefecture of Karafuto. There were an estimated 537,314 adherents at 31 December 2005.

Catholic Bishops' Conference of Japan (Chuo Kyogikai)
2-10-10, Shiomi, Koto-ku, Tokyo 135-8585; tel. (3) 5632-4411; fax (3) 5632-4457; e-mail info@cbcj.catholic.jp; internet www.cbcj.catholic.jp; Pres. Most Rev. AUGUSTINE JUN-ICHI NOMURA (Bishop of Nagoya).

Archbishop of Nagasaki: JOSEPH MITSUAKI TAKAMI, Catholic Centre, 10-34, Uenomachi, Nagasaki-shi 852-8113; tel. (95) 846-4246; fax (95) 848-8310.

Archbishop of Osaka: Most Rev. LEO JUN IKENAGA, Archbishop's House, 2-24-22, Tamatsukuri, Chuo-ku, Osaka 540-0004; tel. (6) 6941-9700; fax (6) 6946-1345.

Archbishop of Tokyo: Most Rev. PETER TAKEO OKADA, Archbishop's House, 3-16-15, Sekiguchi, Bunkyo-ku, Tokyo 112-0014; tel. (3) 3943-2301; fax (3) 3944-8511; e-mail peter2000@nifty.com.

Other Christian Churches

Japan Baptist Convention: 1-2-4, Minami Urawa, Minami-ku, Saitama-shi, Saitama 336-0017; tel. (48) 883-1091; fax (48) 883-1092; f. 1947; Gen. Sec. Rev. MAKOTO KATO; 33,734 mems (March 2003).

Japan Baptist Union: 2-3-18, Nishi Waseda, Shinjuku-ku, Tokyo 169-0051; tel. (3) 3202-0053; fax (3) 3202-0054; e-mail gs@jbu.or.jp; f. 1958; Moderator YOSHIHISA SAWANO; Gen. Sec. KAZUO OYA; 4,600 mems.

Japan Evangelical Lutheran Church: 1-1, Sadohara-cho, Ichigaya-shi, Shinjuku-ku, Tokyo 162-0842; tel. (3) 3260-8631; fax (3) 3268-3589; e-mail s-matsuoka@jelc.or.jp; internet www.jelc.or.jp; f. 1893; Moderator Rev. MASATOSHI YAMANOUCHI; Gen. Sec. Rev. SHUNICHIRO MATSUOKA; 21,967 mems (2000).

Korean Christian Church in Japan: Room 52, Japan Christian Center, 2-3-18, Nishi Waseda, Shinjuku-ku, Tokyo 169-0051; tel. (3) 3202-5398; fax (3) 3202-4977; e-mail kccj@kb3.so-net.ne.jp; f. 1909; Moderator LEE SUNG-WOO; Gen. Sec. PARK SOO-KIL; 7,119 mems (2002).

Among other denominations active in Japan are the Christian Catholic Church, the German Evangelical Church and the Tokyo Union Church.

OTHER COMMUNITIES

Bahá'í Faith

The National Spiritual Assembly of the Bahá'ís of Japan: 7-2-13, Shinjuku, Shinjuku-ku, Tokyo 160-0022; tel. (3) 3209-7521; fax (3) 3204-0773; e-mail nsajp@bahaijp.org; internet www.bahaijp.org.

Judaism

Jewish Community of Japan: 3-8-8, Hiro-o, Shibuya-ku, Tokyo 150-0012; tel. (3) 3400-2559; fax (3) 3400-1827; e-mail office@jccjapan.or.jp; internet www.jccjapan.or.jp; Man. LIOR JACOBI; Leader Rabbi HENRI NOACH.

Islam

Islam has been active in Japan since the late 19th century. There is a small Muslim community, maintaining several mosques, including those at Kobe, Nagoya, Chiba and Isesaki, the Arabic Islamic Institute and the Islamic Center in Tokyo. The construction of Tokyo Central Mosque was completed in 2000.

Islamic Center, Japan: 1-16-11, Ohara, Setagaya-ku, Tokyo 156-0041; tel. (3) 3460-6169; fax (3) 3460-6105; e-mail islamcpj@islamcenter.or.jp; internet www.islamcenter.or.jp; f. 1965; Chair. Dr SALIH M. SAMARRAI.

The New Religions

Many new cults have emerged in Japan since the end of the Second World War. Collectively these are known as the New Religions (Shinko Shukyo), among the most important of which are Tenrikyo, Omotokyo, Soka Gakkai, Rissho Kosei-kai, Kofuku-no-Kagaku, Agonshu and Aum Shinrikyo. (Following the indictment on charges of murder of several members of Aum Shinrikyo, including its leader, Shoko Asahara, the cult lost its legal status as a religious organization in 1996; in January 2000 the cult announced its intention to change its name to Aleph; at that time it named a new leader, TATSUKO MURAOKA.)

Kofuku-no-Kagaku (Institute for Research in Human Happiness): Tokyo; tel. (3) 5750-0771; fax (3) 5750-0782; internet www.irhpress.co.jp; e-mail web-office@irhpress.co.jp; f. 1986; believes its founder to be reincarnation of Buddha; 8.25m. mems; Leader RYUHO OKAWA.

Rissho Kosei-kai: 2-11-1, Wada, Suginami-ku, Tokyo 166-8537; tel. (3) 5341-1641; fax (3) 3381-9792; e-mail info@rk-world.org; internet www.kosei-kai.or.jp; internet www.rk-world.org; f. 1938; Buddhist lay organization based on the teaching of the Lotus Sutra, active inter-faith co-operation towards peace; Pres. Rev. Dr NICHIKO NIWANO; 1.81m. mem households with 253 brs world-wide (2006).

Soka Gakkai: 32, Shinano-machi, Shinjuku-ku, Tokyo 160-8583; tel. (3) 5360-9830; fax (3) 5360-9885; e-mail sgicontact@sgi.org; internet www.sgi.org; f. 1930; society of lay practitioners of the Buddhism of Nichiren; membership of 8.27m. households (2005); group promotes activities in education, international cultural exchange and consensus-building towards peace, based on the humanist world view of Buddhism; Hon. Pres. DAISAKU IKEDA; Pres. MINORU HARADA.

The Press

In December 2004 there were 120 daily newspapers in Japan. Their average circulation was the highest in the world, and the circulation per head of population was also among the highest, at 573 copies per 1,000 inhabitants in 1999. The large number of weekly news journals is a notable feature of the Japanese press. In 2003/04 a total of 4,549 periodicals were produced, 138 of which were weekly publications. Technically the Japanese press is highly advanced, and the major newspapers are issued in simultaneous editions in the main centres.

The two newspapers with the largest circulations are the *Yomiuri Shimbun* and *Asahi Shimbun*. Other influential papers include *Mainichi Shimbun*, *Nihon Keizai Shimbun*, *Chunichi Shimbun* and *Sankei Shimbun*.

NATIONAL DAILIES

Asahi Shimbun: 5-3-2, Tsukiji, Chuo-ku, Tokyo 104-8011; tel. (3) 3545-0131; fax (3) 3545-0358; internet www.asahi.com; f. 1879; also published by Osaka, Seibu and Nagoya head offices and Hokkaido branch office; Pres. KOTARO AKIYAMA; Editor-in-Chief YOICHI FUNABASHI; circ. morning 8.1m., evening 3.7m.

Mainichi Shimbun: 1-1-1, Hitotsubashi, Chiyoda-ku, Tokyo 100-8051; tel. (3) 3212-0321; fax (3) 3211-3598; internet www.mainichi.co.jp; f. 1882; also published by Osaka, Seibu and Chubu head offices, and Hokkaido branch office; Pres. MASATO KITAMURA; Man. Dir and Editor-in-Chief TATSUAKI HASHIMOTO; circ. morning 4.0m., evening 2.0m.

Nihon Keizai Shimbun: 1-9-5, Otemachi, Chiyoda-ku, Tokyo 1008066; tel. (3) 3270-0251; fax (3) 5255-2661; internet www.nikkei.co.jp; f. 1876; also published by Osaka head office and Sapporo, Nagoya and Seibu branch offices; Pres. TSUNEO KITA; Editor-in-Chief YUICHI TAKAHASHI; circ. morning 3.0m., evening 1.6m.

Sankei Shimbun: 1-7-2, Otemachi, Chiyoda-ku, Tokyo 100-8077; tel. (3) 3231-7111; internet www.sankei.co.jp; f. 1933; also published by Osaka head office; Man. Dir and Editor NAGAYOSHI SUMIDA; circ. morning 2.0m., evening 636,649.

Yomiuri Shimbun: 1-7-1, Otemachi, Chiyoda-ku, Tokyo 100-8055; tel. (3) 3242-1111; e-mail webmaster@yomiuri.co.jp; internet www.yomiuri.co.jp; f. 1874; also published by Osaka, Seibu and Chubu head offices, and Hokkaido and Hokuriku branch offices; Pres. and Editor-in-Chief TSUNEO WATANABE; circ. morning 10.0m., evening 4.0m.

PRINCIPAL LOCAL DAILIES

Tokyo

Daily Sports: 1-20-3, Osaki, Shinagawa-ku, Tokyo 141-8585; tel. (3) 5434-1752; internet www.daily.co.jp; f. 1948; morning; Man. Dir HIROHISA KARUO; circ. 400,254.

The Daily Yomiuri: 1-7-1, Otemachi, Chiyoda-ku, Tokyo 100-8055; tel. (3) 3242-1111; internet www.yomiuri.co.jp; f. 1955; morning; English; Man. Editor SHIGEYUKI OKADA; circ. 40,045.

Dempa Shimbun: 1-11-15, Higashi Gotanda, Shinagawa-ku, Tokyo 141-8790; tel. (3) 3445-6111; fax (3) 3444-7515; internet www.dempa.co.jp; f. 1950; morning; Pres. TETSUO HIRAYAMA; Man. Editor TOSHIO KASUYA; circ. 298,000.

The Japan Times: 4-5-4, Shibaura, Minato-ku, Tokyo 108-8071; tel. (3) 3453-5312; internet www.japantimes.co.jp; f. 1897; morning; English; Chair. and Pres. TOSHIAKI OGASAWARA; Dir and Editor-in-Chief YUTAKA MATAEBARA; circ. 61,929.

The Mainichi Daily News: 1-1-1, Hitotsubashi, Chiyoda-ku, Tokyo 100-8051; tel. (3) 3212-0321; internet mdn.mainichi-msn.co.jp; f. 1922; morning; English; also publ. from Osaka; Man. Editor TETSUO TOKIZAWA; combined circ. 49,200.

Naigai Times: 1-3-2, Tsukishima, Chuo-ku, Tokyo 104-0052; tel. (3) 6204-4121; e-mail koukoku@naigai-times.net; internet www.npn.co.jp; f. 1949; evening; Pres. MITSUGU ONDA; Vice-Pres. and Editor-in-Chief KENICHIRO KURIHARA; circ. 410,000.

Nihon Kaiji Shimbun (Japan Maritime Daily): 5-19-2, Shimbashi, Minato-ku, Tokyo 105-0004; tel. (3) 3436-3221; e-mail webmaster@jmd.co.jp; internet www.jmd.co.jp; f. 1942; morning; Man. Editor OSAMI ENDO; circ. 55,000.

Nihon Nogyo Shimbun (Agriculture): 2-3, Akihabara, Taito-ku, Tokyo 110-8722; tel. (3) 5295-7411; fax (3) 3253-0980; internet www.nougyou-shimbun.ne.jp; f. 1928; morning; Man. Editor YASUNORI INOUE; circ. 423,840.

Nihon Sen-i Shimbun (Textile and Fashion): 13-10, Nihonbashi-kobunacho, Chuo-ku, Tokyo 103-0024; tel. (3) 5649-8711; internet www.nissenmedia.com; f. 1943; morning; Man. Editor KIYOSHIGE SEIRYU; circ. 116,000.

Nikkan Kogyo Shimbun (Industrial Daily News): 1-8-10, Kudan-kita, Chiyoda-ku, Tokyo 102-8181; tel. (3) 3222-7111; fax (3) 3262-6031; internet www.nikkan.co.jp; f. 1915; morning; Man. Editor HIDEO WATANABE; circ. 533,145.

Nikkan Sports News: 3-5-10, Tsukiji, Chuo-ku, Tokyo 104-8055; tel. (3) 5550-8888; fax (3) 5550-8901; internet www.nikkansports.com; f. 1946; morning; Man. Editor MOTOHIRO MIURA; circ. 993,240.

Sankei Sports: 1-7-2, Otemachi, Chiyoda-ku, Tokyo 100-8077; tel. (3) 3231-7111; internet www.sanspo.com; f. 1963; morning; Man. Editor YUKIO INADA; circ. 809,245.

Shipping and Trade News: Tokyo News Service Ltd, 6-10, Tsukiji 5-chome, Chuo-ku, Tokyo 104-8004; tel. (3) 3542-68521; fax (3) 3542-5086; e-mail editorial.a@tokyonews.co.jp; internet www.tokyonews.co.jp/marine; f. 1949; English; Man. Editor TAKASHI TAKEDA; circ. 15,000.

Sports Hochi: 4-6-49, Kohnan, Minato-ku, Tokyo 108-8485; tel. (3) 5479-1111; e-mail webmaster@hochi.yomiuri.co.jp; internet hochi.yomiuri.co.jp; f. 1872; fmrly *Hochi Shimbun*; morning; Pres. MASARU FUSHIMI; Man. Editor TATSUE AOKI; circ. 755,670.

Sports Nippon: 2-1-30, Etchujima, Koto-ku, Tokyo 135-8735; tel. (3) 3820-0700; internet www.sponichi.co.jp; f. 1949; morning; Man. Editor SUSUMU KOMURO; circ. 929,421.

Suisan Keizai Shimbun (Fisheries): 6-8-19, Roppongi, Minato-ku, Tokyo 106-0032; tel. (3) 3404-6531; fax (3) 3404-0863; internet www.suikei.co.jp; f. 1948; morning; Man. Editor KOSHI TORINOUMI; circ. 61,000.

Tokyo Chunichi Sports: 2-3-13, Kohnan, Minato-ku, Tokyo 108-8010; tel. (3) 3471-2211; f. 1956; evening; Head Officer TETSUO TANAKA; circ. 330,431.

Tokyo Shimbun: 2-3-13, Kohnan, Minato-ku, Tokyo 108-8010; tel. (3) 3471-2211; fax (3) 3471-1851; internet www.tokyo-np.co.jp; f. 1942; Man. Editor KATSUHIKO SAKAI; circ. morning 655,970, evening 354,191.

Tokyo Sports: 2-1-30, Etchujima, Koto-ku, Tokyo 135-8721; tel. (3) 3820-0801; internet www.tokyo-sports.co.jp; f. 1959; evening; Man. Editor YOSHINOBU EBATA; circ. 1,321,250.

Yukan Fuji: 1-7-2, Otemachi, Chiyoda-ku, Tokyo 100-8077; tel. (3) 3231-7111; fax (3) 3246-0377; e-mail desk@zakzak.co.jp; internet www.zakzak.co.jp; f. 1969; evening; Man. Editor MASAMI KATO; circ. 268,984.

Osaka District

Daily Sports: 1-18-11, Edobori, Nishi-ku, Osaka 550-0002; tel. (6) 6443-0421; f. 1948; morning; Man. Editor TOSHIAKI MITANI; circ. 562,715.

The Mainichi Daily News: 3-4-5, Umeda, Kita-ku, Osaka 530-8251; tel. (6) 6345-1551; internet mdn.mainichi-msn.co.jp; f. 1922; morning; English; Man. Editor KATSUYA FUKUNAGA.

Nikkan Sports: 5-92-1, Hattori-kotobuki-cho, Toyonaka 561-8585; tel. (6) 6867-2811; internet www.nikkansports.com/osaka; f. 1950; morning; Man. Editor KATSUO FURUKAWA; circ. 513,498.

Osaka Shimbun: 2-4-9, Umeda, Kita-ku, Osaka 530-8279; tel. (6) 6343-1221; internet www.osakanews.com; f. 1922; evening; Man. Editor KAORU YURA; circ. 88,887.

Osaka Sports: Osaka Ekimae Daiichi Bldg, 4th Floor, 1-3-1-400, Umeda, Kita-ku, Osaka 530-0001; tel. (6) 6345-7657; f. 1968; evening; Head Officer KAZUOMI TANAKA; circ. 470,660.

Sankei Sports: 2-4-9, Umeda, Kita-ku, Osaka 530-8277; tel. (6) 6343-1221; f. 1955; morning; Man. Editor MASAKI YOSHIDA; circ. 552,519.

Sports Nippon: 3-4-5, Umeda, Kita-ku, Osaka 530-8278; tel. (6) 6346-8500; f. 1949; morning; Man. Editor HIDETOSHI ISHIHARA; circ. 477,300.

Kanto District

Chiba Nippo (Chiba Daily News): 4-14-10, Chuo, Chuo-ku, Chiba 260-0013; tel. (43) 222-9211; internet www.chibanippo.co.jp; f. 1957; morning; Man. Editor NOBORU HAYASHI; circ. 190,187.

Ibaraki Shimbun: 2-15, Kitami-cho, Mito 310-8686; tel. (292) 21-3121; internet www.ibaraki-np.co.jp; f. 1891; morning; Pres. and Editor-in-Chief TADANORI TOMOSUE; circ. 117,240.

Jomo Shimbun: 1-50-21, Furuichi-machi, Maebashi 371-8666; tel. (272) 54-9911; internet www.jomo-news.co.jp; f. 1887; morning; Man. Editor MUTSUO ODAGIRI; circ. 296,111.

Joyo Shimbun: 2-7-6, Manabe, Tsuchiura 300-0051; tel. (298) 21-1780; internet www.tsukuba.com; f. 1948; morning; Pres. MINEO IWANAMI; Man. Editor AKIRA SAITO; circ. 88,700.

Kanagawa Shimbun: 6-145, Hanasaki-cho, Nishi-ku, Yokohama 220-8588; tel. (45) 411-2222; internet www.kanagawa-np.co.jp; f. 1890; morning; Man. Editor NOBUYUKI CHIBA; circ. 238,203.

Saitama Shimbun: 6-12-11, Kishi-cho, Urawa 336-8686; tel. (48) 862-3371; internet www.saitama-np.co.jp; f. 1944; morning; Man. Editor YOTARO NUMATA; circ. 162,071.

Shimotsuke Shimbun: 1-8-11, Showa, Utsunomiya 320-8686; tel. (286) 25-1111; internet www.shimotsuke.co.jp; f. 1884; morning; Man. Dir and Editor-in-Chief EISUKE TODA; circ. 306,072.

Tohoku District
(North-east Honshu)

Akita Sakigake Shimpo: 1-1, San-no-rinkai-machi, Akita 010-8601; tel. (18) 888-1800; fax (188) 23-1780; internet www.sakigake.co.jp; f. 1874; Man. Editor SHIGEAKI MAEKAWA; circ. 263,246.

Daily Tohoku: 1-3-12, Shiroshita, Hachinohe 031-8601; tel. (178) 44-5111; internet www.daily-tohoku.co.jp; f. 1945; morning; Man. Editor TOKOJU YOSHIDA; circ. 104,935.

Fukushima Mimpo: 13-17, Ota-machi, Fukushima 960-8602; tel. (245) 31-4111; internet www.fukushima-minpo.co.jp; f. 1892; Pres. and Editor-in-Chief TSUTOMU HANADA; circ. morning 308,353, evening 9,489.

Fukushima Minyu: 4-29, Yanagi-machi, Fukushima 960-8648; tel. (245) 23-1191; internet www.minyu-net.com; f. 1895; Man. Editor KENJI KANNO; circ. morning 201,414, evening 6,066.

Hokuu Shimpo: 3-2, Nishi-dori-machi, Noshiro 016-0891; tel. (185) 54-3150; internet www.hokuu.co.jp; f. 1895; morning; Chair. KOICHI YAMAKI; circ. 31,490.

Ishinomaki Shimbun: 2-1-28, Sumiyoshi-machi, Ishinomaki 986; tel. (225) 22-3201; f. 1946; evening; Man. Editor MASATOSHI SATO; circ. 13,050.

Iwate Nichi-nichi Shimbun: 60, Minamishin-machi, Ichinoseki 021-8686; tel. (191) 26-5114; internet www.iwanichi.co.jp; f. 1923; morning; Pres. TAKESHI YAMAGISHI; Man. Editor SEIICHI WATANABE; circ. 59,850.

Iwate Nippo: 3-7, Uchimaru, Morioka 020-8622; tel. (196) 53-4111; internet www.iwate-np.co.jp; f. 1876; Man. Editor TOKUO MIYAZAWA; circ. morning 230,073, evening 229,815.

Kahoku Shimpo: 1-2-28, Itsutsubashi, Aoba-ku, Sendai 980-8660; tel. (22) 211-1111; fax (22) 224-7947; internet www.kahoku.co.jp; f. 1897; Exec. Dir and Man. Editor MASAHIKO ICHIRIKI; circ. morning 503,318, evening 133,855.

Mutsu Shimpo: 2-1, Shimo-shirogane-cho, Hirosaki 036-8356; tel. (172) 34-3111; internet www.mutusinpou.co.jp; f. 1946; morning; Man. Editor YUJI SATO; circ. 53,500.

Shonai Nippo: 8-29, Baba-cho, Tsuruoka 997-8691; tel. (235) 22-1480; internet www.shonai-nippo.co.jp; f. 1946; morning; Pres. TAKAO SATO; Man. Editor MASAYUKI HASHIMOTO; circ. 19,100.

To-o Nippo: 78, Kanbayashi, Yatsuyaku, Aomori 030-0180; tel. (177) 39-1111; internet www.toonippo.co.jp; f. 1888; Exec. Dir YOSHIO WAJIMA; Man. Editor TAKAO SHIOKOSHI; circ. morning 262,532, evening 258,590.

Yamagata Shimbun: 2-5-12, Hatagomachi, Yamagata 990-8550; tel. (236) 22-5271; internet www.yamagata-np.co.jp; f. 1876; Man. Editor TOSHINOBU SHIONO; circ. morning 213,057, evening 213,008.

Yonezawa Shimbun: 3-3-7, Monto-cho, Yonezawa 992-0039; tel. (238) 22-4411; internet www.yoneshin.com; f. 1879; morning; Man. Dir and Editor-in-Chief MAKOTO SATO; circ. 13,750.

Chubu District
(Central Honshu)

Chubu Keizai Shimbun: 4-4-12, Meieki, Nakamura-ku, Nagoya 450-8561; tel. (52) 561-5215; internet www.chukei-news.co.jp; f. 1946; morning; Man. Editor NORIMITSU INAGAKI; circ. 91,000.

Chukyo Sports: Chunichi Kosoku Offset Insatsu Bldg, 4-3-9, Kinjo, Naka-ku, Nagoya 460-0847; tel. (52) 982-1911; f. 1968; evening; Head Officer OSAMU SUETSUGU; circ. 289,430.

Chunichi Shimbun: 1-6-1, San-no-maru, Naka-ku, Nagoya 460-8511; tel. (52) 201-8811; internet www.chunichi.ne.jp; f. 1942; Man. Editor NOBUAKI KOIDE; circ. morning 2.7m., evening 748,635.

Chunichi Sports: 1-6-1, San-no-maru, Naka-ku, Nagoya 460-8511; tel. (52) 201-8811; internet chuspo.chunichi.co.jp; f. 1954; evening; Head Officer YASUHIKO AIBA; circ. 631,429.

Gifu Shimbun: 10, Imakomachi, Gifu 500-8577; tel. (582) 64-1151; internet www.jic-gifu.or.jp/np; f. 1881; Exec. Dir and Man. Editor TADASHI TANAKA; circ. morning 170,176, evening 31,775.

Higashi-Aichi Shimbun: 62, Torinawate, Shinsakae-machi, Toyohashi 441-8666; tel. (532) 32-3111; fax (532) 32-3115; e-mail hensyu@higashiaichi.co.jp; internet www.higashiaichi.co.jp; f. 1957; morning; Man. Editor YOSHIYUKI SUZUKI; circ. 52,300.

Nagano Nippo: 3-1323-1, Takashima, Suwa 392-8611; tel. (266) 52-2000; internet www.nagano-np.co.jp; f. 1901; morning; Man. Editor ETSUO KOIZUMI; circ. 73,000.

Nagoya Times: 1-3-10, Marunouchi, Naka-ku, Nagoya 460-8530; tel. (52) 231-1331; internet www.meitai.net; f. 1946; evening; Man. Editor NAOKI KITO; circ. 146,137.

Shinano Mainichi Shimbun: 657, Minamiagata-machi, Nagano 380-8546; tel. (26) 236-3000; fax (26) 236-3197; internet www.shinmai.co.jp; f. 1873; Man. Editor SEIICHI INOMATA; circ. morning 469,801, evening 55,625.

Shizuoka Shimbun: 3-1-1, Toro, Shizuoka 422-8033; tel. (54) 284-8900; e-mail webmaster@shizuokaonline.com; internet www.shizuokaonline.com; f. 1941; Man. Editor HISAO ISHIHARA; circ. morning 730,746, evening 730,782.

Yamanashi Nichi-Nichi Shimbun: 2-6-10, Kitaguchi, Kofu 400-8515; tel. (552) 31-3000; internet www.sannichi.co.jp; f. 1872; morning; Man. Editor KATSUHITO NISHIKAWA; circ. 210,373.

Hokuriku District
(North Coastal Honshu)

Fukui Shimbun: 1-1-14, Haruyama, Fukui 910-8552; tel. (776) 23-5111; internet www.fukuishimbun.co.jp; f. 1899; morning; Man. Editor KAZUO UCHIDA; circ. 206,033.

Hokkoku Shimbun: 2-5-1, Korinbo, Kanazawa 920-8588; tel. (762) 63-2111; internet www.hokkoku.co.jp; f. 1893; Man. Editor WATARU INAGAKI; circ. morning 335,826, evening 93,021.

Hokuriku Chunichi Shimbun: 2-7-15, Korinbo, Kanazawa 920-8573; tel. (762) 61-3111; internet www.hokuriku.chunichi.co.jp; f. 1960; Man. Editor KANJI KOMIYA; circ. morning 107,652, evening 11,373.

Kitanippon Shimbun: 2-14, Azumi-cho, Toyama 930-8680; tel. (764) 45-3300; internet www.kitanippon.co.jp; f. 1884; Dir and Man. Editor MINORU KAWATA; circ. morning 231,509, evening 33,936.

Niigata Nippo: 772-2, Zenku, Niigata 950-1189; tel. (25) 378-9111; internet www.niigata-nippo.co.jp; f. 1942; Dir and Man. Editor MICHIEI TAKAHASHI; circ. morning 499,545, evening 63,790.

Toyama Shimbun: 5-1, Ote-machi, Toyama 930-8520; tel. (764) 91-8111; e-mail admin@hokkoku.co.jp; internet www.toyama.hokkoku.co.jp; f. 1923; morning; Man. Editor SACHIO MIYAMOTO; circ. 42,988.

Kinki District
(West Central Honshu)

Daily Sports: 1-5-7, Higashikawasaki-cho, Chuo-ku, Kobe 650-0044; tel. (78) 362-7100; internet www.daily.co.jp; morning; Man. Editor TAKASHI HIRAI; circ. 584,448.

Ise Shimbun: 34-6, Honmachi, Tsu 514-0831; tel. (592) 24-0003; internet www.isenp.co.jp; f. 1878; morning; Man. Editor FUJIO YAMAMOTO; circ. 108,630.

Kii Minpo: 100, Akizucho, Tanabe 646-8660; tel. (739) 22-7171; internet www.agara.co.jp; f. 1911; evening; Man. Editor KAZUSADA TANIGAMI; circ. 38,526.

Kobe Shimbun: 1-5-7, Higashikawasaki-cho, Chuo-ku, Kobe 650-8571; tel. (78) 362-7100; internet www.kobe-np.co.jp; f. 1898; Man. Editor MASAO MAEKAWA; circ. morning 561,271, evening 259,781.

Kyoto Shimbun: 239, Shoshoi-machi, Ebisugawa-agaru, Karasuma-dori, Nakagyo-ku, Kyoto 604-8577; tel. (75) 241-5430; e-mail kpdesk@mb.kyoto-np.co.jp; internet www.kyoto-np.co.jp; f. 1879; Man. Editor OSAMU SAITO; circ. morning 504,304, evening 319,015.

Nara Shimbun: 606, Sanjo-machi, Nara 630-8686; tel. (742) 26-1331; internet www.nara-shimbun.com; f. 1946; morning; Dir and Man. Editor HISAMI SAKAMOTO; circ. 126,324.

Chugoku District
(Western Honshu)

Chugoku Shimbun: 7-1, Dobashi-cho, Naka-ku, Hiroshima 730-8677; tel. (82) 236-2111; fax (82) 236-2321; e-mail denshi@hiroshima-cdas.or.jp; internet www.chugoku-np.co.jp; f. 1892; Man. Editor NOBUYUKI AOKI; circ. morning 723,981, evening 75,248.

Nihonkai Shimbun: 2-137, Tomiyasu, Tottori 680-8678; tel. (857) 21-2888; internet www.nnn.co.jp; f. 1976; morning; Man. Editor KOTARO TAMURA; circ. 171,120.

JAPAN

Okayama Nichi-Nichi Shimbun: 6-30, Hon-cho, Okayama 700-8678; tel. (86) 231-4211; internet www.okanichi.co.jp; f. 1946; evening; Man. Dir and Man. Editor TAKASHI ANDO; circ. 45,000.

San-In Chuo Shimpo: 383, Tono-machi, Matsue 690-8668; tel. (852) 32-3440; internet www.sanin-chuo.co.jp; f. 1882; morning; Man. Editor MASAMI MOCHIDA; circ. 176,967.

Sanyo Shimbun: 2-1-23, Yanagi-machi, Okayama 700-8634; tel. (86) 231-2210; internet www.sanyo.oni.co.jp; f. 1879; Man. Dir and Man. Editor TAKAMASA KOSHIMUNE; circ. morning 461,876, evening 71,911.

Ube Jiho: 3-6-1, Kotobuki-cho, Ube 755-8557; tel. (836) 31-1511; internet www.ubenippo.co.jp; f. 1912; evening; Exec. Dir and Man. Editor KAZUYA WAKI; circ. 52,300.

Yamaguchi Shimbun: 1-1-7, Higashi-Yamato-cho, Shimonoseki 750-8506; tel. (832) 66-3211; internet www.minato-yamaguchi.co.jp; f. 1946; morning; Pres. MASAAKI INOUE; circ. 89,060.

Shikoku Island

Ehime Shimbun: 1-12-1, Otemachi, Matsuyama 790-8511; tel. (899) 35-2111; internet www.ehime-np.co.jp; f. 1876; morning; Man. Editor RYOJI YANO; circ. 320,278.

Kochi Shimbun: 3-2-15, Honmachi, Kochi 780-8572; tel. (888) 22-2111; internet www.kochinews.co.jp; f. 1904; Dir and Man. Editor KENGO FUJITO; circ. morning 234,347, evening 148,890.

Shikoku Shimbun: 15-1, Nakano-cho, Takamatsu 760-8572; tel. (878) 33-1111; internet www.shikoku-np.co.jp; f. 1889; morning; Man. Editor JUNJI YAMASHITA; circ. 204,999.

Tokushima Shimbun: 2-5-2, Naka-Tokushima-cho, Tokushima 770-8572; tel. (886) 55-7373; fax (866) 54-0165; internet www.topics.or.jp; f. 1944; Dir and Man. Editor HIROSHI MATSUMURA; circ. morning 257,828, evening 52,208.

Hokkaido Island

Doshin Sports: 3-6, Odori-nishi, Chuo-ku, Sapporo 060-8711; tel. (11) 241-1230; internet www.hokkaido-np.co.jp; f. 1982; morning; Pres. KOSUKE SAKAI; circ. 132,445.

Hokkaido Shimbun: 3-6, Odori-nishi, Chuo-ku, Sapporo 060-8711; tel. (11) 221-2111; internet www.hokkaido-np.co.jp; f. 1942; Man. Editor RYOZO ODAGIRI; circ. morning 1.2m., evening 701,934.

Kushiro Shimbun: 7-3, Kurogane-cho, Kushiro 085-8650; tel. (154) 22-1111; internet www.news-kushiro.jp; f. 1946; morning; Man. Editor YUTAKA ITO; circ. 62,600.

Muroran Mimpo: 1-3-16, Hon-cho, Muroran 051-8550; tel. (143) 22-5121; internet www.muromin.mnw.jp; f. 1945; Man. Editor TSUTOMO KUDO; circ. morning 60,300, evening 52,500.

Nikkan Sports: 3-1-30, Higashi, Kita-3 jo, Chuo-ku, Sapporo 060-0033; tel. (11) 242-3900; fax (11) 231-5470; internet www.kita-nikkan.co.jp; f. 1962; morning; Pres. SATOSHI KATO; circ. 160,197.

Tokachi Mainichi Shimbun: 8-2, Minami, Higashi-Ichijo, Obihiro 080-8688; tel. (155) 22-2121; fax (155) 25-2700; internet www.tokachi.co.jp; f. 1919; evening; Dir and Man. Editor TOSHIAKI NAKAHASHI; circ. 90,980.

Tomakomai Mimpo: 3-1-8, Wakakusa-cho, Tomakomai 053-8611; tel. (144) 32-5311; internet www.tomamin.co.jp; f. 1950; evening; Dir and Man. Editor RYUICHI KUDO; circ. 60,676.

Yomiuri Shimbun: 4-1, Nishi, Kita-4 jo, Chuo-ku, Sapporo 060-8656; tel. (11) 242-3111; f. 1959; Head Officer TSUTOMO IKEDA; circ. morning 261,747, evening 81,283.

Kyushu Island

Kumamoto Nichi-Nichi Shimbun: 172, Yoyasu-machi, Kumamoto 860-8506; tel. (96) 361-3111; internet www.kumanichi.com; f. 1942; Man. Editor HIROSHI KAWARABATA; circ. morning 385,784, evening 99,049.

Kyushu Sports: Fukuoka Tenjin Center Bldg, 2-14-8, Tenjin-cho, Chuo-ku, Fukuoka 810-0001; tel. (92) 781-7401; f. 1966; morning; Head Officer HIROSHI MITOMI; circ. 449,850.

Minami Nippon Shimbun: 1-9-33, Yojirou, Kagoshima 890-8603; tel. (99) 813-5001; fax (99) 813-5016; e-mail webmaster@373news.com; internet www.373news.com; f. 1881; Man. Editor YASUSHI MOMIKI; circ. morning 405,795, evening 28,792.

Miyazaki Nichi-Nichi Shimbun: 1-1-33, Takachihodori, Miyazaki 880-8570; tel. (985) 26-9315; e-mail info@the-miyanichi.co.jp; internet www.the-miyanichi.co.jp; f. 1940; morning; Man. Editor MASAAKI MINAMIMURA; circ. 235,759.

Nagasaki Shimbun: 3-1, Mori-machi, Nagasaki 852-8601; tel. (958) 44-2111; internet www.nagasaki-np.co.jp; f. 1889; Dir and Man. Editor SADAKATSU HONDA; circ. morning 196,016.

Nankai Nichi-Nichi Shimbun: 10-3, Nagahama-cho, Naze 894-8601; tel. (997) 53-2121; e-mail web@nankainn.com; internet www.nankainn.com; f. 1946; morning; Man. Editor TERUMI MATSUI; circ. 23,615.

Nishi Nippon Shimbun: 1-4-1, Tenjin, Chuo-ku, Fukuoka 810-8721; tel. (92) 711-5555; internet www.nishinippon.co.jp; f. 1877; Exec. Dir and Man. Editor MEGUMI KIKUCHI; circ. morning 848,656, evening 174,102.

Nishi Nippon Sports: 1-4-1, Tenjin, Chuo-ku, Fukuoka 810; tel. (92) 711-5555; f. 1954; Man. Editor KENJI ISHIZAKI; circ. 198,207.

Oita Godo Shimbun: 3-9-15, Funai-machi, Oita 870-8605; tel. (975) 36-2121; internet www.oita-press.co.jp; f. 1886; Dir and Man. Editor MASAKATSU TANABE; circ. morning 250,300, evening 250,264.

Okinawa Times: 2-2-2, Kumoji, Naha 900-8678; tel. (98) 860-3000; internet www.okinawatimes.co.jp; f. 1948; Dir and Man. Editor MASAO KISHIMOTO; circ. morning 205,624, evening 205,624.

Ryukyu Shimpo: 1-10-3, Izumizaki, Naha 900-8525; tel. (98) 865-5111; internet www.ryukyushimpo.co.jp; f. 1893; Man. Editor TOMOKAZU TAKAMINE; circ. 203,470.

Saga Shimbun: 3-2-23, Tenjin, Saga 840-8585; tel. (952) 28-2111; fax (952) 29-4829; internet www.saga-s.co.jp; f. 1884; morning; Man. Editor TERUHIKO WASHIZAKI; circ. 136,399.

Yaeyama Mainichi Shimbun: 614, Tonoshiro, Ishigaki 907-0004; tel. (9808) 2-2121; internet www.y-mainichi.co.jp; f. 1950; morning; Exec. Dir and Man. Editor YOSHIO UECHI; circ. 14,761.

WEEKLIES

An-An: Magazine House, 3-13-10, Ginza, Chuo-ku, Tokyo 104-03; tel. (3) 3545-7050; fax (3) 3546-0034; internet anan.magazine.co.jp; f. 1970; fashion; Editor MIYOKO YODOGAWA; circ. 650,000.

Asahi Graphic: Asahi Shimbun Publishing Dept, 5-3-2, Tsukiji, Chuo-ku, Tokyo 104-11; tel. (3) 3545-0131; f. 1923; pictorial review; Editor KIYOKAZU TANNO; circ. 120,000.

Diamond Weekly: Diamond Inc, 1-4-2, Kasumigaseki, Chiyoda-ku, Tokyo 100; tel. (3) 3504-6250; e-mail diamondweekly@diamond.co.jp; internet www.diamond.co.jp; f. 1913; economics; Editor YUTAKA IWASA; circ. 78,000.

Focus: Shincho-Sha, 71, Yaraicho, Shinjuku-ku, Tokyo 162; tel. (3) 3266-5271; fax (3) 3266-5390; politics, economics, sport; Editor KAZUMASA TAJIMA; circ. 850,000.

Friday: Kodan-Sha Co Ltd, 2-12-21, Otowa, Bunkyo-ku, Tokyo 112; tel. (3) 5395-3440; fax (3) 3943-8582; current affairs; Editor-in-Chief TETSU SUZUKI; circ. 1m.

Hanako: Magazine House, 3-13-10, Ginza, Chuo-ku, Tokyo 104-03; tel. (3) 3545-7070; fax (3) 3545-7281; internet www.hanako-net.com; f. 1988; consumer guide; Editor AYAKO OTA; circ. 350,000.

Nikkei Business: Nikkei Business Publications Inc, 1-17-3, Shirokane, Minato-ku, Tokyo 108-8646; tel. (3) 6811-8101; fax (3) 5421-9117; internet www.nikkeibp.co.jp; f. 1969; Editor-in-Chief YOSHIYA SATO; circ. 330,000.

Shukan Asahi: Asahi Shimbun Publishing Dept, 5-3-2, Tsukiji, Chuo-ku, Tokyo 104-8011; tel. (3) 3545-0131; f. 1922; general interest; Editor-in-Chief KAZUOMI YAMAGUCHI; circ. 482,000.

Shukan Bunshun: Bungei-Shunju Ltd, 3-23, Kioicho, Chiyoda-ku, Tokyo 102-8008; tel. (3) 3265-1211; fax (3) 3234-3964; e-mail kawabe@bunshun.co.jp; internet www.bunshun.co.jp; f. 1959; general interest; Editor YOJI SUZUKI; circ. 800,000.

Shukan Gendai: Kodan-Sha Co Ltd, 2-12-21, Otowa, Bunkyo-ku, Tokyo 112; tel. (3) 5395-3438; fax (3) 3943-7815; f. 1959; general; Editor-in-Chief TETSU SUZUKI; circ. 930,000.

Shukan Josei: Shufu-To-Seikatsu Sha Ltd, 3-5-7, Kyobashi, Chuo-ku, Tokyo 104; tel. (3) 3563-5130; fax (3) 3563-2073; f. 1957; women's interest; Editor HIDEO KIKUCHI; circ. 638,000.

Shukan Post: Shogakukan Publishing Co Ltd, 2-3-1, Hitotsubashi, Chiyoda-ku, Tokyo 101-01; tel. (3) 3230-5951; internet www.weeklypost.com; f. 1969; general; Editor NORIMICHI OKANARI; circ. 696,000.

Shukan SPA: Fuso-Sha Co, 1-15-1, Kaigan, Minato-ku, Tokyo 105; tel. (3) 5403-8875; f. 1952; general interest; Editor-in-Chief TOSHIHIKO SATO; circ. 400,000.

Shukan ST: Japan Times Ltd, 4-5-4, Shibaura, Minato-ku, Tokyo 108-0023; tel. (3) 3452-4077; fax (3) 3452-3303; e-mail shukanst@japantimes.co.jp; internet www.japantimes.co.jp/shukan-st; f. 1951; English and Japanese; Editor MITSURU TANAKA; circ. 150,000.

Shukan Yomiuri: Yomiuri Shimbun Publication Dept, 1-2-1, Kiyosumi, Koto-ku, Tokyo 135; tel. (3) 5245-7001; e-mail yw@yomiuri.com; internet www.yomiuri.co.jp; f. 1938; general interest; Editor SHINI KAGEYAMA; circ. 453,000.

Sunday Mainichi: Mainichi Newspapers Publishing Dept, 1-1-1, Hitotsubashi, Chiyoda-ku, Tokyo 100-51; tel. (3) 3212-0321; fax (3) 3212-0769; f. 1922; general interest; Editor KENJI MIKI; circ. 237,000.

JAPAN

Tenji Mainichi: Mainichi Newspapers Publishing Dept, 3-4-5, Umeda, Osaka; tel. (6) 6346-8386; fax (6) 6346-8385; f. 1922; in Japanese braille; Editor TADAMITSU MORIOKA; circ. 12,000.

Weekly Economist: Mainichi Newspapers Publishing Dept, 1-1-1, Hitotsubashi, Chiyoda-ku, Tokyo 100-51; tel. (3) 3212-0321; f. 1923; Editorial Chief NOBUHIRO SHUDO; circ. 120,000.

Weekly Toyo Keizai: Toyo Keizai Inc, 1-2-1, Hongoku-cho, Nihonbashi, Chuo-ku, Tokyo 103-8345; tel. (3) 3246-5655; fax (3) 3270-0159; e-mail sub@toyokeizai.co.jp; internet www.toyokeizai.co.jp; f. 1895; business, economics, finance, and corporate information; Editor TOSHIKI OTA; circ. 62,000.

PERIODICALS

All Yomimono: Bungei-Shunju Ltd, 3-23, Kioicho, Chiyoda-ku, Tokyo 102; tel. (3) 3265-1211; fax (3) 3239-5481; f. 1930; monthly; popular fiction; Editor KOICHI SASAMOTO; circ. 95,796.

Any: 1-3-14, Hirakawa-cho, Chiyoda-ku, Tokyo 102; tel. (3) 5276-2200; fax (3) 5276-2209; f. 1989; every 2 weeks; women's interest; Editor YUKIO MIWA; circ. 380,000.

Asahi Camera: Asahi Shimbun Publishing Dept, 5-3-2, Tsukiji, Chuo-ku, Tokyo 104-8011; tel. (3) 3545-0131; fax (3) 5565-3286; f. 1926; monthly; photography; Editor HIROSHI HIROSE; circ. 90,000.

Balloon: Shufunotomo Co Ltd, 2-9, Kanda Surugadai, Chiyoda-ku, Tokyo 101; tel. (3) 3294-1132; fax (3) 3291-5093; f. 1986; monthly; expectant mothers; Dir MARIKO HOSODA; circ. 250,000.

Brutus: Magazine House, 3-13-10, Ginza, Chuo-ku, Tokyo 104-03; tel. (3) 3545-7000; fax (3) 3546-0034; internet www.brutusonline.com; f. 1980; every 2 weeks; men's interest; Editor KOICHI TETSUKA; circ. 250,000.

Bungei-Shunju: Bungei-Shunju Ltd, 3-23, Kioicho, Chiyoda-ku, Tokyo 102-8008; tel. (3) 3265-1211; fax (3) 3221-6623; internet www.bunshun.co.jp; f. 1923; monthly; general; Pres. MASARU SHIRAISHI; Editor KIYONDO MATSUI; circ. 656,000.

Business Tokyo: Keizaikai Bldg, 2-13-18, Minami-Aoyama, Minato-ku, Tokyo 105; tel. (3) 3423-8500; fax (3) 3423-8505; f. 1987; monthly; Dir TAKUO IDA; Editor ANTHONY PAUL; circ. 125,000.

Chuokoron: Chuokoron-Shinsha Inc, 2-8-7, Kyobashi, Chuo-ku, Tokyo 104-8320; tel. (3) 3563-2751; fax (3) 3561-5929; internet www.chuko.co.jp; f. 1887; monthly; general interest; Chief Editor JUN MAYIMA; circ. 90,000.

Croissant: Magazine House, 3-13-10, Ginza, Chuo-ku, Tokyo 104-03; tel. (3) 3545-7111; fax (3) 3546-0034; f. 1977; every 2 weeks; home; Editor MASAAKI TAKEUCHI; circ. 600,000.

Fujinkoron: Chuokoron-Sha Inc, 2-8-7, Kyobashi, Chuo-ku, Tokyo 104; tel. (3) 3563-1866; fax (3) 3561-5920; f. 1916; women's literary monthly; Editor YUKIKO YUKAWA; circ. 185,341.

Geijutsu Shincho: Shincho-Sha, 71, Yarai-cho, Shinjuku-ku, Tokyo 162-8711; tel. (3) 3266-5381; fax (3) 3266-5387; e-mail geishin@shinchosha.co.jp; f. 1950; monthly; fine arts, music, architecture, films, drama and design; Editor-in-Chief KAZUHIRO NAGAI; circ. 50,000.

Gendai: Kodan-Sha Ltd, 2-12-21, Otowa, Bunkyo-ku, Tokyo 112; tel. (3) 5395-3517; fax (3) 3945-9128; f. 1966; monthly; cultural and political; Editor SHUNKICHI YABUKI; circ. 250,000.

Ginza: Magazine House, 3-13-10, Ginza, Chuo-ku, Tokyo 104-8003; tel. (3) 3545-7080; fax (3) 3542-6375; internet ginza.magazine.co.jp; f. 1997; monthly; women's interest; Editor MIYOKO YODOGAWA; circ. 250,000.

Hot-Dog Press: Kodan-Sha Ltd, 2-12-21, Otowa, Bunkyo-ku, Tokyo 112-01; tel. (3) 5395-3473; fax (3) 3945-9128; every 2 weeks; men's interest; Editor ATSUHIDE KOKUBO; circ. 650,000.

Ie-no-Hikari (Light of Home): Ie-no-Hikari Asscn, 11, Ichigaya Funagawaramachi, Shinjuku-ku, Tokyo 162-8448; tel. (3) 3266-9013; fax (3) 3266-9052; e-mail hikari@mxd.meshnet.or.jp; internet www.ienohikari.or.jp; f. 1925; monthly; rural and general interest; Pres. SHUZO SUZUKI; Editor KAZUO NAKANO; circ. 928,000.

Japan Company Handbook: Toyo Keizai Inc, 1-2-1, Nihonbashi Hongoku-cho, Chuo-ku, Tokyo 103-8345; tel. (3) 3246-5621; fax (3) 3246-5473; e-mail sub@toyokeizai.co.jp; internet www.toyokeizai.co.jp; f. 1974; quarterly; English; Editor MASAKI HARA; total circ. 100,000.

Junon: Shufu-To-Seikatsu Sha Ltd, 3-5-7, Kyobashi, Chuo-ku, Tokyo 104; tel. (3) 3563-5132; fax (3) 5250-7081; e-mail junon-voice@mb.shufu.co.jp; internet www.shufu.co.jp/junon; f. 1973; monthly; television and entertainment; circ. 560,000.

Kagaku (Science): Iwanami Shoten Publishers, 2-5-5, Hitotsubashi, Chiyoda-ku, Tokyo 102; tel. (3) 5210-4070; fax (3) 5210-4073; f. 1931; Editor NOBUAKI MIYABE; circ. 29,000.

Kagaku Asahi: Asahi Shimbun Publishing Dept, 5-3-2, Tsukiji, Chuo-ku, Tokyo 104-8011; tel. (3) 5540-7810; fax (3) 3546-2404; f. 1941; monthly; scientific; Editor TOSHIHIRO SASAKI; circ. 105,000.

Keizaijin: Kansai Economic Federation, Nakanoshima Center Bldg, 6-2-27, Nakanoshima, Kita-ku, Osaka 530-6691; tel. (6) 6441-0101; fax (6) 6443-5347; internet www.kankeiren.or.jp; f. 1947; monthly; economics; Editor M. YASUTAKE; circ. 2,600.

Lettuce Club: SS Communications, 11-2, Ban-cho, Chiyoda-ku, Tokyo 102; tel. (3) 5276-2151; fax (3) 5276-2229; internet www.lettuceclub.net; f. 1987; every 2 weeks; cookery; Editor MITSURU NAKAYA; circ. 800,000.

Money Japan: SS Communications, 11-2, Ban-cho, Chiyoda-ku, Tokyo 102; tel. (3) 5276-2220; fax (3) 5276-2229; e-mail mj@sscom.co.jp; internet www.sscom.co.jp/money; f. 1985; monthly; finance; Editor TOSHIO KOBAYASHI; circ. 500,000.

Popeye: Magazine House, 3-13-10, Ginza, Chuo-ku, Tokyo 104-8003; tel. (3) 3545-7160; fax (3) 3545-9026; internet popeye.magazine.co.jp; f. 1976; every 2 weeks; fashion, youth interest; Editor KATSUMI NAMAIZAWA; circ. 320,000.

President: President Inc, Bridgestone Hirakawacho Bldg, 2-13-12, Hirakawa-cho, Chiyoda-ku, Tokyo 102; tel. (3) 3237-3737; fax (3) 3237-3748; internet www.president.co.jp; f. 1963; monthly; business; Editor KAYOKO ABE; circ. 263,308.

Ray: Shufunotomo Co Ltd, 2-9, Kanda Surugadai, Chiyoda-ku, Tokyo 101; tel. (3) 3294-1163; fax (3) 3291-5093; f. 1988; monthly; women's interest; Editor TATSURO NAKANISHI; circ. 450,000.

Ryoko Yomiuri: Ryoko Yomiuri Publications Inc, 2-2-15, Ginza, Chuo-ku, Tokyo 104; tel. (3) 3561-8911; fax (3) 3561-8950; internet www.ryokoyomiuri.co.jp; f. 1966; monthly; travel; Editor TETSUO KINUGAWA; circ. 470,000.

Sekai: Iwanami Shoten Publishers, 2-5-5, Hitotsubashi, Chiyoda-ku, Tokyo 101–8002; tel. (3) 5210-4141; fax (3) 5210-4144; e-mail sekai@iwanami.co.jp; internet www.iwanami.co.jp/sekai; f. 1946; monthly; review of world and domestic affairs; Editor ATSUSHI OKAMOTO; circ. 120,000.

Shinkenchiku: Shinkenchiku-Sha Co Ltd, 2-31-2, Yushima, Bunkyo-ku, Tokyo 113-8501; tel. (3) 3811-7101; fax (3) 3812-8229; e-mail ja-business@japan-architect.co.jp; internet www.japan-architect.co.jp; f. 1925; monthly; architecture; Editor AKIHIKO OMORI; circ. 87,000.

Shiso (Thought): Iwanami Shoten Publishers, 2-5-5, Hitotsubashi, Chiyoda-ku, Tokyo 101-8002; tel. (3) 5210-4055; fax (3) 5210-4037; e-mail shiso@iwanami.co.jp; internet www.iwanami.co.jp/shiso; f. 1921; monthly; philosophy, social sciences and humanities; Editor KIYOSHI KOJIMA; circ. 20,000.

Shosetsu Shincho: Shincho-Sha, 71, Yarai-cho, Shinjuku-ku, Tokyo 162-8711; tel. (3) 3266-5241; fax (3) 3266-5412; f. 1947; monthly; literature; Editor-in-Chief TSUYOSHI MENJO; circ. 80,000.

Shufunotomo: Shufunotomo Co Ltd, 2-9, Kanda Surugadai, Chiyoda-ku, Tokyo 101; tel. (3) 5280-7531; fax (3) 5280-7431; e-mail international@shufunotomo.co.jp; internet www.shufunotomo.co.jp; f. 1917; monthly; home and lifestyle; Editor KYOKO FURUTO; circ. 450,000.

So-en: Bunka Publishing Bureau, c/o Bunka Fashion College, 3-22-1, Yoyogi, Shibuya-ku, Tokyo,151-8522; tel. (3) 3299-2531; fax (3) 3370-3712; internet books.bunka.ac.jp; e-mail info-bpb@bunka.ac.jp; f. 1936; fashion monthly; Editor KEIKO SASAKI; circ. 270,000.

NEWS AGENCIES

Jiji Tsushin (Jiji Press Ltd): 5-15-8, Ginza, Chuo-ku, Tokyo 104-8178; tel. (3) 3591-1111; e-mail info@jiji.co.jp; internet www.jiji.com; f. 1945; Pres. WAKABAYASHI SEIZO; Man. Dir and Man. Editor HIROYUKI YAMAKI.

Kyodo Tsushin (Kyodo News): 2-2-5, Toranomon, Minato-ku, Tokyo 105-8474; tel. (3) 5573-8081; fax (3) 5573-2268; e-mail kokusai@kyodonews.jp; internet home.kyodo.co.jp; f. 1945; Pres. SATOSHI ISHIKAWA; Man. Editor TOSHIEI KOKUBU.

Radiopress Inc: R-Bldg Shinjuku, 5F, 33-8, Wakamatsu-cho, Shinjuku-ku, Tokyo 162-0056; tel. (3) 5273-2171; fax (3) 5273-2180; e-mail rptokyo@oak.ocn.ne.jp; f. 1945; provides news from China, the former USSR, Democratic People's Repub. of Korea, Viet Nam and elsewhere to the press and govt offices; Pres. AKIO IJUIN.

Sun Telephoto: Palaceside Bldg, 1-1-1, Hitotsubashi, Chiyoda-ku, Tokyo 100-0003; tel. (3) 3213-6771; e-mail photo@suntelephoto.com; internet www.suntelephoto.com; f. 1952; Pres. KOZO TAKINO; Man. Editor GORO SHIMAZAKI.

PRESS ASSOCIATIONS

Foreign Correspondents' Club of Japan: 20th Floor, 1-7-1, Yuraku-cho, Chiyoda-ku, Tokyo 100-0006; tel. (3) 3211-3161; fax (3) 3211-3168; e-mail yoda@fccj.or.jp; internet www.fccj.or.jp; f. 1945; 193 cos; Pres. MARTYN WILLIAMS; Man. SEISHI YODA.

Foreign Press Center: Nippon Press Center Bldg, 6th Floor, 2-2-1, Uchisaiwai-cho, Chiyoda-ku, Tokyo 100-0011; tel. (3) 3501-3401; fax (3) 3501-3622; e-mail rr@fpcjpn.or.jp; internet www.fpcj.jp; f. 1976;

JAPAN

est. by the Japan Newspaper Publrs' and Editors' Asscn and the Japan Fed. of Economic Orgs; provides services to the foreign press; Pres. TERUSUKE TERADA.

Nihon Shinbun Kyokai (The Japan Newspaper Publishers and Editors Asscn): Nippon Press Center Bldg, 2-2-1, Uchisaiwai-cho, Chiyoda-ku, Tokyo 100-8543; tel. (3) 3591-3462; fax (3) 3591-6149; e-mail s_intl@pressnet.or.jp; internet www.pressnet.or.jp; f. 1946; mems include 139 cos (108 daily newspapers, 4 news agencies and 27 radio and TV cos); Chair. MASATO KITAMURA; Sec.-Gen. MOTOYOSHI TORII.

Nihon Zasshi Kyokai (Japan Magazine Publishers Asscn): 1-7, Kanda Surugadai, Chiyoda-ku, Tokyo 101-0062; tel. (3) 3291-0775; fax (3) 3293-6239; f. 1956; 85 mems; Pres. HARUHIKO ISHIKAWA; Sec. GENYA INUI.

Publishers

Akane Shobo Co Ltd: 3-2-1, Nishikanda, Chiyoda-ku, Tokyo 101-0065; tel. (3) 3263-0641; fax (3) 3263-5440; e-mail info@akaneshobo.co.jp; internet www.akaneshobo.co.jp; f. 1949; juvenile; Pres. MASAHARU OKAMOTO.

Akita Publishing Co Ltd: 2-10-8, Iidabashi, Chiyoda-ku, Tokyo 102-8101; tel. (3) 3264-7011; fax (3) 3265-5906; e-mail license@akitashoten; internet www.akitashoten.co.jp; f. 1948; social sciences, history, juvenile; Chair. SADAO AKITA; Pres. SADAMI AKITA.

ALC Press Inc: 2-54-12, Eifuku, Suginami-ku, Tokyo 168-0064; tel. (3) 3323-1101; fax (3) 3327-1022; e-mail menet@alc.co.jp; internet www.alc.co.jp; f. 1969; linguistics, educational materials, dictionaries, juvenile; Pres. TERUMARO HIRAMOTO.

Asahi Shimbun Publications Division: 5-3-2, Tsukiji, Chuo-ku, Tokyo 104-8011; tel. (3) 3545-0131; fax (3) 5540-7682; internet opendoors.asahi.com; f. 1879; general; Pres. MUNEYUKI MATSUSHITA; Dir of Publications HISAO KUWASHIMA.

Asakura Publishing Co Ltd: 6-29, Shin Ogawa-machi, Shinjuku-ku, Tokyo 162-8707; tel. (3) 3260-0141; fax (3) 3260-0180; e-mail edit@asakura.co.jp; internet www.asakura.co.jp; f. 1929; natural science, medicine, social sciences; Pres. KUNIZO ASAKURA.

Asuka Publishing Inc: 2-11-5, Suido, Bunkyo-ku, Tokyo 112-0005; tel. (3) 5395-7650; fax (3) 5395-7661; e-mail askaweb@asuka-g.co.jp; internet www.asuka-g.co.jp; f. 1973; sociology, law, economics, languages; Pres. EIICHI ISHINO.

Baifukan Co Ltd: 4-3-12, Kudan Minami, Chiyoda-ku, Tokyo 102-8260; tel. (3) 3262-5256; fax (3) 3262-5276; e-mail bfkeigyo@mx7.mesh.ne.jp; internet www.baifukan.co.jp; f. 1924; engineering, natural and social sciences, psychology; Pres. ITARU YAMAMOTO.

Baseball Magazine-Sha: 3-10-10, Misaki-cho, Chiyoda-ku, Tokyo 101-8381; tel. (3) 3238-0081; fax (3) 3238-0106; internet www.bbm-japan.com; f. 1946; sports, physical education, recreation, travel; Pres. TETSUO IKEDA.

Bensey Publishing Inc: 2-20-6, Kanda-Jimbocho, Chiyoda-ku, Tokyo 101-0051; tel. (3) 5215-9021; fax (3) 5215-9025; e-mail bensey@bensey.co.jp; internet www.bensey.co.jp; f. 1967; philosophy, religion, history, art, languages, literature; Pres. YOJI IKEJIMA.

Bijutsu Shuppan-Sha Ltd: Inaoka Kudan Bldg, 6th Floor, 2-36, Kanda Jimbo-cho, Chiyoda-ku, Tokyo 101-8417; tel. (3) 3234-2151; fax (3) 3234-9451; e-mail artmedia@bijutsu.co.jp; internet www.bijutsu.co.jp; f. 1905; fine arts, graphic design; Pres. KENTARO OSHITA.

Bonjinsha Co Ltd: 1-3-13, Hirakawa-cho, Chiyoda-ku, Tokyo 102-0093; tel. (3) 3263-3959; fax (3) 3263-3116; e-mail info@bonjinsha.com; internet www.bonjinsha.com; f. 1973; Japanese language teaching materials; Pres. HISAMITSU TANAKA.

Bun-eido Publishing Co Inc: 28, Kamitoba, Daimotsucho, Minami-ku, Kyoto 601-8121; tel. (75) 671-3161; fax (75) 671-3165; e-mail fujita@bun-eido.co.jp; internet www.bun-eido.co.jp; f. 1921; reference books, dictionaries, textbooks, juvenile, history; Pres. HIDEOHIRO MASUI.

Bungei Shunju Ltd: 3-23, Kioi-cho, Chiyoda-ku, Tokyo 102-8008; tel. (3) 3265-1211; fax (3) 3265-1363; internet www.bunshun.co.jp; f. 1923; fiction, general literature, recreation, economics, sociology; Dir TOORU UENO.

Bunri Co Ltd: 1-1-5, Sekiguchi, Bunkyo-ku, Tokyo 112-0014; tel. (3) 3268-4110; fax (3) 3268-1462; e-mail tezukatak@bnet.bunri.co.jp; internet www.bunri.co.jp; f. 1950; Pres. SHIRO HATA.

Chikuma Shobo: Chikumashobo Bldg, 2-5-3, Kuramae, Taito-ku, Tokyo 111-8755; tel. (3) 5687-2671; fax (3) 5687-1585; e-mail webinfo@chikumashobo.co.jp; internet www.chikumashobo.co.jp; f. 1940; general literature, fiction, history, juvenile, fine arts; Pres. AKIO KIKUCHI.

Child-Honsha Co Ltd: 5-24-21, Koishikawa, Bunkyo-ku, Tokyo 112-8512; tel. (3) 3813-3785; fax (3) 3813-3765; e-mail ehon@childbook.co.jp; internet www.childbook.co.jp; f. 1930; juvenile; Pres. YOSHIAKI SHIMAZAKI.

Chuo Hoki Publishing Co Ltd: 2-27-4, Yoyogi, Shibuya-ku, Tokyo 151-0053; tel. (3) 3379-3784; fax (3) 5351-7855; e-mail info@chuohoki.co.jp; internet www.chuohoki.co.jp; f. 1947; law, social sciences; Pres. TAKASHI SHOMURA.

Chuo University Press: 742-1, Higashi-Nakano, Hachioji-shi, Tokyo 192-0393; tel. (426) 74-2351; fax (426) 74-2354; e-mail syuppan@tamajs.chuo-u.ac.jp; internet www.2chuo-u.ac.jp/up; f. 1948; law, history, sociology, economics, science, literature; Pres. TAKASHI FUKUDA.

Chuokoron-Shinsha Inc: 2-8-7, Kyobashi, Chuo-ku, Tokyo 104-8320; tel. (3) 3563-1261; fax (3) 3561-5920; internet www.chuko.co.jp; f. 1886; philosophy, history, sociology, general literature; Pres. JUNICHI HAYAKAWA.

Corona Publishing Co Ltd: 4-46-10, Sengoku, Bunkyo-ku, Tokyo 112-0011; tel. (3) 3941-3131; fax (3) 3941-3137; e-mail info@coronasha.co.jp; internet www.coronasha.co.jp; f. 1927; electronics business publs; Pres. TATSUMI GORAI.

Dempa Publications Inc: 1-11-15, Higashi Gotanda, Shinagawa-ku, Tokyo 141-8755; tel. (3) 3445-6111; fax (3) 3447-4666; f. 1950; electronics, personal computer software, juvenile, trade newspapers, English and Japanese language publications; Pres. TETSUO HIRAYAMA.

Diamond Inc: 6-12-17, Jingumae, Shibuya-ku, Tokyo 150-8409; tel. (3) 5778-7203; fax (3) 5778-6612; e-mail mitachi@diamond.co.jp; internet www.diamond.co.jp; f. 1913; business, management, economics, financial; Pres. NORIO TAMURA.

Dohosha Ltd: TAS Bldg, 2-5-2, Nishikanda, Chiyoda-ku, Tokyo 101-0065; tel. (3) 5276-0831; fax (3) 5276-0840; e-mail intl@dohosha.co.jp; internet www.dohosha.co.jp; f. 1997; general works, architecture, art, Buddhism, business, children's education, cooking, flower arranging, gardening, medicine.

East Press Co Ltd: 1-19, Kanda-Jimbocho, Chiyoda-ku, Tokyo 101-0051; tel. (3) 5259-7707; fax (3) 5259-7708; e-mail setsuko@eastpress.co.jp; internet www.eastpress.co.jp; f. 2005; literature, comics, business, self-help, parenting, health, sports, music; Chair. SHINGERU KOBAYASHI; Pres. OSAMU ASOSHINA.

Froebel-Kan Co Ltd: 6-14-9, Honkomagome, Bunkyo-ku, Tokyo 113-8611; tel. (3) 5395-6614; fax (3) 5395-6639; e-mail info-e@froebel-kan.co.jp; internet www.froebel-kan.co.jp; f. 1907; juvenile, educational; Pres. MAMORU KITABAYASHI; Dir YOSHIYUKI ISHII.

Fukuinkan Shoten Publishers Inc: 6-6-3, Honkomagome, Bunkyo-ku, Tokyo 113-8686; tel. (3) 3942-2151; fax (3) 3942-1401; internet www.fukuinkan.co.jp; f. 1952; juvenile; Pres. KAZUTASHI TSUKADA; Chair. KATSUMI SATO.

Fusosha Publishing Inc: 1-15-1, Kaigan, Minato-ku, Tokyo 105-8070; tel. (3) 5403-8851; fax (3) 3578-3078; e-mail gshoseki@fusosha.co.jp; internet www.fusosha.co.jp; f. 1984; social science, business, mystery, magazines, textbooks; Pres. MATSUKI KATAGIRI.

Futabasha Publishers Ltd: 3-28, Higashi-Gokencho, Shinjuku-ku, Tokyo 162-8540; tel. (3) 5261-4811; fax (3) 3267-3560; e-mail general@futabasha.co.jp; internet www.futabasha.co.jp; f. 1948; fiction, non-fiction, comics, guide books; Pres. HIROSHI MOROZUMI.

Gakken Co Ltd: 4-40-5, Kamiikedai, Ota-ku, Tokyo 145-8502; tel. (3) 3726-8111; fax (3) 3493-3338; e-mail personnel@gakken.co.jp; internet www.gakken.co.jp; f. 1946; juvenile, educational, art, encyclopaedias, dictionaries; Pres. YOCHIRO ENDO.

Graphic-sha Publishing Co Ltd: 1-9-12, Kudan Kita, Chiyoda-ku, Tokyo 102-0073; tel. (3) 3263-4318; fax (3) 3263-5297; e-mail info@graphicsha.co.jp; internet www.graphicsha.co.jp; f. 1962; art, design, architecture, manga techniques, hobbies; Pres. SEIICHI SUGAYA.

Gyosei Corpn: 4-30-16, Ogikubo, Suginami-ku, Tokyo 167-8088; tel. (3) 5349-6666; fax (3) 5349-6677; e-mail business@gyosei.co.jp; internet www.gyosei.co.jp; f. 1893; law, education, science, politics, business, art, language, literature, juvenile; Pres. YOHJI ITOH.

Hakusui-Sha Co Ltd: 3-24, Kanda Ogawa-machi, Chiyoda-ku, Tokyo 101-0052; tel. (3) 3291-7821; fax (3) 3291-7810; e-mail hpmaster@hakusuisha.co.jp; internet www.hakusuisha.co.jp; f. 1915; general literature, science and languages; Pres. MASAYUKI KAWAMURA.

Hayakawa Publishing Inc: 2-2, Kanda-Tacho, Chiyoda-ku, Tokyo 101-0046; tel. (3) 3252-3111; fax (3) 3258-0250; e-mail hirohaya@giganet.net; internet www.hayakawa-online.co.jp; f. 1945; wine books, children's books, coffee-table books, drama, comic books, monthly magazines; Pres. HIROSHI HAYAKAWA.

Heibonsha Ltd: 2-29-4 Hakusan, Bunkyo-ku, Tokyo 112-0001; tel. (3) 3818-0641; fax (3) 3818-0830; e-mail shop@heibonsha.co.jp; internet www.heibonsha.co.jp; f. 1914; encyclopaedias, art, history, geography, literature, science; Pres. NAOTO SHIMONAKA.

JAPAN

Hirokawa Publishing Co: 3-27-14, Hongo, Bunkyo-ku, Tokyo 113-0033; tel. (3) 3815-3651; fax (3) 5684-7030; f. 1925; natural sciences, medicine, pharmacy, nursing, chemistry; Pres. SETSUO HIROKAWA.

Hoikusha Publishing Co: 1-6-12, Kawamata, Higashi, Osaka 577-0063; tel. (6) 6788-4470; fax (6) 6788-4970; e-mail ymainishi@hotmail.com; internet www.hoikusha.co.jp; f. 1947; natural science, juvenile, fine arts, geography; Pres. YUKI IMAI.

Hokkaido University Press: 8 Nishi, Kita-Kujo, Kita-ku, Sapporo 060-0809; tel. (11) 747-2308; fax (11) 736-8605; e-mail hupress_2@hup.gr.jp; internet www.hup.gr.jp; f. 1970; social science, natural science, technology, humanities; Pres. HIROSHI SAEKI.

Hokuryukan Co Ltd: 3-8-14, Takanawa, Minato-ku, Tokyo 108-0074; tel. (3) 5449-4591; fax (3) 5449-4950; e-mail hk-ns@mk1.macnet.or.jp; internet www.macnet.or.jp/co/hk-ns/; f. 1891; natural science, medical science, juvenile, dictionaries; Pres. HISAKO FUKUDA.

The Hokuseido Press: 3-32-4, Honkomagome, Bunkyo-ku, Tokyo 113-0021; tel. (3) 3827-0511; fax (3) 3827-0567; e-mail info@hokuseido.com; f. 1914; regional non-fiction, dictionaries, textbooks; Pres. MASAZO YAMAMOTO.

Horitsubunkasha: 71, Iwagakakiuchicho, Kamigamo, Kitaku, Kyoto 603-8053; tel. (75) 791-7131; fax (75) 721-8400; e-mail henshu@hou-bun.co.jp; internet www.hou-bun.co.jp; f. 1947; law, politics, economics, sociology, philosophy; Pres. TSUTOMU OKAMURA.

Hosei University Press: 3-2-7, Kudan-Kita, Chiyoda-ku, Tokyo 102-0073; tel. (3) 5214-5540; fax (3) 5214-5542; e-mail mail@h-up.com; internet www.h-up.com; f. 1948; philosophy, history, economics, sociology, natural science, literature; Pres. CHIMAKE HIRABAYASHI.

Ie-No-Hikari Association: 11, Funagawara-cho, Ichigaya, Shinjuku-ku, Tokyo 162-8448; tel. (3) 3266-9000; fax (3) 3266-9048; e-mail hikari@mxd.mesh.ne.jp; internet www.ienohikari.or.jp; f. 1925; social science, agriculture, cooking; Pres. AKIO IKEBATA.

Igaku-Shoin Ltd: 1-28-23, Hongo, Bunkyo-ku, Tokyo 113-8719; tel. (3) 3817-5610; fax (3) 3815-4114; e-mail info@igaku-shoin.co.jp; internet www.igaku-shoin.co.jp; f. 1944; medicine, nursing; Pres. YU KANEHARA.

Ikubundo Publishing Co Ltd: 5-30-21, Hongo, Bunkyo-ku, Tokyo 113-0033; tel. (3) 3814-5571; fax (3) 3814-5576; e-mail webmaster@ikubundo.com; internet www.ikubundo.com; f. 1899; languages, dictionaries; Pres. TOSHIYUKI OI.

Institute for Financial Affairs Inc (KINZAI): 19, Minami-Motomachi, Shinjuku-ku, Tokyo 160-8519; tel. (3) 3358-1161; fax (3) 3359-7947; e-mail JDI04072@nifty.ne.jp; internet www.kinzai.or.jp; f. 1950; finance and economics, banking laws and regulations, accounting; Pres. MASATERU YOSHIDA.

Ishiyaku Publishers Inc: 1-7-10, Honkomagome, Bunkyo-ku, Tokyo 113-8612; tel. (3) 5395-7600; fax (3) 5395-7606; e-mail webmaster@ishiyaku.co.jp; internet www.ishiyaku.co.jp; f. 1921; medicine, dentistry, rehabilitation, nursing, nutrition and pharmaceutics; Pres. HIDEHO OHATA.

Iwanami Shoten, Publishers: 2-5-5, Hitotsubashi, Chiyoda-ku, Tokyo 101-8002; tel. (3) 5210-4000; fax (3) 5210-4039; e-mail rights@iwanami.co.jp; internet www.iwanami.co.jp; f. 1913; natural and social sciences, humanities, literature, fine arts, juvenile, dictionaries; Pres. AKIO YAMAGUCHI.

Iwasaki Publishing Co Ltd: 1-9-2, Suido, Bunkyo-ku, Tokyo 112-0005; tel. (3) 3812-0151; fax (3) 3812-1381; e-mail ask@iwasakishoten.co.jp; internet www.iwasakishoten.co.jp; f. 1934; juvenile; Pres. HIROAKI IWASAKI.

Japan Broadcast Publishing Co Ltd: 41-1, Udagawa-cho, Shibuya-ku, Tokyo 150-8081; tel. (3) 3464-7311; fax (3) 3780-3353; e-mail kikaka@nhk-book.co.jp; internet www.nhk-book.co.jp; f. 1931; foreign language textbooks, gardening, home economics, sociology, education, art, juvenile; Pres. HARUO OHASHI.

Japan External Trade Organization (JETRO): 2-2-5, Toranomon, Minato-ku, Tokyo 105-8466; tel. (3) 3582-5511; fax (3) 3587-2485; internet www.jetro.go.jp; f. 1958; trade, economics, investment.

Japan Publications Trading Co Ltd: 1-2-1, Sarugaku-cho, Chiyoda-ku, Tokyo 101-0064; tel. (3) 3292-3751; fax (3) 3292-0410; e-mail jpt@po.iijnet.or.jp; internet www.jptco.co.jp; f. 1942; general works, art, health, sports; Pres. SATOMI NAKABAYASHI.

The Japan Times Ltd: 4-5-4, Shibaura, Minato-ku, Tokyo 108-0023; tel. (3) 3453-2013; fax (3) 3453-8023; e-mail jt-books@kt.rim.or.jp; internet bookclub.japantimes.co.jp; f. 1897; linguistics, culture, business; Pres. TOSHIAKI OGASAWARA.

Jikkyo Shuppan Co Ltd: 5, Gobancho, Chiyoda-ku, Tokyo 102-8377; tel. (3) 3238-7700; fax (3) 3238-7719; internet www.jikkyo.co.jp; f. 1941; textbooks; Pres. MASAYUJI SHIMANE.

Jimbun Shoin: 9, Nishiuchihata-cho, Takeda, Fushimi-ku, Kyoto 612-8447; tel. (75) 603-1344; fax (75) 603-1814; e-mail edjimbun@mbox.kyoto-inet.or.jp; internet www.jimbunshoin.co.jp; f. 1922; general literature, philosophy, fiction, social science, religion, fine arts; Pres. MUTSUHISA WATANABE.

Jitsugyo No Nihonsha Ltd: 1-3-9, Ginza, Chuo-ku, Tokyo 104-8233; tel. (3) 3562-1021; fax (3) 3562-2662; e-mail soumu@j-n.co.jp; internet www.j-n.co.jp; f. 1897; general, social sciences, juvenile, travel, business, comics; Pres. YOSHIKAZU MASUDA.

JTB Publishing (Japan Travel Bureau): Urban-net Ichigaya Bldg, 25-5, Haraikatamachi, Shinjuku-ku, Tokyo 162-8446; tel. (3) 6888-7811; fax (3) 6888-7809; e-mail jtbpublishing@rurubu.ne.jp; internet www.jtbpublishing.com; f. 2004; travel, geography, history, fine arts, languages; Pres. MAKOTO EGASHIRA.

Kadokawa Shoten Publishing Co Ltd: 2-13-3, Fujimi, Chiyoda-ku, Tokyo 102-0071; tel. (3) 3238-8611; e-mail k-master@kadokawa.co.jp; internet www.kadokawa.co.jp; fax (3) 3238-8612; f. 1945; literature, history, dictionaries, religion, fine arts, books on tape, compact discs, CD-ROM, comics, animation, video cassettes, computer games; Pres. MINEO FUKUDA.

Kaibundo Publishing Co Ltd: 2-5-4, Suido, Bunkyo-ku, Tokyo 112-0005; tel. (3) 5684-6289; fax (3) 3815-3953; e-mail okadayo@kaibundo.jp; internet www.kaibundo.jp; f. 1914; marine affairs, natural science, engineering, industry; Pres. YOSHIHIRO OKADA.

Kaiseisha Publishing Co Ltd: 3-5, Ichigaya Sadohara-cho, Shinjuku-ku, Tokyo 162-8450; tel. (3) 3260-3229; fax (3) 3260-3540; e-mail foreign@kaiseisha.co.jp; internet www.kaiseisha.co.jp; f. 1936; juvenile; Pres. MASAKI IMAMURA.

Kanehara & Co Ltd: 2-31-14, Yushima, Bunkyo-ku, Tokyo 113-8687; tel. (3) 3811-7185; fax (3) 3813-0288; f. 1875; medical, agricultural, engineering and scientific; Pres. HIROMITSU KAWAI.

Keiso Shobo Publishing Co Ltd: 2-1-1, Suido, Bunkyo-ku, Tokyo 112-0005; tel. (3) 3814-6861; fax (3) 3814-6968; e-mail h-imura@keisoshobo.co.jp; internet www.keisoshobo.co.jp; f. 1948; law, economics, politics, literature, psychology, philosophy, sociology; Pres. HISATO IMURA.

Kenkyusha Ltd: 2-11-3, Fujimi, Chiyoda-ku, Tokyo 102-8152; tel. (3) 3288-7711; fax (3) 3288-7821; e-mail eigyo-bu@kenkyusha.co.jp; internet www.kenkyusha.co.jp; f. 1907; bilingual dictionaries, books on languages; Pres. MASAO SEKIDO.

Kinokuniya Co Ltd: 13-11, Higashi 3-chome, Shibuya-ku, Tokyo 150-8513; tel. (3) 5469-5919; fax (3) 5469-5959; e-mail publish@kinokuniya.co.jp; internet www.kinokuniya.co.jp; f. 1927; humanities, social science, natural science; Pres. OSAMU MATSUBARA.

KK Best Sellers Co Ltd: 2-29-7, Minami-Otsuka, Toshima-ku, Tokyo 170-8457; tel. (3) 5976-9121; fax (3) 5976-9237; e-mail muramatsu@bestsellers.co.jp; internet www.kk-bestsellers.com; f. 1967; non-fiction, general literature; Pres. MIKIO KURIHARA.

Kodansha International Ltd: 1-17-14, Otowa, Bunkyo-ku, Tokyo 112-8652; tel. (3) 3944-6492; fax (3) 3944-6323; e-mail sales@kodansha-intl.co.jp; f. 1963; art, business, cookery, crafts, gardening, language, literature, martial arts; Pres. MITSURU TOMITA.

Kodansha Ltd: 2-12-21, Otowa, Bunkyo-ku, Tokyo 112-8001; tel. (3) 5395-3564; fax (3) 3934-8580; e-mail n-okazaki@kodansha.co.jp; internet www.kodansha.co.jp; f. 1909; fine arts, fiction, literature, juvenile, comics, dictionaries; Pres. SAWAKO NOMA.

Kosei Publishing Co Ltd: 2-7-1, Wada, Suginami-ku, Tokyo 166-8535; tel. (3) 5385-2319; fax (3) 5385-2331; e-mail dharmaworld@kosei-shuppan.co.jp; internet www.kosei-shuppan.co.jp; f. 1966; general works, philosophy, religion, history, pedagogy, social science, art, juvenile; Pres. YUKIO YOKOTA.

Kumon Publishing Co Ltd: Gobancho Grand Bldg, 3-1, Gobancho, Chiyoda-ku, Tokyo 102-8180; tel. (3) 3234-4004; fax (3) 3234-4483; e-mail t_tanaka@kumonshuppan.com; internet www.kumonshuppan.com; f. 1988; juvenile, dictionaries, education; Pres. SHOICHI DOKAI.

Kwansei Gakuin University Press: 1-155, Uegahara-Ichibancho, Nishinomiya-shi, Hyogo 662-0891; tel. (798) 53-5233; fax (798) 53-9592; internet www.kwansei.ac.jp/press; f. 1997; natural science, social science, philosophy, literature; Pres. EIICHI YAMAMOTO.

Kyoritsu Shuppan Co Ltd: 4-6-19, Kohinata, Bunkyo-ku, Tokyo 112-8700; tel. (3) 3947-2511; fax (3) 3947-2539; e-mail general@kyoritsu-pub.co.jp; internet www.kyoritsu-pub.co.jp; f. 1926; scientific and technical; Pres. MITSUAKI NANJO.

Kyoto University Press: Kyodai-Kaikan, 15-9, Yoshidakawaracho, Sakyo-ku, Kyoto 606-8305; tel. (75) 761-6182; fax (75) 761-6190; e-mail ed1-1@kyoto.up.gr.jp; internet www.kyoto.up.or.jp; f. 1989; history, literature, philology, anthropology, sociology, economics, area studies, ecology, architecture, psychology, philosophy, space physics, earth and planetary science; Rep. Prof. YOSHIHIKO MOTOYAMA.

Kyushu University Press: 7-1-146, Hakozaki, Higashi-ku, Fukuoka 812-0053; tel. (92) 641-0515; fax (92) 641-0172; e-mail kup@mocha.ocn.ne.jp; internet www1.ocn.ne.jp/~kup; f. 1975; his-

JAPAN

tory, political science, law, economics, technology, linguistics, literature, psychology, medicine, agriculture; Chief Dir RYUICHIRO TANI.

Maruzen Co Ltd: 3-9-2, Nihonbashi, Chuo-ku, Tokyo 103-8244; tel. (3) 3272-0521; fax (3) 3272-0693; e-mail sitepub@maruzen.co.jp; internet pub.maruzen.co.jp; f. 1869; general works; Dir SHUNJI NAKAMURA.

Meisei University Press: 2-1-1, Hodokubo, Hino-shi, Tokyo 191-8506; tel. (42) 591-9979; fax (42) 593-0192; f. 1975; humanities, education, social science, natural science; Pres. KAZUAKI SAITO.

Minerva Shobo: 1, Tsutsumi dani-cho, Hinooka, Yamashina-ku, Kyoto 607-8494; tel. (75) 581-5191; fax (75) 581-0589; e-mail info@minervashobo.co.jp; internet www.minervashobo.co.jp; f. 1948; general non-fiction and reference; Pres. KEIZO SUGITA.

Misuzu Shobo Ltd: 5-32-21, Hongo, Bunkyo-ku, Tokyo 113-0033; tel. (3) 3815-9181; fax (3) 3818-8497; e-mail info@msz.co.jp; internet www.msz.co.jp; f. 1947; general, philosophy, history, psychiatry, literature, science, art; Pres. TAKASHI ARAI.

Morikita Shuppan Co Ltd: 1-4-11, Fujimi, Chiyoda-ku, Tokyo 102-0071; tel. (3) 3265-8341; fax (3) 3264-8709; e-mail info@morikita.co.jp; internet www.morikita.co.jp; f. 1950; natural science, engineering; Pres. HAJIME MORIKITA.

Nagaoka Shoten Co Ltd: 1-7-14, Toyotama-Kami, Nerima-ku, Tokyo 176-8518; tel. (3) 3992-5155; fax (3) 3948-9161; e-mail jumbo@nagaokashoten.co.jp; internet www.nagaokashoten.co.jp; f. 1963; dictionaries, home economics, sports, recreation, law; Pres. SHUICHI NAGAOKA.

Nakayama-Shoten Co Ltd: 1-25-14, Hakusan, Bunkyo-ku, Tokyo 113-8666; tel. (3) 3813-1100; fax (3) 3816-1015; e-mail eigyo@nakayamashoten.co.jp; internet www.nakayamashoten.co.jp; f. 1948; medicine, biology, zoology; Pres. KUROHIKO NAKAYAMA.

Nanzando Co Ltd: 4-1-11, Yushima, Bunkyo-ku, Tokyo; tel. (3) 5689-7868; fax (3) 5689-7869; e-mail info@nanzando.com; internet www.nanzando.com; medical reference, paperbacks; Pres. HAJIME SUZUKI.

Nigensha Publishing Co Ltd: 2-2, Kanda Jimbo-cho, Chiyoda-ku, Tokyo 101-8419; tel. (3) 5210-4733; fax (3) 5210-4723; e-mail sales@nigensha.co.jp; internet www.nigensha.co.jp; f. 1953; calligraphy, fine arts, art reproductions, cars, watches; Pres. TAKAO WATANABE.

Nihon Hyoronsha: 3-12-4, Minami-Otsuka, Toshima-ku, Tokyo 170-8474; tel. (3) 3987-8611; fax (3) 3987-8590; e-mail hayashi@nippyo.co.jp; internet www.nippyo.co.jp; f. 1919; jurisprudence, economics, science, mathematics, medicine, psychology, business; Pres. KATSUYUKI HAYASHI.

Nihon Keizai Shimbun Inc, Publications Bureau: 1-9-5, Otemachi, Chiyoda-ku, Tokyo 100-0004; tel. (3) 3270-0251; fax (3) 5255-2864; internet www.nikkei-bookdirect.com; f. 1876; economics, business, politics, fine arts, video cassettes, CD-ROM; Pres. SHUNTA KOBAYASHI.

Nihon Vogue Co Ltd: 3-23, Ichigaya Honmura-cho, Shinjuku-ku, Tokyo 162-8705; tel. (3) 5261-5139; fax (3) 3269-8726; e-mail asai@tezukuritown.com; internet www.tezukuritown.com; f. 1954; quilting, needlecraft, handicrafts, knitting, decorative painting, pressed flowers; Pres. NOBUAKI SETO.

Nihonbungeisha Co Ltd: 1-7, Kanda-Jimbocho, Chiyoda-ku, Tokyo 101-0051; tel. (3) 3294-7771; fax (3) 3294-7780; e-mail mmac@nihonbungeisha.co.jp; internet www.nihonbungeisha.co.jp; f. 1959; home economics, sociology, fiction, technical books; Pres. SOUJI NISHIZAWA.

Nippon Jitsugyo Publishing Co Ltd: 3-2-12, Hongo, Bunkyo-ku, Tokyo 113-0033; tel. (3) 3814-5651; fax (3) 3818-2723; e-mail int@njg.co.jp; internet www.njg.co.jp; f. 1950; business, management, finance and accounting, sales and marketing; Chair. and CEO YOICHIRO NAKAMURA.

Nosan Gyoson Bunka Kyokai (Rural Culture Association): 7-6-1, Akasaka, Minato-ku, Tokyo 107-8668; tel. (3) 3585-1141; fax (3) 3589-1387; e-mail rca@mail.ruralnet.or.jp; internet www.ruralnet.or.jp; f. 1940; agriculture, food and health, education, economics, philosophy; Pres. YOSHIHIRO HAMAGUCHI.

NTT Publishing Co Ltd: Arco Tower, 11/F, 1-8-1, Shimo-Meguro, Meguro-ku, Tokyo 153-8928; tel. (3) 5434-1011; fax (3) 5434-1008; internet www.nttpub.co.jp; f. 1987; essays, biography, philosophy, sociology, history, management, economics, technology, telecommunications, picture books, computer game guides; Pres. TAKASAHI SUGIMOTO.

Obunsha Co Ltd: 78, Yarai-cho, Shinjuku-ku, Tokyo 162-0805; tel. (3) 3266-6000; fax (3) 3266-6291; internet www.obunsha.co.jp; f. 1931; textbooks, reference, general science and fiction, magazines, encyclopaedias, dictionaries; software; audio-visual aids; CEO FUMIO AKAO.

Ohmsha Ltd: 3-1, Kanda Nishiki-cho, Chiyoda-ku, Tokyo 101-8460; tel. (3) 3233-0641; fax (3) 3233-2426; e-mail kaigaika@ohmsha.co.jp;

Directory

internet www.ohmsha.co.jp; f. 1914; engineering, technical and scientific; Pres. SEIJI SATO; Sr Man. Dir O. TAKEO.

Ondorisha Publishers Ltd: 11-11, Nishigoken-cho, Shinjuku-ku, Tokyo 162-8708; tel. (3) 3268-3101; fax (3) 3235-3530; f. 1945; knitting, embroidery, patchwork, handicraft books; Pres. HIDEAKI TAKEUCHI.

Ongaku No Tomo Sha Corpn (ONT): 6-30, Kagurazaka, Shinjuku-ku, Tokyo 162-0825; tel. (3) 3235-2111; fax (3) 3235-2119; e-mail home@ongakunotomo.co.jp; internet www.ongakunotomo.co.jp; f. 1941; compact discs, videograms, music magazines, music books, music data, music textbooks; Pres. KUMIO HORIUCHI.

Osaka University of Economics and Law Press: 6-10, Gakuonji, Yao-shi, Osaka 581-8511; tel. (729) 41-8211; fax (729) 41-9979; e-mail kondo-t@keiho-u.ac.jp; internet www.keiho-u.ac.jp/research/syuppan/index.html; f. 1987; economics, law, philosophy, history, natural science, languages, politics; Pres. SHUNKUO KANAZAWA.

Osaka University Press: 1-1, Yamadaoka, Suita-shi, Osaka 565-0871; tel. and fax (6) 6877-1614; e-mail info@osaka-up.or.jp; internet www.osaka.up.or.jp; f. 1993; economics, history, literature, medicine, philosophy, politics, science, sociology, technology; Pres. HIROSHI MATSUOKA.

PHP Institute Inc: 11, Kitanouchi-cho, Nishikujo, Minami-ku, Kyoto 601-8411; tel. (75) 681-4431; fax (75) 681-9921; internet www.php.co.jp; f. 1946; social science; Pres. KATSUHIKO EGUCHI.

Poplar Publishing Co Ltd: 5, Suga-cho, Shinjuku-ku, Tokyo 160-8565; tel. (3) 3357-2216; fax (3) 3351-0736; e-mail henshu@poplar.co.jp; internet www.poplar.co.jp; f. 1947; children's; Pres. HIROYUKI SAKAI.

Sanrio Co Ltd: 1-6-1, Osaki, Shinagawa-ku, Tokyo 141-8603; tel. (3) 3779-8101; fax (3) 3779-8098; internet www.sanrio.co.jp; f. 1960; Pres. SHINTARO TSUJI.

Sanseido Co Ltd: 2-22-14, Misaki-cho, Chiyoda-ku, Tokyo 101-8371; tel. (3) 3230-9411; fax (3) 3230-9547; internet www.sanseido.co.jp; f. 1881; dictionaries, educational, languages, social and natural science; Pres. SUEATSU HACHIMAN.

Sanshusha Publishing Co Ltd: 1-5-34, Shitaya, Taito-ku, Tokyo 110-0004; tel. (3) 3842-1711; fax (3) 3845-3965; e-mail maeda_k@sanshusha.co.jp; internet www.sanshusha.co.jp; f. 1938; languages, dictionaries, philosophy, sociology, electronic publishing (CD-ROM); Pres. KANJI MAEDA.

Seibido Shuppan Co Ltd: 1-7, Shinogawamachi, Shinjuku-ku, Tokyo 162-8445; tel. (3) 5206-8151; fax (3) 5206-8159; internet www.seibidoshuppan.co.jp; f. 1969; sports, recreation, travel guides, music, motor sports, cooking, novels, computer, child care, picture books; Pres. ETSUJI FUKAMI.

Seibundo-Shinkosha Co Ltd: 3-3-1, Hongo, Bunkyo-ku, Tokyo 113-0033; tel. (3) 5800-5775; fax (3) 5800-5773; internet www.seibundo.net; f. 1912; technical, scientific, design, general non-fiction; Pres. YUICHI OGAWA.

Seishun Publishing Co Ltd: 12-1, Wakamatsucho, Shinjuku-ku, Tokyo 162-0056; tel. (3) 3203-5121; fax (3) 3207-0982; e-mail information@seishun.co.jp; internet www.seishun.co.jp; f. 1955; science, education, history, sociology, philosophy, economics, literature; Pres. GENTARO OZAWA.

Seitoku University Press: 550, Iwase, Matsudo-city, Chiba 271-8755; tel. (47) 365-1111; fax (47) 363-1401; e-mail shuppan@seitoku.ac.jp; internet www.seitoku.jp/daigaku/shuppankai; f. 2002; human science, medicine, art; Pres. HIROAKI KAWAKAMI.

Seizando Shoten Publishing Co Ltd: 4-51, Minami-Motomachi, Shinjuku-ku, Tokyo 160-0012; tel. (3) 3357-5861; fax (3) 3357-5867; e-mail publisher@seizando.co.jp; internet www.seizando.co.jp; f. 1954; Pres. MINORU OGAWA.

Sekai Bunka Publishing Inc: 4-2-29, Kudan-Kita, Chiyoda-ku, Tokyo 102-8187; tel. (3) 3262-5111; fax (3) 3221-6843; e-mail m-kanjai@sekeibunka.co.jp; internet www.sekaibunka.com; f. 1946; history, natural science, geography, education, art, literature, juvenile; Pres. TSUTOMU SUZUKI.

Shincho-Sha Co Ltd: 71, Yarai-cho, Shinjuku-ku, Tokyo 162-8711; tel. (3) 3266-5411; fax (3) 3266-5534; e-mail shuppans@shinchosha.co.jp; internet www.shinchosha.co.jp; f. 1896; general literature, fiction, non-fiction, fine arts, philosophy; Pres. TAKANOBU SATO.

Shinkenchiku-Sha Co Ltd: 2-31-2, Yushima, Bunkyo-ku, Tokyo 113-8501; tel. (3) 3811-7101; fax (3) 3812-8229; e-mail ja-business@japan-architect.co.jp; internet www.japan-architect.co.jp; f. 1925; architecture; Pres. AKIHIKO OMORI.

Shinsei Publishing Co Ltd: 4-7-6, Taito, Taito-ku, Tokyo 110-0016; tel. (3) 3831-0743; fax (3) 3831-0758; internet www.shin-sei.co.jp; f. 1944; guidebooks, state examinations, personal computers; Pres. YASUHIRO TOMINAGA.

Shogakukan Inc: 2-3-1, Hitotsubashi, Chiyoda-ku, Tokyo 101-8001; tel. (3) 3230-5526; fax (3) 3288-9653; internet www

JAPAN

.shogakukan.co.jp; f. 1922; juvenile, education, geography, history, encyclopaedias, dictionaries; Pres. MASAHIRO OHGA.

Shokabo Publishing Co Ltd: 8-1, Yomban-cho, Chiyoda-ku, Tokyo 102-0081; tel. (3) 3262-9166; fax (3) 3262-7257; e-mail info@shokabo.co.jp; internet www.shokabo.co.jp; f. 1895; natural science, engineering; Pres. TATSUJI YOSHINO.

Shokokusha Publishing Co Ltd: 25, Saka-machi, Shinjuku-ku, Tokyo 160-0002; tel. (3) 3359-3231; fax (3) 3357-3961; e-mail eigyo@shokokusha.co.jp; f. 1932; architectural, technical and fine arts; Pres. TAKESHI GOTO.

Shueisha Inc: 2-5-10, Hitotsubashi, Chiyoda-ku, Tokyo 101-8050; tel. (3) 3230-6320; fax (3) 3262-1309; internet www.shueisha.co.jp; f. 1925; literature, fine arts, language, juvenile, comics; Pres. and CEO HIDEKI YAMASHITA.

Shufunotomo Co Ltd: 2-9, Kanda Surugadai, Chiyoda-ku, Tokyo 101-8911; tel. (3) 5280-7567; fax (3) 5280-7568; e-mail international@shufunotomo.co.jp; internet www.shufunotomo.co.jp; f. 1916; domestic science, fine arts, gardening, handicraft, cookery and magazines; Pres. KUNIHIKO MURAMATSU.

Shufu-To-Seikatsusha Ltd: 3-5-7, Kyobashi, Chuo-ku, Tokyo 104-8357; tel. (3) 3563-5120; fax (3) 3563-2073; internet www.shufu.co.jp; f. 1935; home economics, recreation, fiction, medicine, comics, cooking, interiors, handicraft, fishing, fashion; Pres. HIDEO MURUYAMA.

Shunju-Sha: 2-18-6, Soto-Kanda, Chiyoda-ku, Tokyo 101-0021; tel. (3) 3255-9614; fax (3) 3255-9370; f. 1918; philosophy, religion, literature, economics, music; Pres. AKIRA KANDA; Man. RYUTARO SUZUKI.

Sony Magazines Inc: 5-1, Gobancho, Chiyoda-ku, Tokyo 102-8679; tel. (3) 3234-5811; fax (3) 3234-5842; internet www.sonymagazines.jp; f. 1979; music books, general literature; Pres. KOICHI HASE.

Taishukan Publishing Co Ltd: 3-24, Kanda-Nishiki-cho, Chiyoda-ku, Tokyo 101-8466; tel. (3) 3294-2221; fax (3) 3295-4107; e-mail kimura@taishukan.co.jp; internet www.taishukan.co.jp; f. 1918; reference, Japanese and foreign languages, sports, dictionaries, audio-visual aids; Pres. KAZUYUKI SUZUKI.

Takahashi Shoten Co Ltd: 1-26-1, Otowa, Bunkyo-ku, Tokyo 112-0013; tel. (3) 3943-4525; fax (3) 3943-4288; e-mail takahashi@takahashishoten.co.jp; internet www.takahashishoten.co.jp; f. 1952; business, food and drink, sport, dictionaries, education, juvenile; Pres. HIDEO TAKAHASHI.

Tamagawa University Press: 6-1-1, Tamagawa-Gakuen, Machida-shi, Tokyo 194-8610; tel. (42) 739-8933; fax (42) 739-8940; e-mail tup@tamagawa.ac.jp; internet www.tamagawa.jp/introduction/press; f. 1929; education, philosophy, religion, arts, juvenile, area studies; Pres. YOSHIAKI OBARA.

Tankosha Publishing Co Ltd: 19-1, Miyanishi-cho Murasakino, Kita-ku, Kyoto 603-8691; tel. (75) 432-5151; fax (75) 432-0273; e-mail tankosha@magical.egg.or.jp; internet tankosha.topica.ne.jp; f. 1949; tea ceremony, fine arts, history; Pres. YOSHITO NAYA.

Teikoku-Shoin Co Ltd: 3-29, Kanda Jimbo-cho, Chiyoda-ku, Tokyo 101-0051; tel. (3) 3262-0834; fax (3) 3262-7770; e-mail kenkyu@teikokushoin.co.jp; internet www.teikokushoin.co.jp; f. 1926; geography, atlases, maps, textbooks, history, civil studies; Pres. MISAO MORIYA.

Tohoku University Press, Sendai: 2-1-1, Katahira, Aoba-ku, Sendai 980-8577; tel. (22) 214-2777; fax (22) 214-2778; e-mail info@tups.jp; internet www.tups.jp; f. 1996; natural science, social science, humanities, history, literature, psychology, philosophy, art, language; Chair. SHIGERU HISAMICHI.

Tokai University Press: 3-10-35, Minami-Yana, Hadano-shi, Kanagawa 257-0003; tel. (463) 79-3921; fax (463) 69-5087; e-mail trem@tsc-u-tokai.ac.jp; internet www.press.tokai.ac.jp; f. 1962; social science, cultural science, natural science, engineering, art; Pres. TATSURO MATSUMAE.

Tokuma Shoten Publishing Co Ltd: 1-1-16, Higashi Shimbashi, Minato-ku, Tokyo 105-8055; tel. (3) 3573-0111; fax (3) 3573-8788; e-mail info@tokuma.com; internet www.tokuma.com; f. 1954; Japanese classics, history, fiction, juvenile; Pres. TAKEYOSHI MATSUSHITA.

Tokyo News Service Ltd: Hamarikyu Park Side Place Bldg, 5-6-10, Tsukiji, Chuo-ku, Tokyo 104-8415; tel. (3) 3542-6511; fax (3) 3545-3628; internet www.tokyonews.co.jp; f. 1947; shipping, trade and television guides; Pres. T. OKUYAMA.

Tokyo Shoseki Co Ltd: 2-17-1, Horifune, Kita-ku, Tokyo 114-8524; tel. (3) 5390-7513; fax (3) 5390-7409; e-mail shoseki@tokyo-shoseki.co.jp; internet www.tokyo-shoseki.co.jp; f. 1909; textbooks, reference books, cultural and educational books; Pres. YOSHIKATSU KAWAUCHI.

Tokyo Sogen-Sha Co Ltd: 1-5, Shin-Ogawa-machi, Shinjuku-ku, Tokyo 162-0814; tel. (3) 3268-8201; fax (3) 3268-8230; internet www.tsogen.co.jp; f. 1954; mystery and detective stories, science fiction, literature; Pres. SHINICHI HASEGAWA.

Toyo Keizai Shinposha: 1-2-1, Nihonbashi-Hongokucho, Chuoku, Tokyo 103-8345; tel. (3) 3246-5661; fax (3) 3231-0906; e-mail tk@toyokeizai.co.jp; internet www.toyokeizai.co.jp; f. 1895; periodicals, economics, business, finance, corporation information; Pres. HIROSHI TAKAHASHI.

Tuttle Publishing Co Inc: RK Bldg, 2nd Floor, 2-12-10, Shimo-Meguro, Meguro-ku, Tokyo, 153 Japan; tel. (3) 5437-0171; fax (3) 5437-0755; e-mail info@tuttlepublishing.com; internet www.tuttlepublishing.com; f. 1948; books on Japanese and Asian religion, history, social science, arts, languages, literature, juvenile, cookery; Pres. ERIC OEY.

United Nations University Press: 5-53-70, Jingumae, Shibuya-ku, Tokyo 150-8925; tel. (3) 3499-2811; fax (3) 3499-2828; e-mail sales@hq.unu.edu; internet www.unu.edu/unupress; f. 1975; social sciences, humanities, pure and applied natural sciences; Head SCOTT MCQUADE.

University of Nagoya Press: 1, Furocho, Chikusa-ku, Nagoya 464-0814; tel. (52) 781-5027; fax (52) 781-0697; e-mail sogo@unp.nagoya-u.ac.jp; internet www.unp.or.jp; f. 1982; social science, humanities, natural science, medicine; Chair. YUICHI KANAI.

University of Tokyo Press: 7-3-1, Hongo, Bunkyo-ku, Tokyo 113-8654; tel. (3) 3811-0964; fax (3) 3815-1426; e-mail info@utp.or.jp; internet www.utp.or.jp; f. 1951; natural and social sciences, humanities; Japanese and English; Chair. KAZUO OKAMOTO; Man. Dir TADASHI YAMASHITA.

Waseda University Press: 1-104-25, Totsukamachi, Shinjuku-ku, Tokyo 169-0071; tel. (3) 3203-1551; fax (3) 3207-0406; e-mail kyw03723@nifty.ne.jp; internet www.waseda-up.co.jp; f. 1886; politics, economics, law, sociology, philosophy, literature; Pres. SHIGENORI WATANABE.

Yama-Kei Publishers Co Ltd: 1-9-13, Akasaka, Minato-ku, Tokyo 107-8410; tel. (3) 6234-1600; fax (3) 6234-1628; e-mail info@yamakei.co.jp; internet www.yamakei.co.jp; f. 1930; natural science, geography, mountaineering, outdoor activity; Pres. YOSHIMITSU KAWASAKI.

Yohan Inc (New Yohan): Akasaka Community Bldg, 1-1-8 Moto-akasaka, Minato-ku, Tokyo 107-0051; tel. (3) 5786-7425; fax (3) 5770-2440; e-mail webinfo@yohan.co.jp; internet www.yohan.co.jp; f. 1953; social science, language, art, juvenile, dictionary; merged with Tuttle Shokai in 2003; Pres. HIROSHI KAGAWA.

Yoshikawa Kobunkan: 7-2-8, Hongo, Bunkyo-ku, Tokyo 113-0033; tel. (3) 3813-9151; fax (3) 3812-3544; e-mail hongo@yoshikawa-k.co.jp; internet www.yoshikawa-k.co.jp; f. 1857; history, biography, art, languages, religion; Pres. HIDEO HAYASHI.

Yuhikaku Publishing Co Ltd: 2-17, Kanda Jimbo-cho, Chiyoda-ku, Tokyo 101-0051; tel. (3) 3264-1312; fax (3) 3264-5030; e-mail susumu-ito@yuhikaku.co.jp; internet www.yuhikaku.co.jp; f. 1877; social sciences, law, economics; Pres. TADATAKA EGUSA.

Yuki Shobo: 3-7-9, Kudan-minami, Chiyoda-ku, Tokyo 102-0074; tel. (3) 5275-8008; fax (3) 5275-8099; e-mail takeshi.nanri@yuskishobo.co.jp; internet www.yukishobo.co.jp; f. 1957; home economics, juvenile, recreation, sociology, sports; Pres. MASAO OKAJIMA.

Yuzankaku Shuppan: 2-6-9, Fujimi, Chiyoda-ku, Tokyo 102; tel. (3) 3262-3231; fax (3) 3262-6938; e-mail info@yuzankaku.co.jp; internet www.yuzankaku.co.jp; f. 1916; history, fine arts, religion, archaeology; Pres. TETSUO MIYATA.

Zen-on Music Co Ltd: 2-13-3, Kami-Ochiai, Shinjuku-ku, Tokyo 161-0034; tel. (3) 3227-6270; fax (3) 3227-6276; e-mail akira@zen-on.co.jp; internet www.zen-on.co.jp; f. 1931; classics, pop, books on music; Pres. TADASHI YOKOKURA.

Zoshindo Juken Kenkyusha Co Ltd: 2-19-15, Shinmachi, Nishi-ku, Osaka 550-0013; tel. (6) 6532-1581; fax (6) 6532-1588; e-mail zoshindo@mbox.inet-osaka.or.jp; internet www.zoshindo.co.jp; f. 1890; educational, juvenile; Pres. AKITAKA OKAMATO.

GOVERNMENT PUBLISHING HOUSE

Government Publications' Service Centre: 1-2-1, Kasumigaseki, Chiyoda-ku, Tokyo 100-0013; tel. (3) 3504-3885; fax (3) 3504-3889.

PUBLISHERS' ASSOCIATIONS

Japan Book Publishers Association: 6, Fukuro-machi, Shinjuku-ku, Tokyo 162-0828; tel. (3) 3268-1303; fax (3) 3268-1196; e-mail rd@jbpa.or.jp; internet www.jbpa.or.jp; f. 1957; 501 mems (1995); Pres. KUNIZO ASAKURA; Exec. Dir TADASHI YAMASHITA.

Publishers' Association for Cultural Exchange, Japan: 1-2-1, Sarugaku-cho, Chiyoda-ku, Tokyo 101-0064; tel. (3) 3291-5685; fax (3) 3233-3645; e-mail office@pace.or.jp; internet www.pace.or.jp; f. 1953; 135 mems; Pres. Dr TATSURO MATSUMAE; Man. Dir YASUKO KORENAGA.

JAPAN

Broadcasting and Communications

TELECOMMUNICATIONS

KDDI Corpn: KDDI Bldg, 2-3-2, Nishi Shinjuku, Shinjuku-ku, Tokyo 163-03; tel. (3) 3347-7111; fax (3) 3347-6470; internet www.kddi.com; f. 2000 by merger of DDI Corpn, Kokusai Denshin Denwa Corpn (KDD) and Nippon Idou Tsuhin Corpn (IDO); major international telecommunications carrier; Pres. TADASHI ONODERA.

Livedoor Co Ltd: Roppongi Hills Mori Tower 38th Floor, 6-10-1 Roppongi, Minato-ku, Tokyo; e-mail info@livedoor.jp; internet www.livedoor.co.jp; f. 1996; 12.75% stake held by Yasuhide Uno, Pres. of Usen Corpn, 12.75% stake held by Fuji Television Network Inc; internet portal; Pres. and CEO KOZO HIRAMATSU.

Nippon Telegraph and Telephone Corpn (NTT): 2-3-1, Otemachi, Chiyoda-ku, Tokyo 100-8116; tel. (3) 5359-2122; internet www.ntt.co.jp; f. 1985; operates local, long-distance and international services; largest telecommunications co in Japan; Pres. and CEO SATOSHI MIURA.

NTT DoCoMo: 2-11-1, Nagatacho, Chiyoda-ku, Tokyo 100-6150; tel. (3) 5156-1111; fax (3) 5156-0271; internet www.nttdocomo.com; f. 1991; operates mobile phone network; Pres. and CEO MASAO NAKAMURA.

SoftBank Telecom Corpn: 1-9-1, Higashi Shimbashi, Minato-ku, Tokyo 105-7316; tel. 0088-41; e-mail tcsc@tm.softbank.co.jp; internet www.softbanktelecom.co.jp; fmrly Japan Telecom; fixed-line business acquired by Ripplewood Holdings Aug. 2003; acquired by Softbank Corpn in 2004; merged with International Digital Communications (IDC) in 2005; name changed as above in 2006; Chair. and CEO MASAYOSHI SON.

Tokyo Telecommunication Network Co Inc (TTNet): 4-9-25, Shibaura, Minato-ku, Tokyo 108; tel. (3) 5476-0091; fax (3) 5476-7625.

Digital Phone and Digital TU-KA also operate mobile telecommunication services in Japan.

BROADCASTING

NHK (Japan Broadcasting Corporation): 2-2-1, Jinnan, Shibuya, Tokyo 150-8001; tel. (3) 3465-1111; fax (3) 3469-8110; e-mail webmaster@www.nhk.or.jp; internet www.nhk.or.jp; f. 1925; fmrly Nippon Hoso Kyokai, NHK (Japan Broadcasting Corpn); Japan's sole public broadcaster; operates five TV channels (incl. two terrestrial services—general TV and educational TV, and three satellite services—BS-1, BS-2 and digital Hi-Vision—HDTV), three radio channels, Radio 1, Radio 2, and FM Radio, and three world-wide services, NHK World TV, NHK World Premium and NHK World Radio Japan; headquarters in Tokyo, regional headquarters in Osaka, Nagoya, Hiroshima, Fukuoka, Sendai, Sapporo and Matsuyama; Pres. GENICHI HASHIMOTO; Exec. Dir-Gen. of Broadcasting TOYOHIKO HARADA.

National Association of Commercial Broadcasters in Japan (NAB-J): 3-23, Kioi-cho, Chiyoda-ku, Tokyo 102-8577; tel. (3) 5213-7727; fax (3) 5213-7730; internet www.nab.or.jp; f. 1951; asscn of 201 companies (133 TV cos, 110 radio cos). Among these companies, 42 operate both radio and TV, with 664 radio stations and 8,315 TV stations (incl. relay stations); Pres. MICHISADA HIROSE; Exec. Dir TOSHIO TAMAGAWA.

In June 2000 there were a total of 99 commercial radio broadcasting companies and 127 commercial television companies operating in Japan.

Some of the most important companies are:

Asahi Hoso—Asahi Broadcasting Corpn: 2-2-48, Ohyodominami, Kita-ku, Osaka 531-8501; tel. (6) 6458-5321; fax (6) 6458-3672; internet www.asahi.co.jp; Chair. TOSHIHARU SHIBATA; Pres. YOSHIRO NISHIMURA.

Bunka Hoso—Nippon Cultural Broadcasting, Inc: 1-31, Hamamatsu-cho, Minato-ku, Tokyo 105-8002; tel. (3) 3357-1111; fax (3) 3357-1140; internet www.joqr.co.jp; f. 1952; Pres. SHIGEKI SATO.

Chubu-Nippon Broadcasting Co Ltd: 1-2-8, Shinsakae, Naka-ku, Nagoya 460-8405; tel. (052) 241-8111; internet hicbc.com; f. 1950; Pres. KAZUYOSHI NATSUME.

Fuji Television Network, Inc: 2-4-8, Daiba, Minato-ku, Tokyo 137-8088; tel. (3) 5500-8888; fax (3) 5500-8027; internet www.fujitv.co.jp; f. 1959; owns Nippon Broadcasting System, Inc; 12.75% stake in internet provider Livedoor; Chair. and CEO HISASHI HIEDA; Pres. KOICHI MURAKAMI.

Kansai TV Hoso (KTV)—Kansai Telecasting Corpn: 2-1-7, Ogimachi, Kita-ku, Osaka 530-8408; tel. (6) 6314-8888; internet www.ktv.co.jp; f. 1958; Pres. SOICHIRO CHIGUSA.

Mainichi Hoso (MBS)—Mainichi Broadcasting System, Inc: 17-1, Chayamachi, Kita-ku, Osaka 530-8304; tel. (6) 6359-1123; fax (6) 6359-3503; internet www.mbs.jp; f. 1950; Pres. MASAHIRO YAMAMOTO.

Nippon Hoso—Nippon Broadcasting System, Inc: 2-4-8, Daiba, Minato-ku, Tokyo 137-8686; tel. (3) 5500-1234; internet www.jolf.co.jp; f. 1954; 49.8% controlling stake acquired by Livedoor Co Ltd in 2005, but subsequently purchased by Fuji Television Network, Inc; Pres. MICHIYASU KAWAUCHI.

Nippon TV Hoso-MO (NTV)—Nippon Television Network Corpn: 1-6-1, Higashi Shimbashi, Minato-ku, Tokyo 105-7444; tel. (3) 6215-3156; fax (3) 6215-3157; internet www.ntv.co.jp; f. 1953; Chair. SEIICHIRO UJIIE; Pres. SHINTARO KUBO.

Okinawa TV Hoso (OTV)—Okinawa Television Broadcasting Co Ltd: 1-2-20, Kumoji, Naha 900-8588; tel. (988) 63-2111; fax (988) 61-0193; internet www.otv.co.jp; f. 1959; Pres. BUNKI TOMA.

Radio Tampa—Nihon Short-Wave Broadcasting Co: 1-9-15, Akasaka, Minato-ku, Tokyo 107-8373; tel. (3) 3583-8151; fax (3) 3583-7441; internet www.tampa.co.jp; f. 1954; Pres. TAMIO IKEDA.

Ryukyu Hoso (RBC)—Ryukyu Broadcasting Co: 2-3-1, Kumoji, Naha 900-8711; tel. (98) 867-2151; fax (98) 864-5732; internet www.rbc-ryukyu.co.jp; f. 1954; Pres. HIROSHI ZAYASU.

Tokyo Hoso (TBS)—Tokyo Broadcasting System, Inc: 5-3-6, Akasaka, Minato-ku, Tokyo 107-8006; tel. (3) 3746-1111; fax (3) 3588-6378; internet www.tbs.co.jp; f. 1951; Chair. YUKIO SUNAHARA; Pres. HIROSHI INOUE.

TV Asahi Corpn: 6-9-1, Roppongi, Minato-ku, Tokyo 106-8001; tel. (3) 6406-1275; fax (3) 3405-3714; internet www.tv-asahi.co.jp; f. 1957; Pres. MASAO KIMIWADA.

TV Osaka (TVO)—Television Osaka, Inc: 1-2-18, Otemae, Chuo-ku, Osaka 540-8519; tel. (6) 6947-0019; fax (6) 6946-9796; internet www.tv-osaka.co.jp; f. 1982; Pres. MAKOTO FUKAGAWA.

TV Tokyo (TX)—Television Tokyo Channel 12 Ltd: 4-3-12, Toranomon, Minato-ku, Tokyo 105-8012; tel. (3) 3432-1212; fax (3) 5473-3447; internet www.tv-tokyo.co.jp; f. 1964; Chair. and Co-CEO SADAHIKO SUGAYA; Pres. and Co-CEO MASAYUKI SHIMADA.

Yomiuri TV Hoso (YTV)—Yomiuri Telecasting Corporation: 2-2-33, Shiromi, Chuo-ku, Osaka 540-8510; tel. (6) 6947-2111; internet www.ytv.co.jp; f. 1958; 20 hrs colour broadcasting daily; Pres. KOJI TAKADA.

Satellite, Cable and Digital Television

In addition to the two broadcast satellite services that NHK introduced in 1989, a number of commercial satellite stations are in operation. Cable television is available in many urban areas, and in 1996/97 there were some 12.6m. subscribers to cable services in Japan. Satellite digital television services, which first became available in 1996, are provided by Japan Digital Broadcasting Services (f. 1998 by the merger of PerfecTV and JSkyB—now Sky Perfect Communications Inc) and DirecTV. Terrestrial digital broadcasting was launched in Japan in December 2003.

Finance

(cap. = capital; p.u. = paid up; res = reserves; dep. = deposits; m. = million; brs = branches; amounts in yen)

BANKING

Japan's central bank and bank of issue is the Bank of Japan. At August 2005 more than one-half of the credit business of the country was handled by 152 private commercial banks, 47 trust banks and three long-term credit banks, collectively designated 'All Banks'.

An important financial role is played by co-operatives and by the many small enterprise institutions. There are also two types of private financial institutions for small business. At August 2005 there were 175 Credit Co-operatives and 297 Shinkin Banks (credit associations), which lend only to members. The latter also receive deposits.

The most popular form of savings is through the post office network. In October 2005 legislation was approved to permit the privatization of Japan Post. Following its initial transfer to a holding company, Japan Post was to be divided into four units (savings, insurance and postal services, along with personnel and property management). The first disposals were scheduled for 2007. Having been established in September 2006, the Japan Post Bank (JPB) commenced operations on 1 October 2007. The Japan Post Bank thus became the world's largest financial institution in terms of deposits; it is also the largest seller of life insurance.

Central Bank

Nippon Ginko (Bank of Japan): 2-1-1, Hongoku-cho, Nihonbashi, Chuo-ku, Tokyo 100-8630; tel. (3) 3279-1111; fax (3) 5200-2256; e-mail prd@info.boj.or.jp; internet www.boj.or.jp; f. 1882; cap. 100m., res 2,527,206m., dep. 63,741,765m. (March 2006); Gov. MASAAKI SHIRAKAWA; Dep. Govs TOSHIRO MUTO, KAZUMASA IWATA; 32 brs.

JAPAN   Directory

Principal Commercial Banks

The Asahi Shinkin Bank: 2-1-2 Higashi-kanda, Chiyoda-ku, Tokyo 101-0031; tel. (3) 3862-0321; fax (3) 5687-6867; f. 1923; est. as Shinyo Kumiai Tomin Kinko, name changed as above after merger in 2002; cap. 20,277m., res 12,005m., dep. 1,609,445m. (Dec. 2006); Chair. YUKIHIKO NAGANO; Pres. KAZURO TSUKAHARA; 70 brs.

Ashikaga Bank Ltd: 4-1-25, Sakura, Utsunomiya, Tochigi 320-8610; tel. (286) 22-0111; e-mail ashigin@ssctnet.or.jp; internet www.ashikagabank.co.jp; f. 1895; nationalized Nov. 2003 owing to insolvency; cap. 147,429m., res 20,169m., dep. 4,369,219m. (March 2005); CEO NORITO IKEDA; 100 brs.

Bank of Fukuoka Ltd: 2-13-1, Tenjin, Chuo-ku, Fukuoka 810-8727; tel. (92) 723-2591; fax (92) 711-1746; internet www.fukuokabank.co.jp; f. 1945; cap. 70,310m., res 293,861m., dep. 7,106,856m. (March 2006); Chair. RYOJI TSUKUDA; Pres. MASAAKI TANI; 167 brs.

Bank of Tokyo-Mitsubishi UFJ Ltd: 2-7-1, Marunouchi, Chiyoda-ku, Tokyo 100-8388; tel. (3) 3240-1111; fax (3) 3240-4197; internet www.bk.mufg.jp; f. 2006 through merger of Bank of Tokyo-Mitsubishi Ltd and UFJ Bank Ltd; specializes in international banking and financial business; subsidiary of Mitsubishi UFJ Financial Group (f. 2005 through merger of Mitsubishi Tokyo Financial Group with UFJ Holdings); cap. 996,973m., res 4,156,935m., dep. 131,295,739m. (March 2006); Pres. SHIGEMITSU MIKI; 785 brs (672 domestic, 113 overseas).

Bank of Yokohama Ltd: 3-1-1, Minatomirai, Nishi-ku, Yokohama, Kanagawa 220-8611; tel. (45) 225-1111; fax (45) 225-1160; e-mail iroffice@hamagin.co.jp; internet www.boy.co.jp; f. 1920; cap. 215,481m., res 312,294m., dep. 10,075,630m. (March 2007); Chair. SADAAKI HIRASAWA; Pres. TADASHI OGAWA; 193 brs.

Chiba Bank Ltd: 1-2, Chiba-minato, Chuo-ku, Chiba 260-8720; tel. (43) 245-1111; e-mail int@chibabank.co.jp; internet www.chibabank.co.jp; f. 1943; cap. 145,069m., res 326,461m., dep. 9,018,016m. (March 2006); Dir KENJI YASUI; Pres. TADASHI TAKEYAMA; Chair. TOSHIAKI ISHII; 160 domestic brs, 3 overseas brs.

The Chiba Kogyo Bank Ltd: 2-1-2, Saiwacho, Mihama-ku, Chiba; tel. (43) 243-2111; fax (43) 244-9203; internet www.chibakogyo-bank.co.jp; f. 1952; cap. 57,941m., res 37,585m., dep. 1,882,554m. (March 2006); Pres. and CEO HIDEO IKEZAWA; 71 brs.

Hachijuni Bank: 178-8, Okada, Nagano-shi, Nagano 380-8682; tel. (26) 227-1182; fax (26) 226-5077; internet www.82bank.co.jp; f. 1931; cap. 52,243m., res 170,977m., dep. 5,294,195m. (March 2006); Chair. KAZUYUKI NARUSAWA; Pres. YOSHIYUKI YAMAURA.

Hokkaido Bank Ltd: 4-1, Odori-Nishi, Chuo-ku, Sapporo 060-8678, Hokkaido; tel. (11) 233-1093; fax (11) 231-3133; internet www.hokkaidobank.co.jp; f. 1951; cap. 93,524m., res 21,856m., dep. 3,602,600m. (March 2006); Pres. YOSHIHIRO SEKIHACHI; 120 brs.

Hokkoku Bank Ltd: 1 Shimotsutsumi-cho, Kanazawa 920-8670, Ishikawa; tel. (762) 631111; fax (762) 233362; internet www.hokkokubank.co.jp; f. 1943; cap. 26,673m., res 48,145m., dep. 2,723,599m. (March 2006); Pres. AKIRA MIYAMA; 130 brs.

Hokuetsu Bank Ltd: 2-2-14, Otedori, Nagaoka 940-8650, Niigata; tel. (258) 353-111; fax (258) 375-113; internet www.hokuetsubank.co.jp; f. 1942; cap. 23,944m., res 41,553m., dep. 1,876,962m. (March 2006); Pres. KUNIAKI NOZAKI; 89 brs.

Hokuriku Bank Ltd: 1-2-26, Tsutsumichodori, Toyama 930-8637; tel. (764) 237-111; fax (764) 915-908; e-mail kokusaibu@hokugin.co.jp; internet www.hokugin.co.jp; f. 1877; cap. 140,409m., res 40,867m., dep. 5,184,175m. (March 2006); Pres. SHIGEO TAKAGI; 176 brs.

Hokuto Bank Ltd: 3-1-41, Nakadori, Akita 010-0001; tel. (188) 833-4211; fax (188) 832-1942; internet www.hokutobank.co.jp; f. 1895; as Masuda Bank Ltd, name changed as above after merger with Akita Akebono Bank in 1993; cap. 12,669m., dep. 1,037,000m. (2007); Pres. TAKEO KAGAYA; 84 brs.

Japan Net Bank: internet www.japannetbank.co.jp; f. 2000; Japan's first internet-only bank.

Joyo Bank Ltd: 2-5-5, Minami-machi, Mito-shi, Ibaraki 310-0021; tel. (29) 231-2151; fax (29) 255-6522; e-mail joyointl@po.net-ibaraki.ne.jp; internet www.joyobank.co.jp; f. 1935; cap. 85,113m., res 378,744m., dep. 6,619,057m. (March 2006); Chair. ISAO SHIBUYA; Pres. KUNIO ONIZAWA; 172 brs.

Juroku Bank Ltd: 8–26, Kandamachi, Gifu 500-8516; tel. (582) 652-111; fax (582) 661-698; internet www.juroku.co.jp; f. 1877; cap. 36,839m., res 117,657m., dep. 3,682,990m. (March 2006); Pres. NOBUO KOJIMA; 147 brs.

Kumamoto Family Bank Ltd: 6-29-20, Suizenji, Kumamoto 862-8601; tel. (96) 385-1111; fax (96) 385-4272; internet www.kf-bank.jp; f. 1992; cap. 34,262m., res 24,610m., dep. 1,205,345m. (March 2006); Pres. KAZUYUKI KAWAGUCHI.

Miyazaki Bank Ltd: 4-3-5, Tachibana-dori, Higashi, Miyazaki 880-0805; tel. (985) 273-131; fax (985) 225-952; e-mail kokusai@miyagin.co.jp; internet www.miyagin.co.jp; f. 1932; cap. 10,662m., res 77,996m., dep. 1,599,614m. (March 2006); Pres. ISAO SATO; 97 brs.

Mizuho Bank Ltd: 1-5 Uchisaiwai-cho, 1-chrome, Chiyoda-ku, Tokyo 100-0011; tel. (3) 3596-1111; fax (3) 3596-2179; internet www.mizuhobank.co.jp; f. 1971 as Dai-Ichi Kangyo Bank; merged with Fuji Bank and Industrial Bank of Japan to form above in 2002; cap. 650,000m., res 1,100,726m., dep. 62,754,614m. (March 2006); Pres. and CEO HIROSHI SAITO; 277 domestic brs, 17 overseas brs.

North Pacific Bank (Hokuyo Bank): 3-11, Odori Nishi, Chuo-ku, Sapporo 060-8661; tel. (11) 261-1416; fax (11) 232-6921; internet www.hokuyobank.co.jp; f. 1917 as Hokuyo Sogo Bank Ltd; assumed present name in 1989; cap. 71,101m., res 129,073m., dep. 5,764,534m. (March 2006); Chair. IWAO TAKAMUKI; Pres. RYUZO YOKOUCHI.

Resona Bank Ltd: 2-2-1, Bingo-machi, Chuo-ku, Osaka 540-8610; tel. (6) 6271-1221; internet www.resona-gr.co.jp; f. 1918; merged with Asahi Bank in 2002 and changed name as above; cap. 279,928m., res 622,973m., dep. 23,765,046m. (March 2007); Chair. EIJI HOSOYA; Pres. MASAAKI NOMURA; 367 brs.

Saitama Resona Bank Limited: 7-41, Tokiwa, Urawa-ku, Saitama 330-0061; tel. (48) 8242411; internet www.resona-gr.co.jp/saitamaresona; f. 2002; cap. 70,000m., res 168,790m., dep. 9,264,861m. (March 2007); Pres. KENJI KAWADA.

San-in Godo Bank Ltd: 10, Uomachi, Matsue 690-0062, Shimane; tel. (852) 551-000; fax (852) 273-398; internet www.gogin.co.jp; f. 1941; cap. 20,705m., res 45,366m., dep. 3,279,741m. (March 2006); Pres. HIROYUKI WAKASA; Chair. IWANE MARU; 153 brs.

Shiga Bank Ltd: 1-38, Hamamachi, Otsu 520-8686, Shiga; tel. (77) 521-2360; fax (77) 521-2892; e-mail sigajpjt@gold.ocn.ne.jp; internet www.shigagin.com; f. 1933; cap. 57,022m., res 192,148m., dep. 3,797,081m. (March 2007); Pres. KOICHI TAKATA; 134 brs.

Shikoku Bank Ltd: 1-1, Minami Harimaya-cho 1, Kochi; tel. (88) 823-2111; fax (88) 873-0322; internet www.shikokubank.co.jp; f. 1873; cap. 25,000m., res 39,192m., dep. 2,297,639m. (March 2006); Chair. MATSUICHI HAMADA; Pres. AKIHIRO AOKI; 121 brs.

Shimizu Bank: 3-1, Fujimi-cho, Shimizu-ku, Shozuoka-shi, Shizuoka 424-8715; tel. (543) 535-151; fax (543) 535-333; internet www.shimizubank.co.jp; f. 1928; cap. 8,670m., res 9,091m., dep. 1,191,821m. (March 2006); Chair. KOICHI SUGIYAMA; Pres. NORIJI YAMADA; 77 brs.

Shizuoka Bank Ltd: 1-10, Gofuku-cho, Shizuoka 420-8760; tel. (54) 261-3131; fax (54) 344-0090; internet www.shizuokabank.co.jp; f. 1943; cap. 90,845m., res 220,888m., dep. 7,441,389m. (March 2006); Chair. YASUO MATSUURA; Pres. and CEO KATSUNORI NAKANISHI; 161 domestic brs, 2 overseas brs.

Sumitomo Mitsui Banking Corpn: 1-2, Yuraku-cho, Chiyoda-ku, Tokyo 100-0006; tel. (3) 3230-8811; fax (3) 3239-4170; internet www.smbc.co.jp; f. 1895; merged with Sakura Bank Ltd in April 2001 and assumed present name; wholly owned subsidiary of Sumitomo Mitsui Financial Group (SMFG—established Dec. 2002); plans for merger between SMFG and Daiwa Securities announced Feb. 2005; cap. 664,986m., res 2,785,672m., dep. 80,711,397m. (March 2007); Chair. TEISUKE KITAYAMA; Pres. MASAYUKI OKU; 425 brs.

Toho Bank Ltd: 3-25, Ohmachi, Fukushima; tel. (24) 523-3131; fax (24) 524-1583; internet www.tohobank.co.jp; f. 1941; cap. 18,684m., res 18,728m., dep. 2,683,313m. (March 2006); Pres. TOSHIO SEYA.

Tokyo Star Bank: 1-6-16 Akasaka, Minato-ku, Tokyo; tel. (3) 3586-3111; fax (3) 3582-8949; internet www.tokyostarbank.co.jp; f. 1950 as Tokyo Sogo Bank, name changed as above in 2001; cap. 102,322m., res 21,478m., dep. 1,480,455m. (March 2007); Chair. HIROSHI OHASHI; Pres. TODD BUDGE; 35 brs.

Tokyo Tomin Bank Ltd: 2-3-11, Roppongi, Minato-ku, Tokyo 106-8525; tel. (3) 3582-8251; fax (3) 3582-1979; e-mail jdu02670@nifty.ne.jp; internet www.tominbank.co.jp; f. 1951; cap. 47,764m., res 24,939m., dep. 2,287,790m. (March 2006); Chair. HIROSHIGE NISHIZAWA; Pres. TETSUYA SHIINA; 72 brs.

Tomato Bank Ltd: 3-4 Bancho, 2-chome, Okayama 700-0811, Ehime; tel. (86) 2211010; fax (86) 2211040; internet www.tomatobank.co.jp; f. 1931 as Sanyo Sogo Bank; 1989 became a commercial bank and the name was changed to Tomato Bank Ltd; cap. 14,310m., res 19,652m., dep. 782,521m. (2006); Pres. TAKANOBU NAKAGAWA.

Principal Trust Banks

Chuo Mitsui Trust and Banking Co Ltd: 3-33-1, Shiba, Minato-ku, Chuo-ku, Tokyo 105-8574; tel. (3) 5232-3331; fax (3) 5232-8879; internet www.chuomitsui.co.jp; f. 1962; as Chuo Trust and Banking Co Ltd, name changed as above in 2000, following merger with Mitsui Trust and Banking Co Ltd; cap. 356,437m., res 239,448m., dep. 10,228,351m. (March 2006); Pres. KAZUO TANABE; 169 brs.

Mitsubishi UFJ Trust and Banking Corporation: 1-4-5, Marunouchi, Chiyoda-ku, Tokyo 100-8212; tel. (3) 3212-1211; fax (3)

3514-6660; internet www.tr.mufg.jp; subsidiary of Mitsubishi UFJ Financial Group; f. 2005 upon merger of parent cos Mitsubishi Tokyo Financial Group and UFJ Holdings to form Mitsubishi UFJ Financial Group; cap. 324,279m., res 949,046m., dep. 14,548,055m. (March 2006); Chair. AKIO UTSUMI; Pres. HARUYA UEHARA; 45 domestic brs, 5 overseas brs.

Mizuho Trust and Banking Co Ltd: 1-2-1, Yaesu, Chuo-ku, Tokyo 103-8670; tel. (3) 3278-8111; fax (3) 3281-6947; internet www.mizuho-tb.co.jp; fmrly Yasuda Trust and Banking Co Ltd; f. 1925; cap. 650,000m., res 1,100,726m., dep. 62,754,614m. (March 2006); Pres. and CEO TERUHIKO IKEDA; 38 brs.

Sumitomo Trust and Banking Co Ltd: 4-5-33, Kitahama, Chuo-ku, Osaka 540-8639; tel. (6) 6220-2121; fax (6) 6220-2043; e-mail ipda@sumitomotrust.co.jp; internet www.sumitomotrust.co.jp; f. 1925; cap. 287,517m., res 569,272m., dep. 15,700,499m. (March 2007); Chair. ATSUSHI TAKAHASHI; Pres. and CEO YUTAKA MORITA; 51 domestic brs, 4 overseas brs.

Long-Term Credit Banks

Aozora Bank: 3-1, Kudan-minami, Chiyoda-ku, Tokyo 102-8660; tel. (3) 3263-1111; fax (3) 3265-7024; e-mail sora@aozora.co.jp; internet www.aozorabank.co.jp; f. 1957; nationalized Dec. 1998, sold to consortium led by Softbank Corpn in Aug. 2000; fmrly The Nippon Credit Bank, name changed as above 2001; 62% owned by Cerberus Group; cap. 419,781m., res 32,714m., dep. 5,087,926m. (March 2006); Pres. and CEO HIROKAZU MIZUKAMI; Chair. MICHAEL E. ROSSI; 17 brs.

Mizuho Corporate Bank Ltd (The Industrial Bank of Japan Ltd): 3-3, Marunouchi, Chiyoda-ku, Tokyo 100-8210; tel. (3) 3214-1111; fax (3) 3201-7643; internet www.mizuhocbk.co.jp; f. 1902; renamed as above in 2002 following merger of the Dai-Ichi Kangyo Bank, the Fuji Bank and the Industrial Bank of Japan; medium- and long-term financing; cap. 1,070,965m., res 1,313,208m., dep. 51,241,476m. (March 2006); Pres. and CEO HIROSHI SAITO; 277 domestic brs, 21 overseas brs.

Shinsei Bank Ltd: 2-1-8, Uchisaiwai-cho, Chiyoda-ku, Tokyo 100-8501; tel. (3) 5511-5111; fax (3) 5511-5505; internet www.shinseibank.co.jp; f. 1952 as The Long-Term Credit Bank of Japan; nationalized Oct. 1998, sold to Ripplewood Holdings (USA), renamed as above June 2000; cap. 180,853m., res 299,442m., dep. 5,785,694m. (March 2006); Chair., Pres. and CEO THIERRY PORTÉ; 29 domestic brs, 1 overseas br.

Co-operative Bank

Shinkin Central Bank: 3-8-1, Kyobashi, Chuo-ku, Tokyo 104-0031; tel. (3) 3563-4111; fax (3) 3563-7553; internet www.shinkin.co.jp; f. 1950; cap. and res 924,458m., dep. 24,769,631m. (March 2007); Chair. YUKIHIKO NAGANO; Pres. and CEO YASUTAKA MIYAMOTO; 13 domestic brs, 2 overseas brs.

Principal Government Institutions

Agriculture, Forestry and Fisheries Finance Corporation: Koko Bldg, 1-9-3, Otemachi, Chiyoda-ku, Tokyo 100-0004; tel. (3) 3270-2261; e-mail intl@afc.go.jp; internet www.afc.go.jp; f. 1953; finances mainly plant and equipment investment; Gov. YUKI TAKAGI; Dep. Gov. SHIGEO OHARA; 22 brs.

Development Bank of Japan: 1-9-1, Otemachi, Chiyoda-ku, Tokyo 100-0004; tel. (3) 3244-1770; fax (3) 3245-1938; e-mail safukas@dbj.go.jp; internet www.dbj.go.jp; f. 1951 as the Japan Development Bank; renamed Oct. 1999 following consolidation with the Hokkaido and Tohoku Development Finance Public Corpn; provides long-term loans; subscribes for corporate bonds; guarantees corporate obligations; invests in specific projects; borrows funds from Govt and abroad; issues external bonds and notes; provides market information and consulting services for prospective entrants to Japanese market; scheduled for privatization in 2008; cap. 1,215,461m., res 1,079,554m., dep. 1,994,801m. (March 2005); Gov. TAKESHI KOMURA; Dep. Govs SUMIHITO OKAWA, KIMIO YAMAGUCHI; 10 domestic brs, 6 overseas brs.

Housing Loan Corporation: 1-4-10, Koraku, Bunkyo-ku, Tokyo 112-8570; tel. (3) 3812-1111; fax (3) 5800-8257; internet www.jyukou.go.jp; f. 1950; provides long-term capital for the construction of housing at low interest rates; cap. 97,200m. (1994); plans announced by Japanese Govt in 2001 to abolish the Housing Loan Corpn; Pres. SUSUMU TAKAHASHI; Vice-Pres. HIROYUKI ITOU; 12 brs.

Japan Bank for International Cooperation (JBIC): 1-4-1, Otemachi, Chiyoda-ku, Tokyo 100-8144; tel. (3) 5218-3101; fax (3) 5218-3955; internet www.jbic.go.jp; f. 1999 by merger of The Export-Import Bank of Japan (f. 1950) and The Overseas Economic Co-operation Fund (f. 1961); governmental financial institution, responsible for Japan's external economic policy and co-operation activities; cap. 7,876,744m., res 761,748m., dep. 1,776,254m. (March 2005); Gov. KYOSUKE SHINOZAWA.

Japan Finance Corporation for Small and Medium Enterprise: 1-9-3, Otemachi, Chiyoda-ku, Tokyo 100-0004; tel. (3) 3270-0505; fax (3) 3279-5910; internet www.jasme.go.jp; f. 1953; promotes long-term growth and devt of small businesses by providing the necessary funds and information on their use in accordance with national policy; cap. 1,479m. (March 2006); wholly subscribed by Govt; Pres. KOICHI MINAGUCHI; 58 brs.

Japan Post Bank Co Ltd: 1-3-2 Kasumigaseki, Chiyoda-ku, Tokyo 100-8798; internet www.jp-bank.japanpost.jp; f. 2006; 100% owned by Japan Post Holdings Co Ltd; cap. 3,500,000m., dep. 182,736,000m. (2007); Chair. and CEO KOJI FURUKAWA; Pres. SHOKICHI TAKAGI.

National Life Finance Corporation: Koko Bldg, 1-9-3, Otemachi, Chiyoda-ku, Tokyo 100-0004; tel. (3) 3270-1361; internet www.kokukin.go.jp; f. 1999 following consolidation of The People's Finance Corpn (f. 1949 to provide business funds, particularly to small enterprises unable to obtain loans from banks and other private financial institutions) and the Environmental Sanitation Business Finance Corpn (f. 1967 to improve sanitary facilities); cap. 369,000m. (March 2006); Gov. NOBUAKI USUI; 152 brs.

Norinchukin Bank (Central Co-operative Bank for Agriculture, Forestry and Fisheries): 1-13-2, Yuraku-cho, Chiyoda-ku, Tokyo 100; tel. (3) 3279-0111; fax (3) 3218-5177; internet www.nochubank.or.jp; f. 1923; main banker to agricultural, forestry and fisheries co-operatives; receives deposits from individual co-operatives, federations and agricultural enterprises; extends loans to these and to local govt authorities and public corpns; adjusts excess and shortage of funds within co-operative system; issues debentures, invests funds and engages in other regular banking business; cap. 1,465,017m., res 2,170,309m., dep. 62,486,080m. (March 2006); Pres. and CEO HIROFUMI UENO; 34 domestic brs, 5 overseas brs.

Shoko Chukin Bank (Central Co-operative Bank for Commerce and Industry): 2-10-17, Yaesu, Chuo-ku, Tokyo 104-0028; tel. (3) 3272-6111; fax (3) 3272-6169; e-mail JDK06560@nifty.ne.jp; internet www.shokochukin.go.jp; f. 1936; provides general banking services to facilitate finance for smaller enterprise co-operatives and other organizations formed mainly by small and medium-sized enterprises; issues debentures; scheduled for privatization in 2008; cap. 517,265m., res 122,916m., dep. 10,345,314m. (March 2005); Pres. TADASHI EZAKI; Dep. Pres. KENICHIRO OTAKE; 99 brs.

Other government financial institutions include the Japan Finance Corpn for Municipal Enterprises, the Small Business Credit Insurance Corpn and the Okinawa Development Finance Corpn.

Foreign Banks

In 2004 there were 84 foreign banks operating in Japan.

Bankers' Associations

Japanese Bankers Association: 1-3-1, Marunouchi, Chiyoda-ku, Tokyo 100-8216; tel. (3) 3216-3761; fax (3) 3201-5608; internet www.zenginkyo.or.jp; f. 1945; fmrly Federation of Bankers Associations of Japan; 128 full mems, 65 associate mems, 62 special mems, 3 bank holding company mems; Chair. TERUNOBU MAEDA.

Tokyo Bankers Association, Inc: 1-3-1, Marunouchi, Chiyoda-ku, Tokyo 100-8216; tel. (3) 3216-3761; fax (3) 3201-5608; f. 1945; 105 mem. banks; conducts the above Association's administrative business; Chair. MASAYUKI OKU.

National Association of Labour Banks: 2-5-15, Kanda Surugadai, Chiyoda-ku, Tokyo 101-0062; tel. (3) 3295-6721; fax (3) 3295-6752; Pres. TETSUEI TOKUGAWA.

Regional Banks Association of Japan: 3-1-2, Uchikanda, Chiyoda-ku, Tokyo 101-0047; tel. (3) 3252-5171; fax (3) 3254-8664; f. 1936; 64 mem. banks; Chair. SADAAKI HIROSAWA.

Second Association of Regional Banks: 5, Sanban-cho, Chiyoda-ku, Tokyo 102-0075; tel. (3) 3262-2181; fax (3) 3262-2339; f. 1989; fmrly National Asscn of Sogo Banks; 65 commercial banks; Chair. MASANAO TAKEI.

STOCK EXCHANGES

Japan Securities Exchange Inc (Jasdaq): 1-5-8, Kayabacho Nihonbashi, Chuo-ku, Tokyo 103-0025; tel. (3) 3669-1199; fax (3) 3669-3308; internet www.jasdaq.co.jp; f. 1976; Chair. TAKASHI FUJIWARA; Pres. and CEO TAKASHI TSUTSUI.

Nagoya Stock Exchange: 3-3-17, Sakae, Naka-ku, Nagoya 460-0008; tel. (52) 262-3172; fax (52) 241-1527; e-mail kikaku@nse.or.jp; internet www.nse.or.jp; f. 1949; Pres. NOBORU KUROYANAGI; Exec. Vice-Pres. SATOSHI NISHIKAWA.

Osaka Securities Exchange: 1-8-16, Kitahama, Chuo-ku, Osaka 541-0041; tel. (6) 4706-0875; fax (6) 6231-2639; e-mail koho@ose.or.jp; internet www.ose.or.jp; f. 1949; 83 regular transaction partners, 5 transaction partners in futures and options trading, 2 IPO transaction partners; Pres. and CEO MICHIO YONEDA.

JAPAN

Sapporo Securities Exchange: 5-14-1, Nishi, Minami Ichijo, Chuo-ku, Sapporo 060-0061; tel. (11) 241-6171; Pres. YOSHIRO ITOH.

Tokyo Stock Exchange, Inc: 2-1, Nihonbashi-kabuto-cho, Chuo-ku, Tokyo 103-8220; tel. (3) 3666-0141; fax (3) 3662-0547; internet www.tse.or.jp; f. 1949; 107 general trading participants, 79 bond futures trading participants, 2 stock index futures trading participants (Nov. 2003); cap. 11,500m., issued shares 2,300,000 (June 2005); Chair. TAIZO NISHIMURO; Pres. and CEO ATSUSHI SAITO; Sr Man. Dir and CFO YASUO TOBIYAMA; 737 employees (June 2005).

Supervisory Body

The Securities and Exchange Surveillance Commission: 3-1-1, Kasumigaseki, Chiyoda-ku, Tokyo 100-8967; tel. (3) 3581-7868; fax (3) 5251-2151; internet www.fsa.go.jp/sesc; f. 1992 for the surveillance of securities and financial futures transactions; Chair. TAKEO TAKAHASHI.

INSURANCE

Principal Life Companies

AIG Edison Life Insurance CXo: 1-12-1, Dogenzaka, Tokyo 150-8674; tel. (3) 5457-8100; internet www.aigedison.co.jp; fmrly GE Edison Life Insurance Co, itself fmrly Toho Mutual Life Insurance Co; acquired by American International Group, Inc (AIG) in 2003; Pres. KAZUNORI KATAOKA.

AIG Star Life Insurance Co Ltd: Triton Square Z, 1-8-2, Harumi, Chuo-ku, Tokyo 104-6231; tel. (3) 6220-0011; internet www.aigstar-life.co.jp; fmrly Chiyoda Mutual Life Insurance Co, acquired by American International Group, Inc (AIG) in 2001.

Aioi Life Insurance Co Ltd: 1-28-1, Ebisu, Shibuya-ku, Tokyo 150-0013; internet www.ioi-life.co.jp.

American Family Life Assurance Co of Columbus AFLAC Japan: Shinjuku Mitsui Bldg, 12th Floor, 2-1-1, Nishishinjuku, Shinjuku-ku, Tokyo 163-0456; tel. (3) 3344-2701; fax (3) 0424-3001; internet www.aflac.co.jp; f. 1974; Chair. YOSHIKI OTAKE; Pres. HIDEFUMI MATSUI.

American Life Insurance Co (Japan): 1-1-3, Marunouchi, Chiyoda-ku, Tokyo 100-0005; tel. (3) 3284-4111; fax (3) 3284-3874; internet www.alico.co.jp; f. 1972; Pres. TOMIO MIYAMOTO.

Asahi Mutual Life Insurance Co: 1-7-3, Nishishinjuku, Shinjuku-ku, Tokyo 163-8611; tel. (3) 3342-3111; fax (3) 3346-9397; internet www.asahi-life.co.jp; f. 1888; Pres. YUZURU FUJITA.

AXA Japan Holding Co Ltd: 1-2-19, Higashi, Shibuya-ku, Tokyo 150-8020; tel. (3) 3407-6210; internet www.axa.co.jp; Pres. and CEO PHILIPPE DONNET.

Cardif Assurance Vie: 9/F Infoss Tower, 20-1, Sakuragaoka-cho, Shibuya-ku, Tokyo 150-0031; internet www.cardif.co.jp/vie; f. 2000; Pres. ATSUSHI SAKAUCHI.

Dai-ichi Mutual Life Insurance Co: 1-13-1, Yuraku-cho, Chiyoda-ku, Tokyo 100-8411; tel. (3) 3216-1211; fax (3) 5221-8139; internet www.dai-ichi-life.co.jp; f. 1902; Chair. TAKAHIDE SAKURAI; Pres. KATSUTOSHI SAITO.

Fuji Life Insurance Co Ltd: 1-18-17, Minamisenba, Chuo-ku, Osaka-shi 542-0081; tel. (6) 6261-0284; fax (6) 6261-0113; internet www.fujiseimei.co.jp; f. 1996; Pres. YOSHIAKI YONEMURA.

Fukoku Mutual Life Insurance Co: 2-2-2, Uchisaiwai-cho, Chiyoda-ku, Tokyo 100-0011; tel. (3) 3508-1101; fax (3) 3597-0383; internet www.fukoku-life.co.jp; f. 1923; Chair. TAKASHI KOBAYASHI; Pres. TOMOFUMI AKIYAMA.

Gibraltar Life Insurance Co Ltd: 4-4-1, Nihonbashi, Hongoku-cho, Chuo-ku, Tokyo 103-0021; tel. (3) 3270-8511; fax (3) 3231-8276; internet www.gib-life.co.jp; f. 1947; fmrly Kyoei Life Insurance Co Ltd, declared bankrupt Oct. 2000; Pres. KAZUO MAEDA.

Hartford Life Insurance K. K.: Kamiyacho MT Bldg, 3/F, 4-3-20, Toranomon, Minato-Ku, Tokyo 105-0001; tel. (3) 5777-8000; fax (3) 5777-8036; internet www.hartfordlife.co.jp; f. 2000.

ING Life Insurance Co Ltd: 26th Floor, New Otani Garden Court, 4-1, Kioi-cho, Chiyoda-ku, Tokyo 102-0094; tel. (3) 5210-0300; fax (3) 5210-0430; internet www.ing-life.co.jp; f. 1985; Pres. MAKOTO CHIBA.

Japan Post Insurance: 1-3-2 Kasumigaseki, Chiyoda-ku, Tokyo 100-8798; tel. (3) 3504-4411; internet www.jp-life.japanpost.jp; f. 2006; 100% owned by Japan Post Holdings Co Ltd; Chair. and CEO JOSUKE SHINDO; Pres. IZUMI YAMASHITA.

Kyoei Kasai Shinrai Life Insurance Co Ltd: Shimbashi 1-18-6, Minato-ku, Tokyo 105-8604; tel. (3) 5372-2100; fax (3) 5372-7701; internet www.kyoeikasai.co.jp; f. 1996; Pres. SUSUMU TAMURA.

Manulife Life Insurance Co: 4-34-1, Kokuryo-cho, Chofu-shi, Tokyo 182-8621; tel. (3) 2442-7120; fax (3) 2442-7977; e-mail craig_bromley@manulife.com; internet www.manulife.co.jp; f. 1999; fmrly Manulife Century Life Insurance Co; absorbed bankrupt Daihyaku Mutual Life Insurance Co in 2001; Pres. and CEO CRAIG BROMLEY.

MassMutual Life Insurance Co: Cerulean Tower, 26-1, Sakuragaoka-cho, Shibuya-ku, Tokyo 150-8512; internet www.massmutual.co.jp; Pres. HIDEO HIRANO.

Meiji Yasuda Life Insurance Co: 2-1-1, Marunouchi, Chiyoda-ku, Tokyo 100-0005; tel. (3) 3283-8111; fax (3) 3215-5219; internet www.meijiyasuda.co.jp; f. 2004 by merger of Meiji Life Insurance Co (f. 1881) and Yasuda Mutual Life Insurance Co (f. 1880); Chair. KENJIRO HATA; Pres. KENJI MATSUO.

Mitsui Life Insurance Co Ltd: 1-2-3, Otemachi, Chiyoda-ku, Tokyo 100-8123; tel. (3) 3211-6111; fax (3) 5252-7265; internet www.mitsui-seimei.co.jp; f. 1927; Chair. KOSHIRO SAKATA; Pres. AKIRA MIYAKE.

Nippon Life Insurance Co (Nissay): 3-5-12, Imabashi, Chuo-ku, Osaka 541-8501; tel. (6) 6209-4500; e-mail hosokawa15560@nissay.co.jp; internet www.nissay.co.jp; f. 1889; Chair. IKUO UNO; Pres. KUNIE OKAMOTO.

Nipponkoa Life Insurance Co Ltd: 3-4-2, Tsukiji, Chuo-ku, Tokyo 104-8407; tel. (3) 5565-8080; fax (3) 5565-8365; internet www.nipponkoa.co.jp/life; f. 1996; formed by merger of Nippon Fire and Marine Insurance and Koa Fire and Marine Insurance.

ORIX Life Insurance Corpn: Shinjuku Monolith, 2-3-1, Nishishinjuku, Shinjuku-ku, Tokyo 163-0923; tel. (3) 5326-2600; fax (3) 5326-2760; internet www.orix.co.jp; f. 1991; Chair. SHOGO KAJINISHI; Pres. IZUMI MIZUMORI.

Prudential Life Insurance Co Ltd: 1-7, Kojimachi, Chiyoda-ku, Tokyo 102-0083; tel. (3) 3221-0961; fax (3) 3221-2305; internet www.prudential.co.jp; f. 1987; Chair. KIYOFUMI SAKAGUCHI; Pres. YUTAKA SAMMORI.

Sompo Japan DIY Life Insurance Co Ltd: 5-68-2, Nakano, Nakano-ku, Tokyo 164-0001; tel. (3) 5345-7603; fax (3) 5345-7608; internet www.diy.co.jp; f. 1999; Pres. HITOSHI KASE.

Sompo Japan Himawari Life Insurance Co Ltd: Shinjuku Mitsui Bldg, 35/F, 1-2-1, Nishi-Shinjuku, Shinjuku-ku, Tokyo; internet www.himawari-life.com; f. 2002; Pres. YASAYUKI TAYAMA.

Sony Life Insurance Co Ltd: 1-1-1, Minami-Aoyama, Minato-ku, Tokyo 107-8585; tel. (3) 3475-8811; fax (3) 3475-8914; internet www.sonylife.co.jp; Chair. TSUNAO HASHIMOTO; Pres. TARO OKUDA.

Sumitomo Life Insurance Co: 7-18-24, Tsukiji, Chuo-ku, Tokyo 104-8430; tel. (3) 5550-1100; fax (3) 5550-1160; internet www.sumitomolife.co.jp; f. 1907; Pres. YOSHIO SATO.

T & D Holdings Inc: 2-7-9, Nihonbashi, Chuo-ku, Tokyo 103-0027; tel. (3) 3231-8685; fax (3) 3231-8893; internet www.td-holdings.co.jp; f. 1895; fmrly Tokyo Mutual Life Insurance Co; T & D Financial Life Insurance Co Holdings company formed in April 2004 through merger of T & D Financial Life Insurance Co, Taiyo Mutual Life Insurance Co and Daido Life Insurance Co; Pres. NAOTERU MIYATO.

Tokio Marine & Nichido Life Insurance Co Ltd: 5-3-16, Ginza, Chuo-ku, Tokyo 106-0041; tel. (3) 5223-2111; fax (3) 5223-2165; internet www.tmn-anshin.co.jp; Pres. SUKEAKI OHTA.

Yamato Mutual Life Insurance Co: 1-1-7, Uchisaiwai-cho, Chiyoda-ku, Tokyo 100-0011; tel. (3) 3508-3111; fax (3) 3508-3118; internet www.yamato-life.co.jp; f. 1911; Pres. TAKEO NAKAZONO.

Zurich Life Insurance Co Ltd: Shinanomachi Rengakan, 35, Shinanomachi, Shinjuku-ku, Tokyo 160-0016; tel. (3) 5361-2700; fax (3) 5361-2728; internet www.zurichlife.co.jp; f. 1996; Pres. KENICHI NOGAMI.

Principal Non-Life Companies

ACE Insurance: Arco Tower, 1-8-1, Shimomeguro, Meguro-ku, Tokyo 153-0064; tel. (3) 5740-0600; fax (3) 5740-0608; internet www.ace-insurance.co.jp; f. 1999; Chair. FUMIO TOKUHIRA; Pres. TAKASHI IMAI.

Aioi Insurance Co Ltd: 1-28-1, Ebisu, Shibuya-ku, Tokyo 150-8488; tel. (3) 5424-0101; internet www.ioi-sonpo.co.jp; f. 2001; from the merger of Dai-Tokyo Fire & Marine Insurance Co Ltd and Chiyoda Fire & Marine Insurance Co Ltd; Pres. TADASHI KODAMA.

Allianz Fire and Marine Insurance Japan Ltd: MITA N. N. Bldg, 4th Floor, 4-1-23, Shiba, Minato-ku, Tokyo 108-0014; tel. (3) 5442-6500; fax (3) 5442-6509; e-mail admin@allianz.co.jp; internet www.allianz.co.jp; f. 1990; Chair. HEINZ DOLLBERG; Pres. ALEXANDER ANKEL.

The Asahi Fire and Marine Insurance Co Ltd: 2-6-2, Kaji-cho, Chiyoda-ku, Tokyo 101-8655; tel. (3) 3254-2211; fax (3) 3254-2296; e-mail asahifmi@blue.ocn.ne.jp; internet www.asahikasai.co.jp; f. 1951; Pres. KAZUHO OYA.

AXA Japan Holding Co Ltd: Ariake Frontier Bldg, Tower A, 3-1-25, Ariake Koto-ku, Tokyo 135-0063; tel. (3) 3570-8900; fax (3) 3570-8911; internet www.axa.co.jp; f. 1998; Pres. GUY MARCILLAT.

The Daido Fire and Marine Insurance Co Ltd: 1-12-1, Kumoji, Naha-shi, Okinawa 900-8586; tel. (98) 867-1161; fax (98) 862-8362; internet www.daidokasai.co.jp; f. 1971; Pres. NAOTO MIRAYA.

JAPAN

The Fuji Fire and Marine Insurance Co Ltd: 1-18-11, Minami-senba, Chuo-ku, Osaka 542-8567; tel. (6) 6271-2741; fax (6) 6266-7115; internet www.fujikasai.co.jp; f. 1918; Pres. Yasuo Oda.

The Japan Earthquake Reinsurance Co Ltd: Kobuna-cho, Fuji Plaza, 4th Floor, 8-1, Nihonbashi, Kobuna-cho, Chuo-ku, Tokyo 103-0024; tel. (3) 3664-6107; fax (3) 3664-6169; e-mail kanri@nihonjishin.co.jp; f. 1966; Pres. Kazumoto Adachi.

JI Accident & Fire Insurance Co Ltd: A1 Bldg, 20-5, Ichiban-cho, Chiyoda-ku, Tokyo 102-0082; tel. (3) 3237-2045; fax (3) 3237-2250; internet www.jihoken.co.jp; f. 1989; Pres. Mitsuhito Minamisawa.

The Kyoei Mutual Fire and Marine Insurance Co: 1-18-6, Shimbashi, Minato-ku, Tokyo 105-8604; tel. (3) 3504-2335; fax (3) 3508-7680; e-mail reins.intl@kyoeikasai.co.jp; internet www.kyoeikasai.co.jp; f. 1942; Pres. Susumu Tamura.

Meiji Yasuda General Insurance Co Ltd: 2-11-1, Kanda-tsukasa-cho, Chiyoda-ku, Tokyo 101-0048; tel. (3) 3257-3111; fax (3) 3257-3295; internet www.meijiyasuda-sonpo.co.jp; f. 1996; Pres. Seiji Nishi.

Mitsui Direct General Insurance Co Ltd: 1-4-27, Koraku Bun-kyou-ku, Tokyo 112-0004; tel. (3) 5804-7711; internet www.mitsui-direct.co.jp; f. 1996; Pres. Toshio Kitamura.

Mitsui Sumitomo Insurance Co Ltd: 27-2, Shinkawa 2-chome, Chuo-ku, Tokyo 104-8252; tel. (3) 3297-1111; internet www.ms-ins.com; f. 2001; formed by merger of Mitsui Marine and Fire Insurance and Sumitomo Marine and Fire Insurance; Pres. and CEO Toshiaki Egashira; Chair. Yoshiaki Shin.

The Nipponkoa Insurance Co Ltd: 3-7-3, Kasumigaseki, Chiyoda-ku, Tokyo 100-8965; tel. (3) 3593-3111; fax (3) 3593-5388; internet www.nipponkoa.co.jp; f. 1892; fmrly The Nippon Fire and Marine Insurance Co Ltd before merging with The Koa Fire and Marine Insurance Co Ltd; acquired Taiyo Fire and Marine Insurance Co Ltd in 2002; Pres. and CEO Ken Matsuzawa.

Nissay Dowa General Insurance Co Ltd: St Luke's Tower, 8-1, Akashi-cho, Chuo-ku, Tokyo 104-8556; tel. (3) 3542-5511; fax (3) 5550-0318; internet www.nissaydowa.co.jp; f. 2001; formed by merger of Nissay General Insurance Co Ltd and Dowa Fire and Marine Insurance Co Ltd; Pres. Ichiro Tateyama; Chair. Masao Okazaki.

The Nisshin Fire and Marine Insurance Co Ltd: 2-3, Kanda Surugadai, Chiyoda-ku, Tokyo 100-8329; tel. (3) 5282-5534; fax (3) 5282-5582; e-mail nisshin@mb.infoweb.ne.jp; internet www.nisshinfire.co.jp; f. 1908; Pres. Hiroshi Miyajima.

Saison Automobile and Fire Insurance Co Ltd: Sunshine 60 Bldg, 3-1-1, Higashi Ikebukuro, Toshima-ku, Tokyo 170-6068; tel. (3) 3988-2572; fax (3) 3980-7367; internet www.ins-saison.co.jp; f. 1982; Pres. Koshin Matuzawa.

Secom General Insurance Co Ltd: 2-6-2, Hirakawa-cho, Chiyoda-ku, Tokyo 103-8645; tel. (3) 5216-6129; fax (3) 5216-6149; internet www.secom-sonpo.co.jp; Pres. Yasuyuki Yoshida.

Sompo Japan Insurance Inc: 26-1, Nishi-Shinjuku 1-chome, Shinjuku-ku, Tokyo 160-8338; tel. (3) 3349-3111; fax (3) 3349-4697; internet www.sompo-japan.co.jp; f. 2002 by merger of Yasuda Fire and Marine Insurance (f. 1888) and Nissan Fire and Marine Insurance (f. 1911); Pres. Matatoshi Sato.

Sonpo 24 Insurance Co Ltd: Sunshine 60 Bldg, 44/F, 3-1-1, Higashi-Ikebukuro, Toshima-ku, Tokyo 170-6044; tel. (3) 5957-0111; internet www.sonpo24.co.jp; Pres. Atsushi Kumanomido.

Sony Assurance Inc: Aromia Square 11/F, 5-37-1, Kamata, Ota-ku, Tokyo 144-8721; tel. (3) 5744-0300; fax (3) 5744-0480; internet www.sonysonpo.co.jp; f. 1999; Pres. Shinichi Yamamoto.

The Sumi-Sei General Insurance Co Ltd: Sumitomo Life Yotsuya Bldg, 8-2, Honshio-cho, Shinjuku-ku, Tokyo 160-0003; tel. (3) 5360-6229; fax (3) 5360-6991; internet www.sumisei-sonpo.co.jp; f. 1996; Chair. Hideo Nishimoto; Pres. Matatoshi Izumi.

The Toa Reinsurance Co Ltd: 3-6, Kanda Surugadai, Chiyoda-ku, Tokyo 101-8703; tel. (3) 3253-3177; fax (3) 3253-5298; internet www.toare.co.jp; f. 1940; Pres. and CEO Teruhiko Ohtani.

Tokio Marine & Nichido Fire Insurance Co Ltd: 1-2-1, Marunouchi, Chiyoda-ku, Tokyo 100-8050; tel. (3) 3212-6211; internet www.tokiomarine-nichido.co.jp; f. 2004; Pres. Kunio Ishihara.

Insurance Associations

The General Insurance Association of Japan Inc (Nihon Songai Hoken Kyokai): Non-Life Insurance Bldg, 2-9, Kanda Awaji-cho, Chiyoda-ku, Tokyo 101-8335; tel. (3) 3255-1439; fax (3) 3255-1234; e-mail kokusai@sonpo.or.jp; internet www.sonpo.or.jp; f. 1946; 23 mems (Jan. 2008); Chair. Toshiaki Egashira; Exec. Dir Katsuo Handa.

The Life Insurance Association of Japan (Seimei Hoken Kyokai): Shin-Kokusai Bldg, 3-4-1, Marunouchi, Chiyoda-ku, Tokyo 100-0005; tel. (3) 3286-2652; fax (3) 3286-2630; internet www.seiho.or.jp; f. 1908; 41 mem. cos (Jan. 2008); Chair. Kunie Okamoto.

Nippon Export and Investment Insurance: Chiyoda First Bldg, East Wing 3/F, 3-8-1, Nishikanda, Chiyoda-ku, Tokyo; internet www.nexi.go.jp; f. 2001; Chair. and CEO Hidahiro Konno.

Non-Life Insurance Rating Organization of Japan: 1-9, Kanda-nishikicho, Chiyoda-ku, Tokyo 101-0054; tel. (3) 3233-4762; fax (3) 3295-9301; e-mail service@nliro.or.jp; internet www.nliro.or.jp; f. 2002; 35 mems (April 2007); Chair. Akio Morishima; Senior Exec. Dir Yasuyuki Tayama.

Trade and Industry

CHAMBERS OF COMMERCE AND INDUSTRY

The Japan Chamber of Commerce and Industry (Nippon Shoko Kaigi-sho): 3-2-2, Marunouchi, Chiyoda-ku, Tokyo 100-0005; tel. (3) 3283-7851; fax (3) 3216-6497; e-mail info@jcci.or.jp; internet www.jcci.or.jp; f. 1922; the central org. of all chambers of commerce and industry in Japan; mems 517 local chambers of commerce and industry; Chair. Tadashi Okamura; Pres. Toshio Nakamura.

Principal chambers include:

Kobe Chamber of Commerce and Industry: 6-1, Minatojima-nakamachi, Chuo-ku, Kobe 650-8543; tel. (78) 303-5806; fax (78) 306-2348; e-mail info@kobe-cci.or.jp; internet www2.kobe-cci.or.jp/index_e.html; f. 1878; 12,000 mems; Chair. Koshi Mizukoshi; Pres. Hitoshi Nakanishi.

Kyoto Chamber of Commerce and Industry: 240, Shoshoi-cho, Ebisugawa-agaru, Karasumadori, Nakakyo-ku, Kyoto 604-0862; tel. (75) 212-6450; fax (75) 251-0743; e-mail kaiinbu@kyo.or.jp; internet www.kyo.or.jp/kyoto; f. 1882; 11,500 mems; Chair. Yoshio Tateisi; Pres. Tuneoki Okuhara.

Nagoya Chamber of Commerce and Industry: 2-10-19, Sakae, Naka-ku, Nagoya, Aichi 460-8422; tel. (52) 223-5722; fax (52) 232-5751; e-mail info@nagoya-cci.or.jp; internet www.nagoya-cci.or.jp; f. 1881; 17,000 mems; Chair. Kunihiko Okada.

Naha Chamber of Commerce and Industry: 2-2-10, Kume Naha, Okinawa; tel. (98) 868-3758; fax (98) 866-9834; e-mail cci-naha@nahacci.or.jp; internet www.nahacci.or.jp; f. 1927; 4,874 mems; Chair. Akira Sakima; Pres. Kosei Yonemura.

Osaka Chamber of Commerce and Industry: 2-8, Hommachi-bashi, Chuo-ku, Osaka 540-0029; tel. (6) 6944-6400; fax (6) 6944-6248; e-mail intl@osaka.cci.or.jp; internet www.osaka.cci.or.jp; f. 1878; 29,908 mems; Chair. Akio Nomura; Pres. Masahiro Nadamoto.

Tokyo Chamber of Commerce and Industry: 3-2-2, Marunouchi, Chiyoda-ku, Tokyo 100-0005; tel. (3) 3283-7523; fax (3) 3216-6497; e-mail kokusai@tokyo-cci.or.jp; internet www.tokyo-cci.or.jp; f. 1878; 83,292 mems; Chair. Tadashi Okamura; Pres. Toshio Nakamura.

Yokohama Chamber of Commerce and Industry: Sangyo Boueki Center Bldg, 8th Floor, Yamashita-cho, Naka-ku, Yokohama 231-8524; tel. (45) 671-7400; fax (45) 671-7410; e-mail info@yokohama-cci.or.jp; internet www.yokohama-cci.or.jp; f. 1880; 14,965 mems; Chair. Masayoshi Takanashi; Pres. Namio Oba.

INDUSTRIAL AND TRADE ASSOCIATIONS
General

The Association for the Promotion of International Trade, Japan (JAPIT): 1-26-5, Toranomon, Minato-ku, Tokyo; tel. (3) 3506-8261; fax (3) 3506-8260; internet www.japitcn.com; f. 1954 to promote trade with the People's Repub. of China; 700 mems; Chair. Yohei Kono.

Industry Club of Japan: 1-4-6, Marunouchi, Chiyoda-ku, Tokyo; tel. (3) 3281-1711; fax (3) 3281-1797; e-mail soumu@kogyoclub.or.jp; internet www.kogyoclub.or.jp; f. 1917 to develop closer relations between industrialists at home and abroad and promote expansion of Japanese business activities; c. 1,600 mems; Pres. Gaishi Hiraiwa; Exec. Dir Kouichirou Shinno.

Japan Commercial Arbitration Association: Taishoseimei Hibiya Bldg, 1-9-1, Yurakucho, Chiyoda-ku, Tokyo 100-1006; tel. (3) 3287-3061; fax (3) 3287-3064; e-mail info@jcaa.or.jp; internet www.jcaa.or.jp; f. 1950; 1,012 mems; provides facilities for mediation, conciliation and arbitration in international trade disputes; Pres. Nobuo Yamaguchi.

Japan External Trade Organization (JETRO): 6/F, Ark Mori Bldg, 1-12-32, Akasaka-cho, Minato-ku, Tokyo 107-6006; tel. (3) 3582-5511; fax (3) 3582-5662; e-mail seh@jetro.go.jp; internet www.jetro.go.jp; f. 1958; information on international trade, investment, import promotion, exhibitions of foreign products; Chair. and CEO Yasuo Hayashi; Pres. Tadashi Izawa.

Japan Federation of Smaller Enterprise Organizations (JFSEO) (Nippon Chusokigyo Dantai Renmei): 2-8-4, Nihonbashi,

Kayaba-cho, Chuo-ku, Tokyo 103-0025; tel. (3) 3669-6862; f. 1948; 18 mems and c. 1,000 co-operative socs; Pres. MASATAKA TOYODA; Chair. of Int. Affairs SEIICHI ONO.

Japan General Merchandise Exporters' Association: 2-4-1, Hamamatsu-cho, Minato-ku, Tokyo; tel. (3) 3435-3471; fax (3) 3434-6739; f. 1953; 40 mems; Pres. TADAYOSHI NAKAZAWA.

Japan Productivity Center for Socio-Economic Development (JPC-SED) (Shakai Keizai Seisansei Honbu): 3-1-1, Shibuya, Shibuya-ku, Tokyo 150-8307; tel. (3) 3409-1112; fax (3) 3409-1986; internet www.jpc-sed.or.jp; f. 1994 following merger between Japan Productivity Center and Social Economic Congress of Japan; 10,000 mems; concerned with management problems and research into productivity; Chair. JIRO USHIO; Pres. TSUNEAKI TANIGUCHI.

Keizai Doyukai (Japan Association of Corporate Executives): 1-4-6, Marunouchi, Chiyoda-ku, Tokyo 100-0005; tel. (3) 3211-1271; fax (3) 3212-3774; e-mail contact@doyukai.or.jp; internet www.doyukai.or.jp; f. 1946; mems: c. 1,400; corporate executives concerned with national and international economic and social policies; Chair. MASAMITSU SAKURAI.

Nihon Boeki-Kai (Japan Foreign Trade Council, Inc): World Trade Center Bldg, 6th Floor, 2-4-1, Hamamatsu-cho, Minato-ku, Tokyo 105-6106; tel. (3) 3435-5959; fax (3) 3435-5969; e-mail mail@jftc.or.jp; internet www.jftc.or.jp; f. 1947; 192 mems; Chair. MIKIO SASAKI; Exec. Man. Dir MASAYOSHI AMANO; Man. Dir TOSHIO SAMPEI.

Chemicals

Japan Chemical Industry Association: Sumitomo Fudosan Rokko Bldg, 4-1, Shinkawa 1-chome, Chuo-ku, Tokyo 104-0033; tel. (3) 3297-2576; fax (3) 3297-2606; e-mail chemical@jcia-net.or.jp; internet www.nikkakyo.org; f. 1948; 266 mems; Chair. RYUICHI TOMIZAWA.

Japan Cosmetic Industry Association: Hatsumei Bldg, 2-9-14, Toranomon, Minato-ku, Tokyo 105-0001; tel. (3) 3502-0576; fax (3) 3502-0829; e-mail info@jcia.org; internet www.jcia.org; f. 1959; 687 mem. cos; Chair. REIJIRO KOBAYASHI.

Japan Gas Association: 1-15-12, Toranomon, Minato-ku, Tokyo 105-0001; tel. (3) 3502-0116; fax (3) 3502-3676; internet www.gas.or.jp; f. 1947; 213 mems; Chair. AKIO NOMURA; Vice-Chair. and Sr Man. Dir HARUKI TAKAHASHI.

Japan Perfumery and Flavouring Association: Saeki No. 3 Bldg, 3/F, 37, Kandakonya-cho, Chiyoda-ku, Tokyo 101-0035; tel. and fax (3) 3526-7855; f. 1947; Chair. YONEJIRO KORAYASHI.

Japan Pharmaceutical Manufacturers' Association: Torii Nihonbashi Bldg, 3-4-1, Nihonbashi Hon-cho, Chuo-ku, Tokyo 103-0023; tel. (3) 3241-0326; fax (3) 3242-1767; internet www.jpma.or.jp; 71 mems; Pres. HATSUO AOKI.

Photo-Sensitized Materials Manufacturers' Association: JCII Bldg, 25, Ichiban-cho, Chiyoda-ku, Tokyo 102-0082; tel. (3) 5276-3561; fax (3) 5276-3563; f. 1948; Pres. SHIGETAKA KOMORI.

Fishing and Pearl Cultivation

Japan Fisheries Association (Dainippon Suisankai): Sankaido Bldg, 1-9-13, Akasaka, Minato-ku, Tokyo 107-0052; tel. (3) 3585-6683; fax (3) 3582-2337; e-mail japan@suisankai.or.jp; internet www.suisankai.or.jp; Pres. ISAO NAKASU.

Japan Pearl Export and Processing Co-operative Association: 3-7, Kyobashi, Chuo-ko, Tokyo; f. 1951; 130 mems.

Japan Pearl Exporters' Association: 122, Higashi-machi, Chuo-ku, Kobe; tel. (78) 331-4031; fax (78) 331-4345; e-mail jpeakobe@lime.ocn.ne.jp; internet www.japan-pearl.com; f. 1954; 56 mems; Pres. YOSHIHIRO SHIMIZU.

Machinery and Precision Equipment

Electronic Industries Association of Japan: 3-2-2, Marunouchi, Chiyoda-ku, Tokyo 100-0005; tel. (3) 3213-5861; fax (3) 3213-5863; e-mail pao@eiaj.or.jp; internet www.eiaj.or.jp; f. 1948; 540 mems; Chair. FUMIO SATO.

Japan Camera Industry Association: JCII Bldg, 25, Ichibancho, Chiyoda-ku, Tokyo 102-0082; tel. (3) 5276-3891; fax (3) 5276-3893; internet www.photo-jcia.gr.jp; f. 1954; Pres. MASATOSHI KISHIMOTO.

Japan Clock and Watch Association: Kudan Sky Bldg, 1-12-11, Kudan-kita, Chiyoda-ku, Tokyo 102-0073; tel. (3) 5276-3411; fax (3) 5276-3414; internet www.jcwa.or.jp; Chair. TSUNEO NAGAI.

Japan Electric Association: 1-7-1, Yuraku-cho, Chiyoda-ku, Tokyo 100-0006; tel. (3) 3216-0551; fax (3) 3214-6005; internet www.denki.or.jp; f. 1921; 4,610 mems; Pres. TATSUO KAWAI.

Japan Electric Measuring Instruments Manufacturers' Association (JEMIMA): 1-2-18, Shiba Daimon, Minato-ku, Tokyo 105-0012; tel. (3) 3408-8113; fax (3) 3408-0575; e-mail o-mitani@jemima.or.jp; internet www.jemima.or.jp; 117 mems; Gen. Man. OSAMU MITANI.

Japan Electrical Manufacturers' Association: 17-4, Ichiban-cho, Chiyoda-ku, Tokyo 102-0082; tel. (3) 3556-5881; fax (3) 3556-5889; internet www.jema-net.or.jp; f. 1948; 284 mems; Chair. ETSUHIKO SHOYAMA; Pres. TOSHIMI HAYANO.

Japan Energy Association: Houwa Mita Tsunasaka Bldg, 2-7-7, Mita, Minato-ku, Tokyo 108-0073; tel. (3) 3451-1651; fax (3) 3451-1360; e-mail common@jea-wec.or.jp; internet www.jea-wec.or.jp; f. 1950; 133 mems; Chair. SHIGE-ETSU MIYAHARA; Exec. Dir HAJIME MURATA.

Japan Machine Tool Builders' Association: Kikai Shinko Bldg, 3-5-8, Shiba Koen, Minato-ku, Tokyo 105-0011; tel. (3) 3434-3961; fax (3) 3434-3763; e-mail intl@jmtba.or.jp; internet www.jmtba.or.jp; f. 1951; 112 mems; Chair. KENICHI NAKAMURA; Pres. TOSHIONI SHONO.

Japan Machinery Center for Trade and Investment (JMC): Kikai Shinko Bldg, 3-5-8, Shiba Koen, Minato-ku, Tokyo 105-0011; tel. (3) 3431-9507; fax (3) 3436-6455; internet www.jmcti.org; f. 1952; 290 mem. cos; Pres. ISAO YONEKURA.

The Japan Machinery Federation: Kikai Shinko Bldg, 3-5-8, Shiba Koen, Minato-ku, Tokyo 105-0011; tel. (3) 3434-5381; fax (3) 3434-2666; e-mail koho@jmf.or.jp; internet www.jmf.or.jp; f. 1952; Pres. SHOICHI SADA; Exec. Vice-Pres. SHINICHI NAKANISHI.

Japan Machine Tools Importers' Association: Toranomon Kogyo Bldg, 1-2-18, Toranomon, Minato-ku, Tokyo 105-0001; tel. (3) 3501-5030; fax (3) 3501-5040; internet www.jmtia.gr.jp; f. 1955; 51 mems; Chair. MICHIHARU CHIKANO.

Japan Microscope Manufacturers' Association: 2-3-1, Nishishinjuku, Shinjuku-ku, Tokyo 163-0914; tel. (3) 6901-4006; fax (3) 6901-4008; e-mail jmma@olympus.co.jp; f. 1954; 25 mems; Chair. T. KIKUKAWA.

Japan Motion Picture Equipment Industrial Association: Kikai Shinko Bldg, 3-5-8, Shiba Koen, Minato-ku, Tokyo 105; tel. (3) 3434-3911; fax (3) 3434-3912; Pres. MASAO SHIKATA; Gen. Sec. TERUHIRO KATO.

Japan Optical Industry Association: Kikai Shinko Bldg, 3-5-8, Shiba Koen, Minato-ku, Tokyo 105-0011; tel. (3) 3431-7073; f. 1946; 7 mems; Chair. SHOICHIRO YOSHIDA; Exec. Sec. SHIRO IWAHASHI.

The Japan Society of Industrial Machinery Manufacturers: Kikai Shinko Bldg, 3-5-8, Shiba Koen, Minato-ku, Tokyo 105-0011; tel. (3) 3434-6821; fax (3) 3434-4767; e-mail obd@jsim.or.jp; internet www.jsim.or.jp; f. 1948; 170 mems; Pres. KENTARO AIKAWA.

Japan Textile Machinery Association: Kikai Shinko Bldg, Room 310, 3-5-8, Shiba Koen, Minato-ku, Tokyo 105; tel. (3) 3434-3821; fax (3) 3434-3043; e-mail am-jtma@jtma.or.jp; internet www.jtma.or.jp; f. 1951; Pres. JUNICHI MURATA.

Metals

Japan Aluminium Association (JAA): Tsukamoto-Sozan Bldg, 4-2-15, Ginza, Chuo-ku, Tokyo 104-0061; tel. (3) 3538-0221; fax (3) 3538-0233; internet www.aluminum.or.jp; f. 1999; est. by merger of Japan Aluminium Federation and Japan Light Metal Association; 146 mems; Chair. KAZUHIKO MASUDA.

Japan Copper and Brass Association: 5/F, Usagiya Bldg, 1-10-10, Ueno, Taito-ku, Tokyo 110-0005; tel. (3) 3836-8801; fax (3) 3836-8808; e-mail jbmajwcc@copper-brass.gr.jp; internet www.copper-brass.gr.jp; f. 1948; 62 mems; Chair. HIROYUKI NAKAYAMA; Sec.-Gen. TOSHINOBU HIDAKA.

The Japan Iron and Steel Federation: Tekko Kaikan Bldg, 3-2-10, Nihonbashi Kayaba-cho, Chuo-ku, Tokyo 103-0025; tel. (3) 3669-4818; fax (3) 3661-0798; internet www.jisf.or.jp; f. 1948; mems 61 mfrs, 61 dealers, six organizations; Chair. AKIO MIMURA.

Japan Stainless Steel Association: 3/F, TMM Bldg, 1-10-5, Iwamoto-cho, Chiyada-ku, Tokyo; tel. (3) 5687-7831; fax (3) 5687-8551; e-mail yabe@jssa.gr.jp; internet www.jssa.gr.jp; f. 1959; 83 mems; Chair. YOICHI SAJI.

Steel Castings and Forgings Association of Japan (JSCFA): Shikoku Bldg Bekkan, 1-14-4, Uchikannda, Chiyoda-ku, Tokyo 101-0047; tel. (3) 5283-1611; fax (3) 5283-1613; e-mail cf@jscfa.gr.jp; internet www.jscfa.gr.jp; f. 1972; mems 42 cos, 44 plants; Exec. Dir TOMOO TAKENOUCHI.

Mining and Petroleum

Japan Cement Association: Shuwa-sakurabashi Bldg, 4-5-4, Hatchobori, Chuo-ku, Tokyo 104-0032; tel. (3) 3523-2704; fax (3) 3523-2700; e-mail international@jcassoc.or.jp; internet www.jcassoc.or.jp; f. 1948; 18 mem. cos; Chair. AKIHIKO IDE.

Japan Coal Energy Center (JCOAL): Meiji Yasuda Seimei Mita Bldg 9/F, 3-14-10, Mita, Minato-ku,Tokyo 108-0073; tel. (3) 6400-5191; fax (3) 6400-5206; e-mail jcoal-qa@jcoal.or.jp; internet www.jcoal.or.jp; formed in 1997 by merger of the Japan Coal Association, Coal Mining Research Centre, and the Japan Technical Cooperation Center for Coal Resources Development; 107 mems; Chair. MASAYA FUJIMURA.

JAPAN

Japan Mining Industry Association: C/o Eiha Bldg, 17-11 Kanda Nishiki-cho 3-chome, Chiyoda-ku, Tokyo 101-0054; tel. (3) 5280-2321; fax (3) 5280-7128; internet www.kogyo-kyokai.gr.jp; f. 1948; 54 mem. cos; Chair. AKIHIKO IDE; Pres. SHINICHI OZEKI.

Japan Petrochemical Industry Association: 2nd Floor, 2-1-1, Uchisaiwai-cho, Chiyoda-ku, Tokyo 100-0011; tel. (3) 3501-2151; internet www.jpca.or.jp; Chair. MITSUO OHASHI.

Japan Petroleum Development Association: Keidanren Bldg, 1-9-4, Otemachi, Chiyoda-ku, Tokyo 100; tel. (3) 3279-5841; fax (3) 3279-5844; e-mail sekkoren@sekkoren.jp; internet www.sekkoren.jp; f. 1961; Chair. TAMOTSU SHOYA.

Paper and Printing

Japan Federation of Printing Industries: 1-16-8, Shintomi, Chuo-ku, Tokyo 104; tel. (3) 3553-6051; fax (3) 3553-6079; internet www.jfpi.or.jp; f. 1985; 10 mems; Pres. MASAHIRO YAMAGUCHI.

Japan Paper Association: Kami Parupu Bldg, 3-9-11, Ginza, Chuo-ku, Tokyo 104-8139; tel. (3) 3248-4801; fax (3) 3248-4826; internet www.jpa.gr.jp; f. 1946; 54 mems; Chair. MASAO KOBAYASHI; Pres. KIYOSHI SAKAI.

Japan Paper Exporters' Association: Kami Parupu Bldg, 3-9-11, Ginza, Chuo-ku, Tokyo 104-8139; tel. (3) 3248-4831; fax (3) 3248-4834; e-mail info@jpeta.or.jp; internet jpeta.or.jp; f. 1952; 33 mems; Chair. IWAO NAKAJIMA.

Japan Paper Importers' Association: Kami Parupu Bldg, 3-9-11, Ginza, Chuo-ku, Tokyo 104-8139; tel. (3) 3248-4832; fax (3) 3248-4834; e-mail info@jpeta.or.jp; internet jpeta.or.jp; f. 1981; 22 mems; Chair. TOSHINORI UMEGAWA.

Japan Paper Products Manufacturers' Association: 4-2-6, Kotobuki, Taito-ku, Tokyo; tel. (3) 3543-2411; f. 1949; Exec. Dir KIYOSHI SATOH.

Textiles

Central Raw Silk Association of Japan: 1-9-4, Yuraku-cho, Chiyoda-ku, Tokyo; tel. (3) 3214-5777; fax (3) 3214-5778.

Japan Chemical Fibers Association: Seni Kaikan, 3-1-11, Nihonbashi-Honcho, Chuo-ku, Tokyo 103-0023; tel. (3) 3241-2311; fax (3) 3246-0823; internet www.jcfa.gr.jp; f. 1948; 21 mems, 1 assoc. mem, 6 supporting mems; Pres. MASANAO KAMBARA; Dir-Gen. MASAO NISHIMURA.

Japan Cotton and Staple Fibre Weavers' Association: 1-8-7, Nishi-Azabu, Minato-ku, Tokyo; tel. (3) 3403-9671; internet www.jcwa.jp; 29 mems.

Japan Silk Spinners' Association: f. 1948; 95 mem. firms; Chair. ICHIJI OHTANI.

Japan Spinners' Association: Mengyo Kaikan Bldg, 2-5-8, Bingomachi, Chuo-ku, Osaka 541-0051; tel. (6) 6231-8431; fax (6) 6229-1590; e-mail spinas@cotton.or.jp; internet www.jsa-jp.org; f. 1948; Exec. Dir HARUTA MUTO.

Transport Machinery

Japan Association of Rolling Stock Industries: Awajicho Suny Bldg, 1-2, Kanda-Sudacho, Chiyoda-ku, Tokyo 101-0041; tel. (3) 3257-1901; e-mail info@tetsushako.or.jp; internet www.tetsushako.or.jp; Chair. HIRAI MASAHARU.

Japan Auto Parts Industries Association: 5/F, Jidosha Buhin Bldg, 1-16-15, Takanawa, Minato-ku, Tokyo 108-0074; tel. (3) 3445-4211; fax (3) 3447-5372; e-mail japiaint@green.am.egg.or.jp; internet www.japia.or.jp; f. 1948; 530 mem. firms; Chair. TSUNEO ISHIMARU; Exec. Dir K. SHIBASAKI.

Japan Automobile Manufacturers Association, Inc (JAMA): Jidosha Kalkan, 1-1-30, Shiba Daimon, Minato-ku, Tokyo 105-0012; tel. (3) 5405-6126; fax (3) 5405-6136; e-mail kaigai_tky@mta.jama.or.jp; internet www.jama.or.jp; f. 1967; 14 mem. firms; Chair. FUJIO CHO; Pres. YOSHIYASU NAO.

Japan Bicycle Manufacturers' Association: 1-9-3, Akasaka, Minato-ku, Tokyo 107; tel. (3) 3583-3123; fax (3) 3589-3125; f. 1955.

Japan Ship Exporters' Association: 5/F, Toranomon 30 Mori Bldg, 3-2-2, Toranomon, Minato-ku, Tokyo 105-0001; tel. (3) 5425-9671; fax (3) 5425-9674; e-mail postmaster@jsea.or.jp; internet www.jsea.or.jp; 34 mems; Pres. TAKASHI NISHIOKA.

Japanese Marine Equipment Association: Kaiyo Senpaku Bldg, 15-16, Toranomon, Minato-ku, Tokyo 105-0001; tel. (3) 3502-2041; fax (3) 3591-2206; e-mail info@jsmea.or.jp; internet www.jsmea.or.jp; f. 1956; 219 mems; Chair. ZENSHICHI ASASAKA.

Japanese Shipowners' Association: Kaiun Bldg, 2-6-4, Hirakawa-cho, Chiyoda-ku, Tokyo 102-0093; tel. (3) 3264-7171; fax (3) 3262-4760; internet www.jsanet.or.jp; Pres. HIROYUKI MAEKAWA.

Shipbuilders' Association of Japan: 5/F, 30 Mori Bldg, 2-2, Toranomon, Minato-ku, Tokyo 105-0001; tel. (3) 3502-2010; fax (3) 3502-2816; internet www.sajn.or.jp; f. 1947; 21 mems; Chair. MASAMOTO TAZAKI.

Society of Japanese Aerospace Companies Inc (SJAC): Toshin-Tameike Bldg, 2nd Floor, 1-1-14, Akasaka, Minato-ku, Tokyo 107-0052; tel. (3) 3585-0511; fax (3) 3585-0541; e-mail itahara-hiroharu@sjac.or.jp; internet www.sjac.or.jp; f. 1952; reorg. 1974; 117 mems, 41 assoc. mems; Chair. MOTOTSUGO ITO; Pres. TAKATOSHI HOSOYA.

Miscellaneous

Communications Industry Association of Japan (CIA-J): 3/F, Shuwa Dai-ichi Hamamatsucho Bldg, 2-2-12, Hamamatsu-cho, Minato-ku, Tokyo 105-0013; tel. (3) 5403-9363; fax (3) 5463-9360; e-mail admin@ciaj.or.jp; internet www.ciaj.or.jp; f. 1948; non-profit org. of telecommunications equipment mfrs; 236 mems; Chair. KAORU YANO; Pres. YOSHIYUKI SUKEMUNE.

Japan Canners' Association: Yurakucho Denki Bldg, 1-7-1, Yuraku-cho, Chiyoda-ku, Tokyo 100-0006; tel. (3) 3213-4751; fax (3) 3211-1430; internet www.jca-can.or.jp; Pres. KEINOSUKE HISAI.

Japan Lumber Importers' Association: Yushi Kogyo Bldg, 3-13-11, Nihonbashi, Chuo-ku, Tokyo 103; tel. (3) 3271-0926; fax (3) 3271-0928; f. 1950; 130 mems; Pres. SHOICHI TANAKA.

Japan Plastics Industry Federation: Kaseihin-Kaikan, 5-8-17, Roppongi, Minato-ku, Tokyo 106-0032; tel. (3) 3586-9761; fax (3) 3586-9760; e-mail info@jpif.gr.jp; internet www.jpif.gr.jp; f. 1950; Chair. KANJI SHONO.

Japan Plywood Manufacturers' Association: Meisan Bldg, 1-18-17, Nishi-Shimbashi, Minato-ku, Tokyo 105; tel. (3) 3591-9246; fax (3) 3591-9240; f. 1965; 92 mems; Pres. KOICHI MATAGA.

Japan Pottery Manufacturers' Federation: Toto Bldg, 1-1-28, Toranomon, Minato-ku, Tokyo; tel. (3) 3503-6761.

The Japan Rubber Manufacturers' Association: 2/F, Tobu Bldg, 1-5-26, Moto Akasaka, Minato-ku, Tokyo 107-0051; tel. (3) 3408-7101; fax (3) 3408-7106; e-mail s-shioya@jrma.gr.jp; f. 1950; 130 mems; Pres. YASUO TOMINAGA.

Japan Spirits and Liquors Makers' Association: Koura Dai-ichi Bldg, 7th Floor, 1-1-6, Nihonbashi-Kayaba-cho, Chuo-ku, Tokyo 103; tel. (3) 3668-4621.

Japan Sugar Refiners' Association: 5-7, Sanban-cho, Chiyoda-ku, Tokyo 102; tel. (3) 3288-1151; fax (3) 3288-3399; internet www.sugar.or.jp; f. 1949; 17 mems; Sr Man. Dir KATSUYUKI SUZUKI.

Japan Tea Exporters' Association: 17, Kitaban-cho, Shizuoka, Shizuoka Prefecture 420-0005; tel. (54) 271-3428; fax (54) 271-2177; e-mail japantea@sound.jp; 44 mems.

Japan Toy Association: 4-22-4, Higashi-Komagata, Sumida-ku, Tokyo 130; tel. (3) 3829-2513; fax (3) 3829-2510; e-mail otoiawase2007@toys.or.jp; internet www.toys.or.jp; 228 mems; Chair. TAKEO TAKASU.

Motion Picture Producers' Association of Japan, Inc: 2nd Floor Nihonbashi Bldg, 1-17-12 Nihonbashi, Chuo-ku, Tokyo 103-0027; tel. (3) 3243-9100; fax (3) 3243-9101; e-mail info@eiren.org; internet www.eiren.org; f. 1945; Pres. ISAO MATSUOKA.

EMPLOYERS' ORGANIZATION

Japan Business Federation (JBF) (Nippon Keidanren): Keidanren Kaikan, 1-9-4, Otemachi, Chiyoda-ku, Tokyo 100-8188; tel. (3) 5204-1500; fax (3) 5255-6255; e-mail webmaster@keidanren.or.jp; internet www.keidanren.or.jp; f. 2002 by merger of Keidanren (f. 1946) and Nikkeiren (f. 1948); 1,343 mem. cos (June 2007); Chair. FUJIO MITARAI; Dir-Gen. YOSHIO NAKAMURA.

UTILITIES

Electricity

Chubu Electric Power Co Inc: 1, Higashi-Shincho, Higashi-ku, Nagoya 461-8680; tel. (52) 951-8211; fax (52) 962-4624; internet www.chuden.co.jp; Chair. KOHEI ABE; Pres. TOSHIO MITA.

Chugoku Electric Power Co Inc: 4-33, Komachi, Naka-ku, Hiroshima 730-8701; tel. (82) 241-0211; fax (82) 523-6185; e-mail angel@inet.energia.co.jp; internet www.energia.co.jp; f. 1951; Chair. TADASHI FUKUDA; Pres. TAKASHI YAMASHITA.

Electric Power Development Co Ltd (J-Power): 6-15-1, Ginza, Chuo-ku, Tokyo 104-8165; tel. (3) 3546-2211; e-mail webmaster@jpower.co.jp; tel. www.jpower.co.jp; f. 1952; Pres. YOSHIHIKO NAKAGAKI.

Hokkaido Electric Power Co Inc: 1-2, Higashi, Odori, Chuo-ku, Sapporo, Hokkaido 060-8677; tel. (11) 251-1111; internet www.hepco.co.jp; Chair. HIDEO MINAMIYAMA; Pres. TATSUO KONDO.

Hokuriku Electric Power Co Inc: 15-1, Ushijima-cho, Toyamashi, Toyama 930-0858; e-mail pub-mast@rikuden.co.jp; internet www.rikuden.co.jp; Chair. FUJIO SHINKI; Pres. ISAO NAGAHARA.

JAPAN

Kansai Electric Power Co Inc: 2-2-2, Uchisaiwai-cho, Chiyoda-ku, Tokyo 100-0011; tel. (6) 6441-8821; fax (6) 6441-8598; e-mail postmaster@kepco.co.jp; internet www.kepco.co.jp; Pres. SHOSUKE MORI.

Kyushu Electric Power Co Inc: 2-1-82, Watanabe-dori, Chuo-ku, Fukuoka 810-8726; tel. (92) 726-1649; fax (92) 731-8719; internet www.kyuden.co.jp; Chair. SHINGO MATSUO; Pres. TOSHIO MANABE.

Okinawa Electric Power Co Inc: 5-2-1, Makiminato, Urasoe, Okinawa 901-2602; tel. (988) 77-2341; fax (988) 77-6017; e-mail ir@okiden.co.jp; internet www.okiden.co.jp; f. 1972; Chair. TSUGIYOSHI TOMA; Pres. DENICHIRO ISHIMINE.

Shikoku Electric Power Co Inc: 2-5, Marunouchi, Takamatsu 760-8573; tel. (878) 21-5061; fax (878) 26-1250; e-mail postmaster@yonden.co.jp; internet www.yonden.co.jp; Chair. ATSUSHI ONISHI; Pres. MOMOKI TOKIWA.

Tohoku Electric Power Co Inc: 1-7-1, Hon-cho, Aoba-ku, Sendai 980-8550; tel. (22) 225-2111; fax (22) 223-6224; e-mail webmaster@tohoku-epco.co.jp; internet www.tohoku-epco.co.jp; Chair. KEIICHI MAKUTA; Pres. HIROAKI TAKAHASHI.

Tokyo Electric Power Co Inc: 1-1-3, Uchisaiwai-cho, Chiyoda-ku, Tokyo 100; tel. (3) 3501-8111; fax (3) 3592-1795; internet www.tepco.co.jp; Chair. SHIGEMI TAMURA; Pres. TSUNEHISA KATSUMATA.

Federation

Federation of Electric Power Companies of Japan (FEPC JAPAN): 1-9-4, Keidanren Kaikan, Ohte-machi, Chiyoda-ku, Tokyo 100-8118; tel. (3) 3279-2182; e-mail webadmin2@fepc.or.jp; internet www.fepc.or.jp; f. 1952; Chair. TSUNEHISA KATSUMATA; Dir and Sec.-Gen. KOJI KAIBE.

Gas

Hokkaido Gas Co Ltd: 7-3-1 Odorinishi, Chuo-ku, Sapporo; tel. (11) 207-7250; internet www.hokkaido-gas.co.jp; Chair. MASASUKE SASAKI; Pres. YOZO MAEIZUMI.

Keiyo Gas Co Ltd: 2-8-8, Ichikawa-minami, Ichikawa, Chiba; tel. (47) 3610211; internet www.keiyogas.co.jp; f. 1927; Chair. TOMO KIKUCHI; Pres. NOBUO SAKUMA.

Osaka Gas Co Ltd: 4-1-2, Hiranomachi, Chuo-Ku, Osaka; tel. (6) 6205-4537; e-mail intlstaff@osakagas.co.jp; internet www.osakagas.co.jp; Chair. AKIO NOMURA; Pres. HIROFUMI SHIBANO.

Saibu Gas Co: 1-17-1 Chiyo, Hakata-ku, Fukuoka; tel. (92) 633-2345; internet www.saibugas.co.jp; f. 1930; Chair. YOSHIAKI HIRAYAMA; Pres. HIROKI OGAWA.

Toho Gas Co Ltd: 19-18, Sakurada-cho, Atsuta-ko, Nagoya 456; tel. (52) 871-3511; internet www.tohogas.co.jp; f. 1922; Chair. TOSHITAKA HAYAKAWA; Pres. KOTARO MIZUNO.

Tokyo Gas Co Inc: 1-5-20, Kaigan, Minato-ku, Tokyo 105; tel. (3) 3433-2111; fax (3) 5472-5385; internet www.tokyo-gas.co.jp; f. 1885; Chair. NORIO ICHINO; Pres. MITSUNORI TORIHARA.

Water

Nagoya City Waterworks & Sewerage Bureau: Sannomaru 3-1-1, Naka-ku, Nagoya 460-8508; tel. (52) 972-3608; fax (52) 972-3710; e-mail mail@water.city.nagoya.jp; internet www.water.city.nagoya.jp.

Osaka City Waterworks Bureau: Osaka; tel. (06) 6616-5404; fax (6) 6616-5409; internet www.city.osaka.jp/suido.

Sapporo City Waterworks Bureau: 23-11, Odori Higashi, Chuo-ku, Sapporo 060-0041; tel. (11) 211-7007; fax (11) 232-1740; e-mail su.somu@suido.city.sapporo.jp; internet www.city.sapporo.jp/suido.

Tokyo Bureau of Waterworks: Tokyo; tel. (3) 5326-1100; internet www.waterworks.metro.tokyo.jp.

Yokohama Waterworks Bureau: 1-1, Minato-cho, Naka-ku, Yokohama; tel. (45) 671-3114; fax (45) 664-6774; internet www.city.yokohama.jp/me/suidou.

Association

Japan Water Works Association (JWWA): 4-8-9, Kudan Minami, Chiyoda-ku, Tokyo 102-0074; tel. (3) 3264-2281; fax (3) 3262-2244; e-mail jnc@jwwa.or.jp; internet www.jwwa.or.jp; f. 1932; Dir-Gen. MASAKAZU AKAGAWA.

TRADE UNIONS

A feature of Japan's trade union movement is that the unions are usually based on single enterprises, embracing workers of different occupations in that enterprise. In June 2006 there were 27,507 unions; union membership stood at 10.0m. workers in that year. In November 1989 the two largest confederations, SOHYO and RENGO, merged to form the Japan Trade Union Confederation (JTUC—RENGO).

Japanese Trade Union Confederation (JTUC–RENGO): 3-2-11, Kanda Surugadai, Chiyoda-ku, Tokyo 101-0062; tel. (3) 5295-0526; fax (3) 5295-0548; e-mail jtuc-kokusai@sv.rengo-net.or.jp; internet www.jtuc-rengo.org; f. 1989; 6.6m. mems; Pres. TSUYOSHI TAKAGI.

Principal Unions

Ceramics Rengo (All-Japan Federation of Ceramics Industry Workers): 3-11, Heigocho, Mizuho-ku, Nagoya-shi, Aichi 467; tel. (52) 882-4562; fax (52) 882-9960; e-mail info@jcw-u.or.jp; internet www.jcw-u.or.jp; 30,083 mems; Pres. TSUNEYOSHI HAYAKAWA.

Denki Rengo (Japanese Electrical, Electronic & Information Union): Denkirengo Bldg, 1-10-3, Mita, Minato-ku, Tokyo 108-8326; tel. (3) 3455-6911; fax (3) 3452-5406; e-mail denki-rengo@jeiu.or.jp; internet www.jeiu.or.jp; f. 1953; 688,436 mems; Pres. NOBUAKI KOGA.

Denryoku Soren (Federation of Electric Power Related Industry Workers' Unions of Japan): TDS Mita 7-13, 3rd Floor, Mita 2-Chome, Minato-ku, Tokyo 108-0073; tel. (3) 3454-0231; fax (3) 3798-1470; e-mail info@denryokusoren.or.jp; internet www.denryokusoren.or.jp; 223,000 mems; Pres. ETSUO NAKAJIMA.

Dokiro (Hokkaido Seasonal Workers' Union): Hokuro Bldg, Kita 4, Nishi 12, Chuo-ku, Sapporo, Hokkaido 060; tel. (11) 261-5775; fax (11) 272-2255; 19,063 mems; Pres. YOSHIZO ODAWARA.

Food Rengo (Federation of All Japan Foods and Tobacco Workers' Unions): Hiroo Office Bldg 8/F, 1-3-18, Hiroo, Shibuya-ku, Tokyo; tel. (3) 3446-2082; fax (3) 3446-6779; internet www.jfu.or.jp; f. 2000 by merger of Shokuhin Rengo and Shokuhin Rokyo to form Shokuhin Renmei; renamed as above 2002; 111,599 mems.

Gomu Rengo (Japanese Rubber Workers' Union Confederation): 2-3-3, Mejiro, Toshima-ku, Tokyo 171; tel. (3) 3984-3343; fax (3) 3984-5862; 60,070 mems; Pres. YASUO FURUKAWA.

Health Care Rokyo (Japanese Health Care Workers' Union): 2-17-20, Shiba, Minato-ku, Tokyo 105-0014; tel. (3) 3451-6025; fax (3) 3451-6040.

Insatsu Roren (Federation of Printing Information Media Workers' Unions): Yuai-kaikan, 7th Floor, 2-20-12, Shiba, Minato-ku, Tokyo 105-0014; tel. (3) 5442-0191; fax (3) 5442-0219; 22,303 mems; Pres. HIROFUMI NAKABAYASHI.

JA Rengo (All-Japan Agriculture Co-operative Staff Members' Union): 218 Nishinomachi, Sanzaemon-bori, Himeji-shi, Hyogo 670-0940; tel. and fax (792) 85-3618; 2,772 mems; Pres. YUTAKA OKADA.

Japan Federation of Service and Distributive Workers' Unions: New State Manor Bldg, 3rd Floor, 2-23-1, Yoyogi, Shibuya-ku, Tokyo 151-0053; tel. (3) 3370-4121; fax (3) 3370-1640; e-mail international@jsd-union.org; internet www.jsd-union.org; f. 2001; 197,000 mems; Pres. TAKAAKI SAKURADA.

Japan Postal Group Union (JPU): 5-2-2, Higashi-Ueno, Taito-ku, Tokyo 110-0015; tel. (3) 5830-2655; fax (3) 5830-2484; internet www.jprouso.or.jp; f. 2007; est. by merger of Japan Postal Workers' Union and All-Japan Postal Labour Union.

JEC Rengo (Japanese Federation of Energy and Chemistry Workers' Unions): Senbai Bldg, 5-26-30, Shiba, Minato-ku, Tokyo 108-8389; tel. (3) 3452-5591; fax (3) 3454-7464; internet www.jec-u.com; formed by merger of Goka Roren and Zenkoku Kagaku; 104,000 mems; Pres. KATUTOSHI KATO.

Jichi Roren (National Federation of Prefectural and Municipal Workers' Unions): 1-15-22, Oji-honcho, Kita-ku, Tokyo 114; tel. and fax (3) 3907-1584; 5,728 mems; Pres. NOBUO UENO.

Jichiro (All-Japan Prefectural and Municipal Workers' Union): Jichiro Bldg, 1, Rokubancho, Chiyoda-ku, Tokyo 102-0085; tel. (3) 3263-0263; fax (3) 5210-7422; internet www.jichiro.gr.jp; f. 1951; 1,004,000 mems; Pres. OKABE KENJI.

Jidosha Soren (Confederation of Japan Automobile Workers' Unions): U-Life Center, 1-4-26, Kaigan, Minato-ku, Tokyo 105-8523; tel. (3) 3434-7641; fax (3) 3434-7428; internet www.jaw.or.jp; f. 1972; 724,000 mems; Pres. YUJI KATO.

Jiunro (Japan Automobile Drivers' Union): 2-3-12, Nakameguro, Meguro-ku, Tokyo 153; tel. (3) 3711-9387; fax (3) 3719-2624; 1,958 mems; Pres. SADAO KANEZUKA.

JR-Rengo (Japan Railway Trade Unions Confederation): TOKO Bldg, 9th Floor, 1-8-10, Nihonbashi-muromachi, Chuo-ku, Tokyo 103; tel. (3) 3270-4590; fax (3) 3270-4429; internet homepage1.nifty.com/JR-RENGO; 78,418 mems; Pres. KAZUAKI KUZUNO.

JR Soren (Japan Confederation of Railway Workers' Unions): Meguro-satsuki Bldg, 3-2-13, Nishi-gotanda, Shinagawa-ku, Tokyo 141-0031; tel. (3) 3491-7191; fax (3) 3491-7192; internet www.jru7.net; 62,300 mems; Pres. YUJI ODA.

Joho Roren (Japan Federation of Telecommunications, Electronic Information and Allied Workers): Zendentsu-rodo Bldg, 3-6, Kanda Surugadai, Chiyoda-ku, Tokyo 101-0062; tel. (3) 3219-2231; fax (3)

3253-3268; e-mail info@joho.or.jp; internet www.joho.or.jp; 265,132 mems; Pres. KAZUO SASAMORI.

Kaiin Kumiai (All-Japan Seamen's Union): 7-15-26, Roppongi, Minato-ku, Tokyo 106-0032; tel. (3) 5410-8330; fax (3) 5410-8336; e-mail iss@jsu.or.jp; internet www.jsu.or.jp; 35,000 mems; Pres. YOUJI FUJISAWA.

Kamipa Rengo (Japanese Federation of Pulp and Paper Workers' Unions): 2-12-4, Kita Aoyama, Minato-ku, Tokyo 107-0061; tel. (3) 3402-7656; fax (3) 3402-7659; e-mail kamipa-rengo@jpw.jtuc-rengo.jp; internet www.jpw.or.jp; 50,858 mems; Pres. TUNEO MUKAI.

Kensetsu Rengo (Japan Construction Trade Union Confederation): Yuai Bldg, 7th Floor, 2-20-12, Shiba, Minato-ku, Tokyo 105; tel. (3) 3454-0951; fax (3) 3453-0582; e-mail vg-sec@krw.jtuc-rengo.jp; internet www.jtuc-rengo.jp/kensetu; 13,199 mems; Pres. MASAYASU TERASAWA.

Kikan Roren (Japan Federation of Basic Industry Workers' Unions—JBU): I & S Riverside Bldg, 4th Floor, 1-23-4, Shinkawa, Chuo-ku, Tokyo 104-0033; tel. (3) 3555-0401; fax (3) 3555-0407; internet www.kikan-roren.or.jp; f. 2003 through merger of Tekko Roren (Japan Federation of Steel Workers' Unions), Zosen Juki Roren (Japan Confederation of Shipbuilding and Engineering Workers' Unions) and Hitetsu Rengo (Japanese Metal Mine Workers' Union); 243,000 mems; Pres. JUNRO NAITO.

JAM (Japanese Association of Metal, Machinery and Manufacturing Workers' Unions): Yuai Kaikan, 2-20-12, Shiba, Minato-ku, Tokyo 105-0014; tel. (3) 3265-2171; fax (3) 3230-0172; e-mail mail@jam-union.or.jp; internet www.jam-union.or.jp; f. 1999; through merger of Kinzoku Kikai (National Metal and Machinery Workers' Union of Japan) and Zenkin Rengo (Japanese Federation of Metal Industry Unions).

Kokko Rengo (Japan Public Sector Union): Hosaka Bldg, 1-10-3, Kanda-ogawamachi, Chiyoda-ku, Tokyo 101-0052; tel. (3) 5209-6205; fax (3) 5209-6209.

Kokko Soren (Japan General Federation of National Public Service Employees' Unions): Hosaka Bldg, Kanda-Ogawamachi, 1-10-3, Chiyoda-ku, Tokyo 101-0052; tel. (3) 5209-6207; fax (3) 5209-6206; e-mail kokko-soren@kokko-soren.jp; internet www.kokko-soren.jp; 33,350 mems; Pres. SEIICHI FUKUDA.

Koku Rengo (Japan Federation of Aviation Industry Unions): 6-5, Haneda-kuko, Ota-ku, Tokyo 144-0041; tel. (3) 5708-7161; fax (3) 5708-7163; e-mail avinet03@jfaiu.gr.jp; internet www.jfaiu.gr.jp.

Kokuzei Roso (Japanese Confederation of National Tax Unions): R154, Okurasho Bldg, 3-1-1, Kasumigaseki, Chiyoda-ku, Tokyo 100; tel. (3) 3581-2573; fax (3) 3581-3843; 40,128 mems; Pres. TATSUO SASAKI.

Kotsu Roren (Japan Federation of Transport Workers' Unions): Yuai Bldg, 3rd Floor, 2-20-12, Shiba, Minato-ku 105-0014; tel. (3) 3451-7243; fax (3) 3454-7393; 97,239 mems; Pres. SHIGEO MAKI.

Koun-Domei (Japanese Confederation of Port and Transport Workers' Unions): 5-10-2, Kamata, Ota-ku, Tokyo 144-0052; tel. (3) 3733-5285; fax (3) 3733-5280; f. 1987; 1,638 mems; Pres. SAKAE IDEMOTO.

NHK Roren (Federation of All-NHK Labour Unions): NHK, 2-2-1, Jinnan, Shibuya-ku, Tokyo 150; tel. (3) 3485-6007; fax (3) 3469-9271; 12,526 mems; Pres. YASUZO SUDO.

Nichirinro (National Forest Workers' Union of Japan): 1-2-1, Kasumigaseki, Chiyoda-ku, Tokyo 100; tel. (3) 3580-8891; fax (3) 3580-1596; Pres. KOH IKEGAMI.

Nikkenkyo (Council of Japan Construction Industry Employees Unions): Moriyama Bldg, 1-31-16, Takadano-baba, Shinjuku-ku, Tokyo 169-0075; tel. (3) 5285-3870; fax (3) 5285-3879.

Nikkokyo (Japan Senior High School Teachers Union): 2-11, Kanda-tacho, Chiyoda-ku, Tokyo 101-0046; tel. (3) 5297-8371; fax (3) 5297-8712; internet www.nikkokyo.org.

Nikkyoso (Japan Teachers' Union): Japan Education Hall, 2-6-2, Hitotsubashi, Chiyoda-ku, Tokyo 101-0003; tel. (3) 3265-2171; fax (3) 3230-0172; internet www.jtu-net.org.jp; f. 1947; 400,000 mems; Pres. NAGAKAZU SAKAKIBARA.

Rosai Roren (National Federation of Zenrosai Workers' Unions): 2-12-10, Yoyogi, Shibuya-ku, Tokyo 151; tel. (3) 3299-0161; fax (3) 3299-0126; internet rosai.roren.jp; 2,091 mems; Pres. TADASHI TAKACHI.

Seiho Roren (National Federation of Life Insurance Workers' Unions): Tanaka Bldg, 3-19-5, Yushima, Bunkyo-ku, Tokyo 113-0034; tel. (3) 3837-2031; fax (3) 3837-2037; internet www.liu.or.jp; 414,021 mems; Pres. YOHTARU KOHNO.

Seiroren (Labour Federation of Government-Related Organizations): Hasaka Bldg, 4th–6th Floors, 1-10-3, Kanda-ogawacho, Chiyoda-ku, Tokyo 101; tel. (3) 5295-6360; fax (3) 5295-6362; e-mail info@lafgo.gr.jp; internet www.lafgo.gr.jp; 27,500 mems; Chair. MITSURU WATANABE.

Shin Unten (F10-Drivers' Craft Union): 4th Floor, 3-25-6, Negishi, Taito-ku, Tokyo 110; tel. (3) 5603-1015; fax (3) 5603-5351; 4,435 mems; Pres. SHOHEI SHINOZAKI.

Shinrin Roren (Japanese Federation of Forest and Wood Workers' Unions): 3-28-7, Otsuka, Bunkyo-ku, Tokyo 112; tel. (3) 3945-6385; fax (3) 3945-6477; 13,928 mems; Pres. ISAO SASAKI.

Shitetsu Soren (General Federation of Private Railway Workers' Unions): 4-3-5, Takanawa, Minato-ku, Tokyo 108-0074; tel. (3) 3473-0166; fax (3) 3447-3927; f. 1947; 160,000 mems; Pres. RYOICHI IKEMURA.

Sonpo Roren (Federation of Non-Life Insurance Workers' Unions of Japan): Kanda MS Bldg, 4th Floor, 27, Kanda-higashimatsushi-tacho, Chiyoda-ku, Tokyo 101; tel. (3) 5295-0071; fax (3) 5295-0073; internet www.fniu.or.jp; Pres. KUNIO MATSUMOTO.

Toshiko (The All-Japan Municipal Transport Workers' Union): 3-1-35, Shibaura, Minato-ku, Tokyo 108; tel. (3) 3451-5221; fax (3) 3452-2977; internet www.toshiko.or.jp; 43,612 mems; Pres. SHUNICHI SUZUKI.

Ui Zensen Domei (Japanese Federation of Textile, Chemical, Food, Commercial, Service and General Workers' Unions): 4-8-16, Kudan-minami, Chiyoda-ku, Tokyo 102-0074; tel. (3) 3288-3723; fax (3) 3288-3728; e-mail kokusai@uizensen.or.jp; internet www.uizensen.or.jp; f. 2002; by merger of CSG Rengo, Zensen Domei and Sen'i Seikatsu Roren; 1,986 affiliates; 790,289 mems (Jan. 2003); Pres. TSUYOSHI TAKAGI.

Unyu Roren (All-Japan Federation of Transport Workers' Union): Zennittsu Kasumigaseki Bldg, 5th Floor, 3-3-3, Kasumigaseki, Chiyoda-ku, Tokyo 100-0013; tel. (3) 3503-2171; fax (3) 3503-2176; internet www.unyuroren.or.jp; f. 1968; 143,084 mems; Pres. KAZUMARO SUZUKI.

Zeikan Roren (Federation of Japanese Customs Personnel Labour Unions): 3-1-1, Kasumigaseki, Chiyoda-ku, Tokyo 100; tel. and fax (3) 3593-1788; Pres. RIKIO SUDO.

Zen Insatsu (All-Printing Agency Workers' Union): 3-59-12, Nishi-gahara, Kita-ku, Tokyo 114; tel. (3) 3910-7131; fax (3) 3910-7155; 5,431 mems; Chair. TOSHIO KATAKURA.

Zenchuro (All-Japan Garrison Forces Labour Union): 3-41-8, Shiba, Minato-ku, Tokyo 105; tel. (3) 3455-5971; fax (3) 3455-5973; Pres. EIBUN MEDORUMA.

Zendensen (All-Japan Electric Wire Labour Union): 1-11-6, Hata-nodai, Shinagawa-ku, Tokyo 142; tel. (3) 3785-2991; fax (3) 3785-2995; e-mail info@densen.or.jp; internet www.densen.or.jp; Pres. NAOKI TOKUNAGA.

Zen-eien (National Cinema and Theatre Workers' Union): Hibiya Park Bldg, 1-8-1, Yurakucho, Chiyoda-ku, Tokyo 100; tel. (3) 3201-4476; fax (3) 3214-0597; Pres. SADAHIRO MATSUURA.

Zengin Rengo (All-Japan Federative Council of Bank Labour Unions): 1-14-12, Higashi-kanda, Chiyoda-ku, Tokyo 101-0031; tel. (3) 5687-5155; fax (3) 5687-5156; e-mail zengin@ceres.ocn.ne.jp; internet www.zengin.jp; 16,474 mems; Pres. YOSHIHIRO KONO.

Zenjiko Roren (National Federation of Automobile Transport Workers' Unions): 3-7-9, Sendagaya, Shibuya-ku, Tokyo 151; tel. (3) 3408-0875; fax (3) 3497-0107; internet www.zenjiko.or.jp; Pres. OSAMU MIMASHI.

Zenkoku Gas (Federation of Gas Workers' Unions of Japan): 5-11-1, Omori-nishi, Ota-ku, Tokyo 143; tel. (3) 5493-8381; fax (3) 5493-8216; internet ws1.jtuc-rengo.or.jp/zenkokugas/index/index.htm; 31,499 mems; Pres. AKIO HAMAUZU.

Zenkoku Keiba Rengo (National Federation of Horse-racing Workers): 2500, Mikoma, Miho-mura, Inashiki-gun, Ibaragi 300-04; tel. (298) 85-0402; fax (298) 85-0416; Pres. TOYOHIKO OKUMURA.

Zenkoku Nodanro (National Federation of Agricultural, Forestry and Fishery Corporations' Workers' Unions): 1-5-8, Hamamatsu-cho, Minato-ku, Tokyo 105; tel. (3) 3437-0931; fax (3) 3437-0681; internet www.nodanro.or.jp; 26,010 mems; Pres. SHIN-ICHIRO OKADA.

Zenkoku Semento (National Federation of Cement Workers' Unions of Japan): 5-29-2, Shimbashi, Minato-ku, Tokyo 105; tel. (3) 3436-3666; fax (3) 3436-3668; Pres. KIYONORI URAKAWA.

Zenkoku Union (Japan Community Workers Union Federation): 7-22-18, Nishi-Shinjuku, Shinjuku-ku, Tokyo 160-0023; tel. (3) 5338-2627; fax (3) 5338-1267.

Zenkoku-Ippan (National Union of General Workers): Zosen Bldg, 5th Floor, 3-5-6, Misakicho, Chiyoda-ku, Tokyo 101-0061; tel. (3) 3230-4071; fax (3) 3230-4360; internet www.zenkoku-ippan.or.jp; 54,708 mems; Pres. YASUHIKO MATSUI.

Zenkyoro (National Race Workers' Union): Nihon Kyoiku Kaikan, 7th Floor, 2-6-2, Hitotsubashi, Chiyoda-ku, Tokyo 100-0003; e-mail zenkoro-honbu@nifty.com; internet homepage2.nifty.com/zenkyoro; tel. (3) 5210-5156; fax (3) 5210-5157; 24,720 mems; Pres. TAKESHI KAWASHIMA.

JAPAN

Zenrokin (Federation of Labour Bank Workers' Unions of Japan): Nakano Bldg, 3rd Floor, 1-11, Kanda-Awajicho, Chiyoda-ku, Tokyo 101; tel. (3) 3256-1015; fax (3) 3256-1045; internet zenrokin.or.jp; Pres. EIICHI KAKU.

Zenshin Roren (All Japan Community Bank Labour Union Association): 2-6-10, Higashi-Shimbashi, Minato-ku, Tokyo 105-0021; tel. (3) 3437-6017; fax (3) 3437-1204.

Zentanko (National Union of Coal Mine Workers): 1162, Ikeshima, Sotome-cho, Nishi-Sonogi-gun, Nagasaki 857-0071; tel. (9) 5926-0004; fax (9) 5926-1000; Pres. NOBORU TAGAWA.

Zenzohei (All-Mint Labour Union): 1-1-79, Temma, Kita-ku, Osaka-shi, Osaka 530; tel. and fax (6) 6354-2389; Pres. CHIKASHI HIGUCHI.

Zenzosen-kikai (All-Japan Shipbuilding and Engineering Union): Zosen Bldg, 6th Floor, 3-5-6, Misakicho, Chiyoda-ku, Tokyo 101; tel. (3) 3265-1921; fax (3) 3265-1870; Pres. YOSHIMI FUNATSU.

Transport

RAILWAYS

Japan Railways (JR) Group: 1-6-5, Marunouchi, Chiyoda-ku, Tokyo 100-0005; tel. (3) 3215-9649; fax (3) 3213-5291; internet www.japanrail.com; fmrly the state-controlled Japanese National Railways (JNR); reorg. and transferred to private sector in 1987; high-speed Shinkansen rail network consists of Tokaido line (Tokyo to Shin-Osaka, 552.6 km), Sanyo line (Shin-Osaka to Hakata, 623.3 km), Tohoku line (Tokyo to Morioka, 535.3 km) and Joetsu line (Omiya to Niigata, 303.6 km); Yamagata Shinkansen (Fukushima to Yamagata, 87 km) converted in 1992 from a conventional railway line and is operated as a branch of the Tohoku Shinkansen with through trains from Tokyo; total railway route length was about 19,955 km in 2008.

Central Japan Railway Co: Yaesu Center Bldg, 1-6-6, Yaesu, Chuo-ku, Tokyo 103-8288; tel. (3) 3274-9727; fax (3) 5255-6780; internet www.jr-central.co.jp; f. 1987; also operates travel agency services, etc.; Chair. YOSHIYUKI KASAI; Pres. MASAYUKI MATSUMOTO.

East Japan Railway Co: 2-2-2, Yoyogi, Shibuya-ku, Tokyo 151-8578; tel. (3) 5334-1151; fax (3) 5334-1110; internet www.jreast.co.jp; privatized in 1987; Chair. MUTSUTAKE OTSUKA; Pres. and CEO SATOSHI SEINO.

Hokkaido Railway Co: West 15-chome, Kita 11-jo, Chuo-ku, Sapporo 060-8644; tel. (11) 700-5717; fax (11) 700-5719; e-mail keieki@jrhokkaido.co.jp; internet www.jrhokkaido.co.jp; Chair. YOSHIHIRO OHMORI; Pres. SHINICHI SAKAMOTO.

Japan Freight Railway Co: 3-13-1, Iidabashi, Chiyoda-ku, Tokyo; internet www.jrfreight.co.jp; Pres. MASAAKI KOYABASHI.

Kyushu Railway Co: 3-25-21, Hakataekimae, Hakata-ku, Fukuoka 812-8566; tel. (92) 474-2501; fax (92) 474-9745; internet www.jrkyushu.co.jp; Chair. KOJI TANAKA; Pres. SUSUMU ISHIHARA.

Shikoku Railway Co: 8-33, Hamano-cho, Takamatsu, Kagawa 760-8580; tel. (87) 825-1622; fax (87) 825-1623; internet www.jr-shikoku.co.jp; Chair. HIROATSU ITO; Pres. TOSHIYUKI UMEHARA.

West Japan Railway Co: 2-4-24, Shibata, Kita-ku, Osaka 530-8341; tel. (6) 6375-8981; fax (6) 6375-8919; e-mail wjr01020@mxy.meshnet.or.jp; internet www.westjr.co.jp/english/global.html; fully privately owned by March 2004; Chair. NORITAKA KARAUCHI; Pres. MASAO YAMAZAKI.

Other Principal Private Companies

Hankyu Hanshin Holdings Inc: 1-16-1, Shibata, Kita-ku, Osaka 530-8389; tel. (6) 6373-5092; fax (6) 6373-5670; e-mail koho@hankyu.co.jp; internet www.hankyu.co.jp; f. 1907; links Osaka, Kyoto, Kobe and Takarazuka; Chair. KOHEI KOBAYASHI; Pres. KAZUO SUMI.

Keihan Electric Railway Co Ltd: 1-2-27, Shiromi, Chuo-ku, Osaka 540; tel. (6) 6944-2521; fax (6) 6944-2501; internet www.keihan.co.jp; f. 1906; Chair. SHIGETAKA SATO; Pres. SEINOSUKE UEDA.

Keihin Express Electric Railway Co Ltd (Keikyu): 2-20-20, Takanawa, Minato-ku, Tokyo 108-8625; tel. (3) 3280-9120; fax (3) 3280-9199; internet www.keikyu.co.jp; f. 1899; Chair. MASARU KOTANI; Pres. TSUNEO ISHIWATA.

Keio Electric Railway Co Ltd: 1-9-1, Sekido, Tama City, Tokyo 206-8052; tel. (42) 337-3106; fax (42) 374-9322; internet www.keio.co.jp; f. 1913; Chair. MASAYUKI SAEGUSA; Pres. KAN KATO.

Keisei Electric Railway Co Ltd: 1-10-3, Oshiage, Sumida-ku, Tokyo 131; tel. (3) 3621-2242; fax (3) 3621-2233; internet www.keisei.co.jp; f. 1909; Chair. HIROSHI OHTSUKA; Pres. TSUTOMU HANADA.

Kinki Nippon Railway Co Ltd (Kintetsu): 6-1-55, Uehommachi, Tennoji-ku, Osaka 543-8585; tel. (6) 6775-3444; fax (6) 6775-3468; internet www.kintetsu.co.jp; f. 1910; Chair. WA TASHIRO; Pres. MITSUHIKO NOGUCHI.

Nagoya Railroad Co Ltd: 1-2-4, Meieki, Nakamura-ku, Nagoya-shi 450; tel. (52) 571-2111; fax (52) 581-6060; e-mail info@meitetsu.co.jp; internet www.meitetsu.co.jp; Chair. MISAO KIMURA; Pres. EIICHI KINOSHITA.

Nankai Electric Railway Co Ltd: 5-1-60, Namba, Chuo-ku, Osaka 542; tel. (6) 6644-7121; internet www.nankai.co.jp; Chair. MAKOTO YAMANAKA; Pres. SHINJI WATARI.

Nishi-Nippon Railroad Co Ltd: 1-11-17, Tenjin-cho, Chuo-ku, Fukuoka 810; tel. (92) 761-6631; fax (92) 722-1405; internet www.nnr.co.jp; serves northern Kyushu; Chair. HIROYOSHI AKASHI; Pres. TSGUO NAGAO.

Odakyu Electric Railway Co Ltd: 1-8-3, Nishi Shinjuku, Shinjuku-ku, Tokyo 160-8309; tel. (3) 3349-2526; fax (3) 3349-2447; e-mail ir@odakyu-dentetsu.co.jp; internet www.odakyu.jp; f. 1948; Chair. TATSUZO TOSHIMITSU; Exec. Pres. YORIHIKO OSUGA.

Sanyo Electric Railway Co Ltd: 3-1-1, Oyashiki-dori, Nagata-ku, Kobe 653; tel. (78) 611-2211; internet www.sanyo-railway.co.jp; Pres. FUMIHIRO AMANO.

Seibu Railway Co Ltd: 1-11-1, Kasunokidai, Tokorozawa-shi, Saitama 359; tel. (429) 26-2035; fax (429) 26-2237; internet www.seibu-group.co.jp/railways; f. 1894; Chair. NAOKI HIRANO; Pres. and CEO TAKASHI GOTOH.

Tobu Railway Co Ltd: 1-1-2, Oshiage, Sumida-ku, Tokyo 131-8522; tel. (3) 3621-5057; internet www.tobu.co.jp; f. 1897; Chair. KAICHIRO NEZU; Pres. YOSHIZUMI NEZU.

Tokyo Express Electric Railway (Tokyu) Co Ltd: 5-6, Nanpei-dai-cho, Shibuya-ku, Tokyo 150; tel. (3) 3477-6111; fax (3) 3496-2965; e-mail public@tokyu.co.jp; internet www.tokyu.co.jp; f. 1922; Pres. KIYOFUMI KANJI.

Principal Subways, Monorails and Tunnels

Subway services operate in Tokyo, Osaka, Kobe, Nagoya, Sapporo, Yokohama, Kyoto, Sendai and Fukuoka. A subway was being planned for Kawasaki by 2010. Most subway lines operate reciprocal through-services with existing private railway lines which connect the cities with suburban areas.

The first commercial monorail system was introduced in 1964 with straddle-type cars between central Tokyo and Tokyo International Airport, a distance of 13 km. Monorails also operate in other cities, including Chiba, Hiroshima, and Kitakyushu.

In 1985 the 54-km Seikan Tunnel (the world's longest undersea tunnel), linking the islands of Honshu and Hokkaido, was completed. Electric rail services through the tunnel began operating in March 1988.

Fukuoka City Subway: Fukuoka Municipal Transportation Bureau, 2-5-31, Daimyo, Chuo-ku, Fukuoka 810-0041; tel. (92) 732-4107; fax (92) 721-0754; internet subway.city.fukuoka.jp; 2 lines of 17.8 km open; Dir KENNICHIROU NISHI.

Kobe Rapid Transit Railway Co Ltd: 6-5-1, Kanocho, Chuo-ku, Kobe 650; tel. (78) 331-8181; 22.7 km open; Dir YASUO MAENO.

Nagoya Subway: Transportation Bureau City of Nagoya, Nagoya City Hall, 3-1-1, Sannomaru, Naka-ku, Nagoya 460-8508; tel. (52) 972-3824; fax (52) 972-3938; internet www.kotsu.city.nagoya.jp; 89.1 km open (2004); Dir-Gen. NOBUO YOSHII.

Osaka Monorail: 5-1-1, Higashi-machi, Shin-Senri, Toyonakashi, Osaka 565; tel. (6) 871-8280; fax (6) 871-8284; internet www.osaka-monorail.co.jp; 113.5 km open; Pres. KATSUNORI HAYAKAWA.

Osaka Underground Railway: Osaka Municipal Transportation Bureau, 1-11-53, Kujominami, Nishi-ku, Osaka 550; tel. (6) 6582-1101; fax (6) 6582-7997; internet www.kotsu.city.osaka.jp; f. 1933; 129.9 km; the 7.9 km computer-controlled 'New Tram' service began between Suminoekoen and Nakafuto in 1981; a seventh line between Kyobashi and Tsurumi-ryokuchi was opened in 1990; Gen. Man. HARUMI SAKAI.

Sapporo Transportation Bureau: Higashi, 2-4-1, Oyachi, Atsubetsu-ku, Sapporo 004; tel. (11) 896-2708; fax (11) 896-2790; internet www.city.sapporo.jp/st; f. 1971; 3 lines of 48 km; Dir T. IKEGAMI.

Sendai City Subway: Sendai City Transportation Bureau, 1-4-15, Kimachidori, Aoba-ku, Sendai-shi, Miyagi-ken 980-0801; tel. (22) 224-5502; fax (22) 224-6839; internet www.kotsu.city.sendai.jp; 15.4 km open; Dir T. IWAMA.

Tokyo Metro Co Ltd: 3-19-6, Higashi Ueno, Taito-ku, Tokyo 110-8614; tel. (3) 3837-7046; fax (3) 3837-7219; internet www.tokyometro.jp; f. 2004; operates eight lines; 186.4 km open (2008); a further 8.9 km under construction; Pres. HISASHI UMEZAKI.

Tokyo Metropolitan Government (TOEI) Underground Railway: Bureau of Transportation, Tokyo Metropolitan Government, 2-8-1, Nishi-Shinjuku, Tokyo 163-8001; tel. (3) 5320-6026; internet www.kotsu.metro.tokyo.jp; operates four underground lines, totalling 105 km.

Yokohama Municipal Subway: Municipal Transportation Bureau, 1-1, Minato-cho, Naka-ku, Yokohama 231-80; tel. (45)

JAPAN — Directory

671-3201; fax (45) 664-3266; internet www.city.yokohama.jp/me/koutuu; 40.4 km open; Dir-Gen. MICHINORI KISHIDA.

ROADS

In April 2004 Japan's road network extended to an estimated 1,248,000 km, including 8,900 km of motorways and 67,000 km of highways. In May 1999 work was completed on a 29-year project to construct three routes, consisting of a total of 19 bridges, between the islands of Honshu and Shikoku across the Seto inland sea, at a cost of some US $25,000m. There is a national omnibus service, 60 publicly operated services and 298 privately operated services.

In October 2005 the major state-owned road authorities were privatized.

Japan Highway Public Corpn: 3-3-2, Kasumigaseki, Chiyoda-ku, Tokyo 100-8979; tel. (3) 3506-0111; internet www.nexco.ne.jp; privatization enacted in Oct. 2005, company divided into East Nippon Expressway Co Ltd (internet www.e-nexco.co.jp), Central Nippon Expressway Co Ltd (internet www.c-nexco.co.jp) and West Japan Nippon Expressway Co Ltd (internet www.w-nexco.co.jp).

SHIPPING

Shipping in Japan is subject to the supervision of the Ministry of Transport. At 31 December 2005 the Japanese merchant fleet (6,842 vessels) had a total displacement of 12,751,477 grt. The main ports are Tokyo, Yokohama, Nagoya and Osaka.

Principal Companies

Daiichi Chuo Kisen Kaisha: 2-14-4, Shintomi-cho, Chuo-ku, Tokyo 104-8544; tel. (3) 5540-1997; fax (3) 3523-8987; internet www.firstship.co.jp; f. 1960; liner and tramp services; Pres. CHIKANOBU NOMURA.

Iino Kaiun Kaisha Ltd: Iino Bldg, 2-1-1, Uchisaiwai-cho, Chiyoda-ku, Tokyo 100; tel. (3) 3506-3037; fax (3) 3508-4121; internet www.iino.co.jp; f. 1918; cargo and tanker services; Chair. SHOJI NOGUCHI; Pres. KATSUYUKI SUGIMOTO.

Kansai Kisen KK: Osaka Bldg, 3-6-32, Nakanoshima, Kita-ku, Osaka 552; tel. (6) 6574-9131; fax (6) 6574-9149; internet www.kanki.co.jp; f. 1942; domestic passenger services; Pres. MAKOTO KUROISHI.

Kawasaki Kisen Kaisha Ltd (K Line): 1-2-9, Nishi Shimbashi, Minato-ku, Tokyo 105-8421; tel. (3) 3595-5082; fax (3) 3595-5001; e-mail otaki@email.kline.co.jp; internet www.kline.co.jp; f. 1919; containers, cars, LNG, LPG and oil tankers, bulk carriers; Chair. of Bd YASUHIDE SAKINAGA; Pres. HIROYUKI MAEKAWA.

Mitsui OSK Lines Ltd: Shosen Mitsui Bldg, 2-1-1, Toranomon, Minato-ku, Tokyo 105-91; tel. (3) 3587-7092; fax (3) 3587-7734; internet www.mol.co.jp; f. 1942; merged with Navix Line Ltd in 1999; world-wide container, liner, tramp, and specialized carrier and tanker services; Chair. KUNIO SUZUKI; Pres. AKIMITSU ASHIDA.

Nippon Yusen Kaisha (NYK) Line: 2-3-2, Marunouchi, Chiyoda-ku, Tokyo 100-0005; tel. (3) 3284-5151; fax (3) 3284-6361; internet www.nykline.co.jp; f. 1885; merged with Showa Line Ltd in 1998; world-wide container, cargo, pure car and truck carriers, tanker and bulk carrying services; Chair. TAKUO KUSAKARI; Pres. KOJI MIYAHARA.

Nissho Shipping Co Ltd: 33, Mori Bldg, 7th Floor, 3-8-21, Toranomon, Minato-ku, Tokyo 105; tel. (3) 3438-3511; fax (3) 3438-3566; internet www.nissho-shipping.co.jp; f. 1943; Pres. TAKEHIKO OKUBO.

Ryukyu Kaiun KK: 1-24-11, Nishi-machi, Naha, Okinawa 900; tel. (98) 868-8161; fax (98) 868-8561; cargo and passenger services on domestic routes; Pres. M. AZAMA.

Taiheiyo Kaiun Co Ltd: Mitakokusai Bldg, 23rd Floor, 1-4-28, Minato-ku, Tokyo 100; tel. (3) 5445-5805; fax (3) 5445-5806; internet www.taiheiyokk.co.jp; f. 1951; cargo and tanker services; Pres. YOSHIHIKO INAMURA.

CIVIL AVIATION

There are international airports at Tokyo (Haneda and Narita), Osaka, Nagoya and Fukuoka. In 1991 the Government approved a plan to build five new airports, and to expand 17 existing ones. In September 1994 the world's first offshore international airport (Kansai International Airport) was opened in Osaka Bay, and a second runway at that airport was due for completion in 2007. In April 2002 a second runway was opened at Narita. In December 2001 plans were approved for a fourth runway at Haneda, scheduled for completion by 2009. Narita airport was privatized in 2004. A further international offshore airport opened at Chubu in February 2005. An international airport at Shizuoka was scheduled to open in 2009.

Air Central: c/o Central Japan International Airport, 1-1, Centrair, Tokoname, Aichi 479-0881; tel. (569) 389-300; fax (569) 389-305; internet www.air-central.co.jp; f. 1988; fmrly Nakanihon Airlines, name changed as above Feb. 2005; regional and domestic services; Pres. YOSHIYUKI IWAMOTO.

Air Do (Hokkaido International Airlines Co Ltd): 1, Nishi, Kita 2, 9-chome, Chuo-ku, Sapporo; tel. (11) 252-5533; fax (11) 252-5580; e-mail postbear@airdo.jp; internet www.airdo.jp; f. 1996; domestic service between Tokyo and Sapporo; Pres. AKIRA NAKAMURA.

Air Nippon (Air Nippon Koku—ANK): 3-5-10, Haneda Airport, Ota-ku, Tokyo 144-0041; tel. (3) 5756-4710; fax (3) 5756-4788; internet www.air-nippon.co.jp; f. 1974; fmrly Nihon Kinkyori Airways; wholly owned subsidiary of All Nippon Airways; domestic passenger services, international service to Taiwan; Pres. and CEO YUZURU MASUMOTO.

All Nippon Airways (ANA): Shiodome City Center, 1-5-2, Higashi-Shimbashi, Minato-ku, Tokyo 105-7133; tel. (3) 6735-1000; fax (3) 6735-1005; internet www.ana.co.jp; f. 1952; operates domestic passenger and freight services; scheduled international services to the Far East, the USA and Europe; charter services world-wide; Chair. YOJI OHASHI; Pres. and CEO MINEO YAMAMOTO.

Hokkaido Air System: New Chitose Airport, Bibi Chitose City, Hokkaido 066-0055; tel. (123) 46-5533; fax (123) 46-5534; internet www.hac-air.co.jp; f. 1997; domestic services on Hokkaido; Pres. YASAYUKI BABA.

Ibex Airlines: Tokyo; internet www.ibexair.co.jp; f. 1999; operates domestic flights from Osaka and Narita International Airports; Chair. TAKAO ASAI; Pres. TOSHINAO MORISAKI.

JALways Co Ltd: Sphere Tower Tennoz 23 F, 2-8, Higashi-Shinagawa 2-chome, Shinagawa-ku, Tokyo 140-0002; tel. (3) 5460-6830; fax (3) 5460-8660; e-mail jazgz.jaz@jal.com; internet www.jalways.co.jp; f. 1990; subsidiary of Japan Airlines Corpn; domestic and international scheduled and charter services; Chair. KAZUNARI YASHIRO; Pres. KATSUMI CHIYO.

Japan Air Commuter: 8-2-2, Fumoto, Mizobe-cho, Aira-gun, Kagoshima 899-64; tel. (995) 582-151; fax (995) 582-673; e-mail info@jac.co.jp; internet www.jac.co.jp; f. 1983; subsidiary of JAL; domestic services; Chair. YOSHITOMI ONO; Pres. TAKAYUKI NAGATSUTA.

Japan Airlines Corpn (JAL): 2-4-11, Higashi-shinagawa, Shinagawa-ku, Tokyo 140-8605; tel. (3) 5769-6476; internet www.jal.com; f. 2002; Pres. and CEO HARUKA NISHIMATSU.

Japan Airlines Domestic Co Ltd: 2-4-11, Higashi-shinagawa, Shinagawa-ku, Tokyo 140-8637; tel. 0120-25-5971; internet www.jal.co.jp; f. 1964 as Japan Domestic Airline; name changed to Japan Air System in 1988; current name adopted 2004; Pres. HARUKA NISHIMATSU.

Japan Airlines International Co Ltd: 2-4-11, Higashi-shinagawa, Shinagawa-ku, Tokyo 140-8637; tel. 0120-25-5931; internet www.jal.co.jp; f. 1951; fmrly Japan Airlines Co Ltd; current name adopted 2004; Pres. HARUKA NISHIMATSU.

Japan Asia Airways Co: JAL Bldg, 19th Floor, 2-4-11, Higashi-shinagawa, Shinagawa-ku, Tokyo 140-0002; tel. (3) 5460-7285; fax (3) 5460-7286; e-mail jaabz@jaa.jalgroup.or.jp; internet www.japanasia.co.jp; f. 1975; subsidiary of Japan Airlines Corpn; international services from Tokyo, Osaka, Nagoya and Okinawa to Hong Kong and Taiwan; Pres. MAMORU ICHIKAWA.

Japan Transocean Air: 3-24, Yamashita-cho, Naha-shi, Okinawa 9000027; tel. (98) 857-2112; fax (98) 857-9396; internet www.jal.co.jp/jta; f. 1967; present name since 1993; subsidiary of Japan Airlines Corpn; domestic passenger services; 8 brs; Chair. and Pres. TAKESHI ICHINOSAWA.

Skymark Airlines: World Trade Center, Bldg 3F, 2-4-1, Hamamatsucho, Minato-ku, Tokyo 105-6103; tel. (3) 5402-6767; fax (3) 5402-6770; e-mail info@skymark.co.jp; internet www.skymark.co.jp; f. 1997; domestic services; Chair. SHINICHI NISHIKUBO; Pres. MASAYUKI INOUE.

Tourism

The ancient capital of Kyoto, pagodas and temples, forests and mountains, traditional festivals and the classical Kabuki theatre are some of the many tourist attractions of Japan. The number of foreign visitors to Japan rose from 7.3m. in 2006 to 8.3m. in 2007. Receipts from tourism (including passenger transport) in 2005 totalled US $15,555m.

Department of Tourism: 2-1-3, Kasumigaseki, Chiyoda-ku, Tokyo 100; tel. (3) 3580-4488; fax (3) 3580-7901; f. 1946; a dept of the Ministry of Land, Infrastructure and Transport; Dir-Gen. KIMITAKA FUJINO.

Japan National Tourist Organization: Tokyo Kotsu Kaikan Bldg, 2-10-1, Yuraku-cho, Chiyoda-ku, Tokyo 100-0006; tel. (3) 3216-1901; fax (3) 3216-1846; internet www.jnto.go.jp; Pres. MINORU NAKAMURA.

JTB Corpn (Japan Travel Bureau Inc): JTB Bldg, 2-3-11 Higashi-Shinagawa, Shinagawa-ku, Tokyo; tel. (3) 3284-7028; internet www.jtb.co.jp; f. 1912; 10,297 mems; Chair. RYUJI FUNAYAMA; Pres. TAKASHI SASAKI.

JORDAN

Introductory Survey

Location, Climate, Language, Religion, Flag, Capital

The Hashemite Kingdom of Jordan is an almost land-locked state in western Asia. It is bordered by Israel and the Palestinian Autonomous Areas to the west, by Syria to the north, by Iraq to the east and by Saudi Arabia to the south. The port of Al-Aqabah (Aqaba), in the far south, gives Jordan a narrow outlet to the Red Sea. The climate is hot and dry. The average annual temperature is about 15°C (60°F) but there are wide diurnal variations. Temperatures in Amman are generally between −1°C (30°F) and 32°C (90°F). More extreme conditions are found in the valley of the River Jordan and on the shores of the Dead Sea (a lake on the Israeli–Jordanian frontier), where the temperature may exceed 50°C (122°F) in summer. The official language is Arabic. More than 90% of the population are Sunni Muslims, while there are small communities of Christians and Shi'i Muslims. The national flag (proportions 1 by 2) has three equal horizontal stripes, of black, white and green, with a red triangle, containing a seven-pointed white star, at the hoist. The capital is Amman.

Recent History

Palestine (including the present-day West Bank of Jordan) and Transjordan (the East Bank) were formerly parts of Turkey's Ottoman Empire. During the First World War (1914–18), when Turkey was allied with Germany, the Arabs under Ottoman rule rebelled. British forces, with Arab support, occupied Palestine and Transjordan in 1917–18, when the Turks withdrew. British occupation continued after the war, when the Ottoman Empire was dissolved. In 1920 Palestine and Transjordan were formally placed under British administration by a League of Nations mandate. In 1921 Abdullah ibn Hussein, a member of the Hashimi (Hashemite) dynasty of Arabia, was proclaimed Amir (Emir) of Transjordan. In the same year his brother, Faisal, became King of neighbouring Iraq. The two new monarchs were sons of Hussein ibn Ali, the Sharif of Mecca, who had proclaimed himself King of the Hedjaz (now part of Saudi Arabia) in 1916. The British decision to nominate Hashemite princes to be rulers of Iraq and Transjordan was a reward for Hussein's co-operation in the wartime campaign against Turkey.

Under the British mandate Transjordan (formally separated from Palestine in 1923) gained increasing autonomy. In 1928 the United Kingdom acknowledged the nominal independence of Transjordan, while retaining certain financial and military powers. Amir Abdullah followed a generally pro-British policy and supported the Allied cause in the Second World War (1939–45). The mandate was terminated on 22 March 1946, when Transjordan attained full independence. On 25 May Abdullah was proclaimed King, and a new Constitution took effect.

When the British Government terminated its mandate in Palestine in May 1948, Jewish leaders there proclaimed the State of Israel. Palestinian Arabs, however, with military support from Arab states, opposed Israeli claims and hostilities continued until July. Transjordan's forces occupied about 5,900 sq km of Palestine, including East Jerusalem, and this was confirmed by the armistice with Israel in April 1949. In June the country was renamed Jordan, and in April 1950, following a referendum, King Abdullah formally annexed the West Bank territory, which contained many Arab refugees from Israeli-held areas.

In July 1951 King Abdullah was assassinated in Jerusalem by a Palestinian belonging to an extremist Islamist organization. Abdullah was succeeded by his eldest son, Talal ibn Abdullah, hitherto Crown Prince. However, in August 1952, because of Talal's mental incapacity, the crown passed to his son, Hussein ibn Talal, then 16 years of age. King Hussein formally came to power in May 1953.

In March 1956, responding to Arab nationalist sentiment, King Hussein dismissed the British army officer who had been Chief of Staff of the British-equipped and -financed Arab Legion (the Jordanian armed forces) since 1939. Jordan's treaty relationship with the United Kingdom was ended in March 1957, and British troops completed their withdrawal from Jordan in July.

The refugee camps in the West Bank became the centre of Palestinian resistance to Israel, and during the 1950s there were numerous attacks on Israeli territory by groups of Palestinian *fedayeen* ('martyrs'). In September 1963 the creation of a unified 'Palestinian entity' was approved by the Council of the League of Arab States (the Arab League, see p. 332), and the first Palestinian congress was held in the Jordanian sector of Jerusalem in May–June 1964, at which it was agreed to form the Palestine Liberation Organization (PLO), which would be financed by the Arab League and would recruit military units to form a Palestine Liberation Army (PLA). The principal Palestinian guerrilla organization within the PLO was the Palestine National Liberation Movement, known as Fatah ('Conquest'), led from 1968 by Yasser Arafat. However, King Hussein regarded the establishment of the PLO as a threat to Jordanian sovereignty, and from the outset refused to allow the PLA to train in Jordan or the PLO to levy taxes from Palestinian refugees residing in his country.

In April 1965 Hussein nominated his brother Hassan ibn Talal to be Crown Prince. During the Six-Day War of June 1967 Israel made substantial military gains, including possession of the whole of Jerusalem (which was incorporated into Israel) and the West Bank; the latter became an Israeli 'administered territory'. The influx of Palestinian refugees into the East Bank bolstered the strength of the PLO, whose continued armed raids on the Israeli-administered territories challenged the personal authority of King Hussein and the sovereignty of the Jordanian Government. King Hussein responded by expelling the guerrilla groups, after a civil war that lasted from September 1970 to July 1971. Aid to Jordan from Kuwait and other wealthy Arab states, suspended after the expulsion of the Palestinian fighters, was only restored following Jordan's military support for Syria during the Arab–Israeli War of October 1973. At an Arab summit meeting in Rabat, Morocco, in October 1974 King Hussein supported a unanimous resolution recognizing the PLO as the 'sole legitimate representative of the Palestinian people' and granting the organization the right to establish an independent national authority on any piece of Palestinian land to be liberated.

In November 1974, as a response to this resolution, both chambers of the Jordanian National Assembly (which had equal representation for the East and West Banks) approved constitutional amendments that empowered the King to dissolve the Assembly and to postpone elections for up to 12 months. The Assembly was dissolved later that month, although it was briefly reconvened in February 1976, when it approved a constitutional amendment giving the King power to postpone elections indefinitely and to convene the Assembly as required. A royal decree of April 1978 provided for the creation of a National Consultative Council, with 60 members appointed for a two-year term by the King, on the Prime Minister's recommendation, to debate proposed legislation.

A proposal put forward by US President Ronald Reagan in September 1982 for an autonomous Palestinian authority on the West Bank, in association with Jordan, was rejected by Yasser Arafat following talks with King Hussein. In January 1984, however, the King responded by dissolving the National Consultative Council and recalling the National Assembly for the first time since 1967—in effect creating the kind of Palestinian forum envisaged by the Reagan initiative. Israel allowed the surviving West Bank deputies to attend the Assembly, which approved constitutional amendments enabling elections to be held in the East Bank, while West Bank deputies would be chosen by the Assembly itself. After discussions with the PLO leader in January 1984 on a joint Palestinian-Jordanian peace initiative, King Hussein's proposals for negotiations, based on UN Security Council Resolution 242 (the resolution, adopted in November 1967, sought to return the region's territorial boundaries to the pre-Six-Day War status, but incorporated implicit recognition of an Israeli state), met with a non-committal response from the Palestine National Council (PNC), which convened in Amman in November 1984. President Hosni Mubarak of Egypt gave his support to Hussein's proposals, following the resumption of diplomatic relations between the two countries in September. In February 1985 King Hussein and Yasser Arafat announced the terms of a Jordanian-Palestinian agreement, proposing a confederated state of Jordan and Palestine to be reached through the convening of a conference of all concerned parties in the Middle East, including the PLO.

In July 1985 Israel rejected a list of seven Palestinians, five of whom were members of the PLO or had links with the PNC, whom King Hussein had presented to the USA as candidates for a joint Jordanian-Palestinian delegation to preliminary peace talks. Further progress was hampered by a series of terrorist incidents in which the PLO was implicated, thereby giving Israel further cause to reject the PLO as a credible partner in peace negotiations. King Hussein came under increasing pressure to advance the peace process, if necessary without PLO participation. In September President Reagan revived his 1984 plan to sell military equipment to the value of some US $1,900m. to Jordan. The proposal was approved by the US Congress on the condition that Jordan enter into direct talks with Israel before 1 March 1986. However, such talks were obstructed by a gradual rapprochement between Jordan and Syria, both of which supported a Middle East peace settlement through an international conference, having rejected 'partial and unilateral' solutions.

Frustrated by the lack of co-operation from Yasser Arafat in advancing the aims of the Jordanian-PLO peace initiative, King Hussein publicly severed political links with the PLO on 19 February 1986. Arafat was subsequently ordered to close his main PLO offices in Jordan by 1 April. The PLO's activities were henceforth to be restricted even further, and a number of Fatah officers loyal to Arafat were expelled. In July the Jordanian authorities closed all 25 Fatah offices in Amman; only 12 bureaux belonging to the PLO remained.

Despite the termination of political co-ordination with the PLO, Jordan continued to reject Israeli requests for direct peace talks that excluded a form of PLO representation. However, Jordan's subsequent efforts to strengthen its influence in the Israeli-occupied territories (Occupied Territories), and to foster a Palestinian constituency there independent of Arafat's PLO, coincided with Israeli measures to grant limited autonomy to Palestinians in the West Bank. In March 1986 the Jordanian House of Representatives approved a draft law increasing the number of seats in the House from 60 to 142 (71 seats each for the East and West Banks), thereby providing for greater representation for West Bank Palestinians in the National Assembly. In August, with Israeli support, Jordan announced a five-year development plan, valued at US $1,300m., for the West Bank and Gaza Strip; the plan was condemned by Arafat and West Bank Palestinians as representing a normalization of relations with Israel. Support for Arafat among Palestinians in the Occupied Territories, and in Jordan, was consolidated as he re-established himself at the head of a reunified PLO at the 18th session of the PNC in April 1987 (when the Jordanian-PLO accord of 1985 was formally abrogated).

In May 1987, following secret meetings with King Hussein, the Israeli Minister of Foreign Affairs, Shimon Peres, claimed to have made significant progress on the crucial issue of Palestinian representation at a Middle East peace conference, and to have the consent of Egypt, Jordan and the USA to convene a conference involving the five permanent members of the UN Security Council and a delegation of Palestinians who rejected terrorism and accepted Security Council Resolutions 242 and 338 (the latter defined the terms of immediate peace following the 1973 Arab–Israeli War) as the basis for negotiations. The Jordanian Prime Minister, Zaid ar-Rifai, confirmed his country's willingness to participate in a joint Jordanian-Palestinian delegation including the PLO, provided that the organization complied with the stated conditions. However, Israel's Prime Minister, Itzhak Shamir, reiterated his alternative proposal of direct regional talks excluding the PLO, and Peres failed to secure the support of a majority of the Israeli Cabinet for his proposals.

At the first full meeting of the Arab League for eight years, convened in Amman in November 1987, King Hussein pursued an agenda of greater Arab unity in support of Iraq in its war with Iran. Prior to the summit, Jordan restored full diplomatic relations with Libya (severed in 1984), which had modified its support for Iran. However, King Hussein's appeal for Egypt to be restored to membership of the League (suspended following the peace treaty with Israel in 1979) was resisted by Libya and Syria, although 11 Arab states subsequently re-established diplomatic relations. Jordan also announced the resumption of co-operation with the PLO.

These achievements were soon overshadowed by the Palestinian *intifada* (uprising), which erupted in the West Bank and Gaza Strip in December 1987, in protest at the continued Israeli occupation and the seemingly indifferent attitude of Arab League states to the Palestinians' plight. The *intifada*, and the increasingly violent Israeli response, increased international support for the PLO and Palestinian national rights. At an extraordinary meeting of the Arab League held in the Algerian capital, Algiers, in June 1988, King Hussein gave the *intifada* his unconditional support and insisted that the PLO must represent the Palestinians at any future peace conference. Furthermore, in accordance with agreements reached at the meeting, on 31 July Jordan cancelled the West Bank development plan and severed its legal and administrative links with the territory.

On 15 November 1988 the PNC, meeting in Algiers, proclaimed the establishment of an independent State of Palestine and, for the first time, endorsed UN Security Council Resolution 242 as a basis for a Middle East peace settlement, thus implicitly recognizing Israel. Jordan and 60 other countries recognized the new state. Addressing a special session of the UN General Assembly in Geneva, Switzerland, in December, Arafat renounced violence on behalf of the PLO. The USA subsequently opened a dialogue with the PLO, making it more probable that Israel would have to do likewise.

In April 1989 there was rioting in several cities, after the Jordanian Government imposed sizeable price increases on basic goods and services. The riots led to the resignation of Prime Minister ar-Rifai and his Cabinet. Field Marshal Sharif Zaid ibn Shaker, a cousin of the King who had been Commander-in-Chief of the Jordanian Armed Forces in 1976–88, was appointed to head a new Government. While King Hussein refused to make any concessions regarding the price increases, he announced that a general election would be held for the first time since 1967. The election to the 80-seat House of Representatives, which proceeded in November 1989, was contested by 647 candidates, mostly independents, as the ban on political parties (in force since 1963) remained. However, the Muslim Brotherhood was able to present candidates for election, owing to its legal status as a charity. At the election the Muslim Brotherhood won 20 seats, while as many as 14 seats were won by independent Islamist candidates who supported the Brotherhood. In December King Hussein appointed former premier Mudar Badran as Prime Minister. The Muslim Brotherhood declined participation in the new Cabinet after its demand for the education portfolio was rejected. However, the Government included three independent Muslim deputies and three 'leftists', all of whom were regarded as members of the opposition. In January 1990 Badran pledged to abolish martial law (which had been suspended in December 1989) within four to six months, and to liberalize the judicial system; he also announced the abolition of the anti-communism law (in force since 1954). In April King Hussein appointed a 60-member commission, under the chairmanship of former premier Ahmad Ubeidat, to devise a national charter that would legalize political parties. The commission's draft national charter was approved by the King in January 1991, and further endorsed by Hussein and leading political figures in June. Also in January the Cabinet was reorganized to include five members of the Muslim Brotherhood.

Iraq's invasion of Kuwait in August 1990, and the consequent imposition of economic sanctions by the UN against Iraq, had a profound impact on Jordan: Iraq was its principal trading partner, and Jordan relied on supplies of Iraqi petroleum. Although King Hussein condemned the Iraqi invasion, he was slow to do so, and advocated an 'Arab solution' to the crisis. There was considerable support for the Iraqi President, Saddam Hussain, among the Jordanian population, particularly among Palestinians. King Hussein was critical of the US-led deployment of multinational military forces in Saudi Arabia and the Persian (Arabian) Gulf, and in the closing months of 1990 he visited numerous Middle East and other capitals in an attempt to avert a war. Jordan's response to the Gulf crisis prompted the USA to review its military and economic assistance to Jordan and led to a deterioration in Jordan's relations with Egypt and Saudi Arabia, both of which contributed to the US-led force. However, diplomatic relations between Jordan and Iran were re-established (having been severed in 1981).

In the months following the Gulf War Jordan concentrated on attempts to revive its shattered economy and on improving relations with its Arab neighbours, particularly Saudi Arabia. In response to Jordanian co-operation in the arrest of a Saudi dissident in Amman, Saudi Arabia revoked a ban on the entry of Jordanian transport vehicles into its territory, and trade between Jordan and Saudi Arabia was resumed. However, high-level ministerial contacts were not renewed until mid-1995.

Meanwhile, Jordan secured the approval of the USA by agreeing to join with a Palestinian delegation at the Middle East peace conference which opened in Madrid, Spain, in October 1991. Subsequent talks in Washington, DC, and Moscow, Russia, between the Israeli and the joint Jordanian-Palestinian delegations remained deadlocked with regard to substantive issues until September 1993, when Israel and the PLO agreed to a declaration of principles regarding Palestinian self-rule in the Occupied Territories. On the signing of the Declaration of Principles, which King Hussein welcomed, the Jordanian-Palestinian delegation was disbanded, and Jordan and Israel concluded an agreement that defined the agenda for subsequent bilateral negotiations within the context of the Middle East peace conference. The talks were to address the following issues: refugees and displaced persons; security; water resources; the demarcation of the border between Jordan and Israel; and future bilateral co-operation.

In 1991 Jordan and the PLO had agreed on the principle of confederation between Jordan and whatever Palestinian entity ultimately emerged from the Middle East peace process, and in July 1993 they undertook to form six committees to discuss relations between Jordan and the Occupied Territories during a period of transitional Palestinian self-rule. Jordan was formally excluded from discussion of some of the issues, however, following the signing of the Declaration of Principles. In January 1994, after King Hussein had twice warned that Jordan might otherwise pursue its own agenda in the ongoing peace talks with Israel, the PLO agreed to sign a comprehensive economic co-operation agreement with Jordan, and to establish a joint committee to co-ordinate financial policy in the Palestinian territories. In the same month Jordan signed a draft security accord with the PLO.

On 25 July 1994 King Hussein and the Israeli Prime Minister, Itzhak Rabin, meeting in the US capital, signed the Washington Declaration, which formally ended the state of war that had existed between Jordan and Israel since 1948. In October 1994 the two countries signed a full peace treaty settling outstanding issues of contention between them and providing, *inter alia*, for the establishment of diplomatic relations and for talks on economic and security co-operation. The official normalization of relations between Jordan and Israel had been completed by 18 January 1996. In Jordan the peace treaty was opposed by Islamist militants, and it was also criticized by Syria. The PLO leadership complained that the treaty undermined Palestinian claims to sovereignty over Jerusalem. None the less, in January 1995 the PLO and Jordan signed an agreement regulating relations between Jordan and the Palestinian Autonomous Areas with regard to economic affairs, finance, banking, education, transport, telecommunications, information and administration. At the same time, the PLO acknowledged Jordan's custodianship of the Muslim holy places in Jerusalem for as long as Jordan recognized and supported Palestinian claims to sovereignty over East Jerusalem.

Meanwhile, in June 1991 Taher al-Masri was appointed to replace Mudar Badran as Prime Minister. However, in the period preceding the opening of the National Assembly in December, it became clear that al-Masri could not command majority support in the legislature; he was forced to resign in November, whereupon Sharif Zaid ibn Shaker again assumed the premiership. In July 1992 the House of Representatives adopted legislation whereby, subject to certain conditions, political parties were formally legalized. In May 1993 King Hussein appointed Abd as-Salam al-Majali, the head of the Jordanian delegation to the Middle East peace conference, to the premiership; his Government was regarded as a transitional administration pending legislative elections to be held before November of that year.

In August 1993 King Hussein unexpectedly dissolved the House of Representatives, provoking criticism from some politicians who had expected the House to debate proposed amendments to Jordan's electoral law. Changes in voting procedures at the general election were announced by the King in that month: voters were to be allowed to cast one vote only, rather than multiple votes equal to the number of candidates contesting a given constituency. Some 68% of the electorate were reported to have participated in Jordan's first multi-party general election, held on 8 November. By far the largest number of deputies returned to the House of Representatives were independent centrists loyal to the King. The Islamic Action Front (IAF, the political wing of the Muslim Brotherhood) emerged as the second largest party in the legislature. A new Senate (House of Notables) was appointed by the King on 18 November, and a new Cabinet, led by al-Majali, was announced in December. Al-Majali was dismissed in January 1995, whereupon Sharif Zaid ibn Shaker once again assumed the premiership at the head of an extensively reorganized Cabinet.

King Hussein implemented a further extensive cabinet reshuffle in February 1996, appointing Abd al-Karim al-Kabariti, hitherto Minister of Foreign Affairs, as Prime Minister. (Kabariti retained the foreign affairs portfolio, and also assumed responsibility for defence.) In August rioting erupted in southern Jordan after the Government imposed a sharp increase on the price of bread. The unrest quickly spread to other parts of the country, including impoverished areas of the capital, and was regarded as the greatest challenge to the King's rule since the rioting over fuel prices in 1989. King Hussein responded by suspending the legislature and deploying the army in order to suppress the worst disturbances. In December 1996 the Government announced its commitment to certain reforms of electoral legislation before the next general election. Kabariti was unexpectedly dismissed by Hussein in March 1997, reportedly as a result of disagreement over issues relating to Jordan's policies towards Israel. Abd as-Salam al-Majali again assumed the premiership, taking the defence portfolio in the new Cabinet.

In July 1997 the IAF announced its intention to boycott the forthcoming parliamentary elections, in protest at what it regarded as the Government's overly concessionary policies towards Israel and at recent restrictive amendments to press legislation. Several other parties also boycotted the polls. Many of the 524 candidates at the elections, which took place on 4 November, were independents or tribal leaders campaigning on local issues. In all, 62 of the 80 seats in the new House of Representatives were won by pro-Government candidates; 10 seats were secured by nationalist and left-wing candidates, and eight by independent Islamists. The overall level of voter participation was reported to have been 54.6%; however, it was reported that the majority of Jordan's Palestinians had not voted. A new Senate was appointed by the King on 22 November, and the Government was reorganized in February 1998. In August Fayez at-Tarawneh was appointed Prime Minister, in place of al-Majali (who had been criticized with regard to a severe water crisis in July); a new Cabinet was subsequently named.

Meanwhile, in July 1998 King Hussein began to undergo treatment for cancer in the USA. In August he issued a royal decree transferring responsibility for certain executive duties to his brother, Crown Prince Hassan. On King Hussein's return to Jordan in January 1999, amid official assurances that his health had been restored, the King prompted renewed speculation about the royal succession by appointing Crown Prince Hassan as his 'deputy'. On 24 January King Hussein issued a royal decree naming his eldest son, Abdullah, as Crown Prince of Jordan. Although Hassan had been regent since 1965, King Hussein was said to have been dissatisfied with his brother's handling of Jordanian affairs during his absence, in particular his attempts to intervene in military matters. Two days later the King left Jordan for emergency treatment in the USA, following a rapid deterioration in his health. King Hussein returned to Amman on 5 February 1999 and was pronounced dead on 7 February. The Crown Prince was sworn in, as King Abdullah ibn al-Hussein of Jordan, on the same day. Prince Hamzeh ibn al-Hussein, the late King's youngest son, became the new Crown Prince.

In March 1999 King Abdullah announced the formation of a new Cabinet. Abd ar-Raouf ar-Rawabdeh, a former Deputy Prime Minister and mayor of Amman, replaced Fayez at-Tarawneh as Prime Minister and Minister of Defence; Abd al-Karim al-Kabariti was appointed Chief of the Royal Court. Ar-Rawabdeh's Cabinet retained eight ministers from the outgoing administration, including those responsible for the key portfolios of the interior, finance and foreign affairs, although several ministers regarded as loyal to Prince Hassan were replaced. King Abdullah charged ar-Rawabdeh with implementing what he termed 'fundamental reforms', including a strengthening of the rule of law and further democratization, as well as economic reforms to address the serious problems of poverty and unemployment in Jordan. Opposition groups expressed cautious loyalty to the new King. The Muslim Brotherhood urged an open dialogue with the Government, and its political wing, the IAF, indicated that it would participate in municipal elections scheduled for July. However, the IAF declined to join the Popular Participation Bloc, a new grouping of 13 leftist, Baathist and pan-Arab parties subsequently formed to contest the elections, owing to a disagreement regarding each party's quota of candidates.

Although in March 1999 King Abdullah had, under a recent amnesty law, released almost 500 prisoners, in April the Arab Human Rights Organization in Jordan criticized the Government for an increase in human rights violations, including arrests of journalists and harsh treatment of prisoners held in detention centres. Nevertheless, censorship of the foreign press was revoked during that month, and in June the Government agreed to amend part of the controversial Press and Publications Law in order to ease certain restrictions on journalists.

The final results of municipal elections held in July 1999 indicated that independent and tribal candidates had secured the most seats. Islamists too were successful in their traditional urban strongholds: the IAF, which notably increased its presence on the Amman municipal council, announced subsequently that it would contest the general election scheduled for late 2001 if the electoral law was amended. The overall level of voter participation was around 59%; voting in some areas was marred by violence, in which two people died. In September 1999 the Government agreed in principle to some of the opposition's demands regarding electoral reform; these included an increase in the number of seats in the House of Representatives from 80 to 120, and the division of the country into 80 electoral districts.

In January 2000 Abd al-Karim al-Kabariti, a long-standing rival of ar-Rawabdeh, resigned as Chief of the Royal Court for unspecified reasons. He was replaced by former premier Fayez at-Tarawneh. A reorganization of the Government followed shortly afterwards: the new Cabinet was dominated by technocrats and supporters of the Prime Minister, and the key ministries remained unchanged. In April a group of deputies in the House of Representatives, among them the Speaker, Abd al-Hadi al-Majali, and the Chairman of the Economic and Finance Committee, Ali Abu ar-Ragheb, urged King Abdullah to dismiss the ar-Rawabdeh Government for its failure to implement reforms and safeguard public freedoms, and demanded the establishment of a 'parliamentary government' of deputies. Although the King responded by expressing his confidence in the Prime Minister, in June Abdullah dismissed ar-Rawabdeh, appointing the more liberal ar-Ragheb in his place; a new Cabinet was duly appointed. King Abdullah stated that the priorities of the new Government were to end corruption, to introduce electoral legislation prior to the next parliamentary elections and to accelerate the economic reform programme.

On 23 April 2001 King Abdullah exercised his constitutional right to extend the current term of the House of Representatives by two years. There was some speculation that the King's decision to postpone legislative elections—scheduled for November—had been taken in an attempt to prevent Islamist opposition parties (which were highly critical of the Government's policies towards Israel) from presenting a serious challenge to his leadership. On 16 June the King ordered the dissolution of the House, which had been sitting in extraordinary session since April, and effected a cabinet reshuffle involving 11 new ministerial appointments (but excluding the key portfolios). The following day King Abdullah set the Government the task of drafting amendments to the electoral law within one month. On 22 July the King approved the new electoral legislation, which provided for the redrawing of electoral boundaries (the number of constituencies was to rise from 21 to 44) in order to increase the number of seats in the House of Representatives from 80 to 104, and a reduction of the age of eligibility to vote from 19 years to 18. The Muslim Brotherhood threatened to boycott the forthcoming parliamentary elections, in view of the Government's failure to meet its demand for the reintroduction of an 'electoral list' system. Critics of the amendments also complained that they failed to address the issue of under-representation in the legislature of Jordanians of Palestinian origin. Nevertheless, the new law did provide for the formation of special committees whose task would be to monitor the electoral process. Shortly afterwards it was reported that the November elections were to be postponed until late 2002 for technical reasons. In August 2001 legislation was enacted imposing a ban on public gatherings and demonstrations. In October, following the suicide attacks on the USA (see below), King Abdullah issued a royal decree amending Jordan's penal code in order to strengthen counter-terrorism measures; he also imposed tougher penalties on those found guilty of 'publication crimes'. Later that month, at the King's request, Prime Minister ar-Ragheb effected a minor reorganization of the Cabinet. In November King Abdullah appointed a new 40-member Senate upon the expiry of its term.

In mid-January 2002 Prime Minister ar-Ragheb again submitted the resignation of his Government, but was asked by King Abdullah to form a new administration capable of initiating economic and social reforms prior to parliamentary elections (now expected by November). A new Cabinet was named shortly afterwards: seven new ministers joined the Government, including Dr Marwan al-Muasher as Minister of Foreign Affairs and Qaftan al-Majali as Minister of the Interior. In late January the King suffered one of the most serious challenges to his rule when two days of violent clashes, in which one policeman died, erupted between protesters and security forces in Ma'an, following the death of a local youth in police custody, who demonstrators alleged had been the victim of police brutality. The Government later announced that two investigations had been launched to determine the causes of both the adolescent's death and the subsequent riots.

King Abdullah announced in mid-August 2002 that legislative elections would be postponed until 2003, owing to the continuing instability in the region. A limited reorganization of the Cabinet was effected in September 2002: the most significant change was the promotion of the Minister of Justice, Faris an-Nabulsi, to a new post of Deputy Prime Minister. In November security forces in Ma'an carried out a large-scale operation aimed at detaining a local Islamist cleric, Muhammad Shalabi (or 'Abu Sayyaf'), and his supporters, who the Government claimed had played an important role in January's riots. Many observers believed that the security operation was linked to the recent assassination of a US diplomat (see below). At least three civilians and two police officers were reportedly killed during the week-long campaign; however, despite the security forces making a large number of arrests, Abu Sayyaf apparently evaded capture. Renewed clashes between police and local gunmen later in November resulted in another civilian death in Ma'an. At the end of the month the Government announced that it would henceforth have the authority to disband any trade union-affiliated committee opposed to the normalization of relations with Israel.

A limited reshuffle of the Cabinet took place in January 2003. King Abdullah approved amendments to draft electoral legislation in February: the amendments, which were to take effect from the next general election (see below), increased the number of seats in the House of Representatives from 104 to 110, in order to provide a quota of six seats for female legislators. In March the King effected several changes to the composition of the Royal Court, including the appointment of a former army general and minister of state, Yousuf ad-Dalabeeh, as Chief of the Royal Court, in place of Fayez at-Tarawneh. The King also appointed Faisal al-Fayez to the new government post of Minister of the Royal Court.

Popular opposition to the US-led military campaign in Iraq (see the chapter on Iraq) manifested itself in government-approved rallies in Amman in February 2003, and in mid-March 14 opposition parties coalesced to protest against the presence of US troops in eastern Jordan. At the end of March 95 prominent establishment figures, including former premiers and security officials, petitioned the King demanding that Jordan refuse to recognize the legality of the conflict in Iraq. A further attempt by 99 prominent Jordanians to petition the King occurred in mid-April, following the capture of Baghdad by US forces on 9 April. At the same time, the IAF issued a *fatwa* (Islamic edict) declaring it a 'great sin' to allow US-led forces to use Jordanian territory. The war in Iraq generally had little impact on Jordan's domestic affairs; however, when up to 12 people were killed by unknown assailants in the bombing of the Jordanian embassy in Baghdad in August, it was widely interpreted as a 'revenge' attack for Jordan's official stance during the conflict.

At the parliamentary elections held on 17 June 2003 tribal representatives and Hashemite loyalists won 80 of the 110 seats in the House of Representatives, while the IAF, the largest opposition party, won 17 seats. Under the legislation approved in February, six seats were reserved for female candidates. Therefore, the new parliament was regarded as largely pro-Government, with some representation for Islamists and those opposed to Jordan's peace treaty with Israel. On 21 July a new 28-member Cabinet was announced, including eight new ministers. Notable appointments included Dr Muhammad al-Halaiqa as Deputy Prime Minister and Minister of Administrative Development, and Samir Habashneh as Minister of the Interior. The composition of the new Cabinet was believed to reflect the increased Islamist presence in the newly elected House of Representatives, which in August rejected a law granting Jordanian women the right to file for divorce.

The new administration of ar-Ragheb proved to be short-lived, however: following considerable criticism of the Government over the slow pace of reform and accusations of corruption, the Prime Minister resigned on 21 October 2003. On 25 October King Abdullah inaugurated a new, reduced 21-member Cabinet under Prime Minister Faisal al-Fayez, who had served as Minister of the Royal Court in the previous administration; al-Fayez was also named as the Minister of Defence. The appointment of three female ministers preceded that of an expanded 55-member Senate in November, in accordance with constitutional guidelines that membership of the Senate must be no larger than one-half that of the House of Representatives.

In April 2004 it was revealed that Jordanian security forces had made a number of arrests that had possibly averted a major terrorist attack in the kingdom. It was alleged that militant Islamists closely linked to the al-Qa'ida (Base) network under the command of Saudi-born Osama bin Laden had planted huge quantities of explosives in trucks, which they had planned to detonate against a number of targets, including the Prime Ministry and the Ministry of the Interior. One of the arrested militants reportedly confessed that the instigator of the plot was Abu Musab az-Zarqawi, the Jordanian national whom US officials believed was directing attacks against the US-led coalition, security forces and civilian targets in Iraq. In December the State Security Court cleared 10 Jordanians and three Saudi fugitives of charges of planning attacks against US interests in Jordan. However, 11 of the men were given prison terms ranging from six to 15 years for possessing explosives; the other two were acquitted owing to a lack of evidence. In February 2006 a military court sentenced to death nine men, including az-Zarqawi (who, together with three other defendants, was charged *in absentia*), for their role in the terrorist plot of April 2004; two defendants received prison terms of up to three years, while another two were acquitted. In March 2006 the General Intelligence Department (GID)—the state agency responsible for internal security—claimed to have disrupted a terrorist cell that was plotting to attack Queen Alia International Airport and several other important civilian installations.

Meanwhile, in September 2004 King Abdullah announced his decision to postpone the reopening of the House of Representatives from 1 October to 1 December, apparently in anticipation of an expected government reshuffle. In October 11 small political parties merged to form the centrist, pro-Government Jordanian National Movement, which sought to encourage national unity and respect for the Constitution and state institutions. Later that month Prime Minister al-Fayez carried out a reorganization of the Cabinet: Dr Marwan al-Muasher assumed the role of Deputy Prime Minister from Dr Muhammad al-Halaiqa, and was also named as Minister of State for Prime Ministry Affairs and Government Performance. Jordan's ambassador to Egypt, Hani Mulki, replaced al-Muasher as Minister of Foreign Affairs. In November King Abdullah took away the title of Crown Prince from his half-brother, Hamzeh ibn al-Hussein, citing the wish to give him more freedom to undertake tasks that this 'symbolic' position did not permit. According to the Constitution, Abdullah's 10-year-old son, Hussein, became heir to the throne; although the position of Crown Prince remained vacant, many commentators expected the King to give the title to his son in the future.

King Abdullah accepted the resignation of al-Fayez's Government in April 2005 and appointed Adnan Badran (a former Minister of Education) as Prime Minister. Two days later a new Government, which was apparently considered more 'reformist' than the previous one, was sworn in. Faruq Kasrawi adopted the foreign affairs portfolio, Dr Bassem Awadallah became Minister of Finance and Awni Yervas was named Minister of the Interior. Badran, like his predecessor, also assumed responsibility for defence. Abdullah had criticized al-Fayez's administration at a summit meeting of Arab countries in the previous month (see below), and the change of Government was believed to be part of an attempt by the King to accelerate political and economic reform. Following Awadallah's resignation in June, however, Badran announced a reshuffle of the Cabinet on 3 July, appointing eight new ministers, including Dr Marwan al-Muasher as Deputy Prime Minister and Adel Qudah as Minister of Finance.

In November 2005 three Iraqi citizens carried out suicide bomb attacks in three hotels frequented by Western businessmen and diplomats in Amman, killing up to 60 people and injuring more than 100. Az-Zarqawi announced that he had instigated the blasts, most of the victims of which were Jordanians, as retaliation for the Government's support for the USA and other Western countries. Within two days over 120 people had been arrested in connection with the attacks, and thousands of Jordanians staged protests against the bombings and az-Zarqawi. Following Badran's resignation from the premiership later in the month, King Abdullah invited Marouf al-Bakhit, who had served as Jordan's ambassador to Israel until his appointment as national security adviser in the aftermath of the bombings, to form a new government. Abdullah insisted that the bombings had only increased Jordan's determination to further the democratization process and pursue its reformist agenda, and called on al-Bakhit to increase security and combat the fundamentalist ideologies behind militant Islamism. The King inaugurated the new Cabinet in late November: al-Bakhit assumed additional responsibility for defence, while the former Governor of the Central Bank, Ziad Fariz, became Deputy Prime Minister and Minister of Finance, Eid al-Fayez was appointed Minister of the Interior and Abd al-Ilah al-Khatib was handed the foreign affairs portfolio (for which he had also been responsible in 1998–2002).

Details were published in January 2006 of a 10-year plan, the principal objectives of which were 'the creation of income-generating opportunities, the improvement of standards of living and the guarantee of social welfare'. As well as outlining plans for economic reform (see Economic Affairs), the so-called National Agenda also included initiatives designed to: safeguard freedom of political activity and of the media; build upon progress already made with regard to the empowerment of women within Jordanian society; and improve both the availability and quality of public services such as education, health care and infrastructure.

In February 2006, following falsified reports that two al-Qa'ida members, one of whom had been convicted for the murder in 2002 of a US diplomat (see below), were to be executed, riots broke out between inmates and staff at a prison in Amman, during which the head of the Jordanian prison system, Col Saad al-Ajrami, and an estimated six police officers were taken hostage by prisoners. Although the situation was defused later that same day and the hostages were released unharmed, the incident marked the beginning of a disquieting series of disturbances within Jordan's prisons. In March 2006 riots erupted in a prison near the northern town of Irbid, and in the following month one prisoner was killed and several police officers were wounded during unrest at Qafqafa prison, also in the north of the country.

In April 2006 Sajida ar-Rishawi, an Iraqi woman reported to be the sister of a close associate of az-Zarqawi, went on trial charged with direct involvement in the November 2005 attacks in Amman. It was alleged that ar-Rishawi had been intended as a fourth bomber but had fled the scene after her device had failed to detonate. Ar-Rishawi had initially admitted to the charges levied against her, but subsequently rescinded her confession, claiming that it had been extracted under torture. Notwithstanding her change of plea, she was convicted and sentenced to death in September 2006; despite an appeal, in January 2007 the Court of Cassation upheld the conviction. A further six people, including at least one other Iraqi woman, were convicted *in absentia* and sentenced to death for their part in the bombings. Meanwhile, having successfully evaded capture for several years, az-Zarqawi was killed in June 2006 during a US air raid near Baquba, approximately 50 km north-east of Baghdad.

The Prevention of Terrorism Act passed into law in November 2006, provoking censure from human rights organizations, including Amnesty International, which alleged that the new legislation failed to comply with international human rights laws and was sufficiently broad in its definition of terrorism to enable it potentially to be abused in order to suppress non-violent opponents of the Government. In June Amnesty International had claimed that the GID routinely indulged in the use of torture as a tool with which to extract false confessions from political detainees, strongly implying that it did so on behalf of the US Administration; furthermore, Jordan's State Security Court was accused of accepting confessions obtained by torture as admissible evidence, and of having based convictions on the grounds of such confessions alone.

On 23 November 2006 Prime Minister Marouf al-Bakhit effected a cabinet reorganization, the stated intention of which was to bolster the Government's programme of economic and political reform. The reshuffle comprised nine changes, including the appointment of Muhammad al-Oran, formerly a member of the opposition, as Minister of Political Development.

It was reported in April 2007 that the Jordanian security services had confiscated from the possession of the Qatar-based television station Al-Jazeera a videotape containing politically sensitive material; the videotape was purported to include footage of King Abdullah's uncle, Prince Hassan, lambasting two of Jordan's firm allies, the US and Saudi Governments, in the wake of news reports alleging that the two administrations had provided financial support to radical Sunni groups in order to offset the influence of Shi'a groups in Iraq and elsewhere in the Middle East.

In late July 2007 the Ministers of Health and of Water and Irrigation tendered their resignations after the contamination of water supplies had affected the health of hundreds of people in the north of the kingdom. In the following month Fariz resigned as Deputy Prime Minister and Minister of Finance, apparently in response to the Cabinet's refusal to acquiesce to his demands for an increase in fuel prices. In September Salah al-Mawajdeh, Muhammad ash-Shatnawi and Hamad al-Kassasbeh were appointed as the new Ministers of Health, of Water and Irrigation and of Finance, respectively.

Nidal Abbadi, one of the IAF's 17 legislators, resigned his parliamentary seat in mid-October 2007, following the IAF leadership's failure to include him on the party list of 22 candidates for the forthcoming parliamentary elections; this prompted suspicions of infighting among members of the main opposition body. In early November a coalition of non-governmental organizations (NGOs) announced that, owing to government restrictions, its members could no longer monitor the polls. The Government had decreed that NGOs intending to observe the elections would have to operate under the direction of the National Centre for Human Rights, a government-regulated organization, and would be prohibited from observing the actual casting and counting of ballots.

Legislative elections were held according to schedule on 20 November 2007, and turn-out was reported at 54% of the registered electorate. According to final results released by the Ministry of the Interior, independents and tribal representatives loyal to King Abdullah dominated the polls, securing 104 of the 110 seats in the House of Representatives. The IAF won just six seats, down from 17 in the 2003 poll, while an alliance of four leftist opposition parties failed to secure representation. Following the publication of the results, the IAF accused the Government of vote-buying and other electoral irregularities, pointing to its apparent failure to win a single seat in the two traditional IAF strongholds of Irbid and Zarqa, an impoverished city approximately 30 km north-east of Amman, as compelling evidence of the widespread prevalence of electoral fraud. The Government strongly refuted such claims, insisting that, aside from a few isolated incidences of vote-buying, the proponents of which had been arrested, the polls had been conducted in a free and fair manner.

On 22 November 2007 King Abdullah appointed Nader ad-Dahabi, hitherto Head of the Special Economic Zone Authority at Aqaba, and a former Minister of Transport, as the new Prime Minister, in place of al-Bakhit, whose mandate had ended with the staging of elections. Shortly thereafter, ad-Dahabi, whose former posts also included that of Assistant Commander of the Jordanian air force, appointed a new 27-member Cabinet, which was formally inaugurated on 25 November. Notable appointments included that of Dr Salah ed-Din al-Bashir as Minister of Foreign Affairs and Amer Hadidi as Minister of Industry and Trade, while Dr Hamad al-Kasasbeh and Eid al-Fayez retained the finance and interior portfolios, respectively; as in previous administrations, responsibility for the defence portfolio was awarded to the Prime Minister.

Meanwhile, in early November 2007 one of the men convicted and sentenced to death *in absentia* for the 2002 murder of the US diplomat Laurence Foley (see below) was also convicted of helping to plan the 2003 attack on the Jordanian embassy in Baghdad. Muammar al-Jaghbeer, who had been captured in Iraq and extradited to Jordan in 2005, was deemed to have acted on the orders of az-Zarqawi and was given a second death sentence, but was expected to appeal against the verdict. In late November al-Jaghbeer's death sentence for the murder of Foley was commuted to a 10-year term of imprisonment after a military court determined that he had had no intention to kill. In March 2008 the Jordanian authorities released Abu Muhammad al-Maqdidi, reported to have been the mentor of az-Zarqawi, without charge. Al-Maqdidi had been arrested in 2005 following a televised interview in which he had urged armed resistance against the US-led coalition forces in Iraq, and had been detained without trial ever since; human rights groups had repeatedly called for him to be either tried or released.

Relations with Israel were severely undermined in September 1997 when the head of the political bureau of the Palestinian Islamist group Hamas, Khalid Meshaal, survived an assassination attempt in Amman by agents of the Israeli intelligence service, Mossad. Intensive negotiations involving Crown Prince Hassan, Israeli Prime Minister Binyamin Netanyahu and US officials resulted in an agreement in October whereby Israel freed the Hamas spiritual leader, Sheikh Ahmad Yassin, in return for Jordan's release of two Mossad agents arrested in connection with the attack on Meshaal. A further 12 Mossad agents were expelled from Jordan following the release from Israeli custody of 23 Jordanian and 50 Palestinian detainees. Israel and Jordan signed several bilateral trade agreements in March 1998, and in the following month King Hussein met with Netanyahu for the first time since the attempt on Meshaal's life. King Hussein's mediation at the US-brokered peace summit held between Israel and the Palestinian (National) Authority (PA) in October was crucial to the signing of the Wye Memorandum (see the chapter on Israel). In December Israel agreed to open its airspace to foreign airlines en route for Jordan.

Upon his accession in February 1999 King Abdullah assured Israel that he would pursue his father's commitment to the Middle East peace process. The issue of how to revive the peace process reportedly dominated talks held in July between Abdullah and the new Israeli Prime Minister, Ehud Barak. The King welcomed the reactivation of the stalled Wye Memorandum by the signing (to which he was a witness) of the Sharm esh-Sheikh Memorandum (Wye Two—see the chapter on Israel) by Barak and Arafat in September.

There was considerable speculation at the time of the Wye Two agreement that recent efforts to bring an end to Hamas's political activities in Jordan had been motivated by a consensus among the Jordanian, Palestinian, Israeli and US authorities on the need to contain potential Islamist opposition to a revival of the peace process. In August 1999 the Jordanian security forces closed down Hamas offices in Amman, on the grounds that these were being used by foreign groups for illegal political activities. The home of Khalid Meshaal was also raided, and in the following months numerous Hamas officials were arrested on various charges including involvement in illicit political activities and the illegal possession of firearms. In November it was reported that Hamas had rejected an offer by the Jordanian Government to release the detained activists provided that they agreed to cease all political activity and that their leaders left the country. Later in the month the Jordanian authorities released some 24 Hamas officials, including four leaders (among them Meshaal and spokesman Ibrahim Ghosheh) who were immediately flown to Qatar. In November 2000, during talks with Khalid Meshaal in Qatar, Jordan's Prime Minister, Ali Abu ar-Ragheb, reportedly reiterated the conditions under which the Hamas leaders would be allowed to return to Jordan. The Jordanian authorities granted permission for Ghosheh to enter the country in June 2001, after he had agreed to end his involvement with Hamas.

Meanwhile, in December 1999 16 alleged al-Qa'ida members were arrested on charges of plotting attacks against US and Israeli tourist targets in Jordan. Trial proceedings began against the detainees in Amman in May 2000, while 12 further alleged militants were tried *in absentia*. In September six of the defendants were sentenced to death, having been convicted of charges including membership of al-Qa'ida and the manufacture of explosives; 16 were condemned to various terms of imprisonment; and six were acquitted. The Jordanian authorities arrested a number of suspected Islamist extremists in July 2000, apparently in response to a warning that the US embassy in Amman was vulnerable to attacks by militant groups; in September four of the defendants received the death sentence. In February 2002 a Jordanian-US national, Raed Hijazi, was sentenced to death, having been convicted of several charges relating to the alleged terrorist plot in late 1999; however, he was cleared of any involvement with al-Qa'ida.

King Abdullah visited Israel for the first time in April 2000, when he held brief discussions with Ehud Barak regarding the peace process, as well as water management and other bilateral issues. In advance of the Israeli-Palestinian peace talks held at the US presidential retreat at Camp David, Maryland, in July, Prime Minister ar-Ragheb emphasized that the Jordanian Government would not accept any more Palestinian refugees and that it supported their right of return to their homeland. (Recent reports had implied that Jordan was being considered as a possible home for those displaced persons currently in refugee camps in Lebanon.) In December 2007 there were 1,903,490 Palestinian refugees in Jordan and a further 745,776 in the West Bank registered with the UN Relief and Works Agency for Palestine Refugees in the Near East (UNRWA, see p. 94). Meanwhile, in August 2000 King Abdullah reiterated that Jordan would not accept Israeli or international sovereignty over the Islamic holy sites in East Jerusalem, an issue that had been a major obstacle to progress at Camp David.

King Abdullah participated in the intense diplomatic efforts aimed at restoring peace in the region following the outbreak of violence in the West Bank and Gaza in September 2000 (see the chapters on Israel and the Palestinian Autonomous Areas). In mid-October the King attended a US-brokered summit meeting between Ehud Barak and Yasser Arafat in Sharm esh-Sheikh, Egypt. As violence between Palestinians and Israeli security forces escalated, Jordan came under growing pressure from other Arab states to sever diplomatic ties with Israel, while large-scale public demonstrations against Israeli and US policies towards the new Palestinian uprising (often termed the al-Aqsa *intifada*) were held in Amman and at Jordan's refugee camps. One 'anti-normalization' protest held in early October resulted in violent confrontations between protesters and police; the Government subsequently issued a ban on public demonstrations. Meanwhile, Jordan delayed the dispatch of its new ambassador to Israel, in response to the deteriorating situation in the West Bank and Gaza. In November the Israeli Vice-Consul in Amman was injured in a gun attack by militant Islamists; another Israeli diplomat was wounded in a similar attack in December.

The convening of a summit meeting of Arab League heads of state in Amman in March 2001 reflected Jordan's prominent role in diplomatic efforts to resolve the Israeli–Palestinian conflict. At the summit Arab leaders pledged to transfer funds to the PA as part of a US $1,000m. fund established in late 2000. Jordan and Egypt both refused to return their ambassadors to Tel-Aviv in protest at Israeli military actions against the Palestinians, although they did not proceed to a formal suspension of diplomatic relations. The summit's final communiqué—the so-called Amman Declaration—repeated demands for Israel to withdraw its armed forces from all occupied territory. It was reported at the end of March 2001 that a joint Egyptian-Jordanian initiative for Middle East peace had been submitted to European Union (EU, see p. 244) and US officials in an attempt to encourage Israel and the PA to revive negotiations.

Further mass demonstrations were held in Jordanian cities and Palestinian refugee camps during late March and April 2002, after public anger had been fuelled by Israel's reoccupation of Palestinian-controlled towns in the West Bank. Jordanian anti-riot police responded forcefully to many unlicensed rallies. In mid-April the Jordanian Minister of Foreign Affairs, Dr Marwan al-Muasher, held talks with Yasser Arafat at his besieged compound in Ramallah, in an apparent demonstration of solidarity with the Palestinian leader. Moreover, in that month the Jordanian authorities began to deliver large consignments of humanitarian aid from Jordan and other Arab states to the West Bank.

On 4 June 2003 King Abdullah hosted a summit meeting between US President George W. Bush, Israeli premier Ariel Sharon and the newly appointed Palestinian Prime Minister, Mahmud Abbas (Abu Mazen). The aim of the summit was to begin the implementation of the 'roadmap' peace plan, an initiative that had been drawn up in late 2002 by the Quartet group (comprising the USA, the UN, Russia and the EU) and unveiled by President Bush in April 2003, following the US-led invasion of Iraq and the removal from power of Saddam Hussain. In September the Governor of the Central Bank of Jordan circulated a letter among the members of the Jordanian Banks Association urging them to suspend transactions involving members of Hamas and also those of five Palestinian non-militant organizations.

In February 2004 a Jordanian delegation travelled to the International Court of Justice (ICJ) in The Hague, Netherlands, to present a 100-page document condemning Israel's construction of a 'security fence' in the West Bank (see the chapters on Israel and the Palestinian Autonomous Areas). The ICJ had been asked by the UN General Assembly to rule on the legality of the barrier, and Jordan was one of 14 countries to present evidence against its construction. It was reported in March that King Abdullah and Ariel Sharon had held secret talks in southern Israel regarding the controversial barrier. In May, following sideline discussions at the World Economic Forum in Amman, Israel and Jordan agreed to upgrade their bilateral trade agreement, which had been signed months after the 1994 peace treaty. In February 2005 King Abdullah attended the summit meeting, held in Sharm esh-Sheikh, between Sharon and Mahmud Abbas—recently elected as Executive President of the PA following the death of Yasser Arafat in November 2004—at which the two leaders issued verbal declarations that Israel and the PA would cease all acts of violence against each other. Later that month Jordan returned an ambassador to Tel-Aviv. However, at an Arab League summit in Algiers in March, King Abdullah failed to secure approval for a proposal for peace with Israel that would not oblige Israel to relinquish all the territories it had occupied in 1967.

Following the victory of Hamas in the Palestinian legislative elections of January 2006, Israeli acting Prime Minister Ehud Olmert informed King Abdullah that his country would not have contact with any administration in which Hamas was represented, insisting that the militant Islamist organization must disarm and annul its covenant, which called for the destruction of the Jewish state. Abdullah argued that Palestinians had to show responsibility and determine the course of their own future, and that the election results should not prevent further peace negotiations from taking place between Israel and the PA. Jordan appeared increasingly supportive of US efforts to coerce the Hamas Cabinet into recognizing Israel through a process of isolation. In April the Government cancelled a planned official visit by Palestinian Minister of Foreign Affairs Dr Mahmud Khalid az-Zahhar, despite Prime Minister al-Bakhit having stated in February that Jordan would extend a warm welcome to a Palestinian delegation. The revocation of the invitation followed the apparent discovery of an arms and explosives cache, allegedly smuggled into Jordan by Hamas from Syria. Hamas officials staunchly denied the claim, which, they alleged, had been crudely fabricated to justify Jordan's decision to cancel the visit. In May Jordanian authorities announced that 20 Hamas members had been arrested on suspicion of plotting terrorist attacks in Jordan. In June Abdullah hosted informal discussions in Petra between Ehud Olmert—who had been confirmed as Prime Minister in April—and Mahmud Abbas, following which the two leaders agreed to conduct more substantial talks.

In May 2007 the ministers responsible for foreign affairs of Jordan, Israel and Egypt convened in the Egyptian capital, Cairo, to discuss an Arab League initiative for peace in the Middle East; the Arab proposal offered Israel peace and normalized relations with all Arab countries, in exchange for an Israeli withdrawal from those lands seized in 1967. The Jordanian Minister of Foreign Affairs, Abd al-Ilah al-Khatib, described the meeting as 'beneficial' and expressed his hope that it might lead to 'tangible results' that might eventually lead to a comprehensive peace in the region. However, the complete blockade of the Hamas-controlled Gaza Strip, imposed by the Israeli Government in mid-January 2008 (see the chapters on Israel and the Palestinian Autonomous Areas), prompted forceful condemnation from King Abdullah, who denounced the 'Israeli policy of aggression' and insisted that meaningful peace negotiations could not be held while Israel persisted with such measures against the Palestinian people.

During the course of 2006 the Jordanian Government repeatedly refused entry to large numbers of Palestinian refugees. In June King Abdullah announced that Jordan would not acquiesce to any deal that discriminated against Palestinians or was disadvantageous to Jordan's own interests, insisting that Jordan would never become a second home for the Palestinians because 'Jordan is Jordan, and Palestine is Palestine'.

Jordan's relations with the USA in the early 1990s were frequently strained by US allegations of Jordanian assistance to Iraq in circumventing the UN trade embargo, as well as Jordan's vocal criticism of US-led policies towards Iraq. However, in September 1993 US President Bill Clinton announced that some US $30m. in economic and military aid to Jordan was to be released in recognition of the country's enforcement of sanctions against Iraq and of its role in the Middle East peace process. In early 1994 renewed tensions emerged with the USA over the Jerusalem issue and the US-led naval blockade of Jordan's only port at Aqaba. Following a sharp deterioration in Jordanian–Iraqi relations in August 1995, when King Hussein granted political asylum to four senior members of the Iraqi regime (see below), Clinton promised to support Jordan in the event of any threat to its security; however, the USA failed to persuade Jordan to sever all economic links with Iraq. In January 1996 the USA offered Jordan $300m. in military assistance, and an expansion of bilateral military co-operation was announced in March. In June 1997 the USA pledged $100m. in economic aid to Jordan, reportedly in recognition of Jordan's contributions to the regional peace process; an assistance fund was established in August. In the same month Jordan signed a debt-rescheduling agreement with the USA, in accordance with a deal reached in May by members of the 'Paris Club' of Western official creditors to reschedule approximately $400m. of Jordanian debt.

In May 1999 King Abdullah began a three-week tour of the USA and several European capitals. Prior to the visit, the King had announced that, in anticipation of a summit of leaders of the Group of Eight (G-8) industrialized countries, due to be held in Germany in June, he would be seeking US support for an agreement by Western countries to write off as much as 50% of Jordan's debt. He achieved some success when the 'Paris Club' agreed, in late May (two days after a meeting with President Clinton), to reschedule about US $800m. of Jordanian debt; in June the G-8 leaders recommended debt reduction arrangements for Jordan. During a visit by King Abdullah to Washington, DC, in October 2000, Jordan and the USA signed a free trade agreement involving the reciprocal removal of all customs duties by 2010. The deal was fully implemented in December 2001.

King Abdullah strongly condemned the September 2001 suicide attacks against New York and Washington, DC, for which the USA held Osama bin Laden's al-Qa'ida network principally responsible, and the King swiftly affirmed Jordan's commitment to the proposed US-led 'war on terror'. Jordanian armed forces joined US and European forces when, from early October, they launched military strikes against al-Qa'ida bases and the Sunni fundamentalist Taliban regime in Afghanistan (which was believed to be harbouring bin Laden). However, Abdullah emphasized that the international community must simultaneously renew efforts to resolve the Israeli–Palestinian conflict. He also warned persistently that any extension of the US-led military action to target any Arab country, such as Iraq, would undermine the international campaign. In April 2002 certain sections of Jordan's business community called on the Government to boycott US products, in protest against perceived US support for Israeli aggression in the West Bank (see above). In July King Abdullah warned that Jordan would not allow its territory to be used by US troops to launch a military attack aimed at ousting the regime of Saddam Hussain in Iraq, and Jordanian officials denied reports in September that the Government had agreed to allow US forces to use Jordanian military bases in return for a guaranteed supply of cheap oil during a potential disruption to Iraq's oil supplies. In October the USA was said to have pledged a further US $85m. to Jordan, apparently in an effort to secure the country's support during a possible US-led military campaign in Iraq and to enable the Jordanian economy to withstand the consequences of a war.

At the end of October 2002 a senior US diplomat, Laurence Foley, became the first Western official to be assassinated in Jordan. The Jordanian security forces detained a large number of suspected Islamist militants following the assassination, and in December two alleged members of al-Qa'ida—one Jordanian and the other Libyan—were arrested on suspicion of involvement in Foley's murder. The trial of 11 suspects charged with involvement in the murder began in July 2003, with six of the defendants, including Abu Musab az-Zarqawi (see above), being tried *in absentia*. At the conclusion of the trial in April 2004, all but one of the defendants were convicted of charges relating to the diplomat's murder: az-Zarqawi and seven others were sentenced to death, and the remaining two were given terms of imprisonment. In February 2003, meanwhile, Jordanian officials confirmed that the USA was to provide the kingdom with an anti-missile defence system in the event of a conflict in Iraq; Jordan had received six F-16 fighter aircraft from the US military in January. King Abdullah met President Bush at Camp David in September. The two leaders discussed issues such as the implementation of the 'roadmap' peace plan and Palestinian militant funds held in Jordan. King Abdullah visited the USA in April 2004, but a meeting with President Bush was cancelled in protest at US support for Israel, particularly following Israel's recent 'targeted killings' of Hamas leaders Sheikh Ahmad Yassin and Abd al-Aziz ar-Rantisi, and at Bush's endorsement of Sharon's plan for an Israeli 'disengagement' from Gaza (see the chapter on Israel). The rescheduled meeting took place in Washington, DC, in May. In November 2006 King Abdullah hosted President Bush and Iraqi Prime Minister Nuri Kamal al-Maliki in Amman for talks that centred on the need to impose stability and security within Iraq; thousands of protesters amassed in the streets of Amman, rallying against US foreign policy, and three Jordanian men were arrested on suspicion of plotting to assassinate the US President during his visit. US Secretary of State Dr Condoleezza Rice visited the kingdom in February 2007 and met with King Abdullah to discuss their shared responsibility to effect a resumption of Israeli-Palestinian peace talks. In the following month the three men accused of plotting to assassinate Bush went on trial in Amman; all three pleaded not guilty and claimed to have been tortured while detained by the Jordanian security services. Court proceedings were adjourned several times during mid-2007 and in September the three defendants were referred for psychiatric assessment; in January 2008 the State Security Court adjourned the trial until February, on the grounds that a psychiatric evaluation had not been received for one of the three men.

After August 1995, when Jordan granted political asylum to the two sons-in-law of the Iraqi President, Saddam Hussain, and their wives (see the chapter on Iraq), King Hussein became more openly critical of the Iraqi regime; however, despite the political rupture, Jordan continued to provide Iraq with a crucial external economic link. In December 1997 Jordan recalled its chargé d'affaires from Baghdad and expelled a number of Iraqi diplomats from Jordan, in protest at the execution of four Jordanians by the Iraqi authorities. Later that month, however, the two countries signed an agreement whereby Iraq was to supply 4.8m. metric tons of crude petroleum and refined petroleum products to Jordan in 1998. In January of that year more than 50 Jordanian detainees were released by Iraq.

In response to critical confrontations between Iraq and the UN during 1998 over the issue of weapons inspections, Jordan indicated that it would not allow its territory or airspace to be used for air-strikes against Iraq. King Hussein consistently advocated a resolution of the crises by diplomatic means, whilst urging Iraq to comply with all pertinent UN resolutions. This position allowed Jordan to improve its relations with some Arab states, notably Egypt. Jordan strongly condemned the air-strikes carried out against Iraq by US and British forces in December, and in early 1999 the Jordanian National Assembly voted in favour of an end to the UN embargo against Iraq.

King Abdullah made attempts to improve Jordan's relations with Iraq following his accession in February 1999. In November 2000 Prime Minister ar-Ragheb undertook an official visit to Iraq—the first visit by a Jordanian premier since 1991—and the two states agreed to increase the value of their trade agreement from US $300m. in 2000 to $450m. in 2001. Jordan condemned the air-strikes launched on Baghdad by US and British forces in February 2001. By mid-2001 Jordan was increasingly concerned that the proposed imposition of so-called 'smart' sanctions against Iraq (the initiative, supported principally by the USA and United Kingdom, was under debate at the UN Security Council—see the chapter on Iraq) would result in the loss of its oil supply from Iraq, in addition to its main regional export market. However, although Jordanian officials declared publicly their opposition to 'smart' sanctions, they were said to have privately assured Western governments that they accepted the policy. The Iraqi leadership, meanwhile, threatened to halt trade with any government that assisted in the implementation of the sanctions regime. In June Royal Jordanian Airline resumed scheduled flights to Iraq for the first time since 1990. At senior-level discussions held in Amman in January 2002, Iraq and Jordan renewed their oil protocol and also agreed to the creation of a free trade zone.

Following discussions held in London, United Kingdom, between the British Prime Minister, Tony Blair, and King Abdullah in February 2003, the two leaders issued a joint statement calling on the Iraqi regime to comply with the terms of UN Security Council Resolution 1441 (see the chapter on Iraq), but stating that both Jordan and the United Kingdom favoured a peaceful solution to the crisis regarding Iraqi disarmament. King Abdullah had asserted in early February that the dispute regarding Iraq's alleged non-compliance with UN weapons inspectors should only be resolved under the umbrella of the UN. During early 2003 Jordan was said to be taking measures to prevent an influx of Iraqi refugees into the kingdom in the event of a US-led military campaign to remove Saddam Hussain's regime from power. However, in September 2007 the UN High Commissioner for Refugees (UNHCR) estimated the number of displaced Iraqis living in Jordan at between 500,000 and 750,000 (some of whom had been displaced prior to the conflict in Iraq from 2003). In an attempt to stem the influx of refugees and thus reduce the likelihood of a humanitarian crisis, Jordan had introduced new legislation in February 2007, rendering mandatory for all Iraqi refugees a recently introduced type of passport, issued only in Baghdad and, it was hoped, difficult to forge. In March the authorities announced that holders of the old passports would, however, be allowed to remain in the kingdom until June of that year. In a change of policy, the Jordanian Government announced in August that all Iraqi children living in the kingdom, even those who were there illegally, would be allowed for the first time to attend government schools; the USA provided financial aid to the sum of US $137m. in order to help the Jordanian education system to cope with the additional drain on its resources. Meanwhile, in June 2003, following the ousting of the Iraqi regime, the establishment was announced of a joint Jordanian-Iraqi business council to facilitate business relations between the two countries and to aid the recovery of the Iraqi economy. In July it was revealed that two daughters of the former Iraqi President had fled to Jordan via the United Arab Emirates (UAE). (In 1995 the women's husbands had been granted asylum in Jordan, but later returned to Iraq where they were executed on the orders of Saddam Hussain.) Official Jordanian sources stated that the two women and their children were being allowed to stay in Jordan for 'humanitarian reasons'.

In July 2004 King Abdullah offered to send troops to Iraq if the recently appointed Iraqi interim President or Prime Minister requested them to assist in restoring security to the country. In November the King held talks in Jordan with Iraq's interim Prime Minister, Dr Ayad Allawi, and Iraqi exiles, in an attempt to win support for elections to a transitional Iraqi legislature, scheduled to be held at the end of January 2005. In early January 2005 Amman hosted a meeting of five of the six countries neighbouring Iraq to discuss the forthcoming elections. The Iranian Minister of Foreign Affairs, Kamal Kharrazi, boycotted the meeting after Jordanian officials accused Iran of seeking to influence Iraqi voting in order to encourage the formation of a Shi'ite-dominated government, which would give largely Shi'ite Iran greater influence in the country. The conference emphasized the need to warn countries against external efforts to influence the outcome of the elections in Iraq. Following reports that a suicide bombing in the Iraqi town of Hillah in February (in which some 125 people died) had been perpetrated by a Jordanian militant, relations between the two countries deteriorated, and large anti-Jordanian protests took place in Baghdad. In the ensuing crisis, during which the Iraqi authorities alleged that Jordan was failing to prevent insurgents from crossing the border into Iraq, in March both countries temporarily withdrew diplomatic envoys from their respective capitals.

President Hafiz al-Assad of Syria led a high-level Syrian delegation at King Hussein's funeral in February 1999, since when Jordan's relations with Syria have improved significantly. It was announced in May that Syria would supply Jordan with water in order to ease the summer drought. In August the first senior Syrian delegation for almost a decade visited Amman for a session of the Jordanian-Syrian Higher Committee; the meeting resulted in an accord that officials hoped might double the volume of bilateral trade. Later in the month Syria reportedly agreed to end the ban (imposed in 1994) on the free circulation of Jordanian newspapers and publications. King Abdullah attended the funeral of President Assad in June 2000, and acted swiftly to forge close relations with the new Syrian President, Bashar al-Assad. In November Syria confirmed that it had upgraded its diplomatic representation in Amman to ambassadorial status, and the Syrian state airline resumed regular flights to Amman after a hiatus of more than 20 years. The Syrian authorities declared in January 2001 that all Jordanian prisoners held in Syria would soon be released; in November Jordanian officials claimed that there were still hundreds of Jordanian nationals being held in Syrian prisons. In August 2002 Jordan and Syria signed an agreement under which Syria was to provide Jordan with water to ease Jordan's water shortages. In December 2005 a Syrian human rights organization accused the Jordanian authorities of having unfairly expelled hundreds of Syrian workers from the country. However, the hostility was short-lived and in February 2006 a Jordanian delegation visited the Syrian capital, Damascus, to express solidarity with Syria and the leadership of President Assad. Despite relations again being threatened in April by the discovery of an arms and explosives cache allegedly smuggled into Jordan from Syria (see above), these were further consolidated by King Abdullah's first visit to Damascus for almost four years, in November 2007, and by the visit to Amman of Walid Moual-lem, the Syrian Minister of Foreign Affairs, in December. Under the terms of a deal concluded between King Abdullah and President Assad in November, 18 Jordanian detainees were released by Syria and returned to Jordan at the end of that month; it was hoped that the formation of a joint committee would secure the subsequent release of all remaining Jordanian prisoners in Syria and of all Syrian prisoners in Jordan.

Meanwhile, King Abdullah sought to strengthen relations with other Arab states. His first major foreign visit was to Egypt for talks with President Mubarak in March 1999. (Jordan and Egypt had signed an agreement in December 1998 providing for the future establishment of a free trade zone.) During April 1999 the new King visited a number of Middle Eastern countries, including Kuwait. Jordan's embassy there had been reopened in March of that year, following the restoration of full diplomatic relations between the two countries (which had been severed in 1990), and in September 1999 the rapprochement was apparently confirmed as King Abdullah again visited Kuwait. Kuwait subsequently announced at the end of a nine-year ban on the sale of Jordanian newspapers. In October Kuwait returned an ambassador to Amman, the post having been vacant since the Gulf crisis. Abdullah became the first Jordanian monarch to visit Lebanon for more than 30 years when, in September 1999, he held discussions with senior Lebanese officials regarding the Middle East peace process and bilateral issues (including a planned free trade agreement). Jordan's relations with Qatar deteriorated in August 2002, after the Jordanian authorities announced a ban on broadcasts in Jordan by Al-Jazeera following criticism of the Government's foreign policy. The Jordanian authorities responded by summoning the Qatari ambassador and later withdrawing its ambassador to Qatar. In October a Jordanian journalist employed by Qatari state television received a death sentence from a court in Qatar, having been convicted of espionage. However, in February 2003 he was granted a pardon by the Amir of Qatar, Sheikh Hamad, in a goodwill gesture to mark the visit to the capital, Doha, of King Abdullah.

Pan-Arab relations were strained as a result of the US-led military campaign in Iraq in early 2003. In March King Abdullah met with President Mubarak to discuss the divisions within the Arab League. Jordan arranged to import oil from Saudi Arabia, Kuwait and the UAE, reportedly at no cost, to circumvent shortages induced by the conflict in Iraq, and in May it was revealed that Jordan was conducting negotiations with the USA and the UN to seek a solution to the problem of interrupted oil supplies from Iraq. In November Minister of Foreign Affairs Dr Marwan al-Muasher visited Iran, primarily to discuss the status of some 1,000 members of the dissident Iranian guerrilla group, the Mujahidin-e-Khalq, who were formerly based in Iraq but who were now being held under Jordanian supervision in the border area between Iraq and Jordan.

In February 2004 Jordan signed a free trade agreement with Egypt, Morocco and Tunisia, which committed each party to removing trade tariffs between them and to intensifying economic co-operation, particularly with regard to legislation concerning customs procedures and standards; the so-called Agadir Agreement was ratified in 2006 and entered into force in 2007. Meanwhile, in January 2007 King Abdullah urged Iran to exercise its influence over its neighbours in a positive manner, imploring the Iranian Government to refrain from adding to existing regional instability, particularly within Iraq, the Palestinian territories and Lebanon.

Relations with Saudi Arabia have improved in recent years, and bilateral ties were further bolstered by reciprocal visits by the two countries' respective monarchs in 2007. In June Saudi Arabia's King Abdullah ibn Abd al-Aziz as-Sa'ud made a two-day visit to Amman, during which he met with his Jordanian counterpart for discussions on a wide range of issues. The two monarchs held further talks when King Abdullah of Jordan visited the Saudi capital, Riyadh, in mid-November; the discussions focused predominantly on consolidating bilateral relations and the respective situations in Iraq and the Palestinian territories, with considerable attention afforded to the forthcoming US-sponsored international Middle East peace summit, which was held at the end of the month in Annapolis, Maryland, USA. In December Jordan and Saudi Arabia signed a border pact on the demarcation of their shared marine border in the Gulf of Aqaba, and in a ceremony to mark the occasion the Saudi Minister of the Interior, Prince Nayef ibn Abd al-Aziz as-Sa'ud, upheld Jordanian-Saudi relations as 'a model for sincere brotherly ties'.

JORDAN

Government

Jordan is a constitutional monarchy. Legislative power is vested in a bicameral National Assembly: the Senate (House of Notables) has 55 members, appointed by the King for eight years (one-half of the members retiring every four years), while the House of Representatives (House of Deputies) has 110 members, elected by universal adult suffrage for four years. Under legislation introduced in February 2003, six seats in the House of Representatives are reserved for women. Executive power is vested in the King, who governs with the assistance of an appointed Cabinet, responsible to the Assembly. There are 12 administrative provinces.

Defence

As assessed at November 2007, the total strength of the Jordanian armed forces was 100,500. The army had 88,000 men, the air force 12,000 and the navy (coastguard) an estimated 500. Reserve forces numbered 65,000 (60,000 in the army). Paramilitary forces numbered an estimated 45,000 men, comprising a Public Security Force (attached to the Ministry of the Interior) of an estimated 10,000 and a Civil Militia of an estimated 35,000 reservists. Military service is based on selective conscription. Defence expenditure for 2007 was budgeted at JD 1,132m.

Economic Affairs

In 2006, according to estimates by the World Bank, the East Bank of Jordan's gross national income (GNI), measured at average 2004–06 prices, was US $14,712m., equivalent to $2,660 per head (or $6,210 per head on an international purchasing-power parity basis). During 1996–2006, it was estimated, the population increased at an average annual rate of 2.6%, while the East Bank's gross domestic product (GDP) per head increased, in real terms, by an average of 2.5% per year. Overall GDP increased, in real terms, by an average annual rate of 5.1% in 1996–2006; growth of 6.4% was recorded in 2006.

Agriculture (including hunting, forestry and fishing) contributed about 3.0% of Jordan's GDP in 2006, according to preliminary figures, and accounted for 9.4% of the country's employed labour force in 2005, according to FAO estimates. The principal cash crops are vegetables, fruit and nuts, and wheat production is also important; vegetables accounted for about 5.1% of export earnings in 2006. The World Bank estimated that the sector's GDP increased at an average annual rate of 3.1% during 1996–2006. Preliminary official data indicated a sectoral growth rate of 0.9% in 2006.

Industry (including mining, manufacturing, construction and power) provided 28.4% of GDP in 2006, according to preliminary figures; about 22.4% of the country's active labour force were employed in the sector in 2005. According to World Bank data, during 1996–2006 industrial GDP increased by an average of 7.6% per year. Preliminary official data indicated that the sector's GDP increased by 8.1% in 2006.

Mining and quarrying contributed 3.1% of GDP in 2006, according to preliminary figures, and accounted for about 0.8% of the employed labour force in 2005. Phosphates and potash are the principal mineral exports, together accounting for around 4.4% of total export earnings in 2006. Jordan also has reserves of oil-bearing shale, but exploitation of this resource is at present undeveloped. Preliminary official figures suggested that mining GDP decreased by an average rate of 5.3% per year during 2002–06, and declined by 9.5% in 2006.

Manufacturing provided 18.4% of GDP in 2006, according to preliminary figures, and engaged some 17.1% of the employed labour force in 2005. The most important branches of manufacturing, measured by gross value of output, are food, beverages and tobacco, refined petroleum products, chemicals, non-metallic mineral products and metal products. World Bank data indicated that manufacturing GDP increased by an average of 10.4% per year in 1996–2006; according to preliminary official figures, the sector recorded growth of 9.5% in 2006.

Energy has traditionally been derived principally from imported petroleum, but attempts are being made to develop alternative sources of power, including wind and solar power. In 2003 petroleum provided 90.1% of total electricity production, but in the following year this declined to just 49.2%; conversely, natural gas accounted for only 9.3% of total electricity production in 2003, but this increased to 50.2% in 2004. Imports of mineral products comprised some 23.3% of the total value of imports in 2006. Following an agreement signed in mid-2001, Egypt commenced exports of gas to Jordan via a high-capacity pipeline in mid-2003; the rate of gas transfer stood at some 1,000m. cu m per year in 2004, and was expected to have doubled by 2008.

Services accounted for some 68.6% of Jordan's GDP in 2006, according to preliminary figures, and engaged an estimated 77.6% of the employed labour force in 2005. During 1996–2006, according to the World Bank, the GDP of the sector increased by an average of 3.8% per year; sectoral growth increased by 6.9% in 2006, according to preliminary official data.

In 2006 Jordan recorded a visible trade deficit of US $5,055.9m., and there was a deficit of $1,909.0m. on the current account of the balance of payments. In 2006 Saudi Arabia was the main source of imports (with 24.9% of the total); other major suppliers were the People's Republic of China, Germany and the USA. The USA was the principal market for exports (with 25.0% of the total); other significant purchasers were Iraq, India and Saudi Arabia. The principal exports in 2006 were textiles, works of art and antiques, and chemical and chemical products, while the principal imports were mineral products, machinery and mechanical appliances, and food, beverages and tobacco.

In 2007 a budget deficit of JD 795.3m. was envisaged. Jordan's external debt totalled US $7,696m. at the end of 2005, of which $6,878m. was long-term public debt. In that year the cost of debt-servicing was equivalent to 6.5% of the value of exports of goods and services. The annual rate of inflation averaged 2.6% in 1996–2006. According to official sources, consumer prices increased by an average of 6.3% in 2007. Unemployment reached some 14.3% in 2006.

Jordan is a member of the Council of Arab Economic Unity (see p. 222), the Arab Monetary Fund (see p. 175) and the World Trade Organization (WTO, see p. 396). In September 1999 the Jordanian parliament ratified the Jordanian-European Partnership Agreement (signed with the EU in November 1997), which provides for the creation of a duty-free zone and the abolition of import duties by 2010.

Despite the outbreak of renewed Israeli–Palestinian conflict in late 2000, which has had a particularly detrimental effect on Jordan's tourism and banking sectors, and the negative impact on the economy of the Iraq conflict in early 2003, the IMF reported in September 2004 that Jordan had achieved substantial economic growth in the aftermath of that war. Growth was driven by buoyant domestic demand and exports, the latter of which was largely attributable to the conclusion of a bilateral free trade agreement with the USA, which took effect in late 2001, and a significant increase in trade with regional neighbours, including Saudi Arabia and the UAE; an association agreement was signed with the EU in 2002. Meanwhile, in 2001 the Aqaba region was accorded the status of a Special Economic Zone, and has since attracted significant levels of foreign investment. The Government has implemented an IMF-supported adjustment and reform programme with the aim of reducing state intervention in industry and, through privatization, raising funds to support the repayment of foreign debt, which since the early 1990s had been a heavy burden upon the Jordanian economy. The problem of external debt has been significantly reduced since the late 1990s, a process facilitated by a series of debt relief measures implemented by Western creditors. However, with extensive development planned in the health and transport sectors, Jordan increased its provision of external debt in 2006, signing up to three debt swap agreements with the 'Paris Club', as well as securing additional loans amounting to an estimated JD 112.3m. from multinational creditors. Total public debt, however, contracted by 2% in that year; according to official data, at October 2006 public debt was equivalent to 72.7% of GDP, well within the 80% limit stipulated by the Public Debt Management Law of 2001. Meanwhile, a year-long petroleum grant subsidized by Saudia Arabia expired in April 2005, requiring Jordan to import crude oil at high international prices. The 2007 budget excluded fuel subsidies from the total planned outlay, and the Government was expected to continue with its privatization programme, the proceeds of which amounted to some US $650m. in 2006. The authorities also planned to extend the provision of tax-free zones to generate much needed investment. In late 2007 the Government upwardly revised its budget deficit forecast, with unofficial sources predicting a deficit of around JD 900m., predominantly owing to increased government spending and the mounting cost of oil subsidies. The 2008 budget forecast a widening of the deficit, attributable in part to the demands of the Jordanian social benefits system; the Government has pledged an annual sum of JD 300m. to compensate the poor for the rising cost of fuel.

JORDAN

In March 2007 the EU pledged some $350m. in aid to Jordan, to be disbursed over a four-year period, to assist the Government in meeting its objectives under the National Agenda, published in January. This ambitious 10-year plan to improve the quality and effectiveness of public administration included as targets the reduction of poverty and unemployment (by creating 600,000 jobs) and the achievement of annual real GDP growth of 7.2%. The IMF estimated GDP growth of 6.0% in 2007, and forecast the same rate for 2008.

Education

Primary education, beginning at six years of age, is free and compulsory. This 10-year preparatory cycle is followed by a two-year secondary cycle. UNRWA provides schooling for Palestinian refugees. There were 39,441 teachers in 2002/03 and 804,904 pupils enrolled in 2004/05 at the primary level. At the secondary level (including both general and vocational institutions), there were 34,543 teachers in 2002/03 and 625,682 pupils in 2004/05. According to UNESCO estimates, in 2004/05 primary enrolment included 88.9% of children in the relevant age-group; in the same year secondary enrolment included 78.7% of children in the relevant age-group. There were 8,251 teachers and 217,823 pupils engaged in higher education in 2004/05. Education in Jordan was provided at 5,167 schools and 22 institutions of higher education in 2003/04. Budgetary expenditure on education by the central Government in 2004 accounted for 11.4% of total spending.

Public Holidays

2008: 10 January*† (Muharram, Islamic New Year), 15 January (Arbor Day), 20 March* (Mouloud, Birth of Muhammad), 22 March (Arab League Day), 25 May (Independence Day), 9 June (King Abdullah's Accession), 30 July* (Leilat al-Meiraj, Ascension of Muhammad), 1 October* (Id al-Fitr, end of Ramadan), 9 December* (Id al-Adha, Feast of the Sacrifice), 29 December*† (Muharram, Islamic New Year).

2009: 15 January (Arbor Day), 9 March* (Mouloud, Birth of Muhammad), 22 March (Arab League Day), 25 May (Independence Day), 9 June (King Abdullah's Accession), 19 July* (Leilat al-Meiraj, Ascension of Muhammad), 20 September* (Id al-Fitr, end of Ramadan), 27 November* (Id al-Adha, Feast of the Sacrifice), 18 December* (Muharram, Islamic New Year).

* These holidays are dependent on the Islamic lunar calendar and may vary by one or two days from the dates given.

† This festival occurs twice (marking the start of the Islamic years AH 1429 and 1430) within the same Gregorian year.

Weights and Measures

The metric system is in force. In Jordan the dunum is 1,000 sq m (0.247 acre).

Statistical Survey

Source: Department of Statistics, POB 2015, Amman 11181; tel. (6) 5300700; fax (6) 5300710; e-mail stat@dos.gov.jo; internet www.dos.gov.jo.

Area and Population

AREA, POPULATION AND DENSITY
(East Bank only)

Area (sq km)	88,778*
Population (census results)	
10–11 November 1979	2,100,019
10 December 1994	
Males	2,160,725
Females	1,978,733
Total	4,139,458
Population (official estimates at 31 December)	
2005	5,473,000
2006	5,600,000
2007	5,723,000
Density (per sq km) at 31 December 2007	64.5

* 34,277 sq miles.

GOVERNORATES
(East Bank only; estimated population at 31 December 2007)

	Area (sq km)	Population	Density (per sq km)
Amman	7,579	2,220,500	293.0
Irbid	1,572	1,018,700	648.0
Az-Zarqa (Zarqa)	4,761	852,700	179.1
Al-Balqa	1,119	383,400	342.6
Al-Mafraq	26,541	269,000	10.1
Al-Karak (Kerak)	3,495	223,200	63.9
Jarash (Jerash)	410	171,700	418.8
Madaba	940	143,100	152.2
Ajloun	420	131,600	313.3
Al-Aqabah (Aqaba)	6,900	120,200	17.4
Ma'an	32,832	108,800	3.3
At-Tafilah	2,209	80,100	36.3
Total	**88,778**	**5,723,000**	**64.5**

PRINCIPAL TOWNS
(population at 1994 census)

Amman (capital)	969,598	Al-Baqa'a	58,592
Az-Zarqa (Zarqa)	350,849	As-Salt	56,458
Irbid	208,329	Madaba	55,749
Ar-Rusayfah (Russeifa)	137,247	Ar-Ramtha	55,022
Wadi as-Sir	89,104	Suwaylih	53,250
Al-Aqabah (Aqaba)	62,773		

Source: Thomas Brinkhoff, *City Population* (internet www.citypopulation.de).

Population at 31 December 2004: Amman 1,053,119; Zarqa 416,270; Russeifa 279,650; Wadi as-Sir 184,600; Ar-Ramtha 106,620; Madaba 85,110; As-Salt 78,790; Suwaylih 65,460.

BIRTHS, MARRIAGES AND DEATHS
(East Bank only)*

	Registered live births		Registered marriages		Registered deaths	
	Number	Rate (per 1,000)	Number	Rate (per 1,000)	Number	Rate (per 1,000)
2002	146,077	29.0	46,873	8.8	17,220	6.4
2003	148,294	28.5	48,784	8.9	16,937	6.7
2004	150,248	28.0	53,754	10.0	17,011	7.0
2005	152,276	28.0	56,418	10.3	17,883	7.0
2006†	163,000	29.1	59,300	10.6	20,400	n.a.

* Data are tabulated by year of registration rather than by year of occurrence. Registration of births and marriages is reported to be complete, but death registration is incomplete. Figures exclude foreigners, but include registered Palestinian refugees.

† Figures are rounded.

Expectation of life (years at birth, WHO estimates): 71.0 (males 69.0; females 73.5) in 2005 (Source: WHO, *World Health Statistics*).

JORDAN

EMPLOYMENT
(economic survey at October, Jordanian employees only, public and private sectors, excl. armed forces)

	2003	2004	2005
Mining and quarrying	6,899	6,582	6,305
Manufacturing	119,442	131,202	132,792
Electricity, gas and water	14,084	13,948	14,260
Construction	14,449	17,009	21,342
Wholesale and retail trade; repair of motor vehicles and motorcycles and personal and household goods	161,973	212,549	187,557
Hotels and restaurants	24,275	29,836	30,367
Transport, storage and communications	25,009	28,638	28,467
Financial intermediation	17,970	17,781	18,463
Real estate, renting and business activities	34,490	33,210	33,281
Public administration and compulsory social security	79,332	74,561	78,065
Education	139,134	141,979	147,248
Health and social work	45,441	47,757	52,074
Other community, social and personal service activities	22,631	21,382	28,605
Total employed	705,130	776,434	778,823
Males	550,331	606,653	595,005
Females	154,799	169,781	183,818

Note: Figures are assumed to exclude data for Jordanians engaged in agriculture and fishing—according to FAO estimates some 194,000 of a total economically active population of 1,975,000 were engaged in the sector at mid-2005. Figures also exclude foreign nationals employed in Jordan, numbering 55,831 in 2003; 75,463 in 2004; 87,295 in 2005.

Health and Welfare

KEY INDICATORS

Total fertility rate (children per woman, 2005)	3.3
Under-5 mortality rate (per 1,000 live births, 2005)	26
HIV/AIDS (% of persons aged 15–49, 2005)	<0.1
Physicians (per 1,000 head, 2004)	2.03
Hospital beds (per 1,000 head, 2005)	1.7
Health expenditure (2004): US $ per head (PPP)	501.7
Health expenditure (2004): % of GDP	9.8
Health expenditure (2004): Public (% of total)	48.4
Access to water (% of persons, 2004)	97
Access to sanitation (% of persons, 2004)	93
Human Development Index (2005): Ranking	86
Human Development Index (2005): Value	0.773

For sources and definitions, see explanatory note on p. vi.

Agriculture

PRINCIPAL CROPS
(East Bank only; '000 metric tons)

	2004	2005	2006
Wheat	13.2	34.4	22.9
Barley	21.0	31.8	18.4
Maize	14.8	30.8	18.4
Potatoes	165.3	172.1	160.0
Olives	160.7	113.1	146.8
Cabbages and other brassicas	28.5	30.6	37.2
Lettuce and chicory	52.6	28.2	37.2
Tomatoes	449.5	598.9	545.6
Cauliflowers and broccoli	92.9	76.0	63.4
Pumpkins, squash and gourds	55.5	72.3	61.8
Cucumbers and gherkins	102.5	166.2	142.7
Aubergines (Eggplants)	82.9	99.3	95.6
Chillies and green peppers	39.1	38.4	38.3
Green onions and shallots	7.5	7.4	3.7
Dry onions	49.4	39.6	28.7
Green beans	12.1	10.0	13.7
Okra	8.7	7.2	4.3

—continued	2004	2005	2006
Watermelons	83.9	85.0	91.9
Cantaloupes and other melons	24.0	32.3	26.8
Bananas	37.1	32.2	42.1
Grapefruit and pomelos	10.4	10.6	4.8
Oranges	41.1	44.2	45.9
Tangerines, mandarins, clementines and satsumas	43.0	45.8	48.2
Lemons and limes	33.3	35.8	32.7
Apples	42.4	45.6	46.4
Peaches and nectarines	13.1	14.4	14.0
Grapes	32.4	34.5	32.2

Aggregate production ('000 metric tons, may include official, semi-official or estimated data): Total cereals 53.4 in 2004, 102.4 in 2005, 61.9 in 2006; Total roots and tubers 165.3 in 2004, 172.1 in 2005, 160.0 in 2006; Total vegetables (incl. melons) 1,176.2 in 2004, 1,399.2 in 2005, 1,305.1 in 2006; Total fruits (excl. melons) 288.6 in 2004, 297.2 in 2005, 303.4 in 2006.

Source: FAO.

LIVESTOCK
(East Bank only; '000 head, year ending September)

	2004	2005	2006
Horses*	4	4	4
Asses, mules or hinnies*	21	21	21
Cattle	69.3	67.5	67.5*
Camels*	18	18	18
Sheep	1,529.1	1,890.4	1,971.5
Goats	501.1	516.1	473.8
Chickens	25,000*	25,000*	25,000

* FAO estimate(s).

Source: FAO.

LIVESTOCK PRODUCTS
(East Bank only; '000 metric tons)

	2004	2005	2006
Cattle meat	3.6	3.7	3.5
Sheep meat*	4.0	4.0	4.0
Goat meat*	1.5	1.5	1.5
Chicken meat	126.7	132.6	115.8
Cows' milk	200.5	196.7	205.1
Sheep's milk	58.4	65.8	84.5
Goats' milk	18.2	15.5	20.2
Hen eggs	46.8	40.6	44.7
Wool: greasy*	2.0	2.0	2.0

* FAO estimates.

Source: FAO.

Forestry

ROUNDWOOD REMOVALS
('000 cubic metres, excluding bark, FAO estimates)

	2004	2005	2006
Industrial wood	4	4	4
Fuel wood	253	262	269
Total	257	266	273

Source: FAO.

Fishing

(metric tons, live weight)

	2003	2004	2005
Capture	481	494	510
Freshwater fishes	350	350	350
Tunas	86	95	109
Aquaculture (Tilapias)	650	487	561
Total catch	1,131	981	1,071

Source: FAO.

Mining

('000 metric tons unless otherwise indicated)

	2003	2004	2005
Crude petroleum ('000 barrels)	9.8	8.5	8.0*
Phosphate rock	6,762	6,223	6,375
Potash salts†	1,190	1,175	1,115
Bromine	—	46.0	50.0*
Feldspar	13.1	13.1	13.0*
Gypsum	63.9	135.3	140.0*

* Estimate.
† Figures refer to the K_2O content.

Source: US Geological Survey.

Industry

SELECTED PRODUCTS
('000 barrels unless otherwise indicated, estimates)

	2003	2004	2005*
Liquefied petroleum gas	1,485	1,299	1,400
Motor spirit (petrol)	5,084	4,938	5,300
Kerosene	1,484	1,252*	1,300
Jet fuels	2,109	1,578	1,700
Distillate fuel oils	8,579	9,116	9,700
Asphalt	1,200	1,300*	1,300
Cement ('000 metric tons)	3,515	3,908	4,046

* Estimate(s).

Electricity (million kWh): 6,921 in 2002; 7,341 in 2003; 8,038 in 2004.

Phosphate fertilizers ('000 metric tons): 435.0 in 2001; 459.0 in 2002.

Source: partly US Geological Survey.

Finance

CURRENCY AND EXCHANGE RATES

Monetary Units
1,000 fils = 1 Jordanian dinar (JD).

Sterling, Dollar and Euro Equivalents (30 November 2007)
£1 sterling = JD 1.465;
US $1 = 709 fils;
€1 = JD 1.047;
JD 10 = £6.83 = $14.10 = €9.56.

Exchange Rate: An official mid-point rate of US $1 = 709 fils (JD 1 = $1.4104) has been maintained since October 1995.

BUDGET
(East Bank only; JD million)*

Revenue†	2005‡	2006‡	2007§
Taxation	1,765.8	2,133.5	2,429.0
Taxes on income and profits	283.7	411.4	488.0
Corporations	197.3	320.1	372.0
Individuals	45.0	47.0	66.0
Taxes on domestic transactions	1,143.3	1,366.6	1,559.0
General sales tax	1,023.4	1,219.1	1,404.0
Taxes on foreign trade	304.9	315.6	338.0
Other revenue	756.0	987.1	1,038.0
Licences	48.2	54.0	67.0
Fees	423.9	502.8	537.0
Interest and profits	97.9	141.5	163.0
Repayment	39.7	43.9	33.0
Total	2,561.8	3,164.5	3,500.0

Expenditure	2005‡	2006‡	2007§
Current	2,908.0	3,118.1	3,839.1
Wages and salaries	489.9	514.3	552.2
Purchases of goods and services	110.1	115.1	147.8
Interest payments	267.1	317.8	393.0
Oil subsidies	530.8	214.0	200.0
Pensions	416.7	490.6	524.7
Decentralized agencies	101.5	167.8	167.6
University and municipalities	42.3	41.0	21.0
Defence and security	698.8	795.1	1,132.6
Capital|	630.9	794.1	1,003.2
Total	3,538.9	3,912.2	4,842.3

* Figures represent a consolidation of the Current, Capital and Development Plan Budgets of the central Government. The data exclude the operations of the Health Security Fund and of other government agencies with individual budgets.
† Excluding foreign grants received (JD million): 500.3 in 2005 (preliminary); 304.6 in 2006 (preliminary); 547.0 in 2007 (budget).
‡ Preliminary figures.
§ Budget.
| Includes overdue settlements and arrears on public sector.

Source: Ministry of Finance, Amman.

INTERNATIONAL RESERVES
(US $ million at 31 December)

	2004	2005	2006
Gold (national valuation)	179.6	212.3	257.1
IMF special drawing rights	1.7	0.6	1.3
Foreign exchange	5,264.8	5,249.5	6,720.4
Total	5,446.1	5,462.4	6,978.8

Source: IMF, *International Financial Statistics*.

MONEY SUPPLY
(JD million at 31 December)

	2004	2005	2006
Currency outside banks	1,414.4	1,657.3	2,027.4
Demand deposits at commercial banks	1,721.1	2,362.8	2,491.6
Total money (incl. others)	3,138.5	4,022.6	4,521.8

Source: IMF, *International Financial Statistics*.

JORDAN

COST OF LIVING
(Consumer Price Index; base: 2002 = 100)

	2005	2006	2007
Food (incl. beverages)	112.8	121.2	132.5
Clothing (incl. footwear)	94.0	96.6	102.7
Housing	105.7	111.6	113.8
Other goods and services	108.4	114.4	117.4
All items	108.7	115.5	121.7

NATIONAL ACCOUNTS
(East Bank only; JD million at current prices)

Expenditure on the Gross Domestic Product

	2002	2003	2004*
Government final consumption expenditure	1,542	1,676	1,723
Private final consumption expenditure	5,196	5,567	6,601
Changes in stocks	78	16	210
Gross fixed capital formation	1,287	1,491	2,005
Total domestic expenditure	8,103	8,750	10,539
Exports of goods and services	3,217	3,419	4,212
Less Imports of goods and services	4,526	4,940	6,670
GDP in purchasers' values	6,794	7,229	8,081
GDP at constant 1994 prices	6,034	6,286	6,816

*Preliminary.

Gross Domestic Product by Economic Activity
(preliminary figures)

	2004	2005	2006
Agriculture, hunting, forestry and fishing	202.1	246.2	274.5
Mining and quarrying	230.4	279.9	281.0
Manufacturing	1,313.6	1,454.7	1,696.8
Electricity and water	189.4	190.2	199.6
Construction	324.4	382.1	435.0
Wholesale and retail trade, restaurants and hotels	746.5	835.9	919.3
Transport, storage and communications	1,188.5	1,256.5	1,342.6
Finance, insurance, real estate and business services	1,444.5	1,747.5	1,998.0
Community, social and personal services	347.8	383.1	425.8
Public administration and defence; compulsory social security	1,338.6	1,424.4	1,531.7
Producers of private non-profit services for households	74.4	75.6	77.7
Private households with employed persons	14.5	16.0	16.9
Sub-total	7,414.7	8,292.1	9,198.9
Less Imputed bank service charge	219.7	312.4	345.9
Gross value added in basic prices	7,195.0	7,979.7	8,853.0
Taxes on products (net)	895.7	961.8	1,144.4
GDP in purchasers' values	8,090.7	8,941.5	9,997.4

Source: Central Bank of Jordan, Amman.

BALANCE OF PAYMENTS
(US $ million)

	2004	2005	2006
Exports of goods f.o.b.	3,882.9	4,301.4	5,204.4
Imports of goods f.o.b.	−7,261.1	−9,317.3	−10,260.2
Trade balance	−3,378.1	−5,015.9	−5,055.9
Exports of services	2,072.8	2,333.6	2,488.9
Imports of services	−2,145.8	−2,542.0	−2,712.3
Balance on goods and services	−3,451.2	−5,224.4	−5,279.3
Other income received	649.2	791.1	1,031.9
Other income paid	−325.5	−382.7	−451.3
Balance on goods, services and income	−3,127.5	−4,815.9	−4,698.7
Current transfers received	3,562.5	3,029.8	3,378.8

—continued	2004	2005	2006
Current transfers paid	−346.3	−441.3	−589.1
Current balance	88.7	−2,227.5	−1,909.0
Capital account (net)	2.1	8.5	62.8
Direct investment (net)	798.2	1,610.8	3,357.4
Portfolio investment assets	−199.0	143.6	−180.4
Portfolio investment liabilities	−89.8	169.1	143.6
Other investment assets	−680.8	−615.9	−1,148.0
Other investment liabilities	68.3	330.6	821.6
Net errors and omissions	192.3	841.6	293.8
Overall balance	179.8	260.8	1,441.7

Source: IMF, *International Financial Statistics*.

External Trade

PRINCIPAL COMMODITIES
(distribution by Harmonized System, JD '000)

Imports c.i.f.	2004	2005	2006
Food, beverages and tobacco	999.5	1,032.7	1,140.2
Live animals and animal products	180.3	207.0	223.7
Vegetable products	393.6	398.5	437.6
Prepared foodstuffs; beverages, spirits and vinegar; tobacco and manufactured tobacco substitutes	279.4	319.5	388.7
Mineral products	1,124.2	1,728.5	1,949.8
Chemicals and related products	406.7	466.2	509.6
Plastics, rubbers, and articles thereof	252.4	296.2	317.2
Textiles and textile articles	564.4	614.1	712.6
Pearls; precious or semi-precious stones; precious metals	117.4	166.9	107.4
Base metals and articles thereof	455.8	566.6	650.6
Machinery and mechanical appliances	784.5	1,151.0	1,199.9
Vehicles, aircraft, vessels and associated transport equipment	527.2	714.8	799.0
Total (incl. others)	5,799.2	7,442.9	8,357.7

Exports f.o.b.	2004	2005	2006
Food, beverages and tobacco	397.4	457.5	515.8
Vegetable products	146.7	183.6	187.2
Animal and vegetable fats, oils and waxes	112.8	85.8	64.4
Prepared foodstuffs; beverages, spirits and vinegar; tobacco and manufactured tobacco substitutes	100.0	113.6	144.8
Mineral products	179.1	145.2	162.9
Chemicals and related products	678.5	774.3	817.3
Textiles and textile articles	751.5	783.2	929.2
Pearls; precious or semi-precious stones; precious metals	126.5	127.0	338.4
Base metals and articles thereof	101.5	142.4	193.7
Machinery and mechanical appliances	210.1	266.6	340.3
Vehicles, aircraft, vessels and associated transport equipment	114.4	106.7	138.0
Works of art, collectors' pieces and antiques	88.0	269.0	905.5
Total (incl. others)	2,753.0	3,049.6	3,689.9

JORDAN

PRINCIPAL TRADING PARTNERS
(countries of consignment, JD million)

Imports c.i.f.	2004	2005	2006
Argentina	57.3	63.0	48.2
Australia	53.1	31.7	47.4
Belgium-Luxembourg	46.0	55.6	56.4
China, People's Republic	489.3	686.7	860.4
Egypt	214.5	261.0	346.4
France	159.9	177.4	198.4
Germany	394.9	597.2	645.2
India	103.2	104.4	26.1
Indonesia	123.7	103.9	102.9
Iraq	45.6	19.7	5.2
Italy	222.2	249.7	298.9
Japan	189.9	210.4	253.4
Korea, Republic	182.2	265.1	256.8
Malaysia	68.2	52.8	50.1
Netherlands	74.2	96.6	81.1
Russia	34.0	94.3	73.0
Saudi Arabia	1,146.6	1,758.4	2,081.0
Spain	68.1	52.0	57.3
Sweden	45.7	43.8	46.1
Switzerland	80.2	99.4	66.1
Syria	147.4	161.6	185.8
Taiwan	114.4	118.9	124.5
Turkey	133.8	181.6	216.2
United Arab Emirates	103.1	150.1	152.4
United Kingdom	150.9	209.2	185.6
USA	393.9	417.0	393.3
Total (incl. others)	5,799.2	7,442.9	8,357.7

Exports f.o.b.	2004	2005	2006
China, People's Republic	27.7	29.4	27.0
Egypt	22.1	32.2	39.7
Germany	6.2	7.5	6.2
India	179.6	247.4	281.4
Indonesia	24.5	9.6	15.3
Iraq	519.5	521.5	449.8
Israel	82.4	83.9	94.0
Kuwait	38.3	51.4	69.0
Lebanon	44.1	48.2	53.2
Malaysia	16.4	17.1	31.8
Pakistan	15.1	15.4	5.1
Qatar	16.7	24.5	37.4
Saudi Arabia	148.2	179.3	281.2
Syria	108.0	143.7	191.1
United Arab Emirates	88.9	121.3	206.6
United Kingdom	9.1	12.0	14.4
USA	724.0	798.1	923.6
Total (incl. others)	2,753.0	3,049.6	3,689.9

Transport

RAILWAYS
(traffic, million)

	2001	2002	2003
Passenger-km	4	3	1
Freight ton-km	371	531	497

Source: UN, *Statistical Yearbook*.

ROAD TRAFFIC
(motor vehicles in use at 31 December)

	2002	2003	2004
Passenger cars	348,783	355,752	387,565
Buses	12,738	13,272	14,084
Lorries and vans	146,372	163,244	176,104
Motorcycles	n.a.	686	800

SHIPPING
Merchant Fleet
(registered at 31 December)

	2004	2005	2006
Number of vessels	26	32	32
Displacement ('000 grt)	222.7	357.5	386.3

Source: Lloyd's Register-Fairplay, *World Fleet Statistics*.

International Sea-borne Freight Traffic
('000 metric tons)

	2000	2001	2002
Goods loaded	7,192	7,791	8,872
Goods unloaded	5,359	5,251	5,286

CIVIL AVIATION
(traffic on scheduled services)

	2001	2002	2003
Kilometres flown (million)	36	37	36
Passengers carried ('000)	1,178	1,300	1,353
Passenger-km (million)	3,848	4,146	4,498
Total ton-km (million)	530	577	602

Source: UN, *Statistical Yearbook*.

Tourism

ARRIVALS BY NATIONALITY
('000)*

	2005	2006	2007†
Egypt	351.9	262.3	370.4
Iraq	773.5	382.7	211.3
Israel	175.7	149.0	205.0
Kuwait	170.4	118.0	120.5
Lebanon	144.2	143.8	152.6
Palestinian Autonomous Areas	113.2	72.8	262.5
Saudi Arabia	924.6	954.1	835.1
Syria	1,655.6	1,599.0	1,585.9
Turkey	104.9	105.1	110.3
United Kingdom	56.8	48.9	68.3
USA	130.1	125.8	126.2
Yemen	33.7	28.6	29.5
Total (incl. others)	5,817.4	4,976.7	5,110.9

* Including pilgrims and excursionists (same-day visitors).
† Preliminary figures.

Tourism receipts (JD million): 803.5 in 2005; 1,055.2 in 2006; 1,291.8 in 2007 (preliminary).

Source: Ministry of Tourism, Amman.

Communications Media

(East Bank only)

	2004	2005	2006
Telephones ('000 main lines in use)	637.8	628.0	614.0
Mobile cellular telephones ('000 subscribers)	1,624.1	3,137.7	4,343.1
Personal computers ('000 in use)	300	n.a.	n.a.
Internet users ('000)	629.5	719.8	796.9
Broadband subscribers ('000)	10.4	24.2	48.6

1996: Book production (titles) 511.

1997: Radio receivers ('000 in use) 1,660; Non-daily newspapers (titles) 13, (average circulation) 154,000.

1998: Facsimile machines ('000 in use) 51.6; Daily newspapers (average circulation) 352,000 copies; Non-daily newspapers (average circulation) 155,000; Periodicals (titles) 270, (average circulation) 148,000 copies.

Daily newspapers (titles): 8 in 1998; 5 in 1999; 5 in 2000; 4 in 2004.

Non-daily newspapers (titles): 13 in 1998; 17 in 1999; 20 in 2000.

Television receivers ('000 in use): 560 in 2000.

Sources: partly International Telecommunication Union; UNESCO, *Statistical Yearbook*; UN, *Statistical Yearbook*.

Education

(East Bank, 2004/05, unless otherwise indicated)

	Schools	Teachers	Pupils
Pre-primary	1,248*	4,526	84,817
Primary	2,877*	39,441†	804,904
Secondary: general	1,002*	30,426†	594,733
Secondary: vocational	40*	4,117*	30,949
Higher	22*	8,251	217,823
of which universities‡	20	3,982	89,010

* 2003/04.
† 2002/03 figure.
‡ 1996/97 figures.

Source: partly UNESCO Institute for Statistics.

Adult literacy rate (UNESCO estimates): 91.1% (males 95.2%; females 87.0%) in 2005 (Source: UNESCO Institute for Statistics).

Directory

The Constitution

The revised Constitution was approved by King Talal I on 1 January 1952.

The Hashemite Kingdom of Jordan is an independent, indivisible sovereign state. Its official religion is Islam; its official language Arabic.

RIGHTS OF THE INDIVIDUAL

There is to be no discrimination between Jordanians on account of race, religion or language. Work, education and equal opportunities shall be afforded to all as far as is possible. The freedom of the individual is guaranteed, as are his dwelling and property. No Jordanian shall be exiled. Labour shall be made compulsory only in a national emergency, or as a result of a conviction; conditions, hours worked and allowances are under the protection of the state.

The Press, and all opinions, are free, except under martial law. Societies can be formed, within the law. Schools may be established freely, but they must follow a recognized curriculum and educational policy. Elementary education is free and compulsory. All religions are tolerated. Every Jordanian is eligible for public office, and choices are to be made by merit only. Power belongs to the people.

THE LEGISLATIVE POWER

Legislative power is vested in the National Assembly and the King. The National Assembly consists of two houses: the Senate and the House of Representatives.

THE SENATE

The number of Senators is one-half of the number of members of the House of Representatives. Senators must be unrelated to the King, over 40, and are chosen from present and past Prime Ministers and Ministers, past Ambassadors or Ministers Plenipotentiary, past Presidents of the House of Representatives, past Presidents and members of the Court of Cassation and of the Civil and *Shari'a* Courts of Appeal, retired officers of the rank of General and above, former members of the House of Representatives who have been elected twice to that House, etc. They may not hold public office. Senators are appointed for four years. They may be reappointed. The President of the Senate is appointed for two years.

THE HOUSE OF REPRESENTATIVES

The members of the House of Representatives are elected by secret ballot in a general direct election and retain their mandate for four years. General elections take place during the four months preceding the end of the term. The President of the House is elected by secret ballot each year by the Representatives. Representatives must be Jordanians of over 30, they must have a clean record, no active business interests, and are debarred from public office. Close relatives of the King are not eligible. If the House of Representatives is dissolved, the new House shall assemble in extraordinary session not more than four months after the date of dissolution. The new House cannot be dissolved for the same reason as the last.

GENERAL PROVISIONS FOR THE NATIONAL ASSEMBLY

The King summons the National Assembly to its ordinary session on 1 November each year. This date can be postponed by the King for two months, or he can dissolve the Assembly before the end of its three-month session. Alternatively, he can extend the session up to a total period of six months. Each session is opened by a speech from the throne.

Decisions in the House of Representatives and the Senate are made by a majority vote. The quorum is two-thirds of the total number of members in each House. When the voting concerns the Constitution, or confidence in the Council of Ministers, 'the votes shall be taken by calling the members by name in a loud voice'. Sessions are public, though secret sessions can be held at the request of the Government or of five members. Complete freedom of speech, within the rules of either House, is allowed.

The Prime Minister places proposals before the House of Representatives; if accepted there, they are referred to the Senate and finally sent to the King for confirmation. If one house rejects a law while the other accepts it, a joint session of the House of Representatives and the Senate is called, and a decision made by a two-thirds majority. If the King withholds his approval from a law, he returns it to the Assembly within six months with the reasons for his dissent; a joint session of the Houses then makes a decision, and if the law is accepted by this decision it is promulgated. The Budget is submitted to the National Assembly one month before the beginning of the financial year.

THE KING

The throne of the Hashemite Kingdom devolves by male descent in the dynasty of King Abdullah ibn al-Hussein. The King attains his majority on his eighteenth lunar year; if the throne is inherited by a minor, the powers of the King are exercised by a Regent or a Council of Regency. If the King, through illness or absence, cannot perform his duties, his powers are given to a Deputy, or to a Council of the Throne. This Deputy, or Council, may be appointed by Iradas (decrees) by the King, or, if he is incapable, by the Council of Ministers.

On his accession, the King takes the oath to respect and observe the provisions of the Constitution and to be loyal to the nation. As Head of State he is immune from all liability or responsibility. He approves laws and promulgates them. He declares war, concludes peace and signs treaties; treaties, however, must be approved by the National Assembly. The King is Commander-in-Chief of the navy, the army and the air force. He orders the holding of elections; convenes, inaugurates, adjourns and prorogues the House of Representatives. The Prime Minister is appointed by him, as are the President and members of the Senate. Military and civil ranks are also granted, or withdrawn, by the King. No death sentence is carried out until he has confirmed it.

MINISTERS

The Council of Ministers consists of the Prime Minister, President of the Council, and of his ministers. Ministers are forbidden to become members of any company, to receive a salary from any company, or to participate in any financial act of trade. The Council of Ministers is entrusted with the conduct of all affairs of state, internal and external.

The Council of Ministers is responsible to the House of Representatives for matters of general policy. Ministers may speak in either House, and, if they are members of one House, they may also vote in that House. Votes of confidence in the Council are cast in the House of Representatives, and decided by a two-thirds' majority. If a vote of 'no confidence' is returned, the ministers are bound to resign. Every newly formed Council of Ministers must present its programme to the House of Representatives and ask for a vote of confidence. The House of Representatives can impeach ministers, as it impeaches its own members.

AMENDMENTS

Two amendments were passed in November 1974 giving the King the right to dissolve the Senate or to take away membership from any of its members, and to postpone general elections for a period not to exceed a year, if there are circumstances in which the Council of Ministers feels that it is impossible to hold elections. A further amendment in February 1976 enabled the King to postpone elections indefinitely. In January 1984 two amendments were passed, allowing elections 'in any part of the country where it is possible to hold them' (effectively, only the East Bank) and empowering the National Assembly to elect deputies from the Israeli-held West Bank. In February 2003 the King ratified legislation according to which six seats in the House of Representatives were, from the next general election, to be reserved for women.

The Government

HEAD OF STATE

King: King ABDULLAH IBN AL-HUSSEIN (succeeded to the throne on 7 February 1999).

CABINET
(March 2008)

Prime Minister and Minister of Defence: NADER AD-DAHABI.
Minister of Finance: Dr HAMAD AL-KASASBEH.
Minister of Foreign Affairs: Dr SALAH ED-DIN AL-BASHIR.
Minister of Justice: AYMAN ODEH.
Minister of the Interior: EID AL-FAYEZ.
Minister of Awqaf (Religious Endowments), Islamic Affairs and Holy Places: ABD AL-FATAH SALAH.
Minister of Health: Dr SALAH AL-MAWAJDEH.
Minister of Industry and Trade: AMER HADIDI.
Minister of Labour: BASSEM AS-SALEM.
Minister of Public Works and Housing: SAHEL AL-MAJALI.
Minister of Energy and Mineral Resources: KHALDOUN QUTEISHAT.
Minister of Education: TAYSEER NUEIMI.
Minister of Higher Education and Scientific Research: Dr OMAR SHDEIFAT.
Minister of Municipal Affairs: SHEHADEH ABU HUDEIB.
Minister of Water and Irrigation: RAED ABU SAUD.
Minister of Planning and International Co-operation: SUHAIR AL-ALI.
Minister of Agriculture: MUZAHIM MUHAISIN.
Minister of Social Development: HALA LATOUF.
Minister of Information and Communications Technology: BASSEM AR-ROUSAN.
Minister of the Environment: KHALID AL-IRANI.
Minister of Transport: ALAA AL-BATAYNEH.
Minister of Tourism and Antiquities: MAHA AL-KHATIB.
Minister of Culture: NANCY BAKIR.
Minister of Political Development and Minister of State for Legal Affairs: KAMAL NASSER.
Minister of Public Sector Development: MAHER MADADHA.
Minister of State for Media and Communications: NASSER JOUDEH.
Minister of State for Prime Ministry Affairs: THOUQAN AL-QUDAH.
Minister of State for Parliamentary Affairs: ABD AR-RAHIM OKOUR.

Note: The Head of Intelligence and the Governor of the Central Bank also have full ministerial status.

MINISTRIES

The Prime Ministry of Jordan: POB 80, Amman 11180; tel. (6) 4641211; fax (6) 4642520; e-mail info@pm.gov.jo; internet www.pm.gov.jo.

Ministry of Administrative Development: Amman; tel. (6) 5654134; e-mail moad94@hotmail.com; internet www.adm.gov.jo.

Ministry of Agriculture: POB 2099, Amman; tel. (6) 5686151; fax (6) 5686310; e-mail agri@moa.gov.jo; internet www.moa.gov.jo.

Ministry of Awqaf (Religious Endowments), Islamic Affairs and Holy Places: POB 659, Amman; tel. (6) 5666141; fax (6) 5602254; e-mail info@awqaf.gov.jo; internet www.awqaf.gov.jo.

Ministry of Culture: POB 6140, Amman; tel. (6) 5696218; fax (6) 5696598; e-mail info@culture.gov.jo; internet www.culture.gov.jo.

Ministry of Defence: POB 80, Amman; tel. (6) 4641211; fax (6) 4642520; e-mail info@jaf.mil.jo; internet www.jaf.mil.jo.

Ministry of Education: POB 1646, Amman 11118; tel. (6) 5607181; fax (6) 5666019; e-mail moe@moe.gov.jo; internet www.moe.gov.jo.

Ministry of Energy and Mineral Resources: POB 2310, Amman; tel. (6) 5863326; fax (6) 5818336; e-mail memr@memr.gov.jo; internet www.memr.gov.jo.

Ministry of the Environment: Amman; tel. (6) 5560113; fax (6) 5560288; e-mail moenv@moenv.gov.jo; internet www.moenv.gov.jo.

Ministry of Finance: POB 85, Amman 11118; tel. (6) 4636321; fax (6) 4618528; e-mail info@mof.gov.jo; internet www.mof.gov.jo.

Ministry of Foreign Affairs: POB 35217, Amman 11180; tel. (6) 5735150; fax (6) 5735163; e-mail inquiry@mfa.gov.jo; internet www.mfa.gov.jo.

Ministry of Health: POB 86, Amman; tel. (6) 5665131; fax (6) 5688373; e-mail info@moh.gov.jo; internet www.moh.gov.jo.

Ministry of Higher Education and Scientific Research: POB 35262, Amman; tel. (6) 5347671; fax (6) 5337616; e-mail mohe@mohe.gov.jo; internet www.mohe.gov.jo.

Ministry of Industry and Trade: POB 2019, 11181 Amman; tel. (6) 5629030; fax (6) 5684692; e-mail info@mit.gov.jo; internet www.mit.gov.jo.

Ministry of Information and Communications Technology: POB 9903, Amman 11191; tel. (6) 5805700; fax (6) 5861059; e-mail moict@moict.gov.jo; internet www.moict.gov.jo.

Ministry of the Interior: POB 100, Amman; tel. (6) 4638849; fax (6) 5606908; e-mail info@moi.gov.jo; internet www.moi.gov.jo.

Ministry of Justice: POB 6040, Amman 11118; tel. (6) 4603630; fax (6) 4643197; e-mail moj@moj.gov.jo; internet www.moj.gov.jo.

Ministry of Labour: POB 8160, Amman 11118; tel. (6) 5802666; fax (6) 5855072; e-mail info@mol.gov.jo; internet www.mol.gov.jo.

Ministry of Municipal Affairs: POB 1799, Amman 11118; tel. (6) 4641393; fax (6) 4640404; e-mail mma3@nic.net.jo; internet www.mma.gov.jo.

Ministry of Planning and International Co-operation: POB 555, Amman 11118; tel. (6) 4644466; fax (6) 4642247; e-mail mop@mop.gov.jo; internet www.mop.gov.jo.

Ministry of Political Development: Amman; tel. (6) 5695216; fax (6) 5686552; e-mail info@mopd.gov.jo; internet www.mopd.gov.jo.

Ministry of Public Sector Development: POB 3575, Amman 11821; tel. (6) 5502530; fax (6) 5502548; e-mail info@mopsd.gov.jo; internet www.mopsd.gov.jo.

Ministry of Public Works and Housing: POB 1220, Amman; tel. (6) 5850470; fax (6) 5857590; internet www.mpwh.gov.jo.

Ministry of Social Development: POB 6720, Amman 11118; tel. (6) 5931391; fax (6) 5932645; e-mail mosd@mosd.gov.jo; internet www.mosd.gov.jo.

Ministry of Tourism and Antiquities: POB 224, Amman 11118; tel. (6) 4603360; fax (6) 4648465; e-mail contacts@mota.gov.jo; internet www.mota.gov.jo.

Ministry of Transport: POB 35214, Amman 11180; tel. (6) 5518111; fax (6) 5527233; e-mail info@mot.gov.jo; internet www.mot.gov.jo.

Ministry of Water and Irrigation: POB 2412, Amman 5012; tel. (6) 5680100; fax (6) 5680075; e-mail info@mwi.gov.jo; internet www.mwi.gov.jo.

JORDAN

Legislature

MAJLIS AL-UMMA
(National Assembly)

Senate

Speaker: ZAID AR-RIFAI.

The Senate (House of Notables) consists of 55 members, appointed by the King. The current Senate was appointed on 16 November 2005.

House of Representatives

Speaker: ABD AL-HADI AL-MAJALI.
General Election, 20 November 2007

Party/Group	Seats
Independents and tribal representatives	104
Islamic Action Front	6
Total	**110***

*Under legislation ratified by King Abdullah in February 2003, six seats are reserved for women. Following the election of November 2007, however, seven seats were held by women.

Political Organizations

With the exception of the officially sanctioned Jordanian National Union (1971–76), political parties were effectively banned for most of the reign of King Hussein. However, a royal commission was appointed in April 1990 to draft a National Charter, one feature of which was the legalization of political parties. In January 1991 King Hussein approved the National Charter, which was formally endorsed in June. In August 1992 legislation allowing the formation of political parties was approved by royal decree, and by March 1993 nine political parties had received official recognition. There were 34 political organizations registered with the Ministry of the Interior in 2006.

Higher Co-ordination Committee for Opposition Parties: Amman; opposition bloc consisting of 15 leftist, pan-Arab and Islamist parties, incl. National Action Party (pan-Arab), Baath Progressive Party, Jordanian Arab Socialist Baath Party, Islamic Action Front, Communist Party, Jordan People's Democratic Party (HASHID) and Popular Unity Party (leftist).

Hizb-ut-Tahrir al-Islami (Party of Islamic Liberation): e-mail info@hizb-ut-tahrir.org; internet www.hizb-ut-tahrir.org; f. 1953; transnational org. prohibited in Jordan and many other countries; aims to establish Islamic caliphate throughout the world; denies claims that it is a militant group; Leader RAMZI SAWALHAH.

Islamic Action Front (Jabhat al-Amal al-Islami—IAF): POB 925310, Abdali, Amman 11110; tel. (6) 5696985; fax (6) 5696987; e-mail info@jabha.net; internet www.jabha.net; f. 1992; seeks implementation of *Shari'a* (Islamic law) and preservation of the *Umma* (Islamic community); mem. of Higher Co-ordination Committee for Opposition Parties; Sec.-Gen. ZAKI SAAD BANI-IRSHEID.

Jordan People's Democratic Party (Hizb ash-Shaab ad-Dimuqrati—HASHID): POB 9966, Luweibdeh, Amman; tel. (6) 5691451; fax (6) 5686857; f. 1993; leftist party, which seeks to establish legal and institutional processes to protect the people, instigate economic, social, democratic and agricultural reform, and organize, unify and protect the working classes; supports the Palestinian cause; mem. of Higher Co-ordination Committee for Opposition Parties; Sec.-Gen. SALEM NAHHAS.

Jordanian Arab New Dawn Party (Al-Fajr al-Jadid al-Arabi al-Urduni): 7th Bldg, Abd ar-Rahman Gharib St, Sweifiyeh, Amman; tel. and fax (6) 5822667; f. 1999; supports the state's Constitution and legal structures; Arab nationalist, pro-Palestinian; mem. of Jordanian National Movement; Sec.-Gen. MUHAMMAD DARWISH SHAHWAN.

Jordanian Arab Socialist Baath Party (Hizb al-Baath al-Arabi al-Ishtiraki al-Urduni): POB 8383, Amman; tel. (6) 4658618; fax (6) 4658617; f. 1993; promotes pan-Arabism; mem. of Higher Co-ordination Committee for Opposition Parties; Sec.-Gen. TAYSEER SALAMEH AL-HOMSI.

Jordanian Democratic Left Party (Hizb al-Yasar ad-Dimuqrati al-Urduni): POB 84545, Abdali, Amman; tel. (7) 9524708; fax (6) 38614; f. 1994; supports the National Charter; pro-Palestinian; Gen. MOUSSA AL-MA'AITAH.

Jordanian Generations Party (Hizb al-Ajyal al-Urduni): Main St, Petrol Station, Russeifa; tel. (5) 3743242; f. 1999; national advocates a comprehensive social system and the of democracy; rejects the current borders of Jordan; ian National Movement; Sec.-Gen. Dr MUHAMMAD

Jordanian National Movement (JNM): pro-Government bloc formed by 11 political parties: Al-Mustaqbal, Amal, al-Ansar, al-Ahd (Pledge), Hizb ar-Risala (Mission Party), ash-Shaab, Rifah, Jordanian Generations Party, Jordanian Renaissance Party, Jordanian Arab New Dawn Party and Muslim Centrist Party; f. 2004; Leader SAMIR AWAMLEH.

Jordanian People's Committees Movement (Harakat Lijan ash-Shaab al-Urduni): f. 2001; moderate; Sec.-Gen. KHALID SHUBAKI.

Jordanian Renaissance Party (Hizb an-Nahda al-Urduni): Wadi Seir Rd, Seventh Circle, Amman; tel. (6) 5829606; fax (6) 5857079; f. 1999; pan-Arab; seeks formation of a Palestinian state, with Jerusalem as its capital; mem. of Jordanian National Movement; Sec.-Gen. MIJHEM AL-KHREISHA.

Muslim Centrist Party (Hizb al-Wasat al-Islami): Haswa Bldg, 3rd Floor, Amman; tel. and fax (6) 5353966; f. 2001 by fmr mems of Islamic Action Front and Muslim Brotherhood; mem. of Jordanian National Movement; Pres. MUHAMMAD ALAWNEH; Sec.-Gen. MARWAN FA'OURI.

Al-Mustaqbal (Future) Party: Shmeisani, Al-Maqdisi St, Amman; tel. (6) 5690911; fax (6) 5690805; f. 1992; advocates the devt of legal, state and social institutions, and the promotion of democracy; pro-Palestinian; mem. of Jordanian National Movement; Sec.-Gen. SULEIMAN ARAR.

National Constitutional Party (Al-Hizb al-Watani ad-Dusturi—NCP): POB 1825237, Amman 11118; tel. (6) 5696256; fax (6) 5686248; f. 1997 by merger of nine parties; Pres. ABD AL-HADI AL-MAJALI; Sec.-Gen. AHMAD SHUNNAQ.

Diplomatic Representation

EMBASSIES IN JORDAN

Algeria: POB 830375, Amman 11183; tel. (6) 4641271; fax (6) 4616552; e-mail ambalg@go.com.jo; Ambassador ALI ARROUDY.

Australia: POB 35201, Amman 11180; tel. (6) 5807000; fax (6) 5807001; e-mail amman.austremb@dfat.gov.au; internet www.jordan.embassy.gov.au; Ambassador TREVOR PEACOCK.

Austria: POB 830795, Jabal Amman, Amman 11183; tel. (6) 4601101; fax (6) 4612725; e-mail amman-ob@bmeia.gv.at; Ambassador FRANZ HÖRLBERGER.

Azerbaijan: Muhammad Ali Bdeir St, Abdoun, Amman; tel. (6) 5935525; fax (6) 5932826; e-mail azerbaijan@azembassy.com.jo; internet www.azembassyjo.org; Ambassador ELMAN ARASLI.

Bahrain: POB 5220, Faris Al-Khoury St, Shmeisani Amman 11183; tel. (6) 5664148; fax (6) 5664190; e-mail bahemb@maktoob.com; Ambassador NASSER RASHID AL-KAABI.

Bangladesh: POB 5685, 10 Muzdalifa St, Ar-Rabiya, Amman 11183; tel. (6) 5529192; fax (6) 5529194; e-mail embangl@wanadoo.jo; Ambassador MUHAMMAD GHULAM.

Belgium: POB 942, Amman 11118; tel. (6) 5932683; fax (6) 5930487; e-mail ambabelamman@wanadoo.jo; internet www.diplomatie.be/amman; Ambassador JOHAN INDEKEU.

Bosnia and Herzegovina: POB 850836, Amman 11185; tel. (6) 5856921; fax (6) 5856923; e-mail ambamman@wanadoo.jo; Ambassador VASILJ KRUNOSLAV.

Brazil: POB 5497, Amman 11183; tel. (6) 4642183; fax (6) 4641328; e-mail jorbrem@wanadoo.jo; Ambassador ANTÔNIO CARLOS COELHO DA ROCHA.

Brunei: POB 851752, Amman 11185; tel. (6) 5928021; fax (6) 5928024; e-mail kbnbdjor@cyberia.jo; Ambassador Pehin Dato HARIMAUPADANG.

Bulgaria: POB 950578, 7 al-Mousel St, Amman 11195; tel. (6) 5529391; fax (6) 5539393; e-mail bulembjord@joinnet.com.jo; Ambassador NIKOLAI NIKOLOV.

Canada: POB 815403, Amman 11180; tel. (6) 5666124; fax (6) 5689227; e-mail amman@dfait-maeci.gc.ca; internet amman.gc.ca; Ambassador MARGARET HUBER.

Chile: POB 830663, 28 Hussein Abu Ragheb St, Abdoun, Amman 11183; tel. (6) 5923360; fax (6) 5924263; e-mail echile@batelco.jo; Ambassador LUIS PALAM.

China, People's Republic: POB 7365, 9 Jakarda St, Amman 11118; tel. (6) 5515151; fax (6) 5518713; e-mail chinaemb_jo@mfa.gov.cn; internet jo.china-embassy.org; Ambassador GONG XIAOSHENG.

Czech Republic: POB 2213, Amman 11181; tel. (6) 5927051; fax (6) 5927053; e-mail amman@embassy.mzv.cz; internet www.mzv.cz/amman; Chargé d'affaires a.i. IVANA HOLOUBKOVA.

Egypt: POB 35178, 14 Riyad el-Mefleh St, Amman 11180; tel. (6) 5605202; fax (6) 5604082; e-mail egypt@embegyptjordan.com; Ambassador AHMAD REZEQ.

France: POB 5348, Amman 11183; tel. (6) 4604630; fax (6) 4604638; e-mail webmestre@mail.com; internet www.ambafrance-jo.org; Ambassador DENYS GAUER.

Georgia: POB 851903, 31 Odeh Abu Tayeh, Shmeisani, Amman 11185; tel. (6) 5603793; fax (6) 5603819; e-mail geoemb@wanadoo.jo; internet www.mfa.gov.ge; Ambassador EKATERINE MEIERING-MIKADZE.

Germany: POB 183, 25 Benghazi St, Jabal Amman 11118; tel. (6) 5930351; fax (6) 5929413; e-mail germaemb@wanadoo.jo; internet www.amman.diplo.de; Ambassador Dr KLAUS BURKHARDT.

Greece: POB 35069, 7 Iskandaronah St, Abdoun, Amman 11180; tel. (6) 5922724; fax (6) 5927622; e-mail greekemb@nol.com.jo; Ambassador TRYPHON PARASKEVOPOULOS.

Holy See: POB 142916, 14 Anton an-Naber St, Amman 11814; tel. (6) 5929934; fax (6) 5929931; e-mail nuntius@nol.com.jo; Apostolic Nuncio Most Rev. FRANCIS ASSISI CHULLIKATT.

Honduras: POB 840526, Amman 33384; tel. (6) 5856414; fax (6) 5853501; Chargé d'affaires a.i. FAIZ ROBERTO ELMADI.

Hungary: POB 3441, Amman 11181; tel. (6) 5925614; fax (6) 5930836; e-mail mission.amm@kum.hu; internet www.mfa.gov.hu/emb/amman; Ambassador Dr GÉZA MIHÁLYI.

India: POB 2168, Amman 11181; tel. (6) 4622098; fax (6) 4659540; e-mail amb.amman@mea.gov.in; Ambassador RATAKONDA DAYAKAR.

Indonesia: POB 811784, Amman 11181; tel. (6) 5538911; fax (6) 5528380; e-mail amman96@go.com.jo; Ambassador ABD AR-RAHMAN SABRAN.

Iran: POB 173, Amman 11118; tel. (6) 4641281; fax (6) 4641383; e-mail pub-rel@iranembassyjordan.org; internet www.iranembassyjordan.org; Ambassador MUHAMMAD IRANI.

Iraq: POB 2025, Amman; tel. (6) 4623175; fax (6) 4619172; e-mail baghdad@nets.com.jo; Ambassador SAAD J. AL-HAYYANI.

Israel: POB 95866, 47 Maysaloon St, Dahiat ar-Rabieh, Amman 11195; tel. (6) 5503500; fax (6) 5524689; e-mail embassy@amman.mfa.gov.il; Ambassador YAAKOV ROSEN.

Italy: POB 9800, Jabal al-Weibdeh, 5 Hafiz Ibrahim St, Amman 11191; tel. (6) 4638185; fax (6) 4659730; e-mail info.amman@esteri.it; internet www.ambamman.esteri.it; Ambassador GIANFRANCO GIORGOLO.

Japan: POB 2835, Ibn al-Furat St, Sweifiyeh, Amman 11181; tel. (6) 5932005; fax (6) 5931006; e-mail mail@embjapan.org.jo; internet www.jordan.emb-japan.go.jp; Ambassador SHIGENOBU KATO.

Kazakhstan: Abu Bakir Nabaty St, Amman; tel. (6) 5927953; fax (6) 5927952; e-mail kazemb@orange.jo; Ambassador BOLAT S. SARSENBAYEV.

Korea, Democratic People's Republic: POB 799, Amman; tel. (6) 4417614; fax (6) 4424735; e-mail dprk-embv@scs-net.org; Ambassador KIM HYONG JUN.

Korea, Republic: POB 3060, Bahjat Homsi St, Amman 11181; tel. (6) 5930745; fax (6) 5930280; e-mail jordan@mofat.go.kr; Ambassador YEON-SUNG SHIN.

Kuwait: POB 2107, Amman 11181; tel. (6) 5675135; fax (6) 5681971; e-mail q8@kuwaitembassyamman.org; Ambassador Sheikh FAISAL AL-HUMOUD AL-MALEK AS-SABAH.

Lebanon: POB 811779, Amman 11181; tel. and fax (6) 5929111; Ambassador ADIB CHARBEL AOUN.

Libya: POB 2987, Amman; tel. (6) 5693101; fax (6) 5693404; Ambassador MUHAMMAD HUSSEIN BARGATHI.

Malaysia: POB 5351, Tayser Na'na'ah St, off Umawiyyeen St, Abdoun, Amman 11183; tel. (6) 5902400; fax (6) 5934343; e-mail mwamman@kln.gov.my; Ambassador HASNUDIN BEN HAMZAH.

Mauritania: POB 851594, Saleh Zakee St, Villa 19, Sweifiyeh, Amman 11185; tel. (6) 5855146; fax (6) 5855148; e-mail muritanyaembassy_amman1@hotmail.com; Ambassador MUHAMMAD AL-AMEEN YAHIA.

Morocco: POB 2175, Amman 11183; tel. (6) 5680591; fax (6) 5680253; e-mail ambmaroc@batelco.jo; Ambassador MUHAMMAD MAEL-AININ.

Netherlands: POB 941361, 22 Ibrahim Ayoub St, 4th Circle, Amman 11194; tel. (6) 5902200; fax (6) 5930161; e-mail amm@minbuza.nl; internet www.netherlandsembassy.com.jo; Ambassador JOANNA MARIA PETRONELLA FRANCISCA VAN VLIET.

Norway: POB 830510, Amman 11183; tel. (6) 5931646; fax (6) 5931650; e-mail emb.amman@mfa.no; internet www.norway.jo; Ambassador METTE RAVN.

Oman: POB 20192, Amman 11110; tel. (6) 5686155; fax (6) 5689404; internet www.ca-oman.org.jo; Ambassador MUSALLAM BEN BAKHIT AL-BARAMI.

Pakistan: POB 1232, Amman 11118; tel. (6) 4622787; fax (6) 4611633; e-mail pakembjo@wanadoo.jo; Ambassador MUHAMMAD AKHTAR TUFAIL.

Philippines: POB 925207, Amman 11190; tel. (6) 5923748; fax (6) 5923744; e-mail ammanpe@wanadoo.jo; Ambassador JOSE DEL ROSARIO, Jr.

Poland: POB 942050, Amman 11194; tel. (6) 5512593; fax (6) 5512595; e-mail polemb@nol.com.jo; Ambassador ANDRZEJ BIERA.

Qatar: POB 831222, Amman 11183; tel. (6) 4659724; fax (6) 4659723; e-mail qataremb@index.com.jo; Ambassador MANA ABD AL-HADI AL-HAJRI.

Romania: POB 2869, 35 Madina Munawwara St, Amman; tel. (6) 5813423; fax (6) 5812521; e-mail roemb@batelco.jo; Ambassador RADU ONOFREI.

Russia: POB 2187, 22 Zahran St, Amman 11181; tel. (6) 4641158; fax (6) 4647448; e-mail rusembjo@mail.ru; internet www.jordan.mid.ru; Ambassador ALEKSANDER KALUGIN.

Saudi Arabia: POB 2133, 5th Circle, Jabal Amman; tel. (6) 5924154; fax (6) 4659853; e-mail joemb@mofa.gov.sa; Ambassador ABD AR-RAHMAN N. AL-OHALY.

South Africa: POB 851508, Sweifiyeh 11185, Amman; tel. (6) 5921194; fax (6) 5920080; e-mail saembjor@index.com.jo; internet www.saembjor.com; Ambassador Dr BOY GELDENHUYS.

Spain: Zahran St, POB 454, Amman 11118; tel. (6) 4614166; fax (6) 4614173; e-mail embespjo@mail.mae.es; Ambassador MANUEL LORENZO GARCÍA-ORMAECHEA.

Sri Lanka: POB 830731, Amman 11183; tel. (6) 5820611; fax (6) 5820615; e-mail slemb@go.com.jo; Ambassador ADNRAYAS WICKRAMACHI MOHOTTALA.

Sudan: POB 3305, Bayader Wadi as-Seer, 7th Circle, Musa Irsheed at-Taib St, Amman 11181; tel. (6) 5854500; fax (6) 5854501; e-mail sudani@nets.com.jo; Ambassador MOHAMMAD OTHMAN MOHAMMAD SAEED.

Sweden: POB 830536, 14 Ibrahim Ayoub St, 4th Circle, Jabal Amman 11183; tel. (6) 5901300; fax (6) 5930179; e-mail ambassaden.amman@foreign.ministry.se; internet www.swedenabroad.com/amman; Ambassador TOMMY ARWITZ.

Switzerland: POB 5341, 19 Ibrahim Ayoub St, 4th Circle, Amman 11183; tel. (6) 5931416; fax (6) 5930685; e-mail amm.vertretung@eda.admin.ch; internet www.eda.admin.ch/amman; Ambassador PAUL WIDMER.

Syria: POB 1733, Amman 11118; tel. (6) 5920684; fax (6) 5920635; e-mail pbox@syrianembassy.jo; internet www.syrianembassy.jo; Ambassador ALI HAMOUD.

Thailand: POB 144329, Amman 11814; tel. (6) 5925410; fax (6) 5926109; e-mail thaibgw@mfa.go.th; Ambassador ISINTHORN SORNVAI.

Tunisia: POB 17185, Amman 11195; tel. (6) 5922746; fax (6) 5922769; e-mail atamman@go.com.jo; Ambassador SALAH AD-DIN AL-JAMMALI.

Turkey: POB 2062, Amman 11181; tel. (6) 4641251; fax (6) 4612353; e-mail ammanbe@nets.com.jo; Ambassador ALI KOPRULU.

Ukraine: 6 Al-Umouma St, As-Sahl, Amman; tel. (6) 5922402; fax (6) 5922405; e-mail ukremb@nets.com.jo; Ambassador IHOR DYACHENKO.

United Arab Emirates: POB 2623, Jawdat Rashid Shama St, 5th Circle, Amman 11181; tel. (6) 5934780; fax (6) 5932666; Ambassador RAHMA HUSSAIN R. AZ-ZA'ABI.

United Kingdom: POB 87, Abdoun, Amman 11118; tel. (6) 5909200; fax (6) 5909279; e-mail info@britain.org.jo; internet www.britain.org.jo; Ambassador JAMES WATT.

USA: POB 354, Amman 11118; tel. (6) 5906000; fax (6) 5920121; e-mail webmasterjordan@state.gov; internet www.usembassy-amman.org.jo; Ambassador DAVID HALE.

Yemen: POB 3085, Prince Hashem Ben Al-Hussain St, Amman 11181; tel. (6) 5923771; fax (6) 5923773; Ambassador Dr HUSSEIN TAHER BIN YAHYA.

Judicial System

With the exception of matters of purely personal nature concerning members of non-Muslim communities, the law of Jordan was based on Islamic Law for both civil and criminal matters. During the days of the Ottoman Empire, certain aspects of Continental law, especially French commercial law and civil and criminal procedure, were introduced. Due to British occupation of Palestine and Transjordan from 1917 to 1948, the Palestine territory has adopted, either by statute or case law, much of the English common law. Since the annexation of the non-occupied part of Palestine and the formation of the Hashemite Kingdom of Jordan, there has been a continuous effort to unify the law.

Court of Cassation (Supreme Court): The Court of Cassation consists of seven judges, who sit in full panel for exceptionally important cases. In most appeals, however, only five members sit to hear the case. All cases involving amounts of more than JD 100 may be reviewed by this Court, as well as cases involving lesser amounts and those which cannot be monetarily valued. However, for the latter types of cases, review is available only by leave of the Court of Appeal, or, upon refusal by the Court of Appeal, by leave of the President of the Court of Cassation. In addition to these functions as final and Supreme Court of Appeal, the Court of Cassation also sits as High Court of Justice to hear applications in the nature of habeas corpus, mandamus and certiorari dealing with complaints of a citizen against abuse of governmental authority.

President of the Court of Cassation (Supreme Court): AHMAD TARAWNEH.

Courts of Appeal: There are three Courts of Appeal, each of which is composed of three judges, whether for hearing of appeals or for dealing with Magistrates Courts' judgments in chambers. Jurisdiction of the three Courts is geographical, with one each in Amman, Irbid and Ma'an. Appellate review of the Courts of Appeal extends to judgments rendered in the Courts of First Instance, the Magistrates' Courts and Religious Courts.

Courts of First Instance: The Courts of First Instance are courts of general jurisdiction in all matters civil and criminal except those specifically allocated to the Magistrates' Courts. Three judges sit in all felony trials, while only two judges sit for misdemeanour and civil cases. Each of the 11 Courts of First Instance also exercises appellate jurisdiction in cases involving judgments of less than JD 20 and fines of less than JD 10, rendered by the Magistrates' Courts.

Magistrates' Courts: There are 17 Magistrates' Courts, which exercise jurisdiction in civil cases involving no more than JD 250 and in criminal cases involving maximum fines of JD 100 or maximum imprisonment of one year.

Religious Courts: There are two types of religious court: the Shari'a Courts (Muslims); and the Ecclesiastical Courts (Eastern Orthodox, Greek Melkite, Roman Catholic and Protestant). Jurisdiction extends to personal (family) matters, such as marriage, divorce, alimony, inheritance, guardianship, wills, interdiction and, for the Muslim community, the constitution of Waqfs (Religious Endowments). When a dispute involves persons of different religious communities, the Civil Courts have jurisdiction in the matter unless the parties agree to submit to the jurisdiction of one or the other of the Religious Courts involved.

Each *Shari'a* (Muslim) Court consists of one judge (*Qadi*), while most of the Ecclesiastical (Christian) Courts are normally composed of three judges, who are usually clerics. *Shari'a* Courts apply the doctrines of Islamic Law, based on the Koran and the *Hadith* (Precepts of Muhammad), while the Ecclesiastical Courts base their law on various aspects of Canon Law. In the event of conflict between any two Religious Courts or between a Religious Court and a Civil Court, a Special Tribunal of three judges is appointed by the President of the Court of Cassation, to decide which court shall have jurisdiction. Upon the advice of experts on the law of the various communities, this Special Tribunal decides on the venue for the case at hand.

Religion

Over 90% of the population are Sunni Muslims, and the King can trace unbroken descent from the Prophet Muhammad. There is a Christian minority, living mainly in the towns, and there are smaller numbers of non-Sunni Muslims.

ISLAM

Chief Justice and President of the Supreme Muslim Secular Council: AHMAD HILAYEL.

Director of Shari'a Courts: Sheikh ISSAM ABD AR-RAZZAQ ARABIYYAT.

Grand Mufti of the Hashemite Kingdom of Jordan: Sheikh Dr NUH ALI SALMAN AL-QUDAH.

CHRISTIANITY

The Roman Catholic Church

Latin Rite

Jordan forms part of the Patriarchate of Jerusalem (see the chapter on Israel).

Vicar-General for Transjordan: Most Rev. SELIM SAYEGH (Titular Bishop of Aquae in Proconsulari), Latin Vicariate, POB 851379, Sweifiyeh, Amman 11185; tel. (6) 5929546; fax (6) 5920548; e-mail regina-pacis2000@yahoo.com.

Melkite Rite

The Greek-Melkite archdiocese of Petra (Wadi Musa) and Philadelphia (Amman) contained 31,300 adherents at 31 December 2005.

Archbishop of Petra and Philadelphia: Most Rev. GEORGES EL-MURR, Archevêché Grec-Melkite Catholique, POB 2435, Jabal Amman 11181; tel. (6) 4624757; fax (6) 4628560.

Syrian Rite

The Syrian Catholic Patriarch of Antioch is resident in Beirut, Lebanon.

Patriarchal Exarchate of Jerusalem (Palestine and Jordan): Mont Achrafieh, POB 510393, Rue Barto, Amman; e-mail stjossc@p-ol.com; Exarch Patriarchal Mgr GRÉGOIRE PIERRE MELKI (Titular Bishop of Batne of the Syrians).

The Anglican Communion

Within the Episcopal Church in Jerusalem and the Middle East, Jordan forms part of the diocese of Jerusalem. The President Bishop of the Church is the Bishop in Cyprus and the Gulf (see the chapter on Cyprus).

Other Christian Churches

The Coptic Orthodox Church, the Greek Orthodox Church (Patriarchate of Jerusalem) and the Evangelical Lutheran Church in Jordan are also active.

The Press

Jordan Press Association (JPA): POB 6788, Abbas Mahmoud al-Aqqad St, Jabal Amman, 2nd Circle, Amman; tel. (6) 5600800; fax (6) 5696183; e-mail info@jpa.jo; internet www.jpa.jo; f. 1953; Chair. TAREQ AL-MOMANI.

DAILIES

Al-Akhbar (News): POB 62420, Amman; f. 1976; Arabic; publ. by the Arab Press Co; Editor RACAN EL-MAJALI; circ. 15,000.

Al-Anbat: POB 962556, Amman 11196; tel. (6) 5200100; fax (6) 5200116; e-mail info@alanbat.net; internet www.alanbat.net; f. 2005; independent; Arabic; political; Editor-in-Chief RULA AL-HROOB.

Al-Arab al-Yawm: POB 962198, Queen Rania St, Amman 11196; tel. (6) 5683333; fax (6) 5620552; e-mail mail@alarab-alyawm.com.jo; internet www.alarabalyawm.net; f. 1997; Arabic; Chief Editor TAHER AL-ODWAN.

Al-Aswaq (Markets): POB 11117, Queen Rania St, Amman 11123; tel. (6) 5157690; fax (6) 5154390; e-mail alaswaq@nets.com.jo; f. 1992; Arabic; business; Man. Editor YAHYA MAHMOUD; Editor-in-Chief MUSTAFA ABU LIBDEH; circ. 40,000.

Ad-Diyar (The Homeland): Amman; f. 2004; Arabic; Chair. of Bd MAHMOUD KHARABSHEH.

Ad-Dustour (The Constitution): POB 591, Amman 11118; tel. (6) 5608000; fax (6) 5667170; e-mail dustour@addustour.com.jo; internet www.addustour.com; f. 1967; Arabic; publ. by the Jordan Press and Publishing Co Ltd; owns commercial printing facilities; Chair. KAMEL ASH-SHARIF; Editor NABIL ASH-SHARIF; Man. Dir SAIF ASH-SHARIF; circ. 70,000.

Al-Ghad (Tomorrow): POB 3535, Amman 11821; tel. (6) 5544000; fax (6) 5544055; e-mail editorial@alghad.jo; internet www.alghad.jo; f. 2004; independent; Arabic; Editor-in-Chief AYMAN AS-SAFADI.

The Jordan Times: POB 6710, Queen Rania Al Abdullah St, Amman 11118; tel. (6) 5600800; fax (6) 5696183; e-mail jotimes@jpf.com.jo; internet www.jordantimes.com; f. 1975; English; publ. by Jordan Press Foundation; Editor-in-Chief SAMIR BARHOUM; circ. 15,000.

Ar-Rai (Opinion): POB 6710, Queen Rania St, Amman 11118; tel. (6) 5667171; fax (6) 5676581; e-mail info@jpf.com.jo; internet www.alrai.com; f. 1971; morning; independent; Arabic; publ. by Jordan Press Foundation; Chair. AHMAD ABD AL-FATTAH; Editor-in-Chief ABD AL-WAHAB ZGHEILAT; circ. 100,000.

Sawt ash-Shaab (Voice of the People): POB 3037, Amman; tel. (6) 5667101; fax (6) 5667993; f. 1983; Arabic; Editor-in-Chief HASHEM KHAISAT; circ. 30,000.

WEEKLIES

Al-Ahali (The People): POB 9966, Amman; tel. (6) 5691452; fax (6) 5686857; e-mail ahali@go.com.jo; internet www.hashd-ahali.org.jo; f. 1990; Arabic; publ. by the Jordan People's Democratic Party; Editor-in-Chief SALEM NAHHAS; circ. 5,000.

Akhbar al-Usbou (News of the Week): POB 605, Amman; tel. (6) 5677881; fax (6) 5677882; f. 1959; Arabic; economic, social, political; Chief Editor and Publr ABD AL-HAFIZ MUHAMMAD; circ. 50,000.

Al-Hadath: Amman; e-mail info@al-hadath.com; internet www.al-hadath.com; Arabic; general news; Man. Editor FATEH MANSOUR.

Al-Haqeqa ad-Duwalia (Fact International): POB 678621, Amman 11171; tel. (6) 5828292; fax (6) 5816646; e-mail info@factjo.com; internet www.factjo.com; f. 1996; independent; Arabic and English; aims to promote moderate image of Islam and to counter conflicts within the faith; Editor-in-Chief HILMI AL-ASMAR.

Al-Liwa' (The Standard): POB 3067, 2nd Circle, Jabal Amman 11181; tel. (6) 5642770; fax (6) 5656324; e-mail info@al-liwa.com; internet www.al-liwa.com; f. 1972; Arabic; Editor-in-Chief HASSAN AT-TAL; circ. 15,000.

Al-Majd (The Glory): POB 926856, Amman 11190; tel. (6) 5530553; fax (6) 5530352; e-mail almajd@almajd.net; internet www.almajd.net; f. 1994; Arabic; political; Editor-in-Chief FAHID NIMER; circ. 8,000.

As-Sabah (The Morning): POB 2396, Amman; Arabic; circ. 6,000.

Shihan: POB 96-654, Amman; tel. (6) 5603585; fax (6) 5696183; Arabic; Editor-in-Chief (vacant); circ. 60,000.

The Star: POB 591, Queen Rania St, Amman 11118; tel. (6) 5653325; fax (6) 5697415; e-mail star@addustour.com.jo; internet www.star.com.jo; f. 1966; English and Russian; political, economic and cultural; publ. by the Jordan Press and Publishing Co; Editor-in-Chief MAHA ASH-SHARIF; circ. 13,200.

Wihda: 6th Floor, Ramallah Bldg, Jamal Abd an-Nasir, Amman; tel. (6) 5655433; fax (6) 5655434; e-mail wihda@nets.com.jo; f. 2002; independent leftist and nationalist; Chair. MUHAMMAD EL-BASHIR; Chief Editor OSAMA RANTISI.

PERIODICALS

Al-Ghad al-Iqtisadi: Media Services International, POB 9313, Amman 11191; tel. (6) 5645380; fax (6) 5648298; fortnightly; English; economic; Chief Editor RIAD AL-KHOURI.

Hatem: POB 6710, Queen Rania St, Amman 11118; tel. (6) 5600800; e-mail info@jpf.com.jo; children's; publ. by Jordan Press Foundation.

Huda El-Islam (The Right Way of Islam): POB 659, Amman; tel. (6) 5666141; f. 1956; monthly; Arabic; scientific and literary; publ. by the Ministry of Awqaf and Islamic Affairs; Editor Dr AHMAD MUHAMMAD HULAYYEL.

Jordan: POB 224, Amman; f. 1969; quarterly; publ. by Jordan Information Bureau, Washington, DC, USA; circ. 100,000.

Jordan Today: Media Services International, POB 9313, Amman 11191; tel. (6) 652380; fax (6) 648298; e-mail star@arabia.com; internet www.jordantoday.com.jo; f. 1995; monthly; English; tourism, culture and entertainment; Editor-in-Chief ZEID NASSER; circ. 10,000.

Military Magazine: Army Headquarters, Amman; f. 1955; quarterly; dealing with military and literary subjects; publ. by Armed Forces.

Royal Wings: POB 341018, Amman 11134; tel. (6) 4875201; fax (6) 4875656; e-mail info@royalwings.com.jo; internet www.royalwings.com.jo; bi-monthly; Arabic and English; magazine for Royal Jordanian Airline; Man. Dir USAMA FARAJ; circ. 40,000.

Shari'a: POB 585, Amman; f. 1959; fortnightly; Islamic affairs; publ. by Shari'a College; circ. 5,000.

Skin: POB 940166, ICCB Centre, Queen Rania Abdullah St, Amman 11194; tel. (6) 5163357; fax (6) 5163257; e-mail huda@neareastmedia.com; internet www.skin-online.com; f. 2006; quarterly; English; publ. by Near East Media Iraq; art, design, fashion, photography, film and music; Editor-in-Chief EDDIE TAYLOR.

World Travel Gazette (WTG): POB 658, Amman; tel. (6) 5665091; fax (6) 5667933; Arabic; Editor A. S. SHREIM.

NEWS AGENCY

Jordan News Agency (PETRA): POB 6845, Amman 11118; tel. (6) 5609700; fax (6) 5682478; e-mail petra@petra.gov.jo; internet www.petra.gov.jo; f. 1965; independent entity since 2004; previously controlled by the Ministry of Information prior to its disbandment in 2001; Dir-Gen. ABDULLAH AL-UTUM.

Publishers

Alfaris Publishing and Distribution Co: POB 9157, Amman 11191; tel. (6) 5605432; fax (6) 5685501; e-mail mkayyali@airpbooks.com; internet www.airpbooks.com; f. 1989; Dir MAHER SAID KAYYALI.

Aram Studies Publishing and Distribution House: POB 997, Amman 11941; tel. (6) 835015; fax (6) 835079; art, finance, health, management, science, business; Gen. Dir SALEH ABOUSBA.

Jordan Book Centre Co Ltd: POB 301, Al-Jubeiha, Amman 11941; tel. (6) 5151882; fax (6) 5152016; e-mail jbc@go.com.jo; f. 1982; fiction, business, economics, computer science, medicine, engineering, general non-fiction; Man. Dir J. J. SHARBAIN.

Jordan Distribution Agency: POB 3371, Amman 11181; tel. (6) 5358855; fax (6) 5337733; e-mail jda@aramex.com; f. 1951; history; subsidiary of Aramex; Chair. FADI GHANDOUR; Gen. Man. WADIE SAYEGH.

Jordan House for Publication: POB 1121, Basman St, Amman; tel. (6) 24224; fax (6) 51062; f. 1952; medicine, nursing, dentistry; Man. Dir MURSI EL-ASHKAR.

Jordan Press and Publishing Co Ltd: POB 591, Amman 11118; tel. (6) 5608000; fax (6) 5667170; e-mail info@addustour.com.jo; internet www.addustour.com; f. 1967 by Al-Manar and Falastin dailies; publishes Ad-Dustour (daily), Ad-Dustour Sport (weekly) and The Star (English weekly); Chair. KAMEL ASH-SHARIF; Dir-Gen. SAIF ASH-SHARIF.

Jordan Press Foundation: POB 6710, Amman 11118; tel. (6) 5667171; fax (6) 5661242; e-mail info@jpf.com.jo; internet www.alrai.com; f. 1971; publishes Ar-Rai (daily), the Jordan Times (daily) and Hatem (monthly); Chair. AHMAD ABD AL-FATAH; Gen. Dir NADER HORANI.

El-Nafa'es: POB 927511, Al-Abdali, Amman 11190; tel. (6) 5693940; fax (6) 5693941; e-mail alnafaes@hotmail.com; f. 1990; education, Islamic; CEO SUFYAN OMAR AL-ASHQR.

At-Tanwir al-Ilmi (Scientific Enlightenment Publishing House): POB 4237, Al-Mahatta, Amman 11131; tel. and fax (6) 4899619; e-mail taisir@yahoo.com; internet www.icieparis.net; f. 1990; affiliated with the International Centre for Innovation in Education; education, engineering, philosophy, science, sociology; Gen. Dir Prof. Dr TAISIR SUBHI YAMIN.

Other publishers in Amman include: Dairat al-Ihsaat al-Amman, George N. Kawar, Al-Matbaat al-Hashmiya and National Press.

Broadcasting and Communications

TELECOMMUNICATIONS

Telecommunications Regulatory Commission (TRC): POB 850967, Amman 11185; tel. (6) 5501120; fax (6) 5863641; e-mail trc@trc.gov.jo; internet www.trc.gov.jo; f. 1995; Chair. and CEO Dr AHMAD HIASAT.

Jordan Mobile Telephone Services Company (Zain): POB 940821, 8th Circle, King Abdullah II St, Amman 11194; tel. (6) 5803000; fax (6) 5828200; e-mail info@jo.zain.com; internet www.jo.zain.com; f. 1994 as Jordan Mobile Telephone Services Co (JMTS—Fastlink); present name adopted Sept. 2007; private co; has operated Jordan's first mobile telecommunications network since 1995; CEO SAAD NASIR.

Jordan Telecom Group: POB 1689, Amman 11118; tel. (6) 4606666; fax (6) 4639200; e-mail info@jordantelecomgroup.jo; internet www.jordantelecomgroup.jo; f. 1971; fmrly Jordan Telecommunications Corpn, Jordan Telecommunications Co and Jordan Telecom; current name adopted in Feb. 2006 following integration of the following cos' operations into a single management structure: Jordan Telecom, MobileCom (mobile cellular telecommunications services), Wanadoo (internet services) and e-Dimension (information technology); in 2007 Jordan Telecom, MobileCom and Wanadoo were all rebranded as Orange; 30.5% govt-owned; 69.5% privately owned: France Télécom SA, France, 51.0%; Social Security Corpn 12.4%; 6.1% of shares listed on Amman Stock Exchange; assets JD 564.4m. (2003). Chair. Dr SHABIB FARAH AMMARI.

Umniah Mobile Company: POB 942481, Amman 11194; tel. (6) 5005000; fax (6) 5622772; e-mail contact@umniah.com; internet www.umniah.com; awarded contract for Jordan's third GSM licence in 2004; commenced operations in June 2005; sole provider of wireless broadband internet services in Jordan; subsidiary of Alghanim Group (Kuwait); 96% owned by Bahrain Telecommunications Co; CEO JOSEPH HANANIA.

BROADCASTING

Radio and Television

Jordan Radio and Television Corporation (JRTV): POB 1041, Amman; tel. (6) 773111; fax (6) 751503; e-mail general@jrtv.gov.jo; internet www.jrtv.jo; f. 1968; govt TV station; broadcasts for 90 hours weekly in Arabic and English; advertising accepted; Dir-Gen. IHSAN RAMZI SHIKIM; Dir of Television NASSER JUDEH; Dir of Radio HASHIM KHURAYSAT.

JORDAN

Finance

(cap. = capital; dep. = deposits; m. = million; res = reserves; brs = branches; amounts in Jordanian dinars unless otherwise indicated)

BANKING

Central Bank

Central Bank of Jordan: POB 37, King Hussein St, Amman 11118; tel. (6) 4630301; fax (6) 4638889; e-mail info@cbj.gov.jo; internet www.cbj.gov.jo; f. 1964; cap. 18.0m., res 140.4m., dep. 4,603.4m. (Dec. 2006); Gov. and Chair. Dr UMAYYA SALAH TOUKAN; 2 brs.

National Banks

Arab Bank PLC: POB 950545, Shmeisani, Amman 11195; tel. (6) 5607231; fax (6) 5606793; e-mail corpcomm@arabbank.com.jo; internet www.arabbank.com; f. 1930; cap. US $525.0m., res $5,209.0m., dep. $25,334.4m. (Dec. 2006); Chair. ABD AL-HAMID SHOMAN; Vice-Chair. MUNIB RASHID MASRI; 84 brs in Jordan, 99 brs abroad.

Bank of Jordan PLC: POB 2140, Shmeisani, Amman 11181; tel. (6) 5696277; fax (6) 5696291; e-mail boj@bankofjordan.com.jo; internet www.bankofjordan.com; f. 1960; cap. 86.0m., res 35.3m., dep. 1,203.6m. (Dec. 2006); Chair. and Gen. Man. TAWFIK SHAKER FAKHOURI; 80 brs and offices.

Cairo Amman Bank: POB 950661, Cairo Amman Bank Bldg, Wadi Saqra St, Amman 11195; tel. (6) 4616910; fax (6) 4642890; e-mail info@cab.jo; internet www.cab.jo; f. 1960; cap. 67.5m., res 70.7m., dep. 983.9m. (Dec. 2006); Chair. and CEO KHALED AL-MASRI; 49 brs in Jordan, 16 brs in the West Bank.

Capital Bank of Jordan: POB 941283, Issam Ajlouni St, Amman 11194; tel. (6) 5100200; fax (6) 5695942; e-mail info@capitalbank.jo; internet www.capitalbank.jo; f. 1996 as Export and Finance Bank; name changed as above 2006; cap. 116.0m., res 24.1m., dep. 549.8m. (Dec. 2006); Chair. and CEO MUHAMMAD ALI AL-HUSARI; Gen. Man. HAYTHAM KAMHIYAH.

Jordan Ahli Bank: POB 3103, Queen Noor St, Shmeisani, Amman 11181; tel. (6) 5622282; fax (6) 5622281; e-mail info@ahlibank.com.jo; internet www.ahli.com; f. 1955 as Jordan National Bank; name changed as above 2006; cap. 110.0m., res 77.5m., dep. 1,462.5m. (Dec. 2006); Chair. Dr RAJAI MOUASHER; CEO and Gen. Man. MARWAN AWAD; 40 brs in Jordan, 6 brs abroad.

Jordan Commercial Bank: POB 9989, Yakoub Sarrouf St, Shmeisani, Amman 11191; tel. (6) 5603931; fax (6) 5603989; e-mail jcb@jcbank.com.jo; internet www.jcbank.com.jo; f. 1977 as Jordan Gulf Bank; name changed as above 2004; cap. 57.5m., res 6.3m., dep. 393.0m. (Dec. 2006); Chair. MICHEL AS-SAYEGH; CEO and Gen. Man. Dr JAWAD AL-HADID; 23 brs in Jordan, 3 brs in West Bank.

Jordan Islamic Bank for Finance and Investment: POB 926225, Shmeisani, Amman 11190; tel. (6) 5677377; fax (6) 5666326; e-mail jib@islamicbank.com.jo; internet www.jordanislamicbank.com; f. 1978; cap. 64.1m., res 37.0m., dep. 1,267.5m. (Dec. 2006); Chair. MAHMOUD J. HASSOUBEH; Vice-Chair. and Gen. Man. MUSA ABD AL-AZIZ SHIHADEH; 56 brs.

Jordan Kuwait Bank: POB 9776, Abdali, Amman 11191; tel. (6) 5629400; fax (6) 5695604; e-mail webmaster@jkbank.com.jo; internet www.jordan-kuwait-bank.com; f. 1976; cap. US $105.8m., res $127.3m., dep. $1,300.0m. (Dec. 2006); Chair. and CEO ABD AL-KARIM AL-KABARITI; Gen. Man. MUHAMMAD YASSER M. AL-ASMAR; 50 brs.

Société Générale de Banque-Jordanie: POB 560, 30 Prince Shaker bin Zeid St, Shmeisani, Amman 11118; tel. (6) 5695470; fax (6) 5693410; e-mail sgbj@sgbj.com.jo; internet www.sgbj.com.jo; f. 1965 as Middle East Investment Bank; became part of the Société Générale Group (France) 1999; name changed as above 2003; cap. 27.0m., res –1.7m., dep. 142.8m. (Dec. 2005); Chair. HASSAN MANGO; Gen. Man. ELIANE TANNOUS; 16 brs.

Specialized Credit Institutions

Agricultural Credit Corporation: POB 77, Amman 11118; tel. (6) 5661105; fax (6) 5668365; e-mail adminacc@go.com.jo; internet www.acc.gov.jo; f. 1959; cap. 24m., res 12.4m., total assets 125.1m. (Dec. 2000); Chair. Eng. MOZAHIM AL-MUHASEN; Vice-Chair. and Dir-Gen. TAWFIQ HABASHNEH; 21 brs.

Arab Jordan Investment Bank: POB 8797, Arab Jordan Investment Bank Bldg, Shmeisani Commercial Area, Amman 11121; tel. (6) 5607126; fax (6) 5681482; e-mail info@ajib.com; internet www.ajib.com; f. 1978; cap. 100m., dep. 374m., total assets 516m. (Dec. 2007); Chair. ABD AL-KADER AL-QADI; CEO HANI AL-QADI; 18 brs and offices in Jordan, 1 br. abroad.

Housing Bank for Trade and Finance: POB 7693, Parliament St, Amman 11118; tel. (6) 5607315; fax (6) 5678121; e-mail info@hbtf.com.jo; internet www.hbtf.com/wps/portal; f. 1973; cap. 250.0m., res 444.7m., dep. 3,143.5m. (Dec. 2006); Chair. Dr MICHEL MARTO; CEO AHMAD ABD AL-FATTAH; 97 brs.

Industrial Development Bank: POB 1982, Al-Kuliah Al-Elmiah, Amman 11118; tel. (6) 4602200; fax (6) 4647821; e-mail idb@indevbank.com.jo; internet www.indevbank.com.jo; f. 1965; cap. 24.0m., res 26.8m., dep. 45.1m. (Dec. 2006); Chair. MUFLEH AKEL; Gen. Man. MARAW AWAD; 3 brs.

Jordan Co-operative Corporation: POB 1343, Amman; tel. (6) 5665171; fax (6) 5695803; internet www.jcc.gov.jo; f. 1995 to replace dissolved Jordan Co-operative Organization; Man. Dir HASSAN AN-NABULSI.

Jordan Investment and Finance Bank (JIFBANK): Issam Ajlouni St, Shmeisani, Amman; tel. (6) 5665145; fax (6) 5681410; e-mail souha@jifbank.com; internet www.jifbank.com; f. 1982 as Jordan Investment and Finance Corpn; name changed 1989; cap. 40.0m., res 19.0m., dep. 1,203.4m. (Dec. 2005); Chair. BASIL JARDANEH; Man. Dir KHALIL NASSER; 5 brs.

Jordan Investment Board (JIB): POB 893, Amman 11821; tel. (6) 5608400; fax (6) 5608421; e-mail info@jib.com.jo; internet www.jordaninvestment.com; f. 1995; CEO Dr MAEN NSOUR.

Rural and Urban Development Bank: POB 1572, Amman 11118; tel. (6) 5682691; fax (6) 5668153; e-mail cvdb100@hotmail.com; f. 1979; 30% state-owned; cap. US $44.561m. (Dec. 2004); Chair. TAWFIQ KRESHAN; Gen. Man. Dr IBRAHIM AS-SOUN; 10 brs.

Social Security Corporation: POB 926031, Amman 11110; tel. (6) 5501880; fax (6) 5501888; e-mail webmaster@ssc.gov.jo; internet www.ssc.gov.jo; f. 1978; Dir-Gen. Dr OMAR AR-RAZZAZ.

Union Bank for Savings and Investment: POB 35104, Prince Shaker Ben Zeid St, Shmeisani, Amman 11180; tel. (6) 5607011; fax (6) 5666149; e-mail retail@unionbankjo.com; internet www.unionbankjo.com; f. 1978 as Arab Finance Corpn; name changed as above 1991; cap. 55.0m., res 27.2m., dep. 769.4m. (Dec. 2006); Chair. and Gen. Man. ISAM SALFITI; 14 brs.

STOCK EXCHANGE

Amman Stock Exchange (ASE): POB 212466, Arjan, nr Ministry of the Interior, Amman 11121; tel. (6) 5664109; fax (6) 5664071; e-mail info@ase.com.jo; internet www.exchange.jo; f. 1978 as Amman Financial Market; name changed as above 1999; Chair. MUHAMMAD SALEH HOURANI; CEO JALIL TARIF.

INSURANCE

There were 25 local and one foreign insurance company operating in Jordan, which employed a collective total of 2,635 people, at the end of 2005.

Jordan Insurance Co Ltd (JIC): POB 279, Company's Bldg, 3rd Circle, Jabal Amman, Amman 11118; tel. (6) 4634161; fax (6) 4637905; e-mail allinsure@jicjo.com; internet www.jicjo.com; f. 1951; cap. 30m. (Dec. 2006); Chair. KHALDUN ABU HASSAN; Gen. Man. IMAD ABD AL-KHALEQ; 7 brs (1 in Jordan, 3 in Saudi Arabia, 3 in the United Arab Emirates) and a marketing agency in Kuwait.

Middle East Insurance Co Ltd (MEICO): POB 1802, Al-Kindi St, Um Uthanina, 5th Circle, Jabal Amman, Amman 11118; tel. (6) 5527100; fax (6) 5527801; e-mail meico@go.com.jo; internet www.meico.com.jo; f. 1962; cap. p.u. US $18.0m. (April 2007); Chair. SAMIR KAWAR; Gen. Man. Dr RAJAI SWEIS; 13 brs.

National Insurance Co: POB 6156-2938, Sayed Qotub St, Shmeisani, Amman 11118; tel. (6) 5671169; fax (6) 5684900; e-mail natinsur@go.com.jo; f. 1965 as above; name changed to National Ahlia Insurance Co in 1986, following merger with Ahlia Insurance Co (f. 1975); reverted to original name July 2007; cap. 2m.; Chair. MUSTAFA ABU GOURA; Gen. Man. GHALEB ABU-GOURA.

United Insurance Co Ltd: POB 7521, United Insurance Bldg, King Hussein St, Amman; tel. (6) 4648513; fax (6) 4629417; e-mail uic@united.com.jo; internet www.united.com.jo; f. 1972; all types of insurance; cap. p.u. 8m.; Gen. Man. MUHAMMAD ABU QUORA.

Insurance Federation

Jordan Insurance Federation (JOIF): POB 1990, Amman 11118; tel. (6) 5689266; fax (6) 5689510; internet www.joif.org; f. 1989 to replace the Jordan Association for Insurance Companies (f. 1956); regulatory and management authority; Chair. WASEEM WAEL ZURUB; Sec.-Gen. MAHER AL-HUSAIN.

Trade and Industry

DEVELOPMENT ORGANIZATIONS

Amman Development Corporation: POB 926621, Amman; tel. (6) 5629471; f. 1979; devt of services in the Amman municipality by constructing and running real estate; industrial and other complexes; Dir-Gen. SAMI AR-RASHID.

Aqaba Development Corporation (ADC): POB 2680, Chamber of Commerce Bldg, Aqaba 77110; tel. (3) 2039100; fax (3) 2039110; e-mail info@adc.jo; internet www.adc.jo; f. 2004 by the Aqaba Special Economic Zone Authority and the Govt of Jordan; Chair. and CEO Eng. IMAD NAJIB FAKHOURY.

Jordan Valley Authority (JVA): POB 2769, Amman 11183; tel. (6) 5689400; fax (6) 5689916; e-mail jvadewan2@mwi.gov.jo; internet www.jva.gov.jo; f. 1977 as a governmental organization responsible for the integrated social and economic development of the Jordan Valley; projects in Stage I of the Jordan Valley Development Plan were completed in 1979. In 1988 the JVA was incorporated into the Ministry of Water and Irrigation. By late 2000 completed infrastructure projects included 2,205 km of roads, 2,223 housing units, 90 schools, 15 health centres, 16 local government buildings, 4 marketing centres, 2 tomato paste factories, 1 cold storage facility and several workshops. Electricity is now provided to all towns and villages in the valley from the national network and potable water is supplied to them from tube wells. Many of the Stage II irrigation projects are now completed. These include the construction of the King Talal, Wadi Arab, Kafrein and Karamah dams; the extension of the King Abdullah Canal to total 110.5 km in length; the construction of major municipal water projects in Amman and Irbid; the construction and conversion of a surface irrigation system into a pressurized pipe system covering an irrigated area of 25,000 ha; the development of groundwater resources and subsurface drainage systems. Projects under way include the construction of the Al-Wehdeh, Tanour and Wala dams, as well as the Mujeb dam and diversion weir. Future developments in tourist and industrial infrastructure will include the development of the Dead Sea East shore, Christ's baptism site on the Jordan river, and industrial free zones; Sec.-Gen. AVEDIS SERPEKIAN.

CHAMBERS OF COMMERCE AND INDUSTRY

Amman Chamber of Commerce: POB 287, Amman 11118; tel. (6) 5666151; fax 5666155; e-mail info@ammanchamber.org.jo; internet www.ammanchamber.org.jo; f. 1923; more than 40,000 regd mems (2007); Chair. HAIDER MURAD; Dir-Gen. MUHANNAD ATTAR.

Amman Chamber of Industry: POB 1800, Amman 11118; tel. (6) 5643001; fax (6) 5647852; e-mail aci@aci.org.jo; internet www.aci.org.jo; f. 1962; approx. 7,500 regd industrial cos (2007); Pres. Dr HATEM H. HALAWANI.

Jordan Chamber of Commerce: POB 7029, Amman 11118; tel. (6) 5665492; fax (6) 5685997; e-mail info@jocc.org.jo; internet www.jocc.org.jo; f. 1955 as Federation of the Jordanian Chambers of Commerce; renamed as above in 2003; intended to promote co-operation between the various chambers of commerce in Jordan, and to consolidate and co-ordinate the capabilities of each; Chair. HAIDAR MURAD; Sec.-Gen. AMIN AL-HUSSEINI.

Professional Associations Council (PAC): Professional Associations Complex, Amman; Pres. HASHIM GHARAIBEH.

UTILITIES

Electricity

Central Electricity Generating Company (CEGCO): POB 2564, Amman 11953; tel. (6) 5340008; fax (6) 5340800; e-mail cegco@cegco.com.jo; internet www.cegco.com.jo; electricity generation; govt-owned; sale pending of 51% of shares to private investors; Dir-Gen. ABD AL-FATTAH AN-NSOUR.

Electricity Distribution Company (EDCO): POB 2310, Orthodox St, 7th Circle, Jabal Amman, Amman; tel. (6) 5858615; fax (6) 5818336; e-mail info@edco.jo; internet www.edco.jo; f. 1999; privatized in Nov. 2007; wholly owned by Kingdom Electricity, a jt venture between Jordan, Kuwait and the United Arab Emirates; electricity distribution for southern, eastern and Jordan Valley regions.

Irbid District Electricity Company (IDECO): POB 46, Amman; tel. (6) 7201500; fax (6) 7245495; e-mail ideco@wanadoo.jo; internet www.ideco.com.jo; f. 1957; 55.4% stake acquired by Kingdom Electricity (see EDCO) in Nov. 2007; electricity generation, transmission and distribution for northern regions; Chair. Prof. WAJEH OWAIS; Gen. Man. Eng. AHMAD THAINAT.

Jordanian Electric Power Company (JEPCO): POB 618, Amman 11118; tel. (6) 5503600; fax (6) 5503619; e-mail jepco@go.com.jo; internet www.jepco.com.jo; f. 1938; privately owned; electricity distribution for Amman, As-Salt, Az-Zarqa and Madaba; Chair. ISSAM BDEIR; Gen. Man. MARWAN BUSHNAQ.

National Electric Power Company (NEPCO): POB 2310, Amman 11118; tel. (6) 5858615; fax (6) 5818336; e-mail info@nepco.com.jo; internet www.nepco.com.jo; f. 1996; fmrly Jordan Electricity Authority; electricity transmission; govt-owned; scheduled for privatization; Chair. Dr HISHAM SALEH GHARAIBEH; Gen. Man. Dr AHMAD HIYASAT.

Water

Water Authority of Jordan (WAJ): POB 2412, Amman 11183; tel. (6) 5680100; fax (6) 5679143; e-mail administrator@waj.gov.jo; internet www.waj.gov.jo; govt-owned; scheduled for privatization; Sec.-Gen. Eng. MUNTHIR KHULIFAT.

TRADE UNIONS

The General Federation of Jordanian Trade Unions: POB 1065, Amman; tel. (6) 5675533; fax (6) 5687911; f. 1954; 17 affiliated unions; 200,000 mems; mem. of Arab Trade Unions Confed; Pres. MAZEN MA'AYTEH.

There are also a number of independent unions, including:

Jordan Engineers' Association (JEA): POB 940188, Professional Associations Center, Shmeisani, Amman 11118; tel. (6) 5607616; fax (6) 5676933; e-mail info@jea.org.jo; internet www.jea.org.jo; f. 1958 under the name Jordan Engineers' Society; present name adopted 1972; 67,000 mems; Pres. WAEL SAQQA; Sec.-Gen. ALI ABU AS-SUKKAR.

General Trade Union of Petroleum and Chemical Employees: POB 305, As-Sa'ada St, Zarqa; tel. (5) 398330; fax (5) 393874; f. 1963; Pres. KHALID ZEYOUD.

Transport

RAILWAYS

Aqaba Railways Corporation (ARC): POB 50, Ma'an; tel. (3) 2132114; fax (3) 2131861; e-mail arc@go.com.jo; internet www.arc.gov.jo; f. 1975; length of track 292 km (1,050-mm gauge); privately owned; Dir-Gen. HUSSEIN KRISHAN.

Formerly a division of the Hedjaz–Jordan Railway (see below), the Aqaba Railway was established as a separate entity in 1972; it retains close links with the Hedjaz but there is no regular through traffic between Aqaba and Amman. It comprises 292 km of 1,050-mm gauge track, consisting in the main of the 169-km line south of Menzil (leased from the Hedjaz–Jordan Railway) and the 115-km extension to Aqaba, opened in October 1975, which serves phosphate mines at el-Hasa and Wadi el-Abyad.

Jordan Hedjaz Railways: POB 4448, Amman 11131; tel. (6) 4895414; fax (6) 4894117; e-mail hji@nets.com.jo; internet www.jhr.gov.jo; f. 1952 as Hedjaz–Jordan Railway; administered by the Ministry of Transport; length of track 496 km (1,050-mm gauge); Chair. Eng. SOUD NSAIRAT; Dir-Gen. ALAA AL-BATAYNEH.

This was formerly a section of the Hedjaz Railway (Damascus, Syria, to Medina) for Muslim pilgrims to Medina and Mecca in Saudi Arabia. It crosses the Syrian border and enters Jordanian territory south of Dera'a, and runs for approximately 366 km to Naqb Ishtar, passing through Az-Zarqa, Amman, Qatrana and Ma'an. Some 844 km of the line, from Ma'an to Medina, were abandoned for more than 60 years. Reconstruction of the Medina line, begun in 1965, was scheduled to be completed in 1971 at a cost of £15m., divided equally between Jordan, Saudi Arabia and Syria. However, the reconstruction work was suspended at the request of the Arab states concerned, pending further studies on costs. The line between Ma'an and Saudi Arabia (114 km) is now completed, as well as 15 km in Saudi Arabia as far as Halet Ammar Station. A new 115-km extension to Aqaba (owned by the Aqaba Railway Corporation—see above) was opened in 1975. In August 1999 an express rail link between Amman and Damascus was inaugurated. In 2006 an international consortium won the contract to carry out a one-year feasibility study into linking Jordan's rail network with neighbouring systems. Five railways were planned: a 450-km route running north–south from Damascus to Aqaba; an 800-km railway running from Baghdad, Iraq, to Zarqa and Mafraq and further west; a 250-km railway from the Dead Sea to the port of Aqaba; a Sinai railway connecting Aqaba to the Egyptian rail network; and a 70-km route connecting Ma'an to Medina. In October 2006 plans to build a 28-km standard gauge rail link between Amman and Zarqa were announced.

ROADS

Amman is linked by road with all parts of the kingdom and with neighbouring countries. All cities and most towns are connected by a two-lane paved road system. In addition, several thousand km of tracks make all villages accessible to motor transport. In 2004 there was a total road network of 7,500 km, of which 3,057 km were highways and 2,078 km were secondary roads.

Iraqi-Jordanian Joint Land Transport Co: POB 5134, Amman 11183; tel. (6) 5930232; fax (6) 5932870; e-mail ijltco@wanadoo.jo; internet www.ijltco.com.jo; f. 1980; jt venture between Govts of Jordan and Iraq; operates a fleet of 150 vehicles; Gen. Man. Eng. HASSAN FARKOUH.

JORDAN

Jordanian-Syrian Land Transport Co: POB 20686, Amman; tel. (6) 5661134; fax (6) 5669645; f. 1976; transports goods between ports in Jordan and Syria; operates 390 trucks; Chair. and Gen. Man. HAMDI AL-HABASHNEH.

SHIPPING

The port of Aqaba is Jordan's only outlet to the sea and consists of a main port, container port (540 m in length) and industrial port, with 25 modern and specialized berths. The port has 761,300 sq m of open and contained storage area, and is used for Jordan's international trade and regional transit trade (mainly with Iraq). Plans to upgrade and expand the port's existing facilities were revealed in 2006. There is a ferry link between Aqaba and the Egyptian port of Nuweibeh.

Ports Corporation of Aqaba: POB 115, Aqaba 77110; tel. (3) 2014031; fax (3) 2016204; e-mail info@aqabaports.gov.jo; internet www.aqabaports.gov.jo; Dir-Gen. AWWAD MAFTAH.

Amman Shipping & Trading Co: POB 213083, 5th Floor, Al-Aqqad Trading Centre, Gardens St, Amman 11121; tel. (6) 5514620; fax (6) 5532324; e-mail astco@albitar.com.

Arab Bridge Maritime Co: POB 989, Aqaba; tel. (3) 2016305; fax (3) 2016312; e-mail info@abmaritime.com.jo; internet www.abmaritime.com.jo; f. 1985; jt venture by Egypt, Iraq and Jordan to improve economic co-operation; commercial shipping of passengers, vehicles and cargo between Aqaba and the Egyptian port of Nuweibeh; transportation of passengers between Jordan and Egypt; Man. Dir Capt. HUSSEIN SOUOB.

Arrow Trans Shipping SA: POB 213083, 5th Floor, Aqad Complex Bldg, Wasfi at-Tal St, Amman 11121; tel. (6) 5512621; fax (6) 5532324; e-mail arrow@albitar.com; f. 1990; Gen. Man. MARWAN JAMAL ED-DIN BITAR.

Assaf Shipping Co SA: POB 2637, Irbid 21110; tel. and fax (2) 7061118; e-mail faisal_assaf@hotmail.com; f. 1998; owned by Assaf Marine Services; marine services, incl. chartering, surveys and management; Gen. Man. FAISAL ASSAF.

Tawfiq Gargour & Fils: POB 419, 4th Floor, Da'ssan Bldg, Wasfi at-Tal St, Amman 11118; tel. (6) 5524142; fax (6) 5530512; e-mail tgf@tgf.com.jo; internet www.tgf.com.jo; f. 1928; shipping agents and owners; CEO Dr DUREID MAHASNEH; Gen. Man. SAMIA ZABANEH (acting).

Hijazi & Ghosheh Co: POB 183292, Amman; tel. (6) 4886166; fax (6) 4886211.

International Ship Management Co Ltd (ISM): POB 941430, 2nd Floor, Noor Centre, Islam Abad St, Ar-Rabeiah, Amman 11194; tel. (6) 5512607; fax (6) 5532083; e-mail ism@go.com.jo; Gen. Man. MOUSTAFA MASSAD.

Jordan National Shipping Lines Co Ltd: POB 5406, Nasir Ben Jameel St, Wadi Saqra, Amman 11183; POB 557, Aqaba; tel. (6) 5511500; fax (6) 5515119; e-mail jnl@go.com.jo; 75% govt-owned; service from Antwerp (the Netherlands), Bremen (Germany) and Tilbury (the United Kingdom) to Aqaba; daily passenger ferry service to Egypt; land transportation to destinations in Iraq and elsewhere in the region; Chair. MUHAMMAD SMADI; Gen. Man. Eng. AKEF ABU TAYEH.

Amin Kawar & Sons Co WLL: POB 222, 24 Abd al-Hamid Sharaf St, Shmeisani, Amman 11118; tel. (6) 5609500; fax (6) 5698322; e-mail kawar@kawar.com.jo; internet www.kawar.com.jo; chartering, forwarding and shipping line agents; Chair. TAWFIQ A. KAWAR; CEO RUDAIN T. KAWAR; Gen. Man. GHASSOUB F. KAWAR.

Al-Mansour Marine Transportation and Trading Co: POB 960359, Amman; tel. (6) 697958; fax (6) 702352.

Orient Shipping Co Ltd: POB 207, Amman 11118; tel. (6) 4641695; fax (6) 4651567; e-mail wah@go.com.jo.

Petra Navigation and International Trading Co Ltd: POB 942502, Amman 11194; tel. (6) 5607021; fax (6) 5601362; e-mail info@petra.jo; internet www.petranav.com.jo; general cargo, ro/ro and passenger ferries; Chair. MAJED ARMOUSH; Man. Dir ANWAR SBEIH.

Red Sea Shipping Agency Co: POB 1248, 24 Sharif Abd al-Hamid Sharaf St, Shmeisani, Amman 11118; tel. (6) 5609501; fax (6) 5688241; e-mail rss@rssa.com.jo; f. 1955.

Salam International Transport and Trading Co: King Hussein St, Abdali, Amman 11121; tel. (6) 5607021.

Syrian-Jordanian Shipping Co: POB 148, rue Port Said, Latakia, Syria; tel. (41) 471636; fax (41) 470250; Chair. OSMAN LEBBADI.

PIPELINES

Two oil pipelines cross Jordan. The former Iraq Petroleum Co pipeline, carrying petroleum from the oilfields in Iraq to Israel's Mediterranean port of Haifa, has not operated since 1967. The 1,717-km (1,067-mile) pipeline, known as the Trans-Arabian Pipeline (Tapline), carries petroleum from the oilfields of Dhahran in Saudi Arabia to Sidon on the Mediterranean seaboard of Lebanon. Tapline traverses Jordan for a distance of 177 km (110 miles) and has frequently been cut by hostile action. Tapline stopped pumping to Syria and Lebanon at the end of 1983, when it was first due to close. It was later scheduled to close in 1985, but in September 1984 Jordan renewed an agreement to receive Saudi Arabian crude oil through Tapline. (This contract was temporarily suspended by Saudi Arabia in 1990 to express its displeasure at what it perceived to be Jordanian support for Iraq during the Gulf War.) Faced with the challenge of meeting rising oil demands, the Jordanian Government has been considering plans to rehabilitate disused sections of Tapline, at an estimated cost of US $200m.–$300m., since early 2005.

CIVIL AVIATION

There are international airports at Amman and Aqaba. The Queen Alia International Airport at Zizya, 40 km south of Amman, was opened in 1983. In October 2006 the Ministry of Transport announced plans for the construction of a new terminal building, at an estimated cost of US $284m.; the new terminal was expected to become operational by 2010 and to increase the airport's annual capacity to approximately 9m. passengers.

Civil Aviation Regulatory Commission (CARC): POB 7547, Amman 11110; tel. (6) 4892282; fax (6) 4891653; e-mail info@carc.gov.jo; internet www.carc.jo; f. 2007, in place of the disbanded Civil Aviation Authority (f. 1950); Chief Commr and CEO Capt. SULEIMAN OBEIDAT.

Aqaba Airports Co: King Hussein International Airport, Special Economic Zone, Aqaba; f. 2007; CEO HANNA NAJJAR.

Arab Wings Co Ltd: POB 341018, Amman 11134; tel. (6) 4899790; fax (6) 4889796; e-mail info@arabwings.com.jo; internet www.arabwings.com.jo; f. 1975; executive jet charter service, air ambulances, priority cargo; Man. Dir AHED QUNTAR; Gen. Man. SAMEER HDAIRIS.

Jordan Aviation (JATE): Fourth Circle Bldg, Um Othayna, Amman; tel. (6) 5501760; fax (6) 5525732; e-mail Commercial@jordanaviation.jo; f. 2000; first privately owned airline in Jordan; operates charter and scheduled flights.

Royal Jordanian Airline: Head Office: POB 302, Housing Bank Commercial Centre, Shmeisani, Amman 11118; tel. (6) 5202000; fax (6) 5672527; e-mail rj@go.com.jo; internet www.rj.com; f. 1963; partially privatized in 2001; further privatization pending; scheduled and charter services to Middle East, North Africa, Europe, USA and Far East; Chair. NASSER A. LOZI; Vice-Chair., Pres. and CEO SAMER MAJALI.

Royal Wings Co Ltd: POB 314018, Amman 11134; tel. (6) 4875206; fax (6) 4875656; e-mail info@royalwings.com.jo; internet www.royalwings.com.jo; f. 1996; subsidiary of Royal Jordanian; operates scheduled and charter regional and domestic services; Man. Dir USAMA FARAJ.

Tourism

The ancient cities of Jarash (Jerash) and Petra, and Jordan's proximity to biblical sites, have encouraged tourism. The development of Jordan's Dead Sea coast is currently under way; owing to the Sea's mineral-rich waters, the growth of curative tourism is anticipated. The Red Sea port of Aqaba is also undergoing a major programme of development, with a view to becoming a centre for diving holidays. In 2005 Jordan received some 5.8m. visitors; however, following the bombings in Amman in November of that year, arrivals declined to 5.0m. in 2006. According to preliminary figures for 2007, tourist numbers increased slightly, to 5.1m., and income from tourism was JD 1,291.8m.

Ministry of Tourism and Antiquities: see Ministries; Sec.-Gen. SULTAN ABU JABER.

Jordan Tourism Board (JTB): POB 830688, Amman 11183; tel. (6) 5678444; fax (6) 5678295; e-mail info@visitjordan.com; internet www.visitjordan.com; f. 1997; Gen. Man. MAZEN HOMOUD.

INDEX OF INTERNATIONAL ORGANIZATIONS

(Main reference only)

ABAC, 177
Abdus Salam International Centre for Theoretical Physics, 141
ACP Council of Ministers, 303
ACP Secretariat, 303
ACP States, 301
ADB Institute, 182
ADF, 163
Aerospace Medical Association, 432
AFESD, 174
African Accounting Council, 169
African Airlines Association, 468
African Association for Public Administration and Management, 422
African Bar Association, 429
African Capacity Building Foundation, 410
African Centre for Monetary Studies, 415
African Civil Aviation Commission, 169
African Commission on Agricultural Statistics, 106
African Commission on Human and Peoples' Rights, 453
African Development Bank, 162
African Development Forum, 41
African Development Fund, 163
African Economic Community, 166
African Export-Import Bank, 163
African Forestry and Wildlife Commission, 106
African Governance Forum, 41
African Groundnut Council, 407
African Guarantee and Economic Co-operation Fund, 416
African Insurance Organization, 415
African Oil Palm Development Association, 407
African Organization of Cartography and Remote Sensing, 459
African Partnership Forum, 348
African Petroleum Producers' Association, 407
African Regional Centre for Technology, 459
African Regional Organization for Standardization, 464
African Reinsurance Corporation, 163
African Social and Environmental Studies Programme, 450
African Society of International and Comparative Law, 429
African Telecommunications Union, 169
African Timber Organization, 402
African Trade Insurance Agency, 206
African Training and Research Centre in Administration for Development, 410
African Union, 164
African Union Mission in Somalia, 168
African Union of Broadcasting, 439
Afro-Asian Peoples' Solidarity Organization, 422
Afro-Asian Rural Development Organization, 410
Agence française de développement, 308
Agence Universitaire de la Francophonie, 417
Agency for the Prohibition of Nuclear Weapons in Latin America and the Caribbean, 422
AGFUND, 411
Agudath Israel World Organisation, 441
Aid to Displaced Persons and its European Villages, 453
AIESEC International, 470
AIIM International, 459
Airports Council International, 468
ALADI, 331
All Africa Conference of Churches, 441
Alliance Israélite Universelle, 441
Alliance of Small Island States, 422
Al-Quds Committee, 369
Amazon Co-operation Treaty Organization, 411
AMISOM, 168
Amnesty International, 453
AMSE-AMCE-WAER, 417
Andean Business Advisory Council, 173
Andean Community of Nations, 170
Andean Development Corporation, 173
Andean Labour Advisory Council, 173
Andrés Bello Agreement, 173
Animal Production and Health Commission for Asia and the Pacific, 106
Anti-Slavery International, 453
ANZUS, 422
AOSIS, 422
APEC, 176
APEC Business Advisory Council, 177

Arab Academy for Science, Technology and Maritime Transport, 333
Arab Administrative Development Organization, 333
Arab Air Carriers' Organization, 468
Arab Atomic Energy Agency, 333
Arab Authority for Agricultural Investment and Development, 402
Arab Bank for Economic Development in Africa, 333
Arab Centre for the Study of Arid Zones and Dry Lands, 333
Arab Company for Drug Industries and Medical Appliances, 223
Arab Company for Electronic Commerce, 223
Arab Company for Industrial Investment, 223
Arab Company for Livestock Development, 223
Arab Co-operative Union, 223
Arab Detergent Chemicals Company, 367
Arab Drilling and Workover Company, 367
Arab Federation for Paper, Printing and Packaging Industries, 223
Arab Federation of Chemical and Petrochemical Industries, 223
Arab Federation of Engineering Industries, 223
Arab Federation of Food Industries, 223
Arab Federation of Leather Industries, 223
Arab Federation of Petroleum, Mining and Chemicals Workers, 427
Arab Federation of Shipping, 223
Arab Federation of Textile Industries, 223
Arab Federation of Travel Agents, 223
Arab Fund for Economic and Social Development, 174
Arab Fund for Technical Assistance to African Countries, 333
Arab Geophysical Exploration Services Company, 367
Arab Gulf Programme for the United Nations Development Organizations, 411
Arab Industrial Development and Mining Organization, 333
Arab Iron and Steel Union, 464
Arab Labour Organization, 333
Arab League, 332
Arab League Educational, Cultural and Scientific Organization, 334
Arab Maritime Petroleum Transport Company, 367
Arab Mining Company, 223
Arab Monetary Fund, 175
Arab Organization for Agricultural Development, 334
Arab Permanent Postal Commission, 439
Arab Petroleum Investments Corporation, 367
Arab Petroleum Services Company, 367
Arab Petroleum Training Institute, 367
Arab Satellite Communications Organization, 334
Arab Seaports Federation, 223
Arab Shipbuilding and Repair Yard Company, 367
Arab Sports Confederation, 457
Arab States Broadcasting Union, 334
Arab Steel Union, 223
Arab Sugar Federation, 223
Arab Telecommunications Union, 439
Arab Towns Organization, 450
Arab Trade Financing Program, 176
Arab Unified Military Command, 333
Arab Union for Cement and Building Materials, 223
Arab Union for Information Technology, 223
Arab Union of Fish Producers, 223
Arab Union of Hotels and Tourism, 223
Arab Union of Land Transport, 223
Arab Union of Railways, 223
Arab Union of the Manufacturers of Pharmaceuticals and Medical Appliances, 223
Arab Union of the Manufacturers of Tyres and Rubber Products, 223
Arab Well Logging Company, 367
Arctic Council, 411
ASEAN, 185
ASEAN Regional Forum, 188
Asia and Pacific Commission on Agricultural Statistics, 106
Asia and Pacific Plant Protection Commission, 106
Asia-Europe Meeting (ASEM), 192
Asia-Pacific Academy of Ophthalmology, 432
Asia-Pacific Broadcasting Union, 439
Asia Pacific Dental Federation, 432
Asia-Pacific Economic Co-operation, 176
Asia-Pacific Fishery Commission, 106
Asia-Pacific Forestry Commission, 106

INDEX

Asia-Pacific Telecommunity, 439
Asia Students Association, 470
Asian-African Legal Consultative Organization, 429
Asian and Pacific Centre for Agricultural Engineering and Machinery, 37
Asian and Pacific Centre for Transfer of Technology, 37
Asian and Pacific Coconut Community, 408
Asian and Pacific Training Centre for ICT for Development, 37
Asian Clearing Union, 415
Asian Confederation of Teachers, 417
Asian Development Bank, 182
Asian Development Fund, 183
Asian-Pacific Postal Union, 439
Asian Productivity Organization, 464
Asian Reinsurance Corporation, 415
Asian South Pacific Bureau of Adult Education, 417
Asian Vegetable Research and Development Center, 402
Asociación de Empresas de Telecomunicaciones de la Comunidad Andina, 172
Asociación del Congreso Panamericano de Ferrocarriles, 470
Asociación Interamericana de Bibliotecarios, Documentalistas y Especialistas en Información Agrícolas, 402
Asociación Interamericana de Ingeniería Sanitaria y Ambiental, 433
Asociación Internacional de Radiodifusión Latinoamericana de Instituciones Financieras para el Desarrollo, 413
Asociación Latinoamericana de Integración, 331
Asociación mundial de ciencias de la educación, 417
Asociación Regional de Empresas de Petróleo y Gas Natural en Latinoamérica y el Caribe, 410
Assembly of Caribbean Community Parliamentarians, 200
Assembly of Western European Union, 426
Associated Country Women of the World, 453
Association des Etats Généraux des Etudiants de l'Europe, 470
Association des universités africaines, 417
Association d'instituts européens de conjoncture économique, 415
Association for Childhood Education International, 417
Association for Paediatric Education in Europe, 432
Association for the Promotion of International Press Distribution (DISTRIPRESS), 439
Association for the Study of the World Refugee Problem, 450
Association for the Taxonomic Study of the Flora of Tropical Africa, 444
Association Générale de Fédérations Internationales de Sports, 457
Association internationale de cybernétique, 460
Association Internationale de la Mutualitétergence et des produits d'entretien, 466
Association internationale de linguistique appliquérature Comparée, 406
Association Internationale de Papyrologues, 419
Association Internationale de Science Politique, 424
Association Internationale des Ecoles Supérieures d'Éducation Physique, 419
Association Internationale des Professeurs et Maîtres de Conférence Universitaires, 419
Association internationale des sciences juridiques, 430
Association internationale des sociétés d'assurance mutuelle, 428
Association mondiale des sciences de l'éducation, 417
Association Montessori Internationale, 417
Association of African Central Banks, 415
Association of African Development Finance Institutions, 163
Association of African Tax Administrators, 415
Association of African Trade Promotion Organizations, 464
Association of African Universities, 417
Association of Agricultural Research Institutions in the Near East and North Africa, 402
Association of Arab Universities, 417
Association of Asia Pacific Airlines, 468
Association of Asian Confederations of Credit Unions, 415
Association of Caribbean States, 411
Association of Caribbean University and Research Institutional Libraries, 417
Association of Commonwealth Newspapers, News Agencies and Periodicals, 213
Association of Commonwealth Universities, 213
Association of Development Financing Institutions in Asia and the Pacific, 411
Association of European Airlines, 468
Association of European Chambers of Commerce and Industry, 464
Association of European Institutes of Economic Research, 415
Association of European Journalists, 439
Association of European Research Libraries, 418
Association of Geoscientists for International Development, 444

International Organizations

Association of National European and Mediterranean Societies of Gastroenterology, 432
Association of Natural Rubber Producing Countries, 408
Association of Pacific Islands Legislatures, 422
Association of Private European Cable Operators, 439
Association of Secretaries General of Parliaments, 422
Association of South East Asian Nations, 185
Association of South Pacific Airlines, 383
Association of South-East Asian Institutions of Higher Learning, 418
Association pour l'Enseignement de la Pédatrie en Europe, 432
Atlantic Treaty Association, 422
AU, 164
Autorité du Bassin du Niger, 413
Aviation sans Frontières, 453

B

BADEA, 333
Bahá'í International Community, 441
Balkan Medical Union, 432
Baltic and International Maritime Council, 469
Baltic Council, 423
Baltic Sea Region Energy Co-operation, 225
Banco Centroamericano de Integración Económica, 203
Banco del Sur, 415
Bank for International Settlements, 194
Banque arabe pour le développement économique en Afrique, 333
Banque centrale des Comores, 307
Banque centrale des états de l'Afrique de l'ouest, 307
Banque de développement des états de l'Afrique centrale, 307
Banque des états de l'Afrique centrale, 307
Banque ouest-africaine de développement, 307
Baptist World Alliance, 441
Basel Committee on Banking Supervision, 195
BCEAO, 307
BCIE, 203
BDEAC, 307
BEAC, 307
Benelux Economic Union, 411
BINUB, 91
BirdLife International, 421
BIS, 194
Black Sea Economic Co-operation, 367
Black Sea Trade and Development Bank, 368
BOAD, 307
BONUCA, 92
Bourse Régionale des Valeurs Mobilières, 307
BSEC, 367
BSEC Business Council, 368
Building and Wood Workers International, 325
Bureau International de la Recupération et du Recyclage, 459
Bureau international des poids et mesures, 446
Bureau of European Policy Advisers, 251
Bureau of International Recycling, 459
BusinessEurope, 464

C

CAB International, 402
CABI Bioscience, 402
CACM, 202
CAEF—The European Foundry Association, 464
CAFTA, 204
Cairns Group, 464
CAN, 170
Capacity 2015, 61
Caribbean Agricultural Research and Development Institute, 200
Caribbean Association of Industry and Commerce, 464
Caribbean-Britain Business Council, 411
Caribbean Centre for Development Administration, 201
Caribbean Community and Common Market, 196
Caribbean Community Climate Change Centre, 201
Caribbean Competition Commission, 201
Caribbean Conference of Churches, 441
Caribbean Court of Justice, 197
Caribbean Development Bank, 201
Caribbean Disaster Emergency Response Agency, 201
Caribbean Environmental Health Institute, 201
Caribbean Examinations Council, 201
Caribbean Food and Nutrition Institute, 201
Caribbean Law Institute, 201
Caribbean Meteorological Organization, 201
Caribbean Plant Protection Commission, 106

INDEX   *International Organizations*

Caribbean Telecommunications Union, 201
Caribbean Tourism Organization, 463
CARICOM, 196
CARICOM Implementing Agency for Crime and Security, 201
CARICOM Regional Organisation for Standards and Quality, 201
Caritas Internationalis, 411
Caspian Environment Programme, 421
Catholic International Education Office, 418
CBSS, 224
CCJ, 197
CIS, 215
CITES, 62
Cedefop, 257
CEEAC, 411
CELADE, 39
Celtic League, 423
CEMAC, 307
CEN-SAD, 411
Central American Air Navigation Services Corporation, 203
Central American Bank for Economic Integration, 203
Central American Common Market, 202
Central American Council of Social Security Institutions, 202
Central American Council on Housing and Human Settlements, 202
Central American Electrification Council, 202
Central American Free-Trade Area, 204
Central American Institute for Business Administration, 466
Central American Institute of Public Administration, 203
Central American Integration System, 201
Central American Monetary Council, 202
Central American University Council, 203
Central Asia Regional Economic Co-operation, 411
Central Commission for the Navigation of the Rhine, 469
Central Emergency Response Fund, 47
Central Europe Pipeline Management Agency, 345
Central European Free Trade Association, 411
Central European Initiative, 423
Centre Africain de Formation et de Recherche Administratives pour le Développement, 410
Centre for Alleviation of Poverty through Secondary Crops' Development in Asia and the Pacific, 38
Centre for Educational Research and Innovation, 350
Centre for International Environmental Law, 429
Centre for Latin American Monetary Studies, 415
Centre for the Development of Enterprise, 303
Centre international de liaison des écoles de cinéma et de télévision, 406
Centre international du film pour l'enfance et la jeunesse, 406
Centre Regional de Formations aux Techniques des leves aerospatiaux, 462
Centrist Democrat International, 423
Centro de Coordinación para la Prevención de Desastres Naturales en América Central, 203
Centro de Estudios de Justicia de las Américas, 366
Centro de Estudios Monetarios Latinoamericanos, 415
Centro Interamericano de Investigación y Documentación sobre Formación Profesional, 418
Centro Internacional de Agricultura Tropical, 403
Centro Latinoamericano y Caribeno de Demografia, 39
CEPOL, 258
CGIAR, 114
Charter of the United Nations, 23
Christian Conference of Asia, 441
Christian Peace Conference, 441
CILSS, 414
CIO, 354
CIOMS, 432
CIS, 215
CITES, 62
CMAG, 208
Coalition Clean Baltic, 421
Cocoa Producers' Alliance, 408
Codex Alimentarius Commission, 106
Collaborative International Pesticides Analytical Council Ltd, 402
Collective Security Treaty Organization, 423
Colombo Plan, 411
Colombo Plan Staff College for Technician Education, 411
COMESA, 205
COMESA Bankers Association, 206
COMESA Leather and Leather Products Institute, 206
COMESA Metallurgical Industries Association, 206
Comisión Centroamericana de Transporte Marítimo, 202
Comisión de Telecomunicaciones de Centroamérica, 203
Comisión Interamericana de Derechos Humanos, 361
Comisión Interamericana de Mujeres, 365

Comisión Interamericana de Puertos, 361
Comisión Interamericana de Telecomunicaciones, 362
Comisión Interamericana para el Control del Abuso de Drogas, 362
Comisión para el Desarrollo Científico y Tecnológico de Centroamérica y Panamán Permanente del Pacífico Sur, 421
Comité Coordinador Regional de Instituciones de Agua Potable y Saneamiento de Centroamérica, Panamá y República Dominicana, 203
Comité européen de normalisation, 465
Comité Européen des Assurances, 415
Comité Interamericano Contra el Terrorismo, 365
Comité International Catholique des Infirmières et Assistantes Médico-Sociales, 434
Comité international de la rayonne et des fibres synthétiques, 468
Comité international de médecine militaire, 434
Comité international des transports ferroviaires, 469
Comité international pour la diffusion des arts et des lettres par le ciné maritime international, 429
Comité permanent inter états de lutte contre la sécheresse au Sahel, 414
Commission de l'Océan Indien, 412
Commission du Golfe de Guinée, 423
Commission for Controlling the Desert Locust in Northwest Africa, 106
Commission for Controlling the Desert Locust in Southwest Asia, 106
Commission for Controlling the Desert Locust in the Central Region, 106
Commission for Inland Fisheries of Latin America, 106
Commission for Labour Co-operation, 339
Commission for Social Development, 20
Commission for Technical Support and Co-operation, 331
Commission for Telecommunications in Central America, 203
Commission Internationale des Irrigations et du Drainage, 460
Commission internationale pour l'exploration scientifique de la mer Méditerranée, 446
Commission Internationale Technique de Sucrerie, 403
Commission on Genetic Resources for Food and Agriculture, 106
Commission on Livestock Development for Latin America and the Caribbean, 106
Commission on the Limits of the Continental Shelf, 324
Commission on the Protection of the Black Sea Against Pollution, 421
Committee for European Construction Equipment, 464
Committee for Inland Fisheries of Africa, 106
Committee for Technical and Economic Studies on Nuclear Development and the Fuel Cycle (Nuclear Development Committee), 352
Committee for the Scientific and Technological Development of Central America and Panama, 202
Committee of the Central American Isthmus for Sport and Recreation, 202
Committee of the Regions, 257
Committee on Nuclear Regulatory Activities, 352
Committee on Radiation Protection, 352
Committee on the Safety of Nuclear Installations, 352
Committee on Trade and Investment, 177
Common Fund for Commodities, 408
Common Market for Eastern and Southern Africa, 205
Commonwealth, 206
Commonwealth Association for Education in Journalism and Communication, 213
Commonwealth Association for Public Administration and Management, 214
Commonwealth Association of Architects, 214
Commonwealth Association of Science, Technology and Mathematics Educators, 213
Commonwealth Broadcasting Association, 213
Commonwealth Business Council, 212
Commonwealth Council for Educational Administration and Management, 213
Commonwealth Countries League, 214
Commonwealth Education Trust, 213
Commonwealth Engineers' Council, 214
Commonwealth Forestry Association, 212
Commonwealth Foundation, 212
Commonwealth Fund for Technical Co-operation, 212
Commonwealth Games Federation, 214
Commonwealth Geological Surveys Forum, 214
Commonwealth Journalists Association, 213
Commonwealth Lawyers' Association, 213
Commonwealth Legal Advisory Service, 213
Commonwealth Legal Education Association, 213
Commonwealth Magistrates' and Judges' Association, 213
Commonwealth Medical Trust, 213

Commonwealth Ministerial Action Group on the Harare Declaration, 208
Commonwealth of Independent States, 215
Commonwealth of Learning, 212
Commonwealth Parliamentary Association, 214
Commonwealth Pharmaceutical Association, 213
Commonwealth Press Union, 213
Commonwealth Secretariat, 8
Commonwealth Society for the Deaf, 213
Commonwealth Telecommunications Organization, 212
Commonwealth War Graves Commission, 214
Commonwealth Youth Exchange Council, 214
Communauté des états Sahelo-Sahariens, 411
Communauté économique des états de l'Afrique centrale, 411
Communauté économique des pays des Grands Lacs, 412
Communauté économique du bétail et de la viande (CEBV) du Conseil de l'Entente, 412
Communauté économique et monétaire de l'Afrique centrale, 307
Community Fisheries Control Agency, 257
Community of Portuguese-Speaking Countries, 423
Community of Sahel-Saharan States, 411
Community Plant Variety Office, 257
Compagnie de réassurance de la Zone d'échanges préférentiels (ZEP-RE), 206
Comparative Education Society in Europe, 418
Comprehensive Nuclear Test Ban Treaty, 109
Comunidad Andina de Naciones, 170
Comunidade dos Países de Língua Portuguesa, 423
Confederación de Organizaciones Turísticas de la América Latino, 463
Confederación Interamericana de Educación Católica, 418
Confederación Latinoamericana y del Caribe de Asociaciones Cristianas de Jóvenes, 471
Confédération européenne des syndicats, 427
Confédération internationale des betteraviers européens, 408
Confederation of Asia-Pacific Chambers of Commerce and Industry, 464
Conference of European Churches, 441
Conference of International Catholic Organizations, 441
Conferencia Interamericano de Seguridad Social, 454
Congress of Local and Regional Authorities of the Council of Europe, 226
Conseil de l'Entente, 412
Conseil International des Femmes, 455
Conseil international des grands réseaux électriques, 460
Conseil international des radios-télévisions d'expression française, 440
Conseil international du cinema de la television et de la communication audiovisuelle, 440
Consejo Centroamericano de Instituciones de Seguridad Social, 202
Consejo Consultivo Empresarial Andino, 173
Consejo Consultivo Laboral Andino, 173
Consejo de Fundaciones Americanas de Desarrollo, 412
Consejo del Istmo Centroamericano de Deportes y Recreación, 202
Consejo Episcopal Latinoamericano, 442
Consejo Interamericano de Música, 405
Consejo Latinoamericano de Iglesias, 442
Consejo Superior Universitario Centroamericano, 203
Consolidated Inter-Agency Appeal Process, 46
Consortium for Oceanographic Research and Education, 421
Consultative Council of Jewish Organizations, 441
Consultative Group on International Agricultural Research, 114
Consultative Group to Assist the Poorest, 114
Consumers International, 464
Convenio Andrés Bello, 173
Convenio Hipólito Unanue, 173
Convenio Simón Rodríguez, 173
Convention on International Trade in Endangered Species of Wild Fauna and Flora, 62
Convention on the Law of the Sea, 323
Convention on the Rights of the Child, 52
Co-operation Council for the Arab States of the Gulf, 219
Co-opération Internationale pour le Développement et la Solidarité, 413
Co-ordinating Committee for International Voluntary Service, 453
Co-ordinator of the Indigenous Organizations of the Amazon Basin, 453
Corporación Andina de Fomento, 173
Corporación Centroamericana de Servicios de Navegación Aérea, 203
Corte Interamericana de Derechos Humanos, 361
Cotonou Agreement, 301
Council for Financial and Monetary Affairs, 331

Council for Research in Values and Philosophy, 450
Council for the Development of Social Science Research in Africa, 450
Council for the International Congresses of Entomology, 444
Council of American Development Foundations, 412
Council of Arab Economic Unity, 222
Council of Commonwealth Societies, 214
Council of Europe, 225
Council of Europe Development Bank, 229
Council of Legal Education, 201
Council of Legal Education, 418
Council of National Customs Directors, 331
Council of the Baltic Sea States, 224
Council of the Bars and Law Societies of Europe, 429
Council of the European Union, 252
Council on International Educational Exchange, 470
Council on Transport for Trade Facilitation, 331
Counterfeiting Intelligence Bureau, 313
Court of First Instance of the European Communities, 255
Court of Justice of the European Communities, 254
CPLP, 423
CropLife International, 464
CSTO, 423
CTC, 17
CTBT, 109
Cystic Fibrosis Worldwide, 432

D

Danube Commission, 469
DDC, 61
Desert Locust Control Organization for Eastern Africa, 402
Developing Eight (D-8), 412
Development Centre, 348
Disarmament Commission, 13
Doha Development Round, 397
Duke of Edinburgh's Award International Association, 214

E

EAC, 412
EAEA, 418
EAPC, 342
Earth Council, 412
East African Community, 412
East African Development Bank, 415
Eastern and Southern African Trade and Development Bank, 206
Eastern Caribbean Central Bank, 415
Eastern Mediterranean Office, 146
Eastern Regional Organisation for Planning and Housing, 450
Eastern Regional Organization for Public Administration, 423
EBRD, 239
ECA, 40
ECE, 33
ECHO, 304
ECLAC, 38
Ecma International, 459
ECO, 238
ECOMOG, 235
Econometric Society, 415
Economic and Social Commission for Asia and the Pacific, 35
Economic and Social Commission for Western Asia, 43
Economic and Social Council, 19
Economic Commission for Africa, 40
Economic Commission for Europe, 33
Economic Commission for Latin America and the Caribbean, 38
Economic Community of Central African States, 411
Economic Community of the Great Lakes Countries, 412
Economic Community of West African States, 232
Economic Co-operation Organization, 238
ECOSOC, 19
ECOWAS, 232
ECOWAS Bank for Investment and Development, 237
Education Action, 418
Education International, 325
EFTA, 412
EI, 325
Energy Charter Secretariat, 464
English-Speaking Union, 450
Entente Council, 412
ESA, 241
ESCAP, 35
ESCAP Pacific Operations Centre, 35
ESCAP/WMO Typhoon Committee, 38
ESCWA, 43

INDEX

ESOMAR—World Association of Opinion and Marketing Research Professionals, 464
EU, 244
EUMETSAT, 459
Eurasian Economic Community (EURASEC), 412
EUREKA, 459
Euro-Atlantic Partnership Council, 342
EUROCHAMBRES, 464
EUROCONTROL, 469
EURO-FER, 465
Eurofound, 258
Euro-Mediterranean Partnership, 295
EUROPOL, 258
Europa Nostra—Pan-European Federation for Cultural Heritage, 405
EuropeAid Co-operation Office, 251
European Agency for Reconstruction, 257
European Agency for Safety and Health at Work, 257
European Agency for the Management of Operational Co-operation at the External Borders of the European Union, 257
European Alliance of News Agencies, 439
European Aluminium Association, 408
European and Mediterranean Plant Protection Organization, 402
European Anti-Fraud Office, 251
European Association for Animal Production, 402
European Association for Cancer Research, 432
European Association for Education of Adults, 418
European Association for Personnel Management, 427
European Association for Population Studies, 450
European Association for Research on Plant Breeding, 402
European Association for the Study of Diabetes, 432
European Association for the Trade in Jute and Related Products, 408
European Association of Communications Agencies, 465
European Association of Conservatoires, Music Academies and Music High Schools, 405
European Association of Electrical Contractors, 465
European Association of Geoscientists and Engineers, 444
European Association of Manufacturers of Radiators, 465
European Association of National Productivity Centres, 465
European Association of Social Medicine, 432
European Astronaut Centre, 241
European Atomic Energy Community, 244
European Atomic Forum, 444
European Aviation Safety Agency, 257
European Bank for Reconstruction and Development, 239
European Baptist Federation, 442
European Brain and Behaviour Society, 432
European Brewery Convention, 465
European Broadcasting Union, 440
European Central Bank, 256
European Centre for Disease Prevention and Control, 257
European Centre for Higher Education, 141
European Centre for the Development of Vocational Training, 257
European Chemical Industry Council, 465
European Chemicals Agency, 257
European Cities Marketing, 427
European Civil Aviation Conference, 469
European Civil Service Federation, 427
European Coal and Steel Community, 244
European Commission, 249
European Commission against Racism and Intolerance, 227
European Commission for the Control of Foot-and-Mouth Disease, 106
European Commission on Agriculture, 106
European Committee for Standardization, 465
European Committee of Associations of Manufacturers of Agricultural Machinery, 465
European Committee of Sugar Manufacturers, 408
European Committee of Textile Machinery Manufacturers, 465
European Community Humanitarian Office, 304
European Confederation of Woodworking Industries, 465
European Conference of Postal and Telecommunications Administrations, 439
European Construction Industry Federation, 427
European Convention for Constructional Steelwork, 459
European Convention for the Protection of Human Rights and Fundamental Freedoms, 226
European Council, 252
European Council of Paint, Printing Ink and Artists' Colours Industry, 465
European Court of Auditors, 255
European Court of Human Rights, 226
European Cultural Foundation, 405
European Defence Agency, 257
European Economic and Social Committee, 256
European Economic Community, 244
European Engineering Industries Association, 468
European Environment Agency, 257
European Evangelical Alliance, 442
European Federation for Catholic Adult Education, 418
European Federation of Associations of Insulation Enterprises, 465
European Federation of Chemical Engineering, 459
European Federation of Corrosion, 459
European Federation of Finance House Associations, 416
European Federation of Financial Analysts Societies, 416
European Federation of Insurance Intermediaries, 465
European Federation of Internal Medicine, 432
European Federation of Lobbying and Public Affairs, 427
European Federation of Management Consultancies' Associations, 465
European Federation of Marketing Research Organisations, 465
European Federation of Materials Handling and Storage Equipment, 465
European Federation of National Engineering Associations, 459
European Federation of Older Persons, 453
European Federation of the Plywood Industry, 465
European Federation of Tile and Brick Manufacturers, 465
European Festivals Association, 407
European Financial Management and Marketing Association, 416
European Food Safety Authority, 258
European Forestry Commission, 106
European Foundation for Management Development, 418
European Foundation for the Improvement of Living and Working Conditions, 258
European Free Trade Association, 412
European Furniture Manufacturers Federation, 465
European General Galvanizers Association, 466
European GNSS Supervisory Authority, 258
European Grassland Federation, 402
European Health Management Association, 432
European Industrial Research Management Association, 427
European Inland Fisheries Advisory Commission, 106
European Investment Bank, 256
European Investment Fund, 256
European Joint Undertaking for ITER and the Development of Fusion Energy, 258
European Judicial Co-operation Unit, 258
European Law Students' Association, 470
European League against Rheumatism, 432
European Livestock and Meat Trading Union, 402
European Maritime Safety Agency, 258
European Medicines Agency, 258
European Metal Union, 459
European Molecular Biology Organization, 444
European Mometary System, 288
European Monitoring Centre for Drugs and Drug Addiction, 258
European Movement, 423
European Network and Information Security Agency, 258
European Ombudsman, 254
European Organisation for the Exploitation of Meteorological Satellites, 459
European Organisation for the Safety of Air Navigation, 469
European Organization for Caries Research, 432
European Organization for Civil Aviation Equipment, 459
European Organization for Nuclear Research (CERN), 444
European Organization for Quality, 466
European Orthodontic Society, 432
European Packaging Federation, 466
European Panel Federation, 466
European Parliament, 253
European Patent Office, 466
European Police College, 258
European Police Office, 258
European Private Equity and Venture Capital Association, 416
European Railway Agency, 258
European Social Charter, 227
European Society for Rural Sociology, 450
European Society of Culture, 405
European Society of Radiology, 432
European Space Agency, 241
European Space Astronomy Centre, 242
European Space Operations Centre, 242
European Space Research and Technology Centre, 242
European Space Research Institute, 242
European Students' Forum, 470
European Telecommunications Satellite Organization, 439
European Trade Union Confederation, 427
European Training Foundation, 258
European Travel Commission, 463

European Union, 244
European Union Agency for Fundamental Rights, 259
European Union Institute for Security Studies, 259
European Union of Arabic and Islamic Scholars, 418
European Union of Medical Specialists, 432
European Union of the Natural Gas Industry, 466
European Union of Women, 423
European Union Satellite Centre, 259
European University Association, 418
European Youth Forum, 471
European-Mediterranean Seismological Centre, 444
EUROPOL, 258
Eurospace, 459
Eurostat, 251
Eurotransplant International Foundation, 433
EUSC, 259

F

Fairtrade Labelling Organizations International, 466
FAO, 102
FATF, 416
FDI World Dental Federation, 433
Federación de Cámaras de Comercio del Istmo Centroamericano, 466
Federación Latinoamericana de Bancos, 417
Federación Latinoamericana de Trabajadores Agrícolas, Pecuarios y Afines, 428
Fédération Aéronautique Internationale, 457
Fédération de la Fonction Publique Européenne, 427
Fédération de l'Industrie Dentaire en Europe, 433
Fédération Démocratique Internationale des Femmes, 427
Fédération des gynécologues et obstetriciens de langue française, 433
Fédération des Professeurs de Langues Vivantes, 419
Federation EIL, 450
Federation Européene pour l'Éducation Catholique des Adultes, 418
Fédération européenne d'associations nationales d'ingénieurs, 459
Fédération européenne de zootechnie, 402
Fédération européenne du lobbying et public afairs, 427
Fédération graphique internationale, 428
Fédération Internationale Catholique d'Education Physique et Sportive, 419
Fédération Internationale de Basketball, 457
Fédération internationale de football association, 457
Fédération internationale de Gymnastique, 458
Fédération Internationale de la Presse Cinématographique, 440
Fédération Internationale de l'Automobile, 457
Fédération internationale de natation, 458
Fédération Internationale de Philatélie, 457
Fédération Internationale de Ski, 458
Fédération internationale de tir à l'arc, 457
Fédération internationale de volleyball, 458
Fédération internationale d'éducation physique, 419
Fédération internationale des acteurs, 428
Fédération Internationale des Archives du Film, 406
Fédération Internationale des associations de Producteurs de Films, 406
Fédération internationale des associations vexillologiques, 450
Fédération internationale des echecs, 459
Federation Internationale des Fonctionnaires Superieures de Police, 430
Fédération Internationale des Hôpitaux, 435
Fédération internationale des ingénieurs-conseils, 461
Fédération internationale des sociétés d'aviron, 458
Fédération internationale d'escrime, 458
Fédération internationale d'universités catholiques, 419
Fédération Internationale Pharmaceutique, 436
Fédération Internationale pour la Recherche Théâtrale, 406
Fédération Internationale pour le Droit Européen, 430
Fédération internationale pour l'éducation des parents, 419
Fédération lanière internationale, 468
Fédération Mondiale des Associations Pour les Nations Unies, 427
Fédération mondiale des travailleurs scientifiques, 429
Fédération mondiale pour l'enseignement de la medicine, 438
Federation of Arab Scientific Research Councils, 444
Federation of Asian Scientific Academies and Societies, 444
Federation of Asia-Pacific Women's Associations, 453
Federation of Central American Chambers of Commerce, 466
Federation of European Biochemical Societies, 444
Federation of French-Language Obstetricians and Gynaecologists, 433
Federation of International Civil Servants' Associations, 427
Federation of Jewish Communities of the CIS, 442
Federation of the European Dental Industry, 433
FIFA, 457
Financial Action Task Force, 416
Financial Investigation Bureau, 313
Financial Stability Forum, 416
Fishery Committee for the Eastern Central Atlantic, 106
Fondation internationale pénale et pénitentiaire, 431
Fondation 'Pour la science', Centre international de synthèse, 444
Fondo Latinoamericano de Reservas, 173
Fonds Africain de Garantie et de Co-opération Economique, 416
Fonds de Solidarité Prioritaire, 308
Food and Agriculture Organization of the United Nations, 102
Foratum, 444
Forum Fisheries Agency, 383
Forum Train Europe FTE, 469
Foundation for International Scientific Co-ordination, 444
Francophonie, 425
Franc Zone, 306
Free Trade Agreement of the Americas (FTAA), 365
Friends of the Earth International, 421
Friends World Committee for Consultation, 442
Fundación Panamericana para el Desarrollo, 366

G

GAFTA, 223
Gambia River Basin Development Organization, 412
Gavi Alliance, 53
GCC, 219
GEF, 61
General Agreement on Tariffs and Trade (GATT), 396
General Arab Insurance Federation, 223
General Assembly, 12
General Association of International Sports Federations, 457
General Association of Municipal Health and Technical Experts, 433
General Fisheries Council for the Mediterranean, 106
General Union of Arab Agricultural Workers and Co-operatives, 223
General Union of Chambers of Commerce, Industry and Agriculture for Arab Countries, 466
Geneva Conventions, 322
GIC, 222
Global Christian Forum, 442
Global Cluster Lead Agencies, 47
Global Commission on International Migration, 454
Global Coral Reef Monitoring Network, 421
Global Elders, 423
Global Environment Facility, 61
Global Fund to Fight AIDS, TB and Malaria, 149
Global Humanitarian Forum, 454
Global Migration Group, 454
Global Programme of Action for the Protection of the Marine Environment from Land-based Activities, 62
Global Strategy for the Progressive Control of Highly Pathogenic Avian Influenza, 147
Graduate Institute of International Studies, 418
Greater Arab Free Trade Area, 223
Greencross International, 421
Greenpeace International, 421
Group of Three (G3), 412
Group of States Against Corruption (GRECO), 229
Group on Earth Observations, 155
Groupe d'action financière, 416
GUAM, 216
Gulf Co-operation Council, 219
Gulf International Bank, 222
Gulf Investment Corporation, 222
Gulf of Guinea Commission, 423
Gulf Organization for Industrial Consulting, 466

H

Hague Conference on Private International Law, 429
Hansard Society, 423
High Commissioner on National Minorities, 355
HIPCs, 113
Hipólito Unanue Agreement, 173
Human Rights Council, 14
Hybrid African Union/UN Operation in Darfur, 46
Hyogo Framework of Action, 46

INDEX

I

IAEA, 107
Ibero-American General Secretariat, 423
IBRD, 112
ICAO, 121
ICDDR, B: Centre for Health and Population Research, 433
ICRC, 320
ICSID, 115
ICTR, 18
ICTY, 18
IDA, 118
IEA, 351
IFAD, 123
IFC, 118
IGAD, 311
ILO, 124
IMF, 129
IMO, 127
IMO International Maritime Law Institute, 128
Inclusion Europe, 454
Indian Ocean Commission, 412
Indian Ocean Fishery Commission, 106
Indian Ocean Rim Association for Regional Co-operation, 413
Industrie Européenne de la Construction, 427
Information Technology Centre for Africa, 43
Initiatives of Change International, 454
INMARSAT, 439
INSOL International, 427
Institut de Droit international, 429
Institut d'émission d'outre-mer, 307
Institut international de philosophie, 420
Institut universitaire de hautes études internationales, 418
Institute for the Integration of Latin America and the Caribbean, 309
Institute of Air Transport, 469
Institute of Commonwealth Studies, 212
Institute of General Semantics, 444
Institute of International Law, 429
Institute of Nutrition of Central America and Panama, 203
Instituto Americano del Niño, la Niña y Adolescentes, 365
Instituto Centroamericano de Administración de Empresas, 466
Instituto Centroamericano de Administración Pública, 203
Instituto de Nutrición de Centroamérica y Panamán para la Agricultura, 366
Instituto Latinoamericano y del Caribe de Planificacion Economica y Social, 39
Instituto Panamericano de Geografía e Historia, 366
Instituto para la Integración de América Latina y el Caribe, 309
INSTRAW, 97
Inter-African Coffee Organization, 408
Inter-African Union of Lawyers, 429
Inter-Agency Standing Committee, 46
Inter-American Association of Agricultural Librarians, Documentalists and Information Specialists, 402
Inter-American Association of Sanitary and Environmental Engineering, 433
Inter-American Bar Association, 429
Inter-American Centre for Research and Documentation on Vocational Training, 418
Inter-American Children's Institute, 365
Inter-American Commercial Arbitration Commission, 466
Inter-American Commission of Women, 365
Inter-American Commission on Human Rights, 361
Inter-American Committee Against Terrorism, 365
Inter-American Committee on Ports, 361
Inter-American Confederation for Catholic Education, 418
Inter-American Conference on Social Security, 454
Inter-American Court of Human Rights, 361
Inter-American Defense Board, 366
Inter-American Development Bank, 308
Inter-American Drug Abuse Control Commission, 362
Inter-American Indigenous Institute, 366
Inter-American Institute for Co-operation on Agriculture, 366
Inter-American Institute for Social Development, 309
Inter-American Investment Corporation, 309
Inter-American Music Council, 405
Inter-American Organization for Higher Education, 418
Inter-American Planning Society, 413
Inter-American Press Association, 440
Inter-American Telecommunication Commission, 362
Inter-American Tropical Tuna Commission, 402
Inter-Arab Investment Guarantee Corporation, 334
Intergovernmental Authority on Development, 311
Intergovernmental Committee of the Universal Copyright Convention, 429
Intergovernmental Oceanographic Commission, 444
Intergovernmental Organization for International Carriage by Rail, 469
International Abolitionist Federation, 454
International Academy for Production Engineering Research, 460
International Academy of Astronautics, 444
International Academy of Aviation and Space Medicine, 433
International Academy of Cytology, 433
International Accounting Standards Board, 416
International Advertising Association Inc, 466
International African Institute, 451
International Agency for Research on Cancer, 152
International Agency for the Prevention of Blindness, 433
International Air Transport Association, 469
International Alliance of Women, 423
International Amateur Athletic Federation, 457
International Amateur Boxing Association, 457
International Amateur Radio Union, 440
International Anatomical Congress, 433
International Archery Federation, 457
International Association for Biologicals, 444
International Association for Bridge and Structural Engineering, 460
International Association for Cereal Science and Technology, 403
International Association for Child and Adolescent Psychiatry and Allied Professions, 433
International Association for Community Development, 423
International Association for Cybernetics, 460
International Association for Dental Research, 433
International Association for Earthquake Engineering, 444
International Association for Ecology, 444
International Association for Education to a Life without Drugs, 454
International Association for Educational and Vocational Guidance, 418
International Association for Group Psychotherapy and Group Processes, 433
International Association for Mathematical Geology, 445
International Association for Mathematics and Computers in Simulation, 445
International Association for Media and Communication Research, 451
International Association for Plant Physiology, 445
International Association for Plant Taxonomy, 445
International Association for Religious Freedom, 442
International Association for Research in Income and Wealth, 416
International Association for Suicide Prevention, 454
International Association for the Development of Documentation, Libraries and Archives in Africa, 418
International Association for the Exchange of Students for Technical Experience, 471
International Association for the History of Religions, 451
International Association for the Physical Sciences of the Ocean, 445
International Association for the Protection of Industrial Property, 429
International Association for the Study of Obesity, 433
International Association for Vegetation Science, 403
International Association of Agricultural Economists, 403
International Association of Agricultural Information Specialists, 403
International Association of Agricultural Medicine and Rural Health, 433
International Association of Applied Linguistics, 451
International Association of Applied Psychology, 433
International Association of Art, 405
International Association of Art Critics, 405
International Association of Asthmology, 434
International Association of Bibliophiles, 405
International Association of Bioethics, 434
International Association of Botanic Gardens, 445
International Association of Broadcasting, 440
International Association of Buddhist Studies, 442
International Association of Buying and Marketing Groups, 466
International Association of Children's International Summer Villages (CISV International Ltd), 454
International Association of Conference Interpreters, 428
International Association of Conference Translators, 428
International Association of Crafts and Small and Medium-Sized Enterprises, 428
International Association of Democratic Lawyers, 429
International Association of Dental Students, 471
International Association of Department Stores, 466
International Association of Deposit Insurers, 416
International Association of Educators for World Peace, 418

International Association of Film and Television Schools, 406
International Association of Geodesy, 445
International Association of Geomagnetism and Aeronomy, 445
International Association of Gerontology and Geriatrics, 434
International Association of Horticultural Producers, 403
International Association of Hydatidology, 434
International Association of Hydraulic Engineering and Research, 460
International Association of Hydrological Sciences, 445
International Association of Insurance Supervisors, 416
International Association of Islamic Banks, 372
International Association of Law Libraries, 430
International Association of Lawyers, 431
International Association of Legal Sciences, 430
International Association of Literary Critics, 406
International Association of Logopedics and Phoniatrics, 434
International Association of Marine Aids to Navigation and Lighthouse Authorities, 460
International Association of Medicine and Biology of the Environment, 434
International Association of Meteorology and Atmospheric Sciences, 445
International Association of Metropolitan City Libraries, 451
International Association of Music Libraries, Archives and Documentation Centres, 407
International Association of Mutual Health Funds, 453
International Association of Mutual Insurance Companies, 428
International Association of Oral and Maxillofacial Surgeons, 434
International Association of Papyrologists, 419
International Association of Penal Law, 430
International Association of Physical Education in Higher Education, 419
International Association of Ports and Harbors, 469
International Association of Public Transport, 469
International Association of Scholarly Publishers, 466
International Association of Schools of Social Work, 454
International Association of Scientific Experts in Tourism, 463
International Association of Sedimentologists, 445
International Association of Social Educators, 454
International Association of Sound and Audiovisual Archives, 440
International Association of Technological University Libraries, 460
International Association of the Soap, Detergent and Maintenance Products Industry, 466
International Association of University Professors and Lecturers, 419
International Association of Volcanology and Chemistry of the Earth's Interior, 445
International Association of Wood Anatomists, 445
International Association of Youth and Family Judges and Magistrates, 429
International Astronautical Federation, 445
International Astronomical Union, 445
International Atomic Energy Agency, 107
International Automobile Federation, 457
International Baccalaureate Organization, 419
International Badminton Federation, 457
International Bank for Reconstruction and Development—IBRD (World Bank), 112
International Bar Association, 430
International Basketball Federation, 457
International Bee Research Association, 403
International Biometric Society, 445
International Board on Books for Young People, 406
International Booksellers Federation
International Botanical Congress, 446
International Brain Research Organization, 434
International Bridge, Tunnel and Turnpike Association, 460
International Bronchoesophagological Society, 434
International Bureau for Epilepsy, 434
International Bureau for the Standardization of Man-Made Fibres, 466
International Bureau of Education, 141
International Bureau of Fiscal Documentation, 416
International Bureau of Weights and Measures, 446
International Butchers' Confederation, 466
International Cadmium Association, 408
International Canoe Federation, 457
International Capital Market Association, 416
International Cargo Handling Co-ordination Association, 460
International Cartographic Association, 446
International Catholic Committee of Nurses and Medico-Social Assistants, 434
International Catholic Federation for Physical and Sports Education, 419
International Catholic Migration Commission, 454
International Catholic Union of the Press, 440
International Cell Research Organization, 434
International Centre for Black Sea Studies, 368
International Centre for Living Aquatic Resources Management, 405
International Centre for Local Credit, 416
International Centre for Migration and Health, 319
International Centre for Settlement of Investment Disputes, 115
International Centre for the Study of the Preservation and Restoration of Cultural Property, 406
International Centre for Tropical Agriculture, 403
International Centre of Films for Children and Young People, 406
International Centre of Insect Physiology and Ecology, 446
International Chamber of Commerce, 312
International Chamber of Shipping, 469
International Chiropractors' Association, 434
International Christian Federation for the Prevention of Alcoholism and Drug Addiction, 454
International Christian Service for Peace, 453
International Civil Aviation Organization, 121
International Civil Defence Organization, 454
International Civil Service Commission, 14
International Cocoa Organization, 408
International Coffee Organization, 408
International College of Surgeons, 434
International Colour Association, 460
International Commission for Optics, 446
International Commission for Plant-Bee Relationships, 446
International Commission for the Conservation of Atlantic Tunas, 403
International Commission for the History of Representative and Parliamentary Institutions, 423
International Commission for the Prevention of Alcoholism and Drug Dependency, 454
International Commission for the Protection of the Rhine, 421
International Commission for the Scientific Exploration of the Mediterranean Sea, 446
International Commission of Agricultural Engineering, 460
International Commission of Jurists, 430
International Commission of Sugar Technology, 403
International Commission on Civil Status, 430
International Commission on Glass, 460
International Commission on Illumination, 460
International Commission on Irrigation and Drainage, 460
International Commission on Large Dams, 460
International Commission on Occupational Health, 434
International Commission on Physics Education, 446
International Commission on Radiation Units and Measurements, Inc, 446
International Commission on Radiological Protection, 434
International Commission on Zoological Nomenclature, 446
International Committee for Animal Recording, 403
International Committee for Social Sciences Information and Documentation, 451
International Committee for the Diffusion of Arts and Literature through the Cinema, 406
International Committee for the History of Art, 451
International Committee of Historical Sciences, 451
International Committee of Military Medicine, 434
International Committee of Museums and Collections of Arms and Military History, 406
International Committee of the Red Cross, 320
International Committee on Aeronautical Fatigue, 460
International Comparative Literature Association, 406
International Confederation for Printing and Allied Industries, 466
International Confederation of Art and Antique Dealers, 467
International Confederation of Catholic Organizations for charitable and social action, 411
International Confederation of European Sugar Beet Growers, 408
International Confederation of Societies of Authors and Composers—World Congress of Authors and Composers, 406
International Conference on the Great Lakes Region, Secretariat, 424
International Congress and Convention Association, 463
International Congress of African Studies, 419
International Container Bureau, 469
International Co-operation for Development and Solidarity, 413
International Co-operative Alliance, 467
International Copyright Society, 430
International Coral Reef Initiative, 421
International Cotton Advisory Committee, 408
International Council for Adult Education, 419
International Council for Commercial Arbitration, 430

INDEX

International Council for Film, Television and Audiovisual Communication, 440
International Council for Health, Physical Education, Recreation, Sport and Dance, 457
International Council for Laboratory Animal Science, 434
International Council for Open and Distance Education, 419
International Council for Philosophy and Humanistic Studies, 451
International Council for Physical Activity and Fitness Research, 435
International Council for Research and Innovation in Building and Construction, 460
International Council for Science, 446
International Council for Scientific and Technical Information, 446
International Council for the Exploration of the Sea, 446
International Council for Traditional Music, 407
International Council of Christians and Jews, 442
International Council of Environmental Law, 430
International Council of French-speaking Radio and Television Organizations, 440
International Council of Graphic Design Associations, 467
International Council of Jewish Women, 442
International Council of Museums, 406
International Council of Nurses, 435
International Council of Psychologists, 446
International Council of Societies of Industrial Design, 467
International Council of Tanners, 467
International Council of the Aeronautical Sciences, 446
International Council of Voluntary Agencies, 454
International Council of Women, 455
International Council on Alcohol and Addictions, 455
International Council on Archives, 451
International Council on Jewish Social and Welfare Services, 455
International Council on Large High-Voltage Electric Systems, 460
International Council on Mining and Metals, 467
International Council on Monuments and Sites, 406
International Council on Social Welfare, 455
International Court of Justice, 20
International Cricket Council, 457
International Criminal Court, 314
International Criminal Tribunal for Rwanda, 18
International Criminal Tribunal for the Former Yugoslavia, 18
International Crops Research Institute for the Semi-Arid Tropics, 403
International Customs Tariffs Bureau, 430
International Cycling Union, 457
International Dachau Committee, 455
International Dairy Federation, 403
International Democrat Union, 424
International Development Association, 118
International Development Law Organization, 430
International Diabetes Federation, 435
International Earth Rotation and Reference Systems Service, 447
International Economic Association, 416
International Electrotechnical Commission, 460
International Emissions Trading Association, 421
International Energy Agency, 351
International Epidemiological Association, 435
International Equestrian Federation, 457
International Ergonomics Association, 451
International Exhibitions Bureau, 467
International Fair Trade Association, 467
International Falcon Movement—Socialist Educational International, 425
International Federation for European Law, 430
International Federation for Housing and Planning, 451
International Federation for Human Rights Leagues, 455
International Federation for Information and Documentation, 461
International Federation for Information Processing, 461
International Federation for Medical and Biological Engineering, 435
International Federation for Medical Psychotherapy, 435
International Federation for Modern Languages and Literatures, 451
International Federation for Parent Education, 419
International Federation for the Promotion of Machine and Mechanism Science, 461
International Federation for Theatre Research, 406
International Federation of Accountants, 416
International Federation of Actors, 428
International Federation of Agricultural Producers, 403
International Federation of Air Line Pilots' Associations, 428

International Organizations

International Federation of Airworthiness, 461
International Federation of Associated Wrestling Styles, 457
International Federation of Association Football, 457
International Federation of Associations of Textile Chemists and Colourists, 467
International Federation of Automatic Control, 461
International Federation of Automotive Engineering Societies, 461
International Federation of Beekeepers' Associations, 403
International Federation of Biomedical Laboratory Science, 428
International Federation of Business and Professional Women, 428
International Federation of Catholic Universities, 419
International Federation of Cell Biology, 447
International Federation of Chemical, Energy, Mine and General Workers' Unions, 325
International Federation of Clinical Chemistry and Laboratory Medicine, 435
International Federation of Clinical Neurophysiology, 435
International Federation of Consulting Engineers, 461
International Federation of Educative Communities, 455
International Federation of Fertility Societies, 435
International Federation of Film Archives, 406
International Federation of Film Critics, 440
International Federation of Film Producers' Associations, 406
International Federation of Freight Forwarders Associations, 469
International Federation of Grocers' Associations, 467
International Federation of Gynecology and Obstetrics, 435
International Federation of Hospital Engineering, 461
International Federation of Institutes for Socio-religious Research, 451
International Federation of Journalists, 325
International Federation of Library Associations and Institutions, 419
International Federation of Medical Students' Associations, 471
International Federation of Musicians, 407
International Federation of Operational Research Societies, 447
International Federation of Ophthalmological Societies, 435
International Federation of Organizations for School Correspondence and Exchange, 419
International Federation of Oto-Rhino-Laryngological Societies, 435
International Federation of Park and Recreation Administration, 458
International Federation of Persons with Physical Disability, 455
International Federation of Pharmaceutical Manufacturers and Associations, 467
International Federation of Philosophical Societies, 451
International Federation of Physical Education, 419
International Federation of Press Cutting Agencies, 440
International Federation of Red Cross and Red Crescent Societies, 322
International Federation of Resistance Movements, 424
International Federation of Science Editors, 447
International Federation of Senior Police Officers, 430
International Federation of Social Science Organizations, 451
International Federation of Social Workers, 455
International Federation of Societies for Microscopy, 447
International Federation of Societies of Classical Studies, 452
International Federation of Surgical Colleges, 435
International Federation of Teachers of Modern Languages, 419
International Federation of the Blue Cross, 455
International Federation of the Periodical Press, 440
International Federation of the Phonographic Industry, 467
International Federation of the Socialist and Democratic Press, 440
International Federation of University Women, 419
International Federation of Vexillological Associations, 450
International Federation of Workers' Education Associations, 419
International Fellowship of Reconciliation, 442
International Fencing Federation, 458
International Fertilizer Industry Association, 467
International Finance Corporation, 118
International Fiscal Association, 416
International Food Information Service, 447
International Food Policy Research Institute, 403
International Foundation of the High-Altitude Research Stations Jungfraujoch and Gornergrat, 447
International Fragrance Association, 467
International Fund for Agricultural Development, 123
International Fur Trade Federation, 467
International Gas Union, 408
International Geographical Union, 447
International Glaciological Society, 447

INDEX — International Organizations

International Grains Council, 408
International Graphical Federation, 428
International Gymnastic Federation, 458
International Hockey Federation, 458
International Hop Growers' Convention, 404
International Hospital Federation, 435
International Hotel and Restaurant Association, 463
International Humanist and Ethical Union, 442
International Hydrographic Organization, 447
International Industrial Relations Association, 428
International Institute for Adult Education Methods, 419
International Institute for Beet Research, 404
International Institute for Children's Literature and Reading Research, 406
International Institute for Conservation of Historic and Artistic Works, 406
International Institute for Democracy and Electoral Assistance, 424
International Institute for Labour Studies, 126
International Institute for Ligurian Studies, 452
International Institute for Peace, 424
International Institute for Strategic Studies, 424
International Institute for the Unification of Private Law (UNIDROIT), 430
International Institute of Administrative Sciences, 452
International Institute of Communications, 440
International Institute of Philosophy, 420
International Institute of Public Finance, 416
International Institute of Refrigeration, 447
International Institute of Seismology and Earthquake Engineering, 461
International Institute of Sociology, 452
International Institute of Space Law, 431
International Institute of Tropical Agriculture, 404
International Institute of Welding, 461
International Iron and Steel Institute, 461
International Islamic News Agency, 372
International Islamic Trade Finance Corporation, 330
International Judo Federation, 458
International Juridical Institute, 431
International Jute Study Group, 408
International Labour Organization, 124
International Law Association, 431
International Law Commission, 13
International Lead and Zinc Study Group, 409
International League against Epilepsy, 435
International League against Racism and Antisemitism, 455
International League for Human Rights, 455
International League of Associations for Rheumatology, 435
International Leprosy Association, 435
International Lesbian and Gay Association, 424
International Livestock Research Institute, 404
International Maize and Wheat Improvement Centre, 404
International Maritime Academy, 128
International Maritime Bureau, 313
International Maritime Organization, 127
International Maritime Radio Association, 440
International Mathematical Union, 447
International Measurement Confederation, 461
International Meat Secretariat, 467
International Metalworkers' Federation, 326
International Mineralogical Association, 447
International Mobile Satellite Organization, 439
International Molybdenum Association, 409
International Monetary Fund, 129
International Movement of Catholic Students, 443
International Music and Media Centre, 407
International Music Council, 406
International Musicological Society, 452
International Narcotics Control Board, 435
International Navigation Association, 462
International Nuclear Law Association, 431
International Numismatic Commission, 452
International Olive Council, 409
International Olympic Committee, 315
International Opticians' Association, 435
International Organisation of Employers, 428
International Organisation of Vine and Wine, 409
International Organization for Biological Control of Noxious Animals and Plants, 404
International Organization for Medical Physics, 436
International Organization for Migration, 317
International Organization for Standardization, 461
International Organization for the Study of the Old Testament, 442
International Organization of Citrus Virologists, 404
International Organization of Experts, 428

International Organization of Legal Metrology, 447
International Organization of Motor Manufacturers, 467
International Organization of Securities Commissions, 417
International Organization of Spice Trading Associations, 409
International Organization of the Flavour Industry, 467
International Palaeontological Association, 447
International Paralympic Committee, 458
International Peace Academy, 452
International Peace Bureau, 424
International Peace Research Association, 452
International Peat Society, 447
International Pediatric Association, 436
International PEN, 407
International Penal and Penitentiary Foundation, 431
International Pepper Community, 409
International Pharmaceutical Federation, 436
International Pharmaceutical Students' Federation, 471
International Philatelic Federation, 457
International Phonetic Association, 447
International Phycological Society, 448
International Planned Parenthood Federation, 455
International Platinum Association, 409
International Police Association, 431
International Political Science Association, 424
International Poplar Commission, 106
International Press Institute, 440
International Press Telecommunications Council, 440
International Primatological Society, 448
International Prisoners' Aid Association, 455
International Psychoanalytical Association, 436
International Public Relations Association, 428
International Publishers' Association, 467
International Radiation Protection Association, 448
International Rail Transport Committee, 469
International Railway Congress Association, 470
International Rayon and Synthetic Fibres Committee, 468
International Reading Association, 420
International Red Cross and Red Crescent Movement, 319
International Red Locust Control Organization for Central and Southern Africa, 404
International Regional Organization of Plant Protection and Animal Health, 203
International Research Group on Wood Protection, 461
International Rhinologic Society, 436
International Rice Commission, 107
International Rice Research Institute, 404
International Road Federation, 470
International Road Safety Organization, 470
International Road Transport Union, 470
International Rowing Federation, 458
International Rubber Research and Development Board, 461
International Rubber Study Group, 409
International Sailing Federation, 458
International Schools Association, 420
International Scout and Guide Fellowship, 471
International Seabed Authority, 323
International Security Assistance Force, 345
International Seed Testing Association, 404
International Sericultural Commission, 404
International Service for National Agricultural Research, 403
International Shipping Federation, 470
International Shooting Sport Federation, 458
International Shopfitting Organisation, 468
International Silk Association, 409
International Skating Union, 458
International Ski Federation, 458
International Social Science Council, 452
International Social Security Association, 455
International Social Service, 456
International Society for Business Education, 420
International Society for Contemporary Music, 407
International Society for Education through Art, 420
International Society for Horticultural Science, 404
International Society for Human and Animal Mycology, 448
International Society for Labour and Social Security Law, 431
International Society for Music Education, 420
International Society for Oneiric Mental Imagery Techniques, 436
International Society for Photogrammetry and Remote Sensing, 461
International Society for Rock Mechanics, 448
International Society for Soil Mechanics and Geotechnical Engineering, 461
International Society for Stereology, 448
International Society for the Psychopathology of Expression and Art Therapy, 436
International Society for the Study of Medieval Philosophy, 420

International Society for Tropical Ecology, 448
International Society for Vascular Surgery, 436
International Society of Audiology, 436
International Society of Biometeorology, 448
International Society of Blood Transfusion, 436
International Society of City and Regional Planners, 428
International Society of Criminology, 448
International Society of Dermatopathology, 436
International Society of Developmental Biologists, 436
International Society of Internal Medicine, 436
International Society of Limnology, 448
International Society of Lymphology, 436
International Society of Neuropathology, 436
International Society of Orthopaedic Surgery and Traumatology, 436
International Society of Physical and Rehabilitation Medicine, 436
International Society of Radiology, 436
International Society of Social Defence and Humane Criminal Policy, 452
International Society of Surgery, 436
International Sociological Association, 452
International Solar Energy Society, 461
International Solid Waste Association, 462
International Special Committee on Radio Interference, 462
International Spinal Cord Society, 436
International Statistical Institute, 452
International Studies Association, 452
International Sugar Organization, 409
International Swimming Federation, 458
International Table Tennis Federation, 458
International Tea Committee Ltd, 409
International Tea Promotion Association, 409
International Telecommunication Union, 135
International Telecommunications Satellite Organization, 439
International Tennis Federation, 458
International Textile, Garment and Leather Workers' Federation, 326
International Textile Manufacturers Federation, 468
International Theatre Institute, 407
International Tobacco Growers' Association, 409
International Trade Centre (UNCTAD/WTO), 400
International Trade Union Confederation, 324
International Training Centre of ILO, 126
International Transport Forum, 470
International Transport Workers' Federation, 326
International Tribunal for the Law of the Sea, 324
International Tropical Timber Organization, 409
International Tungsten Industry Association, 409
International Union against Cancer, 437
International Union against Tuberculosis and Lung Disease, 437
International Union for Electricity Applications, 462
International Union for Health Promotion and Education, 437
International Union for Housing Finance, 417
International Union for Inland Navigation, 470
International Union for Physical and Engineering Sciences in Medicine, 448
International Union for Pure and Applied Biophysics, 448
International Union for Quaternary Research, 448
International Union for the Protection of Industrial Property (Paris Convention), 154
International Union for the Protection of Literary and Artistic Works (Berne Union), 154
International Union for the Protection of New Varieties of Plant, 404
International Union for the Scientific Study of Population, 452
International Union for Vacuum Science, Technique and Applications, 462
International Union of Academies, 452
International Union of Air Pollution Prevention and Environmental Protection Associations, 462
International Union of Anthropological and Ethnological Sciences, 452
International Union of Architects, 428
International Union of Biochemistry and Molecular Biology, 448
International Union of Biological Sciences, 448
International Union of Crystallography, 448
International Union of Family Organisations, 456
International Union of Food, Agricultural, Hotel, Restaurant, Catering, Tobacco and Allied Workers' Associations, 326
International Union of Food Science and Technology, 448
International Union of Forest Research Organizations, 404
International Union of Geodesy and Geophysics, 449
International Union of Geological Sciences, 449
International Union of Immunological Societies, 449
International Union of Latin Notaries, 431
International Union of Marine Insurance, 468
International Union of Microbiological Societies, 449
International Union of Nutritional Sciences, 449
International Union of Pharmacology, 449
International Union of Photobiology, 449
International Union of Physiological Sciences, 449
International Union of Prehistoric and Protohistoric Sciences, 452
International Union of Psychological Science, 449
International Union of Pure and Applied Chemistry, 449
International Union of Pure and Applied Physics, 449
International Union of Radio Science, 449
International Union of Railways, 470
International Union of Socialist Youth, 426
International Union of Soil Sciences, 404
International Union of Students, 471
International Union of Technical Associations and Organizations, 462
International Union of Tenants, 456
International Union of Testing and Research Laboratories for Materials and Structures, 462
International Union of the History and Philosophy of Science, 449
International Union of Theoretical and Applied Mechanics, 449
International Union of Toxicology, 449
International Union of Young Christian Democrats, 424
International Universities Bureau, 419
International Volleyball Federation, 458
International Water Association, 449
International Water Resources Association, 462
International Weightlifting Federation, 458
International Whaling Commission, 404
International Wool Textile Organisation, 468
International World Games Association, 458
International Wrought Copper Council, 468
International Young Christian Workers, 471
International Youth Hostel Federation, 471
International Youth Library, 420
International Zinc Association, 409
Internationale Gesellschaft für Urheberrecht e. V., 430
Internationale Jugendbibliothek, 420
Internationaler Verband für Erziehung zu suchtmittelfreiem Leben, 454
Internationales Institut für Jugendliteratur und Leseforschung, 406
Internet Corporation for Assigned Names and Numbers, 439
Inter-Parliamentary Union, 326
INTERPOL, 430
Inter-University European Institute on Social Welfare, 456
Inuit Circumpolar Conference, 413
Investment Arbitration Board, 333
IOC, 315
IOM, 317
IPU, 326
ISAF, 345
Islamic Centre for the Development of Trade, 372
Islamic Chamber of Commerce and Industry, 373
Islamic Committee for the International Crescent, 373
Islamic Corporation for the Development of the Private Sector, 330
Islamic Corporation for the Insurance of Investment and Export Credit, 330
Islamic Development Bank, 329
Islamic Educational, Scientific and Cultural Organization, 372
Islamic Jurisprudence (Fiqh) Academy, 372
Islamic Research and Training Institute, 330
Islamic Solidarity Fund, 372
Islamic Solidarity Sports Federation, 373
Islamic States Broadcasting Union, 372
Islamic University in Uganda, 372
Islamic University of Niger, 372
Islamic University of Technology, 372
ITCA, 43
ITU, 135
ITUC, 324
IUCN—The World Conservation Union, 421

J

Jeunesses Musicales International, 407
Jewish Agency for Israel, 424
Joint Defence Council, 333
Joint FAO/WHO Food Standards Programme, 106
Joint Parliamentary Assembly, 303
Joint Research Centre, 251
Joint UN Programme on HIV/AIDS, 149
Junior Chamber International, Inc., 471

INDEX

Junta Interamericana de Defensa, 366
Juridicial Commission, 315
Justice Studies Center of the Americas, 366

K

Kagera River Basin Organization, 414
Kosovo Peace Implementation Force (KFOR), 344
Kyoto Protocol, 158

L

La Francophonie, 425
La prevention routière internationale, 470
Labour Advisory Council, 331
LAIA, 331
Lake Chad Basin Commission, 413
Latin American and Caribbean Confederation of Young Men's Christian Associations, 471
Latin American and Caribbean Forestry Commission, 107
Latin American and Caribbean Institute for Economic and Social Planning, 39
Latin American Association of Development Financing Institutions, 413
Latin American Association of National Academies of Medicine, 437
Latin American Banking Federation, 417
Latin American Council of Churches, 442
Latin American Demographic Centre, 39
Latin American Economic System, 413
Latin American Episcopal Council, 442
Latin American Federation of Agricultural Workers, 428
Latin American Integration Association, 331
Latin American Parliament, 424
Latin American Reserve Fund, 173
Latin-American Catholic Press Union, 440
Latin-American Confederation of Tourist Organizations, 463
Latin-American Energy Organization, 462
Latin-American Iron and Steel Institute, 462
Law Association for Asia and the Pacific, 431
Lead Development Association International, 410
League for the Exchange of Commonwealth Teachers, 213
League of Arab States, 332
Liberal International, 424
Ligue des Bibliothèques Européennes de Recherche, 418
Lions Clubs International, 456
Liptako-Gourma Integrated Development Authority, 413
Livestock and Meat Economic Community of the Entente Council, 412
Lomé Conventions, 301
Lutheran World Federation, 442

M

Malacological Union, 450
Mano River Union, 413
MDGs, 58
MDRI, 118
Médecins sans frontières, 456
Medical Women's International Association, 437
Medienzentrum, 407
Mekong River Commission, 413
Mensa International, 453
Mercado Común del Sur/Mercado Comum do Sul (MERCOSUR/MERCOSUL), 391
Middle East Council of Churches, 442
Middle East Neurosurgical Society, 437
MIGA, 120
Millennium Development Goals, 58
MINURCAT, 84
MINURSO, 81
MINUSTAH, 89
Montreal Protocol, 64
MONUC, 85
Mouvement pan-africain de la jeunesse, 471
Multilateral Debt Relief Initiative, 118
Multilateral Investment Fund, 309
Multilateral Investment Guarantee Agency, 120
Multiple Sclerosis International Federation, 437
Muslim World League, 442

N

NADBank, 339
NAFTA, 338
NAM, 424
NATO, 340
NATO Air Command and Control System Management Agency, 346
NATO Airborne Early Warning and Control Programme Management Organisation, 346
NATO CIS Operating and Support Agency, 346
NATO Communications and Information Systems (NCISS) School, 346
NATO Consultation, Command and Control Agency, 346
NATO Defense College, 346
NATO EF 2000 and Tornado Development, Production and Logistics Management Agency, 346
NATO HAWK Management Office, 346
NATO Helicopter Design and Development Production and Logistics Management Agency, 346
NATO Maintenance and Supply Agency, 346
NATO Parliamentary Assembly, 424
NATO (SHAPE) School, 346
NATO Research and Technology Organisation, 346
NATO Standardisation Agency, 346
NATO Undersea Research Centre, 346
NEA, 352
Near East Forestry Commission, 107
New Partnership for Africa's Development (NEPAD), 169
Niger Basin Authority, 413
Nigeria Trust Fund, 163
Nile Basin Initiative, 413
Nomenclature Advisory Commission, 331
Non-aligned Movement, 424
Non-Proliferation Treaty, 109
Nordic Council/Nordic Council of Ministers, 424
Nordic Cultural Fund, 407
Nordic Development Fund, 413
Nordic Environment Finance Corpn, 421
Nordic Industrial Fund—Centre for Innovation and Development, 428
Nordic Industry Workers' Federation, 428
Nordic Investment Bank, 417
Nordic Project Fund, 417
Nordisk InnovationsCenter, 428
Nordisk Kulturfond, 407
Nordisk Skibsrederforening, 470
Nordiska Industriarbetare-Federationen, 428
Nordiska Investeringsbanken, 417
NORDTEST, 462
North Africa, 40
North American Commission for Environmental Co-operation, 339
North American Development Bank, 339
North American Forestry Commission, 107
North American Free Trade Agreement, 338
North Atlantic Council, 340
North Atlantic Treaty Organization, 340
North Pacific Anadromous Fish Commission, 404
North Pacific Regional Office, 378
Northern Forum, 424
Northern Shipowners' Defence Club, 470
Northwest Atlantic Fisheries Organization, 404
NPT, 108
NTF, 163
Nuclear Energy Agency, 347

O

OAPEC, 366
OAS, 360
OAU, 164
OCHA, 46
ODIHR, 355
OEA, 360
OECD, 347
OECD Nuclear Energy Agency, 352
OECS, 425
Office for Democratic Institutions and Human Rights, 355
Office for the Co-ordination of Humanitarian Affairs, 46
Office international de la viande, 467
Office of the High Representative for the Least Developed Countries, Landlocked Developing Countries and Small Island Developing States, 12
Office of the Representative on Freedom of the Media, 355
Office of the Special Representative of the Secretary-General for Children and Armed Conflict, 12
Office of the Special Representative of the UN Secretary-General for West Africa, 90

Office of the United Nations High Commissioner for Human Rights, 49
Office of the United Nations Special Co-ordinator for Lebanon, 90
Office of the United Nations Special Co-ordinator for the Middle East Peace Process, 90
OHCHR, 49
OIC, 369
Olympic Council of Asia, 458
Olympic Games, 315
OPCW, 425
OPEC, 373
OPEC Fund for International Development, 376
Opus Dei, 442
Orgalime, 468
Organisation de coordination pour la lutte contre les endémies en Afrique Centrale, 437
Organisation for Economic Co-operation and Development, 347
Organisation for the Collaboration of Railways, 470
Organisation for the Prohibition of Chemical Weapons, 425
Organisation Internationale de la Francophonie, 425
Organisation Internationale de la Vigne et du Vin, 409
Organisation internationale de protection civile, 454
Organisation Internationale de Recherche sur la Cellule, 434
Organisation internationale des constructeurs d'automobiles, 467
Organisation internationale du caférologie, 438
Organisation Mondiale pour la Systémique et la Cybernétique, 450
Organisation of African Trade Union Unity, 428
Organisation of Eastern Caribbean States, 425
Organisation panafricaine de lutte contre le SIDA, 437
Organisation pour la mise en valeur du fleuve Gambie, 412
Organisation pour la mise en valeur du fleuve Sénégal, 413
Organisation pour l'aménagement et le développement du bassin de la rivière Kagera, 414
Organismo Internacional Regional de Sanidad Agropecuaria, 203
Organismo para la Proscripción de las Armas Nucleares en la América Latina y el Caribe, 422
Organización Centroamericana y del Caribe de Entidades Fiscalizadores Superiores, 202
Organización de Estados Iberoamericanos para la Educación, la Ciencia y la Cultura, 420
Organización de las Cooperativas de América, 414
Organización de los Estados Americanos, 360
Organización de Solidaridad de los Pueblos de Africa, Asia y América Latina, 425
Organización de Universidades Católicas de América Latina, 420
Organización Latino-americana de Energín Panamericana de la Salud, 366
Organization for Co-ordination in the Struggle against Endemic Diseases in Central Africa, 437
Organization for Democracy and Economic Development, 425
Organization for Security and Co-operation in Europe, 354
Organization for the Development of the Senegal River, 413
Organization for the Management and Development of the Kagera River Basin, 414
Organization of African Unity, 164
Organization of American States, 360
Organization of Arab Petroleum Exporting Countries, 366
Organization of Asia-Pacific News Agencies, 441
Organization of Ibero-American States for Education, Science and Culture, 420
Organization of Islamic Capitals and Cities, 373
Organization of Solidarity of the Peoples of Africa, Asia and Latin America, 425
Organization of the Black Sea Economic Co-operation, 367
Organization of the Catholic Universities of Latin America, 420
Organization of the Co-operatives of America, 414
Organization of the Islamic Conference, 369
Organization of the Islamic Shipowners' Association, 373
Organization of the Petroleum Exporting Countries, 373
Organization of World Heritage Cities, 407
OSCE, 354
OSCE Parliamentary Assembly, 355

P

Pacific Agreement on Closer Economic Relations, 381
Pacific Asia Travel Association, 463
Pacific Basin Economic Council, 414
Pacific Community, 377
Pacific Conference of Churches, 442
Pacific Economic Co-operation Council, 414
Pacific Forum Line, 383
Pacific Island Countries Trade Agreement, 381
Pacific Islands Centre, 383
Pacific Islands Forum, 380
Pacific Islands Forum Trade Office, 383
Pacific Islands Private Sector Organization, 383
Pacific Islands Trade and Investment Commission (New Zealand), 383
Pacific Islands Trade and Investment Commission (Sydney), 383
Pacific Science Association, 450
Pacific Telecommunications Council, 439
Pan American Development Foundation, 366
Pan American Health Organization, 366
Pan American Railway Congress Association, 470
Pan-African Association for Literacy and Adult Education, 420
Pan-African Employers' Confederation, 429
Pan-African Institute for Development, 414
Pan-African Institution of Education for Development, 169
Pan-African News Agency, 169
Pan-African Postal Union, 169
Pan-African Railways Union, 169
Pan-African Union of Science and Technology, 450
Pan-African Writers' Association, 407
Pan-African Youth Movement, 471
Pan-American Association of Ophthalmology, 437
Pan-American Institute of Geography and History, 366
Pan-Pacific and South East Asia Women's Association, 456
Pan-Pacific Surgical Association, 437
PAPP, 61
Parlamento Andino, 170
Parlamento Latinoamericano, 424
Parliamentary Assembly of the Black Sea, 368
Parliamentary Association for Euro-Arab Co-operation, 425
Partners in Population and Development, 414
Partnership in Environmental Management for the Seas of East Asia, 128
Party of European Socialists, 425
Pax Romana International Catholic Movement for Intellectual and Cultural Affairs, 443
Peace-building Commission, 14
Peace-building Support Office, 12
Permanent Commission of the South Pacific, 421
Permanent Court of Arbitration, 431
Permanent International Committee of Linguists, 453
Permanent Interstate Committee on Drought Control in the Sahel, 414
Permanent Military Commission, 333
Petrocaribe, 410
PICTA, 381
Population Council, 414
Postal Union of the Americas, Spain and Portugal, 439
Prelature of the Holy Cross and Opus Dei, 442
Press Foundation of Asia, 441
Programme of Assistance to the Palestinian People, 61
PTA Reinsurance Co, 206
Public Relations and Information Department, 373
Public Services International, 326
Puebla-Panamá Plan, 414
Pugwash Conferences on Science and World Affairs, 450

R

Rabitat al-Alam al-Islami, 442
Red Crescent, 319
Red Cross, 319
Regional Association of Oil and Natural Gas Companies in Latin America and the Caribbean, 410
Regional Centre for Mapping of Resources for Development, 462
Regional Centre for Training in Aerospace Surveys, 462
Regional Co-ordinating Unit for East Asian Seas, 62
Regional Co-ordinating Unit for the Caribbean Environment Programme, 62
Regional Council of Co-ordination of Central and East European Engineering Organizations, 462
Regional Marine Pollution Emergency, Information and Training Center for the Wider Caribbean Region, 128
Regional Marine Pollution Emergency Response Centre for the Mediterranean Sea, 128
Regional Science Bureau for Asia and the Pacific, 138
Rehabilitation International, 437
Reporters sans Frontières, 441
Research Centre for Islamic History, Art and Culture, 372
Rotary International, 456
Royal Asiatic Society of Great Britain and Ireland, 407

S

Royal Commonwealth Ex-Services League, 214
Royal Commonwealth Society, 214
Royal Over-Seas League, 214

SAARC, 384
SAARCLAW, 385
SADC, 386
Sahel and West Africa Club, 348
Salvation Army, 443
Schengen Agreement, 277
SDR, 130
SECI, 414
SECI Center, 431
Secretaría de Integración Económica Centroamericana, 202
Secretaría de Integración Turística Centroamericana, 202
Secretaría de la Integración Social Centroamericana, 202
Secretaría del Consejo Agropecuario Centroamericano, 202
Secretaría Ejecutiva de la Comisión Centroamericana de Ambiente y Desarrollo, 202
Secretaría Ejecutiva de la Comisión Regional de Recursos Hidráulicos, 203
Secretaría Ejecutiva del Consejo de Electrificación de América Central, 202
Secretaría Ejecutiva del Consejo Monetario Centroamericano, 202
Secretaría General de la Coordinación Educativa y Cultural Centroamericana, 202
Secretaría General Iberoamericana, 423
Secretariat of the Basel Convention, 63
Secretariat of the Mediterranean Action Plan on the Implementation of the Barcelona Convention, 63
Secretariat of the Multilateral Fund for the Implementation of the Montreal Protocol, 63
Secretariat of the Pacific Community, 337
Secretariat of the Pacific Regional Environment Programme, 421
Secretariat of the UN Framework Convention on Climate Change, 158
Security Council, 14
SELA, 413
Service Civil International, 456
Service social international, 456
Shanghai Co-operation Organization, 425
Shelter-Afrique, 163
SIAP, 38
SICA, 201
SICA Court of Justice, 202
SICA Parliament, 202
SIECA, 202
Sightsavers International, 213
Simón Bolívar Andean University, 173
Simón Rodríguez Agreement, 173
Sistema de la Integración Centroamericana, 201
Sistema Económico Latinoamericano, 413
Socialist International, 425
Socialist International Women, 426
Sociedad Interamericana de Planificación, 413
Sociedad Interamericana de Prensa, 440
Societas Internationalis Limnologiae, 448
Société de neuro-chirurgie de langue française, 437
Société de Transplantation, 437
Société Internationale de Chirurgie Orthopédique et de Traumatologie, 436
Société internationale de criminologie, 448
Société Internationale Financière pour les Investissements et le Développement en Afrique (SIFIDA), 163
Société pour l'habitat et le logement territorial en Afrique, 163
Society for International Development, 414
Society of Comparative Legislation, 431
Society of French-speaking Neuro-Surgeons, 437
Society of Saint Vincent de Paul, 456
SOLIDAR, 456
SOLIDARIOS, 412
Soroptimist International, 456
Sound Seekers, 213
South America, 121
South American Bank, 415
South American Community of Nations, 426
South Asia Co-operative Environment Programme, 421
South Asian Association for Regional Co-operation, 384
South Centre, 414
South West Indian Ocean Fisheries Commission, 107
South-East Asia Office, 146

Southeast Asian Ministers of Education Organization, 420
Southern African Customs Union, 468
Southern African Development Community, 386
Southern Common Market, 391
South Pacific Forum, 380
South Pacific Regional Trade and Economic Co-operation Agreement (SPARTECA), 381
south-pacific.travel, 463
SPC, 337
SPECA, 34
Special Body on Least Developed and Landlocked Developing Countries, 35
Special Body on Pacific Island Developing Countries, 35
Special Bureau for Boycotting Israel, 333
Special Committee on Peace-keeping Operations, 13
Special Committee on the Charter of the United Nations and on the Strengthening of the Role of the Organization, 14
Special Committee on the Implementation of the Declaration on Decolonization, 13
Special Court for Sierra Leone, 19
Special Drawing Rights, 130
Special Programme for the Economies of Central Asia, 34
Standing Committee on Commonwealth Forestry, 212
Statistical, Economic and Social Research and Training Centre for the Islamic Countries, 372
Statistical Office of the European Communities, 251
Stockholm International Peace Research Institute, 426
Sugar Association of the Caribbean (Inc.), 410
Supreme Council for Sports in Africa, 169

T

Technical Centre for Agricultural and Rural Co-operation, 303
Theosophical Society, 443
Third World Forum, 453
Tourism Council, 331
Trade Union Confederation of the Americas, 325
Trade Unions International of Agriculture, Food, Commerce, Textile and Allied Workers, 395
Trade Unions International of Public and Allied Employees, 395
Trade Unions International of Transport Workers, 395
Trade Unions International of Workers in the Energy, Metal, Chemical, Oil and Related Industries, 395
Trade Unions International of Workers of the Building, Wood and Building Materials Industries, 395
Translation Centre for the Bodies of the European Union, 259
Transparency International, 426
Transplantation Society, 437
Treaty on Conventional Armed Forces in Europe, 341
Treaty on the Non-Proliferation of Nuclear Weapons, 109
Tribunal de Justicia de la Comunidad Andina, 170
Trilateral Commission, 426
Trusteeship Council, 19

U

UEMOA, 307
UFI (Global Association of the Exhibition Industry), 468
UMOA, 307
UN Commission on International Trade Law, 14
UN Operation in Darfur, 78
UN Scientific Committee on the Effects of Atomic Radiation, 13
UNAIDS, 149
UNAMA, 90
UNAMI, 90
UNAMID, 78
UNASUR, 426
UNCDF, 61
UNCTAD, 55
UNDCP, 47
UNDG, 10
UNDOF, 78
UNDP, 58
UNDP Development Fund for Women, 61
UNDP Drylands Development Centre, 61
UNEP, 62
UNEP Chemicals, 63
UNEP Division of Technology, Industry and Economics, 63
UNEP International Environmental Technology Centre, 63
UNEP Ozone Secretariat, 63
UNEP Secretariat for the UN Scientific Committee on the Effects of Atomic Radiation, 63

INDEX

UNEP/CMS (Convention on the Conservation of Migratory Species of Wild Animals) Secretariat, 63
UNEP-SCBD (Convention on Biological Diversity—Secretariat), 63
UNESCO, 137
UNESCO Institute for Information Technologies in Education, 142
UNESCO Institute for Life-long Learning, 142
UNESCO Institute for Statistics, 142
UNESCO Institute for Water Education, 142
UNESCO International Centre for Technical and Vocational Education and Training, 141
UNESCO International Institute for Capacity Building in Africa, 141
UNESCO International Institute for Educational Planning, 142
UNESCO International Institute for Higher Education in Latin America and the Caribbean, 142
UNFCCC, 158
UNFICYP, 88
UNFPA, 92
UN-Habitat, 50
UNHCR, 66
UNICEF, 52
UNICEF Innocenti Research Centre, 52
UNICRI, 97
Unidad Coordinadora de la Organización del Sector Pesquero y Acuícola del Istmo Centroamericano, 203
Unidad Técnica del Consejo Centroamericano de Vivienda y Asentamientos Humanos, 202
UNIDIR, 96
UNIDO, 142
UNIFEM, 61
UNIFIL, 80
Union académique internationale, 452
Union catholique internationale de la presse, 440
Unión de Paises Exportadores de Banano, 410
Unión de Universidades de América Latina y el Caribe, 420
Union du Maghreb arabe, 414
Union économique et monétaire ouest-africaine, 307
Union européenne de l'ameublement, 465
Union Européenne des Arabisants et Islamisants, 418
Union Européenne des Médecins Spécialistes, 432
Union interafricaine des avocats, 429
Union internationale contre le cancer, 437
Union internationale des architectes, 428
Union internationale des associations et organismes techniques, 462
Union Internationale des Avocats, 431
Union internationale des chemins de fer, 470
Union Internationale des Syndicats des Travailleurs du Bâtiment, du Bois et des Matériaux de Construction, 395
Union Internationale du Notariat Latin, 431
Union internationale pour la protection des obtentions végétales, 404
Union mondiale des enseignants catholiques, 420
Union mondiale des professions libérales, 429
Union monétaire ouest-africaine, 307
Union Network International, 326
Union of Arab Banks, 417
Union of Arab Contractors, 223
Union of Arab Investors, 223
Union of Arab Jurists, 431
Union of Banana-Exporting Countries, 410
Union of European Beverages Associations, 468
Union of European Football Associations, 458
Union of European Railway Industries, 470
Union of International Associations, 426
Union of South American Nations, 426
Union of the Arab Maghreb, 414
Union of the Electricity Industry, 462
Union of Universities of Latin America and the Caribbean, 420
Unión Postal de las Américas, España y Portugal, 439
UNITAR, 96
Unitas Malacologica, 450
United Bible Societies, 443
United Cities and Local Governments, 426
United Federation of Travel Agents' Associations, 463
United Nations, 3
United Nations Assistance Mission for Iraq, 90
United Nations Assistance Mission in Afghanistan, 90
United Nations Charter, 23
United Nations Children's Fund, 52
United Nations Conference on Trade and Development, 55
United Nations Counter-Terrorism Committee, 17
United Nations Crime Programme, 47
United Nations Development Group, 10
United Nations Development Programme, 58
United Nations Diplomatic Representation, 4
United Nations Disengagement Observer Force, 78
United Nations Drug Programme, 47
United Nations Economic and Social Commission for Asia and the Pacific, 35
United Nations Economic and Social Commission for Western Asia, 43
United Nations Economic Commission for Africa, 40
United Nations Economic Commission for Europe, 33
Untied Nations Economic Commission for Latin America and the Caribbean, 38
United Nations Educational, Scientific and Cultural Organization, 137
United Nations Environment Programme, 62
United Nations Forum on Forests, 20
United Nations Framework Convention on Climate Change, 158
United Nations Fundamental Treaties, 23
Untied Nations General Assembly, 12
United Nations High Commissioner for Human Rights, 49
United Nations High Commissioner for Refugees, 66
United Nations Human Rights Council, 14
United Nations Human Settlements Programme, 50
United Nations Industrial Development Organization, 142
United Nations Institute for Disarmament Research, 96
United Nations Institute for Training and Research, 96
United Nations Integrated Mission in Timor-Leste, 78
United Nations Integrated Office in Burundi, 91
United Nations Integrated Office in Sierra Leone, 91
United Nations Inter-Agency Standing Committee, 46
United Nations Interim Administration Mission in Kosovo, 79
United Nations Interim Force in Lebanon, 80
United Nations International Research and Training Institute for the Advancement of Women, 97
United Nations Interregional Crime and Justice Research Institute, 97
United Nations Military Observer Group in India and Pakistan, 81
United Nations Millennium Development Goals, 58
United Nations Mission for the Referendum in Western Sahara, 81
United Nations Mission in Ethiopia and Eritrea, 82
United Nations Mission in Liberia, 83
United Nations Mission in Nepal, 91
United Nations Mission in Sudan, 84
United Nations Mission in the Central African Republic and Chad, 84
United Nations Mission in the Democratic Republic of the Congo, 85
United Nations Observers, 8
United Nations Observer Mission in Georgia, 86
United Nations Office on Drugs and Crime, 47
United Nations Operation in Côte d'Ivoire, 87
United Nations Peace-building, 89
United Nations Peace-building Commission, 14
United Nations Peace-building Office in the Central African Republic, 92
United Nations Peace-building Support Office in Guinea-Bissau, 92
United Nations Peace-keeping, 77
United Nations Peace-keeping Force in Cyprus, 88
United Nations Political Office for Somalia, 92
United Nations Population Fund, 92
United Nations Relief and Works Agency for Palestine Refugees in the Near East, 94
United Nations Research Institute for Social Development, 97
United Nations Secretariat, 11
United Nations Security Council, 14
United Nations Special System-wide Special Initiative on Africa, 42
United Nations Stabilization Mission in Haiti, 89
United Nations System Staff College, 97
United Nations Training and Research Institutes, 96
United Nations Truce Supervision Organization, 89
United Nations Trusteeship Council, 19
United Nations University, 98
United Nations Volunteers, 62
United World Federation of United Cities, 407
Uniunii Medicale Balcanice, 432
Universal Declaration of Human Rights, 31
Universal Postal Union, 144
Universala Esperanto-Asocio, 420
Universidad Andina Simón Bolívar, 173
University for Peace, 98
UNMEE, 82
UNMIK, 79
UNMIL, 83
UNMIN, 91

UNMIS, 84
UNMIT, 78
UNMOGIP, 81
UNOCI, 87
UNODC, 47
UNOGBIS, 92
UNOMIG, 86
UNOWA, 90
UNPOS, 92
Unrepresented Nations and Peoples Organization, 426
UNRWA, 94
UNSCO, 90
UNSCOL, 90
UNTSO, 89
UNU, 98
UNV, 62
UNWTO, 159
UNWTO Themis Foundation, 160
UPU, 144

V

Victoria League for Commonwealth Friendship, 214
Vienna Institute for International Dialogue and Co-operation, 415

W

War Resisters' International, 426
Watch Tower Bible and Tract Society, 443
WBI, 115
West Africa Rice Development Association, 410
West African Health Organization, 237
West African Monetary Agency, 237
West African Monetary Institute, 237
West African Monetary Union, 307
West Indian Sea Island Cotton Association (Inc.), 410
Western and Central Pacific Fisheries Commission, 405
Western Central Atlantic Fishery Commission, 107
Western European Union (WEU), 426
Western Pacific Office, 146
Wetlands International, 422
WFP, 98
WFTU, 395
WFUNA Youth, 471
WHO, 145
WHO Centre for Health Development, 146
WHO European Office for Investment for Health and Development, 146
WHO Lyon Office for National Epidemic Preparedness and Response, 146
WHO Mediterranean Centre for Vulnerability Reduction, 146
Wiener Institut für internationalen Dialog und Zusammenarbeit, 415
WIPO, 152
WMO, 155
WMO/ESCAP Panel on Tropical Cyclones, 38
Women's International Democratic Federation, 427
World Air Sports Federation, 457
World Airlines Clubs Association, 470
World Allergy Organization, 437
World Alliance of Reformed Churches (Presbyterian and Congregational), 443
World Alliance of Young Men's Christian Associations, 471
World Anti-Doping Agency, 316
World Assembly of Youth, 471
World Association for Animal Production, 405
World Association for Christian Communication, 441
World Association for Disaster and Emergency Medicine, 437
World Association for Educational Research, 417
World Association for Public Opinion Research, 453
World Association of Beet and Cane Growers, 410
World Association of Girl Guides and Girl Scouts, 471
World Association of Industrial and Technological Research Organizations, 462
World Association of Judges, 431
World Association of Law Professors, 431
World Association of Lawyers, 431
World Association of Newspapers, 441
World Association of Nuclear Operators, 463
World Association of Societies of Pathology and Laboratory Medicine, 437
World Association of Travel Agencies, 463
World Association of Veterinary Food Hygienists, 405

World Association of Veterinary Microbiologists, Immunologists and Specialists in Infectious Diseases, 405
World Association of Writers, 407
World Bank, 112
World Bank Institute, 115
World Blind Union, 456
World Boxing Organization, 459
World Bridge Federation, 459
World Bureau of Metal Statistics, 463
World Chess Federation, 459
World Christian Life Community, 443
World Commission on the Ethics of Scientific Knowledge and Technology, 139
World Confederation for Physical Therapy, 438
World Conference of Religions for Peace, 443
World Congress of Faiths, 443
World Council of Churches, 393
World Council of Credit Unions, 417
World Council of Optometry, 438
World Council of Service Clubs, 471
World Crafts Council International, 407
World Customs Organization, 468
World Disarmament Campaign, 427
World Economic Forum, 415
World Education Fellowship, 420
World Energy Council, 463
World Esperanto Association, 420
World Evangelical Alliance, 443
World Federalist Movement, 427
World Federation for Medical Education, 438
World Federation for Mental Health, 438
World Federation of Advertisers, 468
World Federation of Arab-Islamic Schools, 373
World Federation of Associations of Paediatric Surgeons, 438
World Federation of Associations of Poison Centres and Clinical Toxicology Centres, 438
World Federation of Democratic Youth, 472
World Federation of Diamond Bourses, 410
World Federation of Engineering Organizations, 463
World Federation of Exchanges, 417
World Federation of Hydrotherapy and Climatotherapy, 438
World Federation of International Music Competitions, 407
World Federation of Neurology, 438
World Federation of Neurosurgical Societies, 438
World Federation of Occupational Therapists, 438
World Federation of Public Health Associations, 438
World Federation of Scientific Workers, 429
World Federation of Societies of Anaesthesiologists, 438
World Federation of Teachers' Unions, 395
World Federation of the Deaf, 456
World Federation of Trade Unions, 395
World Federation of United Nations Associations, 427
World Fellowship of Buddhists, 443
World Food Programme, 98
World Foundrymen Organization, 463
World Gastroenterology Organization, 438
World Gold Council, 410
World Health Organization, 145
World Heart Federation, 438
World Heritage Programme, 140
World Hindu Federation, 443
World Intellectual Property Organization, 152
World Jewish Congress, 443
World Jurist Association, 431
World Maritime University, 128
World Medical Association, 438
World Meteorological Organization, 155
World Methodist Council, 443
World Movement of Christian Workers, 429
World Ocean Observatory, 422
World Organisation of Animal Health, 405
World Organisation of Systems and Cybernetics, 450
World Organization of the Scout Movement, 472
World ORT, 456
World Packaging Organisation, 468
World Peace Council, 427
World Petroleum Council, 410
World Ploughing Organization, 405
World Psychiatric Association, 438
World Road Association, 463
World Savings Banks Institute, 417
World Self-Medication Industry, 438
World Sephardi Federation, 443
World Social Forum, 456
World Society for Ekistics, 453
World Society for the Protection of Animals, 422
World Squash Federation Ltd, 459

INDEX

World Student Christian Federation, 443
World Sugar Research Organisation, 410
World Summit on the Information Society, 136
World Tourism Organization, 159
World Trade Centers Association, 468
World Trade Organization, 396
World Travel and Tourism Council, 463
World Underwater Federation, 459
World Union for Progressive Judaism, 443
World Union of Catholic Teachers, 420
World Union of Catholic Women's Organisations, 443
World Union of Jewish Students, 472
World Union of Professions, 429
World Urban Forum, 51
World Veterans Federation, 457
World Veterinary Association, 405
World Water Council, 422

World Young Women's Christian Association (World YWCA), 472
WorldFish Center, 405
World's Poultry Science Association, 405
WTO, 396
WWF International, 422

Y

Youth for Development and Co-operation, 472
Youth of the European People's Party, 427

Z

Zone Franc, 306
Zonta International, 457

THE EUROPA REGIONAL SURVEYS OF THE WORLD

'Europa's Regional Surveys of the World are justly renowned for their exceptionally high levels of production, content and accuracy.'
– Reference Reviews

A nine-volume library of historical, political, geographical and economic data, providing an accurate and impartial overview of the major regions of the world.

These exhaustive surveys bring together a unique collection of information, from description and analysis of the principal issues affecting each region, to statistical data and directory information. They provide a combination of contemporary material and important historical perspectives to offer a definitive guide to all regions of the world.

Meticulously researched and updated every year, the *Europa Regional Surveys of the World* are an indispensable information source on which you can rely.

The nine titles that make up the series are as follows:

Africa South of the Sahara; Central and South-Eastern Europe; Eastern Europe, Russia and Central Asia; The Far East and Australasia; The Middle East and North Africa; South America, Central America and the Caribbean; South Asia; The USA and Canada; Western Europe.

To order call: UK & Rest of World Customers: **+44 (0)1235 400524**
North & South American Customers: **1-800-634-7064**

www.routledge.com/reference   Email: reference@routledge.com

EUROPA WORLD *PLUS*

Europa World and the Europa Regional Surveys of the World Online
www.europaworld.com

ALSO AVAILABLE

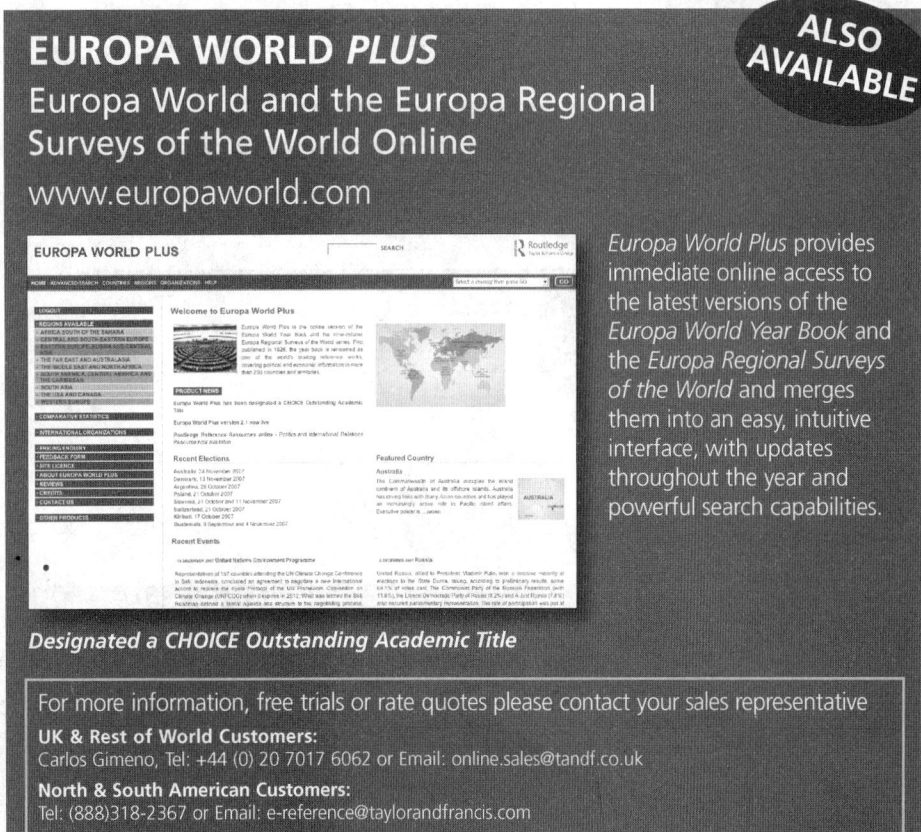

Europa World Plus provides immediate online access to the latest versions of the *Europa World Year Book* and the *Europa Regional Surveys of the World* and merges them into an easy, intuitive interface, with updates throughout the year and powerful search capabilities.

Designated a CHOICE Outstanding Academic Title

For more information, free trials or rate quotes please contact your sales representative

UK & Rest of World Customers:
Carlos Gimeno, Tel: +44 (0) 20 7017 6062 or Email: online.sales@tandf.co.uk

North & South American Customers:
Tel: (888)318-2367 or Email: e-reference@taylorandfrancis.com

Routledge
Taylor & Francis Group

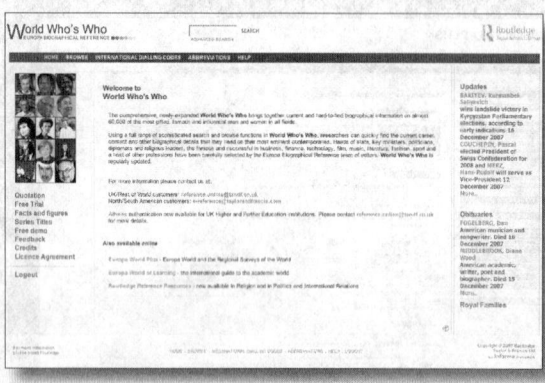